THE OFFICIAL ICAEW LIST OF MEMBERS 2012

Published by Wilmington Publishing & Information Limited
6–14 Underwood Street, London N1 7JQ UK

Editorial enquiries
T +44 (0)20 7324 2399
F +44 (0)20 7324 2366
Contact: Chloé Elliott
E celliott@waterlow.com
icaewfirms.co.uk

Sales enquiries
T +44 (0)20 7566 8227
F +44 (0)20 7324 2341
Contact: Gino De Antonis
E gdeantonis@waterlow.com

A catalogue entry for this book is available from the British Library.

ISBN 978-1-85783-174-0

Typesetting by Data Standards, Frome, Somerset.
Printed in Great Britain by Polestar Wheatons, Exeter.

© ICAEW 2011
Chartered Accountants' Hall, Moorgate Place, London EC2R 6EA UK
T +44 (0)20 7920 8100

The Official ICAEW List of Members is published on behalf of ICAEW by Wilmington Publishing & Information Limited (part of the Wilmington Group), in association with CCH (part of Wolters Kluwer (UK) Limited).

All rights reserved. You may not reproduce, copy or transmit any part of this publication without written permission.

If we find any person, company or firms reproducing or assisting others to produce mailing lists, or machine-readable versions derived from this publication, we will prosecute for copyright infringement.

We make every effort to ensure that the contents of this directory are accurate, but neither the publishers nor ICAEW shall be responsible or liable for any inaccuracy or omission herein. The information in this volume which relates to individuals contains information which was in whole or in part supplied to the publisher (Wilmington Publishing & Information Limited) by, or received by the publisher from, the respective data subject or a third party. If you believe that any information in this volume which relates to you is incorrect or misleading, or if your name has been incorrectly omitted from any section, you should immediately notify the publisher in writing.

Details notified after 1 September 2011 may not be included.

ICAEW
Chartered Accountants' Hall
Moorgate Place
London EC2R 6EA UK
T +44 (0)20 7920 8100
F +44 (0)20 7920 0547

Wolters Kluwer
145 London Road
Kingston upon Thames
KT2 6SR UK
T +44 (0)844 561 8166
F +44 (0)20 8547 2638

CONTENTS

Foreword	5
Analysis of ICAEW members	6
Map of district societies and regions	7
Past presidents	8
Council members 2011–2012	9
Members of principal committees	10
ICAEW honorary membership	13
Honours	13
Regional and district society contacts	14
Student societies and networks	18
ICAEW contact information	19

ICAEW PRODUCTS AND SERVICES

Business Centre	20
Chartered Accountants' Hall	20
Economic Insight	20
Faculties and special interest groups	20
ICAEW.com	20
ICAEW Business Advice Service	20
ICAEW/Grant Thornton UK Business Confidence Monitor (BCM)	20
Library & Information Services (LIS)	20
Mediation	20
Membership offers	20
Practice Support Services	20
President's Appointments Scheme	21
SME Funding Adviser Scheme	21
Support members	21
Technical helpline	21
Technical strategy department	21
UK enterprise survey report	21
Updates	21

ICAEW QUALIFICATIONS AND PROGRAMMES

ACA	22
Certificate in finance, accounting and business (CFAB)	22
IFRSs and financial reporting qualifications and programmes	22
Corporate finance (CF) qualification	22
Diploma in charity accounting (DChA)	22
Forensic accountant accreditation	22
ICAEW ISAs programme	22
ICAEW certificate in insolvency	22
Business sustainability programme (BSP)	22
Pathways to membership	22

MEMBERSHIP INFORMATION

Continuing professional development	23
Member logo	23
Members' helpline	23
Records team	23
CCH	26
Chartered Accountants' Benevolent Association (CABA)	27
Explanatory notes	28
Members: alphabetical	A
Tax Faculty members	B
Members in practice and firms: alphabetical	C

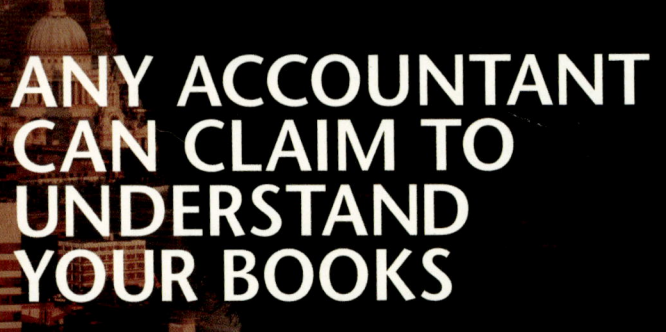

ICAEW members are recognised internationally as some of the world's top finance professionals.

ICAEW Chartered Accountants work at the highest levels of business, across all industry sectors around the world. They are relied upon to provide advice and leadership to the organisations they work for. They are recognised for supporting individuals, organisations and communities to create long-term economic and social value.

The economic recovery is now taking hold in markets around the world, presenting new challenges and opportunities to businesses and governments.

Our members are there to help them make the best possible decisions using knowledge and guidance based on the highest technical and ethical standards.

ICAEW has more than 136,000 members around the world. We are respected internationally with a reputation that is built on technical excellence, thought leadership and clear insight into professional and technical issues. We ensure that our members are at the forefront of their profession by maintaining and developing their skills and knowledge.

Because of us, people can do business with confidence.

Clive Parritt
President

ANALYSIS OF ICAEW MEMBERS

The charts below provide a snapshot of ICAEW membership as at 31 December 2010. Members have been profiled by their sector of work, age and gender.

MEMBERS BY WORK SECTOR

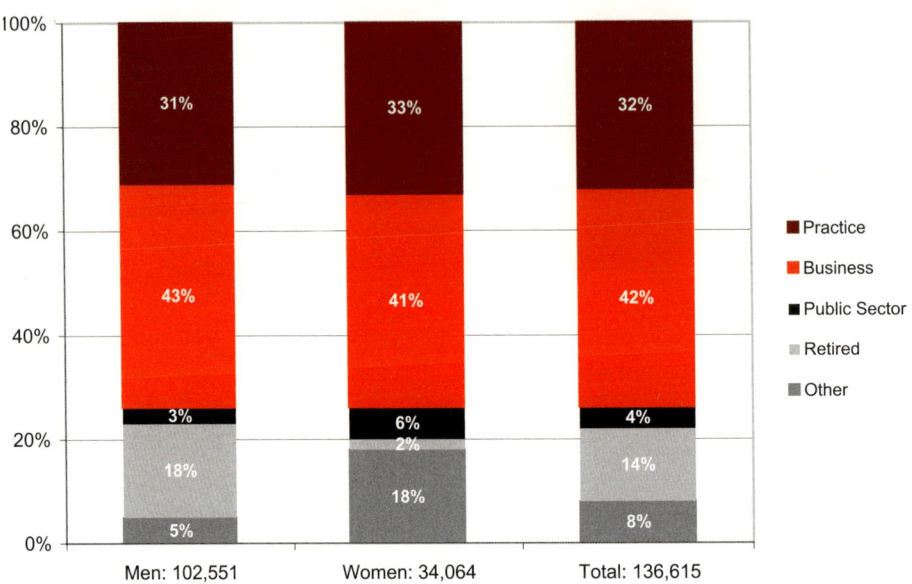

MEMBERS BY AGE AND GENDER

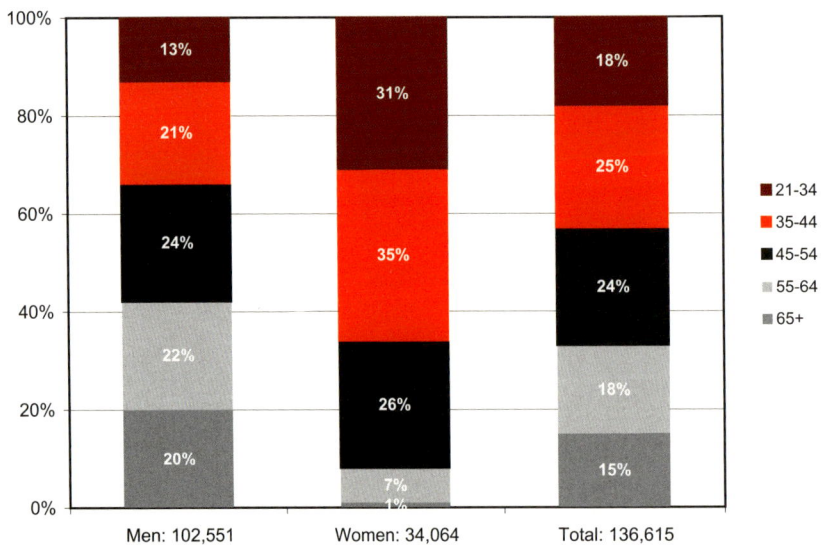

UK DISTRICT SOCIETIES AND REGIONS

	REGIONS	DISTRICT SOCIETIES	NUMBER OF MEMBERS
1	East England	Beds, Bucks & Herts; East Anglian; South Essex	13,681
2	East Midlands	Leicestershire & Northamptonshire; Nottingham, Derby & Lincoln	5,702
3	London	London; Croydon & District	34,378
4	North West	Isle of Man; Liverpool; Manchester; North West	10,890
5	Northern	Northern	3,028
6	South East	South Eastern; Southern; Thames Valley	20,154
7	South West	South Western; West of England	7,639
8	Wales	South Wales	2,327
9	West Midlands	Birmingham & West Midlands; Staffs, Salop & Wolverhampton	7,903
10	Yorkshire & Humber	Humberside & District; Sheffield & District; West Yorkshire	8,030
11	ICAEW members in Scotland		1,451

ICAEW MEMBERS WORLDWIDE

	REGIONS	NUMBER OF MEMBERS
1	Americas	4,544
2	Africa	1,199
3	Australasia	3,422
4	Europe and CIS	120,550
5	Middle East	940
6	North East Asia	3,379
7	South Asia	676
8	South East Asia	1,905

PAST PRESIDENTS

2010-11	Gerald William Russell, London	1954-55	Donald Victor House, London
2009-10	Martin John Hagen, West of England	1953-54	James Blakey, Manchester
2008-09	David Anthony Furst, London	1952-53	Thomas Buston Robson MBE, London
2006-08	Richard George Dyson, London	1951-52	Charles William Boyce MBE, Bradford
2005-06	James Ian Morris, Liverpool	1950-51	Harold Garton Ash OBE MC, London
2004-05	Paul Bryan Druckman, London	1949-50	Sir Russell Kettle, London
2003-04	David Jeremy Illingworth, Manchester	1948-49	Bernhard Heymann Binder, London
2002-03	Peter Lewis Wyman, London	1947-48	Gilbert David Shepherd MBE, Cardiff
2001-02	Michael John Groom, Staffs Salop & Wolv.	1946	Edward Furnival Jones, London
2000-01	Graham Norman Charles Ward MA, London	1945-46	Sir Harold Gibson Howitt GBE DSO MC, London
1999-00	Dame Sheila Valerie Masters DBE LLB FCA, London	1944-45	Harold Montague Barton, London
1998-99	Christopher Swinson MA, London	1938-44	Charles John Geoffrey Palmour, London
1997-98	Christopher Norman Lainé MA, Southern	1937-38	Frank Lindsay Fisher CBE, London
1996-97	Brian Murdoch Currie MA, London	1936-37	Roger Neale Carter MCom, Manchester
1995-96	Keith Spencer Woodley, West of England	1934-36	Arthur Edwin Cutforth CBE, London
1994-95	Roger Hardman Lawson, London	1933-34	Henry Lancelot Hingston Hill, London
1993-94	Michael Aubrey Chamberlain LLD, Leics & Northants	1932-33	Clare Smith, Bristol
1992-93	William Ian David Plaistowe MA, London	1931-32	Henry Lancelot Hingston Hill, London
1991-92	Ian Robert McNeil, South Eastern	1930-31	Harold Fitch Kemp, London
1990-91	Michael Gillam Lickiss BSc(Econ), London	1929-30	Sir William Plender Bt GBE, London
1989-90	Philip Edward Couse, Birmingham & W.Midlands	1928-29	Sir Nicholas Edwin Waterhouse KBE, London
1988-89	Francis Edward Worsley, London	1927-28	Richard Henry March, Cardiff
1987-88	Arthur Green, Liverpool	1926-27	Sir Arthur Francis Whinney KBE, London
1986-87	Derek Arnold Boothman, Manchester	1925-26	George Robert Freeman, London
1985-86	Brian Garton Jenkins MA, London	1924-25	Thomas Galland Mellors, Nottingham
1983-85	Alan John Hardcastle, London	1923	Sir Edward Cecil Moore Bt, London
1982-83	Edward Ernest Ray BCom, London	1921-23	William Cash, London
1981-82	Harry Bruce Singer TD, South Wales	1920-21	John Gordon, Leeds
1980-81	Richard Geoffrey Wilkes OBE TD DL, Leics & Northants	1919-20	John William Woodthorpe, London
1979-80	David Gordon Richards, London	1917-19	Frederic John Young, London
1978-79	Eric Colin Sayers, Birmingham & W. Midlands	1916-17	Arthur Henry Gibson, Birmingham
1977-78	Brian Alfred Maynard MA, London	1915-16	Sir Horace Woodburn Kirby, London
1976-77	Stanley Kitchen, Birmingham & W. Midlands	1913-15	Horace Woodburn Kirby, London
1975-76	John Peter Grenside CBE, London	1912-13	Jarvis William Barber, Sheffield
1974-75	Kenneth Johnston Sharp TD MA, Carlisle	1911-12	Sir William Plender, London
1973-74	Edmund Kenneth Wright MA, London	1910-11	William Plender, London
1972-73	Douglas Spottiswoode Morpeth TD BCom, London	1909-10	Algernon Osmond Miles, London
1971-72	Arthur Halsall Walton, Manchester	1908-09	John Ball Ball, London
1970-71	Claude Croxton-Smith MA LLB, Bristol	1906-08	William Barclay Peat, London
1969-70	Ronald George Leach CBE, London	1905-06	John Gane, London
1968-69	Stanley Dixon MA, Birmingham	1904-05	John Sutherland Harmood-Banner, Liverpool
1967-68	Walter Edmund Parker CBE, London	1903-04	Francis William Pixley, London
1966-67	Sir Henry Alexander Benson CBE, London	1902-03	Alfred Augustus James, London
1965-66	Robert McNeil, Hove	1901-02	Walter Newton Fisher, Birmingham
1964-65	Wilfrid Guy Densem, London	1899-01	Ernest Cooper, London
1963-64	Robert Pearson Winter CBE MC TD DL, Newcastle	1897-99	John George Griffiths, London
1962-63	Percy Frederick Carpenter, London	1896-97	George Walter Knox, Sheffield
1961-62	Paul Francis Granger, Nottingham	1894-96	Charles Fitch Kemp, London
1960-61	Sidney John Pears, London	1892-94	Edwin Waterhouse MA, London
1959-60	Charles Urie Peat MC MA, London	1891-92	Thomas Abercrombie Welton, London
1958-59	William Leonard Barrows LLD, Birmingham	1889-91	Joseph John Saffrey, London
1957-58	William Halford Lawson CBE BA, London	1888-89	William Welch Deloitte, London
1956-57	Arthur Seymour Hamilton Dicker MBE, Norwich	1884-88	Frederick Whinney, London
1955-56	William Speight Carrington, London	1883-84	Arthur Cooper, London
		1882-83	Robert Palmer Harding, London
		1880-82	William Turquand, London

Past presidents are printed as they appear on a stone plaque in ICAEW's Chartered Accountants' Hall main entrance.

INVESTIGATION COMMITTEE
Chairman: Andrew Colquhoun (n) (i) (2009)
Vice-Chairman: Michael Barton (n) (2010)
Accountant members (n): Jeanette Brown; Alan Churchard; Philip Coleman; Paul Dawson; Stuart Diack; Jamie Gleave; Barry Lynch; Michael Pearce; Ali Sadiq
Non-accountant members: Nigel Day; Nigel Dodds; Stewart Goulding; Raj Mehtab; Molly Owen; Jane Rees; Tom Wheare; Ron Whitfield
Staff responsible: Ann Williams +44 (0)1908 546 290

REVIEWERS OF COMPLAINTS
Non-members: Julian Aylmer; Sarah Hannett

DISCIPLINARY COMMITTEE
Chairman: Richard Lea (n) (2011)
Vice-Chairman: Oliver Grundy (n) (2011)
Accountant members (n): Sohail Choudhry; Elliot Harris; David Kaye; Kevin Mawer; Marianne Neuhoff; Michael Swift; Ian Walker; Martin Ward; David Wilton
Non-accountant members: Paul Brooks; Tony Canham; Richard Farrant; Tony Foster; Mary Kelly; Richard Woodman; Peter Williamson
Staff responsible: Tracey Owen +44 (0)1908 546 289

APPEAL COMMITTEE
Chairman: Adrian Brunner (n) (i) (2004)
Vice-Chairman: Peter Susman (n) (i) (2006)
Accountant members (n): Nigel Atkinson; John Brendon; Michael Cox; Jonathan Dennis; John Ellison; Roger Fellows; Chris Harrison; David Ingram; Kaeed Mamujee; Lee Manning; Hasan Mirza; Richard Sweetman; Edward Weiss
Non-accountant members: Susan Bassnett; Peter Brown; Hew Mathewson
Staff responsible: Tracey Owen +44 (0)1908 546 289

MEMBER SUPPORT COMMITTEES

AUDIT AND ASSURANCE FACULTY
Chairman: Charles Bowman (e) (2011)
Vice-Chairman: tba
Council member: Susan Field (e)
Non-council members: Prof Stella Fearnley (c); David Herbinet (e); Sandra Higgins (e); Nigel Johnson (c); Philip Johnson (c); Steve Maslin (e); James Roberts (e); Myles Thompson (c); Peter Upton (e); Richard Wilson (e)
Staff responsible: Henry Irving +44 (0)20 7920 8450

CORPORATE FINANCE FACULTY
Chairman: Jim Keeling (e) (2011)
Vice Chairmen: Ian Leaman (n) (e); Ian Smart (n) (e) (2011)
Non-council members: David Coffman (c); David Collins (c); Nigel Crockford (c); Sachin Date (c); Giles Derry (e); Marc Fecher (c); Richard Green (c); Nigel Guy (c); Mark Hammond; (e); Simon Hawes (c); Mathew Kirk (e); Jon Moulton (c); Maggie Rodriguez-Piza (e); Christopher Searle (c); Nick Standen (c); Chilton Taylor (e); Chris Ward (e)
Staff responsible: David Petrie +44 (0)20 7920 8796

FINANCE AND MANAGEMENT FACULTY
Chairman: Carolyn Bresh (e) (n) (2009)
Deputy-Chairman: Tony Powell (e) (n) (2005)
Council members: Philip Smith (e); Jonathan Teller (c)
Non-council members: Paul Chan (e); John Ferguson (e); Daniel Holden (e); Helen Jesson (e); Leonard Jones (c); Simon Jones (e); Prof Bob Scapens (e); Graeme Scott (e); Judith Shackleton (e); Patricia Spreull (e); Helen Stevens (c); Michaela Talbot (e); Rob Thompson (e)
Staff responsible: Chris Jackson +44 (0)20 7920 8525

FINANCIAL REPORTING FACULTY
Chairman: Andy Simmonds (e) (2008)
Non-council members: Donald Broad (e); Kathryn Cearns (c); Neil Harris (e); Stephanie Henshaw (e); Peter Nicol (c); Brian Shearer (e); Danielle Stewart (e)
Staff responsible: Nigel Sleigh-Johnson +44 (0)20 7920 8793

FINANCIAL SERVICES FACULTY
Chairman: Mark Rhys (e) (n) (2008)
Deputy-Chairman: Alistair Hollows (e) (2008)
Vice-Chairman: Neeraj Kapur (e) (2008)
Non-council members: Richard Bertin (c); Eric Clapton (e); Iain Cummings (c); James Dean (c); Tim Harris (e); Pam Kaur (e); Paul Leech (c); Mike Lloyd (c); Richard Oldfield (c); David Roberts (e); David Symes (e); Daniel Taylor (e)
Staff responsible: Iain Coke +44 (0)20 7920 8674

INFORMATION TECHNOLOGY FACULTY
Chairman: John Oates (e) (n) (2009)
Deputy-Chairman: Nina Robinson (e) (2009)
Vice-Chairman: Simon Hurst (e) (2007)
Council members: Ara Martirossian (e); Jonathan Teller (e)
Non-council members: Jeremy Boss (c); Roland Brook (e); Emily Coltman (c); Piers Clinton-Tarestad (e); David Deaville (c); Steve Fraser (c); Andrew Garforth (e); Michael Hadfield (o); Ben Heald (c); Alan Livesey (e); John Palmer (o); George Quigley (c); Andrew Riley (e); Kevin Salter (e); Ian Whittaker (c)
Staff responsible: Richard Anning +44 (0)20 7920 8635

TAX FACULTY
Chairman: David Heaton (e) (2011)
Deputy-Chairman: Rebecca Bennyworth (n) (e) (2011)
Vice-Chairman: tba
Council members: Paul Aplin (e); Carl Bayley (e); Ian Hayes (e)
Non-council members: Lynnette Bober (e); Susan Gompels (c); Mark Lee (c); Philip Levi (e); Robert Maas (c); Jenny Marks (e); Chris Sanger (e); John Preston (e); Michael Sherry (e); Andrew Tall (e)
Staff responsible: Frank Haskew/Chrissie O'Connor +44 (0)20 7920 8618/8593

PRACTICE CENTRE STEERING COMMITTEE
Chairman: Howard Gross (e) (2010)
Council members: Susan Field; Constantine Ioannou; Rob Millea; Peter Mitchell; Joe Smoczynski; Mark Spofforth
Non-council members: Norman Armstrong; Chris Connor; Steve Corner; Michael Cox; Rachel Davis; Michael Dunham; Keith Ferguson; Peter Hollis; Eric Kench; Nicole Kissun
Head of Practice: Gill Sykes +44 (0)20 7920 8748
Staff responsible: Felicity Nelson +44 (0)20 7920 8678

SPECIALIST ADVISORY COMMITTEES

JOINT AUDIT COMMITTEE
Chairman: Simon Letts (n) (2009)
Non-council members (ICAEW): Peter Upton; Alan Wintersgill
Staff responsible: Tracy Stanhope +44 (0)1908 546 220

JOINT INSOLVENCY COMMITTEE
Member (ICAEW): John Milsom (n)
Staff responsible: Tracy Stanhope +44 (0)1908 546 220

JOINT PROFESSIONAL INDEMNITY INSURANCE COMMITTEE
Chairman: Mick Biles (n) (2010)
Member (ICAEW): tba
Staff responsible: Claire Phillips +44 (0)1908 546 279

BUSINESS LAW COMMITTEE
Chairman: Peter Chidgey (n) (2010)
Council member: Philip Pawson
Non-council members: David Furst; Gwyn Griffiths; John Hitchins; Grant Jones; Susanne Pust Shah; Ken Rigelsford; Alison Ring; Tim Vogel
Non-members: Sally Baker; Neil Barnicoat; Andrew Hobbs
Staff responsible: Felicity Banks +44 (0)20 7920 8413

CORPORATE GOVERNANCE COMMITTEE
Chairman: David Richardson (n) (2010)
Council member: Gerald Russell
Non-council members: Anthony Carey; Richard Clarke; Ian Durant; David Illingworth; Sean O'Hare; David Richardson; Martyn Scrivens; Oliver Tant
Non-members: Roger Barker; Frank Curtiss; George Dallas; Prof Marc Goergen; Susannah Haan; Rosemary Martin; Peter Murray; Ken Rushton
Staff responsible: Vanessa Jones +44 (0)20 7920 8714

CORPORATE RESPONSIBILTY ADVISORY GROUP
Chairman: Gaynor Coley (n) (2010)
Council member: Jan Babiak
Accountant members (n): Paul Druckman; Sir Michael Peat; Richard Reid
Non-members: David Bent; Lawrence Bloom; Will Day; Dame Mary Marsh; Sir Ian McAllister; Sir Mark Moody-Stuart; David Nussbaum; Prof Paul Palmer; Pavan Sukhdev
Staff responsible: Richard Spencer +44 (0)20 7920 8505

SUSTAINABILITY COMMITTEE
Chairman: Shonaid Jemmett-Page (n) (2010)
Vice-Chairman: David Bent (n) (2006)
Council member: tba
Non-council members: Tom Beagent; Martin Bennett; Margaret Bowler; Ian Byrne; Sue Charman; Richard Evans; Melba Foggo; Kathryn Haynes; David Logan; Hugh Parnell; Richard Porter; Peter Wong
Staff member: Richard Spencer
Staff responsible: Rachel Sinha +44 (0)20 7920 8794

INSOLVENCY COMMITTEE
Chairman: Tony Lomas (2003)
Council member: Barrie Harding
Non-council members: Samantha Bewick; Jeremy Knight; Jon Newell; Tony Nygate; Ted Wetton
Staff responsible: Liz Cole +44 (0)20 7920 8746

ETHICS STANDARDS COMMITTEE
Chairman: Iain Lowson (e) (2011)
Council members: Ashish Dave; John Hilton; Robin Liddell; Robert Millea; Fiona Wilkinson
Non-council members: John Acornley; Mike Ashley; Prof Christopher Cowton; Bill Morgan; Sue Nyman; Simon O'Neill; Naima Siddiqi
Staff member: Tony Bromell
Staff responsible: Elizabeth Higgs +44 (0)1908 248 322

TECHNICAL ADVISORY COMMITTEE
Chairman: Derek Haynes (n) (2008)
Vice-Chairman: tba
Council member: Malcolm Bacchus (representing London)
Non-council members: 39 (three from London and one or two from each other district society)
Staff responsible: Andrew Gambier +44 (0)20 7920 8643

OPERATIONAL COMMITTEES

ASSESSMENT COMMITTEE
Chairman: David Blondel (n) (2007)
Vice-Chairman: Prof Ursula Lucas (n) (2010)
Accountant members (n): David Brookfield; Graham Gaddes; Prof Peter Moizer; Paul Robins; Michael Walby
Non-member: Stephen Isherwood
Staff members: Gavin Aspden; Mark Protherough
Staff responsible: Elizabeth Blount +44 (0)1908 248 309

ETHICS ADVISORY COMMITTEE
Chairman: Adrian Keene (2006)
Vice-Chairman: Philip Pawson (2008)
Council members: Michael Hawley; Nathan Steinberg
Non-council members: Mike Arnold; Stephen Cole; Robert Davies; Alison Lally; Heather Lamont; Mark Lee; Kerry Ransley
Staff responsible: Amanda Digne-Malcolm +44 (0)1908 248 332

CACS LTD BOARD
Chairman: John Oyler (n) (2010)
Members (ICAEW) (n): Randal Brew; Bryan Frost
Staff responsible: Ben Jowett +44 (0)1908 546 287

CACS COMPENSATION COMMITTEE
Chairman: John Oyler (n) (2010)
Accountant members (ICAEW) (n): Randal Brew; Brian Frost; Richard Moore
Non-accountant members: Ben Carroll; Razi Shah
Staff responsible: Ben Jowett +44 (0)1908 546 287

RESEARCH ADVISORY BOARD
Chairman: Peter Holgate (n) (2006)
Vice-Chairman: Prof Martin Walker (n) (2004)
Accountant members (n): Andrew Jones; Ray Mackie; Stuart McLeay
Non-members: Prof David Heald; Prof David Otley; Prof Alfred Wagenhofer
Staff members: Prof Richard Macve; Prof Laura Spira
Staff responsible: Gillian Knight +44 (0)20 7920 8478

PRACTICE ASSURANCE COMMITTEE
Chairman: David Cleaver (n) (2011)
Vice-Chairman: Helen Drew (n) (2011)
Accountant members (n): William Duncumb; Jane Fowler; Bipin Kotecha; John Malthouse; Sarah Tuvey; Linda Wiggins
Non-accountant members: David Craig; Alan Nelson; Michael Williams
Staff responsible: Carrie Langridge +44 (0)1908 546 313

PROFESSIONAL INDEMNITY INSURANCE COMMITTEE
Chairman: Mick Biles (n) (2009)
Vice-Chairman: tba
Accountant members (n): Nick Cudmore; Christopher Lawman; Michael Sands; Mike Sturgess; Tony Taylor
Non-member: Ian Joslin
Staff responsible: Claire Phillips +44 (0)1908 546 279

OTHER APPOINTMENTS

ASSOCIATION OF ACCOUNTING TECHNICIANS (AAT)
ICAEW nominated members: Mark Barnish (n); Andrea Dunhill (n); David Walker

ICAEW TRUSTS
CAT Ltd (incl. CALL, CATER, CAPET, ICAEW Foundation, PD Leake)
ICAEW appointed members: Prof Chris Humphrey (n); David Illingworth (n) [Chairman]; Heather Lamont (n); Andrew Pianca (n); Gerald Russell
ACA Ltd
ICAEW appointed members: Roger Lawson (n); Michael Pavia (n) [Chairman]; Martin Robinson (n); Teresa Sienkiewicz (n)
Members appointed from membership: Michael Day; John Hamblin; David Young
FCA Ltd
ICAEW appointed members: Andrew Evans (n); David Illingworth (n) [Chairman]; Andrew Martyn-Johns (n); Jan Weber John Woodman (n)
Members appointed from membership: John O'Donnell (n); Alan Hind (n); John Morton (n); David Young (n)
Staff responsible (ACA Ltd and FCA Ltd): Daria Croker/Liza Elliott +44 (0)1908 248 330/230
Staff responsible (CAT Ltd): Ianthe Alles +44 (0)20 7920 8550

LONDON SOCIETY OF CHARTERED ACCOUNTANTS MAIN COMMITTEE
Council nominees: Malcolm Bacchus; Dennis Cox; Jimmy Daboo; Jan Weber
Staff responsible: Ian Strange +44 (0)20 7920 8788

ICAEW HONORARY MEMBERSHIP

ICAEW gives honorary membership to people who have made an outstanding contribution to the accountancy profession and/or the finance and business world.

Any member can nominate individuals for the accolade. The Nominating Committee considers all nominations then makes a formal proposal to council, which makes the final decision.

HRH The Prince of Wales
Recognised for his commitment to the sustainability agenda; the involvement of the accountancy profession through the *Accounting for Sustainability* project, and the assistance given to young people and businesses generally through the Princes Trust and similar initiatives, which promote business start-ups, personal development and community projects.

Sir Adrian Cadbury
Recognised for his work on corporate governance.

Sir Bryan Nicholson GBE
Recognised for his contribution to the profession and to UK business over many years.

Dr Wang Jun, Vice-Minister of Finance of the People's Republic of China.
Recognised for his contribution to China's accounting reform.

Prof Stephen Zeff, Herbert S. Autrey Professor of Accounting, Jones Graduate School of Management, Rice University, Houston, Texas.
Recognised for his long career as one of the leading accounting and standard setting historians and his contribution to the work of ICAEW.

HONOURS

BIRTHDAY HONOURS 2011

The following ICAEW members were honoured in the Queen's Birthday Honours lists.

Deborah Griffin OBE BSc ACA
Recognised for services to women's rugby

Peter Lloyd CBE LLB FCA
Recognised for services to the defence industry

David Charles Lockwood OBE BSc ACA FRSA
Recognised for services to industry in Scotland

Peter Metcalf MBE FCA DChA
Recognised for services to the community in Preston, Lancashire

Philip John Willoughby OBE FCA
Recognised for services to the City of London Corporation and to charity

NEW YEAR HONOURS 2011

The following ICAEW members were honoured in the Queen's New Year Honours lists.

Vernon Ian Barker OBE BA ACA
Recognised for services to the rail industry

Richard John Boot OBE FCA
Recognised for services to business in the West Midlands

Richard John Bottomley OBE FCA
Recognised for services to the accountancy profession and to business in the North East

Sir Martin Faulkner Broughton FCA
Recognised for services to business

John Arthur Cuthbert OBE DL BSc ACA
Recognised for services to business in the North East

Andrew Fleming Hind CB FCA
Lately chief executive of the Charity Commission for England and Wales

Alistair Dewar Kerr Johnston CMG BSc FCA
Recognised for services to the Foreign and Commonwealth Office Board of Management

Keith Robert Mansell MBE FCA
Recognised for services to gliding

Jonathan Edward Moor CBE BA FCA
Director, Aviation Directorate, Department of Transport

Alexis Jane Redmond MBE BA ACA
Recognised for services to the community in Merseyside

The Hon Philip John Remnant CBE MA ACA
Recognised for services to the financial services industry and to the public sector

Leyland Bradshaw Ridings MBE FCA
Recognised for services to local government

Colin Deverell Smith OBE BCom FCA
Recognised for services to Assured Food Standards

John Leslie Sparkes MBE FCA
Recognised for voluntary service to special needs education and adult services

Kenneth Wild OBE BA FCA
Recognised for services to financial reporting

REGIONAL AND DISTRICT SOCIETY CONTACTS

Our network of 10 regional offices in England and Wales plays a key role in raising our profile around the country. They build relationships with key stakeholders and ensure that members' views on business issues are promoted effectively.

The 22 district societies, along with the Institute Members in Scotland, serve local needs and interests, and supplement locally many of the services which ICAEW provides nationally. They can also help members of the public looking for the services of a chartered accountant. If you are unable to contact the relevant region or district society, you can telephone the regional services department at ICAEW in London, on +44 (0)20 7920 8595.

EAST ENGLAND REGION
REGIONAL DIRECTOR
Phillippa Bourne
PO Box 217, Royston SG8 1AX
T +44 (0)1223 654 681 F +44 (0)1223 654 680
M +44 (0)7876 035 926
E phillippa.bourne@icaew.com; eastengland@icaew.com
DISTRICT SOCIETIES IN THIS REGION
Beds, Bucks & Herts Society of Chartered Accountants
East Anglian Society of Chartered Accountants
South Essex Society of Chartered Accountants

EAST MIDLANDS REGION
REGIONAL DIRECTOR
Tom Madden
PO Box 16025, Henley in Arden B95 8BA
T +44 (0)115 822 1881 F +44 (0)115 822 1880
M +44 (0)7918 739 049
E tom.madden@icaew.com
E eastmidlands@icaew.com
DISTRICT SOCIETIES IN THIS REGION
Leicestershire & Northamptonshire Society of Chartered Accountants
Nottingham, Derby and Lincoln Society of Chartered Accountants

LONDON REGION
REGIONAL OFFICE
Chartered Accountants' Hall
Moorgate Place
London EC2R 6EA
T +44 (0)20 7920 8682 F +44 (0)20 7920 8648
E london@icaew.com
REGIONAL DIRECTOR
Ian Strange
T +44 (0)20 7920 8788
M +44 (0)7876 035 933
E ian.strange@icaew.com
REGIONAL EXECUTIVE
Elizabeth Russell
T +44 (0)20 7920 8562
E elizabeth.russell@icaew.com
DISTRICT SOCIETIES IN THIS REGION
London Society of Chartered Accountants
Croydon and District Society of Chartered Accountants

NORTH WEST REGION
REGIONAL DIRECTOR
Melanie Christie
PO Box 273, Leyland PR26 7WS
T +44 (0)1925 594 283 F +44 (0)1925 594 280
E northwest@icaew.com
DISTRICT SOCIETIES IN THIS REGION
Isle of Man Society of Chartered Accountants
Liverpool Society of Chartered Accountants
Manchester Chartered Accountants
North West Society of Chartered Accountants

NORTHERN REGION
REGIONAL DIRECTOR
Keith Proudfoot
PO Box 417, Newcastle Upon Tyne NE3 9AS
T +44 (0)191 300 0531 F +44 (0)191 300 0530
M +44 (0)7918 194 133
E keith.proudfoot@icaew.com; northern@icaew.com
DISTRICT SOCIETY IN THIS REGION
Northern Society of Chartered Accountants

SOUTH EAST REGION
REGIONAL DIRECTOR
Fay Webster
PO Box 442, Southampton SO31 0AR
T +44 (0)1483 901 821 F +44 (0)1483 901 820
M +44 (0)7918 196 050
E fay.webster@icaew.com; southeast@icaew.com
DISTRICT SOCIETIES IN THIS REGION
South Eastern Society of Chartered Accountants
Southern Society of Chartered Accountants
Thames Valley Society of Chartered Accountants

SOUTH WEST REGION
REGIONAL DIRECTOR
Jon Blake
PO Box 872, Taunton TA1 9GZ
T +44 (0)117 370 1461 F +44 (0)117 370 1460
M +44 (0)7793 834 326
E jon.blake@icaew.com; southwest@icaew.com
DISTRICT SOCIETIES IN THIS REGION
South Western Society of Chartered Accountants
West of England Society of Chartered Accountants

WALES BUSINESS CENTRE
REGIONAL OFFICE
Regus House, Falcon Drive
Cardiff Bay
Cardiff CF10 4RU
T +44 (0)29 2002 1482 F +44 (0)29 2002 1480
E wales@icaew.com; cymru@icaew.com
REGIONAL DIRECTOR
David Lermon
T +44 (0)29 2002 1481 F +44 (0)29 2002 1480
M +44 (0)7876 035 935
E david.lermon@icaew.com
DISTRICT SOCIETY IN THIS REGION
South Wales Society of Chartered Accountants

WEST MIDLANDS REGION
REGIONAL DIRECTOR
Nigel Hastilow
PO Box 255, Evesham WR11 9AT
T +44 (0)121 270 8941 F +44 (0)121 270 8940
M +44 (0)7876 035 940
E nigel.hastilow@icaew.com; westmidlands@icaew.com
DISTRICT SOCIETIES IN THIS REGION
Birmingham and West Midlands Society of Chartered Accountants
Staffs, Salop and Wolverhampton Society of Chartered Accountants

YORKSHIRE & HUMBER REGION
REGIONAL DIRECTOR
Chris Manners
PO Box 504, Keighley BD21 9AW
T +44 (0)113 322 0871 F +44 (0)113 322 0870
M +44 (0)7753 715 812
E chris.manners@icaew.com; yorks-humberside@icaew.com
DISTRICT SOCIETIES IN THIS REGION
Humberside and District Society of Chartered Accountants
Sheffield & District Society of Chartered Accountants
West Yorkshire Society of Chartered Accountants

DISTRICT SOCIETY CONTACTS

1. BEDS, BUCKS & HERTS SOCIETY OF CHARTERED ACCOUNTANTS
President: Liz Perry
Regional Executive: Kim Shield
PO Box 1384, Hemel Hempstead HP1 9NA
T +44 (0)1223 654 682
E kim.shield@icaew.com; bbhsca@icaew.com
Branches: no recognised branches

2. BIRMINGHAM AND WEST MIDLANDS SOCIETY OF CHARTERED ACCOUNTANTS
President: Peter Rees-Steer
Regional Executive: Terry Smythe
PO Box 110, Wellington TF1 6QX
T +44 (0)121 270 8944 F +44 (0)121 270 8940
E terry.smythe@icaew.com; bwmsca@icaew.com
Branches: Warwickshire Society; Worcestershire Branch (contact district society)

3. CROYDON AND DISTRICT SOCIETY OF CHARTERED ACCOUNTANTS
President: Richard Morgan
Regional Executive: Jacquie Fairclough
PO Box 2436, Purley CR8 2NX
T +44 (0)20 8763 6261 F +44 (0)20 7920 8648
E jacquie.fairclough@icaew.com; croydonsca@icaew.com
Branches: no recognised branches

4. EAST ANGLIAN SOCIETY OF CHARTERED ACCOUNTANTS
President: Robert Millea
Regional Executives: Margaret Jackson and Michelle May-Jones
St Andrews Castle, 33 St Andrews Street South, Bury St Edmunds, Suffolk IP33 3PH
T +44 (0)1223 654 686 F +44 (0)1223 654 680
E margaret.jackson@icaew.com; michelle.may-jones@icaew.com; eastangliansca@icaew.com
Branches: Cambridge Society; Ipswich and Colchester Society; Norfolk and Norwich Society (contact district society)

5. HUMBERSIDE AND DISTRICT SOCIETY OF CHARTERED ACCOUNTANTS
President: Jane Mather
Regional Executive: Alexia Bahadur
PO Box 250, Goole DN14 4AA
T +44 (0)113 322 0874 F +44 (0)113 322 0870
E alexia.bahadur@icaew.com
Branches: Grimsby and North Lincolnshire Society (contact district society)

6. LEICESTERSHIRE & NORTHAMPTONSHIRE SOCIETY OF CHARTERED ACCOUNTANTS
President: Brad Revell
Regional Executive: Vicky Nicholas
PO Box 717, Spratton, Northampton NN6 8WP
T +44 (0)115 822 1883 F +44 (0)115 822 1880
E vicky.nicholas@icaew.com; lansca@icaew.com
Branches: no recognised branches

7. LIVERPOOL SOCIETY OF CHARTERED ACCOUNTANTS
President: Martyn Best
Regional Executive: Alex Pilkington
PO Box 471, Wigan WN2 1WY
T +44 (0)1925 594 284 F +44 (0)1925 594 280
E alex.pilkington@icaew.com; liverpoolsca@icaew.com
Branches: Chester and North Wales Society; Southport Society (contact district society); Isle of Man Society T +44 (0)1624 662 788 (independent society)

8. LONDON SOCIETY OF CHARTERED ACCOUNTANTS
President: Grant Jones
Regional Executive: Elizabeth Russell
Chartered Accountants' Hall, Moorgate Place, London EC2R 6EA
T +44 (0)20 7920 8682 F +44 (0)20 7920 8648
E lsca@icaew.com
Branches: North London Society (contact district society)

9. MANCHESTER CHARTERED ACCOUNTANTS
President: Martin Robinson
Regional Executive: Astrid Leather
PO Box 480, Northwich, Cheshire CW9 9AG
T +44 (0)1925 594 282 F +44 (0)1925 594 280
E astrid.leather@icaew.com; manchestersca@icaew.com
Branches: Bolton Society (contact district society)

10. NORTH WEST SOCIETY OF CHARTERED ACCOUNTANTS
President: Leslie Bury
Regional Executive: Clare Parisi
PO Box 1260, Preston PR2 0NY
T +44 (0)1925 594 281 F +44 (0)1925 594 280
E clare.parisi@icaew.com; northwest@icaew.com
Branches: no recognised branches

11. NORTHERN SOCIETY OF CHARTERED ACCOUNTANTS
President: David Swallow
Regional Executive: Marie Rice
PO Box 767, Wallsend NE28 5DQ
T +44 (0)191 300 0532 F +44 (0)191 300 0530
E marie.rice@icaew.com; northernsca@icaew.com
Branches: Cumberland Society; Teesside Society; Tyne and Wear Society (contact district society)

12. NOTTINGHAM, DERBY AND LINCOLN SOCIETY OF CHARTERED ACCOUNTANTS
President: Jeremy Mumby
Regional Executive: Elaine Franklin
PO Box 8543, Nottingham NG16 9AE
T +44 (0)115 822 1882 F +44 (0)115 822 1880
E elaine.franklin@icaew.com; nottinghamsca@icaew.com
Branches: Derby Society; Lincoln Society; Nottingham Society (contact district society)

13. SHEFFIELD & DISTRICT SOCIETY OF CHARTERED ACCOUNTANTS
President: Steve Knowles
Regional Executive: Carmel Smithson
The Blades Enterprise Centre, Greystones Suite, Sheffield United Football Club, John Street, Sheffield S2 4SU
T +44 (0)113 322 0873 F +44 (0)113 322 0870
E carmel.smithson@icaew.com; sheffieldsca@icaew.com
Branches: no recognised branches

14. SOUTH EASTERN SOCIETY OF CHARTERED ACCOUNTANTS
President: Malcolm Kimber
Regional Executive: Katherine Skinner
PO Box 442, Southampton SO31 0AR
T +44 (0)1483 901 822
F +44 (0)1925 901 820
E katherine.skinner@icaew.com
Branches: no recognised branches

15. SOUTH ESSEX SOCIETY OF CHARTERED ACCOUNTANTS
President: Paul Rolison
Regional Executive: Linda Howard
2nd floor, Parker House, 104a Hutton Road, Shenfield, Essex CM15 8NE
T +44 (0)1223 654 684 F +44 (0)1223 654 680
E linda.howard@icaew.com; southessexsca@icaew.com
Branches: no recognised branches

16. SOUTH WALES SOCIETY OF CHARTERED ACCOUNTANTS
President: Nick Toye
Regional Executive: Emma Friedl
PO Box 217, Penarth CF64 9EE
T +44 (0)29 2002 1482 F +44 (0)29 2002 1480
E emma.friedl@icaew.com; wales@icaew.com
Branches: Cardiff and District Society; Gwent and Powys Society; Swansea and West Wales Society (contact district society)

17. SOUTH WESTERN SOCIETY OF CHARTERED ACCOUNTANTS
President: Lucinda Penn
Regional Executive: Trudi Coles
PO Box 80, Launceston PL15 7BB
T +44 (0)117 370 1463 F +44 (0)117 370 1460
E trudi.coles@icaew.com; southwesternsca@icaew.com
Branches: Cornwall and Plymouth Society; Exeter and District Society; Somerset Society (contact district society)

18. SOUTHERN SOCIETY OF CHARTERED ACCOUNTANTS
President: Henry Flint
Regional Executive: Rachel Monk
PO Box 442, Southampton SO31 0AR
T +44 (0)1483 901 823
F +44 (0)1925 901 820
E rachel.monk@icaew.com
Branches: no recognised branches

19. STAFFS, SALOP AND WOLVERHAMPTON SOCIETY OF CHARTERED ACCOUNTANTS
President: Robert Morris
Regional Executive: Terry Smythe
PO Box 110, Wellington TF1 6QX
T +44 (0)121 270 8944 F +44 (0)121 270 8940
E terry.smythe@icaew.com; bwmsca@icaew.com
Branches: Staffordshire Society; Shropshire Society; Wolverhampton Society (contact district society)

20. THAMES VALLEY SOCIETY OF CHARTERED ACCOUNTANTS
President: Michael Cooper
Regional Executive: Sue Pye
PO Box 425, Redhill RH1 2GX
T +44 (0)1483 901 824 F +44 (0)1483 901 820
E sue.pye@icaew.com; thamesvalleysca@icaew.com
Branch: no recognised branches

21. WEST OF ENGLAND SOCIETY OF CHARTERED ACCOUNTANTS
President: Sarah Matthews
Regional Executive: Karen Evans
PO Box 310, Bristol BS16 0BA
T +44 (0)117 370 1464 F +44 (0)117 370 1460
E karen.evans@icaew.com; wesca@icaew.com
Branches: no recognised branches

22. WEST YORKSHIRE SOCIETY OF CHARTERED ACCOUNTANTS
President: Philip Pawson
Regional Executive: Esta Andrews
PO Box 1508, Huddersfield HD1 9HB
T +44 (0)113 322 0875 F +44 (0)113 322 0870
E esta.andrews@icaew.com; westyorkshiresca@icaew.com
Branches: Bradford Society; Huddersfield Society; York Society (contact district society)

23. ICAEW MEMBERS IN SCOTLAND
President: Shelah Dutta
Regional Executive: Fiona Ormiston
PO Box 26198, Dunfermline, Fife KY12 8ZD
T +44 (0)131 202 1251 F +44 (0)131 202 1250
E fiona.ormiston@icaew.com

ACHIEVE YOUR POTENTIAL AND ENHANCE YOUR CAREER

Throughout your career you want to be sure that you get the very best in learning and professional development. To fulfil your potential, choose qualifications and programmes from ICAEW: they represent the highest standards of achievement.

- ACA
- Certificate in Finance, Accounting and Business
- ICAEW Diploma in IFRSs
- IFRSs learning and assessment programme
- Certificate in International Public Sector Financial Reporting
- IFRS for SMEs learning and assessment programme
- Corporate Finance qualification
- Diploma in Charity Accounting
- Forensic Accountant and Expert Witness Accreditation
- ICAEW ISAs programme
- ICAEW Certificate in Insolvency
- Business Sustainability Programme
- Pathways to Membership

+44 (0)1908 248 250

icaew.com/learning

STUDENT SOCIETIES AND NETWORKS

ICAEW STUDENT COUNCIL (ISC) 2011–2012

Chair: Tom Noble
T +44 (0)7766 246 513
E tnoble@deloitte.co.uk

Vice Chair: Matthew Bennett
T +44 (0)7828 939 269
E matthew.s.bennett@uk.pwc.com

ICAEW contact: Mauro Lucrino
T +44 (0)1908 248 108
E mauro.lucrino@icaew.com

STUDENT SOCIETIES AND NETWORKS

BEDS, BUCKS & HERTS
Contact: Kim Shield
T +44 (0)1223 654 682
E kim.shield@icaew.com

BIRMINGHAM
Contact: Anne Hipkiss
T +44 (0)121 258 0245
E annehipkiss@blueyonder.co.uk

BRADFORD & DISTRICT
Contact: Esta Andrews
T +44 (0)1484 428 022
E esta.andrews@icaew.com

BRISTOL & DISTRICT
Contact: Karen Evans
T +44 (0)7876 035 944
E karen.evans@icaew.com

CHESTER & NORTH WALES
Contact: Alex Pilkington
T +44 (0)1925 594 284
E alex.pilkington@icaew.com

CUMBERLAND
Contact: Keith Proudfoot
T (0)191 300 0531
E keith.proudfoot@icaew.com

EAST ANGLIAN
Contact: Michelle May-Jones
T +44 (0)1223 654 686
E michelle.may-jones@icaew.com

HUDDERSFIELD
Contact: Esta Andrews
T +44 (0)113 322 0875
E esta.andrews@icaew.com

HUMBERSIDE
Contact: Alexia Bahadur
T +44 (0)113 322 0874
E alexia.bahadur@icaew.com

ISLE OF MAN
Contact: Cheryl Pryke
T +44 (0)1624 662 788
E cheryl.pryke@icaew.com

LEEDS
Contact: Gillian North
T +44 (0)113 322 0872
E gillian.north@icaew.com

LEICESTERSHIRE & NORTHAMPTONSHIRE
Contact: Vicky Nicholas
T +44 (0)115 822 1883
E vicky.nicholas@icaew.com

LIVERPOOL
Contact: Alex Pilkington
T +44 (0)1925 594 284
E alex.pilkington@icaew.com

LONDON
Contact: Annaliese Shiret
T +44 (0)20 7920 3515
E annaliese.shiret@icaew.com

MANCHESTER
Contact: Astrid Leather
T +44 (0)1925 594 282
E astrid.leather@icaew.com

NORTH WEST
Contact: Clare Parisi
T +44 (0)1925 594 281
E clare.parisi@icaew.com

NORTHERN
Contact: Keith Proudfoot
T +44 (0)191 300 0531
E keith.proudfoot@icaew.com

NOTTINGHAM
Contact: Elaine Franklin
T +44 (0)115 822 1882
E elaine.franklin@icaew.com

SHEFFIELD & DISTRICT
Contact: Carmel Smithson
T +44 (0)113 322 0873
E carmel.smithson@icaew.com

SOUTH & EAST WALES
Contact: Emma Friedl
T +44 (0)29 2002 1482
E emma.friedl@icaew.com

SOUTH EAST
Contact: Katherine Skinner
T +44 (0)1483 901 822
E katherine.skinner@icaew.com

SOUTHERN
Contact: Rachel Monk
T +44 (0)1483 901 823
E rachel.monk@icaew.com

SOUTH WEST SOCIETY
Contact: Trudi Coles
T +44 (0)117 370 1463
E trudi.coles@icaew.com

THAMES VALLEY
Contact: Sue Pye
T +44 (0)1483 901 824
E sue.pye@icaew.com

INTERNATIONAL
China
Contact: Joanna Zhou
E joanna.zhou@cn.ey.com

Cyprus
Contact: Daoud Abulhawa, Chair
E daoud.abulhawa@cy.pwc.com

Middle East
Contact: Nauman Asif, Chair
E nmian@bayt.net

Russia
Contact: Sergei Zaitsev, Chair
E zaitsev@dstadvisors.ru

South East Asia (Malaysia)
Contact: Uqba Jamshaid, Chair
E uqba12@gmail.com

South East Asia (Singapore)
Contact: Lintong Yan, Chair
E yanlintong@hotmail.com

The student representatives from each of the student groups listed on this page are correct at the time of going to press. Any changes after 1 September 2011 may not be incorporated.

ICAEW CONTACT INFORMATION

OUR OFFICES

UK
Chartered Accountants' Hall
Moorgate Place
London EC2R 6EA UK
T +44 (0)20 7920 8100
contactus@icaew.com
icaew.com

Metropolitan House
321 Avebury Boulevard
Milton Keynes MK9 2FZ UK
T +44 (0)1908 248 100
contactus@icaew.com
icaew.com

EUROPE REGION
Europe
227 Rue de la Loi
B-1040 Brussels
Belgium
T +32 (0)2 230 3272
europe@icaew.com
icaew.com/europe

GREATER CHINA REGION
China
Room 706A Tower E1 Oriental Plaza
No.1 East Chang An Avenue Dong Cheng District
Beijing
100738 China
T +86 10 8518 8622
china@icaew.com
icaew.com/china

Hong Kong
27th Floor
Wu Chung House
213 Queen's Road East
Wanchai, Hong Kong
T +852 2287 7277
hongkong@icaew.com
icaew.com/hongkong

SOUTH EAST ASIA REGION
South East Asia
9 Temasek Boulevard
#09-01 Suntec Tower Two
Singapore 038989
T +65 6407 1554
southeastasia@icaew.com
icaew.com/southeastasia

Malaysia
Level 2 Chulan Tower
3 Jalan Conlay
50450 Kuala Lumpur
T +60 3 2171 6022
malaysia@icaew.com
icaew.com/malaysia

MIDDLE EAST REGION
Middle East
Currency House Unit 4, Level 4
Dubai International Financial Centre
PO Box 506836 Dubai
United Arab Emirates
T +971 (0)4 408 0000 (ext 710000)
middleeast@icaew.com
icaew.com/middleeast

OFFICE-HOLDERS
President: Clive Parritt FCA CF FIIA FRSA
Deputy-President: Mark Spofforth BSc FCA CTA FRSA
Vice-President: Martyn Jones BSc FCA CTA FRSA
Chief Executive: Michael Izza BA FCA

USEFUL TELEPHONE NUMBERS

We offer a wide range of services to members so that they can keep up to date professionally. Direct line numbers for some of the most frequently used services are listed below.

ACA training	+44 (0)1908 248 250
Audit and Assurance Faculty	+44 (0)20 7920 8493
Business Centre Reception	+44 (0)20 7920 8800
Communications	+44 (0)20 7920 8633
Continuing Professional Development	+44 (0)1908 248 250
Corporate Finance Faculty	+44 (0)20 7920 8685
Ethics helpline service	+44 (0)1908 248 250
Finance and Management Faculty	+44 (0)20 7920 8508
Financial Reporting Faculty	+44 (0)20 7920 8533
Financial Services Faculty	+44 (0)20 7920 8685
Information Centre	+44 (0)1908 248 250
Insolvency licensing	+44 (0)1908 546 250
IT Faculty	+44 (0)20 7920 8481
Library and Information Service	+44 (0)20 7920 8620
Media relations	+44 (0)20 7920 8630
Membership enquiries and subscriptions	+44 (0)1908 248 250
Money laundering helpline	+44 (0)1908 248 250
One Moorgate Place restaurant	+44 (0)20 7920 8626
Practice Support Services	+44 (0)1908 248 250
Practice Assurance helpline	+44 (0)1908 248 250
President's Appointments Scheme	+44 (0)1908 248 037
Regulatory support	+44 (0)1908 546 302
Special Interest Groups	+44 (0)1908 248 250
Support members	+44 (0)800 917 3526
Tax Faculty	+44 (0)20 7920 8646
Technical enquiries service	+44 (0)1908 248 250

ENQUIRIES
If you have an enquiry and you are not sure who to call, please ring +44 (0)1908 248 250.

SENIOR MANAGEMENT TEAM
Chief Executive
Michael Izza BA FCA T +44 (0)20 7920 8419
Executive Director, Finance and Operations
Robin Fieth BA FCA T +44 (0)20 7920 8464
Executive Director, Technical Strategy
Robert Hodgkinson MA FCA T +44 (0)20 7920 8492
Executive Director, Learning and Professional Development
Mark Protherough MA MBA T +44 (0)20 7920 8563
Executive Director, Professional Standards
Vernon Soare MA MBA ACA CPFA T +44 (0)20 7920 8787

ICAEW PRODUCTS AND SERVICES

BUSINESS CENTRE
The Business Centre at Chartered Accountants' Hall offers members a modern base in the City of London with free access to computers, comfortable work spaces, printers, the internet and WiFi. There is a café and relaxation area, plus bookable meeting rooms.

CHARTERED ACCOUNTANTS' HALL
One Moorgate Place – headquarters of ICAEW – offers a range of elegant and contemporary spaces for meetings and events. Rooms vary from the smallest meeting room for 8 delegates, to the Great Hall, which seats 300. ICAEW members and member firms receive a 10% discount on bookings.

One Moorgate Place Restaurant offers high quality food and a relaxed ambience in sophisticated surroundings. You can also hire it for private dining and receptions.

To find out more, visit **onemoorgateplace.com**
T +44 (0)20 7920 8613 or E events@onemoorgateplace.com

ECONOMIC INSIGHT
Working in partnership with the Centre for Economic and Business Research (Cebr), we provide monthly UK, and quarterly Middle East, South East Asia, and Greater China briefings to ICAEW members and other finance and business professionals. The reports provide global and regionally-focused economic analysis and intelligence.

To find out more or to download the *Economic Insight* briefings, visit: **icaew.com/economicinsight**

FACULTIES AND SPECIAL INTEREST GROUPS
For a small subscription fee, you can further develop your professional knowledge by joining one of our 7 faculties and 12 special interest groups.

With over 30,000 members, the faculties provide an essential source of technical expertise, the latest knowledge of good practice, thought leadership and invaluable networking opportunities. The faculties include audit and assurance; corporate finance; finance and management; financial reporting; financial services; information technology; and tax. To find out more, visit **icaew.com/faculties**

The special interest groups provide practical support, information and the chance to network with your peers when working in, or for, a particular sector. The groups are: charity and voluntary sector; entertainment and media; farming and rural business; forensic; healthcare; insolvency; interim management; non-executive directors; public sector; solicitors; tourism and hospitality; and valuation. To find out more, visit **icaew.com/sigs**

ICAEW.COM
Our website (**icaew.com**) provides a wealth of news and information for anyone with an interest in accountancy. The site includes details on how to become a chartered accountant, the services chartered accountants offer and links to the online edition of the *Directory of Firms*.

If you are a member, you can log into your own dedicated area of the site (**icaew.com/members**) using your membership number and password. Here you will find details of member services, technical helplines, events and personalised information from faculties and regions.

ICAEW BUSINESS ADVICE SERVICE
ICAEW has launched its new Business Advice Service to promote the use of ICAEW Chartered Accountants by businesses. ICAEW firms which join the service will offer SMEs and start-ups an initial meeting at no charge to discuss their business needs.

After the initial meeting, the SME or start-up is free to end its association with the firm. On the other hand, the service may provide the firm with a valuable introduction to a new client.

Firms participating in the service will be identified in the *ICAEW Directory of Firms* with this symbol **BAS**. This will allow SMEs to easily identify participating firms.

Under the ICAEW Business Advice Service, it is made clear that no financial commitment is made by the SME in the first instance.

Full details of the service can be found at **businessadviceservice.com**

ICAEW/GRANT THORNTON UK BUSINESS CONFIDENCE MONITOR (BCM)
The *ICAEW/Grant Thornton UK Business Confidence Monitor* (BCM) provides a regular snapshot of the state of the economy, informed by senior business professionals advising and running all types of business across the UK. The findings are shared with a range of policy-makers at a national and regional level, and are used by the business community, academics and researchers, providing a robust tool on which government and regional authorities can base policy decisions. To find out more, visit **icaew.com/bcm**

LIBRARY & INFORMATION SERVICES (LIS)
The LIS sits within the Business Centre. Our information experts provide members with a range of specialist services, including accountancy, tax, company and business information. The LIS's website provides free online access to premium resources such as market research reports, country profiles, ebooks, international trade and business journals, available worldwide 24/7. We also offer enquiry, book loan and document delivery services, usually with a 24-hour turnaround. To find out more, visit **icaew.com/library**

MEDIATION
Mediation can help resolve disputes, quickly, cost effectively and in confidence. Qualified mediators, including solicitors, barristers and chartered accountants, work as a team with the parties to resolve a wide range of disputes.

We offer two mediation services.

1. For FTSE companies: Resolving Commercial Disputes service

For more information visit **resolvingcommercialdisputes.com**

2. For all other types of dispute: ICAEW's mediation service

To find out more, visit **icaew.com/mediation**

MEMBERSHIP OFFERS
We have partnered with leading companies to provide our members with a range of discounts and offers to support their personal and professional lives. From finance and insurance products to car rental and online retailers, we have selected products and services to suit all your needs. To find out more, visit **icaew.com/memberoffers**

PRACTICE SUPPORT SERVICES
We offer a range of Practice Support Services to assist members in practice, including audit coaching and cold file reviews, Practice Assurance and DPB compliance reviews, practice management consultancy, anti-money laundering coaching, and Bribery Act coaching (also relevant to members in business). The services are provided by a dedicated team of experts who have extensive practice experience and are exempt from the duty to report misconduct.

For more information, T +44 (0)1908 248 250,
E practice.services@icaew.com or visit **icaew.com/practicesupport**

PRESIDENT'S APPOINTMENTS SCHEME

We keep a database of members and others who are specialists in arbitration, mediation and expert determination. If you are looking for an independent valuation of shares in a company, have a partnership dispute or need the services of a forensic accountant as an expert witness, this scheme can help.

For more information or a copy of the scheme guidelines,
T +44 (0)1908 248 037 or visit **icaew.com/presidentsappointments**

SME FUNDING ADVISER SCHEME

ICAEW continues to offer the SME Funding Adviser Scheme for SMEs (small and medium enterprises ie, businesses with up to 250 employees). Firms within this scheme provide independent advice on finance issues to SMEs. Over 2,300 entries were listed in the scheme in the 2011 *Directory of Firms*.

These firms are identified by an icon ◆ in their web and printed directory entries. Entry into this scheme is free, and the firm can receive specific qualified business leads by listing its specialisms. There is no commitment to ICAEW firms to offer advice at no charge under the SME Funding Adviser Scheme.

Full details of the scheme can be found at
icaew.com/smemanagement

SUPPORT MEMBERS

Support members provide immediate, totally confidential and non-judgemental support to all members whenever they are in difficulty. They are all volunteers who give some of their time to help other members. There are support members in each of the regions and district society areas, and they come from a variety of business, practice and other backgrounds.

Experience has shown that in nearly all cases members can benefit from contacting a support member. Just discussing a problem with a support member can often help to identify a way forward. All of the volunteers in this role are exempt from the duty to report misconduct, so you can feel completely at ease in speaking about what might be a difficult or sensitive situation.

Whatever the circumstances, support members are there to help. Freephone +44 (0)800 917 3526 (normal call charges apply if you are calling from outside the UK) or visit **icaew.com/supportmembers**

TECHNICAL HELPLINE

Need technical advice? Call us on +44 (0)1908 248 250 to receive specialist advice on a wide range of topics including ethical, technical and legislative.

Confidentiality: Your enquiry will be treated in strict confidence. If the nature of your enquiry is ethical we will not pass on your details to third parties, including other departments of ICAEW, unless you request or consent to this. We do ask for your membership details and we keep brief details of enquiries on record in case you should ever need to rely on them at a later date.

Ethics Enquiries: Discuss your ethical issues and problems with our experienced advisers. They provide guidance on interpretation and compliance with guidelines, and are exempt from the duty to report misconduct.

Money Laundering Enquiries: Discuss any queries you have about money laundering legislation anonymously. Our team can answer general questions about regulations, and advise you on reporting suspected illegal activity.

Technical Enquiries: Discuss any queries you have about accounting, company law, auditing and other popular specialist areas (eg, charities) with our technical advisers, who are all chartered accountants.

TECHNICAL STRATEGY DEPARTMENT

The Technical Strategy Department maintains and enhances our global reputation for thought leadership and technical excellence. It also develops and promotes technical policy in order to influence the regulatory and professional environments which affect members. The department also supports our work with European and global bodies and provides guidance to members on a wide variety of issues affecting the profession.

To find out more, visit **icaew.com/technical**

UK ENTERPRISE SURVEY REPORT

This annual report provides a unique picture of the opportunities and challenges facing UK businesses. It highlights issues that impact upon business in the UK and some of the key international regions and comments on any trends emerging with particular focus on economic issues, growth, globalisation and regulation.

To find out more or to download a copy, visit **icaew.com/smeresearch** Other survey reports available include: Global; the Asia Pacific; and the Gulf; along with highlights of the UK regions.

UPDATES

We keep members up to date with a monthly email alert, containing accountancy news, events and links to resources, best practice and technical updates.

ICAEW QUALIFICATIONS AND PROGRAMMES

ACA

The ACA is the premier finance-based qualification for business leaders. It is internationally acknowledged as a leading business and finance qualification and inspires business confidence.

Training for the ACA takes between three and five years combining exams, practical experience and skills development. Once you have gained the ACA you can become an ICAEW Chartered Accountant.

The ACA represents achievement across a breadth of financial and business skills to which other qualifications can only aspire. The professional recognition and reputation of ICAEW Chartered Accountants speaks for itself:

84% of UK FTSE 100 companies have an ICAEW Chartered Accountant on their board*.

* Source: ICAEW member data at January 2011, FTSE 350 data at December 2010

To find out more, visit **icaew.com/aca** or T +44 (0)1908 248 250.

CERTIFICATE IN FINANCE, ACCOUNTING AND BUSINESS (CFAB)

Provides essential knowledge for today's business environment that can be used in any industry or financial arena. CFAB consists of the same six modules that make up the first stage of the ACA. Flexible learning assessment and credit for prior learning makes CFAB achievable in less than 12 months.

To find out more, visit **icaew.com/cfab** E cfab@icaew.com or T +44 (0)1908 248 250.

IFRSs AND FINANCIAL REPORTING QUALIFICATIONS AND PROGRAMMES

Understand and confidently meet financial reporting requirements with our range of specialist qualifications and programmes. Select your learning requirements and preferred method of study to acquire the guidance, reassurance and knowledge you need to support your current role or future career.

ICAEW Diploma in IFRSs: Gain an enhanced understanding and the practical knowledge you need to apply IFRSs to best effect in your workplace.

IFRSs learning and assessment programme: Obtain a comprehensive overview of all current international standards in the private sector.

IFRS for SMEs learning and assessment programme: Achieve a detailed understanding of financial reporting for small to medium-sized enterprises.

Certificate in International Public Sector Financial Reporting: Understand and embed the key requirements of financial reporting in the public sector. Developed with CIPFA.

To find out more, visit **icaew.com/fr** E fr@icaew.com or T +44 (0)1908 248 250.

CORPORATE FINANCE (CF) QUALIFICATION

Exclusively designed for corporate finance practitioners by corporate finance practitioners, this qualification has an international focus and has been achieved by more than 1,000 professionals in over 50 countries. It offers a balanced combination of technical knowledge and practical application that you can apply immediately in the workplace. There are two routes to achieving the CF qualification: the experience route or the study route.

To find out more, visit **icaew.com/cfq** E cfqualification@icaew.com or T +44 (0)1908 248 250.

DIPLOMA IN CHARITY ACCOUNTING (DChA)

DChA inspires confidence and shows that you have the expertise to make a real difference to organisations operating in the charity and voluntary sector. It is ideal if you are developing your skills and knowledge or if you are already experienced. There are two ways to obtain the DChA: the experience route in which you reflect on recent experience, or a classroom-based study option.

To find out more, visit **icaew.com/dcha** E dcha@icaew.com or T +44 (0)1908 248 250.

FORENSIC ACCOUNTANT ACCREDITATION

Designed as the benchmark for aspiring and experienced forensic accountants. Accredited individuals are recognised as specialists in their field and their details are listed on a publicly available online register. The scheme is open to all qualified individuals who belong to specified professional bodies, with a suggested five years' minimum experience.

To find out more, visit **icaew.com/forensicaccreditation** E forensicaccreditation@icaew.com or T +44 (0)1908 248 250.

ICAEW ISAs PROGRAMME

This programme will help individuals to expand or update their understanding of the key principles of the clarified international standards on auditing (ISAs) and the audit process.

To find out more, visit **icaew.com/isas** E isas@icaew.com or T +44 (0)1908 248 250.

ICAEW CERTIFICATE IN INSOLVENCY

The most flexible learning programme for insolvency professionals in the UK. It provides finance, legal and other professionals with a practical introduction to corporate and personal insolvency principles and helps to develop the skills they need to apply them. Individuals can choose tuition and assessment options to suit their needs, and those of their employers.

To find out more, visit **icaew.com/insolvencycertificate** E insolvencycertificate@icaew.com or T +44 (0)1908 248 250.

BUSINESS SUSTAINABILITY PROGRAMME (BSP)

An informative and practical e-learning programme designed for users with different levels of knowledge and experience. It will help you to understand the issues that companies face now and in the future and to develop your corporate responsibility action plan. The first two modules are free for all users.

To find out more, visit **icaew.com/bsp** E bsp@icaew.com or T +44 (0)1908 248 250.

PATHWAYS TO MEMBERSHIP

Our Pathways to Membership programme is a route to ICAEW membership which supports succession planning in ICAEW member firms. The programme is open to qualified members of ACCA, CIMA, CIPFA, MICPA, CPA Australia and AICPA who meet the eligibility criteria.

To find out more, including full details of the eligibility criteria and the application process, visit **icaew.com/pathways** E pathways@icaew.com or T +44 (0)1908 248 250.

MEMBERSHIP INFORMATION

CONTINUING PROFESSIONAL DEVELOPMENT

All our members must comply with their CPD obligations; both to maintain 'professionalism by association' and to protect the exceptional reputation of ICAEW in its own right. To meet the requirements, you must:
- reflect on your responsibilities, undertake appropriate development activities, and consider the impact of those development activities on an ongoing basis;
- provide a signed declaration on an annual basis; and
- if asked to do so, submit evidence to back your declaration.

To find out more, visit icaew.com/cpd or T +44 (0)1908 248 250.

MEMBER LOGO

Our members are ICAEW Chartered Accountants. They can be recognised by the designation ACA, or FCA if they have been a member for over 10 years and have applied for Fellowship status.

To become an ICAEW Chartered Accountant they must complete the ACA qualification and be accepted for membership to ICAEW. As members they must comply with our Code of Ethics, are subject to our disciplinary process, and must complete continuing professional development.

By using a firm or individual displaying the logo, you know you are using a financial expert with the knowledge, initiative and judgement you can trust.

MEMBERS' HELPLINE

If you have an enquiry about the current status of a member or member firm, call us on T +44 (0)9066 140 906. Calls cost 60p per minute. If you are contacting us from outside the UK, E contactus@icaew.com. This department also provides:

- validation of membership and registration information including subscription reductions; and
- letters of confirmation of membership, including Notarising and seeking Apostiles from the Foreign & Commonwealth Office and foreign embassies.

Contact us on T +44 (0)1908 248 250 or F +44 (0)1908 248 069 or E contactus@icaew.com

RECORDS TEAM

Members' Registrar: Andrew Fagg
The members' records team maintains the integrity of the ICAEW database. The department also provides the following services:
- admission to membership;
- enquiries about entries in the *List of Members* and *Directory of Firms*;
- applications for reciprocal membership;
- applications for re-admission; and
- resignations.

Contact us by T +44 (0)1908 248 054
F +44 (0)1908 248 064, or E members.records@icaew.com, readmissions@icaew.com, resignations@icaew.com

Individual member logo

Member firm logo

PRACTICE SUPPORT SERVICES

COMPREHENSIVE GUIDANCE TAILORED TO YOU AND YOUR FIRM

We offer a range of coaching and consultancy services to help you in all areas of practice regulation and management. With our expert and confidential advice, we'll provide you with the knowledge and skills necessary to apply standards and regulations correctly, improve audit and practice efficiency, and increase profitability.

For affordable and hands-on guidance, contact us today.

+44 (0)1908 248 250

icaew.com/practicesupport

USE YOUR FACULTIES

In a rapidly changing business environment, the pursuit of competitive advantage is more important than ever. Become a member of one of our seven faculties – giving you a range of powerful tools that will help you stay one step ahead in your specialist area.

Contact us for more information or to join a faculty.

E faculties@icaew.com

icaew.com/faculties

CCH

CCH is part of Wolters Kluwer, a global information services company and number one in tax and accounting worldwide.

CCH is the only company in the UK to offer such a wide range of products and services dedicated to accountants.

CCH ONLINE REFERENCE

Our sole focus is on tax and accountancy, so we understand the profession and the individuals who work in it. The expertise and knowledge we have gained in nearly 100 years of working with accountants has enabled us to build the leading online reference service currently available.

CCH Online is quick and easy to use, is updated in real time and has accurate content from trusted experts. When accuracy and speed of updating are paramount, it is easy to see why CCH Online is the professionals' choice.

CCH BOOKS AND PRINT

CCH publish some of the leading titles in tax and accountancy, including *the British Master Tax Guide, Hardman's Tax Rates and Tables, Schwarz on Tax Treaties, the Red and Green Books, Preparing Company Accounts, Preparing LLP Accounts, the Handbook of Management Accounting and the CCH Master Payroll Guide.*

CCH SOFTWARE

The CCH ProSystem Suite includes all the software you need to run your practice and to provide your clients with the compliance and value-added services on which they rely. Our integrated software makes information about your practice easier to share, see and exploit from a personalised central dashboard.

CCH FEE PROTECTION

Our fee protection products can offer your clients peace of mind knowing that should they be investigated your practice can dedicate the right level of representation without worrying about spiralling expenses.

- **Tax and VAT Telephone Helpline** – up-to-date and accurate information for your practice from our consultants, many of whom are ex-HMRC.

- **Consultancy services** – CCH experts can become directly involved in your cases, at a level that you control. The average accountant deals with fewer than three HMRC enquiries a year; a CCH consultant handles over 50. No wonder we regularly achieve such excellent outcomes on behalf of our clients.

- **Marketing Consultants** – to help you maximise uptake and increase revenue.

CCH PROFESSIONAL DEVELOPMENT

CCH e-CPD® delivers training online so that busy professionals can learn at a place, pace and time that suits them; in bite-size chunks to fit around other professional commitments.

CCH MAGAZINES

As a leading source of news and commentary, CCH helps you stay up to date with developments in the accounting profession through *Accountancy*, the must-read practical magazine written by accountants for accountants.

MORE INFORMATION

To find out more about any of our products and services:
T +44 (0)844 561 8166
E cch@wolterskluwer.co.uk
Visit: **cch.co.uk**

The content on this page has been provided by CCH.

If things aren't right, you can count on us

CABA is here to help when life takes an unexpected turn for the worse.

Whether you are a current or former ICAEW member or dependant, or an active ACA student, we can support you.

For financial, practical and emotional support in confidence
Call +44 (0)1788 556366 *(Mon-Fri, 9-5)*

For free and confidential 24 hour advice and counselling
Call +44 (0)800 1076163
International +44 (0)1455 255 038

Follow us on Twitter @cabacharity

caba.org.uk

Supporting Chartered Accountants since 1886

A Company Limited by Guarantee, registered in England and Wales, No.5970606, Charity No. 1116973

EXPLANATORY NOTES

DESCRIPTION AND DESIGNATORY LETTERS

Members of ICAEW are entitled to describe themselves as chartered accountants and to use the designatory letters FCA (if eligible) or ACA.

ACA denotes associate; **FCA** denotes fellow. **Year** indicates the year of admission to membership of ICAEW or The Society of Incorporated Accountants.

MEMBERS ALPHABETICAL LIST

● denotes members holding a practising certificate and in practice. A member who is not in public practice may hold a practising certificate; some members choose to do this. If this symbol is not shown, it does not necessarily mean that the member is not entitled to engage in practice in his/her country of residence.

Ⓘ denotes members holding an insolvency licence issued by ICAEW.

Where a practising member is a principal in a firm, the name of the firm is given after his/her name followed by the address of the main office at which he/she practises and the name of any other firm in which he/she is a principal. Members who are employed by a firm of accountants appearing in this list are described as being 'with' that firm.

British honours and decorations and the degrees of universities in the UK and Republic of Ireland or of the Council for National Academic Awards (CNAA) are shown in the alphabetical section of the list. The initials DL (Deputy Lieutenant), JP (Justice of the Peace) and MP (Member of Parliament), are shown in the list if requested by a member.

PRACTICE ASSURANCE

Practice Assurance applies to all ICAEW members who hold a practising certificate and who offer accountancy services to the public. These members are required to comply with four published, principles-based standards. ICAEW monitors member firms for compliance with the standards, other relevant regulations and ICAEW's Code of Ethics.

If a practising certificate holder works within a 'mixed' firm, the firm's parent body will undertake the monitoring, under reciprocal arrangements. If there is no parent body, ICAEW will monitor the individual. Member firms that are subject to Practice Assurance monitoring and comply with the principles-based standards are entitled to use ICAEW's logo and Practice Assurance legend.

FIRMS ALPHABETICAL LIST (INCLUDING SOLE PRACTITIONERS)

The names of firms are followed by the names of principals who are members of ICAEW. The address of the main office is followed by the names of the towns in which the firm has offices. Only offices in which members and firms have the exclusive occupation of at least one room, with the daily attendance of a principal or a responsible member of staff, are included.

Firms not marked ▽ or ★ are composed wholly of chartered accountant members of ICAEW.

▽ indicates that the firm is composed wholly of accountants who are members of one or another of the three institutes of chartered accountants in Great Britain and Ireland (namely: ICAEW, The Institute of Chartered Accountants of Scotland and Chartered Accountants Ireland).

★ indicates that the firm is not composed wholly of members of one or another of the three institutes of chartered accountants in Great Britain and Ireland.

Ⓐ indicates a firm registered with ICAEW as a Registered Auditor under the Companies Act 2006.

Ⓕ denotes a firm licensed by ICAEW, in its capacity as a designated professional body under the Financial Services and Markets Act 2000, to carry out a range of investment business activities.

Ⓜ denotes Management Consultants

Ⓟ denotes Corporate Practice

Ⓠ denotes Computer Bureau

Ⓡ denotes Company Registrars

Ⓢ denotes Company Registrars and Computer Bureau

Ⓣ denotes Authorised Training Employer

THE OFFICIAL ICAEW LIST OF MEMBERS 2012

MEMBERS

Members - Alphabetical AALA - ABDUL RAZAK

AALA, Mr. Rosauro, MA FCA *1996;* BPP Professional Education, Apollo Business Centre 2C, Prievozska 4B, 821 09 BRATISLAVA, SLOVAK REPUBLIC.
AALTONEN, Mrs. Elizabeth Ellen, ACA *2008;* 152 Glengall Road, LONDON, NW6 7HH.
AAMIR, Mr. Ali, ACA *1983;* Lotte Pakistan PTA Ltd, EZ/1-P-4, Eastern Industrial Zone, Port Qasim, KARACHI, PAKISTAN.
AARON, Mr. Paul, BA ACA *1997;* 27 Falmouth Gardens, ILFORD, IG4 5JU.
AARONBERG, Mr. Philip, FCA CF *1964;* Capiderm Partners Limited, 6 Grosvenor Street, LONDON, W1K 4PZ.
AARONS, Ms. Nicola Anne, BSc ACA *1986;* 7 Bryniau, Brithdir, DOLGELLAU, GWYNEDD, LL40 2TY.
•AARONS, Mr. Rowland, BA FCA *1987;* Brooks Green, Abbey House, 342 Regents Park Rd, LONDON, N3 2LJ.
AARONS, Mr. Stanley, FCA *1958;* 2 Waltham Avenue, LONDON, NW9 9SJ. (Life Member)
AARONSON, Mr. Colin Paul, BA FCA *1984;* 13 Spencer Drive, LONDON, N2 0QT.
AARONSON, Mr. Edward John, FCA FInstD *1950;* 2 The Paddock, The Street, Bishop's Cannings, DEVIZES, WILTSHIRE, SN10 2LD. (Life Member)
AARTS, Mr. Oscar Anthony Leon, ACA *1994;* c/o Houlihan Lokey, 245 Park Avenue, 20th Floor, NEW YORK, NY 10167, UNITED STATES.
AARVOLD, Mr. John Merriman, FCA *1972;* Thanington, Chichester Road, DORKING, RH4 1LR.
AARVOLD, Ms. Samantha Marie, MA ACA *1995;* 8 Devoil Close, GUILDFORD, SURREY, GU4 7FG.
AB-RAHMAN, Ms. Suria, BSc(Econ) ACA *2000;* 2677 Jalan Permata 23, Taman Permata, Hulu Kelang, 53300 KUALA LUMPUR, FEDERAL TERRITORY, MALAYSIA.
•ABASY, Mr. Waris, FCA ATII *1969;* (Tax Fac), Abasy Yates & Co, 27 Lexham Gardens, LONDON, W8 5JJ.
ABAYAWICKREMA, Mr. Lakshman De Silva, FCA *1965;* Southfields, Main Street, Upton, HUNTINGDON, PE28 5YF. (Life Member)
ABBA, Mr. Glyn Michael, ACA *1984;* 22 Malvern Road, West Bridgford, NOTTINGHAM, NG2 7DG.
ABBABIL, Mr. Darren Nahshon, BEng ACA *1998;* Flat 8 1 Reed Place, LONDON, SW4 7LD.
ABBAS, Mr. Ali Arslan, ACA *2010;* 4172 Bishopstoke Lane, MISSISSAUGA L4Z 1J3, ON, CANADA.
ABBAS, Mr. Arshad Mahmood, BA ACA *1995;* Flat 173 Quadrant Court, Empire Way, WEMBLEY, HA9 0EY.
ABBAS, Mr. Muhammad, BSc(Hons) ACA ACCA *2011;* 239 J EME Housing Society Near Tohkar Niaz Biag Multan Road, LAHORE, PAKISTAN.
ABBAS, Mr. Mustapha, ACA *2011;* 18 Royal Crescent, Newbury Park, ILFORD, IG2 7NH.
ABBAS, Mrs. Rosanne Emily, BA ACA *1986;* 73 Parkgate Road, WATFORD, WD24 7BL.
•ABBAS, Mr. Syed Naveed, ACA ACCA *2008;* AHLN Associates, First Floor, 182-184 Wolverhampton Street, DUDLEY, WEST MIDLANDS, DY1 3AD.
•ABBASAKOOR, Mr. Abdul Wahed Ismail Abdul Karrim, FCA *1975;* De Chazal Du Mee, Frere Felix Valois Street, PORT LOUIS, MAURITIUS.
ABBASAKOOR, Mr. Riyad Rafik, BSc ACA *2001;* Flat 3, Jay Court, 33 Brownlow Road, LONDON, N3 1YT.
ABBASAKOOR, Mr. Umar Noormohamed, FCA *1964;* Umar N. Abbasakoor, Cnr Bernardin De St, Pierre & O.Ernest Streets, QUATRE-BORNES, MAURITIUS.
ABBASBAIKI-VARAMIN, Mr. Hussein, ACA *2008;* The Annexe Rivendell Lawn Avenue, WEST DRAYTON, MIDDLESEX, UB7 7AQ.
ABBASI, Mr. Firdaus Taiyebali, ACA *1979;* 36 Holtspur Top Lane, Holtspur, BEACONSFIELD, HP9 1DR.
ABBASI, Mr. Syed Mohammad Ali, BA(Hons) ACA *2002;* F202 Creek Vista Apartments, Khyaban-e-Shaheen, DHA Phase 8, KARACHI, PAKISTAN.
ABBEY, Mr. Richard John, ACA *1995;* Kroll, 1 Tower Place West, LONDON, EC3R 5BU.
ABBI, Mr. Robin Ranjan, MA FCA *1993;* Immagini Ltd, PO Box 40, Prospect House, HIGH WYCOMBE, BUCKINGHAMSHIRE, HP13 5EX.
ABBIE, Ms. Pauline Margaret, BA FCA *1979;* 61 Southborough Road, LONDON, E9 7EE.
ABBITT, Mrs. Penelope Flora, ACA *1983;* Hadlow College, Hadlow, TONBRIDGE, KENT, TN11 0AL.
ABBONDANZA, Mrs. Stefania, ACA *2002;* 8 Haversham Close, TWICKENHAM, TW1 2JP.
ABBOSH, Mr. Oday Gabriel, BEng ACA *1992;* 38 Blenheim Terrace, St John's Wood, LONDON, NW8 0EG.
ABBOT, Mr. Duncan James Langlands, LLB ACA FSI *1981;* 48 Church Lane, LOUGHTON, IG10 1PD.
ABBOT, Miss. Sarah, LLB ACA *2010;* with Chantrey Vellacott DFK LLP, Russell Square House, 10-12 Russell Square, LONDON, WC1B 5LF.
•ABBOTT, Mr. Adrian Sharrah, FCA *1971;* 31 Cranley Road, GUILDFORD, SURREY, GU1 2JE.
ABBOTT, Mr. Alexander Donald, FCA *1957;* 30 Vibart Road, Yardley, BIRMINGHAM, B26 2AD. (Life Member)
•ABBOTT, Mr. Anthony Richard, BA FCA *1977;* Anthony Abbott Limited, 48 St. Marys Street, BUNGAY, SUFFOLK, NR35 1AX.
ABBOTT, Mr. Anthony Robert, BA ACA *1983;* 9 Thurlow Road, LONDON, W7 2JG.
ABBOTT, Mrs. Barbara Margaret, BA ACA *1985;* 28 Durleston Park Drive, Great Bookham, LEATHERHEAD, KT23 4AJ.
ABBOTT, Mrs. Chai Ming, ACA *1983;* Paccship (UK) Ltd, 19 Buckingham Gate, 3rd Floor, LONDON, SW1E 6LB.
ABBOTT, Mr. Christopher, ACA *2009;* Flat 2 Heaton Moor House, 168 Heaton Moor Road, STOCKPORT, CHESHIRE, SK4 4DH.
ABBOTT, Mr. Christopher John, BA ACA *2010;* Hermitage Waterside, 123 Thomas More Street, LONDON, E1W 1YD.
ABBOTT, Mr. Christopher Michael, FCA *1972;* 15 Woodfield Road, ASHTEAD, SURREY, KT21 2DZ.
ABBOTT, Mr. Christopher Murray, AM FCA *1954;* 20 Rosemont Avenue, WOOLLAHRA, NSW 2025, AUSTRALIA. (Life Member)
ABBOTT, Miss. Clair Denise, ACA *2009;* 3 Rawling Way, LEEDS, LS6 2SB.
ABBOTT, Mr. Clive Paul, FCA *1969;* Flat F/2, Princes Gate, 55 Grove Road, BOURNEMOUTH, BH1 3AW. (Life Member)
ABBOTT, Mr. Daniel James, BA(Econ) ACA *2001;* Flat 2, 13 Randolph Avenue, Maidan Vale, LONDON, W9 1BH.
ABBOTT, Mr. David, FCA *1971;* 20 Churchfield Court, High Street, Girton, CAMBRIDGE, CB3 0XA. (Life Member)
ABBOTT, Mr. David Charles, BA ACA *1989;* Sungbukdong 15-87, Sungbuk-ku, SEOUL, KOREA REPUBLIC OF.
ABBOTT, Mr. David George, BSc FCA CF *1990;* with Solomon Hare Personal Finance Ltd, Oakfield House, Oakfield Grove, Clifton, BRISTOL, BS8 2BN.
•ABBOTT, Mr. David John, FCA *1971;* with Littlestone Martin Glenton, 73 Wimpole Street, LONDON, W1G 8AZ.
•ABBOTT, Mr. David Michael, BEng BCom ACA *1997;* 2 Bomford Hill, Harley Goodacre, WORCESTER, WR4 0PW.
ABBOTT, Mr. David Mortimer, TD BA FCA *1981;* 2 Brockhole Close, Gamston, NOTTINGHAM, NG2 6RT.
ABBOTT, Mr. David Thomas, BA FCA AMCT *1994;* 131 Grandison Road, LONDON, SW11 6LT.
ABBOTT, Mr. David Vivian, FCA *1961;* The Cottage, Highclere Street, Highclere, NEWBURY, RG20 9PY.
ABBOTT, Mr. Derek Harry, FCA *1957;* Clairmont, Chestnut Avenue, Kirby Cross, FRINTON-ON-SEA, CO13 0LA. (Life Member)
•ABBOTT, Mrs. Diane Patricia, BA ACA DChA *1979;* (Tax Fac), R.P. Smith & Co, 28 St Thomas's Rd, CHORLEY, PR7 1HX. See also R P Smith & Co Ltd
ABBOTT, Mr. Douglas James, MA FCA *1973;* 204 Chesterfield Drive, SEVENOAKS, TN13 2EH.
ABBOTT, Miss. Elizabeth, BA(Hons) ACA *2011;* 13 Stanley Avenue, Bishopston, BRISTOL, BS7 9AH.
ABBOTT, Miss. Elizabeth Nash, FCA *1978;* 15 Glyndebourne Avenue, TOORAK, VIC 3142, AUSTRALIA.
•ABBOTT, Mr. Gary Kenneth, BA FCA *1980;* GK Abbott & Co Limited, 25 Wollaton Road, Beeston, NOTTINGHAM, NG9 2NG.
ABBOTT, Mr. Gary William Henry, BSc ACA *1997;* The Cottages, Castle Bernard, BANDON, COUNTY CORK, IRELAND.
ABBOTT, Mr. George William, FCA *1955;* 6 Fyfield Way, Littleton, WINCHESTER, SO22 6PF. (Life Member)
ABBOTT, Mr. Greg John, ACA *2008;* 20 Riding Hill, SOUTH CROYDON, CR2 9LN.
ABBOTT, Mr. Harry, FCA *1952;* 15 Field End Crescent, LEEDS, LS15 0QE. (Life Member)
ABBOTT, Ms. Helen Elizabeth, MA BA ACA *2006;* 34 Salmons Lane, WHYTELEAFE, CR3 0AN.
ABBOTT, Mrs. Helen Jeffrey, LLB ACA *2001;* 14 Holkar Meadows, Bromley Cross, BOLTON, BL7 9NA.
ABBOTT, Miss. Hilary Elizabeth, BA ACA *1983;* 14, Gilpins Ride, BERKHAMSTED, HP4 2PD.
•ABBOTT, Mr. James, ACA FCCA CTA *2011;* Baker Watkin, Middlesex House, Rutherford Close, STEVENAGE, SG1 2EF.
ABBOTT, Mr. John, FCA *1969;* 3 Hollyhocks, Harwell, DIDCOT, OX11 0LX.
ABBOTT, Mr. John, FCA *1958;* 8 Ridgeway Road, Aller Park, NEWTON ABBOT, TQ12 4LS. (Life Member)
ABBOTT, Mr. John Arthur, BA FCA *1976;* 6 Park Avenue, Poynton, STOCKPORT, CHESHIRE, SK12 1QY.
•ABBOTT, Mr. John Gavin Campbell, FCA *1974;* (Tax Fac), J.G.C. Abbott, 6 Stoney Field, Highnam, GLOUCESTER, GL2 8LY.
ABBOTT, Mr. Jonathan James, BEng ACA *2002;* 9 Park Glen, Park Gate, SOUTHAMPTON, SO31 6BZ.
ABBOTT, Mr. Kelvin William, BSc FCA *1977;* AD Astra, Langley Park Road, IVER, BUCKINGHAMSHIRE, SL0 0JQ.
ABBOTT, Mr. Kenneth Robert Mcfarlane, FCA *1964;* 1 Chester Avenue, Hale, ALTRINCHAM, WA15 9DB.
ABBOTT, Mr. Kevin Mark, BA ACA *1998;* Preston North End Plc, Sir Tom Finney Way, Deepdale, PRESTON, PR1 6RU.
ABBOTT, Mrs. Linda Ann, BA ACA *1985;* Wheelgate House, Little Arrow, CONISTON, CUMBRIA, LA21 8AU.
ABBOTT, Miss. Lisa, BSc ACA *2003;* 3 St. James Terrace, Boundaries Road, Balham, LONDON, SW12 8HJ.
ABBOTT, Miss. Louise Pauline, BA(Hons) ACA *2010;* Apartment 803 Millennium Tower, 250 The Quays, SALFORD, M50 3SA.
ABBOTT, Mr. Matthew James, ACA *2009;* 213 Wrotham Road, GRAVESEND, KENT, DA11 7LE.
ABBOTT, Mr. Matthew Stuart, BSc FCA *2001;* 873 Parkridge Dr, MEDIA, PA 19063-1715, UNITED STATES.
ABBOTT, Ms. Melanie, BSc ACA *1995;* 17 Woodstock Street, BOTANY, NSW 2019, AUSTRALIA.
ABBOTT, Mr. Neil, BCom ACA *1988;* The Garden Flat, 94 Westbourne Terrace, Bayswater, LONDON, W2 6QE.
ABBOTT, Mr. Nigel, FCA *1963;* Brookvale, Weir Lane, Hanwood, SHREWSBURY, SY5 8LA.
•ABBOTT, Mr. Paul Richard, FCA *1974;* P.R Abbott, Rushtead House, 66 Woodland Way, Kingswood, TADWORTH, SURREY KT20 6NW.
ABBOTT, Mr. Peter Clive, BA ACA *1984;* ACS International Schools Ltd, Heywood, Portsmouth Road, COBHAM, SURREY, KT11 1BL.
•ABBOTT, Mr. Philip George, BSc FCA CTA *1987;* (Tax Fac), Dickinsons, Enterprise House, Beesons Yard, Bury Lane, RICKMANSWORTH, HERTFORDSHIRE WD3 1DS.
ABBOTT, Miss. Rebecca Clare, ACA *2002;* 23 Banbrook Close, SOLIHULL, WEST MIDLANDS, B92 9NF.
•ABBOTT, Mrs. Rebecca Jane, BSc ACA ATII *1991;* RNS, The Poplars, Bridge Street, BRIGG, NORTH LINCOLNSHIRE, DN20 8NQ.
ABBOTT, Miss. Rebecca Jane, BSc ACA *2010;* 7 Hardwick Close, RIPLEY, DERBYSHIRE, DE5 3SR.
ABBOTT, Mr. Richard, FCA *1970;* 9 Nelson Drive, HUNSTANTON, NORFOLK, PE36 5DU.
ABBOTT, Mr. Robert, BA ACA *2005;* 10 Drayton Close, Bidford-on-Avon, ALCESTER, WARWICKSHIRE, B50 4QD.
•ABBOTT, Miss. Sarah Elizabeth, BSc ACA *2003;* Sarah Abbott and Co Limited, 4 Lancaster Road, IPSWICH, IP4 2NY.
ABBOTT, Mrs. Sarah Jayne, BSc ACA *1992;* 38 Townsend Way, Folksworth, PETERBOROUGH, PE7 3TU.
ABBOTT, Mr. Simon John, LLM LLB ACA *2009;* 150 High Street, LONDON, E17 7JS.
ABBOTT, Mr. Stephen, MA FCA *1980;* 30A Chalcot Road, LONDON, NW1 8LN.
ABBOTT, Mr. Stephen John, FCA *1972;* Coniston, 10 Mount Avenue, Hutton Mount, BRENTWOOD, ESSEX, CM13 2NU. (Life Member)
ABBOTT, Mrs. Susan Elizabeth, BSc ACA *1991;* Somerstone, 11 Richmond Road, GODALMING, GU7 2ET.
ABBOTT, Mr. Timothy Welton, FCA *1966;* 120 Jericho Valley Drive, NEWTOWN, PA 18940-3632, UNITED STATES.
ABBOTT, Miss. Tonnia, ACA *2008;* New Progress Housing Association Sumner House, 21 King Street, LEYLAND, PR25 2LW.
ABBOTT, Mrs. Tracey Anne, LLB FCA *1996;* 9 Park Glen, Park Gate, SOUTHAMPTON, SO31 6BZ.
•ABBOTT, Mr. William John, LLB FCA *1997;* Randall & Payne LLP, 10 Wheatstone Court, Waterwells Business Park, Quedgeley, GLOUCESTER, GL2 2AQ.
ABBOTTS, Mr. David John, BA ACA *1982;* FWB Products Ltd, Whieldon Road, STOKE-ON-TRENT, ST4 4JE.
ABBOTTS, Mr. David Stanley, BSc ACA *1989;* 50 Homefield Road, LONDON, W4 2LW.
ABBOTTS, Mr. Jonathan Laurence, BSc ACA *1990;* 29 Demesne Road, MANCHESTER, M16 8HJ.
ABD RAHMAN, Mr. Daud, BSc ACA *2006;* No.7 Jalan Pulau Angsa U10/32F, Bandar NusaRhu, Seksyen U10, 40170 SHAH ALAM, MALAYSIA.
ABDELMAJEED, Mr. Khalid, ACA *2009;* KPMG, P.O. Box 3800, Level 32 Emirates Towers, DUBAI, UNITED ARAB EMIRATES.
ABDELRAHIM, Mr. Mohamed, ACA *2010;* EPRA, Boulevard de la Woluwe 62, 1200 BRUSSELS, BELGIUM.
ABDELRAHMAN, Mr. Omar, BA ACA *2009;* Flat 43, Stanwick Mansions, Stanwick Road, LONDON, W14 8TP.
ABDI, Mr. Sameer Reza, BEng ACA ACGI *2001;* with Ernst & Young, P.O. Box 140, MANAMA, BAHRAIN.
ABDOOLLAH, Mr. Yusuf Ali, LLB ACA *2002;* 7 Vandermersh Street, ROSE HILL, MAURITIUS.
ABDOU, Mr. Amir, ACA *2009;* Flat 12, Printworks Apartments, 230 Long Lane, LONDON, SE1 4QA.
ABDUL, Miss. Habibah, FCA *1981;* Ernst & Young, Level 23A Menara Milenium, Pusat Bandar Damansara, 50490 KUALA LUMPUR, FEDERAL TERRITORY, MALAYSIA.
ABDUL-AAL, Mr. Jassim Hassan, ACA *1994;* Grant Thorton, Abdulaal Gulf Audit, PO Box 11175 1st Floor, Bahrain Carparks Building, MANAMA, BAHRAIN.
ABDUL AJIB, Mr. Anwar Syahrin, BEng ACA MBA *2002;* MMC Corporation Berhad, Level 11, Kompleks Antarabangsa, Jalan Sultan Ismail, 50250 KUALA LUMPUR, FEDERAL TERRITORY MALAYSIA.
ABDUL ALI, Ms. Nor Afida, BSc ACA *2003;* No 22, Jalan SS15/3A, 47500 SUBANG, SELANGOR, MALAYSIA.
ABDUL AZIZ, Mr. Ahmed Fairuz, BSc ACA *2006;* NO. 44 JALAN 33/70A, DESA SRI HARTAMAS, 50480 KUALA LUMPUR, MALAYSIA.
ABDUL GHANI, Mr. Muhammad Firdaus, ACA CA(AUS) *2008;* 32 Jalan SG 6/3, Taman Sri Gombak, 68100 BATU CAVES, MALAYSIA.
ABDUL HALIM, Mr. Hisyam, BSc ACA *2003;* 3-2-8 Waizuri 1 Apartment Jln 11/27A Seksyen 5, Wangsa Maju, 53300 KUALA LUMPUR, FEDERAL TERRITORY, MALAYSIA.
ABDUL JABAR, Mrs. Nuruluyun, BSc ACA *1992;* 23 Jalan Limau Purut, Bangsar Park, 59000 KUALA LUMPUR, FEDERAL TERRITORY, MALAYSIA.
ABDUL-KADIR, Mr. Ali, FCA *1974;* Financial Reporting Foundation Suite 5-2 5th Floor Wisma UOA Pantai Jalan Pantai Bahru, 59100 KUALA LUMPUR, MALAYSIA.
ABDUL-MAJEED, Mr. Ramzy Mazen, FCA *1997;* PO Box 211752, DUBAI, UNITED ARAB EMIRATES.
ABDUL MALAK, Miss. Cempaka Seri, BA(Hons) ACA CTA *2002;* 42 Barons Keep, Gliddon Road, LONDON, W14 9AU.
ABDUL-MALIK, Mr. El-Azleen, MSc BEng ACA *2001;* No. 16 Jalan Damai Jasa 5, Alam Damai, 56000 CHERAS, MALAYSIA.
ABDUL MANAP, Ms. Nur Azreen, ACA *2008;* 5 Jalan Setiakasih 8, Bukit Damansara, 50490 KUALA LUMPUR, FEDERAL TERRITORY, MALAYSIA.
ABDUL MOHAMMAD, Mr. Samir, ACA *1993;* 132 St. Margarets Road, EDGWARE, MIDDLESEX, HA8 9UX.
ABDUL RAHIM, Mr. Ahmad Zahirudin, BA ACA *1995;* with Ernst & Young, Level 23A Menara Milenium, Pusat Bandar Damansara, 50490 KUALA LUMPUR, FEDERAL TERRITORY, MALAYSIA.
ABDUL RAHIM, Miss. Azlina, BSc ACA *2004;* No 12A Jalan Kenyalang 11/5B, PJU5 Kota Damansara, Petaling Jaya, 47810 KUALA LUMPUR, FEDERAL TERRITORY, MALAYSIA.
ABDUL-RAHIM, Mr. Hisham, BSc ACA *2000;* 13 Bukit Segambut, 51200 KUALA LUMPUR, FEDERAL TERRITORY, MALAYSIA.
ABDUL-RAHIM, Mrs. Joanne Helen, BSc ACA *1991;* Middlesex University Business School, The Burroughs, Hendon, LONDON, NW4 4BT.
ABDUL RAHIM, Mr. Reza, MPhil BSc ACA *2002;* 43 Jalan 14/3, Taman Tun Abdul Razak, 68000 AMPANG, SELANGOR, MALAYSIA.
ABDUL RAZAK, Mr. Mohd Nasiruddin, BA FCA *1999;* 12-2-21 Hartamas Regency Condominium, Persiaran Dutamas, Off Jalan Duta, 50480 KUALA LUMPUR, FEDERAL TERRITORY, MALAYSIA.

ABDUL WAHAB, Miss. Norliwati, MEng ACA *2003;* No 541 Jalan 5, Taman Ampang Utama, 68000 AMPANG, MALAYSIA.
ABDUL WAHEED, Miss. Amina, BSc ACA *2010;* 16 Bridgewater Court, Bridgewater Road, WEMBLEY, MIDDLESEX, HA0 1AU.
ABDUL-WAHID, Mr. Mohamed Redza Shah, BSc ACA *1993;* 6 Lorong Pju 7/21b, Mutiara Damansara, PETALING JAYA, SELANGOR, MALAYSIA.
•①**ABDULALI, Mr. Mustafa Hassanali, FCA** *1980;* Moore Stephens, 6 Ridge House, Ridge House Drive, STOKE-ON-TRENT, ST1 5TL.
ABDULHUSEIN, Mr. Shabbirhusein Jivanji, BSc ACA *1982;* 93 Carrington Drive, RICHMOND HILL L4C 7X8, ON, CANADA.
ABDULLA, Mr. Mohamed Hassanali, FCA *1962;* P O Box 1147, Sarit Centre, NAIROBI, 00606, KENYA.
ABDULLA-JANAHI, Mr. Khalid, BSc FCA *1987;* D M I Administrative Services, P.O. Box 161, 84 Avenue Louis CasaiCointrin, 1216 GENEVA, SWITZERLAND.
ABDULLAH, Mr. Muhammad Shafie Leow Bin, ACA CA(NZ) *2009;* 1103 Casmilla Tower, Jalan Bukit Idaman, 68100 BATU CAVES, MALAYSIA.
ABDULLAH, Mr. Shariq, BSc ACA *1993;* D 74, Clifton Block 5, KARACHI, PAKISTAN.
ABDULLAH, Mr. Tunku Yaacob, BSc FCA *1986;* c/o MAA Holdings Bhd, Penthouse Menara Maa, 12 Jln Dewan Bahasa, 50460 KUALA LUMPUR, FEDERAL TERRITORY, MALAYSIA.
ABDULLAH, Mr. Wan Razly, BA ACA *1999;* 39 Jalan P14A 1/1, Presint 14, Wilayah, 62050 PUTRAJAYA, MALAYSIA.
ABDULREHMAN, Mr. Mohamed Ali, BA FCA *1965;* PO Box 82175, MOMBASA, KENYA. (Life Member)
ABDY, Mr. Richard Martin, ACA *1983;* 8 Anglesey Court Road, CARSHALTON, SM5 3HZ.
ABEDI, Miss. Mana, BEng ACA *1992;* 530 Finchley Road, LONDON, NW11 8DD.
ABEDI, Miss. Rabab, BSc ACA *1998;* 15A St. Mary Abbots Terrace, LONDON, W14 8NX.
ABEDIN, Mr. Joynul, ACA *2010;* Flat 7 Bounty Hall, Gwendolen Avenue, LONDON, SW15 6EZ.
ABEDIN-ZADEH, Mr. Hooman, MSc BA(Hons) ACA *2001;* 3 St. Ronans Avenue, Cotham, BRISTOL, BS6 6EP.
ABEL, Mr. Alan Ralph, FCA *1957;* 21 Ridge Langley, Sanderstead, SOUTH CROYDON, Surrey, CR2 0AP. (Life Member)
ABEL, Mr. Benjamin George, BSc ACA *2003;* 119 Honeywell Road, LONDON, SW11 6ED.
ABEL, Mr. Carl William Emberton, FCA *1958;* 56 Woodhouse Road, Quorn, LOUGHBOROUGH, LE12 8AJ. (Life Member)
ABEL, Miss. Carol Gwynydd, LLB ACA *1983;* Belfast Waterfront Hall, 2 Lanyon Place, BELFAST, BT1 3WH.
ABEL, Miss. Christine Michele, BSc ACA *1986;* 72 Princess May Road, LONDON, N16 8DG.
ABEL, Mrs. Dhana Marie, BSc ACA *1995;* H M Revenue & Customs Custom House, 20 Lower Thames Street, LONDON, EC3R 6EE.
ABEL, Mr. Edward Guy, BA FCA *1969;* 17 Freeburn Road, TAURANGA 3112, NEW ZEALAND.
ABEL, Mr. Geoffrey Charles, BSc ACA *1979;* 26 Armorial Road, Styvechale, COVENTRY, CV3 6GJ.
ABEL, Miss. Helen Louise, ACA *2002;* Butterfield Fulcrum Group (Guernsey) Ltd, PO Box 211, GUERNSEY, GY1 3NQ.
ABEL, Mr. Jeremy Neil, MA ACA *1984;* 103a Station Road, LONDON, NW4 4NT.
•**ABEL, Mr. Lawrence James, BSc ACA** *1991;* (Tax Fac), Alan R. Grey & Co, The Old Forge, Beck Place, Gosforth, SEASCALE, CA20 1AT.
•**ABEL, Mrs. Lynda Julia, BSc ACA** *2000;* Ernst & Young LLP, 1 More London Place, LONDON, SE1 2AF. See also Ernst & Young Europe LLP
ABEL, Mr. Peter William, BSc ACA *1995;* 2 Dublin Crescent, Henleaze, BRISTOL, BS9 4NA.
ABEL, Mr. Philip Mathew, MA ACA *1996;* 4 Acorn Lane, Great Cambourne, CAMBRIDGE, CB23 6GS.
•**ABEL, Mr. Richard Charles, FCA** *1983;* Aggarwal & Co Ltd, 3-5 London Road, Rainham, GILLINGHAM, KENT, ME8 7RG.
•**ABEL, Mr. Richard John, BSc FCA** *1980;* Richard Abel & Co, 14 Shelwick Grove, Dorridge, SOLIHULL, WEST MIDLANDS, B93 8UH.
ABEL, Miss. Sharon Heather, BSc ACA *1993;* 12 Woodlinken Drive, VERWOOD, DORSET, BH31 6BN.
ABEL-DEDMAN, Miss. Jennifer Elizabeth, BA ACA *2010;* Flat 6, Glenroyd House, 26 Cleveland Road, St. Helier, JERSEY, JE2 4PB.
ABELA, Mr. James, MEng ACA *2004;* with Deloitte Touche Tohmatsu, 80 Queen Street, Private Bag 115-033, AUCKLAND 1010, NEW ZEALAND.
ABELES, Mr. Leo, BSc FCA *1963;* 35 Orchard Avenue, LONDON, N3 3NL.
ABELL, Mr. Christopher Andrew, BSc ACA *1984;* rocinante 4 - 5°d, 28034 MADRID, SPAIN.
ABELL, Mr. James Foster, BSc ACA *1987;* Abingworth LLP, 38 Jermyn Street, LONDON, SW1Y 6DN.
ABELL, Mr. Martin James, BSc ACA *2000;* 4 Birds Hill Road, Eastcote, TOWCESTER, NORTHAMPTONSHIRE, NN12 8NF.
ABELL, Mr. Stephen Benedict, BSc ACA *1992;* 18 Hawthorn Road, Hale, ALTRINCHAM, WA15 9RG.
ABELL, Mrs. Victoria, ACA *2003;* 4 Birds Hill Road, Eastcote, TOWCESTER, NORTHAMPTONSHIRE, NN12 8NF.
•**ABERCROMBIE, Mr. Alexander John, FCA** *1962;* Abercrombie & Co, 36 Monmouth Way, HONITON, DEVON, EX14 2GY.
ABERCROMBIE, Mrs. Sarah Michelle, BSc ACA CFA *1998;* Fairmount Branch Road, Hinton Charterhouse, BATH, BA2 7SZ.
ABERNETHY, Miss. Jennifer Elizabeth, MA ACA *2006;* 7 Kells Gardens, Low Fell, GATESHEAD, TYNE AND WEAR, NE9 5XS.
ABERNETHY, Miss. Kate, MA ACA *2007;* 67 Beauval Road, LONDON, SE22 8UH.
ABERSON, Mr. Paul, LLB ACA *2011;* 32 Ruskin, Henley Road, Caversham, READING, BERKSHIRE, RG4 6LE.
ABERY, Miss. Christine, FCA *1977;* (Tax Fac), Aberfield, Coltishall Road, Buxton, NORWICH, NR10 5HB.
ABERY, Mr. David Gary, BA ACA *1991;* PO Box 68613, BRYANSTON, 2021, SOUTH AFRICA.
ABERY, Mr. James Edward, BSc ACA *2010;* D X Network Services Ltd D X House, The Ridgeway, IVER, BUCKINGHAMSHIRE, SL0 9JQ.
ABEYRATNE, Mr. Dilan Amila, BA ACA *2001;* 42A Tower 3, No 8 Bel-air on the Peak, THE PEAK, HONG KONG ISLAND, HONG KONG SAR.
ABEYRATNE, Mr. Jonathan, ACA *2011;* 121 Deacon Road, LONDON, NW2 5NJ.
ABEYSEKERA, Mr. Atula, MSc FCA *1990;* 4 Cotsford Avenue, NEW MALDEN, KT3 5EU.
•**ABHYANKAR, Mr. Amit Hemant, BSc ACA** *1999;* Deloitte LLP, Athene Place, 66 Shoe Lane, LONDON, EC4A 3BQ. See also Deloitte & Touche LLP
ABID, Mr. Adil Farook, BSc ACA *2005;* with KPMG, Falcon Tower, 16th Floor, Al Nasr Street, PO Box 7613, ABU DHABI UNITED ARAB EMIRATES.
•**ABID, Mr. Noorur Rahman, FCA** *1976;* Ernst & Young, P.O. Box 140, MANAMA, BAHRAIN.
•**ABIDIN, Mr. Shaik Alaudin Mohamed, BSc ACA** *1988;* Abidin & Co, 65 Butts Green Road, HORNCHURCH, RM11 2JS.
ABIGAIL, Mrs. Adele Ann, MBS BA ACA *1998;* Flat 28 Connaught Works, 251 Old Ford Road, LONDON, E3 5PS.
ABIGAIL, Mr. Richard, BSc(Econ) ACA *2000;* Flat 28, Connaught Works, 251 Old Ford Road, LONDON, E3 5PS.
ABIOLA, Miss. Aminat Bolanle, BSc ACA *2006;* Flat 4 Block 19, Femi Okunnu Estate III, Lekki Phase 3, Lekki, LAGOS, NIGERIA.
ABIOLA, Mr. Sayeed Olatunji, ACA *2009;* Top floor flat, 662 Fulham Road, LONDON, SW6 5RX.
•**ABJI, Mr. Kurban Ahmed Murji, FCA** *1975;* (Tax Fac), Kurban Abji, 46 Westbourne Road, LUTON, LU4 8JD.
ABLE, Mr. Richard Graham Munro, MA MEng ACA *1999;* Haye Cottage Upper Haye Lane, Fingringhoe, COLCHESTER, CO5 7AB.
ABLETT, Mr. John Robert, FCA *1958;* 25 West Ella Way, Kirk Ella, HULL, HU10 7LN. (Life Member)
ABLETT, Miss. Lisa, BSc(Hons) ACA *2010;* 35 New Town Road, BISHOP'S STORTFORD, HERTFORDSHIRE, CM23 3SB.
ABLETT, Mr. Peter, BSc ACA *1990;* 1 Deanery Crescent, LEICESTER, LE4 2WD.
ABLETT, Mr. Timothy Andrew, FCA *1974;* Benover House, Rectory Lane, Saltwood, HYTHE, CT21 4QA.
•**ABLETT, Mr. William James, BSc FCA** *1976;* Abletts Limited, 7A London Road, ALDERLEY EDGE, CHESHIRE, SK9 7JT.
ABLIN, Mr. Paul Brian, BA(Hons) ACA *2001;* 6 Common Close, Horsell, WOKING, SURREY, GU21 4DB.
ABLITT, Mrs. Carole Elizabeth, ACA *1982;* 39 Woodpecker Copse, Locks Heath, SOUTHAMPTON, SO31 6WS.
•**ABOLINS, Mr. Richard James, BSc ACA** *1983;* Prosper Accounting Services, 6 Arundel Close, Tuffley, GLOUCESTER, GL4 0TW.
ABOOBAKER, Mr. Irfan, BSc ACA *1998;* P.O.Box 45, SALIMA, MALAWI.
ABOOBAKER, Mr. Rizwan Abdul Gaffar, BA ACA *1994;* 70 Kitchener Road, LEICESTER, LE5 4AS.
ABOU-EITA, Mr. Tarek, ACA MBA *1996;* 32 Tag El-Deen El-Sobki Street, The Golf Area, Heliopolis, CAIRO, EGYPT.
ABRAHAM, Mrs. Ann, BA ACA *2005;* 8 Pig Lane, ST. IVES, CAMBRIDGESHIRE, PE27 5QE.
•**ABRAHAM, Ms. Barbara Ann, BA FCA** *1982;* B.A. Abraham, 40A Primrose Gardens, LONDON, NW3 4TP.
•**ABRAHAM, Mr. Edward Charles, FCA** *1963;* (Tax Fac), 18 Pewsey Place, SOUTHAMPTON, SO15 7RX.
ABRAHAM, Mr. Edward Raymond, BA FCA *1975;* Pilpantie 25, KERMA, 79910, FINLAND.
ABRAHAM, Mr. Geoffrey Colin, BSc FCA *1975;* 15 Charnhill Brow, Mangotsfield, BRISTOL, BS16 9JW. (Life Member)
ABRAHAM, Mr. Jonathan William, ACA *2008;* 3 Caraway Court, Meanwood, LEEDS, LS6 4RY.
ABRAHAM, Mrs. Laila Elizabeth, BA(Econ) ACA *2002;* 3806 204th Ave NE, SAMMAMISH, WA 98074, UNITED STATES.
ABRAHAM, Mr. Mark Hill, BA FCA *1993;* Dun Roamin Fambridge Road, Cold Norton, CHELMSFORD, CM3 6NN.
ABRAHAM, Mr. Richard David, FCA *1980;* Flat 19, Meadowcroft House, 16 Trumpington Road, CAMBRIDGE, CB2 8EX.
ABRAHAM, Mr. Richard John, MA ACA *1979;* 179 High Street, AMERSHAM, HP7 0EB.
ABRAHAM, Mrs. Victoria Louise, BSc ACA *2003;* 24 Willow Lane, Stanion, KETTERING, NN14 1DT.
ABRAHAMS, Mr. Alan, FCA *1958;* 18, Crown Hill, SEAFORD, BN25 2XJ. (Life Member)
ABRAHAMS, Mr. Christopher David, BA ACA *1985;* 34a Sunningdale Road, SUTTON, SURREY, SM1 2JS.
•**ABRAHAMS, Mr. Colin Phillip, BA ACA** *1987;* Baker Tilly Tax & Advisory Services LLP, 3 Hardman Street, MANCHESTER, M3 3HF.
ABRAHAMS, Mr. Daniel Henry, BSc ACA *2000;* 3 Derwent Avenue, UXBRIDGE, MIDDLESEX, UB10 8HJ.
ABRAHAMS, Mr. David Reginald, FCA *1980;* Matthew Arnold & Baldwin, PO Box 101, WATFORD, WD17 1HT.
ABRAHAMS, Mr. Ian Charles, MSc FCA *1974;* 1 Baynham Close, BEXLEY, DA5 1RN.
ABRAHAMS, Mr. Jonathan, BSc ACA *1998;* 65 Woodacre, Portishead, BRISTOL, BS20 7EH.
ABRAHAMS, Mr. Malcolm James, ACA CA(SA) *2011;* Great House Cottage, Back Lane, Bradfield, READING, RG7 6DJ.
ABRAHAMS, Mrs. Marguerite, BA ACA *2002;* G V Multi Media Ltd, Unit 1, Inwood Business Centre, Whitton Road, HOUNSLOW, TW3 2EB.
ABRAHAMS, Mr. Mark David, FCA *1976;* 53 Millwell Crescent, CHIGWELL, IG7 5HX.
ABRAHAMS, Mr. Mark Simon, MA FCA *1979;* 140 Clifton, YORK, YO30 6BH.
ABRAHAMS, Mr. Michael Benjamin, BA ACA ATII *1997;* 46 Spencer Road, Chapel-en-le-Frith, HIGH PEAK, DERBYSHIRE, SK23 9SB.
ABRAHAMS, Mr. Michael Bernard, FCA *1972;* 61 Fitzalan Road, LONDON, N3 3PG.
ABRAHAMS, Mr. Samuel Ellis, FCA *1961;* PO Box 641, Northlands, JOHANNESBURG, GAUTENG, 2116, SOUTH AFRICA.
ABRAHAMS, Mr. Tristan Charles Lewis, ACA *2010;* Beggars Roost, Channels End Road, Colmworth, BEDFORD, MK44 2NS.
ABRAHAMSON, Mr. John David, FCA *1969;* 2 New End Square, LONDON, NW3 1LN.
ABRAHAMSON, Mr. William Godfrey, FCA *1968;* 11 Main Street, Stapleton, LEICESTER, LE9 8JN.
ABRAM, Mrs. Melanie Jane Rosalyn, BSc ACA *1992;* Green Side, Swan Lane, Stoke Orchard, CHELTENHAM, GLOUCESTERSHIRE, GL52 7RW.
ABRAM, Mr. Peter James, MA ACA *1995;* 226 Liverpool Road, Longton, PRESTON, PR4 5YB.
•**ABRAM, Mr. Philip George, ACA** *1994;* KPMG LLP, 1 The Embankment, Neville Street, LEEDS, LS1 4DW. See also KPMG Europe LLP
ABRAMS, Mr. Daniel, MA FCA *1982;* Forsyth House, 211-217 Lower Richmond Road, RICHMOND, SURREY, TW9 4LH.
ABRAMS, Mr. Drummond Ernest, FCA *1957;* (Member of Council 1985 - 2001), Old Mill House, Blackboys, UCKFIELD, TN22 5LR. (Life Member)
ABRAMS, Miss. Jane Helen, BA ACA *1993;* Bicester Village, 50 Pingle Drive, BICESTER, OXFORDSHIRE, OX26 6WD.
ABRAMS, Mr. Marc, BSc ACA CTA *2000;* 47A Bramcote Road, Beeston, NOTTINGHAM, NG9 1DW.
•**ABRAMS, Mr. Victor, MA FCA** *1977;* PricewaterhouseCoopers LLP, 1 Embankment Place, LONDON, WC2N 6RH. See also PricewaterhouseCoopers
ABRAMSON, Mr. Anthony Ian Joseph, BA FCA *1973;* 20 Belvedere Avenue, Alwoodley, LEEDS, LS17 8BW.
ABRAMSON, Mrs. Gillian Mary, ACA *2008;* 34 Otley Old Road, LEEDS, LS16 6HW.
•**ABREHART, Mr. David Charles, LLB ACA** *1984;* (Tax Fac), DCA Associates Limited, 3 Great Pitchers, Earls Colne, COLCHESTER, CO6 2SP. See also DCA Associates
ABREHART, Mr. David John, BA ACA *1991;* (Tax Fac), 12 Manor Park, KINGSBRIDGE, DEVON, TQ7 1BB.
ABREW, Mrs. Namalie Apsara, BSc ACA *1998;* Maximastraat 6, 1432 LS AALSMEER, NETHERLANDS.
•**ABREY, Mr. Ian Nicholas, ACA** *1986;* (Tax Fac), 97 Sherwood Avenue, ST. ALBANS, HERTFORDSHIRE, AL4 9PW.
•**ABREY, Mr. Terence John, FCA** *1972;* Varley & Gulliver Ltd, 57 Alfred Street, Sparkbrook, BIRMINGHAM, B12 8JR. See also Abrey T.J.
ABRICHAMI, Mr. Mohammad Hassan, BSc FCA *1967;* 132 Ehteshamieh Street, Koucheh Kambeez, Darrous, TEHRAN, 1946613471, IRAN. (Life Member)
ABRICHAMI, Mr. Mohammad Hossein, BSc FCA *1992;* P O Box 6442, ENOC, ENOC House 1, DUBAI, UNITED ARAB EMIRATES.
ABSALOM, Mr. David, BA BCom FCA *1966;* Hegglefoot, Hesket Newmarket, WIGTON, CA7 8HX.
ABSALOM, Mr. Gareth Owen, BSc ACA *1990;* 31 Wivelsfield Road, Saltdean, BRIGHTON, BN2 8FP.
ABSALOM, Mr. John William, BSc ACA *1987;* 5 Dovehouse Lane, SOLIHULL, B91 2HA.
ABSAR, Mr. Tauseef, CA ACA *2008;* C W Energy Tax Consultants Ltd, 40 Queen Street, LONDON, EC4R 1DD.
ABSOLOM, Mrs. Nicola Caroline, BSc ACA *2000;* Yaffles, Red Shute Hill, Hermitage, THATCHAM, BERKSHIRE, RG18 9QH.
ABSON, Mr. Jeremy Paul, BSc ACA *1996;* Usaha Tegas 8DN Bhd, Level 38 Menara Maris, 50088 KUALA LUMPUR, FEDERAL TERRITORY, MALAYSIA.
ABSOUD, Mr. Amir Ashraf, BSc ACA *2003;* Flat 503 Pacific Wharf, 165 Rotherhithe Street, LONDON, SE16 5QF.
•**ABTAHI, Mr. Nima, MSc ACA** *2007;* 32/1 Shadab Street, Sepahbod Gharani Avenue, PO Box 1115-4731, TEHRAN, IRAN.
ABTAN, Mr. Aziz Jaffar, FCA *1974;* Ministry Of Finance, Office Of The Minister, BAGHDAD, IRAQ.
ABU, Miss. Fuseina Rosalind, BA ACA *2007;* 174 Kingsthorpe Grove, NORTHAMPTON, NN2 6PD.
ABUBACKER, Mrs. Nicola, BA ACA *1993;* 12 Ringwood Road, LUTON, LU2 7BG.
ABULHAWA, Mr. Daoud, ACA *2011;* 5-7 Mikonou, Block D, Flat 106, Strovolos, 2062 NICOSIA, CYPRUS.
ABURROW, Miss. Andrea Jane, BSc FCA *1999;* Terrance Cottage, 47 High Street, Old Oxted, OXTED, SURREY, RH8 9LN.
ACASTER, Mr. Neville Richard, BA ACA *1989;* 75 Highfield Way, RICKMANSWORTH, HERTFORDSHIRE, WD3 7PN.
ACCORDINO, Ms. Marie-Claire, ACA CA(AUS) *2011;* 35 Valencia Avenue, CHURCHLANDS, WA 6018, AUSTRALIA.
•**ACHAL, Mr. Prabhpreet, MSci ACA** *2006;* Achal & Achal Limited, 32 Strathmore Avenue, HITCHIN, HERTFORDSHIRE, SG5 1SN.
ACHARYA, Mr. Sanjay, MA ACA *1999;* 200 E 87TH ST APT 10E, NEW YORK, NY 10128, UNITED STATES.
•**ACHARYA, Mr. Vijay, BA FCA** *1996;* (Tax Fac), Charles Rippin & Turner, Middlesex House, 130 College Road, HARROW, MIDDLESEX, HA1 1BQ.
ACHER, Mr. Gerald, CBE LVO FCA *1967;* (Member of Council 1995 - 2002), Church Stile House, Church Street, COBHAM, SURREY, KT11 3EG.
ACHESON, Mrs. Anne, BA ACA *1984;* 19 Les Bois, Layer De La Haye, COLCHESTER, CO2 0EX.
ACHESON, Mr. Matthew Arthur James, BA ACA *2010;* 73 Bebington Road, Port Sunlight, WIRRAL, MERSEYSIDE, CH62 5BG.
ACHESON, Mr. Michael Peter, BA ACA *1984;* 19 Les Bois, High Road, Layer-De-La-Haye, COLCHESTER, CO2 0EX.
ACHESON, Mrs. Susan Carol, MA ACA *1989;* O'Donnell & Co, 11 Stuart Green, EDINBURGH, EH12 8YF.
•**ACHILLEA, Mr. George, FCA** *1976;* (Tax Fac), George Achillea Limited, 49 Ash Grove, Bush Hill Park, ENFIELD, EN1 2LB.
ACHILLEA, Mr. Michael, BSc FCA *1992;* 13 Queens Avenue, Winchmore Hill, LONDON, N21 3JE.

ACHILLEAS WALLS, Mrs. Erin, BA ACA *2009;* 59 Alric Avenue, NEW MALDEN, SURREY, KT3 4JL.
•**ACKENSON, Mr. Michael, FCA** *1969;* Charterhouse (Accountants) LLP, 88-98 College Road, HARROW, MIDDLESEX, HA1 1RA.
ACKER, Miss. Daniella Elizabeth, MA ACA *1985;* 5 Cornwallis House, Cornwallis Grove, BRISTOL, BS8 4PG.
ACKERLEY, Mrs. Charlotte Julia, BA(Hons) ACA TEP *2000;* Butterfield Bank (Cayman) Ltd, PO Box 705, GEORGETOWN, GRAND CAYMAN, CAYMAN ISLANDS.
ACKERMAN, Mr. Lee Warren, BSc ACA *1988;* The Flower Shop, 35 High Street, EASTLEIGH, HAMPSHIRE, SO50 5LF.
ACKERMAN, Ms. Liesal Jean, BA(Oxon) ACA *2011;* PwC, Via Monte Rosa 91, 20149 MILAN, MI, ITALY.
ACKERS, Mr. Bryan Stephen, BSc ACA *2002;* 1 Oak Gates, Egerton, BOLTON, BL7 9TQ.
ACKERS, Mrs. Diane Marie, BSc ACA *1993;* with PricewaterhouseCoopers LLP, Benson House, 33 Wellington Street, LEEDS, LS1 4JP.
•**ACKERS, Mr. Simon Jonathan, ACA ACCA** *2008;* Simon J Ackers, 37 Brandreth Drive, Parbold, WIGAN, LANCASHIRE, WN8 7HB.
ACKERY, Mr. Graham Bernard, FCA *1963;* 10711 Preston Way, POWELL, OH 43065, UNITED STATES. (Life Member)
ACKLAM-DRURY, Mrs. Ailsa Heather, BA ACA *1992;* 15 Gleneagles Road, Bloxwich, WALSALL, WS3 3UJ.
ACKLAND, Miss. Joanne Louise, BSc ACA *2006;* 8 Rothesay Court, Shrublands Road, BERKHAMSTED, HERTFORDSHIRE, HP4 3HY.
ACKLAND, Dr. Mathew Paul, PhD ACA *2009;* 67 Highmead Avenue, Newton, SWANSEA, SA3 4TY.
ACKLAND, Mr. Richard Granville, FCA *1966;* 3 Ravenswold, Hayes Lane, KENLEY, CR8 5LL. (Life Member)
•**ACKLAND, Mr. Richard James, BSc ACA** *1998;* KPMG LLP, 15 Canada Square, LONDON, E14 5GL. See also KPMG Audit plc
ACKLAND, Mr. Robert Charles, BA ACA *1984;* 21 Weymouth Avenue, DORCHESTER, DORSET, DT1 1QT.
ACKLAND, Mr. Thomas Francis, FCA *1959;* 59 Broadfields Avenue, Winchmore Hill, LONDON, N21 1AG. (Life Member)
ACKRILL, Mr. Gareth John, ACA CA(NZ) *2010;* Financial Services Authority, 25 North Colonnade, LONDON, E14 5HS.
ACKRIM, Mr. Raheel, BSc ACA *1995;* unit 67, 22 notting hill gate, LONDON, w11 3je.
ACKROYD, Mr. Alan, FCA *1969;* 39 Roedhelm Road, East Morton, KEIGHLEY, WEST YORKSHIRE, BD20 5RF.
ACKROYD, Mrs. Angela Diane, BSc ACA *1984;* 28 Pledwick Lane, WAKEFIELD, WF2 6DN.
ACKROYD, Miss. Claire Marie, BA(Hons) ACA *2010;* Apartment 9 Burton Croft, 69 Burton Stone Lane, YORK, YO30 6FG.
ACKROYD, Mr. Gareth Edward, BA ACA *1997;* Adam Fire Surrounds Ltd, St. Thomas's Road, HUDDERSFIELD, HD1 3LF.
ACKROYD, Mr. John Anthony, BA FCA *1978;* CMI Consulting, 11 Beech Grove, CHEPSTOW, NP16 5BD.
ACKROYD, Mr. Matthew, BA ACA *2011;* Flat 4, 309 Harrogate Road, LEEDS, LS17 6PA.
ACKROYD, Mr. Neil James, BSc ACA *2000;* 7 Manor Farm Court, Old Wolverton Road, Old Wolverton, MILTON KEYNES, MK12 5NN.
ACKROYD, Mr. Philip, MA MSc ACA CTA *1989;* Lower Crombleholme Fold Farm, Crombleholme Fold, Goosnargh, PRESTON, PR3 2ES.
ACKROYD, Miss. Rachel Louise, BA(Hons) ACA *2010;* Flat 7, 46 Chillingham Road, NEWCASTLE UPON TYNE, NE6 5BJ.
•**ACLAND, Mr. David Robert, BA FCA** *1989;* Greenways, Ash Brow, Newburgh, WIGAN, WN8 7NG.
ACLOQUE, Mr. David, FCA *1965;* The White House, Mill Lane, Lenwade, NORWICH, NR9 5SQ.
ACOMB, Mr. Norman Mackenzie, FCA *1962;* 32 Grange Park Drive, BINGLEY, BD16 1NR.
ACOMB, Mr. Paul Adam, ACA *1996;* 49 Tallmadge Avenue, CHATHAM, NJ 07928, UNITED STATES.
ACORNLEY, Mr. John Keith, MA FCA *1979;* Rose Cottage, Newton Lane, Odstone, NUNEATON, CV13 0QU.
•**ACOTT, Mr. David Alan, MA FCA** *1978;* (Tax Fac), David A Acott, 12 The Farthings, CROWBOROUGH, TN6 2TW.
ACOTT, Miss. Katherine Emma Louise, BSc ACA *2005;* with Grant Thornton UK LLP, Grant Thornton House, 22 Melton Street, Euston Square, LONDON, NW1 2EP.
ACOTT, Mr. Paul James, BA FCA *1972;* 21 Kitchener Close, DAVENTRY, NORTHAMPTONSHIRE, NN11 9AJ.
ACQUILLA, Mr. Maneesh, MSc(Econ) BL ACA *2006;* with PricewaterhouseCoopers LLP, Benson House, 33 Wellington Street, LEEDS, LS1 4JP.
•**ACQUISTO, Mrs. Vincenza, ACA** *1991;* V. Acquisto, 5 Stafford Drive, BROXBOURNE, HERTFORDSHIRE, EN10 7JT.
•**ACREMAN, Mr. Christopher Ralph, FCA** *1973;* 20 Ashley Meadows, ROMSEY, HAMPSHIRE, SO51 7LT.
ACREMAN, Mrs. Emily, BSc ACA *2006;* 16 North Road, RICHMOND, TW9 4HA.
ACRES, Mrs. Sharon Lesley, ACA *1984;* (Tax Fac), 22 Orchard Way, STUDLEY, WARWICKSHIRE, B80 7NZ.
•**ACTON, Mr. Adrian Harold Alan, FCA** *1972;* (Tax Fac), Adrian H.A. Acton, 25 Ware Lane, Wyton, HUNTINGDON, CAMBRIDGESHIRE, PE28 2AJ. See also Adrian Acton
ACTON, Mr. Carl Thomas, ACA *2008;* 281 Wellington Road North, STOCKPORT, CHESHIRE, SK4 5BP.
•**ACTON, Mr. Keith Lewis, FCA** *1969;* with Bentleys, Hazlemere, 70 Chorley New Road, BOLTON, BL1 4BY.
ACTON, Mr. Kevin John, BCom ACA *2005;* 3 I Group, 16 Palace Street, LONDON, SW1E 5JD.
ACTON, Mr. Thomas Philip, BA ACA *1983;* Garland Hall, Crowley, NORTHWICH, CHESHIRE, CW9 6NS.
ACTON-BROWNE, Mr. Barry Rodney, FCA *1964;* 11 Riddings Road, Hale, ALTRINCHAM, WA15 9DS.
ACUM, Dr. Gillian Amanda, MA ACA CTA *1994;* 2 Tern Drive, Poynton, STOCKPORT, CHESHIRE, SK12 1HR.
ACUTI, Mr. Giovanni Luigi Giorgio, BSc FCA *1988;* 14 Twyford Avenue, LONDON, N2 9NJ.
ADAE-AMOAKOH, Miss. Mame Abena Animah, MSc ACA *1993;* 29 Punchard Crescent, ENFIELD, MIDDLESEX, EN3 6FZ.
ADAIR, Mr. David Anthony John, BSc ACA *1988;* 7 Althorp Road, LONDON, SW17 7ED.
•**ADAIR, Mr. David William, BA FCA** *1986;* PricewaterhouseCoopers LLP, 10-18 Union Street, LONDON, SE1 1SZ. See also PricewaterhouseCoopers
ADAIR, Mr. Gavin Spence, BAcc ACA MBA *1999;* Gondola Holdings Ltd, 2 Balcombe Street, LONDON, NW1 6NW.
ADAIR, Mrs. Kelly Joanne, BSc(Hons) ACA *2000;* 14 Ember Farm Way, EAST MOLESEY, SURREY, KT8 0BL.
ADAIR, Mr. Robert Fredrik Martin, BA ACA *1981;* (Tax Fac), High Leases Farm, Westfields, RICHMOND, NORTH YORKSHIRE, DL10 4SB.
ADAIR, Mr. Stuart Andrew, MA ACA *1988;* Suite 4603, 2045 Lake Shore Blvd. West, TORONTO M8V 2Z6, ON, CANADA.
ADAM, Mr. Alan John, FCA *1975;* 33 Harbour Square, Suite 1232, TORONTO M5J 2G2, ON, CANADA.
ADAM, Mr. Alex, BSc ACA *2007;* with Deloitte LLP, Athene Place, 66 Shoe Lane, LONDON, EC4A 3BQ.
ADAM, Mrs. Austra Emilija, BA ACA *1995;* 11 Parish Ghyll Road, ILKLEY, WEST YORKSHIRE, LS29 9NG.
ADAM, Mr. Craig Alan, ACA *2010;* 30 Linglongs Avenue, Whaley Bridge, HIGH PEAK, DERBYSHIRE, SK23 7DT.
ADAM, Mr. Cyril Louis Ignatius, FCA *1958;* 5 Eylesden Court, Bearsted, MAIDSTONE, KENT, ME14 4BF. (Life Member)
•**ADAM, Mr. David Nicholas Goddard, FCA** *1973;* (Tax Fac), with Lakin Clark, Delandale House, 37 Old Dover Road, CANTERBURY, CT1 3JF.
ADAM, Mr. David William, MA FCA *1970;* 34 Gill Bank Road, Middleton, ILKLEY, WEST YORKSHIRE, LS29 0AU.
ADAM, Mr. Garry Clark, MA ACA *1998;* The Holiday Cottages Group, BARNOLDSWICK, BB94 0AA.
ADAM, Mr. Iftikar Hassen Mohamed, BA ACA *1991;* (Tax Fac), 18 Belgrave Gardens, Oakwood, LONDON, N14 4TT.
ADAM, Mr. James, BSc FCA *1974;* Norland House, Millers Lane, Hornton, BANBURY, OXFORDSHIRE, OX15 6BS.
ADAM, Mrs. Jeanne Rose, MA FCA *1956;* 5 Eylesden Court, Bearsted, MAIDSTONE, KENT, ME14 4BF. (Life Member)
ADAM, Mr. John, FCA *1975;* Truckee Cottage, 45 Simons Walk, Englefield Green, EGHAM, TW20 9SJ.
•**ADAM, Mr. John Alexander, BSc ACA** *1993;* Deloitte LLP, 2 New Street Square, LONDON, EC4A 3BZ. See also Deloitte & Touche LLP
ADAM, Mr. John Cliffe Hamilton, FCA *1964;* Burnt Ash, Gorsewood Road, Hartley, LONGFIELD, KENT, DA3 7DF.
ADAM, Joseph Henri Jerome, Esq OBE FCA *1972;* (Member of Council 2005 - 2008), 44 Chemin Des Ornois, B-1380 LASNE, BELGIUM.
ADAM, Mr. Richard John, BSc FCA *1983;* (Tax Fac), Priory Cottage, Alderton Drive, Little Gaddesden, BERKHAMSTED, HERTFORDSHIRE, HP4 1NB.
ADAM, Mr. Sheryar, LLB CA ACA *2005;* 5 Invergowrie Drive, DUNDEE, DD2 1RD.
ADAM, Mr. Sohail Iqbal, BA(Hons) ACA *2004;* 20 Fishwick Parade, PRESTON, PR1 4XQ.
•**ADAM, Mr. Stuart Mark, BA FCA** *1987;* Thomas Coombs & Son, Century House, 29 Clarendon Road, LEEDS, LS2 9PG.
ADAM, Mr. Thomas Louisson, FCA *1955;* (Member of Council 1992 - 1995), 1 Birch Lea, East Leake, LOUGHBOROUGH, LE12 6LA. (Life Member)
ADAM-SMITH, Mr. Matthew Alexander, BSc FCA *1995;* 15 Brightmore Street, CREMORNE, NSW 2090, AUSTRALIA.
ADAMEK, Mrs. Krystyna, BA(Hons) ACA *2003;* 28/1 Bay Drive, MEADOWBANK, NSW 2114, AUSTRALIA.
•**ADAMIDES, Mr. Chrysostomos Michael, BA ACA** *1989;* CM Adamides & Co, P.O. BOX 57167, 3313 LIMASSOL, CYPRUS.
ADAMIECKI, Miss. Tamzin, ACA *2009;* Games Workshop Ltd, Willow Road, NOTTINGHAM, NG7 2WS.
•**ADAMJEE, Mr. Habel Akberali, FCA** *1972;* (Tax Fac), Christie Buchanan, Bridge House, 11 Creek Road, EAST MOLESEY, SURREY, KT8 9BE. See also Regent Services Ltd
ADAMJEE, Mr. Mazahir, FCA *1972;* Currimjee Jeewanjee & Co Ltd, 38 Royal Street, P.O. Box No. 49, PORT LOUIS, MAURITIUS.
ADAMJEE, Mr. Nicolas Shiraz, BSc(Hons) ACA *2005;* Royal Road, GRAND BAY, MAURITIUS.
ADAMS, Mr. Alan Edward, FCA *1959;* Pebbles, 94 Beer Road, SEATON, EX12 2PT. (Life Member)
ADAMS, Miss. Alexandra, ACA *2011;* 18 Perth Road, LONDON, N4 3HB.
ADAMS, Mr. Andrew Bell, BSc ACA *1981;* 2423 Carrington Place, OAKVILLE L6J 7R6, ON, CANADA.
ADAMS, Mr. Andrew David Bruce, BA ACA *1986;* 2 Larford Farm Barns, Astley, STOURPORT-ON-SEVERN, WORCESTERSHIRE, DY13 0SQ.
ADAMS, Mr. Andrew John, MEng ACA *2004;* #07-01 Novena Suites 200 Moulmein Road, SINGAPORE 308107, SINGAPORE.
ADAMS, Mr. Andrew John, BA ACA *1985;* 711 S. Bowman Avenue, MERION STATION, PA 19066, UNITED STATES.
ADAMS, Mr. Anthony Bruce, FCA *1961;* Abbey House, Foxglove End, Crapstone, YELVERTON, DEVON, PL20 7NY.
ADAMS, Mr. Anthony Frederick, BA FCA *1974;* 28 Granville Road, SEVENOAKS, TN13 1EY.
ADAMS, Mr. Anthony James, FCA *1960;* Cherwell, 17 Staines Close, Appleton, WARRINGTON, WA4 5NP. (Life Member)
ADAMS, Mr. Aubrey John, MA FCA *1975;* Vines Farm, Kidmore End, READING, RG4 9AP.
ADAMS, Mr. Austen Paul, FCA *1971;* 11 Manor Close, Burton in Lonsdale, CARNFORTH, LANCASHIRE, LA6 3NE.
ADAMS, Mr. Ben Norman, BSc ACA *1989;* Adams Group, Oakfield Road, AYLESBURY, BUCKINGHAMSHIRE, HP20 1LJ.
ADAMS, Mr. Benjamin James, BSc(Hons) ACA *2010;* 35 Sheffield Road, SUTTON COLDFIELD, B73 5HD.
ADAMS, Mr. Benjamin Nicholas Christopher, MA ACA *2003;* with Ernst & Young LLP, 1 More London Place, LONDON, SE1 2AF.
ADAMS, Mr. Brian Kenneth, BSc ACA *1982;* 16 Meadowbank Gardens, Glazebury, WARRINGTON, WA3 5LX.
ADAMS, Mr. Bruce Ian Ross, FCA *1976;* Barton Willmore Bean Chief Farm House, Bourne Close Calcot, READING, RG31 7BW.
ADAMS, Mrs. Caroline Julie, BA ACA *1997;* 102 Chertsey Road, TWICKENHAM, TW1 1EW.
ADAMS, Ms. Catherine Jane, BA ACA *1995;* 25 Canning Road, Highbury, LONDON, N5 2JR.
•**ADAMS, Mrs. Cecilia Mary, BSocSc FCA** *1978;* Celia Adams Associates Ltd, Eastham Court, TENBURY WELLS, WR15 8NW.
ADAMS, Miss. Cheryl Anne, BA ACA *2002;* 21 Walsingham, WASHINGTON, TYNE AND WEAR, NE38 7HF.
•**ADAMS, Mrs. Cheryl Diane, BA ACA** *1986;* (Tax Fac), 38 Station Road, Dunham Massey, ALTRINCHAM, CHESHIRE, WA14 5SG.
ADAMS, Mrs. Christina, ACA *2009;* with PricewaterhouseCoopers LLP, Savannah House, 3 Ocean Way, Ocean Village, SOUTHAMPTON, SO14 3TJ.
ADAMS, Mr. Christopher, BSc ACA *2011;* Apartment 3 St. James Court, 4 Moorland Road, MANCHESTER, M20 6AZ.
ADAMS, Mr. Christopher Borlase, FCA *1975;* Belmont House, East Hoathly, LEWES, BN8 6QJ.
•**ADAMS, Mr. Christopher John, FCA** *1971;* 5 Portmore Close, BROADSTONE, DORSET, BH18 8BZ.
•**ADAMS, Mr. Christopher John Heselton, MA FCA** *1975;* Saffery Champness, Sovereign House, 6 Windsor Court, Clarence Drive, HARROGATE, HG1 2PE.
ADAMS, Ms. Claire Abegail, BSc(Hons) ACA *2009;* 37 Newstead Way, LOUGHBOROUGH, LE11 2UA.
ADAMS, Miss. Claire Anna-Marie, BSc ACA *1996;* 9 Eccleston Square, LONDON, SW1V 1NP.
ADAMS, Mr. Colin John, BA FCA *1972;* 27 Burnham Road, WORTHING, WEST SUSSEX, BN13 2NL. (Life Member)
ADAMS, Mr. Colin Raymond, BA ACA *1990;* 36 Pine Grove, Totteridge, LONDON, N20 8LB.
ADAMS, Mr. Daniel Robert Christopher, BSc ACA *2004;* 51 Church Road, RICHMOND, TW10 6LX.
•**ADAMS, Mr. David Charles, FCA** *1966;* Lindley Adams Limited, 28 Prescott Street, HALIFAX, WEST YORKSHIRE, HX1 2LG.
ADAMS, Mr. David Howard, FCA *1967;* 6 Albion Street, Hyde Park, LONDON, W2 2AS.
ADAMS, Mr. David Howson, FCA *1955;* Ranworth, Eccleshall Road, Loggerheads, MARKET DRAYTON, SHROPSHIRE, TF9 4NX. (Life Member)
ADAMS, Mr. David John, FCA *1973;* Bakers Cottage, Whiteleaf, PRINCES RISBOROUGH, BUCKINGHAMSHIRE, HP27 0LL. (Life Member)
ADAMS, Mr. David John, BSc ACA *2004;* 7 Hutton Close, Culcheth, WARRINGTON, WA3 4DW.
ADAMS, Mr. David Kenneth, ACA *1984;* Fermyn Wood, Kings Croft, Allestree, DERBY, DE22 2FP.
ADAMS, Mr. David Laurence, BA ACA *1995;* Geopost UK Ltd, Roebuck Lane, SMETHWICK, B66 1BY.
ADAMS, Mr. David Norman, BA ACA ATII *1986;* (Tax Fac), 34 Silverwood Avenue, Milber, NEWTON ABBOT, TQ12 4LG.
•**ADAMS, Mr. David William, FCA** *1967;* David W. Adams, 12 Epping Close, Rainhill, PRESCOT, L35 0QE.
ADAMS, Mr. Derek Stanley, FCA *1962;* Rockleigh, Devonshire Terrace, CONISTON, CUMBRIA, LA21 8HG.
•**ADAMS, Mr. Derek William, FCA** *1967;* Flat 71, Thomas More House, Barbican, LONDON, EC2Y 8BT.
•**ADAMS, Mr. Donald Frank, FCA** *1993;* Baines Jewitt, Barrington House, 41-45 Yarm Lane, STOCKTON-ON-TEES, CLEVELAND, TS18 3EA. See also Barrington House Solutions Limited
ADAMS, Mr. Donald Raymond, FCA *1952;* Heron Lodge, 63 Osborne Road, WINDSOR, SL4 3EQ. (Life Member)
ADAMS, Mr. Donald Robert John, BSc ACA *1993;* Weeks Land Farm, Biddenden, ASHFORD, KENT, TN27 8JX.
ADAMS, Mr. Douglas Raymond Forsyth, BCom ACA *1981;* Kaim End, Hudnall Common, Little Gaddesden, BERKHAMSTED, HP4 1QJ.
ADAMS, Mrs. Edith Rachel, FCA *1959;* May Cottage, Old London Road, Coldwaltham, PULBOROUGH, RH20 1LF. (Life Member)
ADAMS, Mr. Edward Laurence, ACA *2010;* 2, Ide Hill House Emmetts Lane, Ide Hill, SEVENOAKS, TN14 6BB.
ADAMS, Miss. Eleanor Charlotte, BCom ACA *1999;* Provident Financial, 1 Godwin Street, BRADFORD, BD1 2SU.
ADAMS, Mrs. Eleanor Jane, BA ACA *1997;* 51 Cavendish Road, Colliers Wood, LONDON, SW19 2ET.
ADAMS, Mr. Elliott Paul, BA ACA *2003;* 1a Norrys Road, Cockfosters, BARNET, HERTFORDSHIRE, EN4 9JX.
ADAMS, Mr. Gareth Lee, BSc ACA *2004;* 5 Castellain Road, LONDON, W9 1EY.
ADAMS, Mr. Gary Neil, ACA *2008;* 17 Old School Square, LONDON, E14 7DJ.
ADAMS, Mr. Geoffrey Albert Leonard, FCA *1972;* 116 Mildmay Road, CHELMSFORD, CM2 0EB.
ADAMS, Mr. Geoffrey Rouen, FCA ATII *1969;* Langton Manor, Main Street, Scotton, KNARESBOROUGH, NORTH YORKSHIRE, HG5 9HS.
ADAMS, Mr. George Andrew, BA ACA *1988;* 32 Cross Hayes, MALMESBURY, WILTSHIRE, SN16 9BG.
•**ADAMS, Mrs. Gillian May, FCA** *1976;* (Tax Fac), Derek Young & Co, Estate House, Evesham Street, REDDITCH, B97 4HP.

ADAMS, Mr. Glen Samuel, BSc FCA *1984;* (Tax Fac), Swan Housing, 129 High Street, BILLERICAY, CM12 9AH.
ADAMS, Mr. Graham, FCA *1959;* 4 Crossway Rd, Church Lawton, STOKE-ON-TRENT, ST7 3EY. (Life Member)
ADAMS, Mr. Gregory Bertrand, LLB FCA *1992;* RBC Trust Co (Intl) Ltd, La Motte Chambers, ST HELIER, JE1 1PB.
ADAMS, Mr. Harvey, FCA *1965;* 25 Warren Fields, Valencia Road, STANMORE, MIDDLESEX, HA7 4JQ.
ADAMS, Mrs. Helen, BA ACA *2003;* 3 Crowndale, Edgworth, BOLTON, BL7 0QY.
ADAMS, Mrs. Helen Anna Tansy, BSc FCA CTA *1996;* (Tax Fac), 21 Mallard Close, Twyford, READING, BERKSHIRE, RG10 0BE.
ADAMS, Mrs. Helen Elizabeth, BSc ACA *1987;* 32 Cross Hayes, MALMESBURY, SN16 9BG.
ADAMS, Mrs. Helen Jane, BA ACA *1995;* 33 Royal Mews, LONDON, SW1W 0QH.
•**ADAMS, Ms. Hilary Janet, FCA** *1973;* (Tax Fac), Hilary Adams Ltd, 158 High Street, HERNE BAY, KENT, CT6 5NP. See also Adams Hilary Ltd
ADAMS, Mr. Hubert Theodore, FCA *1954;* 12 Wakefield Road, Oakhill, STOKE-ON-TRENT, ST4 5PT. (Life Member)
•**ADAMS, Mrs. Irene Margaret, FCA** *1975;* 29 Marine Gate Mansions, Promenade, SOUTHPORT, MERSEYSIDE, PR9 0AU.
•**ADAMS, Mrs. Jacqueline Mary, FCA** *1985;* (Tax Fac), Beever and Struthers, St George's House, 215-219 Chester Road, MANCHESTER, M15 4JE.
ADAMS, Mr. James, ACA *2006;* with PKF (UK) LLP, Farringdon Place, 20 Farringdon Road, LONDON, EC1M 3AP.
ADAMS, Mr. James Robert, BSc ACA *2004;* Flat 3, 202 Great Suffolk Street, LONDON, SE1 1NY.
ADAMS, Mr. James Robert, FCA *1975;* Harwood Argos Hill, Rotherfield, CROWBOROUGH, EAST SUSSEX, TN6 3QL.
ADAMS, Mr. Jamie, BA ACA *2009;* 37 Elder Court, Mead Lane, HERTFORD, SG13 7GD.
ADAMS, Miss. Jane McKenzie, BSc ACA *1983;* Thorne Villa, The Thorn, Wrigglebrook, Kingsthorne, HEREFORD, HR2 8AN.
ADAMS, Miss. Jayne Kathryn, BA ACA *1992;* Mountain Trading Company, La Vieille Scierie, 73550 LES ALLUES, FRANCE.
ADAMS, Mr. Jeremy Vernon, FCA *1974;* 3 The Farthings, CROWBOROUGH, EAST SUSSEX, TN6 2TW.
ADAMS, Miss. Jessica Katharine, MA BA ACA *2009;* 4 Church Road, WATFORD, WD17 4PU.
ADAMS, Mrs. Joanna Margaret, BA ACA *1998;* 9 Lilly Street, SHERWOOD, QLD 4075, AUSTRALIA.
ADAMS, Mrs. Joanne, BSc ACA *1999;* 10 Heol Y Cadno, Thornhill, CARDIFF, CF14 9DY.
ADAMS, Mr. John, BA ACA *1994;* 52 Holmwood Avenue, SOUTH CROYDON, SURREY, CR2 9HY.
ADAMS, Mr. John, BSc FCA *1975;* 14 Lisson Grove, Hale, ALTRINCHAM, WA15 9AE.
ADAMS, Mr. John Anthony, BA ACA *1980;* 62 Ritz Cove Drive, DANA POINT, CA 92629, UNITED STATES.
•**ADAMS, Mr. John Blakey, BSc FCA** *1979;* Adams & Co (Ilkley) Limited, Moors House, 11 South Hawksworth Street, ILKLEY, WEST YORKSHIRE, LS29 9DX.
ADAMS, Mr. John Gilbert, BSc FCA *1961;* 3 Paignton Court, Scartho, GRIMSBY, SOUTH HUMBERSIDE, DN33 3DH.
•**ADAMS, Mr. John Peter Antony, BA ACA** *1985;* Wyck Consultancy, Wyck House, Woods Green, WADHURST, EAST SUSSEX, TN5 6QS.
ADAMS, Mr. John Stuart, BCom ACA *1984;* 5 Ashstead Gardens, Broadway Lane, Throop, BOURNEMOUTH, BH8 0AA.
ADAMS, Mr. John Thornton, FCA *1965;* Mountfield, Broomhall Road, Coldharbour, DORKING, RH5 6HF. (Life Member)
ADAMS, Mr. John Trevor, LLB FCA *1964;* (Tax Fac), 4 Grove Road, NORTHWOOD, HA6 2AP.
ADAMS, Mr. John Walter, FCA *1974;* 2 Park Avenue, Wolstanton, NEWCASTLE, ST5 8AU.
ADAMS, Mr. Jonathan Mark, BSc ACA *2005;* Smith & Williamson Ltd, Imperial House, 18-21 Kings Park Road, SOUTHAMPTON, SO15 2AT.
ADAMS, Mr. Joseph Gwyn, ACA *2010;* 44a Thane Villas, LONDON, N7 7PG.
•**ADAMS, Mrs. Josephine Frances, BSc FCA** *1979;* J.F. Adams, 29 Pensford Avenue, RICHMOND, TW9 4HR. See also Adams Tax and Accountancy Services Limited
•**ADAMS, Miss. Julie Barbara, FCA** *1984;* Menzies LLP, Heathrow Business Centre, 65 High Street, EGHAM, SURREY, TW20 9EY.
ADAMS, Miss. Julie Dawn, BA ACA *1987;* 20 Rhonepark Crescent, Crossmichael, CASTLE DOUGLAS, KIRKCUDBRIGHTSHIRE, DG7 3BN.
ADAMS, Miss. Karen Michelle, ACA *2008;* Mericot, Rapsons Road, EASTBOURNE, EAST SUSSEX, BN20 9RJ.
ADAMS, Mrs. Kathryn, BSc ACA *1997;* 6 Beaumont Row, WOTTON-UNDER-EDGE, GLOUCESTERSHIRE, GL12 7AF.
ADAMS, Miss. Kathryn Jane, BSc ACA *1996;* Glebe Cottage, Diddlebury, CRAVEN ARMS, SHROPSHIRE, SY7 9EE.
ADAMS, Mr. Keith Graham, FCA *1966;* Briland, Gorelands Lane, CHALFONT ST.GILES, HP8 4HQ.
•**ADAMS, Mr. Keith Michael, FCA** *1975;* Keith Adams, Tarn Hows, Vinegar Hill, Milford on Sea, LYMINGTON, HAMPSHIRE SO41 0RZ.
ADAMS, Mr. Kevin Gordon, BA ACA *1985;* Capital International Ltd, 40 Grosvenor Place, LONDON, SW1X 7GG.
ADAMS, Mr. Kevin John, BSc ACA *1995;* 33 Grampian Road, SANDHURST, BERKSHIRE, GU47 8NQ.
ADAMS, Mr. Kevin Richard, ACA *1991;* 11 St. Pauls Avenue, Cherry Willingham, LINCOLN, LN3 4LU.
ADAMS, Mrs. Laura Jane, ACA *2008;* (Tax Fac), 61 Fair Close, BICESTER, OXFORDSHIRE, OX26 4YN.
ADAMS, Mr. Lee Thomas, BA ACA *2003;* Rentokil Initial, 2 City Place, Beehive Ring Road, GATWICK, WEST SUSSEX, RH6 0HA.
ADAMS, Miss. Lucy Elizabeth, MChem ACA *2011;* Cleveland House, Gleacher Shacklock Llp, 33 King Street, LONDON, SW1Y 6RJ.
ADAMS, Mrs. Lynne, BSc ACA *1989;* 32 Kendall Court, Southdowns Park, HAYWARDS HEATH, WEST SUSSEX, RH16 4SX.
ADAMS, Mrs. Man Lan, BSc FCA *1995;* 8 Attenborough Close, WIGSTON, LEICESTERSHIRE, LE18 3PR.
ADAMS, Mr. Marcus Ian, MBA BSc FCA *1985;* Goldhawk Barn, Vann Road, Fernhurst, HASLEMERE, GU27 3NJ.
ADAMS, Mrs. Margaret Elizabeth, BSc ACA *1985;* Cunningham Lindsey, 60 Fenchurch Street, LONDON, EC3M 4AD.
ADAMS, Mr. Mark Andrew, BSc ACA *1989;* 2 Swan Court Booths Place, Swan Court, 1 Booth's Place, LONDON, W1T 3AF.
•**ADAMS, Mr. Mark Jonathan Derek, BA ACA CF** *1993;* Deloitte LLP, Athene Place, 66 Shoe Lane, LONDON, EC4A 3BQ. See also Deloitte & Touche LLP
•①**ADAMS, Mr. Mark Keith, BA ACA** *1992;* Deloitte LLP, Athene Place, 66 Shoe Lane, LONDON, EC4A 3BQ. See also Deloitte & Touche LLP
ADAMS, Mr. Martin Charles, BSc ACA *2010;* 9 North East Terrace, TEWKESBURY, GLOUCESTERSHIRE, GL20 5NT.
ADAMS, Mr. Matthew Robert, ACA *2008;* 26 Pryors Road, Galleywood, CHELMSFORD, CM2 8SA.
•**ADAMS, Mr. Michael Edward, LLB FCA** *1981;* (Tax Fac), Adams Tax and Accountancy Services Limited, 29 Pensford Avenue, RICHMOND, SURREY, TW9 4HR.
ADAMS, Mr. Michael James, FCA *1971;* 11 Elmsley Street North, SMITHS FALLS K7A 2G4, ON, CANADA.
ADAMS, Mr. Michael John Paul, MA(Hons) ACA *2010;* with KPMG LLP, 15 Canada Square, LONDON, E14 5GL.
ADAMS, Mrs. Michelle, ACA *2003;* 24 Inglewood Road, Barnehurst, BEXLEYHEATH, KENT, DA7 6JS.
ADAMS, Mr. Neil David, FCA *1984;* 6 Ingarsby Close, Houghton-On-The-Hill, LEICESTER, LEICESTERSHIRE, LE7 9JN.
ADAMS, Mr. Neil Fraser, BSc ACA *1988;* 53 Cottesmore Gardens, LEIGH-ON-SEA, SS9 2TF.
ADAMS, Mr. Nicholas David, BSc ACA *2000;* 60 Pine Grove, LONDON, SW19 7HE.
ADAMS, Mr. Nicholas James, LLB ACA *2006;* Avon and Somerset Police Constabulary, PO Box 37, Valley Road, Portishead, BRISTOL, BS20 8QJ.
ADAMS, Mr. Nicholas William Wareing, ACA *1979;* 348 Billing Road East, NORTHAMPTON, NN3 3LJ.
ADAMS, Mr. Nick Leslie John, ACA *2009;* 16 The Old School, Euclid Street, SWINDON, SN1 2LL.
ADAMS, Mr. Nigel David, BA ACA *1989;* Bank House, Priest Hutton, CARNFORTH, LANCASHIRE, LA6 1JL.
ADAMS, Mr. Nigel Paul, FCA *1976;* Rainbows's End, 439a Topsham Road, EXETER, EX2 7AF.
ADAMS, Miss. Nina Louise, BA ACA *1998;* 11th Floor (CGC-11-53), Citigroup Centre, 33 Canada Square, LONDON, E14 5LB.
•**ADAMS, Mr. Paul, BSc FCA** *1977;* Richard Matthew Ltd, 17 Broomfield Park, Westcott, DORKING, RH4 3QQ.
ADAMS, Mr. Paul Alistair, BSc FCA *1992;* 17 Worcester Lane, Pedmore, STOURBRIDGE, DY8 2PA.
ADAMS, Mr. Paul Christopher, BEng ACA *1999;* 72 Quintilis, Roman Hill, BRACKNELL, BERKSHIRE, RG12 7QQ.
ADAMS, Mr. Paul Ernest, FCA *1964;* 30 Elwyn Road, SUTTON COLDFIELD, B73 6LB. (Life Member)
ADAMS, Mr. Paul Francis, FCA *1971;* Chez Martine, 24320 VERTEILLAC, DORDOGNE, FRANCE.
ADAMS, Mr. Paul James, ACA *2010;* Midtown, F T I Consulting, 322 High Holborn, LONDON, WC1V 7PB.
ADAMS, Mr. Paul Quentin, MA ACA *1987;* 2 Manor Farm, Culham, ABINGDON, OXFORDSHIRE, OX14 4NP.
ADAMS, Mr. Paul Robert James, ACA *2009;* 78 Devonshire Gardens, Tilehurst, READING, RG31 6FP.
ADAMS, Mr. Paul William, BSc ACA *2007;* 43 Woodborough Street, BRISTOL, BS5 0JA.
•**ADAMS, Mr. Peter Charles, FCA** *1979;* 10 Southerland Close, Oatlands Drive, WEYBRIDGE, KT13 9EN.
ADAMS, Mr. Peter David, PhD ACA *2006;* 891 Holderness Road, HULL, HU8 9DA.
ADAMS, Mr. Peter John, FCA *1970;* Leicester Lesbian Gay Bisexual & Transgender Centre, 15 Wellington Street, LEICESTER, LE1 6HH.
ADAMS, Mr. Peter John, FCA *1966;* with Baker Tilly Tax & Advisory Services LLP, Lancaster House, 7 Elmfield Road, BROMLEY, BR1 1LT.
•**ADAMS, Mr. Peter Mark Chegwyn, FCA** *1978;* Adams & Co, Pullman House, 7 Battle Road, Heathfield Industrial Estate, NEWTON ABBOT, DEVON TQ12 6RY.
ADAMS, Mr. Peter Raymond, FCA *1961;* The Pightle Barn, The Pightle, Finchingfield, BRAINTREE, ESSEX, CM7 4LB. (Life Member)
•**ADAMS, Mr. Peter Robert Noel, BSc FCA** *1975;* Saffery Champness, Lion House, Red Lion Street, LONDON, WC1R 4GB.
ADAMS, Mr. Peter Stephen, MA FCA *1970;* 36 Greening Drive, Edgbaston, BIRMINGHAM, B15 2XA. (Life Member)
ADAMS, Mr. Philip Christopher, BA ACA *1996;* 15 Harrop Road, Hale, ALTRINCHAM, WA15 9BY.
ADAMS, Mr. Philip James, BA(Hons) ACA *2010;* 95 Claremount Road, WALLASEY, MERSEYSIDE, CH45 3JG.
ADAMS, Mrs. Philippa Ruth, BA(Hons) ACA *2002;* 15 Nettleton Road, Ickenham, UXBRIDGE, MIDDLESEX, UB10 8ER.
•**ADAMS, Mrs. Rachel Anne, BA(Hons) ACA** *2002;* Dolphin Tax LLP, 195 Loughborough Road, LEICESTER, LE4 5PL.
ADAMS, Mrs. Rachel Diane, PhD BSc ACA *2004;* Royal & Sunalliance, PO Box 144, LIVERPOOL, L69 3EN.
•**ADAMS, Mr. Raymond David, BA FCA** *1983;* BDO LLP, 66 Broomfield Road, CHELMSFORD, ESSEX, CM1 1SW. See also BDO Stoy Hayward LLP
•**ADAMS, Mr. Raymond John, ACA** *1982;* Ray Adams, Wellington House, 273-275 High Street, London Colney, ST. ALBANS, HERTFORDSHIRE AL2 1HA. See also RJA Accountants Ltd
ADAMS, Mr. Reza Sherron, MEng ACA *2004;* 1306 Broadmoor Lane, IRVING, TX 75061, UNITED STATES.
ADAMS, Mr. Rhoderic Gavin Iain, BSc FCA *1977;* APT Controls Ltd, The Power House, Chantry Place, Headstone Lane, HARROW, MIDDLESEX HA3 6NY.
ADAMS, Mr. Richard, FCA *1959;* 3 The Ridings, Sendmarsh, WOKING, SURREY, GU23 6JJ. (Life Member)
ADAMS, Mr. Richard Arthur, FCA *1964;* 77 Eastern Road, Selly Park, BIRMINGHAM, B29 7JX.
ADAMS, Mr. Richard Michael, BSc FCA *1972;* The Imagination Group Ltd, 25 Store Street, South Crescent, LONDON, WC1E 7BL.
ADAMS, Mr. Richard William, BSc ACA *1987;* 3 Courtenwell, Speldhurst Road, Langton Green, TUNBRIDGE WELLS, KENT, TN3 0JQ.
ADAMS, Mr. Robert, MA FCA *1965;* Avenue de L'Epervier 13, Boite 4, 1640 RHODE ST GENESE, BELGIUM.
ADAMS, Mr. Robert Frank, BA FCA *1972;* The Hall, Main Street, Shangton, LEICESTER, LE8 0PG.
ADAMS, Mr. Robert John, BA ACA *1995;* with Grant Thornton UK LLP, Royal Liver Building, Pier Head, LIVERPOOL, L3 1PS.
ADAMS, Mr. Rodney Dickey, LLB ACA *2009;* 4 High Royd Cottages, High Royd Lane Hoylandswaine, SHEFFIELD, S36 7JR.
•**ADAMS, Mr. Roland John, BSc FCA** *1981;* (Tax Fac), Percy Westhead & Company, Greg's Buildings, 1 Booth Street, MANCHESTER, M2 4AD.
•**ADAMS, Mrs. Rosalind Anne, BSc FCA** *1992;* Cooper Adams Limited, 12 Payton Street, STRATFORD-UPON-AVON, WARWICKSHIRE, CV37 6UA.
ADAMS, Mr. Ross Geoffrey, MA ACA *2007;* Edwards & Keeping Unity Chambers, 34 High East Street, DORCHESTER, DORSET, DT1 1HA.
•**ADAMS, Mr. Roy William, FCA** *1980;* (Tax Fac), Beresfords, Castle House, Castle Hill Avenue, FOLKESTONE, CT20 2TQ. See also C-BAS Accountancy and Taxation Services Ltd
ADAMS, Miss. Ruth, BA FCA *1988;* with KPMG LLP, 1 The Embankment, Neville Street, LEEDS, LS1 4DW.
ADAMS, Ms. Sally Ann, BA ACA *1994;* R S Components Ltd, PO Box 99, CORBY, NORTHAMPTONSHIRE, NN17 9RS.
ADAMS, Mr. Samuel Charles Burney, MA BA ACA *2008;* 9 Victoria Street, LEAMINGTON SPA, CV31 3PU.
ADAMS, Mrs. Sandra Christine, MEng ACA *2000;* 98 Fennel Close, MAIDSTONE, KENT, ME16 0XT.
•**ADAMS, Mrs. Sharon Aideen Mei Mei, BSc FCA CTA** *1992;* (Tax Fac), Waltons Clark Whitehill LLP, Oakland House, 40 Victoria Road, HARTLEPOOL, CLEVELAND, TS26 8DD. See also Horwath Clark Whitehill (North East) LLP
ADAMS, Miss. Sharon Lynette, BSc ACA *2005;* 13 Wintney Street, FLEET, HAMPSHIRE, GU51 1AL.
ADAMS, Mr. Simon Charles Rouen, BA ACA *1998;* 9 Foxwood Walk, WETHERBY, WEST YORKSHIRE, LS22 7XS.
ADAMS, Mr. Simon John, LLB(Hons) ACA *2010;* 100 Northstand Apartments, Highbury Stadium Square, LONDON, N5 1FL.
ADAMS, Mr. Simon Keith, BEng ACA *1998;* Elsevier, 3251 Riverport Lane, MARYLAND HEIGHTS, MO 63043, UNITED STATES.
ADAMS, Mr. Stan Nicholas, ACA *2009;* 32 Sharples Green, LUTON, LU3 4BB.
ADAMS, Mr. Stephen Christopher, BA ACA *1985;* 1 Shakespeare Road, WIMBORNE, DORSET, BH21 1NZ.
ADAMS, Mrs. Susan Jennifer, BSc ACA *1991;* 42 Long Rede Lane, Barming, MAIDSTONE, ME16 9LB.
ADAMS, Mr. Thomas, MA(Cantab) ACA *2011;* Flat 3, 95 Downton Avenue, LONDON, SW2 3TU.
ADAMS, Mr. Thomas Eric, FCA *1952;* Breach House, Little Berkhamsted, HERTFORD, SG13 8LU. (Life Member)
ADAMS, Mr. Timothy James, BSc ACA *2005;* with Smith & Williamson Ltd, 25 Moorgate, LONDON, EC2R 6AY.
ADAMS, Mr. Timothy Lawrence, FCA *1968;* 7 Southlands Crescent, LEEDS, LS17 5NX.
•**ADAMS, Mr. Timothy Prideaux Legh, BSc ACA** *1992;* Saffery Champness, Lion House, Red Lion Street, LONDON, WC1R 4GB.
ADAMS, Miss. Tracy Ann, BSc ACA *2002;* 45 Victoria Road, LONDON, N4 3SJ.
ADAMS, Mr. William Joseph, BCom ACA *1987;* 1 Harmony Crescent, BONNYRIGG, MIDLOTHIAN, EH19 3NZ.
ADAMSON, Mr. Alan Ralston, BA ACA *1993;* Digges Barn, Out Elmstead Lane, Barham, CANTERBURY, CT4 6PH.
ADAMSON, Mr. Charles Bertram, FCA *1951;* Gemini, Langham Lane, WINCHESTER, HAMPSHIRE, SO22 5JS. (Life Member)
ADAMSON, Mr. Christopher William, BSc ACA *1989;* 2 Gilpin Avenue, LONDON, SW14 8QY.
ADAMSON, Mr. Daniel Manus, BA(Hons) ACA *2001;* 114 Newport Road, MANCHESTER, M21 9WN.
ADAMSON, Mr. Edward Kenyon, FCA *1961;* 162 Chemin de Guichan, Oeyregave, 40300 PEYREHORADE, FRANCE.
ADAMSON, Miss. Elizabeth Jane, ACA *2011;* 23 Malmesbury Road, LONDON, E3 2EB.
ADAMSON, Mr. Ian William, BSc ACA *1999;* Kerneos Aluminate Technologies, Dolphin Way, PURFLEET, ESSEX, RM19 1NZ.
ADAMSON, Mr. James, BSc ACA *2009;* 18 Patterdale Avenue, Urmston, MANCHESTER, M41 7DW.
ADAMSON, Mr. John Percival, ACA *1981;* Cambria, Greenstiles Lane, Swanland, NORTH FERRIBY, HU14 3NH.
ADAMSON, Mr. Mark Andrew, JP BSc FCA *1988;* Sanderson Ltd Poplar Way, Catcliffe, ROTHERHAM, SOUTH YORKSHIRE, S60 5TR.
ADAMSON, Mr. Mark Duncan, BA ACA *1991;* Formica Corporation, 10155 Reading Road, CINCINNATI, OH 45241, UNITED STATES.
ADAMSON, Mr. Max, BA(Hons) ACA *2004;* 13 Vinegar Street, LONDON, E1W 2QQ.
ADAMSON, Mr. Michael, FCA *1974;* 2 Boundary Way, Shoeburyness, SOUTHEND-ON-SEA, SS3 9QF. (Life Member)

ADAMSON, Mr. Michael Robert, ACA MAAT *1994;* Cherry Tree House, 38 Brantingham Road, Elloughton, BROUGH, NORTH HUMBERSIDE, HU15 1HX.
ADAMSON, Mr. Neil John, BSc ACA *1996;* 18 Oak Ridge, WETHERBY, WEST YORKSHIRE, LS22 6GT.
•**ADAMSON, Mrs. Rebecca, ACA FCCA** *2008;* Harris Lacey and Swain, 8 Waterside Business Park, Livingstone Road, HESSLE, NORTH HUMBERSIDE, HU13 0EN.
ADAMSON, Mr. Richard Joseph, FCA *1956;* Old Coach House, Southfield Road, Woodchester, STROUD, GLOUCESTERSHIRE, GL5 5PA. (Life Member)
ADAMSON, Mr. Richard Mark, BSc ACA *1998;* 13 East Hill, OXTED, SURREY, RH8 9AF.
ADAMSON, Mr. Robert Nicholas, BA FCA *1973;* 34 Ridgeview Road, Whetstone, LONDON, N20 0HJ.
•**ADAMSON, Mr. Roland John, BA FCA** *1977;* (Tax Fac), Roland J. Adamson, 1 North Parade Passage, BATH, BA1 1NX.
ADAMSON, Mr. Rory Beaton, BA ACA *1995;* P.O. Box 18648, MANAMA, BAHRAIN.
ADAMSON, Mr. Ross Ian Charles, ACA *2008;* 1 Dudley Mews, LONDON, SW2 2YE.
ADAMSON, Mrs. Ruth Alison, BA ACA *2004;* AEGIS London, 33 Gracechurch Street, LONDON, EC3V 0BT.
•**ADAMSON, Mrs. Sarah Louise, BSc ACA** *1992;* Sarah Adamson, Digges Barn, Out Elmstead Lane, Barham, CANTERBURY, KENT CT4 6PH.
ADAMSON, Stephen James Lister, Esq CBE CA *1979; (CA Scotland 1966);* Englewood, Ridgemead Road, Englefield Green, EGHAM, TW20 0YG.
ADAMSON, Mr. Stuart Victor, ACA CA(SA) *2009;* 9 Fyfield Way, Littleton, WINCHESTER, HAMPSHIRE, SO22 6PB.
ADAMSON, Mr. Stuart William John, FCA *1963;* Moons Farm, Sharpsbridge Lane, Piltdown, UCKFIELD, EAST SUSSEX, TN22 3XE.
ADAT, Mr. Mahmud Anverali, BCom FCA *1991;* 34 Anthony Road, BOREHAMWOOD, HERTFORDSHIRE, WD6 4NG.
ADATIA, Mrs. Elizabeth Jane, ACA *2010;* Cognita Ltd, 5-7 Diamond Court, Opal Drive, Fox Milne, MILTON KEYNES, MK15 0DU.
ADATYA, Miss. Yasmin, ACA *1982;* Y.Adatya, 73 Lily Close, LONDON, W14 9YA.
ADBY, Mr. David, FCA *1959;* 39 Farm Close, SEAFORD, EAST SUSSEX, BN25 3RY. (Life Member)
ADCOCK, Mr. Christopher John, MA ACA *1988;* Duchy of Lancaster, 1 Lancaster Place, Strand, LONDON, WC2E 7ED.
ADCOCK, Mr. Mark Nicholas, BSc ACA *1996;* 30 Kingsdale Drive, Menston, ILKLEY, WEST YORKSHIRE, LS29 6QN.
ADCOCK, Mr. Nigel Charles, FCA *1981;* 30 The Fields, Tacolneston, NORWICH, NR16 1DG.
•**ADCOCK, Mr. Oliver John Willamot, FCA** *1959;* John Adcock & Co, 7 Marlborough Road, EXETER, EX2 4TJ.
ADCOCK, Mrs. Sarah Elizabeth, BA ACA *2002;* 7 Cherry Hill Avenue, Barnt Green, BIRMINGHAM, B45 8LA.
•**ADCOCK, Mr. Simon Mark Peter, BSocSc ACA** *2001;* Deloitte LLP, 4 Brindley Place, BIRMINGHAM, B1 2HZ. See also Deloitte & Touche LLP
•**ADCOCK, Mr. Stephen Robert, FCA** *1978;* Somersby Consulting Limited, 100 Somersby Road, Woodthorpe, NOTTINGHAM, NG5 4LT.
ADDA, Mr. Michael Elie Smouha, MA FCA *1971;* La Rouquette, 24510 LIMEUIL, DORDOGNE, FRANCE.
ADDERLEY, Lord James Nigel Arden, FCA *1971;* Chalet Petrus, Rue de Patier 24, ch-1936 VERBIER, VALAIS, SWITZERLAND. (Life Member)
•**ADDERLEY, Mr. Melvyn William Thorpe, BA ACA** *1990;* Adderley & Co., Heathcot, Abbotskerswell, NEWTON ABBOT, DEVON, TQ12 5PW.
•**ADDERLEY, Mr. Paul Richard, MSc BSc(Hons) ACA** *2002;* Sustainable Opportunity Solutions Limited, 14 Ravensheugh Road, Levenhall, MUSSELBURGH, MIDLOTHIAN, EH21 7PU.
ADDEY, Mr. Edward James Beaumont, FCA *1968;* 20 bis Rue Raspail, 92300 LEVALLOIS, FRANCE.
ADDIS, Mr. Adam Richard, ACA *2009;* Flat 28 Forsyth House, Tachbrook Street, LONDON, SW1V 2LE.
ADDIS, Mr. Christopher Paul, BSc FCA *1992;* 20 Sidney Gardens, Muscliff, BOURNEMOUTH, BH9 3SG.
ADDIS, Mr. Jonathan Peter, BSc ACA *1996;* 98 Park Hill, Moseley, BIRMINGHAM, B13 8DS.
ADDIS, Mr. Keith John, BSc ACA *1992;* Lyndon Scaffolding Plc Garretts Green Trading Estate, Valepits Road, BIRMINGHAM, B33 0TD.
ADDIS, Mr. William Dickon, BSc ACA MBA *1988;* 47 Emerald Hill Road, SINGAPORE 229323, SINGAPORE.
ADDIS-FULLER, Mrs. Julie Elizabeth, BA(Hons) ACA *2004;* with Deloitte LLP, 2 New Street Square, LONDON, EC4A 3BZ.
ADDISCOTT, Mr. Mark Peter, BSc(Hons) ACA *2002;* 15 Saughall Close, Kingsmead, NORTHWICH, CW9 8GS.
ADDISON, Mrs. Alina Dana, BA ACA *2001;* 2 Maldon Close, Champion Grove, LONDON, SE5 8DD.
ADDISON, Mr. Barry Raymond, FCA *1972;* Flat 27 Paper Mill Wharf, 50 Narrow Street, LONDON, E14 8BZ.
ADDISON, Mr. Christopher John, BSc ACA *1995;* Seatoller, St. Helens Avenue, HASTINGS, EAST SUSSEX, TN34 2JT.
ADDISON, Ms. Clare Nicola, MA ACA *1990;* 67 St Albans Avenue, LONDON, W4 5JS.
•**ADDISON, Mr. David John, BA FCA** *1989;* (Tax Fac), Addison & Co (Teesdale) Limited, Ebor House, 91 Galgate, BARNARD CASTLE, COUNTY DURHAM, DL12 8ES.
ADDISON, Mr. David John, ACA *2003;* 13 Maidwell Close, WIGSTON, LEICESTERSHIRE, LE18 3WU.
ADDISON, Mr. Derek Edward, FCA *1963;* 'Quennel', 84 Oaktree Drive, NORTHALLERTON, DL7 8FG.
ADDISON, Mr. James Richard, BA ACA *2005;* Flat 11 Berwick Court, 10 Swan Street, LONDON, SE1 1BG.
•**ADDISON, Mr. Jonathan Charles, ACA MAAT** *1998;* Collards, 2 High Street, KINGSTON UPON THAMES, KT1 1EY.
ADDISON, Ms. Katherine, MSci ACA *2010;* K P M G, 100 Temple Street, BRISTOL, BS1 6AG.
ADDISON, Mr. Michael, FCA *1968;* 7 Julian Close, WOKING, SURREY, GU21 3HD. (Life Member)
ADDISON, Mr. Peter Ian, FCA *1948;* 14 Brook Crescent, West Hagley, STOURBRIDGE, DY9 0QE. (Life Member)
ADDISON, Mr. Philip, MA FCA *1972;* 8 Spencers Orchard, BRADFORD-ON-AVON, BA15 1TJ.
ADDISON, Miss. Rachel Bernadette, BSc ACA *1996;* 109 Selby Road, West Bridgford, NOTTINGHAM, NG2 7BB.
ADDISON, Mr. Robert John, FCA *1955;* Abbeyfield House, 17 Herbert Road, NEW MILTON, HAMPSHIRE, BH25 6BX. (Life Member)
ADDISON, Mr. Stephen John, BSocSc BSS FCA *1983;* 2 Tibbets Lane, Harborne, BIRMINGHAM, B17 0SX.
ADDISON SMITH, Mr. John, FCA *1952;* 6a North Pallant, CHICHESTER, WEST SUSSEX, PO19 1TJ. (Life Member)
ADDISON SMITH, Mr. Nigel James, BSc ACA *1991;* Oakdene Melrose Place, Storrington, PULBOROUGH, WEST SUSSEX, RH20 3HH.
ADDLEY, Mr. Mark, DPhil ACA *2009;* 20 The Orchards, CAMBRIDGE, CB1 9HD.
ADDO, Mrs. Cheryl, BSc(Hons) ACA *2000;* 45 Harlesden Road, ST. ALBANS, HERTFORDSHIRE, AL1 4LE.
ADDO, Mr. John Kpakpo, BSc FCA *1993;* P.O. Box CT 4680, Cantoments, ACCRA, GHANA.
ADDO-KUFUOR, Mr. Kwame, FCA *1995;* AngloGoldAshanti Ghana Ltd, Gold House, 1 Patrice Lumumba Road, Box 2665, Accra, ACCRA GHANA.
ADDRISON, Mr. John Trevelyan, BA ACA *1993;* Flat 33 Datchet Meadows, Datchet Road, SLOUGH, SL3 7FR.
•**ADDY, Mr. Christopher, BA FCA** *1986;* 1 Cliff Hill Close, Maltby, ROTHERHAM, SOUTH YORKSHIRE, S66 8BF.
ADDY, Mr. Christopher James, BA FCA *1994;* 1850 Panama Bureau 415, BROSSARD J4W 3C6, QC, CANADA.
ADDY, Mrs. Gillian Anne, BA ACA *1991;* 11 Carnarvon Road, SOUTHEND-ON-SEA, SS2 6LR.
ADDY, Mr. Neville, BA FCA *1972;* C R A Consulting Recruitment Specialists, 6 Paradise Street, SHEFFIELD, S1 2DF.
ADDY, Miss. Rachel Joanne, ACA *2009;* 4 Upper Ozzings, Shelley, HUDDERSFIELD, HD8 8LZ.
ADDY, Mr. Richard Martin, BA ACA *1982;* 57 Bradfield Avenue, Hadleigh, IPSWICH, IP7 5EX.
ADDY, Miss. Sarah Elizabeth, BSc ACA *2000;* Lansdown, Gorse Way, Hartley, LONGFIELD, KENT, DA3 8AE.
ADEBOYE, Mrs. Ezirenua, LLB ACA *2007;* with PricewaterhouseCoopers, Plot 252E Muri Okunola Street, Victoria Island, P O Box 2419, LAGOS, NIGERIA.
ADEBOYE, Mrs. Oyeyimika Omosanya, BSc FCA *1990;* House G23 Road 2, Victoria Garden City, Lekki Expressway, LAGOS, LAGOS STATE, NIGERIA.
ADEBULEHIN, Mrs. Tracy, MSc BA ACA *2010;* 2 Egret House, 108 Wraysbury Drive, WEST DRAYTON, MIDDLESEX, UB7 7FN.
ADEDOYIN, Mr. Adeniyi, ACA *1994;* 300 North Canal Street Apt. 3105, CHICAGO, IL 60606, UNITED STATES.
ADEEL, Mr. Kamran, ACA ACCA *2011;* House No 631, Street No 39, National Police Foundation, E-11, ISLAMABAD 44000, PAKISTAN.
ADEFOPE, Mr. Michael Olufemi, MSc FCA *1983;* P.O.Box 71931, Victoria Island, LAGOS, NIGERIA.
ADEFUYE, Mr. Modupe Adewale, MSc ACA *1992;* 51 Hening Avenue, IPSWICH, IP3 9QJ.
•**ADEGBILE, Mrs. Cynthia Julie, BA FCA** *2001;* Cindy & Co Limited, The Weston Centre M6, Weston Road, CREWE, CHESHIRE, CW1 6FL.
ADEGBITE, Mr. Ademola Olumide, BA ACA *2005;* 37 Bickenhall Mansions, Bickenhall Street, LONDON, W1U 6BR.
ADEGBITE, Mr. Adewale Michael, BA FCA *1992;* P.O. Box 2095, IKEJA, NIGERIA.
ADEGHE, Mr. Iyobosa, BSc ACA *2010;* 11 Muchall Road, Penn, WOLVERHAMPTON, WV4 5SE.
ADEKOYA, Miss. Modinat, BSc ACA *2006;* 31 Redwood Way, BARNET, HERTFORDSHIRE, EN5 2RU.
ADELMAN, Mr. Laurence Stuart, BCom FCA *1975;* 677 Old South Head Road, VAUCLUSE, NSW 2030, AUSTRALIA.
ADELMANN, Mr. Frederick Gustaf Birger, BSc FCA *1974;* Bank for Int.Settlements, Centralbahnplatz 2, CH-4052, BASEL, SWITZERLAND.
ADEMOLA, Mr. Adedotun Babatunde, MA ACA *1994;* 100 St. Albans Avenue, LONDON, E6 6HQ.
ADENIBI, Mr. Babatunde Erinoso, FCA *1986;* 119 Hazel Avenue, GUILDFORD, SURREY, GU1 1NU.
ADENIJI, Mr. Aderemi, MEng ACA *2010;* 27 Tulyar Court, BINGLEY, WEST YORKSHIRE, BD16 3ND.
ADENIJI-ADELE, Mr. Adelowo Oladoke Sheu, ACA *2008;* Apartment 207 Westgate Apartments, 14 Western Gateway, LONDON, E16 1BP.
ADENIYI, Mr. Adeyemi Mogbolade, MA ACA *1991;* 12 Rokeby Road, LONDON, SE4 1DE.
ADEOSUN, Mrs. Folakemi, BSc ACA *1995;* Chapel Hill Denham, Necom House, 15 Manna, LAGOS, NIGERIA.
ADEOSUN, Mrs. Olamide Abimbola, BA ACA *2003;* 47 Beechwood Avenue, RUISLIP, MIDDLESEX, HA4 6EG.
ADERYN, Mrs. Diane, MA ACA *1984;* University Of Bath, Finance Office, Claverton Down, BATH, BA2 7AY.
•**ADESANYA, Mr. Emmanuel Adekunle, FCA** *1971;* Adekunle Adesanya & Co, 12 Ogundana Street, Off Allen Avenue, IKEJA, NIGERIA.
ADETONA, Prince Abdul-Rasheed Adesupo, FCA *1967;* 3 Tokunbo Omisore Street, Lekki Penninsula Scheme I, PO Box 55018, Falomo, LAGOS, NIGERIA. (Life Member)
ADEY, Mr. Geoffrey Howard, BCom FCA *1976;* 12 Leadbetter Drive, BROMSGROVE, B61 7JG.
ADEY, Mr. John Brian, FCA *1962;* 19 Spa Garth, CLITHEROE, LANCASHIRE, BB7 1JD. (Life Member)
ADEY, Mr. John Victor, FCA *1964;* The Old Cellar, Back Lane, Stoney Stratton, SHEPTON MALLET, BA4 6EA.
ADEY, Mr. Keith Derek, BSc(Hons) ACA *2004;* 151 Featherstone Grove, NEWCASTLE UPON TYNE, NE3 5RF.
•**ADEY, Mr. Leslie Brian, BCom FCA** *1974;* Horder Adey, 13 Princeton Court, 53-55 Felsham Road, Putney, LONDON, SW15 1AZ.
ADEY, Mr. Matthew John, BSc ACA *2000;* 5 Pentney Road, LONDON, SW12 0NZ.
ADEY, Mr. Michael Robert, BSc ACA *2002;* 16 Winsham Grove, LONDON, SW11 6ND.
ADEY, Mr. Patrick Charles Victor, BSc ACA *2003;* Flat 75 Viridian Apartments, 75 battersea Park Road, LONDON, SW8 4DA.
ADEY, Mr. Paul Alan, BA ACA *1997;* The Chestnuts, Danes Green, Claines, WORCESTER, WR3 7RU.
ADEY, Mr. Philip Jeremy, BSc ACA *1992;* 44 Ringwood Avenue, LONDON, N2 9NS.
ADEYEMI, Mr. Olayemi, MEng ACA *2009;* 24 Spitfire Road, WALLINGTON, SURREY, SM6 9GL.
ADEYEYE-OLUKOYA, Mrs. Modupe Iyabo, FCA *1974;* P.O. Box 8784, LAGOS, NIGERIA.
ADIBE, Mr. Pius Nwachukwu, BSc FCA *1973;* PKF Professional Services, Gidan Shehu Ahmed, Bank Road, KANO, NIGERIA. See also PKF S.A.R.L (Life Member)
ADIE, Miss. Alison Barbara, MA ACA *1989;* S & A Foods Ltd, 37 Shaftesbury Street South, DERBY, DE23 8YH.
ADIE, Mr. Andrew Mark Devonald, BA ACA *1987;* 6 Coulter Close, Cuffley, POTTERS BAR, EN6 4RR.
ADIKARAM, Mr. Sanka Haripriya Bandara, BSc ACA *2010;* 53 Shillingford Close, LONDON, NW7 1HQ.
•**ADIL, Mr. Ahmad, FCA** *1978;* Ernst & Young, P.O. Box 140, MANAMA, BAHRAIN.
ADIL, Mr. Mustafa, ACA *2008;* with Ernst & Young, P.O. Box 140, MANAMA, BAHRAIN.
ADJEI-TWUM, Miss. Nana Akosua, MA ACA *1999;* Flat 1, 32 Emperors Gate, South Kensington, LONDON, SW7 4JA.
ADJEPONG, Mr. Samuel Francis, ACA *2009;* Flat 4, 96 Palatine Road, MANCHESTER, M20 3YB.
•**ADKIN, Mr. Christopher Colin, BA FCA** *1990;* Adkin Sinclair LLP, Sterling House, 32 St. John Street, MANSFIELD, NOTTINGHAMSHIRE, NG18 1QJ.
ADKINS, Mr. Bernard James, BSc FCA *1968;* 2 Vicars Close, CHICHESTER, WEST SUSSEX, PO19 1PT.
•**ADKINS, Mr. Clive, FCA** *1975;* Kilby Fox, 4 Pavilion Court, 600 Pavilion Drive, NORTHAMPTON, NN4 7SL.
ADKINS, Mrs. Laura Claire, ACA *2008;* 11 Grey Lane, WITNEY, OXFORDSHIRE, OX28 1FN.
•**ADKINS, Mr. Mark, BSc ACA** *1992;* 17 Higher Port View, SALTASH, CORNWALL, PL12 4BU.
ADKINS, Mr. Michael John, FCA *1968;* Stoke on Trent Boat Building Ltd, Longport Wharf, STOKE-ON-TRENT, ST6 4NA.
ADKINS, Mr. Michael Robert, FCA *1968;* 10 First Avenue, FRINTON-ON-SEA, CO13 9EZ.
ADKINS, Mr. Paul David, BA ACA *2006;* 10 Greenland Avenue, WYMONDHAM, NORFOLK, NR18 0ER.
ADKINS, Roy Ewart, Esq OBE FCA *1963;* Friary House, Nethertown, HAMSTALL RIDWARE, STAFFORDSHIRE, WS15 3QH. (Life Member)
ADKINS, Mr. Simon Paul, FCA *1987;* (Tax Fac), Water End Cottage, Wrestlingworth, SANDY, SG19 2HA.
•**ADL, Miss. Manuela, BSc ACA ATII** *1988;* Adam & Co, 8 St Clare Court, Foxgrove Avenue, BECKENHAM, BR3 5BG.
ADLAM, Miss. Marie Suzanne, BSc(Hons) ACA *2002;* 12 Chapel Square, VIRGINIA WATER, GU25 4SZ.
ADLAM, Mr. Thomas Richard, MA FCA *1988;* PCP Uganda Ltd, PO Box 15373, KAMPALA, UGANDA.
ADLARD, Miss. Emma Jane, BSc ACA *1995;* McCormick (UK) Plc Haddenham Business Park, Pegasus Way Haddenham, AYLESBURY, BUCKINGHAMSHIRE, HP17 8LB.
ADLARD, Miss. Katharine Sarah Elizabeth, ACA *2009;* The Annexe, 54 Apsley Road, BRISTOL, BS8 2ST.
ADLEM, Mr. Blake Thomas, BSc(Hons) ACA *2011;* 41 Newlands Avenue, Cheadle Hulme, CHEADLE, CHESHIRE, SK8 6NE.
•**ADLER, Mr. Barry David, BA ACA** *1991;* Adlers, 349 Bury Old Road, Prestwich, MANCHESTER, M25 1PY.
•**ADLER, Mr. Bernard, FCA** *1960;* 46 Balfern Grove, LONDON, W4 2XJ.
ADLER, Mr. Daniel Andrew, BCom ACA *1997;* 25 Parkside, Mill Hill, LONDON, NW7 2LJ.
ADLER, Mr. David Harold, FCA *1966;* 29 Ipswich Road, NORWICH, NR2 2LN.
ADLER, Mr. David Mark Edgar, BSc(Econ) ACA *1999;* 5 Stormont Road, LONDON, N6 4NS.
ADLER, Mr. Gideon, ACA *2011;* 20 Christchurch Crescent, RADLETT, HERTFORDSHIRE, WD7 8AH.
•**ADLER, Mr. Joseph Benjamin, FCA** *1974;* Ben Adler Associates, 4c Unity House, 3-5 Accommodation Road, LONDON, NW11 8ED.
ADLER, Mr. Michael Alan, BSc FCA *1991;* A. Oppenheimer & Co Ltd, 20 Vanguard Way, Shoeburyness, SOUTHEND-ON-SEA, ESSEX, SS3 9RA.
ADLER, Mr. Philip Michael, BSc FCA *1976;* 40 Silverdale Road, Earley, READING, RG6 7LS.
•**ADLER, Mr. Stephen Paul, BA FCA** *1982;* Shelley Stock Hutter LLP, 7-10 Chandos Street, LONDON, W1G 9DQ.
ADLEY, Miss. Samantha Jane Angela, BA ACA *1999;* 65 Cleaveland Road, SURBITON, SURREY, KT6 4AJ.
ADLINGTON, Mr. Christopher, FCA *1963;* 274 Degraw Street, BROOKLYN, NY 11231, UNITED STATES.

ADLINGTON, Mr. David James, BA ACA *1999;* 258 Trinity Road, LONDON, SW18 3RQ.

ADLINGTON, Mr. Simon John, MA ACA *1998;* Bet365 Ltd Unit 2, Hillside Festival Way, STOKE-ON-TRENT, ST1 5SH.

ADNAN, Mr. Adeel, ACA *2008;* 46 Field Lane, DEWSBURY, WEST YORKSHIRE, WF13 3DU.

ADNETT, Mr. Richard Charles, ACA *2009;* Apartment 12, The Firs, 1 New Hawthorne Gardens, LIVERPOOL, L18 8FE.

ADNETT, Mr. Richard John, BSc ACA *1999;* The Co-operative Financial Services Limited, 20th floor Miller Street, MANCHESTER, M60 0AL.

ADNITT, Mr. Graham Arthur Haddon, FCA *1971;* Haddon House, 49 New Street, Chagford, NEWTON ABBOT, DEVON, TQ13 8BB.

•ADOLPHUS, Mrs. Joanne, FCA *1982;* Joanne Adolphus FCA, Aigburth, 1 Seymour Place, Mile Path, WOKING, SURREY GU22 0JX.

ADOLPHUS, Mr. Peter Kim, ACA *1981;* 18 Hacketts Lane, WOKING, SURREY, GU22 8PP.

ADOLPHUS, Mr. Stephen James, ACA *1982;* Unit 2 Morston Court, Aisecome Way, WESTON-SUPER-MARE, AVON, BS22 8NG.

ADOMAKOH, Mrs. Penelope Le Messurier, BA ACA *1986;* 23 Hanover Gardens, LONDON, SE11 5TN.

ADRIAN, Mr. Carl Sheldon, BSc ACA *1997;* United Business Media Plc Ludgate House, 245 Blackfriars Road, LONDON, SE1 9UY.

ADRIAN, Mr. David Stuart, BA ACA *1997;* Windmill Farm, Otley Road, Beckwithshaw, HARROGATE, NORTH YORKSHIRE, HG3 1QL.

•ADSHEAD, Mrs. Christine Maria, BA ACA *1990;* PricewaterhouseCoopers LLP, 101 Barbirolli Square, Lower Mosley Street, MANCHESTER, M2 3PW. See also PricewaterhouseCoopers

ADSHEAD, Miss. Janette Clare, BAcc FCA *1998;* Holly Croft, Knolls Green, Mobberley, KNUTSFORD, WA16 7BW.

ADSHEAD, Mr. Neil William, MSc ACA *1991;* 21 Halifax Road, Ainsdale, SOUTHPORT, PR8 3JU.

•ⓘADSHEAD, Mr. Stephen John, BSc ACA FABRP *1985;* Smith & Williamson Ltd, 25 Moorgate, LONDON, EC2R 6AY.

ADSHEAD-GRANT, Mr. Douglas Byron, BA ACA *1995;* Hawbush House, Mill Lane, Cressing, BRAINTREE, ESSEX, CM77 8NX.

ADU, Mr. Dominic Kwame, BA ACA *1994;* P.O. Box CT3125, Cantoments, ACCRA, GHANA.

ADUBIFA, Mrs. Abimbola, BSc ACA *2006;* 21/22 Marina, LAGOS, NIGERIA.

ADVANI, Mr. Anil Gobind, ACA *1980;* 17 Brinley Place, Sinnamon Park, BRISBANE, QLD 4073, AUSTRALIA.

ADVANI, Mr. Ram Awatrai, FCA *1975;* 146 Princess Park Manor, Royal Drive, LONDON, N11 3FQ.

ADVANI, Mr. Suresh Pritam Singh, FCA *1965;* 2 Mayfield Drive, KENILWORTH, WARWICKSHIRE, CV8 2SW.

ADWALPALKAR, Mr. Shailendra Bholanath, ACA *1978;* Brandis Sarl, 44 Avenue Des F.A.R, CASABLANCA, 20000, MOROCCO.

AELLIG, Mr. Martin, ACA CA(AUS) *2011;* (Tax Fac), Macquarie Bank Limited, Level 11, Ropemaker Place, 28 Ropemaker Street, LONDON, EC2Y 9HD.

AERI, Miss. Neena, BA ACA AITI *1986;* 25 Springvale, Edmundstown Road, Rathfarnham, DUBLIN D14, COUNTY DUBLIN, IRELAND.

AERON-THOMAS, Mr. David, MA FCA *1989;* 24 Manville Road, LONDON, SW17 8JN.

AF FORSELLES, Mr. Bernard, MPhil BSc ACA *2000;* 5 Parker Close, Hamstreet, ASHFORD, KENT, TN26 2JQ.

AFAMI, Miss. Eleni, ACA *2011;* 44C STADIOU STREET, AGLANDJIA, 2103 NICOSIA, CYPRUS.

AFFARKA, Mr. Abdul Naser, BA ACA *1990;* 1249 Rose Galaxy Landing, Apt 301, VIRGINIA BEACH, VA 23456, UNITED STATES.

AFFLECK, Mr. Paul Gabriel, FCA *1975;* 54 Kings Avenue, WOODFORD GREEN, IG8 0JF.

•AFFLECK, Mr. Robert Arthur, BSc FCA *1975;* Robert Affleck FCA, 3 The Knoll, COBHAM, SURREY, KT11 2PN.

AFFLEY, Mr. Martin Gerard, BSc ACA *1999;* 38 St. Georges Square, LONDON, E14 8DL.

•AFFLICK, Mr. Ian, BA FCA *1972;* Ian Afflick, 336A Wellington Road North, Heaton Chapel, STOCKPORT, CHESHIRE, SK4 5DA.

AFGHAN, Mr. Rajinder, BSc ACA *1997;* Credit Suisse Securities (Japan) Ltd, Izumi GardenTower, 1-6-1 Roppongi, Minato-ku, TOKYO, 106-6024 JAPAN.

•AFRIDI, Mr. Ali Akbar, BSc ACA *2003;* Cisco Systems International BV, Saudi Arabia Branch, Abraj Atta'uneyya Building, (NCCI Tower), 11th Floor, North Tower King Fahad Road Olaya Street P O Box 295200 RIYADH 11351 SAUDI ARABIA.

AFRIDI, Mr. Javed Khan, ACA *2009;* 4 St. Johns Road, SLOUGH, SL2 5EY.

AFXENTIOU, Miss. Athanasia, BA ACA *2010;* Flat 104, Near Chou Court 10, Kyriakou & Sotiri, Papalazarou, 4300 LIMASSOL, CYPRUS.

•AFXENTIOU, Mr. Costas, BSc FCA *1983;* HLB Afxentiou Limited, Palaceview House, Corner of Prodromos St & Zinonos Kitieos, POBox 16006, CY-2085 NICOSIA, CYPRUS.

AFXENTIOU, Mrs. Zaharoulla, BSc ACA *2003;* 6A KOLOKOTRONI STREET, 2235 LATSIA, CYPRUS.

AFZAL, Miss. Humera, MEng ACA MBA *2003;* Flat 23 Grove Hall Court, Hall Road, LONDON, NW8 9NR.

•AFZAL, Mr. Javed, FCA *1968;* J. Afzal & Co, 23 Grove Hall Court, Hall Road, LONDON, NW8 9NR.

AFZAL, Mr. Mohammad, FCA *1974;* 21-A, Street 30, Sector F-8/1, ISLAMABAD 44000, PAKISTAN. (Life Member)

AFZAL, Mr. Muhammad Sanaullah, ACA *2007;* PO Box 4722, Abu Dhabi UAE, ABU DHABI, UNITED ARAB EMIRATES.

•AFZAL, Mr. Nadir, BA ACA *2001;* Flat 17a, Etchingham Court, Etchingham Park Road, LONDON, N3 2EA.

AFZAL, Mr. Sulaiman, FCA *1969;* US Data Solutions LLC, 41801Echo Forest Drive, CANTON, MI 48188, UNITED STATES.

•AFZAL, Mr. Taheer, MSc ACA *2002;* Darlaston Taxshop Ltd, 210a-212a Darlaston Road, Darlaston, WEDNESBURY, WEST MIDLANDS, WS10 7TQ.

AFZAL, Mr. Talib, ACA *2009;* Abu Dhabi Commercial Bank, Head Office, 6th Floor Internal Audit Department, ABU DHABI, 939, UNITED ARAB EMIRATES.

AFZAL, Mr. Tayyeb, ACA FCCA *2010;* D-28 Block 4, Clifton, KARACHI 75600, PAKISTAN.

AGA, Mr. Kekobad, FCA *1975;* 2211 Dunvegan Avenue, OAKVILLE L6J 6P7, ON, CANADA.

AGACE, Mr. James Jonathan, BSc ACA *1993;* Harboury, Linchmere Ridge, HASLEMERE, SURREY, GU27 3PS.

AGAH-TEHRANI, Mr. Hossein, FCA *1975;* 1 Springpark Drive, BECKENHAM, BR3 6QD. (Life Member)

AGAR, Mrs. Christine Ruth, BSc ACA *1990;* 10A Clements Gate, Diseworth, DERBY, DE74 2QE.

AGAR, Mr. Christopher Forrester, BSc FCA MCT *1990;* Flat 1, 19 Frognal Lane, LONDON, NW3 7DB.

AGAR, Mr. Frank Edward, BA ACA *1984;* 10A Clements Gate, Diseworth, DERBY, DE74 2QE.

•AGAR, Mr. Ian Conyers Fletcher Shelton, FCA *1985;* Robert Whowell & Partners, 78 Loughborough Road, Quorn, LOUGHBOROUGH, LEICESTERSHIRE, LE12 8DX.

AGAR, Mr. Richard Brian, FCA *1956;* Hazelville, 24 Park Road, Menston, ILKLEY, LS29 6EN.

AGARWAL, Mr. Ajey Rajan, BSc ACA *2002;* 70 Kenton Road, Gosforth, NEWCASTLE UPON TYNE, NE3 4NP.

AGARWAL, Mrs. Nidhi, ACA *2010;* Flat 47, Naxos Building, 4 Hutchings Street, LONDON, E14 8JR.

AGARWAL, Mr. Vinay, ACA *2008;* Flat 5 Kinlock Court, 22 Beckenham Grove, BROMLEY, BR2 0XB.

AGATE, Mr. Robert Michael, FCA *1958;* 20 Bermuda Road, WESTPORT, CT 06880, UNITED STATES. (Life Member)

AGATHANGELOU, Miss. Chloe Maria, BSc ACA *2003;* Flat 3 Elderberry Lodge, 28 Christchurch Avenue, LONDON, N12 0DE.

AGATHANGELOU, Ms. Christina, BSc ACA *2010;* 1 King Paul Street, Ayios Dhometios, 2360 NICOSIA, CYPRUS.

•AGATHANGELOU, Mr. Marios, BA(Hons) ACA *2002;* with Horwath DSP Ltd, 1st Floor, Photiades Business Centre, 8 Stassinos Avenue, PO Box 22545, 1522 NICOSIA CYPRUS.

AGATHANGELOU, Mr. Stavros, BSc ACA *1995;* PO Box 24429, 1704 NICOSIA, CYPRUS.

AGATHANGELOU, Miss. Xanthe, BSc(Hons) ACA *2006;* Flat 5, Mulberry Lodge, 46 The Ridgeway, ENFIELD, MIDDLESEX, EN2 8QS.

•AGATHOCLEOUS, Mr. Alexis, BSc(Econ) FCA *1998;* Maximos Plaza Tower A 3rd floor, 213 Arch. Makarios III Avenue, CY-3105 LIMASSOL, CYPRUS. See also Deloitte Hadjipavlou Sofianos & Cambanis S.A

•AGATHOCLEOUS, Mr. Nicolas, BA ACA *2007;* Interquality Ltd, 4 Isavellas Katholikis, Office 2, Anavargos, 8025 PAFOS, CYPRUS.

AGATHOCLEOUS, Mr. Tassos, BA(Hons) ACA *2010;* 29A Vassileos Georgiou B street, Kapsalos, cy3077 LIMASSOL, CYPRUS.

AGER, Mr. David Mark, LLB ACA *1990;* 669 Woolwich Road, LONDON, SE7 8SL.

•AGER, Mr. Eddie Paul, BSc FCA *1992;* 4 Redgrove Park, CHELTENHAM, GLOUCESTERSHIRE, GL51 6QY.

AGER, Miss. Felicity Gillian Clare, BSc(Hons) ACA *2010;* 51 Ashley Park Avenue, WALTON-ON-THAMES, SURREY, KT12 1EU.

AGER, Mrs. Helen Rosemary, BA ACA *1991;* (Tax Fac), 25 Bentley Road, CAMBRIDGE, CB2 8AW.

AGER, Mr. Jonathan Christopher, ACA *1995;* 7 Orchard Lands, Burstall, IPSWICH, IP8 3DZ.

•AGER, Mr. Jonathan Peter, FCA CTA *1975;* (Tax Fac), Buzzacott LLP, 130 Wood Street, LONDON, EC2V 6DL.

AGG, Mr. Andrew Jonathan, BA ACA *1996;* National Grid Plc, 1-3 Strand, LONDON, WC2N 5EH.

AGG, Mr. Christopher Charles William, BA ACA *1978;* Grays Farm, West End Lane, HENFIELD, WEST SUSSEX, BN5 9RF.

AGG, Mrs. Jacqueline Sarah, BSc FCA CTA *1997;* (Tax Fac), 13 Ox Lane, HARPENDEN, HERTFORDSHIRE, AL5 4HH.

AGGARWAL, Mr. Amit, MA ACA *2000;* Level 5, Australia Centre, Australian High Commission, Australia House, Strand, LONDON WC2B 4LA.

AGGARWAL, Miss. Amita, ACA *1994;* Well House, 3 Darland Cottages, Pear Tree Lane, GILLINGHAM, KENT, ME7 3PP.

•AGGARWAL, Mr. Anil, FCA *1983;* Aggarwal & Co Ltd, 3-5 London Road, Rainham, GILLINGHAM, KENT, ME8 7RG.

AGGARWAL, Mr. Anil Kumar, BSc ACA *2006;* with PricewaterhouseCoopers LLP, 1 Embankment Place, LONDON, WC2N 6RH.

AGGARWAL, Mr. Arjun, BSc ACA *1992;* 535 Warren Terrace, HINSDALE, IL 60521, UNITED STATES.

AGGARWAL, Mr. Arun, BSc FCA *1982;* 39 Dennis Lane, STANMORE, MIDDLESEX, HA7 4JS.

•AGGARWAL, Mr. Ashok Kumar, FCA *1983;* Clifton House Partnership, Clifton House, Four Elms Road, CARDIFF, CF24 1LE.

•AGGARWAL, Mr. Ashwani Kumar, BSc FCA *1993;* (Tax Fac), Ash & Associates, 2 London Wall Buildings, London Wall, LONDON, EC2M 5PP.

AGGARWAL, Mr. Deepak, FCA *1975;* 57 Wellesley Avenue, Richings Park, IVER, SL0 9BP.

AGGARWAL, Mr. Deepak Kumar, BSc ACA *1994;* 20 Delacourt Road, Fallowfield, MANCHESTER, M14 6BX.

•AGGARWAL, Mr. Eesh Kumar, FCA *1990;* (Tax Fac), Appleby Windsor, 100 Hibernia Road, HOUNSLOW, TW3 3RN. See also Aggarwal Eesh

•AGGARWAL, Mrs. Gita Harilal, ACA *1979;* (Tax Fac), Gee Aggar & Co Limited, 10A Osram Road, East Lane Business Park, WEMBLEY, MIDDLESEX, HA9 7NG.

AGGARWAL, Mr. Neal, ACA *2008;* with Deloitte LLP, 2 New Street Square, LONDON, EC4A 3BZ.

AGGARWAL, Mr. Nitin, ACA *1988;* Seawatch, 47 South Road, SOUTHAMPTON SN01, BERMUDA.

AGGARWAL, Mr. Pran Chand, MA FCA *1971;* 39 Dennis Lane, STANMORE, HA7 4JS. (Life Member)

AGGARWAL, Mr. Rajendra Paul, BSc ACA *1993;* 68 Dorothy Road, LONDON, SW11 2JP.

•AGGARWAL, Mr. Rakesh Kumar, BSc FCA *1983;* 31 Queens Road, SOUTHEND-ON-SEA, SS1 1LT.

AGGARWAL, Mr. Ravi, BSc ACA *1983;* 28 Derwent Avenue, Ickenham, UXBRIDGE, MIDDLESEX, UB10 8HJ.

AGGARWAL, Mr. Sanjay, BEng ACA *1999;* 92 Parkside Drive, WATFORD, WD17 3AZ.

AGGARWAL, Mr. Sheil William, BSc ACA *1992;* 19 Pinecroft, Gidea Park, ROMFORD, RM2 6DG.

AGGARWAL, Mr. Sumeer Prakash, BSc(Econ) ACA *2003;* 1 Churchdale Court, Harvard Road, LONDON, W4 4EE.

AGGARWAL, Mr. Sunil, BSc ACA *1987;* 16 Daymer Gardens, PINNER, HA5 2HP.

AGGARWAL, Mr. Sunil Kumar, FCA *1981;* P.O.BOX 66700 NAIROBI KENYA, NAIROBI, 00800, KENYA.

•AGGARWAL, Ms. Surekha, ACA *1988;* Carnelian Business Services Limited, 7a Wyndham Place, LONDON, W1H 1PN.

•ⓘAGGARWAL, Mr. Suresh Kumar, BSc ACA *1992;* SKA IP Ltd, Boundary House, Boston Road, LONDON, W7 2QE.

AGGARWAL, Mr. Vijay Kumar, FCA *1965;* 2 Church Road, Delhi Cantonment, NEW DELHI 110010, INDIA.

•AGGARWAL, Mr. Viman Kumar, BSc FCA *1982;* 24 Courtfield Avenue, HARROW, MIDDLESEX, HA1 2JX.

AGGARWAL, Mr. Vinesh, BSc ACA *1997;* (Tax Fac), 61 Wolverhampton Street, WILLENHALL, WV13 2NF.

AGGARWAL, Mr. Vishal, ACA *2011;* Flat 46, 30 St. James's Road, LONDON, SE16 4QJ.

AGGARWALL, Mr. Kamal, MA(Oxon) ACA *2010;* (Tax Fac), 9 Bridle Road, PINNER, HA5 2SL.

AGGAS, Mrs. Marion, BEng ACA *1992;* Moortoft, The Moor, Coleorton, COALVILLE, LE67 8GE.

•AGGETT, Mr. Stephen Michael, ACA CPFA *2008;* with KPMG LLP, St. James's Square, MANCHESTER, M2 6DS.

AGGLETON, Mr. Paul James, BA ACA *1996;* 45 Windsor Road, WORTHING, WEST SUSSEX, BN11 2LZ.

AGGREY, Mr. Martin, MEng ACA *2007;* 6 Glen Drive, BRISTOL, BS9 1SB.

AGGREY, Miss. Michelle Jane, BSc ACA *2000;* 2 Panorama Court, RURAL VIEW, QLD 4740, AUSTRALIA.

AGHA, Mr. Ayaz Azim, BSc ACA FCCA *2002;* PO BOX 26222, DOHA, QATAR.

AGHA, Mr. Salman Ali, BSc(Hons) ACA *2002;* The Association of Chartered Certified Accountants, 29 Lincoln's Inn Fields, LONDON, WC2A 3EE.

AGHAIZU, Mr. Denis Chionye, BSc(Econ) ACA *2002;* Argoneo Real Estate GmbH, An der Welle 3, 60322 FRANKFURT AM MAIN, GERMANY.

AGHAJANI, Mrs. Azadeh, BA ACA *2010;* 13 Hillcroome Road, SUTTON, SM2 5EL.

AGHOGHOVBIA, Miss. Oghenevona Cynthia, ACA *2009;* Flat 31 Block B, Ardmore Lane, BUCKHURST HILL, IG9 5RY.

AGISILAOU, Miss. Chrysanthie, ACA *2011;* Charalambou Mouskou 10, 2220 NICOSIA, CYPRUS.

AGIUS, Miss. Isabel Gillian, ACA *2009;* PricewaterhouseCoopers, 167 Merchants Street, VALLETTA VLT 1174, MALTA.

AGNEW, Mr. Alistair Robert, LLB ACA *2000;* 9 Clarence Road, Hersham, WALTON-ON-THAMES, KT12 5JU.

AGNEW, Mr. Anthony John, FCA *1967;* Merryfields, West Street, Corfe Castle, WAREHAM, BH20 5HE.

AGNEW, Miss. Caroline Helen, LLB ACA *2002;* Ranier Technology Ltd, Greenhouse Park, Newmarket Road, Teversham, CAMBRIDGE, CB5 8AA.

AGNEW, Mr. John David, BA ACA *1992;* 19 Redvers Grove, PLYMOUTH, PL7 1HU.

•AGNEW, Mr. John Raymond, FCA *1975;* John R. Agnew, 11 Waterloo Drive, Scartho Top, GRIMSBY, NORTH LINCOLNSHIRE, DN33 3SQ.

AGNEW, Mr. Justin, ACA *2011;* 7a Beresford Court, Somerhill Road, HOVE, EAST SUSSEX, BN3 1RH.

AGNEW, Miss. Kayleigh, ACA *2010;* 45 Church House Road, Berrow, BURNHAM-ON-SEA, SOMERSET, TA8 2NQ.

•AGNIHOTRI, Mr. Inderjit, MSc BEng ACA *2000;* 91 Cannon Lane, PINNER, MIDDLESEX, HA5 1HP.

AGNOLI, Mrs. Catherine Amy Elisabeth, BSc ACA *2011;* 9 Bloomfield Lane, Kingseat, AUCKLAND, NEW ZEALAND.

AGOMBAR, Mr. Michael George, FCA *1971;* 14 Pemberton Avenue, Gidea Park, ROMFORD, RM2 6EX. (Life Member)

AGOSTINI, Mr. John Charles, FCA *1984;* 221 Hagley Road, Hayley Green, HALESOWEN, B63 1ED.

AGOSTINI, Mr. Richard Arthur Ralph, FCA *1971;* Flat 2 53 St. Georges Drive, LONDON, SW1V 4DF.

AGRAN, Mr. Norman, MA ACA *1980;* 111 Century Court, Grove End Road, LONDON, NW8 9LD.

AGRAWAL, Mrs. Anjali, ACA *1993;* 13 Dogwood Drive, PLAINSBORO, NJ 08536, UNITED STATES.

AGRAWAL, Mr. Anup Gopal, ACA *2005;* 25 Brushwood Drive, Chorleywood, RICKMANSWORTH, HERTFORDSHIRE, WD3 5RS.

AGRAWAL, Miss. Bharti, BA(Hons) ACA *2002;* with KPMG LLP, 15 Canada Square, LONDON, E14 5GL.

AGRAWAL, Mr. Manish, ACA *2011;* 19 Donne Close, CRAWLEY, WEST SUSSEX, RH10 3AP.

AGRAWAL, Miss. Sheila, BA ACA *2006;* 30 Buxton Avenue, Caversham, READING, RG4 7BU.

AGRAWAL, Mrs. Sudha, FCA *1989;* B Davis & Co, 158-160 Arthur Road, Wimbledon Park, LONDON, SW19 8AQ.

AGRAWAL, Mr. Vikas, MA ACA *1997;* 3 Rudd Close, Wynyard, BILLINGHAM, CLEVELAND, TS22 5TG.

AGRAWALA, Mr. Javed Piyarali, ACA *1981;* Annexe 84/2/1 21st Street Kh-e-Hilal, KARACHI, SINDH, PAKISTAN.

AGROTIS, Mrs. Christiana, ACA *2011;* 1 Presidential Avenue, Flat 501, 1300 NICOSIA, CYPRUS.

AGROTIS, Mrs. Demetra, BSc ACA *2004;* 26 Osidge Lane, LONDON, N14 5JE.

AGUDA, Mr. Adeyemi Richard, BA ACA *1998;* Flat 12 Editha Mansions, Edith Grove, LONDON, SW10 0NN.

AGUIAR, Mrs. Michelle Sarah Zoe, BA ACA *1999;* 1 The Pennards, SUNBURY-ON-THAMES, MIDDLESEX, TW16 5JZ.

•AGUSS, Mr. Martyn James, FCA *1981;* 10 Eriswell Crescent, Hersham, WALTON-ON-THAMES, KT12 5DS.

•AGUTTER, Miss. Helen Elizabeth, BA ACA *1999;* (Tax Fac), Agutter Helen ACA, 48 Albany Villas, HOVE, EAST SUSSEX, BN3 2RW. See also MM Bookkeeping Ltd

AGUTTER, Mr. Richard Devenish, FCA *1964;* Leabridge Farmhouse, Westburton, PULBOROUGH, WEST SUSSEX, RH20 1HD.

•AGYEI-BOAMAH, Mr. Ransford, ACA FCCA *2010;* Harmer Slater Limited, Salatin House, 19 Cedar Road, SUTTON, SURREY, SM2 5DA.

AH-CHING, Mr. Cheong Shaow Woon, FCA *1992;* Morcellement Coprim, TOMBEAU BAY, MAURITIUS.

AH CHIP, Mr. Jean Laval, BSc(Econ) ACA *2003;* Laimin Family, Royal Road, Palm Lane, Telfair, MOKA, MAURITIUS.

AH-CHIP, Mr. Patrice Chung Yuen Cheong, BSc ACA *2010;* Iceland Wharf, Flat 25, 1 Yeoman Street, LONDON, SE8 5DP.

AH-CHUEN, Mr. Donald, FCA MBA *1961;* ABC Motors Co Ltd, Military Road, PORT LOUIS, MAURITIUS.

AH-HEE, Miss. Li Yin Yin, BSc ACA *2004;* Lot 54 Rue Montpellier, Residences Trianon, Petit Camp, PHOENIX, MAURITIUS.

•AH-HEN, Miss. Clairette Fy-Thin, BA FCA *1986;* Sinclair House, 4 Raoul Rivet Street, Square Petricher, PORT LOUIS, PL1, MAURITIUS.

AH-KANG, Mr. Jean France Gaetan, ACA *1992;* C/o Notre Dame Store, Loreto Convent Street, Curepipe Road, CUREPIPE, MAURITIUS.

AH LIM, Miss. Annabel Priscille, ACA *2007;* 5 Albert Road, LONDON, E18 1LE.

AH-PIANG, Mr. Shane Robert, BSc FCA *1991;* Residence Marguerite, 285 rue de Cessange, L1321 LUXEMBOURG, LUXEMBOURG.

AH-SEE, Miss. Marie-Michele, MA ACA *1993;* MEDINE MEWS - LEVEL 6, CHAUSSEE ST, PORT LOUIS, MAURITIUS.

AH-YOONG, Mr. Georges, FCA *1972;* 88 Hendon Road, MARKHAM L3R 0P7, ON, CANADA.

AH-YOONG, Miss. Jeannette, ACA *1979;* Canada Revenue Agency, Toronto East Tax Services Office, 200 Town Centre Court, SCARBOROUGH M1P 4YE, ON, CANADA.

AH YOW, Miss. Karen Melanie, MSc ACA *2010;* Apartment 7, 2 The Dale, SHEFFIELD, S8 0PW.

AHAMED, Mr. Mohamed Faizal, MEng ACA *1999;* R C I Europe Ltd Kettering Parkway, Kettering Venture Park, KETTERING, NORTHAMPTONSHIRE, NN15 6EY.

•AHAMMAD, Mrs. Ursula Castillo, FCA *1976;* (Tax Fac), Chowdhury Ahammad & Co, 4th Floor, 36 East Castle Street, LONDON, W1W 8DP.

AHEARNE, Mr. Stephen James, FCA *1963;* Dovehouse Place, Cromwell Park, Felsted, DUNMOW, CM6 3DD. (Life Member)

AHERN, Miss. Charlotte Jane, BSc ACA *2004;* 62 Tankerton Road, WHITSTABLE, CT5 2AF.

AHERN, Mr. Dominic David, ACA *2009;* Flat 10, 60 Sinclair Road, LONDON, W14 0NH.

AHERN, Mr. Edward George, FCA *1958;* Penn View, Fair Place, Chiselborough, STOKE-SUB-HAMDON, SOMERSET, TA14 6TL. (Life Member)

AHERN, Mr. Julian Mark, BA ACA *1989;* Tuckswood, Etchingwood, Buxted, UCKFIELD, EAST SUSSEX, TN22 4PL.

AHERNE, Mr. Brian Joseph Michael, BSc FCA *1978;* Carroll & Kinsella Motors, 48 Upper Churchtown Road, Churchtown, DUBLIN 14, COUNTY DUBLIN, IRELAND.

AHERNE, Mrs. Joanne Elizabeth, BSc ACA *1993;* (Tax Fac), Orchard House, Beesley Green, Worsley, MANCHESTER, M28 2QW.

AHERNE, Mr. Stephen, MPhil BSc ACA *2002;* 2 Bullfinch Close, SEVENOAKS, TN13 2BB.

AHFONG WAN, Mrs. Marie Lisette Florise Choytiane, FCA *1984;* United Business Media Ludgate House, 245 Blackfriars Road, LONDON, SE1 9UY.

AHKINE, Mr. Suie Sen Hockmeen, ACA *1991;* Harel Mallac & Co. Ltd, 18 Edith Cavell Street, PORT LOUIS, MAURITIUS.

AHKONG, Mr. Ian, ACA *2009;* 20 Renmuir Street, LONDON, SW17 9SS.

AHLUWALIA, Mr. Ajeet Singh, MSc BSc(Eng) DIC FCA CF MBA ACGI *1986;* Apt A16-3A Zehn Bukit Pantai, 12 Jalan Bukit Pantai, 59100 KUALA LUMPUR, FEDERAL TERRITORY, MALAYSIA.

AHLUWALIA, Miss. Amrita, MA ACA *2007;* 34 / 42 First Floor, West Punjabi Bagh, New Delhi - 110026, India, NEW DELHI 110026, INDIA.

•AHLUWALIA, Mr. Davinder Singh, ACA *1978;* D.S A-Walia & Co, 5 Amery Road, HARROW, HA1 3UH.

AHLUWALIA, Mr. Harminder Singh, BSc ACA *2008;* 2 The Hollies, LONGFIELD, KENT, DA3 7HU.

AHLUWALIA, Mr. Lalit, FCA *1978;* G3/15 DLF PHASE 1, GURGAON 122002, HARYANA, INDIA.

AHLUWALIA, Mr. Madan Mohan Singh, FCA *1970;* 23 Canons Drive, EDGWARE, HA8 7RB.

AHLUWALIA, Mrs. Neelu, BSc FCA *1985;* 47445 Greenwich Drive, NOVI, MI 48374, UNITED STATES.

AHLUWALIA, Mr. Rajiv Mohan Singh, BA ACA *1996;* 23 Canons Drive, EDGWARE, MIDDLESEX, HA8 7RB.

AHMAD, Mr. Abdul Rahim, BA(Hons) ACA *2004;* 109/E Mira Khan Road, Lahore Cantonment, LAHORE 54810, PAKISTAN.

AHMAD, Mr. Abdul Rahman, BA ACA *1996;* 1A Lorong 14/47B, 46100 PETALING JAYA, SELANGOR, MALAYSIA.

AHMAD, Mr. Aftab, FCA *1966;* Aftab Nabi & Co, Alshajar, Nila Gubad, Anarkali, LAHORE, PAKISTAN.

AHMAD, Mr. Ajaz, FCA *1967;* Plot No.29-A, Vegetable & Poultry Farm, Scheme No. II Chakshahzad, ISLAMABAD, PAKISTAN. (Life Member)

•AHMAD, Mr. Akbar, BSc FCA *2000;* with Deloitte & Touche (M.E), 1001 City Tower 2, Sheikh Zayed Rod, PO Box 4254, DUBAI, UNITED ARAB EMIRATES.

AHMAD, Ms. Ameena, ACA *2010;* Flat 3, 161 Gloucester Place, LONDON, NW1 6DX.

AHMAD, Mr. Anees, FCA *1966;* 35 Chemin Moise-Duboule, 1209 GENEVA, SWITZERLAND. (Life Member)

•AHMAD, Mr. Arif, ACA *1999;* Henton & Co LLP, St. Andrews House, St. Andrews Street, LEEDS, LS3 1LF.

•AHMAD, Mr. Arif Mahtab, BA FCA *1999;* PricewaterhouseCoopers LLP, Benson House, 33 Wellington Street, LEEDS, LS1 4JP. See also PricewaterhouseCoopers

AHMAD, Mr. Ather Jawed, FCA *1965;* 32/D Jhelum Road, Lalazar I Morgah, RAWALPINDI 46600, PAKISTAN. (Life Member)

AHMAD, Mr. Basharat, ACA *1983;* 6010 Sumner Road, ALEXANDRIA, VA 22310, UNITED STATES.

•AHMAD, Mr. Ejaz, FCA *1970;* Al Qahtani Group, PO Box 20, DAMMAM, 31411, SAUDI ARABIA.

AHMAD, Mr. Faisal Aziz, MEng ACA *2007;* 124 Princes Gardens, LONDON, W3 0LJ.

AHMAD, Miss. Hafsa Asmaa, BSc ACA *2006;* 438 Bath Road, HOUNSLOW, TW4 7RP.

AHMAD, Mr. Haroon, BSc ACA *2000;* Capinvest, PO Box 31303, Level 41, Emirates Tower, DUBAI, UNITED ARAB EMIRATES.

AHMAD, Mr. Ijaz, FCA *1968;* 5101 Bladensburg Way, ARLINGTON, TX 76017, UNITED STATES.

AHMAD, Mr. Imtiaz, MA ACA *2010;* 21/3 Stuart Crescent, EDINBURGH, EH12 8XR.

AHMAD, Mr. Isar, FCA *1974;* 140/I 12th Street, Off Khayaban-e-Bokhari, Phase 6 DHA, KARACHI 75500, PAKISTAN.

AHMAD, Mrs. Josephine Ann, FCA *1968;* 5101 Bladensburg Way, ARLINGTON, TX 76017, UNITED STATES.

AHMAD, Mr. Kaisar, FCA *1961;* Apt 9B The Brussels, 9801 67th Avenue, NEW YORK, NY 11374, UNITED STATES. (Life Member)

•AHMAD, Mr. Mahmood, FCA *1976;* (Tax Fac), Ahmad Accountancy Services Limited, 232 Whitchurch Road, CARDIFF, CF14 3ND.

AHMAD, Mr. Mahmood Shafiq, FCA *1994;* Shipowners Protection Ltd St. Clare House, 30-33 Minories, LONDON, EC3N 1BP.

AHMAD, Mr. Mansoor, BA(Hons) ACA *2010;* with PricewaterhouseCoopers LLP, 1 Embankment Place, LONDON, WC2N 6RH.

AHMAD, Mr. Mobashar, FCA *1975;* Provincial Auditors Office, 1500 Chateau Tower, 1920 Broad Street, REGINA S4P3V2, SK, CANADA.

AHMAD, Mr. Mohamed Abdul Halim, BSc ACA *1986;* No 70 Lakeview Bungalow, Saujana Resort, Section U2, 4015 0 SHAH ALAM, SELANGOR, MALAYSIA.

AHMAD, Mr. Mohammad Ijaz, FCA *1972;* 19 Norman Crescent, PINNER, HA5 3QQ.

AHMAD, Mr. Mohammad Arif, BSc ACA *2010;* 14 Percy Street, NELSON, LANCASHIRE, BB9 0AA.

AHMAD, Mr. Moyeen, FCA *1975;* Flat 1, 69 Finchley Lane, LONDON, NW4 1BY.

AHMAD, Miss. Muna, MSc(Econ) ACA *1999;* 37 Dunmore Road, LONDON, SW20 8TN.

AHMAD, Mr. Nadeem, BSc ACA ATII *1992;* 28 West Parish Road, WESTPORT, 06880, UNITED STATES.

AHMAD, Mr. Naeem Ud Din, FCA *1976;* 9510 Valley Lake Ln, IRVING, TX 75063, UNITED STATES.

•AHMAD, Mr. Nasim, BA FCA *1983;* Nasim Ahmad & Co, 48 Woodend, Handsworth Wood, BIRMINGHAM, B20 1EN.

AHMAD, Mr. Nizam Uddin, FCA *1973;* 40 Wychwood Avenue, EDGWARE, HA8 6TH.

AHMAD, Mr. Qazi Zubair, BSc ACA *2005;* 13 Church Avenue, PINNER, HA5 5JA.

AHMAD, Mr. Rafique, FCA *1975;* D-106, Saima Pride, Rashid Minhas Road GULSAN-E-IQBAL, KARACHI, SINDH, PAKISTAN.

AHMAD, Mr. Rashid, FCA *1963;* The Launderette, 13 Parkstone Parade, HASTINGS, EAST SUSSEX, TN34 2PS. (Life Member)

AHMAD, Mr. Rashid, FCA *1966;* 36 Avenue de la Chardonniers, 78124 MAREIL-SUR-MAULDRE, FRANCE.

AHMAD, Miss. Reema Rehman, ACA *2009;* 170 Hartfield Road, LONDON, SW19 3TQ.

AHMAD, Miss. Saira, BSc(Hons) ACA *2011;* Flat 5, 31 Seward Street, LONDON, EC1V 3PD.

AHMAD, Mr. Sajjad, FCA *1966;* Managing Director, United Kaipara Dairies Ltd., P.O. Box 6424, DUBAI, UNITED ARAB EMIRATES.

AHMAD, Mrs. Shamail, BA ACA *2005;* 9 Helena Close, BARNET, HERTFORDSHIRE, EN4 0JA.

AHMAD, Miss. Shazia, BA ACA *2000;* Financial Reporting Council Aldwych House, 71-91 Aldwych, LONDON, WC2B 4HN.

•AHMAD, Mrs. Syma, BA ACA *2003;* Heathcoates Limited, Carr Chambers, 24-26 Carr Road, NELSON, LANCASHIRE, BB9 7JS.

AHMAD, Mr. Waheed, BSc ACA *2001;* 29 Whinmoor Gardens, LEEDS, LS14 1AF.

AHMAD, Mr. Waqqas, BSc ACA *2004;* Flat 41 Neville Court, Abbey Road, LONDON, NW8 9DA.

AHMAD, Mr. Yousuf Zia, BSc ACA *1990;* Hillrise, 142 Pepys Road, West Wimbledon, LONDON, SW20 8NR.

AHMAD HAMAD, Mr. Ismail Osman, ACA *2010;* 18 Omar Ibn Al Hussain Street, DOHA, QATAR.

AHMAD-SUFIAN, Mr. Muffriezal, BSc(Econ) ACA *2003;* 46 Riverview Kemensah, Jalan Melawati 5A, 53100 KUALA LUMPUR, MALAYSIA.

AHMED, Mr. Abid Zamir, BSc(Hons) ACA *2009;* 98 York Road, WOKING, SURREY, GU22 7XR.

•AHMED, Mr. Abmr, FCA *1979;* (Tax Fac), R Ahmed & Co., 37 New Road, LONDON, E1 1HE.

AHMED, Mr. Aftab, BSocSc ACA MBA *1999;* ConocoPhillips, HU-2012E, 600 N Dairy Ashford, HOUSTON, TX 77079, UNITED STATES.

AHMED, Mr. Aftab, FCA *1966;* 10/11 6 Zamzama Street, Clifton, KARACHI 75600, PAKISTAN.

AHMED, Mr. Ajaz, ACA FCCA *2011;* 240 Hedge Lane, LONDON, N13 5DA.

AHMED, Mr. Akhlaq, MSc BSc ACA *2002;* 52 Havelock Road, Saltley, BIRMINGHAM, B8 1RT.

AHMED, Mr. Amjad Iqbal, ACA *1986;* Iqbalsons, 224-B-1Block 2, PECHS, KARACHI, PAKISTAN.

AHMED, Mr. Anwar Yaseen, BSc ACA *1991;* with PepsiCo UK & Ireland, 1600 Arlington Business Park, Theale, READING, RG7 4SA.

AHMED, Mr. Anwaruddin, FCA *1964;* 30/A Road No. 8 Sector No. 3, Uttara Model Town, DHAKA 1230, BANGLADESH. (Life Member)

•AHMED, Mr. Ashraf Uddin, FCA *1974;* Ashraf Ahmed & Co, 112 Dickenson Road, Rusholme, MANCHESTER, M14 5HS.

AHMED, Miss. Asifa, ACA *2010;* 65 Moor Lane, Hutton, PRESTON, PR4 5SE.

AHMED, Mr. Atif, ACA *2009;* 14 Goodman Park, SLOUGH, SL2 5NN.

AHMED, Mrs. Farzana, BSc ACA *2004;* 64 Cavendish Gardens, BARKING, IG11 9DX.

•AHMED, Mr. Forhad, BSc ACA *1997;* (Tax Fac), F.Ahmed, 232 Perth Road, ILFORD, ESSEX, IG2 6DY.

AHMED, Mr. Fuad, MA(Oxon) ACA *2004;* 22 Fairmead Rise, Kings Norton, BIRMINGHAM, B38 8BS.

AHMED, Mr. Helaluddin, BSc ACA *1998;* 47 High View, PINNER, MIDDLESEX, HA5 3PE.

•AHMED, Mr. Hussain, ACA ACCA *2008;* Ahmed-Cliffords Limited, 153 Beehive Lane, ILFORD, ESSEX, IG4 5DX.

AHMED, Mr. Iftikhar, FCA *1964;* F23 Block 4, Kehkashan, Clifton, KARACHI, PAKISTAN.

AHMED, Mr. Ijaz, FCA *1968;* 127 J, Model Town, LAHORE 54700, PAKISTAN. (Life Member)

AHMED, Mr. Irfan, BSc ACA *2007;* 50 Cambridge Road, Seven Kings, ILFORD, IG3 8LX.

AHMED, Mr. Irfan, MSc ACA *2010;* 146 Malmesbury Road, BIRMINGHAM, B10 0JJ.

•AHMED, Mr. Jalal Uddin, FCA *1972;* Islam & Ahmed Ltd, 68 Seymour Grove, Old Trafford, MANCHESTER, M16 0LN.

•AHMED, Mr. Kashif Masud, BSc ACA *2004;* with Ahmad Accountancy Services Limited, 232 Whitchurch Road, CARDIFF, CF14 3ND.

AHMED, Mr. Khizer Khurshid, BSc ACA *1999;* 3 Foskett Road, LONDON, SW6 3LY.

AHMED, Mr. Khurshid, FCA *1969;* 36 Strathfield Gardens, BARKING, IG11 9UL.

AHMED, Mr. Mahmood, BA FCA *1996;* 14 Linden Lea, Finchfield, WOLVERHAMPTON, WV3 8BD.

•AHMED, Mr. Maqbool, MPhil ACA *1990;* M. Ahmed & Co, 83 Park Road, Chilwell, NOTTINGHAM, NG9 4DE.

•AHMED, Mr. Massroor, ACA *2005;* Advantage, 240 Gain Lane, BRADFORD, WEST YORKSHIRE, BD3 7DW.

•AHMED, Mr. Maudood, FCA *1984;* 4 Chave Croft, Broadwalk, EPSOM, SURREY, KT18 5TT.

AHMED, Mr. Menir, BSc ACA AMCT *1992;* Oasis Capital Bank B.S.C (c), PO Box 991 BFH West Tower - 20, MANAMA, BAHRAIN.

•AHMED, Mr. Mesbah Uddin, FCA *1971;* M.U. Ahmed & Co, 28 Christian Fields, Norbury, LONDON, SW16 3JZ.

AHMED, Mr. Mohammad Ibrahim, FCA *1950;* F89 Block 7, Kehkashan, Clifton, KARACHI 75600, PAKISTAN. (Life Member)

•AHMED, Mr. Mohammed Faroque, BA(Hons) ACA *2003;* Acctech Consulting, 51Basement Fashion Street, LONDON, E1 6PX.

AHMED, Mr. Mohammed Gohir, ACA *2004;* 155 Wells Road, Knowle, BRISTOL, BS4 2BU.

AHMED, Mr. Moinuddin, BSc FCA *1999;* 113 Mildmay Road, CHELMSFORD, CM2 0DS.

AHMED, Mr. Mostaque, MA(Cantab) ACA *2000;* 119 Dudden Hill Lane, LONDON, NW10 1BN.

AHMED, Mr. Muneeb, ACA *2011;* 68 Claremont Street, BRISTOL, BS5 0UJ.

AHMED, Mr. Munir, MBA BA FCA CTA *1993;* Melrose, 127 Wilmer Road, Heaton, BRADFORD, BD9 4AG.

AHMED, Mr. Muntazar Bashir, BSc FCA *1980;* 35-A Block B, New Muslim Town, LAHORE, PAKISTAN.

AHMED, Mr. Mushfiq Uddin, BSc(Hons) ACA *2004;* 64 Cavendish Gardens, BARKING, IG11 9DX.

•AHMED, Mr. Nadeem, MBA BSc FCA *1994;* Henton & Co LLP, St. Andrews House, St. Andrews Street, LEEDS, LS3 1LF.

AHMED, Miss. Nadia Naureena, BSc ACA *2005;* 134 Benson Close, Bramingham Woods, LUTON, LU3 3QR.

•AHMED, Mr. Naim, FCA *1975;* (Tax Fac), Naim Ahmed & Co, 79 College Road, HARROW, MIDDLESEX, HA1 1BD.

AHMED, Mr. Nauman, ACA CF *1986;* (Tax Fac), Deloitte & Touche Bakr Abulkhair & Co, PO Box 182, DAMMAM, 31411, SAUDI ARABIA.

AHMED, Mr. Naveed, LLM LLB ACA CTA *2006;* with Saffery Champness, Lion House, Red Lion Street, LONDON, WC1R 4GB.

AHMED, Miss. Nimat, MSc BSc ACA *2011;* 5 Temple Close, LUTON, LU2 7XZ.

AHMED, Mr. Noveed, BSc ACA *2007;* 7 Fairlop Road, Leytonstone, LONDON, E11 1BL.

AHMED, Mr. Nufel, ACA *2008;* 4 Cleveland Road, SOUTHSEA, HAMPSHIRE, PO5 1SG.

AHMED, Mr. Omar, MSc BA ACA *2010;* 246 Farndale Road, NEWCASTLE UPON TYNE, NE4 8TY.

AHMED, Mr. Raza, BA FCA *1991;* 204-4879 Kimbermount Avenue, MISSISSAUGA L5M 7R8, ON, CANADA.

AHMED, Mr. Riazuddin, BSc ACA *1992;* 1818 H Street NW, MC 6-611, WASHINGTON, DC 20433, UNITED STATES.

AHMED, Miss. Sabrina Tahseen, BSc ACA *2010;* Flat 8, Northlands, 165 Widmore Road, BROMLEY, BR1 3AN.

•AHMED, Mr. Sajjad, ACA *2010;* 37 Calmont Road, BROMLEY, BR1 4BY.

AHMED, Mr. Salim, ACA FCCA *2010;* 33 Dorrington Close, LUTON, BEDFORDSHIRE, LU3 1XL.

•AHMED, Mr. Salman, ACA CF *1983;* PO Box 5475, MANAMA, BAHRAIN. See also PricewaterhouseCoopers

AHMED, Mr. Samar, ACA *1989;* (Tax Fac), Safestore Brittanic House, Stirling Way, BOREHAMWOOD, HERTFORDSHIRE, WD6 2BT.

AHMED, Mr. Samiuddin, BSc ACA *1982;* 5268 CASTLEFIELD DRIVE, MISSISSAUGA L5V 1T5, ON, CANADA.

AHMED, Mrs. Sandhya, BSc ACA *1992;* 4 Chave Croft, Broadwalk, EPSOM, SURREY, KT18 5TT.

AHMED, Mr. Saqib, BA ACA *2008;* 58/1A, 22nd Street Khyban-e-Mujahid, DHA Phase V, KARACHI, PAKISTAN.

AHMED, Mr. Sarfaraz, FCA *1981;* 2155 Granite Street, VICTORIA V8S 3G8, BC, CANADA.

AHMED, Mr. Sebah, FCA *1975;* House # 28-S, Defence Housing Authority, Phase-II, Lahore Cantt, LAHORE, PAKISTAN.

AHMED, Miss. Shabana, ACA *2008;* 39 Canterbury Avenue, ILFORD, ESSEX, IG1 3NA.

•**AHMED, Miss. Shabana Naaz, BSc ACA** *2007;* Accounts Tax and VAT Ltd, 49 Northfield Road, BARNET, HERTFORDSHIRE, EN4 9DW.

AHMED, Mr. Shawkat, ACA *1981;* 652 Overlook Wood Way, LAWRENCEVILLE, GA 30043-6258, UNITED STATES.

AHMED, Mrs. Sheeba, BA ACA MBA *2006;* The Brae, Nicholas Road, LIVERPOOL, L23 6TS.

AHMED, Mr. Sherjeel, BSc ACA *2005;* 76 Brisbane Road, ILFORD, ESSEX, IG1 4SL.

AHMED, Mr. Siraj Shujaat, BSc ACA *1998;* 32 Southborough Road, BROMLEY, BR1 2EB.

AHMED, Miss. Sunbal, MSc BSc ACA *2006;* 9 Holm Grove, UXBRIDGE, MIDDLESEX, UB10 9LZ.

AHMED, Mr. Syed Nadir, ACA *2010;* 70 Warwick Road, LONDON, W5 5PT.

•**AHMED, Mr. Tahir, ACA ACMA** *2010;* Business Consulting & Accounting Limited, 161 Elm Grove, SOUTHSEA, HAMPSHIRE, PO5 1LU. See also Business Consulting & Accounting Limited

•**AHMED, Mr. Tofail, MCom FCA ATII** *1989;* Ahmed & Co, Ferrari House, 2nd Floor, 102 College Road, HARROW, HA1 1ES.

AHMED, Mr. Umer Farooq, MSc FCA *1994;* 58 The Vale, LONDON, NW11 8SJ.

AHMED, Mr. Usman, ACA FCCA *2010;* 9 Fishguard Way, LONDON, E16 2RG.

AHMED, Mr. Waseem, BCom ACA *1999;* 28 Kemperleye Way, Bradley Stoke, BRISTOL, BS32 8EB.

AHMED, Mr. Zakir, BSc ACA *2010;* 67 Blackstock Road, LONDON, N4 2JW.

AHMED RAZAK, Mrs. Alya, BSc ACA *1993;* 5 Pickering Gardens, LONDON, N11 3PP.

AHMEDABADI, Mrs. Seema, ACA CTA MAAT *2001;* (Tax Fac), 40 Cornish Crescent, NUNEATON, CV10 7JD.

•**AHMEDANI, Mr. Mohammad Tahir, FCA** *1979;* (Tax Fac), Ahmedani & Co, 46 Wycliffe Road, LONDON, SW11 5QR.

AHMEDBHAI, Miss. Yasmin Shamshudin, FCA *1975;* 4800 Kingsway ste 454, BURNABY V5H 4J2, BC, CANADA.

•**AHMEDI, Mr. Mohammed Azhar, LLB ACA** *1980;* M A Ahmedi, 1 Marlow Copse, Walderslade, CHATHAM, KENT, ME5 9DP. See also Ahmedi & Co Limited

AHMEDJI, Mr. Dawood, BA(Hons) ACA *2001;* with Deloitte Middle East, Currency House, Building 1 Level 5, DIFC, PO Box 282056, DUBAI UNITED ARAB EMIRATES.

AHMUN, Mrs. Emma Jane, BA ACA *2007;* 16 Chamomile Close, Pontprennau, CARDIFF, CF23 8RE.

•**AHRENS, Mr. Richard John, BA FCA** *1971;* Richards Ahrens, Croham House, Croham Road, CROWBOROUGH, EAST SUSSEX, TN6 1NY.

•**AHSON, Dr. Mahmood Umar, ACA ACMA** *2009;* (Tax Fac), A2Z Associates Limited, 639 Green Lanes, LONDON, N8 0RE.

AHUJA, Mr. Ajay, BSc ACA *1998;* 2 Fen View, Doddington, MARCH, CAMBRIDGESHIRE, PE15 0SN.

AHUJA, Mr. Anjit, BSc ACA *1993;* Emirates Aluminium, PO Box 111023, ABU DHABI, UNITED ARAB EMIRATES.

AHUJA, Mr. Naveen, FCA *1975;* 3 The Limes, Nightingale Road, RICKMANSWORTH, HERTFORDSHIRE, WD3 7SX.

AHUJA, Mr. Nikhil, ACA *2009;* 1 Siglap Road, Apt 08-03, Mandarin Gardens, SINGAPORE 448906, SINGAPORE.

AHUJA, Miss. Tina, MSci ARCS ACA *2010;* 45 Gledwood Drive, HAYES, MIDDLESEX, UB4 0AH.

AHYE, Mr. Peter David, BA ACA *1992;* Upper West End Farm, Gale Lane, Stainburn, OTLEY, WEST YORKSHIRE, LS21 2LX.

AIBARA, Mr. Hormaz Sorab, FCA *1978;* Mahajan & Aibara, 1 Chawla House, 62 Wodehouse Road Colaba, MUMBAI 400 005, INDIA.

AIDIN, Mr. Michael Read, MA FCA *1963;* The Old Rectory, Wiggonholt, PULBOROUGH, RH20 2EL. (Life Member)

AIFAN, Mr. Talib Hassan, FCA *1973;* 645 2 150, Aladel Noughborhood, BAGHDAD, 6452150, IRAQ.

•**AIGBE, Mr. Festus Olushola, FCA** *1971;* Olusola Aigbe & Co, 21 Fagbile Street, Surulere, PO Box 432 Yaba, LAGOS, NIGERIA.

AIK, Miss. Lucretia, ACA *2011;* 40B Zion Road, SINGAPORE 247774, SINGAPORE.

AIKEN, Mr. Andrew John Alexander, MA FCA *1975;* 164 Walm Lane, Willesden Green, LONDON, NW2 4RX.

•**AIKEN, Mr. Andrew Peter, FCA** *1972;* Parkside, 12 Stuart Road, BARNET, HERTFORDSHIRE, EN4 8XG.

AIKEN, Mr. Jason Neil, ACA *2008;* 25 Chigwell Park Drive, CHIGWELL, IG7 5BD.

AIKEN, Mr. William John, BSc ACA *1986;* 55 Lynch Hill Park, WHITCHURCH, HAMPSHIRE, RG28 7NF.

AIKEN-JONES, Mrs. Emma, BSc ACA *2005;* with PricewaterhouseCoopers LLP, 31 Great George Street, BRISTOL, BS1 5QD.

AIKMAN, Mrs. Elizabeth Jane, BEng ACA *1992;* Monks Pool, Rectory Road, Meppershall, SHEFFORD, BEDFORDSHIRE, SG17 5NB.

AIKMAN, Mr. John Kenneth Gresham, FCA *1971;* 29 Cartmel Drive, BURNLEY, BB12 8UX.

AILLES, Mr. Ian, BA ACA *1991;* 84 Beaumont Avenue, ST. ALBANS, HERTFORDSHIRE, AL1 4TP.

AILLES, Mrs. Susan Mary, BA ACA *1989;* 84 Beaumont Avenue, ST. ALBANS, AL1 4TP.

AINDOW, Mr. David, ACA *2011;* 36 Croftgate, Fulwood, PRESTON, PR2 8LS.

AINDOW, Mr. Peter Gerard, BCom FCA *1958;* 39 Red Lane, Claygate, ESHER, KT10 0ES.

AINDOW, Mr. Richard, BA(Hons) ACA *2009;* 1 Weaver Avenue, Burscough, ORMSKIRK, LANCASHIRE, L40 4LE.

AINGER, Mrs. Anna Elizabeth, ACA *1999;* 41 Baring Road, BEACONSFIELD, BUCKINGHAMSHIRE, HP9 2NB.

AINLEY, Mr. Adam Harry, BA ACA *1989;* 2034 Armacost Avenue, 1st Floor, LOS ANGELES, CA 90025, UNITED STATES.

AINLEY, Mr. Andrew John Hirst, FCA *1972;* Beck House, Grafton, YORK, YO51 9QJ.

AINLEY, Miss. Caroline Vanessa, BA ACA *2009;* Flat 3, 36 Clarendon Drive, LONDON, SW15 1AE.

AINLEY, Mr. Harvey Bertenshaw, BA ACA *1991;* 1st Floor Havell House, 62-66 Queens Road, READING, RG1 4AP.

AINLEY, Mr. James, BA ACA *2007;* Ground Floor Flat, 162 Sheen Road, RICHMOND, TW9 1UU.

AINLEY, Mr. John Stuart, FCA *1965;* 27 Fallowfield, STANMORE, MIDDLESEX, HA7 3DF. (Life Member)

AINLEY, Ms. Joy Rosalind, BA ACA *1986;* Ivy Croft, 52 Moreland Drive, GERRARDS CROSS, SL9 8BE.

•**AINLEY, Mr. Mark William, BSc FCA** *1984;* Mark Ainley Limited, Regent House, Heaton Lane, STOCKPORT, CHESHIRE, SK4 1BS. See also Ainley Limited

AINLEY, Mr. Miles Jasper, BSc ACA *1998;* 39 Holt Park Road, LEEDS, LS16 7QS.

•**AINLEY, Mr. Paul Frederick, FCA** *1973;* Ainley Cookson & Co, 102 Market Street, Hoylake, WIRRAL, MERSEYSIDE, CH47 3BE.

•**AINLEY, Mr. Simon Walter, BA ACA** *1984;* Forward Financial Accounting Ltd, Catalyst House, 720 Centennial Court, Centennial Park, Elstree, BOREHAMWOOD HERTFORDSHIRE WD6 3SY.

AINLEY, Mr. Simon William, BA ACA *2007;* Flat 203, Pierpoint Building, 16 Westferry Road, LONDON, E14 8NQ.

•**AINLEY, Mrs. Susan Elizabeth, FCA** *1975;* Susan E. Ainley, 39 Fourth Avenue, HOVE, BN3 2PN.

•①**AINSCOUGH, Mr. Christopher Hugh, BA ACA** *1982;* Bourton Farm, Bourton Lane, Compton Bishop, AXBRIDGE, BS26 2EP.

AINSCOUGH, Mrs. Irene, BSc ACA *1996;* 10 Claremont Avenue, CHORLEY, PR7 2HL.

AINSCOUGH, Mr. James Martin, BA ACA *2000;* 4 The Conifers, 81a Pinkneys Road, MAIDENHEAD, SL6 5DT.

AINSCOUGH, Mr. Philip, FCA *1972;* 1 Aston Way, Leyland, PRESTON, PR26 7UX.

•**AINSCOUGH, Mr. Richard Anthony, FCA** *1974;* PM+M Solutions for Business LLP, Greenbank Technology Park, Challenge Way, BLACKBURN, BB1 5QB. See also PM & M Corporate Finance Limited

AINSCOW, Mr. Richard Raymond, FCA *1975;* 42 Bowes Hill, ROWLAND'S CASTLE, HAMPSHIRE, PO9 6BP.

AINSLEY, Miss. Charlotte Louise, ACA *2008;* PwC, Dorchester House, HAMILTON HM11, BERMUDA.

AINSLEY, Mr. Nicholas Wilhelm, BSc ACA *1981;* Hillview House, Contlaw Road, Milltimber, ABERDEEN, AB13 0EL.

AINSLEY, Mr. Stanley, BSc FCA *1981;* 10 Bukit Sedap Rd, SINGAPORE 279912, SINGAPORE.

AINSLIE, Mr. Michael Robert Arthur, BSc ACA *1988;* 11 Westbury Road, LONDON, W5 2LE.

AINSWORTH, Mr. Allan, FCA *1953;* Hibisous Retirement Resort, 84/52 University Way, CHANCELLOR PARK, QLD 4556, AUSTRALIA. (Life Member)

AINSWORTH, Mr. Ashley Clive, BA ACA *2009;* Brookfield, The Willows, DYMOCK, GL18 4AY.

AINSWORTH, Mr. Brian Thomas, FCA *1955;* 13 Emerson Road, POOLE, DORSET, BH15 1QS. (Life Member)

AINSWORTH, Miss. Chloe, BA(Hons) ACA *2011;* 157 Simpkin Street, Abram, WIGAN, LANCASHIRE, WN2 5PS.

AINSWORTH, Mr. David, BA ACA *1991;* Woodhouse Grove School Apperley Lane, Apperley Bridge, BRADFORD, BD10 0NR.

AINSWORTH, Mr. David Michael Godfrey, ACA *2007;* Weinmanngasse 84, CH - 8700, KUESNACHT, SWITZERLAND.

AINSWORTH, Mr. Desmond Robert William, BSc FCA *1975;* Woodcroft, Willington Road, Willington, TARPORLEY, CW6 0ND.

AINSWORTH, Mr. Edward Peter Richard, FCA *1954;* (Member of Council 1985 - 1997), New Cottage, Davey Lane, ALDERLEY EDGE, CHESHIRE, SK9 7NZ.

AINSWORTH, Mr. Eric Stephen, FCA *1970;* Flat 144 Compass House, Smugglers Way, LONDON, SW18 1DB.

AINSWORTH, Dr. Godfrey Howard Harrison, PhD BSc FCA *1983;* Kingscote House, Kingscote, TETBURY, GL8 8XY.

•**AINSWORTH, Mrs. Helen Mavis, BSc FCA** *1989;* HMA Accountancy Services, Ranmore, Waterhouse Lane, Kingswood, TADWORTH, SURREY KT20 6DT.

AINSWORTH, Mr. Ian Harry, FCA *1953;* 101 Hazlehurst Road, Worsley, MANCHESTER, M28 2SW. (Life Member)

•**AINSWORTH, Miss. Janet, BA FCA** *1980;* Janet Ainsworth Accountancy Services, 18 Weylands Grove, Pendleton, SALFORD, M6 7WU.

AINSWORTH, Mrs. Joan Elizabeth, BSc ACA *1989;* 25 Huntingdon Gardens, Chiswick Place, LONDON, W4 3HX.

AINSWORTH, Miss. Joanne Lesley, BA(Hons) ACA *2000;* 7 Sandpiper Crescent, St Benedicte Gardens, Bamber Brook, PRESTON, PR5 6ZG.

AINSWORTH, Mr. Jonathan, BA ACA *2000;* 4 Woodchester Road, Dorridge, SOLIHULL, B93 8EW.

AINSWORTH, Mrs. Julie Lisa, BA FCA *2000;* with Luckmans Duckett Parker Limited, 44-45 Queens Road, COVENTRY, CV1 3EH.

AINSWORTH, Miss. Lyn Helen, BA(Hons) ACA *2003;* Foxley Kingham Prospero House, 46-48 Rothesay Road, LUTON, LU1 1QZ.

AINSWORTH, Mr. Paul Anthony, BSc FCA FSI *1996;* 81 White Oak Shade Road, NEW CANAAN, CT 06840, UNITED STATES.

•**AINSWORTH, Mr. Paul Ralph, BA ACA** *1984;* Ainsworth Accountants Limited, 19 Sandringham Park Drive, New Longton, PRESTON, PR4 4ZS.

AINSWORTH, Mr. Robert David, BA FCA *1976;* 16 Wakeling Road, Denton, MANCHESTER, M34 6ES.

AINSWORTH, Mr. Robert David, BA FCA *1976;* Turner House, Station Road, Elsenham, BISHOP'S STORTFORD, CM22 6LA. (Life Member)

AINSWORTH, Mr. Robert Desmond, BA ACA *1983;* 75 Hemdean Road, Caversham, READING, RG4 7SS.

AINSWORTH, Mrs. Sarah Helen, MA FCA *1992;* E D & F Man Holdings Ltd, Cottons Centre, Hays Lane, LONDON, SE1 2QE.

AIRD, Mr. Alastair Gordon Stephen, BSc ACA *1995;* 12 Veronica Road, LONDON, SW17 8QL.

AIRD, Mrs. Josephine Lorraine, BA ACA *2004;* 1 Alwinton Terrace, NEWCASTLE UPON TYNE, NE3 1UB.

AIRD, Mr. Michael Stewart, MA ACA CTA *1997;* 47 Halton Way, NEWCASTLE UPON TYNE, NE3 5RQ.

AIRD, Mr. Robert William Service, BA ACA *1993;* 10 building 1 1st Volokolamsky proyezd, 123060 MOSCOW, RUSSIAN FEDERATION.

AIREY, Mr. Desmond Frederick, FCA *1965;* Flat 2 Geoffrey Court, 39 Alpha Road, BIRCHINGTON, CT7 9EG.

AIREY, Mrs. Helen Elizabeth, BA ACA *2006;* Directorbank Group, 8 St. Pauls Street, LEEDS, LS1 2LE.

•**AIREY, Mr. John Charles, FCA** *1972;* Holywell Cottage, Hodsoll Street, SEVENOAKS, TN15 7LE.

AIREY, Mr. Paul Graham, BSc ACA *2006;* 15 Fairfield Link, Sherburn in Elmet, LEEDS, LS25 6LT.

•**AIREY, Mr. Richard Antony, BSc FCA** *1985;* Richard Airey Limited, 2 Church Lane, Clayton West, HUDDERSFIELD, HD8 9LY.

AIREY, Mr. Russell Robert, BA(Hons) ACA *1991;* 33 Sailsbury Road, Flitwick, BEDFORD, MK45 1UD.

AIREY, Mr. Thomas Mattinson, BSc FCA *1978;* 39 Delamere Road, Ealing, LONDON, W5 3JL.

AIRTON, Mr. Robert Charles John, BA FCA *1986;* Hedges Silver Street, Chalford Hill, STROUD, GLOUCESTERSHIRE, GL6 8ES.

AISBITT, Mr. Jonathan Robert, MA FCA *1981;* Lunces Hall, Church Lane, Wivelsfield, HAYWARDS HEATH, WEST SUSSEX, RH17 7RD.

AISTHORPE, Mr. Andrew Liam, ACA *2004;* 27 Felstead Road, GRIMSBY, DN34 4EU.

AISTON, Mr. John James, ACA *2011;* 50 Lower Wardown, PETERSFIELD, HAMPSHIRE, GU31 4PA.

AITCHESON, Mr. Joseph, BA FCA *1979;* Tyson H Burrisdge Ltd, Old Coachworks, Distington, WORKINGTON, CUMBRIA, CA14 5XJ.

AITCHISON, Mr. James Douglas, MA FCA CTA *1987;* 38 High Oaks Road, WELWYN GARDEN CITY, HERTFORDSHIRE, AL8 7BS.

•**AITCHISON, Mr. Mark Christopher Charles, BSc FCA CF** *1993;* Colten Care Ltd, 16 Western Road, LYMINGTON, HAMPSHIRE, SO41 9HL.

AITKEN, Mr. Anthony, BA ACA ATII *1998;* 5 Martins Hill, Carlton, NOTTINGHAM, NG4 1AZ.

•**AITKEN, Mrs. Beverley Ann, FCA** *1977;* (Tax Fac), Day Smith & Hunter, Globe House, Eclipse Park, Sittingbourne Road, MAIDSTONE, KENT ME14 3EN.

AITKEN, Mr. Bruce, BSc ACA *1996;* 26 Oakleigh Avenue, Whetstone, LONDON, N20 9JH.

AITKEN, Mr. Charles, MA ACA *2004;* PricewaterhouseCoopers, 21/F Edinburgh Tower, 15 Queen's Road, CENTRAL, HONG KONG ISLAND, HONG KONG SAR.

AITKEN, Mr. Donald Wilfred, FCA *1947;* Cornerways, 16 Manor Road, PAIGNTON, DEVON, TQ 3 2HS. (Life Member)

•**AITKEN, Mr. Euan Robert, BA ACA DChA** *1989;* Baker Tilly UK Audit LLP, Number One Old Hall Street, LIVERPOOL, L3 9SX. See also Baker Tilly Tax and Advisory Services LLP

AITKEN, The Countess of Carnarvon Fiona Jane Mary, ACA *1994;* Field House, Highclere Park, Highclere, NEWBURY, RG20 9RN.

•**AITKEN, Mr. Glenn Malcolm, BTech FCA** *1976;* G M Aitken, 18 High Street, NORTH FERRIBY, NORTH HUMBERSIDE, HU14 3JP. See also Aitken Corporate Finance Limited

AITKEN, Mr. Hamish Bruce Christian, BSc ACA *1986;* BT, PP HWM 502, Virutal Postbox, PO Box 400, LONDON, N18 1XU.

AITKEN, Mrs. Jane Katherine Reid, BA ACA *1993;* Gallic Books Ltd, Worlds End Studios, 134 Lots Road, LONDON, SW10 0RJ.

AITKEN, Mr. John, ACA *2008;* 29 Barnmead, HAYWARDS HEATH, WEST SUSSEX, RH16 1UY.

AITKEN, Mr. John Robin, BSc FCA *1974;* Sevington Cottages, Acton Beauchamp, WORCESTER, WR6 5AF. (Life Member)

AITKEN, Mr. Jonathan Guthrie, ACA CA(SA) *2010;* 16 The Mall, SURBITON, SURREY, KT6 4ER.

AITKEN, Mr. Kenneth George, FCA *1962;* Willowmead, Glendene Avenue, East Horsley, LEATHERHEAD, KT24 5AY.

AITKEN, Mr. Lyle Douglas, FCA *1975;* Simmonds The Green, Sarratt, RICKMANSWORTH, HERTFORDSHIRE, WD3 6AT.

AITKEN, Ms. Melanie, ACA *2008;* 56 Casewick Road, LONDON, SE27 0SY.

AITKEN, Mr. Neil David Robertson, BSc ACA *1997;* Kester Cunningham & John Chequers House, 77-81 Newmarket Road, CAMBRIDGE, CB5 8EU.

AITKEN, Mr. Neill, BSc ACA *1998;* 7 Laburnum Road, BIRMINGHAM, B30 2BA.

•**AITKEN, Mr. Paul David, FCA** *1983;* PricewaterhouseCoopers LLP, 1 Embankment Place, LONDON, WC2N 6RH. See also PricewaterhouseCoopers

AITKEN, Miss. Penelope Sophie Victoria, BA ACA *2001;* 1 Gwalior Road, LONDON, SW15 1NP.

AITKEN, Miss. Rebecca Kirsty, ACA *2011;* Apartment 28, 6-9 Canute Road, SOUTHAMPTON, SO14 3FH.

AITKEN, Mr. Robert Nicholas Reid, ACA *1981;* 104 Coleraine Road, Blackheath, LONDON, SE3 7NZ.

AITKEN, Mr. Robin Douglas, BSc FCA *1990;* Grafton House, High Street, Norton St. Philip, BATH, BA2 7LG.

•**AITKEN, Mrs. Roopa, BSc ACA** *1995;* (Tax Fac), Grant Thornton UK LLP, Grant Thornton House, 22 Melton Street, Euston Square, LONDON, NW1 2EP. See also Grant Thornton LLP

AITKEN, Miss. Sally, MEng ACA *2000;* 54 Seaview Terrace, EDINBURGH, EH15 2HE.

AITKEN, Mr. William John, LLB ACA *1992;* 15 Blanchland Circle, Monkston, MILTON KEYNES, MK10 9GQ.

AITKENHEAD, Mr. Leslie Allan, BA FCA *1976;* Gartmore Investment Management Gartmore House, 8 Fenchurch Place, LONDON, EC3M 4PB.

AIZLEWOOD, Mr. Gregory James, ACA *2011;* 24 Glastonbury Drive, Milnsbridge, HUDDERSFIELD, HD3 4SA.

AIZLEWOOD, Mr. John Henry, BSc ACA *1994;* Weeping Ash Farm, North End Road, Yatton, BRISTOL, BS49 4AW.

AIZLEWOOD, Mrs. Sarah Jane, BSc ACA *1993;* Weeping Ash Farm, North End Road, Yatton, BRISTOL, BS49 4AW.

AJAM-HASSANI, Miss. Azadeh, BSc ACA *2006;* 44 Brompton Park Crescent, LONDON, SW6 1SW.

AJANIA, Mr. Noordin Gulamhussein, FCA *1963;* PO Box 44488, NAIROBI, 00100, KENYA. (Life Member)

AJIBOLA, Mr. Omoniyi, BEng ACA *2004;* Vitol Services Ltd Belgrave House, 76 Buckingham Palace Road, LONDON, SW1W 9TQ.

AKAM, Mr. Johnson Cyril, FCA *1970;* 93 Hundred Acres Lane, AMERSHAM, BUCKINGHAMSHIRE, HP7 9BP.

AKAMATSU, Miss. Fusae, ACA *1997;* Shiba Park Tower, 411 3-34-1 Shiba, Minatoku, TOKYO 105-0014, JAPAN.

AKANDE, Mrs. Ayoyinka Mobolaji, BSc FCA *1987;* (Tax Fac), 4 The Coppice, Villiers-Sur-Marne Avenue, BISHOP'S STORTFORD, HERTFORDSHIRE, CM23 4HX.

AKBAR, Mrs. Amrah, BA ACA *2005;* Flat 5 Ravenscar Lodge, 22 The Downs, LONDON, SW20 8HT.

•**AKBAR, Mr. Farrukh, ACA** *1981;* 32 Brighton Road, PURLEY, CR8 3AD.

AKBAR, Mrs. Gabrielle Mary, BEng ACA *1998;* Cleveland House, Sydney Road, BATH, BA2 6NR.

AKBAR, Mr. Jamil, BEng ACA MBA *2001;* 61 10th Street, Off Khayaban-e-Badban, DHA Phase 5, KARACHI 75500, PAKISTAN.

AKBAR, Mr. Javid Razwan, BA FCA *1996;* 27 Baileys Mead Road, Stapleton, BRISTOL, BS16 1AE.

AKBAR, Mr. Khaliq, ACA *2011;* Flat 2, 32 Brighton Road, PURLEY, SURREY, CR8 3AD.

AKBAR, Mr. Khurram, ACA *1980;* 32 Brighton Road, PURLEY, CR8 3AD.

AKBAR, Mr. Mohammed Atheeq, BA ACA *2011;* 6 Evington Valley Gardens, LEICESTER, LE5 5LW.

AKBAR, Mr. Rafi, ACA *1979;* National Bank of Kuwait S.A.K., Internal Audit Division, PO Box 95, SAFAT, 13001, KUWAIT.

AKBAR, Mr. Razzak, ACA *2009;* with Deloitte & Touche, P.O.Box HM 1556, Corner House, Church & Parliament Streets, HAMILTON HM FX, BERMUDA.

AKBAR, Miss. Sabeen, BSc(Hons) ARCS ACA *2002;* 54 Barn Hill, WEMBLEY, HA9 9LQ.

AKBAR, Mr. Sahir, BSc BSc(Hons) ACA *2011;* 6 The Charter Road, WOODFORD GREEN, ESSEX, IG8 9QU.

•**AKBAR, Mr. Shafeen Ramjan, FCA** *1985;* S. Akbar & Co, 1st Floor Rear, Hamilton House, 84-86 High Street, Rainham, GILLINGHAM KENT ME8 7JH. See also Economize Accounting & Tax Solutions Limited

AKBARALI, Mr. Sadrudin, FCA *1971;* Flat 33, Petersham House, 29-37 Harrington Road, LONDON, SW7 3HD.

AKBER, Mr. Mohammad Fawad, ACA *2004;* 60 Georgia Road, THORNTON HEATH, CR7 8DR.

•**AKDAG, Mr. Metin, BSc(Hons) FCA** *2001;* (Tax Fac), Akdag & Co Limited, 1st Floor South, 332-336 Holloway Road, LONDON, N7 6NJ. See also Metin Akdag

•**AKDENIZ, Mr. Alper, MSc FCA** *1990;* 34 Al-Farabi Avenue, Building A 4th Floor, ALMATY 050059, KAZAKHSTAN.

AKE, Mr. Christopher David, BSc ACA *1995;* Litton House, Litton Somererset, BATH, BA3 4PW.

AKED, Mrs. Gemma Louise, BA ACA *2002;* Johnson Controls Ltd, 2-3 The Briars, Waterberry Drive, WATERLOOVILLE, HAMPSHIRE, PO7 7YH.

AKED, Mr. John Martin, MA FCA *1975;* Chemin des Cassivettes 23, CH-1173 FECHY, SWITZERLAND.

AKEHURST, Mr. Jonathan, MEng ACA *2011;* 21 Manor Green, STRATFORD-UPON-AVON, WARWICKSHIRE, CV37 7ES.

AKEHURST, Mr. Stephen, BA(Econ) FCA *1968;* 24 Barnfield Avenue, SHEFFIELD, S10 5TA.

AKERMAN, Mr. Andrew Christopher, BA FCA *1977;* Diamond Light Source Ltd Diamond House, Harwell Science & Innovation Campus Road Four Chilton, DIDCOT, OXFORDSHIRE, OX11 0DE.

AKERMAN, Mr. Christopher James, BSc ACA *1989;* 4 High Path Road, GUILDFORD, SURREY, GU1 2QG.

AKERMAN, Mrs. Helen Christine, BSc ACA *1993;* 430 Longford Road, Thornford, SHERBORNE, DT9 6QQ.

AKERMAN, Mr. Stephen Richard, FCA *1953;* 54 Norwood Gardens, HAYES, UB4 9LU. (Life Member)

AKEROYD, Mr. Ashley, BA(Hons) ACA *2011;* 22 Homefield Avenue, Arnold, NOTTINGHAM, NG5 8GA.

AKEROYD, Mr. Charles Ernest, VRD FCA *1932;* 3 Copenhagen Court, Denmark Grove, Alexandra Park, NOTTINGHAM, NG3 4LF. (Life Member)

•**AKEROYD, Mr. David Edward George, FCA** *1963;* C.E. Akeroyd, Sherwood House, 7 Gregory Boulevard, NOTTINGHAM, NG7 6LB.

AKEROYD, Mr. Philip Denman, FCA *1974;* 237 Alexandra Road, #02-01 The Alexcier, SINGAPORE 159929, SINGAPORE.

•**AKERS, Mr. Duncan John, ACA** *2008;* with Easterbrook Eaton Limited, Cosmopolitan House, Old Fore Street, SIDMOUTH, DEVON, EX10 8LS.

AKERS, Mr. Mark David, BA ACA *1988;* East Copse Icehouse Wood, OXTED, SURREY, RH8 9DW.

AKERS, Mr. Peter James, FCA *1956;* Hatch House, Upton Lovell, WARMINSTER, WILTSHIRE, BA12 0JP. (Life Member)

•①**AKERS, Mr. Stephen John, BSc ACA** *1980;* Grant Thornton UK LLP, 30 Finsbury Square, LONDON, EC2P 2YU. See also Grant Thornton LLP

•**AKERS-DOUGLAS, Mr. Francis Alexander Moreton, FCA** *1971;* Smith & Williamson Ltd, 25 Moorgate, LONDON, EC2R 6AY.

•**AKESTER, Mr. David Howard, BSc FCA** *1983;* Auker Rhodes Tax & Financial Planning Ltd, Sapphire House, Albion Mills, Albion Road, Greengates, BRADFORD WEST YORKSHIRE BD10 9TQ. See also Auker Rhodes Accounting Ltd

AKHAVAN, Mr. Bijan, BA ACA *1982;* 15456 Ventura Boulevard, Suite 300, SHERMAN OAKS, CA 91401, UNITED STATES.

AKHNIOTIS, Mr. Georgios, BSc ACA *1992;* Dioskouridi 5, 14671 NEA ERITHREA, GREECE.

AKHRAS, Mr. Edward Jonathan, ACA *2009;* FAO Akhras, Finansinspektionen, Box 7821 SE-103 97, STOCKHOLM, SWEDEN.

AKHTAR, Mr. Ahsan Ahmad, BSc ACA *1994;* A/56 Gulshan-E-Faisal, Street 12/A, Bath Island, KARACHI, PAKISTAN.

AKHTAR, Miss. Forida, ACA *2009;* 19 Wells Green Road, SOLIHULL, B92 7PF.

AKHTAR, Mr. Kamran Javid, BSc(Hons) ACA *2004;* 10 Rosebury Square, Repton Park, WOODFORD GREEN, ESSEX, IG8 8GT.

•**AKHTAR, Mr. Mirza Hasnain, FCA** *1969;* (Tax Fac), Akhtar & Co Limited, 11 Regent Place, RUGBY, WARWICKSHIRE, CV21 2PJ.

AKHTAR, Mr. Muhammad, ACA *2007;* Aghaadir Building, DUBAI, 3366, UNITED ARAB EMIRATES.

AKHTAR, Mr. Muhammad, BSc FCA *1980;* M. Akhtar, 171 Shah Jamal, Colony, LAHORE, PAKISTAN.

•**AKHTAR, Mr. Naeem, FCA** *1986;* Akhtar & Co, 454-458 Chiswick High Road, LONDON, W4 5TT.

•**AKHTAR, Mrs. Nahid, BA(Hons) ACA** *2008;* AA Accountants Ltd, 6 Blenheim Court, Peppercorn Close, PETERBOROUGH, PE1 2DU.

AKHTAR, Mr. Qaiser Abbas, BA(Hons) ACA *2010;* 17 Cheltenham Close, Great Sankey, WARRINGTON, WA5 3PX.

AKHTAR, Mr. Saeed, FCA *1967;* A-56. Gulshan-e-Faisal, Street 12-A, Bath Island, KARACHI, PAKISTAN. (Life Member)

•**AKHTAR, Mr. Sajjad Ahmad, FCA MBA** *1974;* PKF-CAP LLP, 146 Robinson Road #08-01, SINGAPORE 068909, SINGAPORE.

AKHTAR, Mr. Shahid Yaseen, BEng ACA *1995;* #19-20, 808 Thomson Road, Thomson 800, SINGAPORE 298190, SINGAPORE.

AKHTAR, Mr. Suleman, BSc ACA *1992;* The Bungalow, Ash Island, Molesey Lock, EAST MOLESEY, KT8 9AX.

AKHTAR, Mr. Syed Irshad, BEng ACA *1992;* HSBC Building 7601 Olaya Street North (Al Murooj Area P O Box 9084, RIYADH, 11413, SAUDI ARABIA.

AKHTAR, Miss. Zarnigar, ACA *1982;* 1 Cherry Drive, Bordesley Village, BIRMINGHAM, B9 4JL.

•**AKHTARUZZAMAN, Mr. Mohammed, ACA** *1981;* (Tax Fac), Fordhams & Co, Second Floor, 61 Old Street, LONDON, EC1V 9HX.

AKHTERUZZAMAN, Mr. Abu Khaled Mohammad, FCA *1972;* House No 4B, Road No 118, Gulshanz, DHAKA, BANGLADESH.

AKHURST, Mr. Neil James, ACA *2008;* 128 Cranworth Gardens, LONDON, SW9 0NU.

AKHURST, Mr. Thomas Kenneth, BSc FCA *1972;* 8 Knights Ridge, Pembury, TUNBRIDGE WELLS, TN2 4HP.

AKI-SAWYERR, Mrs. Denise Yvonne, ACA *1994;* 112 Copse Hill, LONDON, SW20 0NL.

AKIN, Mr. Barrie Simon, LLB FCA *1982;* (Tax Fac), Grays Inn Tax Chambers, 3rd floor Grays Inn Chambers, Gray's Inn, LONDON, WC1R 5JA.

•**AKINDELE, Chief Olukayode Oladipo, BSc FCA** *1980;* Olukayode Akindele & Co, 208/ 212 Broad Street, P.O. Box 70828, LAGOS, NIGERIA. See also Akindele Olukayode & Co

AKINGBADE, Mrs. Margaret Regina Adoley, BSc ACA *2006;* with KPMG LLP, 1 Forest Gate, Brighton Road, CRAWLEY, WEST SUSSEX, RH11 9PT.

AKINLEMIBOLA, Miss. Tiwa, ACA *2011;* Flat 12 Balmoral House, Lanark Square, LONDON, E14 9QD.

AKINS, Mrs. Anoushka Charlotte, LLB ACA *2001;* with KPMG LLP, St. Nicholas House, 31 Park Row, NOTTINGHAM, NG1 6FQ.

AKINSOYINU, Mr. Disu Oluremi, FCA *1974;* Idris Akinsoyinu, 7 Ayinde Giwa Street, IRE Akari Estate, Isolo, LAGOS, NIGERIA. (Life Member)

AKISTER, Mrs. Louise Helen, BA ACA *1988;* Harvestore Systems LTD, Newnham Court Shopping Village, Bearsted Road, MAIDSTONE, KENT ME14 5LH.

AKIWUMI-TANOH, Mrs. Karen AyodeleAbiola, ACA *1989;* rua dos coqueiros No 13, bairo dos coqueiros INGOMBOTA, LUANDA, ANGOLA.

AKKELIDES, Mr. Christos, BEng ACA *1999;* 5 Dionysou Street, Aglantzia, 2123 NICOSIA, CYPRUS.

AKKIDOU, Ms. Anastasia, BSc ACA *2008;* 29 Ayiou Georgiou, Pallouriotissa, 1040 NICOSIA, CYPRUS.

AKLE, Miss. Caroline Assad, BSc ACA *1992;* Flat 8, Bentinck Mansions, 12-16 Bentinck Street, LONDON, W1U 2ER.

AKRAM, Mr. Aamir, BA ACA *1996;* 599 High Road, WOODFORD GREEN, ESSEX, IG8 0RE.

•**AKRAM, Mr. Adeel Shahzad, BSc ACA** *2007;* M Akram & Co, 413 Lea Bridge Road, LONDON, E10 7EA. See also Muhammad Akram & Company

AKRAM, Mr. Aftab Muhammad, LLB ACA *2004;* (Tax Fac), 65 Kingslea Road, SOLIHULL, B91 1TJ.

AKRAM, Mr. Athar, ACA *1979;* British Petroleum Co Plc, 1 St. James's Square, LONDON, SW1Y 4PD.

AKRAM, Mr. Imran Muhammad, BSc(Econ) ACA *1998;* 37 Milton Avenue, LONDON, N6 5QF.

AKRAM, Miss. Mehvash Naseem, BA ACA *2005;* 16 Castle Hills Drive, BIRMINGHAM, B36 9BP.

AKRAM, Mr. Mohammed Arif, ACA *2009;* 20 Granville Gardens, LONDON, SW16 3LL.

•**AKRAM, Mr. Muhammad, BA FCA** *1974;* (Tax Fac), M Akram & Co, 413 Lea Bridge Road, LONDON, E10 7EA. See also Muhammad Akram & Company

AKRAM, Mr. Muhammad Sheraz, ACA FCCA *2010;* 184 Canterbury Road, LONDON, E10 6EH.

AKRAM, Mr. Nabil Muhammad, BSc(Hons) ACA *2008;* 109 Farmilo Road, Walthamstow, LONDON, E17 8JN.

AKRAM, Mr. Osman, BSc ACA *2005;* 3 Ryecroft Avenue, ILFORD, ESSEX, IG5 0UQ.

AKRAM, Miss. Salma, MA ACA *2009;* 27 Croxley Road, LONDON, W9 3HH.

AKRAM, Miss. Umerah, MEng ACA *2005;* Flat 5, 46 Stanhope Road, LONDON, N6 5AJ.

AKRIGG, Mr. Stephen, FCA *1975;* WRB Enterprises, Suite 201, 1414 Swann Avenue, TAMPA, FL 33606, UNITED STATES.

•**AKRILL, Mr. James Edward, FCA CF MBA** *1980;* PM & M Corporate Finance Limited, Greenbank Technology Park, Challenge Way, BLACKBURN, BB1 5QB. See also PM&M Solutions for Business LLP

AKRILL, Mrs. Sarah Jane, BA ACA *1992;* IT Telemarketing, Earle House, Atlantic Street, Broadheath, ALTRINCHAM, CHESHIRE WA14 5DD.

AKRITIDES, Mr. Kyrillos, ACA *2008;* Skiathou 11 Block 2 Flat 203, LIMASSOL, CYPRUS.

AKROYD, Mr. Gregory Thomas, BSc ACA *2001;* 14a Norton Close, HALIFAX, WEST YORKSHIRE, HX2 7RD.

AKUSHIE, Mrs. Rita Kuukua, ACA *1995;* 37 Wallenger Avenue, Gidea Park, ROMFORD, RM2 6EP.

AKWAEZE, Mr. Chinedu Nnamdi, ACA *2010;* 20 Sandwick Close, LONDON, NW7 2AX.

•**AKWAEZE, Mr. Chukwuemeka Jideofor, MSc BA ACA** *2006;* Financial Strategists Limited, 20 Sandwick Close, LONDON, NW7 2AX.

AKWAEZE, Mr. Gabriel Chukwuemeka, BSc(Econ) FCA *1965;* 20 Sandwick Close, Mill Hill, LONDON, NW7 2AX. (Life Member)

AL-ADHAMY, Mr. Abdul Hakim, FCA *1977;* PO BOX 30194, BUDAIYA, BAHRAIN.

AL-ALAWI, Mr. Hameed Ahmed Mohamed, FCA *1974;* 5223 Fairford Cres Unit (86), MISSISSAUGA L5V 2M6, ON, CANADA.

AL-AMIN, Mr. Abdul Karim Mahmod, BCom FCA *1971;* Investment Group Ltd, P O Box 3755, SHARJAH, UNITED ARAB EMIRATES.

AL-ATTAR, Miss. Sara, ACA *2008;* with Deloitte LLP, Athene Place, 66 Shoe Lane, LONDON, EC4A 3BQ.

•**AL-AZZAWI, Mr. Rafid Wathik, BEng ACA** *1992;* Al Jaber Group, Mussafah, ABU DHABI, POBox 2175, UNITED ARAB EMIRATES.

•**AL-BAYAA, Mr. Islam Ahmad, MA ACA** *1998;* KPMG Al Fozan Al Sadhan, PO Box 55078, JEDDAH, 21534, SAUDI ARABIA. See also KPMG Europe LLP

AL BAYAA, Mr. Israa Ahmad, BSc ACA MBA *1997;* 11 Queens Grove, LONDON, NW8 6EL.

AL-BAYOUK, Mr. Ata Hamad Mohamed, FCA *1973;* Albayouk Chartered Accountants POB 250514 Riyadh 11391 Office 4101 1st Floor Alsafwa Commercia, RIYADH, 11391, SAUDI ARABIA.

AL-DAHHAN, Mr. Rashid Abdul Hamid, FCA *1973;* Apartment B1 Montevetro, 100 Battersea Church Road, LONDON, SW11 3YL.

AL-FADHILI, Mr. Firas, BA(Hons) ACA *2010;* P.O. Box 7817, Galleries 2 Downtown Jebel Ali, DUBAI, 7817, UNITED ARAB EMIRATES.

AL-HALABI, Mr. Abdul Wahab, BSc(Econ) FCA *1999;* PO Box 53629, DUBAI, 53629, UNITED ARAB EMIRATES.

AL-HASSO, Mr. Abdulelah Abdullah, BSc FCA *1975;* P O Box 18474, DUBAI, 00, UNITED ARAB EMIRATES.

AL-HAWIZ, Mr. Nezhet Mohamed Tayib, BCom FCA *1954;* 21 Hyde Park Gate, LONDON, SW7 5DH. (Life Member)

AL-IDID, Mr. Syed Razif, BSc ACA *1997;* 15b Belmont Road, SINGAPORE 269861, SINGAPORE.

•**AL JADIR, Mrs. Rebecca Amy, ACA** *1987;* Jadir & Co Ltd, 23 Parkway, CROWTHORNE, BERKSHIRE, RG45 6EP.

AL-JANABI, Mr. Bustam Abood, BSc FCA *1970;* Al-janabi Al-rubaie, No 66, St 14 Ave 902, Al -Wathiq Sq, BAGHDAD, IRAQ.

AL-JEBOURI, Mr. Gati Saadi, BEng ACA *1995;* Flat 101, Devonport, 23 Southwick Street, LONDON, W2 2QH.

AL-KAMIL, Mr. Abdulrehman Amir, FCA *1975;* AR Al-Kamil, PO Box 13, Kumeu, AUCKLAND 0841, NEW ZEALAND.

AL-KHALILI, Mr. Nazar Sadik, BSc ACA *1990;* Origin Housing Group, St. Richards House, 110 Eversholt Street, LONDON, NW1 1BS.

AL PAIDATHALLY, Mr. Subramaniam, ACA *1992;* Sylvester Grove & Co, 27 Jalan Perisai, Taman Sri Trebrau, 80050 JOHOR BAHRU, JOHOR, MALAYSIA.

AL-RAHWANJI, Mr. Issam Mohammed Said Masallam, BSc FCA *1997;* Aujan Industries, PO Box 102743, DUBAI, UNITED ARAB EMIRATES.

•**AL-RUBAIE, Mr. Abdul Munaim Jawad, BCom FCA** *1971;* Baker Tilly MKM, P.O. Box 46283, ABU DHABI, UNITED ARAB EMIRATES.

AL-SAMADI, Mr. Moyassar Adeeb, BA FCA *1971;* 7111 Appleby Line, MILTON L9T 2Y1, ON, CANADA.

AL-SHABIBI, Mr. Ali Najib, BSc ACA *1995;* PO Box 9267, DUBAI, 9267, UNITED ARAB EMIRATES.

AL-TAHAN, Mr. Sayf, ACA *2011;* 19 Highclere Drive, HEMEL HEMPSTEAD, HERTFORDSHIRE, HP3 8BY.

AL-TAJER, Ms. Reem Mohamed Saeed, ACA *2003;* House 1112, Road 3223 Block 332, MANAMA, 26270, BAHRAIN.

AL-TIMIMI, Mr. Hadi Abbas, BA FCA *1964;* 1700 Rene-levesque O, Apt 707, MONTREAL H3H 2V1, QUE, CANADA. (Life Member)

ALA, Mr. Quazi Mohammad Shariful, BSc ACA *1984;* House 37 Road - 7, Block G, Banani, DHAKA, BANGLADESH.

ALABI, Mr. Christopher Olawale, MSc BEng ACA *2009;* Flat 35, Regents Plaza Apartments, 8 Greville Road, LONDON, NW6 5HU.

ALAGAPPA, Miss. Jane, BSc ACA *2004;* Flat 24/A, Kensington Mansions, Trebovir Road, LONDON, SW5 9TF.

•**ALAHI, Mr. Ghulam, MSc BA FCA** *1999;* Vision Consulting, 555 Cranbrook Road, ILFORD, ESSEX, IG2 6HE.

ALALADE, Mr. Evans Durodola, FCA *1960;* Private Mail Bag 5213, IBADAN, NIGERIA. (Life Member)
ALAM, Mr. Chaklader Mahboob-Ul, FCA *1969;* Idioma Esperanto 8, 28017 MADRID, SPAIN. (Life Member)
ALAM, Mr. Chaklader Nasir-Ul, ACA *2001;* c/ Castello 19, 28001 MADRID, SPAIN.
ALAM, Mr. Foizul, BCom FCA *1952;* Flat 10, Braemar, 12 Kersfield Road, LONDON, SW15 3HG. (Life Member)
ALAM, Mr. Habib, FCA *1969;* Habib Alam & Co., 249 Jinnah Colony Rehman Hospital Road, Opposite Pakistan Academy, FAISALABAD, PAKISTAN.
ALAM, Mr. Iftekhar, FCA *1975;* Alam House, C-105 Block I, North Nazimabad, KARACHI 74700, PAKISTAN.
•**ALAM, Mr. Iftekhar, BSc FCA** *1985;* I Alam, 7 Tash Place, New Southgate, LONDON, N11 1PA.
ALAM, Mr. Khan Mohammad Rahat, BA FCA *1961;* 416 Wallace Street, EDISON, NJ 08817, UNITED STATES. (Life Member)
•**ALAM, Mr. Mahboob, FCA** *1973;* M S & K Financial Services Limited, 144 Motspur Park, NEW MALDEN, SURREY, KT3 6PF.
ALAM, Mr. Mahbub, FCA *1973;* 28 Mount Drive, HARROW, MIDDLESEX, HA2 7RP.
ALAM, Mr. Mirza Zaki-Ul, ACA *1988;* 10828 - 6 Ave. SW, EDMONTON T6W 1G3, AB, CANADA.
ALAM, Mr. Mohammed Ishtiaq, BA ACA *2002;* 55 Hillingdon Avenue, Nuthall, NOTTINGHAM, NG16 1RA.
ALAM, Mr. Mohammed Safdar, BSc ACA *1998;* 66 Ringinglow Road, SHEFFIELD, S11 7PQ.
ALAM, Mr. Nasr, MSc ACA *1995;* Royal Mail, 35-50 Rathbone Place, LONDON, W1T 1HQ.
ALAM, Mr. Nurul, FCA *1971;* 181 Abbotts Drive, WEMBLEY, MIDDLESEX, HA0 3SH.
ALAM, Mr. Raf, MBA BA ACA *1993;* 23 Foxbourne Road, LONDON, SW17 8EN.
ALAM, Mr. Shahzad, ACA *1994;* 45 Amberley Road, LONDON, N13 4BH.
ALAM, Mr. Shahzad, ACA *2011;* Deloitte & Touche Abbots House, Abbey Street, READING, RG1 3BD.
ALAM, Mr. Shamsul, FCA *1961;* G.P.O. Box 3068, DHAKA 1000, BANGLADESH. (Life Member)
ALAMBRITIS, Mr. Marios, BSc ACA *2004;* 70 Foti Pitta Avenue, Aradippou, 7103 LARNACA, CYPRUS.
ALAMBRITIS, Mr. Prodromos, BSc ACA *2011;* 26 Macariou Avenue, Aradippou, 7104 LARNACA, CYPRUS.
ALAN, Miss. Hayley Anne, BA ACA *1996;* Adrian Alan, 66-67 South Audley Street, LONDON, W1K 2QX.
ALANSARI, Mr. Sameer Kamal, BSc FCA *1988;* Emirates Towers, Level 28, PO Box 31045, DUBAI, UNITED ARAB EMIRATES.
•**ALANTHWAITE, Mr. Timothy Robin, BA ACA** *1987;* Alanthwaite & Co, The Linden Building, Regent Park, Booth Drive, WELLINGBOROUGH, NORTHAMPTONSHIRE NN8 6GR.
ALAOUI, Mrs. Anne-Kathrin, BA(Hons) ACA *2001;* 42 Esmond Road, LONDON, NW6 7HE.
ALASADY, Mrs. Elaine Ann, BSc ACA *1991;* 48 St. Kenelms Avenue, HALESOWEN, WEST MIDLANDS, B63 1DN.
ALBANS, Mr. Gareth Anthony, FCA *1975;* Hanborough Business Park, OXFORD, OXFORDSHIRE, OX298SJ.
ALBERS, Mr. Patrick Oliver, ACA *1993;* Lear Corporation GmbH, Am Ziegelwerk 1, 85391 ALLERSHAUSEN, GERMANY.
ALBERT, Mr. Colin Robert, MA BTh ACA ACII *1979;* Criminal Cases Review Commission Alpha Tower, Suffolk Street Queensway, BIRMINGHAM, B1 1TT.
ALBERT, Mr. Philip John, BA ACA *2004;* 13 Deerings Drive, Eastcote, PINNER, HA5 2NZ.
ALBON, Mr. Philip Ian, BSc FCA *1984;* John Holman & Sons Ltd, 22 Billiter Street, LONDON, EC3M 2RY.
ALBORNO, Mr. Nabil Emran Mousa, FCA *1991;* (Tax Fac), Flat 3 Hanover House, St. Johns Wood High Street, LONDON, NW8 7DX.
ALBOROUGH, Mr. John Warman, FCA *1970;* Rushton, Ockham Road South, East Horsley, LEATHERHEAD, KT24 6RZ. (Life Member)
ALBRECHT, Miss. Marie-Christin, BSc(Hons) ACA *2011;* Flat 9, Clarendon Mansions, 80 East Street, BRIGHTON, BN1 1NF.
ALBRIGHT, Mr. Mark Stephen, BA ACA *1993;* UBS AG, 100 Liverpool Street, LONDON, EC2M 2RH.
ALBRIGHTON, Dr. Lewis Mark, ACA *2003;* 58 Balmoral Drive, Bramcote, NOTTINGHAM, NG9 3FU.
ALBRIGHTON, Mr. Simon James, BSc ACA *2001;* KPMG, One Snowhill, BIRMINGHAM, B4 6GH.
ALBUTT, Mrs. Nicola Helen, BSc ACA *1981;* 11 Tulip Tree Lane, DARIEN, CT 06820, UNITED STATES.
ALBUTT, Mr. Roy, FCA *1971;* Rethink Severe Mental Illness Castlemill, Burnt Tree, TIPTON, DY4 7UF.
ALBUTT, Mr. Stephen John, ACA *1994;* 74 Headland Drive, DISCOVERY BAY, HONG KONG SAR.
ALCANTARA, Mr. Julian James, BSc ACA *1996;* Flat 28 Harrold House, Finchley Road, LONDON, NW3 6JX.
ALCOCK, Miss. Brenda Cecilia, FCA *1970;* 7 Trapstyle Road, WARE, SG12 0BA.
ALCOCK, Mr. Brian Alan, FCA *1959;* 55 Morven Road, SUTTON COLDFIELD, B73 6NE. (Life Member)
ALCOCK, Mr. David Andrew, BA FCA *1987;* Dennathorne Cottage, Moorshop, TAVISTOCK, DEVON, PL19 9JU.
ALCOCK, Mr. David Glyn, BSc ACA *1986;* GARDEN COTTAGE OAKMERE HALL, CHESTER ROAD, OAKMERE, NORTHWICH, CW8 2EG.
ALCOCK, Mr. Derek Arnold, FCA *1952;* 30 South Avenue, Littleover, DERBY, DE23 6BA. (Life Member)
ALCOCK, Mrs. Helen Frances, BA FCA *1987;* Dennathorne Cottage, Moorshop, TAVISTOCK, DEVON, PL19 9JU.
ALCOCK, Mr. James Alfred, FCA ACIS *1958;* Ramsden, 4 Meadway, Weston Favell, NORTHAMPTON, NN3 3BP. (Life Member)
ALCOCK, Mr. John, BSc FCA *1977;* 16 Crooked Usage, Finchley, LONDON, N3 3HB.
ALCOCK, Miss. Justine, ACA *2010;* K P M G St. Nicholas House, 31 Park Row, NOTTINGHAM, NG1 6FQ.
ALCOCK, Mrs. Louise Helen, BSc(Hons) ACA *2002;* 59 Moorgate Road, Carrbrook, STALYBRIDGE, CHESHIRE, SK15 3NF.
ALCOCK, Mr. Mark Julius, BSc FCA *1979;* Chalet Aramis, 4:02 Süd-Ost, 3906 SAAS FEE, SWITZERLAND.
ALCOCK, Mr. Martin, BSc ACA *2004;* 50a Oakmead Road, Balham, LONDON, SW12 9SJ.
•**ALCOCK, Mr. Peter Arthur, FCA CF** *1987;* Wilson Henry LLP, 145 Edge Lane, Edge Hill, LIVERPOOL, L7 2PF.
ALCOCK, Mr. Philip Michael, BA ACA *1999;* Top Floor Flat 4 Blenheim Road, BRISTOL, BS6 7JW.
ALCOCK, Mr. Stephen David, BA(Hons) ACA *2004;* 14 Baslow Drive, Heald Green, CHEADLE, SK8 3HP.
ALCOTT, Mr. Donald Alec, MBA FCA *1959;* 40 Tanworth Lane, Shirley, SOLIHULL, WEST MIDLANDS, B90 4DR. (Life Member)
ALCRAFT, Mr. Matthew James, BSc ACA *2006;* 12 York Road, RICHMOND, TW10 6DR.
ALCRAFT, Mr. Nicholas John, BSc ACA *1993;* The Old School, The Green, Upper Heyford, OXFORD, OX6 3LG.
ALCULUMBRE, Mr. Michael Haim, BSc ACA *1983;* 29 Tillingbourne Gardens, LONDON, N3 3JJ.
ALDA, Mrs. Pamela Russell, BA ACA *1982;* 2 Langbourne Ave, Highgate, LONDON, N6 6AL.
ALDAM, Mr. Anthony, FCA *1969;* 3700 Massachusetts Avenue NW, Apt # 413, WASHINGTON, DC 20016, UNITED STATES.
ALDCROFT, Mr. Christopher Stuart, FCA *1975;* Senior Response Ltd, Business Innovation Centre, Blythe Valley Park, Shirley, SOLIHULL, WEST MIDLANDS B90 8AJ.
ALDEN, Mrs. Alison Jane, BA ACA *1997;* 8 The Waggonway, PRUDHOE, NE42 5QN.
ALDEN, Mr. David John, FCA *1959;* 2441 NW 114 Avenue, CORAL SPRINGS, FL 33065, UNITED STATES. (Life Member)
ALDEN, Mr. Galen Derek, BA ACA *1996;* 3 Brenchwood Close, Downley, HIGH WYCOMBE, HP13 5UP.
ALDEN, Mr. Michael Victor, FCA *1972;* Barden Lodge, Barden Lane, BURNLEY, BB12 0DY.
ALDEN, Mr. Richard David, BA ACA *1990;* Calle Atalayuela 27, Ciudad Sto Domingo, Algete, 28120 MADRID, SPAIN.
•**ALDER, Mr. Andrew Mark, BSc FCA** *1979;* with RSM Tenon Audit Limited, Highfield Court, Tollgate, Chandlers Ford, EASTLEIGH, SO53 3TY.
ALDER, Mr. David John, ACA *1984;* Dairy Cottage, Digswell Place Farm, WELWYN GARDEN CITY, AL8 7SU.
ALDER, Mr. John, BA ACA *1992;* 5731 Brookstone Drive, ACWORTH, GA 30101, UNITED STATES.
•**ALDER, Mr. John Welsh Blackwood, FCA** *1985;* Nash Harvey LLP, The Granary, Hermitage Court, Hermitage Lane, MAIDSTONE, KENT ME16 9NT. See also Nash Harvey Payroll Services Ltd and Nash Harvey Taxation Services Ltd
ALDER, Mr. Julian Craig, BSc ACA *2002;* PricewaterhouseCoopers, Darling Park Tower 2, 201 Sussex Street, SYDNEY, NSW 2000, AUSTRALIA.
•**ALDER, Mr. Nicholas John, FCA** *1980;* (Tax Fac), Reeves & Co LLP, 37 St. Margarets Street, CANTERBURY, KENT, CT1 2TU.
ALDER, Mr. Robert Geoffrey, BA ACA *1993;* 1 Holmes Drive, Ketton, STAMFORD, LINCOLNSHIRE, PE9 3YB.
•**ALDER, Mr. Samuel George, BA FCA** *1971;* Alder Dodsworth & Co, 22 Athol Street, Douglas, ISLE OF MAN, IM1 1JA.
ALDERDICE, Mr. Keith, FCA *1953;* 4 Wharnley Way, Castleside, CONSETT, DH8 9QN. (Life Member)
•**ALDERMAN, Mrs. Anne, BSc ACA** *1979;* Anne Alderman, 13 Mill Vale Meadows, Milland, LIPHOOK, HAMPSHIRE, GU30 7LZ.
ALDERMAN, Mr. Christopher Peter, ACA *2009;* 2 Keswick Place, NEWCASTLE, STAFFORDSHIRE, ST5 3QN.
ALDERMAN, Mrs. Clare Elizabeth, BSc(Hons) ACA *2001;* 360 Elizabeth Street, MELBOURNE, VIC 3000, AUSTRALIA.
ALDERMAN, Mr. Frederick Alan, FCA *1956;* The Old Stables, Moreton Morrell, WARWICK, CV35 9AL. (Life Member)
ALDERMAN, Mr. Nicholas, BSc ACA *1997;* 8 Wessex Gardens, Twyford, READING, RG10 0AY.
ALDERMAN, Mr. Nicholas Guy, BSc(Hons) ACA *2002;* Alderman Consulting Ltd, 321 Beacon Road, LOUGHBOROUGH, LEICESTERSHIRE, LE11 2RA.
ALDERMAN, Mr. Nigel John, FCA *1975;* 42 Port Lion, Llangwm, HAVERFORDWEST, SA62 4JT.
ALDERMAN, Mr. Roger, FCA *1969;* 100 Epping Way, WITHAM, CM8 1NQ.
ALDERSLEY, Miss. Sandra June, BA ACA *1992;* Alexander Cottage, Kimpton, ANDOVER, HAMPSHIRE, SP11 8PG.
ALDERSON, Mr. Adam David, BEng FCA *1993;* 37 Haden Hill Road, HALESOWEN, WEST MIDLANDS, B63 3NE.
ALDERSON, Mr. Alan Thompson, FCA *1946;* 10 Graylands, High Rickleton, WASHINGTON, TYNE AND WEAR, NE38 9HF. (Life Member)
ALDERSON, Mr. David John, FCA *1966;* 6 Weaverthorpe, Nunthorpe, MIDDLESBROUGH, CLEVELAND, TS7 0PU.
ALDERSON, Mr. Jason John Wells, ACA *2008;* Flat 4 Elms Court, 46 New Dover Road, CANTERBURY, KENT, CT1 3DT.
ALDERSON, Mr. Jeffrey, BSc FCA *1979;* Le Soleil D'Or, 20 Bd Rainier III, MONACO, MONACO.
ALDERSON, Mrs. Julie Anne, BA ACA *1986;* 11 Collingwood Road, Wellfield, WHITLEY BAY, NE25 9HR.
ALDERSON, Mr. Kevin Paul, BA(Hons) ACA *2004;* 3 Albion Terrace, London Road, READING, RG1 5BG.
ALDERSON, Mr. Stephen, BSc ACA *2004;* (Tax Fac), 37 Basil Way, SOUTH SHIELDS, TYNE AND WEAR, NE34 8UA.
•**ALDERSON, Mr. Stephen John, ACA** *1981;* (Tax Fac), Aldersons, 4 The Moorings, Mossley, ASHTON-UNDER-LYNE, LANCASHIRE, OL5 9BZ.
ALDERSON, Mr. Timothy, BA FCA *1985;* Stone Trough Cottage, Back Street, Castleton, HOPE VALLEY, S33 8WE.
ALDERTON, Mr. Dennis Allen, FCA *1958;* 4803 Havenwoods Drive, HOUSTON, TX 77066, UNITED STATES. (Life Member)
ALDERTON, Miss. Kay, BSc ACA *2011;* 57 Harwood Road, MARLOW, BUCKINGHAMSHIRE, SL7 2AR.
•**ALDERTON, Mr. Kevin Robert, BA ACA** *1983;* Kevin Alderton & Team Ltd, 14 South Way, NEWHAVEN, EAST SUSSEX, BN9 9LL.
ALDERTON, Mr. Mark John, MA FCA *1987;* HM Revenue & Customs Warwick House, 67 Station Road, REDHILL, SURREY, RH1 1QU.
ALDERTON, Mrs. Rosalind Sara, BA ACA *1982;* 9 Coppice Close, St. Ives, RINGWOOD, BH24 2LB.
•**ALDERWICK, Mr. George Alexander Matthew, MSc FCA CTA** *1974;* (Tax Fac), Alderwick James & Co Limited, 4 The Sanctuary, 23 Oak Hill Grove, SURBITON, SURREY, KT6 6DU.
ALDHAM, Mr. Jonathan Mark, BA ACA *1989;* 40 Queens Road, Hersham, WALTON-ON-THAMES, KT12 5LP.
ALDINGTON, Mr. Richard Nicholas, ACA *1993;* 178 Wimbledon Park Road, LONDON, SW18 5RL.
ALDINGTON, Mr. Timothy Richard, FCA *1962;* Stable House, White Waltham, MAIDENHEAD, SL6 3RU. (Life Member)
ALDISS, Mr. Thomas Edward, FCA *1972;* 83 Offington Avenue, WORTHING, WEST SUSSEX, BN14 9PR.
ALDONS, Mrs. Lesley Jane, BSc ACA *2000;* 16 Squirrels Field, Mile End, COLCHESTER, CO4 5YA.
ALDOUS, Mr. Bryan James, FCA *1961;* (Tax Fac), 18 Eastern Avenue, Thorpe St Andrew, NORWICH, NR7 0UQ.
ALDOUS, Mr. David Alan, FCA *1967;* Church Hill Cottage, Church Hill, Hoxne, EYE, SUFFOLK, IP21 5AT.
ALDOUS, Mr. Geoffrey, FCA *1951;* Apartment 7, Toddbrook House, 20 Whaley Lane, Whaley Bridge, HIGH PEAK, DERBYSHIRE SK23 7BA. (Life Member)
ALDOUS, Mr. Hugh Graham Cazalet, BCom FCA *1970;* Flat 8/B, Portman Mansions, Porter Street, LONDON, W1U 6DE.
ALDOUS, Mr. Stephen David, BA ACA *1992;* 139 Epsom Road, GUILDFORD, SURREY, GU1 2PP.
ALDRED, Mr. Douglas Joseph, FCA *1958;* 31 Wilfreds Road, Bessacarr, DONCASTER, DN4 6AA. (Life Member)
ALDRED, Mr. Duncan, BSc ACA *1987;* Penwood, Penwood End, Hook Heath, WOKING, GU22 0JU.
ALDRED, Miss. Faye Amber, BSc(Hons) ACA *2004;* GE Money Building 4, Igroup Ltd Building 4, Hatters Lane, WATFORD, WD18 8YF.
ALDRED, Mr. Hugh, MA FCA *1950;* 14 The Anchorage, Waverton, CHESTER, CH3 7PL. (Life Member)
ALDRED, Mr. Ian Alexander, FCA *1965;* Cromwell House, The Lane, West Deeping, PETERBOROUGH, PE6 9HS.
ALDRED, Mrs. Jennifer Anne, BA(Hons) FCA *2000;* Yattendon Investment Trust Plc Barn Close, Burnt Hill Yattendon, THATCHAM, RG18 0UX.
ALDRED, Mr. Jonathan, BA ACA *1980;* 41 The Mallards, Langstone, HAVANT, HAMPSHIRE, PO9 1SS.
ALDRED, Miss. Karen Lesley, BSc ACA CTA MCT *1990;* Swiss Reinsurance Company, Mythen Quai 50/60, 8022 ZURICH, SWITZERLAND.
ALDRED, Mr. Martin, FCA *1970;* Flat 2, Barrie House, St. Edmunds Terrace, LONDON, NW8 7QH.
ALDRED, Miss. Paula Mary, BA ACA *2000;* Bates Weston Chartered Accountants The Mill, Canal Street, DERBY, DE1 2RJ.
ALDRED, Mr. Ralph Harry Charles, FCA *1956;* Swiss House, Shoreham Road, Otford, SEVENOAKS, TN14 5RN. (Life Member)
ALDRED, Mr. Steven John, BSc ACA *1992;* 8 Alder Grove, Bromley Cross, BOLTON, BL7 9YL.
ALDREN, Mr. Marcus Ashley, BSc ACA *1991;* Windy Ridge, Thorpe Road, Haddiscoe, NORWICH, NR14 6PP.
ALDREN, Mr. Michael Stephen, ACA *2009;* Flat 8, Spring Firs, 221 Spring Road, SOUTHAMPTON, SO19 2NY.
ALDREN, Mr. Stephen, FCA *1975;* 59 Seward Road, Badsey, EVESHAM, WR11 7HQ.
ALDRICH, Mr. Andrew William, BSc(Hons) ACA *2005;* University of the Arts London, 5 Richbell Place, LONDON, WC1N 3LA.
ALDRICH, Mr. Christopher Raymond, BSc(Hons) ACA *2005;* Ballantyne McKean & Sullivan Ltd, 1 America Square, LONDON, EC3N 2LS.
•**ALDRIDGE, Mrs. Amanda Jane, BSc FCA** *1987;* KPMG LLP, 15 Canada Square, LONDON, E14 5GL. See also KPMG Europe LLP
ALDRIDGE, Mr. Andrew Charles, BSc ACA *1990;* 14-1001 Central Park, 6 Chaowai Street, BEIJING 100020, CHINA.
ALDRIDGE, Mr. Anthony Francis, MA ACA *1981; (ACA Ireland 1967);* 29 Hollingbourne Gardens, LONDON, W13 8EN. (Life Member)
ALDRIDGE, Mr. Geoffrey David, MA BSc ACA *2010;* 25 Glendale Road, HOVE, EAST SUSSEX, BN3 6ES.
ALDRIDGE, Mrs. Helen Louise, BA ACA *1997;* Close Wealth Management Ltd, Nelson House, Gadbrook Business Centre, Rudheath, NORTHWICH, CHESHIRE CW9 7TN.
ALDRIDGE, Mr. Ian Douglas Bowers, BA FCA CF *1983;* 15 Newalls Rise, Wargrave, READING, RG10 8AY.
ALDRIDGE, Mrs. Jacqueline, BA FCA ATII *1985;* The Lynchets, Coombe, WOTTON-UNDER-EDGE, GL12 7NB.
ALDRIDGE, Mr. James Francis, ACA *1993;* 43b Fermor Road, Tarleton, PRESTON, PR4 6AP.
ALDRIDGE, Mr. James Richard, BSc ACA *1991;* with KPMG LLP, Two Financial Center, 60 South Street, BOSTON, MA 02111, UNITED STATES.
ALDRIDGE, Mrs. Joanne Alexandra, BSc ACA *1997;* 2 Second Avenue, GLASGOW, G44 4TE.
ALDRIDGE, Mr. John, FCA *1961;* The Old Jallow School House Ballajora Hill, Ballajora Ramsey, ISLE OF MAN, IM7 1AY. (Life Member)

ALDRIDGE, Mrs. Karen Jane, ACA DChA *1990;* 64 Old Hadlow Road, TONBRIDGE, TN10 4EX.
ALDRIDGE, Mrs. Kylie Louise, ACA *2011;* 2 Wenlock Close, CRAWLEY, WEST SUSSEX, RH11 8NH.
•**ALDRIDGE, Mr. Mark Leonard, BSc ACA ATII** *1985;* Grant Thornton UK LLP, Hartwell House, 55-61 Victoria Street, BRISTOL, BS1 6FT. See also Grant Thornton LLP
•**ALDRIDGE, Mr. Mark Lionel, FCA** *1981;* (Tax Fac), Mark L. Aldridge & Co, Woodlands Lodge, 2 Penfold Drive, Great Billing, NORTHAMPTON, NN3 9EQ. See also Aldridge Taxation & Accountancy Services Ltd
•**ALDRIDGE, Mr. Mark Nicholas Kennedy, BA ACA** *1992;* Better Capital LLP, 39-41 Charing Cross Road, LONDON, WC2H0AR.
ALDRIDGE, Mr. Matthew Richard, BSc ACA *2006;* 1 Willow Lane, Great Cambourne, CAMBRIDGE, CB23 6AB.
ALDRIDGE, Mrs. Mavis, BA FCA *1969;* 25 Glendale Road, HOVE, BN3 6ES.
ALDRIDGE, Mr. Michael James, MA BA(Hons) ACA *2002;* 67 Milson Road, LONDON, W14 0LH.
•**ALDRIDGE, Mr. Michael Reginald, FCA** *1972;* M.R. Aldridge, 2a Crown Street, Redbourn, ST. ALBANS, HERTFORDSHIRE, AL3 7JX.
ALDRIDGE, Mrs. Patricia Mary, BA FCA TEP *1978;* 13 Southdown Avenue, BRIGHTON, BN1 6EG.
ALDRIDGE, Mr. Paul Stephen, BA ACA *1998;* Flat 1, 65 Mayville Road, LONDON, E11 4PH.
ALDRIDGE, Mr. Richard Charles, FCA *1965;* Old Whitstone, Bovey Tracey, NEWTON ABBOT, DEVON, TQ13 9NA. (Life Member)
•**ALDRIDGE, Mr. Richard Weston, FCA** *1972;* Henn & Westwood, Rumbow House, Rumbow, HALESOWEN, B63 3HU.
ALDRIDGE, Dr. Roger Dennis, PhD FCA *1966;* 64 Polwarth Terrace, EDINBURGH, EH11 1NJ.
ALDRIDGE, Mr. Sam, ACA *2008;* 12 Louisville Road, LONDON, SW17 8RW.
•**ALDRIDGE, Mr. Trevor Alfred, FCA** *1980;* Trevor Aldridge, 64 Old Hadlow Road, TONBRIDGE, TN10 4EX. See also Trevor Aldridge Limited
ALDWORTH, Miss. Jenny Kay, BA ACA *2010;* Flat 8, Faraday Lodge, Renaissance Walk, LONDON, SE10 0QL.
•**ALDWORTH, Mrs. Sandra, ACA** *1987;* (Tax Fac), Sandra Aldworth, The School House, Clayhidon, CULLOMPTON, DEVON, EX15 3PL.
ALEEM, Mr. Shezad, LLB ACA *2009;* 33 The Circle, LONDON, NW2 7QR.
ALEKSANDROV, Mr. Nikolas, ACA *2007;* 60 Bywater Place, LONDON, SE16 5NE.
ALEKSEEVA, Ms. Yulia, ACA *2009;* 9 Rodou street Flat 2, Agios Omologites, 1086 NICOSIA, CYPRUS.
ALEM, Mr. Yirga, FCA *1971;* P O Box 4186, ADDIS ABABA, ETHIOPIA.
ALEMANY, Mr. Juan-Carlos, BA ACA *2001;* Fieldgate House Tubbs Lane, Highclere, NEWBURY, BERKSHIRE, RG20 9PW.
ALERS-HANKEY, Mr. Andrew Richard, FCA *1966;* 10 Hammersmith Terrace, LONDON, W6 9TS.
ALERS-HANKEY, Mr. Ian Raymondd, FCA *1964;* 59 Limerston Street, LONDON, SW10 0BL.
•**ALESBURY, Mr. David Norman Edwin, BA FCA** *1990;* (Tax Fac), Pumphrey Dasalo Limited, 1 The Green, RICHMOND, SURREY, TW9 1PL.
ALETE, Mr. Christopher Uchegbu, BA ACA *1994;* The Granary, Ryton Village, RYTON, NE40 3QQ.
ALETE, Miss. Rachel Ngozi, BA ACA *1993;* Rue de Zurich 41, 1201 GENEVA, SWITZERLAND.
ALETRARIS, Mr. Demetrios Soterios, BSc ACA *1992;* 4 A Ainstain Street, Agioi Omologitai, 1065 NICOSIA, CYPRUS.
•**ALEXANDER, Mr. Adrian John, CA FCA CF** *1987;* Mazars LLP, 37 Frederick Place, BRIGHTON, BN1 4EA.
ALEXANDER, Mrs. Alison Jane England, MA ACA *1998;* C M G Law, 94 Chorley New Road, BOLTON, BL1 4DH.
•**ALEXANDER, Mr. Andrew Robin, FCA** *1973;* A.R. Alexander FCA, 6 The Sparlings, Kirby-le-Soken, FRINTON-ON-SEA, ESSEX, CO13 0HD. See also Andrew Alexander
ALEXANDER, Mr. Angus, ACA *1989;* 39 Athol Street, Douglas, ISLE OF MAN, IM99 1HN.
ALEXANDER, Mr. Anthony George Laurence, FCA *1962;* Crafnant, Gregories Farm Lane, BEACONSFIELD, BUCKINGHAMSHIRE, HP9 1HJ. (Life Member)
ALEXANDER, Mr. Anthony John, FCA *1988;* 1 Hillside, Cumnor Hill, OXFORD, OX2 9HS.
ALEXANDER, Mr. Barry Howard, FCA *1974;* (Member of Council 2001 - 2007), 15 Ravenscroft Avenue, LONDON, NW11 0SA.
ALEXANDER, Mr. Benjamin, BEng ACA *2002;* 8 South Close, IPSWICH, IP4 2TH.
ALEXANDER, Mr. Bernard, BCom FCA *1958;* 3 Regency Lawn, Croftdown Road, LONDON, NW5 1HF. (Life Member)
ALEXANDER, Mrs. Catherine Helen, ACA *1985;* 29 Junction Road, BRENTWOOD, ESSEX, CM14 5JH.
ALEXANDER, Mr. Cecil Mark, FCA *1968;* 51 Oakley Drive, New Eltham, LONDON, SE9 2HQ. (Life Member)
•**ALEXANDER, Mr. Charles Philip, BSc ACA** *1997;* Ernst & Young LLP, 1 More London Place, LONDON, SE1 2AF. See also Ernst & Young Europe LLP
ALEXANDER, Mr. Charles Stuart, LLB FCA *1973;* Peartree House, The Green, Cropredy, BANBURY, OXFORDSHIRE, OX17 1NH.
ALEXANDER, Mr. Charles Victor, FCA CF *1968;* Loyola, 14 Orinoco Street, PYMBLE, NSW 2073, AUSTRALIA.
ALEXANDER, Mr. Christopher Ian, BSc FCA *1987;* 59 Telford Avenue, LONDON, SW2 4XL.
ALEXANDER, Mrs. Claire Louise, BSc ACA *1992;* Newcastle United Football Co Ltd St. James Park, Strawberry Place, NEWCASTLE UPON TYNE, NE1 4ST.
ALEXANDER, Mr. Colin Michael, BA ACA *1981;* 1 Windy Bank, Middle Road, SMITHS FL 02, BERMUDA.
ALEXANDER, Mr. Daniel David, BA ACA MBA *1995;* IVO Business Solutions, 42 Glisson Road, CAMBRIDGE, CB1 2HF.
ALEXANDER, Mr. Daniel James, LLB ACA *2010;* 63 Carrick Point, Falmouth Road, LEICESTER, LE5 4WN.
ALEXANDER, Mr. David Anthony, ACA *1978;* 49 Parkside, Mill Hill, LONDON, NW7 2LN.
ALEXANDER, Mr. David John, BA FCA *1990;* (Tax Fac), 24 QUALICUM STREET, NEPEAN K2H 7G8, ON, CANADA.
ALEXANDER, Prof. David John Anthony, BSc FCA *1971;* Routen Syke Farm, Arlecdon, FRIZINGTON, CA26 3UW.
ALEXANDER, Mr. David Martin, BSc ACA *1997;* with Ernst & Young LLP, 1 More London Place, LONDON, SE1 2AF.
•**ALEXANDER, Mr. David Peter, BSc FCA** *1989;* Smith & Williamson Ltd, 25 Moorgate, LONDON, EC2R 6AY.
ALEXANDER, Mr. Donald James, BSc ACA *1996;* 8 Greenwood Drive, WILMSLOW, CHESHIRE, SK9 2RW.
ALEXANDER, Mr. Douglas Moray, MA ACA *1989;* Shell International Petroleum Co Ltd Shell Centre, York Road, LONDON, SE1 7NA.
ALEXANDER, Mr. Duncan Peter, BA ACA *2003;* 1 Victoria Terrace, Victoria Road, HITCHIN, HERTFORDSHIRE, SG5 2LW.
•**ALEXANDER, Mr. Duncan Strother, FCA** *1983;* Strother Alexander, 5 Ballyshannon Road, KILLARNEY HEIGHTS, NSW 2087, AUSTRALIA.
ALEXANDER, Mr. Edward Michael Fiddymont, BSc FCA *1972;* 28 rue de L'Ouest, 44100 NANTES, FRANCE. (Life Member)
ALEXANDER, Mrs. Elizabeth, BA(Hons) ACA *2002;* 8 The Poplars, Gosforth, NEWCASTLE UPON TYNE, NE3 4AE.
ALEXANDER, Mrs. Gillian Ann Mary, BSc ACA *1999;* 9 Learmonth Terrace, EDINBURGH, EH4 1PG.
ALEXANDER, Mr. Graeme Mark, BA ACA *2000;* 7 Reserve Street, SEAFORTH, NSW 2092, AUSTRALIA.
ALEXANDER, Mrs. Helen Alexis, BSc ACA *1991;* De Lane Lea (Post Production) Ltd, 75 Dean Street, LONDON, W1D 3PU.
ALEXANDER, Mr. Hugo Alliott Lighton, BSc ACA *1992;* Mole End Wormley Lane, Hambledon, GODALMING, GU8 4HB.
•**ALEXANDER, Mr. Iain James, BA ACA** *1989;* with KPMG LLP, 15 Canada Square, LONDON, E14 5GL.
ALEXANDER, Mrs. Jacqueline Hazel, BSc ACA *2000;* 26-28 Bristol Road, Keynsham, BRISTOL, BS31 2BQ.
ALEXANDER, Mr. James Ross, BA ACA *2000;* 1 Kidmore Court, Hunters Chase, Caversham, READING, RG4 7XL.
ALEXANDER, Miss. Jenny Anne, BA ACA *1991;* 83 Putney Bridge Road, LONDON, SW15 2PA.
•①**ALEXANDER, Mr. John Alfred George, FCA** *1975;* Carter Backer Winter LLP, Enterprise House, 21 Buckle Street, LONDON, E1 8NN.
ALEXANDER, Mr. John Martin, FCA *1959;* 50 Orchard Way, Cogenhoe, NORTHAMPTON, NN7 1LZ. (Life Member)
ALEXANDER, Mr. John Patrick Richard, ACA *2001;* Upper Floor Flat, 2 Huntingdon Road, LONDON, N2 9DU.
•**ALEXANDER, Mr. Jon Steven, BA FCA** *2000;* Duncan & Toplis, 27 Lumley Avenue, SKEGNESS, LINCOLNSHIRE, PE25 2AT.
•**ALEXANDER, Mrs. Katharine Ann, MA ACA CTA** *2004;* Ernst & Young LLP, 1 More London Place, LONDON, SE1 2AF. See also Ernst & Young Europe LLP
ALEXANDER, Mr. Keith David Rennie, BSc FCA *1979;* Mill House, Badsell Road, Five Oak Green, TONBRIDGE, TN12 6QU.
ALEXANDER, Mr. Kenneth George, FCA *1949;* El Zoco de Nerja Box 77, Avda. de Chimenea 37, Nerja, 29780 MALAGA, SPAIN. (Life Member)
•**ALEXANDER, Miss. Lesley Ellen, MA ACA** *1987;* Lesley Alexander, 36 Ferrymans Quay, William Morris Way, LONDON, SW6 2UT. See also Du Gua Limited
ALEXANDER, Mr. Malcolm James, BA(Hons) ACA *2002;* 49 Whieldon Grange, Church Langley, HARLOW, CM17 9WG.
ALEXANDER, Mr. Mark Charles Hugh Orbell, BA FCA *1989;* Building 5, D S T L, Porton Down, SALISBURY, SP4 0JQ.
ALEXANDER, Mr. Martin, MSc ACA *1999;* (Tax Fac), 39 Herbert Road, BEXLEYHEATH, KENT, DA7 4QF.
•①**ALEXANDER, Mr. Michael David, FCA** *1972;* Lewis Alexander & Connaughton, Second Floor, Boulton House, 17-21 Chorlton Street, MANCHESTER, M1 3HY. See also Lewis Alexander & Collins
ALEXANDER, Mr. Michael James, FCA *1969;* 57 Common Road, North Leigh, WITNEY, OXFORDSHIRE, OX29 6RE.
ALEXANDER, Mr. Nathaniel Timothy, MA ACA *2003;* 568 Julu Lu, Building 1 Apartment 2C, Jing'An District, SHANGHAI 200040, CHINA.
ALEXANDER, Mr. Neil Ross, BEng ACA *1995;* Avondale Route de Farras, Forest, GUERNSEY, GY8 0EA.
ALEXANDER, Mr. Nicholas, BSc ACA *1998;* 5 Morganti Court, RIDGEFIELD, CT 06877, UNITED STATES.
ALEXANDER, Mr. Nicholas Jonathan, BSc FCA *1974;* Prime Estates Ltd, 64 Wilbury Way, HITCHIN, HERTFORDSHIRE, SG4 0TP.
ALEXANDER, Miss. Nicole Angelique, BA ACA *1995;* 145 Fox Lane, LONDON, N13 4AU.
ALEXANDER, Mr. Paul Andrew, BCom ACA *1988;* 26 Briton Crescent, Sanderstead, SOUTH CROYDON, Surrey, CR2 0JF.
•**ALEXANDER, Mr. Paul David, FCA** *1992;* (Tax Fac), Accountancy Management Services Ltd, South Street House, 51 South Street, ISLEWORTH, MIDDLESEX, TW7 7AA.
ALEXANDER, Mr. Peter David, FCA *1973;* 17 Swallow Road, DRIFFIELD, NORTH HUMBERSIDE, YO25 5JY.
ALEXANDER, Mr. Peter Leslie, FCA *1973;* 12 Leicester Close, HENLEY-ON-THAMES, OXFORDSHIRE, RG9 2LD.
ALEXANDER, Mr. Peter William, BA ACA *1983;* 10 Ospringe Place, FAVERSHAM, ME13 8TB.
•**ALEXANDER, Mr. Philip, BA ACA MBA** *1983;* Littlejohn LLP, 1 Westferry Circus, Canary Wharf, LONDON, E14 4HD.
ALEXANDER, Miss. Rachel Elizabeth, BA ACA *1989;* 63 Priory Road, Chiswick, LONDON, W4 5JA.
ALEXANDER, Mr. Raymond John, BSc FCA *1974;* Pretty Corner, 1 Knowle Village, BUDLEIGH SALTERTON, EX9 6AL.
ALEXANDER, Mr. Robert Gordon, BSc ACA *1989;* Parkgate, Piggottshill Lane, HARPENDEN, HERTFORDSHIRE, AL5 1AB.
ALEXANDER, Mr. Robert James, BA(Hons) ACA *2003;* Allen & Overy Llp One, Bishops Square, LONDON, E1 6AD.
ALEXANDER, Mr. Roger, BA ACA *1998;* B A E Systems Warton Aerodrome, Warton, PRESTON, PR4 1AX.
ALEXANDER, Mr. Roger John Blake, FCA *1965;* 3 Millers Point, 18c Mayfield Road, WEYBRIDGE, KT13 8XD.
ALEXANDER, Mrs. Rosemary Ann, BSc FCA *1989;* St. Hugh's College, St. Margaret's Road, OXFORD, OX2 6LE.
ALEXANDER, Ms. Rosemary Elizabeth, LLB ACA *1993;* 5 Church Terrace, RICHMOND, TW10 6SE.
ALEXANDER, Mr. Roy Ernest, FCA *1956;* 87 Falmouth Road, Springfield, CHELMSFORD, CM1 6JA. (Life Member)
ALEXANDER, Miss. Sarah, BA ACA *1998;* 11 The Gowers, AMERSHAM, BUCKINGHAMSHIRE, HP6 6ER.
•**ALEXANDER, Mrs. Sarah Marie, ACA FCCA** *2010;* Lewis Brownlee, Avenue House, Southgate, CHICHESTER, WEST SUSSEX, PO19 1ES. See also Lewis Brownlee Sherlock
•**ALEXANDER, Mr. Simon Leonard, BSc FCA** *1992;* (Tax Fac), Alexander & Co (Accountancy) Ltd, 7 Murray Crescent, PINNER, MIDDLESEX, HA5 3QF.
ALEXANDER, Mr. Stephen Fillmer, BA ACA *1979;* 13 Lannoweth Road, PENZANCE, CORNWALL, TR18 3AB.
ALEXANDER, Mr. Stephen Mark, FCA *1969;* Green Park Reading Road, Mattingley, HOOK, HAMPSHIRE, RG27 8JZ.
ALEXANDER, Mr. Stephen Thomas Norman, FCA *1970;* 5 Cole Park View, St. Margarets, TWICKENHAM, TW1 1JW.
ALEXANDER, Miss. Tracy Catherine, MA(Hons) MSc ACA *2006;* Royal Bank of Canada, 20 King Street West, 8th Floor, TORONTO M5H 1C4, ON, CANADA.
ALEXANDER, Miss. Victoria Rosemary, ACA *2008;* (Member of Council 2008 - 2010), 62 Havelock Road, River Place Tower B1, #03-03, SINGAPORE 169659, SINGAPORE.
ALEXANDER, Mr. William Norman, BSc ACA *1983;* 21 Alexandra Road, LONDON, W4 1AX.
ALEXANDER, Mr. William Simon, BSc ACA *1996;* Stagden Cross House, Stagden Cross, High Easter, CHELMSFORD, ESSEX, CM1 4QY.
ALEXANDER-CLAYTON, Mrs. Marisa, BSc ACA *2009;* with KPMG LLP, 1 The Embankment, Neville Street, LEEDS, LS1 4DW.
ALEXANDER-MARSH, Mr. Andrew Howard, BSc FCA *1977;* 1 Church Court, 134 High Street, EGHAM, SURREY, TW20 9HU. (Life Member)
•**ALEXANDER-PASSE, Miss. Gabriella, ACA FCCA** *2011;* Alexander-Passe Ltd, 44 North Crescent, LONDON, N3 3LL.
ALEXANDERIAN, Mr. Masiss Nikoghossian, BCom FCA *1967;* Massis Alexandrian, PO Box 11-8169, Riad Solh, BEIRUT, LEBANON. (Life Member)
ALEXANDRE, Mr. Keith John, FCA *1962;* 17 Rushfield Road, LISS, GU33 7LW.
ALEXANDROFF, Mr. Olivier, BSc ACA *1997;* 15 North Salem Road, RIDGEFIELD, CT 06877, UNITED STATES.
ALEXANDROU, Mr. Andrew, FCA *1990;* 30 Blackacre Road, Theydon Bois, EPPING, ESSEX, CM16 7LU.
ALEXANDROU, Ms. Antigoni, BSc ACA *2009;* 4A Tarsou Street, Lakatahia, 2300 NICOSIA, CYPRUS.
ALEXANDROU, Mr. Charalambos Loizou, BSc FCA *1985;* 21 Makedonitissis Street, 2369 Ayios Dhometios, NICOSIA, CYPRUS.
ALEXANDROU, Mr. Marios, BSc ACA *2004;* Ippokratous 19, Flat 302, 2006 STROVOLOS, CYPRUS.
ALEXANDROU, Mr. Photos, ACA *1979;* (Tax Fac), 5 Marias Siglitikis Road, Strovolos, CY 2036 NICOSIA, CYPRUS.
•**ALEXANDROU, Mr. Pieris, BA FCA** *1989;* The Mudd Partnership, Lakeview House, 4 Woodbrook Crescent, BILLERICAY, ESSEX, CM12 0EQ.
ALEYAN, Mr. Shawket Abdul Hadi, BA ACA *1981;* Arab Monetary Fund, P.O. Box 2818, ABU DHABI, UNITED ARAB EMIRATES.
ALFARADHI, Mr. Raihan, ACA *2010;* with PricewaterhouseCoopers LLP, 1 Embankment Place, LONDON, WC2N 6RH.
ALFLATT, The Revd. Hilary, BD FCA *1957;* 1 Farndon Cottages, Romanby, NORTHALLERTON, DL7 8HE. (Life Member)
ALFLATT, Mr. John Neal, BSc FCA *1993;* 1 Grove Hill Road, HARROW, MIDDLESEX, HA1 3AA.
ALFLATT, Mr. Mark Robert William, BSc ACA AMCT *1994;* 3 Seymour Drive, BROMLEY, BR2 8RE.
ALFONSO, Mr. Robin Jay, LLB ACA *2004;* 36 Yallop Avenue, Gorleston, GREAT YARMOUTH, NORFOLK, NR31 6HD.
•**ALFORD, Mr. Anthony Paul Robin, MA MSc FCA** *1971;* Anthony Alford, Shepherd's Crook, Netherbury, BRIDPORT, DT6 5LY.
ALFORD, Mr. Christopher, ACA *2011;* Basement Flat, 154 Old Woolwich Road, LONDON, SE10 9PR.
ALFORD, Mr. David Peter, BA ACA *1996;* Harper Collins, 77-87 Fulham Palace Road, Hammersmith, LONDON, W6 8JA.
ALFORD, Dr. Elizabeth Anne, PhD FCA *1988;* (Tax Fac), 26 Mount Road, Southdown, BATH, BA2 1LE.
ALFORD, Mr. Nicholas David, BSc ACA *1978;* Cedars, Little Lane, East Common, HARPENDEN, HERTFORDSHIRE, AL5 1DF.
ALFORD, Mr. Philip John, BA FCA *1978;* 1382 Piedra Morada, PACIFIC PALISADES, CA 90272, UNITED STATES.
ALFORD, Mr. Philip Roy, BSc ACA *1988;* 54 Creighton Road, Ealing, LONDON, W5 4SJ.
ALFORD, Miss. Rachel Eve, BA ACA *2006;* Les Hirondelles Rue Du Pre Bourdon, St. Saviour, GUERNSEY, GY7 9JS.
ALFORD, Mr. Raymond John, FCA *1971;* 5 Beckenham Drive, Allingham, MAIDSTONE, KENT, ME16 0TG. (Life Member)
ALFORD, Mr. Stuart William, BSc ACA *1990;* Lanford Lea, 42 Pecche Place, Chineham, BASINGSTOKE, HAMPSHIRE, RG24 8AA.
ALFREDSON, Mr. Anders Olof, MSc ACA *2000;* 151 Wapping High Street, LONDON, E1W 3NQ.

ALFS, Mrs. Julie Ann, BA ACA *1994;* Autumn House, The Street, Tendring, CLACTON-ON-SEA, ESSEX, CO16 0BW.

ALGAR, Mr. Julian Francis, MEng ACA *1999;* 88 Arthur Road, WINDSOR, BERKSHIRE, SL4 1RX.

ALGAR, Mr. Leslie Walter, FCA *1972;* I S P, Tunstall Court, 4 Gore Court Road, SITTINGBOURNE, KENT, ME10 1QL.

ALGEO, Mr. Anthony James, BSc ACA *1998;* 33 Pickhurst Mead, BROMLEY, BR2 7QP.

ALGEO, Mr. Steven John, ACA *1999;* 51 Sparrow Drive, ORPINGTON, BR5 1RY.

ALI, Mr. Abdihakim Mohammed, BA(Hons) ACA *2010;* 17 Palmer Close, NORTHOLT, MIDDLESEX, UB5 5TY.

ALI, Mr. Aftab, BA(Hons) ACA *2002;* Toyota Financial Services (UK) PLC, Great Burgh, Yew Tree Bottom Road, EPSOM, SURREY, KT18 5UZ.

ALI, Mr. Ahmad Fariz, BSc ACA *2009;* 9 Jalan SS 19/4, 47500 SUBANG, SELANGOR, MALAYSIA.

ALI, Mr. Ahmed, ACA *2009;* Specialised Finance Group, National Commercial Bank, P.O.Box 3555, JEDDAH, 21481, SAUDI ARABIA.

ALI, Mr. Ahsan, BEng ACA *2002;* with PricewaterhouseCoopers LLP, 1 Embankment Place, LONDON, WC2N 6RH.

ALI, Mr. Ahsan, BSc ACA *2006;* 62 Lisle Close, LONDON, SW17 6LD.

ALI, Mr. Akbar Allan, ACA CA(SA) *2009;* 2277 LAKEVILLE ROAD, APOPKA, FL 32703, UNITED STATES.

ALI, Mr. Ali Mohammed Ridha, MEng ACA ASI *2006;* Royal Bank of Scotland, 135 Bishopsgate, LONDON, EC2M 3UR.

ALI, Mr. Amjid, ACA *2008;* 150 Crewe Street, DERBY, DE23 8QP.

ALI, Mr. Arsalan, BSc ACA *2007;* 62 Lisle Close, LONDON, SW17 6LD.

ALI, Mr. Ashraf-Uz-Zaman, BSc ACA *2005;* 39 Studley Road, LONDON, E7 9LU.

ALI, Mr. Asif, ACA *1997;* 13867 Stonecreek Place, CHINO HILLS, CA 91709, UNITED STATES.

ALI, Mr. Asker, BA ACA *2001;* Flat 1 Clayton House, 50 Trinity Church Road, LONDON, SW13 8EL.

ALI, Mr. Eron, BSc ACA *2000;* 67 Carlton Crescent, LUTON, BEDFORDSHIRE, LU3 1EP.

ALI, Mr. Fawad, BCom ACA ACCA *2001;* 3 College Road, F-7/3, ISLAMABAD 44000, PAKISTAN.

ALI, Mr. Firasat, FCA *1966;* PO BOX 211299, DUBAI, UNITED ARAB EMIRATES.

ALI, Mr. Furquan, ACA ACCA *2010;* Flat 1, Kinsale Grange, 57 Langley Park Road, SUTTON, SURREY, SM2 5GZ.

ALI, Mr. Hason, ACA *2009;* 68 Icknield Drive, ILFORD, IG2 6SD.

ALI, Mr. Hossam Amin Fahmy Mohamed, MA ACA *1992;* with KPMG Mesa, P O BOX 28653, SHARJAH, 28653, UNITED ARAB EMIRATES.

ALI, Mr. Ibrahim, BSc ACA DipFS *2004;* 42 Kensington Gardens, Cranbrook, ILFORD, IG1 3EL.

ALI, Mr. Imran Gulzar, BA(Hons) ACA *2011;* 442 Kingsway, Burnage, MANCHESTER, M19 1QJ.

ALI, Mr. Issifu, MA FCA *1963;* Issifu Ali & Co., PO Box 6037, ACCRA, GHANA.

ALI, Mrs. Jan, FCA *1982;* 20 Oaklands Avenue, Adel, LEEDS, LS16 8NR.

•ALI, Mr. Khurshid Mian, ACA CPA *2011;* Kamran Tax & Financial Services Inc., 818 Wagon Trail Suite 101, AUSTIN, TX 78758, UNITED STATES.

ALI, Miss. Kiran, BSc ACA *2006;* 1 Camrose Close, CROYDON, CR0 7XP.

ALI, Mr. Majid, ACA *2008;* 128 Westridge Road, BIRMINGHAM, B13 0EE.

ALI, Miss. Maleeha, MSc BSc ACA *2007;* Flat 28c, Randolph Crescent, LONDON, W9 1DR.

ALI, Mr. Masroor Anwar, BA ACA *1987;* 5 Paines Orchard, Cheddington, LEIGHTON BUZZARD, LU7 0SN.

ALI, Mr. Mir Yasin, ACA *1979;* c/o T P McCarthy, 2 The Paddocks Offord D'Arcy, St. Neots, ST. NEOTS, PE19 5GE.

ALI, Mr. Mohammad Bilal, BA ACA *2009;* 6-8 Ross Street, Brierfield, NELSON, LANCASHIRE, BB9 5LQ.

ALI, Mr. Mohammad Najam, ACA *1992;* 161 Kh. Hafiz Phase 6 DHA, KARACHI, PAKISTAN.

ALI, Mr. Mohammed Mojahid, BSc ACA *2011;* 1 Elmhurst Road, Forest Gate, LONDON, E7 9PQ.

ALI, Mr. Mostafa, BSc ACA *2001;* 1 Brookside, LONDON, N21 1JT.

•ALI, Mr. Mozam, ACA *2009;* 68 Heatherfield Road, HUDDERSFIELD, HD1 4QJ.

ALI, Mr. Muhammad Abraham, ACA *2010;* 159 Ramsey Road, ST. IVES, CAMBRIDGESHIRE, PE27 3TZ.

ALI, Mr. Muhammad Mansoor, BA ACA *2007;* Mubadala Development Company, 7th Floor, Al-Mamoura Building, PO Box 45005, ABU DHABI, UNITED ARAB EMIRATES.

ALI, Mr. Muhammed Vaqas, ACA *2008;* 103 Ludwick Way, WELWYN GARDEN CITY, HERTFORDSHIRE, AL7 3PL.

ALI, Mr. Musharif, BA ACA *2004;* Flat 9, 12 Maud Road, Leyton, LONDON, E10 5QS.

ALI, Mr. Mushtaque, BCom ACA *2006;* PricewaterhouseCoopers LLP, North American Centre, 5700 Yonge Street Suite 1900, NORTH YORK M2M 4K7, ON, CANADA.

ALI, Miss. Najma Sultana, BA ACA *1994;* 7 Robertsons Gardens, Nechells, BIRMINGHAM, B7 5NL.

•ALI, Mr. Nasir, FCA *1999;* PricewaterhouseCoopers, Stand No 2374, P O Box 30942, Thabo Mbeki Road, LUSAKA, 10101 ZAMBIA.

ALI, Mr. Nesawar, ACA MAAT *2004;* 32 Dallington Road, NORTHAMPTON, NN5 7BQ.

ALI, Mr. Pear, ACA *1979;* Baree Pear & Khan, 154KA Mohammadpur, Pisciculture, Housing Society Ltd, 2nd Floor, Syamolly DHAKA 1207 BANGLADESH.

ALI, Mr. Raza, ACA *2008;* Triple Point Llp, 4-5 Grosvenor Place, LONDON, SW1X 7HJ.

ALI, Miss. Rehana Begum, MA BA(Hons) ACA *2002;* 77 Lullingstone Lane, LONDON, SE13 6UH.

ALI, Mr. Rooful Amin, BA ACA *2000;* 15 St. Marys Paddock, WELLINGBOROUGH, NORTHAMPTONSHIRE, NN8 1HJ.

ALI, Mr. Safdar Syed, BSc(Econ) ACA *1998;* 245 Woodmansterne Road, LONDON, SW16 5TY.

ALI, Miss. Saffeena, BA ACA *2010;* 38 Horndean Road, SHEFFIELD, S5 6UL.

ALI, Miss. Saima, BA ACA *2008;* 32 Wyverne Road, MANCHESTER, M21 0ZN.

ALI, Mr. Saiyid Mohammed, FCA *1969;* 9 Basing Hill, WEMBLEY, MIDDLESEX, HA9 9QS.

ALI, Mr. Shahzad, BSc(Econ) FCA *1996;* HSBC Private Bank (Suisse) SA, PO Box 358, Rue du Rhone 82-84, GENEVA, SWITZERLAND.

ALI, Mr. Shakil Mohammed, BA ACA *2005;* 895 Oldham Road, ROCHDALE, OL16 4RY.

•ALI, Mr. Shamshad, MA ACA CF *1997;* PricewaterhouseCoopers LLP, 7 More London Riverside, LONDON, SE1 2RT. See also PricewaterhouseCoopers

ALI, Mr. Sheikh Ghulam, ACA *1980;* 47 Maple Road, SURBITON, SURREY, KT6 4AF.

ALI, Miss. Sobia, BSc ACA *2007;* 128 Westridge Road, BIRMINGHAM, B13 0EE.

ALI, Mr. Suleman, LLB ACA CTA *2003;* Nortel Ltd 2-3 Maidenhead Office Park, Westacott Way Littlewick Green, MAIDENHEAD, BERKSHIRE, SL6 3QH.

ALI, Mr. Syed Fazle, FCA *1965;* S.F.Ahmed & Co., House No 25D, Road No 13A, Block D, Banani, DHAKA 1213 BANGLADESH.

ALI, Mr. Syed Feisal, FCA *1984;* 34/1/1 Khyaban Shaheen, Defence Housing Society, KARACHI 75500, PAKISTAN.

ALI, Mr. Syed Iftikhar, FCA *1966;* 103/II Khayaban-e-Badar Phase VI Defence Housing Authority, KARACHI 75500, PAKISTAN. (Life Member)

ALI, Mr. Tahir Iqbal, BA ACA *1991;* 35 Princes Meadow, Gosforth, NEWCASTLE UPON TYNE, NE3 4RZ.

ALI, Mr. Tayseer, ACA *2011;* 360 Route de Longwy, L-1940 LUXEMBOURG, LUXEMBOURG.

ALI, Mr. Tehseen, BA(Hons) ACA *2004;* 17 Brierfield Drive, BURY, LANCASHIRE, BL9 5JJ.

ALI, Mr. Vazeer, FCA *1967;* D4/1 Clifton, Block 7, KARACHI 75600, PAKISTAN. (Life Member)

ALI, Mr. Yasir Syed, BA ACA *2004;* 97 Shelley Crescent, HOUNSLOW, TW5 9BH.

ALI-KHAN, Mr. Moazzam, FCA *1982;* Zuidplein 216, World Trade Center, Tower H 27th Floor, 1077 XV AMSTERDAM, NETHERLANDS.

ALI-KHAN, Mr. Shahrukh, FCA *1975;* 262 Woodmansterne Road, LONDON, SW16 5UA.

ALIAS, Miss. Maizatul Azura, BAcc ACA *2002;* No 31 Jalan SM 9, Taman Sunway Batu Caves, 68100 BATU CAVES, SELANGOR, MALAYSIA.

•ALIBHAI, Mr. Hussein, BSc FCA *1976;* (Tax Fac), Leftley Rowe & Company, The Heights, 59-65 Lowlands Road, HARROW, MIDDLESEX, HA1 3AW. See also Mountsides Limited

ALIBO, Ms. Mia, ACA *2008;* Flat 15, 31 Three Colt Street, LONDON, E14 8HH.

•ALIDINA, Mr. Bakerali Hassanali Rajabali, ACA FCCA *2008;* BFCA Limited, Barbican House, 26-34 Old Street, LONDON, EC1V 9QQ. See also Blevin Franks Limited

ALIDINA, Mr. Hasnein Abdulrasul Fazal, ACA *1985;* 1 Holmdene Avenue, HARROW, HA2 6HP.

ALIDINA, Mr. Shabir Abdulrasul Fazal, ACA *1980;* 7 Roseleigh Blvd, SYDENHAM, VIC 3037, AUSTRALIA.

•ALIMCHANDANI, Mr. Naresh Jaikrishin, BSc ACA *1988;* with Ernst & Young LLP, 1 More London Place, LONDON, SE1 2AF.

ALIMOHAMED, Mr. Iqbal, FCA *1968;* 36-F Block-6, P.E.C.H.S., KARACHI 75400, SINDH, PAKISTAN.

ALIMOHAMED, Mr. Tariq Sadik, BSc(Hons) ACA *2009;* P O Box 214298, DUBAI, UNITED ARAB EMIRATES.

ALIMONDA, Miss. Jane Louise, ACA *2008;* Ground Floor Flat, 11 Gladstone Terrace, BRIGHTON, BN2 3LB.

•ALIMORADIAN, Mr. Bahram, BSc FCA *1980;* Bahram Alimoradian & Co, 76 Braithwaite Tower, Hall Place, LONDON, W2 1LR.

•ALINEK, Mr. Michael Stuart, BA FCA *1972;* M.S.Alinek, 7 Upton Lodge Close, BUSHEY, WD23 1AG.

ALING, Mr. Oliver Lee Kian Lioong, BSc ACA *2004;* La Hausse De La Louviere, Curepipe, FLOREAL, MAURITIUS.

ALING, Mr. Teddy Kian Lim, BSc ACA CFA *1998;* c/o AHLING WORLD, Royal Road, BEAU BASSIN, MAURITIUS.

ALINGTON, Mrs. Amanda, BSc ACA *1992;* 6 Riverview Gardens, TWICKENHAM, TW1 4RT.

ALISTOUN, Mr. Neil Murray, ACA *2008;* 29 Elms Drive, Marston, OXFORD, OX3 0NN.

ALIX, Mr. Patrick Thomas Gerald, BA(Hons) ACA *2002;* 78 avenue du Général De Gaulle, 94160 SAINT MANDE, FRANCE.

ALKER, Mr. Andrew Stephen, MA ACA *1991;* Stotherds Farm, Goosnargh Lane, Goosnargh, PRESTON, PR3 2JU.

ALLADINA, Mr. Latif Muradally, FCA *1976;* 16 Wood Thrush Avenue, MARKHAM L3S 4A8, ON, CANADA.

ALLAM, Mr. Jonathan, BSc FCA *1992;* 34 Meiros Way, Ashington, PULBOROUGH, WEST SUSSEX, RH20 3QB.

ALLAM, Mr. Matthew, BA ACA *1998;* Genworth Financial, 101 Miller Street, NORTH SYDNEY, NSW 2060, AUSTRALIA.

ALLAN, Miss. Alexandra, MSc ACA *2006;* 9/11 Amherst St, Cammeray Square - Building B, CAMMERAY, NSW 2062, AUSTRALIA.

ALLAN, Mr. Alistair John, MA FCA *1985;* Alistair Allan, The Lindens, 94 Drymen Road, Bearsden, GLASGOW, G61 2SY.

ALLAN, Mr. Andrew John, BA ACA *1995;* Bruntwood Estates Alpha Portfolio Ltd City Tower, Piccadilly Plaza, MANCHESTER, M1 4BT.

ALLAN, Mr. Andrew Robert, BA(Hons) ACA *2011;* Flat 2, 35 Alderbrook Road, LONDON, SW12 8AD.

•ALLAN, Mr. Angus Ian, BA FCA CF *1992;* Clive Owen & Co LLP, 140 Coniscliffe Road, DARLINGTON, DL3 7RT.

ALLAN, Miss. Charlotte, BSc(Hons) ACA *2001;* (Tax Fac), 1a Fitzroy Mews, LONDON, W1T 6DE.

ALLAN, Mr. Christopher John, ACA *1983;* 81 Melton Road, West Bridgford, NOTTINGHAM, NG2 6EN.

•ALLAN, Mr. Christopher John, FCA *1975;* 2 The Green, Little Neston, NESTON, CH64 4BZ.

ALLAN, Mr. Christopher John, FCA *1965;* 29 Woodland Avenue, HOVE, BN3 6BH.

ALLAN, Mr. Christopher Robert, FCA *1974;* 5 Ravenhurst Drive, Great Barr, BIRMINGHAM, B43 7RS.

ALLAN, Mr. Christopher Roy, BSc ACA *1997;* 24 Tailors, St Michaels Mead, BISHOP'S STORTFORD, CM23 4FQ.

•ALLAN, Mr. Daniel Garland, LLB ACA *1987;* Accountantsandtax Ltd, 15 Quarry Hill Road, Borough Green, SEVENOAKS, KENT, TN15 8RQ. See also Allan AS Limited

ALLAN, Miss. Fiona Elizabeth, MA ACA *2002;* 70 Sternhold Avenue, LONDON, SW2 4PW.

ALLAN, Mr. Gerald, FCA *1960;* 54 Oakland Road, WHITLEY BAY, NE25 8LX. (Life Member)

ALLAN, Mr. Gerard, MBA BSc FCA *1978;* Rolls-Royce Plc, P.O. Box 31, Moor Lane (ML-3), DERBY, DE24 8BJ.

ALLAN, Mr. James Stuart, BA ACA *2005;* 10 Haymoor, LICHFIELD, STAFFORDSHIRE, WS14 9SS.

ALLAN, Mrs. Jane Edith, FCA *1973;* (Member of Council 1979 - 1985), Heim im Wald Waldferiendorf 18, 94209 REGEN, GERMANY.

ALLAN, Miss. Jemma Louise, BSc ACA *2011;* 55 Avebury Road, BRISTOL, BS3 2QQ.

ALLAN, Mr. John Hamilton Birkett, MA FCA *1964;* 4 Church Bank, Richmond Road, ALTRINCHAM, WA14 3NW.

ALLAN, Mrs. Julie Ann, BSc ACA CTA *1991;* 6 Oakfield Gardens, Ormesby, MIDDLESBROUGH, CLEVELAND, TS7 9RH.

•ALLAN, Mrs. Julie Louise, BSc ACA *2002;* JLA Accounting, 32 Collingsway, West Park, DARLINGTON, COUNTY DURHAM, DL2 2FD.

ALLAN, Mr. Kenneth Alfred, FCA *1950;* Brackenridge, Dalesway, Heswall, WIRRAL, CH60 4RU. (Life Member)

ALLAN, Mr. Mark Christopher, ACA *1997;* The Unite Group plc, The Core, 40 St Thomas Street, BRISTOL, BS1 6JX.

ALLAN, Mr. Melville David, FCA *1955;* 16 Spring Walk, Brayton, SELBY, YO8 9DS. (Life Member)

ALLAN, Mr. Michael Arthur, BA FCA *1963;* 1 The Woods, Ickenham, UXBRIDGE, UB10 8NN. (Life Member)

ALLAN, Mr. Michael Kingsley, FCA *1970;* Greenwood Cottages, 106 New Ridley Road, STOCKSFIELD, NE43 7EQ. (Life Member)

ALLAN, Miss. Natalie Julia, ACA *2010;* Laundry Cottage Whitecross Road, East Harptree, BRISTOL, BS40 6AA.

ALLAN, Mr. Nicholas James, ACA *1997;* PO BOX 171, CLAREMONT, WA 6910, AUSTRALIA.

•ALLAN, Mr. Paul, BSocSc ACA *2002;* F.W. Berringer & Co, Lygon House, 50 London Road, BROMLEY, BR1 3RA. See also Berringer F.W. & Co

ALLAN, Mr. Peter Frederick, BA FCA *1974;* Les osierettes, Malataverne, 30480 CENDRAS, FRANCE. (Life Member)

ALLAN, Mr. Peter Robert, BA FCA *1971;* Doxbond Cambridge, 7 Vicarage Close Dullingham, NEWMARKET, SUFFOLK, CB8 9XA.

ALLAN, Mr. Richard Bellerby, MA FCA *1966;* 8 Northampton Park, LONDON, N1 2PJ.

ALLAN, Mr. Robert Alastair Liston, MA FCA *1981;* 19 King Edward Avenue, Moordown, BOURNEMOUTH, BH9 1TY.

ALLAN, Mr. Robert Andrew, BA ACA *1989;* Premium Credit House, 60 East Street, EPSOM, KT17 1HB.

ALLAN, Mr. Robert Jeremy, MA FCA *1968;* Poplars, Fitzgeorge Avenue, NEW MALDEN, KT3 4SH. (Life Member)

ALLAN, Mr. Roy Maclaren, FCA *1959;* The Garth, 9 Blundell Drive, Birkdale, SOUTHPORT, PR8 4RG. (Life Member)

•ALLAN, Mr. Simon Roger, BSc ACA *1981;* J.& A.W. Sully & Co, The Old Wagon House, Bullocks Lane, Kingston Seymour, North Somerset, CLEVEDON AVON BS21 6XA.

ALLAN, Mr. Stephen James, BSc(Hons) ACA *2000;* Singer & Friedlander Ltd, 21 New Street, LONDON, EC2M 4HR.

ALLAN, Miss. Suzanne Frances, BSc ACA CF *1991;* Manorbier, Linden Chase Road, SEVENOAKS, KENT, TN13 3JU.

ALLAN-SMITH, Mr. John Neville, BSc(Hons) ACA *2001;* RBS Non Core Division, 9th Floor, 600 Washington Blvd, STAMFORD, CT 06901, UNITED STATES.

ALLANA, Mr. Mehboob Bahadurali, ACA *1980;* 115 Knoll Crescent, NORTHWOOD, MIDDLESEX, HA6 1HX.

ALLANBY, Mr. Edward Gordon Clarendon, BA ACA *1986;* Leman Management Limited, 2nd Floor Wessex House, 45 Reid Street, HAMILTON HM 1L, BERMUDA.

ALLANSON, Mrs. Julie, BSc ACA *2005;* with Ernst & Young LLP, 1 Bridgewater Place, Water Lane, LEEDS, LS11 5QR.

ALLANSON, Mr. Kenneth, FCA *1960;* 22 Hemwood Road, WINDSOR, SL4 4YU. (Life Member)

ALLARD, Dr. Emma, PhD BSc ACA *2011;* 62 Freshfield Gardens, WATERLOOVILLE, HAMPSHIRE, PO7 7TL.

ALLARD, Miss. Gillian Clare, BA ACA *1999;* 13 Riverdale Drive, LONDON, SW18 4UR.

ALLARD, Mr. Michael John, FCA *1955;* Gialda Cottage, 12 Maes Y Mynach, St Davids, HAVERFORDWEST, SA62 6QG. (Life Member)

ALLARD, Miss. Victoria Sarah, BSc ACA *1991;* 201 Broad Street, Apartment 2502, STAMFORD, CT 06901, UNITED STATES.

ALLARDICE, Mr. James Brian, FCA *1957;* 185 London Road, Appleton, WARRINGTON, WA4 5BX. (Life Member)

ALLARDICE, Mr. Michael Graham, BCom FCA *1990;* 19th Floor IFC 2, 8 Finance Street, CENTRAL, HONG KONG ISLAND, HONG KONG SAR.

ALLARDICE, Mr. Richard Steven, BCom ACA *1990;* Ground Floor Flat, 15 Strathearn Road, EDINBURGH, EH9 2AE.

ALLARIE, Mr. Randy James, ACA *2002;* 191 Rhatigan Road East, EDMONTON T6R 1N6, AB, CANADA.

•ALLATSON, Mr. Timothy, BA FCA *1991;* Tim Allatson Limited, 4 Brompton Way, West Bridgford, NOTTINGHAM, NG2 7SU.

ALLATT, Mr. John David, FCA *1962;* Lerida, Haughton Lane, SHIFNAL, TF11 8HW.

ALLATT, Mr. John Graham, MA FCA *1977;* 9 Longcroft Avenue, HARPENDEN, AL5 2RB.

ALLATT, Mr. Jonathan, BA(Econ) FCA *1998;* 33 Partition Street, BRISTOL, BS1 5QJ.

ALLATT, Miss. Sarah Elizabeth Claire, ACA *2004;* 12 Woodland Crescent, LONDON, SE16 6YP.
ALLAWAY, Mr. Stuart David, ACA MBA *1991;* 46 Claremont Road, TUNBRIDGE WELLS, TN1 1TF.
•ALLBUT, Mr. John Gwilym, FCA *1958;* J.G. Allbut & Co., Stonefield Lodge, Newcastle Road, STONE, STAFFORDSHIRE, ST15 8LB.
•ALLCHILD, Mr. Maurice Bernard, FCA *1972;* Allchild Accounting Limited, 4 Howland Court, 20 The Avenue, Hatch End, PINNER, MIDDLESEX HA5 4ET. See also Allchild M.B.
•ALLCHIN, Mr. Andrew Philip, BA FCA *1997;* Baker Tilly Tax & Advisory Services LLP, Hartwell House, 55-61 Victoria Street, BRISTOL, BS1 6AD. See also Baker Tilly UK Audit LLP
ALLCHURCH, Mr. Marcus Nicol Strachan, BSc ACA *2005;* Lustleigh, Poyle Lane, Burnham, SLOUGH, SL1 8LA.
ALLCOCK, Mr. Alistair John, BSc ACA *2007;* with PricewaterhouseCoopers LLP, Benson House, 33 Wellington Street, LEEDS, LS1 4JP.
•ALLCOCK, Mr. Andrew Clive, BA FCA *1986;* A Allcock Corporate Finance, 59 Granary Way, SALE, CHESHIRE, M33 4GF.
•ALLCOCK, Mr. David Lee, FCA *1985;* Twentyone Twelve Ltd, 2 Coal Cart Road Birstall, LEICESTER, LE4 3BY.
ALLCOCK, Mr. Dean Joseph, BA ACA *2000;* 15 Meadow Way, Kinoulton, NOTTINGHAM, NG12 3RE.
ALLCOCK, Miss. Jennifer Louise, BSc ACA *1999;* P P D Development Granta Park, Great Abington, CAMBRIDGE, CB21 6GQ.
ALLCOCK, Mr. John Frank, FCA *1961;* 1 Holyoake Cottages, Defford Road, PERSHORE, WR10 1HZ. (Life Member)
ALLCOCK, Mr. John William, BA(Econ) FCA *1982;* P J Livesey Group Limited, Ashburton Park, Ashburton Road West, Trafford Park, MANCHESTER, M17 1AF.
ALLCOCK, Mr. Michael Lewis, BSc ACA *1992;* Foxhouse, Rowe Lane, Pirbright, WOKING, GU24 0LX.
ALLCOCK, Mrs. Rebecca Louise, BA ACA *2009;* 14 Avonbridge Close, Arnold, NOTTINGHAM, NG5 8DE.
ALLCOCK, Miss. Sarah Gayle Alexandra, BSc ACA DChA *2000;* 48 Poplar Road, Dorridge, SOLIHULL, WEST MIDLANDS, B93 8DB.
•ALLCOCK, Mr. Stephen Paul, FCA *1977;* Rogers Spencer Limited, Newstead House, Pelham Road, NOTTINGHAM, NG5 1AP.
ALLCROFT, Mr. Jason Matthew, BA FCA *1997;* with Cassons, St Crispin House, St. Crispin Way, Haslingden, ROSSENDALE, LANCASHIRE BB4 4PW.
ALLCROFT, Mr. Mark Anthony, BSc ACA *2000;* with KPMG LLP, 15 Canada Square, LONDON, E14 5GL.
ALLCROFT, Mrs. Mira Rosa, BA FCA *1982;* 4 Gorse Corner, Townsend Drive, ST. ALBANS, AL3 5SH.
ALLCROFT, Mr. Robert Neil, BA ACA *1979;* Sunnybank, Lanehead Road, Totley, SHEFFIELD, S17 3BD.
ALLCUTT, Mr. David Alastair, MSc BSc ACA *2009;* 27 Musbury Avenue, Cheadle Hulme, CHEADLE, CHESHIRE, SK8 7AT.
ALLDAY, Mr. David John, BSc FCA *1964;* Green House, Dale Road South, Darley Dale, MATLOCK, DERBYSHIRE, DE4 3BP.
ALLDAY, Mr. John Philip, FCA *1963;* The Old Farm House, Bullocks Lane, Kingston Seymour, CLEVEDON, BS21 6XA. (Life Member)
ALLDIS, Mr. James, BA(Hons) ACA *2010;* 9 Barham Close, BOURNEMOUTH, DORSET, BH14BZ.
ALLDRIDGE, Mrs. Christine, BSc ACA *1992;* Sycamore House, 2 Thorp Arch Park, Thorp Arch, WETHERBY, WEST YORKSHIRE, LS23 7AN.
ALLDRIDGE, Mr. Stephen Alexander, BSc ACA *1992;* Sycamore House, 2 Thorp Arch Park, Thorp Arch, WETHERBY, WEST YORKSHIRE, LS23 7AN.
ALLDRITT, Mrs. Claire, MSc ACA *2005;* with Deloitte LLP, 2 New Street Square, LONDON, EC4A 3BZ.
ALLELY, Mrs. Helen Margaret, FCA *1964;* 2 Chalk Paddock, EPSOM, KT18 7AT. (Life Member)
ALLELY, Mr. Ian William, FCA *1964;* 2 Chalk Paddock, EPSOM, KT18 7AT.
•ⓘALLEN, Mr. Adrian David, BA ACA *1988;* Baker Tilly Tax & Advisory Services LLP, 2 Whitehall Quay, LEEDS, LS1 4HG. See also Baker Tilly Restructuring and Recovery LLP
ALLEN, Mr. Adrian John, ACA *1982;* Haylors Cottage, London Road, Balcombe, HAYWARDS HEATH, RH17 6PY.
ALLEN, Mr. Adrian Keith, FCA *1981;* 16 Radnor Road, DUDLEY, DY3 3TW.
•ALLEN, Mr. Adrian Michael, BSc FCA *1989;* Sowerby FRS LLP, Beckside Court, Annie Reed Road, BEVERLEY, NORTH HUMBERSIDE, HU17 0LF.
ALLEN, Mr. Adrian Roger, FCA *1970;* Hill Farm, Hill, RUGBY, CV23 8DX.
ALLEN, Mrs. Alison Janet, BSc ACA ATII *1989;* (Tax Fac), with BDO LLP, Kings Wharf, 20-30 Kings Road, READING, RG1 3EX.
ALLEN, Mr. Andrew, BSc ACA *2007;* 22 Parsonage Road, TUNBRIDGE WELLS, TN4 8TA.
ALLEN, Mr. Andrew Charles, ACA *2009;* Apartment 9 Lyon 2 Kenwood Court, SHEFFIELD, S7 1NT.
•ALLEN, Mr. Andrew Greenwood, BSc FCA *2000;* Winter Rule LLP, Lowin House, Tregolls Road, TRURO, CORNWALL, TR1 2NA. See also Francis Clark LLP
•ALLEN, Mr. Andrew James, BSc FCA *1979;* A.J. Allen & Co, Orchard House, Alhampton, SHEPTON MALLET, SOMERSET, BA4 6PZ.
ALLEN, Mr. Andrew Mark, BSc ACA *2010;* with RSM Tenon Limited, Cedar House, Breckland, Linford Wood, MILTON KEYNES, MK14 6EX.
ALLEN, Mr. Andrew Vernon Moor, BA ACA *1985;* Elco S.P.A, Via Marconi 1, 20065 INZAGO, MI, ITALY.
ALLEN, Miss. Annabel Lucy, BSc ACA *2005;* 5 Ellesmere Road, Windsor, MELBOURNE, VIC 3181, AUSTRALIA.
ALLEN, Mr. Anthony David, FCA *1966;* H04, 47 Leigh Rd, COBHAM, KT11 2LF.
ALLEN, Mr. Anthony Douglas, FCA *1973;* 3 The Shires, WOKINGHAM, BERKSHIRE, RG41 4SZ.
ALLEN, Mr. Anthony Joseph, BSc ACA *1992;* Norwich Union Life, PO Box 285, Wellington Row, YORK, YO90 1YB.
ALLEN, Mr. Anthony Russell, FCA *1958;* 42 Station Road, BILLERICAY, CM12 9DR. (Life Member)
ALLEN, Mr. Anthony Steven, MA FCA *1976;* The Coach House, Kemnal Road, CHISLEHURST, BR7 6LT.
ALLEN, Mr. Antony William, FCA *1951;* The Walled Garden, Wadhurst Road, Frant, TUNBRIDGE WELLS, TN3 9EH. (Life Member)
ALLEN, Miss. Barbara Melanie, FCA *1976;* 12 Blackett Close, STAINES, MIDDLESEX, TW18 3NW.
ALLEN, Mr. Barrie John, BSc FCA *1979;* Target Loan Servicing Ltd Picture House, Imperial Way Coedkernew, NEWPORT, GWENT, NP10 8UH.
ALLEN, Mr. Barry, FCA *1960;* Sandcroft, 61 Etherley Lane, BISHOP AUCKLAND, DL14 7QZ. (Life Member)
ALLEN, Mr. Benjamin, ACA *2008;* 18 Evenden Road, Meopham, GRAVESEND, DA13 0HA.
ALLEN, Mr. Benjamin James, MA FCA *1962;* 2 Wargrave Hall, High Street, Wargrave, READING, RG10 8DA.
ALLEN, Mr. Bernard, FCA *1955;* 11 Belmont Close, Cockfosters, BARNET, EN4 9LS. (Life Member)
ALLEN, Mr. Brian James, BEng ACA *2001;* 61 Gurney Court Road, ST. ALBANS, HERTFORDSHIRE, AL1 4QU.
ALLEN, Mr. Brian Richard, BSc FCA *1978;* Carlton Lodge, Rue Du Presby Tere, Castel, GUERNSEY, GY5 7NE.
ALLEN, Mr. Bruce John, ACA *1992;* Apartment 8 Strines House, 2 Holyrood Avenue, SHEFFIELD, S10 4NW.
ALLEN, Miss. Caroline, ACA *2011;* 5 Stratton Court, Marlborough Drive, DARLINGTON, COUNTY DURHAM, DL1 5YQ.
ALLEN, Mrs. Caroline Elizabeth, BA ACA *1992;* 8 Saxon Road, WINCHESTER, SO23 7DJ.
ALLEN, Miss. Carolyn Sarah, LLB ACA *1990;* (Tax Fac), 43 Tudor Close, Churchdown, GLOUCESTER, GL3 1AW.
ALLEN, Mrs. Catharine Anne, BA ACA *1993;* with PricewaterhouseCoopers LLP, 31 Great George Street, BRISTOL, BS1 5QD.
ALLEN, Mrs. Catherine Jane, BA ACA *2002;* 140 South Park Road, LONDON, SW19 8TA.
ALLEN, Miss. Catherine Louise, BSc ACA *2003;* Flat 26, Caversham Place, Richfield Avenue, READING, RG1 8BY.
ALLEN, Mrs. Charmain Siew Yong, BSc ACA *1998;* School of Technology, University of Cambridge, 17 Mill Lane, CAMBRIDGE, CB2 1RX.
ALLEN, Mr. Christian Philip Quentin, BSc ACA *1988;* Og House, Marlborough Road, Ogbourne St. George, MARLBOROUGH, SN8 1TF.
ALLEN, Mr. Christian Thomas, BA ACA *2003;* The Grove Cottage Grove Road, Penshurst, TONBRIDGE, TN11 8DU.
ALLEN, Mr. Christopher David, BSc ACA *1991;* Blackrock Investment Managers, 33 King William Street, LONDON, EC4R 9AS.
ALLEN, Mr. Christopher James, BA FCA *1969;* 6 Fishermans Wharf, ABINGDON, OX14 5RX.
ALLEN, Mr. Christopher John, ACA *1983;* Forrester Boyd, 26 South St. Marys Gate, GRIMSBY, SOUTH HUMBERSIDE, DN31 1LW.
ALLEN, Mr. Christopher Lawrence Edgar, FCA *1975;* 22 Marston Close, Walderslade, CHATHAM, ME5 9BY.
ALLEN, Mr. Christopher Michael, MSc BA ACA *2001;* 38 Arethusa House, Gunwharf Quays, PORTSMOUTH, PO1 3TQ.
ALLEN, Miss. Clare Elizabeth, BSc ACA *2006;* 96 Penshurst Way, NUNEATON, CV11 4XN.
ALLEN, Mr. Colin, ACA *1979;* 14 Oxford Gardens, Whetstone, LONDON, N20 9AG.
ALLEN, Mr. Colin William Mewes, FCA CPFA *1953;* 9 Green Walk, Norwood Green, SOUTHALL, UB2 5QX. (Life Member)
ALLEN, Mr. Daniel, BSc ACA *1989;* 74 Birdhurst Road, SOUTH CROYDON, SURREY, CR2 7EB.
•ALLEN, Mr. David, BSc FCA *1988;* PricewaterhouseCoopers LLP, 80 Strand, LONDON, WC2R 0AF. See also PricewaterhouseCoopers
ALLEN, Mr. David, FCA *1953;* 15 Silvas Court, MORPETH, NORTHUMBERLAND, NE61 1HQ. (Life Member)
ALLEN, Mr. David Christoper, BA FCA *1971;* Orange Tree Lodge Kings Mills Road, Castel, GUERNSEY, GY5 7JT.
•ALLEN, Mr. David John, BA FCA *1991;* (Tax Fac), Mabe Allen LLP, 3 Derby Road, RIPLEY, DERBYSHIRE, DE5 3EA.
ALLEN, Mr. David John, BA ACA *2007;* (Tax Fac), 74 Leslie Road, ST. HELENS, MERSEYSIDE, WA10 3EU.
ALLEN, Mr. David John Drysdale, BSc FCA *1975;* Wood Cottage, Sample Oak Lane, Chilworth, GUILDFORD, GU4 8QP.
•ALLEN, Mr. David Keith, ACA ACCA *2008;* (Tax Fac), Allen Mills Howard Ltd, 56 Manchester Road, ALTRINCHAM, WA14 4PJ.
ALLEN, Mr. David Lomax, FCA *1956;* 15 Tor Avenue, Greenmount, BURY, BL8 4HG. (Life Member)
ALLEN, Mr. David Michael, MSci ACA *2003;* 34 Centurion Square, Skeldergate, YORK, YO1 6DP.
ALLEN, Mr. David Nicholas, ACA *1987;* 2 Stanstead Road, CATERHAM, CR3 6AA.
ALLEN, Mr. David Owen, MA ACA *1998;* 8 Oakhill Road, SEVENOAKS, KENT, TN13 1NP.
•ALLEN, Mr. David Stewart, BSc FCA *1973;* (Tax Fac), David Allen Associates, 122 Hill Top Road, Thornton, BRADFORD, BD13 3QX.
ALLEN, Mr. Dennis Wright, FCA *1965;* 36 Ladycroft Road, Armthorpe, DONCASTER, DN3 3RP.
ALLEN, Ms. Diana Gabrielle, BSc ACA *1990;* Enigma Grosvenor Road, Chobham, WOKING, GU24 8DZ.
ALLEN, Mr. Edmund, MSci BA ACA *2004;* Chemin de la Blonde 27, 1253 Vandoeuvres, GENEVA, SWITZERLAND.
ALLEN, Mr. Edward, MEng ACA *2010;* Old Hill House Old Hill, Winford, BRISTOL, BS40 8DX.
ALLEN, Miss. Elizabeth Anne, BSc ACA *1997;* Brynawelon, 26 Clos-Y-Cwarra, St Fagans, CARDIFF, CF5 4QT.
ALLEN, Mrs. Elsa Rachel, BA FCA *2000;* Trinity Wiring Ltd, 1a Mayflower Way, HARLESTON, NORFOLK, IP20 9EB.
•ALLEN, Mr. Frederick Roy, FCA *1965;* Parkfield House, Parkfield, SEVENOAKS, TN15 0HX.
ALLEN, Mr. Frederick William, FCA *1962;* Fairlands, Oxshott Road, LEATHERHEAD, SURREY, KT22 0EN. (Life Member)
•ALLEN, Mr. Gary David, FCA *1995;* 5 Charnwood Court, Pinner View, HARROW, MIDDLESEX, HA1 4RD.
ALLEN, Mrs. Gaynor Fee, BSc ACA *1989;* 6 Oakston Avenue Rainhill, PRESCOT, MERSEYSIDE, L35 0QN.
ALLEN, Mr. Geoffrey William, FCA *1982;* (Tax Fac), North Stoke Farm, North Stoke, WALLINGFORD, OX10 6BL.
ALLEN, Mr. Giles Derek, ACA *1983;* Computer Accounting Services Ltd, West Way, Walworth Ind Estate, ANDOVER, SP10 5JG.
ALLEN, Mr. Graham Andrew, BSc ACA *1999;* The London Stock Exchange Plc The London Stock Exchange, 10 Paternoster Square, LONDON, EC4M 7LS.
ALLEN, Mr. Graham Kevin, BSc ACA *1991;* 13 Woodlands Road, ORPINGTON, BR6 6EB.
ALLEN, Mr. Greg, BSc ACA *2011;* Les Galets, Route des Chatillons, Mies, 1295 VAUD, SWITZERLAND.
ALLEN, Mrs. Halina Anne, BA ACA *1989;* Russett Glade, Hollybush Ride, Finchampstead, WOKINGHAM, RG40 3QP.
ALLEN, Mr. Harry, FCA *1954;* 10 Priory Orchard, Flamstead, ST. ALBANS, HERTFORDSHIRE, AL3 8BU. (Life Member)
ALLEN, Mr. Henry John, BA ACA *1999;* Hamlet House Kelvedon Road, Coggeshall, COLCHESTER, CO6 1RQ.
ALLEN, Mrs. Hilary Jane, BSc ACA *1990;* Brook House, Bayleys Hill Road, Bough Beech, EDENBRIDGE, KENT, TN8 7AS.
ALLEN, Mr. Howard William Habberfield, BEng ACA *1998;* 15 Elnathan Mews, LONDON, W9 2JE.
ALLEN, Mr. Ian Yarwood, FCA *1969;* 22 Ely Gardens, TONBRIDGE, TN10 4NZ. (Life Member)
ALLEN, Mrs. Isabelle Stephanie Marie, ACA *1995;* 41 rue du Bois de boulogne, 92200 NEUILLY-SUR-SEINE, FRANCE.
•ALLEN, Miss. Jacquelyn, BA ACA *1993;* J Allen & Co, Suite 3&4 Rood End House, 6 Stortford Road, DUNMOW, ESSEX, CM6 1DA. See also Accountancy Professionals Ltd
ALLEN, Mr. James, BA ACA *2007;* Flat 41, Augustine Bell Tower, 7 Pancras Way, LONDON, E3 2SU.
ALLEN, Mr. James Anthony, BSc ACA *2008;* with Menzies LLP, Woking Office, Midas House, 62 Goldsworth Road, WOKING, SURREY GU21 6LQ.
ALLEN, Mr. James Stephen, MA ACA *1985;* 30 The Green, Great Bowden, MARKET HARBOROUGH, LEICESTERSHIRE, LE16 7EU.
ALLEN, Mr. Jamie Lee, MSc BSc ACA *2006;* 109 Kipling Drive, LONDON, SW19 1TL.
ALLEN, Miss. Jane Louise, MA ACA DChA *1999;* Cumbria Community Foundation Dovenby Hall, Dovenby, COCKERMOUTH, CUMBRIA, CA13 0PN.
ALLEN, Mrs. Janet Ann, BSc FCA *1977;* Staffordlodge Ltd, Yeldon, Higher Eype, BRIDPORT, DORSET, DT6 6AT.
ALLEN, Mr. Jeffrey Beynon, BSc ACA *1983;* Castle Sound & Vision Ltd, 48-50 Maid Marian Way, NOTTINGHAM, NG1 6GF.
ALLEN, Mrs. Jennifer Margaret, MA ACA *1999;* 69 Marlpit Lane, COULSDON, SURREY, CR5 2HF.
ALLEN, Miss. Jenny, ACA *2009;* 16 Oakham Way, ILKESTON, DERBYSHIRE, DE7 8TF.
•ALLEN, Mrs. Joanna Claire, BA(Hons) ACA *2002;* with PricewaterhouseCoopers LLP, 1 East Parade, SHEFFIELD, S1 2ET.
ALLEN, Mrs. Joanne Rose, BSc ACA *2004;* 91 Lavender Walk, EVESHAM, WORCESTERSHIRE, WR11 2LN.
ALLEN, Mr. John Albert, FCA *1966;* 60 Dorchester Road, LEICESTER, LE3 0UF.
ALLEN, Mr. John David, FCA *1973;* 5 Bishops Wood, Cuddesdon, OXFORD, OX44 9HA.
ALLEN, Mr. John Edward, FCA *1980;* Garth House Bell Lane, Cocking, MIDHURST, WEST SUSSEX, GU29 0HU.
ALLEN, Mr. John Frederick, FCA *1950;* Osborne House, The Avenue, TARPORLEY, CW6 0BA. (Life Member)
ALLEN, Mr. John Godfrey, BCom FCA *1965;* 7 Little Gaddesden House, Little Gaddesden, BERKHAMSTED, HERTFORDSHIRE, HP4 1PL.
ALLEN, Mr. John Hanson, FCA *1970;* 5 Regal Drive, Rishworth, SOWERBY BRIDGE, HX6 4RW.
ALLEN, Mr. John Kenneth, FCA *1968;* 17 Inglemere Gardens, Arnside, CARNFORTH, LANCASHIRE, LA5 0BX.
ALLEN, Mr. John Meirion, BSc ACA *1986;* 4 Moser Grove, Sway, LYMINGTON, SO41 6GA.
•ALLEN, Mr. John Nigel, FCA CTA *1983;* John N. Allen, 15 Ellis Avenue, Onslow Village, GUILDFORD, GU2 7SR.
•ALLEN, Mr. John Philip, FCA *1964;* Mabe Allen LLP, 50 Osmaston Road, DERBY, DE1 2HU.
ALLEN, Mr. John William, BSc FCA *1979;* 12 Rosebury Vale, RUISLIP, MIDDLESEX, HA4 6AQ.
ALLEN, Mr. Jonathan, BA ACA *1996;* 15 Summerhill Grange, Lindfield, HAYWARDS HEATH, WEST SUSSEX, RH16 1RQ.
ALLEN, Mr. Jonathan, BA ACA *2006;* PWC First Point, Buckingham Gate Gatwick Airport, LONDON, WEST SUSSEX, RH60NT.
ALLEN, Mr. Jonathan Mark, BA ACA *2005;* 112 Blackburn Crescent, Chapeltown, SHEFFIELD, S35 2EF.
ALLEN, Mr. Jonathon Michael Peter, BSc ACA *1986;* The Mount, Mount Gawne Road, Port St. Mary, ISLE OF MAN, IM9 5LX.
ALLEN, Miss. Josephine, BA(Hons) ACA *2009;* Flat 20 Anchor Terrace, 3-13 Southwark Bridge Road, LONDON, SE1 9HQ.
ALLEN, Mrs. Julie Carolyn, BSc ACA *2004;* Legal and General House, Legal & General Assurance Society Ltd Legal & General House, St. Monicas Road, TADWORTH, SURREY, KT20 6EU.

ALLEN, Miss. Julie Elizabeth, FCA *1983;* Glebe House, Hosey Hill, WESTERHAM, TN16 1TA.
ALLEN, Mrs. Julie Michelle, ACA *1994;* The Mallows, 15A West Road, Dibden Purlieu, SOUTHAMPTON, SO45 4RH.
ALLEN, Mrs. Karen Elizabeth, BA ACA *1996;* 7 Hilltop Gardens Horndean, WATERLOOVILLE, HAMPSHIRE, PO8 0AT.
ALLEN, Mrs. Katherine Jennifer, BA ACA *2003;* with RSM Tenon Audit Limited, Stoughton House, Harborough Road, Oadby, LEICESTER, LE2 4LP.
ALLEN, Miss. Kathryn, ACA *2009;* PO Box 10729, GEORGETOWN, KY1-1007, CAYMAN ISLANDS.
ALLEN, Miss. Katie, LLB ACA *2011;* 19 Tatton Lane, Thorpe, WAKEFIELD, WEST YORKSHIRE, WF3 3FF.
ALLEN, Mrs. Katie Ilana, BSc ACA *2006;* 14 Claybury, BUSHEY, WD23 1FT.
ALLEN, Mr. Keith, BSc FCA *1988;* The Farrelly's, 7a Over Lane, Almondsbury, BRISTOL, BS32 4BL.
•ALLEN, Mr. Keith Cyril, FCA *1975;* K.C. Allen, 49B Post Street, Godmanchester, HUNTINGDON, PE29 2AQ.
•ALLEN, Mr. Keith Gaskell, FCA *1969;* Allen Mills Howard Ltd, 56 Manchester Road, ALTRINCHAM, WA14 4PJ.
ALLEN, Mr. Kenneth, FCA *1972;* 25 Millmount, Charroterie, St. Peter Port, GUERNSEY, GY1 1EL.
ALLEN, Mrs. Kerena, BSc ACA CTA *1994;* 6 Christies Avenue, Badgers Mount, SEVENOAKS, TN14 7AN.
ALLEN, Mr. Kevin David, BSc FCA *1989;* The NMB Group Ltd, 3rd Floor, Warwick House, 737 Warwick Road, SOLIHULL, WEST MIDLANDS B91 3DG.
ALLEN, Mr. Kevin John, BSc FCA *1980;* 41 Green Lane, Bovingdon, HEMEL HEMPSTEAD, HERTFORDSHIRE, HP3 0JZ.
ALLEN, Mr. Kevin Michael, BSc ACA *1983;* 9 Woodgate Close, Charlton Kings, CHELTENHAM, GL52 6UW.
ALLEN, Mrs. Kirsteen, BSc ACA *1996;* 9 Kippington Road, SEVENOAKS, KENT, TN13 2LH.
ALLEN, Miss. Kitty Ann, ACA *2009;* 13 Handen Road, LONDON, SE12 8NP.
ALLEN, Mr. Kris, BEng ACA *2004;* Akumal Grandes Maisons Road, St. Sampson, GUERNSEY, GY2 4JS.
•ALLEN, Mr. Lawrence Graham Gunstone, LLB FCA FCCA *1974;* Marriot Gibbs Rees Wallis, 13-17 Paradise Square, SHEFFIELD, S1 2DE. See also Marriott Gibbs Rees Wallis
ALLEN, Mr. Lindsey James, FCA *1968;* 5 Barn Meadow, Staplehurst, TONBRIDGE, KENT, TN12 0SY. (Life Member)
ALLEN, Miss. Linzi Kristina, ACA *2009;* KPMG, Level 3, 100 Melville Street, Tasmania, HOBART, TAS 7000 AUSTRALIA.
ALLEN, Miss. Louise Tracey Ann, BSc ACA *1991;* 33 Millbrook Mews, LYTHAM ST.ANNES, FY8 5AU.
ALLEN, Mr. Luke, ACA *1997;* F R M Investment Management Ltd, PO Box 173, GUERNSEY, GY1 4HG.
ALLEN, Mr. Marcus William Kendrick, BA ACA *2000;* 2 Primrose Cottages, 31 Victoria Road, Mortimer Common, READING, RG7 3SJ.
ALLEN, Mr. Mark Anthony, BSc ACA *1992;* Goldman Sachs Peterborough Court, 133 Fleet Street, LONDON, EC4A 2BB.
ALLEN, Mr. Mark David, BSc(Hons) ACA *2003;* with B & P Accounting, Kingsley House, Church Lane, Shurdington, CHELTENHAM, GL51 4TQ.
ALLEN, Mr. Mark Jonathan, BSc ACA *2000;* with Deloitte LLP, Abbots House, Abbey Street, READING, RG1 3BD.
ALLEN, Miss. Martha Louise, BSc ACA *2002;* 15a Montrose Way, Nollamara, PERTH, WA 6061, AUSTRALIA.
ALLEN, Mr. Martin Cross, MA FCA *1961;* 520 Endsleigh Court, Upper Woburn Place, LONDON, WC1H 0HJ. (Life Member)
ALLEN, Mr. Martin Derek, BA ACA *1982;* Apple Tree Lodge, 3 The Green, Park Lane, Old Knebworth, KNEBWORTH, HERTFORDSHIRE SG3 6QN.
•ALLEN, Mr. Matthew, ACA *2006;* Synergee Limited, 2nd Floor, 8 Lonsdale Gardens, TUNBRIDGE WELLS, KENT, TN1 1NU.
ALLEN, Mr. Matthew Robert, BSc ACA *2001;* Rosecote, 15 Station Road, Huyton, LIVERPOOL, L36 4HU.
ALLEN, Mr. Melvyn James, BSc ACA *1999;* 69 Marlpit Lane, COULSDON, SURREY, CR5 2HF.
ALLEN, Mr. Michael, BA ACA *1997;* 1 High Ash Avenue, LEEDS, LS17 8RS.
ALLEN, Mr. Michael Derek, BSc FCA *1977;* Manor Cottage, Farley Lane, Braishfield, ROMSEY, SO51 0QL.
ALLEN, Mr. Michael James, ACA *2010;* 106 Queen Elizabeths Drive, LONDON, N14 6RE.
ALLEN, Mr. Michael James Wilfred, FCA *1969;* Varclin House, Le Varclin, St. Martin, GUERNSEY, GY4 6AL. (Life Member)
ALLEN, Mr. Michael John, BA ACA *1981;* Advanced Interactive Systems Inc., 665 Andover Park West, TUKWILA, WA 98188, UNITED STATES.
•ALLEN, Mr. Michael John, FCA *1973;* (Tax Fac), 31 St. James's Place, LONDON, SW1A 1NR.
ALLEN, Mr. Michael Phillip, MA FCA *1972;* C/o Deloitte & Touche, Lit K Gustaf Bus Centre, 36/40 Sredniy Prospect, 199004 ST PETERSBURG, RUSSIAN FEDERATION.
•ALLEN, Mr. Michael Robert, FCA *1973;* Gorings, 34 Station Road, Sandiacre, NOTTINGHAM, NG10 5BG.
•ALLEN, Mr. Michael Stuart, BSc ACA *1996;* Allen Consulting Limited, 9 St. Helier Close, WOKINGHAM, BERKSHIRE, RG41 2HA.
ALLEN, Mrs. Michelle Katie, BA ACA CTA *2006;* with Wright Vigar Limited, 15 Newland, LINCOLN, LN1 1XG.
ALLEN, Ms. Miranda Clare, BA ACA ACCA *2001;* with PricewaterhouseCoopers LLP, 1 Embankment Place, LONDON, WC2N 6RH.
ALLEN, Mr. Neal, MA BA ACA *2001;* Caird Capital 3rd Floor Exchange Place 3, 3 Semple Street, EDINBURGH, EH3 8BL.
ALLEN, Mr. Neil Adrian, BA ACA *1995;* 41 rue du Bois de Boulogne, 92200 NEUILLY-SUR-SEINE, FRANCE.
•ALLEN, Mr. Neil Angus, FCA *1968;* N.A. Allen, 2 Dewhurst Terrace, Sunniside, NEWCASTLE UPON TYNE, NE16 5LP.
ALLEN, Mr. Nicholas, BSc(Econ) ACA *1998;* 6 Lamberhurst Road, MAIDSTONE, ME16 0NS.
ALLEN, Mr. Nicholas Charles, MA FCA *1987;* with PricewaterhouseCoopers, omladinskih brigada 88a, 11070 BELGRADE, SERBIA.
ALLEN, Mr. Nicholas Charles, BA FCA *1981;* Flat 0995, 9/F Block 18, HONG KONG SAR Parkview, 88 Tai Tam Reservoir Road, TAI TAM, HONG KONG ISLAND HONG KONG SAR.
ALLEN, Mr. Nicholas Chatterton, FCA *1960;* 13 Caledonia Place, Clifton, BRISTOL, BS8 4DJ. (Life Member)
ALLEN, Mr. Nicholas John, BSc ACA *1990;* with PricewaterhouseCoopers GmbH, Elsenheimerstrasse 31-33, D-80687 MUNICH, GERMANY.
ALLEN, Mr. Nigel Craig, FCA *1982;* 215 Mudford Road, YEOVIL, BA21 4NL.
ALLEN, Mr. Norman Stanley, FCA *1961;* Fairview, 37 Clarence Road, RAYLEIGH, SS6 8TA. (Life Member)
ALLEN, Mr. Patrick Guy, FCA *1953;* Normandie, 9 Sandy Lane, Charlton Kings, CHELTENHAM, GL53 9BS. (Life Member)
ALLEN, Mr. Patrick William, FCA *1971;* 293 Castle Road, SALISBURY, SP1 3SB. (Life Member)
ALLEN, Mr. Paul, FCA *1975;* Dingle House, Blackburn Road, Edgworth Turton, BOLTON, BL7 0QE.
ALLEN, Mr. Paul Ross, ACA *2009;* 14 St. Michaels Lane, Longstanton, CAMBRIDGE, CB24 3DD.
ALLEN, Mr. Pelham Brian, MA FCA FIFT *1976;* Staffordlodge Ltd, Yeldon, Higher Eype, BRIDPORT, DORSET, DT6 6AT.
ALLEN, Mr. Peter, BA FCA *1979;* PACIFIC CENTURY REGIONAL DEVELOPMENTS LIMITED, 6 BATTERY ROAD, #38-02, SINGAPORE 049909, SINGAPORE.
ALLEN, Mr. Peter James, BA(Hons) ACA *2004;* 57 Millais Road, ENFIELD, EN1 1EF.
ALLEN, Mr. Peter James Russell, BA ACA *1988;* Olympic Gymnasium Services, Greatworth Park, Welsh Lane, Greatworth, BANBURY, OXFORDSHIRE OX17 2HB.
ALLEN, Mr. Peter John, BSc ACA *1987;* Pedley House, Pedley Hill, Adlington, MACCLESFIELD, CHESHIRE, SK10 4LB.
ALLEN, Mr. Peter John, BCom FCA *1972;* Lindens, 19 Berwick Road, MARLOW, SL7 3AR.
ALLEN, Mr. Peter John, BA ACA *1986;* 42 Silver Crescent, LONDON, W4 5SE.
•ALLEN, Mr. Peter John, FCA *1996;* (Tax Fac), Meades Consulting LLP, 39 The Metro Centre, Tolpits Lane, WATFORD, WD18 9SB.
ALLEN, Mr. Peter Richard, MA FCA *1969;* 38 Blunts Wood Road, HAYWARDS HEATH, RH16 1NB. (Life Member)
ALLEN, Mr. Peter Richard, BA ACA *1984;* 25 King Edwards Gardens, Acton Hill, LONDON, W3 9RF.
ALLEN, Mr. Peter Robert, BSc FCA *1976;* Mercer & Hole, 72 London Road, ST. ALBANS, HERTFORDSHIRE, AL1 1NS.
ALLEN, Mr. Peter Robert, FCA *1949;* Bankside, Chandos Street, Winchcombe, CHELTENHAM, GL54 5HX. (Life Member)
ALLEN, Mr. Peter Vance, BA ACA *1981;* 24 Charnham Street, HUNGERFORD, BERKSHIRE, RG17 0EJ.
ALLEN, Mr. Peter William, FCA *1971;* 4 Fields End Farm Cottages, Pouchen End Lane, HEMEL HEMPSTEAD, HERTFORDSHIRE, HP1 2SD. (Life Member)
ALLEN, Mr. Peter William, MA FCA *1966;* Great Torr Barn, Kingston, KINGSBRIDGE, DEVON, TQ7 4HA.
ALLEN, Mr. Philip, BSc ACA *1983;* 405 Brighton Avenue, SPRING LAKE, NJ 07762, UNITED STATES.
ALLEN, Mr. Philip John, MA ACA *1995;* Hays Personnel Services, (Australia) Pty Ltd, Level 11 Chifley Tower, Chifley Square, SYDNEY, NSW 2001 AUSTRALIA.
ALLEN, Mr. Philip Richmond John, ACA *1984;* 30 Breakspear Avenue, ST. ALBANS, AL1 5EL.
•①ALLEN, Mr. Phillip Hartland, BSc FCA *1982;* Debt Lifeboat Limited, Centre City Tower, 7 Hill Street, BIRMINGHAM, B5 4UU. See also Baker Tilly Restructuring and Recovery LLP
•ALLEN, Mrs. Priscilla Jane, BA ACA *1988;* (Tax Fac), Smartie & Co Limited, Rosewood, Gt. Ponton Road, Boothby Pagnell, GRANTHAM, NG33 4DH.
ALLEN, Mrs. Rachel Elizabeth, BA ACA *1995;* PO Box 522, DUBAI, UNITED ARAB EMIRATES.
ALLEN, Mr. Richard Andrew, ACA *2008;* 13 Buxton Avenue, Caversham, READING, RG4 7BT.
ALLEN, Mr. Richard Anthony, FCA *1972;* The Long Barn, Bainton, BICESTER, OXFORDSHIRE, OX27 8RL.
ALLEN, Mr. Richard Batley, FCA *1976;* 2 Burton Acres Way, Kirkburton, HUDDERSFIELD, HD8 0RF.
•ALLEN, Mr. Richard James, FCA *1987;* Jamesons Ltd, Jamesons House, Compton Way, WITNEY, OXFORDSHIRE, OX28 3AB.
•ALLEN, Mr. Richard James, BA ACA *1997;* Bag End, 2 Les Ozouets Farm Court Skins Lane, St Peter Port, GUERNSEY, GY1 1SA.
•ALLEN, Mr. Richard John, BCom FCA ATT *1970;* (Tax Fac), Richard J Allen, Glengarry Lodge, INVERGARRY, INVERNESS-SHIRE, PH35 4HG.
ALLEN, Mr. Richard Keith, MA ACA *1990;* 144 Ramsden Road, LONDON, SW12 8RE.
ALLEN, Mr. Richard Martin, FCA *1967;* 22 Cornwallis Avenue, Clifton, BRISTOL, BS8 4PP.
•ALLEN, Mr. Richard Myrddin Vaughan, FCA *1979;* Fawcetts, Windover House, St Ann Street, SALISBURY, SP1 2DR.
ALLEN, Mr. Richard Nigel, BA FCA *1968;* 156a Westbury Road, Westbury-on-Trym, BRISTOL, BS9 3AL.
ALLEN, Mr. Richard Nigel De Garrs, ACA *1979;* (Tax Fac), Hydrainer Holdings Ltd, Rotherham Close, Norwood Industrial Estate, Killamarsh, SHEFFIELD, S21 2JU.
ALLEN, Mr. Richard Oliver, BCom ACA *2004;* Tate & Lyle Ltd Sugar Quay, Lower Thames Street, LONDON, EC3R 6DQ.
ALLEN, Mr. Richard Paul, BA(Hons) ACA *2002;* 170 Fawe Park Road, LONDON, SW15 2EQ.
ALLEN, Mr. Richard Thomas, FCA *1957;* 28 Victoria Road, DORCHESTER, DT1 1SB. (Life Member)
ALLEN, Mr. Robert John, ACA *1986;* 54A Dornton Road, Balham, LONDON, SW12 9NE.
ALLEN, Mr. Robert John, BSc ACA *1991;* Victoria Cottage, Oakfield Road, Hatherleigh, OKEHAMPTON, DEVON, EX20 3JT.
ALLEN, Mr. Robert Michael, BCom FCA *1989;* 30 Lyttelton Road, DROITWICH, WORCESTERSHIRE, WR9 7AB.
•ALLEN, Mr. Robert Michael John, FCA *1966;* Allen Thornton Springer, 67 Westow Street, Upper Norwood, LONDON, SE19 3RW.
•①ALLEN, Mr. Robert Preston James, BSc ACA *1991;* Vantage, Lower Ground Floor, 20-24 Kirby Street, LONDON, EC1N 8TS.
ALLEN, Mr. Robert William Edward, BSc FCA *1976;* (Tax Fac), Salem House, Salem, Long Buckby, NORTHAMPTON, NN6 7QD.
•①ALLEN, Mr. Robin David, BA FCA *1990;* with Deloitte LLP, 3 Rivergate, Temple Quay, BRISTOL, BS1 6GD.
ALLEN, Mr. Roger, FCA *1966;* 8 Dauphine Close, COALVILLE, LE67 4QQ.
ALLEN, Mr. Roger David, BSc FCA *1991;* 11 Ruskin Drive, ORPINGTON, KENT, BR6 9RP.
ALLEN, Mrs. Rosalyn Margaret Dorothy, BSc ACA *1991;* 76 Palace Road, LONDON, SW2 3JX.
ALLEN, Mr. Ross Hopwood, FCA *1957;* Rasterac, 32480 BERRAC, FRANCE. (Life Member)
ALLEN, Mrs. Samantha Marie, BSc ACA *1994;* 5 Hall Park Gate, BERKHAMSTED, HERTFORDSHIRE, HP4 2NL.
ALLEN, Mr. Samuel David, BSc ACA *2010;* 43d Windsor Road, TEDDINGTON, MIDDLESEX, TW11 0SG.
ALLEN, Mrs. Sara Elizabeth, BCom ACA *1992;* Warwick International Ltd Coast Road, Mostyn, HOLYWELL, CLWYD, CH8 9HE.
ALLEN, Mrs. Sarah Elizabeth, BA ACA *1997;* Berry Barn, Paradise, Painswick, STROUD, GLOUCESTERSHIRE, GL6 6TN.
ALLEN, Mrs. Sarah Lillian, BSc ACA *1989;* 90 Glenridge Drive, COOROIBAH, QLD 4565, AUSTRALIA.
ALLEN, Mrs. Sian Elise, BA(Hons) ACA *2001;* (Tax Fac), with PricewaterhouseCoopers LLP, 9 Greyfriars Road, READING, RG1 1JG.
ALLEN, Mrs. Sian Elizabeth, BSc(Hons) ACA *2001;* 38 Park Avenue, WREXHAM, CLWYD, LL12 7AH.
ALLEN, Mr. Simon Lucien, FCA *1974;* 49 Belmore Lane, LYMINGTON, HAMPSHIRE, SO41 3NR.
ALLEN, Miss. Stephanie, BSc(Hons) ACA *2010;* Deloitte Llp, 4 Brindley Place, BIRMINGHAM, B1 2HZ.
•ALLEN, Mr. Stephen Albert, FCA CTA *1964;* Payne & Co, 76 Grove Vale Avenue, Great Barr, BIRMINGHAM, B43 6BZ.
ALLEN, Mr. Stephen Charles, FCA *1989;* 1 Craig Street, WEMBLEY DOWNS, WA 6019, AUSTRALIA.
ALLEN, Mr. Stephen Graham Stafford, FCA *1976;* Brown & Co, The Atrium, St. Georges Street, NORWICH, NR3 1AB.
•ALLEN, Mr. Stephen James, ACA *1999;* Allen Accounting, 57 Dartmouth Road, RUISLIP, MIDDLESEX, HA4 0DE.
ALLEN, Mr. Stephen John, BSc FCA *1974;* 8 Long Road, CAMBRIDGE, CB2 8PS.
ALLEN, Mr. Stephen John, MSc BSc ACA *2004;* 52b Church Road, Wootton, BEDFORD, MK43 9HF.
ALLEN, Mr. Stephen Nicholas, BA ACA *1992;* 29 Ryelands Close, MARKET HARBOROUGH, LEICESTERSHIRE, LE16 7XE.
•ALLEN, Mr. Stephen Raymond, FCA *1982;* (Tax Fac), Stephen R. Allen & Co, Appletree Court, 2A Vicarage Lane, HESSLE, HU13 9LQ.
•ALLEN, Mr. Steven David, BEng FCA *1995;* (Tax Fac), David Allen, Dalmar House, Barras Lane Estate, Dalston, CARLISLE, CA5 7NY. See also David Allen & Co
ALLEN, Mrs. Suzanne Jane, ACA *2003;* Alliance & Leicester Plc, Bridle Road, BOOTLE, MERSEYSIDE, L30 4GB.
•ALLEN, Mrs. Tanya Louise, BA ACA *1999;* (Tax Fac), Allen Accountancy Services, Unit 13 Gwenfro Units, Wrexham Technology Park, WREXHAM, CLWYD, LL13 7YP.
ALLEN, Mr. Thomas Alexander, BA ACA *2003;* 40 High Street, Otford, SEVENOAKS, TN14 5PQ.
ALLEN, Mr. Thomas William, FCA *1955;* Willowside, Elmstead Road, WEST BYFLEET, KT14 6JB. (Life Member)
ALLEN, Mr. Tim, BA ACA CF *2002;* with PricewaterhouseCoopers LLP, Pricewaterhousecoopers, 12 Plumtree Court, LONDON, EC4A 4HT.
•ALLEN, Mr. Timothy Andrew Mark, ACA CTA MAAT *1993;* Bennett Jones & Co, 22 Victoria Road, ST AUSTELL, CORNWALL, PL25 4QD.
ALLEN, Mr. Timothy Charles, BEng ACA CTA *2004;* 6th Floor, K P M G Llp, 15 Canada Square, LONDON, E14 5GL.
•ALLEN, Mr. Timothy James, BSc FCA *1989;* Flat B, 7 Charles Street, LONDON, W1J 5DQ.
ALLEN, Mr. Timothy Paul, BSc ACA *1994;* Motorola Limited Unit A2 Linhay Business Park, Eastern Road, ASHBURTON, DEVON, TQ13 7UP.
ALLEN, Mr. Timothy Peter, BSc FCA *1980;* Crusader Wing Brocksford, Doveridge, ASHBOURNE, DERBYSHIRE, DE6 5PA.
•ALLEN, Mr. Timothy Peter Graystoke, FCA *1977;* C.B. Heslop & Co, 1 High Street, THATCHAM, RG19 3JG.
ALLEN, Mrs. Vanessa Michelle, BSc ACA *1999;* 1 Abell Way, Chelmer Village, CHELMSFORD, CM2 6WU.
•ALLEN, Miss. Vivien Margaret, FCA *1973;* Allen Consulting, 96a Hillside Road, Portishead, BRISTOL, BS20 8LJ.
ALLEN, Mr. Wilfred Jonathan, MA FCA *1968;* 14 Newland Park Close, YORK, YO10 3HW.
ALLEN, Mr. William Edmund, FCA *1947;* 9 The Firs, Fulshaw Park, WILMSLOW, CHESHIRE, SK9 1QH. (Life Member)
ALLEN, Mr. William George, FCA *1960;* 7 Wendover Lodge, Church Street, WELWYN, HERTFORDSHIRE, AL6 9LR.
ALLEN, Mrs. Yvette Heather, ACA *1989;* with Deloitte LLP, Athene Place, 66 Shoe Lane, LONDON, EC4A 3BQ.
ALLEN-CHITWA, Mrs. Audrey Marie, BSc ACA *1993;* (Tax Fac), National Union of Teachers Hamilton House, Mabledon Place, LONDON, WC1H 9BD.
ALLENBY, Miss. Kirstie, BSc ACA *2003;* 710 Beverley Road, HULL, HU6 7JG.

ALLENBY, Mr. Michael, ACA *1993;* Fun Life Sports Ltd, Street 6, Villa 19, DUBAI, UNITED ARAB EMIRATES.

•**ALLENBY, Mr. Simon Michael, BA FCA** *1993;* Clifford Fry & Co LLP, St. Marys House, Netherhampton, SALISBURY, SP2 8PU. See also Clifford Fry & Co (Payroll) Limited

ALLENSTEIN, Mr. Spencer Jonathan, BSc ACA *1983;* POB 23601, 91236 JERUSALEM, ISRAEL.

ALLERTON, Mr. Neil Richard, BA ACA *1994;* 24 Sudeley Street, LONDON, N1 8HP.

ALLERTON, Mr. Thomas, BA ACA *2004;* 80 Albert Road, LONDON, N22 7AH.

ALLERTON-AUSTIN, Miss. Caroline Victoria, BAcc ACA *2005;* 5 Gerard Place, Groombridge Road, LONDON, E9 7DG.

ALLES, Mr. Francis Leonard Cuthbert, FCA *1966;* 167 Preston Hill, Kenton, HARROW, MIDDLESEX, HA3 9UY. (Life Member)

ALLEWELL, Mr. Jonathan Richard, BSc ACA *1994;* Augusta, Long Mill Lane, Platt, SEVENOAKS, KENT, TN15 8LZ.

ALLEWELL, Mrs. Sarah Jane, BA ACA *1995;* Augusta Long Mill Lane, Platt, SEVENOAKS, TN15 8LZ.

•**ALLEY, Mr. Charles Robert Trystram, BSc FCA** *1986;* Tryall Ltd, 2 Lower Mount Street, Elvertham Heath, FLEET, HAMPSHIRE, GU51 1BN. See also Trystram Alley & Co

ALLEYNE, Mr. Austin Scott, FCA *1975;* 4th floor Victoria House, Victoria Road, CHELMSFORD, CM1 1JR.

ALLEYNE, Mr. Hugo Sean, BA ACA *1998;* 6 Manor Road, RICHMOND, TW9 1YB.

ALLEYNE, Miss. Kelda Perdita, BSc FCA *1993;* 4 Westwood Place, Westwood Hill, LONDON, SE26 6PF.

ALLFORD, Mr. Rodger Francis, FCA *1970;* Cucarres 2-A-2, BP 21006, 03710 CALPE, ALICANTE, SPAIN.

ALLFORD, Mr. Simon John, MA ACA ACIS *1993;* The Childrens Mutual, Brockbourne House, 77 Mount Ephraim, TUNBRIDGE WELLS, KENT, TN4 8GN.

ALLFORD, Mr. Trevor Godfrey, FCA *1960;* La Corbiere, 27 Copse Edge, CRANLEIGH, SURREY, GU6 7DU. (Life Member)

ALLFREY, Mr. Mark David John, BSc FCA *1989;* 16 The Strand, Gladesville, SYDNEY, NSW 2111, AUSTRALIA.

ALLFREY, Mr. Peter Charles Scudamore, FCA *1965;* Dolphin Lodge, Rowdefield, DEVIZES, WILTSHIRE, SN10 2JD.

ALLGOOD, Mr. Glen, BA ACA *1997;* 16 Central Way, OXTED, RH8 0LS.

ALLI, Mr. Andrew, MBA BEng ACA *1992;* 9160 Carriage House Lane, SILVER SPRING, MD 21045, UNITED STATES.

ALLI, Mr. Khalil Gibran, MSc FCA *2000;* Jack A. Alli Sons & Co, 145 Crown Street, GEORGETOWN, 6, GUYANA.

•**ALLI, Mr. Ronald Muntaz, FCA** *1972;* (Tax Fac), Jack A. Alli Sons & Co, 145 Crown Street, GEORGETOWN, 6, GUYANA.

•**ALLIBAN, Mr. Richard Douglas, FCA** *1964;* (Tax Fac), Stacey & Partners, 30 Bridge Street, THETFORD, NORFOLK, IP24 3AG.

ALLIBHAI, Mr. Salim Sadrudin, FCA *1977;* 1620 96 Avenue sw, CALGARY T2V 5E5, AB, CANADA.

ALLIBONE, Mrs. Jennifer Elaine, BSc ACA *1993;* 115 Lakeside Way, Nantyglo, EBBW VALE, GWENT, NP23 4EN.

•**ALLIBONE, Mr. Rupert Henry, FCA** *1957;* Rupert H Allibone FCA, Hunters View, Stemborough Lane, Leire, LUTTERWORTH, LE17 5EX.

ALLIN, Mr. Brian Reginald, FCA *1968;* 19a Luton Road, Wilstead, BEDFORD, MK45 3EP.

ALLIN, Mr. Robert Edward, ACA *1993;* 35 Dunstal Field, Cottenham, CAMBRIDGE, CB4 8UH.

ALLINGHAM, Mr. David Spencer, FCA *1970;* Cuttinglye Hophurst Hill, Crawley Down, CRAWLEY, RH10 4LP. (Life Member)

ALLINGHAM, Mr. William, BSc FCA *1973;* Scope Medical Ltd, Tubs Hill House, London Road, SEVENOAKS, KENT, TN13 1BL.

ALLINSON, Mr. Iain, ACA *2011;* 105 Engadine Street, Southfields, LONDON, SW18 5DU.

ALLINSON, Mr. Nicholas Mark, BA ACA *1997;* Daisy House, Daisy Communications Ltd, 1 Lindred Road Brierfield, NELSON, BB9 5SR.

•**ALLINSON, Mr. Richard George, FCA** *1979;* Rippington House, Hemington, PETERBOROUGH, PE8 5QJ.

ALLISON, Mr. Alan, FCA *1954;* 45 Bushbys Lane, Formby, LIVERPOOL, L37 2DY. (Life Member)

ALLISON, Mr. Alec James, FCA *1949;* Kettles, Kinsbourne Green Lane, Kinsbourne Green, HARPENDEN, HERTFORDSHIRE, AL5 3PF. (Life Member)

ALLISON, Mrs. Anna Frances, BA FCA *1992;* 44 Chapel Road, Morley St. Botolph, WYMONDHAM, NORFOLK, NR18 9TF.

ALLISON, Mr. Anthony Richard, BA ACA *1990;* Bilsdale Properties Ltd, 12 Bruntcliffe Way, Morley, LEEDS, LS27 0JG.

ALLISON, Mrs. Caroline Ann, ACA *1996;* Brookfield, Ipswich Road, Brantham, MANNINGTREE, ESSEX, CO11 1PB.

ALLISON, Mr. Colin, FCA *1955;* 56 St. Johns Street, YORK, YO31 7QT. (Life Member)

ALLISON, Mr. David, BSc FCA *1995;* UK Head Office, Adey Ltd, Gloucester Road, CHELTENHAM, GL51 8NR.

ALLISON, Mr. David Martin, FCA *1965;* Allison & Associates, 31 Mentone Road, PO Box 30, PORT ALFRED, 6170, SOUTH AFRICA.

ALLISON, Mr. Douglas Forbes, BSc ACA *1980;* 77 Gracechurch Street, LONDON, EC3V 0AS.

ALLISON, Mr. Harold, MA FCA *1954;* 25 Algarth Road, Pocklington, YORK, YO42 2HP. (Life Member)

ALLISON, Mrs. Jane Elizabeth, BSc ACA *1987;* 59 Harrow View, HARROW, MIDDLESEX, HA1 1RF.

•**ALLISON, Mr. Jeremy Neil, BSc FCA CF** *1987;* Smailes Goldie, Regents Court, Princess Street, HULL, HU2 8BA.

ALLISON, Mr. John, FCA JDipMA *1956;* 16 Urquhart Drive, GOUROCK, PA19 1JG. (Life Member)

ALLISON, Mr. John Clive, BA ACA *1980;* 55 Midwood Street, BROOKLYN, NY 11225, UNITED STATES.

ALLISON, Mr. John James, MEng ACA *2005;* 18 Kay Road, LONDON, SW9 9DE.

ALLISON, Mr. John Michael, FCA *1974;* Greenloanin, Balchristie, Colinsburgh, LEVEN, FIFE, KY9 1HE.

ALLISON, Mr. John Richard, FCA *1968;* 11741 NW 11th Street, Plantation, FORT LAUDERDALE, FL 33323, UNITED STATES.

ALLISON, Mrs. Julie Anne, BSc ACA *1995;* 34 Broadlands, Cleadon, SUNDERLAND, SR6 7RD.

ALLISON, Mr. Mark Stuart, ACA *1983;* 1 Felix Manor, Old Perry Street, CHISLEHURST, KENT, BR7 6PL.

ALLISON, Mr. Neil Marvin, BA ACA *1994;* Brookfield, Ipswich Road, Brantham, MANNINGTREE, ESSEX, CO11 1PB.

•**ALLISON, Mr. Nigel Douglass, FCA** *1980;* (Tax Fac), Nigel Allison Ltd, Bridge Farmhouse, Crowfield Road, Coddenham, IPSWICH, IP6 9PX.

ALLISON, Mr. Raymond Tollit, FCA *1970;* 3 Palmerston Court, 48 Palmerston Road, BUCKHURST HILL, IG9 5LJ.

ALLISON, Mr. Richard John, BSc ACA *1982;* 15 The Avenue, WEST WICKHAM, BR4 0DX.

ALLISON, Mr. Richard Lewis, BSc FCA *1976;* 651 Bury Road, Bamford, ROCHDALE, OL11 4AU.

ALLISON, Mr. Robert Andrew, BSc FCA *1975;* Mill House, Nutbourne, PULBOROUGH, RH20 2HE.

ALLISON, Mr. Rodney, FCA *1969;* Walnut Barn, Gussage St Michael, WIMBORNE, DORSET, BH21 5HX.

ALLISON, Mr. Simon Christian, BSc ACA *2004;* Smith & Nephew Ltd, 101 Hessle Road, HULL, HU3 2BN.

ALLISON, Mr. Simon George, BSc ACA *1990;* 21 College Glen, MAIDENHEAD, SL6 6BL.

•**ALLISTON, Mr. James Douglas Edward, BA FCA** *1990;* CFO Services Asia Pte Limited, 114 Taman Permata, Yew Lian Park, SINGAPORE 575237, SINGAPORE.

ALLISTON, Mr. Paul Frederick, FCA *1968;* 1201 Botany Hill, OAKVILLE L6J 6J5, ON, CANADA.

•**ALLISTON-GREINER, Mr. Clement Richard, BA ACA** *1986;* Moore Stephens LLP, 150 Aldersgate Street, LONDON, EC1A 4AB. See also Moore Stephens & Co

ALLISTONE, Mr. Peter William, FCA *1975;* 6 Faraday House, Queenswood Avenue, HAMPTON, TW12 3AP.

ALLITT, Mr. David John, FCA *1973;* Porch Cottage, Elmhurst, LICHFIELD, STAFFORDSHIRE, WS13 8HA.

ALLIX, Mr. Ian James Louis, FCA *1977;* 31 Treesmill Drive, Cox Green, MAIDENHEAD, SL6 3HR.

ALLIX, Mr. Stephen Robert, BSc(Econ) ACA *2000;* 20 Harlington Road, BEXLEYHEATH, DA7 4AS.

ALLKINS, Mr. Thomas Stewart, BSc ACA *2001;* 23 Kingswood Court, Brewery Road, WOKING, SURREY, GU21 4LJ.

ALLMAN, Mr. Andrew John, BSc ACA *1990;* 5 The Green, Diseworth, DERBY, DE74 2QN.

ALLMAN, Mr. Benjamin, MA(Hons) ACA *2010;* Whitley Stimpson Llp Penrose House, 67 Hightown Road, BANBURY, OXFORDSHIRE, OX16 9BE.

ALLMAN, Mr. Christopher Alan, BSc FCA *1976;* 14 Reedley Drive, Worsley, MANCHESTER, M28 7XR.

•**ALLMAN, Mr. David Malcolm, FCA** *1991;* (Tax Fac), Pheonix Consultancy Limited, 17 Collinbrook Avenue, CREWE, CHESHIRE, CW2 6PN.

ALLMAN, Mr. Eric Brian, BSc ACA *1981;* 24 Frog Lane, Titchfield, FAREHAM, PO14 4DU.

ALLMAN, Mr. Geoffrey Colin, FCA *1950;* 31 Arley Road, SOLIHULL, B91 1NJ. (Life Member)

ALLMAN, Mr. George Ernest, FCA *1960;* 1 Boscombe Drive, Hazel Grove, STOCKPORT, SK7 5JA. (Life Member)

ALLMAN, Mr. Ian James, MPhys MSc ACA *2006;* 9 Plateau Close, HORNSBY HEIGHTS, NSW 2077, AUSTRALIA.

ALLMAN, Mrs. Jeanette Lynne, BSc ACA *1997;* 5 Chelney Walk, Binley, COVENTRY, CV3 2XR.

ALLMAN, Mr. Michael Edward, ACA *2008;* with PricewaterhouseCoopers LLP, 1 Embankment Place, LONDON, WC2N 6RH.

ALLMAN, Mr. Michael William, FCA *1963;* 12 Mill Green Court, LYME REGIS, DORSET, DT7 3PJ. (Life Member)

ALLMAN, Mr. Richard Kenneth, MA FCA *1997;* National Grid, National Grid House, Warwick Technology Park, Gallows Hill, WARWICK, CV34 6DA.

ALLMAN, Mr. Robert Holker, FCA *1959;* Stadbury Grange, Aveton Gifford, KINGSBRIDGE, TQ7 4PD. (Life Member)

ALLMAN, Mr. Timothy John, FCA *1991;* with PricewaterhouseCoopers, Riverside Centre, 123 Eagle Street, GPO Box 150, BRISBANE, QLD 4001 AUSTRALIA.

ALLMAN-WARD, Mr. Antony Peter, BSc FCA *1973;* 800 West First St, Apt 2508, LOS ANGELES, CA 90012-2433, UNITED STATES.

ALLMAND-SMITH, Mr. Timothy Paull, FCA *1965;* Hilltop House, Chichester Road, MIDHURST, WEST SUSSEX, GU29 9PZ.

ALLMARK, Miss. Erica Gillian, BSc ACA *1981;* 201 Walter Havill Drive, Suite 405, HALIFAX B3N 3J4, NS, CANADA.

ALLMOND, Mr. Richard, ACA *1982;* 27 Braybourne Drive, ISLEWORTH, TW7 5EL.

ALLNER, Mr. Andrew James, BA FCA *1979;* 9 The Crescent, LONDON, SW13 0NN.

ALLNER, Mrs. Susan Isabel, BA ACA *1982;* 9 The Crescent, Barnes, LONDON, SW13 0NN.

ALLNER, Mr. Thomas Charles, BSc ACA *2011;* 11 Chalkpit Lane, DORKING, SURREY, RH4 1EZ.

ALLNUTT, Mr. Derek Peter, FCA *1969;* 19 Arun Way, West Wellow, ROMSEY, HAMPSHIRE, SO51 6GT.

ALLNUTT, Mrs. Julia Anne, ACA *2003;* 41 Crane Drive, VERWOOD, DORSET, BH31 6QB.

ALLON, Mr. Sebastian George Anthony, BSc ACA *1998;* 24 Clavering Avenue, LONDON, SW13 8DY.

ALLPASS, Mr. James Rodney, BSc ACA *1992;* Imago Publishing Ltd, Albury Court, Albury, THAME, OXFORDSHIRE, OX9 2LP.

•**ALLPORT, Mr. James Askew, FCA** *1972;* Orchard House, Houghton, STOCKBRIDGE, SO20 6LT.

ALLPORT, Mr. Jeremy Cole, BA ACA *2001;* The Lodge, Casewick, STAMFORD, LINCOLNSHIRE, PE9 4RX.

ALLPORT, Mr. Peter James, MA ACA *2000;* 71c Nightingale Lane, LONDON, SW12 8LY.

•①**ALLPORT, Mr. Simon, BSc ACA** *1988;* Ernst & Young LLP, 100 Barbirolli Square, MANCHESTER, M2 3EY. See also Ernst & Young Europe LLP

ALLSEBROOK, Miss. Claire Lucy, ACA *1988;* 5326 Ruperts Gate Drive, MISSISSAUGA L5M 5C4, ON, CANADA.

ALLSEBROOK, Mr. David Jeffrey, BSc ACA *1994;* 4 Repton Close, BACUP, LANCASHIRE, OL13 9TF.

ALLSHIRE, Mr. Andrew William, MA BBS ACA *1991;* Chemin des Vignes 10, CH-1806 ST LEGIER, SWITZERLAND.

ALLSO, Mr. Nigel Harry, BSc FCA *1981;* Personal Touch Financial Services Ltd, Trinity 3, Trinity Park, Station Way, BIRMINGHAM, B37 7ES.

ALLSOP, Mrs. Abigail, ACA *2009;* 26 Queenscourt, WEMBLEY, MIDDLESEX, HA9 7QU.

ALLSOP, Mr. Andrew, BA ACA *1990;* Rosemary Hill Farm, Park Lane, HALIFAX, WEST YORKSHIRE, HX3 9JZ.

ALLSOP, Miss. Deborah Joanne Louise, BA(Hons) ACA *2010;* 58 Dorothy Road, LONDON, SW11 2JP.

ALLSOP, Mr. John Myles Lonsdale, BA ACA *2000;* 3 Grove Lane, KINGSTON UPON THAMES, KT1 2SU.

•**ALLSOP, Mr. John Roger, FCA** *1968;* J.R. Allsop, 32 Bryanston Avenue, Whitton, TWICKENHAM, TW2 6HP.

ALLSOP, Mr. Malcolm John, FCA *1968;* 15 Dauphine Close, COALVILLE, LE67 4QQ.

•**ALLSOP, Mr. Mark, BSc ACA** *1993;* Pound House, 55 High Street, Great Barford, BEDFORD, MK44 3JJ.

ALLSOP, Mrs. Melanie Jane, BSc ACA *1994;* Pound House, 55 High Street, Great Barford, BEDFORD, MK44 3JJ.

ALLSOP, Mr. Michael Robert, BA FCA *1975;* 6 Southfield Gardens, Strawberry Hill, TWICKENHAM, TW1 4SZ.

ALLSOP, Mr. Paul David, BA ACA *1987;* (Tax Fac), 7 Fairbourne, COBHAM, SURREY, KT11 2BT.

•**ALLSOP, Mr. Philip Charles, BA FCA** *1986;* Barber Harrison & Platt, 2 Rutland Park, SHEFFIELD, S10 2PD.

ALLSOP, Mrs. Rachel Louise, BA ACA *2008;* 53 Station Road, Penshaw, HOUGHTON LE SPRING, TYNE AND WEAR, DH4 7PS.

ALLSOP, Mr. Richard Leonard, FCA *1976;* 94 Colehill Lane, LONDON, SW6 5EH.

ALLSOP-GUEST, Mrs. Lyn Elizabeth, BA ACA *1992;* 9 Beamish Street, PADSTOW, NSW 2211, AUSTRALIA.

ALLSOPP, Mr. Arthur Leonard, FCA *1946;* 77 Washford Road, Meole Brace, SHREWSBURY, SY3 9HW. (Life Member)

ALLSOPP, Mr. Darren, BA ACA *1993;* 6 Low Farm, Ellington, MORPETH, NE61 5PA.

ALLSOPP, Mr. David Michael, FCA *1969;* Lindrick Cottage, Lindrick Common, WORKSOP, S81 8BA. (Life Member)

ALLSOPP, Mrs. Laura Emily, BA ACA *2007;* 10 Graham Hill Road, TOWCESTER, NORTHAMPTONSHIRE, NN12 7AB.

ALLSOPP, Mr. Michael, BSc ACA *1991;* 2 Broom Lea, Loggerheads, MARKET DRAYTON, TF9 4RE.

ALLSOPP, Mrs. Rachel Elizabeth, BA ACA *1995;* Glanbia Cheese Ltd 4 Royal Mews, Gadbrook Park, NORTHWICH, CW9 7UD.

ALLSOPP, Mr. Richard Malcolm, FCA *1960;* 3 Moss Close, Wickersley, ROTHERHAM, SOUTH YORKSHIRE, S66 1ET. (Life Member)

ALLSOPP, Mr. Steven John, BSc ACA *1996;* 9 Elizabeth Way, KENILWORTH, CV8 1QP.

•**ALLSOPP, Mr. William Doyle, FCA** *1971;* WD & GR Allsopp Ltd, 7 Daisy Close, Bagworth, COALVILLE, LEICESTERSHIRE, LE67 1HP. See also W D Allsopp

ALLUM, Mr. Anthony Restal, FCA *1962;* Bunbury, Dobley Cottages, Redlynch, BRUTON, BA10 0NH.

ALLUM, Mr. Peter Gordon, FCA *1971;* 54 Primrose Path Crescent, MARKHAM L3S 4A9, ON, CANADA.

•**ALLUM, Mrs. Sheila, FCA** *1978;* Turner Peachey, Column House, London Road, SHREWSBURY, SY2 6NN. See also Ridgeway Wall & Co

ALLVEY, Mr. David Philip, FCA *1977;* Flat 1019, Point West, 116 Cromwell Road, Kensington, LONDON, SW7 4XN.

ALLWEIS, Mr. Neil Robert, BA FCA *1977;* 84 Carrwood, Hale Barns, ALTRINCHAM, WA15 0ES.

ALLWELL-BROWN, Mr. Senibo, FCA *1966;* Allwell Brown & Co, 73 Ikwerre Road, P.O. Box 242, PORT HARCOURT, NIGERIA.

•**ALLWOOD, Mr. Andrew Michael, ACA** *1985;* A.M. Allwood, 73 Hallam Road, Moorgate, ROTHERHAM, SOUTH YORKSHIRE, S60 3ED.

•**ALLWOOD, Mrs. Catherine Margaret, BSc FCA** *1977;* (Tax Fac), Cate Allwood, 12 Church Close, Pulham St. Mary, DISS, NORFOLK, IP21 4RR.

ALLWOOD, Mr. Charles John, BA FCA *1977;* 3 Charles Street, BERKHAMSTED, HERTFORDSHIRE, HP4 3DG.

ALLWOOD, Mr. David, BSc ACA *1993;* 3 Orchard Avenue, Bingham, NOTTINGHAM, NG13 8GD.

ALLWOOD, Mr. Mark Stephen, BSc ACA CTA *2002;* with haysmacintyre, Fairfax House, 15 Fulwood Place, LONDON, WC1V 6AY.

ALLWOOD, Miss. Sarah Lucy, ACA *2010;* Flat 12 Spectrum Place, Lytham Street, LONDON, SE17 2GP.

ALLYBOKUS, Mr. Mamode Aniff Elias, FCA *1975;* 16 Pyecombe Corner, Woodside Park, LONDON, N12 7AJ.

ALMAHI, Ms. Tasnim, ACA CA(SA) *2011;* 13 Newfeldt Street, Gelvan Park, PORT ELIZABETH, 6020, SOUTH AFRICA.

ALMAND, Mr. Barry, BCom FCA *1977;* Ridings House, 28-30 West Barnes Lane, LONDON, SW20 0BP.

ALMANDRAS, Mr. Michael, BSc ACA *2009;* Flat 30 Denton House, Halton Road, LONDON, N1 2AE.

ALMANZA, Mr. Ashley Martin, ACA CA(SA) *2008;* B G Group, 100 Thames Valley Park Drive, READING, RG6 1PT.

ALMARRI, Mr. Helal Saeed Salem Khalfan, BA ACA *2001;* Jumeira, PO Box 333419, DUBAI, UNITED ARAB EMIRATES.

ALMEIDA, Mr. Geoffrey William, FCA *1977;* White Lodge, 2 Furze Field, Oxshott, LEATHERHEAD, KT22 0UR.

ALMOND, Mr. Benjamin James, BA ACA *1993;* 1 Upland Drive, Brookmans Park, HATFIELD, AL9 6PS.

ALMOND, Mrs. Carole, ACA *1992;* 21 Ambleside Terrace, SUNDERLAND, SR6 8NP.

ALMOND, Mr. Christopher, BSc ACA *1984;* The American School in London, 1 Waverley Place, LONDON, NW8 0NP.

ALMOND, Mr. David William, FCA *1967;* 11 Oakwood Drive, Sewalls Point, STUART, FL 34996, UNITED STATES.

ALMOND, Mr. Edward Lawrence, MSc FCA MBA *1993;* Kwetu Maiden Street Weston, HITCHIN, HERTFORDSHIRE, SG4 7AA.

ALMOND, Mr. Graeme, BA ACA *1996;* 8 Main Street, Monk Fryston, LEEDS, NORTH YORKSHIRE, LS25 5EG.

•**ALMOND, Mr. Graham John, FCA** *1968;* GJ Almond, 3 Topfield, Popes Lane, COLCHESTER, CO3 3JR.

ALMOND, Mr. Jonathan Mark, BA ACA *1989;* 103 Drayton Road, SUNDERLAND, SR6 8ES.

ALMOND, Mr. Luke, BSc ACA *2011;* 33 West Way, Holmes Chapel, CREWE, CW4 7DG.

ALMOND, Mr. Mark, BSc ACA *2008;* Flat 1, Azura Court, 48 Warton Road, LONDON, E15 2JS.

•**ALMOND, Dr. Martin John, DBA MSc FCA** *1973;* Hatherton Farm, Sampford Courtenay, OKEHAMPTON, DEVON, EX20 2SW.

ALMOND, Mr. Michael David, ACA *2008;* 71 Pine Grove, Church Crookham, FLEET, GU52 6BQ.

ALMOND, Mr. Michael James, BA FCA *1977;* 13-14 Bourton, MUCH WENLOCK, SHROPSHIRE, TF13 6QF.

ALMOND, Dr. Michael Richard, FCA *1983;* The Old Forge, Long Lane Village, Dalbury Lees, ASHBOURNE, DERBYSHIRE, DE6 5BJ.

ALMOND, Mr. Peter, FCA *1964;* Oak Tree Cottage, 4 Chapel Close, Corfe Mullen, WIMBORNE, BH21 3SH.

ALMOND, Mr. Phillip John, BSc ACA *1986;* Groenlaan 3, 3080 TERVUREN, BELGIUM.

•**ALMOND, Mr. Stephen, BA FCA** *1981;* Deloitte LLP, 2 New Street Square, LONDON, EC4A 3BZ. See also Deloitte & Touche LLP

ALMOND, Ms. Susan Christina, BSc FCA *1983;* 5 Honey Hill, Emberton, OLNEY, BUCKINGHAMSHIRE, MK46 5LT.

ALNER, Mr. Brian John, BSc FCA *1987;* 21 Manse Road, Coylton, AYR, KA6 6LD.

ALNER, Mr. Christopher David, BA(Hons) ACA *2000;* 5 Moreton Road, WORCESTER PARK, KT4 8EY.

ALNER, Mr. Michael Geoffrey, BA ACA *1993;* The Cedars Tile Barn, Woolton Hill, NEWBURY, RG20 9UZ.

ALNUAIMI, Mr. Awni Omar, BSc FCA *1975;* PO Box 20074, DOHA, QATAR.

ALOYSIUS, Mr. Jonathan, BSc ACA *2009;* 40 Christie Road, STEVENAGE, HERTFORDSHIRE, SG2 0NG.

ALOYSIUS, Mr. Neil, BEng ACA *2006;* 25 Spirit Quay, LONDON, E1W 2UT.

ALPAR, Mr. Steven Antal, BSc ACA *1995;* 32 Elmete Drive, Oakwood, LEEDS, LS8 2LA.

ALPE, Mr. James Oliver, BA ACA *1988;* Chaldwell Cottage, Church Street, Micheldever, WINCHESTER, HAMPSHIRE, SO21 3DB.

ALPHEY, Dr. Nina, MA DPhil BA FCA *1990;* 65 The Moors, Kidlington, KIDLINGTON, OXFORDSHIRE, OX5 2AJ.

ALPIN, Mrs. Janet, BA FCA *1981;* Thornton & Ross Ltd, Linthwaite Laboratories, Linthwaite, HUDDERSFIELD, HD7 5QH.

ALPIN, Mr. Peter Richard, BSc FCA *1982;* 66 Lightridge Road, Fixby, HUDDERSFIELD, HD2 2HS.

ALRAWI, Mr. Yasir, MSc ACA *2011;* Flat 152 Compass House, Smugglers Way, LONDON, SW18 1DB.

ALS-MCCLEAN, Mr. Merlon Dacosta, BSc FCA *1992;* 14 Rosslyn Crescent, LUTON, LU3 2AU.

ALSAGOFF, Mr. Syed Ahmad B Syed Yusof, ACA *1989;* Block 601 Elias Road, #16-250, SINGAPORE 510601, SINGAPORE.

ALSAGOFF, Mr. Syed Hassan S A B, FCA *1980;* 18-14-2 Sri Mahligai Condominium Jalan Tengku Ampuan Rahimah 9/20, 40100 SHAH ALAM, MALAYSIA.

ALSBURY, Mr. Michael Richard, ACA *2009;* 25 Tanners Mead, EDENBRIDGE, TN8 5JY.

ALSEGAF, Mr. Husin, BSc FCA *1962;* 6008 River Road, BETHESDA, MD 20816-3420, UNITED STATES. (Life Member)

ALSEPT, Mrs. Nicola, BSc ACA *1992;* 58 Kings Field, SEAHOUSES, NORTHUMBERLAND, NE68 7PA.

•**ALSEPT, Mr. Richard James, BA ACA** *1991;* Richard Alsept Limited, 58 Kings Field, Seahouses, SEAHOUSES, NORTHUMBERLAND, NE68 7PA.

ALSFORD, Mr. Michael, BA(Hons) ACA *2003;* 64 Manchuria Road, Battersea, LONDON, SW11 6AE.

ALSOP, Mr. David, FCA *1972;* Chandlers, Church Street, Woodhurst, HUNTINGDON, CAMBRIDGESHIRE, PE28 3BN.

ALSOP, Mrs. Elaine, BA ACA *1998;* Corbiere, 1 Rosebery Place, DUNBAR, EAST LOTHIAN, EH42 1AQ.

ALSOP, Miss. Emma, ACA *2009;* 18 Hopps Lodge Drive, RUGBY, CV21 3UW.

ALSOP, Mr. John William, FCA *1957;* 67 The Fairway, Brunton ParkGosforth, NEWCASTLE UPON TYNE, NE3 5AQ. (Life Member)

ALSOP, Mr. Michael D, BSc FCA *1990;* 9 Frith View, Chapel-En-Le-Frith, HIGH PEAK, SK23 9TL.

ALSOP, Mr. Robert James, BSc(Hons) ACA *2000;* 48 College Avenue, MAIDENHEAD, SL6 6AY.

ALSOP, Mr. Simon James, BA ACA *1994;* 76 Abinger Road, LONDON, W4 1EX.

ALSOP, Mr. Stephen James, BSc ACA *2003;* Johnson & Johnson Medical Ltd Pinewood Campus, Nine Mile Ride, WOKINGHAM, RG40 3EW.

ALSTEAD, Mr. Robert Geoffrey, ACA *1992;* International Greetings UK Limited, Scandinavian Design Ltd 10-12 North Road, Penallta Industrial Estate Penallta, HENGOED, MID GLAMORGAN, CF82 7SS.

ALSTON, Mr. David George, BSc ACA *1991;* Rose Cottage, North Street Village, Nr Theale, READING, RG7 5EZ.

ALSTON, Mr. James Michael Rowland, BA ACA *1992;* Sutton Park House, 15 Carshalton Road, SUTTON, SM1 4LD.

ALSTON, Mr. Rupert Donald, MSc ACA *2001;* 25 Iveley Road, LONDON, SW4 0EN.

ALSTON, Mr. Timothy John, MBE FCA *1976;* 1 Marshlands, Priors Hill Road, ALDEBURGH, IP15 5EP.

ALSTON, Miss. Zena, ACA *2010;* Flat 9, 52 West End Lane, West Hampstead, LONDON, NW6 2NE.

ALTENDORFF, Mr. Frank Russell, BA ACA *1979;* 2 Downland Close, BRIGHTON, BN2 6DN.

ALTHAM, Mr. Richard David, BA ACA ACCA *1996;* PO Box 143, 7 Pearl Street, KENNEBUNKPORT, ME 04046, UNITED STATES.

ALTHASEN, Mr. Gerald Hyman, FCA *1958;* 11 Heathfield House, 2/5 Westcliff Parade, WESTCLIFF-ON-SEA, SS0 7QZ. (Life Member)

ALTINI, Mr. Claudio Massimo, ACA CA(SA) *2010;* 24 Saddleback Way, FLEET, HAMPSHIRE, GU51 2US.

ALTMAN, Mr. Alexander Craig, BA ACA *1995;* 32 Cotton Road, POTTERS BAR, EN6 5JG.

•**ALTMAN, Mr. Jeffrey Allen, FCA** *1977;* (Tax Fac), Jeffrey Altman & Company, Wayman House, 141 Wickham Road, Shirley, CROYDON, CR0 8TE.

•**ALTMAN, Miss. Mikaela Deborah, ACA** *2008;* Jeffrey Altman & Company, Wayman House, 141 Wickham Road, Shirley, CROYDON, CR0 8TE.

ALTMAN, Mrs. Sarah Elizabeth, ACA *1992;* 11 Kewferry Drive, NORTHWOOD, MIDDLESEX, HA6 2NT.

ALTMAN, Mr. Stephen Louis, BA FCA CF *1987;* 77 Dennis Lane, STANMORE, MIDDLESEX, HA7 4JU.

ALTOFT, Mr. Philip James, BSc ACA *1999;* 10 Tiffany Close, WOKINGHAM, RG41 3BN.

ALTOFT, Mr. Robert Derek, BSc ACA *2006;* 49 Emmanuel Road, LONDON, SW12 0HN.

•**ALTON, Mr. Albert Geoffrey Robinson, FCA CTA** *1961;* Hunter Jones Alton, 36 Bridge Street, BELPER, DERBYSHIRE, DE56 1AX.

ALTON, Mr. Brian Walter Barnett, FCA *1959;* 68 Quai Louis Bleriot, 75016 PARIS, FRANCE. (Life Member)

ALTON, Mrs. Esther Miriam, BA ACA *2000;* Bahnrainstrasse 36, 8708 MAENNEDORF, SWITZERLAND.

•**ALTON, Miss. Fiona Elaine Claire, ACA** *2004;* Hunter Jones Alton, 36 Bridge Street, BELPER, DERBYSHIRE, DE56 1AX.

ALTON, Mr. John Philip Parkin, BA ACA *2000;* Bahnrainstrasse 36, 8708 MANNEDORF, SWITZERLAND.

•**ALTON, Mr. Paul, BSc FCA** *1981;* Paul Alton, Admin House, 6 North Street, DROITWICH, WORCESTERSHIRE, WR9 8JB.

ALTON, Mr. Paul Alan, ACA *2009;* 57 The Oval, HARTLEPOOL, CLEVELAND, TS26 9QH.

ALTON, Mr. Richard, FCA *1966;* Old Bank House, Windley, BELPER, DE56 2LP.

ALTON, Mr. Roger David, FCA *1967;* 107 Bramcote Lane, Wollaton, NOTTINGHAM, NG8 2NJ. (Life Member)

ALTON, Mr. Russell Alexander, MA ACA *1997;* Beech House Private Road, Balcombe, HAYWARDS HEATH, WEST SUSSEX, RH17 6PS.

ALTON, Mrs. Sadie Jane, BA(Hons) ACA *2001;* with KPMG LLP, 1 The Embankment, Neville Street, LEEDS, LS1 4DW.

ALTOUNIAN, Mrs. Hera, BSc(Hons) ACA *2001;* PO Box 28532, 2080 NICOSIA, CYPRUS.

ALTY, Mr. Philip William, BA ACA *1989;* Lifeline Ltd, 101-103 Oldham Street, MANCHESTER, M4 1LW.

•**ALUKO, Bishop Joseph Folusho, FCA** *1971;* Joseph Anderson Beadle & Co, 196 High Road, LONDON, N22 8HH.

•**ALUWIHARE, Mr. Duleep Arjuna, BSc FCA** *1983;* Ernst & Young Audit Sp. z.o.o., Rondo ONZ 1, 00-124 WARSAW, POLAND. See also Ernst & Young Europe LLP

•**ALVAREZ, Mr. Harry Lewis, FCA** *1970;* Harry Alvarez FCA, 51 Ranelagh Road, Ealing, LONDON, W5 5RP.

ALVAREZ, Mr. Robin Julian, BSc FCA *1976;* 20 Norfolk Road, LONDON, NW8 6HG.

ALVES GOMES, Miss. Joane Maria, ACA *2011;* Flat 3, 40 Englands Lane, LONDON, NW3 4UE.

ALVEY, Ms. Jane Elizabeth, BA ACA *1991;* 33 St Marys Road, Sindlesham, WOKINGHAM, RG41 5DA.

ALVEY, Miss. Kathryn, BA(Hons) ACA *2002;* 29a Dupree Road, LONDON, SE7 7RR.

ALVEY, Mr. Philip Antony, MA ACA *1999;* Level 36, H S B C, 8-16 Canada Square, LONDON, E14 5HQ.

ALVI, Mr. Ahsan Mahmood, FCA *1974;* 18/II Khayaban-E-Shahbaz, Phase VI Defence Housing Auth, KARACHI 75500, PAKISTAN.

ALVI, Mr. Atif Rahim, BA ACA MBA *2002;* 11-11 Punjab Town, Garden East, KARACHI 74400, PAKISTAN.

ALVI, Mr. Yasser, BSc(Hons) ACA *2001;* c/o Nakheel PJSC, PO Box 17777, DUBAI, UNITED ARAB EMIRATES.

•**ALVIS, Mr. Raymond Blair, FCA** *1977;* (Tax Fac), Sloan & Co, Granite Buildings, 6 Stanley Street, LIVERPOOL, L1 6AF.

ALVIS, Mr. William, BA ACA *2011;* Grove End House, Grove End, BAGSHOT, SURREY, GU19 5HY.

ALWAN-WALKER, Mrs. Kay, MA ACA *2004;* with KPMG LLP, 1 The Embankment, Neville Street, LEEDS, LS1 4DW.

ALWAR, Miss. Karuna, ACA *2011;* 69 Portland Avenue, GRAVESEND, KENT, DA12 5HJ.

ALWEISS, Mr. Manfred, FCA *1951;* 22 Middleton Road, LONDON, NW11 7NS. (Life Member)

AMAH, Mr. Evarist Chukwuma, ACA FCCA *2008;* 40 Memorial Highway, Apt. 19H, NEW ROCHELLE, NY 10801, UNITED STATES.

AMAN, Mr. Raja, FCA *1974;* No 12 Jalan 1, Taman Tun Abdul Razak, Ampang Jaya, 68000 AMPANG, SELANGOR, MALAYSIA.

AMANATIDOU, Miss. Marina, BSc ACA *2004;* 10 Grammou Street, Flat 101, 2006 NICOSIA, CYPRUS.

AMANULLAH, Mr. Najib, ACA *1984;* PO Box 121307, DUBAI, UNITED ARAB EMIRATES.

AMAR, Miss. Alpna, BA ACA *2007;* 140 New City Road, Plaistow, LONDON, E13 9PY.

AMARAWANSA, Miss. Ana, BA(Hons) ACA *2011;* 14 Holborn Walk, LEEDS, LS6 2RA.

AMARSHI, Mr. Husein Sadrudin, BSc(Econ) ACA *1995;* P O Box 41865, MOMBASA, KENYA.

AMAT, Mrs. Christine Bridget, BSc ACA *1986;* 49 Mount View Road, LONDON, N4 4SS.

AMAT, Mr. Richard James Antony, BSc ACA *1989;* Lehman Bros, 25-30 Bank Street, LONDON, E14 5LE.

AMATYA, Mr. Prashant, BSc ACA *2004;* 104 Clarence Close, BARNET, HERTFORDSHIRE, EN4 8AN.

AMBANPOLA, Mr. Ekanayaka Mudiyanselage Karunaratne Banda, BSc FCA *1962;* 9 Skelton Gardens, 5 COLOMBO, SRI LANKA. (Life Member)

AMBLER, Mrs. Julia Graham, BSc FCA *1981;* 39 Du Maurier Close, Church Crookham, FLEET, GU52 0YA.

AMBLER, Mr. Keith, FCA *1962;* 7 Badby Leys, RUGBY, CV22 5RB.

AMBLER, Mr. Stephen Michael, ACA *1982;* 1995 Vincent Drive, SAN MARTIN, CA 95046-9659, UNITED STATES.

AMBLER, Mrs. Susan Jane, BA ACA *1999;* 14 Millersdale Avenue, MANSFIELD, NG18 5HS.

AMBLER, Mrs. Tracy Susan, BSc ACA *1992;* South East Health Ltd Kingston House, The Long Barrow Orbital Park, ASHFORD, TN24 0GP.

AMBROSE, Mr. Alexander Lancaster, BA ACA *2002;* 18 South Bank, Sutton Valence, MAIDSTONE, KENT, ME17 3BE.

AMBROSE, Mrs. Alison Jane, BA ACA *1988;* 47 Leighton Road Toddington, DUNSTABLE, BEDFORDSHIRE, LU5 6AL.

AMBROSE, Mr. David Michael Taylor, LLB FCA *1965;* Bridge House, Whitefield Lane, GREAT MISSENDEN, BUCKINGHAMSHIRE, HP16 0BH.

AMBROSE, Mr. Gary, BSc ACA *1995;* West View, Sandy Lane, Newburgh, WIGAN, WN8 7TT.

AMBROSE, Mr. John Maurice Timothy, MA FCA *1979;* Arnewood, 8 Cleveden Road, Kelvinside, GLASGOW, G12 0NT. (Life Member)

AMBROSE, Mr. Keith Charles, BSc FCA *1993;* Newport House, Field End, Brooke Road, Braunston, OAKHAM, RUTLAND LE15 8QR.

AMBROSE, Miss. Keren Stephanie, BA ACA *1993;* 6 Smithers Cottages, Guildford Road, Rudgwick, HORSHAM, WEST SUSSEX, RH12 3BX.

•**AMBROSE, Mrs. Laura Annette, BA(Hons) ACA** *2004;* Haslers, Old Station Road, LOUGHTON, ESSEX, IG10 4PL.

•**AMBROSE, Mr. Michael Lewis, BSc FCA** *1988;* 5 The Mews, Breadcroft Lane, HARPENDEN, HERTFORDSHIRE, AL5 4TF.

AMBROSE, Mr. Robert Peter, MMath ACA *2009;* 29 Ashbrook Crescent, SOLIHULL, B91 3TD.

AMBROSE, Mrs. Susan Elizabeth, ACA ACCA *2008;* 70 Upper Broadmoor Road, CROWTHORNE, BERKSHIRE, RG45 7DF.

AMBROSE-GRIFFITH, Mrs. Alice, BA(Hons) ACA *2011;* 36 Wakenshaw Road, DURHAM, DH1 1EW.

AMBROSIO, Mr. Giuseppe, ACA *2011;* KPMG GLD ET Associes, 2 rue de las lujerneta, Athos Palace, 98000 MONACO, MONACO.

AMBROZIE, Mrs. Susan Louise, BSc ACA *1993;* 702 N Lisbon Dr, CHANDLER, AZ, 85226, UNITED STATES.

AMEEN, Mr. Hamidul Haque Mansurul, FCA *1972;* 3334 Fenwick Crescent, MISSISSAUGA L5L 5N1, ON, CANADA.

AMEEN, Ms. Mahjabeen, BSc ACA *1992;* Contra S. Francesco 94, 36100 VICENZA, ITALY.

AMEEN, Mr. Nasratul, FCA *1971;* Tax Assist, P O Box 19962, LONDON, N3 1ZH.

AMEER, Mr. Rana Gul, MSc ACA *2006;* One Canada Square, One Canada Square Canary Wharf, LONDON, E14 5FA.

AMEL-AZIZPOUR, Mr. Davoud Reza, BSc(Hons) ACA *2004;* 22 Cross Road, KINGSTON UPON THAMES, SURREY, KT2 6HG.

AMEL-AZIZPOUR, Mrs. Julie, BSc ACA *2004;* Aviva UK Central Services St. Helens, 1 Undershaft, LONDON, EC3P 3DQ.

AMELSBARG-BUSWELL, Mrs. Iris, BA(Hons) ACA *2010;* Flat 40 Meyrick Court, 22 St. Winifreds Road, BOURNEMOUTH, BH2 6PH.

AMER, Mr. Colin George, FCA *1961;* Le Petit Coin, Les Tracheries, L'Islet, St. Sampson, GUERNSEY, GY2 4SW. (Life Member)

AMER, Mr. Robin Jonathan, BSc FCA *1991;* Tregassa, 23 Goldcrest Avenue, Vale, GUERNSEY, GY6 8HP.

AMER MUSHTAQ, Mr. Mohammed Amer, BA(Econ) ACA *2001;* 85 Denison Road, Victoria Park, MANCHESTER, M14 5RN.

AMERICA, Mr. Julian Charles, BA ACA *1992;* 5 The Avenue, Spinney Hill, NORTHAMPTON, NN3 6BA.

AMERICANOS, Mr. Antonio, BA ACA FSI *1994;* (Tax Fac), 78 Cambridge Gardens, LONDON, W10 6HS.

AMERSEY, Mr. Atul Nanalal, FCA *1972;* 33 Honeyman Close, Brondesbury Park, LONDON, NW6 7AZ.

AMERSI, Mr. Salim, MSc ACA *1991;* Ernst & Young Llp, 1 More London Place, LONDON, SE1 2AF.

AMERY, Mr. James David, BSc ACA *2003;* 62-64 Loughborough Road, Mountsorrel, LOUGHBOROUGH, LEICESTERSHIRE, LE12 7AU.

AMERY, Mr. Robert Henry, FCA *1959;* 7 The Garth, Waterford Road, PRENTON, MERSEYSIDE, CH43 6US. (Life Member)

AMES, Mr. Christopher Brian, FCA *1964;* Winterfold, Tyrrells Wood, LEATHERHEAD, KT22 8QW.

AMES, Mr. Christopher John, MA FCA *1979;* Heathfield, 97 Howards Lane, LONDON, SW15 6NZ.

AMES, Mr. Colin, FCA *1969;* Brook Farm Cottage, Dorrington, SHREWSBURY, SY5 7JD.

•**AMES, Mr. David John, FCA** *1974;* Manningtons, 7-9 Wellington Square, HASTINGS, EAST SUSSEX, TN34 1PD.

AMES, Mr. Jeremy Peter, MA ACA *1989;* British Petroleum Co Plc, Chertsey Road, SUNBURY-ON-THAMES, MIDDLESEX, TW16 7LN.

AMES, Mr. Malcolm John, FCA *1967;* Destiny, Monxton Road, Grateley, ANDOVER, HAMPSHIRE, SP11 8JH. (Life Member)

AMES, Mrs. May Wen, BSc ACA *1993;* 5 Pandan Valley, #06-702, SINGAPORE 597629, SINGAPORE.

AMES, Mrs. Rebecca Jane, LLB ACA *2001;* 19 Dunnock Close, STOWMARKET, SUFFOLK, IP14 5UA.

AMES, Mr. Richard Adam, BA ACA *1997;* 2 Chatsworth Avenue, CHESTERFIELD, DERBYSHIRE, S40 3JU.

Members - Alphabetical AMES - ANDERES

AMES, Mr. Roger Simon Nicholas, BA FCA *1992;* Rose Barton, Stockleigh Pomeroy, CREDITON, DEVON, EX17 4AU.

AMES, Mrs. Sharon Tracey Dawn, BSc ACA *1992;* Homewaters, Pitt Court, North Nibley, DURSLEY, GLOUCESTERSHIRE, GL11 6EH.

AMESBURY-PAGE, Mr. Richard John, ACA *1995;* 35 Redworth Drive, Amesbury, SALISBURY, SP4 7YD.

AMESS, Mr. Simon Alec, BA ACA *1998;* 69 Beningfield Drive, London Colney, ST. ALBANS, HERTFORDSHIRE, AL2 1UX.

AMESSIS, Mrs. Harriet Louise, BSc ACA *2003;* 2 Parkside Cottages, The Street West Clandon, GUILDFORD, GU4 7ST.

AMESUR, Miss. Anup Hemantkumar, BSc ACA *1985;* 19a Kingdon Road, LONDON, NW6 1PJ.

AMEY, Mr. John Richard, FCA *1973;* 20 Hollowood Avenue, Littleover, DERBY, DE23 6JD.

•AMEY, Ms. Sarah Louise, BSc(Hons) ACA *2004;* Amey & Associates, 32a St. Benedicts Street, NORWICH, NR2 4AQ.

AMFO-AGYEI, Miss. Harriet, BSc ACA *2005;* 23 Alexandra Road, MITCHAM, CR4 3LT.

•AMICO, Mr. Salvador Insua, FCA *1989;* Menzies LLP, Woking Office, Midas House, 62 Goldsworth Road, WOKING, SURREY GU21 6LQ.

AMIEE, Mr. Bradley Lloyd Robert, MA ACA *2000;* 36 Castle Hill Avenue, BERKHAMSTED, HERTFORDSHIRE, HP4 1HJ.

•AMIES, Mr. Jonathan Stephen, FCA *1978;* Amies & Co., 205 High Street, Brownhills, WALSALL, WS8 6HE.

AMIES, Mr. Thomas George Timothy, MA FCA *1998;* 34 Owlstone Road, CAMBRIDGE, CB3 9JH.

AMIJEE, Mr. Afzal, MSc BA FCA *1994;* 42 Rue d'Avon, 77300 FONTAINEBLEAU, FRANCE.

AMIN, Mr. Ajay, BA ACA *2009;* with PricewaterhouseCoopers LLP, 7 More London Riverside, LONDON, SE1 2RT.

•AMIN, Mr. Arif, BSc FCA *1975;* 2 Kingsley Drive, Adel, LEEDS, LS16 7PB.

AMIN, Miss. Arma, ACA *2009;* with PricewaterhouseCoopers LLP, 1 Embankment Place, LONDON, WC2N 6RH.

AMIN, Mr. Azad, BA ACA *1996;* 171 New Church Road, HOVE, BN3 4DB.

•AMIN, Mr. Bilal, BSc ACA *2009;* Almas Consulting Ltd, 195 Stoke Pages Lane, SLOUGH, BERKSHIRE, SL1 3LU.

AMIN, Mr. Biren Kumar, MSc BA FCA AMCT *1991;* 14 Radcliffe Road, Park Hill, CROYDON, CR0 5QE.

AMIN, Mr. Farhan Javaid, MSc ACA *2003;* 9b Wedderburn Road, LONDON, NW3 5QS.

AMIN, Mr. Ferhat, ACA *1998;* 33 Horn Park Lane, LONDON, SE12 8UX.

AMIN, Mr. Himanshu Jashbhai, FCA *1978;* Lunkad Skylounge, Apt A 1004, Lane No 7, Kalyaninagar, PUNE 411 006, INDIA.

AMIN, Mrs. Jaimini, BA ACA *1991;* with PricewaterhouseCoopers, 250 Howe Street, Suite 700, VANCOUVER V6C 3S7, BC, CANADA.

AMIN, Mr. Jitendra, FCA *1964;* 315 rue Moge, SOREL-TRACY J3P 6X1, QUE, CANADA.

AMIN, Mr. Kamran, BSc FCA *1984;* 33 Queen's Gate Gardens, LONDON, SW7 5RR.

AMIN, Mrs. Lubna, BSc(Hons) ACA *2003;* Ernst & Young, 1 Colmore Square, BIRMINGHAM, B4 6HQ.

AMIN, Mr. Mahendra Manibhai, BA FCA *1976;* 30 Rylett Crescent, Stamford Brook, LONDON, W12 9RL.

AMIN, Mr. Mohammed, MA FCA *1977;* 32 Wellington Road, Whalley Range, MANCHESTER, M16 8EX.

AMIN, Mr. Mohammed Sameer, BSc ACA *1998;* Possingworth Barn, Blackboys, UCKFIELD, EAST SUSSEX, TN22 5HE.

AMIN, Mr. Muhammad, FCA *1965;* Amin Mudassar & Co, 4th Floor 97-B/D-I, Main Building, Gulberg III, LAHORE, PAKISTAN.

AMIN, Mr. Muhammad Athar, BSc FCA *1989;* 1 Blackett Street, LONDON, SW15 1QG.

AMIN, Mr. Mukund, ACA *1983;* 8 Graveney Road, LONDON, SW17 0EQ.

AMIN, Mr. Nikhil, BSc(Econ) ACA *2009;* 70 Orion Point, 7 Crews Street, LONDON, E14 3TX.

•AMIN, Mrs. Nina, ACA *1981;* KPMG LLP, 15 Canada Square, LONDON, E14 5GL. See also KPMG Europe LLP

AMIN, Miss. Nita, BEng ACA *1998;* Flat 2, 80A St Johns Wood, High Street, LONDON, NW8 7SH.

•AMIN, Mr. Nitin Shantilal, ACA *1980;* Amin Patel & Shah, 1st Floor, 334-336 Goswell Road, LONDON, EC1V 7RP. See also Amin N.S. & Co

•AMIN, Mr. Pratapbhanu Ambalal, FCA *1971;* (Tax Fac), Amin & Co, 781-783 Harrow Road, Sudbury Town, WEMBLEY, MIDDLESEX, HA0 2LP.

•AMIN, Mr. Rajesh, BA FCA *1992;* (Tax Fac), Body Dubois Associates LLP, The Belbourne, 103 High Street, ESHER, KT10 9QE. See also Body Dubois Limited and The R & M Partnership

AMIN, Mr. Rajul Ramesh, BA ACA *1985;* 75 Draycott Avenue, HARROW, MIDDLESEX, HA3 0DD.

AMIN, Miss. Saeeda Naz, BA ACA *1993;* 18 Iddlesleigh Terrace, Bondgate Green, Boroughbridge Road, RIPON, HG4 1QW.

AMIN, Mr. Sanjay Peter, BSc(Econ) ACA *1993;* 46 Bancroft Avenue, LONDON, N2 0AS.

AMIN, Ms. Sapna, MEng ACA *2001;* 50 Chestnut Grove, LONDON, SW12 8JJ.

•AMIN, Mr. Sheeten Ratilal, BSc ACA *1985;* Sheeten Amin, 8 Langley Grove, NEW MALDEN, KT3 3AL.

AMIN, Mrs. Shima, BA ACA *1992;* (Tax Fac), Beechcroft, 1 Fairlawn Close, KINGSTON UPON THAMES, KT2 7JW.

•AMIN, Mr. Shirishkumar Prahladbhai, ACA *1982;* S. Amin & Co., 10 The Covert, NORTHWOOD, HA6 2UD.

AMIN, Mr. Siddharth Natverlal, MA ACA *1982;* Flat 342 Shakespeare Tower, Barbican, LONDON, EC2Y 8NJ.

AMIN, Mr. Suneel Mahadev, BSc ACA *1985;* Pissaro F-1003, Maestros, Salunkhe Vihar Road, PUNE 411040, MAHARASHTRA, INDIA.

AMIN, Miss. Tejal, BA ACA *2002;* 329 Havering Road, ROMFORD, RM1 4BY.

•AMIN, Mrs. Yogini, BA ACA *1995;* Magus, 140 Buckingham Palace Road, LONDON, SW1W 9SA.

AMINI, Miss. Nina, BSc ACA *1986;* 5 Brightwen Grove, STANMORE, MIDDLESEX, HA7 4WH.

•AMINIAN, Mr. Massoud, FCA *1976;* (Tax Fac), Aminian & Co, Unit 2 Edison Business Centre, 52 Edison Road, AYLESBURY, HP19 8TE.

AMINULLAH, Mr. Shehrzad, BSc FCA *1999;* 17-A/1 North Central Avenue, Defence Housing Authority, Phase I, KARACHI 75500, PAKISTAN.

•AMIRI, Mr. Iraj, MSc FCA *1982;* 200 Woodford Road, Woodford, STOCKPORT, CHESHIRE, SK7 1QF.

•AMIRI, Mr. Said Amin, BSc FCA CF *1980;* A2E Venture Catalyst Limited, 57 Princess Street, MANCHESTER, M2 4EQ. See also Amiri Associates

AMIS, Mr. Alan Stephen, FCA *1951;* 1 Larks Rise, Holton Road, HALESWORTH, IP19 8JZ. (Life Member)

AMIS, Mr. Robert Henry Charles, BA ACA *1985;* 50 Englewood Road, LONDON, SW12 9NZ.

•AMISS, Ms. Stella Claire, BA ACA *1997;* PricewaterhouseCoopers LLP, 1 Embankment Place, LONDON, WC2N 6RH. See also PricewaterhouseCoopers

AMITRANO, Mrs. Elizabeth Ann, BSc ACA *1997;* Briar Close, 16 Latchmoor Avenue, Chalfont St. Peter, GERRARDS CROSS, BUCKINGHAMSHIRE, SL9 8LJ.

•AMITRANO, Mr. Marco, MEng ACA *1997;* PricewaterhouseCoopers LLP, The Atrium, 1 Harefield Road, UXBRIDGE, UB8 1EX. See also PricewaterhouseCoopers

AMJAD, Miss. Michelle, ACA *2009;* Pricewaterhousecoopers, 1 Embankment Place, LONDON, WC2N 6RH.

AMJAD, Miss. Nayab, BSc ACA *2010;* Flat 18, Rossmore Court, Park Road, LONDON, NW1 6XX.

AMJAD, Mr. Syed Perwaiz, FCA *1972;* Naqi Arcade, 2nd Floor, 71 Shahrah-e-Quaid-e-Azam, LAHORE MAIN 54000, PAKISTAN. (Life Member)

AMLANI, Mr. Anil Kassam Kanji, FCA *1975;* 1644 The Chase, MISSISSAUGA L5M 5A2, ON, CANADA.

AMLANI, Mr. Kushil, BA ACA *1993;* (Tax Fac), 5 Callerton Court, Ponteland, NEWCASTLE UPON TYNE, NE20 9EN.

•AMLOT, Mr. Antony Richard, FCA *1981;* Lakin Clark, Delandale House, 37 Old Dover Road, CANTERBURY, CT1 3JF. See also Lakin Clark Limited

AMNER, Mrs. Anne Belinda, BA ACA *1994;* 4 Queen Street, MALDON, ESSEX, CM9 5DP.

AMOA, Mr. Apeawusu, MSc ACA *2005;* Flat 612 California Building, Deals Gateway, LONDON, SE13 7SF.

AMOO-ASANTE, Mr. Kwaku, FCA *1985;* 320 Mercer Lane, WINDSOR, CT 06095, UNITED STATES.

AMOR, Miss. Caroline, ACA *2011;* 165 Reading Road, WOKINGHAM, BERKSHIRE, RG41 1LJ.

AMOR, Mr. John Stewart, FCA *1968;* Gully Cottage, Nempnett Thrubwell, Chew Stoke, BRISTOL, BS40 8YS. (Life Member)

AMOR, Mr. Kevin Martin, BSc FCA *1986;* 3 Wootton Lane, Dinton, AYLESBURY, BUCKINGHAMSHIRE, HP17 8UY.

•AMOR, Mrs. Margaret Winifred, ACA *1979;* M.W. Amor, 4 The Colliers, Heybridge Basin, MALDON, CM9 4SE.

AMOR, Mr. Nicolas John, BA ACA *1982;* West Compton House, West Compton, DORCHESTER, DT2 0EY.

AMOS, Mr. Alexander, FCA *1962;* A31-01 Kiaramas Ayuria, Jalan Desa Kiara, Mont Kiara, 50480 KUALA LUMPUR, FEDERAL TERRITORY, MALAYSIA. (Life Member)

AMOS, Mr. Charles Anthony, MA FCA *1978;* Pensions Secretariat Services Ltd 3rd Floor, 38 Lombard street, LONDON, EC3V 9BS.

AMOS, Mr. Colin Philip, BSc ACA *1990;* Volumatic Ltd, Taurus House, Endemere Road, COVENTRY, CV6 5PY.

AMOS, Mr. David Stephen, BSS ACA *1991;* 5 Plymouth Drive, Barnt Green, BIRMINGHAM, B45 8JB.

AMOS, Mr. Gareth, BSc ACA *2006;* Flat 6 Guildown Court, Stoke Road, GUILDFORD, GU1 4HQ.

AMOS, Mr. John Ernest, FCA *1975;* 6 Llewellyn Close, CHELMSFORD, CM1 7RE.

AMOS, Mrs. Lisa Wyn, MSc LLB ACA *2006;* 90 Park Road, Whitchurch, CARDIFF, CF14 7BR.

AMOS, Miss. Margaret Elaine, ACA *1985;* Rathmore House, Whateley, TAMWORTH, B78 2ET.

AMOS, Mr. Melvyn Edward, FCA *1973;* Y Goedlan, 26 Cwrt Y Cadno, CARDIFF, CF5 4PJ.

•AMOS, Mr. Michael, FCA *1987;* Cooper Dawn Jerrom Limited, Units SCF 1 & 2, Western International Market, Hayes Road, SOUTHALL, MIDDLESEX UB2 5XJ.

AMOS, Mr. Michael Ralph, FCA *1963;* 59 Wroughton Road, LONDON, SW11 6AY.

AMOS, Mr. Michael William, BSc ACA *1981;* Hideaway, Cherry Tree Lane, Chalfont St. Peter, GERRARDS CROSS, BUCKINGHAMSHIRE, SL9 9DQ.

AMOS, Mr. Richard John, BA ACA *1992;* 22 Collens Road, HARPENDEN, HERTFORDSHIRE, AL5 2AJ.

AMOS, Mrs. Sheriden Frances, BSc ACA *1995;* Church Cottage, Church Road, Crowle, WORCESTER, WR7 4AX.

AMOS, Mr. Simon David, BCom ACA *1986;* 44 Rebekah Gardens, DROITWICH, WR9 8UG.

AMOS, Mr. Timothy David, BSc ACA CTA *2002;* Room 2B-E18, Ford Research & Engineering Centre, Laindon, BASILDON, SS15 6EE.

AMOS, Ms. Valerie Heather, BSc ACA *1993;* 18 Hermitage Close, LONDON, E18 2BW.

AMPALAVANAR, Mr. Segarajah, FCA *1975;* 26 Jalan 12/16, 46200 PETALING JAYA, MALAYSIA.

AMPOMAH, Mr. Jamil Yaw Okyere, BA(Hons) ACA *2001;* P.O.Box MP1119, LAGOS, GHANA.

AMROHI, Miss. Meghna, ACA *2011;* 9 Parkleigh Road, LONDON, SW19 3BU.

AMSDEN, Mr. Christopher Norman, BSc ACA *1996;* 31 Lyttelton Road, DROITWICH, WORCESTERSHIRE, WR9 7AB.

AMSTERDAM, Mr. David, FCA *1953;* 1801 Century Park East, Suite 1080, LOS ANGELES, CA 90067, UNITED STATES. (Life Member)

AMUSAN, Mr. Kunle, BSc ACA *2004;* 36 Compton Road, CROYDON, CR0 7JA.

AMY, Mr. Arthur Rodney, MA FCA TEP *1971;* Le Boulivot, La Rue Du Boulivot, Grouville, JERSEY, JE3 9DP. (Life Member)

AMY, Mr. George Crosby, FCA *1954;* The Pines, Hammerwood Road, Ashurst Wood, EAST GRINSTEAD, RH19 3TG. (Life Member)

AMY, Mrs. Sabrina, BSc ACA *2005;* Windermere 13 La Mielle Clement, La Route Des Quennevais St. Brelade, JERSEY, JE3 8FW.

AMY, Mr. Thomas, BSc ACA *2003;* Windermere, 13 La Mielle Clement, St. Brelade, JERSEY, JE3 8FW.

AMY, Mr. William Patrick, FCA *1967;* American International Underwriters, American International Building 2-8 Altyre Road, CROYDON, CR9 2LG.

AN, Ms. Katherine, ACA CA(AUS) *2011;* Flat 36, Turner House, Townshend Estate, LONDON, NW8 6LN.

ANA, Mrs. Tolulope Veronica, BSc ACA *2009;* 15 Yarrow Close, THATCHAM, BERKSHIRE, RG18 4BQ.

ANAND, Mr. Aneil, BA ACA *1999;* Duet Mena Limited, Office 10 Level 4 Al Fattan Currency House, DIFC, P.O. Box 482011, DUBAI, UNITED ARAB EMIRATES.

ANAND, Mr. Arun, FCA *1969;* 16 Nizamyddin East, NEW DELHI 13, INDIA.

ANAND, Mr. Gurbir Singh, BA ACA *2007;* 6 Georgian Way, HARROW, MIDDLESEX, HA1 3LF.

ANAND, Mr. Harpreet Singh, MA LLM ACA *2001;* 220 Sixth Street South, Suite 1400, MINNEAPOLIS, MN 55402, UNITED STATES.

ANAND, Mrs. Jyotika Kaur, BSc(Hons) ACA *2003;* 116 Station Road, HARPENDEN, HERTFORDSHIRE, AL5 4RH.

ANAND, Mr. Karan, BA(Hons) FCA *1973;* Anands, E-282 1st Floor, Greater Kailash Part II, NEW DELHI 110 048, INDIA.

ANAND, Mr. Lalit Mohan, FCA *1967;* 14 Ascot Close, MACCLESFIELD, SK10 2UH.

ANAND, Mr. Ravinder Singh, BSc ACA *1993;* 151A King Henrys Road, LONDON, NW3 3RD.

ANAND, Mr. Vimal Kumar, BSc ACA *1982;* 2072 Kingspointe Drive, Clarkson Valley, CHESTERFIELD, MO 63005, UNITED STATES.

ANANDA-RAJAH, Mr. Robert Anton, FCA *1971;* 41 Waratah Street, CROYDON PARK, NSW 2133, AUSTRALIA.

ANARFI, Mr. Robert, BSocSc ACA *2001;* 1 CYPRUS ROAD, FAREHAM, HAMPSHIRE, PO14 4JY.

ANASTASI, Mrs. Maria, BA ACA *2001;* 10 Costaki Mardapitta, Pano Lakatamia, CY - 2313 NICOSIA, CYPRUS.

ANASTASI, Mr. Marios, BSc ACA *2006;* 4 Michael Nikolaou, 2236 LATSIA, CYPRUS.

ANASTASIADES, Mr. Evangelos Andreou, FCA *1986;* 17 Gt CONSTANTINE STREET, AGLANJIA, 2121 NICOSIA, CYPRUS.

ANASTASIOU, Mr. Andreas, BA(Hons) ACA *2003;* 7A Thoukididou Street, Strovolos, 2006 NICOSIA, CYPRUS.

ANASTASIOU, Ms. Christina, BSc ACA *2006;* 3 Skra Street, 3077 LIMASSOL, CYPRUS.

ANASTASIOU, Miss. Chrystalla, BSc ACA *2010;* 10 Olgas Street, Flat 102, 2304 LAKATAMIA, CYPRUS.

ANASTASIOU, Miss. Ioanna, BA ACA *2009;* PO Box 61109, Kato-Pafos, PAPHOS, CYPRUS.

ANASTASIOU, Mr. Kleanthis, BA(Econ) ACA *2004;* 4 Timokreontos street, 3076 LIMASSOL, CYPRUS.

ANASTASIOU, Mr. Lambro Michael, ACA *2008;* 1 Hainfield Drive, SOLIHULL, WEST MIDLANDS, B91 2PL.

ANASTASIOU, Mr. Loukas, ACA *2011;* P.O.BOX 53480, 3303 LIMASSOL, CYPRUS.

ANASTASIOU, Mr. Marios Costa, BA ACA *1995;* 11 Dionyson Str, Cybc Area, 2123 NICOSIA, CYPRUS.

ANASTASIOU, Miss. Natasa, BSc ACA *2007;* 39 Themistocleous street Strovolos, Aliada Apartment 102, 2060 NICOSIA, CYPRUS.

ANASTASIOU, Mr. Panagiotis, BSc ACA *2008;* POB 58267, 3732 LIMASSOL, CYPRUS.

ANASTASIOU, Mr. Panayiotis, BA(Hons) ACA *2003;* Flat 21 Acropolis Court, 6 Aristofanouj Street, 3031 LIMASSOL, CYPRUS.

ANASTASIOU, Mr. Stavros, BA ACA *2009;* iras 2 c204 ayios tychonas amathusa coastal heights, 4532 LIMASSOL, CYPRUS.

ANASTASIOU, Mr. Stylianos, BA ACA *2006;* 40 Nicosia Avenue, Peristerona, 2731 NICOSIA, CYPRUS.

ANASTASIOU, Mr. Tasos, BSc(Econ) FCA CF *1999;* The Cyprus Cement Plc, PO Box 50019, CY 3600 LIMASSOL, CYPRUS.

ANASTASIOU, Mr. Themis A, BA(Hons) ACA *2009;* Aiyptou 13, Faneromeni, 6030 LARNACA, CYPRUS.

ANASTASSIADES, Mr. Andreas, BA ACA *1994;* 10 Elpinikis Street, Acropolis, NICOSIA, CYPRUS.

ANASTASSIADES, Mr. Gabriel George, BA ACA *1994;* No.1 Andreas Stavrides Street, Strovolos, 2015 NICOSIA, CYPRUS.

ANASTASSIOU, Mr. Demosthenis Christaki, BA(Econ) ACA *1996;* Georgiou Lapithi 1, Engomi, 2407 NICOSIA, CYPRUS.

ANASTASSIOU, Mr. Stelios, BA(Econ) ACA *1999;* 9 Kyrenia Street, Acropolis, 2008 STROVOLOS, CYPRUS.

ANASTASSIS, Mr. Christos, MSc ACA *2010;* 322 Patission Str, 11141 ATHENS, GREECE.

ANATHAKUMAR, Mr. Hari Govind, ACA *2010;* 19 Venus Colony, 2nd Street, Alwarpet, CHENNAI 600018, INDIA.

•ANAYI, Mr. Frank, MA FCA *1973;* FJA, 1 Shalford Road, GUILDFORD, SURREY, GU1 3XL.

ANAYIOTOS, Mr. Christophoros, BSc(Econ) ACA CF *2000;* PO Box 21121, 1502 NICOSIA, CYPRUS.

•ANAYIOTOS, Mr. Nicos, FCA *1974;* N Anayiotos & Co, 20 Bishops Avenue, ELSTREE, WD6 3LZ.

ANCELL, Mr. Paul, BA FCA *1990;* 41 Snowdonia Road, Walton Cardiff, TEWKESBURY, GLOUCESTERSHIRE, GL20 7RN.

ANCHORS, Mr. Matthew James, BA ACA *2001;* 97 Waterloo Road, NORTH RYDE, NSW 2113, AUSTRALIA.

ANCLIFF, Miss. Lesley Jayne, ACA *1992;* Tanners Pembury Grange, Sandown Park, TUNBRIDGE WELLS, KENT, TN2 4RP.

ANDERES, Mr. Rolf, BSc FCA *1977;* chemin de la Colline 4, CH-1197 PRANGINS, VAUD, SWITZERLAND.

ANDERS, Mr. Paul Francis, FCA *1963;* Northall, Stag Lane, Chorleywood, RICKMANSWORTH, WD3 5HD.
ANDERS, Mr. Philip William, MBA BA ACA *1988;* 5 Fitzwilliams Court, Greatford, STAMFORD, PE9 4QQ.
ANDERSEN, Mr. Brian Anthony, BA FCA *1978;* South Barn, Church Farm, Chartway Street, Sutton Valence, MAIDSTONE, KENT ME17 3JB.
ANDERSEN, Mr. David Peter, ACA CA(SA) *2009;* with Deloitte LLP, Athene Place, 66 Shoe Lane, LONDON, EC4A 3BQ.
ANDERSEN, Mr. Jeremy, BA ACA *1990;* Prudhoe Floor 2, Northern Rock Plc Northern Rock House, Regent Centre Gosforth, NEWCASTLE UPON TYNE, NE3 4PL.
ANDERSEN, Mr. Mark Lykke, BSc ACA *2007;* Apartment O S 604 Royal Mills, 2 Cotton Street, MANCHESTER, M4 5BW.
ANDERSEN, Mr. Reginald Ernest, FCA *1959;* 7 Garners Road, Chalfont St. Peter, GERRARDS CROSS, SL9 0HA. (Life Member)
ANDERSEN, Mr. Stian Bowes, MSc ACA *2003;* 37 Euston Road, Sandringham, AUCKLAND, NEW ZEALAND.
ANDERSON, Miss. Adanta Loreign Marion, BA ACA *2008;* 50 Sheriff Way, WATFORD, WD25 7QG.
•ANDERSON, Miss. Adele Helen, BSc ACA *1989;* Long Barn, Crook Road, Brenchley, TONBRIDGE, KENT, TN12 7BE.
ANDERSON, Mr. Alan John, FCA *1958;* 14 Birchalls, High Lane, STANSTED, CM24 8LQ. (Life Member)
ANDERSON, Mr. Alan John, FCA *1947;* 40 Tiddington Court, Knights Lane, Tiddington, STRATFORD-UPON-AVON, WARWICKSHIRE, CV37 7BP. (Life Member)
ANDERSON, Mrs. Alexia, BSc ACA *1992;* 29 Keith Road, BOURNEMOUTH, BH3 7DS.
ANDERSON, Mrs. Alison Jane, BSc ACA *1982;* 75 Manor Way, BECKENHAM, BR3 3LW.
ANDERSON, Mrs. Angela Wendy, BSc ACA *1988;* Redmile Farm, 45 Main Street, Dyke, BOURNE, PE10 0AF.
ANDERSON, Mr. Angus Firby, BSc ACA MBA *1987;* McGill Services 14 Chapell Lane, Wynyard Park Business Village Wynyard, BILLINGHAM, CLEVELAND, TS22 5FG.
ANDERSON, Miss. Antonia Frances, ACA *2008;* with Deloitte LLP, City House, 126-130 Hills Road, CAMBRIDGE, CB2 1RY.
ANDERSON, Mr. Ariel George Vernon, FCA *1960;* 6985 Waite Drive #75, LA MESA, CA 91941, UNITED STATES. (Life Member)
ANDERSON, Mr. Benjamin James, MSci ACA *2006;* V T B Bank, 14 Cornhill, LONDON, EC3V 3ND.
ANDERSON, Mrs. Camille Ninon, MSc ACA *2001;* with BDO LLP, 55 Baker Street, LONDON, W1U 7EU.
ANDERSON, Ms. Catherine Jane, BSc ACA *1999;* 46 Shelley Way, LONDON, SW19 1TS.
ANDERSON, Miss. Charlotte, BSc ACA *2007;* 1 Court Cottage, West Green Common Hartley Wintney, HOOK, RG27 8JD.
ANDERSON, Mrs. Charlotte Emma, BSc ACA *2004;* 383 Bideford Green, LEIGHTON BUZZARD, BEDFORDSHIRE, LU7 2TY.
•ANDERSON, Mr. Christopher Geoffrey, ACA CA(AUS) *2010;* Oak Tree, 6 Oak Tree Road, MARLOW, BUCKINGHAMSHIRE, SL7 3EE.
ANDERSON, Miss. Claire Helen, BSc ACA *1992;* Total Flow Ltd, 28 Park Hill, HARPENDEN, AL5 3AT.
ANDERSON, Miss. Claire Jean, ACA *1988;* 10 Altenburg Gardens, LONDON, SW11 1JJ.
ANDERSON, Miss. Clare, MEng ACA ACGI *2010;* Flat 2 Dene Mansions, Dennington Park Road, LONDON, NW6 1AY.
ANDERSON, Mr. Colin, FCA *1973;* Lanes End, Red Lion Lane, FARNHAM, SURREY, GU9 7QW.
ANDERSON, Mr. Colin Clive, BSc FCA CTA *1972;* (Tax Fac), with Davey Grover Limited, 4 Fenice Court, Phoenix Business Park, Eaton Socon, ST. NEOTS, CAMBRIDGESHIRE PE19 8EP.
ANDERSON, Mr. David, ACA *1980;* 27 Bradman Drive, CHESTER LE STREET, COUNTY DURHAM, DH3 3QS.
ANDERSON, Mr. David Anthony, BA FCA *1964;* 20 Kelvon Close, Glenfield, LEICESTER, LE3 8AT. (Life Member)
ANDERSON, Mr. David Campbell, BSc ACA *1999;* 8D Elizabeth Bay Gardens, 15-19 Onslow Avenue, Elizabeth Bay, SYDNEY, NSW 2021, AUSTRALIA.
ANDERSON, Mr. David John, FCA *1971;* Hall Farm, Hall Lane, Shenfield, BRENTWOOD, CM15 0SH.
ANDERSON, Mr. David John, BSc ACA *2001;* 2 Victor Road, WINDSOR, BERKSHIRE, SL4 3JU.
•ANDERSON, Mr. David Mark, BSc ACA *1990;* Crowe Clark Whitehill LLP, Carrick House, Lypiatt Road, CHELTENHAM, GLOUCESTERSHIRE, GL50 2QJ. See also Horwath Clark Whitehill LLP
•ANDERSON, Mr. David Paul, FCA *1976;* Moore Stephens Enfield Limited, 57 London Road, ENFIELD, MIDDLESEX, EN2 6SW.
ANDERSON, Mr. David Peet, FCA *1956;* Bendyke House, 22 Willow Close, Burton Joyce, NOTTINGHAM, NG14 5FF. (Life Member)
ANDERSON, Mr. David Stephen, BA ACA *2007;* 7/47-53 Dudley Street, COOGEE, NSW 2034, AUSTRALIA.
ANDERSON, Mrs. Deborah Ann, BA ACA *1985;* 68 Crawley Road, WITNEY, OX28 1HU.
•ANDERSON, Miss. Deborah Jane, BA ACA *1989;* with Smith & Williamson Ltd, 25 Moorgate, LONDON, EC2R 6AY.
ANDERSON, Miss. Deborah Louise, BA ACA *2009;* 33 Central Road, Rudheath, NORTHWICH, CHESHIRE, CW9 7EN.
ANDERSON, Mr. Dennis John George, FCA *1974;* (Tax Fac), 64 Colebourne Road, Kings Heath, BIRMINGHAM, B13 0EY.
ANDERSON, Mr. Derek John, FCA *1966;* Bramleys, Muss Lane, Kings Somborne, STOCKBRIDGE, HAMPSHIRE, SO20 6PE. (Life Member)
•ANDERSON, Mr. Detlev Ronald, BSc FCA DChA *1987;* Ryecroft Glenton, 32 Portland Terrace, Jesmond, NEWCASTLE UPON TYNE, NE2 1QP.
ANDERSON, Mr. Donald Neil Keith, BA FCA *1980;* 17 Clos St Anne, B 1332 GENVAL, BELGIUM.
ANDERSON, Mr. Douglas Davidson, FCA *1972;* Woodlands, Greatford Gardens, Greatford, STAMFORD, PE9 4PX.
•ANDERSON, Mr. Duncan Ross, FCA *1978;* (Tax Fac), Duncan Anderson & Company, Temple Chambers, 4 Abbey Road, GRIMSBY, DN32 0HF. See also Anderson Duncan & Company
ANDERSON, Miss. Elaine Alison, BA(Hons) ACA *2011;* Pricewaterhousecoopers, 7 More London Riverside, LONDON, SE1 2RT.
•ANDERSON, Miss. Elizabeth Lesley, MA FCA CTA *1991;* Community Accountancy Service Ltd, The Grange, Pilgrim Drive, Beswick, MANCHESTER, M11 3TQ.
ANDERSON, Dr. Elizabeth Sara Llewelyn, PhD MSc ACA *2005;* 8 Higher Shapter Street, Topsham, EXETER, EX3 0AW.
ANDERSON, Miss. Eloise Kate, ACA *2010;* 20 Parkers Road, Starcross, EXETER, EX6 8QL.
ANDERSON, Mrs. Emily Jane, BA(Hons) ACA *2002;* 7 Lon Wynne, DENBIGH, CLWYD, LL16 5YD.
ANDERSON, Mrs. Emma Jane, BSc ACA *1996;* 4 Brightmore Street, CREMORNE, NSW 2090, AUSTRALIA.
ANDERSON, Miss. Emma Louise, BA ACA *2006;* Bahnhofstrasse 22, 6301 ZUG, SWITZERLAND.
•ANDERSON, Mr. Eric Hatty, FCA *1971;* AIMS - Eric Anderson, Rhos Fach Farm, Cross Hands, LLANELLI, DYFED, SA14 6DG.
ANDERSON, Miss. Erin Marie, BA(Hons) ACA *2011;* 12 Dalton Close, DRIFFIELD, NORTH HUMBERSIDE, YO25 6YE.
ANDERSON, Mr. Fergus Grant, MA ACA *2005;* 62K, 3/1 62 Hilton Gardens, GLASGOW, G13 1DB.
•ANDERSON, Mr. Frederick John Haiste, BSc FCA *1984;* (Tax Fac), Anderson & Co, Sumpter House, 8 Station Road, Histon, CAMBRIDGE, CB24 9LQ.
ANDERSON, Mrs. Gabrielle, ACA CA(AUS) *2009;* 1 Golf Street, ALFREDTON, VIC 3350, AUSTRALIA.
•ANDERSON, Mr. Gareth, MA ACA CTA *1999;* Ernst & Young LLP, Wessex House, 19 Threefield Lane, SOUTHAMPTON, SO14 3QB. See also Ernst & Young Europe LLP
ANDERSON, Mr. Gareth Jon, BSc ACA *1999;* 20 Monkseaton Drive, WHITLEY BAY, TYNE AND WEAR, NE26 1SZ.
ANDERSON, Miss. Gayle, BSc ACA *2005;* 39 Manton Road, HITCHIN, HERTFORDSHIRE, SG4 9NP.
•ANDERSON, Mr. Gerald Charles De Grey, BA FCA *1960;* Ansons, Parker House, 104a Hutton Road, Shenfield, BRENTWOOD, ESSEX CM15 8NB.
•ANDERSON, Mr. Gerard Francis, MA FCA *1981;* Ernst & Young, Al-Farabi 77/7, Essentai Tower, ALMATY 050059, KAZAKHSTAN.
•ANDERSON, Mr. Graham, BSc FCA *1973;* Graham Anderson, Holwell, Stainfield Road, Kirkby Underwood, BOURNE, LINCOLNSHIRE PE10 0SG. See also Peasemore Business Services Ltd
•ANDERSON, Mr. Hamish, MSc BAcc ACA *2001;* PricewaterhouseCoopers LLP, Hays Galleria, 1 Hays Lane, LONDON, SE1 2RD. See also PricewaterhouseCoopers
ANDERSON, Mrs. Hannah Louise, ACA *2010;* 6 Bishop Rise, Drayton, NORWICH, NR8 6UX.
ANDERSON, Miss. Hazel Anne, ACA *2003;* 34 Broughtons Field, WIGSTON, LEICESTERSHIRE, LE18 3LJ.
ANDERSON, Miss. Helen Joy, MSci ACA *2005;* with Deloitte LLP, Hill House, 1 Little New Street, LONDON, EC4A 3TR.
•ANDERSON, Mrs. Helen Louise, LLB ACA *2000;* HLA Accounting, The Gleanings, Church Road, Glatton, HUNTINGDON, CAMBRIDGESHIRE PE28 5RR.
ANDERSON, Mr. Henry, FCA *1963;* 1 Parklands, Spofforth, HARROGATE, HG3 1DB.
ANDERSON, Mr. Hugh Moncrieff, MBA FCA *1973;* Mill Race Cottage, Adel Mill, LEEDS, LS16 8BF.
ANDERSON, Mr. Ian, FCA *1967;* Rosedale Cottage, 39 Barmoor Lane, Scalby, SCARBOROUGH, NORTH YORKSHIRE, YO13 0PG. (Life Member)
ANDERSON, Mr. Ian, BSc ACA *2005;* with KPMG LLP, 15 Canada Square, LONDON, E14 5GL.
•ANDERSON, Mr. Ian Alexander, FCA *1969;* I.A. Anderson & Co, 1 Three Pears Road, Merrow, GUILDFORD, GU1 2XU.
ANDERSON, Mr. Ian Henry, BA FCA *1987;* (Tax Fac), 31 Carrwood, KNUTSFORD, CHESHIRE, WA16 8NE.
ANDERSON, Mr. Ian Lee Mackay, FCA *1970;* 79 Bedford Court Mansions, Bedford Avenue, LONDON, WC1B 3AE.
•ANDERSON, Mr. Ian Mackenzie, BA ACA *1980;* Ian Anderson, 24 Leigh View, Tingley, WAKEFIELD, WEST YORKSHIRE, WF3 1NJ. See also Aims Accountants
•ANDERSON, Mr. Ian Stephen, BA FCA *1980;* (Tax Fac), Ian S Anderson, Chartam House, 16 College Avenue, MAIDENHEAD, BERKSHIRE, SL6 6AX.
ANDERSON, Mr. Ian Wallace, FCA *1966;* PO Box 61278, FORT MYERS, FL 33906-1278, UNITED STATES.
ANDERSON, Mrs. Jacqueline, BA ACA *1993;* 149 Whitley Road, WHITLEY BAY, TYNE AND WEAR, NE26 2DS.
ANDERSON, Mr. James David, BA ACA *1999;* 10 Butyrsky Val, 125047 MOSCOW, RUSSIAN FEDERATION.
ANDERSON, Dr. James Lloyd, PhD MA BA FCA *1966;* Phillimore Cottage, Thorncombe Street, Bramley, GUILDFORD, GU5 0LU. (Life Member)
ANDERSON, Mr. James Marcus, BA ACA *2001;* 79 Houses Hill, HUDDERSFIELD, HD5 0PA.
ANDERSON, Mr. James Robert, FCA *1947;* 4 Vardon Drive, WILMSLOW, SK9 2AQ. (Life Member)
ANDERSON, Mr. James Robert Bullock, ACA *2009;* 26 Scarborough Road, LONDON, N4 4LT.
ANDERSON, Miss. Jane Alison, BSc ACA *1983;* 5 Ladyhaugh Drive, Whickham, NEWCASTLE UPON TYNE, NE16 5TE.
•ANDERSON, Mrs. Jaqueline Anne, LLB ACA *1991;* AKA Consulting Limited, 6 Esplanade Crescent, SCARBOROUGH, NORTH YORKSHIRE, YO11 2XB.
ANDERSON, Mr. Jason Mark, BA ACA *1996;* Carlisle Brass, Parkhouse Road, CARLISLE, CA3 0JU.
ANDERSON, Mr. Jeffrey James, BEng ACA *1994;* The Old Station, Station Road, Stow-cum-Quy, CAMBRIDGE, CB25 9AJ.
ANDERSON, Miss. Jennifer Alexandra, MA ACA *1990;* 1 Orchard Cottages, St Giles Road, Swanton Novers, MELTON CONSTABLE, NORFOLK, NR24 2RD.
ANDERSON, Mrs. Jennifer Grace, BSc ACA *1979;* 9 Acacia Drive, Melbourne, DERBY, DE73 8LT.
ANDERSON, Mrs. Joanna Helen, BSc(Hons) ACA CTA *2002;* 10 Hall Hurst Close, Loxwood, BILLINGSHURST, WEST SUSSEX, RH14 0BE.
ANDERSON, Mr. John Campbell, FCA *1968;* 28 Temple Rhydding Drive, Baildon, SHIPLEY, WEST YORKSHIRE, BD17 5PU.
ANDERSON, Mr. John Kenneth, FCA *1949;* Medburn, 51 Jubilee Close, LEDBURY, HR8 2XA. (Life Member)
ANDERSON, John Victor Ronald, Esq OBE DL MA FCA *1962;* (Member of Council 1995 - 2003), Caer Rhun Hall Company, CONWY, LL32 8HX. (Life Member)
•ANDERSON, Mr. Jonathan Edward Leslie, BA ACA *1992;* Ernst & Young LLP, 1 More London Place, LONDON, SE1 2AF. See also Ernst & Young Europe LLP
ANDERSON, Mr. Jonathan Trevor, MA ACA *1982;* 31 Manor Rd, DORCHESTER, DT1 2AX.
ANDERSON, Mr. Joseph Edward Robert, ACA *2008;* Flat 7 Brook House, Cranleigh Street, LONDON, NW1 1NU.
ANDERSON, Miss. Judy, BA(Hons) ACA *2001;* 6-8 Dewar Place Lane, EDINBURGH, EH3 8EF.
ANDERSON, Mrs. Julia Beverley, BSc ACA *1987;* Braeside, Beardwood Brow, BLACKBURN, BB2 7AT.
•ANDERSON, Mrs. Karen, BA ACA *1989;* Karen Anderson, 18 Brampton Chase, Lower Shiplake, HENLEY-ON-THAMES, OXFORDSHIRE, RG9 3BX.
ANDERSON, Mrs. Karen, BA ACA *1998;* Town Farm House, Ryton Village, RYTON, NE40 3QQ.
ANDERSON, Mrs. Karen Dawn, BA ACA *1992;* 290 Blackburn Road, Egerton, BOLTON, BL7 9TB.
•ANDERSON, Mrs. Karen Jane, BSc(Hons) ACA *2001;* Oak Tree, 6 Oak Tree Road, MARLOW, BUCKINGHAMSHIRE, SL7 3EE.
ANDERSON, Miss. Karen Margaret, BSc ACA *1992;* 1 Rothbury Gardens, Old London Road, HYTHE, KENT, CT21 4DG.
ANDERSON, Mrs. Katharine Mary, BA ACA *1990;* 25 Killaloe Crescent, GEORGETOWN L7G 5N2, ON, CANADA.
ANDERSON, Mr. Keith Michael, BA ACA *1991;* 20a Arterberry Road, LONDON, SW20 8AJ.
•ANDERSON, Mr. Keith Richard, BA FCA *1986;* KPMG LLP, One Snowhill, Snow Hill Queensway, BIRMINGHAM, B4 6GN. See also KPMG Europe LLP
•ANDERSON, Mr. Kenneth Andrew, FCA *1971;* (Tax Fac), Astacx Limited, Longcroft Farmhouse, 31 Derby Road, Aston-on-Trent, DERBY, DE72 2AE.
ANDERSON, Mr. Kenneth Arthur, FCA *1949;* 8 Darbie Close, New Earswick, YORK, YO32 4DJ. (Life Member)
ANDERSON, Mr. Laurence Keith, BA ACA *1980;* The Villas, 10 Church Road, Kibworth, LEICESTER, LE8 0NB.
ANDERSON, Mrs. Lina, BSc(Hons) ACA *2002;* 87/89 High Street, Hanging Heaton, BATLEY, WF17 6DR.
ANDERSON, Mrs. Margaret Elizabeth, FCA *1972;* Woodlands, Greatford Gardens, Greatford, STAMFORD, PE9 4PX.
ANDERSON, Mr. Mark, MA DMS FCA *1998;* 27 St. Vigeans Gardens, ARBROATH, ANGUS, DD11 4EB.
ANDERSON, Mr. Mark Graham Whitelaw, BSc ACA *1995;* Carnival UK Carnival House, 100 Harbour Parade, SOUTHAMPTON, SO15 1ST.
ANDERSON, Mr. Mark Ian, BA ACA *1984;* Essar Steel Processing & Distribution UK Ktd, Pensnett Road, DUDLEY, DY1 2HA.
•ANDERSON, Mr. Mark Jeremy, ACA *1990;* Crowe Clark Whitehill LLP, Jaeger House, 5 Clanricarde Gardens, TUNBRIDGE WELLS, KENT, TN1 1PE. See also Horwath Clark Whitehill LLP and Crowe Clark Whitehill
•ANDERSON, Mr. Mark Raymond, BCom FCA *1989;* (Tax Fac), Mark Anderson Limited, 68 Crawley Road, WITNEY, OXFORDSHIRE, OX28 1HU. See also Mark Anderson
ANDERSON, Mr. Martin James, FCA *1969;* 39 Barkers Lane, Wythall, BIRMINGHAM, B47 6BY.
•ANDERSON, Mr. Martin John, BSc FCA *1980;* Haslers, Old Station Road, LOUGHTON, ESSEX, IG10 4PL.
ANDERSON, Mr. Martin John, BSc ACA *1992;* RBC Dexia, George's Quay House, 43 Townsend Street, DUBLIN 2, COUNTY DUBLIN, IRELAND.
•ANDERSON, Mrs. Mary, BSc ACA *1980;* Agincourt Practice Limited, 6 Agincourt Street, MONMOUTH, GWENT, NP25 3DZ.
•ANDERSON, Mr. Matthew Curtis, BSc FCA *1995;* with UHY Hacker Young LLP, Quadrant House, 4 Thomas More Square, LONDON, E1W 1YW.
ANDERSON, Miss. Maxine Ann, BSc ACA *1989;* 14 Belgrave Road, Barnes, LONDON, SW13 9NS.
ANDERSON, Miss. Melody Ruth, ACA MAAT *2010;* 84 Lexicon Apartments, Mecury Gardens, ROMFORD, ESSEX, RM1 3HG.
ANDERSON, Mr. Michael Alan, FCA *1952;* 17 Godolphin House, Fellows Road, LONDON, NW3 3LG. (Life Member)
•ANDERSON, Mr. Michael Braid, BA FCA *1987;* Bell Anderson Ltd, 264-266 Durham Road, GATESHEAD, NE8 4JR. See also M B Anderson & Co
ANDERSON, Mr. Michael Robert, BA ACA *2002;* 31 Richmond Avenue, LONDON, SW20 8LA.
ANDERSON, Mrs. Michelle, BSc ACA *1991;* 72 Brock End, Portishead, BRISTOL, BS20 8AS.
ANDERSON, Mrs. Michelle Marie, BSc ACA *2005;* 3 Harefield Drive, MANCHESTER, M20 2SZ.
•ANDERSON, Miss. Muriel Elizabeth, FCA *1986;* (Tax Fac), Anderson & Shepherd, Shepson House, Stockwell Street, LEEK, STAFFORDSHIRE, ST13 6DH.
ANDERSON, Dr. Neil David, BSc(Hons) ACA *2002;* 26 Gardens Close, Stokenchurch, HIGH WYCOMBE, BUCKINGHAMSHIRE, HP14 3SP.

ANDERSON, Mr. Neil Edward, BSc FCA *1988;* Kellys Bay, Barnageeragh, SKERRIES, COUNTY DUBLIN, IRELAND.
ANDERSON, Mr. Neil Fraser, BSc ACA *2002;* 78 Boulevard Barbes, 75018 PARIS, FRANCE.
•**ANDERSON, Mr. Neville, BSc ACA** *2001;* with PricewaterhouseCoopers GmbH, Olof-Palme-Strasse 35, 60439 FRANKFURT AM MAIN, GERMANY.
ANDERSON, Mr. Nicholas Geoffrey, BA FCA *1991;* American Appraisal (UK) Ltd, Aldermary House, 10-15 Queen Street, LONDON, EC4N 1TX. (Life Member)
ANDERSON, Mr. Nicholas Jonathan Bruce, MA FCA *1989;* UBS AG, GPO BOX 5251, BRISBANE, QLD 4001, AUSTRALIA.
•**ANDERSON, Ms. Nicola Jane, FCA FCIE MACIE** *1980;* Nicola Anderson FCA FCIE, 189 Baldwins Lane, Croxley Green, RICKMANSWORTH, HERTFORDSHIRE, WD3 3LL.
ANDERSON, Mr. Nigel, BA ACA *1987;* 290 Blackburn Road, Egerton, BOLTON, BL7 9TB.
ANDERSON, Mr. Nigel Charles, FCA *1955;* Thornlea, 37 Elmfield Road, Gosforth, NEWCASTLE UPON TYNE, NE3 4BA. (Life Member)
ANDERSON, Mr. Nigel Sean, BSc FCA *1993;* The Hawthorns, Barton Road, Welford On Avon, STRATFORD-UPON-AVON, CV37 8EY.
ANDERSON, Mrs. Nina, BA ACA *1999;* 9 Crawford Road, Milngavie, GLASGOW, G62 7LE.
ANDERSON, Mr. Patrick Leonard, BA ACA *1983;* 41 Copperfield Drive, KINGSTON K7M 1M3, ON, CANADA.
ANDERSON, Mr. Paul, FCA *1962;* Gerald Duthie & Co, 525 Windsor Avenue, WINDSOR N9A 1J4, ON, CANADA.
ANDERSON, Mr. Paul Andrew, BA(Hons) ACA *2001;* 20 Challum Drive, Chadderton, OLDHAM, OL9 0LY.
ANDERSON, Mr. Paul Stuart, BA ACA *2005;* 10 Woodham Park Drive, BENFLEET, SS7 5EH.
ANDERSON, Mr. Paul Stuart, BSc ACA AMCT *1999;* Peterborough Services Great North Road, Haddon, PETERBOROUGH, PE7 3UQ.
ANDERSON, Mrs. Penelope Claire, BA ACA *1993;* Unit 9 The Bell Centre, Newton Road, CRAWLEY, WEST SUSSEX, RH10 9FZ.
ANDERSON, Mr. Peter John Ronald, MA FCA *1990;* 2 Blenheim Drive, OXFORD, OX2 8DG.
ANDERSON, Miss. Rachel Elizabeth, BA FCA *1982;* 15 Burbage Road, LONDON, SE24 9HJ.
ANDERSON, Mr. Raymond Keith, FCA *1971;* 11 Helen Close, WEST MOLESEY, SURREY, KT8 2PU.
ANDERSON, Mr. Richard, ACA *1981;* La Providence., Ruette Braye, St. Peter Port, GUERNSEY, GY1 1PJ.
ANDERSON, Mr. Richard, LLB ACA ATII *1991;* M R P Development Services Ltd, 20 Fletcher Gate, NOTTINGHAM, NG1 2FZ.
ANDERSON, Mr. Richard Alec Douglas, BSc ACA *1994;* 16 Hampden Grove, Beeston, NOTTINGHAM, NG9 1FG.
ANDERSON, Mr. Richard Charles, BSc FCA *1983;* The Thatched House, Bisham Road, MARLOW, SL7 1RL.
ANDERSON, Mr. Richard James, BA ACA *1997;* High Trees House, Main Street, Greatford, STAMFORD, LINCOLNSHIRE, PE9 4QA.
ANDERSON, Mr. Richard John, BSc ACA *1991;* The Schoolhouse, The Green, Wolviston, BILLINGHAM, TS22 5LN.
•**ANDERSON, Mr. Richard John, FCA** *1963;* with Anderson Barrowcliff, Waterloo House, Teesdale South, Thornaby Place, STOCKTON-ON-TEES, TS17 6SA.
ANDERSON, Mr. Richard Neil, BA ACA *2006;* 30 Seymour Road, EAST MOLESEY, SURREY, KT8 0PB.
ANDERSON, Mr. Richard Philip, BEng ACA *2005;* 31 Marchant Way, Churwell, Morley, LEEDS, LS27 7GF.
•**ANDERSON, Mr. Robert, FCA** *1988;* (Tax Fac), Fox Evans Limited, Abbey House, 7 Manor Road, COVENTRY, CV1 2FW.
ANDERSON, Mr. Robert, MA ACA *2011;* 3 Herondale Avenue, LONDON, SW18 3JN.
ANDERSON, Mr. Robert, FCA *1962;* Hamilton House, 11 Marquis Way, Aldwick, BOGNOR REGIS, PO21 4AT. (Life Member)
ANDERSON, Mr. Robert Andrew, BA(Hons) ACA *2009;* 43/10 Deanhaugh Street, EDINBURGH, EH4 1LR.
ANDERSON, Mr. Robert Charles Bruce, BSc FCA *1977;* 6 Kilfillan Gardens, BERKHAMSTED, HERTFORDSHIRE, HP4 3LU.
•**ANDERSON, Mr. Robert David, FCA** *1974;* (Tax Fac), R. David Anderson, West Gables, Westgate, Thornton-le-Dale, PICKERING, YO18 7SG.
ANDERSON, Mr. Robert David, FCA *1966;* The Coach House, Well Place, CHELTENHAM, GLOUCESTERSHIRE, GL50 2PJ.
ANDERSON, Mr. Robert Gavin Stewart, FCA *1964;* 205 Hillspoint Road, WESTPORT, CT 06880, UNITED STATES.
•**ANDERSON, Mr. Robert Henry, FCA FCCA** *1974;* Andersons Accountants Limited, Bank Chambers, Market Place, Melbourne, DERBY, DE73 8DS.
ANDERSON, Mr. Robert James, BSc ACA *1992;* 28 Knutsford Road, WILMSLOW, SK9 6JB.
ANDERSON, Mr. Robert James Hazley, BSc ACA *1992;* The Willows, Beech Hill, Headley Down, BORDON, HAMPSHIRE, GU35 8HS.
ANDERSON, Mr. Robert John, FCA *1973;* R V Anderson Ltd, The Limes, Avon Dassett, SOUTHAM, CV47 2AR.
ANDERSON, Mr. Robert Llewellyn, BSc ACA *2002;* 7 Bells Court, Carlton-le-Moorland, LINCOLN, LN5 9JL.
ANDERSON, Mr. Robert Neil, BSc ACA *1987;* West Manor, Robins Nest Hill, Little Berkhamsted, HERTFORD, SG13 8LS.
ANDERSON, Mr. Robert Oswald, FCA *1951;* 66 Dartmouth Ave, Westlands, NEWCASTLE, ST5 3PA. (Life Member)
ANDERSON, Mr. Robin John, MA FCA *1967;* 57 High Street, Bridge, CANTERBURY, KENT, CT4 5LA.
ANDERSON, Dr. Roderick Alan, ACA *1985;* Flat 23, Normandy Court, West Parade, WORTHING, WEST SUSSEX, BN11 3QY.
ANDERSON, Mr. Roger Bruce, FCA *1977;* Far Hills, 16 Hesitation Lane, DEVONSHIRE DV 03, BERMUDA.
ANDERSON, Mr. Roland Edwin, BA ACA *2006;* 10 Albert Square, LONDON, SW8 1BT.
ANDERSON, Mrs. Rosemary Annie, BA FCA ATII *1992;* (Tax Fac), Bride Cross Granary, Dob Park, OTLEY, WEST YORKSHIRE, LS21 2NA.
ANDERSON, Mr. Ross Kenyon, MA FCA *1963;* 12 The Park, LONDON, NW11 7SU. (Life Member)
•**ANDERSON, Miss. Ruth, BA FCA CTA** *1980;* 10 Knox Street, LONDON, W1H 1FY.
ANDERSON, Miss. Ruth, BSc ACA *1993;* New Farm House, Crostwight, NORTH WALSHAM, NORFOLK, NR28 9PA.
ANDERSON, Miss. Ruth Elizabeth, MA ACA *1988;* University of Surrey, GUILDFORD, GU2 7XH.
•**ANDERSON, Mrs. Sarah, BSc FCA** *1994;* (Tax Fac), King Hope & Co, 34 Romanby Road, NORTHALLERTON, DL7 8NF.
ANDERSON, Mr. Sean McAdam, BAcc ACA *2000;* 47 Mulberry Drive, DUNFERMLINE, KY11 8BZ.
ANDERSON, Mrs. Selina, BSc ACA *2009;* 1 Bowling Green, Compton, GUILDFORD, GU3 1JT.
ANDERSON, Mr. Simon Nicholas, FCA *1964;* Newlyn, 14 West Green, Barrington, CAMBRIDGE, CB22 7SA. (Life Member)
•**ANDERSON, Mr. Stephen, BSc ACA** *2000;* PricewaterhouseCoopers - Qatar LLC, 3rd Floor, Al Amadi Business Centre, P O Box 6689, DOHA, QATAR. See also PricewaterhouseCoopers LLP
•**ANDERSON, Mr. Stephen Mark, BA FCA** *1989;* PM+M Solutions for Business LLP, Greenbank Technology Park, Challenge Way, BLACKBURN, BB1 5QB. See also PM & M Corporate Finance Limited
•**ANDERSON, Mr. Stuart, BSc FCA** *1986;* (Tax Fac), Stuart Anderson Accountants Limited, Newland, Ely Valley Road, Talbot Green, PONTYCLUN, MID GLAMORGAN CF72 8AP.
ANDERSON, Mr. Stuart Edward, ACA *2008;* 7 Powell Gardens, REDHILL, RH1 1TQ.
ANDERSON, Miss. Susan Clare Frances, BSc ACA *1990;* 94 Greenway, Totteridge, LONDON, N20 8EJ.
•**ANDERSON, Mrs. Susan Jane, BA ACA** *1988;* S J Anderson BA ACA, Walton House, 10 Mapperley Road, Mapperley Park, NOTTINGHAM, NG3 5AA.
•**ANDERSON, Mrs. Tara Ann, BA ACA** *1993;* Andersons, 53 Wellhall Road, HAMILTON, LANARKSHIRE, ML3 9BY. See also Anderson Brownlie Ltd
ANDERSON, Mr. Thomas Robert, ACA *2008;* 58 Chapel Lane, WILMSLOW, CHESHIRE, SK9 5HZ.
ANDERSON, Mr. Timothy David, BA ACA *2001;* 10 Haversham Close, CRAWLEY, WEST SUSSEX, RH10 1LB.
ANDERSON, Mr. Timothy John, BA ACA *1994;* Winder's Wood Cottage Howden Dene, CORBRIDGE, NORTHUMBERLAND, NE45 5LT.
•**ANDERSON, Mr. Timothy Ross, FCA** *1975;* Tim R Anderson, 56 Glebelands Road, KNUTSFORD, CHESHIRE, WA16 9DZ.
ANDERSON, Miss. Tracey Jane, BSc ACA *1997;* 40 Broadfern Road, Knowle, SOLIHULL, B93 9DD.
ANDERSON, Miss. Tracy Marie, ACA *2011;* Jandine, Main Road, Stickney, BOSTON, LINCOLNSHIRE, PE22 8AD.
ANDERSON, Mr. Trevor John, FCA *1972;* The Gables, 52 Brockham Lane, BETCHWORTH, RH3 7EH.
ANDERSON, Mrs. Victoria Anne, BA ACA *1994;* Primrose Cottage, 40 Church Street, Thriplow, ROYSTON, SG8 7RE.
•**ANDERSON, Mrs. Victoria Mary Ross, BA FCA DChA** *1992;* Clark Brownscombe Limited, 2 St. Andrews Place, Southover Road, LEWES, EAST SUSSEX, BN7 1UP.
ANDERSON, Mr. William Eamonn, BSc FCA *1981;* 43 Main Street, Wheldrake, YORK, YO19 6AE.
ANDERSON, Mr. William Robert, BA ACA *1986;* 6 The Green, Park Lane Old Knebworth, KNEBWORTH, HERTFORDSHIRE, SG3 6QN.
ANDERSON, Mr. William Wallace, FCA *1973;* Henderson Global Investors, 201 Bishopsgate, LONDON, EC2M 3AE.
ANDERSON BROWN, Mr. Duncan John, BSc ACA *1994;* 2 The Crescent, Chapel Field Road, NORWICH, NR2 1SA.
•**ANDERSON-RILEY, Mr. John Harry, FCA** *1983;* Trudgeon Halling, The Platt, WADEBRIDGE, PL27 7AE. See also Trudgeon Halling Limited
ANDERSON TYRER, Mrs. Yana, BSc ACA *1991;* 4 Hunt Road, THAME, OX9 3LG.
ANDERSSON, Mr. Christopher Frej, BA ACA *1998;* Gateway House, 28 The Quadrant, RICHMOND, SURREY, TW9 1DN.
ANDERTON, Mr. Christopher James, BA(Hons) ACA *2003;* 15 Poplar Road, LONDON, SE24 0BN.
ANDERTON, Mr. Colin James, BSc ACA *2002;* Egg Financial Products, Riverside Road, Pride Park, DERBY, DE99 3GG.
ANDERTON, Mrs. Elizabeth Ruth, BSc ACA *2000;* 93 Elthorne Park Road, LONDON, W7 2JH.
ANDERTON, Mrs. Erin Elizabeth, MSc BA ACA *2009;* Apartment 417 The Box Works, 4 Worsley Street, MANCHESTER, M15 4NU.
ANDERTON, Mr. Ian Leeming, BSc ACA *1992;* 7 Tormore Close, Heapey, CHORLEY, PR6 9BP.
ANDERTON, Miss. Lesley Jayne, BA ACA *1988;* 3 Rackham Drive, LUTON, LU3 2AF.
ANDERTON, Miss. Michelle, BBA ACA *2006;* 11 Wye Street, LONDON, SW11 2SN.
ANDERTON, Mr. Paul Robert, BA FCA *1982;* PricewaterhouseCoopers, Strathvale House, PO Box 258, GEORGE TOWN, GRAND CAYMAN, KY1-1104 CAYMAN ISLANDS.
•**ANDERTON, Mr. Roger John, FCA** *1983;* R J Anderton Limited, Suite 110, First Floor, Malthouse Business Centre, 48 Southport Road, ORMSKIRK LANCASHIRE L39 1QR.
ANDIC, Mr. Stephen George, FCA *1981;* (Tax Fac), with MacIntyre Hudson LLP, Peterbridge House, The Lakes, NORTHAMPTON, NN4 7HB.
ANDO, Mr. Alexander Francis Carlo, MA ACA *1982;* Via G. Severano 28, 00161 ROME, ITALY.
•**ANDO, Mr. Roderic David Clarence, BA FCA CTA** *1990;* (Tax Fac), The New Villas, Sopworth, CHIPPENHAM, SN14 6PR.
•**ANDOW, Mr. Ian George, ACA** *1985;* Shinewood Ltd, 4 Orchard Place, Harvington, EVESHAM, WORCESTERSHIRE, WR11 8NF.
ANDRADE, Miss. Amber Louise, ACA *2008;* Deloitte & Touche Hill House, 1 Little New Street, LONDON, EC4A 3TR.
ANDRASOVSKY, Mr. Robert, MSc ACA *2005;* Lipnicka 1448, 19800 PRAGUE, CZECH REPUBLIC.
ANDRAWES, Mr. Sherif, BEng FCA *1991;* 38 Station Street, SUBIACO, WA 6008, AUSTRALIA.
ANDRE, Mr. Dillon, ACA CA(SA) *2009;* 6 Bushy Close, OXFORD, OX2 9SH.
ANDREA, Mr. Andrew, MA ACA *1996;* Brook Farm Yoxall Road, Newborough, BURTON-ON-TRENT, STAFFORDSHIRE, DE13 8SU.
ANDREA, Mr. Andros, BA FCA *1996;* MacIntyre Hudson, Euro House, 1394 High Road, LONDON, N20 9YZ.
ANDREADES, Mr. Andreas, BA ACA *1992;* Voulgaroktonou 25, Voula, 16673 ATHENS, GREECE.
ANDREADOU, Miss. Despina, BSc ACA *1990;* 24 Al Panagouli Street, Glyfada, 16675 ATHENS, GREECE.
ANDREAE, Mrs. Aimee Rebecca, ACA *2008;* Financial Services Audit 4th Floor, K P M G Llp, 15 Canada Square, LONDON, E14 5GL.
•**ANDREAE, Miss. Vivien Rona, FCA ATII** *1977;* V.R. Andreae, 57a Chilkwell Street, GLASTONBURY, BA6 8DE.
ANDREAS, Mr. Anthony, ACA *2011;* Flat 13 Thatcham Court, High Road, LONDON, N20 9QU.
ANDREOU, Mr. Andreas, ACA *2009;* Griva Digeni 31, #8220 Dali #8221, 2540 NICOSIA, CYPRUS.
•**ANDREOU, Mr. Andreas, BA ACA** *2001;* Deloitte Limited, 24 Spyrou Kyprianou Avenue, P.O.Box 21675 CY-1512, 1075 NICOSIA, CYPRUS.
ANDREOU, Mr. Andreas, ACA *2009;* 3 Nearchou St, Ormidhia, 7530 LARNACA, CYPRUS.
ANDREOU, Mr. Andreas Kyprou, BSc ACA *1996;* P O Box 51555, 3506 LIMASSOL, CYPRUS.
ANDREOU, Mr. Andrew, BSc ACA *1983;* U M E Investment Co, Tavistock House, Tavistock Square, LONDON, WC1H 9LG.
ANDREOU, Miss. Anna, BSc ACA *2001;* Archiepiskopoy Kyprianoy 4, Peristerona, 2731 NICOSIA, CYPRUS.
ANDREOU, Mr. George, BSc ACA *2006;* 9 Bellapais Street, 8049 PAPHOS, CYPRUS.
•**ANDREOU, Mr. Marios Solonos, BSc(Econ) ACA** *1996;* PricewaterhouseCoopers Limited, Julia House, 3 Themistocles Dervis Street, CY-1066 NICOSIA, CYPRUS.
ANDREOU, Mr. Stylianos Savva, MSc BA(Hons) ACA *2002;* Spyridona, Trikoupy 3, 6053 LARNACA, CYPRUS.
ANDRESEN, Mr. Oivind, BSc ACA *2007;* 124 Brondesbury Villas, LONDON, NW6 6AE.
ANDRESS, Mr. William Graham, FCA *1960;* Apartdo De Correos 191, Alhavrin El Grande, 29120 MALAGA, SPAIN. (Life Member)
ANDREW, Mrs. Annabel, MSci ACA *2002;* 54 Pembridge Road, LONDON, W11 3HN.
ANDREW, Mrs. Ceri Elizabeth, BA ACA *1996;* 11 Maes Brith y Garn, Pontprennau, CARDIFF, CF23 8QE.
ANDREW, Mr. Christopher John, FCA *1972;* (Tax Fac), 42 Green Street, Hazlemere, HIGH WYCOMBE, HP15 7RA.
ANDREW, Mr. David John, MBA BSc ACA CTA *1992;* Flat 111 Bishops Mansions, Bishops Park Road, Fulham, LONDON, SW6 6DY.
ANDREW, Mr. Derek Norman, BA FCA *1957;* Walnut House, Old Coach Road, Cross, AXBRIDGE, BS26 2EH. (Life Member)
ANDREW, Ms. Elizabeth Clare, MA ACA *1998;* SEPSR Moscow. c/o expat mail, Shell International Petroleum Co Ltd Shell Centre, York Road, LONDON, SE1 7NA.
ANDREW, Mr. Glenn Paul, BSc ACA *1998;* 11 Maes Brith y Garn, Pontprennau, CARDIFF, CF23 8QE.
ANDREW, Mr. Graham Pentreath, MA ACA *1990;* 185 Popes Lane, Ealing, LONDON, W5 4NH.
ANDREW, Mr. Guy Anthony Bevis, MBA BA FCA *1977;* PO Box 372, PARAP, NT 0804, AUSTRALIA.
ANDREW, Miss. Heather Elizabeth, BA(Hons) ACA *2011;* Selwyn Croft, 175 Whittingham Lane, Goosnargh, PRESTON, PR3 2JJ.
ANDREW, Mr. Ian, FCA *1966;* 58 Tomline Road, FELIXSTOWE, SUFFOLK, IP11 7PA.
•**ANDREW, Mr. John, BSc ACA** *1992;* (Tax Fac), John Andrew, Green Tree Barn, Faraday Road, KIRKBY STEPHEN, CUMBRIA, CA17 4QL.
ANDREW, Mr. John Charles, BA ACA *1993;* 41 Home Farm Way, Penllergaer, SWANSEA, SA4 9HF.
ANDREW, Mr. John Christopher, FCA *1973;* Maroy Inchgarth Road, Pitfodels Cults, ABERDEEN, AB15 9NX.
•**ANDREW, Mr. John Duncan, FCA** *1988;* Duncan & Toplis, 3 Castlegate, GRANTHAM, LINCOLNSHIRE, NG31 6SF.
ANDREW, Mr. John Keith, ACA *1996;* 34 Sanderstead Court Avenue, SOUTH CROYDON, SURREY, CR2 9AG.
ANDREW, Mr. Jonathan Charles, BSc ACA *1992;* Bromlea, 49 Bowes Road, WALTON-ON-THAMES, SURREY, KT12 3HU.
•**ANDREW, Mr. Jonathan Garnett, FCA** *1970;* (Tax Fac), Jonathan Andrew, 1A The Homend, LEDBURY, HR8 1BN.
ANDREW, The Revd. Jonathan William, MA FCA *1975;* Orchard, 6 Westacres, ESHER, KT10 9JE.
ANDREW, Mrs. Marisa Helen, BEd ACA *1992;* 34 Church Road, Stanfree Bolsover, CHESTERFIELD, S44 6AQ.
•**ANDREW, Mr. Mark Stephen Rees, MA FCA** *1987;* 47 Oxenden Wood Road, Chelsfield Park, ORPINGTON, BR6 6HP.
•**ANDREW, Mr. Nicholas Anthony Samuel, MA FCA** *1974;* (Tax Fac), Nicholas Andrew & Co Limited, 49 Berkeley Square, LONDON, W1J 5AZ.
ANDREW, Mr. Nigel Lee, BSc FCA *1983;* 2 St. Austell Drive, Greenmount, BURY, LANCASHIRE, BL8 4EY.

ANDREW, Mr. Richard, ACA *2009;* with Hawsons, Jubilee House, 32 Duncan Close, Moulton Park, NORTHAMPTON, NN3 6WL.
ANDREW, Mr. Richard Stephen, ACA *2005;* First Floor East Bridge Mills, Stramongate, KENDAL, CUMBRIA, LA9 4UB.
ANDREW, Mr. Robert St J, FCA *1965;* The Old Manse, Kirkmichael, BLAIRGOWRIE, PH10 7NY. (Life Member)
ANDREW, Mrs. Rosemary Winifred, BSc(Econ) FCA *1957;* 74 Elizabeth Avenue, North Hykeham, LINCOLN, LN6 9RR. (Life Member)
ANDREW, Mrs. Sally Elizabeth, BSc ACA *1992;* 49 Bowes Road, WALTON-ON-THAMES, SURREY, KT12 3HU.
•**ANDREW, Mrs. Samantha, BSc ACA** *1992;* Samantha Adnrew BSc ACA, 1 Knighton Road, Wembury, PLYMOUTH, PL9 0EA.
ANDREW, Mr. Stephen John, BSc ACA *1992;* 14 Beckside, Elvington, YORK, YO41 4BE.
•**ANDREW, Mrs. Victoria Elizabeth, MA(Oxon) FCA FRSA** *1989;* (Tax Fac), HBA Accountancy, 47 Oxenden Wood Road, Chelsfield Park, ORPINGTON, KENT, BR6 6HP. See also VE Andrew (Incorporating Hollamby & Co)
ANDREWARTHA, Mrs. Elaine Bridget, BSc ACA *1994;* (Tax Fac), Lanteague, Two Burrows, Blackwater, TRURO, TR4 8HN.
ANDREWES, Mr. John David, MA FCA *1964;* 8 Murray Road, Wimbledon, LONDON, SW19 4PB. (Life Member)
ANDREWES, Mr. Peter Michael, BSc FCA *1973;* 19 Hendy Close, Derwen Fawr, SWANSEA, SA2 8BB.
•**ANDREWS, Mr. Adrian Ronald, FCA** *1979;* Adrian Andrews, 42 Bushey Way, BECKENHAM, BR3 6TB.
ANDREWS, Mr. Alfred George, FCA *1950;* Whitecroft, 31 Carroll Hill, LOUGHTON, IG10 1NL. (Life Member)
ANDREWS, Mrs. Alison, BA ACA *1998;* Association of Investment Companies, 24 Chiswell Street, LONDON, EC1Y 4YY.
ANDREWS, Mr. Alun Leslie, FCA *1970;* 24 Cathedral Road, CARDIFF, CF11 9LJ.
ANDREWS, Mr. Anthony Mark, MA FCA ATII *1989;* 4 Bradshaws Close, LONDON, SE25 4EN.
ANDREWS, Mr. Anthony Neil, MA FCA *1975;* 15 Wentworth Road, SUTTON COLDFIELD, B74 2SD.
•**ANDREWS, Mr. Bowker Roy, BSc FCA** *1980;* PricewaterhouseCoopers LLP, 1 Embankment Place, LONDON, WC2N 6RH. See also PricewaterhouseCoopers
ANDREWS, Mr. Brian, FCA *1958;* Cherries, 6 Sytche Close, MUCH WENLOCK, SHROPSHIRE, TF13 6JJ.
ANDREWS, Mr. Brian Samuel, FCA *1958;* 136 Church Road, Sandford On Thames, OXFORD, OX4 4YB. (Life Member)
ANDREWS, Mr. Brian Trevor, BA FCA *1962;* Tynewydd, 20 The Beeches, Middleton St. George, DARLINGTON, COUNTY DURHAM, DL2 1GD.
ANDREWS, Mr. Carl, BSc ACA *2005;* 15 Treharne Road, TREHARRIS, CF46 5NY.
ANDREWS, Mrs. Carmel Ann, BSc ACA *1988;* 64 Blackhills Place, DANVILLE, CA 94506-2103, UNITED STATES.
ANDREWS, Miss. Carolyn Ann, BA ACA *1981;* 38 Lancaster Avenue, LONDON, SE27 9DZ.
ANDREWS, Mr. Charles James, BA ACA *1992;* Hill View, 46 Castle Street, Cranborne, WIMBORNE, DORSET, BH21 5QA.
ANDREWS, Mr. Charles Robert James, MA ACA *2001;* The Laurels, 2A Southern Road, LONDON, N2 9LN.
•**ANDREWS, Mr. Christopher John, BA(Econ) ACA** *2004;* (Tax Fac), Leftley Rowe & Company, The Heights, 59-65 Lowlands Road, HARROW, MIDDLESEX, HA1 3AW. See also Mountsides Limited
ANDREWS, Mr. Christopher John, BSc ACA *1998;* 50 Elizabeth Drive, WANTAGE, OX12 9YG.
ANDREWS, Mr. Christopher John Francis, BA ACA *1987;* Sortridge Manor, Horrabridge, YELVERTON, DEVON, PL20 7UA.
ANDREWS, Mr. Christopher Stewart, BA ACA *1986;* Elmhurst, Zig-Zag Road, KENLEY, CR8 5EL.
ANDREWS, Mr. Colin, FCA *1970;* 30 Leveller Road, Newick, LEWES, EAST SUSSEX, BN8 4PL.
•**ANDREWS, Mr. Colin Charles, FCA** *1982;* Colin C Andrews Limited, 44 Armingford Crescent, Melbourn, ROYSTON PARK, HERTFORDSHIRE, SG8 6NG.
ANDREWS, Mr. Colin Sidney, FCA *1974;* 10 Kemnal Park, HASLEMERE, GU27 2LF.
ANDREWS, Mr. Colin William, FCA *1957;* Fairmead, 146 Cooden Sea Road, Cooden, BEXHILL-ON-SEA, TN39 4TE. (Life Member)
ANDREWS, Mr. Daniel Paul, BA ACA *2004;* K P M G, 1 The Embankment, LEEDS, LS1 4DW.
•**ANDREWS, Mr. David Hugh, FCA** *1969;* (Tax Fac), Richard Place & Co, Here House, Second Avenue, Batchmere, CHICHESTER, WEST SUSSEX PO20 7LF.
ANDREWS, Mr. David Hunter, BA FCA *1954;* Cefn Bryn House, Penmaen, Gower, SWANSEA, SA3 2HQ. (Life Member)
ANDREWS, Mr. David James, BA ACA *1998;* 5 Bramley Road, STREET, SOMERSET, BA16 0QE.
ANDREWS, Mr. David Norman Martindale, MA FCA *1967;* Highlands, EtchingWood Lane, Framfield, UCKFIELD, EAST SUSSEX, TN22 5SA. (Life Member)
•**ANDREWS, Mr. David Ross, BSc FCA** *1979;* (Tax Fac), D.R. Andrews, Northacre, Deerleap Road, Westcott, DORKING, RH4 3LE.
ANDREWS, Mr. David William, MA FCA *1971;* Xchanging, Lilly House, 13 Hanover Square, LONDON, W1S 1HN.
•**ANDREWS, Mr. Dean Michael, FCA** *1984;* Mackenzie Field, Hyde House, The Hyde, Edgware Road, LONDON, NW9 6LA.
ANDREWS, Mrs. Deborah Jane, ACA *1990;* B & P Accounting Partnership, Kingsley House, Church Lane, Shurdington, CHELTENHAM, GLOUCESTERSHIRE GL51 4TQ.
ANDREWS, The Revd. Dennis Arthur, DD FCA *1952;* 3019 Old Sambro Road, WILLIAMSWOOD B3V 1E6, NS, CANADA. (Life Member)
ANDREWS, Mrs. Emma Julia, ACA *2005;* 48 Berridge Road, SHEERNESS, ME12 2AD.
ANDREWS, Miss. Esta Louise, BSc(Hons) *2001;* 191 Bradley Road, HUDDERSFIELD, HD2 1QF.
ANDREWS, Mr. Francis Stanley, FCA *1965;* 1 Frith Knowle, Hersham, WALTON-ON-THAMES, KT12 5EW.
ANDREWS, Mr. Gary Richard, BSc FCA *1992;* Westwood, Bradford Road, BINGLEY, WEST YORKSHIRE, BD16 1NQ.
ANDREWS, Miss. Gemma Marie, ACA *2010;* K P M G Alteus House, 1 North Fourth Street, MILTON KEYNES, MK9 1NE.
ANDREWS, Mr. Glenn Martin, BSc(Econ) FCA CTA *1978;* (Tax Fac), Kwik-Fit: Divisional Office, 216 East Main Street, BROXBURN, WEST LOTHIAN, EH52 5AS.
ANDREWS, Mr. Graham Derek, BA(Hons) ACA *2001;* 144 Woodside Road, AMERSHAM, HP6 6NP.
ANDREWS, Mr. Gregory Edward, FCA *1990;* Timberline, Oak Way, REIGATE, RH2 7ES.
ANDREWS, Miss. Hannah Louise, BSc ACA *2006;* 47 Ferry Road, KIDWELLY, DYFED, SA17 5EQ.
ANDREWS, Mr. Henrique Alves, MA BSc ACA *2006;* 44 Overbury Avenue, BECKENHAM, BR3 6PY.
ANDREWS, Mr. Hugh Christopher, BSc FCA *1990;* Conocophillips, 2 Portman Street, LONDON, W1H 6DU.
ANDREWS, Mr. Hugh Martin John, BSc ACA *1990;* 4 rue Maurice Berteaux, 78780 MAURECOURT, FRANCE.
ANDREWS, The Revd. Ian Arthur, FCA *1963;* Snowdon Cottage, Snowdon Cottage Lane, CHARD, TA20 1LN.
ANDREWS, Mr. Ian William, BCom FCA *1977;* 308 Upton Lane, WIDNES, WA8 9AG.
ANDREWS, Mr. James John, MA MEng ACA *2010;* 64 Bullimore Grove, KENILWORTH, CV8 2QF.
ANDREWS, Mr. James Robert John, BSc ACA *1997;* 22 The Esplanade, HOLYWOOD, COUNTY DOWN, BT18 9JP.
•**ANDREWS, Mrs. Jane Margaret, ACA** *1987;* (Tax Fac), Jane M. Andrews, 9 Nimrod Close, Sandpit Lane, ST. ALBANS, AL4 9XY. See also Prolific Payroll Limited
ANDREWS, Miss. Janet Frances, ACA *2009;* Pricewaterhousecoopers, 101 Barbirolli Square, MANCHESTER, M2 3PW.
•**ANDREWS, Mr. Jeremy Marc, BSc ACA** *1985;* (Tax Fac), Jeremy Marc Andrews, Milroy House, Sayers Lane, TENTERDEN, KENT, TN30 6BW.
•**ANDREWS, Miss. Jill, BA ACA** *1994;* Ashbys Business Consultants Limited, Morton House, 9 Beacon Court, Pitstone Green Business Park, Pitstone, LEIGHTON BUZZARD BEDFORDSHIRE LU7 9GY.
ANDREWS, Mrs. Joan Rosalind, FCA *1967;* 6 Spring Shaw Road, ORPINGTON, BR5 2RH.
ANDREWS, Mr. John Anthony, BSc ACA *1993;* 69 St. Andrews Road, CAMBRIDGE, CB4 1DH.
ANDREWS, Mr. John Derek, BA ACA *1986;* 10 Ryecroft Lane, BRIGHOUSE, HD6 3TQ.
ANDREWS, Mr. John Malcolm, OBE FCA *1974;* Martello Tower, Hospital Hill, Sandgate, FOLKESTONE, KENT, CT20 3TB. (Life Member)
ANDREWS, Mr. John Michael Geoffrey, MA FCA *1956;* 80 Palace Gardens Terrace, LONDON, W8 4RS. (Life Member)
ANDREWS, Mr. John Miles, FCA *1963;* 7 The Moat, Charing, ASHFORD, KENT, TN27 0JH.
ANDREWS, Mr. John Robert, BCom FCA *1975;* Ash Tree House 3 The Woodlands Lathom, ORMSKIRK, LANCASHIRE, L40 5RS.
ANDREWS, Mr. John Robert, FCA *1953;* 17 Cockersand Avenue, Hutton, PRESTON, PR4 5FN. (Life Member)
ANDREWS, Mr. Jonathan David, FCA *1974;* Netlearn Services Inc, Seabird House, 1 Midwood Road, VICTORIA V9B 1L4, BC, CANADA.
ANDREWS, Mrs. Judith Elizabeth, BA ACA *1986;* Rumbold's Holding, Woodhouse Lane, Botley, SOUTHAMPTON, SO30 2EZ.
ANDREWS, Mrs. Kate Elizabeth, BSc ACA *1994;* Stamford Investment Trusts, 36 Broadway, LONDON, SW1H 0BH.
ANDREWS, Mrs. Kate Louise, BA ACA *1995;* 41 Wantage Road, DIDCOT, OXFORDSHIRE, OX11 0BS.
ANDREWS, Mr. Kenneth Douglas, FCA *1956;* 11 Robin Drive, Steeton, KEIGHLEY, BD20 6TF. (Life Member)
ANDREWS, Miss. Kirsty Rachel, BSc ACA *2003;* (Tax Fac), 9 Windsor Court, Kings Road, FLEET, HAMPSHIRE, GU51 3BD.
ANDREWS, Mrs. Leanne Claire, BSc(Hons) ACA *2000;* Ark End, Mallows Green Road, Manuden, BISHOP'S STORTFORD, HERTFORDSHIRE, CM23 1BP.
ANDREWS, Mr. Lee Michael, BSc FCA *1976;* 3708 - 221st Place SE, SAMMAMISH, WA 98075, UNITED STATES.
ANDREWS, Mr. Leslie Vincent, FCA *1973;* Abbeymead Guest House, 39a Victoria Road, CIRENCESTER, GL7 1ES.
ANDREWS, Dr. Lynn Marie, PhD BSc ACA *2005;* 4 Avondale Road, LONDON, N3 2EP.
ANDREWS, Mrs. Margaret Ann, ACA *1982;* 8 Earls Close, Webheath, REDDITCH, B97 5QQ.
ANDREWS, Mr. Mark Christian, MA ACA *1998;* 36 Chemin des Bleds, Hameau de Watterdal, 62380 SENINGHEM, FRANCE.
•**ANDREWS, Mr. Mark Richard, ACA FCCA** *2009;* (Tax Fac), Broadhead Peel Rhodes Ltd, 27a Lidget Hill, PUDSEY, WEST YORKSHIRE, LS28 7LG.
•**ANDREWS, Mr. Mark Stuart, BSc(Hons) ACA** *2000;* KPMG LLP, 15 Canada Square, LONDON, E14 5GL.
ANDREWS, Mr. Mark Thomas Beadle, BA ACA *2004;* 10 Weavers Mead, Bolnore Village, HAYWARDS HEATH, WEST SUSSEX, RH16 4FR.
ANDREWS, Mr. Martin John, BSc ACA *1990;* Hazy Hill Farm, 248 Old Birmingham Road, Marlbrook, BROMSGROVE, WORCESTERSHIRE, B60 1NU.
ANDREWS, Ms. Melinda Jane, BA ACA *1985;* 2 Wollaston Villas, 7 Hardy Road, LONDON, SE3 7NS.
ANDREWS, Ms. Melinda Josephine, BSc FCA *1982;* 3 Cornpoppy Avenue, MONMOUTH, GWENT, NP25 5SD.
ANDREWS, Mr. Michael David, BSc ACA *1993;* 62 Reedley Road, Westbury-on-Trym, BRISTOL, BS9 3SU.
•**ANDREWS, Mr. Michael John, BSc FCA** *1996;* Stephenson Smart, 22-26 King Street, KING'S LYNN, NORFOLK, PE30 1HJ.
ANDREWS, Mr. Michael John, ACA *1990;* Global Immersion Limited, The Barn Hurstwood Grange Hurstwood Lane, HAYWARDS HEATH, WEST SUSSEX, RH17 7QX.
ANDREWS, Mr. Neil Thomas, FCA *1957;* 2 Mossley Court, The Rank, Gnosall, STAFFORD, ST20 0BU. (Life Member)
ANDREWS, Mr. Nicholas, BSc ACA ATII *1984;* Tumbling Water Cakeham Road, West Wittering, CHICHESTER, WEST SUSSEX, PO20 8EB.
ANDREWS, Mr. Nicholas Charles, BSc ACA *1986;* Rumbolds Holding, Woodhouse Lane, Botley, SOUTHAMPTON, SO30 2EZ.
•**ANDREWS, Mr. Nicholas David, MA FCA** *1985;* KPMG LLP, 15 Canada Square, LONDON, E14 5GL. See also KPMG Europe LLP
ANDREWS, Mr. Patrick John, BSc FCA ATII *1975;* Poppyfield, 2 Hansby Close, Tickhill, DONCASTER, DN11 9RP.
ANDREWS, Mr. Peter John, MA MSc ACA MSI *1982;* 2 Wollaston Villas, 7 Hardy Road, LONDON, SE3 7NS.
ANDREWS, Mr. Peter Reginald, FCA *1959;* 114 Seacliff Drive, APTOS, CA 95003-4425, UNITED STATES. (Life Member)
ANDREWS, Mr. Peter Spencer, FCA *1967;* Pond House, Thurlow Road, Great Bradley, NEWMARKET, SUFFOLK, CB8 9LW.
ANDREWS, Mr. Phillip Steven, ACA *2009;* 4 Dunster Close, SOUTHAMPTON, SO16 8DF.
ANDREWS, Mrs. Rachel Claire, MA ACA *2000;* 38 Nepcote Lane, Findon, WORTHING, WEST SUSSEX, BN14 0SG.
ANDREWS, Mrs. Rachel Jane, BEng ACA *1998;* 28 Westwood Road, RYDE, ISLE OF WIGHT, PO33 3BJ.
ANDREWS, Mr. Raymond Maurice, FCA *1961;* 2 Northampton Road, Blisworth, NORTHAMPTON, NN7 3DN. (Life Member)
ANDREWS, Mrs. Rhona Ellen, BSc FCA *1993;* Porsche Cars GB, Bath Road, Calcot, READING, BERKSHIRE, RG31 7SE.
ANDREWS, Mr. Richard Charles Arthur, FCA *1970;* 7 Hill Drive, HOVE, EAST SUSSEX, BN3 6QN.
ANDREWS, Mr. Richard Desmond, BSc ACA *1982;* 13 Stott Close, Windmill Green, LONDON, SW18 2TG.
•**ANDREWS, Mr. Richard John, ACA** *1984;* RJN Associates Ltd, 28 Penny Croft, HARPENDEN, AL5 2PB.
•**ANDREWS, Mr. Richard John, MA ACA** *2000;* 48 Brokesley Street, LONDON, E3 4QJ.
ANDREWS, Mr. Richard John, BA ACA *1979;* 107 St Mary's Lane, Ballsbridge, DUBLIN 4, COUNTY DUBLIN, IRELAND.
ANDREWS, Mr. Robert David, MA ACA *1998;* 7 Parsonage Lane, WINDSOR, SL4 5EW.
ANDREWS, Mr. Robert David, FCA *1965;* 60 Longdown Lane North, EPSOM, SURREY, KT17 3JG.
ANDREWS, Mr. Robert Gary King, BA ACA *2006;* Hanson Aggregates The Ridge, Chipping Sodbury, BRISTOL, BS37 6AY.
ANDREWS, Mr. Robert Mario John, MA FCA *1970;* 15 Court Lane Gardens, Dulwich, LONDON, SE21 7DZ.
•**ANDREWS, Mr. Roger David, FCA CTA** *1971;* Andrews & Palmer Limited, 32 The Square, GILLINGHAM, DORSET, SP8 4AR.
ANDREWS, Mr. Roger Stephen, FCA *1977;* 3016 25A Street SW, CALGARY T3E 1Z7, AB, CANADA.
•**ANDREWS, Mrs. Rosemarie Ann, BA(Hons) ACA** *1988;* Whittles LLP, 1 Richmond Road, LYTHAM ST. ANNES, LANCASHIRE, FY8 1PE. See also Whittles
ANDREWS, Mr. Ross, ACA *2011;* 1 Stone Cottages, Heath Road, Boughton Monchelsea, MAIDSTONE, KENT, ME17 4JD.
ANDREWS, Mr. Ross Malcolm, BA ACA *1990;* Succinct Communications Ltd 1 Burton House, Repton Place White Lion Road, AMERSHAM, BUCKINGHAMSHIRE, HP7 9LP.
•**ANDREWS, Mr. Roy Stephen, ACA** *1981;* Prolific Payroll Limited, 9 Nimrod Close, Sandpit Lane, ST. ALBANS, HERTFORDSHIRE, AL4 9XY.
ANDREWS, Mr. Simon Patrick, ACA *1986;* 4 Sadberge Court, Osbaldwick, YORK, YO10 3DB.
ANDREWS, Mr. Simon Richard, BA ACA *2005;* 3 Clements Mews, West Street, ROCHFORD, ESSEX, SS4 1FZ.
ANDREWS, Mr. Stephen, BSc FCA *1974;* 249 Winsley Road, BRADFORD-ON-AVON, BA15 1QS.
ANDREWS, Mr. Stephen Charles, BA ACA *1988;* 28 Plympton Street, NEW PLYMOUTH, NEW ZEALAND.
ANDREWS, Mr. Stephen John, BSc FCA *1983;* 6 Highworth Way, Tilehurst, READING, RG31 6GP.
ANDREWS, Mr. Stephen Richard, BSocSc ACA *1997;* 45 Denton Avenue, LEEDS, LS8 1LE.
ANDREWS, Mr. Steven James, BSc ACA *1993;* 42 Mirfield Road, SOLIHULL, B91 1JD.
ANDREWS, Mr. Stuart Anthony, MA ACA *2000;* Ark End, Mallows Green Road, Manuden, BISHOP'S STORTFORD, HERTFORDSHIRE, CM23 1BP.
ANDREWS, Mrs. Susan Joan, BA ACA *1995;* Ryecroft Barn, 10 Ryecroft Lane, BRIGHOUSE, HD6 3TQ.
ANDREWS, Mrs. Suzannah Jane, BEng ACA *1999;* 15 John Street, WILLIAMSTOWN, VIC 3016, AUSTRALIA.
ANDREWS, Mr. Timothy Keith, BSc ACA *1988;* 133 Harbord Street, LONDON, SW6 6PN.
ANDREWS, Mr. Trevor Stephen, BA FCA *1980;* 1 Den Close, BECKENHAM, BR3 6RP.
ANDREWS, Miss. Victoria Clare, BA ACA *1986;* 12 Gayton Road, LONDON, NW3 1TX.
ANDREWS, Mrs. Victoria Lucy, BSc ACA *1999;* 61 Blunts Wood Road, HAYWARDS HEATH, WEST SUSSEX, RH16 1ND.
ANDREWS, Mr. Yiannakis, BSc(Hons) ACA *2004;* 7 Brook Farm Close, Wymington, RUSHDEN, NORTHAMPTONSHIRE, NN10 9NQ.
ANDREWS-FAULKNER, Mr. John Oliver, FCA *1951;* 6 Home Ground, Cricklade, SWINDON, SN6 6JG. (Life Member)
ANDREWS MERCER, Mrs. Emma Louise, BSc ACA *1999;* with Carillion plc, Carillion Services, Construction House, 24 Birch Street, WOLVERHAMPTON, WV1 4HY.

ANDRIJASEVIC, Mrs. Stephanie Jane, BA ACA *1997;* Jardin de Devant, Rue A L'Eau, St. Pierre Du Bois, GUERNSEY, GY7 9HB.
ANDROKLI, Mr. Lefteris, BSc ACA *2006;* 3 Andrea Zakoy, Akrounta, 4522 LIMASSOL, CYPRUS.
ANDRONICOU, Mr. Andreas, MSc BSc ACA *2009;* 25 Dhigenis Akritas Street, 2045 STROVOLOS, CYPRUS.
•ⓘ**ANDRONIKOU, Mr. Andrew, BA ACA** *1990;* UHY Hacker Young LLP, Quadrant House, 4 Thomas More Square, LONDON, E1W 1YW.
ANDRONOWSKI, Miss. Mary Monica, BA FCA *1984;* 9 Merryfield, Pannal Ash, HARROGATE, HG2 9DH.
•**ANEIZI, Mr. Ali, BSc ACA CF** *2001;* Baker Tilly Tax and Advisory Services LLP, 25 Farringdon Street, LONDON, EC4A 4AB. See also Baker Tilly Corporate Finance LLP
ANEJA, Mr. Anil, ACA *1979;* Anil Aneja & Co, F213C Lado Sari, 1st Floor, NEW DELHI 110030, INDIA.
•**ANFIELD, Mrs. Elizabeth Margaret, BSc FCA** *1974;* Elizabeth M Anfield, 6 Tudor Road, NEWBURY, RG14 7PU.
ANFIELD, Mrs. Susannah Kate, BSc ACA *1998;* with PricewaterhouseCoopers LLP, Pricewaterhousecoopers, 12 Plumtree Court, LONDON, EC4A 4HT.
ANG, Miss. Ai Hoon, ACA *1983;* 1305 Block A Ehsan Ria Condo, Jalan Bukit 11/2, 46200 PETALING JAYA, SELANGOR, MALAYSIA.
ANG, Mr. Boo Chong, BA FCA *1980;* 14 Delaware Street, EPPING, NSW 2121, 2121, AUSTRALIA.
ANG, Mr. Chin Soon, FCA *1977;* Adams & Soanes, 49 High Street, SAFFRON WALDEN, ESSEX, CB10 1AR.
ANG, Mr. Eugene Hui Tiong, ACA *1997;* Vanke Blue Mountain (Wanke Lanshan), Jin Hai Road Lane 3333, House 208, SHANGHAI 201209, CHINA.
ANG, Ms. Jessie Poh Heo, ACA *1983;* 2 Mei Hwan Road, SINGAPORE 568312, SINGAPORE.
ANG, Mr. Julius Soo Beng, ACA *1994;* 207 Old Hall Lane, Fallowfield, MANCHESTER, M14 6HJ.
ANG, Ms. Su Yi, BSc(Econ) ACA *2002;* No. 1 Jln PJS 3/2 Petaling Jaya Selatan, 46000 PETALING JAYA, MALAYSIA.
ANGEL, Mr. Alexander Morris, FCA *1948;* 38 Park Grove, EDGWARE, HA8 7SJ. (Life Member)
ANGEL, Mr. Barry Paul, ACA *1979;* 41 Frampton Way, Totton, SOUTHAMPTON, SO40 9AD.
ANGEL, Mr. Brett, BEng ACA *2006;* Flat 8-11, 47 Bennett Park, LONDON, SE3 9RA.
ANGEL, Mr. Harold Bernard, FCA *1972;* Menachem Begin 52/15, KFAR YONA, ISRAEL. (Life Member)
•**ANGEL, Mr. Leon, FCA** *1980;* Hazlems Fenton LLP, Palladium House, 1-4 Argyll Street, LONDON, W1F 7LD. See also Argyll Street Management Services Ltd
•**ANGEL, Mrs. Pamela, BSc FCA** *1996;* Angel Accountancy Services, 3 Stobart Avenue, Prestwich, MANCHESTER, M25 0AJ.
•**ANGEL, Mr. Peter Brian, FCA** *1979;* Peter Angel & Co Ltd, Finance House, 77 Queens Road, BUCKHURST HILL, IG9 5BW. See also Angel P.B.
ANGEL, Mr. Robert Gilbert, FCA *1966;* The Gilford Group Limited, 1 Balmoral Avenue Suite 617, TORONTO M4V 3B9, ON, CANADA.
ANGEL, Mrs. Sally Ann Elizabeth, MA ACA *1987;* 10 Achnacone Drive, Braiswick, COLCHESTER, CO4 5AZ.
ANGEL, Miss. Sophie Farrah Amy, ACA *2006;* 12 Avon Buildings, CHRISTCHURCH, DORSET, BH23 1QS.
ANGELI, Mr. George, ACA FCCA *2010;* 7 Northpoint Close, SUTTON, SURREY, SM13SQ.
ANGELIDES, Mr. George, MSc BSc ACA *2005;* NATIONAL BANK OF GREECE, 6-10 CHARILAOU TRIKOUPI Str., 5th Floor, 106 79 ATHENS, GREECE.
ANGELINI, Mr. Kevin, BSc ACA *2006;* 35/F Shell Tower Times Square, 1 Matheson Street, CAUSEWAY BAY, HONG KONG ISLAND, HONG KONG SAR.
•**ANGELIS, Mr. Anthony George, BA ACA** *1991;* (Tax Fac), with RSM Tenon Audit Limited, 66 Chiltern Street, LONDON, W1U 4JT.
ANGELL, Mr. Ian Hugh Arthur, FCA *1975;* Praesta Partners LLP, Dentsu Holdings Europe Ltd Berger House, 36-38 Berkeley Square, LONDON, W1J 5AH.
•**ANGELL, Mr. Malcolm, FCA** *1976;* Angell Pinder Limited, 1 Victoria Street, DUNSTABLE, BEDFORDSHIRE, LU6 3AZ.
ANGELL, Mrs. Paula Joy, FCA *1978;* Chase Acres, Parrotts Lane, Buckland Common, TRING, HP23 6NY.
ANGELL, Mr. Peter George, FCA *1959;* 29 Bow Field, HOOK, RG27 9SA. (Life Member)
ANGELL, Mr. Philip, BSc FCA *1975;* 201 Vanderpool Lane #127, HOUSTON, TX 77024, UNITED STATES.
ANGELL, Mr. Rodney Albert, FCA *1972;* 12 Barley Way, Rothley, LEICESTER, LE7 7RL.
ANGELL-PAYNE, Mrs. Jane, BSc ACA DChA *1987;* Priory Cottage, Romford Road, Pembury, TUNBRIDGE WELLS, TN2 4JD.
ANGERS, Mr. Brian Mason, FCA *1959;* 11 St. Joseph's Mews, Greyfriars Lane Storrington, PULBOROUGH, WEST SUSSEX, RH20 4GJ.
ANGLE, Mr. Martin David, BSc FCA FRSA MSI *1975;* Cantorist House, Childrey, WANTAGE, OX12 9UT.
ANGLES, Miss. Alison Jane, BSc ACA *1990;* 21 Ormonde Road, LONDON, SW14 7BE.
ANGLISS, Mr. Keith Edward, FCA *1963;* 122 Parkway, LONDON, SW20 9HG. (Life Member)
•**ANGLISS, Mr. Roy Alan, BA FCA** *1985;* Saffery Champness, P O Box 141, La Tonnelle House, Les Banques, St. Sampson, GUERNSEY GY1 3HS.
ANGOOD, Mr. John, ACA *2007;* 52 Lower White Road, BIRMINGHAM, B32 2RT.
ANGRAVE, Mr. Leon Francis, FCA *1979;* Lower Ambion House, Ambion Lane, Sutton Cheney, NUNEATON, CV13 0AD.
ANGSEESING, Mr. Hugh Nathaniel, BSc ACA *2009;* 13 East Crescent, Beeston, NOTTINGHAM, NG9 1PZ.
ANGUS, Mr. Brian Lambert, FCA *1960;* 26 Somersby Close, London Road, LUTON, LU1 3XB. (Life Member)
ANGUS, Mrs. Catherine Ann, BA FCA DChA *1990;* with Mazars LLP, 45 Church Street, BIRMINGHAM, B3 2RT.
ANGUS, Mr. Charles James Nicholas, BSc ACA *1986;* 21 Wood End Hill, HARPENDEN, AL5 3EZ.
ANGUS, Ms. Cynthia Louise, ACA *2007;* 17 Burrow Road, LONDON, SE22 8DU.
•**ANGUS, Mr. Gordon Peter, FCA** *1983;* HLB Jackson Fox Limited, PO Box 264, Union House, Union Street, JERSEY, JE4 8TQ. See also HLB Jackson Fox
ANGUS, Mr. Ian Malcolm, FCA *1965;* Leonor de Castilla 8, Sotogrande, San Roque, 11310 CADIZ, SPAIN. (Life Member)
ANGUS, Mr. Martin Graeme, BA ACA *1992;* PO Box 3331, General Post Office, CENTRAL, HONG KONG SAR.
ANGUS, Mrs. Melisa Joy, BSc ACA *1990;* Opsec Security Group Inc 535 16th Street, Suite 920, DENVER, CO 80202, UNITED STATES.
ANGUS, Mr. Michael William, BA ACA *1989;* 60 South Dahlia Street, DENVER, CO 80246, UNITED STATES.
ANGUS, Mrs. Rachel Louise, BA ACA *2007;* 9 Lea Walk, HARPENDEN, HERTFORDSHIRE, AL5 4NG.
ANGUS, Mr. Ralph Neill Stewart, MA ACA *1991;* Honiton Queens Road, Port St. Mary, ISLE OF MAN, IM9 5EN.
ANGUS, Mr. Richard Barton, BA ACA *1980;* 11, Old Jewry, LONDON, EC2R 8DU.
ANGUS, Mr. Robert Stewart, BA ACA *1990;* Emirate Airlines, PO Box 686, DUBAI, UNITED ARAB EMIRATES.
ANGUS, Mr. Robert Trevor, ACA *2007;* 1 Lea Walk, HARPENDEN, HERTFORDSHIRE, AL5 4NG.
ANGUS, Mr. Roger Mildon, MA BPhil FCA *1978;* The Glade, Woodland Walk, FERNDOWN, BH22 9LP.
ANGUS, Mr. Stephen, BA ACA *2002;* with KPMG LLP, Quayside House, 110 Quayside, NEWCASTLE UPON TYNE, NE1 3DX.
ANGUS, Mr. Stephen Donald, BSc ACA *1987;* Hyde Park Property Services Ltd, 6 Albert Court, Prince Consort Road, LONDON, SW7 2BE.
ANGUS, Ms. Susan Mary Elizabeth, FCA *1974;* 11 Upper Green Road, Tewin, WELWYN, HERTFORDSHIRE, AL6 0LE.
ANIBABA, Mr. Olufemi, MA BSc ACA *2002;* Zain Nigeria, Plot L2, Banana Island, LAGOS, NIGERIA.
ANILIONIS, Mr. Deividas, BSc ACA *2010;* 57a Prospect Road, ST. ALBANS, HERTFORDSHIRE, AL1 2AT.
ANIMASHAUN, Mr. Wahab Kolawole Idris, FCA *1972;* P O Box 50197, Falomo, Ikoyi, LAGOS, NIGERIA. (Life Member)
•**ANJOUS, Chief Babatunde, KJW FCA** *1962;* Anjous Uku Eweka & Co, 4 Ladipo Labinjo Crescent, Off Bode Thomas Street, Suru Lere, LAGOS, PMB 12020 NIGERIA.
ANJUM, Mr. Abdul Jalil, FCA *1972;* 106/1 Khayabane Ghazi, Defence Housing Authority, KARACHI, PAKISTAN. (Life Member)
ANKERS, Miss. Clare Stephanie, BA ACA *2003;* Hillcote Cottage Homefield Lane, Rugby Road Dunchurch, RUGBY, CV22 6QS.
ANKERS, Mr. James William, BA(Hons) ACA *2001;* 4 Roughlands, Pyrford, WOKING, SURREY, GU22 8PT.
ANKERS, Mr. Jonathan Roy, BA ACA *1979;* Clegg Group Bishops House, 42 High Pavement, NOTTINGHAM, NG1 1HN.
ANKERS, Mrs. Katharine, BA(Hons) ACA *2002;* 4 Roughlands, Pyrford, WOKING, SURREY, GU22 8PT.
ANKERS, Mrs. Katie Elizabeth, ACA *2005;* Flat 8 Kelsey Court, 66 Wickham Road, BECKENHAM, BR3 6LY.
ANKRAH, Miss. Lucille Houda, BSc ACA CF *1998;* with Ernst & Young LLP, 1 More London Place, LONDON, SE1 2AF.
ANNAN, Mr. Christopher Graham, BSc FCA *1990;* The Old Dairy, Main Street, Sudbrook, GRANTHAM, NG32 3RY.
ANNAN, Mr. Malcolm Reid, FCA *1978;* with Reads & Co Limited, PO Box 179, 40 Esplanade, St Helier, JERSEY, JE4 9RJ.
ANNANDALE, Mr. Brett Richard, ACA CA(SA) *2008;* 5 Viceroy Lodge, Claremont Road, SURBITON, SURREY, KT6 4RQ.
ANNANDSINGH, Mr. Joseph, MSc BSc ACA *2010;* Apartment 206, 21-33 Worple Road, LONDON, SW19 4BH.
ANNANDSINGH, Miss. Sarah, ACA *2009;* Flat 13, Northways, College Crescent, LONDON, NW3 5DR.
ANNELLS, Miss. Deborah, BSc ACA *1985;* (Tax Fac), Apartment 6B, South Tower 7, Residence Bel-Air, POK FU LAM, HONG KONG ISLAND, HONG KONG SAR.
•**ANNESLEY, Mr. Mark, BA ACA** *1982;* (Tax Fac), Mark Annesley & Co, Heather Lodge, Kingston Hill, KINGSTON UPON THAMES, SURREY, KT2 7LX.
ANNESLEY, Mr. Richard Bruce, FCA *1962;* Stonebridge, Wolvershill Road, BANWELL, AVON, BS29 6DR.
ANNET, Mr. Rodney Michael Chester, BA ACA *1989;* Pinpoint Group Unit 35 Meridian House, Road One Winsford Industrial Estate, WINSFORD, CHESHIRE, CW7 3QG.
ANNETT, Mr. Peter, FCA *1961;* 3 Friary Gardens, Shepherds Hill, Alnmouth, ALNWICK, NE66 3NL. (Life Member)
ANNETT, Mrs. Sophie Dominique, BSc ACA *1997;* Sunny View, Palestine, ANDOVER, SP11 7ES.
ANNETTE, Mrs. Gillian Elizabeth, BA ACA *1999;* 13 Teddington Park Road, TEDDINGTON, MIDDLESEX, TW11 8NB.
ANNETTS, Mr. David Charles, ACA *1983;* Cim Management Ltd, Whittington Hall, WORCESTER, WR5 2ZX.
ANNETTS, Mr. Sean, BSc ACA *1992;* 19 Portobello Close, Barton-Le-Clay, BEDFORD, MK45 4SN.
ANNFIELD, Mr. Alastair Graeme, BA FCA *1969;* Le Brugeau, 24500 ST AUBIN DE CADELECH, FRANCE.
ANNIBLE, Mrs. Liesel Denise, BA FCA *1992;* 1 Bermerside House, Greenroyd Close, HALIFAX, WEST YORKSHIRE, HX3 0JY.
ANNING, Mr. David Colin, FCA *1969;* Swallowfield, 203 Old Dover Road, CANTERBURY, CT1 3ER.
ANNING, Mr. David Edward, FCA *1964;* 76 Nut Bush Lane, Chelston, TORQUAY, TQ2 6SD. (Life Member)
ANNING, Mr. Eric Stuart, FCA *1969;* 36 Llantillio Drive, PLYMOUTH, DEVON, PL2 3RX.
ANNING, Miss. Katie, ACA *2007;* Snowdrop Cottage Ball Lane, Kennington, ASHFORD, TN25 4EB.
•**ANNING, Mr. Paul Anthony, BSc FCA** *1983;* Anning and Co, 5 High Street, Westbury-On-Trym, BRISTOL, BS9 3BY.
ANNING, Mr. Richard Mark, BA FCA MCIM DipM *1986;* Harewood, Crab Tree Lane, Stoke, ANDOVER, SP11 0LX.
•**ANNIS, Mr. Christopher David, ACA** *2000;* LB Group Ltd, 6 Pegasus, Orion Court, Addison Way, Great Blakenham, IPSWICH IP6 0LW.
ANNIS, Mr. Mark Richard, BA ACA *1990;* 17 Denholm Close, Poulner, RINGWOOD, BH24 1TF.
ANNISS, Mr. Darren James, BSc ACA *2004;* Mace Ltd Atelier House, 64 Pratt Street, LONDON, NW1 0LF.
ANNISS, Mrs. Louise Patricia, BSc(Hons) ACA *2001;* Voramar, Villa 28, Santa Maria, Lavimia, 07181 BLANES, MALLORCA SPAIN.
ANNISS, Mr. Richard Guy, BSc FCA *1973;* Limehurst, Shipley, HORSHAM, RH13 8PR.
ANNUAR, Ms. Azzahraa, LLB ACA *2011;* No 10, Jalan Setiabakti 3, Bukit Damansara, 50490 KUALA LUMPUR, FEDERAL TERRITORY, MALAYSIA.
ANONUEVO, Miss. Elizabeth, BSc ACA *2006;* 7 Poppy Close, Yarnton, KIDLINGTON, OXFORDSHIRE, OX5 1GZ.
•**ANSARI, Mr. Akbar, FCA** *1969;* Ansari & Associates, 126 Sepehr Street, Farahzadi Boulevard, Shahrak Goods, TEHRAN, 1468673951 IRAN.
ANSARI, Mr. Asad Anis, FCA *1975;* Habib Bank Ltd, 63 Mark Lane, LONDON, EC3R 7NQ.
ANSARI, Mr. Israr Illahi, FCA *1969;* Bungalow No. D-14, C.A.A. Colony, Karachi Airport, KARACHI 75200, SINDH, PAKISTAN.
ANSARI, Mr. Khalid Masud, FCA *1985;* KPMG, 4th Floor HSBC Building, Muttrah Business District, PO Box 641, 112 MUSCAT, OMAN.
ANSARI, Mr. Misbahuddin, FCA *1965;* BRDB, 609 Continental Trade Centre, Main Clifton Road, KARACHI 75600, PAKISTAN.
ANSARI, Mr. Mohammed Fayyaz, ACA FCCA *2006;* 37 Somerset Road, Walthamstow, LONDON, E17 8QN.
ANSARI, Mr. Naseem Khalid, BSc ACA *2011;* 50 Spencer House, Whitelands Crescent, LONDON, SW18 5QY.
ANSARI, Mr. Shehryar, ACA *1993;* 14-A 14th Office Floor Executive Towers Dolmen City Block-4 Clifton, KARACHI 75600, PAKISTAN.
ANSCOMBE, Mrs. Alison Jane, BSc ACA *1998;* Temple House, 27 High Street, Meldreth, ROYSTON, HERTFORDSHIRE, SG8 6JU.
ANSCOMBE, Mr. Dennis Terence, FCA *1969;* The Saddlers, Grittleton, CHIPPENHAM, SN14 6AP.
ANSDELL, Mr. Peter, FCA *1959;* PO Box 2029, WALNUT CREEK, CA 94595, UNITED STATES. (Life Member)
ANSELL, Mr. Anthony Arnold, FCA *1971;* 158 Kingshill Drive, Kenton, HARROW, HA3 8QS.
ANSELL, Mr. David Thomas, FCA *1960;* 6 Madgeways Close, Great Amwell, WARE, HERTFORDSHIRE, SG12 9RU. (Life Member)
ANSELL, Mr. James Edward, MEng ACA *2004;* 31 Pelham Road, BECKENHAM, BR3 4SQ.
ANSELL, Mr. James Paul, BSc ACA CF *2005;* The Lodge, Raleigh Drive, Claygate, ESHER, SURREY, KT10 9DE.
ANSELL, Mr. Marcus Alexander, BSc FCA *1972;* 24 Methuen Ave, TORONTO M6S 1Z6, ON, CANADA. (Life Member)
ANSELL, Mr. Mark John, FCA *1973;* The Spinney, 2 Rosewood Close, Little Aston, SUTTON COLDFIELD, WEST MIDLANDS, B74 3UZ.
ANSELL, Mr. Michael John, FCA *1966;* 19 The Highlands, RICKMANSWORTH, HERTFORDSHIRE, WD3 7EW. (Life Member)
ANSELL, Mr. Nicholas Paul, BA ACA *1990;* Hetlee Farm, Leigh Road, WILMSLOW, SK9 6DS.
ANSELL, Mr. Peter Donald, FCA *1968;* 8 Coombe Gardens, BERKHAMSTED, HP4 3PA.
ANSELL, Mr. Philip Thomas, BSc(Hons) ACA *2010;* Hartlands, Silver Street, Sway, LYMINGTON, HAMPSHIRE, SO41 6DF.
ANSELL, Mr. Richard David, ACA *1993;* 4 Cassandra Grove, WARWICK, CV34 6XD.
ANSELL, Mrs. Samantha Jane, BA ACA *2002;* 93 Martens Avenue, BEXLEYHEATH, DA7 6AB.
ANSELL, Mrs. Sheila Mary, FCA *1974;* The Spinney, 2 Rosewood Close, Little Aston, SUTTON COLDFIELD, WEST MIDLANDS, B74 3UZ.
ANSELL, Mr. Terence John, FCA *1972;* Elm Cottage, Asheridge Road, CHESHAM, HP5 2XD.
ANSELL, Mr. Tom William, BA(Hons) ACA *2001;* 12 Guernsey Farm Drive, WOKING, GU21 4BE.
ANSELL, Mr. Trevor James, FCA *1972;* 83 The Green, Ewell, EPSOM, SURREY, KT17 3JX. (Life Member)
ANSELM, Mrs. Ewa, MA ACA *2006;* 5 Ymittou Street, Flat 101, Platy Aglantzia, 2113 NICOSIA, CYPRUS.
ANSLEY, Mr. Charles William, BA ACA *1979;* 7 Sinclair Gardens, LONDON, W14 0AU.
ANSLEY-YOUNG, Mr. Martin James, MA ACA *1993;* Ove Arup & Partners, 13 Fitzroy Street, LONDON, W1T 4BQ.
ANSLOW, Mr. David Keith, MA FCA *1967;* 4 Warblers Green, Water Lane, COBHAM, KT11 2NY.
•**ANSLOW, Mr. Mark Ashley, BSc FCA** *1989;* BDO LLP, 125 Colmore Row, BIRMINGHAM, B3 3SD. See also BDO Stoy Hayward LLP
ANSON, Mr. Alexander Lothian, MA FCA *1976;* (Tax Fac), 29 Bernard Avenue, LONDON, W13 9TG.
ANSON, Mrs. Alison Clare, ACA *1991;* Holly Cottage, North Side, Steeple Aston, BICESTER, OXFORDSHIRE, OX25 4SE.
ANSON, Miss. Amelia Jane, BSc ACA *1994;* 124 Waldegrave Road, BRIGHTON, EAST SUSSEX, BN1 6GG.
ANSON, Mr. Anthony Ross, ACA *1984;* with Langtons, The Plaza, 100 Old Hall Street, LIVERPOOL, L3 9QJ.
•**ANSON, Mr. Bernard Llewelyn, FCA** *1972;* Hillier Hopkins LLP, Charter Court, Midland Road, HEMEL HEMPSTEAD, HERTFORDSHIRE, HP2 5GE. See also Bernie Anson Limited

ANSON, Mr. John Patrick, FCA *1955;* The Bower Laceys Farm, Long Road, Colby, NORWICH, NR11 7EF. (Life Member)
ANSON, Mr. John Robert, FCA *1970;* Anson Care Services, Tremethick House, Meadowside, REDRUTH, CORNWALL, TR15 3AL.
•ANSON, Mr. Martin John, FCA *1992;* Whitley Stimpson LLP, Penrose House, 67 Hightown Road, BANBURY, OXFORDSHIRE, OX16 9BE.
•ANSON, Mrs. Nicola, MSc ACA *1992;* N Anson, 3 Swan Grove, Exning, NEWMARKET, SUFFOLK, CB8 7HX.
ANSTAY, Miss. Catherine, ACA *2010;* 8 Byron Court, Swalwell, NEWCASTLE UPON TYNE, NE16 3JU.
ANSTEAD, Mr. Hamilton Douglas, BSc FCA *1982;* 10 St. Michael's Mews, LONDON, SW1W 8JZ.
•ANSTEE, Mr. Eric Edward, FCA FFA *1974;* City of London Group Plc, 30 Cannon Street, LONDON, EC4M 6XH.
ANSTEE, Mr. Neil Keith, FCA *1958;* Beech Corner, Hudnall Common, Little Gaddesden, BERKHAMSTED, HP4 1QJ. (Life Member)
•ANSTEE, Mr. Nicholas John, FCA CF *1982;* S J Berwin Llp, 10 Queen Street, LONDON, EC4R 1BE.
ANSTEE, Mr. Samuel James, BSc(Hons) ACA *2009;* 167 Henry Doulton Drive, LONDON, SW17 6DH.
ANSTEE, Mr. Stephen St John, MA ACA *1987;* I D J Ltd, 81 Piccadilly, LONDON, W1J 8HY.
ANSTEY, Mr. Adam, BSc ACA *2007;* 12 Cotswold Drive, STEVENAGE, HERTFORDSHIRE, SG1 6GT.
ANSTEY, Mr. Brian David, FCA *1976;* 341 Bukit Timah Road, Honolulu Tower Apt 1101, SINGAPORE 259719, SINGAPORE.
ANSTEY, Mrs. Terina, BSc(Hons) ACA *2010;* 12 Cotswold Drive, STEVENAGE, HERTFORDSHIRE, SG1 6GT.
ANSTIS, Mr. David Guy, BSc ACA *1991;* 1 The Slype, Wheathampstead, ST. ALBANS, HERTFORDSHIRE, AL4 8RY.
ANSTIS, Miss. Katy Lauren, BA(Hons) ACA *2010;* Arcadia Group Plc Colegrave House, 68-70 Berners Street, LONDON, W1T 3NL.
ANSTISS, Mr. Simon Marshall, BSc ACA *2002;* 34 Buckerell Avenue, St Leonard, EXETER, EX2 4RD.
ANSTRUTHER-NORTON, Mr. Quentin James Anstruther, BSc ACA *1986;* 34 Millside, Hales, NORWICH, NR14 6SW.
ANTCLIFF, Miss. Tracey, BA ACA *2003;* 606 Gateway South, Marsh Lane, LEEDS, LS9 8BD.
ANTCLIFFE, Mr. Richard William, MA ACA DChA *2003;* 1 Balfour Road, HARROW, MIDDLESEX, HA1 1RJ.
ANTHIS, Mr. Stamatios, MSc BA ACA *2011;* Rue Belliard 165, 1040 BRUSSELS, BELGIUM.
•ANTHISTLE, Mr. Michael Peter, FCA *1975;* (Tax Fac), Anthistle Craven Ltd, 31 High Street, BUCKINGHAM, MK18 1NU.
ANTHONEY, Mr. Alan, FCA *1960;* Duntarvie, Audmore, Gnosall, STAFFORD, ST20 0HF. (Life Member)
ANTHONISZ, Mr. Christopher Sean, BSc ACA *2000;* 4 Salisbury Court, Hoppers Road Winchmore Hill, LONDON, N21 3NN.
•ANTHONISZ, Mr. Ian Haig, FCA *1971;* Anthonisz Neville LLP, 1st Floor, 105-111 Euston Street, LONDON, NW1 2EW.
•ANTHONISZ, Mr. Mark, BA ACA *1992;* Wesley Pemberton LLP, 89 Vicars Moor Lane, LONDON, N21 1BL.
ANTHONY, Mr. Alan Henry, FCA *1969;* 4 Kingsbridge Avenue, Mapperley Plains, NOTTINGHAM, NG3 5SA.
ANTHONY, Mr. Andre, LLB ACA *2009;* 14 Church Lane, HATFIELD, HERTFORDSHIRE, AL9 5HX.
•ANTHONY, Mrs. Anna, MA ACA *2003;* Ernst & Young LLP, 1 More London Place, LONDON, SE1 2AF. See also Ernst & Young Europe LLP
ANTHONY, Mr. Audy Moningha, BSc ACA *1982;* Audy Anthony & Co, 41 Muyibat Oyefusi Crescent, Omole Estate Phase One, Lagos State, IKEJA, 2525 IKEJA NIGERIA.
ANTHONY, Miss. Catrin Hefina, BA(Hons) FCA *1995;* 18 Dogo Street, Pontcanna, CARDIFF, CF11 9JJ.
ANTHONY, Mr. Christopher Michael, BA ACA *2010;* 5 Longford Drive, SHEFFIELD, S17 4LN.
ANTHONY, Mr. David Gwilym, MA FCA *1973;* Hitachi Capital (UK) Plc, Wallbrook Business Centre, Green Lane, HOUNSLOW, TW4 6NW.
ANTHONY, Mr. David Vivian, BA FCA *1978;* Carmel House, 2a Penallta Villas, Ystrad Mynach, HENGOED, MID GLAMORGAN, CF82 7GH.
•ANTHONY, Ms. Deborah Susan, MA ACA *1985;* (Member of Council 2003 - 2005), Deloitte LLP, Hill House, 1 Little New Street, LONDON, EC4A 3TR. See also Deloitte & Touche LLP
•ANTHONY, Mr. Dominic, ACA FCCA *2009;* Ashcroft Anthony Ltd, Heydon Lodge, Flint Cross, Newmarket Road, Heydon, ROYSTON HERTFORDSHIRE SG8 7PN. See also Ashcroft Anthony
ANTHONY, Mrs. Ellen Brigitte, BSc ACA *1979;* Retreat, Church Lane, Stoke Poges, SLOUGH, SL2 4NZ.
ANTHONY, Miss. Helen Rose, ACA *2008;* 32 Fields Park Road, NEWPORT, GWENT, NP20 5BB.
•ANTHONY, Mr. Hugh Dene, FCA *1958;* 15 Dane Court, WOKING, SURREY, GU22 8SX.
ANTHONY, Mr. Ian, BSc ACA *1991;* 9 Barlings Road, HARPENDEN, HERTFORDSHIRE, AL5 2AL.
•ANTHONY, Mr. John Michael, FCA *1980;* 2 Victorian Stables, Syerston Hall Park, Syerston, NEWARK, NOTTINGHAMSHIRE, NG23 5NL.
ANTHONY, Mr. John Morgan, BA FCA *1954;* 6 rue Geurny Chambaudrie, Lussais, 79110 CHEF BOUTONNE, FRANCE. (Life Member)
ANTHONY, Mr. John Stuart Frazer, BA ACA *1992;* (Tax Fac), 62 London Road, Twyford, READING, RG10 9EY.
ANTHONY, Mr. Julian Charles Cohen, BSc ACA *1993;* 3 Silverdale Road, BUSHEY, WD23 2LY.
ANTHONY, Mr. Julian Peter, BSc ACA *1984;* Fairbourne, 4 Oathall Road, HAYWARDS HEATH, WEST SUSSEX, RH16 3EA.
ANTHONY, Mr. Keith Moncur, FCA *1968;* En-Dah-Win, Spring Lane, Farnham Royal, SLOUGH, SL2 3EH. (Life Member)
ANTHONY, Mrs. Lucy Victoria, BSc ACA *2001;* with DLA Piper UK LLP, 1 St. Pauls Place, SHEFFIELD, S1 2JX.
•ANTHONY, Mrs. Margaret Jill, BA FCA DChA *1990;* Hardcastle Burton, 166 Northwood Way, NORTHWOOD, MIDDLESEX, HA6 1RB.
ANTHONY, Mrs. Maria Anne, BA ACA *1982;* West Law, Meadway, Oxshott, LEATHERHEAD, KT22 0LZ.
ANTHONY, Mr. Michael, BSc(Hons) ACA *2009;* 26 Beachway, CANVEY ISLAND, ESSEX, SS8 0BD.
•ANTHONY, Mr. Michael Andrew, FCA CTA *1975;* (Tax Fac), Randall & Payne LLP, Rodborough Court, Walkley Hill, STROUD, GLOUCESTERSHIRE, GL5 3LR.
ANTHONY, Mr. Michael John, FCA *1971;* 104 Prinsep Street, Apt 03-02, SINGAPORE 0719, SINGAPORE.
ANTHONY, Mr. Nigel, BSc ACA *1986;* Flat 33 Maxime Court, Gower Road Sketty, SWANSEA, SA2 9FB.
•ANTHONY, Mr. Paul Neville, BA ACA *1998;* BDO LLP, Arcadia House, Maritime Walk, Ocean Village, SOUTHAMPTON, SO14 3TL. See also BDO Stoy Hayward LLP
ANTHONY, Miss. Philippa Jane, ACA *1988;* Flat 4, 42 Rusholme Road, LONDON, SW15 3LG.
ANTHONY, Dr. Richard Forbes, MA ACA *1997;* Hunters Lodge, 37 Dullingham Ley Dullingham, NEWMARKET, SUFFOLK, CB8 9XG.
•ANTHONY, Mr. Robert Neil, BSc ACA *1985;* Robert Anthony, 36 Merdon Avenue, Chandlers Ford, EASTLEIGH, SO53 1EP.
ANTHONY, Mr. Robin David, BA ACA *1995;* 6 The Chestnuts, Lindfield, HAYWARDS HEATH, RH16 2AS.
ANTHONY, Mr. Roderick James, BSc ACA *1986;* 100 Dorridge Road, Dorridge, SOLIHULL, WEST MIDLANDS, B93 8BS.
ANTHONY, Mr. Simon David, LLB ACA *1992;* 1 Fife Court, COWES, ISLE OF WIGHT, PO31 7LW.
ANTHONY, Mr. Simon James, MA MPhil ACA *1999;* Court Lodge, 3 Layhams Road, WEST WICKHAM, BR4 9HJ.
•ANTHONY, Mr. Steven Ronald, FCA *1975;* (Tax Fac), S.R. Anthony, 26 Beachway, CANVEY ISLAND, SS8 0BD.
ANTHONY, Mr. Stuart Grant, BSc ACA *1990;* 29 Belvedere Road, Crystal Palace, LONDON, SE19 2HJ.
ANTHONY, Mr. Thomas Owen, BSc ACA *1999;* 18 Sibley Avenue, HARPENDEN, HERTFORDSHIRE, AL5 1HF.
ANTHONY, Mr. Wayne George, BA FCA *1993;* Pricewaterhousecoopers, 12 Plumtree Court, LONDON, EC4A 4HT.
ANTIAN, Mr. Raymond Joseph, FCA *1983;* 14 Old Rectory Gardens, EDGWARE, MIDDLESEX, HA8 7LS.
ANTILL, Mrs. Amanda Fiona, BA ACA CTA AMCT *1993;* 51 Glyndebourne Gardens, CORBY, NORTHAMPTONSHIRE, NN18 0QA.
•ANTIPPA, Mr. Angelo George, BSc FCA *1987;* (Tax Fac), Antippa & Company Ltd, 17 Copthall Gardens, TWICKENHAM, TW1 4HH. See also A. G. Antippa
ANTKOWIAK, Miss. Natalie Emilia, ACA *2008;* The Grange, 271 Birstall Road, Birstall, LEICESTER, LE4 4DJ.
ANTON, Mr. David, FCA *1958;* 21b Highgate Close, LONDON, N6 4SD. (Life Member)
ANTON, Mr. Keith Gordon, BSc FCA CTA *1977;* 10 Church Road, Bengeo, HERTFORD, SG14 3DP.
ANTON, Mr. Nicholas John, BA ACA *1982;* 16 Amis Way, STRATFORD-UPON-AVON, CV37 7JF.
ANTONAKI, Miss. Maria-Evgenia, BA ACA *2005;* Ippokratous 16, Galatsi, 11146 ATHENS, GREECE.
•ANTONIA, Mr. David John, BSc(Econ) FCA CTA TEP *1976;* (Tax Fac), Mitchell Charlesworth, 5 Temple Square, Temple Street, LIVERPOOL, L2 5RH.
ANTONIADES, Mr. Andreas, BA ACA *2003;* 12 rue Alcide De Gasperi, 1615 LUXEMBOURG, LUXEMBOURG.
ANTONIADES, Mr. Andrew, BA ACA *2007;* 6 Glenfield Road, LONDON, W13 9JZ.
ANTONIADES, Miss. Aphrodite, BSc ACA *2011;* 11 Oriole Drive, Cringleford, NORWICH, NR4 7LU.
ANTONIADES, Mr. Chris, ACA *2008;* 31 Overton Road, LONDON, N14 4SX.
ANTONIADES, Mr. Christoforos, BA ACA *1995;* Ayioy Dometioy 11, Engomi, NICOSIA, CYPRUS.
ANTONIADES, Mr. Costakis Philippou, FCA *1974;* 253 Great Cambridge Road, ENFIELD, MIDDLESEX, EN1 1SQ.
•ANTONIADES, Mr. Michael, BA FCA ACA *1993;* KPMG, 14 Esperidon Street, 1087 NICOSIA, CYPRUS. See also KPMG Metaxas Loizides Syrimis
ANTONIADES, Mr. Soteris Michael, MSc FCA *1989;* 262 Green Lanes, Norbury, LONDON, SW16 3BA.
ANTONIADES, Mr. Thomas Demetriou, FCA *1976;* Moore Stephens, 150 Aldersgate Street, LONDON, EC1A 4AB.
ANTONIADOU, Miss. Elena, BA ACA *1992;* 60 Westbury Road, LONDON, N12 7PD.
•ANTONIAZZI, Mr. John Lawrence, FCA *1986;* Deloitte LLP, 5 Callaghan Square, CARDIFF, CF10 5BT. See also Deloitte & Touche LLP
ANTONIOU, Mr. Andreas, BSc ACA *2004;* Korytsas 12 Ayios Andreas, 1107 NICOSIA, CYPRUS.
ANTONIOU, Mr. Anthony, BA ACA *2007;* 13 Abercrombie Street, LONDON, SW11 2JB.
ANTONIOU, Mr. Antonios Theodosio, BSc ACA *1986;* PricewaterhouseCoopers, Griffon House, 19/21 Dostoyevskogo ul., 191126 ST PETERSBURG, RUSSIAN FEDERATION.
ANTONIOU, Mr. Antonis, BSc ACA *2010;* 6 Ayiou Eftichiou, Archangelos, 2055 NICOSIA, CYPRUS.
•ANTONIOU, Mr. Christakis Demou, FCA *1984;* PKF Savvides & Co Ltd, Meliza Court, 4th & 7th Floor, 229 Arch Makorious III Avenue, 3105 LIMASSOL, CYPRUS.
ANTONIOU, Mr. Christos, BA ACA *2004;* 46 Selinis Street, Ayll Anargyri II, 6053 LARNACA, CYPRUS.
ANTONIOU, Miss. Ioanna, BA ACA *1997;* 43 Thessalonikis Str, 6035 LARNACA, CYPRUS.
ANTONIOU, Mr. Jack, ACA *2009;* Flat 1, 103 Overhill Road, LONDON, SE22 0NA.
ANTONIOU, Miss. Katerina Andrea, MSc ACA *1995;* Evrou 5, Pania Court 2, Flat 302, 6031 LARNACA, CYPRUS.
ANTONIOU, Mr. Kyriacos, BA FCA *1993;* 2 Queen Frederica Street, 2063 NICOSIA, CYPRUS.
ANTONIOU, Miss. Marina, MSc BSc ACA *2002;* 1805 Cascades Tower, 2-4 Westferry Road, LONDON, E14 8JW.
•ANTONIOU, Mr. Marios, BA FCA *1991;* Barron & Co, 175 Cole Valley Road, Hall Green, BIRMINGHAM, B28 0DG.
•ANTONIOU, Mr. Michael Joseph, ACA *1981;* Michael J. Antoniou, Flat 7, 29 Aeschylus Street, 1011 NICOSIA, CYPRUS.
ANTONIOU, Mr. Nicholas, BA(Hons) ACA *2004;* Cypriana, Radfall Road, Chestfield, WHITSTABLE, KENT, CT5 3EN.
ANTONIOU, Mr. Paraskevas Spiros, BA ACA *1989;* P O Box 23314, CY 1681 NICOSIA, CYPRUS.
ANTONIOU, Mrs. Wendy Jane, BSc ACA PGCE *1999;* 39 Hutton Road, Shenfield, BRENTWOOD, ESSEX, CM15 8NF.
•ANTONIS, Mr. Simon Maughan, ACA CA(SA) *2011;* (Tax Fac), Maughan, 9/2 Viewforth Square, EDINBURGH, EH10 4LW.
•ANTONIUS, Mr. Antonio, BSc FCA *1983;* KPMG LLP, 100 Temple Street, BRISTOL, BS1 6AG. See also KPMG Europe LLP
ANTOUN, Mr. Antoun Rene, ACA *2011;* PO Box 70032, Victoria Island, LAGOS, NIGERIA.
ANTRAM, Mr. Peter John, FCA *1977;* Cargill Europe BVBA, Bedrijvenlaan 9, B-2800 MECHELEN, BELGIUM.
ANTRIM, Mr. Carl James, BA(Hons) ACA *2002;* 8 Bythorne Court, Rainham, GILLINGHAM, ME8 8TN.
•ANTROBUS, Mrs. Barbara Ann, FCA CTA *1980;* (Tax Fac), BA Taxation Services Ltd, Lyndhurst, Main Street, Peasmarsh, RYE, EAST SUSSEX TN31 6YA.
•ANTROBUS, Mr. Colin Paul, FCA *1972;* (Tax Fac), CP Antrobus FCA, 20 North Meade, Green Park, Maghull, LIVERPOOL, L31 8DP.
ANTROBUS, Mr. Graham Paul, BSc(Hons) ACA *2004;* with Bruce Sutherland & Co, Moreton House, MORETON-IN-MARSH, GL56 0LH.
ANTROBUS, Mr. Paul David, BA ACA *1989;* Ernst & Young, Karlovo Namesti 10, 1200 PRAGUE, CZECH REPUBLIC.
ANTROBUS, Mr. Roger Arthur, BA ACA *1978;* 15 Batchelor's Way, AMERSHAM, HP7 9AQ.
•ANTROBUS, Mrs. Sally Maria, BSc(Econ) ACA *2001;* Equal Accounting, 22 Cranmere Road, PLYMOUTH, PL3 5JY.
ANTWI-BOASIAKO, Mrs. Okobea Akosua, BSc ACA *2002;* 41 Willows Avenue, MORDEN, SURREY, SM4 5SG.
ANUAR, Miss. Azferina, ACA *2008;* No. 9 Jalan 4B, Ampang Jaya, 68000 AMPANG, MALAYSIA.
ANUAR, Mr. Shamsul Bin, BSc FCA *2001;* South Hook Gas Co Ltd, Two, London Bridge, LONDON, SE1 9RA.
ANUP, Mr. Yesh, BSc ACA *2010;* 2 Douglas Walk, MILTON KEYNES, BUCKINGHAMSHIRE, MK10 7DF.
ANUWAR, Miss. Sherrina Eveline, BSc(Econ) ACA *2003;* with Nomura International Plc, 1 Angel Lane, LONDON, EC4R 3AB.
ANVAR, Mr. Jamshid, BA FCA *1968;* 6 Route De Commugny, 1296 COPPET, SWITZERLAND.
ANVER KHAN, Miss. Taisheen, BSc ACA *2010;* Flat 27 Melina Court, Grove End Road, LONDON, NW8 9SB.
ANWAR, Mr. Imran, ACA *2009;* 60 Brooklawn Drive, MANCHESTER, M20 3GZ.
•ANWAR, Mr. Javed, BSc FCA *1980;* (Tax Fac), JA, 9 Hudswell Close, Whitefield, MANCHESTER, M45 7UD.
ANWAR, Mr. Naeem, BA ACA *2005;* 1 Castlemere Street, ROCHDALE, OL11 3SW.
ANWAR, Mr. Naveed, ACA *1989;* 6829 W Briles Road, PEORIA, AZ 85383, UNITED STATES.
ANWAR, Mrs. Reehana, BSc ACA *1994;* 23 Eden Way, BECKENHAM, BR3 3DN.
ANWAR, Mr. Salman, FCA *1990;* 24 M.T.Khan Road, 4th Floor, Bahria Complex, KARACHI 74000, PAKISTAN.
ANWAR, Miss. Shimaela, LLB ACA *2002;* Flat 22, West End Court, Priory Road, LONDON, NW6 3NU.
ANWAR, Mr. Shoaib, ACA ACCA *2010;* 6 Stratford Road, Shirley, SOLIHULL, WEST MIDLANDS, B90 3LT.
ANWAR, Mrs. Tahseen, BSc ACA *2006;* 72 Anderson Avenue, READING, RG6 1HB.
ANWARRUDIN, Miss. Arni Laily, BSc ACA *2002;* 92 Pinggir Zaaba Taman Tun, Dr Ismail, 60000 KUALA LUMPUR, FEDERAL TERRITORY, MALAYSIA.
ANWELL, Mrs. Hazel Anne, BSc FCA *1982;* with RSM Tenon Limited, Vantage, Victoria Street, BASINGSTOKE, RG21 3BT.
ANYON, Mr. Neil Andrew, ACA *2008;* Flat 1 11, Rochester Terrace, LONDON, NW1 9JN.
AOLAD, Mr. Mustafa Alim, BSc ACA *2004;* Flat 3B, House 68/A, Road 5, DHAKA, BANGLADESH.
APEDAILE, Mr. Steven James, ACA *1981;* Sprintex, 73 Resource Wa 6090, MALAGA, WA 6090, AUSTRALIA.
APLIN, Mr. David Charles, BSc FCA *1992;* (Tax Fac), with PricewaterhouseCoopers LLP, The Atrium, 1 Harefield Road, UXBRIDGE, UB8 1EX.
APLIN, Mr. Eric Charles, FCA *1962;* Pastoral, Churchway, Sutton St. Nicholas, HEREFORD, HR1 3BD.
APLIN, Mrs. Isabel Christine, FCA *1969;* 22 Park Hall Close, WALSALL, WS5 3HQ. (Life Member)
APLIN, Mrs. Lucy Gail Hammonds, BSc ACA *1993;* Dell Computers, Dell House, Dell Campus, Cain Road, BRACKNELL, BERKSHIRE RG12 1BF.
•APLIN, Mr. Paul Stephen, OBE BSc FCA ATII *1985;* MEMBER OF COUNCIL, (Tax Fac), A.C. Mole & Sons, Stafford House, Blackbrook Park Avenue, TAUNTON, SOMERSET, TA1 2PX.
APLIN, Mr. Peter David, BSc(Hons) ACA *2003;* 1 Old Chapel Close, Little Kimble, AYLESBURY, BUCKINGHAMSHIRE, HP17 0RA.

Members - Alphabetical APLIN - ARCHER

APLIN, Mr. Philip Henry, BSc FCA *1974;* 10 Malleson Road, Gotherington, CHELTENHAM, GLOUCESTERSHIRE, GL52 9ER.
APLIN, Miss. Sarah, ACA *2009;* 33 Alverton, Great Linford, MILTON KEYNES, MK14 5EF.
APOSTOLI, Mr. Tasos, BSc ACA *1993;* 2 Morven Close, POTTERS BAR, HERTFORDSHIRE, EN6 5HE.
APOSTOLIDES, Mr. George, BSc ACA *2010;* 10Vasily MichailidhPeristerona, 2731 NICOSIA, CYPRUS.
APOSTOLOU, Mr. Antonis, BA ACA *1996;* 147 Inderwick Road, LONDON, N8 9JR.
APOSTOLOVA, Mrs. Maria Georgieva, MA ACA *2002;* 121 Waverley Road, EPSOM, SURREY, KT17 2LN.
APPAIAH, Miss. Shalini Machimada, BSc(Hons) ACA *2002;* 617 Fulton Street, MEDFORD, MA 02155, UNITED STATES.
APPARICIO, Miss. Donna Ann, ACA *1987;* Shepherds Building Central, Charecroft Way, LONDON, W14 0EH.
APPAVOO, Mr. Soondra Moorthi, MA FCA MBA *1998;* Punter Southall & Co, 126 Jermyn Street, LONDON, SW1Y 4UJ.
APPEL, Mr. Jason Ian, BSc ACA *2006;* Solsana, 1 Abbotshall Avenue, Southgate, LONDON, N14 7JU.
APPELBE, Mr. Paul, MA FCA *1977;* 69 Hale Road, Hale, ALTRINCHAM, WA15 9HP.
APPELGREN, Mr. Johan, MSc BA ACA *2008;* 008 / 8B10030, Credit Suisse, 1 Cabot Square, LONDON, E14 4QJ.
•**APPELL, Mr. Simon Jonathan, BA FCA** *1990;* Zolfo Cooper LLP, 10 Fleet Place, LONDON, EC4M 7RB.
APPIAH SHIPPEY, Mrs. Angela Arabella, BA ACA *1999;* 10 Theresa Avenue, BRISTOL, BS7 9EP.
APPIOS, Mr. George, MSc ACA *1993;* Piraeus Bank (Cyprus) Ltd, 1 Spryros Cyprianou Avenue, 1065 NICOSIA, CYPRUS.
APPLEBEE, Mr. John Walter, FCA *1961;* 2 Oaklands Park Drive, Rhiwderin, NEWPORT, GWENT, NP10 8RB.
APPLEBY, Mr. Alan Roderick, FCA *1958;* 210 Stockton Lane, YORK, YO31 1EY. (Life Member)
APPLEBY, Mr. Andrew Gordon, FCA *1966;* 17 Little Hill, Long Lane, RICKMANSWORTH, WD3 5BX. (Life Member)
APPLEBY, Mr. Andrew Richard, BSc ACA *2002;* 8 Tinglesfield, CIRENCESTER, GL7 2JL.
•**APPLEBY, Mr. Christopher John, BA ACA CF** *1992;* BTG Financial Consulting LLP, 2 Collingwood Street, NEWCASTLE UPON TYNE, NE1 1JF. See also BTG McInnes Corporate Finance LLP
APPLEBY, Mrs. Deborah Margaret, FCA DChA *1987;* (Tax Fac), 5 Bramble Hill, Chandler's Ford, EASTLEIGH, SO53 4TP.
APPLEBY, Ms. Deborah Suzanne, BA ACA *1988;* 3 Chapel Close, Broadmayne, DORCHESTER, DORSET, DT2 8XB.
APPLEBY, Mr. Douglas Edward Marrison, BSc FCA *1957;* (Member of Council 1971 - 1975), 5 The Roost, Heather Lane, Hathersage, HOPE VALLEY, DERBYSHIRE, S32 1DQ. (Life Member)
APPLEBY, Mr. George, FCA *1950;* 67 Millview Drive, Tynemouth, NORTH SHIELDS, NE30 2QD. (Life Member)
APPLEBY, Mr. Ian, MA FCA MPMI *1991;* with PricewaterhouseCoopers, 1 East Parade, SHEFFIELD, S1 2ET.
APPLEBY, Mrs. Jacqueline Anne, MA MSc BSc ACA *1982;* Biocity Nottingham Ltd, Pennyfoot Street, NOTTINGHAM, NG1 1GF.
APPLEBY, Miss. Jane Elizabeth, BSc ACA *1986;* 24 Princes Meadow, Gosforth, NEWCASTLE UPON TYNE, NE3 4RZ.
APPLEBY, Mr. John Alexander, FCA *1952;* 19 Bittersweet Lane, DARIEN, CT 06820, UNITED STATES. (Life Member)
•**APPLEBY, Mr. John Ernest, FCA** *1971;* AIMS - John E Appleby FCA, 82 Upper Hanover Street, SHEFFIELD, S3 7RQ.
APPLEBY, Mr. John Kevin, BSc(Econ) FCA *1986;* Reivers Rest, Burn View Drive, Otterburn, NEWCASTLE UPON TYNE, NE19 1BA.
APPLEBY, Mrs. Louise Helen, BA ACA *2002;* 8 Oaklands Drive, Hazel Grove, STOCKPORT, CHESHIRE, SK7 6LL.
APPLEBY, Mrs. Lynn Frances, BSc ACA *1989;* Russell House, 1 West Hill, Portishead, BRISTOL, BS20 6LF.
APPLEBY, Mr. Mark James, MSc FCA *1999;* 174 Florence Road, LONDON, SW19 8TN.
APPLEBY, Mr. Mark John Crowther, BA FCA *1992;* PricewaterhouseCoopers, No. 12 Aviation Road, Una Home, 3rd Floor, Airport City, ACCRA PMB CT 42 GHANA.
•**APPLEBY, Mr. Nigel Francis, FCA** *1974;* NFCA Limited, Brookside Farm, Forest Road, Burley, RINGWOOD, HAMPSHIRE BH24 4DQ.
APPLEBY, Mr. Ralph Graham, ACA *1981;* Proudfoot Plc, 49 Church Road, Gosforth, NEWCASTLE UPON TYNE, NE3 1UE.
APPLEBY, Mr. Richard, BEng ACA *1996;* 37 Tuena Street, MUDGEERABA, QLD 4213, AUSTRALIA.
APPLEBY, Mr. Robert Ian, BSc FCA *1990;* 10/ 21 Moruben Road, BALMORAL, NSW 2088, AUSTRALIA.
•**APPLEBY, Mr. Robert Paul, MA FCA** *1984;* (Tax Fac), Newton Willows Glen Road, Newton Harcourt, LEICESTER, LE8 9FH.
APPLEBY, Ms. Sarah Helen, ACA *2006;* The Cabin High Street, Stonesfield, WITNEY, OXFORDSHIRE, OX29 8PU.
APPLEBY, Mr. Simon John, BA ACA *1986;* Russell House, 1 West Hill, Portishead, BRISTOL, BS20 6LF.
APPLEBY, Mr. Stephen Mark, MA ACA *1983;* Appleby Consulting Ltd, Green Gates, Cresswell, MORPETH, NORTHUMBERLAND, NE61 5JT.
APPLEBY, Mr. Stephen Robert, FCA *1972;* 94 Lavender Hill, ENFIELD, MIDDLESEX, EN2 0RQ.
APPLEBY, Miss. Tracy Anne, MChem ACA *2007;* 67 Silverthorne Road, LONDON, SW8 3HH.
APPLEBY, Mr. William Peter, BA ACA *1997;* 14 Alderbrook Road, LONDON, SW12 8AG.
APPLEFORD, Mr. Clive Nugent, FCA *1969;* Kibo, 22 Oaks Way, Heswall, WIRRAL, CH60 3SP.
APPLEFORD, Mrs. Llinos Haf, BSc ACA *2005;* 11 Spottiswoode Street, EDINBURGH, EH9 1EP.
APPLEFORD, Mr. Nigel Alan, BA ACA *1986;* 15 Golden Oak Dell, SHEFFIELD, S6 6FN.
APPLEGATE, Mr. Christopher John, FCA *1981;* 71 Berry Way, ANDOVER, SP10 3RZ.
APPLEGATE, Miss. Heidi Louise, BSc ACA *2005;* Flat 7, 70 Wapping High Street, LONDON, E1W 2NN.
APPLEGATE, Mr. Jeffrey, ACA *1981;* Low Swinton House Low Swinton, Masham, RIPON, NORTH YORKSHIRE, HG4 4JP.
APPLEGATE, Mr. Martin Peter, BA FCA *1983;* Owl House, 115 Cornbrash Rise, Hilperton, TROWBRIDGE, BA14 7TS.
APPLEGATE, Mr. Martin Trevor, BA ACA *1992;* 8 Brambridge, EASTLEIGH, SO50 6HZ.
APPLESON, Mr. Peter William, MSc FCA *1974;* Frauenlobstrasse 28, 80337 MUNICH, GERMANY.
APPLETON, Mr. Adrian Pegler, FCA *1973;* 8 Mounton Close, CHEPSTOW, NP16 5EG.
APPLETON, Mr. Anthony Frederick, FCA *1958;* Copper Beeches, Fairway, GODALMING, SURREY, GU7 1PG. (Life Member)
APPLETON, Mr. Anthony William, BA ACA *1999;* Pinfold Cottage, 40 Tong Lane, BRADFORD, WEST YORKSHIRE, BD4 0RP.
APPLETON, Mr. Arthur Herbert, FCA *1955;* 2544 Whaley Drive, MISSISSAUGA L5B 1X2, ON, CANADA. (Life Member)
APPLETON, Mrs. Barbara Mary, FCA *1956;* (Member of Council 1997 - 2001), Woodland, Hall Lane, Broxton, CHESTER, CH3 9JE. (Life Member)
APPLETON, Mr. Brian Phillip, FCA *1971;* 4 Drewery Drive, Rainham, GILLINGHAM, KENT, ME8 0NX.
APPLETON, Mrs. Caroline Elizabeth, BSc ACA *2010;* Flat 5, Albanian Court, 85 Camp Road, ST. ALBANS, HERTFORDSHIRE, AL1 5EA.
APPLETON, Mr. David John, FCA *1966;* 3 Rathbone Road, Hightown, LIVERPOOL, L38 0BR.
APPLETON, Mr. David Kendrew, BSocSc ACA *1988;* 6 Ridgely Close, Ponteland, NEWCASTLE UPON TYNE, NE20 9BN.
•**APPLETON, Mr. Edward George, FCA** *1970;* Appletons, Suite 1, Armcon Business Park, London Road South, Poynton, STOCKPORT CHESHIRE SK12 1LQ. See also Compliant Accounting Limited
APPLETON, Mr. Guy, MA ACA *1999;* Talisman Energy (UK) Ltd Talisman House, 163 Holburn Street, ABERDEEN, AB10 6BZ.
APPLETON, Mr. John, FCA *1968;* 1 Chemin de la Vie, Hameau de Montfort, 21500 MONTIGNY MONTFORT, FRANCE.
•**APPLETON, Mr. John Christopher, MSc FCA CF** *1978;* Nexia Smith & Williamson Audit Limited, Imperial House, 18-21 Kings Park Road, SOUTHAMPTON, SO15 2AT. See also Smith & Williamson Ltd and Nexia Audit Limited
APPLETON, Mr. Jonathan David, BA ACA *1992;* 30 Pretoria Road, CAMBRIDGE, CB4 1HE.
APPLETON, Mr. Keith Edward, BSc ACA *1989;* 17 Lime Lane, Failsworth, MANCHESTER, M35 9WA.
APPLETON, Mr. Marcus, ACA *2011;* 42c Foxley Road, LONDON, SW9 6ES.
APPLETON, Mr. Matthew, MA ACA *2001;* Doughty Hanson & Co, 45 Pall Mall, LONDON, SW1Y 5JG.
APPLETON, Miss. Patricia Mary, BSc ACA *1985;* 5 Ormathwaites Corner, Warfield, BRACKNELL, RG42 3XX.
•①**APPLETON, Mr. Paul Robert, BA FCA** *1993;* (Tax Fac), David Rubin & Partners LLP, 26-28 Bedford Row, LONDON, WC1R 4HE. See also David Rubin & Partners
APPLETON, Mr. Peter Dominic, BA ACA *1998;* 12 Dartmouth Drive, Windle, ST. HELENS, MERSEYSIDE, WA10 6BP.
APPLETON, Mr. Philip Charles Carlton, BA ACA *1984;* KPMG Kenya, P.O. Box 40612, 16 Floor Lonrho HS, Standard Street, NAIROBI, 00100 KENYA.
APPLETON, Mrs. Sally, BA(Hons) ACA *2002;* with Saffery Champness, Sovereign House, 6 Windsor Court, Clarence Drive, HARROGATE, HG1 2PE.
•**APPLEYARD, Mr. Andrew, LLB ACA** *1989;* Amington Hall, Ashby Road, TAMWORTH, STAFFORDSHIRE, B79 0BX.
APPLEYARD, Mr. Brian Walmsley, FCA *1960;* Garden House, Mill Lane Calcot, READING, BERKSHIRE, RG31 7RS. (Life Member)
APPLEYARD, Miss. Gemma Jane, ACA *2009;* First Floor Flat, 3 Shirlock Road, LONDON, NW3 2HR.
APPLEYARD, Miss. Gillian Susan, ACA *2010;* Flat 1, 88 Greencroft Gardens, LONDON, NW6 3JQ.
APPLEYARD, Ms. Helen Katrine, BA ACA *1992;* 11 Blackwell Close, Higham Ferrers, RUSHDEN, NORTHAMPTONSHIRE, NN10 8PJ.
APPLEYARD, Miss. Jane Louise, BA ACA *2002;* Unit 6, The Breakers, 26 South Shore Road, WARWICK WK02, BERMUDA.
APPLEYARD, Mr. Mark, BA ACA *2002;* Apartment 225, Market Buildings, 87 High Street, MANCHESTER, M4 1BF.
APPLEYARD, Mr. Paul, BA ACA *1987;* H I Weldrick Ltd, Leedale House, Railway Court, DONCASTER, SOUTH YORKSHIRE, DN4 5FB.
APPLEYARD, Mr. Peter Russell, BCom FCA *1956;* 10 Craigendarroch Walk, BALLATER, AB35 5ZB. (Life Member)
APPLEYARD, Mr. Richard, BSc(Hons) ACA *2010;* Armida Limited, Bell Walk House, High Street, UCKFIELD, EAST SUSSEX, TN22 5DQ.
•**APPLIN, Mr. Trevor, FCA** *1977;* Alwyns LLP, Crown House, 151 High Road, LOUGHTON, ESSEX, IG10 4LG.
APPS, Mr. Adrian Linley, BSc FCA *1978;* 26 Warwick Drive, Hale, ALTRINCHAM, WA15 9DY.
APPS, Mr. Andrew Peter, BEng ACA *1997;* 24 Wells Close, TONBRIDGE, TN10 4NW.
•**APPS, Mrs. Deborah Elizabeth, ACA MAAT** *2000;* Apps Accountancy Services Ltd, 130 - 140 Old Shoreham Road, BRIGHTON, EAST SUSSEX, BN3 7BD. See also Deborah Turner Accountancy Services Ltd
APPS, Mr. Jonathan Michael Charles, BCom ACA *1989;* 8 Paines Close, PINNER, HA5 3BN.
•**APPS, Mr. Richard Victor, BA ACA** *1994;* Richard Apps, 3 Strickland Avenue, Shadwell, LEEDS, LS17 8JX.
APPS, Mr. Simon James, BA(Hons) ACA *2006;* A B N Amro Bank NV, 250 Bishopsgate, LONDON, EC2M 4AA.
APPS, Miss. Susan Elizabeth, FCA *1983;* 11 Honiton Way, BEDFORD, BEDFORDSHIRE, MK40 3AN.
APPUHAMY, Mr. Ion Francis, BSc ACA *1993;* 72 Staunton Road, KINGSTON-UPON-THAMES, KT2 5TL.
APSEY, Mr. Robert, BA(Hons) ACA *1999;* 8 Crest Way, Portslade, BRIGHTON, BN41 2EY.
APTE, Mr. Prakash Vinayak, FCA *1969;* 7 Prailash CHS, Relief Road, Daulatnagar, Santa Cruz West, MUMBAI 400054, INDIA. (Life Member)
•**APTED, Mr. Roger George, FCA** *1975;* Griffiths Marshall, Beaumont House, 172 Southgate Street, GLOUCESTER, GL1 2EZ.
•**AQUINO, Mr. David James, FCA** *1985;* (Tax Fac), Berkeley Townsend, Hunter House, 150 Hutton Road, Shenfield, BRENTWOOD, CM15 8NL.
ARAIM, Mr. Jaffer, ACA *2011;* Flat C, 23 Queens Road, TWICKENHAM, TW1 4EZ.
ARAIN, Mr. Suhail Afzal, LLB ACA CFA *1997;* 342 London Road, ST. ALBANS, HERTFORDSHIRE, AL1 1EA.
ARAM, Mr. Behzad, MBA FCA *1973;* 4139-121 Street, EDMONTON T6J 1Y7, AB, CANADA.
ARAM, Mr. Borzou, BSc ACA *1985;* Borzou Aram, Samco Shipholding Pte. Ltd., 20 Science Park Road, #02-23/24 TeleTech Park, SINGAPORE 117674, SINGAPORE.
ARAM, Mr. Jeffrey, FCA *1969;* 20 Delph Lane, Netherton, HUDDERSFIELD, HD4 7HH.
•**ARANIYASUNDARAN, Ms. Sundareswary, ACA FCCA** *2010;* (Tax Fac), Brooks & Co, Mid-Day Court, 20-24 Brighton Road, SUTTON, SM2 5BN.
ARASARATNAM, Miss. Anandi Aida, BA ACA *2005;* 75 Peascroft Road, HEMEL HEMPSTEAD, HP3 8ER.
ARASARATNAM, Mr. Arunasalam Rasaratnam, FCA *1970;* 2154 Pineview Drive, OAKVILLE L6H 5M3, ON, CANADA.
ARASARATNAM, Ms. Christine Roshana, BA(Hons) ACA *2002;* 15 Southey Road, LONDON, SW19 1NN.
ARBAB, Mr. Faisal Habib, ACA CA(NZ) *2009;* Saeed Methani Mushtaq & Co, Suite 23c Block B, Cantonment Board Plaza, PESHAWAR, PAKISTAN.
ARBAB-SOLEIMANI, Mr. Abbas, FCA *1973;* Audit Organization, 31 Beihaqi Blvd., TEHRAN, 1514746417, IRAN.
ARBABHA, Ms. Sahba, ACA *1991;* 204 Addison House, Grove End Road, LONDON, NW8 9EJ.
•**ARBENZ, Mr. Christopher John, FCA** *1972;* Parker Business Services Ltd, Cornelius House, 178-180 Church Road, HOVE, EAST SUSSEX, BN3 2DJ. See also Parkers Business Services Limited
ARBER, Mr. Christopher Charles, BA FCA *1993;* 7 Wiley Terrace, Wilton, SALISBURY, SP2 0HN.
ARBERY-JONES, Mrs. Sian, ACA *2009;* 46 Woodlands Park, Kenfig Hill, BRIDGEND, MID GLAMORGAN, CF33 6EB.
ARBIB, Mr. James Ashley, MA ACA *1999;* 49 Campden Hill Road, LONDON, W8 7DY.
ARBIB, Sir Martyn, Kt FCA *1962;* The Old Rectory, 17 Thameside, HENLEY-ON-THAMES, OXFORDSHIRE, RG9 1LH. (Life Member)
ARBUCKLE, Mr. Daryl Clive, ACA CA(SA) *2011;* Springs 15, Street 9, Villa 8, DUBAI, UNITED ARAB EMIRATES.
ARBUTHNOT, Mr. James, ACA *2010;* 5 Egerton Place, LONDON, SW3 2EF.
ARBUTHNOTT, Mr. Dominic Hugh, BA ACA *1992;* KAZMER LEJTO 2, 1121 BUDAPEST, HUNGARY.
ARBUTHNOTT, Mr. Robert Keith, MA ACA *1993;* Barclays Capital, Level 27, One Raffles Quay South Tower, SINGAPORE 048583, SINGAPORE.
ARCA, Mr. Carlos, BA ACA MBA *2005;* Flat 19 Thornycroft Court, 214-216 Kew Road, RICHMOND, TW9 2AN.
•**ARCH, Mr. Brian Frank, FCA** *1970;* Griffiths & Pegg, 42-43 Reddal Hill Road, CRADLEY HEATH, B64 5JS.
ARCH, Mr. David Andrew, BA *1984;* Oriel Securities Ltd, 125 Wood Street, LONDON, EC2V 7AN.
ARCH, Mr. Jonathan David, BSc ACA *1998;* Rolls-Royce Brazil, Rua Dr Cincanto Braga 47, SAO BERNARDO DO CAMPO, 09600-000, BRAZIL.
ARCH, Mr. Martin Antony, BSc ACA *2006;* 141 Oakway, WOKING, GU21 8TR.
•**ARCH, Mr. Philip John, ACA FCCA FMAAT** *2009;* Wilkes Tranter & Co Limited, Brook House, Moss Grove, KINGSWINFORD, WEST MIDLANDS, DY6 9HS.
ARCHARD, Mr. John David, BSc FCA *1984;* 71 St. Johns Avenue, WATERLOOVILLE, PO7 5QZ.
ARCHARD, Mr. Tim Paul Lenfestey, BA ACA *2006;* Plaisance Villa, Route de Plaisance, St Pierre du Bois, GUERNSEY, GY7 9SJ.
ARCHBOLD, Mr. Douglas, FCA *1952;* 7 Rock Lodge Road, Roker, SUNDERLAND, SR6 9NX. (Life Member)
ARCHBOLD, Mr. John Keith, FCA *1955;* Ashgate, Golf Lane, Church Brampton, NORTHAMPTON, NN6 8AY. (Life Member)
•**ARCHBOLD, Mr. Michael Gibson, FCA** *1970;* M.G Archbold, 63 Castlefields, Bournmoor, HOUGHTON LE SPRING, DH4 6HJ.
ARCHBOLD, Mr. Richard Brian, BA ACA *2004;* 29 Lumiere Court, 209 Balham High Road, LONDON, SW17 7BQ.
ARCHEOU, Miss. Aliki, ACA *2008;* 8 Nelsonos Street, Strovolos, 2021 NICOSIA, CYPRUS.
ARCHEOU, Mrs. Elizabeth, BA ACA *2004;* Kerkyras 17, 2640 NICOSIA, CYPRUS.
ARCHER, Mrs. Alexandra Louise, BSc ACA *1990;* 11 Arlington, Woodside Park, LONDON, N12 7JR.
ARCHER, Ms. Amanda, BA ACA *1992;* 7844 E. 9th Avenue, DENVER, CO 80230, UNITED STATES.
ARCHER, Miss. Amy Louise, BA(Hons) ACA *2010;* Ernst & Young, PO Box 510, GEORGE TOWN, GRAND CAYMAN, KY1-1106, CAYMAN ISLANDS.
ARCHER, Mr. Anthony, ACA *2011;* 50 Murray Way, New Forest Village, LEEDS, WEST YORKSHIRE, LS10 4GA.
ARCHER, Mr. Anthony William, LLB ACA *1979;* Barn Cottage Little Gaddesden, BERKHAMSTED, HERTFORDSHIRE, HP4 1PH.

ARCHER, Mr. Benedict John Patrick, BSc ACA *2001;* 23 Denmark Road, Wimbledon, LONDON, SW19 4PG.

ARCHER, Miss. Cheryl Jane, BSc ACA *1995;* 407 Goffs Lane, Goffs Oak, WALTHAM CROSS, HERTFORDSHIRE, EN7 5HQ.

ARCHER, Mr. Chris, ACA *2007;* 4 Cameron Close, LEAMINGTON SPA, WARWICKSHIRE, CV32 7DZ.

ARCHER, Mr. Christopher, BSc FCA *1997;* Sancroft International Ltd, 46 Queen Annes Gate, LONDON, SW1H 9AP.

ARCHER, Mr. Christopher John, BCom ACA *1992;* Yorkshire Bank Plc, 4 Victoria Place Holbeck, LEEDS, LS11 5AE.

•**ARCHER, Mr. Clive Philip, FCA ACCA** *1976;* (Tax Fac), Howards, Newport House, Newport Road, STAFFORD, ST16 1DA. See also Howards Limited

ARCHER, Mr. Colin Robert Hill, BA FCA *1974;* 6 Rectory Road, Barnes, LONDON, SW13 0DT. (Life Member)

ARCHER, Mr. David Jan Richard, MA ACA *2002;* Flat 721 Willoughby House, Barbican, LONDON, EC2Y 8BN.

ARCHER, Mr. Dudley Ian, FCA *1955;* Barbrona, Coppice Lane, REIGATE, RH2 9JF. (Life Member)

ARCHER, Mr. Edwin Aisah, ACA *2009;* 13 Timothy Close, BEXLEYHEATH, DA6 8JB.

ARCHER, Mr. Gilbert Simon Henry, PhD MA FCA *1964;* 5 Cavendish Court, Cardigan Road, RICHMOND, SURREY, TW10 6BL.

•**ARCHER, Mr. Howard Simon, BA FCA** *1984;* Archer Associates, 1 Olympic Way, WEMBLEY, MIDDLESEX, HA9 0NP. See also Archer Associates (Finchley) Ltd

ARCHER, Mr. James, BSc ACA *2009;* 2 Callingham Place, BEACONSFIELD, BUCKINGHAMSHIRE, HP9 2BT.

ARCHER, Mr. James Norman, BA ACA *1987;* 59 Portland Street, ST. ALBANS, HERTFORDSHIRE, AL3 4RA.

ARCHER, Miss. Jayne Louise, BA(Hons) ACA *2001;* 115 Woodman Road, Warley, BRENTWOOD, ESSEX, CM14 5AU.

ARCHER, Mr. John Allerton, BA FCA *1962;* 3 Ash Terrace, Whitcliffe, CLECKHEATON, BD19 3DB. (Life Member)

ARCHER, Mr. Jonathan, BA ACA *2002;* 61 Warkworth Woods, NEWCASTLE UPON TYNE, NE3 5RB.

ARCHER, Mr. Joseph Campbell, BA(Hons) ACA *2004;* 14 Kingsley Road, LONDON, N13 5PL.

ARCHER, Miss. Kathryn Clare, ACA *2010;* 9 Nova Scotia Place, BRISTOL, BS1 6XJ.

ARCHER, Mrs. Kay Elizabeth, FCA *1987;* 5 Western Avenue, LINCOLN, LINCOLNSHIRE, LN6 7SR.

•**ARCHER, Mr. Kelvin, ACA** *1983;* Kelvin Archer, Cob Suite Old Swan House, 29 High Street, HEMEL HEMPSTEAD, HP1 3AA. See also Kelvin Archer Limited, Pension Accounts Limited and Archer Kelvin

•**ARCHER, Mr. Lawrence Charles, BA FCA** *1992;* (Tax Fac), Harold Smith, Unit 32, Llys Edmund Prys, St. Asaph Business Park, ST. ASAPH, LL17 0JA.

ARCHER, Mr. Marc Stephen, BA ACA ATII *1991;* 53 Truesdale Gardens, Langtoft, PETERBOROUGH, PE6 9QQ.

ARCHER, Mr. Marcus Paul, BSc ACA *1998;* 9 Lexington Court, PURLEY, SURREY, CR8 1JA.

ARCHER, Mr. Martin Walker, LLB FCA *1982;* 5 Slayleigh Lane, SHEFFIELD, S10 3RE.

ARCHER, Mrs. Natalie Jane, BA ACA *2000;* 22a Long Park, AMERSHAM, BUCKINGHAMSHIRE, HP6 5LA.

ARCHER, Mr. Nicholas James, BSc FCA *1981;* 10 Hillcrest Waye, GERRARDS CROSS, BUCKINGHAMSHIRE, SL9 8DN.

ARCHER, Mr. Oliver Carl, BSc(Econ) ACA *1998;* 22a Long Park, Chesham Bois, AMERSHAM, BUCKINGHAMSHIRE, HP6 5LA.

ARCHER, Mr. Paul, BA ACA *1986;* 13 Lockwood Street, YORK, YO31 7QY.

ARCHER, Mr. Paul Anthony, BA FCA *1977;* 39 bis Rue Rousselle, 92800 PUTEAUX, FRANCE.

ARCHER, Mr. Paul Duncan, BA FCA *1983;* Mar Lodge, High Street, Little Chesterford, SAFFRON WALDEN, CB10 1TS.

•**ARCHER, Mr. Paul Michael, BSc FCA** *1975;* (Tax Fac), Carpenter Box LLP, Amelia House, WORTHING, WEST SUSSEX, BN11 1QR.

ARCHER, Mr. Richard David, BSc(Hons) ACA *2003;* 12 Bambrook Close, Desford, LEICESTER, LE9 9FY.

ARCHER, Mr. Robert Charles, ACA *2009;* 3 St. Francis Road, LONDON, SE22 8DE.

ARCHER, Mr. Robin Thomas Edward, BA ACA *1999;* (Tax Fac), Zurich Insurance Co, The Zurich Centre, 3000 Parkway, Whiteley, FAREHAM, PO15 7JZ.

ARCHER, Miss. Rosalind Amy Spencer, BSc ACA *2011;* 86 Cromwell Road, Wimbledon, LONDON, SW19 8NA.

ARCHER, Mr. Sam Richard Douglas, BSc ACA *2003;* 22 Leopold Avenue, LONDON, SW19 7ET.

ARCHER, Mrs. Sarah Jane, ACA *1983;* Sydney Mitchell, 346 Stratford Road, Shirley, SOLIHULL, B90 3DN.

ARCHER, Mr. Stephen Charles, BSc ACA *1992;* c/o Eesti Raudtee, Pikk 36, TALLINN 15073, ESTONIA.

•**ARCHER, Mr. Steven John, FCA** *1987;* Geens, 68 Liverpool Road, STOKE-ON-TRENT, ST4 1BG.

ARCHER, Mr. Terence, MBA FCA *1975;* P4, Broad Fold Hall, Luddenden, HALIFAX, WEST YORKSHIRE, HX2 6TW.

•**ARCHER, Mr. Timothy William, MBA FCA** *1995;* Deloitte LLP, Abbots House, Abbey Street, READING, RG1 3BD. See also Deloitte & Touche LLP

ARCHER, Mr. William Alan, FCA *1957;* 75 Aylestone Hill, HEREFORD, HR1 1HX. (Life Member)

ARCHER, Mr. William Richard Valentine, FCA *1962;* 6 Brookfield close, ASHTEAD, SURREY, KT21 2GA.

ARCHER-PERKINS, Mr. Richard Charles, FCA *1970;* 23 Wangjiao Plaza 175 East Yanan Road, SHANGHAI 200002, CHINA.

ARCHER-SMITH, Mrs. Helen Elizabeth, ACA DChA *2005;* 41 Farleigh Road, PERSHORE, WORCESTERSHIRE, WR10 1LB.

ARCHIBALD, Mr. Robin Andrew Crawford, FCA *1977;* 69 Park Lane, CROYDON, CR0 1JD.

ARCHIBALD, Ms. Valerie Jane, MA FCA *1982;* 13 Ranelagh Crescent, ASCOT, SL5 8LW.

ARCHIBOLD, Mrs. Lisa Martine, BA ACA *1997;* 20 Leybourne Avenue, BOURNEMOUTH, BH10 6HF.

ARCIDIACONO, Miss. Concetta Maria Luisa, BSc ACA *1992;* The Old Rectory, Churchfield Road, Tewin, WELWYN, HERTFORDSHIRE, AL6 0JN.

ARCKLESS, Mrs. Jane Alison, ACA *1991;* Hill House, Orton, PENRITH, CUMBRIA, CA10 3RG.

ARCULUS, Mr. Robin Gilman, MA FCA CMC *1963;* The Warren, Pudding Hill, Warren Row, WARGRAVE, BERKSHIRE RG10 8QZ.

ARDEN, Mr. David John, FCA *1974;* The Post Box, Buzon No 156, D.J. & R.I. Arden, Commercial Local No7, URB. Dona Pepa, Cuidad Quesada Rojales 03170 ALICANTE SPAIN.

ARDEN, Mr. Richard Brian, BA ACA *2001;* 71 Firvale, Harthill, SHEFFIELD, S26 7XP.

•**ARDEN-DAVIS, Mr. James Dalley, BSc ACA** *1991;* PricewaterhouseCoopers LLP, 7 More London Riverside, LONDON, SE1 2RT. See also PricewaterhouseCoopers

ARDEN-DAVIS, Mrs. Rachel, ACA *2001;* 3 Moreton Avenue, HARPENDEN, HERTFORDSHIRE, AL5 2EU.

ARDERN, Mr. Derek Percival George, FCA *1953;* 3 Southway, CHESTER, CH1 5NW. (Life Member)

ARDILES, Mrs. Sarah Helen, BA ACA *2005;* 16 Chestnut Grove, FLEET, HAMPSHIRE, GU51 3LW.

ARDILL, Mr. Ian Leslie, BSc ACA *1992;* Biocompatibles UK Ltd Chapman House, Farnham Business Park Weydon Lane, FARNHAM, GU9 8QL.

ARDLEY, Mr. John Anthony, FCA *1970;* Anerley, Horn Cote Lane, New Mill, Holfirth, HUDDERSFIELD, HD9 7DG.

ARDOUIN, Mr. James Matthew, BA ACA AMCT *1999;* Mimosa, Monarchs Way, RUISLIP, MIDDLESEX, HA4 7BS.

•**ARDREY, Mr. Raymond, BSc(Econ) FCA** *1979;* Birchlea, Bosbury, LEDBURY, HEREFORDSHIRE, HR8 1PR.

ARDRON, Mr. John Stuart, BCom ACA *1995;* 15 Wood Ride, Petts Wood, ORPINGTON, KENT, BR5 1PZ.

ARDRON, Mr. William Dean, BCom FCA *1990;* 2 Middlewood Drive, Scholes, ROTHERHAM, S61 2XY.

AREFPOUR, Mr. Mohamad Reza, ACA *1990;* 2 Hocroft Road, LONDON, NW2 2BL.

AREH, Mr. Mudasiru Olaloye, FCA *1968;* 60A Apapa Road, Ebute Metta PO Box 53637, Falomo Ikoyi, LAGOS, NIGERIA. (Life Member)

ARGENT, Mr. Christopher Lee, FCA *1971;* 16 ROSE LANE, CANTERBURY, CT1 2UR.

ARGENT, Miss. Julia Lois, BA ACA *1994;* 9 The Stables, Great Hyde Hall, Hatfield Heath Road, SAWBRIDGEWORTH, HERTFORDSHIRE, CM21 9JA.

ARGENT, Mr. Michael, BSc ACA *1988;* 77 Downs Hill, BECKENHAM, BR3 5HD.

•**ARGENT, Mr. Stephen, ACA** *1981;* Argent & Company, 20 Burgess Hill, LONDON, NW2 2DA.

•**ARGYLE, Mr. Andrew Iain, BCom FCA** *1989;* KPMG LLP, One Snowhill, Snow Hill Queensway, BIRMINGHAM, B4 6GN. See also KPMG Europe LLP

ARGYLE, Mr. Anthony, FCA *1956;* 18 Spencefield Lane, Evington, LEICESTER, LE5 6PS. (Life Member)

ARGYLE, Mr. James Alexander, BA(Hons) ACA *2000;* 47 Broadway, CHEADLE, CHESHIRE, SK8 1LB.

•**ARGYLE, Mr. Michael John, BSc ACA** *1989;* Duncan & Toplis, 3 Castlegate, GRANTHAM, LINCOLNSHIRE, NG31 6SF. See also Fidentia Services LLP

ARGYLE, Mrs. Rachel Mary, BA ACA *1999;* with Deloitte LLP, PO Box 500, 2 Hardman Street, MANCHESTER, M60 2AT.

ARGYLE, Mr. Robert Anthony, BA(Hons) ACA *2001;* Daniels Chilled Foods Unit 4, Killingbeck Drive, LEEDS, LS14 6UF.

ARGYROPOULOS, Mr. Iordanis, BA ACA *2009;* 50 Golgon Street, 3027 LIMASSOL, CYPRUS.

ARGYROU, Mr. Agathoclis, BSc ACA *1997;* 3 Pelopos St, Delfi, 2107 NICOSIA, CYPRUS.

ARGYROU, Mr. Andreas, BSc ACA *2010;* 12 Vasili H Yianni, Strovolos, 2042 NICOSIA, CYPRUS.

ARGYROU, Mr. Theo, BA ACA *2009;* 20 Athanasiou Christodoulou Street, Mesa Yitonia, 4002 LIMASSOL, CYPRUS.

ARGYTAKIS, Mr. Georgios, BSc ACA *2009;* P.O. Box 62236, 8062 PAPHOS, CYPRUS.

ARHEL, Mr. Christophe John, MSc BSc ACA *2004;* 65 The Oaks, Milton, CAMBRIDGE, CB24 6ZG.

•**ARIAN, Mr. Imtiaz Ali, FCA** *1973;* (Tax Fac), The Gallagher Partnership LLP, PO Box 698, 2nd Floor, Titchfield House, 69/85 Tabernacle Street, LONDON EC2A 4RR.

•**ARIARATNAM, Mr. Namasivayam, BSc FCA** *1963;* (Tax Fac), Siva Yogan & Co, Hounslow Business Park, Unit 6, HOUNSLOW, TW3 3UD.

ARIEL, Mrs. Carol Anne, BSc ACA *1983;* 6 Tadorne Road, TADWORTH, KT20 5TD.

•①**ARIEL, Mr. John David, BSc ACA** *1982;* Baker Tilly Tax & Advisory Services LLP, 12 Gleneagles Court, Brighton Road, CRAWLEY, WEST SUSSEX, RH10 6AD. See also Baker Tilly Restructuring and Recovery LLP

ARIES, Mr. Edmund Roland, BSc ACA *1985;* 9675 Sunderson Road, ORLANDO, FL 32825, UNITED STATES.

ARIES, Mr. Mark Anthony, BCom ACA *1994;* 27 Cumberford Close, Bloxham, BANBURY, OX15 4HN.

ARIF, Miss. Fatimah, ACA *2008;* 23 The Drive, BUCKHURST HILL, ESSEX, IG9 5RB.

ARIF, Mr. Luqman, MSc BSc ACA *2011;* 3 Lyndon Avenue, Great Harwood, BLACKBURN, BB6 7TP.

ARIF, Mr. Mohammad, FCA *1967;* 44 Masson Road, LAHORE, PAKISTAN. (Life Member)

ARIF, Mr. Mohammed, BA ACA CTA *2002;* Cummins Ltd. c/o Cummins Turbo Technologies Limited, St Andrews Road, HUDDERSFIELD, WEST YORKSHIRE, HD1 6RA.

ARIF, Mr. Nafees, BSc(Hons) FCA *2000;* 53a Murray Road, LONDON, W5 4XR.

ARIF, Mr. Talah, BSc(Hons) ACA AMCT *2004;* Floor 24, 60 Wall Street, NEW YORK, NY 10005, UNITED STATES.

ARIF, Mr. Usman, ACA *1998;* 75 Compayne Gardens, LONDON, NW6 3RS.

ARIF, Mr. Zeeshan, MSc ACA *2010;* Flat 5 Bentley House, 21 Wellington Way, LONDON, E3 4XE.

ARIFF, Mr. Abbas, ACA *2010;* 4b Mid Stocket Road, ABERDEEN, AB15 5NE.

ARIFULIN, Mr. Alexey, ACA *2008;* c. Usovo 48, Odintsovskiy Rayon, 143084 MOSCOW, RUSSIAN FEDERATION.

•**ARIS, Mr. Menelaos Aristodemou, FCA FCMI** *1971;* (Tax Fac), M.Aris & Co, Northway House, 1379 High Road, Whetstone, LONDON, N20 9LP.

•**ARIS, Ms. Natalie, BA FCA** *1997;* (Tax Fac), with M.Aris & Co, Northway House, 1379 High Road, Whetstone, LONDON, N20 9LP.

ARIS, Mr. Peter James Perkins, FCA *1958;* 23 Hill Rise, Woodhouse Eaves, LOUGHBOROUGH, LEICESTERSHIRE, LE12 8QX. (Life Member)

ARIS, Mr. Richard Stephen, FCA *1973;* Stream Cottage, 70 Dukes Wood Drive, GERRARDS CROSS, BUCKINGHAMSHIRE, SL9 7LF.

ARISTIDOU, Mr. Andrew, BSc FCA *1995;* 15 Buckingham Avenue, LONDON, N20 9BU.

ARISTIDOU, Mr. Aristides, BSc ACA *2010;* 5 Iacovos Patatsos Street, Palouriotissa, 1040 NICOSIA, CYPRUS.

ARISTIDOU, Mrs. Inderjit Kaur, BSc ACA *1995;* 15 Buckingham Avenue, Whetstone, LONDON, N20 9BU.

ARISTIDOU, Mr. Moisis, BSc ACA *2011;* 18 Onisilou Str, V.Polos Kaimakli, 1026 NICOSIA, CYPRUS.

ARISTIDOU, Mr. Paris, BSc ACA *2010;* 5 IACOVOS PATATSOS STREET, PALOURIOTISSA, 1040 NICOSIA, CYPRUS.

ARISTIDOU, Miss. Vicky, ACA *2008;* P.O. Box 51524, 3506 LIMASSOL, CYPRUS.

ARISTODEMOU, Miss. Androula, BSc ACA *2006;* 43 Nicosias Street, Strovolos, 2018 NICOSIA, CYPRUS.

ARISTODEMOU, Mr. Nicolas, BA ACA *2010;* Ntinou Pavlou9, 8020 PAPHOS, CYPRUS.

ARISTODEMOU, Ms. Sotia, BBA ACA *2005;* Naiadon 97, Palaio Faliro, Attiki, 175 62 ATHENS, GREECE.

ARISTOTELOUS, Mr. Demetris, BSc ACA *1998;* Flat 12 Green Park Mansions A 29 Panayiotis Kaspis Str., 2008 STROVOLOS, CYPRUS.

ARISTOTELOUS, Mr. Panayiotis, MPhil ACA *1993;* Nikiphorou Phoka 5, K Lakatamia, 2334 NICOSIA, CYPRUS.

•**ARISTOTELOUS, Mr. Robert Phaidonos, FCA FCCA MCIArb** *1974;* Paris & Co UK Limited, 9 Leys Gardens, Cockfosters, BARNET, EN4 9NA.

ARIYADASA, Mr. Channa Saman, BA ACA *1992;* 49 Ashburton Road, RUISLIP, HA4 6AA.

ARIYASENA, Mr. Janaka Ishan, ACA *2009;* 35 Grove Road, LONDON, E3 4PE.

•**ARK, Mr. Balvinder Singh, BSocSc FCA** *1995;* (Tax Fac), Ark Aurora Ltd, Capital House, 172-176 Cape Hill, BIRMINGHAM, WEST MIDLANDS, B66 4SJ. See also Ark Associates Ltd

•**ARK, Mr. Gurnek, BCom FCA** *1992;* (Tax Fac), with Ark Aurora Ltd, Capital House, 172-176 Cape Hill, BIRMINGHAM, WEST MIDLANDS, B66 4SJ.

ARKELL, Mrs. Caroline Olivia, BA(Hons) ACA *2004;* with Grant Thornton UK LLP, 1 Dorset Street, SOUTHAMPTON, SO15 2DP.

ARKELL, Mr. David Lewis, BSc ACA *2004;* 84 Wilton Gardens, SOUTHAMPTON, SO15 7QR.

ARKELL, Mrs. Eleanor Julia, BA ACA *2006;* Flat C, 226 Earlsfield Road, LONDON, SW18 3DX.

ARKINSTALL, Mr. Donald Edward, FCA *1954;* 5 Cefn Morfa, Cefnllys Lane, LLANDRINDOD WELLS, LD1 5NP. (Life Member)

ARKINSTALL, Mrs. Sara Jean, BA ACA *1983;* Lateral, 2nd Floor, 8 City Walk, LEEDS, LS11 9AT.

ARKLE, Miss. Jane, MA FCA *1980;* (Tax Fac), 45 Clapham Common West Side, Battersea, LONDON, SW4 9AR.

ARKLE, Mr. Richard Manning, FCA *1975;* Oakwood, Manor Road, Baldwins Gate, NEWCASTLE, ST5 5ET.

ARKLE, Mr. Richard Sidney, LLB ACA *2011;* Ground floor flat, 2 Effie Place, LONDON, SW6 1TA.

•**ARKLEY, Mr. David Robert, FCA** *1976;* (Tax Fac), Leonard Bye, 80 Borough Road, MIDDLESBROUGH, TS1 2JN.

ARKLEY, Mr. Derek Wilfred, FCA *1958;* 26 Blackthorn Close, BIRMINGHAM, B30 1SB.

ARKWRIGHT, Mr. James Richard Edward, BSc(Hons) ACA *2000;* 8 Litherland Road, SALE, CHESHIRE, M33 2PE.

ARLETT, Mrs. Carolyn Helen, BSc(Hons) ACA *2001;* 65 Regency Gardens, WALTON-ON-THAMES, SURREY, KT12 2BE.

ARLETT, Mr. Julian, BA ACA *2001;* 8 Hanover Street, LONDON, W1S 1YE.

ARLIDGE, Miss. Tandy, ACA *1983;* ACA Apex Ltd, Unit 21, Harmill Industrial Estate, LEIGHTON BUZZARD, BEDFORDSHIRE, LU7 4FF.

ARMAND SMITH, Mr. Colin Walter, FCA *1972;* 2 The Green, Marston, DEVIZES, SN10 5SW.

•**ARMER, Mrs. Annette Patricia, FCA** *1982;* (Tax Fac), Smith Hodge & Baxter, Thorpe House, 93 Headlands, KETTERING, NN15 6BL.

ARMER, Mrs. Elizabeth Joy, MA ACA *2000;* Applegarth White House Lane Great Eccleston, PRESTON, PR3 0XB.

ARMER, Mrs. Fiona Mary, BSc ACA *1995;* Park View Offices, Royal Blackburn Hospital, Haslingden Road, BLACKBURN, BB2 3HH.

•**ARMES, Mr. Nicholas, BA ACA** *1993;* (Tax Fac), N Armes & Co Ltd, 1 Pelmark House, 11 Amwell End, WARE, HERTFORDSHIRE, SG12 9HP.

ARMES-REARDON, Mr. Simon Patrick John Francis, BA ACA *1982;* The Red House, 2 Apperley Road, STOCKSFIELD, NORTHUMBERLAND, NE43 7PE.

•**ARMFIELD, Mr. Griffiths Ian Ashley, BSc FCA** *1980;* PricewaterhouseCoopers LLP, 7 More London Riverside, LONDON, SE1 2RT. See also PricewaterhouseCoopers

•**ARMISTEAD, Mr. John Gerald Herbert Lewis, FCA** *1970;* G A Pindar & Son Ltd, Thornburgh Road, Eastfield, SCARBOROUGH, NORTH YORKSHIRE, YO11 3UY. See also Armistead John

ARMISTEAD, Mr. Rupert Burnie, MA ACA *1988;* 52 Hamilton Street, Riverview, LANE COVE, NSW 2066, AUSTRALIA.

ARMITAGE, Mr. Alan Mason, FCA *1969;* Sandwath Cottage, Water Lane, Eyam, HOPE VALLEY, DERBYSHIRE, S32 5RB.

ARMITAGE, Mr. Anthony David, BA ACA *2000;* U B S AG, 100 Liverpool Street, LONDON, EC2M 2RH.

ARMITAGE, Mr. Anthony Giles, BSc FCA *1980;* 8 Sarum View, WINCHESTER, SO22 5QF.

ARMITAGE, Mr. Brian Crowther, FCA *1963;* 12 Congreve Way, Bardsey, LEEDS, LS17 9BG.

ARMITAGE, Mr. Christian, ACA *2007;* 1 Union Street, SOWERBY BRIDGE, WEST YORKSHIRE, HX6 2PB.

ARMITAGE, Mr. Christopher Edward Michael, FCA *1966;* The Granary, Hawthorne House Farm, Dunkeswick, LEEDS, LS17 9LP.

ARMITAGE, Mr. Christopher Michael, BSc FCA *1974;* Sowbury House, High Street, Chieveley, NEWBURY, BERKSHIRE, RG20 8UR.

ARMITAGE, Mr. Christopher Nigel, BEng ACA *1999;* 61 The Drive, BECKENHAM, BR3 1EE.

ARMITAGE, Mr. Daniel Robert, BA(Hons) ACA *2002;* Bessie Garth, Egton Grange, WHITBY, NORTH YORKSHIRE, YO22 5AU.

ARMITAGE, Mr. David Gordon, FCA *1955;* 23 Thurlaston House, Thurlaston Drive, Cawston, RUGBY, WARWICKSHIRE, CV22 7SB. (Life Member)

ARMITAGE, Mr. David U, FCA *1966;* Sellers International Ltd, International House, Chapel Hill, HUDDERSFIELD, HD1 3EE.

ARMITAGE, Mr. Edward John, BA(Hons) ACA *2002;* Oaktree Cottage, Lilac Close, Willington, TARPORLEY, CHESHIRE, CW6 0PL.

ARMITAGE, Mrs. Elizabeth Jane, MA ACA *1993;* 54 Bradstock Road, Stoneleigh, EPSOM, KT17 2LQ.

ARMITAGE, Miss. Emma, BSc ACA *2011;* 7 Ash Close, Beeston, SANDY, BEDFORDSHIRE, SG19 1GE.

ARMITAGE, Mr. Eric Davies, FCA *1956;* 19 Pinewood Avenue, Bolton Le Sands, CARNFORTH, LA5 8AS. (Life Member)

ARMITAGE, Mr. Eric Leslie, FCA *1951;* 27 Grenville Court, Chorleywood, RICKMANSWORTH, WD3 5PZ. (Life Member)

•**ARMITAGE, Miss. Gaynor, BSc FCA** *1993;* Giess Wallis Crisp LLP, 10-12 Mulberry Green, HARLOW, ESSEX, CM17 0ET.

ARMITAGE, Mr. George Michael, FCA *1950;* 99 Overstand Road, CROMER, NR27 0DJ. (Life Member)

•**ARMITAGE, Mr. Graham Paul, MA ACA** *1994;* KPMG LLP, 15 Canada Square, LONDON, E14 5GL. See also KPMG Europe LLP

ARMITAGE, Mr. Harry Douglas, BSc FCA *1979;* Experian Finance Plc, Suite 3.1.4, Universal Square, Devonshire Street North, MANCHESTER, M12 6JH.

ARMITAGE, Mr. Hugh Jeremy Hazeland, MA FCA *1963;* 375 Chemin Des Puits, 83136 NEOULES, FRANCE. (Life Member)

ARMITAGE, Mrs. Jennifer Anne Sarah, BA ACA *1999;* 27 Oak Court, Woodfield Plantation, Balby, DONCASTER, SOUTH YORKSHIRE, DN4 8TT.

ARMITAGE, Mr. John, FCA *1973;* 2 Orwell Close, Albert Road, Caversham Heights, READING, RG4 7PU.

•**ARMITAGE, Mr. John Stuart, FCA** *1973;* P.O. Box 67498, NAIROBI, KENYA.

ARMITAGE, Mr. Jonathan Spencer, BA FCA CF *1991;* 20 New Road, Rufford, ORMSKIRK, L40 1SR.

ARMITAGE, Mr. Julian, FCA *1968;* 2 Chestnut Garth, Quarmby, HUDDERSFIELD, HD3 4FH.

ARMITAGE, Mr. Matthew, ACA *2011;* Flat under the newsagents, 30 Essex Road, LONDON, N1 8LN.

ARMITAGE, Mr. Michael, FCA *1974;* 44 Townparks, SKERRIES, COUNTY DUBLIN, IRELAND.

ARMITAGE, Mr. Michael Paul, BA ACA *1995;* 50 Canal Street, DERBY, DE1 2RJ.

ARMITAGE, Mr. Michael Robert, BA(Econ) ACA *1996;* RTE (Stage 7), Nutley Lane, Donnybrook, DUBLIN 4, COUNTY DUBLIN, IRELAND.

ARMITAGE, Mr. Nicholas James, BSc(Hons) ACA *2002;* with BDO LLP, 55 Baker Street, LONDON, W1U 7EU.

ARMITAGE, Mr. Peter Dickson, FCA *1970;* Les Oliviers, 18 La Rue de la Forge, Grouville, JERSEY, JE3 9BH. (Life Member)

ARMITAGE, Mr. Peter Lockhart, BA FCA *1973;* O C S Group Ltd, 79 Limpsfield Road, SOUTH CROYDON, SURREY, CR2 9LB.

ARMITAGE, Mr. Peter Robert, ACA *1981;* 19A Lower Busker Farm, Busker Lane, Scissett, HUDDERSFIELD, HD8 9JU.

•**ARMITAGE, Mr. Philip David, FCA** *1976;* Armitage & Co Limited, 1 New Street, Slaithwaite, HUDDERSFIELD, HD7 5AB. See also Daggerlux Limited

ARMITAGE, Mr. Raymond George, FCA *1965;* c/o Mrs K Armitage, 13 Acomb Wood Close, Woodthorpe, YORK, YO24 2SN. (Life Member)

ARMITAGE, Mrs. Rebecca Victoria Yorke, BSc ACA *1997;* Maythorne, Northcote Road, West Horsley, LEATHERHEAD, SURREY, KT24 6LT.

ARMITAGE, Mr. Richard Simon, BA ACA *2000;* 26 St. Swithun Street, WINCHESTER, HAMPSHIRE, SO23 9HU.

ARMITAGE, Mr. Robert John, BSc ACA *1986;* 7 Grosvenor Avenue, RICHMOND, SURREY, TW10 6PD.

ARMITAGE, Mr. Roger Stuart, FCA *1965;* 191 Gillroyd Lane, Linthwaite, HUDDERSFIELD, HD7 5SR.

ARMITAGE, Mr. Roy, FCA *1961;* Apt 512, 10 Delisle Avenue, TORONTO M4V 3C6, ON, CANADA. (Life Member)

ARMITAGE, Mr. Simon James, BA FCA *1986;* Universities Superannuation Scheme Ltd Royal Liver Building, Pier Head, LIVERPOOL, L3 1PY.

ARMITAGE, Mr. Simon Nicholas, BA ACA *1995;* 5 Polynesia Grove, WEST LAKES, SA 5021, AUSTRALIA.

ARMITAGE, Mrs. Susan Mary, BA ACA *1987;* 7 Grosvenor Avenue, RICHMOND, TW10 6PD.

ARMITAGE, Mr. Terence Peter, FCA *1971;* Paddock View, 8 Duke's Field, Down Ampney, CIRENCESTER, GLOUCESTERSHIRE, GL7 5PQ.

ARMITSTEAD, Mr. Christopher John, ACA *1983;* brewchem house, Brewchem International Ltd Brewchem House, Steeton Grove Steeton, KEIGHLEY, WEST YORKSHIRE, BD20 6TT.

ARMITSTEAD, Mrs. Katrina Louise, BA ACA *1998;* 60 Castle Grove, KENDAL, CUMBRIA, LA9 7AZ.

ARMITT, Mr. Matthew, BSc ACA *2006;* 125 Old Broad Street, LONDON, EC2N 1AR.

ARMITT, Mr. Michael William, ACA *2011;* Flat 9, Tyseley House, Swanwick Lane, Broughton, MILTON KEYNES, MK10 9NS.

ARMITT, Mr. Philip John, BA ACA *1978;* 2 Elgin Avenue, Holmes Chapel, CREWE, CW4 7JE.

ARMOUR, Mrs. Amelia, BSc ACA *2001;* The Old House High Street, Newport, SAFFRON WALDEN, CB11 3QX.

ARMOUR, Mr. John Andrew Stuart, BSc ACA *1998;* The Old House, High Street, Newport, SAFFRON WALDEN, ESSEX, CB11 3QX.

ARMOUR, Mr. Mark Henry, MA FCA *1980;* Reed Elsevier, 1-3 Strand, LONDON, WC2N 5JR.

ARMOUR, Mrs. Tanya Chivonne Anne, BSc FCA *1993;* Mullberry Cottage, 145 Forest Road, LISS, HAMPSHIRE, GU33 7BU.

•**ARMSBY, Mr. Adam John, BA ACA** *1990;* Howarth Armsby, New Broad Street House, 35 New Broad Street, LONDON, EC2M 1NH.

ARMSTRONG, Mr. Alan Vincent, FCA *1960;* Woodlands, School Road, Conon Bridge, DINGWALL, IV7 8AB. (Life Member)

ARMSTRONG, Mr. Alistair Paul, BA ACA *2005;* Primary Capital Ltd, Augustine House, 6a Austin Friars, LONDON, EC2N 2HA.

ARMSTRONG, Miss. Amy Claire Maxwell, ACA *2009;* 105 Sherbrooke Road, LONDON, SW6 7QL.

ARMSTRONG, Mr. Andrew John, BSc ACA *1996;* 103 Silver Birch Avenue, TORONTO M4E 3L3, ON, CANADA.

ARMSTRONG, Mr. Andrew Leslie, ACA *1987;* 3 Leys Road, Timperley, ALTRINCHAM, WA14 5AT.

ARMSTRONG, Mr. Andrew Mark, BSc ACA *1988;* 24 Rutland Road, RETFORD, DN22 7HF.

ARMSTRONG, Miss. Ann-Marie, BA ACA *2007;* Thorntons Plc Thornton Park, Somercotes, ALFRETON, DERBYSHIRE, DE55 4XJ.

•**ARMSTRONG, Mr. Anthony Daniel, BA ACA** *1985;* (Tax Fac), Armstrong & Co, Unit 4A, Printing House Yard, Hackney Road, LONDON, E2 7PR.

ARMSTRONG, Mr. Benjamin James, BA ACA *2002;* 27 Royton Drive, Whittle-le-Woods, CHORLEY, PR6 7HJ.

ARMSTRONG, Mr. Bruce Fraser, BSc FCA *1973;* Crosshills, 7 Pine Coombe, Shirley, CROYDON, CR0 5HS.

ARMSTRONG, Mrs. Caroline Frances Margaret, BA ACA *2005;* 2 Kent Place, KETTERING, NORTHAMPTONSHIRE, NN15 6JU.

•**ARMSTRONG, Ms. Christine Carole, BA ACA** *1983;* 13 Downs Way, TADWORTH, KT20 5DH.

ARMSTRONG, Mr. Christopher Paul, BSc FCA *1990;* Christison Particle Technologies Ltd, Albany Road, GATESHEAD, NE8 3AT.

ARMSTRONG, Miss. Claire, ACA *2005;* G & J Peck Ltd, Lisle Lane, ELY, CAMBRIDGESHIRE, CB7 4PU.

ARMSTRONG, Mr. Colin, FCA *1982;* Talland House, Wylam Wood Road, WYLAM, NE41 8HX.

ARMSTRONG, Mr. David, BSc *1988;* with Francis Clark, North Quay House, Sutton Harbour, PLYMOUTH, PL4 0RA.

•**ARMSTRONG, Mr. David, FCA** *1977;* Ryecroft Glenton, 32 Portland Terrace, Jesmond, NEWCASTLE UPON TYNE, NE2 1QP.

ARMSTRONG, Mr. David Guy, BA ACA MCT *1995;* 16 Belle Vue Road, READING, RG1 7TX.

ARMSTRONG, Mr. David James, BA FCA *1990;* The Malt House, Ockham Road North, East Horsley, LEATHERHEAD, KT24 6PX.

•**ARMSTRONG, Mr. David Maurice, FCA** *1992;* (Tax Fac), Ribchesters, 67 Saddler Street, DURHAM, DH1 3NP.

•**ARMSTRONG, Mr. David Neil, FCA** *1985;* 31 Denwick Close, CHESTER LE STREET, COUNTY DURHAM, DH2 3TL.

ARMSTRONG, Mr. David Peter, FCA *1962;* 20 Longview, Hethersett, NORWICH, NR9 3JN.

ARMSTRONG, Mr. Denis Edmund, FCA *1957;* Tordene, Dean Place, Newstead, MELROSE, ROXBURGHSHIRE, TD6 9RL. (Life Member)

ARMSTRONG, Miss. Dominique Margaret, LLB ACA *2003;* 13 Westhorpe Road, LONDON, SW15 1QH.

ARMSTRONG, Mr. Douglas Patrick, BA(Hons) ACA *2004;* Flat 15 Westside, Ravenscourt Park, LONDON, W6 0TY.

ARMSTRONG, Mrs. Elizabeth Miranda, BA ACA *1996;* The Manor House Church Street, Great Shefford, HUNGERFORD, RG17 7DZ.

ARMSTRONG, Miss. Emma Louise, BSc ACA *2009;* K P M G Edward VII Quay, Navigation Way Ashton-on-Ribble, PRESTON, PR2 2YF.

•**ARMSTRONG, Mrs. Faye, MA(Hons) ACA AIIT DChA** *2003;* Dodd & Co., Fifteen Rosehill, Montgomery Way, Rosehill Estate, CARLISLE, CA1 2RW. See also Dodd & Co

ARMSTRONG, Mr. Geoffrey Read, ACA *2008;* Woodland House, Woodland Lane, Colgate, HORSHAM, WEST SUSSEX, RH13 6HU.

ARMSTRONG, Mrs. Hayley Carron, BSc ACA *1991;* 258 Station Road, Knowle, SOLIHULL, B93 0ES.

ARMSTRONG, Mr. Hugh Clayton Alexander, FCA *1959;* The Corner House, 17 Buckland Gardens, LYMINGTON, HAMPSHIRE, SO41 8QL. (Life Member)

ARMSTRONG, Mr. James, BA ACA *1998;* 46 Sandstone Drive, Whiston, PRESCOT, MERSEYSIDE, L35 7NJ.

ARMSTRONG, Mr. James, BSc(Hons) ACA *2003;* Bain Capital Ltd Devonshire House, 1 Mayfair Place, LONDON, W1J 8AJ.

ARMSTRONG, Mr. James Henry, ACA *1991;* 1st Floor, 50 - 54 Clerkenwell Road, LONDON, EC1M 5PS.

ARMSTRONG, Mr. John Anthony, FCA *1970;* 4 The Limes, Standish, WIGAN, LANCASHIRE, WN6 0BJ. (Life Member)

ARMSTRONG, Mr. John Osborne William, BA FCA *1975;* 72 Dominies Close, ROWLANDS GILL, TYNE AND WEAR, NE39 1PB.

ARMSTRONG, Mr. John Philip, BSc ACA *1979;* 31 Canada Way, Lower Wick, WORCESTER, WR2 4DJ.

•**ARMSTRONG, Mr. John Richard Maxwell, BSc FCA** *1976;* The Stone Barn Ufton Fields, Ufton, LEAMINGTON SPA, CV33 9PE.

ARMSTRONG, Mr. Jonathan David, ACA *2009;* 20 Evesham Road, Middleton, MANCHESTER, M24 1PY.

ARMSTRONG, Mr. Jonathan Kendal, BSc ACA *1993;* 5 Highcliffe Edge, Winston, DARLINGTON, DL2 3RX.

ARMSTRONG, Miss. Judith Sarah, BSc ACA *2000;* Pricewaterhousecoopers Cornwall Court, 19 Cornwall Street, BIRMINGHAM, B3 2DT.

ARMSTRONG, Mr. Justin, BA(Hons) ACA *2007;* C/o Close Brothers (Cayman) Limited, 4th Floor Harbour Place, 103 South Church Street, GEORGETOWN, GRAND CAYMAN, KY1-1104 CAYMAN ISLANDS.

ARMSTRONG, Mrs. Karen Heather, ACA *2008;* 26 Cotts Wood Drive, GUILDFORD, GU4 7RB.

ARMSTRONG, Miss. Kate, BA ACA *2004;* 5 Bennett Road, NOTTINGHAM, NG3 6BQ.

ARMSTRONG, Miss. Katherine Ann, BSc ACA *2002;* Lloyds TSB Bank Plc, Canons House, Canons Way, BRISTOL, BS1 5LL.

ARMSTRONG, Mrs. Lesley Denise, BSc ACA *1989;* Silverdale, The Ridgeway, Oxshott, LEATHERHEAD, SURREY, KT22 0LG.

ARMSTRONG, Miss. Lucy Alexandra, ACA *2009;* Flat 14, 120 Wimbledon Hill Road, LONDON, SW19 7QU.

ARMSTRONG, Mr. Malcolm John, MA ACA CTA *1988;* 9 Ashcroft Avenue, STOKE-ON-TRENT, ST4 6LZ.

ARMSTRONG, Mr. Mark Franklin, BA ACA *2000;* (Tax Fac), 9 Sandringham Road, Birkdale, SOUTHPORT, MERSEYSIDE, PR8 2JZ.

ARMSTRONG, Mrs. Melanie Clare, BSc ACA *2000;* HMRC, Albert Bridge House, 1 Bridge Street, MANCHESTER, M60 9AL.

ARMSTRONG, Ms. Melanie Jane, BSc ACA *1990;* 6 Richmond Close, AMERSHAM, HP6 6UY.

ARMSTRONG, Miss. Melissa Claire, BSc ACA *2007;* Pets at Home Ltd, Epsom Avenue, Stanley Green Trading Estate, Handforth, WILMSLOW, CHESHIRE SK9 3RN.

ARMSTRONG, Mr. Michael Edward, LLB ACA *2010;* 14 Scotts Way, TUNBRIDGE WELLS, KENT, TN2 5RG.

ARMSTRONG, Mr. Michael Gordon William, BSc ACA *1982;* with KPMG, P O Box 641, 112 MUSCAT, OMAN.

ARMSTRONG, Mr. Michael Pattison, MA FCA *1973;* Westbrook House, Bromham, CHIPPENHAM, SN15 2EE.

ARMSTRONG, Mr. Neil Robert, BSc ACA *1989;* 107 Woodhead Drive, CAMBRIDGE, CB4 1FG.

•**ARMSTRONG, Mr. Nick James, BA(Hons) ACA** *2004;* Howsons, 50 Broad Street, LEEK, ST13 5NS. See also Howsons Accountants Limited

•**ARMSTRONG, Mr. Nigel James, BSc FCA** *1977;* (Tax Fac), Alliotts, Imperial House, 15 Kingsway, LONDON, WC2B 6UN.

•**ARMSTRONG, Mr. Norman Michael, BSc FCA** *1996;* Grant Thornton UK LLP, 1 Dorset Street, SOUTHAMPTON, SO15 2DP. See also Grant Thornton LLP

•①**ARMSTRONG, Mr. Philip Lewis, BSc ACA** *1998;* FRP Advisory LLP, 10 Furnival Street, LONDON, EC4A 1YH.

ARMSTRONG, Miss. Rachel, BSc ACA *2011;* Flat 4, 71 St. Margarets Road, TWICKENHAM, TW1 2LL.

ARMSTRONG, Mr. Richard Charles, BA(Hons) ACA *2001;* Rosehill, 16 South Road, Bowdon, ALTRINCHAM, CHESHIRE, WA14 2LB.

ARMSTRONG, Mr. Richard Michael, BA FCA *1968;* 68 Knowsley Road, LONDON, SW11 5BL. (Life Member)

ARMSTRONG, Mr. Robert Thomas Maxwell, BSc ACA MBA *1996;* 40 Leigh Road, Hale, ALTRINCHAM, CHESHIRE, WA15 9BD.

ARMSTRONG, Mr. Robin William Alexander, ACA *2008;* Flat 14 Robins Court, Kings Avenue, LONDON, SW4 8EE.

ARMSTRONG, Mr. Russell, BA ACA *1985;* 7 Castleton Road, Hazel Grove, STOCKPORT, CHESHIRE, SK7 6LB.

ARMSTRONG, Mr. Simon Peter, ACA *2008;* 3 Hayling Grove, WICKFORD, ESSEX, SS12 9LQ.

ARMSTRONG, Mrs. Sinead Eithne, BCom ACA *1992;* Malt House, Ockham Road North, East Horsley, LEATHERHEAD, SURREY, KT24 6PX.

ARMSTRONG, Mr. Stephen, BA(Hons) ACA *2010;* 24 Curzon Place, Half Noon Lane, GATESHEAD, TYNE AND WEAR, NE8 2ER.

•**ARMSTRONG, Mr. Stephen William, BSc ACA** *1985;* Armstrong Rose Limited, 21 Langholm Road, EAST BOLDON, TYNE AND WEAR, NE36 0ED.

ARMSTRONG, Miss. Susan Elizabeth, BSc ACA *1995;* 75 Kitchener Street, Trigg, PERTH, WA 6029, AUSTRALIA.

ARMSTRONG, Mr. Terence Michael, BSc FCA *1971;* 42 Selborne Road, CROYDON, CR0 5JQ. (Life Member)

ARMSTRONG, Mr. Tim, BSc ACA *2010;* Walnut Farm, The Street, Bodham, HOLT, NORFOLK, NR25 6NW.

ARMSTRONG, Mr. Timothy James, BA ACA *2005;* Flat 2, 68 Westbere Road, LONDON, NW2 3RU.

ARMSTRONG, Mr. Trevor George, ACA *1984;* Sterling Court, Norton Rd, STEVENAGE, HERTFORDSHIRE, SG1 2JY.

ARMSTRONG-FLEMMING, Mr. Nigel Hugh Gordon, FCA *1964;* Winchmore, Chalk Lane, East Horsley, LEATHERHEAD, KT24 6TH. (Life Member)

ARMSTRONG-HOLDEN, Ms. Caroline Margaret, MA ACA *1985;* Notting Hill Preparatory School, 95 Lancaster Road, LONDON, W11 1QQ.

ARMSTRONG NASH, Mr. Neil Stewart, BSc FCA *1991;* Avenue Blanc 46, 1202 GENEVA, SWITZERLAND.

ARMSTRONG-TAYLOR, Mrs. Sarah Wendy, BSc ACA *2000;* 5 The Close, LONDON, SE3 0UR.

ARNALL, Mr. Andrew Nigel, BSc FCA *1991;* 14 Lessar Avenue, Clapham, LONDON, SW4 9HJ.

ARNAUTOVIC, Mr. Eduard Parnell, BA ACA *2002;* 41 Hiley Road, LONDON, NW10 5PT.

ARNETT, Mr. Peter Richard, MA ACA *1989;* c/o Elena Filippova, Ulitsa Akademika Chelomeya 4, KB. 22, 117630 MOSCOW, RUSSIAN FEDERATION.

ARNEY, Mr. John Andrew, BSc ACA *1994;* Candover Partners Plc, 20 Old Bailey, LONDON, EC4M 7LN.

ARNEY, Mr. Nicholas John, BSS ACA *1991;* 60 Great Portland Street, LONDON, W1W 7RT.

ARNFIELD, Mr. Norman Fennell, FCA *1959;* The Old Forge, 104 Christchurch Lane, LICHFIELD, WS13 8AL. (Life Member)

ARNFIELD, Mr. Peter Philip, BSc ACA *1995;* Banstraat 25, 2517 GH, DEN HAAG, NETHERLANDS.

ARNISON-NEWGASS, Mr. Michael, FCA *1975;* Gambledown Farm, Gambledown, Sherfield English, ROMSEY, SO51 6JU.

ARNOLD, Mr. Adrian Paul, BSc ACA *1991;* Greystones, Quarry Road, SWINDON, SN1 4EW.

ARNOLD, Miss. Alice Jane, MA ACA *2002;* Dune London, 9 Hatton Street, LONDON, NW8 8PL.

ARNOLD, Ms. Andrea Leslie, MA ACA *1992;* Flat C, 13, Westbourne Terrace, LONDON, W2 3UL.

ARNOLD, Mr. Andrew John, BSc ACA *1995;* 54 Alexandra Road, WINDSOR, BERKSHIRE, SL4 1HU.

ARNOLD, Mr. Andrew Robert, MEng ACA *1990;* 5 The Mapletons, Odiham, HOOK, HAMPSHIRE, RG29 1DJ.

ARNOLD, Mr. Arthur Jeremy, FCA *1962;* Furze Cottage, Les Nouvelles Charrieres, St. John, JERSEY, JE3 4DJ.

ARNOLD, Mr. Barry, BA FCA *1973;* Beech House, 71 Greenhill Main Road, SHEFFIELD, S8 7RE.

ARNOLD, Mr. Barry, BSc ACA *1985;* 8 Monkshood Close, WOKINGHAM, RG40 5YE.

ARNOLD, Mr. Ben Ian, ACA *2009;* Flat 505 Queens Quay, 58 Upper Thames Street, LONDON, EC4V 3EH.

ARNOLD, Mr. Benjamin Edward, BEng ACA *1998;* 5 Radlet Avenue, LONDON, SE26 4BZ.

ARNOLD, Mr. Bruce Anthony, BA ACA *2004;* 574 Flemmington Street, Kyalami Estates, KYALAMI, GAUTENG, 1684, SOUTH AFRICA.

ARNOLD, Ms. Catherine, BA ACA *2003;* with Deloitte LLP, Stonecutter Court, 1 Stonecutter Street, LONDON, EC4A 4TR.

ARNOLD, Mr. Charles William Geoffrey, FCA *1973;* 8 Ramshill, PETERSFIELD, GU31 4AP.

ARNOLD, Mr. Christopher Mark, BSc ACA *1985;* 4 Holly Close, Alveston, BRISTOL, BS35 3PW.

ARNOLD, Mrs. Clare Anne, BA(Hons) ACA *1992;* Unit 1 Temple House Estate, 6 West Road, HARLOW, ESSEX, CM20 2DU.

•**ARNOLD, Mr. Clement Brian, FCA** *1957;* 6 Ribble Avenue, Oadby, LEICESTER, LE2 4NZ.

ARNOLD, Mr. Clifford Roy, FCA *1956;* 21 Maple Close, SHIFNAL, SHROPSHIRE, TF11 8HA. (Life Member)

ARNOLD, Mr. Daniel Rhys, BA ACA *2009;* 48 Maypole Road, Ashurst Wood, EAST GRINSTEAD, WEST SUSSEX, RH19 3QY.

ARNOLD, Mr. David, FCA *1974;* 11 Fennels Farm Road, Flackwell Heath, HIGH WYCOMBE, BUCKINGHAMSHIRE, HP10 9BP.

ARNOLD, Mr. David Christopher Evans, FCA *1970;* The Croft, 14 Broad Oak Road, WESTON-SUPER-MARE, BS23 4NW.

ARNOLD, Mr. David Matthew, FCA *1977;* 203 Mayfield Crescent, WINNIPEG R3R 3L7, MB, CANADA.

•**ARNOLD, Mr. David Philip James, BSc FCA** *1979;* Ernst & Young LLP, 1 More London Place, LONDON, SE1 2AF. See also Ernst & Young Europe LLP

ARNOLD, Mr. Derek Michael, FCA *1955;* Wild Orchard, North Lane, South Harting, PETERSFIELD, HAMPSHIRE, GU31 5PY. (Life Member)

ARNOLD, Mrs. Elizabeth, BSc ACA *1993;* with BDO LLP, Arcadia House, Maritime Walk, Ocean Village, SOUTHAMPTON, SO14 3TL.

ARNOLD, Mr. Geoffrey, BA ACA *2004;* (Tax Fac), Le Petit Creg-na-Baa La Pouquelaye, St. Helier, JERSEY, JE2 3GG.

ARNOLD, Mr. Geoffrey Charles, MA FCA *1977;* South Riding, Maidenhatch, Pangbourne, READING, RG8 8HH.

•**ARNOLD, Mr. Graham, MBA BSc FCA MIMgt** *1981;* Flat 2, Cromwell House, Irving Mews Islington, LONDON, N1 2FP.

ARNOLD, Mr. Harry Stephenson, FCA *1965;* The Leys, Blackhill Lane, Pulloxhill, BEDFORD, MK45 5HQ. (Life Member)

ARNOLD, Mr. Henry Michael George, MChem ACA *2003;* Flat 12 Block 38, Celestial Heights, 80 Sheung Shing Street, HO MAN TIN, HONG KONG SAR.

ARNOLD, Mr. Ian Philip Howard, BSc FCA *1981;* 28 Sandelswood End, BEACONSFIELD, HP9 2AE.

ARNOLD, Mrs. Ingrid, BSc ACA *1997;* 10 Shouldham Street, LONDON, W1H 5FH.

ARNOLD, Mr. James Matthew, BA ACA MBA *1995;* 15 Sheridan Road, LONDON, SW19 3HW.

ARNOLD, Mrs. Jean Dorothy, BA FCA *1982;* 10 Mill Close, Bookham, LEATHERHEAD, SURREY, KT23 3JX.

ARNOLD, Mr. Jeffrey William, FCA *1973;* 4 Turton Close, Birchwood, WARRINGTON, WA3 7LU.

ARNOLD, Mrs. Jill Anita, BSc ACA ATII *1988;* (Tax Fac), KPMG, Level 7, 147 Collins Street, MELBOURNE, VIC 3000, AUSTRALIA.

ARNOLD, Mr. John, FCA *1955;* 34 Brae Road, WINSCOMBE, AVON, BS25 1LJ. (Life Member)

•**ARNOLD, Mr. John, FCA** *1973;* (Tax Fac), J.W. Arnold & Co., 59A Station Road, Winchmore Hill, LONDON, N21 3NB.

ARNOLD, Prof. John Andre, MSc FCA *1967;* (Member of Council 1984 - 1988), 3 Green Meadows, Marple, STOCKPORT, SK6 6QF.

•**ARNOLD, Mr. John Brian, BA FCA** *1978;* Bapindo Plaza, Citibank Tower 20th floor, Jl Jend Sudirman Kav 54-55, JAKARTA, 12190, INDONESIA.

•**ARNOLD, Mr. John Harold Eveleigh, MA FCA FRSA** *1977;* (Tax Fac), Generaal Spoorlaan 22, 2252TA VOORSCHOTEN, NETHERLANDS.

ARNOLD, Mr. Jonathan Sean, BSc ACA *1991;* 23 Belton Park Drive, North Hykeham, LINCOLN, LN6 9XW.

ARNOLD, Miss. Josephine Eleanor, BSc ACA *2011;* First Floor Flat, 195 Upper Richmond Road, LONDON, SW15 6SG.

•**ARNOLD, Mr. Julian Cary, BSc ACA** *1995;* (Tax Fac), John Davis & Co, 172 Gloucester Road, BRISTOL, BS7 8NU.

ARNOLD, Ms. Julie Louise, BA ACA *1999;* 3 Quantock Mews, LONDON, SE15 4RG.

ARNOLD, Mrs. Katie Jane, BA ACA *2005;* 10 Acers, Park Street, ST. ALBANS, HERTFORDSHIRE, AL2 2BJ.

ARNOLD, Dr. Kenny, ACA *2011;* Apartment 147 Skyline, 165 Granville Street, BIRMINGHAM, B1 1JX.

ARNOLD, Mr. Lawrence Kenneth, FCA *1970;* 42 Raglan Road, REIGATE, SURREY, RH2 0DP.

ARNOLD, Miss. Lindsay Jayne, ACA *2006;* 117 Kinross Close Fearnhead, WARRINGTON, WA2 0UT.

ARNOLD, Miss. Louise Rebecca, ACA *2009;* 18 Eastern Road, Lindfield, HAYWARDS HEATH, WEST SUSSEX, RH16 2LP.

ARNOLD, Mr. Marc Adam, ACA *2008;* 1 Brockley Avenue, STANMORE, MIDDLESEX, HA7 4LX.

ARNOLD, Mr. Marc Jason, BA ACA *1990;* 4 Armour Close, North Lakes, BRISBANE, QLD 4509, AUSTRALIA.

ARNOLD, Miss. Marie Claire, ACA *2004;* (Tax Fac), 28 Station Road, Lowdham, NOTTINGHAM, NG14 7DW.

ARNOLD, Mr. Matthew John Tarrant, BSc ACA *1995;* Flat 7, Lenton House, 27 Lenton Road, The Park, NOTTINGHAM, NG7 1DS.

ARNOLD, Mr. Michael John, FCA *1974;* (Member of Council 2005 - 2011), 25 Sergison Road, HAYWARDS HEATH, RH16 1HX.

ARNOLD, Mr. Michael John, FCA *1957;* Brockhill, Naunton, CHELTENHAM, GLOUCESTERSHIRE, GL54 3BA. (Life Member)

ARNOLD, Mrs. Natalie Jane, BSc ACA *1997;* Willington Rise Common Lane, Kelsall, TARPORLEY, CHESHIRE, CW6 0PY.

ARNOLD, Mr. Neill, BSc ACA *1997;* 30a Grand Drive, LEIGH-ON-SEA, SS9 1BG.

ARNOLD, Mr. Nicholas Saul, BA ACA *2002;* 95 Theobald Street, BOREHAMWOOD, HERTFORDSHIRE, WD6 4PS.

ARNOLD, Mrs. Nicola Jane, BA(Hons) ACA FPC *2001;* 152 Whitton Road, TWICKENHAM, TW1 1DE.

ARNOLD, Miss. Nicola Jane, ACA *1994;* 79 Lower Mortlake Road, RICHMOND, TW9 2LW.

ARNOLD, Mr. Nigel Kenneth, BSc ACA *1994;* (Tax Fac), Double Negative Ltd, 77 Shaftesbury Avenue, LONDON, W1D 5DU.

•**ARNOLD, Mr. Nigel William, ACA** *1980;* Nigel Arnold & Co, 18 Norfolk House, Courtlands Sheen Road, RICHMOND, TW10 5AT.

•**ARNOLD, Mrs. Patricia Jillian Ruth, BA FCA** *1981;* (Tax Fac), Patricia J Arnold & Co Ltd, Black House, Dipton Mill Road, HEXHAM, NORTHUMBERLAND, NE46 1RZ.

ARNOLD, Mr. Paul Robert, BSc ACA *2003;* The Orchard, Olchfa Lane, Gower Road, SWANSEA, SA2 8QQ.

ARNOLD, Mr. Peter David, FCA *1963;* 28 Dorchester Road, CANNOCK, STAFFORDSHIRE, WS11 1QF. (Life Member)

ARNOLD, Mr. Philip John, BSc FCA FIMC CDir *1983;* The Firs, Cadsden Road, PRINCES RISBOROUGH, BUCKINGHAMSHIRE, HP27 0NB.

ARNOLD, Mr. Raymond Terry, FCA *1958;* 16 Eastfields, PINNER, HA5 2SR. (Life Member)

•**ARNOLD, Mr. Rhydian Lloyd, FCA** *1979;* Griffiths Green Arnold, 11 New Street, Pontnewydd, CWMBRAN, NP44 1EE.

•**ARNOLD, Mr. Richard Francis, BA ACA** *1983;* Resolve - Tax and Accounts Limited, 7 Braybrooke Road, Wargrave, READING, RG10 8DU.

ARNOLD, Mr. Richard Neil, BSc ACA *1997;* Willington Rise Common Lane, Kelsall, TARPORLEY, CHESHIRE, CW6 0PY.

ARNOLD, Mr. Robert Antony, BSc ACA *1997;* Swallowtail House Grenadier Road, Exeter Business Park, EXETER, EX1 3LH.

ARNOLD, Mr. Robert Kingsley, MSc ACA *2002;* Little Reynoldston Farm, Reynoldston, SWANSEA, SA3 1AQ.

ARNOLD, Mr. Robert Michael Roland, BCom FCA *1976;* Clasemont Limited, 42 Apthorpe Street, Fulbourn, CAMBRIDGE, CB21 5EY.

ARNOLD, Mr. Rodney David, FCA *1962;* Flat 7, Earlswood, 21 Clarendon Road, Westbourne, BOURNEMOUTH, BH4 8AL.

ARNOLD, Mr. Roger Henry Philip, FCA *1971;* 32 West Parade, HYTHE, KENT, CT21 6DE.

ARNOLD, Miss. Sapna Jyotini, BSc FCA *2001;* 31a Old Kennels Lane, Olivers Battery, WINCHESTER, HAMPSHIRE, SO22 4JR.

ARNOLD, Mrs. Sarah Ann, ACA *2003;* (Tax Fac), R M T Financial Management Unit 2, Gosforth Park Avenue, NEWCASTLE UPON TYNE, NE12 8EG.

•**ARNOLD, Mr. Selwyn Jeffrey, BA(Hons) FCA** *1983;* Sobell Rhodes LLP, Monument House, 215 Marsh Road, PINNER, MIDDLESEX, HA5 5NE.

ARNOLD, Mr. Shane, BSc ACA *1998;* 33 Clover Avenue, STOCKPORT, CHESHIRE, SK3 8QA.

ARNOLD, Mrs. Sharron Margaret, BSc FCA *1977;* 42 Effingham Road, Harden, BINGLEY, BD16 1LQ.

ARNOLD, Mr. Simon Kenneth, BSc ACA *2002;* T U I UK Wigmore House, Wigmore Place Wigmore Lane, LUTON, LU2 9TN.

ARNOLD, Mr. Stephen Martin, BA ACA *2003;* 6 St. Ann's Park Road, LONDON, SW18 2RW.

ARNOLD, Mr. Thomas George, BA ACA *1985;* The Beeches, Raby Drive, Raby Mere, WIRRAL, MERSEYSIDE, CH63 0NL.

ARNOLD, Mr. Thomas Robert, MChem ACA *2010;* 23d Cricklewood Lane, LONDON, NW2 1HN.

ARNOLD, Mrs. Victoria Louise, BSc ACA *2001;* 9 Swinnow Garth, Bramley, LEEDS, LS13 4TB.

ARNOLD, Mr. William Charles, BA ACA *2002;* with BTG Financial Consulting LLP, 9th Floor, Bond Court, LEEDS, LS1 2JZ.

ARNOLD, Mr. William John, ACA *1979;* Moorevale Properties Limited, 45 Clarges Street, LONDON, W1J 7EP.

ARNOLD-BOAKES, Mr. Anthony Michael, BA FCA *1970;* 7 Westpark, 39/43 Eaton Rise, LONDON, W5 2HH. (Life Member)

ARNOLL, Mr. Andrew Michael, BA ACA *1994;* 1 ALLEE DES TUILERIES, 91370 VERRIERES-LE-BUISSON, FRANCE.

ARNOT, Mr. Keith James, BSc ACA *1984;* 43 Cromwell Avenue, Highgate, LONDON, N6 5HP.

ARNOT, Mrs. Lynne Patricia, BSc ACA *1991;* Lyndene, Mobberley Road, Morley, WILMSLOW, SK9 5NR.

ARNOT, Mr. Miles Roger, BCom ACA *1983;* 25 Glan Aber Park, Hough Green, CHESTER, CH4 8LE.

•**ARNOTT, Mr. Andrew George David, FCA** *1977;* (Tax Fac), Saffery Champness, Lion House, Red Lion Street, LONDON, WC1R 4GB.

ARNOTT, Mr. Arthur Barry, FCA *1957;* 8 Grosvenor Mews, Rawdon, LEEDS, LS19 6SD. (Life Member)

ARNOTT, Mrs. Claire Judy, BSc(Hons) ACA *1990;* 49 Thellusson Way, RICKMANSWORTH, HERTFORDSHIRE, WD3 8RL.

•**ARNOTT, Ms. Katharine Jane, BSc ACA** *2003;* MacIntyre Hudson LLP, 31 Castle Street, HIGH WYCOMBE, BUCKINGHAMSHIRE, HP13 6RU.

ARNOTT, Mr. Russell John, ACA *1993;* Caterpillar (UK) Ltd, The Phoenix Building, Central Boulevard, Blythe Valley Park, Shirley, SOLIHULL WEST MIDLANDS B90 8BG.

ARNSTEIN, Mrs. Monica Jane, BSc ACA *1985;* BLG Claims LLP, Chancery Place, 50 Brown Street, MANCHESTER, M2 2JT.

AROKIASAMY, Mr. Jean-Marc, ACA *2011;* 3 Blackley Close, WATFORD, WD17 4TE.

ARONCHIKOVA, Ms. Vera, ACA *2010;* Dorchester House, 7 Church Street, HAMILTON HM11, BERMUDA.

ARONSON, Mr. Christopher James, ACA *2008;* PricewaterhouseCoopers Chile, Avenida Andrés Bello 2711 - piso 5, Las Condes, SANTIAGO, CHILE.

•**ARONSON, Mr. Rees, BSc FCA** *1994;* KPMG LLP, 15 Canada Square, LONDON, E14 5GL. See also KPMG Europe LLP

ARORA, Mr. Amit, BA ACA *2006;* 241 Boston Manor Road, BRENTFORD, Middlesex, TW8 9LF.

ARORA, Mr. Davinder Paul Singh, ACA *1981;* Flat 3, 14 Bramham Gardens, LONDON, SW5 0JJ.

•**ARORA, Mr. Devender, ACA** *1989;* The Corporate Practice Limited, 65 Delamere Road, HAYES, MIDDLESEX, UB4 0NN.

ARORA, Mr. Hanish Kumar, BSc ACA *2008;* 4 Bear Pit Apartments, 14 New Globe Walk, LONDON, SE1 9DR.

•**ARORA, Mr. Harish Chandra, ACA** *1980;* 66 Primrose Court, Ty Canol, CWMBRAN, GWENT, NP44 6JL.

ARORA, Mr. Hemant Kumar, ACA *1979;* PO BOX 212451, DUBAI, UNITED ARAB EMIRATES.

ARORA, Mr. Manvinder Singh Swaraj Singh, FCA *1977;* 10 Parkgate Crescent, Hadley Wood, BARNET, EN4 0NP.

•**ARORA, Miss. Monte, ACA** *1992;* M A Financial & Tax Consultants, 1 Ramsey House, Fawley Road, LONDON, NW6 1SN.

ARORA, Mr. Sandeep, BSc ACA *1995;* 33 Edgarley Terrace, LONDON, SW6 6QE.

ARORA, Mrs. Shalni, BA ACA *1996;* 54 Carrwood, Hale Barns, ALTRINCHAM, WA15 0EW.

ARORA, Mr. Sonal Kumar, BSc ACA *2010;* 6 Barossa Place, BRISTOL, BS1 6SU.

ARORA, Mr. Sukhvinder Singh, BA(Econ) ACA *1997;* Columbia Pictures Corp Ltd, 25 Golden Square, LONDON, W1F 9LU.

AROTSKY, Mr. Victor, BSc ACA *2000;* 36 Foscote Road, LONDON, NW4 3SD.

ARRAM, Mr. Benjamin Ian, MEng ACA *2005;* 32 Clifton Avenue, LONDON, N3 1BN.

ARRAND, Mr. Andrew, FCA *1963;* 9 Netherfields, ALDERLEY EDGE, CHESHIRE, SK9 7EH.

ARRAND, Mr. David Robert, FCA *1975;* 1 Walkers Way, Coleshill, BIRMINGHAM, B46 3DA.

ARRAND, Miss. Jennifer Lisa, BA ACA *2007;* The Shades, Sutton, THIRSK, NORTH YORKSHIRE, YO7 2PU.

ARRAND, Mr. Norman, FCA *1964;* Croft Farm, 38 Cross Street, Crowle, SCUNTHORPE, DN17 4LH.

•**ARRANDALE, Mr. Stuart Leslie, BA ACA** *1985;* Stuart Arrandale, 23-25 Gwydir Street, CAMBRIDGE, CB1 2LG.

ARRATOON, Mr. Christopher Peter Gregoris, FCA *1967;* 22 St Leonard's Road, Ealing, LONDON, W13 8PW.

ARRATOON, Mr. David Gregory, FCA *1971;* 36 Hungerford Place, SANDBACH, CW11 4PP.

ARRIENS, Mrs. Christine, ACA *1996;* 31 Northwood Drive, SITTINGBOURNE, KENT, ME10 4QR.

ARRIGAN, Mrs. Nicola Marion Rohana, BSc(Hons) ACA FCCA *2002;* ACCA UK, 29 Lincoln's Inn Fields, LONDON, WC2A 3EE.

ARRIGHI, Miss. Rebecca Anne, BA ACA *2005;* 23 Loop Road South, WHITEHAVEN, CUMBRIA, CA28 7TW.

ARROW, Mr. Anthony, BA ACA *2000;* Lautze + Lautze, 303 Second Street, Suite 950, SAN FRANCISCO, CA 94107, UNITED STATES.

ARROWSMITH, Mr. Anthony Ronald, FCA *1969;* 281 Wingrove Road North, NEWCASTLE UPON TYNE, NE4 9EE. (Life Member)

ARROWSMITH, Mr. Aubrey Tobias, MEng ACA *2001;* 17 Oak Way, Walmley, SUTTON COLDFIELD, WEST MIDLANDS, B76 2PG.

ARROWSMITH, Mrs. Catherine Jane, BA ACA *2001;* Le Vauguerin, 44110 ST AUBIN DES CHATEAUX, FRANCE.

ARROWSMITH, Mr. Fred, FCA *1956;* Helmshore, 40 Duporth Bay, Duporth, ST AUSTELL, CORNWALL, PL26 6AQ. (Life Member)

ARROWSMITH, Mr. John James, FCA *1973;* Downing Smiths Lane, Snitterfield, STRATFORD-UPON-AVON, CV37 0JY.

ARROWSMITH, Mr. John Michael, BSc FCA *1971;* Flat 6, Goldsmiths House, 50 Hough Green, CHESTER, CH4 8JQ. (Life Member)

ARROWSMITH, Mr. Jonathan David, BSc ACA *2002;* D C Advisory Partners Ltd, 60 Threadneedle Street, LONDON, EC2R 8HP.

•**ARROWSMITH, Mr. Peter, FCA** *1979;* (Tax Fac), Peter Arrowsmith, Office 4 Knights Farm, Newton Road, RUSHDEN, NORTHAMPTONSHIRE, NN10 0SX. See also Peter Arrowsmith FCA

ARROWSMITH, Mr. Robert George, FCA *1977;* 8 Brendon Drive, ESHER, KT10 9EQ.

ARROWSMITH, Mr. Stephen David, BEng ACA *1992;* JLT Insurance Management (Bermuda) Ltd., PO Box HM 1838, HAMILTON HM HX, BERMUDA.

ARSCOTT, Miss. Philippa, BSc ACA *2010;* 14 Mill Lane, STOCKTON-ON-TEES, CLEVELAND, TS20 1LG.

ARSHAD, Mr. Muhammad Akhtar, BA ACA *2000;* Flat 7 Warwick Mansions, Lower Richmond Road, LONDON, SW15 1ES.

ARSHAD, Mr. Ryan Aaron, ACA *2008;* 29 Cissbury Hill, CRAWLEY, WEST SUSSEX, RH11 8TJ.
ARTEAGA-KACZMARZ, Mrs. Aneta Joanna, ACA *2009;* Flat 14 167 Pampisford Road, SOUTH CROYDON, SURREY, CR2 6LS.
ARTEMI, Mr. Panayiotis K, ACA *2010;* Loizou Andrea 38, 7520 LARNACA, CYPRUS.
ARTER, Mr. Kai, MBA ACA *1996;* Badgequo Ltd, Number 8 Belton Road, SILSDEN, WEST YORKSHIRE, BD20 0EE.
•**ARTERTON, Mr. Alexander James, BSc ACA** *1989;* Deloitte LLP, Hill House, 1 Little New Street, LONDON, EC4A 3TR. See also Deloitte & Touche LLP
ARTERTON, Mrs. Lucy Elizabeth, BSc ACA *1990;* Claremont Dower, Pollards Wood Hill, Limpsfield, OXTED, SURREY, RH8 0QX.
•**ARTHUR, Mr. Alan David, BSc(Econ) FCA** *1974;* Alan David Arthur BSc (Econ), 76 Hallowes Park Road, Cullingworth, BRADFORD, WEST YORKSHIRE, BD13 5AR.
ARTHUR, Mrs. Amanda, BA ACA *1993;* (Tax Fac), 3 Pumphouse Close, Longford, COVENTRY, CV6 6RE.
ARTHUR, Mr. Andrew Brian, BA ACA *1998;* 25 Kanyaka Road, ALDGATE, SA 5154, AUSTRALIA.
ARTHUR, Mr. Ben James, BA ACA *1999;* 42 Kiparra Street, WEST PYMBLE, NSW 2073, AUSTRALIA.
ARTHUR, Mr. Brian John, FCA *1962;* 339 Woodlands Road, Woodlands, SOUTHAMPTON, SO40 7GE. (Life Member)
•**ARTHUR, Mr. David Robson, FCA** *1976;* (Tax Fac), Tait Walker LLP, Bulman House, Regent Centre, Gosforth, NEWCASTLE UPON TYNE, NE3 3LS. See also Tait Walker Management Limited
ARTHUR, Mr. Gerald, BA ACA *1995;* 6 Milling Street, Hunters Hill, SYDNEY, NSW 2110, AUSTRALIA.
ARTHUR, Mrs. Helen, BA ACA *1987;* Roadlink International Ltd, Strawberry Lane, WILLENHALL, WEST MIDLANDS, WV13 3RL.
ARTHUR, Mr. Hugh Robert Foster, BSc ACA *1982;* Save the Children International St. Vincent House, 30 Orange Street, LONDON, WC2H 7HH.
ARTHUR, Mr. John Stewart, FCA *1971;* 192 Turney Road, Dulwich, LONDON, SE21 7JL.
ARTHUR, Mr. Kevin McCabe, BA ACA *1987;* 704 Tram Road, RD2 Kaiapoi, CHRISTCHURCH, NEW ZEALAND.
ARTHUR, Mr. Matthew David, BA ACA *2009;* 70 Coity Road, BRIDGEND, MID GLAMORGAN, CF31 1LT.
ARTHUR, Mr. Michael John, BCom FCA *1959;* 17 West Common Close, GERRARDS CROSS, BUCKINGHAMSHIRE, SL9 7QR. (Life Member)
ARTHUR, Mr. Nigel John, BSc ACA *1986;* Diageo Plc Lakeside Drive, Park Royal, LONDON, NW10 7HQ.
ARTHUR, Mr. Rhys Anthony, FCA *1981;* Actuate (Management Services (Ltd, 2 Llys ty Mawr, Treoes, BRIDGEND, MID GLAMORGAN, CF35 5EQ.
•**ARTHUR, Mr. Richard David, FCA** *1986;* Old Cadet House Le Mont Mallet, St. Martin, JERSEY, JE3 6DX.
ARTHUR, Mr. Robert, ACA *2011;* 29 Marlowe Road, WALLASEY, MERSEYSIDE, CH44 3DA.
•**ARTHUR, Mr. Roy Neil, BSc FCA** *1973;* TMF Management (UK) Limited, 400 Capability Green, LUTON, BEDFORDSHIRE, LU1 3AE.
•**ARTHUR, Mrs. Susan Jane, FCA ATII** *1984;* Clifton House Partnership, Clifton House, Four Elms Road, CARDIFF, CF24 1LE.
•**ARTHUR, Mr. Timothy, BSc FCA** *1988;* IFD Consulting Ltd, 10 Perry Court, CAMBRIDGE, CB3 0RS.
•**ARTHURS, Mr. Henry Lonsdale, BA FCA** *1993;* Baker Tilly Tax & Advisory Services LLP, Lancaster House, 7 Elmfield Road, BROMLEY, BR1 1LT. See also Baker Tilly UK Audit LLP
ARTHURS, Mr. William Magowan, MA FCA ACMA ACIS FRSA CISA *1991;* PO Box 635, AMERSHAM, HP6 9AH.
ARTHURTON, Mr. Anthony William, BCom ACA *1997;* Flat 2, Isis Court, Grove Park Road, LONDON, W4 3SA.
ARTHURTON, Mrs. Laura Natalie, ACA *1998;* Flat 2 Isis Court, Grove Park Road, LONDON, W4 3SA.
ARTINDALE, Mr. Gerard William, BSc FCA *1979;* 4 New Bells Cottages, Haughley Green, STOWMARKET, SUFFOLK, IP14 3RN.
ARTINGSTALL, Miss. Eve, ACA *2008;* Flat 18 Ravensworth Court, Fulham Road, LONDON, SW6 5NN.
ARTLEY, Mr. Gordon, ACA *1983;* Swift Group Ltd, Dunswell Road, COTTINGHAM, NORTH HUMBERSIDE, HU16 4JX.
ARTLEY, Mr. John Graham, FCA *1957;* 14 Village Fold, Kirkby Fleetham, NORTHALLERTON, DL7 0TX. (Life Member)
ARTLEY, Mr. Julian Frederick, FCA *1966;* 3 Maple Close, BRIDLINGTON, YO16 6TD.
ARTT, Miss. Catherine Louise, BCom ACA *2005;* 33 Mayhill Road, LONDON, SE7 7JG.
ARTT, Mr. Michael William, BA ACA *2006;* Flat 14 Leeside Court, 169 Rotherhithe Street, LONDON, SE16 5SZ.
ARTYUKHOV, Mr. Konstantin, ACA *2009;* Okhotnichiy proezd 10, 143500 ISTRA, MOSCOW REGION, RUSSIAN FEDERATION.
ARULIAH, Mr. Thurairatnam, FCA *1962;* 7 Sydney Road, LONDON, N10 2LR. (Life Member)
ARULNAYAGAM, Mr. Anthony Barnabas, BSc FCA *1967;* 10 Lynngrove Crescent, RICHMOND HILL L4B 2B7, ON, CANADA. See also Arul & Associates
ARULVEL, Mr. Mathan, MSc ACA *2008;* 9 Worcester Road, Walthamstow, LONDON, E17 5QR.
ARUMUGAM, Mr. Alvin, BA ACA *2010;* 158 Bordesley Road, MORDEN, SURREY, SM4 5LT.
ARUMUGAM, Mr. Ravinthran, BBA FCA *1992;* 6 Stevens Drive, Apt 01-05, SINGAPORE 257902, SINGAPORE.
ARUNASALAM, Mr. Pariasamy, BSc FCA *1974;* Lot 1804 Plot 6Jalan Arunamari off Jalan Senyum BintangCountry Heights Kajang, 43000 KAJANG, SELANGOR, MALAYSIA. (Life Member)
ARUNDALE, Mr. George Herbert, FCA *1938;* Tall Trees, 6 Wharncliffe Road, Highcliffe, CHRISTCHURCH, BH23 5DD. (Life Member)
•**ARUNDALE, Mr. Keith, MSc BSc FCA FCIM** *1980;* Keith Arundale, 8 Chestnut Drive, St Leonards Hill, WINDSOR, BERKSHIRE, SL4 4UT.
ARUNDALE, Mr. Mark, ACA *2011;* 30 Milton Avenue, MALTON, NORTH YORKSHIRE, YO17 7LD.
ARUNDALE, Mr. Roger Leigh, FCA *1969;* Le Carrefour Les Prevosts Road, St. Saviour, GUERNSEY, GY7 9UH.
ARUNDEL, Mrs. Charlotte Jane, BSc ACA *1991;* 35 Nasturtium Way, Pontprennau, CARDIFF, CF23 8SF.
ARUNDEL, Mr. Kenneth Julian, FCA *1974;* 2 Church Lane, CawthorneNr, BARNSLEY, S75 4DW.
ARUNDEL NEWELL, Mrs. Sasha Maree, BSc ACA *2001;* 1 Firgrove, St. Johns, WOKING, SURREY, GU21 7RD.
ARUNDELL, Mr. Colin David, BSc(Hons) ACA *2001;* 67 Portland Avenue, GRAVESEND, KENT, DA12 5HJ.
ARWAS, Mr. Elliot Samuel Joseph, ACA *2008;* Flat E Welford House, 114 Shirland Road, LONDON, W9 2BT.
ARYA, Mr. Rajeev, ACA *2008;* Working Links, 57-59 Long Acre, LONDON, WC2E 9JL.
ARZENTON, Mr. Nicola, ACA *2004;* 55 Sussex Square, LONDON, W2 2SR.
ARZHANGI, Mr. Kamak, ACA *1998;* with The Postal Services Commission, Hercules House, 6 Hercules Road, LONDON, SE1 7DB.
ASAD, Mr. Mohammad Aamir, ACA *2009;* 12 Finland Street, LONDON, SE16 7TP.
ASAD, Mr. Nauman, ACA *2009;* 327 Aylsham Drive, UXBRIDGE, MIDDLESEX, UB10 8UJ.
ASADULLINA, Ms. Aysylu, ACA *2011;* ZAO Raiffeisenbank, 180 Melodogvardeyskaya Street, 443010 SAMARA, RUSSIAN FEDERATION.
ASANTE-WIREDU, Mr. Kwabena, BSc FCA *1973;* Asante-Wiredu & Associates, 4 Feo Eyeo Link, off Dadeban Road, North Industrial Area, PO Box AN 19196, ACCRA GHANA.
ASARDAG, Mrs. Ayse, ACA *1993;* Zeytinoglu Caddesi, Fenerli Hristo Sokak Cevre St, 15C Blk D9 Akatlar, ISTANBUL, TURKEY.
ASARDAG, Mr. Mustafa Kursat, MA ACA *1992;* Zeytinoglu Caddesi, Fenerli Hristo Sokak, Cevre Sitesi15CBlk D9Akatlar, ISTANBUL, TURKEY.
ASARIA, Mr. Mohamed Jaffer Gulamhussein, FCA *1974;* 67 Morley Crescent West, STANMORE, MIDDLESEX, HA7 2LL.
ASBURY, Mrs. Diane Janet, BSc(Hons) ACA CTA *2000;* 21 Old Farm Drive, Codsall, WOLVERHAMPTON, WV8 1GF.
ASBURY, Mr. Gregory Malcolm, BSc DipLP ACA *2000;* 21 Old Farm Drive Codsall, WOLVERHAMPTON, WV8 1GF.
ASBURY, Mr. Leonard Stuart, FCA *1955;* 7 Stonehurst Drive, SHREWSBURY, SY2 6DF. (Life Member)
ASCH, Prof. David Conrad, MSc FCA *1971;* 9 Barnards Way, Kibworth Harcourt, LEICESTER, LE8 0RS.
•**ASCOTT, Mr. David Paul, ACA CF** *1983;* Grant Thornton UK LLP, 30 Finsbury Square, LONDON, EC2P 2YU. See also Grant Thornton LLP
ASCOTT, Mr. David Spencer, ACA *1989;* 14 Herbert Street, ALBERT PARK, VIC 3206, AUSTRALIA.
ASCOTT, Mr. Geoffrey John, FCA *1960;* 4 Garrad House, Rockliffe Avenue, KINGS LANGLEY, HERTFORDSHIRE, WD4 8DR. (Life Member)
•**ASCOTT, Mr. Robert David, FCA** *1980;* 3 Barley Close, Sibford Gower, BANBURY, OX15 5RZ.
ASCOUGH, Mr. Ian Johnson, FCA *1958;* 117 Wells Road, MALVERN, WR14 4PD. (Life Member)
ASCROFT, Mrs. Clare Angela, BSc ACA *1993;* 2 Spurwood Cottage, Morris Lane, Halsall, ORMSKIRK, L39 8SX.
•**ASCROFT, Mrs. Jane, MA FCA** *2000;* (Tax Fac), Jane Ascroft Accountancy Limited, Dale House, Hutton Magna, RICHMOND, NORTH YORKSHIRE, DL11 7HH.
ASCROFT, Mr. Mark John, BA ACA *1995;* 3 Cleadon Drive South, BURY, BL8 1EJ.
ASCROFT, Mr. Peter Anthony, BSc ACA *1986;* PNR Construction Ltd, 19 Reading Road, Pangbourne, READING, RG8 7LT.
ASEERVATHAM, Mr. Jonathan, BSc ACA *2011;* 13 Brooklands Avenue, SIDCUP, KENT, DA15 7PE.
•**ASFOUR, Ms. Thelma Mary, MA FCA** *1980;* Mary Asfour, 21 Fremantle Road, BRISTOL, BS6 5SY.
•**ASGHAR, Mr. Sajjad, FCA** *1966;* (Tax Fac), S.Asghar & Co, 69 Headstone Road, HARROW, MIDDLESEX, HA1 1PQ.
ASGHAR, Mr. Tariq Ali, MA ACA *1997;* 93 Bankes Road, Small Heath, BIRMINGHAM, B10 9PW.
ASH, Mr. Alan Johnn, FCA *1963;* 7 Downs Bridge Road, BECKENHAM, BR3 5HX. (Life Member)
ASH, Mr. Ben, BSc ACA *2007;* 3 The Brook, Old Alresford, ALRESFORD, HAMPSHIRE, SO24 9DQ.
ASH, Miss. Colette Mary, BA ACA *1992;* 3 Letheren Place, EASTBOURNE, BN21 1HL.
ASH, Mr. David Anthony, BA ACA *2009;* KPMG, Crown House, 4 Par la Ville, HAMILTON HM 08, BERMUDA.
•**ASH, Mr. Desmond Anthony, FCA** *1965;* Guard D'Oyly, 4 Mansell Street, STRATFORD-UPON-AVON, WARWICKSHIRE, CV37 6NR.
ASH, Mr. Edward Barry, FCA *1958;* Flat One The Laurels, 1 Homefield Road, BROMLEY, BR1 3LA. (Life Member)
ASH, Mr. Graham Charles, BSc ACA *1987;* 3 Harcourt Hill, Redland, BRISTOL, BS6 7RB.
ASH, Mr. Grant Robert, BA ACA *1996;* 75 Cairns Road, SHEFFIELD, S10 5NA.
ASH, Mr. Ian George Claudius, FCA *1965;* The Old Stables, Horsemoor, Chieveley, NEWBURY, BERKSHIRE, RG20 8XD. (Life Member)
ASH, Mr. John Garton, MC MA FCA *1949;* Fairfield, 14 Highdown Road, Roehampton, LONDON, SW15 5BU. (Life Member)
ASH, Mr. Julian Vincent, BA ACA *1985;* The Homestead, Dunsley Bank, Kinver, STOURBRIDGE, DY7 6NA.
ASH, Miss. Michelle Louise, LLB ACA *2006;* 1 Tushingham Close, Great Boughton, CHESTER, CH3 5RD.
ASH, Dr. Nicholas Watson, PhD BSc ACA *2000;* 32 Trevor Road, West Bridgford, NOTTINGHAM, NG2 6FT.
ASH, Mr. Robin Adrian, FCA *1969;* 12 Grantham Drive, Low Fell, GATESHEAD, NE9 6HQ.
ASH, Mr. Roderick Martin, BCom FCA *1981;* 18 Whinbrook Grove, LEEDS, LS17 6AF.
ASH-EDWARDS, Mr. Christopher John Peter, FCA *1974;* 45 Turners Mill Road, HAYWARDS HEATH, WEST SUSSEX, RH16 1NW.
ASHALL, Miss. Katherine Jane, MChem ACA *2005;* Flat 6, 9-11 Belsize Grove, LONDON, NW3 4UU.
•**ASHALL, Miss. Rosemary Denise, BSc FCA** *1978;* (Tax Fac), Ashall & Co, 4 Locksley Close, Heaton Norris, STOCKPORT, SK4 2LW.
ASHAR, Mr. Kalpesh, BSc ACA *2003;* 238 Chamberlayne Road, LONDON, NW10 3LN.
ASHARIA, Mr. Sajjad, ACA *2008;* Flat 69, Solent Court, 1258 London Road, LONDON, SW16 4EZ.
ASHARY, Mr. Shan-E-Abbas, FCA *1973;* Al-Jomaih Holding Co, P.O. Box 54308, RIYADH, 11514, SAUDI ARABIA.
ASHBEE, Mr. Hedley Paul, BA FCA *1974;* The Coach House, Wardes Moat Vicarage Road, Yalding, MAIDSTONE, ME18 6DY.
ASHBEE, Mr. Nicholas Hedley, BA ACA *2002;* Pricewaterhousecoopers, 12 Plumtree Court, LONDON, EC4A 4HT.
①**ASHBOURNE, Mr. Darryl Marcus, FCA** *1982;* with KPMG LLP, 15 Canada Square, LONDON, E14 5GL.
ASHBRIDGE, Mr. Anthony Frederick, LLB FCA *1984;* (Tax Fac), 4 Burnaby Close, Molescroft, BEVERLEY, HU17 7ET.
•**ASHBROOK, Mr. Michael Keith, BA ACA** *1980;* (Tax Fac), M.K. Ashbrook, 59-61 Sea Lane, Rustington, LITTLEHAMPTON, WEST SUSSEX, BN16 2RQ.
ASHBURNER, Mr. Robert William, BSc ACA *1997;* 4932 Blue Meadow Lane, CINCINNATI, OH 45251, UNITED STATES.
ASHBY, Mr. Anthony James, FCA *1960;* 36 West Common, HAYWARDS HEATH, RH16 2AH. (Life Member)
ASHBY, Mrs. Claire Elizabeth, BA ACA *2001;* AlixPartners Ltd, 20 North Audley Street, LONDON, W1K 6WE.
ASHBY, Miss. Claire Louise, BSc FCA *2000;* 10 Wycliffe Road, Wimbledon, LONDON, SW19 1ER.
ASHBY, Mrs. Della Margaret, FCA *1958;* 22 Roundwood Grove, Hutton, BRENTWOOD, CM13 2NE. (Life Member)
ASHBY, Mr. Geoffrey Frank, FCA *1959;* (Tax Fac), 2 Brighton Court, 73 West Hill, LONDON, SW15 2UL. (Life Member)
ASHBY, Mr. Gideon, ACA *2009;* 66 Haven Lane, LONDON, W5 2HN.
ASHBY, Mrs. Janet Elizabeth, BA ACA ATII *1990;* Water Mill Court Dearne Hall Road Barugh Green, BARNSLEY, SOUTH YORKSHIRE, S75 1LX.
•**ASHBY, Mr. John Frederick Dixon, FCA** *1976;* John F.D. Ashby, Braeside, 39 Silverdale Road, EASTBOURNE, EAST SUSSEX, BN20 7AT.
•**ASHBY, Mr. John William Newland, FCA** *1974;* Ashby & Company, North Bank, 14 Bishearne Gardens, LISS, HAMPSHIRE, GU33 7SB.
ASHBY, Miss. Laura Jayne, ACA *2009;* Flat 29 The Mill Apartments, East Street, COLCHESTER, CO1 2QT.
ASHBY, Mrs. Leona Burnall, ACA *1995;* 92 Moor Lane, RICKMANSWORTH, WD3 1LQ.
ASHBY, Mr. Mark, FCA *1973;* 22 Ullswater Road, LONDON, SW13 9PJ.
ASHBY, Mr. Mark Edward, BA ACA *1998;* 16 Carnoustie Close, SUTTON COLDFIELD, B75 6UW.
ASHBY, Mr. Matthew James, ACA *2009;* 8 Rose Walk, ST. ALBANS, HERTFORDSHIRE, AL4 9AF.
ASHBY, Mr. Matthew James, ACA *2009;* Genesis Investment Management Llp, 21 Knightsbridge, LONDON, SW1X 7LY.
ASHBY, Mr. Neil Anthony, ACA *2001;* DMGT plc, Northcliffe House, Derry Street, LONDON, W8 5TT.
ASHBY, Mr. Nicholas James, BSc ACA *1990;* 6 Sibleys Rise, South Heath, GREAT MISSENDEN, BUCKINGHAMSHIRE, HP16 9QQ.
ASHBY, Mr. Norman Charles, FCA *1962;* 11 Newleaze Gardens, TETBURY, GL8 8BY.
ASHBY, Mr. Simon Michael, BA ACA *1995;* Nad Rybnicky 24, Praha 4, Kunratice, 148 00 PRAGUE, CZECH REPUBLIC.
ASHBY, Ms. Sonia, BSc ACA *2003;* 20 Waldegrave Road, LONDON, W5 3HT.
ASHCROFT, Mr. Andrew Jonathan, BSc ACA *1995;* Amika, Broad Lane, Tanworth-in-Arden, SOLIHULL, WEST MIDLANDS, B94 5DY.
ASHCROFT, Mr. Christopher Mark, BSc(Econ) ACA *2001;* 2 Penman Way, LEICESTER, LEICESTERSHIRE, LE19 1ST.
ASHCROFT, Mrs. Joanne Christine, BA ACA *1998;* Royal Oak Cottage, 173 Lower Luton Road, Wheathampstead, ST. ALBANS, HERTFORDSHIRE, AL4 8HQ.
ASHCROFT, Mr. Jonathan Richard, MA ACA *1987;* Harvey Nash Plc, 13 Bruton Street, LONDON, W1J 6QA.
ASHCROFT, Mrs. Julie, BA ACA *1987;* The Merrows, Todenham Road, MORETON-IN-MARSH, GL56 9NJ. (Life Member)
ASHCROFT, Mr. Keith Anthony, BA ACA *1994;* 14 Weymouth House, Hill House Mews, BROMLEY, BR2 0DD.
ASHCROFT, Mr. Kenneth, FCA FCMA *1957;* Fendley Corner, Sauncy Wood, HARPENDEN, AL5 5DW. (Life Member)
ASHCROFT, Mr. Martin Roy, BSc ACA *1996;* Hill Top Barn, 2 Ayerfield Road, Roby Mill, Upholland, SKELMERSDALE, WN8 0QP.
•**ASHCROFT, Mr. Martin Spencer, BSc FCA** *1992;* (Tax Fac), 4 Elton Cottages, Littleworth Road, Downley, HIGH WYCOMBE, BUCKINGHAMSHIRE, HP13 5UZ.
ASHCROFT, Mr. Matthew David, ACA *2009;* 2 Repton Avenue, WOLVERHAMPTON, WV6 7TD.
ASHCROFT, Mr. Matthew Gethyn, ACA *2010;* 25 Dartington Drive, Pontprennau, CARDIFF, CF23 8SA.

ASHCROFT, Mr. Paul Michael, LLB ACA *2000;* (Tax Fac), W Brindley (Garages) Ltd, 55 Penn Road, WOLVERHAMPTON, WV2 4WW.
ASHCROFT, Mr. Paul Stuart, BSc ACA *1989;* 11 Parkway, WILMSLOW, SK9 1LS.
ASHCROFT, Mrs. Rebecca Louise, BA(Hons) ACA *2000;* 7 Sunnybank Close Aldridge, WALSALL, WS9 0YR.
ASHCROFT, Mr. Robert, ACA *2008;* 15 Haddon Road, Goose Green, WIGAN, LANCASHIRE, WN3 6RP.
ASHCROFT, Mr. Robert John, BEng ACA MIET *2003;* 10 East Ontario Street, Apartment 3501, CHICAGO, IL 60611, UNITED STATES.
ASHCROFT, Mr. William Donald, FCA *1955;* Woodcroft, Seymour Plain, MARLOW, SL7 3DA. (Life Member)
ASHDOWN, Miss. Helen Elizabeth, BA ACA *2011;* 35 Warneford Road, OXFORD, OX4 1LU.
ASHDOWN, Mr. John Callum Torquil, ACA *2005;* J P Morgan Chase, 125 London Wall, LONDON, EC2Y 5AJ.
ASHDOWN, Mr. Kenneth Graeham, FCA *1981;* 11 Lees Road, Bramhall, STOCKPORT, SK7 1BT.
ASHDOWN, Mr. Nigel Stanley, FCA *1976;* 303 Norton Way South, LETCHWORTH GARDEN CITY, HERTFORDSHIRE, SG6 1SU.
•**ASHDOWN, Mr. Robert Victor, MBA BSc(Econ) LLB ACA** *1979;* Robert V. Ashdown, 75 Brookville Road, LONDON, SW6 7BH. See also R Ashdown & Company Limited
ASHE, Mr. Christopher Robin, FCA *1973;* Hannays, Farthing Green, Geldeston, BECCLES, NR34 0LW.
ASHE, Mr. David Rupert Armstrong, BSc ACA *1986;* Wall House Consulting, Wall House, 1 The Green, LONDON, SW19 5AZ.
ASHE, Mrs. Lisa Marie, BA ACA *1996;* 122 Peperharow Road, GODALMING, GU7 2PN.
ASHE, Mr. Oliver, LLB ACA *2004;* EBERSWALDER STR 16, 10437 BERLIN, GERMANY.
ASHE, Mr. Vincent, FCA *1978;* Woodside, Farm Lane, ASHTEAD, SURREY, KT21 1LR.
ASHELBY, Mrs. Helen, ACA *2008;* with Deloitte LLP, 1 City Square, LEEDS, WEST YORKSHIRE, LS1 2AL.
ASHELFORD, Mr. Andrew James, BA ACA *1992;* 2 The Maltings, Midford, BATH, BA2 7DE.
ASHELFORD, Mrs. Mei, BBA ACA *2005;* 27 Ronald Road, BEACONSFIELD, BUCKINGHAMSHIRE, HP9 1AJ.
ASHER, Miss. Carolyn Amanda, BSc FCA *1990;* with PKF (UK) LLP, 4th Floor, 3 Hardman Street, MANCHESTER, M3 3HF.
ASHER, Mr. David James, BSc ACA *1992;* 14 Priory Close, LONDON, N20 8BB.
ASHER, Miss. Hema, BA ACA *1992;* 171-365 Kent Street, SYDNEY, NSW 2000, AUSTRALIA.
ASHER, Mr. Stuart Roger, FCA *1975;* 9 Deacons Hill Road, BOREHAMWOOD, WD6 3HY.
ASHER-RAJDA, Mrs. Jesal, BSc ACA *2001;* 1500 Hudson Street, Apt 8M, Hoboken, NEW JERSEY, NJ 07030, UNITED STATES.
ASHER-RELF, Mr. Samuel Niall, BSc ACA *2005;* Ingram Micro UK Ltd, 7 Clarendon Drive Wymbush, MILTON KEYNES, MK8 8ED.
ASHFAQ, Mr. Ali, FCA *1983;* Rahman Rahman Huq, 9 Mohakhali Commercial Area, 11th & 12th Floors, DHAKA 1212, BANGLADESH.
ASHFIELD, Mrs. Jessica, BA(Hons) ACA *2009;* 10 Marryat Square, Wyfold Road, LONDON, SW6 6UA.
•**ASHFIELD, Mr. Mark, BA FCA** *1998;* Harrison Beale & Owen, Highdown House, 11 Highdown Road, Sydenham, LEAMINGTON SPA, WARWICKSHIRE CV31 1XT. See also Harrison Beale & Owen Limited
ASHFIELD, Mr. Nigel Bruce, LLB ACA *2000;* 47 Waldemar Avenue, LONDON, SW6 5LN.
ASHFIELD, Mr. Robert Mark, BSc ACA *1992;* (Tax Fac), 3805 Rockbrook Drive, CARROLLTON, TX 75007, UNITED STATES.
ASHFIELD, Mrs. Samantha Jane Lowe, BSc ACA *1999;* Highfield, Battenhall Avenue, WORCESTER, WR5 2HW.
ASHFORD, Mr. Damien, BSc ACA *2001;* 2 Fiennes Road, Thorpe St Andrew, NORWICH, NR7 0YP.
•**ASHFORD, Mr. Derek Francis, FCA** *1980;* (Tax Fac), Ashford & Co, 95A High Street, Lees, OLDHAM, OL4 4LY.
•**ASHFORD, Mr. Graham Robert, FCA** *1979;* Mayer Brown JSM, 16th-19th Floors, Prince's Building, 10 Chater Road, CENTRAL, HONG KONG SAR.
ASHFORD, Mr. John Charles Portlock, FCA *1952;* 50 Manor Road, Alcombe, MINEHEAD, TA24 6EJ. (Life Member)
•**ASHFORD, Mr. Jon Gardiner, FCA** *1974;* (Tax Fac), Ashford & Co, 186 Reservoir Road, GLOUCESTER, GL4 6SB.
ASHFORD, Dr. Lynette Mary, PhD MA(Hons) ACA *2003;* 9 Campden Grove, Hatton Park, WARWICK, CV35 7TY.
ASHFORD, Mr. Nicholas Geoffrey Neale, FCA FSI *1967;* Windy Bank Cottage, Bighton, ALRESFORD, SO24 9RE. (Life Member)
ASHFORD, Mr. Peter Desmond, FCA *1961;* 1 Kiln Field, LISS, HAMPSHIRE, GU33 7SW. (Life Member)
ASHFORD, Mr. Philip, MEng ACA *2011;* 61 Hollinwell Avenue, Wollaton, NOTTINGHAM, NG8 1JY.
ASHFORD, Miss. Samantha Jane, BSc ACA *1992;* Buckley & Co, 41 Park Road, SOUTHAMPTON, SO15 3AW.
ASHFORD, Mrs. Sarah-Jane, BSc(Econ) ACA *2002;* Pitkin & Ruddock Ltd, Unit 1, Capital Estate, Whapload Road, LOWESTOFT, SUFFOLK NR32 1TY.
ASHFORD-HODGES, Mr. John Nicholas, MA FCA *1976;* British American Eon House, 138 Piccadilly, LONDON, W1J 7NR.
•**ASHFORTH, Mrs. June Guat Imm, BSc ACA** *1991;* (Tax Fac), Ashforth LLP, 93 Bramley Road, Ealing, LONDON, W5 4ST.
ASHFORTH, Mr. Phillip John, BA FCA *1980;* Woodside, 17 Garth Road, SEVENOAKS, TN13 1RT.
ASHFORTH, Mr. Stephen James, MA FCA *1976;* PO Box 1068, GILLITTS, KWAZULU NATAL, 3603, SOUTH AFRICA.
ASHIAGBOR, Mr. Wyczynsky, MEng FCA *1994;* PO Box 01313, ACCRA, GHANA.
•**ASHING, Mr. Darryl Douglas, BSc FCA** *1991;* (Tax Fac), Ashings Limited, Northside House, Mount Pleasent, BARNET, HERTFORDSHIRE, EN4 9EB.
ASHING, Mr. Martin Paul, MA ACA ACCA *1996;* 8 Glencairn Crescent, EDINBURGH, EH12 5BS.
ASHIOTIS, Mr. Demetris, BSc ACA *1998;* 33 Nicodemou Mylona, Marina Court, PO Box 60159, 8101 PAFOS, CYPRUS.
ASHIQ, Mr. Michael Irfan, FCA *1962;* 225 Plymouth Street, OTTAWA K1S 3E4, ON, CANADA.
ASHKEN, Mr. Ian Guy Handley, BA ACA *1987;* Marlin Cpital LP, 555 Theodore Fremd Avenue, Suite B-302 Rye, NEW YORK, NY 10580, UNITED STATES.
ASHKEN, Mr. Richard Lawrence, FCA *1975;* City Endowments The Stables, Church Lane Lewknor, WATLINGTON, OXFORDSHIRE, OX49 5TP.
ASHLEY, Mr. Alan Maurice, FCA *1959;* 11 Letchworth Close, BROMLEY, KENT, BR2 9BD. (Life Member)
ASHLEY, Mr. Allan Kenneth, BSc ACA *1979;* Marketforce (UK) Ltd, Blue Fin Building, 110 Southwark Street, LONDON, SE1 0SU.
ASHLEY, Mr. Andrew Robert, BSc ACA *1994;* 22 Carlton Place, ABERDEEN, AB15 4BQ.
ASHLEY, Mr. Cedric Walter, FCA *1956;* 360 Watson Road, Sailwinds, Unit 106, WHITBY L1N 9G2, ON, CANADA. (Life Member)
ASHLEY, Mrs. Charlotte Roisin, BA ACA *1999;* 22 Wellington Road, Edgbaston, BIRMINGHAM, B15 2EU.
ASHLEY, Mr. Darren Eric, ACA *2009;* 17 Caldbeck, WALTHAM ABBEY, EN9 1UR.
ASHLEY, Mrs. Deborah Nixon, ACA *1983;* with RSM Tenon Audit Limited, Charterhouse, Legge Street, BIRMINGHAM, B4 7EU.
ASHLEY, Miss. Fiona Elizabeth, BSc ACA *1998;* with National Audit Office, 157-197 Buckingham Palace Road, Victoria, LONDON, SW1W 9SP.
ASHLEY, Mr. Gordon Robert, BSc FCA *1976;* Rozelle, Pilgrims Way, Boughton Lees, ASHFORD, KENT, TN25 4JD.
ASHLEY, Miss. Helen, BSc ACA *1979;* 9 Allcock Street, BIRMINGHAM, B9 4DY.
ASHLEY, Miss. Jackie Ursula, BSc ACA *1990;* 324 W20th Street, NORTH VANCOUVER V7M 1Y5, BC, CANADA.
•**ASHLEY, Mr. John Andrew, BSc FCA** *1972;* (Tax Fac), John Ashley, Oake House, The Tolleys, Mill Street, CREDITON, DEVON EX17 1HG.
ASHLEY, Mr. John Bedford, BA ACA *1983;* 18 Primrose Hill, BATH, BA1 2UT.
ASHLEY, Miss. Katherine Ruth, ACA *2008;* 24 Southview Drive, WORTHING, WEST SUSSEX, BN11 5HT.
ASHLEY, Ms. Louise, BSc ACA *1991;* University House, University of Warwick, COVENTRY, CV4 8UW.
ASHLEY, Mr. Mark Reginald, BSc ACA *1987;* Russetts, Halsfordwood Lane, Nadderwater, EXETER, EX4 2LD.
ASHLEY, Mr. Matthew Edward, BA ACA *1999;* 22 Wellington Road, Edgbaston, BIRMINGHAM, B15 2EU.
ASHLEY, Mr. Michael Derek, ACA *1980;* 27 Bilberry Close, Locks Heath, SOUTHAMPTON, SO31 6XX.
•**ASHLEY, Mr. Michael St John, MA FCA** *1979;* KPMG LLP, 15 Canada Square, LONDON, E14 5GL. See also KPMG Europe LLP, KPMG Audit plc
ASHLEY, Mr. Paul James, BA ACA *2003;* 33 St. Peters Road, ST. ALBANS, HERTFORDSHIRE, AL1 3SA.
ASHLEY, Mr. Simon Haydon, BSc ACA *1990;* 90 Tambourine Bay Road, RIVERVIEW, NSW 2066, AUSTRALIA.
ASHLEY, Mr. Stuart, BSc FCA *1993;* 1 Hofheim Drive, TIVERTON, DEVON, EX16 5QD.
ASHLEY, Mr. William George, FCA *1950;* Sandiway House, 14 Archery Fields, Odiham, HOOK, HAMPSHIRE, RG29 1AE. (Life Member)
ASHLEY BACH, Mr. Charles Michael Digby, FCA *1970;* C.M.D. Ashley Bach, 82 Kings Road, RICHMOND, SURREY, TW10 6EE.
ASHLEY-JONES, Mr. Robert Mylles Evan, FCA *1972;* 8 Canning Road, Highbury, LONDON, N5 2JS.
ASHLEY-SMITH, Mrs. Diane Louise, FCA *1970;* 27 Richmond Road, CAMBRIDGE, CB4 3PP.
ASHLIN, Mr. Timothy James West, BA ACA *2003;* Phoenix Equity Partners, 33 Glasshouse Street, LONDON, W1B 5DG.
•**ASHMAN, Mr. Andrew Russell, BA FCA** *1975;* 7 Prince Arthur Mews, LONDON, NW3 1RD.
ASHMAN, Miss. Christina Stephanie, BSc ACA *2007;* 81 Burwell Road, Exning, NEWMARKET, SUFFOLK, CB8 7DU.
•**ASHMAN, Mr. David James, FCA DChA** *1975;* (Tax Fac), Reeves & Co LLP, 37 St. Margarets Street, CANTERBURY, KENT, CT1 2TU.
•**ASHMAN, Mr. Duncan Mark, FCA** *1991;* BDO LLP, Fourth Floor, One Victoria Street, BRISTOL, BS1 6AA. See also BDO Stoy Hayward LLP
•**ASHMAN, Mr. Gerald Henry William, FCA** *1975;* (Tax Fac), G.H.W.Ashman, 109a North Street, Burwell, CAMBRIDGE, CB25 0BB.
ASHMAN, Mr. John William, MA FCA *1962;* Flat 3, Beaupre, 3 Woodville Road, Bowdon, ALTRINCHAM, CHESHIRE WA14 2AN. (Life Member)
ASHMAN, Mr. Jonathan, BSc ACA *2007;* 69 Comyn Road, LONDON, SW11 1QB.
ASHMAN, Mr. Laurence John, MSc FCA *1967;* Hedera House, Bushy Cross Lane, Ruishton, TAUNTON, TA3 5JY.
ASHMAN, Mr. Leslie Brian, FCA *1965;* 32 St. Mary's Walk, MIRFIELD, WF14 0QB. (Life Member)
ASHMAN, Miss. Ruth Elizabeth, BA(Hons)Oxon ACA *2011;* 154 Campbell Road, OXFORD, OX4 3NR.
ASHMAN, Mrs. Susan Mary, MA MBA ACA *1992;* 33 Woodlands, Gosforth, NEWCASTLE UPON TYNE, NE3 4YL.
ASHMEAD, Ms. Elise Ann, ACA CA(AUS) *2008;* Young & Co Brewery Plc, 26 Osiers Road, LONDON, SW18 1NH.
•**ASHMORE, Mr. Brendan Paul, BSc ACA** *1996;* Tingle Ashmore Ltd, Enterprise House, Broadfield Court, SHEFFIELD, S8 0XF.
ASHMORE, Mr. David Grenville, FCA *1968;* 20 Troed Y Garth, Pentyrch, CARDIFF, CF15 9AB.
ASHMORE, Mr. Edward, BA ACA *2011;* 95a Mortimer Road, LONDON, N1 4LB.
•**ASHMORE, Mr. Gary James, FCA** *1983;* Austral Ryley Limited, 416-418 Bearwood Road, SMETHWICK, WEST MIDLANDS, B66 4EZ.
•**ASHMORE, Mr. Howard Charles Selby, FCA** *1986;* (Tax Fac), Godfrey Laws & Co Limited, 69 Knowl Piece, Wilbury Way, HITCHIN, HERTFORDSHIRE, SG4 0TY.
ASHMORE, Miss. Jane Louise, BA ACA *2000;* 57 Deykin Road, LICHFIELD, STAFFORDSHIRE, WS13 6PS.
ASHMORE, Mr. Neil, LLB ACA *2000;* 542 Parkside Drive, WATERDOWN L0R 2H1, ON, CANADA.
ASHMORE, Mrs. Rachel Louise, BA ACA *1998;* Jarretts Carlton Road, South Godstone, GODSTONE, RH9 8LE.
•**ASHMORE, Mr. Richard Jonathan, BA ACA** *1990;* Altus Business Consulting, 76 High Street, STOURBRIDGE, WEST MIDLANDS, DY8 1DX.
ASHMORE, Miss. Susan Elizabeth, BA ACA ATII *1991;* 126 Cherry Crescent, Rawtenstall, ROSSENDALE, LANCASHIRE, BB4 6DS.
ASHOUR, Miss. Hannah Jane, ACA *2010;* 13 Hunter Court, Sandy Mead, EPSOM, SURREY, KT19 7NG.
ASHPLANT, Mrs. Victoria Jane, BA ACA *2009;* PwC, Corner Bryce & Anglesea Streets, PO Box 191, HAMILTON 3240, NORTH ISLAND, NEW ZEALAND.
ASHPOLE, Miss. Noel, BSc ACA *1993;* with PricewaterhouseCoopers, 15th Floor, Bangkok City Tower, 179/74-80 South Sathorn Road, BANGKOK 10120, THAILAND.
ASHPOOL, Miss. Wendy, BSc ACA *2005;* 10 Brackendale Grove, HARPENDEN, HERTFORDSHIRE, AL5 3EJ.
ASHRAF, Miss. Fareeha Ambar, ACA *2009;* 81 Drury Road, HARROW, MIDDLESEX, HA1 4BT.
•**ASHRAF, Miss. Fatima, MSc BSc ACA** *2008;* Azlan & Co, 55 Sherwood Avenue, GREENFORD, MIDDLESEX, UB6 0PQ.
ASHRAF, Mr. Kamran, BSc ACA *2006;* with Merrill Lynch Europe Plc, 2 King Edward Street, LONDON, EC1A 1HQ.
ASHRAF, Ms. Masheed, ACA *2010;* (Tax Fac), Flat 306, Balmoral Apartments, 2 Praed Street, LONDON, W2 1JL.
•**ASHRAF, Mr. Mohammad, FCA** *1975;* Ashraf & Co., 30 Crescent Road, SHEFFIELD, S7 1HL.
ASHRAF, Mr. Mohammad, FCA *1974;* BDO Dunwoody, 60 Columbia Way, Suite 400, MARKHAM L3R 0C9, ON, CANADA. See also BDO International
ASHTON, Mr. Ben James, BA ACA *2004;* 8 Tracy Drive, NEWTON-LE-WILLOWS, MERSEYSIDE, WA12 8PX.
ASHTON, Miss. Carrie-Ann, BSc ACA *2007;* with Smith & Williamson Ltd, 1 Bishops Wharf, Walnut Tree Close, GUILDFORD, SURREY, GU1 4RA.
ASHTON, Mr. Cedric Herbert, FCA *1947;* 18 Springfield Street, MARKET HARBOROUGH, LE16 8BD. (Life Member)
ASHTON, Mr. Charles James, BA ACA *1988;* 10 Paternoster Square, Paternoster Square, LONDON, EC4M 7AL.
ASHTON, Mr. Charles Kenneth, FCA *1944;* 54 Longhouse Lane, POULTON-LE-FYLDE, FY6 8DF. (Life Member)
•**ASHTON, Mrs. Charlotte Ann Myfanwy, FCA** *1963;* C.A.M.Ashton, Marwood, 8 Townsend, Curry Rivel, LANGPORT, SOMERSET TA10 0HN.
ASHTON, Mrs. Christine Anne, BSc ACA *2003;* 25 Branksome Close, NORWICH, NR4 6SP.
ASHTON, Mr. Christopher Edward, BSc FCA *1975;* 16 Rydal Road, BOLTON, BL1 5LQ.
ASHTON, Mr. Christopher John Robert, BSc ACA *1992;* 2 Jowitt Road, SHEFFIELD, S11 9FJ.
ASHTON, Mr. Clive Geoffrey, FCA *1964;* PO Box 6977, MOSHI, TANZANIA.
ASHTON, Mr. David James, FCA *1958;* Glebe Cottage, Escrick, YORK, YO19 6LN. (Life Member)
ASHTON, Mr. David Jeremy, MA ACA *2004;* with Grant Thornton UK LLP, Grant Thornton House, 22 Melton Street, Euston Square, LONDON, NW1 2EP.
•**ASHTON, Mr. David Julian, BSc FCA** *1973;* FTI Consulting Limited, Davidson Building, 5 Southampton Street, LONDON, WC2E 7HA. See also LECG
ASHTON, Mr. David Keith, FCA *1970;* 18 Barrett Road, SOUTHPORT, PR8 4PG.
ASHTON, Mr. Edward Laurence, MA FCA *1950;* 39 Dowhills Road, Blundellsands, LIVERPOOL, L23 8SJ. (Life Member)
ASHTON, Miss. Elizabeth, BA ACA *2009;* 3 Archers Farm, Peel Road, BLACKPOOL, FY4 5JX.
ASHTON, Miss. Faye Louise, ACA *2009;* 17 Foxhill Drive, Glen Parva, LEICESTER, LE2 9NR.
•**ASHTON, Mr. Frank Martin Scott, FCA** *1974;* (Tax Fac), HW Westernshare Limited, 48 Totteridge Drive, HIGH WYCOMBE, BUCKINGHAMSHIRE, HP13 6JJ. See also Westernshare Limited
ASHTON, Mr. Gordon, FCA *1973;* Rowan House, Brown Edge Farm, Newcastle Road South, Brereton, SANDBACH, CHESHIRE CW11 1SB. (Life Member)
ASHTON, Mr. Guy Julian Claude, BSc FCA *1990;* Colebrook House, 27 Colebrook Street, WINCHESTER, HAMPSHIRE, SO23 9LH.
ASHTON, Mr. Hubert Gaitskell, DL MA FCA *1956;* Abbey View, 59 East Street, Coggeshall, COLCHESTER, ESSEX, CO6 1SJ. (Life Member)
ASHTON, Mr. James Edward Simon, MBA ACA *1995;* Suite 1302, Tower 4, Lane 1199 Fu Xing Zhong Road, Xu Hui Qu, SHANGHAI 200031, CHINA.
ASHTON, Miss. Jane Christine, BSc ACA *1984;* 18 Grove Park Terrace, LONDON, W4 3QG.
ASHTON, Mr. Jason, ACA CA(AUS) *2010;* 2 Elm Close, Wheatley, OXFORD, OX33 1UW.
ASHTON, Mr. Jason Russel, BA(Econ) ACA *1996;* 33 Angrave Road, East Leake, LOUGHBOROUGH, LE12 6JA.
ASHTON, Mr. John Gavin, BTech FCA *1973;* 7 Grove Drive, WOODHALL SPA, LINCOLNSHIRE, LN10 6RT. (Life Member)

ASHTON, Mr. Jonathan Richard, BSc ACA *1982;* 285 Vista View Drive, MAHWAH, NJ NJ 07430, UNITED STATES.
ASHTON, Miss. Julie, BA ACA *2000;* 46 Laitwood Road, LONDON, SW12 9QJ.
ASHTON, Mrs. Kay Elizabeth, MA ACA *1989;* Silverfleet Capital Partners Llp, 1 New Fetter Lane, LONDON, EC4A 1HH.
ASHTON, Miss. Kirsten Margaret, MA ACA *1998;* Primrose Cottage, Upper Hartfield, HARTFIELD, EAST SUSSEX, TN7 4AL.
•ASHTON, Mr. Malcolm Geoffrey, ACA *1980;* Rawcliffe & Co, 13 Poulton Street, Kirkham, PRESTON, PR4 2AA.
ASHTON, Mrs. Marie, BA(Hons) ACA *2001;* with KPMG LLP, 15 Canada Square, LONDON, E14 5GL.
•ASHTON, Mr. Mark, ACA FCCA *2009;* (Tax Fac), Lancaster & Co, Granville House, 2 Tettenhall Rd, WOLVERHAMPTON, WV1 4SB. See also Lancaster Haskins LLP
ASHTON, Mr. Mark Christopher, BA FCA *1998;* 185 Queens Park Road, BRIGHTON, BN2 9ZA.
ASHTON, Mr. Michael, FCA FCMA JDipMA *1955;* 11 Albert Avenue, Penton Park, CHERTSEY, KT16 8QG. (Life Member)
ASHTON, Mr. Michael Nicholas, BSc ACA *1989;* Leimenstrasse 80, 4051 BASEL, SWITZERLAND.
ASHTON, Mr. Neil Marshall, BA ACA *2001;* 122 St. Leonards Road, LONDON, SW14 7NJ.
ASHTON, Mr. Nicholas Gerard Anthony, BA ACA *2011;* 64 Brayburne Avenue, LONDON, SW4 6AA.
•ASHTON, Mr. Nicholas Lewis, BPharm FCA *1982;* (Tax Fac), Harold Smith, Unit 32, Llys Edmund Prys, St. Asaph Business Park, ST. ASAPH, LL17 0JA.
ASHTON, Mr. Nigel Mark, LLB ACA *1990;* Flat 14 Arundel Court, 16 Beckenham Grove, Shortlands, BROMLEY, BR2 0XN.
•ASHTON, Mr. Paul Kerr, FCA *1975;* Beavis Morgan LLP, 82 St. John Street, LONDON, EC1M 4JN.
ASHTON, Mrs. Pauline Margaret, BSc ACA *1984;* 15 Cedar Court Road, TORQUAY, TQ1 3HH.
ASHTON, Mr. Peter Maurice, FCA *1966;* po box f42683, FREEPORT, BAHAMAS.
ASHTON, Mr. Peter Thomas, ACA *2008;* PO Box 25883, St Heliers, AUCKLAND, NEW ZEALAND.
ASHTON, Mr. Philip James, BSocSc ACA *1994;* 64 Valley Road, HENLEY-ON-THAMES, OXFORDSHIRE, RG9 1RR.
ASHTON, Mr. Philip Priestley, BA FCA *1973;* West Barn, Wandales Lane, Bulmer, YORK, YO60 7ES.
ASHTON, Mr. Phillip Christopher, BSc ACA *1984;* 18 Hawkesley Court, Watford Road, RADLETT, HERTFORDSHIRE, WD7 8HH.
•ASHTON, Dr. Raymond Keighley, PhD LLM MSc BSc FCA ACMA FTII ACIS *1973;* (Tax Fac), Dr R K Ashton, Upton Cottage, Nairdwood Lane, Prestwood, GREAT MISSENDEN, BUCKINGHAMSHIRE HP16 0QH.
ASHTON, Mr. Richard, BCom ACA *2004;* Blackwood Group, 6 Gracechurch Street, LONDON, EC3V 0AT.
ASHTON, Mr. Richard, FCA *1950;* The Knoll, Priestley Road, CAERNARFON, LL55 1HP. (Life Member)
ASHTON, Mr. Richard Ian, BA ACA *1997;* 27 Vine Brook Road, LEXINGTON, MA 02421, UNITED STATES.
ASHTON, Mr. Richard John, BSc ACA *1992;* 42 Woodall Close, Middleton, MILTON KEYNES, MK10 9JZ.
ASHTON, Mr. Robin James, BA ACA *1983;* Clifford Lodge, Clifford Road, Middleton, ILKLEY, LS29 0AL.
ASHTON, Mr. Rodney Blake Williams, FCA *1973;* West End Farm, Thornholme, DRIFFIELD, YO25 4NN. (Life Member)
ASHTON, Mr. Roy Alfred, FCA *1959;* 211 East 70th Street, Suite 24H, NEW YORK, NY 10021, UNITED STATES. (Life Member)
ASHTON, Ms. Sara Helen May, BSc ACA CPA *1995;* with PricewaterhouseCoopers LLP, 300 Madison Avenue, NEW YORK, NY 10017, UNITED STATES.
ASHTON, Miss. Sarah Jane, ACA *2008;* 53a Parkhurst Road, LONDON, N7 0LR.
•ASHTON, Mrs. Sarah Louise, BA ACA *1998;* with Garbutt & Elliott LLP, Arabesque House, Monks Cross Drive, Huntington, YORK, YO32 9GW.
ASHTON, Miss. Sharon Mary, BA ACA *1989;* Ivy Cottage, Upper Hulme, LEEK, STAFFORDSHIRE, ST13 8TY.
ASHTON, Mr. Simon Dudley Keith Shaw, BSc ACA *1995;* British American Tobacco Plc Globe House, 4 Temple Place, LONDON, WC2R 2PG.
ASHTON, Mr. Simon Mark, BSc ACA MBA *1986;* Catalysa Limited, Moseley Farmhouse, Smithy Lane, LEEDS, LS16 7NG.
ASHTON, Mr. Stephen David, BEng ACA *1989;* Field End, Loosley Hill, Loosley Row, PRINCES RISBOROUGH, HP27 0PB.
ASHTON, Mr. Steven James, FCA *1974;* Unichem Nigeria Ltd, P.O. Box 303 Apapa, LAGOS, NIGERIA.
ASHTON, Mrs. Susan Mary, BSc FCA *1991;* 58 Noel Road, LONDON, N1 8HB.
ASHTON, Mr. Timothy James, MA ACA CFA *1998;* Orbis Investment Advisory Ltd Orbis House, 5 Mansfield Street, LONDON, W1G 9NG.
ASHTON, Mr. William Wilson, FCA *1957;* 2 Manor House Drive, NORTHWOOD, HA6 2UJ. (Life Member)
ASHTON, Mrs. Yvonne Margaret, MA ACA *1987;* 9 Stoke Park Road, Stoke Bishop, BRISTOL, BS9 1LE.
ASHTON-JONES, Miss. Amelia Jane, BSc FSS ACA *2006;* with Deloitte LLP, Hill House, 1 Little New Street, LONDON, EC4A 3TR.
ASHUN, Miss. Roberta Abena, BA ACA *2001;* 121a Vaughan Road, HARROW, MIDDLESEX, HA1 4EF.
•ASHURST, Mr. Adrian John, FCA *1969;* Graham Associates AG, Breitackerstr 1, 8702 ZOLLIKON, SWITZERLAND.
ASHURST, Mr. Christopher Peter, BSc FCA *1981;* 34 Moreton End Lane, HARPENDEN, HERTFORDSHIRE, AL5 2HD.
ASHURST, Mr. John Richard, MA FCA *1985;* 29 Broadhurst, ASHTEAD, SURREY, KT21 1QB.
ASHURST, Miss. Kim Jayne, BA(Hons) ACA *2003;* with Feist Hedgethorne Limited, Preston Park House, South Road, BRIGHTON, BN1 6SB.
ASHURST, Mr. Mark Laurence Robert, BA FCA *1985;* 15 Bolingbroke Grove, Battersea, LONDON, SW11 6EP.
•ASHURST, Mr. Michael David, FCA *1972;* 93 Houghton Lane, Swinton, MANCHESTER, M27 0BR.
ASHWELL, Mr. Anthony, BA FCA *1999;* 30 Redwood Drive, HUDDERSFIELD, HD2 1PW.
ASHWELL, Mr. Anthony Harbour, BSc FCA ACMA *1971;* 51 Summerleaze Road, MAIDENHEAD, BERKSHIRE, SL6 8ER. (Life Member)
ASHWELL, Mr. David, BA ACA *2005;* 61 Jersey Drive, Winnersh, WOKINGHAM, BERKSHIRE, RG41 5GQ.
ASHWELL, Miss. Emily, BSc ACA *2007;* 69 Fairacres Road, OXFORD, OX4 1TQ.
ASHWELL, Mrs. Fay, BSc(Hons) ACA *2000;* 1 Manor Villas, Manor Road Kilsby, RUGBY, WARWICKSHIRE, CV23 8XS.
ASHWELL, Mr. James, MChem ACA *2003;* Morgan Stanley, 23 Church Street, 16-01 Capital Square, SINGAPORE 049481, SINGAPORE.
ASHWELL, Mr. Peter Michael Campbell, FCA *1975;* White Lodge, 77 Bayham Road, SEVENOAKS, KENT, TN13 3XA.
ASHWELL, Mrs. Sonia Claire, ACA *1996;* 11 Chesterfield Drive, Hinchley Wood, ESHER, KT10 0AH.
ASHWELL, Miss. Suzanne Munro, BA(Hons) ACA *2003;* Orchard View, 119 Norman Road, WEST MALLING, KENT, ME19 6RW.
ASHWIN, Mr. Michael David, ACA *2009;* 6 Griffin Drive, Penallta, HENGOED, MID GLAMORGAN, CF82 6AH.
ASHWIN, Miss. Sarah Elizabeth, BA ACA *2000;* 20 Nuns Road, WINCHESTER, HAMPSHIRE, SO23 7EF.
ASHWOOD, Mr. Perry Colin, FCA *1971;* 96, Dropmore Road, Burnham, SLOUGH, SL1 8EL.
ASHWORTH, Mrs. Alison Joanne, BA ACA *1989;* The Grove, Spurgrove Lane, Frieth, HENLEY-ON-THAMES, BUCKINGHAMSHIRE, RG9 6NU.
ASHWORTH, Mr. Craig Mark, BSc ACA *1993;* 5 Letchworth Place, WHEELERS HILL, VIC 3150, AUSTRALIA.
ASHWORTH, Mr. David, BSc ACA *1990;* 11 Nevill Road, Bramhall, STOCKPORT, CHESHIRE, SK7 3ET.
ASHWORTH, Mr. David Robert, FCA *1970;* Royche Farm, Malcoff, Chapel-en-le-Frith, High Peak, SK23 0QR.
ASHWORTH, Mr. Francis George, FCA *1953;* 9 Windrush Quay, WITNEY, OXFORDSHIRE, OX28 1YL. (Life Member)
ASHWORTH, Mr. Garth Edwin, FCA *1961;* Via Ipparco di Nicea 35, Casalpalocco, 00124 ROME, ITALY.
ASHWORTH, Mr. Gerald, FCA *1948;* 5 Linden Road, STALYBRIDGE, SK15 2SL. (Life Member)
ASHWORTH, Mr. Iain Michael, BEng ACA *2001;* 44 Henwood Road, MANCHESTER, M20 4XG.
•ASHWORTH, Miss. Jennifer Rose, BSc ACA *2005;* Ashworth Accountancy & Bookkeeping Services, 7 Stanford Hall Crescent, Ramsbottom, BURY, LANCASHIRE, BL0 9FD.
ASHWORTH, John Brian, Esq OBE FCA *1961;* Woodside, Upper Colquhoun Street, HELENSBURGH, G84 9AJ.
ASHWORTH, Mr. John Stephen, BA ACA *1991;* PT Hutchison Ports Indonesia, Graha Rekso Building, 7th Floor Suite 7 A-B, Jl. Bulevar Artha Gading Kav.A1, Kelapa Gading, JAKARTA 14240 INDONESIA.
ASHWORTH, Mrs. Julia Kathryn Anne, BSc ACA *1993;* Grey Stoke, Cross Oak Road, BERKHAMSTED, HERTFORDSHIRE, HP4 3NA.
ASHWORTH, Miss. Karen Deborah, BSc ACA *2002;* 73 St. Albans Avenue, LONDON, W4 5JS.
ASHWORTH, Mr. Mark Andrew, ACA *1994;* 16 Warwick Avenue, Cheadle, STOKE-ON-TRENT, ST10 1WD.
•ASHWORTH, Mr. Mark Anthony, BA FCA *1995;* Kendall Wadley LLP, Granta Lodge, 71 Graham Road, MALVERN, WORCESTERSHIRE, WR14 2JS.
ASHWORTH, Mr. Mark James, BA(Hons) ACA *2002;* 5 Thodays Close, Willingham, CAMBRIDGE, CB24 5LE.
ASHWORTH, Mr. Martin William, BA ACA *1991;* Warwick Court, 5 Paternoster Square, LONDON, EC4M7DX.
ASHWORTH, Mr. Michael James, ACA *2010;* Flat 5, 12 Clarendon Street, LEAMINGTON SPA, CV32 5ST.
ASHWORTH, Mr. Michael Philip, BA ACA CFA *1998;* 1 Church Walk, Crowton, NORTHWICH, CHESHIRE, CW8 2SA.
ASHWORTH, Ms. Michelle Louise, LLB ACA *2002;* Floor 5 Municipal Offices, Rochdale Metropolitan Borough Council, PO Box 39, ROCHDALE, LANCASHIRE, OL16 1LQ.
ASHWORTH, Mrs. Pamela Ruth, FCA *1969;* 4 Blue Meadow, Kingsclere, NEWBURY, BERKSHIRE, RG20 5ST.
ASHWORTH, Mr. Paul Richard, BSc ACA *1993;* 118 St. Anns Hill, LONDON, SW18 2RR.
ASHWORTH, Mr. Richard Findlay, FCA *1975;* Incommunities Trust House, 5 New Augustus Street, BRADFORD, WEST YORKSHIRE, BD1 5LL.
ASHWORTH, Miss. Sarah, ACA *2011;* 51 Thornhill Square, LONDON, N1 1BE.
ASHWORTH, Miss. Sharon Jayne, BA ACA *2007;* 98 Alma Road, LONDON, SW18 1AH.
ASHWORTH, Mr. Simon Holmes, FCA *1960;* Underhill Farm, Underhill, East Knoyle, SALISBURY, SP3 6BP. (Life Member)
ASHWORTH, Mr. Stephen Charles, BSc ACA *1992;* Grey Stoke, Cross Oak Road, BERKHAMSTED, HERTFORDSHIRE, HP4 3NA.
ASHWORTH, Mrs. Susan Elizabeth, BA ACA *1988;* The Lawn, 93 Aylesbury Road, Aston Clinton, AYLESBURY, BUCKINGHAMSHIRE, HP22 5AJ.
ASIF, Mr. Mohammed Ikram, BSc(Hons) ACA *2002;* 983 Alum Rock Road, Ward End, BIRMINGHAM, B8 2LY. See also Syedain & Co
ASIF SEDOO, Mrs. Reyhana, BSc ACA *2003;* 50 Mansfield Road, Walthamstow, LONDON, E17 6PJ.
ASIMENOU, Mrs. Chrystalla, ACA *1982;* Audit Office of the Republic of Cyprus, Deligiorgi 6, 1406 NICOSIA, CYPRUS.
ASKAROFF, Mr. Nikolai Fawley, FCA *1980;* EMC Ltd, 49 Gildredge Road, EASTBOURNE, EAST SUSSEX, BN21 4RY.
ASKE, Mr. Jeremy John, FCA *1973;* 11 Broadleaze Way, WINSCOMBE, SOMERSET, BS25 1JX.
ASKE, Mr. Nicholas James, BA ACA *1979;* 156a Russell Drive, Wolllaton, NOTTINGHAM, NG8 2BE.
ASKEW, Mr. Anthony Edward, FCA *1964;* 25 Stockwood Rise, CAMBERLEY, SURREY, GU15 2EA.
ASKEW, Mr. David, ACA *2011;* Fallowfield, Lower Washwell Lane, Painswick, STROUD, GLOUCESTERSHIRE, GL6 6XW.
•ASKEW, Miss. Elizabeth Anne, ACA *2006;* 5 Palmar Road, Allington, MAIDSTONE, KENT, ME16 0DL.
ASKEW, Mr. James Dennis, FCA *1948;* 4 Queens Court, Queens Road, CHELTENHAM, GLOUCESTERSHIRE, GL50 2LU. (Life Member)
•ASKEW, Mr. Jonathan, MA ACA *2002;* Hartley Fowler LLP, 4th Floor, Tuition House, 27-37 St. Georges Road, Wimbledon, LONDON SW19 4EU.
ASKEW, Mr. Jonathan Christopher, BA ACA *2007;* 13 Burnelli Building, 352 Queenstown Road, LONDON, SW8 4NG.
ASKEW, Mr. Karl James, BA ACA DChA *2002;* 27a Codrington Hill, LONDON, SE23 1LR.
ASKEW, Mr. Richard, BA ACA *2006;* 5 Ellenborough Old Road, MARYPORT, CUMBRIA, CA15 7PG.
ASKEW, Mr. Robert John Irving, FCA *1970;* Sunnymede, 10 Nab Lane, Nab Wood, SHIPLEY, BD18 4EH.
•ASKEW, Mr. Stephen James Thomas, FCA *1981;* (Tax Fac), Burns Waring, Roper Yard, Roper Road, CANTERBURY, CT2 7EX. See also SME Payroll Services Limited, Waring & Partners. and Burns Waring & Partners Ltd
•ASKEY, Mr. James Stephen, FCA *1968;* Askey & Co, 25 Whitebridge Parkway, Gosforth, NEWCASTLE UPON TYNE, NE3 5LU. See also Askey Stephen & Co
ASKEY, Mr. Richard Stephen, BSc ACA *2006;* DTE, Hollins Mount, Hollins Lane, BURY, LANCASHIRE, BL9 8AT.
ASKHAM, Mr. Francis Guy Lewis, FCA *1955;* Ashton House, 12 The Precinct, Winchester Road, Chandler's Ford, EASTLEIGH, HAMPSHIRE SO53 2GB. (Life Member)
ASKHAM, Mr. Paul David, BA ACA *1986;* Unit 1 Trinity Business Centre, Brunel Road Totton, SOUTHAMPTON, SO40 3WX.
ASKHAM, Mrs. Sara Ann, ACA *1989;* 7 Pilkington Road, ORPINGTON, KENT, BR6 8HR.
•①ASKHAM, Mr. Timothy Alan, FCA *1978;* Mazars LLP, The Lexicon, Mount Street, MANCHESTER, M2 5NT.
ASKWITH, Mr. Nelson Mark, FCA *1952;* Island Reach, River Gardens, Bray, MAIDENHEAD, SL6 2BJ. (Life Member)
ASLAM, Mr. Ammad, MS BCom ACA *2009;* P. O. Box 50115, HIDD, BAHRAIN.
ASLAM, Mr. Imran, ACA FCCA *2010;* 220 Perry Drive, NORTH BRUNSWICK, NJ 08902, UNITED STATES.
•ASLAM, Mr. Jahanzeb, ACA *2008;* Pearl Accountants Ltd, 359 Willington Road South, HOUNSLOW, TW4 5HU. See also Pearl Accountants
ASLAM, Mr. Kabeer, BSc ACA *1996;* 70 Cambridge Drive, LONDON, SE12 8AJ.
ASLAM, Mr. Mohammad, FCA *1962;* Unit No 4, 12689 - 72 Ave, SURREY V3W 2M7, BC, CANADA.
•ASLAM, Mr. Mohammad, FCA *1963;* M. Aslam, 259 Mansfield Road, NOTTINGHAM, NG1 3FT.
ASLAM, Mr. Muhammad, FCA *1974;* Baad-E-Saba, 84 Khayaban-e-Rahat, Phase VI Defence Housing Auth, KARACHI, 75500, PAKISTAN.
ASLAM, Mr. Nadeem, BSc ACA *1996;* 24 Warwick Gardens, ILFORD, IG1 4LE.
ASLAM, Mr. Naveed, BSc FCA *1985;* 9 Campaspe Street, BOX HILL, VIC 3129, AUSTRALIA.
ASLAM, Ms. Saaima Tasleem, BSc ACA *2004;* 18 Bodmin Road, Woodley, READING, RG5 3RZ.
ASLAM, Miss. Saima Razia, ACA *2008;* 27 Highgate, NELSON, LANCASHIRE, BB9 0DU.
ASLAM, Mrs. Shazia, ACA *2010;* 7th Floor, Dashwood House, 69 Old Broad Street, LONDON, EC2M 1QT.
ASLAM, Mr. Sheikh Mohommad, FCA *1966;* 12-B, 7th East Street, Phase 1 DHA, KARACHI 75500, PAKISTAN. (Life Member)
ASLAM, Mr. Ziad Irfan, BSc ACA *1997;* Flat P/ 11 Cavalier House, 46-50 Uxbridge Road, LONDON, W5 2SU.
•ASLAM KHAN, Mr. Mohammad, FCA *1973;* (Tax Fac), AKC Limited, 42 Charles Street, MANCHESTER, M1 7DB. See also KKMJ Limited
ASLETT, Mr. Albert Edward, FCA *1958;* 16 Richmond Avenue, Raynes Park, LONDON, SW20 8LA. (Life Member)
ASLETT, Mr. Brian Robert, BSc FCA *1973;* 18 Maclear Road, CLAREMONT, 7708, SOUTH AFRICA.
ASLIN, Mr. Thomas, BSc ACA *2002;* with Kingston Smith LLP, Devonshire House, 60 Goswell Road, LONDON, EC1M 7AD.
ASPBURY, Mr. Dominic, ACA *2011;* 36 Walton Road, WOKING, SURREY, GU21 5DL.
ASPDEN, Mr. Gavin John, BSc FCA *1998;* Institute of Chartered Accountants in England & Wales, Metropolitan House 4 Rillaton Walk, MILTON KEYNES, MK9 2FZ.
ASPDEN, Mr. Peter Graham, FCA *1974;* Sandholme, Walton Road, Kimcote, LUTTERWORTH, LE17 5RU.
ASPDEN, Mrs. Susan, FCA *1974;* Sandholme, Walton Road, Kimcote, LUTTERWORTH, LE17 5RU.
ASPDIN, Mr. Nigel Slater, FCA *1975;* 19 Vernon Street, DERBY, DE1 1FT. (Life Member)
ASPEY, Mr. Rupert Laurence, MA ACA *1992;* 11 Kelham Gardens, MARLBOROUGH, SN8 1PW.
ASPIN, Mr. Geoffrey, FCA *1958;* 26 Cleeve Lawns, SWINDON, SN3 1LE. (Life Member)
ASPIN, Mrs. Judith Clare, BA FCA *1994;* 3 The Paddock, Greenfield, OLDHAM, OL3 7PU.
ASPIN, Mr. Philip Anthony, BSc ACA MCT *1992;* United Utilities PLC, haweswater House, Lingley Mere Business Park, Great Sankey, WARRINGTON, WA5 3LP.
ASPINALL, Mr. Allan, FCA *1969;* 33 Glenalla Road, RUISLIP, HA4 8DW. (Life Member)

ASPINALL, Mr. Anthony Breese, FCA *1955;* 9 The Moorlands, Four Oaks Park, SUTTON COLDFIELD, WEST MIDLANDS, B74 2RF. (Life Member)
ASPINALL, Miss. Brenda, FCA *1969;* 7 Otho Court, Augustus Close, BRENTFORD, TW8 8PX.
ASPINALL, Mrs. Clair Delyth Ann, BSc ACA *1997;* 68 Cluny Gardens, EDINBURGH, EH10 6BR.
ASPINALL, Mr. David Charles, FCA *1967;* Shingle Quay Green Lane, Hamble, SOUTHAMPTON, SO31 4GB. (Life Member)
ASPINALL, Mr. Ian, BA FCA *1989;* Consilium Partners Ltd, 14 The Embankment, Heaton Mersey, STOCKPORT, CHESHIRE, SK4 3GN.
ASPINALL, Mrs. Jacqueline Mary, BA FCA *1989;* 9 Beechfield Drive, MIDDLEWICH, CW10 9QE.
ASPINALL, Mr. James Eric, BSc ACA *1989;* Centro Centro House, 16 Summer Lane, BIRMINGHAM, B19 3SD.
ASPINALL, Miss. Jane Louise, BA ACA *1994;* 38 Buckingham Road, WILMSLOW, CHESHIRE, SK9 5LB.
ASPINALL, Mrs. Kathleen Elsie, FCA *1970;* 1 West Garleton Holdings, HADDINGTON, EH41 3SJ.
ASPINALL, Mr. Keith Wilton, MA MBA FCA *1977;* 160 Dartmouth Street, NEWTON, MA 02465, UNITED STATES.
ASPINALL, Mr. Lawrence, BSc ACA *1978;* Clover Bank The Ridgeway, Shorne, GRAVESEND, DA12 3LW.
ASPINALL, Mrs. Marguerite Helen, ACA *1981;* 505 High Road, HARROW, HA3 6HL.
•ASPINALL, Mr. Matthew, BA(Hons) ACA *2004;* Aspinall Accountancy Limited, 5 Hockery View, Hindley, WIGAN, LANCASHIRE, WN2 3JX.
ASPINALL, Mr. Michael Stuart, MEng ACA *2001;* 20 Links Road, Flackwell Heath, HIGH WYCOMBE, BUCKINGHAMSHIRE, HP10 9LY.
ASPINALL, Mr. Peter, ACA *2008;* 34 Lynette Avenue, LONDON, SW4 9HD.
ASPINALL, Mr. Philip John, BA ACA *1992;* 6 Octavian Drive, Bancroft, MILTON KEYNES, MK13 0PW.
ASPINALL, Mr. Robert Neil, BA(Hons) ACA CFE *2003;* 4th Floor, Citrus Grove Building, P.O. Box 993 GT, GEORGETOWN, GRAND CAYMAN, KY1-1109 CAYMAN ISLANDS.
ASPINALL, Mr. Roy, FCA *1971;* 117 George Lane, Notton, WAKEFIELD, WF4 2NE.
ASPINALL, Mrs. Samantha Helen, BA(Hons) ACA MBA *2000;* 20 Links Road, Flackwell Heath, HIGH WYCOMBE, BUCKINGHAMSHIRE, HP10 9LY.
ASPINWALL, Mr. Roger Stableford, FCA *1960;* Cornerstones, Church Road, Yapton, ARUNDEL, WEST SUSSEX, BN18 0EN. (Life Member)
ASPINWALL, Mr. Thomas, ACA *2011;* 1 Kensington Villas, Royal Park, BRISTOL, BS8 3AJ.
ASPLAND, Mr. Jason Robert, BSc ACA *1995;* Val Pre, La Rue Du Maupertuis, St. Clement, JERSEY, JE2 6NG.
ASPLET, Mr. John Robert, BSc FCA *1989;* La Reverie Avenue Du Petit Mont, St. Helier, JERSEY, JE2 4UT.
ASPLET, Mr. Matthew, BSc ACA *2005;* Flat 6, 86 Westbourne Terrace, LONDON, W2 6QE.
ASPLIN, Mrs. Laura May Elizabeth, BSc(Hons) ACA *2004;* with Deloitte LLP, Athene Place, 66 Shoe Lane, LONDON, EC4A 3BQ.
•ASPLIN, Mr. Mark, BCom FCA CF *1984;* Jasper CF Limited, 80 Caroline Street, BIRMINGHAM, B3 1UP.
ASPRAY, Mr. Rodney George, FCA *1960;* Kambara, 4 Green Lane, Poynton, STOCKPORT, SK12 1TJ. (Life Member)
ASPROU, Mr. George Demetriou, FCA *1975;* (Tax Fac), 2 Ty Parc Close, Aradur Park Llandaff, CARDIFF, CF5 2RG.
ASQUITH, Mr. Antony James, MEng ACA *2002;* Barclays Capital, 41/F Cheung Kong Centre, 2 Queens Road, CENTRAL, HONG KONG ISLAND, HONG KONG SAR.
ASQUITH, Mr. David, FCA *1973;* Little London Farm, Triangle, SOWERBY BRIDGE, HX6 3EY.
ASQUITH, Mr. Paul Matthew, ACA *2008;* 9 Evelina Road, MELBOURNE, VIC 3142, AUSTRALIA.
ASQUITH, Mr. Stephen Richard, BSc ACA *2006;* Indorama Polymers Workington Ltd, Lowca Lane, WORKINGTON, CUMBRIA, CA141LG.
ASQUITH-EVANS, Mrs. Penelope Jane, BSc ACA *1992;* 19 Augusta Drive, Tytherington, MACCLESFIELD, CHESHIRE, SK10 2UR.
ASSAD, Miss. Philippa Sandra, ACA *2009;* 1 Colonel Road, Betws, AMMANFORD, DYFED, SA18 2HB.
•ASSADIAN, Mrs. Tessa, BA(Hons) ACA *2004;* 15 Beaconsfield Close, Beumont Park, WHITLEY BAY, TYNE AND WEAR, NE25 9UW.
ASSAN, Mr. Imran, BEng ACA *2010;* 22D Jalan Ulu Siglap, SINGAPORE 457169, SINGAPORE.
ASSEFJAH, Mr. Ali-Reza, FCA *1972;* 20563 Hatteras Street, WOODLAND HILLS, CA 91367, UNITED STATES.
ASSENDER, Mr. Richard David, ACA *1980;* GPO box 4055, SYDNEY, NSW 2001, AUSTRALIA.
ASSER, Miss. Simone Rachel, BSc ACA *1995;* 422 Mola Avenue, FORT LAUDERDALE, FL 33301, UNITED STATES.
ASSHETON, Mrs. Joanne Louise, BSc ACA *1999;* Hameau Le Roy, 14240 SALLEN, FRANCE.
ASSIOTIS, Mr. Kyriakos, BSc(Hons) ACA *2011;* 5A Manis Street, Makedonitissa, Engomi, 2415 NICOSIA, CYPRUS.
•ASSMAN, Mr. Matthew Alexander, BEng ACA *1999;* AJH Limited, Trinity House, Bath Street, St. Helier, JERSEY, JE2 4ST.
ASSOMULL, Mr. Vashdev Kishinchand, FCA *1969;* Mesk Towers, Unit 2103, P.O. Box 48748, Dubai Marina, DUBAI, UNITED ARAB EMIRATES. (Life Member)
•ASSUMALL, Mr. Jagdish Gobindram, FCA *1973;* Pantrade & Investment Co Ltd, 33 Main Street, PO Box 34, GIBRALTAR, GIBRALTAR.
ASTALL, Mrs. Janet, MA ACA *1999;* 28 Mexfield Road, LONDON, SW15 2RQ.
ASTALL, Mr. John, FCA *1975;* 3 Swallowfield Gardens, Appleton, WARRINGTON, WA4 5QY.
ASTALL, Miss. Marise Alexa Sophia Joyce, MSc ACA *2010;* Wilderspool House, 3 Park Drive, CREWE, CW2 8EW.
•ASTBURY, Mr. Craig, BSc ACA *2002;* Astbury Accountants Limited, Regent House, Bath Avenue, WOLVERHAMPTON, WV1 4EG. See also BSS & Co (Bridgnorth) Limited
ASTBURY, Miss. Elisabeth Louise, BSc ACA *2008;* Armajaro Trading Ltd, 16 Charles Street, LONDON, W1J 5DS.
ASTBURY, Miss. Elizabeth Anne, BA ACA *1992;* 47 Victoria Ct Leicester Rd, Oadby, LEICESTER, LE2 4AG.
ASTBURY, Mr. Ivor Charles, FCA *1962;* 35 Pine Crescent, Chandlers Ford, EASTLEIGH, SO53 1LN. (Life Member)
ASTBURY, Mr. James Robert, BSc(Hons) ACA *2003;* Buckcroft Braintree Road, Felsted, DUNMOW, CM6 3DX.
•ASTBURY, Mr. Stephen John, BSc ACA *1991;* Steve Astbury Ltd, 379 Stitch-Mi-Lane, Harwood, BOLTON, BL2 3PR. See also Steve Astbury & Partners Ltd
ASTELL, Mr. Philip, FCA *1977;* Jontree House, Church Lane, Challock, ASHFORD, KENT, TN25 4BS.
ASTELL - CROCKER, Mrs. Claire Louise, BSc(Hons) ACA *2003;* 198 Derby Road, Chellaston, DERBY, DE73 6RQ.
ASTHANA-PATEL, Mrs. Jemini, BCom ACA *2003;* 17 Warden Road, SUTTON COLDFIELD, WEST MIDLANDS, B73 5SB.
ASTILL, Mr. John Trevor, FCA *1967;* 30 Barn Close, Cumnor Hill, OXFORD, OX2 9JP.
ASTILL, Mr. Julian Mark, FCA *1964;* 17 Strathearn Avenue, Whitton, TWICKENHAM, TW2 6JT.
ASTILL, Mr. Peter William, FCA *1955;* 33 Luckley Wood, WOKINGHAM, RG41 2EW. (Life Member)
ASTILL, Dr. Tom Patrick, PhD BSc ACA *2009;* 10 Waltham Close, West Bridgford, NOTTINGHAM, NG2 6LE.
ASTIN, Mr. Clive Donald Claud, FCA *1968;* Gubberhill Farm, Ripple, TEWKESBURY, GLOUCESTERSHIRE, GL20 6HB. (Life Member)
ASTIN, Mr. Colin Paul, FCA *1969;* 40 Hauxton Road, Little Shelford, CAMBRIDGE, CB22 5HJ.
ASTLES, Mr. George Robert, FCA *1959;* 1 Annisgarth Park, WINDERMERE, CUMBRIA, LA23 2HX. (Life Member)
•ASTLES, Mrs. Judith Mary, BSc ACA *1986;* JMA Solutions Ltd, 22 Dunmow Hill, FLEET, HAMPSHIRE, GU51 3AN.
ASTLEY, Mr. Carl Daniel, BSc(Hons) ACA *2003;* 82 Willian Road, HITCHIN, HERTFORDSHIRE, SG4 0LT.
ASTLEY, Mrs. Claire Joanne, BSc(Hons) ACA CTA *2001;* 5 Smith Lane, Egerton, BOLTON, BL7 9ET.
ASTLEY, Mr. Ian Peter, BA ACA *1992;* Privet Capital LLP, 18B Charles Street, LONDON, W1J 5DU.
ASTLEY, Mr. James Michael Harry, ACA *2009;* 87 Windmill Drive, Croxley Green, RICKMANSWORTH, HERTFORDSHIRE, WD3 3FB.
ASTLEY, Mrs. Joanna Marie, ACA *1995;* 20 Claremont Avenue, Stony Stratford, MILTON KEYNES, MK11 1HH.
ASTLEY, Mr. Paul, LLB ACA *1992;* Vodafone Group Plc Vodafone House, The Connection, NEWBURY, RG14 2FN.
ASTLEY, Mr. Rupert Haydon, MA FCA *1990;* High Gates, 21 The Ballands North, Fetcham, LEATHERHEAD, SURREY, KT22 9HU.
ASTLEY, Mr. Shaun Derek, BSc ACA *1981;* 107 Maidenhall, Higham, GLOUCESTER, GL2 8DJ.
ASTLEY, Mr. Trevor Roy, FCA *1950;* Sleepy Hollow, Castle Hill, Prestbury, MACCLESFIELD, SK10 4AS. (Life Member)
ASTON, Mr. Anthony Lynn, BSc FCA *1964;* Eildon, Seal Hollow Road, SEVENOAKS, TN13 3SF. (Life Member)
ASTON, Mr. Anthony Peter Charles, FCA *1964;* Broomfield, The Street, East Preston, LITTLEHAMPTON, WEST SUSSEX, BN16 1HT.
ASTON, Mr. Christopher James, BA ACA *1996;* Quarry Offices, Tarmac Ltd Croxden Quarry, Freehay Cheadle, STOKE-ON-TRENT, ST10 1RH.
ASTON, Mr. Craig, BSc ACA *1998;* 1A, Welton Drive, WILMSLOW, SK9 6HF.
•ASTON, Mr. David John William, BA FCA *1993;* with Barnes Roffe LLP, 3 Brook Business Centre, Cowley Mill Road, Cowley, UXBRIDGE, MIDDLESEX UB8 2FX.
•ASTON, Mr. David William, BSc FCA *1973;* (Tax Fac), Aston & Co, 132 Walham Green Court, Moore Park Road, Fulham, LONDON, SW6 2PX. See also Preston Accountants Limited
•ASTON, Mr. Geoffrey Leonard, FCA *1970;* G.L. Aston, 23 Church Lane, Old Arley, COVENTRY, CV7 8FW.
ASTON, Mrs. Helen, ACA *2002;* 15 Meyrick Close, Winstanley, WIGAN, LANCASHIRE, WN3 6DW.
ASTON, Mr. Ian, BCom FCA CF *1990;* Rainbow House Polecat Road, Cressing, BRAINTREE, CM77 8PH.
•ASTON, James, Esq MBE BSc FCA *1992;* BDO LLP, Emerald House, East Street, EPSOM, SURREY, KT17 1HS. See also BDO Stoy Hayward LLP
•ASTON, Mr. James Bernard, BSc ACA *1998;* Aston Business Consultancy, 69 Bolton Avenue, RICHMOND, DL10 4BA.
ASTON, Mr. John Anthony, ACA *1987;* 187 Elsinge Road, ENFIELD, EN1 4NZ.
ASTON, Mr. John Christopher, OBE MA ACA *1979;* 18 Barrow Road, CAMBRIDGE, CB2 8AS.
ASTON, Mr. Lee, BA(Hons) FCA *2000;* 14 Friendship Road, BRISTOL, BS4 2RN.
ASTON, Mrs. Linda Christine, BA ACA *1980;* 11 Dorset Avenue, Walton-le-Dale, PRESTON, PR5 4GJ.
ASTON, Mr. Nicholas, MSc BSc(Hons) ACA *2011;* 4 Cot Lane, STOURBRIDGE, WEST MIDLANDS, DY8 5PP.
ASTON, Mrs. Petra Barbara, BA ACA *1993;* 13 The Avenue, PETERSFIELD, HAMPSHIRE, GU31 4JQ.
ASTON, Mr. Raymond, FCA *1957;* 33 Longsight Road, Holcombe Brook, BURY, BL0 9SL. (Life Member)
ASTON, Mr. Richard, BA(Hons) ACA *2002;* 15 Meyrick Close, Winstanley, WIGAN, LANCASHIRE, WN3 6DW.
ASTON, Mr. Richard Michael, ACA *2008;* Albion Ventures Llp, 1 Kings Arms Yard, LONDON, EC2R 7AF.
ASTON, Mr. Ronald Peter, BA ACA *1980;* Talisman (Sageri) Ltd, Indonesia Stock Exchange Building, Tower 1, 11th Floor, Jl. Jend Sudirman Kav. 52-53, JAKARTA 12190 INDONESIA.
ASTON, Miss. Scarlett Natillya, BSc ACA *2005;* 11 Mill Drive, North Rocks, SYDNEY, NSW 2151, AUSTRALIA.
ASTON, Mr. Stephen Mark, BCom ACA *1988;* The Gables, Rowley Avenue, STAFFORD, ST17 9AA.
ASTON, Mr. Stephen Richard, ACA *1982;* Beechwood Lodge, 6 Beechwood Croft, Little Aston, SUTTON COLDFIELD, WEST MIDLANDS, B74 3UU.
•ASTON, Mr. Tom, BA ACA ATII *1995;* KPMG LLP, 15 Canada Square, LONDON, E14 5GL. See also KPMG Europe LLP
ASTOR, Mr. Cedric Alexander, MA FCA *1981;* Route de la Dent de Bonavau 27, 1874 CHAMPERY, SWITZERLAND.
ASWANI, Mr. Joseph, ACA *2010;* 33 The Crescent, WEST WICKHAM, KENT, BR4 0HB.
•ASWANI, Mr. Pershotum, BSc(Econ) ACA FCCA *2007;* with Hazlems Fenton LLP, Palladium House, 1-4 Argyll Street, LONDON, W1F 7LD.
ATACK, Mr. Gregory Spencer, BSc ACA *1991;* 43 Whitecroft Way, BECKENHAM, BR3 3AQ.
ATACK, Mrs. Helen Ann, BSc ACA *1996;* 134 Hawes Lane, WEST WICKHAM, KENT, BR4 9AF.
ATACK, Miss. Kathryn Elizabeth, BA ACA *1999;* 34 West Park Crescent, LEEDS, LS8 2EQ.
ATACK, Mr. Robert Daniel, FCA *1970;* Pen-y-Waen, Bryniau, Dyserth, RHYL, LL18 6BY.
ATACK, Mr. Scott Michael, BA ACA *2004;* 35 Tamesis Place, Patrick Road Caversham, READING, RG4 8ET.
ATACK-LEE, Mrs. Jayne Louise, BSc ACA *1996;* Walnut Tree Health Centre, Blackberry Court, Walnut Tree, MILTON KEYNES, BUCKINGHAMSHIRE, MK7 7NR.
ATAII, Mr. Bahman, BSc ACA *1980;* Melli Bank Plc, 1 London Wall, LONDON, EC2Y 5EA.
ATAII, Mr. Edward Nicholas Giles, ACA *2009;* K P M G Llp, 15 Canada Square, LONDON, E14 5GL.
ATAILER, Mr. Tayfun, ACA *2006;* Flat 19, Space Apartments, 419 High Road, Wood Green, LONDON, N22 8JS.
ATAL, Mr. Aditya Kumar, ACA *1983;* RPG Enterprises, 6th Floor, Agarwal House, 2 St George's Gate, Hastings, KOLKATA 700022 WEST BENGAL INDIA.
ATAL, Mr. Deepak, ACA *1979;* PO Box 320, Al Harthy Complex, 118 MUSCAT, OMAN.
ATAL, Mr. Pavan, ACA *1996;* 366C Xian Jiang Hua Yuan 1 Xiang Jiang Bei Lu Chaoyang Qu, BEIJING 100102, CHINA.
ATAL, Mr. Vikram Anand, BSc FCA *1981;* 525 East 80th Street, Apt 10f, NEW YORK, NY 10075, UNITED STATES.
•ATALIANIS, Mr. Cleanthis, FCA *1981;* Aston Draycott, Caprini House, 163/173 Praed Street, LONDON, W2 1RH.
ATALLA, Mr. Mahmoud Shawki Abdel Hamid, FCA *1960;* 14 Abd El Hamid Lofti Street, Dokki, GIZA, EGYPT. (Life Member)
•ATASHROO, Mr. Abel, BSc ACA *1984;* Abel Atashroo & Co, 3 Elm Grove Road, Ealing, LONDON, W5 3JH.
ATCHA, Mr. Idris, BSc FCA *1994;* 147 Gibbon Street, BOLTON, BL3 5LW.
ATCHA, Miss. Mariyah, BSc(Hons) ACA *2011;* 50 High Street, BOLTON, BL3 6SZ.
ATCHISON, Mr. Derek James, FCA *1957;* Whispers, Shirleys, Ditchling, HASSOCKS, BN6 8UD. (Life Member)
ATCHLEY, Ms. Catherine Margot, BA FCA *1980;* Anasmara, ACHARACLE, ARGYLL, PH36 4JX. (Life Member)
ATEFI, Mr. Paul, BA ACA *2007;* Flat C, 14 Cavendish Road, LONDON, SW12 0DG.
•ATHA, Ms. Carol Ann, BSc FCA *1991;* Deloitte LLP, Athene Place, 66 Shoe Lane, LONDON, EC4A 3BQ. See also Deloitte & Touche LLP
ATHA, Mrs. Karen, BSc ACA *1994;* 15 Cranleigh Road, ESHER, KT10 8DF.
•ATHANASIADES, Mr. Anastasios Nicos, BA FCA *1995;* A.N. Athanasiades & Co Limited, 46 Stassinos Street, 1st Floor Office 28, 2002 NICOSIA, CYPRUS.
ATHANASIOU, Miss. Andri, BA ACA *2003;* 84 Kleisthenous Road, Archangelos, Lakatamia, 2335 NICOSIA, CYPRUS.
•ATHANASIOU, Mr. Athanasios Manoli, BSc FCA *1986;* (Tax Fac), BSG Valentine, Lynton House, 7/12 Tavistock Square, LONDON, WC1H 9BQ. See also BSG Valantine
•ATHANASIOU, Mr. Miltiades, FCA *1977;* (Tax Fac), M. Athanasiou, PO Box 54320, 3723 LIMASSOL, CYPRUS.
ATHANASSIADES, Mr. Aristos, BA ACA *2007;* Maximos Michaelides Street, 3310 LIMASSOL, CYPRUS.
ATHANASSOPOULOS, Mr. Athanasios, MSc ACA *2004;* Flat B310 Flat 310 Peninsula Apartments 4 Praed Street, LONDON, W2 1JE.
•ATHAWES, Mr. Auden Kenway, FCA *1974;* Athawes & Company Limited, Stirling House, Sunderland Quay, Culpeper Close, Medway City Estate, ROCHESTER KENT ME2 4HN.
ATHENODOROU, Mr. Georgios, MSc BSc ACA *1999;* 10 Spyrou Kyprianou Flat G1 Mesa Yitonia, 4001 LIMASSOL, CYPRUS.
•ATHERDEN, Mr. John Edward, FCA *1980;* (Tax Fac), Atherden & Co, PO Box 660, ALTRINCHAM, CHESHIRE, WA14 3UZ.
ATHERLEY, Mr. Stephen Walter, BA ACA *1992;* La Chaumiere, La Rue Jutize, Grouville, JERSEY, JE3 9UQ.
ATHERSMITH, Mr. Joseph Ernest, FCA *1938;* 815 Sutton Road, Aldridge, WALSALL, WS9 0QJ. (Life Member)
ATHERTON, Mr. Andrew Joseph, BA ACA *1993;* 5 Sayer Close, GREENHITHE, DA9 9PZ.
ATHERTON, Mr. Anthony James, FCA *1972;* 44 Felden Street, LONDON, SW6 5AF.
ATHERTON, Mr. Arthur Dewhurst, FCA *1938;* 3 Grosvenor Court, 22 Grove Road, BOURNEMOUTH, BH1 3DB. (Life Member)
ATHERTON, Mr. Ashley Edwin, FCA *1978;* 9 Anstey Brook, Weston Turville, AYLESBURY, HP22 5RT.
ATHERTON, Mr. Christopher Nigel, BA FCA *1993;* 2 Drake Street, FEILDING, NEW ZEALAND.

ATHERTON, Miss. Danielle, BA ACA *2006;* with PricewaterhouseCoopers LLP, 1 Embankment Place, LONDON, WC2N 6RH.

ATHERTON, Ms. Emma Jane, BSc ACA *1997;* Edelweiss, 1 Between The Walls, PEMBROKE HM06, BERMUDA.

ATHERTON, Mr. James Patrick, BSc ACA *1991;* Copperfield House, Curridge, THATCHAM, RG18 9DL.

ATHERTON, Miss. Jane, BSc ACA *2004;* 10 Greystead Road, South Wellfield, WHITLEY BAY, TYNE AND WEAR, NE25 9HL.

ATHERTON, Miss. Joanne, BSc ACA *2007;* 11 Blackburn Gardens, Palatine Road, MANCHESTER, M20 3YH.

ATHERTON, Mr. John Philip, BSc ACA *2002;* East of England Tourist Board, Dettingen House, Dettingen Way, BURY ST. EDMUNDS, SUFFOLK, IP33 3TU.

ATHERTON, Mr. Jonathan, BA ACA *1987;* 2 Lorrimore Close, MT ELIZA, VIC 3930, AUSTRALIA.

ATHERTON, Mr. Julian James, BA ACA *2004;* 28 Boundary Lane South, Cuddington, NORTHWICH, CHESHIRE, CW8 2PG.

ATHERTON, Dr. Kate, ACA *2011;* 41 Kingston Road, COVENTRY, CV5 6LP.

ATHERTON, Miss. Katherine Sally, BA ACA *1983;* 10 Woodcrest Road, PURLEY, CR8 4JB.

•ATHERTON, Mr. Michael Andrew, BA ACA *1993;* 2 Spofforth Hill, WETHERBY, WEST YORKSHIRE, LS22 6SE.

•ATHERTON, Mr. Michael Francis, BA ACA *1986;* Michael F. Atherton, 12 Hollies Close, Feniscowles, BLACKBURN, BB2 5AJ.

ATHERTON, Mr. Morgan Edward, BA ACA *1993;* Swarbourne Cottage, Newborough End, BURTON-ON-TRENT, STAFFORDSHIRE, DE13 8SR.

ATHERTON, Mr. Neil Gordon, BA FCA *1989;* The Millstone, 45 Mill Road, Sharnbrook, BEDFORD, MK44 1NX.

ATHERTON, Mr. Paul Richard, BSc ACA *1989;* Quennevais House, La Route Orange, St. Brelade, JERSEY, JE3 8GP.

•ATHERTON, Mr. Philip Andrew, BA ACA *1984;* Chaytor Steele & Co, 9a Derby Street, ORMSKIRK, L39 2BJ.

ATHERTON, Mr. Richard John, FCA *1977;* Little Meadows, Ashford Hill Road, Headley, THATCHAM, RG19 8AL.

ATHERTON, Miss. Sarah Elizabeth, BA ACA *1997;* Cadbury Kenya Ltd, Ol Kalou Road, P.O. Box 45466, 00100, NAIROBI, KENYA.

ATHERTON, Mr. Thomas Alexander, BSocSc ACA *1996;* Dairy Crest Ltd, Claygate House, Littleworth Road, ESHER, SURREY, KT10 9PN.

ATHEY, Mr. Martin John, ACA *2004;* 10 Laburnum Grove, Gomersal, CLECKHEATON, WEST YORKSHIRE, BD19 4SQ.

•ATHINODOROU, Mr. Andreas, BSc FCA *1994;* Athinodorou & Zevedeou Ltd, Elia House, 77 Limassol Avenue, 2121 NICOSIA, CYPRUS.

ATIQ, Mr. Zeeshan, ACA *2008;* 4BFirst Central Lane, Phase 2, Dha Karachi, KARACHI 75500, SINDH, PAKISTAN.

ATKAR, Mr. Amarjit Singh, BA FCA *1980;* Birchgrove, 50 Fulmer Drive, GERRARDS CROSS, SL9 7HL.

ATKIN, Mr. Andrew Neil, BSc FCA *1998;* SMEC Holdings Ltd, Level 5, 71 Queens Road, MELBOURNE, VIC 3004, AUSTRALIA.

•ATKIN, Miss. Catherine Elizabeth, LLB ACA *1980;* (Tax Fac), Atkin & Co, 75 The Chase, Clapham, LONDON, SW4 0NR.

ATKIN, Mr. Christopher David, BA ACA *1999;* 21 Blondin Avenue, LONDON, W5 4UL.

ATKIN, Mr. Colin, FCA *1965;* 18 Bull Pasture, South Cave, BROUGH, NORTH HUMBERSIDE, HU15 2HT. (Life Member)

ATKIN, Mr. David Gerard, FCA *1965;* 39 Chemin Des Caves, F30340 ST PRIVAT DES VIEUX, FRANCE.

ATKIN, Miss. Elizabeth Katherine, BSc ACA *2004;* 8 Whitchurch Road, FLEET, HAMPSHIRE, GU51 1ED.

•ATKIN, Mr. Graham, FCA *1980;* Crane & Partners, Leonard House, 5-7 Newman Road, BROMLEY, BR1 1RJ. See also Armada Computer Accounting Ltd

ATKIN, Mr. John Dudley, BSc FCA *1989;* Brookside Cottage, Marston St. Lawrence, BANBURY, OXFORDSHIRE, OX17 2DA.

ATKIN, Mr. John Duncan, BSc FCA *1977;* 20 Hallside Park, KNUTSFORD, CHESHIRE, WA16 8NQ.

ATKIN, Mrs. Miriam Therese, BA ACA *1991;* Discovery House, Serco Group Plc Form Two, 18 Bartley Wood Business Park Bartley Way, HOOK, RG27 9XA.

•ATKIN, Mr. Neil Warren, BA FCA *1992;* Foster & Co Ltd, 80 Lytham Road, Fulwood, PRESTON, PR2 3AQ.

ATKIN, Mr. Paul Christopher, BA FCA *1986;* 1 Sketchley Hall Gardens, Burbage, HINCKLEY, LE10 3JP.

ATKIN, Mr. Robert Victor, BSc ACA *2004;* Apartment, Flat 36, 7 Merchants Court, BINGLEY, BD16 1DL.

ATKIN, Mrs. Sarah Jane, BA ACA *1997;* 13 Edward Road, West Bridgford, NOTTINGHAM, NG2 5GE.

ATKIN, Mr. Stephen Edward, FCA FRSA *1981;* 70 Sea Lane, East Preston, LITTLEHAMPTON, WEST SUSSEX, BN16 1ND.

ATKINS, Mrs. Alison Rachel, BSc ACA *2001;* 7 Normandy Road, Wroughton, SWINDON, SN4 0UJ.

ATKINS, Mrs. Amanda Jane, BA ACA *1983;* 17 Telfords Yard, LONDON, E1W 2BQ.

•ATKINS, Mr. Andrew James, FCA *1987;* Crompton & Co Financial Solutions Ltd, 42 Queens Road, COVENTRY, CV1 3DX.

ATKINS, Mr. Andrew John, FCA *1969;* 199 Norsey Road, BILLERICAY, CM11 1BZ.

•ATKINS, Mr. Andrew Robert, BA FCA *1997;* Bulley Davey, 1-4 London Road, SPALDING, LINCOLNSHIRE, PE11 2TA. See also Bulley Davey & Co

•ATKINS, Mr. Bernard, FCA ATII *1965;* Bernard Atkins Limited, Eight Bells House, 14 Church Street, TETBURY, GLOUCESTERSHIRE, GL8 8JG.

ATKINS, Mr. Christoph Paul, ACA *2007;* 58 Providence Square, LONDON, SE1 2EB.

ATKINS, Mr. Christopher Paul, BA(Hons) ACA *2009;* Flat 54 Bramber House, Royal Quarter Seven Kings Way, KINGSTON UPON THAMES, KT2 5BU.

ATKINS, Mr. Christopher Roy, ACA *1978;* Yew House, Barnet Wood Road, BROMLEY, KENT, BR2 8HJ.

ATKINS, Miss. Clare Rebecca, BSc(Hons) ACA *2009;* with PricewaterhouseCoopers, Private Bag 92162, AUCKLAND 1142, NEW ZEALAND.

ATKINS, Mr. Darren John, BA ACA *1996;* 67 Henley Road, IPSWICH, IP1 3SW.

ATKINS, Mr. David Edmund, BSc(Econ) FCA *1967;* 10 Broxbournebury Mews, BROXBOURNE, HERTFORDSHIRE, EN10 7JA. (Life Member)

•ATKINS, Ms. Deborah, ACA *2004;* (Tax Fac), Atkins Accountancy Services Limited, 15 Yarbury Way, WESTON-SUPER-MARE, AVON, BS24 7EP.

ATKINS, Mr. Eric James George, FCA *1955;* 198 Chislehurst Road, Petts Wood, ORPINGTON, BR5 1NR. (Life Member)

ATKINS, Mrs. Frances Joan, BA ACA *1991;* 18 Mill Gardens, Powmill, DOLLAR, CLACKMANNANSHIRE, FK14 7LQ.

ATKINS, Mr. Graham Nigel, BA ACA *1984;* 28 Prospect Road, Kibworth Beauchamp, LEICESTER, LE8 0HX.

•ATKINS, Mr. Graham Paul, BSc FCA *1989;* Deloitte LLP, Abbots House, Abbey Street, READING, RG1 3BD. See also Deloitte & Touche LLP

•ATKINS, Mr. Howard Timothy, FCA *1968;* Howard Atkins Limited, 49 The Drive, RICKMANSWORTH, WD3 4EA. See also Howard Atkins Partnership

•ATKINS, Mr. Ian Clark, BA FCA *1981;* (Tax Fac), Holborn Accountancy Tuition Limited, 12 Cock Lane, LONDON, EC1A 9BU.

ATKINS, Mr. James Edward Julian, MA ACA *1993;* Vertis Environmental Finance, Alkotas U 39/C, 1123 BUDAPEST, HUNGARY.

ATKINS, Mrs. Jennifer Lisa, LLB ACA *2009;* 74 Dacre Road, HITCHIN, HERTFORDSHIRE, SG5 1QL.

ATKINS, Mr. Jonathan Lloyd, ACA *1992;* Adams House, 54 Trinity Street, HALSTEAD, CO9 1GB.

ATKINS, Mr. Julian Cedric Clive, BA FCA *1976;* Interserve Project Services Lt, 395 George Road, Erdington, BIRMINGHAM, B23 7RZ.

ATKINS, Mr. Keith William, BSc(Econ) FCA *1975;* 36 Shenley Avenue, Woodsetton, DUDLEY, DY1 4LR. (Life Member)

ATKINS, Mr. Kevin Francis, BA ACA *1994;* Gate House Farm House, Eastbourne Road, Newchapel, LINGFIELD, RH7 6LF.

ATKINS, Mrs. Louise, BSc ACA *2003;* 167 Somerset Avenue, Yate, BRISTOL, BS37 7SL.

ATKINS, Mr. Mark Houghton Roger, BA ACA *1990;* 16a Cadogan Square, LONDON, SW1X 0JU.

•①ATKINS, Mr. Martin John, FCA ATII FABRP *1993;* Harris Lipman LLP, 2 Mountview Court, 310 Friern Barnet Lane, LONDON, N20 0YZ.

ATKINS, Mr. Michael, FCA *1974;* Chy-an-Vre, Gwealhellis Warren, HELSTON, CORNWALL, TR13 8PQ.

ATKINS, Mr. Michael Kent, FCA *1963;* Wallop Brook Lodge, Heathman Street, Nether Wallop, STOCKBRIDGE, HAMPSHIRE, SO20 8EW.

ATKINS, Mr. Michael Nigel, BSc FCA FCMA *1972;* 16 Waterloo Road, Bidford-on-Avon, ALCESTER, B50 4DL.

•ATKINS, Mr. Morgwn Duncan, BA ACA *2002;* Morgwn Atkins Limited, Eight Bells House, 14 Church Street, TETBURY, GLOUCESTERSHIRE, GL8 8JG.

ATKINS, Mr. Philip Lawrence, LLB FCA *1989;* Alte Schulstrasse 4, 21521 AUMUEHLE, GERMANY.

ATKINS, Mr. Richard, BSc(Hons) ACA AMCT *2002;* 33 Club Street #03-11 Emerald Garden, SINGAPORE 069415, SINGAPORE.

ATKINS, Mr. Richard Charles, BA FCA *1976;* 7 The Quillott, Burwood Park, WALTON-ON-THAMES, KT12 5BY.

•ATKINS, Mr. Richard Farquhar, FCA *1962;* (Tax Fac), Eric Nabarro & Co, 4th Floor, Erico House, 93-99 Upper Richmond Road, LONDON, SW15 2TG. See also Nabarro

•ATKINS, Mr. Robin Vaughan, FCA *1967;* Robin Atkins Limited, 7 Lindley Gardens, ALRESFORD, SO24 9PU.

ATKINS, Mr. Rowan Rhodri Andrew, ACA *2009;* 149 Priests Lane, Shenfield, BRENTWOOD, CM15 8HS.

•ATKINS, Mr. Simon, BSc FCA *2001;* Clement Keys, 39/40 Calthorpe Road, Edgbaston, BIRMINGHAM, B15 1TS. See also Professional Link Limited

ATKINS, Mrs. Stephanie Louise, BA(Hons) ACA *2001;* (Tax Fac), Burberry Limited, Horseferry House, Horseferry Road, LONDON, SW1P 2AW.

ATKINS, Mr. Stuart, BSc ACA *1997;* Welcome Foods, Brookside Way, Huthwaite, SUTTON-IN-ASHFIELD, NOTTINGHAMSHIRE, NG17 2NL.

•ATKINS, Mrs. Susan Jane, ACA *1986;* (Tax Fac), Susan Atkins, Yew House, Barnet Wood Road, BROMLEY, BR2 8HJ.

ATKINS, Mrs. Susan Mary, BSc FCA ACA *1984;* En Bajon, 32300 IDRAC RESPAILLES, FRANCE.

ATKINS, Mr. Thomas William, BA ACA *2002;* with PricewaterhouseCoopers LLP, First Point, Buckingham Gate, London Gatwick Airport, GATWICK, WEST SUSSEX RH6 0NT.

ATKINS, Mr. William Giles, MA FCA *1965;* Brambly, Clunie, BLAIRGOWRIE, PERTHSHIRE, PH10 6RG.

ATKINSON, Mr. Alan Keith, FCA *1965;* 6 Deacons Way, HITCHIN, HERTFORDSHIRE, SG5 2UF. (Life Member)

ATKINSON, Mr. Alexander Bruce, MA ACA *2007;* 409 Ditchling Road, BRIGHTON, BN1 6XB.

ATKINSON, Ms. Ann, BA ACA *1998;* 37 Chester Terrace, BRIGHTON, BN1 6GB.

ATKINSON, Mr. Anthony, FCA *1972;* 37 Randall Road, Chandler's Ford, EASTLEIGH, SO53 5AJ. (Life Member)

ATKINSON, Mr. Anthony, JP MA(Cantab) ACA *1981;* 2 Washingwell Park, Whickham, NEWCASTLE UPON TYNE, NE16 4QW.

ATKINSON, Miss. Birgitta Alexandra, MSc BEng ACA *1998;* with Deloitte LLP, Athene Place, 66 Shoe Lane, LONDON, EC4A 3BQ.

ATKINSON, Mr. Brian Francis, BSc FCA *1970;* 3 Links Road, EPSOM, SURREY, KT17 3PP. (Life Member)

ATKINSON, Miss. Caroline Mary, BA(Hons) ACA *2003;* 9 St. Christophers Walk, WAKEFIELD, WEST YORKSHIRE, WF1 2UP.

ATKINSON, Mrs. Caroline Zoe, BSc ACA *2005;* 20 Hazel Court, BROUGH, NORTH HUMBERSIDE, HU15 1TS.

•ATKINSON, Mrs. Carolyn, FCA *1990;* Sheards Accountancy Limited, Vernon House, 40 New North Road, HUDDERSFIELD, HD1 5LS. See also Sheards

ATKINSON, Miss. Catherine Elizabeth, BSc ACA *1995;* P O Box 380, KANGAROO GROUND, VIC 3097, AUSTRALIA.

ATKINSON, Mr. Charles Martin, MA FCA *1984;* 19 Southwood Avenue, LONDON, N6 5SA.

ATKINSON, Ms. Charlotte Sarah, MA BSc ACA *2003;* 12301 Mika Lane, BOWIE, MD 20715-2945, UNITED STATES.

•ATKINSON, Mr. Christopher John, BSc FCA *1992;* Simpson Wreford & Partners, Suffolk House, George Street, CROYDON, CR0 0YN.

ATKINSON, Mr. Clive, BA ACA *1990;* 74 Popes Grove, Strawberry Hill, TWICKENHAM, TW1 4JX.

ATKINSON, Mr. Daniel Edward, BA ACA *1997;* 4 The Coppice, Rothwell Road, HALIFAX, WEST YORKSHIRE, HX1 2HF.

•ATKINSON, Mr. David Blythe, FCA *1971;* David Atkinson LLP, 25 Harley Street, LONDON, W1G 9BR. See also Gerald Edelman Transaction Services Ltd

ATKINSON, Mr. David Charles, ACA *1978;* 37 Pheasant Walk, Littlemore, OXFORD, OX4 4XX.

ATKINSON, Mr. David Eric, BSc ACA *1979;* Cotteswold House, Market Place, Northleach, CHELTENHAM, GLOUCESTERSHIRE, GL54 3EG.

ATKINSON, Mr. David Ian, FCA *1963;* 14 Oaklands Avenue, Tattenhall, CHESTER, CH3 9QU. (Life Member)

ATKINSON, Mr. David John, BA ACA *1994;* 68/F Cheung Kong Center, 2 Queens Road, CENTRAL, HONG KONG ISLAND, HONG KONG SAR.

ATKINSON, Mr. David Michael, FCA *1958;* Brambles, Winterpit Lane, Mannings Heath, HORSHAM, RH13 6LZ. (Life Member)

•ATKINSON, Mr. David Nigel, ACA *1983;* Atkinsons, The Red House, 10 Market Square, AMERSHAM, HP7 0DQ.

ATKINSON, Mr. David Rowland, FCA *1957;* Russetts, 124 The Ridings, Rothley, LEICESTER, LE7 7SL. (Life Member)

ATKINSON, Mr. David Steven, FCA *1982;* Link Building Products, P O Box 2616, BLANTYRE, MALAWI.

ATKINSON, Miss. Dawn, BA ACA *2005;* Flat 4, 11 Portland Street, YORK, YO31 7EH.

ATKINSON, Mr. Derek George Lawrence, BSc ACA *2004;* 119 Kensington Road, PORTSMOUTH, PO2 0QD.

•ATKINSON, Mr. Edward Joseph, BA ACA *1994;* Johnston Carmichael, Bishops Court, 29 Albyn Place, ABERDEEN, AB10 1YL.

•ATKINSON, Mr. Edward Peter, BA FCA *1992;* Jackson Stephen LLP, James House, Stonecross Business Park, 5 Yew Tree Way, Golborne, WARRINGTON CHESHIRE WA3 3JD. See also JS Outsource Solutions Limited

ATKINSON, Mr. Ernest Norman, FCA *1950;* Flat 6, Mayfield Court, Broad Oak, HEATHFIELD, EAST SUSSEX, TN21 8SW. (Life Member)

•ATKINSON, Mr. Francis, BA FCA *1977;* Alexander & Co, 17 St Ann's Square, MANCHESTER, M2 7PW.

•ATKINSON, Mr. Gareth, BA ACA *2007;* Atkinson Accountancy Limited, 137 Manor Road North, SOUTHAMPTON, SO19 2DX.

ATKINSON, Mr. Geoffrey Dayot, MA FCA *1959;* Greylands, Rue Des Grons, St. Martin, GUERNSEY, GY4 6JP. (Life Member)

•ATKINSON, Mr. Geoffrey Robert, BA FCA *1972;* Purcross, Wayford, CREWKERNE, SOMERSET, TA18 8QL.

ATKINSON, Mr. Gerald, FCA *1961;* Leathley Cottage, Leathley Lane, Leathley, OTLEY, WEST YORKSHIRE, LS21 2JY.

ATKINSON, Mrs. Gillian, BSc ACA *1986;* 31 Burgess Wood Road South, BEACONSFIELD, BUCKINGHAMSHIRE, HP9 1EL.

•ATKINSON, Miss. Gillian Heather, FCA *1983;* (Tax Fac), M D Coxey & Co Limited, 25 Grosvenor Road, WREXHAM, CLWYD, LL11 1BT.

ATKINSON, Mr. Gordon Smith, FCA *1966;* C/ La Guardia 151, Costa Nova, Javea, 03730 ALICANTE, SPAIN. (Life Member)

ATKINSON, Mr. Graham Andrew, MA MEng ACA *1997;* Flat 7, 5 Onslow Square, LONDON, SW7 3NJ.

•ATKINSON, Mr. Graham David, BA FCA *1992;* Walter Dawson & Son, 7 Wellington Road East, DEWSBURY, WF13 1HF.

ATKINSON, Mr. Guy Thomas, MA ACA *1995;* No 04-02, 27 Stevens Drive, SINGAPORE 257919, SINGAPORE.

ATKINSON, Mr. Henry John, MA FCA *1962;* Piet Heinstraat 1, 2041 HH ZANDVOORT, NETHERLANDS. (Life Member)

ATKINSON, Mr. Ian, BSc ACA *1988;* 60 Upton Grange, CHESTER, CH2 1BF.

ATKINSON, Mr. Ian Philip, BSc FCA *1978;* Orchard End, Barnfield Manor Lodge Lane, Singleton, POULTON-LE-FYLDE, FY6 8LJ.

ATKINSON, Mr. James Matthew, BA ACA *2010;* Pricewaterhousecoopers, 33 Wellington Street, LEEDS, LS1 4JP.

ATKINSON, Mr. James Richard, BSc ACA *1995;* The Coach House, Cleobury North, BRIDGNORTH, SHROPSHIRE, WV16 6RW.

ATKINSON, Mr. James Stuart, FCA *1964;* 1 Sedber Lane, Grassington, SKIPTON, BD23 5LQ. (Life Member)

ATKINSON, Mr. James Wilson, FCA *1971;* 12 Bewdley Close, HARPENDEN, AL5 1QX.

•ATKINSON, Mr. Jeffrey Eden, BSc FCA *1995;* Afford Bond LLP, 31 Wellington Road, NANTWICH, CHESHIRE, CW5 7ED. See also Afford Astbury Bond LLP

ATKINSON, Mr. John, FCA *1958;* 44 Blackwell, DARLINGTON, DL3 8QT. (Life Member)

•ATKINSON, Mr. John, FCA *1973;* Atkinsons (Bishopstone) Ltd, The Old Chapel, Chapel Lane, Bishopstone, SALISBURY, SP5 4BT.

ATKINSON, Mr. John Alexander, FCA *1970;* Ribby Hall Village Ribby Road, Wrea Green, PRESTON, PR4 2PR.

ATKINSON, Mr. John Anthony, FCA *1954;* 11 Westbourne Grove, DARLINGTON, DL3 8LS. (Life Member)

ATKINSON, The Revd Canon John Dudley, FCA *1960;* 48 Prince Rupert Road, LEDBURY, HEREFORDSHIRE, HR8 2FA. (Life Member)

•**ATKINSON, Mr. John Spencer, BA FCA** *1974;* (Tax Fac), Accord Tax and Accountancy Ltd, 16a Bon Accord Square, ABERDEEN, AB11 6DJ. See also Optima Tax and Accountancy Ltd

•**ATKINSON, Mr. John William, FCA** *1981;* (Tax Fac), J W Atkinson Ltd, First Floor, Gloucester House, Clarence Court, Rushmore Hill, ORPINGTON KENT BR6 7LZ.

ATKINSON, Mr. John Wilson, FCA *1960;* 8305 Chinaberry Road, INDIAN RIVER SHORES, FL 32963-4202, UNITED STATES. (Life Member)

ATKINSON, Mr. Joseph Beaumont, FCA *1970;* 8 Wolds End Close, CHIPPING CAMPDEN, GLOUCESTERSHIRE, GL55 6JW.

ATKINSON, Miss. Karen Jane, BSc FCA *1997;* Top Floor Flat, 27 Moring Road, LONDON, SW17 8DN.

ATKINSON, Ms. Karen Jane, BA ACA DChA *1995;* 4th Floor, Great Ormond Street Hospital Childrens Charity, 40 Bernard Street, LONDON, WC1N 1LE.

ATKINSON, Mrs. Karen Lesley, BA FCA ATII *1991;* 38 Valley Road, WELWYN GARDEN CITY, HERTFORDSHIRE, AL8 7DN.

ATKINSON, Miss. Karina, MMath ACA *2004;* with PricewaterhouseCoopers LLP, 89 Sandyford Road, NEWCASTLE UPON TYNE, NE1 8HW.

ATKINSON, Mrs. Katherine Margaret, BSc FCA *1996;* Southern Cross Health Care Southgate House, Archer Street, DARLINGTON, COUNTY DURHAM, DL3 6AH.

ATKINSON, Mr. Keith, FCA *1971;* 2 Willow Park, Barnoldby-le-Beck, GRIMSBY, DN37 0YP.

ATKINSON, Mr. Keith Andrew, BA FCA *1987;* Metnor Group Plc Metnor House, Mylord Crescent, NEWCASTLE UPON TYNE, NE12 5YD.

ATKINSON, Mr. Kevin Matthew, BSc FCA *1977;* El Rodeo Interior 1833, Lo Barnechea, SANTIAGO, CHILE.

ATKINSON, Mr. Lee Mark, BA ACA CF *1997;* 102 Kirby Drive, Bramley, TADLEY, HAMPSHIRE, RG26 5FN.

ATKINSON, Miss. Mandy Elizabeth, BSc ACA *1994;* 6 Rectory Court, Kirk Smeaton, PONTEFRACT, WEST YORKSHIRE, WF8 3SP.

•**ATKINSON, Mrs. Margaret Dorothy Forrest, FCA** *1972;* Atkinsons, 32 Hiltingbury Road, EASTLEIGH, SO53 5SS.

•**ATKINSON, Mrs. Margaret Joan, FCA** *1975;* MJ Accountants, 43 Gloucester Road, WALSALL, WS5 3PL.

ATKINSON, Mr. Mark Roger, MMath ACA *2005;* 67 Westfield Road, Caversham, READING, RG4 8HL.

ATKINSON, Mr. Martin, MEng ACA CTA *2004;* 8 Ullswater Road, LONDON, SW13 9PJ.

•**ATKINSON, Mr. Martyn Stuart, BA FCA** *1991;* with Sopher + Co, 5 Elstree Gate, Elstree Way, BOREHAMWOOD, WD6 1JD.

ATKINSON, Mr. Matthew John, ACA *2008;* National Audit Office, 157-197 Buckingham Palace Road, LONDON, SW1W 9SP.

•**ATKINSON, Mrs. Melinda Nicola Patricia Amanda, LLB FCA** *1986;* Lucentum Limited, Kensal House, 77 Springfield Road, CHELMSFORD, CM2 6JG.

•**ATKINSON, Mr. Michael, FCA** *1975;* 143 Harecroft, Wilsden, BRADFORD, BD15 0BP.

ATKINSON, Mr. Michael, BA(Hons) ACA *2002;* 2 Fergus Road, LONDON, N5 1JS.

•**ATKINSON, Mr. Michael, FCA** *1974;* Wright & Co Partnership Ltd, 9 Stafford Street, Brewood, STAFFORD, ST19 9DX.

ATKINSON, Mr. Michael, ACA *2010;* Flat G Floor 55, Tower 6 Grand Promenade, 38 Tai Hong Street, SAI WAN HO, HONG KONG ISLAND, HONG KONG SAR.

ATKINSON, Mr. Michael Adrian, FCA *1970;* Higher Barn, Higher Rocombe, Stokeinteignhead, NEWTON ABBOT, TQ12 4QL.

ATKINSON, Mr. Michael Norman, BA FCA *1970;* Ash Brow, Caraway Close, ULVERSTON, LA12 9NF.

ATKINSON, Mr. Michael Simon, BA ACA *1991;* Ballkeirn, Port Soderick, Douglas, ISLE OF MAN, IM4 1AY.

ATKINSON, Mrs. Natalie, BSc ACA *1996;* Begonialaan 21, 3080 TERVUREN, BELGIUM.

ATKINSON, Mr. Neil, BA ACA *1997;* Grenaby, Balla Collister Lane, Fairy Cottage, Laxey, ISLE OF MAN, IM4 7JP.

•**ATKINSON, Mr. Nicholas Alexander, BA ACA** *1995;* PricewaterhouseCoopers LLP, 7 More London Riverside, LONDON, SE1 2RT. See also PricewaterhouseCoopers

ATKINSON, Mrs. Nicola Jane, BSc ACA *2004;* 42 Bennerley Road, LONDON, SW11 6DS.

ATKINSON, Mr. Nigel, FCA *1968;* Cowden House, Grately Road, Cholderton, SALISBURY, SP4 0DJ. (Life Member)

•①**ATKINSON, Mr. Nigel Geoffrey, BSc FCA CF MSTP** *1977;* Begbies Traynor, 32 Cornhill, LONDON, EC3V 3BT. See also Begbies Traynor(Central) LLP and Begbies Traynor Limited

•**ATKINSON, Mr. Nigel Peter, BA FCA** *1989;* (Tax Fac), Hunter Gee Holroyd, Club Chambers, Museum Street, YORK, YO1 7DN. See also Hunter Gee Holroyd Limited

ATKINSON, Mr. Oliver, BSc ACA *2006;* 409 Ditchling Road, BRIGHTON, BN1 6XB.

ATKINSON, Mr. Patrick John, MA ACA CF *1998;* Torre PwC, Paseo de la Castellana 259B, 28046 MADRID, SPAIN.

•**ATKINSON, Mr. Paul, FCA** *1991;* Atkinson Accounts, The Grange, 1 Hoole Road, CHESTER, CH2 3NQ. See also Atkinson & Co

ATKINSON, Mr. Paul Alan, BSc ACA *1985;* (Tax Fac), Lima, Milverton, SKERRIES, COUNTY DUBLIN, IRELAND.

ATKINSON, Mr. Paul Anthony, BA ACA *1992;* Knowle Top, Pendleton, CLITHEROE, BB7 1PU.

ATKINSON, Mr. Paul David Hugh, BA ACA *2002;* ADT Fire & Security Plc, Security House, The Summit, Hanworth Road, SUNBURY-ON-THAMES, TW16 5DB.

ATKINSON, Mr. Paul Robert, BSc FCA *1986;* 4 Victoria Road, SIDCUP, DA15 7HD.

ATKINSON, Mr. Paul Russell, FCA *1973;* Ctra. Villaverde a Vallecas 265, Edif. Hormigueras 1° izda, 28031 MADRID, SPAIN, 28031 MADRID SPAIN.

ATKINSON, Mr. Peter, ACA *2008;* 63 Brampton Gardens, GATESHEAD, TYNE AND WEAR, NE9 6PT.

ATKINSON, Mr. Peter, MChem ACA *2007;* 16 Corinthian Avenue, LIVERPOOL, L13 3DP.

•**ATKINSON, Mr. Peter Graham, FCA** *1975;* (Tax Fac), Atkinsons Consulting Limited, Innovation Centre, University Road, Heslington, YORK, YO10 5DG. See also Finance Mix LLP

ATKINSON, Mr. Peter Miles, MSc ACA *1979;* 7-2369 Ontario St., OAKVILLE L6L 1A6, ON, CANADA.

•**ATKINSON, Mr. Peter Richard, FCA** *1971;* Atkinsons, 32 Hiltingbury Road, EASTLEIGH, SO53 5SS.

ATKINSON, Mr. Philip John, BA ACA *1994;* 750 5A Street NW, CALGARY T2N 1R4, AB, CANADA.

ATKINSON, Mr. Philip Roger, BA FCA *1991;* BDO, 10th & 11th Floors GBCORP Tower, Bahrain Financial Harbour, PO Box 787, MANAMA, BAHRAIN.

ATKINSON, Mr. Raymond Fraser, BSc ACA *1989;* 3 Shorehill Court, Kemsing, SEVENOAKS, TN15 6BF.

ATKINSON, Mrs. Rebecca, BSc ACA *1992;* 8 Thurleigh Road, LONDON, SW12 8UG.

ATKINSON, Mr. Richard Duncan, BSc ACA *1990;* (Tax Fac), 61 Weybridge Street, SURREY HILLS, VIC 3127, AUSTRALIA.

•**ATKINSON, Mr. Richard John, BA ACA** *1999;* Waterton Park Accountancy, Holly Cottage, Brockswood Court, Walton, WAKEFIELD, WEST YORKSHIRE WF2 6RU.

•**ATKINSON, Mr. Richard Mark, ACA** *1983;* Atkinson Saul Fairholm Limited, 21a Newland, LINCOLN, LN1 1XP.

•**ATKINSON, Mr. Robert Bruce, FCA** *1962;* (Tax Fac), Atkinsons, Palmeira Avenue Mansions, 19 Church Road, HOVE, BN3 2FA.

ATKINSON, Mr. Robert Michael James, BA FCA *1978;* 31A Cherry Crest, 3 Kui in Fong, MID LEVELS, HONG KONG ISLAND, HONG KONG SAR.

ATKINSON, Mr. Robin Keith, FCA *1964;* The Willows, 20 Green Drive, CLITHEROE, BB7 2BB.

ATKINSON, Mr. Roy Wilfred, FCA *1961;* 14 Knights End Road, Great Bowden, MARKET HARBOROUGH, LE16 7EY. (Life Member)

ATKINSON, Miss. Sarah Elizabeth, BSc FCA *1984;* 13 Milverton Drive, Bramhall, STOCKPORT, SK7 1EY.

ATKINSON, Mr. Simon, ACA *2002;* 40 Beech Road, Hale, ALTRINCHAM, CHESHIRE, WA15 9HX.

ATKINSON, Mr. Simon Andrew, MA FCA *1981;* 81 Lonsdale Road, Barnes, LONDON, SW13 9DA.

ATKINSON, Mr. Simon James, BSc ACA *1993;* Ashen Grove Cottage, Steventon, BASINGSTOKE, RG25 3BL.

ATKINSON, Miss. Sophie Elizabeth Sinton, BSc ACA *1997;* 15 Crondace Road, LONDON, SW6 4BB.

ATKINSON, Mr. Steven, BA FCA *1977;* Lindisfarne, West Road, Bowdon, ALTRINCHAM, WA14 2JS.

•**ATKINSON, Mr. Stuart Arnold, FCA** *1965;* Atkinsons (Hull) Ltd, 60 Commercial Road, HULL, HU1 2SG.

ATKINSON, Mr. Stuart David, BA ACA *2000;* with Royal Bank of Scotland, 135 Bishopsgate, LONDON, EC2M 3TP.

ATKINSON, Mr. Stuart James, BSc ACA *1994;* 8 Thurleigh Road, LONDON, SW12 8UG.

•**ATKINSON, Mr. Thomas Andrew, FCA** *1982;* (Tax Fac), Wm Fortune & Son, Collingwood House, Church Square, HARTLEPOOL, TS24 7EN.

•**ATKINSON, Mrs. Victoria Jane, BA FCA** *1996;* Riley & Co Limited, 52 St.Johns Lane, HALIFAX, HX1 2BW.

ATKINSON, Mr. Walter John, BCom FCA *1958;* 237 Chapel Lane, New Longton, PRESTON, PR4 4AD. (Life Member)

ATKINSON, Mr. William Silver, FCA *1961;* 1 Eton College Road, LONDON, NW3 2BS.

ATTAR, Mr. Raphael, FCA *1966;* Corso di Porta Romana 46, 20122 MILAN, ITALY.

ATTAR-ZADEH, Mr. Reza, BSc ACA *1999;* 5 Sherborne Place, NORTHWOOD, MIDDLESEX, HA6 2BH.

ATTAVAR, Mrs. Nita Dayananda, BSc ACA *1996;* 4 Hollybush Lane, AMERSHAM, BUCKINGHAMSHIRE, HP6 6EB.

•**ATTAWAR, Mr. Krishan Chand, BSc(Hons) FCA** *1984;* Indus Gold Limited, 17 Belmont Close, MAIDSTONE, KENT, ME16 9DY.

ATTENBOROUGH, Miss. Katie Louise Christine, MSc BEng ACA *2010;* 7 Bradbury Gardens, Ruddington, NOTTINGHAM, NG11 6AX.

ATTENBOROUGH, Mr. Richard Edgar, FCA *1979;* Urb La Capellania, Calle Gredos 4, Benalmadena, 29639 MALAGA, SPAIN. (Life Member)

ATTER, Mr. Douglas John, FCA *1976;* Dairy Pipe lines Ltd, Unit 6 Ashdon Road Commercial Centre, SAFFRON WALDEN, ESSEX, CB10 2NH.

ATTERBURY, Mr. David Ashley, BSc ACA *1998;* Fairways, Coulsdon Lane, Chipstead, COULSDON, SURREY, CR5 3QG.

ATTERBURY, Mr. George Marriott, BSc FCA *1980;* Woodstock Elm, Little Chesterford, SAFFRON WALDEN, CB10 1TS.

ATTERBURY THOMAS, Mr. David, BSc FCA *1974;* 47 St. Johns Park, LONDON, SE3 7JW.

ATTESLIS, Mr. Alexis, ACA *2008;* 5 Tudor Close, LONDON, NW3 4AB.

ATTESLIS, Mr. Marios George, BA ACA *1995;* P.O.Box 51245, 3503 LIMASSOL, CYPRUS.

ATTEWELL, Mrs. Beverley Jane, BSc ACA *1995;* 6 Grange Close, WINCHESTER, SO23 9RS.

ATTEWELL, Mr. Leonard James, MA MBA ACA *1983;* 25 St. Johns Road, GUILDFORD, GU2 7UQ.

ATTFIELD, Mr. Andrew John, FCA *1974;* Caxton CottageAshford Road, Bethersden ASHFORD, Kent, TN26 3AP.

ATTFIELD, Mr. Dennis Vincent, FCA *1952;* 3 The Gardens, Evesham Road, Pittville, CHELTENHAM, GL50 4QE. (Life Member)

ATTFIELD, Mr. Julian Michael Stuart, BA ACA *1994;* 37 Hartington Grove, CAMBRIDGE, CAMBRIDGESHIRE, CB1 7UA.

ATTFIELD, Mr. Philip James, FCA *1951;* 26 Churchfield Road, WALTON-ON-THAMES, SURREY, KT12 2SY. (Life Member)

ATTIS, Mr. Martin Charles, BA ACA *1983;* Sundial House, Sundial Magazines, 17 Wickham Road, BECKENHAM, BR3 5JS.

•**ATTLE, Mr. Craig Edward, MA(Hons) ACA ACCA** *2003;* Numera Partners LLP, 6th Floor, Charles House, 108-110 Finchley Road, LONDON, NW3 5JJ.

ATTLEY, Mr. David John, BA ACA *1983;* Waterend House, 11 Dunstable Road, Redbourn, ST. ALBANS, HERTFORDSHIRE, AL3 7BE.

•**ATTREE, Mr. Alan Howard, FCA** *1960;* Howard Attree Smith & Co, 12 Park Court, Park Road, BURGESS HILL, RH15 8EY.

ATTREE, Mr. Peter Robert, FCA *1966;* 71 Shelldale Road, Portslade, BRIGHTON, BN41 1LE. (Life Member)

ATTREE, Mrs. Sophie Ellen Catherine, BA ACA *2001;* 16 Ridgmont Road, ST. ALBANS, HERTFORDSHIRE, AL1 3AF.

ATTREE, Mr. Thomas Glenn, BA(Hons) ACA *2002;* 16 Ridgmont Road, ST. ALBANS, HERTFORDSHIRE, AL1 3AF.

ATTRIDGE, Miss. Catherine, BA ACA *2007;* 51 Dover Street, NORWICH, NR2 3LG.

ATTRIDGE, Mrs. Lisa Karen, ACA *1993;* (Tax Fac), 33 Bloemfontein Avenue, LONDON, W12 7BJ.

ATTRIDGE, Miss. Samantha Kathleen, MSc BA ACA *2001;* 4 Pellatt Road, LONDON, SE22 9JA.

ATTRILL, Mr. Christopher Richard, BA FCA *1979;* 9 The Chines, Delamere Park Cuddington, NORTHWICH, CW8 2XA.

ATTRILL, Miss. Sally Lynne, ACA *2009;* Flat 4 Amberley House, Kennedy Road, HORSHAM, WEST SUSSEX, RH13 5TG.

ATTRYDE, Mrs. Sally Ann, BSc ACA *1996;* 18 St. Helena Road, Westbury Park, BRISTOL, BS6 7NR.

ATTWELL, Mr. Colin Frost, FCA *1956;* 34 Greenfield Avenue, Spinney Hill, NORTHAMPTON, NN3 2AF. (Life Member)

ATTWELL, Mr. David Charles, BSc ACA *1984;* Montagu Evans Llp, Clarges House, 6-12 Clarges Street, LONDON, W1J 8HB.

ATTWELL, Ms. Erica, BA ACA *2007;* Flat A-f, 24 Randolph Crescent, LONDON, W9 1DR.

ATTWELL, Mr. Simon John, FCA *1973;* 19 Hardcastle Gardens, BOLTON, BL2 4NZ.

ATTWELL, Mr. William Arthur, FCA *1968;* 3 Dunlin Rise, Fairways, Tytherington, MACCLESFIELD, CHESHIRE, SK10 2SP. (Life Member)

ATTWELL THOMAS, Mr. Christopher Paul, MA ACA *1988;* Dolgoy, Blaencelyn, LLANDYSUL, DYFED, SA44 6DF.

ATTWELL THOMAS, Mr. Kerry Mark, MA ACA MCT *1985;* 16 St. Martins Church Street, SALISBURY, SP1 2HY.

ATTWOOD, Mr. Anthony Richard, FCA *1971;* 96 Rue Principale, Rameldange, 6990 LUXEMBOURG, LUXEMBOURG.

ATTWOOD, Mr. Christopher, BA ACA AMCT *1999;* Flat 15 Thomas More House, Barbican, LONDON, EC2Y 8BT.

ATTWOOD, Mr. Christopher Raymond, FCA *1970;* Southwinds, 1 The Drive, Warwick Park, TUNBRIDGE WELLS, KENT, TN2 5ER.

•**ATTWOOD, Mr. David, BA ACA** *1980;* Attwood & Co, Harrison House, Marston Road, WOLVERHAMPTON, WV2 4NJ.

ATTWOOD, Mr. David, BSc ACA *2011;* Grant Thornton UK Llp, Kingfisher House, 1 Gilders Way, NORWICH, NR3 1UB.

ATTWOOD, Mr. David John George, MBA LLB ACA *2006;* NORMAWIND, Trav. de Gràcia 58 Entresuelo 3ª, 08006 BARCELONA, SPAIN.

•**ATTWOOD, Mr. Frank Albert, BSc FCA** *1968;* 21 Woodside Road, NEW MALDEN, KT3 3AW.

ATTWOOD, Mrs. Helen Suzanne, BSc ACA *2002;* 1 Linden Rise, Warley, BRENTWOOD, CM14 5UB.

ATTWOOD, Mr. James Robert, BA ACA *2004;* 1 Holmfield Close, Toddington, DUNSTABLE, BEDFORDSHIRE, LU5 6JA.

ATTWOOD, Mr. Jeremy, BSc ACA *1990;* Total Computer Networks Ltd Unit 1-2, Brooklands Court Kettering Venture Park, KETTERING, NORTHAMPTONSHIRE, NN15 6FD.

ATTWOOD, Miss. Joanne, ACA *2002;* 141 Farleigh Road, PERSHORE, WORCESTERSHIRE, WR10 1JX.

•**ATTWOOD, Mr. Martin Percival, ACA** *1982;* (Tax Fac), Attwoods, 12 Palfrey Close, ST. ALBANS, HERTFORDSHIRE, AL3 5RE.

ATTWOOD, Mr. Richard Steven, BA(Hons) ACA *2002;* 40 Brendon Avenue, East Kilbride, GLASGOW, G75 9GT.

ATTWOOD, Miss. Sally Louise, BSc ACA *2010;* 15 Aster Way, CAMBRIDGE, CB4 2DT.

ATTWOOD, Mr. William Antony, ACA *1982;* Kirschenstr. 33, 15566 SCHOENEICHE, GERMANY. (Life Member)

•**ATWAL, Mr. Harminder Singh, MSc BSc ACA** *2003;* with PricewaterhouseCoopers LLP, The Atrium, 1 Harefield Road, UXBRIDGE, UB8 1EX.

ATWELL, Miss. Elizabeth Anne Burnett, BSc ACA *2006;* Room 5E10, Department for International Development, 1 Palace Street, LONDON, SW1E 5HE.

ATWELL, Mr. George Edward Charles, BSc ACA *1987;* 5 Brackenwood, Naphill, HIGH WYCOMBE, HP14 4TD.

ATWELL, Mr. Gerald Rex, MA BSc FCA CTA *1981;* with Thompson Taraz LLP, 35 Grosvenor Street, Mayfair, LONDON, W1K 4QX.

ATWOOD, Mr. Paul Anthony, MA ACA *1981;* 62 Tulloh Street, Willoughby, SYDNEY, NSW 2068, AUSTRALIA.

ATWOOD, Mr. Robert Charles, FCA *1966;* Temple Grove Schools Trust Limited, Breakstones Speldhurst Road, Langton Green, TUNBRIDGE WELLS, TN3 0JL.

ATYEO, Mr. Henry Paul Bingham, MA FCA *1956;* Vine Cottage, Church Hanborough, Freeland, WITNEY, OX29 8AA. (Life Member)

AU, Mr. Alex Shiu Leung, BCom ACA *1990;* Flat 8A, 70 Sing Woo Road, HAPPY VALLEY, HONG KONG ISLAND, HONG KONG SAR.

AU, Mr. Alexander Siu Kee, ACA *2006;* No. 1 Po Shan Road, Tower 1, Flat 9b, MID LEVELS, HONG KONG ISLAND, HONG KONG SAR.

AU, Mr. Alvin Yiu Kwan, BA ACA *1992;* with Grant Thornton, 6th Floor, Nexus Building, 41 Conaught Road, CENTRAL, HONG KONG ISLAND HONG KONG SAR.

AU, Mr. Andrew, BSc ACA *2006;* 10 Yew Walk, HARROW, HA1 3EJ.

AU, Ms. Angela Yin-Chiu, MA ACA *1993;* 6 Perry Court Clerk Maxwell Road, CAMBRIDGE, CAMBRIDGESHIRE, CB3 0RS.

AU, Mr. Barry Wen Jie, ACA *2011;* 78 Weston Drive, STANMORE, MIDDLESEX, HA7 2EN.

AU, Miss. Caroline Ka Ling, BSc ACA *1990;* Block 137 Sunset Way #03-09, Clementi Park Condominium, SINGAPORE 597159, SINGAPORE.

AU, Mr. Daniel Sek Bong, BA ACA *1996;* 71D Sun Tower, The Arch, 1 Austin Road West, TSIM SHA TSUI, KOWLOON, HONG KONG SAR.
AU, Mr. David, BSc ACA *2002;* 5 The Old Works, Old London Road, ST. ALBANS, HERTFORDSHIRE, AL1 1QU.
AU, Miss. Fiona Siu Kwan, BSc(Econ) ACA *2001;* 92 Southover, Woodside Park, LONDON, N12 7HD.
AU, Mr. Jason, BA(Hons) ACA *2004;* PROPERTY ALLIANCE GROUP LTD, Alliance House, Westpoint Enterprise Park, Clarence Avenue, Trafford Park, MANCHESTER M17 1QS.
AU, Mr. Kien, BSc ACA *2000;* 22 Humphrys Street, PETERBOROUGH, PE2 9RH.
AU, Miss. Melanie, BSc ACA *2010;* 50 College Fields, Woodhead Drive, CAMBRIDGE, CB4 1YZ.
AU, Dr. Mo Ying Mary, ACA *2005;* 8B Shun On Building, 2 Sands Street, KENNEDY TOWN, HONG KONG ISLAND, HONG KONG SAR.
AU, Mr. Moon Ying Henry, ACA *2007;* GPO Box 3488, General Post Office, CENTRAL, HONG KONG ISLAND, HONG KONG SAR.
AU, Mr. Ngui Ming, MSc ACA *1987;* 128 Stainburn Crescent, LEEDS, LS17 6NG.
AU, Mr. Pui Lam, ACA *2005;* Ronald W.F. Ko & Co, 4th Floor Winbase Centre, 208 Queen's Road Central, CENTRAL, HONG KONG ISLAND, HONG KONG SAR.
AU, Mr. Quincy Hoe Kye, ACA *2005;* 1560 Caoyang Road, Putuo District, SHANGHAI 200333, CHINA.
AU, Mr. Steven Yu Chiu, MBA BA ACA *1987;* 7 Coronado Avenue, Royal Palms, YUEN LONG, NEW TERRITORIES, HONG KONG SAR.
AU, Mr. Tin Po, ACA *2008;* T P Au & Co, Units B-C, 15th Floor Sun House, 90 Connaught Road, CENTRAL, HONG KONG ISLAND HONG KONG SAR.
AU, Mr. Wai Keung, ACA *2008;* Unit A 15/F, Block 3, Sun Yuen Long Centre, YUEN LONG, NEW TERRITORIES, HONG KONG SAR.
•AU, Mr. Wilson Pui-Shing, BA ACA *1988;* Flat B 10th Floor, Tower 5 Hoi Ning Court, South Horizons, AP LEI CHAU, HONG KONG ISLAND, HONG KONG SAR.
AU, Mr. Yan Alfred, ACA *2007;* 24/F, Hang Wai Commercial Building, No 231-233, Queen's Road East, WAN CHAI, HONG KONG SAR.
AU, Mr. Yiu Wing, FCA *1972;* 110 Cassiobury Park Avenue, WATFORD, WD18 7LF. (Life Member)
AU-FERRIS, Mrs. Sokha Au, ACA *2001;* 9 Cawdor Burn Road, BROOKFIELD, CT 06804, UNITED STATES.
AU YEUNG, Mr. Chi Wai, ACA *2008;* Flat C, 13/F Hang King Garden, 9 Wing Fong Road, KWAI CHUNG, NEW TERRITORIES, HONG KONG SAR.
AU-YEUNG, Miss. Emily, ACA *2008;* Flat 20D Tower 1, Scenecliff, No.33 Conduit Road, MID LEVELS, HONG KONG ISLAND, HONG KONG SAR.
AU-YEUNG, Mr. Huen Ying, ACA *2006;* Au Yeung Huen Ying & Co, 8th Floor, Shum Tower, 268 Des Vouex Road, CENTRAL, HONG KONG ISLAND HONG KONG SAR.
AU YEUNG, Ms. Lai Sheung Lisa, ACA *2005;* Au Yeung & Au Yeung CPA Limited, Room C 18/F, Nathan Commericial Bldg, 430-436 Nathan Road, YAU MA TEI, KOWLOON HONG KONG SAR.
AU-YEUNG, Miss. Marianna Man-Chong, BSc ACA *2004;* Flat 61, Merganser Court, Star Place, LONDON, E1W 1AQ.
AU YEUNG, Mr. Po Fung, ACA *2005;* Flat F 36/F Two Robinson Place, 70 Robinson Road, MID LEVELS, HONG KONG ISLAND, HONG KONG SAR.
AU-YEUNG, Miss. Pui Yiu, BA ACA *2002;* B G L Group Pegasus House Southgate Park, Bakewell Road Orton Southgate, PETERBOROUGH, PE2 6YS.
AU YEUNG, Mr. Shiu Kuen Steve, ACA *2005;* Steve Au Yeung & Co, Room 1901 19/F, Ka Nin Wah Commercial Building, 423-425 Hennessy Road, CAUSEWAY BAY, HONG KONG ISLAND HONG KONG SAR.
AU YEUNG, Ms. Sin Ming Cindy, ACA *2008;* Pegasus & Co, 7/F Chuang's Enterprises Building, 382 Lockhart Road, WAN CHAI, HONG KONG SAR.
AU YEUNG, Ms. Wing Sze, ACA *2005;* FLAT 1905 BLOCK 46 HENG FA CHUEN, CHAI WAN, HONG KONG SAR.
AU YONG SU LIN, Miss. Christine, BSc(Hons) ACA *2002;* E-2-8 OUG Villa, 2 Jalan Awan Dandan, Taman Yarl, 58200 KUALA LUMPUR, FEDERAL TERRITORY, MALAYSIA.
AU YOUNG, Mr. Rudolf Man, ACA *1980;* Au Young Tse & Wu, 3500 Yorkshire Road, PASADENA, CA 91107, UNITED STATES.
•AUBER, Mr. John Richard Gerratt, FCA *1971;* (Tax Fac), JRG Auber Limited, 2 Castle Business Village, Station Road, HAMPTON, MIDDLESEX, TW12 2BX.
•AUBIN, Mrs. Donna Joy Hurd, BA ACA *1990;* J. Aubin Ltd, 4 Old Barn Close, CHRISTCHURCH, BH23 2QZ.
AUBIN, Mr. Nicholas Charles, BSc ARCS ACA *1984;* Nos Y V la, Mont Felard, St.Lawrence, JERSEY, JE3 1JA.
AUBIN, Mr. Stephane Hugues, MSc ACA *2004;* Flat 4, 28 Cheniston Gardens, LONDON, W8 6TH.
•AUBREY, Mr. Alan John, BA ACA *1987;* The Cottage The Village, Skelton, YORK, YO30 1XX.
AUBREY, Mrs. Caroline Margaret, BA ACA *1988;* 24 St. Barnabas Road, Emmer Green, READING, BERKSHIRE, RG4 8RA.
AUBUSSON, Mr. John Walter, MA ACA *1993;* Flat 1A, 34-35 Newman Street, LONDON, W1T 1PZ.
AUCHIMOWICZ, Ms. Belinda Ann, BA(Hons) ACA *1996;* Mercia Group Ltd, Best House, Grange Business Park, Enderby Road, Whetstone, LEICESTER LE8 6EP.
AUCKLAND, Mr. David Charles, BSc(Hons) ACA CTA *2001;* 59 Berriedale Avenue, HOVE, EAST SUSSEX, BN3 4JG.
•AUCKLAND, Mr. Keith Howard, MA ACA *1981;* Aucland & Associates Limited, Guppys Lodge, Fishpond Bottom, BRIDPORT, DORSET, DT6 6NN. See also Auckland Keith ACA
AUCKLOO, Mr. Jaysen Vikash, BA(Hons) ACA *2004;* 65c Stephens Road, SUTTON COLDFIELD, B76 2TT.
AUCOTT, Mr. Grenville Stuart, FCA *1986;* 81 Broughton Road, Croft, LEICESTER, LE9 3EB.
AUCOTT, Miss. Jacqueline Louise, BSc ACA *1996;* 9 Devon Close, CHIPPENHAM, WILTSHIRE, SN14 0YL.
AUCOTT, Mr. Terence Bernard, FCA *1970;* 3 Rickard Close, Knowle, SOLIHULL, B93 9RD.
AUCOTT, Mr. Thomas Harold, FCA *1962;* Carlton Cottage, High Street, Angmering Village, LITTLEHAMPTON, BN16 4AW. (Life Member)
AUDCENT, Mr. Justin David, BA ACA *1993;* Ernst & Young Building, 11 Mounts Bay Road, PERTH, WA 6000, AUSTRALIA.
AUDCENT, Mr. Martin Richard, BA(Hons) ACA *2001;* 91 Highclove Lane, Boothstown, MANCHESTER, M28 1GZ.
AUDIN, Mr. Mark Ian, BSS FCA CF *1993;* Spring Acres House, Abdon, Near Ditton Priors, CRAVEN ARMS, SHROPSHIRE, SY7 9HU.
AUDLEY-MILLER, Miss. Gail Shirley, BA ACA *1986;* 49 Burlington Avenue, Kew, RICHMOND, TW9 4DG.
AUDLEY-MILLER, Mr. Tomas James, BA ACA *2007;* Fujitsu Observatory House, Windsor Road, SLOUGH, SL1 2EY.
AUER, Mrs. Julia Christine, BSc(Hons) ACA *2001;* with Ernst & Young LLP, 1 More London Place, LONDON, SE1 2AF.
AUER, Mr. Martin Graeme, MA ACA *1998;* 17 Agates Lane, ASHTEAD, KT21 2NG.
AUER, Mr. Nicholas, BA ACA *1997;* 12 Lankester Square, OXTED, SURREY, RH8 0LJ.
AUERBACH, Mr. Cyril James, FCA *1942;* Flat E, 53 Fitzjohns Avenue, LONDON, NW3 6PH. (Life Member)
AUERBACH, Mr. Daniel, FCA *1959;* with Arithma LLP, 9 Mansfield Street, LONDON, W1G 9NY.
AUERO-FOX, Mrs. Heidi Marina, BSc ACA *1984;* (Tax Fac), 2 Weston's Yard, Eton College, WINDSOR, SL4 6DB.
AUFRANC, Miss. Colette, BA ACA *1994;* 5 Hill Top Road, WELLESLEY, MA 02482, UNITED STATES.
AUGER, Mr. David, BA ACA *1994;* East Lodge Lees Hill, South Warnborough, HOOK, RG29 1RQ.
AUGER, Mr. David James Frank, BSc FCA *1983;* 4 Heathfield Road, PETERSFIELD, GU31 4DG.
AUGER, Mr. Lee John, ACA *2010;* 67 Springfield Park, Twyford, READING, RG10 9JG.
AUGER, Mr. Paul William, FCA *1968;* EWhurst, 61 Linersh Wood Road, Bramley, GUILDFORD, GU5 0EF.
•AUGHTERSON, Mr. James Richard, LLB ACA ATII *1994;* (Tax Fac), Aughtersons, 1 Wheatsheaf Close, WOKING, SURREY, GU21 4BL. See also Silbury Woking Ltd
AUGHTON, Mrs. Juliette Anne, BA ACA ATII *1997;* Astrazeneca Plc, Alderley House, Alderley Park, Alderley Edge, MACCLESFIELD, SK10 4TF.
AUGIER, Mr. Martin Kenneth, FCA *1973;* 17 Hove Park Way, HOVE, BN3 6PT.
•AUGUSTE, Mr. Peter, FCA *1971;* (Tax Fac), Peter Auguste & Co, 1 Dukes Passage, Off Duke Street, BRIGHTON, EAST SUSSEX, BN1 1BS.
AUGUSTIN, Mr. Bruno Bernard, LLB FCA *1992;* 44 Elmroyd Avenue, POTTERS BAR, EN6 2EE.
AUGUSTIN, Mr. Eugene Desmond, ACA *1981;* 5 Highfield Park, MARLOW, SL7 2DE.
AUJLA, Mr. Amarjit, BSc FCA FRSA *1983;* 1 Limmer Close, WOKINGHAM, BERKSHIRE, RG41 4DF.
AUJLA, Miss. Balvinder Kaur, BCom ACA *2003;* 58 Bellot Street, LONDON, SE10 0AH.
AUJLA, Mr. Gurjit Singh, BA ACA ATII *1998;* 4 Alder Lane, Balsall Common, COVENTRY, CV7 7DZ.
AUJLA, Miss. Hardeep Kaur, ACA *2009;* 38 Vernon Avenue, BIRMINGHAM, B20 1DF.
•AUJLA, Mr. Jasbant Singh, BA FCA *1993;* Oak, 4 Hampton Close, SUTTON COLDFIELD, WEST MIDLANDS, B73 6RQ.
AUJLA, Mr. Ravi, BSc ACA *2010;* 4 Mitchell Close, SLOUGH, SL1 9DY.
•AUKETT, Mr. Bryan Courtney, FCA *1972;* Blue Spire South LLP, Cawley Priory, South Pallant, CHICHESTER, WEST SUSSEX, PO19 1SY.
•AUKETT, Mr. David Roger, FCA *1980;* Aukett & Co, Gildredge House, 5 Gildredge Road, EASTBOURNE, EAST SUSSEX, BN21 4RB.
AUKETT, Mr. Tony James, FCA *1971;* Continental Paper Grading Co., 1623 S. Lumber St., CHICAGO, IL 60616, UNITED STATES.
AUL, Miss. Anita, BA(Hons) ACA *2000;* with Deloitte LLP, Stonecutter Court, 1 Stonecutter Street, LONDON, EC4A 4TR.
AULAK, Mr. Ajay, ACA *2010;* 189 Syon Lane, ISLEWORTH, MIDDLESEX, TW7 5PU.
AULAK, Miss. Gagandeep, BSc ACA *2011;* 31 Brooklands Road, BIRMINGHAM, B28 8LA.
•AULAK, Mr. Sukhjinder Singh, ACA FCCA *2008;* Chantrey Vellacott DFK LLP, 35 Calthorpe Road, Edgbaston, BIRMINGHAM, WEST MIDLANDS, B15 1TS.
AULD, Mr. Emile, BA ACA *1993;* 1 Wroxham Avenue, Urmston, MANCHESTER, M41 5TE. (Life Member)
AULT, Mrs. Diane Clare, BA ACA *1998;* 47 Applin Green, Emersons Green, BRISTOL, BS16 7ES.
AULT, Mr. Geoffrey Richard, BSc FCA *1978;* 6 Stone Hall Road, Winchmore Hill, LONDON, N21 1LP.
AULT, Mr. Michael John, BSc FCA *1998;* Peveril, One Pin Lane, Farnham Common, SLOUGH, BUCKINGHAMSHIRE, SL2 3RA.
AULT, Mr. Stephen William, BSc ACA *2006;* with Ernst & Young, The Ernst & Young Building, 680 George Street, SYDNEY, NSW 2000, AUSTRALIA.
AULT, Mrs. Virginia Velma, BA ACA *1987;* Ernst & Young, 100 Barbirolli Square, MANCHESTER, M2 3EY.
AULT, Mr. William Duncan, BSc FCA *1972;* 7 Menston Old Lane, Burley-in-Wharfedale, ILKLEY, LS29 7QA.
AULTON, Mr. John Stuart, FCA *1955;* Littleworth House Farm, Alkmonton, ASHBOURNE, DE6 3DG. (Life Member)
•AULUK, Mr. Ranjit Singh, BSc ACA *1995;* PricewaterhouseCoopers LLP, Cornwall Court, 19 Cornwall Street, BIRMINGHAM, B3 2DT. See also PricewaterhouseCoopers
AUMANN, Mr. Michael James, ACA CA(AUS) *2011;* with PricewaterhouseCoopers LLP, 1 Embankment Place, LONDON, WC2N 6RH.
AUMEERALLY, Miss. Anissa Bibi Shenaz, BA(Hons) ACA *2000;* Top Flat, 18 Glen Drive, Stoke Bishop, BRISTOL, BS9 1SB.
AUMEERALLY, Ms. Feriel Jabeen, BSc FCA *1996;* 157 SSR Avenue, QUATRE-BORNES, MAURITIUS.
AUMEERALLY, Miss. Juvaria, ACA *2010;* Flat 2, 102 Warwick Gardens, LONDON, W14 8PR.
AUNDHIA, Mr. Bharat Kumar Ghelabhai, FCA *1973;* Aundhia & Parikh, 265 Rimrock Road, Suite 1, NORTH YORK M3J 3C6, ON, CANADA.
AUNGIER, Mrs. Kathryn Louise, BSc ACA *2005;* M J Bushell Limited, 8 High Street, BRENTWOOD, CM14 4AB.
AUNGLES, Mr. Glenn, BSc FCA *1992;* 1 Chaworth Road, West Bridgford, NOTTINGHAM, NG2 7AE.
•AUREN, Mr. Johan, BSc ACA CTA *2005;* (Tax Fac), Auren & Co Limited, Sweden House, 5 Upper Montagu Street, LONDON, W1H 2AG.
AURORA, Mr. Gautam Anthony, BSc(Hons) ACA *2002;* The Living Room, 2nd Floor, 31 Hauz Khas Village, DELHI, INDIA.
AURORA, Mr. Paramjit Singh, BSc FCA *1999;* 27 Bassett Green Road, SOUTHAMPTON, SO16 3DJ.
AUSAF, Mr. Sohail, BA FCA *1993;* Sohail Ausaf, Vice President-Finance, Etisalat Corp, P O Box 300, ABU DHABI, 300 UNITED ARAB EMIRATES.
AUSDEN, Mr. Richard Charles, FCA *1975;* PO BOX 423, BEECHWORTH, VIC 3747, AUSTRALIA.
AUSTEN, Mrs. Claire Louise, BA ACA *2006;* 1 Oakmont Close, CONGLETON, CHESHIRE, CW12 3GU.
AUSTEN, Mr. Derek, MA FCA *1971;* 41 Strand on The Green, Chiswick, LONDON, W4 3PB. (Life Member)
AUSTEN, Mr. Jonathan Martin, BSc FCA *1981;* Lygon Croft, Sandy Way, COBHAM, KT11 2EY.
AUSTEN, Mrs. Kim, BSc ACA *1993;* 37 Downsmead, Baydon, MARLBOROUGH, WILTSHIRE, SN8 2LQ.
AUSTEN, Mr. Mark David, BA FCA *1991;* with James Cowper LLP, Mill House, Overbridge Square, Hambridge Lane, NEWBURY, BERKSHIRE RG14 5UX.
•AUSTEN, Mr. Paul James, BA(Hons) ACA *2003;* Paul Austen Associates, Charter House, 7-9 Wagg Street, CONGLETON, CHESHIRE, CW12 4BA.
AUSTEN, Mr. Peter David, BA ACA *1983;* Pippins, Popes Lane, Cookham, MAIDENHEAD, BERKSHIRE, SL6 9NY.
AUSTEN, Mr. Robert Nigel, FCA *1978;* 128 Sandy Lane, Cheam, SUTTON, SM2 7ES.
AUSTERBERRY, Ms. Judith Caroline, BA ACA *2000;* 28 Woolpitch Wood, CHEPSTOW, GWENT, NP16 6DW.
AUSTIN, Miss. Alison Ann, BA ACA *1991;* 64 Beechwood Road, Sanderstead, SOUTH CROYDON, Surrey, CR2 0AA.
•AUSTIN, Mr. Anthony Julian, FCA *1977;* (Tax Fac), 17 Lacey Drive, COULSDON, SURREY, CR5 1ER.
AUSTIN, Mr. Brian William, FCA *1960;* 1050 Melton Road, Syston, LEICESTER, LE7 2NN. (Life Member)
•AUSTIN, Mrs. Carolyn Suzanne, BA ACA *1991;* Carolyn Austin, 5 Barnfield Close, Cookham, MAIDENHEAD, BERKSHIRE, SL6 9DY.
AUSTIN, Mr. Christian, MSci ACA *2011;* 121 Whyteladyes Lane, Cookham, MAIDENHEAD, BERKSHIRE, SL6 9LF.
AUSTIN, Mrs. Christine Mary, BCom ACA *1992;* Centralis Ltd Centralis House Upper Wawensmoor, Wawensmere Road Wootton Wawen, HENLEY-IN-ARDEN, B95 6BS.
AUSTIN, Mr. Christopher Sebastian, MA(Cantab) ACA CTA *2001;* 4 Dartmouth Row, Greenwich, LONDON, SE10 8AN.
AUSTIN, Ms. Clare Serena, BSc ACA DChA *1985;* 19 Holly Park Gardens, LONDON, N3 3NG.
AUSTIN, Mr. Clive, FCA *1955;* Athelney, Rickmansworth Road, NORTHWOOD, MIDDLESEX, HA6 2RF. (Life Member)
•AUSTIN, Mr. Darren Philip, ACA *1995;* Synergee Limited, 2nd Floor, 8 Lonsdale Gardens, TUNBRIDGE WELLS, KENT, TN1 1NU.
AUSTIN, Mr. David, FCA *1963;* 26 Brookside, Witton Gilbert, DURHAM, DH7 6RT.
AUSTIN, Mr. David George, FCA *1958;* Erquy, Brigsteer Road, Levens, KENDAL, LA8 8NU. (Life Member)
AUSTIN, Mr. David Michael, LLB ACA *1981;* Julian Hodge Bank Plc, 29-30 Windsor Place, CARDIFF, CF10 3BZ.
AUSTIN, Mr. David Norman, FCA *1975;* 21 Park Road, WALLINGTON, SURREY, SM6 8AA. (Life Member)
AUSTIN, Mr. David Trevor, BA ACA *1994;* Meadow Barn, Bulwick Road, Laxton, CORBY, NORTHAMPTONSHIRE, NN17 3AX.
AUSTIN, Mr. Edward David, FCA *1957;* 103 Nanpantan Road, LOUGHBOROUGH, LE11 3YB. (Life Member)
AUSTIN, Mrs. Fiona Jane, BSc ACA *1992;* c/o Lashmars, Palamos House, 66-67 High Street, LYMINGTON, HAMPSHIRE, SO41 9AL.
AUSTIN, Mr. Gary Scott, ACA *1980;* Wayside Group Ltd, Denbigh House, Denbigh Road, Bletchley, MILTON KEYNES, MK1 1DF.
AUSTIN, Mr. Graham, BSc ACA *1987;* 8 Shenden Way, SEVENOAKS, KENT, TN13 1SE.
•AUSTIN, Mrs. Helen Louise, BSc ACA *2003;* Austin & Co, 18 Angram Drive, SUNDERLAND, SR2 7RD.
AUSTIN, Mr. James Haldane, BA(Hons) *2010;* Doughty Hanson & Co, 45 Pall Mall, LONDON, SW1Y 5JG.
AUSTIN, Mr. James Paul, ACA *2004;* TMF Managment (UK) Ltd, Pellipar House, 9 Cloak Lane, LONDON, EC4R 2RU.
•AUSTIN, Mr. James Peter, BA ACA CF FSI *1993;* BDO LLP, 55 Baker Street, LONDON, W1U 7EU. See also BDO Stoy Hayward LLP
•AUSTIN, Mr. James Robert, FCA *1970;* 38 Clevedon Road, KINGSTON-UPON-THAMES, KT1 3AD.
AUSTIN, Miss. Jennifer Margaret, BA ACA *2007;* Flat 6, Bedford Court, Mowbray Road, LONDON, SE19 2RW.

AUSTIN, Mrs. Joanne, BA ACA *1991;* with KPMG LLP, 1 The Embankment, Neville Street, LEEDS, LS1 4DW.
•**AUSTIN, Mr. John, FCA** *1985;* Phipps Henson McAllister, 22/24 Harborough Road, Kingsthorpe, NORTHAMPTON, NN2 7AZ.
AUSTIN, Mr. John, FCA *1974;* The Croft, Highland Avenue, BRENTWOOD, ESSEX, CM15 9DD.
AUSTIN, Mr. John Dennis Dean, FCA *1954;* P.O. Box 486, APSLEY K0L 1A0, ON, CANADA. (Life Member)
•**AUSTIN, Mr. John Eric, FCA** *1952;* Austins, Pine House, Chandlers Way, SOUTHEND-ON-SEA, SS2 5SE.
AUSTIN, Mr. John George, FCA *1968;* Fenemore Fir Tree Lane, Little Baddow, CHELMSFORD, CM3 4SS. (Life Member)
AUSTIN, Mr. John Haldane, BA FCA *1961;* The Lodge, 10 Glebelands Road, TIVERTON, DEVON, EX16 4EB.
•**AUSTIN, Mr. John Jeremy Robison, FCA** *1975;* (Tax Fac), Rushton Osborne & Co Limited, Ringley Park House, 59 Reigate Road, REIGATE, SURREY, RH2 0QJ.
AUSTIN, Mr. John Marley, FCA *1953;* 8 Norbury Close, Norbury, LONDON, SW16 3ND. (Life Member)
AUSTIN, Miss. Karen, BA ACA *1985;* 42 Marshalswick Lane, ST. ALBANS, AL1 4XG.
AUSTIN, Miss. Kathryn Louise, BSc ACA *2010;* 22 Briar Road, SHEFFIELD, S7 1SA.
AUSTIN, Miss. Kathryn Mary, FCA CTA *1992;* (Tax Fac), 74 High Street, Shoreham, SEVENOAKS, KENT, TN14 7TE.
AUSTIN, Mr. Kevin Douglas, BSc FCA FCCA FCMI *1976;* Access Financial Services Sarl, CP 2123, Chemin de Precossy 7, CH 1260 NYON, VAUD, SWITZERLAND.
AUSTIN, Mr. Kevin Gerard, BSc ACA *1988;* unit 43, Argyle Business Centre Ltd, 39 North Howard Street, BELFAST, BT13 2AP.
AUSTIN, Mr. Leonard Alfred, FCA *1956;* High Gables, Stylecroft Road, CHALFONT ST.GILES, HP8 4HY. (Life Member)
AUSTIN, Mrs. Marianne Therese, MA BSc ACA *1986;* 19 Burlington Avenue, Kew, RICHMOND, SURREY, TW9 4DF.
AUSTIN, Mr. Mark Stedman, BSc ACA *1985;* 365 BRIDGE STREET APT 6A, BROOKLYN, NY 11201-3805, UNITED STATES.
•**AUSTIN, Mr. Maurice Piercy Gardiner, BSc FCA** *1979;* Goodman Jones LLP, 29-30 Fitzroy Square, LONDON, W1T 6LQ.
AUSTIN, Mrs. Meryl, FCA *1983;* Ron Coates & Co, 374 Cowbridge Road East, CARDIFF, CF5 1JJ.
AUSTIN, Mr. Michael, FCA *1964;* Shornfield Wood House, Shrub Lane, Burwash, ETCHINGHAM, TN19 7ED.
•**AUSTIN, Michael, Esq MBE FCA** *1964;* PO Box 692, GEORGE TOWN, GRAND CAYMAN, KY1 1107, CAYMAN ISLANDS.
AUSTIN, Mr. Michael Hayman, FCA *1953;* 4 Beauchamps Place, Ravens Way, Milford on Sea, LYMINGTON, HAMPSHIRE, SO41 0PX. (Life Member)
AUSTIN, Mr. Michael John, BSc FCA *1977;* 15/F Tower A, Manulife Financial Centre, 223-231 Wai Yip Street, KWUN TONG, HONG KONG SAR.
•**AUSTIN, Mr. Michael John Charles, BSc ACA** *1986;* (Tax Fac), Blue Dot Consulting Limited, Riverbank House, Business Centre, 1 Putney Bridge Approach, LONDON, SW6 3JD.
•**AUSTIN, Mr. Neil, MA FCA** *2000;* with PricewaterhouseCoopers LLP, 89 Sandyford Road, NEWCASTLE UPON TYNE, NE1 8HW.
AUSTIN, Mr. Paul, BSc ACA *1991;* Stone Court, Greenhill Lane, Denbury, NEWTON ABBOT, DEVON, TQ12 6DN.
AUSTIN, Mr. Paul Antony, BSc ACA *2003;* 26 Crown Walk, HEMEL HEMPSTEAD, HERTFORDSHIRE, HP3 9WS.
AUSTIN, Mr. Paul Michael, BA ACA *1998;* 27a Love Walk, LONDON, SE5 8AD.
AUSTIN, Mr. Peter Kenneth, BSc ACA *1993;* 78 Kennel Lane, Fetcham, LEATHERHEAD, SURREY, KT22 9PW.
•**AUSTIN, Mr. Philip, ACA** *1979;* Simmons Gainsford LLP, 5th Floor, 7-10 Chandos Street, Cavendish Square, LONDON, W1G 9DQ.
AUSTIN, Mr. Philip Edward, BA(Hons) ACA *2003;* 13 Park Avenue, ST. ALBANS, HERTFORDSHIRE, AL1 4PB.
AUSTIN, Mrs. Rachel, MA ACA CTA *2001;* with Deloitte LLP, 2 New Street Square, LONDON, EC4A 3BZ.
AUSTIN, Mr. Reginald David Fryer, FCA *1955;* Flat 5, Carlisle Grange, 22a Grange Road, EASTBOURNE, EAST SUSSEX, BN21 4HF. (Life Member)
AUSTIN, Mr. Reginald Edward, FCA *1970;* 54 Downs Wood, Epsom Downs, EPSOM, KT18 5UL. (Life Member)
•**AUSTIN, Mr. Richard, BSc(Econ) ACA CTA** *1998;* Crowe Clark Whitehill LLP, Carrick House, Lypiatt Road, CHELTENHAM, GLOUCESTERSHIRE, GL50 2QJ. See also Horwath Clark Whitehill LLP and Crowe Clark Whitehill
AUSTIN, Mr. Richard Neil, BSc FCA *1979;* 29 Pemberley Avenue, BEDFORD, MK40 2LE.
AUSTIN, Mr. Robert, BA BSc(Econ) FCA *1972;* 9 Fanshawe Rd, THAME, OX9 3LF.
AUSTIN, Mr. Robert John, BSc ACA *1992;* (Tax Fac), Gappe Stones, 4 Lothersdale Road, Glusburn, KEIGHLEY, NORTH YORKSHIRE, BD20 8JN.
AUSTIN, Mrs. Ruth Christina, BA FCA *1982;* Woodlands, Marley Lane, BATTLE, TN33 0RB.
•**AUSTIN, Mr. Shaun George, BA FCA** *1995;* Deloitte LLP, 4 Brindley Place, BIRMINGHAM, B1 2HZ. See also Deloitte & Touche LLP
AUSTIN, Mr. Simon David, BA ACA *1994;* 35 Hastings Road, SOUTHPORT, MERSEYSIDE, PR8 2LN.
•**AUSTIN, Mr. Simon John, FCA** *1980;* (Tax Fac), Austins, Pine House, Chandlers Way, SOUTHEND-ON-SEA, SS2 5SE.
AUSTIN, Mr. Stephen Arthur, ACA *1992;* 3531 Crossgate Circle North, COLLEYVILLE, TX 76034, UNITED STATES.
AUSTIN, Mr. Stephen Thomas, FCA *1978;* 2 Bertram Drive North, Meols, WIRRAL, CH47 0LW.
AUSTIN, Mr. Terence Nigel, FCA *1967;* Longwall Barn, Bircham Road, Stanhoe, KING'S LYNN, NORFOLK, PE31 8PT.
AUSTIN, Mr. Terence Philip, BA FCA *1977;* 19 Carolyn Drive, ORPINGTON, BR6 9ST.
AUSTIN, Mr. Thomas James, ACA *2008;* 24 Trafalgar Terrace, BRISTOL, BS3 2SW.
AUSTIN, Mr. Toby Edward, BA(Hons) ACA *2001;* 8 Deyncourt Close, Darras Hall, Ponteland, NEWCASTLE UPON TYNE, NE20 9JY.
AUSTIN, Mr. Warren Stuart, BSc ACA *1992;* Hammerson Plc, 10 Grosvenor Street, LONDON, W1K 4BJ.
AUSTIN-BAILEY, Mr. Peter George, BA ACA ATII Bar(NP) *1998;* (Tax Fac), 5 Meadow Gardens, Measham, SWADLINCOTE, DERBYSHIRE, DE12 7EA.
AUSTIN-HOGG, Mrs. Gayle, BA(Hons) ACA *2004;* 2 Chestnut Court, Angmering, LITTLEHAMPTON, WEST SUSSEX, BN16 4FT.
•**AUSTRENG, Mr. Trevor, FCA** *1979;* (Tax Fac), Fawcetts, Windover House, St Ann Street, SALISBURY, SP1 2DR.
•**AUSTWICK, Mr. Steven John, BSc ACA** *1992;* (Tax Fac), KPMG, Vesetas iela 7, RIGA LV 1013, LATVIA.
AUTERSON, Miss. Georgina, ACA *2011;* 65 Eland Road, Battersea, LONDON, SW11 5JZ.
AUTIN, Ms. Florence, ACA *1995;* 80 route de Biot, 06560 VALBONNE, FRANCE.
AUTON, Mr. Marcus, BSc ACA *1994;* Apartment 14, 12 Pond Street, LONDON, NW3 2PS.
AUTON, Mr. Michael Colin, FCA *1966;* (Tax Fac), The Coach House, Main Street, Hotham, YORK, YO43 4UF.
AUTON, Mr. Robert Timothy, BSc ACA MSI *2001;* 61 St. Albans Road, KINGSTON UPON THAMES, SURREY, KT2 5HH.
AUTY, Mr. David, BA ACA *1980;* 21 Beeches End, Boston Spa, WETHERBY, WEST YORKSHIRE, LS23 6HL.
AUTY, Mr. Gilbert Ainsworth, FCA *1938;* 2 Hellifield, Fulwood, PRESTON, PR2 9SY. (Life Member)
AUTY, Dr. James Michael Alexander, ACA *2009;* Farways, South Munstead Lane, GODALMING, GU8 4AG.
AUTY, Mr. Robert Andrew, ACA *2010;* 8 Carlbury Crescent, DARLINGTON, COUNTY DURHAM, DL3 9QL.
AUW, Mr. Gim-Tiem, FCA *1974;* Cidex 452, 766 Chemin de Peire Luche, 06330 ROQUEFORT LES PINS, FRANCE.
AVAIS, Mr. Wiqar, FCA *1974;* Avais Hyder Liaquat Nauman, 1/C-5 Avais Chambers, Sikander Malhi Road, Canal Park, Gulberg 2, LAHORE PAKISTAN.
•**AVANN, Mr. Andrew Raymond, MA FCA CertPFS AMCT** *1983;* A R Avann and Co Ltd, 33 Wood Lane, Sonning Common, READING, RG4 9SJ.
AVERILL, Mrs. Caroline Elizabeth, BA ACA *1999;* 54 Broad Oaks Road, SOLIHULL, B91 1JB.
AVERILL, Mr. Peter James, BSc ACA *2001;* 26B Block 3, Pacific View, 38 Tai Tam Road, STANLEY, HONG KONG ISLAND, HONG KONG SAR.
•**AVERILLO, Miss. Dawn Louisa, FCA** *1989;* Averillo & Associates, 16 South End, CROYDON, CR0 1DN. See also Averillo Taxation Services Limited
AVERIS, Mr. Benjamin James, ACA *2011;* Flat 8, St. Johns Court, 144-146 St. John's Hill, Battersea, LONDON, SW11 1SN.
AVERKIOU, Mrs. Nadine Martha, ACA CA(SA) *2010;* 29 Deerings Drive, PINNER, MIDDLESEX, HA5 2NZ.
AVERRE, Mrs. Katherine Louise, BSc ACA *1992;* 21 Buxton Gardens, Acton, LONDON, W3 9LF.
AVERTY, Mrs. Joanne Kim, FCA *1983;* The Barn House Midland, La Grande Route de St. Jean Trinity, JERSEY, JE3 5FN.
AVERY, Mrs. Alison Jane, BA ACA *1996;* 6509 Torrey Pines Cv, AUSTIN, TX 78746, UNITED STATES.
AVERY, Mr. David Robert Arthur, MEng ACA *1993;* 11 Rollo Road, Hextable, SWANLEY, KENT, BR8 7RD.
AVERY, Mr. Dennis, FCA *1956;* Apartado 2125, Quinta Do Lago, 8135-024 ALMANCIL, PORTUGAL. (Life Member)
AVERY, Mr. John Leonard, BA ACA *1985;* Summerhill, Clifton Road, Newton Blossomville, BEDFORD, MK43 8AS.
AVERY, Mr. Jonathan William, BA ACA *1993;* 24 Britten Close, Chandos Way, Off Wellgarth Road Golders Gr, LONDON, NW11 7HQ.
AVERY, Miss. Keiley, BA(Hons) ACA *2011;* 16 Jeffcut Road, CHELMSFORD, CM2 6XN.
AVERY, Mrs. Linda, ACA *1992;* 31 Barrow Green Road, OXTED, RH8 0NJ.
AVERY, Mr. Michael Paul, FCA *1971;* 10 Osterley Lane, Norwood Green, SOUTHALL, UB2 4LB.
AVERY, Mr. Paul John, BSc ACA *2005;* with Deloitte LLP, 2 New Street Square, LONDON, EC4A 3BZ.
AVERY, Mr. Richard Alan, BSc FCA *2000;* with Ernst & Young LLP, 1 More London Place, LONDON, SE1 2AF.
AVERY, Miss. Rosslyn Dawn, MSc FCA *1991;* 115 Mill Street, KIDLINGTON, OX5 2EE.
AVERY, Mr. Russell Paul, ACA *2008;* 3 Curtis Road, Shrivenham, SWINDON, SN6 8AY.
AVERY, Mrs. Sally Ann, BSc ACA *1992;* Route du Jura 37, CH-1700 FRIBOURG, SWITZERLAND.
AVERY, Mrs. Sally Rachel, MMath ACA *2009;* 104a Brookmill Road, LONDON, SE8 4JJ.
AVERY, Mr. Stephen, MBA BA FCA *1987;* 393 Stroude Road, VIRGINIA WATER, GU25 4BY.
AVERY, Mr. William Francis, BCom FCA *1963;* 138 Stonegate Drive, FURRY CREEK V0N3Z2, BC, CANADA.
•①**AVERY-GEE, Mr. Jonathan Elman, FCA** *1973;* Kay Johnson Gee, Griffin Court, 201 Chapel Street, MANCHESTER, M3 5EQ.
AVES, Mr. John Daniel, BSc ACA *2001;* 27 Durnsford Avenue, LONDON, SW19 8BH.
AVES, Mr. Peter Nicholas, BA ACA *1986;* 26 Sidney Square, LONDON, E1 2EY.
AVGHERINOS, Miss. Helen, BA ACA *2003;* SDHFT, Regents House, Regent Close, TORQUAY, TQ2 7AN.
AVGOUSTI, Dr. Avgoustinos Petros, ACA *1993;* PO Box 54529, 3725 LIMASSOL, CYPRUS.
AVGOUSTI, Mr. Christos, BSc(Hons) ACA *2002;* 73 Demokratias Street, CY-2331 NICOSIA, CYPRUS.
AVIGNON, Mrs. Emma Jane, BA ACA *2001;* Ernst & Young Llp, 1 More London Place, LONDON, SE1 2AF.
AVIS, Mr. Ian Paul, FCA *1978;* Gulf International Bank, Al-Dowali Building King, Faisal Highway, PO Box 1017, MANAMA, BAHRAIN.
AVIS, Miss. Joanne Christine, LLB ACA *1992;* 42 Linden Road, BRISTOL, BS6 7RP.
AVIS, Mrs. Melanie Jane, BSc ACA *1991;* Henshaws College, Bogs Lane, HARROGATE, NORTH YORKSHIRE, HG1 4ED.
•**AVIS, Mr. Nicholas John, BSc FCA** *1984;* (Tax Fac), Place Campbell, Wilmington House, High Street, EAST GRINSTEAD, RH19 3AU.
AVIS, Mrs. Penelope Jane, LLB ACA *1993;* Iffley Lodge, 22 Oxford Road, LONDON, SW15 2LF.
AVIS, Mr. Peter David, BSc ACA *1991;* 11 Kirkhills, Thorner, LEEDS, LS14 3JD.
AVIS, Mr. Philip David, BSc ACA *2004;* 37 Drewery Drive, GILLINGHAM, ME8 0NP.
AVISON, Mr. Barry John, FCA *1978;* 62 Arnesby Avenue, SALE, M33 2NF.
AVISON, Mr. Gerald Edwin, FCA *1956;* 15 Grennan Court, St Georges Mount, WALLASEY, CH45 9NZ. (Life Member)
AVISON, Mrs. Harriet Linda, BA(Hons) ACA *2001;* 35 George Road, West Bridgford, NOTTINGHAM, NG2 7PT.
AVISON, Mrs. Lynn, MA BA FCA *1982;* 20 Moor View, MIRFIELD, WEST YORKSHIRE, WF14 0JH.
AVRAAM, Mr. Alkis, BSc ACA *2011;* 2 Iouliou, Tipaldou, Agios Athanasios, 4104 LIMASSOL, CYPRUS.
AVRAAM, Mr. Andreas, BSc ACA *2004;* 14 Chrysoulas Malaktou Street, Ayios Athanasios, 4108 LIMASSOL, CYPRUS.
•**AVRAAM, Mr. Costas Loizos, BSc FCA** *1993;* (Tax Fac), Avraam Associates, 495 Green Lanes, Palmers Green, LONDON, N13 4BS.
AVRAAM, Mrs. Karolina, BSc ACA *2006;* 110 St. Margarets Road, EDGWARE, MIDDLESEX, HA8 9UX.
AVRAAM, Mr. Michael, BA ACA *1993;* 8 DIGENIS AKRITAS AVENUE, OFFICE 403 P.O.BOX 29127, 1621 NICOSIA, CYPRUS.
AVRAAM, Mr. Paraskevas, BSc ACA *2006;* (Tax Fac), 110 St. Margarets Road, EDGWARE, MIDDLESEX, HA8 9UX.
•**AVRAAMIDES, Mr. Andreas, BSc ACA** *1998;* Ernst & Young Cyprus Limited, Nicosia Tower Centre, 36 Byron Avenue, P.O Box 21656, 1511 NICOSIA, CYPRUS.
AVRAMOVIC, Mr. Adam Novak, ACA *2009;* Integra House Floor 2, Vicarage Road, EGHAM, TW20 8JZ.
AVWUNU, Mr. George Akpobo, BCom ACA *1986;* 27 Southwell Road, CROYDON, CR0 3QD.
AW, Mr. Allan, BSc FCA *1976;* Apt C-2, 78-80 Repulse Bay Road, REPULSE BAY, HONG KONG ISLAND, HONG KONG SAR.
AW, Mr. Hong Boo, FCA *1974;* No.15, SS 21/17, Damansara Utama, 47400 PETALING JAYA, SELANGOR, MALAYSIA.
AW, Miss. Melanie Mei Hooi, ACA *2009;* with Larkings (S.E) LLP, Cornwallis House, Pudding Lane, MAIDSTONE, KENT, ME14 1NH.
AW, Mr. Tuan-Jin, BSc ACA *2003;* 37 Seafield Road, LONDON, N11 1AR.
•**AW, Mr. Tudor, BA ACA** *1990;* KPMG LLP, 15 Canada Square, LONDON, E14 5GL. See also KPMG Europe LLP
AWAAN, Mr. Tahir Farooq, ACA *2009;* 65 Belper Avenue, Carlton, NOTTINGHAM, NG4 3SE.
AWAIS, Miss. Aaysha Arjumand, ACA *2009;* 2 Chichester Gardens, ILFORD, ESSEX, IG1 3NB.
AWAL, Miss. Sonia, BA ACA *2007;* 31 Orchard Way, CROYDON, CR0 7NP.
AWAN, Mr. Ahsan, BSc ACA *2006;* Cable & Wireless, Worldwide House, Western Road, BRACKNELL, BERKSHIRE, RG12 1RW.
AWAN, Mr. Iftikhar Ahmad, FCA CF *1978;* The Samar, 16 Spath Road, Didsbury, MANCHESTER, M20 2FA. (Life Member)
AWAN, Miss. Natasha Anisa, ACA *2006;* 24 Water Meadow Way, IBSTOCK, LE67 6GY.
AWAN, Mr. Qamar Sayeed, FCA *1968;* House No 3, Street 58, F10/3, ISLAMABAD, PAKISTAN. (Life Member)
•**AWAN, Mr. Tahir Masood, BSc FCA ARPS** *1977;* Deloitte LLP, Athene Place, 66 Shoe Lane, LONDON, EC4A 3BQ. See also Deloitte & Touche LLP
AWAN, Mr. Zahir, BSc ACA *2000;* with RSM Tenon Audit Limited, 66 Chiltern Street, LONDON, W1U 4JT.
AWANG MAMAT, Mr. Ismail Yusoff, BA(Hons) ACA *2001;* with PricewaterhouseCoopers, P.O.Box 10192, Level 10 1 Sentral, Jalan Travers, 50470 KUALA LUMPUR, FEDERAL TERRITORY MALAYSIA.
AWATAR, Mr. Vishal, BSc ACA *2001;* 222 Wellington Road, ENFIELD, EN1 2RL.
AWOYINKA, Miss. Seyi, BSc ACA *2010;* 432c Fulham Road, LONDON, SW6 1DU.
AWTY, Mr. Edward Samuel, BSc FCA *1975;* 42 St. Peters Square, LONDON, W6 9NR.
AWTY, Miss. Julia Ruth, BSc ACA *2004;* 7 Wolseley Road, LONDON, N8 8RR.
•**AWTY, Mrs. June, BA FCA** *1986;* 42 St. Peters Square, LONDON, W6 9NR.
AWUONDO, Mr. Isaac Odundo, ACA CF *1984;* P.O. Box 30437 - 00100, GPO, NAIROBI, KENYA.
•**AXCELL, Mr. Paul Steven, FCA** *1977;* (Tax Fac), Paul S Axcell, Kiln Cottage, Fourstones, HEXHAM, NE47 5DH.
AXCELL, Mr. Stephen John, MMath ACA *2005;* with Jacob Cavenagh & Skeet, 5 Robin Hood Lane, SUTTON, SURREY, SM1 2SW.
AXELBY, Mr. James, BSc(Hons) ACA *2000;* 18 Whielden Street, AMERSHAM, BUCKINGHAMSHIRE, HP7 0HT.
AXELRAD, Mr. Nigel Gideon, BA ACA *1981;* Bank Farm, Carlton, NUNEATON, CV13 0BU.
•**AXELROD, Mrs. Kate, BA ACA** *1995;* Axel Consulting, 6 Upper Heath Road, ST. ALBANS, HERTFORDSHIRE, AL1 4DN.
AXELROD, Mr. Michael Clifford, BA FCA *1980;* 26 Raglan Road, REIGATE, RH2 0DP.
AXELROD, Mr. Philip Jacob, BSc FCA *1974;* 316 Park Boulevard North, WINNIPEG R3P 0G7, MB, CANADA. (Life Member)
•**AXELSEN, Mr. Andrew John, FCA** *1985;* Amlbenson Limited, AML Maybrook House, 97 Godstone Road, CATERHAM, CR3 6RE.
AXFORD, Mr. Eric Sidney, FCA *1973;* La Pierre Blanche, 72 Mont Es Croix, La Rue de la Pointe, St. Brelade, JERSEY, JE3 8EN.
AXFORD, Mrs. Frances, BSc ACA *1997;* 24 Water Perry, Nr Wheatley, OXFORD, OX33 1LB.
AXFORD, Mr. Richard Frederick, BA ACA *2000;* 9 Alnwick Close, Whickham, NEWCASTLE UPON TYNE, NE16 5ZD.

AXON, Mrs. Emma Louise, ACA *2002;* 21 Brook Lane Cottages, Swan Lane Sellindge, ASHFORD, KENT, TN25 6HG.
AXON, Mr. John Temperley, FCA *1972;* South Cottage, Hog Lane, Ashley Green, CHESHAM, BUCKINGHAMSHIRE, HP5 3PS.
AXON, Mr. Malcolm, ACA *1984;* 514 Manhattan Beach Blvd, MANHATTAN BEACH, CA 90266, UNITED STATES.
AXON, Mr. Martin Nolan, BA ACA *1993;* Wellington School, South Street, WELLINGTON, SOMERSET, TA21 8NT.
AXON, Mr. Paul, BSc ACA *1994;* 17 Carradale Glen, Hillarys, PERTH, WA 6025, AUSTRALIA.
AXON, Mr. Peter, ACA *2007;* 7 Church Farm Way, Arthingworth, MARKET HARBOROUGH, LEICESTERSHIRE, LE16 8NP.
AXTELL, Mr. Michael Paul, MEng ACA *2001;* Wood View Broad Street, Wrington, BRISTOL, BS40 5LA.
•AXTON, Mr. Christopher John, BSc ACA *1987;* Axtons, The Mews, St Nicholas Lane, LEWES, BN7 2JZ.
AXUP, Mr. David Andrew, BA ACA *1987;* Pinhaw House, 1 Jenkins Close, Pocklington, YORK, YO42 2PA.
AXUP, Mrs. Julie Elizabeth, BSc ACA *1987;* Pinhaw House, 1 Jenkins Close, Pocklington, YORK, YO42 2PA.
AYAZ, Mr. Badar, BSc ACA *2007;* 18 Higher Downs, BRADFORD, BD8 0NA.
AYDINER, Mr. Ismail, BSc FCA *1981;* Highview, 2a Croydon Road, KESTON, BR2 6EB.
AYENI, Mr. Ayodeji, BA ACA *2010;* Apartment 96, Burford Wharf Apartments, 3 Cam Road, LONDON, E15 2SL.
AYENI, Mrs. Mojisola Oluyemisi, BA ACA *1990;* The Shell Petroleum Development, Company of Nigeria Ltd, Freeman House, 21/22 Marina PMB 2418, LAGOS, NIGERIA.
AYERST, Mr. Richard John, BSc FCA *1979;* 24 Friary Avenue, LICHFIELD, WS13 6QQ.
AYERST, Mr. Thomas Hedley, BA ACA *1999;* with PricewaterhouseCoopers LLP, 1 Embankment Place, LONDON, WC2N 6RH.
•AYEW, Mr. John Kwaku, FCA *1961;* Ayew Agyeman Turkson & Co, Mobil House, P.O. Box 3599, ACCRA, GHANA.
AYIOMAMITIS, Mr. Emilios, BSc ACA *2007;* P.O Box 70726, 3802 LIMASSOL, CYPRUS.
AYIOMAMITIS, Mr. Nicholas, ACA *2007;* PO Box 5-3276, 3 Nikis, Mesa Yitonia, 4003 LIMASSOL, CYPRUS.
AYKROYD, Mr. Bryan Timothy, BA FCA *1973;* 15 rue montorgueil, 75001 PARIS, FRANCE.
AYLEN, Mr. Charles Eric, BCom FCA *1956;* 8 Elmtree Grove, Gosforth, NEWCASTLE UPON TYNE, NE3 4BG. (Life Member)
AYLES, Mrs. Claudine Odette, BSc ACA *1998;* 2 Langdale Close, WOKING, SURREY, GU21 4RS.
AYLETT, Mr. Boydin Stuart, FCA *1967;* Boydin Aylett, Level 2, 135 Fullarton Road, ROSE PARK, SA 5067, AUSTRALIA.
AYLETT, Mr. Peter Geoffrey, FCA *1971;* 95 Windmill Avenue, WOKINGHAM, BERKSHIRE, RG41 3XG.
AYLIFFE, Mr. Angus Hugh, BA ACA *1995;* Ariel Reinsurance Company Ltd, PO Box HM 1727, HAMILTON HM GX, BERMUDA.
AYLIFFE, Mr. George David, BA ACA *1989;* Long Meadow, Claremont Lane, Bishop Monkton, HARROGATE, HG3 3RE.
AYLIFFE, Mr. Robert William, BA ACA *1997;* The Beech House La Rue Des Alleurs, St. Martin, JERSEY, JE3 6AZ.
AYLING, Miss. Emma Jane, BSc(Hons) ACA *2003;* 10a Bolehill Road, Bolehill, MATLOCK, DERBYSHIRE, DE4 4GQ.
AYLING, Dr. Joanna Rebecca, BSc ACA *1999;* 8 Troutbeck Avenue, LEAMINGTON SPA, CV32 6NE.
AYLING, Miss. Linda Mary, BA FCA *1990;* Dacres Chelmsford Road, White Roding, DUNMOW, CM6 1RG.
AYLING, Ms. Louise Georgina, BA ACA *1999;* Kingston College, Kingston Hall Road, KINGSTON UPON THAMES, SURREY, KT1 2AQ.
AYLING, Miss. Louise Grace, BA ACA *2006;* 2 Valley Court, LEEDS, LS17 6LU.
AYLING, Mr. Michael Ramon, BA ACA *1992;* Laguna Resorts & Hotels plc, 390/1 Mool, Srisoon Thorn Road, Cherngtalay, Thalang, PHUKET 83110 THAILAND.
AYLING, Mr. William, MChem ACA *2011;* 18d Warrington Crescent, LONDON, W9 1EL.
AYLING-ROUSE, Mr. Julian David, BSc ACA *2007;* St. Anthonys Cottage, High Street, HENFIELD, WEST SUSSEX, BN5 9HP.
AYLMER, Mr. John Philip, FCA *1972;* 20 The Cedars, Milton Road, HARPENDEN, HERTFORDSHIRE, AL5 5LQ.
AYLMER, Mr. Patrick Anthony Richard, BSc FCA *1988;* British American Tobacco, Globe House, 4 Temple Place, LONDON, WC2R 2PG.
AYLOTT, Mr. Christopher James, BSc ACA *2003;* with Deloitte LLP, Hill House, 1 Little New Street, LONDON, EC4A 3TR.
•AYLOTT, Mr. Colin Paul, BSc FCA *1987;* (Tax Fac), Smith & Williamson Ltd, 25 Moorgate, LONDON, EC2R 6AY.
AYLOTT, Mr. Martin James, BA ACA *1979;* 30 Stradmore Avenue, Templestowe, MELBOURNE, VIC 3106, AUSTRALIA.
•AYLWARD, Mr. Brian Stewart Millett, BA FCA *1975;* (Tax Fac), Stewart Aylward FCA, Isbourne, Chandos Street, Winchcombe, CHELTENHAM, GLOUCESTERSHIRE GL54 5HX.
•AYLWARD, Mr. John Hopkin Thomas, FCA *1974;* (Tax Fac), with Broomfield & Alexander Limited, Ty Derw, Lime Tree Court, Cardiff Gate Business Park, CARDIFF, CF23 8AB.
AYLWARD, Mr. Justin Philip, BA ACA CFA *1981;* 29 Marlborough Street, VICTORIA V8V 4A6, BC, CANADA.
AYLWARD, Mr. Peter Nunn, FCA *1972;* 6183 Swainland Road, OAKLAND, CA 94611, UNITED STATES.
AYLWIN, Mr. Andrew Charles, FCA *1971;* The Red House, Terrace Road North, Binfield, BRACKNELL, RG42 5PH.
AYLWIN, Mr. Andrew Richard, BA ACA *1998;* Lyceum Capital Partners Llp, 357 Strand, LONDON, WC2R 0HS.
AYLWIN, Mr. Nicholas Claude, FCA *1967;* 27 Ellerton Road, Wimbledon, LONDON, SW20 0EW.
AYLWIN, Mr. Richard Talbot, BEng ACA *1994;* Warren Bank, Warren Lane, Cross in Hand, HEATHFIELD, EAST SUSSEX, TN21 0TE.
AYNSLEY, Miss. Hannah Sophy, BSc ACA *2007;* with BDO LLP, 55 Baker Street, LONDON, W1U 7EU.
AYODEJI, Miss. Olufunlola, BA ACA *2007;* Flat 124 Alpine Court, Alpine Road, REDHILL, RH1 2LF.
•AYRE, Mr. Andrew Nicholas, FCA *1983;* (Tax Fac), Greaves West & Ayre, 1-3 Sandgate, BERWICK-UPON-TWEED, TD15 1EW.
AYRE, Mr. Duncan Terence, BSc ACA *1989;* 5 Oasthouse Spinney, Church Meadows Bocking, BRAINTREE, CM7 5GX.
AYRE, Mr. Graham John, MA ACA *1987;* Haselmere, Park Road, STROUD, GL5 2JG.
AYRE, Mrs. Joanne Kay, BSc(Hons) ACA *2002;* 56 Canberra Road, Marton-in-Cleveland, MIDDLESBROUGH, CLEVELAND, TS7 8ER.
•AYRE, Mr. John Laurence, ACA *1979;* John Ayre Limited, 29a Shaw Lane, Holbrook, BELPER, DERBYSHIRE, DE56 0TG.
AYRE, Mr. John Victor, FCA *1965;* 4 The Paddock, Swanland, NORTH FERRIBY, NORTH HUMBERSIDE, HU14 3QW. (Life Member)
•AYRE, Mr. Peter Barrowford, MA ACA *1980;* (Tax Fac), Greaves West & Ayre, 1-3 Sandgate, BERWICK-UPON-TWEED, TD15 1EW.
AYRE, Miss. Tracey, BA ACA *1999;* Woodcroft, Birch Tree Lane, Goostrey, CREWE, CW4 8NS.
AYRE, Mrs. Trudy Gail, BSc ACA *1988;* Haselmere, Park Road, STROUD, GL5 2JG.
AYRES, Mr. Arthur John, BSc FCA *1983;* Integrity Print Ltd, Westfield Trading Estate Midsomer Norton, BATH, BA3 4BS.
AYRES, Mr. Christopher John Julian, ACA *2011;* 43 Peacock Place, LONDON, N1 1YG.
•AYRES, Mr. Christopher Robert, ACA *2005;* (Tax Fac), Longdon Asset Management Ltd, The Old Barrel Store, Draymans Lane, MARLOW, BUCKINGHAMSHIRE, SL7 2FF.
AYRES, Mrs. Claire Louise, LLB ACA *2007;* 4 Wellington Court, ASHFORD, MIDDLESEX, TW15 3RR.
AYRES, Mr. John, FCA *1954;* 50 Cumberland Avenue, Goring-by-Sea, WORTHING, BN12 6JX. (Life Member)
AYRES, Mr. John David, BA ACA *1990;* with PricewaterhouseCoopers, Level 2, 139 Main Street, ROAD TOWN, TORTOLA ISLAND, VIRGIN ISLANDS (BRITISH).
AYRES, Mr. Jonathan James, MA MSc ACA *1999;* C Hoare & Co, PO Box 146, LONDON, EC4P 4DQ.
AYRES, Mr. Mark Andrew, BSc ACA *2005;* with Moore Stephens LLP, 150 Aldersgate Street, LONDON, EC1A 4AB.
AYRES, Mrs. Melissa Jane, BSc ACA *1995;* Firefly, 34 High Street, Silkstone, BARNSLEY, SOUTH YORKSHIRE, S75 4JW.
AYRES, Mr. Michael, BSc FCA *1977;* 96 Old Rectory Drive, HATFIELD, HERTFORDSHIRE, AL10 8FE.
AYRES, Mr. Michael David, BA ACA *1991;* Ashtree House, 4 Rotherby Lane, Frisby On The Wreake, MELTON MOWBRAY, LE14 2NW.
AYRES, Mr. Nigel Paul, MA ACA *1983;* 39 Portsmouth Wood Close, Lindfield, HAYWARDS HEATH, WEST SUSSEX, RH16 2DQ.
AYRES, Mr. Preston Thomas, FCA *1968;* 2 Tudor Gardens, Stony Stratford, MILTON KEYNES, MK11 1HX. (Life Member)
AYRES, Mr. Rhydian John, MSci ACA *2001;* 19 Maes Cefn Mabley, Llantrisant, PONTYCLUN, MID GLAMORGAN, CF72 8GA.
AYRES, Mrs. Rosemary Anne, BSc FCA *1962;* 6 Rue Pierre Crin, 60200 COMPIEGNE, FRANCE.
AYRES, Mr. Stephen George, BSc ACA *1994;* Firefly, 34 High Street, Silkstone, BARNSLEY, SOUTH YORKSHIRE, S75 4JW.
•AYRES, Mr. Stephen Norman, FCA *1978;* Tyas & Company, 5 East Park, CRAWLEY, RH10 6AN.
AYRES, Mr. Terence Arthur, FCA *1972;* BP 15151, Magenta, NOUMEA, 98804, NEW CALEDONIA.
AYRTON, Mr. Grant, ACA *1982;* 18 Alders Avenue, Chinley, HIGH PEAK, SK23 6DS.
•AYRTON, Mr. Jawahar Bomi, ACA *1997;* (Tax Fac), KPMG LLP, 15 Canada Square, LONDON, E14 5GL. See also KPMG Europe LLP
AYRTON, Mr. Mark Nicholas, BA ACA *2000;* NXP Semiconductors, Bramhall Moor Lane, Hazel Grove, STOCKPORT, CHESHIRE, SK7 5BJ.
AYSCOUGH, Mrs. Helen Mary, BSc ACA *1997;* 7 The Greenwood, GUILDFORD, SURREY, GU1 2ND.
AYTON, Mr. David Neil, MSc BSc(Hons) ACA *2001;* Matchtech Group Plc, 1450 Parkway Whiteley, FAREHAM, PO15 7AF.
•AYTON, Mr. David Nigel, BA ACA *1982;* (Tax Fac), D N Ayton, 5 Jenkins Drive, BISHOP AUCKLAND, COUNTY DURHAM, DL14 6XJ.
•AYTON, Mr. John Robert, FCA *1970;* AGM Partners LLP, Suite 9, Innovation Centre, 23 Cambridge Science Park, CAMBRIDGE, CB4 0EY.
AYTON, Mr. Peter George, FCA *1971;* Birds House, 26 Bengal Lane, Greens Norton, TOWCESTER, NN12 8BE.
AYTON, Mr. Ronald Benjamin, FCA *1955;* 20 Homefield Avenue, Newbury Park, ILFORD, IG2 7JG. (Life Member)
AYTON, Mr. Rupert Harry Derrick, FCA *1965;* (Tax Fac), 22 Dukes Road, Lindfield, HAYWARDS HEATH, WEST SUSSEX, RH16 2JQ.
AYUB, Mr. Ijaz, FCA *1980;* Ijaz Ayub CPA, 3521 Brewster Drive, PLANO, TX 75025, UNITED STATES.
AYUB, Mrs. Sameena, BSc ACA *1995;* 1 Wheatfield Avenue, HARPENDEN, HERTFORDSHIRE, AL5 2NU.
AYUB, Mr. Samir, ACA *2009;* Polar Capital, 4 Matthew Parker Street, LONDON, SW1H 9NP.
AYUB, Mr. Tahir, BA ACA *1990;* with PricewaterhouseCoopers, 250 Howe Street, Suite 700, VANCOUVER V6C 3S7, BC, CANADA.
AYUB, Mr. Umer, ACA *1998;* Flat 5, 33-35 Lancaster Gate, LONDON, W2 3LP.
AZAD, Mr. Abul Kalam, FCA *1968;* 188 Perth Road, ILFORD, IG2 6DZ.
AZAD, Mr. Harvinder Singh, BA FCA *1995;* Tall Timbers, 14 Maesmawr Road, LLANGOLLEN, LL20 7PG.
AZADEHDEL, Mr. Robert, BA ACA *2007;* 5 Windermere Road, Beeston, NOTTINGHAM, NG9 3AS.
AZAM, Mr. Ahmar, BSc ACA *1999;* 7 Chipwood Lane, NORTH BRUNSWICK, NJ 08902, UNITED STATES.
•AZAM, Mr. Ammar, BCom FCA *1992;* 9 East Pathway, BIRMINGHAM, B17 9DN.
AZAM, Mr. Farooq, FCA *1968;* P O Box 34833, JEDDAH, 21478, SAUDI ARABIA.
AZAM, Mr. Mohammad, FCA *1971;* 164-165 Badar Block, Allama Iqbal Town, LAHORE, PAKISTAN.
AZAM, Mr. Nasim, MSc BSc(Hons) FCA *2001;* 98 Whitchurch Gardens, EDGWARE, MIDDLESEX, HA8 6PB.
AZAM, Mr. Usman, LLB ACA *2011;* Flat 91 Kimble House, 1 Lilestone Street, LONDON, NW8 8TQ.
•AZARANG, Mrs. Alison Jane, BSc ACA *2004;* Brackman Chopra LLP, 8 Fairfax Mansions, Finchley Road Swiss Cottage, LONDON, NW3 6JY.
AZEMIAN-HEATH, Mrs. Neda, BSc(Hons) ACA *2003;* c/o La Pezerie, 37600 BETZ-LE-CHATEAU, FRANCE.
AZFAR, Mr. Shahab, FCA *1960;* No 27 8th Floor, Sasi Boat View Apartments, Clifton Block #2, KARACHI 75600, PAKISTAN. (Life Member)
AZHAR, Miss. Nadia Anila, BSc ACA *2003;* 17 Jordan Court, Upper Richmond Road, LONDON, SW15 6TJ.
AZIM, Mr. Mohammad Azhar, ACA *2011;* 38 Agrics Town, 4 KM Raiwind Road, LAHORE, PAKISTAN.
AZIM, Mr. Mohammed Aamir Aamir, ACA ACCA CISA *2008;* Floor 23-24 Arraya Tower II Al-Shuhada Street Sharq Safat 13018, KUWAIT CITY, KUWAIT.
AZIZ, Mr. Akhtar Hanif, FCA *1990;* House No. 476 Street No. 10, F-10/2, ISLAMABAD, PAKISTAN.
AZIZ, Mrs. Cathryn Christine, MSc ACA *2004;* 4 Adelaide Terrace, Barrack Road, NORTHAMPTON, NN2 6AH.
AZIZ, Mr. Daniel Hartyun, BSc(Hons) ACA *2004;* 12 Demesne Road, Douglas, ISLE OF MAN, IM1 3EA.
AZIZ, Mr. Fahad Abdul, ACA *2005;* B.A.T Plc, Globe House, 4 Temple Place, LONDON, WC2R 2PG.
AZIZ, Mr. Ghorzang, ACA *2011;* 34 Townsend Way, NORTHWOOD, MIDDLESEX, HA6 1TF.
•AZIZ, Mr. Ibrahim Ismail, BA(Hons) ACA *2006;* (Tax Fac), Numerion Associates LLP, 2 London Wall Buildings, London Wall, LONDON, EC2M 5UU.
AZIZ, Mr. Kamran, FCA *1986;* 104 Western Way, Ponteland, NEWCASTLE UPON TYNE, NE20 9LY.
AZIZ, Mr. Masud-Ul, FCA *1963;* 31/12B Abubakar Block, New Garden Town, LAHORE 54600, PAKISTAN. (Life Member)
AZIZ, Mr. Muhammad Saqib, ACA *2008;* 3 Dorney Place, Bradwell Common, MILTON KEYNES, MK13 8EJ.
AZIZ, Mrs. Naheed, ACA *1978;* 346 Whitewood Drive, ROCKY HILL, CT 06067, UNITED STATES.
AZIZ, Mr. Noordad, ACA *2009;* 19 Greaves Street, Great Harwood, BLACKBURN, BB6 7DY.
AZIZ, Mr. Owais Farid, BA ACA *2004;* Flat 2, 36 Kingsend, RUISLIP, MIDDLESEX, HA4 7DA.
AZIZ, Mr. Rashid Akhtar, FCA *1976;* 2775 West 31st Avenue, VANCOUVER V6L 1Z9, BC, CANADA.
•AZIZ, Mr. Robert Simon, BA ACA *1992;* BDO LLP, 55 Baker Street, LONDON, W1U 7EU. See also BDO Stoy Hayward LLP
AZIZ, Miss. Sana, BSc ACA *2011;* 111 Russell Road, Moseley, BIRMINGHAM, B13 8RS.
•AZIZ, Mrs. Shahjahan, BSc ACA *1994;* Numerion Associates LLP, 2 London Wall Buildings, London Wall, LONDON, EC2M 5UU.
AZIZ, Mr. Tengku Azmil Zahruddin, MA ACA ACT *1997;* 17 Jalan Beverly Heights, Beverly Heights, 68000 AMPANG, SELANGOR, MALAYSIA.
AZIZ, Mr. Tengku Taufik, BA(Hons) ACA *2002;* 21 Jalan Tiara Kemensah 1, Tiara Kemensah, Saujana Melawati, 53100 KUALA LUMPUR, FEDERAL TERRITORY, MALAYSIA.
AZIZ, Mr. Umar Usman, BA(Hons) ACA *2010;* 32 Valley Drive, Handforth, WILMSLOW, CHESHIRE, SK9 3DW.
AZIZUDDIN, Mr. Abid Fauvad, BEng ACA *1993;* 34 Derwent Drive, PURLEY, SURREY, CR8 1EQ.
AZLAN, Mr. Adam Malik, BEng ACA *2004;* ECM Libra Investment Bank, 3rd Floor Wisma Genting, Jalan Sultan Ismail, 50250 KUALA LUMPUR, FEDERAL TERRITORY, MALAYSIA.
AZMI, Mr. Mohammad Faiz, BA FCA *1990;* PricewaterhouseCoopers, P.O.Box 10192, Level 10 1 Sentral, Jalan Travers, 50470 KUALA LUMPUR, FEDERAL TERRITORY MALAYSIA.
AZOOR, Mr. Godfrey Amin, BEng ACA *1993;* 45 Huntley Road, Bentleigh, MELBOURNE, VIC 3204, AUSTRALIA.
AZOOR-HUGHES, Ms. Sufiya Dianne, ACA *1983;* Pitcher Partners, Level 19, 15 William Street, MELBOURNE, VIC 3000, AUSTRALIA.
AZOULAY, Mr. Richard Andrew, MA ACA *1999;* 16 Capital Wharf, Wapping High Street, LONDON, E1W 1LY.
AZOUZ, Mr. Edward, FCA *1973;* Permanent House, 133 Hammersmith Road, LONDON, W14 0QL.
AZZI, Mr. William Peter, BSc ACA *1990;* 8 Sheppy Place, GRAVESEND, KENT, DA12 1BT.
AZZOPARDI, Mrs. Clare, BA(Hons) ACA *2002;* 13 Melaleuca Avenue, Templestowe Lower, MELBOURNE, VIC 3107, AUSTRALIA.
AZZOPARDI, Mr. Stefan John, BSc ACA *1995;* 13 Grantham Road, GLENDOWIE 1071, AUCKLAND, NEW ZEALAND.
•AZZOPARDI-HOLLAND, Mr. Mark, FCA *1990;* Mark Azzopardi-Holland, Valletta Buildings Flat 20, South Street, VALLETTA VLT 1103, MALTA.
BABA, Miss. Lauren, BSc ACA *2011;* Flat C, 84 Edgeley Road, LONDON, SW4 6HB.

BABA, Mr. Sahibzada Muhammed Masood Ahmad, FCA *1973;* 62 Thirlmere Gardens, WEMBLEY, MIDDLESEX, HA9 8RE.
BABAR, Mr. Nauman, BSc(Hons) ACA *2010;* 14 Mallard Row, READING, RG1 6QA.
BABARIYA, Mr. Firoj, BA(Hons) ACA *2002;* 755 Blackburn Road, BOLTON, BL1 7JJ.
BABB, Mr. Colin, ACA *1984;* Wintry Park House, Thornwood Road, EPPING, ESSEX, CM16 6SZ.
BABB, Mr. Robert Alan, FCA *1967;* 6 Woodlands, Mullion, HELSTON, TR12 7RN. (Life Member)
BABBAGE, Mr. Ian James, BSc FCA *1979;* 10 Prior Park Buildings, BATH, BA2 4NP.
BABBAGE, Mrs. June Elizabeth, BSc ACA *1984;* 8 Sauncey Wood, HARPENDEN, AL5 5DP.
BABBAGE, Mr. Stephen Robert, FCA MICM *1980;* Allegra, Real Club Maritim de Barcelona, Moll d'Espanya s/n, 08039 BARCELONA, SPAIN.
BABBE, Mrs. Fiona Sarah, ACA *2010;* 82 Avenue Road, LONDON, N15 5DN.
BABBRA, Mr. Jagpal Singh, BSc(Hons) ACA *2011;* 7 Eltham Lodge, 9a Apsley Close, HARROW, HA2 6DP.
BABBS, Mr. Daniel Colin, BSc(Hons) ACA *2002;* 25 Oxford Court, CHELMSFORD, CM2 6AX.
BABBS, Mr. Graham, ACA *2008;* 20/5 Gooch St., PRAHRAN, VIC 3181, AUSTRALIA.
BABCOCK, Mrs. Stephanie Joanna Susan, BSc ACA *1998;* Woodside, Woodside Church Road, Cookham, MAIDENHEAD, BERKSHIRE, SL6 9PJ.
•BABER, Mrs. Karen Susan, BA ACA *1993;* Karen Baber, 18 Mariners Drive, Backwell, BRISTOL, BS48 3HS.
BABER, Miss. Rachel Lucy, ACA CTA *1992;* Smith & Williamson (Bristol) Llp, Portwall Place Portwall Lane, BRISTOL, BS1 6NA.
BABER, Mr. Ralph Peter, BSc FCA *1983;* Oaklands, 5 Queenborough Gardens, CHISLEHURST, BR7 6NP.
BABER, Miss. Samantha, BSc(Econ) ACA *1998;* Oxford Psychologists Press Elsfield Hall, 15-17 Elsfield Way, OXFORD, OX2 8EP.
BABESHKO, Ms. Anna, ACA *2010;* 15th floor, Canary Wharf Ltd, 1 Canada Square, LONDON, E14 5AB.
BABIAK, Ms. Jan May, CA *2007;* Scotland 1994); MEMBER OF COUNCIL, PO Box 68-1119, FRANKLIN, TN 37068, UNITED STATES.
BABILON-HARRISON, Mrs. Gabriele, BA ACA *1994;* Zum Bruhlsgarten 8, 66706 PERL-NENNIG, GERMANY.
BABINGTON, Mr. Christopher David, LLB ACA *1993;* Tall Pines, Park Grove, CHALFONT ST. GILES, BUCKINGHAMSHIRE, HP8 4BG.
BABINGTON, Mr. Mark, BA FCA *1999;* with National Audit Office, 157-197 Buckingham Palace Road, Victoria, LONDON, SW1W 9SP.
BABLA, Mr. Yogesh Himatsinh, BSc ACA *1992;* 3124 Carnegie Court, SAN DIEGO, CA 92122, UNITED STATES.
BABONEAU, Mr. Michael Gerald, FCA *1972;* ABORIGINAL AFFAIRS AND NORTHERN DEVELOPMENT CANADA, 630 CANADA PLACE 9700 JASPER AVENUE, EDMONTON T5J 4G2, AB, CANADA.
BABOOLALL, Mr. Kabirsingh, BSc ACA *2007;* 29 Masefield Avenue, SOUTHALL, UB1 2NE.
BACCHUS, Mr. Anthony Graham, FCA *1970;* Upton Grey, 4 Bourne Grove, Lower Bourne, FARNHAM, GU10 3QT. (Life Member)
BACCHUS, Ms. Lamia, BSc(Hons) ACA *1991;* NNS Capital, 4 Cork Street, LONDON, W1S 3LG.
•BACCHUS, Mr. Malcolm Graham, MA FCA *1981;* MEMBER OF COUNCIL, Baccma Consulting (MG Bacchus), 92 Jerningham Road, Telegraph Hill, LONDON, SE14 5NW.
BACCHUS, Mr. Peter James, MA ACA *1995;* The White House, Hampton Court Road, EAST MOLESEY, SURREY, KT8 9BS.
•BACCUS, Mr. Alam, ACA *1995;* Baccus, 391 Cranbrook Road, ILFORD, ESSEX, IG1 4UH.
•BACH, Mr. Alan Rene, BMus FCA *1973;* (Tax Fac), Henry Bach & Co, Suite 2, 15 Broad Court, Covent Garden, LONDON, WC2B 5QN.
BACH, Mr. Geoffrey David Benham, FCA *1961;* 6610 Marine Crescent, VANCOUVER V6P 5X1, BC, CANADA.
BACH, Mrs. Karen, BA ACA *1995;* Potts Cottage, Kent Street, Cowfold, HORSHAM, WEST SUSSEX, RH13 8BE.
•BACH, Mrs. Melissa Lisanne Scott, BA ACA *1986;* Gowers Limited, The Old School House, Bridge Road, Hunton Bridge, KINGS LANGLEY, HERTFORDSHIRE WD4 8SZ.
BACH, Mr. Michael Alan, BA ACA *1979;* 12 Colorado Avenue, READING, PA 19608, UNITED STATES.
BACH, Mr. Michael Vaughan, MEng FCA *1988;* 14 Lincoln Street, NORWICH, NR2 3LA.
BACH, Mr. Roger Andrew, BA ACA *1985;* The Cedars, Wayside, LONDON, NW11 8QY.
BACH, Ms. Susannah Mary, MA CA ACA *1989;* Canadian Direct Insurance, Suite 600-750 Cambie Stree, VANCOUVER V6B OA2, BC, CANADA.
BACHA, Mr. Poorendranath, FCA *1977;* Bacha & Co, 62 S.S.R. Avenue, QUATRE-BORNES, MAURITIUS.
BACHA, Mr. Rubendranath, BA ACA *2006;* 9th Floor, Bacha Building, Cathedral Square, PORT LOUIS, MAURITIUS.
BACHA, Mr. Toshlen Anil, BSc ACA *2011;* 9th Floor, Les Bacha, Cathedral Sqaure, PORT LOUIS, MAURITIUS.
•BACHA, Mr. Yogendranath, BA(Hons) ACA *2002;* Bacha and Bacha, Steamhouse, 555 White Hart Lane, LONDON, N17 7RP.
•BACHA, Mr. Yogendranath, FCA *1973;* Bacha and Bacha, Steamhouse, 555 White Hart Lane, LONDON, N17 7RP.
BACHADA, Mr. Ajit Singh, MSc BSc ACA *2008;* 18 Redlake Drive, STOURBRIDGE, DY9 0RX.
BACHE, Mr. Mark John Thomas, BSc FCA *1989;* 4 Silhill Hall Road, SOLIHULL, B91 1JU.
BACHE, Mr. Matthew, BSc ACA *1993;* 39 Wellington Road, RAYLEIGH, ESSEX, SS6 8EX.
BACHE, Mrs. Nicola Mary, BCom ACA CTA *1989;* 4 Silhill Hall Road, SOLIHULL, B91 1JU.
BACHE, Mr. Richard Henry, FCA *1971;* 4 Oldfields, Hagley, STOURBRIDGE, WEST MIDLANDS, DY9 0QG. (Life Member)
BACHELOR, Mr. Mark Alan, MEng ACA *2008;* 55 Great Meadow, TIPTON, WEST MIDLANDS, DY4 7NF.
•BACHRACH, Mr. Simon Mark, FCA *1986;* Chalmers & Co (SW) Limited, 6 Linen Yard, South Street, CREWKERNE, SOMERSET, TA18 8AB.
BACK, Mr. Graeme Andrew, BA ACA *1999;* Hill Dickinson Co Ltd, 1 St. Pauls Square, LIVERPOOL, L3 9SJ.
BACK, Mr. Jonathan David, BSc ACA *1989;* Darland Hall Farm Darland Lane, Rossett, WREXHAM, CLWYD, LL12 0BA.
BACK, Mr. Martin Howard, BSc FCA *1976;* 6a Church Road, Wickham Bishops, WITHAM, ESSEX, CM8 3LA.
BACK, Mr. Nicholas John, MA ACA *2001;* Murco Petroleum Ltd, 4 Beaconsfield Road, ST. ALBANS, HERTFORDSHIRE, AL1 3RH.
BACK, Mr. Nigel Barry Quarles, FCA *1974;* Washingford House, Cookes Road, Bergh Apton, NORWICH, NR15 1AA.
BACK, Mr. Oliver Watson Maillard, ACA *2008;* 20 Solent Road, LONDON, NW6 1TU.
BACK, Mr. Simon Richard, BA ACA *2002;* 124 Dower Road, SUTTON COLDFIELD, WEST MIDLANDS, B75 6TL.
•BACK, Mr. Terence Alan James, FCA *1980;* Grant Thornton UK LLP, Grant Thornton House, 22 Melton Street, Euston Square, LONDON, NW1 2EP. See also Grant Thornton LLP
BACKER, Mr. Thomas Alfred, BA FCA *1975;* La Michele, Les Hubits, St. Martin, GUERNSEY, GY4 6NB. (Life Member)
BACKES, Mr. David Grahame, ACA *1982;* Howard Garages (Weston) Ltd, Searle Crescent, WESTON-SUPER-MARE, BS23 3YX.
•BACKES, Miss. Natalie, BA(Hons) ACA ATT *2002;* Natalie Backes, 93 Listria Park, LONDON, N16 5SP.
BACKHOUSE, Mr. Anthony Douglas, FCA *1972;* 33 Sutherland Chase, ASCOT, BERKSHIRE, SL5 8TE.
BACKHOUSE, Mr. Benjamin Geoffrey, MA ACA *1998;* Backhouse Solicitors Ltd Carlton House, 101 New London Road, CHELMSFORD, CM2 0PP.
BACKHOUSE, Mr. Bernard John, FCA *1960;* 40 Beatrice Road, Worsley, MANCHESTER, M28 2TN.
BACKHOUSE, Mr. Christopher Mark, BA FCA *1981;* 21 Dettingen Crescent, Deepcut, CAMBERLEY, GU16 6GN.
•BACKHOUSE, Mr. Clive John, BA FCA *1981;* NCR Accountants Ltd, Miller House, Rosslyn Crescent, HARROW, MIDDLESEX, HA1 2RZ.
BACKHOUSE, Mr. David Ian, BEng ACA *1998;* 36 Netherbury Road, LONDON, W5 4SP.
BACKHOUSE, Mr. David Wynter, MA FCA *1981;* Thames Valley Police, Force Training Centre, Sulhamstead, READING, RG7 4DX.
BACKHOUSE, Mr. Edward Andrew, BSc ACA *1985;* Dodsleigh Grange, Dodsleigh, Leigh, STOKE-ON-TRENT, ST10 4QA.
BACKHOUSE, Mrs. Joanna Alice Roxby, BSc FCA *1983;* Croft Ends, Maulds Meaburn, PENRITH, CUMBRIA, CA10 3HN.
BACKHOUSE, Mr. Michael, BA ACA *1981;* 20 Clifton Green, YORK, YO30 6LN.
BACKHOUSE, Mr. Neil Vivian, FCA *1970;* ExxonMobil Qatar Inc. ExxonMobil House, Ermyn Way, LEATHERHEAD, KT22 8UX.
BACKHOUSE, Mr. Nicholas Paul, MA ACA *1988;* Tidemark, Spinney Lane, Itchenor, CHICHESTER, WEST SUSSEX, PO20 7DJ.
BACKHOUSE, Mr. Robert John, FCA *1964;* Alucast Ltd, Western Way, WEDNESBURY, WEST MIDLANDS, WS10 7BW.
BACKHOUSE, Mrs. Wendy Margaret, ACA *1984;* 23 York Road, MALTON, NORTH YORKSHIRE, YO17 6AX.
BACKLER, Mrs. Catherine Naomi, LLB ACA *2000;* Charles White Ltd, 92 Morningside Road, EDINBURGH, EH10 4BY.
BACKMAN, Mr. John Martin, ACA *2008;* Gallåkersvägen 37, 239 32 SKANOR, SWEDEN.
BACKMAN, Ms. Katie Eve, BSc ACA *2000;* 27 Hogarth Hill, LONDON, NW11 6AY.
BACKWELL, Mrs. Kate Louise, BSc ACA *1997;* 85 Prospect Hill Road, CAMBERWELL, VIC 3124, AUSTRALIA.
BACON, Mr. Alan James, ACA *1986;* 7 Orchard Way, Keinton Mandeville, SOMERTON, SOMERSET, TA11 6EX.
BACON, Mr. Charles Philip, FCA *1960;* 107 Hummersknott Avenue, DARLINGTON, DL3 8RR. (Life Member)
BACON, Mr. David Michael, FCA *1957;* 3 York Terrace West, Regents Park, LONDON, NW1 4QA. (Life Member)
BACON, Mr. David Philip, MBA BA ACA *1986;* 5 Millers Gardens, MARKET HARBOROUGH, LE16 9FE.
BACON, Mr. Gerard Dominic Andrew, BSc ACA *1987;* Little Heath, Crays Pond, READING, RG8 7QG.
BACON, Mr. Iain James, BSc ACA *1990;* Veterinary Laboratories Agency, Woodham Lane, New Haw, ADDLESTONE, SURREY, KT15 3NB.
BACON, Ms. Jenifer Judite, BSc ACA *1996;* ASCO Trinidad Limited, 52 New Street, PORT OF SPAIN, TRINIDAD AND TOBAGO.
BACON, Mr. John, BA(Hons) ACA *2001;* Keys Hill Park Park Road, Wroxham, NORWICH, NR12 8SB.
BACON, Mrs. Juliana Elisabeth, BA ACA *1999;* 12 Princes Avenue, CARSHALTON, SURREY, SM5 4NZ.
BACON, Mrs. Karen Jayne, BA ACA *1992;* 1 Halls Lane, Keelby, GRIMSBY, DN41 8DE.
•BACON, Mr. Michael Albert, BSc ACA *1984;* (Tax Fac), KPMG LLP, 15 Canada Square, LONDON, E14 5GL. See also KPMG Europe LLP
BACON, Mr. Michael John, BSc ACA *1985;* 3 Greenview Drive, TOWCESTER, NN12 6DL.
BACON, Miss. Michelle Louise, BSc ACA *2005;* 54 Mossvale Drive, WAKERLEY, QLD 4154, AUSTRALIA.
•BACON, Mr. Nicholas, BA ACA ATII *1990;* Ernst & Young LLP, 1 More London Place, LONDON, SE1 2AF. See also Ernst & Young Europe LLP
•BACON, Mr. Nicholas Robert, BA ACA *1982;* N R Bacon Ltd, 19 Queens Road, Sketty, SWANSEA, SA2 0SD.
•BACON, Mr. Nigel Douglas, BSc FCA *1984;* Secantor Limited, Forward House, 17 High Street, HENLEY-IN-ARDEN, WEST MIDLANDS, B95 5AA.
BACON, Mr. Philip Anthony, MA ACA *1987;* Velázquez 119 5A, 28043 MADRID, SPAIN.
•BACON, Mr. Richard Francis, BSc FCA *1979;* (Tax Fac), 47 Deepdene Avenue, DORKING, RH5 4AA.
•BACON, Mr. Richard Francis, BSc FCA *1991;* PricewaterhouseCoopers, Cornwall Court, 19 Cornwall Street, BIRMINGHAM, B3 2DT. See also PricewaterhouseCoopers LLP
BACON, Mr. Richard William, FCA *1968;* 24 Tweed Way, Rise Park, ROMFORD, RM1 4AZ. (Life Member)
BACON, Mr. Robert Arthur, FCA *1972;* Visage Imports Ltd, 56 Shaftesbury Avenue, SOUTH SHIELDS, TYNE AND WEAR, NE34 9PH.
BACON, Mr. Rodney Martyn, FCA *1961;* Jan Van Ruusbroeclaan 35, B-3080, TERVUREN, BELGIUM.
BACON, Mr. Roger, FCA *1966;* 6 Howlett Drive, HAILSHAM, EAST SUSSEX, BN27 1QW.
BACON, Mr. Roger Philip, FCA *1971;* Hernshaw, Knowle Lane, CRANLEIGH, GU6 8JN.
BACON, Dr. Sarah Louise, PhD ACA *2004;* 6 Colyton Road, LONDON, SE22 0NE.
BACON, Mrs. Sharon Jane, BSc ACA *2001;* 6 Wensum Crescent, NORWICH, NR6 5DL.
BACON, Mrs. Suzanne Patricia, ACA *2010;* Flat 3, 1 Alma Road, Clifton, BRISTOL, BS8 2BZ.
BACON, Mr. Theodore Sidney, FCA *1956;* 8 Manley Close, New Earswick, YORK, YO32 4DN. (Life Member)
BACON, Mr. Timothy Reginald, FCA *1973;* Applegarth, Somers Road, LYME REGIS, DORSET, DT7 3EX.
BACQUIE, Mr. Peter Jermyn, BA ACA *1978;* 19820 SW 7th Place, PEMBROKE PINES, FL 33029, UNITED STATES.
BADALA, Mr. Pervinder Singh, ACA *2011;* 141 Headley Drive, Gants Hill, ILFORD, ESSEX, IG2 6QJ.
BADAMI, Mr. Baqir, ACA *1995;* P O Box 339, DAMMAM, 31411, SAUDI ARABIA.
BADAR, Mr. Mohamed Ashraf, FCA *1975;* 77 Hillend Road, Clarkston, GLASGOW, G76 7XT.
BADAT, Mr. Osman Mahmad, FCA *1998;* with British American Investment Co. (MTIUS) Ltd, BAI Building, 25 Pope Hennessy Street, PO Box 331, PORT LOUIS, MAURITIUS.
BADCOCK, Mr. Benjamin Edward, BA ACA *1997;* Interserve Plc Interserve House, Ruscombe Park Ruscombe, READING, RG10 9JU.
•BADCOCK, Mr. Ian Leslie, BA FCA *1987;* (Tax Fac), Badcock Business Solutions Limited, 4 Prince William Close, WORTHING, WEST SUSSEX, BN14 0AZ.
BADCOCK, Mr. James David, BSc ACA *1996;* 92 Kyrle Road, LONDON, SW11 6BA.
BADCOCK, Mr. Peter George, FCA *1964;* 15 Lowndes Avenue, CHESHAM, HP5 2HH. (Life Member)
•BADCOCK, Mrs. Sophia Belinda, BSc ACA *1991;* (Tax Fac), The Tax Advisor Ltd, 1 Adam Business Centre, Henson Way, Industrial Estate, KETTERING, NORTHAMPTONSHIRE NN16 8PX.
BADDELEY, Mr. Andrew Martin, FCA *1987;* Shepherds Hey, Clenches Farm Lane, SEVENOAKS, TN13 2LX.
BADDELEY, Miss. Anna Louise, MSc ACA *2004;* 4 Hartside Close, Gamston, NOTTINGHAM, NG2 6NW.
BADDELEY, Mr. David Martin, BA ACA *2009;* 146 Totley Brook Road, SHEFFIELD, S17 3QU.
BADDELEY, Mr. Hugh Frame, FCA *1972;* Farn Brakes, Rudgwick, HORSHAM, RH12 3EJ. (Life Member)
BADDELEY, Mr. Kevin David, LLB ACA *2010;* 44 Flanders Court, 12-14 St Albans Road, WATFORD, HERTFORDSHIRE, WD17 1BN.
BADDELEY, Mr. Robert Gregory, BA FCA *1980;* 71 Park Road, Hale, ALTRINCHAM, CHESHIRE, WA15 9LN.
BADDELEY, Mr. Simon Irvine, FCA *1972;* 24 Queen Annes Grove, Bedford Park, LONDON, W4 1HN.
BADDELEY, Mr. Stuart David, BSc ACA *1994;* 290 Reading Road, Winnersh, WOKINGHAM, BERKSHIRE, RG41 5AH.
BADDELEY-CHAPPELL, Mr. Andrew David, BSc ACA *1990;* Nationwide Building Society, Nationwide House, Pipers Way, SWINDON, SN38 1NW.
BADDI, Mr. Aftab Farooq, ACA *2008;* Premier Group W.L.L., 4th Floor, Bahrain Commercial Complex, Government Avenue, PO Box 836, MANAMA PO Box 836 BAHRAIN.
BADDILEY, Mr. Peter, ACA *1986;* Bluebell Cottage, 3-4 School Lane, Peatling Magna, LEICESTER, LE8 5US.
BADDILEY, Mrs. Stephanie Jayne, BA ACA *1991;* Bluebell Cottage, 3-4 School Lane, Peatling Magna, LEICESTER, LE8 5US.
BADEN, Mr. Anthony David, BA FCA DChA *1991;* Flat 17 Rosemount Park, Rosemount Close, PRENTON, MERSEYSIDE, CH43 2LR.
BADEN, Mr. Tej Singh, ACA *2008;* Rexall Chemist, 204 Penn Road, WOLVERHAMPTON, WV4 4AA.
BADENOCH, Mr. Alexander Brunton, FCA *1970;* 77 Addison Road, LONDON, W14 8EB.
BADENOCH-JONES, Mr. Paul Harwood, FCA *1977;* 179/280 Supalai Place Condominium, Sukhumvit Soi 39, Klongton, Wattana, BANGKOK 10110, THAILAND.
BADERMAN, Mrs. Catherine Emma, BA ACA *1993;* 233 South Wacker Drive, Suite 4200, CHICAGO, IL 60606, UNITED STATES.
BADESHA, Mrs. Harbinder, BA ACA *2005;* 11 Beaver Close, COLCHESTER, CO3 9DZ.
BADETHALAV, Mr. Gopal Sundarraj, ACA *1986;* 41 Kimberley Avenue, Lane Cove, SYDNEY, NSW 2066, AUSTRALIA.
BADGER, Mr. Adam Douglas, BSc(Hons) ACA *2004;* European Space Agency, 8-10 rue Mario-Nikis, F75738, Cedex 15 PARIS, FRANCE.
BADGER, Mr. James Colin Thomas, BSc ACA *2004;* 8 Fowlmere Road, Thriplow, ROYSTON, HERTFORDSHIRE, SG8 7QU.
BADGER, Mr. John Stuart, FCA *1959;* PO Box 250, Udorn Thani Post Office, UDON THANI 41000, THAILAND. (Life Member)
BADGER, Mr. Kevin John, BSc ACA *2010;* 148 Bladindon Drive, BEXLEY, KENT, DA5 3BW.
BADGER, Mr. Roger Gregory, FCA *1970;* Yew Tree House, 27 Warwick Road, BISHOP'S STORTFORD, CM23 5NH.

•**BADGER, Mr. Ross Wyndham, FCA** *1980;* (Tax Fac), Hillier Hopkins LLP, Dukes Court, 32 Duke Street, LONDON, SW1Y 6DF.
BADGER, Mr. Stephen Nicholas, BSc ACA *2002;* 53 All Saints Close, WOKINGHAM, RG40 1WE.
•**BADHWAR, Mr. Sharad, BSc ACA CTA** *1992;* (Tax Fac), Sharad Badhwar BSc ACA CTA, 17 Balmoral Road, HARROW, MIDDLESEX, HA2 8TF.
BADHWAR, Mr. Varisht, FCA *1984;* Badhwar & Co, C-28 East of Kailash, NEW DELHI 110065, INDIA.
BADHWAR, Mr. Vivek, BA ACA *1991;* 17 Balmoral Road, HARROW, HA2 8TF.
BADIANI, Mr. Aman, BSc ACA *2007;* Woodgate Healthcare, 3 Grace House, Bessborough Road, HARROW, MIDDLESEX, HA1 3EX.
BADIANI, Mr. Arvind Premjibhai, FCA *1971;* 1074 DEACON DRIVE, MILTON L9T 5S7, ON, CANADA.
BADIANI, Mr. Chandu Nanji, FCA *1973;* 18 The Mount, WEMBLEY, MIDDLESEX, HA9 9EE.
BADIANI, Mr. Sunit Hasmukhkant, ACA *2009;* 32 Beechcroft Gardens, WEMBLEY, MIDDLESEX, HA9 8EP.
•**BADIANI, Mr. Tony, BSc ACA** *1996;* Calder & Co, 1 Regent Street, LONDON, SW1Y 4NW.
•**BADMAN, Mr. John, FCA** *1966;* Coope Badman & Co., 209 Church Street, BLACKPOOL, FY1 3TE.
BADMAN, Mr. Matthew Philip, BSc ACA *2008;* 56 Youghal Close, CARDIFF, CF23 8RN.
BADMAN, Mr. Nicholas Jeremy Rupert, MA ACA *1994;* Penfida Partners LLP, 1 Carey Lane, LONDON, EC2V 8AE.
BADMAN, Mr. Paul Woodland, MA FCA *1972;* Southways, Burkes Crescent, BEACONSFIELD, HP9 1PD.
BADRICK, Mr. Simon Francis Charles, ACA *1989;* 1 Park Road, SUDBURY, CO10 2QB.
BADROCK, Mr. Kevin, FCA *1985;* 21 Oak Road, Saltney, CHESTER, CH4 8NR.
BADSHAH, Mrs. Christina, BSc ACA *1993;* 46 Beech Hill, Hadley Wood, BARNET, HERTFORDSHIRE, EN4 0JJ.
BAEHR, Mr. Laurence Josef, FCA *1981;* TP Suite 309, Ctra.Moraira Teulada 62, Centro Commercial Barclays, 03724 MORAIRA, ALICANTE, SPAIN.
BAER, Miss. Lucy Alix St Clair, BA FCA *1987;* (Tax Fac), with Moore Stephens LLP, 150 Aldersgate Street, LONDON, EC1A 4AB.
BAGARIA, Miss. Ambika, MSc BSc(Hons) ACA *2011;* Flat 177, Chiltern Court, Baker Street, LONDON, NW1 5SG.
BAGARY, Mr. Balwinder Singh, LLB ACA *1994;* 21 Boscombe Road, SINGAPORE 439765, SINGAPORE.
BAGARY, Mrs. Jasbir Kaur, BA ACA *1990;* Priors, Doggetts Wood Lane, CHALFONT ST. GILES, BUCKINGHAMSHIRE, HP8 4TH.
BAGASRAWALLA, Miss. Tarifa Mohmed, BSc ACA *2007;* Apartment 18, 874 Wilmslow Road, MANCHESTER, M20 5AB.
BAGBY, Mr. Graham, ACA *1993;* 2 Dryersfie, Boughton, CHESTER, CH3 5RQ.
BAGBY, Mrs. Mary Caroline, BSc ACA *1996;* 2 Dryersfield, Boughton, CHESTER, CH3 5RQ.
BAGDADES, Mrs. Marina Andrea, BSc ACA *1990;* P.O. Box 23303, 1681 NICOSIA, CYPRUS.
BAGE, Mr. Alan William, FCA *1971;* Middlesbrough Football Club Riverside Stadium, Middlehaven Way, MIDDLESBROUGH, CLEVELAND, TS3 6RS.
BAGE, Miss. Helen Louise, BA ACA *2004;* 2 Westfield Terrace, LEEDS, LS7 3QG.
BAGE, Mrs. Katherine Louise, BSc ACA *2009;* 26 Broadacres, GUILDFORD, SURREY, GU3 3AZ.
BAGGA, Miss. Monika, BSc ACA *1998;* Beech Lodge, Snowball Hill, MAIDENHEAD, SL6 3LU.
BAGGA, Mrs. Somali, BSc ACA *1999;* Freshfields BD, 65 Fleet Street, LONDON, EC4Y 1HT.
•**BAGGALEY, Mr. Brian Samuel, FCA** *1974;* Hardings, 6 Marsh Parade, NEWCASTLE, ST5 1DU.
•**BAGGALEY, Mr. John Anthony, FCA** *1968;* William Harling & Co, 23 Abingdon Street, BLACKPOOL, FY1 1DG.
BAGGALEY, Miss. Joy Elizabeth, BA FCA *1984;* The Maples, 19a Willowtree Road, ALTRINCHAM, WA14 2EQ.
•**BAGGALEY, Miss. Michelle Jennifer, FCA** *1975;* Michelle Baggaley, 17 Walsingham Road, Childwall, LIVERPOOL, L16 3NR.
BAGGE, Sir John Jeremy Picton, Bt FCA *1968;* Stradsett Estate Office, Stradsett, KING'S LYNN, PE33 9HA.
BAGGETT, Mrs. Elizabeth Abigail, BSc ACA *1995;* Finance, The University of Buckingham Yeomanry House, Hunter Street, BUCKINGHAM, MK18 1EG.
•**BAGGOTT, Mr. Andrew Duncan, BA ACA ATII** *1994;* Clarke Nicklin LLP, Clarke Nicklin House, Brooks Drive, Cheadle Royal Business Park, CHEADLE, CHESHIRE SK8 3TD.
BAGGOTT, Mr. David Ian, BSocSc ACA *1999;* Windsor Life Assurance Company Ltd, Windsor House, Ironmasters Way, Town Centre, TELFORD, SHROPSHIRE TF3 4NB.
BAGGOTT, Mr. David John, BA ACA *2011;* 9 Kinder Drive, Marple, STOCKPORT, CHESHIRE, SK6 7BU.
BAGGOTT, Miss. Elizabeth Jane, ACA *2009;* 9 Kinder Drive, Marple, STOCKPORT, CHESHIRE, SK6 7BU.
BAGGOTT, Mr. Joseph George, ACA *2009;* 84 Moorland Road, CARDIFF, CF24 2LP.
BAGGOTT, Mr. Laurence Ingram, FCA *1968;* 7 Blandford Road, LONDON, W4 1DU.
BAGGOTT, Mr. Martin, FCA CTA *1964;* 9 Kinder Drive, Marple, STOCKPORT, CHESHIRE, SK6 7BU. (Life Member)
BAGGOTT, Mr. Peter, BA FCA *1979;* 1 Beech Road, Hollywood, BIRMINGHAM, B47 5QS.
BAGGOTT, Mr. Robert David, FCA *1951;* 40 Hallam Grange Road, SHEFFIELD, S10 4BJ. (Life Member)
BAGGS, Mr. David John, ACA *1992;* 11 Seymour Gardens, Hanworth, FELTHAM, MIDDLESEX, TW13 7PQ.
BAGGS, Mr. David Richard, FCA *1969;* Teigncombe Park View Road, Woldingham, CATERHAM, CR3 7DL.
•**BAGGS, Mrs. Deborah Jane, ACA** *1991;* 50 Alleyn Road, Dulwich, LONDON, SE21 8AL.
•**BAGGS, Mr. Ian Jonathan Jordan, BSc FCA** *1991;* Ernst & Young LLP, 1 More London Place, LONDON, SE1 2AF. See also Ernst & Young Europe LLP
BAGGS, Mr. Shawn, BSc ACA *2003;* 15 Greenway, BERKHAMSTED, HERTFORDSHIRE, HP4 3JD.
BAGHERI, Mr. Shahriar, BSc ACA *1985;* 7502 Brickyard Road, POTOMAC, MD 20854, UNITED STATES.
BAGIER, Mr. Gordon Duncan, BA(Hons) ACA *2003;* 148 Holyfields, West Allothent, NEWCASTLE UPON TYNE, NE27 0EX.
•**BAGINSKY, Mr. Sidney, FCA** *1966;* (Tax Fac), 10 Derwent Avenue, Mill Hill, LONDON, NW7 3DZ.
BAGLEY, Mr. Andrew Charles, BSc(Hons) ACA *2004;* 27 Meadow Rise, Townhill, SWANSEA, SA1 6RG.
•**BAGLEY, Mr. David John, BA FCA CF** *1981;* 12 Welburn, 222 Graham Road, SHEFFIELD, S10 3GS.
•**BAGLEY, Mrs. Gaenor Anne, MA ACA** *1990;* PricewaterhouseCoopers LLP, 1 Embankment Place, LONDON, WC2N 6RH. See also PricewaterhouseCoopers
•**BAGLEY, Mr. James Oliver John, ACA** *2007;* Smith Cooper, Wilmot House, St James Court, Friar Gate, DERBY, DE1 1BT.
BAGLEY, Mr. Laurence William, BCom ACA *1987;* 40 Coltbeck Avenue, Narborough, LEICESTER, LE19 3EJ.
BAGLEY, Mr. Mark Edmund, BA ACA *2007;* 5 Ambleside Drive, Headington, OXFORD, OX3 0AG.
BAGLEY, Mr. Peter Anthony, MA FCA *1990;* Beggar's Roost, Priorsfield Road, GODALMING, SURREY, GU7 2RG.
BAGLIN, Mr. Edward Andrew, FCA *1975;* 23 The Vale, Stock, INGATESTONE, CM4 9PW.
BAGLIN, Miss. Lisa Claire, MA ACA *1996;* 42 Roderick Road, LONDON, NW3 2NL.
BAGLOW, Mr. Guy, BSc ACA *1993;* 9 Skimmington Cottages, Reigate Heath, REIGATE, RH2 8RL.
•**BAGNALL, Mr. Andrew Mark, FCA** *1992;* Johnstone Howell & Co, Fairfield House, 104 Whitby Road, ELLESMERE PORT, CHESHIRE, CH65 0AB.
•**BAGNALL, Mr. Charles Andrew St John, FCA** *1968;* Andrew Bagnall, Wyndham House, The Street, Market Weston, DISS, IP22 2NZ.
BAGNALL, Mr. Christopher John, BA ACA *2006;* 135 Graham Road, SHEFFIELD, S10 3GP.
BAGNALL, Mr. David Leonard, FCA *1964;* 2 Meadway, Bramhall, STOCKPORT, SK7 1LA.
BAGNALL, Mrs. Gillian, BA ACA *1994;* PO Box 181, WITNEY, OX28 6WD.
BAGNALL, Mr. Ian Russell, BSc FCA *1991;* 40 St. Andrews Park, Tarragon Road, MAIDSTONE, ME16 0WD.
BAGNALL, Mr. James, FCA *1956;* 34-50 Fiddlers Green Road, LONDON N6H 4T4, ON, CANADA. (Life Member)
BAGNALL, Mr. John Keith, FCA *1965;* Shackleton House Farm, North Walk, Long Lane, Harden, BINGLEY, WEST YORKSHIRE BD16 1RY.
BAGNALL, Mr. John Leonard, FCA *1965;* 5 Grange Court, Eynsham Road, Cumnor, OXFORD, OX2 9BJ.
BAGNALL, Mrs. Julie, BSc ACA *2006;* 1 Oberon Way, BLYTH, NORTHUMBERLAND, NE24 3RU.
BAGNALL, Mr. Paul Andrew, BA ACA *1989;* 10 Glastonbury Close, Nailsea, BRISTOL, BS48 2SP.
BAGNALL, Mr. Robin Anthony, FCA *1972;* 5 Five Oaks Close, Seabridge, NEWCASTLE, ST5 3BE.
BAGNALL, Mrs. Sara Alexandra, BA ACA *1995;* 92 St. Johns Road, ISLEWORTH, MIDDLESEX, TW7 6PG.
BAGOL, Miss. Sabeena Kaur, BSc ACA *1998;* 33 Sunderland Road, LONDON, W5 4JY.
BAGOT, Mr. Neil David, BSc ACA *2007;* Apartment 21 Dukes Wharf, Wharf Road, NOTTINGHAM, NG7 1GD.
BAGOT, Mr. Peter James Cornelius, FCA *1960;* Five Oaks, Moss Side Lane, Wrea Green, PRESTON, PR4 2PE. (Life Member)
BAGOT JEWITT, Mrs. Phillippa Louise Margaret, MA ACA *1993;* Diocesan Board of Finance St Marys House, The Close, LICHFIELD, STAFFORDSHIRE, WS13 7LD.
BAGREE, Mr. Prashant Kumar, BA(Hons) ACA *2011;* 100 Warwick Road, LONDON, N11 2ST.
BAGRI, Mr. Jaspaul, BA ACA *1991;* 1 RUE AMIEL, 1203 GENEVA, SWITZERLAND.
BAGRI, Mr. Pavanjeet Singh, BA ACA *2007;* 21 Alder Drive, PUDSEY, WEST YORKSHIRE, LS28 8RD.
BAGSHAW, Mr. David Lorraine, MSc FCA *1967;* 4 Sandford Drive, Woodley, READING, RG5 4RR.
BAGSHAW, Mrs. Elisabeth Anne, BSc ACA *1982;* Chiltington International Ltd Holland House, 1-4 Bury Street, LONDON, EC3A 5AW.
BAGSHAW, Mr. Guy Robert Thomas, BEng ACA *2004;* Flat 3, 69 Stockport Road, Timperley, ALTRINCHAM, WA15 7LH.
BAGSHAW, Ms. Katharine Elizabeth, BA FCA *1990;* Hillock Cottage, Grindsbrook Booth, Edale, HOPE VALLEY, S33 7ZD.
BAGSHAW, Mr. Michael John, BSc FCA *1978;* 30 Moffats Lane, Brookmans Park, HATFIELD, AL9 7RU.
BAGSHAW, Mr. Nigel Charles, BA ACA *1992;* 3 Kempsford Close, Baguley, MANCHESTER, M23 1LH.
BAGSHAW, Mr. Paul Jonathan, BSc FCA *1973;* Birchrun, Hill Road, HASLEMERE, GU27 2NH.
•**BAGSHAW, Mr. Roger David, ACA** *1980;* Bonham Bagshaw, 25 Greenfield Avenue, NORTHAMPTON, NN3 2AA.
BAGSHAW, Ms. Sarah, BA(Hons) ACA *1995;* 11 Nelson Gardens, Inskip, PRESTON, PR4 0TR.
BAGSHAWE, Mr. James Richard, BSc FCA *1983;* Dene Manor, Meopham, GRAVESEND, DA13 0BS.
•**BAGSHAWE, Mr. Rohan Eric, FCA** *1979;* (Tax Fac), Potter & Pollard Ltd, Richmond Court, 216 Capstone Road, BOURNEMOUTH, BH8 8RX. See also Stephen Penny and Parnters
•**BAGULEY, Mr. Andrew Mark, BSc ACA** *1996;* 30 Macrae Road, Ham Green, BRISTOL, BS20 0EB.
BAGULEY, Mr. Robert David Arthur, BSc ACA *1980;* Neubadrain 69, 4102 BINNINGEN, SWITZERLAND.
BAGULEY, Mr. Robert Harold, FCA *1957;* 10 Leawood Croft, Holloway, MATLOCK, DE4 5BD. (Life Member)
BAGULEY, Mr. Roy, FCA *1953;* 11 Hasley Road, Burley in Wharfedale, ILKLEY, WEST YORKSHIRE, LS29 7PW. (Life Member)
•**BAGWORTH, Mr. Steven Michael, BA ACA** *1992;* with Ernst & Young LLP, 1 Colmore Square, BIRMINGHAM, B4 6HQ.
BAHADUR, Miss. Meghna, ACA *2009;* with Deloitte LLP, Hill House, 1 Little New Street, LONDON, EC4A 3TR.
BAHAJ, Mr. Bashir, BSc ACA *2007;* Flat 3, 21 Hamilton Road, LONDON, W5 2EE.
BAHAL, Mr. Anuj, BSc ACA *1995;* FTI Consulting, 3 Times Square, 11th Floor, NEW YORK, NY 10036, UNITED STATES.
BAHAL, Mrs. Ritu, BSc ACA *1996;* 20 Shawnee Road, SHORT HILLS, NJ 07078, UNITED STATES.
BAHARIL, Mr. Imran, ACA *2009;* 2 Pavillion Court, 7 Nursery Road Wimbledon, LONDON, SW19 4JA.
BAHARUDIN, Mr. Zifri, BEng ACA *2005;* 37 Prospect House, Frean Street, LONDON, SE16 4AE.
BAHARUM-REMIL, Mrs. Siti Asriah, BSc(Hons) ACA *2001;* 14 rue Juge, Appart 23, 75015 PARIS, FRANCE.
•**BAHEMIA, Mr. Ismael Ibrahim, FCA** *1975;* Fideco Global Business Services Ltd, 44 St George Street, PORT LOUIS, MAURITIUS. See also BDO International
BAHEMIA, Mr. Mohammad Riyaz Abubakar Hassam, BSc ACA *1999;* Patel Street, Mare Gravier, BEAU BASSIN, MAURITIUS.
BAHEMIA, Mr. Muhammad Osman, ACA *1992;* Deloitte & Touche, P O Box 431, DOHA, QATAR.
BAHER, Miss. Ralda, BSc ACA *1993;* Flat E, 10 Daleham Gardens, LONDON, NW3 5DA.
BAHIA, Mr. Satbinder Singh, BA ACA *1994;* 7 Stoke Court Drive, Stoke Poges, SLOUGH, SL2 4LT.
•**BAHL, Mr. Ajay Kumar, BA ACA** *1995;* (Tax Fac), Wenn Townsend, 30 St Giles', OXFORD, OX1 3LE. See also Wenn Townsend Accountants Limited
BAHL, Mr. Ashok, FCA *1966;* MSG Advisers P Ltd, 9 Prithiraj Road, NEW DELHI 110011, INDIA.
BAHL, Mrs. Kim Elaine, ACA CTA *2000;* 15 Kilnside, Claygate, ESHER, SURREY, KT10 0HS.
BAHL, Mr. Navin, FCA *1966;* N. Bahl & Co, A 9/34 Vasant Vihar, NEW DELHI 110057, INDIA.
BAHL, Mrs. Parmjeet Kaur, BA ACA *1997;* 23 London Road, Headington, OXFORD, OX3 7RE.
BAHL, Mr. Rajeev, BSc(Hons) ACA *2001;* 12 Northolme Road, LONDON, N5 2UZ.
•**BAHRA, Mr. Jaspal, BSc FCA** *1998;* 43 Burlington Road, ISLEWORTH, MIDDLESEX, TW7 4LX.
BAHRA, Mr. Kanwaljit Singh, BSc ACA *1993;* Flat 402, May Tower 1, 7 May Road, MID LEVELS, HONG KONG SAR.
BAHREE, Mrs. Anshu, MA ACA *1998;* Flat 1, 33 Inner Park Road, LONDON, SW19 6DF.
BAHREE, Mr. Vidur, BEng ACA *1996;* Flat 1, 33 Inner Park Road, LONDON, SW19 6DF.
BAHRIN, Mr. Pengiran Izam Ryan, BA ACA *2006;* Deloitte & Touche LLP, DBS Building Tower Two, 6 Shenton Way #32-00, SINGAPORE 068809, SINGAPORE.
BAHT, Mr. Rashpal Singh, BSc ACA *1993;* Wychwood, 22 The Greenway, GERRARDS CROSS, BUCKINGHAMSHIRE, SL9 8LX.
BAI, Mr. Guang-Ji, MSc BSc ACA *2010;* Flat 36 Wingfield Court, 4 Newport Avenue, LONDON, E14 2DR.
BAIG, Mr. Azhar, BA ACA CISA *2003;* 67 Arundel Road, LUTON, LU4 8DY.
BAIG, Mr. Mirza Arshed, FCA *1971;* Mirza Arshed Baig, 190-R, LCCHS, LAHORE 54792, PAKISTAN.
BAIG, Mr. Mirza Taimur, BSc FCA *1990;* Standard Chartered, 1 Basinghall Avenue, LONDON, EC2V 5DD.
BAIG, Mrs. Muneeza, BSc ACA *2005;* 90 Shirley Way, CROYDON, CR0 8PD.
BAIG, Mrs. Shakila Jabeen, BA ACA *2008;* 60 Broadmark Road, SLOUGH, SL2 5PR.
BAIG, Miss. Sorraya Anna, BSc(Hons) ACA *2004;* Sony Music, 9 Derry Street, LONDON, W8 5HY.
BAIGEL, Mr. Jonathan Charles Mayer, BA ACA *1996;* 43 The Drive, EDGWARE, MIDDLESEX, HA8 8PS.
BAIGEL, Mr. Michael Neil Woolf, BA CIRP FCA FIPA *1994;* A Farber & Partners Inc, Suite 1600, 150 York Street, TORONTO M5H 3S5, ON, CANADA.
BAIGENT, Mr. Andrew David, BA FCA *1995;* MEMBER OF COUNCIL, National Audit Office, 157-197 Buckingham Palace Road, LONDON, SW1W 9SP.
BAIGENT, Mr. Gareth, BA ACA *2006;* 21 Burton Crescent, LEEDS, LS6 4DN.
BAIJAL, Mr. Shalabh, BA(Hons) ACA *2001;* 30 Sunnyside Road, LONDON, W5 5HU.
BAIKIE, Miss. Hilary Ann, BSc(Hons) ACA *2000;* 17 Snarsgate Street, LONDON, W10 6QP.
BAILEFF, Mrs. Nicola, BSc(Hons) ACA CTA *2000;* (Tax Fac), 140 Barnett Wood Lane, ASHTEAD, KT21 2LL.
BAILES, Mr. Alan, LLB ACA *2003;* Astrazeneca, Alderley House, Alderley Park, MACCLESFIELD, CHESHIRE, SK10 4TF.
BAILES, Mr. Arthur Geoffrey, FCA *1966;* Tebay Ghyll, Tebay, PENRITH, CUMBRIA, CA10 3XZ.
BAILES, Mrs. Caroline Michelle, MA ACA *1996;* 2B Brampton Road, ST. ALBANS, AL1 4PW.
BAILES, Mr. Philip Alan, MSc ACA *1980;* 69 King Edwards Grove, TEDDINGTON, TW11 9LZ.
BAILES, Mrs. Sarah-Jane, MA(Hons) ACA *2003;* 305 East 85th Street, Apt 16B, NEW YORK, NY 10028, UNITED STATES.
BAILES, Mrs. Vicky Joanne, BSc ACA *2005;* 16 Oakworth Drive, Belmont Park, Sharples, BOLTON, BL1 7BB.
BAILEY, Miss. Abigail, BA(Hons) ACA *2003;* 64 Church Way, SOUTH CROYDON, CR2 0JR.
•**BAILEY, Mr. Adrian, BSc FCA** *1985;* H.I. Associates Limited, 17 The Orchards, Cheswick Green, Shirley, SOLIHULL, WEST MIDLANDS B90 4HP.
BAILEY, Mr. Adrian John, BA(Hons) ACA *2002;* The Finance Unit, Metrodome, Queens Ground, Queens Road, BARNSLEY, SOUTH YORKSHIRE S71 1AN.

BAILEY - BAILEY **Members - Alphabetical**

BAILEY, Mr. Aidan, BSc ACA *1995;* Basement Flat, 41 Palace Court, LONDON, W2 4LS.

BAILEY, Mr. Alan, FCA *1970;* (Tax Fac), with Morris & Co (2011) Limited, Chester House, Lloyd Drive, Chesire Oaks Business Park, ELLESMERE PORT, CHESHIRE CH65 9HQ.

BAILEY, Mr. Alan James, FCA *1969;* 5 Clear Vista Drive, ROLLING HILLS ESTATES, CA 90274, UNITED STATES.

BAILEY, Mr. Alan Roland, FCA *1958;* 6 Boston Vale, LONDON, W7 2AP. (Life Member)

BAILEY, Mr. Albert Maurice, FCA *1959;* 5 Newstead Road, HOUGHTON-LE-SPRING, DH4 5LW. (Life Member)

BAILEY, Mr. Alec, FCA *1976;* Greenacres, Winterbourne Abbas, DORCHESTER, DT2 9LJ.

BAILEY, Mrs. Alice Mary Prosser, BSc ACA *1990;* Orchard House, Dunnington, ALCESTER, B49 5NX.

BAILEY, Miss. Alison Siobhan, ACA *1981;* 4655 Vantreight Drive, VICTORIA V8N 3W8, BC, CANADA.

BAILEY, Mrs. Andrea Marie, BA ACA *2002;* 11 Charnley Court, Cottage Lane, Bamber Bridge, PRESTON, PR5 6ZJ.

BAILEY, Mr. Andrew, ACA *1982;* 14 Austen Court, Cubbington, LEAMINGTON SPA, CV32 7LJ.

BAILEY, Mr. Andrew Douglas, BA ACA *1990;* Forge Cottage, Herm Island, GUERNSEY, GY1 3HR.

BAILEY, Mr. Andrew Ian, BA ACA CTA *1999;* with Deloitte LLP, 4 Brindley Place, BIRMINGHAM, B1 2HZ.

BAILEY, Mr. Andrew Richard, BA(Econ) ACA CFE CIA *2001;* with Deloitte & Touche, 185 avenue Charles de Gaulle, 92524 NEUILLY-SUR-SEINE, FRANCE.

BAILEY, Mrs. Angela, FCA *1983;* 77 Keith Road, BOURNEMOUTH, BH3 7DT.

BAILEY, Miss. Angela Jane, BSc ACA *2002;* 15 Bethersden Road, WIGAN, LANCASHIRE, WN1 2RL.

BAILEY, Miss. Ann Jeannette, BA FCA ATT CTA *1986;* (Tax Fac), 7 Church Lane, TEDDINGTON, TW11 8PA.

BAILEY, Mrs. Anne, BA ACA *1991;* (Tax Fac), 4 Haining Valley, Steading, LINLITHGOW, EH49 6LN.

BAILEY, Mr. Anthony James, FCA *1971;* 30 Dale Road, SWANLEY, KENT, BR8 7HR.

•BAILEY, Mr. Anthony Joseph, ACA FCCA *2007;* ARCD Associates Ltd, 42 Wright Lane, Kesgrave, IPSWICH, IP5 2FA. See also Dallas (East Anglia) Ltd

BAILEY, Mr. Barrie Carr, FCA *1962;* Idle Rocks, Clare Valley, The Park, NOTTINGHAM, NG7 1BU.

BAILEY, Mr. Brian, FCA *1974;* Stockenerstrasse 85, 8405 WINTERTHUR, SWITZERLAND.

BAILEY, Mr. Brian John, FCA *1969;* Genworth Financial, Building 11, Chiswick Park, Chiswick High Road, LONDON, W4 5XR.

BAILEY, Mr. Bryan, BCom ACA *1993;* Rye Brook, Woodfield, ASHTEAD, SURREY, KT21 2RL.

BAILEY, Mrs. Catharine Helen, BA ACA *1993;* Allington, Gonalston, NOTTINGHAM, NG14 7JA.

BAILEY, Mrs. Ceri, BA ACA *1998;* Focus Solutions Group PLC, Cranford House, Kenilworth Road, LEAMINGTON SPA, WARWICKSHIRE, CV32 6RQ.

BAILEY, Mr. Charles Howard, FCA *1958;* Beeches, Frank's Field, Peaslake, GUILDFORD, GU5 9SR.

BAILEY, Mr. Christopher, ACA *2008;* 4 Netherfield Road, LONDON, SW17 8AZ.

BAILEY, Mr. Christopher James Cecil, MA FCA *1965;* The Hall, Shotesham Park, Shotesham St Mary, NORWICH, NR15 1XA.

BAILEY, Mr. Christopher John, ACA *1979;* 20 Mansfield Avenue, Eldwick, BINGLEY, BD16 3HJ.

•BAILEY, Mr. Christopher Keith, FCA *1982;* Stephenson & Co, Ground Floor Austin House, 43 Poole Road, Westbourne, BOURNEMOUTH, BH4 9DN.

•BAILEY, Mr. Christopher Neil, BSc ACA *1993;* Christopher Bailey, Yoden House, 30 Yoden Way, PETERLEE, COUNTY DURHAM, SR8 1AL.

BAILEY, Mr. Christopher Stuart, FCA *1969;* Stone House, Westmancote, TEWKESBURY, GLOUCESTERSHIRE, GL20 7EU.

BAILEY, Mrs. Claire Helen, LLB ACA *2001;* 4 Old Harpenden Road, ST. ALBANS, HERTFORDSHIRE, AL3 6AX.

BAILEY, Mrs. Claire Louise, BSc ACA *1993;* 3 Elm Drive Blakedown, KIDDERMINSTER, WORCESTERSHIRE, DY10 3NF.

BAILEY, Mrs. Claire Louise, FCA *1983;* Fort View Cottage, The Plain, Whiteshill, STROUD, GLOUCESTERSHIRE, GL6 6AA.

BAILEY, Mr. Clive Vernon Austin, MA FCA MBA *1976;* 64 Bosworth Road, BARNET, HERTFORDSHIRE, EN5 5LP.

•BAILEY, Mr. Colin Frederick, FCA *1985;* The Bailey Partnership, Sterling House, 27 Hatchlands Road, REDHILL, RH1 6RW.

•BAILEY, Mr. Colin John, BCom FCA *1971;* C J Bailey & Co, 145 High Street, NEWTON-LE-WILLOWS, WA12 9SQ.

BAILEY, Mr. Cyrus, BA ACA *2005;* 3 Bryanstone, Mews, COLCHESTER, CO3 9XZ.

•BAILEY, Mr. Darren Jonathan, BSc ACA *1992;* Bailey Philpott Limited, 30 Medlicott Way, Swanmore, SOUTHAMPTON, SO32 2NE.

BAILEY, Mr. Daryl Sherwin, BSc ACA *1991;* Open International Limited, Buckholt Drive, WORCESTER, WR4 9SR.

•BAILEY, Mr. David, BA(Econ) ACA *1997;* Afford Bond LLP, 31 Wellington Road, NANTWICH, CHESHIRE, CW5 7ED. See also Afford Astbury Bond LLP

•BAILEY, Mr. David, FCA *1974;* Radford Bailey, First Floor, 2a Lord Street, Douglas, ISLE OF MAN, IM99 1HP.

BAILEY, Mr. David Alan, LLB ACA *1996;* 33 The Great Hall Kingsway Square, 96 Battersea Park Road, LONDON, SW11 4LP.

BAILEY, Mr. David Brian, FCA *1957;* Little Orchard, Mill Lane, Beckington, FROME, SOMERSET, BA11 6SN. (Life Member)

BAILEY, Mr. David John, BA ACA *1995;* The Cottage, St Andrews Close, Finchley, LONDON, N12 8BA.

BAILEY, Mr. David John William, MA MSc ACA *1990;* Maxillia Consultants Limited, 1 The Magpies, Maulden, BEDFORD, MK45 2EG.

BAILEY, Mr. Devan Richard, MChem ACA *2010;* Flat 3 Darcy Court, 71 Westhall Road, WARLINGHAM, SURREY, CR6 9HG.

•①BAILEY, Mr. Donald, BA FCA *1980;* with Baker Tilly Restructuring & Recovery LLP, 3 Hardman Street, MANCHESTER, M3 3HF.

BAILEY, Mr. Donald Stuart, BSc FCA *1973;* 16 Old Gardens Close, TUNBRIDGE WELLS, TN2 5ND.

BAILEY, Mr. Duncan Nicholls, FCA *1962;* 32 The Avenue, SALE, M33 4PH.

BAILEY, Mrs. Elaine, BSc ACA *1990;* Beeches, Trout Rise, Loudwater, RICKMANSWORTH, HERTFORDSHIRE, WD3 4JS.

BAILEY, Mr. Eric Sidney, FCA *1952;* 39 Greenmount Drive, Greenmount, BURY, BL8 4HA. (Life Member)

BAILEY, Mrs. Felicia Mary Joanne, BA ACA *1994;* 28 Scotts Road, SINGAPORE 228223, SINGAPORE.

BAILEY, Mr. Forbes Anthony Barnes, BSc FCA *1976;* (Tax Fac), 18 Elfindale Road, LONDON, SE24 9NW.

BAILEY, Mrs. Frances Lai-Ling, BA ACA *1989;* Somerville House, Chenies Road, Chorleywood, RICKMANSWORTH, HERTFORDSHIRE, WD3 5LU.

BAILEY, Mr. Frank Lewis, FCA *1958;* P.O.Box 5078, Lambton Quay, WELLINGTON 6145, NEW ZEALAND. (Life Member)

BAILEY, Mr. Frederick Arthur, FCA *1948;* 27a Moss Lane, Timperley, ALTRINCHAM, WA15 6LQ. (Life Member)

BAILEY, Mr. Gareth Scot, BSc ACA *1995;* Eden Cottage, Faringdon Road, Southmoor, ABINGDON, OXFORDSHIRE, OX13 5AF.

BAILEY, Mr. Gary Leon, BA ACA *1993;* 34 Danvers Road, LONDON, N8 7HH.

BAILEY, Mr. Geoffrey Stuart, BA FCA *1986;* The Limes, Heathside Park Road, WOKING, GU22 7JF.

•BAILEY, Mr. Gerald, FCA *1958;* (Tax Fac), Gerald Bailey, 6 St Martins Close, Firbeck, WORKSOP, S81 8JU.

BAILEY, Mrs. Gillian Mary, BA(Hons) ACA *2003;* 36 Pursey Drive Bradley Stoke, BRISTOL, BS32 8DJ.

•BAILEY, Mr. Gordon, FCA *1968;* Ashworth Bailey Limited, 20a Racecommon Road, BARNSLEY, SOUTH YORKSHIRE, S70 1BH.

BAILEY, Mr. Gyles, MA(Hons) ACA *2000;* 4 Old Harpenden Road, ST. ALBANS, HERTFORDSHIRE, AL3 6AX.

BAILEY, Mrs. Heather Alison, BSc ACA *2005;* Trader Media Group Limited, Thames Valley Auto Trader Auto Trader House, Danehill Lower Earley, READING, RG6 4UT.

BAILEY, Mrs. Helen Claire, BSc FCA *1986;* The Barn, Edingale Fields Farm, Lullington Road Edingale, TAMWORTH, B79 9JA.

BAILEY, Miss. Helen Louise, BA ACA *2005;* 21 Featherstone Grove, BEDLINGTON, NORTHUMBERLAND, NE22 6NU.

BAILEY, Mr. Ian, BSc ACA *1992;* Kmart, 690 Springvale Road, MULGRAVE, VIC 3170, AUSTRALIA.

•BAILEY, Mr. Ian Charles, BSc FCA *1992;* with Curo Professional Services Limited, Curo House, Greenbox, Westonhall Road, Stoke Prior, BROMSGROVE WORCESTERSHIRE B60 4AL.

BAILEY, Mr. Ian Michael, BA ACA *1992;* 4 Lane End, Midgley, HALIFAX, HX2 6TU.

BAILEY, Mr. Ivan Martin, ACA *1981;* PO BOX 375, RYDALMERE, NSW 1701, AUSTRALIA.

BAILEY, Mr. James, BSc ACA *2002;* 52 St. Margarets Road Horsforth, LEEDS, LS18 5BG.

BAILEY, Mr. James Edward, ACA *2011;* 16 Bywater Road, South Woodham Ferrers, CHELMSFORD, CM3 7AJ.

BAILEY, Mr. James William, ACA *2008;* 2 Marylands Avenue, HOCKLEY, SS5 5AQ.

BAILEY, Miss. Jane, ACA *2006;* 42 Park Mount Drive, MACCLESFIELD, CHESHIRE, SK11 8NT.

BAILEY, Mrs. Jane Clare, ACA *2009;* Deloitte & Touche, 4 Brindley Place, BIRMINGHAM, B1 2HZ.

BAILEY, Ms. Jane Elizabeth, BA(Hons) ACA *2001;* 10 Farrer Road, 06-07 Waterfall Gardens, SINGAPORE 268822, SINGAPORE.

•BAILEY, Mrs. Jenny, ACA *1993;* Claverley Accountancy Services, 22 The Wold, Claverley, WOLVERHAMPTON, WV5 7BD.

BAILEY, Miss. Joanne, ACA *2011;* Meadow Rise, Bettiscombe, BRIDPORT, DORSET, DT6 6HP.

BAILEY, Mr. John, MA ACA *1996;* 5 Chatsworth AVENUE, Cosham, PORTSMOUTH, PO6 2UG.

BAILEY, Mr. John, ACA CPA *1981;* 301 Portabello Way, SIMPSONVILLE, SC 29681, UNITED STATES.

BAILEY, Mr. John, FCA *1968;* The Hayloft, Old Carlton Farm, Warthill, YORK, YO19 5XS.

BAILEY, Mr. John, BA ACA *1986;* 21 The Croft, Kirby Hill, Boroughbridge, YORK, YO51 9YA.

BAILEY, Mr. John Arthur, FCA *1971;* 1234 Mission Ridge Road, KELOWNA V1W 3B2, BC, CANADA.

•BAILEY, Mr. John Edward, BSc FCA *1977;* HW, 7-11 Station Road, READING, BERKSHIRE, RG1 1LG. See also HW Corporate Finance LLP and Haines Watts

BAILEY, Mr. John Francis, MA ACA *1986;* McLaren Construction McLaren House, 100-102 Kings Road, BRENTWOOD, CM14 4EA.

BAILEY, Mr. John Frederick Michael Porter, LLM MA FCA *1960;* 7 Oakwood Court, BELFAST, BT9 6DF. (Life Member)

BAILEY, Mr. John Marcus, MEng ACA *1998;* 12 Low Fold The Village Thurstonland, HUDDERSFIELD, HD4 6XX.

BAILEY, Mr. John Philip, ACA *1988;* 107 St. Helens Avenue, Benson, WALLINGFORD, OXFORDSHIRE, OX10 6RU.

BAILEY, Mrs. Karen Jane, ACA *1991;* Larchwood, 2 Beech Dell, KESTON, BR2 6EP.

BAILEY, Mrs. Katharine Jane, BA FCA *1994;* Fortis Lease UK, 133 Finnieston Street, GLASGOW, G3 8HB.

BAILEY, Mrs. Katherine Natalia, BA ACA *1987;* 9 Wheeler Avenue, Penn, HIGH WYCOMBE, HP10 8EN.

BAILEY, Mrs. Kay Tracey, ACA *1987;* 396 Unthank Road, NORWICH, NR4 7QE.

BAILEY, Mr. Keith Andrew, BA ACA *1983;* Tree Top, Main Road, Little Haywood, STAFFORD, ST18 0TR.

•BAILEY, Mr. Keith Martin, FCA *1977;* Bailey Phillips, 17 Hanbury Close, Cheshunt, WALTHAM CROSS, HERTFORDSHIRE, EN8 9BZ.

BAILEY, Mr. Kenneth Malcolm, MA ACA *1989;* Heogh Capital Partners, 5 Young Street, LONDON, W8 5EH.

•BAILEY, Mr. Lawrence Richardd, BSc FCA CF *1975;* 14 Lotfield Street, Orwell, ROYSTON, HERTFORDSHIRE, SG8 5QT.

BAILEY, Mrs. Lindsay Jane, BSc ACA *2003;* 16 Coulter Mews, BILLERICAY, ESSEX, CM11 1LN.

BAILEY, Miss. Lisa Suzanne, BA ACA *1997;* Brown Forman Beverages Ltd, 45 Mortimer Street, LONDON, W1W 8HJ.

BAILEY, Mrs. Lorna Caroline, MA ACA *1999;* 53 Grierson Road, LONDON, SE23 1PF.

BAILEY, Miss. Louise Helen, BSc ACA *1999;* Flat 4, 23 Royal Crescent, LONDON, W11 4SN.

BAILEY, Miss. Lynsey, BA ACA *2007;* Flat 114, 118 Southwark Bridge Road, LONDON, SE1 0BQ.

BAILEY, Mr. Mark Robert, BSc ACA *2001;* 14 Brooklands Drive, Simmondley, GLOSSOP, SK13 6PT.

BAILEY, Mr. Mark Roy, BSc ACA *1991;* 16 Brownlow Avenue, Bitterne, SOUTHAMPTON, SO19 7BY.

•BAILEY, Mr. Mark Simon, FCA *1990;* Citroen Wells, Devonshire House, 1 Devonshire Street, LONDON, W1W 5DR.

BAILEY, Mr. Martin Bryan, BA ACA *2000;* Shawbrook Farm Keepers Lane, Antrobus, NORTHWICH, CHESHIRE, CW9 6NP.

BAILEY, Mr. Martin John, BA ACA *2009;* Flat 2, 6 Shinfield Street, LONDON, W12 0HN.

BAILEY, Mrs. Melissa, BSc ACA *1990;* 3 Russell Road, Moor Park, NORTHWOOD, HA6 2LJ.

BAILEY, Mr. Michael, BSc ACA *1990;* Larchwood, 2 Beech Dell, KESTON, BR2 6EP.

BAILEY, Mr. Michael Henry, FCA *1973;* 14 Bonney Grove, Goffs Oak, WALTHAM CROSS, EN7 5LS. (Life Member)

BAILEY, Mr. Michael James, BSc ACA *2007;* 4 Bradstone Brook Cottages, New Road Chilworth, GUILDFORD, GU4 8LS.

BAILEY, Mr. Michael Patrick, BA FCA *1982;* Rafters, Heathlands Road, WOKINGHAM, RG40 3AR.

BAILEY, Mr. Michael Paul, FCA *1977;* 72 Dunstall Road, HALESOWEN, B63 1BE.

•BAILEY, Mr. Michael William, BA FCA *1978;* with Beavis Morgan Audit Limited, 82 St. John Street, LONDON, EC1M 4JN.

BAILEY, Mr. Michael William John, FCA *1975;* Day's Eye, 4 Newtons Orchard, Kilmington, AXMINSTER, DEVON, EX13 7UG.

BAILEY, Mrs. Naomi Roshini, BSc ACA *2006;* 30 Aston Road, LONDON, SW20 8BE.

BAILEY, Mr. Neil, BA ACA CTA *1991;* Allington, Gonalston, NOTTINGHAM, NG14 7JA.

BAILEY, Mr. Neil Henry, BSc FCA *1983;* 36 Keswick Road, High Lane, STOCKPORT, SK6 8AP.

BAILEY, Mr. Neill, ACA *2004;* 20 Malsbury Street, BICTON, WA 6157, AUSTRALIA.

BAILEY, Mr. Nicholas, OBE FCA *1971;* Flat 11 County Wharf, Pier Road, LITTLEHAMPTON, WEST SUSSEX, BN17 5AF.

BAILEY, Mr. Nicholas Gordon, FCA *1972;* Ghyll House, Coxham Lane, STEYNING, WEST SUSSEX, BN44 3LG.

BAILEY, Miss. Nicola Jane, BSc ACA *2010;* Apartment 6, 77-81 Wright Street, HULL, HU2 8JS.

•BAILEY, Mr. Nigel Hugh, FCA *1975;* 12 Oakdene Close, WIMBORNE, DORSET, BH21 1TJ.

BAILEY, Mr. Noel Caladine, MA FCA *1988;* NG Bailey Ltd, Denton Hall, ILKLEY, WEST YORKSHIRE, LS29 0HH.

BAILEY, Mrs. Pamela Sharples, BA ACA *1986;* 32 Stonebreaks Road, Springhead, OLDHAM, OL4 4BZ.

BAILEY, Mr. Patrick Edgar, FCA *1954;* Apartment 17, The Arena, Standard Hill, NOTTINGHAM, NG1 6GL. (Life Member)

BAILEY, Mr. Paul, BSc(Econ) FCA MIQA RC *1974;* Corn Exchange, Transatlantic Reinsurance Co, 55 Mark Lane, LONDON, EC3R 7NE.

•BAILEY, Mr. Paul Michael, FCA *1969;* Winton Cottage, High Street, Bishopstone, SWINDON, SN6 8PH.

BAILEY, Mr. Paul Michael John, BSc ACA *1999;* 4 Walnut Grove, Nounsley Road, Hatfield Peverel, CHELMSFORD, CM3 2RF.

•BAILEY, Mr. Paul Richard, BA ACA *2006;* John Belford & Co Ltd, 14a Main Street, COCKERMOUTH, CUMBRIA, CA13 9LQ.

BAILEY, Mr. Paul Roger, FCA *1966;* 1 Willowbrook Gardens, Douglas, ISLE OF MAN, IM2 2QQ.

BAILEY, Mr. Peter Arthur Neil, FCA *1985;* Cedar Cottage, La Rue Du Cimetiere, St. John, JERSEY, JE3 4AH. (Life Member)

BAILEY, Mr. Peter Charles Kingsley, BSc FCA *1974;* 49 Bury Green, Wheathampstead, ST. ALBANS, AL4 8DB.

BAILEY, Mr. Peter David, FCA *1954;* The Cottage, St Andrew's Close, LONDON, N12 8BA. (Life Member)

BAILEY, Mr. Peter Edwin, BA ACA *1999;* Fletcher King, St. Georges House, 61 Conduit Street, LONDON, W1S 2GB.

BAILEY, Mr. Peter John, BSc FCA *1975;* 52 Roundhey, Heald Green, CHEADLE, CHESHIRE, SK8 3JR.

BAILEY, Mr. Peter Stewart, MBA BSc ACA *1986;* Rowan Tree Cottage, 1 Ridgway Hill Road, FARNHAM, GU9 8LS.

BAILEY, Mr. Peter William, FCA *1970;* The Laurels, Evendine Court, MALVERN, WR13 6DT.

BAILEY, Mr. Peter William, BSc ACA *1997;* 20 Newbridge Hill, BATH, BA1 3PU.

•BAILEY, Mr. Philip, BSc(Econ) FCA CF *1980;* Robertshaw Myers, Number 3, Acorn Business Park, Keighley Road, SKIPTON, NORTH YORKSHIRE BD23 2UE. See also Robertshaw & Myers

BAILEY, Mr. Philip Atkinson, BEng FCA ATII *1999;* Ernst & Young, 100 Barbirolli Square, MANCHESTER, M2 3EY.

BAILEY, Miss. Philippa, ACA *1998;* 37 Southgate, Fulwood, PRESTON, PR2 3HX.

BAILEY, Mr. Raymond William, FCA *1956;* Flat 9, 5 The Avenue, BECKENHAM, BR3 5DG. (Life Member)

BAILEY, Mr. Richard Anthony John, BA ACA *2000;* Daniel Thwaites Plc, PO Box 50, Star Brewery, BLACKBURN, BB1 5BU.

•BAILEY, Mr. Richard Charles, FCA *1978;* (Tax Fac), Barron & Barron, Bathurst House, 86 Micklegate, YORK, YO1 6LQ.

BAILEY, Mr. Richard James, BA ACA *2010;* 5 Queens Gate, Stoke Bishop, BRISTOL, BS9 1TZ.

•**BAILEY, Mr. Robert, FCA** *1962;* Robert Bailey, Slater House, Meadowcroft Business Park, Pope Lane, Whitestake, PRESTON PR4 4BA.
BAILEY, Mr. Robert Christian, BSc FCA *1989;* (Tax Fac), with Bishop Fleming, Chy Nyverow, Newham Road, TRURO, TR1 2DP.
•**BAILEY, Mr. Robert Ian, FCA** *1982;* (Tax Fac), Allchurch Bailey Limited, 93 High Street, EVESHAM, WORCESTERSHIRE, WR11 4DU.
BAILEY, Mr. Robert Malcolm, BSc FCA *1975;* Burnham House, Market Place, Burnham Market, KING'S LYNN, NORFOLK, PE31 8HD.
BAILEY, Mr. Robert Michael, FCA *1971;* Bailey Management Services Ltd, 3 Beacon Court, Birmingham Road, Great Barr, BIRMINGHAM, B43 6NN.
BAILEY, Mr. Robin John, BSc(Econ) ACA *2002;* 26 Chivalry Road, LONDON, SW11 1HT.
BAILEY, Mr. Roger, ACA *1979;* Lang & Potter Galileo Close, Newnham Industrial Estate Plympton, PLYMOUTH, PL7 4JW.
BAILEY, Mr. Ross Alan, BA ACA *2010;* 28 Hermitage Drive, Twyford, READING, RG10 9HS.
BAILEY, Mr. Roy Anthony, FCA *1955;* Rosehill, Saxmundham Road, ALDEBURGH, IP15 5PD. (Life Member)
BAILEY, Mr. Samuel Adam, ACA *2008;* Richard J Smith & Co, 53 Fore Street, IVYBRIDGE, DEVON, PL21 9AE.
BAILEY, Mrs. Sarah Alexandra, MSc ACA *1992;* 36 Ivy Lane, MACCLESFIELD, SK11 8NR.
BAILEY, Mr. Sean, BSc ACA *1995;* 36 Ivy Lane, MACCLESFIELD, SK11 8NR.
BAILEY, Mr. Simon Alexander Farquhar, ACA *1984;* (Tax Fac), 9 Sixacres, Slinfold, HORSHAM, RH13 0TH.
BAILEY, Mr. Simon Benjamin, BSc ACA *2002;* 5 Shepherds Walk, Oakley, BASINGSTOKE, RG23 7BF.
BAILEY, Mr. Simon James, BSc ACA *2004;* 30 Aston Road, Raynes Park, LONDON, SW20 8BE.
BAILEY, Mr. Simon James, MM ACA *2007;* 26 Pier Avenue, HERNE BAY, CT6 8PQ.
BAILEY, Mr. Simon Timothy, BSc ACA *1995;* 16 William Kirby Close, Tile Hill, COVENTRY, CV4 9AD.
BAILEY, Mr. Simon Unsworth, BA ACA *1992;* 12 Chesterfield Drive, ESHER, SURREY, KT10 0AH.
BAILEY, Mr. Stephen, BA BTP FCA *1984;* 4 Abbotsfield Close, TAVISTOCK, PL19 8EX.
BAILEY, Mr. Stephen Geoffrey, BA ACA *1997;* South Staffordshire College, The Friary, LICHFIELD, STAFFORDSHIRE, WS13 6QG.
•**BAILEY, Mr. Stephen Graham, BA ACA** *1991;* Connect Financial Management Ltd, 29 Beverley Rise, ILKLEY, WEST YORKSHIRE, LS29 9DB.
BAILEY, Mr. Stephen John, BSc ACA *1990;* Rosier Bailey Associates Ltd, The Rock, Richards Castle, LUDLOW, SHROPSHIRE, SY8 4ES.
BAILEY, Mr. Stephen John, MA BA ACA *2005;* 300 Constitution Avenue (Apt 421), BAYONNE, NJ 07002, UNITED STATES.
BAILEY, Mr. Stephen Mark, BA ACA *1986;* Vertex Data Science Ltd, 1050 Europa Boulevard Westbrook, WARRINGTON, WA5 7ZD.
BAILEY, Mr. Stephen Richard, FCA *1979;* 53 Malden Hill, NEW MALDEN, SURREY, KT3 4DS.
BAILEY, Mr. Stephen Roy Patrick, BSc ACA *1985;* 10 Jevington Drive, SEAFORD, EAST SUSSEX, BN25 2NX.
BAILEY, Mr. Steven Andrew, ACA *2009;* Flat E, 28 Harold Road, LONDON, SE19 3PL.
BAILEY, Mr. Steven Clive, BSc ACA *1988;* PO Box 909, UXBRIDGE, MIDDLESEX, UB8 9FH.
•**BAILEY, Mr. Steven Graham, FCA** *1980;* 11 Wingfield Court, BINGLEY, WEST YORKSHIRE, BD16 4TE.
BAILEY, Mr. Stuart Alistair, BSc ACA *1993;* 19 Parklands, Royton, OLDHAM, OL2 5YN.
BAILEY, Mr. Stuart John William, MA ACA *1978;* 4A Little Cloister, Westminster Abbey, LONDON, SW1P 3PL.
BAILEY, Mrs. Sue-Ann, BA ACA *2008;* 19 Juniper Close, WORTHING, WEST SUSSEX, BN13 3PR.
BAILEY, Ms. Susan Angela, MA ACA *1990;* 15 Brockwell Avenue, BECKENHAM, KENT, BR3 3GE.
BAILEY, Miss. Susan Helen, ACA *2008;* K P M G, 100 Temple Street, BRISTOL, BS1 6AG.
BAILEY, Mrs. Susan Ida, BA FCA *1988;* 21 The Croft, Kirby Hill, Boroughbridge, YORK, YO51 9YA.
BAILEY, Ms. Suzanne Nicola, BA ACA *1997;* 5 Broadway, Duffield, BELPER, DERBYSHIRE, DE56 4BT.
•**BAILEY, Mr. Thomas Patrick John, FCA** *1977;* Chestnuts, Lanham Green, Cressing, BRAINTREE, CM77 8DT. See also Paradigm Accountancy Services
•**BAILEY, Mr. Timothy, FCA** *1959;* (Tax Fac), Lemans, 29 Arboretum Street, NOTTINGHAM, NG1 4JA.
BAILEY, Mr. Timothy James, BA(Hons) ACA *2002;* 36 Pursey Drive, Bradley Stoke, BRISTOL, BS32 8DJ.
BAILEY, Mr. Timothy Robert, BA ACA *1984;* Mansfield Cottage, 5 The Mews The Common, Dunsfold, GODALMING, GU8 4LJ.
BAILEY, Mr. Timothy William, BSc ACA *1998;* The Old Parsonage, Shackleford Road, Shackleford, GODALMING, SURREY, GU8 6AE.
BAILEY, Mr. Tom William, ACA *2010;* 109 Welbeck Avenue, Highfield, SOUTHAMPTON, SO17 1SP.
BAILEY, Mr. Trevor Arthur, FCA *1955;* 69 Whitestone Road, NUNEATON, CV11 4SY. (Life Member)
•**BAILEY, Mrs. Veronica Fay, BA FCA** *1992;* 4 Chipping Hill, WITHAM, ESSEX, CM8 2DE.
BAILEY, Miss. Victoria Claire, MEng ACA *2007;* 21 Emu Road, LONDON, SW8 3PS.
BAILEY, Mrs. Vivienne Irene, BA ACA *1993;* Greenergy International, Egerton House, Towers Business Park, Wilmslow Road, MANCHESTER, M20 2DX.
BAILEY, Mr. William Arthur, FCA FFA *1969;* MEMBER OF COUNCIL, Oaklands, Birks Drive, Ashley Heath, MARKET DRAYTON, TF9 4PX.
BAILEY, Mr. William David, BSc ACA *1990;* 10 Woodside Close, Chiddingfold, GODALMING, GU8 4RH. See also PricewaterhouseCoopers
BAILEY, Mrs. Zoe Elizabeth, BA ACA *2004;* 8 Woodall Road, LISBURN, COUNTY ANTRIM, BT28 3ND.
BAILHAM, Mr. Mark Michael, BSc ACA *1988;* 3 Hereward Mount, Stock, INGATESTONE, ESSEX, CM4 9PS.
BAILIE, Mr. Fergus, LLB ACA *2006;* 5 Academy Drive, Dringhouses, YORK, YO24 1UJ.
BAILIE, Mr. Mark McCracken, BA ACA *1999;* 9 Stradella Road, Herne Hill, LONDON, SE24 9HN.
BAILIE, Mr. Robert, BA ACA *1998;* Tilda Ltd, Coldharbour Lane, RAINHAM, RM13 9YQ.
BAILIE, Mr. Thomas Jeremy, BSc FCA *1982;* 9 Carrowcrin Road, Armoy, BALLYMONEY, COUNTY ANTRIM, BT53 8YL.
BAILKOSKI, Mr. Robert Broncho, LLB ACA *2001;* Furlongs, Peasemore, NEWBURY, RG20 7JE.
•**BAILLACHE, Mr. Mark Robert, BA FCA** *1995;* KPMG LLP, 15 Canada Square, LONDON, E14 5GL. See also KPMG Europe LLP
BAILLIE, Mr. Mark, ACA *2008;* 199 Highbury Hill, LONDON, N5 1TB.
BAILLIE, Mr. Scott Anthony, ACA *2009;* (Tax Fac), 68 Clarinda House, Clovelly Place, GREENHITHE, DA9 9FB.
BAILLIEUL, Mr. Derek Charles, FCA *1971;* 382 Windermere, BEACONSFIELD H9W 6C1, QC, CANADA.
•**BAILUR, Mr. Sanjay Gurudas, BSc FCA ACT** *1993;* AlixPartners UK LLP, 20 North Audley Street, LONDON, W1K 6WE.
BAILY, Mr. Patrick Alexander Highett, FCA *1956;* 15 Peppard Road, Caversham, READING, RG4 8JP. (Life Member)
•**BAILY, Mr. Stephen, BSocSc FCA** *1986;* (Tax Fac), Kingscott Dix Limited, 60 Kings Walk, GLOUCESTER, GL1 1LA.
•**BAIN, Mr. Andrew Edward, ACA** *1983;* Andrew E. Bain, 8 Scotland Bridge Road, New Haw, ADDLESTONE, KT15 3HD.
BAIN, Miss. Charlotte Amy, ACA *2008;* 37 Caernarvon Road, NORWICH, NR2 3HZ.
BAIN, Mr. David Graham Shenton, BSc FCA *1976;* Rua Alberto de Oliveira 42, 4150-034 PORTO, PORTUGAL.
BAIN, Mr. David Nicholas, MA ACA *1983;* c/o Royal Danish Embassy, PO Box 9171, DAR ES SALAAM, TANZANIA.
BAIN, Mr. Duncan Howard, BSc FCA *1989;* Pinfold Barn, 1 Pinfold Lane, Plumtree, NOTTINGHAM, NG12 5EZ.
BAIN, Mr. Duncan Whiteford Taylor, FCA *1977;* The Baltic Exchange Ltd, The Baltic Exchange, 38 St. Mary Axe, LONDON, EC3A 8BH.
BAIN, Mrs. Emma Caroline, BSc ACA *1997;* Sterling Insurance Co Ltd, 50 Kings Hill Avenue, Kings Hill, WEST MALLING, KENT, ME19 4JX.
BAIN, Mrs. Lisa Michelle, BA ACA ATII *1992;* The Laurels, 3 Willow Walk, Bookham, LEATHERHEAD, SURREY, KT23 4ER.
BAIN, Mrs. Margaret, BMus ACA *2002;* 52 Beaconsfield Road, LONDON, SE3 7LG.
BAIN, Mr. Matthew John Curtis, BSc ACA *1999;* 20B Bledisloe Street, Cockle Bay, AUCKLAND 2014, NEW ZEALAND.
BAIN, Mr. Michael, ACA *2009;* Reuter Weg 91, 60323 FRANKFURT AM MAIN, GERMANY.
BAIN, Mr. Neville Charles, FCA *1958;* Queenscourt Hospice, 1 Alma Road, SOUTHPORT, MERSEYSIDE, PR8 4AN. (Life Member)
BAIN, Mr. Peter Scott, BSc ACA *1995;* Geopost UK Ltd, Roebuck Lane, SMETHWICK, B66 1BY.
BAIN, Mr. Richard John Shenton, FCA *1964;* 39 Hartwell Road, Hanslope, MILTON KEYNES, MK19 7BY.
BAIN, Mr. Robert Simpson, BA ACA *1992;* Flat 15 Downings House 21 Southey Road, LONDON, SW19 1ND.
BAIN, Mrs. Sarah Caroline, FCA *1991;* Les Granges, 36140 LA BUXERETTE, FRANCE.
•**BAIN, Mr. Toby Bramwell Findlater, BA ACA** *1980;* with RSM Tenon Limited, Vantage, Victoria Street, BASINGSTOKE, RG21 3BT.
BAIN, Mr. William Edmond Adam, FCA *1971;* Hatchgate Farm, Pennypot Lane, Chobham, WOKING, GU24 8DL.
BAINBRIDGE, Mr. Alan Gerard, MA FCA MBA *1975;* 2 Haythrop Close, Downhead Park, MILTON KEYNES, MK15 9DD.
BAINBRIDGE, Mrs. Allison Margaret, BSocSc ACA *1990;* V P Plc Beckwith Knowle, Otley Road Beckwithshaw, HARROGATE, NORTH YORKSHIRE, HG3 1UD.
BAINBRIDGE, Mr. Anthony David, BSc FCA FSI FRM *1995;* 22 Keats Road, BASKING RIDGE, NJ 07920, UNITED STATES.
BAINBRIDGE, Miss. Christine, BCom ACA *1991;* 9 Stephen Close, Twyford, READING, RG10 0XN.
BAINBRIDGE, Miss. Elizabeth Melanie, ACA CTA *1998;* 12 Grange View, WIGTON, CUMBRIA, CA7 9EZ.
•**BAINBRIDGE, Miss. Gail Andrea, BA ACA** *2004;* Bainbridge Lewis Limited, 13 Kingsway House, 134-140 Church Road, HOVE, EAST SUSSEX, BN3 2DL.
•**BAINBRIDGE, Mr. Guy Lawrence Tarn, MA ACA** *1986;* KPMG LLP, 15 Canada Square, LONDON, E14 5GL. See also KPMG Europe LLP
BAINBRIDGE, Mr. Harold Anthony, FCA *1952;* Old Mill House, Burton, WIRRAL, CHESHIRE, CH64 5TD. (Life Member)
BAINBRIDGE, Mr. John Philip, FCA *1972;* Baltic House, The Common, CRANLEIGH, SURREY, GU6 8SL. (Life Member)
BAINBRIDGE, Mr. John Richard, PhD ACA *1987;* Four Walls, High Knott Road, Arnside, CARNFORTH, LANCASHIRE, LA5 0AW.
BAINBRIDGE, Mr. Jonathan Michael, BSc ACA *1990;* 12 Gorsehill Grove Littleover, DERBY, DE23 3ZE.
BAINBRIDGE, Mr. Leigh, BEng ACA *1992;* The Bay Tree, Fee Farm Road, Claygate, ESHER, SURREY, KT10 0JX.
BAINBRIDGE, Mr. Matthew, BA ACA *2005;* 1 Sycamore Court, Fyfe Lane Baildon, SHIPLEY, WEST YORKSHIRE, BD17 6EJ.
BAINBRIDGE, Mr. Peter John, FCA *1973;* 47 Alexandra Road, PUDSEY, LS28 8BX.
BAINBRIDGE, Mrs. Rachel Mary, BSc ACA *1989;* 16 Red Post Hill, Dulwich, LONDON, SE24 9JQ.
BAINBRIDGE, Mr. Richard Charles, BA ACA *1988;* 14 York Road, LEAMINGTON SPA, CV31 3PR.
BAINBRIDGE, Mr. Robert Adam, BSc ACA *1988;* 16 Red Post Hill, Dulwich, LONDON, SE24 9JQ.
BAINBRIDGE, Mrs. Sarah Hayley, ACA *2008;* with A P Robinson LLP, 107 Cleethorpe Road, GRIMSBY, SOUTH HUMBERSIDE, DN31 3ER.
BAINBRIDGE, Mr. Stephen Ronald, BCom ACA *2002;* 3a Havelock Road, MAIDENHEAD, SL6 5BJ.
BAINBRIDGE, Mr. Steven John, BSc ACA *2004;* Sapphire Building Albion Mills, Albion Road, BRADFORD, BD10 9TQ.
BAINBRIDGE, Mr. Stuart James, BSc ACA *2003;* St James House, 26 Bridge Street, LEATHERHEAD, SURREY, KT22 8BZ.
BAINBRIGGE, Miss. Mari-Carmen Philippa, BA ACA *1994;* Telegraph House, 133 Sydenham Hill, LONDON, SE26 6LW.
•**BAINES, Mr. Alan Leonard, FCA** *1970;* Alan Baines, Church House, Thorpe, ASHBOURNE, DERBYSHIRE, DE6 2AW.
BAINES, Miss. Alexandra, ACA *2011;* Flat 1, 49 Lewin Road, LONDON, SW16 6JZ.
BAINES, Miss. Catherine Ann, BSc ACA *1991;* 27 Osbaldeston Gardens, NEWCASTLE UPON TYNE, NE3 4JE.
BAINES, Mr. Charles Joseph, BSc ACA *1990;* Holly House, Franks Lane, Whixley, YORK, YO26 8AP.
BAINES, Mr. Colin, BSc ACA *2010;* 49 East Lane, Cuddington, NORTHWICH, CHESHIRE, CW8 2QQ.
BAINES, Mr. David Richard, BSc ACA *1993;* Palmstead Hill House, Bekesbourne Lane, CANTERBURY, CT3 4AD.
BAINES, Mr. Edward, FCA *1973;* Fairview, Kirkenong Road, Delegate River, BONANG, VIC 3888, AUSTRALIA.
BAINES, Mr. Gerald Charles, BCom FCA *1965;* 26 Buckles Way, BANSTEAD, SM7 1HD.
•**BAINES, Mrs. Hilary Pauline, FCA** *1982;* (Tax Fac), Hill & Roberts, 50 High Street, MOLD, CH7 1BH.
•**BAINES, Mrs. Janet Lesley, FCA** *1967;* J.L. Baines & Co, Chalklands, Hatherden, ANDOVER, SP11 0HJ.
BAINES, Mrs. Joanne Sheila, BA ACA *1986;* The Royal Bank of Scotland Plc 2 & A Half, Devonshire Square, LONDON, EC2M 4BA.
BAINES, Mr. John Duncan, BA ACA *1988;* 6 The Ridgeway, RADLETT, HERTFORDSHIRE, WD7 8PR.
BAINES, Mr. John Wilfrid, FCA *1952;* 14 Oasthouse Court, SAFFRON WALDEN, ESSEX, CB10 1DX. (Life Member)
BAINES, Mr. Jonathan Piers, BSc ACA *2000;* Flat 4, 5a Station Road, Hampton Wick, KINGSTON UPON THAMES, KT1 4HG.
BAINES, Mr. Joseph William, FCA *1970;* JPC Limited, Brundall Harbour, Riverside Estate, Brundall, NORWICH, NR13 5PL.
BAINES, Mrs. Josine Elizabeth, MA ACA *1998;* 17 Hilden Avenue, Hildenborough, TONBRIDGE, KENT, TN11 9BY.
BAINES, Miss. Kathryn Alison, BSc ACA *1991;* Apartment 6, Monterey, Deganwy Road, Deganwy, CONWY, GWYNEDD LL31 9DL.
BAINES, Dr. Malcolm Ian, MA ACA *1994;* (Tax Fac), 1 West Garden Place, Kendal Street, LONDON, W2 2AQ.
•**BAINES, Mr. Mark, BA ACA** *1988;* Arbor Grange, Babraham Road, CAMBRIDGE, CB22 3AY.
BAINES, Mr. Ranjeev, BSc(Hons) ACA *2000;* British Petroleum Co Plc, Witan Gate House, 500-600 Witan Gate West, MILTON KEYNES, MK9 1ES.
BAINES, Mrs. Rebecca Helen, BSc ACA *1998;* 69 Barkham Ride, Finchampstead, WOKINGHAM, RG40 4HA.
BAINES, Mr. Richard Andrew, MA ACA MCT *1985;* 6 Honeysuckle Gardens, ANDOVER, SP10 3DD.
BAINES, Mr. Robert Harrison, FCA *1973;* 20 Eldon Road, LONDON, W8 5PT.
•**BAINES, Mr. Roger John, BA FCA** *1983;* Maynard Heady LLP, Matrix House, 12-16 Lionel Road, CANVEY ISLAND, ESSEX, SS8 9DE. See also Kiloview Ltd and Maynard Heady
BAINES, Mr. Stephen Paul, BA ACA *1996;* Green Barn, 2 Telegraph Lane, Claygate, ESHER, KT10 0DU.
BAINES, Mrs. Susan Toni, BA ACA *1993;* The Sherard Building, Edmund Halley Road, OXFORD, OXFORDSHIRE, OX4 4DQ.
•**BAINES, Mr. Thomas Charles, MSc FCA** *1986;* (Tax Fac), Berkeley Hamilton LLP, 5 Pullman Court, Great Western Road, GLOUCESTER, GL1 3ND.
•**BAINES, Mr. Timothy John, BSc FCA DChA** *1984;* Crowe Clark Whitehill LLP, St Bride's House, 10 Salisbury Square, LONDON, EC4Y 8EH. See also Horwath Clark Whitehill LLP and Crowe Clark Whitehill
BAINES, Mr. Vivian Muspratt, FCA *1959;* 1782-2 Senoh, Imaichi-Shi, TOCHIGI-SHI, 321-1264 JAPAN. (Life Member)
BAINS, Mr. Chunpreet Singh, BA ACA *2009;* 8 Edinburgh Road, WALSALL, WS5 3PQ.
BAINS, Mr. David, BSc ACA *2007;* Flat B, 141 Lavender Sweep, LONDON, SW11 1EA.
BAINS, Mr. Harbinder Singh, BA ACA *1991;* 1 Lascelles Road, SLOUGH, SL3 7PS.
BAINS, Mrs. Jane Elizabeth, MA ACA *1985;* 37 The Moor, Melbourn, ROYSTON, SG8 6ED.
BAINS, Mr. Mukhtiar Singh, BSc ACA *1990;* H M P Hewell, Hewell Lane, REDDITCH, WORCESTERSHIRE, B97 6QS.
BAINS, Mrs. Parmjit, BA FCA *1995;* 397 Brookfield Road, KENMORE HILLS, QLD 4069, AUSTRALIA.
BAINS, Mr. Parmjit Singh, BA ACA *1990;* 20 Jourdain Park, Heathcote, WARWICK, CV34 6FJ.
BAINS, Mrs. Rajbir Kaur, BA(Hons) ACA *2010;* 86 Old Road East, GRAVESEND, KENT, DA12 1PE.
BAINS, Mr. Richard Leonard, BA ACA *1996;* 36 Rutland Drive, MORDEN, SM4 5QH.
BAINS, Mr. Rupinder Singh Mike, BA(Hons) ACA *2002;* 16 Longford Gardens, HAYES, UB4 0JW.
BAINS, Mr. Satwant Singh, BSc ACA *1991;* 9 Brailsford Road, LONDON, SW2 2TB.
BAINS, Miss. Sundeep, MEng ACA *2006;* 60 Wall Street, (29th Floor), NEW YORK, NY 10005-2836, UNITED STATES.
BAINS, Mr. Tarloke, BSc ACA *1997;* 1 Lutton Terrace, LONDON, NW3 1HB.
BAIRD, Mr. Adam John, BA(Hons) ACA *2001;* Flat 73, Bernhard Baron House, Henriques Street, LONDON, E1 1LZ.

BAIRD, Mr. Andrew Allan, BSc ACA *1990;* PriceWaterhouseCoopers LDA, Palacio Sottomayor, Rue Sousa Martins, No 1 - 2 Esq, 1050-217 LISBON, PORTUGAL.

BAIRD, Mr. Christopher Robert, LLB FCA *1977;* 99 Grove Park, LONDON, SE5 8LE.

BAIRD, Mr. Christopher St Clair, BSc FCA CF *1995;* Flat 9, 62 Inverness Terrace, LONDON, W2 3LB.

BAIRD, Mr. Colin William Graham, MA FCA *1960;* 2 Cartmel Close, REIGATE, SURREY, RH2 0LS. (Life Member)

BAIRD, Mr. Craig, ACA *2004;* 19 Hilberry Rise, NORTHAMPTON, NN3 5ER.

BAIRD, Mr. Douglas Murray, MA FCA *1962;* Les Surelles, 50480 GOURBESVILLE, FRANCE. (Life Member)

BAIRD, Miss. Eileen Patricia, MA FCA *1994;* Flat 3/2, 5 Fairlie Park Drive, Partick, GLASGOW, G11 7SS.

BAIRD, Mr. Guy Martin, FCA *1970;* 19 Castle Street, WALLINGFORD, OXFORDSHIRE, OX10 8DW.

BAIRD, Mr. Harry, FCA *1961;* Harry Baird, 32 Brownsholme Close, Crag Bank, CARNFORTH, LA5 9UW. (Life Member)

•BAIRD, Mr. James Walter Forrester, MA ACA *1990;* Deloitte LLP, General Guisan-Quai 38, PO Box 2232, 8022 ZURICH, SWITZERLAND. See also Deloitte & Touche LLP

BAIRD, Miss. Laura Jane, BSc ACA *2010;* Flat 50 Boss House, 2 Boss Street, LONDON, SE1 2PS.

BAIRD, Mr. Matthew James, MEng ACA *2000;* 67 Chiltern Court, Baker Street, LONDON, NW1 5SQ.

BAIRD, Mr. Michael, FCA *1970;* 29 Field Lane, Appleton, WARRINGTON, WA4 5JR.

BAIRD, Mr. Neil Douglas Lockhart, BSc ACA MBA *1983;* 7 Helena Rd, COOLOONGUP, WA 6168, AUSTRALIA.

BAIRD, Mr. William Brand, FCA *1964;* Neuk O'Hedge, West Plean, STIRLING, FK7 8AS. (Life Member)

•BAIROLIYA, Mr. Rajib, MBA BSc FCA *1989;* (Tax Fac), FTI Forensic Accounting Limited, 322 High Holborn, LONDON, WC1V 7PB.

BAIROLIYA, Miss. Veena, BSc ACA *1996;* Kempton Investments Ltd, Wigmore Lane, LUTON, LU2 9JA.

•BAIRSTOW, Mrs. Emma Louise Sinclair, BA ACA CTA *1997;* Deloitte LLP, Global House, High Street, CRAWLEY, RH10 1DL. See also Deloitte & Touche LLP

BAIRSTOW, Mr. John David, BA(Hons) ACA *2004;* 17 Smallman Street, BULIMBA, QLD 4171, AUSTRALIA.

•BAIRSTOW, Mr. John Martin, FCA *1974;* Sutcliffe & Riley, 3 Central Street, HALIFAX, HX1 1HU.

BAIRSTOW, Miss. Katharine Selina, ACA *2008;* with Deloitte LLP, Stonecutter Court, 1 Stonecutter Street, LONDON, EC4A 4TR.

•BAIRSTOW, Mr. Nicholas John, BA FCA *1995;* Moore Stephens, Oakley House, Headway Business Park, 3 Saxon Way West, CORBY, NORTHAMPTONSHIRE NN18 9EZ.

•BAIRSTOW, Mr. Vivian Murray, FCA FIPA FABRP *1969;* Englewick, Barley Mow Road, Englefield Green, EGHAM, SURREY, TW20 0NX.

BAISH, Mr. David John, BA ACA *1978;* 59 Cardinals Way, ELY, CAMBRIDGESHIRE, CB7 4GF.

BAISH, Mrs. Jennifer Mary, BA ACA *1994;* Kentwood Milley Road, Waltham St. Lawrence, READING, RG10 0JP.

BAISHNAB, Mr. Neil Utpaul, BSc(Econ) ACA *2002;* Brook House, 137 Chatsworth Road, Worsley, MANCHESTER, M28 2WR.

BAISTER, Mr. David John, BCom FCA *1970;* 10 Lower Road, Higher Denham, UXBRIDGE, UB9 5EA. (Life Member)

BAISTER, Miss. Heather Margaret, LLB ACA *2003;* 4116 Warner Boulevard, Apt B, BURBANK, CA 91505, UNITED STATES.

BAITUP, Mr. Maurice Aubrey, FCA *1950;* 2 Buckingham Road, Poynton, STOCKPORT, CHESHIRE, SK12 1JH. (Life Member)

BAITUP, Mr. Peter Robin, FCA *1962;* Temple Farmhouse, Chapel Street, Broadwell, MORETON-IN-MARSH, GLOUCESTERSHIRE, GL56 0TW.

BAJAJ, Mr. Gulshan Kumar, FCA *1977;* 563 Military Trail, SCARBOROUGH M1E 4S7, ON, CANADA.

BAJAJ, Mr. Nikhil, BSc ACA *2009;* M-70 Greater Kailash 1, NEW DELHI 110048, INDIA.

•BAJAJ, Mr. Parminder Kumar, ACA *1981;* Bajaj & Company., 111 Imperial Drive, North Harrow, HARROW, MIDDLESEX, HA2 7HW.

BAJAJ, Mr. Rahul, BA ACA *1993;* 15 Rees Drive, STANMORE, HA7 4YN.

BAJAJ, Mr. Suvinder Singh, BSc ACA *2001;* 515 Dunman Road, #16-02, SINGAPORE 439204, SINGAPORE.

•BAJARIA, Mr. Chandrasinh Hansraj, FCA *1960;* (Tax Fac), C. Bajaria & Co, 42 Bromley Common, BROMLEY, BR2 9PD.

BAJER, Mr. David Alan, BA FCA *1984;* (Tax Fac), 77 Malford Grove, South Woodford, LONDON, E18 2DH.

BAJPAI, Mr. Ashish, BSc ACA *1993;* 46 Clifton Gardens, LONDON, W9 1AU.

BAJWA, Miss. Neeta, MSc BSc ACA *2003;* 37 Wall Street, Apt 14Q, NEW YORK, NY 10005, UNITED STATES.

BAK, Mr. Andrew Roman, ACA *1997;* Birchwood, 8 Compton Avenue, Hutton, BRENTWOOD, ESSEX, CM13 2HH.

BAK, Mr. Paul Mario, BA FCA *1981;* 5th Floor, 77 Grosvenor Street, LONDON, W1K 3JR.

BAKAR ALI, Miss. Faridah, BA(Hons) ACA *2002;* No 17 Jalan 45/70A, Desa Sri Hartamas, 50480 KUALA LUMPUR, FEDERAL TERRITORY, MALAYSIA.

BAKARANIA, Miss. Roopal, BSc(Hons) ACA *2010;* 19 Rosslyn Crescent, HARROW, HA1 2SA.

BAKELS, Mr. Teunis Friso, ACA *1994;* Hemsterhuisstraat 28, 1065 KB AMSTERDAM, NETHERLANDS.

BAKER, Mr. Adrian Harry, BSc ACA *1983;* 16 Cavendish Drive, Claygate, ESHER, SURREY, KT10 0QE.

BAKER, Mr. Alexander, BA(Hons) ACA *2010;* Flat 11 Quilting Court, Garter Way, LONDON, SE16 6XF.

BAKER, Mrs. Alexandra Louise, BSc ACA *2005;* 10 Harbutts View, MIDDLEWICH, CHESHIRE, CW10 9PL.

•BAKER, Mrs. Alison Claire, BSc ACA *1997;* Cobham House High Street, Twyford, WINCHESTER, SO21 1RG.

BAKER, Dr. Alison Elizabeth, MSc ACA *2005;* 17 Woodlands Grove, Caversham, READING, RG4 6NB.

BAKER, Mr. Allan Harrison, FCA *1960;* April Cottage, 7 Blackborough Close, REIGATE, SURREY, RH2 7BZ. (Life Member)

BAKER, Mrs. Andrea, BSc ACA *1993;* 33 Orange Grove Road, 04-08 Orange Grove Residences, SINGAPORE 258359, SINGAPORE.

BAKER, Mrs. Andrea, ACA *1994;* 7 Marine Close, Wroughton, SWINDON, WILTSHIRE, SN4 9SG.

•BAKER, Mr. Andrew Douglas, BA FCA *1993;* Potter Baker, 20 Western Road, LAUNCESTON, PL15 7BA.

•BAKER, Mr. Andrew Howard, ACA CTA *1990;* Baker Tilly UK Audit LLP, Number One Old Hall Street, LIVERPOOL, L3 9SX. See also Baker Tilly Tax and Advisory Services LLP

•BAKER, Mr. Andrew Peter, MA FCA *1981;* Connolly & Callaghan Ltd, 80 Stokes Croft, BRISTOL, BS1 3QY.

BAKER, Mrs. Anne-Marie Elizabeth, BA ACA *1993;* 57 Wood Lane, LONDON, N6 5UD.

BAKER, Mr. Anthony Chantrey, FCA *1965;* Travessa SR., Dos Aflitos 51, 4410-066 SERZEDO VNG, PORTUGAL.

BAKER, Mr. Anthony Frank, FCA *1966;* 10 Elm Gardens, West End, SOUTHAMPTON, SO30 3SA. (Life Member)

BAKER, Mr. Anthony Michael, FCA *1959;* 47 Bantock Gardens, Finchfield, WOLVERHAMPTON, WV3 9LP. (Life Member)

•BAKER, Mr. Anthony Peter, BSc ACA *1980;* A.P. Baker & Co, 493a Caerphilly Road, Rhiwbina, CARDIFF, CF14 4SN.

BAKER, Mr. Anthony Philip, FCA *1955;* Highlands, 3 Great Lane, SHAFTESBURY, DORSET, SP7 8ET. (Life Member)

BAKER, Mr. Anthony Roy, FCA *1966;* 5 Berrylands, LONDON, SW20 9HB. (Life Member)

BAKER, Mr. Antony John, FCA *1961;* 12 Penman Close, Chiswell Green, ST. ALBANS, AL2 3DJ.

BAKER, Mr. Arthur Henry Claude, FCA *1957;* 5 Edale Drive, Kelsall, TARPORLEY, CW6 0RB. (Life Member)

BAKER, Mrs. Bernadette Anne, BSc ACA *1994;* Gatehouse, Nantwich Road, Wimboldsley, MIDDLEWICH, CHESHIRE, CW10 0LL.

BAKER, Mr. Charles Edward Fenn, BSc ACA *1986;* Alternative Networks Plc, Chatfield Court, 56 Chatfield Road, LONDON, SW11 3UL.

•BAKER, Mr. Charles Stephen, BSc FCA *1975;* Underwood Barron LLP, Monks Brook House, 13-17 Hursley Road, Chandler's Ford, EASTLEIGH, HAMPSHIRE SO53 2FW. See also Underwood Barron Associates Limited

BAKER, Mr. Chris, ACA *2009;* 118 Offord Road, LONDON, N1 1PF.

BAKER, Mr. Christopher, FCA *1968;* P.O. Box F-42498, Suite One, Stac House, Corner Settlers Way & Oak Street, FREEPORT, GRAND BAHAMA ISLAND 00000 BAHAMAS.

BAKER, Mr. Christopher James, BA ACA *2005;* 31 Girton Road, LONDON, SE26 5DJ.

•BAKER, Mr. Christopher John, BSS FCA *1982;* PricewaterhouseCoopers LLP, 1 Embankment Place, LONDON, WC2N 6RH. See also PricewaterhouseCoopers

BAKER, Mr. Christopher John, FCA *1970;* 27 Whitegates, West Hunsbury, NORTHAMPTON, NN4 9XA.

BAKER, Mr. Christopher John Stanley, MSc FCA *1973;* The Red House, 2a Princes Road, Kew, RICHMOND, TW9 3HP.

•BAKER, Mr. Christopher Terence, ACA *2004;* MacIntyre Hudson LLP, Euro House, 1394 High Road, Whetstone, LONDON, N20 9YZ.

BAKER, Mr. Christopher William, FCA *1965;* 87 Avenue Road, ERITH, KENT, DA8 3AT. (Life Member)

•BAKER, Mr. Clifford John, FCA *1979;* (Tax Fac), ST Hampden Limited, 57 London Road, HIGH WYCOMBE, BUCKINGHAMSHIRE, HP11 1BS. See also Seymour Taylor Audit Ltd

BAKER, Mr. Clifford Malcolm, BA ACA *1981;* 36 Queen Anne Street, LONDON, W1G 8HF.

BAKER, Mr. Clive, FCA *1982;* Armogain Ltd, 31 Oakbark House, High Street, BRENTFORD, MIDDLESEX, TW8 8LF.

BAKER, Mr. Clive Darren, BSc ACA *1990;* 41 Donnington Road, BRIGHTON, BN2 6WH.

BAKER, Mr. Clive John, FCA *1976;* 8 Short Drove, DOWNHAM MARKET, NORFOLK, PE38 9PT. (Life Member)

•BAKER, Mr. Colin Anthony, FCA *1972;* Building 3, Appartment 4, Zalman Shazar, 42493 NETANYA, ISRAEL.

BAKER, Mr. Colin William, ACA *1981;* 11 Love Lane, Cheam, SUTTON, SM3 8PS.

•BAKER, Mr. Colin William, BA ACA *1987;* 3 Hawthorne Mews, MAGHERA, COUNTY LONDONDERRY, BT46 5FS.

BAKER, Mr. Craig, BA ACA *2006;* 21Hornbeam Way, Kirkby-in-Ashfield, NOTTINGHAM, NG17 8RL.

BAKER, Mr. Craig Fenton, BSc ACA *1997;* 1A Darell Road, Caversham Heights, READING, RG4 7AY.

BAKER, Mr. Daniel, ACA MAAT *2011;* 25a Border Road, POOLE, DORSET, BH16 5EE.

BAKER, Mr. Daniel John, BSc ACA *1994;* Wildfell House Church Lane, Worplesdon, GUILDFORD, GU3 3RU.

BAKER, Mr. Daniel John, MSc BSc ACA *2008;* 2 Oxenford Street, LONDON, SE15 4DE.

BAKER, Mr. Daniel John, BSc ACA *2005;* with Deloitte LLP, 3 Victoria Square, Victoria Street, ST. ALBANS, HERTFORDSHIRE, AL1 3TF.

BAKER, Mr. David Ingram, FCA *1957;* Bridge House, Earl Soham, WOODBRIDGE, SUFFOLK, IP13 7RT. (Life Member)

BAKER, Mr. David John, BA FCA *1972;* 5 Acresdale, Beaumont ParkLostock, BOLTON, BL6 4PJ.

BAKER, Mr. David Richard, ACA *1986;* 2 Layters Avenue, Chalfont St. Peter, GERRARDS CROSS, SL9 9HP.

BAKER, Mr. David Ronald, BSc ACA *1988;* 30 Lower Hill Road, EPSOM, KT19 8LT.

BAKER, Mr. David William, FCA *1968;* Norcros Plc Baileys House, Central Walk, WOKINGHAM, BERKSHIRE, RG40 1AZ.

•BAKER, Ms. Dawn Julia, BSc ACA *1993;* (Tax Fac), Muras Baker Jones, Regent House, Bath Avenue, WOLVERHAMPTON, WV1 4EG.

BAKER, Mrs. Deborah Claire, BSc FCA *1992;* 64 Waller Drive, BANBURY, OXFORDSHIRE, OX16 9NR.

BAKER, Mr. Denis, BA ACA *1984;* 312 Coppergate House, 16 Brune Street, LONDON, E1 7NJ.

BAKER, Mr. Dennis Henry, FCA *1959;* Larchdene, 3A Hillcrest Road, HYTHE, CT21 5EX. (Life Member)

BAKER, Mr. Derek John, FCA *1977;* 51 Meadway, Southgate, LONDON, N14 6NJ.

BAKER, Mrs. Diane Mary, ACA *1985;* 18 Lower Wilton Road, MALVERN, WORCESTERSHIRE, WR14 3RJ.

•BAKER, Mr. Donald Matthew Burton, FCA *1976;* (Tax Fac), Bland Baker, 21 Lodge Lane, GRAYS, RM17 5RY.

BAKER, Mr. Duncan Charles, BA ACA *2006;* 34 Fairfields, Cawston, NORWICH, NR10 4AS.

BAKER, Mr. Edmund Anthony, BA ACA *1999;* Fools Syke House, Coal Pit Lane, Gisburn, CLITHEROE, LANCASHIRE, BB7 4JH.

BAKER, Mr. Edward, FCA *1957;* 21 Murton Close, Burwell, CAMBRIDGE, CB25 0DT. (Life Member)

•BAKER, Mr. Edward James, FCA *1970;* (Tax Fac), Edward J. Baker Ltd, Badgers Bank, Hastings Hill, Churchill, CHIPPING NORTON, OX7 6NA.

BAKER, Mr. Edward Joseph Christopher, MA ACA *1988;* 11 Cecilia Court, TIBURON, CA 94920, UNITED STATES.

•BAKER, Mr. Edward William, BA(Hons) ACA *1995;* with KPMG LLP, 8 Princes Parade, LIVERPOOL, L3 1QH.

BAKER, Mrs. Elaine Beryl, BSc ACA *1992;* 7 Willes Terrace, LEAMINGTON SPA, WARWICKSHIRE, CV31 1DL.

BAKER, Miss. Elizabeth, BSc ACA *1998;* 2 Britannia Square, Fairview Street, CHELTENHAM, GLOUCESTERSHIRE, GL52 2JQ.

BAKER, Mrs. Elizabeth Jane, LLB FCA *1986;* Oak Barn, Pettiphers Farm, Pebworth, STRATFORD-UPON-AVON, WARWICKSHIRE, CV37 8AW.

BAKER, Mrs. Emma, BSc ACA *2005;* 10 Stubley Gardens, LITTLEBOROUGH, OL15 8JD.

BAKER, Mrs. Emma Louise Mary, BSc ACA *2005;* 2 Badgers Rise, Badgers Mount, SEVENOAKS, KENT, TN14 7AW.

BAKER, Mr. Errol Benjamin, FCA *1966;* 23 School Close, HIGH WYCOMBE, BUCKINGHAMSHIRE, HP11 1PH.

BAKER, Mrs. Fay, BA ACA *2003;* 9 Barton Copse, Chieveley, NEWBURY, BERKSHIRE, RG20 8RN.

BAKER, Ms. Frances Chloe, BSc ACA *1989;* Le Bistrot Pierre Ashbourne House, 49-51 Forest Road East, NOTTINGHAM, NG1 4HT.

BAKER, Mr. Francis John, FCA *1966;* Inglenook, The Butts, Rodborough, STROUD, GL5 3UN. (Life Member)

BAKER, Mr. Gary Paul, BA ACA *1993;* 59 West 76th Street, Apartment 6E, NEW YORK, NY 10023, UNITED STATES.

•BAKER, Mrs. Gayle Alexandra, BA ACA *1994;* Chris Reid Ltd, Brick House, 150A Station Road, Woburn Sands, MILTON KEYNES, MK17 8SG.

BAKER, Mr. Geoffrey Freame, FCA *1973;* 4 Hamble Close, Warsash, SOUTHAMPTON, SO31 9GT.

BAKER, Mr. Gilbert Joseph, FCA *1955;* 3 Claremont Gardens, TUNBRIDGE WELLS, TN2 5DD. (Life Member)

BAKER, Mrs. Gillian, BA ACA *1992;* 11 Iredale Crescent, Standish, WIGAN, WN6 0UD.

BAKER, Mr. Gordon Spencer, FCA *1966;* 2 The Granary, Northwick Park, Blockley, MORETON-IN-MARSH, GL56 9RJ. (Life Member)

BAKER, Mr. Graham, BSc ACA *1986;* Ashcroft Vicarage Hill, Tanworth-in-Arden, SOLIHULL, B94 5EA.

BAKER, Mr. Graham James, BA ACA *1985;* Frontline, 1 America Square, LONDON, EC3N 2LB.

BAKER, Mr. Graham John, FCA *1968;* 2 Lamberts Close, Morcott, OAKHAM, LE15 9DE. (Life Member)

BAKER, Mr. Graham Peter, ACA *1978;* 26 New England Close, Bicknacre, CHELMSFORD, CM3 4XA.

BAKER, Mr. Graham Stuart, FCA *1963;* 82 Holbeach Drive, Kingsway, QUEDGELEY, GLOUCESTERSHIRE, GL2 2BF. (Life Member)

BAKER, Mr. Graham Timothy, BA ACA *1994;* 57 Wood Lane, LONDON, N6 5UD.

BAKER, Mr. Grahame Charles, BA FCA *1969;* Landscapes Rise, Cross Lane, Ticehurst, WADHURST, TN5 7HQ.

BAKER, Mr. Guy Christopher Scott, FCA *1968;* Scott - Baker Consulting, 66 Main Street, Thorpe Satchville, MELTON MOWBRAY, LEICESTERSHIRE, LE14 2DQ.

BAKER, Mrs. Helen, BA ACA *1981;* 5A Chapel Street, Hagley, STOURBRIDGE, DY9 0NL.

BAKER, Mr. Herbert Daniel, FCA FIIA *1971;* 17 Walnut Way, Hyde Heath, AMERSHAM, HP6 5SB. (Life Member)

BAKER, Mrs. Hilary, BSc ACA *1997;* 6 Sorrel Drive, LIGHTWATER, SURREY, GU18 5PB.

•BAKER, Mr. Hilary David, FCA *1980;* (Tax Fac), Hilary D Baker, 28 Lansdowne Road, STANMORE, MIDDLESEX, HA7 2SA.

•BAKER, Mr. Howard Lindon, FCA *1967;* (Tax Fac), Howard Baker Limited, 30 Christchurch Road, BOURNEMOUTH, BH1 3PD. See also Baker Howard Limited

•BAKER, Mr. Huw Lance, FCA *1984;* BTP Associates Limited, 84-86 High Street, MERTHYR TYDFIL, MID GLAMORGAN, CF47 8UG. See also BTP Associates

BAKER, Mr. Ian Alexander, BSc ACA *2002;* 20 Tolson Road, ISLEWORTH, MIDDLESEX, TW7 7AE.

BAKER, Mr. Ian Edward, BA ACA *1986;* Rockspring Property Investment Managers, 166 Sloane Street, LONDON, SW1X 9QF.

BAKER, Mr. Ian Howard, FCA *1981;* 25 Poplar Drive, Hutton, BRENTWOOD, CM13 1YU.

•BAKER, Mr. Ian Richard, FCA *1988;* Bache Brown & Co Ltd, Swinford House, Albion Street, BRIERLEY HILL, WEST MIDLANDS, DY5 3EE. See also Swinford House LLP

BAKER, Mr. Ian Seymour, BA ACA *1994;* 19b Pemberton Avenue, Bayview, NORTH SHORE CITY 0629, AUCKLAND, NEW ZEALAND.

BAKER, Mr. James Anthony, BSc ACA *1998;* Credit Suisse, 1 Cabot Square, LONDON, E14 4QJ.

BAKER, Mr. James Christopher, BA(Hons) ACA *2010;* 2a Princes Road, Kew, RICHMOND, SURREY, TW9 3HP.
BAKER, Mr. James Francis Christopher, ACA *2008;* 62 Brooklyn House, 31 Rillaton Walk, MILTON KEYNES, MK9 2BN.
BAKER, Mr. James Lawrence, BSc ACA *2011;* Riverdale Seaford Road, Alfriston, POLEGATE, EAST SUSSEX, BN26 5TR.
BAKER, Mr. James Robert, BA ACA *1992;* 68 Dorothy Road, LONDON, SW11 2JP.
•ⓘ**BAKER, Mr. Jason Daniel, BA ACA** *1999;* FRP Advisory LLP, 10 Furnival Street, LONDON, EC4A 1YH.
BAKER, Mr. Jason Sean, ACA MAAT *1998;* Plovers, Pilgrims Way, WESTERHAM, KENT, TN16 2DU.
•**BAKER, Mr. Jeffrey Alan, FCA** *1970;* 4 Imperial Place, Maxwell Road, BOREHAMWOOD, HERTFORDSHIRE, WD6 1JN.
BAKER, Miss. Joanna, BSc ACA DChA *2010;* B D O Stoy Hayward, Emerald House, East Street, EPSOM, SURREY, KT17 1HS.
BAKER, Miss. Joanne Clare, BA ACA *1996;* 59 Longfield Drive, AMERSHAM, BUCKINGHAMSHIRE, HP6 5HE.
•**BAKER, Mrs. Joanne Marie, ACA** *1996;* Baker & Co, Golden Meadow, 21 Dennyview Road, Abbots Leigh, BRISTOL, BS8 3RD. See also Tax Partner Ltd
BAKER, Mr. John, BSc ACA *1992;* Wales Audit Office, 24 Cathedral Road, CARDIFF, CF11 9LJ.
BAKER, Mr. John Charles, BSc FCA *1988;* Braye House, The Glebefield, Riverhead, SEVENOAKS, TN13 3DR.
BAKER, Mr. John David, BSc ACA *2010;* Pricewaterhousecoopers, 12 Plumtree Court, LONDON, EC4A 4HT.
BAKER, Mr. John Derek, JP FCA FRSA *1954;* 28 Gorway Road, WALSALL, WS1 3BG.
BAKER, Mr. John Frederick, BSc ACA *1981;* 49 Avenue Road, LONDON, SE20 7RR.
BAKER, Mr. John George, FCA *1977;* 31 Netherby Road, Forest Hill, LONDON, SE23 3AL.
•**BAKER, Mr. John Kenneth, BA FCA** *1987;* PricewaterhouseCoopers LLP, 1 Embankment Place, LONDON, WC2N 6RH. See also PricewaterhouseCoopers
•**BAKER, Mr. John Miller Buchanan, FCA** *1974;* 7 Rockleigh, North Road, HERTFORD, SG14 1LS.
BAKER, Mr. John Raymond, FCA *1955;* Thameside, Vicarage Walk, Bray, MAIDENHEAD, BERKSHIRE, SL6 2AE. (Life Member)
BAKER, Mr. John Samuel George, FCA *1972;* Seven Oaks, Forest Drive, Cross Keys, NEWPORT, NP11 7FA.
BAKER, Mr. John Simon, ACA *2007;* 5/1 Bennett Street, BONDI, NSW 2026, AUSTRALIA.
BAKER, Mr. Jon Phillip, BSc ACA *2006;* 82 Bronsart Road, LONDON, SW6 6AB.
BAKER, Mr. Jonathan, BSc(Hons) ACA *2004;* Financial Services Authority, 25 North Colonnade, LONDON, E14 5HS.
BAKER, Mr. Jonathan Alan, ACA *1995;* Arnold House, St Julian's Avenue, St Peter Port, GUERNSEY, GY13NF.
BAKER, Mr. Jonathan Patrick, FCA *1979;* 130 Worcester Road, Hagley, STOURBRIDGE, DY9 0NR.
BAKER, Mr. Jonathan Philip, MA FCA *1968;* Casilla No. 11-01-454, Correos del Ecuador, LOJA, ECUADOR. (Life Member)
BAKER, Mr. Jonathan Southgate, MA ACA *1986;* 2 Nethercourt Hill, RAMSGATE, CT11 0RX.
•**BAKER, Mr. Jonathan Stanley, FCA FCCA** *1980;* Hill Osbourne Limited, Tower House, Parkstone Road, POOLE, BH15 2JH.
BAKER, Mrs. Juliette Micaela, BA(Hons) ACA *2002;* 7 Hocombe Drive, Chandler's Ford, EASTLEIGH, SO53 5QE.
BAKER, Mrs. Karen Nicola, BA(Hons) ACA *2003;* 12 Station Lane, Lapworth, SOLIHULL, B94 6LT.
BAKER, Miss. Katherine Rose, ACA *2008;* (Tax Fac), Flat 5 Monmouth House, 44 West Hill Road, LONDON, SW18 5HS.
BAKER, Miss. Katie Louise, ACA *2009;* 37 Fullerton Road, Byfleet, WEST BYFLEET, SURREY, KT14 7TA.
BAKER, Mr. Keith Andrew, BA ACA *1982;* Brook House, Lower Frith Common, Eardiston, TENBURY WELLS, WR15 8JU.
BAKER, Mr. Keith George, FCA *1962;* 66a Granary Lane, BUDLEIGH SALTERTON, DEVON, EX9 6ES.
BAKER, Miss. Kerri Helen, ACA *2008;* Garden Flat, 81 Kingsdown Parade, BRISTOL, BS6 5UJ.
•**BAKER, Mr. Kevin, ACA** *1985;* Parkwood Financial Solutions Ltd, Madon & Co, 8th Floor Tolworth Tower, Ewell Road, SURBITON, SURREY KT6 7EL.
BAKER, Miss. Laura Elizabeth, BSc ACA *2006;* Paper House, Waterwells Drive, GLOUCESTER, GL2 2PH.
BAKER, Mr. Lee James, ACA *2009;* with Wenn Townsend, 30 St Giles', OXFORD, OX1 3LE.
BAKER, Mr. Leslie William, FCA *1965;* Victoria House, St. Catherines Hill, LAUNCESTON, CORNWALL, PL15 7EJ.
BAKER, Mrs. Louise Anne, ACA *2008;* Horwath Clark Whitehill Oakland House, 38-42 Victoria Road, HARTLEPOOL, CLEVELAND, TS26 8DD.
BAKER, Mr. Mark Leslie, BSc ACA *1992;* 43 Woodruff Way Thornhill, CARDIFF, CF14 9FP.
BAKER, Mr. Mark Stewart, BSc ACA *1982;* 14 The Street, Brettenham, IPSWICH, IP7 7QP.
BAKER, Mr. Mark Sydney, BA ACA *1988;* Eltek House, Maxted Road, HEMEL HEMPSTEAD, HERTFORDSHIRE, HP2 7DX.
BAKER, Mr. Martin Richard, BA ACA *1987;* xoserve Limited, National Grid, 31 Homer Road, SOLIHULL, B91 3LT.
BAKER, Mr. Matthew James, BSc ACA *2007;* 429a Chertsey Road, TWICKENHAM, TW2 6LS.
BAKER, Mr. Matthew James, BEng ACA *1994;* Wickens Barn, Bleasdale, PRESTON, PR3 1UX.
BAKER, Mr. Maurice Edward, BA ACA *1978;* 213 Turncroft Lane, STOCKPORT, CHESHIRE, SK1 4BN.
BAKER, Mr. Maurice Keith, FCA *1987;* 68 Tatnam Road, POOLE, BH15 2DS.
•**BAKER, Mr. Mervyn Ronald, FCA** *1978;* Wheelers, 16 North Street, WISBECH, CAMBRIDGESHIRE, PE13 1NE.
BAKER, Mr. Michael Andrew, BA ACA *1988;* 19 Park Hill, HARPENDEN, HERTFORDSHIRE, AL5 3AT.
BAKER, Mr. Michael Charles, BSc ACA *2001;* Eddy's Dream, 1 Upper Unit, 21 Music Heights, SOUTHAMPTON SN03, BERMUDA.
•**BAKER, Mr. Michael George, BA FCA** *1985;* Charcroft Baker, 5 West Court, Enterprise Road, MAIDSTONE, KENT, ME15 6JD.
BAKER, Mr. Michael John, MBA BSc FCA AMCT *1984;* Wisteria Cottage, 8 Higher Polsham Road, PAIGNTON, TQ3 2SY.
BAKER, Miss. Natalie Susan, MSci ACA *2007;* Barclays Capital, 5 The North Colonnade, Canary Wharf, LONDON, E14 4BB.
BAKER, Mr. Nathan Michael, BSc ACA *2010;* 235 Ludlow Road, SOUTHAMPTON, SO19 2EL.
BAKER, Mr. Neil Graham, BA ACA *1986;* NewSmith Capital Partners Lansdowne House, 57 Berkeley Square, LONDON, W1J 6ER.
BAKER, Mr. Neil Martin, BA ACA *1990;* Lancotbury Manor, Castle Hill Road, Totternhoe, DUNSTABLE, BEDFORDSHIRE, LU6 1RG.
BAKER, Mr. Nicholas James, BA(Hons) ACA *2000;* with PricewaterhouseCoopers LLP, Donington Court, Pegasus Business Park, Castle Donington, DERBY, DE74 2UZ.
BAKER, Mr. Nigel David, BSc FCA *1978;* 58 Hampton Park, Redland, BRISTOL, BS6 6LJ.
BAKER, Mrs. Nina Ann, BSc ACA *2006;* (Tax Fac), 34 Fairfields, Cawston, NORWICH, NR10 4AS.
BAKER, Mr. Norman Keith, FCA *1970;* 19 Fleming Close, Biddenham, BEDFORD, MK40 4QZ.
BAKER, Mr. Paul, ACA *1980;* 9 Lonsdale Promenade, WESTBURY, TAS 7303, AUSTRALIA.
•**BAKER, Mr. Paul Albert, BA FCA** *1987;* R M Chancellor & Company Ltd, Lewis House, Great Chesterford Court, Great Chesterford, SAFFRON WALDEN, ESSEX CB10 1PF. See also HSA Bookkeeping Limited
BAKER, Mr. Paul Andrew, BA ACA *1985;* 4 Honeysgreen Lane, West Derby, LIVERPOOL, L12 9EW.
•**BAKER, Mr. Paul Anthony, FCA FCCA** *1989;* (Tax Fac), P Baker & Associates, Grover House, Grover Walk, Corringham, STANFORD-LE-HOPE, ESSEX SS17 7LS. See also PBA Ltd
•**BAKER, Mr. Paul Arthur, MA ACA CTA** *1991;* Rawlinson & Hunter, Eighth Floor, 6 New Street Square, New Fetter Lane, LONDON, EC4A 3AQ.
•**BAKER, Mr. Paul David, BSc ARCS FCA** *1999;* Greenstones, Rookery Way, HAYWARDS HEATH, WEST SUSSEX, RH16 4RE.
BAKER, Mr. Paul Edward Simon, BA(Hons) ACA *2002;* 34 Hillcrest Avenue, EDGWARE, MIDDLESEX, HA8 8PA.
BAKER, Mr. Paul Francis, FCA *1973;* 2 Thorpe Court, Thorpe Waterville, KETTERING, NN14 3ED.
BAKER, Mr. Paul Hartley, BA ACA *1979;* 11 Swinton Terrace, Masham, RIPON, HG4 4HS.
BAKER, Mr. Paul Martin, BA ACA *1985;* Troux Technologies, 8601 FM2222, Building 3, Suite 300, AUSTIN, TX 78730 UNITED STATES.
•**BAKER, Mr. Paul Stuart, FCA** *1975;* McKenzies, 14-16 Station Road West, OXTED, SURREY, RH8 9EP. See also Professional Financial Consultants(Purley)Limited
BAKER, Mr. Paul William, BA ACA *2003;* with PricewaterhouseCoopers LLP, Cornwall Court, 19 Cornwall Street, BIRMINGHAM, B3 2DT.
BAKER, Mr. Paul William, BA ACA *1998;* 35 Turnstone Close, LONDON, E13 0HN.
BAKER, Mr. Peter Charles, MA FCA *1966;* 10A Kirkwick Avenue, HARPENDEN, AL5 2QL. (Life Member)
BAKER, Mr. Peter Garry, BA FCA *1971;* Nockolds Solictors, 6 Market Square, BISHOP'S STORTFORD, CM23 3UZ.
BAKER, Mr. Peter Norman, FCA *1965;* 19 Studland Park, WESTBURY, BA13 3HQ. (Life Member)
•**BAKER, Mr. Philip Jefferay, FCA** *1974;* Construction Industry Solutions Ltd, The Coins Building, The Grove, SLOUGH, SL1 1QP.
BAKER, Mr. Philip Richmond, FCA *1972;* 5A Chapel Street, Hagley, STOURBRIDGE, DY9 0NL.
•**BAKER, Mrs. Rachael, BA(Hons) ACA** *2001;* Baker Accounting, Knutcroft, Knutscroft Lane, Thurloxton, TAUNTON, TA2 8RL.
BAKER, Mr. Ramsey Karim, BSc(Hons) ACA *2010;* Flat 6 15 Croxteth Road, LIVERPOOL, L8 3SE.
•**BAKER, Mr. Richard, FCA** *1986;* Condy Mathias, 6 Houndiscombe Road, PLYMOUTH, PL4 6HH.
BAKER, Mr. Richard Calverley, BA ACA *1989;* 27 East Parkside, WARLINGHAM, SURREY, CR6 9PY.
•**BAKER, Mr. Richard Charles, ACA FCCA ATII** *2008;* (Tax Fac), Tax Partner Ltd, 21 Dennyview Road, Abbots Leigh, BRISTOL, BS8 3RD.
BAKER, Mr. Richard Clive Jonathan, BA ACA *1982;* Boxworth House High Street, Boxworth, CAMBRIDGE, CB23 4LZ.
•**BAKER, Mr. Richard Francis, ACA** *2002;* Crowe Clark Whitehill LLP, Hatherton House, Hatherton Street, WALSALL, WS1 1YB. See also Horwath Clark Whitehill LLP and Crowe Clark Whitehill
BAKER, Mr. Richard Harley, FCA *1968;* 9 Slipper Road, EMSWORTH, HAMPSHIRE, PO10 8BS.
•**BAKER, Mr. Richard James Malcolm Louis, BSc FCA** *1987;* (Tax Fac), Crowe Clark Whitehill LLP, St Bride's House, 10 Salisbury Square, LONDON, EC4Y 8EH. See also Horwath Clark Whitehill LLP and Crowe Clark Whitehill
BAKER, Mr. Richard Shane, ACA CA(AUS) *2011;* Flat 76, 6 Rossetti Road, Bermondsey, LONDON, SE16 3EZ.
BAKER, Mr. Robert Brian, FCA *1960;* 27 Rowney Gardens, SAWBRIDGEWORTH, CM21 0AT. (Life Member)
BAKER, Mr. Robert Frederick, MSc FCA *1975;* Lakes Rise, Fawsley, DAVENTRY, NORTHAMPTONSHIRE, NN11 3BA. (Life Member)
BAKER, Mr. Robert James, BSc ACA *1998;* Eastview 184 Wigan Road Euxton, CHORLEY, LANCASHIRE, PR7 6JW.
BAKER, Mr. Robert James Stephenson, BA ACA *2004;* Dolphin House, Garth Road, LETCHWORTH GARDEN CITY, SG6 3NG.
BAKER, Mr. Robert John, BA FCA *1980;* Moonrakers Corner, Harewood Road, CHALFONT ST. GILES, HP8 4UB.
BAKER, Mr. Robert Leslie David, BEng ACA *2000;* 79 Woodland Drive, ST. ALBANS, AL4 0EN.
•**BAKER, Mr. Robin Dudley, FCA** *1964;* Turner & Ellerby, The Guildhall, Framlingham, WOODBRIDGE, IP13 9AZ.
BAKER, Mr. Roger Christopher, FCA *1974;* 10 Devereux Drive, WATFORD, WD17 3DE.
BAKER, Mr. Roger Owen, BSc ACA *1989;* Ampfield House, Blackheath, GUILDFORD, GU4 8RD.
BAKER, Mr. Ronald, FCA *1963;* Braemar, 2 Livesay Crescent, WORTHING, BN14 8AS.
•**BAKER, Mrs. Rowan Clare, MA ACA CTA** *2003;* (Tax Fac), 92 Sandbanks Road, POOLE, DORSET, BH14 8BY.
•**BAKER, Mr. Roy Buchanan, ACA** *1979;* Baker Watkin, Middlesex House, Rutherford Close, STEVENAGE, SG1 2EF.
BAKER, Mr. Russell Edward James, BSc ACA *1991;* 38 Chestnut Way, Repton, DERBY, DE65 6FQ.
BAKER, Miss. Sally Louise, BSc ACA *1999;* Flat 7 Wilbury Lodge, Dry Arch Road, ASCOT, BERKSHIRE, SL5 0DB.
BAKER, Mrs. Sarah Ann Elizabeth, BA FCA *1988;* Fiander Tovell & Co, 63-64 The Avenue, SOUTHAMPTON, SO17 1XS.
BAKER, Miss. Sarah Elizabeth, BSc ACA *2010;* Monks Cottage, Monks Lane, Dedham, COLCHESTER, CO7 6DP.
BAKER, Miss. Sarah Louise, BA(Hons) ACA FCILA *1991;* 20 The Downs, Aldridge, WALSALL, WS9 0YT.
BAKER, Mrs. Sarah Louise, LLB ACA *1998;* 9 Grosvenor Gardens, LONDON, SW14 8BY.
BAKER, Mr. Shaun, BA ACA *1998;* The Orchard Upper Street, Stratford St. Mary, COLCHESTER, CO7 6JW.
BAKER, Mr. Simon, BA ACA *1992;* 7 Willes Terrace, LEAMINGTON SPA, WARWICKSHIRE, CV31 1DL.
BAKER, Mr. Simon Edward, ACA *2009;* 1 Hampden Hill, WARE, HERTFORDSHIRE, SG12 7JT.
BAKER, Mr. Stephen Dennis, BA FCA *1983;* with Alwyns LLP, Crown House, 151 High Road, LOUGHTON, ESSEX, IG10 4LG.
BAKER, Mr. Stephen George, BSc ACA *1993;* The Old Vicarage, Church Road, Shackerstone, NUNEATON, WARWICKSHIRE, CV13 6NN.
•**BAKER, Mr. Stephen Roy, BSc FCA CF** *1980;* Grant Thornton UK LLP, 30 Finsbury Square, LONDON, EC2P 2YU. See also Grant Thornton LLP
•**BAKER, Mr. Steven Anthony, BA FCA** *1991;* 28 Marion Road, Furnace Green, CRAWLEY, RH10 6QH.
BAKER, Mr. Stewart Frank Bradley, BSc ACA *2009;* Experian Ltd Riverleen House, Electric Avenue, NOTTINGHAM, NG80 1RH.
BAKER, Mrs. Susan Elizabeth, MA ACA *1997;* 61a Monkhams Avenue, WOODFORD GREEN, IG8 0EX.
BAKER, Miss. Susan Louise, BSc ACA *2007;* 28 Piernik Close, SWINDON, SN25 1AS.
BAKER, Miss. Susan Margaret, BA ACA *1980;* 99 Cambridge Road, NEW MALDEN, KT3 3QP.
BAKER, Mrs. Suzanne Elizabeth, BSc ACA *1992;* Clos Des Seux, Le Mont Du Coin, St. Brelade, JERSEY, JE3 8BE.
BAKER, Mr. Terence, BSc FCA CTA *1956;* Old Garden, Maresfield Park, UCKFIELD, TN22 3ER. (Life Member)
•**BAKER, Mr. Thomas, BSc ACA** *2006;* The Fresh Accountancy Company Limited, 1 Brownings End, Ogwell, NEWTON ABBOT, DEVON, TQ12 6YZ.
BAKER, Mr. Thomas Grigg, BSc ACA PGCE *2005;* 2 Wath Lane Cottages Burton Grange, Helperby, YORK, YO61 2RY.
BAKER, Mr. Timothy Michael Matthew, MA ACA *1987;* 56 Kingsley Street, LONDON, SW11 5LE.
BAKER, Mr. Timothy Simon, BA ACA *1990;* Ballamenaugh, Glen Auldyn, Lezayre, ISLE OF MAN, IM7 2AG.
BAKER, Mrs. Tracy Anne, BSc ACA *1993;* Ladle Hill Cottage, Old Burghclere, NEWBURY, BERKSHIRE, RG20 9NR.
BAKER, Mr. Vivian, FCA *1951;* Harry Bower Cottage, 150 Paddock Road, Kirkburton, HUDDERSFIELD, HD8 0TT. (Life Member)
BAKER, Mr. Warren Bryce Rezvan, MA ACA *1992;* 3 Arundel Court, Raymond Road, Wimbledon, LONDON, SW19 4AF.
•**BAKER, Mr. Warren Edward, BCom FCA** *1988;* Wilson Wright LLP, First Floor, Thavies Inn House, 3-4 Holborn Circus, LONDON, EC1N 2HA.
BAKER, Mr. Wayne William, ACA *2004;* Rickard Keen, 9 Nelson Street, SOUTHEND-ON-SEA, SS1 1EH.
BAKER, Mrs. Wendy, BA ACA *2005;* 10 Chiltern Close, STAINES, MIDDLESEX, TW18 2BU.
BAKER, Mr. William, BEng ACA *2002;* 66 Downlands Road, PURLEY, CR8 4JF.
BAKER, Mr. William, FCA *1959;* 16 Alpraham Crescent, Upton, CHESTER, CH2 1QX. (Life Member)
•**BAKER, Mr. William John, FCA** *1970;* W. John Baker, 4 Corbar Road, STOCKPORT, SK2 6EP.
BAKER-BATES, Mr. Rodney Pennington, BA FCA AIMC *1972;* Ancient House, Church Street, Peasenhall, SAXMUNDHAM, SUFFOLK, IP17 2HL.
BAKER-HIRST, Mrs. Jennifer, BSc FCA *1992;* 9 The Glebe Field, Shoreham Lane, SEVENOAKS, TN13 3DR.
BAKER-JOHNSON, Mr. Roderick Michael, MEng FCA *1997;* 6 Teasel Way, CARTERTON, OXFORDSHIRE, OX18 1JD.
BAKERMAN, Mr. Warner, FCA *1958;* 2 Glenside, LIVERPOOL, L18 9UJ. (Life Member)
BAKES, Miss. Philippa Jane, BSc FCA *1991;* WHK, L1 200 Malop Street, PO Box 1, GEELONG, VIC 3220, AUSTRALIA.
BAKEWELL, Miss. Annemarie Jacqueline, BSc ACA *1989;* 1 Asmara Road, LONDON, NW2 3SS.
BAKEWELL, Mrs. Sarah Jane, BSc(Hons) ACA MSI *2003;* Vine Cottage, 1 Orchard Close, Barkestone, NOTTINGHAM, NG13 0HU.

•**BAKEWELL, Mrs. Sharon Louise, BSc ACA** *1997;* Bakewell Accountancy Services, 4 Coed Terfyn, Penymynydd, CHESTER, CH4 0XB. See also Bakewll Accountancy Services
BAKHAI, Mr. Amish, BSc ACA *2005;* 3 Coney Close, Langley Green, CRAWLEY, WEST SUSSEX, RH11 7QA.
BAKHAI, Mrs. Hansa Ramesh, FCA *1975;* 22 Alderton Hill, LOUGHTON, IG10 3JB.
BAKHDA, Mr. Brijesh, MSc ACA *2000;* PO Box 29913, DUBAI, UNITED ARAB EMIRATES.
BAKHSHI, Miss. Reeva, BSc(Hons) ACA *2002;* 10 Ramillies Road, LONDON, W4 1JN.
BAKHSHI, Mr. Sangdeep, MSc ACA *2010;* 32 Crosthwaite Way, SLOUGH, SL1 6EX.
BAKHTIAR, Mr. Ramin Sacha, BSc ACA *2009;* Carbon Trust UK, 5 New Street Square, LONDON, EC4A 3BF.
BAKOS, Mr. Stephen, BCom BAcc ACA CA(SA) *2009;* Stonehage Financial Services Limited, 56 Conduit Street, LONDON, W1S 2YZ.
BAKRAN, Mr. Adam, ACA *2011;* 25 Kensington Hall Gardens, Beaumont Avenue, LONDON, W14 9LS.
BAKRANIA, Mr. Rajesh, BSc ACA *1999;* 129 Mill Road, WELLINGBOROUGH, NN8 1PH.
BAKRANIA, Mr. Rajnikant Kababhai, FCA *1966;* 27 Burlington Rise, East Barnet, BARNET, HERTFORDSHIRE, EN4 8NH.
BAKRIDAN, Miss. Clara, BSc ACA *2003;* 82 Lyndhurst Gardens, LONDON, N3 1TD.
•**BAKSHI, Mr. Pankaj Shantilal, FCA CTA** *1979;* (Tax Fac), Hodge Bakshi Limited, Churchgate House, 3 Church Road, Whitchurch, CARDIFF, CF14 2DX.
•**BAKST, Mr. Aron Joseph, FCA** *1973;* Suite 1203 Twin Towers, 35 Jabotinsky Street, 52511 RAMAT GAN, ISRAEL.
•**BAL, Mr. Jastinder Singh, LLB FCA** *2000;* (Tax Fac), Evergreen, 2 London Wall Buildings, London Wall, LONDON, EC2M 5UU.
BAL, Mr. Raj Paul Singh, MA FCA *1993;* Castle Dene, 11 Burgess Wood Road, BEACONSFIELD, BUCKINGHAMSHIRE, HP9 1EQ.
BAL, Mr. Rajpal Singh, ACA *2011;* 8 Sutton Avenue, SLOUGH, SL3 7AW.
BALA, Miss. Seetha, BSc ACA *2011;* 12 Manning Gardens, HARROW, MIDDLESEX, HA3 0PF.
BALA, Miss. Zohra Ismail, ACA *2005;* Pricewaterhousecoopers, 33 Wellington Street, LEEDS, LS1 4JP.
BALAAM, Mr. Martin Anthony, BSc ACA *1995;* The Laurels, Coole Lane, Newhall, NANTWICH, CW5 8AY.
BALABAN, Mr. Graham Daniel, FCA *1973;* 4 Sheepfoot Lane, Prestwich, MANCHESTER, M25 0BL.
BALACHANDRAN, Mr. Sacha, BA ACA CF *1998;* The Old House, 1 Broughton Road, Salford, MILTON KEYNES, MK17 8BH.
BALACHANDRAN, Mrs. Tracy Michelle, BSc ACA *1999;* The Old House, 1 Broughton Road, Salford, MILTON KEYNES, MK17 8BH.
BALAKRISHNAN, Mrs. Ka Yan Claudia, PhD MA BA ACA *2010;* 2 Franklin Place, LONDON, SE13 7ES.
•**BALAKRISHNAN, Mr. Venkatesha, BSc FCA MCT FSI** *1993;* Ernst & Young LLP, 1 More London Place, LONDON, SE1 2AF. See also Ernst & Young Europe LLP
BALAS, Mr. Heskel Jacob, ACA *2009;* 21 Highview Gardens, EDGWARE, MIDDLESEX, HA8 9UB.
BALAS, Mrs. Ruth Anne, FCA *1974;* 21 Highview Gardens, EDGWARE, HA8 9UB.
BALAS, Mr. Solomon, BSc FCA *1974;* 21 Highview Gardens, EDGWARE, HA8 9UB.
BALASBURAMANIAM, Mr. Rajeesh, ACA *2011;* BDO International, 12th Floor Menara Uni. Asia, Jalan sultan Ismail, 1008 KUALA LUMPUR, FEDERAL TERRITORY, MALAYSIA.
•**BALASINGHAM, Mr. Joseph Ravindrasingham, BSc FCA** *1992;* Joseph R Balasingham, 46 Mount Stewart Avenue, HARROW, MIDDLESEX, HA3 0JU. See also Shanthini Business and Management Consultancy Limited
•**BALASOUPRAMANIEN, Miss. Pamela, BA FCA** *1997;* Apartment B20 Diplomat Garden La Hausse de la Louviere, FLOREAL, MAURITIUS.
BALASUBRAMANIAM, Miss. Rashmir, BSc ACA *1998;* 1406 N 38th Street, SEATTLE, WA 98103, UNITED STATES.
BALASUBRAMANIAN, Mr. Jayaraman, MSc ACA *2004;* Old Number 35, New Number 5, Lock Street, Kottur villa, Flat No D-6, Varadapuram Kotturpuram CHENNAI 600085 INDIA.
BALASUNDARAM, Ms. Dheepa, BSc ACA *2001;* 22 Brocklebank Road, LONDON, SW18 3AU.
BALAWAJDER, Mr. Martin John, BSc ACA *1992;* IPOPEMA Securities S.A., ul. Walicow 11, 00-851 WARSAW, POLAND.
BALAZS, Mr. Arpad, ACA *2008;* with PricewaterhouseCoopers KFT, Wesselenyi u 16, BUDAPEST, H-1077, HUNGARY.
BALBAN, Mr. Nathan, BSc FCA *2000;* with Deloitte Touche Tohmatsu, Grosvenor Place, 225 George Street, P.O. Box N 250, SYDNEY, NSW 2000 AUSTRALIA.
BALBI, Mr. Anthony Stuart Galileo, BSc ACA *1992;* b.p. 2587, L-1025 LUXEMBOURG, LUXEMBOURG.
BALBI, Mr. David Charles, BSc ACA *1993;* St Catherines, 4 Crag Lane, KNARESBOROUGH, NORTH YORKSHIRE, HG5 8EE.
BALBI, Mrs. Rachel Helen, BA ACA *1993;* St Catherines, 4 Crag Lane, KNARESBOROUGH, NORTH YORKSHIRE, HG5 8EE.
BALBOA, Mrs. Virna De Los Santos, ACA CA(AUS) *2011;* 67 Clonmel Road, Teddington, LONDON, TW11 0ST.
BALCAM, Mr. Robert Edward Schofield, BA FCA *1977;* Lemming House, Woodsome Park, Fenay Bridge, HUDDERSFIELD, HD8 0JW.
BALCH, Miss. Catherine Susan, BSc ACA *1999;* 53 East Dulwich Road, LONDON, SE22 9AP.
BALCH, Mr. David Thomas, BA ACA *2007;* 5 Percy Road, EXETER, EX2 8JY.
•**BALCH, Mrs. Denise Margaret, ACA** *1987;* (Tax Fac), Thompson Balch Limited, Sovereign House, 15 Towcester Road, Old Stratford, MILTON KEYNES, MK19 6AN.
•**BALCH, Mr. Shaun Alexander, FCA** *1991;* Thompson Balch Limited, Sovereign House, 15 Towcester Road, Old Stratford, MILTON KEYNES, MK19 6AN.
BALCHIN, Mr. Andrew Mark, ACA *1984;* Springfield Butts Lane, Stour Provost, GILLINGHAM, DORSET, SP8 5RU.
BALCHIN, Mr. John, FCA *1947;* PO Box 19, YZERFONTEIN, 7351, SOUTH AFRICA. (Life Member)
BALCHIN, Miss. Rachel, ACA *2010;* Green 1, National Audit Office, 157-197 Buckingham Palace Road, LONDON, SW1W 9SP.
BALCHIN, Mrs. Victoria Jane, BA ACA *2000;* Stanway, Ashwood Road, WOKING, SURREY, GU22 7JN.
•**BALCOMBE, Mr. Adrian Kenneth, BA ACA** *1987;* Alvarez & Marsal Transaction Advisory Group Europe LLP, 1 Finsbury Circus, LONDON, EC2M 7EB.
BALD, Miss. Denise Yvonne, BA ACA *1996;* 45 Leamington Road, SOUTHPORT, MERSEYSIDE, PR8 3JZ.
BALDACCHINO, Mr. Hugo John, BA ACA *1997;* 9 Wisteria Close, YEOVIL, BA22 8UT.
BALDACCHINO, Mr. Raymond, FCA *1964;* 8 The Patchins, 333 Sandbanks Road, POOLE, BH14 8HZ. (Life Member)
BALDEN, Mr. Robert Shaw, TD FCA *1952;* 34 Northfield Court, SHEFFIELD, S10 1QR. (Life Member)
BALDERSON, Mr. Nicholas, ACA *2011;* 41 Kings Avenue, WATFORD, WD18 7SB.
BALDERSON, Mr. Trevor, ACA *1979;* 46 Gramfield Road, Crosland Moor, HUDDERSFIELD, HD4 5QD.
BALDERSTON, Mr. David James, MBA BA FCA *1989;* 20 Wedgwood Close, Wombourne, WOLVERHAMPTON, WV5 8EL.
•**BALDING, Mr. Charles Leonard, FCA** *1972;* (Tax Fac), Clarke Dowzall & Balding, 6 Old Main Street, BINGLEY, WEST YORKSHIRE, BD16 2RH.
BALDING, Mrs. Kerry Celine, BA ACA *1993;* Hampton Cottage, Main Street, Bishampton, PERSHORE, WR10 2NH.
BALDING, Mr. Simon Andrew, BSc ACA *1993;* 15 Avondale Road, BROMLEY, BR1 4HT.
•**BALDOCK, Mr. Andrew James, FCA** *1982;* 5 Glanmead, Shenfield, BRENTWOOD, ESSEX, CM15 8ER.
BALDOCK, Mr. Geoffrey Martin, BSc ACA *1994;* 85 Chiltern Road, Caversham, READING, RG4 5HS.
•**BALDOCK, Mr. Peter Jeremy, BA FCA CF** *1973;* Deloitte & Touche, 6 Shenton Way, 32-00, DBS Building Tower Two, SINGAPORE 068809, SINGAPORE.
BALDOCK, Mr. Simon Paul, BSc(Econ) ACA *1997;* 15 ROMAN CLOSE, BLUE BELL HILL, CHATHAM, ME5 9DJ.
BALDREY, Miss. Clare, BSc ACA *2003;* 4 Laslett Street, WORCESTER, WR3 8JR.
BALDREY, Mr. Philip Nigel, FCA *1980;* Evergreen Rising Lane, Lapworth, SOLIHULL, B94 6HP.
BALDRIDGE, Mr. Michael, FCA *1971;* 240 Abbey Lane, Beauchief, SHEFFIELD, S8 0BW.
BALDRY, Mr. David Howard, BA(Hons) ACA *2001;* Postnet Suite 49, Private Bag X12, Cresta, JOHANNESBURG, 2118, SOUTH AFRICA.
BALDRY, Mr. Matthew William, BSc ACA *2009;* 16 Treetop Close, LUTON, LU2 0JZ.
•**BALDRY, Mr. Neville William, FCA** *1986;* Clive Owen & Co LLP, 140 Coniscliffe Road, DARLINGTON, DL3 7RT.
BALDRY, Mr. Simon James, ACA *1995;* Norwich Union, 3rd FloorWillow House, Peachman Way, Broadland Business Park, NORWICH, NR7 0WF.
•**BALDRY, Mr. Trevor, FCA** *1974;* Brookside, 36 Bell Hill, Finedon, WELLINGBOROUGH, NORTHAMPTONSHIRE, NN9 5ND.
BALDWIN, Mr. Andrew Michael, ACA *2008;* 40 Scott Street, YORK, YO23 1NS.
BALDWIN, Mrs. Ann Shirley, FCA *1972;* Cardene Professional Development, 125 Bridge House, 18 St George Wharf, LONDON, SW8 2LQ.
•**BALDWIN, Ms. Anne Louise, BSc FCA CTA** *1991;* (Tax Fac), Ansax Business Solutions, Brickfield Cottage, Hurn, CHRISTCHURCH, DORSET, BH23 6AR.
BALDWIN, Mr. Antony William Wells, MA FCA *1961;* Beechcroft, 7 Upper Hollis, GREAT MISSENDEN, BUCKINGHAMSHIRE, HP16 9HP. (Life Member)
BALDWIN, Mr. Christopher, BSc FCA *1992;* 4 Robins Grove, WARWICK, WARWICKSHIRE, CV34 6RF.
BALDWIN, Mr. Christopher, BSc ACA *1990;* 13 Fawn Road, CHIGWELL, IG7 4HG.
BALDWIN, Mr. David Peter, BA FCA *1975;* 14 Bennys Way, Coton, CAMBRIDGE, CB3 7PS.
BALDWIN, Mrs. Diana Mary, MA ACA *1988;* Dover Town Council, Maison Dieu House, Biggin Street, DOVER, KENT, CT16 1DW.
BALDWIN, Mr. Edwin George, BSc FCA *1971;* Alexander Forbes Financial Services Ltd, Leon House, 233 High Street, CROYDON, CR9 9AF.
•**BALDWIN, Mrs. Fiona Christine, BMus ACA** *1996;* with Grant Thornton UK LLP, 4 Hardman Square, Spinningfields, MANCHESTER, M3 3EB.
BALDWIN, Mr. Gary Richard, BSc ACA *1989;* STFC, Polaris House, North Star Avenue, SWINDON, SN2 1ET.
BALDWIN, Miss. Hannah Elizabeth, BSc ACA *2006;* 103 Lincolns Mead, LINGFIELD, SURREY, RH7 6TA.
BALDWIN, Mr. Iain Andrew, BSc ACA *1991;* Allsop Residential Investment Ltd, 33 Park Place, LEEDS, LS1 2RY.
BALDWIN, Mr. Ian, BSc(Hons) ACA *2001;* Transfield Services, Level 10, 111 Pacific Highway, NORTH SYDNEY, NSW 2060, AUSTRALIA.
BALDWIN, Mrs. Janet Enid, ACA *1985;* Hawkwell Business Consultants Ltd, 55b Victor Gardens, HOCKLEY, SS5 4DS.
BALDWIN, Miss. Joanna Fay, MA ACA *1996;* Ground Floor Flat, 13 Burstock Road, LONDON, SW15 2PW.
BALDWIN, Mr. John Frederick, FCA *1965;* 8 St. Peters Close, Lugwardine, HEREFORD, HR1 4AT. (Life Member)
BALDWIN, Miss. June Imelda, BA ACA *1993;* 55 Middle Street, Brockham, BETCHWORTH, RH3 7JT.
BALDWIN, Mr. Leslie John, FCA *1966;* Glenroy, 1 Well Close, WINSCOMBE, BS25 1HG.
BALDWIN, Mr. Mark Christopher, BA ACA *1985;* Pattonair (Derby) Ltd, 50 Longbridge Lane, DERBY, DE24 8UJ.
BALDWIN, Mrs. Marla, LLB ACA *2001;* (Tax Fac), with PricewaterhouseCoopers LLP, 1 Embankment Place, LONDON, WC2N 6RH.
BALDWIN, Mr. Matthew Ian, BSc ACA *2004;* CPI, 98-102 rue de Paris, 92100 BOULOGNE BILLANCOURT, FRANCE.
BALDWIN, Mrs. Michelle Joanne, BSc ACA *2001;* 1/11 Hardie Street, NEUTRAL BAY, NSW 2089, AUSTRALIA.
BALDWIN, Mr. Neil Richard, BA ACA *1988;* Brewin Dolphin Ltd, 34 Lisbon Street, LEEDS, LS1 4LX.
BALDWIN, Mr. Nicholas Charles, ACA *1981;* Nick. C. Baldwin, 80 Pilford Heath Road, WIMBORNE, DORSET, BH21 2ND.
BALDWIN, Mr. Nicholas James, BA(Hons) ACA *2011;* Langholme, The Drive, BOURNE END, BUCKINGHAMSHIRE, SL8 5RE.
•**BALDWIN, Mr. Nicholas Mark, BA FCA DChA** *1987;* Baldwin Scofield & Co, 3 New House Farm Business Centre, Old Crawley Road, HORSHAM, WEST SUSSEX, RH12 4RU.
BALDWIN, Mrs. Patricia Mary, BA ACA *1985;* 259 Hyde End Road, Spencers Wood, READING, RG7 1DA.
BALDWIN, Mr. Paul, MEng ACA ACGI *1999;* (Tax Fac), Top Floor Flat, 39 Tonsley Hill, LONDON, SW18 1BE.
BALDWIN, Mr. Paul Graham, ACA *1984;* 324 Park AveAPT 2, HOBOKEN, NJ 07030, UNITED STATES.
BALDWIN, Mr. Paul John, ACA CTA *2001;* 42 Oakwood Hill, LOUGHTON, ESSEX, IG10 3EW.
BALDWIN, Mr. Peter Frederick, BA FCA *1967;* 9 Willaston Avenue, Blacko, NELSON, BB9 6LU.
BALDWIN, Mr. Philip Edward, BCom FCA *1972;* Orchard Cottage, Brook End, Longdon, RUGELEY, WS15 4PD. (Life Member)
BALDWIN, Mr. Richard John, MA ACA *1996;* 5 Curlew Close, MACCLESFIELD, CHESHIRE, SK10 2SX.
•**BALDWIN, Mr. Richard Kenneth, BCom FCA CTA** *1972;* RK Baldwin FCA CTA - Consultant, Tanglewood, Long Bottom Lane, Seer Green, BEACONSFIELD, BUCKINGHAMSHIRE HP9 2UL.
BALDWIN, Mr. Robert Patrick, BSc ACA *2000;* 7 Southcote Rise, RUISLIP, MIDDLESEX, HA4 7LN.
BALDWIN, Mr. Robert Paul, MA FCA CTA *1989;* (Tax Fac), with KPMG LLP, 15 Canada Square, LONDON, E14 5GL.
BALDWIN, Miss. Sarah Ruth, ACA *2004;* with BDO Binder, Level 19, 2 Market Street, SYDNEY, NSW 2000, AUSTRALIA.
BALDWIN, Mr. Steven John, BA ACA *1994;* 53 Albert Drive, LONDON, SW19 6LA.
•**BALDWIN, Mr. Steven Robert, FCA** *1985;* (Tax Fac), Venthams Limited, Millhouse, 32-38 East Street, ROCHFORD, SS4 1DB.
•**BALDWIN, Mr. Terence, FCA** *1979;* McBrides Accountants LLP, Nexus House, 2 Cray Road, SIDCUP, KENT, DA14 5DA. See also McBrides Corporate Finance Limited
BALDWIN, Dr. Trevor John Leslie, PhD MSc FCA *1965;* Woodlands, Balnaskeag, Kenmore, ABERFELDY, PERTHSHIRE, PH15 2HB. (Life Member)
BALE, Mr. Andrew Paul, ACA *1981;* 157 York Road, WOKING, GU22 7XS.
BALE, Mrs. Catherine Davies, ACA *2008;* 66 Newport Road, MANCHESTER, M21 9NN.
BALE, Mr. Christopher, BSc ACA *2006;* with Ernst & Young LLP, 100 Barbirolli Square, MANCHESTER, M2 3EY.
BALE, Mr. Craig David, BSc ACA CF *1997;* Shanacloon, KILDARE, COUNTY KILDARE, IRELAND.
•**BALE, Mr. David George, FCA** *1968;* Smith Hodge & Baxter, Thorpe House, 93 Headlands, KETTERING, NN15 6BL.
BALE, Mr. Graham Stewart, BA FCA *1973;* 12 Carlton Road, Ainsdale, SOUTHPORT, PR8 2PG.
•**BALE, Mr. Mark Peter Bryan, MA FCA** *1980;* Mark Bale Limited, 106 Staunton Road, Headington, OXFORD, OX3 7TN.
BALE, Mr. Nicholas Malyn, PhD BSc FCA *1978;* (Tax Fac), 5 Edgeborough Court, Upper Edgeborough Road, GUILDFORD, SURREY, GU1 2BL.
BALE, Mr. Oliver, ACA *2009;* 26 Crofton Square, Sherfield-on-Loddon, HOOK, RG27 0SX.
BALE, Mr. Robert Michael, BA FCA *1957;* 21 Waverley Avenue, BASINGSTOKE, RG21 3JN. (Life Member)
BALEM, Mrs. Ruth Sarah, BSc ACA *2001;* 52 Sentry Way, SUTTON COLDFIELD, B75 7HT.
BALEM, Mr. Simon Grant, BA ACA *1999;* 52 Sentry Way, SUTTON COLDFIELD, B75 7HT.
BALENDRAN, Mrs. Srivathana, ACA *1996;* Cedarwood, 15a Langley Avenue, Southborough, SURBITON, KT6 6QN.
BALENTHIRAN, Mr. Kerry Kumar, BSc ACA *2003;* F M Global, 1 Windsor Dials Arthur Road, WINDSOR, BERKSHIRE, SL4 1RS.
•**BALES, Mr. Christopher Roy, FCA** *1967;* Bales, 15 Cheddar Close, Nailsea, BRISTOL, BS48 4YA.
BALES, Mrs. Deborah Lois, BSc ACA *1984;* 3 Kerwin Drive, Dore, SHEFFIELD, S17 3DG.
BALES, Mr. Michael Howard, BSc FCA *1980;* 3 Kerwin Drive, Dore, SHEFFIELD, S17 3DG.
BALES, Miss. Victoria Mary Elizabeth, MA ACA *2001;* Oak Garth, High Lane, HASLEMERE, GU27 1BD.
BALES, Miss. Zoe Claire, BA ACA *2003;* 9 Soulbury Road, Burcott, LEIGHTON BUZZARD, BEDFORDSHIRE, LU7 0JU.
BALESTRIERI, Mrs. Lara Jayn, ACA *1999;* Via Rimini 1/A, 31021 MOGLIANO VENETO, ITALY.
BALFE, Mr. Maurice Edward, FCA *1970;* 116 Southover, LONDON, N12 7HD.
BALFOUR, Miss. Anna-Liza, ACA *2008;* St. Breock, Bronshill Road, TORQUAY, TQ1 3HD.
BALFOUR, Mr. David Charles Creighton, FCA *1969;* Craigy, Fulmer Road, GERRARDS CROSS, SL9 7EE. (Life Member)
•**BALFOUR, Mr. Mark David, BA FCA** *1986;* (Tax Fac), Larking Gowen, King Street House, 15 Upper King Street, NORWICH, NR3 1RB.

BALFOUR, Mr. Michael Selby, FCA *1956;* 10 Rue Metchnikoff, 92310, 92310 SEVRES, FRANCE. (Life Member)

BALFOUR, Mr. Michael William, OBE FCA *1973;* The Hideaways Club, 136 Sloane Street, LONDON, SW1X 9AY. (Life Member)

•**BALFOUR, Mr. Nigel Laurence, FCA** *1972;* Sanson Limited, 17 Bourne Court, Southend Road, WOODFORD GREEN, ESSEX, IG8 8HD.

BALFOUR, Mr. Richard George Edward, BSc ACA *2002;* Level 46, 680 George Street, SYDNEY, NSW 2000, AUSTRALIA.

BALFOUR, Miss. Sarah Louise, ACA *2008;* Romney House, Apt 215, 47 Marshan Street, LONDON, SW1P 3DP.

BALGOBIN, Mr. Sooraj Lall, BEng ACA *1997;* 2398 Dorchester Street West, FURLONG, PA 18925, UNITED STATES.

BALI, Mr. Atul, BA ACA *1997;* 7571 Mulholland Drive, LOS ANGELES, CA 90046, UNITED STATES.

BALI, Mr. Shubh Ashish, FCA *1981;* 91 Maple Ave, MORRIS PLAINS, NJ 07950, UNITED STATES.

BALKWILL, Mr. Roger Norman, ACA *1979;* Soditic Ltd, Wellington House, 125 Strand, LONDON, WC2R 0AP.

•**BALL, Mr. Adrian, ACA** *1983;* (Tax Fac), Adrian Ball, 130 High Street, Boston Spa, WETHERBY, WEST YORKSHIRE, LS23 6BW.

BALL, Mr. Alan Edward, FCA *1964;* Cherry Gate, Kiln Lane, Stokenham, KINGSBRIDGE, TQ7 2SF. (Life Member)

BALL, Mr. Alexander George, FCA ACGI *1995;* 115 Benson Road, REMUERA, AUCKLAND, NEW ZEALAND.

•**BALL, Mr. Alfred Arthur, FCA** *1973;* A.A. Ball, 4 Lidgate Walk, Westbury Park, Clayton, NEWCASTLE, STAFFORDSHIRE ST5 4LT.

•**BALL, Mr. Andrew, BA(Hons) ACA** *2003;* haysmacintyre, Fairfax House, 15 Fulwood Place, LONDON, WC1V 6AY.

BALL, Dr. Andrew Derek, PhD BSc ACA *1992;* The Barn, 3 Devonshire House Farm, Lothersdale, KEIGHLEY, NORTH YORKSHIRE, BD20 8EU.

BALL, Mr. Andrew James, MA ACA *1988;* York House, Bunzl Plc York House, 45 Seymour Street, LONDON, W1H 7JT.

•**BALL, Mr. Andrew John, BA ACA** *1992;* Cowgill Holloway LLP, Regency House, 45-51 Chorley New Road, BOLTON, BL1 4QR. See also Cowgill Holloway Liverpool LLP and Cowgill Holloway Care 1 Limited

BALL, Mr. Andrew Michael, BSc ACA *1990;* Country Garden Cakes, 12 Fairview Estate, Newtown Road, HENLEY-ON-THAMES, OXFORDSHIRE, RG9 1HG.

BALL, Mr. Anthony, FCA *1967;* 7550 Colleen Street, BURNABY V5A 2A6, BC, CANADA. (Life Member)

BALL, Mr. Anthony Gerard, BSc ACA *1999;* 21 Woodlands Parkway, Timperley, ALTRINCHAM, CHESHIRE, WA15 7QT.

•**BALL, Mr. Anthony Martin Jackson, BA FCA** *1974;* A M J Ball, 75 Banner Cross Road, Ecclesall, SHEFFIELD, S11 9HQ.

BALL, Miss. Barbara Ethel, FCA *1954;* 45 Manor Lane, SUNBURY-ON-THAMES, TW16 5EB. (Life Member)

BALL, Mrs. Beverley Ann, BA FCA *1985;* C H2 M Hill Ltd, Avon House, Kensington Village, Avonmore Road, LONDON, W14 8TS.

BALL, Mrs. Carol, BSc ACA *1985;* Maple House, Wantage Road, Streatley, READING, RG8 9LB.

BALL, Mrs. Caroline Fiona, BSc ACA *2004;* 24 Gordon Avenue, TWICKENHAM, TW1 1NQ.

BALL, Mr. Chris, BA ACA *2005;* with KPMG, 27/F Alexandra House, 18-20 Chater Road, CENTRAL, HONG KONG ISLAND, HONG KONG SAR.

BALL, Mr. Christopher, BA ACA *1994;* Overdale, Tofts Lane, Follifoot, HARROGATE, NORTH YORKSHIRE, HG3 1DY.

BALL, Mr. Christopher Henry, FCA *1970;* 9 Brooklands Road, Ramsbottom, BURY, LANCASHIRE, BL0 9SW. (Life Member)

BALL, Mr. Christopher Henry, FCA *1964;* 2 Laurence Allison Mews, The Warren, Caversham, READING, RG4 7TQ. (Life Member)

BALL, Mr. Christopher John, BSc ACA *1981;* Woodend Cottage, 12 New Lane, Sutton Green, GUILDFORD, GU4 7QF.

BALL, Mr. Christopher John, BA ACA *1994;* 16 Rectory Road, SOLIHULL, WEST MIDLANDS, B91 3RP.

BALL, Mr. Darren, ACA MAAT *2001;* 18 Kisdon Avenue, STOKE-ON-TRENT, ST6 8GW.

BALL, Mr. David Edward, FCA *1960;* Shawsmead, 4 Manor Farm, Little Wenlock, TELFORD, TF6 5BZ. (Life Member)

BALL, Mr. David Ian, BA ACA *1992;* 23 Boleyn Close, Grange Park, SWINDON, SN5 6JZ.

BALL, Mr. David John, LLB ACA *1987;* Bedfordshire Pilgrims Housing Association Ltd Pilgrims Hous, Horne Lane, BEDFORD, MK40 1NY.

BALL, Mr. David Lewis, FCA *1965;* Limestones Harewood Road, East Keswick, LEEDS, LS17 9HG.

BALL, Mr. David Offord James, MA ACA *1991;* 22 Viscount Drive, Beckton, LONDON, E6 5XQ.

BALL, Mr. David Owen, FCA *1965;* Rose Cottage, HARTFIELD, TN7 4DR.

•**BALL, Mr. David Philip, MA ACA** *1995;* with Ernst & Young LLP, 1 More London Place, LONDON, SE1 2AF.

BALL, Mr. David William Dawson, MA MEng ACA *1994;* Tudor Great Burgh, Yew Tree Bottom Road, EPSOM, SURREY, KT18 5XT.

BALL, Mr. Dylan, BA ACA *1997;* 44 The Village, Archerfield Dirleton, NORTH BERWICK, EAST LOTHIAN, EH39 5HT.

BALL, Mrs. Elizabeth Alice, BSc ACA *1992;* Controls Division, Ultra Electronics Ltd, 417 Bridport Road, GREENFORD, MIDDLESEX, UB6 8UE.

BALL, Mrs. Elizabeth Ann, BA ACA *1986;* Spital House, Paxton, BERWICK-UPON-TWEED, TD15 1TD.

BALL, Miss. Emma Louise, BA ACA *2002;* Alexander & Co, 17 St. Anns Square, MANCHESTER, M2 7PW.

BALL, Mrs. Frances, BSc ACA *2007;* 32 Sparkford House, Battersea Church Road, LONDON, SW11 3NQ.

BALL, Mr. Geoffrey Anthony, FCA *1974;* Minyrafon, 4 High Street, Pontardawe, SWANSEA, SA8 4HU.

BALL, Mr. Geoffrey Arthur, FCA *1967;* 26 Hermitage Drive, EDINBURGH, EH10 6BY.

BALL, Mr. Geoffrey William, BSc ACA *1988;* Toke House, 11 Wilton Road, BEACONSFIELD, HP9 2BS.

BALL, Mr. George William, BA ACA *2010;* Basement Flat, 27 Charlwood Street, LONDON, SW1V 2DZ.

BALL, Mr. Graham Arthur Ridgeway, BCom FCA *1975;* Rosebank, River Lane, RICHMOND, TW10 7AG.

•**BALL, Mr. Graham George, FCA** *1986;* Ward Goodman Limited, 4 Cedar Park, Cobham Road, Ferndown Industrial Estate, WIMBORNE, DORSET BH21 7SF. See also Ward Goodman

BALL, Mr. Graham Wakely, FCA *1965;* Hoeland House, Watersfield, PULBOROUGH, RH20 1NJ.

BALL, Mrs. Helen, BSc ACA *2007;* 65 Cheltenham Road, GLOUCESTER, GL2 0JG.

BALL, Mrs. Helen, BA ACA *1994;* 77 Elder Drive, DAVENTRY, NORTHAMPTONSHIRE, NN11 0XE.

BALL, Mrs. Helen Elizabeth, BSc ACA *1992;* Mulberry House, Trumps Green Road, VIRGINIA WATER, GU25 4JA.

•**BALL, Mr. Hywel William, BSc ACA** *1987;* Ernst & Young LLP, Ten George Street, EDINBURGH, EH2 2DZ. See also Ernst & Young Europe LLP

BALL, Mr. Ian Robert, BSocSc ACA *2001;* Top Floor Flat, 14 Strathblaine Road, LONDON, SW11 1RJ.

BALL, Mrs. Jacqueline Margaret, ACA *1988;* N A Slack & Co Llp, 50 London Road, NEWCASTLE, STAFFORDSHIRE, ST5 1LL.

BALL, Mr. Jasbinder Singh, LLB ACA *2000;* 29 Elbe Street, LONDON, SW6 2QP.

BALL, Mrs. Jennifer, BSc(Econ) ACA *2001;* 43 Lakeside Avenue, Rownhams, SOUTHAMPTON, SO16 8DP.

BALL, Miss. Jennifer Elizabeth, BA(Hons) ACA *2009;* Sims Barn, Offley Hay, Bishops Offley, STAFFORD, ST21 6HJ.

BALL, Mr. Jeremy Christopher, BSc ACA *1990;* Gwynedd, Southampton Road, Cadnam, SOUTHAMPTON, SO40 2NF.

BALL, Miss. Joanne Clare, BA ACA *1995;* National Audit Office, 157-197 Buckingham Palace Road, Victoria, LONDON, SW1W 9SP.

BALL, Mr. John, FCA *1979;* (Member of Council 2007 - 2011), 23 Caroline Close, Alvaston, DERBY, DE24 0QX.

BALL, Mr. John Colin, BA ACA *1997;* 26a Danehurst Street, LONDON, SW6 6SD.

BALL, Mr. John Martin, BA ACA *1990;* 56 Boileau Road, Ealing, LONDON, W5 3AJ.

•**BALL, Mr. John Morris, BSc FCA** *1976;* Gotham Erskine LLP, Friendly House, 52-58 Tabernacle Street, LONDON, EC2A 4NJ. See also MacIntyre Hudson LLP

BALL, Miss. Judith Mary Anne, BSc ACA *1998;* Thames View Windsor Road, Datchet, SLOUGH, SL3 9BT.

BALL, Mr. Julian Robert Steven, BA FCA CF *1989;* House 152, Tai hang Hau Village, Clear Water Bay, SAI KUNG, NEW TERRITORIES, HONG KONG SAR.

BALL, Miss. Juliet, BSc(Hons) ACA *2000;* Chancellor House, Easynet Ltd, 5 Thomas More Square, LONDON, E1W 1YW.

BALL, Mrs. Kathryn Jane, MA ACA *1987;* 16 Firdale Road, Sea Point, CAPE TOWN, C.P., 8005, SOUTH AFRICA.

BALL, Mr. Keith Martyn, BA FCA *1973;* 27 Rollscourt Avenue, Herne Hill, LONDON, SE24 0EA.

BALL, Mr. Kenneth, BSc ACA *1993;* 59 Earlswood Street, LONDON, SE10 9ET.

BALL, Mr. Kevin Michael, BA ACA *2006;* 78 Tachbrook Street, LONDON, SW1V 2NA.

•**BALL, Mr. Leslie Richard, FCA** *1973;* Leslie R. Ball, 28 Dunkirk Road, Birkdale, SOUTHPORT, PR8 4RQ.

BALL, Miss. Lucia Carmel Anne, ACA *2010;* 11 Acacia Road, Hordle, LYMINGTON, HAMPSHIRE, SO41 0YG.

BALL, Mr. Martin Jon, BSc ACA *2003;* with KPMG LLP, 15 Canada Square, LONDON, E14 5GL.

BALL, Mr. Michael, BSc ACA *2011;* 5 Wycliffe Road, LEEDS, LS13 1LY.

BALL, Cllr Michael Anthony, BSc ACA *1998;* 7 Percivale Road, Chandler's Ford, EASTLEIGH, HAMPSHIRE, SO53 4TS.

BALL, Mr. Michael David, BCom ACA *1991;* McCarthy & Stone (Plc), 26-32 Oxford Road, BOURNEMOUTH, BH8 8EZ.

•**BALL, Mr. Michael Edward, BSc ACA** *1983;* Michael Ball, James House, Newport Road, Albrighton, WOLVERHAMPTON, WV7 3FA.

•**BALL, Mr. Michael Edward, FCA** *1969;* M.E. Ball & Associates Limited, Global House, 1 Ashley Avenue, EPSOM, SURREY, KT18 5AD.

BALL, Mr. Michael James, BSc FCA *1974;* Farchynys Hall, Bontddu Barmouth, BARMOUTH, LL42 1TN.

•**BALL, Mr. Michael Jonathan, BA ACA** *2002;* MacIntyre Hudson LLP, Lyndale House, Ervington Court, Harcourt Way, Meridian Business Park, LEICESTER LE19 1WL.

BALL, Mrs. Michelle Jennifer, BSc ACA *1991;* 4 Marlborough Road, Ealing, LONDON, W5 5NY.

BALL, Mr. Nicholas, BSc FCA *1993;* Flat 6D, Yuan Kung Mansion, 1 Tai Koo Shing Road, TAIKOO SHING, HONG KONG ISLAND, HONG KONG SAR.

BALL, Mr. Nicholas Martin, BSc ACA *1998;* 30 Alderside Walk, Englefield Green, EGHAM, SURREY, TW20 0LY.

BALL, Miss. Nicola Fiona, BA(Hons) ACA *2003;* Ground Floor Flat, 6 Redland Park, BRISTOL, BS6 6SB.

BALL, Mr. Nigel Robert, BSc ACA *1992;* 20 Aykley Green, DURHAM, DH1 4LN.

BALL, Mr. Peter Alexander, BA ACA *2005;* with Ernst & Young LLP, 1 Bridgewater Place, Water Lane, LEEDS, LS11 5QR.

BALL, Mr. Peter Francis, BA ACA *1986;* Humphrey Farms Ltd, Hazeley Road, Twyford, WINCHESTER, HAMPSHIRE, SO21 1QA.

•**BALL, Mr. Peter James, FCA** *1967;* Peter J. Ball, 25 Kersteman Road, BRISTOL, BS6 7BX.

•**BALL, Mr. Philip John, BSc FCA** *1991;* with PricewaterhouseCoopers LLP, Hays Galleria, 1 Hays Lane, LONDON, SE1 2RD.

BALL, Mrs. Rachel Jane, BA ACA *1997;* St. Helens High Street, Laxfield, WOODBRIDGE, SUFFOLK, IP13 8DU.

BALL, Mr. Raymond John Charles, BSc(Hons) ACA *2001;* Godscroft House, Godscroft Lane, FRODSHAM, WA6 6XU.

BALL, Mr. Richard, BA FCA *1977;* 8 Eaton Park, Eaton Bray, DUNSTABLE, BEDFORDSHIRE, LU6 2SR.

BALL, Mr. Richard Alexander, BA ACA *1985;* Newhouse Farm, Washbourne, TOTNES, DEVON, TQ9 7UD.

BALL, Mr. Richard David, BSc ACA *1994;* Barrick Gold Corporation Brookfield Place TD Canada Trust Tower Suite 3700 161 Bay St P.O. Box, TORONTO M5J2S1, ON, CANADA.

BALL, Mr. Richard Graham, ACA *1987;* Manhattan Associates, 2 The Arena Downshire Way, BRACKNELL, RG12 1PU.

BALL, Mr. Richard John Alexander, FCA *1973;* 76 Buckingham Avenue, Craighall Park, JOHANNESBURG, GAUTENG, 2196, SOUTH AFRICA.

BALL, Mr. Richard William, FCA *1967;* 160 Kauri Road, Whenuapai Village, AUCKLAND, NEW ZEALAND.

BALL, Mr. Robert Kenneth, FCA *1958;* 42 Downs Hill, BECKENHAM, KENT, BR3 5HB. (Life Member)

BALL, Mrs. Rosalind Jane, BSc ACA *2001;* 40 Wordsworth Road, HARPENDEN, HERTFORDSHIRE, AL5 4AF.

BALL, Miss. Rosalyn Margaret, BA ACA *1985;* 3 Sweetings Road, Godmanchester, HUNTINGDON, CAMBRIDGESHIRE, PE29 2JS.

•**BALL, Mr. Russell Mark, BA FCA** *1990;* (Tax Fac), D E Ball & Co Ltd, 15 Bridge Road, Wellington, TELFORD, SHROPSHIRE, TF1 1EB.

BALL, Ms. Sally Jane, BSc ACA *1993;* Kaplan Financial, Lowgate House, Lowgate, HULL, HU1 1EL.

BALL, Mr. Simon Peter, BSc FCA *1985;* 23 Denbigh Gardens, RICHMOND, SURREY, TW10 6EL.

BALL, Mrs. Sonya, BA ACA *2004;* 45 St. Kingsmark Avenue, CHEPSTOW, GWENT, NP16 5LY.

BALL, Miss. Stephanie, BSc ACA *2007;* Flat 1, 89 Norwood Road, LONDON, SE24 9AA.

•**BALL, Mr. Stephen James, FCA** *1977;* Sphere Management Limited, PO Box 587, St Peter Port, GUERNSEY, GY1 6LS.

•**BALL, Mr. Stephen Thomas Lintern, BA FCA** *1976;* (Tax Fac), Maxwells, 4 King Square, BRIDGWATER, SOMERSET, TA6 3YF.

BALL, Miss. Susan Elisabeth, BA FCA *1986;* Nutwood, 25 Silver Birch Drive, Hollywood, BIRMINGHAM, B47 5RB.

BALL, Mr. Thomas, FCA *1952;* 30 Dunbar Road, SOUTHPORT, PR8 4RD. (Life Member)

BALL, Mr. Thomas William, BSc ACA *2001;* 5 Hacienda Grove, No 04-04, Siglap, SINGAPORE 457911, SINGAPORE.

•①**BALL, Mr. Timothy Colin Hamilton, BA ACA** *1986;* Mazars LLP, Clifton Down House, Beaufort Buildings, Clifton Down, Clifton, BRISTOL BS8 4AN.

BALL, Mr. Timothy Steven, MA FCA *1976;* Tinker Coppice, Poles Lane, Otterbourne, WINCHESTER, SO21 2DS. (Life Member)

BALL, Mr. Timothy Walder, BSc ACA *1993;* #3949 411 Walnut Street, GREEN COVE SPRINGS, FL 32043, UNITED STATES.

BALL, Mr. Tom James, ACA *2009;* 76 Eton Wick Road, Eton Wick, WINDSOR, BERKSHIRE, SL4 6JL.

•**BALL, Mr. Trevor Mackenzie, FCA** *1960;* Trevor M Ball & Co, 46 The Close, NORWICH, NR1 4EG.

BALL, Mr. Warwick James Dillon, BA ACA *1993;* 26 Wood Lane, LONDON, N6 5UB.

BALLADON, Mrs. Shirley Anne, ACA *1983;* 10 Heath Road, Berea, DURBAN, 4001, SOUTH AFRICA.

BALLAH, Mr. Kristy Kumar, ACA *2009;* 23 Avenue Louvet, Morc St Espirit, QUATRE-BORNES, MAURITIUS.

•**BALLAMY, Mr. Mark Elroy, BA FCA** *1983;* Ballamy Woodhouse, Albert Buildings, 49 Queen Victoria Street, LONDON, EC4N 4SA.

BALLAN-WHITFIELD, Mrs. Joanne, BSc ACA *1990;* Upper Ford House, Henton, WELLS, SOMERSET, BA5 1PD.

•**BALLAN-WHITFIELD, Mr. Philip Anthony, BA FCA** *1989;* Chalmers HB Limited, 20 Chamberlain Street, WELLS, BA5 2PF.

BALLANCE, Mr. Anthony Nevill Peter, BSc ACA *1990;* (Tax Fac), Coach House College Road, Clifton, BRISTOL, BS8 3HZ.

BALLANCE, Miss. Morag McIntyre, BA ACA *1986;* (Tax Fac), with PricewaterhouseCoopers LLP, Lennox House, 7 Beaufort Buildings, Spa Road, GLOUCESTER, GL1 1XD.

•**BALLANDS, Mr. Simon, BSc FCA** *1992;* Baker Homyard, Ingouville House, Ingouville Lane, St Helier, JERSEY, JE2 4SG.

•**BALLANTINE, Mr. Alan Thomas, BSc ACA** *1987;* (Tax Fac), Fala Accounting Limited, Haughhead House, Fala Dam, PATHHEAD, MIDLOTHIAN, EH37 5SW.

BALLANTINE, Mrs. Charlotte Angela, ACA *2008;* 567 Basingstoke Road, READING, RG2 0SJ.

BALLANTINE, Miss. Helen Jane, BA ACA *2000;* 2032 Condolea Drive, Leawood, OVERLAND PARK, KS 66209, UNITED STATES.

BALLANTINE, Mr. Mark Edward, MA ACA *1990;* Affinity Sutton Group Ltd, 6 More London Place, LONDON, SE1 2DA.

•**BALLANTINE, Mr. Stuart Douglas, FCA** *1980;* Stuart Ballantine, 9 Oak Avenue, Ickenham, UXBRIDGE, MIDDLESEX, UB10 8LP.

BALLANTYNE, Mr. Alistair James, MSci ACA *2007;* 10 Rum Close, LONDON, E1W 3QX.

BALLANTYNE, Mr. Andrew James Motyer, BA ACA *1999;* with BDO LLP, 6th Floor, 3 Hardman Street, Spinningfields, MANCHESTER, M3 3AT.

BALLANTYNE, Mrs. Christine Margaret, BA ACA *1986;* 38 Dreyer Way, BULL CREEK, WA 6149, AUSTRALIA.

BALLANTYNE, Mr. David Henry, MA ACA *1986;* 38 Dreyer Way, BULL CREEK, WA 6149, AUSTRALIA.

BALLANTYNE, Mr. Howard Eric, BA ACA *1989;* Echo Beach, 2 Taunton Avenue, Bamford, ROCHDALE, OL11 5LD. (Life Member)

BALLANTYNE, Miss. Julie Anne, BA(Hons) ACA *2004;* National Express Ltd, Mill Lane, BIRMINGHAM, B5 6DD.

BALLANTYNE, Mr. Robert Leigh, FCA *1959;* Pig Oak Cottage, Holt Lane, WIMBORNE, DORSET, BH21 7DQ. (Life Member)

BALLANTYNE, Mr. Ronald Young, FCA *1961;* Westway, Albert Square, Bowdon, ALTRINCHAM, WA14 2ND.
BALLANTYNE, Mrs. Sarah Louise, BSc ACA *1996;* with PricewaterhouseCoopers LLP, 101 Barbirolli Square, Lower Mosley Street, MANCHESTER, M2 3PW.
BALLARD, Mr. Brian Ivan, FCA *1959;* Wooton Manor Farm, 70 Church Road, Wootton Bridge, RYDE, ISLE OF WIGHT, PO33 4PZ. (Life Member)
BALLARD, Mr. Christopher James, BSc ACA *2006;* Flat 8, 79 Bramley Road, LONDON, W10 6SY.
BALLARD, Mr. Denis George William, BA FCA *1949;* 253 Shakespeare Tower, Barbican, LONDON, EC2Y 8DR. (Life Member)
BALLARD, Mr. Geoffrey Leonard, FCA *1968;* Bracken Hill House, Wrington Hill, Wrington, BRISTOL, BS40 5PN. (Life Member)
•BALLARD, Mr. Geoffrey William, BSc FCA *1979;* (Tax Fac), Ballard Dale Syree Watson LLP, Oakmoore Court, Kingswood Road, Hampton Lovett, DROITWICH, WORCESTERSHIRE WR9 0QH.
BALLARD, Mr. Ian Malcolm, BA ACIB FCA *1980;* Gateway House, Gargrave Road, SKIPTON, NORTH YORKSHIRE, BD23 1UD.
•BALLARD, Mr. Jonathan, BA ACA *1998;* Ballard Evans Corporate Finance Limited, Lowry House, 17 Marble Street, MANCHESTER, M2 3AW.
BALLARD, Mr. Jonathan, BSc ACA *2005;* 7 Jennings Way, HORLEY, RH6 9SF.
•BALLARD, Mr. Jude, BA ACA *1995;* JB Accountancy Solutions Limited, 28 Deane Croft Road, PINNER, MIDDLESEX, HA5 1SR.
BALLARD, Mr. Karl, MMath ACA *2010;* 249 Burton Road, MANCHESTER, M20 2WA.
•BALLARD, Mr. Keith Bryan, FCA *1970;* (Tax Fac), Hetherington & Co, Second Floor, 289 Green Lane, Palmers Green, LONDON, N13 4XS. See also CSG Accountancy Limited
BALLARD, Mr. Leslie Kim Michael, BA ACA *1980;* Artbay Ltd, The Sycamores Sycamore Drive, Wrecclesham, FARNHAM, GU10 4RY.
•BALLARD, Miss. Linda Jane, FCA *1984;* Baker Tilly Tax & Advisory Services LLP, The Clock House, 140 London Road, GUILDFORD, SURREY, GU1 1UW.
BALLARD, Mr. Michael Terence, BSc ACA *1996;* 12 Parkside Walk, SLOUGH, SL1 2BL.
BALLARD, Mr. Peter, BA ACA *1979;* Compton Developments Ltd, 45/51 Wychtree Street, Morriston, SWANSEA, SA6 8EX.
•BALLARD, Mr. Peter Charles, FCA *1960;* David Beagent & Co, The Old Rectory, Mill Lane, Tempsford, SANDY, SG19 2AT.
BALLARD, Mr. Philip Terence, BSc ACA *1998;* 114 Lichfield Road, SUTTON COLDFIELD, B74 2TA.
BALLARD, Mr. Thomas Henry, FCA *1980;* 48 Downsway, SHOREHAM-BY-SEA, BN43 5GN.
BALLARDIE, Mr. John Dougald, FCA *1972;* The Rest, Northbrook, Market Lavington, DEVIZES, WILTSHIRE, SN10 4AP.
BALLAUFF, Mr. Christopher Anthony, FCA *1972;* 19 Cross Street, PYMBLE, NSW 2073, AUSTRALIA.
BALLENDEN, Mr. Quinton Douglas, ACA CA(SA) *2010;* 31 Stockmen Field, BISHOP'S STORTFORD, HERTFORDSHIRE, CM23 4GP.
BALLENTINE, Mr. Iain Robert, MA(Hons) ACA *2003;* Flat 20 Brookfield Highgate West Hill, LONDON, N6 6AS.
BALLESTY, Mrs. Annemiek, BSc ACA *1992;* B6 Habitat, Mang Kung Wo Road, Pak Sha Wan, SAI KUNG, NEW TERRITORIES, HONG KONG SAR.
BALLIN, Mr. Jonathan Guy, BA FCA *1985;* Clock House The Avenue, Tisbury, SALISBURY, SP3 6JG.
BALLINGER, Mr. Brian Anthony, FCA *1971;* 1 Cotton Mill Spinney, Coventry Road, Cubbington, LEAMINGTON SPA, WARWICKSHIRE, CV32 7XH. (Life Member)
BALLINGER, Mr. David Bruce, BSc ACA *1989;* Acorn Cottage, Rays Lane, Penn, HIGH WYCOMBE, HP10 8LH.
BALLINGER, Miss. Elizabeth Anne, BA ACA *2001;* 86 Cotton Lane, BIRMINGHAM, B13 9SE.
BALLINGER, Mr. Julian Aubrey, BCom ACA *1981;* Builders Supply Stores (Coventry) Ltd, Archways House, 45 Spon End, COVENTRY, CV1 3HG.
•BALLINGER, Mr. Michael Vivian, FCA *1975;* Bakers, Arbor House, Broadway North, WALSALL, WS1 2AN. See also Baker (Midlands) Limited
BALLINGER, Miss. Rebecca, BSc ACA *1994;* 2/2 18 Glencairn Drive, GLASGOW, G41 4QN.
BALLS, Mr. Graham Francis, BA ACA *1984;* Alfred-Ulrich Strasse 69, 71711, STEINHEIM, GERMANY.
BALLS, Mr. Herbert James, FCA *1952;* 17 Waveney Drive, Hoveton, NORWICH, NR12 8DP. (Life Member)
BALLS, Mr. John Harris, FCA *1953;* Balls Brothers Limited, 313 Cambridge Heath Road, LONDON, E2 9LQ. (Life Member)
BALLS, Mr. Matthew, BA ACA *2010;* 16 Ennismore Avenue, GUILDFORD, SURREY, GU1 1SP.
BALLS, Mr. Richard Chiesman, FCA *1977;* Balls Brothers Limited, 313 Cambridge Heath Road, LONDON, E2 9LQ.
BALLSDON, Mr. Andrew James, MA ACA *1992;* 10 Fernbrook Road, Caversham, READING, RG4 7HG.
BALM, Mr. Christopher, BSc FCA AMCT *1985;* PO Box 22664, DOHA, QATAR.
BALME, Mr. Anthony David Nettleton, FCA *1972;* Po Box 74, ALRESFORD, SO24 9YU.
BALME, Mrs. Jennifer Ann, BA FCA *1984;* 19 Welham Road, Gt. Bowden, MARKET HARBOROUGH, LE16 7HS.
BALMER, Mr. Adam David, MSc BCom ACA *1998;* 43 Flowerscroft, NANTWICH, CHESHIRE, CW5 7GN.
BALMER, Mrs. Alison Margaret, BSc FCA *1984;* 7 The Cot, St. Arvans, CHEPSTOW, GWENT, NP16 6HL.
BALMER, Mr. Jon Robert, BA ACA *2004;* 6 Windsor Court, Felling, GATESHEAD, NE10 9UA.
BALMER, Mr. Jonathan Griffith Toby, ACA *1986;* Gai Tronics Ltd, Brunel Drive, Stretton, BURTON-ON-TRENT, STAFFORDSHIRE, DE13 0BZ.
•BALMER, Mr. Ronald George, FCA *1965;* 138 West Way, BROADSTONE, BH18 9LN.
BALMFORD, Mr. James Norman, FCA *1959;* 4 The Grove, UPMINSTER, RM14 2ER. (Life Member)
BALMFORTH, Mrs. Helen Louise, BSc ACA *2007;* Lloyds TSB Bank Plc Canons House, Canons Way, BRISTOL, BS1 5LL.
BALMFORTH, Mrs. Jane Maria, ACIB ACA *2000;* 1a Heath Mount Road, BRIGHOUSE, WEST YORKSHIRE, HD6 3RS.
BALMFORTH, Mr. Keith, FCA *1962;* Bar Croft, Bar House Lane, Utley, KEIGHLEY, BD20 6HQ. (Life Member)
BALMFORTH, Mrs. Nicola Susan, BSc ACA *1990;* Bolling Coffee Ltd, The Roastery, Bent Ley Industrial Estate, Meltham, HOLMFIRTH, HD9 4EP.
BALMFORTH, Mr. Peter Anthony, BA(Hons) ACA *2010;* Apartment 161 Whitehall Waterfront, 2 Riverside Way, LEEDS, LS1 4EG.
BALMOND, Miss. Felicity Claire, ACA *2011;* 49 Kings Drive, Hanham, BRISTOL, BS15 3JJ.
•BALMONT, Mr. Stephen John, BA FCA *1988;* S J Balmont, 11 Lodge Road, Fetcham, LEATHERHEAD, KT22 9QY.
BALNAVES, Dr. Andrew Stuart, ACA *2009;* Standard Bank, 3 Simmonds Street, JOHANNESBURG, 2107, SOUTH AFRICA.
BALO, Miss. Georgina Maria, MSc BSc(Hons) ACA *2003;* 26 Watson's Close, Broughton, CHESTER, CH4 0SS.
BALOCH, Mr. Wajahat Hussain, ACA FCCA *2011;* 76 Freeman Road North, LEICESTER, LE5 4NA.
BALOO, Mr. Nizar Karmali, FCA *1975;* 22 Church Hill, PURLEY, SURREY, CR8 3QN.
BALOO, Mrs. Yasmin, FCA *1978;* 22 Church Hill, PURLEY, SURREY, CR8 3QN.
•BALOUCH, Mr. Asim Ali Akbar, BA ACA ACCA *2004;* Hammond Knight, 2nd Floor, 145-157 St. John Street, LONDON, EC1V 4PY.
BALROOP, Mr. Marlon Krisen, BSc ACA *1992;* 9 Montenotte Road, Crouch End, LONDON, N8 8RL.
BALSARA, Mr. Cyrus Keki, FCA *1972;* 423/424 Samudra Mahal, Dr A Beasant Road, Worli, MUMBAI 400 018, MAHARASHTRA, INDIA.
BALSARA, Mr. Darayus Jal, FCA *1978;* 20 Rubislaw Drive, ABERDEEN, AB15 4BX.
BALSEKAR, Mr. Shivdas Ramesh, FCA *1971;* 41B Diamond Court, 40 Nepean Sea Road, MUMBAI 400 036, MAHARASHTRA, INDIA.
•BALSHAW, Mr. John Frederick, FCA *1967;* (Tax Fac), J. F. Balshaw & Co, 20 Old Kiln Lane, Heaton, BOLTON, BL1 5PD.
BALSHAW, Mr. Richard Thomas, FCA *1964;* 35 Darwen Close, Longridge, PRESTON, PR3 3TP.
BALSIGER, Mrs. Alison Miranda, BSc ACA *2002;* 69 Ribblesdale Avenue, LONDON, N11 3AQ.
•BALSOM, Mr. Peter James, FCA *1970;* (Tax Fac), with Simpkins Edwards LLP, Michael House, Castle Street, EXETER, EX4 3LQ.
BALSTON, Mrs. Claire, ACA MAAT *2010;* 76 Cutlers Place, WIMBORNE, DORSET, BH21 2HX.
BALSTON, Mr. Harry Jethro, ACA *2008;* Maslens Farm Brown's Lane, Alton Barnes, MARLBOROUGH, SN8 4JZ.
BALTAIAN, Mr. Boghos, BA FCA *1964;* 35 Iroon Street, Ay. Andreas Quarter, 1105 NICOSIA, CYPRUS.
BALTAO, Miss. Catherine, ACA *2011;* 2 Vesta Court, City Walk, LONDON, SE1 3BP.
BALTSOUCOS, Mr. Dimitri, ACA CA(SA) *2010;* 3 Chrysoulas Malaktou, Agios Athansios, 4108 LIMASSOL, CYPRUS.
BALUJA, Mr. Samir, ACA *1986;* W15/27 (Old J19), Western Avenue, Sainik Farms, NEW DELHI 110062, INDIA.
BALY, Mr. Patrick Thomas, FCA *1951;* 5 Essendene Close, CATERHAM, CR3 5PD. (Life Member)
BALZAN, Mr. John Martin, BA FCA *1993;* 1 Mawsley Lodge, Mawsley, KETTERING, NORTHAMPTONSHIRE, NN14 1SW.
BALZER, Mr. Thomas, BSc ACA *2010;* 41 Streetly End, West Wickham, CAMBRIDGE, CB21 4RP.
•BAMBER, Mr. Christopher, FCA *1975;* Berwell Consultancy, Bowbridge House, 23 Kings Drive, Bishopston, BRISTOL, BS7 8JW. See also Bamber Chris & Co
BAMBER, Mr. Harry Arthur, BSc FCA *1985;* West Holdings Ltd, PO Box 16 Analyst House, Douglas, ISLE OF MAN, IM99 1AP.
BAMBER, Miss. Laura Jane, ACA *2008;* 72 Hastings Parade, NORTH BONDI, NSW 2026, AUSTRALIA.
BAMBER, Mr. Matthew Alan, MA BA ACA *2002;* 25 Leigh Woods House, Church Road Leigh Woods, BRISTOL, BS8 3PQ.
•BAMBER, Mr. Neil, BA FCA *1975;* Livesey Spottiswood Limited, 17 George Street, ST.HELENS, WA10 1DB. See also Livesey Spottiswood Holdings Ltd
•BAMBER, Mr. Norman, FCA *1980;* (Tax Fac), Bush & Co, 2 Barnfield Crescent, EXETER, EX1 1QT. See also Westcountry Payroll Ltd
BAMBER, Mr. Paul Daniel, MA ACA *2004;* 19 Ambrose Drive, MANCHESTER, M20 2YE.
BAMBER, Mr. Scott Anthony, BSc(Hons) ACA *2004;* Akzo Nobel (Asia) Co Ltd, 5F The Exchange, No 299 Tong Ren Road, SHANGHAI 200040, CHINA.
BAMBERGER, Mr. Jonathan, BSc ACA *1980;* Redpath Sugar Ltd, 95 Queens Quay East, TORONTO M5E 1A3, ON, CANADA.
BAMBERGER, Mr. Louis David John, BSc ACA *2010;* Hillfoot House, Beenham, READING, RG75LS.
BAMBERY, Mr. Matthew James, MSc ACA *2004;* Foxlands, 162 Falcondale Road, BRISTOL, BS9 3JF.
BAMBRICK, Mrs. Wendy Elizabeth, BA ACA DChA *1993;* 29 Kingfisher Road, SHEFFORD, BEDFORDSHIRE, SG17 5YQ.
•BAMBRIDGE, Mr. Alistair John, ACA *2008;* (Tax Fac), Bambridge Accountants Ltd, 34 South Molton Street, LONDON, W1K 5RG.
BAMBRIDGE, Mr. Lee Frederick, BA ACA AMCT *1988;* Evergreen, 8 Peatmoor Close, FLEET, HAMPSHIRE, GU51 4LE.
BAMBROUGH, Mr. James Benjamin, MA ACA *2001;* 3 Farm Road, BRISTOL, BS16 6DD.
BAMBROUGH, Mr. Roger Arthur, FCA *1963;* Brookhampton Farmhouse, North Cadbury, YEOVIL, SOMERSET, BA22 7DD.
BAMBURY, Mr. Cyril Frank, FCA *1955;* Wychwood, 17a Sole Farm Rd, Great Bookham, LEATHERHEAD, KT23 3DW. (Life Member)
BAMBURY, Mr. Mark, BSc ACA *1996;* 14 Wilton Crescent, SOUTHAMPTON, SO15 7QP.
BAMBURY, Mrs. Nichola, BA ACA *1999;* PO Box 487085, DUBAI, UNITED ARAB EMIRATES.
BAMENT, Miss. Sara Jayne, BSc ACA *2001;* 26 Heyford Avenue, Eastville, BRISTOL, BS5 6UE.
BAMFIELD, Mr. Nicholas Mark Hargrave, BA ACA *1985;* 5A Hollybush Lane, SEVENOAKS, TN13 3UN.
BAMFIELD, Mr. Vargo Michael Leon, BSc ACA *2004;* 5 Ballard Place, FIG TREE POCKET, QLD 4069, AUSTRALIA.
•BAMFORD, Mr. Brian Ronald, BSc ACA *1989;* B.R. Bamford, Old School Cottage, 6-7 Moulton Road, Pitsford, NORTHAMPTON, NN6 9AU.
BAMFORD, Miss. Ciara, BA(Hons) ACA *2010;* Basement, 71 Sinclair Road, LONDON, W14 0NR.
BAMFORD, Mrs. Claire Louise, BSc ACA *2006;* Enteraction TV Unit 7 Park Place, 10-12 Lawn Lane, LONDON, SW8 1UD.
BAMFORD, Mr. James William, BA ACA *2010;* Deloitte & Touche, 2 New Street Square, LONDON, EC4A 3BZ.
•BAMFORD, Mr. Miles Oliver, FCA *1974;* (Tax Fac), H.V.Bamford & Co, 99 Main Street, Wilsden, BRADFORD, BD15 0DZ.
BAMFORD, Mr. Niall Richard, BSc ACA *1993;* Invicta Capital Limited, 33 St. James's Square, LONDON, SW1Y 4JS.
BAMFORD, Mr. Patrick Charles, ACA *2008;* Basement Flat, 1a Ranelagh Gardens, LONDON, SW6 3PA.
BAMFORD, Mr. Philip Ian, BA ACA *1984;* Premier Foods, 2 Woolgate Court St. Benedicts Street, NORWICH, NR2 4AP.
BAMFORD, Miss. Rachael, ACA MAAT *2010;* 35 Pear Tree Road, Bignall End, STOKE-ON-TRENT, ST7 8NH.
BAMFORD, Mr. Richard John, ACA *1988;* Dairy House, Ashford Hill, THATCHAM, BERKSHIRE, RG19 8BL.
BAMFORD, Mr. Richard John Edward, FCA *1966;* 9 Peter Avenue, OXTED, RH8 9LG.
BAMFORD, Mrs. Ruth Elizabeth, ACA *2000;* 1 Elm Terrace, Hawkley Road, LISS, HAMPSHIRE, GU33 6JH.
BAMFORD, Mrs. Wendy Esmee, BSc ACA *2005;* Midsummer Place Tangmere Road, Tangmere, CHICHESTER, WEST SUSSEX, PO20 2HW.
•BAMFORTH, Mr. Adam Lee, BSc ACA *1996;* Bamforth & Co, Douglas House, 24 Bridge Street, Slaithwaite, HUDDERSFIELD, HD7 5JN. See also Business Advantage Limited
•BAMFORTH, Miss. Andrea, ACA *2001;* Bairstow & Atkinson, Carlton House, Bull Close Lane, HALIFAX, HX1 2EG.
BAMFORTH, Mr. Ian Peter, FCA *1978;* 15 Cote Green Road, Marple Bridge, STOCKPORT, CHESHIRE, SK6 5EH.
•BAMFORTH, Mr. Jay Darren, BSc FCA *1993;* Atraxa Consulting Limited, Brooke's Mill, Armitage Bridge, HUDDERSFIELD, HD4 7NR.
BAMFORTH, Mr. John Richard, BSc FCA *1990;* 26 Seascale Park, SEASCALE, CA20 1HD.
BAMFORTH, Mr. Matthew John, MChem ACA *2005;* 18 Gloucester Court, Kew Road, RICHMOND, SURREY, TW9 3EB.
BAMFORTH, Mr. Peter John, BSc(Econ) FCA *1980;* Foxbury, Giddy Horn Lane, MAIDSTONE, KENT, ME16 0EE.
BAMFORTH, Mr. Robert, BSc ACA *2005;* Richer Sounds Plc, Unit 4, Richer House, Hankey Place, LONDON, SE1 4BB.
•BAMJI, Mr. Khurshed Jehangir, BSc(Hons) ACA FCCA *2011;* Hodge Bakshi Limited, Churchgate House, 3 Church Road, Whitchurch, CARDIFF, CF14 2DX.
BAMJI, Mr. Pervez Dossabhoy, FCA *1977;* 420 Park Place, Apt. 3A, FORT LEE, NJ 07024, UNITED STATES.
BAMKIN, Mr. Nicholas Carl, ACA *1995;* 10 Bosworth Close, ASHBY-DE-LA-ZOUCH, LEICESTERSHIRE, LE65 1LB.
BAMRAH, Mr. Malkiat, BA ACA *1995;* 21 Harlech Gardens, PINNER, MIDDLESEX, HA5 1JT.
BANATVALA, Mr. Phiroze Edal, FCA *1971;* 19 Pewterers Avenue, BISHOP'S STORTFORD, HERTFORDSHIRE, CM23 4GR.
•BANBROOK, Mr. John Anthony, FCA *1975;* Fox Evans Limited, Abbey House, 7 Manor Road, COVENTRY, CV1 2FW.
BANBURY, Mr. James Bray, FCA *1956;* Lake, Bondleigh, NORTH TAWTON, EX20 2AQ. (Life Member)
•BANBURY, Miss. Rosalind Janet Manuela, MA ACA *1981;* (Tax Fac), R J M Banbury, 44 Bounds Oak Way, TUNBRIDGE WELLS, TN4 0TN. See also Banbury Rosalind.J.M.
BANCE, Mr. Nicholas Herbert, MA MEng ACA *2002;* PO box 71189, BRYANSTON, GAUTENG, 2021, SOUTH AFRICA.
•BANCE, Mr. Sunil, MSc ACA *1999;* Bance Consultants Limited, 46a Station Road, North Harrow, HARROW, MIDDLESEX, HA2 7SE. See also Fetherstones Ltd and Bruce Consultants Limited
BANCHETTI, Mr. Lamberto Vincenzo Albino, FCA *1961;* Casella Postale N 70, Poste Narni, 05035 NARNI, TR, ITALY. (Life Member)
BANCROFT, Mr. Andrew John Leonard, MMath ACA *2002;* 44 All Saints Drive, Four Oaks, SUTTON COLDFIELD, WEST MIDLANDS, B74 4AG.
BANCROFT, Miss. Caroline Gail, MEng FCA *2001;* 27 Helen Street, NORTHCOTE, VIC 3070, AUSTRALIA.
BANCROFT, Mrs. Catherine Victoria, BCom ACA *2005;* Danaher, Central Boulevard Blythe Valley Business Park, SOLIHULL, B908AG.
BANCROFT, Mr. Colum Sebastian Joseph, BA FCA *1992;* 1701-02 Central Plaza, 18 Harbour Road, WAN CHAI, HONG KONG ISLAND, HONG KONG SAR.
•BANCROFT, Mr. Donald George, BSc FCA *1988;* PKF (UK) LLP, 4th Floor, 3 Hardman Street, MANCHESTER, M3 3HF.
BANCROFT, Mr. Ian Richard, BSc ACA *1998;* Spring House, Seven Springs, CHELTENHAM, GL53 9NG.
BANCROFT, Mrs. Janet, BA ACA *1989;* 4 Sandside Road, Alsager, STOKE-ON-TRENT, ST7 2XJ.

BANCROFT, Mr. John Hudson, BSc FCA *1967;* 6 Hop Pocket Close, Sissinghurst, CRANBROOK, TN17 2LB. (Life Member)
BANCROFT, Ms. Lynne Deborah, BSc ACA *1993;* Playstole, Chapel Lane, Sissinghurst, CRANBROOK, TN17 2JN.
BANCROFT, Mr. Martin James, BA ACA *1986;* Britannia Building Society, Britannia House, LEEK, STAFFORDSHIRE, ST13 5RG.
BANCROFT, Mr. Matthew John, ACA *2009;* 27 Charnwood Bank, BATLEY, WEST YORKSHIRE, WF17 8PY.
•BANCROFT, Mr. Michael Emmanuel, FCA *1954;* Michael E Bancroft, 19 Hurricane Court, Hurricane Drive, International Business Park, Speke, LIVERPOOL L24 8RL.
BANCROFT, Mr. Michael Henson, FCA *1964;* The Nuttery, Over Stratton, SOUTH PETHERTON, TA13 5LQ. (Life Member)
BANCROFT, Mr. Paul, MA ACA *1986;* 9 Brook Road, GLENBROOK, NSW 2773, AUSTRALIA.
•BANCROFT, Mr. Peter Linton, BA FCA *1981;* HW (Leeds) LLP, Sterling House, 1 Sheepscar Court, Meanwood Road, LEEDS, WEST YORKSHIRE LS7 2BB.
BANCROFT, Mr. Richard Anthony, BA BSc ACA *1989;* Haines Watts (Lancashire) LLP, Northern Assurance Buildings, 9-21 Princess Street, MANCHESTER, M2 4DN.
BANCROFT, Mr. Richard Lee, MA FCA *1975;* Moorcourt Farm, Moorside, STURMINSTER NEWTON, DORSET, DT10 1HH.
BANCROFT, Mr. Stuart Charles, BSc ACA *1995;* Citigroup Centre, 33 Canada Square, LONDON, E14 5LB.
BANCROFT, Mr. Thomas, BA ACA *2011;* 21 Mitchell Road, Grange Park, ST. HELENS, MERSEYSIDE, WA10 3EX.
BANCROFT-JONES, Mrs. Helen Louise, BSc ACA *2005;* 5 Garden Close, Shamley Green, GUILDFORD, SURREY, GU5 0UW.
BANCROFT-JONES, Mr. Neil, BA ACA *2005;* B O C Ltd, The Priestley Centre, 10 Priestley Road, Surrey Research Park, GUILDFORD, SURREY GU2 7XY.
•BAND, Mr. Andrew Roy, BA FCA *1998;* Whiting & Partners, The Old School House, Dartford Road, MARCH, PE15 8AE.
BAND, Mr. John Oliver, MA FCA *1976;* 1801 B Wing Lokhandwala Residency, Manjrekar Lane, WORLI 400 018, INDIA.
•BAND, Mr. Peter Charles, FCA *1968;* 5 Vixen Close, SUTTON COLDFIELD, B76 1JY.
BANDALI, Mr. Navroz Nurmohamed Darvesh, FCA *1974;* 919 KING GEORGES WAY, WEST VANCOUVER V7S 1S6, BC, CANADA.
•BANDAY, Mr. Arif Saleem, ACA *1988;* (Tax Fac), Banday Limited, 47 Park Chase, WEMBLEY, MIDDLESEX, HA9 8EQ.
BANDEL, Mr. Martin Howard, ACA *1982;* Gable End, 29 Christchurch Crescent, RADLETT, HERTFORDSHIRE, WD7 8AQ.
BANDELE, Mr. David Anla Llewellyn, BA ACA *1999;* Aasengata 6B, 0480 OSLO, NORWAY.
•BANDOPADHYAY, Mr. Kishalay, BSc FCA *1980;* P O Box 31876, DUBAI, UNITED ARAB EMIRATES.
BANDURA, Mr. Frank, BSc ACA *1992;* Carluccios Plc, 35 Rose Street, LONDON, WC2E 9EB.
BANDY, Mr. Clive Russell, BA ACA *2003;* 46 Charnley Drive, LEEDS, LS7 4ST.
•BANE, Mr. Michael Roland, BA ACA *1986;* Ernst & Young LLP, PO Box 9, Royal Chambers, St Julian's Avenue, St Peter Port, GUERNSEY GY1 4AF. See also Ernst & Young Europe LLP
BANERJEE, Dr. Bhaskar, ACA *2008;* Bukhatir Group, PO Box 88, SHARJAH, UNITED ARAB EMIRATES.
BANERJEE, Mr. Gautam, BSc FCA *1981;* PricewaterhouseCoopers LLP, 17-00 PWC Building, 8 Cross Street, SINGAPORE 048424, SINGAPORE.
BANERJEE, Ms. Indrani, MSc ACA *1999;* 32 Melliss Avenue, RICHMOND, SURREY, TW9 4BQ.
BANERJEE, Mr. Pradip, MBA FCA *1973;* 37 Kingfisher Drive, Ham, RICHMOND, TW10 7UF.
BANERJEE, Mr. Pranoy, ACA *2010;* Flat 13, Fabian Bell Tower, 2 Pancras Way, LONDON, E3 2SD.
•BANERJEE, Mr. Ronojit, BA ACA *2007;* Banner & Associates Ltd, 29 Byron Road, HARROW, HA1 1JR.
•BANERJEE, Mr. Subarna, BSc(Econ) ACA *1996;* 61 Osier Crescent, LONDON, N10 1QS.
BANERJEE, Mr. Suvobroto, BSc(Econ) ACA *2001;* Flat 8 The Glass House, 51-57 Lacy Road, LONDON, SW15 1PR.
BANERJI, Mr. Abhijit Bobby, BA ACA *1988;* Bnp Paribas, 10 Harewood Avenue, LONDON, NW1 6AA.
BANFIELD, Mr. Colin Dennis, BSc ACA *1990;* 9B Pinecrest, 65 Repulse Bay Road, REPULSE BAY, HONG KONG ISLAND, HONG KONG SAR.
BANFIELD, Mr. Craig Michael John, MA FCA *1992;* 27 Mill Mead, Wendover, AYLESBURY, HP22 6BY.
BANFIELD, Dr. Darren, MA ACA *2000;* CQS Management Ltd, 33 Chester Street, LONDON, SW1X 7BH.
BANFIELD, Mr. John Clayton, FCA *1961;* The Mews, 3 Penn Hill, YEOVIL, SOMERSET, BA20 1SF. (Life Member)
BANFIELD, Mr. Jonathan David Alexander, BSc ACA *2010;* Park House, Park Corner, Nettlebed, HENLEY-ON-THAMES, OXFORDSHIRE, RG9 6DR.
•BANFIELD, Mr. Lewis John, BA ACA *1998;* Francis Clark, Vantage Point, Woodwater Park, Pynes Hill, EXETER, EX2 5FD. See also Francis Clark LLP
BANFIELD, Mr. Simon Philip, BA ACA *1991;* Moat Homes Ltd, Mariner House, Galleon Boulevard, Crossways Business Park, DARTFORD, DA2 6QE.
BANFIELD, Mr. Stephen John, BA ACA *1999;* 27 Stanbury Street, GLADESVILLE, NSW 2111, AUSTRALIA.
BANFIELD, Mr. Vivian Wyn, FCA *1974;* Clarke International Limited, Hemnall Street, EPPING, ESSEX, CM16 4LG.
BANFORD, Mrs. Margaret, FCA *1955;* 60 Cunningham Drive, BURY, BL9 8PD. (Life Member)
BANFORD, Mr. Nigel Anthony Howard, ACA *1981;* Oak Farm Hotel, Watling Street, Hatherton, CANNOCK, WS11 1SB.
•BANG, Mr. Christian Francis Lanyon, FCA *1973;* 15 Bowfell Road, LONDON, W6 9HE.
•BANGA, Mr. Rajinder Singh, FCA *1990;* (Tax Fac), The Zane Partnership, 925 Finchley Road, LONDON, NW11 7PE. See also Zane Accounting Services Limited and Zane Partnership
BANGASH, Mr. Waleed Qassim Zakaria Khan, BA ACA *2003;* House no. 3585, Road no. 5773, Area 0457, Bu Quwah, MANAMA, BAHRAIN.
BANGAY, Miss. Natalie, BA(Hons) ACA *2004;* Flat 5, Carlton Place, 37 Carlton Drive, LONDON, SW15 2BH.
BANGEE, Mr. Omar, MA FCA *1997;* SAMCO, PO Box 8755, JEDDAH, 21492, SAUDI ARABIA.
BANGHAM, Mr. Arran, BA FCA *1992;* The Rockeries, 114 Mossley Road, Grasscroft, OLDHAM, OL4 4HA.
•ⒹBANGHAM, Mr. John Ivor, BSc ACA MABRP *1983;* with KPMG LLP, 100 Temple Street, BRISTOL, BS1 6AG.
BANGHARD, Mr. Satwinder, BA ACA *2007;* 49 Woodlands Road, SURBITON, SURREY, KT6 6PR.
BANGOR-JONES, Mr. Charles Stephen, BA FCA *1998;* Le Moigne Cottage, La Rue Des Bergers, Castel, GUERNSEY, GY5 7AP.
BANGOR-JONES, Ms. Fiona Ann, ACA CA(SA) *2009;* Gibbs Building, The Wellcome Trust, 183-193 Euston Road, LONDON, NW1 2BE.
BANGOR-JONES, Mr. Richard Stephen, FCA *1962;* Brookwood, Water Lane, Tarbock Green, PRESCOT, L35 1RE. (Life Member)
BANGS, Mr. Martin Graham, BSc ACA *1991;* Winton, 4 Kiln Lane, Brockham, BETCHWORTH, RH3 7LX.
BANHAM, Mrs. Christine, BSc ACA *2003;* 58 Nunthorpe Crescent, YORK, YO23 1DU.
BANHAM, Mr. Edward, BA ACA *2006;* 206 West End Lane Horsforth, LEEDS, LS18 5RU.
•BANHAM, Mr. James Arthur, FCA CF *1984;* Banham Graham, Windsor Terrace, 76-80 Thorpe Road, NORWICH, NR1 1BA. See also Banham Graham Corporate Limited
BANHAM, Mr. Peter Douglas, BA ACA *1999;* 67, Dulverton Road, LEICESTER, LE3 0SB.
BANHAM, Mr. Richard Anton, BSc(Hons) ACA *2004;* Flat 1, 112 Church Road, RICHMOND, TW10 6LW.
BANHAM, Mr. Robert George, LLB ACA *1999;* with PricewaterhouseCoopers LLP, 1 Embankment Place, LONDON, WC2N 6RH.
•BANHAM, Mrs. Sarah Louise, BA ACA *1999;* with PricewaterhouseCoopers LLP, 1 Embankment Place, LONDON, WC2N 6RH.
BANIM, Dr. Amanda Jane, PhD BSc(Hons) ACA *2001;* 8 Charleston Court, Bailick Road, MIDLETON, COUNTY CORK, IRELAND.
BANINAJAR, Mr. Ali, MSc BA ACA *2005;* 95 Winnipeg Way, BROXBOURNE, HERTFORDSHIRE, EN10 6FH.
BANISTER, Mr. Adam Frederick, FCA *1955;* 2 McKenzie Close, BUCKINGHAM, MK18 1SS. (Life Member)
BANISTER, Mr. Ian Arthur, FCA *1958;* 2 Church Lane, Cheddington, LEIGHTON BUZZARD, LU7 0RU. (Life Member)
BANISTER, Mr. Michael Robert, BA ACA *1985;* Banister Bros. & Co. Ltd., Bee Mill, Ribchester, PRESTON, PR3 3XJ.
BANKER, Mr. Rajnikant Shantikumar, BSc FCA *1968;* 61 Forest Ridge Road, WESTON, MA 02493, UNITED STATES.
BANKES, Mr. Rhydian, MA ACA *2010;* Ty Ucha Llan, Mountain Road, Cilcain, MOLD, CLWYD, CH7 5PA.
BANKIER, Mr. Hugh Charles Macdonald, BA ACA *1996;* 130 Upper Grosvenor Road, TUNBRIDGE WELLS, KENT, TN1 2EX.
BANKS, Mr. Adrian, BA(Hons) ACA *2002;* Tunstall Group Ltd Whitley Lodge, Doncaster Road Whitley, GOOLE, NORTH HUMBERSIDE, DN14 0HR.
BANKS, Mr. Alan Edward, BSc FCA *1970;* 65a Chesterfield Drive, IPSWICH, IP1 6DN.
•BANKS, Mr. Alan Peter, FCA *1969;* A.P. Banks & Co, Bodwannick Lodge, Nanstallon, BODMIN, CORNWALL, PL30 5LN.
BANKS, Miss. Alison Dawn, BSc CA ACA *1997;* 8 La Place Du Puits, La Rue de la Capelle St. Ouen, JERSEY, JE3 2DQ.
BANKS, Mr. Andrew, BA FCA *1990;* Downs Cottage, Melton Avenue, Storrington, PULBOROUGH, RH20 4BH.
BANKS, Mr. Andrew David, BSc ACA *1980;* St Mary's, Cowl Lane, Winchcombe, CHELTENHAM, GL54 5RA.
BANKS, Mr. Andrew John, BSc ACA *1999;* Rolls-Royce Plc, PO Box 31, DERBY, DE24 8BJ.
BANKS, Mr. Andrew John Greenwood, BA FCA *1967;* The Nuttery, Newnham, DAVENTRY, NN11 3EU. (Life Member)
BANKS, Mrs. Anne Hilary, MA ACA *1980;* 7 Anglesmede Way, PINNER, HA5 5SS.
BANKS, Mrs. Carol Elizabeth, BA ACA *1986;* 1 Linden Crescent, Hutton Rudby, YARM, CLEVELAND, TS15 0HU.
BANKS, Miss. Carolyne Jane, BSc FCA *1989;* The Granary, Throop Road, BOURNEMOUTH, BH8 0DH.
BANKS, Mrs. Catherine, BA FCA *1979;* 11 Thornbury Drive, WHITLEY BAY, NE25 9XN.
BANKS, Mr. Christopher, BSc(Hons) ACA *2010;* 39 Alexandra Road, Wesham, PRESTON, PR4 3JE.
BANKS, Mr. Christopher John, FCA *1980;* Cornerstones, 16 High Street, Glinton, PETERBOROUGH, PE6 7LS.
BANKS, Mrs. Claire Louise, BA ACA *1999;* 10 Brookdale Drive, Littleover, DERBY, DE23 3YY.
BANKS, Mrs. Claire Louise Jane, BSc ACA *1997;* 7 Pewley Bank, GUILDFORD, SURREY, GU1 3PU.
BANKS, Mrs. Dale, BA ACA *1993;* PO Box 22827, DUBAI, UNITED ARAB EMIRATES.
BANKS, Mr. David Bernard, MA FCA *1973;* London Waste Ltd, Advent Way, Edmonton, LONDON, N18 3AG.
•BANKS, Mr. David Eric, BA FCA *1977;* David Banks Associates, Douelis House, 49 Ben Rhydding Road, ILKLEY, WEST YORKSHIRE, LS29 8RN.
•BANKS, Mr. Derek Arthur, FCA *1955;* 70 Scrub Rise, BILLERICAY, CM12 9PE.
•BANKS, Mr. Euan Charles, FCA *1989;* Baker Tilly Tax and Advisory Services LLP, 25 Farringdon Street, LONDON, EC4A 4AB. See also Baker Tilly UK Audit LLP
BANKS, Mrs. Felicity Jane, MSc FCA *1977;* with ICAEW, Chartered Accountants' Hall, Moorgate Place, LONDON, EC2P 2BJ.
BANKS, Dr. Frank David, FCA *1957;* 3 Adams Close, Ampthill, BEDFORD, MK45 2UB. (Life Member)
BANKS, Mr. Gareth Edward, BSc ACA *1999;* Champ Ventures, L4 Customs House, 31 Alfred Street, SYDNEY, NSW 2096, AUSTRALIA.
BANKS, Mr. Garth Nigel John, FCA *1959;* Penmere House, Millefleurs, Boslowick Road, FALMOUTH, TR11 4EZ. (Life Member)
•BANKS, Mr. Geoffrey Laurence, FCA *1969;* (Tax Fac), Castle Park Services Limited, 39 Castle Street, LEICESTER, LE1 5WN. See also Hayles & Partners Limited
BANKS, Mr. George Frederick, FCA *1949;* Pandora, West Street, Hunton, MAIDSTONE, ME15 0SA. (Life Member)
BANKS, Miss. Gillian, BA ACA *2011;* Flat 5, 171 Fleet Street, LONDON, EC4A 2EA.
BANKS, Mrs. Gillian Morag, BSc FCA *1986;* (Tax Fac), with PricewaterhouseCoopers, 101 Barbirolli Square, Lower Mosley Street, MANCHESTER, M2 3PW.
BANKS, Mrs. Helen Elizabeth, MMath ACA *2005;* Informa Publishing Group Ltd, Sheepen Place, COLCHESTER, CO3 3LP.
BANKS, Mrs. Helen Jane, ACA *1982;* Cornerstones, 16 High Street, Glinton, PETERBOROUGH, PE6 7LS.
•BANKS, Mr. James Robert, BSc FCA *1998;* Williamson Morton Thornton LLP, 47 Holywell Hill, ST. ALBANS, HERTFORDSHIRE, AL1 1HD.
BANKS, Mrs. Jenny, ACA MAAT *2003;* C L B Fleet House, New Road, LANCASTER, LA1 1EZ.
BANKS, Mr. Jeremy Loch Mansell, BSc ACA CF *1996;* Watergate House, 13-15 York Buildings, LONDON, WC2N 6JU.
BANKS, Miss. Joanna Claire, BA ACA *2010;* Garden Flat, 114 Redland Road, BRISTOL, BS6 6QT.
BANKS, Mr. John Christopher, FCA *1973;* Copyhold, Lock Lane, Partridge Green, HORSHAM, RH13 8EF.
•BANKS, Mr. John Frederick, MBA BSc FCA *1979;* J.F. Banks & Co, 76 Huddersfield Road, BRIGHOUSE, WEST YORKSHIRE, HD6 3RD.
BANKS, Mr. John Loch Curtis, FCA *1964;* Little Barns, Blackboys, UCKFIELD, TN22 5JE. (Life Member)
•BANKS, Mr. John Peter, FCA CF *1973;* Baker Tilly Tax & Advisory Services LLP, Hartwell House, 55-61 Victoria Street, BRISTOL, BS1 6AD. See also Baker Tilly Corporate Finance LLP
BANKS, Mr. John Robert, BA FCA *1979;* 11 Thornbury Drive, WHITLEY BAY, NE25 9XN.
BANKS, Mr. John Rodney, FCA *1969;* 3127 Indigobush Way, NAPLES, FL 34105, UNITED STATES. (Life Member)
BANKS, Mr. Joseph Lionel, BSc ACA *2004;* 60 Threadneedle Street, LONDON, EC2R 8AP.
BANKS, Ms. Julia Mary, BEng ACA CTA *1991;* 49 Fontmell Close, ST. ALBANS, HERTFORDSHIRE, AL3 5HU.
BANKS, Mr. Julian Charles, FCA *1972;* Crockett & Jones Ltd, Perry Street, NORTHAMPTON, NN1 4HN.
BANKS, Miss. Katie, ACA *2009;* 176 Miller Way, Brampton, HUNTINGDON, CAMBRIDGESHIRE, PE28 4UA.
BANKS, Mrs. Lynette Susan, FCA *1975;* (Tax Fac), 112a St. Johns Road, CANNOCK, STAFFORDSHIRE, WS11 0AN.
BANKS, Mr. Matthew Clayton, BSc ACA *2005;* 37 Riversmead, HODDESDON, EN11 8DP.
•BANKS, Mr. Nicholas Leslie, ACA FCCA *2009;* Scrutton Bland, Sanderson House, Museum Street, IPSWICH, IP1 1HE.
•BANKS, Mr. Nigel Neal, BA FCA *1975;* 9 Turner Road, TAUNTON, SOMERSET, TA2 6DT.
BANKS, Mr. Patrick John, BA ACA *1988;* 16 John Street, LONDON, WC1N 2DL.
BANKS, Mr. Peter, FCA *1966;* 5 Fairways, LYTHAM ST. ANNES, LANCASHIRE, FY8 3NB.
BANKS, Mr. Peter Hitchen, MA ACA *1986;* 1 Homefield Close, Woodham, ADDLESTONE, SURREY, KT15 3QH.
BANKS, Mr. Peter John, BA FCA *1972;* 7 Croftson Avenue, ORMSKIRK, LANCASHIRE, L39 1NJ.
BANKS, Mr. Peter William, BSc ACA *1984;* 12 Brodrick Rd, LONDON, SW17 7DZ.
BANKS, Miss. Rachel, BA ACA *2001;* Flat 3, 32 Eton Avenue, LONDON, NW3 3HL.
BANKS, Mr. Richard David William, FCA *1968;* 9 Algernon Street, Stockton Heath, WARRINGTON, WA4 6EA.
BANKS, Mr. Richard Kirkwood, BSc ACA *1991;* Aubrigstrasse 23a, 8800 THALWIL, SWITZERLAND.
BANKS, Mr. Roger Howard, FCA *1969;* 49 Richter Close, FADDEN, ACT 2904, AUSTRALIA.
BANKS, Mr. Seymour Peter Maurice, MA ACA *1993;* Signet Capital Management, 3 St. James's Square, LONDON, SW1Y 4JU.
BANKS, Mr. Simon Richard Gerwin, FCA *1966;* Ridgacre Cottage, West Street, Burghclere, NEWBURY, BERKSHIRE, RG20 9LB. (Life Member)
BANKS, Mr. Simon Timothy, BSc ACA *1979;* UK Greetings Ltd, Mill Street East, DEWSBURY, WEST YORKSHIRE, WF12 9AW.
•BANKS, Mr. Stephen Craig, FCA *1995;* (Tax Fac), Lubbock Fine, Russell Bedford House, City Forum, 250 City Road, LONDON, EC1V 2QQ.
BANKS, Mr. Steven Coaker, BA ACA *1994;* The Poplars, Main Street, West Ilsley, NEWBURY, BERKSHIRE, RG20 7AW.
BANKS, Mr. Steven Paul, BSc FCA *1989;* 88 Mill Road, Pelsall, WALSALL, WS4 1BU.
BANKS, Mr. Stuart Keith, FCA *1968;* 15 Springpool, Winstanley, WIGAN, WN3 6DE.
•BANKS, Mr. Stuart Paul, BSc FCA *1990;* (Tax Fac), Banks Sheridan Limited, Datum House, Electra Way, CREWE, CW1 6ZF.
BANKS, Mr. Timothy Paul, BA(Hons) ACA *2010;* 26 Cloister Avenue, SOUTH SHIELDS, TYNE AND WEAR, NE34 9AQ.
BANKS, Mr. Timothy Richard, BA ACA *1987;* 11 Hawthorn Way, Sonning, READING, RG4 6TG.
BANKS, Mr. Tony, ACA *1997;* Le Douaire La Rue Es Philippes, Grouville, JERSEY, JE3 9UZ.
BANKS, Mr. William Robert, MA FCA *1977;* Tutchens, Sheepcote Lane, Paley Street, MAIDENHEAD, SL6 3JU.

BANNATYNE, Mr. Alan Robert, BA ACA *1998;* Stanbrook Cottage, Sailing Club Road, BOURNE END, BUCKINGHAMSHIRE, SL8 5QS.

•**BANNATYNE, Mr. Iain Robert, ACA** *1993;* KPMG LLP, 15 Canada Square, LONDON, E14 5GL. See also KPMG Europe LLP

BANNER, Mr. Anthony Gerard, BSc ACA *1991;* 230 Station Road, Wythall, BIRMINGHAM, B47 6ES.

BANNER, Mr. Brendon James, BA ACA *1998;* William Hare Ltd Brandlesholme House, Brandlesholme Road, BURY, BL8 1JJ.

BANNER, Mr. Roger, BSc FCA *1973;* Cae Nant, The Hendre, MONMOUTH, NP25 5NL. (Life Member)

BANNER, Mr. Simon Paul, MSc ACA *1994;* Green 1, National Audit Office, 157-197 Buckingham Palace Road, LONDON, SW1W 9SP.

BANNERMAN, Mr. Andrew Hamish, MA ACA *1997;* 15 Leigh Drive, Elsenham, BISHOP'S STORTFORD, HERTFORDSHIRE, CM22 6BY.

BANNERMAN, Mr. Nigel Arnold, BSc ACA *1993;* Flat 17 Langbourne Mansions, Langbourne Avenue, LONDON, N6 6PR.

•**BANNING, Mrs. Janet Rose, FCA** *1971;* Janet R. Banning, 11 Teresa Walk, Muswell Hill, LONDON, N10 3LL.

BANNING, Mr. Paul Christopher, BSc ACA *1990;* Eaton Aerospace Ltd, Abbey Park, Southampton Road, Titchfield, FAREHAM, HAMPSHIRE PO14 4QA.

BANNINGTON, Mr. Adrian John, FCA CDir *1980;* 9 Chapel Road, EPPING, CM16 5DS.

BANNISTER, Mr. Andrew Charles, FCA *1998; (CA Scotland (Tax Fac),* Barloworld Holdings PLC, Ground Floor, Statesman House, Stafferton Way, MAIDENHEAD, BERKSHIRE SL6 1AD.

BANNISTER, Mr. Brian, BCom FCA *1962;* 2 Pilgrims Way, Standish, WIGAN, WN6 0AJ.

BANNISTER, Mr. Christopher John, BCom ACA *1993;* 26 Renshaw Road, Ecclesall, SHEFFIELD, S11 7PD.

BANNISTER, Mr. Derek William, BSc ACA *1981;* 7 Kings Acre, Bowdon, ALTRINCHAM, CHESHIRE, WA14 3SE.

BANNISTER, Mrs. Evelyn Ceri Nora, FCA *1975;* Camden Electrical Wholesalers, Ltd, 37 Lower City Road, Tividale, OLDBURY, B69 2HA.

•**BANNISTER, Miss. Jacqueline Roma, FCA** *1978;* 74 Henhurst Hill, BURTON-ON-TRENT, DE13 9TD.

BANNISTER, Mrs. Jean Ruth, BSc ACA *1980;* 19 Clarke Place, MOUNT WAVERLEY, VIC 3149, AUSTRALIA.

BANNISTER, Miss. Jennifer Anne, BSc ACA *2010;* 43 Cavendish Road, LONDON, NW6 7XS.

BANNISTER, Mr. John Francis, ACA *1980;* 19 Clarke Place, MOUNT WAVERLEY, VIC 3149, AUSTRALIA.

BANNISTER, Mr. John Raymond, FCA *1970;* 28 Hambrook Street, SOUTHSEA, HAMPSHIRE, PO5 3BE.

BANNISTER, Ms. Kate Emma, BA ACA *1989;* (Tax Fac), K P M G Llp, 15 Canada Square, LONDON, E14 5GL.

•**BANNISTER, Mr. Keith Ian Robert, BSc FCA** *1992;* KPMG LLP, 15 Canada Square, LONDON, E14 5GL. See also KPMG Europe LLP

BANNISTER, Miss. Lisa Clare, BSc ACA *2010;* Ferrier Hodgson, Level 13, 225 George Street, SYDNEY, NSW 2000, AUSTRALIA.

BANNISTER, Mr. Michael Brian, FCA *1967;* 78 Rugby Road, Cubbington, LEAMINGTON SPA, CV32 7JF.

BANNISTER, Mr. Michael Thomas, FCA *1969;* 27 Box Ridge Avenue, PURLEY, SURREY, CR8 3AS. (Life Member)

BANNISTER, Mr. Neil, BSc(Econ) FCA *1999;* 49 Milldown Road, Goring, READING, RG8 0BA.

•**BANNISTER, Mr. Paul, BSc FCA** *1992;* Haywards, 4 Bridgeman Terrace, WIGAN, LANCASHIRE, WN1 1SX.

BANNISTER, Mr. Paul Andrew, BSc ACA *2005;* Taylor Wimpey Chase House, Park Plaza Heath Hayes, CANNOCK, STAFFORDSHIRE, WS12 2DD.

BANNISTER, Mr. Stephen David, FCA *1984;* Ash Tree Farm, Cross Lane, Kermincham, CONGLETON, CW12 2LJ.

BANNON, Mr. Eugene Christopher, BCom FCA *1972;* Ship to Shore, PO Box 400, WINCHESTER, HAMPSHIRE, SO22 4RU.

BANNON, Miss. Lindy, BA ACA *2011;* 20 Bonningtons, BRENTWOOD, ESSEX, CM13 2TN.

BANNON, Ms. Lynne, BA FCA ATII *1984;* Quastina, Leddington, DYMOCK, GL18 2EA.

BANNON, Miss. Michelle Frances, LLB ACA AITI *1997;* 45 Gainsborough Green, MALAHIDE, COUNTY DUBLIN, IRELAND.

BANOS, Mr. Theo, BA ACA *2007;* 9 Peterborough Close, GRANTHAM, LINCOLNSHIRE, NG31 8SH.

BANSAL, Mr. Avnish Kumar, BSc ACA *2004;* Independence House, Flat 15, 6 Chapter Way, LONDON, SW19 2RX.

BANSAL, Mrs. Caroline Tina, MA(Oxon) ACA CTA *1998;* 11 Scott Avenue, LONDON, SW15 3PA.

BANSAL, Mrs. Harjean Kaur Ghatoray, LLB ACA *2000;* 19 Breamore Crescent, DUDLEY, DY1 3DA.

BANSAL, Mr. Harkamal Singh, BA(Hons) ACA *2004;* C/- PricewaterhouseCoopers, Darling Park Tower 2 Level 16, 201 Sussex Street, GPO Box 2650, SYDNEY, NSW 1171 AUSTRALIA.

BANSAL, Miss. Sarita, BA(Hons) ACA *2004;* 35 Parklands Way, HARTLEPOOL, TS26 0AP.

•**BANSAL, Mr. Tejinder Singh, BA FCA** *1993;* (Tax Fac), Jamen Jones, 77 Manor Way, HARROW, MIDDLESEX, HA2 6BZ.

BANSZKY, Mrs. Caroline Janet, BA FCA *1978;* 6 Rylett Crescent, Stamford Brook, LONDON, W12 9RL.

BANTIN, Mr. David, FCA *1979;* 154a Nelson Road, Whitton, TWICKENHAM, TW2 7BU.

BANTIN, Mr. Owen Michael, BA(Hons) ACA *2009;* 32D South Villas, LONDON, NW1 9BT.

BANTING, Mr. Darren James, BSc(Hons) ACA *2001;* 9 Tower Drive, BROMSGROVE, B61 0TZ.

BANTING, Mrs. Louise Kathryn, BSc(Hons) ACA *2001;* 9 Tower Drive, Woodland Grange, BROMSGROVE, WORCESTERSHIRE, B61 0TZ.

BANTOCK, Mr. Angus Graham Granville, BSc ACA *1989;* 11 The Green, EPSOM, KT17 3JS.

BANTON, Mr. Antony John, MA FCA *1982;* with KPMG International, 159 avenue de la Marne, B P 5035, 59705 MARCQ EN BAROEUL, FRANCE.

BANTON, Mr. James Edward, BSc FCA *1991;* R. Delamore Ltd, Station Road, Wisbech St. Mary, WISBECH, CAMBRIDGESHIRE, PE13 4RY.

BANTON, Mr. Matthew Richard, BA ACA *1999;* 9 Earl Road, LONDON, SW14 7JH.

BANWAIT, Mr. Balwinder Singh, MA BSc ACA *1997;* Centrica Plc Millstream, Maidenhead Road, WINDSOR, SL4 5GD.

BANWAITT, Mr. Leigh, ACA *2009;* 44 Woodall Close, Middleton, MILTON KEYNES, MK10 9JZ.

•**BANWELL, Mr. Gary Paul, BA(Hons) ACA** *2002;* (Tax Fac), Peregrine Accountants & Business Advisors Ltd, The Old Bank, The Triangle, Paulton, BRISTOL, BS39 7LE.

BANWELL, Mr. Geoffrey Wilfrid, BSc FCA ATII TEP *1972;* (Tax Fac), The Willows, Marsh Road, Rode, FROME, BA11 6PE.

BANWELL, Mrs. Karey Judith Lesley, BA ACA *2005;* 21a Mountside, GUILDFORD, SURREY, GU2 4JD.

BANYARD, Mrs. Susanne Clare, BSc ACA *1993;* BMT Hi-Q Sigma Ltd, Taylormade Court, Jays Close, BASINGSTOKE, HAMPSHIRE, RG22 4BS.

BANYDEEN, Mr. Mohunlall, ACA *1982;* AZUR BLEU, ST FRANCOIS DEBARCADERE ROAD, CALODYNE, MAURITIUS.

BANYMANDHUB, Mr. Kishore, BSc ACA *1980;* Impasse des Tourterelles, Morcellement Swan, PEREYBERE, MAURITIUS.

BAO, Mr. Jingming, MSc ACA *2010;* KPMG, 8/F Office Tower E2, Oriental Plaza No. 1 East Chang An Ave., Beijing 100738 China, BEIJING 100738, CHINA.

BAO, Mr. Matthew, MA ACA *1993;* Business Giant Holdings Ltd, GUANGZHOU, CHINA.

BAO, Mr. Raymond King To, ACA *2005;* Avenida de Almeida Ribeiro No. 37-61, 21/F Central Plaza, MACAU, MACAO.

BAO, Ms. Sihan, ACA *2011;* 177 Elgar Road, READING, RG2 0DH.

BAO, Mr. Wei, ACA *2011;* 11 Park West, Edgware Road, LONDON, W2 2QG.

BAPORIA, Mr. Mohamed Anwar Unus, ACA *1987;* 402 Petal Homes, 165-J PECHS Block III, KARACHI, PAKISTAN.

BAQA, Mr. Muhammad, ACA ACCA *2011;* Flat 8, Paddle Steamer House, Pettacre Close, LONDON, SE28 0PD.

BAR, Mr. Geoffrey, FCA *1950;* Thatchers, Lyndhurst Road, Bransgore, CHRISTCHURCH, BH23 8LB. (Life Member)

BAR, Mr. Timothy Simon Gordon, BSc ACA *1982;* 59 Addison Road, GUILDFORD, GU1 3QQ.

BARACZEWSKI, Mr. George Witold, BSocSc ACA *1979;* Galliford UK Ltd Leicester Road, Wolvey, HINCKLEY, LE10 3JF.

BARADAR, Mr. Ali Reza, MSc ACA *2000;* Flat 69 Durrels House, Warwick Gardens, LONDON, W14 8QB.

BARAGWANATH, Mr. Guy Richard, MPhys ACA *2010;* C & GB Associates, 8-10 Millgate, THIRSK, NORTH YORKSHIRE, YO7 1AA.

BARAKBAH, Mr. Syed Fahkri, FCA *1975;* 33 Jalan Kelab Golf 13/7, Seksyen 13, 40000 SHAH ALAM, SELANGOR, MALAYSIA.

BARANOWSKI, Mr. Christopher John, MSc FCA *1987;* 21 Avenue Road, Dorridge, SOLIHULL, B93 8LD.

BARANY, Miss. Bernadett, ACA *2010;* 181 Northgate, Almondbury, HUDDERSFIELD, HD5 8US.

BARBAREZ, Mr. Merrell Keith, PhD BSc ACA *1979;* 12 Holmesdale Road, TEDDINGTON, TW11 9LF.

BARBER, Mr. Adam James, ACA *2005;* 4 The Berets, SUTTON COLDFIELD, WEST MIDLANDS, B75 7HS.

•**BARBER, Mr. Alan John, BSc FCA** *1972;* The Limes, 14 Portsmouth Lane, Lindfield, HAYWARDS HEATH, RH16 1SD.

BARBER, Mr. Alexander Samuel, BA ACA *1989;* 304 1281 Parkgate Avenue, NORTH VANCOUVER V7H 3A3, BC, CANADA.

BARBER, Mr. Alistair Michael, BSocSc ACA *1987;* 13 Foley Road East, Streetly, SUTTON COLDFIELD, B74 3HN.

BARBER, Mr. Allan, FCA *1965;* Inglenook, Hill Top Road, Oakworth, KEIGHLEY, WEST YORKSHIRE, BD22 7PY.

BARBER, Mr. Andrew, ACA *2008;* 45 Tudor Road, West Bridgford, NOTTINGHAM, NG2 6EB.

BARBER, Mr. Anthony, BSc FCA *1978;* 4982 Olde Towne Way, MARIETTA, GA 30068, UNITED STATES.

BARBER, Mr. Anthony James, FCA *1970;* 11 Commonwealth Way, Thorpe St Andrew, NORWICH, NR7 0UR.

BARBER, Mr. Bryan Clifford, BA ACA *1996;* 4 Lea Road, HARPENDEN, HERTFORDSHIRE, AL5 4PG.

BARBER, Mr. Carl, ACA *2009;* 38 Cranbrook Road, MANCHESTER, M18 7JW.

BARBER, Miss. Caroline, BSc ACA *2009;* 12 Stanhope Gardens, LONDON, N6 5TS.

BARBER, Miss. Charlotte Amanda, BSc ACA *2011;* 5 Moat Road, EAST GRINSTEAD, WEST SUSSEX, RH19 3JZ.

BARBER, Mr. Chris, ACA *2011;* 78 Southgate Road, LONDON, N1 3JD.

BARBER, Mr. Christopher Derek, BSc ACA *2004;* 24 Horsley Court, Montaigne Close, LONDON, SW1P 4BF.

BARBER, Mr. Christopher James Courtney, ACA *1980;* 6 Merrydown, Downley, HIGH WYCOMBE, HP13 5NQ.

BARBER, Mrs. Clare, BA ACA *1987;* Unique Digital Marketing Ltd, 53 Corsica Street, Highbury, LONDON, N5 1JT.

BARBER, Mr. Colin Thomas, BSc FCA *1972;* Bidborough Close, Franks Hollow Road, Bidborough, TUNBRIDGE WELLS, TN3 0UD.

BARBER, Mr. David Duncan, FCA *1975;* P.O. Box 47035, PARKLANDS, 2121, SOUTH AFRICA.

BARBER, Mr. Dean Anthony, BA(Econ) ACA *2002;* Jarvis Facilities Ltd Meridian House, The Crescent, YORK, YO24 1AW.

BARBER, Mr. Donald Stewart, FCA *1973;* 29 Forest End, FLEET, HAMPSHIRE, GU52 7XE.

•**BARBER, Mrs. Elizabeth Marian, BSc FCA** *1992;* The Old Farm, Otley Road, Burley in Wharfedale, ILKLEY, WEST YORKSHIRE, LS29 7DY.

BARBER, Miss. Fiona, BA ACA *1993;* 15 Tanfield Lane, NORTHAMPTON, NORTHAMPTONSHIRE, NN1 5RN.

BARBER, Mrs. Gabrielle Mary, BSc ACA *1984;* The Limes, Thornfield, Bailey Hills Road, BINGLEY, BD16 2RJ.

•**BARBER, Mr. Geoffrey, FCA** *1960;* 20 Astley Crescent, HALESOWEN, WEST MIDLANDS, B62 9SX.

BARBER, Mrs. Gina Anne, BSc ACA *1995;* 5 Penshurst Close, CHALFONT ST. PETER, BUCKINGHAMSHIRE, SL9 9HB.

•**BARBER, Mr. Graham Colin, BA ACA** *1986;* Graham Barber Accountancy Limited, Westcross House, 73 Midford Road, BATH, BA2 5RT.

•**BARBER, Ms. Gwyneth Mary, BA ACA** *1985;* 130 Pontefract Road, High Ackworth, PONTEFRACT, WF7 7EE.

BARBER, Miss. Helen Louise, BCom ACA *2007;* with John Yelland & Company, 22 Sansome Walk, WORCESTER, WR1 1LS.

•**BARBER, Mr. Ian, BSc FCA** *1997;* (Tax Fac), M + A Partners (North Norfolk) Limited, 12 Church Street, CROMER, NORFOLK, NR27 9ER.

BARBER, Mr. Ian David, FCA *1993;* H M Revenue & Customs Inspector of Taxes Cambridge House, 47 Clarendon Road, WATFORD, WD17 1HN.

•**BARBER, Mr. Ian Graham, FCA** *1969;* 14 Burrows Close, Penn, HIGH WYCOMBE, BUCKINGHAMSHIRE, HP10 8AR.

BARBER, Mr. James Michael Garston, LLB ACA *1993;* 13 Trinity Road, RAYLEIGH, ESSEX, SS6 8QD.

•**BARBER, Mr. Jeffrey Miller, BSc ACA CF** *1980;* BTG Corporate Finance, 340 Deansgate, MANCHESTER, M3 4LY. See also BTG McInnes Corporate Finance LLP

BARBER, Mrs. Joanne Cowburn, BSc ACA *2004;* 4 The Berets, SUTTON COLDFIELD, WEST MIDLANDS, B75 7HS.

BARBER, Dr. John Philip, ACA *1991;* Personal Assurance Plc, John Ormond House, 899 Silbury Boulevard, MILTON KEYNES, BUCKINGHAMSHIRE, MK9 3XL.

•**BARBER, Mr. Jonathan Stephen, BSc ACA** *1980;* (Tax Fac), 12 Heather Close, New Haw, ADDLESTONE, SURREY, KT15 3PF.

BARBER, Mrs. Julia Margaret, ACA *1994;* Westways, Mill Lane, CHALFONT ST. GILES, BUCKINGHAMSHIRE, HP8 4NX.

BARBER, Miss. Kathryn, ACA MAAT *2004;* B M S Computer Solutions Ltd Sproughton House, Sproughton, IPSWICH, IP8 3AW.

•**BARBER, Mrs. Katia, BSc ACA** *1979;* Katia Barber Associates, West View, Wood Lane, Bardsey, LEEDS, LS17 9AW.

BARBER, Mr. Keith John, BSc FCA *1999;* The Bluebells, Park Road, FOREST ROW, EAST SUSSEX, RH18 5BX.

BARBER, Mr. Kevin David, BA FCA *1984;* Barbican GMBU, Schillerstr 6, 69242, MUHLHAUSEN, GERMANY.

BARBER, Mr. Lionel John, FCA *1961;* Cedar House, 18 Silver Lane, PURLEY, CR8 3HG. (Life Member)

•**BARBER, Mr. Michael George, FCA** *1963;* Barber & Co, 57 Downs Court Road, PURLEY, SURREY, CR8 1BF.

BARBER, Mr. Michael John, ACA *2008;* 23 Cape Yard, LONDON, E1W 2JU.

BARBER, Mr. Michael John Luke, BA(Hons) ACA *2003;* 4 The Courtyard, Upper Seagry, CHIPPENHAM, SN15 5JZ.

•**BARBER, Mr. Michael Robert, BA ACA** *1998;* Deloitte LLP, Abbots House, Abbey Street, READING, RG1 3BD. See also Deloitte & Touche LLP

BARBER, Mr. Michael Vernon, FCA *1978;* 37 Rothley Close, SHREWSBURY, SY3 6AN.

BARBER, Mr. Miles Winston, FCA *1973;* Becketts, East Dean, CHICHESTER, WEST SUSSEX, PO18 0JG.

BARBER, Mrs. Natasha, BAcc ACA *2010;* 28 Kinnoul Road, LONDON, W6 8NQ.

BARBER, Mr. Paul Romney, FCA *1971;* The Old Cottage, Well, HOOK, HAMPSHIRE, RG29 1TL. (Life Member)

BARBER, Mrs. Penelope Jane, BSc FCA *1990;* The Seasons, Hawthorn Close, Micheldever, WINCHESTER, HAMPSHIRE, SO21 3DQ.

•**BARBER, Mr. Peter John, FCA** *1983;* (Tax Fac), Barber & Co, 2 Jardine House, The Harrovian Bus' Village, Bessborough Road, HARROW, HA1 3EX. See also PC Accounting Services Limited

BARBER, Mr. Robert Paul, BSc ACA CTA *2004;* with PricewaterhouseCoopers LLP, The Atrium, 1 Harefield Road, UXBRIDGE, UB8 1EX.

BARBER, Miss. Sarah Jane, BSc ACA *1999;* 21 Thynne Road, BILLERICAY, ESSEX, CM11 2HH.

BARBER, Miss. Sarah Louise, BA(Hons) ACA *2002;* 16 Manor Lane Terrace, LONDON, SE13 5QL.

BARBER, Mr. Simon John, BA FCA *1973;* Spring Grove, 16 Digley Road, Holmbridge, HOLMFIRTH, HD9 2QN.

BARBER, Mr. Simon John, ACA ACMA *2011;* HMT Assurance LLP, 5 Fairmile, HENLEY-ON-THAMES, OXFORDSHIRE, RG9 2JR.

BARBER, Mr. Simon John, BA ACA *1992;* Westview, 1 Tern Drive, Poynton, STOCKPORT, SK12 1HR.

BARBER, Mr. Simon Keith, BA FCA *1993;* 3 Birch Croft, Elloughton, BROUGH, NORTH HUMBERSIDE, HU15 1AT.

BARBER, Mrs. Sophie Odile, BA ACA *1998;* 38 Homewood Road, ST. ALBANS, HERTFORDSHIRE, AL1 4BQ.

BARBER, Mr. Stanley Vernon, FCA *1952;* High Ridge, Kemberton, SHIFNAL, TF11 9LW. (Life Member)

•**BARBER, Mr. Stephen David, BSc(Econ) FCA** *1976;* The Objectivity Partnership LLP, 12 York Gate, Regent's Park, LONDON, NW1 4QS.

BARBER, Miss. Susan, ACA *2011;* 8 Boothcote, Audenshaw, MANCHESTER, M34 5NF.

BARBER, Mr. Thomas, BA ACA *2006;* 11 Marsh Grove Road, HUDDERSFIELD, HD3 3AQ.

BARBER, Mrs. Yvette Mavis, BSc ACA *1996;* 4 Lea Road, HARPENDEN, HERTFORDSHIRE, AL5 4PG.

BARBERIS, Mrs. Janet, BSc ACA *1989;* 44 Malvern Drive, WOODFORD GREEN, IG8 0JP.

BARBINI, Mr. Nicola, ACA *2005;* Flat 54 Ionian Building, 45 Narrow Street, LONDON, E14 8DW.

BARBINI, Mr. Tomaso, BSc ACA *1989;* Via San Maurilio 19, 20123 MILAN, ITALY.

•BARBOUR, Mr. Alastair William Stewart, BSc FCA *1978;* 5 King's Cramond, EDINBURGH, EH4 6RL.

BARBOUR, Mrs. Ann Elizabeth, BA ACA *1997;* 20 Vincent Avenue, SOUTHAMPTON, SO16 6PQ.

BARBOUR, Mr. Brian William, FCA *1951;* 20 Wolseley Grove, BRIGHTON, VIC 3186, AUSTRALIA. (Life Member)

BARBOUR, Mr. Dominic James, BA ACA *1986;* 57a Highbury Hill, LONDON, N5 1SU.

BARBOUR, Mrs. Julia Kumari, BA ACA *1985;* Middle House, 57A Highbury Hill, LONDON, N5 1SU.

BARBOUR, Mr. Paul Nicholas, LLB ACA *1992;* 136 Bridge House, Wandsworth Road St George Wharf, LONDON, SW8 2LQ.

BARBOUR, Mr. Peter William, BEng ACA *1999;* Auchengibbert, Crocketford, DUMFRIES, DG2 8RQ.

BARBOUR, Mrs. Sarah Elizabeth, BA ACA *1997;* 45 Littleton Street, LONDON, SW18 3SZ.

BARBROOK, Dr. Laura Sophie Scudamore, ACA *2001;* Chapel House, Frogge Street, Ickleton, SAFFRON WALDEN, CB10 1SH.

BARBROOKE-GRUBB, Mr. Andrew, FCA *1971;* Broads House, Beech Road, Wroxham, NORWICH, NR12 8TP. (Life Member)

BARCHAM, Mr. Paul, FCA *1969;* with McCranors Limited, Clifford House, 38-44 Binley Road, COVENTRY, CV3 1JA.

BARCHHA, Mr. Rashmikant Odhavji, ACA *1978;* 7 Chemin du Parc, 1297 FOUNEX, SWITZERLAND.

•BARCIA, Mr. Michael Gregory, BA ACA CF *1995;* Meridian Corporate Finance LLP, The Coach House, Rownhams House, Rownhams, SOUTHAMPTON, SO16 8LS.

BARCLAY, Mr. Alastair Robert Christopher, FCA *1965;* Jewells Thatch, Chapel Row, Bucklebury, READING, RG7 6PB.

•BARCLAY, Mr. Alistair, FCA *1974;* Alistair Barclay, 28 Cartha Place, DUMFRIES, DG1 4LW.

BARCLAY, Mr. Andrew, ACA *2010;* Brocks Rew, Broomers Hill Lane, PULBOROUGH, WEST SUSSEX, RH20 2HZ.

BARCLAY, Mr. Andrew David, BSc ACA *2002;* 40 West 86th Street Apartment 2D, NEW YORK, NY 10024, UNITED STATES.

BARCLAY, Mr. Gavin Dunbar, ACA *2011;* 28 Sacombe Green, LUTON, LU3 4EW.

BARCLAY, Mr. Ian, BSc ACA *1986;* 36 Lancaster Avenue, HITCHIN, SG5 1PB.

•BARCLAY, Mr. Jack Kelvin, FCA *1979;* Everett & Son, 35 Paul Street, LONDON, EC2A 4UQ.

BARCLAY, Mr. John Christopher, LLB ACA *1982;* 4305 office tower, convention plaza, 1 harbour road, hong kong island, WAN CHAI, HONG KONG SAR.

•BARCLAY, Mr. Peter James, FCA *1978;* Peter Barclay Limited, 1st Floor, 11 Church Street, MELKSHAM, WILTSHIRE, SN12 6LS.

BARCLAY, Mr. Rupert George Maxwell Lothian, MA ACA MBA *1985;* Victory House, 99-101 Regent Street, LONDON, W1B 4RS.

BARCLAY, Mr. Stephen John, FCA *1965;* 71 Raynham, Norfolk Crescent, LONDON, W2 2PQ.

BARCLAY, Mr. Stuart, BSc FCA *1980;* 9 Allbrook Close, TEDDINGTON, MIDDLESEX, TW11 8TY.

BARCLAY, Miss. Theola, BSc ACA *1998;* PO Box 32396, LUSAKA, ZAMBIA.

BARCLAY, Mr. William Alan Gordon, FCA *1969;* 98 Norwich Road, CHICHESTER, WEST SUSSEX, PO19 5DF. (Life Member)

BARCLAY-WHITE, Mr. Adam Meredith, ACA MBA *2003;* 52 Dartnell Avenue, WEST BYFLEET, KT14 6PH.

BARCO, Mr. Colin Anthony John, ACA *1992;* Penwith Community Development Trust The Penwith Centre, Parade Street, PENZANCE, CORNWALL, TR18 4BU.

BARCOCK, Mrs. Amanda Jane, BCom ACA *2000;* 29 Brockhurst Lane, Shirley, SOLIHULL, WEST MIDLANDS, B90 1RG.

BARCOCK, Mr. Andrew Alan Richard, LLB ACA *2001;* 29 Brockhurst Lane, Shirley, SOLIHULL, WEST MIDLANDS, B90 1RG.

BARCROFT, Mr. Colin Ian, FCA *1976;* Spring Villa, 76 Station Road, Alsager, STOKE-ON-TRENT, ST7 2PD. (Life Member)

•BARCROFT, Mr. Stephen John, FCA *1990;* Barcrofts, 157 Bolton Road, BURY, LANCASHIRE, BL8 2NW.

BARCZOK, Miss. Kate Louise, ACA *2006;* 4 West Street, Bishopsteignton, TEIGNMOUTH, DEVON, TQ14 9QU.

BARD, Mr. Andrew David, BA ACA *1998;* Burnthorne Farm, Dunley, STOURPORT-ON-SEVERN, WORCESTERSHIRE, DY13 0TU.

BARD, Mr. Jeremy Laurence, BA ACA *1987;* Corner Croft, Loudwater Heights, Loudwater, RICKMANSWORTH, HERTFORDSHIRE, WD3 4AX.

•BARD, Mr. Laurence David, MA FCA CTA *1975;* (Tax Fac), BTG Tax LLP, 11 Haymarket, LONDON, SW1Y 4BP.

BARD, Miss. Sarah, ACA *2008;* The Estate Office The Rama Building, 32-38 Scrutton Street, LONDON, EC4A4RQ.

•BARDELL, Mr. David, FCA *1982;* Baker Tilly Tax & Advisory Services LLP, Marlborough House, Victoria Road South, CHELMSFORD, CM1 1LN. See also Baker Tilly UK Audit LLP

BARDELL, Mr. Geoffrey Thomas, FCA *1952;* 3 The Limes House, 15 Beverley Road, LEAMINGTON SPA, WARWICKSHIRE, CV32 6PH. (Life Member)

BARDELL-COX, Mr. Timothy Arthur, MBA BSc(Econ) MCMI MAPM ACA *2008;* 29 St. Marys Grove, Nailsea, BRISTOL, BS48 4NQ.

BARDEN, Miss. Angela, BA ACA *1994;* Laburnum Cottage School Hill, Lamberhurst, TUNBRIDGE WELLS, KENT, TN3 8DF.

•BARDEN, Mr. James Douglas, BSc FCA *1982;* Barlow Andrews LLP, Carlyle House, 78 Chorley New Road, BOLTON, BL1 4BY. See also Beech Business Services Limited

BARDEN, Miss. Jennifer, ACA *2009;* 22 Marina Drive, Upton, CHESTER, CH2 1RJ.

BARDEN, Mr. Peter James, FCA *1965;* Furzedown Cottage, Grub Street, OXTED, RH8 0SH.

•BARDEN, Mr. Philip John, BA ACA *1990;* with Deloitte LLP, 2 New Street Square, LONDON, EC4A 3BZ.

BARDGETT, Mr. John Edward, FCA *1968;* 3 The Garden Houses, Whalton, MORPETH, NE61 3UZ.

BARDIN, Mr. Christopher Neil, BA FCA *1993;* 1 Loxwood Close, Walton Park, PRESTON, PR5 4NQ.

BARDIN, Mrs. Gillian Mary, MA FCA *1999;* 1 Loxwood Close Walton-le-Dale, PRESTON, PR5 4NQ.

•BARDLE, Mrs. Helen Louise, BA ACA *1990;* Helen Bardle, 7 Cliff Street, CHEDDAR, SOMERSET, BS27 3PT.

BARDO, Mr. Campbell Rowland, ACA *1987;* Linc - Cymru Housing Association Limited, 387 Newport Road, CARDIFF, CF24 1GG.

BARDOEL, Miss. Henneke, ACA *2003;* Korte Prinsengracht 99 HS, 1013 GR AMSTERDAM, NETHERLANDS.

BARDRICK, Mr. Donald Joseph Woolston, FCA *1954;* 30 Waterslade, Elm Road, REDHILL, RH1 6AJ. (Life Member)

BARDSLEY, Mrs. Alison Elizabeth, MA ACA *1991;* 24 Shortbutts Lane, LICHFIELD, WS14 9BT.

BARDSLEY, Ms. Jacqueline Margaret, BA FCA *1978;* PO Box 22439, SEATTLE, WA 98122, UNITED STATES.

BARDSLEY, Mr. John, FCA *1966;* 23 Peakdale Avenue, Heald Green, CHEADLE, SK8 3QL. (Life Member)

BARDSLEY, Mrs. Lisa Ann, BA ACA *1999;* with Grant Thornton UK LLP, 4 Hardman Square, Spinningfields, MANCHESTER, M3 3EB.

BARDSLEY, Mr. Martin John, BEng FCA ATII *1990;* (Tax Fac), 47 Undine Road, Clippers Quay, Isle of Dogs, LONDON, E14 9UW.

BARDSLEY, Mr. Matthew Alexander, ACA *2009;* Flat 1, 50 Cannon Street Road, LONDON, E1 0BH.

BARDSWELL, Mr. Charles Leslie Geoffrey, BA ACA *2007;* 36b Harbut Road, LONDON, SW11 2RB.

BARDWELL, Mr. Andrew William, MSc ACA *1981;* 22 Cherry Way, Upper Halliford, SHEPPERTON, TW17 8QG.

•BARDWELL, Mrs. Dawn Belinda, BA FCA *1986;* Upper Reach House, 36 Vantorts Road, SAWBRIDGEWORTH, CM21 9NB.

BARDWELL, Mr. John Edward, FCA FCT *1956;* Mill Stream House, Hockley Mill, Church Lane Twyford, WINCHESTER, SO21 1PJ. (Life Member)

BAREE, Mr. Mohamed Abdul, MSc ACA *1980;* Hoda Vasi Chowdury & Co], Chartered Accountants, BTMG Bhavan (8th Floor), Kawran Bazar, DHAKA, BANGLADESH.

BAREE, Mr. Ridwan, BA(Hons) ACA *2009;* 26 Summerfield Street, LONDON, SE12 0NQ.

•BAREHAM, Mr. Colin Anthony, FCA *1969;* (Tax Fac), Raedan, Maple House, High Street, POTTERS BAR, HERTFORDSHIRE, EN6 5BS.

BAREHAM, Mr. James Robert, BSc(Hons) ACA *2001;* 7 Mona Terrace, Castletown, ISLE OF MAN, IM9 1BH.

BAREHAM, Mr. Jonathan James, ACA *2009;* 5 Edmund Mews, KINGS LANGLEY, HERTFORDSHIRE, WD4 8GB.

BAREHAM, Mr. Robert Edward, FCA *1972;* 267 Southlands Road, BICKLEY, BR1 2EG.

BAREN, Mr. Peter Anthony, BA FCA *1985;* Emerson Developments, Emerson House, Heyes Lane, ALDERLEY EDGE, CHESHIRE, SK9 7LF.

•BARFIELD, Mrs. Lesley Anne, FCA *1975;* 119 Purley Oaks Road, SOUTH CROYDON, SURREY, CR2 0NY.

BARFIELD, Mr. Richard John, BSc FCA CMC FIBC *1979;* 59 Vernon Road, East Sheen, LONDON, SW14 8NU.

BARFIELD, Mr. Richard Timothy, BA FCA FRSA *1985;* Wymondham House, 18 Brooklands Avenue, CAMBRIDGE, CAMBRIDGESHIRE, CB2 8BB.

•BARFOOT, Miss. Carol Elizabeth, BSc FCA *2000;* (Tax Fac), Gibbons Mannington & Phipps, 20-22 Eversley Road, BEXHILL-ON-SEA, EAST SUSSEX, TN40 1HE.

BARFORD, Mr. Andrew, BSc ACA *2007;* with PricewaterhouseCoopers LLP, 1 Embankment Place, LONDON, WC2N 6RH.

BARFORD, Mr. Michael Thomas, BA FCA *1978;* 9 Ashley Park Road, WALTON-ON-THAMES, SURREY, KT12 1JU. (Life Member)

BARFORD, Miss. Nicola Ann, BA FCA *1993;* 132 Tanjong Rhu Road #09-06, SINGAPORE 436919, SINGAPORE.

BARFORD, Mrs. Sarah, LLM LLB PGDL ACA *2005;* 30 Shakespeare Avenue, RAYLEIGH, SS6 8YA.

BARFORD, Mr. Thomas, ACA *2011;* Flat 95, Albert Palace Mansions, Lurline Gardens, LONDON, SW11 4DH.

BARGENT, Mr. Brian Gerald, ACA CA(NZ) *2010;* 1 Haldon Close, Topsham, EXETER, EX3 0LW.

BARGER, Mr. Raymond Frederick, FCA *1972;* 43 Erpingham Road, Putney, LONDON, SW15 1BQ.

BARGERY, Mr. Stuart James, BA ACA *1989;* (Tax Fac), with PricewaterhouseCoopers LLP, 10-18 Union Street, LONDON, SE1 1SZ.

BARGH, Mr. Brian, FCA *1959;* 10a Greendale Avenue, CHESTERFIELD, S42 7DT. (Life Member)

BARGH, Mr. Derek William, FCA *1975;* 6 Rawcliffe Close, WIDNES, CHESHIRE, WA8 9FZ.

BARGUS, Mr. Geoffrey Kenneth, FCA *1976;* 66 Tarragon Way, Burghfield Common, READING, RG7 3YU.

BARHAM, Mr. Andrew Paul, MA ACA *1990;* 3 Lancot Place, DUNSTABLE, BEDFORDSHIRE, LU6 2AR.

BARHAM, Mr. Dean James Alan, ACA *1992;* Hotham House, 14 Hotham Close, SWANLEY, KENT, BR8 7UX.

•BARHAM, Mrs. Helen Lyn, ACA *1995;* Ash Tree Accounting Limited, 1 Ash Tree Close, HEATHFIELD, EAST SUSSEX, TN21 8BF.

BARHAM, Mr. Mark, BA ACA *2002;* 55 W Delaware Pl Apt 1010, CHICAGO, IL 60610, UNITED STATES.

BARHAM, Mr. Paul Leslie, FCA *1976;* 5331 Spring Valley Road, DALLAS, TX 75254, UNITED STATES.

BARHAM, Mr. Richard Charles, BSc FCA *1974;* 807 10045-118 Street, EDMONTON T5K 2K2, AB, CANADA.

BARHAM, Mr. Scott William, BSc(Econ) ACA *2002;* 15 Scott Avenue, Putney, LONDON, SW15 3PA.

BARHEY, Mr. Sukhraj Singh, BSc ACA *1991;* 7 Hawthorn Way, Bilton, RUGBY, CV22 7LS.

BARI, Mr. Faisal, ACA *1988;* Olayan Financing Company, Al Hassa Street, Near Pepsi Factory, Malaz District, PO Box 8772, RIYADH 11492 SAUDI ARABIA.

BARI, Miss. Laila, BA(Hons) ACA *2011;* 103 Gigg Lane, BURY, LANCASHIRE, BL9 9JB.

•BARI, Miss. Yasmin, BSc ACA *2003;* Pullan Barnes Limited, Stephenson House, Richard Street, Hetton-le-Hole, HOUGHTON LE SPRING, TYNE AND WEAR DH5 9HW.

BARK-JONES, Mr. Timothy James, BA ACA *2002;* 28 Quoitings Drive, MARLOW, BUCKINGHAMSHIRE, SL7 2PE.

BARKAS, Miss. Nina Christine, BSc ACA *2005;* 21 Riverside Court, 4 Quayside Road, Bitterne Manor, SOUTHAMPTON, SO18 1EP.

BARKE, Mrs. Anna Louise Sarah, ACA *2007;* 73 Amity Grove, West Wimbledon, LONDON, SW20 0LQ.

BARKE, Miss. Karen, BA ACA *1992;* BY Design (UK) Ltd, Newcombe House, 43-45 Notting Hill Gate, LONDON, W11 3LQ.

BARKE, Mr. Thomas, MBiochem ACA *2011;* 34 Valley Road, Burghfield Common, READING, RG7 3NF.

BARKEL, Mrs. Maxime Isabelle, BA ACA *1985;* Cherry Trees, Kingswood Road, Penn, HIGH WYCOMBE, BUCKINGHAMSHIRE, HP10 8JL.

BARKER, Mrs. Abigail Louise, ACA *2009;* 23 Plumian Way, Balsham, CAMBRIDGE, CB21 4EG.

BARKER, Mrs. Adele, BSc ACA *1994;* O M F International 6 Station Court, Station Approach Borough Green, SEVENOAKS, TN15 8BG.

•BARKER, Mr. Adrian John, BA ACA *1997;* Combined Business Solutions Limited, Rowan House North, 1 The Professional Quarter, Shrewsbury Business Park, SHREWSBURY, SY2 6LG. See also CBSL Group Limited and CBSL Accountants Limited

•BARKER, Alan Douglas, Esq OBE FCA *1964;* (Tax Fac), Alan Barker & Co, Barnhill, Wetherby Road, Collingham, WETHERBY, LS22 5AY.

BARKER, Mr. Alan Marcus, FCA *1957;* Flat 5 The Croft, Pages Croft, Easthampstead Road, WOKINGHAM, BERKSHIRE, RG40 2HN. (Life Member)

BARKER, Mr. Alan Michael, BA ACA *1992;* 48 Weir Road, Milnrow, ROCHDALE, LANCASHIRE, OL16 3UX.

BARKER, Mr. Alexander John, BSc ACA *2010;* Buzzacott LLP, 130 Wood Street, LONDON, EC2V 6DL.

BARKER, Mrs. Alice May, FCA *1975;* 4 Gardiner Drive, Goms Mill, STOKE-ON-TRENT, ST3 2RQ.

BARKER, Miss. Alison, BA(Hons) ACA *2010;* 2 Belgravia Gardens, MANCHESTER, M21 9JJ.

BARKER, Miss. Alison Michelle, LLB ACA *2001;* 346 Congress Street # 209, BOSTON, MA 02210, UNITED STATES.

BARKER, Mrs. Amanda Helen, BA ACA *2004;* 4 Finchale Priory, BEDFORD, MK41 0WB.

•BARKER, Ms. Angela Mary, ACA *1979;* (Tax Fac), A.M. Barker, 1B Singlets Lane, Flamstead, ST. ALBANS, AL3 8EN.

BARKER, Mrs. Anita Louise, BA(Hons) ACA *2003;* with PricewaterhouseCoopers, Emirates Towers Offices, PO Box 11987, Level 40, Sheikh Zayed Road, PO Box 11987 DUBAI UNITED ARAB EMIRATES.

BARKER, Mrs. Anita Marie, BA ACA *1989;* 80 Sheepwalk Lane, Ravenshead, NOTTINGHAM, NG15 9FB.

BARKER, Mrs. Anna Bridget, MA CA ACA *1989;* PO Box 7109, Fitzroy, NEW PLYMOUTH, TARANAKI, NEW ZEALAND.

BARKER, Miss. Annabel Sarah, MSc ACA *2000;* Level 16 - Group Finance, Aviva UK Central Services St. Helens, 1 Undershaft, LONDON, EC3P 3DQ.

BARKER, Mrs. Annette Louise, BA FCA *1998;* 25 Nether Way, Nether Poppleton, YORK, YO26 6HW.

•BARKER, Mr. Anthony John, FCA *1982;* (Tax Fac), Caerwyn Jones, Emstrey House, Shrewsbury Business Park, SHREWSBURY, SY2 6LG.

BARKER, Mr. Brian Geoffrey, BSc FCA *1968;* 7 Magnolia Place, Montpelier Road, Ealing, LONDON, W5 2QQ. (Life Member)

•BARKER, Mr. Bryan John, FCA *1984;* Townends, 11 The Crescent, SELBY, YO8 4PD.

BARKER, Mrs. Caroline Annette, BSc FCA *1986;* 78A Elwill Way, Park Langley, BECKENHAM, BR3 6RX.

BARKER, Ms. Catherine Jane, BA ACA *1984;* Springfort Lodge, 2 Stoke Hill, Stoke Bishop, BRISTOL, BS9 1JE.

BARKER, Mr. Charles Peter, BA ACA *2007;* Pine Trees, Bilton-in-Ainsty, YORK, YO26 7NN.

BARKER, Mr. Charles Richard, BSc FCA *1976;* Hill Top House, Main Street, Burley in Wharfedale, ILKLEY, WEST YORKSHIRE, LS29 7JW.

BARKER, Mr. Christopher, FCA *1968;* with Harben Barker Limited, Drayton Court, Drayton Road, SOLIHULL, WEST MIDLANDS, B90 4NG.

BARKER, Mr. Christopher Albion, BSc FCA *1975;* with Ian Pickup & Co, 123 New Road Side, Horsforth, LEEDS, LS18 4QD.

BARKER, Mr. Christopher Lawrence, BA ACA *1995;* 43 Chine Walk, West Parley, FERNDOWN, DORSET, BH22 8PR.

BARKER, Mrs. Claire Louise, BSc ACA *2004;* 97 Lichfield Road, SUTTON COLDFIELD, WEST MIDLANDS, B74 2RR.

BARKER, Mr. Clifford Anthony, BA FCA *1986;* 5 Lady Close, Newnham, DAVENTRY, NN11 3HN.

•BARKER, Mr. Colin Andrew, BSc FCA *1985;* Brookes & Company(UK) Limited, Trafalgar House, Fullbridge, MALDON, ESSEX, CM9 4LE.

•BARKER, Mr. Colin Stephen, ACA *1985;* Colin Barker, 11 Felton Close, Hollins, BURY, BL9 8BJ.

BARKER, Mr. Cyril Charles, FCA *1952;* Amberley, 5 Raven Close, EXETER, EX4 4SR. (Life Member)

BARKER, Mr. Daniel, MSci ACA *2011;* PricewaterhouseCoopers, 22/F Prince's Building, CENTRAL, HONG KONG ISLAND, HONG KONG SAR.

BARKER, Mr. David Eric, FCA *1952;* Chandelle, 79 Bownham Park, STROUD, GL5 5BZ.

BARKER, Mr. David Robert, BA ACA *1993;* Cinven, Warwick Court, Paternoster Square, LONDON, EC4M 7AG.

BARKER, Mr. Dominic Clive, BSc(Hons) ACA *2004;* with Magus Partners LLP, 101 Wigmore Street, LONDON, W1U 1QU.
•**BARKER, Mr. Douglas Andrew, FCA** *1968;* Armitage Davis & Co., 81b High Street, WARE, SG12 9AD.
BARKER, Mr. Edward Peter, BSocSc ACA *1999;* 45 Cavell Way, Knaphill, WOKING, SURREY, GU21 2TJ.
BARKER, Mrs. Eva-Marie, ACA *1981;* 56 Charlwood Road, Putney, LONDON, SW15 1PZ.
BARKER, Mr. George Edward Alexander, FCA *1961;* Windways, 1 Stancombe View, Lower House Lane, North Nibley, DURSLEY, GLOUCESTERSHIRE GL11 6BP. (Life Member)
BARKER, Mr. Gerald Cecil, FCA *1959;* 35 Sissinghurst Drive, Thrapston, KETTERING, NORTHAMPTONSHIRE, NN14 4XQ. (Life Member)
•**BARKER, Mr. Glyn Anthony, BSc ACA** *1978;* PricewaterhouseCoopers LLP, 1 Embankment Place, LONDON, WC2N 6RH. See also PricewaterhouseCoopers
BARKER, Mr. Godfrey William, FCA *1966;* Frogmore Cottage, Penelewey, Feock, TRURO, TR3 6RD.
BARKER, Mr. Gordon Howard, FCA *1968;* Benfield, Warren Corner, Froxfield, PETERSFIELD, GU32 1BJ.
BARKER, Mr. Graham Richard, BA FCA *1977;* Wildlife Art Gallery, Phoenix House, 97 High Street, Lavenham, SUDBURY, SUFFOLK CO10 9PZ.
BARKER, Miss. Hannah Elizabeth, ACA *2009;* 20 Ernest Street, CHEADLE, CHESHIRE, SK8 1PN.
BARKER, Mrs. Hannah Jane, BSc(Hons) ACA *2009;* Deloitte, 1 City Square, LEEDS, LS1 2AL.
BARKER, Miss. Hazel Anne, MA(Oxon) FCA CTA *1986;* Evans Property Group, Millshaw, Ring Road, Beeston, LEEDS, LS11 8EG.
BARKER, Mrs. Heather Louise, ACA *1986;* Clayhill Cottage, Fairford Road, LECHLADE, GL7 3DS.
•**BARKER, Mrs. Helen Dorothy, TD BSc ACA ATII** *1988;* (Tax Fac), Mezaprospekts 40, RIGA LV-1014, LATVIA.
BARKER, Miss. Helen Elizabeth, BSc(Hons) ACA *2007;* 18 Beaumont Road, Flitwick, BEDFORD, MK45 1WD.
BARKER, Mrs. Helena, BA ACA *2010;* 4 Coton Road, WELLING, DA16 3PL.
BARKER, Mrs. Hilary Jane, BSc ACA *1984;* Trinity Healthcare Ltd, Grosvenor House, 100-102 Beverley Road, HULL, HU3 1YA.
•**BARKER, Mr. Iain David, FCA** *1994;* Page Kirk LLP, Sherwood House, 7 Gregory Boulevard, NOTTINGHAM, NG7 6LB.
BARKER, Mr. Ian David George, ACA *2009;* Santander UK Plc, 2-3 Triton Square, LONDON, NW1 3AN.
BARKER, Mr. James Alan, BSc FCA TEP *1993;* 224 Broadway, GRIMSBY, DN34 5QU.
•**BARKER, Mr. James Alan, FCA** *1973;* 20 Crabtree Park, FAIRFORD, GLOUCESTERSHIRE, GL7 4LT.
BARKER, Mr. James Nicholas William, BSc ACA *1996;* 1325 N Lemon Ave, MENLO PARK, CA 94025, UNITED STATES.
BARKER, Mr. James Paul, BSc ACA *1999;* Sheppard Robson, 77 Parkway, LONDON, NW1 7PU.
BARKER, Mrs. Jane Victoria, BSc FCA *1974;* Equitas Limited, 33 St Mary Axe, LONDON, EC3A 8LL.
BARKER, Miss. Jillian Ann, BSc FCA *1986;* 27 Calle Fondeo, Sotogrande, San Roque, 11310 CADIZ, SPAIN.
•**BARKER, Mr. John Arthur, FCA** *1973;* (Tax Fac), Hillier Hopkins LLP, 64 Clarendon Road, WATFORD, WD17 1DA.
BARKER, Mr. John Ernest Ridley, BSc FCA *1977;* 14 Glebe Meadow, Overton, BASINGSTOKE, RG25 3ER.
BARKER, Mr. John Granville, FCA *1973;* Warren Point, Rhoslan, ABERDOVEY, LL35 0NT.
BARKER, Mr. John Kirk, BCom FCA *1972;* Field House, Cranham, GLOUCESTER, GL4 8HB.
•**BARKER, Mr. John Leonard, FCA** *1977;* BDO LLP, Prospect Place, 85 Great North Road, HATFIELD, HERTFORDSHIRE, AL9 5BS. See also BDO Stoy Hayward LLP
BARKER, Mr. John William, BSc FCA *1978;* Lees of Grimsby Ltd, 222 Victoria Street, GRIMSBY, SOUTH HUMBERSIDE, DN31 1BJ.
•**BARKER, Mr. John-Paul, BA ACA** *1999;* PricewaterhouseCoopers LLP, 7 More London Riverside, LONDON, SE1 2RT. See also PricewaterhouseCoopers
BARKER, Mr. Jonathan, BSc ACA *1993;* 36 Glenferrie Road, ST. ALBANS, HERTFORDSHIRE, AL1 4JU.
BARKER, Mrs. Julie Faith, BA ACA *1988;* 7 Spencer Road, EAST MOLESEY, KT8 0SP.
BARKER, Mrs. Katharine Frances, BSc ACA *1997;* 40 St. Johns Road, Penn, HIGH WYCOMBE, BUCKINGHAMSHIRE, HP10 8HU.
BARKER, Miss. Katherine, BA ACA *2007;* Pearl Group Limited, Juxon House 100 St. Pauls Churchyard, LONDON, EC4 8BU.
BARKER, Miss. Katherine Anne, BSc ACA *2005;* 19 Bath Road, WELLS, SOMERSET, BA5 3HP.
BARKER, Mrs. Kathleen, BSc ACA *1998;* 39 Chishill Road, Heydon, ROYSTON, SG8 8PP.
BARKER, Miss. Kathleen Elizabeth, BSc FCA *1992;* Enstar (EU) Limited America House, 2 America Square, LONDON, EC3N 2LU.
•**BARKER, Mr. Keith Dennis, FCA** *1982;* Cook & Partners Limited, 108 High Street, STEVENAGE, HERTFORDSHIRE, SG1 3DW. See also Cook & Partners
•**BARKER, Mr. Kenneth, FCA** *1969;* (Tax Fac), Barkers Accountants Limited, Street Ashton Farm House, Stretton Under Fosse, RUGBY, WARWICKSHIRE, CV23 0PH.
•**BARKER, Mrs. Kirsten Jean, BA(Hons) ACA** *2004;* Russell Smith Tax & Accountancy Services Limited, G3 Round Foundry, Media Centre, Foundry Street, LEEDS, LS11 5QP.
BARKER, Miss. Kirsten Louise, ACA *2010;* 26 Kendal Close, LONDON, SW9 6EW.
BARKER, Mrs. Kirstin Marie, BA(Hons) ACA *2001;* Canterbury College, Finance Department, New Dover Road, CANTERBURY, KENT, CT1 3AJ.
BARKER, Miss. Louise Claire, BA ACA *2007;* (Tax Fac), 4 Havanna, Killingworth, NEWCASTLE UPON TYNE, NE12 5BL.
BARKER, Mr. Mark, ACA *2008;* Thomson Reuters Thomson Reuters Building, 30 South Colonnade, LONDON, E14 5EP.
BARKER, Mr. Mark Anthony, BA ACA *1992;*. 529 Felsham Way, Taverham, NORWICH, NR8 6HQ.
BARKER, Mr. Matthew Howard, BSc(Hons) ACA *2004;* 8 West Pasture Close, Horsforth, LEEDS, LS18 5PB.
BARKER, Mr. Matthew Richard, MEng ACA *1996;* 40 St. Johns Road Penn, HIGH WYCOMBE, BUCKINGHAMSHIRE, HP10 8HU.
BARKER, Miss. Melanie Jane, BA ACA *1987;* Bishop Douglass RC High School, Hamilton Road, LONDON, N2 0SQ.
BARKER, Mr. Michael David Latta, ACA *1983;* Palos de la Frontera 42, 04007 ALMERIA, SPAIN.
•**BARKER, Mr. Michael Denis, BSc ACA** *2001;* Noviga Consulting, 28 Woodbine Road, Gosforth, NEWCASTLE UPON TYNE, NE3 1DD.
BARKER, Mr. Michael Humphrey, FCA *1973;* 2 Herons Brook, Naccolt Road, Brook, ASHFORD, KENT, TN25 5NX. (Life Member)
BARKER, Mr. Neal, MA ACA *2007;* Ingenious Media Plc, 15 Golden Square, LONDON, W1F 9JG.
BARKER, Mr. Nicholas Charles Lawrence, ACA *1983;* 201 Tatton Road, RD9, WHANGAREI 0179, NEW ZEALAND.
BARKER, Mr. Nicholas James, BSc ACA *2005;* J W P Creers Foss Place, Foss Islands Road, YORK, YO31 7UJ.
BARKER, Miss. Nicola Kate, BA ACA *2010;* Deloitte & Touche, 2 New Street Square, LONDON, EC4A 3BZ.
BARKER, Mr. Nigel Anthony, BA FCA *1991;* 24 Scott Lane, Gomersal, CLECKHEATON, BD19 4JY.
BARKER, Mr. Nigel Davidson, FCA *1962;* 5 Clonway, YELVERTON, DEVON, PL20 6EG.
BARKER, Mr. Nigel John, BSc ACA *1993;* 37 Telegraph Lane, Four Marks, ALTON, GU34 5AX.
BARKER, Mr. Nigel Kenyon, BA ACA *1992;* Blackdown Cottage, Forest Road, WOKING, SURREY, GU22 8LU.
BARKER, Mr. Oliver, BA ACA *2003;* Merrill Lynch Europe Plc, 5 Paternoster Square, LONDON, EC4M 7DX.
BARKER, Mrs. Pamela Joy, BSc ACA *1983;* 13 The Paddocks, Stapleford Abbotts, ROMFORD, RM4 1HG.
BARKER, Mr. Paul Andrew, BA ACA *2005;* Kier Group Plc, Tempsford Hall, SANDY, BEDFORDSHIRE, SG19 2BD.
BARKER, Mr. Peter, BA ACA *2006;* Basement Flat, 3 Christchurch Road, BRISTOL, BS8 4EF.
BARKER, Mr. Philip Anthony, BA ACA *1986;* Old Timbers, Church Street, Naseby, NORTHAMPTON, NN6 6DA.
BARKER, Mr. Philip John Newton, BSc ACA *1988;* Talk Me Through It, Corsley Garage, Corsley Heath, Corsley, WARMINSTER, WILTSHIRE BA12 7PL.
BARKER, Mr. Philip Nigel Helm, BSc ACA *1986;* with Cavendish Corporate Finance, 40 Portland Place, LONDON, W1B 1NB.
BARKER, Mr. Phillip David, MBA BSc ACA *1988;* 26 Somerset Avenue, Baildon, SHIPLEY, BD17 5LS.
BARKER, Mrs. Rachel Helen, BA(Hons) ACA *2003;* 61 Chipping Vale, Emerson Valley, MILTON KEYNES, MK4 2HT.
BARKER, Mr. Richard Alan, ACA *2008;* 32 Cherry Drive, ROYSTON, HERTFORDSHIRE, SG8 7DL.
BARKER, Mr. Richard Edward, BA ACA *1998;* Credit Suisse, The Gate Building, 9th Floor East, Dubai International Financial Centre, DUBAI, 33660 UNITED ARAB EMIRATES.
BARKER, Mr. Richard Lloyd, FCA *1975;* Ashbrook House, Quarry Close, Slitting Mill, RUGELEY, STAFFORDSHIRE, WS15 2YB.
BARKER, Mr. Richard Simon, BA ACA *1989;* PURAC America Inc, 111 Barclay Blvd, LINCOLNSHIRE, IL 60069, UNITED STATES.
BARKER, Mr. Robert Andrew, BA ACA ATII *1997;* with Deloitte LLP, 3 Rivergate, Temple Quay, BRISTOL, BS1 6GD.
BARKER, Mr. Robert Anthony, FCA *1970;* 46 Meadowfield, Stokesley, MIDDLESBROUGH, CLEVELAND, TS9 5HH.
BARKER, Mr. Robert Edwin, BA FCA *1983;* 1 Ellesmere Grove, CHELTENHAM, GL50 2QQ.
•①**BARKER, Mr. Robert Henry, MA FCA** *1979;* RH Barker & Co, T/A Cambridge Recovery Services, St John's Innovation Centre, Cowley Road, CAMBRIDGE, CB4 0WS. See also Cambridge Recovery Services Limited
BARKER, Mr. Robert Holme, BA FCA *1969;* Meadow Cottage, 5 Grange Farm Close, Menston, ILKLEY, LS29 6QG.
BARKER, Mr. Robert John Swinburn, FCA *1968;* (Tax Fac), Remenham House, 12 The Chipping, TETBURY, GLOUCESTERSHIRE, GL8 8ET. (Life Member)
BARKER, Mr. Robert Michael, BA FCA *1980;* Greenwood & Coope Ltd Brookhouse Mill, Holcombe Road Greenmount, BURY, BL8 4HR.
BARKER, Mr. Robert Michael, BSc ACA *1989;* Colefax & Fowler Ltd, 19-23 Grosvenor Hill, LONDON, W1K 3QD.
BARKER, Mr. Roger Thomas, FCA *1955;* 27 Spinney Hill Drive, LOUGHBOROUGH, LE11 3LB. (Life Member)
BARKER, Miss. Rosemary Ann, FCA *1993;* Box Tree Cottage Three Ashes Stoke St. Michael, RADSTOCK, BA3 5JF.
BARKER, Miss. Rosemary Jayne, BA ACA *2009;* Beechwood, Slapton, KINGSBRIDGE, DEVON, TQ7 2QD.
BARKER, Mr. Russell, BSc ACA *2010;* with Baker Tilly Tax & Advisory Services LLP, 1st Floor, 46 Clarendon Road, WATFORD, WD17 1JJ.
•**BARKER, Mrs. Sarah Blanche, FCA** *1983;* Barkers, Council Offices, College Road, CAMELFORD, PL32 9TL.
BARKER, Miss. Sarah Georgina, MTh ACA *1992;* Grove House Grove Road, Old Buckenham, ATTLEBOROUGH, NORFOLK, NR17 1PJ.
BARKER, Miss. Sarah Jane, ACA *1993;* 12 rue M Weistroffer, Kockelscheuer, L-1898 LUXEMBOURG, LUXEMBOURG.
BARKER, Mr. Simon Charles, FCA *1975;* 47 Priory Road, Kew, RICHMOND, TW9 3DQ.
•**BARKER, Mr. Simon Charles, BSc ACA** *1992;* KPMG LLP, Arlington Business Park, Theale, READING, RG7 4SD. See also KPMG Europe LLP
BARKER, Mr. Simon George Harry, QC FCA *1976;* The Birmingham Civil Justice Centre, The Priory Courts, 33 Bull Street, BIRMINGHAM, B4 6DS.
BARKER, Mr. Simon Peter, BA ACA *1993;* 202 New Road Side, Horsforth, LEEDS, LS18 4DT.
BARKER, Mr. Simon Peter Dudley, BA ACA *1984;* Campion House Cleves Lane, Upton Grey, BASINGSTOKE, HAMPSHIRE, RG25 2RG.
BARKER, Miss. Stacey, BSc ACA *2010;* 9 Celandine Mead, TAUNTON, SOMERSET, TA1 3XF.
•**BARKER, Mr. Stephen, FCA** *1975;* (Tax Fac), Morris & Co (2011) Limited, Chester House, Lloyd Drive, Chesire Oaks Business Park, ELLESMERE PORT, CHESHIRE CH65 9HQ.
BARKER, Mr. Stephen James, BBA ACA *2010;* 180 Carronade Court, Eden Grove, LONDON, N7 8GP.
•**BARKER, Mr. Stephen Philip, FCA** *1987;* Masons Audit Limited, 4 Hadleigh Business Centre, 351 London Road,. Hadleigh, BENFLEET, ESSEX SS7 2BT.
BARKER, Mr. Stuart Paul, ACA *1991;* 11 Ingram Road, LONDON, N2 9QA.
BARKER, Mrs. Susan Caroline, BSc ACA *1997;* 1325 N Lemon Avenue, MENLO PARK, CA 94025, UNITED STATES.
BARKER, Miss. Suzanne, BA FCA *1990;* Baines Jewitt, Barrington House, 43-45 Yarm Lane, STOCKTON-ON-TEES, CLEVELAND TS18 3EA.
BARKER, Mrs. Suzanne Margaret, BSc FCA *1987;* Old Timbers, Church Street, Naseby, NORTHAMPTON, NN6 6DA.
BARKER, Mr. Terrence, FCA *1964;* Sowerby Grange, Green Lane East, THIRSK, NORTH YORKSHIRE, YO7 1NA.
BARKER, Mr. Thomas, FCA *1961;* Acre Nook, Lower Withington, Nr Chelford, MACCLESFIELD, SK11 9AA.
BARKER, Mr. Thomas Ian Helm, BSc ACA *1991;* St. Anslem Development Co, 128 Mount Street, LONDON, W1K 3NU.
BARKER, Mr. Timothy Guy, BA FCA *1974;* Rhos y Gwaliau, Longnor, SHREWSBURY, SY5 7QH.
BARKER, Mr. Timothy James, ACA *1988;* (Tax Fac), 19 Epsom Road, Toton, NOTTINGHAM, NG9 6HQ.
BARKER, Mr. Timothy Roger, BCom ACA *1991;* 306 Bristol Road, Edgbaston, BIRMINGHAM, B5 7SN.
BARKER, Ms. Tracy Ann, BSc(Econ) ACA *1995;* 25 Magpie Hall Lane, BROMLEY, BR2 8ED.
BARKER, Mr. Travis James, BA ACA *1996;* 113 Bellenden Road, Peckham Rye, LONDON, SW15 4QY.
BARKER, Mr. Trevor, FCA *1957;* PO Box 711, COMO, PERTH, WA 6952, AUSTRALIA. (Life Member)
BARKER, Mrs. Una Mary, BSc ACA *1991;* 33 Maple Park, CRUMLIN, COUNTY ANTRIM, BT29 4WZ.
BARKER, Mr. Vernon Ian, OBE BA ACA *1986;* 7 Cherington Crescent, MACCLESFIELD, CHESHIRE, SK11 8LA.
BARKER, Mr. Warren James, BSc(Hons) ACA *2009;* Flat 5 Chinnocks Wharf, 42 Narrow Street, LONDON, E14 8DJ.
BARKER, Mrs. Wendy Frances, BA ACA *1992;* 40 Victor Gardens, Hawkwell, HOCKLEY, SS5 4DS.
BARKER, Mr. William, FCA *1967;* Bishops Move London, Unit B Davis Road Industrial Park, Davis Road, CHESSINGTON, SURREY, KT9 1TQ.
BARKER, Mr. William Ernest, FCA *1958;* 17 Woodlands Avenue, Cheadle Hulme, CHEADLE, SK8 5DD. (Life Member)
BARKER, Mr. William Francis, FCA *1971;* O Comitti & Sons Four Wantz Corner, Fyfield Road, ONGAR, CM5 0AH.
•**BARKER-BENFIELD, Mr. Charles Vere, FCA** *1981;* (Tax Fac), Morchard Bishop & Co, 4 Dene Walk, Lower Bourne, FARNHAM, SURREY, GU10 3PL.
BARKES, Mrs. Helen, BSc(Hons) ACA *2005;* 16 Hillside Grove, LONDON, NW7 2LR.
BARKES, Mr. Tom Richard, BA(Hons) ACA *2002;* 16 Hillside Grove, LONDON, NW7 2LR.
•**BARKESS, Mr. Christopher, FCA** *1974;* Barkess & Co Limited, Stockton Business Centre 70-74, Brunswick Street, STOCKTON-ON-TEES, CLEVELAND, TS18 1DW. See also AIMS - Chris Barkess
BARKHAM, Mr. Michael Richard, BSc FCA *1983;* 19 King Harry Lane, ST. ALBANS, HERTFORDSHIRE, AL3 4AS.
•**BARKUS, Mr. Paul Andrew, BSc FCA** *1991;* PricewaterhouseCoopers LLP, 1 Embankment Place, LONDON, WC2N 6RH. See also PricewaterhouseCoopers
BARKWITH, Mr. Antony John, MPhys ACA *2010;* 130 Bridge Avenue, UPMINSTER, ESSEX, RM14 2LR.
BARKWORTH, Mr. Paul Raymond Braithwaite, FCA *1972;* 43 Indian Ridge Road, EAST HAMPSTEAD, NH 03826-2472, UNITED STATES.
BARLASS, Mr. Mohammad Mosa, ACA *2011;* Flat 28, Kersfield House, 11 Kersfield Road, LONDON, SW15 3HJ.
BARLEY, Miss. Jessica Elizabeth, BA(Hons) ACA *2009;* Flat 4 Skipton Court, Skipton Road, HARROGATE, NORTH YORKSHIRE, HG1 3EX.
BARLEY, Mr. Michael, MBA BSc(Eng) FCA *1981;* 28 Peel Avenue, Frimley, CAMBERLEY, GU16 8YT.
BARLEY, Mr. Paul, BSc ACA *1994;* Great Enton, Enton, GODALMING, SURREY, GU8 5AH.
BARLEY, Mr. Richard, BA(Hons) ACA *2003;* 29b Longbeach Road, LONDON, SW11 5SS.
BARLEY, Mr. Stephen, BA ACA *2002;* 54/8 Cook Street, Southbank, MELBOURNE, VIC 3006, AUSTRALIA.
BARLING, Mr. Brett, BSc FCA *1982;* L'Hirondelle, 15 Rue Princesse Antoinette, MONTE CARLO, MONACO.
•**BARLING, Mrs. Lisa Marie, ACA** *2008;* MacIntyre Hudson LLP, Boundary House, 4 County Place, CHELMSFORD, CM2 0RE.
•**BARLING, Mrs. Lynette, MA FCA** *1975;* Lynette Barling, 4 Wych Elm Rise, GUILDFORD, SURREY, GU1 3TH. See also Barling Lynette
•**BARLING, Mr. Matthew, BSc ACA** *1992;* PricewaterhouseCoopers LLP, Hays Galleria, 1 Hays Lane, LONDON, SE1 2RD. See also PricewaterhouseCoopers

BARLING, Mr. Peter Gilbert Bonnor, FCA 1964; 29 Wansunt Road, BEXLEY, DA5 2DQ.
BARLOW, Mr. Adam, ACA 2008; 20 Mal Bay Court, MINDARIE, WA 6030, AUSTRALIA.
BARLOW, Mr. Andrew James, BEng FCA 1996; with PricewaterhouseCoopers, 2 Southbank Boulevard, Southbank, MELBOURNE, VIC 3006, AUSTRALIA.
BARLOW, Mr. Arthur David Patrick, BSc ACA 1989; 1 Priestwell Court, East Haddon, NORTHAMPTON, NN6 8BT.
•BARLOW, Mr. Barry Craig, BA(Hons) ACA 2001; Butterworth Barlow, Prescot House, 3 High Street, PRESCOT, MERSEYSIDE, L34 3LD.
BARLOW, Mr. Bernard Paul, BSc ACA 1992; 2175 Coastland Ave, SAN JOSE, CA 95125, UNITED STATES.
BARLOW, Mr. Christopher, MSc BSc ACA 2002; 3 Alden Rise, ROSSENDALE, BB4 4LZ.
•BARLOW, Mr. Christopher, ACA FCCA 2009; Bloomer Heaven Limited, Rutland House, 148 Edmund Street, BIRMINGHAM, B3 2FD.
BARLOW, Mr. Christopher Howard, FCA 1965; 1 Cranesbill Drive, BURY ST. EDMUNDS, SUFFOLK, IP32 7JU. (Life Member)
BARLOW, Mr. Christopher Mark, FCA 1969; Ohamanui, School Road, Risby, BURY ST. EDMUNDS, SUFFOLK, IP28 6RG.
BARLOW, Mr. Christopher Raymond, MEng ACA 2004; London School of Business & Finance, 9 Holborn, LONDON, EC1N 2LL.
BARLOW, Ms. Claire Louise, BSc ACA 1995; 20 Willow Close, Unsworth, BURY, BL9 8NU.
BARLOW, Mr. Colin John, FCA 1969; 9 Sandwich Road, Eccles, MANCHESTER, M30 9HD.
BARLOW, Mr. Colin Ronald, BEng ACA 1994; 14 Little Wolf Road, SUMMIT, NJ 07901, UNITED STATES.
BARLOW, Mr. David Garth, BA ACA 1993; 67 Morrab Road, PENZANCE, TR18 2QT.
BARLOW, Mr. David Jonathan, BSc ACA 1992; 15 Fennels Way, Flackwell Heath, HIGH WYCOMBE, BUCKINGHAMSHIRE, HP10 9BX.
BARLOW, Mrs. Debbie-Anne, ACA 1995; 3 Lawn Cottages, The Planks, SWINDON, SN3 1QR.
BARLOW, Mr. Dudley John, FCA 1955; 6 Kenlay Close, New Earswick, YORK, YO32 4DW. (Life Member)
BARLOW, Mr. Edgar, FCA 1958; Joseph Adamson (Hyde) Ltd, Estate Office, Adamson Industrial Estate, Croft Street, HYDE, CHESHIRE SK14 1EE.
BARLOW, Mr. Gavin Rosewarne, FCA 1969; 18 Staveley Road, LONDON, W4 3ES.
BARLOW, Henry Sackville, Esq OBE MA FCA 1969; P.O. Box 10139, 50704 KUALA LUMPUR, FEDERAL TERRITORY, MALAYSIA.
BARLOW, Mr. Ian Edward, MA FCA FTII 1976; c/o BHA, 75 High Holborn, LONDON, WC1V 6LS.
BARLOW, Mr. James Nevile Disney, BSc ACA 1992; 39 Riverside, CAMBRIDGE, CB5 8HL.
BARLOW, Mrs. Joanne Clare, BA ACA 2005; Britannia Bldg Soc, PO Box 20, LEEK, STAFFORDSHIRE, ST13 5RG.
BARLOW, Mr. John Charles, BA ACA 1983; 4 Granby Lane, Plungar, NOTTINGHAM, NG13 0JJ.
BARLOW, Mr. Kenneth Charles, FCA 1953; Tabor Hill Farm, Heasley Mill, SOUTH MOLTON, DEVON, EX36 3LQ. (Life Member)
BARLOW, Mrs. Laura Jane, BA ACA 1993; The Royal Bank of Scotland, 10th Floor, 280 Bishopsgate, LONDON, EC2M 4RB.
BARLOW, Mr. Leigh Anthony, ACA 2006; 109 Cranleigh Road, BOURNEMOUTH, BH6 5JY.
BARLOW, Mrs. Line Bolt, BSc ACA 1996; 14 Little Wolf Rd, SUMMIT, NJ 07901, UNITED STATES.
BARLOW, Mrs. Louise, BA ACA 1995; Ernst & Young Llp, 1 More London Place, LONDON, SE1 2AF.
BARLOW, Dr. Lyndsey Jane, BSc ACA 2006; 12 Moorfield Drive, WILMSLOW, CHESHIRE, SK9 6DL.
BARLOW, Mrs. Lynne Alison, BSc ACA 1992; Manchester Science Park, Kilburn House, Lloyd Street North, Manchester Science Park, MANCHESTER, M15 6SE.
BARLOW, Mr. Mark Thomas Duncan, BSc(Econ) ACA 1995; The Seckford Foundation Marryott House, Burkitt Road, WOODBRIDGE, SUFFOLK, IP12 4JJ.
BARLOW, Mr. Michael Jonathan, BSc ACA 2010; Flat 3 Arley Court, 21 Arley Hill, BRISTOL, BS6 5PH.
BARLOW, Miss. Naomi, ACA 2010; Flat 38 Garand Court, Eden Grove, LONDON, N7 8EB.
BARLOW, Miss. Nicola Helen, BSc ACA 2007; 1 Alfred Street, Eccles, MANCHESTER, M30 9QF.
BARLOW, Mr. Paul Michael, BSc ACA 2005; Hargreaves Services PLC, West Terrace, Esh Winning, DURHAM, DH7 9PT.
BARLOW, Mr. Paul Richard, BA ACA 1994; Network Rail, 1 Sheldon Square, PADDINGTON, W2 6TT.
BARLOW, Mr. Peter Charles, BA ACA CTA 1996; Fieldside Swellshill, Brimscombe, STROUD, GLOUCESTERSHIRE, GL5 2SW.
BARLOW, Mr. Peter David, BSc ACA 1996; 15 Sherwood Grove, Meols, WIRRAL, CH47 9SL.
BARLOW, Mr. Peter Douglas, FCA 1969; 8 The Walk, ABERDARE, MID GLAMORGAN, CF44 0RQ.
•BARLOW, Mr. Peter John, ACA 1980; Hadley & Co, Adelphi Chambers, 30 Hoghton Street, SOUTHPORT, PR9 0NZ.
•BARLOW, Mr. Roger William, BA FCA 1978; 35 Bower Road, Hale, ALTRINCHAM, CHESHIRE, WA15 9DU.
BARLOW, Mr. Ryan, BA(Hons) ACA 2009; with Ensors, Cardinal House, 46 St Nicholas Street, IPSWICH, IP1 1TT.
BARLOW, Miss. Sara Elizabeth Amy, ACA 2011; 131 Bury Road, Radcliffe, MANCHESTER, M26 2UT.
BARLOW, Mrs. Sarah Helen, ACA 2009; 101 Sprotbrough Road, DONCASTER, SOUTH YORKSHIRE, DN5 8BW.
BARLOW, Mr. Simon Christopher, BSc ACA 2005; 45A Route de L'Uche, 1255 VEYRIER, SWITZERLAND.
BARLOW, Mr. Simon Frank, BSc ACA 1991; 7 Tenter Drive, Standish, WIGAN, LANCASHIRE, WN6 0BN.
BARLOW, Mr. Stanley Lyon, FCA 1962; 28 Crabtree Close, BEACONSFIELD, HP9 1UQ. (Life Member)
BARLOW, Mr. Stephen, MBA BA ACA 1989; 37 Weeping Cross, STAFFORD, ST17 0DG.
BARLOW, Mr. Steven Foreshew, BA ACA 1980; c/o Dubai Holding, PO BOX 66000, DUBAI, UNITED ARAB EMIRATES.
BARLOW, Mr. Thomas Michael, FCA 1959; Goldby House, High Street, Mickleton, CHIPPING CAMPDEN, GLOUCESTERSHIRE, GL55 6SA. (Life Member)
•BARLTROP, Mr. Christopher Charles, FCA 1983; (Tax Fac), Beauchamp Charles, 145a Ashley Road, Hale, ALTRINCHAM, WA14 2UW.
BARMA, Mr. Abid, BSc ACA 2009; Flat 41 Harvard Court, Honeybourne Road, LONDON, NW6 1HL.
BARMA, Mr. Hanif, BSc ACA 1987; 70 Carlton Hill, LONDON, NW8 0ET.
BARMA, Dr. Hussein, MA BCL ACA 1992; Antofagasta Plc, 5 Princes Gate, LONDON, SW7 1QJ.
BARMA, Mr. Shabbir Yahya, FCA 1972; 3441 Riverplace Drive, EUGENE, OR 97401-1585, UNITED STATES. (Life Member)
BARMAKY, Mr. Mohammad Shariq Sayeed, FCA 1995; Deloitte & Touche, 6 Shenton Way, 32-00, DBS Building Tower Two, SINGAPORE 068809, SINGAPORE.
BARMAN, Mr. Jonathan Henry, FCA 1957; Three Gables, Nimms Meadow, Wantage Road, Great Shefford, HUNGERFORD, BERKSHIRE RG17 7BZ. (Life Member)
BARMBY, Mr. Mark Stephen, BSc ACA 1993; 24 Mill Grove, Lead Syke Hove Edge, BRIGHOUSE, HD6 2FA.
BARNABY, Mr. Ross Ashley, MA ACA 1998; 9 Avondale Avenue, LONDON, N12 8EP.
BARNACLE, Mr. Dennis George, FCA 1966; 3200 Binnacle Drive, Apt A4, NAPLES, FL 34103, UNITED STATES.
BARNACLE, Mr. Keith, FCA 1969; 14 Tudor Court, Prestwich, MANCHESTER, M25 0EP.
BARNACLE, Mr. Roger, FCA 1973; 27 Archery Fields, Odiham, HOOK, HAMPSHIRE, RG29 1AE.
•BARNACLE, Mr. Vaughan, BA(Hons) ACA 2002; Anchorage, 17 Red Lion Court, Victoria Street, HEREFORD, HR4 0BZ.
BARNARD, Miss. Anne Trevenen, BA ACA 1986; 37 Percy Road, Shepherds Bush, LONDON, W12 9PX.
BARNARD, Mr. Bruce Peter, ACA 1996; Michelmersh House Northfield Avenue, Lower Shiplake, HENLEY-ON-THAMES, OXFORDSHIRE, RG9 3PD.
•BARNARD, Mrs. Catherine Natasha, ACA FCCA 2007; with Wellden Turnbull LLP, 78 Portsmouth Road, COBHAM, SURREY, KT11 1PP.
BARNARD, Mr. Christopher John, FCA 1975; 175 Tessall Lane, Northfield, BIRMINGHAM, B31 5ED. (Life Member)
BARNARD, Mrs. Felicity, ACA 2010; 17 Frances Gibbs Gardens, Whitnash, LEAMINGTON SPA, WARWICKSHIRE, CV31 2TN.
BARNARD, Mr. Glenn Norman, BSc ACA 1996; 18 Ivel Close, Langford, BIGGLESWADE, BEDFORDSHIRE, SG18 9RW.
BARNARD, Mr. James Alan, MSc ACA 2005; State Street Bank & Trust, 20 Churchill Place, LONDON, E14 5HJ.
BARNARD, Mrs. Joannah, BA(Hons) ACA 2007; Calle Fatiga 42, 11310 SOTOGRANDE, CADIZ, SPAIN.
•BARNARD, Mr. John Charles, FCA 1973; J. Barnard, Brelston Court, Marstow, ROSS-ON-WYE, HEREFORDSHIRE, HR9 6HF.
BARNARD, Mr. John Raymond, FCA 1973; The Yellow House, c/o Island Rentals The Anchorage, Dockyard Drive, ENGLISH HARBOUR, ANTIGUA AND BARBUDA.
BARNARD, Mr. Jonathan James, ACA 2009; 9 South Road, Portishead, BRISTOL, BS20 7DW.
•BARNARD, Ms. Julia, ACA 1983; Ford Campbell Freedman LLP, 34 Park Cross Street, LEEDS, LS1 2QH.
BARNARD, Mr. Justin, MA ACA 1988; 9 Lion Lane, Thurton, NORWICH, NR14 6HL.
•BARNARD, Mr. Keith, ACA 1984; K. Barnard, 25 Rosemary Drive, Napsbury Park, ST. ALBANS, HERTFORDSHIRE, AL2 1UD.
BARNARD, Mr. Kevin, BSc FCA 1999; 26 Grousemoor Drive, ASHINGTON, NE63 8LU.
BARNARD, Mrs. Margaret Lynne, BA ACA 1980; 1 Shirley Road, WALLINGTON, SM6 9QB.
•BARNARD, Mr. Martin Trevor, FCA 1982; 89 West Common Gardens, SCUNTHORPE, SOUTH HUMBERSIDE, DN17 1EJ.
BARNARD, Mr. Michael John, FCA CTA 1964; 195 Normanston Drive, LOWESTOFT, SUFFOLK, NR32 2PY.
BARNARD, Miss. Patricia Angela, BA ACA 1995; 53 Elizabeth Road, HENLEY-ON-THAMES, OXFORDSHIRE, RG9 1RA.
BARNARD, Mr. Philip John, BSc ACA 1979; Flat 143, Taplow, Thurlow Street, LONDON, SE17 2UJ.
•BARNARD, Mr. Roger Leslie, LLM LLB FCA 1971; with RSM Tenon Limited, Vantage, Victoria Street, BASINGSTOKE, RG21 3BT.
BARNARD, Mr. Samuel, ACA 2011; Armida Ltd, Bell Walk House, Bell Walk, UCKFIELD, EAST SUSSEX, TN22 5DQ.
BARNARD, Miss. Tracy Jane, BA ACA 1997; 166 Watford Road, Chiswell Green, ST. ALBANS, AL2 3EB.
•BARNARD, Mrs. Victoria Carol, BSc(Hons) ACA 2000; Victoria Barnard Accountancy, 13 Pitfold Avenue, HASLEMERE, SURREY, GU27 1PN.
BARNARD, Mr. William Sedgwick, MA FCA 1969; 2/63 Muston Street, MOSMAN, NSW 2088, AUSTRALIA.
BARNARD, Mr. William Thomas, FCA 1968; (Tax Fac), Unit 7a Wootton Business Park, Whiterails Road Wootton Bridge, RYDE, ISLE OF WIGHT, PO33 4RH.
•BARNASIUK, Mr. Stephen Anthony, BSc FCA 1983; 37 Juniper Close, Cufaude Village Chineham, BASINGSTOKE, RG24 8XH.
•BARNBROOK, Mr. Gareth Neil, FCA 1975; (Tax Fac), Barnbrook Sinclair Limited, 1 High Street, Knaphill, WOKING, SURREY, GU21 2PG. See also The Barnbrook Sinclair Partnership LLP
BARNBROOK, Mr. John, BA FCA 1965; Las Margaritas 4, Avenida Fuerteventura, 35660 CORRALEJO, SPAIN.
BARNBY, Mr. David George, FCA 1948; P.O. Box 1229, NORTH RIDING, 2162, SOUTH AFRICA. (Life Member)
BARNBY, Mr. Ian Eager Guy, FCA 1954; Tamaroa, Blacksmith Lane, Chilworth, GUILDFORD, GU4 8NF. (Life Member)
BARNES, Mr. Adam Robert, BA ACA 1991; British Petroleum Co Ltd, 4 Longwalk Road Stockley Park, UXBRIDGE, UB11 1FE.
BARNES, Mrs. Alexandra, BA ACA 2006; 16 Robins Hill, HITCHIN, HERTFORDSHIRE, SG4 9FE.
BARNES, Mrs. Alison Mackie, FCA 1975; 5 The Links, Burleigh Road, ASCOT, SL5 7TN.
BARNES, Mrs. Alison Mary, BSc ACA 1988; 29 Hambledon Vale, EPSOM, KT18 7DA.
BARNES, Miss. Alison Mary, BSc ACA 1990; Baker Tilly, 2 Whitehall Quay, LEEDS, LS1 4HG.
BARNES, Mrs. Andrea Karen, BA ACA 1996; (Tax Fac), Cadhay, 2 Coton Road, Walton-On-Trent, SWADLINCOTE, DE12 8NL.
BARNES, Mr. Andrew James, BA ACA 1995; Investec Bank (UK) Ltd, 2 Gresham Street, LONDON, EC2V 7QP.
BARNES, Mr. Andrew John, MBA BA FCA 1989; Argent Holdings Ltd, 9 Hatton Street, LONDON, NW8 8PL.
BARNES, Mr. Andrew Paul, ACA 2008; Barnes Roffe Llp Leytonstone House, Hanbury Drive, LONDON, E11 1GA.
BARNES, Mr. Andrew Thomas, BA ACA 2000; 58 Eastgrove Avenue, Sharples, BOLTON, BL1 7HA.
BARNES, Miss. Angela Vilma, ACA 1989; 33 Winterberry Way, Caversham Heights, READING, RG4 7XA.
BARNES, Mrs. Ann, ACA 1980; Thorneyknowe, Penton, CARLISLE, CA6 5RY.
BARNES, Mrs. Ann Louise, ACA 2006; Marcussen Consulting LLP, Bath Brewery, Toll Bridge Road, BATH, BA1 7DE.
BARNES, Mrs. Anna Elisabeth, BA ACA 2006; 4S.3 Redgrave Court, Health & Safety Executive Redgrave Court, Merton Road, BOOTLE, MERSEYSIDE, L20 7HS.
BARNES, Ms. Anna Marie, BA ACA 2002; Ove Arup & Partners 13 Fitzroy Street, LONDON, W1T 4BQ.
•BARNES, Mr. Anthony Gwynne Black, FCA 1973; A.G. Barnes & Co, 147 Forest Road, TUNBRIDGE WELLS, TN2 5EX. See also AGB Services Ltd
BARNES, Mr. Anthony Richard, BCom ACA 1997; Cadhay, 2 Coton Road, Walton-On-Trent, SWADLINCOTE, DE12 8NL.
BARNES, Mr. Antony Jonathan Ward, BSc FCA FCT 1989; Experian Group Services Ltd, Newenham House, Northern Cross, Malahide Road, DUBLIN, COUNTY DUBLIN IRELAND.
•BARNES, Mr. Arthur Rennie, BA FCA 1970; A R Barnes, P O Box 15046, Lankata, NAIROBI, 00509, KENYA.
BARNES, Mrs. Barbara Joyce, FCA 1987; (Tax Fac), Deodar, 35 Townend, CATERHAM, CR3 5UJ.
BARNES, Mr. Bradley John, ACA 2006; 42 Seaforth Avenue, Somerton Park, ADELAIDE, SA 5044, AUSTRALIA.
•BARNES, Mrs. Caroline Joanne, BSc ACA 1990; Caroline Barnes, College Farm, Creeting Hills, Creeting St. Mary, IPSWICH, IP6 8PX.
BARNES, Mrs. Caroline Marie, BA ACA 1998; Paddock View Middle Road, Great Plumstead, NORWICH, NR13 5EG.
BARNES, Mrs. Catrin Jane, BA ACA 1993; 4 Righton Close, Charvil, READING, RG10 9UN.
BARNES, Mr. Charles Antony, FCA 1950; (Member of Council 1981 - 1991), 3 Selwyn House, Manor Fields, LONDON, SW15 3LR. (Life Member)
BARNES, Mrs. Charlotte Alixandra, BSc ACA 2006; 14 Thomas Road, North Baddesley, SOUTHAMPTON, SO52 9PT.
•BARNES, Mr. Christopher David, FCA 1974; with Hunter Accountants Limited, 3 Kings Court, Little King Street, BRISTOL, BS1 4HW.
BARNES, Mr. Christopher Howard, FCA 1969; 11 Hepplewhite Close, Baughurst, TADLEY, RG26 5HD. (Life Member)
BARNES, Mr. Christopher James, BA ACA 1995; Terra Firma Capital Partners, 2 More London Riverside, LONDON, SE1 2AP.
BARNES, Mr. Christopher John, BSc ACA 2004; with KPMG LLP, 1 The Embankment, Neville Street, LEEDS, LS1 4DW.
BARNES, Mrs. Claire Elizabeth Mary, MA FCA 1989; 10 The Croft, East Hagbourne, DIDCOT, OXFORDSHIRE, OX11 9LS.
BARNES, Miss. Claire Marguerite, BSc ACA 1994; 26 Orlando Road, LONDON, SW4 0LF.
BARNES, Mr. Colin Cooper, FCA 1943; 8 Alston Road, Bessacarr, DONCASTER, DN4 7HB. (Life Member)
BARNES, Mr. David Chapman, FCA 1967; with TTR Barnes Financial Services Limited, 3-5 Grange Terrace, Stockton Road, SUNDERLAND, SR2 7DG.
BARNES, Mr. David John, FCA 1966; Hunters Dene, 8 Croydon Lane, BANSTEAD, SM7 3AS.
•BARNES, Mr. David John, BSc ACA 1989; Deloitte LLP, Hill House, 1 Little New Street, LONDON, EC4A 3TR. See also Deloitte & Touche LLP
BARNES, Mr. David John Delacourt, FCA 1971; (Tax Fac), with Wheatley Pearce Limited, 11 Winchester Place, North Street, POOLE, DORSET, BH15 1NX.
•BARNES, Mr. David Leonard, FCA 1965; Edwin Smith, 32 Queens Road, READING, RG1 4AU.
•BARNES, Mr. David Lionel, BA FCA 1986; Grant Thornton UK LLP, Grant Thornton House, 22 Melton Street, Euston Square, LONDON, NW1 2EP. See also Grant Thornton LLP
BARNES, Mrs. Deborah Anne May, BSc ACA 1995; 64 Kings Road, CHATHAM, NJ 07928-2109, UNITED STATES.
BARNES, Mr. Derek Talbot, FCA 1968; Rua Santa Cristina 322, Jardim Paulistano, SAO PAULO, 01443-020 SP, BRAZIL. (Life Member)
BARNES, Mrs. Diana Clare, BSc FCA 1970; Westwood Garth, Brough Sowerby, KIRKBY STEPHEN, CUMBRIA, CA17 4EG.
BARNES, Mrs. Diane Patricia, BSc ACA 1998; Hill House, Hook Heath Road, WOKING, GU22 0LB.

•**BARNES, Mr. Duncan Jonathan, MA FCA MAE QDR** *1980;* Haines Watts Exeter LLP, 3 Southernhay West, EXETER, EX1 1JG.

BARNES, Mrs. Elizabeth Kathleen, BA ACA *1988;* 91 Rigdale Close, Eggbuckland, PLYMOUTH, PL6 5PR.

BARNES, Mr. Ernest William, FCA *1952;* 12 Forest Park, Maresfield, UCKFIELD, EAST SUSSEX, TN22 2NA. (Life Member)

BARNES, Mrs. Fiona Constance, ACA *1990;* Howard de Walden Estates Ltd, 23 Queen Anne Street, LONDON, W1G 9DL.

•**BARNES, Mr. Geoffrey Frederick, FCA FCCA** *1977;* (Member of Council 2002 - 2004), 17 Perivale Lodge, Perivale Lane, GREENFORD, UB6 8TW.

•**BARNES, Mr. Geoffrey Kenneth, FCA** *1976;* (Tax Fac), Langley Associates, Milton Heath House, Westcott Road, DORKING, SURREY, RH4 3NB.

•**BARNES, Mr. Geoffrey Norman, FCA** *1980;* (Tax Fac), Geoffrey N. Barnes, 12 Fratton Road, PORTSMOUTH, PO1 5BX.

BARNES, Mr. Gerald William, FCA *1956;* Sweynes, 1 Church Crescent, Sproughton, IPSWICH, IP8 3BJ. (Life Member)

BARNES, Mr. Graham, BSc ACA *1996;* 20 Vicarage Park, Redlynch, SALISBURY, SP5 2JZ.

BARNES, Mr. Graham Leslie, BSc ACA *1980;* 104 Tressillian Road, LONDON, SE4 1XX.

•**BARNES, Mr. Graham Paul, FCA** *1984;* (Tax Fac), Graham Barnes, 19A The Nook, Anstey, LEICESTER, LE7 7AZ.

BARNES, Miss. Hannah Kate, BSc ACA *2007;* with PricewaterhouseCoopers LLP, 9 Greyfriars Road, READING, RG1 1JG.

•**BARNES, Mrs. Heather Jane, ACA** *1986;* Heather Barnes, 1 Nottingham Road, Ravenshead, NOTTINGHAM, NG15 9HG.

BARNES, Mr. Hugh Edward Michael, FCA *1958;* Hamgate Farm House, Penny Street, STURMINSTER NEWTON, DORSET, DT10 1DF. (Life Member)

•**BARNES, Mr. Ian James, BSc ACA** *2003;* Deloitte LLP, 3 Victoria Square, Victoria Street, ST. ALBANS, HERTFORDSHIRE, AL1 3TF. See also Deloitte & Touche LLP

BARNES, Mr. Ian Kenneth, BA FCA *1998;* 100 Glapthorn Road, Oundle, PETERBOROUGH, PE8 4PS.

BARNES, Mr. Ian Sinclair, BSc FCA *1991;* 39 Smiths Way, Water Orton, BIRMINGHAM, B46 1TW.

BARNES, Mr. James Jackson, FCA *1966;* 2 Worden Close, LEYLAND, PR25 1FL.

BARNES, Mr. James William, BSc FCA *1975;* Claverstone, Coombe, WOTTON-UNDER-EDGE, GL12 7ND. (Life Member)

BARNES, Mrs. Jane Michelle, BA ACA *1997;* Wreaks End House, Wreaks End, BROUGHTON-IN-FURNESS, CUMBRIA, LA20 6BS.

BARNES, Mr. Jeffrey John, BA ACA *2002;* 14 Thomas Road, North Baddesley, SOUTHAMPTON, SO52 9PT.

BARNES, Mrs. Jennifer, BSc ACA *2003;* 5 Tutnall Grange, Tutnall, BROMSGROVE, WORCESTERSHIRE, B60 1NN.

•**BARNES, Mrs. Jenny Christine, FCA ATII** *1987;* Jenny Barnes & Co Limited, 1st Floor Offices, 2A Highfield Road, RINGWOOD, HAMPSHIRE, BH24 1RQ.

•**BARNES, Mr. Jeremy, BA FCA** *1986;* Smith & Williamson Ltd, Portwall Place, Portwall Lane, BRISTOL, BS1 6NA.

•**BARNES, Mr. Jeremy John Kentish, FCA** *1970;* Jeremy Barnes & Co, Outmoor Barn, Hale House Lane, Churt, FARNHAM, GU10 2NG.

BARNES, Mr. Jeremy Richard Delano, BEng FCA *1998;* 1510 Granada Blvd, CORAL GABLES, FL 33134, UNITED STATES.

BARNES, Mr. Jeremy Ronald Talbot, BSc ACA *2010;* Rua Santa Cristina, 322 Jardim Paulistano, SAO PAULO, 01443-020, BRAZIL.

BARNES, Mrs. Joanna Louise, ACA *2007;* Grant Thornton, 5th Floor Bermuda House, Dr Roys Drive, PO Box 1044, GEORGETOWN, GRAND CAYMAN KY1-1102 CAYMAN ISLANDS.

•**BARNES, Mr. John Charles Radcliffe, ACA** *1981;* (Tax Fac), Barnes Business Services Ltd, 30 Blake Hall Road, MIRFIELD, WEST YORKSHIRE, WF14 9NS.

BARNES, Mr. John Christopher, BSc ACA *1985;* Lanner Group Ltd The Oaks, Clews Road, REDDITCH, WORCESTERSHIRE, B98 7ST.

BARNES, Mr. John Down, MA FCA *1959;* 9 Ingham Close, MIRFIELD, WF14 9NP. (Life Member)

•**BARNES, Mr. John Terry, FCA** *1982;* Baker Tilly Tax & Advisory Services LLP, Marlborough House, Victoria Road South, CHELMSFORD, CM1 1LN. See also Baker Tilly UK Audit LLP

BARNES, Mr. Jonathan William, BA ACA *1979;* Brightside, Middle Common, Kington Langley, CHIPPENHAM, SN15 5NW.

BARNES, Mr. Joseph Harry George, FCA *1953;* Tudor Court, 29 Grimwade Avenue, CROYDON, CR0 5DJ. (Life Member)

BARNES, Mrs. Josephine Margaret, BSc ACA *1990;* Limebeers Oakwell Farm, Kings Nympton, UMBERLEIGH, EX37 9TE.

BARNES, Ms. Julie Elizabeth, BA ACA *2002;* 23 Leyland Avenue, MANCHESTER, M20 6EW.

BARNES, Mrs. Katherine, BA ACA *2002;* 76 Woodfield Lane, Lower Cambourne, CAMBRIDGE, CB23 6DS.

BARNES, Mr. Kenneth, FCA *1951;* New House, Oxenden Square, HERNE BAY, CT6 8TN. (Life Member)

•**BARNES, Mr. Leslie Clifton, ACA** *1979;* CK, No 4 Castle Court 2, Castlegate Way, DUDLEY, WEST MIDLANDS, DY1 4RH.

BARNES, Mrs. Linda Mary, FCA *1983;* with ICAEW, Metropolitan House, 321 Avebury Boulevard, MILTON KEYNES, MK9 2FZ.

BARNES, Mr. Marc Christopher, BSc(Econ) ACA *1998;* 38 Wolseley Road, GODALMING, SURREY, GU7 3EA.

BARNES, Mrs. Maria Luisa, BSc ACA *1992;* 30 Park Road, Chiswick, LONDON, W4 3HH.

BARNES, Mr. Matthew, BSc ACA *2004;* with Deloitte LLP, Hill House, 1 Little New Street, LONDON, EC4A 3TR.

•**BARNES, Mr. Michael, BA ACA** *1990;* Pullan Barnes Limited, Stephenson House, Richard Street, Hetton-le-Hole, HOUGHTON LE SPRING, TYNE AND WEAR DH5 9HW.

•**BARNES, Mr. Michael John, ACA** *1978;* (Tax Fac), Mike Barnes Ltd, Unit 3 Waterford Industrial Estate, Mill Lane, Great Massingham, KING'S LYNN, NORFOLK PE32 2HT. See also AIMS - Mike Barnes

BARNES, Mr. Michael Wayne, FCA *1969;* 14 Grange Park, Westbury-On-Trym, BRISTOL, BS9 4BP.

BARNES, Mrs. Muriel, BEng ACA *2000;* 3 Chipstead Park Close, SEVENOAKS, KENT, TN13 2SJ.

BARNES, Mr. Paul Edward, BSc ACA *1993;* McIntyre Hudson, Moulsham Court, 39 Moulsham Street, CHELMSFORD, ESSEX, CM2 0HY.

BARNES, Mr. Paul Edward, BSc ACA *1991;* Budecska 44, 12000 2 PRAGUE, CZECH REPUBLIC.

BARNES, Mr. Peter Alan, ACA *1995;* Flat 5, 28 Belsize Park, LONDON, NW3 4DX.

BARNES, Mr. Peter Anthony, BSc ACA MCT *1988;* 29 Hambledon Vale, EPSOM, KT18 7DA.

BARNES, Mr. Peter Michael, FCA *1970;* 15 Eccles Road, Chapel-en-le-Frith, HIGH PEAK, DERBYSHIRE, SK23 9RP. (Life Member)

BARNES, Mr. Philip Andrew, ACA *1984;* Cove Nest, 5 Rocky Ridge Road, SMITHS HS02, BERMUDA.

•**BARNES, Mr. Philip Michael, FCA** *1957;* (Tax Fac), Philip Barnes & Co Ltd, The Old Council Chambers, Halford Street, TAMWORTH, B79 7RB.

BARNES, Mrs. Rachel Elisabeth, BA ACA *2006;* 58 Highfield Road, LYMM, CHESHIRE, WA13 0EE.

BARNES, Mr. Raymond George Lennie, FCA *1969;* Le Chalet Rosat, La Frasse, 1660 CHATEAU -D'OEX, SWITZERLAND.

BARNES, Mr. Riccardo George, FCA CTA *1972;* 5 The Links, Burleigh Road, ASCOT, SL5 7TN. (Life Member)

BARNES, Mr. Richard John, MEng ACA *2002;* 83 Claughton Avenue, LEYLAND, LANCASHIRE, PR25 5TN.

BARNES, Mr. Richard John, BA ACA *1995;* Copse Edge, Forest Road, East Horsley, LEATHERHEAD, SURREY, KT24 5DH.

BARNES, Mr. Richard Nigel, FCA *1967;* 42 Victoria Avenue, SURBITON, KT6 5DW.

BARNES, Mr. Robert Bruce, BSc FCA *1976;* Flat 14 Fielding Court, 28 Earlham Street, LONDON, WC2H 9LN.

BARNES, Mr. Robert Edward, FCA *1969;* The Old House Carters Green, Matching, HARLOW, CM17 0NX.

BARNES, Mr. Robert Ogle Ball, MA FCA *1970;* 14 Chishill Road, Heydon, ROYSTON, HERTFORDSHIRE, SG8 8PW.

•**BARNES, Mr. Robin Richard, BA FCA** *1990;* J W Hinks, 19 Highfield Road, Edgbaston, BIRMINGHAM, B15 3BH.

BARNES, Mr. Ronald Henry, FCA *1957;* 51 Vinery Road, BURY ST.EDMUNDS, IP33 2LB. (Life Member)

BARNES, Dr. Ronnie, MA MSc ACA *1990;* Apartment G/3 Belgrave Court, 36 Westferry Circus, LONDON, E14 8RJ.

BARNES, Mrs. Rosemary Sarah, BSc ACA *2003;* with BDO LLP, 55 Baker Street, LONDON, W1U 7EU.

BARNES, Mrs. Ruth Elma, BA ACA *1993;* 29 Spinfield Park, MARLOW, BUCKINGHAMSHIRE, SL7 2DD.

BARNES, Mrs. Sarah Caroline, BA ACA *1993;* Trevone, 86 Lady Lane, Shirley, SOLIHULL, WEST MIDLANDS, B90 1RJ.

BARNES, Mrs. Sarah Louise, BSc ACA *2006;* Smartfocus, 1 Redcliff Street, BRISTOL, BS1 6NP.

•**BARNES, Mr. Scott, MA FCA** *1982;* Grant Thornton UK LLP, Grant Thornton House, 22 Melton Street, Euston Square, LONDON, NW1 2EP. See also Grant Thornton LLP

BARNES, Mr. Simon Royston, BA FCA *1987;* Badgers End, Dog Lane, Witcombe, GLOUCESTER, GL3 4UG.

•**BARNES, Mr. Simon William Stewart, MA FCA** *1973;* Walcot House, 139 Kennington Road, LONDON, SE11 6SF.

•**BARNES, Mr. Stephen, MA ACA** *1988;* PricewaterhouseCoopers LLP, Hays Galleria, 1 Hays Lane, LONDON, SE1 2RD. See also PricewaterhouseCoopers

•**BARNES, Mr. Stephen Charles, BSc FCA** *1979;* (Tax Fac), Warr & Co, Mynshull House, 78 Churchgate, STOCKPORT, SK1 1YJ. See also Warr & Co Limited

BARNES, Mr. Stephen John, ACA *1992;* 85 Woodhurst Drive, Standish, WIGAN, LANCASHIRE, WN6 0RW.

BARNES, Mr. Stephen John, BA ACA *1992;* Sovereign House, Howard Smith Paper Ltd Rhosili Road, Brackmills Industrial Estate, NORTHAMPTON, NN4 7JE.

BARNES, Mr. Thomas William, ACA *2008;* 9 Pear Tree Avenue, Long Ashton, BRISTOL, BS41 9FF.

BARNES, Mr. Timothy James, BEng ACA *1993;* 64 Kings Road, CHATHAM, NJ 07928-2109, UNITED STATES.

BARNES, Mr. Timothy Michael James, BA(Hons) ACA *2009;* 79 Bromedale Avenue, Mulbarton, NORWICH, NORFOLK, NR14 8GG.

BARNES, Mr. Timothy Miles Henry, BSc ACA *1992;* Waterlands, Meadows Road, Brookfields Park, Manvers, ROTHERHAM, SOUTH YORKSHIRE S63 5DJ.

BARNES, Ms. Tracey Anne, BA ACA *1989;* Diageo Plc Lakeside Drive, Park Royal, LONDON, NW10 7HQ.

BARNES, Mr. Trevor Colin, BA ACA *1986;* 54a Freshfield Road, Formby, LIVERPOOL, L37 3HW.

BARNES, Mr. Trevor George Enwright, FCA *1968;* Yarbury, The Park, Yatton, BRISTOL, BS49 4AB. (Life Member)

BARNES, Mr. Victor John, FCA *1955;* 17 Long Rede Lane, Barming, MAIDSTONE, ME16 9LB. (Life Member)

BARNES, Mrs. Wendy Ann, BA FCA *1989;* 175 London Road, Wollaston, WELLINGBOROUGH, NORTHAMPTONSHIRE, NN29 7QS.

BARNES, Mr. Wilfred Stuart Delano, FCA *1957;* Herondel, Ferry Lane, St Catherines, GUILDFORD, SURREY, GU2 4EE. (Life Member)

BARNES, Mr. William Albert, FCA *1956;* 83 The Grove, WEST WICKHAM, BR4 9LA. (Life Member)

•**BARNES, Mr. William David, BSc ACA** *1984;* College Farm, Creeting Hills, Creeting St. Mary, IPSWICH, IP6 8PX.

BARNES, Mr. William Peter, FCA *1975;* Barmanco Ltd, The Grange, Neston Road, NESTON, CH64 7TL.

BARNES, Mr. William Robert, BCom FCA *1982;* The Pines, 60 Kneeton Road, East Bridgford, NOTTINGHAM, NG13 8PJ.

BARNES-AUSTIN, Mr. James David, BA ACA *1997;* Ogilvy Group UK, 10 Cabot Square, LONDON, E14 4QB.

BARNES-CLAY, Ms. Catherine Emma, MSc BEng ACA *2004;* 55 Malham Drive, KETTERING, NORTHAMPTONSHIRE, NN16 9FS.

BARNET, Mr. Bernard, FCA *1967;* 98 Stradbroke Grove, Clayhall, ILFORD, ESSEX, IG5 0DL.

BARNETT, Miss. Alice, BA ACA *2007;* 142a Tachbrook Street, LONDON, SW1V 2NE.

BARNETT, Mr. Andrew, FCA *1974;* Avenue Soret 25, 1203 GENEVA, SWITZERLAND. (Life Member)

BARNETT, Mr. Andrew John, BA FCA *1974;* 42 Firle Court, Yeomanry Close, EPSOM, KT17 4DD.

•**BARNETT, Mr. Anthony John, FCA** *1976;* Barnett Spooner, The Old Steppe House, Brighton Road, GODALMING, SURREY, GU7 1NS.

BARNETT, Mr. Bernard Howard, FCA *1973;* 16 South View Crescent, Gants Hill, ILFORD, IG2 6DG.

BARNETT, Mr. Brian John, FCA *1959;* Bramblewood Cottage, Pains Hill, OXTED, RH8 0RG. (Life Member)

BARNETT, Mr. Carl Jonathan, ACA *2003;* 158 Apperley Road, Apperley Bridge, BRADFORD, BD10 9TP.

•**BARNETT, Mrs. Carole Julie, FCA** *1977;* (Tax Fac), Carole J. Barnett, 102 Kimberley Park Road, FALMOUTH, TR11 2DQ.

BARNETT, Miss. Catherine Lucy, BA ACA *2007;* Grant Thornton UK Llp, 30 Finsbury Square, LONDON, EC2A 1AG.

•**BARNETT, Mr. Christopher, MChem ACA CTA** *2003;* Rees Pollock, 35 New Bridge Street, LONDON, EC4V 6BW.

BARNETT, Mr. David James, BSc ACA *2003;* 20 Thorncroft Avenue, Astley, Tyldesley, MANCHESTER, M29 7TA.

BARNETT, Mr. David Jeffrey, BSc FCA *1980;* (Tax Fac), 2 Moore Close, CAMBRIDGE, CB4 1ZP.

•**BARNETT, Mr. David John, FCA** *1984;* David J Barnett, The Point, Granite Way, Mountsorrel, LOUGHBOROUGH, LEICESTERSHIRE LE12 7TZ.

BARNETT, Mr. David Victor, MA FCA *1983;* 39 Charney Avenue, ABINGDON, OX14 2NY.

BARNETT, Dr. Eric Charles, MBChB ACA *1992;* 303 Crabtree Crossing, CARY, NC 27513, UNITED STATES.

BARNETT, Mr. Gareth, BSc ACA *2007;* 1 Shrewbridge Road, NANTWICH, CHESHIRE, CW5 5TG.

BARNETT, Mr. Gerald Nelson, FCA *1956;* 57 Wychwood Avenue, EDGWARE, HA8 6TQ. (Life Member)

BARNETT, Mr. Gerald Robert, FCA *1981;* 92 Gordon Avenue, STANMORE, HA7 3QS.

BARNETT, Mr. Glenn Stuart, BA FCA *1978;* P.O. Box 3354, ROAD TOWN, TORTOLA ISLAND, VIRGIN ISLANDS (BRITISH).

BARNETT, Mr. Guy, ACA *2009;* 4 Hollybank, Guiseley, LEEDS, LS20 8RA.

•**BARNETT, Mr. Ian David, FCA** *1980;* 12 Hobson Road, Selly Park, BIRMINGHAM, B29 7QA.

BARNETT, Mr. Ian Duncan, FCA *1965;* The Bungalow, Alveston Road, Old Down Tockington, BRISTOL, BS32 4PH.

BARNETT, Mr. Ian Richard, ACA *1988;* Brandlesholme Old Hall, Brandlesholme Road, BURY, BL8 4LS.

BARNETT, Mrs. Jane Mary, BA ACA *1990;* 10 Water House Lane, Shirley, SOUTHAMPTON, SO15 8QD.

•①**BARNETT, Mr. Jeremy William, FCA** *1975;* 32 Tunbridge Lane, Bottisham, CAMBRIDGE, CB5 9DU.

BARNETT, Mr. John Robert, FCA *1967;* Rothmans Benson & Hedges Inc, 1500 Don Mills Road, TORONTO M3B 3L1, ON, CANADA.

BARNETT, Miss. Julia Christina, BA ACA *2010;* 53 Derwent Road, Stretford, MANCHESTER, M32 0EB.

BARNETT, Mr. Keith Malcolm, BA FCA *1963;* Riesensessel 17, 29308 WINSEN-ALLER, GERMANY.

BARNETT, Miss. Laura, BA ACA *2007;* with PricewaterhouseCoopers, 9 Greyfriars Road, READING, RG1 1JG.

BARNETT, Mr. Lionel Philip John, FCA *1966;* Seven Springs, Latteridge Road, Iron Acton, BRISTOL, BS37 9TL. (Life Member)

BARNETT, Mr. Luke, BSc ACA *2011;* Wychelm, 15 Glenrose Avenue, Ravensden, BEDFORD, MK44 2SB.

•**BARNETT, Mr. Malcolm Arthur, FCA** *1975;* Barnett & Co, 19-21 New Road, WILLENHALL, WV13 2BG. See also JPO Associates Limited

BARNETT, Mr. Marc James, BSc(Hons) ACA *2001;* 10 Constable Way, College Town, SANDHURST, BERKSHIRE, GU47 0FE.

BARNETT, Mr. Michael, FCA CTA *1961;* Urb Lomas de Sierra, Blanca Blq Jaen Apt 2a, Ctr Istan, 29602 MARBELLA, MALAGA, SPAIN. (Life Member)

•**BARNETT, Mr. Michael Stuart, BA FCA** *1985;* Richard Anthony & Company, 13 Station Road, Finchley, LONDON, N3 2SB.

BARNETT, Ms. Natasha Faye, BSc ACA *2001;* 23 Fawn Drive, North Lane, ALDERSHOT, HAMPSHIRE, GU12 4FW.

BARNETT, Mr. Nicholas James, BSc ACA *1999;* 12 Rythe Close, Claygate, ESHER, SURREY, KT10 9DD.

BARNETT, Mr. Nicholas Peter, ACA *2009;* Flat K/5, Du Cane Court, Balham High Road, LONDON, SW17 7JY.

BARNETT, Mr. Paul Andrew Hannington, BSc(Hons) ACA *2004;* Millennium Inorganic Chemicals Limited, PO Box 26, GRIMSBY, SOUTH HUMBERSIDE, DN41 8DP.

BARNETT, Mr. Paul David, BSc ACA *2005;* 34a Lucerne Road, LONDON, N5 1TZ.

BARNETT, Mr. Paul Wakefield, BSc ACA *1994;* 12 Manor Green, STRATFORD-UPON-AVON, CV37 7ES.

BARNETT, Mr. Peter Denzil, MBE BA FCA *1978;* 12 Seville Street, Lane Cove, SYDNEY, NSW 2066, AUSTRALIA.

BARNETT, Mr. Peter William, BSc FCA *1974;* 50 Tithby Road, Bingham, NOTTINGHAM, NG13 8GP.

•**BARNETT, Mr. Philip Anthony, FCA** *1967;* Barnett Ravenscroft LLP, 13 Portland Road, Edgbaston, BIRMINGHAM, B16 9HN.

BARNETT, Mrs. Rachael Jane, BSc ACA *2005;* 52 Salop Road, LONDON, E17 7HT.

•BARNETT, Mr. Richard James, LLB ACA 2004; RB Chartered Accountant Ltd, Offices 1 & 2 Top Corner, Market Street, PENKRIDGE, STAFFORDSHIRE, ST19 5DH.
BARNETT, Mr. Ronald, FCA 1975; The Blakeney Hotel, The Quay, Blakeney, HOLT, NORFOLK, NR25 7NE.
BARNETT, Miss. Sarah Louise, BA ACA 2001; 1 Southcliffe Cottage, Southcliffe Road, STOCKPORT, CHESHIRE, SK5 7EE.
BARNETT, Mr. Spencer, BA ACA 2007; with Mazars LLP, 8 New Fields, 2 Stinsford Road, Nuffield, POOLE, DORSET BH17 0NF.
BARNETT, Mr. Stuart James, BSc ACA 1998; 21 Teddington Road, Hampton, MELBOURNE, VIC 3188, AUSTRALIA.
•BARNETT, Mr. Stuart William, BSc FCA 1977; Deloitte LLP, Hill House, 1 Little New Street, LONDON, EC4A 3TR. See also Deloitte & Touche LLP
BARNETT, Mr. Wayne, FCA ACIS 1975; (Tax Fac), Dwr Cymru Welsh Water, Pentwyn Road, Nelson, TREHARRIS, CF46 6LY.
•BARNETT, Mr. Wayne Richard, FCA 1976; Actinium Ltd, Protex House, 25-27 School Lane, Bushey Heath, BUSHEY, HERTFORDSHIRE WD23 1SS.
BARNEY, Mr. Christopher Keith, ACA 1994; 9 Warwick Road, READING, RG2 7AX.
BARNEY, Mr. John Milward, FCA 1954; 7 Church Farm, Colney, NORWICH, NR4 7TX. (Life Member)
BARNFATHER, Miss. Anna Elizabeth, MA ACA 1998; Jefferies International Ltd Vintners Place, 68 Upper Thames Street, LONDON, EC4V 3BJ.
BARNFATHER, Mr. Michael, FCA 1966; 45 Washington Avenue, Bispham, BLACKPOOL, FY2 0PT.
BARNFATHER, Mr. Russell Harold, BSc ACA 1993; 22 Orchard Avenue, Worsley, MANCHESTER, M28 1FT.
BARNFATHER, Miss. Valentina Jane, MA ACA 1999; 35 Rowan Road, LONDON, W6 7DT.
BARNFIELD, Mr. Peter Dion, ACA 1982; 9 Marlborough Road, SALE, M33 3AF.
BARNFIELD, Mr. Roger Alan, ACA 1981; 18 Whitecourt, Uley, DURSLEY, GL11 5TG.
BARNFIELD, Mr. Stephen Gerald, MA FCA 1984; (Tax Fac), 39 Madeira Park, TUNBRIDGE WELLS, TN2 5SY.
BARNHURST, Mr. Graham John, FCA 1960; 3 Highwoods Avenue, Little Common, BEXHILL-ON-SEA, TN39 4NN.
BARNIKEL, Mr. Peter Humphry Wyatt, BA ACA 2003; 20 Julian Street, WILLOUGHBY, NSW 2068, AUSTRALIA.
BARNISH, Mr. David John, MBA BA FCA JDipMA 1969; (Tax Fac), Spinney Rise, Ashurst Drive, Boxhill, TADWORTH, KT20 7LN.
BARNISH, Mr. Mark William, BA FCA DChA 1980; (Member of Council 2007 - 2011), St. John of God Hospitaller Service, Morton Park Way, DARLINGTON, COUNTY DURHAM, DL1 4XZ.
BARNLEY, Mr. Nicholas John, BSc ACA 2006; Audi UK - Network Development, Volkswagen Group UK Ltd Yeomans Drive, Blakelands, MILTON KEYNES, MK14 5AN.
•BARNSDALL, Mr. Stuart John, BA ACA 1986; PKF (UK) LLP, Farringdon Place, 20 Farringdon Road, LONDON, EC1M 3AP.
BARNSLEY, Mr. John Corbitt, LLB FCA 1973; with American Appraisal (UK) Ltd, Aldermary House, 10 - 15 Queen Street, LONDON, EC4N 1TX.
BARNSLEY, Mr. Kenneth, FCA 1971; The Staithe, Ivy Lodge Road, Great Horkesley, COLCHESTER, CO6 4EN.
BARNSLEY, Mr. Paul Geoffrey, BA ACA 1982; 125, Crossefield Road, Cheadle Hulme, CHEADLE, SK8 5PF.
•BARNWELL, Mr. Alistair, FCA 1977; Bird Luckin Limited, Gateway House, 42 High Street, DUNMOW, ESSEX, CM6 1AH.
•BARNWELL, Miss. Susan Mary, BSc ACA 1985; (Tax Fac), Susan Barnwell, The Former Vicarage, Much Marcle, LEDBURY, HEREFORDSHIRE, HR8 2NL. See also Susan Barnwell ACA
BARON, Mr. Alan Rickard Warwick, MA FCA 1958; 5 Rue Georges Risler, 94320 THIAIS, FRANCE. (Life Member)
BARON, Mr. David Michael, FCA 1978; The Oxford Academy, Littlemore, OXFORD, OX4 6JZ.
BARON, Mr. Gary Lee, BSc ACA 2006; 52 Chatterton Drive, ACCRINGTON, LANCASHIRE, BB5 2TD.
BARON, Mr. John Edward, FCA 1969; Philton Aututrim (Pty) Ltd, PO Box 70118, BRYANSTON, GAUTENG, 2021, SOUTH AFRICA.
BARON, Mr. Keith, FCA 1971; e-Financial Management Ltd, 14 Maxet House, Liverpool Road, LUTON, LU1 1RS.
BARON, Mr. Luke Christian, BA(Hons) ACA 2009; 231 London Road, NORTHWICH, CHESHIRE, CW9 8AN.
BARON, Mr. Mark, BSc ACA 2005; Linklaters, 1 Silk Street, LONDON, EC2Y 8HQ.
BARON, Mr. Stuart David, ACA 2008; 63 Clough Lea, Marsden, HUDDERSFIELD, HD7 6DN.
BARON-COHEN, Mr. Gerald, BA FCA 1957; 70 Wildwood Road, LONDON, NW11 6UJ. (Life Member)
BARON COHEN, Mr. Hyman Vivian, BA FCA 1959; 20 The Meadway, LONDON, NW11 7AS. (Life Member)
•BARR, Mr. Alan Murray, FCA 1955; (Tax Fac), Alan Barr & Co, 146/148 Bury Old Road, Whitefield, MANCHESTER, M45 6AT.
BARR, Mrs. Amanda Jane, BA ACA 1997; 23 Garrick Lane, New Waltham, GRIMSBY, DN36 4WD.
BARR, Miss. Carolyn Mary, MA FCA CPA 1991; 1544 River Road, TEANECK, NJ 07666, UNITED STATES.
BARR, Mr. David Howard, BSc ACIB FCA 1975; Moorbrook Textiles Ltd, March Street, PEEBLES, EH45 8ER.
•BARR, Mr. David John Cyril, BSc FCA 1989; Martin and Company, 25 St Thomas Street, WINCHESTER, SO23 9HJ. See also Martin and Company Accountants Limited
•BARR, Mr. Duncan Charles Alexander, BA FCA 1986; Duncan Barr Associates Limited, Canalside Buildings, Graingers Way, Roundhouse Business Park, LEEDS, LS12 1AH.
BARR, Mr. Graham Duncan James, BA ACA 1992; T T International Moor House, 120 London Wall, LONDON, EC2Y 5ET.
BARR, Mr. Gregor James, BA(Hons) ACA 2010; 50 Meadowvale Road, Lickey End, BROMSGROVE, WORCESTERSHIRE, B60 1JY.
BARR, Mrs. Hayley, ACA 1996; 6 Harlaw Terrace, ABERDEEN, AB15 4YU.
BARR, Mr. James Walter, FCA 1973; Goldeneye, Broughton Crescent, Barlaston, STOKE-ON-TRENT, ST12 9DB.
BARR, Mr. Jeremy Miles, MSc FCA 1970; P O Box 89175, Kowloon City Post Office, KOWLOON CITY, KOWLOON, HONG KONG SAR. (Life Member)
BARR, Mr. Lloyd, FCA 1969; 45 Avenue Close, Avenue Road, LONDON, NW8 6DA.
BARR, Mrs. Nicola Joan, BA(Hons) ACA 2002; Betfred, Spectrum, 56-58 Benson Road, Birchwood, WARRINGTON, WA3 7PQ.
BARR, Mr. Patrick Bartholomew, BSc ACA 1984; 187 Tolcarne Drive, PINNER, HA5 2DN.
•BARR, Mrs. Penelope Ann, BA FCA 1990; (Tax Fac), Barr & Associates, 22 Westcott, WELWYN GARDEN CITY, HERTFORDSHIRE, AL7 2PP.
BARR, Mr. Robert James, BA FCA 1984; 109 London Road, REDHILL, RH1 2JG.
BARR, Mr. Robert Nicolas, MA FCA 1984; Lindfield, Faringdon Road, ABINGDON, OX14 1BD.
•BARR, Mr. Roger, ACA 1981; (Tax Fac), Lithgow Nelson & Co, Unit F/1, Moor Hall, Sandhawes Hill, EAST GRINSTEAD, WEST SUSSEX RH19 3NR.
•BARR, Mr. Steven Maxwell, ACA 1987; CCW Limited, 295-297 Church Street, BLACKPOOL, FY1 3PJ.
BARRABLE, Mr. Colin Michael, FCA 1967; The New Barn, 16a High Street, Clare, SUDBURY, SUFFOLK, CO10 8NY.
BARRABLE, Mr. Simon, BSc ACA 1979; 26 Holmbury Avenue, CROWTHORNE, RG45 6TQ.
BARRACLOUGH, Mr. Andrew, BA ACA 1994; Tesco Personal Finance, 22 Haymarket Yards, EDINBURGH, EH12 5BH.
BARRACLOUGH, Mr. Andrew Richard, BA(Hons) ACA 2001; 22 Louis Fields, Fairlands, GUILDFORD, SURREY, GU3 3JQ.
BARRACLOUGH, Mr. Anthony, FCA 1966; 9 Chelsea Mansions, Northowram, HALIFAX, HX3 7HG.
BARRACLOUGH, Mrs. Catherine, BA(Hons) ACA 2001; 33 Castle Lodge Avenue, Rothwell, LEEDS, LS26 0ZD.
BARRACLOUGH, Mr. Ian, BSc ACA 1995; 51 Pledwick Crescent, Sandal, WAKEFIELD, WF2 6DG.
BARRACLOUGH, Mr. James Jonathan, MA BSc ACA 2002; with BDO LLP, 1 Bridgewater Place, Water Lane, LEEDS, LS11 5RU.
•BARRACLOUGH, Mrs. Jean Anne, BA FCA 1982; 36 Victoria Road, Fulwood, PRESTON, PR2 8NE.
BARRACLOUGH, Mr. Keith, FCA 1962; Holme View Barn, Main Street, Burton Agnes, DRIFFIELD, NORTH HUMBERSIDE, YO25 4NG. (Life Member)
BARRACLOUGH, Mr. Keith Clayton, BA FCA 1964; Loetschenmattstrasse 25, 8912 Obfelden, ZURICH, SWITZERLAND.
•BARRACLOUGH, Mr. Malcolm John, BSc FCA 1992; 16 Brownberrie Crescent, Horsforth, LEEDS, LS18 5PT.
BARRACLOUGH, Mr. Mark, BSc ACA 2010; 49 South Cliff, BEXHILL-ON-SEA, EAST SUSSEX, TN39 3ED.
BARRACLOUGH, Ms. Melanie Jane, MA ACA RA 1991; Grote Bickersstraat 96, 1013 KS AMSTERDAM, NETHERLANDS.
BARRACLOUGH, Mr. Neil Keith, ACA 2003; 2 Arden Lodge, Haugh Shaw Road, HALIFAX, HX1 3AB.
BARRACLOUGH, Mr. Nigel Mark, ACA 1988; Y F M Group, 210-212 Chapeltown Road, LEEDS, LS7 4HZ.
BARRACLOUGH, Mr. Raymond John, FCA 1970; Little Willow, Birch Close, HAYWARDS HEATH, RH17 7ST.
BARRACLOUGH, Mr. Robert James, FCA 1965; The Ballroom, Hawkswick, SKIPTON, NORTH YORKSHIRE, BD23 5QA.
•BARRACLOUGH, Mr. Roy, FCA 1974; Roy Barraclough, 36 Victoria Road, Fulwood, PRESTON, PR2 8NE.
BARRADELL, Mrs. Julie Margaret, ACA 1985; 5 Bell Farm Green, BILLERICAY, CM12 9RW.
•BARRADELL, Mr. Michael Francis, BEng ACA 1997; KPMG LLP, 15 Canada Square, LONDON, E14 5GL. See also KPMG Europe LLP
BARRADELL, Mr. Peter Ian, BSc DipArb ACA 1986; Neo Operations SA, Akti Themistokleous 20, 18536 PIRAEUS, GREECE.
BARRALET, Mr. Peter Adrian, BSc FCA 1973; Needle Cottage, 74 Bath Road, Longwell Green, BRISTOL, BS30 9DG.
BARRAND, Mr. Nicholas Charles, BA ACA 1999; 16 Trefoil Close, WOKINGHAM, BERKSHIRE, RG40 5YQ.
•BARRAND, Mr. Peter John, BSc ACA 1995; Hurst Morrison Thomson Corporate Finance LLP, The Hub, 14 Station Road, HENLEY-ON-THAMES, OXFORDSHIRE, RG9 1AY.
BARRAND, Mr. Roger Woolrych, FCA 1964; 17 Kingsway, Petts Wood, ORPINGTON, KENT, BR5 1PL. (Life Member)
BARRAND, Mrs. Susan Elizabeth, BSc ACA 1998; 16 Trefoil Close, WOKINGHAM, BERKSHIRE, RG40 5YQ.
BARRAS, Miss. Dorothy Jean, BSc FCA 1976; 62 Trajan Walk, HEDDON-ON-THE-WALL, NORTHUMBERLAND, NE15 0BL.
BARRASS, Mr. Craig, ACA 2010; Colebrook & Burgess, Colebrook House, First Avenue, Tyne Tunnel Trading Estate, NORTH SHIELDS, TYNE AND WEAR NE29 7SU.
BARRASS, Miss. Sarah Jane, ACA 2009; 15 Murray Drive, LEEDS, WEST YORKSHIRE, LS10 4GE.
BARRASS, Mr. Simon, LLB ACA 2005; with Deloitte LLP, Athene Place, 66 Shoe Lane, LONDON, EC4A 3BQ.
BARRATT, Mrs. Beverley Janet, BSc ACA 1998; Crawford T H G (UK) Ltd, 30-32 St. Pauls Square, BIRMINGHAM, B3 1QZ.
BARRATT, Miss. Catherine, MPhil ACA 2011; Flat 41, Farthing Court, 60 Graham Street, BIRMINGHAM, B1 3JR.
BARRATT, Mr. Christopher John, BSc FCA 1986; The Coach House, Brightwell Farm, Brightwell Baldwin, WATLINGTON, OXFORDSHIRE, OX49 5NP.
•BARRATT, Mr. Colin Edward, FCA 1981; (Tax Fac), Wheawill & Sudworth, P.O. Box B30, 35 Westgate, HUDDERSFIELD, HD1 1PA.
BARRATT, Mr. David John, FCA 1972; Kilbracken, 5 Meadow Road, ASHTEAD, SURREY, KT21 1QR.
BARRATT, Mr. Geoffrey Michael, BA ACA 1981; The Gables, 74 High Street, Littleton Panell, DEVIZES, SN10 4EU.
BARRATT, Mr. Graham Paul, BSc FCA 1977; 1 Colton Close, Baston, PETERBOROUGH, PE6 9QH.
BARRATT, Mrs. Helen, MSc BEng FCA 1999; 5 Wharfedale, Crofters Fold, Galgate, LANCASTER, LA2 0RS.
BARRATT, Miss. Helen Jayne, BA ACA 1990; Fair Oaks, Slitting Mill, RUGELEY, WS15 2UU.
BARRATT, Miss. Kate Elizabeth, ACA 2008; 59 Mercia Drive, Ancaster, GRANTHAM, LINCOLNSHIRE, NG32 3QQ.
•BARRATT, Mr. Mark Andrew, BA ACA 1992; Harrisaccounts LLP, Marland House, 13 Huddersfield Road, BARNSLEY, SOUTH YORKSHIRE, S70 2LW. See also M A Barratt Limited
BARRATT, Mr. Nigel Paul, FCA 1970; Gaul House, 3a Thoroughfare, WOODBRIDGE, SUFFOLK, IP12 1AA.
•BARRATT, Mr. Peter Douglas, FCA 1972; (Tax Fac), Barramsgate Limited, 105 London Road, RAMSGATE, KENT, CT11 0DR.
•BARRATT, Mr. Peter Nigel, BA FCA 1987; Hurst & Company Accountants LLP, Lancashire Gate, 21 Tiviot Dale, STOCKPORT, CHESHIRE, SK1 1TD.
BARRATT, Mr. Peter William, FCA 1959; Sandy Acre, The Paddocks, Whitegate, NORTHWICH, CHESHIRE, CW8 2DD. (Life Member)
•BARRATT, Mrs. Susan Jane, BA ACA 1987; Deloitte LLP, Abbots House, Abbey Street, READING, RG1 3BD. See also Deloitte & Touche LLP
BARRATT, Miss. Susan Verity, BA ACA 1990; Natures Way Park Farm Barn, Chichester Road Selsey, CHICHESTER, WEST SUSSEX, PO20 9HP.
BARRATT, Mrs. Yvonne Michelle, BSc(Hons) ACA 2001; 1 Ivybank, Long Cross Hill Headley, BORDON, GU35 8BS.
•①BARRELL, Mr. Anthony Steven, BCom FCA 1994; 52 Wentworth Road, BIRMINGHAM, B17 9TA.
BARRELL, Mr. James William, BSc ACA 1995; 7 Cheriton Place, Westbury-on-Trym, BRISTOL, BS9 4AW.
BARRELL, Ms. Lisanne, BSc(Hons) FCA 2001; 16 Honeycroft Hill, UXBRIDGE, MIDDLESEX, UB10 9NH.
BARRELL, Mr. Richard Jason, BCom ACA 1998; K P M G, 100 Temple Street, BRISTOL, BS1 6AG.
BARRELL, Mr. Roger Alexander, FCA 1954; 52 Old Fort Road, SHOREHAM-BY-SEA, BN43 5RJ. (Life Member)
•BARRELL, Mr. Simon Gregory, FCA 1983; SGB Consulting, Woodridings, Landscape Road, WARLINGHAM, SURREY, CR6 9JB.
BARRELL, Mr. Simon Lee, MA ACA 2009; (Tax Fac), 61 Thornhill Road, CARDIFF, CF14 6PE.
BARRERA REGUEIRO, Miss. Sonia Maria, BA ACA 2003; Brambledene, Maybury Hill, WOKING, GU22 8AB.
BARRETT, Mr. Alan Roger, FCA 1963; 2 Oakwood Park, LEEDS, LS8 2PJ.
BARRETT, Mrs. Amerjit Kaur, BSc FCA 1991; 14 Lon-Ysgubor, CARDIFF, CF14 6SG.
BARRETT, Mr. Andrew John, BSc ACA 1979; 22 Wolsey Close, WELLS, BA5 2ET.
BARRETT, Mr. Andrew John, BA ACA 1992; (Tax Fac), The Old Byre, Crickham, WEDMORE, SOMERSET, BS28 4JT.
BARRETT, Mr. Andrew Thomas, FCA 1967; Albion Cottage, Wheelers Lane, Brockham, BETCHWORTH, SURREY, RH3 7LA.
BARRETT, Miss. Anna Louise, BA ACA 2005; 19a Duntshill Road, LONDON, SW18 4QN.
BARRETT, Mr. Anthony Charles, BA ACA CTA 1992; Little Berkhamsted House, Robins Nest Hill, Little Berkhamsted, HERTFORD, SG13 8LS.
BARRETT, Mr. Anthony John, FCA 1967; 30 St. Augustines Avenue, Thorpe Bay, SOUTHEND-ON-SEA, SS1 3JH.
BARRETT, Mr. Austin Francis, FCA 1964; (Tax Fac), Chaffcombe Lodge, West Hill Road, West Hill, OTTERY ST. MARY, DEVON, EX11 1TY.
BARRETT, Mr. Brian John, MA ACA 1992; 2BS Consulting Ltd, 1 Robins Close, Great Rollright, CHIPPING NORTON, OXFORDSHIRE, OX7 5RT.
BARRETT, Mrs. Cara Lindsay, BA ACA 2000; 34 College Drive, ILKLEY, WEST YORKSHIRE, LS29 9TY.
BARRETT, Mr. Chris, BSc ACA 2010; 36/1 Addison Road, MANLY, NSW 2095, AUSTRALIA.
BARRETT, Mr. Christopher David, FCA 1970; The Ford, Ford Lane, Alresford, COLCHESTER, CO7 8BB.
BARRETT, Mr. Christopher Mark, BSc ACA 2006; 12a Amherst Road, LONDON, W13 8ND.
•BARRETT, Mr. Christopher Paul, FCA 1982; Armstrong Watson, Central House, 47 St Pauls Street, LEEDS, LS1 2TE.
BARRETT, Mr. Christopher Philip, MA BA(Hons) ACA 2010; 2 Hall Green Manor, West Boldon, EAST BOLDON, TYNE AND WEAR, NE36 0PD.
BARRETT, Mr. Colin, BSc ACA 1982; Dewi Sant Hospital, Albert Street, PONTYPRIDD.
BARRETT, Mr. David Anthony, BA FCA 1979; 32 Dyne Road, LONDON, NW6 7XE.
BARRETT, Mr. David Geoffrey, FCA 1969; Mulberry House Oldfield Lane, Ombersley, DROITWICH, WORCESTERSHIRE, WR9 0JL.
BARRETT, Mr. David Michael, BA ACA 1983; PSI Advertising Limited, 20-22 Grosvenor Garden Mews, LONDON, SW1W 0JP.
BARRETT, Mr. David William, BSc ACA 1991; 72 Bd Prince Felix, 1513 KIRCHBERG, LUXEMBOURG.
BARRETT, Mr. Denis Patrick, BA ACA 1981; 2114 Veranda Residences, Princess Drive, Grace Bay Beach, PROVIDENCIALES, TURKS AND CAICOS ISLANDS.
BARRETT, Mr. Donald John, BA FCA 1977; 39 Park Road, Hampton Hill, HAMPTON, TW12 1HG.
BARRETT, Mrs. Dorothy, ACA 1980; 8 East Croft, BRISTOL, BS9 4PJ.
BARRETT, Mr. Duncan Miles, BSc ACA 2005; 32 Cowper Road, LONDON, SW19 1AB.

BARRETT, Mr. Edward, FCA *1966;* 7 Willowborne Gardens, Winfrith Newburgh, DORCHESTER, DORSET, DT2 8JR. (Life Member)
BARRETT, Mr. Edward William, ACA *2008;* 67 Hillside Road, BILLERICAY, CM11 2BX.
BARRETT, Miss. Fiona Clare, BSc ACA *2004;* Flat 8 Highover House, The Beeches, West Didsbury, MANCHESTER, M20 2BG.
BARRETT, Mr. George Henry, BSc ACA *1992;* Tekelec Ltd Wacker House, 85 High Street, EGHAM, TW20 9HF.
BARRETT, Mr. George Wilson, FCA *1954;* Heath Croft, Cardrona Road, GRANGE-OVER-SANDS, LA11 7EW. (Life Member)
BARRETT, Mrs. Gillian, LLB ACA *1980;* 1 Hillside, Abbotts Ann, ANDOVER, SP11 7DF.
•BARRETT, Mrs. Gillian Ann, BA FCA *1987;* (Tax Fac), GRS Accounting Limited, 17 Birley Brook Drive, Newbold, CHESTERFIELD, S41 8XN.
•BARRETT, Miss. Gillian Ruth, BMus FCA *1992;* Gillian Barrett, 34 Greenfield Avenue, SURBITON, SURREY, KT5 9HR.
BARRETT, Mr. Gordon Bridge, FCA *1954;* 39 Stone Road, BROMLEY, BR2 9AX. (Life Member)
BARRETT, Mrs. Helen, ACA *1985;* 10 Capesthorne Road, Christleton, CHESTER, CH3 7GA.
BARRETT, Miss. Helen, JP BA ACA *2007;* 34 High Street, Hampton-in-Arden, SOLIHULL, B92 0AA.
•BARRETT, Mrs. Hilary Denise, MA(Hons) ACA CTA *2002;* Roger Lugg & Co, 12/14 High Street, CATERHAM, CR3 5UA. See also Roger Lugg & Co Limited
BARRETT, Mr. Ian, ACA *1979;* Medlar House, Church Street, Thornham, HUNSTANTON, NORFOLK, PE36 6NJ.
•BARRETT, Mr. Ian Peter, FCA *1980;* (Tax Fac), Barretts, 22 Union Street, NEWTON ABBOT, DEVON, TQ12 2JS. See also Check Book Ltd
BARRETT, Miss. Jacqueline Louise, BSc ACA *1993;* Cherry Trees, 136 Main Street, Burley in Wharfedale, ILKLEY, WEST YORKSHIRE, LS29 7JP.
BARRETT, Mr. James, BA(Hons) ACA *2004;* 17 Trelawny Road, TAVISTOCK, PL19 0EN.
BARRETT, Mr. James, ACA *2003;* 4 Harewood Crest, BROUGH, NORTH HUMBERSIDE, HU15 1QD.
BARRETT, Mr. James Shepherd, MA FCA *1980;* Higher Fold, Worlds End Lane, Synwell, WOTTON-UNDER-EDGE, GL12 7HD.
BARRETT, Mr. John, FCA *1962;* 28 Melbury Gardens, LONDON, SW20 0DJ. (Life Member)
BARRETT, Mr. John Joseph, ACA ACCA *2011;* Flat 1, Silvester House, 192 Joel Street, Eastcote, PINNER, MIDDLESEX HA5 2RB.
BARRETT, Mr. Jonathan Matthew, BA ACA *1999;* 1 Kings Road, ST. ALBANS, HERTFORDSHIRE, AL3 4TQ.
BARRETT, Mr. Jonathan Paul, BSc ACA *2006;* 134 Westbourne Avenue, Princes Avenue, HULL, HU5 3HZ.
BARRETT, Mrs. Marie Clare, ACA *2004;* 4 Harewood Crest, BROUGH, NORTH HUMBERSIDE, HU15 1QD.
BARRETT, Mr. Martin Guy Victor, BA ACA *1992;* Aemtlerstrasse 26, 8003 ZURICH, SWITZERLAND.
•BARRETT, Mr. Michael, FCA *1967;* (Tax Fac), Barrett & Co (Carlisle) Ltd, 56 Warwick Road, CARLISLE, CA1 1DR. See also Barrett & Co
BARRETT, Mr. Michael Charles, BSc ACA *1994;* 9428 Gunbarrel Ridge Road, BOULDER, CO 80301, UNITED STATES.
BARRETT, Mr. Michael Down, MA FCA *1965;* Merriefields, 5 Hillside, East Dean, EASTBOURNE, EAST SUSSEX, BN20 0HE. (Life Member)
•BARRETT, Mr. Michael Russell, FCA *1973;* M. R. Barrett Limited, 1 Commonside Cottages, Salle, NORWICH, NR10 4EP.
BARRETT, Mr. Michael William, FCA *1963;* 4 Sycamore Close, Hurworth, DARLINGTON, COUNTY DURHAM, DL2 2EY. (Life Member)
BARRETT, Mr. Neil, BSc ACA *1982;* Carlisle Diocesan Board of Finance, Church House, West Walls, CARLISLE, CA3 8UE.
BARRETT, Mr. Neil, ACA *2010;* 9 Aldeburgh Way, CHELMSFORD, CM1 7PB.
BARRETT, Mr. Neil Alan, BSc ACA *1992;* Arbury Peugeot, Goodfellows Garage Ltd Walsall Road, Aldridge, WALSALL, WS9 0GG.
BARRETT, Mr. Paul, BA ACA *1991;* 22 Wellcarr Road, SHEFFIELD, S8 8QQ.
BARRETT, Mr. Paul Carl, MA FCA *1972;* 254 Chemin Du Riou, 06140 VENCE, FRANCE.
BARRETT, Mr. Paul Marcus, BA FCA *1989;* Sydney Packett & Sons Ltd Salts Wharf, Ashley Lane, SHIPLEY, WEST YORKSHIRE, BD17 7DB.
BARRETT, Mr. Paul Michael, BA FCA FRSA *1986;* 89 Elms Crescent, LONDON, SW4 8QF.
•BARRETT, Mr. Peter Charles, BSc FCA *1970;* Peter Barrett, The Manor, Little Clanfield, BAMPTON, OX18 2RX.
•BARRETT, Mr. Peter John, FCA *1966;* Barretts, 1 St.Marys House, St.Marys Road, SHOREHAM-BY-SEA, BN43 5ZA.
BARRETT, Mr. Peter John Alexander, BSc FCA *1993;* 10 Lamerton Way, WILMSLOW, CHESHIRE, SK9 3UN.
•BARRETT, Mr. Peter Mervyn, BA FCA *1975;* PMB, Maseru Book Centre Building, P.O. Box 1252, Kingsway, MASERU, 100 LESOTHO.
•BARRETT, Mr. Philip John, BA FCA *1990;* (Tax Fac), Grant Thornton UK LLP, Grant Thornton House, 202 Silbury Boulevard, MILTON KEYNES, BUCKINGHAMSHIRE, MK9 1LW. See also Grant Thornton LLP
BARRETT, Mr. Philip Mathew, BSc ACA *1994;* 18 Calbourne Road, Balham, LONDON, SW12 8LP.
BARRETT, Mr. Raymond Alexander Holden, BA ACA *1994;* Vicarage End, Sydenham Road, Sydenham, CHINNOR, OXFORDSHIRE, OX39 4NE.
BARRETT, Miss. Rebecca, BSc ACA *2006;* A B S Industrial Resources Ltd, The Brickworks, Kilnhurst Road, Kilnhurst, MEXBOROUGH, SOUTH YORKSHIRE S64 5TE.
BARRETT, Mrs. Renee Teresa, BSc ACA *1992;* (Tax Fac), The Old Byre, Crickham, WEDMORE, SOMERSET, BS28 4JT.
BARRETT, Mr. Rex William Norman, FCA *1951;* 33 Wycombe Road, Prestwood, GREAT MISSENDEN, BUCKINGHAMSHIRE, HP16 0NZ. (Life Member)
BARRETT, Mr. Richard James, BSc ACA *1996;* 14 Larke Rise, MANCHESTER, M20 2UL.
•BARRETT, Mr. Richard Mark, BA FCA *1985;* The Old Granary Evesham Road, Inkberrow, WORCESTER, WR7 4LJ.
BARRETT, Mr. Richard William, BSc FCA *1985;* 15 Ford End, Denham Village, UXBRIDGE, UB9 5AL.
•BARRETT, Mr. Roger Francis, BCom FCA *1972;* Horgan Barrett & Co, Evergreen House, Congress Road, CORK, COUNTY CORK, IRELAND.
BARRETT, Mr. Ronan Joseph, BSc ACA *2011;* 13 Forest Close, Crawley Down, CRAWLEY, WEST SUSSEX, RH10 4LT.
BARRETT, Mr. Roy, FCA *1969;* 15 Soi 16, Seri 2, Suan Luang, BANGKOK 10250, THAILAND.
BARRETT, Mrs. Samantha, BA FCA ATII *1994;* with Deloitte LLP, PO Box 500, 2 Hardman Street, MANCHESTER, M60 2AT.
BARRETT, Mr. Simon Christopher, BA FCA *1990;* XL Insurance Co Ltd, XL House, 70 Gracechurch Street, LONDON, EC3V 0XL.
•BARRETT, Mr. Stephen Andrew, BSc ARCS FCA *1999;* (Tax Fac), R C Barrett & Co (Wokingham) Ltd, Tithe House, 15 Dukes Ride, CROWTHORNE, BERKSHIRE, RG45 6LZ.
•BARRETT, Mrs. Susan Marie, FCA *1983;* (Tax Fac), Barrett & Co, Cheriton, Basingstoke Road, Riseley, READING, RG7 1QL.
BARRETT, Mr. Terence, FCA *1965;* 5255 Lakeshore Road, Unit #34, BURLINGTON L7L 5X8, ON, CANADA. (Life Member)
BARRETT, Mr. Thomas Hubert John, FCA *1951;* The Nutshell, Robinswood Crescent, PENARTH, CF64 3JF. (Life Member)
BARRETT, Mr. Thomas Patrick, BSc FCA *1985;* 54 Deynecourt Gardens, LONDON, E11 2BU.
BARRETT, Ms. Victoria Anne, BA ACA *1992;* 88 Park Road, Stevington, BEDFORD, MK43 7QG.
BARRETT-MILES, Mr. James, BA ACA *2001;* Lark Rise, West Hill, OTTERY ST. MARY, DEVON, EX11 1TZ.
•BARRETT ROGERS, Mrs. Marianne Patricia, FCA CTA *1979;* (Tax Fac), Barretts, 22 Union Street, NEWTON ABBOT, DEVON, TQ12 2JS. See also Check Book Ltd
BARRETTO, Mr. Peter James, BA(Hons) ACA *2009;* 92 Knighton Road, PLYMOUTH, PL4 9DA.
BARRICK, Mr. Graham Michael, BSc ACA *1981;* 2a Carlton Road, SHIPLEY, WEST YORKSHIRE, BD18 4NE.
BARRICK, Mr. Simon John, BSc ACA *1992;* Cyndene House, Main Street, Asselby, GOOLE, DN14 7HE.
•BARRIE, Mrs. Carol Hazel, FCA *1971;* 7 Carnoustie Close, SUTTON COLDFIELD, WEST MIDLANDS, B75 6UW.
BARRIE, Mr. Christopher Winston, FCA *1970;* 5 Lewis Close, Headington, OXFORD, OX3 8JD.
BARRIE, Mr. Duncan Colin, BA FCA *1998;* 35 Rosemount, DURHAM, DH1 5GA.
BARRIE, Mr. Ian Melvyn, FCA *1966;* 2 Chemin du Grand Camp, Margon, 34320 HERAULT, FRANCE. (Life Member)
BARRIE, Mr. John Michael, FCA *1954;* 31a Foxley Lane, PURLEY, SURREY, CR8 3EH. (Life Member)
BARRIE, Mr. Stephen, ACA *2009;* 59 Crescent Lane, DUNDEE, DD4 6DP.
•BARRIGAN, Mr. Robert, BA FCA *1980;* (Tax Fac), Rob Barrigan Consulting, Stoer House, 1 Polam Road, DARLINGTON, COUNTY DURHAM, DL1 5NW.
BARRINGTON, Mr. Charles Peter, FCA *1970;* The Lodge, Great Bealings, WOODBRIDGE, IP13 6NW.
•BARRINGTON, Mr. Christian Mark, BSc ACA *1989;* (Tax Fac), Jackson Stephen LLP, James House, Stonecross Business Park, 5 Yew Tree Way, Golborne, WARRINGTON CHESHIRE WA3 3JD.
BARRINGTON, Mr. James Edward, MA(Hons) ACA *2002;* 12 Southcroft Road, BIGGAR, LANARKSHIRE, ML12 6AJ.
BARRINGTON, Mr. Jeremy Frank Newland, BSc ACA *1985;* 23 Westfield Avenue, SOUTH CROYDON, Surrey, CR2 9JY.
BARRINGTON, Mr. Justin, BSc ACA *1993;* 11 Belsize Avenue, LONDON, NW3 4BL.
•BARRINGTON, Mr. Michael John, BA FCA *1973;* Deloitte & Touche, Al Jana Pawla 19, 00854 WARSAW, POLAND.
BARRINGTON, Mr. Raymond Lewis, FCA *1963;* Lukes Farm, Addlehole, KINGSBRIDGE, TQ7 2DX. (Life Member)
BARRINGTON, Ms. Sara Jane, BA ACA *1993;* 31194 La Baya Drive, Suite 100, WESTLAKE VILLAGE, CA 91362, UNITED STATES.
BARRINGTON HAYNES, Mr. Edward Graham, BSc FCA *1979;* Westbrook House, Langham, GILLINGHAM, DORSET, SP8 5NQ.
BARRINGTON-WELLS, Mr. James, BSc(Hons) ACA *2010;* 11 Burnsall Street, LONDON, SW3 3SR.
•BARRITT, Mr. John, BA(Hons) FCA *1985;* 40 Princes Avenue, Petts Wood, ORPINGTON, BR5 1QS.
BARRITT, Mr. Martin John, FCA *1969;* P O Box 40, North Side, GEORGE TOWN, GRAND CAYMAN, KY1-1701, CAYMAN ISLANDS.
BARRITT, Mr. Oliver Philip, BSc(Hons) ACA *2001;* 24 Francis Street, FAIRLIGHT, NSW 2094, AUSTRALIA.
BARRON, Mr. Adrian, BSc(Econ) ACA *2009;* The Hermitage Cottage, Bath Road, Taplow, MAIDENHEAD, BERKSHIRE, SL6 0AR.
BARRON, Mr. Alexander Paul, ACA FMAAT *2001;* Estate Office, West Dean College, West Dean Park, CHICHESTER, PO18 0QZ.
BARRON, Mr. Arthur David, MA FCA *1973;* 36 Lytton Grove, Putney, LONDON, SW15 2HB.
BARRON, Miss. Beth Louise, MSc BSc ACA *2011;* Flat 3, 34 Mossbury Road, LONDON, SW11 2PB.
BARRON, Mr. Daniel, BA ACA *2006;* Flat 11, Wych End, 49 Copers Cope Road, BECKENHAM, KENT, BR3 1NX.
BARRON, Mr. David Fred, FCA CTA *1952;* 2 Studland View, 49 Montague Road, BOURNEMOUTH, BH5 2EW. (Life Member)
BARRON, Miss. Elizabeth Ann, BA ACA *1991;* BMS Finance, C/O 11 Trinity Rise, LONDON, SW2 2QP.
BARRON, Mrs. Gillian Elizabeth, BA ACA *2001;* Hawksmere Ltd Elizabeth House, 39 York Road, LONDON, SE1 7NQ.
BARRON, Mr. Graeme Mackintosh, ACA *1992;* 108 Edith Road, LONDON, W14 9AP.
BARRON, Mr. James Andrew, BA FCA *1971;* 110 The Avenue, Ealing, LONDON, W13 8JX.
BARRON, Mr. James David, BSc ACA *1999;* with Deloitte & Touche LLP, P.O.Box 49279, Bentall Cntr., 1055 Dunsmuir Street, VANCOUVER V7X 1P4, BC CANADA.
BARRON, Miss. Jo-Ann Louise, ACA *2010;* 8 Ashbourne Avenue, Douglas, ISLE OF MAN, IM2 1NW.
BARRON, Mrs. Joan, BSc ACA CTA *1978;* (Tax Fac), with PKF (UK) LLP, 5 Temple Square, Temple Street, LIVERPOOL, L2 5RH.
BARRON, Mr. John Michael, MA FCA *1961;* 35 Bourne Gardens, Chingford, LONDON, E4 9DX. (Life Member)
BARRON, Mr. John Stewart, BA ACA *1983;* Balfour Beatty Ltd, 86 Station Road, REDHILL, RH1 1PQ.
•BARRON, Mr. Jonathan Mark, FCA MAE *1984;* Hazlems Fenton LLP, Palladium House, 1-4 Argyll Street, LONDON, W1F 7LD.
•BARRON, Mr. Keith William, BA FCA *1990;* K W Barron Limited, 27 Grove Road, LEE-ON-THE-SOLENT, HAMPSHIRE, PO13 9JA.
BARRON, Miss. Kerry Anne, ACA *2010;* PricewaterhouseCoopers, Darling Park Tower 2, 201 Sussex Street, GPO Box 2650, SYDNEY, NSW 1171 AUSTRALIA.
BARRON, Mr. Martin David, FCA *1972;* (Tax Fac), Mosley & Co, 14 Market Place, Ramsbottom, BURY, LANCASHIRE, BL0 9HT.
BARRON, Mr. Martin John, BA ACA *1997;* with Deloitte LLP, 1 City Square, LEEDS, WEST YORKSHIRE, LS1 2AL.
BARRON, Mrs. Micayla Louise, BSc ACA *1998;* 43 Merrivale Gardens, WOKING, GU21 3LX.
BARRON, Mr. Michael, FCA *1970;* 25 Hawley Close, HAMPTON, MIDDLESEX, TW12 3XX.
BARRON, Mr. Michael, ACA *2011;* 148 Newland Gardens, HERTFORD, SG13 7WY.
•BARRON, Mr. Nicholas Roger Burdett, FCA *1973;* Underwood Barron LLP, Monks Brook House, 13-17 Hursley Road, Chandler's Ford, EASTLEIGH, HAMPSHIRE SO53 2FW. See also Underwood Barron Associates Limited
BARRON, Mr. Paul, BA(Hons) ACA *2010;* 148 Newland Gardens, HERTFORD, SG13 7WY.
BARRON, Mrs. Rachel Jane, BA ACA *1986;* Ernst & Young, 1 Colmore Square, BIRMINGHAM, B4 6HQ.
BARRON, Mr. Richard Patrick, BSocSc ACA *1988;* 17 Sandhills Lane, Barnt Green, BIRMINGHAM, B45 8NU.
BARRON, Mr. Shaun Robert, LLB ACA *2000;* 8 Royston Park Road, PINNER, HA5 4AD.
BARRONS, Mr. Anthony Peter George, BSc ACA *1988;* 3rd Floor, 30 Gresham Street, LONDON, EC2P 2XY.
BARROTT, Mr. Michael Anthony Cooper, MA MBA FCA *1980;* Michael Barrott, 126 Kennington Road, LONDON, SE11 6RE.
BARROW, Miss. Alison Elizabeth, BSc ACA *1992;* East End Farm, Bentworth, ALTON, HAMPSHIRE, GU34 5JT.
BARROW, Mrs. Amanda Helen, BSc ACA *1998;* (Tax Fac), Chipstead, Blackdown Avenue, WOKING, GU22 8QH.
BARROW, Mr. Andrew Stephen, BSc ACA *1993;* 10 Linderbreck Lane, POULTON-LE-FYLDE, LANCASHIRE, FY6 8FJ.
BARROW, Mr. David, ACA *2008;* 45 Highbury Road East, LYTHAM ST. ANNES, LANCASHIRE, FY8 2RW.
BARROW, Mr. David, FCA ACMA *1962;* 6 Hawthorn Close, Clifton, BRIGHOUSE, HD6 1RG.
BARROW, Miss. Elisabeth Jane, BA ACA *2003;* 33 Milner Road, LIVERPOOL, L17 0AB.
BARROW, Mrs. Elizabeth Maryse, FCA *1976;* 16 Moana Road, Days Bay, WELLINGTON 6008, NEW ZEALAND.
BARROW, Mr. Frederick, FCA *1955;* 13 Framingham Road, Brooklands, SALE, M33 3ST. (Life Member)
BARROW, Mr. Geoffrey, LLB ACA *1986;* Balmer Cottage, The Balmer, Welshampton, ELLESMERE, SY12 0PP.
BARROW, Mr. Howard Lonsdale, FCA *1968;* 17 Keep Hill Road, HIGH WYCOMBE, BUCKINGHAMSHIRE, HP11 1DW. (Life Member)
BARROW, Mr. John David, FCA *1970;* 50 Station Lane, Birkenshaw, BRADFORD, BD11 2JE. (Life Member)
BARROW, Mr. John Philip, FCA *1963;* 37 Gravel Hill, HENLEY-ON-THAMES, RG9 2EF.
BARROW, Mr. John William, BD FCA *1980;* Plas y Coed Heath Road, Bradfield, MANNINGTREE, CO11 2UZ.
BARROW, Mrs. Julie Lyndora, BA ACA *2002;* 128 Westwick Road, Greenhill, SHEFFIELD, S8 7BX.
BARROW, Mr. Karl Richard, BSc ACA *1994;* The Cottage Main Street, Gumley, MARKET HARBOROUGH, LE16 7RU.
BARROW, Miss. Kate, ACA *2008;* 84 Trevore Drive, Standish, WIGAN, WN1 2QE.
BARROW, Mrs. Kathryn Ann, MA ACA *1992;* Hollybank House, Church Place, Limekilns, DUNFERMLINE, KY11 3HR.
•BARROW, Miss. Kathryn Lucy, BSc ACA *1996;* Ernst & Young LLP, 1 More London Place, LONDON, SE1 2AF. See also Ernst & Young Europe LLP
BARROW, Miss. Laura, MA ACA *2009;* 18 Lindsay Road, BRISTOL, BS7 9NP.
BARROW, Mr. Paul James, MBA FCA *1974;* 18 Ashcroft Gardens, CIRENCESTER, GLOUCESTERSHIRE, GL7 1RB.
BARROW, Mr. Paul William, BA(Hons) ACA *2001;* 200 The Broadway, NORTH SHIELDS, TYNE AND WEAR, NE30 3RY.
•BARROW, Mr. Peter Victor, BSc ACA *1986;* PricewaterhouseCoopers LLP, Hays Galleria, 1 Hays Lane, LONDON, SE1 2RD. See also PricewaterhouseCoopers
•BARROW, Mr. Robert Malcolm, FCA *1972;* Barrow LLP, Jackson House, Station Road, Chingford, LONDON, E4 7BU.
BARROW, Mr. Roderick Guy, BSc FCA *1990;* Paddock House Churt Road, Churt, FARNHAM, SURREY, GU10 2NY.
BARROW, Mr. Simon Peter, FCA *1977;* 16 Moana Road, Days Bay, LOWER HUTT 5013, NEW ZEALAND.

BARROW, Mr. Steven George, BSc ACA *1992;* Apple Tree House, Lamyatt, SHEPTON MALLET, SOMERSET, BA4 6NP.
BARROW, Mr. Steven Trevor, BA ACA *2006;* 7 Wren Close, Biddulph, STOKE-ON-TRENT, ST8 7UB.
BARROWCLIFF, Mrs. Alina, BA ACA *1995;* Home Farm, Britwell Salome, WATLINGTON, OX49 5LH.
•BARROWCLOUGH, Mr. Richard Ashley, BSc FCA *1984;* Balance Accountants Limited, Victoria Court, 91 Huddersfield Road, HOLMFIRTH, HD9 3JA. See also Alexa-Rae Ltd
BARROWMAN, Mr. Andrew Kenneth, BCom FCA *1973;* 6 Vale Croft, Claygate, ESHER, KT10 0NX.
BARROWMAN, Mr. David Alexander, BSc FCA *1983;* (Tax Fac), Flat 4, 30 Colinton Road, EDINBURGH, EH10 5DG.
BARROWS, Mr. Charles William, BCom ACA *1988;* Flat 3, Osprey Court, Star Place, LONDON, E1W 1AG.
BARROWS, Mr. Lloyd Aston, BA ACA *2006;* 8 Stapleford Road, WEMBLEY, HA0 4RN.
BARROWS, Mr. Peter William, FCA *1954;* Elm Tree Farm, Chapmore End, WARE, SG12 0HF. (Life Member)
•BARRS, Mr. Michael, FCA *1973;* Michael Barrs and Company, 395 Hoe Street, Walthamstow, LONDON, E17 9AP.
•BARRS, Mr. Roger Geoffrey, FCA *1977;* Crowe Clark Whitehill Audit LLC, 6th Floor, Victory House, Prospect Hill, Douglas, ISLE OF MAN IM1 1EQ. See also Horwath Clark Whitehill Audit LLC and Horwath Clark Whitehill LLC
BARRS, Mrs. Sally Anne Penelope, BSc ACA *1994;* 14 Salisbury Avenue, COLCHESTER, CO3 3DN.
BARRY, Mr. Andrew, BA ACA *1996;* 1 Goddard Close, GUILDFORD, SURREY, GU2 9AG.
BARRY, Mr. Angus Michael, BSc ACA MSI MCMI *1999;* 5 Sunnybank, MARLOW, BUCKINGHAMSHIRE, SL7 3BL.
BARRY, Mr. Bernard Anthony, FCA *1976;* B G S Industrial Ltd, 242 Whitchurch Road, CARDIFF, CF14 3ND.
•BARRY, Mr. Christopher David Gordon, BEng ACA *2000;* 8 Le Clos de Sargeant, Le Chemin Des Maltieres Grouville, JERSEY, JE3 9EQ.
BARRY, Mr. David James, BEng ACA *2002;* Wirral Sensory Services Limited, 37 Allport Lane, Bromborough, WIRRAL, MERSEYSIDE, CH62 7HH.
BARRY, Mr. David John, BSc ACA *1995;* Chapel Cottage, Green Lane, Stutton, TADCASTER, NORTH YORKSHIRE, LS24 9BW.
BARRY, Mr. David Julian, BA(Hons) ACA *2001;* 24 Coales Gardens, MARKET HARBOROUGH, LEICESTERSHIRE, LE16 7NY.
BARRY, Dr. Hugh, DPhil BSc ACA *2009;* 188 Crow Lane East, NEWTON-LE-WILLOWS, MERSEYSIDE, WA12 9UA.
BARRY, Mr. Ian Charles, BSc FCA *1978;* CAB International, Nosworthy Way, Mongewell, WALLINGFORD, OXFORDSHIRE, OX10 8DE.
BARRY, Mrs. Jacqueline, BSc ACA *2000;* 19 Gerald Road, PRENTON, MERSEYSIDE, CH43 2LA.
BARRY, Mrs. Joanne, BSc ACA *1992;* 4 Holly Bank Court, Crich, MATLOCK, DERBYSHIRE, DE4 5HZ.
BARRY, Mr. John Paul, BEng ACA *1998;* 137 Waterson Vale, CHELMSFORD, CM2 9GG.
BARRY, Mr. John Richard, BSc ACA *1993;* Hillview House, Manor Road, Off Ricketts Hill Lane, Tatsfield, WESTERHAM, TN16 2ND.
BARRY, Mr. John Sean, BSc ACA *1995;* 136.22 Riant -Coteau, 1196 GLAND, VAUD, SWITZERLAND.
•BARRY, Mrs. Katherine Rebecca, BSc ACA *1996;* KPB Limited, 30 Broadwalk, Caerleon, NEWPORT, GWENT, NP18 1NQ.
BARRY, Mr. Kevin Paul, MA BA DipPTC FCA *1978;* 33 Hillcroft Crescent, Ealing, LONDON, W5 2SG.
BARRY, Mr. Kevin Richard, ACA *1993;* Oast Hatch, Harvel, Meopham, GRAVESEND, DA13 0DE.
BARRY, Mrs. Lorraine Kate, BSc FCA *1988;* (Tax Fac), 36 Hillydeal Road, Otford, SEVENOAKS, KENT, TN14 5RU.
•BARRY, Mr. Louis, FCA *1975;* Ford Bull Watkins, Clerks Well House, 20 Britton Street, LONDON, EC1M 5TU.
BARRY, Mr. Matthew Cameron, BA(Hons) ACA *2009;* 12 Discovery Walk, LONDON, E1W 2JG.
BARRY, Mr. Michael Bailor, ACA *2008;* Flat 12, Tavern Court, 95 New Kent Road, LONDON, SE1 6RY.
•BARRY, Mr. Michael Edward, BA FCA *1994;* (Tax Fac), Rock Insurances, 6 Magellan Terrace Gatwick Road, CRAWLEY, WEST SUSSEX, RH10 9PJ.
BARRY, Miss. Michelle Dawn, BSc(Hons) ACA *2002;* with PricewaterhouseCoopers, Abacus House, Castle Park, CAMBRIDGE, CB3 0AN.
BARRY, Mrs. Nichola Yvette, ACA *1996;* 1 Goddard Close, GUILDFORD, SURREY, GU2 9AG.
BARRY, Mr. Owen David Conor Brian, BSc ACA *2007;* Logica Plc, Keats House, The Office Park, Springfield Drive, LEATHERHEAD, SURREY KT22 7LP.
BARRY, Mr. Paul Anthony, FCA *1975;* 5 Cornflower Close, Lisvane, CARDIFF, CF14 0BD.
BARRY, Mr. Paul Stephen, BA ACA *1987;* Tsurumaki 4-17-11, Setagaya-ku, TOKYO, JAPAN.
•BARRY, Mr. Philip Anthony, BSc(Hons) ACA *2001;* Hollingdale Pooley Limited, Bramford House, 23 Westfield Park, Clifton, BRISTOL, BS6 6LT.
BARRY, Mr. Quintin John, BSc ACA *1990;* 9 Mill Lane, SHOREHAM-BY-SEA, WEST SUSSEX, BN43 5AG.
BARRY, Mrs. Sonia Claire, ACA CA(AUS) *2010;* Cayzer Trust Co Ltd, 30 Buckingham Gate, LONDON, SW1E 6NN.
BARRY, Mr. Stephen Jeffrey, BA FCA *1967;* Limecourt Ventures Plc, 19 Newman Street, LONDON, W1T 1PF. (Life Member)
BARRY, Mr. Timothy Donal, FCA *1960;* Innishannon House, INNISHANNON, COUNTY CORK, IRELAND. (Life Member)
BARRY, Mr. Timothy Mark, BSc FCA *1994;* Tomigaya 2-39-3, Shibuyaku, TOKYO, 1510063 JAPAN.
BARSBY, Miss. Alison Pauline, BSc(Hons) ACA *2001;* 39 Yateley Drive, Barton Seagrave, KETTERING, NORTHAMPTONSHIRE, NN15 6BN.
BARSHAM, Mr. Michael Keith, BSc ACA *1982;* Jurby Watertech International, Northway House, 1379 High Road, LONDON, N20 9LP.
BARSHAM, Mr. Ronald Andrew, FCA *1949;* Cliff House, Bay View, Amble, MORPETH, NE65 0AZ. (Life Member)
BARSTOW, Mr. Michael James, MA FCA *1978;* 48 Redan Street, LONDON, W14 0AB.
BARSTOW, Mr. Oliver George, FCA *1966;* 3 Mount Beacon, BATH, BA1 5QP. (Life Member)
BART-WILLIAMS, Miss. Ruth, BSc ACA *2004;* Torosay, 106 Kippington Road, SEVENOAKS, TN13 2LL.
BARTARYA, Mr. Ajeet, MSc BA ACA *2006;* (Tax Fac), S N Bartarya, First floor, Chartwell House, 292-294 Hale Lane, EDGWARE, MIDDLESEX HA8 8NP.
•BARTARYA, Mr. Shailendra Nath, FCA *1968;* S.N. Bartarya, 75 Weston Street, LONDON, SE1 3RS.
•BARTARYA, Mr. Shubendra Nath, FCA *1966;* S.N. Bartarya, Chartwell House 1st Floor, 292 Hale Lane, EDGWARE, HA8 8NP.
BARTELLA, Ms. Nancy, BSc(Hons) ACA *2000;* 4 Vassilikos Street, Strovolos, 2060 NICOSIA, CYPRUS.
BARTER, Mrs. Angela Jane, BA ACA *1988;* 11 Pindari Road, DOVER HEIGHTS, NSW 2030, AUSTRALIA.
BARTER, Mrs. Audrey, BSc ACA *1995;* Green Acres, KENTSTOWN, COUNTY MEATH, IRELAND.
•BARTER, Mr. James Terence, FCA *1972;* (Tax Fac), 2 Howard Bowen Close, Osbaston, MONMOUTH, GWENT, NP25 3AU.
BARTER, Mr. John Harry, BSc FCA *1958;* 18 Warnham Court Mews, Warnham Court, Warnham, HORSHAM, WEST SUSSEX, RH12 3QE. (Life Member)
BARTER, Ms. Lisa, ACA MAAT *1997;* 7 Grazeley Road, Three Mile Cross, READING, RG7 1BL.
BARTER, Mrs. Patricia Anne, BA ACA DChA *1988;* Society for Endocrinology, 22 Apex Court, Woodlands, Bradley Stoke, BRISTOL, BS32 4JT.
BARTER, Mr. Philip, BSc ACA *1987;* 11 Pindari Road, DOVER HEIGHTS, NSW 2030, AUSTRALIA.
BARTER, Mr. Philip Jon, BSc(Hons) ACA *2000;* Riddy House, 28 Riddy Lane, Bourn, CAMBRIDGE, CB23 2SP.
BARTER, Mr. Robert Jon, BA ACA *1995;* Green Acres, KENTSTOWN, COUNTY MEATH, IRELAND.
BARTER, Mr. Robert William, FCA *1975;* Home Farm House, Holton, OXFORD, OX33 1QA.
BARTER, Mr. Roger Albert, FCA *1974;* Rhodes Rogers & Jolly Ltd, 21 Worcester Road, MALVERN, WORCESTERSHIRE, WR14 4QY.
BARTER, Mrs. Sharon Louise, BSc ACA *1993;* Thomas Cook Ltd, 13-16 Coningsby Road, PETERBOROUGH, PE3 8AB.
BARTFIELD, Mr. William, FCA *1954;* 8775 Killians Green Drive, LAS VEGAS, NV 89131, UNITED STATES. (Life Member)
BARTHOLOMEUSZ, Mr. Michael Allan, BSc ACA *1983;* K P M G Llp, 15 Canada Square, LONDON, E14 5GL.
BARTHOLOMEW, Mr. Alex Daniel Henry, BA ACA *2005;* Independent Regulator of NHS Foundation Trust, 4 Matthew Parker Street, LONDON, SW1H 9NP.
BARTHOLOMEW, Mrs. Alison Elizabeth, BSc ACA *1993;* (Tax Fac), 2 West View, ASHTEAD, KT21 2JD.
BARTHOLOMEW, Mrs. Andrea, BA ACA *1986;* 18 Mill Race Drive, Wistaston, CREWE, CW2 6XG.
BARTHOLOMEW, Mrs. Annabella Margarita, FCA *1996;* Gossamer Cottage Reynolds Lane Slindon, ARUNDEL, WEST SUSSEX, BN18 0QT.
BARTHOLOMEW, Mr. Charles Geoffrey, MA FCA *1972;* UK Athletics, Central Boulevard Blythe Valley Park, SOLIHULL, B90 8AJ.
BARTHOLOMEW, Mr. Grant David, ACA *2010;* 6 Meyrick Road, PORTSMOUTH, PO2 8JN.
BARTHOLOMEW, Mr. Lee Barry Andrew, ACA *2001;* (Tax Fac), 5 Kynance Terrace, The Lizard, HELSTON, CORNWALL, TR12 7NH.
BARTHOLOMEW, Mr. Philip Andrew, BA ACA *2004;* Electronic Data Systems Ltd Yorktown House, 8 Frimley Road, CAMBERLEY, SURREY, GU15 3BA.
BARTHOLOMEW, Mrs. Ruth Helena, BA ACA *1990;* 53 The Avenue, SUNBURY-ON-THAMES, MIDDLESEX, TW16 5HY.
BARTHRAM, Miss. Jill, BA ACA *2005;* Bartham Funeral Services, 5 The Wynd Hutton Rudby, YARM, CLEVELAND, TS15 0ES.
BARTHRAM, Mr. Timothy, ACA *1986;* Crella Farm, Crows-An-Wra, St. Buryan, PENZANCE, TR19 6HT.
BARTLAM, Mr. David John, BSc ACA *2007;* 68 Elworth Road, SANDBACH, CW11 3HN.
BARTLAM, Mr. Neil Keith, ACA *1981;* 34 Browns Lane, Knowle, SOLIHULL, B93 9BE.
BARTLAM, Mr. Thomas Hugh, MA FCA *1973;* Blounce House, South Warnborough, HOOK, RG29 1RX.
BARTLE, Mr. Matthew Thomas, BA ACA *2002;* 4 Birch View, Barrow, CLITHEROE, LANCASHIRE, BB7 9BB.
BARTLETT, Mr. Anthony David, FCA *1975;* Skelbo House, Skelbo, DORNOCH, SUTHERLAND, IV25 3QG.
•BARTLETT, Anthony Henry Peter, Esq MA FCA *1958;* (Tax Fac), A.H.P. Bartlett & Co, 24 Swaylands House, Penshurst, TONBRIDGE, KENT, TN11 8DZ.
BARTLETT, Mr. Anthony John, FCA *1972;* 2 Turks Head Court, Eton, WINDSOR, BERKSHIRE, SL4 6AL.
BARTLETT, Mr. Brian James, FCA *1957;* 4 The Gardens, Evesham Road, CHELTENHAM, GL50 4QE. (Life Member)
•BARTLETT, Mrs. Catherine Jane, BA ACA *1997;* Bartlett Platt & Company, 1 Oak Farm, Long Lane, Haughton, TARPORLEY, CHESHIRE CW6 9RN.
BARTLETT, Mr. Charles Edward Nicholas, BA ACA *1999;* 1 Oak Farm, Haughton, TARPORLEY, CHESHIRE, CW6 9RN.
BARTLETT, Mr. Christopher John, FCA *1963;* The Bridge Trust, 7 Bridge Chambers, BARNSTAPLE, DEVON, EX31 1HB.
BARTLETT, Mr. Colin Roger, FCA *1975;* Treyford House, Leycester Road, KNUTSFORD, CHESHIRE, WA16 8QR.
BARTLETT, Mr. David Arthur, FCA *1971;* 9 Mount Court, Mount Road, WALLASEY, CH45 9JS.
BARTLETT, Mr. David Graham, BSc ACA *1990;* Farsound Engineering Ltd Ashton Road, Harold Hill, ROMFORD, RM3 8UH.
•BARTLETT, Mr. David John, FCA *1982;* Daly Hoggett & Co, 5-11 Mortimer Street, LONDON, W1T 3HS.
BARTLETT, Mr. David John, BA ACA *1992;* Collector's Office, The Honourable Society of the Inner Temple, 3 King's Bench Walk Temple, LONDON, EC4Y 7DQ.
BARTLETT, Mr. David Kenneth, BSc ACA *2007;* Flat 10, 23 Nightingale Lane, LONDON, SW4 9AH.
BARTLETT, Miss. Elizabeth, ACA *2009;* Flat A, 99 Victoria Road, LONDON, N22 7XG.
BARTLETT, Miss. Emma Katherine, BA(Hons) ACA *2003;* 6A Jubilee Avenue, Devonport, AUCKLAND 0642, NEW ZEALAND.
BARTLETT, Miss. Faith Lesley, BA ACA *1996;* Handpost Basingstoke Road, Swallowfield, READING, RG7 1PU.
BARTLETT, Mr. Graham Philip, FCA *1957;* 21 Reyntiens View, Odiham, HOOK, RG29 1AF. (Life Member)
BARTLETT, Mr. Guy Paul, ACA CA(SA) *2011;* (Tax Fac), 24 Tantallon Road, LONDON, SW12 8DG.
BARTLETT, Miss. Hayley Lynn, BA ACA *2006;* Desk EP 7.195G, Pricewaterhousecoopers Legal Llp, 1 Embankment Place, LONDON, WC2N 6DX.
BARTLETT, Miss. Holly Pledger, BSc ACA *2007;* Deloitte & Touche, 1 City Square, LEEDS, LS1 2AL.
BARTLETT, Mr. James Carnegy, BSc ACA *1991;* The Old Bakery, Drift Hill, Ashampstead, READING, RG8 8RG.
BARTLETT, Mr. James David, BSc(Hons) FCA *2001;* 69 Church Avenue, PINNER, MIDDLESEX, HA5 5JE.
•BARTLETT, Mr. James Michael Gilbert, FCA *1971;* (Tax Fac), Bartlett Kershaw Trott, 4 Pullman Court, Great Western Road, GLOUCESTER, GL1 3ND.
BARTLETT, Mr. Jeremy Guy, BSc ACA *2000;* UPL, Prennau House, Copse Walk, Cardiff Gate Business Park, CARDIFF CF23 8XH.
BARTLETT, Mr. John Charles Harold, BA FCA *1981;* Greenhayes, Tilford Road, FARNHAM, GU9 8HX.
BARTLETT, Mr. John Dominic Timothy, BSc ACA *1991;* 8 Fairmead Rise, Kings Norton, BIRMINGHAM, B38 8BS.
BARTLETT, Mr. John Samuel Guest, FCA *1968;* Kawarty Red Sea Ltd., P.O. Box 71, Cairo International Airport, CAIRO, 11776, EGYPT.
BARTLETT, Mr. Joshua Edward, BSc ACA *2010;* with PricewaterhouseCoopers LLP, 1 Embankment Place, LONDON, WC2N 6RH.
BARTLETT, Miss. Julia, BSc ACA *2011;* Flat 2, 28a Old Devonshire Road, Balham, LONDON, SW12 9RB.
•BARTLETT, Mr. Julian Antony, BSc FCA *1989;* Grant Thornton UK LLP, 30 Finsbury Square, LONDON, EC2P 2YU. See also Grant Thornton LLP
•BARTLETT, Miss. Karen Teresa, FCA *1984;* (Tax Fac), Saffery Champness, Fox House, 26 Temple End, HIGH WYCOMBE, HP13 5DR.
BARTLETT, Mr. Kenneth David, FCA *1969;* (Tax Fac), The Brook House, 1 Hemming Way, Chaddesley Corbett, KIDDERMINSTER, WORCESTERSHIRE, DY10 4SF.
BARTLETT, Mr. Lee, ACA *2009;* 12 Cranborne Walk, FAREHAM, HAMPSHIRE, PO14 1JU.
BARTLETT, Mr. Leigh James, BEng ACA *1997;* Churchill Insurance Co Ltd Churchill Court, Westmoreland Road, BROMLEY, BR1 1DP.
BARTLETT, Miss. Lucy, ACA *2009;* 2 Westacre Close, BRISTOL, BS10 7DQ.
BARTLETT, Mr. Michael John Richard, BSc FCA *1985;* with Crowe Clark Whitehill LLP, Arkwright House, Parsonage Gardens, MANCHESTER, M3 2HP.
BARTLETT, Mr. Nicholas, MPhys ACA ACCA *2010;* 10 Kingswood Close, DARTFORD, DA1 3AD.
BARTLETT, Mr. Patrick David, MA FCA *1992;* AEGON, Edinburgh Park, EDINBURGH, EH12 9SE.
BARTLETT, Mr. Paul William, BA FCA AIIT *1991;* Imber, Cheeseman's Green Lane, Sevington, ASHFORD, KENT, TN24 0LJ.
•BARTLETT, Mr. Peter Michael Arnold, FCA *1981;* (Tax Fac), Lewis Knight, Suite D, Pinbrook Court, Venny Bridge, Pinhoe, EXETER EX4 8JQ. See also LKCA Limited
BARTLETT, Mr. Philip Anthony, FCA *1964;* 40 Eton Road, STRATFORD-UPON-AVON, CV37 7ER. (Life Member)
BARTLETT, Mr. Richard Frederick, ACA *2008;* 1615 Green Street, Pat C, PHILADELPHIA, PA 19130, UNITED STATES.
BARTLETT, Mr. Robert, ACA *2009;* Flat 458 Anchor House, Smugglers Way, LONDON, SW18 1EX.
BARTLETT, Mr. Robert Wilson, BSc FCA *1971;* 11 Berkeley Avenue, Bishopston, BRISTOL, BS7 8HH.
BARTLETT, Mr. Roger Anthony John, BCom FCA *1971;* Tir Artair, By Killin, KILLIN, FK21 8TX. (Life Member)
BARTLETT, Mr. Ronald William, FCA *1953;* 186 Beckenham Hill Road, BECKENHAM, BR3 1SZ. (Life Member)
BARTLETT, Miss. Samantha, BSc(Hons) ACA *2010;* Flat 2, 35 Culverden Road, LONDON, SW12 9LT.
BARTLETT, Miss. Sarah Elizabeth, BA ACA *1999;* Roonstrasse 31, 50674 COLOGNE, GERMANY.
BARTLETT, Mr. Simon Charles, BA ACA *1993;* British Film Institute, 21 Stephen Street, LONDON, W1T 1LN.
BARTLETT, Mr. Stephen Geoffrey, BSc FCA *1993;* Yew Tree Farm House, Behoes Lane, Woodcote, READING, RG8 0PP.
BARTLETT, Miss. Susan Elizabeth, BSc ACA *1991;* Lloyds TSB Asset Finance Division, St. William House, Tresillian Terrace, CARDIFF, CF10 5BH.
BARTLETT, Mrs. Voon Pow Cathy, ACA *1979;* (Tax Fac), 29 Ridley Road, LONDON, SW19 1ET.
BARTLETT-RAWLINGS, Mr. Richard Alan, ACA *2009;* 28 London Road, BRAINTREE, ESSEX, CM7 2LG.

BARTLEY, Mr. Gerard Paul, BEng ACA *1995;* Diependaalsedrift 3, 1213CM HILVERSUM, NETHERLANDS.
BARTLEY, Miss. Helen Julie, BA ACA *1997;* Willow House, 19 Knutsford Road, WILMSLOW, SK9 6JB.
BARTLEY, Mrs. Nicola Louise, MA MSt ACA *2002;* Westcroft, 14 Wychall Park Grove, BIRMINGHAM, B38 8AQ.
BARTLEY, Mr. Roger Denton, BA ACA *1983;* Orchard Cottage, Warren Road, Chelsfield Village, ORPINGTON, KENT, BR6 6EP.
BARTMAN, Mr. Barry David, BSc(Econ) FCA *1965;* 11 Park Avenue South, HARPENDEN, HERTFORDSHIRE, AL5 2DZ.
BARTOLACCI, Mrs. Suzanne Claire, BSc(Econ) ACA *1997;* 67 Miller Avenue, TARRYTOWN, NY 10591, UNITED STATES.
BARTOLI, Mr. David Albert, ACA *1983;* Casa Del Monte, 32 Sacred Heart Avenue, ST JULIANS, MALTA.
BARTOLO, Miss. Pamela, ACA *2008;* 232 East 64th Street, Apt 10, NEW YORK, NY 10065, UNITED STATES.
BARTON, Miss. Abigail Jane, BA ACA *2000;* 65 Horseshoe Road, Pangbourne, READING, RG8 7JL.
BARTON, Mr. Adam, ACA *2011;* 217 Leeds Road, Kippax, LEEDS, LS25 7EA.
BARTON, Mr. Alan, BSc ACA *1979;* (Tax Fac), Samworth Brothers Ltd, Chetwode House, 1 Samworth Way, MELTON MOWBRAY, LEICESTERSHIRE, LE13 1GA.
BARTON, Mr. Alan John, BA FCA *1975;* 141 Alwoodley Lane, Alwoodley, LEEDS, LS17 7PG. (Life Member)
BARTON, Mr. Allen, BSc ACA *2002;* Flat 26 Wollaton House, 7 Batchelor Street, LONDON, N1 0EY.
BARTON, Dr. Amanda Jane, PhD BSc ACA *1995;* Tilefield, Tilebarn Lane, BROCKENHURST, SO42 7UE.
BARTON, Mr. Andrew Mark, ACA *2008;* 16 Park Road, Worsley, MANCHESTER, M28 7DA.
BARTON, Mr. Andrew Ronald, BA FCA *1980;* Fernbank, 7 Mayfield Road, HERNE BAY, KENT, CT6 6EJ.
BARTON, Mr. Arthur Christopher Frank, MBA BSc FCA *1978;* Theodor-Storm-Str. 7a, 81245 MUNICH, GERMANY.
BARTON, Mr. Ashley, ACA *2009;* with KPMG LLP, 15 Canada Square, LONDON, E14 5GL.
BARTON, Mr. Brian Henry, FCA *1960;* 14 High Street, Hunsdon, WARE, HERTFORDSHIRE, SG12 8NZ. (Life Member)
BARTON, Mr. Bruce Oliver, FCA *1970;* 1 Lodge Walk, Greatpark, WARLINGHAM, SURREY, CR6 9PS. (Life Member)
•BARTON, Miss. Carole Ann, FCA *1991;* Carole A Barton FCA, 5 Grange Park Road, CHEADLE, CHESHIRE, SK8 1HQ.
BARTON, Mr. Christopher Alexander, MEng ACA *1998;* Conifers, 70a Harrow Lane, MAIDENHEAD, SL6 7PA.
BARTON, Mr. Christopher Synge, FCA *1966;* Compton Cottage, Compton Pauncefoot, YEOVIL, BA22 7EN.
•BARTON, Mr. Clive Neil Stewart, FCA *1974;* (Tax Fac), Moore Stephens, P O Box 236, First Island House, Peter Street, St. Helier, JERSEY JE4 8SG. See also Moore Stephens Limited
BARTON, Mr. Daniel, ACA *2010;* 14 Darwell Avenue, Eccles, MANCHESTER, M30 7AB.
BARTON, Mr. David, FCA *1969;* Flat 5, 12 Lennox Gardens, LONDON, SW1X 0DG.
•BARTON, Mr. David John, BA FCA *1975;* David Barton, 8 Bevan Street, Islington, LONDON, N1 7DY.
•BARTON, Mr. David Robert, BSocSc ACA CTA *1993;* Baker Tilly Tax & Advisory Services LLP, The Pinnacle, 170 Midsummer Boulevard, MILTON KEYNES, MK9 1BP.
•BARTON, Mrs. Deborah Marjorie, ACA *1981;* RFW Rutherfords Ltd, Ardenham Court Oxford Road, AYLESBURY, BUCKINGHAMSHIRE, HP19 8HT.
BARTON, Mr. Derek Hugh, FCA *1955;* 5 Holbrook Park, Old Holbrook, HORSHAM, RH12 4TW. (Life Member)
BARTON, Ms. Elizabeth, BSc ACA *1995;* Little Bowden, Bowden Green, PANGBOURNE, BERKSHIRE, RG8 8JJ.
BARTON, Mr. Eric Lancaster, FCA *1967;* 9 Foxglove Gardens, Merrow Park, GUILDFORD, GU4 7ES.
BARTON, Mr. Ernest Raymond, FCA *1957;* Crawford House, London Street, Whissonsett, DEREHAM, NORFOLK, NR20 5ST. (Life Member)
BARTON, Mr. Geoffrey Peter, FCA *1969;* 40 Rayneham Road, Shipley Common Lane, ILKESTON, DE7 8RJ.
BARTON, Mr. Gerald, FCA *1975;* Deer Park Farm Rectory Lane, Combe Martin, ILFRACOMBE, DEVON, EX34 0LP.
BARTON, Ms. Helen, ACA *2008;* Swallow Barns Mobberley Road, Ashley, ALTRINCHAM, CHESHIRE, WA15 0QL.
BARTON, Mrs. Helen Pauline, BA ACA *1992;* 8 Green Close, Stanbridge, LEIGHTON BUZZARD, BEDFORDSHIRE, LU7 9JL.
BARTON, Mr. Ian Mark, BSc ACA *1989;* Hopecote, 11 St. Stephens Hill, LAUNCESTON, CORNWALL, PL15 8HN.
•BARTON, Mr. Ian Robert, BA ACA CF *1996;* with Deloitte LLP, Abbots House, Abbey Street, READING, RG1 3BD.
BARTON, Mr. Jake Woodrow, BA ACA *1996;* Kantar Group, Research International Ltd, 6 More London Place, LONDON, SE1 2QY.
BARTON, Mr. James, BSS ACA *1994;* with PPM Capital Limited, 1 New Fetter Lane, LONDON, EC4A 1HH.
•BARTON, Mr. James Christopher, FCA *1967;* J.C. Barton & Co, Martland Buildings, Mart Lane, Burscough, ORMSKIRK, L40 0SD.
BARTON, Mr. James Ian, MA FCA *1997;* 13 Cockerell Street, FERNTREE GULLY, VIC 3156, AUSTRALIA.
BARTON, Mrs. Janet Loyd, BSc FCA ACA *1980;* 4 Dellcroft Way, HARPENDEN, HERTFORDSHIRE, AL5 2NG.
BARTON, Mr. Jeremy Gordon, FCA *1962;* 83 Stanley Gardens Road, TEDDINGTON, TW11 8SY.
BARTON, Mr. Jeremy John Orr, MA ACA *2001;* 14 Hansler Road, LONDON, SE22 9DJ.
BARTON, Mr. Jeremy Phillip Laurence, BA(Hons) ACA *2004;* Highfield The Street, Knapton, NORTH WALSHAM, NORFOLK, NR28 0AD.
BARTON, Mr. John Raymond, FCA *1956;* 98 Balmoral Drive, SOUTHPORT, PR9 8PY. (Life Member)
•BARTON, Mr. John Victor, FCA *1969;* (Tax Fac), John V. Barton, 29 Garstang Road, PRESTON, PR1 1LA.
BARTON, Mr. Jonathan Christopher, BSc ACA *1999;* Imtech ICT Ltd, Units B & C Oakcroft Business Centre Oakcroft Road, CHESSINGTON, KT9 1RH.
BARTON, Mr. Jonathan James, MA ACA *1998;* 6th Floor - L20, U B S AG, 100 Liverpool Street, LONDON, EC2M 2RH.
BARTON, Mrs. Judith Helen, BSc ACA *1988;* (Tax Fac), with PricewaterhouseCoopers LLP, 1 Embankment Place, LONDON, WC2N 6RH.
BARTON, Miss. Julia, BSc ACA *2009;* Unipart Group of Companies Unipart House, Garsington Road Cowley, OXFORD, OX4 2PG.
BARTON, Miss. Julie Dawn, BA ACA *1994;* 39 Ledborough Lane, BEACONSFIELD, BUCKINGHAMSHIRE, HP9 2DB.
BARTON, Mr. Justin Glenn, BSc ACA *1989;* 2 Stevenage Road, Fulham, LONDON, SW6 6ER.
BARTON, Mrs. Karen Elizabeth, BSc ACA *2002;* 7 Manor Walk, WEYBRIDGE, SURREY, KT13 8SD.
BARTON, Mrs. Katherine Jane, BSc ACA *2004;* Barclays Capital, 200 Park Avenue, NEW YORK, NY 10166, UNITED STATES.
BARTON, Mr. Kenneth, BSc FCA *1981;* (Tax Fac), Edgerley Loosley Hill, Loosley Row, PRINCES RISBOROUGH, BUCKINGHAMSHIRE, HP27 0NT.
BARTON, Mr. Kenneth Callum Orr, BA FCA *1973;* 16 route de Credery, 1242 SATIGNY, SWITZERLAND.
BARTON, Mrs. Lisa Ann, BA ACA *1998;* 38 Silvester Way, Church Crookham, FLEET, HAMPSHIRE, GU52 0TP.
BARTON, Mr. Martin, FCA *1968;* 15 Ty Gwyn Crescent, CARDIFF, CF23 5JL.
BARTON, Mr. Matthew, BA(Hons) ACA *2011;* 79 Argie Avenue, Burley, LEEDS, LS4 2QN.
BARTON, Mr. Michael, BSc ACA *2004;* Feldweg 24, 6415 ARTH, SWITZERLAND.
BARTON, Mr. Michael Stuart, BSc ACA *1995;* Skimbles Swinbrook Road, Shipton-under-Wychwood, CHIPPING NORTON, OXFORDSHIRE, OX7 6DX.
•BARTON, Mr. Michael William, BSc FCA *1981;* (Tax Fac), Titus Thorp & Ainsworth Limited, 1 Church Street, Adlington, CHORLEY, LANCASHIRE, PR7 4EX. See also Rotherham Taylor Limited
BARTON, Mrs. Michelle, BA(Hons) ACA *2004;* 24 Edgecote Close, MANCHESTER, M22 4UT.
•BARTON, Mr. Neil Christopher, LLB ACA *2001;* with BDO LLP, 6th Floor, 3 Hardman Street, Spinningfields, MANCHESTER, M3 3AT.
BARTON, Dr. Nina Elizabeth Mariam, PhD BSc ACA *2010;* 32 Wootton Road, BRISTOL, BS4 4AL.
BARTON, Mr. Paul Alexander, MBA BSc FCA *1971;* 68 Tippings Lane, Woodley, READING, RG5 4RY.
BARTON, Mr. Paul Edward, BSc FCA *1990;* 3 Low Pastures, Levens, KENDAL, CUMBRIA, LA8 8QH.
•BARTON, Mr. Peter Francis, FCA *1975;* (Tax Fac), Barton Little & Co, 1 Fernhurst Road, LONDON, SW6 7JN.
•BARTON, Mr. Peter John, FCA *1976;* Wilkins Kennedy, Greytown House, 221-227 High Street, ORPINGTON, BR6 0NZ.
BARTON, Mr. Peter John, FCA *1989;* (Tax Fac), with Reeves & Co LLP, 37 St. Margarets Street, CANTERBURY, KENT, CT1 2TU.
BARTON, Mr. Richard Alistair, BSc FCA *1991;* Hawks View, Paley Street, MAIDENHEAD, SL6 3JS.
BARTON, Mr. Richard Robert, BSc ACA *1994;* 33 Harbour Way, Victoria Dock, HULL, HU9 1PL.
BARTON, Mr. Robert Andrew, BA ACA *1979;* 111 Aberdale Gardens, POTTERS BAR, EN6 2JG.
BARTON, Mr. Robert John, BSc ACA *1983;* Birchwood, 35 Sheepwalk Lane, Ravenshead, NOTTINGHAM, NG15 9FD.
•BARTON, Mr. Roy, FCA *1971;* (Tax Fac), Bright Brown Limited, Exchange House, St. Cross Lane, NEWPORT, ISLE OF WIGHT, PO30 5BZ.
BARTON, Miss. Sarah Anne, BSc ACA *2004;* 15 Trelawne Drive, CRANLEIGH, GU6 8BS.
BARTON, Mrs. Sarah Elizabeth, MA ACA *1998;* 48 Clapham Manor Street, Clapham, LONDON, SW4 6DZ.
BARTON, Mrs. Sarah Louise, BA(Hons) ACA *2001;* Ashlands Ballinger Road South Heath, GREAT MISSENDEN, BUCKINGHAMSHIRE, HP16 9QJ.
BARTON, Mrs. Shirley Elaine, BA ACA *1989;* 56 Derwent Road, HARPENDEN, AL5 3NX.
BARTON, Mr. Simon Charles Robert, MA ACA *1990;* 27 Pickford Road, Markyate, ST ALBANS, AL3 8RS.
BARTON, Mr. Simon James, BA BA(Hons) ACA *2011;* 9 Silverburn Drive, Oakwood, DERBY, DE21 2JJ.
BARTON, Mr. Stephen Charles, BA ACA *1996;* Finance House, Park Street, GUILDFORD, GU1 4XB.
BARTON, Mr. Stephen Paul, BA(Hons) ACA *2001;* 38 Silvester Way, Church Crookham, FLEET, GU52 0TP.
BARTON, Mr. Thomas Wulstan, FCA *1954;* 4 Berkeley Close, CHORLEY, PR7 3JS. (Life Member)
BARTON, Mr. Timothy Peter, BSc ACA *1998;* 10 Lexden Road, West Bergholt, COLCHESTER, CO6 3BT.
BARTON, Mr. Warren Stride, FCA *1974;* 28 Rue Du Paillet, 69570 DARDILLY, FRANCE.
BARTON-SMITH, Mr. Colin, FCA *1971;* Victoria House Station Road, Ditton Priors, BRIDGNORTH, SHROPSHIRE, WV16 6SS.
BARTON-WOOD, Mr. Richard Oliver, BSc ACA *1998;* East Acre, 156 Lovedon Lane, Kings Worthy, WINCHESTER, SO23 7NJ.
BARTOSIK, Mr. Robert Matthew, ACA *2007;* Flat C, 7 Lansdown Crescent, CHELTENHAM, GL50 2JY.
BARTRAM, Mr. Lucien Osborne, MA ACA *1996;* Globe Microsystems Ltd, Unit D7, Sandown Industrial Park, Mill Road, ESHER, SURREY KT10 8BL.
BARTRAM, Ms. Natalie Anne, BA ACA *1997;* 39 Taylor Row, Wilmington, DARTFORD, DA2 7DU.
BARTRAM, Mrs. Sarah, BA(Hons) ACA *2003;* 3 Cambalt Road, LONDON, SW15 6EL.
•BARTRAM, Mrs. Wendy Patricia, ACA *1990;* (Tax Fac), Ian R. Collins & Co., The Bridge House, Mill Lane, DRONFIELD, S18 2XL.
•BARTROP, Mr. Peter John, FCA *1974;* (Tax Fac), Deep Roofs, Hay Green Lane, Hook End, BRENTWOOD, ESSEX, CM15 0NX.
BARTSCH, Mr. David Karl, BCom ACA *2007;* Schlumberger Ltd, Parkstraat 83, 2514JG THE HAGUE, ZUID HOLLAND, NETHERLANDS.
•BARTY, Mrs. Emma Louise, BSc ACA *2000;* AJS & Associates, 43 Battery Hill, Fairlight, HASTINGS, EAST SUSSEX, TN35 4AP.
BARTY, Mr. Ian Christopher, ACA MBA *1991;* Unilever Asia Private Limited, 20 Pasir Panjang Road #06-22, Mapletree Business Centra, SINGAPORE 117439, SINGAPORE.
BARUA, Mr. Deba Prasad, BA FCA *1956;* 6th Floor, 4 Grosvenor Place, LONDON, SW1X 7DG.
BARUA, Mr. Goutam Swapan Kumar, FCA *1971;* 23 Ripley Road, Seven Kings, ILFORD, ESSEX, IG3 9HA. (Life Member)
BARUAH, Mr. Dean, BA(Hons) ACA *2004;* 7/ 11 Lang Street, MOSMAN, NSW 2088, AUSTRALIA.
BARUAH, Mr. Rangam, BSc ACA *1995;* 9605 Tree Bend Dr, AUSTIN, TX 78750, UNITED STATES.
•BARVE, Mrs. Rubina, ACA *1997;* YG Eaton & Co Limited, Alpine House, Unit 2, 1st Floor, Honeypot Lane, LONDON NW9 9RX.
•BARWELL, Mrs. Jane Frances, BA ACA *1994;* with Ernst & Young LLP, The Paragon, Counterslip, BRISTOL, BS1 6BX.
•BARWELL, Mr. Nicholas Mark, FCA *1982;* (Tax Fac), Nicholas Barwell & Co Ltd, Stirling House, Carriers Fold, Church Road, Wombourne, WOLVERHAMPTON WV5 9DJ.
BARWICK, Mr. Christopher John, ACA *1983;* Fir Tree Lodge, Ashby Lane, Bitteswell, LUTTERWORTH, LE17 4LS.
BARWICK, Mr. David John, FCA *1961;* 11 Woodview, Langdon Hills, BASILDON, ESSEX, SS16 6TZ.
•BARWICK, Mr. Kevin Arthur, FCA *1980;* Baker Tilly Tax & Advisory Services LLP, Spring Park House, Basing View, BASINGSTOKE, HAMPSHIRE, RG21 4HG. See also Baker Tilly UK Audit LLP
BARWICK, Mr. Paul James, LLB ACA *2010;* 20 Seren Park Gardens, LONDON, SE3 7RP.
•BARWICK, Mr. Richard John, FCA *1966;* R J Barwick, Maybury Copse, The Ridge, WOKING, SURREY, GU22 7EQ.
BARWICK, Mr. Roger William, FCA *1970;* 6 Western Esplanade, BROADSTAIRS, KENT, CT10 1TG.
BARWICK, Mr. William Alfred, FCA *1958;* 60 Alexandra Road, EPSOM, KT17 4BZ. (Life Member)
BARWISE, Mr. Anthony Jevon, BA FCA *1995;* 2 Shetland Close, Fearnhead, WARRINGTON, WA2 0UW.
BARWOOD, Mrs. Jacqueline Ann, ACA *1993;* The School House, Emery Down, LYNDHURST, SO43 7DY.
BARZEGAR, Mr. Roland, BSc ACA *2007;* 23 Sussex Avenue, Horsforth, LEEDS, LS18 5NP.
•BASADDIQ, Mr. Abdulrahman Sadiq Salim, FCA *1978;* Flat 39 Stafford Court, Kensington High Street, LONDON, W8 7DL.
BASAK, Mr. Arun Kumar, BCom FCA *1954;* Kahlenberger Strasse 61/9, A-1190 VIENNA, AUSTRIA. (Life Member)
•BASANTA LALA, Mr. Couldiplall, FCA *1975;* International Financial Services Limited, IFS Court, TwentyEight, Cybercity, Ebene, REDUIT MAURITIUS. See also Interantional Financial Services
BASANTA LALA, Miss. Divya, ACA *2010;* 495 Yio Chu Kang Road, #01-03 Seasons' Park Condonium, SINGAPORE 787080, SINGAPORE.
•BASCH, Mr. Richard, BA(Hons) ACA *2006;* Richard Ian & Co, Suite 7, 2nd Floor Elstree House, Elstree Way, BOREHAMWOOD, HERTFORDSHIRE WD6 1SD.
•BASCOMBE, Mr. Ian Charles, FCA *1989;* Sully Partnership, 8 Unity Street, College Green, BRISTOL, BS1 5HH. See also Sully Partnership Limited
BASCOMBE, Mr. Mark Rodney, BA FCA *1988;* 24 Somers Street, Bentleigh, MELBOURNE, VIC 3204, AUSTRALIA.
BASDEN, Mr. Brian Edward, MA FCA *1951;* (Member of Council 1977 - 1981), The Bolt, 11 East Common, GERRARDS CROSS, SL9 7AD. (Life Member)
BASDEN-SMITH, Mr. Hugh Philipp, FCA *1959;* 6 Selmeston Court, Surrey Road, SEAFORD, BN25 2NQ. (Life Member)
BASDEN-SMITH, Mr. Ian, FCA *1973;* The Garden House, Chart lane, Brasted n' Westerham, WESTERHAM, KENT, TN16 1LW.
BASE, Mr. Trevor John, FCA *1956;* 11 Padwick Road, HORSHAM, RH13 6BN. (Life Member)
BASELEY, Mr. Clive William, FCA *1974;* The Old Stables, Monument Lane, Hagley, STOURBRIDGE, DY9 9JX.
BASEY, Mr. Paul, BA ACA *1991;* 1 Farnacres Cottages, Coach Road, GATESHEAD, TYNE AND WEAR, NE11 0HJ.
BASEY, Mr. Phillip Victor, BA ACA *1981;* 52 St. Giles Avenue, UXBRIDGE, MIDDLESEX, UB10 8RL.
BASFORD, Mr. Anthony Dian, MA BA ACA *2009;* 57 Ashley Gardens, Ambrosden Avenue, LONDON, SW1P 1QG.
BASFORD, Mr. Hedley Richard, MBA FCA *1968;* Chapter Seven, Old Tree, Hoath, CANTERBURY, KENT, CT3 4LE. (Life Member)
BASFORD, Mr. Stuart Arthur, BSc ACA *1992;* 2 Little Lane, Blisworth, NORTHAMPTON, NN7 3BS.
BASFORD, Mr. Wayne, BSc ACA *1992;* with BDO International, G.P.O. Box 2551, SYDNEY, NSW 2001, AUSTRALIA.
BASGEET, Mr. Yogesh Rai, ACA FCCA *2007;* 7(i) Lislet Geoffroy Street, CUREPIPE, MAURITIUS.
•BASGER, Mr. Andrew Grant, BA FCA *1999;* Edwards Veeder (Oldham) LLP, Block E, Brunswick Square, Union Street, OLDHAM, OL1 1DE.
BASHALL, Mr. Godfrey Francis, FCA *1953;* 87 Victoria Road, Fulwood, PRESTON, PR2 8NL. (Life Member)
BASHAM, Mr. Paul, BSc FCA *1999;* Horticultural Trades Association, 19 High Street Theale, READING, RG7 5AH.
BASHEER, Mr. Rafi Haroon, ACA *1997;* 2nd Floor, SHELL HOUSE, SHELL PAKISTAN LIMITED, Near Frere Police Station, 6 Chaudary Khaliquzzaman Road, KARACHI 75530 PAKISTAN.

BASHFORTH, Miss. Amy, ACA *2011;* 83 Scholes View, Ecclesfield, SHEFFIELD, S35 9YQ.
BASHFORTH, Mr. Edward Michael, BA FCA CF *1998;* 102 Harrow Road, NOTTINGHAM, NG8 1FN.
BASHIR, Mr. Fahim, BSc ACA *2006;* KPMG Safi Al-Mutawa & Partners, 18th Floor Rakan Tower, Fahad Al-Salem Street, KUWAIT CITY, KUWAIT.
BASHIR, Mr. Paul Wayne, BA(Hons) ACA *2001;* Aggmore Properties Ltd, 35 Dover Street, LONDON, W1S 4NQ.
BASHIR, Mrs. Rahat, ACA *2008;* 7 Alnmouth Drive, NEWCASTLE UPON TYNE, NE3 1YF.
BASHIR, Mr. Shahzad, ACA *1982;* 2929 Allen Parkway Suite 2700, HOUSTON, TX 77019, UNITED STATES.
BASHIR, Mr. Zaheer, ACA *2010;* Flat 4 Heckford House, Grundy Street, LONDON, E14 6AE.
BASIRDIN, Mr. Steve Shaiful Hamidi, MSc BSc ACA *2003;* Flat 16 Earls House, 10 Strand Drive, RICHMOND, SURREY, TW9 4DZ.
BASIS, Mr. Rawi, *2009;* 12C York Mews, LONDON, NW5 2UJ.
BASKARAN, Mr. Angelo Karunalingam, ACA *1982;* 3038 Military Road, ARLINGTON, VA 22207, UNITED STATES.
BASKER, Miss. Namrata, ACA *2009;* Flat 73, Building 45, Hopton Road, LONDON, SE18 6TJ.
BASKERVILLE, Mr. David John, BSc ACA *1990;* Hepplewhite, Headcorn Road, Frittenden, CRANBROOK, TN17 2EJ.
BASKERVILLE, Mrs. Fiona Claire, BA(Hons) ACA *2003;* with Ernst & Young LLP, Wessex House, 19 Threefield Lane, SOUTHAMPTON, SO14 3QB.
BASKERVILLE, Mr. George Edward, FCA *1965;* Dewsbury Cottage, Grub Lane, Kelsall, TARPORLEY, CHESHIRE, CW6 0QU.
BASKERVILLE, Miss. Jennifer, BSc ACA *2011;* Flat 3, 6 Old Station Way, LONDON, SW4 6DA.
BASKERVILLE, Mr. Malcolm Stuart, FCA *1973;* 257 Chester Road, Helsby, FRODSHAM, WA6 0AN.
BASKERVILLE, Mr. Mark, MSc BSc ACA *2007;* 12a Mayfair Gardens, SOUTHAMPTON, SO15 2TW.
BASKERVILLE, Mr. Richard, BSc ACA *2001;* The Royal Bank of Scotland, 38/F Cheung Kong Center, 2 Queens Road, CENTRAL, HONG KONG ISLAND, HONG KONG SAR.
BASKEYFIELD, Mr. Alex, ACA *2008;* with Mazars LLP, Mazars House, Gelderd Road, Gildersome, LEEDS, LS27 7JN.
BASKEYFIELD, Mrs. Joanna Kay, BSc(Hons) ACA *2003;* 8 St. Johns Way, Sandiway, NORTHWICH, CHESHIRE, CW8 2LX.
BASKIN, Mr. Ronald Joel, MSc FCA *1952;* 15 Sandwich Road, WORTHING, BN11 5NT. (Life Member)
BASKIN, Mr. Stanley, FCA *1966;* 2 Maya Road, East Finchley, LONDON, N2 0PP.
BASMA, Mr. Amar Joseph, BA ACA ATII *1998;* 6 Head Croft, Farleigh Green, Flax Bourton, BRISTOL, BS48 1US.
BASON, Miss. Caroline Anne, BSc ACA *1996;* Carter Jonas Llp, South Pavilion, Sansaw Business Park, Hardwicke Stables, Hadnall, SHREWSBURY SY4 4AS.
BASON, Mr. John George, MA ACA *1985;* Associated British Foods Plc, Weston Centre, 10 Grosvenor Street, LONDON, W1K 4QY.
BASON, Mr. Keith Martin, BSc FCA *1990;* Chalton House, Love Lane, PETERSFIELD, GU31 4BU.
BASON, Mr. Roger Esmond, MA FCA *1966;* 234 Queen Elizabeth Driveway, OTTAWA K1S 3M4, ON, CANADA. (Life Member)
BASON, Mr. Thomas Peter, ACA *2008;* Flat A, 88 Sheen Road, RICHMOND, TW9 1UF.
BASRA, Mrs. Amandeep Kaur, BSc ACA *2007;* 12 Blackberry Close, KETTERING, NORTHAMPTONSHIRE, NN16 9JQ.
BASRA, Mr. Bhaljinder Singh, LLB ACA *2004;* 330 London Road, Langley, SLOUGH, SL3 7HU.
BASRA, Mr. Davinderpal Singh, BSc ACA *1999;* 32 Arboretum Road, WALSALL, WS1 2QH.
•**BASRA, Mr. Hera, BA FCA** *1993;* Basra & Basra Ltd, 9 London Road, SOUTHAMPTON, SO15 2AE.
•**BASRA, Mr. Rajinder Singh, BSc FCA** *1991;* Cameron & Associates Ltd, 35-37 Lowlands Road, HARROW, MIDDLESEX, HA1 3AW.
BASRA, Mr. Satvinder Singh, BA ACA *1993;* BB-27-02, 10 Mont Kiara, Jalan Kiara 1, Mont Kiara, 50480 KUALA LUMPUR, FEDERAL TERRITORY MALAYSIA.
•**BASRA, Mr. Steven, BSc ACA** *1995;* 1st Finance Solutions Limited, Acorn House, Broomfield Park, Sunningdale, ASCOT, BERKSHIRE SL5 0JT.
BASRAI, Mr. Abbas, BSc ACA *2007;* 14 Chatsworth Court, Pembroke Road, LONDON, W8 6DG.
•**BASRAI, Mr. Abdul Husain, FCA** *1976;* KPMG Taseer Hadi & Co, 1st Floor, Sheikh Sultan Trust Bldg Apt 2, Beaumont Road, KARACHI 75530, PAKISTAN.
BASRAN, Mr. Surinder Singh, ACA *2005;* 20 Edward Road, OLDBURY, WEST MIDLANDS, B68 0LY.
•**BASS, Mr. Anthony John, FCA** *1968;* Bass & Co, 123 Riddlesdown Road, PURLEY, CR8 1DL.
BASS, Mr. Arthur Norman, FCA *1950;* Four Winds, 13 Queens Park Rd, CATERHAM, CR3 5RB. (Life Member)
BASS, Miss. Caroline, BA(Hons) ACA *2011;* 19 Firacre Road, Ash Vale, ALDERSHOT, HAMPSHIRE, GU12 5JR.
BASS, Mr. Clive John, BA ACA *1996;* Francis House, 11 Francis Street, LONDON, SW1P 1DE.
BASS, Mr. Craig Darren, BA(Hons) ACA *2003;* 15 Rue De Luxembourg, L8140 Bridel, LUXEMBOURG, LUXEMBOURG.
BASS, Mr. Derek Michael, FCA *1978;* (Tax Fac), 9 Helford Way, UPMINSTER, RM14 1RJ.
BASS, Mr. John David, MA FCA *1965;* York House, 85 Green Lane, Burnham, SLOUGH, SL1 8EG. (Life Member)
BASS, Mrs. Karen Ruth, BA ACA *1996;* 21 Clement Road, Marple Bridge, STOCKPORT, CHESHIRE, SK6 5AF.
BASS, Mrs. Keren Joy Irene, BSc ACA *1992;* (Tax Fac), 10 Cam Green, Cam, DURSLEY, GL11 5HN.
•**BASS, Mr. Malcolm Roy, ACA** *1982;* Malcolm Bass & Co, 53 Bentfield Causeway, STANSTED, ESSEX, CM24 8HU.
BASS, Mr. Matthew James, BSc ACA *1994;* 1 Celandine Close, RUSHDEN, NORTHAMPTONSHIRE, NN10 0GJ.
•**BASS, Mr. Robert James, BA FCA** *1975;* (Tax Fac), Robert J. Bass & Co, 339 High Street, WEST BROMWICH, B70 9QG.
BASS, Ms. Rowena Ann Cordelia, BSc ACA *1989;* 36 Dickerage Road, KINGSTON-UPON-THAMES, KT1 3SS.
BASS, Mr. Simon Charles, BA ACA *1985;* Yew Tree Farmhouse, The Street, Wormshill, SITTINGBOURNE, KENT, ME9 0TU.
BASS, Mr. Stewart Richard, BSc ACA *2009;* 44 Forest Avenue, ASHFORD, TN25 4GB.
BASSAS, Mr. Henry Ejaz, BCom FCA FCCA ATII *1964;* 110 Netherlands Road, New Barnet, BARNET, HERTFORDSHIRE, EN5 1BX. (Life Member)
BASSET, Mr. Thomas Mark, BA ACA *2008;* Marwyn Capital LLP, 11 Buckingham Street, LONDON, WC2N 6DF.
BASSETT, Mr. Adam David, BSc ACA *1993;* R S P B The Lodge, Potton Road, SANDY, SG19 2DL.
•**BASSETT, Mr. Andrew Graham, FCA** *1968;* (Tax Fac), 24 Northumberland Avenue, Forest Hall, NEWCASTLE UPON TYNE, NE12 9NR.
BASSETT, Miss. Anna, BA ACA *2003;* with PricewaterhouseCoopers LLP, 1 Embankment Place, LONDON, WC2N 6RH.
BASSETT, Mr. Anthony Wyn, BSc ACA *1990;* AXA Insurance, 1 Aldgate, LONDON, EC3N 1RE.
•**BASSETT, Mr. Christopher Lyn, FCA DChA** *1979;* Izod Bassett, 105 High Street, Needham Market, IPSWICH, IP6 8DQ.
BASSETT, Mr. Clive Warren, FCA MAAT *1992;* 46 Okus Road, SWINDON, SN1 4JQ.
BASSETT, Mr. Colin Michael, ACA *1988;* Apartment 11, Kings Wharf, GIBRALTAR, GIBRALTAR.
•**BASSETT, Ms. Elisabeth Anne, MA ACA** *1985;* KPMG LLP, 15 Canada Square, LONDON, E14 5GL. See also KPMG Europe LLP
BASSETT, Mr. Ervin John, MA FCA *1977;* Sussex Downs College, Cross Levels Way, EASTBOURNE, EAST SUSSEX, BN21 2UF.
BASSETT, Mr. Ian, BSc FCA MBA *1991;* Highfield House Lower Mountain Road, Penyffordd, CHESTER, CH4 0EU.
BASSETT, Ms. Jacqueline Sian, ACA *1994;* 59 Barton Avenue, Heretaunga, UPPER HUTT 5018, NEW ZEALAND.
BASSETT, Mrs. Janie Ellen, ACA *2006;* Fairleys Way Badwell Green, Badwell Ash, BURY ST. EDMUNDS, SUFFOLK, IP31 3JG.
BASSETT, Mr. John Peter Cecil, FCA *1975;* P.O. Box 47740, GREYVILLE, KWAZULU NATAL, 4023, SOUTH AFRICA.
BASSETT, Mr. Laurence, ACA *2009;* K P M G, 37 Hills Road, CAMBRIDGE, CB2 1XL.
BASSETT, Mr. Leslie, BA ACA *1981;* Camino El Callao 1, NO 70, La Asomada, Final Del Camino, Las Palmas, 35571 LANZAROTE SPAIN.
•**BASSETT, Mr. Nicholas Wathen, BSc FCA** *1984;* Harris Bassett Limited, 5 New Mill Court, Phoenix Way, Enterprise Park, SWANSEA, SA7 9FG.
BASSETT, Mr. Philip Simon Lloyd, MA ACA *1992;* The Old Rectory, Brightwell Baldwin, WATLINGTON, OXFORDSHIRE, OX49 5NW.
BASSFORD, Mr. Ian, BSc ACA *2003;* (Tax Fac), 36 Carston Close, LONDON, SE12 8DZ.
•①**BASSFORD, Mr. Mark Philip, BA FCA MABRP** *1994;* Guardian Business Recovery LLP, 6-7 Ludgate Square, LONDON, EC4M 7AS. See also Sentinel Trustees Limited and Guardian Business Recovery (VA) Ltd
BASSI, Mr. Alvin, LLB ACA *2001;* 31 Tewkesbury Avenue, PINNER, MIDDLESEX, HA5 5LQ.
BASSI, Mr. Anuj Cyrus, BSc(Hons) ACA *2000;* 31 Davenport, HARLOW, ESSEX, CM17 9TF.
BASSI, Mrs. Jasvinder, LLB ACA *2003;* 191 Ringway, SOUTHALL, UB2 5SU.
BASSI, Ms. Naveen, BSc ACA *2009;* 1 Clydesdale Close, ISLEWORTH, TW7 6ST.
BASSI, Mr. Ramneet, BSc(Hons) ACA *2003;* 1 Clydesdale Close, ISLEWORTH, MIDDLESEX, TW7 6ST.
BASSI, Miss. Simneet Kaur, ACA *2008;* with PricewaterhouseCoopers LLP, 1 Embankment Place, LONDON, WC2N 6RH.
BASSI, Ms. Sudesh, BA ACA MBA *1990;* 30 Cambridge Road, HOUNSLOW, TW4 7BS.
BASSI, Mr. Sunil, BA ACA *1992;* International Power Senator House, 85 Queen Victoria Street, LONDON, EC4V 4DP.
BASSI, Miss. Tanya, ACA *2004;* 25 Pavilion Square, LONDON, SW17 7DN.
•**BASSIL, Mr. John Edward, FCA** *1971;* (Tax Fac), Thatchers, 13 Dunstable Road, Studham, DUNSTABLE, LU6 2QG.
BASSILL, Mr. Neil Christopher, ACA *2008;* PriceWaterhouse Coopers, Freshwater Place, 2 Southbank Boulevard, Southbank, MELBOURNE, VIC 3141 AUSTRALIA.
BASSINDALE, Mr. Graham John, FCA *1972;* 7 Saxon Way, SAFFRON WALDEN, CB11 4EQ.
BASSOM, Mrs. Catherine Grace, BA ACA *1993;* 70 Missenden Acres, Hedge End, SOUTHAMPTON, SO30 2RE.
BASSOM, Mr. Mark William, BA ACA *1992;* 70 Missenden Acres, Hedge End, SOUTHAMPTON, SO30 2RE.
BASSON, Miss. Leanne Louise, ACA *2010;* 150 Mosley Common Road, Worsley, MANCHESTER, M28 1AF.
BASSON, Ms. Tinecke, ACA *2011;* 69 Tooting Bec Road, LONDON, SW17 8BP.
BASTABLE, Mr. Mark Graham, BA ACA *1990;* 68 Norton Road, Norton, STOURBRIDGE, DY8 2AQ.
•**BASTABLE, Mr. Stephen John, BSc FCA** *1976;* SJB Accountancy Limited, 41 Lochaber Street, Roath, CARDIFF, CF24 3LS.
BASTEN, Mr. Jonathan, ACA *2008;* Trevor Jones & Co Central House, 582-586 Kingsbury Road Erdington, BIRMINGHAM, B24 9ND.
BASTERFIELD, Mr. Brian Roy, FCA *1962;* 33 Holland Avenue, Knowle, SOLIHULL, B93 9DW.
BASTIANPILLAI, Miss. Shalini, BA ACA *2008;* 52 Queens Gardens, LONDON, W2 3AA.
BASTIBLE, Mr. Brian James, BA ACA MCT *1993;* IDA Ireland, Finiskin Business Park, SLIGO, COUNTY SLIGO, IRELAND.
BASTICK, Dr. Liam, DPhil MPhil MSc BA(Hons) FCA *1998;* 261 Sayers Road, TRUGANINA, VIC 3029, AUSTRALIA.
BASTIMAN, Mr. Nicholas Andrew, BA ACA *1992;* Royal Bank of Canada (Jersey) Ltd, PO Box 194, 19-21 Broad Street, St Helier, JERSEY, JE4 8RR.
BASTIN, Mr. Clive David, FCA *1960;* Penny Farthing, Stortford Road, Hatfield Heath, BISHOP'S STORTFORD, HERTFORDSHIRE, CM22 7DL. (Life Member)
BASTING, Mrs. Joanne Elizabeth, BSc ACA *2004;* G4S Security Services (UK) Ltd, Sutton Park House 15 Carshalton Road, SUTTON, SURREY, SM1 4LD.
BASTOCK, Mr. James, ACA *2010;* 7 Bishop Lonsdale Way, Mickleover, DERBY, DE3 9DF.
BASTOCK, Mrs. Lyndsey, BCom ACA *2001;* 30a Belgrave Road, HALESOWEN, WEST MIDLANDS, B62 9EY.
BASTON, Mr. Leonard Alfred John, FCA *1956;* 58 Grangewood Road, Wollaton, NOTTINGHAM, NG8 2SW. (Life Member)
BASTON, Mr. Timothy James Saint Clair, BSc ACA *1988;* 9 Gannet Close, SOUTHAMPTON, SO16 8ET.
BASTOW, Mr. Mark Andrew, BSc ACA *2002;* 17 Mayhall Avenue, East Morton, KEIGHLEY, WEST YORKSHIRE, BD20 5WF.
BASTOW, Mr. Mark David, BA ACA *1990;* En Bois-Billens 1, 1162 ST PREX, SWITZERLAND.
BASTOW, Mr. Richard Mark, BA ACA *1995;* 3 Earl Crag View, Cowling, KEIGHLEY, WEST YORKSHIRE, BD22 0NG.
BASU, Mr. Bhuban, FCA *1970;* KS Aiyar & Co, 9 Syed Amir Ali Avenue, 4th Floor, KOLKATA 700017, INDIA.
BASU, Mr. Kalyan, BA ACA *1992;* 12-06 Block D, Astoria Park, Kembangan, SINGAPORE, SINGAPORE.
BASU, Mr. Nihar Kumar, MA LLB FCA *1953;* Flat 6F Regent Tower, 121/1 N.S.C. Bose Road, CALCUTTA 700040, INDIA. (Life Member)
BASU, Mr. Nikhil, BA ACA *1990;* 24 Sunswyck Road, DARIEN, CT 06820, UNITED STATES.
BASU, Mr. Praphulla Chandra, FCA *1948;* Plot 372, Block G, New Alipore, CALCUTTA 53, INDIA. (Life Member)
BASU, Mr. Rajiv, FCA *1986;* Deloitte & Touche LLP, Two World Financial Center, NEW YORK, NY 10281-1414, UNITED STATES.
•**BASU, Mr. Romit, FCA** *1990;* with Sinclairs Carston Ltd, 32 Queen Anne Street, LONDON, W1G 8HD.
BASU, Mr. Ronit, MSc BSc ACA *2011;* 31e Fitzjohns Avenue, LONDON, NW3 5JY.
BASU, Mr. Shekhar, FCA *1975;* I.T.C. Ltd., Virginia House, 37 J.L. Nehru Road, KOLKATA 700 012, INDIA.
BASU, Mr. Shomit, ACA *1994;* 18 St. Michaels Close, North Finchley, LONDON, N12 9NB.
•**BASU, Mrs. Tracy Jane, BA(Hons) ACA** *2001;* Abasus Accounting Limited, 22 Chapel Lane, LEEDS, LS6 3BW.
BASUNIA, Mr. Tahzeen Hossain, BSc ACA *2004;* Voice Connections (UK) Ltd, 46 Graveney Road, LONDON, SW17 0EH.
•**BASUNIA, Mr. Tamjid Hossain, FCA** *1968;* 48 The Gallop, SUTTON, SURREY, SM2 5RY.
•**BATAVIA, Mr. Hasmukh Jagmohandas, FCA** *1979;* 19 Woodlawn Road, MARKHAM L3P 7G7, ON, CANADA.
BATCHELDOR, Mr. James Brook, BSc(Hons) ACA *2001;* 7 Golden Cross Mews, LONDON, W11 1DZ.
BATCHELOR, Mr. Andrew Charles, BSc ACA *1995;* C K Batchelor Ltd, Cold Bath Place, HARROGATE, HG2 0PH.
BATCHELOR, Mr. Andrew John, ACA CA(SA) *2010;* 30 Pensford Avenue, Kew, RICHMOND, SURREY, TW9 4HP.
BATCHELOR, Mr. Charles Richard, ACA *1995;* 25 Vale Coppice, Ramsbottom, BURY, LANCASHIRE, BL0 9FJ.
BATCHELOR, Mrs. Christine Alton, BSc ACA *1978;* Rozel House, 16 Oast Road, Hurst Green, OXTED, RH8 9DU.
BATCHELOR, Mr. David Frank, FCA *1981;* The Beeches, Packhorse Road, Bessels Green, SEVENOAKS, TN13 2QP.
BATCHELOR, Miss. Dawn Michelle, BSc FCA *1991;* Atlantic Compliance Ltd, Rose Cottage, 20 Folly Hill, FARNHAM, SURREY, GU9 0BD.
BATCHELOR, Mr. Francis George Ritchie, FCA *1950;* 56 West Park Road, LEEDS, LS8 2DZ. (Life Member)
BATCHELOR, Mr. Harvey Clive, BSc ACA *1994;* Loughane East, Loughane, BLARNEY, COUNTY CORK, IRELAND.
BATCHELOR, Mr. Horace George, FCA *1948;* 20 Stanley Close, Gidea Park, ROMFORD, RM2 5DP. (Life Member)
BATCHELOR, Mr. John Allison, BSc ACA *1987;* Wood Peckers, Main Street, Stoke Row, HENLEY-ON-THAMES, OXFORDSHIRE, RG9 5PL.
BATCHELOR, Mr. Mark, ACA MAAT *2011;* 2 Midanbury Crescent, SOUTHAMPTON, SO18 4FN.
•**BATCHELOR, Mr. Mark Alan, BSc FCA** *1989;* Batchelor Coop Ltd, The New Barn, Mill Lane, Eastry, SANDWICH, CT13 0JW.
•**BATCHELOR, Mr. Martyn Kenneth, BA ACA** *1989;* Batchelor & Co, 14 Wellington Square, HASTINGS, EAST SUSSEX, TN34 1PB. See also Abacus
BATCHELOR, Mr. Nigel Maurice, MA ACA *1985;* 3 The Green, LONDON, SW19 5AZ.
BATCHELOR, Mr. Paul Walter, BSc ACA *1993;* Walkeliweg 1, 6210 SURSEE, SWITZERLAND.
BATCHELOR, Mr. Peter Andrew, BA FCA *1987;* (Tax Fac), Fourth Floor, 110 Wigmore Street, LONDON, W1U 3RW.
BATCHELOR, Mr. Philip Frederick, BSc ACA *1980;* 30 Church Side, Methley, LEEDS, LS26 9EE.
•**BATCHELOR, Mr. Richard Mark, FCA** *1992;* R M Batchelor ACA, 70 Chesterton Avenue, HARPENDEN, HERTFORDSHIRE, AL5 5SU. See also Dodd R.M.
•**BATCHELOR, Mr. Roland Patrick, BSc ACA** *1995;* Tax Partner Ltd, 21 Dennyview Road, Abbots Leigh, BRISTOL, BS8 3RD.
BATCHELOR, Mrs. Ruth Catherine, MA ACA CTA *2003;* The Gables Windmill Hill, Platt, SEVENOAKS, TN15 8QR.
•**BATCHELOR, Miss. Sarah Louise, ACA MAAT** *1999;* Baker Tilly Restructuring And Recovery LLP, 25 Farringdon Street, LONDON, EC4A 4AB. See also Baker Tilly Tax and Advisory Services LLP

BATCHELOR, Mr. Simon Richard, BA ACA RC *1987;* BP Europa SE - BP Nederland, Rivium Boulevard 301, 2909 LK CAPELLE AAN DEN IJSSEL, NETHERLANDS.
BATCHELOR, Mr. Stephen John, ACA *1991;* 21 Red Hill, Wateringbury, MAIDSTONE, KENT, ME18 5NN.
BATCHEN, Mr. Iain, BA ACA *2007;* with KPMG LLP, Bureau 1500, 600 boul De Maisonneuve Ouest, MONTREAL H3A OA3, QUE, CANADA.
BATCHEN, Mr. Iain, ACA *2010;* 4 The Straits, Astley, Tyldesley, MANCHESTER, M29 7RR.
•**BATE, Mr. Andrew Joseph, ACA** *1981;* (Tax Fac), ABA, 49 Park Lane, FAREHAM, PO16 7LE.
BATE, Miss. Arianne Claire, ACA *2008;* FLAT 5, 10 Smedley Street, LONDON, SW4 6PG.
BATE, Mr. Christopher, ACA *2011;* 6 Dresser Road, Prestwood, GREAT MISSENDEN, BUCKINGHAMSHIRE, HP16 0NA.
BATE, Mr. Dominic, ACA *2005;* 23 Heol Peredur, Thornhill, CARDIFF, CF14 9HP.
•**BATE, Mr. Geoffrey Clifford, ACA** *1981;* Muras Gill Ltd, Thomas House, Croxstalls Place, Bloxwich, WALSALL, WS3 2PP.
•**BATE, Miss. Janice Susan, FCA** *1983;* Berkeley Bate Limited, 27-28 Monmouth Street, BATH, BA1 2AP.
BATE, Mr. John Clyde, BPharm ACA *1991;* 65 Tudor Way, UXBRIDGE, UB10 9AA.
BATE, Mr. Mark, ACA *2008;* 8 Foreland Road, CARDIFF, CF14 7AR.
BATE, Mr. Matthew Giles, BA(Hons) ACA *2001;* 12 Quarry Terrace, Quarry Road, HASTINGS, EAST SUSSEX, TN34 3SA.
BATE, Mr. Peter Charles Balfour, FCA *1971;* The Long House, 17 High Road, Ashton Keynes, SWINDON, SN6 6NL.
BATE, Mr. Philip John, BSc FCA *1978;* 7 Ridgeway Road, Timperley, ALTRINCHAM, WA15 7HA.
BATE, Mr. Richard, ACA *2009;* with PKF (UK) LLP, 4th Floor, 3 Hardman Street, MANCHESTER, M3 3HF.
BATE, Mr. Richard, BA ACA *2006;* Canons House, Canons Way, BRISTOL, BS1 5LL.
BATE, Mr. Richard Geoffrey, BA ACA *2002;* 66 The Quadrant, 258 Fog Lane, Burnage, MANCHESTER, M19 1AT.
BATE, Ms. Susan Ann, ACA *1992;* Pauls Farm Barn, Ensfield Road, Leigh, TONBRIDGE, KENT, TN11 8RX.
BATE, Mr. Thomas John, FCA *1955;* 20 Barrington Road, Olton, SOLIHULL, B92 8DP. (Life Member)
BATEMAN, Mr. Arthur John Forster, FCA *1973;* 5 Lowes Rise, DURHAM, DH1 4NS.
BATEMAN, Mr. Brian Ronald, BA FCA *1977;* 34 Harvest Drive, Whittle-le-Woods, CHORLEY, LANCASHIRE, PR6 7QL.
BATEMAN, Miss. Catherine Ellen, BA ACA *1986;* with Deloitte & Touche LLP, Suite 1400, 181 Bay Street, TORONTO M5J 2V1, ON, CANADA.
BATEMAN, Mrs. Claire Rachel, BA ACA *2007;* 1 Mill Lane, Caistor, MARKET RASEN, LINCOLNSHIRE, LN7 6UA.
BATEMAN, Miss. Clare Marie, BA ACA *1999;* 29 Melbourn Road, SHEFFIELD, S10 1NR.
BATEMAN, Mr. Darren Neil, BA ACA *2005;* Weybourne House, Lenten Street, ALTON, HAMPSHIRE, GU34 1HH.
BATEMAN, Mr. Duncan Paul, FCA *1968;* 55 Marshall's Drive, ST. ALBANS, AL1 4RD.
BATEMAN, Mr. Edwin Charles Howard, FCA *1967;* Rectory Grange, 1 Watnall Road, Nuthall, NOTTINGHAM, NG16 1DT. (Life Member)
BATEMAN, Mrs. Emma Sarah, BA ACA *1999;* 36 Engadine Street, LONDON, SW18 5BH.
BATEMAN, Mr. Graham, DPh MA MBA FCA *1976;* 22 The Cobbles, Cuddington, NORTHWICH, CW8 2XH.
BATEMAN, Mr. Ian Michael, MEng BA ACA *2001;* Elsevier Ltd Bewlay House, 32 Jamestown Road, LONDON, NW1 7BY.
BATEMAN, Mrs. Julia, ACA *2009;* 4/1091 Burke Road, HAWTHORN EAST, VIC 3123, AUSTRALIA.
BATEMAN, Mr. Justin Miles, MA ACA *2000;* BC Partners Inc, 667 Madison Avenue, NEW YORK, NY 10065, UNITED STATES.
BATEMAN, Mrs. Kaye, MA ACA *1999;* Meadow Ridge, The Drove, Horton Heath, EASTLEIGH, SO50 7DR.
BATEMAN, Mr. Malcolm Richard, MA ACA *1992;* 57 Bond Street, Englefield Green, EGHAM, TW20 0PL.
BATEMAN, Mr. Martin James, BA ACA *1999;* Snarestone Lodge, Measham Road, Snarestone, SWADLINCOTE, DERBYSHIRE, DE12 7DA.
•**BATEMAN, Mr. Peter Richard, BSc FCA CPFA** *1973;* P.R Bateman, 9 Pembroke Close, CHESTER, CH4 7BS.
BATEMAN, Mr. Robin John, FCA *1970;* CARAVAN, 2 Lakeside Business Park, Swan Lane, SANDHURST, BERKSHIRE, GU47 9DN.
BATEMAN, Mr. Rodney Leslie, BCom FCA *1983;* 3 La Pepiniere, La Rue Du Boulay, Trinity, JERSEY, JE3 5JE.
BATEMAN, Mr. Samuel Ian, BA ACA *2007;* with PricewaterhouseCoopers LLP, 1 Embankment Place, LONDON, WC2N 6RH.
BATEMAN, Mr. Stephen Leonard, FCA *1968;* Underley, The Cliff Path, Bonchurch, VENTNOR, PO38 1RL.
BATER, Mr. Campbell Paul, LLB ACA *1979;* (Tax Fac), 58 Hanover Gate Mansions, Park Road, LONDON, NW1 4SN.
•**BATES, Mr. Adam David, BSc ACA** *1986;* KPMG LLP, 15 Canada Square, LONDON, E14 5GL. See also KPMG Europe LLP
BATES, Mr. Adrian David, FCA *1975;* Yana Aspley Heath Lane, Tanworth-in-Arden, SOLIHULL, B94 5HU.
BATES, Mr. Alan Eric Hamilton, FCA ATII *1964;* Third Floor, Kings Court, Bay Street, PO Box N63, NASSAU, BAHAMAS.
BATES, Mr. Alec John, FCA *1972;* Suite 199, Postnet X51, Bryanston, JOHANNESBURG, GAUTENG, 2021 SOUTH AFRICA.
BATES, Mr. Andrew Guy, MEng ACA *2007;* 17 Yr Efail, Treoes, BRIDGEND, MID GLAMORGAN, CF35 5EG.
BATES, Mr. Andrew Jonathan, BA(Hons) ACA *2000;* 150a Maney Hill Road, SUTTON COLDFIELD, B72 1JU.
BATES, Mr. Andrew Michael, FCA *1984;* 71 Hereford Way, Maryville Downs, LOWER CHITTERING, WA 6084, AUSTRALIA.
•**BATES, Mr. Andrew William Allen, BSc ACA** *1980;* Ceilic Ltd, 5 Miles Garth, Bardsey, LEEDS, LS17 9BW.
BATES, Mr. Antony Jeffrey, BSc FCA *1980;* One Reading Central, Yell, 23 Forbury Road, READING, RG1 3YL.
•**BATES, Mr. Beavon George Joseph, FCA** *1964;* Bates Accountants, Wulfrun Chambers, 17 Lawton Road, Alsager, STOKE-ON-TRENT, ST7 2AA. See also Bates
•**BATES, Mr. Brian, ACA** *1980;* Stephens Paul, 24 Cuddington Avenue, WORCESTER PARK, KT4 7DA.
•**BATES, Mr. Brian Michael, FCA** *1973;* Bates & Company Shrewsbury Limited, 10 Park Plaza, Battlefield Enterprise Park, SHREWSBURY, SY1 3AF.
BATES, Mrs. Carrie, BA ACA *2004;* 1 Preston Road, Beacon Heights, NEWARK, NG24 2GE.
BATES, Mr. Christopher, BA ACA *1993;* 214 Madison Road, SCARSDALE, NY 10583, UNITED STATES.
BATES, Mr. Christopher Carl, BSc ACA *1986;* Currie & Warner Ltd Summer Hill Works, Powell Street, BIRMINGHAM, B1 3DH.
BATES, Mr. Christopher Elliot, MEng ACA *2005;* 55D Dartmouth Road, LONDON, NW2 4EP.
BATES, Mr. Christopher Mark, ACA *1982;* Andrej Sacharovstraat 15, 2332 AB LEIDEN, NETHERLANDS.
BATES, Mr. Christopher Ralph, BSc FCA *1990;* Fairfield, 12 Beech Road, REIGATE, RH2 9LR.
BATES, Mr. Christopher Sean, BSc ACA *2007;* with Begbies Chettle Agar, Epworth House, 25 City Road, LONDON, EC1Y 1AR.
BATES, Miss. Claire Melanie, BA(Hons) ACA *2001;* 53 Hornbeam Road, Theydon Bois, EPPING, ESSEX, CM16 7JU.
BATES, Mrs. Clare, BA ACA *2000;* Twopenny Hay, 22 Townsend, Lower Almondsbury, BRISTOL, BS32 4EN.
•**BATES, Mr. Colin Adrian, BSc ACA** *2000;* PricewaterhouseCoopers LLP, 31 Great George Street, BRISTOL, BS1 5QD. See also PricewaterhouseCoopers
BATES, Mr. Colin George Llewellyn, FCA *1973;* Butts Cottage, Rhinefield Road, BROCKENHURST, SO42 7SR. (Life Member)
BATES, Mr. Daniel Alan, BA(Hons) ACA *2001;* 17 Bushy Park Road, TEDDINGTON, MIDDLESEX, TW11 9DQ.
BATES, Miss. Danielle, BSc(Hons) ACA *2011;* School House, Barston Lane, Barston, SOLIHULL, WEST MIDLANDS, B92 0JU.
BATES, Mr. David Arthur, FCA *1951;* Kilgobbin House, Wotton Road, Rangeworthy, BRISTOL, BS37 7NB. (Life Member)
BATES, Mr. David Charles, FCA *1963;* Flat 28, Tower Bridge Wharf, 86 St. Katharines Way, LONDON, E1W 1UR.
BATES, Mr. David Christopher, BSc FCA *1977;* 24 Norwich Road, Newton Hall, DURHAM, DH1 5QA.
•**BATES, Mr. David George, FCA CTA** *1962;* George Bates Consultancy, 79 Tempest Avenue, POTTERS BAR, HERTFORDSHIRE, EN6 5LD.
BATES, Mr. David John, FCA *1957;* 1 The Bungalows, Ashley Road, Uffculme, CULLOMPTON, EX15 3AY. (Life Member)
BATES, Mr. David John, FCA *1960;* 11 The Laurels, Potten End, BERKHAMSTED, HP4 2SP. (Life Member)
•**BATES, Mr. David Leslie, BSc FCA ATII** *1987;* Willow House, PO Box 5, Heswall, WIRRAL, MERSEYSIDE, CH60 0FW.
BATES, Mr. David William, ACA *2009;* 73 Queens Road, RICHMOND, SURREY, TW10 6HJ.
BATES, Mrs. Denise Andrea, MA FCA DChA *1984;* 104 Mottram Old Road, STALYBRIDGE, SK15 2TE.
BATES, Mr. Edward Arthur, MA FCA *1964;* Downlands, Clandon Rd, West Clandon, GUILDFORD, GU4 7UW.
BATES, Mr. Edward Laurence, BA FCA *1952;* 1 Blacksmiths Lane, Smeeton Westerby, LEICESTER, LE8 0QB. (Life Member)
BATES, Mr. Eric, MSc FCA *1961;* Westcott Orchard, Bonnington, ASHFORD, KENT, TN25 7BN.
•**BATES, Mrs. Faith, ACA FCCA** *2009;* Philip Barnes & Co Ltd, The Old Council Chambers, Halford Street, TAMWORTH, B79 7RB.
BATES, Dr. George Benjamin, PhD ACA *2000;* Schlucht Strasse 41, 4142 MUNCHENSTEIN, SWITZERLAND.
•**BATES, Mr. Giles Langley, BSc ACA** *1989;* (Tax Fac), Wingrave Yeats Partnership LLP, 101 Wigmore Street, LONDON, W1U 1QU.
BATES, Mr. Graham Christopher, FCA *1974;* 4 Belle Avenue, READING, RG6 7BL.
BATES, Mr. Graham Colin, ACA *2005;* 12 Cronk Y Berry Beg, Douglas, ISLE OF MAN, IM2 6HA.
BATES, Mr. Gregor John, BSc ACA *1996;* 6 Beech Close, Effingham, LEATHERHEAD, KT24 5PQ.
BATES, Mrs. Heather Marr, BSc(Hons) ACA *2004;* 36 Upper Broadmoor Road, CROWTHORNE, RG45 7DB.
BATES, Mr. Ian, FCA *1982;* Butterfield Morris Bushell Ltd, Bute Mills, Mill Yard, Guildford Street, LUTON, BEDFORDSHIRE LU1 2NH.
BATES, Mr. Ian Leslie, BSc FCA *1979;* Kingsfold Cottage Farm Marringdean Road, BILLINGSHURST, WEST SUSSEX, RH14 9HD.
•**BATES, Mr. James Andrew, MA(Cantab) ACA** *2000;* Ernst & Young LLP, 1 More London Place, LONDON, SE1 2AF. See also Ernst & Young Europe LLP
•**BATES, Mr. James Anthony, BSc ACA** *1998;* Deloitte LLP, 2 New Street Square, LONDON, EC4A 3BZ. See also Deloitte & Touche LLP
BATES, Mr. James Higson, FCA *1951;* 81 Earlsway, Curzon Park, CHESTER, CH4 8AZ. (Life Member)
•**BATES, Mrs. Jane Challoner, BA FCA** *1982;* (Tax Fac), Goodman Jones LLP, 29-30 Fitzroy Square, LONDON, W1T 6LQ.
BATES, Mr. Jeffrey, BSc ACA *1998;* 37 RoseBerry Avenue, BirkenHead, AUCKLAND 0626, NEW ZEALAND.
BATES, Mr. John, FCA *1963;* 1 Ridley Close, Cropston, LEICESTER, LE7 7HB.
BATES, Mr. John Michael, FCA *1958;* 21 Greshams Way, EDENBRIDGE, TN8 5NY. (Life Member)
BATES, Mr. Jonathan Guy, BSc ACA *1986;* N H S Medway Fifty Pembroke Court, Pembroke Chatham Maritime, CHATHAM, ME4 4EL.
•**BATES, Mr. Joseph Richard, FCA DChA** *1981;* Clement Keys, 39/40 Calthorpe Road, Edgbaston, BIRMINGHAM, B15 1TS.
BATES, Miss. Julia Clare, BA ACA *1998;* 18 Cornfield Close, Chandler's Ford, EASTLEIGH, HAMPSHIRE, SO53 4HD.
BATES, Mr. Keith Michael Logan, FCA *1974;* Granary Barn, Blagrave Farm, Upper Woodcote RoadCaversham, READING, RG4 7JX.
BATES, Mr. Kenneth, BA FCA *1980;* School of Accounting and Commercial Law, 105 Grant Road, Thorndon, WELLINGTON 6011, NEW ZEALAND.
•**BATES, Mr. Kevin George, BSc ACA** *1992;* Rosscot Limited, Thomas Edge House, Tunnell Street, St Helier, JERSEY, JE2 4LU. See also Rosscot Assurance Limited
BATES, Mr. Kevin Robert, ACA *2009;* 30 Holly Street, MANCHESTER, M11 3BN.
BATES, Mr. Leon, BSc ACA *2011;* 92 Hertford Road, ENFIELD, MIDDLESEX, EN3 5AL.
BATES, Mr. Lionel John Daniel, FCA *1972;* 13 Beverley Heights, REIGATE, SURREY, RH2 0DL.
BATES, Mr. Mark D'arcy, ACA *1995;* 52 Sycamore, Wilnecote, TAMWORTH, B77 5HB.
BATES, Mr. Mark Richard, BSc ACA *1983;* 46 St Michaels Avenue, Bramhall, STOCKPORT, SK7 2PL.
BATES, Mr. Martin Anthony, BA ACA *1995;* The Farmhouse, 1 Southall Green Farm, Beighton, SHEFFIELD, S20 1FU.
BATES, Mr. Martin Colin, MA FCA *1955;* Brackenhurst, Wonham Way, Gomshall, GUILDFORD, GU5 9NZ. (Life Member)
BATES, Mr. Martin John Graham, BSc ACA *1979;* Elta Lighting Ltd, Roman Way, Coleshill, BIRMINGHAM, B46 1HQ.
BATES, Mr. Matthew John, BCom ACA *1992;* 95 Cubberla Street, Fig Tree Pocket, BRISBANE, QLD 4069, AUSTRALIA.
BATES, Miss. Melissa Carolyn, BA ACA *1999;* 14 Fieldfare Avenue, PORTISHEAD, BS20 7NL.
BATES, Mr. Michael Edward, FCA *1974;* Latimers Lodge, Hipsley Lane, Baxterley, ATHERSTONE, WARWICKSHIRE, CV9 2HS.
BATES, Mr. Michael John, BA ACA *1991;* 9 Westmorland Drive, CAMBERLEY, GU15 1EW.
BATES, Miss. Nicola, BA ACA *2004;* 22 Wood Walk, Wombwell, BARNSLEY, SOUTH YORKSHIRE, S73 0NG.
BATES, Mr. Nigel Allan, FCA *1977;* 17 Chiltern Walk, TUNBRIDGE WELLS, TN2 3NJ.
BATES, Mr. Nigel William Munro, FCA *1975;* Easterling, Kingswood Road, TUNBRIDGE WELLS, TN2 4UJ.
BATES, Mr. Paul Andrew, BA FCA *1977;* Ascesis Consulting Ltd, 11 Cranley Road, Burwood Park, WALTON-ON-THAMES, KT12 5BX.
BATES, Mr. Paul David Oldham, MA ACA *1995;* 78 Chelverton Road, LONDON, SW15 1RL.
•**BATES, Mr. Paul James, BA(Hons) ACA** *2002;* BDO LLP, 1 Bridgewater Place, Water Lane, LEEDS, LS11 5RU. See also BDO Stoy Hayward LLP
BATES, Mr. Paul Richard, ACA CA(SA) *2009;* Charles Taylor Adjusting, 88 Leadenhall Street, LONDON, EC3A 3BA.
BATES, Mr. Paul Terence, BSc ACA *1997;* 15 Eccles Road, LONDON, SW11 1LY.
•**BATES, Mr. Peter William, BSc FCA** *1973;* Business Information Systems, 11 Upper Church Park, Mumbles, SWANSEA, SA3 4DD. See also Bizis Limited
•**BATES, Mr. Phillip Neil, BA FCA** *1980;* Phillip Bates & Co Limited, 1-3 Chester Road, NESTON, CH64 9PA.
BATES, Mr. Raymond, FCA *1953;* 12 Meadow Court, Darras Hall, NEWCASTLE UPON TYNE, NE20 9RB. (Life Member)
BATES, Mr. Richard Alan, FCA *1969;* 54 Church Road, HAYLING ISLAND, HAMPSHIRE, PO11 0NX.
BATES, Mr. Richard Logan, BA(Hons) ACA *2001;* 46 Newcastle Avenue, COLCHESTER, CO3 9XE.
BATES, Mr. Richard Milner, FCA *1971;* Court House, 15 Main Street, Cold Overton, OAKHAM, LE15 7QA.
BATES, Mr. Robert Alexander, FCA *1965;* 24 Lucastes Avenue, HAYWARDS HEATH, RH16 1JX.
BATES, Dr. Robert William, BA ACA *1997;* 9 Kingston Road, TEDDINGTON, MIDDLESEX, TW11 9JX.
BATES, Mr. Roger Alfred, FCA *1968;* Mapsedge Knolls View, Totternhoe, DUNSTABLE, BEDFORDSHIRE, LU6 2BT.
BATES, Miss. Sarah Jane, BA(Hons) ACA *2010;* 25 Werneth Avenue, HYDE, CHESHIRE, SK14 5NL.
BATES, Mrs. Sheryl, BSc(Hons) ACA *2010;* Flat 2, 49 Addison Gardens, LONDON, W14 0DP.
BATES, Miss. Simone Rosetta, BA(Hons) ACA *2003;* Institute of Chartered Accountants in England & Wales, Metropolitan House, 4 Rillaton Walk, MILTON KEYNES, MK9 2FZ.
BATES, Mr. Stephen Alexander, BBus ACA CA(AUS) *2009;* KPMG, Badenerstrasse 170, CH 8026 ZURICH, SWITZERLAND.
BATES, Mr. Stephen Charles, BSc ACA *1990;* 8 Chester Road, POOLE, BH13 6DD.
BATES, Mr. Stuart Edward, BA ACA *1996;* 5 Marquis Gardens, Chellaston, DERBY, DE73 5WD.
•**BATES, Mr. Stuart John, BA ACA** *1996;* (Tax Fac), Wenn Townsend, Victoria House, 10 Broad Street, ABINGDON, OX14 3LH. See also Wenn Townsend Accountants Limited
BATES, Mr. Stuart William, ACA *2010;* Flat 18 Headbourne House, Law Street, LONDON, SE1 4DY.
BATES, Mrs. Thandi Eve, ACA CA(SA) *2009;* 31 Thorndon Gardens, EPSOM, KT19 0QB.
•**BATES, Mr. Thomas Henry, FCA** *1956;* T.H. Bates, 27 Clarendon Road, Boston Spa, WETHERBY, LS23 6NG.
•**BATES, Mr. Timothy John, BEng FCA ATII** *1995;* Clarkson Mayer Limited, Queensgate House, 48 Queen Street, EXETER, EX4 3SR.
BATESON, Mrs. Deborah Joy, BSc FCA *1986;* 5 Broadfield Crescent, FOLKESTONE, CT20 2PH.
BATESON, Mr. Nicholas, BSc ACA *2005;* Flat 3 4 Dalmeny Road, LONDON, N7 0HH.
BATESON, Mr. Peter Daniel, LLB ACA *1980;* Rodings, 13 The Warren, HARPENDEN, AL5 2NH.
BATESON, Miss. Rachel Lucy, BA ACA *2004;* with Buzzacott LLP, 130 Wood Street, LONDON, EC2V 6DL.

BATESON, Mr. Timothy George, BEng ACA *2010;* Flat 11, Binding House, Binding Close, NOTTINGHAM, NG5 1RG.

BATEY, Mr. Robert Geoffrey, FCA *1970;* Welton Plains, Welton, CARLISLE, CA5 7ET.

BATEY, Mr. Simon George, MA FCA *1979;* Higher Heyes Farm, Ball Lane, Kingsley, FRODSHAM, WA6 8HP.

BATH, Mr. Alan William, BSc FCA *1980;* Glengarth Port Soderick Glen, Port Soderick, ISLE OF MAN, IM4 1BE.

BATH, Mr. Aled Spencer James, MEng ACA *2003;* Shill Lodge, Main Road, Alvescot, BAMPTON, OXFORDSHIRE, OX18 2PU.

BATH, Mr. Charles Roger, FCA *1979;* (Tax Fac), H M Revenue & Customs, 100 Parliament Street, LONDON, SW1A 2BQ.

BATH, Mr. Christopher Paul Singh, BA ACA *2002;* Sainsbury Asia, Suite 1 - 7 & 12, 14th Floor Tower 1, The Gateway, 25 Canton Road, TSIM SHA TSUI KOWLOON HONG KONG SAR.

BATH, Mr. Christopher William, MA ACA *1999;* 13 Crooms Hill Grove, LONDON, SE10 8HB.

BATH, Mrs. Julie Ann, BSc ACA *1984;* (Tax Fac), Oakwood, 13 Brushwood Drive, Chorleywood, RICKMANSWORTH, WD3 5RS.

BATH, Mr. Michael John, BSc FCA *1998;* 27 Lime Gardens, West End, SOUTHAMPTON, SO30 3RG.

BATH, Mr. Paul, BSc(Hons) ACA *2010;* Flat 520 Falcon Wharf, 34 Lombard Road, LONDON, SW11 3RF.

BATH, Mr. Rajinder Singh, BSc ACA *2010;* 8 Hibernia Gardens, HOUNSLOW, TW3 3SD.

BATH, Mr. Richard Neil, PhD BSc FCA *1983;* Bequia House, Wharf Hill, WINCHESTER, SO23 9NQ.

•BATH, Mr. Robert Nicholas, BA ACA *1991;* R Bath & Co Ltd, 8 Northwood Park Road, Hanley, STOKE-ON-TRENT, ST1 2DT.

BATH, Mr. Stephen Alexander Glanville, MA FCA *1988;* with IBM UK Ltd, 40 Hanover Gardens, LONDON, SE11 5TN.

BATH, Mr. Sukhdeep Singh, BSc(Hons) ACA *2000;* 22 Long Drive, Burnham, SLOUGH, SL1 8AL.

•BATHAM, Mr. Matthew Nicholas, BSc ACA *1999;* Deloitte LLP, 2 New Street Square, LONDON, EC4A 3BZ. See also Deloitte & Touche LLP

BATHER, Miss. Alexandra Louise, MEng ACA *1997;* 11 Beconsfield Close, Dorridge, SOLIHULL, WEST MIDLANDS, B93 8QZ.

BATHFIELD, Mr. Pierre Raoul Sydney, FCA *1963;* St Antoine, GOODLANDS, MAURITIUS.

BATHGATE, Mr. Mark George, BA ACA *1997;* Denjean & Associés, 35 avenue Victor Hugo, 75116 PARIS, FRANCE.

•BATHIA, Mr. Arun Maganlal, FCA *1974;* with Burford and Partners LLP, Suite 75, London Fruit Exchange, Brushfield Street, LONDON, E1 6EP.

BATHIA, Mr. Kamlesh, BA ACA *1992;* 6a Trebeck Street, LONDON, W1J 7RB.

•BATHIA, Mr. Kaushik, FCA *1983;* Thomas May & Co, Allen House, Newarke Street, LEICESTER, LE1 5SG.

BATHIA, Mrs. Kirti Nilesh, BA FCA *1989;* Tabora Lodge, 32 Rowley Green Road, BARNET, HERTFORDSHIRE, EN5 3HJ.

•BATHIA, Mr. Nishit, BSc FCA *1985;* PKF (UK) LLP, Pannell House, 159 Charles Street, LEICESTER, LE1 1LD.

BATHIJA, Mr. Dhiraj, ACA *2009;* 90 Peters Court, Porchester Road, LONDON, W2 5DR.

BATHO, Mr. Jonathan Adam, FCA MBA *1994;* 9 Elmsway, Bramhall, STOCKPORT, CHESHIRE, SK7 2AE.

•BATHO, Mr. Roger Denis, FCA *1969;* RD Batho & Co, 12A West Beach, LYTHAM ST. ANNES, FY8 5QH.

BATHURST, Mr. Benjamin Edward, MA ACA *2011;* 80 Phillips Lane, Formby, LIVERPOOL, L37 4BQ.

BATKI, Mr. Malcolm Dosabhai, MA FCA *1984;* 58 Glendon Way, Dorridge, SOLIHULL, WEST MIDLANDS, B93 8SY.

BATKI-BRAUN, Mr. David AlexanderDonath, BA ACA *1987;* 146 Harestone Valley Road, CATERHAM, CR3 6HG.

BATLEY, Mr. Alan Stuart, FCA *1972;* Klein Moddergat Estate, Cnr Main Road & Chesnut Drive, HOUT BAY, 7806, SOUTH AFRICA. (Life Member)

BATLEY, Mr. John Albert William, FCA *1974;* 18 Blackbrook Lane, Bickley, BROMLEY, KENT, BR2 8AY.

BATLEY, Mrs. Lisa Victoria, ACA *2008;* 27 Aspen Close, Gomersal, CLECKHEATON, WEST YORKSHIRE, BD19 4NY.

BATLEY, Mr. Rees James, ACA *2011;* Second Floor Flat, 1 Richmond Terrace, Clifton, BRISTOL, BS8 1AB.

BATO, Mr. Michael John, FCA *1959;* House 2, 85 Raglan Street, Mosman, SYDNEY, NSW 2008, AUSTRALIA. (Life Member)

BATORIJS, Mrs. Sarah, BSc ACA FIBC *1991;* 51 Kewstoke Road, Stoke Bishop, BRISTOL, BS9 1HE.

BATRA, Mr. Anil, FCA *1991;* 15 Campden Crescent, North Wembley, WEMBLEY, HA0 3JH.

•BATRA, Mr. Anil Kumar, BA ACA *1984;* Durrants, 24 Wellington Business Park, Dukes Ride, CROWTHORNE, RG45 6LS.

•BATSFORD, Mr. Colin Lionel, BA FCA *1988;* C.L. Batsford, 69 Grange Park Avenue, Winchmore Hill, LONDON, N21 2LN. See also Centrecourt Limited

BATSVIK-MILLER, Mr. Magnus, BSc ACA *2006;* First Floor 71 Altenburg Gardens, LONDON, SW11 1JQ.

BATT, Mr. David Wayne, ACA CTA *1992;* 2 Annandale Way, HARRISDALE, WA 6112, AUSTRALIA.

BATT, Mrs. Helen Claire, ACA CTA *1992;* 2 Annandale Way, HARRISDALE, WA 6112, AUSTRALIA.

•BATT, Mr. Ian Gregory, FCA *1970;* (Tax Fac), Batt & Co, 11 Woolaston Drive, Alsager, STOKE-ON-TRENT, ST7 2PL.

BATT, Mr. John Robert, MSc FCA *1975;* 1 Oak Barn Close, Cranfield, BEDFORD, MK43 0TW.

BATT, Mr. Michael Sinclair, FCA *1967;* 9 Grange Park, Henleaze, BRISTOL, BS9 4BU. (Life Member)

BATT, Mr. Nigel Paul, FCA *1969;* 5 The Close, SEVENOAKS, KENT, TN13 2HE.

•BATT, Mr. Terence Stanley, FCA *1975;* T.S. Batt, Crown House, Home Gardens, DARTFORD, DA1 1DZ.

•BATTARBEE, Mr. Edward, BA(Hons) FCA *1968;* (Tax Fac), Edward Battarbee, 195 Longlands Road, SIDCUP, KENT, DA15 7LB.

BATTEN, Miss. Elizabeth, ACA *2011;* Flat 3, 2 Eaton Crescent, BRISTOL, BS8 2EJ.

BATTEN, Mr. Ivor Richard, FCA *1974;* Flat 1, 97 Rope Street, LONDON, SE16 7TQ.

BATTEN, Mr. John Roger, FCA *1966;* West Hill Farm, 3 Shepreth Road, Foxton, CAMBRIDGE, CB22 6SU.

•①BATTEN, Mr. Mark Charles, BA ACA *1983;* PricewaterhouseCoopers LLP, Pricewaterhousecoopers, 12 Plumtree Court, LONDON, EC4A 4HT. See also PricewaterhouseCoopers

•BATTEN, Mr. Mark Edward, BA ACA *1999;* PricewaterhouseCoopers, 2 Southbank Boulevard, Southbank, MELBOURNE, VIC 3006, AUSTRALIA. See also PricewaterhouseCoopers LLP

BATTERBEE, Mr. Clive William Beardwell, FCA *1976;* 58 Arthurdon Road, Brockley, LONDON, SE4 1JU.

BATTERBEE, Mr. Gareth, BA ACA *2002;* Hawksmere Ltd Elizabeth House, 39 York Road, LONDON, SE1 7NQ.

BATTERBEE, Mr. Stephen Mark, MA ACA *1992;* 97 Silhill Hall Road, SOLIHULL, B91 1JT.

BATTERHAM, Mr. Christopher Michael, MA FCA *1979;* Vale Farm House, Hawridge Vale, CHESHAM, HP5 2UG.

BATTERS, Mr. Michael Christopher, BA ACA *1992;* 17 Eliot Court, Fulford, YORK, YO10 4LP.

BATTERS, Mr. Royce, FCA *1962;* 28 Church Lane, Henbury, MACCLESFIELD, CHESHIRE, SK11 9NN. (Life Member)

BATTERSBY, Mr. Geoffrey Brian, BA ACA *1985;* 13-15 Westcombe Park Road, LONDON, SE3 7RE.

BATTERSBY, Mr. Graham, BCom ACA *1982;* 290 Northenden Road, SALE, M33 2PA.

BATTERSBY, Mr. Harry, FCA *1949;* 252 Rosemont Garden, LEXINGTON, KY 40503, UNITED STATES. (Life Member)

BATTERSBY, Mrs. Joanne, BA ACA *1990;* 279 Carterknowle Road, Ecclesall, SHEFFIELD, S11 9FX.

BATTERSBY, Mr. Jonathan Simon, BSc ACA *1989;* 279 Carter Knowle Road, SHEFFIELD, S11 9FX.

BATTERSBY, Mr. Michael George, BSc FCA *1977;* 8 Moorcroft, Edenfiled, Ramsbottom, BURY, BL0 0LL.

BATTERSBY, Mr. Richard Godfrey, BA FCA JDipMA *1966;* St. Jacques House St. Jacques, St. Peter Port, GUERNSEY, GY1 1SP.

•BATTERSBY, Mr. Richard Michael, BSc FCA *1996;* Ernst & Young LLP, 1 More London Place, LONDON, SE1 2AF. See also Ernst & Young Europe LLP

BATTERSBY, Mr. Steven, BA ACA *1982;* 5 Applewood, Firwood Park, OLDHAM, OL9 9UD.

BATTERSHELL, Mr. John Vesey, FCA *1975;* 6 Coed yr Esgob, Llantrisant, PONTYCLUN, MID GLAMORGAN, CF72 8EL.

BATTERSON, Mr. Michael Adrian Seymour, BSc ACA *1990;* 105 Longfleet Road, POOLE, DORSET, BH15 2HP.

BATTEY, Mr. David Nicholas, ACA *2008;* Flat 12 Chenies Street Chambers, 9 Chenies Street, LONDON, WC1E 7ET.

BATTEY, Mr. Richard Alleyne Duncan, BSc ACA *1995;* SAGARD, 24-32 Rue Jean Goujon, 75008 PARIS, FRANCE.

BATTEY, Mr. Richard John, BA FCA *1977;* Woodgrange, Fort Road, St. Peter Port, GUERNSEY, GY1 1ZW.

BATTIN, Mr. David Ian, BSc ACA *1993;* Lyndene, Sytchampton, STOURPORT-ON-SEVERN, WORCESTERSHIRE, DY13 9TA.

BATTISON, Mr. Mark, BA ACA *2007;* 25 Faraday Avenue, SIDCUP, DA14 4JB.

BATTISON, Mr. Roy, BA FCA *1971;* Kimberley, 34 Hermitage Road, KENLEY, CR8 5EB.

BATTISSON, Mr. Nicholas Samuel, ACA *2009;* National Air Traffic Services Ltd, 4000 Parkway Whiteley, FAREHAM, PO15 7FL.

BATTLE, Mrs. Annabel, BSc ACA *2000;* Im Musli 8, CH, 6315 OBERAEGERI, SWITZERLAND.

BATTLE, Mr. Peter Jonathan, BA ACA *2003;* The Old Cottage, Church Road, Crowle, WORCESTER, WR7 4AX.

BATTLE, Mr. Richard, ACA *2011;* 6 Willows Edge, Eynsham, WITNEY, OXFORDSHIRE, OX29 4QD.

BATTLE, Mr. Simon Robin Vulliamy, FCA *1976;* Regional Holdings Ltd, 197A New Kings Road, LONDON, SW6 4SR.

BATTRICK, Mrs. Deborah Elizabeth, BA ACA *1991;* Cheltenham & Gloucester Plc Barnett Way, Barnwood, GLOUCESTER, GL4 3RL.

BATTRUM, Mr. Andrew, MA ACA *1983;* Woobine Cottage, Whitbourne, WORCESTER, WR6 5RT.

•①BATTRUM, Mr. Derek, BSc ACA *1987;* 38 Sidmouth Road, Brondesbury Park, LONDON, NW2 5HJ.

BATTSON, Mrs. Heather Anne, BA ACA *1996;* Greenbank, Bredons Norton, TEWKESBURY, GL20 7EZ.

BATTY, Mr. Andrew John, BA(Hons) ACA *2001;* MEMBER OF COUNCIL, with PricewaterhouseCoopers LLP, Hays Galleria, 1 Hays Lane, LONDON, SE1 2RD.

BATTY, Mr. Collin Martin, FCA *1962;* Rockstone, La Grande Route Des Sablons, Grouville, JERSEY, JE3 9BB. (Life Member)

BATTY, Mr. David Manning, BSc ACA *1986;* Bear Cottage, 63 Swanland Hill, NORTH FERRIBY, HU14 3JL.

BATTY, Mr. Graham David, BSc ACA CTA *1983;* with Baker Tillly Tax & Advisory Services LLP, St Philips Point, Temple Row, BIRMINGHAM, B2 5AF.

BATTY, Mr. James Kevin, FCA *1981;* 9 Sunways, MIRFIELD, WF14 9TN.

BATTY, Mr. John Francis, FCA *1956;* Ravenswood, 8 Third Avenue, Denvilles, HAVANT, PO9 2QS. (Life Member)

BATTY, Miss. Kathryn, ACA *2010;* Marl Villa, Mottram Road, HYDE, CHESHIRE, SK14 3AR.

BATTY, Miss. Lesley Anne, BA FCA *1989;* 32 Rosebank Close, TEDDINGTON, MIDDLESEX, TW11 9BW.

BATTY, Mr. Marcus John, LLB FCA *1975;* Yew Tree House, North Street Rogate, PETERSFIELD, GU31 5HG.

•BATTY, Mr. Mark William, BSc ACA *1986;* MB Consulting, 21 Oakland Close, Glais, SWANSEA, SA7 9EW.

BATTY, Mr. Michael James, BA(Econ) ACA *1999;* 3 Parklands Road, LONDON, SW16 6TB.

•①BATTY, Mr. William Antony, BA FCA *1988;* Antony Batty & Company LLP, 3 Field Court, Gray's Inn, LONDON, WC1R 5EF.

•BATTYE, Mr. Anthony Charles Norton, BA ACA *1994;* (Tax Fac), Anthony Battye, 8 Ashlyns Road, FRINTON-ON-SEA, ESSEX, CO13 9ED.

BATTYE, Mrs. Michelle Louise, BSc ACA *2007;* with Dutton Moore, 6 Silver Street, HULL, HU1 1JA.

BATTYE, Mrs. Sarah, BSc ACA *2000;* Urban Splash Group Ltd, Timber Wharf, 16-22 Worsley Street, Castlefield, MANCHESTER, M15 4LD.

BATY, Mr. Christopher, MSc ACA *1998;* Ruadean, Highford Lane, HEXHAM, NORTHUMBERLAND, NE46 2DP.

BATY, Mrs. Emily Ann, BSc ACA *2002;* 1 Cranley Gardens, Flat C, Muswell Hill, LONDON, N10 3AA.

•BATY, Mr. John Alistair, FCA *1972;* Baty Casson Long, 23 Moorhead Terrace, SHIPLEY, WEST YORKSHIRE, BD18 4LB.

BATY, Mr. John Clifford, BA ACA *1997;* Flat C, 1 Cranley Gardens, LONDON, N10 3AA.

BATY, Mrs. Monika Anna, ACA CTA *1993;* 20 West Park Apartments, La Route de St. Aubin St. Helier, JERSEY, JE2 3PZ.

BATY, Mr. Richard Jonathan Charles, BSc ACA *2001;* 29 Jocelyn Road, RICHMOND, TW9 2TJ.

BAUCKHAM, Mr. Philip Timothy, BSc ACA *1993;* Inflight Productions Ltd, 15 Stukeley Street, LONDON, WC2B 5LT.

BAUDAINS, Mrs. Sandra Elizabeth, BSc ACA *1984;* 37 Langton Road, Bishops Waltham, SOUTHAMPTON, SO32 1GF.

BAUER, Mr. Donald Clive, BA FCA *1979;* Holly Bank Ixworth Road Norton, BURY ST. EDMUNDS, SUFFOLK, IP31 3LJ.

BAUER, Mr. John William, BSc ACA *1986;* 9 Regent Street, BRIGHTON EAST, VIC 3187, AUSTRALIA.

BAUERMEISTER, Mr. George Craufurd, CA *1976; (CA Scotland 1965);* 78 Avenue de Suffren, 75015 PARIS, FRANCE. (Life Member)

BAUERNFEIND, Mr. David Gregory, BSc ACA *1993;* Xchanging, 34 Leadenhall Street, LONDON, EC3A 1AX.

BAUGH, Mrs. Susan Margaret, BSc ACA *1985;* 53 Glendale, SWANLEY, KENT, BR8 8TP.

BAUGHAN, Mrs. Iliana, MBA BSc ACA *2006;* Arena Leisure Plc, 408 Strand, LONDON, WC2R 0NE.

•BAUGHAN, Mr. Stephen William, ACA *1978;* Stephen Baughan, 3 Ormond Drive, HAMPTON, MIDDLESEX, TW12 2TP.

BAUGHEN, Miss. Carly, ACA *2010;* 45 Francis Way, SLOUGH, SL1 5PH.

BAUGHEN, Miss. Philippa Joanne, ACA *2008;* Flat 8 Tollgate Lodge, 82 Chislehurst Road, CHISLEHURST, BR7 5NP.

BAUGHMAN, Mrs. Caroline Anne, BA ACA *1996;* 399 Park Avenue, NEW YORK, NY 10022, UNITED STATES.

•BAUJI, Mr. Hassan Abdul Latif, FCA *1972;* (Tax Fac), Summerhill, Hunting Close, ESHER, SURREY, KT10 8PB.

BAULF, Mr. Adrian John, FCA FCCA *1967;* (Tax Fac), 16 St. Michaels, Limpsfield, OXTED, SURREY, RH8 0QL.

BAULK, Mr. Roger Edward, FCA CTA *1959;* 19 Summer Hill Avenue, KIDDERMINSTER, WORCESTERSHIRE, DY11 6BY. (Life Member)

•BAUM, Mr. Daniel Ian, BSc FCA *1987;* Cameron Baum Limited, 88 Crawford Street, LONDON, W1H 2EJ. See also Cameron Baum

BAUM, Miss. Naomi, FCA *1977;* The Lodge, Upton Leigh, Overton Road, CHELTENHAM, GLOUCESTERSHIRE, GL50 3BL.

BAUM-DIXON, Mr. Timothy James, BA(Hons) ACA *2010;* 19 Goosecarr Lane, Todwick, SHEFFIELD, S26 1HG.

BAUMANN, Mr. Leonard George, FCA *1946;* P.O. Box 1513, WESTVILLE, KWAZULU NATAL, 3630, SOUTH AFRICA. (Life Member)

BAUMANN, Miss. Tamsin Katrina, BA ACA *2000;* 108 Westfields Avenue, LONDON, SW13 0AZ.

BAUMBER, Mr. David Charles Adrian, BSc ACA *1999;* 24 Widney Manor Road, SOLIHULL, B91 3JQ.

BAURA, Mr. Harjeet Singh, LLB ACA *2000;* with PricewaterhouseCoopers, 33/F Cheung Kong Center, 2 Queen's Road, CENTRAL, HONG KONG ISLAND, HONG KONG SAR.

BAURA, Mr. Mandeep Singh, BA ACA *2005;* 8/10 Raymond Road, NEUTRAL BAY, NSW 2089, AUSTRALIA.

BAUSCH, Ms. Anja, BA ACA *1997;* Am Angerfeld 18a, 82362 WEILHEIM, GERMANY.

BAVAGE, Mr. Mark Andrew, FCA *1979;* Sheen Stickland, 4 High Street, ALTON, HAMPSHIRE, GU34 1BU.

•BAVEJA, Mr. Jagdish, BA(Hons) FCA *1983;* (Tax Fac), 51 Park Close, HOUNSLOW, TW3 2HN.

BAVERSTOCK, Mr. Anthony Robert, BA FCA *1983;* 6 Erick Avenue, CHELMSFORD, CM1 7BX.

BAVERSTOCK, Mr. Gavin James, BSc ACA *1999;* 7 Mythop Road, LYTHAM ST. ANNES, LANCASHIRE, FY8 4JD.

BAVERSTOCK, Mr. William Joslyn, MEng ACA *2003;* Cirrus B, Shire Park, WELWYN GARDEN CITY, HERTFORDSHIRE, AL7 1AB.

BAVEYSTOCK, Mr. John Christian Murray, BA ACA *1989;* 31 The Parapet, Castlecrag, SYDNEY, NSW 2068, AUSTRALIA.

•BAVILL, Mr. Ian Michael, ACA *2007;* Year End Accounting Limited, 1st Floor, 9 East Parade, LEEDS, LS1 2AJ.

BAVIN, Mr. Clive Nicholas, BSc ACA *1993;* 1 Levens Close, West Bridgford, NOTTINGHAM, NG2 6SN.

BAVIN, Mrs. Nicola Ann, FCA *1995;* with Maynard Heady, Matrix House, 12-16 Lionel Road, CANVEY ISLAND, SS8 9DE.

•BAVINGTON-JONES, Mr. Robin Frederick, FCA *1964;* R.F. Bavington-Jones, 1 Oak Cottages, Cox Hill, Shepherdswell, DOVER, KENT CT15 7NB.

BAVIS, Mr. Stephen, BA ACA *1984;* 12 Brier Hill View, Bradley, HUDDERSFIELD, HD2 1JQ.

BAVISHI, Mr. Kishor Labhshanker Harilal, FCA *1973;* 258 Harrow Road, WEMBLEY, MIDDLESEX, HA9 6QL.
BAVISTER, Mr. John Howard, FCA *1974;* Donnington, Ryde Road, SEAVIEW, ISLE OF WIGHT, PO34 5AB.
BAVISTER, Mr. Stephen Charles, BSc FCA *1973;* Waterfall Nind Lane, Kingswood, WOTTON-UNDER-EDGE, GL12 7QU.
BAWA, Mrs. Akrishek Kaur, ACA *2007;* 55 Syon Park Gardens, ISLEWORTH, MIDDLESEX, TW7 5NE.
BAWA, Mr. Navtaj Singh, LLB ACA *2010;* 47 Greenock Crescent, WOLVERHAMPTON, WV4 6BH.
•**BAWA, Mr. Sukhpreet Singh, BSc FCA** *1999;* SB & Company, 55 Syon Park Gardens, ISLEWORTH, MIDDLESEX, TW7 5NE.
BAWANY, Mr. Sulaiman, BSc ACA *2010;* Escribir College of Advance Studies, 5th Floor The Plaza Plot no G7Block 9, KDA Scheme no 5, Clifton, KARACHI, SINDH PAKISTAN.
BAWDEN, Mr. Clive Lewis, BA(Hons) FCA MCIM DipM *1998;* 18 Wise Grove, WARWICK, CV34 5JW.
•**BAWDEN, Mr. Richard Ian, BA FCA** *1981;* 57 Winchester Street, LONDON, SW1V 4NY.
BAWDEN, Mr. Ronald Charles, FCA *1957;* 135 Ember Lane, ESHER, KT10 8EH. (Life Member)
BAWLER, Mr. John William Kenneth, FCA *1970;* 30 East Drive, Angmering, LITTLEHAMPTON, WEST SUSSEX, BN16 4JH.
BAWN, Mrs. Ailsa Lesley Clare, BSc ACA *1989;* 56 Browning Road, ENFIELD, EN2 0EW.
•**BAWS, Mr. Anthony Roy, FCA** *1974;* Baws and Co, 70 Elm Road, LEIGH-ON-SEA, SS9 1SJ.
BAWS, Mr. Graham Keith, FCA MBA *1969;* Mosaic Management & Financial Services, 1 Fox Green, FLOREAT, WA 6014, AUSTRALIA.
•**BAWTREE, Mr. Christopher Ormsby, FCA** *1963;* Chris Bawtree FCA, 8 Kingsmill Road, BASINGSTOKE, RG21 3JJ.
•**BAWTREE, Mr. Donald Edgar, MA FCA** *1983;* BDO LLP, Emerald House, East Street, EPSOM, SURREY, KT17 1HS. See also BDO Stoy Hayward LLP
BAX, Mr. Richard Graham, FCA *1972;* Municipal Mutual Insurance Ltd, 29 Buckingham Gate, Westminster, LONDON, SW1E 6NF.
BAX, Mr. Richard William, ACA *2008;* 1 Langstone Gardens, Nutbourne, CHICHESTER, WEST SUSSEX, PO18 8SY.
BAXENDALE, Mr. Brian Michael, FCA *1968;* Sunbeams, South Drive, Littleton, WINCHESTER, HAMPSHIRE, SO22 6PY. (Life Member)
BAXENDALE, Mr. David James, MA ACA *1995;* (Tax Fac), with Ernst & Young LLP, 1 More London Place, LONDON, SE1 2AF.
•①**BAXENDALE, Mr. David Robert, BCom ACA** *2002;* 3 The Green, EPSOM, KT17 3JP.
BAXENDALE, Miss. Lisa, BSc(Hons) ACA *2004;* Kaplan Financial, 10-14 White Lion Street, LONDON, N1 9PD.
•**BAXENDALE, Mr. Nicholas Leo, ACA** *1983;* Donnellys C.A. Limited, Peel House, 2 Chorley Old Road, BOLTON, BL1 3AA.
BAXENDALE, Mrs. Sarah Frances, BSc ACA *2002;* 3 The Green, EPSOM, KT17 3JP.
•**BAXENDALE, Mr. Simon John, BSc ACA** *1989;* Pierce C A Ltd, Mentor House, Ainsworth Street, BLACKBURN, BB1 6AY. See also Pierce Group Limited
BAXENDALE, Mr. Terence, FCA *1972;* 16 Churchill Crescent, Sonning Common, READING, RG4 9RX.
BAXENDINE, Mr. Andrew John, ACA *1987;* Elm Cottage, Pilley Bailey, Pilley, LYMINGTON, HAMPSHIRE, SO41 5QT.
BAXI, Mrs. Daxa Jawahar, BA FCA *1977;* 122 Poornanand, Dongersi Road, Walkeshwar, MUMBAI 400 006, MAHARASHTRA, INDIA.
BAXTER, Mr. Alan, FCA *1959;* 4 Meadows Road, Cheadle Hulme, CHEADLE, SK8 6EJ. (Life Member)
BAXTER, Miss. Alice Lepine, BA ACA *1983;* 3 Grosvenor Road, BANBURY, OX16 5HN.
BAXTER, Mrs. Andrea Mary, BSc(Econ) ACA *1997;* Lowermeade, Bromsgrove Road, Clent, STOURBRIDGE, WORCESTERSHIRE, DY9 9RH.
•**BAXTER, Mr. Andrew Geoffrey, FCA** *1980;* Baxters, 3 Nightingale Place, Pendeford Business Park, Wobaston Road, WOLVERHAMPTON, WV9 5HF.
BAXTER, Mr. Andrew Paul, BCom ACA *2002;* Coach & Horses Cottage, London Road, LICHFIELD, STAFFORDSHIRE, WS14 0PS.
BAXTER, Mr. Anthony, ACA *1982;* C.P. Group Ltd, Parkgate House, Hesslewood Country Office Park, Ferriby Road, HESSLE, NORTH HUMBERSIDE HU13 0QF.
•**BAXTER, Mr. Barry Phillip, FCA** *1976;* BPB (Accountants) Limited, The Gatehouse, Gloucester Lane, Mickleton, CHIPPING CAMPDEN, GLOUCESTERSHIRE GL55 6SD.
BAXTER, Mrs. Catherine Wendy Perdue, ACA *2008;* 32 Sherlock Close, CAMBRIDGE, CB3 0HP.
•**BAXTER, Mr. Christopher John, FCA** *1981;* (Tax Fac), Christopher Baxter Limited, 7 Ashby Road, SPILSBY, LINCOLNSHIRE, PE23 5DS.
•**BAXTER, Mr. Christopher Raymond, FCA** *1982;* Roffe Swayne, Ashcombe Court, Woolsack Way, GODALMING, GU7 1LQ.
BAXTER, Mr. Clive Martin, MA FCA *1987;* (Tax Fac), A.P. Moller - Maersk A/S, Tax Dept, Esplanaden 50, DK-1098 COPENHAGEN, DENMARK.
BAXTER, Mr. Craig, BSc ACA *1995;* Rivermead, Cartford Lane, Little Eccleston, PRESTON, PR3 0YP.
BAXTER, Mr. David Andrew, BA ACA *2000;* 34 Fir Road, Bramhall, STOCKPORT, SK7 2NP.
BAXTER, Mr. David Lomas, MA FCA *1979;* Sullington Warren, Heather Way, Storrington, PULBOROUGH, RH20 4DD.
BAXTER, Mr. David Malcolm, BSc FCA *1973;* Flat 5, Stratton House, Westcliff Parade, WESTCLIFF-ON-SEA, ESSEX, SS0 7QD.
•**BAXTER, Mr. David Nicholas, FCA** *1981;* Baxters, Mill Road Farmhouse, Low Road, North Tuddenham, DEREHAM, NR20 3AB.
BAXTER, Mr. David Tennant Harry, FCA *1975;* (Tax Fac), with Rupert King & Company Limited, Stanton House, 31 Westgate, GRANTHAM, LINCOLNSHIRE, NG31 6LX.
BAXTER, Mr. David William, BA FCA *1963;* 45 Adela Avenue, NEW MALDEN, KT3 6LF. (Life Member)
BAXTER, Mr. David William, BSc ACA *2001;* 125 Elsley Road, LONDON, SW11 5LH.
BAXTER, Mrs. Elaine Rose, FCA ATII *1991;* Trenchard, Cross Street, Hoxne, EYE, IP21 5AH.
BAXTER, Geoffrey Albert Edward, Esq OBE BCom FCA *1958;* Bernard Shaw 10-801, POLANCO DF 11560, MEXICO. (Life Member)
BAXTER, Mr. Graham James, FCA *1977;* 41 River Gardens, CARSHALTON, SM5 2NH.
BAXTER, Mr. Harold, LLB FCA CTA *1969;* (Tax Fac), 486 Street Lane, LEEDS, LS17 6HA.
BAXTER, Mrs. Helen Alexis, BSc FCA *1979;* 52 Hastings Avenue, WHITLEY BAY, TYNE AND WEAR, NE26 4AG.
BAXTER, Mrs. Helen Catherine, BSc ACA *1996;* 2 Croft Gardens, Grappenhall Heys, WARRINGTON, CHESHIRE, WA4 3LH.
BAXTER, Mr. Ian Anthony, BA ACA *1996;* Promethean Ltd Promethean House, Lower Philips Road Whitebirk Industrial Estate, BLACKBURN, BB1 5TH.
BAXTER, Mrs. Jennifer, ACA *2002;* 24 Anglian Way, MARKET RASEN, LN8 3RP.
BAXTER, Mr. John Anthony, BSc ACA *2008;* 32 Sherlock Close, CAMBRIDGE, CB3 0HP.
BAXTER, Mr. John Collinge, FCA *1952;* Chesters, 1a Erneston Crescent, CORSHAM, WILTSHIRE, SN13 9DH. (Life Member)
BAXTER, Mr. Jonathan Mark, BA ACA *2002;* 23 Oaklands Avenue, LEEDS, LS13 1LH.
BAXTER, Miss. Katherine Sarah, BA ACA *1997;* 6 Ings View, Tollerton, YORK, YO61 1PR.
BAXTER, Mrs. Laura, ACA *2011;* 25 Longmead Avenue, BRISTOL, BS7 8QB.
BAXTER, Miss. Lisa Carmen, MA ACA CTA *1993;* Griffins, 12 Bereweeke Close, WINCHESTER, SO22 6AR.
BAXTER, Mr. Neil, ACA *2011;* 24 Brooklyn Works, Green Lane, SHEFFIELD, S3 8SH.
BAXTER, Mr. Paul, BSc ACA *1989;* Todhunter Earle Ltd, 1st Floor Chelsea Reach, 79-89 Lots Road, LONDON, SW10 0RN.
BAXTER, Mr. Peter John, FCA *1970;* Oyster Beds, 56 Sutherland Chase, ASCOT, SL5 8TF.
BAXTER, Mr. Robert Edward, BA ACA *1985;* Arts Building, University of Birmingham, Edgbaston, BIRMINGHAM, B15 2TT.
BAXTER, Mr. Robin Tristram, MA FCA *1964;* 112 Thurleigh Road, Balham, LONDON, SW12 8TT.
BAXTER, Mr. Roger Ian, MA FCA FRSA *1971;* 25 Newlands Avenue, THAMES DITTON, SURREY, KT7 0HD.
BAXTER, Mr. Roy William, FCA *1951;* 3 Laurel Close, Glenfield, LEICESTER, LE3 8AW. (Life Member)
•**BAXTER, Mr. Simon John Robert, BA ACA** *1994;* with KPMG LLP, Arlington Business Park, Theale, READING, RG7 4SD.
BAXTER, Mr. Stephen Richard, MA ACA *1990;* 5 Elm Court, Elmdon, SAFFRON WALDEN, ESSEX, CB11 4NP.
BAXTER, Mrs. Susan, BA ACA *1986;* 20 Hampshire Drive, Edgbaston, BIRMINGHAM, B15 3NZ.
BAXTER, Mrs. Susan Patricia, BSc ACA *1995;* 42 St Johns Road, SEVENOAKS, TN13 3LP.
BAXTER, Mrs. Suzanne Claire, BSc ACA *1992;* Mitie Group Plc, 1 Harlequin Office Park, Fieldfare, Emersons Green, BRISTOL, BS16 7FN.
•**BAXTER, Mrs. Sylvie Gabrielle, BA ACA** *1995;* (Tax Fac), with Mayes Business Partnership Ltd, 22-28 Willow Street, ACCRINGTON, LANCASHIRE, BB5 1LP.
BAXTER, Ms. Victoria, BA ACA *2007;* Top Floor Flat, 131 Chadwick Road, LONDON, SE15 4PY.
BAXTER-BRAND, Mrs. Kerstin, ACA *1998;* 45 Fitzjames Avenue, CROYDON, CR0 5DN.
BAXTER-JONES, Mr. Mark, ACA *2010;* 106 Thingwall Park, BRISTOL, BS16 2AT.
•**BAY, Mrs. Lorraine Maria, ACA** *1988;* Moore Stephens LLP, 150 Aldersgate Street, LONDON, EC1A 4AB. See also Moore Stephens & Co
•**BAYAT, Mr. Manoochehr, BSc FCA** *1968;* KPMG Bayat Rayan, 3rd Floor, 239 Motahari Ave, TEHRAN, 15876, IRAN.
BAYAT MOKHTARI, Mr. Mohsen, BSc FCA *1988;* 5 Brightwen Grove, STANMORE, MIDDLESEX, HA7 4WH.
BAYCROFT, Mr. Mark Anthony, BSc ACA CTA *2001;* (Tax Fac), The Pound, Saddlers Scarp, Grayshott, HINDHEAD, GU26 6DZ.
BAYER, Mr. Ian William, FCA *1968;* Lower Farm, Rimpton, YEOVIL, BA22 8AB.
BAYER, Mr. Michael Jonathan, BSc ACA CF *1996;* 1 Old Convent, Moat Road, EAST GRINSTEAD, WEST SUSSEX, RH19 3RS.
•**BAYER, Mr. Michael Moshe, FCA** *1983;* (Tax Fac), Harold Everett Wreford LLP, 1st Floor, 44-46 Whitfield Street, LONDON, W1T 2RJ.
BAYES, Mr. David Graham, FCA *1969;* 7 Dybdale Crescent, WELLINGBOROUGH, NN8 5EX.
BAYES, Mr. Matthew James, MA(Oxon) BA ACA *2006;* 11 Cheney Court, Husbands Bosworth, LUTTERWORTH, LEICESTERSHIRE, LE17 6LX.
•**BAYES, Mr. Maxwell William, FCA** *1969;* Max Bayes, 33 Main Road, Hackleton, NORTHAMPTON, NN7 2AD.
•**BAYES, Mr. Paul, FCA** *1973;* Baymor, 14 Valley Walk, Croxley Green, RICKMANSWORTH, WD3 3SY.
BAYFIELD, Mr. Gary, MEng ACA *2006;* 51 Hill Road, Tividale, OLDBURY, WEST MIDLANDS, B69 2LN.
BAYFORD, Mr. Robin Alec, BA FCA *1975;* Cob House, Crawley, WINCHESTER, SO21 2PZ.
BAYLARBAYOV, Mr. Teymur, ACA *2010;* A71, Albion Riverside Building, 8 Hester Road, LONDON, SW11 4AJ.
BAYLES, Mr. Nigel, BSc ACA *2003;* Sage (UK) Ltd, North Park Avenue, NEWCASTLE UPON TYNE, NE13 9AA.
•**BAYLEY, Mr. Carl, BSc ACA** *1987;* MEMBER OF COUNCIL (Member of Council 2003 - 2005), (Tax Fac), Bayley Miller Ltd, 16b Queen Street, EDINBURGH, EH2 1JE.
BAYLEY, Mr. Darren, BSc ACA *1993;* 47 Denman Lane, Huncote, LEICESTER, LE9 3AL.
BAYLEY, Mr. Edward Derek, BA ACA *1985;* 8a Links Road, EPSOM, KT17 3PS.
BAYLEY, Mr. Graeme Charles Roger, BSc FCA CF *1993;* (Tax Fac), 31 Bidborough Ridge, TUNBRIDGE WELLS, KENT, TN4 0UT.
BAYLEY, Mr. Hugh Sheppard, BA FCA *1948;* Room 25, Milner House, Ermyn Way, LEATHERHEAD, SURREY, KT22 8TX. (Life Member)
BAYLEY, Mr. James Peter, ACA *2009;* Flat 7, 156 High Street, HUNTINGDON, CAMBRIDGESHIRE, PE29 3TF.
BAYLEY, Mr. Nicholas Charles, BA ACA *1989;* 296 North Auburn Road, AUBURN, ME 04210, UNITED STATES.
BAYLEY, Mr. Norman, FCA *1963;* with Gilchrist Tash, Cleveland Bldgs., Queen's Square, MIDDLESBROUGH, TS2 1PA.
BAYLEY, Mr. Peter Jack, BSc ACA *2007;* 27 Curzon Drive, Church Crookham, FLEET, HAMPSHIRE, GU52 6JL.
BAYLEY, Ms. Rowan, BA FCA ATII *1980;* (Tax Fac), Chevron Ltd, 1 Westferry Circus, Canary Wharf, LONDON, E14 4HA.
BAYLEY, Mrs. Susan, FCA *1972;* Orchard House, White Ladies Aston, WORCESTER, WR7 4QQ.
BAYLEY, Mr. Trevor John, OBE FCA *1974;* Woodside, Clay Lake, ENDON, STOKE-ON-TRENT, ST9 9DD.
BAYLIFF, Mrs. Leanne Jane, BA ACA *2006;* R F Miller & Co Bellevue, Princes Street, ULVERSTON, CUMBRIA, LA12 7NB.
BAYLIS, Miss. Catherine Elizabeth, MA ACA *2000;* 17 Fawe Park Road, LONDON, SW15 2EB.
•**BAYLIS, Mr. Christopher Edward, BA ACA** *1997;* Silbury Business Advisers Ltd, Venture House, Calne Road, Lyneham, CHIPPENHAM, WILTSHIRE SN15 4PP. See also Silbury Woking Ltd
BAYLIS, Mr. George Miles Sarjeant, MA FCA *1963;* 19 Ernle Road, LONDON, SW20 0HH.
BAYLIS, Mrs. Gillian Margaret, BA ACA *1983;* 25 Moorfield Avenue, Knowle, SOLIHULL, B93 9RA.
BAYLIS, Mr. Mark, BSc ACA *1998;* 6 Freedom Trl, MANSFIELD, MA 02048, UNITED STATES.
BAYLIS, Dr. Richard Mark, PhD BSc ACA *2010;* 40 Ger y Nant, Birchgrove, SWANSEA, SA7 0HD.
BAYLIS, Mr. Robert John, BA FCA *1993;* Abbey Warehouse, Abbey Slip, PENZANCE, CORNWALL, TR18 4AR.
•**BAYLIS, Mr. Simon John, BA ACA CTA** *1998;* Moore Stephens LLP, 150 Aldersgate Street, LONDON, EC1A 4AB.
BAYLISS, Mrs. Allison Sandra, BA ACA *1991;* 12 The Village, Keele, NEWCASTLE, STAFFORDSHIRE, ST5 5AR.
BAYLISS, Mr. Gareth John, BCom ACA *2001;* Baywood Cottage, The Stocks, Beenham, READING, RG7 5NA.
BAYLISS, Mr. Howard Mark Robert, BSc ACA *1996;* 16 Winchester Road, ALTON, HAMPSHIRE, GU34 1RX.
BAYLISS, Mr. John William, FCA *1956;* Pump House, Church Street, Great Burstead, BILLERICAY, CM11 2TR. (Life Member)
BAYLISS, Mrs. Kate Louise, BSc ACA *1993;* with Chris Duckett, Thorn Office Centre, Straight Mile Road, Rotherwas, HEREFORD, HR2 6JT.
BAYLISS, Mrs. Laura Jane, ACA *2004;* 20 Thackeray Close, UXBRIDGE, MIDDLESEX, UB8 3DW.
BAYLISS, Miss. Leanne Marie, BA(Hons) ACA *2010;* 40 Beaudesert Road, Hollywood, BIRMINGHAM, B47 5DP.
BAYLISS, Mr. Mark, BA ACA *2011;* 124 Cuffley Hill, Goffs Oak, WALTHAM CROSS, HERTFORDSHIRE, EN7 5EY.
BAYLISS, Mr. Mark Richard, BSc ACA *1987;* 162 Paddington Street, PADDINGTON, NSW 2021, AUSTRALIA.
BAYLISS, Mr. Paul Anthony, BSc FCA *1983;* Chelmsford College, 102 Moulsham Street, CHELMSFORD, ESSEX, CM2 0JQ.
•**BAYLISS, Mr. Paul Dennis, BA ACA** *1981;* Bayliss & Co, 25 Lordswood Road, Harborne, BIRMINGHAM, B17 9RP.
•**BAYLISS, Mr. Perry, BA ACA** *1986;* Bayliss Ware Ltd, 9 Stratfield Park, Elettra Avenue, WATERLOOVILLE, HAMPSHIRE, PO7 7XN.
BAYLISS, Mr. Peter Herbert, BA ACA *1985;* Windy Ridge, Ladder Hill, Wheatley, OXFORD, OX33 1HY.
BAYLISS, Mr. Richard Anthony, BSc ACA *1995;* 28 Redcrest Gardens, CAMBERLEY, GU15 2DU.
BAYLISS, Mr. Robert James, BSc ACA *2006;* Apartment 1, 72 Brunswick Street, LEAMINGTON SPA, WARWICKSHIRE, CV31 2EQ.
BAYLISS, Mr. Royston Alexander, MBA BSc FCA *1996;* Flagstone Reassurance Suisse, Rue du Collège 1, CH-1920 MARTIGNY, SWITZERLAND.
BAYLISS, Mr. Samuel John, BA(Hons) ACA *2009;* 19 Turbary Avenue, WORCESTER, WR4 0PS.
BAYLISS, Miss. Sian, BA ACA *1992;* The Cottage Selsey Road, North Woodchester, STROUD, GL5 5NG.
BAYLY, Mrs. Caroline, BA ACA *2000;* 5 Hotham Road, Putney, LONDON, SW15 1QL.
BAYMAN, Mr. David Paul, ACA *1998;* 40 Aldworth Close, BRACKNELL, BERKSHIRE, RG12 7AW.
•**BAYMAN, Mrs. Vicki, ACA** *2003;* Lime Accountancy Limited, 10 Upper Bourne Lane, Wrecclesham, FARNHAM, SURREY, GU10 4RQ.
BAYNE, Mr. Alastair Grahame Mountjoy, FCA *1969;* The Farmhouse, 188 Moo 7, T Banlao A Bangfang, KHON KAEN 40279, THAILAND.
BAYNE, Mr. John Robert, FCA *1969;* 15 Falcon Lane, STOCKTON-ON-TEES, CLEVELAND, TS20 1LS.
BAYNE, Mr. Michael, BSc ACA *2000;* Ridley Cottage High Street Chalford, STROUD, GLOUCESTERSHIRE, GL6 8DS.
BAYNE, Mr. Scott, BSc ACA *2005;* 38 Montgomery Close, Great Sankey, WARRINGTON, WA5 8DL.
BAYNE, Mr. Thomas Justin Everard, BA ACA *1988;* The Cottage, 21 St. Anns Villas, LONDON, W11 4RT.
BAYNES, Miss. Alyson Claire, ACA *2009;* 12 Southey Mews, LONDON, E16 1TN.
BAYNES, Mrs. Catherine Anne-Marie, BA ACA *1996;* 242 Locks Road, Locks Heath, SOUTHAMPTON, SO31 6LB.
•**BAYNES, Mr. Charles Bruce, FCA** *1983;* Wilkins Kennedy, Bridge House, London Bridge, LONDON, SE1 9QR. See also W K Corporate Finance LLP

BAYNES, Mr. Christopher Rory, BSc ACA *1982;* Greywalls, 52 The High Street, Findon Village, WORTHING, BN14 0SZ.
BAYNES, Mr. David, BA ACA *1992;* P & M M Ltd Rockingham Drive, Linford Wood, MILTON KEYNES, MK14 6LY.
BAYNES, Mr. David Graham, BA ACA *1992;* The Lodge, Station Road, Haddenham, ELY, CB6 3XD.
BAYNES, Mr. Quentin Arthur, BSc(Hons) ACA *2004;* 54 The Street, Alburgh, HARLESTON, IP20 0DN.
BAYNHAM, Miss. Emma, ACA *2011;* Four Bells, The Street, East Langdon, DOVER, KENT, CT15 5JF.
BAYNHAM, Mr. Haydn Thomas, FCA *1959;* 33 Cae Mawr Road, Rhiwbina, CARDIFF, CF14 6NY. (Life Member)
BAYNHAM, Mr. Peter Frederick, BA FCA *1980;* Marsh Ltd, 1 Tower Place West, LONDON, EC3R 5BU.
BAYNTON, Mr. Cyril Joseph, FCA *1969;* 13 Wootton Road, Finchfield, WOLVERHAMPTON, WV3 8EG.
BAYS, Mr. David Charles, FCA *1972;* 15 Woodhall Avenue, PINNER, HA5 3DY.
BAYS, Mr. Ian Thomas, BSc ACA *1989;* c/o Freshfields Bruckhaus Deringer, 11th Floor, 2 Exchange Square, CENTRAL, HONG KONG ISLAND, HONG KONG SAR.
BAYS, Mr. John Newton, FCA *1964;* The Stable House, Hampnett, Nr Northleach, CHELTENHAM, GL54 3NN.
BAZALGETTE, Mr. Simon Louis, BSc ACA *1988;* 57 Kings Road, RICHMOND, TW10 6EG.
BAZELEY, Mrs. Cathryn Ann, FCA *1983;* 14 The Paddock, LICHFIELD, STAFFORDSHIRE, WS14 9BZ.
BAZELKOVA, Ms. Stefka Hristeva, BA ACA *2001;* Flat 34 New Caledonian Wharf, 6 Odessa Street, LONDON, SE16 7TN.
BAZELL, Mr. Barnaby Piercy, MPhil BSc ACA *1980;* Greenfield Manor Cottage, Greenfield, Christmas Common, WATLINGTON, OX49 5HF.
BAZELL, Mr. Robert Hugh, FCA *1956;* Turves FarmBilsington Road, Ruckinge ASHFORD, Kent, TN26 2PB. (Life Member)
BAZIRE, Mrs. Susan Carol, BA ACA *1986;* 5 Coldwaltham Lane, BURGESS HILL, WEST SUSSEX, RH15 0EL.
BAZLEY, Mr. William John David, FCA *1968;* 95 Heath End Road, Flackwell Heath, HIGH WYCOMBE, BUCKINGHAMSHIRE, HP10 9ES. (Life Member)
BAZZAZ, Miss. Shobna, BA ACA *1995;* 65 Derby Road, Bramcote, NOTTINGHAM, NG9 3GW.
BEABLE, Mr. Thomas, ACA *2011;* 15 Passage Leaze, BRISTOL, BS11 9QL.
BEACH, Mr. Andrew William, BA ACA *2000;* 39 Randall Place, LONDON, SE10 9LA.
•BEACH, Mr. Graham Stephen John, BA ACA CTA *1992;* Leigh Graham Associates, 10 John Street, STRATFORD-UPON-AVON, WARWICKSHIRE, CV37 6UB.
BEACH, Mr. Jonathan Stuart, ACA *2002;* 72 Wisteria Drive, Healing, GRIMSBY, SOUTH HUMBERSIDE, DN41 7JS.
BEACH, Mr. Martin David, BSc ACA *1983;* Harrison Castings Ltd, Gough Road, LEICESTER, LE5 4AP.
BEACH, Mr. Stephen Charles, BSc FCA *1983;* PricewaterhouseCoopers, Anz Haus, Central Avenue, LAE, PAPUA NEW GUINEA.
BEACHAM, Mr. Bruce Henry, BA CA *1980; (CA Scotland 1975);* The Lowman Group, The Island, Lowman Green, TIVERTON, EX16 4LA.
BEACHAM, Miss. Clare Elizabeth, BA ACA *2005;* 20 Tiny Meadows, South Petherwin, LAUNCESTON, CORNWALL, PL15 7JD.
BEACHAM, Mrs. Jennifer Louise, ACA *2008;* 17 Henrietta Grove, PRESCOT, MERSEYSIDE, L34 1PZ.
BEACHAM, Mr. Mark Derrick, BSc FCA *1984;* 11 Austwick Lane, Emerson Valley, MILTON KEYNES, MK4 2DR.
BEACHAM, Mr. Mark Richard, LLB ACA *2005;* 17 Killarney Road, LONDON, SW18 2DU.
BEACHAM, Mr. Richard Alexander, BEng ACA *1992;* 48 Remington Drive West, HIGHLAND VILLAGE, TX 75077, UNITED STATES.
BEACHAM, Mr. Robin Paul, MA ACA *1987;* Batch Orchard, Back Lane, Batcombe, SHEPTON MALLET, SOMERSET, BA4 6AA.
•BEACHELL, Miss. Clare Louise, LLB ACA *1993;* (Tax Fac), Smith Cooper, Wilmot House, St James Court, Friar Gate, DERBY, DE1 1BT. See also Smith Cooper LLP
BEACHELL, Mr. Peter, BSc ACA *2004;* 15 Hopefield Chase, Rothwell, LEEDS, LS26 0XX.
BEACHER, Mr. Richard Lawrence, BA FCA *1983;* 23 Nam Shan Village, SAI KUNG, NEW TERRITORIES, HONG KONG SAR.
BEACOCK, Mr. Patrick, BSc ACA *1989;* 41 Northwood Falls, Woodlesford, LEEDS, LS26 8PD.
BEACOM, Mr. Brian Edward, FCA *1956;* 39 Well Road, Otford, SEVENOAKS, TN14 5PS. (Life Member)
BEACOM, Mrs. Hannah Mercedes, ACA *1998;* Island Coachways Les Banques, St. Peter Port, GUERNSEY, GY1 2HZ.
BEADEN, Mr. Andrew Michael, BA FCA *1994;* Luxfer Group, The Victoria, Harbour City, Salford Quays, SALFORD, M50 3SP.
BEADLE, Mrs. Charlotte Jayne, BSc ACA *1998;* Barrwood, Hildenborough Road, Shipbourne, TONBRIDGE, TN11 9QA.
BEADLE, Mr. Clive Richard, BA FCA *1985;* 12 Risborrow Close, Etwall, DERBY, DE65 6HY.
•BEADLE, Mr. Mark Ronald Sydney, BA FCA *1993;* The Objectivity Partnership LLP, 12 York Gate, Regent's Park, LONDON, NW1 4QS.
•BEADLE, Mr. Michael, FCA *1970;* (Tax Fac), M Beadle & Co Limited, 53 Peacocks Close, Cavendish, SUDBURY, SUFFOLK, CO10 8DA.
BEADLE, Mr. Michael John, BA ACA *2001;* 5 Townley Road, LONDON, SE22 8SW.
BEADLE, Mr. Richard Alan, BSc ACA *1996;* 60 Folly Lane, ST. ALBANS, HERTFORDSHIRE, AL3 5JJ.
BEADLE, Mr. Roy Bernard, FCA *1956;* 42 Parkfield Crescent, TAUNTON, SOMERSET, TA1 4SA. (Life Member)
BEADLE, Mr. Simon Mark, BSc ACA *1990;* 10 Doveleat, CHINNOR, OXFORDSHIRE, OX39 4DW.
BEADMAN, Mr. Nigel Stuart William, FCA *1971;* Level 1, 370 Pitt Street, SYDNEY, NSW 2000, AUSTRALIA.
BEADMAN, Mrs. Pamela, BSc FCA *1996;* 24 Strother Close, Pocklington, YORK, YO42 2GR.
•BEADMAN, Mr. Paul Martin Frank, FCA *1971;* Beadman & Co, Maple Lodge, Paines Hill, Steeple Aston, BICESTER, OXFORDSHIRE OX25 4SQ.
BEADMAN, Mr. Robert Stuart, BA(Hons) ACA *2003;* 19 Grove Crescent, KINGSTON UPON THAMES, SURREY, KT1 2DD.
•BEADSMOORE, Mr. Phillip Harry John, ACA *1991;* Palmer Moore Limited, C/O Harwoods, 1 Trinity Place, Midland Drive, SUTTON COLDFIELD, WEST MIDLANDS B72 1TX. See also Quantum Solutions Limited
•BEAGENT, Mr. David John, FCA *1959;* David Beagent & Co, The Old Rectory, Mill Lane, Tempsford, SANDY, SG19 2AT.
BEAGENT, Mr. Thomas Benjamin John, BSc ACA *2003;* with PricewaterhouseCoopers LLP, 1 Embankment Place, LONDON, WC2N 6RH.
BEAGLEY, Mr. Richard Tregurtha, FCA *1975;* 135 Holmwood Road, Cheam, SUTTON, SM2 7JS.
•BEAHAN, Mr. Michael Peter, FCA *1982;* (Tax Fac), M. P. Beahan & Co, 57 Laughton Road, Dinnington, SHEFFIELD, S25 2PN.
BEAK, Miss. Catherine Helen, ACA *2006;* Apartment 17, 77 Musters Road West Bridgford, NOTTINGHAM, NG2 7PY.
BEAK, Mr. Colin Emeil, BA ACA *1979;* 14 Linsdale Gardens, Gedling, NOTTINGHAM, NG4 4GY.
BEAK, Mr. David William, BA FCA *1980;* 36 Rousebarn Lane, Croxley Green, RICKMANSWORTH, WD3 3RL.
•BEAK, Mr. Geoffrey Alan, FCA *1975;* (Tax Fac), Harold Duckworth & Co, 41 Houndiscombe Road, Mutley, PLYMOUTH, PL4 6EX.
•BEAK, Mr. Terence John, FCA *1964;* (Tax Fac), Terry Beak & Co, 5 Hamilton Close, Littlestone, NEW ROMNEY, TN28 8NU.
BEAL, Mr. Derek George, BA FCA *1977;* 1 Highview Place, Arterberry Road, LONDON, SW20 8AL.
•BEAL, Miss. Elaine Lynne, ACA *2007;* Gary Sargeant + Company, 5 White Oak Square, London Road, SWANLEY, BR8 7AG.
BEAL, Mr. John Francis, BA FCA *1977;* 9 St. Johns Avenue, Warley, BRENTWOOD, CM14 5DF.
•BEAL, Mrs. Linda Janice, BSc ACA *1986;* PricewaterhouseCoopers LLP, 1 Embankment Place, LONDON, WC2N 6RH. See also PricewaterhouseCoopers
BEAL, Mr. Michael, BA FCA *1963;* 2 Toller Road, Quorn, LOUGHBOROUGH, LE12 8AH. (Life Member)
BEAL, Mr. Richard Easton, BSc FCA *1978;* 1 High Ash Avenue, LEEDS, LS17 8RS.
BEALCH, Ms. Jane Anne, BSc(Econ) ACA *1995;* Heronwood Soldridge Road, Medstead, ALTON, GU34 5JF.
BEALE, Mr. Alan Paul, BSc ACA *1984;* Woodside, Broomfield Road, Kingswood, MAIDSTONE, ME17 3NY.
BEALE, Mr. Andrew, ACA *2008;* 12 Manor Park Close, Tilehurst, READING, RG30 4PS.
BEALE, Mr. Ashley Ross, ACA *2009;* Flat 4, 2 Manstone Road, LONDON, NW2 3XG.
BEALE, Mr. Bertram George, FCA *1949;* 36 Kinloch Drive, Heaton, BOLTON, BL1 4LZ. (Life Member)
BEALE, Mr. Colin James, FCA *1968;* 35 Fieldgate Lane, KENILWORTH, WARWICKSHIRE, CV8 1BT.
BEALE, Mr. Crispin John, BSc ACA *1998;* Facts International Ltd Unit 3, Henwood Henwood Industrial Estate, ASHFORD, TN24 8FL.
BEALE, Mr. David Robert, BSc ACA *1982;* 16 Barlings Road, HARPENDEN, AL5 2AN.
BEALE, Mr. Edward John, MA ACA *1987;* 16 Strathearn Rd, Wimbledon, LONDON, SW19 7LH.
BEALE, Mr. Gerald Montague, FCA *1954;* 55 Chelsea Towers, Chelsea Manor Gardens, LONDON, SW3 5PN. (Life Member)
BEALE, Mr. Graham Harold, FCA *1961;* 7 chemin des Epines, 1222 Vesenaz, GENEVA, SWITZERLAND. (Life Member)
BEALE, Mr. Graham John, BSc ACA *1986;* 8 St. James's Square, BATH, BA1 2TR.
BEALE, Mr. Mark Ernest, BA FCA MBA *1986;* 6 Mulberry Gardens, PETERBOROUGH, PE4 6SY.
BEALE, Mr. Matthew Terence, ACA *2010;* 40 Hartledon Road, BIRMINGHAM, B17 0AD.
BEALE, Mr. Nicholas John, BA FCA *1968;* 10 Austen Close, EAST GRINSTEAD, RH19 1RZ. (Life Member)
BEALE, Mr. Ralph John, BSc CIRM FCA PIIA *1980;* 851 Kingsway, East Didsbury, MANCHESTER, M20 5PA.
•BEALE, Mr. Robert Andrew, BA FCA CTA *1993;* (Tax Fac), Morris Owen, 43-45 Devizes Road, SWINDON, SN1 4BG.
•BEALE, Mr. Sidney Arthur, FCA *1964;* Sidney A. Beale & Co., 338 Yardley Road, Yardley, BIRMINGHAM, B25 8LT. See also Wellborne Limited
•BEALE, Mr. Stephen George John, FCA *1975;* (Tax Fac), S.G. Beale & Co., 3 Redman Court, Bell Street, PRINCES RISBOROUGH, HP27 0AA.
BEALER, Mr. Christopher James, BA ACA *2001;* 1766 Mallard Court, LIVERMORE, CA 94551, UNITED STATES.
BEALER, Mr. Robert Charles, BA FCA *1974;* 4123A Purdue St, HOUSTON, TX 77005, UNITED STATES.
BEALES, Mr. Allan John, BA ACA *1992;* PO Box HM 2209, HAMILTON HMJX, BERMUDA.
BEALES, Miss. Christina Margaret, MA FCA *1991;* 1 Millington Close, READING, RG2 7LR.
•BEALES, Mr. David, FCA *1972;* Beales & Co, Oaken Coppice, Bears Den, Kingswood, TADWORTH, KT20 6PL.
BEALES, Mr. Graeme, BA ACA *1992;* Helena Labs UK Ltd, Queensway South, Team Valley Trading Estate, GATESHEAD, TYNE AND WEAR, NE11 0SD.
BEALEY, Mr. Martin David, BSc ACA *1981;* 18 South Road, AMERSHAM, HP6 5LU.
BEAMAN, Mr. Matthew, ACA *2011;* Apartment 323, City Gate 3, 5 Blantyre Street, MANCHESTER, M15 4JS.
BEAMAN, Mr. Michael Stanley, FCA *1966;* Kenilworth, 20 Port Hill Drive, SHREWSBURY, SY3 8RS.
BEAMAN, Mr. Paul Robert, FCA *1988;* 5 Sherbrook Road, CANNOCK, WS11 1HJ.
BEAMER, Mr. David Bryan, MA ACA *1993;* Jabil Circuit Inc, 10560 Dr Martin Luther King Jr St N, ST PETERSBURG, FL 33716, UNITED STATES.
•BEAMES, Mr. John Charles, FCA *1972;* J.C Beames & Co., 4 The Crossway, Mottingham, LONDON, SE9 4JJ.
•BEAMES, Mr. John Walter, FCA MCIArb *1974;* Wilkins Kennedy, Parmenter House, 57 Tower Street, WINCHESTER, HAMPSHIRE, SO23 8TD.
BEAMES, Miss. Phillida Alicia Kyrene, ACA *2008;* Lower Flat, 80B North Street, Clapham, LONDON, SW4 0HE.
BEAMISH, Mr. Adrian David, BA ACA *1996;* 544 Roxbury Lane, LOS GATOS, CA 95032, UNITED STATES.
BEAMISH, Mr. Peter Howard, BA FCA *1973;* Blue Water, Rue De La Blanche Pierre, St Lawrence, JERSEY, JE3 1EA.
BEAMISH, Mr. Richard Barnard, ACA *1978;* PO BOX 163, SUMMER HILL, NSW 2130, AUSTRALIA.
BEAMISH, Mrs. Valerie Anne, BSc FCA *1976;* Blue Water, Rue de la Blanche Pierre, St. Lawrence, JERSEY, JE3 1EA.
BEAN, Dr. David Geoffrey, FCA *1969;* Green Lane Cottage, Green Lane, Over Peover, KNUTSFORD, CHESHIRE, WA16 8UH. (Life Member)
BEAN, Miss. Erica, BA(Hons) ACA *2011;* 35 Dells Lane, BIGGLESWADE, BEDFORDSHIRE, SG18 8LJ.
BEAN, Mr. Hubert Kenneth, FCA *1953;* Park Cottage, Hatchet Lane, Stonely, ST. NEOTS, PE19 5EG. (Life Member)
BEAN, Mr. James Garry, BCom FCA *1963;* 201 Billesley Lane, Moseley, BIRMINGHAM, B13 9RR. (Life Member)
BEAN, Miss. Jennifer Elaine, MBA BSc ACA CMC *1984;* H B Consulting, PO Box 21660, LONDON, SW16 1WJ.
BEAN, Mrs. Joanne Louise Bernadette, BSc ACA *2004;* 12 Highfield Drive, Urmston, MANCHESTER, M41 7AF.
BEAN, Mr. John Clifford, FCA *1968;* 21 Brookfields, West Wellow, ROMSEY, HAMPSHIRE, SO51 6GS.
BEAN, Mr. Jonathan Willoughby, FCA *1970;* Penpont Farmhouse, Penpont, BRECON, POWYS, LD3 8ES.
•BEAN, Mr. Lawrence Philip, FCA *1971;* (Tax Fac), Forster Stott & Co, Langton House, 124 Acomb Road, Holgate, YORK, NORTH YORKSHIRE YO24 4EY.
•BEAN, Mrs. Mary Ann, BA FCA *1988;* Ernst & Young Audit & Associados SROC S.A, Avenida da Republica 90-6, 1600-206 LISBON, PORTUGAL.
BEAN, Mr. Nicholas David, ACA *1992;* May Gurney Ltd, Trowse, NORWICH, NR14 8SZ.
BEAN, Mr. Richard James, MA ACA *2002;* 12 Highfield Drive, Urmston, MANCHESTER, M41 7AF.
•BEAN, Mr. Robert David, BA ACA *1995;* Grunberg & Co., 10-14 Accommodation Road, Golders Green, LONDON, NW11 8ED. See also Grunberg & Co Limited
BEANE, Mrs. Jennifer, BSc ACA *2005;* HSBC, c/o Andrew Beane, PO Box 242, ABU DHABI, UNITED ARAB EMIRATES.
BEANEY, Miss. Catherine Louise, BA ACA *2006;* 33 Jedburgh Street, LONDON, SW11 5QA.
BEANEY, Mrs. Margaret Valerie, BSc ACA *1980;* (Tax Fac), 5 Old Gannon Close, NORTHWOOD, MIDDLESEX, HA6 2LU.
BEANEY, Mr. Nigel John, BA ACA *1986;* Knoll House, Loudhams Wood Lane, CHALFONT ST. GILES, BUCKINGHAMSHIRE, HP8 4AR.
•BEANLAND, Mr. Daniel Charles, BSc FCA *1996;* Deloitte LLP, Athene Place, 66 Shoe Lane, LONDON, EC4A 3BQ. See also Deloitte & Touche LLP
BEANLAND, Mrs. Jacqueline Anne, LLB ACA *1998;* Flat 1, 51 Eton Avenue, LONDON, NW3 3EP.
BEANLAND, Mr. Richard John Charles, BA ACA *1984;* 3535 Gillespie Street, Apt 203, DALLAS, TX 75219, UNITED STATES.
BEANLANDS, Mr. Philip Darnborough, BA ACA *1993;* 1 Victoria Gardens, ILKLEY, LS29 9EQ.
BEARCROFT, Mr. Jeffrey John, ACA *1980;* 12 Charnley Drive, LEEDS, LS7 4ST.
BEARD, Mr. Adrian Alexander, BA FCA *1975;* Hameau Du Colin, 59 Chemin Du Colin, 69370 ST DIDIER AU MONT D'OR, FRANCE.
BEARD, Miss. Amanda Katherine, BSc ACA *2005;* C/O PricewaterhouseCoopers, Lvl 21, QV1 Building, 250 St Georges Terrace, PERTH, WA 6000 AUSTRALIA.
•BEARD, Mr. Brian Michael, FCA *1971;* Seetru Ltd, Albion Dockside Works, Hanover Place, BRISTOL, BS1 6UT.
BEARD, Mrs. Carolyn Elaine, BA ACA *1987;* with PricewaterhouseCoopers LLP, 1 Embankment Place, LONDON, WC2N 6RH.
BEARD, Mr. Christopher Paul, BA FCA *1963;* Flat 4, 29 Ladbroke Gardens, LONDON, W11 2PY.
BEARD, Mr. David Benjamin Thomas, ACA *2008;* 123 Common Lane, Thundersley, BENFLEET, ESSEX, SS7 3RY.
BEARD, Miss. Elizabeth, BSc ACA *1998;* 38 High Street, Wing, LEIGHTON BUZZARD, LU7 0NR.
BEARD, Mrs. Emer Catherine, BA ACA *1990;* 5 Chepping Close, Tylers Green, Penn, HIGH WYCOMBE, HP10 8JH.
BEARD, Mr. Gary, FCA *2000;* 7 Blyth Way, Laceby Park, GRIMSBY, SOUTH HUMBERSIDE, DN37 7FD.
BEARD, Miss. Jacqueline, BSc ACA *1989;* (Tax Fac), 85 Chassen Road, Urmston, MANCHESTER, M41 9DZ.
BEARD, Mr. James Daniel, MA(Hons) ACA *2000;* 1 Kinnego Park, Cleenagh, Ballymagan, BUNCRANA, COUNTY DONEGAL, IRELAND.
BEARD, Mr. James Ian, FCA *1977;* The Walnuts, High Street, Shingay Cum Wendy, ROYSTON, SG8 0HG. (Life Member)
•BEARD, Mr. Jeremy Royston, ACA *1992;* haysmacintyre, Fairfax House, 15 Fulwood Place, LONDON, WC1V 6AY.
BEARD, Mr. John Michael, FCA *1954;* (Member of Council 1980 - 1989), 2 Croft Road, Great Longstone, BAKEWELL, DERBYSHIRE, DE45 1PA. (Life Member)
BEARD, Mr. Jonathan Peter, ACA *1992;* with C.J. Lucking & Co, 34 Cross Street, Long Eaton, NOTTINGHAM, NG10 1HD.

BEARD, Mr. Keith Paul, BSc ACA *1992;* 28 Ringlet Way, AYLESBURY, BUCKINGHAMSHIRE, HP19 9BS.
BEARD, Mr. Matthew Andrew, BCom ACA *1997;* Intrepid Travel, 11 Spring Street, FITZROY, VIC 3065, AUSTRALIA.
BEARD, Mr. Michael John, ACA *1985;* Master John's Farmhouse, Thoby LaneMountnessing, BRENTWOODEssex, CM15 0SY.
•BEARD, Mr. Michael Walter, FCA *1964;* Michael W. Beard, 62 Hermitage Road, SOLIHULL, B91 2LP.
BEARD, Mr. Paul Edward, BSc FCA *1993;* 3 Merton Road, BEDFORD, MK40 3AF.
BEARD, Mr. Paul Leonard, FCA *1958;* 64 Anstruther Road, Edgbaston, BIRMINGHAM, B15 3NP. (Life Member)
BEARD, Mr. Richard, ACA *2011;* 2 Statham Fold, HYDE, CHESHIRE, SK14 4UA.
•BEARD, Mr. Richard Frank, FCA *1972;* Crowthers Accountants Limited, 10 The Southend, LEDBURY, HEREFORDSHIRE, HR8 2EY.
BEARD, Mr. Richard James, BA ACA *1997;* 34 Hillway, WESTCLIFF-ON-SEA, SS0 8QA.
BEARD, Mr. Robert James, FCA *1968;* 76A Asquith Road, Wigmore, GILLINGHAM, Kent, ME8 0JB.
•BEARD, Mr. Robert Morgan Tansley, ACA *1980;* Francis Clark LLP, Sigma House, Oak View Close, Edginswell Park, TORQUAY, TQ2 7FF.
BEARD, Mr. Roger Leonard, BSc FCA *1974;* 5 St James Close, EVESHAM, WR11 5PZ.
BEARD, Mr. Sebastian James, ACA *2009;* (Tax Fac), 26 Clifden Close, NEWQUAY, CORNWALL, TR7 2EZ.
BEARD, Mr. Simon Mark, BSc ACA *1989;* 8 Park Avenue, LYTHAM ST. ANNES, LANCASHIRE, FY8 5QU.
BEARD, Mr. Stephen Andrew, MEng ACA *1999;* 70 Brooklyn Avenue, LOUGHTON, IG10 1BN.
BEARD, Mr. Timothy David, BA FCA *1982;* Tranters Cottage, 18 Doctors Hill, Bournheath, BROMSGROVE, WORCESTERSHIRE, B61 9JE.
•BEARDALL, Mr. Ian Malcolm, MA FCA *1984;* (Tax Fac), PKIB Accounting LLP, 132 Leicester Road, LOUGHBOROUGH, LEICESTERSHIRE, LE11 2AQ.
BEARDER, Mr. Anthony Peter, BA ACA *1980;* Hogalidsgatan 44B, 1tr, 11730 STOCKHOLM, SWEDEN.
BEARDER, Mr. Robert Michael, FCA *1977;* Torr House, Chagford, NEWTON ABBOT, TQ13 8DX.
BEARDMORE, Mrs. Anne-Marie, BA(Hons) ACA *2010;* 4 Terrington Drive, Westbury Park, NEWCASTLE, STAFFORDSHIRE, ST5 4NB.
•BEARDMORE, Mr. David William, ACA *1991;* Dean Statham LLP, 29 King Street, NEWCASTLE, STAFFORDSHIRE, ST5 1ER.
BEARDMORE, Mr. John Denis, BSc FCA *1978;* 8 Oakley Close, SANDBACH, CW11 1RQ.
BEARDMORE, Mr. Russell Trevor Michael, LLB ACA *1986;* Standard Chartered Bank, Structured Finance, 4-4a Des Voeux Road, CENTRAL, HONG KONG SAR.
BEARDMORE, Mrs. Sara Elizabeth, MA ACA *1986;* 71 Felsham Road, LONDON, SW15 1AZ.
BEARDMORE-GRAY, Mr. John Duncan Invernairn, MA FCA *1960;* 103 Woodlands Lane, CHICHESTER, WEST SUSSEX, PO19 5PF. (Life Member)
BEARDMORE-GRAY, Mr. Thomas, MA ACA *1991;* De Beers UK Ltd D T C Research Centre, Belmont Road, MAIDENHEAD, SL6 6JW.
•BEARDON, Mr. Douglas, MA LLM FCA *1972;* (Tax Fac), Barcant Beardon LLP, 8 Blackstock Mews, Islington, LONDON, N4 2BT. See also Genial Systems Ltd
BEARDOW, Mrs. Catherine Ann, BA ACA *1996;* 33 Carlotta Street, GREENWICH, NSW 2065, AUSTRALIA.
BEARDOW, Mr. John Ernest, FCA *1962;* 53 Merynton Avenue, COVENTRY, CV4 7BL. (Life Member)
BEARDS, Mr. Graham, BSc ACA *1983;* Oakdale House, Vernon Drive, BAKEWELL, DE45 1FZ.
BEARDSELL, Mr. Jonathan, ACA *2011;* with RSM Tenon Audit Limited, Arkwright House, Parsonage Gardens, MANCHESTER, M3 3BB.
BEARDSLEY, Mr. Christopher Alan, MA BA ACA *2006;* with Dains LLP, 1st Floor, Gibraltar House, First Avenue, BURTON-ON-TRENT, STAFFORDSHIRE DE14 2WE.
BEARDSLEY, Mrs. Jenny Clare, BSc ACA *2006;* 45 Grace Avenue, MAIDSTONE, ME16 0BS.
BEARDSLEY, Mr. Michael Robert, FCA *1982;* Chevin Lodge, Farnah Green, BELPER, DE56 2UP.
•BEARDSMORE, Mr. Michael John, FCA *1969;* C K Consulting, 193 Wolverhampton Street, DUDLEY, WEST MIDLANDS, DY1 1DU.
BEARDSMORE, Mr. Paul Christopher, BSc(Hons) ACA *2002;* 3 Foxhill Cotgrave, NOTTINGHAM, NG12 3QQ.
BEARDSMORE, Mr. Philip Raymond, MA ACA *1993;* White House, Nunton, SALISBURY, SP5 4HZ.
BEARDSMORE, Mr. Robert Horatio, MA ACA *1996;* 17 Parsonage Barns, Bottisham, CAMBRIDGE, CB25 9EG.
•BEARDSWORTH, Mr. Allan William, MA ACA *1988;* Deloitte LLP, PO Box 500, 2 Hardman Street, MANCHESTER, M60 2AT. See also Deloitte & Touche LLP
BEARDSWORTH, Miss. Harriet Jane, ACA *2009;* AstraZeneca, 2 Kingdom Street, LONDON, W2.
BEARDSWORTH, Mrs. Lindsay Jane, PhD BSc FCA *1994;* Ebnetstrasse 14, CH 4106 THERWIL, SWITZERLAND.
BEARDWELL, Mr. Edward, BEng ACA *1994;* Pinewood Lower Kingsdown Road, Kingsdown, CORSHAM, WILTSHIRE, SN13 8BD.
BEARE, Mr. David Jonathan Elliott, BSc ACA *1993;* 3 Tay Close, Dronfield Woodhouse, DRONFIELD, DERBYSHIRE, S18 8ZS.
•BEARE, Mr. Kevin Leslie, FCA *1972;* (Tax Fac), Invest in UK Limited, Forest House, 3-5 Horndean Road, BRACKNELL, BERKSHIRE, RG12 0XQ.
BEARE, Mr. Patrick John, BSS ACA *1991;* 34 Devonshire Buildings, BATH, BA2 4SU.
BEARMAN, Mr. Alan Peter, FCA ATII *1956;* Flat 23 Portland Court, 101 Hendon Lane, LONDON, N3 3SH. (Life Member)
BEARMAN, Mr. Marcus Paul, BA ACA *1990;* Orion Publishing Group, 5 Upper St. Martin's Lane, LONDON, WC2H 9EA.
BEARN, Mr. Philip Arthur, BSc ACA *1993;* 32 Oakfield Road, Poynton, STOCKPORT, CHESHIRE, SK12 1AS.
BEARNE, Mr. Colin Charles Fraser, FCA *1964;* Box 3399, PARKLANDS, GAUTENG, 2121, SOUTH AFRICA.
BEARPARK, Miss. Jennifer Kathryn, MSc ACA *2001;* (Tax Fac), Shell International Petroleum Co Ltd, Shell Centre, York Road, LONDON, SE1 7NA.
•BEARPARK, Mr. Neville, BSc FCA CF *1985;* UNW LLP, Citygate, St. James Boulevard, NEWCASTLE UPON TYNE, NE1 4JE.
BEARPARK, Mr. Stephen David, BA ACA *1999;* 60 Blacka Moor Road, SHEFFIELD, S17 3GJ.
BEART, Ms. Jill Elizabeth, PhD BSc ACA *1989;* with MA Partners LLP, 7 The Close, NORWICH, NORFOLK, NR1 4DJ.
BEART, Mr. Michael, ACA *2007;* 30 Gaveston Road, LEAMINGTON SPA, CV32 6EU.
BEART, Mr. Nicholas Anthony, BA ACA *1991;* 50 Elsynge Road, LONDON, SW18 2HN.
BEART, Mr. Simon Delaval, BA ACA *1984;* 63 Albert Bridge Road, LONDON, SW11 4QA.
•BEASANT, Mr. Adam Keith, BSc ACA *2005;* with PricewaterhouseCoopers LLP, 9 Greyfriars Road, READING, RG1 1JG.
•BEASANT, Mr. Jonathan James, BSc FCA *1988;* Waterford, St Helens Gardens, The Pitchens, Wroughton, SWINDON, WILTSHIRE SN4 0RD.
BEASANT, Mrs. Lynn Joanne, BA ACA *2005;* White Rose House Water Street, Hampstead Norreys, THATCHAM, RG18 0SG.
BEASHEL, Mr. Mark Nicholas, BA FCA *1995;* 2 Oakview Close, HARPENDEN, HERTFORDSHIRE, AL5 2PP.
BEASHEL, Mrs. Sheila Maria, BA ACA *1996;* 2 Oakview Close, HARPENDEN, HERTFORDSHIRE, AL5 2PP.
BEASLEY, Mr. Alan Walter, FCA *1958;* 694 Chatsworth Road, CHESTERFIELD, S40 3PB. (Life Member)
•BEASLEY, Mrs. Alison, BSc ACA *1992;* HBD Accountancy Services LLP, Gladstone House, 2 Church Road, Wavertree, LIVERPOOL, L15 9EG.
BEASLEY, Mr. Christopher Andrew, BA FCA *1992;* 16 Mount Road, West Kirby, WIRRAL, MERSEYSIDE, CH48 2HL.
BEASLEY, Mrs. Georgina Heather, BA ACA *1991;* 31 Park Rise, Campbells Bay, AUCKLAND, NEW ZEALAND.
BEASLEY, Miss. Jennifer Frances, BA ACA *2007;* with Baker Tilly Restructuring And Recovery LLP, 25 Farringdon Street, LONDON, EC4A 4AB.
BEASLEY, Mr. Jonathan Alan, BSc ACA *2008;* 64 Sandmere Road, LONDON, SW4 7QH.
BEASLEY, Mrs. Lorraine Vanessa, BSc ACA *1983;* 9 Bunyan Close, Gamlingay, SANDY, BEDFORDSHIRE, SG19 3JD.
•BEASLEY, Mr. Michael Keith, BSc ACA *1986;* H L Plastics Ltd Denby Hall Industrial Estate, Derby Road Marehay, RIPLEY, DERBYSHIRE, DE5 8JX.
•BEASLEY, Mr. Paul John, FCA *1974;* Paul Beasley, Dampier House, Dampier Street, LEEK, STAFFORDSHIRE, ST13 5PF.
BEASLEY, Mr. Robert Anthony, ACA *2008;* 36 Gloster Drive, BOGNOR REGIS, WEST SUSSEX, PO21 3JN.
BEASLEY, Mrs. Shirley Anne, BSc ACA *1986;* Coven, Longfield Drive, AMERSHAM, HP6 5HE.
BEASLEY, Mr. Timothy Carlton, ACA *2009;* 12 Walton Terrace, WOKING, GU21 5EL.
BEASLEY, Miss. Wendy Jane, BSc ACA *1994;* 14 Moorview, Methley, LEEDS, LS26 9AP.
BEASLEY-SUFFOLK, Mr. Adrian Brendan, BSc FCA *1975;* Sarn House Main Street Cropthorne, PERSHORE, WORCESTERSHIRE, WR10 3LT.
BEASLEY-SUFFOLK, Mr. Jack Philip, ACA *2008;* Seestrasse 6, 8803 RUESCHLIKON, SWITZERLAND.
BEASLEY-SUFFOLK, Mrs. Susan Jane, BA(Hons) ACA *2003;* Crisis UK, 66 Commercial Street, LONDON, E1 6LT.
BEASLEY-SUFFOLK, Mrs. Sylvia, ACA *2008;* Seestrasse 6, 8803 RUSCHLIKON, SWITZERLAND.
BEASTALL, Mr. Ian Howard, MEng ACA *1998;* 37 Kelsey Lane, Balsall Common, COVENTRY, CV7 7GR.
BEASTALL, Mr. John Reginald, FCA *1972;* Clover Bank Maple View, Starkholmes Road, MATLOCK, DERBYSHIRE, DE4 3AD.
BEASTALL, Mr. Mark Francis, BA ACA *2003;* 29 Albany Road, LONDON, W13 8PQ.
BEASTALL, Mr. Paul Warren, BA FCA *1997;* 8 Brett Drive, Bromham, BEDFORD, MK43 8RF.
BEASTALL, Mrs. Susan Caroline, BSc ACA *1996;* 37 Kelsey Lane, Balsall Common, COVENTRY, CV7 7GR.
BEATH, Mr. Andrew Antony, BA ACA *1994;* Garland Serviced Apartments(Unit 603), 1188 Kai Xuan Road, Chang Ning district, SHANGHAI 200052, CHINA.
BEATHAM, Mrs. Ann, BSc ACA *1992;* 3 Santon Close, Wesham, PRESTON, PR4 3HF.
BEATON, Mr. Arthur, FCA *1955;* Studlands, Milch Hill Lane, Great Leighs, CHELMSFORD, CM3 1QF. (Life Member)
BEATON, Mr. Bruce Mount, FCA *1957;* 19 Hooke Court, LIPHOOK, HAMPSHIRE, GU30 7GF. (Life Member)
BEATON, Mrs. Catherine Anne, BA ACA *1983;* Guiseley School, Fieldhead Road, Guiseley, LEEDS, LS20 8DT.
BEATON, Miss. Helen Jane, BA ACA *1991;* South Tyneside College, St. Georges Avenue, SOUTH SHIELDS, TYNE AND WEAR, NE34 6ET.
BEATON, Mr. Malcolm Iain, MA ACA *2001;* Gervase, Bulwick, CORBY, NORTHAMPTONSHIRE, NN17 3DY.
BEATON, Mr. Paul Gordon, BSc(Econ) ACA *2002;* 5 Cornwall Road, ST. ALBANS, HERTFORDSHIRE, AL1 1SQ.
•BEATON, Mr. Roger Alan, FCA *1975;* BG Audit LLP, 2/4 York Road, FELIXSTOWE, IP11 7QG. See also Beatons Limited
BEATON, Mr. Scott Alexander, BA ACA *1991;* 3 Freshwater Close, Great Sankey, WARRINGTON, WA5 3PU.
•BEATON, Mrs. Susan, BA ACA *1988;* Coveney Nicholls Limited, The Old Wheel House, 31/37 Church Street, REIGATE, RH2 0AD.
BEATSON, Mr. Neil Robert, BA ACA *2004;* 151a Western Road, SHEFFIELD, S10 1LD.
BEATSON, Miss. Paula Louise, ACA *1997;* Edf Club Puerto Atlantico, Avenida Los Canarios 3, Arguineguin, 35120 MOGAN, SPAIN.
BEATTIE, Mr. Andrew Charles, BSc ACA *1991;* Zurich Financial Services, P.O.Box, 8022 ZURICH, SWITZERLAND.
BEATTIE, Mr. Arnold Robin William, FCA *1965;* 51 Gills Hill Lane, RADLETT, WD7 8DG.
BEATTIE, Mr. Arthur, FCA *1960;* Pendle View, Long Preston, SKIPTON, BD23 4PS. (Life Member)
BEATTIE, Miss. Charlotte, ACA *2010;* Apartment 502, East Block, Forum Magnum Square, LONDON, SE1 7GN.
BEATTIE, Mr. Clive Diarmid, ACA *1982;* The Butts, 154 Slade Road, Portishead, BRISTOL, BS20 6AP.
BEATTIE, Mr. Dylan Joseph, ACA *2009;* Olveston Ville Au Roi, St. Peter Port, GUERNSEY, GY1 1NZ.
BEATTIE, Miss. Elizabeth Ruth, BA(Hons) ACA *2003;* 6 Blackthorn Way, NEWTOWNABBEY, COUNTY ANTRIM, BT37 0GW.
BEATTIE, Miss. Emma Clare, BA(Hons) ACA *2004;* Lombard, Zone 5.1, 3 Princess Way, REDHILL, RH1 1NP.
BEATTIE, Mr. Giles Edward Ramsay, BSc(Hons) ACA *2004;* Baker & McKenzie, 100 New Bridge Street, LONDON, EC4V 6JA.
•BEATTIE, Mrs. Imogen Mary, BA ACA *1988;* (Tax Fac), Imogen Beattie & Co, 5 Douglas Drive, Cambuslang, GLASGOW, G72 8NG.
BEATTIE, Mr. James, BA ACA *2010;* 46 Heathfield Road, CARDIFF, CF14 3JY.
•BEATTIE, Mrs. Joanne Lindsey, BSc ACA *1989;* (Tax Fac), S.B.T.S Limited, 72a Thornbury Wood, Chandler's Ford, EASTLEIGH, HAMPSHIRE, SO53 5DQ.
•BEATTIE, Mr. John, FCA *1972;* (Tax Fac), J. Beattie & Co, 23 Bowling Green Road, KETTERING, NN15 7QW.
•BEATTIE, Mr. John Michael, FCA *1973;* JMBt Limited, The Old Studio, High Street, West Wycombe, HIGH WYCOMBE, HP14 3AB.
BEATTIE, Mrs. Julia, MA ACA *1993;* 48 Garrett Close, Kingsclere, NEWBURY, RG20 5SD.
•BEATTIE, Mr. Michael George, FCA *1973;* (Tax Fac), M G Beattie & Co Limited, 6 Main Avenue, Moor Park, NORTHWOOD, HA6 2HJ.
BEATTIE, Mr. Richard Cameron Farquharson, BSc ACA *1983;* 46 Lanesborough Court, NEWCASTLE UPON TYNE, NE3 3BZ.
•BEATTIE, Miss. Roslyn, BSc FCA *1980;* (Tax Fac), Company Solutions Limited, 2 Festival Square, Little Germany, BRADFORD, WEST YORKSHIRE, BD1 5BD.
BEATTIE, Mr. Scott James, BSc ACA *2002;* Flat 3 Pipers House, Collington Street, LONDON, SE10 9LU.
BEATTON, Mr. David John, FCA *1968;* Bartonwood, Rolvenden, CRANBROOK, KENT, TN17 4ND.
BEATTY, Mr. Adam George, BSS ACA *1994;* Willis Re Inc, One World Financial Center, Third Floor, 200 Liberty Street, NEW YORK, NY 10281 UNITED STATES.
BEATTY, Mr. Roderick Anthony Hume, BA ACA *2001;* 16, Whittle Close, Finchampstead, WOKINGHAM, RG40 4JH.
BEATTY, Mr. Sean Antony, BSc ACA *1991;* 16124 North Point Road, HUNTERSVILLE, NC 28078, UNITED STATES.
BEATTY, Mr. Stephan Christoph, MA BA ACA *2002;* (Tax Fac), Flat 123, Flat 121-126 Elmhurst Mansions, Edgeley Road, LONDON, SW4 6EX.
BEATY, Mr. James Hamilton, BSocSc ACA *1995;* 4 Mildred Road, Walton, STREET, BA16 9QP.
BEATY, Mrs. Kathleen Mary, BSc ACA *1987;* Pine View, Townhead, Hayton, BRAMPTON, CA8 9JQ.
•BEATY-POWNALL, Mr. Michael Christopher, FCA *1970;* (Tax Fac), Beaty-Pownall Associates Limited, 5 Fir Close, WALTON-ON-THAMES, SURREY, KT12 2SX. See also Freeport Management Ltd
BEAUCHAMP, Mr. Keith Maurice, BA ACA *2001;* Branded Media Ltd Unit A Lutyens Industrial Centre, 2 Bilton Industrial Estate Bilton Road, BASINGSTOKE, RG24 8LJ.
BEAUCHAMP, Mr. Russell James, BA(Hons) ACA *2002;* Central Networks, Pegasus Business Park, Castle Donington, DERBY, DE74 2TU.
BEAUCHAMP, Mr. Simon Richard Thorpe, BEng ACA *2000;* Skanska UK Ltd, Condor House, 5-10 St. Paul's Churchyard, LONDON, EC4M 8AL.
BEAUCHAMP, Ms. Sophie Joy, BA ACA *1983;* 43 Richmond Avenue, Islington, LONDON, N1 0NB.
BEAUCHAMP, Mr. Stuart Edward, BSc ACA *2000;* 20 Moxhull Drive, SUTTON COLDFIELD, B76 1LZ.
BEAUCHAMP, Mr. Timothy Douglas, BA ACA *1999;* 6 The Drive, BECKENHAM, BR3 1EQ.
BEAUCLAIR, Mr. Jonathan, ACA *1982;* 26 Stoatley Rise, HASLEMERE, GU27 1AG.
•BEAUCLERK, The Duke of St Alban Murray de Vere, FCA *1962;* Burford and Partners LLP, Suite 75, London Fruit Exchange, Brushfield Street, LONDON, E1 6EP.
BEAUFRERE, Mr. Paul Harvey, FCA *1965;* Quinces, The Street, Sheering, BISHOP'S STORTFORD, CM22 7LU. (Life Member)
BEAUGIE, Mrs. Pamela Jane Skjalm, BA ACA *1996;* Simon Beaugie Picture Frames LTD, Manor Farm Hamstreet Road, Shadoxhurst, ASHFORD, TN26 1NW.
BEAULAH, Mr. Carl Richard, ACA *1982;* G.K Beaulah & Co Ltd, 23 Park Street, HULL, HU2 8RU.
BEAUMONT, Mrs. Abigail Jane Hannah, BSc ACA *2006;* Ye Halfpennies, High Street, MARLBOROUGH, WILTSHIRE, SN8 1LZ.
BEAUMONT, Mr. Alan Storey, FCA *1954;* Burford House, Bluntington, Chaddesley Corbett, KIDDERMINSTER, DY10 4NR. (Life Member)
BEAUMONT, Mrs. Angela Jane, ACA *1985;* 26 Church Street, Hundon, SUDBURY, CO10 8EW.
BEAUMONT, Mr. Bryan Kenneth, FCA *1950;* 20 York Avenue, East Sheen, LONDON, SW14 7LG. (Life Member)
BEAUMONT, Mr. Charles Hugh Richard, BSc FCA *1978;* Dartmeet, 1 Mill Lane, Stock, INGATESTONE, CM4 9RY.
•BEAUMONT, Mr. Christopher Donald, BA FCA *1986;* Lakin Rose Limited, Pioneer House, Vision Park, Histon, CAMBRIDGE, CB24 9NL.

•**BEAUMONT, Mr. Christopher Paul, BA(Hons) FCA DChA** *1995;* Clive Owen & Co LLP, 140 Coniscliffe Road, DARLINGTON, DL3 7RT.

BEAUMONT, Mr. Colin Campbell, FCA *1949;* 5 Alder Lane, Balsall Common, COVENTRY, CV7 7DZ. (Life Member)

BEAUMONT, Mr. Daniel William, ACA *2009;* Flat 203, Park South, Austin Road, LONDON, SW11 5JN.

•**BEAUMONT, Mr. David, FCA** *1968;* (Tax Fac), David Beaumont Ltd, 58 Valley Prospect, NEWARK, NG24 4QW.

•**BEAUMONT, Mr. David Ryder, BA ACA** *1990;* Greenhead, Ridgewood, 7 Park Drive South, Greenhead, HUDDERSFIELD, HD1 4HT.

BEAUMONT, Mr. Edward Alan, FCA *1959;* PO Box 20773, The Quarry, EAST LONDON, C.P., 5200, SOUTH AFRICA. (Life Member)

•**BEAUMONT, Miss. Elaine, ACA ACCA** *2011;* Sutcliffe & Riley, 3 Central Street, HALIFAX, HX1 1HU.

BEAUMONT, Mrs. Elizabeth Anne, BSc ACA *1995;* 10 Hugill Close, YARM, CLEVELAND, TS15 9SS.

BEAUMONT, Mr. Elliot, BSc ACA *2010;* 55a Caistor Road, Laceby, GRIMSBY, SOUTH HUMBERSIDE, DN37 7JA.

BEAUMONT, Mr. Ewan, BSc(Hons) ACA *2001;* 55 Oatlands Avenue, WEYBRIDGE, SURREY, KT13 9SS.

BEAUMONT, Mr. Fred, FCA *1959;* 1225A Rochdale Road, Blackley, MANCHESTER, M9 2EG.

•**BEAUMONT, Mrs. Gayle Elizabeth, FCA** *1993;* 8 Purshall Close, REDDITCH, WORCESTERSHIRE, B97 4PD.

•**BEAUMONT, Mr. Geoffrey David, FCA** *1982;* Firth Parish, 1 Airport West, Lancaster Way, Yeadon, LEEDS, LS19 7ZA.

BEAUMONT, Miss. Hannah Claire, ACA *2009;* 6 The Meadows, Halstead, SEVENOAKS, KENT, TN14 7HD.

BEAUMONT, Mrs. Helen Lesley, MA ACA *2003;* 55 Oatlands Avenue, WEYBRIDGE, KT13 9SS.

•**BEAUMONT, Mrs. Helen Vivienne, BA FCA** *1989;* Wheawill & Sudworth, P.O. Box B30, 35 Westgate, HUDDERSFIELD, HD1 1PA.

•**BEAUMONT, Mr. Ian, BA FCA** *1993;* BDO LLP, 1 Bridgewater Place, Water Lane, LEEDS, LS11 5RU. See also BDO Stoy Hayward LLP

BEAUMONT, Mr. James Edward Day, BSc ACA *2002;* 23 Elliscombe Road, Charlton, LONDON, SE7 7PF.

BEAUMONT, Mr. James Nicholas, BA(Hons) ACA *2001;* 4 Geraldine Road, LONDON, SW18 2NU.

•**BEAUMONT, Mr. John, FCA FCCA** *1974;* John Beaumont & Co, 159 Stamford Street, ASHTON-UNDER-LYNE, LANCASHIRE, OL6 6XW.

BEAUMONT, Mr. John Geoffrey, BA ACA *1988;* 5 Linden Park Road, TUNBRIDGE WELLS, TN2 5QL.

•**BEAUMONT, Mr. John Harvey, FCA** *1973;* (Tax Fac), Beaumonts, 8 Navigation Court, Calder Park, WAKEFIELD, WEST YORKSHIRE, WF2 7BJ.

BEAUMONT, Mr. Julian John Bromhead, FCA *1971;* P.O.Box 1138, DOUBLE BAY, NSW 1360, AUSTRALIA.

BEAUMONT, Mrs. Katherine Jane Victoria, LLB ACA *1986;* (Tax Fac), 2 Denstead Manor, Denstead Lane, Chartham Hatch, CANTERBURY, CT4 7NL.

BEAUMONT, Ms. Kathryn Louise, ACA *2008;* 14 White Hart Wood, SEVENOAKS, TN13 1RR.

BEAUMONT, Miss. Katie Joanna, ACA *2009;* 23 Kingswood Avenue, NEWCASTLE UPON TYNE, NE2 3NS.

•**BEAUMONT, Mrs. Kerstin Anne, BA FCA** *1998;* 12 Draytons View, Greenham, THATCHAM, BERKSHIRE, RG19 8SA.

•**BEAUMONT, Mr. Lee, BSc ACA** *2006;* 6 Drovers Way, Barnham, BOGNOR REGIS, WEST SUSSEX, PO22 0DD.

BEAUMONT, Mr. Martin Dudley, MA FCA *1977;* Handgreen House Pudding Lane, Tiverton, TARPORLEY, CHESHIRE, CW6 9SN.

BEAUMONT, Michael Day, Esq CBE FCA *1958;* Rowangarth, Kirklington Road, Eakring, NEWARK, NG22 0DA.

•**BEAUMONT, Mr. Michael Robert, FCA** *1973;* M.R. Beaumont & Co, The Birches, 28A High Street, Standlake, WITNEY, OX29 7RY.

BEAUMONT, Mr. Neil Geoffrey, LLB ACA *1983;* 4 Tamarisk Close, Claines, WORCESTER, WR3 7LE.

BEAUMONT, Mr. Peter Stuart, BSc ACA *1995;* The Cornish Mutual Assurance Co Ltd C M A House, Newham Road Newham, TRURO, CORNWALL, TR1 2SU.

BEAUMONT, Mr. Richard, BA ACA *2007;* 123 Sugden Road, LONDON, SW11 5ED.

BEAUMONT, Ms. Sarah Louise, MA BCom FCA *1980;* 10 Leicester Road, BARNET, HERTFORDSHIRE, EN5 5DA.

BEAUMONT, Ms. Stephanie Ann, BA ACA *2007;* with Ernst & Young LLP, Citygate, St James' Boulevard, NEWCASTLE UPON TYNE, NE1 4JD.

•**BEAUMONT, Mr. Steven, BA(Hons) ACA** *2004;* The Taylor Cocks Partnership Limited, Arena Business Centre, 9 Nimrod Way, WIMBORNE, DORSET, BH21 7SH. See also Taylor Cocks Medical LLP

BEAUMONT, Mr. Steven, BSc ACA *1988;* 34 Moorway, Hawkshaw, BURY, BL8 4LF.

BEAUMONT, Miss. Victoria Helen, BSc ACA *2006;* 7 Topliff Road, Chilwell Beeston, NOTTINGHAM, NG9 5AS.

BEAUMONT-KERRIDGE, Mrs. Christine Julie, MA ACIB ACA *1994;* 10 Valencia Road, STANMORE, MIDDLESEX, HA7 4JH.

BEAUPREZ, Mr. Richard Joseph, FCA *1968;* Firwood, Kent Street, Selescombe, BATTLE, TN33 0SG.

BEAUTYMAN, Mrs. Sally Anne, BA ACA *2000;* 25 Beverley Gardens, NORTH SHIELDS, TYNE AND WEAR, NE30 4NS.

BEAVAN, Mr. Christopher Chamney Purves, FCA *1969;* Via Ramazzotti 30, 20052 MONZA, ITALY.

•**BEAVAN, Mr. Christopher Philip, FCA** *1974;* Kilby Fox, 4 Pavilion Court, 600 Pavilion Drive, NORTHAMPTON, NN4 7SL.

•**BEAVAN, Mr. Dean, BSc ACA** *1984;* 35 Sea Parade, MENTONE, VIC 3194, AUSTRALIA.

BEAVAN, Miss. Gillian, BA ACA *1995;* Luxwell Ltd, 239 Deansgate, MANCHESTER, M3 4EN.

BEAVAN, Ms. Sally Helen, BSc ACA *2000;* Langdale, 108 Park Hill, BIRMINGHAM, B13 8DS.

BEAVEN, Mrs. Amanda Jane, BA ACA *1996;* Fletcher & Partners, Crown Chambers, Bridge Street, SALISBURY, SP1 2LZ.

BEAVEN, Mrs. Helen Frances, BA ACA *1999;* 10 Farmway, Feniton, HONITON, DEVON, EX14 3BX.

BEAVEN, Mr. Matthew James, BA ACA *2005;* Eschenring 4, 6300 Zug ZUG, SWITZERLAND.

•**BEAVEN, Mr. Peter Francis, FCA** *1974;* (Tax Fac), Marshall Beaven, Christchurch Business Centre, Grange Road, CHRISTCHURCH, DORSET, BH23 4JD.

BEAVEN, Mr. Stephen Andrew, ACA *2006;* Pearson Plc, 80 Strand, LONDON, WC2R 0RL.

BEAVER, Mr. Andrew John, BSc(Hons) ACA *2003;* 17 Ellesmere Road, ALTRINCHAM, CHESHIRE, WA14 1JG.

BEAVER, Miss. Jennifer Louise, ACA *2008;* First Floor Flat, 76 Upper Tollington Park, LONDON, N4 4NB.

BEAVER, Mrs. Johan Louise, LLB ACA *2007;* Coppice Cottage, Walk Mills, CHURCH STRETTON, SY6 6NJ.

BEAVER, Mr. Michael James, ACA CA(AUS) *2011;* 25 Drayton Road, LONDON, W13 0LD.

•**BEAVER, Mr. Michael John, BA FCA** *1975;* Beavers, 3 The Shrubberies, George Lane, LONDON, E18 1BD.

BEAVIS, Mrs. Caren Rachael, BSc ACA *1991;* 10 Torre Abbey, BEDFORD, MK41 0UJ.

BEAVIS, Mrs. Emily Charlotte, BA ACA *2004;* 4 Campion Way, WOKINGHAM, BERKSHIRE, RG40 5YF.

BEAVIS, Mr. John James, FCA *1953;* 38 Sandy Lodge Road, RICKMANSWORTH, WD3 1LJ. (Life Member)

BEAVIS, Prof. John Royston Seaford, FCA *1961;* Aveley Cottage, 9 Frensham Road, FARNHAM, GU9 8HD. (Life Member)

BEAVIS, Mr. Michael John, BA ACA *1992;* Northern Motors, 333 Pinner Road, HARROW, MIDDLESEX, HA1 4JR.

BEAVIS, Mr. Nigel William, BA ACA *1992;* Baxi Potterton Brooks House, Coventry Road, WARWICK, CV34 4LL.

•**BEAVIS, Mrs. Stephanie Jean, BSc ACA** *1994;* with KPMG LLP, 6 Lower Brook Street, IPSWICH, IP4 1AP.

BEAVON, Miss. Louise Elen, BA(Hons) ACA *2002;* PO Box 1313, Humpty Doo, DARWIN, NT 0836, AUSTRALIA.

BEAZER, Mr. Anthony Hadyn, BA ACA *1999;* 14a Rusholme Road, Putney, LONDON, SW15 3JZ.

BEAZER, Mr. Trevor Anthony, FCA *1973;* Manoir de Guervihan, 56300 Kergrist, PONTIVY, BRITTANY, FRANCE.

BEAZLEIGH, Mr. Brian Anthony, FCA *1964;* 17 Stickens Lane, East Malling, WEST MALLING, ME19 6BT. (Life Member)

BEAZLEY, Mr. Christopher Wills, BA ACA *1989;* Triodos Bank Brunel House, 11 The Promenade Clifton Down, BRISTOL, BS8 3NN.

BEAZLEY, Ms. Clare Louise, BSc ACA *1989;* Cherry Tree House The Hill, Little Somerford, CHIPPENHAM, WILTSHIRE, SN15 5BQ.

BEAZLEY, Mr. James Anthony John, BSc ACA *1984;* Coston Manor, Aston-on-Clun, CRAVEN ARMS, SHROPSHIRE, SY7 8EJ.

BEAZLEY, Mr. James Henry Tetley, BA ACA *1987;* 62 Telford Avenue, Streatham Hill, LONDON, SW2 4XF.

BEAZLEY, Mr. John Ivor, BA ACA *1988;* 2311 Connecticut Avenue, Apt 402, WASHINGTON, DC 20008, UNITED STATES.

•**BEAZLEY, Mr. Kim Michael George, BSc FCA** *1975;* CW Fellowes Limited, Carnac Place, Cams Hall Estate, Fareham, PORTSMOUTH, PO16 8UY.

BEBB, Mr. Haydn William, FCA *1960;* Flat 1, Longworth House, 9 Woodhayes Road, Wimbledon, LONDON, SW19 4RG. (Life Member)

BEBB, Miss. Sarah Chandra, BSc ACA *1992;* 24 Marine Drive, Ogmore-by-Sea, BRIDGEND, MID GLAMORGAN, CF32 0PJ.

BEBBINGTON, Mr. Andrew Charles, BSc ACA *1985;* 4035 Reynolds Blvd, GREEN COVE SPRINGS, FL 32043, UNITED STATES.

•**BEBBINGTON, Mr. Andrew John Price, FCA** *1976;* Bebbington & Co, 13 Rushside Road, Cheadle Hulme, CHEADLE, SK8 6NW. See also Borderbay Limited and A J P Bebbington

•**BEBBINGTON, Mr. Frank David, FCA** *1972;* Frank Bebbington Accountants Ltd, Bridge House, 9 Fowley Common Lane, Glazebury, WARRINGTON, WA3 5JJ.

BEBBINGTON, Mr. Ian, BSc ACA *1991;* 18 Stanfell Road, LEICESTER, LE2 3GA.

BEBBINGTON, Mrs. Pauline Margaret, BSc FCA CTA *1986;* (Tax Fac), with Grant Thornton UK LLP, Grant Thornton House, Kettering Parkway, Kettering Venture Park, KETTERING, NORTHAMPTONSHIRE NN15 6XR.

•**BEBBINGTON, Mr. Roger, BSc FCA** *1973;* Ropas Limited, PO Box 63531, NAIROBI, 00619, KENYA.

•**BEBER, Mr. Paul Aaron Cohen, BA FCA** *1978;* Fisher Corporate plc, Acre House, 11/15 William Road, LONDON, NW1 3ER. See also H.W. Fisher & Company and H W Fisher & Company Limited

•**BECHER, Mr. Jonathan Michael Richard, FCA** *1974;* Matrix Corporate Capital LLP, 1 Vine Street, LONDON, W1J 0AH.

BECHMAN, Mr. Theodor Robert, BA ACA *1984;* 14 Conway Road, West Wimbledon, LONDON, SW20 8PA.

BECK, Mr. Alan Karl, ACA *2009;* Ernst & Young Llp, 1 More London Place, LONDON, SE1 2AF.

BECK, Mrs. Andrea Patricia, ACA *1982;* 4 Old Hall Gardens, CHESTER, CHESHIRE, CH2 3AB.

BECK, Mr. Andrew Charles, BA ACA *2006;* 27 Finchley Avenue, CHELMSFORD, CM2 9BX.

BECK, Mrs. Anna, MSc ACA *2001;* 23 Crawford Compton Close, HORNCHURCH, ESSEX, RM12 6UA.

BECK, Mrs. Anna Clare, BSc ACA *2004;* 2 Liddiards Way, Purbrook, WATERLOOVILLE, PO7 5QW.

BECK, Mr. Brian Trevor, FCA *1959;* 76 High Street, Ecton, NORTHAMPTON, NN6 0QB. (Life Member)

BECK, Mrs. Bryony, BEng ACA *2000;* 7-9 Lottage Road, Aldbourne, MARLBOROUGH, WILTSHIRE, SN8 2DL.

BECK, Mr. Charles William Henry, FCA *1976;* 4 Old Hall Gardens, Flookersbrook, CHESTER, CH2 3AB.

BECK, Mr. Dudley Stephen, FCA *1970;* Old Acres Farm, Stour Provost, GILLINGHAM, DORSET, SP8 5LT. (Life Member)

BECK, Mrs. Gemma Louise, ACA *2009;* Ernst & Young Llp The Paragon, Counterslip, BRISTOL, BS1 6BX.

BECK, Miss. Jacquelyn Susan, BA ACA *1991;* Digby Morgan Consulting Ltd Roxburghe House, 273-287 Regent Street, LONDON, W1B 2HA.

BECK, Mr. John Maurice, BA ACA *1988;* Coniston, 89 Ack Lane East, Bramhall, STOCKPORT, SK7 2BH.

BECK, Mr. John Michael, MA FCA *1975;* 4 St. Marys Avenue, HARROGATE, HG2 0LP. (Life Member)

BECK, Mr. Jonathan David, BSc FCA *1977;* Flat 4 Rowbottom House, New Mill Stile, LIVERPOOL, L25 6JY.

BECK, Mr. Martin Christopher, FCA *1971;* Summerfields, Ironchurch Lane, Blackham, TUNBRIDGE WELLS, KENT, TN3 9TS.

•**BECK, Mr. Martin William, FCA** *1975;* Martin Beck, 7 Hurnard Drive, COLCHESTER, CO3 3SH.

BECK, Mr. Michael Leslie, BA ACA *1986;* Ladbrokes Ltd Imperial House, Imperial Drive, HARROW, MIDDLESEX, HA2 7JW.

BECK, Mr. Michael Walter Cornford, FCA *1956;* Tern Cottage, 14 Sea Drive, Felpham, BOGNOR REGIS, WEST SUSSEX, PO22 7NE. (Life Member)

BECK, Mr. Michael William, BSc ACA *2000;* 23 Crawford Compton Close, HORNCHURCH, ESSEX, RM12 6UA.

•**BECK, Mr. Neil Spencer, BA ACA** *1992;* (Tax Fac), Wellers, Stuart House, 55 Catherine Place, LONDON, SW1E 6DY. See also Wellers Contractors Limited

•**BECK, Mr. Nigel Robin, FCA** *1966;* (Tax Fac), Nigel Beck Taxation Consultant, Ashfield, Rookery Lane, Broughton, STOCKBRIDGE, HAMPSHIRE SO20 8AZ.

•**BECK, Mr. Philip Alexander, MA ACA MABRP** *1992;* Philip Beck Limited, 41 Kingston Street, CAMBRIDGE, CB1 2NU.

BECK, Miss. Rachael Claire, BSc ACA *1995;* 16 The Crescent, Robswall, Malahide, DUBLIN 15, COUNTY DUBLIN, IRELAND.

BECK, Mr. Stephen James, LLB FCA *1999;* 16 Glendon Way, Dorridge, SOLIHULL, B93 8SY.

BECK, Mr. Stephen Michael, BSc ACA *2001;* Andelain, Brookfield Lane, BUCKINGHAM, MK18 1AU.

•**BECK, Mr. Stephen Michael, FCA** *1979;* Cladd Beck Limited, 56a London Road, Apsley, HEMEL HEMPSTEAD, HERTFORDSHIRE, HP3 9SB. See also Cladd Beck

BECK, Mr. Timothy Kenneth, BA(Hons) ACA *2002;* Mill Haven, Chestnut Avenue, GUILDFORD, GU2 4HF.

BECKAYA, Mr. Alok, BSc(Hons) ACA *2009;* 68 Commonfield Road, BANSTEAD, SURREY, SM7 2JZ.

BECKENSALL, Mr. Michael John, BSc FCA *1977;* 1 Birkdale Drive, Kidsgrove, STOKE-ON-TRENT, ST7 4SL.

BECKER, Miss. Cassandra, BSc(Hons) ACA *2004;* Thomson Reuters Ltd Aldgate House, 33 Aldgate High Street, LONDON, EC3N 1DL.

•**BECKER, Mr. David Daniel, BA ACA** *2000;* with Deloitte LLP, PO Box 137, Regency Court, Glategny Esplanade, St Peter Port, GUERNSEY GY1 3HW.

BECKER, Mr. David Stanley Frederick, FCA *1957;* Room 28, Farnham Common House, Beaconsfield Road, Farnham Common, SLOUGH, SL2 3HU. (Life Member)

BECKER, Mrs. Lisa Sara, BA ACA *1988;* 101 College Street, Suite 350, TORONTO M5G 1L7, ON, CANADA.

BECKER, Mrs. Louise Mary, BSc ACA *1988;* Straussweg 12, 71640 LUDWIGSBURG, GERMANY.

BECKER, Mrs. Louise Rachael Elizabeth, BSc ACA *2003;* La Tournel, Retot Lane, Castel, GUERNSEY, GY5 7EG.

•**BECKER, Mr. Roy Anthony, BA FCA** *1969;* Crawfords Accountants LLP, Stanton House, 41 Blackfriars Road, SALFORD, M3 7DB.

BECKER, Mr. Walter, LLB FCA *1960;* Gerhard-Domagk Str 7, 67071 LUDWIGSHAFEN, GERMANY. (Life Member)

BECKET, Ms. Lydia Katherine, MA BSocSc ACA *2002;* 132 Topstreet Way, HARPENDEN, HERTFORDSHIRE, AL5 5TS.

BECKETT, Mrs. Andrea Clare, FCA *1982;* The Stables, Upper Ferry Lane, Callow End, WORCESTER, WR2 4TL.

BECKETT, Mr. Andrew, MSc BA ACA *1990;* Maxey Moverly Ltd, 4 Broad Ground Road, REDDITCH, WORCESTERSHIRE, B98 8YP.

•**BECKETT, Mr. Andrew Richard Harley, BA FCA** *1987;* Becketts, Unit 1 Waterside, Old Boston Road, WETHERBY, WEST YORKSHIRE, LS22 5NB.

BECKETT, Mr. Brian Philip, FCA *1974;* 39 Grove End Road, FARNHAM, GU9 8RB.

BECKETT, Mrs. Claire Louise, ACA *2009;* 61 Ashdene Close, Willerby, HULL, HU10 6LW.

BECKETT, Dr. Clare Alison, BSc ACA *1997;* 14 sherwood ave, RUISLIP, HA4 7XL.

BECKETT, Mr. David, BA(Hons) ACA *2002;* 290B Sheung Sze Wan, CLEARWATER BAY, NEW TERRITORIES, HONG KONG SAR.

•**BECKETT, Mr. David Edward, BSc ACA** *1980;* Becketts, Suite 8, 12 Devon Place, NEWPORT, GWENT, NP20 4NN.

BECKETT, Mrs. Dawn Lesley, BSc ACA *1991;* 1 Gilbertsoun Loan, EDINBURGH, EH15 2RQ.

BECKETT, Mr. Gary Derek, BA ACA *1996;* 19 Hall Drive, Mottram, HYDE, CHESHIRE, SK14 6LH.

BECKETT, Mr. Graham Charles, FCA *1971;* with ICAEW, Metropolitan House, 321 Avebury Boulevard, MILTON KEYNES, MK9 2FZ.

BECKETT, Mrs. Juliette Elizabeth, BA ACA *1991;* 43 Edgeley Road, Countesthorpe, LEICESTER, LE8 5QN.

BECKETT, Mrs. Kate, BSc ACA *2007;* with Deloitte LLP, 1 City Square, LEEDS, WEST YORKSHIRE, LS1 2AL.

BECKETT, Mr. Martin Richard, BA ACA *2005;* 17 Carr Manor Mount, LEEDS, LS17 5DG.

•**BECKETT, Mr. Michael Alexander, BA FCA** *2000;* Forrester Boyd, 26 South Saint Mary's Gate, GRIMSBY, NORTH LINCOLNSHIRE, DN31 1LW.

BECKETT, The Revd. Michael Shaun, ACA *1979;* St Pauls Vicarage, 15 St Paul's Road, CAMBRIDGE, CB1 2EZ.
BECKETT, Mr. Nathan Jon, BSc(Hons) ACA *2006;* 74 Victoria Road, Bradmore, WOLVERHAMPTON, WV3 7EU.
BECKETT, Mr. Paul George, BSc ACA *1992;* Briar Dene, 22 The Rise, CARDIFF, CF14 0RD.
•BECKETT, Mr. Paul Gregory, FCA *1979;* Baker Tilly Tax & Advisory Services LLP, 3rd Floor Preece House, Davigdor Road, HOVE, EAST SUSSEX, BN3 1RE.
BECKETT, Mr. Richard Alexander, BSc FCA *1980;* with MacIntyre Hudson LLP, Boundary House, 4 County Place, CHELMSFORD, CM2 0RE.
•BECKETT, Mr. Simon William, BA FCA *1989;* 37 Le Strange Close, NORWICH, NR2 3PW.
BECKETT, Mr. Stephen John, BA FCA CTA *1993;* Headmoor Farmhouse, Headmoor Lane, Four Marks, ALTON, GU34 3ES.
BECKETT, Mr. Steven John, FCA *1969;* 830 Sailaway Ln, APT 102, NAPLES, FL 34108-0700, UNITED STATES.
BECKETT, Mr. Trevor Russell, BA ACA *1987;* 70 Bridge Road, GLEBE, NSW 2037, AUSTRALIA.
BECKFORD, Mr. Christopher James, BA ACA *1997;* 5 Highmoor Cross, HENLEY-ON-THAMES, RG9 5DP.
BECKHAM, Mr. Leo Tristram, BA ACA *2007;* Keefe Bruyette & Woods Ltd, 1 Broadgate, LONDON, EC2M 2QS.
•BECKHURST, Mr. Neville Clive, FCA *1978;* Plummer Parsons, 18 Hyde Gardens, EASTBOURNE, BN21 4PT. See also Plummer Parsons Accountants Ltd
•①BECKINGHAM, Mr. Andrew Howard, MA FCA *1989;* BDO LLP, 55 Baker Street, LONDON, W1U 7EU. See also BDO Stoy Hayward LLP
•BECKINSALE, Mr. Anthony William, FCA *1972;* A W. Beckinsale & Co, 1 St. Peters Road, BRAINTREE, CM7 9AN.
BECKLEY, Mr. Andrew, ACA *2007;* 72 Cottingham Drive Pontprennau, CARDIFF, SOUTH GLAMORGAN, CF23 8QG.
BECKLEY, Mr. Bruce Maurice, ACA *2003;* GPO Box 3015, SYDNEY, NSW 2001, AUSTRALIA.
BECKLEY, Mr. Daniel, BSc ACA *2001;* 467 Footscray Road, LONDON, SE9 3UH.
BECKLEY, Mr. John Arthur, FCA *1960;* 22 Sheridan Road, Oxhey, WATFORD, WD19 4QL. (Life Member)
BECKLEY, Mr. John Howard, FCA *1952;* 2 Brookside Way, Blakedown, KIDDERMINSTER, DY10 3NE. (Life Member)
•BECKLEY, Mr. Matthew Nicholas, BA ACA *1992;* DTE Business Advisory Services Limited, 1 North Parade, MANCHESTER, M3 2NH. See also DTE Risk and Financial Management Ltd
BECKLEY, Mr. Percy, FCA *1975;* 15 Stoneacre Gardens, Appleton, WARRINGTON, WA4 5ET.
BECKLEY, Mr. Robert John, BA FCA *1983;* Priors Court School Priors Court, Hermitage, THATCHAM, RG18 9NU.
•BECKMAN, Mr. David John, BA ACA *1990;* David Beckman & Co Ltd, 62 The Street, ASHTEAD, SURREY, KT21 1AT. See also David Beckman & Co
•BECKMAN, Mr. John Neville, FCA *1951;* J.Neville Beckman & Co, 7 Osidge Lane, LONDON, N14 5JD.
•BECKMAN, Mrs. Lindsay, BSc FCA *1983;* (Tax Fac), Lindsay Beckman & Co Limited, 8 Bloxham Road, BROADWAY, WR12 7EU.
BECKMAN, Mr. Peter David Joseph, FCA *1981;* (Tax Fac), 45 West Heath Drive, LONDON, NW11 7QG.
BECKRAM, Mr. Mark Anthony, ACA *1995;* 34 Holmefield Close, Brayton, SELBY, NORTH YORKSHIRE, YO8 9LR.
•BECKSMITH, Mr. Derrick Paul, FCA *1984;* Paul Becksmith FCA, 14 Oldfield Wood, WOKING, GU22 8AN.
BECKSMITH, Mrs. Jennifer Anne, BSc ACA *2005;* Al Claims Solutions Plc Viscount Court, Sir Frank Whittle Way, BLACKPOOL, FY4 2FB.
BECKWITH, Mr. David, BSc ACA *1995;* 15 Old College Road, NEWBURY, BERKSHIRE, RG14 1TB.
•BECKWITH, Mr. David Martin, FCA *1975;* (Tax Fac), BBK Partnership, 1 Beauchamp Court, Victors Way, BARNET, HERTFORDSHIRE, EN5 5TZ.
BECKWITH, Sir John Lionel, CBE FCA *1970;* Pacific Investments Plc, 124 Sloane Street, LONDON, SW1X 9BW.
BECKWITH, Miss. Linda Mary, BSc ACA *2001;* Cobwebs Keeling Hall Road Foulsham, DEREHAM, NORFOLK, NR20 5PR.
BECKWITH, Mr. Piers, BSc ACA *2006;* 50 Onslow Gardens, LONDON, SW7 3QA.
BECTOR, Mr. Rakesh, BSc ACA *1993;* 40 Dudding Road, Goldthorn Park, WOLVERHAMPTON, WV4 5DN.
BEDDALL, Mr. James Henry Maitland, BSc ACA *2006;* 10 South Worple Way, LONDON, SW14 8ST.
BEDDARD, Mr. Darren James, MA ACA *2001;* 46 Falconers Green, Burbage, HINCKLEY, LEICESTERSHIRE, LE10 2SX.
•BEDDARD, Mr. Peter Alan, FCA *1979;* Arundales, Stowe House, 1688 High Street, Knowle, SOLIHULL, B93 0LY.
BEDDOE, Mr. Robert Gerard, BA FCA *1978;* 3 Herringshaw Croft, SUTTON COLDFIELD, WEST MIDLANDS, B76 1HT.
BEDDOE, Mr. Russell Steven, FCA *1970;* Shakespeare Birthplace Trust Shakespeare Centre, Henley Street, STRATFORD-UPON-AVON, WARWICKSHIRE, CV37 6QW.
BEDDOES, Miss. Christina, BA ACA *1990;* (Tax Fac), 33 St Mellion Drive, Biddenham, BEDFORD, MK40 4BF.
BEDDOW, Mr. Barnabas Towne, BSc ACA *1980;* Cheverell Mill, The Green, Great Cheverell, DEVIZES, SN10 5UP.
BEDDOW, Mr. James Edward, ACA *2008;* 27 Vernon Road, LEIGH-ON-SEA, ESSEX, SS9 2RD.
BEDDOW, Mr. Peter Raymond, BA ACA *1993;* 54 Lakeridge Drive, SCARBOROUGH M1C 5E3, ON, CANADA.
BEDDOWS, Mr. Peter Richard, BCom ACA *1983;* Austcliffe House Farm, Cookley, KIDDERMINSTER, DY10 3UR.
BEDDOWS, Mr. Roy John, BA ACA *1983;* Investec Bank (UK) Ltd, 2 Gresham Street, LONDON, EC2V 7QP.
BEDE, Mr. Jarvis John, FCA *1957;* Box 6056, Station D, CALGARY T2P 2C7, AB, CANADA.
BEDENHAM, Mr. Martin James, FCA *1965;* 24 Wrenwood Way, PINNER, HA5 2HS.
BEDER, Mr. Andrew Justin, FCA ACII ACILA *1984;* 23 Bishops Road, Prestwich, MANCHESTER, M25 0HT.
BEDEWELL, Mr. Simon Philip, BEng ACA *2001;* Flat 4, 200-201 Grange Road, LONDON, SE1 3AA.
BEDFORD, Mrs. Alison Jane Christina, BA ACA *1990;* 3 Rattray Loan, EDINBURGH, EH10 5TQ.
BEDFORD, Miss. Anne Margaret, BSc ACA *1996;* 9 Randolph Close, Barnehurst, BEXLEYHEATH, DA7 6HY.
BEDFORD, Mr. Anthony Charles, FCA *1967;* 11410 SW 112 Terrace, MIAMI, FL 33176, UNITED STATES.
BEDFORD, Mr. Anthony Douglas, FCA *1972;* 1 Greenway, Honley, HOLMFIRTH, HD9 6NQ.
•BEDFORD, Mr. Anthony Lawrence, FCA *1966;* 103 Spencefield Lane, LEICESTER, LE5 6HH.
•BEDFORD, Mrs. Barbara Jane, BA FCA *1982;* BJB Tax, The Hayloft, Grange Farm, Gartree Road, STOUGHTON, LEICESTERSHIRE LE2 2FB.
•BEDFORD, Mrs. Caroline Joan, BA(Hons) ACA CFE *1998;* with RGL LLP, 8th Floor, Dashwood, 69 Old Broad Street, LONDON, EC2M 1QS.
BEDFORD, Mr. Christopher, ACA *2008;* 107 Griffiths Drive, WOLVERHAMPTON, WV11 2JW.
BEDFORD, Mr. David Michael, BSc ACA *1994;* Damson Cottage, Hadley End, Yoxall, BURTON-ON-TRENT, DE13 8PF.
BEDFORD, Mr. Edward Michael Octavius, BSc ACA *2004;* 20 Gracechurch Street, LONDON, EC3V 0BG.
BEDFORD, Miss. Elizabeth Jane, BA ACA *2006;* 34 Forge Place, LONDON, NW1 8DQ.
•BEDFORD, Mr. Howard Martin, BA FCA *1989;* (Tax Fac), Howard M Bedford & Co, 1st Floor, 27 Norton Road, STOCKTON-ON-TEES, CLEVELAND, TS18 2BW.
BEDFORD, Miss. Janet Elizabeth, BSc ACA *1997;* 5 Avondale Villas, Thorner, LEEDS, LS14 3DQ.
BEDFORD, Mr. Michael John, BSc ACA *1987;* Anglia Meat Products Ltd, 1-2 Threxton Road Industrial Estate Watton, THETFORD, NORFOLK, IP25 6NG.
BEDFORD, Mr. Nicholas Stuart James, BSc ACA *2003;* 777 Sixth Avenue, 31c, NEW YORK, NY 10001, UNITED STATES.
BEDFORD, Mr. Nicolas Norman, BA ACA *1986;* Flat 1 Victoria Gardens, 15 Marston Ferry Road, OXFORD, OX2 7EF.
BEDFORD, Mr. Nigel Jonathan, BSc ACA *1988;* Strathcona, Icknield Lane, WANTAGE, OXFORDSHIRE, OX12 8EF.
BEDFORD, The Revd. Paul Michael, BSc FCA *1976;* 17 Burnham Wood, FAREHAM, PO16 7UD.
•BEDFORD, Mr. Paul Nicholas, ACA *1982;* Paul Bedford, 36 Princes Road, TEDDINGTON, MIDDLESEX, TW11 0RW.
•BEDFORD, Mr. Philip Henry, FCA *1981;* Lentells Limited, Ash House, Cook Way, Bindon Road, TAUNTON, SOMERSET TA2 6BJ.
BEDFORD, Mrs. Rhiannon Bridget, BA ACA *1999;* Somerville, 2 Somerset Road, SANDYS MA02, BERMUDA.
BEDFORD, Mr. Richard Bruce, FCA *1992;* 5 Bluebell Close, HERTFORD, SG13 7UP.
BEDFORD, Mr. Richard William, BA ACA *1992;* 3 Rattray Loan, EDINBURGH, EH10 5TQ.
•BEDFORD, Mr. Robert James, BSc FCA *1994;* Miller Davies, Unit A3, Broomsleigh Business Park, Worsley Bridge Road, LONDON, SE26 5BN.
BEDFORD, Mr. Robin James, BA ACA *1998;* Somerville, 2 Mangrove Bay Road, SANDYS MA01, SOMERSET, BERMUDA.
•BEDFORD, Mrs. Sharon Lesley, MA FCA CTA *1988;* James Cowper LLP, Willow Court, 7 West Way, Botley, OXFORD, OX2 0JB. See also JC Payroll Services Ltd
BEDFORD, Mr. Simon Jeffrey, BSc ACA *2001;* 21 South Road, West Bridgford, NOTTINGHAM, NG2 7AG.
BEDFORD, Mr. Simon Nicholas, BSc ACA *1986;* Dixons Stores Group Plc Maylands Avenue, Hemel Hempstead Industrial Estate, HEMEL HEMPSTEAD, HERTFORDSHIRE, HP2 7TG.
BEDFORD, Mr. Stephen Valentine, BSc ACA *1992;* 3 Spring Gardens, NEWBURY, BERKSHIRE, RG20 0PR.
BEDFORD, Mr. Thomas Anthony Joshua, FCA *1961;* 8 Adel Pasture, Adel, LEEDS, LS16 8HU. (Life Member)
BEDFORD, Dr. Wendy Margaret, PhD BSc FCA *1977;* Blaen-y-Cwm, Abergorlech Road, CARMARTHEN, CARMARTHENSHIRE, SA32 7LA.
BEDFORD SMITH, Mr. Philip Theodore, BA FCA *1973;* 77 Troy Court, Kensington High Street, LONDON, W8 7RB.
•BEDI, Mr. Davinder Pal Singh, BSc ACA *1979;* Clearly Read Limited, 18 Neofytou Nicolaidi Avenue, 8011 PAPHOS, CYPRUS.
BEDI, Mrs. Harpreet Sonia, BA ACA *2001;* 47 The Stream, Ditton, AYLESFORD, ME20 6AG.
BEDINGFIELD, Mr. Alastair, MS BSc ACA *2003;* 7 St Davids Close, BECCLES, SUFFOLK, NR34 9PX.
•BEDINGFIELD, Mr. Geoffrey James, FCA *1983;* (Tax Fac), Baker Tilly Tax & Advisory Services LLP, 1st Floor, 46 Clarendon Road, WATFORD, WD17 1JJ. See also Baker Tilly UK Audit LLP
•BEDLOW, Mr. Mark Richard, BA ACA *1989;* with PricewaterhouseCoopers, Abacus House, Castle Park, CAMBRIDGE, CB3 0AN.
BEDNALL, Mr. Jonathan Albert, BA ACA *1996;* 6 Cherrington Way, SOLIHULL, WEST MIDLANDS, B91 3TH.
BEDNALL, Mrs. Justine, BSc ACA *1997;* 6 Cherrington Way, SOLIHULL, B91 3TH.
BEDNALL, Mr. Wallace James, FCA *1965;* 1 Walker Close, LONDON, N11 1AQ. (Life Member)
•①BEDNASH, Mr. Lane Gary, BA(Hons) ACA *1990;* with Valentine & Co, 4 Dancastle Court, 14 Arcadia Avenue, LONDON, N3 2HS.
BEDOUET, Mrs. Anne-Laure, ACA *2002;* 18 Anley Road, LONDON, W14 0BY.
BEDSER, Mrs. Barbara Elizabeth, BSc FCA *1982;* 4 Beechwood Close, Long Ditton, SURBITON, SURREY, KT6 6PF.
BEDWELL, Mr. Bryan Frederick Edward, FCA *1957;* 31 Sandy Lane, Cheam, SUTTON, SM2 7PQ. (Life Member)
BEDWIN, Mr. Charles Mark, FCA *1969;* 3 Elms Lea Avenue, BRIGHTON, BN1 6UG.
BEDWIN, Mr. Stuart Alexander, BA ACA *2005;* 2 Russell Road, BUCKHURST HILL, ESSEX, IG9 5QJ.
BEDWORTH, Mrs. Lisa Joanne, BSc FCA *1991;* Long Acre, Boughton Hall Avenue, Send, WOKING, SURREY, GU23 7DF.
BEDWORTH, Mr. Paul William, BA FCA *1991;* Jubilee House, Waitrose Ltd, Doncastle Road, BRACKNELL, BERKSHIRE, RG12 8YA.
BEDWORTH, Mr. William Douglas, FCA *1964;* Sheeling House, Bickington Road, Bickington, BARNSTAPLE, EX31 2LR. (Life Member)
BEE, Mrs. Caroline Joan, ACA *2000;* 10 Halfway Close, TROWBRIDGE, WILTSHIRE, BA14 7HQ.
BEE, Mr. Christopher Raynor, FCA *1969;* 96 Otter Crescent, TORONTO M5N 2W8, ON, CANADA.
BEE, Mr. Eric Raymond, FCA *1959;* 9a Fen Road, Heighington, LINCOLN, LN4 1JL. (Life Member)
BEE, Mr. Henry Peter, MA FCA *1964;* 64 Lawsons Road, THORNTON-CLEVELEYS, FY5 4DD.
BEE, Mr. John Derek, MA FCA *1965;* Westfield, Bennet Head, Watermillock, PENRITH, CA11 0LT. (Life Member)
BEE, Mr. Paul William, BA ACA *1989;* 54 Etherington Street, GAINSBOROUGH, DN21 2EW.
BEE, Mr. Richard James, LLB FCA *1993;* Diageo, 5 Lochside Way, EDINBURGH, EH12 9DT.
BEE, Mr. Steven Graham, BSc ACA *1993;* 15 Cromwell Court, Cromwell Road, HOVE, EAST SUSSEX, BN3 3EF.
BEEBEEJAUN, Mr. Asif, ACA FCCA *2000;* Seneck Road, PLAINE DES ROCHES, RIVIERE DU REMPART, MAURITIUS.
BEEBY, Mrs. Amy Victoria, BA ACA *2004;* with Deloitte LLP, 2 New Street Square, LONDON, EC4A 3BZ.
BEEBY, Mr. David Albert, BSc FCA *1977;* Finance Department, Glasgow Caledonian University City Campus, 70 Cowcaddens Road, GLASGOW, G4 0BA.
BEEBY, Mr. David George, FCA *1975;* The Ghyll, COCKERMOUTH, CA13 0NJ.
BEEBY, Mr. John Edward, FCA *1961;* 23A Abington Park Crescent, NORTHAMPTON, NN3 3AD.
BEEBY, Mr. Jonathan Derek, BSc FCA CTA *1999;* (Tax Fac), 44 Geers Wood, HEATHFIELD, TN21 0AR.
BEECH, Mr. Alan Derek, ACA *1986;* Camellia Plc, Linton Park, Linton, MAIDSTONE, ME17 4AB.
BEECH, Mr. Henry Nicholas, ACA *2009;* 23 Empire Square East, Empire Square, LONDON, SE1 4NB.
•BEECH, Mr. Ian, FCA *1982;* Accountancy 4 Growth Ltd, 33 Wolverhampton Road, CANNOCK, WS11 1AP.
BEECH, Mr. Michael, ACA *2008;* Skipton Building Society, The Bailey, SKIPTON, NORTH YORKSHIRE, BD23 1DN.
BEECH, Miss. Orla, LLB ACA *2011;* 28a Springfield Road, BRIGHTON, BN1 6DA.
BEECH, Mrs. Patricia, BSc ACA *1984;* BOX 145, MASTERTON 5840, NEW ZEALAND.
•BEECH, Mr. Sean James, BA ACA *1990;* 18 Gladstone Road, CHESTER, CH1 4BY. See also Deloitte & Touche LLP
BEECH, Mr. Sydney John, BA FCA *1972;* (Tax Fac), 8 Woodland Avenue, NANTWICH, CW5 6JE.
BEECH, Mr. Timothy Paul, BA FCA *1980;* 31 East Avenue, Talbot Woods, BOURNEMOUTH, BH3 7BS.
BEECH, Mr. Walter, FCA *1967;* 14 Mackinnon Avenue, Kiveton Park, SHEFFIELD, S26 6QB.
BEECHAM, Mr. Colin Robert, BA FCA MCT *1984;* Danesfort, Killiney Hill Road, Killiney, DUBLIN, COUNTY DUBLIN, IRELAND.
BEECHAM, Mr. Eric Mark, FCA *1949;* Flat A, 52 Maresfield Gardens, LONDON, NW3 5RX. (Life Member)
BEECHAM, Mr. Julian Mark, FCA *1976;* Howard Tenens Associates Ltd, Kingfisher Business Park, London Road, STROUD, GLOUCESTERSHIRE, GL5 2BY.
BEECHAM, Mr. Martin, BA FCA *1973;* Larchmount, Chew Magna, BRISTOL, BS40 8RU.
BEECHAM, Mr. Miles, BSc(Hons) ACA *2000;* 19 Harness Lane, Boroughbridge, YORK, YO51 9PF.
•BEECHER, Mr. Alistair Arthur, BSc FCA *1987;* Ernst & Young LLP, 1 More London Place, LONDON, SE1 2AF. See also Ernst & Young Europe LLP
BEECHER, Mr. David Rowland, BA FCA *1967;* Box 398, UNLEY, SA 5061, AUSTRALIA.
•BEECHER, Mr. James Russell, BA ACA *2000;* Midgley Snelling, Ibex House, Baker Street, WEYBRIDGE, SURREY, KT13 8AH.
BEECHER, Miss. Tracy Ann, BSc ACA *1989;* Holly Tree Farm Ham Lane, Oldbury-on-Severn, BRISTOL, BS35 1PZ.
BEECHES, Mr. Trevor Andrew, BA ACA *1984;* 15f/Block C, Olympian Mansion, 9 Conduit Road, MID LEVELS, HONG KONG ISLAND, HONG KONG SAR.
BEECHEY, Mr. David Richard, FCA *1968;* Touchwood House, Royston Road, Wendens Ambo, SAFFRON WALDEN, ESSEX, CB11 4JX.
•BEECHING, Mr. Barrie Francis, FCA *1975;* Holly House, Hoath, CANTERBURY, KENT, CT3 4JT.
BEECHING, Mr. Guy Anthony, FCA *1967;* 5 The Oaks, Woodside Avenue, LONDON, N12 8AR.
BEECHINOR, Mr. Paul Michael, BSc ACA *1992;* 14 Heather Close, Lynham Chase, Hopwood, HEYWOOD, OL10 2PE.
BEECRAFT, Mr. Brian Gordon, FCA *1973;* Brook Cottage, The Millham, West Hendred, WANTAGE, OXFORDSHIRE, OX12 8RN.
BEECROFT, Mrs. Amy, BSc *2004;* 19 Newton Road, Lindfield, HAYWARDS HEATH, WEST SUSSEX, RH16 2NB.
BEECROFT, Mr. David, MMath ACA *2002;* 19 Newton Road Lindfield, HAYWARDS HEATH, WEST SUSSEX, RH16 2NB.
BEECROFT, Mr. Kenner Stanley, FCA *1952;* 24 Islington Park St, LONDON, N1 1PX. (Life Member)
BEECROFT, Mr. Martin, ACA *2005;* 9 Oldfield Court, LEEDS, LS7 4SZ.

Members - Alphabetical BEECROFT - BEH

•**BEECROFT, Mr. Robert Dearnley, FCA** *1975;* Beecroft & Associates, The Laurels, Wickham Heath, NEWBURY, BERKSHIRE, RG20 8PG.
BEECROFT, Mr. Thomas Michael, FCA *1973;* (Tax Fac), 20 Castle Rise, Ridgewood, UCKFIELD, TN22 5UN.
BEECROFT, Mr. William Andrew, BA(Hons) ACA *2000;* Flat 2, 27 Belsize Park, LONDON, NW3 4DU.
BEED, Mr. Christopher Martin Vermulen, BSc ACA *1993;* 4 Teasel Close, ROYSTON, HERTFORDSHIRE, SG8 9NG.
BEEDASSY, Mr. Visharad Pranav, ACA CA(AUS) *2009;* 11B Sleight Street, ST JAMES, WA 6102, AUSTRALIA.
BEEDEN, Mr. Alistair John, BA ACA *1992;* 86 Ruffs Furze, Oakley, BEDFORD, MK43 7RT.
•**BEEDHAM, Mr. Peter John Geoffrey, BA FCA** *1979;* (Tax Fac), P J Beedham Limited, Graffix House, Newtown Road, HENLEY-ON-THAMES, OXFORDSHIRE, RG9 1HG.
BEEDIE, Miss. Lucy, BA(Hons) ACA *2010;* #8 Inwood Close, PAGET PG 05, BERMUDA.
BEEDLE, Mr. Andrew Craig, BSc ACA *1997;* 5 Anning Fold, Garforth, LEEDS, LS25 2PQ.
BEEDLE, Mrs. Elaine Margaret, BSc ACA *1993;* The Cottage, Gants Mill, Gants Mill Road, BRUTON, SOMERSET, BA10 0DB.
BEEDLE, Mr. Gregory Merrick, BA FCA *1992;* The Cottage Gants Mill, Gants Mill Road, BRUTON, SOMERSET, BA10 0DB.
BEEDLE, Mr. Simon Scott, BA ACA *1992;* Pantheon Ventures Ltd, Norfolk House, 31 St. James's Square, LONDON, SW1Y 4JR.
BEEFORTH, Mrs. Deborah, BSocSc FCA *1997;* Broadland Properties Ltd, 137 Scalby Road, SCARBOROUGH, NORTH YORKSHIRE, YO12 6TB.
•**BEEFORTH, Mr. Michael Allan, BA FCA** *1983;* (Tax Fac), S V Bye, New Garth House, Upper Garth Gardens, GUISBOROUGH, TS14 6HA.
•**BEEGUN, Mr. Ravi Kumar, BEng FCA** *1995;* KPMG Audit, 9 Allee Scheffer, 2520 LUXEMBOURG, LUXEMBOURG. See also KPMG Europe LLP
•**BEEHARRY, Mr. Tej, MA(Hons) ACA** *2006;* Raffingers Stuart, 19/20 Bourne Court, Southend Road, WOODFORD GREEN, ESSEX, IG8 8HD.
BEEKARRY, Mrs. Nundeeta, ACA *2010;* 8 Jevington Way, LONDON, SE12 9NE.
BEEKARRY, Mr. Satyajeet, BSc ACA *2007;* with PricewaterhouseCoopers, Strathvale House, PO Box 258, GEORGE TOWN, GRAND CAYMAN, KY1-1104 CAYMAN ISLANDS.
•**BEELAM, Mrs. Sheila Margaret, BSc ACA** *2005;* Beelams Accountancy Limited, 93 Burlescoombe Road, Thorpe Bay, SOUTHEND-ON-SEA, SS1 3PT. See also Beelams
BEELEY, Mr. Anthony Christopher, BSc FCA *1990;* The Barn Green Lane, Darley, HARROGATE, NORTH YORKSHIRE, HG3 2QG.
•**BEELEY, Mr. Graham Michael, MSc ACA** *2002;* Beeley Hawley & Co Ltd, 44 Nottingham Road, MANSFIELD, NOTTINGHAMSHIRE, NG18 1BL.
•**BEELEY, Mr. Philip Michael, FCA** *1965;* (Tax Fac), Beeley Hawley & Co Ltd, 44 Nottingham Road, MANSFIELD, NOTTINGHAMSHIRE, NG18 1BL.
BEELS, Mr. Mark Daniel, BSc ACA *2003;* Canadian Imperial Bank of Commerce, Cottons Lane, LONDON, SE1 2QL.
BEEMAN, Miss. Philippa Jane, BSc ACA *2007;* 39 Woodlands Road, ALTRINCHAM, CHESHIRE, WA15 8EZ.
BEENEY, Mr. Robert George, BSc ACA *1999;* 201a Camberwell Grove, LONDON, SE5 8JU.
BEENHAM, Mr. Christopher Gordon, FCA *1965;* Quylters, Nethergate Street, Clare, SUDBURY, SUFFOLK, CO10 8NP.
BEENSTOCK, Mr. Mark, ACA *1980;* 5 Wildwood Road, LONDON, NW11 6UL.
BEENSTOCK, Mr. Richard, BCom ACA *2005;* 7 Holly Park, LONDON, N3 3JA.
BEENSTOCK, Mr. Robert Hyman, MSc ACA *2005;* with Grant Thornton UK LLP, 30 Finsbury Square, LONDON, EC2P 2YU.
•**BEENY, Mr. David John, FCA** *1962;* (Tax Fac), 48 Wellington Terrace, CLEVEDON, AVON, BS21 7BJ.
BEENY, Mr. Richard John, BA ACA *2000;* Apartment No.2, 124 Neville Park Boulevard, TORONTO M4E 3P8, ON, CANADA.
BEER, Miss. Allison Kaye, ACA *2010;* Harney Westwood & Riegels, Craigmuir Chambers, PO Box 71, Road Town, TORTOLA, VIRGIN GORDA 1110 VIRGIN ISLANDS (BRITISH).
BEER, Mr. Andrew Keith, BA ACA *1984;* 16 Wimbledon Road, Henleaze, BRISTOL, BS6 7YA.
BEER, Mrs. Anne Patricia, BSc ACA *1988;* 17 St. James's Avenue, Hampton Hill, HAMPTON, MIDDLESEX, TW12 1HH.
BEER, Miss. Carol Ann, BSc ACA *1995;* Bridle Way, 52a Well House Drive, Penymynydd, CHESTER, FLINTSHIRE, CH4 0LB.
BEER, Mrs. Caroline Mary Rachael, BA ACA *1999;* 3 Abbots Close, Shenfield, BRENTWOOD, CM15 8LT.
BEER, Mr. Charles, BA ACA *1998;* 7 Bude Close, Bramhall, STOCKPORT, CHESHIRE, SK7 2QP.
BEER, Mr. Christopher Trevor, BSc FCA *1990;* Flat 9, Tideway Wharf, 153 Mortlake High Street, Mortlake, LONDON, SW14 8SW.
BEER, Mrs. Claire Philippa, BSc ACA *1989;* Hollowdene Court, Frensham, FARNHAM, GU10 3BW.
•**BEER, Mr. David Andrew, BSc ACA** *1999;* PricewaterhouseCoopers, 1 Embankment Place, LONDON, WC2N 6RH. See also PricewaterhouseCoopers LLP
•**BEER, Mr. Gordon Robert, MA FCA** *1973;* Blue Spire South LLP, Unit E1, Cumberland Business Centre, Northumberland Road, SOUTHSEA, HAMPSHIRE PO5 1DS.
•**BEER, Mr. Ian Scott, BSc ACA** *1999;* Ernst & Young Europe LLP, 1 More London Place, LONDON, SE1 2AF. See also Ernst & Young LLP
BEER, Mr. James, BSc ACA *2005;* 2/14 Chester street, WOOLLAHRA, NSW 2025, AUSTRALIA.
BEER, Miss. Joanne Elizabeth, BSc ACA *2007;* Warner Bros, 98 Theobalds Road, LONDON, WC1X 8WB.
BEER, Mr. Martin Francis Stafford, MA ACA *1989;* Hollowdene Court, Frensham, FARNHAM, GU10 3BW.
BEER, Mr. Michael John, LLB FCA *1955;* Tawny Ridge, Middlefield, West Wittering, CHICHESTER, WEST SUSSEX, PO20 8AP. (Life Member)
BEER, Mr. Nicholas Simon, BSc FCA *1999;* 4E Le Zodiaque, 15 Avenue Crovetto Freres, 98000 MONACO, MONACO.
BEER, Mr. Nigel Jonathan, BA FCA *1978;* Southdene, Thames Road, Goring, READING, RG8 9AL.
•**BEER, Mr. Paul Allan, FCA** *1970;* H W Fisher & Company, Acre House, 11-15 William Road, LONDON, NW1 3ER. See also Fisher Corporate Plc and H W Fisher & Company Limited
BEER, Mr. Richard Stewart, BA ACA *1986;* S E A C Ltd, 46 Chesterfield Road, LEICESTER, LE5 5LP.
BEER, Mr. Robert William, MBA BA FCA *1977;* 1 Parsonage Farm Barns, High Easter, CHELMSFORD, CM1 4QZ.
BEER, Miss. Tanya Louise, BA ACA *1992;* Canons House, PO Box 112 Canons Way, BRISTOL, BS99 7LB.
BEER, Mr. Thomas Jeffrey Tempest, ACA *2010;* First Floor Flat, 55 Inglethorpe Street, LONDON, SW6 6NU.
BEER, Miss. Victoria Mary Louise, BSc ACA *2008;* Pitcher Partners, Level 19 MLC Centre, 19 Martin Place, SYDNEY, NSW 2000, AUSTRALIA.
BEERAJE, Mr. Jason, BSc ACA *2003;* Commerzbank, PO Box 52715, LONDON, EC2P 2XY.
BEERE, Mr. Howard, ACA *1993;* The Lodge Mitford Hall, Mitford, MORPETH, NORTHUMBERLAND, NE61 3PU.
BEERE, Mr. Julian, MA ACA *1997;* The Manor House, Park Lane, Harbury, LEAMINGTON SPA, WARWICKSHIRE, CV33 9HX.
BEERE, Mr. Liam James, BSc ACA *1992;* UBS Limited, 1 Finsbury Avenue, LONDON, EC2M 2PP.
BEERE, Mrs. Sarah Louise, BA ACA *1992;* Greyfriars, The Common, Redbourn, ST. ALBANS, AL3 7LX.
BEERH, Mr. Surinder Kumar, ACA *1980;* Meadow View, Rhymers Gate, Wyton, HUNTINGDON, CAMBRIDGESHIRE, PE28 2JR.
BEERJERAZ, Mrs. Penny Judith, BSc ACA *1992;* 22 Pereira Road, Harborne, BIRMINGHAM, B17 9JN.
BEERLING, Mr. Kevin Michael, BSc FCA *1995;* 14 Firside Grove, SIDCUP, DA15 8WB.
BEERMAN, Mr. Ian, ACA *2011;* 71 Woodfield Drive, East Barnet, BARNET, HERTFORDSHIRE, EN4 8PD.
BEES, Mr. Timothy Henry, MA FCA *1964;* Keepers Oak Cottage, Wedds Farm, Ticehurst, WADHURST, TN5 7DP.
BEESE, Mr. Derek Alfred, FCA *1958;* Rodborough Manor, Bear Hill, Rosborough, STROUD, GL5 5DH. (Life Member)
BEESE, Mr. Robert Ian, BSc FCA *1975;* Bilton Dene, Bilton Lane, HARROGATE, HG1 4DH.
•**BEESLEY, Mr. Andrew Stephen, FCA FRSA MBA** *1971;* 55 Westover Road, Downley, HIGH WYCOMBE, HP13 5HX.
BEESLEY, Miss. Clare Marie, BSc ACA *2007;* Rodings, 65 Mill Road, Great Totham, MALDON, CM9 8DH.
BEESLEY, Mrs. Jacqueline Anne, BSc ACA *1994;* 3 Fernyhalgh Court, Fulwood, PRESTON, PR2 9NJ.
•**BEESLEY, Mr. James, FCA FCCA** *1969;* Whitnalls, 1st Floor, Cotton House, Old Hall Street, LIVERPOOL, L3 9TX.
BEESLEY, Miss. Joanna Elizabeth, BSc ACA *2006;* 8 Appleby Close, Petts Wood, ORPINGTON, BR5 1GA.
BEESLEY, Miss. Julie Patricia, BSc FCA *1994;* 74 Nandi Avenue, FRENCHS FOREST, NSW 2086, AUSTRALIA.
BEESLEY, Mr. Mark Christopher, FCA *1973;* Rodings, 65 Mill Road, Great Totham, MALDON, CM9 8DH.
BEESLEY, Mr. Martin Geoffrey, BSc ACA *1991;* Morrison Utility Services Morrison House, Primett Road, STEVENAGE, HERTFORDSHIRE, SG1 3EE.
•**BEESLEY, Mr. Stuart Nicholas, BSc FCA** *1977;* (Tax Fac), Lancaster & Co, Granville House, 2 Tettenhall Rd, WOLVERHAMPTON, WV1 4SB. See also Lancaster Haskins LLP
BEESON, Mr. Andrew James, BA ACA *1985;* 6 Briggs Street, Mont Albert North, MELBOURNE, VIC 3129, AUSTRALIA.
BEESON, Mr. Benedick, ACA *2011;* 154 Arlington Road, LONDON, NW1 7HP.
BEESON, Mr. Edward, ACA *1995;* Beesons Ltd Bradeley Abattoir, Bradeley Hall Road Haslington, CREWE, CW1 5QF.
BEESON, Mr. James Gerard, BSocSc ACA *2001;* 34 Pursers Cross Road, LONDON, SW6 4QX.
•**BEESON, Miss. Nicola Dorothy, BSc ACA FCCA** *2009;* NB Consulting Limited, 2 Foxglove Close, BUCKINGHAM, MK18 1FU. See also Silverstone Audit Limited
•**BEESON, Mr. Paul David, FCA** *1977;* (Member of Council 2003 - 2007), Shorts, 6 Fairfield Road, CHESTERFIELD, DERBYSHIRE, S40 4TP.
BEESON, Mr. Paul Robert, BSc FCA DChA *1987;* 13 Digswell Road, WELWYN GARDEN CITY, HERTFORDSHIRE, AL8 7PD.
BEESON, Mr. Philip George, ACA *1991;* 1 The Albany, IPSWICH, IP4 2TP.
BEESON, Mr. Russell Bruce Clifford, MA FCA *1971;* 29 Meadow Rise, BROADSTONE, BH18 9ED.
•**BEESTON, Mr. Christopher James, FCA** *1974;* C.J. Beeston, The Laurels, Reeth, RICHMOND, DL11 6TX.
BEESTON, Mr. Guy Antony, BA ACA *1994;* Windmill Farm, Benhall Mill Road, TUNBRIDGE WELLS, EAST SUSSEX, TN2 5JW.
BEESTON, Miss. Jennifer Eileen, BSc ACA *1988;* G A M Ltd, 12 St. James's Place, LONDON, SW1A 1NX.
BEESTON, Mr. John Keith, BSc(Hons) ACA *2002;* 61 Belgrave Road, DARWEN, LANCASHIRE, BB3 2SF.
•**BEESTON, Mrs. Julie Veronica, BA FCA FCCA** *1983;* J.V. Botterell, 10 Congleton Road, SANDBACH, CHESHIRE, CW11 1HJ.
BEESTON, Mr. Richard, BSc ACA *1991;* 25 Clovelly Road, Ealing, LONDON, W5 5HF.
BEESTON, Mr. Richard Geoffrey, BSc ACA *2007;* 2 Milksey Cottages, Great Wymondley, HITCHIN, HERTFORDSHIRE, SG4 7EZ.
BEESTON, Miss. Tara Louise, ACA *2010;* 34a Lincoln Road, North Hykeham, LINCOLN, LN6 8HB.
•**BEET, Mr. Andrew Michael, BSc(Hons) FCA** *1999;* Rice Associates Ltd, Market Chambers, 3-4 Market Place, WOKINGHAM, BERKSHIRE, RG40 1AL.
•**BEET, Mr. Steven William, ACA** *1983;* PricewaterhouseCoopers LLP, 101 Barbirolli Square, Lower Mosley Street, MANCHESTER, M2 3PW. See also PricewaterhouseCoopers
BEETHAM, Mrs. Claire Emilie, ACA *2008;* 25 Royd Moor Road, BRADFORD, WEST YORKSHIRE, BD4 0TR.
BEETHAM, Mr. Philip James, FCA *1959;* Back Lane Farm, Shirley, ASHBOURNE, DE6 3AS. (Life Member)
BEETLESTONE, Mr. Andrew, FCA *1973;* 147 Te Whau Drive, Te Whau Peninsular Estate, WAIHEKE ISLAND 1240, AUCKLAND, NEW ZEALAND.
BEETON, Miss. Emily Kate, MA ACA *2003;* 15 Drayton Gardens, LONDON, N21 2NR.
BEETON, Mr. Kenneth George, FCA *1976;* 1 Mulberry Gardens, PETERBOROUGH, PE4 6SY.
BEETON, Miss. Mandy Louise, BSc FCA *1990;* 13 Rivercherry Street, Trinity Grove, SMITHFIELD, QLD 4878, AUSTRALIA.
BEETUL, Mr. Kaviraj, ACA ACCA *2010;* Ernst & Young Ltd, 62 Forum Lane, Camana Bay, GEORGE TOWN, GRAND CAYMAN, 510 CAYMAN ISLANDS.
•**BEEVER, Mr. Gordon James, MA FCA** *1972;* Larchcroft Limited, 12 Market Street, HEBDEN BRIDGE, WEST YORKSHIRE, HX7 6AD.
BEEVER, Ms. Margaret Mary, BSc ACA *2004;* Provident Financial, 1 Godwin Street, BRADFORD, BD1 2SU.
BEEVER, Miss. Sarah Jayne, BSc ACA *2008;* with BDO LLP, 55 Baker Street, LONDON, W1U 7EU.
BEEVER, Mr. Stephen Michael, ACA *2009;* 31 Observatory Street, OXFORD FALLS, OX2 6EW.
BEEVERS, Miss. Clare Louise, BSc ACA *2009;* with Hornbeam Accountancy Services Ltd, Hornbeam House, Bidwell Road, Rackheath, NORWICH, NR13 6PT.
BEEVERS, Mr. Graham Martyn, FCA *1968;* 4 Shrublands, Brookmans Park, HATFIELD, AL9 7AL.
•**BEEVERS, Mr. John, BA FCA** *1995;* (Tax Fac), Sagars LLP, Gresham House, 5-7 St. Pauls Street, LEEDS, LS1 2JG.
BEEVERS, Mr. Michael William, FCA *1965;* Little Chub Tor, YELVERTON, DEVON, PL20 6JA. (Life Member)
BEEVERS, Mr. Neal Stuart, ACA *2001;* with Deloitte LLP, 1 City Square, LEEDS, WEST YORKSHIRE, LS1 2AL.
BEEVERS, Mr. Thomas, MA BA ACA *2003;* The Bank of New York Mellon, 160 Queen Victoria Street, LONDON, EC4V 4LA.
•**BEEVERS, Mr. Timothy, BA FCA** *1986;* (Tax Fac), Beevers & Moreno LLP, 44 Chatsworth Gardens, LONDON, W3 9LW. See also Beevers Accounting Services Ltd
BEEVOR, Mr. Alan John, BCom FCA *1975;* 2 Regent Terrace, PENZANCE, CORNWALL, TR18 4DW.
BEEVOR, Mr. David Nigel, MA FCA *1968;* Ratling House, Ratling Road, Aylesham, CANTERBURY, CT3 3HN. (Life Member)
BEG, Mr. Masood Mirza, ACA *2008;* 65 Ansell Road, LONDON, SW17 7LT.
BEG, Miss. Tasnim, FCA *1975;* D-162/A ROJHAN STREET, BLOCK V CLIFTON, KARACHI, PAKISTAN.
•**BEGBEY, Mr. Simon Martyn, BSc(Econ) ACA** *2002;* A Team Finance Limited, 34 Beaufort Crescent, Stoke Gifford, BRISTOL, BS34 8QY.
BEGG, Mr. Duncan Kenneth, ACA *1982;* 10 Hathaway Close, RUISLIP, HA4 6PY.
BEGGAN, Ms. Ciara Mary, BCom ACA *1999;* 50 Alexander Ave, YONKERS, NY 10704, UNITED STATES.
BEGGEROW, Mr. Gary Karl, MA ACA *1992;* 36 Luttrell Avenue, LONDON, SW15 6PE.
•**BEGGEROW, Mr. Roy Edmund, BSocSc ACA** *1981;* Dancers Hill Road, BARNET, HERTFORDSHIRE, EN5 4RP.
BEGGS, Mr. Douglas Arthur, FCA *1963;* 6307 Rideau Valley Drive North, MANOTICK K4M 1B3, ON, CANADA. (Life Member)
BEGH, Mr. Adnan, ACA FCCA *2011;* 12 Berberry Close, BIRMINGHAM, B30 1TB.
BEGLEY, Miss. Joanne Michelle, BSc ACA *2005;* 22 Linnet Mews, LONDON, SW12 8JE.
•**BEGLEY, Mr. Kevin George, BSc FCA** *1986;* (Tax Fac), Walker Begley Limited, 207 Knutsford Road, Grappenhall, WARRINGTON, WA4 2QL.
BEGLEY, Mr. Michael Joseph, BSc FCA *1988;* 57 Ashley Way, Balsall Common, COVENTRY, CV7 7UP.
BEGLEY, Ms. Stephanie Anne, BSc FCA *1990;* Poplar Harca, 167a East India Dock Road, LONDON, E14 0EA.
BEGLEY, Mrs. Wendy, FCA *1961;* Chillerton Farm Cottage, Main RoadChillerton, NEWPORTIsle of Wight, PO30 3HA.
BEGLIN, Miss. Michelle Clare, BSc ACA *1995;* 4 Bryanstone Road, Crouch End, LONDON, N8 8TN.
BEGUM, Miss. Afidah, ACA *2009;* 130 Mantilla Drive, COVENTRY, CV3 6LJ.
BEGUM, Ms. Farhana, BSc ACA ADIT *2009;* with Ernst & Young LLP, 1 More London Place, LONDON, SE1 2AF.
BEGUM, Miss. Jahanara Munna, BSc ACA *2005;* 14 Poppy Drive, WALSALL, WS5 4RB.
BEGUM, Miss. Marjana, BSc(Hons) ACA *2011;* 32 Cambridge Road, SMETHWICK, WEST MIDLANDS, B66 2HS.
BEGUM, Miss. Moirom Leena, ACA *2009;* Thorpe-Bradleys, Mill Lane, WORTHING, WEST SUSSEX, BN13 3DH.
BEGUM, Miss. Ruhina, BSc ACA *2010;* Flat 10 Macclesfield House, Central Street, LONDON, EC1V 8BA.
BEGUM, Miss. Shabana, ACA *2009;* 54 Brecon Road, BIRMINGHAM, B20 3RW.
BEH, Miss. Chian Tyng, ACA *2010;* 6 Lorong Kemaris 5 Bukit Bandaraya., 59100 BANGSAR, SELANGOR, MALAYSIA.
BEH, Miss. Lee Peng, ACA *1980;* 20 English Avenue, CASTLE HILL, NSW 2154, AUSTRALIA.
BEH, Dato' Lye Huat, FCA *1975;* Beh L.H. & Co, Suite B-2-1A, North Point Office, Mid Valley City, 1 Medan Syed Putra Utara, 59200 KUALA LUMPUR FEDERAL TERRITORY MALAYSIA.
BEH, Miss. Meng Ni, BCom ACA *2000;* 99 Meridian Place, LONDON, E14 9FF.

BEHAN, Miss. Katherine Maria, BA ACA *2004;* 1 Sycamore Street, SALE, CHESHIRE, M33 2HD.

BEHAN, Mr. Matthew Hayes, BSc FCA *1998;* with KPMG LLP, 500 East Middlefield Road, MOUNTAIN VIEW, CA 94043, UNITED STATES.

BEHAN, Mr. Richard Michael, ACA *2008;* 25 Bowland Close, STOCKPORT, CHESHIRE, SK2 5NW.

•**BEHAN, Mr. Robert Sean, BSc FCA** *1993;* BBA Limited, Beachside Business Centre, La Rue du Hocq, St Clement, JERSEY, JE2 6LF.

BEHARRY, Mr. Boodlal, FCA *1967;* 11 Knights Court, CASCADE, TRINIDAD AND TOBAGO.

BEHBAHANI, Mr. Khosrow, BSc ACA *1981;* 4 Redbourne Avenue, LONDON, N3 2BS.

BEHL, Mr. Nitin, ACA *2011;* Route De L' Aurore 2C, 1700 FRIBOURG, SWITZERLAND.

BEHL, Mr. Vinay Narjit Singh, ACA *2010;* 350 Bombay Circle, SACRAMENTO, CA 95835, UNITED STATES.

BEHNAM, Mr. Shahrokh, BSc FCA *1964;* (Tax Fac), 36 Campden Hill Court, Campden Hill Road, LONDON, W8 7HS.

BEHR, Mr. Gabriel Simon, MSc BA(Hons) ACA *2001;* Flat 1, Haddon House, 10 Hanson Street, LONDON, W1W 6TZ.

BEHREND, Mr. David Michael, MA FCA *1955;* New Rocklands, Rocklands Lane, WIRRAL, CH63 4JX. (Life Member)

BEHRENS, Mr. Charles William Dalrymple, BEng ACA *1991;* Weston Hill Farm, Moreton Pinkney, DAVENTRY, NN11 3SN.

•**BEHRMAN, Mr. John, BSc FCA** *1977;* Behrman Swindell & Co., 4b Shenley Road, BOREHAMWOOD, HERTFORDSHIRE, WD6 1DL.

BEHZAD, Mr. Aman, ACA *2008;* Citigroup, Suite 701, Building 2 Floor 7, DIFC, DUBAI, UNITED ARAB EMIRATES.

BEIGHTON, Mrs. Fiona Jane, BA ACA *1990;* 1 Westbury Avenue, Claygate, ESHER, SURREY, KT10 0DN.

BEIGHTON, Mr. Jonathan Hugh, LLB ACA CFE *1990;* 1 Westbury Avenue, Claygate, ESHER, KT10 0DN.

•①**BEIGHTON, Mr. Kris, BA ACA** *2000;* KPMG, P O Box 493 Century Yard, Cricket Square, GEORGE TOWN, GRAND CAYMAN, KY1-1106 CAYMAN ISLANDS. See also KPMG (BVI) Limited

BEIGHTON, Mr. Nicholas Timothy, FCA *1995;* Asos, Second floor, Greater London House, Hampstead Road, LONDON, NW1 7FB.

BEIGHTON, Mr. Philip, MA FCA *1962;* 13 Sandygate, Wath-Upon-Dearne, ROTHERHAM, S63 7LN.

BEIRNE, Mr. Andrew, BSc ACA *2006;* (PF778436) BFPO 5203, Foreign & Commonwealth Office, West End Road, RUISLIP, MIDDLESEX, HA4 6EP.

BEIRNE, Mrs. Caroline, BA ACA *2001;* 36 The Course, LEWES, EAST SUSSEX, BN7 1JL.

BEIRNE, Mr. John, FCA *1952;* Urchins, 3 Alfrey Close, Southbourne, EMSWORTH, HAMPSHIRE, PO10 8ET. (Life Member)

BEIRNE, Mr. Paul, BA ACA *1993;* 40 Gainsborough Gardens, EDGWARE, HA8 5TB.

BEIRNE, Mr. Peter Joseph, BA FCA *1972;* Langdown, Golden Acre, East Preston, LITTLEHAMPTON, BN16 1QR.

BEKENN, Ms. Geraldine, BA(Hons) ACA *2010;* Flat A, 5 Meath Street, LONDON, SW11 4JA.

BEKENN, Mr. Jonathan Paul, FCA *1966;* 7 Albany Close, ESHER, SURREY, KT10 9JR. (Life Member)

BEKHOR, Mr. David Hai, FCA *1961;* 26 Spencer Close, Regents Park Road, LONDON, N3 3TX. (Life Member)

BEKHOR, Mr. Jonathan Elia Sassoon, FCA *1969;* 8712 Gregory Way Apt 401, LOS ANGELES, CA 90035, UNITED STATES.

BEKHOR, Mrs. Julia Ruth, BSc ACA *1984;* 8 Acacia Road, LONDON, NW8 6AB.

•**BEKISZ, Mr. Paul Daren, BA(Hons) ACA** *1999;* Begbies Traynor (Central) LLP, Omega Court, 368 Cemetery Road, SHEFFIELD, S11 8FT.

BELBEN, Mrs. Christina Gillian, FCA ACA *1983;* 6 Pine Shaw, Pound Hill, CRAWLEY, RH10 7TN.

BELBEN, Mr. Timothy Devereux, FCA *1955;* Church Farm, Wookey, WELLS, BA5 1JX. (Life Member)

BELBIN, Mr. David Julian, BA ACA *1991;* 18 Mulberry Close, West Bridgford, NOTTINGHAM, NG2 7SS.

•**BELBIN, Mr. David Mark, BSc FCA DChA** *1989;* (Tax Fac), CBHC LLP, Riverside House, 1-5 Como Street, ROMFORD, RM7 7DN.

BELBIN, Mr. Donald Roy James, FCA *1963;* 78 Brackendale Road, Queen's Park, BOURNEMOUTH, BH8 9HZ. (Life Member)

BELCHEM, Mr. Gary, BSc ACA *1998;* 17 Turkey Oak Close, Upper Norwood, LONDON, SE19 2NZ.

BELCHER, Mr. Anthony William, ACA *1979;* Yarningale Cottage, Buttermilk Lane, Yarningale Common, WARWICK, CV35 8HP.

BELCHER, Prof. Claire Alice, FCA *1986;* 24 Boase Avenue, ST. ANDREWS, FIFE, KY16 8BX.

BELCHER, Mr. David Colin, ACA *1981;* Baumatic Ltd, 6 Bennet Road, READING, RG2 0QX.

BELCHER, Miss. Mary Frances, FCA *1966;* The Withies, Sackmore Lane, Marnhull, STURMINSTER NEWTON, DORSET, DT10 1PJ.

BELCHER, Mr. Richard Alan, BA ACA *1996;* Ansys UK Ltd, 6 Europa View, SHEFFIELD, S9 1XH.

BELCHER, Mr. Robert Allan, BA ACA *1988;* 56 Highland Drive, Lightwood, STOKE-ON-TRENT, ST3 4TB.

•**BELCHER, Mr. Robert William, ACA** *1980;* Robert W. Belcher, 26 Station Approach, Hayes, BROMLEY, BR2 7EH. See also Robert W Belcher Limited

BELCHER, Mrs. Rosamund Lesley, ACA *1980;* Yarningale Cottage, Buttermilk Lane, Yarningale Common, WARWICK, CV35 8HP.

BELCHER, Mr. Simon Donald, BSc ACA *1992;* 247 Mereside Way, Olton, SOLIHULL, WEST MIDLANDS, B92 7AY.

BELCHER, Miss. Suzanne Marie, ACA *2009;* K P M G Quayside House, 110 Quayside, NEWCASTLE UPON TYNE, NE1 3DX.

•**BELCHER, Mr. William George, FCA** *1981;* W.G. Belcher & Co, 9 Queens Road, Westbourne, BOURNEMOUTH, BH2 6BA. See also The Accountancy Fellowship Limited

BELCHIER, Mr. Paul, ACA *2009;* Flat 2-4, 13 Lyndhurst Road, LONDON, NW3 5NL.

BELDERBOS, Mr. Stephen Joseph, BSc(Hons) ACA *2002;* 158 St. Clements Hill, NORWICH, NR3 4DG.

•**BELEJ, Mr. Andrew Eugene, ACA** *1984;* Abel Associates Ltd, 16 The Grangeway, LONDON, N21 2HG. See also Andy Belej

BELFER, Mr. Daniel Walter, FCA *1955;* Flat 29, 45 Marlborough Place, LONDON, NW8 0PX. (Life Member)

BELFER, Mr. Simon Leo, MA ACA *1990;* 1 St. Margarets Road, EDINBURGH, EH9 1AZ.

BELFIELD, Mr. David Phillip, BA ACA *2004;* Irwin Mitchell Riverside East, 2 Millsands, SHEFFIELD, S3 8DT.

•**BELFIELD, Mr. Richard Craig, BEng ACA** *1989;* (Tax Fac), Belfield & Co Ltd, 15 Medlock Road, Woodhouses, Failsworth, MANCHESTER, M35 9UA.

BELFIELD, Mr. Richard James, BA FCA *1984;* 2 Aplins Close, HARPENDEN, AL5 2QD.

BELFIELD, Mr. Ross Graham, BSc ACA *1991;* 12 Beech Road, Hale, ALTRINCHAM, WA15 9HX.

•**BELFORD, Mr. John, FCA** *1975;* John Belford & Co Ltd, 14a Main Street, COCKERMOUTH, CUMBRIA, CA13 9LQ.

BELGAUMKAR, Mr. Harish Bindu, BCom ACA *1993;* Subindu, 560 Ist Main R.M.V. Extension, Stage II Block III, BANGALORE 560094, INDIA.

BELHAM, Mr. Martin David, ACA *1985;* Mayfield Farm Green Lane, Althorne, CHELMSFORD, CM3 6BQ.

BELILO, Mr. Ariel Samuel, BA ACA *2005;* F&C REIT Asset Management Worldwide Ltd, 23 Engineer Lane, GIBRALTAR, GIBRALTAR.

BELING, Mr. Jeremy Charles, MA ACA *1983;* 46 Forest Edge Road, Sandford, WAREHAM, DORSET, BH20 7BX.

•**BELINGER, Mr. John Joseph Robert, BSc FCA** *1974;* (Tax Fac), Princecroft Willis LLP, Towngate House, 2-8 Parkstone Road, POOLE, DORSET, BH15 2PW. See also PW Business Solutions

BELINSKAYA, Mrs. Anastasia Markovna, ACA *1997;* 55 King George Street, LONDON, SE10 8QB.

BELK, Mr. Andrew John, BSc ACA *1992;* Pen Plannau, Moelfre, Llansilin, OSWESTRY, SY10 7QL.

•**BELK, Mr. Brian Henry, FCA** *1962;* (Tax Fac), B.H. Belk & Co, 35 Hainton Avenue, GRIMSBY, DN32 9AY.

BELKIN, Mr. Jeffrey Philip, BA ACA *1987;* 10A Sherriff Road, West Hampstead, LONDON, NW6 2AU.

•**BELL, Mr. Alan Douglas, MA FCA CTA** *1968;* (Tax Fac), Adbell International Limited, Finsgate, 5-7 Cranwood Street, LONDON, EC1V 9EE.

•**BELL, Mr. Alexander James, LLB ACA** *1990;* Day Smith & Hunter, Batchworth House, Batchworth Place, Church Street, RICKMANSWORTH, HERTFORDSHIRE WD3 1JE.

•**BELL, Mr. Alexander William John, ACA MAAT** *2003;* (Tax Fac), Studholme-Bell Limited, Vantage House, East Terrace Business Park, Euxton Lane, Euxton, CHORLEY PR7 6TB.

BELL, Mrs. Alexandra Jane, BSc ACA *2003;* Suite 28, 125 Oxford Street, Bondi Junction, SYDNEY, NSW 2022, AUSTRALIA.

BELL, Mrs. Alison, BMus ACA *1991;* L'Ancien Bistrot, Beauregard, 46310 CONCORES, FRANCE.

•**BELL, Miss. Amanda Faye, MA FCA** *1996;* Amanda Bell MA (Cantab) FCA, Suite 122, 5 High Street, MAIDENHEAD, BERKSHIRE, SL6 1JN.

BELL, Mr. Andrew Alan Jeremy, BA ACA *1992;* 19 Yewhurst Close, Twyford, READING, RG10 9PW.

BELL, Mr. Andrew Christopher, BA FCA *1989;* 1 Wellington Road, Bollington, MACCLESFIELD, CHESHIRE, SK10 5JR.

BELL, Mr. Andrew David, BA ACA *2001;* 67 Mossway, Middleton, MANCHESTER, M24 1WS.

BELL, Mr. Andrew Finlay, BSc(Hons) ACA *2009;* 51 Spring Vale Garden Village, DARWEN, LANCASHIRE, BB3 2HJ.

BELL, Mr. Andrew James, BSc ACA *1999;* 15 Main Street, Scopwick, LINCOLN, LN4 3NR.

BELL, Mr. Andrew Malcolm, ACA *1998;* 18 Lamplighters Close, Hempstead, GILLINGHAM, KENT, ME7 3NZ.

BELL, Mr. Andrew Michael, BA ACA *2004;* 9 St Michaels Avenue, Aylsham, NORWICH, NR11 6YA.

•**BELL, Mr. Andrew Nicholas, BA FCA** *1990;* PricewaterhouseCoopers LLP, 1 Embankment Place, LONDON, WC2N 6RH. See also PricewaterhouseCoopers

BELL, Mr. Andrew Richard, BA ACA *1987;* 1 Southfields Farm Cottages, Micheldever Road, WHITCHURCH, HAMPSHIRE, RG28 7JL.

BELL, Mrs. Annette Karen, BSc ACA *1990;* Real Star Group, 161 Brompton Road, LONDON, SW3 1QP.

•**BELL, Mr. Arthur Robert, FCA** *1977;* Hopper Williams & Bell Limited, Highland House, Mayflower Close, Chandler's Ford, SOUTHAMPTON, HAMPSHIRE SO53 4AR. See also HWB Holdings Limited

BELL, Mr. Benjamin Thornton, MA ACA *1997;* 34 Grandison Road, LONDON, SW11 6LW.

BELL, Mr. Brian, BA FCA *1962;* Gainsford Bell & Co., 111 Arlosoroff St, TEL AVIV, 62098, ISRAEL.

BELL, Mr. Bruce Mather, BA ACA *1990;* Kimberley, Rue De L'arquet, St. Saviour, GUERNSEY, GY7 9NE.

BELL, Miss. Cara Elizabeth, BA(Hons) ACA *2010;* Standard Bank Plc, 20 Gresham Street, LONDON, EC2V 7JE.

BELL, Miss. Caroline Louise, BSc ACA *2006;* 55 Long Breech, Mawsley, KETTERING, NORTHAMPTONSHIRE, NN14 1TR.

•**BELL, Mr. Charles Richard, BCom ACA** *1992;* Deloitte LLP, PO Box 500, 2 Hardman Street, MANCHESTER, M60 2AT. See also Deloitte & Touche LLP

•**BELL, Mr. Christopher, ACA** *1982;* (Tax Fac), B M Howarth Limited, West House, Kings Cross Road, HALIFAX, WEST YORKSHIRE, HX1 1EB.

BELL, Mr. Christopher, FCA *1973;* 22 Garfield Road, LONDON, SW11 5PN.

•**BELL, Mr. Christopher David Charles, BA FCA** *2000;* PCJ Solictiors Ltd, 2 Moorfields, LIVERPOOL, L2 2BS.

BELL, Mr. Christopher John, BSc FCA *1975;* Yew Tree Barn, Chilson, CHIPPING NORTON, OX7 3HU.

BELL, Mr. Christopher Michael, FCA *1987;* 33 Chapel Road, Earith, HUNTINGDON, PE28 3PU.

BELL, Mr. Craig Anthony, BA ACA *1997;* Ladhar Leisure Unit G13-G14, Stockholm Close Tyne Tunnel Trading Estate, NORTH SHIELDS, TYNE AND WEAR, NE29 7SF.

BELL, Mr. Daniel John, BA ACA *2008;* 17 Snowdonia Way, Great Ashby, STEVENAGE, HERTFORDSHIRE, SG1 6GU.

BELL, Mr. David, BSc ACA *1979;* Tithegrove Ltd Marshgate House, Marshgate, SWINDON, SN1 2PA.

BELL, Mr. David, BSc ACA *1980;* 49 Brassey Avenue, EASTBOURNE, BN22 9QG.

BELL, Mr. David Alexander, BA(Hons) ACA *2002;* Shell International Ltd, Shell Centre, LONDON, SE1 7NA.

BELL, Mr. David Craig, BSc ACA *1998;* 2 Tame Close, TAMWORTH, STAFFORDSHIRE, B77 5FW.

BELL, Mr. David Maurice, MA FCA *1986;* 23 Dolphin Lane, Melbourn, ROYSTON, SG8 6AE.

•**BELL, Mr. David Michael, BA ACA** *1990;* 17 Greenheys Drive, South Woodford, LONDON, E18 2HA.

BELL, Mr. David Peter, BSc ACA *1993;* 129 Derbeth Grange, Kingswells, ABERDEEN, AB15 8UD.

BELL, Mr. David Robert, FCA *1969;* 1 Dunkeld Road, Talbot Woods, BOURNEMOUTH, BH3 7EN. (Life Member)

BELL, Mr. David Thomas, ACA *2009;* (Tax Fac), 32a Hazelbourne Road, LONDON, SW12 9NS.

BELL, Mr. David William, BSc ACA *1992;* Summerfield, Back Lane, Shirley, ASHBOURNE, DE6 3AS.

BELL, Miss. Deborah Stacy, BA(Hons) ACA *2010;* Ryedene Main Street, Hensall, GOOLE, NORTH HUMBERSIDE, DN14 0RA.

•**BELL, Mr. Donald, FCA** *1966;* Noy & Partners Accountants Ltd, 144 Nottingham Road, Eastwood, NOTTINGHAM, NG16 3GE.

BELL, Mr. Duncan James, BSc ACA *1979;* 2a Hangmans Lane, WELWYN, HERTFORDSHIRE, AL6 0TJ.

BELL, Mr. Edward Snelson, MA FCA *1949;* Sandy Knoll, Wood Lane South, Adlington, MACCLESFIELD, SK10 4PJ. (Life Member)

BELL, Ms. Elaine Ee Leng, MA ACA *1993;* 71 Wheeleys Road, Edgbaston, BIRMINGHAM, B15 2LN.

BELL, Mrs. Eleanor Katherine Ann, MSci ACA *2004;* 1/37-39 Sir Thomas Mitchell Road, BONDI BEACH, NSW 2026, AUSTRALIA.

BELL, Mrs. Elisabeth, ACA *2005;* Steffensvägen 28A, HOLLVIKEN, SWEDEN.

BELL, Ms. Elizabeth Karen, BA ACA *1998;* 90 Potternewton Lane, LEEDS, LS7 3DH.

BELL, Mrs. Elizabeth Margaret, BA ACA *1983;* 11 Claremont Avenue, SUNBURY-ON-THAMES, TW16 5LX.

BELL, Miss. Emma Patricia, BA(Hons) ACA *2004;* 47 Nutfield Road, Merstham, REDHILL, RH1 3EN.

BELL, Miss. Erica, ACA *2008;* Apartment 9, 91 Liverpool Road, MANCHESTER, M3 4JN.

BELL, Mrs. Fiona, BA ACA *2006;* 110 Clonmore Street, LONDON, SW18 5HB.

BELL, Mrs. Fiona Mary, BA ACA *2000;* La Maison Des Buttes, La Rue Des Buttes, St. John, JERSEY, JE3 4ER.

BELL, Mr. Fraser, BAcc ACA *2002;* 14 Ellesmere Drive, CHEADLE, SK8 2JB.

BELL, Mr. Garry James, LLB(Hons) ACA CTA *1997;* (Tax Fac), 2 Homestill, La Grande Route De St. Martin, St. Saviour, JERSEY, JE2 7GT.

•**BELL, Mr. Gary Michael, ACA MAAT** *2008;* Faust Loveday Bell LLP, 5 Curfew Yard, Thames Street, WINDSOR, BERKSHIRE, SL4 1SN.

•**BELL, Mr. Gavin Mckenzie Andrew, BA ACA** *1987;* Bartfields (UK) Limited, Burley House, 12 Clarendon Road, LEEDS, LS2 9NF. See also Bartfields Business Services LLP

•**BELL, Mr. Geoffrey Alfred, FCA** *1967;* Fryers Bell & Co, 27 Athol Street, Douglas, ISLE OF MAN, IM1 1LB.

BELL, Mr. Geoffrey Arthur William, BSc FCA *1974;* 26 Meadow Road, RINGWOOD, BH24 1RU.

BELL, Mr. Geoffrey Malcolm, BSc FCA MIoD *1971;* D S F Refractories Ltd Friden, Newhaven, BUXTON, SK17 0DX.

BELL, Mr. Geoffrey Martin, BA ACA *1982;* 11 Hunt Lea, Fellside Park, Whickham, NEWCASTLE UPON TYNE, NE16 5TU.

BELL, Mr. George, ACA *1979;* Wiltons, Newnham Lane, Eastling, FAVERSHAM, ME13 0AS.

BELL, Mr. George, FCA *1967;* 7 Sundown Road, SHEFFIELD, S13 8UD.

BELL, Mr. George Corbet, FCA *1952;* 18 Asquith Boulevard, LEICESTER, LE2 6FA. (Life Member)

BELL, Mr. George Eric, FCA *1972;* 36 Beach Road, Newton, PORTHCAWL, CF36 5NH.

BELL, Mr. George John Raymond, MA FCA ATII *1982;* Scarrow Beck Farm, Scarrow Beck, Erpingham, NORWICH, NR11 7QU.

BELL, Mr. Gordon Lawrence, BSc ACA *1992;* Windsor House, 56 Harcourt Road, Dorney Reach, MAIDENHEAD, BERKSHIRE, SL6 0DU.

BELL, Mr. Graeme Clive, BA ACA *1990;* 98 Symphony Court, BIRMINGHAM, B16 8AF.

BELL, Mr. Graham, BA(Hons) ACA *2001;* 32 Horton Crescent, EPSOM, SURREY, KT19 8AA.

BELL, Mr. Graham Mitchell, FCA *1974;* 5 Falcon Court, Nimrod House, 5 Falcon Court Preston Farm Industrial Estate, STOCKTON-ON-TEES, CLEVELAND, TS18 3TS.

BELL, Mr. Guy Anthony John, MA ACA *1987;* 6 Badminton Road, LONDON, SW12 8BN.

BELL, Mrs. Helen Alexandra, MA ACA *1992;* Farncotes, 3a Green Lane Cottages, Churt, FARNHAM, SURREY, GU10 2PB.

BELL, Mrs. Helen Margaret, BA(Hons) ACA *2003;* 120 Drakefield Road, LONDON, SW17 8RR.

•**BELL, Mrs. Hilary, BSc ACA** *1988;* Hilary Bell Limited, North Mosses, Asby, WORKINGTON, CA14 4RP.

BELL, Mr. Iain Edward, BSc ACA CTA *1990;* 31 Plovers Lane, Helsby, FRODSHAM, WA6 0QA.

BELL, Mr. Iain James Charles Duncan, BA FCA *1991;* 12 Reedsmere Walk, Comberbach, NORTHWICH, CHESHIRE, CW9 6BZ.
•**BELL, Mr. Ian Alexander, FCA** *1990;* Baker Tilly Tax & Advisory Services LLP, 12 Gleneagles Court, Brighton Road, CRAWLEY, WEST SUSSEX, RH10 6AD. See also Baker Tilly UK Audit LLP
BELL, Mr. Ian Daniel, ACA *2008;* Flat 1, 15 Kent Road, LONDON, W4 5EY.
BELL, Mr. Ian Howard, MBA BSc FCA *1990;* 10 Riverside, Felton, MORPETH, NE65 9EA.
BELL, Ms. Jacqueline Swee Chin, ACA *1995;* 1862 Sagu Street Dasmarinas Village, MAKATI CITY 1200, METRO MANILA, PHILIPPINES.
BELL, Mr. James, BA(Hons) ACA *2011;* 33 The Royal, Wilton Place, SALFORD, M3 6WP.
BELL, Mr. James Alan Russell, FCA *1976;* C/o Dar es Salaam Yacht Club, P O Box 1280, Msasani Peninsula, DAR ES SALAAM, TANZANIA.
•**BELL, Mr. James Douglas, FCA** *1977;* (Tax Fac), Bell & Co (Accountancy Services) Ltd, 4 Jermyns Lane, Ampfield, ROMSEY, SO51 0QA.
BELL, Mr. James Martin Graham, BSc(Hons) ACA *2000;* 10b Solesbridge Close, Chorleywood, RICKMANSWORTH, HERTFORDSHIRE, WD3 5SP.
BELL, Mr. James William Robert, BSc ACA *2004;* Shell Aviation, Shell Centre, York Road, LONDON, SE1 7NA.
BELL, Ms. Janice Theresa Margaret, BA ACA *1991;* 47 Gossoms End, BERKHAMSTED, HERTFORDSHIRE, HP4 1DF.
BELL, Mr. Jason Mark, MEng ACA *1998;* 85 Marsland Road, SALE, M33 3JA.
BELL, Mrs. Joanna, BA ACA *1992;* 6 Tredington Park, Hatton Park, WARWICK, CV35 7TT.
BELL, Mrs. Joanna Jane, BSc ACA *1989;* 10 Riverside, Felton, MORPETH, NE65 9EA.
BELL, Mr. John, BSc FCA *1975;* Carlton House, Carlton Road, South Godstone, GODSTONE, SURREY, RH9 8LG.
BELL, Mr. John, BA ACA *1990;* Gutch 21, Allenwinden, 6319 BAAR, SWITZERLAND.
•①**BELL, Mr. John, BA FCA** *1978;* (Tax Fac), Bell Tindle Williamson LLP, The Old Post Office, 63 Saville Street, NORTH SHIELDS, TYNE AND WEAR, NE30 1AY. See also BTW LLP and Bell Tindle Williamson Services Limited
BELL, Mr. John Christopher, FCA *1964;* Gerwyn Hall, Cross Lanes, WREXHAM, LL13 0TD. (Life Member)
BELL, Mr. John Gordon, FCA *1961;* PO Box 25104, NAIROBI, KENYA.
•**BELL, Mr. John Graham Kearton, BA FCA** *1962;* (Tax Fac), J.G.K. Bell, 1 Westwood Gardens, Barnes, LONDON, SW13 0LB.
•①**BELL, Mr. John Paul, BA FCA** *1989;* Clarke Bell Limited, Parsonage Chambers, 3 The Parsonage, MANCHESTER, M3 2HW.
BELL, Mr. Jonathan Andrew, BA ACA *1991;* 28 Llwyn Arian, Margam Village, PORT TALBOT, SA13 2UP.
BELL, Mr. Jonathan James, ACA DChA *2001;* Manor Farm, 165 Fitton Road, St. Germans, KING'S LYNN, NORFOLK, PE34 3AY.
•**BELL, Mr. Jonathan Leslie Turner, ACA** *2000;* KPMG LLP, 15 Canada Square, LONDON, E14 5GL. See also KPMG Audit plc
BELL, Mr. Jonathan Marc, BA ACA *1997;* Casal Ribeiro 35, Casal Ribeiro, Carregueiros, 2305-224 TOMAR, PORTUGAL.
BELL, Mr. Jonathan Matthew, BA ACA *2000;* 25 Poynton Close, Grappenhall, WARRINGTON, WA4 2NG.
BELL, Mr. Jonathan Richard, BSc ACA *1997;* 96a Netherwood Road, West Kensington, LONDON, W14 0BQ.
BELL, Mr. Jonathan Scott, BA(Hons) ACA *2001;* LDC 8th Floor, 1 Marsden Street, MANCHESTER, M2 1HW.
BELL, Mr. Julian Ingress, FCA *1958;* The Little Gate House, Burfield Road, Old Windsor, WINDSOR, SL4 2LH. (Life Member)
BELL, Mrs. Justine, BA ACA *1991;* 1 The West Lawns, SOUTHWELL, NOTTINGHAMSHIRE, NG25 0JW.
BELL, Mrs. Kate, BSc(Hons) ACA CTA *2001;* 19 Greatfield Close, HARPENDEN, HERTFORDSHIRE, AL5 3HP.
BELL, Mrs. Kathleen Margaret, BA FCA *1976;* 128A Skipton Road, ILKLEY, LS29 9BQ.
BELL, Miss. Katie, BSc ACA *2002;* 23 Stockdale Walk, KNARESBOROUGH, NORTH YORKSHIRE, HG5 8DZ.
BELL, Mr. Keith James, BA FCA *1981;* 10 Scott Road, WALSALL, WS5 3JN.
•**BELL, Mr. Keith Rushforth, FCA** *1981;* Ryans, 67 Chorley Old Road, BOLTON, BL1 3AJ.
BELL, Mr. Kelvin James, BA FCA *1972;* 6 The Banks, Bingham, NOTTINGHAM, NG13 8BL.
BELL, Mr. Kevin Gerard, BSc FCA *1977;* British Petroleum Co Plc, 1 St. James's Square, LONDON, SW1Y 4PD.
BELL, Miss. Kimberley Jane, BA ACA *2004;* 16 Flood Street, CLOVELLY, NSW 2031, AUSTRALIA.
BELL, Mrs. Linda, BA ACA ACIS *1986;* 8 Wentworth Grove, MORLEY, WA 6062, AUSTRALIA.
BELL, Mrs. Lisa Jane, MBS BA(Hons) ACA *2002;* Queen Elizabeth Hospital, Gayton Road, KING'S LYNN, NORFOLK, PE30 4ET.
BELL, Mrs. Lucinda Margaret, MA FCA *1990;* The British Land Co Ltd York House, 45 Seymour Street, LONDON, W1H 7LX.
BELL, Mrs. Lucy Jane, BSocSc ACA *2001;* Punch Taverns Ltd Jubilee House, Second Avenue Centrum One Hundred, BURTON-ON-TRENT, STAFFORDSHIRE, DE14 2WF.
BELL, Mr. Macdonald Gilbert, BCom ACA *1987;* SG Fleet UK Ltd, Warwick Mill Business Centre, Warwick Bridge, CARLISLE, CA4 8RR.
BELL, Mrs. Margaret, BSc ACA *1984;* 45 Waterloo Road, Bramhall, STOCKPORT, CHESHIRE, SK7 2NS.
BELL, Mr. Mark, BA ACA *2002;* 1 Gorse Ridge, Over Lane Baslow, BAKEWELL, DERBYSHIRE, DE45 1RT.
BELL, Mr. Mark Alan, BSc ACA *2008;* 206 Buckland Way, WORCESTER PARK, SURREY, KT4 8NP.
BELL, Mr. Martin, BA(Hons) ACA *2003;* Flat 6, Tudor House, 8 Olive Shapley Avenue, MANCHESTER, M20 6QA.
•**BELL, Mr. Martin Thomas, BA FCA** *1976;* Greystoke, Wansbeck Road, ASHINGTON, NORTHUMBERLAND, NE63 8JE.
BELL, Mr. Matthew James, MEng ACA *2005;* AOG Advisory Services, 63 Brook Street, LONDON, W1K 4HS.
BELL, Mr. Maurice Allen, FCA *1961;* 14 Bronescombe Avenue, Bishopsteignton, TEIGNMOUTH, TQ14 9SR. (Life Member)
BELL, Mr. Michael, BSc FCA *1990;* 19 Silverthorn Drive, HEMEL HEMPSTEAD, HERTFORDSHIRE, HP3 8BU.
BELL, Mr. Michael Brian, BSc ACA *1996;* 61 Van Tassel Lane, ORINDA, CA 94563, UNITED STATES.
BELL, Mr. Michael David, BA ACA *1995;* Zurich Insurance Co The Zurich Centre 3000b, Parkway Whiteley, FAREHAM, HAMPSHIRE, PO15 7JZ.
•**BELL, Mr. Michael Ernest, BSc FCA ATII** *1984;* (Tax Fac), Michael Bell & Co, 4 Greenfield Road, HOLMFIRTH, WEST YORKSHIRE, HD9 2JT. See also Practical Tax Consultants Limited and Bell Michael & Co
BELL, Mr. Michael Graham, MA ACA *1983;* Catholic Marriage Care Ltd, 1 Blythe Mews, Blythe Road, LONDON, W14 0NW.
BELL, Mr. Michael Hugh, ACA CA(SA) *2010;* 4 Hugh de Port Lane, FLEET, HAMPSHIRE, GU51 1HT.
•**BELL, Mr. Michael John, ACA** *1982;* (Tax Fac), Tax Consulting Solutions, 53 The Business Centre, Metcalf Way, CRAWLEY, WEST SUSSEX, RH11 7XX.
•**BELL, Mr. Michael Roy, ACA MAAT** *1996;* Deloitte LLP, 16 High Holborn, LONDON, WC1V 6BX. See also Deloitte & Touche LLP
BELL, Mrs. Morna Elizabeth Mary, MA ACA *1988;* 1A Woodpecker Close, Ewshot, FARNHAM, GU10 5TH.
BELL, Miss. Natalie, BA(Hons) ACA CFA *2002;* 14 Battledean Road, Highbury, LONDON, N5 1UZ.
BELL, Mr. Neil Andrew, BSc ACA *1989;* Essential Vivendi Limited, South Lodge, 1 The Parade, Moor Road, FILEY, NORTH YORKSHIRE YO14 9GA.
BELL, Mrs. Nellia, BSc ACA *1997;* 7 Montague Terrace, Durham Road, BROMLEY, BR2 0SZ.
BELL, Mr. Nicholas John, BA FCA *1977;* 29 Daniell Way, Great Boughton, CHESTER, CH3 5XH.
•**BELL, Mr. Nicholas William, BSc(Hons) ACA** *2007;* (Tax Fac), Orwin Oliver Ltd, 24 King Street, ULVERSTON, CUMBRIA, LA12 7DZ.
BELL, Mrs. Nicola, LLB ACA *2002;* 175a Oatlands Drive, WEYBRIDGE, SURREY, KT13 9JY.
BELL, Mr. Nigel Howard, BSc ACA *1988;* 7 Burns Court, BATLEY, WEST YORKSHIRE, WF17 9JZ.
BELL, Mrs. Nina Anne, BA ACA *1993;* 11 The Burlings, ASCOT, BERKSHIRE, SL5 8BY.
BELL, Mr. Norman, BSc FCA *1972;* Petersen Stainless Rigging Ltd, Cowen Road, BLAYDON-ON-TYNE, TYNE AND WEAR, NE21 5TW.
•**BELL, Mr. Norman Alan, FCA** *1963;* Bell & Co, 37 The Vale, Southgate, LONDON, N14 6HR.
BELL, Mr. Norman William, FCA *1960;* 20 Moorland Drive, LEEDS, LS17 6JP. (Life Member)
BELL, Mr. Oliver William, ACA *2011;* 26 Newlands Quay, LONDON, E1W 3QZ.
BELL, Mr. Patrick Daniel, BSc ACA *2006;* 17 Greenbank Road, WATFORD, WD17 4JJ.
•**BELL, Mr. Patrick John, FCA** *1974;* (Tax Fac), Bell Dinwiddie & Co, Glenavon House, 39 Common Road, Claygate, ESHER, SURREY KT10 0HG.
BELL, Mr. Paul, BA ACA *1997;* Apt. 1102 at Amber, Tiara Residences, The Palm Jumeirah, PO Box 215118, DUBAI, UNITED ARAB EMIRATES.
BELL, Mr. Peter Duncan, BSc ACA *1990;* Jam Magazine, PO Box 138, Bramhall, STOCKPORT, CHESHIRE, SK7 2WS.
BELL, Mr. Peter Johnston, FCA *1951;* 35 Halstead Road, COLCHESTER, CO3 9AD. (Life Member)
BELL, Mr. Peter Joseph, ACA *1983;* Peter Symonds College, Owens Road, WINCHESTER, HAMPSHIRE, SO22 6RX.
BELL, Mr. Phillip William, BA ACA *1987;* West Hillborough Farm, Hillborough Lane, Bidford-on-Avon, ALCESTER, WARWICKSHIRE, B50 4LS.
BELL, Miss. Rachel Angharad, MA BA ACA *2007;* (Tax Fac), 32 The Yonne, St Martins, CHESTER, CH1 2NH.
BELL, Miss. Rachel Caroline, BSc ACA CTA *1995;* 1 Crosspath Cottages, Magpie Lane, Coleshill, AMERSHAM, HP7 0LT.
BELL, Miss. Rachel Tamsin, BA ACA *1992;* 15 Milland Road, WINCHESTER, HAMPSHIRE, SO23 0QA.
BELL, Mr. Raymond Vincent, FCA *1951;* with Lubbock Fine, Russell Bedford House, City Forum, 250 City Road, LONDON, EC1V 2QQ. (Life Member)
BELL, Mr. Richard Andrew, BA ACA *1992;* Desguinlei 90 11E, 2018 ANTWERP, BELGIUM.
BELL, Mr. Richard Dominic, BSc ACA *1999;* 2 Pearl Cottage, Over Wallop, STOCKBRIDGE, HAMPSHIRE, SO20 8HR.
BELL, Mr. Richard Gordon Osborne, FCA *1968;* 147/491 Moo 2 Soi 8/1, Baan Roongaroon, CHIANG MAI 50230, THAILAND.
BELL, Mr. Richard William, BSc FCA *1976;* Bedingham Bell Ltd, 128a Skipton Road, ILKLEY, WEST YORKSHIRE, LS29 9BQ.
•**BELL, Mr. Robert, ACA** *2010;* consult.Autus Limited, 5 Eskdale Avenue, Bramhall, STOCKPORT, CHESHIRE, SK7 1DS.
BELL, Mr. Robert, BSc ACA *2005;* 205 West End, Costessey, NORWICH, NR8 5AW.
BELL, Mr. Robert Pierre, BSc ACA *2009;* with Smith & Williamson Ltd, 25 Moorgate, LONDON, EC2R 6AY.
BELL, Mr. Rodney George, FCA *1958;* Shillbrook, Barn End, Weald, BAMPTON, OX18 2HL. (Life Member)
BELL, Mr. Roger Thomas, BA FCA *1972;* Windmill House, 1 Windmill Lane, Wheatley, OXFORD, OX33 1TA. (Life Member)
•**BELL, Mr. Roger Wallace, FCA** *1966;* (Tax Fac), Roger Bell & Co, 25 Purfield Drive, Wargrave, READING, RG10 8AP.
•**BELL, Mr. Ronald Edward, BA FCA** *1983;* Glendevon, 1a Woodpecker Close, Ewshot, FARNHAM, SURREY, GU10 5TH.
BELL, Mr. Rowell, FCA *1969;* (Tax Fac), Osborne House, 8 Henley Road, IPSWICH, IP1 3SL.
BELL, Mrs. Sally Rachel, BCom ACA *1993;* 10 Park Road, MANCHESTER, M8 4HU.
BELL, Mrs. Samantha Louise, BA ACA *2003;* 12 Chandos Road, Keynsham, BRISTOL, BS31 2DB.
BELL, Miss. Sarah Jayne, ACA *2008;* Flat 2, 41 Waterfront Avenue, EDINBURGH, EH5 1JD.
BELL, Mrs. Sarah Louise, BSc ACA *1992;* 104 Langham Road, TEDDINGTON, TW11 9HJ.
BELL, Miss. Sharon Elaine, BA(Hons) ACA *2001;* 7 Roe Gardens, Ruddington, NOTTINGHAM, NG11 6AQ.
BELL, Mr. Simon James, BSc ACA *1991;* 17 Rayleigh Road, Stoke Bishop, BRISTOL, BS9 2AU.
•**BELL, Mr. Simon Jeremy, BA FCA ATII** *1989;* (Tax Fac), SJB & Co, 8 Barnfield, Feering, COLCHESTER, CO5 9HP.
BELL, Mr. Simon Leonard Lawrance, BA FCA *1974;* 32A, Evelyn Gardens, LONDON, SW7 3BJ.
BELL, Mrs. Sophie Helen, BSc ACA *2008;* Ground Floor Flat, 32 Hazelbourne Road, LONDON, SW12 9NS.
BELL, Mr. Stephen, BA ACA *2006;* Flat 39, 17 Hardwicks Square, LONDON, SW18 4AG.
•**BELL, Mr. Stephen Alan, BA FCA** *1986;* Montgomery & Co, Norham House, Mountenoy Road, Moorgate, ROTHERHAM, S60 2AJ.
BELL, Mr. Stephen Alexander, ACA *2008;* 33 Peatey Court, Princes Gate, HIGH WYCOMBE, BUCKINGHAMSHIRE, HP13 7AY.
BELL, Mr. Stephen John, FCA *1970;* (Tax Fac), with KPMG LLP, 15 Canada Square, LONDON, E14 5GL.
•**BELL, Mr. Stephen Richard, FCA** *1973;* (Tax Fac), Stephen R. Bell, 30 Avon Way, South Woodford, LONDON, E18 2AR.
•**BELL, Mr. Steven David, BA ACA** *1991;* Ernst & Young LLP, 1 More London Place, LONDON, SE1 2AF. See also Ernst & Young Europe LLP
BELL, Mr. Steven William, BA ACA *1993;* 6 Kenwood Park Road, SHEFFIELD, S7 1NF.
BELL, Mr. Stewart William, BA FCA *1974;* 9 Stratford Court, Avenue Road, STRATFORD-UPON-AVON, WARWICKSHIRE, CV37 6UF.
•**BELL, Mr. Thomas Leonard, BA FCA** *1979;* Bellanco Limited, 32 The Yonne, CHESTER, CH1 2NH.
BELL, Mr. Timothy Francis, FCA *1969;* Pixton Park House, DULVERTON, SOMERSET, TA22 9HW. (Life Member)
BELL, Mrs. Tinuke Eniola, BA ACA *1992;* Hampton House, 16 The Avenue, TWICKENHAM, TW1 1RY.
BELL, Mr. Travers John Stuart, BSc ACA *1983;* Apartment 37, 10 Wild Street, LONDON, WC2B 4RL.
BELL, Mrs. Victoria Jill, MA ACA *1997;* R P M I, Stooperdale Offices, Brinkburn Road, DARLINGTON, COUNTY DURHAM, DL3 6EH.
BELL, Mr. William Laurence, BA FCA *1969;* 72 Court Orchard, WOTTON-UNDER-EDGE, GLOUCESTERSHIRE, GL12 7JE. (Life Member)
BELL, Mr. William Michael, FCA *1967;* Apple Acre, Park Lane, Leverington, WISBECH, PE13 5EH. (Life Member)
BELL, Mr. William Robert Geoffrey, FCA *1973;* Langcliffe Hall, SETTLE, BD24 9LY.
•**BELL-RICHARDS, Mr. Thomas Adam Mark, MA ACA** *1987;* Thomas Bell-Richards Ltd, Bowman & Hillier Building, The Old Brewery, Priory Lane, BURFORD, OX18 4SG.
•**BELL-SCOTT, Miss. Fiona Victoria, BA ACA** *2006;* Houghton Stone, The Conifers, Filton Road, Hambrook, BRISTOL, BS16 1QG.
•**BELLAIRS, Mr. Christian Terence, BSc FCA** *2001;* with PricewaterhouseCoopers LLP, 7 More London Riverside, LONDON, SE1 2RT.
BELLAMY, Ms. Alice Elizabeth, MA ACA *2001;* The Old Farmhouse, 2a Monument Lane, Lickey, BIRMINGHAM, B45 9QQ.
BELLAMY, Mr. Anthony Stuart, FCA *1974;* 12 Tabors Road, Margate, HOBART, TAS 7054, AUSTRALIA.
BELLAMY, Mr. Carlton Alexander, BA FCA *1992;* Yew Tree House Apeton, Church Eaton, STAFFORD, ST20 0AE.
BELLAMY, Ms. Catherine Elizabeth, MBChB ACA ATII *1996;* 9 Byfield, Combe Down, BATH, BA2 5JD.
BELLAMY, Mr. David Edward, BA(Hons) ACA *2011;* 1 Drury Lane, Dore, SHEFFIELD, S17 3GG.
BELLAMY, Mr. Edward Gordon, FCA MBA *1967;* (Tax Fac), 5 High Street, Carlton, BEDFORD, MK43 7JX.
•**BELLAMY, Mr. Glynn Michael, BA ACA** *1998;* KPMG LLP, 15 Canada Square, LONDON, E14 5GL.
BELLAMY, Mrs. Helen Marie, BA ACA *1991;* Yew Tree House, Apeton, Church Eaton, STAFFORD, ST20 0AE.
BELLAMY, Mrs. Isabel Emma, BSc ACA *2009;* 59 Island Apartment, 30 Colmfield, LONDON, N1 7BY.
•**BELLAMY, Mr. Jeffrey, BSc FCA** *1985;* (Tax Fac), Colman Whittaker & Roscow, The Close, Queen Square, LANCASTER, LA1 1RS.
BELLAMY, Mr. Kristan David, BSc ACA *2006;* Barclays Capital, 5 North Colonnade, LONDON, E14 4BB.
BELLAMY, Mr. Malcolm George, FCA *1968;* 254 Cottingham Road, HULL, HU6 8QA.
BELLAMY, Mr. Martin William, BSc ACA *1994;* Holmleigh, Lothersdale, KEIGHLEY, BD20 8EL.
•**BELLAMY, Mr. Martyn Frank, BSc FCA** *1975;* with Grant Thornton UK LLP, 30 Finsbury Square, LONDON, EC2P 2YU.
BELLAMY, Mr. Murdo Alec James, BA FCA *1980;* Bristol Rugby Club Ltd, Station Road, Henbury, BRISTOL, BS10 7TT.
BELLAMY, Mr. Nicholas Donald, ACA *1992;* KPMG Phoomchai Audit Limited, 48th Floor Empire Tower, 195 South Sathorn Road, BANGKOK 10120, THAILAND.
BELLAMY, Mr. Nicholas James, BSc ACA *2010;* 10 Wellingborough Road, Mears Ashby, NORTHAMPTON, NN6 0DZ.
BELLAMY, Mrs. Nicola Karen, BSc FCA *1987;* (Tax Fac), White Steading, Station Road, AMERSHAM, HP7 0AW.
BELLAMY, Mr. Northcote Miles, FCA *1951;* 53 Plumstead Road, Thorpe End, NORWICH, NR13 5BS. (Life Member)
BELLAMY, Mr. Steven, BA ACA *1979;* 123 Pierpont Avenue, PO Box 656, SUMMERLAND, CA 93067, UNITED STATES.
BELLARD, Mr. Derek, FCA *1952;* 107 Marsh Lane, Shepley, HUDDERSFIELD, HD8 8AS. (Life Member)

BELLARD, Mrs. Jacqueline, BSc ACA *1981;* 21 Lowstern Close, Egerton, BOLTON, BL7 9XW.

•**BELLARS, Mr. Simon, ACA** *1986;* PricewaterhouseCoopers LLP, 1 Embankment Place, LONDON, WC2N 6RH. See also PricewaterhouseCoopers

BELLENIE, Mr. Reginald Alan, FCA *1971;* Tara, Sandy Lane, REDRUTH, TR16 5SU. (Life Member)

•**BELLERBY, Miss. Nicola Jane, BSc FCA CTA** *1997;* Clive Owen & Co LLP, Aire House, Mandale Business Park, Belmont Ind Estate, DURHAM, DH1 1TH.

BELLERBY, Mr. Robert Edward, ACA *2009;* Cherry Tree House, 1 Victoria Road, Cross Hills, KEIGHLEY, BD20 8SY.

BELLETTY, Mr. Nigel Patrick, BA FCA *1980;* 29 Old Sneed Avenue, BRISTOL, BS9 1SD.

•**BELLEW, Miss. Joanne Louise, ACA** *1995;* Joanne Bellew, 1 Pier Close, Portishead, BRISTOL, BS20 7BU.

BELLEW, Mr. Patrick Seamus Anthony, LLB ACA *1994;* with Deloitte & Touche LLP, One Illinois Center, 111 S Wacker Drive, CHICAGO, IL 60606-4301, UNITED STATES.

BELLEW, Mr. Robert Edward Colin, BA ACA *1980;* 68 Willington Road, Cople, BEDFORD, MK44 3TN.

BELLHOUSE, Mr. Donald Geoffrey, FCA *1956;* The Triangle, 20a Orchard Close, Wendover, AYLESBURY, BUCKINGHAMSHIRE, HP22 6LN. (Life Member)

BELLI, Mr. David Bernard George, BSocSc ACA *1989;* Medstrom Ltd, Millhouse Business Centre, Station Road, Castle Donington, DERBY, DE74 2NJ.

BELLING, Mrs. Charlotte Faye, BSc ACA *2003;* 21 Cobourg Road, BRISTOL, BS6 5HT.

BELLINGHAM, Mr. Brian Hugh Mayberry, FCA *1963;* Burrows Cottage, Kilfield Road, Bishopston, SWANSEA, SA3 3DW.

BELLINGHAM, Mr. David Ridney, BSc ACA *1991;* Suite 86, Private Bag X1, MELKBOSSTRAND, 7437, SOUTH AFRICA.

BELLINI, Mr. Peter Joseph, BSc ACA *1991;* (Tax Fac), Turnpike House, Aylesbury Road, PRINCES RISBOROUGH, BUCKINGHAMSHIRE, HP27 0JP.

BELLIS, Mr. John Alan, FCA *1958;* 21 Macefin Avenue, Chorlton, MANCHESTER, M21 7QQ. (Life Member)

BELLIS, Mr. Nicholas James Manning, BA ACA *1999;* Stephen Baxter, 4 Cleveland Road, LONDON, SW13 0AB.

BELLIS, Mr. Thomas Paul, BSc(Hons) ACA *2009;* 62 Maple Crescent, Penketh, WARRINGTON, WA5 2LG.

BELLO, Mr. Anthony Joseph Michael, BA ACA *1980;* T X Group Europe Ltd, 1000 Great West Road, BRENTFORD, MIDDLESEX, TW8 9DW.

BELLO GARCIA, Miss. Esther Helena, BSc ACA *1989;* Goteley Manor, Church Lane, Northiam, RYE, TN31 6NW.

BELLONI, Mrs. Claire Elizabeth, BA(Hons) ACA *2004;* 18 Applecroft, Park Street, ST. ALBANS, HERTFORDSHIRE, AL2 2AP.

BELLRINGER, Mr. Charles Albert John, MSc ACA *1981;* Tenchleys Manor, Itchingwood Common Road, Limpsfield, OXTED, RH8 0RL.

BELLRINGER, Mr. David Roy, FCA *1974;* 3A Dok Beyers Street, Heuwelsig, BLOEMFONTEIN, FREE STATE, 9301, SOUTH AFRICA.

•**BELLWOOD, Mr. David Dean, FCA** *1973;* 116 Oakhill Road, SEVENOAKS, TN13 1NU.

BELLWOOD, Mr. Mark David, ACA *2009;* with Northcott Trumfield, Devonshire Villa, 52 Stuart Road, Stoke, PLYMOUTH, PL3 4EE.

BELLWOOD, Mr. Simon Mark, BSc ACA *1988;* 6 Heathmoor Close, Idle, BRADFORD, BD10 8QE.

BELMAN, Mr. Jeffrey Lewis, FCA *1969;* 6 Datchworth Court 22, Village Road, ENFIELD, EN1 2DS.

BELMORE, Mrs. Frances McInnes Muir McLaren, BA ACA *1984;* County Hall, Norfolk County Council Children Services, County Hall Martineau Lane, NORWICH, NR1 2DL.

BELOW, Mrs. Erica, ACA *1984;* 24 Wheatley Road, ILKLEY, LS29 8TS.

BELOW, Mr. Paul Kay, BA FCA *1984;* 24 Wheatley Road, ILKLEY, LS29 8TS.

BELOW, Mrs. Rachel Catherine Christie, MA ACA *1991;* Hillcote, Doctors Commons Road, BERKHAMSTED, HP4 3DR.

BELSEY, Mr. Craig, ACA *2008;* UNITS 23 & 24, Wrotham Business Park, BARNET, HERTFORDSHIRE, EN5 4SZ.

•**BELSEY, Mr. John Edward, BSc ACA** *1999;* Gotwick Farm, Holtye Road, EAST GRINSTEAD, WEST SUSSEX, RH19 3PP.

BELSEY, Mr. Peter John, BA ACA *1986;* The Woodlands, 34 Dearnside Road, Denby Dale, HUDDERSFIELD, HD8 8TL.

BELSHAM, Mr. Christopher James, BSc ACA *1999;* with KPMG LLP, St. James's Square, MANCHESTER, M2 6DS.

BELSHAM, Mr. William John, BA ACA *1984;* 21 Sevenoaks Road, ORPINGTON, BR6 9JH.

BELSHAW, Mr. Andrew Scott James, MA FCA MBA *1998;* Gamma Telecom, Unit 1, The Pentangle, Park Street, NEWBURY, BERKSHIRE RG14 1EA.

BELSHAW, Mr. Brian Edward, FCA *1964;* Hillcrest, 113 Barton Road, Barton Seagrave, KETTERING, NN15 6RT. (Life Member)

BELSHAW, Mr. Gordon Richard, BSc FCA *1962;* Autumn Retreat, 1 Burdon View, Aislaby Road, Eaglescliffe, STOCKTON-ON-TEES, CLEVELAND TS16 0GZ.

BELSHAW, Mrs. Rachel Amanda, MA ACA CTA *1999;* 3 Swan Drive, Aldermaston, READING, RG7 4UZ.

BELSHAW, Mr. Thomas Robert, FCA *1970;* 54 Cromwell Road, BECKENHAM, BR3 4LN.

BELSMAN, Mr. Paul Simon, MA FCA CTA *1982;* (Tax Fac), 16a The Warren, RADLETT, WD7 7DX.

•**BELTON, Mrs. Alexandra Justine, MA ACA** *1994;* Ernst & Young LLP, 1 More London Place, LONDON, SE1 2AF. See also Ernst & Young Europe LLP

BELTON, Mr. Christian Mathew, BA ACA *1997;* 1/30 Prosser Avenue, NORWOOD, SA 5067, AUSTRALIA.

BELTON, Mrs. Claire Louise, BA(Hons) ACA *2004;* 22 Montbelle Road, LONDON, SE9 3PB.

BELTON, Mr. John Patrick, FCA *1971;* The Haywain, Hill Farm Road, MARLOW, BUCKINGHAMSHIRE, SL7 3LX.

BELTON, Mr. Kevin Alan, BSc FCA *1982;* 153 Manygate Lane, SHEPPERTON, TW17 9EP.

BELTON, Mr. Mark Robert, BA ACA *1994;* Trifast plc, Trifast House, Bellbrook Park Industrial Estate, UCKFIELD, EAST SUSSEX, TN22 1QW.

BELTON, Mr. Neil Andrew, BSc ACA *2005;* with PKF (UK) LLP, Pannell House, 6 Queen Street, LEEDS, LS1 2TW.

BELTOWSKI, Mr. Wojciech Jerzy, BSc FCA *1973;* 3/30 Percy Street, SEMAPHORE, SA 5019, AUSTRALIA.

BELWARD, Mr. David Patrick Thomas, LLB ACA *1991;* Highstone Group Ltd Beech Villa, 1 Esplanade, HARROGATE, NORTH YORKSHIRE, HG2 0LN.

BEM, Mr. Alexander, ACA *2009;* 9 Stratford Avenue, UXBRIDGE, MIDDLESEX, UB10 0JW.

•**BEMAN, Mr. David Garrick, MA BSc FCA** *1975;* (Tax Fac), Beman & Co, The Bungalow, Llantrithyd House, Llantrithyd, COWBRIDGE, CF71 7UB. See also Astonworth Limited and Berman & Co

BEMAN, Mr. Kim, ACA *1981;* with Parkhurst Hill, Torrington Chambers, 58 North Road East, PLYMOUTH, PL4 6AJ.

BEMBRIDGE, Miss. Emma Jayne, BSc ACA *1999;* Ernst & Young, 925 Euclid Avenue, CLEVELAND, OH 44115, UNITED STATES.

BEMBRIDGE, Miss. Laura, BSc ACA *2010;* Flat 4 Pochard House, 7 Millward Drive Bletchley, MILTON KEYNES, MK2 2BW.

BEMBRIDGE, Mrs. Sarah Anna-Louise, BA ACA *2001;* 76 Cranbourne Drive, Otterbourne, WINCHESTER, SO21 2ET.

BEMBRIDGE, Mr. William Harry, BA ACA *2000;* (Tax Fac), 76 Cranbourne Drive, Otterbourne, WINCHESTER, SO21 2ET.

•**BEMMENT, Mr. Anthony Peter, ACA** *1980;* (Tax Fac), A P Bemment & Co Limited, 101 Bridge Road, Oulton Broad, LOWESTOFT, SUFFOLK, NR32 3LN.

•**BEMMENT, Mr. Gregory Paul, FCA** *1982;* Wheatley Pearce Limited, 11 Winchester Place, North Street, POOLE, DORSET, BH15 1NX.

BEMPAH, Miss. Maame-Yaa, BSc ACA *2006;* 6 Sarsen Avenue, HOUNSLOW, TW3 4JN.

BEMROSE, Mr. David Richard, FCA *1968;* 36 Devonshire Avenue, GRIMSBY, SOUTH HUMBERSIDE, DN32 0BW.

BEMROSE, Miss. Jill, BA FCA *1977;* 27 Cornflower Drive, RUGBY, CV23 0UG.

•**BEN-NATHAN, Mr. Colin Victor, MA FCA CTA** *1989;* (Tax Fac), KPMG LLP, 15 Canada Square, LONDON, E14 5GL. See also KPMG Europe LLP

BEN-NATHAN, Mr. Martin Joseph, MA FCA *1962;* 1 Hillside Gardens, HARROW, MIDDLESEX, HA3 9UW.

BEN REAZ, Mr. Abdullah, FCA CPA *1975;* Apt. 503, House 10 Road 6, Gulshan 1, DHAKA 1212, BANGLADESH.

•**BENADY, Mr. Mark Mordejay, BSc FCA** *1990;* Benady Cohen & Co, 21 Engineer Lane, GIBRALTAR, GX11 1AA, GIBRALTAR.

BENADY, Ms. Ruth, BA ACA *2002;* 6 Kingsley Close, LONDON, N2 0ES.

BENADY, Mr. Solomon, ACA *2010;* Flat 29 West Heath Court, North End Road, LONDON, NW11 7RG.

BENAIM, Mr. Michael Raphael, BA ACA *1998;* 59 Finchley Lane, LONDON, NW4 1BY.

BENAIM, Mr. Shalom, BA ACA *1995;* (Tax Fac), 11 Parklands Drive, LONDON, N3 3HA.

•**BENAIM, Mr. Solomon Benjamin, BSc FCA** *1980;* BDO LLP, 55 Baker Street, LONDON, W1U 7EU. See also BDO Stoy Hayward LLP

BENATTAR, Mr. Iver Edmund Jacob, FCA *1966;* 223 Pitshanger Lane, Ealing, LONDON, W5 1RG.

BENAVIDES, Mrs. Joanne Elizabeth, BA ACA *2003;* Flat 54 Watermans Quay, William Morris Way, LONDON, SW6 2UU.

BENAZETH, Mr. Jean-Paul Leonce Antoine, FCA *1963;* 29 Chemin de Clamarquier, 06650 LE ROURET, FRANCE.

BENBOW, Mr. Christopher John, BSS ACA *1994;* 10 Kings Drive, Heaton Moor, STOCKPORT, CHESHIRE, SK4 4DZ.

BENBOW, Mr. John Andrew, FCA *1957;* 11 The Mount, LEATHERHEAD, KT22 9EB. (Life Member)

BENBOW, Mr. John Buie, FCA *1975;* P O Box 923, GEORGE TOWN, GRAND CAYMAN, KY1-1102, CAYMAN ISLANDS.

BENBOW, Mr. John Leslie, BA ACA *1991;* 11 The Brackens Westbury Park, Clayton, NEWCASTLE, ST5 4JL.

BENBOW, Mr. Nicholas John, MA FCA *1977;* The Sheepcote, Frith Common, Eardiston, TENBURY WELLS, WORCESTERSHIRE, WR15 8JX.

BENCARD, Mr. Robin Louis Henning, BA FCA *1990;* L3, H S B C, 8-16 Canada Square, LONDON, E14 5HQ.

BENCE, Mr. David Edward, BA(Hons) ACA *2001;* The Old Bakery, 2 St. Peters Street, Duxford, CAMBRIDGE, CB22 4RP.

BENCE, Mr. David John, PhD BA ACA *1988;* Bristol Business School, UWE, Frenchay, BRISTOL, BS16 1QY.

•**BENCE, Mr. Thomas How, FCA** *1973;* Concept Hotels Ltd, Sheep Street, Stow on the Wold, CHELTENHAM, GLOUCESTERSHIRE, GL54 1AU.

BENCH, Mr. Iain George Peter, BA FCA *1986;* 14 Fordhook Avenue, Ealing, LONDON, W5 3LP.

BENCH, Miss. Lisa Jane, ACA *2009;* Atkey Goodman Chartered Accountants Prudence House, Langage Park Office Campus Ashleigh Way Langage Business P, PLYMOUTH, PL7 5JX.

BENDA, Mr. David Karel, BSc ACA *1994;* 38 Coniger Road, LONDON, SW6 3TA.

BENDALL, Mr. Adam James, BSc ACA *2004;* 12 Northlands Way, TETBURY, GLOUCESTERSHIRE, GL8 8YT.

•**BENDALL, Mr. Christopher Rodney, ACA** *2000;* Balanced Accounting LLP, Unit Q, The Brewery, Bells Yew Green, TUNBRIDGE WELLS, KENT TN3 9BD.

BENDALL, Mr. Dudley Hockney, FCA *1958;* The Old Cottage, Main Street, Aslockton, NOTTINGHAM, NG13 9AB. (Life Member)

BENDALL, Mr. George Peter, BA(Hons) ACA *2010;* 4 Manor Close, Tockington, BRISTOL, BS32 4NT.

BENDALL, Mr. Peter Harry, FCA *1971;* St Petroc, Rock Road, Rock, WADEBRIDGE, PL27 6JZ.

BENDALL, Mr. Peter Stanley, BA FCA *1977;* (Tax Fac), Cannon Cottage, 4 Cannongate Close, HYTHE, KENT, CT21 5PZ.

BENDASIUK, Mr. Aaron Michael, ACA *2011;* 18 Medlock Drive, OLDHAM, OL8 2TZ.

•**BENDEL, Mr. Allan Paul, FCA** *1964;* Bendel & Company, 5 Whitegate Gardens, Harrow Weald, HARROW, HA3 6BW.

•**BENDELL, Mr. Robert Keith, BSc FCA** *1983;* Robert K. Bendell, 10 Holmesdale Road, BEXHILL-ON-SEA, TN39 3QE.

BENDER, Dr. Ruth Frances, PhD MBA BA FCA *1980;* Cranfield School of Management, Cranfield University, College Road, Cranfield, BEDFORD, MK43 0AL.

BENDER, Mr. Stephen David, BA FCA *1990;* Bidvest, 3rd floor, 11 Hill Street, LONDON, W1J 5LQ.

BENDER, Ms. Tatjana, BA(Hons) ACA *2001;* 65 Mayfield Road, LONDON, W12 9LT.

BENDESH, Mr. Ian, BA ACA *2006;* 50B Valerie Street, DIANELLA, WA 6059, AUSTRALIA.

BENDIG, Mr. Maurice, JP FCA *1956;* 26 Canford Drive, Allerton, BRADFORD, WEST YORKSHIRE, BD15 7AU. (Life Member)

•**BENDING, Mrs. Delyth Clare, BA FCA** *1994;* (Tax Fac), Delyth Bending Accountancy Limited, 4 The Paddock, Lower Boddington, DAVENTRY, NORTHAMPTONSHIRE, NN11 6YF.

BENDING, Mr. Lawrence Charles, FCA *1976;* Child-Beale Trust, Beale Park, Reading Road, Lower Basildon, Pangbourne, READING RG8 9NH.

BENDING, Mrs. Tania Estelle, BSc ACA *1998;* 3 Cwrt y Cadno, Pen-y-Fai, BRIDGEND, MID GLAMORGAN, CF31 4GL.

BENDING, Mr. Timothy Mark, BSc FCA MCT *1989;* School House, Fewston, HARROGATE, NORTH YORKSHIRE, HG3 1SS.

BENDIT, Mrs. Frances Katherine, BSc ACA *1986;* Endlewick House, Arlington, POLEGATE, EAST SUSSEX, BN26 6RU.

BENDIT, Mr. Paul Jonathan, ACA *1985;* Endlewick House Wilbees Road, Arlington, POLEGATE, EAST SUSSEX, BN26 6RU.

BENDLE, Mr. Douglas Jonathan, ACA *2008;* 19a Westgate Terrace, LONDON, SW10 9BT.

BENDLE, Mr. Frederick Ivor, BA ACA *1983;* Rubec Wick Hill, Finchampstead, WOKINGHAM, RG40 3SW.

BENDRE, Mr. Rajiv Ratnakar, MA ACA *1985;* 337 WITHELLS ROAD, AVONHEAD, CHRISTCHURCH, NEW ZEALAND.

BENDRE, Mr. Sanjiv Ratnakar, MCom ACA *1993;* 19 Surrey Road, HARROW, MIDDLESEX, HA1 4NJ.

BENEDETTI, Mr. Stefan, BSc ACA *1993;* 7 Sutherland House, Marloes Road, LONDON, W8 5LG.

•**BENEDICT, Mr. Anthony Peter Mcqueen, FCA** *1972;* Benedict Mackenzie, The Old Coach House, Croydon Lane, BANSTEAD, SURREY, SM7 3AT. See also Benedict Mackenzie LLP

BENEDICT, Mr. Elmo Jeganathan, ACA *1982;* 1603 Islington Ave, TORONTO M9A 3M7, ON, CANADA.

BENEDICT, Mr. Neil Paton, FCA *1971;* PO Box 691, SHARON, CT 06069, UNITED STATES.

•**BENEDICT, Mr. Peter Harry, FCA** *1958;* Reed Taylor Benedict, First Floor, Trinominis House, 125-129 High Street, EDGWARE, HA8 7DB.

BENEST, Mr. Brian Peter Voisin, FCA *1971;* Chevaux de Bois, La Route De St Jean, St John, JERSEY, JE3 4EA.

BENEST, Mr. Dale Ian Anthony, BA ACA ACOI MSI *1992;* 3 Clos D'Edouard, Rue Des Pres, St. Saviour, JERSEY, JE2 7RE.

BENET BARRIOS, Miss. Blanca, MA ACA *2001;* 21 Bennerley Road, LONDON, SW11 6DR.

BENEY, Mr. Ralph Martin, ACA *1984;* August Pitts Farmhouse, Churn Lane, Horsmonden, TONBRIDGE, TN12 8HW.

BENFIELD, Mr. James Oliver, BEng ACA *2000;* 73 Athenlay Road, LONDON, SE15 3EN.

BENFOLD, Mr. Andy, BSc ACA *2007;* Lipco Engineering Ltd, Forest House, Hightown Industrial Estate, RINGWOOD, HAMPSHIRE, BH24 1ND.

BENFOLD, Mr. John Michael, FCA *1979;* Troy Cottage, Horsell Park, WOKING, SURREY, GU21 4LY.

•**BENFORD, Mr. Jonathan Richard, MA FCA** *1990;* (Tax Fac), Dixon Wilson, 19 avenue de L'Opera, 75001 PARIS, FRANCE.

BENFORD, Mr. Michael John, BSc ACA *2000;* 8 Kenton Avenue, Nuthall, NOTTINGHAM, NG16 1PX.

BENFORD, Miss. Suzanne Marie, BA(Hons) ACA *2001;* 7 Ashbrooke Close, WHITLEY BAY, TYNE AND WEAR, NE25 8EQ.

•**BENG, Mr. Kian Phee Philip, FCA** *1973;* 46 Chee Hoon Avenue, SINGAPORE 299765, SINGAPORE.

BENGANI, Mr. Sanjay Kumar, BA ACA *1998;* Flat 303 Summit 2, Opp. Reliance Petrol Pump, Off Anand Nagar Road, Satellite, AHMEDABAD 380 051, INDIA.

BENGE, Mr. Geoffrey Peter Alfred, BA ACA *1985;* with Rayner Essex LLP, Faulkner House, Victoria Street, ST. ALBANS, HERTFORDSHIRE, AL1 3SE.

BENGE, Mr. Roger Brace, FCA *1962;* BDO Patel, P.O. Box 25836, ABU DHABI, UNITED ARAB EMIRATES. See also BDO International

BENGE, Miss. Samantha, ACA *2011;* 56 Minster Way, HORNCHURCH, ESSEX, RM11 3TD.

•**BENGSTON, Mr. Malcolm, BSc FCA** *1979;* Malcolm Bengston, 27 Partridge Close, Ayton Green, WASHINGTON, NE38 0ES.

BENHAM, Mr. Daniel Douglas, BSc ACA *1991;* 23 ruesonnex, Grand saconnex, 1218 GENEVA, SWITZERLAND.

BENHAM, Mr. Ian John, BSc ACA *2004;* 48 Hogarth Road, HOVE, EAST SUSSEX, BN3 5QH.

BENHAM, Mr. Mark Steven, BSc ACA *1990;* 51 Sugarloaf Crescent, CASTLECRAG, NSW 2068, AUSTRALIA.

BENHAM, Mr. Stephen John, BA FCA *1979;* 90 Long Acre, LONDON, WC2E 9RA.

BENHAM, Miss. Victoria Jane, BSc ACA *2003;* 29A Limesford Road, Nunhead, LONDON, SE15 3BX.

BENISCHKE, Mr. Reinhard Gunther, BSc ACA *1982;* Boldman Ltd, Unit 4, Britannia Way, BOLTON, BL2 2HH.

BENISO, Mr. Raphael Abraham, BA ACA *2007;* with Deloitte Limited, PO Box 758, Merchant House, 22-24 John Mackintosh Square, GIBRALTAR, GIBRALTAR.
BENISTON, Mr. Paul, BA FCA *1978;* 14 Park Meadow, Doddinghurst, BRENTWOOD, Essex, CM15 0TT.
BENJAMIN, Mr. David, BSc ACA *1992;* Asteys, 8 Camlet Way, BARNET, HERTFORDSHIRE, EN4 0LH.
•BENJAMIN, Mr. Ian Joseph, BA FCA *1980;* McGladrey & Pullen LLP, 1185 Avenue of the Americas, Suite 500, NEW YORK, NY 10036, UNITED STATES.
•BENJAMIN, Mr. Jeremy Daniel, BA FCA *1992;* Jeremy Benjamin, Ground Floor Flat, 47 Bynes Road, SOUTH CROYDON, SURREY, CR2 0PY.
BENJAMIN, Mrs. Joanne, BSc ACA *2003;* 10 Francklyn Gardens, EDGWARE, MIDDLESEX, HA8 8RY.
BENJAMIN, Mr. Philip Gregory, BSc ACA *1986;* 19 St. Catherine Drive, Hartford, NORTHWICH, CHESHIRE, CW8 2FE.
BENJAMIN, Mr. Theodore Toby, BCom FCA *1956;* 4 Arlington Court, Kenton Avenue, NEWCASTLE UPON TYNE, NE3 4JR. (Life Member)
BENJAMIN-WARDLE, Miss. Eirlys, ACA *2011;* 13 rue Navier, 75017 PARIS, FRANCE.
BENKEL, Mr. Julian Christopher William, ACA *1986;* 8 St. Heliers Avenue, HOVE, EAST SUSSEX, BN3 5RE.
BENN, Mr. Christopher, BA ACA *1995;* 95 West End Lane, PINNER, MIDDLESEX, HA5 3NU.
BENN, Mr. David, ACA *1981;* 11 Manor Park Road, CLECKHEATON, WEST YORKSHIRE, BD19 5BL.
BENN, Mr. David, LLB FCA *1974;* Hillcroft, High Street, TARPORLEY, CW6 0AX.
BENN, Mr. Michael Arthur, FCA *1963;* 11 Yew Tree Lane, Spratton, NORTHAMPTON, NN6 8HL.
•BENN, Mr. Peter, BSc FCA *1983;* East Riding Accounts, 48 New Village Road, COTTINGHAM, HU16 4NA.
•BENN, Mr. Richard John, ACA CA(SA) *2010;* Cheetah Management Services, Rua 31 de Janiero 81A - 3E, 9050-011 FUNCHAL, MADEIRA, PORTUGAL.
BENN, Mr. Robert Ernest, MA FCA *1989;* 15 Northumberland Street, EDINBURGH, EH3 6LL.
BENN, Mr. Travis Aggrey, BSc ACA *2010;* 6 Shipton Hill, Bradville, MILTON KEYNES, MK13 7EE.
BENNELL, Mrs. Maureen Brenda, BSc ACA *1980;* 6 Holloway Place, Curl Curl, SYDNEY, NSW 2096, AUSTRALIA.
BENNELL, Mr. Stafford John, ACA *1986;* 4 Oakhill Close, ASHTEAD, SURREY, KT21 2JQ.
BENNER, Mr. John Edward, LLB ACA *2003;* 12 Brewery Lane, Bridge, CANTERBURY, KENT, CT4 5LD.
BENNER, Mr. Richard Matthew, MA ACA AMCT *1993;* 10 Birch End, WARWICK, CV34 5GQ.
BENNET, Ms. Alison Ruth, MA ACA *1991;* 24 Kings Avenue, LONDON, N10 1PB.
BENNET, Mr. Gordon Iain, MA FCA *1984;* 152 East Clyde Street, HELENSBURGH, DUNBARTONSHIRE, G84 7AX.
BENNET, The Revd. Mark David, MA ACA *1989;* The Rectory St. James Church Perry Road, HARLOW, ESSEX, CM18 7NP.
BENNET, Mrs. Teresa Shirley, BSc ACA *1990;* 29 Stratton Way, BIGGLESWADE, SG18 0NS.
•BENNET-SMITH, Mr. Andrew, FCA *1975;* Ross Bennet-Smith, Charles House, 5-11 Regent Street, St James, LONDON, SW1Y 4LR.
BENNETT, Mr. Adam Edward Spencer, BA FCA MBA *1981;* Shernover House, Windmill Hill, Brenchley, TONBRIDGE, KENT, TN12 7NP.
•BENNETT, Dr. Adrian James, BSc(Hons) ACA *2002;* with PricewaterhouseCoopers LLP, Abacus House, Castle Park, CAMBRIDGE, CB3 0AN.
BENNETT, Mr. Adrian Nigel, BA FCA *1979;* The Coach House, London Road, Rake, LISS, GU33 7PE.
BENNETT, Mr. Alan Gordon, BA FCA *1984;* Smith Nicholas, 2 Friarsgate, Grosvenor Street, CHESTER, CH1 1XG.
BENNETT, Mrs. Aleksandra, BSc ACA *1991;* 33 Elmsleigh Road, Cove, FARNBOROUGH, Hampshire, GU14 0ET.
BENNETT, Mr. Alexander Solomon, FCA *1958;* Silver Birches Cromer Road High Kelling, HOLT, NORFOLK, NR25 6QZ. (Life Member)
BENNETT, Mrs. Alison, BSc ACA *1991;* Ridge House, Beaulieu Road, LYNDHURST, HAMPSHIRE, SO43 7DA.
•BENNETT, Mrs. Amanda Louise, FCA *1989;* Target Consulting Limited, Lawrence House, Lower Bristol Road, BATH, BA2 9ET. See also Target Winters Limited
BENNETT, Mr. Andrew, ACA *2011;* Top Floor Flat, 35 Palace Court, LONDON, W2 4LS.
BENNETT, Mr. Andrew Charles, ACA *1979;* c/o Mrs S N Bennett, 3 Wedgewood Court, Parkhill Road, BEXLEY, KENT, DA5 1HL.
BENNETT, Mr. Andrew David, BA ACA *1995;* Bowhill Bagatelle Road, St. Saviour, JERSEY, JE2 7TZ.
BENNETT, Mr. Andrew Geoffrey, BSc ACA CFA HKICPA *1991;* c/o Ernst & Young, 18/F Two Interational Finance Centre, 8 Finance Street, CENTRAL, HONG KONG ISLAND, HONG KONG SAR.
BENNETT, Mr. Andrew Mark, BSc ACA *1989;* Ashfield Extrusion Ltd, Clover Street, Kirkby-in-Ashfield, NOTTINGHAM, NG17 7LH.
BENNETT, Mr. Andrew Michael, BSc(Hons) FCA *2001;* MRO, Meggitt Aerospace Limited, Holbrook Lane, COVENTRY, CV6 4AA.
•BENNETT, Mr. Andrew Neil, BSc FCA CTA *1990;* (Tax Fac), Southwinds Consulting Limited, 2nd Floor, Nadine House, 13 North Quay, Douglas, ISLE OF MAN IM1 4LE.
BENNETT, Mr. Andrew Nicholas, MA ACA *1988;* 52 Normandy Road, ST. ALBANS, AL3 5PW.
•BENNETT, Mr. Andrew William, BSc FCA CF CTA *1980;* (Tax Fac), Rothman Pantall LLP, Fryern House, 125 Winchester Road, Chandler's Ford, EASTLEIGH, HAMPSHIRE SO53 2DR.
BENNETT, Mrs. Angela, BSc ACA *1992;* 78 Ottways Lane, ASHTEAD, SURREY, KT21 2PW.
•BENNETT, Miss. Anna Elizabeth, BSc ACA *1991;* Hallidays LLP, Riverside House, Kings Reach Business Park, Yew Street, STOCKPORT, CHESHIRE SK4 2HD. See also Hallidays Accountants LLP
BENNETT, Mrs. Anna Louise, BSc ACA DChA *2002;* 109 Puller Road, BARNET, HERTFORDSHIRE, EN5 4HQ.
BENNETT, Miss. Anne Elizabeth, BSc ACA *1993;* 7th Floor 5NC, Barclays Capital, 5 North Colonnade, LONDON, E14 4BB.
BENNETT, Mrs. Anne Marie, BCom ACA *1992;* Fernau Avionics Ltd Unit C, Airport Executive Park President Way, LUTON, LU2 9NY.
BENNETT, Mr. Anthony David, BA ACA *1990;* Ladova 460, 273 45 HREBEC, CZECH REPUBLIC.
BENNETT, Mr. Anthony Herbert Mansel, PhD MSc BSc FCA *1958;* 23 Barn Way, Wembley Park, WEMBLEY, HA9 9NT. (Life Member)
BENNETT, Mr. Anthony Joseph, FCA *1972;* Furnace Place, Killinghurst Lane, HASLEMERE, SURREY, GU27 2EJ.
BENNETT, Mr. Barrie John Arthur, FCA *1951;* 316 Blossomfield Road, SOLIHULL, B91 1TF. (Life Member)
BENNETT, Mrs. Bethan, BSc ACA *2003;* 28 Maynard Terrace, Clutton, BRISTOL, BS39 5PW.
BENNETT, Mr. Bruce Leonard, MA ACA *1993;* 39 Ramsbury Road, ST. ALBANS, HERTFORDSHIRE, AL1 1SN.
BENNETT, Mr. Calum John, BA FCA *1995;* (Tax Fac), Smiths Consulting Ltd Fabriam Centre, Cobalt Business Exchange Cobalt Park Way, WALLSEND, TYNE AND WEAR, NE28 9NZ.
BENNETT, Mrs. Carol Heather, FCA *1976;* The Oaks, Exeter Road, TEIGNMOUTH, DEVON, TQ14 9JG.
•BENNETT, Mrs. Catherine, BSc(Hons) ACA *2005;* Catherine Bennett, 6 Green Lane, Redruth, CORNWALL, TR15 1JT.
BENNETT, Mrs. Christine Margaret, BSc FCA *1976;* 5 Admirals Walk, ST. ALBANS, AL1 5SH.
BENNETT, Mr. Christopher Edwin, MA ACA *1979;* Ruelle de l'Eglise 10, CH 1143 APPLES, SWITZERLAND.
BENNETT, Mr. Christopher James Philip, BSc(Hons) ACA *2010;* 48 Maldon Road, BRIGHTON, BN1 5BE.
BENNETT, Mr. Christopher John, BA ACA *1991;* 27 Sundew Road, HEMEL HEMPSTEAD, HERTFORDSHIRE, HP1 2DQ.
BENNETT, Mr. Christopher Mark, BSc ACA *1992;* 125 Old Broad Street, D T Z Debenham Tie Leung, PO Box 274, LONDON, EC2N 2BQ.
BENNETT, Mr. Christopher Midwood, FCA *1971;* 7 Pool Drive, BRIDGNORTH, WV16 5DL.
•BENNETT, Mr. Christopher Richard Edward, FCA *1963;* Christopher Bennett, Summer Pool Meadow, High Street, Bramley, GUILDFORD, SURREY GU5 0HB.
BENNETT, Mr. Clive Frank, FCA *1968;* Pine Lodge, Church Hill, Kingswear, DARTMOUTH, DEVON, TQ6 0BX. (Life Member)
BENNETT, Mr. Damian Jonathan, BSc ACA *1997;* 2 Newhall Cottages, Stocks Lane, Over Peover, KNUTSFORD, CHESHIRE, WA16 9HA.
BENNETT, Mrs. Danielle Louise, BA(Hons) ACA *2002;* Val Claret, Juas Lane, Vale, GUERNSEY, GY3 5RB.
BENNETT, Mr. David, MA FCA *1973;* 63 Pasture Close, SWINDON, SN2 2UJ.
•BENNETT, Mr. David Alastair, BA FCA CTA *1988;* (Tax Fac), Moore and Smalley LLP, Priory Close, St Mary's Gate, LANCASTER, LA1 1XB.
•BENNETT, Mr. David Anthony, BA FCA *1978;* (Tax Fac), David Bennett BA FCA, 46 Old Wool Lane, Cheadle Hulme, CHEADLE, CHESHIRE, SK8 5JA.
BENNETT, Mr. David Christopher, BA FCA *1976;* The Old School House, Ley Green, Kings Walden, HITCHIN, HERTFORDSHIRE, SG4 8LX.
BENNETT, Mr. David John, FCA *1975;* 40 Long Park, Chesham Bois, AMERSHAM, HP6 5LA.
•BENNETT, Mr. David John, BA ACA *1984;* (Tax Fac), 21 Highnam Business Centre, Highnam, GLOUCESTER, GL2 8DN.
BENNETT, Mr. David John, FCA *1975;* Timberly House, Moreton-on-lugg, HEREFORD, HR4 8DQ.
•BENNETT, Mr. David Paul, FCA *1982;* (Tax Fac), Whitakers, Bryndon House, 5-7 Berry Road, NEWQUAY, TR7 1AD.
BENNETT, Mr. David Richard, BA ACA *1992;* 5 Canterbury Park, Didsbury, MANCHESTER, M20 2UQ.
BENNETT, Miss. Dawn Marie, BSc ACA *2007;* 59 Arcot Park, SIDMOUTH, EX10 9HT.
BENNETT, Mr. Derek Basil, FCA *1952;* 18 Russell Road, West Wittering, CHICHESTER, WEST SUSSEX, PO20 8EF. (Life Member)
BENNETT, Mr. Derek Clinton, FCA *1960;* 38 Westfield Road, Edgbaston, BIRMINGHAM, B15 3QG. (Life Member)
BENNETT, Mr. Derek John, FCA *1974;* Founders Insurance Consultants, 855 Laguna Drive, FERNANDINA BEACH, FL 32034, UNITED STATES.
BENNETT, Miss. Diane Rosemary, ACA *1983;* H E Simm & Son, Spinnaker House, 141 Sefton Street, Toxteth, LIVERPOOL, L8 5SN.
BENNETT, Mr. Dougal, BA BSc(Hons) ACA *2011;* K P M G Llp, 15 Canada Square, LONDON, E14 5GL.
BENNETT, Mr. Douglas William, FCA *1970;* 19 Offas Green, Norton, PRESTEIGNE, POWYS, LD8 2NX.
BENNETT, Mr. Douglas William Warburton, FCA *1959;* Heathersett, Downsview Road, Headley Down, BORDON, GU35 8JH. (Life Member)
BENNETT, Miss. Emma Jane, BA ACA *2001;* Newsquest Media Group Ltd, 58 Church Street, WEYBRIDGE, SURREY, KT13 8DP.
BENNETT, Ms. Fiona Rosalyn Vivienne, BA ACA *1981;* PO Box 9083, Were Street, BRIGHTON, VIC 3186, AUSTRALIA.
BENNETT, Miss. Frances, MEng ACA *2005;* Flat 63, Percy Laurie House, 217 Upper Richmond Road, Putney, LONDON, SW15 6SY.
BENNETT, Mr. Gary Roger, BA(Hons) ACA *2000;* 14 Chapel Lane, LEICESTER, LE2 3WE.
BENNETT, Mr. Geoffrey, FCA *1967;* Toad Hole Stables, Toad Lane, Epperstone, NOTTINGHAM, NG14 6AJ.
BENNETT, Mrs. Gillian Mary, BA ACA *1995;* Aviva UK, 2 Rougier Street, YORK, YO90 1UU.
BENNETT, Mr. Gordon, BSc FCA *1974;* 16 Sandgate Lane, LONDON, SW18 3JP.
BENNETT, Mr. Gordon Scott, BSc ACA *1999;* Spectron Gas & Electricity Ltd, 4-5 Grosvenor Place, LONDON, SW1X 7DL.
BENNETT, Mr. Graham Cyril, FCA *1959;* 21 The Rise, Llanishen, CARDIFF, CF14 0RB. (Life Member)
BENNETT, Mr. Graham David, FCA *1961;* 17A Montpellier Villas, CHELTENHAM, GL50 2XE.
BENNETT, Mr. Graham John, FCA *1953;* 13 Buckingham Grove, KINGSWINFORD, DY6 9ED. (Life Member)
BENNETT, Mr. Graham Vine, BA ACA *1988;* Y.B.A. KANOO, P.O. Box 45, MANAMA, BAHRAIN.
BENNETT, Mr. Gregory Nicholas Brian, BA ACA *1994;* 19 Astell Street, LONDON, SW3 3RT.
BENNETT, Mr. Guy Matthew, BSc(Hons) ACA *2008;* 27 Lyndale Road, Eldwick, BINGLEY, BD16 3HE.
•BENNETT, Mr. Harry, FCA *1973;* (Tax Fac), H. Bennett, East Park, Woodland Road, ST AUSTELL, CORNWALL, PL25 4QZ.
BENNETT, Miss. Hazel Ann, BSc ACA *1985;* Unit 404, 19 Cadigal Avenue, Pyrmont, SYDNEY, NSW 2000, AUSTRALIA.
BENNETT, Mrs. Helen Mary, BSc FCA *1977;* Hurst Hill Churt Road, HINDHEAD, GU26 6HT.
BENNETT, Mr. Ian Lewis, BA ACA *2002;* Tilney Investment Management, Royal Liver Building Pier Head, LIVERPOOL, L3 1NY.
•BENNETT, Mr. Ian Malcolm, FCA *1976;* 77 Appledore Crescent, SIDCUP, KENT, DA14 6RG.
BENNETT, Mr. Ian Rhys, BSc ACA *2002;* with PricewaterhouseCoopers, Darling Park Tower 2, 201 Sussex Street, GPO Box 2650, SYDNEY, NSW 1171 AUSTRALIA.
BENNETT, Mrs. Jacqueline Ann, BSc ACA *1990;* The White House, Partridge Lane, Newdigate, DORKING, SURREY, RH5 5EE.
BENNETT, Mr. James Hywel, BSc ACA *2002;* 77 Britten Road, SWINDON, SN25 2HQ.
BENNETT, Mr. James Ogilvy John, BA ACA *1994;* Kingswood Farm Kingswood, Stogumber, TAUNTON, SOMERSET, TA4 3TP.
BENNETT, Mrs. Jane Marie, BA FCA *1991;* 88 Ings Road, REDCAR, CLEVELAND, TS10 2DF.
BENNETT, Mr. Jason, BSc ACA *2010;* 71 Berwick Road, MARLOW, BUCKINGHAMSHIRE, SL7 3AS.
•BENNETT, Mr. Jason Spenser, MSc BA FCA *1999;* Kleinman Graham, Turnberry House, 1404 -1410 High Road, Whetstone, LONDON, N20 9BH. See also Howard Frank Limited and Graham Kleinman
BENNETT, Mr. Jeffrey Simon, FCA *1979;* Burlington Associates Ltd, 61 Cheapside, LONDON, EC2V 6AX.
BENNETT, Mrs. Jennifer Priscilla, ACA *1991;* 145 Blackdown View, ILMINSTER, SOMERSET, TA19 0BG.
BENNETT, Mrs. Joanne, BA ACA *1988;* 27 Warwick Road, LONDON, W5 3XH.
BENNETT, Miss. Joanne Clare, ACA *2002;* The Tall Barn, 407 Walton Road, WEST MOLESEY, SURREY, KT8 2EG.
•BENNETT, Mr. John, BSc FCA *1983;* RSM Tenon Audit Limited, Cedar House, Breckland, Linford Wood, MILTON KEYNES, MK14 6EX.
BENNETT, Mr. John, BSc FCA *1997;* The Financial Training Co Ltd Cotton House, Old Hall Street, LIVERPOOL, L3 9TP.
BENNETT, Mr. John Alfred, MA FCA *1970;* 29 Kenilworth Road, LONDON, W5 5PA. (Life Member)
BENNETT, Mr. John Charles Quentin, PhD ACA *2004;* 2 Thorpe Gardens, ALTON, HAMPSHIRE, GU34 2BQ.
BENNETT, Mr. John Edward, BA(Hons) ACA *2001;* 5 Ramsey Lodge Court, Hillside Road, ST. ALBANS, HERTFORDSHIRE, AL1 3QY.
BENNETT, Mr. John Edward Nicholas, BA ACA *1986;* 55 Southlands Drive, West Cross, SWANSEA, SA3 5RJ.
BENNETT, Mr. John Henry, FCA *1970;* Sandiford House, Van Diemens Lane, BATH, BA1 5TW.
•BENNETT, Mr. John Stuart, FCA *1969;* (Tax Fac), Southfield Bungalow, Kippax Lane End, Garforth, LEEDS, LS25 2AA.
BENNETT, Mr. John Watson, FCA *1967;* The Barn, Hazel Bank, Rosthwaite, KESWICK, CA12 5XB.
BENNETT, Mr. Jonathan James Albion, BSc ACA *1992;* 147 Fordham Avenue, CAMBERWELL, VIC 3124, AUSTRALIA.
BENNETT, Mrs. Judith Claire, FCA *1975;* 11 Woodford Way, WITNEY, OXFORDSHIRE, OX28 6GF.
BENNETT, Miss. Judith Helen, BA ACA *1995;* 9 Bassett Drive, REIGATE, SURREY, RH2 9JT.
BENNETT, Mrs. Julia Claire, BA ACA *1997;* 42 Portland Road, Edgbaston, BIRMINGHAM, B16 9HU.
BENNETT, Mrs. Julia Lesley, BA ACA *1987;* Hedderly House, Old Boars Hill, OXFORD, OXFORDSHIRE, OX1 5JQ.
BENNETT, Mr. Julian Philip, BSc ACA *1987;* Sunnyview, Lower Meend, St Briavels, LYDNEY, GLOUCESTERSHIRE, GL15 6RJ.
BENNETT, Mrs. Kathryn Jean, BSc ACA *1993;* 31 Cricketers Approach, Wrenthorpe, WAKEFIELD, WEST YORKSHIRE, WF2 0JH.
BENNETT, Mr. Keith, FCA *1966;* Thornhill, Linton Common, Linton, WETHERBY, LS22 4JD. (Life Member)
BENNETT, Mr. Keith Lester, FCA *1953;* 17 Grove Park, Wanstead, LONDON, E11 2DN. (Life Member)
BENNETT, Mr. Leonard James, FCA *1956;* 14 Rosedale, ASHTEAD, KT21 2JJ. (Life Member)
BENNETT, Mrs. Lesley, BSc ACA *1982;* 56 Court Meadow, Stone, BERKELEY, GL13 9LR.
BENNETT, Mrs. Lisa Rosamund, BSc FCA *1994;* 2 Buttercup Close, Groby, LEICESTER, LE6 0AY.
BENNETT, Mrs. Lisako, BA(Hons) ACA *2003;* 40 Bewley Street, LONDON, SW19 1XD.
•BENNETT, Mr. Luke Mervyn, FCA *1987;* Winter Rule LLP, Lowin House, Tregolls Road, TRURO, CORNWALL, TR1 2NA. See also Francis Clark LLP
•BENNETT, Mr. Lyndon Paul Hargreaves, MA FCA *1963;* L.P.H. Bennett, 11 Daisy Road, HILTON, KWAZULU NATAL, 3245, SOUTH AFRICA.

•BENNETT, Mr. Marc Stephen, BA(Hons) FCA FFA 1992; (Tax Fac), AEL Partners LLP, 2nd Floor, 201 Haverstock Hill, LONDON, NW3 4QG.
BENNETT, Mrs. Marina Lilian Alexandra, BSc ACA 1993; 99 Chaplin Crescent, TORONTO M5P 1A4, ON, CANADA.
BENNETT, Mr. Mark Ian, FCA 1977; 6 Muirfield Close, Holmer, HEREFORD, HR1 1QB.
BENNETT, Mr. Mark Richard, BSc ACA 2002; 20 Deller Street, Binfield, BRACKNELL, BERKSHIRE, RG42 4UU.
BENNETT, Mr. Mark Robert, BSc ACA 1989; Milliken Industrials Limited, Beech Hill Plant, Gidlow Lane, WIGAN, WN6 8RN.
BENNETT, Mr. Martin David, BA FCA 1975; 27a Napleton Lane, Kempsey, WORCESTER, WR5 3PT.
BENNETT, Mr. Martin John, BCom FCA 1995; St. Peters Manor, St. Peters Church Lane, DROITWICH, WORCESTERSHIRE, WR9 7AN.
•BENNETT, Mr. Matthew, BSc ACA 2005; Coveney Nicholls Limited, The Old Wheel House, 31/37 Church Street, REIGATE, RH2 0AD.
BENNETT, Mr. Matthew, ACA 2011; 13 Broxholm Road, Heaton, NEWCASTLE UPON TYNE, NE6 5RL.
BENNETT, Mr. Matthew Edward, BA(Hons) ACA 2001; 22 Oaks Way, Long Ditton, SURBITON, SURREY, KT6 5DS.
BENNETT, Mr. Michael Christopher, BSc ACA 1986; 20A Nim Green, SINGAPORE 807640, SINGAPORE.
BENNETT, Mr. Michael John Raymond, FCA 1966; Fernecumbe House, Sherbourne Hill, WARWICK, CV35 8AG.
BENNETT, Mr. Michael Karl, ACA 2009; Flat 2/A Campden Mansions, 9 Kensington Mall, LONDON, W8 4DU.
BENNETT, Mr. Michael Peter, FCA 1981; Unite Group Plc The Core, 40 St. Thomas Street, BRISTOL, BS1 6JX.
BENNETT, Miss. Michelle, ACA 2010; Rawlinson & Hunter, The Lower Mill, Kingston Road, EPSOM, SURREY, KT17 2AE.
BENNETT, Mrs. Michelle Lee-Ann, BSc ACA 2004; 11 Horner Avenue, Fradley, LICHFIELD, WS13 8TR.
•BENNETT, Mr. Nicholas Brian, MA ACA 1990; Scott-Moncrieff, Exchange Place 3, Semple Street, EDINBURGH, EH3 8BL.
BENNETT, Mrs. Nicola Tracey, BA ACA 1991; 32 Hallhead Road, EDINBURGH, EH16 5QJ.
•BENNETT, Mr. Nigel Andrew, FCA 1992; Glover Stanbury & Co, 30 Bear Street, BARNSTAPLE, DEVON, EX32 7DD.
•BENNETT, Mr. Nigel David, BA FCA 1986; Hallidays LLP, Riverside House, Kings Reach Business Park, Yew Street, STOCKPORT, CHESHIRE SK4 2HD. See also Hallidays Accountants LLP
BENNETT, Mr. Nigel Gordon, MA FCA 1975; 4921 N Bell Ave, CHICAGO, IL 60625, UNITED STATES.
BENNETT, Mr. Owen Michael, ACA 2008; 9 Capilano Park, Aughton, ORMSKIRK, L39 5HA.
BENNETT, Mrs. Patricia, BA ACA 1986; 54 Sturdee Gardens, High West Jesmond, NEWCASTLE UPON TYNE, NE2 3QT.
•BENNETT, Mr. Paul, BA FCA 1982; David Owen & Co, 17 Market Place, DEVIZES, SN10 1BA.
BENNETT, Mr. Paul, BEng ACA 1996; 15 Devonport Close, Walton Le Dale, PRESTON, PR5 4LW.
BENNETT, Mr. Paul David, BA ACA 1986; with PricewaterhouseCoopers, 1 Embankment Place, LONDON, WC2N 6RH.
BENNETT, Mr. Paul John, ACA 2009; 20 Radcliffe Road, WINSFORD, CHESHIRE, CW7 1RE.
BENNETT, Mr. Paul John, BA FCA 1985; 4 Chirton Walk, WOKING, GU21 3RD.
BENNETT, Mr. Paul Michael, BSc ACA CISA 1993; 3 Park Lane, Harvington, KIDDERMINSTER, WORCESTERSHIRE, DY10 4LW.
BENNETT, Mr. Paul Michael, BSc ACA 2010; 57 Park Terrace, Stump Cross, HALIFAX, WEST YORKSHIRE, HX3 7AF.
BENNETT, Mr. Paul Richard, BA FCA 1996; with Grant Thornton UK LLP, Enterprise House, 115 Edmund Street, BIRMINGHAM, B3 2HJ.
BENNETT, Mr. Paul St John, MA FCA ATII 1987; 2 Townfield Road, WIRRAL, MERSEYSIDE, CH48 7EZ.
BENNETT, Mr. Paul William John, BSc FCA 1978; 9 Hadrian Way, Corfe Mullen, WIMBORNE, DORSET, BH21 3XF.
BENNETT, Mr. Peter Edwin, LLB ACA 2003; 148 Chester Road, ILFORD, ESSEX, IG3 8PY.
BENNETT, Mr. Peter George, FCA 1969; Ashridge Cottage, Pebblemoor, Edlesborough, DUNSTABLE, LU6 2HZ. (Life Member)
BENNETT, Mr. Peter John, FCA 1972; 7 Hurley House, 70 Broom Rd, TEDDINGTON, TW11 9NP. (Life Member)
BENNETT, Mr. Peter John, FCA 1957; 19 Falkland Drive, NEWBURY, RG14 6JQ. (Life Member)
BENNETT, Mr. Peter Richard, FCA 1967; The Penthouse The Mansion, Ottershaw Park, Ottershaw, CHERTSEY, KT16 0QG. (Life Member)
BENNETT, Mr. Philip Edward, ACA 2008; 35 Highfield Road, West Bridgford, NOTTINGHAM, NG2 6DR.
BENNETT, Mr. Phillip James, BSc ACA 1993; 38 Elm Street, Borrowash, DERBY, DE72 3HP.
BENNETT, Mr. Piers Antony, BA ACA 1989; Whitehaven, Oldwich Lane West, Chadwick End, SOLIHULL, B93 0BQ.
BENNETT, Mr. Richard Charles, BSc ACA 2001; 45a Adelaide Road, SURBITON, KT6 4SR.
BENNETT, Mr. Richard John Jacques, BSc FCA 1976; 37 Woodhill Road, COLWYN BAY, CLWYD, LL29 7ES.
BENNETT, Mr. Richard Vaughan, BSc FCA 1986; 30 Boltons Lane Binfield, BRACKNELL, BERKSHIRE, RG42 4UB.
BENNETT, Mr. Robert Boyd, BSc FCA 1990; Alcentra Ltd, 10 Gresham Street, LONDON, EC2V 7JD.
•BENNETT, Mr. Robert Charles, FCA 1955; Robert C. Bennett, Willow House, 69 Ridgeway Road, Long Ashton, BRISTOL, BS41 9EZ.
•BENNETT, Mr. Robert Frederick, FCA 1970; The Granary, Foggett Farm, HEXHAM, NE46 1YB.
BENNETT, Mr. Robert Geoffrey, FCA 1970; 10 Barricane, St Johns, WOKING, SURREY, GU21 7RB.
BENNETT, Mr. Robin Thomas Hendley, OBE FCA 1966; Hyatt Tower III, 1033 Izmir Street, BAKU AZ1065, AZERBAIJAN.
BENNETT, Mr. Roger, FCA 1964; 7 Meadow Heights, St. Owens Cross, HEREFORD, HR2 8NP. (Life Member)
BENNETT, Mr. Roger, FCA 1966; 10 Normanton Avenue, BOGNOR REGIS, WEST SUSSEX, PO21 2TX.
BENNETT, Mr. Roger Andrew, BA ACA 1989; 10-14, Duke Street, READING, RG1 4RU.
BENNETT, Mr. Roland Sinclair, ACA 1992; 1325 Powers Run Road, PITTSBURGH, PA 15238, UNITED STATES.
BENNETT, Mr. Ronald Wallace, FCA 1960; The Fields, St. Briavels Common, LYDNEY, GL15 6SW. (Life Member)
•BENNETT, Mrs. Roseanne Marie, BSc ACA 2007; Greaves West & Ayre, 1-3 Sandgate, BERWICK-UPON-TWEED, TD15 1EW.
BENNETT, Mr. Russell, BSc ACA 1999; C/O Gulf International Bank, 3 Palace Avenue, PO Box 1017, MANAMA, BAHRAIN.
BENNETT, Mrs. Ruth, BA(Hons) ACA 2002; Cancer Research UK, Robinson Way, CAMBRIDGE, CB2 0RE.
BENNETT, Mr. Ryan Philip, LLB ACA 2000; with BDO LLP, 125 Colmore Row, BIRMINGHAM, B3 3SD.
BENNETT, Miss. Sandiya, BSc ACA 2004; 1827 N Sedgwick, CHICAGO, IL 60614, UNITED STATES.
BENNETT, Miss. Sarah Elizabeth, BA AIBA FCA 1989; (Tax Fac), 22 Eastway, SALE, CHESHIRE, M33 4DX.
BENNETT, Miss. Sarah Ruth, BA ACA 1991; 16 Foxcote, WOKINGHAM, BERKSHIRE, RG40 3PE.
BENNETT, Mr. Sean Douglas, BSc ACA 1996; Postnet Suite 256, Private Bag X 87, Bryanston, JOHANNESBURG, 2021, SOUTH AFRICA.
•BENNETT, Mr. Simon Charles, ACA 1981; Fairfax I S Plc, 46 Berkeley Square, LONDON, W1J 5AT.
BENNETT, Mr. Simon Miles, BA ACA 1992; 78 Ottways Lane, ASHTEAD, SURREY, KT21 2PW.
•BENNETT, Mr. Simon Russell, BSc FCA 1993; The Hutchinson Partnership Limited, The Bull Pen, Amberley Court, Sutton St. Nicholas, HEREFORD, HR1 3BX.
BENNETT, Mr. Stephen Gerard, BA ACA 1981; 2 Linden Grove, MATLOCK, DE4 3EN.
BENNETT, Mr. Stephen Guy, BSc ACA 1991; Ridge House, Beaulieu Road, LYNDHURST, HAMPSHIRE, SO43 7DA.
BENNETT, Mr. Stephen Robert, BSc FCA 1988; 19 Hatherden Drive, Walmley, SUTTON COLDFIELD, B76 2RB.
•BENNETT, Mr. Stephen Scott, FCA 1969; Buckingham Corporate Finance Limited, 57A Catherine Place, LONDON, SW1E 6DY.
BENNETT, Mr. Steven John, ACA 1982; Stocks Farm Swan Lane, Leigh, SWINDON, SN6 6RD.
•ⓓBENNETT, Mr. Stewart Trevor, FCA 1975; S T Bennett & Co, 36 Bracken Drive, CHIGWELL, ESSEX, IG7 5RF.
BENNETT, Mrs. Susan Elizabeth, BSc ACA 1991; 3A Church Lane, Bisbrooke, OAKHAM, LE15 9EL.
BENNETT, Mrs. Susan Meriel, FCA 1959; 8 Westminster Close, Hartford, NORTHWICH, CHESHIRE, CW8 1GQ.
BENNETT, Mrs. Suzanne, BA ACA 1992; 148 Hawthorne Way, Shelley, HUDDERSFIELD, HD8 8PX.
BENNETT, Mr. Sydney Roy, FCA 1966; The Moorings, Chapel Hill, Gweek, CORNWALL, TR12 7AE. (Life Member)
BENNETT, Mr. Terry Curtis, BSc ACA 1996; D, 72 Randolph Avenue, LONDON, W9 1BG.
BENNETT, Mr. Thomas, ACA 2011; 115 Stainburn Crescent, Moortown, LEEDS, LS17 6NQ.
•BENNETT, Mr. Thomas, ACA 1981; Towers & Gornall, Suites 5 & 6, The Printworks, Hey Road, Barrow, CLITHEROE LANCASHIRE BB7 9WB.
BENNETT, Mr. Timothy John, MA ACA 1994; 40b-40c Lavender Gardens, LONDON, SW11 1DN.
BENNETT, Mr. Timothy John, FCA 1978; Lowena Homes Ltd Unit 1 Lowena House Glenthorne Court, Truro Business Park Threemilestone, TRURO, CORNWALL, TR4 9NY.
BENNETT, Mrs. Tracy Anne, BCom ACA 1998; Croft Cottage, 22 Horsepool, Burbage, HINCKLEY, LEICESTERSHIRE, LE10 2DH.
•BENNETT, Mr. Vaughan William, FCA 1976; 21 Fownhope Road, SALE, CHESHIRE, M33 4RF.
•BENNETT, Mr. William Lloyd, FCA 1970; Baker Tilly Isle of Man LLC, PO Box 95, 2a Lord Street, Douglas, ISLE OF MAN, IM99 1HP. See also Baker Tilly Bennett Roy LLC
BENNETT-BAGGS, Mr. Charles Martin, FCA 1976; Weldtite Products Ltd, Unit 9 Harrier Road, Humber Bridge Industrial Estate, BARTON-UPON-HUMBER, SOUTH HUMBERSIDE, DN18 5RP.
BENNETT-BLACKLOCK, Miss. Nicola Caroline, BA ACA 2006; Crosshorn Shelderton, Clungunford, CRAVEN ARMS, SHROPSHIRE, SY7 0PD.
BENNETTS, Miss. Anne, ACA 2008; PO Box 905, GEORGETOWN, KY1-1103, CAYMAN ISLANDS.
BENNETTS, Mr. David Hugh, FCA 1958; Pol Brandy, The Ropewalk, Penpol, Devoran, TRURO, TR3 6NS. (Life Member)
BENNETTS, Mrs. Geraldine Patricia, BSc ACA 1980; 27 Kinghorn Park, MAIDENHEAD, SL6 7TX.
BENNETTS, Miss. Katie Alison, BA ACA 2010; 27 Kinghorn Park, MAIDENHEAD, SL6 7TX.
BENNETTS, Miss. Nicola Jane, BSc(Econ) ACA 1996; 103/67 Carabella Street, Kirribilli, SYDNEY, NSW 2061, AUSTRALIA.
•BENNETTS, Mr. Peter Lawrence, FCA 1978; (Tax Fac), Peter Bennetts Ltd, 51 Albert Street, LONDON, NW1 7LX.
BENNETTS, Mr. Stephen Roy, ACA 1979; 27 Kinghorn Park, MAIDENHEAD, SL6 7TX.
•BENNEWITH, Mr. Anthony John, FCA FFA FRSA 1968; MEMBER OF COUNCIL, (Tax Fac), A.J. Bennewith & Co., Hitherbury House, 97 Portsmouth Road, GUILDFORD, GU2 4YF.
BENNEWITH, Mr. John William, FCA 1959; 13 Parkway, EASTBOURNE, EAST SUSSEX, BN20 9DX. (Life Member)
•BENNEY, Mr. Paul, ACA 2009; (Tax Fac), St James Consultancy, 1 Emperor Way, Exeter Business Park, EXETER, DEVON, EX1 3QS.
•BENNEYWORTH, Mr. John Ernest, FCA 1965; J.E. Benneyworth, 7 Broome Close, YATELEY, GU46 7SY.
•BENNEYWORTH, Mrs. Rebecca Anne, BSc FCA 1981; (Tax Fac), Rebecca Benneyworth, Woodhouse, Rodborough Lane, Rodborough, STROUD, GL5 2LN.
BENNFORS, Mr. Ulf Peter Dundas, BSc ACA 1987; 65 Garfield Avenue, MADISON, NJ 07940, UNITED STATES.
BENNIE, Miss. Anne Bridges, LLB ACA 1990; Lilac Cottage, Westerfield Road, Westerfield, IPSWICH, IP6 9AJ.
BENNIE, Miss. Giselle, BSc ACA 1996; with PricewaterhouseCoopers LLP, 1 Embankment Place, LONDON, WC2N 6RH.
BENNIE, Mr. Robert Edward, BA ACA 2009; 2 Meadows Croft, West Bradford, CLITHEROE, LANCASHIRE, BB7 4TJ.
BENNING-PRINCE, Mr. Nicholas Arthur Dawe, LLB ACA CTA 2001; Hanson UK, Hanson House, 14 Castle Hill, MAIDENHEAD, BERKSHIRE, SL6 4JJ.
BENNINGTON, Mr. David John, FCA 1958; 29 Morford Way, Eastcote, RUISLIP, HA4 8SL. (Life Member)
BENNINGTON, Mr. Ian James, BSc ACA 2003; 11 Little Ox, Colwick, NOTTINGHAM, NG4 2DA.
BENNION, Mr. Matthew James, BA ACA 1997; Careks Lodge The Street, Shotesham All Saints, NORWICH, NR15 1YW.
BENNISON, Miss. Ann, ACA 2008; 19 King Edward Street, HALIFAX, HX1 1BW.
BENNISON, Mr. George Michael, FCA 1976; 100 Ridgeway, Wrose, SHIPLEY, WEST YORKSHIRE, BD18 1PN.
BENNISON, Mrs. Joanna Louise, BSc FCA 1993; 31 Festing Road, LONDON, SW15 1LW.
BENNISON, Mr. Matthew Edward, BA ACA 1998; Copthorne, Marton cum Grafton, YORK, YO51 9QJ.
BENNISON, Mr. Peter Andrew, BSc ACA 2005; 48 Kipling Drive, Wimbledon, LONDON, SW19 1TW.
•BENNISON, Mr. Richard, FCA 1981; KPMG LLP, 15 Canada Square, LONDON, E14 5GL. See also KPMG Europe LLP, KPMG Audit plc, KPMG Holding plc
BENNY, Mr. Paul Andrew, BSc FCA 1988; 19 Goughs Lane, KNUTSFORD, WA16 8QL.
BENOSIGLIO, Mr. Adrian Howard, MSc BA(Econ) ACA CTA 1996; (Tax Fac), with BDO LLP, 55 Baker Street, LONDON, W1U 7EU.
•BENOSIGLIO, Mr. Anthony Ivor, BSc ACA 1987; Goldwins Limited, 75 Maygrove Road, West Hampstead, LONDON, NW6 2EG.
BENOSIGLIO, Miss. Lisa Vanessa, BSc(Econ) ACA 1996; with BDO LLP, 55 Baker Street, LONDON, W1U 7EU.
•BENOY, Mr. William Oscar Robin, BSc ACA 1993; (Tax Fac), Morris & Co (2011) Limited, Chester House, Lloyd Drive, Chesire Oaks Business Park, ELLESMERE PORT, CHESHIRE CH65 9HQ.
BENSELIN, Mr. Adrian Gerard, BA ACA 1982; Rivermead House, 7 Lewis Court, Grove Park, Enderby, LEICESTER, LE19 1SD.
BENSI, Mr. Marco, BA ACA 1999; 50 Chestnut Grove, Balham, LONDON, SW12 8JJ.
BENSON, Mr. Adrian Kevin, BSc ACA 2007; 90 Kentsford Road, GRANGE-OVER-SANDS, CUMBRIA, LA11 7BB.
BENSON, Mr. Andrew, ACA 2009; 30 Norfolk Place, PENRITH, CUMBRIA, CA11 9BE.
BENSON, Mrs. Anita Julie Sheelagh, BA ACA 1982; (Tax Fac), 32 Charles Crescent, Lenzie Kirkintilloch, GLASGOW, G66 5HG.
BENSON, Miss. Annie, LLB ACA 2005; Transport for London Windsor House, 42-50 Victoria Street, LONDON, SW1H 0TL.
BENSON, Mrs. Cynthia Sin Yi, BSc ACA 1988; (Tax Fac), Flat 12/F Hyde Park Mansions Cabbell Street, LONDON, NW1 5BB.
BENSON, Mr. David, ACA 2011; K P M G, Salisbury Square House, 8 Salisbury Square, LONDON, EC4Y 8BB.
BENSON, Mr. David Clayton, FCA 1965; 5 Greenhill Road, Wylde Green, SUTTON COLDFIELD, B72 1DS.
BENSON, Mr. David Henry, FCA 1968; 20 Longmeads, Rusthall, TUNBRIDGE WELLS, TN3 0AX. (Life Member)
BENSON, Mr. David John, BSc ACA 1990; Extra Care Charitable Trust Abbey Park, Humber Road, COVENTRY, CV3 4AQ.
BENSON, Mr. David Neville, BSc ACA 1997; Keller Group Plc Capital House, 25 Chapel Street, LONDON, NW1 5DH.
BENSON, Mrs. Eileen Joan, FCA 1960; 31 West Park Avenue, Roundhay, LEEDS, LS8 2EB. (Life Member)
BENSON, Miss. Elizabeth Ann, ACA 2008; 316 Molesey Road, Hersham, WALTON-ON-THAMES, KT12 4SQ.
BENSON, Miss. Elizabeth Jane, BSc ACA 2000; 32 Manchester Road, WILMSLOW, SK9 1BG.
BENSON, Miss. Felicity Margaret Mary, BSc FCA 1978; E F G Private Bank, Leconfield House, Curzon Street, LONDON, W1J 5JB.
•BENSON, Mr. Frank, FCA 1977; Frank Benson, 199 Carr Lane, Tarleton, PRESTON, PR4 6BY.
BENSON, Mr. Gareth Paul, ACA 2008; with Armstrong Watson, Bute House, Montgomery Way, Rosehill, CARLISLE, CA1 2RW.
•BENSON, Mr. Geoffrey Alan, MA FCA 1980; Midsummer House, Chailey Rise, Clutton, CHESTER, CHESHIRE, CH3 9SL.
BENSON, Mr. Harry Peter Neville, CBE MC FCA 1946; The Gate House, Little Chesters Nursery Road, Walton-on-the-Hill, TADWORTH, KT20 7TX. (Life Member)
BENSON, Mr. Henry Charles, FCA 1973; 6/ 111 Jersey Road, WOOLLAHRA, NSW 2025, AUSTRALIA.
BENSON, Mr. James Peter, FCA 1975; The White House, Brockley, Nr Backwell, BRISTOL, BS48 3AU.

•**BENSON, Mr. John Alexander, FCA** *1989;* JBC Accountants Ltd, First Floor, Swift House, 26 Falcon Court, Preston Farm Industrial Estate, STOCKTON-ON-TEES CLEVELAND TS18 3TX.

BENSON, Mr. John Anthony, FCA *1957;* Woodleigh, Station Road, Hoghton, PRESTON, PR5 0DD. (Life Member)

•**BENSON, Mr. Laurence Michael, FCA** *1980;* Laurence Benson & Co, 19 Southerton Way, Shenley, RADLETT, HERTFORDSHIRE, WD7 9LJ.

BENSON, Miss. Lesley Margaret, MBA BSc ACA *1985;* 90 Andlers Ash Road, LISS, GU33 7LR.

BENSON, Mr. Mark Charles, BSc ACA *2003;* with PricewaterhouseCoopers, Darling Park Tower 2, 201 Sussex Street, GPO Box 2650, SYDNEY, NSW 1171 AUSTRALIA.

BENSON, Mr. Mark Henry, BEng FCA *1975;* 33 St Keyna Avenue, HOVE, BN3 4PN.

BENSON, Mr. Mark Peter, BA(Hons) ACA *2003;* W R Refrigeration Ltd, Bridge Park Plaza, Bridge Park Road, Thurmaston, LEICESTER, LE4 8BL.

•**BENSON, Mr. Matthew Duncan, BSc ACA** *1998;* Ernst & Young Gmbh, Mergenthaleralle 10-12, 65760 ESCHBORN, GERMANY. See also Ernst & Young Europe LLP

•**BENSON, Dr. Michael Gerard, ACA** *1991;* Murray Smith LLP, Darland House, 44 Winnington Hill, NORTHWICH, CHESHIRE, CW8 1AU.

•**BENSON, Mr. Michael Howard, FCA** *1973;* BSG Valentine, Lynton House, 7/12 Tavistock Square, LONDON, WC1H 9BQ.

•**BENSON, Mr. Neil Winston, OBE FCA** *1961;* Lewis Golden & Co, 40 Queen Anne Street, LONDON, W1G 9EL.

BENSON, Mrs. Patricia Jane, BA ACA *1979;* The White House, Brockley, Nr Backwell, BRISTOL, BS48 3AU.

BENSON, Mr. Paul Duncan, FCA *1973;* 4 Meadow Croft, Barkisland, HALIFAX, WEST YORKSHIRE, HX4 0FB.

BENSON, The Hon. Peter Macleod, LVO MA FCA *1965;* 2 King's Quay, Chelsea Harbour, LONDON, SW10 0UX.

•**BENSON, Mr. Robert Miles, ACA MAAT** *2004;* Mazars LLP, The Atrium, Park Street West, LUTON, LU1 3BE.

•**BENSON, Mr. Roger Scholes, FCA** *1954;* R.S. Benson, Bell Lane House, Bell Lane, Minchinhampton, STROUD, GL6 9BP.

BENSON, Mrs. Sally Jane, BSc ACA *1989;* 650 Yarm Road, Eaglescliffe, STOCKTON-ON-TEES, CLEVELAND, TS16 0DH.

•**BENSON, Mr. Simon Quinn, BSc ACA** *2002;* 8 Scott Street, HAMPTON EAST, VIC 3188, AUSTRALIA.

BENSON, Miss. Tinuade Abiodun Sylvia, BSc ACA *1999;* International Finance Corporation, 12th Floor, Millbank Tower, 21-24 Millbank, LONDON, SW1P 4QP.

BENSON COPE, Mrs. Jane, BSc ACA *1990;* The Forge, Piltdown, UCKFIELD, EAST SUSSEX, TN22 3XA.

BENSTEAD, Mr. Graham John, FCA *1957;* Gippeswyk, 44 Heathfield, ROYSTON, SG8 5BN. (Life Member)

BENSTEAD, Mr. William George Henry, FCA *1965;* 7 Bournemouth Road, Holland-on-Sea, CLACTON-ON-SEA, ESSEX, CO15 5TD.

BENSUSAN, Mr. Stuart Michael, BSc FCA *1975;* Rehov Shvo 3, Apt 2, MEVASSERET ZION, 90805, ISRAEL.

BENT, Mr. David Ross, ACA *1980;* 24218 Saint Edens Circle, WEST HILLS, CA 91307, UNITED STATES.

BENT, Mr. David Timothy, ACA *2001;* 36b Devonshire Road, LONDON, SE23 3SR.

BENT, Miss. Katherine Sarah, BA(Hons) ACA *2006;* 1 Rushes Lane, Lubenham, MARKET HARBOROUGH, LEICESTERSHIRE, LE16 9TN.

BENT, Mr. Simon James, BA(Hons) ACA *2002;* CMGRP Pty Ltd, 166 William Street, WOOLLOOMOOLOO, NSW 2011, AUSTRALIA.

BENTALL, Mrs. Jane Elizabeth, BSc ACA *1998;* (Tax Fac), 1 Park Lane, HEMEL HEMPSTEAD, HP2 4YL.

BENTALL, Mr. Leonard Edward, DL FCA *1964;* Heneage Farm, Windlesham Road, Chobham, WOKING, SURREY, GU24 8QR. (Life Member)

•**BENTALL, Mr. Timothy Charles, BSc FCA** *1979;* with BDO LLP, Arcadia House, Maritime Walk, Ocean Village, SOUTHAMPTON, SO14 3TL.

BENTALL, Mr. William Edward Glen, ACA *2009;* Hillborough, Mill Lane, CHALFONT ST. GILES, BUCKINGHAMSHIRE, HP8 4NX.

BENTALL-LYNCH, Mrs. Rebecca, ACA *2007;* with National Audit Office, 157-197 Buckingham Palace Road, Victoria, LONDON, SW1W 9SP.

BENTATA, Mrs. Clare, LLB FCA *1999;* 280 Kidmore Road, Caversham, READING, RG4 7NF.

BENTHALL, Mr. Edward Anfrid Pringle, MA ACA *1989;* Little Dartmouth, DARTMOUTH, DEVON, TQ6 0JP.

BENTHAM, Mr. Alan, BA MCD ACA CMC FIBC *1986;* with Microguide CCC, Wyndham House, 82 Shortlands Road, KINGSTON UPON THAMES, SURREY, KT2 6HE.

BENTHAM, Mr. Eric, FCA *1953;* 90 Manor Drive, BINGLEY, BD16 1PN. (Life Member)

BENTHAM, Mr. Nicolas Peter, MPhil BSc(Hons) ACA *2002;* 11 Ridgewood Gardens, HARPENDEN, AL5 3NN.

•**BENTHAM, Mr. Peter Joseph, FCA** *1972;* Topping Partnership, 40 Church Street, LEIGH, WN7 1BB.

BENTHAM, Mr. Timothy Philip, BA ACA *1999;* 119 Henry st apt 1, BROOKLYN, NY 11201, UNITED STATES.

•**BENTHAM, Mrs. Tracey Norma, ACA** *1981;* PricewaterhouseCoopers LLP, 31 Great George Street, BRISTOL, BS1 5QD. See also PricewaterhouseCoopers

•**BENTLEY, Mr. Adrian Alan, BSc ACA** *1985;* E T Peirson & Sons, 21 The Point, Rockingham Road, MARKET HARBOROUGH, LEICESTERSHIRE, LE16 7NU.

BENTLEY, Mr. Alan William, FCA *1956;* with E T Peirson & Sons, 21 The Point, Rockingham Road, MARKET HARBOROUGH, LEICESTERSHIRE, LE16 7NU.

•**BENTLEY, Mrs. Amanda Jane, BSc ACA** *1992;* Brockhurst Davies Limited, 11 The Office Village, North Road, LOUGHBOROUGH, LEICESTERSHIRE, LE11 1QJ.

BENTLEY, Mr. Andrew David, ACA *1997;* 167 Liverpool Road, NEWCASTLE, STAFFORDSHIRE, ST5 9HF.

BENTLEY, Mr. Andrew James, LLB ACA *2001;* 4 Bury Mews, Bury Lane, RICKMANSWORTH, HERTFORDSHIRE, WD3 1FR.

BENTLEY, Mrs. Anne Susannah, BA ACA CPA *1990;* 9839 NE 33rd Street, BELLEVUE, WA 98004, UNITED STATES.

BENTLEY, Mr. Bruce Michael, BSc(Econ) FCA *1967;* 35 Hudson Road, Woodley, READING, RG5 4EN.

BENTLEY, Mr. Cameron, BA ACA *1995;* 26 Long Meadows, Burley in Wharfedale, ILKLEY, WEST YORKSHIRE, LS29 7RX.

BENTLEY, Mr. Christopher James, MA ACA *1990;* Holiday Break Plc Hartford Manor, Greenbank Lane, NORTHWICH, CHESHIRE, CW8 1HW.

BENTLEY, Mr. Christopher John, MA CA ACA *2006;* with PricewaterhouseCoopers LLP, 101 Barbirolli Square, Lower Mosley Street, MANCHESTER, M2 3PW.

BENTLEY, Miss. Claire, BSc ACA *1996;* 12 Graylands, Theydon Bois, EPPING, CM16 7LB.

BENTLEY, Mrs. Claire Amanda, BSc ACA *1994;* 6 Sawbrook, Fleckney, LEICESTER, LE8 8TR.

•**BENTLEY, Mr. David, BA FCA** *1999;* Wyatt Morris Golland & Co, Park House, 200 Drake Street, ROCHDALE, OL16 1PJ.

•**BENTLEY, Mr. David George, BA FCA** *1977;* with RSM Tenon Limited, 1 Hollinswood Court, Stafford Park 1, TELFORD, SHROPSHIRE, TF3 3DE.

BENTLEY, Mr. Douglas, MA BA(Hons) ACA *2011;* 7 Dart Close, ST. IVES, CAMBRIDGESHIRE, PE27 3JA.

BENTLEY, Miss. Gemma Elaine, BA(Hons) ACA *2003;* with KPMG LLP, 333 Bay Street, Suite 4600, TORONTO M5H 2S5, ON, CANADA.

BENTLEY, Mrs. Ginnette, BSc(Hons) FCA *2001;* 36 Cleveland Road, SUNDERLAND, SR4 7JR.

BENTLEY, Mr. Harold Gordon, MA FCA *1974;* 24 Brompton Road, KENSINGTON, NSW 2033, AUSTRALIA.

BENTLEY, Miss. Heather Rowena, BSc ACA *2010;* 33 Farleigh Road, WARLINGHAM, CR6 9EG.

BENTLEY, Mrs. Helen Margaret, BSc ACA *1984;* Ridge Cottage, 36 Ridgeway Tranmere Park, Guiseley, LEEDS, LS20 8JA.

BENTLEY, Mr. Ian Richard, BA(Hons) ACA *2003;* 58 Highfield Road, PURLEY, CR8 2JG.

BENTLEY, Mrs. Irene Elizabeth, LLB FCA *1981;* Pool House, Vicarage Lane, Little Budworth, TARPORLEY, CW6 9BY.

BENTLEY, Mrs. Isobel Ann, BA FCA *1978;* Long View, 151 Prestbury Road, MACCLESFIELD, CHESHIRE, SK10 3DF.

BENTLEY, Ms. Jennifer Elaine, MA ACA *1989;* 56 Eagle Wharf Court, 43 Lafone Street, LONDON, SE1 2LZ.

BENTLEY, Mr. Jeremy George, BA ACA *1995;* Four Oaks, Swan Lane, EDENBRIDGE, TN8 6BA.

BENTLEY, Mr. Jeremy Tudor Gregory, BA ACA *1996;* Comptons Lea Cottage, Comptons Brow Lane, HORSHAM, WEST SUSSEX, RH13 6BX.

•**BENTLEY, Miss. Joanne Carol, BA ACA ATII** *1992;* Deloitte LLP, 2 New Street Square, LONDON, EC4A 3BZ. See also Deloitte & Touche LLP

BENTLEY, Mr. John, MA FCA *1976;* 151 Prestbury Road, MACCLESFIELD, CHESHIRE, SK10 3DF.

BENTLEY, Mr. John David Greer, FCA *1959;* 18 Ryalls Court, SEATON, EX12 2HJ. (Life Member)

BENTLEY, Mr. John Henry, FCA *1970;* 58 Highfield Road, PURLEY, CR8 2JG.

BENTLEY, Mr. John Paul, BA ACA *1991;* 19 Ouseley Road, LONDON, SW12 8ED.

BENTLEY, Mr. John Russell, FCA *1977;* Pool House, Vicarage Lane, Little Budworth, TARPORLEY, CW6 9BY.

BENTLEY, Mrs. Katherine Elaine, BSc ACA *1989;* with E T Peirson & Sons, 21 The Point, Rockingham Road, MARKET HARBOROUGH, LEICESTERSHIRE, LE16 7NU.

BENTLEY, Ms. Kathryn, MSc ACA *1987;* 17 Copperclay Walk, Easingwold, YORK, YO61 3RU.

BENTLEY, Mrs. Katie Victoria, ACA *2010;* 84 Brook Meadow Road, Shard End, BIRMINGHAM, B34 6QP.

•**BENTLEY, Mr. Laurence John, FCA** *1977;* (Tax Fac), BFE Brays Ltd, Building Society Chambers, Wesley Street, OTLEY, WEST YORKSHIRE, LS21 1AZ.

BENTLEY, Mrs. Lois, BSc FCA *1983;* 24 West Court, Roundhay, LEEDS, LS8 2JP.

BENTLEY, Mrs. Lone Vestergaard, BA ACA *1993;* 6 Cornwall Crescent, Diggle, OLDHAM, OL3 5PW.

BENTLEY, Mr. Malcolm Kenneth Sharp, BSc ACA *1979;* Old Ford House, Bournemouth Road, Blandford St.Mary, BLANDFORD FORUM, DT11 9LN.

BENTLEY, Mr. Mark, BA ACA *1996;* 27 Nutter Lane, LONDON, E11 2HZ.

BENTLEY, Mr. Matthew David Jeremy, ACA *2008;* 17 Monmouth Road, BRISTOL, BS7 8LF.

BENTLEY, Mr. Michael David, ACA *1982;* 10 Park Grove, EDGWARE, HA8 7SJ.

•**BENTLEY, Mr. Michael Philip, BSc ACA** *1990;* Ernst & Young, 999 Third Avenue, Suite 3500, SEATTLE, WA 98104, UNITED STATES.

•**BENTLEY, Mr. Michael Scott, ACA DChA** *1995;* (Tax Fac), Winter Rule LLP, Lowin House, Tregolls Road, TRURO, CORNWALL, TR1 2NA. See also Francis Clark LLP

BENTLEY, Ms. Nadya Lynne, BSc ACA *1999;* 262 Hyde End Road, Spencers Wood, READING, RG7 1DL.

BENTLEY, Mr. Nicolas Bryan, FCA *1965;* Bentley Reid & Co (Pacific) Ltd, 24th Floor, Diamond Exchange Building, 8-10 Duddell Street, CENTRAL, HONG KONG ISLAND HONG KONG SAR.

•**BENTLEY, Mr. Peter John, FCA** *1971;* The Wolery, 15 Coldharbour Lane, Hildenborough, TONBRIDGE, TN11 9JT.

BENTLEY, Mr. Peter John, FCA *1966;* 10 Myln Meadow, Stock, INGATESTONE, CM4 9NE.

BENTLEY, Mr. Peter Joseph, FCA *1972;* 96 Dingwall Drive, Greasby, WIRRAL, MERSEYSIDE, CH49 1SQ.

BENTLEY, Miss. Ria, ACA *2009;* Back Flat, 24 Cross Street, LONDON, N1 2BG.

BENTLEY, Mr. Robert Duncan Bartlett, LLM FCA *1989;* Pro Vice-Chancellor, Curtin Business School, Curtin University of Technology, GPO Box U1987, PERTH, WA 6845 AUSTRALIA.

BENTLEY, Mr. Roger David, BSc FCA *1991;* Eaton Manor, Lightfoot Lane, Eaton, TARPORLEY, CHESHIRE, CW6 9AF.

•**BENTLEY, Mr. Rupert James, BSc ACA** *1995;* R J Bentley, Milsons Cottage, Wellhouse, Hermitage, THATCHAM, BERKSHIRE RG18 9UG.

BENTLEY, Mr. Simon Anthony, FCA *1980;* Regents Park Estates Limited, Summit House, 12 Red Lion Square, LONDON, WC1R 4QD.

BENTLEY, Miss. Siobhan Maria, ACA *2008;* Marks & Spencer Plc Waterside House, 35 North Wharf Road, LONDON, W2 1NW.

BENTLEY, Mr. Stephen, BA ACA *1980;* The Grange, 87 Gores Lane, Freshfield, LIVERPOOL, L37 7DE.

•**BENTLEY, Mr. Stephen, BA FCA** *1985;* 39A Financial Direction, 38 Strother Close, Pocklington, YORK, YO42 2GR. See also 39a Business Solutions LLP

BENTLEY, Mr. Stephen Graham, BA FCA MCT *1978;* Waterside, Little Heath Lane, Dunham Massey, ALTRINCHAM, WA14 4TS.

•**BENTLEY, Mr. Stephen Johnson, BA FCA** *1986;* (Tax Fac), Financial Management Solutions UK Limited, 42a High Street, SUTTON COLDFIELD, B72 1UJ.

BENTLEY, Mr. Stephen Peter, LLB ACA *1998;* 11 Covington, Elloughton, BROUGH, HU15 1FD.

BENTLEY, Mr. William Arnold Royston, BSc ACA *1988;* 8 Atkinson Court, ALBANY CREEK, QLD 4035, AUSTRALIA.

BENTLEY-JONES, Mrs. Michelle Sarah, ACA *2008;* 86 Westminster Road, Hoole, CHESTER, CH2 3AP.

BENTON, Mr. Alan, FCA *1974;* (Tax Fac), 5 Gregory Mews, Beaulieu Drive, WALTHAM ABBEY, EN9 1JX.

•**BENTON, Mr. David Arthur, FCA** *1977;* Kingston Smith LLP, Orbital House, 20 Eastern Road, ROMFORD, RM1 3PJ. See also Kingston Smith Limited Liability Partnership, Devonshire Corporate Services LLP and Kingston Smith Consulting LLP

BENTON, Mr. Gary Miles, BA FCA *1977;* 8 Kestrel Way, Kenrock Estate, Valley Road, Hout Bay, CAPE TOWN, WESTERN CAPE PROVINCE 7806 SOUTH AFRICA.

BENTON, Mr. John Barnsley, FCA *1948;* 24A Eggington Road, Wollaston, STOURBRIDGE, DY8 4QJ. (Life Member)

BENTON, Mr. Julian Roger, BA ACA *1999;* 2/ 160 Charman Road, MENTONE, VIC 3194, AUSTRALIA.

BENTON, Mr. Leslie David, FCA *1972;* 52 Kiln Lane, Headington, OXFORD, OX3 8EY.

BENTON, Mr. Mark Ian, BA(Hons) ACA CTA *2001;* Woodbury, 50 Beaumont Park Road, HUDDERSFIELD, HD4 5JP.

•**BENTON, Mr. Martin Jeremy, FCA** *1981;* (Tax Fac), 12 Lawrence Gardens, Mill Hill, LONDON, NW7 4JT.

BENTON, Mrs. Mary Theresa, FCA *1988;* 46 Main Street, PAKENHAM, VIC 3810, AUSTRALIA.

BENTON, Mr. Michael Roy, BA FCA *1985;* 15 Woodland Drive, HOVE, EAST SUSSEX, BN3 6DH.

BENTON, Mr. Nicholas Charles, ACA *2009;* 67 Thomas Baines Road, LONDON, SW11 2HH.

BENTON, Mr. Paul Leslie, BA FCA *1985;* 39 Roy Terrace, CHRISTIES BEACH, SA 5165, AUSTRALIA.

BENTON, Mr. Paul Walter, FCA *1967;* 2 Numbers Farm, Egg Farm Lane, Station Road, KINGS LANGLEY, HERTFORDSHIRE, WD4 8LS.

BENTON, Mr. Raymond Arthur, FCA *1972;* Flat 5, The Cedars, Albert Park Road, MALVERN, WORCESTERSHIRE, WR14 1HW.

BENTON, Mr. Thomas Christopher, BSc ACA *1998;* 16 Northcote Road, TWICKENHAM, TW1 1PA.

BENTS, Mrs. Anita Jane, BA FCA *1989;* Blue Planet Web Ltd, Honey Cottage, Thorndown Lane, WINDLESHAM, SURREY, GU20 6DJ.

BENTWOOD, Mr. Paul Robert, BA ACA *1985;* Otep Technologies Ltd Oakdale House, Cale Lane Aspull, WIGAN, WN2 1HB.

•**BENVENISTE, Mr. Barry Phillip, FCA** *1972;* (Tax Fac), Barry P. Bennis & Co, 9 Chilton Road, EDGWARE, MIDDLESEX, HA8 7NJ.

BENVENUTI, Mr. Francesco Giovanni, FCA *1993;* Via Tristano Calco 2, 20123 MILAN, ITALY.

BENWELL, Mr. David Ian, BA FCA *1965;* 13 St. Anns Close, Goodworth Clatford, ANDOVER, SP11 7RW.

BENYON, Mr. David John, BSc FCA *1991;* Angliskaya Nabrezhnaya 20-11, 190000 ST PETERSBURG, RUSSIAN FEDERATION.

BENYON, Mrs. Kay Alexandra, BCom ACA *1989;* Brayton, North Road, The Reddings, CHELTENHAM, GL51 6RD.

BENYON, Mr. Martin, ACA *1980;* Rosebank, Shawhead, DUMFRIES, DG2 9UQ.

BENYON, Miss. Patricia Ann, BSc FCA *1991;* with RSM Tenon Audit Limited, Highfield Court, Tollgate, Chandlers Ford, EASTLEIGH, SO53 3TY.

BENYON, Mr. Sean Adrian, BSocSc ACA *1989;* Deloitte & Touche Llp, 66 Shoe Lane, LONDON, EC4A 3BQ.

BENZECRY, Mr. Michael Raphael, FCA *1955;* Tanners, Old Lane, Martyr's Green, COBHAM, KT11 1NQ. (Life Member)

BENZIE, Mr. Alan Athol Emslie, FCA *1971;* Oakbarn, Higher House Farm, Hocker Lane, Over Alderley, MACCLESFIELD, CHESHIRE SK10 4SD.

BENZIE, Mr. Paul John, BA ACA *1994;* 1489 29th Place NE, ISSAQUAH, WA 98029, UNITED STATES.

BENZIKIE, Mr. Peter Andrew, FCA *1974;* 585 Estates Place, LONGWOOD, FL 32779-2857, UNITED STATES. (Life Member)

BERARWALLA, Miss. Jasmine, ACA *1989;* 23 Kensington Gate, LONDON, W8 5NA.

BERBER, Miss. Glynis, ACA *2002;* 3 Ardglass Gardens, RIDGEWOOD, WA 6030, AUSTRALIA.

BERENDT, Mr. Paul Francis, FCA *1974;* Gerald Edelman, Edelman House, 1238 High Road, Whetstone, LONDON, N20 0LH.

•**BERENS, Mr. Andrew Wayne, FCA** *1976;* (Tax Fac), Andrew W Berens FCA, 48 Ringley Drive, Whitefield, MANCHESTER, M45 7LR.

BERESFORD, Mrs. Carol Frances, BSc ACA *1986;* HSBC Bank Plc, 12 Calthorpe Road, Edgbaston, BIRMINGHAM, B15 1QT.

BERESFORD, Mr. Daniel, MA(Hons) ACA *2010;* The Prudential Assurance Co Ltd, 12 Arthur Street, LONDON, EC4R 9AQ.

•BERESFORD, Mr. Gary Lewis, BA FCA *1987;* 93 Little Aston Lane, SUTTON COLDFIELD, B74 3UE.

BERESFORD, Mrs. Kathryn Toni, BA FCA *1993;* Goodband Viner Taylor Ellin House, 42 Kingfield Road, SHEFFIELD, S11 9AS.

BERESFORD, Mr. Nicholas Keith, BA ACA *1995;* C/O UNDP Somalia, GARROWE, PUNTLAND STATE, SOMALIA.

BERESFORD, Mr. Richard Jonathan, BSc FCA *1984;* 41 Shaftesbury Crescent, Laleham, STAINES, TW18 1QL.

•BERESSI, Mr. Julian Leon Victor, BSc FCA *1984;* Kay Johnson Gee, Griffin Court, 201 Chapel Street, MANCHESTER, M3 5EQ.

BEREZAI, Mrs. Amanda Sarah Louise, MA(Hons) ACA *2001;* with Deloitte LLP, PO Box 500, 2 Hardman Street, MANCHESTER, M60 2AT.

•BERG, Mr. Adrian Harvey, BSc FCA *1973;* Alexander & Co, 17 St Ann's Square, MANCHESTER, M2 7PW.

BERG, Mr. Antony Benjamin, BA ACA *2006;* Flat C, Flat C 32 Priory Road, LONDON, NW64SJ.

•BERG, Mr. Brian, BSc FCA *1972;* Brian Berg Limited, 35 Ballards Lane, LONDON, N3 1XW.

BERG, Miss. Corinne Rachelle, BA MSt ACA *2005;* 12 High Mount, Station Road, LONDON, NW4 3SS.

BERG, Mr. Elliot Lawrence, BA(Hons) ACA *2011;* 47 Linton Rise, Alwoodley, LEEDS, LS17 8QW.

BERG, Mr. Jonathan Graham, BSc FCA *1993;* 22 Westminster Road, MIDDLESBROUGH, CLEVELAND, TS5 6NA.

BERG, Ms. Julie, BA(Hons) ACA *2001;* Grimsrød Gate 8, 1515 MOSS, NORWAY.

BERG, Mr. Norman Maurice, BA FCA *1961;* The Timbers Church Lane, Old St. Mellons, CARDIFF, CF3 5UP. (Life Member)

BERG, Mr. Per Christian, ACA *2008;* 20 Parkgate Road, WALLINGTON, SURREY, SM6 0AH.

BERG, Mr. Robert Lee, BA(Hons) ACA *2010;* 13 Bradfords Close, BUCKHURST HILL, IG9 6ED.

BERG, Mr. Robert Vivian Nathaniel, MA FCA *1973;* Mail Boxes Etc, 28 Old Brompton Road, LONDON, SW7 3SS. (Life Member)

BERG, Mr. Sidney, FCA *1948;* 25 Tower Court, Westcliff Parade, WESTCLIFF-ON-SEA, SS0 7QQ. (Life Member)

BERG, Mr. Timothy Edward, BA FCA *1987;* 7a Britwell Road, Burnham, SLOUGH, SL1 8AF.

BERGER, Miss. Alexa Kate, BA ACA *2010;* Flat 2/A, Exeter Mansions, Exeter Road, LONDON, NW2 3UG.

BERGER, Mr. Geoffrey David, FCA *1967;* Po Box 12162, LONDON, NW11 7WR.

BERGER, Mr. Harvey, FCA *1961;* 18 Chalk Lane, Cockfosters, BARNET, HERTFORDSHIRE, EN4 9HJ. (Life Member)

•BERGER, Mr. John, FCA *1982;* Courtland Ltd, Courtlands Cottage, 62 Copsem Lane, Oxshott, LEATHERHEAD, KT22 0NT. See also J. Berger

BERGER, Mr. Jonathan Paul Stuart, BSc FCA *1984;* Brackenfell, Colmore Lane, Kingwood, HENLEY-ON-THAMES, OXFORDSHIRE, RG9 5LX.

BERGER, Mr. Lawrence, FCA *1966;* 14F Avda Generalife, Nueva Andalucia, MARBELLA, SPAIN.

BERGER, Mr. Michael Kenneth, FCA *1959;* 34 Selhurst Close, Wimbledon, LONDON, SW19 6AZ. (Life Member)

BERGER, Mr. Michael Norman, FCA *1971;* 39 Hogarth Drive, Shoeburyness, SOUTHEND-ON-SEA, SS3 9TH. (Life Member)

BERGER, Mr. Michael Stanley, FCA *1954;* Quinta Da Coroa, PO Box 114, Sta Barbara de Nexe, 8000 FARO, ALGARVE, PORTUGAL. (Life Member)

BERGER, Mr. Patrick Beverley Stuart, FCA *1951;* Bakers Yard, 27 Castle Square, Benson, WALLINGFORD, OX10 6SD. (Life Member)

•BERGER, Mr. Stephen Howard, MSc BSc FCA *1970;* (Tax Fac), Baker Tilly Tax and Advisory Services LLP, 25 Farringdon Street, LONDON, EC4A 4AB.

BERGESEN, Miss. Linda Beathe, ACA CA(AUS) *2008;* Nedrelia 9, 5231 PARADIS, NORWAY.

BERGHS, Mr. Alexander Alec Hubert, MBA FCA *1995;* First Floor, 178 Sutherland Avenue, LONDON, W9 1HR.

BERGIN, Mr. Jonathan Patrick, BA ACA *1998;* 23 Manor Crescent, Pool in Wharfedale, OTLEY, WEST YORKSHIRE, LS21 1ND.

BERGIN, Mr. Michael Gerard, BA ACA *1992;* 32 Crescent Road, BURGESS HILL, RH15 8EG.

BERGIN, Mr. Patrick Joseph, BA ACA *1995;* Rose Cottage, Rowly Drive, Rowly, CRANLEIGH, GU6 8PJ.

BERGIN, Mr. Paul Geoffrey, BA ACA *1990;* Centrepoint, McBride Plc Centre Point, 103 New Oxford Street, LONDON, WC1A 1DD.

BERGMAN, Mr. James Henry Richard, FCA CertPFS FCMI *1961;* J.B. Financial Services, Copse Meade, 3 Kentish Lane, Brookmans Park, HATFIELD, AL9 6NG. (Life Member)

BERI, Mr. Karan, ACA *2011;* E-539 Greater Kailash - 2, New Delhi, NEW DELHI 110048, INDIA.

BERI, Mr. Suneel, BA ACA *1987;* 74 Burnt Ash Road, LONDON, SE12 8PY.

BERINGER, Mr. David John, BEng FCA *1998;* Eastwood Cottage, 14 Eastfield, BRISTOL, BS9 4BQ.

BERISTAIN, Mr. Josu, ACA *1998;* 75 Potter Street, NORTHWOOD, HA6 1QH.

BERJAOUI, Miss. Natalie, BA(Hons) ACA *2004;* with Vincent Clemas, Cornerways House, School Lane, RINGWOOD, BH24 1LG.

BERKE, Mr. David Maurice, FCA *1957;* Flat 53, 8-D Nitza Boulevard, NETANYA, 42262, ISRAEL. (Life Member)

BERKELEY, Mr. David James, FCA *1968;* Higher Hutcherleigh, Blackawton, TOTNES, DEVON, TQ9 7AD.

BERKELEY, Mr. Edward, ACA *2011;* Flat 6, 2 Spencer Hill, LONDON, SW19 4NY.

•BERKELEY, Mr. Rodney Guy, FCA *1970;* Cranfield Associates Ltd, Church Street House, Church Street, Rudgwick, HORSHAM, WEST SUSSEX RH12 3EH.

BERKELEY, Mr. Thurstan Timothy Edward, BA ACA *1990;* 44 Winners Circle, TORONTO M4L 3Z7, ON, CANADA.

BERKIN, Mr. Antony, BA FCA *1989;* 2 Cleopatra Close, STANMORE, MIDDLESEX, HA7 4PR.

BERKIN, Mr. John Alastair Geoffrey, BSc FCA *1972;* City Consulting Associates, 54 Clarendon Road, WATFORD, WD17 1DU.

•BERKLEY, Mr. Andrew Philip Crowley, MA ACA AMCT *1999;* Ambitious Minds Limited, 4 Shaw Green Lane, Prestbury, CHELTENHAM, GLOUCESTERSHIRE, GL52 3BP.

BERKLEY, Mr. David Jonathan, FCA *1969;* 36 Hill Crescent, LONDON, N20 8HD.

BERKLEY, Mr. James Robert, BSc ACA *2004;* with PricewaterhouseCoopers LLP, Pricewaterhousecoopers, 12 Plumtree Court, LONDON, EC4A 4HT.

BERKLEY, Mr. John Richard, ACA *1981;* 2 The Lymes, View Road, LYME REGIS, DT7 3AA.

BERKLEY, Mr. Leigh George, BA ACA *1987;* Maitland House, Tessera Group 5th Floor Maitland House Warrior Square, SOUTHEND-ON-SEA, SS1 2JS.

•BERKLEY, Mr. Trevor Frederick, FCA *1982;* The KBSP Partnership, Harben House, Harben Parade, Finchley Road, LONDON, NW3 6LH. See also Stardata Business Services Limited

•BERKO, Mr. Laurence, FCA *1977;* Complete Audit and Accounting Solutions Ltd, Unit 203, China House, 401 Edgware Road, LONDON, NW2 6GY.

BERKOFF, Mr. Stuart Charles, BA ACA *1997;* Floor 4, D P World, 16 Palace Street, LONDON, SW1E 5JQ.

•BERKOVI, Mr. Anthony Joseph, FCA *1973;* 5 The Downsway, SUTTON, SURREY, SM2 5RL.

BERKOVI, Mr. Paul Lewis, BSc ACA *2010;* 3 Templeton Court, 12 Kingsbridge Drive, LONDON, NW7 1HL.

BERKOVITS, Mr. Jeremy, BA ACA *1981;* 1 Rechov Matityahu, JERUSALEM, 93504, ISRAEL.

BERKS, Mr. Colin Edward, BSc(Hons) FCA ACMA *1962;* Brekonridge, 20 The Peak, ROWLAND'S CASTLE, HAMPSHIRE, PO9 6AH.

BERKS, Mr. Graham Leslie, BSc FCA *1981;* 8 Fulford Chase, YORK, YO10 4QP.

•BERLYN, Mr. Gerald, FCA *1960;* Gerald Berlyn FCA, Flat 10 Elderberry Court, 39b Bycullah Road, ENFIELD, MIDDLESEX, EN2 8FF.

•BERLYN, Mr. Paul Philip, BSocSc FCA *1988;* Arram Berlyn Gardner, 30 City Road, LONDON, EC1Y 2AB.

BERMAN, Mr. Andrew Colin, BSc ACA *1996;* 16 Holmfield Avenue, Hendon, LONDON, NW4 2LN.

BERMAN, Mr. Barry Jules, FCA *1955;* Frithwood, Far Oakridge, STROUD, GL6 7PG. (Life Member)

•①BERMAN, Mr. Jeremy Hugh, FCA *1981;* Berley, 76 New Cavendish Street, LONDON, W1G 9TB. See also Berley Accountants Limited

BERMAN, Mr. John David, FCA *1958;* 68 Richmond Road, New Barnet, BARNET, HERTFORDSHIRE, EN5 1SE. (Life Member)

BERMAN, Mr. Neil David, BA ACA *2003;* 160 Front St, Apartment 3G, NEW YORK, NY 10038, UNITED STATES.

•BERMAN, Mr. Sidney, FCA *1955;* Sidney Berman FCA, 24 Riverside Gardens, LONDON, N3 3GR.

BERMAN-WALD, Mr. Michael Keith, FCA *1968;* Flat 37, Sunflower Court, 173 Granville Road, LONDON, NW2 2BF.

BERMEL, Mr. Hans Roland, BSc ACA *1983;* Investec Bank (UK) Ltd, 2 Gresham Street, LONDON, EC2V 7QP.

BERMINGHAM, Mr. Jerome, BCom FCA *1980;* 2 Holbein Close, CHESTER, CH4 7EU.

BERNAL, Mr. Paul Alexander, BA ACA *1991;* 54 Highsett, CAMBRIDGE, CB2 1NZ.

BERNARD, Mr. Andrew Robert, FCA *1981;* The Old COttage, Broadham Green, OXTED, RH8 9PF.

BERNARD, Mr. Harvey Geoffrey, FCA *1965;* Buzon 1155, Pintor Sorolla 21, Urb Monte Pego, Pego, 03780 ALICANTE, SPAIN.

•BERNARD, Mr. Keith Murray, FCA *1971;* K.M Bernard, PO Box 999, MANAMA, BAHRAIN.

BERNARD, Mr. Nicolas Raymond Thomas, BA ACA *1989;* Flat 2, Lords Wood House, 18 Cayton Road, COULSDON, SURREY, CR5 1LT.

•BERNARD, Mrs. Patricia Joan, FCA *1979;* Patricia Bernard, 1 Chapel Close, Leigh Sinton, MALVERN, WR13 5BP.

BERNARD, Ms. Rosemary Jane, BSc FCA *1983;* 37 Windsor Avenue, Radyr, CARDIFF, CF15 8BX.

BERNARD, Mr. Thomas Mackenzie Firth, RD JP FCA *1952;* Blackawton House, Brook Street, Dedham, COLCHESTER, CO7 6AD. (Life Member)

BERNASCONI, Miss. Jessica May, ACA *2010;* 5 Lancaster Avenue, Whitefield, MANCHESTER, M45 6DX.

BERNASKO, Miss. Dorothy Sophia, MEng ACA *2006;* 1307 E. 60TH STREET APT 234, CHICAGO, IL 60637-3283, UNITED STATES.

BERNAU, Mr. Christopher Gordon, BSc ACA *2006;* 4 Regency Gardens, WEYBRIDGE, KT13 0DY.

BERNE, Mr. Herbert Kurt Ralph Wolfgang, BCom FCA *1955;* 133 Citation Drive, TORONTO M2K 1T3, ON, CANADA. (Life Member)

BERNE, Mr. Paul Michael, BA ACA *2000;* 7 Ealand Chase, Horwich, BOLTON, BL6 5HJ.

BERNERS PRICE, Mr. Michael, BA FCA *1977;* with Audit Inspection Unit, Financial Reporting Council, 5th Floor, Aldwych House, 71-91 Aldwych, LONDON WC2B 4HN.

BERNEY, Mrs. Carol Jane, MA BA ACA *1989;* Thistlethwaite, Littlebury Green, SAFFRON WALDEN, ESSEX, CB11 4XB.

BERNEY, Mr. Gareth Mark, BA ACA *1991;* Standard Chartered, 1 Basinghall Avenue, LONDON, EC2V 5DD.

BERNEY, Mr. John Michael, BSc ACA *1980;* CIO Plus Ltd, 90 Leamington Road, KENILWORTH, CV8 2AA.

BERNIE, Mr. Peter Raymond James, MA FCA MCT *1982;* Liverpool & London Unit 17, Junction 8 Business Centre Rosscliffe Road, ELLESMERE PORT, CH65 3AS.

BERNSEN, Mr. Christopher, FCA *1975;* Beech House, 39 Amos Hill, TOTLAND BAY, ISLE OF WIGHT, PO39 0DP.

•BERNSTEIN, Mr. Anthony Julian, FCA *1971;* H W Fisher & Company, Acre House, 11-15 William Road, LONDON, NW1 3ER. See also H W Fisher & Company Limited

BERNSTEIN, Mrs. Carol Beverley Kathleen, FCA *1990;* 13 Purley Knoll, PURLEY, CR8 3AF.

BERNSTEIN, Mr. Daniel Lipman, FCA *1969;* 3 Chartridge Close, Arkley, BARNET, EN5 3LX.

BERNSTEIN, Mr. David Alan, FCA *1966;* 48 Fitzalan Road, Finchley, LONDON, N3 3PE.

BERNSTEIN, Mr. Henry Alan, FCA *1971;* 37 Abbotswood Gardens, Clayhall, ILFORD, IG5 0BG.

BERNSTEIN, Mr. Mark Jonathan, BA ACA *1985;* The Old Rectory, Nock Verges, Stoney Stanton, LEICESTER, LE9 4LR.

BERNSTEIN, Mr. Mark Simon, BA FCA *1988;* 13 Purley Knoll, PURLEY, CR8 3AF.

•BERNSTEIN, Mr. Michael David Tobias, BA FCA *1976;* Harris Lipman LLP, 2 Mountview Court, 310 Friern Barnet Lane, LONDON, N20 0YZ.

•BERNSTEIN, Mr. Raymond Philip, BA FCA *1989;* I Count Limited, 26 Boundary Road, PINNER, MIDDLESEX, HA5 1PN.

BERNSTEIN, Mr. Richard Philip, BSc ACA *1989;* 18 Russell Close, LONDON, W4 2NU.

BERNSTEIN, Mr. Robert Steven, BA ACA *2001;* 83 Clarence Way, Camden, LONDON, NW1 8DG.

BERNSTEIN, Mr. Simon Laurence, BA ACA *1989;* SJR Properties Ltd, 5th Floor, 94-96 Wigmore Street, LONDON, W1U 3RF.

BERO, Mr. Maxwell, ACA *2006;* 7 Famet Close, PURLEY, SURREY, CR8 2DX.

BERRA, Mr. Derek Peter, ACA *1980;* 9 Church Hill, Cheddington, LEIGHTON BUZZARD, BUCKINGHAMSHIRE, LU7 0SX.

BERRECLOTH, Mr. James Henry, BSc ACA *1995;* 1 Upper Lattimore Road, ST. ALBANS, HERTFORDSHIRE, AL1 3UD.

BERRESFORD, Mr. Derren Michael, BSc ACA *1999;* 10 Chaworth Road, West Bridgford, NOTTINGHAM, NG2 7AB.

BERRESFORD, Mrs. Dorothy Ann, BSc ACA *1985;* Greystone Court, Little Sodbury Common, Chipping Sodbury, BRISTOL, BS37 6QF.

•BERRIDGE, Mrs. Amanda Mary, FCA *1986;* (Tax Fac), PricewaterhouseCoopers LLP, 1 Embankment Place, LONDON, WC2N 6RH. See also PricewaterhouseCoopers

BERRIDGE, Mrs. Helena Bryony, MA ACA *1994;* 64 Compton Road, LONDON, SW19 7QD.

BERRIDGE, Mr. Paul Francis, BEng FCA *1991;* Global Process Systems Inc., 4th Floor Spectrum Building, Oud Metha PO Box 30953, DUBAI, UNITED ARAB EMIRATES.

BERRIDGE, Mr. Scott James, BSc ACA *2005;* 42 Berridge Mews, LONDON, NW6 1RF.

BERRIDGE, Mrs. Susan Joy, BA ACA *1992;* 2 Kingston Way, MARKET HARBOROUGH, LE16 7XB.

BERRIE, Mr. James Douglas, CA *1975; (CA Scotland 1961);* Brown McLeod & Berrie, 12 Spring Lane, Bottisham, CAMBRIDGE, CB25 9BL.

BERRIGAN, Mr. Sean Daniel, MChem ACA *2010;* 98 Holt Lane, Rainhill, PRESCOT, MERSEYSIDE, L35 8NH.

BERRILL, Mr. Colin John, FCA *1975;* Sterling House, 32 St. John Street, MANSFIELD, NOTTINGHAMSHIRE, NG18 1QJ.

•BERRIMAN, Mr. John Robert Lloyd, FCA *1979;* PricewaterhouseCoopers LLP, 7 More London Riverside, LONDON, SE1 2RT. See also PricewaterhouseCoopers

BERRIMAN, Mr. Robin Bielby, BCom FCA *1977;* 124 Moor Lane, Woodford, STOCKPORT, SK7 1PJ.

•BERRIMAN, Mr. Stuart Graham, ACA FCCA *2007;* (Tax Fac), Chater Allan LLP, Beech House, 4a Newmarket Road, CAMBRIDGE, CB5 8DT.

BERRINGTON, Mr. Richard Norman, FCA *1953;* Summerbank, 10 Willow Way, Prestbury, MACCLESFIELD, CHESHIRE, SK10 4XB. (Life Member)

BERRINGTON, Mr. William Nicholas Huggonson, FCA *1976;* The Coach House Ayot House, Ayot St. Lawrence, WELWYN, HERTFORDSHIRE, AL6 9BP.

BERRISFORD, Mr. Andrew, BSc ACA *2001;* Amcor Flexibles Winterbourne Winterbourne Road, Bradley Stoke, BRISTOL, BS34 6PT.

BERRISFORD, Mr. Andrew Steven, FCA *1976;* 2 Lemon Grove, Whitehill, BORDON, HAMPSHIRE, GU35 9BE.

BERRISFORD, Mr. Daniel, BSc ACA *1996;* Heat Trace Ltd Meres Edge, Chester Road Helsby, FRODSHAM, WA6 0DJ.

BERRISFORD, Mr. Michael Henry, BA ACA *1981;* Rue Marcel Marien, 18 BRUSSELS, BELGIUM.

BERROW, Miss. Charlotte Elizabeth Georgina, BA ACA *2003;* Flat 24, 18 Lloyd Square Niall Close, BIRMINGHAM, B15 3LX.

BERROW, Mr. John Ronald, FCA *1965;* RR1 Site 2 Comp 49, NARAMATA V0H 1N0, BC, CANADA.

BERROW, Mr. Rupert William Leslie, BA ACA *1987;* Mascolo Limited, 58-60 Stamford Street, LONDON, SE1 9LX.

BERROW, Mr. Stephen, MA(Oxon) ACA *2010;* 8 Victoria Road, Bishops Waltham, SOUTHAMPTON, SO32 1DJ.

•①BERRY, Mr. Adrian Peter, BA FCA *1992;* Cherry Trees, 1 Newfield Drive, Menston, ILKLEY, WEST YORKSHIRE, LS29 6JQ.

BERRY, Prof. Aidan Joseph, BA FCA *1976;* 21 Modena Road, HOVE, EAST SUSSEX, BN3 5QF.

BERRY, Mrs. Alison Dawn, BAcc ACA *1996;* 16 Wylam Avenue, Holywell, WHITLEY BAY, TYNE AND WEAR, NE25 0TR.

BERRY, Mrs. Alison Katharine, BA(Hons) ACA *2001;* Strategic Thought Group plc, 1 Grenfell Road, MAIDENHEAD, SL6 1HN.

BERRY, Mr. Andrew John, BSc ACA *1993;* Trelleborg Sealing Solutions, Handwerkstrasse 5-7, 70565 STUTTGART, GERMANY.

BERRY, Mr. Andrew John Sutherland, BA ACA *1991;* 11 Webb Close, Oundle, PETERBOROUGH, NORTHAMPTONSHIRE, PE8 4HS.

BERRY, Mrs. Anna Kate, BSc ACA *1996;* Teutonenstrasse 12, 70771 LEINFELDEN-ECHTERDING, GERMANY.

BERRY, Mr. Anthony Edward John, FCA *1955;* 16 Hopstone Gardens, Penn, WOLVERHAMPTON, WV4 4DD. (Life Member)

BERRY, Miss. Barbara Ann, BA ACA *1984;* 7 Beechcroft, Galsworthy Road, KINGSTON-UPON-THAMES, KT2 7BL.

BERRY, Mr. Christopher, BSc ACA *2005;* 18 Pulross Road, LONDON, SW9 8AF.

BERRY, Mr. Christopher, FCA *1977;* Russell Hobbs Ltd Fir Street, Failsworth, MANCHESTER, M35 0HS.

BERRY, Mrs. Claire Jane, BA ACA *1997;* with PricewaterhouseCoopers LLP, 1 Embankment Place, LONDON, WC2N 6RH.

BERRY, Miss. Claire Louise, BSc ACA *2011;* 122a Towngate, Eccleston, CHORLEY, LANCASHIRE, PR7 5QS.

BERRY, Mr. David Arthur, BA ACA *1989;* National Grid Plc Grand Buildings, 1-3 Strand, LONDON, WC2N 5EH.

BERRY, Mr. David Charles, FCA *1961;* Portland Dene, Valley Way, GERRARDS CROSS, SL9 7PN. (Life Member)

BERRY, Mr. David Jonathan, ACA *2008;* 28 Edwards Road, CHESTER, CH4 8HW.

•**BERRY, Mr. Derek, FCA** *1955;* D. Berry, 41 Elmstead Lane, CHISLEHURST, KENT, BR7 5EG.

BERRY, Mr. Douglas Mark, BA FCA *1984;* (Tax Fac), 9 Daffodil Close, Hatfield Garden Village, HATFIELD, HERTFORDSHIRE, AL10 9FF.

BERRY, Mr. Duncan Andrew, BSc ACA *1997;* 6 Meadow End, LIPHOOK, GU30 7UA.

•**BERRY, Mrs. Elaine Louise, ACA** *1982;* Finnieston Berry Partnership Limited, Europa House, 72-74 Northwood Street, BIRMINGHAM, B3 1TT.

BERRY, Mrs. Esther Ruth, BSc(Hons) ACA *2000;* Penralt, Avenue Road, FLEET, HAMPSHIRE, GU51 4NG.

BERRY, Mrs. Eve Marcia, BA ACA *1991;* 33 Lyndhurst Gardens, LONDON, N3 1TA.

BERRY, Mr. Frank Thurstan, BA FCA *1980;* (Tax Fac), 5 Church Meadows, Harwood, BOLTON, BL2 3PB.

BERRY, Mr. Geoffrey Arthur, FCA *1970;* 252 Station Road, Knowle, SOLIHULL, WEST MIDLANDS, B93 0ES.

BERRY, Miss. Gillian, BSc ACA *1997;* 24 Windsor Road, CHORLEY, LANCASHIRE, PR7 1LN.

BERRY, Mr. Graeme Jonathan, MA(Oxon) FCA *1982;* 21 Eastmearn Road, West Dulwich, LONDON, SE21 8HA.

BERRY, Mr. Graham Vivian, FCA *1961;* 10 St. Annes Close, WINCHESTER, HAMPSHIRE, SO22 4LQ.

BERRY, Mr. Grant Rostron, BA ACA *1995;* 54 Carrwood Road, WILMSLOW, CHESHIRE, SK9 5DT.

BERRY, Mr. Harry, FCA *1966;* P07, 36 Beechfields, Eccleston, CHORLEY, PR7 5RE. (Life Member)

BERRY, Mrs. Helen Jane, MPhil BSc ACA *2005;* (Tax Fac), 79 Masefield Road, Little Lever, BOLTON, BL3 1NG.

BERRY, Ms. Helen Jean, MA ACA *2000;* 48 Meadowbank, Primrose Hill, LONDON, NW3 3AY.

BERRY, Mr. Ian, BSc ACA *2004;* The Co-operative Group (C W S) Ltd Dantzic Building, Dantzic Street, MANCHESTER, M60 0AF.

•**BERRY, Mr. Ian, BSc FCA** *1977;* Berry & Hotson LLP, Cherrytree Suite 2, Union Road, Nether Edge, SHEFFIELD, S11 9EF.

BERRY, Mr. Ian Norman, FCA *1972;* 23 Holly Way, KALAMUNDA, WA 6076, AUSTRALIA.

BERRY, Mr. Idris Lawton, DFC FCA *1948;* 40 Thornway, High Lane, STOCKPORT, SK6 8EL. (Life Member)

•**BERRY, Ms. Jacqueline Mary, BA ACA** *1993;* Mazars LLP, The Atrium, Park Street West, LUTON, LU1 3BE.

BERRY, Mr. James Arthur, FCA *1961;* 145-10451 Shellbridge Way, VANCOUVER V6X 2W8, BC, CANADA.

BERRY, Mr. James David, BSc(Hons) ACA *2011;* Flat 60, Ionian Building, 45 Narrow Street, LONDON, E14 8DW.

BERRY, Mr. James Donald, BA(Hons) ACA *2002;* KPMG, Crown House, 4 Par La Ville Road, HAMILTON HM08, BERMUDA.

BERRY, Mr. James Lindsay, BA ACA *1999;* with Berry Accountants, Bowden House, 36 Northampton Road, MARKET HARBOROUGH, LEICESTERSHIRE, LE16 9HE.

BERRY, Mr. James Robert, BSc FCA *1977;* Flex Recruitment Plus Ltd Unit 4, Salisbury House Wheatfield Way, HINCKLEY, LE10 1YG.

BERRY, Mr. Jeffrey William, MA FCA *1991;* 23 Stoke Park Road, BRISTOL, BS9 1JF.

BERRY, Mrs. Jenny Clare, BA ACA *2006;* Meillionydd, Derwen, CORWEN, CLWYD, LL21 9SG.

BERRY, Miss. Jillian Ruth, ACA *2008;* Flat 3, 30 Romberg Road, LONDON, SW17 8UA.

•**BERRY, Mrs. Joanna Katherine, BA ACA** *2005;* Berrys Business Services Limited, Caddywell Yard, Caddywell Lane, TORRINGTON, DEVON, EX38 7EL.

BERRY, Miss. Jodie, BSc ACA *2005;* 7 Longford Road, Chorlton cum Hardy, MANCHESTER, M21 9WP.

BERRY, Mr. John, BA FCA *1968;* 4 Weald Way, CATERHAM, CR3 6EG. (Life Member)

BERRY, Mr. John Alexander, FCA *1960;* The Linhay Court Barton, Coffinswell, NEWTON ABBOT, TQ12 4SS. (Life Member)

BERRY, Mr. John Paul, BA ACA *2007;* 50 Thorpehall Road, Edenthorpe, DONCASTER, SOUTH YORKSHIRE, DN3 2NZ.

BERRY, Mr. John Russell Whiteway, FCA FCCA *1960;* 6 Gregson Gardens, Toton, NOTTINGHAM, NG9 6LR. (Life Member)

BERRY, Mr. John Trevor, FCA *1971;* Box 682, 29600 MARBELLA, SPAIN.

BERRY, Mr. Johnathan Andrew, BSc ACA *2002;* 1 Alderminster Road, SOLIHULL, WEST MIDLANDS, B91 3UN.

BERRY, Mr. Jonathan Michael, BA FCA *1985;* 14 Devonshire Buildings, BATH, BA2 4SP.

BERRY, Mr. Joseph Thomas, MEng ACA *2001;* 43 First Avenue, LONDON, SW14 8SP.

BERRY, Mrs. Karen Elizabeth, BA ACA *2005;* 16 Elder Way, Hazlemere, HIGH WYCOMBE, BUCKINGHAMSHIRE, HP15 7UE.

BERRY, Mrs. Katharine Denise, BSc ACA *2001;* 36 Cheviot Close, TONBRIDGE, KENT, TN9 1NH.

BERRY, Miss. Katherine Elizabeth, BSc ACA *2000;* Warren, Beacon Farm, Beaconside, STAFFORD, ST18 0AE.

BERRY, Miss. Kathryn Charlotte, MA ACA *1981;* (Tax Fac), Seb Merchant Banking, 2-6 Cannon Street, LONDON, EC4M 6XX.

BERRY, Mrs. Kathryn Mary, BA ACA *1991;* Hedgerows, Forest Road, East Horsley, LEATHERHEAD, KT24 5BD.

•**BERRY, Mr. Keith Julian, FCA** *1993;* (Tax Fac), Berrys Business Services Limited, Caddywell Yard, Caddywell Lane, TORRINGTON, DEVON, EX38 7EL.

•**BERRY, Mr. Lawrence Alfred Gordon, FCA** *1974;* Lawrie Berry FCA, Oakleigh, Paynes Lane, Nazeing, WALTHAM ABBEY, ESSEX EN9 2EU.

BERRY, Mr. Mark, BA ACA *1995;* 16 Wylam Avenue, Holywell, WHITLEY BAY, TYNE AND WEAR, NE25 0TR.

BERRY, Mr. Mark Edward Michael, BA ACA *1999;* 25 Langford Lane, Burley in Wharfedale, ILKLEY, LS29 7ER.

BERRY, Mr. Mark Ian James, BSc ACA *2000;* with Hays plc, 250 Euston Road, LONDON, NW1 2AF.

BERRY, Miss. Martha Carys, BSc ACA *2002;* 98 Scholes Lane, Prestwich, MANCHESTER, M25 0AU.

•**BERRY, Mr. Martin Curtis, BA FCA** *1977;* (Tax Fac), Hobsons, Alexandra House, 43 Alexandra Street, NOTTINGHAM, NG5 1AY.

BERRY, Mr. Martin Smith, FCA *1956;* 10 Evelyn Croft, SUTTON COLDFIELD, WEST MIDLANDS, B73 5LF. (Life Member)

BERRY, Mr. Martin Steven, BA FCA HKICPA *1994;* Flat C 19/F Block 3, Baycrest, 8 Hang Ming Street, Ma On Shan, SHA TIN, NEW TERRITORIES HONG KONG SAR.

BERRY, Mrs. Mary Rose, BA ACA *2000;* Villa 18, Street 4, Savannah, Arabiao Ranches, DUBAI, UNITED ARAB EMIRATES.

BERRY, Mr. Michael Francis, FCA *1960;* 119 Leafy Glade Place, WINDSOR, CA 95492, UNITED STATES. (Life Member)

BERRY, Mr. Michael James, BA ACA *2010;* 41a Lodge Avenue, ROMFORD, RM2 5AB.

BERRY, Mr. Michael James, BA FCA *1986;* La Brecque, La Verte Rue, St. Mary, JERSEY, JE3 3DA.

BERRY, Mr. Michael Kim, BSc ACA *1985;* High Oaks, Yorkley Wood Road, Yorkley, LYDNEY, GL15 4TT.

BERRY, Mr. Michael Peter, FCA *1979;* Panaz Ltd, Spring Mill, Wheatley Lane Road, Fence, BURNLEY, LANCASHIRE BB12 9HP.

BERRY, Mr. Michael Philip, MA ACA *1979;* Versatus Advisers LLP, 30-34 Moorgate, LONDON, EC2R 6DN.

•①**BERRY, Mr. Michael Richard, FCA CTA FABRP** *1970;* (Tax Fac), Maxwells, 4 King Square, BRIDGWATER, SOMERSET, TA6 3YF.

BERRY, Mr. Michael Richard, BA ACA *1984;* P.O. Box 32, Wendywood, JOHANNESBURG, 2144, SOUTH AFRICA.

BERRY, Mr. Neil, ACA *2009;* London & Scandinavian Metallurgical Co Ltd, Fullerton Road, ROTHERHAM, SOUTH YORKSHIRE, S60 1DL.

BERRY, Mr. Neil Jonathan, BA ACA AMCT *1992;* Hertford House, B A E Systems, PO Box 87, FARNBOROUGH, GU14 6YU.

BERRY, Mr. Neil Malcolm, BA ACA *1990;* Marks & Spencer Money, F.A.O Finance Department, Kings Meadow, Chester Business Park, CHESTER, CH99 9FB.

BERRY, Mr. Nigel Andrew, BA ACA *1984;* Littlecote, Rideaway, Hemingford Abbots, HUNTINGDON, PE28 9AG.

BERRY, Mr. Norman Frank, FCA *1957;* Walnut Tree Cottage, 203 Main Road, Gt. Leighs, CHELMSFORD, CM3 1NS. (Life Member)

BERRY, Ms. Patricia Rosemary, BA FCA *1989;* F B R McGarry Harvey Unit 38-39, New Forest Enterprise Centre Chapel Lane Totton, SOUTHAMPTON, SO40 9LA.

BERRY, Mr. Paul David, MSc ACA *1998;* Penralt, Avenue Road, FLEET, HAMPSHIRE, GU51 4NG.

BERRY, Mr. Paul David, BA ACA *1992;* 17 Manor Close, Bramhope, LEEDS, LS16 9HQ.

BERRY, Mr. Paul Gerald, ACA CA(SA) *2010;* Flat 13, Ross Apartments, 23 Seagull Lane, LONDON, E16 1DE.

BERRY, Mr. Paul Stephen, BA ACA *1990;* Smithy Cottage Newcastle Road South, Brereton, SANDBACH, CHESHIRE, CW11 1RS.

BERRY, Mr. Peter James, BSc ACA *2005;* Ernst & Young, 680 George Street, SYDNEY, NSW 2026, AUSTRALIA.

BERRY, Mr. Peter John, FCA *1956;* 113 Hackness Road, Scalby, SCARBOROUGH, NORTH YORKSHIRE, YO13 0QY. (Life Member)

BERRY, Mrs. Rachael Jeanette, BA ACA *2006;* 18 Downs Close, Headcorn, ASHFORD, KENT, TN27 9UG.

BERRY, Mr. Raymond Phillip, BCom ACA *2007;* 4 Cloister Walk, HEMEL HEMPSTEAD, HERTFORDSHIRE, HP2 5UE.

BERRY, Mr. Raymond William, FCA *1973;* 263 Luton Road, HARPENDEN, AL5 3LN.

BERRY, Mr. Richard, BA FCA *1984;* Ridgemount, 44 Uplands Way, SEVENOAKS, TN13 3BW.

BERRY, Mr. Richard John, BCom FCA *1963;* Old School House, 37 Germain Street, CHESHAM, BUCKINGHAMSHIRE, HP5 1LW. (Life Member)

BERRY, Mr. Richard Leyland, BA ACA *1986;* 129 Geary Road, LONDON, NW10 1HS.

BERRY, Mr. Robert Joseph, BSc ACA *1978;* 13 East Lennox Drive, HELENSBURGH, DUNBARTONSHIRE, G84 9JD.

•**BERRY, Mr. Robin Seymour, BA ACA** *2002;* Wilder Coe, Oxford House, Campus 6, Caxton Way, STEVENAGE, HERTFORDSHIRE SG1 2XD. See also Wilder Coe LLP, Artaius Ltd

BERRY, Mrs. Sarah, BSc ACA *1999;* 25 Lark Rise, Bussage, STROUD, GL6 8FF.

BERRY, Mrs. Sarah, BSc ACA *2005;* 5 Brancaster Drive, LONDON, NW7 2SQ.

BERRY, Mrs. Sarah Elizabeth, BA ACA *1993;* 14 Greenhills, Rawdon, LEEDS, LS19 6NP.

BERRY, Mr. Simon Andrew, BA ACA *1999;* 14 Polwarth Crescent, NEWCASTLE UPON TYNE, NE3 2EE.

BERRY, Mr. Simon John, BSc FCA *1996;* Orchard Cottage, Blackhorse Road, WOKING, GU22 0RE.

•**BERRY, Mr. Steven, BA FCA** *1982;* Wood Berry & Co, 5 Anderson Court, Sullart Street, COCKERMOUTH, CUMBRIA, CA13 0EB.

BERRY, Mr. Thomas Richard, MSc BSc(Hons) ACA *2006;* with Deloitte LLP, Athene Place, 66 Shoe Lane, LONDON, EC4A 3BQ.

BERRY, Mr. Timothy Paul, MSc ACA *2000;* 19 Range Meadow Close, LEAMINGTON SPA, WARWICKSHIRE, CV32 6RU.

BERRY, Mrs. Victoria, BSc ACA *2006;* 6 Meadow End, LIPHOOK, HAMPSHIRE, GU30 7UA.

BERRY, Mr. Zair David, FCA *1978;* Flat 17, Price's Court, Cotton Row, LONDON, SW11 3YR.

BERRYMAN, Mr. Brian Arthur Charles, FCA *1952;* 47A Eynsham Road, OXFORD, OX2 9BS. (Life Member)

BERRYMAN, Mr. Douglas John Bliss, MMath ACA *2005;* Flat 2 Alwyn Court, Barnpark Road, TEIGNMOUTH, DEVON, TQ14 8PJ.

BERRYMAN, Miss. Jane Philippa, BPharm ACA *1992;* Vue du Port, Rue Des Vignes, St Peter, JERSEY, JE3 7BE.

BERRYMAN, Mr. Jonathan Richard William, BSc(Hons) ACA MBCS *1991;* Micklebeck, Burtons Lane, CHALFONT ST. GILES, BUCKINGHAMSHIRE, HP8 4BN.

•**BERRYMAN, Mrs. Katherine, BSc ACA** *1991;* Kate Berryman, Micklebeck, Burtons Lane, CHALFONT ST. GILES, BUCKINGHAMSHIRE, HP8 4BN.

BERRYMAN, Mr. Marc, ACA *2009;* 2 Churchfields, LONDON, SE10 9JZ.

•**BERRYMAN, Mr. Scott, BSc ACA** *2000;* PricewaterhouseCoopers LLP, Hays Galleria, 1 Hays Lane, LONDON, SE1 2RD.

BERTHOUD, Mr. Charlton James, BSc ACA *1991;* 1st floor Cromwell House, 14 Fulwood Place, LONDON, WC1V 6HZ.

BERTI, Mr. Mario, MA ACA *2001;* 29 Westcombe Park Road, LONDON, SE3 7RE.

BERTIN, Mr. Richard Gerard, ACA *1991;* F F P Services Ltd, 15 Suffolk Street, LONDON, SW1Y 4HG.

BERTIN, Mrs. Sara, FCA *1976;* Shorefields Holidays Ltd Shorefield Country Park, Shorefield Road Downton, LYMINGTON, SO41 0LH.

•**BERTOLOTTI, Mr. Alex Jonathan, BA ACA** *1997;* PricewaterhouseCoopers LLP, Hays Galleria, 1 Hays Lane, LONDON, SE1 2RD. See also PricewaterhouseCoopers

BERTOLOTTI, Mr. Nicholas Paul, BSc ACA *1987;* C S First Credit Suisse Financial Products, 1 Cabot Square, LONDON, E14 4QJ.

BERTOLOTTI, Ms. Sarah Elizabeth, BCom ACA *1997;* 1 Wensley Close, LONDON, N11 3GU.

BERTORELLI, Miss. Caroline Anne, ACA *1987;* Hikarigaoka 7-7-4-205, Nerima-Ku, TOKYO, 179-0072 JAPAN.

BERTORELLI, Mr. Joseph Romeo Bartolomeo, FCA *1966;* Chatsworth Lodge, 13 Woodland Road, WESTON-SUPER-MARE, BS23 4HF.

BERTORELLO, Miss. Valerie-Maryse, MSc ACA *2009;* 106 Saltram Crescent, LONDON, W9 3JX.

BERTRAM, Mr. Anthony David Weguelin, FCA *1966;* (Tax Fac), 20 Fraser Avenue, Caversham, READING, RG4 6RT.

BERTRAM, Mr. Peter John Andrew, FCA *1955;* 5 Guild Close, Cropston, LEICESTER, LE7 7HT. (Life Member)

BERTRAM, Mr. Peter Michael, BA FCA *1981;* Torrells, Pursers Lane, Peaslake, GUILDFORD, GU5 9RE.

BERTRAM, Mr. Richard James Wilson, BSc FCA *1974;* 12 St. Helen's Road, Norbury, LONDON, SW16 4LB.

BERTRAM, Mr. Timothy Charles Andrew, BA ACA *1992;* Miele Co Ltd Fairacres, Marcham Road, ABINGDON, OXFORDSHIRE, OX14 1TW.

BERTRAM GREGORY, Mr. Christopher Robin, FCA *1974;* 47 Hartwell Road, Long StreetHanslope, MILTON KEYNES, MK19 7BY.

•**BERTRAND, Mr. Eric John, ACA** *1989;* KPMG Channel Islands Limited, 5 St. Andrew's Place, Charing Cross, St. Helier, JERSEY, JE4 8WQ.

BERTSCH, Mr. Timothy, BSc FCA *1990;* 337 Rae Street, FITZROY NORTH, VIC 3068, AUSTRALIA.

BERTWISTLE, Mr. Mark, BA(Hons) ACA *2002;* 10 Bundoran Road, Aigburth, LIVERPOOL, L17 0AX.

BERWICK, Mr. Gerald Richard Gray, BA FCA *1963;* Garden Lodge, Hill House, Burgage Lane, SOUTHWELL, NOTTINGHAMSHIRE, NG25 0ER. (Life Member)

BERY, Mr. Anil, FCA *1969;* 61 Hemkunt Colony, NEW DELHI 110048, INDIA. (Life Member)

BERY, Mr. Brij Lal, BCom FCA *1953;* S-17 Panchshila Park, NEW DELHI 110017, INDIA. (Life Member)

BERY, Mr. Vikram, ACA *1990;* Bago Laboratories Pvt Ltd, 512 Meridian Plaza, Ameerpet, HYDERABAD 500016, ANDHRA PRADESH, INDIA.

BERZINS, Mr. Andrey Charles, BSc ACA *1985;* 24 RAFFLES PLACE, #25-03A CLIFFORD CENTRE, SINGAPORE 048621, SINGAPORE.

•**BESANT-ROBERTS, Miss. Helen Ann, BA FCA** *1999;* Hurst & Company Accountants LLP, Lancashire Gate, 21 Tiviot Dale, STOCKPORT, CHESHIRE, SK1 1TD.

•**BESHAHWRED, Mr. Getachew, MBA FCA** *1996;* (Tax Fac), GB & Co, Brent House, 214 Kenton Road, HARROW, MIDDLESEX, HA3 8BT.

•**BESKINE, Mr. Michael Donald Bernard, BA ACA** *1985;* Office 203. Edf MBC, Avda De las Cumbres Sin/ No., Elviria, 29604 MARBELLA, MALAGA, SPAIN.

BESLEY, Mr. John, FCA *1955;* Barley House, Holton, OXFORD, OX33 1PZ. (Life Member)

BESS, Mr. Matthew Peter, ACA *2008;* 16 Delfryn, Miskin, PONTYCLUN, MID GLAMORGAN, CF72 8SS.

BESSANT, Mr. David Thomas, BSc ACA *1997;* 40 Ryland Road, Edgbaston, BIRMINGHAM, B15 2BN.

BESSANT, Mr. Gavin George, BA ACA *2007;* The Maynard Centre, G E Healthcare Ltd Cardiff Laboratories, Forest Farm Road Whitchurch, CARDIFF, CF14 7YT.

BESSANT, Mrs. Helen, BA ACA *1998;* 40 Ryland Road, Edgbaston, BIRMINGHAM, B15 2BN.

•**BESSANT, Mr. Ian Victor, LLB ACA** *1986;* Durrants, 24 Wellington Business Park, Dukes Ride, CROWTHORNE, RG45 6LS.

BESSANT, Mrs. Kathryn Mary, ACA *1983;* 2 Paddocks End, Reading RoadBurghfield Com, READING, RG7 3BH.

BESSELL-MARTIN, Mrs. Laura, BA ACA *2003;* 49A Sotheby Road, LONDON, N5 2UP.

•**BESSLER, Mr. Peter Arnold, FCA** *1969;* Bessler Hendrie, Albury Mill, Mill Lane, Chilworth, GUILDFORD, SURREY GU4 8RU. See also J P Consulting

BEST - BEVAN — **Members - Alphabetical**

BEST, Mr. Alan, FCA *1972;* 20 Selkirk Way, NORTH SHIELDS, TYNE AND WEAR, NE29 8DD.

BEST, Mr. Andrew, BSc ACA *1987;* 20 Waverley Road, KENILWORTH, CV8 1JN.

•**BEST, Mr. Charles Leslie Mark, ACA** *1987;* Charles Best Limited, 12 Henley Close, Rawdon, LEEDS, LS19 6QB.

BEST, Mr. Christopher John, BA FCA *1982;* 3 Drury Park, Snape, SAXMUNDHAM, IP17 1TA.

BEST, Mr. David Edward Michael, BA FCA *1997;* 11 Broomfield Road, SURBITON, KT5 9AZ.

BEST, Mr. David Graham, FCA *1973;* Toftwood, East Common, HARPENDEN, AL5 1DD.

BEST, Mr. David Martin, BA ACA *1985;* 34 Vicarage Meadow, MIRFIELD, WF14 9JL.

•①**BEST, Mr. Dickon John, BSocSc ACA** *2001;* with PricewaterhouseCoopers, Cornwall Court, 19 Cornwall Street, BIRMINGHAM, B3 2DT.

•**BEST, Mr. Eddie John, BA ACA** *1998;* Grant Thornton UK LLP, 30 Finsbury Square, LONDON, EC2P 2YU. See also Grant Thornton LLP

BEST, Mr. Francis Paul, BA ACA *1988;* April Cottage Cardeston, Ford, SHREWSBURY, SY5 9NN.

•**BEST, Mr. Graham Roy, FCA** *1974;* Graham Best & Co, 189 Lynchford Road, FARNBOROUGH, HAMPSHIRE, GU14 6HD.

•①**BEST, Mr. Ian, BSc ACA** *1987;* Ernst & Young LLP, 1 Colmore Square, BIRMINGHAM, B4 6HQ. See also Ernst & Young Europe LLP

•**BEST, Mrs. Jaine, FCA** *1994;* (Tax Fac), Accountably Limited, First Floor, Unit 12, Compass Point, Ensign Way, Hamble SOUTHAMPTON SO31 4RF.

BEST, Mr. John David, FCA *1970;* 43 Lady Byron Lane, Knowle, SOLIHULL, WEST MIDLANDS, B93 9AX.

BEST, Mrs. Karen Elizabeth, BSc ACA *1997;* Vodafone Group Plc, Vodafone House, The Connection, NEWBURY, BERKSHIRE, RG14 2FN.

•**BEST, Mr. Keith Michael, BA FCA** *1975;* The Chiltern Partnership Ltd, Grafton House, Bulls Head Yard, ALCESTER, WARWICKSHIRE, B49 5BX.

BEST, Mr. Lloyd Stephen, BSc FCA ATII *1989;* 14 Litton Court, 2 Jackson Walk, Menston, ILKLEY, WEST YORKSHIRE, LS29 6BS.

BEST, Mr. Malcolm, FCA *1976;* Glenquay Farm, Glendevon, DOLLAR, CLACKMANNANSHIRE, FK14 7JX.

BEST, Mr. Martyn James, FCA *1980;* 24 Dowhills Drive, LIVERPOOL, L23 8SU.

BEST, Mr. Michael John, FCA *1981;* 15 Oak Close, OTTERY ST. MARY, DEVON, EX11 1BB.

BEST, Miss. Natalie, BA(Hons) ACA *2011;* 22 Skye Close, Alwalton, PETERBOROUGH, PE2 6DT.

BEST, Mr. Nicholas Anthony, BSc ACA *1995;* Keepers Cottage, Blatchbridge, FROME, SOMERSET, BA11 5EJ.

BEST, Mr. Peter, LLB FCA *1964;* 126 Roe Lane, SOUTHPORT, PR9 7PJ. (Life Member)

BEST, Mr. Peter Michael, ACA *1982;* 2 Clent Drive, Hagley, STOURBRIDGE, DY9 9LN.

BEST, Mr. Raymond Merrik, FCA *1957;* High View, 9 The Coppice, Starrs Mead, BATTLE, TN33 0UJ. (Life Member)

BEST, Mr. Redvers Peter Alan, BA FCA *2000;* 4 Badminton Villas, Bridge Street, CHEPSTOW, NP16 5HB.

BEST, Mr. Richard William John, LLB ACA *1995;* The Gables, Castle Road, PEVENSEY, EAST SUSSEX, BN24 5LG.

BEST, Mr. Robin James, BA FCA *1984;* The Old Orchard Tunworth Road, Mapledurwell, BASINGSTOKE, RG25 2LU.

BEST, Mr. Roger George, BCom FCA ATII *1967;* 2913 Kitchums Pond Road, WILLIAMSBURG, VA 23185, UNITED STATES. (Life Member)

•**BEST, Mr. Roger Thomas, FCA** *1973;* 201 Seabee Lane, DISCOVERY BAY, NEW TERRITORIES, HONG KONG SAR.

BEST, Miss. Sarah Elizabeth, ACA *1980;* with F.W. Berringer & Co, Lygon House, 50 London Road, BROMLEY, BR1 3RA.

BESTFORD, Miss. Clare Marie, BA ACA *1993;* Hazel Cottage, Hale House Lane, Churt, FARNHAM, GU10 2JQ.

BESTLEY, Miss. Sarah Elizabeth, BSc ACA *1992;* (Tax Fac), Carter Nicholls Limited, Victoria House, Stanbridge Park, Staplefield Lane, Staplefield, HAYWARDS HEATH WEST SUSSEX RH17 6AS.

BESTON, Mr. Ronald Mathieson Hamilton, FCA *1956;* 15 Kings Mill Park, DRIFFIELD, YO25 6UZ.

BESTWICK, Mr. Christopher Robert, FCA *1980;* 21 Les Arches, La Route de la Cote, St. Martin, JERSEY, JE3 6LA.

BESTWICK, Mr. Edward Alfred, FCA *1969;* 33 Sapcote Road, Stoney Stanton, LEICESTER, LE9 4DW.

BESTWICK, Mr. Matthew, ACA *2011;* 7a Savile Park, HALIFAX, WEST YORKSHIRE, HX1 3EA.

BESTWICK, Mr. Robert Gordon, BA ACA *2005;* 1308 788 12th Ave SW, CALGARY T2R 0H1, AB, CANADA.

BESTWICK, Mr. Stephen Charles, FCA *1972;* 1 Redbarn Close, LEEDS, LS10 4SZ.

BESTWICK, Mr. Timothy Bembridge, FCA *1962;* 27 Elgin Avenue, Littleover, DERBY, DE23 7SE.

BESWETHERICK, Mr. Nigel Phillips, FCA *1952;* The Cottage, Says Lane, Langford, BRISTOL, BS40 5DZ. (Life Member)

BESWETHERICK, Mrs. Sara Jane, BSc ACA *1990;* Serena, Warren Road, Chelsfield, ORPINGTON, BR6 6JB.

BESWICK, Mr. Graham Edward, BA ACA *1990;* Fisher Productions Ltd, 118 Garratt Lane, LONDON, SW18 4DJ.

BESWICK, Mr. Graham John, BCom FCA *1967;* 33 Blandy Road, HENLEY-ON-THAMES, OXFORDSHIRE, RG9 1QB.

BESWICK, Mr. John Kenneth, BSc(Hons) ACA *2002;* 19 Broadfields Avenue, Winchmore Hill, LONDON, N21 1AB.

BESWICK, Mrs. Kirsty Fiona, BSc ACA *1999;* 3 Lomond View, Symington, KILMARNOCK, AYRSHIRE, KA1 5QS.

BESWICK, Mr. Nigel Lloyd, BA FCA *1989;* Mitie Client Service Ltd Cottons Centre, Cottons Lane, LONDON, SE1 2QG.

BESWICK, Mr. Richard Noel, ACA *1985;* GPO Box 1571, HOBART, TAS 7001, AUSTRALIA.

BESWICK, Miss. Sarah, BSc ACA *2001;* 1 Wood Lane, Harborne, BIRMINGHAM, B17 9AY.

BESWITHERICK, Mr. David Peter, FCA *1980;* 12 Horncastle Close, Woodbank, BURY, BL8 1XE.

BETESH, Mr. Daniel Joseph, FCA *1960;* Kennedy Street Enterprises Ltd, Kennedy House, 31 Stamford Street, ALTRINCHAM, CHESHIRE, WA14 1ES.

BETHEL, Mr. Peter David, FCA *1969;* (Tax Fac), Tingrith, Ashburton Road, TOTNES, TQ9 5JU.

BETHELL, Mrs. Clare Anne, ACA *1993;* 2 St Johns Avenue, CHELMSFORD, ESSEX, CM2 0UA.

BETHELL, Mr. Jonas Sanderson, FCA *1954;* 24 Glebe Park, Eyam, HOPE VALLEY, DERBYSHIRE, S32 5RH. (Life Member)

BETHELL, Mr. Mark David, LLB ACA *1991;* Informa Telecoms, Mortimer House, 37-41 Mortimer Street, LONDON, W1T 3JH.

BETHELL, Mr. Peter John, FCA *1954;* 3 Westmorland Grove, Norton, STOCKTON-ON-TEES, TS20 1PA. (Life Member)

BETHENCOURT, Mrs. Angela Rich, FCA *1976;* 3c Julian Mansions, Julian Road, BRISTOL, BS9 1NQ. (Life Member)

BETHUNE, Mr. Richard, ACA *2007;* 11 Violet Hill, LONDON, NW8 9EB.

•**BETLEY, Mr. Anthony Derek, BA FCA** *1982;* Guidewise Ltd, 27 Redwood Glade, LEIGHTON BUZZARD, BEDFORDSHIRE, LU7 3JT. See also Betley A.D.

BETT, Mr. Darren Brian, BSc ACA *1999;* Grønnegade 41 1, 7100 VEJLE, DENMARK.

BETT, Mr. James Wilson, ACA CA(AUS) *2009;* Rose Farm Cottage The Front, Potten End, BERKHAMSTED, HERTFORDSHIRE, HP4 2QR.

BETT, Mrs. Katie Jane, BA ACA *2000;* Rose Farm Cottage The Front, Potten End, BERKHAMSTED, HERTFORDSHIRE, HP4 2QR.

BETT, Miss. Lara, ACA *2010;* Flat 5, 165 Kings Road, READING, RG1 4EX.

BETT, Mr. Timothy John, FCA *1969;* 21 Welcombe Grove, SOLIHULL, B91 1PD.

•**BETTAM, Mrs. Belinda Carol, BSc ACA** *1991;* Belinda Bettam ACA, 16 Sandy Lane, Little Neston, NESTON, CH64 4DR.

•**BETTANEY, Mrs. Sheila Helen, BA FCA CTA** *1978;* (Tax Fac), S.H. Bettaney, 78 Harrowes Meade, EDGWARE, HA8 8RP.

BETTANY, Ms. Jane, ACA *2011;* Amex House UMC 52-01-024, American Express Europe Ltd, 154-155 Edward Street, BRIGHTON, BN88 1AH.

BETTANY, Mr. Nicholas Paul Pyatt, BA ACA MBA MSI *2002;* The Hideaways Club (UK) Ltd, 136 Sloane Street, LONDON, SW1X 9AY.

•**BETTANY, Mr. Ralph Christopher, BSc FCA** *1986;* Ralph Bettany Associates Limited, 1st Floor, 13 Vardre Road, Clydach, SWANSEA, SA6 5LP. See also Diamond RBA Ltd

BETTELEY, Mr. Ian Stewart, BA(Hons) ACA *2002;* 12 North Brook Road, Utkinton, TARPORLEY, CHESHIRE, CW6 0LS.

BETTELEY, Mr. Mark John, BA ACA *1998;* 44 Batchwood Drive, ST. ALBANS, HERTFORDSHIRE, AL3 5SB.

•**BETTERIDGE, Mrs. Deborah Emma, ACA** *1999;* Sycamore Accounting Services, 42 New Lane, Huntington, YORK, YO32 9NT.

•**BETTERIDGE, Mr. Ian Clark, FCA** *1974;* MacIntyre Hudson LLP, Lyndale House, Ervington Court, Harcourt Way, Meridian Business Park, LEICESTER LE19 1WL.

BETTERIDGE, Mr. Lee Anthony, LLB ACA *2006;* 13 Kew Avenue, SINGAPORE 466302, SINGAPORE.

BETTERIDGE, Mr. Paul Anthony Andrew, LLB ACA *2001;* 69 Freegrounds Road, Hedge End, SOUTHAMPTON, SO30 0HS.

BETTERIDGE, Mr. Robert Stefan Cowley, BSc FCA *1976;* John Smith & Son (Glasgow) Ltd Unit 19, Headlands Business Park Salisbury Road Blashford, RINGWOOD, HAMPSHIRE, BH24 3PB.

BETTERIDGE, Mr. Simon Richard, BA ACA *2007;* 4 Brockley Road, West Bridgford, NOTTINGHAM, NG2 5JY.

•**BETTESWORTH, Mr. David Sean, BSc ACA** *1997;* Deloitte LLP, 2 New Street Square, LONDON, EC4A 3BZ. See also Deloitte & Touche LLP

BETTIN, Mr. Christoph Markus, BA ACA *1997;* Lower Milltown, Milltown, LOSTWITHIEL, CORNWALL, PL22 0JL.

•**BETTINSON, Mr. Michael Charles Edgar, FCA** *1976;* (Tax Fac), Cole & Co, 400 Harrow Rd, LONDON, W9 2HU.

BETTINSON, Mr. Paul Robert, BA FCA *1999;* Theldew, 11 Doran Drive, REDHILL, RH1 6AX.

BETTISON, Miss. Emily Margaret, ACA *2009;* Scaramanga, 80 Royal Avenue, Onchan, ISLE OF MAN, IM3 1LB.

BETTISON, Mr. Richard Thomas, BA ACA *2006;* 21 Chyandour, REDRUTH, CORNWALL, TR15 3AB.

BETTLES, Mr. Clive Douglas, ACA *1993;* 9 Devonshire Park Road, Davenport, STOCKPORT, SK2 6JZ.

BETTLES, Mr. Kurt James, ACA *2004;* 1st Floor, Carston & Co (Cardiff) Ltd Tudor House, 16 Cathedral Road, CARDIFF, CF11 9LJ.

BETTLEY, Dr. Richard Matthew, MA DPhil ACA *2001;* Room 252, Cardiff County Council, County Hall, Atlantic Wharf, CARDIFF, CF10 4UW.

BETTLEY, Mr. Terence, FCA *1957;* 59 Wood Street, South Hiendley, BARNSLEY, SOUTH YORKSHIRE, S72 9BJ. (Life Member)

BETTNEY, Mrs. Dawn Sharon, BSc ACA *1989;* 22 Oak Grove, Easton In Gordano, BRISTOL, BS20 0LN.

BETTON, Miss. Alice Miranda, ACA *2009;* with H W, Sterling House, 5 Buckingham Place, Bellfield Rd West, HIGH WYCOMBE, HP13 5HQ.

BETTON, Mr. Andrew David Norman, BA ACA *1997;* 2 Howitt Lodge, 6 Eversley Park Road, LONDON, N21 1JX.

BETTON, Mrs. Madeleine Christine, BSc ACA *1996;* 60 Lowther Drive, Oakwood, ENFIELD, EN2 7JP.

•**BETTRIDGE, Mrs. Catherine Louise, BA ACA** *1993;* James, 6 Beaconsfield Road, Clifton, BRISTOL, BS8 2TS.

•**BETTRIDGE, Mr. Michael Graham, BSc ACA** *1996;* Bettridge & Co, 28 Broad Street, WOKINGHAM, BERKSHIRE, RG40 1AB. See also Windows Bookkeeping Ltd

BETTS, Mr. Andrew John, BA ACA *2004;* 73 Mackie Avenue, BRIGHTON, BN1 8RD.

BETTS, Mr. Anthony George, BSc FCA *1964;* 23 Boundary Drive, Moseley, BIRMINGHAM, B13 8NY. (Life Member)

BETTS, Mr. Arthur Selby, FCA *1963;* 7 Pilkington Avenue, SUTTON COLDFIELD, B72 1LA.

BETTS, Mrs. Caron, ACA FCCA *2011;* 34 Copplestone Close, Worlingham, BECCLES, SUFFOLK, NR34 7SF.

BETTS, Mrs. Emma Louise, ACA *2011;* 6 Martin Crescent, Ruddington, NOTTINGHAM, NG11 6AG.

BETTS, Miss. Georgina Louise Michelle, BSc ACA *2006;* 2 Langham Way, ELY, CAMBRIDGESHIRE, CB6 1DZ.

BETTS, Mr. Graham Louis, FCA *1981;* Anchors Wood, Hindhead Road, HASLEMERE, GU27 1LR.

BETTS, Mrs. Hayley Ann, BSc ACA *1992;* 7 The Belfry, Bushmead, LUTON, LU2 7GA.

•**BETTS, Mr. John Arthur, BA FCA** *1973;* with Philip Hudson & Co, 454-458 Chiswick High Road, LONDON, W4 5TT.

BETTS, Mr. Jonathan Martin, BA ACA *1990;* Tesco Stores Ltd Tesco House, Delamare Road Cheshunt, WALTHAM CROSS, HERTFORDSHIRE, EN8 9SL.

BETTS, Miss. Katie, ACA *2010;* 324 Feltham Hill Road, ASHFORD, MIDDLESEX, TW15 1LW.

BETTS, Mrs. Laura Clare, BSc ACA *2004;* 16 Lime Avenue, HIGH WYCOMBE, BUCKINGHAMSHIRE, HP11 1DP.

BETTS, Mr. Martin Brian, BA FCA DipM *1999;* 18 Mill Hey Lane, Rufford, ORMSKIRK, L40 1SJ.

BETTS, Mr. Martin John, ACA *1986;* Rio Tinto Iron & Tatanium Ltd, 2 Eastbourne Terrace, LONDON, W2 6LG.

BETTS, Ms. May, ACA *1991;* 8 Talbot Road, East Dulwich, LONDON, SE22 8EH.

BETTS, Mr. Michael Andrew, ACA *2009;* 16 Bennett Court, Gordon Road, CAMBERLEY, SURREY, GU15 2JJ.

BETTS, Mr. Michael Robert, BA ACA *1994;* Coolmore Lodge, Bethesda Street, Upper Basildon, READING, RG8 8NU.

BETTS, Mr. Nicholas David, ACA *1991;* 28a St. Leonards Road, Claygate, ESHER, SURREY, KT10 0EL.

BETTS, Miss. Nicola Alexa, ACA *2009;* Flat B, 190 Bedford Hill, LONDON, SW12 9HL.

•**BETTS, Mr. Nigel Rolf, MIEM BA ACA** *2002;* (Tax Fac), Professional Tax & Accounting Services Ltd, 44 Squires Lane, Finchley, LONDON, N3 2AT.

BETTS, Mr. Paul Aaron, BA ACA *2002;* 289 Lidgett Lane, LEEDS, LS17 6PD.

BETTS, Mr. Paul Alex, ACA *1980;* 11 Gleaners Close, Grove Green, MAIDSTONE, ME14 5ST.

BETTS, Mr. Paul Wickham, ACA *1980;* The Old Parsonage, The Common, Mellis, EYE, SUFFOLK, IP23 8EE.

BETTS, Mr. Richard, BSc ACA *2009;* Flat 23, Tyndal Court, Transom Square, LONDON, E14 3TQ.

BETTS, Mr. Richard John, ACA *1986;* (Tax Fac), 9 Greylag Close, Salhouse, NORWICH, NR13 6SD.

BETTS, Mr. Stephen, ACA *2010;* Associated British Foods Plc, 10 Grosvenor Street, LONDON, W1K 4QY.

BETTS, Mr. Timothy Alexander, BSc ACA *2007;* 41 Moors Ley, Walkern, STEVENAGE, HERTFORDSHIRE, SG2 7NQ.

BETTS, Mrs. Toni Jayne, BA(Hons) ACA *2003;* 73 Mackie Avenue, BRIGHTON, BN1 8RD.

BETTY, Mr. David Rex, FCA *1961;* RSM Betty & Dickson, PO Box 1734, RANDBURG, GAUTENG, 2125, SOUTH AFRICA.

BEUDEN, Mr. Kenneth William Illtyd, MA LLB FCA *2001;* Brooklands, 99 Glaziers Lane, Normandy, GUILDFORD, SURREY, GU3 2EA.

BEUSCH, Dr. Danny, PhD MA BA(Hons) ACA *2011;* 241 Station Road, Kings Heath, BIRMINGHAM, B14 7TF.

BEUTLICH, Mrs. Lynne, MA(Oxon) ACA ATII *1989;* Loretohoehe 16, 6300 ZUG, SWITZERLAND.

BEUTLICH, Mr. Matthew, BA ACA *1992;* Loretohoehe 16, CH - 6300 ZUG, SWITZERLAND.

BEVAN, Mr. Alan James, BSc FCA *1972;* 19A Fulmer Drive, GERRARDS CROSS, SL9 7HH.

BEVAN, Mr. Alexander, BA ACA *1999;* Ealing Abbey, Charlbury Grove, LONDON, W5 2DY.

BEVAN, Mr. Anthony William, BSc ACA *1990;* 32 Dyfed, Northcliffe, PENARTH, CF64 1DX.

BEVAN, Miss. Caroline, BA ACA CTA *1999;* with PricewaterhouseCoopers LLP, 1 Embankment Place, LONDON, WC2N 6RH.

BEVAN, Mrs. Caroline Sela, BSc ACA CTA *1987;* 18 Cintra Avenue, READING, BERKSHIRE, RG2 7AU.

BEVAN, Miss. Charlotte Ann, ACA *2009;* 10 Coronation Terrace, PONTYPRIDD, MID GLAMORGAN, CF37 4DP.

•**BEVAN, Mr. Christopher John, BA ACA** *1987;* (Tax Fac), Addicus, 1 Winchester Place, North Street, POOLE, BH15 1NX.

BEVAN, Mr. Christopher Stuart, BA ACA ATII *1994;* 16 Keswick Close, Ainsdale, SOUTHPORT, PR8 3QR.

BEVAN, Mr. David, MA ACA *2000;* 6 Parkfield Road, LONDON, NW10 2BJ.

BEVAN, Mr. David Charles, BSc FCA *1991;* (Tax Fac), 1 Oakland Drive, NEATH, WEST GLAMORGAN, SA10 7ED.

BEVAN, Mr. David John, FCA *1966;* 1 Walnut Way, Hyde Heath, AMERSHAM, BUCKINGHAMSHIRE, HP6 5SB.

BEVAN, Mr. Francis Leslie, ACA *1987;* 45 Maple Drive, EXMOUTH, DEVON, EX8 5NR.

BEVAN, Mr. Hugh Charles, FCA *1987;* Manor House, Church Road, Upper Farringdon, ALTON, GU34 3EG.

BEVAN, Mr. Hywel Richard, BSc ACA *2010;* Sundorne Holdernesse Road, LONDON, SW17 7RG.

•**BEVAN, Mr. John David, FCA** *1980;* Guy Walmsley & Co, 3 Grove Road, WREXHAM, LL11 1DY.

•**BEVAN, Mr. John Garnett, FCA** *1958;* John Bevan, Underhill, SOUTH BRENT, TQ10 9DZ.

BEVAN, Mr. Jonathan David, BSc ACA *1996;* with Clear Channel Outdoor, 33 Golden Square, LONDON, W1F 9JT.

BEVAN, Mr. Jonathan Mark, BA ACA *1979;* 2 Stoneybridge Court, Stoneybridge, Belbroughton, STOURBRIDGE, WEST MIDLANDS, DY9 9XT.
BEVAN, Miss. Karen Michelle, BSc ACA *2004;* 15 Hillside Avenue, Carrbrook, STALYBRIDGE, CHESHIRE, SK15 3NE.
BEVAN, Mr. Keith Andrew, BSc ACA *1988;* 4 The Sanctuary, Hulme, MANCHESTER, M15 5TR.
BEVAN, Mr. Luke Andrew John, MSc ACA *2010;* 62 Havendale, Hedge End, SOUTHAMPTON, SO30 0FD.
BEVAN, Mr. Malcolm Leslie, FCA *1964;* 8 Fulmar Crescent, Boxmoor, HEMEL HEMPSTEAD, HP1 1SG.
BEVAN, Mr. Martin, BSc FCA *1983;* Cygnet House, Swan Yard, East Street, Coggeshall, COLCHESTER, CO6 1SJ.
BEVAN, Mr. Matthew Armstrong, BA(Hons) ACA CIA *2001;* 73 Northcote Street, NAREMBURN, VIC 2065, AUSTRALIA.
BEVAN, Mr. Paul, BA ACA *1983;* 1485 Holyoak Lane, LUCAS, TX 75002, UNITED STATES.
BEVAN, Mr. Peter Harrison, FCA *1957;* The Creel, Back Lane, Clive, SHREWSBURY, SY4 3LA. (Life Member)
•BEVAN, Mr. Peter Joseph, BA ACA *1995;* 11 Patch Lane, Bramhall, STOCKPORT, CHESHIRE, SK7 1JB.
BEVAN, Mr. Richard Charles, BA ACA *1998;* (Tax Fac), Flat 1a, 15 Chelsea Embankment, LONDON, SW3 4LA.
BEVAN, Mr. Richard Peter Alexander Wilmot, BSc ACA *1989;* 24 Portsmouth Avenue, THAMES DITTON, SURREY, KT7 0RT.
BEVAN, Mr. Roger, MBA LLB ACA *1984;* The Shires, 20 Woodbank, Loosley Row, PRINCES RISBOROUGH, BUCKINGHAMSHIRE, HP27 0TS.
BEVAN, Miss. Sarah, ACA *2010;* Flat 5, 49 Fog Lane, MANCHESTER, M20 6AR.
BEVAN, Mrs. Sarah Louise, MA ACA *2005;* 31 Wherretts Well Lane, SOLIHULL, B91 2SD.
BEVAN, Miss. Shanie Leanne, ACA MAAT *2002;* 18 Mabel Grove, West Bridgford, NOTTINGHAM, NG2 5GT.
•BEVAN, Mr. Simon Bruce, BA FCA *1985;* 4 Nelsons Yard, LONDON, NW1 7RN.
•BEVAN, Mr. Simon James Platel, FCA *1971;* Simon Bevan, Cheviot View, Holy Island, BERWICK-UPON-TWEED, TD15 2SQ.
•BEVAN, Mrs. Sophia, BA FCA *1991;* BDO LLP, 55 Baker Street, LONDON, W1U 7EU. See also BDO Stoy Hayward LLP
BEVAN, Mr. Timothy John, BA ACA *2000;* Little Plummerden Ardingly Road, Lindfield, HAYWARDS HEATH, WEST SUSSEX, RH16 2QY.
BEVAN-JONES, Mr. Julian David William, FCA *1974;* Box LY 23, LAYOU, SAINT VINCENT AND THE GRENADINES.
•BEVAN-JONES, Mr. Richard Ian, FCA *1977;* Owen John & Co Ltd, Mardy Chambers, 6 Wind Street, SWANSEA, SA1 1DH.
•BEVENS, Mrs. Stella, BA ACA *1989;* Bennett Brooks & Co Ltd Maple Court, Davenport Street, MACCLESFIELD, CHESHIRE, SK10 1JE.
•BEVERIDGE, Mr. Alastair Paul, BEng FCA *1991;* with Zolfo Cooper Ltd, 10 Fleet Place, LONDON, EC4M 7RB.
BEVERIDGE, Mr. Andrew Alexander, FCA *1954;* Greystones, High Callerton, Ponteland, NEWCASTLE UPON TYNE, NE20 9TT. (Life Member)
BEVERIDGE, Mr. Christopher, ACA *2007;* 41 Page Hill, WARE, HERTFORDSHIRE, SG12 0RZ.
BEVERIDGE, Mr. David Mark Andrew, BSc ACA *1987;* Holly Lodge, The Green, Croxley Green, RICKMANSWORTH, WD3 3HN.
BEVERIDGE, Mr. Duncan Jeremy Graham, BSc ACA *1987;* Jarvis Hotels Ltd Castle House, 71-75 Desborough Road, HIGH WYCOMBE, BUCKINGHAMSHIRE, HP11 2PR.
BEVERIDGE, Mr. Glen Thomas, BSc FCA *1977;* 5 Firbank Avenue, Torrance, GLASGOW, G64 4EJ. (Life Member)
BEVERIDGE, Mr. Ian, BSc ACA *1983;* 12 Elmwood, MAIDENHEAD, SL6 8HX.
BEVERIDGE, Mr. James John, BA ACA *1991;* 25 Kelsey Way, BECKENHAM, KENT, BR3 3LP.
BEVERIDGE, Mr. John Alan, BA ACA *1990;* 19 Kings Road, WHITLEY BAY, NE26 3BD.
BEVERIDGE, Mr. Robert James, BA ACA *1980;* 81 Kidmore Road, Caversham, READING, RG4 7NQ.
BEVERLEY, Mr. Eric Robert, FCA *1976;* 7 Park View, HOLMFIRTH, HD9 3BT.
BEVERLEY, Mr. Gerald, FCA *1954;* Flat 7, High Sheldon, Sheldon Avenue, Highate, LONDON, N6 4NJ. (Life Member)
BEVERLEY, Mrs. Lucy Catherine Lindsey, BSc ACA *1998;* 71 Horniman Drive, LONDON, SE23 3BU.
BEVERLEY, Mr. Michael, DL BA FCA FRSA *1976;* One Medical, Black Hill Road, Arthington, OTLEY, WEST YORKSHIRE, LS21 1PY.
BEVERLEY, Mr. Nathan Francis, BSc ACA *2011;* 17a London Road South, Merstham, REDHILL, RH1 3AZ.
BEVERLEY-HOLE, Mr. Clive Patrick, FCA *1970;* 30 rue des Sablons, 78750 MAREIL MARLY, FRANCE.
BEVERTON, Mr. John Davey, FCA *1965;* c/o Beverton & Co, 3 Old Print House, Russell Street, DOVER, KENT, CT16 1PX. (Life Member)
•BEVERTON, Mr. Neil David, ACA *1985;* Beverton & Co., 3 The Old Print House, Russell Street, DOVER, CT16 1PX.
•BEVINGTON, Mr. Mark, BA ACA *1998;* Ernst & Young LLP, 1 More London Place, LONDON, SE1 2AF. See also Ernst & Young Europe LLP
BEVINGTON, Miss. Romana Jane, BA ACA *2005;* with PricewaterhouseCoopers LLP, 31 Great George Street, BRISTOL, BS1 5QD.
BEVINGTON, Mr. Ryan Scott, LLB ACA *2002;* Maven Capital Partners UK LLP, St. James House, 7 Charlotte Street, MANCHESTER, M1 4DZ.
BEVINGTON, Mrs. Thida, BSc ACA *2000;* The Old Rectory, Foulsham, DEREHAM, NORFOLK, NR20 5SF.
BEVIS, Mr. Alexander Peter, BA(Hons) ACA *2001;* 3 Home Close, Histon, CAMBRIDGE, CB24 9JL.
•BEVIS, Mr. Christopher John, FCA *1974;* Bevis & Co, Apex House, 6 West Street, EPSOM, SURREY, KT18 7RG. See also Music Business Associates Limited
•BEVIS, Mr. Geoffrey David, FCA *1969;* (Tax Fac), Bevis Accountants Ltd, First Floor, 32-34 High Street, RINGWOOD, HAMPSHIRE, BH24 1AG.
•BEVIS, Mr. Michael Andrew, BSc FCA *1979;* 89 Dunyeats Road, BROADSTONE, DORSET, BH18 8AF.
•BEVIS, Mr. Philip Leslie, ACA FCCA *2010;* Andrews & Palmer Limited, 32 The Square, GILLINGHAM, DORSET, SP8 4AR.
BEWERS, Mrs. Heather, BA ACA *1993;* with KPMG LLP, 15 Canada Square, LONDON, E14 5GL.
BEWERS, Mr. John Stuart Leslie, FCA *1957;* 15 Packsaddle Park, Prestbury, MACCLESFIELD, SK10 4PU. (Life Member)
•BEWERS, Mr. Paul Anthony, BSc FCA *1976;* Bewers Turner & Co Ltd, Portland House, Station Road, KETTERING, NORTHAMPTONSHIRE, NN15 7HH.
BEWES, Mr. Jonathan Michael Arundell, BA ACA *1991;* U B S Limited, 2 Finsbury Avenue, LONDON, EC2M 2PP.
BEWES, Mrs. Lorraine, MA(Oxon) ACA *1987;* 32 Allfarthing Lane, Wandsworth, LONDON, SW18 2PQ.
BEWICK, Mr. Alastair James, BSc ACA *2007;* 4b Elsie Road, LONDON, SE22 8DX.
•BEWICK, Mr. Brian Neville, FCA *1965;* B.N. Bewick, 5 Radway Close, Whiteholme, THORNTON-CLEVELEYS, FY5 3EZ.
BEWICK, Mrs. Pamela Jayne, BA ACA *1998;* Arriva Plc, 1 Admiral Way, Doxford International Business Park, SUNDERLAND, SR3 3XP.
•ⒹBEWICK, Miss. Samantha Rae, BA FCA *1993;* with KPMG LLP, 15 Canada Square, LONDON, E14 5GL.
BEWLEY, Miss. Louisa Mary, BSc ACA *1988;* Flat 3, 356 Camden Road, LONDON, N7 0LG.
BEWLEY, Mr. Mark William, BSc ACA *1986;* HKEX, Listing Division, 11/F One Int'l Finance Centre, CENTRAL, HONG KONG ISLAND, HONG KONG SAR.
BEWLEY, Mrs. Natalie Louise, ACA *2008;* 79 Matlock Close, Great Sankey, WARRINGTON, WA5 3PZ.
BEWS, Mr. Colin Innes, BA ACA *1986;* 7 Metford Road, Redland, BRISTOL, BS6 7LA.
BEWS, Mr. Paul Anthony, FCA *1972;* 10 Beechwood Close, Church Crookham, FLEET, GU51 5PT.
BEWSHER, Miss. Clare Elizabeth, BSc ACA ATII *1993;* 7/11A Oyama Ave, MANLY, NSW 2095, AUSTRALIA.
BEXFIELD, Mrs. Alison Margaret, MA FCA *1993;* B B C Trust, 180 Great Portland Street, LONDON, W1W 5QZ.
BEXFIELD, Mr. Henry Simon, BA FCA *1968;* 1 Turret Lodge, Bents Road, SHEFFIELD, S11 9RG. (Life Member)
•BEXLEY, Mr. Kevin Howard, BSc ACA ATII *1991;* (Tax Fac), Optima Financial Solutions Limited, Elms Farm, Upper Minety, MALMESBURY, WILTSHIRE, SN16 9PR.
•BEXON, Mr. Adam James Scott, MChem ACA *2008;* Stewart Fletcher and Barrett, Manor Court Chambers, 126 Manor Court Road, NUNEATON, CV11 5HL.
BEXON, Mrs. Caroline Zoe, BA ACA *2008;* 24 Cedar Avenue, Ryton on Dunsmore, COVENTRY, CV8 3QB.
•BEXON, Mr. John Philip, BA FCA *1984;* Bexons Accountants Limited, 24 Rectory Road, West Bridgford, NOTTINGHAM, NG2 6BG.
BEYER, Mr. Arthur Riaan, ACA CA(SA) *2009;* 53 Meridian Place, LONDON, E14 9FE.
BEYER, Mr. Holger, MA ACA *1999;* 4 Sandels Way, BEACONSFIELD, BUCKINGHAMSHIRE, HP9 2AB.
BEYHUM, Miss. Maya, BA ACA *1998;* Morgan Stanley, 20 Cabot Square Canary Wharf, LONDON, E14 4QW.
BEYNON, Mr. David Owen, BEd ACA *1985;* David Benyon Financial Consultant, 40 South Road, SAFFRON WALDEN, CB11 3DN.
BEYNON, Mr. David Richard, BSc FCA *1975;* Tegfan, Pwllmeyric, CHEPSTOW, GWENT, NP16 6LA.
BEYNON, Mr. Desmond Michael, BSc(Econ) ACA *1998;* Finance Office, University College Cork, College Road, CORK, COUNTY CORK, IRELAND.
BEYNON, Dr. Emma Margaret, BA ACA *2001;* (Tax Fac), 6 Sugworth Close, HAYWARDS HEATH, WEST SUSSEX, RH16 1PN.
BEYNON, Mr. John Hill, BSc ACA *1980;* P.O. Box 902, CROWS NEST, NSW 2065, AUSTRALIA.
•BEYNON, Mr. Michael John, FCA *1969;* M J Beynon Limited, 7 Pennard Drive, Pennard, SWANSEA, SA3 2BL.
BEYNON, Mr. Paul Adams, BSc ACA *1988;* 24 Glen Road, Norton, SWANSEA, SA3 5PR.
BEYNON, Mr. Peter, BSc FCA *1981;* Level 27 Al Moosa Tower 11, Sheikh Zayeed Road, PO Box 113341, DUBAI, UNITED ARAB EMIRATES.
BEYNON, Mr. Raymond John, FCA *1960;* 375 Clydach Road, Ynysforgan, SWANSEA, SA6 6QN. (Life Member)
BEYNON, Mr. Robert Charles, BSc ACA *1991;* (Tax Fac), 202 Riverside Drive, Apt 4C, NEW YORK, NY 10025, UNITED STATES.
BEYNON, Mr. Thomas, ACA *2008;* Flat 5 Pinehurst House, 43 Springfield Road, DORKING, SURREY, RH4 3PB.
BEYNON, Mr. Warren David Clarke, BA ACA *2000;* Pilgrims, 3 Charles Hankin Close, IVYBRIDGE, DEVON, PL21 0WF.
BEYNON, Mr. William Brian, FCA *1954;* 61 Moore Street, Howick, AUCKLAND, NEW ZEALAND. (Life Member)
BEYNON-NUR, Miss. Caroline Jane, BA ACA *1992;* 68 Trematon Place, TEDDINGTON, MIDDLESEX, TW11 9RG.
BEZANT, Mr. Colin David, ACA *1989;* with PricewaterhouseCoopers LLP, 9 Greyfriars Road, READING, RG1 1JG.
•BEZANT, Mr. Mark, BA FCA *1991;* Tall Trees, Priory Close, CHISLEHURST, KENT, BR7 5LB.
BEZEM, Mr. David Charles, BSc ACA *1985;* 3 Sharon Road, CHISWICK, LONDON, W4 4PD.
BEZZANT, Mr. John William, BSc FCA *1996;* 28 Silhill Hall Road, SOLIHULL, B91 1JU.
BHABHA, Mr. Homi Cooverji Hormasji, FCA *1981;* 49 Cuffe Parade, MUMBAI 400 005, MAHARASHTRA, INDIA.
BHABUTA, Mrs. Varinder, BA(Econ) ACA *2003;* 203 Parr Lane, BURY, BL9 8JW.
BHACHU, Mr. Tarnjeet Singh, MSci ACA *2010;* 10 Roxholme Terrace, LEEDS, LS7 4JH.
BHADHAL, Mrs. Rita, BSc ACA *1994;* 32 London Road, New Balderton, NEWARK, NG24 3AJ.
BHADOO, Mr. Kunal, MSc ACA *2003;* House No. 1054, Street No.3, Circular Road, ABOHAR 152116, PUNJAB, INDIA.
BHADRA, Mr. Santanu, BSc ACA *1993;* 8 Bradmore Way, Lower Earley, READING, RG6 4DS.
•BHADURI, Mr. Sanjay Kumar, BSc FCA *1979;* SME Accountancy Limited, 46-48 High Street, BARNET, HERTFORDSHIRE, EN5 5SJ.
BHAGANI, Mr. Ashok Babulal, FCA *1976;* 14 Penn House, Main Avenue, NORTHWOOD, MIDDLESEX, HA6 2HH.
BHAGAT, Miss. Bhavna, BA ACA *1996;* 83 Marlborough Road, SLOUGH, SL3 7JS.
BHAGAT, Mr. Kishor, BSc ACA *1979;* 24 Dickinson Road, KENDALL PARK, NJ 08824, UNITED STATES.
BHAGAT, Mr. Sanjiv, ACA *1980;* 28 Swan Gardens, Tetsworth, THAME, OXFORDSHIRE, OX9 7BN.
BHAGCHANDANI, Mr. Rajeev, ACA *2008;* Flat 111 Maurer Court, Mudlarks Boulevard, LONDON, SE10 0SY.
BHAGDEV, Mr. Malav Himanshu, ACA *2009;* Deloitte & Touche Llp, 2 Hardman Street, MANCHESTER, M3 3HF.
•BHAGEERUTTY, Mr. Sanroy Shiv, BSc FCA *1994;* 10 Sedlescombe Road, LONDON, SW6 1RD.
•BHAGI, Mr. Anil Kumar, FCA *1984;* (Tax Fac), Anil K. Bhagi, 91 Soho Hill, Hockley, BIRMINGHAM, B19 1AY.
BHAGRATH, Mr. Mandeep Singh, BA ACA CF *1990;* Kapitalize LLP, Cherry Cottage, 28 Chipperfield Road, KINGS LANGLEY, HERTFORDSHIRE, WD4 9JA.
BHAIJI, Mr. Imran, BSc(Hons) ACA *2009;* 254 Revidge Road, BLACKBURN, BB1 8DJ.
BHAIJI, Mr. Inayat Ali Mansurali, FCA *1977;* P.O BOX 82220, MOMBASA, 80100, KENYA.
BHAIWALA, Mr. Danish Zoeb, BA(Hons) ACA *2000;* Flat 19, Longstone Court, 22 Great Dover Street, LONDON, SE1 4LB.
BHAKAR, Mr. Gurdeep Singh, ACA *2009;* 57 St. Andrews Road, ILFORD, IG1 3PF.
BHAKTA, Mr. Divyesh, BSc ACA *1998;* 2 - 14th Street, Apt 812, HOBOKEN, NJ 07030, UNITED STATES.
BHALERAO, Mr. Vibhas Hari, BSc ACA *1987;* 37 Stanhope Avenue, Finchley, LONDON, N3 3LX.
BHALLA, Mr. Amit Kumar, BA ACA *2006;* with PricewaterhouseCoopers LLP, 89 Sandyford Road, NEWCASTLE UPON TYNE, NE1 8HW.
BHALLA, Mr. Hitesh Nand, MSci ACA *2010;* 6 Clevedon Gardens, HOUNSLOW, TW5 9TS.
BHALLA, Miss. Krisma, BSc ACA *2010;* 3 Chapman Crescent, HARROW, MIDDLESEX, HA3 0TG.
BHALLA, Mr. Puneet, BSc(Hons) ACA *2001;* 16 Park Drive, North Harrow, HARROW, MIDDLESEX, HA2 7LT.
BHALLA, Mr. Victor Vinod, ACA *1979;* Fairfield, The Village, Upper Basildon, READING, RG8 8LU.
BHALOO, Mr. Amirali Kamrudin Nurmohamed, BA FCA *1975;* 143 Hampstead Rise NW, CALGARY T3A 6B4, AB, CANADA.
BHALOO, Mr. Karim, BSc(Hons) ACA *2009;* Flat 5, 166 Gloucester Terrace, LONDON, W2 6HR.
BHALOO, Mr. Nurali Valli, FCA *1964;* Apt 1001, 2024 Fullerton Avenue, North Vancouver, VANCOUVER V7P 3G4, BC, CANADA.
•BHAMM, Mr. Anup Kumar, FCA *1981;* (Tax Fac), Carringtons Ltd, 6 Maple Grove Business Centre, Lawrence Road, HOUNSLOW, TW4 6DR.
•BHAMRA, Mr. Ravinder Singh, BA ACA *1989;* (Tax Fac), Coombs (Bedford) Limited, 164 Bedford Road, Kempston, BEDFORD, MK42 8BH.
•BHANA, Mr. Ishwar Ooka, FCA *1965;* Bhana & Co, 410 Raheja Chambers, Plot No 213Nariman Point, MUMBAI 400 021, MAHARASHTRA, INDIA.
BHANDAL, Mrs. Seema, BSc ACA *2000;* 11 Ash Close, STANMORE, MIDDLESEX, HA7 3RH.
BHANDAL, Mrs. Sukhdeep Kaur, ACA *2008;* 26 Bessemer Close, HITCHIN, HERTFORDSHIRE, SG5 1AG.
BHANDARI, Mrs. Anna Jane, ACA ATII *1992;* 28 Binns Road, LONDON, W4 2BS.
BHANDARI, Mr. Arvind, FCA *1971;* Panorama, 203 Walkeshwar Road, MUMBAI 400 006, MAHARASHTRA, INDIA.
BHANDARI, Mr. Deepak, FCA *1977;* B/12 Vasant Marg, Vasant Vihar, NEW DELHI 110057, INDIA.
BHANDARI, Mr. Nitin, ACA *1995;* 9 Jaipur Estate, Nizamuddin east, NEW DELHI 110013, NATIONAL CAPITAL DISTRICT, INDIA.
BHANDARI, Mr. Raghbar Dayal, FCA *1971;* 2 Ludlow Way, Croxley Green, RICKMANSWORTH, WD3 3SH.
BHANDARI, Mr. Rajinder Mohan, FCA *1953;* A 231, New Friends, Colony, DELHI 110065, INDIA. (Life Member)
BHANDARI, Mr. Sunil Datt, BA ACA *1987;* Apartment 455, King Edwards Wharf, 25 Sheepcote Street, BIRMINGHAM, B16 8AB.
•BHANDARI, Mr. Vikrant, BSc FCA *1993;* Maya's, 11 Bunyana Avenue, WAHROONGA, NSW 2076, AUSTRALIA.
BHANDARY, Mr. Sova Ram, FCA *1972;* Pass de la Fin 8, 1217 GENEVA, SWITZERLAND. (Life Member)
BHANJI, Mr. Abdul Fazal, BA FCA *1980;* 15 Wallside, Monkwell Square Barbican, LONDON, EC2Y 8BH.
BHANJI, Miss. Zeenat Tina, BSc FCA *1996;* Flat 58 Capital East Apartments, 21 Western Gateway, LONDON, E16 1AS.
•BHANOT, Mr. Anil Kumar, BSc FCA *1984;* (Tax Fac), Bhanot & Co, First Floor, 126-128 Uxbridge Road, Ealing, LONDON, W13 8QS.
BHANSALI, Mr. Rahul, ACA *2009;* 106 Greencroft Gardens, LONDON, NW6 3PH.
BHANSHALY, Mr. Rupendra, BA ACA *1992;* 178 Portland Crescent, STANMORE, HA7 1LU.
BHARADIA, Mr. Vijay Vithal, BSc ACA *1994;* 44 Waltham Drive, EDGWARE, HA8 5PE.
BHARADWA, Mr. Sunil, BA ACA *1995;* 34 Clarendon Road, ASHFORD, MIDDLESEX, TW15 2QE.

BHARAJ, Miss. Amarjit, ACA *2007;* 41b Byrne Road, LONDON, SW12 9HZ.
BHARAJ, Mr. Sudharshan Singh, BSc(Eng) ACA *2006;* BSMHFT, B1 50 Summerhill Road, BIRMINGHAM, B1 3RB.
•BHARAKDA, Mr. Ashok Damji, BA FCA *1990;* Ashley Nathoo & Co Ltd, 250 High Road, HARROW, MIDDLESEX, HA3 7BB.
•BHARAKHADA, Mr. Harshad, BA ACA *1996;* with Grant Thornton UK LLP, Enterprise House, 115 Edmund Street, BIRMINGHAM, B3 2HJ.
BHARAT HIRANI, Mrs. Heena, ACA *2011;* 17 Broadcroft Avenue, STANMORE, MIDDLESEX, HA7 1NT.
•BHARATH, Mr. Adrian Martin, BA FCA *1992;* Apt. 107 East Bayside Towers, Cocorite, PORT OF SPAIN, TRINIDAD AND TOBAGO.
BHARDWAJ, Miss. Rashmi, MBA BSc FCA *1987;* 40 Whitehall Lane, BUCKHURST HILL, IG9 5JG.
BHARDWAJA, Mr. Surinder Kumar, FCA *1973;* 10 Cobbetts Avenue, Redbridge, ILFORD, IG4 5JR.
•BHARGAVA, Mr. Rakesh Narain, BPhil ACA *1982;* Levy + Partners Limited, 86-88 South Ealing Road, LONDON, W5 4QB.
•BHARKHADA, Mr. Rajnikant Nanji, FCA *1976;* Somerton & Co, Challenge House, 616 Mitcham Road, CROYDON, CR0 3AA.
BHARKHDA, Mr. Hitesh, BSc FCA *1988;* 61 Castle Avenue, Ewell, EPSOM, KT17 2PJ.
BHARMAL, Mrs. Pauline Joan, BA ACA *1987;* P O Box 283, DAR ES SALAAM, TANZANIA.
BHARMAL, Mr. Zainul, BA ACA *1988;* Soap & Allied Industries Ltd, PO Box 283, DAR ES SALAAM, TANZANIA.
BHARTIA, Mr. Shishir, BA ACA *2008;* Bhartia House, Opp 4 Bunglows., Gorakshan Road, AKOLA 444001, MAHARASHTRA, INDIA.
BHARUCHA, Mr. Pesi Shavakshaw, FCA *1975;* 111 Atur Apartments, Minoo desai Marg, Opp Fariyas Hotel Colaba, MUMBAI 400005, MAHARASHTRA, INDIA.
BHARWANI, Mr. Muslim Gulamabbas Merali Dharamsi, FCA *1974;* 117 Streathbourne Road, LONDON, SW17 8RA.
BHASIN, Miss. Joshika, MSc ACA *2009;* 35 Sussex Place, LONDON, W2 2TH.
•BHASIN, Mr. Praveen Kumar, FCA *1979;* Horwath Dafinone, Ceddi Towers 16 Wharf Road, Apapa PO Box 2151, Marina, LAGOS, NIGERIA.
BHASIN, Mr. Uday, BA(Econ) FCA CF *2001;* P.O.Box 5155, DUBAI, UNITED ARAB EMIRATES.
BHATARA, Mr. Mukesh, FCA *1995;* JJ Gallagher Limited, Gallagher House, Gallagher Way, Gallagher Business Park, Heathcote, WARWICK CV34 6AF.
BHATHENA, Mr. Rushad, ACA *1995;* Apt 1202, 100 Upper Madison Avenue, NORTH YORK M2N 9M4, ON, CANADA.
BHATIA, Mr. Kamal, BA ACA *2005;* 2a Windsor Court, Moscow Road, LONDON, W2 4SN.
BHATIA, Mr. Kirit, BA ACA *2001;* 8 Berkeley Road, LOUGHBOROUGH, LEICESTERSHIRE, LE11 3SJ.
BHATIA, Mr. Mohit, BAcc ACA *2002;* 4 Playford Road, IPSWICH, IP4 5RH.
BHATIA, Miss. Natasha, BSc ACA *1991;* Second Floor Flat, 42 Ladbroke Grove, LONDON, W11 2PA.
BHATIA, Mrs. Savita, BSc ACA *2007;* 5 Coniston Gardens, WEMBLEY, MIDDLESEX, HA9 8SE.
•BHATIA, Mr. Vikram, FCA *1972;* Bhatia Sonnadara & Co, Tower House, 17 Tower Road, Strawberry Hill, TWICKENHAM, TW1 4PD.
BHATIA, Mr. Vishesh Lal, FCA *1971;* 28 Level, Festival Tower, Dubai Festival City, DUBAI, UNITED ARAB EMIRATES.
BHATIA UDESHI, Mr. Jeetendra Ganeshlal, FCA ACA *2010;* Range Hospitality, PO Box 450341, DUBAI, 450341, UNITED ARAB EMIRATES.
BHATNAGAR, Mr. Akshay, ACA *1998;* 4 Sandy Lane, Hightown, LIVERPOOL, L38 3RR.
BHATT, Mrs. Gayatri, BSc(Hons) ACA *2003;* 6 Station Crescent, WEMBLEY, MIDDLESEX, HA0 2LB.
BHATT, Mr. Kirit Mahendra, FCA *1982;* 11990 South Aviary Drive, COOPER CITY, FL 33026, UNITED STATES.
BHATT, Mr. Mainak, BSc ACA *1992;* 27 Beechwood Park, South Woodford, LONDON, E18 2EH.
BHATT, Mr. Piyush, BSc FCA *1977;* 9 Grace Avenue, Beecroft, SYDNEY, NSW 2119, AUSTRALIA.
•BHATT, Mr. Sanjiv Kumudchandra, BCom ACA *1990;* S.K. Bhatt, 178 Stroud Road, GLOUCESTER, GL1 5JX.
BHATT, Ms. Sonya Rani, BSc(Econ) ACA *1998;* 20 Hillside Road, NORTHWOOD, MIDDLESEX, HA6 1QA.
•BHATT, Mr. Sureshkumar Liladhar, FCA *1972;* Bhatt & Co, 20 College Close, Harrow Weald, HARROW, MIDDLESEX, HA3 7BZ.
BHATTACHARJEE, Miss. Archana, BSc(Econ) ACA *2001;* 65 Mildmay Road, LONDON, N1 4PU.
BHATTACHARJEE, Mr. Partha Sarathy, FCA *1994;* 527 Jodhpur Park, KOLKATA 700068, WEST BENGAL, INDIA.
BHATTACHARYA, Mr. Shamir Pramod, FCA *1979;* 110 Country Club Drive, MOORESTOWN, NJ 08057, UNITED STATES.
BHATTACHARYA, Mr. Sujit, FCA *1968;* 52C Ballygunge Circular Road, KOLKATA 700 019, INDIA.
BHATTACHARYYA, Mr. Biplab Bijay, FCA *1973;* 47 Thellusson Way, RICKMANSWORTH, WD3 8RL. (Life Member)
BHATTACHARYYA, Miss. Paula Debasree, BSc ACA *1999;* 21 Sussex Way, Cockfosters, BARNET, EN4 0BQ.
BHATTACHARYYA, Miss. Rina, BSc ACA *2007;* 1285 Avenues of the Americas, FL 3, NEW YORK, NY 10019, UNITED STATES.
BHATTAD, Mr. Aashish Hiralal, BA FCA *1999;* 27 The Spinneys, BROMLEY, BR1 2NT.
BHATTI, Mr. Abdul Hafiz, FCA *1971;* 23 Twickenham Gardens, GREENFORD, MIDDLESEX, UB6 0LU.
BHATTI, Mr. Adil Hussain, BCom ACA *1996;* 10 Spring Lane, Erdington, BIRMINGHAM, B24 9BU.
BHATTI, Mr. Arslan, BSc ACA *2007;* 36 Vista Drive, ILFORD, IG4 5JF.
BHATTI, Miss. Ayesha, MSc ACA *2003;* 10 Spring Lane, Erdington, BIRMINGHAM, B24 9BU.
BHATTI, Mr. Davinder Singh, BA ACA *1992;* CCSS (Europe) Ltd, Unit 6, The Courtyard, Campus Way, Gillingham Business Park, GILLINGHAM KENT ME8 0NZ.
BHATTI, Mr. Mohamed Asif, BSc FCA *1996;* 10 Green Park, Prestwood, GREAT MISSENDEN, BUCKINGHAMSHIRE, HP16 0PZ.
BHATTI, Mr. Mohammad Saqib, LLB ACA *2011;* 42 Greaves Avenue, WALSALL, WS5 3QG.
•BHATTI, Mr. Mohammad Younis, FCA *1975;* Younis Bhatti & Co Ltd, 1st Floor, 93 Broad Street, BIRMINGHAM, B15 1AU.
•BHATTI, Mr. Paramjit, FCA *1991;* (Tax Fac), Bhatti & Co, 60 Waterloo Road, WOLVERHAMPTON, WV1 4QP.
BHATTI, Mr. Pardeep, BSc ACA *2003;* 16 Tregaron Avenue, Crouch End, LONDON, N8 9EY.
BHATTI, Mr. Raheel Sharif, BA ACA *1992;* 5 Manor Road Extension, Oadby, LEICESTER, LE2 4FG.
•BHATTI, Mr. Rashad Ali, BCom ACA *1993;* Ingle Bhatti & Co, RAB House, 102-104 Park Lane, CROYDON, CR0 1JB.
BHATTI, Mr. Sajjad Younis, ACA *2008;* Product Control, H S B C, 8-14 Canada Square, LONDON, E14 5HQ.
BHATTI, Mr. Tanveer, DPhil ACA *1993;* BHATTI, 51 Harrowes Meade, EDGWARE, MIDDLESEX, HA8 8RR.
•BHATTI, Mr. Tauqeer Ahmed, MA ACA ATII *1990;* MMTI Limited, 44 Carlton Avenue West, WEMBLEY, HA0 3QU.
BHATTI, Mr. Zahid Iqbal, ACA *1981;* A.F. Ferguson & Co, State Life Building 1C, Off I.I. Chundrigar Road, P.O. Box 4716, KARACHI 74000, PAKISTAN.
BHAVANANI, Mr. Anil Narain, ACA *1980;* 102 Olympus Apartments, Altamount Road, MUMBAI 400026, MAHARASHTRA, INDIA.
BHAVNANI, Mr. Manjeet, BSc FCA ATII MSI *1995;* (Tax Fac), 88 Natal Road, New Southgate, LONDON, N11 2HY.
BHAVNANI, Mr. Sunil, BSc ACA *1997;* 103 Old Church Lane, STANMORE, MIDDLESEX, HA7 2RT.
BHAVSAR, Mr. Amit Jayprakash, BSc ACA *2011;* 16 Durham Road, Manor Park, LONDON, E12 5AX.
•BHAVSAR, Mr. Bhasker Dev Ambalal, FCA *1978;* Bhaskar Bhavsar Limited, 36 Tottenhall Road, LONDON, N13 6HX.
BHAYANI, Mr. Dilesh Narandas, BSc ACA *1991;* P.O.Box 66394., Post Code 00800, Westlands., NAIROBI, KENYA.
•BHAYAT, Mr. Ismail Mohammed, BA(Hons) FCA *1994;* 24 Rosemary Drive, Redbridge, ILFORD, ESSEX, IG4 5JD.
BHEENICK, Mr. Krishna, BSc ACA *2002;* Flat 4 Earls House, 10 Strand Drive, RICHMOND, TW9 4DZ.
BHIMANI, Mr. Vimal Liladhar, BSc ACA *1995;* Machine Mart Ltd, 211, Lower Parliament Street, NOTTINGHAM, NG1 1GN.
•BHIMJEE, Mr. Anwar Ali, FCA *1975;* (Tax Fac), 244 Juanita Way, SAN FRANCISCO, CA 94127, UNITED STATES.
BHIMJEE, Mr. Daanish, BSc ACA *2006;* Flat 7, 69 Harrington Gardens, LONDON, SW7 4JZ.
BHIMJI, Mr. Mohamed Gulamhusein Punja, FCA *1971;* 16 St Peters Close, RUISLIP, HA4 9JT.
•BHIMJIYANI, Mr. Pradipkumar Trikamlal, FCA ATII *1974;* P.T. Bhimjiyani & Co, 124 Chatsworth Road, LONDON, NW2 5QU.
BHINDI, Mr. Vinay Zaverilal, BSc(Hons) ACA *2001;* 80 Cranley Drive, ILFORD, ESSEX, IG2 6AJ.
•BHOGADIA, Mr. Mahmood Reza, BSc ACA *1986;* (Tax Fac), 6 Alder Close, Hollywood Grange, BIRMINGHAM, B47 5RA.
BHOGAITA, Mr. Chavan, BA FCA *1999;* National Bank of Abu Dhabi, Financial Markets Division, P O Box 4, ABU DHABI, UNITED ARAB EMIRATES.
BHOGAITA, Mr. Vishal Shivshanker, ACA *2009;* Flat 41 Priory Heights, 2a Wynford Road, LONDON, N1 9SL.
BHOGAL, Mr. Dupinder Singh, BEng ACA *1993;* S A P (UK) Ltd Clockhouse Place, Bedfont Road, FELTHAM, MIDDLESEX, TW14 8HD.
BHOGAL, Mr. Joginder Singh, BSc ACA *1997;* 11 Knoll Drive, COVENTRY, CV3 5BT.
BHOJANI, Mr. Sohail Raza, FCA *1995;* ICI Pakistan Limited, Paints Business, 346 Ferozepur Road, P O Box 273, LAHORE 54600, PAKISTAN.
BHOJANI, Mr. Vasant Dhanji Naran, BA(Hons) ACA *2001;* 60 Ravenscroft Avenue, WEMBLEY, MIDDLESEX, HA9 9TL.
BHOJWANI, Mr. Kiran Ramchand, ACA *1982;* 11 East Close, LONDON, W5 3HE.
BHOLAH, Mr. Mohammad Abdool Rahman, BA ACA *1989;* 23 Beedassy Lane, FLOREAL, MAURITIUS.
BHOPAL, Mr. Rajinderpal Singh, BSc ACA *2008;* 58 Hollywood Lane, Wainscott, ROCHESTER, ME3 8AR.
•BHOPAL, Mr. Runjit Singh, BEng ACA *1992;* Mancini Limited, 10 Shallowford Grove, Furzton, MILTON KEYNES, MK4 1ND.
BHOTE, Mr. Cyrus Homi, FCA *1981;* Tata Consultancy Services, 26th Floor, 101 Park Avenue, NEW YORK, NY 10178, UNITED STATES.
BHOTI, Miss. Shila, BSc ACA *1997;* 45a Stapleton Road, LONDON, SW17 8BA.
BHOVAN, Mr. Prashant, BSc ACA CTA *1996;* (Tax Fac), 4 Lancaster Road, HARROW, HA2 7NL.
•BHUCHAR, Mr. Rishi, BSc ACA *2000;* Ernst & Young LLP, 1 More London Place, LONDON, SE1 2AF. See also Ernst & Young Europe LLP
BHUCHAR, Miss. Sangeeta, BSc ACA *1991;* 45 Holland Avenue, Cheam, SUTTON, SURREY, SM2 6HT.
BHUDIA, Miss. Dipa Bhimji, ACA *2010;* 30 Delta Grove, NORTHOLT, UB5 6DX.
BHUGALOO, Mr. Asraf, BSc ACA *1994;* 7 Tanglewood Drive, NASHUA, NH 03062, UNITED STATES.
BHUIYAN, Mrs. Nazma Ali, BSc ACA *2003;* 58 Beattyville Gardens, ILFORD, IG6 1JY.
BHULLAR, Mr. Kulwinder Singh, BSc(Hons) ACA *2004;* 148 Martindale Road, HOUNSLOW, TW4 7HQ.
BHULLAR, Mr. Sandip, BA(Hons) ACA *2008;* 15a Ecclesbourne Road, LONDON, N1 3RP.
BHUNDIA, Mr. Bharat, BA ACA *1983;* 65 Chandos Avenue, LONDON, N20 9EG.
BHUNDIA, Mr. Hitan Dayalal, BA ACA *1997;* Aspect Education Ltd, Shepherds West, Rockley Road, LONDON, W14 0DA.
•BHUNDIA, Mr. Prakash Dahyalal, BA ACA *1982;* Crane Court Properties Ltd, 22-24 Red Lion Court, Fleet Street, LONDON, EC4A 3EB.
BHUTRA, Mr. Deepak, BA ACA *2006;* Skanska UK Plc, Maple Cross House, Denham Way, Maple Cross, RICKMANSWORTH, HERTFORDSHIRE WD3 9SW.
BHUVA, Mr. Jitendra Shantilal, FCA *1973;* 5 Runnelfield, South Hill Avenue, HARROW, HA1 3NY.
BHUVA, Mr. Pritesh Ratilal, BSc ACA *2004;* 94 The Drive, ILFORD, ESSEX, IG1 3JH.
BHUWANIA, Miss. Ruchi, BSc(Hons) ACA *2007;* 16 Tudor Close, LONDON, NW3 4AB.
BI, Mrs. Zamiran, ACA *2007;* 21 Fisher Road, Foleshill, COVENTRY, CV6 5HU.
BIAGIONI, Mr. Mauro Andrea, BSc(Hons) ACA *2003;* NVM Private Equity, Northumberland House, Princess Square, NEWCASTLE UPON TYNE, NE1 8ER.
BIALKOWSKA, Mrs. Ewa Renata, ACA *1983;* 33 Popes Grove, Strawberry Hill, TWICKENHAM, TW1 4JZ.
BIANCHI, Mr. Jason, BSc ACA *2010;* 37 Manor Road, BECKENHAM, BR3 5JB.
BIANCHI, Mr. Stefano, ACA *2004;* Viale Venezia 22, 36061 BASSANO DEL GRAPPA, ITALY.
BIANCHI, Mrs. Teresa Catherine, BSc ACA *2002;* Willow House Buckley Hill Lane, Milnrow, ROCHDALE, OL16 4BU.
BIANCO, Mr. Carmine, BA ACA *1992;* Ernst & Young, 400 Capability Green, LUTON, LU1 3LU.
BIANCO, Mr. Edward James, BA ACA *2010;* Foreign Currency Direct Plc, Currencies Mews, 2b Badminton Court, Church Street, AMERSHAM, BUCKINGHAMSHIRE HP7 0DD.
BIBBY, Mr. David John, BCom ACA *1985;* Sports & Leisure Management, 3 Watling Drive, Sketchley Meadows, HINCKLEY, LEICESTERSHIRE, LE10 3EY.
BIBBY, Mr. Derek William, FCA *1950;* 29 Osborne Parade, CLAREMONT, WA 6010, AUSTRALIA. (Life Member)
BIBBY, Miss. Elizabeth Ann, BEng ACA *1996;* 15 Carlton Rise, BEVERLEY, NORTH HUMBERSIDE, HU17 8UR.
BIBBY, Mr. Geoffrey Frank Harold, BA ACA *1991;* South Dalton, Willington Lane, Clotton, TARPORLEY, CW6 0HQ.
BIBBY, Mr. John, BA FCA *1960;* 15 Sanderstead Hill, SOUTH CROYDON, SURREY, CR2 0HD. (Life Member)
BIBBY, Mr. Mark Damien, BA ACA *1996;* 53 Station Road, Marple, STOCKPORT, CHESHIRE, SK6 6AJ.
BIBBY, Mr. Michael Andrew, BSc ACA *1993;* Kall Kwik Printing, 19b St. Petersgate, STOCKPORT, CHESHIRE, SK1 1EB.
BIBBY, Mr. Peter William, FCA *1970;* B M S Super Factors Ltd, 249-251 Oldham Road, ROCHDALE, LANCASHIRE, OL16 5RD.
BIBBY, Mr. Philip James, BA ACA *2006;* 5 Neston Way, Handforth, WILMSLOW, CHESHIRE, SK9 3BX.
BIBBY, Mrs. Rebecca Charlotte, ACA *2008;* Tsys International, Fulford Moor House, Fulford Road, YORK, YO10 4EY.
•BIBBY, Mr. Richard Norman, FCA *1984;* Bibby & Legge Limited, Unit 3D, Dreadnought Trading Estate, Magdalen Lane, BRIDPORT, DT6 5BU.
•BIBBY, Mr. Stephen Edward, BA FCA *1973;* S.E. Bibby & Co, 1 Wych Elm Close, HORNCHURCH, RM11 3AJ.
BIBI, Miss. Safina, BA ACA *2006;* 3 Norfolk Farm Close, WOKING, SURREY, GU22 8LL.
BIBI, Mrs. Zoohera, LLM ACA *2002;* 20 Upney Lane, BARKING, ESSEX, IG11 9LW.
BICHARD, Mrs. Beatrix Bridget, BSc(Hons) ACA *2002;* 2 Kensington Gardens, Titchfield Common, FAREHAM, PO14 4RJ.
•BICHARD, Mr. James William Edward, BSc ACA *2007;* PricewaterhouseCoopers LLP, Hays Galleria, 1 Hays Lane, LONDON, SE1 2RD.
BICHARD, Mrs. Lynne, ACA *1993;* Hunts Hall Farm House, Leigh Road, Holt, TROWBRIDGE, WILTSHIRE, BA14 6PP.
•BICK, Mr. James David, FCA *1981;* (Tax Fac), Bick Accountants Ltd, 18a Littleham Road, EXMOUTH, DEVON, EX8 2QG.
BICKART, Mr. Marc, ACA *2007;* 38 rue Lamarck, 75018 PARIS, FRANCE.
BICKEL, Mr. David Charles, BA ACA *1987;* 34 Wroughton Road, LONDON, SW11 6BG.
BICKELL, Mr. Brian, FCA *1976;* Shaftesbury plc, Pegasus House, 37/43 Sackville Street, Piccadilly, LONDON, W1S 3DL.
BICKENSON, Miss. Sarah Joanne, MA ACA *2009;* Flat 9 Princess Court, 105 Hornsey Lane, LONDON, N6 5XD.
•BICKENSON, Mrs. Teresa Ellen, BA FCA *1976;* (Tax Fac), Terry Bickenson, 96 Broadmoor Lane, BATH, BA1 4LB.
BICKER, Mr. Adrian Hedley, ACA *1980;* 9 Barn Rd, BROADSTONE, BH18 8NH.
BICKERSTAFF, Miss. Mary Elizabeth, MSc FCA *1976;* Flat 13, 63 West Smithfield, LONDON, EC1A 9DY.
BICKERSTAFF, Mr. Michael, BEng ACA *1994;* 3 Woodland Street, Coogee, SYDNEY, NSW 2034, AUSTRALIA.
BICKERSTAFF, Ms. Penelope Tracey, LLB FCA CMC *1985;* MEMBER OF COUNCIL, 9 Fitzgerald Road, Wanstead, LONDON, E11 2ST.
BICKERSTAFFE, Mr. Mark, BSc ACA *2004;* London Business School, Sussex Place, Regents Park, LONDON, NW1 4SA.
BICKERTON, Mr. Andrew Alan, BA ACA *2004;* West End House, Gladstone Place, Penkhull, STOKE-ON-TRENT, STAFFORDSHIRE, ST4 5HP.
BICKERTON, Mr. Barry Garth, BA FCA *1970;* St Mary's Cottage, Hardwick, AYLESBURY, HP22 4DZ. (Life Member)
BICKERTON, Mr. Richard Henry Cheetham, FCA *1968;* Send Grove, Church Lane, Send, WOKING, GU23 7JL.
BICKERTON, Mr. Roger, FCA *1958;* Applewood, Brook Street, Fovant, SALISBURY, SP3 5JB. (Life Member)
BICKFORD, Mr. David Philip, BSc ACA *1994;* c/o Mr & Mrs G Bickford, 36 South View Park, PLYMOUTH, PL7 4JE.

BICKFORD, Mr. Robert William, BA FCA *1972;* with PricewaterhouseCoopers, Plot 252E Muri Okunola Street, Victoria Island, P O Box 2419, LAGOS, NIGERIA.

BICKFORD-SMITH, Mr. Michael Rupert David, BEng ACA *2010;* Flat A-b, 670 Fulham Road, LONDON, SW6 5RX.

BICKLE, Mr. David John, MPhil BSc ACA *2003;* Deloitte Tohmatsu Tax Co, Shin Tokyo Building 5F, 3-3-1 Marunouchi Chiyoda ku, TOKYO, 100-8305 JAPAN.

BICKLEY, Mrs. Alison Sian, BA ACA *1995;* Edwards & Keeping, Unity Chambers, 34 High East Street, DORCHESTER, DORSET, DT1 1HA.

BICKLEY, Mr. Alistair James, BA ACA *1991;* 21 Romeyn Road, LONDON, SW16 2NU.

BICKLEY, Mr. Anthony John, ACA *1982;* 5 Rowley Hall Close, STAFFORD, ST17 9AH.

BICKLEY, Mr. Douglas William Ronald, FCA *1976;* Aggregates Industries UK Ltd, Bardon Hill, COALVILLE, LEICESTERSHIRE, LE67 1TL.

•**BICKLEY, Mr. Peter Charles, BSc FCA** *1981;* (Tax Fac), 4 Maplehurst Road, CHICHESTER, WEST SUSSEX, PO19 6QL.

BICKLEY, Mr. Richard Matthew, BSc ACA *1986;* 2 Woodland View, Threshfield, SKIPTON, BD23 5EX.

BICKNELL, Mr. Anthony Guy Kirsten, MA ACA *1979;* 59 Chelverton Road, LONDON, SW15 1RW.

BICKNELL, Mr. Christopher Guy, FCA *1962;* with Bloomer Heaven, 33 Lionel Street, BIRMINGHAM, B3 1AB.

BICKNELL, Mr. Christopher Thomas, FCA *1950;* Trevose, Kithurst Park, Storrington, PULBOROUGH, RH20 4JH. (Life Member)

BICKNELL, Mr. Geoffrey James, FCA *1966;* 1300. Ben Franklin Drive, The Beach Residence No.503, SARASOTA, FL FL 34236, UNITED STATES.

BICKNELL, Mr. Marc Andrew, BA(Hons) ACA *2002;* Rotherham Metropolitan Borough Council:, Internal Audit, Civic Building, ROTHERHAM, SOUTH YORKSHIRE, S65 1UF.

•**BICKNELL, Mr. Ralph, FCA** *1961;* R. Bicknell & Co, 71 Bedford Road, READING, RG1 7EY.

BICKNELL, Mr. Robert Sabin Alexander, BA ACA *1998;* Computer Associates, Ditton Park, Riding Court Road, Datchet, SLOUGH, SL3 9LL.

BICKNELL, Mr. Simon David, BSc ACA *1998;* 3 Samworths Close, Castor, PETERBOROUGH, PE5 7BQ.

BIDD, Mrs. Saryu Ilesh, BSc ACA *1985;* 24 Hauxton Road, Little Shelford, CAMBRIDGE, CB22 5HJ.

•**BIDDEL, Mr. David, FCA** *1972;* 12 The Newlands, Frenchay, BRISTOL, BS16 1NQ.

BIDDELL, Mr. Vaughan Alan, BSc FCA *1974;* (Tax Fac), Chalet Revau, Route D'Anzere 66, 1972 ANZERE, SWITZERLAND.

BIDDER, Mr. Andrew John, MBA MSc BSc FCA *1988;* 2221 Caledonia Avenue, NORTH VANCOUVER V78 1TG, BC, CANADA.

BIDDER, Mr. David, FCA *1970;* 23 Endfield Close, Heavitree, EXETER, EX1 3BB.

BIDDER, Ms. Jane Patricia, BA ACA *1992;* Chandlers, Seaway Lane, TORQUAY, TQ2 6PW.

BIDDISCOMBE, Mr. Simon, BA FCA *1993;* 20 Arlington Close, NEWPORT, NP20 6QF.

BIDDLE, Mr. Adrian Charles, ACA *1989;* Home Farm, Station Road, WINSFORD, CW7 3DP.

•**BIDDLE, Mr. Andrew John, BA(Hons) ACA** *2000;* Dufton Kellner Limited, Barnston House, Beacon Lane, Heswall, WIRRAL, CH60 0EE.

BIDDLE, Mr. Anthony Garry, BA FCA *1974;* 55 Upper Tilehouse Street, HITCHIN, HERTFORDSHIRE, SG5 2EF.

BIDDLE, Mrs. Apryl Elizabeth, BCom ACA *1990;* Minsups Ltd, Road One, Winsford Industrial Estate, WINSFORD, CHESHIRE, CW7 3RG.

BIDDLE, Mr. Donald Frank, FCA *1956;* Vernon House, Duver Road, St. Helens, RYDE, ISLE OF WIGHT, PO33 1XY. (Life Member)

BIDDLE, Mr. Henry, BA ACA *2010;* Flat 1, Exeter Mansions, 106 Shaftesbury Avenue, LONDON, W1D 5EQ.

BIDDLE, Mr. James, MA ACA *2005;* Westways Farm, Gracious Pond Road, Chobham, WOKING, GU24 8HH.

BIDDLE, Mr. Paul Richard, FCA *1968;* Westways Farm, Gracious Pond Road, Chobham, WOKING, GU24 8HH.

•**BIDDLE, Mrs. Pauline, BSc ACA** *1996;* Deloitte LLP, Abbots House, Abbey Street, READING, RG1 3BD. See also Deloitte & Touche LLP

•**BIDDLE, Mr. Richard James, BSc ACA** *1993;* Biddle Matthews, Mulberry House, 18a Ashfield Lane, CHISLEHURST, KENT, BR7 6LQ.

BIDDLE, Mr. Stephen John, BSc ACA *1979;* British Heart Foundation, Crown House, Church Road, Claygate, ESHER, KT10 0BF.

BIDDLE, Mr. Thomas, ACA *2008;* Ground Floor Flat, 5 Kendoa Road, LONDON, SW4 7ND.

BIDDLECOMBE, Mr. Darren Jon, BA ACA *1993;* Kays Medical, 3-7 Shaw Street, LIVERPOOL, L6 1HH.

BIDDLECOMBE, Miss. Elizabeth Cecilia, BSc ACA *2006;* 31 Disraeli Gardens, LONDON, SW15 2QB.

BIDDLECOMBE, Mrs. Rowena Jane Naomi, BSc ACA *2007;* 2 Buckenhoe Road, SAFFRON WALDEN, CB10 2DE.

BIDDLECOMBE, Mr. Sean Michael, BA ACA *1990;* 18 Church Lane, ROMSEY, HAMPSHIRE, SO51 8EP.

BIDDLECOMBE, Mr. Steven, BA ACA *1991;* Combe End, 15 Vincent Close, Fetcham, LEATHERHEAD, KT22 9PB.

BIDDULPH, Mr. David Paul, BSc ACA *1990;* Robinson Way & Co Ltd, London Scottish House, Carolina Way, SALFORD, M50 2ZY.

BIDDULPH, Miss. Emily Louise, ACA *2008;* Flat 5 Butterfield Court, 1b Nevill Road, LONDON, N16 8SH.

BIDEAU, Miss. Tracy Jane, BA ACA *1998;* Veue Du Jaon, L'ancresse Road, Vale, GUERNSEY, GY3 5AJ.

•**BIDGOOD, Mr. Christopher Glen, BA(Hons) ACA** *2002;* CG Lee Ltd, Ingram House, Meridian Way, NORWICH, NR7 0TA.

BIDGOOD, Mr. Stuart, BA FCA *1981;* 3 Aitken Close, Sprowston, NORWICH, NR7 8BB.

BIDGWAY, Mr. Simon Marcus, BA ACA *1992;* 30 Harvest Hill, EAST GRINSTEAD, WEST SUSSEX, RH19 4BT.

•**BIDMEAD, Mr. Ian Trevor, FCA** *1988;* (Tax Fac), Stanley Yule, Beaconsfield House, 26 Belvidere Road, WALSALL, WS1 3AU. See also Stanley Yule Ltd

BIDNELL, Mrs. Jennifer Frances, BA(Hons) ACA *2009;* Apartment 5, 6 Third Avenue, HOVE, EAST SUSSEX, BN3 2PD.

BIDSTON, Mr. Michael John, BSc(Econ)Hons FCA *1974;* Copper Heights, 10 Redstone Drive, Lower Heswall, WIRRAL, CH60 9HH.

BIEBUYCK, Miss. Caroline Mary, BSc ACA *1991;* 1 Manor Close Freshford, BATH, BA2 7WS.

BIEL, Mr. Desmond Thomas, FCA *1962;* 25 Gomshall Road, SUTTON, SM2 7JZ. (Life Member)

•**BIELBY, Miss. Anna Catherine, ACA** *2001;* Flat 2, 21 Burton Crecent, LEEDS, LS6 4DN.

•**BIELCKUS, Mr. Colin David, BSc FCA** *1981;* Avenue Business Services, 1 Silvertrees, Lady Bettys Drive, Titchfield, FAREHAM, HAMPSHIRE PO15 6RJ.

•**BIELICH, Mr. Basil Dean, ACA CA(SA)** *2008;* Browne Craine Associates Limited, Burleigh Manor, Peel Road, Douglas, ISLE OF MAN, IM1 5EP.

BIENEN, Ms. Stefanie, ACA *2010;* High View, Windsor Road, TORQUAY, TQ1 1SW.

BIENFAIT, Mr. Richard Antoine, BA ACA AMCT *1995;* 86 Marshals Drive, ST. ALBANS, HERTFORDSHIRE, AL1 4RE.

BIER, Mr. Jonathan, ACA *2011;* Flat 15, 153 Regents Park Road, LONDON, NW1 8BB.

BIER, Mr. Manfred, BCom FCA *1955;* 8 The Gateways Sprimont Place, LONDON, SW3 3JA. (Life Member)

BIERER, Miss. Serina, MSc ACA *2008;* Falkland Oil & Gas Ltd, 32-34 Wigmore Street, LONDON, W1U 2RR.

BIERRUM, Mr. Alexander Milne, MA MSc LLB FCA FCIArb *1971;* Tudor Cottage, Back Lane, Preston, HITCHIN, HERTFORDSHIRE, SG4 7UJ. (Life Member)

BIEZANEK, Mr. Nicholas Campbell, MA FCA *1977;* PO Box 5356, Weltevreden Park, JOHANNESBURG, GAUTENG, 1715, SOUTH AFRICA.

•**BIFFEN, Mr. John Leslie, FCA** *1984;* Menzies LLP, Victoria House, 50-58 Victoria Road, FARNBOROUGH, HAMPSHIRE, GU14 7PG.

•**BIFULCO, Mr. Vincent, BA FCA** *1971;* (Tax Fac), Vincent Bifulco & Co Ltd, 47 Cumberland Park, LONDON, W3 6SX.

•**BIGAIGNON, Mr. Noel Maurice Robert, FCA** *1976;* (Tax Fac), Societe Roger, De Chazal, 6th Floor, Cerne House, Chaussee, PORT LOUIS MAURITIUS.

BIGFORD, Mr. Philip Jonathan, BEng ACA *1993;* The Porch House, Green Lane, MALVERN, WR14 4HU.

BIGG, Mr. Derek Charles, DFC FCA *1950;* Ronas, 16 Crown Drive, INVERNESS, IV2 3NL. (Life Member)

BIGG, Miss. Julia Rhiannon, BA ACA DChA *2006;* with Littlejohn, 1 Westferry Circus, Canary Wharf, LONDON, E14 4HD.

BIGGART, Mr. Andrew John, MEng FCA *1991;* with Deloitte LLP, General Guisan-Quai 38, PO Box 2232, 8022 ZURICH, SWITZERLAND.

BIGGART, Mr. Malcolm William, BA ACA *1992;* Mavahraun 12, 220 HAFNARFJORDUR, ICELAND.

•**BIGGIN, Mr. Alan Keith, FCA** *1972;* (Tax Fac), Bostocks Boyce Welch, The Counting House, Tower Buildings, Wade House Road, Shelf, HALIFAX WEST YORKSHIRE HX3 7PB.

BIGGIN, Mr. Charles Arnold John, FCA *1962;* 4 Ranmoor Crescent, SHEFFIELD, S10 3GU. (Life Member)

BIGGINS, Miss. Rebecca Helen, ACA *2010;* 22 Fletcher Court, MANCHESTER, M26 1PZ.

BIGGINS, Mr. Steven William, MA FCA *1983;* 44 Hawksley Rise, Oughtibridge, SHEFFIELD, S35 0JB.

BIGGS, Mr. Andrew James, BA ACA *1992;* Attends Healthcare, 3rd Floor, The Old Post Office, St. Nicholas Street, NEWCASTLE UPON TYNE, NE1 1RH.

BIGGS, Mr. Andrew Leslie, BA ACA *1994;* Hoppe (UK) Ltd, Gailey Park, Standeford, WOLVERHAMPTON, WV10 7GW.

BIGGS, Mr. Anthony Gerald, FCA *1962;* Siltint Industries Ltd, 124 Longley Lane, MANCHESTER, M22 4SP.

BIGGS, Mr. Anthony Mark, MSc BSc ACA AMCT *1984;* Lime Tree Hous, Braddens Furlong, Off Jesses Lane, Long Crendon, AYLESBURY, BUCKINGHAMSHIRE HP18 9BL.

•**BIGGS, Mr. Carl, ACA CA(NZ)** *2009;* C Biggs, 1 Malcolm Drive, SURBITON, SURREY, KT6 6QS.

BIGGS, Mrs. Carolynn Marie, BA ACA *1992;* 17 Elm Way, Hackleton, NORTHAMPTON, NN7 2BT.

BIGGS, Mr. Christopher James Derham, MEng ACA *2008;* S Notaro Ltd, Huntworth, BRIDGWATER, SOMERSET, TA7 0AJ.

BIGGS, Mr. Christopher Kenneth Edeford, FCA *1970;* The Coach House St. Ibbs, London Road St. Ippolyts, HITCHIN, HERTFORDSHIRE, SG4 7NL.

BIGGS, Mr. Christopher Paul, BA ACA *1987;* 43A Sandy Lane, Cheam, SUTTON, SURREY, SM2 7PQ.

BIGGS, Mr. Christopher Robert, FCA *1998;* 474 Upper Richmond Road, LONDON, SW15 5JG.

BIGGS, Mr. Colin Charles, FCA *1966;* 30 Stacey Rd, TONBRIDGE, TN10 3AR.

•**BIGGS, Mr. Colin Leslie, FCA** *1977;* Waugh Haines Rigby Limited, 18 Miller Court, Severn Drive, Tewkesbury Business Park, TEWKESBURY, GLOUCESTERSHIRE GL20 8DN.

BIGGS, Mrs. Constance Helen, BSc ACA *1996;* 474 Upper Richmond Road, LONDON, SW15 5JG.

BIGGS, Mr. Cyril Eric, FCA *1948;* 5 Lidford Tor Avenue, PAIGNTON, TQ4 7ED. (Life Member)

BIGGS, Mr. David Robert, BSc FCA *1986;* 64 Beaumont Avenue, ST. ALBANS, HERTFORDSHIRE, AL1 4TN.

BIGGS, Mr. Ian Malcolm, BA ACA *1983;* 1525 River Road, DE FOREST, WI 53532, UNITED STATES.

BIGGS, Mr. Jeremy, BSc ACA *1986;* The Essendine, Essendine, STAMFORD, PE9 4LD.

BIGGS, Mr. John Simon, BA(Hons) ACA *2000;* (Tax Fac), 65 Sandown Lodge, Avenue Road, EPSOM, KT18 7QU.

BIGGS, Mr. Jonathan Michael Arthur, BSc ACA *1994;* Accel Partners, 16 St James Street, LONDON, SW1A 1ER.

BIGGS, Mrs. Kathryn Tracy, MA ACA *1990;* 64 Beaumont Avenue, ST. ALBANS, HERTFORDSHIRE, AL1 4TN.

•**BIGGS, Mr. Kenneth Alan, FCA** *1977;* (Tax Fac), Princep Pardoe, 794 High Street, KINGSWINFORD, WEST MIDLANDS, DY6 8BQ.

BIGGS, Mr. Michael Allan, BSc ACA *2001;* 58 Kingsmead Avenue, WORCESTER PARK, KT4 8XA.

BIGGS, Mr. Michael Nicholas, MA ACA *1979;* Resolution Limited, 23 Savile Row, LONDON, W1S 2ET.

BIGGS, Mr. Michael Richard, FCA *1966;* Hill House, High Street, Meonstoke, SOUTHAMPTON, SO32 3NH. (Life Member)

•**BIGGS, Mr. Paul, BA(Hons) ACA ACCA** *2011;* Biggs Doran, 55 Irene Avenue, LANCING, WEST SUSSEX, BN15 9NY.

BIGGS, Miss. Phillippa Catherine, MSc BA(Hons) ACA *2000;* 33 chemin des Pirris, 74310 PARIS, SAVOIE, FRANCE.

BIGGS, Miss. Rachel Helen, BSc ACA *2000;* 30 Alderside Walk, Englefield Green, EGHAM, TW20 0LY.

BIGGS, Mr. Roger Norman, ACA *1979;* PO Box 137, SOUTHBROOM, 4277, SOUTH AFRICA.

BIGGS, Mrs. Sarah Britland, BA FCA *1988;* 43a Sandy Lane, SUTTON, SM2 7PQ.

BIGGS, Miss. Sarah Louise, ACA *2009;* 18 Bethel Road, SEVENOAKS, TN13 3UE.

BIGGS, Mr. Simon Andrew, ACA *2006;* 4 Vyrnwy Road, OSWESTRY, SHROPSHIRE, SY11 1NP.

BIGHAM, Mr. Andrew John, BA ACA *1986;* 3 Sprigg Place, MOUNT COLAH, NSW 2079, AUSTRALIA.

BIGHAM, Mr. Thomas Robert, ACA *2008;* Flat 2, 20 Twickenham Drive, MOSELEY, BIRMINGHAM, B13 8LY.

•**BIGLAND, Mr. David Harry, FCA** *1968;* (Tax Fac), Gorings, The Laurels, St. Mary Street, ILKESTON, DE7 8BQ.

BIGLEY, Mr. Alastair James, MA(Hons) ACA *2003;* 133 Honor Oak Road, LONDON, SE23 3SL.

•**BIGLEY, Mr. Michael Robert, BA FCA** *1983;* Baines Jewitt, Barrington House, 41-45 Yarm Lane, STOCKTON-ON-TEES, CLEVELAND, TS18 3EA. See also Barrington House Solutions Limited

BIGLEY, Mr. Robert Hilton, MA ACA *1986;* B & R Ice Cream Ltd Plews Way, Leeming Bar Industrial Estate, NORTHALLERTON, NORTH YORKSHIRE, DL7 9UL.

BIGLEY, Mrs. Sandra Jacqueline, FCA *1973;* 10 St Leonards Road West, LYTHAM ST. ANNES, LANCASHIRE, FY8 2PF.

BIGMORE, Mr. Daren Christopher, BSc ACA *1998;* 43 Milldown Road, Goring, READING, RG8 0BA.

BIGNAL, Miss. Rachel Ann, BA ACA *1992;* 65 Wadham Grove, Emersons Green, BRISTOL, BS16 7DX.

BIGNELL, Mrs. Beverley Jane, BEng ACA *1999;* Northside, Bull Hill, Bethersden, ASHFORD, KENT, TN26 3LB.

BIGNELL, Mr. James Graham, BA ACA *2003;* Cadogan Management Kingsbury House, 15-17 King Street, LONDON, sw1y 6qu.

BIGNELL, Miss. Laura Elizabeth Hilary, ACA *2009;* Deloitte & Touche Abbots House, Abbey Street, READING, RG1 3BD.

BIGNELL, Mr. Philip Alwyn, MA ACA *1979;* 22 Birdhurst Rise, SOUTH CROYDON, CR2 7ED.

•**BIGNOLD, Mr. Roger Charles, FCA** *1973;* Bignold & Co, Lester House, 7 Bridge Street, STURMINSTER NEWTON, DT10 1AP.

BIGWOOD, Mrs. Penelope Ann, MA FCA *1973;* (Tax Fac), Charts Edge, Hosey Hill, WESTERHAM, TN16 1PL.

BIJA, Mr. Kenneth Lee, BA ACA *1992;* 59 West Cross Avenue, West Cross, SWANSEA, SA3 5TX.

BIJLANI, Miss. Ravina Gopal, BA ACA *2008;* 53 Prince George Road, LONDON, N16 8DL.

BILAL, Mr. Mohammad Amin, BEng ACA *1995;* 52 St Marys Crescent, Hendon, LONDON, NW4 4LH.

BILBIE, Miss. Janet Elizabeth, FCA *1977;* 9 De Montfort Road, Streatham, LONDON, SW16 1NF.

BILBOA, Mr. David Frederick Charles, MSci ACA *2010;* Flat 3, 71a Stroud Green Road, LONDON, N4 3EG.

BILBY, Mr. Colin Thomas, FCA *1961;* 1 Callaways Road, SHIPSTON-ON-STOUR, CV36 4HB.

BILDING, Mr. Leslie Alfred, FCA *1970;* Edgefields, 4 Factory Lane, Chevington, BURY ST. EDMUNDS, SUFFOLK, IP29 5QF.

BILES, Mr. Andrew John, BA FCA *1976;* Gerber Juice Co Ltd Mallard Court, Express Park Bristol Road, BRIDGWATER, SOMERSET, TA6 4RN.

BILES, Mr. John Anthony, TD BSc FCA *1972;* The Old Manor, Cliftons Lane, REIGATE, RH2 9RA.

•**BILES, Mr. John Christopher Morris, BSc FCA** *1965;* Llanmaes, St.Fagans, CARDIFF, CF5 6DU.

BILES, Mr. Jonathan David Frederick, BSc ACA *1993;* Park House, Wellington Square, CHELTENHAM, GLOUCESTERSHIRE, GL50 4JZ.

BILES, Miss. Louise Elizabeth, BA ACA *2007;* 67c Radbourne Road, LONDON, SW12 0ED.

BILES, Mr. Michael James, BA FCA *1970;* Hartland House, 4 Parkfield Rise, PRINCES RISBOROUGH, BUCKINGHAMSHIRE, HP27 0DW.

BILGRAMI, Mr. Ali Hyder, FCA *1968;* 15A Street No.6, P&V Scheme No.2, Off Park Road, Chak Shahzad Farms, ISLAMABAD, PAKISTAN.

BILGRAMI, Mr. Syed Zahid Hussain, BSc ACA *1997;* 8 Woodstead Grove, EDGWARE, MIDDLESEX, HA8 6PQ.

BILHAM, Miss. Deborah Patricia, ACA *2006;* Expro International Group Davidson House, The Forbury, READING, RG1 3EU.

BILIMORIA, Mr. Ardeshir Minoo, FCA *1979;* 28 Etheldene Avenue, Muswell Hill, LONDON, N10 3QH.

•**BILIMORIA, Mr. Jehangir Dinyar, ACA** *1981;* Bilimoria & Co Limited, 171 Raeburn Avenue, SURBITON, KT5 9DE.

BILIMORIA, Mr. Jimmy Soli, FCA *1974;* 5 Battery House, 74 Bhulabhai Desai Road, MUMBAI 400 026, MAHARASHTRA, INDIA.
BILIMORIA, Lord Karan Faridoon, CBE DL FCA *1987;* Cobra Partnership, 37 Stokenchurch Street, LONDON, SW6 3TS.
BILIMORIA, Mr. Yazdi Phiroz, FCA *1974;* 6 Ashburnham Close, LONDON, N2 0NH.
BILKHU, Mr. Randhir Singh, ACA *2009;* Global Aerospace Underwriting Managers Ltd Fitzwilliam Hous, 10 St. Mary Axe, LONDON, EC3A 8EQ.
BILL, Mr. Christopher Ian, BSc FCA *1992;* 9 Clear View, KINGSWINFORD, DY6 9XQ.
BILL, Mr. David, MA ACA *1981;* Boxtree, Beech Drive, Kingswood, TADWORTH, KT20 6PP.
BILL, Mr. Francis, FCA *1955;* 11 Egg Hall, EPPING, CM16 6SA. (Life Member)
BILL, Mr. John, FCA *1964;* 7 Milford Close, Wordsley, STOURBRIDGE, WEST MIDLANDS, DY8 5RB.
•BILL, Mr. John Leslie, FCA *1974;* Trafalgar Accountancy & Tax Limited, Trafalgar House, 261 Alcester Road South, BIRMINGHAM, B14 6DT.
BILL, Miss. Joyce Margaret Rose, LLB ACA *1998;* Social Security Agency 5th Floor, The Lighthouse, 1 Cromac Place, BELFAST, BT7 2JB.
BILL, Miss. Julia Carole, BSc ACA *1994;* PO Box 66539, 8590 Peyia, PAPHOS, CYPRUS.
BILL, Mr. Julian Michael, BA FCA *1993;* Berwyn, 87 Fairwater Road, Llandaff, CARDIFF, CF5 2LG.
•BILL, Miss. Susan Nicola, LLB ACA *1988;* Moore Stephens LLP, 150 Aldersgate Street, LONDON, EC1A 4AB. See also Moore Stephens & Co
BILLAM, Miss. Phebe, ACA *2011;* 56 Malthouse Meadows, LIPHOOK, HAMPSHIRE, GU30 7BG.
BILLARD, Mrs. Lynda Jane, BSc ACA *1985;* 1 Webster Crescent, Kimberworth, ROTHERHAM, S61 2BS.
•BILLARD, Mr. Trevor, MA ACA *1986;* Trevor Billard and Company Limited, 1 Webster Crescent, Kimberworth, ROTHERHAM, SOUTH YORKSHIRE, S61 2BS.
BILLEN, Mr. Guy, BSc ACA *2005;* 38 Barnard Way, Church Village, PONTYPRIDD, MID GLAMORGAN, CF38 1DQ.
BILLEN, Mr. Robin George, FCA *1969;* Horton International, Level 9, 52 Collins Street, MELBOURNE, VIC 3000, AUSTRALIA.
BILLEN, Mrs. Ruth, BA ACA *2006;* 38 Barnard Way, Church Village, PONTYPRIDD, MID GLAMORGAN, CF38 1DQ.
BILLER, Mr. Ian Geoffrey, MA ACA *1998;* 25 Lollards Close, AMERSHAM, BUCKINGHAMSHIRE, HP6 5JL.
BILLER, Mrs. Louise Margaret, BSc ACA *1998;* 25 Lollards Close, AMERSHAM, BUCKINGHAMSHIRE, HP6 5JL.
•BILLETT, Mr. James Geoffrey, MA MSc(Econ) ACA *2003;* James Billett Ltd, 2 Bowbank Cottage, Eddleston, PEEBLES, PEEBLESSHIRE, EH45 8QR.
BILLETT, Mr. Paul, BA ACA *1993;* Flat 1, 26 Byrne Road, LONDON, SW12 9JD.
BILLETT, Mr. Paul Nigel, BSc ACA *1999;* Imperium Corporate Finance Limited, 22 Roman Avenue, Angmering, LITTLEHAMPTON, WEST SUSSEX, BN16 4GH.
BILLIALD, Mrs. Rachel Louise, BSc ACA *2003;* 11 Mount Way, CHEPSTOW, GWENT, NP16 5NF.
BILLIALD, Ms. Sarah Margaret, BA ACA *2000;* 8 Leslie Road, DORKING, RH4 1PS.
BILLIMORIA, Mr. Furrokh Burjor, FCA *1974;* 11 Futura House, 168 Grange Road, LONDON, SE1 3BN.
BILLIMORIA, Mr. Hoshang Shavaksha, FCA *1976;* B221Grand Paradi, 572 Dadyseth Hill, August Kranti Marg, MUMBAI 400036, INDIA.
BILLIMORIA, Mr. Jemshed Homi, BSc FCA *1962;* 106 Great Valley Road, GLEN IRIS, VIC 3146, AUSTRALIA.
BILLIMORIA, Mr. Jimmy Phiroze, FCA *1975;* 401 Orchids, Riverside Estates, 12 Boat Club Road, PUNE 411001, INDIA.
BILLIMORIA, Mr. Kaiyoze Beji, BA ACA *1982;* Sunita 10B, Ridge Road, Malabar Hill, MUMBAI 400 006, INDIA.
BILLIMORIA, Mrs. Nargis Farokh, ACA *1981;* Unit 94, 183 St John's Avenue, GORDON, NSW 2072, AUSTRALIA.
BILLIN, Mr. Christopher Melbourne, ACA CA(SA) *2008;* 1a High Street, Sutton Courtenay, ABINGDON, OXFORDSHIRE, OX14 4AW.
BILLING, Mr. Andrew David, BSc ACA *1996;* 12 Symeon Place, St Peters Hill, Caversham, READING, RG4 7AS.
BILLING, Mrs. Caroline, ACA *1991;* Winton House, Ashampstead, READING, RG8 8RG.
BILLING, Mr. George James, FCA *1966;* East Wing Trenley Hall, Trenley Drive, CANTERBURY, CT3 4AW.
BILLING, Mr. Graham Stephen, BSc ACA *2009;* Windrush, 11 Pannatt Hill, MILLOM, CUMBRIA, LA18 5DB.
BILLING, Ms. Katherine Anne, ACA *1993;* British Petroleum Co Plc, 20 Canada Square, LONDON, E14 5NJ.
BILLING, Mr. Keith Bernard, BSc ACA *1984;* The Auditing Practices Board, Financial Reporting Council Aldwych House, 71-91 Aldwych, LONDON, WC2B 4HN.
BILLING, Mr. Navroz, BSc ACA *1997;* 25 Balder Rise, LONDON, SE12 9PF.
BILLING, Mr. Stephen Eric Charles, ACA *1984;* 36 Garfield Street, WATFORD, WD24 5HB.
BILLING, Mrs. Victoria Henrietta Louise, BA ACA *2002;* with Ernst & Young LLP, 1 More London Place, LONDON, SE1 2AF.
BILLINGE, Mr. Andrew John, BSc ACA *1989;* 48 Old Deer Park Gardens, RICHMOND, TW9 2TL.
BILLINGE, Mr. John Malcolm, FCA *1973;* 10 Swallows Acre, DAWLISH, DEVON, EX7 0RU.
BILLINGHAM, Mr. Adam, BA(Hons) ACA *2010;* 27 Euston Road, Far Cotton, NORTHAMPTON, NN4 8DT.
•BILLINGHAM, Mr. Barry John, FCA *1974;* (Tax Fac), Billingham & Co Limited, 4 Masons Yard, Mill Street, KIDDERMINSTER, WORCESTERSHIRE, DY11 6UY.
BILLINGHAM, Mr. Brian Michael, FCA *1955;* PO Box 689, Milsons Point, SYDNEY, NSW 2061, AUSTRALIA. (Life Member)
BILLINGHAM, Mr. David John, FCA *1958;* Road Green House, North Nibley, DURSLEY, GL11 6BA. (Life Member)
BILLINGHAM, Mr. Mark, ACA *2011;* 31 Jardine Close, STOURBRIDGE, DY8 4AT.
BILLINGHAM, Mr. Mark Robert, ACA *1995;* 45 Westdene Drive, BRIGHTON, BN1 5HE.
BILLINGHAM, Mr. Paul Andrew, ACA *1993;* Grant Thornton, Level 17, 383 Kent Street, SYDNEY, NSW 2000, AUSTRALIA.
BILLINGHAM, Mrs. Penelope, BSc ACA ACCA *1998;* Lowethorpe, Lowe Lane, Wolverley, KIDDERMINSTER, WORCESTERSHIRE, DY11 5QR.
•BILLINGHAM, Mr. Robert, FCA *1973;* Robert Billingham Limited, Spring Fields, Leasowes Lane, Lapal, HALESOWEN, WEST MIDLANDS B62 8QE.
BILLINGHURST, Mr. Cyril George, FCA *1950;* 36 Broadhurst Road, NORWICH, NR4 6RD. (Life Member)
BILLINGHURST, Mr. Michael Richard, BSc ACA *1986;* Cumbria Partnership NHS Foundatio Trust, Cumberland House, Carleton Clinic, Cumwhinton Road, CARLISLE, CA1 3SX.
•BILLINGHURST, Mr. Richard Brian, BA ACA *1992;* with Knox Cropper, 8-9 Well Court, LONDON, EC4M 9DN.
BILLINGHURST, Mr. Ronald Frank, FCA *1958;* Flat 4, 9904 Third Street, SIDNEY V8L 3B2, BC, CANADA. (Life Member)
•BILLINGHURST, Mr. Stephen Graham, BA ACA *1995;* with Deloitte & Touche, The Old Courthouse, PO Box 250, Athol Street, Douglas, ISLE OF MAN IM99 1XJ.
BILLINGHURST, Mrs. Susan Janet, BA ACA *1995;* Ardane Ballakillowey Road, Colby, ISLE OF MAN, IM9 4BD.
•BILLINGS, Mr. John Graham, BA FCA CTA *1987;* (Tax Fac), Carpenter Box LLP, Amelia House, WORTHING, WEST SUSSEX, BN11 1QR.
BILLINGS, Mr. Mark, BA FCA *1985;* 26 Cavendish Road, Hazel Grove, STOCKPORT, CHESHIRE, SK7 6HY.
BILLINGS, Mr. Paul Richard, BA ACA *1990;* 23 Edward Street, LOUTH, LINCOLNSHIRE, LN11 9LA.
BILLINGS, Mrs. Philippa Susan, MEng ACA *2001;* c/o Mr K Billings, 11 Calderstone Court, Middlestown, WAKEFIELD, WEST YORKSHIRE, WF4 4UE.
BILLINGS, Mr. Robert Nigel, BA ACA *1999;* 58 Worminghall Road, Ickford, AYLESBURY, BUCKINGHAMSHIRE, HP18 9JD.
BILLINGS, Mr. Roger Anthony, MA FCA *1963;* 4 Fairfield Heights, SHERBORNE, DORSET, DT9 4HH.
BILLINGSLEY, Mr. Simon Hugh, BA ACA *1987;* 63 Tanfield Lane, NORTHAMPTON, NN1 5RN.
•BILLINGTON, Mrs. Caroline Anne, BSc ACA *1992;* A-Count-A-Bility Ltd, Brook House, 60-62 Northbrook Street, NEWBURY, BERKSHIRE, RG14 1AH.
•BILLINGTON, Mr. Christopher, ACA *1986;* PricewaterhouseCoopers LLP, 1 Embankment Place, LONDON, WC2N 6RH. See also PricewaterhouseCoopers
BILLINGTON, Mr. Christopher William, BA ACA *1992;* Bird & Bird, Finance, 15 Fetter Lane, LONDON, EC4A 1JP.
BILLINGTON, Mr. Daniel Robert, BSc ACA *2010;* Flat 67 Kittiwake House, High Street, SLOUGH, SL1 1AG.
BILLINGTON, Mr. David John, BSc(Hons) FCA *2000;* with BDO LLP, 125 Colmore Row, BIRMINGHAM, B3 3SD.
BILLINGTON, Mr. Derek Julian, FCA *1975;* Ashworth Billington, 23 King Street, BLACKPOOL, FY1 3EJ.
BILLINGTON, Mr. Edward William, BSc ACA *1991;* Edward Billington & Son Ltd, Cunard Building, LIVERPOOL, L3 1EL.
BILLINGTON, Mrs. Emma Louise, BSc(Hons) ACA *2001;* 42 Harvest Fields Way, SUTTON COLDFIELD, WEST MIDLANDS, B75 5RB.
BILLINGTON, Mr. Frank, FCA *1973;* 17 Cleveland Grove, Royton, OLDHAM, OL2 5EX.
BILLINGTON, Mrs. Gemma Katharine Louise, MA ACA *1996;* 28 Dunstall Road, LONDON, SW20 0HR.
BILLINGTON, Mr. Jonathan, BSc ACA *1986;* Coventry Bldg Soc Orchard Court, Binley Business Park Harry Weston Road, COVENTRY, CV3 2TQ.
BILLINGTON, Mr. Kris Philip, ACA FCCA *2009;* with McEwan Wallace, 68 Argyle Street, Birkenhead, WIRRAL, CH41 6AF.
BILLINGTON, Mrs. Linda, MBA BA FCA *1992;* 2 Waltham Croft, CHESTERFIELD, DERBYSHIRE, S41 0UZ.
•BILLINGTON, Mr. Malcolm Harold, BSc FCA *1985;* CFO Partners Ltd, PO Box 28560, Remuera, AUCKLAND 1541, NEW ZEALAND.
BILLINGTON, Mr. Mark Anthony, BA FCA *1991;* (Tax Fac), 130A Yuk Tong Ave, SINGAPORE 596437, SINGAPORE.
BILLINGTON, Mrs. Mary Margaret, BSc ACA *1985;* 28 Captains Hill, ALCESTER, B49 6QW.
•BILLINGTON, Mr. Michael Christopher, FCA *1972;* M.C. Billington & Co, 17 Barford Close, SOUTHPORT, PR8 2RS.
BILLINGTON, Mr. Neville Cooper, FCA *1937;* Dreemskella, St Judes Road, Sulby, ISLE OF MAN, IM7 2ET. (Life Member)
BILLINGTON, Miss. Sophie Kathleen, BA ACA *1998;* Trerose, Mylor, FALMOUTH, CORNWALL, TR11 5SU.
BILLON, Mr. Eric, ACA *2009;* 66 rue de la Verrie, 44120 VERTOU, FRANCE.
•BILLS, Mr. David John, BA ACA *1993;* KPMG LLP, St. James's Square, MANCHESTER, M2 6DS. See also KPMG Europe LLP
BILLS, Mrs. Susan Jane, BA ACA *1989;* 45 Calool Cr, BELROSE, NSW 2085, AUSTRALIA.
BILLSBOROUGH, Mr. Stanley Thomas, FCA *1967;* 70 Dowbridge, Kirkham, PRESTON, PR4 2YL.
BILLUPS, Mr. Craig, BSc ACA *1999;* 185 Roughwood Road, ROTHERHAM, SOUTH YORKSHIRE, S61 3AB.
•BILLUPS, Mr. Russell John, FCA *1990;* RJB, Warlingham Court Farm, Tithepit Shaw Lane, WARLINGHAM, CR6 9AT.
BILSLAND, Mr. Andrew Stuart, BA ACA *1988;* 53 Oxford Drive, LONDON, SE1 2FB.
BILSLAND, Mr. Benjamin John, BA(Hons) ACA *2009;* 9 Nova Scotia Place, BRISTOL, BS1 6XJ.
BILSLAND, Mrs. Janice Amelia, BSc ACA *1981;* 9 Templeton Way, Penlan, SWANSEA, SA5 7JY.
BILSLAND, Mr. Nicholas James Philip, BSc ACA *1992;* Littleworth Corner Common Lane Burnham, SLOUGH, SL1 8PP.
BILSLAND, Mr. Ross Tomas, BA ACA *2005;* 227 Fulham Palace Road, LONDON, SW6 6UB.
BILTON, Mr. Andrew Stephen, FCA *1979;* 290 Warminster Road, SHEFFIELD, S8 8PT.
BILTON, Miss. Elizabeth Sarah, BA(Hons) ACA *2002;* Rose Cottage Withersdane, Wye, ASHFORD, TN25 5DL.
BILTON, Mr. Michael Andrew, FCA *1982;* 55 Lime Grove, NEW MALDEN, KT3 3TP.
BILTON, Mr. Paul Stephen, MA FCA *2001;* National Audit Office, 157-197 Buckingham Palace Road, LONDON, SW1W 9SP.
BILTON, Mr. Thomas Daniel Michael, LLB ACA *2007;* Flat 5, 18 St Neot Avenue, Pott Point, SYDNEY, NSW 2011, AUSTRALIA.
BILTOO, Mr. Huns, MA ACA *2004;* KPMG Mauritius, KPMG Centre, Cybercity, EBENE, MAURITIUS.
BIMSON, Mr. Michael, ACA *2010;* Basement Flat, 80 Morton Road, LONDON, N1 3BE.
BIN JAAFAR, Mr. Anuar, FCA *1975;* SEQU GROUP OF COMPANIES, SUITE 626 BLOCK A KELANA CENTRE POINT, JALAN SS7/9 KELANA JAYA, 47301 PETALING JAYA, MALAYSIA.
BIN MOHAMMED NOOR, Mr. Azizan, FCA *1973;* Yayazan, Aminuddin Baki, 79 Jalan Datuk Haji Eusoff, Kompleks Damai, 50400 KUALA LUMPUR, FEDERAL TERRITORY MALAYSIA.
BIN OMAR, Mr. Abdul Aziz, ACA *1981;* 60 Jalan Damai, 55000 KUALA LUMPUR, FEDERAL TERRITORY, MALAYSIA.
BINDER, Mr. Alan George, FCA *1957;* Spurlands House, Spurlands End Road, Great Kingshill, HIGH WYCOMBE, HP15 6PE. (Life Member)
BINDER, Mr. David John, BSc ACA *1988;* 50th floor, citibank tower, CENTRAL, HONG KONG SAR.
BINDICS, Mrs. Judit, BSc ACA *1992;* with Ernst & Young Advisory Ltd, Vaci ut 20, 1132 BUDAPEST, HUNGARY.
BINDING, Ms. Clare, BSc ACA *1999;* 65 Downsway, CHELMSFORD, CM1 6TT.
BINDING, Mr. Hector Arthur, FCA *1956;* 100 Wedgwood Drive, POOLE, DORSET, BH14 8EX. (Life Member)
BINDLISH, Mr. Raj Kumar, FCA *1964;* 1384 Wendigo Trail, MISSISSAUGA L5G 2W2, ON, CANADA. (Life Member)
BINDLOSS, Mr. Thomas Henry, MSc ACA *2001;* 34 Shire Lane, Chorleywood, RICKMANSWORTH, HERTFORDSHIRE, WD3 5NP.
BINDMAN, Mr. Bernard Alan, BSc FCA *1973;* 59 Kenilworth Avenue, LONDON, SW19 7LP.
BINDRA, Ms. Anita, BA ACA *1998;* 9 Disraeli Road, Ealing, LONDON, W5 5HS.
BINDRA, Mr. Deepak Raj, FCA *1971;* 63 Elliot Road, Hendon, LONDON, NW4 3DN.
BINDRA, Miss. Devika, BSc ACA *2005;* 63 Elliot Road, LONDON, NW4 3DN.
BINDRA, Mrs. Harinder, MMath ACA *2004;* 17a Norfolk Road, BIRMINGHAM, B15 3PZ.
BINDRA, Mr. Jasbir Singh, BA ACA *1993;* Treasury Control Department, HSBC Bank Middle East Ltd, Level 5 Building No 5 Emaar Square, DUBAI, pob 502601, UNITED ARAB EMIRATES.
BINDRA, Mr. Manraj Singh, FCA *1983;* PO Box 191531, DUBAI, UNITED ARAB EMIRATES.
BINEFA, Mr. Dominic Antonio, BSc ACA *2010;* 2 Windermere Court, 44 Park Road, KENLEY, SURREY, CR8 5AR.
BINEFA, Mrs. Genevieve Frances, BA ACA *2010;* 2 Windermere Court, 44 Park Road, KENLEY, SURREY, CR8 5AR.
BINES, Mr. Edward Robert, ACA MAAT MABRP *2001;* 4 Nicholson Grove, WICKFORD, SS12 9PL.
BINES, Mr. Kenneth Arthur, FCA *1960;* 4 Bury Lane, Bratton, WESTBURY, BA13 4RD. (Life Member)
BINFIELD, Mr. Paul Andrew, BA ACA *1990;* 55 Erica Avenue, GLEN IRIS, VIC 3146, AUSTRALIA.
•BINFIELD, Mr. Robert Frederick, ACA *1989;* Crabtree House, Crabtree Lane, Headley, BORDON, HAMPSHIRE, GU35 8QB.
BINGE, Mrs. Fiona Campbell, BA ACA *1988;* Knysna, 14a Mayfield Road, WEYBRIDGE, KT13 8XD.
•BINGE, Mr. Laurence, FCA *1986;* Woolford & Co LLP, Hillbrow House, Hillbrow Road, ESHER, SURREY, KT10 9NW. See also Dixcart International Limited
BINGEL, Mr. Peter Paul, BA ACA *2007;* Flat 1-6, 126 Bedford Hill, LONDON, SW12 9HW.
BINGER, Mrs. Karin, ACA *2007;* Flat H, 2 Hopton Road, LONDON, SW16 2EQ.
BINGHAM, Mrs. Amy, BSc ACA *2007;* ICAP Plc, 2 Broadgate, LONDON, EC2M 7UR.
BINGHAM, Mr. Anthony John, FCA *1972;* 37a Alleyn Park, Dulwich, LONDON, SE21 8AT. (Life Member)
BINGHAM, Mr. Christopher Philip, BSc(Hons) ACA *2004;* 25 Cumberland Mills Square, LONDON, E14 3BH.
BINGHAM, Mr. David Paul, BSc FCA CTA *1994;* (Tax Fac), 3 Whistley Court Farm, Lodge Rd, Whistley Green, READING, RG10 0EJ.
BINGHAM, Mr. Dennis Edward, FCA *1961;* The Old Farmhouse, 38 Highlands Road, HORSHAM, RH13 5LU. (Life Member)
•BINGHAM, Mrs. Elizabeth Eleanor, FCA *1979;* AIMS - Elizabeth Bingham, The Thatched House, The Downs, LEATHERHEAD, SURREY, KT22 8LH.
BINGHAM, Miss. Grainne Roisin, ACA *2010;* 15 Hoylake Close, Bletchley, MILTON KEYNES, MK3 7RH.
•BINGHAM, Mr. Howard, BSc FCA *1974;* H. Bingham & Co, 39 Andrew Avenue, Rawtenstall, ROSSENDALE, BB4 6EU.
•BINGHAM, Mr. Ian Anthony, FCA *1988;* (Tax Fac), PKF (UK) LLP, 4th Floor, 3 Hardman Street, MANCHESTER, M3 3HF.
•BINGHAM, Mr. Jonathan, BSc ACA *2000;* KPMG LLP, 15 Canada Square, LONDON, E14 5GL.
BINGHAM, Miss. Karen Alison, BA ACA *2004;* 21 Valerie Avenue Chatswood, SYDNEY, NSW 2067, AUSTRALIA.
BINGHAM, Miss. Kimberley, ACA *2010;* 26 Tolethorpe Square, STAMFORD, LINCOLNSHIRE, PE9 1LD.
BINGHAM, Mr. Mark Charles, BSc ACA *1995;* 2 Albany Woods, Shanganagh Road, KILLINEY, COUNTY DUBLIN, IRELAND.

BINGHAM, Mr. Mark William, BA ACA *1985;* Coca-Cola Hellas S.A., 26 Kifissias Av. & 2 Paradissou Street, 151 25 ATHENS, GREECE.

BINGHAM, Mr. Michael Christopher, FCA *1972;* Fbh Partners, Po Box 434, LINDFIELD, NSW 2070, AUSTRALIA.

BINGHAM, Mrs. Nicola, BSc ACA *2002;* 67 Cracknell Road, Annerley, BRISBANE, QLD 4103, AUSTRALIA.

BINGHAM, Mr. Oliver John Geoffrey, MEng BSc ACA *2004;* 57 Southborough Road, LONDON, E9 7EE.

BINGHAM, Mr. Richard Austin, BA ACA *1987;* 2 Whipling Close, Whatton, NOTTINGHAM, NG13 9EA.

BINGHAM, Mr. Richie David, BA ACA *2001;* E D F Energy, 40 Grosvenor Place, LONDON, SW1X 7EN.

BINGHAM, Mr. Simon, ACA ACMA *2010;* Headley Brothers Holdings Ltd, Queens Road, ASHFORD, KENT, TN24 8HH.

BINGHAM, Mr. Steven, BA ACA *1994;* 5 Avebury Avenue, LUTON, LU2 7DT.

•**BINGLEY, Mr. Giles William, BSc FCA** *1975;* Wills Bingley Limited, St. Denys House, 22 East Hill, ST. AUSTELL, CORNWALL, PL25 4TR. See also Eric Wills & Co Ltd

BINGLEY, Miss. Naomi, BSc ACA *2003;* 63 New Road Side, Horsforth, LEEDS, LS18 4JX.

BINKS, Mr. Allan William Spence, FCA *1964;* Liston House Liston Gardens, Liston, SUDBURY, SUFFOLK, CO10 7HY.

BINKS, Mr. Andrew, MA FCA *1978;* Holywell Farm, Caynton, NEWPORT, TF10 8NF.

BINKS, Mr. David John, BSc ACA *1987;* 1 Church Hill, Washingborough, LINCOLN, LN4 1EH.

•**BINKS, Mr. Phillip Andrew, BA ACA** *1998;* TTP Business Services Limited, 84 Manor Road, LANCING, WEST SUSSEX, BN15 0HD.

BINKS, Mr. Robin Paul, MA ACA *1979;* 6 Liskeard Gardens, Blackheath, LONDON, SE3 0PN.

•**BINKS, Mr. Samuel George, BA FCA** *1975;* Sam Binks, Coombe Farm Cottage, Canford Lane, BRISTOL, BS9 3PE.

•**BINLEY, Mrs. Amanda Jane, ACA** *1980;* A.J. Binley, 44 Hill Grove, Henleaze, BRISTOL, BS9 4RQ.

BINLEY, Mr. Harold Frederick, FCA *1976;* 44 Hill Grove, BRISTOL, BS9 4RQ.

BINLEY, Miss. Miranda, ACA *2011;* Garden Flat, 166 Westbury Road, Westbury-on-Trym, BRISTOL, BS9 3AH.

BINMORE, Mr. Andrew John, MA MEng ACA *1995;* Bleak House, Robinsons Hill, Melbourne, DERBY, DE73 8DJ.

BINMORE, Mr. John Simpson, FCA *1962;* Bleak House, Melbourne, DERBY, DE73 8DJ.

BINNER, Mr. Raymond Allan, MA FCA *1976;* 28 Chiltern Road, MAIDENHEAD, SL6 1XA.

BINNEY, Mr. Adrian Philip, FCA *1977;* Aldby House, Stackhouse Lane, Giggleswick, SETTLE, BD24 0DW.

BINNEY, Mr. David John, BSc FCA *1975;* Malt House, 39 New Street, HENLEY-ON-THAMES, OXFORDSHIRE, RG9 2BP.

BINNEY, Mr. Hibbert Atkin Hardman, BA FCA *1954;* St. Johns Almshouse, Half Moon Street, SHERBORNE, DORSET, DT9 3LJ. (Life Member)

•**BINNEY, Mr. Mark, BA FCA** *1999;* PricewaterhouseCoopers LLP, 7 More London Riverside, LONDON, SE1 2RT. See also PricewaterhouseCoopers

BINNEY, Mr. Michael Andrew Barclay, FCA *1983;* C/O Transearch Executive Search Co.Ltd., 34th Floor Abdulrahim Place, 990 Rama IV Road, BANGKOK 10500, THAILAND.

BINNEY, Mr. Paul, BSc ACA *1983;* Hayward Road, RD 8, WHANGAREI, NEW ZEALAND.

BINNEY, Mr. Paul Francis, BCom ACA *1984;* No 1 Dormer Villa, The Square, Portscatho, TRURO, CORNWALL, TR2 5HW.

•**BINNIE, Mr. Christopher Evan, FCA** *1994;* Clouders (Audit & Accounts) Limited, Charter House, 103-105 Leigh Road, LEIGH-ON-SEA, ESSEX, SS9 1JL. See also Clouders

BINNING, Mrs. Beverley Jean, BA ACA *1983;* 26 Selcroft Road, PURLEY, CR8 1AD.

BINNING, Mr. Simon Kenneth, MA ACA *1984;* 26 Selcroft Road, PURLEY, CR8 1AD.

BINNINGTON, Miss. Alisa Jane, BA ACA *1992;* Elms Farmhouse Upper End, Salford, CHIPPING NORTON, OXFORDSHIRE, OX7 5YU.

BINNINGTON, Mr. Benjamin, BA FCA *1990;* 40 Woodsome Road, LONDON, NW5 1RZ.

BINNINGTON, Mrs. Elizabeth Caroline, MA FCA AMCT *1993;* 9 Dalkeith Road, HARPENDEN, AL5 5PP.

BINNS, Mr. Adam John, BSc ACA *1990;* 15 Langhams Way, Wargrave, READING, RG10 8DX.

•**BINNS, Mr. Andrew Geoffrey, ACA** *1992;* Andrew G Binns, 5 Kings Croft, Ealand, SCUNTHORPE, DN17 4GA.

BINNS, Mr. Brian, FCA *1971;* Home Services, 17 Lisle Court, Dagger Lane, HULL, HU1 2LX.

BINNS, Mr. Jack, FCA *1956;* Scoatfell, Hill Top Road, Hainworth, KEIGHLEY, BD21 5QN. (Life Member)

BINNS, Mr. John Christopher, FCA *1970;* 52 Moorfield Drive, Baildon, SHIPLEY, WEST YORKSHIRE, BD17 6LL.

BINNS, Mr. Simon Andrew, LLB ACA *1986;* Trumpf Ltd Unit A, President Way, LUTON, LU2 9NL.

BINNS, Mr. Thomas, ACA *2009;* 22 Printers Park, Hollingworth, HYDE, CHESHIRE, SK14 8QH.

BINNY, Ms. Rachel Elizabeth, BSc ACA *2006;* 68 Crescent Lane, LONDON, SW4 9PU.

BINSTEAD, Mr. Michael Terence Hugh, FCA *1964;* 90 Glengall Road, WOODFORD GREEN, IG8 0DL.

BINSTEAD, Mrs. Sarah Helen, BEng ACA *1998;* 14 Gaunts Road, Pawlett, BRIDGWATER, SOMERSET, TA6 4SF.

•**BINSTED, Mr. John Wadkin, FCA** *1951;* J.W. Binsted & Co, Brueton House, 34 Brueton Avenue, SOLIHULL, B91 3EN.

BINSTOCK, Mr. Daniel Solomon, BA ACA *2006;* 56 Golders Gardens, LONDON, NW11 9BU.

BINT, Mr. David Michael, BSc ACA *2002;* 47 Longacres, ST. ALBANS, HERTFORDSHIRE, AL4 0SL.

•**BINT, Mr. Richard Sidney, MA ACA** *1979;* PKF (UK) LLP, Farringdon Place, 20 Farringdon Road, LONDON, EC1M 3AP.

BINTI SA'AD, Miss. Fadzilah, FCA *1968;* 38 Jalan 7, Kemansah HeightsHulu Kelang, 68000 AMPANG, SELANGOR, MALAYSIA. (Life Member)

•**BINTLIFF, Miss. Joanna Kathryn Victoria, ACA** *2004;* 8 Clough Head, SOWERBY BRIDGE, WEST YORKSHIRE, HX6 3QH.

BINYON, Ms. Claire Margaret, BSc ACA *1993;* Maplins, Munstead View Road, Bramley, GUILDFORD, SURREY, GU5 0DA.

BINYON, Mr. James Edward Charles, MA ACA *1987;* 156 Calle Reina Ana, La Villa de Torrimar, GUAYNABO, 00969, PUERTO RICO.

BIOJOUT, Mr. Alexandre Denis, MSc ACA *2010;* Top Floor, 57 Moreton Street, LONDON, SW1V 2NY.

BIRCH, Mr. Alan Francis, BA FCA *1976;* Canberra, Churchill Close, Ettington, STRATFORD-UPON-AVON, CV37 7SP.

BIRCH, Mr. Anthony Laurence Hamilton, FCA *1980;* P O Box 250, REDLYNCH, QLD 4870, AUSTRALIA.

BIRCH, Ms. Cherry Janet, FCA *1978;* 1/251 Barkly Street, St Kilda, MELBOURNE, VIC 3182, AUSTRALIA.

BIRCH, Mr. Christopher Charles, FCA *1960;* P.O. Box SS 5017, NASSAU, BAHAMAS.

BIRCH, Mr. Christopher Charles, BSc FCA *1977;* (Tax Fac), 7 Campden Way, Handforth, WILMSLOW, SK9 3JA.

•**BIRCH, Mr. Christopher Leo, BSc FCA** *1988;* Perrins Limited, Custom House, The Strand, BARNSTAPLE, DEVON, EX31 1EU.

BIRCH, Mr. Clive Hedley William, FCA *1978;* 6 School Lane, Haslingfield, CAMBRIDGE, CB3 7JL.

•**BIRCH, Mr. David Clifford, ACA** *1980;* (Tax Fac), Mazars LLP, The Pinnacle, 160 Midsummer Boulevard, MILTON KEYNES, MK9 1FF.

BIRCH, Mr. Edward, BA ACA *2007;* 169a Clapham Manor Street, LONDON, SW4 6DB.

BIRCH, Mrs. Emma Elizabeth, BA ACA *1999;* 154 Oldfield Road, ALTRINCHAM, CHESHIRE, WA14 4BJ.

•**BIRCH, Mr. Graham Nicholas, FCA** *1982;* Birch Riddle & Co Limited, Pond House, Weston Green, THAMES DITTON, SURREY, KT7 0JX.

BIRCH, Miss. Hannah Victoria, ACA *2009;* 10 Brook Terrace, Slaithwaite, HUDDERSFIELD, HD7 5BU.

BIRCH, Mr. Ian, BA ACA *1999;* 47 Longmore Road, Shirley, SOLIHULL, B90 3DZ.

•**BIRCH, Mr. James William, FCA** *1988;* (Tax Fac), Dickinsons, Enterprise House, Beesons Yard, Bury Lane, RICKMANSWORTH, HERTFORDSHIRE WD3 1DS.

BIRCH, Mrs. Jennifer Charlotte, BSc ACA *2000;* Holborn College, Woolwich Road, LONDON, SE7 8LN.

BIRCH, Miss. Jenny, ACA *2011;* 260 Heath Road, WIRRAL, MERSEYSIDE, CH63 2HQ.

BIRCH, Mr. Jeremy Mark, BSc(Hons) ACA *2001;* 9 Church Street, Whittington, LICHFIELD, STAFFORDSHIRE, WS14 9LE.

BIRCH, Mr. Jonathan Mark, BSc ACA *1991;* Capital One Bank (Europe) Plc Trent House, Station Street, NOTTINGHAM, NG2 3HX.

•**BIRCH, Mr. Jonathan Mark, BA FCA MABRP** *1978;* with FRP Advisory LLP, 10 Furnival Street, LONDON, EC4A 1YH.

BIRCH, Miss. Kathryn Anne, BA ACA *2011;* 114 Stapleton Hall Road, Flat B, LONDON, N4 4QA.

BIRCH, Mr. Kevin Paul, FCA *1967;* 6 Yarborough Terrace, Stedham, MIDHURST, WEST SUSSEX, GU29 0NP.

•**BIRCH, Mr. Leslie Michael, OBE MA FCA** *1973;* PricewaterhouseCoopers KFT, Wesselenyi u 16, BUDAPEST, H-1077, HUNGARY.

BIRCH, Miss. Margaret Lindsay, ACA *1988;* Smiley Knows, 71 Dirleton Avenue, NORTH BERWICK, EH39 4QL.

BIRCH, Mr. Nicholas Alan, BA ACA *1985;* Express Group Ltd College Business Park, Kearsley Road, RIPON, NORTH YORKSHIRE, HG4 2RN.

•**BIRCH, Mr. Nigel Milne, BSc FCA** *1973;* (Tax Fac), Kingston Smith & Partners LLP, 105 St. Peters Street, ST. ALBANS, HERTFORDSHIRE, AL1 3EJ. See also Kingston Smith Limited Liability Partnership, Kingston Smith LLP, Devonshire Corporate Services LLP and Kingston Smith Consulting LLP

•**BIRCH, Mrs. Patricia Gwynn, BA ACA** *1990;* 15 Chestnut Green, Monk Fryston, LEEDS, LS25 5PN.

BIRCH, Mr. Paul Jonathan, BA ACA *1997;* 55 Frith View, Chapel-en-le-Frith, HIGH PEAK, DERBYSHIRE, SK23 9TT.

•**BIRCH, Mr. Peter Michael, BA ACA** *2003;* Deloitte LLP, PO Box 500, 2 Hardman Street, MANCHESTER, M60 2AT. See also Deloitte & Touche LLP

BIRCH, Mr. Robert Gray, BA ACA *1982;* 90 Rua Elvira Niemeyer, Sao Conrado, 22610-370 RIO DE JANEIRO, BRAZIL.

BIRCH, Mr. Robert James, BA(Hons) ACA CPA *2002;* Ernst & Young LLP, Building 1, Suite 200, 1001 Page Mill Road, PALO ALTO, CA 94304 UNITED STATES.

•**BIRCH, Mr. Robert William, BSc FCA** *1992;* with KPMG LLP, One Snowhill, Snow Hill Queensway, BIRMINGHAM, B4 6GN.

•**BIRCH, Mr. Robin David Mortland, BA ACA** *1994;* Ernst & Young LLP, 1 More London Place, LONDON, SE1 2AF. See also Ernst & Young Europe LLP

BIRCH, Mr. Robin Francis Dickens, BA FCA *1980;* 35 Waterhouse Lane, Gedling, NOTTINGHAM, NG4 4BP.

BIRCH, Mr. Ronald, FCA *1951;* Idle Hour, Caddington Common, Markyate, ST ALBANS, AL3 8QF. (Life Member)

BIRCH, Mr. Scott, ACA *2003;* Eden House, Ridley Mill, STOCKSFIELD, NORTHUMBERLAND, NE43 7QU.

BIRCH, Mr. Simon Charles, BA ACA *1993;* 123 Arthur Road, LONDON, SW19 7DR.

BIRCH, Mr. Simon Mark, BSc ACA *1989;* Cornwall Farmers Ltd, 44 Threemilestone Industrial Estate Threemilestone, TRURO, CORNWALL, TR4 9LD.

BIRCH, Mrs. Susan Margaret, BSc ACA *2003;* Hazelwoods Staverton Court, Staverton, CHELTENHAM, GLOUCESTERSHIRE, GL51 0UX.

•①**BIRCH, Mr. Trevor Nigel, BA FCA** *1987;* PKF (UK) LLP, Farringdon Place, 20 Farringdon Road, LONDON, EC1M 3AP.

BIRCH, Miss. Victoria Faith, BSc ACA *2010;* 9 Longwood Avenue, BINGLEY, WEST YORKSHIRE, BD16 2RX.

BIRCH, Mr. Walter Alfred, FCA *1958;* 30 Corfe Avenue, WORCESTER, WR4 0EB. (Life Member)

BIRCH, Mr. William Gareth, BA ACA *1987;* ADS, Alcohol & Drug Services, 87 Oldham Street, MANCHESTER, M4 1LW.

BIRCH-EVANS, Mrs. Katherine Rose, BSc ACA *2007;* 359 St. Albans Road West, HATFIELD, HERTFORDSHIRE, AL10 9RU.

BIRCHALL, Mr. Alfred Henry, FCA *1951;* 8 Meadowbank Lane, GRANGE-OVER-SANDS, CUMBRIA, LA11 6AT. (Life Member)

BIRCHALL, Mr. Charles William David, FCA *1964;* Barrick Gold Corporation, 161 Bay Street, Suite 3700, TORONTO M5J 2S1, ON, CANADA.

BIRCHALL, Mr. Christopher John, ACA *1983;* B.C. Securities Commission, PO Box 10142 Pacific Centre, 701 West Georgia Street, VANCOUVER V7Y 1L2, BC, CANADA.

BIRCHALL, Miss. Eloise, BA ACA *2004;* 62 Park Road, WILMSLOW, CHESHIRE, SK9 5BT.

BIRCHALL, Miss. Erica, BA ACA *2005;* 321/6 Cowper Wharf Road, WOOLLOOMOOLOO, NSW 2011, AUSTRALIA.

•**BIRCHALL, Mr. Francis John, ACA** *1984;* Birchall & Co, 5 Penrhos Road, Hoylake, WIRRAL, MERSEYSIDE, CH47 1HU.

BIRCHALL, Miss. Kim Lisa, BA FCA *1987;* Quantum, PO Box 2643, CALNE, SN11 9ZX.

BIRCHALL, Mr. Paul Peter, BA ACA *2003;* with Synergy Health PLC, Ground Floor Stella, Windmill Hill Business Park, Whitehill Way, SWINDON, SN5 6NX.

BIRCHALL, Mr. Robert William, BA ACA *1984;* Rivington, Holly Bank Road, WOKING, GU22 0JW.

•①**BIRCHALL, Mr. Robert William, BSc FCA** *1978;* with Pricewaterhousecoopers, 12 Plumtree Court, LONDON, EC4A 4HT.

BIRCHALL, Mr. Roger Julian, FCA *1969;* Hazelmere, 5 St. John's Road, KNUTSFORD, WA16 0DL.

•**BIRCHALL, Mr. Sean Robert, BA(Hons) ACA** *2002;* Birchall & Co, 42 Church Street, LEIGH, LANCASHIRE, WN7 1AZ.

BIRCHALL, Mrs. Susan Elizabeth, MA ACA *1989;* 2 Avenue South, SURBITON, KT5 8PJ.

BIRCHALL, Mr. Tristan Paul, BSc ACA *2001;* 41 In der Steinkaul, D 54441 WELLEN, GERMANY.

•**BIRCHELL, Mr. Christopher Stuart, BSc ACA** *2006;* with Lancaster Haskins LLP, Granville House, 2 Tettenhall Road, WOLVERHAMPTON, WV1 4SB.

BIRCHENOUGH, Mr. Adrian Hugh, BA ACA *1981;* 15 Clement Road, Marple Bridge, STOCKPORT, SK6 5AF.

BIRCHENOUGH, Mr. Mark Andrew, BSc FCA DChA *1993;* 10 Church Lane, Backwell, BRISTOL, BS48 3PQ.

BIRCHER, Miss. Caroline, BSc ACA *2010;* Richard C Bircher (Holdings) Ltd, Quarkhill, Crowcombe, TAUNTON, SOMERSET, TA4 4BJ.

BIRCHER, Dr. Christopher Paul, MA ACA *1982;* 38c Parliament Hill, Hampstead, LONDON, NW3 2TN.

BIRD, Mr. Adam Sean, BSc ACA *2010;* 13 Crow Park Drive, Burton Joyce, NOTTINGHAM, NG14 5AS.

BIRD, Mr. Alan Geoffrey, BSocSc ACA *1985;* 13 Crow Park Drive, Burton Joyce, NOTTINGHAM, NG14 5AS.

BIRD, Mrs. Amanda Jane, BSc ACA *1993;* 153 Beaumaris Way, Grove Park, BLACKWOOD, NP12 1DF.

BIRD, Mr. Anthony Malcolm David, FCA *1967;* Failand Hill House Horse Race Lane Failand, BRISTOL, BS8 3TY. (Life Member)

BIRD, Mr. Anthony Michael, BSc ACA *1990;* 58 Squires Bridge Road, SHEPPERTON, TW17 0QA.

BIRD, Mr. Brian John Kidman, FCA *1951;* The Royal British Legion, Mais House, 18 Hastings Road, BEXHILL-ON-SEA, EAST SUSSEX, TN40 2HH. (Life Member)

BIRD, Ms. Caroline Louise, BMus ACA *1990;* 41 Capron Road, DUNSTABLE, BEDFORDSHIRE, LU5 5AG.

BIRD, Mrs. Caroline Natalie, ACA *2002;* 17 The Glade, Fetcham, LEATHERHEAD, KT22 9TQ.

BIRD, Mrs. Carolyn, BSc LLB ACA *1985;* 9 Highfields Mead, East Hanningfield, CHELMSFORD, CM3 8XA.

BIRD, Ms. Celia Alice, ACA CPA *1989;* 366 Woodland Ridge, LOS GATOS, CA 95033, UNITED STATES.

BIRD, Miss. Charlotte Elizabeth, ACA *2009;* ABF The Soldiers Charity, Mountbarrow House, 6-20 Elizabeth Street, LONDON, SW1W 9RB.

•**BIRD, Mr. Christopher Donald, BSc ACA** *1986;* Chris Bird, Porth Y Castell, Ravenspoint Road, Trearddur Bay, HOLYHEAD, GWYNEDD LL65 2AQ.

BIRD, Mr. Christopher Howard, BA FCA *1973;* Ladybird Inns Ltd, Ladybird Barn, Old Burcot Lane, BROMSGROVE, WORCESTERSHIRE, B60 1PH.

•**BIRD, Mr. Christopher Paul, BSc FCA** *1992;* Stapletons, 4 Market Street, CREDITON, EX17 2AJ.

BIRD, Mr. Christopher Robert, ACA *1985;* unit 7, 14 redeness street, YORK, yo31 7uu.

•**BIRD, Mr. Colin Graham, FCA** *1973;* The Oak House, 140 North Road, HERTFORD, SG14 2BZ.

BIRD, Mr. Damien Michael, BA ACA *2002;* 9 Clearsprings, LIGHTWATER, SURREY, GU18 5YJ.

BIRD, Mr. David Alan, FCA MCT *1984;* Leasedrive Ltd, Crowthorne House, Nine Mile Ride, WOKINGHAM, BERKSHIRE, RG40 3GA.

BIRD, Mr. David Richard, ACA *2008;* with PricewaterhouseCoopers LLP, 1 Embankment Place, LONDON, WC2N 6RH.

BIRD, Miss. Fiona Louise, ACA *2005;* 1/72 Lang Street, South Yarra, MELBOURNE, VIC 3141, AUSTRALIA.

BIRD, Miss. Fiona Mary, LLB ACA *1993;* (Tax Fac), 2 Grantley Close, Shalford, GUILDFORD, GU4 8DL.

BIRD, Mr. Frederick Thomas George, FCA *1958;* 268a Main Road, Duston, NORTHAMPTON, NN5 6PP. (Life Member)

BIRD, Mr. Frederick William, FCA *1953;* Flat 8, Beacon Court, 77 Telegraph Road, Heswall, WIRRAL, MERSEYSIDE CH60 0AR. (Life Member)
BIRD, Mr. George Simon, BSc ACA *1983;* 6 Sydney Road, Muswell Hill, LONDON, N10 2LP.
BIRD, Miss. Georgina Helen, BA(Hons) ACA *2004;* with BDO LLP, Prospect Place, 85 Great North Road, HATFIELD, HERTFORDSHIRE, AL9 5BS.
BIRD, Mr. Graham John, MA ACA *1998;* Little Cowlands, Collops Road, Stebbing, DUNMOW, ESSEX, CM6 3SZ.
BIRD, Mr. James Derek, FCA *1955;* 1 Sudbrooke Road, LONDON, SW12 8TG. (Life Member)
BIRD, Mr. James Edward, ACA *2011;* 147 Willingdon Road, LONDON, N22 6SE.
BIRD, Mr. James Graham Lyster, BSc ACA *2005;* Royal & Sunalliance Leadenhall Court, 1 Leadenhall Street, LONDON, EC3V 1PP.
BIRD, Mr. James Robert, MA ACA *1995;* 153 Beaumaris Way, Grove Park, BLACKWOOD, GWENT, NP12 1DF.
BIRD, Mr. Jeffrey Mark, BA FCA *1992;* 28 The Crescent, Welton, BROUGH, NORTH HUMBERSIDE, HU15 1NS.
BIRD, Miss. Joanne, BSc ACA *2009;* Penlan, Coventry Road, Fillongley, COVENTRY, CV7 8BZ.
BIRD, Mr. John, ACA *2006;* 4 Garsdale Close, Walton-Le-Dale, PRESTON, PR5 4BU.
•BIRD, John Leslie, Esq OBE FCA *1951;* (Member of Council 1974 - 1991), John L Bird, The Old Vicarage, Loves Green, Highwood, CHELMSFORD, CM1 3QG.
BIRD, Mr. John Richard, MA FCA *1976;* 11678 Havenner Rd, Fairfax Station, FAIRFAX, VA 22039, UNITED STATES.
BIRD, Mr. John Richard, FCA *1969;* 1861 Tolmie St., VANCOUVER V6R 4B9, BC, CANADA.
•BIRD, Mr. John William, BSc FCA *1976;* John Bird, 38 Northgate Street, LEICESTER, LE3 5BY.
•BIRD, Mr. John William, BSc FCA *1988;* Deloitte LLP, 2 New Street Square, LONDON, EC4A 3BZ. See also Deloitte & Touche LLP
BIRD, Mr. Jon Harvey, FCA *1992;* Ingenix, 3100 Lake Center Drive, SANTA ANA, CA 92714, UNITED STATES.
BIRD, Mrs. Karen Anne, ACA *1982;* 248a Stourbridge Road, Catshill, BROMSGROVE, WORCESTERSHIRE, B61 9LQ.
BIRD, Mr. Kevin Anthony, FCA *1981;* Furlong View Town Lane, Bradwell, HOPE VALLEY, DERBYSHIRE, S33 9JY.
BIRD, Mr. Lawrence, BSc ACA *2011;* Flat 7, 11 Woodside Avenue, LONDON, N12 8AN.
BIRD, Mrs. Louise, BA(Hons) ACA *2003;* with BDO LLP, 1 Bridgewater Place, Water Lane, LEEDS, LS11 5RU.
•BIRD, Mr. Malcolm Kenneth, FCA CTA *1975;* Malcolm Bird, 1 Kendals Close, RADLETT, WD7 8NQ.
BIRD, Mr. Mark Jeremy, BA ACA *2003;* 1 Henslow Mews, CAMBRIDGE, CB2 8BX.
BIRD, Mr. Martin Clive, FCA *1956;* Applegarth House, Terrace Road North, Binfield, BRACKNELL, RG42 5JJ. (Life Member)
•BIRD, Mrs. Meinir Elaine, BSc ACA *1992;* with Clifton-Crick Sharp & Co, 40 High Street, PERSHORE, WORCESTERSHIRE, WR10 1DP.
BIRD, Mrs. Melissa Janine, BA ACA *2003;* with Menzies LLP, Victoria House, 50-58 Victoria Road, FARNBOROUGH, HAMPSHIRE, GU14 7PG.
BIRD, Mr. Michael, ACA *2008;* Morgan Stanley International, 25 Cabot Square, LONDON, E14 4QA.
BIRD, Mr. Michael James, BA ACA *1990;* Dial House, Chislehurst Road, BICKLEY, KENT, BR1 2NJ.
BIRD, Mr. Michael Thomas, FCA *1969;* 115 Crabtree Lane, HARPENDEN, AL5 5RQ.
BIRD, Mr. Neville, FCA *1976;* 221 Cressex Road, Booker, HIGH WYCOMBE, HP12 4QE.
•BIRD, Mr. Nicholas Charlton Penrhys, FCA *1974;* (Tax Fac), Finrob Limited, Suite 5b, Brook House, 77 Fountain Street, MANCHESTER, M2 2EE.
BIRD, Mr. Nigel James, MA FCA *1976;* Pembroke College, St. Aldates, OXFORD, OX1 1DW.
BIRD, Mr. Paul Michael, BSc ACA *1990;* 68 Strathnaver Avenue, STRATHMORE, VIC 3041, AUSTRALIA.
BIRD, Mr. Peter Anthony, FCA *1966;* 5 Park Road, Heswall, WIRRAL, CH60 2SL. (Life Member)
•BIRD, Mr. Peter Charles John, FCA *1959;* Philip Barnes & Co Ltd, The Old Council Chambers, Halford Street, TAMWORTH, B79 7RB.
BIRD, Mr. Peter Newton, ACA CA(SA) *2010;* PO Box 727, HAYWARDS HEATH, WEST SUSSEX, RH16 9FH.
•BIRD, Ms. Phaedra Selina, BSc FCA *1995;* Crowe Clark Whitehill Audit LLC, 6th Floor, Victory House, Prospect Hill, Douglas, ISLE OF MAN IM1 1EQ. See also Horwath Clark Whitehill Audit LLC and Horwath Clark Whitehill LLC
BIRD, Mr. Philip Trevor, BA ACA *1988;* 46 Rue St Martin, 27150 ETREPAGNY, FRANCE.
•BIRD, Mr. Phillip John, BSc ACA *2005;* Online Accounting Solutions Limited, 65A Liverpool Road, Penwortham, PRESTON, PR1 9XD. See also My Online Accountants Limited
BIRD, Mrs. Rebecca Mary, BSc(Hons) ACA *2003;* 7 Denton Road, NORWICH, NR3 4DP.
BIRD, Mr. Richard William, BSc FCA *1996;* 61 Hill Rise, RICKMANSWORTH, HERTFORDSHIRE, WD3 7NY.
BIRD, Mr. Robert Andrew, BA ACA *2000;* 5/9 The Crescent, MANLY, NSW 2095, AUSTRALIA.
BIRD, Mr. Robert Edward, BA ACA *2003;* Ladybird Barn, Old Burcot Lane, BROMSGROVE, WORCESTERSHIRE, B60 1PH.
BIRD, Mr. Robert John, BSc ACA *1992;* Charles Kendall Group, 7 Albert Court, Prince Consort Road, LONDON, SW7 2BJ.
BIRD, Mr. Robert Nigel, BSc ACA *1990;* 39 Wychwood Grove, Chandler's Ford, EASTLEIGH, HAMPSHIRE, SO53 1FQ.
•BIRD, Mr. Roger Hughes, FCA *1970;* R.H. Bird & Co, Spencer House, 114 High Street, Wordsley, STOURBRIDGE, DY8 5QR.
BIRD, Mr. Roger Leslie, FCA *1961;* Fairhaven, 24 Berks Hill, Chorleywood, RICKMANSWORTH, WD3 5AQ.
BIRD, Mr. Roger Nicholas, MA(Oxon) FCA *1999;* 20 Newbery Close, CATERHAM, SURREY, CR3 6GD.
BIRD, Mrs. Sarah Anne, BSc ACA *1997;* Hays House, 4 St. Georges Square, High Street, NEW MALDEN, SURREY, KT3 4JQ.
•BIRD, Mr. Simon Christopher, FCA *1979;* (Tax Fac), Freeman Baker Associates, The Old Church, 48 Verulam Road, ST. ALBANS, AL3 4DH.
BIRD, Mr. Simon John, BSc(Hons) ACA MAAT *2010;* 1 Overdale Close, Glenfield, LEICESTER, LE3 8GR.
BIRD, Mr. Stephen, BSc ACA *2002;* PO Box 905, GEORGE TOWN, GRAND CAYMAN, KY1-1103, CAYMAN ISLANDS.
BIRD, Mr. Stephen Ronald, BSc ACA *1990;* 3 Clos Y Fran, Thornhill, CARDIFF, CF14 9JJ.
BIRD, Mr. Stuart Charles, BA ACA *1994;* 12a Oak Gardens, Bredon, TEWKESBURY, GLOUCESTERSHIRE, GL20 7LS.
BIRD, Miss. Sylvia Anne, FCA *1958;* c/o Malcolm Taylor, 15 Woodland Way, WOODFORD GREEN, ESSEX, IG8 0QG. (Life Member)
BIRD, Miss. Tanya Marie, BA ACA *2001;* 19 Berryfield Close, The Downs, SUNDERLAND, SR3 2XU.
BIRD, Mr. Terence Albert, BA FCA *1973;* The Beck, 333 Tonbridge Road, Wateringbury, MAIDSTONE, ME18 5PA.
BIRD, Mr. Wesley Thomas George, ACA *2005;* with BDO LLP, Arcadia House, Maritime Walk, Ocean Village, SOUTHAMPTON, SO14 3TL.
BIRD, Mr. William Leslie, FCA *1951;* 10 Alexandra Court, Alexandra Road, BURTON-ON-TRENT, STAFFORDSHIRE, DE15 0JF. (Life Member)
•BIRDITT, Mr. Gary Richard, FCA *1974;* Burchill & Co, Reed House, 16 High Street, West Wratting, CAMBRIDGE, CB21 5LU.
•BIRDSALL, Mr. Eric Graham, FCA *1964;* (Tax Fac), Birdsall & Bennett LLP, 1 Tranquility, Crossgates, LEEDS, LS15 8QU.
•BIRDSALL, Mr. Nicholas James, FCA *1993;* Birdsall & Bennett LLP, 1 Tranquility, Crossgates, LEEDS, LS15 8QU.
BIRDSALL, Mr. Paul, JP FCA *1969;* The Orchard, 37 Main Street, Scholes, LEEDS, LS15 4DQ.
BIRKBECK, Miss. Caroline, BSc ACA *1992;* 3 Kirkfell Drive High Lane, STOCKPORT, CHESHIRE, SK6 8JB.
BIRKBY, Mr. David James, BA ACA *1996;* Recticel Manufacturing Bluebell Close, Clover Nook Industrial Park, Somercotes, ALFRETON, DERBYSHIRE, DE55 4RD.
BIRKBY, Mr. David Matthew, BSc ACA *2009;* Flat 6, 54 Anglesea Road, IPSWICH, IP1 3PW.
BIRKE, Mr. Michael Russell, FCA *1973;* 73 Poplar Grove, MAIDSTONE, KENT, ME16 0AN.
BIRKE, Mrs. Pritibala, BSc ACA *1989;* 12 Oakhill Road, ORPINGTON, BR6 0AE.
BIRKENHEAD, Mr. Paul, BSc ACA MSI *1999;* Corporate Horizons, 27 Beckman Road, STOURBRIDGE, WEST MIDLANDS, DY9 0TZ.
•BIRKETT, Mr. Aidan, FCA *1977;* 44 Oakhill Road, SEVENOAKS, KENT, TN13 1NS.
BIRKETT, Mr. Alexander James, BSc ACA *2010;* Deloitte & Touche, 2 New Street Square, LONDON, EC4A 3BZ.
BIRKETT, Miss. Allison, BA ACA *1997;* Lower Flat, 70 Gloucester Terrace, LONDON, W2 3HH.
BIRKETT, Mrs. Catherine, BA ACA *1999;* 2 St. Pauls Close, HARPENDEN, HERTFORDSHIRE, AL5 5UH.
BIRKETT, Mr. David Alston, FCA *1971;* Maylands, Chelveston Road, Raunds, WELLINGBOROUGH, NN9 6DA.
BIRKETT, Mrs. Jacqueline Elaine, BA ACA *1986;* 113 The Park, Sallins Road, NAAS, COUNTY KILDARE, IRELAND.
BIRKETT, Miss. Joanna Minturn, BA FCA *1989;* Elia Cottage, Wareside, WARE, HERTFORDSHIRE, SG12 7RB.
•BIRKETT, Mrs. Jodi Elizabeth, BSc(Hons) ACA *2000;* Deloitte LLP, PO Box 500, 2 Hardman Street, MANCHESTER, M60 2AT. See also Deloitte & Touche LLP
BIRKETT, Mr. Joseph William, BA FCA *1971;* The Gables, Chinthurst Lane, Shalford, GUILDFORD, SURREY, GU4 8JS.
BIRKETT, Miss. Julienne Louise, BSc ACA *2004;* 19 Brooklands Avenue, LONDON, SW19 8EP.
BIRKETT, Dr. Martin John, PhD BSc ACA *2001;* 63 Lancaster Avenue, GUILDFORD, GU1 3JR.
BIRKETT, Mr. Michael David, BA ACA *1997;* 2 St. Pauls Close, HARPENDEN, HERTFORDSHIRE, AL5 5UH.
BIRKETT, Mr. Michael John, FCA *1956;* Frensham House, Headley Road, LEATHERHEAD, SURREY, KT22 8PT. (Life Member)
BIRKETT, Mr. Nigel Carl, ACA CF *1999;* 40 Clearwater Drive, Didsbury Point, MANCHESTER, M20 2ED.
BIRKETT, Mr. Richard Henry Struan, MA ACA *1991;* 5 Abbey Cottages Ferry Lane Medmenham, MARLOW, BUCKINGHAMSHIRE, SL7 2HB.
BIRKETT, Mr. Simon James, MA FCA *1981;* (Tax Fac), with The Professional Training Partnership, Cherwell Innovation Centre, 77 Heyford Park, Camp Road, Upper Heyford, BICESTER OXFORDSHIRE OX25 5HD.
BIRKETT, Mr. Stuart Paul, BSc ACA *1998;* 99 Higher Lane, LYMM, CHESHIRE, WA13 0BZ.
BIRKETT, Mr. Timothy Lloyd, BA ACA *1988;* 17 Padstow Drive Bramhall, STOCKPORT, CHESHIRE, SK7 2HU.
•BIRKIN, Mr. David William Thomas, FCA *1979;* (Tax Fac), D W T Birkin & Co, Ivy House, Nantwich Road, Audley, STOKE-ON-TRENT, ST7 8DW. See also David W T Birkin Ltd, North Staffs Accountancy Services Ltd
BIRKIN, Mr. John Richard, FCA *1957;* 8 Doddington Road, LINCOLN, LN6 7EN. (Life Member)
BIRKIN, Mr. Michael John, LLB ACA *1984;* BKN Partners, 60 Greene Street, Apt 4, NEW YORK, NY 10012, UNITED STATES.
•BIRKINSHAW, Mr. Charles Stephen, MA FCA *1977;* Birkinshaw Raven Limited, 54a Lightfoot Lane, Fulwood, PRESTON, PR2 3LR.
BIRKINSHAW, Mrs. Evelyn Christina, BA BPhil ACA *1981;* 9 Beechwood Grove, WOTTON-UNDER-EDGE, GLOUCESTERSHIRE, GL12 7NH.
BIRKINSHAW, Mr. Richard Mark, MA ACA *2005;* 4 Knole Road, NOTTINGHAM, NG8 2DB.
BIRKLE, Mr. Christopher William, BA ACA *1992;* 104 Addison Gardens, LONDON, W14 0DS.
BIRKMIRE, Mr. John Charles, BSc FCA *1980;* Le Paradou, Forest, GUERNSEY, GY8 0AE.
BIRKS, Mr. Christopher, ACA *1980;* Control Techniques Ltd, Pool Road, NEWTOWN, POWYS, SY16 3BE.
BIRKS, Mr. Nigel Francis, BSc ACA *1987;* Meetingzone Ltd, Oxford House, Oxford Road, THAME, OXFORDSHIRE, OX9 2AH.
BIRKWOOD, Mr. Gregory James, BA(Hons) ACA *2001;* 12 The Pennings, Wendover, AYLESBURY, BUCKINGHAMSHIRE, HP22 6JE.
BIRKWOOD, Mr. Peter Alexander, BSc ACA *1996;* 2 Brackendale Grove, HARPENDEN, HERTFORDSHIRE, AL5 3EJ.
BIRKWOOD, Mrs. Rachael Claire, BA(Hons) ACA *2001;* 12 The Pennings, Wendover, AYLESBURY, BUCKINGHAMSHIRE, HP22 6JE.
BIRLEY, Mr. David Geoffrey, BA ACA *1997;* 24 Tulworth Road, Poynton, STOCKPORT, CHESHIRE, SK12 1BL.
BIRLEY, Mr. John Keith, MA FCA *1961;* Aspen Lodge Boreham Hill, Boreham Street, HAILSHAM, EAST SUSSEX, BN27 4SH. (Life Member)
BIRLEY, Miss. Lesley-Ann, BSc ACA *1996;* Sandown 11 Wolseley Place, MANCHESTER, M20 3LR.
BIRLEY, Mr. Terence, FCA *1974;* R. Swain & Sons Ltd, Medway Freight Centre, Priory Road, Strood, ROCHESTER, KENT ME2 2BD.
•BIRLEY, Mr. Thomas Spencer, ACA ATII *1997;* (Tax Fac), TS Birley, West Suite, Level 5, Mill Court, La Charroterie, St. Peter Port GUERNSEY GY1 1EJ.
BIRMINGHAM, Mr. Michael Ernest, FCA *1961;* Truckells Cottage East, Harding Shute, Ashey Brading, RYDE, ISLE OF WIGHT, PO33 4AP.
BIRMINGHAM, Mr. Stephen John, FCA *1982;* 29 Claybank Drive, Tottington, BURY, LANCASHIRE, BL8 4BU.
BIRN, Mr. Edward Mark, BA FCA *1976;* 29 Lyon, NEWPORT COAST, CA 92657-1101, UNITED STATES.
•①BIRNE, Mr. David Lawrence, BSc FCA *1993;* Fisher Partners, Acre House, 11-15 William Road, LONDON, NW1 3ER. See also H.W. Fisher & Company and H W Fisher & Company Limited
BIRNEY, Mr. James Charles David, ACA *2010;* Hindrigg, Wark, HEXHAM, NORTHUMBERLAND, NE48 3BN.
BIRNEY, Mr. John David, MA FCA *1970;* Kelmscott House, 26 Upper Mall, LONDON, W6 9TA.
BIRNEY, Mrs. Sarah, BSc ACA *2002;* 28 Columbine Road, Widmer End, HIGH WYCOMBE, BUCKINGHAMSHIRE, HP15 6BP.
BIRNIE, Mr. Andrew James, BSc ACA *1993;* Ashburnham, 69 Coombe Lane, BRISTOL, BS9 2AZ.
•BIRNS, Mr. David Martin, FCA *1967;* Cohen Arnold, New Burlington House, 1075 Finchley Road, Temple Fortune, LONDON, NW11 0PU. See also Cohen Arnold & Co
•BIRNS, Mr. Raymond, FCA *1958;* (Tax Fac), Raymond Birns, 20 Woodstock Avenue, LONDON, NW11 9SL.
BIRRELL, Mr. Christopher Ros Stewart, MA FCA *1981;* 25 Turret Grove, Clapham, LONDON, SW4 0ES.
BIRRELL, Sir James Drake, Kt FCA *1955;* 4 Marlin End, BERKHAMSTED, HP4 3GB. (Life Member)
BIRRELL, Mr. Norman Alistair, FCA *1949;* Willards Hill, ETCHINGHAM, TN19 7DB. (Life Member)
BIRRELL-GRAY, Mr. Jonathan Michael, BA ACA *1985;* 26 Winterbourne, HORSHAM, RH12 5JW.
BIRRI, Mr. Mark, BSc ACA *2009;* Catalyst Corporate Finance LLP, 5th Floor, 12-18 Grosvenor Gardens, LONDON, SW1W 0DH.
BIRRING, Mr. Kulvinder, BSc ACA *1996;* Watsons Personal Care Stores, 20th Floor central Plaza, 34 Jalan Sultan Ismail, 50250 KUALA LUMPUR, FEDERAL TERRITORY, MALAYSIA.
BIRT, Mr. Adam John, BSc FCA *1989;* with ICAEW, Metropolitan House, 321 Avebury Boulevard, MILTON KEYNES, MK9 2FZ.
BIRT, Mr. Giles Stewart, BA ACA *1990;* Lowe & Fletcher Ltd, Westwood Granary, Oldbury, BRIDGNORTH, SHROPSHIRE, WV16 5LP.
BIRT, Mrs. Julia Margaret, BA ACA *1988;* ASOS 2nd Floor Greater London House, Hampstead Road, LONDON, NW1 7FB.
BIRT, Mr. Leslie, FCA *1970;* 4 Dunnockswood, Alsager, STOKE-ON-TRENT, ST7 2XU.
BIRT, Mrs. Rebecca Louise, BA ACA *2004;* 45 Wellcroft Gardens, LYMM, CHESHIRE, WA13 0LU.
BIRT, Mr. Tim, BA(Hons) ACA *2002;* Sportfive Limited, 1st Floor, 50 Alderley Road, WILMSLOW, CHESHIRE, SK9 1NY.
BIRTCHNELL, Mr. Kevin John, BSc FCA *1993;* 425 1st Street, Apartment 3403, SAN FRANCISCO, CA 94105, UNITED STATES.
BIRTLE, Mr. Robert, ACA *2009;* 8 Silverwood Close, HARTLEPOOL, CLEVELAND, TS27 3QF.
•BIRTLES, Mr. Eric Roydon, BSc ACA *1984;* (Tax Fac), KTS Owens Thomas Limited, The Counting House, Dunleavy Drive, CARDIFF, CF11 0SN.
BIRTLES, Miss. Hayley Louise, BSc ACA *2005;* 4 Waltham Close, West Bridgford, NOTTINGHAM, NG2 6LE.
•BIRTLES, Mr. John Matthew Anthony, FCA *1988;* Stubbs Parkin South, The Manse, Dodington, WHITCHURCH, SHROPSHIRE, SY13 1DZ.
BIRTLES, Mr. Peter Alan, BSc ACA *1989;* 7 Coral Pea Close, WARNER, QLD 4500, AUSTRALIA.
BIRTLES, Mr. Ronald Andrew, FCA *1966;* 4 Ave de la Resistance, B-4053 EMBOURG, BELGIUM.
BIRTLES, Mr. Simon Fiddian, ACA *1986;* Defence Estates, Kingston Road, SUTTON COLDFIELD, WEST MIDLANDS, B75 7RL.

BIRTWISTLE, Mr. Andrew George, BSc ACA *1989;* Sunset House Arlington, Bibury, CIRENCESTER, GL7 5ND.
BIRTWISTLE, Mr. Christopher John, FCA *1974;* 29 Brookmans Avenue, Brookmans Park, HATFIELD, AL9 7QH.
BIRTWISTLE, Mr. Ian Andrew, BA ACA *1995;* United Business Media Plc Ludgate House, 245 Blackfriars Road, LONDON, SE1 9UY.
BIRTWISTLE, Mr. Mark Derek Astley, ACA *1984;* Ruskin Hay, 3 Ruskin Drive, Kirkby Lonsdale, CARNFORTH, LA6 2DB.
BIRTWISTLE, Mrs. Sharon Liesel, BA ACA CTA *1998;* Oaklea, 8 Oakway, Studham, DUNSTABLE, BEDFORDSHIRE, LU6 2PE.
•BISCHOFF, Mr. Andre Desmond, BA ACA *1990;* Broadlands, 9 Amersham Road, Chesham Bois, AMERSHAM, BUCKINGHAMSHIRE, HP6 5PD.
BISCOE, Mrs. Catherine Helen, MEng ACA *2006;* 51 Esher Road, EAST MOLESEY, SURREY, KT8 0AH.
BISHNOI, Mr. Rahul, ACA *1990;* 4 Netherhall Gardens, LONDON, NW3 5RR.
BISHOP, Mrs. Aimee Elise, BSc ACA *2002;* 80 St. James Road, SOUTHAMPTON, SO15 5HJ.
BISHOP, Mr. Alan, BSc ACA *2001;* 80 St. James Road, SOUTHAMPTON, SO15 5HJ.
BISHOP, Mr. Andrew Arthur, MEng ACA *2007;* 23 Eleanor Grove, LONDON, SW13 0JN.
•BISHOP, Mr. Andrew Geoffrey, FCA *1973;* Andrew G. Bishop, 24 Ebley Road, Ryeford, STONEHOUSE, GL10 2LQ.
•BISHOP, Mr. Andrew John, BSc FCA *1993;* AJB Accounting Services Ltd, 2 Ruskin Lodge, 20 Victor Drive, LEIGH-ON-SEA, SS9 1PP.
BISHOP, Miss. Anna Mary, ACA *2003;* c/o Anna Cullinane, PO Box 5170, GREENWICH, NSW 2065, AUSTRALIA.
BISHOP, Mr. Anthony David, FCA *1958;* 45 Harfield Road, SUNBURY-ON-THAMES, MIDDLESEX, TW16 5PT. (Life Member)
BISHOP, Miss. Carol Claire, BSc ACA *2000;* 9 The Meadows, SAWBRIDGEWORTH, CM21 9PY.
•BISHOP, Mrs. Catherine Antoinette, BA ACA *1991;* Bishop CLS Limited, 93 Beaumont Road, Petts Wood, ORPINGTON, KENT, BR5 1JH.
BISHOP, Miss. Charlotte, BSc ACA *2011;* 18 Harley Street, LEIGH-ON-SEA, ESSEX, SS9 2NJ.
BISHOP, Mr. Christopher David, FCA *1963;* Spratsbourne Farmhouse, Goudhurst Road, CRANBROOK, TN17 2PY.
BISHOP, Mr. Clive, BA FCA *1975;* 26 Stanley Road, Whalley Range, MANCHESTER, M16 8HS.
•BISHOP, Mr. David Charles, BA FCA *1989;* PricewaterhouseCoopers LLP, 1 Embankment Place, LONDON, WC2N 6RH. See also PricewaterhouseCoopers
•BISHOP, Mr. David George Windsor, BSc FCA *1976;* Walker Moyle, 3 Chapel Street, REDRUTH, TR15 2BY.
•BISHOP, Mr. David Glyn, BSc(Econ) FCA *1975;* Hilton Sharp & Clarke, 30 New Road, BRIGHTON, BN1 1BN.
BISHOP, Mr. David John, FCA *1968;* 51 Stoke Road, LEIGHTON BUZZARD, LU7 2SP. (Life Member)
BISHOP, Mr. Dennis John, FCA *1960;* 6 St James Gardens, Bulkington, Bedworth, NUNEATON, CV12 9NT. (Life Member)
BISHOP, Mr. Derick Robin, FCA *1970;* 2 Kelburn Road, ROSEVILLE, NSW 2069, AUSTRALIA.
BISHOP, Miss. Elizabeth Anne, BA FCA *1977;* 2 Westwood Road, COULSDON, CR5 1AH.
BISHOP, Mrs. Elizabeth Mary, BSc FCA *1990;* 1910 North Eyre Road, RD5, RANGIORA 7475, NEW ZEALAND.
•BISHOP, Mrs. Elizabeth Mary Ann, BSc FCA DChA *1983;* Chessman Limited, Wrenfield, The Chase, Oxshott, LEATHERHEAD, SURREY KT22 0HR.
BISHOP, Mr. Fabian, BCom ACA *2004;* Enstar Limited, Windsor Place 3rd Floor, 18 Queen Street, HAMILTON HM JX, BERMUDA.
BISHOP, Mr. Gavin Charles, BSc(Hons) ACA ARe AIS AIT OV CPCU ARM *2002;* Validus Reinsurance Limited, Suite # 1790, 48 Par-la-ville Road, HAMILTON HM11, BERMUDA.
BISHOP, Mr. Gerald, FCA *1961;* 30 Gore Court Road, SITTINGBOURNE, ME10 1QP. (Life Member)
•BISHOP, Mr. Gerald John, BSc FCA MSFA *1979;* G.J. Bishop, 16 Stewarts Close, ABBOTS LANGLEY, WD5 0LU.
BISHOP, Mr. Hugh William, MA FCA PIIA *1973;* 50 High Street, Sharnbrook, BEDFORD, BEDFORDSHIRE, MK44 1PF.
BISHOP, Mr. Ian Alan, BSc ACA *1992;* Hirzbodenpark 16, CH 4052 BASEL, SWITZERLAND.
BISHOP, Mr. James Ian, MC ACA *2002;* 28 Ellesmere Road, LONDON, E3 5QX.
BISHOP, Mr. Jason Gareth, ACA *1996;* Bay Lodge, Pembroke Road, WOKING, SURREY, GU22 7DS.
BISHOP, Mrs. Jennifer Louise, ACA *2010;* 35 Beechgate, WITNEY, OXFORDSHIRE, OX28 4JL.
BISHOP, Mr. Jeremy Marshall, FCA *1966;* Villa Magnol, Fosse Andre, St. Peter Port, GUERNSEY, GY1 1XB. (Life Member)
BISHOP, Mrs. Jill Mary, FCA *1973;* Villa Magnol, Fosse Andre, St. Peter Port, GUERNSEY, GY1 1XB. (Life Member)
BISHOP, Mr. John Andrew, BSc FCA *1991;* (Tax Fac), 8 Emsworth Road, HAVANT, HAMPSHIRE, PO9 2SS.
BISHOP, Mr. John Edwin, BSc ACA *1993;* 115 Hay Street, Steeple Morden, ROYSTON, HERTFORDSHIRE, SG8 0PD.
BISHOP, Mr. John Nathan, FCA *1982;* 1st Floor, Dorey Court, Admiral Park, St Peter Port, GUERNSEY, GY1 6HJ.
BISHOP, Mr. John Robert Anthony, FCA *1960;* 2 Whitehall Barns, Kings Walden, HITCHIN, HERTFORDSHIRE, SG4 8NQ. (Life Member)
BISHOP, Mr. John William, BSc FCA *1962;* Beeston, 91 Cassiobury Drive, WATFORD, WD17 3AG.
BISHOP, Mr. Jonathan Huw, MA FCA *1989;* Flat 1, 98 Maida Vale, LONDON, W9 1PS.
BISHOP, Mr. Julian Kenneth, MA FCA *1983;* Wrenfield, The Chase, Oxshott, LEATHERHEAD, KT22 0HR.
BISHOP, Mr. Julian Roger, BSc ACA *1992;* with KPMG, 10 Shelley Street, SYDNEY, NSW 2000, AUSTRALIA.
BISHOP, Mrs. Kathy Lee Carol, BA ACA *1993;* (Tax Fac), 8 Emsworth Road, HAVANT, HAMPSHIRE, PO9 2SS.
BISHOP, Mr. Kenneth Godfrey, FCA *1955;* (Member of Council 1974 - 1981), Quai Maria Belgia 6, CH 1800 VEVEY, SWITZERLAND. (Life Member)
•BISHOP, Mr. Kevin Mark, FCA *1983;* Bishops Accountancy Practice Limited, 2 Water End Barns, Water End, Eversholt, MILTON KEYNES, MK17 9EA.
BISHOP, Mr. Laurence, BSc ACA *1984;* E C Group Europa Park, London Road, GRAYS, RM20 4DN.
BISHOP, Mr. Mark Edward, ACA *2007;* with Grant Thornton UK LLP, 3140 Rowan Place, John Smith Drive, Oxford Business Park South, OXFORD, OX4 2WB.
BISHOP, Mr. Mark John Charles, ACA *2008;* 5 Thomas Street, YORK, YO10 3DH.
BISHOP, Mr. Martin Allan, ACA *1984;* St. Albans Diocesan Office, 41 Holywell Hill, ST. ALBANS, AL1 1HE.
BISHOP, Mr. Martyn Cuthbert, BSc FCA *1982;* Charles Kendall & Partners (Holdings) Ltd, 7 Albert Court, Prince Consort Road, LONDON, SW7 2BJ.
•BISHOP, Mr. Martyn John, FCA *1970;* Mint Cottage, Bolton By Bowland, CLITHEROE, BB7 4NN.
BISHOP, Mr. Matthew John, ACA *2008;* PricewaterhouseCoopers, Dorchester House, 7 Church Street, HAMILTON HM11, BERMUDA.
•BISHOP, Mr. Michael, FCA *1974;* Cole Bishop & Co Limited, Market Square Chambers, BROMYARD, HEREFORDSHIRE, HR7 4BP.
BISHOP, Mr. Michael Alan, BA ACA *1992;* 2 Forest View, BROCKENHURST, HAMPSHIRE, SO42 7YX.
•BISHOP, Mr. Michael David, FCA *1975;* BPU Limited, Radnor House, Greenwood Close, Cardiff Gate Business Park, CARDIFF, CF23 8AA.
•BISHOP, Mr. Michael David, BA ACA *1983;* Smith & Williamson Ltd, 25 Moorgate, LONDON, EC2R 6AY. See also Nexia Audit Limited
BISHOP, Mr. Michael Frederick, FCA *1973;* 19 Phillpotts Avenue, BEDFORD, MK40 3UF.
BISHOP, Mr. Michael Geoffrey, MEng ACA *1992;* 7 Albemarle Gardens, NEW MALDEN, KT3 5BB.
•BISHOP, Mr. Michael Ian, FCA *1971;* MBA Michael Bishop & Associates, Elderns, 19b Kings Weston Road, Henbury, BRISTOL, BS10 7QT.
BISHOP, Mr. Michael John Venables, BSc ACA *1986;* Oak Cottage, Park Lane, BROXBOURNE, EN10 7PQ.
BISHOP, Mr. Michael Richard, ACA *2008;* 27 Victoria Road, Formby, LIVERPOOL, L37 7AQ.
BISHOP, Mr. Michael Robert, BSc ACA *1997;* Webworks, Sovereign House, Vision Park, Chivers Way, Histon, CAMBRIDGE CB24 9BY.
•BISHOP, Miss. Michele Elaine, ACA ATT CTA FMAAT *2004;* Bishop Jones, 13a Broad Street, WELLS, SOMERSET, BA5 2DJ. See also Payroll Specialist Limited and Accountancy Training Partnership Limited
BISHOP, Mrs. Natalie Lisa, BSc(Hons) ACA *2003;* 4 Barley Drive, Burton Latimer, KETTERING, NORTHAMPTONSHIRE, NN15 5YU.
BISHOP, Mr. Nicholas David Charles, BA ACA *1999;* Fitch Design Consultants Ltd, 121-141 Westbourne Terrace, LONDON, W2 6JR.
BISHOP, Mr. Nicholas John, BSc(Hons) ACA *2003;* 169 South Park Road, LONDON, SW19 8RX.
BISHOP, Mr. Nicholas John, BA ACA *1994;* Fernbank, Lower North Street, CHEDDAR, BS27 3HA.
BISHOP, Mrs. Nicola Leonie, BSc ACA *1982;* Clovelly, Rue Robin, Vale, GUERNSEY, GY3 5ND.
BISHOP, Mrs. Nicola Margaret, BA ACA *1993;* 4 Derby Road, Heaton Moor, STOCKPORT, SK4 4NE.
BISHOP, Mr. Nigel Christopher Peter, FCA *1974;* 1 Chilcrofts Road, Kingsley Green, HASLEMERE, GU27 3LS.
•BISHOP, Mr. Paul, MA ACA *1980;* KPMG LLP, 15 Canada Square, LONDON, E14 5GL. See also KPMG Europe LLP
•BISHOP, Mr. Paul Anthony, BSc ACA *1997;* PA Bishop & Co Limited, Unit 316, Ettrick Riverside Business Centre, Dunsdale Road, SELKIRK, TD7 5EB. See also Paul A Bishop
BISHOP, Mr. Paul Peter, CEng ACA CPhys *2009;* 57 Lincoln Wood, HAYWARDS HEATH, WEST SUSSEX, RH16 1LH.
BISHOP, Mr. Philip Mark, BSc ACA *1994;* 52 Northborough Road, SLOUGH, SL2 1PS.
BISHOP, Mr. Reginald William, FCA *1958;* Parkside, Park Road, Stevington, BEDFORD, MK43 7QG. (Life Member)
•BISHOP, Mr. Ronald Earl, FCA *1961;* R E Bishop, Little Orchard, 97 Westbury Road, NORTHWOOD, HA6 3DA.
•BISHOP, Mrs. Sally Elizabeth Mary, ACA *1987;* Accountability FD Limited, The Warren, Wychbold Court, Worcester Road, Wychbold, DROITWICH WORCESTERSHIRE WR9 7PF. See also BDWM Limited
BISHOP, Mr. Scott Raymond, ACA MAAT *2009;* 40 Henry Warby Avenue, Elm, WISBECH, CAMBRIDGESHIRE, PE14 0BT.
•BISHOP, Mr. Simon Andrew, BSc FCA *1991;* (Tax Fac), David Howard, 1 Park Road, Hampton Wick, KINGSTON UPON THAMES, KT1 4AS.
BISHOP, Mr. Stephen James, BSc FCA CF *2001;* 38 Bowden Green, DROITWICH, WORCESTERSHIRE, WR9 8WZ.
BISHOP, Mr. Stephen Michael, ACA *1982;* DP World, 5th Floor, LOB 17 JAFZA, PO Box 17000, DUBAI, UNITED ARAB EMIRATES.
BISHOP, Mrs. Susan Diane, BSc ACA *1990;* 29 St Cuthberts Lane, Locks Heath, SOUTHAMPTON, SO31 6QR.
BISHOP, Mrs. Susan Keren, ACA *1982;* LAKESIDE HOUSE, Leicestershire Health Authority PO Box 2, Grove Park Enderby, LEICESTER, LE19 1SS.
BISHOP, Mrs. Suzanne, BA ACA *1994;* 30 Edward Road South, CLEVEDON, AVON, BS21 7JA.
BISHOP, Mr. Timothy, BSc ACA *1992;* Aviva UK Central Services, PO Box 6, NORWICH, NR1 3NS.
BISHOP, Mr. Timothy Stuart, BSc ACA *1986;* 21 Roseacre Gardens, Chilworth, GUILDFORD, GU4 8RQ.
BISHOP, Mr. Tobias Julian Felce, MA FCA CPA CFE *1985;* Deloitte FAS LLP, 111 S Wacker Dr, CHICAGO, IL 60606-4301, UNITED STATES.
BISHOP, Mrs. Victoria, BSc(Hons) ACA *2011;* 37 Green Lane, SEAFORD, EAST SUSSEX, BN25 1EG.
BISHOPP, Mrs. Corinna Jayne, BA ACA *1998;* 4 Queens Court, Queens Road, RICHMOND, TW10 6LA.
BISHOPP, Mr. Michael, MA FCA *1975;* The Old Forge, 45 North Road, Highgate, LONDON, N6 4BE. (Life Member)
BISHTON, Mrs. Lisa, BSc ACA *2001;* 18 Crabtrees, SAFFRON WALDEN, ESSEX, CB11 3BH.
BISHTON, Mr. Peter James, BSc ACA *2001;* 15 Elmbridge Drive, RUISLIP, MIDDLESEX, HA4 7XD.
BISHTON, Mrs. Reena Chunilal, BSc(Econ) ACA *2001;* oakview, 15 Elmbridge Drive, RUISLIP, MIDDLESEX, HA4 7XD.
BISHTON, Mr. Roger John, LLB FCA *1993;* 96 Argyle Road, Ealing, LONDON, W13 8EL.
BISHTON, Mr. Timothy Edward, BSc ACA *2001;* 18 Crabtrees, SAFFRON WALDEN, ESSEX, CB11 3BH.
BISMAL, Mr. Anuraj, BSc ACA *1991;* 165 Midland Avenue, UPPER MONTCLAIR, NJ 07042, UNITED STATES.
BISMAL, Mrs. Babita, BSc ACA *1993;* 15 Compton Road, LONDON, N21 3NU.
BISMAL, Mr. Vineet, BSc ACA *1999;* 32 Stassinos Str, 2003 NICOSIA, CYPRUS.
BISNATH, Mr. David Matthew Kiran, MA(Cantab) MSc FCA *2001;* 155 Falloden Way, LONDON, NW11 6LG.
BISPHAM, Mr. Stephen Donald, FCA *1977;* P.O. Box 443, GORDON, NSW 2072, AUSTRALIA.
•BISS, Mr. Alan Raymond, FCA *1974;* Llandaff Accountancy & Business Services, 5 Insole Close, CARDIFF, CF5 2HQ.
BISSEKER, Mr. Justin John, BA ACA *1997;* 35 Prospect Lane, West Common, HARPENDEN, HERTFORDSHIRE, AL5 2PL.
BISSEKER, Mr. Tilden John, MA FCA *1971;* (Tax Fac), Ede & Ravenscroft Ltd, 93 Chancery Lane, LONDON, WC2A 1DU.
BISSELL, Mrs. Alison Christine, BA ACA *1989;* 18 East Street, Turners Hill, CRAWLEY, WEST SUSSEX, RH10 4PU.
•BISSELL, Mrs. Ceri Sian, FCA *1991;* (Tax Fac), PBA Accountants, 130 High Street, HUNGERFORD, BERKSHIRE, RG17 0DL.
BISSELL, Mrs. Lorraine Mary, BSc ACA *1993;* 11 Woodavon Gardens, THATCHAM, BERKSHIRE, RG18 4DN.
BISSELL, Mrs. Louise Virginia Anne, BA ACA *1989;* 3 Cranford Road, Urmston, MANCHESTER, M41 8PS.
BISSET, Mr. Andrew Patrick, BA ACA *1995;* (Tax Fac), International Personal Finance Plc, 3 Leeds City Office Park, Meadow Lane, LEEDS, LS11 5BD.
•BISSET, Mrs. Claire, BA ACA *2000;* Claire Bisset, Beech Tree Cottage, The Street, Bacton, STOWMARKET, SUFFOLK IP14 4LF.
BISSET, Mr. James Gordon, BA ACA *1995;* Linklaters, 1 Silk Street, LONDON, EC2Y 8HQ.
BISSET, Mr. John, FCA *1970;* Ivor House, Bridge Street, CARDIFF, CF10 2EE.
BISSET, Mr. Niel Stewart George, MA ACA *1986;* 57 Lillishall Street, LONDON, SW4 0LW.
BISSET, Mr. Peter, BA ACA *2008;* 31 Regency Court, Jesmond Road, NEWCASTLE UPON TYNE, NE2 1JN.
BISSET, Mrs. Victoria, BSc ACA *2006;* 31 Regency Court, Jesmond Road, NEWCASTLE UPON TYNE, NE2 1JN.
BISSETT, Mrs. Anne Elizabeth, BSc ACA *1991;* Shawtop House, 3 Rookdean, Chipstead, SEVENOAKS, KENT, TN13 2RT.
BISSETT, Mr. Ashley Raymond, BSc ACA *1989;* Prospect House, Chaucer Business Park, Thanet Way, WHITSTABLE, CT5 3FD.
BISSETT, Mr. Keith, BSc ACA *2006;* 48 Leaver Gardens, Western Avenue, GREENFORD, MIDDLESEX, UB6 8ER.
BISSETT, Mrs. Kelly, BA(Hons) ACA *2001;* 31 Weymouth Bay Avenue, WEYMOUTH, DORSET, DT3 5AE.
BISSEX, Mr. Michael Douglas, FCA *1971;* 3 Ffordd Celyn, Sychdyn, MOLD, CLWYD, CH7 6SS.
•BISSEX, Mr. Raymond Arthur, FCA *1981;* Raymond Bissex, The Vicarage, 4 St. Andrews Road, BOOTLE, MERSEYSIDE, L20 5EX.
BISSICKS, Mr. Paul Kenneth, MA ACA *1979;* 26 Lime Avenue, Heworth, YORK, YO31 1BT.
BISSLAND, Mr. Donald Joseph, FCA *1949;* 20 Geffery's House, London Road, HOOK, RG27 9EF. (Life Member)
BISSMIRE, Miss. Catrin Helen, ACA *2009;* 17 Aspen Gardens, LONDON, W6 9JD.
BISSON, Mrs. Anneliese Caroline Laura, BA ACA *1999;* Southern Cross Venture Partners, Level 5, 80 Mount Street, North Sydney, PO Box 1743, SYDNEY NSW 2059 AUSTRALIA.
BISSON, Miss. Jane Emily, BSc ACA *2003;* Skipton Building Society, The Bailey, SKIPTON, NORTH YORKSHIRE, BD23 1DN.
•BISSON, Mrs. Julie Angela, ACA *1993;* with Ernst & Young LLP, PO Box 9, Royal Chambers, St Julian's Avenue, St Peter Port, GUERNSEY GY1 4AF.
BISSON, Mrs. Lousia Jane, BSc ACA *1999;* Oakley Cottage, 23 Sedgewell Road, Sonning Common, READING, RG4 9TA.
BISSON, Mr. Michael Paul, BA ACA *2005;* Mayfield La Rue de la Petite Falaise, Trinity, JERSEY, JE3 5AR.
BISSON, Mr. Paul John, FCA *1969;* 30 Coronet Court, NORTH ROCKS, NSW 2151, AUSTRALIA.
BISTER, Mr. Roger Alan, FCA *1964;* 39 Gloster Gardens Wellesbourne, WARWICK, CV35 9TQ. (Life Member)
BISWAS, Miss. Anusua, BSc ACA *2009;* 96 Dorset Road, LONDON, SW19 3HD.
BISWAS, Mr. Debashish, MA(Oxon) ACA DipCII ALCM *2009;* (Tax Fac), 144 Grove Lane, LONDON, SE5 8BP.
BISWAS, Mr. Neil, MA ACA *2001;* 41 Hopewell Street, PADDINGTON, NSW 2021, AUSTRALIA.
BISWAS, Mr. Shanu, MA FCA *1986;* 9915 Bald Cypress Drive, ROCKVILLE, MD 20850, UNITED STATES.

BISWAS, Mr. Subhashis, MEng ACA MSI *2001;* Mailstop: NYC60-2412, 24th Floor, 60 Wall Street, NEW YORK, NY 10005, UNITED STATES.
•**BITAR, Mr. Samir Nakhleh, FCA** *1982;* Mazars, Al Nassr Plaza, Offices 218 219 220, PO Box 6212, DUBAI, UNITED ARAB EMIRATES.
•**BITCON, Miss. Ann, BA ACA DChA** *1989;* Ad Hoc Accountancy Services, 12-14 Hall Square, DENBIGH, CLWYD, LL16 3NU. See also Ann Bitcon
BITHELL, Mr. Charles Peter, MA ACA *1995;* The Hawthorns, 78 The Common, Parbold, WIGAN, LANCASHIRE, WN8 7EA.
BITHELL, Mr. David, MA FCA *1982;* 89 North Road, RICHMOND, TW9 4HQ.
BITHELL, Mrs. Lesley Jill, MA ACA *1994;* The Hawthorns, 78 The Common, Parbold, WIGAN, LANCASHIRE, WN8 7EA.
BITHELL, Mr. Michael John, MA CEng FCA *1996;* 59 Aylesford Street, LONDON, SW1V 3RY.
•**BITHRAY, Mr. Andrew, BSc ACA CTA** *2004;* with WSM Partners LLP, Pinnacle House, 17/25 Hartfield Road, Wimbledon, LONDON, SW19 3SE.
•**BITHREY, Mr. Paul M, ACA ACCA** *2009,* FKCA Limited, Prospero House, 46-48 Rothesay Road, LUTON, LU1 1QZ. See also Foxley Kingham Medical LLP
BITMEAD, Mr. Martin Paul, BA ACA *1997;* 18 Highgrove Avenue, ASCOT, SL5 7HR.
BITSI, Miss. Athina, MSc ACA *2010;* 69 N. Kazantzaki Street, Zografou, ATHENS, GREECE.
BITTER, Mr. Peter Carl, FCA *1974;* Lascelles deMercado & Co. Ltd., 23 Dominica Drive, KINGSTON 5, JAMAICA.
BITTINER, Mr. Alan Howard, BSc FCA *1968;* 29 Chemin des Rannaux, Coppet, 1296 VAUD, SWITZERLAND. (Life Member)
BITTINER, Mr. Richard John Garside, BA FCA TEP *1968;* Maitland Switzerland S.A, 12 Rue de L'arquebuse, 1211 GENEVA, SWITZERLAND.
BITTLESTONE, Mr. Anthony John, MBA FCA *1969;* 2 Milton Drive, Ravenshead, NOTTINGHAM, NG15 9BB.
BITTNER, Mrs. Sarah Louise, BEng ACA *2002;* 33 Commerce Street, Melbourne, DERBY, DE73 8FT.
BITYUTSKAYA, Miss. Yulia, ACA *2010;* Spyrou Kyprianou Avenue Elenion Building 85 office 204, 6051 LARNACA, CYPRUS.
BIYANI, Mr. Rohit, BSc ACA *2010;* 11 Harrow Fields Gardens, HARROW, MIDDLESEX, HA1 3SN.
BJELK, Mr. Kevin, BA ACA *1996;* Concrete Developments Ltd Unit 12, Barnsley Business & Innovation Centre Innovation Way, BARNSLEY, SOUTH YORKSHIRE, S75 1JL.
BJORKHOLT-BOILING, Mr. Ben Graham, ACA *2007;* Halvorsplass, 4824 BJORBEKK, NORWAY.
BLABER, Mrs. Barbara Louise, BA FCA *1978;* 16 Christchurch Road, SALE, CHESHIRE, M33 5JL.
BLABER, Mr. Nicholas John, BA ACA *1997;* 4 Boderton Mews, Burton Park, Duncton, PETWORTH, WEST SUSSEX, GU28 0LS.
BLABER, Mr. Roger Bryant, FCA *1975;* Abbey Life Assurance Co.Ltd., 80 Holdenhurst Road, BOURNEMOUTH, BH8 8ZQ.
BLABY, Mr. Timothy Benwell, BSc FCA *1996;* 3 South Close, Tranmere Park, Guiseley, LEEDS, LS20 8JD.
BLACAS, Mr. Robert William, ACA *1992;* Badgers Croft Intack Lane, High Legh, KNUTSFORD, CHESHIRE, WA16 0SE.
BLACK, Mr. Alan Robert, ACA *1981;* 22 history row, THE WOODLANDS, TX 77380, UNITED STATES.
BLACK, Mr. Alex, BA ACA *2003;* with National Audit Office, 157-197 Buckingham Palace Road, Victoria, LONDON, SW1W 9SP.
BLACK, Mr. Alexander William Francis, BSc ACA *1992;* 422 Ocean Drive West, STAMFORD, CT 06902, UNITED STATES.
BLACK, Mr. Alistair, BSc ACA *2006;* 2 Hind Place, CHIPPING NORTON, NSW 2170, AUSTRALIA.
BLACK, Mr. Andrew Nicholas, BA ACA *1995;* Sunset Crest, 180 South Road, PAGET DV04, BERMUDA.
BLACK, Mr. Andrew Peter, BSc ACA *1992;* Higher Trethem, Trethem, St. Just In Roseland, TRURO, TR2 5JF.
BLACK, Mr. Andrew Ross, BSc ACA *1984;* 18 Canonbury, SHREWSBURY, SY3 7AH.
BLACK, Mr. Christopher Charles, BSc ACA *2005;* Stirling Square Capital Partners Ltd Liscartan House, 127 Sloane Street, LONDON, SW1X 9AS.
BLACK, Mr. Christopher Latham, BSc FCA DChA *1994;* Ryecroft Glenton, 32 Portland Terrace, Jesmond, NEWCASTLE UPON TYNE, NE2 1QS.
BLACK, Mrs. Cindy Elaine, BSc(Econ) ACA *1996;* 33 Annes Walk, CATERHAM, CR3 5EL.
BLACK, Mr. Colin, BSc FCA *1979;* Sykes House, Queen Street, Halford, SHIPSTON-ON-STOUR, WARWICKSHIRE, CV36 5BT.
BLACK, Dr. Daniel, BSc ACA *2000;* 70 Shaw Road, STOCKPORT, CHESHIRE, SK4 4AN.
BLACK, Mr. David, BA FCA *1995;* PO Box 487, BEROWRA, NSW 2081, AUSTRALIA.
•**BLACK, Mr. David Iain, BSc ACA** *1995;* Monahans, 38-42 Newport Street, SWINDON, SN1 3DR.
BLACK, Mr. David Ian, FCA *1968;* Foxlease, Broadwell, MORETON-IN-MARSH, GLOUCESTERSHIRE, GL56 0TJ.
•**BLACK, Mr. David Peter, FCA** *1979;* (Tax Fac), Jack Ross, Barnfield House, The Approach, MANCHESTER, M3 7BX.
•**BLACK, Mr. Derek G, BSc FCA** *1978;* Black & Co, Gorse Cottage, Harborough Hill, West Chiltington, PULBOROUGH, RH20 2PW.
BLACK, Mr. Douglas Buller, BSc ACA *1982;* 54a Oaklands Grove, LONDON, W12 0JB.
BLACK, Mrs. Ella Maxine, BSc(Econ) FCA *1977;* 7 Althorp Road, ST. ALBANS, AL1 3PH.
BLACK, Mrs. Emma, BA ACA *2010;* 131 Thirlmere Avenue, Tilehurst, READING, RG30 6XG.
BLACK, Mr. Eon Hamilton, FCA *1959;* 154 Main Road North, PARAPARAUMU 5036, NEW ZEALAND. (Life Member)
BLACK, Mr. Francis Rokeby, FCA *1959;* The Old Vicarage, Wing, LEIGHTON BUZZARD, LU7 0NU. (Life Member)
BLACK, Mr. Geoffrey Howard, FCA *1971;* 4 Shelton Park, SHREWSBURY, SY3 8BL.
BLACK, Mr. Geoffrey Ian, FCA *1963;* 4 Beech Park Drive, Barnt Green, BIRMINGHAM, B45 8LZ.
•**BLACK, Mr. Gilmour Buchan, BSc FCA** *1975;* Gil Black Ltd, 28 Chaise Meadow, LYMM, CHESHIRE, WA13 9UP.
BLACK, Mr. Graeme Michael, BSc ACA *1998;* Pavillion Capital Management LLP c.o/G M Black, Flat 202 Pavilion Apartments, 34 St. Johns Wood Road, LONDON, NW8 7HB.
BLACK, Mr. Hugo Marcus Vernon, MSc BSc(Hons) ACA MSI ASI MRICS *2006;* Flanchford Farm House, Flanchford Road, REIGATE, RH2 8RB.
•**BLACK, Mr. Ian Alexander, ACA** *1992;* Sterling 2000 Ltd, Sterling House, 810 Mandarin Court, Centre Park, WARRINGTON, WA1 1GG. See also AGP
BLACK, Mr. Ian Spencer, MBA BSc FCIB FCA *1984;* 402 Birkby Road, HUDDERSFIELD, HD2 2DN.
BLACK, Mr. Ian Stuart, BSc ACA *1997;* 47 Woodhead Drive, CAMBRIDGE, CB4 1YY.
BLACK, Mr. James David, BSc FCA *1977;* 11 Winchester Road, FRINTON-ON-SEA, ESSEX, CO13 9JB. (Life Member)
•**BLACK, Mr. Jeremy Maurice, MA ACA** *1997;* with Deloitte LLP, 2 New Street Square, LONDON, EC4A 3BZ.
BLACK, Mrs. Joanne Elizabeth, BSc ACA CTA *1997;* 47 Woodhead Drive, CAMBRIDGE, CB4 1YY.
BLACK, Mr. John Robert Couper, FCA *1953;* Lower Woodhouse, Milebrook, KNIGHTON, LD7 1LR. (Life Member)
BLACK, Mr. Julian Robin, BA ACA *1995;* Canon Europe Ltd, 3 The Square, Stockley Park, UXBRIDGE, MIDDLESEX, UB11 1ET.
BLACK, Mrs. Kate Mary, BSc ACA *2007;* 9 Firtree Close, SANDHURST, GU47 8HU.
BLACK, Miss. Katherine Margaret, BA ACA *1997;* 11 Woodridings, The Firs, Bowdon, ALTRINCHAM, CHESHIRE, WA14 2TF.
BLACK, Miss. Kathryn Faye, BA ACA *2005;* 110 Lakeside Road, Governors Hill, Douglas, ISLE OF MAN, IM2 7DF.
BLACK, Miss. Lyndsey Anne, BA(Hons) ACA *2010;* 33 Rushmore Grange, WASHINGTON, TYNE AND WEAR, NE38 7LF.
BLACK, Mr. Marcus William, BA ACA *1995;* 3 Scarah Bank Cottages, Ripley, HARROGATE, HG3 3EE.
BLACK, Mr. Martin Ian, BSc ACA *1989;* 51A Highbury Hill, LONDON, N5 1SU.
•**BLACK, Mr. Michael Anthony, FCA** *1967;* (Tax Fac), Mike Black, 9 Crockwell Close, BICESTER, OXFORDSHIRE, OX26 2HG.
BLACK, Miss. Moira Elizabeth, CBE MA FCA *1976;* 60 Beaufort Road, LONDON, W5 3EA.
BLACK, Mr. Nicholas Branfoot, ACA CA(SA) *2010;* 47 Kingham Close, LONDON, SW18 3BX.
BLACK, Mr. Oliver Vernon, FCA *1948;* 28 Vicarage Street, Woburn Sands, MILTON KEYNES, MK17 8RE. (Life Member)
BLACK, Mr. Peter Malcolm, BSc FCA *1990;* 93 Langthorne Street, LONDON, SW6 6JU.
BLACK, Mrs. Philippa Mary, BA ACA *1999;* 30 Cranley Gardens, LONDON, N10 3AP.
BLACK, Mr. Richard Henry, ACA *1981;* P.O. Box HM 2592, HAMILTON HM KX, BERMUDA.
BLACK, Mr. Richard John Peploe, FCA *1968;* Brook Royde, Park Street, FAIRFORD, GLOUCESTERSHIRE, GL7 4JL.
BLACK, Mr. Robin Kennedy, BA ACA *1983;* Nevergood Farmhouse, Brick Kiln Lane, HORSMONDEN, TN12 8ES.
•**BLACK, Mr. Ronald, BSc ACA** *1980;* R. Black & Co, 11 Vernon Road, SALFORD, M7 4NW.
•**BLACK, Mr. Russell, BSc FCA** *1983;* Glazers, 843 Finchley Road, LONDON, NW11 8NA. See also Glazers Ltd
BLACK, Mr. Simon Douglas, ACA *2008;* Heldrew House First Floor extn 51611, Tesco Stores Ltd Tesco House, Delamare Road Cheshunt, WALTHAM CROSS, HERTFORDSHIRE, EN8 9SL.
BLACK, Mr. Stuart David, MA ACA *1989;* Absolute Zero, Gweneth Cottages, Mead Road, EDGWARE, HA8 6LJ.
BLACK, Mr. Stuart John, BA ACA *2000;* 52 Kedleston Road, LEEDS, LS8 2BJ.
BLACK, Mrs. Sue J, BA ACA *1983;* Mizrahi Tefahot Limited, 30 Old Broad Street, LONDON, EC2N 1HQ.
BLACK, Miss. Susan Elizabeth, LLB ACA *2007;* Greyleys Old Lane, St. Johns, CROWBOROUGH, EAST SUSSEX, TN6 1RX.
BLACK, Mr. Terence Ignatius, FCA *1972;* 53 Greenacres, Fulwood, PRESTON, PR2 7DB.
BLACK, Mr. William Daniel, ACA *2010;* with KPMG LLP, 1 Forest Gate, Brighton Road, CRAWLEY, WEST SUSSEX, RH11 9PT.
BLACK, Mr. William Findlay, FCA *1973;* Les Melezes 114, Ch de Medieres 50, 1936 VERBIER, SWITZERLAND.
BLACKAH, Mr. James Herbert, FCA *1961;* 6 Castle Meadows, Snape, BEDALE, NORTH YORKSHIRE, DL8 2TT.
BLACKBOURN, Mrs. Sarah Janine, BA ACA *1993;* 21 Sorrel Close, Wootton, NORTHAMPTON, NN4 6EY.
BLACKBROW, Miss. Louise Joan, BA ACA *1992;* 191 Priests Lane, Shenfield, BRENTWOOD, ESSEX, CM15 8LF.
BLACKBURN, Mr. Alastair Richard Michael, BA ACA *1982;* 3 Red House Lane, WALTON-ON-THAMES, SURREY, KT12 1EF.
BLACKBURN, Mr. Alfred, FCA *1969;* 18 Castlegate, RICHMOND, TW9 2HJ.
BLACKBURN, Mr. Alistair James, MA ACA MBA *1997;* 192 Wedgewood Drive, OAKVILLE L6J 4R7, ON, CANADA.
BLACKBURN, Mr. Angus, ACA *2007;* 40 High Street, Wingham, CANTERBURY, CT3 1AB.
•**BLACKBURN, Mr. Barrie, BCom FCA** *1973;* (Tax Fac), Yew Trees, Wantage Road, Streatley, READING, RG8 9LD.
BLACKBURN, Mr. Charles Andrew, BA ACA *1980;* Gelpke & Bate Ltd Camomile House, Kings Cross Lane South Nutfield, REDHILL, RH1 5NG.
•**BLACKBURN, Mr. Colin Andrew, FCA** *1974;* (Tax Fac), Blackburn & Blackburn Ltd, Glenroyd, Keighley Road, COLNE, LANCASHIRE, BB8 7HF.
BLACKBURN, Mr. David Glanville, BSc ACA *1988;* 21 Parsonage Road, HORSHAM, WEST SUSSEX, RH12 4AW.
BLACKBURN, Mrs. Deborah Jayne, BA ACA *1990;* 20 Kings Close, Bramhall, STOCKPORT, CHESHIRE, SK7 3BN.
•**BLACKBURN, Mr. Gary Edgar, FCA FICM FIPA FABRP** *1980;* BWC Business Solutions Limited, 8 Park Place, LEEDS, LS1 2RU.
BLACKBURN, Mr. Geoffrey Reginald, FCA *1962;* 3 Boldrewood, School Lane, Burghfield Common, READING, RG7 3LR. (Life Member)
BLACKBURN, Mr. Graeme, BA(Hons) ACA *2000;* 2 Wheatfields, Seaton Delaval, WHITLEY BAY, NE25 0PZ.
BLACKBURN, Mr. Harold William, PhD MA ACA ACCA *2002;* with Youngman & Co, 163 Mill Road, CAMBRIDGE, CB1 3AN.
BLACKBURN, Mr. Ian Marcel, FCA *1981;* Zetar Plc Highgate Studios, 53-79 Highgate Road, LONDON, NW5 1TL.
BLACKBURN, Mr. Kieron Francis, BSc ACA *1994;* 5 Beresford Gardens, BATH, BA1 4NX.
BLACKBURN, Miss. Laura Helen, BA ACA *2003;* 24 Herons Place, MARLOW, BUCKINGHAMSHIRE, SL7 3HP.
BLACKBURN, Mr. Ludovic Neil Charles, BSc ACA *2003;* Laverstock House, Laverstock, BRIDPORT, DORSET, DT6 5PE.
BLACKBURN, Mr. Martin Lawrence, BA ACA *1994;* 2b Pelham Road, LONDON, SW19 1SX.
BLACKBURN, Mr. Michael, MA MSci ACA *2011;* 4 Livingstone Mews, Stanley Street South, BRISTOL, BS3 3PU.
BLACKBURN, Mr. Michael David Neil, BSc ACA *1990;* 49 Park Hill, CARSHALTON, SM5 3SD.
BLACKBURN, Mr. Michael Francis, BSc FCA *1984;* Frensham House, London Road, ASCOT, BERKSHIRE, SL5 7EH.
BLACKBURN, Mr. Michael John, FCA *1953;* White Gates, 7 Princes Drive, Oxshott, LEATHERHEAD, KT22 0UL. (Life Member)
BLACKBURN, Mr. Paul Adrian, BSc ACA *1996;* (Tax Fac), 2 Brushwood Road, HORSHAM, RH12 4PE.
BLACKBURN, Mr. Peter, BA ACA *1990;* 20 Charlton Close, WOKINGHAM, RG40 4YQ.
BLACKBURN, Mr. Peter, FCA *1975;* 10 Kistvaen Gardens, Meltham, HOLMFIRTH, HD9 5NQ.
BLACKBURN, Mr. Peter Duncan, FCA *1954;* Cobblers, Culross Avenue, HAYWARDS HEATH, RH16 1JF. (Life Member)
BLACKBURN, Mr. Peter Hugh, BA FCA *1966;* Watersmeet, 12 Promenade Square, HARROGATE, HG1 2PH.
BLACKBURN, Mr. Richard Francis, BA(Hons) ACA *2011;* 34 Oulton Avenue, SALE, CHESHIRE, M33 2WA.
BLACKBURN, Mr. Richard John, MA FCA *1965;* Maypoles, Cole Hill, Soberton, SOUTHAMPTON, SO32 3PJ. (Life Member)
BLACKBURN, Mr. Robert Allan, BSc FCA *1968;* 39 Pasturegate, BURNLEY, BB11 4DE.
•**BLACKBURN, Mr. Robin Bell, FCA** *1975;* Robin Blackburn, Field House, 29 Adlington Road, WILMSLOW, SK9 2BJ.
BLACKBURN, Mr. Robin Kay, BA ACA *1980;* Badgers, Village Road, Dorney, WINDSOR, BERKSHIRE, SL4 6QJ.
BLACKBURN, Mr. Roderick John Philip, BCom FCA *1972;* 3 Chanonry Crescent, FORTROSE, IV10 8RH.
BLACKBURN, Mr. Roger Arthur, BSc FCA *1978;* Abbey Hill, Nags Head, Naul Co, DUBLIN, COUNTY DUBLIN, IRELAND.
BLACKBURN, Mrs. Sally-Anne, BA ACA *1991;* 30 Laundry Lane, Thorpe St. Andrew, NORWICH, NR7 0XF.
BLACKBURN, Dr. Sarah Kaye, DBA MA FCA FIIA *1989;* Rombourne, 130 Aztec West Almondsbury, BRISTOL, BS32 4UB.
•**BLACKBURN, Mr. Stuart Peter, FCA** *1970;* 4 V. Dimech Street, FLORIANA FRN 1504, MALTA.
•**BLACKBURN, Mr. Vernon Frederick Neil, FCA** *1969;* (Tax Fac), Pelican Consultancy Ltd, 6 Cockhaise Cottages, Monteswood Lane, Lindfield, HAYWARDS HEATH, WEST SUSSEX RH16 2QP.
BLACKBURN, Mr. William, FCA *1964;* 43 Gleneagles Drive, Penwortham, PRESTON, PR1 0JT. (Life Member)
BLACKEBY, Mrs. Claire, BSc(Hons) ACA *2002;* 32 Protheroe Field, Old Farm Park, MILTON KEYNES, MK7 8QS.
BLACKER, Mrs. Alison June, BA FCA *1975;* 13 Greatchesters, Bancroft, MILTON KEYNES, MK13 0PA.
BLACKER, Mr. John Steven, BSc ACA CTA *2004;* 8 Gledhow Wood Grove, LEEDS, LS8 1NZ.
BLACKER, Mr. Keith, DBA MBA BSc FCA FIIA *1977;* 5 Rewlands Drive, WINCHESTER, SO22 6PA.
BLACKER, Miss. Nicola, BSc ACA *2006;* 131 Hanson Street, Newtown, WELLINGTON 6021, NEW ZEALAND.
BLACKET, Mr. David Ronald, FCA *1972;* 27 Rose Walk, ST. ALBANS, AL4 9AA.
BLACKETT, Mr. Andrew Christopher, ACA *2008;* 5 Esperley Lane, Cockfield, BISHOP AUCKLAND, COUNTY DURHAM, DL13 5AN.
BLACKETT, Mr. Anthony David, BA FCA *1967;* 27 Willow Meadow Road, ASHBOURNE, DERBYSHIRE, DE6 1HT. (Life Member)
BLACKETT, Mrs. Claire Angela, BA ACA *1998;* Northern Rock plc, Northern Rock House, Gosforth, NEWCASTLE UPON TYNE, NE3 4PL.
BLACKETT, Mr. Mark Alexander, BA ACA *1993;* c/o Oxfam Great Britain, PO Box 2333, Megenaga-Bole Ring Road, Near Imperial Hotel, ADDIS ABABA, ETHIOPIA.
BLACKETT, Miss. Samantha, BSc(Hons) ACA *2011;* 30 Victoria Avenue, Douglas, ISLE OF MAN, IM2 4AN.
BLACKETT, Mr. Stuart, BSc ACA *2001;* 41 Wellington Drive, Wynyard, BILLINGHAM, CLEVELAND, TS22 5QJ.
•**BLACKFORD, Ms. Caroline Jane, MA ACA** *1993;* (Tax Fac), Hillside Cottage, Rhodyate, Blagdon, BRISTOL, BS40 7TP.
BLACKFORD, Mr. Mark, BSc ACA *1993;* Medecins Sans Frontieres Hollande, Avenue Des Martyrs, BANGUI, BP 1793, CENTRAL AFRICAN REPUBLIC.
BLACKFORD, Mr. Robert Martin Lindsey, BSc FCA *1989;* 71 The Toose, YEOVIL, BA21 3SN.
BLACKHALL, Mr. Anthony Marcus, FCA *1952;* 30 Ash Way, Woodford Halse, DAVENTRY, NORTHAMPTONSHIRE, NN11 3SS. (Life Member)

BLACKHAM, Ms. Holly Emma, BA ACA *2003;* 82 Westbourne Road, LONDON, N7 8AB.
BLACKHAM, Mr. Nigel Malin, BSc FCA *1977;* The Laurels, Mill Road, Thurleigh, BEDFORD, MK44 2DL.
BLACKHURST HILL, Mrs. Mary Olive, BA ACA *1991;* The Long Barns, 15 Snowy Way, Hartford, HUNTINGDON, PE29 1LQ.
BLACKIE, Mr. Craig Mac Pherson, BA(Hons) ACA *2003;* 54 Well Lane, Heswall, WIRRAL, MERSEYSIDE, CH60 8NG. (Life Member)
•BLACKIE, Mr. Jon George, BA ACA *1998;* Ernst & Young Europe LLP, 1 More London Place, LONDON, SE1 2AF. See also Ernst & Young LLP
BLACKIE, Mrs. Louise Maria, BA(Hons) ACA *2003;* 54 Well Lane, Heswall, WIRRAL, MERSEYSIDE, CH60 8NG.
BLACKIE, Mr. Peter Antony, BSc FCA *1968;* (Member of Council 2002 - 2008), 7 Rue Vervloesem, 1200 BRUSSELS, BELGIUM.
•BLACKLER, Mr. Antony Lawrence, MBE FCA *1970;* Blackler & Co, The Barn Office, Tredivett Mill, Little Comfort, LAUNCESTON, PL15 9NA.
BLACKLER, Mr. Fernley Percy George, ACA *1994;* 20 Bunbury Way, EPSOM, SURREY, KT17 4JP.
BLACKLEY, Mrs. Joanna Victoria, ACA *1994;* 1 Rose Cottages, Summers Lane, TOTLAND BAY, PO39 0HL.
BLACKLIDGE, Mr. David, FCA FCMA *1965;* 11 Barrington Avenue, NORTH SHIELDS, TYNE AND WEAR, NE30 3HG.
BLACKMAN, Mr. Benjamin, BSc ACA *2002;* 261 Boldmere Road, SUTTON COLDFIELD, B73 5LL.
BLACKMAN, Mrs. Helen Felicity, BSc ACA *2004;* 53 Rashwood Close, Hockley Heath, SOLIHULL, B94 6SD.
•BLACKMAN, Mr. Ian Charles, BA FCA *1985;* Chantrey Vellacott DFK LLP, Russell Square House, 10-12 Russell Square, LONDON, WC1B 5LF. See also CV Capital LLP
BLACKMAN, Dr. James Michael, ACA *2009;* Pricewaterhousecoopers Savannah House, 3 Ocean Way, SOUTHAMPTON, SO14 3TJ.
BLACKMAN, Mr. Jason Lee Peter, BA(Hons) ACA *2003;* 18 Stour Green, ELY, CAMBRIDGESHIRE, CB6 2WR.
BLACKMAN, Mrs. Joanne Irene, BSc ACA *1991;* Accord Management Services, 170 Tonbridge Road Wateringbury, MAIDSTONE, ME18 5NS.
BLACKMAN, Mr. Philip John, MA ACA *1990;* Oakwood Lodge, Oakwood Close, CHISLEHURST, KENT, BR7 5DD.
BLACKMAN, Mr. Stephen David, BSc ACA *1984;* 22 Gladsmuir Road, LONDON, N19 3JX.
BLACKMAN, Mr. Steven Robert, BA FCA *1976;* Chatwood, Llansannor, COWBRIDGE, CF71 7RX.
BLACKMAN, Miss. Trudy Janelle, ACA *2008;* Barclays Bank Plc, Level 10, 1 Churchill Place, LONDON, E14 5HP.
BLACKMORE, Mrs. Alison Judith, BSc ACA *1985;* New Greenham Park Ltd, Liberty House, New Greenham Park, NEWBURY, BERKSHIRE, RG19 6HW.
•BLACKMORE, Mr. Andrew David, BSc FCA *1992;* The Lowe, Fen Road, Pakenham, BURY ST. EDMUNDS, SUFFOLK, IP31 2JS.
BLACKMORE, Mr. Andrew Robert, BSc ACA *2003;* with Ernst & Young LLP, 1 More London Place, LONDON, SE1 2AF.
BLACKMORE, Miss. Aneen, BA ACA *2007;* 63 Jenner Road, LONDON, N16 7RB.
BLACKMORE, Mr. Cory Mark Bradford, BA(Hons) ACA CTA *2003;* Glenfield Borough Green Road, Ightham, SEVENOAKS, TN15 9HS.
BLACKMORE, Miss. Deborah Clare, BSc ACA *1994;* 10 Plymouth Road, TOTNES, TQ9 5PH.
BLACKMORE, Mr. Francis Andrew, BSc ACA *2006;* 100 Old Road, NEATH, WEST GLAMORGAN, SA11 2BU.
BLACKMORE, Mr. Gary Fenton, BSc(Econ) ACA *2002;* (Tax Fac), 6 Hurst Hill, POOLE, DORSET, BH14 8LF.
•BLACKMORE, Mr. Mark Rupert, FCA *1966;* (Tax Fac), Blackmore & Company, Pier Cottage, Pier Road, Portishead, BRISTOL, BS20 7HG.
BLACKMORE, Mr. Peter Stewart, FCA *1966;* 15 Peachley Gardens, Lower Broadheath, WORCESTER, WR2 6QS. (Life Member)
BLACKMORE, Mr. Philip, ACA *2011;* Flat 3, 72 Rowfant Road, Balham, LONDON, SW17 7AS.
BLACKMORE, Mr. Steven Mark, BA FCA *1987;* (Tax Fac), Elver Consultancy, 1 Smallshaw Close, Ashton-in-Makerfield, WIGAN, WN4 9LW.
BLACKMORE, Mr. Warner Keith James, FCA *1974;* 36 Rathdown Drive, Terenure, DUBLIN, COUNTY DUBLIN, IRELAND.
BLACKMUN, Mr. Stephen, BA ACA *1981;* 15011 Turkey Trail Court, HOUSTON, TX 77079, UNITED STATES.
BLACKSHAW, Mrs. Catherine, BA ACA *1990;* Caw House, Tutin Road, Leeming Bar Industrial Estate, NORTHALLERTON, NORTH YORKSHIRE, DL7 9UJ.
BLACKSHAW, Mr. David, BA ACA *1991;* C/ Guinardó 4, 08530 LA GARRIGA, SPAIN.
BLACKSHAW, Mr. Julian James, BSc ACA *2003;* 31 Wakehurst Road, LONDON, SW11 6DB.
BLACKSHAW, Mr. Keith Fielden, FCA *1955;* Mayville, 2 Vicarage Lane, Wilpshire, BLACKBURN, BB1 9HX. (Life Member)
BLACKSHAW, Mr. Robert Michael, FCA *1969;* N.T Blackshaw Holdings Ltd, Cedar Wood, Burton Road, Repton, DERBY, DE65 6FN.
BLACKSHAW, Mr. Steven, BA ACA *1987;* First Response Finance Ltd, 5 Regan Way, Chilwell, Beeston, NOTTINGHAM, NG9 6RZ.
BLACKSHAW, Mr. Terry, FCA *1968;* 7 New Tame, Denshaw Road, Delph, OLDHAM, OL3 5TS. (Life Member)
BLACKSTAFF, Mr. Michael, FCA *1963;* The Malt House, 34 Main Road, Colden Common, WINCHESTER, HAMPSHIRE, SO21 1RR.
BLACKSTAFFE, Mr. Peter John, FCA *1971;* 72 Brim Hill, Hampstead Garden Suburb, LONDON, N2 0HQ.
•BLACKSTOCK, Mr. Anthony Brian, MA FCA *1975;* Anthony Blackstock Limited, 37 High Street, Eydon, DAVENTRY, NN11 3PP.
•BLACKSTONE, Mr. Andrew Simon, BSc FCA *1994;* (Tax Fac), Andy Blackstone, 106 Chatsworth Road, LONDON, NW2 5QU. See also Blackstone
BLACKSTONE, Mr. Christopher John Rickwood, FCA *1963;* Le Vallet, Le Mont De Gouray, JERSEY, JE3 6ET.
•BLACKSTONE, Mr. Lance Roy, BCom FCA *1970;* (Tax Fac), Blackstone Franks LLP, Barbican House, 26-34 Old Street, LONDON, EC1V 9QR.
BLACKTON, Mr. John Reader, FCA *1954;* Hill Pasture, Sutton Lane, Etwall, DERBY, DE65 6LQ. (Life Member)
BLACKTOP, Mrs. Nancy Joan, BSc(Hons) ACA *2001;* The Royal Bank of Scotland Plc, 4th Floor, 1 Spinningfields Square, MANCHESTER, M3 3AP.
•BLACKWELL, Mr. Anthony Richard, BA ACA *1982;* 5 Stepping Stones, East Morton, KEIGHLEY, BD20 5UG.
BLACKWELL, Miss. Charlotte Leanne, ACA *2008;* Moore Stephens, 150 Aldersgate Street, LONDON, EC1A 4AB.
BLACKWELL, Mr. Christopher Michael, MA FCA *1984;* (Tax Fac), 78 Camberwell Grove, LONDON, SE5 8RF.
BLACKWELL, Mr. David Nicholas, FCA *1965;* Tomorrow's Net Ltd, PO Box 7677, HUNGERFORD, RG17 0FX. (Life Member)
BLACKWELL, Mrs. Deirdre Philomena, FCA *1983;* Garden House, EPPING, CM16 5HS.
BLACKWELL, Mr. Glen Richard, BA ACA *2005;* 7 Wilbye Close, BURY ST. EDMUNDS, SUFFOLK, IP32 7DT.
BLACKWELL, Mr. Graeme Martin, BA(Econ) ACA *1998;* 5 Priory Lea, Walford, ROSS-ON-WYE, HR9 5RT.
BLACKWELL, Miss. Hayley Jayne, BSc ACA *2011;* 4 Blenheim View, Park Lane, Long Hanborough, WITNEY, OXFORDSHIRE, OX29 8RD.
BLACKWELL, Mr. John David, BSc ACA *1991;* Hima-Sella Ltd, Carrington Field Street, STOCKPORT, CHESHIRE, SK1 3JN.
•BLACKWELL, Mr. John William George, FCA *1966;* (Tax Fac), J.W.G. Blackwell, 6 Hallfields, Radford Semele, LEAMINGTON SPA, CV31 1TS.
BLACKWELL, Mr. Mark Charles, BSc ACA *1989;* Staplehay Lodge, Staplehay, Trull, TAUNTON, TA3 7HR.
BLACKWELL, Mr. Mark Robert, MSc FCA *1992;* Thomson Reuters (Legal) Ltd, Monmouth House, 58-64 City Road, LONDON, EC1Y 2AL.
BLACKWELL, Mr. Martin, FCA *1976;* Hertogenweg 14, 3080 TERVUREN, BELGIUM.
BLACKWELL, Mr. Michael, FCA *1961;* Spinneyfield, 13 Highlands, TAUNTON, SOMERSET, TA1 4HP.
BLACKWELL, Mr. Nicholas Adam, BSc ACA ALCM *2000;* Flat 5, 58 Hogarth Road, LONDON, SW5 0PX.
BLACKWELL, Mr. Paul, BSc FCA *1977;* 5 Nydd Vale Terrace, HARROGATE, NORTH YORKSHIRE, HG1 5HA.
•BLACKWELL, Mr. Paul Bryan, FCA *1965;* Blackwell P.B., 8 Bramley Close, LYMINGTON, HAMPSHIRE, SO41 3TE.
•BLACKWELL, Mr. Peter Kendal, BTech FCA *1975;* Peter K Blackwell FCA, 11 Farndale, WIGSTON, LEICESTERSHIRE, LE18 3XP.
BLACKWELL, Mrs. Philippa Jane, BA ACA *1984;* The Coach House, Burcot, ABINGDON, OX14 3DJ.
•BLACKWELL, Mr. Richard John, BA ACA *1991;* Deloitte LLP, City House, 126-130 Hills Road, CAMBRIDGE, CB2 1RY. See also Deloitte & Touche LLP
BLACKWELL, Mr. Ross Fraser John, BA ACA *1996;* Fuenkhgasse 16, 3021 PRESSBAUM, AUSTRIA.
BLACKWELL, Mrs. Sarah Elizabeth, BSc ACA *2000;* 27 Petersham Drive, Appleton, WARRINGTON, WA4 5QF.
BLACKWELL, Mr. Terrence George, FCA *1959;* Badgers Hollow House, 37 Hawkley Way, Elvetham Heath, FLEET, HAMPSHIRE, GU51 1AX. (Life Member)
BLACKWELL, Mr. Timothy Charles, BA ACA *1986;* 5 Garden Street, BENALLA, VIC 3672, AUSTRALIA.
BLACKWELL, Mr. Timothy Mark, BSc ACA *1995;* 63 Cloncurry Street, LONDON, SW6 6DT.
BLACKWELL, Mr. William Samuel, MA ACA *2003;* 16 Melrose Terrace, LONDON, W6 7RL.
BLACKWELL, Mrs. Yvonne, BSc ACA *1989;* 3 Orchid Court, PARK ORCHARDS, VIC 3114, AUSTRALIA.
BLACKWELL-FRIER, Mr. Geoff, ACA *1993;* Sphere Recruitment Consultants Unit 1 Brooklyn Chambers, 1 Brooklyn Road, CHEADLE, CHESHIRE, SK8 1BS.
BLACKWOOD, Mr. Andrew Robert, BA ACA *1986;* (Tax Fac), Southernwood, Manor Park, CHISLEHURST, BR7 5QD.
BLACKWOOD, Mr. David Charles, BSc ACA *1984;* Yule Catto & Co Ltd, Central Road, HARLOW, ESSEX, CM20 2BH.
BLACKWOOD, Miss. Heather Mary, BSc ACA *1987;* South Buckinghamshire Hospitals NHS Trust, Amersham Hospital, Finance Department, Whielden Street, AMERSHAM, BUCKINGHAMSHIRE HP7 0JD.
•BLACKWOOD, Mr. Iain Stuart, ACA CTA *1995;* (Tax Fac), Blackwood Futcher & Co, 9 St. Georges Yard, Castle Streeet, FARNHAM, SURREY, GU9 7LW.
BLACKWOOD, Mrs. Irene Sally, BSc ACA *1988;* Highclere, 7 Mizen Close, COBHAM, KT11 2RJ.
BLACKWOOD, Mr. Michael John, BA FCA *1963;* 129 Village Way, BECKENHAM, BR3 3NL. (Life Member)
•BLACKWOOD, Mr. Nicholas Geoffrey, BSc ACA *1986;* PricewaterhouseCoopers LLP, 1 Embankment Place, LONDON, WC2N 6RH. See also PricewaterhouseCoopers
BLADEN, Mr. James Henry, LLB ACA FHKSA FHKICPA *1988;* Walford House, Walford, Standon, STAFFORD, ST21 6QS.
BLADEN, Miss. Kathleen, BSc ACA *2011;* with BDHC, 11 Moor Street, CHEPSTOW, GWENT, NP16 5DD.
•BLADEN, Mr. Richard Warwick, FCA *1976;* Dean Statham LLP, 29 King Street, NEWCASTLE, STAFFORDSHIRE, ST5 1ER.
BLADEN, Mr. Simon Luke, ACA *2008;* 15 Glencroft, Dobbin Hill, SHEFFIELD, S11 7JB.
•BLADES, Mr. Peter George, BCom FCA *1976;* CW Fellowes Limited, Carnac Place, Cams Hall Estate, Fareham, PORTSMOUTH, PO16 8UY.
BLADES, Mr. Simon James, BSc ACA *1991;* Devon Pct Devon County Hall, Topsham Road, EXETER, EX2 4QL.
BLADES, Mr. Timothy John, BA FCA *1982;* Tudor House, 21 Manor Road, Great Bowden, MARKET HARBOROUGH, LEICESTERSHIRE, LE16 7HE.
BLADON, Mr. David, FCA *1974;* 4 Park Meadow, BRENTWOOD, Essex, CM15 0TT.
BLADON, Mr. Keith Victor, JP BCom FCA *1957;* Sunnymead, Blakemere, HEREFORD, HR2 9JY. (Life Member)
BLAGBURN, Mr. Peter Charles, FCA *1956;* 34 Mulberry Close, WELLINGBOROUGH, NORTHAMPTONSHIRE, NN8 3JU. (Life Member)
BLAGBURN, Mr. Robin James, FCA *1973;* 17 Fernwood, Clayton Road, NEWCASTLE UPON TYNE, NE2 1TL.
BLAGDEN, Mr. Ronald Peter, MA FCA *1982;* Anselm, White Edge Dr, Baslow, BAKEWELL, DE45 1SJ.
BLAGG, Charles William, Esq MBE BA FCA CTA *1947;* White Gables, Milford Road, Brocton, STAFFORD, ST17 0UD. (Life Member)
BLAGG, Mr. Graham James, FCA *1972;* 15 Old Sopwell Gardens, ST. ALBANS, AL1 2BY. (Life Member)
•BLAIKIE, Lord Paul John, BA FCA *1992;* (Tax Fac), CCW Limited, 295-297 Church Street, BLACKPOOL, FY1 3PJ.
BLAIKLOCK, Mr. Anthony Michael, MA ACA *1981;* 10 Longwood Drive, LONDON, SW15 5DL.
BLAIN, Mr. David Jonathan, ACA *1985;* Primrose Hill, Priory Road, ULVERSTON, LA12 9QE.
•BLAIN, Mr. Michael Louis Ian, FCA *1982;* Baker Tilly Tax & Advisory ServicesLLP, Spring Park House, Basing View, BASINGSTOKE, HAMPSHIRE, RG21 4HG.
BLAIN, Mr. Nicholas Joseph, MA FCA FSI CFA *1995;* Royal London House, 22-25 Finsbury Square, LONDON, EC2A 1DX.
BLAIN, Mr. Phillip Nigel, BSc ACA *1992;* 8 Ladyrigg, Ponteland, NEWCASTLE UPON TYNE, NE20 9QS.
BLAIN, Dr. Sharon Ann, BA ACA *2000;* 46 Craiglockhart Dell Road, EDINBURGH, EH14 1JP.
BLAIR, Mr. Alan Robert, FCA *1938;* Mill Cottage, 48 Mill Road, BURNHAM-ON-CROUCH, CM0 8PZ. (Life Member)
BLAIR, Mr. Andrew Peter, BA ACA *1989;* Ennismore Fund Management Ltd, Kensington Cloisters, 5 Kensington Church Street, LONDON, W8 4LD.
BLAIR, Miss. Anna, BSc(Hons) ACA *2011;* 33 Midfield Road, SHEFFIELD, S10 1SU.
BLAIR, Mr. Benjamin William, ACA *2008;* C/O KPMG, PO Box 493, GEORGE TOWN, GRAND CAYMAN, KY1-1106, CAYMAN ISLANDS.
BLAIR, Mrs. Caroline Anne, BSc ACA *1992;* Global Integration, 75 Nine Mile Ride, Finchampstead, WOKINGHAM, BERKSHIRE, RG40 4ND.
BLAIR, Mr. David Colin, BSc ACA *1993;* 6 Wolfram Court, ANULA, NT 0812, AUSTRALIA.
BLAIR, Mr. David Leslie, ACA *2009;* Flat 13 Deuchar House, 158 Sandyford Road, NEWCASTLE UPON TYNE, NE2 1XG.
•BLAIR, Mr. David Mckay, MA MBA FCA CF *1988;* DBA Group Limited, 6 Varrier Jones Drive, Papworth Everard, CAMBRIDGE, CB23 3GJ. See also David Blair Associates
BLAIR, Mr. David Peter Martin, FCA *1974;* Cranwell, Rockville Crescent, BLACKROCK, COUNTY DUBLIN, IRELAND.
•BLAIR, Mr. Derek Andrew, BA FCA *1994;* Pinkham Blair, 87A High Street, The Old Town, HEMEL HEMPSTEAD, HERTFORDSHIRE, HP1 3AH.
BLAIR, Mrs. Gemma, BA(Hons) ACA *2011;* 1 Priory Crescent, AYLESBURY, BUCKINGHAMSHIRE, HP19 9NZ.
•BLAIR, Mr. Graeme James, BSc FCA *1994;* (Tax Fac), Goodman Jones LLP, 29-30 Fitzroy Square, LONDON, W1T 6LQ.
BLAIR, Mr. Graeme Thomas, ACA *2008;* Apartment 18 Pershore House, 9 Prenton Lane, BIRKENHEAD, MERSEYSIDE, CH42 8LA.
BLAIR, Mrs. Hayley, ACA CA(SA) *2009;* C/O Paul Blair, PO BOX 502050, DUBAI, UNITED ARAB EMIRATES.
BLAIR, Mrs. Helen Joanne, MA ACA AIIMR *1996;* Rushworth House, 21 Eaton Park Road, COBHAM, SURREY, KT11 2JJ.
BLAIR, Mrs. Helen Margaret, BA FCA CTA *1992;* (Tax Fac), Isallt Rowen, CONWY, GWYNEDD, LL32 8YW.
BLAIR, Mr. James David, FCA *1950;* 91 Uplands Road, Oadby, LEICESTER, LE2 4NT. (Life Member)
BLAIR, The Revd. Jonathan Lewis, MA BA ACA *1989;* St. Pauls Vicarage, Pembroke Road, WOKING, SURREY, GU22 7ED.
BLAIR, Mrs. Kirsty Marie, LLB ACA *2005;* Inmarsat, 99 City Road, LONDON, EC1Y 1AX.
BLAIR, Mr. Martin Incledon, ACA *1982;* Pilat Media Global plc, 19th Floor, Wembley Point, 1 Harrow Road, WEMBLEY, MIDDLESEX HA9 6DE.
BLAIR, Mrs. Michelle Angela, BSc ACA *1992;* 4 Carolside Avenue, Clarkston, GLASGOW, G76 7AE.
BLAIR, Mr. Paul Anthony, ACA CA(SA) *2009;* 86 Carlton Park Avenue, Raynes Park, LONDON, SW20 8BL.
BLAIR, Mr. Peter Alexander, LLB(Hons) ACA CTA *2005;* Hess Corporation, 1185 Avenue of the Americas, NEW YORK, NY 10036, UNITED STATES.
BLAIR, Mr. William Bell, FCA *1938;* Highlands Village, 68 Aberfeldy Avenue Howick, Pakuranga, AUCKLAND, NEW ZEALAND. (Life Member)
•BLAKE, Mr. Alan Ronald, BSc FCA *1978;* Streets, Charter House, 62-64 Hills Road, CAMBRIDGE, CB2 1LA. See also Streets Whitmarsh Sterland
BLAKE, Mr. Andrew James, BSc ACA *2002;* 33 The Crunnis, Bradley Stoke, BRISTOL, BS32 8AD.
BLAKE, Mrs. Anna Mariola, ACA CA(AUS) *2010;* 88 Boulevard De La Tour Maubourg, 75007 PARIS, FRANCE.
BLAKE, Mr. Anthony Martin, FCA *1969;* 15 Manor Gardens, SOUTH CROYDON, Surrey, CR2 7BU.
BLAKE, Mr. Benjamin John, MEng ACA *2002;* Pond Yard Cottage Ketton Road, Collyweston, STAMFORD, LINCOLNSHIRE, PE9 3PS.
BLAKE, Miss. Cheryl, ACA *2010;* Flat 6, 7 Steele Road, LONDON, W4 5AD.

BLAKE, Mr. David George Bennett, MA(Cantab) ACA *1998;* Boardworks Ltd, The Gallery, 54 Marston Street, OXFORD, OX4 1LF.
BLAKE, Mr. David John, BSc FCA *1986;* Chantry Corporate Finance, Parallel House, 32 London Road, GUILDFORD, SURREY, GU1 2AB.
BLAKE, Mr. David Jonathan, BSc ACA *1995;* The Chestnuts, 2 Thrapston Road, Kimbolton, HUNTINGDON, PE28 0HW.
BLAKE, Mr. David Michael, BA FCA *1991;* 1 High Street, Haslingfield, CAMBRIDGE, CB23 1JW.
BLAKE, Mr. David Richard, BA ACA *1989;* Tassiloweg 16, 82319 STARNBERG, GERMANY.
BLAKE, Mr. Desmond Anthony, BSc ACA *1991;* 14 Stanley Road, LONDON, E12 6RJ.
•**BLAKE, Mr. Douglas, FCA** *1973;* (Tax Fac), Blake & Co, Rasdens, The Street, Halvergate, NORWICH, NR13 3AJ.
•**BLAKE, Mrs. Elizabeth Jane, ACA** *2002;* Elizabeth Blake ACA, 27 Tudor Road, Ainsdale, SOUTHPORT, MERSEYSIDE, PR8 2RY.
BLAKE, Mrs. Emma Maria, BA ACA *1997;* (Tax Fac), Woodland Hyde, Stowting, ASHFORD, TN25 6BD.
BLAKE, Mrs. Fiona Cathrine, BA ACA *1989;* C/o KPMG, PO Box 493, Century Yard, GEORGETOWN, GRAND CAYMAN, KY1-1106 CAYMAN ISLANDS.
BLAKE, Mr. Gavin Jonathan Metcalf, BEng ACA *1998;* 16 Weston Park, LONDON, N8 9TJ.
BLAKE, Mr. George Lovewell, FCA FTII *1957;* (Member of Council 1989 - 1999), The Charters, Town Road, Fleggburgh, GREAT YARMOUTH, NR29 3AB. (Life Member)
BLAKE, Mr. Harold Joseph, FCA *1952;* 1 Blenheim Court, Belnheim WayGreat Barr, BIRMINGHAM, B44 8LF. (Life Member)
BLAKE, Mrs. Helen, BA ACA DChA *2006;* The National Deaf Childrens Society, 15-16 Dufferin Street, LONDON, EC1Y 8UR.
BLAKE, Mr. Ian Robert, BCom ACA *1984;* P.O Box 882, KIMBERTON, PA 19442, UNITED STATES.
•**BLAKE, Mr. James, BSc ACA** *2006;* with The Taylor Cocks Partnership Limited, 3 Acorn Business Centre, Northarbour Road, Cosham, PORTSMOUTH, PO6 3TH.
•**BLAKE, Mr. James Samuel, BSc FCA** *1980;* (Tax Fac), Kelsey Lodge, Kelsey Square, BECKENHAM, BR3 1AF.
BLAKE, Mrs. Jayne Caroline, BSc ACA *1999;* 23 St. Giles Close, Wendlebury, BICESTER, OXFORDSHIRE, OX25 2PZ.
BLAKE, Mr. John Martin, FCA *1968;* 1 Somerton Avenue, RICHMOND, TW9 4QP.
BLAKE, Mr. Jonathan Rupert Bowden, BSc ACA *1988;* The Hawthornes, Cowesfield, Whiteparish, SALISBURY, SP5 2QZ.
BLAKE, Mrs. Katherine Marie, BSc ACA *1997;* 44 Southview Road, High Brooms, TUNBRIDGE WELLS, TN4 9BX.
•**BLAKE, Mr. Kevin Neil, BA FCA** *1988;* (Tax Fac), Carpenter Box LLP, Amelia House, WORTHING, WEST SUSSEX, BN11 1QR.
BLAKE, Mr. Laurence Alexander, FCA *1972;* 7 Ashlyn Close, BUSHEY, WD23 2EJ.
BLAKE, Mrs. Louise Margaret, MEng ACA *1994;* 30 Rosamond Drive, Bradway, SHEFFIELD, S17 4LW.
BLAKE, Mrs. Lucy Catherine Adamson, BA(Hons) ACA *2001;* St. Clares Oxford, 139 Banbury Road, OXFORD, OX2 7AL.
BLAKE, Mr. Matthew James, BSc ACA *2001;* 15 Oak Stubbs Lane, Dorney Reach, MAIDENHEAD, BERKSHIRE, SL6 0DW.
BLAKE, Mr. Matthew Jon, BA FCA *1993;* (Tax Fac), 27 Tudor Road, SOUTHPORT, MERSEYSIDE, PR8 2RY.
BLAKE, Mr. Michael Anthony, BSc ACA *1991;* 4 Ropeland Way, HORSHAM, RH12 5NY.
•**BLAKE, Mr. Michael David, BSc FCA CTA** *1979;* (Tax Fac), The TACS Partnership, Graylaw House, Mersey Square, STOCKPORT, CHESHIRE, SK1 1AL.
•**BLAKE, Mr. Michael David, BA FCA** *1980;* Great Copse House, Brickhouse Lane, Eversley, HOOK, HAMPSHIRE, RG27 0PY.
•**BLAKE, Mr. Michael Edward, FCA** *1971;* Michael E. Blake & Co, Evans Corner, Woodmansterne Lane, CARSHALTON, SURREY, SM5 4DQ.
•**BLAKE, Mr. Michael Ian, BSc FCA** *1991;* Coates and Partners Limited, 51 St. John Street, ASHBOURNE, DERBYSHIRE, DE6 1GP.
BLAKE, Mr. Michael Orlando, BSc FCA *1973;* 36 Grafton Road, WORTHING, WEST SUSSEX, BN11 1QT.
•**BLAKE, Miss. Nathalie Helen, BSc(Hons) ACA** *2001;* Ford Campbell Corporate Finance LLP, Bass Warehouse, 4 Castle Street, Castlefield, MANCHESTER, M3 4LZ. See also Ford Campbell Corporate Finance Ltd
BLAKE, Mr. Nicholas Charles, FCA *1973;* A G N International Ltd, Tuition House, 5-6 Francis Grove, LONDON, SW19 4DT.
BLAKE, Mr. Paul Anthony, FCA *1975;* Field Offshore Designs LLC, Suite 3-148, 100010 York Road, JENKINTOWN, PA 19046, UNITED STATES.
BLAKE, Mr. Paul Owen, BSc ACA MBA *2010;* 9/73 Grasmere Road, CREMORNE, NSW 2090, AUSTRALIA.
BLAKE, Miss. Pauline Lorraine, BSc ACA *2005;* 67A Elms Road, Clapham Common, LONDON, SW4 9EP.
•**BLAKE, Mr. Peter Richard, ACA** *1991;* 9 Wallis Drive, SWINDON, SN25 4GA.
BLAKE, Mr. Peter Robert, FCA *1969;* 4 River View, ENFIELD, EN2 6PX. (Life Member)
•**BLAKE, Mrs. Rebecca Louise, BSc FCA CTA** *1990;* with Rebecca Blake, The Studio, 2 Kings End Road, Powick, WORCESTER, WR2 4RA. See also Rebecca Blake & Co
BLAKE, Mr. Richard, FCA *1962;* The Cottage, South Road, Lympsham, WESTON-SUPER-MARE, BS24 0DX.
BLAKE, Mr. Richard John Bowden, FCA *1960;* Bakers House, Brokenborough, MALMESBURY, WILTSHIRE, SN16 0HY.
BLAKE, Mr. Roger Michael, BA(Hons) ACA *2003;* Greyholme, Skinburness, WIGTON, CUMBRIA, CA7 4QY.
BLAKE, Mr. Russell Adrian, BA ACA *1991;* 17 Holbeche Road, Knowle, SOLIHULL, B93 9PE.
BLAKE, Mrs. Ruth Elizabeth, BEd ACA *1992;* 20 Butlers Close, Broomfield, CHELMSFORD, CM1 7BE.
BLAKE, Miss. Sarah Louise, BSc ACA *1994;* 5 Meadow Close, HOVE, BN3 6QQ.
BLAKE, Mrs. Sarah Melanie, BA ACA *2004;* 15 Oak Stubbs Lane, Dorney Reach, MAIDENHEAD, BERKSHIRE, SL6 0DW.
BLAKE, Mrs. Sharon Patricia, BA ACA *1984;* 4 Theed Street, LONDON, SE1 8ST.
BLAKE, Mr. Simon, BSc ACA *1993;* 30 Rosamond Drive, Bradway, SHEFFIELD, S17 4LW.
•**BLAKE, Mr. Simon James, FCA CF** *1997;* Price Bailey LLP, 7th Floor Dashwood House, 69 Old Broad Street, LONDON, EC2M 1QS. See also Price Bailey Private Client LLP
BLAKE, Mr. Simon Peter, BSc ACA *1984;* Bathwick Corporation Ltd, Bathwick House, London Road, RICKMANSWORTH, WD3 1JT.
BLAKE, Mr. Simon Robert Austin, BA FCA *1980;* 8 Birchwood Avenue, LONDON, N10 3BE.
BLAKE, Mr. Stanley Samuel, BSc FCA CTA *1980;* Robson Welsh, 7th Floor, Silkhouse Court, Tithebarn Street, LIVERPOOL, L2 2LZ.
•**BLAKE, Mrs. Susan Ruth, BSc FCA** *1980;* (Tax Fac), Hunt Blake Ltd, Jubilee House, The Oaks, RUISLIP, MIDDLESEX, HA4 7LF.
•**BLAKE, Mr. Timothy John, BA ACA** *1996;* (Tax Fac), KPMG LLP, 15 Canada Square, LONDON, E14 5GL. See also KPMG Europe LLP
•**BLAKE, Mr. Vincent Charles, BCom FCA** *1979;* Vincent Blake, The Old Farmhouse, Town Row Green, CROWBOROUGH, TN6 3QU.
BLAKE, Mr. William Charles, FCA *1957;* 29 Bartram Road, Totton, SOUTHAMPTON, SO40 9JL. (Life Member)
BLAKE-THOMAS, Mr. Hugh Clay, FCA *1986;* Prospects Services Ltd, 19 Elmfield Road, BROMLEY, BR1 1LT.
BLAKE-WILSON, Mr. Tom, BA ACA *2009;* 58 Nightingale Road, RICKMANSWORTH, HERTFORDSHIRE, WD3 7BT.
•**BLAKEBOROUGH, Mr. John Vincent, BA FCA** *1978;* John V Blakeborough, 5 Adel Park Croft, LEEDS, LS16 8HT.
BLAKEBROUGH, Mr. David Charles, FCA *1962;* The Roothings, Valley Road, SWANAGE, DORSET, BH19 3DX. (Life Member)
BLAKELEY, Mr. Christopher Mark, BSc ACA *1993;* Wayside, North Road, Yate, BRISTOL, BS37 7LQ.
BLAKELEY, Mrs. Lorna, BSc(Hons) ACA *2004;* Canons House, P0 Box 112 Canons Way, BRISTOL, BS99 7LB.
BLAKELEY, Mr. Paul Norman, BSc ACA *1996;* 37 Southill Road, BOURNEMOUTH, DORSET, BH9 1SH.
BLAKELEY, Mr. Stephen, BA ACA CTA *1992;* 608 SW 8th Street, BENTONVILLE, AR 72716, UNITED STATES.
BLAKELEY, Mr. Stephen Thomas, LLM BSc ACA *2004;* with KPMG LLP, 15 Canada Square, LONDON, E14 5GL.
BLAKELY, Mr. Michael John, FCA *1968;* 1 Norfolk Wing, Tortington Manor, Ford Road, Tortington, ARUNDEL, WEST SUSSEX BN18 0FD. (Life Member)
BLAKEMAN, Mr. Andrew Peter Matthew, MSc BSc(Econ) FCA CF *1992;* 10 Cecil Park, PINNER, HA5 5HH.
BLAKEMORE, Mr. Christopher Martin, BA ACA *1986;* 5 Cross Barn, English Bicknor, COLEFORD, GL16 7PP.
•**BLAKEMORE, Mr. Dominic William, BA ACA** *1997;* 40 Winterbrook Road, LONDON, SE24 9JA.
BLAKEMORE, Mr. Jonathan, BSc ACA *1991;* Spring Cottage, Porteynon, SWANSEA, SA3 1NL.
•**BLAKEMORE, Mr. Mark Allen, BSc FCA MAE MCIArb** *1991;* Baker Tilly Tax & Advisory Services LLP, 3 Hardman Street, MANCHESTER, M3 3HF. See also Baker Tilly Restructuring and Recovery LLP
BLAKEMORE, Mr. Neil James, BSc ACA *1993;* Moor Farm, High Street, Pavenham, BEDFORD, MK43 7NU.
BLAKEMORE, Mr. Paul Roland, BA FCA *1976;* 21 Hollytree Close, Hoton, LOUGHBOROUGH, LE12 5SE.
BLAKEMORE, Mr. Robert Iain, ACA *2008;* Landin Wilcock & Co Queen Street Chambers, 68 Queen Street, SHEFFIELD, S1 1WR.
BLAKER, Mrs. Kerrie Louise, LLB ACA CTA *2002;* 25 King George Street, LONDON, SE10 8QJ.
BLAKER, Mr. Nicholas William Hermann, MA ACA *2002;* Greys Piece, Rotherfield Greys, HENLEY-ON-THAMES, RG9 4QG.
BLAKESLEY, Mr. Andrew Laurence, FCA *1958;* Midsummer Lodge, Gatesdene, Little Gaddesden, BERKHAMSTED, HERTFORDSHIRE, HP4 1PB. (Life Member)
BLAKESTONE, Miss. Karen, BSc ACA *1992;* 8 Willow Tree Garth, BEVERLEY, NORTH HUMBERSIDE, HU17 9UR.
•**BLAKEY, Mr. Andrew Malcolm, BA(Hons) FCA** *1991;* with Henton & Co LLP, St. Andrews House, St. Andrews Street, LEEDS, LS3 1LF.
•**BLAKEY, Mrs. Beverley Susan, BA FCA** *1988;* Anderson Barrowcliff LLP, Waterloo House, Thornaby Place, Thornaby on Tees, STOCKTON-ON-TEES, CLEVELAND TS17 6SA. See also Anderson Barrowcliff
BLAKEY, Mr. David John, FCA *1974;* 24 Dowhills Road, Crosby, LIVERPOOL, L23 8SW.
BLAKEY, Ms. Fiammetta Iole Maria, LLB ACA *1999;* 92 King George Street, LONDON, SE10 8QB.
BLAKEY, Mr. Frederick Robert, FCA *1957;* 5 Vihiers Close, Whalley, CLITHEROE, BB7 9UH. (Life Member)
BLAKEY, Miss. Laura Jane, BA(Hons) ACA *2004;* 34 Birchfield Drive, Worsley, MANCHESTER, M28 1ND.
BLAKEY, Mr. Michael Vincent, BA ACA *1994;* The Hayloft, Mitford, MORPETH, NORTHUMBERLAND, NE61 3QW.
BLAKEY, Mr. Sam Robert James, BSc(Hons) ACA *2011;* 19 Keswick Close, Ainsdale, SOUTHPORT, MERSEYSIDE, PR8 3QR.
BLAKISTON, Mr. John, BCom ACA ACMA *1995;* Rose Cottage, Spring Grove, Bewdley Bypass, BEWDLEY, WORCESTERSHIRE, DY12 1LG.
BLAMEY, Mr. Matthew Hind, FCA *1935;* Flat 3, Saumarez Park Manor Res Home, Route de SaumarezCastel, GUERNSEY, GY5 7TH. (Life Member)
BLAMIRE-BROWN, Miss. Heather, BSc ACA *2010;* 4 Dalton Street, ST. ALBANS, HERTFORDSHIRE, AL3 5QQ.
•**BLAMIRE-BROWN, Mr. Mark James, BSc FCA** *1977;* Thomas & Young LLP, 240-244 Stratford Road, Shirley, SOLIHULL, WEST MIDLANDS, B90 3AE.
•**BLAMIRE-BROWN, Mr. Stephen John, BSc FCA** *1973;* Brown & Co, Maple House, Bayshill Road, CHELTENHAM, GLOUCESTERSHIRE, GL50 3AW.
BLAMIRES, Mrs. Sarah Louise, BSc ACA *2010;* 13 Phillida Terrace, MIDDLESBROUGH, CLEVELAND, TS5 6LU.
BLAMPIED, Mr. Charles Richard, BA FCA *1974;* St Clair, Coast Road, St. Clement, JERSEY, JE2 6FQ.
BLAMPIED, Miss. Katrina, BSc ACA *2006;* 7 Beachside Mews, La Rue Du Hocq, St. Clement, JERSEY, JE2 6LF.
BLAMPIED, Peter Gilroy, Esq OBE FCA *1952;* The Croft, La Grande Route de la Cote, St. Clement, JERSEY, JE2 6FT. (Life Member)
BLANC, Mr. Paul Edward, BSc ACA *1991;* 39 Priory Drive, REIGATE, SURREY, RH2 8AF.
BLANCH, Mr. Stuart Harding, BA ACA *1994;* Intel Corporation (UK) Ltd, Pipers Way, SWINDON, SN3 1RJ.
BLANCHARD, Mrs. Angela, BCom ACA DChA *1985;* Sayer Vincent Unit 8 Angel Gate, 326 City Road, LONDON, EC1V 2SJ.
BLANCHARD, Mr. Charlie Edward David, MSc ACA MBCS CISA CISM CISSP *2005;* 4233 McConnell Blvd, LOS ANGELES, CA 90066, UNITED STATES.
BLANCHARD, Mr. David William Forbes, FCA *1966;* 74 Chemin des Hauts de Grisy, 78860 ST NOM LA BRETECHE, FRANCE.
BLANCHARD, Mr. John Cyril, FCA *1957;* 21 Totnes Road, NEWTON ABBOT, TQ12 1LY. (Life Member)
BLANCHARD, Mr. Kevin Peter, BSc ACA *1993;* 32 Garrett Road, RD5, TAURANGA 3175, NEW ZEALAND.
BLANCHARD, Mr. Peter, FCA *1964;* 131 Chemin Des Marais, 1255 VEYRIER, SWITZERLAND.
BLANCHARD, Mr. Peter Vernon, FCA *1965;* Asholme, 372 Station Road, Dorridge, SOLIHULL, B93 8ES.
BLANCHARD, Mr. Scott, MSc BA FCA *2000;* 6 Leverholme Gardens, Eltham, LONDON, SE9 3DG.
BLANCHET, Miss. Annette Georgine, BAcc ACA *1996;* 3 Le Perquage, Sandybrook, St. Lawrence, JERSEY, JE3 1EZ.
BLANCHFIELD, Mrs. Julia Margaret, ACA *1988;* 8 Hunters Park Avenue, Clayton, BRADFORD, BD14 6EG.
BLANCHFIELD, Mrs. Tracy, MBA ACA *1992;* Bicknells Farm, East Street, Drayton, LANGPORT, SOMERSET, TA10 0JZ.
BLANCHFLOWER, Mr. Nicholas, BSc(Hons) ACA *2001;* 6F Hana Bank Extension Building, 9-10 2Ga Euljiro, Jung-Gu, SEOUL, KOREA REPUBLIC OF.
BLANCHFLOWER, Mr. Philip Ronald, FCA *1964;* 1 Broadmead Green, Thorpe End, NORWICH, NR13 5DE. (Life Member)
BLAND, Mrs. Alison Jane, BSc ACA *1991;* The Old Mill, Kennell Hill, Sharnbrook, BEDFORD, MK44 1PS.
•①**BLAND, Mr. Andrew Mark, BA FCA** *1997;* DMC Recovery Ltd, 41 Greek Street, STOCKPORT, CHESHIRE, SK3 8AX. See also Downham Mayer Clarke Limited
BLAND, Mr. Andrew Michael, BSocSc ACA *1995;* 67 Island Row, Commercial Wharf, Limehouse, LONDON, E14 7HU.
BLAND, Miss. Carolyn, ACA *2003;* 85 Leicester Road, Fleckney, LEICESTER, LE8 8BG.
BLAND, Mr. David Roger, FCA *1977;* Victory House, Westgate Street, Shouldham, KING'S LYNN, PE33 0BL.
•**BLAND, Mr. David Victor, FCA** *1977;* (Tax Fac), Leesing Marrison Lee & Co, P O Box 341, Oldcotes, WORKSOP, NOTTINGHAMSHIRE, S80 4HW. See also Leesing Marrison Lee Limited
BLAND, Mrs. Helen Elizabeth, BSc ACA *2001;* 2 St Philips Court, Buddle Lane, EXETER, EX4 1JB.
BLAND, Mr. Hugh Valentine Thomas, BSc ACA *1985;* The Warren, Aldbourne, MARLBOROUGH, SN8 2LE.
BLAND, Mr. James, BSc(Hons) ACA *2004;* with Deloitte LLP, 4 Brindley Place, BIRMINGHAM, B1 2HZ.
BLAND, Miss. Jane Louise, BA ACA *2000;* Flat 6, 44 Mortimer Street, LONDON, W1W 7RJ.
BLAND, Mr. John Nigel, BSocSc FCA *1986;* 14 Rodborough Road, Dorridge, SOLIHULL, WEST MIDLANDS, B93 8ED.
BLAND, Mr. Karl Alexander, BA ACA *2000;* 85 Montague Close, WOKINGHAM, BERKSHIRE, RG40 5PH.
BLAND, Mr. Martin Allan Gill, BA FCA *1984;* Church View, 17A Bluehouse Lane, OXTED, SURREY, RH8 0AA.
•**BLAND, Mr. Maurice Nathan, FCA** *1965;* (Tax Fac), Maurice Bland & Co, Suite One First Floor, Blue Pit Business Centre, Queensway, ROCHDALE, LANCASHIRE OL11 2PG.
•**BLAND, Mr. Michael Stuart, ACA** *1991;* Wheawill & Sudworth, P.O. Box B30, 35 Westgate, HUDDERSFIELD, HD1 1PA.
BLAND, Mr. Paul Neil, BA(Hons) ACA *2010;* 3 Apple Tree Drive, BARROW-IN-FURNESS, CUMBRIA, LA13 0LA.
BLAND, Mr. Peter, BSc FCA *1992;* 55 Stumperlowe Crescent Road, SHEFFIELD, S10 3PR.
BLAND, Mr. Philip, BA ACA *1986;* White Lodge, Gravel Path, BERKHAMSTED, HP4 2PJ.
BLAND, Mrs. Rachel Ann, BA ACA *1991;* 55 Stumperlowe Crescent Road, SHEFFIELD, S10 3PR.
BLAND, Mr. Richard, BA ACA *1999;* 4 Rosedale Drive, Tingley, WAKEFIELD, WF3 1WG.
BLAND, Mr. Stephen Joseph, FCA *1971;* 32 Patching Way, HAYES, MIDDLESEX, UB4 9YD.
BLAND, Mrs. Wendy Michelle, BA(Hons) ACA *2001;* 26 St. Cuthberts Way, Holystone, NEWCASTLE UPON TYNE, NE27 0UZ.
BLAND, Mr. William, FCA *1964;* 73 Ailsa Avenue, St Margarets, TWICKENHAM, TW1 1NF. (Life Member)
•**BLAND, Mr. William Lymbery, FCA** *1973;* W.L. Bland & Co, 141 High Street, AMERSHAM, BUCKINGHAMSHIRE, HP7 0DY.
BLANDFORD, Mrs. Maxene Danielle Gemma, BSc ACA *2010;* Flat 8, Sandringham Court, King & Queen Wharf, Rotherhithe Street, LONDON, SE16 5SQ.

BLANDFORD, Mr. Thomas, BA ACA *2008;* 1 Woodside Lane, Grenoside, SHEFFIELD, S35 8RW.
•①**BLANE, Mr. Alan, FCA** *1965;* Altman Blane & Co, Middlesex House, 29/45 High Street, EDGWARE, HA8 7LH.
BLANEY, Mr. Martin Robert Charles, FCA *1982;* Res Choo Choy, Rue Jaundally No. 22, ROCHES BRUNES, MAURITIUS.
BLANEY, Mr. Stephen John Digby, BCom FCA *1974;* The Old Stables, Main St., Sicklinghall, WETHERBY, LS22 4BD.
BLANFORD, Mr. Julian Michael, MA FCA *1966;* 13 Larchcroft, CHATHAM, ME5 0NL.
BLANK, Mr. Derek, BA ACA *1981;* 5 Higher Croft, Whitefield, MANCHESTER, M45 7LY.
BLANK, Mr. Samuel, BSc ACA *2011;* 65 Woodburn Close, Brent Street, LONDON, NW4 2NF.
•**BLANK, Mr. Stephen Martin, MA MSc FCA** *1976;* Manchester Industrial Finance Limited, c/o SM Blank, 26 Grey Road, ALTRINCHAM, CHESHIRE WA14 4BU.
BLANKENSHIP, Mrs. Alexandra Kate, BCom ACA *1990;* Portoi, Arzens, 11290 CARCASSONNE, FRANCE.
BLANKLEY, Mr. John Harrower, MA FCA *1972;* Flagship Networks Inc, 10 Doverton Drive, GREENWICH, CT 06831, UNITED STATES.
BLANKSBY, Mrs. Sheree Anne, BSc ACA *1992;* 11 The Meads, Northchurch, BERKHAMSTED, HERTFORDSHIRE, HP4 3QX.
BLANKSON, Mr. Robert, MEng ACA *2011;* 62a Bramley Road, Ealing, LONDON, W5 4SS.
BLANKSTONE, Mr. Stephen Jonathan, BA ACA *1993;* Jack Blankstone Ltd, Picton House, Kitling Road, Knowsley Business Park, PRESCOT, MERSEYSIDE L34 9JA.
•**BLANNIN, Mr. Nigel Andrew, BSc FCA** *1977;* Maxwells, 4 King Square, BRIDGWATER, SOMERSET, TA6 3YF.
BLANSHARD, Mr. Mark, BA ACA *1994;* 15 Park Avenue, Wynyard Village, BILLINGHAM, CLEVELAND, TS22 5RU.
BLASEBY, Mrs. Kirsten Fiona, ACA *2008;* 1 Furzefield Road, LONDON, SE3 8TU.
BLASI, Mr. Dimitry Mark, ACA *2000;* 1 Ismona Street, NEWPORT, NSW 2106, AUSTRALIA.
•**BLASKEY, Mr. Roger Waldo, BSc FCA** *1975;* Kay Johnson Gee, Griffin Court, 201 Chapel Street, MANCHESTER, M3 5EQ.
BLASTLAND, Mr. James, BSc ACA *2010;* 84 Beaconsfield Road, SURBITON, KT5 9AP.
BLATCH, Miss. Sarah, BA(Hons) ACA *2001;* 44 Albemarle Road, MANCHESTER, M21 9HZ.
BLATCHFORD, Mr. Eric David, FCA *1979;* 21 Thornbrook, Naas, KILDARE, COUNTY KILDARE, IRELAND.
BLATCHFORD, Mr. Trevor Paul, BSc FCA *1976;* Kylesku, Houmtel Lane, Vale, GUERNSEY, GY3 5LG.
BLATCHLY, Mr. Christopher Nigel, BA ACA *1983;* Old Comptons, Comptons Lane, HORSHAM, RH13 6BP.
BLATHERWICK, Mr. John, ACA *1980;* 132 Ogley Hay Road, Chase Terrace, BURNTWOOD, STAFFORDSHIRE, WS7 2HX.
BLATHWAYT, Mr. Arthur Tobin, MBA BSc ACA *1994;* 1/11 Hororata Road, TAKAPUNA 0622, AUCKLAND, NEW ZEALAND.
BLATT, Mr. Jeffrey Malcolm, FCA *1971;* Lambourne, Bournebridge Lane, Stapleford Abbotts, ROMFORD, RM4 1LT.
BLATT, Mrs. Kamala Valentina Mary, ACA CTA AMCT *1990;* 22 Brokes Crescent, REIGATE, RH2 9PS.
BLATT, Miss. Mary Jocelyn, BA ACA *1985;* 13 Cedar Grove, Copnor, PORTSMOUTH, PO3 6HH.
BLATT, Mr. Timothy John, BA ACA *1992;* West Sussex Primary Care Trust, 1 The Causeway Goring By Sea, WORTHING, WEST SUSSEX, BN12 6BT.
•**BLAXALL, Mr. Christopher Stanley, BSc ACA** *1981;* CLPC Limited, 41 Shaws Park, HEXHAM, NORTHUMBERLAND, NE46 3BJ.
•**BLAXILL, Mr. Keith Douglas, FCA** *1970;* Keith Blaxill Limited, 12 Stevenage Road, KNEBWORTH, SG3 6AW.
BLAXLAND, Mr. Andrew Richard, BSc ACA *1984;* Swife House, Swife Lane, Broad Oak, HEATHFIELD, TN21 8UR.
BLAXLAND, Mr. Richard Bryan, FCA *1952;* Gleamingwood, 10 Walderslade Road, CHATHAM, ME4 6NX. (Life Member)
•**BLAXLAND, Mrs. Rowan Fiona, FCA** *1992;* (Tax Fac), Rowan Blaxland, Grove Lodge, Grove Road, Brockdish, DISS, IP21 4JP.
•**BLAXTER, Mr. David, FCA** *1961;* David Blaxter, Wood Cottage, Barton Hartshorne, BUCKINGHAM, MK18 4JT.
BLAY, Mr. Paul Richard, MSc FCA *1971;* 9 Marple Hall Drive, Marple, STOCKPORT, SK6 6JN.
BLAYDES, Mr. Simon Richard, BSc ACA *1993;* Altius Petroleum, Nurly Tau, Al Farabi, Korpus 2B Office 604, ALMATY 050010, KAZAKHSTAN.
BLAYNEY, Mr. Mark Richard, ACA MBA *1991;* Turnaroundhelp Ltd, High Turney Shield, Carrshield, HEXHAM, NORTHUMBERLAND, NE47 8AW.
BLAYNEY, Mr. Simon Robert, MBA BA ACA *1993;* Chellomedia Ltd, 4th Floor, Michelin House, 81 Fulham Road, LONDON, SW3 6RD.
BLAZEBY, Mr. Crispin Anthony Leigh, BA FCA *1965;* Rose Cottage, Blackstone Lane, Albourne, HASSOCKS, BN6 9JD.
BLAZEBY, Mr. Jonathan Paul, BA FCA *1993;* Flat 28B Caperidge Drive, DISCOVERY BAY, NEW TERRITORIES, HONG KONG SAR.
•**BLEACH, Mr. Christopher Ray, BSc ACA CTA** *1990;* Lautrec, 11 Thorpe Road, Chacombe, BANBURY, OXFORDSHIRE, OX17 2JW.
•**BLEACH, Mrs. Jane Catherine, BSc ACA** *1989;* Baker Tillly Tax & Advisory Services LLP, St Philips Point, Temple Row, BIRMINGHAM, B2 5AF. See also Baker Tilly UK Audit LLP
BLEAKLEY, Mr. Ian Alexander, BSc ACA *2001;* 2 Hawthorn Grove, BATH, BA2 5QA.
BLEARS, Ms. Anne Elizabeth, BSc ACA *1988;* 41 Buxton Road, Chinley, HIGH PEAK, SK23 6DJ.
•**BLEARS, Mr. Kenneth Herbert, FCA** *1952;* Kenneth H. Blears, Church Green, 4 Church Lane, BROMSGROVE, B61 8RB.
BLEASDALE, Mr. Christopher James, FCA CTA *1966;* The Grain Store, Wenham Manor, Rogate, PETERSFIELD, HAMPSHIRE, GU31 5AY.
BLEASDALE, Mr. David Michael, BA FCA *1983;* 1 Bali Place, Berowra, SYDNEY, NSW 2081, AUSTRALIA.
BLEASDALE, Ms. Pamela Jane, BA FCA *1989;* 15 Lanark Gardens, WIDNES, CHESHIRE, WA8 9DT.
BLEASE, Mrs. Catherine Ann, BSc FCA *1989;* 18 Eastway, Nailsea, BRISTOL, BS48 2NH.
BLEATHMAN, Miss. Carly Lorraine, ACA *2008;* with Whale Rock Professional Services Group, 4th Floor, 15 Basinghall Street, LONDON, EC2V 5BR.
BLEATHMAN, Mr. Charles Richard, BA ACA *1992;* Orchard Cottage, Church Street, Woolley, BATH, BA1 8AS.
BLEAZARD, Mr. Ian Robert, MSc ACA *1998;* 14 North Lodge Road, Penn Hill, POOLE, DORSET, BH14 9BB.
•**BLEAZARD, Mr. Keith, FCA** *1959;* (Tax Fac), Bleazard K, 5 Chapel Street, POULTON-LE-FYLDE, FY6 7BQ.
BLEAZARD, Mrs. Rachel Louise, BSocSc ACA *1998;* 14 North Lodge Road, Penn Hill, POOLE, DORSET, BH14 9BB.
BLECH, Mr. Neville Franklin, FCA *1959;* 57 Pelham Street, LONDON, SW7 2NJ. (Life Member)
BLECH, Mr. Nicholas, MA ACA *1992;* 21 The Linnets, Cottenham, CAMBRIDGE, CB24 8XZ.
•**BLECHER, Mr. Kenneth, BSc FCA** *1989;* Pepper Ideas Limited, 18a Rothschild Road, LONDON, W4 5HS.
BLEE, Mr. Martin Robert, ACA *1986;* 4 Tobias Grove, STAMFORD, LINCOLNSHIRE, PE9 4BD.
BLEE, Mr. Simon Andrew, BA(Hons) ACA *2002;* University of Oxford, 23-38 Hythe Bridge Street, OXFORD, OX1 2EP.
BLELLOCH, Mr. Ian James Stevenson, LLB ACA *1988;* Chaco Ltd, Chapel Cottage, Kingston Road, Frilford, ABINGDON, OXFORDSHIRE OX13 5NX.
BLENCOWE, Mr. Andrew, LLM BCom ACA CFP *2008;* Andrew Blencowe, 18 Pleasant Avenue, PO Box 108, ERSKINEVILLE, NSW 2043, AUSTRALIA.
BLENCOWE, Miss. Carla Marie, ACA *2008;* Kaplan Financial, Block 2 4th Floor, 1 Torrens Street, Angle Square, LONDON, EC1V 1NY.
•**BLENCOWE, Mr. Robert Francis, BSc FCA** *1979;* Blencowe & Partners Limited, 15 High Street, BRACKLEY, NORTHAMPTONSHIRE, NN13 7DH.
BLEND, Mr. Derek Keith, FCA *1975;* Calle Campillo 36, 29752 SAYALONGA, MALAGA, SPAIN.
•①**BLENKARN, Mr. David John, BA FCA** *1982;* Smith & Williamson Ltd, Imperial House, 18-21 Kings Park Road, SOUTHAMPTON, HAMPSHIRE, SO15 2AT.
BLENKARN, Mr. George Milner, FCA *1975;* Aou Carde, Lagarde Hachan, Mirande, 32300 GERS, FRANCE.
BLENKHARN, Miss. Katie, BSc ACA *2011;* Brookleigh, Eppleby, RICHMOND, NORTH YORKSHIRE, DL11 7AZ.
BLENKINSHIP, Mrs. Sally, MA MBA ACA *2000;* Moor Roods, Grindleton Road, West Bradford, CLITHEROE, BB7 4QH.
BLENKINSOP, Miss. Catherine, BSc(Hons) ACA *2003;* H S B C Bank plc, 8 Canada Square, LONDON, E14 5HQ.
BLENKINSOP, Mr. Gordon Penrhyn, ISO FCA *1957;* Carlton Hayes, Convent Road, SIDMOUTH, EX10 8RB. (Life Member)
BLENKINSOP, Mr. Ian Stewart, MSc ACA *1984;* 17 Canynge Square, Clifton, BRISTOL, BS8 3LA.
•**BLENKINSOP, Mr. John, BSc FCA** *1978;* Blenkinsop & Co, 1 Shardlow Gardens, Bessacarr, DONCASTER, DN4 6UB.
BLENKINSOP, Mr. Peter John, FCA *1969;* Colchester House, 26 High Street, OLNEY, BUCKINGHAMSHIRE, MK46 4BB.
BLENKIRON, Mrs. Joanne Lesley, BA ACA *2000;* 59 Marlpit Lane, SUTTON COLDFIELD, B75 5PJ.
BLESSED, Mr. Roger, BA FCA *1968;* 57 Thames Street, WEYBRIDGE, SURREY, KT13 8LA.
BLESSINGTON, Mr. Thomas Paul, BSc(Hons) ACA ATT *2011;* Flat 11, Keswick Heights, Keswick Road, LONDON, SW15 2JR.
BLESSITT, Mr. Malcolm, FCA *1958;* Hollyburn, 64 Willowmead Drive, Prestbury, MACCLESFIELD, SK10 4DD. (Life Member)
•**BLESSLEY, Mr. Colin Peter, BA FCA** *1973;* 16 Ildersly Grove, LONDON, SE21 8EU.
BLETCHER, Mr. John Roland, BSc FCA *1972;* Sheepcote House, South Street, North Kelsey, MARKET RASEN, LN7 6ET.
BLETSO, Mr. David Roy, BSc ACA *1995;* Ember Place, Carleton Close, ESHER, SURREY, KT10 8EE.
BLETSOE-BROWN, Mrs. Eleanor Mary, BSc ACA ATII *1984;* The Croft, Naseby Road, Haselbech, NORTHAMPTON, NN6 9LH.
•**BLEWETT, Mr. Brian Frederick, FCA** *1971;* B. Blewett, 13 Cedar Avenue, Blackwater, CAMBERLEY, GU17 0JE.
BLEWETT, Mrs. Fiona Katherine, ACA *1995;* Trevarrack Manor, Lelant, ST.IVES, CORNWALL, TR26 3HA.
BLEWITT, Mr. Jason Lee, BA(Hons) ACA *2004;* 19 Dukes Meadow, Pendine, CARMARTHEN, DYFED, SA33 4UH.
BLEWITT, Miss. Joanna Maria, BA ACA *1989;* 35 Vallis Way, Ealing, LONDON, W13 0DD.
BLEYTHING, Mrs. Alison Jane, BA ACA *1991;* 12 Charles Close, Thornbury, BRISTOL, BS35 1LN.
BLEZARD, Mr. Adam Jon, ACA *2009;* 19 Arbuthnot Road, LONDON, SE14 5LS.
BLIAULT, Miss. Joanna Clare, ACA *2009;* Wilkins Kennedy & Co, Bridge House, 4 Borough High Street, LONDON, SE1 9QR.
BLIGH, Mr. Andrew William, BSc ACA *1992;* 18 Stanley Hill Avenue, AMERSHAM, BUCKINGHAMSHIRE, HP7 9BD.
BLIGH, Mrs. Caroline Jane, BSc ACA *1993;* 144 Military road, Dover Heights, SYDNEY, NSW 2030, AUSTRALIA.
BLIGH, Mr. Peter Robin, FCA *1962;* 2 Penarth Place, CAMBRIDGE, CB3 9LU. (Life Member)
BLIGH, Mr. Simon Dominic, BA ACA *1993;* 144 Military Road, Dover Heights, SYDNEY, NSW 2030, AUSTRALIA.
•**BLIGH, Mr. Stephen Gerard, BSc FCA** *1983;* KPMG LLP, 15 Canada Square, LONDON, E14 5GL. See also KPMG Europe LLP, KPMG Audit plc
BLIGHT, Mr. Andrew John, BSc FCA *1996;* 3 Bracken Court, Maulden, BEDFORD, MK45 2AN.
BLIGHT, Mrs. Carolyn Jane Amy, LLB ACA *1991;* Willow Cottage, Portskewett, CALDICOT, GWENT, NP26 5TR.
BLIGHT, Mr. Daniel Robert, BSc ACA *2002;* 15 Bloomfield Road, HARPENDEN, HERTFORDSHIRE, AL5 4DD.
BLIGHT, Miss. Samantha, ACA *2007;* 90a Church Road, FOLKESTONE, CT20 3EN.
BLIGNAUT, Mrs. Amrusta, ACA CA(SA) *2010;* 35 Kettlewell Close, WOKING, SURREY, GU21 4HY.
BLINKHORN, Mr. Phillip Steel, BA FCA *1978;* 1 Blundell Close, Unsworth, BURY, BL9 8LH.
•**BLISS, Mr. Christopher Jan Andrew, BSc FCA** *1981;* (Tax Fac), Rawlinson & Hunter, Eighth Floor, 6 New Street Square, New Fetter Lane, LONDON, EC4A 3AQ.
BLISS, Mrs. Jacqueline Charmaine, BA ACA *1989;* 3 Maitland Place, Shoeburyness, SOUTHEND-ON-SEA, SS3 8UF.
BLISS, Mr. John, FCA *1967;* 17 Rosslyn Crescent, LUTON, LU3 2AT.
BLISS, Mr. John Cecil, JP FCA *1951;* 3 Brick Kiln Cottage, Mount Road, OSWESTRY, SY10 7PJ. (Life Member)
BLISS, Dr. John Gerald, MSc BA FCA *1975;* 1817 Madden Avenue, SASKATOON S7H 3M7, SK, CANADA. (Life Member)
BLISS, Mr. Jonathan, FCA *1972;* Bramble Way, Clease Way, Compton Down, WINCHESTER, SO21 2AL. (Life Member)
BLISS, Miss. Julia Anne, BSc ACA *2011;* 7 Heatherways, Formby, LIVERPOOL, L37 7HL.
BLISS, Mrs. Karen, BA FCA *1992;* 108 Beech Walk, Standish, WIGAN, WN6 0YE.
BLISS, Mr. Nigel Graham, BSc ACA *1989;* 71 Devonshire Road, LONDON, W5 4TS.
BLISS, Mr. Richard John, FCA *1965;* Arboleda 6, Lomas Bellavista, 52994 ATIZAPAN, MEXICO. (Life Member)
•**BLITZ, Mr. Samuel, FCA** *1972;* SMB Total Accounting Limited, 14 Greenleafe Drive, ILFORD, ESSEX, IG6 1LL. See also Samuel Blitz & Company Limited
BLIZARD, Mr. Christopher John, MA ACA ATII *1983;* Coxfold, Cox Green, Rudgwick, HORSHAM, RH12 3DD.
BLOCH, Mr. Alan Geoffrey, FCA *1968;* 54 Fairgreen, BARNET, EN4 0QS. (Life Member)
BLOCK, Mr. Nicholas, BSc ACA *2005;* with Bishop Fleming, Chy Nyverow, Newham Road, TRURO, TR1 2DP.
•**BLOCK, Mr. Paul Robert, BA ACA** *1990;* Blocks, Roseworth, Roseworth Crescent, Gosforth, NEWCASTLE UPON TYNE, NE3 1NR.
BLOCKLEY, Mrs. Keeley Rae, BSc ACA AMCT *1997;* 5 Rectory Close Swinford, LUTTERWORTH, LEICESTERSHIRE, LE17 6BR.
BLOCKLEY, Miss. Pippa Helen, BA ACA *2010;* Pricewaterhousecoopers, 1 Embankment Place, LONDON, WC2N 6RH.
BLOCKSIDGE, Mr. Peter Anthony, MBA FCA *1969;* (Tax Fac), 63 Victoria Mansions, Navigation Way, Ashton-On-Ribble, PRESTON, PR2 2YY.
•**BLOFIELD, Mr. David Charles, BSc FCA** *1990;* Caerwyn Jones, Emstrey House, Shrewsbury Business Park, SHREWSBURY, SY2 6LG.
•**BLOGG, Mr. Ian David, BA ACA** *1986;* 20 Vinten Close, HERNE BAY, CT6 7TG.
BLOGG, Mr. Michael John, MA ACA FSI *1980;* 54 Westfields Avenue, LONDON, SW13 0AU.
•**BLOGGS, Mr. Christopher Andrew Jervis, FCA** *1974;* Northumberland House, 230 High Street, BROMLEY, BR1 1PQ.
BLOIS, Mr. Timothy Michael, BA FCA CF *1992;* 1 Pryors Orchard, Melbourn, ROYSTON, SG8 6UT.
BLOIS-BROOKE, Mr. Edward, ACA *2011;* 156a Columbia Road, LONDON, E2 7RG.
BLOKHUIS, Mr. Hendrik Jacob, ACA *2003;* 3 Hill Rise, RICKMANSWORTH, HERTFORDSHIRE, WD3 7NY.
BLOM, Mrs. Laura Muriel, BSc FCA DipPsych *1989;* The Clockcase, Christchurch Road, VIRGINIA WATER, GU25 4PX.
•**BLOMELEY, Mr. Peter Paul, FCA MBCS MCSI** *1973;* Peter P Blomeley FCA, 6 Christopher Acre, ROCHDALE, LANCASHIRE, OL11 5FE.
BLOMFIELD, Mr. Nick John, BSc ACA *2006;* 52 Marlborough Gardens, Hedge End, SOUTHAMPTON, SO30 2UT.
BLOMFIELD, Mr. Paul Richard, BA ACA *1999;* UCB, 208 Bath Road, SLOUGH, BERKSHIRE, SL1 3WE.
BLONDEL, Mr. David, BA ACA *1991;* 29 Canonbury Grove, LONDON, N1 2HR.
BLOODWORTH, Ms. Helen Lucy, BA ACA *2000;* with Baker Tilly Tax and Accounting Limited, Spring Park House, Basing View, BASINGSTOKE, HAMPSHIRE, RG21 4HG.
BLOODWORTH, Mrs. Julie Nicola, BA FCA *1999;* with Rawlinsons, Ruthlyn House, 90 Lincoln Road, PETERBOROUGH, PE1 2SP.
•**BLOOM, Mr. Alan Neale, FCA** *1970;* Steele Robertson Goddard, 28 Ely Place, LONDON, EC1N 6AA.
•①**BLOOM, Mr. Alan Robert, FCA** *1979;* Ernst & Young LLP, 1 More London Place, LONDON, SE1 2AF. See also Ernst & Young Europe LLP
BLOOM, Mr. Andrew Johnathan, BA ACA *2001;* 98 Millway, Mill Hill, LONDON, NW7 3JJ.
BLOOM, Mr. Charles Neil, ACA *1980;* 16 Mallards Road, Bursledon, SOUTHAMPTON, SO31 8EJ. (Life Member)
BLOOM, Mr. David Edward, BA FCA *1995;* 24 Greville Street, LONDON, EC1N 8SS.
BLOOM, Mr. Gordon Lionel, BA FCA *1950;* The Hamlet, Coggeshall Hamlet, Kelvedon Road Coggeshall, COLCHESTER, CO6 1RJ. (Life Member)
BLOOM, Mr. Nicholas Mark, BA FCA *1986;* 35 Carr Street, WAVERTON, NSW 2060, AUSTRALIA.
BLOOM, Mr. Nicholas Roy, ACA *1989;* 15F Hillcrest Villas, Hillcrest Road, SINGAPORE 286756, SINGAPORE.
BLOOM, Mr. Norman, FCA *1953;* 28204 Plantation Drive, ATLANTA, GA 30324, UNITED STATES. (Life Member)
BLOOM, Mr. Paul Alan, BA FCA *1994;* Flat 14, 9 Devonhurst Place, Heathfield Terrace, LONDON, W4 4JB.
•**BLOOM, Mr. Peter Graham, BA ACA** *1985;* BM Samuels Finance Group Plc, 314 Regents Park Road, Finchley, LONDON, N3 2JX.

•BLOOM, Mr. Peter John, MA FCA *1971;* 37 Felcote Avenue, Dalton, HUDDERSFIELD, HD5 8DR.
BLOOM, Mr. Robert Simon, BSc ACA *1991;* 62C Sackville Street, Grey Lynn, AUCKLAND 1021, NEW ZEALAND.
•BLOOMBERG, Mr. Joseph Morris, ACA *1982;* (Tax Fac), Joseph Morris & Co Ltd, Suite 109, Atlas Business Centre, Imex House, Oxgate Lane, LONDON NW2 7HJ.
BLOOMBERG, Mr. Spencer Adam, BSc ACA *1995;* 1 Little Potters, Bushey Heath, BUSHEY, WD23 4QT.
BLOOMER, Mr. Harry Raymond, FCA *1949;* Kingsgate, 15 Richard Pl, Brookhouse, WALSALL, WS5 3QP. (Life Member)
BLOOMER, Mr. James William Jonathan, BSc ACA *2010;* 13 Fleming House, St. Georges Grove, LONDON, SW17 0BF.
BLOOMER, Mr. Jonathan William, BSc FCA *1977;* Cerberus, 84 Grosvenor Street, LONDON, W1K 3JZ.
BLOOMER, Mrs. Lynda Jane, BA ACA *1993;* (Tax Fac), 8 Meadowcourt Road, LEICESTER, LE2 2PB.
BLOOMER, Mr. Mark Duncan, BSc ACA *1992;* 8 Meadowcourt Road, LEICESTER, LE2 2PB.
BLOOMER, Miss. Rachel Anne, BSc ACA *2007;* Sunnyside Broad Street, KINGSWINFORD, WEST MIDLANDS, DY6 9LR.
•BLOOMER, Mr. Roger Charles, FCA *1981;* (Tax Fac), AccounTax Services (Swindon) Limited, 2 Charnwood Court, Newport Street, SWINDON, SN1 3DX.
BLOOMER, Mr. Stephen, BSc ACA ATII *1990;* Tresgyrch Farm, Rhyd-Y-Fro, Pontardawe, SWANSEA, SA8 4RU.
BLOOMFIELD, Mr. Alan Malcolm, FCA MBA *1971;* Flat 34 Northpoint, Sherman Road, BROMLEY, BR1 3JN.
BLOOMFIELD, Mr. Andrew John, BA FCA *1977;* Thistle, Heath Ride, Finchampstead, WOKINGHAM, RG40 3QE.
BLOOMFIELD, Mr. Andrew Thomas, BSc ACA *2004;* 26 Chalk Hill Road, NORWICH, NR1 1SL.
BLOOMFIELD, Mr. Aston Samuel, FCA *1957;* 517 Lake Forest Drive, COPPELL, TX 75019, UNITED STATES. (Life Member)
BLOOMFIELD, Mr. Darren, BA ACA *1995;* with PricewaterhouseCoopers LLP, Donington Court, Pegasus Business Park, Castle Donington, DERBY, DE74 2UZ.
BLOOMFIELD, Mrs. Gaye, BSc ACA *1998;* 2 Ridgeway Farm Cottages, Peel Road, BLACKPOOL, FY4 5LN.
BLOOMFIELD, Mr. Ian Andrew, BA ACA *1988;* 8 Emsworth Drive, Brooklands, SALE, M33 3PR.
BLOOMFIELD, Mr. James Peter, MMath ACA CTA *2005;* 1b Bentcliffe Mount, LEEDS, LS17 6QW.
•BLOOMFIELD, Mr. Jonathan Charles, FCA *1975;* (Tax Fac), Bloomfield Business Services Limited, 9 Queen Street, GREAT YARMOUTH, NORFOLK, NR30 2QP.
BLOOMFIELD, Mrs. Karen Margaret, MSc FCA *1992;* with KPMG LLP, 15 Canada Square, LONDON, E14 5GL.
BLOOMFIELD, Mr. Mark Andrew, BSc ACA *2002;* 9 Southvale Road, LONDON, SE3 0TP.
BLOOMFIELD, Mr. Mark Christopher Bowen, BA ACA *1987;* 37 Hotham Road, LONDON, SW15 1QL.
BLOOMFIELD, Mr. Peter Randolph, FCA *1968;* 17 Wellesley Drive, Wellington Park, CROWTHORNE, BERKSHIRE, RG45 6AL.
•BLOOMFIELD, Mr. Philip, BA ACA *1989;* PricewaterhouseCoopers LLP, 1 Embankment Place, LONDON, WC2N 6RH. See also PricewaterhouseCoopers
BLOOMFIELD, Mr. Richard Jeffery, FCA *1982;* 6 Highfield Gardens, off Boley Cottage Lane, LICHFIELD, WS14 9JA.
BLOOMFIELD, Mr. Robert, BSc ACA *2002;* 375 Haslingden Old Road, Rawtenstall, ROSSENDALE, BB4 8RR.
BLOOMFIELD, Mr. Simon Crispin, ACA *1982;* 93 Kenilworth Avenue, LONDON, SW19 7LP.
BLOOMFIELD, Mr. Timothy John, MA ACA *1987;* C Aiano & Sons Ltd, 64-70 Chrisp Street, Poplar, LONDON, E14 6LR.
BLOOR, Mr. Charles Richard, BA ACA *1996;* Shoe Zone Haramead Business Centre, Humberstone Road, LEICESTER, LE1 2LH.
BLOOR, Mr. Christopher Charles, FCA *1975;* 8 Kingsoe Leys, Middleton, MILTON KEYNES, BUCKINGHAMSHIRE, MK10 9BG.
BLOOR, Mr. Graham Ernest, MPhil FCA *1992;* 12 Janes Meadow, Tarleton, PRESTON, PR4 6ND.
BLOOR, Mr. John Charles Anthony Rawson, FCA *1953;* 3 The Cobs, Woodbury Lane, TENTERDEN, TN30 6JH. (Life Member)
BLOOR, Mr. John Derek, FCA *1958;* 17 Dorchester Court, Brooklands Road, SALE, CHESHIRE, M33 3GJ. (Life Member)
BLOORE, Mr. John Richard, FCA *1973;* Alex Lawrie Factors Ltd, 1 Brookhill Way, BANBURY, OX16 3EL.
BLOTT, Mrs. Janet Diane, ACA *1969;* Howe, St. Fergus, PETERHEAD, AB42 3HH.
BLOTT, Mr. Peter James, BA ACA *1988;* 27086 Ironwood Drive, LAGUNA HILLS, CA 92653, UNITED STATES.
BLOUNT, Mr. Edward James, BA ACA *2010;* 9 Poplars Way, MANSFIELD, NOTTINGHAMSHIRE, NG18 4UX.
•BLOW, Mr. Denis Stephen, FCA *1960;* Blow Abbott Ltd, 36 High Street, CLEETHORPES, SOUTH HUMBERSIDE, DN35 8JN.
BLOW, Miss. Katharine Anne Helen, BSc ACA *2003;* 67 Green Street, SUNBURY-ON-THAMES, TW16 6RD.
BLOW, Mr. Michael Roy, FCA *1962;* 120 Langley Road, WATFORD, WD17 4RR.
BLOW, Mr. Stephen Paul, BA ACA *1996;* Centrica Plc, Millstream, Maidenhead Road, WINDSOR, BERKSHIRE, SL4 5GD.
BLOWER, Mr. Charles Peter, FCA *1975;* 20 Sandfield Lane, Hartford, NORTHWICH, CW8 1PU.
BLOWER, Mr. Graham Victor, FCA *1974;* Church Cottage, Harbridge, RINGWOOD, BH24 3PS.
BLOWER, Mrs. Joanne Lyn, MSc(Econ) ACA *2001;* 9 Hogarth Close, LONDON, W5 2JT.
BLOWER, Mrs. Mary Ellen, BSc ACA *2000;* 11 Warbeck Road, LONDON, W12 8NS.
•BLOWER, Mr. Nicholas Ralph Neilson, BCom FCA *1992;* PricewaterhouseCoopers KFT, Wesselenyi u 16, BUDAPEST, H-1077, HUNGARY.
BLOWER, Mr. Robert Gordon, BSc ACA *1985;* 26 Legh Road, Prestbury, MACCLESFIELD, CHESHIRE, SK10 4HX.
BLOWER, Miss. Susan, BA ACA *1999;* with BDO LLP, 55 Baker Street, LONDON, W1U 7EU.
BLOWERS, Mrs. Sarah Kate, BSc ACA *2004;* Landis & Gyr Ltd, 1 Lysander Drive, Northfields Industrial Estate, Market Deeping, PETERBOROUGH, PE6 8FB.
BLOWFIELD, Mr. Glenn Richard, BA ACA *2001;* 1 East View, Summerhouse, DARLINGTON, COUNTY DURHAM, DL2 3UD.
BLOWS, Mr. John Alexander, BSc(Hons) ACA *2002;* 48 Leigh Road, COBHAM, KT11 2LD.
BLOWS, Mr. Jonathan Darcy Blything, BA ACA *1991;* Old Cider Mill Castle Street, Winchcombe, CHELTENHAM, GL54 5JA.
•BLOWS, Mr. Philip Clive, BA FCA *1975;* Hansard Trust Co Ltd, Granary House, The Grange, St Peter Port, GUERNSEY, GY1 2QG.
BLOXHAM, Miss. Carina Louise, BSc(Hons) ACA *2010;* 29 Royal Close, BASINGSTOKE, HAMPSHIRE, RG22 4XE.
BLOXSIDGE, Mrs. Nicola Dawn, ACA *1999;* Michaelmas Lodge, 73 Lakewood Road, Chandler's Ford, EASTLEIGH, SO53 5AD.
BLOXSOME, Mr. John Richard, MA FCA *1976;* Home Farm, Fennes Road, BRAINTREE, ESSEX, CM7 5PJ.
BLOXWICH, Mr. Rupert Benjamin, ACA *2009;* 88 Knavesmire Crescent, YORK, YO23 1EU.
•BLOY, Mr. Andrew Richard, BSc(Hons) ACA *2002;* Hornbeam Accountancy Services Ltd, Hornbeam House, Bidwell Road, Rackheath, NORWICH, NR13 6PT.
•BLOY, Mrs. Susan Anne, BSc FCA *1992;* (Tax Fac), Lakes Accountancy Limited, 11 Church Street, WINDERMERE, CUMBRIA, LA23 1AQ. See also Lakes Accountancy
BLOYE, Mrs. Amanda Julie, BSc ACA *1989;* 41 Gregories Drive, Wavendon Gate, MILTON KEYNES, MK7 7RN.
BLOYE, Mr. Ronald Brian, FCA *1959;* 4 Lion Court, Haddenham, ELY, CB6 3XL. (Life Member)
BLUCK, Mr. Steven Francis, BA FCA *1987;* 63 Longley Lane, Northenden, MANCHESTER, M22 4JD.
•BLUEITT, Mr. Anthony, BA ACA *1989;* (Tax Fac), 37 Roundhaven, DURHAM, DH1 3TX.
BLUES, Mr. Ernest Thomson, BA FCA *1986;* PO Box N-713, One Silver Palm Lane, NASSAU, N-713, BAHAMAS.
•BLUESTONE, Mr. Steven David, BA FCA DChA *1989;* 52 St. Edmunds Drive, STANMORE, MIDDLESEX, HA7 2AU.
BLUETT, Mr. Timothy Mark, BSc FCA *1989;* TELECOM NEW ZEALAND, PRIVATE BAG 92028, AUCKLAND, NEW ZEALAND.
BLUFF, Mrs. Alison Mary, ACA *1991;* Linden House, Church Walk, Bruntingthorpe, LUTTERWORTH, LEICESTERSHIRE, LE17 5QH.
•BLUFF, Mrs. Karen Lesley, BSc ACA *1983;* with PricewaterhouseCoopers LLP, 101 Barbirolli Square, Lower Mosley Street, MANCHESTER, M2 3PW.
BLUFF, Miss. Zoey, ACA *2011;* Flat 2, 50 Atherley Road, SOUTHAMPTON, SO15 5DS.
•BLUH, Mr. Roderick, FCA *1981;* Banks Limited, 14 Devizes Road, Old Town, SWINDON, SN1 4BH.
BLUM, Mr. Simon, ACA *2004;* 56 Princes Park Avenue, LONDON, NW11 0JT.
BLUM, Mr. Simon Jeffrey, LLB ACA *1991;* 4 Willow Way, RADLETT, WD7 8DX.
BLUMENTHAL, Mr. Harry, BA ACA *1991;* Dancastle Ltd 1 Dancastle Court, 14 Arcadia Avenue, LONDON, N3 2JU.
BLUMER, Mr. Charles Robert Colville, FCA *1957;* 1 Beadon Road, SALCOMBE, DEVON, TQ8 8LX. (Life Member)
BLUMSOM, John David, Esq OBE TD FCA *1959;* 25 Shrublands Rd., BERKHAMSTED, HP4 3HX. (Life Member)
BLUNDELL, Ms. Amy, ACA *2011;* Oaks End, Exeter Road, HONITON, DEVON, EX14 1AT.
BLUNDELL, Mr. Andrew Arthur Gordon, MA ACA *1989;* Fernside House, Bobbin Mill Hill, Fritchley, BELPER, DE56 2HN.
BLUNDELL, Mr. Andrew Colin, BSc ACA *2000;* 101 Broad Street, BROMSGROVE, WORCESTERSHIRE, B61 8LR.
BLUNDELL, Miss. Caroline Anne, BSc ACA *2010;* 10 Waterside, BOOTLE, MERSEYSIDE, L30 0RA.
BLUNDELL, Mrs. Catherine, MSci ACA *2006;* (Tax Fac), with PKF (UK) LLP, 5 Temple Square, Temple Street, LIVERPOOL, L2 5RH.
•BLUNDELL, Mrs. Helen Janet, LLB FCA FCIE DChA *1997;* with Bloomer Heaven Limited, Rutland House, 148 Edmund Street, BIRMINGHAM, B3 2FD.
BLUNDELL, Mr. Mark David Giles, BSc ACA *1987;* Wood Top Farm, Creskeld Lane, Bramhope, LEEDS, LS16 9ER.
BLUNDELL, Mr. Mark Stuart, MSc ACA *1987;* Bearscombe, Ballinger Road, South Heath, GREAT MISSENDEN, BUCKINGHAMSHIRE, HP16 9QH.
•BLUNDELL, Mr. Michael Kevin, FCA *1980;* M.K. Blundell & Co., 15 Carlton Croft, Sandal, WAKEFIELD, WEST YORKSHIRE, WF2 6DA.
BLUNDELL, Mr. Nicholas Christopher John, LLB ACA *2002;* 69 Waresley Park Hartlebury, KIDDERMINSTER, WORCESTERSHIRE, DY11 7XF.
BLUNDELL, Mr. Peter Derrick Howard, FCA *1956;* Mallard House, 9 The Moorings, Woodford, KETTERING, NN14 4HN. (Life Member)
BLUNDELL, Mr. Phillip Edward Frank, BA ACA *2010;* 138 Salcott Road, LONDON, SW11 6DG.
BLUNDELL, Mr. Phillip Robert, BSc ACA *1988;* 121 Cambridge Road, TEDDINGTON, TW11 8DF.
BLUNDELL, Mr. Richard Charles, BSc ACA *1992;* Seefeldstrasse 168, 8008 ZURICH, SWITZERLAND.
•BLUNDELL, Mr. Robert Andrew, BSc FCA *2000;* Creaseys LLP, 12 Lonsdale Gardens, TUNBRIDGE WELLS, KENT, TN1 1PA.
BLUNDELL, Mr. Roger Frederick Crawford, BSc ACA *1989;* 61 Vineyard Hill Road, LONDON, SW19 7JL.
BLUNDELL, Mrs. Rosemary, MA ACA CTA *1990;* (Tax Fac), Mazars, Cartwright House, Tottle Road, NOTTINGHAM, NG2 1RT.
BLUNDELL, Mrs. Sarah Rachel, BA(Hons) ACA *2002;* 11 Hillside, Tarleton, PRESTON, PR4 6DW.
BLUNDELL, Mr. Stephen James, BA ACA *1996;* 21 Darby Vale, Warfield, BRACKNELL, RG42 2PH.
BLUNDELL, Mrs. Suzanne Marie, BSc ACA *2003;* 69 Waresley Park, Hartlebury, KIDDERMINSTER, WORCESTERSHIRE, DY11 7XF.
BLUNDEN, Mr. Dean Anthony, ACA *2007;* 145 Paramount, Beckhampton Street, SWINDON, SN1 2SJ.
BLUNDEN, Mr. Lee David, LLB FCA *1995;* (Member of Council 2005 - 2009), 9 The Laurels, FERNDOWN, BH22 9TB.
BLUNDEN, Mrs. Lynne Marie, BSc ACA *1998;* 8 South View Place, Blowhorn Street, MARLBOROUGH, SN8 1DD.
BLUNDEN, Mr. Paul James, MEng ACA *2004;* 25 Randalls Road, LEATHERHEAD, KT22 7TQ.
BLUNDEN, Mr. Paul John, BSc ACA *1999;* 15a West Close, VERWOOD, DORSET, BH31 6PS.
BLUNDEN, Mr. Richard John, BSc ACA *2006;* 5 Johnson Way, Chilwell Beeston, NOTTINGHAM, NG9 6RJ.
BLUNDEN, Mr. Terence John, FCA *1974;* Flow Control Co Ltd, 4a Cooper Drive Springwood Industrial Estate, BRAINTREE, CM7 2RF.
BLUNDY, Mr. Darren William, BA ACA *1999;* 85, Newman Street, LONDON, W1T 3EX.
BLUNN, Mrs. Anne Elizabeth, BSc ACA *1990;* Becatech Ltd, Becatech House, Sharpham Road, CHEDDAR, SOMERSET, BS27 3DR.
BLUNN, Mr. David Howard, BSc FCA *1975;* Sterling Industries Plc, DL Group Building, George Smith Way, YEOVIL, SOMERSET, BA22 8QR.
BLUNSTONE, Mr. Lee John, BA(Hons) ACA *2003;* 12 Chapman Court, BARNOLDSWICK, LANCASHIRE, BB18 5EE.
BLUNT, Mr. Brian Frederick, FCA *1966;* 64 St. Lawrence Avenue, WORTHING, BN14 7JG.
BLUNT, Mrs. Claire Jacqueline, BEng ACA *1997;* Staples, Westfields, London Road, HIGH WYCOMBE, BUCKINGHAMSHIRE, HP11 1HA.
BLUNT, Mr. Philip Richard, FCA *1961;* 133 Lower Blandford Road, BROADSTONE, BH18 8NT. (Life Member)
BLURTON, Mr. Andrew Francis, FCA *1976;* Old Cedar House, Guildford Road, CRANLEIGH, SURREY, GU6 8LT.
BLY, Mr. Roger Anthony, FCA *1972;* 252 Cator Lane North, Beeston, NOTTINGHAM, NG9 4BP.
BLYDE, Miss. Zoe, ACA *2009;* B, 210 Stewarts Road, LONDON, SW8 4UB.
•BLYTH, Mr. Christopher John Julian, FCA *1963;* Blyth & Co, Sental House, 66 Waldeck Road, Strand-on-the-Green, LONDON, W4 3NU.
•BLYTH, Mr. Crispin Richard, BSc FCA *1987;* (Tax Fac), Blyth & Co Corporate Services Ltd, Church View Cottage, Fordon Road, Burton Fleming, DRIFFIELD, YO25 3PS.
BLYTH, Mrs. Cristina, BSocSc ACA *2002;* 140 Pineapple Road, BIRMINGHAM, B30 2TX.
BLYTH, Mr. David, FCA *1968;* 48 Sunny Road, Churchtown, SOUTHPORT, MERSEYSIDE, PR9 7LX. (Life Member)
BLYTH, Mrs. Katharine Elizabeth Tara, BA ACA *2002;* 34 Chatto Road, Battersea, LONDON, SW11 6LL.
BLYTH, Mrs. Lucy Caroline, BA ACA *1992;* 75 Culverden Down, TUNBRIDGE WELLS, KENT, TN4 9SL.
BLYTH, Mr. Paul Barnabas, BA ACA *1997;* 4 Nansen Road, LONDON, SW11 5NT.
BLYTH, Mr. Robert, BA ACA *1998;* Deloitte & Touche, 2 New Street Square, LONDON, EC4A 3BZ.
BLYTH, Mr. Robert Graham Charles, MA DPhil FCA *1985;* 10 Colegrove Down, OXFORD, OX2 9HT.
BLYTH, Mr. Stephen Michael, BA FCA *1973;* Browns Lodge, 6 Church End, Roade, NORTHAMPTON, NN7 2NP.
BLYTH, Mr. Stephen William, ACA *1980;* Block 22, Apt 101, Portomaso, ST JULIANS, MALTA.
BLYTH, Mr. Steven Arthur, BA FCA *1977;* 50 Marriotts Close, Felmersham, BEDFORD, MK43 7HD.
•BLYTH, Mr. William Charles, BA FCA *1973;* 11 Nightingale Drive, TOWCESTER, NORTHAMPTONSHIRE, NN12 6RA.
BLYTHE, Mr. Alastair Neil, MSc ACA *2003;* Johnson Matthey Plc, Orchard Road, ROYSTON, HERTFORDSHIRE, SG8 5HE.
•BLYTHE, Mr. David William, BSc FCA *1989;* DWB Limited, 41 Oldfields Road, SUTTON, SURREY, SM1 2NB. See also Blythe & Co
BLYTHE, Mrs. Deirdre Frances, BSc FCA *1988;* 45 Fitzgerald Street, SOUTH YARRA, VIC 3141, AUSTRALIA.
BLYTHE, Mr. Dominic James, BSc FCA *2000;* The Acorns, Slaugham, HAYWARDS HEATH, WEST SUSSEX, RH17 6AL.
BLYTHE, Mr. Edwin Charles, BSc ACA *1996;* Quark Expeditions, 49 Jackes Ave First Floor, TORONTO M4T 1E2, ON, CANADA.
BLYTHE, Mrs. Elizabeth Anne, BSc ACA *1992;* Skipton Bldg Soc, The Bailey, SKIPTON, NORTH YORKSHIRE, BD23 1DN.
•BLYTHE, Mr. Jonathan David, BSc FCA *1982;* (Tax Fac), Blythe Financial Ltd, 206 Upper Richmond Road West, East Sheen, LONDON, SW14 8AH. See also Blythe & Co
BLYTHE, Mr. Paul James, MA(Hons) ACA CF *2001;* with Mazars LLP, Tower Bridge House, St. Katharines Way, LONDON, E1W 1DD.
•BLYTHE, Mr. Philip Patrick, MA FCA *1989;* PricewaterhoseCoopers Co Ltd, Sumitomo Fudosan Shiodome Hamarikyu Bldg 19F, 8-21-1 Ginza Chuo-ku, TOKYO, 104-0061 JAPAN.
BLYTHE, Mr. Richard Christopher Kenneth, FCA *1981;* 21 Wren Close, Badger Farm, WINCHESTER, SO22 4HX.
BLYTHE, Miss. Stephanie June, BA FCA FCIPD *1976;* 2 Willow Clough, Oldham Road, Ripponden, SOWERBY BRIDGE, WEST YORKSHIRE, HX6 4SA.
•BLYTHE-BARTRAM, Mrs. Katharine, ACA *1997;* KP Accounting Limited, 25 Broad View, Thorpe End, NORWICH, NR13 5DZ.
•BLYTHE-BARTRAM, Mr. Philip Jeremy, ACA FCCA *2008;* Lovewell Blake LLP, 102 Prince of Wales Road, NORWICH, NORFOLK, NR1 1NY.
BLYTHE-BROOK, Mrs. Carolyn Elizabeth, BA FCA *1985;* 5 Melbourne Close, ORPINGTON, BR6 0BJ.
BLYTHE-BROOK, Mr. Graeme Howard, FCA *1981;* EA Gibson Shipbrokers Ltd, Audrey House, 16-20 Ely Place, LONDON, EC1P 1HP.

BLYTHIN, Miss. Elizabeth Ann, ACA *2008;* 38 St. Lukes Court, HATFIELD, HERTFORDSHIRE, AL10 0FD.

BLYTHIN, Mr. Simon Roger, ACA *2008;* 16 Greyfort Crescent, SOLIHULL, B92 8DW.

BLYTON, Mrs. Charlotte June, BA ACA *1997;* with PricewaterhouseCoopers LLP, 1 Embankment Place, LONDON, WC2N 6RH.

BOA, Mr. William Andrew, BA ACA *1992;* The Saddlers, High Street, Yetminster, SHERBORNE, DT9 6LF.

•BOADLE, Mr. Jeremy Tristan, FCA *1980;* Smith & Williamson Trust Corporation Ltd, 25 Moorgate, LONDON, EC2R 6AY. See also Smith & Williamson Ltd

•BOADLE, Mr. Simon Hunter, ACA *1983;* PricewaterhouseCoopers LLP, 7 More London Riverside, LONDON, SE1 2RT. See also PricewaterhouseCoopers

BOAG, Mr. Andrew Steven, ACA *2010;* Flat C, 23 Hornsey Lane Gardens, LONDON, N6 5NX.

BOAG, Mr. Steven George, MA FCA *1978;* 38 Stevenage Road, KNEBWORTH, HERTFORDSHIRE, SG3 6NN.

•BOAGE, Mr. Ian Neal, ACA *1985;* (Tax Fac), with Ian Boage & Co, Rookery Barn, Yew Tree Farm, Low Ham, LANGPORT, SOMERSET TA10 9DW.

•BOAGEY, Mr. Graeme Richard, BA FCA CTA *1987;* Chipchase Manners, 384 Linthorpe Road, MIDDLESBROUGH, TS5 6HA. See also Chipchase, Manners & Co

BOAK, Mr. Stephen John, HND FCA AMCT BEng(Hons) *1994;* 49 Irwell Close, OAKHAM, LEICESTERSHIRE, LE15 6SX.

BOAK, Mr. Stephen Noel, FCA *1968;* The Old Barn House, Settrington Road, Norton, MALTON, YO17 9PJ.

BOAKES, Miss. Carla, ACA *2008;* Flat 15, Ashley Court, Ashley Road, EPSOM, SURREY, KT18 5AJ.

BOAKES, Mr. Simon Alexander, BSc ACA *1993;* 9 Bushetts Grove, Merstham, REDHILL, RH1 3DX.

BOALER, Mrs. Lucie Margaret, BA ACA *2006;* 25 Lodge Hill Lane, Chattenden, ROCHESTER, KENT, ME3 8PN.

BOALER, Mr. Martin John, BSc ACA *1990;* The Croft, 104 High Street, Great Cheverell, DEVIZES, SN10 5XR.

BOAM, Mr. Michael, BSc ACA *1998;* Flat 35 Capstan Court, 24 Wapping Wall, LONDON, E1W 3SE.

BOAMAH, Miss. Amma, ACA *2008;* Flat 2, 125 Elderfield Road, LONDON, E5 0AY.

BOAMPONG, Mr. Samuel Apeagyei, FCA *1964;* PO Box 510935, KUMASI, GHANA. (Life Member)

BOANAS, Mrs. Helen Annabelle, BSc ACA *2008;* 59 Northen Grove, West Didsbury, MANCHESTER, M20 2NN.

BOAR, Mr. Graham, BA ACA *2007;* (Tax Fac), with WKH, PO Box 501, The Nexus Building, Broadway, LETCHWORTH GARDEN CITY, HERTFORDSHIRE SG6 9BL.

BOARD, Mr. Andrew Charles, BSc ACA *2006;* 3 Elderberry Way, Almondsbury, BRISTOL, BS32 4FH.

•BOARD, Mrs. Rebecca Anne, ACA *2006;* Simply Accounting, 39 Barnfield, CREDITON, DEVON, EX17 3HS.

BOARD, Mrs. Sarah, BSc ACA *2007;* 3 Elderberry Way, Almondsbury, BRISTOL, BS32 4FH.

BOARDALL, Mr. Keith, FCA *1957;* The Old Parsonage, Baldersby St.James, THIRSK, YO7 4PT.

BOARDALL, Mr. Marcus Keith, BSc ACA *1987;* Reed Boardall Group, Cod Beck Mill Industrial Estate, Dalton Lane, Dalton, THIRSK, NORTH YORKSHIRE YO7 3HR.

BOARDMAN, Mr. Allan Neville, ACA CA(SA) *2011;* House 3, Hailey Hall School, Hailey Lane, HERTFORD, SG13 7PB.

BOARDMAN, Mr. Andrew James, BA ACA *1995;* 6 The Cressinghams, EPSOM, KT18 5DJ.

BOARDMAN, Mr. Andrew Thomas, BSc ACA *1995;* 49 Westbourne Road, SOUTHPORT, MERSEYSIDE, PR8 2HY.

BOARDMAN, Mr. Andrew Timothy, ACA *1981;* Dearie Contracting Inc., 128 Hedgedale Rd, BRAMPTON L6T 5L2, ON, CANADA.

BOARDMAN, Mrs. Belinda Rhian, BA ACA *1991;* Littlewoods Shop Direct Home Shopping Ltd Skyways House, Speke Road Speke, LIVERPOOL, L70 1AB.

BOARDMAN, Miss. Clare, BSc ACA *2002;* 22 Cringle Drive, CHEADLE, CHESHIRE, SK8 1JJ.

BOARDMAN, Mr. Dennis Charles, BSc FCA *1956;* Hillside, Crathes, BANCHORY, AB31 5JH. (Life Member)

BOARDMAN, Mr. Francis Michael, MA ACA *1992;* 54 Madrid Road, LONDON, SW13 9PG.

BOARDMAN, Miss. Gemma Melisssa, BSc ACA *2008;* 144 Crow Green Road, BRENTWOOD, Essex, CM15 9RP.

•BOARDMAN, Mr. Geoffrey Alan, BA FCA *1973;* Lakeside, 36 Reynards Road, WELWYN, AL6 9TP.

BOARDMAN, Mrs. Heidi Eleanor, BSc ACA *1990;* Wings School, Whassett, MILNTHORPE, CUMBRIA, LA7 7DN.

•BOARDMAN, Mrs. Jane Alexandra, BSc ACA *2000;* Deloitte LLP, PO Box 500, 2 Hardman Street, MANCHESTER, M60 2AT. See also Deloitte & Touche LLP

BOARDMAN, Mrs. Janice Anne, ACA CA(SA) *2010;* 5 Pineneedle Lane, SEVENOAKS, KENT, TN13 3JY.

BOARDMAN, Mrs. Joanne Pauline, BSc ACA *1993;* 49 Westbourne Road, SOUTHPORT, MERSEYSIDE, PR8 2HY.

•BOARDMAN, Mr. Mark, ACA *1995;* Accountancy Summit Limited, Riverbank, Laskey Farm, Laskey Lane, Thelwall, WARRINGTON WA4 2TF.

BOARDMAN, Mr. Neil, BSc(Hons) ACA *2002;* Ashdawn Barn Breach House Lane, Mobberley, KNUTSFORD, CHESHIRE, WA16 7NT.

BOARDMAN, Miss. Nicola, BSc(Hons) ACA *2003;* Turner Broadcasting System Europe Ltd, 16 Great Marlborough Street, LONDON, W1F 7HS.

BOARDMAN, Mr. Peter John, FCA *1962;* Holly Cottage, 2 Spring Court Spring Hill, Bubbenhall, COVENTRY, CV8 3BD.

BOARDMAN, Mr. Philip Edward, BA FCA *1980;* Centurion House, 129 Deansgate, MANCHESTER, M3 3WR.

BOARDMAN, Mr. Richard, BA ACA *1988;* 69b Northlands Road, SOUTHAMPTON, SO15 2LP.

BOARDMAN, Mr. Robert Philip, BA ACA *1998;* Luccombe, Ockham Road South, East Horsley, LEATHERHEAD, SURREY, KT24 6SL.

BOARDMAN, Mrs. Sally Elisabeth, ACA *1995;* Stephenson Smart & Co, 22-26 King Street, KING'S LYNN, NORFOLK, PE30 1HJ.

BOARDMAN, Mrs. Sharon Marie, BSc ACA *1996;* 2 Naburn Drive, Orrell, WIGAN, LANCASHIRE, WN5 8SB.

•BOARDMAN, Mrs. Sheila, MA FCA *1989;* Paterson Boyd & Co Limited, 18 North Street, GLENROTHES, KY7 5NA.

•BOARDMAN, Mrs. Susan, FCA *1975;* Boardman & Co, Lakeside, 36 Reynards Road, WELWYN, AL6 9TP.

BOARDMAN, Mr. Thomas Aldridge Wilson, BA ACA *2004;* 63 Tennyson Street, LONDON, SW8 3SU.

BOARDMAN-WESTON, Mrs. Pamela Susan, MA ACA CTA *1982;* Lakeview, 26 Measham Road, ASHBY-DE-LA-ZOUCH, LE65 2PF.

•BOARDWELL, Mr. David Neil, BA FCA *1977;* Boardwell & Company, Oakdene, Barrowford Road, BURNLEY, BB12 9AT.

BOARER, Miss. Carole Dawn, BPharm ACA *1994;* St. Jude, Ravenscroft Close, Ash, ALDERSHOT, HAMPSHIRE, GU12 6BW.

BOAST, Mr. Christopher John, BSc FCA *1991;* 41 St. Lawrence Road, GLOUCESTER, GL4 3QS.

BOAST, Mr. Clive Richard, FCA *1970;* Lorne House, 22 The Croft, Sutton Park Road, KIDDERMINSTER, DY11 6LX.

BOATENG, Miss. Leona Asaah, BA ACA CTA *1982;* (Tax Fac), Asamani Villa, Avenue Road, Bray, MAIDENHEAD, SL6 1UG.

•BOATFIELD, Miss. Joanna Laura, ACA *2010;* Dixon Wilson, 22 Chancery Lane, LONDON, WC2A 1LS.

BOATFIELD BELL, Mr. Christopher David, BSc ACA *1998;* 11c St. Johns Park, LONDON, SE3 7TD.

BOATH, Mr. Douglas William, BSc FCA *1958;* 7 Encombe Road, WAREHAM, DORSET, BH20 4PS. (Life Member)

BOATMAN, Miss. Helen Juliet, BA ACA *1996;* Flat 4 Caversham Lodge, Grove Avenue, LONDON, N10 2AJ.

BOATMAN, Mr. Timothy Geoffrey, FCA *1965;* The Lodge, Mildenhall Road, Worlington, BURY ST.EDMUNDS, IP28 8RX.

BOBATH, Mr. Anthony John, BA ACA *1991;* 25 Northumberland Road, LEAMINGTON SPA, CV32 6HE.

BOBBETT, Mr. Michael Jonathan, BSc ACA *2006;* Graelyn, 16 Risca Road, Rogerstone, NEWPORT, GWENT, NP10 9FZ.

BOBBIN, Mrs. Jane, BSc(Hons) ACA *2002;* 126 Bradenham Beeches, Walters Ash, HIGH WYCOMBE, BUCKINGHAMSHIRE, HP14 4XN.

BOBER, Miss. Lynnette Joy Christina Margaret Therese, MA ACA CTA TEP *2000;* (Tax Fac), 14 Goodey Road, BARKING, IG11 9PB.

BOBKER, Dr. David Siegfried, MA DPhil ACA FRM *1987;* A23A-6 Hampshire Residences, 2A Persiaran Hampshire, 50450 KL, KUALA LUMPUR, FEDERAL TERRITORY, MALAYSIA.

BOBROFF, Mr. Philippe Edward, FCA *1977;* 6 St. Marys Avenue, NORTHWOOD, MIDDLESEX, HA6 3AZ.

•BOBY, Mr. Alan Richard, BA FCA *1981;* (Tax Fac), Ellacotts LLP, Countrywide House, 23 West Bar Street, BANBURY, OXFORDSHIRE, OX16 9SA.

BOCALANDRO, Ms. Paula Maria, BSc ACA *1996;* Oakhill Farm House, Roundhay Park Lane, LEEDS, LS17 8AR.

BOCK, Mr. Lionel Leslie, FCA *1965;* 36 Grove Park, Wanstead, LONDON, E11 2DL.

BOCRESION HAILE, Mr. Suhul, BSc ACA *1998;* 48 Brodrick Road, LONDON, SW17 7DY.

BOCSKEI, Miss. Selina Jane, ACA *2008;* 11 Lees Bank Road, Cross Roads, KEIGHLEY, BD22 9EN.

BODALIA, Mr. Rakesh, BSc ACA *2003;* 213 White Road, Quinton, BIRMINGHAM, B32 2SZ.

BODDEN, Mr. Alexander Stephen, ACA *1991;* McGladrey & Pullen Cayman, PO Box 10311, GEORGE TOWN, GRAND CAYMAN, KY1-1003, CAYMAN ISLANDS.

BODDICE, Mr. Benjamin James, BA ACA *2001;* P Z Cussons (UK) Ltd, 3500 Aviator Way, MANCHESTER, M22 5TG.

BODDIE, Mr. Paul Nicholas, BSc ACA *2005;* 23 Hobb Lane, Hedge End, SOUTHAMPTON, SO30 0GG.

BODDIE, Mr. Richard Leigh, FCA *1969;* 26 Pensford Avenue, RICHMOND, SURREY, TW9 4HP.

BODDIE, Mr. Simon, BA ACA *1986;* Flint Cottage, Park Corner, Nettlebed, HENLEY-ON-THAMES, RG9 6DR.

•BODDINGTON, Mr. Christopher Elliot, BEng FCA *1994;* Suite 2104 21st Floor Tower B, Ping An International Finance Centre, 1-3 Xinyuan Lu, Chaoyang District, BEIJING 100027, CHINA.

BODDINGTON, Mrs. Valerie June, JP FCA *1966;* 9 Owston, Lower Earley, READING, RG6 3DX.

•BODDIS, Mr. Peter, FCA *1973;* Thompson Jones LLP, 2 Heap Bridge, BURY, LANCASHIRE, BL9 7HR. See also Thompson Jones Business Solutions Limited

•BODDY, Mr. Alan David, FCA *1987;* Alan Boddy & Co, Damer House, Meadoway, WICKFORD, SS12 9HA.

BODDY, Mr. David Julian, MSc FCA *1987;* Aldridge House, 23 Ilkley Road, Caversham Heights, READING, RG4 7BD.

BODDY, Mrs. Emma Catherine, BSc(Hons) ACA *2003;* PO Box 5604, Wellesley Street, AUCKLAND 1141, NEW ZEALAND.

BODDY, Mr. John, FCA *1965;* 1 Broadley Avenue, Anlaby, HULL, HU10 7HH.

BODDY, Mr. Lewis Daniel, BSc ACA *1996;* Old Rectory, 4 Hastings Road, Pembury, TUNBRIDGE WELLS, KENT, TN2 4PD.

BODDY, Mr. Martyn Alan, BSc FCA MSI *1977;* Lady's Wood, 47 Woodside Lane, Poynton, STOCKPORT, CHESHIRE, SK12 1BB.

BODDY, Mr. Matthew James, BSc ACA *2005;* 45 Greenway Avenue, Alveley, BRIDGNORTH, WV15 6PB.

BODDY, Dr. Rachel Elaine, PhD BEng ACA *2002;* Well Cottage, Main Street, East Haddon, NORTHAMPTON, NORTHAMPTONSHIRE, NN6 8BU.

BODDY, Mr. Richard Paul, BEng ACA *1994;* c/o AXA Insurance, Kanoo Building, 2nd Floor, PO Box 45, MANAMA, BAHRAIN.

BODDY, Mr. Simon Noel, ACA *1984;* Hurtis Hill House, Hurtis Hill, CROWBOROUGH, EAST SUSSEX, TN6 3BL.

•BODDYE, Mr. Robert Charles Tatton, BSc FCA *1988;* with PricewaterhouseCoopers LLP, 101 Barbirolli Square, Lower Mosley Street, MANCHESTER, M2 3PW.

BODEK, Mr. Darren Leigh, BA ACA *2007;* BBC White City Room 4500, 201 Wood Lane, LONDON, W12 7TS.

BODEK, Mrs. Hannah, BSc ACA *2006;* 40 Wellesley Road, LONDON, E11 2HF.

BODEN, Mrs. Beverley Dawn, BA ACA *1989;* 32 Selmans Hill, Bloxwich, WALSALL, WS3 3RL.

BODEN, Miss. Emma Louise, BSc ACA *1995;* 15 Hack Drive, Colden Common, WINCHESTER, SO21 1UD.

BODEN, Ms. Jennifer, BSc ACA *2000;* Kohler Mira Ltd, Cromwell Road, CHELTENHAM, GLOUCESTERSHIRE, GL52 5EP.

BODEN, Mr. John David, FCA *1960;* Woodbourne Trustees Ltd, P O Box HM 1475, HAMILTON HM FX, BERMUDA.

BODEN, Miss. Laura, ACA *2008;* 17 Greenhill Way, WALSALL, WS9 8SQ.

BODEN, Mr. Martin Brett, BA FCA *1985;* South House The Green, Adderbury, BANBURY, OXFORDSHIRE, OX17 3NE.

BODEN, Mr. Martin Richard, BA ACA *2001;* 11 Cross Street, PRESTON, PR1 3LT.

•BODEN, Mr. Nicholas William Edward, BA ACA *1990;* PricewaterhouseCoopers LLP, 101 Barbirolli Square, Lower Mosley Street, MANCHESTER, M2 3PW. See also PricewaterhouseCoopers

•BODEN, Mr. Paul Steven, BSc ACA *1979;* Atkin Macredie & Co Ltd, Westbourne Place, 23 Westbourne Road, SHEFFIELD, S10 2QQ.

BODEN, Mr. Stephen Mark, ACA *1984;* 18 Leeds Road, Kippax, LEEDS, LS25 7HQ.

•BODENHAM, Mr. Martin Philip, BA FCA CF *1984;* Advantage Corporate Finance, 14 Main Street, Ayston, OAKHAM, RUTLAND, LE15 9AE.

BODEY, Mr. Jeremy John, BSc ACA *1999;* 1 Abington Road, SALE, CHESHIRE, M33 3DL.

BODEY, Mrs. Nicola Jayne, BSc ACA *2007;* 1 Abington Road, SALE, CHESHIRE, M33 3DL.

BODGER, Mr. Stephen Graham, MA FCA *1975;* Tanyard House, Horsmonden, TONBRIDGE, TN12 8JU.

BODGER, Mr. Thomas, BSc ACA *2003;* 52/32 Carabella Street, KIRRIBILLI, NSW 2061, AUSTRALIA.

BODHA, Mr. James Sanjay, BSc ACA *1993;* Myriad Group Tower House, Towers Business Park Wilmslow Road, MANCHESTER, M20 2SL.

BODICOAT, Mr. Alan Charles, FCA *1962;* The Spinney, 5 Maes Bache, LLANGOLLEN, LL20 8AQ. (Life Member)

BODICOAT, Mr. Richard, BA FCA *1991;* 20 Ivor Place, LONDON, NW1 6EU.

BODILY, Mr. Richard Thomas, BSc ACA *1987;* Borneo Linnells, Dixon House, 77-97 Harpur Street, BEDFORD, MK40 2SY.

•BODIMEADE, Mr. Colin Peter, FCA MBA *1968;* (Tax Fac), Green Corporates Limited, Brandon House, King Street, KNUTSFORD, CHESHIRE, WA16 6DX. See also Solution 121 Limited

BODIO, Mrs. Victoria Jane, BA ACA *2007;* 6 Coronation Avenue, BOURNEMOUTH, BH9 1TN.

•BODKIN, Mr. Andrew Michael, BA FCA *1995;* Haines Watts, 2nd Floor, Argyll House, 23 Brook Street, KINGSTON UPON THAMES, SURREY KT1 2BN.

BODKIN, Mrs. Marie, BA ACA *1995;* 58b Cross Road, TADWORTH, SURREY, KT20 5ST.

BODKIN, Mr. Raymond, FCA *1959;* 23 Derwent Close, HAILSHAM, BN27 3DA.

BODNAR, Mr. Stephen Paul, BSc ACA *1978;* 19 Clifton Road, Ben Rhydding, ILKLEY, LS29 8TU.

BODNAR-HORVATH, Mr. Robert Edmund Paul, BSc FCA *1981;* 20 Harold Road, LONDON, SE19 3PL.

•BODOANO, Mr. Robert Archer, FCA *1962;* R.A Bodoano, Rowanberries, Linton, ROSS-ON-WYE, HR9 7RY.

BODOSSIAN, Mr. Haig, MA ACA *1983;* 12 Popham Gardens, Lower Richmond Road, RICHMOND, TW9 4LJ.

BODSWORTH, Mrs. Emma, BA ACA *2007;* 46 Woodlark Drive, Cottenham, CAMBRIDGE, CB24 8XT.

•BODSWORTH, Mr. Peter, FCA *1973;* Bodsworth & Co, 55 Mowbray Street, SHEFFIELD, S3 8EZ.

•BODY, Mr. Christopher Charles, FCA *1983;* The Old Church, Quicks Road, Wimbledon, LONDON, SW19 1EX.

BODY, Mr. Peter Joseph, FCA *1948;* 31 Townscliffe Lane, Marple Bridge, STOCKPORT, SK6 5AW. (Life Member)

BOEHM, Miss. Sandra Christine, BSc ACA *1999;* with PricewaterhouseCoopers SA, Birchstrasse 160, 8050 ZURICH, SWITZERLAND.

BOETTGER, Mr. John George, ACA *1989;* 53 Ulting Way, WICKFORD, SS11 8ND.

BOETTGER, Mrs. Kasey Ann, BA ACA *1994;* 53 Ulting Way, WICKFORD, SS11 8ND.

BOFFEY, Miss. Anna Katherine, BSc ACA *2002;* Lloyds TSB Asset Finance Division, St. William House, Tresillian Terrace, CARDIFF, CF10 5BH.

BOFFEY, Mr. Christopher, BSc ACA *1987;* House 1 Horizon Crest, 22 Stanley Village Road, Stanley STANLEY, Hong Kong Island, HONG KONG SAR.

BOFFIN, Mr. John William, FCA *1954;* 57 Hilton Grange, Hilton Crescent, West Bridgford, NOTTINGHAM, NG2 6UG. (Life Member)

BOFKIN, Mr. Brian Ashley, FCA *1969;* 95 Wise Lane, LONDON, NW7 2BD.

•BOGARD, Mr. Montague Charles, MSc BCom FCA *1964;* M.C. Bogard, 22 Dukes Avenue, LONDON, W4 2AE.

BOGATYREV, Mr. Alexei, ACA *2010;* with ZAO Deloitte & Touche CIS, 5 Lesnaya Street, Building B, 125047 MOSCOW, RUSSIAN FEDERATION.

BOGGISS, Mr. Stanley Amos, FCA *1954;* Flat 9, Ravens House, Charter Quay, Wadbrook Street, KINGSTON UPON THAMES, SURREY KT1 1HR. (Life Member)

•BOGGON, Mr. Roland John, BA FCA *1973;* (Tax Fac), Roland J. Boggon, Moorea, Pitchcombe, STROUD, GL6 6LJ.

BOGGS, Mr. Jason Alexander, BCom ACA *2001;* PricewaterhouseCoopers, Suite 3000 Box 82, Royal Trust Tower TD Centre, TORONTO M5K 1G8, ON, CANADA.
BOGHANI, Miss. Munira, BSc ACA *2005;* Candover Investments Plc, 20 Old Bailey, LONDON, EC4M 7LN.
BOGHANI, Mr. Nashir Nurmohamed, ACA *1981;* (Tax Fac), 37 Bedford Road, Moor Park, NORTHWOOD, MIDDLESEX, HA6 2AX.
BOGHANI, Mr. Shirazali Noormohamed, FCA *1975;* Haydon House, 296 Joel Street, PINNER, HA5 2PY.
BOGIE, Miss. Gillian Margaret, BSc(Hons) ACA *2000;* The Edinburgh Cyrenian Trust, Norton Park, 57 Albion Road, EDINBURGH, EH7 5QY.
BOGLE, Mr. Paul Hempstead, MA FCA *1976;* 3 Mynchen Road, BEACONSFIELD, HP9 2AS.
BOGLE, Mr. Peter Douglas, FCA *1956;* The Pound, Holcot Road, Walgrave, NORTHAMPTON, NN6 9QN. (Life Member)
BOGLE, Mr. Philip Garth, FCA *1968;* 7 Greenmount Close, Off Clevelands Drive, Heaton, BOLTON, BL1 5GX.
•BOGOD, Mr. Anthony Harry, BA FCA *1983;* 4 Marsh Close, LONDON, NW7 4NY.
BOGUES, Mr. James George, BSc ACA *1991;* 19214 Noah Arbor Lane, HOUSTON, TX 77094, UNITED STATES.
BOGUZAS, Mr. Patrick Edward, BA ACA *2007;* 34 Stavordale Road, LONDON, N5 1NE.
BOHAN, Ms. Adrienne Maureen, BCom ACA *1992;* 114 Crescent Road, BARNET, EN4 9RJ.
BOHAN, Mrs. Isabel Mary Catherine, BA ACA *2001;* 95 Sandringham Gardens, North Finchley, LONDON, N12 0PA.
BOHAN, Mr. Nicholas John, BSc FCA *1973;* 4026 West 39th Avenue, VANCOUVER V6N 3B2, BC, CANADA.
BOHM, Mr. Anthony Robert, FCA *1974;* 25 Stanley Road, North Chingford, LONDON, E4 7DB.
BOHM, Mr. Jeremy Leo, ACA *2009;* 11 Rowben Close, LONDON, N20 8QR.
BOHM, Mr. Justin Antony, BA(Hons) ACA *2000;* 40 Theobald Street, BOREHAMWOOD, HERTFORDSHIRE, WD6 4SE.
BOHM, Mr. Wolfgang Peter, FCA *1996;* Institut der Wirtschaftsprufer, Wirtschaftspruferhaus, Tersteegenstrasse 14, 40474 DUSSELDORF, GERMANY.
BOHNEL, Mrs. Elaine Ann, BSc ACA *1987;* 12 The Leys, Chesham Bois, AMERSHAM, BUCKINGHAMSHIRE, HP6 5NP.
BOILING, Mr. David, ACA *1992;* 61 Manitou Bay, WINNIPEG R3K 0V5, MB, CANADA.
BOILING, Mr. Martin Eric, BSc FCA *1980;* 4 Kenilworth Avenue, LONDON, SW19 7LW.
BOIVIN, Mr. Andrew John, ACA *2009;* with Deloitte Touche Tohmatsu, 80 Queen Street, Private Bag 115-033, AUCKLAND 1010, NEW ZEALAND.
BOJARSKA, Miss. Monika Malgorzata, BSc ACA *1995;* AT Capital Ltd, 50 Brook Street, LONDON, W1K 5DR.
BOJKOVIC, Mr. Milan, BSc ACA *1993;* The Carphone Warehouse, 1 Portal Way, LONDON, W3 6RS.
BOKHARI, Mr. Harris, ACA CertPFS *2004;* 115 Thorndon Gardens, Stoneleigh, EPSOM, KT19 0QE.
BOKHARI, Mr. Sabeeh Mohsan, MSc BSc ACA *2010;* 368 Mortlake Road, ILFORD, ESSEX, IG1 2TG.
BOKHARI, Mr. Syed Ahfar Hussain, BSc ACA *1998;* Premium Credit Ltd, Premium Credit House, 60 East Street, EPSOM, SURREY, KT17 1HB.
•BOKHARI, Mr. Syed Zahir Hassan, FCA *1994;* Deloitte LLP, Hill House, 1 Little New Street, LONDON, EC4A 3TR. See also Deloitte & Touche LLP
BOKIL, Ms. Pravda, BSc ACA *1997;* 1 Ashcombe Street, LONDON, SW6 3AW.
BOLA, Mr. Navraj Singh, MEng ACA *2010;* Flat 3, 1 Paddington Street, LONDON, W1U 5QA.
•BOLAM, Mr. Eric Gordon, FCA *1970;* Eric G. Bolam, 14 Fox Covert, River View Park, Colwick, NOTTINGHAM, NG4 2DD.
BOLAN, Mr. Christopher Norman, BSc ACA *1993;* 29 Tamarind Way, Earley, READING, RG6 5GR.
BOLAND, Mr. Darren, BSc ACA *2002;* 104a Cumberland Road, BROMLEY, BR2 0PW.
BOLAND, Mr. Jason Paul, BSc ACA *1995;* 30 Walsingham Avenue, Middleton, MANCHESTER, M24 1SR.
BOLAND, Mr. Michael Thomas, ACA *2010;* 32 Shakespeare Road, BEDFORD, MK40 2ED.
BOLAND, Dr. Robert George Alfred, MD FCA *1949;* Chemin De la Garenne, Prevessin, 01280 FERNEY VOLTAIRE, FRANCE. (Life Member)
BOLAS, Mr. Timothy Peter, BA ACA *1984;* Pilkington Automotive, Hall Lane, Lathom, ORMSKIRK, LANCASHIRE, L40 5UF.
BOLCHOVER, Mr. Jeremy William, BCom ACA *1988;* Nova Chambers, A J Estates, 1a Wilmslow Road, CHEADLE, CHESHIRE, SK8 1DW.
BOLD, Mrs. Ann Olive, FCA *1971;* Charnwood House, Burtons Lane, Swannington, COALVILLE, LEICESTERSHIRE, LE67 8QA. (Life Member)
BOLD, Mr. Christopher Paul, ACA *2009;* with Ernst & Young LLP, PO Box 9, Royal Chambers, St Julian's Avenue, St Peter Port, GUERNSEY GY1 4AF.
BOLD, Mr. John, BA ACA *2004;* 26 Langs Road, IVANHOE, VIC 3079, AUSTRALIA.
BOLD, Mr. Simon Mercer, FCA *1970;* (Tax Fac), Charnwood House, Burtons Lane, Swannington, COALVILLE, LEICESTERSHIRE, LE67 8QA. (Life Member)
BOLDEN, Mr. Jamie, BSc ACA *2006;* Gleacher Shacklock Llp, Cleveland House, 33 King Street, LONDON, SW1Y 6RJ.
•BOLDEN, Mr. John Charles, FCA *1981;* (Tax Fac), Bolden & Long, 36a Goring Road, Goring-by-Sea, WORTHING, BN12 4AD.
•BOLDERO, Mr. Ian Gordon McDonald, MA BSc(Hons) FCA *2000;* Boldero & Co, Ivy House, The Market Place, Reepham, NORWICH, NR10 4LZ.
BOLDERO, Mr. Michael Herbert Andrew, FCA *1961;* The White House, Mill Street, Swanton Morley, DEREHAM, NR20 4QB. (Life Member)
BOLDERSTON, Mr. David Paul, ACA *2009;* PWC, 201 Sussex Street, SYDNEY, NSW 2001, AUSTRALIA.
•BOLDY, Mr. Anthony David, FCA *1965;* David Boldy, 6 Spring Farm Mews, Wilsden, BRADFORD, BD15 0EF.
BOLE, Mr. John, BSc ACA IMC *2007;* 6 Scholars Road, LONDON, SW12 0PG.
•BOLEAT, Mr. Richard Michael, FCA *1988;* Loraine & Boleat, First Floor, 7 Bond Street, St. Helier, JERSEY, JE2 3NP.
BOLER, Mr. James Richard, LLB ACA *2011;* 33 Black Rock Way, MANSFIELD, NOTTINGHAMSHIRE, NG18 4YE.
BOLER, Mr. John Mark, BA ACA *1994;* 96 St. Albans Avenue, ASHTON-UNDER-LYNE, OL6 8UR.
BOLEY, Mr. Stephen David, MA ACA *1980;* 5 Beauchamp Terrace, LONDON, SW15 1BW.
BOLGER, Mr. Michael Anthony, FCA *1960;* 9 Belvedere Court, 1 Paulin Drive, Winchmore Hill, LONDON, N21 1AZ. (Life Member)
BOLIER, Mr. Robert Jan, ACA *2008;* 115 Marlow Bottom, MARLOW, BUCKINGHAMSHIRE, SL7 3PJ.
BOLINGBROKE, Mr. Michael James, BA ACA *1991;* 31 Bollin Hill, WILMSLOW, CHESHIRE, SK9 4AN.
BOLITHO, Mr. Mark Alan, BA ACA *1994;* 147 The Ryde, HATFIELD, AL9 5DP.
BOLITHO, Mr. Michael David, BA ACA *1993;* 731 Alexander Rd, Building 2, PRINCETON, NJ 08540, UNITED STATES.
BOLITHO, Mr. Simon, MA ACA *1993;* 47 Trevarthian Road, ST AUSTELL, CORNWALL, PL25 4BT.
BOLLAND, Mr. Anthony John Lee, BA ACA *1991;* Cable & Wireless Global, 26 Red Lion Square, LONDON, WC1R 4HQ.
BOLLAND, Mr. Brian, FCA *1957;* 10, 151 - 153 Darley Street West, MONA VALE, NSW 2103, AUSTRALIA. (Life Member)
BOLLAND, Mr. Charles Joshua Fenton, BSc ACA *1994;* PricewaterhouseCoopers, Strathvale House, PO Box 258, GEORGE TOWN, GRAND CAYMAN, KY1-1104 CAYMAN ISLANDS.
•BOLLAND, Mr. Ian Arthur, BA FCA *1983;* Denham Hall, Denham Lane, Brindle, CHORLEY, PR6 8PR.
BOLLAND, Mr. Julian Raymond Fearne, FCA *1969;* J B Offshore Ltd, West Hamstead Farm East Close, Cranmore, YARMOUTH, ISLE OF WIGHT, PO41 0XX.
BOLLAND, Mrs. Lorraine Brenda Marie, BA(Hons) ACA *2001;* Meadow View, The Old Orchard, Green Lane, ILMINSTER, SOMERSET, TA19 9DF.
•BOLLAND, Mr. Lynn Murray, MBA BA(Econ) FCA *1981;* Flat E/10, Elizabeth Court, Grove Road, BOURNEMOUTH, BH1 3DT.
BOLLAND, Mr. Martin Keith, BA ACA *1981;* 6 Whittaker Street, LONDON, SW1W 8JQ.
BOLLAND, Mr. Peter Willoughby Spence, BSc ACA *1990;* Coutts & Co, 33-35 Queen Square, BRISTOL, BS1 4LU.
BOLLAND, Mr. Robin Anthony, FCA *1966;* 36 Whitehall Road, HARROW, MIDDLESEX, HA1 3AJ. (Life Member)
BOLLAND, Mr. Stephen Michael, BA ACA *1993;* 10 Southfield, CHEDDAR, SOMERSET, BS27 3HT.
BOLLAND, Miss. Valerie, BA ACA *2006;* Flat 2, 21 Blake Hall Road, LONDON, E11 2QQ.
BOLLARD, Mrs. Janet Grace, BSc ACA *1994;* St. Swithuns School, Alresford Road, WINCHESTER, SO21 1HA.
BOLLE-JONES, Mr. Huw Maurice, BSocSc FCA *1979;* Bachauderie Cottage, La Rue de la Bachauderie, St. Martin, JERSEY, JE3 6JE.
BOLLEN, Mr. Philip, FCA *1973;* 33 Selborne Drive, Douglas, ISLE OF MAN, IM2 3NJ.
•BOLLEN, Mr. Trevor Brian, BSc FCA *1974;* T.B. Bollen, 89 Groundwell Road, SWINDON, SN1 2NA.
BOLLING, Miss. Gillian Helen, BA ACA *1997;* 7 Paxton Court, East Kilbride, GLASGOW, G74 4GG.
BOLOT, Mr. Timothy James, ACA *1996;* Bolt Partners LLP, 5th Floor Sussex House, 143 Long Acre, LONDON, WC2E 9AD.
BOLS, Captain Peter Heinrich Charles, BEng ACA *1995;* The Manor, 19 Green End, Comberton, CAMBRIDGE, CB3 7DY.
BOLSHAW, Mr. Keith, MA FCA *1977;* Cleeves, Castle Street, Bletchingley, REDHILL, RH1 4QA.
•BOLSOM, Mr. Alan Norman, MA FCA *1963;* (Tax Fac), H. Rainsbury & Co., 15 Duncan Terrace, LONDON, N1 8BZ.
BOLSOVER, Ms. Dawn Louise, BSc ACA *2005;* 9 St. Michaels Drive, Sheepcot Lane, WATFORD, WD25 7JN.
BOLSOVER, Ms. Sarah Janet, ACA MCT *1982;* 5 Temple Fortune Lane, LONDON, NW11 7UB.
BOLSTER, Mr. Jack Ronald, FCA *1958;* 2433 Brazilia Drive, Apt 49, CLEARWATER, FL 33763, UNITED STATES. (Life Member)
BOLSTER, Mr. Patrick Charles, BA ACA *1999;* Beachcroft Llp Portwall Place, Portwall Lane, BRISTOL, BS1 6NA.
BOLT, Mr. Benjamin Alexis, BA ACIB ACA *1998;* 413 Lichfield Road, Four Oaks, SUTTON COLDFIELD, B74 4DJ.
BOLT, Mr. Brian Michael, BA ACA *1982;* 31 Longwater Lane, Costessey, NORWICH, NR5 0TB.
BOLT, Mrs. Caroline, BSc ACA *2001;* Eversheds, 1 Royal Standard Place, NOTTINGHAM, NG1 6FZ.
BOLT, Mrs. Claire Ann, BA ACA *2003;* 33 Allt-yr-yn Close, NEWPORT, GWENT, NP20 5ED.
BOLT, Mr. Colin Arthur, BA ACA *1989;* 46 Chatsworth Heights, CAMBERLEY, GU15 1NH.
•BOLT, Mr. John Oxton, FCA *1968;* Plumtree Cottage, 216 Bramhall Moor Lane, Hazel Grove, STOCKPORT, CHESHIRE, SK7 5JJ.
BOLT, Miss. Karen, ACA *1980;* 40 Peel Avenue, Frimley, CAMBERLEY, GU16 8YT.
•BOLT, Mr. Nigel Ivan, FCA *1978;* Bessler Hendrie, Albury Mill, Mill Lane, Chilworth, GUILDFORD, SURREY GU4 8RU.
BOLT, Mr. Roy Brian Stuart, FCA *1960;* 55 Kingsdown Crescent, DAWLISH, EX7 0HJ. (Life Member)
BOLTER, Mr. Andrew Christopher, BA(Hons) ACA *1997;* 14 Dalton Drive, SHREWSBURY, SY3 8DA.
BOLTER, Mr. Roger Christopher, BSc FCA *1981;* Sheepleys, Llandow, COWBRIDGE, SOUTH GLAMORGAN, CF71 7PA.
•BOLTON, Mr. Alan Keith, BA FCA DChA *1979;* (Tax Fac), A Bolton and Co. Business Advisers Limited, 14 Warrington Street, Ashton-Under-Lyne, MANCHESTER, OL6 6AS.
BOLTON, Mr. Alastair Maxwell, FCA *1964;* Thyme House, 4 Somerset Close, Seend, MELKSHAM, WILTSHIRE, SN12 6QH. (Life Member)
BOLTON, Miss. Alice, BA ACA *1990;* 33 Palmer Avenue, CHEADLE, SK8 2DE.
BOLTON, Mr. Andrew Stephen, FCA *1977;* 140 Adel Lane, LEEDS, LS16 8BX.
BOLTON, Miss. Bridget Katherine, BSc ACA *1989;* 6 Ashbury Place, LONDON, SW19 8TQ.
BOLTON, Miss. Carol Elizabeth, MPhil BSc ACA *1981;* (Tax Fac), Robins Wood, Aldworth Road, Upper Basildon, READING, RG8 8NG.
BOLTON, Mr. Christopher Alan, MA FCA *1976;* Garden Flat, 53 Woodland Gardens, LONDON, N10 3UE.
BOLTON, Mr. Christopher Richard, MA FCA *1983;* Chemin de Sorecot 16, Les Echères, 1134 VUFFLENS-LE-CHATEAU, VAUD, SWITZERLAND.
BOLTON, Mr. Daniel John, BA ACA *2002;* Working Links, 57-59 Long Acre, LONDON, WC2E 9JL.
BOLTON, Mr. David Edward, ACA *2008;* Deloitte Llp, 4 Brindley Place, BIRMINGHAM, B1 2HZ.
BOLTON, Mr. David Edward, LLB FCA *1965;* 3 Belgrave Pl, Birkdale, SOUTHPORT, PR8 2EF.
BOLTON, Mr. David George, MA FCA *1977;* Aldwyn, Greenroyd Avenue, Skircoat Green, HALIFAX, HX3 0LP.
BOLTON, Mr. David John, BSc FCA *1975;* Kensington House, 69 Borrowcop Lane, LICHFIELD, STAFFORDSHIRE, WS14 9DG.
BOLTON, Mr. David Richard, FCA *1968;* 10 Westmeare, Hemingford Grey, HUNTINGDON, PE28 9BZ. (Life Member)
•BOLTON, Mr. David Trevor Sproule, FCA *1969;* D T S Bolton, Laurels Back Lane, Goudhurst, CRANBROOK, TN17 1AN.
•BOLTON, Mr. Dominic George Noel, MA ACA CF *1993;* Grant Thornton UK LLP, 30 Finsbury Square, LONDON, EC2P 2YU. See also Grant Thornton LLP
BOLTON, Ms. Elizabeth Ann, BA ACA *1988;* Trawsmawr Hall, Henfwich Road, CARMARTHEN, SA33 6AE.
BOLTON, Miss. Emily Frances, ACA *2008;* Flat 3, 58 Kenilworth Road, LEAMINGTON SPA, CV32 6JW.
BOLTON, Mr. Frederick George Edwin, FCA CTA *1951;* 36 Rosedale Road, Stoneleigh, EPSOM, SURREY, KT17 2JQ. (Life Member)
•BOLTON, Mr. Gerald Rodney, FCA *1961;* Atkinson Finch & Co, Central Chambers, 45-47 Albert St, RUGBY, CV21 2SG.
BOLTON, Ms. Gillian Elizabeth, BA ACA *1986;* 15 Freesia Close, LOUGHBOROUGH, LEICESTERSHIRE, LE11 2FD.
BOLTON, Mr. Gregg, BA ACA *1991;* 4 Lakeland Drive, Calderstones Park, Whalley, CLITHEROE, LANCASHIRE, BB7 9XD.
•BOLTON, Mrs. Helen, BSc FCA *1989;* Bolton Consulting Ltd, 16 Lee Fold, Tyldesley, MANCHESTER, M29 7FQ.
BOLTON, Mr. Henry Alan, MA FCA *1989;* (Tax Fac), 44 Littlebury Road, LONDON, SW4 6DN.
BOLTON, Mr. Hugh Malcolm, BA ACA *1999;* Aberdeen Asset Management Plc Bow Bells House, 1 Bread Street, LONDON, EC4M 9HH.
BOLTON, Mr. James Richard, BA ACA *1993;* 51 Woodside, LONDON, SW19 7AF.
•BOLTON, Miss. Jill Helen, BEng ACA *2002;* Jill Bolton Professional Services, 69 Broomfield, LEEDS, LS16 7AD.
BOLTON, Mr. John Clifford Fairhurst, BA FCA *1955;* 3 Pinewood Court, South Downs Road, Hale, ALTRINCHAM, CHESHIRE, WA14 3HY. (Life Member)
BOLTON, Mr. John Douglas, FCA *1961;* Whitehouse, Main Road, Kirk Michael, ISLE OF MAN, IM6 2HH.
BOLTON, Mr. John Kenneth, FCA *1969;* No 38 Jalan Bukit Indah 2/1, Taman Bukit Indah, 68000 AMPANG, SELANGOR, MALAYSIA.
BOLTON, Mr. John Stansfeld, FCA *1956;* 21 Cedar Grove, Vicarage Meadows, KENDAL, LA9 5BL. (Life Member)
BOLTON, Mr. Jonathan Charles, BA ACA *1994;* 7 Barrow Hall Farm, Village Road, Great Barrow, CHESTER, CH3 7JH.
BOLTON, Mr. Jordan Mark, ACA *2004;* Building Materials Ltd, Leeward Highway, PROVIDENCIALES, PO Box 559, TURKS AND CAICOS ISLANDS.
BOLTON, Miss. Julie Joy, MBA BSc ACA *1988;* 1810 Woods Hollow Lane, ALLENTOWN, PA 18103, UNITED STATES.
BOLTON, Mrs. Katherine Anne, MBA BSc ACA *1992;* Hill House, Hill House Lane, Needham Market, IPSWICH, IP6 8EA.
BOLTON, Mrs. Kathleen Margaret, FCA *1955;* Springfield House, Babylon Lane, Heath Charnock, CHORLEY, PR6 9EU. (Life Member)
•BOLTON, Dr. Lina Wai Yue, PhD MA ACA *2002;* (Tax Fac), 6 Kennet Road, Keynsham, BRISTOL, BS31 1NZ.
BOLTON, Mrs. Lucy Caroline, ACA *2008;* Hare Cottage, 5 Green Lane, Ledston, CASTLEFORD, WEST YORKSHIRE, WF10 2BD.
•BOLTON, Mr. Malcolm John, FCA *1982;* 98 Waxwell Lane, PINNER, MIDDLESEX, HA5 3ES.
BOLTON, Mrs. Margaret Ann, BA ACA *2006;* 33 Halifax Road, CAMBRIDGE, CB4 3QB.
BOLTON, Mrs. Margaret Elizabeth, FCA *1966;* 15 Spinney Close, Pelsall, WALSALL, WS3 4LB.
•BOLTON, Mr. Mark Neil, BSc ACA *1997;* PricewaterhouseCoopers LLP, 7 More London Riverside, LONDON, SE1 2RT. See also PricewaterhouseCoopers
BOLTON, Mr. Martin Joseph John, FCA *1973;* 75 Twyford Avenue, LONDON, N2 9NP. (Life Member)
•BOLTON, Mrs. Mary Clare, BA FCA CTA *1976;* PricewaterhouseCoopers LLP, 101 Barbirolli Square, Lower Mosley Street, MANCHESTER, M2 3PW. See also PricewaterhouseCoopers
BOLTON, Mr. Michael, FCA *1961;* New Wood House, 21 New Wood Lane, Blakedown, KIDDERMINSTER, DY10 3LD.
BOLTON, Mr. Michael John, BCom ACA *1984;* 2502 N. Clark St, Suite 207, CHICAGO, IL 60614, UNITED STATES.
•BOLTON, Mr. Michael John, FCA *1961;* (Tax Fac), Michael John Bolton FCA, 2 St. Andrews Drive, DROITWICH, WORCESTERSHIRE, WR9 8BS.

BOLTON, Mr. Nicholas John Canning, BSc(Hons) ACA CTA *2001;* (Tax Fac), 7 Portland Close, WORCESTER PARK, SURREY, KT4 8BW.
BOLTON, Mr. Peter Graham Hickman, FCA CPA *1974;* The Old Vicarage, Main Road, St. Johns, ISLE OF MAN, IM4 3LU. (Life Member)
•**BOLTON, Mr. Philip Charles, FCA** *1976;* (Tax Fac), Clifton House Partnership, Clifton House, Four Elms Road, CARDIFF, CF24 1LE.
BOLTON, Mr. Philip David, BA(Hons) ACA *2002;* 115 Stormont Road, LONDON, SW11 5EJ.
BOLTON, Ms. Rebecca Elizabeth, BA(Hons) ACA *2002;* 27 Corinthian Way, HULL, HU9 1UF.
BOLTON, Mr. Richard Douglas, FCA *1969;* Rosary Priory Convent, 93 Elstree Road, Bushey Heath, BUSHEY, WD23 4EE.
•**BOLTON, Mr. Richard Gareth, BSc FCA** *1995;* Riches & Company, 34 Anyards Road, COBHAM, SURREY, KT11 2LA.
BOLTON, Mr. Richard James, BA ACA *2007;* Apartment 8 Bridge Place, 1 Troy Road Horsforth, LEEDS, LS18 5NQ.
BOLTON, Mr. Roland John, FCA *1962;* 6 Rockhill, LONDON, SE26 6SW.
BOLTON, Mr. Roy Percy, FCA *1952;* Faraway Lodge, Spilsby Road, Thorpe St. Peter, SKEGNESS, PE24 4PS. (Life Member)
BOLTON, Mr. Stephen Peter, BA FCA *1982;* The Conifers The Green, Hickling, MELTON MOWBRAY, LE14 3AE.
BOLTON, Mr. Stewart John, FCA *1969;* The Pines, 11 Graveney Drive, Caversham Heights, READING, RG4 7EG. (Life Member)
•**BOLTON, Mr. Stuart Gerald, FCA** *1987;* Atkinson Finch & Co, Central Chambers, 45-47 Albert St, RUGBY, CV21 2SG.
•**BOLTON, Mrs. Suzanne Julie, BSc ACA** *2004;* Geoffrey Ellis & Co., Kirby Grange, Cold Kirby, THIRSK, NORTH YORKSHIRE, YO7 2HL.
•**BOLTON, Mrs. Theresa, ACA** *1984;* Theresa M. Bolton, 32 Granville Road, BARNET, EN5 4DS.
•**BOLTON, Mr. Timothy David, FCA** *1992;* (Tax Fac), Bolton & Co Accountants Ltd, Squirrels Wood, Reigate Road, LEATHERHEAD, SURREY, KT22 8QY.
•**BOLTON, Mr. Timothy Patrick, FCA** *1967;* Timothy P. Bolton, Latchmere House, Watling Street, CANTERBURY, CT1 2UD.
BOLTON, Mr. Trevor George Walter, FCA *1962;* 16 The Green, Southwick, BRIGHTON, BN42 4GF.
BOLTON, Mr. William Andrew, FCA *1956;* The Willows, 5 Foxwood Drive, Over Peover, KNUTSFORD, WA16 8TS. (Life Member)
•**BOLTSA, Mr. Michael, FCA** *1956;* (Tax Fac), M. Boltsa, Premier House, 112-114 Station Road, EDGWARE, HA8 7BJ.
BOLUS, Mr. Edward Robert, BSc(Hons) ACA *2004;* 164 Tythe Barn Lane, Dickens Heath, Shirley, SOLIHULL, WEST MIDLANDS, B90 1PF.
BOLUS, Mr. Jonathan William, BA ACA *2000;* Hermes Pensions Management Ltd, Lloyds Chambers, 1 Portsoken Street, LONDON, E1 8HZ.
BOMBA, Mrs. Kathryn Alison, BSc ACA *1989;* 29 Framingham Road, SALE, M33 3ST.
•**BOMBER, Miss. Jennifer Ann, FCA** *1976;* (Tax Fac), J W Hinks, 19 Highfield Road, Edgbaston, BIRMINGHAM, B15 3BH.
•**BOMBER, Mr. Trevor Anthony, FCA** *1968;* Trevor A. Bomber FCA, 59 King Street, Darlaston, WEDNESBURY, WS10 8DE. See also TAB Associates Ltd
•**BOMER, Mr. Mark, BA ACA** *1990;* BDO LLP, 55 Baker Street, LONDON, W1U 7EU. See also BDO Stoy Hayward LLP
BOMFORD, Mrs. Alison Jane, BA ACA *1988;* Far Upton Wold Farm, Springhill, MORETON-IN-MARSH, GLOUCESTERSHIRE, GL56 9TG.
BOMFORD, Mr. Jonathan Galton, FCA *1973;* Springhill House, Salters Lane, Lower Moor, PERSHORE, WR10 2PE.
BOMPHREY, Mr. Andrew David, FCA *1975;* Tyn y Ddol Farm, Pontfadog, LLANGOLLEN, CLWYD, LL20 7AR.
BONAR, Mr. David Charles, MA ACA MCT *1998;* National Grid Transco, Grand Buildings, 1-3 Strand, LONDON, WC2N 5EH.
BONCEY, Mrs. Susan, LLB FCA *1983;* 17 Chemin De Paris, 77760 RECLOSES, FRANCE.
•**BOND, Mr. Adrian William, ACA** *1982;* with Bond Associates Ltd, 62a Belgrave Court, 36 Westferry Circus, LONDON, E14 8RL.
BOND, Mr. Alan, FCA *1959;* 15 Otterburn Gardens, Low Fell, GATESHEAD, TYNE AND WEAR, NE9 6HE. (Life Member)
BOND, Mr. Alfred Anthony, MA FCA *1974;* Westcott, Dimmocks Lane, Sarratt, RICKMANSWORTH, HERTFORDSHIRE, WD3 6AP.
•**BOND, Ms. Alison Linda, LLB ACA** *1998;* Deloitte LLP, 2 New Street Square, LONDON, EC4A 3BZ. See also Deloitte & Touche LLP
BOND, Miss. Amanda Jane, BA ACA *1999;* 35 The Crescent, MAIDENHEAD, BERKSHIRE, SL6 6AG.
•**BOND, Mr. Andrew David, BA ACA** *1989;* Smith & Williamson Ltd, 25 Moorgate, LONDON, EC2R 6AY. See also Nexia Audit Limited
•**BOND, Mr. Andrew John, BA(Hons) ACA** *2002;* Deloitte LLP, Abbots House, Abbey Street, READING, RG1 3BD. See also Deloitte & Touche LLP
BOND, Mr. Barry Christopher, BSc ACA *1979;* Springvale, Clatford Lodge, Abbots Ann, ANDOVER, SP11 7DL.
BOND, Miss. Catherine Jane, BA ACA *1990;* Dynamite Baits Ltd The Development Centre, Wolds Farm The Fosse, Cotgrave, NOTTINGHAM, NG12 3HG.
BOND, Mr. Christopher Barrie, FCA *1961;* 24 Newton Park, Newton Solney, BURTON-ON-TRENT, DE15 0SX.
•**BOND, Mr. Christopher Paul, BA(Hons) ACA** *2001;* SBCA, Park House, 17 Moor Park Avenue, PRESTON, PR1 6AS. See also Crystal Securities Practice Limited
BOND, Mr. Christopher William, BSc FCA *1971;* 16 South Drive, Sonning, READING, RG4 6GB.
BOND, Mrs. Claire Louise, MMath ACA *2005;* Valad Property Group, 2nd Floor, 3125 Century Way, Thorpe Park, LEEDS, LS15 8ZB.
BOND, Mr. Colin Michael, MBA BSc FCA MRPharmS *1991;* Hasenbüelstr.11, CH-8123 EBMATINGEN, SWITZERLAND.
BOND, Mr. Craig, BA ACA *2007;* 10 Minster Close, DONCASTER, SOUTH YORKSHIRE, DN4 6RR.
BOND, Mr. Darren James, BA FCA *1994;* 20 Marston Drive, FARNBOROUGH, HAMPSHIRE, GU14 8JL.
BOND, Mr. David John, FCA MBA *1976;* 24 Lodge Close, COBHAM, KT11 2SQ.
BOND, Mr. David McGregor, BA ACA *1989;* 17 Peacock Parkway, BONNYRIGG, MIDLOTHIAN, EH19 3RQ.
BOND, Mr. David Theodore, BSc FCA *1978;* 67 Sidmouth Road, Springfield, CHELMSFORD, CM1 6LS.
•**BOND, Mr. David William, FCA** *1983;* (Tax Fac), Morris Owen, 43-45 Devizes Road, SWINDON, SN1 4BG.
BOND, Mr. Denis Joseph Christopher, MA ACA *1982;* Cricket Cottage, Churchfields, Cradley, MALVERN, WR13 5LJ.
BOND, Mr. Derek Arthur, MA ACA *1982;* 51 St Olafs Road, Fulham, LONDON, SW6 7DN.
BOND, Mr. Edward Henry, FCA *1952;* Moyglare Farm, Stoney Heath, Baughurst, TADLEY, RG26 5SN. (Life Member)
BOND, Miss. Emily Anne, ACA *2009;* Arla Foods Plc, 4 Savannah Way Leeds Valley Park, LEEDS, LS10 1AB.
BOND, Prof. Francis Michael, MA BCom FCA *1969;* Heathayne Farm, COLYTON, EX24 6RS.
BOND, Mr. Graham Derek, MSc BA FCA FCT *1976;* 7 Sadler Close, LEEDS, LS16 8NN.
BOND, Mr. Graham Paul, LLB ACA *2001;* 50 Rothiemay Road, Urmston, MANCHESTER, M41 6JY.
•**BOND, Mr. Graham Peter, BA FCA** *1991;* Baker Tilly Tax & Advisory Services LLP, 3 Hardman Street, MANCHESTER, M3 3HF. See also Baker Tilly UK Audit LLP
BOND, Miss. Helen Clare, MSc ACA *1993;* Old Meadow, Chestnut Avenue, CHICHESTER, WEST SUSSEX, PO19 5QD.
BOND, Mrs. Helen Louise, BSc(Hons) ACA *2001;* 5 Marlborough Drive, Fulwood, PRESTON, PR2 9UE.
BOND, Mrs. Helen Louise, BA ACA *2005;* GE Oil & Gas, Range Road Cody Technology Park, FARNBOROUGH, GU14 0FG.
BOND, Mr. Henry Gordon, FCA *1953;* Heyeswood House, Bolney Road, Lower Shiplake, HENLEY-ON-THAMES, RG9 3NS. (Life Member)
①**BOND, Mr. Ian Douglas Barker, FCA** *1963;* The Coach House, Littley Green, CHELMSFORD, CM3 1BX.
BOND, Miss. Jane Louise, BSc ACA *2003;* Flat 6, Milton House, Abbey Park, BECKENHAM, KENT, BR3 1PW.
BOND, Mr. Jeremy David, BSc ACA *1987;* Suite 704, 48 Par-La-Ville Road, HAMILTON HM11, BERMUDA.
•**BOND, Mr. Jeremy Simon, FCA** *1977;* Hollows Davies Crane, Hoghton Chambers, Hoghton Street, SOUTHPORT, PR9 0TB.
BOND, Mrs. Joanna Gail, MSc ACA *1995;* Bryher Cottage, 4 Oast Road, Hurst Green, OXTED, RH8 9DX.
BOND, Mrs. Joanne Marie, BA ACA *1999;* AUBOURG, 82400 PERVILLE, FRANCE.
BOND, Miss. Johanna Elizabeth Sarah, BA ACA *1999;* 9 Pyotts Hill, Old Basing, BASINGSTOKE, RG24 8AR.
BOND, Mr. John Michael, FCA *1955;* Poolehill Cottage, Poole Hill Road, Poole, NANTWICH, CW5 6AH. (Life Member)
BOND, Mr. Jonathan Richard, BSc FCA *1972;* 104 Nottingham Drive, ALAMEDA, CA 94502, UNITED STATES.
•**BOND, Mr. Joseph Aloysius, FCA** *1965;* with Hollows Davies Crane, Hoghton Chambers, Hoghton Street, SOUTHPORT, PR9 0TB.
BOND, Mr. Keith Douglas, BSc ACA *1982;* Suite No 478, 48 Par-la-Ville Road, HAMILTON HM11, BERMUDA.
BOND, Mr. Keith William, FCA *1976;* 9 Glebe Field Garth, WETHERBY, LS22 6WH.
BOND, Mr. Kenneth Andrew, BA ACA *1995;* Uplands Rear, Timothy Lane, BATLEY, WF17 0AJ.
BOND, Mr. Leon Barrie Leslie, MEng ACA *2010;* 41 Lexham Gardens, AMERSHAM, BUCKINGHAMSHIRE, HP6 5JP.
BOND, Mrs. Maureen Frances, BSc ACA DChA *1979;* Marlborough College, MARLBOROUGH, WILTSHIRE, SN8 1PA.
BOND, Miss. Melanie, ACA *2010;* 186 Tottington Road, BURY, BL8 1RU.
BOND, Mr. Michael Gerard, BCom FCA *1982;* Taymount Grange, Hall Drive, Hanbury, BURTON-ON-TRENT, DE13 8TF.
BOND, Miss. Michelle Julie, BSc ACA *1995;* 16 Freehold Street, Quorn, LOUGHBOROUGH, LE12 8AY.
•**BOND, Mrs. Monica Joyce, ACA** *1991;* with Bond Associates Ltd, 62a Belgrave Court, 36 Westferry Circus, LONDON, E14 8RL.
BOND, Miss. Naomi, BSc ACA *2004;* with Ernst & Young LLP, 1 More London Place, LONDON, SE1 2AF.
BOND, Mr. Nicholas John Everett, FCA *1973;* 34b Ayston Road, Uppingham, OAKHAM, LEICESTERSHIRE, LE15 9RL.
BOND, Mr. Nigel David, BA ACA *1999;* Nike (UK) Ltd, Camberwell Way, Doxford International Business Park, SUNDERLAND, SR3 3XN.
BOND, Mr. Nigel Phillip, MA FCA *1975;* The White House, The Street, South Stoke, READING, RG8 0JS.
BOND, Mr. Nigel Robert, BSc ACA *1983;* Dutmoss House, Hawstead Road, Whepstead, BURY ST. EDMUNDS, SUFFOLK, IP29 4TG.
•**BOND, Mr. Paul Anthony, BSc FCA** *1975;* 109 Kingsway, Chandler's Ford, EASTLEIGH, HAMPSHIRE, SO53 5DU.
•**BOND, Mr. Phillip Raymond, FCA** *1969;* (Tax Fac), Bond & Co, 110 Kenilworth Road, COVENTRY, CV4 7AH.
BOND, Mr. Richard Andrew, ACA *2004;* Communisis Plc, Wakefield Road, LEEDS, LS10 1DU.
BOND, Mr. Richard Mark, BEng ACA *1997;* 37 Mill Lane, Acaster Malbis, YORK, YO23 2UJ.
BOND, Mr. Robin, ACA *2011;* 34 Byron Road, CHELTENHAM, GLOUCESTERSHIRE, GL51 7HD.
BOND, Miss. Rosemary Anne Louise, BA FCA CTA *1975;* (Tax Fac), 5A St James Road, ILKLEY, LS29 9PY.
•**BOND, Mr. Stewart Frederick, FCA** *1968;* Crystal Securities Practice Limited, Park House, 17 Moor Park Avenue, PRESTON, PR1 6AS.
BOND, Mr. Timothy Conor David, MA ACA MCT *1997;* 3 Grange Park, BISHOP'S STORTFORD, HERTFORDSHIRE, CM23 2HX.
BOND, Mr. Trevor John, BSc ACA *1986;* Lindbergh-Allee 1, 8152 GLATTPARK, SWITZERLAND.
•**BONDS, Mr. Graham Baynard, BSc FCA** *1995;* (Tax Fac), Buchanan Bonds Limited, 39 Braehead Crescent, STONEHAVEN, KINCARDINESHIRE, AB39 2PP.
BONDS, Mr. Michael Jonathan, BA ACA *1990;* Caledon Capital Partners LLP, 7 Old Park Lane, LONDON, W1K 1QR.
•**BONE, Mr. Barry John, FCA** *1975;* B.J. Bone, 14 Hurst Farm Road, Weald, SEVENOAKS, TN14 6PE.
BONE, Mr. David Russell, BSc ACA *2006;* Henry Schein UK Holdings Ltd Whatman House, St. Leonards Road Allington, MAIDSTONE, ME16 0PF.
•**BONE, Mr. Eric, BA FCA** *1959;* Eric Bone, Offshore House, Euroseas Centre, Albert Street, BLYTH, NORTHUMBERLAND NE24 1LZ.
•**BONE, Mr. Ian Keith, BA ACA** *1991;* KPMG Audit plc, 15 Canada Square, LONDON, E14 5GL. See also KPMG Europe LLP and KPMG LLP
BONE, Mrs. Jane Margaret, BA ACA *1998;* 42 Pattison Road, LONDON, NW2 2HJ.
BONE, Mr. Kenneth William, FCA *1974;* The Cottage, 11 Chapel Road, Rowledge, FARNHAM, GU10 4AW.
•**BONE, Mr. Nicholas Clement, BA FCA** *1979;* BBA Limited, Beachside Business Centre, La Rue du Hocq, St Clement, JERSEY, JE2 6LF.
BONE, Mr. Paul, BSc ACA *2002;* 155 Humber Road, LONDON, SE3 7EG.
BONE, Mr. Peter William, FCA MP *1976;* 17 Magnolia Drive, RUSHDEN, NORTHAMPTONSHIRE, NN10 0XD.
•**BONE, Mr. Shawn, BSc CA ACA CF** *1992;* BTG Financial Consulting LLP, 2 Collingwood Street, NEWCASTLE UPON TYNE, NE1 1JF. See also BTG McInnes Corporate Finance LLP
BONE, Mrs. Susan Mary, ACA *1985;* 2 Santa Rosa, La Ruette de Patier, St Saviour, JERSEY, JE2 7LQ.
BONEHAM, Mrs. Carolyn Mary, BSc ACA *1989;* 14 Fairlawn Park, WOKING, GU21 4HT.
BONEHAM, Mr. David Edmund, MA(Oxon) ACA ATII MCT *1984;* 14 Fairlawn Park, WOKING, SURREY, GU21 4HT.
•**BONEHILL, Mr. Robert Mark, BA ACA** *2000;* RJ Accountancy, Crows Cottage, Low Road, Friskney, BOSTON, LINCOLNSHIRE PE22 8NW.
•**BONELLA, Mrs. Jacqueline Ann, BSc ACA** *1988;* Aims- Jackie Bonella Ltd, Avonlea, Bush Lane, Send, WOKING, SURREY GU23 7HP.
•**BONELLE, Mr. Andrew David, FCA** *1979;* Bonelle & Co Limited, 1 Wyecliffe Terrace, Bath Street, HEREFORD, HR1 2HG.
•**BONELLO, Mr. John Louis, FCA** *1972;* 2 Oleander Street, The Gardens, ST JULIANS STJ 1910, MALTA.
BONES, Mr. Andrew Stephen, BA BSc ACA *2006;* 95 Great King Street, MACCLESFIELD, CHESHIRE, SK11 6PW.
BONES, Miss. Rachael, ACA *2011;* 29 Eland Way, CAMBRIDGE, CB1 9XQ.
BONES, Mr. Richard Neville, FCA *1960;* 44/107 M0012, Thepprasit 17, Jomtien, Nongprue, Banglamung, CHON BURI 20260 THAILAND. (Life Member)
BONES, Mr. Stephen Robert, BSc FCA *1981;* Gullacombe, Station Road, SOUTH MOLTON, DEVON, EX36 3EA.
BONESS, Mr. Jon, MMath ACA *2004;* B Z W, 10 South Colonnade, LONDON, E14 4PU.
BONFIELD, Mr. Matthew, ACA *2003;* 13 Pound Lane, MARLOW, BUCKINGHAMSHIRE, SL7 2AH.
BONFIGLIO SCOTT, Mrs. Natalie Marie, BA ACA *1995;* 2 Birkdale Close, Edwalton, NOTTINGHAM, NG12 4FB.
BONG, Mr. Ian, BSc(Hons) ARCS ACA *2004;* 4 Brambling Close, RUGBY, CV23 0WR.
BONG, Mr. Peter Jin Fah, FCA *1982;* No 29 Jalan USJ 11/2C, 47620 SUBANG, SELANGOR, MALAYSIA.
•**BONHAM, Mr. Alan John, MA FCA** *1978;* Alan Bonham, 2 Crabtree Lane, HARPENDEN, AL5 5TB.
BONHAM, Mr. Arthur Keith, MBE DL BA FCA *1966;* Serchio, 38 Old Sneed Avenue, Stoke Bishop, BRISTOL, BS9 1SE.
BONHAM, Mrs. Louise Jane, BA ACA *2006;* 1 Salvin Road, LONDON, SW15 1DR.
BONHAM, Mr. Mark James, ACA *2009;* 21 Littleton Street, LONDON, SW18 3SZ.
BONHAM, Mr. Michael James, BA FCA *1989;* 10 Crawfurd Gardens, Rutherglen, GLASGOW, G73 4JP.
BONHAM, Mr. Robert John, BA ACA *2002;* MOLINS PLC, ROCKINGHAM DRIVE LINFORD WOOD EAST, MILTON KEYNES, BUCKINGHAMSHIRE, MK14 6LY.
BONHAM, Mr. Robert Walker, BSc ACA *1994;* Lucknow, 34 Station Road, Fernhill Heath, WORCESTER, WR3 7UJ.
BONIEUX, Mr. Robert Marie Andre, BA ACA *1985;* PricewaterhouseCoopers, 18 CyberCity, EBENE, MAURITIUS.
BONIFACE, Mr. David Peter, ACA *2008;* 9 Albion Close, FAREHAM, HAMPSHIRE, PO16 9EW.
BONIFACE, Mr. Richard Alistair, BA ACA *1989;* 8 The Copse, Marple Bridge, STOCKPORT, CHESHIRE, SK6 5QQ.
BONIFACE, Mr. Thomas, BSc(Econ) ACA *2002;* 1914 22nd Avenue, SAN FRANCISCO, CA 94116, UNITED STATES.
BONIN, Mrs. Caroline Anne, BA ACA *1994;* 8 Winchester Grove, SEVENOAKS, KENT, TN13 3BL.
BONING, Mr. Roger Charles, MA FCA *1977;* The Old Rectory, Church Westcote, CHIPPING NORTON, OXFORDSHIRE, OX7 6SF.
BONNAR, Mr. Anthony David, FCA *1974;* 1 Highstone House, 21 Highbury Crescent, LONDON, N5 1RX.
•**BONNELL, Mr. Peter, FCA** *1976;* Barnes Roffe LLP, Leytonstone House, Leytonstone, LONDON, E11 1GA.
BONNELLO, Mr. Nicholas William, MSc BSc ACA *2008;* with RWB CA Limited, Northgate House, North Gate, Basford, NOTTINGHAM, NG7 7BE.

•**BONNELLO, Mr. Richard William, FCA** *1971;* RWB CA Limited, Northgate House, North Gate, Basford, NOTTINGHAM, NG7 7BE.
BONNER, Mr. Michael, FCA *1971;* 1 Fell View, Branthwaite, WORKINGTON, CA14 4SY.
BONNER, Mr. Peter Anthony, BSc(Hons) ACA *2001;* 16 Sharpe Road, GRANTHAM, LINCOLNSHIRE, NG31 9BN.
BONNER, Mr. Peter Martin, BA FCA *2000;* 11 Riverside Drive, West Yorkshire, OTLEY, LS21 2RU.
•**BONNER, Mrs. Sally Jayne, FCA DChA** *1983;* Chantrey Vellacott DFK LLP, Russell Square House, 10-12 Russell Square, LONDON, WC1B 5LF.
BONNER, Mr. Stephen Geoffrey, BCom FCA *1974;* 20 Oaklands Avenue, WEST WICKHAM, BR4 9LE.
BONNER, Trevor Courtney, Esq CBE FCA *1965;* Brae House, 17 Lovelace Avenue, SOLIHULL, B91 3JR. (Life Member)
•**BONNERT, Mr. David Victor, FCA** *1969;* (Tax Fac), Higson & Co, White House, Wollaton St, NOTTINGHAM, NG1 5GF.
BONNETT, Mr. Christopher Alfred Herbert, BA FCA *1972;* 12 Church Close, Staveley, CHESTERFIELD, S43 3LU.
BONNETT, Mr. John Reginald, BSc FCA *1977;* 3 Oakfield Close, Menston, ILKLEY, LS29 6QE.
•**BONNETT, Mr. Robert James, FCA** *1975;* (Tax Fac), with Claytons, 39 Harewood Avenue, NORTHOLT, MIDDLESEX, UB5 5DB.
BONNEY, Mr. George Thomas, ACA *2008;* 10 Abbey Gardens, Natland, KENDAL, CUMBRIA, LA9 7SP.
•**BONNEY, Mrs. Joyce Elizabeth, BSc FCA** *1978;* Joyce E. Bonney & Co., 30 Basin Approach, Limehouse, LONDON, E14 7JA.
•**BONNEY, Mr. Keith Philip, FCA** *1983;* K.P. Bonney & Co LLP, 50 Cleasby Road, Menston, ILKLEY, WEST YORKSHIRE, LS29 6JA. See also 8M3 Limited
BONNEY, Mrs. Louisa Peta, ACA *2002;* Rose Cottage St. Sampsons Avenue, Le Pont Du Val St. Brelade, JERSEY, JE3 8FF.
BONNEY, Mr. Richard James, MSc BSc ACA *2002;* T. Bailey Asset Management Ltd, 64-66 St. James's Street, NOTTINGHAM, NG1 6FJ.
BONNEY, Mr. Stephen Andrew, BSc ACA *1994;* (Tax Fac), 40 Harwood Point, 307 Rotherhithe Street, LONDON, SE16 5HD.
BONNEY, Mr. Stephen Robert, BCom FCA *1976;* Avondale Farm, 183 South Road, Bretherton, LEYLAND, PR26 9AJ.
•**BONNEY, Miss. Susan Philippa, BSc FCA** *1987;* (Tax Fac), KPMG LLP, 15 Canada Square, LONDON, E14 5GL. See also KPMG Europe LLP
BONNIER, Mr. Philip, MA FCA *1983;* 49 Ringwood Road, OXFORD, OX3 8JB.
BONNINGTON, Mr. Darren Neil, BSc ACA *2000;* 10 Rona Road, Hampstead, LONDON, NW3 2JA.
BONNOR, Mr. Richard Henry, BA ACA *1988;* Halfords Group plc, Icknield Street Drive Washford West, REDDITCH, WORCESTERSHIRE, B98 0DE.
BONNOR-MORIS, Mrs. Caroline, BA ACA *1996;* 87 Sterndale Road, LONDON, W14 0HX.
BONNOR-MORIS, Mr. Ian David, BSc ACA *1993;* RBS Global Banking & Markets, 135 Bishopsgate, LONDON, EC2M 3UR.
BONNY, Mr. Robert Paul, BSc(Hons) ACA *2002;* 39 Hythe Park Road, EGHAM, SURREY, TW20 8BW.
BONSER, Mr. Anthony Martin Henry, FCA *1964;* 6 Greystoke Avenue, PINNER, MIDDLESEX, HA5 5SL.
BONSER, Miss. Carrie-anne, ACA *2009;* 182 Cardiff Road, Llandaff, CARDIFF, CF5 2AD.
BONSER, Mr. David William, FCA *1955;* Marsh House, 6 The Marsh, Crick, NORTHAMPTON, NN6 7TN. (Life Member)
BONSER, Mr. John Richard, BA FCA *1977;* 78 Cedar Terrace, RICHMOND, SURREY, TW9 2BZ.
BONSER, Mr. Timothy David, MEng ACA *2011;* 52 Albert Road, RICHMOND, SURREY, TW10 6DP.
BONSEY, Mr. Colin Peter, FCA *1969;* 127 Guildford Road, West End, WOKING, GU24 9LS.
BONSOR, Mr. Alexander Cosmo Walrund, BSc ACA *2003;* 26-02 Centennial Tower, 3 Temasek Avenue, SINGAPORE 039190, SINGAPORE.
BONTE, Miss. Marie-Fleur, ACA *2001;* 13 Rue du Portugal, 35500 VITRE, FRANCE.
•**BONVOISIN, Mr. Peter Fitzroy, MA FCA** *1982;* The Court House, Llanvair Discoed, CHEPSTOW, GWENT, NP16 6LX.
•**BOOBBYER, Mr. David Nicholas Alexander, BA FCA** *1989;* McCabe Ford Williams, Bank Chambers, High Street, CRANBROOK, TN17 3EG.
BOOBYER, Miss. Ella Marie, ACA *2010;* 5A Glycena Road, LONDON, SW11 5TP.
•**BOOCOCK, Mr. Darren Neil, BA ACA CF** *1996;* Deloitte LLP, 4 Brindley Place, BIRMINGHAM, B1 2HZ. See also Deloitte & Touche LLP
BOOCOCK, Mr. John, FCA *1981;* 21 Boothstown Drive, Worsley, MANCHESTER, M28 1UF.
BOODHNA, Miss. Karuna, ACA *2008;* 20 Perch Street, LONDON, E8 2EG.
BOODHOO, Mr. Ambar, BSc(Econ) FCA CF CFA *1999;* 400 East 52nd Street, Apartment 11GJ, NEW YORK, NY 10022, UNITED STATES.
BOODHOO, Mr. Hunsraj, MBA ACA FCCA *2007;* Lyndale, Woodhouse Lane, East Ardsley, WAKEFIELD, WEST YORKSHIRE, WF3 2JS.
BOODHUN, Mr. Dheeraj, ACA *2008;* 9 Battle Square The West Village, READING, RG30 1BF.
BOOHAN, Mr. Michael Daniel, FCA *1964;* 34 Crescent West, BARNET, HERTFORDSHIRE, EN4 0EJ.
BOOKER, Miss. Catherine Joan, BA ACA *1998;* The Old Orchard, Nobold Court, Gold Street, Clipston, MARKET HARBOROUGH, LEICESTERSHIRE LE16 9RR.
BOOKER, Mr. Christopher James, ACA *1995;* with Deloitte LLP, Abbots House, Abbey Street, READING, RG1 3BD.
BOOKER, Mr. David Francis, BA FCA *1975;* (Tax Fac), Whitethorns, 63 Stumperlowe Crescent Road, SHEFFIELD, S10 3PR.
BOOKER, Mr. Eric Sidney Hayes, FCA *1953;* 30 Rutland Close, Highlight Park, BARRY, SOUTH GLAMORGAN, CF62 8AR. (Life Member)
BOOKER, Miss. Jacqueline Elizabeth Kilgour, MA ACA *1987;* Boyer Allan Investment Management LLP, 12-18 Grosvenor Gardens, LONDON, SW1W 0DH.
•**BOOKER, Mr. Jeremy Charles, BSc ACA** *1980;* PricewaterhouseCoopers LLP, 1 Embankment Place, LONDON, WC2N 6RH. See also PricewaterhouseCoopers
BOOKER, Mrs. Leona, BSc ACA *2004;* 17 Woburn Close, Caversham, READING, RG4 7HB.
BOOKER, Mr. Malcolm Colin, BSc ACA *1995;* 7 Lime Walk, MAIDENHEAD, BERKSHIRE, SL6 6QB.
•**BOOKER, Mr. Malcolm Marc, FCA** *1991;* (Tax Fac), Deloitte & Touche, Deloitte Place, Mriehel Place, Mriehel Bypass, MRIEHEL BKR3000, MALTA.
BOOKER, Mr. Martyn Paul, BA(Hons) ACA *1991;* 13 Musgrave Avenue, EAST GRINSTEAD, WEST SUSSEX, RH19 4BP.
BOOKER, Mrs. Rachael Mary, BSc ACA *2003;* 14 Burmoor Close, HUNTINGDON, CAMBRIDGESHIRE, PE29 6GE.
BOOKER, Mr. Robert Carlton, BSc ACA *1992;* 10 Pipistrelle Way, Charvil, READING, RG10 9WA.
BOOKER, Mr. Roger Denys, BA FCA *1974;* (Tax Fac), Warner Music, 28 Kensington Church Street, LONDON, W8 4EP.
BOOKER, Mr. Roger Ian, BA ACA *1984;* Sevacare, Unit 9, Sidestrand, Pendeford Business Park, WOLVERHAMPTON, WV9 5HD.
BOOKER, Mrs. Sarah Louise, BSc ACA *1999;* Parkwood Project Management Ltd, Parkwood House, Berkeley Drive, Bamber Bridge, PRESTON, PR5 6BY.
•**BOOKEY, Mr. Bernard Sidney, FCA** *1956;* Bookey & Co, 319 Trafalgar House, Grenville Place, LONDON, NW7 3SA.
BOOL, Mrs. Caroline, BSc ACA *1996;* Im Marbach 25, 8800 THALWIL, SWITZERLAND.
BOOL, Mr. Malcolm Colin, FCA ACMA *1956;* 26 Queens Road, KINGSTON UPON THAMES, SURREY, KT2 7SN. (Life Member)
•**BOOLAKY, Dr. Pran Krishansing, PhD ACA ACCA MBA** *2007;* University of Southern Queensland, Faculty of Business, Level 3, Room T317, TOOWOOMBA, QLD AUSTRALIA.
BOOME, Miss. Helen Venetia, MA ACA *2002;* Pricewaterhousecoopers Llp, 1 Hays Lane, LONDON, SE1 2RD.
•**BOOMLA, Mr. Mark Adam, ACA FCCA** *2010;* Prager and Fenton LLP, 8th Floor, Imperial House, 15-19 Kingsway, LONDON, WC2B 6UN.
BOON, Mr. Alfred Brian, FCA *1962;* 35 Jacklin Drive, Finham Park, COVENTRY, CV3 6QG. (Life Member)
BOON, Miss. Genieve Lucinda, BA ACA *2003;* 181a Iffley Road, OXFORD, OX4 1EL.
BOON, Mr. Gerald William, LLB FCA *1977;* 6 Sandringham Road, Birkdale, SOUTHPORT, MERSEYSIDE, PR8 2JZ.
BOON, Mr. John David, BA ACA *1988;* Pinecroft, Henley Road, MARLOW, BUCKINGHAMSHIRE, SL7 2DG.
BOON, Mr. Michael Charles Mcmillan, BA(Hons) FCA MSt(Cantab) *1969;* Hill House, 5 Addison Road, Gorleston, GREAT YARMOUTH, NR31 0PA.
BOON, Mr. Philip Richard, FCA *1969;* Holly Tree Cottage, 85 Lane End, Corsley, WARMINSTER, BA12 7PF.
BOON, Mrs. Ruth Elizabeth, MSci ACA *2003;* 59 Fox Hollies Road, SUTTON COLDFIELD, B76 2RL.
BOON, Mr. Simon Trevor Seymour, BA ACA CTA *2003;* 59 Fox Hollies Road, SUTTON COLDFIELD, B76 2RL.
BOON, Mr. Steven Paul, BCom ACA *1988;* 64 Park Road, WOKING, SURREY, GU22 7BZ.
BOON, Mr. Terence Kristian, MMath BA ACA *2002;* with PricewaterhouseCoopers LLP, Hays Galleria, 1 Hays Lane, LONDON, SE1 2RD.
BOON, Mr. Timothy Walter, BSc ACA *1995;* 71 Holland Road, LONDON, E6 2EP.
BOON KANG, Mr. Tang, BAcc ACA *2004;* Block 290C, Compassvale Cresent #03-34, SINGAPORE 543290, SINGAPORE.
BOONE, Ms. Amanda Louise, BA ACA *1999;* Little Gables, Foundry Lane, Copford, COLCHESTER, CO6 1BH.
BOONMAHANARK, Mr. Chinnarat, ACA *1998;* 4388 Rama 4 Road, BANGKOK 10110, THAILAND.
BOONZAAIER, Mr. Ivan Coenraad, BA ACA *2006;* Flat 1601 Wharfside Point South, 4 Prestons Road, LONDON, E14 9EX.
BOORA, Miss. Nimrata, ACA *2010;* 16 Aspen Way, Red Lodge, BURY ST. EDMUNDS, SUFFOLK, IP28 8GU.
BOORE, Mr. Rhys Thomas, BSocSc ACA *1995;* 65 Bishops Road, Whitchurch, CARDIFF, CF14 1LW.
BOORE, Dr. Roger Pryse, PhD MA FCA *1965;* 28 Church Road, Whitchurch, CARDIFF, CF14 2EA.
BOORER, Miss. Jennifer Louise, ACA *2008;* 20b Victoria Road, LONDON, E18 1LG.
BOORMAN, Mr. Alastair James, BSc ACA *2004;* 15 Church Road, Almondsbury, BRISTOL, BS32 4DT.
BOORMAN, Mrs. Christiane Mary, MA ACA *1982;* Spylaw Cottage, 3 Spylaw Park, EDINBURGH, EH13 0LS.
BOORMAN, Mr. Ian Hugh, ACA *1983;* (Tax Fac), 3 Alderwick Grove, Kings Hill, WEST MALLING, KENT, ME19 4GB.
BOORMAN, Mr. Jeremy Stuart, BA ACA *1998;* New Street Research, 145 Leadenhall Street, LONDON, EC3V 4QT.
BOORMAN, Mrs. Kate Patricia Janet, MSc ACA *2004;* Church house, 15 Church Road, Almondsbury, BRISTOL, BS32 4DT.
BOORMAN, Mr. Michael John Charles, BA ACA *1983;* Blackrock, 40 Torphichen Street, EDINBURGH, EH3 8JB.
•**BOORMAN, Mr. Paul, BSc FCA** *1978;* PricewaterhouseCoopers LLP, 10-18 Union Street, LONDON, SE1 1SZ. See also PricewaterhouseCoopers
BOORMAN, Miss. Rebecca Jane, ACA *2008;* Ivy House, 35 High Street, BUSHEY, HERTFORDSHIRE, WD23 1BD.
BOORMAN, Mr. Victor Douglas, FCA *1942;* 39 Worthing Road, East Preston, LITTLEHAMPTON, BN16 1DF. (Life Member)
BOORNE, Mr. Simon, BSc ACA *2011;* 46 Golden Avenue, East Preston, LITTLEHAMPTON, WEST SUSSEX, BN16 1QX.
BOOROFF, Mr. Christopher Johnathon, BSc ACA *2006;* 19 Cheriton Close, LONDON, W5 1TR.
BOOS, Mr. Peter Neville, FCA *1969;* Hillcrest, Golf Club Road, CHRISTCHURCH, BB15120, BARBADOS.
BOOSEY, Miss. Mary Cecilia, BA ACA *1998;* 100 Huntingdon Road, East Finchley, LONDON, N2 9DU.
BOOT, Mr. Andrew Simon, BSc ACA *1995;* St Clair, 2 West End Grove, FARNHAM, GU9 7EG.
•**BOOT, Mr. George Robert, FCA** *1971;* Robert Boot & Co, Cotleigh, 6A Windermere Way, REIGATE, RH2 0LW.
BOOT, Miss. Lyn, BSc ACA *1979;* Orchard Lodge, Brickyard Lane, Farnsfield, NEWARK, NG22 8JS.
BOOT, Mrs. Melanie, BSc ACA *1995;* 403 Tandur Road, TANDUR, QLD 4570, AUSTRALIA.
•**BOOT, Mr. Nicholas, LLB FCA** *1998;* Bullimores LLP, Old Printers Yard, 156 South Street, DORKING, SURREY, RH4 2HF.
BOOT, Mr. Nicholas Peter William, MA ACA *1995;* 403 Tandur Road, TANDUR, QLD 4570, AUSTRALIA.
BOOT, Mr. Nigel Richard, BTech ACA *1980;* Stonecroft, 4 Beechwood Grove, ILKLEY, WEST YORKSHIRE, LS29 9AX.
BOOT, Mr. Richard John, OBE FCA *1973;* Churchill Grange, Churchill, KIDDERMINSTER, DY10 3LZ.
BOOT-HANDFORD, Miss. Victoria, ACA *2010;* 10 Weston Road, BROMLEY, BR1 3RH.
BOOTE, Mr. Charles Richard Michael, TD DL FCA *1963;* Business Development International, Enson Moor House, Enson, STAFFORD, ST18 9TA.
BOOTE, Mr. Gervase William Alexander, FCA *1967;* The Willows, Brook, GODALMING, GU8 5UJ.
BOOTE, Mr. Nicholas Rupert Edmund, FCA *1973;* 7 Forthbridge Road, Battersea, LONDON, SW11 5NU.
BOOTE, Mr. Paul Michael, BSc ACA *2003;* Pennon Group Plc, Peninsula House, Rydon Lane, EXETER, EX2 7HR.
•**BOOTE, Mr. Stephen Thomas, BSc FCA** *1979;* Mapus-Smith & Lemmon LLP, 48 King Street, KING'S LYNN, NORFOLK, PE30 1HE.
BOOTH, Mr. Adam Charles, MA ACA *2001;* 10 Hallside Court, Mosborough, SHEFFIELD, S20 5EP.
BOOTH, Mr. Alan, FCA *1971;* (Tax Fac), Hallcroft, 54 Chesterfield Road, Tibshelf, ALFRETON, DE55 5NL.
BOOTH, Mr. Alan Frederick, FCA *1954;* 28 Highway Lane, Keele, NEWCASTLE, ST5 5AN. (Life Member)
BOOTH, Mr. Alan Hoggarth, FCA *1961;* The Willows, 13 St. Lawrence Avenue, Bidborough, TUNBRIDGE WELLS, KENT, TN4 0XA. (Life Member)
BOOTH, Mr. Andrew Arnold, BSc FCA *1977;* 13 Cedar Gardens, SANDY, SG19 1EY.
•**BOOTH, Mr. Andrew Ernest, ACA** *1988;* Moss & Williamson, 3 Mellor Road, Cheadle Hulme, CHEADLE, SK8 5AT. See also Moss & Williamson Ltd
BOOTH, Dr. Andrew James, PhD MA BA ACA *2001;* iCount Training, Portland Tower, Portland Street, MANCHESTER, M1 3LF.
BOOTH, Mr. Andrew Philip, ACA *1993;* The Farmhouse, Stainton Cotes, Coniston Cold, SKIPTON, NORTH YORKSHIRE, BD23 4EQ.
BOOTH, Mr. Andrew William, LLB ACA *1992;* 48 Green Lane, Formby, LIVERPOOL, L37 7BH.
BOOTH, Mr. Anthony, FCA *1973;* 35 Burnbridge Oval, Burn Bridge, HARROGATE, NORTH YORKSHIRE, HG3 1LP.
BOOTH, Mr. Anthony Miles Philip, BSc ACA *1990;* with Grant Thornton UK LLP, 4 Hardman Square, Spinningfields, MANCHESTER, M3 3EB.
BOOTH, Mr. Anthony Stuart, FCA *1965;* 6 Second Avenue, Douglas, ISLE OF MAN, IM2 6AW.
BOOTH, Arthur Thomas, Esq CBE FCA *1959;* Lee Wood, Reservoir Road, Whaley Bridge, HIGH PEAK, SK23 7BW. (Life Member)
BOOTH, Mrs. Carmel, BA(Hons) ACA *2001;* Amion Consulting Ltd, Horton House, Exchange Flags, LIVERPOOL, L2 3YL.
BOOTH, Miss. Caroline Jane, BSc ACA *2006;* 14 Brook Avenue, ASCOT, SL5 7SG.
BOOTH, Mrs. Catherine Alice, BSc ACA *1990;* 47 Jamestown Way, LONDON, E14 2DE.
BOOTH, Miss. Catherine Jane, BSc FCA *1999;* 16 Hemdean Hill, Caversham, READING, RG4 7SB.
BOOTH, Mr. Charles Jonathan Norleigh, FCA *1966;* Hudworth Cottage, The Village, Castle Eden, HARTLEPOOL, CLEVELAND, TS27 4SJ.
BOOTH, Mr. Christopher, BA(Hons) ACA ATT *2010;* 25 Roman Terrace, LEEDS, LS8 2DU.
•**BOOTH, Mr. Christopher Paul, BA FCA** *1982;* 65 Hall Ing Lane, HOLMFIRTH, WEST YORKSHIRE, HD9 6QW.
•**BOOTH, Mr. Christopher Raymond, BSc ACA** *1988;* McKellens Ltd, 11 Riverview, The Embankment Business Park, Heaton Mersey, STOCKPORT, CHESHIRE SK4 3GN. See also McKellens Outsourcing LLP
BOOTH, Mr. Christopher Warren, ACA *2009;* British American Tobacco Plc Globe House, 4 Temple Place, LONDON, WC2R 2PG.
BOOTH, Mrs. Claire Julia, BA ACA *1990;* Kerrera, 15 Stream Farm Close, Lower Bourne, FARNHAM, GU10 3PD.
BOOTH, Miss. Clare Rosemary, BA(Hons) ACA *2002;* Tenwick Financial Services, 11 Kennedy Close, London Colney, ST. ALBANS, HERTFORDSHIRE, AL2 1GR.
BOOTH, Mr. David Andrew, BSocSc ACA *1986;* CDB Management Ltd, 32 Ray Lea Road, MAIDENHEAD, SL6 8QE.
•**BOOTH, Mr. David Nigel, BSc FCA** *1990;* Booth Parkes & Associates Limited, Southolme, Trinity Street, GAINSBOROUGH, DN21 2EQ.
BOOTH, Mr. David Patrick Ian, BA ACA *2000;* British American Tobacco Plc Globe House, 4 Temple Place, LONDON, WC2R 2PG.
•**BOOTH, Miss. Deirdre Lilian, FCA** *1970;* Deirdre L Booth, Fairview, Marley Lane, Hoath, CANTERBURY, CT3 4JY.

BOOTH, Mr. Derek Malcolm, BA FCA *1963;* The Old Vicarage, Newton Hall, Newton, STOCKSFIELD, NE43 7UH. (Life Member)
BOOTH, Mr. Dominic, ACA *2009;* Flat 24 Nichols Court, 10 Cremer Street, LONDON, E2 8HR.
BOOTH, Mr. Donald Barrie, FCA *1959;* 12 Grange Road, Bessacarr, DONCASTER, DN4 6SA. (Life Member)
•BOOTH, Mr. Douglas Steele, FCA *1974;* D.S Booth & Co, 19 Tower Estate, Point Clear, St Osyth, CLACTON-ON-SEA, ESSEX CO16 8NG.
BOOTH, Mr. Edward Lawrence, FCA *1962;* 10 Westbrook Avenue, WESTVILLE, 3629, SOUTH AFRICA.
BOOTH, Mrs. Eleanor Jane, LLB ACA *2002;* Financial Services Centre, B O C Ltd Rother Valley Way, Holbrook, SHEFFIELD, S20 3RP.
BOOTH, Mr. Francis David, FCA *1977;* Homefield Barn, Speldhurst Hill, Speldhurst, TUNBRIDGE WELLS, KENT, TN3 0NE.
BOOTH, Mr. Frank Andrew, FCA *1966;* Griffins Cottage, Lyme Park, Disley, STOCKPORT, CHESHIRE, SK12 2NT.
BOOTH, Mr. Gary Stephen, BA(Hons) ACA *2004;* WHITEFRIARS HOUSING GROUP, 9 Little Park Street, COVENTRY, CV1 2UR.
•BOOTH, Mr. Geoffrey Charles, BSc FCA *1985;* (Tax Fac), Taxsavers Direct Ltd, 26 Orchard Way, OXTED, SURREY, RH8 9DJ.
BOOTH, Mr. Geoffrey Graham, MA ACA *1980;* 2 Glenside, Castle Bytham, GRANTHAM, LINCOLNSHIRE, NG33 4SS.
BOOTH, Mr. George Charles Robin, FCA *1969;* London Chamber Of Commerce, & Industry, 33 Queen Street, LONDON, EC4R 1AP.
BOOTH, Mr. Gerald Edward, FCA *1961;* 10 Kelvin Grove, Cleadon, SUNDERLAND, SR6 7SW.
BOOTH, Miss. Hayley, BSc ACA *2006;* Blackbrook Farm, Blackbrook, Hanbury, BURTON-ON-TRENT, DE13 8TX.
BOOTH, Miss. Helen Jane, BSc FCA *1994;* 35 Sharket Head Close, Queensbury, BRADFORD, WEST YORKSHIRE, BD13 1PD.
BOOTH, Mr. Iain Nelson, BA ACA *2002;* 25 Calderstones Avenue, LIVERPOOL, L18 6HX.
BOOTH, Mr. Ian Gordon, FCA *1957;* Ashmead, Hillhead, COLYTON, EX24 6NJ. (Life Member)
BOOTH, Mr. James, MSc ACA *2010;* 50 Charwood Road, WOKINGHAM, RG40 1RY.
BOOTH, Mr. James Michael, BSc ACA *1999;* 9 Lancaster Mews, RICHMOND, SURREY, TW10 6RG.
BOOTH, Mrs. Janet Lesley, BSc ACA *1983;* Bretton Woods, Barley Mow Field, Craig Penllyn, COWBRIDGE, CF71 7RT.
BOOTH, Miss. Joanne Sarah, BCom FCA *1992;* 30 Kew Green, RICHMOND, TW9 3BH.
BOOTH, Mr. John, FCA *1967;* 5 Priory Road, Manton, OAKHAM, LE15 8ST.
BOOTH, Mr. Jonathan, ACA *1986;* Unit 3 Block C Axis Point, Hill Top Road, HEYWOOD, OL10 2RQ.
BOOTH, Mrs. Katherine Sarah, BA(Hons) ACA *2003;* 38 George Road, WARWICK, CV34 5LX.
BOOTH, Mrs. Katy Leigh, BSc(Hons) ACA *2002;* 16 Hollybush Close, Whitley, GOOLE, NORTH HUMBERSIDE, DN14 0FF.
BOOTH, Mr. Kenneth, FCA *1954;* 23 Falcon Road, BINGLEY, BD16 4DP. (Life Member)
BOOTH, Mrs. Laura Jane, MA ACA *1995;* 63 Browns Road, SURBITON, SURREY, KT5 8SP.
BOOTH, Mrs. Lianne Marie, BSc ACA *1995;* Castle Court Consulting Ltd, 3 Park Court Mews, CARDIFF, CF10 3DQ.
BOOTH, Miss. Lorna, BSc ACA *1997;* 3 Buttermere Drive, Ramsbottom, BURY, LANCASHIRE, BL0 9YG.
BOOTH, Mrs. Lorna Margaret, BSc(Hons) ACA *2004;* Central Midlands Co-operative Society Ltd Central House, Hermes Road, LICHFIELD, STAFFORDSHIRE, WS13 6RH.
BOOTH, Mr. Malcolm Frederick, FCA *1957;* 12 Moor Lane, East Ayton, SCARBOROUGH, NORTH YORKSHIRE, YO13 9EW. (Life Member)
BOOTH, Mr. Malcolm Kevin, FCA *1979;* 36 Crawshaw Ave, BEVERLEY, HU17 7QW.
BOOTH, Mr. Mark Richard, MEng ACA *2000;* 12 Cranford Avenue, KNUTSFORD, CHESHIRE, WA16 0EB.
BOOTH, Mr. Martin Kershaw, BA ACA *1992;* 7 Lodge Gardens, HARPENDEN, AL5 4JE.
BOOTH, Mr. Martin Stuart, FCA *1971;* 35 Station Road, Rearsby, LEICESTER, LE7 4YY.
BOOTH, Mr. Matthew Stephen, BSc(Hons) ACA *2010;* Hetlands, Markland Hill, BOLTON, BL1 5AF.
BOOTH, Mr. Michael, ACA *2011;* 88 York Gardens, WALTON-ON-THAMES, SURREY, KT12 3EW.
•BOOTH, Mr. Michael Alan, ACA *1983;* Hanley & Co, 25 Main Street, Staveley, KENDAL, LA8 9LU.
BOOTH, Mr. Michael David, FCA *1973;* The Coach House, 28 Humber Road, NORTH FERRIBY, HU14 3DW.
BOOTH, Mr. Michael John, FCA *1973;* 43 Station Road, KINGS LANGLEY, WD4 8RU.
•BOOTH, Mr. Michael Sinclair, BA ACA *1983;* Booth Ainsworth LLP, Alpha House, 4 Greek Street, STOCKPORT, CHESHIRE, SK3 8AB.
BOOTH, Mrs. Morag, MA ACA *1988;* 34 Bromley Road, SHIPLEY, BD18 4DT.
BOOTH, Mr. Neil Douglas, FCA *1964;* Rivendell, 1114 Bolton Road, BRADFORD, BD2 4HS.
BOOTH, Mrs. Patricia Anne, BA ACA *1992;* Loreto Grammar School, Dunham Road, ALTRINCHAM, CHESHIRE, WA14 4AH.
•BOOTH, Mr. Paul Nigel, MPhil BA FCA MICM DChA *1992;* Mitchell Charlesworth, Centurion House, 129 Deansgate, MANCHESTER, M3 3WR.
BOOTH, Mr. Peter David, BSc ACA *1989;* M C Truck & Bus Ltd, Beddow Way, Forstal Road, AYLESFORD, ME20 7BT.
BOOTH, Mr. Peter James, FCA *1978;* Windy Ridge Hermitage Road, Higham, ROCHESTER, ME3 7NF.
BOOTH, Mr. Philip Martin, ACA *2008;* 18 Binley Close, Shirley, SOLIHULL, B90 2RB.
•BOOTH, Mrs. Philippa Louise, BSc(Hons) ACA CTA *1999;* Deloitte LLP, Hill House, 1 Little New Street, LONDON, EC4A 3TR. See also Deloitte & Touche LLP
BOOTH, Miss. Rachael Ann, BA ACA *2004;* Myriad Group Tower House, Towers Business Park Wilmslow Road, MANCHESTER, M20 2SL.
BOOTH, Mr. Richard, FCA *1970;* 29 West Park Grove, LEEDS, LS8 2DX. (Life Member)
BOOTH, Mr. Richard, BA ACA *2007;* 42 Linkway, LONDON, SW20 9AU.
BOOTH, Mr. Richard James, BSocSc ACA *2003;* H M Revenue & Customs, 4th Floor, City Centre House, 30 Union Street, BIRMINGHAM, WEST MIDLANDS B2 4AD.
BOOTH, Mr. Richard John, ACA *1992;* 117 Dartmouth Avenue, NEWCASTLE, STAFFORDSHIRE, ST5 3NR.
•BOOTH, Mr. Richard Mark Sinclair, BA FCA *1984;* (Tax Fac), LMDB Limited, Railview Lofts, 19c Commercial Road, EASTBOURNE, EAST SUSSEX, BN21 3XE.
BOOTH, Mr. Robert, ACA *2011;* 24 Thirstin Road, Honley, HOLMFIRTH, HD9 6JG.
BOOTH, Mr. Robert Brian, FCA *1956;* 10 Overdene Close, Lostock, BOLTON, BL6 4DY. (Life Member)
BOOTH, Mr. Robert Edward, BSc FCA *1992;* 9 Brownlow Street, LEAMINGTON SPA, CV32 5XH.
BOOTH, Mr. Robert Frank, BA FCA *1990;* 36 Ashgrove Avenue, Ashley Down, BRISTOL, BS7 9LL.
BOOTH, Mr. Robin, BSc ACA *1991;* Weston Centre, Associated British Foods Plc, 10 Grosvenor Street, LONDON, W1K 4QY.
BOOTH, Mr. Ronald Parkyn, VRD FCA *1948;* 5 The Finney, Caldy, WIRRAL, CH48 2LL. (Life Member)
BOOTH, Mr. Roy William, FCA *1960;* Old Stables, Greys Hill, HENLEY-ON-THAMES, OXFORDSHIRE, RG9 1SW. (Life Member)
BOOTH, Mr. Russell, MA ACA *1982;* (Tax Fac), Dept 662 Taxes International, Deutsche Post DHL, Charles-De-Gaulle-Strasse 20, 53113 BONN, GERMANY.
BOOTH, Mrs. Ruth Margaret, BA ACA *1990;* 3 Beckets Square, BERKHAMSTED, HP4 1BZ.
BOOTH, Mrs. Samantha Jane, BA ACA *2010;* 25 Roman Terrace, LEEDS, LS8 2DU.
BOOTH, Mrs. Samantha Rosemary Jane, BSc ACA *1998;* 1 Brownhills Close, Tottington, BURY, BL8 3LF.
BOOTH, Mrs. Sarah Alexandra, BA(Econ) ACA *1996;* 32 Willesley Gardens, ASHBY-DE-LA-ZOUCH, LEICESTERSHIRE, LE65 2QF.
BOOTH, Mrs. Sarah Elizabeth, ACA *2008;* Rolls-Royce Plc, PO Box 31, DERBY, DE24 8BJ.
BOOTH, Mrs. Sarah Elizabeth, BA ACA *1993;* Bullhouse Mill Cottage, Lee Lane, Millhouse Green, SHEFFIELD, S36 9NN.
BOOTH, Mr. Sean, BA ACA *2004;* 49 Olive Lane, LIVERPOOL, L15 8LR.
BOOTH, Mr. Simon Andrew, BA ACA *1989;* Newcastle Bldg Soc, Portland House, New Bridge Street West, NEWCASTLE UPON TYNE, NE1 8AL.
BOOTH, Mr. Simon Edward, MA ACA *1996;* 1 Birch Gardens, AMERSHAM, BUCKINGHAMSHIRE, HP7 9TH.
•BOOTH, Mr. Stephen Charles Edward, FCA *1974;* Stephen Booth, 17 Ivyhouse Road, Ickenham, UXBRIDGE, UB10 8NF.
BOOTH, Mr. Stephen Edward, ACA *1983;* Trelayne, Chalk Road, Ifold Loxwood, BILLINGSHURST, RH14 0UD.
BOOTH, Mr. Stephen Gerald, BSc FCA *1979;* 160c Hoppers Road, LONDON, N21 3LA.
•BOOTH, Mr. Stephen Graham, BSc ACA *1991;* Booth Finance Consulting Limited, 2 Bradley Drive, WOKINGHAM, BERKSHIRE, RG40 3HZ.
BOOTH, Mr. Stephen John, BA ACA *1986;* 14 Dunchurch Crescent, SUTTON COLDFIELD, B73 6QN.
•BOOTH, Mr. Steven John, FCA *1980;* (Tax Fac), Graham H. Wood & Co, 225 Market Street, HYDE, CHESHIRE, SK14 1HF. See also Graham Wood Partnership
BOOTH, Mr. Thomas Damian, MA ACA *1988;* 111a Liverpool Road, Cadishead, MANCHESTER, M44 5BG.
BOOTH, Miss. Tineke Jarine Hinke, ACA *2005;* with KPMG LLP, One Snowhill, Snow Hill Queensway, BIRMINGHAM, B4 6GN.
BOOTH, Miss. Victoria, MChem ACA *2000;* 18 Lawn Crescent, Kew, RICHMOND, TW9 3NR.
•BOOTH, Mr. William John, BA FCA *1988;* Armstrong Watson, Central House, 47 St Pauls Street, LEEDS, LS1 2TE.
BOOTH, Mr. William Thomas, FCA *1973;* (Tax Fac), Peter Brett Associates, Caversham Bridge House, Waterman Place, READING, BERKSHIRE, RG1 8DN.
BOOTH, Mrs. Zoe Abigail, MPhys ACA *2010;* Flat 17 Ship Canal House, 29 Slate Wharf, MANCHESTER, M15 4SX.
•BOOTHBY, Mr. Geoffrey Guy, FCA *1981;* (Tax Fac), Boothby Baker & Co, 12 Mountway Close, WELWYN GARDEN CITY, HERTFORDSHIRE, AL7 4JZ.
•BOOTHBY, Mr. Terence Guy, FCA *1974;* Griffins, Griffins Court, 24-32 London Road, NEWBURY, RG14 1JX. See also Griffins Business Advisers LLP
BOOTHBY, Mrs. Treena, BA ACA *1996;* 7 Cornet Close, Lindley, HUDDERSFIELD, HD3 3QQ.
BOOTHMAN, Mrs. Anne, ACA *1981;* Flat 4, Bladon Lodge, Boltons Place, LONDON, SW5 0LQ.
BOOTHMAN, Mr. Clive Nicholas, BA ACA *1981;* 331 Riverside West, Smugglers Way, LONDON, SW18 1ED.
•BOOTHMAN, Mr. David Alexander, BSc FCA *1977;* Boothmans, Millennium House, Summerhill Business Park, Victoria Road, Douglas, ISLE OF MAN IM2 4RW.
BOOTHMAN, Mr. Derek Arnold, CBE FCA *1954;* (President 1986 - 1987) (Member of Council 1969 - 1991), Ashworth Dene, Wilmslow Road, Mottram St. Andrew, MACCLESFIELD, SK10 4QH. (Life Member)
BOOTHMAN, Mr. Richard, FCA *1953;* 879 Blackpool Road, Lea, PRESTON, PR2 1QS. (Life Member)
BOOTHROYD, Mr. Brian, BA FCA *1962;* 52 Belvedere Court, Alwoodley, LEEDS, LS17 8NF. (Life Member)
•BOOTHROYD, Mr. Paul, BSc FCA *1978;* Paul Boothroyd, 1 Potters Walk, Golcar, HUDDERSFIELD, HD7 4HH.
BOOTHROYD, Mr. Paul Stuart, FCA *1975;* 113 Victoria Road, ELLAND, HX5 0QF.
•BOOTHROYD, Mr. Peter Alexander John, FCA *1985;* (Tax Fac), Saint & Co., Sterling House, Wavell Drive, Rosehill, CARLISLE, CA1 2SA.
BOOTHROYD, Mr. Richard Alan, MBA BA ACA *1988;* Zenos Ltd Aynho Park House, Aynhoe Park Aynho, BANBURY, OXFORDSHIRE, OX17 3BQ.
BOOTHROYD, Mr. Stephen Robert, ACA *2010;* 21 Westwood Avenue, Timperley, ALTRINCHAM, CHESHIRE, WA15 6QF.
BOOTLAND, Mr. Harvey Douglas, LLB ACA *2004;* Shell International Petroleum Co Ltd, C4014 Shell Centre, York Road, LONDON, SE1 7NA.
BOOTON, Mr. Joseph Stanley, TD FCA *1950;* 152 Lauderdale Tower, LONDON, EC2Y 8BY. (Life Member)
BOOTY, Miss. Jill Alexandra, BA ACA *1989;* The Dower House, 52 High Street, Bugbrooke, NORTHAMPTON, NN7 3PG.
BOPARAI, Mr. Raminder Singh, BSc ACA *1997;* 46 Woodville Gardens, LONDON, W5 2LQ.
•BOR, Mr. Jeffrey Anthony, BSc FCA *1975;* (Tax Fac), Shacter Cohen & Bor, 29-31 Sackville Street, MANCHESTER, M1 3LZ. See also SCB (Accountants) Limited
BORALESSA, Mr. Harsha, BSc ACA *1997;* (Tax Fac), Flat 24, Circus Lodge, Circus Road, St Johns Wood, LONDON, NW8 9JL.
BORAM, Mrs. Alison Joyce, BSc ACA *1983;* Simpson Wreford & Partners Suffolk House, George Street, CROYDON, CR0 0YN.
BORAM, Mr. Kevin, BSc ACA *1983;* 48 Buckingham Road, SHOREHAM-BY-SEA, BN43 5UD.
BORASTON, Ms. Joanna Pamela, BSc ACA *1992;* The Granary, Ileden, Kingston, CANTERBURY, CT4 6HP.
BORBAS, Mr. Mark Attila, BA ACA *1994;* 8 Ostlers Way, KETTERING, NORTHAMPTONSHIRE, NN15 6GJ.
BORCHART, Mr. Andrew Neil, BA FCA *1988;* 55 The Gables, Haddenham, AYLESBURY, HP17 8AD.
BORDER, Mr. Robin David, ACA *1978;* Leawood, Tanners Lane, Chalkhouse Green, READING, OXFORDSHIRE, RG4 9AD.
BORDERICK, Miss. Rebecca, ACA *2007;* 480 Aureole Walk, NEWMARKET, SUFFOLK, CB8 7BQ.
•BORDOLEY, Mr. Michael, FCA *1964;* (Tax Fac), Wilder Coe LLP, 233-237 Old Marylebone Road, LONDON, NW1 5QT. See also Wilder Coe
•BOREHAM, Mr. Christopher John, MA ACA *1999;* with PricewaterhouseCoopers LLP, 9 Greyfriars Road, READING, RG1 1JG.
BOREHAM, Mr. John Stokes, FCA *1960;* Silver Birch, Lyle Park, Linden Chase, SEVENOAKS, KENT, TN13 3JX. (Life Member)
BORG, Miss. Rosina, BSc ACA *1999;* Box 441, WALKERVILLE, SA 5081, AUSTRALIA.
BORGENICHT, Mr. Nathan, BSc ACA *1983;* 93 Woodlands, LONDON, NW11 9QT.
BORKETT, Mr. William Richard, BSc FCA CPA *1976;* 65 Palatine, Apartment 423, IRVINE, CA 92612, UNITED STATES.
BORKHATARIA, Mr. Nirmal-Kumar, BSc ACA *1986;* The Lodge, Northaw Park, Firs Wood Close Northaw, POTTERS BAR, EN6 4BY.
BORKOWSKI, Mr. Andre Nicholas, BA ACA *1979;* 26 Wassell Drive, BEWDLEY, WORCESTERSHIRE, DY12 1EE.
•BORLAND, Mr. Andrew Herbert, FCA *1976;* (Tax Fac), Andrew Borland, 75 Newnham Street, ELY, CB7 4PQ.
BORLAND, Mr. Robert David, FCA *1975;* 26 Copse Hill, Braddan, ISLE OF MAN, IM2 1NE.
BORLENGHI, Miss. Lara Marianne Elizabeth, MA ACA *1998;* 65 Finsbury Park Road, LONDON, N4 2JY.
•BORLEY, Mr. Ian James, FCA *1989;* KPMG LLP, 1 Waterloo Way, LEICESTER, LE1 6LP. See also KPMG Europe LLP
BORLEY, Mrs. Rachel Elizabeth, ACA *2006;* 1 Sheridan Close, STOWMARKET, SUFFOLK, IP14 1UL.
BORMAN, Mr. Colin Andrew, BEng FCA *1997;* La Franchette, La Petite Route Des Mielles, St. Brelade, JERSEY, JE3 8FA.
BORMAN, Miss. Rebecca Claire, BA(Hons) ACA *2003;* 9a Kings Road, Bramhope, LEEDS, LS16 9JW.
BORMANN, Mr. Matthias, ACA *2001;* 67 Bolingbroke Road, LONDON, W14 0AH.
BORN, Ms. Annette Elizabeth, BSc ACA *1995;* Bournemouth & Poole College of Further Education, North Road, POOLE, BH14 0LS.
BORN, Miss. Carolyn Louise, BSc ACA *2004;* 9 Churchward Mews, Somerset Close, MARTOCK, SOMERSET, TA12 6DQ.
•①BORN, Mr. Graham Irvine, FCA ACIArb ATII FABRP *1963;* Born Associates Limited, 4 Bloomsbury Place, LONDON, WC1A 2QA.
•BORN, Mr. Simon Henry Graham, BA(Hons) ACA *2002;* (Tax Fac), Born Associates Limited, 4 Bloomsbury Place, LONDON, WC1A 2QA.
BORNER, Ronald Stewart, Esq OBE VRD FCA *1936;* 14 Gange Mews, Middle Row, FAVERSHAM, KENT, ME13 7ED. (Life Member)
BORNOFF, Mr. Timothy Anthony, BSc(Hons) ACA MBA *2001;* 207 1A Tusculum Street, Potts Point, SYDNEY, NSW 2011, AUSTRALIA.
•BORONTE, Mr. Anthony Lee, BSc ACA *1991;* BRAL Limited, 12 York Gate, Regents Park, LONDON, NW1 4QS. See also Tick Accountancy Limited
BOROS, Mr. Anthony, BA ACA *1992;* 12 Malton Close, Monkston, MILTON KEYNES, MK10 9HR.
BOROS, Mr. Leon David, BA FCA *1990;* Wychcross, 14 Briar Hill, PURLEY, CR8 3LE.
•BOROWSKI, Mrs. Karen Gale, BA FCA *1995;* Revell Ward LLP, 7th Floor, 30 Market Street, HUDDERSFIELD, HD1 2HG.
BORRELL, Mr. Arthur James Peter, BA ACA *1983;* Pinedale, Wallace Avenue, Whickham, NEWCASTLE UPON TYNE, NE16 4SX.
BORRELLI, Mr. Michael Alexander, BA FCA *1982;* 40 Dukes Avenue, Chiswick, LONDON, W4 2AE.
BORRETT, Miss. Angela Seema, BSc(Hons) ACA *2002;* Shiraz, No.1 Bungalow Stanbury Road, Thruxton, ANDOVER, HAMPSHIRE, SP11 8NR.
BORRETT, Mrs. Anneke Helena, BA ACA *1995;* 1 Homechurch, Baylham, IPSWICH, IP6 8RF.
BORRETT, Mr. Paul Leo, BA FCA *1996;* with Deloitte & Touche LLP, 2000 ManuLife Place, 10180-101 Street, EDMONTON T5J 4E4, AB, CANADA.

BORRETT, Miss. Tracey, BSc ACA *1998;* 604 Timble Beck, Neptune Street, LEEDS, LS9 8AR.
BORRILL, Mr. Edwin Neil, FCA *1963;* 106 Thoresby Road, Bramcote Hills, NOTTINGHAM, NG9 3EP.
BORRILL, Miss. Helen Elizabeth, BSc ACA *2005;* 16 Cooke Close, WARWICK, CV34 5YG.
BORROTT, Mr. Andrew Robert, DPhil BSc ACA *2002;* 27 Archer Court, Longwell Green, BRISTOL, BS30 7DW.
BORROWDALE, Mr. John Arthur James, ACA *2010;* Flat 15 Chatsworth Court, Stanhope Road, ST. ALBANS, HERTFORDSHIRE, AL1 5BA.
BORROWDALE, Miss. Julie Anne, BA ACA *1984;* Cleveland Potash Ltd Boulby Mine, Loftus, SALTBURN-BY-THE-SEA, CLEVELAND, TS13 4UZ.
BORROWS, Mr. Matthew Philip, BA ACA *2003;* 50 Bracadale Drive, STOCKPORT, CHESHIRE, SK3 8RY.
BORSBOOM, Mrs. Francoise Claudia Germaine, ACA *1996;* Avenue Francine 1, 1640 RHODE ST GENESE, BELGIUM.
BORSOI, Mrs. Claire Jane, FCA *1986;* with Humphrey & Co, 7-9 The Avenue, EASTBOURNE, EAST SUSSEX, BN21 3YA.
BORTCOSH, Ms. Siham, ACA *1992;* 15 Campbell Road, Bow, LONDON, E3 4DS.
BORTHWICK, Mr. Alistair Trond, BSc FCA *1996;* 17 Quarry Gardens, LEATHERHEAD, SURREY, KT22 8UE.
BORTHWICK, Mr. Brian Livsey Fairlie, FCA *1965;* Drift House, Ockham Road North, East Horsley, LEATHERHEAD, KT24 6NU. (Life Member)
BORTHWICK, Mr. Christopher Michael, FCA *1973;* 9 The Park, Bookham, LEATHERHEAD, KT23 3JL.
BORTHWICK, Mr. Colin Stewart, BA ACA *1989;* 23 Swinbourne Gardens, WHITLEY BAY, TYNE AND WEAR, NE26 3AZ.
BORTHWICK, Mr. Graeme Ronald, BSc ACA *1998;* 4 Caldwell Road, WINDLESHAM, SURREY, GU20 6JJ.
BORTHWICK, Mr. Hugh Edward Grant, FCA *1977;* Barnum, 15 Barnfield Road, PETERSFIELD, GU31 4DQ.
BORTHWICK, Mr. Michael, ACA *2002;* 49 Sudlow Road, LONDON, SW18 1HP.
BORTHWICK, Mr. Nigel Brian Alexander, BCom FCA *1986;* Mizuho International Plc, Bracken House, 1 Friday Street, LONDON, EC4M 9JA.
•BORTHWICK, Mr. Patrick James Joseph, FCA *1971;* (Tax Fac), James Borthwick FCA, 35 Anxey Way, Haddenham, AYLESBURY, BUCKINGHAMSHIRE, HP17 8DJ.
BORTHWICK, Miss. Pippa Margaret, LLB ACA *2001;* 4/15 Lochend Road, EDINBURGH, EH6 8BR.
BORTHWICK, Mr. William Martin S, ACA *2008;* Pricewaterhousecoopers, 1 Embankment Place, LONDON, WC2N 6RH.
BORTON, Miss. Amanda, ACA *2011;* 20 Chapel House Street, LONDON, E14 3AS.
•BORTON, Mr. Richard Edward Timothy, FCA DChA *1990;* Bishop Fleming, Stratus House, Emperor Way, Exeter Business Park, EXETER, EX1 3QS.
•BORUCKI, Mr. Jerzy Ignacy Eugeniusz, FCA *1974;* Keith Vaudrey & Co, First Floor, 15 Young Street, LONDON, W8 5EH.
BORZOMATO, Mr. Mark, BSc ACA *1998;* Cowgill Holloway, 49 Peter Street, MANCHESTER, M2 3NG.
BOSANQUET, Mr. Richard Peter, FCA *1975;* 15a Dunsfold Rise, COULSDON, SURREY, CR5 2ED.
•BOSCH, Mr. Xavier, MBA BSc FCA *1990;* 1 Lower Park Road, MANCHESTER, M14 5RS.
BOSCHAT, Mr. Denzil Maurice, FCA *1983;* with RBC cees Fund Managers (Jersey) Limited, Le Motte Chambers, St Helier, JERSEY, JE1 1BJ.
BOSCHER, Mr. Paul Stanley, ACA *1994;* Apartment 8 Canichers House Royal Garden Bosq Lane St. Peter Port, GUERNSEY, GY1 2JE.
BOSCHI, Mr. Nigel Guy James, FCA *1962;* 11 Norris Gardens, HAVANT, PO9 2TT. (Life Member)
BOSCOTT, Mrs. Rebecca Jane, BSc ACA *1999;* 52 Peplins Way, Brookmans Park, HATFIELD, HERTFORDSHIRE, AL9 7UU.
BOSE, Mr. Basu Deb, FCA *1969;* 39 Pauline Court, CONCORD L4K 3G3, ON, CANADA.
BOSE, Miss. Bonani Sanjita, BSc ACA *2000;* Sandy Lodge, 17a Dollis Avenue, LONDON, N3 1UD.
BOSE, Mr. Dipak Kanti, BA FCA *1964;* 601 Daisylea, 17A Mount Pleasant Road, Malabar Hill, MUMBAI 400006, MAHARASHTRA, INDIA. (Life Member)
BOSE, Mr. Goutam Deb, BSc ACA *1985;* 19 Lebanon Gardens, LONDON, SW18 1RQ.
•BOSE, Mr. Kalyan, FCA *1978;* A-52, Sector 34, NOIDA 201307, UTTAR PRADESH, INDIA.
BOSE, Mr. Mihir Kiran, FCA *1974;* 30 Poplar Grove, LONDON, W6 7RE.
BOSE, Mr. Philip, FCA *1963;* Inglenook Cottage, Tedburn Road, Whitestone, EXETER, EX4 2HF. (Life Member)
BOSE, Mr. Pranab Kumar, FCA *1969;* 113 Block C, Bangur Avenue, KOLKATA, WEST BENGAL, INDIA. (Life Member)
BOSE, Mr. Radha Bhusan, FCA *1938;* 2-2 Keyatala Road, CALCUTTA 700 029, INDIA. (Life Member)
•BOSE, Miss. Roshni, MSc ACA *2007;* BOSeCo, 309 Regents Park Road, LONDON, N3 1DP.
•BOSE, Mr. Samar, FCA *1975;* (Tax Fac), BOSeCo, 309 Regents Park Road, LONDON, N3 1DP.
BOSHELL, Mrs. Ffion Lowri, BA ACA *2007;* 3 I Group, 16 Palace Street, LONDON, SW1E 5JD.
BOSIACKI, Miss. Jennifer Louise, BSc ACA *2009;* 15 Priory Gardens, WATERLOOVILLE, HAMPSHIRE, PO7 7RS.
BOSKOVIC, Miss. Jelena, MChem ACA *2011;* 79 Eastwick Drive, Bookham, LEATHERHEAD, SURREY, KT23 3NS.
BOSLEY, Miss. Catherine Ellen, BSocSc ACA *2001;* Thomas River Capital, 51 Berkeley Square, LONDON, W1J 5BB.
BOSLEY, Mrs. Eleanor Catherine Rose, MA ACA *2003;* (Tax Fac), K P M G Llp, 15 Canada Square, LONDON, E14 5GL.
BOSLEY, Mr. Peter Barry, FCA *1966;* with Eden Currie Limited, Pegasus House, Solihull Business Park, SOLIHULL, WEST MIDLANDS, B90 4GT.
•BOSLEY, Mr. Steven John, ACA MAAT *2009;* Collinsonsplus Limited, 55 Newhall Street, BIRMINGHAM, B3 3RB.
BOSLEY, Mr. Stuart Duncan, FCA *1975;* Southwood House, Woodpecker Way, Mayford, WOKING, GU22 0SG.
BOSMAN, Mrs. Birka Thordis Reinhild, ACA CA(SA) *2011;* (Tax Fac), Easy Limited, 1st Floor, Highlands House, 165 The Broadway, LONDON, SW19 1NE.
BOSMAN, Mrs. Lesley Jane, BSc ACA *1987;* The Grove, Avon Dassett Road, Fenny Compton, SOUTHAM, WARWICKSHIRE, CV47 2XX.
BOSONNET, Paul Graham, Esq CBE FCA *1955;* The Old House Cottage, Pyrford Road, Pyrford, WOKING, GU22 8UE. (Life Member)
BOSS, Mr. Jeremy Charles, BA *1986;* Audit Commission, Westward House, Lime Kiln Close, Stoke Gifford, BRISTOL, BS34 8SR.
BOSS, Mr. Jonathan Robin, BSc FCA *1993;* E Office Prudential Building, Wine Street, BRISTOL, BS1 2PH.
•BOSS, Mrs. Linda Ann, BSc FCA DChA *1986;* Monahans, Clarks Mill, Stallard Street, TROWBRIDGE, BA14 8HH. See also Monahans Limited
BOSS, Mr. Peter Henry, BA FCA *1977;* Tower House, 131 London Road West, BATH, BA1 7JF.
BOSSHARD, Mr. Laurence Nicholas, BSc(Hons) FCA *2000;* The Corner House, 22 Marwell, WESTERHAM, KENT, TN16 1SB.
BOSSHARD, Mr. Robert Martin, BA ACA *1980;* PricewaterhouseCoopers, Royal Trust Tower, Suite 3000 TD Centre, Box 82, 77 King Street West, TORONTO M5K 1G8 ON CANADA.
BOSSICK, Mr. Michael Philip, ACA *1985;* 82 Worlds End Lane, ORPINGTON, BR6 6AG.
BOSSICK, Mrs. Sarah Louise, ACA *1989;* 82 Worlds End Lane, ORPINGTON, BR6 6AG.
BOSSON, Mr. Charles, ACA MCT *1995;* Coventry Bldg Soc Orchard Court, Binley Business Park Harry Weston Road, COVENTRY, CV3 2TQ.
BOSSON, Mr. Paul Francis, MBA BSc(Eng) ACA *1988;* Sophis Technology Ireland Ltd, 61-62 Fitzwilliam Lane, DUBLIN 2, COUNTY DUBLIN, IRELAND.
BOSSONS, Mr. Anthony James, BSc ACA *1989;* Rotherdene, Withyham Road, Groombridge, TUNBRIDGE WELLS, TN3 9QT.
•BOSTELMANN, Mr. Michael John, FCA *1970;* Arnold Hill & Co, Craven House, 16 Northumberland Ave, LONDON, WC2N 5AP. See also Arnold Hill Sp zoo
BOSTEN, Mr. John Herbert, FCA *1957;* 62 Couchmore Avenue, ESHER, SURREY, KT10 9AU. (Life Member)
•BOSTOCK, Mr. Antony Charles, FCA CF *1986;* Bostock White Limited, Unit 1, Cabourn House, Station Street, Bingham, NOTTINGHAM NG13 8AQ.
BOSTOCK, Christopher Ingram, Esq OBE MA FCA *1951;* 12 Pensioners Court, Charterhouse, LONDON, EC1M 6AU. (Life Member)
BOSTOCK, Mr. Christopher Paul, BSc ACA *1993;* 17 Willow Park Way, Aston-on-Trent, DERBY, DE72 2DF.
BOSTOCK, Miss. Emma Kate, BEng ACA *2007;* Flat 34 Arnold House, Doddington Grove, LONDON, SE17 3SU.
BOSTOCK, Miss. Emma Mary, BSc ACA *1999;* 7 Chiswick Lane, LONDON, W4 2LR.
BOSTOCK, Mr. Jeremy Peter, BA FCA *1998;* Thompson Wright, Ebeneezer House, Ryecroft, NEWCASTLE, STAFFORDSHIRE, ST5 2BE.
BOSTOCK, Mr. Jonathan Howard, BSc ACA *1997;* Birch Cottage Belper Road, Stanley Common, ILKESTON, DERBYSHIRE, DE7 6FY.
BOSTOCK, Mr. Karl Robert, BSc(Hons) ACA *2002;* Paragon Labels Ltd, Enterprise Way, Pinchbeck, SPALDING, LINCOLNSHIRE, PE11 3YR.
BOSTOCK, Mr. Michael Edward, BA(Hons) ACA *2001;* 31 Turner Road, LONDON, E17 3JG.
BOSTOCK, Mr. Nathan Mark, BSc ACA *1986;* Abbey National Plc, 2-3 Triton Square, LONDON, NW1 3AN.
BOSTOCK, Mr. Nicholas Stephen Godfrey, DL FCA *1969;* Tixall House, Tixall, STAFFORD, ST18 0XT.
•BOSTOCK, Mr. Nigel David, BA FCA *1995;* Crowe Clark Whitehill LLP, St Bride's House, 10 Salisbury Square, LONDON, EC4Y 8EH. See also Horwath Clark Whitehill LLP and Crowe Clark Whitehill
BOSTOCK, Mr. Paul, FCA *1975;* Palletways UK Ltd Fradley Distribution Park, Wood End Lane Fradley, LICHFIELD, STAFFORDSHIRE, WS13 8NE.
BOSTOCK, Mrs. Paula-Jayne, BA(Hons) ACA *2001;* Birch Cottage, Belper Road, Stanley Common, ILKESTON, DE7 6FY.
BOSTOCK, Miss. Rebecca, BSc ACA *2006;* 7 Elmsfield Avenue, HEANOR, DERBYSHIRE, DE75 7BD.
BOSTOCK, Mr. Richard, BA FCA *1953;* 6 Avalon, Lilliput, POOLE, DORSET, BH14 8HT. (Life Member)
BOSTOCK, Mr. William Richard, FCA *1966;* 6 Lakenheath, Oakwood, LONDON, N14 4RN.
•BOSTON, Mr. Andrew Roy, BSc FCA *1978;* Robert S. Boys, 28-30 Grange Road West, BIRKENHEAD, CH41 4DA.
BOSTON, Mrs. Bernadette Elaine, BA ACA *2000;* 1 St. Clements Court, Weston, CREWE, CW2 5NS.
BOSTON, Mr. David James, BSc ACA *1999;* 88 Brocksparkwood, BRENTWOOD, ESSEX, CM13 2TJ.
BOSTON, Miss. Gillian Carol, BSc FCA *1998;* Flat 3/1, 191 Hyndland Road, GLASGOW, G12 9HT.
BOSTON, Mrs. Helen Louise, BSc ACA *2000;* 5 Chalcroft Road, LONDON, SE13 5RE.
•BOSTON, Mr. James Henry, ACA MAAT *2003;* JH Boston & Co Limited, Ebor Cottage, 80 High Street, Bempton, BRIDLINGTON, YO15 1HP.
BOSTON, Mr. John Arthur, BA ACA *1989;* 2 Meavy Villas, YELVERTON, PL20 6AQ.
BOSTON, Mr. Jonathan Charles, BSc ACA *1990;* P P D Development Granta Park, Great Abington, CAMBRIDGE, CB21 6GQ.
BOSTON, Mr. Nicholas Ian, MA ACA *1985;* Chestnuts, Mark Way, GODALMING, GU7 2BW.
BOSTON, Mrs. Nicola Elizabeth, BSc ACA *2005;* 88 Brocksparkwood, Ingrave, BRENTWOOD, ESSEX, CM13 2TJ.
BOSTON, Mr. Simon Atwell, BA(Hons) ACA *2002;* 53 Barrier Point Road, LONDON, E16 2SB.
BOSTROM, Miss. Caroline Louise, BSc ACA *2003;* 16 Gainsborough Road, BRAINTREE, ESSEX, CM77 8DU.
BOSTWICK, Mr. Timothy Paul, BA ACA *1985;* Splash Cottage, Norton, MALMESBURY, WILTSHIRE, SN16 0JP.
•BOSU, Mr. Aloke, FCA *1960;* Aloke Bosu, 17880 Skypark Circle, Suite 120, IRVINE, CA 91614-4498, UNITED STATES.
BOSWELL, Mr. Brian Peter, BA(Hons) FCA *1966;* (Member of Council 2001 - 2007), Ashdown, Bell Close, Hallow, WORCESTER, WR2 6QA.
BOSWELL, Mr. John Roderick, FCA *1960;* Peacock Farm, Holywell, Shrewley, WARWICK, CV35 7BJ.
•BOSWELL, Ms. Joy Rosalind, ACA ACCA *2007;* Four Fifty Partnership Limited, 34 Boulevard, WESTON-SUPER-MARE, AVON, BS23 1NF. See also T P Lewis & Partners (WSM) Limited
BOSWORTH, Mr. Christopher Michael, BA ACA *1998;* Kwik Fit Ltd, 216 East Main Street, BROXBURN, WEST LOTHIAN, EH52 5AS.
BOSWORTH, Mrs. Lydia Jane, MA ACA *2005;* 17 Torrington Drive, POTTERS BAR, HERTFORDSHIRE, EN6 5HU.
BOSWORTH, Mr. Michael, FCA *1968;* Monkstone House, Main Street, Mowsley, LUTTERWORTH, LEICESTERSHIRE, LE17 6NU.
BOTCHERBY, Mrs. Jane Suzanne, BSocSc ACA *1990;* 28 Oak Tree Road, Eccleston, ST.HELENS, MERSEYSIDE, WA10 5LH.
BOTCHERBY, Miss. Sally, BA(Hons) ACA *2011;* Flat 16, Maycroft Court, Hulse Road, SOUTHAMPTON, SO15 2LB.
BOTCHERBY, Mr. Serge Pierre Vincent, BSc ACA *1992;* 28 Oaktree Road, ST.HELENS, WA10 5LH.
BOTELER, Mr. Andrew Norman, BA ACA *1994;* 22 Parkelands, Bovey Tracey, NEWTON ABBOT, DEVON, TQ13 9BJ.
BOTES, Mr. Jan Hendrik Louis, ACA CA(SA) *2010;* with PricewaterhouseCoopers LLP, 1 Embankment Place, LONDON, WC2N 6RH.
BOTETER, Mrs. Lindsay Marie, BA ACA *1992;* 22 Parkelands, Bovey Tracey, NEWTON ABBOT, DEVON, TQ13 9BJ.
BOTFISH, Mr. Neil Philip, BA ACA *1986;* Southway Housing Trust, Level 1, Heron House, 3638 Brazennose Street, MANCHESTER, M2 5ED.
BOTHA, Mr. Andrew James, BA ACA *1992;* No 7 SQAQ 14, Triq Santa Lucija, NAXXAR NXR 1641, MALTA.
BOTHA, Mr. Anton Christiaan, ACA CA(SA) *2009;* 33 Raymond Road, MAIDENHEAD, BERKSHIRE, SL6 6DF.
BOTHA, Mrs. Barbara Ann, ACA CA(SA) *2009;* 33 Raymond Road, MAIDENHEAD, BERKSHIRE, SL6 6DF.
BOTHA, Mrs. Linda Colleen, ACA *2009;* 5th floor, 89 New Bond Street, LONDON, W1S 1DA.
BOTHA, Mr. Michael Andrew, ACA CA(SA) *2010;* Domino's Pizza, Domino's House, Lasborough Road, Kingston, MILTON KEYNES, MK10 0AB.
•BOTHAM, Mr. Andrew John, BSc ACA *1996;* Botham Accounting Limited, 14 Clarendon Street, NOTTINGHAM, NG1 5HQ.
BOTHAM, Mr. John, BSc ACA *1989;* Padmall House, 22 Oakfield Lane, KESTON, BR2 6BY.
BOTHAM, Mr. Neil Roderick, FCA *1967;* 11/73 Grasmere Road, CREMORNE, NSW 2090, AUSTRALIA. (Life Member)
BOTHAMLEY, Mr. Andrew James, BSc CA ACA *1998;* 2915 Glenwood Avenue, WINDSOR N9E 2X7, ON, CANADA.
BOTHAMLEY, Mr. Brian Michael, FCA *1968;* 4 Manor Farm Mews, High Street, Colsterworth, GRANTHAM, LINCOLNSHIRE, NG33 5JA. (Life Member)
BOTHAMLEY, Mr. Paul Justin Robert, BSc ACA CTA *1990;* (Tax Fac), Knowle Hill Park, Fairmile Lane, COBHAM, KT11 2PD.
BOTHWELL, Miss. Kimberley Marie, BSc ACA *2010;* 3 Dene Court Road, SOLIHULL, WEST MIDLANDS, B92 8DG.
BOTHWELL, Mrs. Pamela Ann, BSc FCA *1976;* Kells Cottage, Smugglers Way, The Sands, FARNHAM, GU10 1NB.
BOTHWELL, Mr. Robert James, BA ACA *2008;* 39 Bush Farm Drive, Portslade, BRIGHTON, BN41 2GY.
BOTHWELL, Miss. Stephanie Elizabeth, ACA *2011;* 23b Beauchamp Road, LONDON, SW11 1PG.
BOTKHOLOVA, Miss. Dina, ACA *2009;* 22 Kefallinias Str., Sakyrco 1 apt 102, 3107 LIMASSOL, CYPRUS.
BOTLEY, Mr. John Peter, FCA *1975;* 29 Grays Lane, HITCHIN, HERTFORDSHIRE, SG5 2HH.
•BOTROS, Mr. Samir Ezzy, BCom FCA *1969;* Botros & Co, 4 Northwest Business Park, Servia Hill, LEEDS, LS6 2QH.
BOTROS, Mrs. Victoria, BA(Hons) ACA CTA *1999;* (Tax Fac), 4 Rue de Veraye, 1820 TERRITET, SWITZERLAND.
BOTT, Mr. Andrew, BA ACA *1995;* 1120 Avenue of Americas, 5th Floor, NEW YORK, NY 10036, UNITED STATES.
•BOTT, Mr. David Richard Arden, FCA *1988;* Mazars LLP, Clifton Down House, Beaufort Buildings, Clifton Down, Clifton, BRISTOL BS8 4AN.
BOTT, Mr. Geoffrey Brian, FCA *1964;* May House, Woodland View, RYDE, ISLE OF WIGHT, PO33 2DG.
BOTT, Mr. Glen Andrew, ACA *2010;* 12 Aster Close, NORTHAMPTON, NN3 3XG.
BOTT, Mr. Phillip Paul, BSc ACA *2006;* with Mark J Rees, Granville Hall, Granville Road, LEICESTER, LE1 7RU.
BOTT, Mr. Richard Phillip, FCA *1976;* 24 Ridgeway, Tranmere Park, Guiseley, LEEDS, LS20 8JA.
BOTTERILL, Mr. David William, BEng ACA *2005;* Polar on Lighting Ltd Usk House, Lakeside Llantarnam Industrial Park, CWMBRAN, GWENT, NP44 3HD.
BOTTERILL, Mr. Deryck, FCA *1956;* 28 Pendour Park, LOSTWITHIEL, CORNWALL, PL22 0PQ. (Life Member)

•**BOTTING, Mr. Anthony Ernest William, FCA** *1965;* (Tax Fac), Botting & Co Ltd, 8 Clifton Moor Bus.Village, James Nicolson Link, YORK, YO30 4XG. See also Botting & Co
BOTTING, Mr. Hugh Derek, BA ACA *1987;* 7th Floor Senate House, University of Surrey, GUILDFORD, SURREY, GU2 7XH.
BOTTING, Mr. Nigel Hugh, BSc FCA *1985;* 101 Heol Isaf, Radyr, CARDIFF, CF15 8DW.
BOTTING, Mr. Richard Anthony, BA ACA *1994;* 9 Bancroft Avenue, Cheadle Hulme, CHEADLE, CHESHIRE, SK8 5BA.
BOTTING, Mr. Ronald Dennis James, FCA *1948;* Stockwells, Thorpe Street, Aston Upthorpe, DIDCOT, OXFORDSHIRE, OX11 9EG. (Life Member)
BOTTINI, Mr. Riccardo Francesco Enrico, BSc ACA *1994;* Via Cocquo 45/D, SESTO CALENDE, 21018 MILAN, ITALY.
BOTTINO, Miss. Joanna Elaine, LLB ACA *2003;* 16 Dawson Road, KINGSTON UPON THAMES, SURREY, KT1 3AT.
BOTTJER, Mr. Mark, BSc FCA *1988;* Boxperfect Presentation Packaging Ltd, 7 Faraday Close, Oakwood Business Park, CLACTON-ON-SEA, ESSEX, CO15 4TR.
•**BOTTOM, Mr. Alexander Michael, ACA** *2001;* Hillier Hopkins LLP, 64 Clarendon Road, WATFORD, WD17 1DA.
BOTTOME, Mr. Phillip James, MA ACA *1998;* 37 St. James's Square, BATH, BA1 2TT.
BOTTOMLEY, Miss. Charlotte, ACA *2011;* Flat 3, 6 Old Station Way, LONDON, SW4 6DA.
BOTTOMLEY, Mr. Clifford Andrew, BSc ACA *1996;* Carval Investors UK Ltd, Knowle Hill Park, Fairmile Lane, COBHAM, KT11 2PD.
•①**BOTTOMLEY, Mr. David Halstead, FCA** *1971;* Bottomley and Co, Glenwood House, 5 Arundel Way, Cawston, RUGBY, WARWICKSHIRE CV22 7TU.
•**BOTTOMLEY, Mr. David Robert, BSc ARCS FCA CTA** *1988;* (Tax Fac), David Bottomley, The Old Rectory, Owmby Cliff Road, Owmby-by-Spital, MARKET RASEN, LINCOLNSHIRE LN8 2HL.
BOTTOMLEY, Mrs. Jill, BA ACA *1996;* 26 Park Avenue, Old Basing, BASINGSTOKE, HAMPSHIRE, RG24 7HJ.
BOTTOMLEY, Mr. John Mark, BSc FCA *1989;* 74 Helsinki Road, Sutton Fields, HULL, HU7 0YW.
BOTTOMLEY, Miss. Julie Anne, BA ACA *1990;* PO Box 10268, The Terrace, WELLINGTON 6143, NEW ZEALAND.
BOTTOMLEY, Miss. Lisa Jane, BSc ACA *2009;* Flat 4 Dryburgh Court, 1 Dryburgh Road, LONDON, SW15 1BN.
BOTTOMLEY, Mr. Matthew, BA ACA *1992;* 43 Court Lane, Dulwich, LONDON, SE21 7DP.
•**BOTTOMLEY, Mr. Michael David, FCA** *1979;* Robertshaw Myers, Number 3, Acorn Business Park, Keighley Road, SKIPTON, NORTH YORKSHIRE BD23 2UE. See also Robertshaw & Myers
BOTTOMLEY, Mr. Nigel Derek, BA ACA *1996;* 14 New Street, Stainland, HALIFAX, WEST YORKSHIRE, HX4 9QL.
BOTTOMLEY, Mr. Richard John, OBE FCA *1980;* Willow Beck, Greenacres, Burley-in-Wharfedale, ILKLEY, LS29 7SE.
BOTTOMLEY, Mr. Simon Hugh, MA ACA *1989;* Woodside, Caneheath, Arlington, POLEGATE, BN26 6SL.
BOTTOMLEY, Mr. Stuart, BSc ACA *1992;* 5 Golden End Drive, Knowle, SOLIHULL, B93 0JP.
BOTTOMLEY, Mrs. Susan Mary, BSc ACA *1992;* 43 Court Lane, Dulwich, LONDON, SE21 7DP.
BOTTOMLEY, Mr. Terence, FCA *1962;* 130 New Adel Lane, Lawnswood, LEEDS, LS16 6BB.
BOTTOMLEY, Mr. Thomas Alexander Max, MA ACA *1993;* MMS, Melbourne House, Melbourne Street, Farsley, PUDSEY, WEST YORKSHIRE LS28 5BT.
BOTTOMLEY, Mrs. Tracy Jane, BSc FCA ACT *1989;* 35 Wheatlands Road East, HARROGATE, HG2 8QS.
BOTTOMLEY, Mrs. Velma Elizabeth, ACA *1980;* Howgill Cottage, Bolton Low Houses, WIGTON, CA7 8PF.
BOTTOMLEY, Mr. Walter Leslie, FCA *1952;* 71 Wicks Crescent, Formby, LIVERPOOL, MERSEYSIDE, L37 1PD. (Life Member)
BOTTOMORE, Mr. Ian, ACA *2002;* 20 Ryedale Avenue, MANSFIELD, NOTTINGHAMSHIRE, NG18 3GT.
BOTTOMORE, Mrs. Karen, BA ACA *2003;* 20 Ryedale Avenue, MANSFIELD, NOTTINGHAMSHIRE, NG18 3GT.
•①**BOTWOOD, Mr. Mark Jonathan, BA ACA** *1994;* Muras Baker Jones, Regent House, Bath Avenue, WOLVERHAMPTON, WV1 4EG.
BOTWRIGHT, Mr. Stuart Richard, BA FCA *1994;* 7 Rue des Geraniums, MC98000 MONTE CARLO, MONACO.
BOTY, Mr. John William, FCA *1958;* West Wing St George's, Mill Lane, North Chailey, LEWES, BN8 4EG. (Life Member)
BOTY, Mr. Paul Albert, BSc ACA *1986;* 11 Becketts Avenue, ST. ALBANS, HERTFORDSHIRE, AL3 5RT.
BOUCAULT, Mr. Denis Francis, FCA *1968;* 5 La Rocquaise, La Route Des Genets, St. Brelade, JERSEY, JE3 8HY. (Life Member)
•**BOUCH, Mr. Clive, BSc FCA** *1985;* 52 Burges Road, Thorpe Bay, SOUTHEND-ON-SEA, SS1 3AX.
BOUCH, Mr. Howard Heskett, FCA *1968;* Howard H. Bouch, Grove House, 13 Low Seaton, Seaton, WORKINGTON, CA14 1PR.
BOUCH, Mr. Simon Andrew Ross, BA ACA *2006;* Hi-Q Tyre Services Tyre Fort, 94-98 Wingfoot Way Erdington, BIRMINGHAM, B24 9HY.
BOUCH, Mr. Thomas Philip, BA ACA *2010;* 10 Parklands Close, Loddington, KETTERING, NORTHAMPTONSHIRE, NN14 1LG.
BOUCHARD, Mr. David Charles, BSc ACA *1996;* Oak House, The Green, Gt Hockham, THETFORD, IP24 1NH.
•**BOUCHER, Mr. Andrew Paul, BSc ACA** *1992;* (Tax Fac), PricewaterhouseCoopers LLP, 1 Embankment Place, LONDON, WC2N 6RH. See also PricewaterhouseCoopers
BOUCHER, Mr. Charles Andre, FCA FCT *1966;* 52 Dartmouth Road, LONDON, NW2 4EX.
BOUCHER, Mr. Charles Patrick, FCA *1970;* Oak Tree Cottage Crawley Road, HORSHAM, WEST SUSSEX, RH12 4RX.
BOUCHER, Mr. Geoffrey John, BA ACA *1988;* The Rectory, West Monkton, TAUNTON, TA2 8QT.
BOUCHER, Mr. John Francis Charles, FCA *1967;* 19 Highmoor Road, Caversham, READING, RG4 7BL.
BOUCHER, Mr. Jonathan Mark, BA ACA *1998;* Tarmac Ltd, Millfields Road, Ettingshall, WOLVERHAMPTON, WV4 6JP.
BOUCHER, Mr. Joseph, ACA *2009;* 72 St. Olaf's Road, LONDON, SW6 7DN.
BOUCHER, Mrs. Reinette Rivers, ACA *1994;* Fernleigh House, Barkestone Le Vale, NOTTINGHAM, NG13 0HA.
BOUCHER, Mr. Roderick Martin, MA FCA *1978;* New Century Place, 1 Marie Davis Court, East Street, READING, RG1 4QH.
BOUCHER, Mr. Thomas Greer, BA ACA *1996;* Data Explorers Ltd, 2 Seething Lane, LONDON, EC3N 4AT.
BOUCHER, Mr. Timothy James, BA ACA *1998;* 44 Cathles Road, LONDON, SW12 9LD.
BOUCHER, Mr. Timothy Montfort, BA FCA *1992;* 38 Atalanta Street, Fulham, LONDON, SW6 6TR.
BOUCHERAT, Mrs. Angela, BSc FCA *1976;* 3 Somerstown, CHICHESTER, WEST SUSSEX, PO19 6AG. (Life Member)
BOUCHIER, Mr. Richard John Wallace, BSc ACA *1992;* General Mills International Sarl, Avenue Reverdil 8-10, 1260 NYON, SWITZERLAND.
BOUCKLEY, Mr. John Kenneth, FCA *1966;* 12470 Collier's Reserve Drive, NAPLES, FL 34110-0913, UNITED STATES. (Life Member)
BOUCKLEY, Mr. Mark Jonathan, BA ACA *1997;* 101 Sanborn Avenue, WEST ROXBURY, MA 02132, UNITED STATES.
BOUD, Mr. Douglas William George, FCA *1960;* Pentland Dell, Horseshoe Lane, ASH VALE, SURREY, GU12 5LJ. (Life Member)
BOUD, Mr. Ian David, BSc ACA *1979;* Apt C506, Les Naturelles, Gribelier St 37, CH 3954 LEUKERBAD, SWITZERLAND.
BOUD, Mr. Trevor Edward, FCA *1962;* 8, Oak Grove, Grove Road, CRANLEIGH, GU6 7JR.
BOUGAN, Mr. Surinder Singh, LLB ACA *2000;* Ernst & Young LLP, 1 Colmore Square, BIRMINGHAM, B4 6HQ.
BOUGH, Mr. Anthony Herbert, FCA *1963;* 33 Saltdean Way, BEXHILL-ON-SEA, TN39 3SS.
BOUGH, Mr. Graham Arthur, FCA *1975;* Mission Aviation Fellowship Operations Centre, Henwood, ASHFORD, TN24 8DH.
•①**BOUGHEY, Mr. Mark, ACA FCCA** *2008;* with Ernst & Young LLP, The Paragon, Counterslip, BRISTOL, BS1 6BX.
•**BOUGHTON, Mr. Derek Mark, BA FCA** *1985;* Ellacotts LLP, Countrywide House, 23 West Bar Street, BANBURY, OXFORDSHIRE, OX16 9SA.
BOUGHTON, Ms. Jocelyn Moira, BA ACA *1988;* Flat 32, 416 Manchester Road, LONDON, E14 3FD.
BOUGHTON, Mr. John Brian, FCA *1957;* 61 Havers Lane, BISHOP'S STORTFORD, CM23 3PA.
BOUGHTON, Mr. Marc, BA ACA *1989;* Wonham Hill, Wonham Lane, BETCHWORTH, SURREY, RH3 7AD.
•**BOUGHTON, Mr. Michael Aubrey John, MA FCA** *1977;* The Sanderum Partnership, Sanderum House, 38 Oakley Road, CHINNOR, OXFORDSHIRE, OX39 4TW.
BOUGHTON, Mr. Neil Charles, MEng&Man ACA *1993;* Bramleys, Roman Road, INGATESTONE, CM4 9EX.
BOUGHTON, The Revd. Paul Henry, BSc ACA *1985;* Fetcham Rectory, 10A The Ridgeway, Fetcham, LEATHERHEAD, KT22 9AZ.
BOUGHTON, Mr. Paul Victor, BSc FCA *1981;* 11 Esher Place Avenue, ESHER, SURREY, KT10 8PU.
BOUGHTON, Mrs. Siobhan Mary Elizabeth, BSc ACA *1993;* Wonham Hill, Wonham Lane, BETCHWORTH, SURREY, RH3 7AD.
BOUGHTON, Mr. Stephen Brian, FCA *1975;* 13 Highbury Crescent, BURY ST.EDMUNDS, IP33 3RS.
BOUGOURD, Mr. Mark Peter, BA(Hons) ACA *2010;* Cleland & Co Ltd First Floor Harbour Court, Les Amballes St. Peter Port, GUERNSEY, GY1 1WU.
BOUIC, Mr. Joseph Gaetan, FCA *1961;* Poste Lafayette, POSTE DE FLACQ, MAURITIUS. (Life Member)
BOUILLAUD, Miss. Adeline, ACA *2010;* 54 Rotherfield Way, Emmer Green, READING, RG4 8PL.
BOUKRABA-OULANOVA, Miss. Natalia, BSc(Hons) ACA *2010;* 3 Ormsby Gardens, GREENFORD, MIDDLESEX, UB6 9NR.
BOULBY, Mr. Philip Andrew, BSc ACA *2009;* The Beeches, 25 Highfield Park, MARLOW, BUCKINGHAMSHIRE, SL7 2DE.
BOULD, Mr. David Charles, FCA *1968;* 21 Glenholme Park, Clayton, BRADFORD, BD14 6NF:
BOULD, Mrs. Rachel, BA ACA *2007;* 8 Rook Hill, Worsbrough, BARNSLEY, SOUTH YORKSHIRE, S70 4QS.
BOULDIN, Mr. Jonathan Richard, BA ACA *2007;* Flat 37 Drive Mansions, Fulham Road, LONDON, SW6 5JD.
BOULDING, Mr. Alasdair James Jesse Boyd, BSc ACA *1986;* 1607 Southorn Gardens, 2 O'Brien Road, WAN CHAI, HONG KONG ISLAND, HONG KONG SAR.
BOULDING, Mr. Guy Richard, BEng ACA *2007;* 24 Red Lane, Burton Green, KENILWORTH, CV8 1NZ.
BOULDING, Mr. John Egerton, MA FCA *1961;* 4 The Ridgeway, TONBRIDGE, TN10 4NQ. (Life Member)
BOULDING, Mr. Robert Mark, ACA *2003;* with PricewaterhouseCoopers LLP, 1 Embankment Place, LONDON, WC2N 6RH.
BOULT, Mr. Richard David, BA ACA *1990;* 22 Geneva Road, KINGSTON-UPON-THAMES, KT1 2TW.
BOULTER, Mr. Arthur Robert, BSc FCA *1977;* 8 Maythorn Grove, SOLIHULL, B91 3JS.
BOULTER, Mr. Brian David, FCA *1955;* 24 Cradock Drive, Quorn, LOUGHBOROUGH, LE12 8ER. (Life Member)
•**BOULTER, Mrs. Deirdre Elizabeth, FCA** *1971;* D.E. Boulter, New Mills Cottage, Ermington, IVYBRIDGE, PL21 0LH.
BOULTER, Mr. Harvey Eric, BSc FCA *1994;* PO Box 38255, DUBAI, UNITED ARAB EMIRATES.
BOULTER, Mrs. Jennifer, LLB ACA *2003;* (Tax Fac), 55 Musard Road, LONDON, W6 8NR.
BOULTER, Mrs. Katie Victoria, ACA *2003;* 5 Prykes Drive, CHELMSFORD, CM1 1TP.
•**BOULTER, Mr. Mark, ACA ACCA** *2010;* THP Limited, 34-40 High Street, Wanstead, LONDON, E11 2RJ. See also THP Wealth Structuring LLP
BOULTER, Mr. Roy Eric, FCA *1957;* Apartment 2, Broad Oaks, Chessetts Wood Road, Lapworth, SOLIHULL, WEST MIDLANDS B94 6ES. (Life Member)
BOULTER, Mr. Simon Andrew, BSc ACA *1989;* 72 Waterside, EXETER, EX2 8GY.
•**BOULTON, Mr. Graham David, BSc FCA** *1989;* Robinson Reed Layton, Peat House, Newham Road, TRURO, CORNWALL, TR1 2DP. See also DCN & Co. Limited
BOULTON, Mrs. Henrietta Winstan, BA ACA *1998;* 94 Fildyke Road, Meppershall, SHEFFORD, BEDFORDSHIRE, SG17 5LU.
BOULTON, Mr. Ian Stuart, BA ACA *1999;* 13 Cedar Avenue, Kirkby-in-Ashfield, NOTTINGHAM, NG17 8BD.
BOULTON, Mr. James Leslie, BSc(Hons) ACA *2004;* 4 Weyacres, Borrowash, DERBY, DE72 3QT.
BOULTON, Mr. John, BA ACA *2005;* 223a New North Road, LONDON, N1 7BG.
BOULTON, Mr. Mark, BA ACA *1992;* Foxcote, Church Road, Winkfield, WINDSOR, BERKSHIRE, SL4 4SF.
BOULTON, Mr. Richard, TD JP FCA *1950;* Whitegates, Homefield Paddock, BECCLES, SUFFOLK, NR34 9NE. (Life Member)
BOULTON, Mr. Richard Edward Stanley, MA FCA *1986;* Chambers of Anthony Grabiner Q C, 1 Essex Court, Temple, LONDON, EC4Y 9AR.
•**BOULTON, Mr. Robert William, BSc ACA** *1992;* Gillani & Co, Conduit House, Conduit Lane, HODDESDON, EN11 8EP.
BOULTON, Mr. Roy Joseph, BSc ACA *1979;* 12 Springmount, Lowton, WARRINGTON, WA3 2QH.
BOULTON, Madam Susan Gillian, BA ACA *1995;* CHAMP Cargosystems S.A., Lux Tech Center Building, 2 rue Edmond Reuter, Z.A. Weiergewan, L-5326 CONTERN, LUXEMBOURG.
BOULTON-HEMMINGS, Mrs. Sharon Lorna, BA ACA *1994;* 3 Manton Close, Ampthill, BEDFORD, MK45 2XQ.
BOULTON-JONES, Mr. Nicholas Meyrick, ACA *2009;* Downsview, 28 Valley Close, Goring, READING, RG8 0AN.
BOULTWOOD, Mrs. Merrony Jane, MSc ACA *2003;* 41-45 London Road, ST. ALBANS, HERTFORDSHIRE, AL1 1LJ.
•**BOUND, Mr. Jonathan David, MPhys FCA** *2000;* with PricewaterhouseCoopers, One Kingsway, CARDIFF, CF10 3PW.
BOUND, Mr. Michael Alan, FCA MCT *1983;* Smartswell, Willow Wents, Mereworth, MAIDSTONE, ME18 5NF.
BOUNDS, Mr. Kevin Charles, MA MBA ACA *1979;* The Chantry, Shirenewton, CHEPSTOW, NP16 6RL.
•**BOUNDY, Mr. Michael Alexander, FCA** *1967;* Leach & Co, Ashley House, 136 Tolworth Broadway, SURBITON, SURREY, KT6 7LA.
BOUNSALL, Mr. Lee Keith, ACA *2005;* 7 Swale Close, STEVENAGE, HERTFORDSHIRE, SG1 6DF.
BOUNTRA, Mrs. Hemlata, BSc ACA *1993;* 104c Cumnor Hill, OXFORD, OX2 9HY.
•**BOURCHIER, Mr. Harry Holland, FCA** *1978;* Coates and Partners Limited, 51 St. John Street, ASHBOURNE, DERBYSHIRE, DE6 1GP.
•**BOURDEAUX, Mr. John Stephen, MA ACA** *1991;* PricewaterhouseCoopers LLP, Cornwall Court, 19 Cornwall Street, BIRMINGHAM, B3 2DT. See also PricewaterhouseCoopers
BOURGAIZE, Mr. Owen Edward, FCA *1959;* 35 Les Blancs Bois, Rue Cohu, Castel, GUERNSEY, GY5 7SY.
BOURGET, Mr. Darren Moreton, MA ACA *1997;* 72 Elborough Street, LONDON, SW18 5DN.
BOURKE, Mrs. Alice, ACA *2009;* 58 Malvern Road, CAMBRIDGE, CB1 9LD.
BOURKE, Mr. John Edward, BA ACA *1987;* Alliance One Tobacco (Malawi) Ltd, PO Box 30522, Lilongwe 3, LILONGWE, MALAWI.
BOURKE, Mr. Michael William, BA ACA *1992;* 10 Essex Rise, Warfield, BRACKNELL, RG42 3XG.
BOURLET, Mr. Charles Thomas, FCA *1950;* Milford, 90A Bluehouse Lane, Limpsfield, OXTED, RH8 0AJ. (Life Member)
BOURN, Prof. Alan Michael, BSc FCA *1958;* 83 Cranbourne Drive, Otterbourne, WINCHESTER, SO21 2ES.
•**BOURN, Mr. Robin David Laurence, BA FCA** *1973;* 72 Bryanston Road, SOLIHULL, WEST MIDLANDS, B91 1BS.
BOURNE, Mr. Adrian John, BSc FCA *1988;* Spring Lodge, Mellersh Hill Road, Wonersh, GUILDFORD, GU5 0QL.
BOURNE, Miss. Anna, ACA *2008;* 54 Montfitchet Walk, STEVENAGE, HERTFORDSHIRE, SG2 7DT.
BOURNE, Mr. Anthony Alexander, FCA *1972;* Lanesfield, Hoden Lane, Cleeve Prior, EVESHAM, WORCESTERSHIRE, WR11 8LH.
•**BOURNE, Mr. Anthony Charles Arthur, FCA** *1967;* Bourne & Company, 19 High Street, LEATHERHEAD, SURREY, KT23 4AA. See also Bourne & Co
BOURNE, Mr. Charles Peter, FCA *1970;* Weavers, Friezley Lane, CRANBROOK, KENT, TN17 2LL. (Life Member)
BOURNE, Mr. Charles Richard, FCA *1974;* Radwood Hall Farm, Baldwins Gate, NEWCASTLE, ST5 5ER.
•**BOURNE, Mr. Christopher John, FCA FCCA** *1986;* (Tax Fac), Griffiths Marshall, Beaumont House, 172 Southgate Street, GLOUCESTER, GL1 2EZ.
BOURNE, Mr. David, MA FCA *1969;* The Knoll Belbroughton Road, Clent, STOURBRIDGE, DY9 0EW. (Life Member)
BOURNE, Mr. David George Frank, FCA *1969;* 1 Cleveland, 29 Beech Rd, REIGATE, RH2 9ND. (Life Member)
BOURNE, Mr. David John, BA ACA *1999;* 35 Prince William Drive, Tilehurst, READING, RG31 5WD.
BOURNE, Mr. David Mark, BA ACA *2007;* 30 Southgate Road, TENTERDEN, TN30 7BS.
BOURNE, Mr. Harry Brooks, ACA *2008;* Flat 5, 50-52 Warriner Gardens, LONDON, SW11 4DU.

BOURNE, Mr. Henry Graham Stanley, FCA *1963;* Barley Mow House, Spratts Hatch Lane, Winchfield, HOOK, RG27 8DD. (Life Member)
BOURNE, Miss. Jayne Lesley, BSc ACA *1987;* 48 Long Compton Drive, Hagley, STOURBRIDGE, DY9 0PD.
•**BOURNE, Mr. Jonathan, BSc FCA** *1986;* Ernst & Young LLP, 1 More London Place, LONDON, SE1 2AF. See also Ernst & Young Europe LLP
•**BOURNE, Mr. Jonathan Hartle, MA FCA** *1983;* (Tax Fac), Buelstrasse 26, 8132 HINTEREGG-ZH, SWITZERLAND.
BOURNE, Mr. Jonathan Mark William, BA FCA *1993;* 3 Kingston Avenue, Didsbury, MANCHESTER, M20 2SP.
BOURNE, Mrs. Judith Evelyn, ACA *1982;* 4 Burleigh View, Bussage, STROUD, GL6 8DD.
BOURNE, Mr. Kevin, BA ACA MBA *1998;* 15 Thorntree Lane, GOOLE, NORTH HUMBERSIDE, DN14 6LJ.
BOURNE, Miss. Laura Patience, BSc ACA *2003;* Radwood Hall Farm, Baldwins Gate, NEWCASTLE, ST5 5ER.
BOURNE, Mr. Michael Gerald, BSc ACA *1983;* 6 Wolsey Close, Coombe Lane West, KINGSTON-UPON-THAMES, KT2 7ER.
BOURNE, Mr. Michael John, FCA *1952;* Bourne Properties Limited, 4 Hailwood Avenue, Douglas, ISLE OF MAN, IM2 7AB. (Life Member)
BOURNE, Mr. Miles Barrington Charles, BSc ACA *2002;* 34 Scholey Close, Halling, ROCHESTER, ME2 1JZ.
BOURNE, Mr. Paul Howard, FCA *1974;* 11 Connaught Circuit, KELLYVILLE, NSW 2155, AUSTRALIA.
BOURNE, Mr. Richard Anthony, FCA *1974;* 439 Crewe Road, Wistaston, CREWE, CW2 6QU.
BOURNE, Mr. Robert Anthony, FCA *1973;* 117 Waterloo Road, LONDON, SE1 8UL.
BOURNE, Mr. Robert Sidney, FCA *1966;* 18 Burton Road, Rosliston, SWADLINCOTE, DE12 8JU.
BOURNE, Miss. Sarah Alice, ACA *2006;* Radwood Hall Farm Radswood, Baldwins Gate, NEWCASTLE, STAFFORDSHIRE, ST5 5ER.
BOURNE, Mrs. Sarah Louise, BA ACA CTA *2000;* 44 Gravel Hill, LUDLOW, SHROPSHIRE, SY8 1QR.
BOURNE, Mr. Stephen Charles, BA FCA *1982;* Brook Cottage, Moreton, THAME, OXFORDSHIRE, OX9 2HX.
BOURNE, Mr. Stephen Charles, BA ACA *2008;* with PricewaterhouseCoopers, Avenida Andres Bello 2711, Torre Costanera Piso 5, SANTIAGO, CHILE.
BOURNE, Mr. Stephen Michael, FCA *1975;* 5 Holmdene Avenue, LONDON, NW7 2LY.
BOURNE, Mr. Stephen Robert Richard, MA FCA *1977;* Falmouth Lodge, Snailwell Road, NEWMARKET, SUFFOLK, CB8 7DN.
BOURNE, Mr. Steven Brian, BSc ACA *1996;* Volvo Group UK Ltd, Wedgnock Industrial Estate, WARWICK, CV34 5YA.
BOURNE, Mrs. Susan Joyce, BSc ACA *1986;* Eagles Nest, Bayleys Hill, SEVENOAKS, KENT, TN14 6HS.
BOURNE, Mr. Walter, FCA *1961;* 142 Woodland Drive, HOVE, BN3 6DE. (Life Member)
BOURNE-HALLETT, Mr. Christopher Mark, BA ACA *1989;* Alexander Comley Ltd, Building 1b, Dandy Bank Road, Pensnett Trading Estate, KINGSWINFORD, WEST MIDLANDS DY6 7ND.
BOURNER, Mr. David Edward, ACA *2008;* 2 Carrick House, Hotwell Road, BRISTOL, BS8 4NF.
BOURNER, Mrs. Hannah, BSc ACA *2010;* 2 Carrick House, Hotwell Road, BRISTOL, BS8 4NF.
BOURNER, Mr. Roger Alan John, FCA *1968;* Label Express Unit 8, Beddington Trading Estate Bath House Road, CROYDON, CR0 4TT.
BOURNER, Mrs. Sarah Roxanne, FCA *1990;* 7 West Lane, North Baddesley, SOUTHAMPTON, SO52 9GB.
•**BOURQUIN, Mr. Dominic Bruce, LLB ACA** *2000;* Monahans, Lennox House, 3 Pierrepont Street, BATH, BA1 1LB.
•**BOURTON, Mr. Anthony Victor, BA ACA** *1989;* 1 Tryes Cottages, Brandon Place, CHELTENHAM, GL50 2HE.
BOUSFIELD, Miss. Clare Jane, BSc FCA *1993;* Aegon Plc, Edinburgh Park, 1 Lochside Crescent, EDINBURGH, EH12 9SE.
BOUSFIELD, Mr. Merrik, ACA *2008;* 11 College Glen, MAIDENHEAD, SL6 6BL.
BOUSFIELD, Mr. Raymond Delabere, FCA *1948;* Follyfoot, Hadlow Castle, Hadlow, TONBRIDGE, TN11 0EG. (Life Member)
•**BOUSTEAD, Mr. Ian Bryan, FCA** *1975;* (Tax Fac), 71 Beechcroft Avenue, NEW MALDEN, KT3 3EE.
BOUSTEAD, Mr. John Richard, FCA *1964;* 4426 Striped Maple Court, CONCORD, CA 94521, UNITED STATES. (Life Member)
BOUTCHER, Miss. Emma Charlotte, BA ACA *2005;* 24 Grenville Close, Churchdown, GLOUCESTER, GL3 1LY.
BOUTLAND, Mr. Richard Anthony William, BSc ACA CFA *1993;* Apt 10B Breezy Court, 2A Park Road, MID LEVELS, HONG KONG SAR.
BOUTLE, Mr. Grahame Charles, FCA *1958;* 36 Elwill Way, BECKENHAM, BR3 6RZ. (Life Member)
BOUTON, Mrs. Angela Ruth, BA FCA *1993;* Imperial Tobacco Ltd Technical Divisions, PO Box 525, BRISTOL, BS99 1LQ.
BOUTTELL, Mr. Brian, FCA *1966;* Rockwell, 25 Margerison Road, Ben Rhydding, ILKLEY, LS29 8QY. (Life Member)
•**BOUTTELL, Mr. Keith Charles, ACA** *1996;* Hardcastle Burton LLP, Lake House, Market Hill, ROYSTON, HERTFORDSHIRE, SG8 9JN.
BOUVIER, Mr. Stephane, BA(Hons) ACA *2002;* 119 Hempstead Road, WATFORD, WD17 3HF.
BOUZARELOU, Miss. Paraskevi, MSc BA ACA *2010;* 10 Gimnastiriou 10, Ilioupous, 16346 ATHENS, GREECE.
BOUZAYEN, Mr. Dhia, BSc ACA *1993;* 65 Avenue Taieb Mehiri, MARSA, 2070, TUNISIA.
BOVAIRD, Mr. James Alexander, BA(Hons) ACA *2001;* 7 Forebury Avenue, SAWBRIDGEWORTH, HERTFORDSHIRE, CM21 9BG.
BOVILL, Mrs. Sarah Helen, BA ACA *1991;* Sightsavers International, Grosvenor Hall, Bolnore Road, HAYWARDS HEATH, RH16 4BX.
BOVINGDON, Mr. Sean, BA ACA *1992;* 251 Silverhill Way NW, CALGARY T3B 4K9, AB, CANADA.
BOW, Mr. Christopher John, BSc ACA *1978;* 3 Sternes Way, Stapleford, CAMBRIDGE, CB22 5DA.
BOWACK, Miss. Claire, ACA *2011;* Flat 4, 66 Lillieshall Road, LONDON, SW4 0LP.
BOWACK, Mr. Michael Hamilton, FCA *1966;* Pathways, 53 Fairmile Lane, COBHAM, KT11 2DH. (Life Member)
BOWATER, Mr. Christopher Mark, ACA *2011;* 11 Leveson Road, WOLVERHAMPTON, WV11 2HF.
BOWATER, Mrs. Jennifer, ACA *2011;* 11 Leveson Road, WOLVERHAMPTON, WV11 2HF.
•**BOWATER, Mr. Paul Matthew, ACA** *1983;* with Grant Thornton UK LLP, Hartwell House, 55-61 Victoria Street, BRISTOL, BS1 6FT.
BOWCOCK, Mr. Simon John, MA ACA *1996;* 9 Broomville Avenue, SALE, M33 3DD.
BOWD, Mr. Philip Adrian, BA ACA *2002;* Brock Meadow, Myddle, SHREWSBURY, SY4 3RX.
BOWDEN, Mr. Andrew Gary, BSc ACA *1994;* 8 Top Manor Close, Ockbrook, DERBY, DE72 3TN.
BOWDEN, Mrs. Anne-Marie, BSc ACA *1984;* Ecton Lee House, Ecton, ASHBOURNE, DERBYSHIRE, DE6 2AH.
BOWDEN, Mr. Charles Edward, BA ACA *1999;* 56 Fielding Road, LONDON, W4 1HL.
BOWDEN, Mr. Clive Frederick Ernest, BSc FCA *1972;* Jerusalem, Pickard Way, BUDE, CORNWALL, EX23 8PE. (Life Member)
•**BOWDEN, Mr. Darren Richard, ACA** *2008;* James de Frias Limited, Llanover House, Llanover Road, PONTYPRIDD, CF37 4DY.
BOWDEN, Mr. David Andrew, MSc BA ACA *2000;* 37 Grasmere Road, Gatley, CHEADLE, CHESHIRE, SK8 4RS.
BOWDEN, Mr. David Bertram, FCA *1963;* 41 Above Town, DARTMOUTH, TQ6 9RG.
BOWDEN, Mr. David Christopher, FCA *1964;* 28 Warnham Court, Warnham, HORSHAM, WEST SUSSEX, RH12 3QE. (Life Member)
BOWDEN, Mr. David Huw, MA ACA *2001;* 22 The Coppice, ENFIELD, MIDDLESEX, EN2 7BY.
BOWDEN, Mrs. Dawn Lorraine, BSc ACA *1997;* 31 Rata Road, Hataitai, WELLINGTON 6021, NEW ZEALAND.
BOWDEN, Mrs. Donna Patricia, BA ACA *1999;* 56 Fielding Road, Chiswick, LONDON, W4 1HL.
BOWDEN, Miss. Emily-Ann Harriet, BA ACA *2006;* Flat 3, Coachmans Terrace, 80-86 Clapham Road, LONDON, SW9 0JR.
•**BOWDEN, Mr. Gareth John, FCA** *1977;* Curtis Bowden & Thomas, 101 Dunraven Street, TONYPANDY, MID GLAMORGAN, CF40 1AR.
BOWDEN, Mr. Geoffrey, FCA *1951;* 51 Leighlands, Pound Hill, CRAWLEY, RH10 3DN. (Life Member)
BOWDEN, Mr. George James, FCA *1969;* 40 Ricardo Crescent, Mudeford, CHRISTCHURCH, DORSET, BH23 4BX. (Life Member)
BOWDEN, Mr. Graham Francis, FCA *1967;* 4 Elven Close, East Dean, EASTBOURNE, EAST SUSSEX, BN20 0LJ.
BOWDEN, Mr. Ian Lewis, BA FCA *1968;* 9 Boscastle Road, LONDON, NW5 1EE. (Life Member)
•**BOWDEN, Mrs. Jacqueline, BSc ACA** *1990;* (Tax Fac), Pearson May, 37 Great Pulteney Street, BATH, BA2 4DA.
BOWDEN, Mr. James Edward Blake, MA(Oxon) MBA ACA *2002;* 29 Pullman Lane, GODALMING, GU7 1XY.
BOWDEN, Mr. Jeremy John, MA ACA *1983;* Cedar Cottage Dean, Sparsholt, WINCHESTER, SO21 2LP.
BOWDEN, Mr. John Anthony, FCA *1956;* Apt 9-180 Victor Lewis Drive, WINNIPEG R3P 2E1, MB, CANADA. (Life Member)
BOWDEN, Mr. Jonathan Christopher, BSc ACA *1997;* 31 Rata Road, WELLINGTON, NEW ZEALAND.
BOWDEN, Miss. Julie Ann, BSc ACA *1993;* 37 Grasmere Road, Gatley, CHEADLE, CHESHIRE, SK8 4RS.
BOWDEN, Miss. Karen Julie, BSc(Hons) ACA *2004;* Diageo Plc Lakeside Drive, Park Royal, LONDON, NW10 7HQ.
BOWDEN, Mr. Karl, BA ACA *1990;* Task Force Movement & Storage Ltd, 1-2 Moss Road, WITHAM, ESSEX, CM8 3UQ.
BOWDEN, Mr. Kenneth Henry, BCom FCA *1955;* Uplands, Hastings Road, Kirby Muxloe, LEICESTER, LE9 2EE. (Life Member)
BOWDEN, Mrs. Leann Frances, BSc ARCS ACA FSI *1988;* 26 Blacketts Wood Drive, Chorleywood, RICKMANSWORTH, WD3 5QH.
BOWDEN, Mrs. Lesley, BSc ACA *1992;* Wild Acre, Wansdyke, MORPETH, NORTHUMBERLAND, NE61 3RL.
BOWDEN, Mrs. Mandy Marene, BSc ACA *1992;* 5 St John's Drive, NELSON 7010, NEW ZEALAND.
BOWDEN, Mr. Michael Paul, BSc ACA *1986;* National Blood Service Leeds Centre, Bridle Path, LEEDS, LS15 7TW.
BOWDEN, Mrs. Natasha Leigh, BA ACA *1998;* 22 Grange Farm Road, Yatton, BRISTOL, BS49 4RB.
BOWDEN, Mr. Paul Anthony, BSc ACA *2004;* 16 Rhodfa'r Wennol, Cwmrhydyceirw Morriston, SWANSEA, SA6 6SP.
•**BOWDEN, Mr. Paul Henry, BSc ACA** *1987;* Paul Howley & Co Limited, 42 Pitt Street, BARNSLEY, SOUTH YORKSHIRE, S70 1BB.
BOWDEN, Mr. Peter Rowley, FCA *1962;* Burnaby House, 8 Church Street, North Marston, BUCKINGHAM, MK18 3PH. (Life Member)
•**BOWDEN, Mr. Robert Stanley, FCA** *1970;* Robert S Bowden, Apple Tree, White Gritt, Minsterley, SHREWSBURY, SY5 0JN.
BOWDEN, Mr. William Lee, FCA *1960;* 15 St. Davids Avenue, Romiley, STOCKPORT, SK6 3JT. (Life Member)
•**BOWDEN-SMITH, Mr. Robert William, FCA** *1971;* Bowden Smith, 6 Roedeer Copse, HASLEMERE, SURREY, GU27 1RF. See also R W Bowden-Smith
•**BOWDEN-WILLIAMS, Mr. Julian, BSc FCA CTA AMCT** *1997;* Ernst & Young LLP, 1 Colmore Square, BIRMINGHAM, B4 6HQ. See also Ernst & Young Europe LLP
BOWDEN-WILLIAMS, Mrs. Melissa Jane, LLB ACA CTA *2001;* 36 Eglamour Way, Heathcote, WARWICK, CV34 6GE.
BOWDER, Mr. Donald, FCA *1958;* The Granary, 100 Lakeshore Road E Apt 301, OAKVILLE L6J 6M9, ON, CANADA. (Life Member)
BOWDERY, Mrs. Angela, BSc ACA *1990;* 26 Swiss Pine Gardens, Foxwoods, ST. HELENS, WA9 5UE.
BOWDITCH, Mr. David John, BSc FCA *1978;* 156 Westwick Road, SHEFFIELD, S8 7BX.
BOWE, Mr. Joseph Edward, BA ACA *1997;* Lakes Leisure, Burton Road, KENDAL, CUMBRIA, LA9 7HX.
BOWE, Ms. Sarah, BSc ACA *1993;* 43/45 Portman Square, LONDON, W1A 3BG.
BOWELL, Mr. Lee, BSc ACA *2004;* 1 Overton Drive, Caversham, READING, RG4 5DN.
BOWELL, Mr. Ross Alexander, MA(Oxon) ACA *2004;* Ringwood School, Parsonage Barn Lane, RINGWOOD, BH24 1SE.
BOWEN, Mr. Alfred William, MA FCA *1949;* Boyke Folly, Boyke Lane, Ottinge, CANTERBURY, CT4 6XL. (Life Member)
•**BOWEN, Mrs. Alison Frances, BSc ACA** *1993;* Accounts and More Ltd, 10 Copperfields, BEACONSFIELD, BUCKINGHAMSHIRE, HP9 2NS.
BOWEN, Mrs. Amanda Jane, LLB ACA *2003;* 52 Kestrel Avenue, LONDON, SE24 0EB.
BOWEN, Mr. Andrew Lawrence, BA ACA *1995;* The Global Draw, 99 Green Lane, HOUNSLOW, TW4 6BW.
BOWEN, Mrs. Bridget Claire, BSc FCA *1993;* 86 High Street, Weston, BATH, BA1 4DD.
BOWEN, Miss. Catrin Wyn, BSc ACA *1997;* Machlud Llanddarog Road, Capel Dewi, CARMARTHEN, DYFED, SA32 8AJ.
BOWEN, Mr. Christopher Alan, BSc ACA *1981;* 6 Englewood Road, LONDON, SW12 9NZ.
BOWEN, Mrs. Claire Louise, ACA *2008;* 19 Woodcombe Close, BRIERLEY HILL, DY5 3PQ.
BOWEN, Mrs. Claire Louise, ACA *2006;* 3 Marloo Lane, QUINNS ROCKS, WA 6030, AUSTRALIA.
BOWEN, Mr. Clive, FCA *1982;* Kingsleigh, 13 Carrwood Avenue, Bramhall, STOCKPORT, SK7 2PX.
BOWEN, Mr. Craig Roy, MMath ACA *2010;* Apartment 10, 1 Langley Walk, BIRMINGHAM, B15 2EF.
•**BOWEN, Mr. David Alexander, BSc FCA** *1993;* with KPMG LLP, 1 Forest Gate, Brighton Road, CRAWLEY, WEST SUSSEX, RH11 9PT.
•**BOWEN, Mr. David Alun, MA FCA** *1980;* KPMG Audit LLC, 180 Dostyk Avenue, ALMATY 050051, KAZAKHSTAN. See also KPMG Europe LLP
BOWEN, Mr. David Brian, FCA *1969;* Roberts & Ball, 4 High Street, Pontardawe, SWANSEA, SA8 4HU.
BOWEN, Mr. David Iain, BA ACA *1988;* Via Montecrescenzio 30, 00047 MARINO, ITALY.
BOWEN, Mr. David Manery, FCA *1982;* Illuminate Consulting, 37 Edenside Road, Gt Bookham, LEATHERHEAD, SURREY, KT23 3JB.
BOWEN, Mr. David Mark, BA(Hons) ACA *2003;* Arthur J Gallagher (UK) Ltd, 9 Alie Street, LONDON, E1 8DE.
•**BOWEN, Mr. Delme Roger, BSc ACA** *1982;* (Tax Fac), H & W Jones & Co., 81 Bridge Street, LAMPETER, SA48 7AB.
BOWEN, Mr. Gareth, BSc ACA *2000;* 43 Lincoln Crescent, ENFIELD, MIDDLESEX, EN1 1JZ.
BOWEN, Mr. Graham Michael Glazebrook, BCom ACA *1986;* Horsley Hall, Horsley Lane, Eccleshall, STAFFORD, ST21 6JD.
•**BOWEN, Mr. Howel Isaac, FCA** *1971;* (Tax Fac), H. I. Bowen, Llwynbedw, Bethlehem Road, St. Clears, CARMARTHEN, DYFED SA33 4AN.
•**BOWEN, Mr. Ian David, LLB ACA** *1982;* (Tax Fac), I.D. Bowen & Co, 19 Alexandra Road, Gorseinon, SWANSEA, SA4 4NW.
BOWEN, Mr. James Thomas, BSc ACA *2000;* Tullymet, 29 Kincardine Road, Torphins, BANCHORY, KINCARDINESHIRE, AB31 4GH.
BOWEN, Mrs. Jane Louise, FCA *1997;* with BDO LLP, 55 Baker Street, LONDON, W1U 7EU.
•**BOWEN, Mr. John, FCA** *1968;* Conradi Morrison & Co, 4 Summerhill Road, DARTFORD, DA1 2LP.
BOWEN, Mr. John Arnold, FCA *1957;* 30 Albany Court, Beach Road, PENARTH, CF64 1JU. (Life Member)
BOWEN, Mr. John Harry, FCA *1962;* Goosecroft, 5 Wood Gardens, Swardeston, NORWICH, NR14 8QU.
BOWEN, Mr. John Murray, FCA *1950;* 3 Airthrey Court, 5 Wilderton Road, Branksome Park, POOLE, BH13 6EB. (Life Member)
BOWEN, Mr. John Neil, FCA *1958;* 3 Severn Drive, MALVERN, WORCESTERSHIRE, WR14 2SZ. (Life Member)
BOWEN, Mr. John Nigel, FCA *1965;* Maunu Road, RD 9, WHANGAREI, NEW ZEALAND. (Life Member)
BOWEN, Mrs. Kate Lyndsey Jane, MBiochem ACA *2007;* 2 Hillview Crescent, ORPINGTON, BR6 0SL.
BOWEN, Mr. Peter Mark, BA ACA *1987;* 12 Arthur Street, LONDON, EC4R 9AQ.
BOWEN, Mr. Richard Gareth, FCA DChA *1980;* St Bride's House, 10 Salisbury Square, LONDON, EC4Y 8EH.
•**BOWEN, Mr. Robert William Peter, BA(Hons) FCA** *1994;* H.L. Barnes & Sons, Barclays Bank Chambers, Bridge Street, STRATFORD-UPON-AVON, WARWICKSHIRE, CV37 6AH.
BOWEN, Mr. Ronald Eric William, FCA *1964;* Inshalla, 132 Main Road, Naphill, HIGH WYCOMBE, HP14 4PZ.
BOWEN, Mr. Ross James, ACA *2008;* K P M G, 2 Cornwall Street, BIRMINGHAM, B3 2DL.
BOWEN, Mrs. Sharon Jean, ACA *1991;* The Capita Group Plc, Dean Bradley House, 52 Horseferry Road, LONDON, SW1P 2AF.
BOWEN, Mr. Stephen Andrew, BSc ACA *1987;* 60 South Eden Park Road, BECKENHAM, BR3 3BG.
•**BOWEN, Mr. Thomas Graham Howell, ACA** *1980;* H & W Jones & Co., 81 Bridge Street, LAMPETER, SA48 7AB.
•**BOWEN, Mr. William Charles Rodney, ACA** *1983;* (Tax Fac), Bowen Accountants Ltd, Griffon House, Seagry Heath, Great Somerford, CHIPPENHAM, WILTSHIRE SN15 5EN.

BOWEN, Mr. William John, FCA *1962;* Chestnut Cottage, Pitchcombe, STROUD, GL6 6LW. (Life Member)

•**BOWEN-DAVIES, Mr. David Ian, FCA** *1973;* (Tax Fac), D Bowen-Davies & Co, 67 Elmcroft Close, FELTHAM, TW14 9HJ.

BOWEN-JONES, Mr. Richard, FCA *1974;* Cruck Barn, Bryn Yorkin Manor, Caergwrle, WREXHAM, LL12 9HT.

BOWENS, Mr. Martin John, BSc ACA *1996;* 53 Chimera Wood, Helens Bay, BANGOR, COUNTY DOWN, BT19 1XX.

BOWER, Mr. Alan John, FCA *1978;* 10 Park Avenue, ILKESTON, DE7 5DH.

BOWER, Mr. Andrew James, MEng ACA *1996;* 7 Knox Street, Yarraville, MELBOURNE, VIC 3013, AUSTRALIA.

BOWER, Mr. Brian Ralph, FCA *1957;* 33 Brookfield Av, Poynton, STOCKPORT, SK12 1JE. (Life Member)

BOWER, Mrs. Charlotte Victoria, BSc ACA *1997;* 185A Old Birmingham Road, Marlbrook, BROMSGROVE, B60 1DQ.

BOWER, Mr. Christopher David, FCA *1962;* 39 Low Wood, Wilsden, BRADFORD, BD15 0JS.

BOWER, Mr. Daniel Austin, BSc ACA *2011;* 69 Kilcoby Avenue, Swinton, MANCHESTER, M27 8AD.

BOWER, Mr. Daniel Peter, ACA *2007;* 6 Teak Place, CHERRYBROOK, NSW 2126, AUSTRALIA.

BOWER, Mr. David John, BA FCA *1994;* 18 Hazelwood Drive, BOURNE, PE10 9SZ.

BOWER, Mr. David Jonathan, BSc FCA MBA *1996;* 185a Old Birmingham Road Marlbrook, BROMSGROVE, WORCESTERSHIRE, B60 1DQ.

BOWER, Mr. Julian Thurstan Syndercombe, FCA *1961;* 159 Ebury Street, LONDON, SW1W 9QN. (Life Member)

•**BOWER, Mr. Leighton Michael, BA ACA** *2000;* Rouse Audit LLP, 55 Station Road, BEACONSFIELD, BUCKINGHAMSHIRE, HP9 1QL. See also Rouse Partners LLP

BOWER, Mr. Mark Richard, BA FCA *1985;* 16 Burnt Stones Close, Sandygate, SHEFFIELD, S10 5TS.

BOWER, Mr. Martin Leslie, FCA *1960;* 11 Goodwood Close, Furnace Green, CRAWLEY, RH10 6NG. (Life Member)

BOWER, Mr. Michael John, BSc ACA *1993;* 2 Glendale Road, TURRAMURRA, NSW 2074, AUSTRALIA.

BOWER, Miss. Rebecca Margaret, OBE BSc ACA *1983;* 54 Ramillies Road, Chiswick, LONDON, W4 1JN.

•①**BOWER, Mr. Simon Peter, BA ACA** *1990;* Zenith Hygiene Systems Plc, Zenith House, A1(M) Business Centre, Dixons Hill Road, HATFIELD, HERTFORDSHIRE AL9 7JE.

BOWER, Mrs. Suzanne Helen, BA(Hons) ACA *2002;* 14 Cherry Street, STRATFORD-UPON-AVON, WARWICKSHIRE, CV37 6DF.

BOWER-SLOANE, Mr. Christian, LLB LLB(Hons) ACA *2011;* 10 Cranbourne Avenue, Hoylake, WIRRAL, MERSEYSIDE, CH47 7BW.

BOWERMAN, Mrs. Sarah Fiona, BSc ACA *1994;* West Morden House, Morden, WAREHAM, BH20 7EA.

BOWERS, Mr. Alan Christopher, BSc ACA *1997;* 114 New Road, MARLOW, SL7 3NW.

BOWERS, Mr. Anthony David, BA ACA *1990;* 3638 Lorimer Lane, ENCINITAS, CA 92024, UNITED STATES.

BOWERS, Mr. Anthony James, FCA *1982;* 4 Great Auclum Place, Burghfield Common, READING, RG7 3ED.

BOWERS, Mr. Bryan Andrew, MA FCA *1976;* 32 Court Street Suite 2200, BROOKLYN, NY 11201, UNITED STATES.

BOWERS, Mrs. Catherine Elisabeth Annabel, BA ACA *1988;* 17 Manor Park Drive, Finchampstead, WOKINGHAM, RG40 4XE.

BOWERS, Miss. Charlotte, BSc(Hons) ACA *2011;* 8 Bampton Court, Hursley Road, Chandler's Ford, EASTLEIGH, HAMPSHIRE, SO53 2TA.

BOWERS, Mr. Christopher Conway, FCA *1969;* 17 Woodham Park Road, Woodham, ADDLESTONE, KT15 3ST. (Life Member)

BOWERS, Mr. David, BCom FCA *1975;* 29 Grenville Court, Blacketts Wood Drive, Chorleywood, RICKMANSWORTH, HERTFORDSHIRE, WD3 5PZ.

•**BOWERS, Mr. David Findlow, FCA** *1976;* Warr & Co, Mynshull House, 78 Churchgate, STOCKPORT, SK1 1YJ. See also Warr & Co Limited

BOWERS, Mr. Edward David, BA ACA *1993;* 2200 Scarlet Rose Drive, LAS VEGAS, NV 89134, UNITED STATES.

•**BOWERS, Mr. Edward Norman, ACA** *1979;* Bowers & Co, 13 Peel Road, Douglas, ISLE OF MAN, IM1 4LR.

•**BOWERS, Mrs. Fiona Mary, MA(Hons) ACA** *2002;* Cansdales, Bourbon Court, Nightingales Corner, Little Chalfont, AMERSHAM, HP7 9QS. See also Cansdales Ltd

BOWERS, Mrs. Florence Isobel, BSc FCA *1963;* 35 Mowbray Road, FLEETWOOD, FY7 7JJ. (Life Member)

BOWERS, Mr. Ian Francis, FCA *1980;* with James Worley & Sons, 9 Bridle Close, Surbiton Road, KINGSTON UPON THAMES, SURREY, KT1 2JW.

BOWERS, Miss. Karen, BA ACA *2002;* 84 Foulser Road, LONDON, SW17 8UD.

BOWERS, Miss. Lucy, BA ACA *2011;* 7 Parade Bank, Moulton, NORTHAMPTON, NN3 7ST.

BOWERS, Mr. Paul Graham, BA ACA *1999;* 4 Larches Road, KIDDERMINSTER, WORCESTERSHIRE, DY11 7AA.

•**BOWERS, Mr. Paul Michael, BA FCA CTA** *1980;* Paul M Bowers, 3 Herewood Close, NEWBURY, BERKSHIRE, RG14 1PY.

BOWERS, Mr. Peter, BA ACA *1982;* Flat 21, Kildare Court, Barcombe Close, EASTBOURNE, EAST SUSSEX, BN20 8HU.

BOWERS, Mr. Stephen, BA ACA CTA *1986;* 2/4 Hilton Street, MOUNT WAVERLEY, VIC 3149, AUSTRALIA.

BOWERS, Mr. Steven John, BSc ACA *1998;* Thornbury Cottage, Chalk Hill, Coleshill, AMERSHAM, BUCKINGHAMSHIRE, HP7 0LY.

BOWES, Mrs. Anne, BSc ACA *1980;* 8 Meadow Sweet Road, STRATFORD-UPON-AVON, WARWICKSHIRE, CV37 0TH.

BOWES, Miss. Chloe Mary, MSc BSc ACA *2009;* Council House, Derby City Council Corporate Services Department, Council House Corporation Street, DERBY, DE1 2FS.

BOWES, Mr. Christopher John Lincoln, BA FCA FCMA JDipMA *1959;* 19 Beech Grove Court, Beech Grove, HARROGATE, NORTH YORKSHIRE, HG2 0EU. (Life Member)

BOWES, Mr. David Geoffrey, BA ACA *2001;* 22 Mead Close, KNUTSFORD, WA16 0DU.

BOWES, Mr. Gary, BA ACA *1998;* Chatterley House, Clifton, BANBURY, OXFORDSHIRE, OX15 0PA.

BOWES, Mr. John Michael Charles, ACA *1991;* Cook & Partners Solicitors, 241 Lower Addiscombe Road, CROYDON, CR0 6RD.

BOWES, Mr. Patrick Norton, MA ACA *1992;* Old Mutual Plc, Old Mutual Place, 2 Lambeth Hill, LONDON, EC4V 4GG.

•**BOWES, Mr. Paul Rodney, BSc FCA** *1982;* Paul R Bowes, 57 Centurion Road, BRIGHTON, BN1 3LN.

BOWES, Mr. Ronald Turner, FCA *1948;* 8 Beech Court, Woodlands Apartments, La Rue Des Cotils, Grouville, JERSEY, JE3 9AY. (Life Member)

BOWES, Mr. Thomas, BA FCA *1976;* Greycroft, Croft Place, ALNWICK, NORTHUMBERLAND, NE66 1XU.

BOWES LYON, Sir Simon Alexander, BA FCA *1959;* St. Paul's Walden Bury, HITCHIN, SG4 8BP. (Life Member)

BOWESMAN, Mr. Raymond Handley, FCA *1958;* 62 Hawk Close, Abbeydale, GLOUCESTER, GL4 4WE. (Life Member)

BOWEY, Mr. Thomas James, BA ACA *2011;* 12 Beckhall, Welton, LINCOLN, LN2 3LJ.

•**BOWGEN, Mr. John Steven, BA FCA** *1990;* 274 Ipswich Road, COLCHESTER, CO4 0ES.

BOWHILL, Mr. Gareth, BSc ACA *2009;* 16 Wilberforce Road, SOUTHSEA, HAMPSHIRE, PO5 3DR.

BOWHILL-MANN, Mrs. Carol Ann, BA ACA CTA *1998;* Larking Gowen, Larking Gowen Kingstreet House, 15 Upper King Street, NORWICH, NR3 1RB.

BOWIE, Mr. Graham, LLM BAcc ACA *2007;* 14 Swallow Close, Pool in Wharfedale, OTLEY, WEST YORKSHIRE, LS21 1RR.

BOWKER, Mr. Anthony James, FCA *1975;* 1941 Maud Avenue, CHICAGO, IL 60614, UNITED STATES.

BOWKER, Mr. David Geoffrey, BSc ACA *1987;* Upper Flat, Riverbank, High Street, Hamble, SOUTHAMPTON, SO31 4HA.

BOWKER, Mr. Ian Patrick, BSc FCA *1989;* Greenbank, Priestlands, SHERBORNE, DT9 4HN.

BOWKER, Mr. Julian John, FCA *1970;* 6 Fairbourne Close, WILMSLOW, CHESHIRE, SK9 6JG.

•**BOWKER, Mrs. Nicola Jane, FCA** *1990;* Nicola Bowker & Co Limited, Alexanda Houses, 37 New Road, Laxey, ISLE OF MAN, IM4 7BQ.

BOWKER, Mr. Richard, BEng ACA *1997;* Cobblers Cottage, 12 The Nook, Bolton le Sands, CARNFORTH, LANCASHIRE, LA5 8DR.

BOWLAND, Mr. Ian Alexander, BA FCA MSI *1980;* 14 Linton Avenue, SOLIHULL, B91 3NN.

BOWLAND, Mr. Nigel Graham, BSc ACA *1987;* Surgical Innovations, Unit 6, Clayton Wood Bank, LEEDS, LS16 6QZ.

BOWLBY, Mr. Henry Alverey Salvin, BA ACA *1991;* Spitfire Technology Group, Unit 6/7, Southbank Business Centre, Ponton Road, LONDON, SW8 5BL.

BOWLER, Mr. Andrew Miles, BSc ACA *1992;* 18a Springbank Road, Gildersome Morley, LEEDS, LS27 7DJ.

•**BOWLER, Mr. Graham William, ACA** *1981;* Gorrie Whitson Limited, 18 Hand Court, LONDON, WC1V 6JF.

•**BOWLER, Mr. Jeremy James, FCA** *1975;* Cooper Parry LLP, 3 Centro Place, Pride Park, DERBY, DE24 8RF. See also Cooper Parry Wealth Strategies Limited

•**BOWLER, Mr. John, BA FCA** *1979;* Grant Thornton UK LLP, Regent House, 80 Regent Road, LEICESTER, LE1 7NH. See also Grant Thornton LLP

BOWLER, Mr. Jonathan, BA FCA *1994;* 19 Kilmory Fold, GLOSSOP, DERBYSHIRE, SK13 7PH.

•**BOWLER, Mr. Kim David, FCA** *1977;* Kim Bowler & Co Limited, 32 Clarence Street, YORK, YO31 7EW.

•**BOWLER, Miss. Margaret Mary, BSc ACA** *1980;* 14 Cambridge Cottages, RICHMOND, TW9 3AY.

BOWLER, Mr. Mark Richard, BSc FCA *1983;* Hatters Barn, Cutthorpe, CHESTERFIELD, S42 7AJ.

BOWLER, Mr. Peter Bruce, BA FCA *1964;* (Tax Fac), The Meadows, Townfield Lane, Mollington, CHESTER, CH1 6NJ.

BOWLER, Ms. Rhona, ACA *1986;* 17 Beechwood, Tabley Road, KNUTSFORD, CHESHIRE, WA16 0PQ.

BOWLER, Mr. Richard Anthony, ACA *1979;* 4 Waterfield Road, Cropston, LEICESTER, LE7 7HN.

•**BOWLER, Mr. Timothy Gordon, FCA** *1985;* Harrop Marshall, Ashfield House, Ashfield Road, CHEADLE, CHESHIRE, SK8 1BB.

BOWLES, Mr. Andrew Martin, BSc FCA *1989;* Rose Builders Ltd Riverside House, Riverside Avenue East Lawford, MANNINGTREE, CO11 1US.

BOWLES, Mr. Christopher Mark, BA FCA *1992;* with Old Mill Accountancy LLP, The Old Mill, Park Road, SHEPTON MALLET, SOMERSET, BA4 5BS.

•**BOWLES, Mr. Christopher Stephen, BA ACA** *1987;* Ernst & Young LLP, 1 More London Place, LONDON, SE1 2AF. See also Ernst & Young Europe LLP

BOWLES, Mr. David Victor, FCA *1960;* 36 Kings Avenue, EASTBOURNE, EAST SUSSEX, BN21 2PF. (Life Member)

BOWLES, Mrs. Elfride Ng, BA ACA *1995;* 48 Duchy Road, HARROGATE, NORTH YORKSHIRE, HG1 2EY.

BOWLES, Mr. Huw Martin Richard, BSc ACA *1994;* Ridgeway House, Easton Town, Sherston, MALMESBURY, WILTSHIRE, SN16 0PT.

•**BOWLES, Mr. Martin James, FCA** *1996;* Haines Watts (East Midlands) Limited, 10 Stadium Business Court, Millennium Way, Pride Park, DERBY, DE24 8HP.

BOWLES, Mr. Marven Anthony, BSc FCA *1974;* 8 Caribbean Villas, 81 Sheung Sze Wan Road, Clear Water Bay, SAI KUNG, HONG KONG SAR.

•**BOWLES, Mr. Michael Benjamin, FCA** *1972;* Bowles & Co., 14 Westerham Road, SEVENOAKS, TN13 2PU.

BOWLES, Mr. Michael Ian, BSc FCA *1972;* P O Box 369, WA 6065 NEROO, WA 6065, AUSTRALIA. (Life Member)

BOWLES, Mr. Philip Bryan, FCA *1978;* St. Martin of Tours H A Ltd, 318-320 St. Pauls Road, Highbury, LONDON, N1 2LF.

BOWLES, Mr. Robert Nigel, BA ACA *1988;* 48 Duchy Road, HARROGATE, NORTH YORKSHIRE, HG1 2EY.

BOWLES, Ms. Sally Jane, MA ACA *1984;* 2 Watson Garth, Appleton Roebuck, YORK, YO23 7EE.

BOWLES, Miss. Sarah, MA ACA *1989;* c/o Rachel Hearn-Phillips, 93 Fairway Avenue, Tilehurst, READING, BERKSHIRE, RG30 4QB.

BOWLES, Mr. Sidney Theodore, FCA *1955;* 6 Grange Road, Christchurch Road, NORWICH, NR2 3NH. (Life Member)

BOWLES, Mr. Simon Alan, MA FCA FCT *1983;* H M Revenue & Customs, 100 Parliament Street, LONDON, SW1A 2BQ.

BOWLES, Mr. Stephen, BA ACA *2000;* 25 Roman Way, Warfield, BRACKNELL, RG42 7UT.

BOWLES, Mr. Stephen Graham, FCA *1969;* Church View, The Common, Mulbarton, NORWICH, NR14 8JQ.

BOWLEY, Mr. Andrew Douglas, BSc ACA *1995;* The Gatehouse, Dunnings Road, EAST GRINSTEAD, RH19 4AA.

BOWLEY, Mr. Andrew James, BEng ACA *1998;* Po Box 1821, WELLINGTON 6140, NEW ZEALAND.

BOWLEY, Mr. Brian Allan, FCA *1952;* 4 Pagasvlei Rd, Constantia, CAPE TOWN, C.P., 7806, SOUTH AFRICA. (Life Member)

BOWLEY, Mr. Christopher Earl, BA FCA *1970;* 2 Stoke Green Cottages, Stoke Green, Stoke Poges, SLOUGH, SL2 4HR.

BOWLEY, Mrs. Deirdre Margaret, BEng ACA *1999;* 5 Wensley Road, HARROGATE, NORTH YORKSHIRE, HG2 8AQ.

BOWLEY, Mr. Geoffrey Francis, FCA *1974;* Woodlands, Newdigate Road, Beare Green, DORKING, SURREY, RH5 4QD.

BOWLEY, Mr. James Edward, BSc(Hons) ACA *2001;* Urenco Ltd, 18 Oxford Road, MARLOW, BUCKINGHAMSHIRE, SL7 2NL.

BOWLEY, Mrs. Jane Alicia, BA ACA *1989;* 6 Marys Close, Wymeswold, LOUGHBOROUGH, LE12 6TH.

BOWLEY, Mrs. Jennifer Marion, BA ACA *1983;* 10 Church Crescent, LONDON, N10 3ND.

BOWLEY, Mrs. Mary Paula, BA ACA *1989;* 11 Gerrard Close, Arnold, NOTTINGHAM, NG5 9QL.

BOWLEY, Mr. Mervyn Welford, FCA *1950;* 56 Upton Lane, Upton, CHESTER, CH2 1EE. (Life Member)

BOWLEY, Mr. Paul Robert, BA ACA *1999;* 41 Royal Lane, Hillingdon, UXBRIDGE, UB8 3QU.

BOWLEY, Mr. Richard Anthony, BSc ACA *1986;* 10 Church Crescent, LONDON, N10 3ND.

BOWLEY, Mr. Richard John, BA ACA *1985;* C2C Rail Limited, 207 Old Street, LONDON, EC1V 9NR.

BOWLEY, Mr. Robert Keith Lyon, FCA *1972;* 1 Forbes Place, King George Gardens, CHICHESTER, WEST SUSSEX, PO19 6LF. (Life Member)

BOWLING, Mr. David John, BSc(Hons) ACA *2002;* Crompton Farm York Road, Haxby, YORK, YO32 3HN.

BOWLING, Mr. James, ACA *2008;* 106 Parkville Road, MANCHESTER, M20 4TZ.

BOWLING, Mr. James Nicholas, BA ACA *1995;* Roseacre, Bighton Road, Medstead, ALTON, HAMPSHIRE, GU34 5ND.

BOWLING, Mr. Keith Michael, BA(Econ) ACA *2001;* 3/33 Hood Street, SUBIACO, WA 6008, AUSTRALIA.

BOWLING, Mr. Stephen Eric, BSc ACA *1992;* 6 Scholars Way, ROMFORD, ESSEX, RM2 5US.

BOWLING, Mrs. Susan Aileen, BSc ACA *1993;* Springfield Rough Lane, Shirley, ASHBOURNE, DERBYSHIRE, DE6 3AZ.

BOWLING, Mr. Thomas Anthony, BA FCA *1985;* 22 Greystoke Avenue, NEWCASTLE UPON TYNE, NE2 1PN.

BOWMAN, Mr. Alasdair Rutledge Roy, FCA *1975;* High House, 79 High Road, RAYLEIGH, SS6 7SE.

BOWMAN, Mrs. Angela Michele, BSc FCA CTA *1995;* (Tax Fac), H M Revenue & Customs St. Johns House, Merton Road, LIVERPOOL, L75 1BB.

BOWMAN, Mrs. Cara Elise, BA ACA *1998;* 27 Brackenfield Road, Gosforth, NEWCASTLE UPON TYNE, NE3 4DX.

•**BOWMAN, Mr. Charles Edward Beck, BA FCA** *1986;* MEMBER OF COUNCIL, PricewaterhouseCoopers LLP, 1 Embankment Place, LONDON, WC2N 6RH. See also PricewaterhouseCoopers

BOWMAN, Mr. Christopher Nigel, BA(Hons) ACA *2001;* 61 Lubbock Road, CHISLEHURST, KENT, BR7 5JG.

BOWMAN, Mr. Colin Roy, BSc FCA *1976;* 37 Summers Way, KNUTSFORD, CHESHIRE, WA16 9AR.

BOWMAN, Mr. Daniel Robin, ACA *2007;* 55 Madison Walk, Ackworth, PONTEFRACT, WEST YORKSHIRE, WF7 7ER.

•**BOWMAN, Mr. David, BA FCA** *1982;* David Bowman, 40 Hurdeswell, Long Hanborough, WITNEY, OX29 8DH.

BOWMAN, Mr. David Andrew, BSc ACA IMC CFA *1989;* 65 Catharine Close, Chafford Hundred, GRAYS, RM16 6QH.

BOWMAN, Mr. David Neil, BA ACA *1998;* 27 Brackenfield Road, Gosforth, NEWCASTLE UPON TYNE, NE3 4DX.

BOWMAN, Mr. Edward, FCA *1971;* with G J Jackson Accountants Limited, 5 Victoria Avenue, BISHOP AUCKLAND, COUNTY DURHAM, DL14 7JH.

BOWMAN, Miss. Emma Louise, BCom ACA *2007;* with Asda Stores Ltd, Asda House, Great Wilson Street, LEEDS, LS11 5AD.

BOWMAN, Mr. Graham Reavley, FCA *1968;* (Tax Fac), Crossgates House, 70 Wyke Lane, Wyke, BRADFORD, BD12 9BA.

BOWMAN, Mrs. Hazel Jean, BA ACA *1987;* 40 Hurdeswell, Long Hanborough, WITNEY, OX29 8DH.

BOWMAN, Mr. Ian, ACA *2009;* Benson House, Pricewaterhousecoopers, 33 Wellington Street, LEEDS, LS1 4JP.

BOWMAN, Sir Jeffery Haverstock, FCA *1962;* (Member of Council 1986 - 1990), The Old Rectory, Church Road, Boreham, CHELMSFORD, CM3 3EP. (Life Member)

BOWMAN, Mr. John Edward Beck, MA FCA *1954;* Colneford House, White Colne, COLCHESTER, CO6 2PJ. (Life Member)
•**BOWMAN, Mrs. Kathryn Jane, BA ACA** *1990;* (Tax Fac), Kates Accountancy Services, 1 Woodridge Close, Edgmond, NEWPORT, SHROPSHIRE, TF10 8JF. See also Kate Accountancy Services and Bowmans Accountants Limited
BOWMAN, Mr. Keith Raymond, FCA *1958;* 10 Burr Tree Drive, Colton LaneWhitkirk, LEEDS, LS15 9ED. (Life Member)
BOWMAN, Mr. Neil Robert, FCA *1967;* (Tax Fac), Lavender Cottage School Road, Bursledon, SOUTHAMPTON, SO31 8BW.
BOWMAN, Mr. Neville James, PhD BSc FCA AIIT MCT *1980;* Ambleside, 2 Meadway, Prestbury, MACCLESFIELD, CHESHIRE, SK10 4DF.
•**BOWMAN, Mr. Nicholas John, ACA** *1981;* (Tax Fac), Bowman & Co, Bowman & Hillier Building, The Old Brewery, Priory Lane, BURFORD, OX18 4SG. See also N J Bowman Ltd
BOWMAN, Mr. Peter Drummond, BSc ACA *1986;* 97 Palewell Park, East Sheen, LONDON, SW14 8JJ.
BOWMAN, Mr. Philip, MA FCA *1977;* Smiths Group Plc, 80 Victoria Street, LONDON, SW1E 5JL.
BOWMAN, Mr. Russell, BSc FCA *1989;* Lavender Cottage, Warborne Lane, Portmore, LYMINGTON, SO41 5RJ.
BOWMAN, Mrs. Samira, BSc ACA *2001;* 61 Lubbock Road, CHISLEHURST, KENT, BR7 5JG.
BOWMAN, Mr. Stephen, ACA *1978;* 33 Fleet Lane, Oulton, LEEDS, LS26 8HT.
•**BOWMAN, Mr. Stephen Lindsay, FCA** *1975;* (Tax Fac), Blackborn Limited, 131 High Street, Chalfont St. Peter, GERRARDS CROSS, BUCKINGHAMSHIRE, SL9 9QJ. See also Blackborn Services
BOWMAN, Mr. Terence Patrick Edward, FCA *1974;* Ryburn, Barkisland Mill, Beestonley Lane, Barkisland, HALIFAX, WEST YORKSHIRE HX4 0HF.
BOWMAN, Mr. William John, FCA *1970;* Aptdo de Correos 1015, Can Andrauet, 07840 SANTA EULALIA, IBIZA, SPAIN.
BOWMAR, Mr. Alan, BA ACA *2005;* 19 Swinburne Avenue, Adwick-le-street, DONCASTER, DN6 7DH.
BOWN, Mr. Andrew, BSc ACA *2004;* Harmatinger Str. 12, 81377 MUNICH, GERMANY.
BOWN, Miss. Corinne, BSc FCA *1978;* 4 Fishersdene, Claygate, ESHER, KT10 0HT.
BOWN, Miss. Helen Louise, BA ACA *2007;* 58 Bullcote Green, Royton, OLDHAM, OL2 6NJ.
•**BOWN, Mr. John Anthony, FCA** *1962;* Shorts, 6 Fairfield Road, CHESTERFIELD, DERBYSHIRE, S40 4TP.
BOWN, Mr. Michael Ryan, FCA *1963;* Kelly Parc, Harrowbarrow, CALLINGTON, CORNWALL, PL17 8JN. (Life Member)
BOWN, Mr. Nicholas Neville, FCA *1964;* 76 Botley Road, CHESHAM, HP5 1XG. (Life Member)
BOWN, Mrs. Nicola Claire, BA ACA *1991;* Ruby Cottage, 126 Ownham, NEWBURY, RG20 8PJ.
BOWN, Mr. Peter John, BSc ACA *1981;* 13 Park Close, Oakley, BASINGSTOKE, RG23 7LE.
BOWN, Philip Arnold, Esq MBE FCA *1957;* Uplands, Itton Road, CHEPSTOW, MONMOUTHSHIRE, NP16 6BQ. (Life Member)
BOWN, Mr. Raymond John, BSc FCA *1975;* 1 Poplar Way, High Lane, STOCKPORT, SK6 8ES.
BOWN, Mrs. Rebecca, BSc ACA *2005;* Harmatinger Strasse 12, 81377 MUNICH, GERMANY.
•**BOWN, Mr. Simon Edgar, FCA** *1968;* Simon Bown Associates, Highfield Court, Highfield Park, Creaton, NORTHAMPTON, NN6 8NT.
BOWN, Mr. Steven Michael, BSc FCA *1991;* 126 Ownham, NEWBURY, RG20 8PJ.
•**BOWNAS, Mr. Mark David, MA FCA** *1991;* KPMG Advisory Kft, Vaci ut 99, BUDAPEST, H-1139, HUNGARY. See also KPMG Hungaria Kft
BOWNES, Miss. Anna Ellen, BA(Hons) ACA *2001;* AAPT, 680 George St, SYDNEY, NSW 2000, AUSTRALIA.
•**BOWNESS, Mrs. Angela Elaine, FCA** *1971;* Angela Bowness, 44 Stoughton Drive, LEICESTER, LE5 6AN.
BOWNESS, Mr. Ian Francis, BA FCA *1982;* United Carpets Moorhead House, Moorhead Way Bramley, ROTHERHAM, SOUTH YORKSHIRE, S66 1YY.
BOWNESS, Miss. Rebecca, ACA *2005;* with PricewaterhouseCoopers LLP, 89 Sandyford Road, NEWCASTLE UPON TYNE, NE1 8HW.
BOWRAN, Mrs. Amanda Jane, BSc ACA *1994;* 5 Park Rise Close, HARPENDEN, AL5 3AW.
•**BOWRAN, Miss. Clare Louise, ACA FCCA** *2011;* Louise Bowran Accountancy, 14 Kendal Close, PETERBOROUGH, PE4 7GN.
BOWRING, Mr. Ian Stuart, BCom ACA *1995;* 13 Glenview Street, SYDNEY, NSW 2065, AUSTRALIA.
BOWRING, Mr. Stewart Edward, BSc ACA *2011;* 32 Redwood Drive, AYLESBURY, BUCKINGHAMSHIRE, HP21 7TN.
BOWRON, Mr. Henry Colin, MA FCA *1953;* Rectory Farm, Arlingham, GLOUCESTER, GL2 7JL. (Life Member)
BOWRON, Mr. Simon Martin, BSc ACA *1995;* 495 Birmingham Road, Marlbrook, BROMSGROVE, WORCESTERSHIRE, B61 0HY.
BOWRON, Mrs. Susan Lorraine, BSc ACA *1999;* Old School House The Village, Chaddesley Corbett, KIDDERMINSTER, WORCESTERSHIRE, DY10 4SA.
BOWRY, Mr. John Clement, FCA *1963;* 37 Downs Way, EPSOM, KT18 5LU.
BOWSER, Mr. Richard Julian, BSocSc ACA *1986;* Bankfield, Arden Road, Dorridge, SOLIHULL, WEST MIDLANDS, B93 8LJ.
BOWSHER, Miss. Sally, MEng ACA *2010;* Flat 20, Stephen Sanders Court, Salcott Road, LONDON, SW11 6DD.
BOWSHER, Mrs. Sandra Jayne, BSc ACA *1988;* 44 Treatts Road, LINDFIELD, NSW 2070, AUSTRALIA.
BOWSHER, Mrs. Sarah Jane, BSc ACA *1999;* 21 Carston Grove, Calcot, READING, RG31 7ZN.
BOWSKILL, Mr. Daniel James, BSc(Hons) ACA *2000;* 1806/168 Kent Street, SYDNEY, NSW 2000, AUSTRALIA.
BOWSTEAD, Mr. Stephen, BA ACA *2005;* Flat 23 Vanguard House, 70 Martello Street, LONDON, E8 3QQ.
BOWTELL, Mr. Daniel Adam, BSc(Hons) ACA *2001;* Amberley, 10 Main Street, Caythorpe, NOTTINGHAM, NG14 7ED.
BOWTELL, Mr. John Paul Maurice, MA ACA *1995;* Pardons, 78 East End Lane, Ditchling, HASSOCKS, WEST SUSSEX, BN6 8UR.
BOWTELL, Mr. Michael Andrew, MBA ACA *1984;* 5 Harrier Close, Hartford, HUNTINGDON, PE29 1XA.
BOWTELL, Mr. Raymond Charles, FCA *1953;* 83 Boundstone Road, Rowledge, FARNHAM, GU10 4AT. (Life Member)
BOWTELL, Mr. Richard Scott, BSc FCA *1981;* 7 The Mayflowers, Bassett Crescent East, SOUTHAMPTON, SO16 7PD.
BOWTELL, Mr. Robert James, BSc ACA *1986;* The Kantar Group, 501 Kings Highway East, FAIRFIELD, CT 06825, UNITED STATES.
BOWTHORPE, Mr. Jonathan Richard, FCA *1967;* Sunnymead, Heath Lane, Blackheath, LONDON, SE3 0UT.
BOWYER, Mrs. Alison Margaret, BSc ACA *1989;* 45 Old Kirk Road, EDINBURGH, EH12 6JU.
BOWYER, Mr. Andrew, ACA *2010;* 178 Dalmally Road, CROYDON, CR0 6LX.
BOWYER, Mr. Christopher Garry, FCA *1973;* 41 Northbrook Rd, WORTHING, BN14 8PS. (Life Member)
•**BOWYER, Mr. David Clive, ACA** *1982;* (Tax Fac), Clive Bowyer Limited, 18 Old Well Gardens, PENRYN, CORNWALL, TR10 9LF.
BOWYER, Mr. David Thomas, FCA *1978;* Windward House, Arden Road, Dorridge, SOLIHULL, B93 8LJ.
BOWYER, Miss. Evie Marjorie, FCA *1972;* MEMBER OF COUNCIL (Member of Council 2000 - 2009), EVB Training Consultancy Ltd, 92 Valiant House, Vicarage Crescent, LONDON, SW11 3LX.
BOWYER, The Revd. Geoffrey, BA FCA CTA *1980;* (Tax Fac), 36 Bakers Close, Bishops Hull, TAUNTON, TA1 5HD.
BOWYER, Mr. James Anthony, ACA *1980;* 43 Old House Road, RD2 Upper Moutere, NELSON 7175, NEW ZEALAND.
BOWYER, Mrs. Julia Mary, MA ACA *2002;* with PricewaterhouseCoopers LLP, 1 Embankment Place, LONDON, WC2N 6RH.
BOWYER, Ms. Kate Ann, BSc ACA *1995;* Bramley Cottage, Back Lane, Horsmonden, TONBRIDGE, TN12 8NH.
BOWYER, Mr. Peter Damian, MA FCA *1966;* 323 Conrad Tower, Bollo LaneActon, LONDON, W3 8QS.
BOWYER, Mr. Richard Charles, BSc ACA *1996;* 12 Heathfield, ROYSTON, HERTFORDSHIRE, SG8 5BW.
BOWYER, Mr. Russell Adrian, ACA ATII *1989;* Custom World Ltd, 38 Cobham Road, Ferndown Industrial Estate, WIMBORNE, DORSET, BH21 7NP.
BOWYER, Mrs. Sally Ann, BSc ACA *1993;* 16 Northcote Road, Bramhall, STOCKPORT, SK7 2HJ.
BOWYER, Mrs. Sarah Louise, BA ACA *1997;* 25 Marlborough Avenue, Hawarden, DEESIDE, CLWYD, CH5 3SA.
BOWYER, Mr. Simon, BSc ACA *2007;* 10 Brigantine Court, 7 Spert Street, LONDON, E14 8EB.
BOWYER, Mr. Stephen William, BSc ACA *1979;* 9 Thurlow Close, Oadby, LEICESTER, LE2 4TG.
BOWYER, Mr. William Walter, MA ACA *1981;* with BDO LLP, 55 Baker Street, LONDON, W1U 7EU.
BOX, Mr. Colin William, BA ACA *1979;* Harrison Clark, 5 Deansway, WORCESTER, WR1 2JG.
BOX, Mrs. Elaine Mary, BSc ACA *1986;* Refugee and Migrant Justice, 153-157 Commercial Road, LONDON, E1 2DA.
BOX, Mr. George Henry, FCA *1976;* Homefield, 10 St Mary's Road, Portishead, BRISTOL, BS20 6QW.
BOX, Mr. Nicholas James, MSci ACA *2010;* 54a Honeybrook Road, LONDON, SW12 0DW.
BOX, Mr. Nicholas Simon, BA(Hons) ACA *2006;* with Deloitte LLP, City House, 126-130 Hills Road, CAMBRIDGE, CB2 1RY.
BOX, Ms. Sarah Penelope Charlotte, MA CA ACA *1996;* 54 Montvale Drive, TORONTO M1M 3E7, ON, CANADA.
BOXALL, Mr. Christopher Alfred, ACA *1990;* 3 High Close, RICKMANSWORTH, HERTFORDSHIRE, WD3 4DZ.
BOXALL, Mrs. Hannah Lucy, BSc ACA *2001;* 18 Richelieu Park, Tower Road St. Helier, JERSEY, JE2 3HT.
BOXALL, Ms. Hayley Ann, BSc ACA *2001;* Pinsent Masons, 1 Park Row, LEEDS, LS1 5AB.
BOXALL, Mr. John Duncan, FCA *1939;* Green Acres, Hancocks Lane, Little Malvern, MALVERN, WR14 4JP. (Life Member)
BOXALL, Mr. John Harold, FCA *1967;* Orchard Croft, Eversleigh Rise, Darley Bridge, MATLOCK, DERBYSHIRE, DE4 2JW. (Life Member)
BOXALL, Mr. John Phillip, BA FCA *1977;* Flat 3, 97 Cromwell Road, HOVE, BN3 3EG.
•**BOXALL, Mr. Malcolm James, FCA** *1971;* (Tax Fac), Wagstaff Rowland & Huntley, 27 Lewisham High St, LONDON, SE13 5AF.
BOXALL, Mr. Mark, BA ACA *2010;* 2 Priory Court, Stanford Avenue, BRIGHTON, BN1 6AB.
BOXALL, Mr. Philip Stephen, BA ACA AMCT *1986;* Brita House, Brita Water Filter Systems Ltd, Granville Way, BICESTER, OX26 4JT.
BOXALL, Mrs. Susan Mary, BA ACA *1993;* 95 Reedley Road, BRISTOL, BS9 3TB.
BOXALL, Mr. Timothy Graham Kent, BSocSc ACA *1986;* 34 Ray Mercer Way, KIDDERMINSTER, WORCESTERSHIRE, DY10 1NY.
BOXFORD, Mr. James Alan, BA(Hons) ACA *2000;* 45 Ewhurst Avenue, SOUTH CROYDON, SURREY, CR2 0DH.
BOXFORD, Mr. Steven Keith, ACA *1979;* 49 Fairfax Road, TEDDINGTON, MIDDLESEX, TW11 9DA.
BOXHALL, Mr. Richard Charles, FCA *1960;* Cedar Rose, Court Lane, Thurlestone, KINGSBRIDGE, DEVON, TQ7 3ND. (Life Member)
•**BOXWELL, Mr. Duncan Harvey, FCA** *1973;* Duncan Boxwell & Company Limited, Montrose House, Clayhill Industrial Park, NESTON, CH64 3RU.
BOYALL, Mr. Laurence Richard, FCA *1956;* 126 Bodmin Road, CHELMSFORD, CM1 6LL. (Life Member)
BOYCE, Mr. Benjamin Matthew, BSc ACA *2005;* 16 Folly Road, Darley Abbey, DERBY, DE22 1ED.
BOYCE, Ms. Charlotte Alice, BA ACA *1999;* 44 Water Lane, TIVERTON, DEVON, EX16 6RB.
BOYCE, Mr. Ian Duncan, FCA *1968;* Sir Elly Kadoorie & Sons Ltd, St Georges Building, 24th Floor, CENTRAL, HONG KONG ISLAND, HONG KONG SAR.
BOYCE, Mrs. Janet Rosemary Zillah, ACA *1985;* 56 Alleyn Road, LONDON, SE21 8AH.
BOYCE, Ms. Julia Louise, BSc ACA *1995;* 10 Blenheim Way, Southmoor, ABINGDON, OX13 5NQ.
BOYCE, Mrs. Katrina Ann, FCA *1969;* 28 Lime Grove, Linslade, LEIGHTON BUZZARD, BEDFORDSHIRE, LU7 2SU. (Life Member)
BOYCE, Mrs. Nicola Louise, ACA *2005;* 28 The Paddocks, RAYLEIGH, SS6 8NF.
BOYCE, Mr. Richard Edward, BA(Econ) ACA AMCT *1996;* NHS South East Coast Strategic Health Authority Yorke House, 18-20 Massetts Road, HORLEY, RH6 7DE.
BOYCE, Mr. Timothy James, MSc ACA *1989;* 56 Alleyn Road, LONDON, SE21 8AH.
BOYCE, Mrs. Vivienne Janette, BSc ACA *2001;* 31 Fidlas Avenue, Llanishen, CARDIFF, CF14 0NY.
BOYCOTT, Mr. Douglass Peter, BA FCA *1975;* 45 Mayfield Close, WALTON-ON-THAMES, KT12 5PR.
BOYCOTT, Mr. Peter Michael, MA FCA *1969;* Swalcliffe House, Grange Lane, Swalcliffe, BANBURY, OXFORDSHIRE, OX15 5EY.
BOYCOTT, Mr. Robin David, BSc FCA *1975;* Whittonditch House, Ramsbury, MARLBOROUGH, WILTSHIRE, SN8 2PZ. (Life Member)
BOYD, Mr. Adrian, MA MEng ACA *1998;* 4 The Meadway, ORPINGTON, BR6 6HH.
BOYD, Mr. Alistair, MA ACA *2005;* Ernst & Young Llp, 1 More London Place, LONDON, SE1 2AF.
BOYD, Mr. Anthony Morgan, BCom FCA *1952;* 26 Darras Road, Ponteland, NEWCASTLE UPON TYNE, NE20 9PA. (Life Member)
BOYD, Mr. Ari Jason, ACA CA(SA) *2011;* Flat 9, Regal Court, 195 Holders Hill Road, LONDON, NW7 1ND.
BOYD, Miss. Brenda, BA ACA *1997;* 17 Glen Douglas Drive, Craigmarloch, Cumbernauld, GLASGOW, G68 0DW.
BOYD, Mr. Christopher Alan, BSc ACA *1995;* 115 Connaught Road, NORWICH, NR2 3BS.
•**BOYD, Mr. Christopher Nigel, MA FCA** *1982;* (Tax Fac), TWY Limited, 20 Sansome Walk, WORCESTER, WR1 1LR.
BOYD, Mrs. Claire Margaret, BA ACA *1998;* Yew Tree Cottage, Main Street, Houston, JOHNSTONE, PA6 7EL.
BOYD, Mr. Colin George, FCA *1963;* Finch House, The Street, Sedlescombe, BATTLE, EAST SUSSEX, TN33 0QW.
BOYD, Mr. David Henry, BSc ACA *1980;* Bardsey, 11 Derby Road, HASLEMERE, GU27 1BS.
BOYD, Mr. David Marc, LLB ACA CTA *2002;* 89 Hale Drive, Mill Hill, LONDON, NW7 3EL.
•**BOYD, Mr. Derek Roger, FCA** *1983;* Waltons Clark Whitehill, Oakland House, 40 Victoria Road, HARTLEPOOL, CLEVELAND, TS26 8DD. See also Horwath Clark Whitehill (North East) LLP
BOYD, Mr. Dermot Robert James, MA ACA *1986;* The Shopping Channel, Q V C, Marco Polo House, 346 Queenstown Road, LONDON, SW8 4NQ.
BOYD, Miss. Gillian Carole, BA ACA *1991;* Two Castles Housing Association, 3 Paternoster Row, CARLISLE, CA3 8TT.
BOYD, Mr. Gregory Francis Joseph, FCA *1976;* 24 Scaffog Avenue, ENNISKILLEN, COUNTY FERMANAGH, BT74 7JJ.
BOYD, Mr. Iain Ker, BA ACA *2004;* 8 The Street, Snailwell, NEWMARKET, SUFFOLK, CB8 7LX.
BOYD, Mr. Ian Leslie, FCA *1974;* 3 The Fellside, Kenton, NEWCASTLE UPON TYNE, NE3 4LJ.
BOYD, Mrs. Jacqueline Gail, BSc ACA *1989;* 17 Airedale Road, LONDON, SW12 8SQ.
BOYD, Mr. James David, BA ACA *1998;* Ladywood, The Avenue, AMERSHAM, BUCKINGHAMSHIRE, HP7 0AB.
BOYD, Mr. James Wilfred, BA ACA *2007;* with Buzzacott LLP, 12 New Fetter Lane, LONDON, EC4A 1AG.
BOYD, Mr. Jeremy John, FCA *1980;* 14 Fewston Close, Elwick Rise, HARTLEPOOL, TS26 0QN.
BOYD, Ms. Joanna Jane, BA ACA *1995;* Zweierhof 18, 8824ZH SCHONENBERG, SWITZERLAND.
•**BOYD, Mrs. Judith Helen, BA ACA** *1994;* (Tax Fac), Dolphin Tax LLP, 195 Loughborough Road, LEICESTER, LE4 5PL.
BOYD, Mrs. Julie Elizabeth, BSc ACA *1997;* Ivy House, 35 Goodwyns Vale, LONDON, N10 2HA.
BOYD, Mr. Kevin James, BEng CEng FCA FIET *1996;* Mews Close, 48 The Crescent, Pattishall, TOWCESTER, NORTHAMPTONSHIRE, NN12 8NA.
BOYD, Mr. Leslie Robert, FCA *1961;* 71 Waterloo Road, Birkdale, SOUTHPORT, PR8 2NW.
BOYD, Mrs. Lisa Jane, BA ACA *1998;* 4 The Meadway, ORPINGTON, BR6 6HH.
BOYD, Mr. Malcolm John, BA ACA *1994;* 19 Arlington Road, TEDDINGTON, MIDDLESEX, TW11 8NL.
BOYD, Mr. Mark Elliot Kerr, BSc(Hons) ACA *2002;* 11 Myaree Way, DUNCRAIG, WA 6023, AUSTRALIA.
•**BOYD, Mr. Matthew John, BSc FCA** *1994;* Jones Boyd, 16/17 Marshall Terrace, Gilesgate Moor, DURHAM, DH1 2HX.
BOYD, Mrs. Melanie, ACA *2008;* Sachsenstr. 16, 54295 TRIER, GERMANY.
BOYD, Mr. Michael Andrew, BSc FCA *1986;* Butts Dell House Free Street, Bishops Waltham, SOUTHAMPTON, SO32 1EE.
BOYD, Mr. Michael Iain Macbryde, BA FCA *1973;* (Tax Fac), 17 Southwell Park Road, CAMBERLEY, GU15 3PU.
BOYD, Mr. Michael Neil Murray, FCA *1970;* Pirbright House, Whites Lane, Pirbright, WOKING, SURREY, GU24 0LN.
BOYD, Mr. Michael Richard, FCA *1973;* 31 Westmoor Park, TAVISTOCK, DEVON, PL19 9AA.

BOYD, Mrs. Pauline Ann, BSc ACA *1980;* 8 Menlo Close, Noctorum, PRENTON, CH43 9YD.
BOYD, Mr. Pippin Jeremy Roxburgh, BA ACA *1995;* 8 Hinton Avenue, CAMBRIDGE, CB1 7AS.
BOYD, Mr. Quentin James Francis, MA ACA *1989;* LCF Edmond De Rothschild, Securities Limited, Orion House, 5 Upper St. Martin's Lane, LONDON, WC2H 9EA.
BOYD, Mr. Richard Ian, LLB ACA ATII *2001;* Games Workshop Group plc, Willow Road, Lenton, NOTTINGHAM, NG7 2WS.
BOYD, Mr. Richard Marshall, BA ACA *1998;* Kingfisher Plc, 3 Sheldon Square, LONDON, W2 6PX.
BOYD, Mr. Richard William, BSc FCA *1988;* Shadingfield, 11a Rookery Close, Fetcham, LEATHERHEAD, KT22 9BG.
BOYD, Mr. Robert Ian, BSc ACA *1996;* 16 Crackley Hill, Coventry Road, KENILWORTH, WARWICKSHIRE, CV8 2FP.
BOYD, Mr. Robert Ian Walter, FCA *1968;* Willow Green, Slingsby Walk, HARROGATE, NORTH YORKSHIRE, HG2 8LL.
BOYD, Mr. Robert Stephen, BA ACA *1993;* Rose Cottage, 5 Church Lane, Long Clawson, MELTON MOWBRAY, LE14 4ND.
BOYD, Mr. Roland Wheatley, BA FCA *1980;* Chiltern International Ltd, 171 Bath Road, SLOUGH, SL1 4AA.
BOYD, Mr. Simon James, BA(Hons) ACA *2002;* T T International, Moor House, Level 13, 120 London Wall, LONDON, EC2Y 5ET.
BOYD, Mr. Steven Clive, BSc FCA *1987;* Hundred Way, Hundred Lane, Portmore, LYMINGTON, SO41 5RG.
BOYD, Mrs. Tania Louise, BSc ACA *1998;* 8 Glenhurst Road, Henley-In-Arden, SOLIHULL, B95 5HZ.
BOYD, Mr. Timothy David, BSc ACA *1991;* 147 Southborough Lane, BROMLEY, BR2 8AP.
BOYD, Mr. William Michael, BA ACA *1982;* (Tax Fac), 16 Purley Knoll, PURLEY, CR8 3AE.
BOYD, Mrs. Yvonne, BSc ACA *1983;* 16 Purley Knoll, PURLEY, CR8 3AE.
•**BOYDE, Mr. Geoffrey Callin, FCA** *1965;* Callin & Co, 6-7 Fort William, Head Road, Douglas, ISLE OF MAN, IM1 5BG.
BOYDE, Mr. Martin Robert Cameron, BEng ACA *2003;* Roskilly Pont Vaillant Lane, Vale, GUERNSEY, GY6 8BN.
BOYDE, Mr. Neil, BA FCA *1990;* David Woods & Associates, 16-18 Kirby Street, LONDON, EC1N 8TS.
BOYDELL, Mr. David, FCA *1970;* Lilac Cottage, 24 Lower Stanton St Quintin, CHIPPENHAM, SN14 6DB.
BOYDELL, Mrs. Joanna, BA ACA *1993;* Mothercare UK Ltd, Cherry Tree Road, WATFORD, WD24 6SH.
•**BOYDELL, Mr. Malcolm Barry, FCA** *1970;* Boydell & Co, 89 Chiswick High Road, LONDON, W4 2EF.
BOYDELL, Mr. Stephen John, BA ACA *1997;* 22 Lorne Road, SOUTHSEA, HAMPSHIRE, PO5 1RR.
BOYDELL, Miss. Susannah, ACA *2008;* 20 New Beech Road, STOCKPORT, CHESHIRE, SK4 3DD.
•**BOYDEN, Mr. Jeremy Ashley, BA FCA** *1995;* CBHC LLP, Riverside House, 1-5 Como Street, ROMFORD, RM7 7DN.
BOYER, Ms. Claire Virginia, BSc ACA *1990;* Mount Green Housing Association, 33 Bridge Street, LEATHERHEAD, KT22 8BN.
BOYER, Mr. David John, BA ACA *1990;* 32 Longlands Court, Winslow, BUCKINGHAM, MK18 3QA.
BOYER, Miss. Janine Carolyn, ACA *1997;* 6 Barn Rise, BRIGHTON, BN1 5EE.
BOYER, Mr. John Paul, BSc ACA *1994;* 238 Carmel Road North, DARLINGTON, COUNTY DURHAM, DL3 9TG.
BOYER, Mr. Nicholas, BSc ACA *1996;* 4 Cumbria Grange, Gamston, NOTTINGHAM, NG2 6LZ.
BOYER, Ms. Siobhan Elisabeth, FCA *1991;* 64 South Way, LEWES, EAST SUSSEX, BN7 1LY.
BOYERS, Ms. Faith Gillian, MA FCA *1982;* LLoyds TSB Commercial Finance, Ltd, 1 Brookhill Way, BANBURY, OX16 3EL.
•**BOYERS, Mr. Jonathan Mark, BA FCA CF** *1992;* KPMG LLP, St. James's Square, MANCHESTER, M2 6DS. See also KPMG Europe LLP
BOYERS, Mrs. Victoria Claire, ACA *2008;* Dorset Cereals Ltd Peverell Avenue East, Poundbury, DORCHESTER, DORSET, DT1 3WE.
BOYES, Mr. Christopher, BA ACA *1988;* South Coombe Farm, Witheridge, TIVERTON, DEVON, EX16 8QL.
•**BOYES, Mr. Graham Gardner, FCA** *1970;* (Tax Fac), Pierce C A Ltd, Mentor House, Ainsworth Street, BLACKBURN, BB1 6AY. See also Pierce Group Limited
BOYES, Mr. Raymond, FCA *1960;* 18 Solent Heights, 23 Marine Parade East, LEE-ON-THE-SOLENT, PO13 9BW. (Life Member)
•**BOYES, Mr. Stephen, BA FCA** *1985;* Beever and Struthers, Central Buildings, Richmond Terrace, BLACKBURN, BB1 7AP.
BOYES-WATSON, Mr. Timothy Crispin, MA ACA *1996;* 2 The Green, Hook Norton, BANBURY, OXFORDSHIRE, OX15 5LE.
BOYFIELD, Mr. Stephen Andrew, FCA *1969;* Fir Trees, 1a Beechwood Lane, Culcheth, WARRINGTON, WA3 4HJ.
BOYLAN, Mr. Mark Gerard, MA MBA FCA *1971;* 69 Woodsford Square, LONDON, W14 8DS.
BOYLAN, Mr. Robert, MA ACA *2010;* Ordnance House, 31 Pier Road, ST HELIER, JE1 8PW.
BOYLAN, Miss. Siobhan Geraldine, BA ACA *1996;* Aviva Investors Holdings Ltd, 1 Poultry, LONDON, EC2R 8EJ.
BOYLAND, Mr. Allan Ian, BSc ACA *1994;* 25 rue Schlammeste, L-5770 WEILER LA TOUR, LUXEMBOURG.
BOYLAND, Mr. Brian Robert, MA FCA *1969;* 32 Castle Hill, MAIDENHEAD, SL6 4JJ.
BOYLAND, Mr. Roger Michael, FCA *1968;* 18 Chemin du Nant-d'Argent, Cologny, 1223 GENEVA, SWITZERLAND.
BOYLE, Mr. Alexander Donald, BSc FCA *1991;* Mills & Reeve Solicitors Francis House, 112 Hills Road, CAMBRIDGE, CB2 1PH.
BOYLE, Mrs. Alexandra Helen, BSc ACA *2000;* (Tax Fac), 17 Everest Road, LONDON, SE9 6PX.
BOYLE, Mr. Alistair David, LLB ACA *2001;* The Russels Alana Clos, 4 Route Militaire St. Sampson, GUERNSEY, GY2 4DZ.
•**BOYLE, Mr. Andrew John, BA ACA** *2004;* GBAC Limited, Old Linen Court, 83-85 Shambles Street, BARNSLEY, SOUTH YORKSHIRE, S70 2SB.
BOYLE, Mr. Andy Iain, BA ACA *1994;* 6 Hilton Court, Bramhope, LEEDS, LS16 9LG.
BOYLE, Miss. Barbara Ann, BSc ACA *1986;* Castlebar Park Ltd, 5g Castlebar Park, Ealing, LONDON, W5 1DD.
BOYLE, Miss. Claire, ACA *2011;* 88 Gander Drive, BASINGSTOKE, RG24 9JR.
BOYLE, Mr. Damian Joseph, ACA *1986;* 14 Weymouth Avenue, Ealing, LONDON, W5 4SA.
BOYLE, Mr. Denis, BSc FCA *1983;* Cami Vell de Sarria 23 4 3, 08029 BARCELONA, SPAIN.
•①**BOYLE, Mr. Edward George, MA ACA** *1999;* with KPMG LLP, 15 Canada Square, LONDON, E14 5GL.
•**BOYLE, Mr. Gerald Patrick, BA FCA** *1992;* (Tax Fac), G P Boyle & Co, Old Fire Station, Cecil Street, NEWRY, COUNTY DOWN, BT35 6AU.
BOYLE, Miss. Hilary Jane, BSc ACA *1989;* 33 Tanglewood Street, Middle Park, BRISBANE, QLD 4074, AUSTRALIA.
BOYLE, Mr. Ian Timothy, ACA *1985;* 46 Camelot Crescent, Middle Park, BRISBANE, QLD 4074, AUSTRALIA.
BOYLE, Miss. Jennifer, BA(Hons) ACA *2011;* 198 Baltic Quay, Mill Road, GATESHEAD, TYNE AND WEAR, NE8 3QZ.
BOYLE, Miss. Joanna, BSc ACA *2011;* 48 Beechcroft Avenue, HARROW, MIDDLESEX, HA2 7JF.
BOYLE, Mr. John Edward, BA ACA *1989;* Alexon International, 40-48 Guildford Street, LUTON, LU1 2PB.
BOYLE, Mr. Jonathan Charles Mason, MBA BA FCA FCT *1980;* Merriewood, Ockham Road South, East Horsley, LEATHERHEAD, KT24 6SL.
BOYLE, Mr. Kevin, BA ACA *1991;* The Coach House, Moorend Park Road, CHELTENHAM, GLOUCESTERSHIRE, GL50 2XW.
BOYLE, Mr. Lee Stuart, BA ACA *1998;* 6 Ferndale Drive, Appley Bridge, WIGAN, LANCASHIRE, WN6 9BB.
•**BOYLE, Mr. Marcus Jarlath, BSc ACA** *1990;* Deloitte LLP, Stonecutter Court, 1 Stonecutter Street, LONDON, EC4A 4TR. See also Deloitte & Touche LLP
BOYLE, Miss. Maria, BSc ACA *2010;* 24 Grey Street, St Kilda Beach, MELBOURNE, VIC 3182, AUSTRALIA.
BOYLE, Mr. Mark Gregory, BSc ACA *1995;* HSBC, Asia Pacific Finance, 21/F Citibank Tower, 3 Garden Road, CENTRAL, HONG KONG ISLAND HONG KONG SAR.
BOYLE, Mr. Mark Robert, BSc ACA *1992;* (Tax Fac), WH Smith, 180 Wardour Street, LONDON, W1F 8FY.
BOYLE, Mr. Michael James, FCA *1966;* Anthedon, 9 Clarendon Way, CHISLEHURST, BR7 6RE.
BOYLE, Mr. Nicholas Joseph, FCA *1973;* Tall Trees, 22a Compstall Road, Marple Bridge, STOCKPORT, SK6 5HH.
BOYLE, Mrs. Nicola, BA ACA *1994;* 29 Chestnut Way, Repton, DERBY, DE65 6FQ.
BOYLE, Mr. Paul Anthony, BA FCA *1977;* High Trees, 14 Pembroke Road, Moor Park, NORTHWOOD, HA6 2HR.
BOYLE, Mr. Peter David, BSc(Hons) ACA *2001;* 101/85 Reynolds Street, BALMAIN, NSW 2041, AUSTRALIA.
BOYLE, Mr. Robert William, MA FCA *1972;* St. Andrews House, Kilmeston, ALRESFORD, HAMPSHIRE, SO24 0NL.
BOYLE, Mr. Terence John, BSc FCA *1976;* 19 Merton Close, Lordswood, CHATHAM, ME5 8YX.
BOYLE, Mr. Tobias Humphrey James, BSc FCA *1983;* Wharfedale Capital LLP, 67 Carlton Hill, St. John's Wood, LONDON, NW8 0EN.
BOYLE, Mr. Vincent Charles, BA ACA *1992;* 49 Elton Road, Bishopston, BRISTOL, BS7 8DG.
BOYLIN, Miss. Lisa June, BSc ACA *2010;* Pricewaterhousecoopers Savannah House, 3 Ocean Way, SOUTHAMPTON, SO14 3TJ.
BOYLIN, Ms. Sarah Jane, MA ACA *1990;* Port Lion, Horsleys Green, HIGH WYCOMBE, HP14 3UX.
BOYLING, Mr. Roger Frank, FCA *1975;* Briars Croft, Heathwood Road, Higher Heath, WHITCHURCH, SY13 2HG.
BOYNE, Mrs. Isobel Louise, BSc ACA *1996;* 29 Vincent Drive, CHESTER, CH4 7RQ.
BOYNE-MANCHEE, Mr. Simon Richard Stephen, BSc ACA *1993;* 5 Swaffield Gardens, WEYMOUTH, DT4 9PE.
BOYNS, Mr. Richard, BA ACA *1996;* with HSBC, 8-14 Canada Square, LONDON, E14 5HQ.
BOYNTON, Dr. Andrew Ian, MA DPhil FCA CTA *1984;* PO Box 4066, Tyger Valley, BELLVILLE, 7536, SOUTH AFRICA.
BOYO, Mr. Alexander Olumoye, BA ACA *1993;* 141 Landscape Road, Mount Eden, AUCKLAND, NEW ZEALAND.
BOYS, Mr. Adam Michael Bacher Palm, MA ACA *1994;* c/o ICMP, Alipasina 45a, 71000, 71000 SARAJEVO, BOSNIA AND HERZEGOVINA.
BOYS, Mr. David Charles, ACA *1980;* Vermont Bury Gate, Bury, PULBOROUGH, WEST SUSSEX, RH20 1NL.
BOYS, Miss. Matilda Emma Louise, ACA *2010;* 38 Fentiman Road, LONDON, SW8 1LF.
BOYS, Mr. Peter George, BA FCA *1974;* 2 Cadnam Close, CANTERBURY, CT2 7SD.
BOYS, Mr. Robert Douglas, FCA *1972;* 14 West End, Bugbrooke, NORTHAMPTON, NN7 3PF.
•**BOYS, Mr. Robert Stewart, FCA** *1974;* Robert S. Boys, 28-30 Grange Road West, BIRKENHEAD, CH41 4DA.
•①**BOYS-STONES, Mr. Richard Claude, BSc FCA** *1980;* PricewaterhouseCoopers LLP, Pricewaterhousecoopers, 12 Plumtree Court, LONDON, EC4A 4HT. See also PricewaterhouseCoopers
•**BOYTON, Mr. John Leonard, FCA** *1972;* (Tax Fac), Ingenious Media Plc, 15 Golden Square, LONDON, W1F 9JG.
BOYTON, Mr. Michael Stephen, ACA *2011;* 2 Chaplin Close, Galleywood, CHELMSFORD, ESSEX, CM2 8QW.
BOZORGI, Mr. Rustom Ardeshir Irani, ACA *1979;* 30 Farrington Drive, TORONTO M2L 2B6, ON, CANADA.
BOZZINO, Mr. Julius Manuel, BSc(Econ) ACA *1996;* Lombard Bank Malta p.l.c., 59 Republic Street, VALLETTA VLT1872, MALTA.
BRAATHEN, Mr. Antony Julian, BA FCA *1977;* 147 Overmount Avenue, Apt E, WOODLAND PARK, NJ 07424, UNITED STATES.
•**BRABAZON, Mr. Andrew Dennis, BA(Hons) ACA** *2002;* Garratts Wolverhampton Limited, 29 Waterloo Road, WOLVERHAMPTON, WV1 4DJ.
BRABAZON, Mr. Vincent Francis Mary, BSc ACA *1987;* 281 Ocean Drive #11-01, The Oceanfront @ Sentosa Cove, SINGAPORE 098527, SINGAPORE.
BRABBS, Mr. Steven Jeffrey, BA ACA *1988;* Merrydown Ellis Avenue, Chalfont St. Peter, GERRARDS CROSS, BUCKINGHAMSHIRE, SL9 9UB.
BRABIN, Mr. Matthew Edward Stanley, BA FCA *1992;* I S S Pest Control I S S House, 1 Genesis Business Park Albert Drive, WOKING, GU21 5RW.
BRABON, Mrs. Jacqueline Fettes, BEd ACA *1981;* PO Box 142, KOROR, 96940, PALAU.
BRABYN, Dr. Caroline Jane, PhD BSc ACA *1987;* 1567 Baker Road, CASSELMAN K0A 1M0, ON, CANADA.
BRACE, Mr. Allan John, MSc FCA *1967;* Rooftop Housing Group, 70 High Street, EVESHAM, WORCESTERSHIRE, WR11 4YD.
BRACE, Mr. Christopher Simon, ACA *1987;* Chemin Du Mas Fourcade, 66480 MAUREILLAS, FRANCE.
BRACE, Mr. Henry, MA ACA *2001;* 76 Stonor Park Road, SOLIHULL, B91 1EG.
BRACE, Mr. Ian, ACA *2009;* 17 Thistle Bank, East Leake, LOUGHBOROUGH, LE12 6RS.
BRACE, Mr. John, BSc ACA *1985;* Aster Group, Sarsen Housing Association Ltd Sarson Court, Horton Avenue, DEVIZES, SN10 2AZ.
BRACE, Mrs. Katharine Alexandra, MA(Hons) ACA *2002;* 76b Alderbrook Road, Clapham, LONDON, SW12 8AB.
BRACE, Mr. Paul Spencer, FCA *1977;* 63 Parkside, LONDON, SW19 5NL.
BRACE, Mr. Robert Paul, BSc FCA *1975;* 4417 Fox Brook Lane, CHARLOTTE, NC 28211, UNITED STATES. (Life Member)
BRACE, Mr. Roger William George, FCA *1971;* 48 Kilfield Road, Bishopston, SWANSEA, SA3 3DN.
BRACE, Mr. Timothy David, ACA *2008;* Flat 6, 227 St. John's Hill, LONDON, SW11 1TH.
BRACEGIRDLE, Mr. Andrew, BA ACA *2009;* 12/6 Campbell Parade, MANLY VALE, NSW 2093, AUSTRALIA.
BRACEGIRDLE, Mr. David Howard, BA FCA *1982;* 10 Burrs Close, Brandlesholme, BURY, LANCASHIRE, BL8 1JU.
BRACEGIRDLE, Mr. John Mark, BA ACA *1997;* Le Haut Courtil Route de Pleinmont, Torteval, GUERNSEY, GY8 0RH.
BRACEGIRDLE, Mrs. Lindsay Anne, BA ACA *1991;* Ingouville House, Ingouvulle Lane, ST HELIER, JE2 4SG.
BRACEGIRDLE, Mr. Peter Harold, BA ACA *1990;* 13 Castle Street, ST HELIER, JE4 5UT.
BRACEGIRDLE, Mr. Richard Peter, LLB ACA *1993;* 20 Foxcover Road, Heswall, WIRRAL, CH60 1YB.
•**BRACEINER, Mr. Abraham Jacob, FCA** *1971;* A.J. Braceiner & Co, Park House, Russell Gardens, Golders Green, LONDON, NW11 9NJ.
•**BRACEWELL, Mr. Alan Peter, BSc FCA** *1982;* Colman Whittaker & Roscow, 118 Thornton Road, MORECAMBE, LANCASHIRE, LA4 5PL.
BRACEWELL, Mr. David Watson, FCA *1972;* Apple Tree Yard, Church Lane, Winmarleigh, PRESTON, PR3 0LA.
BRACEWELL, Mr. James Andrew, BA ACA *2004;* 27b Alma Lane, WILMSLOW, CHESHIRE, SK9 5EY.
BRACEWELL, Ms. Katherine, BA ACA *1980;* 72 Carr Road, Calverley, PUDSEY, LS28 5RH.
BRACEWELL, Mr. Mark Andrew, BA FCA *1995;* 2 Fossards Close, Bramham, WETHERBY, LS23 6WD.
BRACEY, Miss. Dawn, BA ACA *1990;* Urbanizacion Valdesol, Chalet 4, c/Angel De La Hoz, Valdecilla, Medio Cudeyo, 39724 CANTABRIA SPAIN.
BRACEY, Mr. John Paul, BSc ACA *2006;* with Ernst & Young LLP, 1 More London Place, LONDON, SE1 2AF.
BRACEY, Mr. Myles Neville, BSc ACA *1999;* 37 Green Lane, EDGWARE, MIDDLESEX, HA8 7PS.
BRACHER, Mrs. Margaret Helen, BA FCA *1975;* M.H. Bracher, Fox Cottage, 1a Abingdon Road, Tubney, ABINGDON, OXFORDSHIRE OX13 5QL.
•**BRACHER, Mr. Matthew James, BSc FCA** *1994;* HW Bristol Limited, Hyland, 21 High Street, Clifton, BRISTOL, BS8 2YF.
BRACHER, Mr. Simon Lawrence, ACA *2006;* 32 Badgers Close, WOKING, GU21 3JF.
BRACK, Mr. Rodney Lee, FCA *1968;* 3 Redcliffe Road, Chelsea, LONDON, SW10 9NR.
BRACKEN, Mrs. Barbara Merial Jacqueline, BSc(Eng) ACA *2006;* 24 Woodlands Terrace, LEEDS, LS28 6QD.
BRACKEN, Mr. Derek Andrew, LLB ACA *1996;* Independent News & Media (UK) Ltd Northcliffe House, 2 Derry Street, LONDON, W8 5HF.
BRACKEN, Mr. James, BSc ACA *1992;* 15 Broad St, Apt 3710, NEW YORK, NY 10005, UNITED STATES.
BRACKEN, Mr. Jonathan Robert, MA ACA *1989;* 152 Manor Green Road, EPSOM, KT19 8LL.
BRACKEN, Miss. Lisa Jayne, ACA *2009;* 91 Stockdale Drive, Great Sankey, WARRINGTON, WA5 3RU.
BRACKEN, Miss. Louise Victoria, MA ACA *2004;* 8 Enid Close, Bricket Wood, ST. ALBANS, HERTFORDSHIRE, AL2 3EL.
BRACKEN, Mr. Peter William, FCA *1958;* 3 Hampton Court, PO Box No 337, NIAGARA-ON-THE-LAKE L0S 1J0, ON, CANADA. (Life Member)
•**BRACKEN-SMITH, Mrs. Louise Martha Mary, BA FCA** *1999;* HLB Jackson Fox Limited, PO Box 264, Union House, Union Street, JERSEY, JE4 8TQ. See also HLB Jackson Fox
•**BRACKENBORO, Mr. Douglas William, FCA** *1972;* Barons Farm, 7 Angle Lane, Shepreth, ROYSTON, HERTFORDSHIRE, SG8 6QJ.
BRACKENBURY, Mr. Allan Willshaw, FCA *1963;* 127 Glandon Drive, Cheadle Hulme, CHEADLE, SK8 7HD. (Life Member)

BRACKENBURY, Mrs. Anne Elizabeth, BA FCA *1980;* 17 Horncastle Road, LOUTH, LINCOLNSHIRE, LN11 9LB.

BRACKENBURY, Mr. Charles Edward, MA FCA *1936;* 22 rue de la Dole, 1203 GENEVA, SWITZERLAND. (Life Member)

BRACKENBURY, Mr. Paul, FCA *1979;* West Lawn, 17 Horncastle Rd., LOUTH, LINCOLNSHIRE, LN11 9LB.

BRACKENRIDGE, Mr. Peter, FCA *1968;* 2 Tall Trees, ROYSTON, SG8 7EG. (Life Member)

BRACKIN, Mr. Austen John, BA FCA *1961;* 3 Hill Grove, Henleaze, BRISTOL, BS9 4RL. (Life Member)

BRACKIN, Mr. Russell, BSc ACA *1992;* 24 Ashbourne Drive, High Lane, STOCKPORT, CHESHIRE, SK6 8DB.

BRACKIN, Mr. Timothy John, MA ACA *1993;* 4 Pirton Close, HITCHIN, HERTFORDSHIRE, SG5 2BU.

BRACKLEY, Mrs. Maria, BA(Hons) ACA *2001;* Hermes Fund Managers, Lloyds Chambers, 1 Portsoken Street, LONDON, E1 8AW.

BRACKLO, Mr. Marcus Huascar, MSc ACA *1990;* Baigo Capital, Bockenheimer Anlage 4, 60322 FRANKFURT AM MAIN, GERMANY.

•**BRACKMAN, Mr. Stephen, BSc FCA** *1983;* First Floor, 421A Finchley Road, LONDON, NW3 6HJ. See also Brackman & Co LLP

BRACKSTONE, Mr. Neil Robert, LLB ACA CTA *2001;* with BDO LLP, Kings Wharf, 20-30 Kings Road, READING, RG1 3EX.

BRACKWELL, Miss. Lara Jane, BA(Hons) ACA *2010;* 37 Arethusa House, Gunwharf Quays, PORTSMOUTH, PO1 3TQ.

BRADBERY, Mr. David Alexander, BA ACA *1999;* U B S AG, 100 Liverpool Street, LONDON, EC2M 2RH.

•**BRADBROOK, Mr. Charles John, FCA** *1974;* with Deloitte LLP, 2 New Street Square, LONDON, EC4A 3BZ.

BRADBROOK, Mr. Michael Anthony, LLM FCA *1999;* 1 Meadow Way, Melbourn, ROYSTON, HERTFORDSHIRE, SG8 6EA.

BRADBROOK, Mr. Paul Nigel, MA FCA *1971;* The Lodge Keepers Walk, VIRGINIA WATER, GU25 4RU.

BRADBURN, Mr. Arthur John, FCA *1965;* 4 Greylands Close, Moss Lane, SALE, M33 6GS.

BRADBURN, Mr. Jeremy Royston Paul, BSc ACA *1992;* 16 Bellcast Close, Appleton, WARRINGTON, WA4 5SA.

BRADBURN, Mr. Richard James, FCA *1974;* 68 Middle Wall, WHITSTABLE, CT5 1BN.

BRADBURN, Mr. Robert John, BSc FCA *1984;* NHS Blood and Transplant, Oak House, Reeds Crescent, WATFORD, WD24 4QN.

BRADBURN, Mr. Simon James, MA FCA *1979;* The Priory Knaresborough Road, Follifoot, HARROGATE, NORTH YORKSHIRE, HG3 1DT.

BRADBURY, Mr. Adrian John, BSc FCA *1989;* Quam Capital Limited, 3204 Gloucester Tower, The Landmark, CENTRAL, HONG KONG ISLAND, HONG KONG SAR.

BRADBURY, Mr. Andrew Michael, BSc ACA *1998;* with Ernst & Young, P.O. Box 74, SAFAT, 13001, KUWAIT.

BRADBURY, Mr. Arnold Needham, FCA *1949;* Lynfield, Upper Langwith, Collingham, WETHERBY, LS22 5DQ. (Life Member)

BRADBURY, Mrs. Briony Gwendolin, BA ACA *1989;* Alliotts Friary Court, 13-21 High Street, GUILDFORD, GU1 3DL.

BRADBURY, Miss. Ceri, ACA *2009;* 24 Newland Gardens, HERTFORD, SG13 7WN.

BRADBURY, Mrs. Clare Louise, BSc(Hons) ACA *2003;* 39 Mayors Road, ALTRINCHAM, CHESHIRE, WA15 9RW.

BRADBURY, Mr. Denis Carlos, FCA *1949;* 6 Dovehouse Close, BRACKLEY, NN13 7HJ. (Life Member)

BRADBURY, Mr. George Leland, MA FCA *1961;* Squirrels Leap, 4 Beech Close Court, Stoke D'Abernon, COBHAM, KT11 2HA. (Life Member)

BRADBURY, Mr. Guy, MSc ACA *2003;* 3 Thorngrove Road, WILMSLOW, SK9 1DD.

BRADBURY, Mr. James Thomas, BA FCA *1969;* 35 Walnut Walk, LICHFIELD, STAFFORDSHIRE, WS13 8FA.

BRADBURY, Miss. Janet Carol, ACA *1983;* 64 Northleigh Road, Stretford, MANCHESTER, M16 0EQ.

BRADBURY, Mr. John Fletcher, BAcc ACA *2001;* with Reckitt Benckiser plc, 103-105 Bath Road, SLOUGH, SL1 3UH.

BRADBURY, Ms. Katharine Sarah, BSc ACA *1995;* 2 Henleaze Avenue, BRISTOL, BS9 4ET.

BRADBURY, Mr. Kenneth Walter, BA ACA *1983;* 18 Bernard Road, WORTHING, WEST SUSSEX, BN11 5EL.

BRADBURY, Mr. Lee Jonathan, ACA *2006;* 36 Bolle Road, LOUTH, LINCOLNSHIRE, LN11 0GR.

BRADBURY, Mr. Matthew Roland, BEng ACA *2001;* 8 Malting Lane, Aldbury, TRING, HERTFORDSHIRE, HP23 5RH.

BRADBURY, Mr. Michael James, BA(Hons) ACA *2003;* 39 Mayors Road, ALTRINCHAM, CHESHIRE, WA15 9RW.

BRADBURY, Mr. Miles Arthur, BA(Hons) ACA *2001;* with KPMG LLP, 15 Canada Square, LONDON, E14 5GL.

BRADBURY, Mr. Neil Simon, ACA *2008;* 9 Great Northern Court 63 Walsworth Road, HITCHIN, HERTFORDSHIRE, SG4 9FH.

BRADBURY, Mrs. Nicola, BA ACA *1994;* The Mount, Bolton Road, CHORLEY, PR7 4AJ.

•**BRADBURY, Mr. Paul Andrew, BA FCA** *1986;* Ashdown Hurrey LLP, 28 Wilton Road, BEXHILL-ON-SEA, EAST SUSSEX, TN40 1EZ.

•**BRADBURY, Mr. Paul James, BA ACA** *1984;* Booth Ainsworth LLP, Alpha House, 4 Greek Street, STOCKPORT, CHESHIRE, SK3 8AB.

BRADBURY, Mr. Peter William, FCA *1967;* 7 North Street, Nafferton, DRIFFIELD, NORTH HUMBERSIDE, YO25 4JW.

BRADBURY, Mr. Robert, ACA *1980;* 4 Carrock Close, KENDAL, LA9 7HW.

•①**BRADBURY, Mr. Robert Andrew, MA ACA** *1991;* Deloitte LLP, Athene Place, 66 Shoe Lane, LONDON, EC4A 3BQ. See also Deloitte & Touche LLP

BRADBURY, Mrs. Seema, BSc ACA *2000;* Beazley, 60 Great Tower Street, LONDON, EC3R 5AD.

BRADBURY, Miss. Sharon Ann, BSc ACA *1992;* Belvoir View, Thoroton, NOTTINGHAM, NG13 9DS.

BRADBURY, Mr. Simon John, BA ACA *1992;* 10 Wycombe Road, MARLOW, BUCKINGHAMSHIRE, SL7 3HU.

BRADBURY, Mr. Simon Tatterson, BSc(Econ) FCA *1988;* The World Bank, 1818 H Street, WASHINGTON, DC 20433, UNITED STATES.

BRADBURY, Mrs. Susan Patricia, BSc ACA *1981;* Causeway Foot, Outlane, HUDDERSFIELD, HD3 3FQ.

BRADBURY, Ms. Victoria Eleanor, BA CA ACA CMC *1992;* 334 Pumpridge Place SW, CALGARY T2V 5E3, AB, CANADA.

BRADBY, Mrs. Pamela, BSc ACA *1990;* Home Farm House, 36 Richmond Road, Brompton On Swale, RICHMOND, DL10 7HE.

BRADD, Dr. Kerry Joy, PhD BSc ACA *2005;* 73 Tilkey Road Coggeshall, COLCHESTER, CO6 1QN.

BRADDICK, Miss. Donna Christina, BSc ACA *2004;* Merrill Lynch Financial Centre, 2 King Edward Street, LONDON, EC1A 1HQ.

BRADDICK, Mr. Jason Spencer, BSc ACA *1996;* 17 Quintin Avenue, Wimbledon, LONDON, SW20 8LD.

BRADDICK, Mr. Raymond, FCA *1957;* 28 Heol St Denys, Lisvane, CARDIFF, CF14 0RU. (Life Member)

BRADDOCK, Mrs. Julie-Anne, BA ACA *1990;* 9 Chemin Alois, Pictet, CH-1234 VESSY, SWITZERLAND.

BRADDOCK, Mr. Martin Joseph, LLB ACA *1990;* 9 Chemin Alois Pictet, CH-1234 VESSY, SWITZERLAND.

BRADDY, Mr. Eric Charles, FCA *1949;* 17 Petersfield Drive, Lower Street, Horning, NORWICH, NR12 8FB. (Life Member)

BRADEN, Mr. Stephen Francis, FCA *1963;* The OastGates Farm, High Halden ASHFORD, Kent, TN26 3HL. (Life Member)

BRADES, Mrs. Diane Margaret, FCA *1985;* Ernst & Young, 1 Colmore Square, BIRMINGHAM, B4 6HQ.

BRADESCU, Mr. John Robert, BA ACA *1992;* 1 Westhorpe Road, Putney, LONDON, SW15 1QH.

BRADFIELD, Mr. Nicholas Alan, BSc ACA *1984;* HB Professionals Ltd, 143A Queens Road, Wimbledon, LONDON, SW19 8NS.

BRADFIELD, Mr. Robert Andrew Richard, MA FCA *1977;* Howe Hall, Littlebury Green, SAFFRON WALDEN, CB11 4XB.

BRADFIELD, Mr. Simon David, BA ACA *1997;* 63 Colwell Drive, WITNEY, OXFORDSHIRE, OX28 5NN.

BRADFORD, Mr. Andrew Peter Francis, BA ACA *2004;* Transport for London Windsor House, 42-50 Victoria Street, LONDON, SW1H 0TL.

BRADFORD, Mr. Charles Lowther, FCA *1977;* 34 Old Camp Road, EASTBOURNE, EAST SUSSEX, BN20 8DL.

BRADFORD, Mr. Graeme Robert, BSc ACA *2000;* 16 Westcott Drive, Durham Moor, DURHAM, DH1 5AG.

•**BRADFORD, Mr. James Peter Blunden, FCA** *1966;* (Tax Fac), JPB Bradford & Co, Walnut Lodge, 31 Beaumont Avenue, ST. ALBANS, HERTFORDSHIRE, AL1 4TL.

BRADFORD, Miss. Jennifer, BSc(Hons) ACA *2010;* 171 Mongeham Road, Great Mongeham, DEAL, KENT, CT14 9LL.

BRADFORD, Mr. Jonathan David, BSc FCA *1995;* North Cottage, Middle Lipwood Barns, Haydon Bridge, HEXHAM, NORTHUMBERLAND, NE47 6EB.

BRADFORD, Mr. Justin Nicholas, BA ACA AMCT *1993;* (Tax Fac), 6 Woodlands Road, SURBITON, KT6 6PS.

BRADFORD, Mr. Mark Andrew, BA ACA *1999;* 6 Luckley Wood, WOKINGHAM, BERKSHIRE, RG41 2EW.

BRADFORD, Mr. Martin Major, BA FCA *1969;* 10 Edenhurst Avenue, LONDON, SW6 3PB.

BRADFORD, Mr. Michael, FCA *1962;* Mews House, The Old Stables, Ingestre Hall, Ingestre, STAFFORD, ST18 0RE. (Life Member)

BRADFORD, Mr. Paul Charles Leonard, ACA *2008;* Top Flat, 28 Hampstead High Street, LONDON, NW3 1QA.

•**BRADFORD, Mr. Peter Antony, ACA** *1981;* P. Bradford, Abbey Cottage, Kings Road, MALVERN, WR14 4HL.

BRADFORD, Mr. Richard John Charles, BSc ACA *1990;* 76 St Andrews Road, Bebington, WIRRAL, CH63 9JQ.

•**BRADFORD, Ms. Sarah Diane, BA(Hons) ACA CTA(Fellow)** *1990;* (Tax Fac), WriteTax Consultancy Services Limited, 6 Eider Close, BUCKINGHAM, MK18 1GL.

BRADFORD, Mrs. Shirley Ann, MBA BA ACA *1985;* with HSBC, 8-14 Canada Square, LONDON, E14 5HQ.

BRADFORD, Mr. Simon James, BA(Hons) ACA *2004;* 23 Church View Drive, Baslow, BAKEWELL, DERBYSHIRE, DE45 1RA.

BRADFORD, Mr. Thomas Celeste, FCA *1965;* 4b Newtown Gardens, HENLEY-ON-THAMES, OXFORDSHIRE, RG9 1EH.

BRADFORD, Mr. Timothy, FCA *1974;* Father Hudson's Society, Coventry Road, Coleshill, BIRMINGHAM, B46 3ED.

•**BRADING, Mr. Alan Jeffrey, FCA** *1994;* Hamilton Brading, 1 Sopwith Crescent, WICKFORD, SS11 8YU.

•**BRADING, Mr. Ian, BSc FCA** *1972;* (Tax Fac), Brading & Co, 5 Kilncroft, HEMEL HEMPSTEAD, HP3 8HH.

BRADING-MILES, Mr. Malcolm Ian, BSc ACA *2002;* 7 Springfield Crescent, HARPENDEN, HERTFORDSHIRE, AL5 4LJ.

•**BRADISH, Mr. Martyn Henry Stewart, FCA FCIArb** *1973;* (Tax Fac), Martyn Bradish, 31 Dugdale Hill Lane, POTTERS BAR, EN6 2DP.

BRADLEY, Mr. Adrian Paul, BA ACA *1990;* The Spinney Misbourne Avenue, Chalfont St. Peter, GERRARDS CROSS, BUCKINGHAMSHIRE, SL9 0PF.

BRADLEY, Mrs. Amanda Jane, BA ACA *1993;* Blackberry House, Priestlands, SHERBORNE, DORSET, DT9 4HW.

BRADLEY, Mrs. Amanda Kay Marianne, BA(Hons) ACA *2002;* Glaxo Smithkline Plc G S K House, 980 Great West Road, BRENTFORD, TW8 9GS.

BRADLEY, Mr. Andrew David, BA ACA *1998;* Bank House, Barmby-on-the-Marsh, GOOLE, NORTH HUMBERSIDE, DN14 7HX.

•**BRADLEY, Mr. Andrew Robert, BSc FCA** *1983;* Cantium Consulting Limited, 162 High Street, TONBRIDGE, KENT, TN9 1BB.

BRADLEY, Mr. Anthony Michael, FCA *1972;* 8 Setts Green, BOURNE, LINCOLNSHIRE, PE10 0FZ.

•**BRADLEY, Mr. Ben, BSc ACA** *2005;* with Barnes Roffe LLP, 16-19 Copperfields, Spital Street, DARTFORD, DA1 2DE.

BRADLEY, Mr. Brian William, FCA *1965;* The Firs, Chapel Lane, ASHBOURNE, DERBYSHIRE, DE6 2GL.

•**BRADLEY, Mr. Christopher, BSc FCA** *1981;* F D Consultancy, 113 North Road, Stoke Gifford, BRISTOL, BS34 8PE.

BRADLEY, Mr. Christopher Norman, FCA *1969;* 55 Pillory Hill Noss Mayo, PLYMOUTH, PL8 1ED.

BRADLEY, Mr. Christopher William, BSc ACA *1990;* C-Mac Microcircuits Ltd, South Denes, Great Yarmouth, GREAT YARMOUTH, NORFOLK, NR30 3PX.

BRADLEY, Mrs. Claire Marie, BSc(Hons) ACA *2002;* 10 Cloverhill Drive, RYTON, TYNE AND WEAR, NE40 4TG.

BRADLEY, Mr. Colin Edward, BA ACA *1989;* Mothercare plc, Cherry Tree Road, WATFORD, WD24 6SH.

BRADLEY, Mr. Colin George, BSc ACIB ACA *1981;* 1 Lockton Close, ASHBY-DE-LA-ZOUCH, LE65 1AY.

BRADLEY, Mr. Colin Walter, BA ACA *1981;* Horseshoe Cottage, Mill Lane, Llanarmon-yn-Ial, MOLD, CLWYD, CH7 4QF.

BRADLEY, Mr. David, BSc FCA *1980;* East Lodge, Upsall, THIRSK, YO7 2QH.

BRADLEY, Mr. David, BSc ACA *2002;* 17 Alwyn Gardens, Upton, CHESTER, CH2 1LW.

•**BRADLEY, Mr. David Peter, ACA** *1981;* PM+M Solutions for Business LLP, 83 Bank Parade, BURNLEY, LANCASHIRE, BB11 1UG. See also PM & M Corporate Finance Limited

BRADLEY, Mr. Derek John, BSc FCA *1992;* 6 Stanhope Road, CROYDON, CR0 5NS.

BRADLEY, Mr. Edward, ACA *2011;* 88 Lexden Road, COLCHESTER, CO3 3SR.

BRADLEY, Mrs. Elizabeth Ann, ACA *2002;* 23 Ashley Road, RICHMOND, SURREY, TW9 2TG.

BRADLEY, Mr. Eric Gordon, FCA *1959;* 769 Santa Barbara Rd, BERKELEY, CA 94707, UNITED STATES. (Life Member)

BRADLEY, Mr. George Peter, FCA *1962;* 140 Hale Road, Hale, ALTRINCHAM, WA15 8SQ. (Life Member)

BRADLEY, Miss. Helen Catherine Taylor, MSc ACA *2001;* with KPMG LLP, 15 Canada Square, LONDON, E14 5GL.

BRADLEY, Mrs. Helen Elizabeth, BSc ACA *2005;* 89 Coxs End, Over, CAMBRIDGE, CB24 5TY.

BRADLEY, Mr. Ian David, BA(Hons) ACA *2002;* Marsh Ltd, Victoria House, Queens Road, NORWICH, NR1 3QQ.

BRADLEY, Mr. James Hylton, ACA *2008;* 4 Kings Walk, Leicester Forest East, LEICESTER, LE3 3JP.

BRADLEY, Mr. Jason Garner Craven, BSc ACA *1993;* Greensleeves, Chalk Hill, Harpsden, HENLEY-ON-THAMES, OXFORDSHIRE, RG9 4HN.

BRADLEY, Mr. Jason John, BSc ACA *1990;* 25 Cambrian Close, CAMBERLEY, GU15 3LD.

BRADLEY, Miss. Jennifer Ann, MA ACA *1978;* Electoral Reform Services Ltd, The Election Centre, 33 Clarendon Road, LONDON, N8 0NW.

•**BRADLEY, Mrs. Jennifer Ruth, BA FCA** *1979;* (Tax Fac), George Arthur, 5 Wigmores South, WELWYN GARDEN CITY, HERTFORDSHIRE, AL8 6PL.

BRADLEY, Miss. Joanne, ACA *2002;* 17 Borle Brook Court, Highley, BRIDGNORTH, SHROPSHIRE, WV16 6LY.

BRADLEY, Mr. John Andrew, BA ACA *1992;* 65 Westgate, Guiseley, LEEDS, LS20 8HH.

BRADLEY, Mr. John Gerard, FCA *1981;* Heatherstone House, Annaslee, BURNFOOT, COUNTY DONEGAL, IRELAND.

•**BRADLEY, Mr. John Philip, FCA** *1981;* Bradley & Co, 110 High Street, ALFRETON, DERBYSHIRE, DE55 7HH.

•**BRADLEY, Mr. John Stephen, BA FCA ATII** *1985;* PKF (Channel Islands) Ltd, PO Box 296, Sarnia House, Le Truchot, St Peter Port, GUERNSEY GY1 4NA. See also PKF Guernsey Ltd

BRADLEY, Mr. John Stewart, FCA *1958;* Oregon, Avenue Road, COBHAM, KT11 3HW. (Life Member)

BRADLEY, Mr. Julian Anthony, MA ACA *1979;* 15 River View, WELWYN GARDEN CITY, AL7 1UA.

BRADLEY, Mrs. Karen Anne, BSc ARCS ACA *1995;* (Tax Fac), 4 Southfields, LEEK, STAFFORDSHIRE, ST13 5LR.

BRADLEY, Mrs. Kerry Denise, BA ACA *1995;* Tangaroa House, Busk Lane, Church Fenton, TADCASTER, LS24 9RJ.

BRADLEY, Miss. Leila Katherine, ACA *2010;* Deloitte SA, Route de Pré Bois 20, PO Box 1808, CH 1215 GENEVA, SWITZERLAND.

BRADLEY, Mr. Marc, MA ACA *2001;* Baxter Storey The Waterfront, 300 Thames Valley Park Drive, READING, RG6 1PT.

BRADLEY, Mr. Mark, BA ACA *2008;* 5 East Central Drive, Swinton, MANCHESTER, M27 4FE.

BRADLEY, Mr. Mark Eric, MA ACA *1992;* Cross Manufacturing Co Ltd, Midford Road, BATH, BA2 5RR.

•**BRADLEY, Mr. Mark Mason, FCA** *1992;* (Tax Fac), Stokoe Rodger, St Matthews House, Haugh Lane, HEXHAM, NORTHUMBERLAND, NE46 3PU.

BRADLEY, Mr. Martin, FCA *1977;* 1098 Colony Drive, ALPHARETTA, GA 30009, UNITED STATES.

BRADLEY, Mr. Martin Barker, FCA *1976;* 22 Woodvale Close, Higham, BARNSLEY, SOUTH YORKSHIRE, S75 1PP.

BRADLEY, Mr. Matthew Gurney, MA ACA *1983;* (Tax Fac), 17 Thamespoint, Fairways Broom Road, TEDDINGTON, TW11 9PP.

BRADLEY, Mr. Maurice Graham, FCA *1956;* 30 Florence Road, OLDBURY, B69 2DN. (Life Member)

BRADLEY, Mr. Michael Colin, ACA *2009;* 38 New Windsor Street, UXBRIDGE, MIDDLESEX, UB8 2TU.

BRADLEY, Mr. Michael James, BCom ACA *2006;* Willow Dene Fleece Road, Long Ditton, SURBITON, SURREY, KT6 5JN.

BRADLEY, Mr. Michael Paul, ACA *2008;* 51 Broadhurst, ASHTEAD, SURREY, KT21 1QD.

BRADLEY, Mr. Neil James, BEng ACA *2000;* 57 Old Fold View, BARNET, HERTFORDSHIRE, EN5 4EA.

BRADLEY, Mr. Nicholas James, MSc BSc ACA *2003;* NYK Logistics, Common Road, SUTTON-IN-ASHFIELD, NOTTINGHAMSHIRE, NG17 2JK.

BRADLEY, Mr. Nigel Anthony, BSc ACA *1987;* 41 Hovis Mill, Union Road, MACCLESFIELD, CHESHIRE, SK11 7BF.

•**BRADLEY, Mr. Paul Andrew, BA ACA** *1999;* Ernst & Young Gmbh, Mergenthalerallee 3 - 5, Eschborn, D65760 FRANKFURT AM MAIN, GERMANY.
•**BRADLEY, Mr. Paul Edward, FCA** *1980;* (Tax Fac), DEKM Limited, 5 Trinity Terrace, London Road, DERBY, DE1 2QS.
BRADLEY, Mr. Paul Gerard, BSc FCA *1979;* Lee House Frensham Court, Gardeners Hill Road, Lower Bourne, FARNHAM, GU10 3JB.
•**BRADLEY, Mr. Peter, FCA** *1964;* Peter Bradley, 63 Kingswood Road, TADWORTH, KT20 5EF.
BRADLEY, Mr. Peter, BSc ACA *1992;* 9 Vernon Avenue, CONGLETON, CW12 3AZ.
•**BRADLEY, Mr. Philip, ACA** *1992;* Bradley & Co, 4b Christchurch House, Beaufort Court, ROCHESTER, KENT, ME2 4FX. See also Company Secretarial Services UK Ltd
BRADLEY, Mr. Philip Stephen, FCA *1971;* Sunstone Uk Ltd, Panbrook House, Llangarron, ROSS-ON-WYE, HEREFORDSHIRE, HR9 6NW.
BRADLEY, Mr. Raymond, BSc ACA *1991;* Namco Europe Ltd Namco House Unit 7-8, Acton Park Estate The Vale, LONDON, W3 7QE.
BRADLEY, Mr. Richard, MA FCA *1992;* 53 St. Johns Road, SEVENOAKS, TN13 3NA.
BRADLEY, Mr. Richard John, FCA *1968;* Highmoor Stables, Highmoor, HENLEY-ON-THAMES, RG9 5DH. (Life Member)
BRADLEY, Mr. Richard Simon, BA ACA *2006;* Flat A, 170 Putney Bridge Road, LONDON, SW15 2NG.
BRADLEY, Mr. Robin Derek, BSc(Hons) ACA *2001;* 77 Cranbrook Road, LONDON, W4 2LJ.
BRADLEY, Mr. Roger Adrian, FCA *1955;* 37 Worrall Hill, LYDBROOK, GL17 9QE. (Life Member)
BRADLEY, Mr. Ross, BSc ACA *2011;* Flat 3, 12 Worcester Terrace, BRISTOL, BS8 3JW.
•**BRADLEY, Mr. Ross Paul, ACA** *2004;* Austral Ryley Limited, 416-418 Bearwood Road, SMETHWICK, WEST MIDLANDS, B66 4EZ.
BRADLEY, Mrs. Ruth Elizabeth, BSc ACA *2003;* with Bulley Davey, 4 Cyrus Way, Cygnet Park, Hampton, PETERBOROUGH, PE7 8HP.
•**BRADLEY, Miss. Sally Ann, BA ACA** *1988;* PricewaterhouseCoopers LLP, 1 Embankment Place, LONDON, WC2N 6RH. See also PricewaterhouseCoopers
BRADLEY, Ms. Sarah Elizabeth, MA MBA FCA ATII *1992;* Transport for London, Windsor House, 42-50 Victoria Street, LONDON, SW1H 0TL.
BRADLEY, Mrs. Sharon Margaret, BSc ACA *1988;* with Grant Thornton UK LLP, 11-13 Penhill Road, CARDIFF, CF11 9UP.
BRADLEY, Mr. Simon Peter, ACA *2011;* 147 Tavistock Crescent, LONDON, W11 1AE.
BRADLEY, Mr. Thomas Stuart, ACA *2010;* 22 Moorland Close, Locks Heath, SOUTHAMPTON, SO31 6WE.
BRADLEY, Mrs. Vanessa-Jayne, BSc ACA CPA *2001;* with BDO LLP, 55 Baker Street, LONDON, W1U 7EU.
BRADLEY, Mr. William Mark Campbell, FCA *1958;* Tudor Farm, Catesby Lane, Lapworth, SOLIHULL, B94 5QU. (Life Member)
•**BRADLEY-HOARE, Mr. Jonathan, MA** *1988;* Welbeck Associates Limited, 31 Harley Street, LONDON, W1G 9QS. See also Bradley-Hoare & Co
•**BRADLY RUSSELL, Mr. Michael John, FCA** *1975;* Ashleys (Hitchin) Limited, Invision House, Wilbury Way, HITCHIN, HERTFORDSHIRE, SG4 0TY. See also Ashleys
BRADMAN, Mr. Avram Michael Richard, MPhil BSc ACA *1999;* 24 Parklands Drive, LONDON, N3 3HA.
BRADMAN, Mr. Godfrey Michael, FCA *1961;* 1 Berkeley Street, LONDON, W1J 8DJ.
BRADMAN, Mr. Neil Nathan, FCA *1969;* The London City Group of, Companies Russell House, 28-30 Little Russell Street, LONDON, WC1A 2HN.
•**BRADNEY, Mr. James Preston, ACA** *1990;* Bridge Business Recovery LLP, 3rd Floor, 39-45 Shaftesbury Avenue, LONDON, W1D 6LA. See also The Counting House Partnership LLP and BKL Business Recovery LLP
BRADSHAW, Mr. Alastair Michael, MSc ACA *1998;* Robin Hill, South Drive, DORKING, RH5 4AG.
BRADSHAW, Mr. Alistair John, BEng ACA *1995;* Flat 10 Chimney Court, 23 Brewhouse Lane, Wapping, LONDON, E1W 2NU.
BRADSHAW, Miss. Amanda Jane, BSc ACA *1994;* 71 Bishop Road, CHELMSFORD, CM1 1PY.
•**BRADSHAW, Mr. Andrew James, ACA** *1987;* Bradshaws Ltd, Charter Court, 2 Well House Barns, Chester Road, Bretton, CHESTER CH4 0DH.
BRADSHAW, Mr. Andrew John, BA ACA *2005;* 7 Heatherway, Fulwood, PRESTON, PR2 6QZ.
BRADSHAW, Mrs. Angela Jayne, BA ACA *1994;* Whippenscott Farm, Rose Ash, Bishops Nympton, SOUTH MOLTON, EX36 4PP.
BRADSHAW, Mr. Chris John, BA ACA *1994;* Disa Cottage, 22a Frognall, Deeping St James, PETERBOROUGH, LINCOLNSHIRE, PE6 8RR.
BRADSHAW, Mr. Christopher David, BSc ACA *1992;* Cae Gwenith, Corntown Road, Corntown, BRIDGEND, CF35 5BG.
•**BRADSHAW, Mr. David, BSc FCA** *1981;* BLA Consulting LLP, 264-266 Durham Road, GATESHEAD, TYNE AND WEAR, NE8 4JR.
BRADSHAW, Mr. Edward David, BA ACA *2009;* 5 Wychwood Close, EDGWARE, MIDDLESEX, HA8 6TE.
BRADSHAW, Mr. Edward John, BA ACA *1991;* Denner Hill Studio, Hampden Road, Prestwood, GREAT MISSENDEN, BUCKINGHAMSHIRE, HP16 0JL.
BRADSHAW, Mr. Eric, FCA *1964;* Romany, 100 Druids Cross Road, LIVERPOOL, L18 3HN. (Life Member)
BRADSHAW, Mr. Geoffrey James, BA ACA *1983;* Pinnacle Accountancy & Consultancy Services Ltd, 20 Bennett Drive, Vicarage Gardens, Orrell, WIGAN, LANCASHIRE WN5 7AR.
•**BRADSHAW, Mr. Graham Martin, BSc(Econ) ACA** *1996;* 61 Lytton Road, Clarendon Park, LEICESTER, LE2 1WL.
BRADSHAW, Mrs. Hayley, ACA *2010;* 23 Summerbank Close, Drighlington, BRADFORD, WEST YORKSHIRE, BD11 1LQ.
•**BRADSHAW, Mr. Ian, FCA** *1982;* (Tax Fac), CC Accountants Limited, Business Suite 5, 3rd Floor, Castle Circus House, 136 Union Street, TORQUAY TQ2 5QG.
•**BRADSHAW, Miss. Jacqueline Ann, BA FCA** *1994;* PricewaterhouseCoopers, Cornwall Court, 19 Cornwall Street, BIRMINGHAM, B3 2DT. See also PricewaterhouseCoopers LLP
•**BRADSHAW, Mr. Jeffrey Roy, FCA** *1964;* (Tax Fac), Batesons, 2 Statham Court, Statham Street, MACCLESFIELD, SK11 6XN.
•**BRADSHAW, Mr. John, LLB ACA** *1990;* Burrowmoor Consulting Limited, 200 Broadway, PETERBOROUGH, PE1 4DT.
BRADSHAW, Miss. Kate Victoria, BA ACA *2003;* 8 Rosemary Way, CLEETHORPES, SOUTH HUMBERSIDE, DN35 0SR.
•**BRADSHAW, Mr. Keith, ACA FCCA** *2010;* (Tax Fac), Certax Accounting Ltd, Maynard House, 40 Clarence Road, CHESTERFIELD, DERBYSHIRE, S40 1LQ.
BRADSHAW, Mr. Keith George, FCA *1968;* The Chase, Nurton Hill Road, Pattingham, WOLVERHAMPTON, WV6 7HG.
•**BRADSHAW, Mr. Kenneth Morton, BA FCA** *1957;* (Tax Fac), Kenneth M. Bradshaw, 44 Pashley Road, EASTBOURNE, BN20 8EA.
BRADSHAW, Miss. Laura Joanne, BSc ACA *2006;* 54 Denbigh Street, LONDON, SW1V 2EU.
BRADSHAW, Mr. Laurence Brian, BA FCA *1960;* Orchard House, Bulmer, YORK, YO60 7BL. (Life Member)
BRADSHAW, Miss. Lynsey Karen, MA(Cantab) ACA *2009;* (Tax Fac), Flat 12/A Gloucester Court, 33 Gloucester Avenue, LONDON, NW1 7TJ.
BRADSHAW, Mr. Mark Alexander, BA(Hons) ACA *1999;* Hill Dickinson Co Ltd, 1 St. Pauls Square, LIVERPOOL, L3 9SJ.
BRADSHAW, Mr. Mark Anthony James, LLB ACA *1983;* Highlands, Clock Barn Lane, Hydestile, GODALMING, GU8 4AZ.
•**BRADSHAW, Mr. Mark Philip, BA(Hons) ACA** *2004;* (Tax Fac), Streets, St.Peters Chambers, 2 Bath Street, GRANTHAM, LINCOLNSHIRE, NG31 6EG. See also Streets LLP
BRADSHAW, Mr. Michael, FCA *1968;* 38 Helted Way, Almondbury, HUDDERSFIELD, HD5 8XZ. (Life Member)
BRADSHAW, Mr. Michael Peter, BSc ACA *2004;* 4 Waltham Road, BUCKSHAW VILLAGE, PR7 7EE.
BRADSHAW, Mrs. Nicola, BA ACA *2006;* 21 Brickenell Road, Calverton, NOTTINGHAM, NG14 6PL.
BRADSHAW, Mr. Paul David James, BSc(Hons) ACA *2001;* 20 Bluebell Road, Walsall Wood, WALSALL, WEST MIDLANDS, WS9 9EU.
BRADSHAW, Miss. Paula, BSc(Hons) ACA *2001;* 18 Godmond Hall Drive, Worsley, MANCHESTER, M28 1YF.
•**BRADSHAW, Mr. Peter David, BA(Econ) FCA ACA** *1983;* (Tax Fac), Dains LLP, Unit 306, Third Floor, Fort Dunlop, Fort Parkway, BIRMINGHAM B24 9FD.
BRADSHAW, Mr. Peter Hamilton, BA ACA *1992;* Lynton Ampfield Hill, Ampfield, ROMSEY, HAMPSHIRE, SO51 9BD.
•**BRADSHAW, Mr. Raymond James, FCA** *1971;* (Tax Fac), R.J.Bradshaw & Co, 98 Westbury Lane, BUCKHURST HILL, IG9 5PW.
BRADSHAW, The Revd. Raymond John, FCA *1959;* 2 Cliffside Drive, BROADSTAIRS, CT10 1RX. (Life Member)
BRADSHAW, Miss. Rebecca Ann, ACA *2008;* (Tax Fac), 33 Hillcrest Avenue, Longridge, PRESTON, PR3 3NU.
•**BRADSHAW, Mr. Roger Harold, BSc FCA** *1971;* (Tax Fac), R. H. Bradshaw, Mill Brow, Brookfield Park Road, COWBRIDGE, CF71 7HJ.
BRADSHAW, Mrs. Sara, BSc(Hons) ACA *2011;* Mazars Unit 7-8, 2 New Fields Business Park Stinsford Road, POOLE, BH17 0NF.
BRADSHAW, Miss. Sarah Louise, BSc(Hons) ACA *2004;* Flat 1 Corinne Court, Sotherby Drive, CHELTENHAM, GLOUCESTERSHIRE, GL51 0FW.
•**BRADSTOCK, Mr. Alan Stuart, FCA FCCA FABRP** *1979;* Accura Partners LLP, Langley House, Park Road, East Finchley, LONDON, N2 8EY. See also Langley Group LLP
BRADSTREET, Mr. Philip Lionel Stanton, MA FCA *1972;* 38 Avenue Maurice, 1050 BRUSSELS, BELGIUM.
BRADSWORTH, Miss. Emma, ACA *2011;* 22 Neptune Court, Trafalgar Square, Poringland, NORWICH, NR14 7WQ.
BRADWELL, Mrs. Ginette Louise, BSc ACA *1997;* 1 Dovedale, Bushmead, LUTON, LU2 7FQ.
BRADY, Mrs. Alison Mary, BA ACA *1985;* Carnegie Investment Bank A B, 24 Chiswell Street, LONDON, EC1Y 4UE.
BRADY, Mr. Anthony Pierre Patrick, ACA *1987;* Metlife Insurance Ltd, 1 Canada Square, LONDON, E14 5AA.
BRADY, Mr. Austin, BA ACA *1995;* 48 Longhurst Lane, Marple Bridge, STOCKPORT, SK6 5AE.
BRADY, Miss. Beverley Helen, MA ACA *1988;* 23 Harbour Street, MOSMAN, NSW 2088, AUSTRALIA.
BRADY, Mr. Calvin Robert, BSc ACA *1996;* 29 Austenway, Chalfont St. Peter, GERRARDS CROSS, BUCKINGHAMSHIRE, SL9 8NN.
BRADY, Mr. Christopher Connell, BA(Hons) ACA *2010;* Apartment 245, 5 Blantyre Street, MANCHESTER, M15 4JJ.
BRADY, Mr. David Anthony, BA(Hons) ACA *2003;* 14 Elstree Court, WIDNES, CHESHIRE, WA8 3EP.
BRADY, Mr. David Richard, FCA *1973;* 37 Duck End, Cranford, KETTERING, NORTHAMPTONSHIRE, NN14 4AD.
BRADY, Mr. Edward, ACA *2009;* Hawks Nest Farm House, Mislingford, FAREHAM, HAMPSHIRE, PO17 5AS.
BRADY, Mr. John Vincent, FCA *1963;* Derrynaseera, COOLRAIN, COUNTY LAOIS, IRELAND. (Life Member)
BRADY, Mr. Mark David, LLB ACA *1989;* The Timbers, 37 Queens Drive, ILKLEY, LS29 9QW.
BRADY, Mr. Matthew Lyndon, BA ACA *1998;* 1500 Ave at Port Imperial, Rivers Edge Apt 720, WEEHAWKEN, NJ 07086, UNITED STATES.
•**BRADY, Mr. Michael James, BA FCA** *1996;* Infinitude Services Limited, 24 Fernham Road, FARINGDON, OXFORDSHIRE, SN7 7LB.
BRADY, Mr. Michael Peter James, BA FCA *1990;* 4 Whitelake Road, TONBRIDGE, KENT, TN10 3TJ.
BRADY, Mr. Nicholas James, FCA *1970;* Rookswood, Seven Devils Lane, SAFFRON WALDEN, ESSEX, CB11 4BB.
BRADY, Miss. Paula, BA ACA *1993;* 3 Dewberry Fields, Upholland, SKELMERSDALE, WN8 0BQ.
BRADY, Mr. Peter, FCA *1969;* 42 Dukes Wood Drive, GERRARDS CROSS, BUCKINGHAMSHIRE, SL9 7LR.
BRADY, Mr. Peter Francis, ACA *1979;* 6 Culmore Road, Hurst Green, HALESOWEN, B62 9HP.
BRADY, Mr. Philip Dominic, LLB ACA *1999;* The Farmhouse Langford Lane, Oxford Airport, KIDLINGTON, OXFORDSHIRE, OX5 1QT.
BRADY, Mr. Scott Michael, BSc(Hons) ACA *2009;* 19 Wentworth Crescent, LEEDS, LS17 7TW.
BRADY, Mr. Stephen Brian, FCA *1963;* 31 Larkhill Lane, Formby, LIVERPOOL, L37 1LT. (Life Member)
BRADY, Mrs. Susan Jayne, BSc ACA *1989;* The Timbers, 37 Queens Drive, ILKLEY, LS29 9QW.
•**BRADY, Mr. Wayne Michael, ACA** *1983;* Brady & Co, 19 Wentworth Crescent, Alwoodley, LEEDS, LS17 7TW.
BRADY, Mr. William Joseph, BSc ACA *1982;* 17 Esher Drive, Brooklands, SALE, M33 3PE.
BRADY COLLINS, Mrs. Danielle, BSc ACA *2004;* Estee Lauder Unit 3, Kites Croft Business Park, FAREHAM, HAMPSHIRE, PO14 4FL.
BRAGANZA, Mr. Francis Anthony, FCA *1980;* Forest Mount, 12 Amersham Road, HIGH WYCOMBE, HP13 6PL.
•**BRAGANZA, Mr. Maurice Arnold, FCA** *1968;* (Tax Fac), Maurice Braganza & Co, 1 Lancaster Place, LONDON, WC2E 7ED. See also MABCO Limited
BRAGANZA, Mr. Michael Anthony, BSc FCA *1980;* Michael Braganza Consultancy, Hoppingwood Farm, Robin Hood Way, LONDON, SW20 0AB.
•**BRAGAZZI, Mr. Marco, BSc ACA** *2005;* 212 Balvernie Grove, LONDON, SW18 5RW.
BRAGG, Mr. Andrew Stewart, ACA ATII *1991;* (Tax Fac), 67 Egremont Drive, Lower Earley, READING, RG6 3BS.
•**BRAGG, Mrs. Clare Jane, BA FCA** *1993;* C Bragg & Co Ltd, Rose Villa, Cherry Chase, Tiptree, COLCHESTER, CO5 0AE.
BRAGG, Mr. Gordon, FCA *1973;* 24 The Crescent, SOLIHULL, B91 1JR.
•**BRAGG, Mrs. Jane, ACA CTA** *1997;* Jane Bragg ACA, 59 Nelson Road, RAYLEIGH, ESSEX, SS6 8HQ. See also Kiloview Ltd
BRAGG, Mr. Jeremy David, BA(Hons) ACA *2003;* Flat 28, 2 Battle Bridge Lane, LONDON, SE1 2HL.
BRAGG, Mrs. Lisa Jayne, BA ACA *1994;* Moorville Tamworth Road, Keresley End, COVENTRY, CV7 8JJ.
BRAGG, Mrs. Lorna Jayne, BSc ACA *1993;* 67 Egremont Drive, Lower Earley, READING, RG6 3BS.
BRAGG, Miss. Marie Clare, BA ACA *2003;* Flat 9 Aldermen Court, Friern Barnet, LONDON, N11 3GW.
BRAGG, Mr. Nicholas Christopher John, BSc ACA *1986;* 322 Barkham Road, WOKINGHAM, RG41 4DA.
•**BRAGG, Mr. Nicholas John, ACA** *1990;* Maynard Heady LLP, Matrix House, 12-16 Lionel Road, CANVEY ISLAND, ESSEX, SS8 9DE. See also Maynard Heady
BRAGG, Mr. Paul Roger, ACA *1996;* Tower 1, Computer Science Corporation Royal Pavilion, Wellesley Road, ALDERSHOT, HAMPSHIRE, GU11 1PZ.
BRAGG, Mrs. Sarah Jane, BSc ACA *2005;* 74 Billingsley Road, Sheldon, BIRMINGHAM, B26 2EA.
BRAGG, Mr. Simon Ewing, BSc ACA *1995;* 67 Penningtons, BISHOP'S STORTFORD, CM23 3TG.
BRAGG, Mr. Simon William, BSc ACA *1989;* Oriel Securities Ltd, 125 Wood Street, LONDON, EC2V 7AN.
BRAGG, Mrs. Sophie Clare, BA ACA CTA *1999;* (Tax Fac), Francis Clark Chartered Accountants Sigma House, Oak View Close, TORQUAY, TQ2 7FF.
BRAGG, Mr. William Frederick Edmund, FCA *1966;* 20 Gardenia Street, Morningside Ext 40, SANDTON, GAUTENG, 2196, SOUTH AFRICA.
BRAGGER, Mr. Ian, ACA *2009;* 12 Ridgestone Avenue, Hemsworth, PONTEFRACT, WEST YORKSHIRE, WF9 4JH.
BRAGGIOTTI, Mr. Gerardo, ACA *1979;* Via Fiori Oscuri 3, 20121 MILAN, ITALY.
BRAGGS, Mr. Steven John, MA ACA *1992;* 13 Fogwell Road, Botley, OXFORD, OX2 9SA.
BRAHAM, Mr. Darren Spencer, BSc ACA *1990;* Holly House, 20a Hartsbourne Avenue, Bushey Heath, BUSHEY, HERTFORDSHIRE, WD23 1JL.
BRAHAM, Mr. David Stewart, BA ACA *1999;* 4 Old School Yard, Sapcote, LEICESTER, LE9 4ND.
BRAHAM, Mr. Geoffrey Ernest, BSc FCA *1985;* Baxter Healthcare Ltd, Wallingford Road, Compton, NEWBURY, RG20 7QW.
BRAHAM, Miss. Hannah Gail, BA ACA *2000;* 286 Coombe Lane, LONDON, SW20 0RW.
BRAHAM, Mr. John Leslie, FCA *1972;* 3 Ladies Mile, KNUTSFORD, CHESHIRE, WA16 0ND.
BRAHAM, Mr. Michael Alan, FCA *1961;* Flat 2 Rossanne House, 2 Etchingham Park Road, Finchley, LONDON, N3 2UJ.
BRAHAM, Mr. Raymond Peter, FCA *1961;* 45 Kelvin Road, Bramley, JOHANNESBURG, GAUTENG, 2090, SOUTH AFRICA. (Life Member)
BRAHAM, Mr. Simon Benjamin, BA ACA *2003;* Flat 8, 9 Airlie Gardens, LONDON, W8 7AJ.
•**BRAHAM, Mr. Stephen Charles, FCA** *1981;* with RSM Tenon Audit Limited, 66 Chiltern Street, LONDON, W1U 4JT.
•**BRAHAMS, Mr. Barry Philip, FCA** *1967;* Brahams & Co, 43 Wren Crescent, BUSHEY, WD23 1AN.
BRAHMBHATT, Mr. Avinash Jaydev, BSc ACA *1996;* 45 Rowan Drive, Cheadle Hulme, CHEADLE, CHESHIRE, SK8 7DU.
BRAHMBHATT, Mr. Harish Amulakhray, ACA *1985;* 34 Gair Road, South Reddish, STOCKPORT, SK5 7LH.

BRAHMBHATT, Mrs. Hetal Rajesh, ACA *2009;* 185 Bourne Vale, BROMLEY, BR2 7LX.

BRAHMBHATT, Mr. Milin Sunnil Kumar, ACA *2011;* 185 Bourne Vale, BROMLEY, BR2 7LX.

BRAHO, Mrs. Ilva, ACA *2011;* 46 Marmion Avenue, Chingford, LONDON, E4 8EP.

BRAID, Mr. Alexander Charles, BSc ACA *2007;* 20a St. Quintin Avenue, LONDON, W10 6NU.

BRAID, Mr. Darryl Paul, ACA *2008;* with PricewaterhouseCoopers LLP, 1 Embankment Place, LONDON, WC2N 6RH.

BRAID, Miss. Nancy Barnes, LLB ACA *1986;* 2/1 16 Falkland Street, GLASGOW, G12 9PR.

BRAID, Mr. Simon, MA FCA DChA *1979;* Petresfield, Fordcombe Road, Penshurst, TONBRIDGE, TN11 8DL.

BRAID, Mr. William Robert, FCA *1962;* Cobblestones, Sandy Lane, Milford, GODALMING, SURREY, GU8 5BL. (Life Member)

BRAIDE, Mr. Thomas John, BA(Hons) ACA *2010;* 120 Meadway, Bramhall, STOCKPORT, CHESHIRE, SK7 1NL.

BRAIDE, Mr. William Gordon, FCA *1962;* Sandal Lodge, Walton Lane, Sandal, WAKEFIELD, WF2 6NG.

•BRAIDEN, Mr. Brian Anthony, BA(Hons) ACA *2005;* Brian A Braiden ACA, 59 Lansdowne Place, HOVE, EAST SUSSEX, BN3 1FL.

•BRAIDWOOD, Mrs. Christine Elizabeth, FCA *1973;* (Tax Fac), Braidwood & Company, Willow Grange, The Street, BETCHWORTH, SURREY, RH3 7DJ.

BRAIDWOOD, Mr. Rodger Gordon, FCA *1970;* Cherry Trees Farnham Lane, Langton Green, TUNBRIDGE WELLS, TN3 0JT.

•BRAILEY, Mr. Colin William, FCA *1971;* (Tax Fac), Cocke Vellacott & Hill, Unit 3, Dock Offices, Surrey Quays Road, Surrey Quays, LONDON SE16 2XU.

BRAILEY, Mr. James Ashley, MA BA ACA *2006;* 41 Chaffers Mead, ASHTEAD, KT21 1NA.

BRAILSFORD, Ms. Alice, BA ACA *2011;* Andola, Trunk Road, FARNBOROUGH, HAMPSHIRE, GU14 9TX.

BRAILSFORD, Mr. Antony James, MEng ACA *2003;* Flat 1 Marlow House, 29, Cranes Park, SURBITON, KT5 8AG.

BRAILSFORD, Mr. James Andrew, BSc ACA *2002;* 43 Moulsham Drive, CHELMSFORD, CM2 9PX.

BRAILSFORD, Mr. Robert Ian, BSc FCA *1979;* 19 Prospect Place, Old Town, SWINDON, SN1 3LQ.

BRAIME, Mr. Alan, BA ACA *2007;* The Tithe Barn, Newton Kyme, TADCASTER, LS24 9LS.

BRAIN, Mr. Anthony James, BA FCA *1986;* 191 Proctor Road, Old Catton, NORWICH, NR6 7EJ.

•BRAIN, Mr. Damon Alec, ACA FMAAT *2002;* Duncan & Toplis, 4 Henley Way, Doddington Road, LINCOLN, LN6 3QR.

BRAIN, Mr. David Vernon, FCA *1957;* 29 Little Aston Hall, Aldridge Road, Little Aston, SUTTON COLDFIELD, B74 3BH. (Life Member)

BRAIN, Ms. Eunice Barbara Emma, BA ACA *2002;* 5 Goodall Terrace, Kesgrave, IPSWICH, IP5 2TX.

BRAIN, Mr. Fergus Andrew, BSc ACA *2002;* P O Box 188, KENTHURST, NSW 2156, AUSTRALIA.

•BRAIN, Mr. John, FCA *1969;* (Tax Fac), J. Brain, 8 Whitegates, Shopping Centre, Flaxpits Lane Winterbourne, BRISTOL, BS36 1JX.

BRAIN, Mr. John Richard, BCom ACA *1983;* Busigen Ltd, 7 Jervis Crescent, Streetley Four Oaks, SUTTON COLDFIELD, B74 4PW.

BRAIN, Miss. Judith Mary, BA ACA *1995;* 674 Blueridge Avenue, NORTH VANCOUVER V7R 2J3, BC, CANADA.

•BRAIN, Mrs. Laura Ruth, BSc ACA *2001;* Firth Parish, 1 Airport West, Lancaster Way, Yeadon, LEEDS, LS19 7ZA.

•BRAIN, Mr. Malcolm Henry, FCA FCCA *1976;* Palmer McCarthy, Toronto House, 49a South End, CROYDON, CR9 1LT.

BRAIN, Mr. Mark Edward Langton, BA ACA *1997;* 1 The Meadows, Portsmouth Road, GUILDFORD, SURREY, GU2 4DT.

•BRAIN, Mr. Raymond Howard, BA FCA *1988;* (Tax Fac), James Todd & Co, Greenbank House, 141 Adelphi Street, PRESTON, PR1 7BH.

BRAIN, Mr. Stuart, BA ACA *2004;* with Mazars LLP, Tower Bridge House, St. Katharines Way, LONDON, E1W 1DD.

BRAIN, Mrs. Susan Jane, BSc ACA *1987;* Clearwater, Chapel Road, Rowledge, FARNHAM, GU10 4AN.

BRAIN, Mr. Thomas Michael, BA ACA *2003;* with haysmacintyre, Fairfax House, 15 Fulwood Place, LONDON, WC1V 6AY.

BRAINCH, Miss. Jatinder Kaur, BA ACA *1999;* 1 Wetherall Mews, ST. ALBANS, HERTFORDSHIRE, AL1 1AS.

BRAINE, Mr. Stephen Richard, MA FCA *1979;* Tradex Insurance Co Ltd, 7 Selsdon Way, LONDON, E14 9GL.

BRAINES, Mr. John Joseph, BA FCA *1971;* 58 Kipling Road, KETTERING, NN16 9JZ.

BRAINT, Mr. Richard Brian, FCA *1959;* 1378 South Arm Road, SANDFORD, TAS 7020, AUSTRALIA. (Life Member)

BRAITHWAITE, Mrs. Alison Jane, BSc ACA *1994;* St Lawrence, Bazehill Road, Rottingdean, BRIGHTON, BN2 7DB.

BRAITHWAITE, Mr. Andrew, ACA *2011;* The Bungalow, Wickham Hall, Hadham Road, BISHOP'S STORTFORD, HERTFORDSHIRE, CM23 1JG.

BRAITHWAITE, Mrs. Claire Elizabeth, MA(Oxon) ACA *1999;* Forest Villa, Blakemere Lane, Delamere Forest, FRODSHAM, WA6 6NS.

BRAITHWAITE, Mr. Denis Alan, FCA *1968;* P O Box 1125, MORNINGSIDE, GAUTENG, 2057, SOUTH AFRICA. (Life Member)

BRAITHWAITE, Mrs. Elaine Marie, BA ACA *2001;* 32 Bedfords Fold, Hillam, LEEDS, LS25 5HZ.

BRAITHWAITE, Mr. Geoffrey Doncaster, FCA *1962;* 102 Oakwood Drive, ST. ALBANS, HERTFORDSHIRE, AL4 0XA. (Life Member)

BRAITHWAITE, Mr. Howard Proctor, FCA *1964;* Brooklands, New Road, Prestbury, MACCLESFIELD, CHESHIRE, SK10 4HT. (Life Member)

BRAITHWAITE, Miss. Jennifer, BSc ACA *2003;* Flat 3, 30 Lytton Grove, LONDON, SW15 2HB.

BRAITHWAITE, Mr. John Paul, BA ACA *1992;* 16 Queenswood Gate, SHEFFIELD, S6 1RL.

BRAITHWAITE, Miss. Laura, BA(Hons) ACA *2004;* TUI Travel PLC, Crawley Business Quarter, Fleming Way, CRAWLEY, WEST SUSSEX, RH10 9QL.

BRAITHWAITE, Mrs. Lindsay Anne, BA ACA *2003;* 7 Barley Drive, Burton Latimer, KETTERING, NORTHAMPTONSHIRE, NN15 5YU.

BRAITHWAITE, Mrs. Lucy Rebecca, BA ACA *1997;* Church Barn High Street, Yardley Hastings, NORTHAMPTON, NN7 1ER.

BRAITHWAITE, Mr. Mark Franklin, BSc ACA *1999;* Dückersgatan 9, 254 54 HELSINGBORG, SWEDEN.

BRAITHWAITE, Mr. Mark William, BSc FCA MCT *1992;* Thames Water Utilities Ltd Clearwater Court, Vastern Road, READING, RG1 8DB.

BRAITHWAITE, Mr. Michael Edward, BSc ACA *1996;* PO Box 144GT, GEORGETOWN, CAYMAN ISLANDS.

BRAITHWAITE, Mr. Michael Elliott, MA FCA *1966;* Clarilaw Farm House, Clarilaw, HAWICK, ROXBURGHSHIRE, TD9 8PT. (Life Member)

BRAITHWAITE, Mr. Michael John, FCA *1965;* 18 Bars Lane, BROXBOURNE, HERTFORDSHIRE, EN10 7EH.

BRAITHWAITE, Mrs. Monica Laura, BSc ACA *1998;* 45 Vespasian Road, MARLBOROUGH, SN8 2FB.

BRAITHWAITE, Mr. Nathan, BA(Econ) ACA *2004;* 25 Chalmers Avenue, WAIKIKI, WA 6169, AUSTRALIA.

BRAITHWAITE, Mr. Neil, BA ACA *1983;* 74 Stockton Lane, YORK, YO31 1BN.

•BRAITHWAITE, Mr. Peter Gordon, FCA *1968;* Peter Braithwaite FCA, 40 Kingswood Avenue, Shortlands, BROMLEY, BR2 0NY.

BRAITHWAITE, Ms. Rosemary Elisabeth, MSc FCA *2000;* 43 Embleton Road, LONDON, SE13 7DQ.

BRAITHWAITE, Mr. Thomas, ACA *2011;* 4 Gibson Street, LONDON, SE10 9AD.

BRAITHWAITE, Mrs. Tracy Ann, BSc ACA *1994;* 16 Queenswood Gate, Wadsley, SHEFFIELD, S6 1RL.

•BRAJKOVICH, Mr. Nikola, BSc FCA *1993;* (Tax Fac), Nick Brajkovich Limited, 29 Withers Avenue, Orford, WARRINGTON, WA2 8EU.

•BRAKE, Mr. Brian, FCA *1969;* Breakthrough Finance Limited, Suite 303 Princess House, 50-60 East Castle Street, LONDON, W1W 8EA.

BRAKE, Mrs. Sarah Jane, BA ACA *1998;* The Gables, Bartley Road, Woodlands, SOUTHAMPTON, SO40 7GP.

BRAKELL, Mr. John Russell, BA FCA *1962;* 19 Willow Path, EPSOM, SURREY, KT18 7TD. (Life Member)

BRAKEWELL, Mrs. Jessie Kok Nam, BA ACA *1984;* Central Power Services ltd, Garstang Road, Claughton-On-Brock, PRESTON, PR3 0PH.

BRAL, Mr. Marc, BSc FCA CPA *1979;* 1801 Avenue of the Stars, Suite 704, LOS ANGELES, CA 90067, UNITED STATES.

BRALEY, Mr. Mark Peter L'estrange, BA ACA *1998;* 5 St. Martin's Road, Stockwell, LONDON, SW9 0SP.

BRALSFORD, Mr. David Martin, MSc FCA FCT *1970;* PO Box 321, 2nd Floor 6 Vine Street, Royal Square, St Helier, JERSEY, JE4 9XP.

BRAMAH, Mr. John Philip, MEng ACA *2002;* No 11, Castellon Crescent, COOGEE, WA 6166, AUSTRALIA.

BRAMALL, Mr. Colin Stephen, LLB FCA *1982;* The Old Rectory, Newton Blossomville, BEDFORD, MK43 8AL.

BRAMALL, Mr. Douglas Charles Antony, FCA *1959;* Blamall & Janes Ltd, 12 Cardale Court, Cardale Park, Beckwith Head Road, HARROGATE, NORTH YORKSHIRE HG3 1RY.

BRAMALL, Mr. Gareth David, BSc ACA *2005;* 4 Fryston, Elloughton, BROUGH, NORTH HUMBERSIDE, HU15 1SH.

•BRAMALL, Mr. George Michael, FCA *1975;* (Tax Fac), Mike Bramall & Co. Limited, Mayfield View, 60 School Green Lane, SHEFFIELD, S10 4GR.

BRAMALL, Mr. George Robert, MM FCA *1950;* Stonecrest, Mumbery Hill, Wargrave, READING, RG10 8EE. (Life Member)

BRAMALL, Mr. Graham Stuart, BA FCA *1964;* The Hawthorns, 67 Clifford Road, Poynton, STOCKPORT, CHESHIRE, SK12 1JA.

BRAMALL, Miss. Janine, BSc ACA *1999;* Tyco, Wormald Ansul UK Ltd Wormald Park, Grimshaw Lane, MANCHESTER, M40 2WL.

•BRAMALL, Mr. Paul John, BSc FCA *1981;* (Tax Fac), with BDO LLP, 55 Baker Street, LONDON, W1U 7EU.

•BRAMALL, Mr. Philip Michael, BSc FCA *1990;* Tenbury Ltd, Brenchley Mews, School Road, Charing, ASHFORD, KENT TN27 0JW.

BRAMALL, Mr. Stephen Thomas, BSc ACA *2006;* 7 Langdale Crescent, COTTINGHAM, HU16 5DL.

BRAMALL, Mr. Thomas John, BSc ACA *1991;* Well House Farm, Waverton, CHESTER, CH3 7QN.

BRAMBLE, Mrs. Teresa Margaret Ann, BA ACA *2004;* 12 Fushia Close, HAVANT, HAMPSHIRE, PO9 2FR.

BRAME, Mr. Alan Frederick, FCA *1986;* KPMG, KPMG Centre, 18 Viaduct Harbour Avenue, P.O. Box 1584, AUCKLAND 1140, NEW ZEALAND.

BRAME, Miss. Rachel Elizabeth, BSc ACA *2007;* with Goodman Jones LLP, 29-30 Fitzroy Square, LONDON, W1T 6LQ.

BRAME, Miss. Susan, ACA *2011;* 24 Birch Spinney, Mawsley, KETTERING, NORTHAMPTONSHIRE, NN14 1QW.

BRAME, Mrs. Susan Helen, BSc ACA *1994;* Apatec 350-370 Centennial Avenue, Centennial Park Elstree, BOREHAMWOOD, HERTFORDSHIRE, WD6 3TJ.

BRAMELD, Mr. Ian, BA ACA *1991;* 49 Grosvenor Road, Langely Vale, EPSOM, SURREY, KT18 6JG.

BRAMFORD, Mr. Paul William, FCA *1972;* 9 Gilmore Close, OAKHAM, LE15 6FR.

BRAMHALL, Mr. John James, BA ACA *1986;* 42 Stapleton Road, Formby, LIVERPOOL, L37 2YT.

BRAMHAM, Miss. Hannah, BSc ACA *2006;* 13 Grangefield Avenue, Burley in Wharfedale, ILKLEY, WEST YORKSHIRE, LS29 7HA.

BRAMHAM, Mrs. Joanne Helen, BA(Hons) ACA *2003;* Hornby Green Cottage, Hornby, NORTHALLERTON, NORTH YORKSHIRE, DL6 2JN.

BRAMHILL, Mr. Martin Paul, BA ACA *2000;* 26 Holmesdale Road, North Holmwood, DORKING, RH5 4HT.

BRAMLEY, Mr. Alan Kenneth, BA FCA *1977;* 8 Park Farm Close, Finchley, LONDON, N2 0PU.

BRAMLEY, Ms. Anne, FCA *1974;* 380 Ecclesall Road South, SHEFFIELD, S11 9PY.

BRAMLEY, Mrs. Belinda, BA ACA *1991;* Global Canopy Programme Field Station Office, Wytham, OXFORD, OX2 8QJ.

BRAMLEY, Mr. Christopher Nigel, BA FCA *1985;* Hickory Place, 5 Dickens Wynd, Elvet Moor, DURHAM, DH1 3QR.

BRAMLEY, Mr. Dennis Scott, FCA *1953;* 18 Crossfell Darras Hall, Ponteland, NEWCASTLE UPON TYNE, NE20 9EA. (Life Member)

BRAMLEY, Mr. Duncan Giles, MA CEng ACA *2000;* Woodhouse of Dardarroch, Dunscore, Auldgirth, DUMFRIES, DG2 0TF.

BRAMLEY, Mr. George, ACA *2011;* Apartment 28, 2 Hardwicks Square, LONDON, SW18 4HU.

BRAMLEY, Mr. Keith Ralph, FCA *1973;* Quintins Gap, Frome St. Quintin, DORCHESTER, DORSET, DT2 0HG.

BRAMLEY, Mr. Kevin, BA ACA *1991;* (Tax Fac), 11 Raby Close, BEDLINGTON, NE22 6NL.

BRAMLEY, Mr. Nigel Charles, FCA *1977;* 31 Park Way, Meols, WIRRAL, CH47 7BS.

BRAMLEY, Mr. Paul Julian, MA ACA MCT *1990;* 35 Ingham Road, West Hampstead, LONDON, NW6 1DG.

BRAMLEY, Mr. Simon Gareth, MBA BSc ACA *1993;* 950 Southview Trail, SOUTHLAKE, TX 76092, UNITED STATES.

BRAMLEY, Mrs. Susan Carolyn, BA FCA *1990;* 31 Park Way, Meols, WIRRAL, CH47 7BS.

BRAMLEY, Mr. Thomas John, MA FCA *1967;* 4 Priory Lodge, Priory Park, Blackheath, LONDON, SE3 9UY.

•BRAMLEY, Mr. William Nigel, FCA *1969;* Bramleys, 380 Ecclesall Rd South, SHEFFIELD, S11 9PY.

•BRAMMAN, Mr. Paul Frederick, BSc FCA *1978;* 7 Radstone Close, Oakwood, DERBY, DE21 2PT.

BRAMMER, Mr. David John, FCA *1979;* Unit 204, 95 Spencer Street, BIRMINGHAM, B18 6DA.

•BRAMPTON, Mr. Stuart Russell, BSc ACA CTA *1991;* Stuart Brampton, 95 Hollywood Lane, Hollywood, BIRMINGHAM, B47 5PY.

•①BRAMSTON, Mr. Timothy James, BA FCA *1987;* Griffins, Tavistock House South, Tavistock Square, LONDON, WC1H 9LG.

BRAMWELL, Mrs. Ann Helen, BSc ACA *1980;* (Tax Fac), Manor House Barn, Hudswell, RICHMOND, NORTH YORKSHIRE, DL11 6BL.

BRAMWELL, Mr. Clifford, FCA *1960;* 4A Lichfield Road, CAMBRIDGE, CB1 3SS. (Life Member)

BRAMWELL, Mr. David Nicholas, BA ACA *1986;* The Quality Furniture Co Ltd, Alma Park Road, GRANTHAM, NG31 9SE.

BRAMWELL, Mr. Derek, FCA *1959;* 4, Hazel Close, MARLBOROUGH, SN8 2AD. (Life Member)

BRAMWELL, Mr. Harold Keith, FCA *1957;* Byways, 1 Martin Avenue, Kirby Muxloe, LEICESTER, LE9 2JH. (Life Member)

BRAMWELL, Mr. John Edwin Crighton Byrom, FCA *1978;* Olympia Tools (UK) Ltd, 69 Honey End Lane, Tilehurst, READING, BERKSHIRE, RG30 4EL.

BRAMWELL, Mr. John William Ellis, FCA *1958;* 8 Convent Road, CANVEY ISLAND, ESSEX, SS8 9DH. (Life Member)

•BRAMWELL, Mr. Kenneth, FCA *1977;* (Tax Fac), Holmes Beaumont & Holroyd, 15 Ropergate End, PONTEFRACT, WF8 1JT.

•BRAMWELL, Mrs. Marie, BA(Hons) ACA *2002;* Dyke Yaxley Limited, 1 Brassey Road, Old Potts Way, SHREWSBURY, SY3 7FA.

•BRAMWELL, Mr. Neville Stanley, BA ACA *1992;* Deloitte LLP, 2 New Street Square, LONDON, EC4A 3BZ. See also Deloitte & Touche LLP

BRAMWELL, Mr. Peter John, FCA ATII *1975;* Manor House Barn, Hudswell, RICHMOND, NORTH YORKSHIRE, DL11 6BL.

BRAMWELL, Mr. Richard, BSc ACA *2003;* 3 Crossford Close, highfield, WIGAN, LANCASHIRE, WN3 6BT.

BRANAGAN MATTHEWS, Mrs. Gillian Amy Louise, ACA *2010;* (Tax Fac), 19 Taylor Drive, Bramley, TADLEY, RG26 5XB.

BRANAGH, Mrs. Rebecca Jayne, BCom ACA *2001;* Remarkable Pencils Limited, Midland Road, WORCESTER, WR5 1DN.

BRANCH, Mr. Alan Charles, BSc ACA *1991;* 75 Church Road, Bebington, WIRRAL, MERSEYSIDE, CH63 3EA.

BRANCH, Miss. Camille, BSc ACA *2011;* 11d Oakhill Road, LONDON, SW15 2QJ.

BRANCH, Mrs. Diane Mary, BSc ACA *1984;* Tanglewood, 8 Aldersey Road, GUILDFORD, GU1 2ES.

BRANCH, Mr. Dudley William, BSc FCA *1972;* 3742 Carrall Road, WESTBANK V4T 2C6, BC, CANADA.

BRANCH, Mrs. Emily Victoria, ACA *2008;* 61 Rosebery Road, NORWICH, NR3 3AB.

•BRANCH, Mr. Gregory John, BSc FCA *1984;* Deloitte LLP, PO Box 403, Lord Coutanche House, 66-68 Esplanade, St Helier, JERSEY JE4 8WA. See also Deloitte & Touche LLP

BRANCH, Mr. Henry Christopher, BCom FCA *1960;* 2 Pine View, Fairmile Park Road, COBHAM, KT11 2PG. (Life Member)

BRANCH, Mr. Nicholas Stuart Thomas, BSc FCA *1984;* 8 Aldersey Road, GUILDFORD, SURREY, GU1 2ES.

•BRANCH, Mr. Robert John, ACA MAAT *1997;* Moore Stephens, 30 Gay Street, BATH, BA1 2PA.

BRANCH, Mr. Stewart John, ACA *2008;* 61 Rosebery Road, NORWICH, NR3 3AB.

BRANCH, Mr. Stuart Thomas Peter, FCA *1953;* Red Tiles, 10 Pit Farm Road, GUILDFORD, GU1 2JH. (Life Member)

BRANCHDALE, Mr. Harry Gideon, MA FCA *1961;* 25 Ventnor Drive, Totteridge, LONDON, N20 8BT. (Life Member)

BRANCHER, Mr. Carl David Monnington, BSc ACA *1981;* 26 Western Road, ABERGAVENNY, GWENT, NP7 7AD.

BRANCHFLOWER, Mr. Andrew James, ACA *2008;* 59 Casino Avenue, LONDON, SE24 9PJ.

BRANCHFLOWER, Mr. David William, BSc ACA *2006;* Quintrel, Chase Road West, Great Bromley, COLCHESTER, CO7 7UA.

BRANCHFLOWER, Mr. Joseph William, BA FCA *1975;* 92 Woodhurst Avenue, Petts Wood, ORPINGTON, BR5 1AT.

•①**BRANCHFLOWER, Mr. Paul James, BA FCA** *1984;* 358 Mumbles Road, West Cross, SWANSEA, SA3 5TW.

BRANCHFLOWER, Mrs. Rebecca Jayne, BA ACA ATII *1999;* Unit 1, Harlequin Office Park, Fieldfare, Emersons Green, BRISTOL, BS16 7FN.

•**BRAND, Mr. Anthony David, BA FCA** *1982;* Haines Watts Kent LLP, 4-5 Kings Row, Armstrong Road, MAIDSTONE, KENT, ME15 6AQ.

BRAND, Mr. Barnaby James, MEng ACA *2005;* Pant-y-Gored Farm Heol Pant-y-Gored, Creigiau, CARDIFF, CF15 9NF.

BRAND, Mr. Christopher Anthony, BA ACA *1995;* 26 Glenhurst Avenue, LONDON, NW5 1PS.

BRAND, Mr. Derek Jack, FCA *1979;* (Tax Fac), 102 Kenneth Road, Chadwell Heath, ROMFORD, RM6 6LP.

BRAND, Mrs. Elina Claire, BA ACA *2002;* T B W A, Bryan House, 76-80 Whitfield Street, LONDON, W1T 4EZ.

BRAND, Mr. Geoffrey, BA ACA *2005;* 41 Calbourne Road, LONDON, SW12 8LW.

BRAND, Ms. Georgina Charlotte, BA(Hons) ACA *2003;* 32 The Sanctury, Hulme, MANCHESTER, M15 5TR.

BRAND, Mrs. Gillian Elizabeth, BSc ACA *1979;* Boxwood, 6 Polston Road, Kirkton of Maryculter, ABERDEEN, AB12 5GY.

BRAND, Mr. James Christopher, BSc ACA *2006;* 105 Holmwood Road, SUTTON, SURREY, SM2 7JS.

BRAND, Mr. Malcolm Arthur, FCA *1964;* Dodfield Horn, Colletts Green, Powick, WORCESTER, WR2 4RQ.

•**BRAND, Mr. Neal, ACA FCCA** *2010;* NJB, 40 Lawrence Avenue, WARE, HERTFORDSHIRE, SG12 8JL.

BRAND, Mr. Nicholas Richard, BA ACA *2001;* Goat Hill Farm, Well Hill Lane, ORPINGTON, BR6 7QJ.

BRAND, Mr. Paul John, BSc ACA *1989;* Highley House Wheatley Lane, Upton-upon-Severn, WORCESTER, WR8 0QS.

BRAND, Mr. Richard Walter, FCA *1954;* 10 Granville Road, Limpsfield, OXTED, RH8 0DA. (Life Member)

BRAND, Mr. Ronald Arthur Harry, FCA *1960;* 20 Houndsden Road, Winchmore Hill, LONDON, N21 1LT. (Life Member)

BRAND, Mr. Ronald Henry Albert, FCA *1952;* 113 Ranger Road, FISH HOEK, 7975, SOUTH AFRICA. (Life Member)

BRAND, Mr. Stephen, ACA *1980;* PO Box 4141, Tsufit 24, TEL MOND, 40600, ISRAEL.

BRAND-BONNES, Ms. Karin, ACA *2000;* 1010 N State Street, MONTICELLO, IL 61856, UNITED STATES.

BRANDER, Mrs. Sarah Carolyn, FCA ATII *1991;* 11A Woodside Road, Coalpit Heath, BRISTOL, BS36 2QP.

BRANDER BROWN, Dr. Jacqueline Caroline Fiona, BA FCA FBHA *1987;* The Herbery, 39 Cresswell Grove, West Didsbury, MANCHESTER, M20 2NH.

BRANDES, Miss. Suzy, MA ACA *2006;* 6 Dacre Green, ROYSTON, SG8 7LH.

BRANDIE, Miss. Shona-Maree, BA(Hons) ACA *2003;* 11 Troon Close, NORMANTON, WEST YORKSHIRE, WF6 1WA.

•**BRANDL, Mr. Peter Leonard Joseph, FCA** *1970;* (Tax Fac), Peter Brandl FCA, 30 St Cuthberts Lane, Locks Heath, SOUTHAMPTON, HAMPSHIRE, SO31 6TE.

BRANDLER, Mr. Andrew Clifford Winawer, MA MBA ACA *1981;* CLP Holdings, 147 Argyle Street, MONG KOK, KOWLOON, HONG KONG SAR.

BRANDLEY, Mrs. Hannah Jane, BSc(Hons) ACA *2003;* 28 Finsbury Rise, Roche, ST. AUSTELL, CORNWALL, PL26 8FN.

BRANDMAN, Mr. Samuel Mark, ACA *2008;* 14 Canal Boulevard, LONDON, NW1 9AQ.

BRANDMAN, Mr. Stephen Philip, FCA *1968;* 415-1 W. Duarte Road, ARCADIA, CA 91007-6823, UNITED STATES.

BRANDON, Miss. Amanda Jane, MA ACA *1992;* 50 The Ridgeway, TONBRIDGE, KENT, TN10 4NJ.

BRANDON, Mr. Andrew James, BA ACA *1996;* 38 Martineau Lane, Hurst, READING, RG10 0SF.

BRANDON, Mr. James Roderick Vivian, LLB ACA *1987;* 35a Trinity Road, Wimbledon, LONDON, SW19 8QS.

BRANDON, Mrs. Janet Yvonne, LLB ACA *1999;* 13 Barley Croft, BRISTOL, BS9 3TG.

BRANDON, Mr. Mark Stewart, LLB ACA *2001;* Deloitte Tohmatsu Tax Co Shin-Tokyo Building 5F 3-3-1 Marunouchi Chiyoda-Ku, TOKYO, 100-8305 JAPAN.

BRANDON, Mr. Stewart Ian Hamilton, BA ACA *2007;* Moore Stephens Llp City Gates, 2-4 Southgate, CHICHESTER, WEST SUSSEX, PO19 8DJ.

BRANDON, Miss. Wendy, BA ACA MAAT *2002;* 4 Handel Cossham Court, BRISTOL, BS15 1LU.

BRANDON-TRYE, Mr. Christopher Philip, BA FCA *1974;* Lavender Cottage, 37 Wellhouse Road, Beech, ALTON, GU34 4AQ. (Life Member)

•**BRANDRETH, Mr. Stuart, FCA** *1973;* (Tax Fac), Stuart Brandreth, 41 Chestnut Drive, Berry Hill, MANSFIELD, NOTTINGHAMSHIRE, NG18 4PW.

BRANDRICK, Mr. Garry Joseph Edward, ACA *2008;* 55 Pinewoods Avenue, Hagley, STOURBRIDGE, DY9 0JF.

BRANDT, Mr. Jan Arild, ACA *2001;* Arnulf Overlandsvei 175, N-0763 OSLO, NORWAY.

BRANDT, Mr. Karl-Alex Peter, BCom ACA *1993;* 19 Andrews Road, MALVERN, PA 19355, UNITED STATES.

BRANDT, Mr. Richard, MA FCA *1957;* The Anchorage, Ryde Road, SEAVIEW, PO34 5AB. (Life Member)

BRANDWOOD, Mrs. Rosalind Jane, FCA *1977;* Woodcote, Newtown Common, NEWBURY, BERKSHIRE, RG20 9BE.

BRANIFF, Ms. Gillian Elaine, ACA *1980;* Greylake House, Middlezoy, BRIDGWATER, TA7 0PJ.

BRANKIN, Ms. Jennifer, LLB(Hons) ACA *2010;* Bankbrae Farm, BRIDGE OF WEIR, RENFREWSHIRE, PA11 3SH.

BRANN, Mr. Nicholas Stephen, MA ACA *1987;* 8 Southfields Road, LONDON, SW18 1QN.

BRANN, Mr. Stephen John, BA ACA *1997;* 3 Summerhill Grange, Summerhill Lane, HAYWARDS HEATH, WEST SUSSEX, RH16 1RQ.

BRANNAN, Mr. Christopher Lorraine, ACA *2003;* 4735 N. Artesian Avenue, CHICAGO, IL 60625, UNITED STATES.

BRANNAN, Miss. Giselle Hope, BA ACA *1992;* 20 Main Street, Great Casterton, STAMFORD, PE9 4AP.

BRANNAN, Mr. James Cameron, ACA *2009;* with KPMG LLP, 757 Third Avenue, NEW YORK, NY 10017, UNITED STATES.

•**BRANNIGAN, Mr. Eric, FCA** *1972;* (Tax Fac), Rowlands, Rowlands House, Portobello Road, Birtley, CHESTER LE STREET, COUNTY DURHAM DH3 2RY. See also Rowlands Limited

•①**BRANNON, Mr. Andrew, BA FCA** *1986;* 22 Elm Bank Gardens, Barnes, LONDON, SW13 0NT.

BRANSBURY, Mr. Alan, FCA *1966;* 3 Lannesbury Crescent, ST. NEOTS, CAMBRIDGESHIRE, PE19 6AG. (Life Member)

•**BRANSBURY, Mr. David, BSc FCA** *1996;* (Tax Fac), CBHC LLP, Riverside House, 1-5 Como Street, ROMFORD, RM7 7DN.

•**BRANSBURY, Mr. Richard Edward, FCA** *1977;* CBHC LLP, Riverside House, 1-5 Como Street, ROMFORD, RM7 7DN.

BRANSBY, Mr. Leonard James, MBA ACA FCCA FCMA FCIS FRSA FCIM *2007;* 18 Lapwing Drive, Hampton-in-Arden, SOLIHULL, WEST MIDLANDS, B92 0BF.

•**BRANSBY, Mr. Roger James, BA FCA** *1974;* Bransby & Co, 5 Bedales, Lewes Road, HAYWARDS HEATH, RH17 7TE.

•**BRANSBY-ZACHARY, Mr. Stefan Victor Henri, FCA** *1975;* (Tax Fac), B.Z. Alexander, The Old Post Cottage, Denston, NEWMARKET, Suffolk, CB8 8PW.

•**BRANSON, Mr. Andrew David, BSc ACA CTA** *1993;* (Tax Fac), WBD Accountants Ltd, Norton House, Fircroft Way, EDENBRIDGE, KENT, TN8 6EJ. See also Added Business Solutions LLP

BRANSON, Mr. Andrew Nicholas, BSc ACA *1985;* Ardencaple, 89 Bottrells Lane, CHALFONT ST.GILES, HP8 4EH.

BRANSON, Mr. Anthony, FCA *1973;* The Great Barn, Old Delaware, Hever Road, EDENBRIDGE, TN8 7LD.

BRANSON, Miss. Julie Belinda, BA ACA *1995;* 15 Moor Close, Finchampstead, WOKINGHAM, RG40 4EZ.

BRANSON, Ms. Maria Teresa, BSc ACA *1991;* 2 Craigs Avenue, EDINBURGH, EH12 8HR.

BRANSON, Mr. Robert John, BSc FCA *1987;* 20 Hartshill Road, Olton, BIRMINGHAM, B27 6PB.

BRANSTON, Mr. Paul Richard, BCom FCA *1977;* 20 Kings Road, TWICKENHAM, TW1 2QS.

BRANTER, Mr. Martin John, MSc ACA *1989;* Danehurst, The Drive, Cheam, SUTTON, SM2 7DH

BRANTINGHAM, Mr. Mark, BCom FCA *1983;* 60 New Penkridge Road, CANNOCK, STAFFORDSHIRE, WS11 1HW.

BRANTON, Mrs. Elizabeth Jane, BSc ACA *1996;* Walter Wright & Co, 89 High Street Hadleigh, IPSWICH, IP7 5EA.

BRAR, Mr. Adrian Baldip Singh, BSc ACA *1991;* The Leas 16 Ings View Tollerton, YORK, YO61 1PR.

BRAR, Mr. Ragveer Singh, BSc ACA *2000;* Timber Grange, Bangors Road South, Iver Heath, IVER, SL0 0BB.

BRASH, Mr. Raymond Cantril, BA ACA *1993;* Ramblers, Tarrant Launceston, BLANDFORD FORUM, DORSET, DT11 8BY.

BRASHAW, Mr. Marc James, BA ACA *2006;* Compass Plc, Parklands Court, 24 Parklands, Rubery, BIRMINGHAM, B45 9PZ.

BRASHAW, Mr. Nigel Paul, MSc BA ACA CPA *2002;* with PricewaterhouseCoopers LLP, 125 High Street, BOSTON, MA 02110, UNITED STATES.

BRASHER, Mr. James Guy Richard, BA FCA *1995;* Petits Hiboux, Le Mont Isaac, St. Lawrence, JERSEY, JE3 1GB.

BRASHER, Mr. Richard Imre, MA FCA *2000;* Coca-Cola HBC Romania SRl, Global City Business Park, 10th Bucuresti Nord StreetBuilding 02, Voluntari, 077190 BUCHAREST, ROMANIA.

BRASIER, Mr. Peter Edward, FCA *1966;* The Dreys, Station Road, Crowhurst, BATTLE, TN33 9DB. (Life Member)

BRASS, Mr. Brian David, FCA *1955;* Orchard House, 130 Hampstead Way, LONDON, NW11 7XJ. (Life Member)

BRASS, Mr. James Michael, ACA *2008;* 12 Fanshawe Street, HERTFORD, SG14 3AT.

BRASS, Miss. Joanna Jayne, ACA *2009;* 74 Straightsmouth, LONDON, SE10 9LD.

BRASS, Mr. Peter Thomas, MA FCA *1964;* Maple Lodge, Moulsford, WALLINGFORD, OX10 9JD. (Life Member)

BRASS, Mr. Richard, BSc ACA *2000;* 20 Briarwood Road, LONDON, SW4 9PX.

•**BRASS, Mrs. Stephanie Ruth, FCA CTA** *1981;* Stephanie Brass, 12 Snowdrop Grove, Winnersh, WOKINGHAM, RG41 5UP.

•**BRASS, Mr. Thomas Francis, LLB FCA** *1973;* Dolphins, Elmstead Road, WEST BYFLEET, KT14 6JB.

BRASSETT, Mr. Peter George, FCA *1964;* 100 Shenfield Place, Shenfield, BRENTWOOD, ESSEX, CM15 9AJ. (Life Member)

BRASSEY, Mr. Timothy Robert Geoffrey, BA ACA *1990;* 132 Eastcote Road, PINNER, HA5 1EZ.

BRASSIL, Mr. Michael Coleman, MBS BCom ACA *1994;* 1751 Vermont Court, ALLEN, TX 75013, UNITED STATES.

BRASSILL, Mr. Michael Thomas, BCom ACA *1984; (ACA Ireland 1973);* 27 St Helens Road, Booterstown, BLACKROCK, COUNTY DUBLIN, IRELAND. (Life Member)

BRASSINGTON, Mr. David John, BA ACA *1989;* Compass Group Plc Compass House, Guildford Street, CHERTSEY, KT16 9BQ.

•**BRASSINGTON, Mr. Ian Robert, FCA** *1979;* Brassington & Co, 600 High Rd, WOODFORD GREEN, IG8 0PS.

BRASSINGTON, Mr. Jeremy Guy, MA FCA *1977;* Selacourt, Heathfield Close, WOKING, GU22 7JQ.

BRASSINGTON, Mr. John, BSc FCA *1972;* 20 Manor Way, Todwick, SHEFFIELD, S26 1HR.

BRASSINGTON, Mr. Joseph Paul, BSc ACA *2010;* 14 Broxash Road, LONDON, SW11 6AB.

BRASSINGTON, Mr. Matthew John, BA ACA *1995;* 32 Glen Street, Hawthorn, MELBOURNE, VIC 3122, AUSTRALIA.

BRASSINGTON, Mrs. Penelope Sian Louise, BSc FCA *1992;* 32 Glen Street, Hawthorn, MELBOURNE, VIC 3122, AUSTRALIA.

•**BRASSINGTON, Miss. Victoria, BA FCA** *1995;* (Tax Fac), Price Pearson Ltd, Finch House, 28-30 Wolverhampton Street, DUDLEY, DY1 1DB. See also Finch House Properties Limited

BRATCH, Mr. Jasvir Singh, BA ACA *2003;* 4 Osborne Road, WOLVERHAMPTON, WV4 4AY.

BRATCHELL, Mr. Duncan John Timothy, BSc FCA *1982;* 16 Green End Road, Boxmoor, HEMEL HEMPSTEAD, HP1 1QW.

BRATHERTON, Mr. Roger, FCA *1961;* 9 Devon Gardens, Childwall, LIVERPOOL, L16 9JR. (Life Member)

BRATT, Mrs. Clare, BSc ACA *2005;* Britannia Building Society, Britannia House, Cheadle Road, LEEK, STAFFORDSHIRE, ST13 5RG.

BRATT, Mr. David, BSc ACA *2007;* 3 The Paddock, Helsby, FRODSHAM, WA6 9PY.

BRATTESANI, Mrs. Ingrid, BA ACA *1986;* 19 Hanningtons Way, Burghfield Common, READING, RG7 3BE.

BRATTON, Mr. Adam Evans, BSc FCA *1995;* 60 Warren Road, CROYDON, CR0 6PF.

•**BRATTON, Mr. Andrew James, FCA** *1968;* Bratton A.J., 2 Priory Court, Priory Farm, STUDLEY, B80 7BB.

BRATTON, Mr. Nigel David, FCA *1970;* Cranford Court, Greenstiles Lane, Swanland, NORTH FERRIBY, HU14 3NH.

BRAUN, Mr. Alexander Stefan, BSc ACA *1986;* 15a Wilson Road, Jardines Lookout, HAPPY VALLEY, HONG KONG ISLAND, HONG KONG SAR.

•**BRAUN, Mr. Philip, BSc FCA** *1997;* with BDO Alto Limited, Windward House, La Route de la Liberation, St Helier, JERSEY, JE1 1BG.

BRAUN, Mr. Richard, BSc ACA *1997;* Flat 4 Madison Court, 202A West Hill, Putney, LONDON, SW15 3JA.

BRAUND, Mr. Jonathan Robin, MA ACA *1987;* 78 Pilford Heath Rd, Colehill, WIMBORNE, BH21 2ND.

BRAUND, Miss. Tamsin Elizabeth, BA ACA *2007;* 5 Lydwell Park Road, TORQUAY, TQ1 3TQ.

BRAUNTON, Mr. Oliver John, ACA *2008;* R T Marke & Co, 69 High Street, BIDEFORD, DEVON, EX39 2AT.

BRAVENBOER, Mrs. Melanie Ann, BSc ACA *2001;* 116 Mayfield Road, SOUTH CROYDON, SURREY, CR2 0BD.

BRAVERY, Mr. Paul Brian, BSc ACA *1990;* International Finance Corporation, 2121 Pennsylvania Avenue, NW, WASHINGTON, DC 20433, UNITED STATES.

BRAVINER, Mr. Anthony, BSc ACA *1996;* The Larches, 4b Mill Hill Lane, SANDBACH, CHESHIRE, CW11 4PN.

BRAVINER, Mrs. Melanie Jane, BSc ACA *1994;* The Larches, 4b Mill Hill Lane, SANDBACH, CHESHIRE, CW11 4PN.

BRAVINER, Father William Edward, BA BSc DMS ACA *1992;* St Peters House, Parish Office St. Peters Church Centre, York Avenue, JARROW, TYNE AND WEAR, NE32 5LP.

BRAVINGTON, Mr. Adrian Mark, BSc ACA *1994;* Elan Homes Ltd, Oak House, Lloyd Drive, Cheshire Oaks Business Park, ELLESMERE PORT, CH65 9HQ.

•**BRAVO, Mr. Graham Philip, FCA** *1964;* Graham Bravo & Co, 27 Tudor Manor Gardens, WATFORD, WD25 9TQ.

BRAWN, Mr. Gerald Mark Frederick, BSc ACA *1989;* Flat 24 Corriander Court, 20 Gainsford Street, Shad Thames, LONDON, SE1 2PG.

•**BRAWN, Mr. Martin Austin, FCA** *1977;* M.A. Brawn & Company Limited, 2a Acland Road, BRIDGEND, MID GLAMORGAN, CF31 1TF.

BRAWN, Mr. Richard James, MA ACA *1994;* B H Brawn & Co Ltd, 14 Bradfield Close Finedon Road Industrial Estate, WELLINGBOROUGH, NORTHAMPTONSHIRE, NN8 4RQ.

•**BRAWN, Mr. Richard William, FCA** *1979;* (Tax Fac), King Morter Proud & Co, Bank House, 11 West Street, BUILTH WELLS, LD2 3AH.

BRAXTON, Mr. Donald William, FCA *1974;* Rue des 4 Fontaines, 1278 LA RIPPE, SWITZERLAND.

BRAXTON, Mr. Giles David, BSc ACA *1995;* Court Lodge Farm, Ashburnham, BATTLE, EAST SUSSEX, TN33 9PJ.

BRAXTON, Mr. Nicholas Charles, BA(Hons) ACA *2000;* Waterside, 18 St. Johns Terrace, Devoran, TRURO, CORNWALL, TR3 6NE.

BRAY, Mr. Adam, BSc ACA *2011;* Flat 1, 9 Dennington Park Road, West Hampstead, LONDON, NW6 1BB.

BRAY, Mr. Adrian Paul, ACA ATII *1988;* 7 Webbs Court, Lyneham, CHIPPENHAM, WILTSHIRE, SN15 4TR.

BRAY, Mr. Alan John Neil, FCA *1968;* Ashdowns, Copyhold Lane, Cuckfield, HAYWARDS HEATH, RH17 5EB.

BRAY, Miss. Alexandra, BA(Hons) ACA *2011;* G12 Pine Grange, Bath Road, BOURNEMOUTH, BH1 2PW.

BRAY, Mr. Andrew Francis, MA ACA *1982;* 31 Oxted Green, Milford, GODALMING, GU8 5DD.

BRAY, Mr. Andrew James, MSc BSc ACA *2002;* XL House, One Bermudiana Road, PO Box HM 2245, HAMILTON HM JX, BERMUDA.

BRAY, Mr. Andrew Paul, BA ACA *2002;* 54 Tinney Drive, TRURO, CORNWALL, TR1 1AQ.

BRAY, Mr. Anthony John, MA FCA *1953;* Sandpipers, 8 Wheatsheaf Close, BURGESS HILL, RH15 8UT. (Life Member)

BRAY, Mrs. Catharine Rachel Elisabeth, BA ACA *1990;* Morgan Cole, Bradley Court, Park Place, CARDIFF, CF10 3DP.

BRAY, Mrs. Celine Sze Ling, ACA *2010;* 71 The Deans, Portishead, BRISTOL, BS20 6EQ.

BRAY, Mr. Christopher John, BA FCA *1990;* BDO, PO Box 1839, GABORONE, BOTSWANA. See also BDO International

BRAY, Mr. David Andrew, FCA *1977;* 3 The Avenue, Blaby, LEICESTER, LE8 4GW.

•**BRAY, Mrs. Dawn Susan, BSc ACA ATII** *1991;* (Tax Fac), DHB Accountants Limited, 110 Whitchurch Road, CARDIFF, CF14 3LY.

BRAY, Mrs. Deborah Faith, BSc ACA CTA *1997;* (Tax Fac), 16 Honor Link, CHELMSFORD, CM1 6BB.

BRAY, Mr. Douglas Charles, FCA *1958;* 4 Nash Croft, GRAVESEND, DA11 8SY. (Life Member)

BRAY, Mrs. Eleanor Grace, BSc ACA CTA *1983;* BP (Building G Floor 2 TAX), British Petroleum Co Plc, Chertsey Road, SUNBURY-ON-THAMES, MIDDLESEX, TW16 7LN.
•**BRAY, Mr. Iain Myles, FCA** *1983;* (Tax Fac), Bray Giffin LLP, Langford Hall Barn, Witham Road, Langford, MALDON, ESSEX CM9 4ST.
BRAY, Mr. Jacob William, ACA *2009;* 71 The Deans, Portishead, BRISTOL, BS20 6EQ.
BRAY, Miss. Joanne, BA ACA *1992;* 18 Marchmont Road, RICHMOND, SURREY, TW10 6HQ.
BRAY, Miss. Louise, BSc ACA *2011;* 80 Parsonage Lane, ENFIELD, EN2 0AH.
BRAY, Mr. Matthew Charles, MA ACA *2009;* 26 The Avenue, Claygate, ESHER, SURREY, KT10 0RY.
BRAY, Mr. Michael, FCA *1960;* The Old Forge, 12 Meeting Street, Quorn, LOUGHBOROUGH, LEICESTERSHIRE, LE12 8EX. (Life Member)
BRAY, Mr. Michael Charles, BSc ACA *1978;* 7 Westfield, Brays Green, Hyde Heath, AMERSHAM, BUCKINGHAMSHIRE, HP6 5RE.
•**BRAY, Mr. Michael William, FCA** *1972;* M W Bray, Byndes Farn, Pebmarsh, HALSTEAD, ESSEX, CO9 2LZ.
BRAY, Mr. Nicholas James, BA ACA *2001;* Serramalte Limited, 676 Fulham Road, LONDON, SW6 5SA.
BRAY, Mr. Nicholas Paul, BSc ACA *1991;* 143 Pack Lane, BASINGSTOKE, HAMPSHIRE, RG22 5HN.
BRAY, Mrs. Nicola, ACA *2010;* 54 Tinney Drive, TRURO, CORNWALL, TR1 1AQ.
BRAY, Mr. Paul Baron, BSc ACA *1990;* Frogmore Property Co Ltd, 11-15 Wigmore Street, LONDON, W1A 2JZ.
BRAY, Mr. Richard Veysey, BSc ACA DChA *1985;* Cancer Research UK, 61 Lincoln's Inn Field, LONDON, WC2A 3PX.
BRAY, Mr. Timothy Jack, FCA *1970;* Smithriding, Ramsden Mill Lane, Linthwaite, HUDDERSFIELD, HD7 5QZ.
BRAYAM, Mr. Robert, ACA *2007;* 40 Woodville Road, LONDON, NW11 9TN.
BRAYBROOK, Mr. James, BSc(Hons) ACA *2003;* Euromoney Publications Plc, Nestor House, 4 Playhouse Yard, LONDON, EC4V 5EX.
BRAYE, Mr. Paul Graham, FCA CTA *1989;* with BDO LLP, Arcadia House, Maritime Walk, Ocean Village, SOUTHAMPTON, SO14 3TL.
BRAYN, Mr. Warren Peter, BSc(Hons) ACA *2004;* Highfield, Colton Road, Honingham, NORWICH, NR9 5BB.
BRAYNE, Mr. Philip Ross, BA(Hons) ACA *2002;* 12 The Windings, MIDDLEWICH, CHESHIRE, CW10 9GW.
BRAYSHAW, Mrs. Angela Wai-Kuen, BSc ACA *1983;* 501 Westlake Park, HOUSTON, TX 77079, UNITED STATES.
BRAYSHAW, Mr. Colin Bertram, FCA *1970;* PO Box 652643, Benmore 2010, SANDTON, GAUTENG, 2010, SOUTH AFRICA.
BRAYSHAW, Mr. Edward Michael, FCA *1964;* 14 Gainsborough Avenue, Adel, LEEDS, LS16 7PG.
BRAYSHAW, Mr. Jonathan Alexander, BA ACA *2010;* 87 Main Street, Lyddington, OAKHAM, LE15 9LS.
BRAYSHAW, Mr. Keith, BCom FCA *1975;* 33 St. Barnabas Drive, Swanland, NORTH FERRIBY, NORTH HUMBERSIDE, HU14 3RL.
BRAYSHAW, Mr. Martin John, LLB FCA *1982;* 87 Main Street, Lyddington, OAKHAM, LE15 9LS.
BRAYSHAW, Mr. Michael Howard, BA ACA *1989;* Miller Homes - East Midlands, 2 Centro Place, Pride Park, DERBY, DE24 8RF.
BRAYSHAW, Mr. Michael Stanley, FCA *1958;* Chanor, Greenhill, Wombourne, WOLVERHAMPTON, WV5 0LD. (Life Member)
BRAYSHAW, Mr. Robert Edward, FCA *1962;* Poachers Cottage, Springhill Lane, Lower Penn, WOLVERHAMPTON, WV4 4UF.
BRAYSHAW, Mr. Roger Spencer, FCA *1972;* HAF & RC, 61 Moordown, LONDON, SE18 3NA.
BRAYSHAW, Mrs. Samantha Jayne, BSc ACA *2000;* Sandy Point, 22a The Esplanade, FRINTON-ON-SEA, ESSEX, CO13 9AU.
BRAYSHAW, Mr. Simon Martyn Terry, MBA BSc(Hons) FCA *1988;* Wards End, Langbar, ILKLEY, LS29 0ET.
BRAYSHAW, Miss. Victoria Anne, ACA *2011;* Flat 9, Walter Langley Court, 14 Brunel Road, LONDON, SE16 7HT.
•**BRAYSHER, Mr. Richard Peter, FCA** *1975;* Richard P Braysher, 2 High Road, Eastcote, PINNER, MIDDLESEX, HA5 2EW. See also R P Braysher
BRAYSON, Mr. William Richard, FCA *1969;* 5 Birk Crag Court, HARROGATE, HG3 2GH.
BRAZEL, Mr. Paul Richard Gerard, BA ACA *1988;* CommVault Ltd, Apex Plaza, Forbury Road, READING, RG1 1AX.
BRAZELL, Mr. Andrew Thomas, BA(Hons) ACA *2002;* British Red Cross Society, 44 Moorfields, LONDON, EC2Y 9AL.
BRAZELL, Mr. Raymond, FCA *1978;* (Tax Fac), 16a Oakridge Avenue, RADLETT, HERTFORDSHIRE, WD7 8EP.
BRAZENDALE, Mr. Alan Courtenay, FCA *1950;* 8 The Orchard, Whickham, NEWCASTLE UPON TYNE, NE16 4HD. (Life Member)
BRAZENOR, Mr. Timothy James, BSc(Hons) ACA *2011;* Crowe Clark Whitehill LLP, Aquis House, 49-51 Blagrave Street, READING, RG1 1PL.
BRAZIER, Mr. Anthony Benjamin, FCA *1981;* (Tax Fac), 25 The Oaklands, DROITWICH, WR9 8AD.
BRAZIER, Mr. Christopher John, BA ACA *2010;* 64 Berrall Way, BILLINGSHURST, WEST SUSSEX, RH14 9PG.
•**BRAZIER, Mrs. Debbie Ann, BCom ACA** *1993;* Signet Accounting Services Limited, 7 Gloucester Road, BARNET, HERTFORDSHIRE, EN5 1RS. See also Signet Accounting Services
BRAZIER, Mrs. Elizabeth Anne, BSc ACA *1994;* 9 Duglynch Lane, Gretton, CHELTENHAM, GLOUCESTERSHIRE, GL54 5EX.
BRAZIER, Mrs. Paola, BSc ACA *2007;* 184 Hill End Lane, ST. ALBANS, HERTFORDSHIRE, AL4 0AB.
BRAZIER, Mr. Peter John, MA ACA *1988;* 522 East Coast Rd., # 09-04, Nasus Block, Ocean Park, SINGAPORE 458966, SINGAPORE.
BRAZIER, Mr. Ralph Ian, BSc ACA MIoD *1992;* 17 Basing Close, THAMES DITTON, SURREY, KT7 0NY.
BRAZIER, Mr. Richard John, BSc ACA *1990;* 98 Ewart Street, BRIGHTON, BN2 9UQ.
BRAZIER, Mr. Stanley Leonard, FCA *1955;* 31 Aplins Close, HARPENDEN, AL5 2PZ. (Life Member)
BRAZIER, Mr. Stephen Harvey, BSc FCA *1987;* Russett House, 8 Main Drive, GERRARDS CROSS, SL9 7PS.
BRAZIER, Mr. Stephen Peter, ACA *1990;* 42 Gateley Avenue, South Beach Estate, BLYTH, NORTHUMBERLAND, NE24 3HG.
BRAZIL, Mrs. Adrienne Mary, BSc FCA *1982;* 15 Knowlys Drive, Heysham, MORECAMBE, LA3 2PD.
BRAZIL, Mrs. Diane Elizabeth, MA ACA *1991;* 11 Wike Ridge Fold, Alwoodley, LEEDS, LS17 9NT.
BRAZINGTON, Mr. Phillip Ernest, FCA *1968;* 30 Inglis Road, COLCHESTER, CO3 3HU.
•**BREACH, Mr. Jonathan Hugh Mackenzie, FCA** *1995;* with BDO Corporate Finance (Middle East) LLP, DIFC, Gate Village 10, Level 03, Office 33, PO Box 125115 DUBAI UNITED ARAB EMIRATES.
BREACH, Mr. Peter John Freeman, BA FCA *1966;* 7 Park Street, BRISTOL, BS1 5NF.
BREACH, Mr. Stephen Derrick, BSc ACA *1993;* Tribal Group Plc, 87-91 Newman Street, LONDON, W1T 3EY.
BREADEN, Mr. Paul William, ACA *2009;* E.on Ruhrgas UK E & P Ltd, 129 Wilton Road, LONDON, SW1V 1JZ.
BREAKS, Mr. Jonathan Michael, BSc ACA CTA *1999;* Bramble Patch, Plaisters Lane, Sutton Poyntz, WEYMOUTH, DORSET, DT3 6LQ.
BREAKSPEAR, Mr. Adrian Patrick, BA ACA *1994;* 7 Maysfield Close, Portishead, BRISTOL, BS20 6RL.
BREAKSPEAR, Mr. Bill Nicholas George, BA ACA *2008;* 36 High Street, Sherston, MALMESBURY, WILTSHIRE, SN16 0LQ.
BREAKSPEAR, Miss. Katherine, MEng ACA *2011;* 13 Patrick Road, Caversham, READING, RG4 8DD.
BREAKWELL, Mr. Francis Roy, FCA *1957;* Ewell, St. Johns Avenue, Thorner, LEEDS, LS14 3BZ. (Life Member)
BREAKWELL, Mr. Paul Stephen, BSc FCA *1986;* 16 Mornington Drive, WINCHESTER, HAMPSHIRE, SO22 5LR.
BREALEY, Mr. Christopher Paul, MA FCA ATII *1996;* c/o FIL (Luxembourg) S.A., 2a rue Albert Borschette, BP2174, L-1021 LUXEMBOURG, LUXEMBOURG.
•**BREALEY, Mr. Keith Leonard, FCA** *1963;* K.L. Brealey & Co., 26 Market Place, Huthwaite, SUTTON-IN-ASHFIELD, NG17 2QX.
•**BREALEY, Mr. Peter Ian, BSc FCA** *1985;* Brealey Foster & Co, Edwards Centre, The Horsefair, HINCKLEY, LE10 0AN.
BREALEY, Mr. Roger William, BSc FCA *1977;* Fairways, 29 Church Road, KENLEY, SURREY, CR8 5DW.
•**BREAM, Mrs. Nicola Aileen, BSc ACA** *1995;* Money Partner, 29 Kings Road, EMSWORTH, HAMPSHIRE, PO10 7HN.
BREAM, Mr. Peter Edward, MA ACA *1991;* Victrex Plc, Hillhouse Industrial Site, Fleetwood Road North, THORNTON-CLEVELEYS, LANCASHIRE, FY5 4QD.
BREAR, Mr. Christopher Roy, LLB ACA *1998;* 1 Bafford Lane, Charlton Kings, CHELTENHAM, GL53 8DN.
•**BREAR, Mr. John Westwood, ACA** *1987;* Brown Butler, Leigh House, 28-32 St Paul's Street, LEEDS, LS1 2JT.
BREARE, Mr. Nicholas Anthony, BSc ACA *1998;* Wilderness House, Rendcomb, CIRENCESTER, GL7 7HD.
BREARLEY, Mr. Andrew Timothy, BSc FCA *1978;* Wilkinson & Co, 10a Boroughgate, OTLEY, WEST YORKSHIRE, LS21 3AL.
BREARLEY, Mr. Colin James, MMath ACA *2003;* 216 Dower Road, SUTTON COLDFIELD, B75 6SZ.
BREARLEY, Mr. Jeffrey Gordon, MA ACA *1983;* Antony Hodari & Co, 34 High Street, MANCHESTER, M4 1AH.
BREARLEY, Mr. John David, MA FCA *1979;* 29 Micklefield Lane, Rawdon, LEEDS, LS19 6AZ.
BREARLEY, Mr. John Paul, BA FCA *1971;* Smugglers Way, Adlams Lane, Sway, LYMINGTON, SO41 6EG. (Life Member)
BREARLEY, Mr. John Richard, BSc ACA *1986;* The Northumberland Estates, Estates Office, Alnwick Castle, ALNWICK, NORTHUMBERLAND, NE66 1NQ.
BREARLEY, Mr. Peter James, FCA *1971;* 41 Burnbridge Oval, Burnbridge, HARROGATE, HG3 1LP.
BREARLEY, Mr. Peter James, MBA BA FCA *1979;* Wyndhams, St. Josephs Place, DEVIZES, SN10 1DD.
BREARLEY, Mr. Richard William, FCA *1975;* 20 Borrowcop Lane, LICHFIELD, WS14 9DF.
BREARLEY, Mr. Robert David Foord, FCA *1948;* The Wicket, Potterne Road, DEVIZES, SN10 5DD. (Life Member)
•**BREARLEY, Mr. Thomas, BA FCA** *1978;* (Tax Fac), Avery West Ltd, 334 Blossomfield Road, SOLIHULL, WEST MIDLANDS, B91 1TF.
•**BREARTON, Mr. John Christopher, FCA** *1973;* Paylings, 40-42 Castleford Road, NORMANTON, WEST YORKSHIRE, WF6 2EE.
BREATHWICK, Mr. Leslie, FCA *1965;* Hanbury House, West Langton Hall, MARKET HARBOROUGH, LEICESTERSHIRE, LE16 7TY. (Life Member)
BREBBIA, Mr. Alexander Carlos, BSc ACA *1997;* Burley Hill House, Burley, RINGWOOD, HAMPSHIRE, BH24 4HE.
BREBBIA, Mrs. Alix, BSc ACA *1998;* GAAP & GAAS Solutions Ltd, Burley Hill House, Burley Hill, Burley, RINGWOOD, HAMPSHIRE BH24 4HE.
BREBNER, Mr. Gary, BSc ACA *1986;* 7 Broughton Close, WARRINGTON, WA4 3DR.
•**BRECHT, Mr. Christopher Iceton Teal, BA FCA** *1992;* Griffin Stone Moscrop & Co., 41 Welbeck Street, LONDON, W1G 8EA.
BRECKENRIDGE, Mrs. Gwen, BA FCA *1991;* 72A Andover Road, NEWBURY, BERKSHIRE, RG14 6JR.
BRECKENRIDGE, Mr. John Alexander, MA ACA *1990;* 72A Andover Road, NEWBURY, BERKSHIRE, RG14 6JR.
BRECKIN, Mr. Alan Leslie, ACA *1982;* 10 Prospect Place, BURY, LANCASHIRE, BL9 8EX.
BRECKMAN, Mr. Robert Michael, FCA *1961;* 49 South Molton Street, LONDON, W1K 5LH.
BRECKNELL, Mr. Edmund Robert George, BA ACA *2007;* Basement Flat, 100 Harleyford Road, LONDON, SE11 5SN.
•**BRECKNELL, Mr. Michael Anthony, BSc FCA** *1961;* M.A. Brecknell, Flat 72, 8 New Crane Place, LONDON, E1W 3TX.
BRECKNOCK, Mr. Anthony Bernard Page, FCA CTA *1963;* The Old Gig House, Blackliffe Farm Mews, Loughborough Rd Bradmore, NOTTINGHAM, NG11 6PD. (Life Member)
BRECKNOCK, Mr. Jeremy Robert, FCA *1976;* 2 Danemere Street, LONDON, SW15 1LT.
BREDEN, Miss. Julie, BA ACA *2007;* 44 Pennsylvania Road, LIVERPOOL, L13 9BA.
BREDEN, Ms. Paula, MMath ACA *2004;* 85 October Drive, LIVERPOOL, MERSEYSIDE, L6 4ET.
BREDENKAMP, Mr. Robert, BA FCA *1989;* 690 chemin du Caladou, 06560 VALBONNE, FRANCE.
BREE, Miss. Catherine Ann, ACA *2008;* 15 / 107 Macpherson Street, Bronte, SYDNEY, NSW 2024, AUSTRALIA.
BREE, Mr. Jamie Robert, MA BSc ACA *2007;* Equity Trust, 6 St. Andrew Street, LONDON, EC4A 3AE.
BREE, Ms. Orla, *2010; (ACA Ireland 2009);* Scarden Court, Strandhill Road, SLIGO, COUNTY SLIGO, IRELAND.
BREED, Mr. Thomas Graham, ACA *2009;* 107 Downton Avenue, LONDON, SW2 3TX.
BREEDS, Mr. Iain David, ACA *1986;* 14 Overhill Drive, BRIGHTON, BN1 8WH.
BREEDYK, Mr. Martin Philip, BA ACA *1998;* 4 Peacocks Close, BERKHAMSTED, HERTFORDSHIRE, HP4 1TH.
•**BREEN, Mr. Jeremy Mark, FCA** *1979;* (Tax Fac), Breen & Co, 12 Church Square, LEIGHTON BUZZARD, BEDFORDSHIRE, LU7 1AE.
BREEN, Miss. Louise Mary, BCom ACA *1996;* The Oast House, Elliotts Lane, Brasted, WESTERHAM, KENT, TN16 1JD.
BREEN, Mr. Martin Gerard, BA ACA *1981;* Willow Tree Barn, Grange Road, TENTERDEN, TN30 6EE.
BREEN, Mr. Paul, FCA *1961;* 1 Paddock Close, Blundellsands, LIVERPOOL, L23 8UX.
BREENEY, Mr. David Bernard, BA(Hons) ACA *2010;* 17 Fawcett Crescent, Woodley, READING, RG5 3HX.
BREESE, Mr. Bernard Arthur, FCA *1960;* 25 Mount Pleasant Road, LINGFIELD, SURREY, RH7 6BH. (Life Member)
BREESE, Mr. Charles Jonathon, FCA *1969;* Steane Grounds, Nr Farthinghoe, BRACKLEY, NN13 5NP.
BREESE, Mr. Henry Strother Colquhoun, BSS ACA *1994;* Portland House, 101 Main Street, Ebberston, SCARBOROUGH, YO13 9NJ.
BREESE, Mr. Iain Charles Dempster, BSc FCA *1968;* Westler Foods Ltd., Amotherby, MALTON, YO17 6TQ.
BREESE, Mr. Richard Quentin, ACA *1985;* Field House, 24 Avenue Road, STRATFORD-UPON-AVON, CV37 6UN.
BREESE, Mr. Steven, ACA *1989;* Stephen James Aftersales 1 Martinbridge Industrial Estate, 240-242 Lincoln Road, ENFIELD, EN1 1SP.
•**BREEZE, Mr. Alan Leonard, FCA** *1973;* (Tax Fac), Breeze & Associates Ltd, 5 Cornfield Terrace, EASTBOURNE, EAST SUSSEX, BN21 4NN.
•**BREEZE, Mrs. Carol, ACA FCMA** *2009;* Callow & Holmes, Tattershall House, 19 St Catherine's Road, GRANTHAM, NG31 6TT.
BREEZE, Miss. Elizabeth, BSc ACA *2005;* with KPMG, Crown House, 4 Par-la-Ville Road, HAMILTON HM 08, BERMUDA.
BREEZE, Mrs. Ellen Claire, BA ACA *1998;* 17 Penn Road, Park Street, ST. ALBANS, HERTFORDSHIRE, AL2 2QT.
BREEZE, Mrs. Nicola Leigh Jarvis, ACA *1998;* Hauiti Farm, P O Box 8385, Haverlock North, HASTINGS, NEW ZEALAND.
BREEZE, Mr. Peter, FCA *1964;* Eriska, Rectory Road, Taplow, MAIDENHEAD, SL6 0ET. (Life Member)
BREEZE, Mr. Robert Andrew, BA ACA AMCT *1997;* Eisai Europe Ltd, Mosquito Way, HATFIELD, HERTFORDSHIRE, AL10 9SN.
BREEZE, Mr. Shaun Martin, BA ACA *1990;* Johnston International Ltd, P O Box 70, PROVIDENCIALES, TURKS AND CAICOS ISLANDS.
•**BREEZE, Mr. Thomas George, MA ACA** *2001;* (Tax Fac), Luminary Finance LLP, PO Box 135, LONGFIELD, KENT, DA3 8WF.
BREGENZER, Ms. Deborah Elizabeth, BA ACA *1995;* Hornweg 13, 8700 KUESNACHT, SWITZERLAND.
•**BREGER, Mr. David Wayne, BA FCA** *1978;* H W Fisher & Company, Acre House, 11-15 William Road, LONDON, NW1 3ER. See also FisherEase Limited, VAT Assist Limited, and H W Fisher & Company Limited
•**BREGMAN, Mr. Jonathan David, BSc FCA FCCA** *2000;* J. D. Bregman & Co, 25a York Road, ILFORD, ESSEX, IG1 3AD.
BREHENY, Mr. John Paul James, ACA *2009;* 4 Tansybrook Way, West Timperley, ALTRINCHAM, CHESHIRE, WA14 5ZB.
BRELSFORD, Mrs. Elspeth Anne, BA ACA *1981;* Y Gorlan, Trefnant, DENBIGH, LL16 5AG.
BREMAKUMAR, Mr. Sivasampu, FCA *1983;* Westfield, 6 Meadway, ESHER, KT10 9HF.
BREMNER, Mr. George Alan, MA FCA *1976;* Yattendon Group Plc, Barn Close, Burnt Hill, Yattendon, THATCHAM, BERKSHIRE RG18 0UX.
BREMRIDGE, Mr. John Charles Godfrey, MA FCA *1986;* John Swire & Sons (S.E. Asia) Pte Limited, 300 Beach Road, No. 12-01 The Concourse, SINGAPORE 199555, SINGAPORE.
BRENA LAJAS, Mr. Fernando-Borja, ACA *2010;* Barclays Capital, 5 North Colonnade, LONDON, E14 4BB.
BRENAN, Mr. Patrick, OBE FCA *1950;* (Member of Council 1976 - 1995), Colwood House, Cuckfield Lane, Warninglid, HAYWARDS HEATH, RH17 5SP. (Life Member)
BRENCHER, Mr. Paul Carey, BSc ACA *1996;* Aviva UK Insurance, Wellington Row, YORK, YO90 1WR.
BRENCHLEY, Miss. Christine Margaret, BA ACA *1985;* 6b Cedarberry Drive, Hamilton Parish, HAMILTON CR04, BERMUDA.
BRENCHLEY, Mr. Clive Russell, BA ACA *1993;* Endsleigh Faris Lane, Woodham, ADDLESTONE, SURREY, KT15 3DJ.

BRENCHLEY, Mr. John, ACA *1981;* 18 Torridon Loop, WANNEROO, WA 6065, AUSTRALIA.
BRENCHLEY, Mrs. Nicola Maria, BSc ACA *1995;* Endsleigh Faris Lane, Woodham, ADDLESTONE, SURREY, KT15 3DJ.
BRENCHLEY, Mr. Paul James, BA(Hons) ACA *2003;* 1 Ashgrove House, 28 Lindsay Square, LONDON, SW1V 2HW.
BRENDON, Mr. John Patrick, BA FCA *1972;* Flat 91, Princes House, 50 Kensington Park Road, LONDON, W11 3BW.
BRENER, Mr. Alan Howard, LLB(Hons) ACA FCIBS *1982;* 18 Gilray House, Gloucester Terrace, LONDON, W2 3DF.
BRENIG, Mr. Benny, ACA *2007;* 5 Leeside Crescent, LONDON, NW11 0DA.
•BRENNAN, Mr. Aidan Joseph, BA ACA *1992;* KPMG LLP, 15 Canada Square, LONDON, E14 5GL. See also KPMG Europe LLP
BRENNAN, Mr. Andrew Michael, BSc ACA *1989;* with Deloitte LLP, Athene Place, 66 Shoe Lane, LONDON, EC4A 3BQ.
BRENNAN, Mrs. Ann, BA(Hons) ACA *2002;* 29 Kyrle Road, LONDON, SW11 6BB.
BRENNAN, Mrs. Anna, BA(Hons) ACA *2003;* 31 The Wick, HERTFORD, SG14 3HP.
BRENNAN, Mrs. Anne-Marie, BA ACA *1987;* Marstons Plc, Marstons House, Brewery Road, WOLVERHAMPTON, WEST MIDLANDS, WV1 4JT.
BRENNAN, Miss. Caroline Elizabeth, BA ACA *2001;* 30 Felden Street, LONDON, SW6 5AF.
BRENNAN, Mr. Christopher David, BA FCA *1996;* 8 Farrar Street, BALGOWLAH HEIGHTS, NSW 2093, AUSTRALIA.
BRENNAN, Mr. Ciaran, BA FCA MBA CPA *1970;* SM 92 MZ 22 Lt24Ed 24Calle 18 DP 7Fr La Forida, 77511 CANCUN, MEXICO. (Life Member)
BRENNAN, Mrs. Claire, BSc ACA DChA *2003;* with PricewaterhouseCoopers LLP, First Point, Buckingham Gate, London Gatwick Airport, GATWICK, WEST SUSSEX RH6 0NT.
BRENNAN, Mr. Daniel, BSc ACA *2011;* 5a (Upper) Ord Road, WARWICK WK09, BERMUDA.
BRENNAN, Mr. Daniel James, ACA *2008;* PricewaterhouseCoopers, 250 Howe Street Suite 700, VANCOUVER V6C 3S7, BC, CANADA.
BRENNAN, Mr. David John, FCA *1969;* 215 Woodlands Road, BATLEY, WF17 0QS.
BRENNAN, Miss. Emma Louise, BA ACA *2000;* Ogier & le Masurier, PO Box 404, JERSEY, JE4 9WG.
BRENNAN, Mrs. Helen Rahman, BA ACA *1999;* 1 Mitchison Road, LONDON, N1 3NJ.
BRENNAN, Mr. James Anthony, ACA *2004;* 54a Halliford Street, LONDON, N1 3EQ.
BRENNAN, Mrs. Jennifer Louise, BSc(Hons) ACA *2003;* 1 Priory Lodge, Priory Road Bowdon, ALTRINCHAM, CHESHIRE, WA14 3BT.
BRENNAN, Mr. Joseph James, ACA *2008;* 12b Hillgate Place, LONDON, SW12 9ES.
BRENNAN, Mr. Leslie, BSc FCA *1975;* Cohuman Inc, 632 Commercial Street Fl 3, SAN FRANCISCO, CA 94111, UNITED STATES.
BRENNAN, Mr. Liam Patrick, BSc(Hons) ACA *2002;* Halifax Plc, Trinity Road, HALIFAX, WEST YORKSHIRE, HX1 2RG.
•BRENNAN, Mrs. Lucy, ACA *2001;* Saffery Champness, Lion House, Red Lion Street, LONDON, WC1R 4GB.
•BRENNAN, Mr. Michael Edward, FCA *1972;* Brennan Neil & Leonard, 32 Brenkley Way, Blezard Business Park, Seaton Burn, NEWCASTLE UPON TYNE, NE13 6DS.
BRENNAN, Mrs. Moira Elizabeth, BSc FCA ATII *1989;* 46 Warminster Road, BATH, BA2 6RX.
•BRENNAN, Mr. Nicholas John, BA FCA *1986;* (Tax Fac), Citroen Wells, Devonshire House, 1 Devonshire Street, LONDON, W1W 5DR.
BRENNAN, Mrs. Pamela Anne, BA ACA *1987;* (Tax Fac), 6 Burford Road, SALISBURY, SP2 8AN.
BRENNAN, Mr. Patrick Gerard, ACA FCCA *2010;* Fothergill Engineered Fabrics Ltd, Summit, LITTLEBOROUGH, LANCASHIRE, OL15 0LR.
BRENNAN, Mr. Paul Anthony, BSc ACA *1989;* William Mitchell Sinkers, Tram Way, Oldbury Road, SMETHWICK, WEST MIDLANDS, B66 1NY.
BRENNAN, Mr. Peter John, BA FCA *1979;* Martel, Dancing Lane, WINCANTON, SOMERSET, BA9 9DE.
BRENNAN, Mrs. Rachel Anne, BSc ACA *1991;* 6 Mount Park Crescent, LONDON, W5 2RN.
BRENNAN, Mr. Robert John, BSc(Hons) ACA *2009;* Flat 1, 2a Sumatra Road, LONDON, NW6 1PU.
•BRENNAN, Mr. Roger Fergus, FCA *1989;* (Tax Fac), Hebblethwaites, Westbrook Court, Sharrow Vale Road, SHEFFIELD, S11 8YZ.
BRENNAN, Mrs. Sally Joan, BA ACA *1988;* 8-11 St. John's Lane, LONDON, EC1M 4BF.
BRENNAN, Mrs. Suzanne Margaret, BSc ACA *1994;* 23 Savernake Road, LONDON, NW3 2JT.
BRENNAN, Dr. Tessa, BSc ACA *2006;* 13 Downs View, BRADFORD-ON-AVON, WILTSHIRE, BA15 1PN.
•BRENNAND, Mr. Colin, FCA *1967;* 6 St. Anthonys Road, Blundellsands, LIVERPOOL, L23 8TP.
BRENNAND, Mr. Jonathan Mark, BSc ACA *2000;* 6 St. Anthonys Road, Crosby, LIVERPOOL, L23 8TP.
BRENNAND, Mr. Theo James Mathew, BA ACA *2006;* Flat 53 Buckingham Court, 78 Buckingham Gate, LONDON, SW1E 6PE.
BRENNAND, Mrs. Victoria, BA ACA *1998;* 17 Blackwood Avenue, LIVERPOOL, L25 4RN.
BRENNAND, Mr. William Richard John, ACA *2008;* with JWPCreers, 20-24 Park Street, SELBY, NORTH YORKSHIRE, YO8 4PW.
•BRENNER, Mr. Alan Maurice, FCA *1956;* Brenner & Co, 7 Pavilion Court, Mount Vernon, Frognal Rise, LONDON, NW3 6PZ.
BRENT, Mr. Alan Robert, FCA *1967;* 16 Peakfield, Denmead, WATERLOOVILLE, HAMPSHIRE, PO7 6YP.
BRENT, Mr. David Michael, FCA *1976;* B A E Systems, PO Box 87, FARNBOROUGH, HAMPSHIRE, GU14 6YU.
BRENT, Mrs. Deborah Jane, BSc FCA *1977;* 188 Whyteleafe Road, CATERHAM, CR3 5ED.
BRENT, Mr. Elliot Daniel, BSc ACA *2009;* Flat 17 Maystocks Court, 59 Chigwell Road, LONDON, E18 1NL.
BRENT, Mr. Guy Jonathan, BSc ACA *1994;* 9 Montpelier Street, Neutral Bay, SYDNEY, NSW 2089, AUSTRALIA.
•BRENT, Mr. Robert John, BA ACA *1994;* KPMG LLP, 15 Canada Square, LONDON, E14 5GL. See also KPMG Europe LLP
BRENT, Mr. Russell Stuart, BA ACA *2008;* 16 Angelica Road, Bisley, WOKING, GU24 9EY.
BRENT, Mrs. Sarah, BA(Hons) ACA *2011;* Garden Flat, 97 Richmond Road Montpelier, BRISTOL, BS6 5EP.
BRENTFORD, Viscountesse Gillian Evelyn, OBE FCA *1965;* Springhill, Tottingworth Park, Broad Oak, HEATHFIELD, EAST SUSSEX, TN21 8XJ.
BRENTNALL, Mr. Andrew, BSc FCA *1974;* Flat 40, Grand Ocean, Longridge Avenue, Saltdean, BRIGHTON, BN2 8BU.
BRENTNALL, Mr. Christopher Neal, BCom ACA *1985;* Ouseley Farm, Aston Eyre, BRIDGNORTH, WV16 6XD.
•BRENTNALL, Mr. Edward James, BA(Hons) ACA *2004;* Dow Schofield Watts Transaction Services LLP, 7700 Daresbury Park, Daresbury, WARRINGTON, WA4 4BS.
BRENTNALL, Mr. Philip, DFC FCA *1943;* Brentnall, 1 Long Wood Drive, Jordans, BEACONSFIELD, HP9 2SS. (Life Member)
•BRERETON, Mr. Anthony John Patrick, BA FCA *1975;* Spittle House, Bollin Grove, Prestbury, MACCLESFIELD, SK10 4JJ.
BRERETON, Mr. David Charles, FCA *1958;* 2 Beech Close, Ollerton, KNUTSFORD, WA16 8TD. (Life Member)
•BRERETON, Miss. Magdalene, BSc ACA *1997;* KPMG LLP, 15 Canada Square, LONDON, E14 5GL.
BRERETON, Mr. Mark Charles, BSc ACA *1999;* 37 Dover Drive, ROME, GA 30161, UNITED STATES.
BRERETON, Mr. Martyn Ian, BA ACA *1986;* 35 Hawthorne Way, Shelley, HUDDERSFIELD, HD8 8PX.
BRERETON, Mr. Piers William, FCA *1968;* Firethorn, Aylesford Way, Stapleford, CAMBRIDGE, CB22 5DP.
BRESH, Mrs. Carolyn Mary, MBA BSc ACA ACT *1991;* 45 Narcissus Road, West Hampstead, LONDON, NW6 1TL.
•BRESKAL, Mr. Gregory, BA FCA *1992;* Mawson Breskal & Co, Bishops House, Monkville Avenue, LONDON, NW11 0AH.
BRESLAW, Mr. David Lewis Barry, FCA *1975;* Regency Estates, 2 Frognal Parade, LONDON, NW3 5HH.
BRESLER, Mr. Ben Lewis, BA ACA *2009;* 9 Dartmouth Road, LONDON, NW2 4ET.
•BRESLIN, Mr. Paul James, FCA *1984;* Breslins, Albion Court, 18-20 Frederick Street, BIRMINGHAM, B1 3HE. See also Breslins Birmingham Ltd
BRESLIN, Mr. Steven, BSc ACA *2002;* 45 Silhill Hall Road, SOLIHULL, B91 1JX.
BRESLIN, Mrs. Victoria, BSc ACA *2002;* St. Modwen Properties PLC, Sir Stanley Clarke House, 7 Ridgeway, Quinton Business Park, Quinton, BIRMINGHAM B32 1AF.
BRETHERTON, Mr. Alex James, BA ACA *2000;* 33 North Street, Castlethorpe, MILTON KEYNES, MK19 7EW.
BRETHERTON, Dr. Derek Edward, PhD BSc ACA *2011;* 25 Hazlewood Avenue, Karori, WELLINGTON 6012, NEW ZEALAND.
BRETHERTON, Mr. Michael Anthony, BA ACA *1983;* 25 Great Lawn, Chipping, ONGAR, CM5 0AA.
BRETHERTON, Mr. Thomas, FCA *1941;* Tudor Way, 29 Gravel Hill, WIMBORNE, BH21 1RW. (Life Member)
BRETON, Mr. Gerald David, FCA *1954;* Holbeck Cottage, 10 Carr Bank Bottom, OTLEY, LS21 2AJ. (Life Member)
BRETT, Mr. Adam James Austen, BA *1999;* 8 Langland Gardens, LONDON, NW3 6PY.
BRETT, Mr. Alistair David, FCA *1978;* Warden Barns, Low Warden, HEXHAM, NE46 4SN.
•BRETT, Mr. Andrew, BA ACA *1992;* KPMG Europe LLP, 15 Canada Square, LONDON, E14 5GL.
BRETT, Mr. Andrew Crawford, FCA *1965;* 55 The Dales, COTTINGHAM, NORTH HUMBERSIDE, HU16 5JS.
BRETT, Mrs. Anne Luise, BSc ACA *2003;* 4 Beacon Close, Chalfont St. Peter, GERRARDS CROSS, BUCKINGHAMSHIRE, SL9 0AW.
BRETT, Mr. David Anthony, BSc ACA *1988;* 43 Juniper Drive, Allesley Green, COVENTRY, CV5 7QH.
•BRETT, Mr. David John, FCA *1986;* Flat 6 Foster Court, 62 York Avenue, HOVE, EAST SUSSEX, BN3 1PJ.
BRETT, Mr. David Richard, BSc CEng FCA FIET *1975;* 18 Ledbury, Great Linford, MILTON KEYNES, MK14 5DS.
BRETT, Miss. Emily Rebecca, ACA *2010;* 51a Monmouth Road, PORTSMOUTH, PO2 8BT.
BRETT, Mrs. Emma, ACA *1993;* 26 Westbury Lane, BUCKHURST HILL, ESSEX, IG9 5PL.
BRETT, Miss. Heather Jane, ACA *1998;* 38 Mallard Way, STOWMARKET, IP14 1UN.
BRETT, Mrs. Helen Margaret, FCA *1982;* 10 Woodville Gardens, Lovelace Road, SURBITON, KT6 6NN.
BRETT, Mr. Jeremy Richard, BCom ACA *1989;* Industrial & Financial Systems I F S UK Ltd Artisan, Hillbottom Road Sands Industrial Estate, HIGH WYCOMBE, BUCKINGHAMSHIRE, HP12 4HJ.
BRETT, Mr. John, FCA *1965;* Beech House, 3A Christchurch Road, NORWICH, NR2 2AD. (Life Member)
BRETT, Miss. Kaye Heather, ACA *2011;* 81 Hillsborough Drive, BURY, BL9 8LF.
BRETT, Mr. Kevin Charles Darney, MSc BSc ACA *1992;* 20 Longs View, Charfield, WOTTON-UNDER-EDGE, GL12 8HZ.
•BRETT, Mrs. Margaret Jean, BA FCA DChA *1978;* (Tax Fac), Bullimores LLP, Old Printers Yard, 156 South Street, DORKING, SURREY, RH4 2HF.
BRETT, Mr. Mathew Anthony, BA ACA *1996;* 22 College Avenue, MAIDENHEAD, BERKSHIRE, SL6 6AX.
•BRETT, Mr. Michael Joseph, BA FCA *1986;* Brett Pittwood Limited, Suite 8, Bourne Gate, 25 Bourne Valley Road, POOLE, DORSET BH12 1DY.
BRETT, Mr. Nathanael, ACA *2011;* 2 Belvedere Court, IPSWICH, IP4 4AW.
BRETT, Mrs. Nicola, ACA MAAT *1997;* 3 Lotus Close, IPSWICH, IP1 5QH.
•BRETT, Mr. Raymond Michael Ashby, FCA FCCA ATII *1958;* (Tax Fac), Raymond M A Brett, Woodside, Westfields, Whiteleaf, PRINCES RISBOROUGH, HP27 0LH.
BRETT, Mr. Richard John, FCA *1970;* 3 The Hamiltons, Torquay Road, Shaldon, TEIGNMOUTH, DEVON, TQ14 0AY.
BRETT, Mr. Richard Mark, BSc ACA *2010;* 10 Kembold Close, BURY ST. EDMUNDS, SUFFOLK, IP32 7EF.
BRETT, Mr. Richard Michael, FCA *1966;* North Brunton House, North Brunton, NEWCASTLE UPON TYNE, NE3 5HD.
BRETT, Mr. Robert Alastair Parker, BSc ACA *1992;* PO Box 75157, Al Qasr Hotel, DUBAI, UNITED ARAB EMIRATES.
BRETT, Miss. Rosalind, BA(Hons) ACA *2004;* 1 Tamarisk Gardens, Woodley, READING, RG5 3BW.
BRETT, Mrs. Sally Georgina, ACA *1984;* 5 Old School Orchard, Watton At Stone, HERTFORD, SG14 3SS.
BRETT, Mrs. Sheenagh Marlene Moira, BSc ACA *1984;* 21 Sommerville Estate Road, SINGAPORE 258025, SINGAPORE.
BRETT, Mr. Simon Robert, BSocSc ACA *2000;* 26 Westbury Lane, BUCKHURST HILL, IG9 5PL.
BRETT, Mr. Stephen Kenneth, BSc ACA *1982;* L P A Niphan Systems Tudor Works, Debden Road, SAFFRON WALDEN, CB11 4AN.
BRETTELL, Mr. Stephen Leslie, BCom ACA *1979;* 3 Glen Park Road, WALLASEY, CH45 5JQ.
BRETTON, Mr. Nigel Paul, BCom ACA *1988;* The Royal Bank of Scotland Plc, 10th Floor, 280 Bishopsgate, LONDON, EC2M 4RB.
BREUER, Mr. Mark Andrew, ACA *1987;* J P Morgan Cazenove, 20 Moorgate, LONDON, EC2R 6DA.
BREW, Mr. Alistair Jeremy, BA ACA *1999;* Business Growth Fund, 21 Palmer Street, LONDON, SW1H 0AD.
BREW, Mrs. Cheryl Christine, BA ACA *1998;* The Old Courthouse, Deloitte & Touche PO Box 250, Douglas, ISLE OF MAN, IM99 1XJ.
•BREW, Mr. Joseph Edward, FCA *1974;* (Tax Fac), Littlejohn LLP, 1 Westferry Circus, Canary Wharf, LONDON, E14 4HD.
•BREW, Mr. Kenneth Taylor, BA FCA DChA *1979;* Ken Brew & Co, 32 Hallville Road, Mossley Hill, LIVERPOOL, L18 0HR.
BREW, Mr. Lawrence Guy, MA ACA *1982;* 3 St. James Close, NEW MALDEN, KT3 6DU.
•BREW, Randal Anthony Maddock, Esq OBE FCA *1968;* 127 Bunbury Road, Northfield, BIRMINGHAM, B31 2NB.
BREWER, Mr. Alexander Charles, BSc ACA *1989;* 22 Masefield Way, TONBRIDGE, KENT, TN9 2PY.
BREWER, Mrs. Amanda, BA(Hons) ACA *2011;* 15 Nelson Road, Freemantle, SOUTHAMPTON, SO15 3DX.
BREWER, Mr. Arnold James, FCA *1975;* 2 London Road, Headington, OXFORD, OX3 7PA.
BREWER, Mr. Charles, BSc ACA *2006;* 31a Barnard Road, LONDON, SW11 1QT.
BREWER, Mr. Christopher John, BA ACA *1982;* 65 chemin du Boullidou, 13510 EGUILLES, FRANCE.
•BREWER, Mr. Colin William, FCA *1972;* Brewer & Company Limited, 1 Abbotsleigh House, 3 Dalton Road, EASTBOURNE, EAST SUSSEX, BN20 7NP.
BREWER, Mr. Damian Frazer, MSc BA ACA *1996;* Flat 19, 53 Britton Street, LONDON, EC1M 5UQ.
BREWER, Mr. Daniel, BSc(Hons) ACA *2009;* 4 Perseus Terrace, PORTSMOUTH, HAMPSHIRE, PO1 3TG.
BREWER, Mr. David Douglas, BSc ACA *1994;* (Tax Fac), Phoenix Luxury Co Ltd, 9, Hurlingham Business Park, Sulivan Road, LONDON, SW6 3DU.
BREWER, Miss. Helen Sian, BSc ACA *1989;* International Crisis Group, 149 Avenue Louise, 1050 BRUSSELS, BELGIUM.
BREWER, Mrs. Holly Gwenllian Anne, BSc ACA *2004;* Masters Cottage, Sandroyd School Rushmore Park, Tollard Royal, SALISBURY, SP5 5QD.
BREWER, Mr. Ian Patrick, BA ACA *1992;* 10 Garden Walk, ROTHERHAM, SOUTH YORKSHIRE, S60 3HY.
•BREWER, Miss. Jacqueline Ruth, BSc FCA *1988;* Jackie Brewer, 71 Elgin Road, Pwll, LLANELLI, CARMARTHENSHIRE, SA15 4AF.
BREWER, Mrs. Jane Michelle, MEng ACA *1992;* Chestnut House, Broadway Lane, Fladbury, PERSHORE, WORCESTERSHIRE, WR10 2QG.
BREWER, Mrs. Joanne, BSc ACA *2000;* 114 Sandringham Drive, DARTFORD, DA2 7WL.
BREWER, Mr. John Charles, MA ACA *1980;* 40 Sandringham Road, NORWICH, NR2 3RZ.
•BREWER, Mr. Keith Paul Merrick, BSc FCA CTA *1979;* Rouse Partners LLP, 55 Station Road, BEACONSFIELD, BUCKINGHAMSHIRE, HP9 1QL.
BREWER, Mrs. Marion Ann, BA ACA *1991;* Oak Villa, Mill Lane, Goosnargh, PRESTON, PR3 2JX.
BREWER, Mr. Mark Andrew, BA ACA *1996;* The Co-Operative Group, 1st Floor, Old Bank, New Century House, Corporation Street, MANCHESTER M60 4ES.
BREWER, Mr. Matthew Graham, BSc FCA *1999;* 10 Pasture View, Sherburn In Elmet, LEEDS, LS25 6LZ.
BREWER, Ms. Natalie Ann, ACA CA(AUS) *2011;* Flat 3, 341 Baker Street, LONDON, NW1 6XE.
•BREWER, Mr. Neil Tod, FCA *1993;* with Rickard Keen LLP, 7 Nelson Street, SOUTHEND-ON-SEA, SS1 1EH.
BREWER, Mr. Peter Raymond, FCA *1955;* Springfield, Llantrisant Road, Groesfaen, PONTYCLUN, CF72 8NJ. (Life Member)
BREWER, Miss. Rebecca Mary, MSc BSc ACA *2006;* PricewaterhouseCoopers, PO Box 11987, DUBAI, UNITED ARAB EMIRATES.
BREWER, Mr. Robert John, FCA *1979;* Tanners Farm Bran End, Stebbing, DUNMOW, ESSEX, CM6 3RS.
BREWER, Mr. Simon Paul Alan, BA FCA TEP *1989;* Sanne Trust Company Ltd, PO Box 539, JERSEY, JE4 5UT.
•BREWER, Mr. Stephen Paul, FCA *1979;* (Tax Fac), Berkeley Lifford Hall, Greengate House, Pickwick Road, CORSHAM, SN13 9BY.

BREWER, Mr. Steven Roger, BA ACA *1997;* Swale Heating Ltd, Heard Way, Enrolink Industrial Estate, SITTINGBOURNE, ME10 3SA.
BREWER, Mr. Trevor James, BSc ACA *2006;* Apartment 5 Belgravia House, 65 Thorpe Road, PETERBOROUGH, PE3 6DF.
•**BREWERTON, Mr. John Charles, FCA** *1975;* (Tax Fac), J.C. Brewerton & Co, Ashcombe House, 4 Morville Close, Dorridge, SOLIHULL, B93 8SZ.
BREWILL, Mr. Robert David, BSc FCA *1989;* 29 Leicester Road, Quorn, LOUGHBOROUGH, LE12 8BA.
BREWIN, Mr. Craig Andrew, LLB ACA *2002;* 24 Elmhurst Close, Slaid Hill, LEEDS, LS17 8BD.
•**BREWIN, Mr. David, BSc ACA** *1989;* Ernst & Young LLP, 100 Barbirolli Square, MANCHESTER, M2 3EY. See also Ernst & Young Europe LLP
BREWIN, Mr. David Richard, BSc ACA *1988;* 1 Hawtrey Road, LONDON, NW3 3SS.
BREWIN, Mrs. Elizabeth, ACA *2008;* Block 7 Commonwealth Avenue, 12 - 650, SINGAPORE 140007, SINGAPORE.
BREWIN, Mr. Gareth, ACA *2007;* 14 Gabriel Court, LEEDS, LS10 1DH.
BREWIN, Mrs. Jane Elizabeth, BSc ACA *1997;* 9 Hogarth Road, Nr Thurcaston, LEICESTER, LE4 2SA.
BREWIN, Mrs. Joanne Jayne, BA ACA *2006;* Dyson Ltd, Tetbury Hill, MALMESBURY, WILTSHIRE, SN16 0RP.
BREWIN, Mr. Nicholas John, BA ACA *1992;* 15 Davenport, HARLOW, CM17 9TF.
BREWIN, Mr. Peter, BSc ACA *2006;* 2683 Oak Road, No.240, WALNUT CREEK, CA 94597, UNITED STATES.
BREWIN, Mr. Richard Neil, BSc FCA *1985;* 8 Plantagenet Way, ASHBY-DE-LA-ZOUCH, LEICESTERSHIRE, LE65 1LE.
BREWIS, Mr. Robert Goodchild, BSc ACA *1982;* Coney Grey, Gun Lane, Sherington, NEWPORT PAGNELL, MK16 9PE.
BREWOOD, Mr. Andrew Colin, BA ACA *2000;* 91 Boundary Road, CHEADLE, SK8 2EW.
•**BREWSTER, Mr. Charles Thomas, BA FCA** *1980;* Brewster & Co (NE) Ltd, 5a Station Terrace, EAST BOLDON, TYNE AND WEAR, NE36 0LJ. See also Bond Partners LLP
BREWSTER, Mr. Christopher James, BSc ACA *2004;* Findus Group, Ross House, Wickham Road, GRIMSBY, SOUTH HUMBERSIDE, DN31 3SW.
BREWSTER, Mr. David, BA FCA *1984;* (Tax Fac), with Hardcastle France, 30 Yorkersgate, MALTON, YO17 7AW.
BREWSTER, Mr. Ian Christopher, FCA *1975;* Alnafetgata 8a, 0192 OSLO, NORWAY.
BREWSTER, Mr. Michael Ernest, FCA *1969;* April Cottage, Green Road, Woolpit, BURY ST. EDMUNDS, SUFFOLK, IP30 9RF.
BREWSTER, Mr. Nigel David, BSc ACA *1989;* Lynden Hall, Langworthy Lane, MAIDENHEAD, BERKSHIRE, SL6 2HH.
BREWSTER, Mr. Richard David, FCA *1968;* 180 Kew Road, RICHMOND, TW9 2AS.
BREWSTER, Mr. Richard Mark, BSc ACA *1980;* 37 Titus Way, COLCHESTER, CO4 9WH.
BREWSTER, Mr. Roy Burnett, FCA *1952;* 40 Catherine Road, WOODBRIDGE, IP12 4JP. (Life Member)
BREWSTER, Miss. Sophia Warren, ACA *2008;* The Financial Times, One Southwark Bridge, LONDON, SE1 9HL.
BRIAN, Mr. Andrew John, ACA *2003;* with Deloitte Touche Tohmatsu, Grosvenor Place, 225 George Street, P.O. Box N 250, SYDNEY, NSW 2000 AUSTRALIA.
BRIAN, Mr. Carl Adrian, BSc ACA *1992;* 26 Theberton Street, LONDON, N1 0QX.
BRIAN, Mr. Michael John, BSc ACA *2006;* 6 Marsh Brook Close, Rixton, WARRINGTON, WA3 6LR.
BRIAN-DAVIS, Miss. Helen Elizabeth, BA ACA *1992;* Highlands, 13 The Ridgeway, Friston, EASTBOURNE, BN20 0EU.
BRIANT, Mr. Daren Raymond Jonathan, BSc ACA *1991;* 8 Redburn Street, LONDON, SW3 4BX.
•**BRIANT, Mr. Ian Thomas John, BCom ACA** *2007;* with Briants, Maritime House, Discovery Quay, FALMOUTH, CORNWALL, TR11 3XA.
BRIANT, Miss. Jennifer, BSc ACA *1980;* 21 Main Street, Huncote, LEICESTER, LE9 3AU.
BRIANT, Mr. Kenneth Vincent, BA ACA *1987;* 20 Prescelly Place, EDGWARE, MIDDLESEX, HA8 6DH.
BRIANT, Mr. Matthew, BSc ACA *1993;* 7 Laburnum Close, Rogerstone, NEWPORT, NP10 9JQ.
BRIANT, Mr. Michael John, ACA *1984;* Furze House, Fyning Lane, Rogate, PETERSFIELD, HAMPSHIRE, GU31 5DF.
BRIANT, Mr. Paul Francis, FCA *1968;* 93 Willingdon Rd., EASTBOURNE, BN21 1TZ.
BRIANT, Mr. Peter James, MA ACA CTA *1992;* Societe Generale, S G House, 41 Tower Hill, LONDON, EC3N 4SG.
BRIANT, Mr. Terence George Malcolm, BSc ACA *1980;* c/o Billiton Marketing AG, Jochlerweg 2, 6340 BAAR, SWITZERLAND.
•**BRIANT, Mr. Thomas Arthur Clyde, FCA** *1975;* Briants, Maritime House, Discovery Quay, FALMOUTH, CORNWALL, TR11 3XA.
BRIANT, Mr. Timothy, BSc(Econ) ACA *1997;* 116 Chanctonbury Way, LONDON, N12 7AB.
BRIANT, Mrs. Yasemin, BSc ACA *1998;* 116 Chanctonbury Way, LONDON, N12 7AB.
•**BRIANTI, Mr. Roberto Vittorio Francis, FCA** *1990;* (Tax Fac), Daly Hoggett & Co, 5-11 Mortimer Street, LONDON, W1T 3HS.
BRIAR, Mr. Michael Edward, FCA *1970;* 2 Mace Walk, CHELMSFORD, CM1 2GE.
BRIARS, Miss. Joanna Clair, ACA *1994;* The Coach House, Arrow, ALCESTER, WARWICKSHIRE, B49 5PP.
BRIARS, Mr. Mark Anthony, BA ACA *1990;* 21 Galleydene, BENFLEET, SS7 2QA.
BRICE, Mrs. Denise Joanna, BSc ACA *1987;* The Old Rectory, Free Street, BISHOPS WALTHAM, HAMPSHIRE, SO32 1EE.
BRICE, Mr. John Roger Simpson, BSc ACA *1987;* 34 Peninsula Heights, 93 Albert Embankment, LONDON, SE1 7TY.
BRICE, Mr. Jonathan Andrew, BA ACA ACT *1992;* Northern General Hospital N H S Trust, Herries Road, SHEFFIELD, S5 7AU.
BRICE, Mr. Michael Stephen, BA ACA *1992;* 50 Boston Avenue, READING, RG1 6JU.
BRICE, Mr. Nicholas Lawrence, BSc FCA *1989;* County House, Conway Mews, LONDON, W1T 6AA.
•**BRICE, Mr. Nigel Alan, FCA** *1985;* Finerty Brice, Endeavour House, 78 Stafford Road, WALLINGTON, SM6 9AY.
BRICE, Mr. Patrick Andrew, MA ACA *1996;* 53 Carlisle Avenue, ST. ALBANS, HERTFORDSHIRE, AL3 5LX.
•**BRICE, Mr. Paul Francis, BA FCA CTA MSI** *1991;* Whitelands House, Pishill, HENLEY-ON-THAMES, OXFORDSHIRE, RG9 6HH.
BRICE, Miss. Sarah Elizabeth, BSc(Hons) ACA *2003;* 128 Harbut Road, LONDON, SW11 2RE.
BRICE, Mrs. Sian Helen, BA ACA *1995;* 53 Carlisle Avenue, ST. ALBANS, AL3 5LX.
BRICE, Mr. Stephen John, ACA *2008;* 3 Brackley Drive, Middleton, MANCHESTER, M24 1SS.
•**BRICE, Mr. Steven Ayrton, BSc(Econ) ACA** *1995;* Mazars LLP, Tower Bridge House, St. Katharines Way, LONDON, E1W 1DD.
•**BRICHIERI-COLOMBI, Mr. Thomas Leslie Alistair, MA ACA** *2004;* Mazars LLP, Tower Bridge House, St. Katharines Way, LONDON, E1W 1DD.
BRICK, Mrs. Linda Jayne, BA ACA *1992;* D V Marlow, 72 West Street Portchester, FAREHAM, HAMPSHIRE, PO16 9UN.
•**BRICKELL, Mr. Christopher William, FCA** *1965;* Kendall Wadley LLP, Granta Lodge, 71 Graham Road, MALVERN, WORCESTERSHIRE, WR14 2JS.
BRICKELL, Mr. Michael James Brindley, FCA *1965;* Brindleys Barn, Quay Lane, Hanley Castle, WORCESTER, WR8 0BS.
BRICKHILL, Mr. Timothy David, FCA *1964;* Beech Farm, Whitchurch Hill, READING, RG8 7NZ.
•**BRICKLEY, Mrs. Karen Elizabeth, BSc ACA CertPFS** *1999;* Langdon West Williams plc, Curzon House, 24 High Street, BANSTEAD, SM7 2LJ.
BRICKMAN, Mr. Andrew Leon, BA ACA *1996;* 1 Maxted Park, HARROW, HA1 3BB.
BRICKMAN, Mrs. Fiona Gay, BA FCA CTA *1986;* 72 East Avenue, Talbot Woods, BOURNEMOUTH, BH3 7DB.
BRICKMAN, Mrs. Rosalind Serena, BA(Econ) ACA *1997;* with PKF (UK) LLP, Farringdon Place, 20 Farringdon Road, LONDON, EC1M 3AP.
•**BRICKNELL, Mr. Paul, FCA** *1983;* with BDO LLP, Arcadia House, Maritime Walk, Ocean Village, SOUTHAMPTON, SO14 3TL.
BRICOLA, Mrs. Sonali, LLB ACA *2003;* 47 St. Albans Road, WOODFORD GREEN, IG8 9EQ.
BRIDDOCK, Mr. Paul Thomas, BA ACA *1993;* 15 Hockley Lane, Wingerworth, CHESTERFIELD, DERBYSHIRE, S42 6QG.
BRIDDON, Mr. John David, FCA *1972;* (Tax Fac), 6 Bosley Drive, Poynton, STOCKPORT, CHESHIRE, SK12 1UX.
•**BRIDDON, Mr. Paul, BSc FCA** *1991;* Lovewell Blake LLP, 89 Bridge Road, Oulton Broad, LOWESTOFT, NR32 3LN.
BRIDE, Mr. Andrew Neal, BA ACA *1987;* Spa House, Middlehill, Box, CORSHAM, WILTSHIRE, SN13 8QS.
BRIDEL, Mr. Jonathan Ronald Lucien, MBA FCA *1987;* Chevalier House, Belmont Rise, St. Peter Port, GUERNSEY, GY1 1PZ.
BRIDEL, Mr. Ronald Albert Heyward, FCA *1961;* Hilltop, Route De L'Eglise, Castel, GUERNSEY, GY5 7NB. (Life Member)
BRIDER, Mrs. Lisa, ACA CA(SA) *2008;* 147a St. Andrews Road, COULSDON, CR5 3HL.
BRIDEWELL, Mr. Jack William, FCA *1952;* 45 Rue Vautier, 1227 Carouge, GENEVA, SWITZERLAND. (Life Member)
•**BRIDGE, Mr. Andrew Mark, BA FCA** *1990;* Barringtons Limited, 570-572 Etruria Road, NEWCASTLE, ST5 0SU.
BRIDGE, Mr. David, BSc ACA *1988;* 1 Artlett Street, EDGECLIFF, NSW 2027, AUSTRALIA.
BRIDGE, Mr. David George, BSc ACA *1982;* Villa 5 895 Rue Jean de Gingins, 01220 DIVONNE-LES-BAINS, FRANCE.
BRIDGE, Mr. David Shaw, MA FCA *1986;* 43 Sedley Taylor Road, CAMBRIDGE, CB2 8PN.
BRIDGE, Miss. Elizabeth Thelma Anne, MA ACA *1988;* Generali Worldwide Insurance Company Limited, Generali House, Hirzel Street, St Peter Port, GUERNSEY, GY1 4PA.
BRIDGE, Mr. Gordon Wilson, FCA *1968;* Primrose Cottage Farm, Kirkedge Road, High Bradfield, SHEFFIELD, S6 6LJ.
BRIDGE, Mr. John Nicholas, BSc FCA *1981;* 113 Greenfield Road, Harborne, BIRMINGHAM, B17 0EH.
BRIDGE, Miss. Judith Mary, BA ACA *1993;* Alston Church Road, Hartley, LONGFIELD, DA3 8DL.
BRIDGE, Miss. Katie, ACA *2009;* Flat 1, Frome House, Sandalwood Road, WESTBURY, WILTSHIRE, BA13 3TY.
BRIDGE, Mr. Mark, BA FCA *1992;* 10 The Bramblings, LONDON, E4 6LU.
•**BRIDGE, Mr. Michael, FCA** *1974;* PKF (UK) LLP, Pannell House, Park Street, GUILDFORD, SURREY, GU1 4HN.
BRIDGE, Mr. Michael Andrew, BA FCA *1984;* PricewaterhouseCoopers, GPO Box 1331L, MELBOURNE, VIC 3001, AUSTRALIA.
BRIDGE, Miss. Susan Rosemary, BSc FCA *1977;* 5 Bulls Copse Lane, WATERLOOVILLE, HAMPSHIRE, PO8 9QX.
BRIDGE, Mrs. Tania Jeannette Amanda, BA ACA *1995;* 3 Southington Lane, Overton, BASINGSTOKE, RG25 3DT.
•**BRIDGE, Mr. Thomas Edward, FCA** *1967;* (Tax Fac), Edward Bridge, Oak Cottage, London Road, Walgherton, NANTWICH, CHESHIRE CW5 7LA.
BRIDGEHOUSE, Mr. Edward, FCA *1962;* Trefin, Hilda Road, Gee Cross, HYDE, SK14 5EY.
BRIDGEMAN, Mr. Alan John, FCA *1974;* PO Box 1060, DUNEDIN 9054, NEW ZEALAND.
BRIDGEMAN, Mr. Alexander Howard, BSc FCA *1988;* 23 Arthur Road, WOKINGHAM, BERKSHIRE, RG41 2SS.
•**BRIDGEMAN, Mr. Peter, FCA** *1969;* Bridgeman, Dell House, Lower Buckland Road, LYMINGTON, HAMPSHIRE, SO41 9DS.
BRIDGEN, Mrs. Belinda Ann, BSc FCA *1978;* Mishcon de Reya Solicitors Summit House 12 Red Lion Square, LONDON, WC1R 4QD.
BRIDGEN, Mr. Nicholas John, BSc FCA *1978;* Apartment 26, Kourmangazi 66, ALMATY, KAZAKHSTAN.
BRIDGEN, Mrs. Rebecca Joanne, BA FCA *1989;* with PricewaterhouseCoopers LLP, Savannah House, 3 Ocean Way, Ocean Village, SOUTHAMPTON, SO14 3TJ.
•**BRIDGEN, Mr. Richard Charles, FCA** *1968;* Bridgen Watkins & Wainwright, 10 Dashwood Avenue, HIGH WYCOMBE, HP12 3DN.
BRIDGENS, Mr. Stephen Christopher, FCA *1976;* 18 Park Lane, Weston-on-Trent, DERBY, DE72 2BR.
BRIDGER, Mr. Ben, BA ACA *2010;* 42 Moor End Lane, Silkstone Common, BARNSLEY, SOUTH YORKSHIRE, S75 4QS.
BRIDGER, Mr. Colin Henry, FCA *1958;* Westbourne House, 31A Chesham Road, AMERSHAM, HP6 5HN. (Life Member)
BRIDGER, Mr. David, ACA *2011;* 43 Paignton Avenue, PORTSMOUTH, PO3 6LL.
BRIDGER, Mr. David Wilson, BA FCA *1970;* Byways, 160 Worlds End Lane, ORPINGTON, BR6 6AS. (Life Member)
BRIDGER, Mr. Gary William, ACA *1983;* 32 Woodgreen Road, Upshire, WALTHAM ABBEY, EN9 3SD.
BRIDGER, Mr. John Lawrence, BSc ACA *1979;* 1449 London Road, LEIGH-ON-SEA, SS9 2SB.
BRIDGER, Mr. Lawrence Dudley, ACA *1983;* T D Bridger Limited, Avenue One, LETCHWORTH GARDEN CITY, HERTFORDSHIRE, SG6 2WP.
BRIDGER, Mr. Mark David, BSc ACA *2003;* 40 Rochester Avenue, CANTERBURY, CT1 3YE.
BRIDGER, Mr. Peter Anthony, FCA *1947;* 8 Brand Close, P.O.Box 181, DUNSBOROUGH, WA 6281, AUSTRALIA. (Life Member)
•**BRIDGER, Mr. Robert George Cameron, BSc(Hons) ACA CTA** *2002;* (Tax Fac), Place Campbell, Wilmington House, High Street, EAST GRINSTEAD, RH19 3AU.
BRIDGES, Mrs. Carol Barbara, LLB FCA *1986;* 12 Dinch Hill, Undy, CALDICOT, GWENT, NP26 3JL.
BRIDGES, Mrs. Charlotte Louise, BA ACA *1992;* 24a Amersham Road, HIGH WYCOMBE, BUCKINGHAMSHIRE, HP13 6QU.
•**BRIDGES, Mr. Colin Leslie, FCA** *1977;* 69 Ramsbury Road, ST. ALBANS, HERTFORDSHIRE, AL1 1SN.
BRIDGES, Mr. David Graham, ACA *1983;* 106 Repton Road, Hartshorne, SWADLINCOTE, DERBYSHIRE, DE11 7AE.
BRIDGES, Mrs. Karen Louise, BSc ACA *1995;* Severn Trent Plc, 2297 Coventry Road, BIRMINGHAM, B26 3PU.
BRIDGES, Mr. Mark Royston, BSc FCA *1983;* P O Box FL 669, FLATTS FL BX, BERMUDA.
BRIDGES, Mr. Matthew James, BA(Econ) ACA *2003;* 12/6 Braid Road, EDINBURGH, EH10 6AD.
BRIDGES, Mrs. Patricia Ann, BA ACA *1982;* 1 Elm Grove, Thorpe Bay, SOUTHEND-ON-SEA, SS1 3EY.
BRIDGES, Mr. Paul Malcolm, BA ACA *1982;* 1 Elm Grove, Thorpe Bay, SOUTHEND-ON-SEA, SS1 3EY.
BRIDGES, Mrs. Penelope Jane Phoebe, BA ACA *1994;* Loth Lorien, Faircrouch Road, WADHURST, TN5 6PN.
•**BRIDGES, Mr. Peter Anthony, FCA** *1975;* (Tax Fac), John Crook & Partners, 255 Green Lanes, Palmers Green, LONDON, N13 4XE.
BRIDGES, Mr. Simon Gerard, BCom ACA *1998;* 22 Kingscliffe Gardens, LONDON, SW19 6NR.
BRIDGES, Mr. Stuart John, MA ACA *1987;* Hiscox Plc, 1 Great St. Helen's, LONDON, EC3A 6HX.
BRIDGES, Mrs. Zoe Ann, BSc ACA *2004;* 14 Montrose Park, Brisington, BRISTOL, BS4 4JF.
BRIDGEWATER, Mr. Peter Jeremy, BA FCA *1989;* 25 Combrook, WARWICK, CV35 9HP.
BRIDGEWATER, Mr. Simon Paul, BSc ACA *1993;* 2 Long Ridge, Green Road Rickling Green, SAFFRON WALDEN, ESSEX, CB11 3BZ.
BRIDGEWATER, Mr. Sydney Tyndale, FCA *1948;* Blue Jay Way, Lawnswood Drive, STOURBRIDGE, DY7 5QW. (Life Member)
BRIDGFORD, Mr. David John Martin, BA ACA *1989;* 4 Gosmere Farm Barns, Newhouse Lane Sheldwich, FAVERSHAM, ME13 9PR.
BRIDGFORD, Mr. David Peter, FCA *1974;* Radley College, Radley, ABINGDON, OXFORDSHIRE, OX14 2HR.
•**BRIDGFORD, Ms. Julie Margaret, BSc FCA** *1985;* (Tax Fac), Keith Bridgford & Co, 17 The Grove, ILKLEY, LS29 9LW.
BRIDGLAND, Mr. David Vernon, MA ACA *1992;* Ivy House Farm, Berrick Salome, WALLINGFORD, OX10 6JP.
•**BRIDGLAND, Mrs. Lindsay Evelyn, BSc ACA** *1992;* 26 Alice Street, TURRAMURRA, NSW 2074, AUSTRALIA.
•**BRIDGLAND, Mrs. Sally Jane, FCA** *1988;* Richmond House, 10 St. Martins Avenue, EPSOM, SURREY, KT18 5HS.
BRIDGMAN, Mr. Donald Alfred, FCA *1973;* 12 Langford Green Hutton, BRENTWOOD, ESSEX, CM13 1YJ.
BRIDGMAN, Miss. Joanna Tracy, BA ACA *1997;* 26 Austin Edwards Drive, WARWICK, CV34 5GW.
BRIDGMAN, Miss. Joanne Elizabeth, BSc ACA *1995;* Annscott, Halls Lane, Waltham St. Lawrence, READING, RG10 0JD.
BRIDGMAN, Mrs. Karen Nina, BSc ACA *1992;* 4 The Nurseries, Balcombe, HAYWARDS HEATH, RH17 6JD.
BRIDGMAN, Mr. Kenneth Alwyn, FCA *1950;* Martlets, Connaught Close, SIDMOUTH, EX10 8TU. (Life Member)
BRIDGMAN, Mr. Peter Alwyn, BSc FCA *1976;* PepsiCo Inc, 700 Anderson Hill Road, PURCHASE, NY 10577, UNITED STATES.
BRIDGMAN, Mr. Robert Edward, ACA *2009;* with Deloitte Middle East, Currency House, Building 1 Level 5, DIFC, PO Box 282056, DUBAI UNITED ARAB EMIRATES.
BRIDGWATER, Mr. Howard Guy, BSc ACA *1989;* 3rd Floor Regal house, 70 London Road, TWICKENHAM, TW1 3QS.
BRIDGWATER, Miss. Lesley Philippa, BSc ACA *1992;* F T Morrell & Co Ltd Wellington Works, Woodley, STOCKPORT, CHESHIRE, SK6 1RN.
BRIDLE, Mr. Nigel Anthony, FCA *1982;* 11 Park Close, Middleton Stoney, BICESTER, OXFORDSHIRE, OX25 4AS.

BRIDSON, Mr. Brian James, LLB ACA *1982;* Southmead, Long Hey Road, Caldy, WIRRAL, CH48 1LY.
•BRIDSON, Mr. Robert John, BSc FCA *1992;* PricewaterhouseCoopers LLP, 7 More London Riverside, LONDON, SE1 2RT. See also PricewaterhouseCoopers
BRIEN, Mr. Desmond Patrick, ACA *1995;* 4 Shelbourne Place, Shelbourne Road, Ballsbridge, DUBLIN 4, COUNTY DUBLIN, IRELAND.
BRIEN, Mr. John, BA FCA *1985;* with Wilkins Kennedy, Parmenter House, 57 Tower Street, WINCHESTER, HAMPSHIRE, SO23 8TD.
BRIEN, Mr. Michael Anthony, BSc FCA ACII *1980;* with Deloitte LLP, Hill House, 1 Little New Street, LONDON, EC4A 3TR.
•BRIER, Mr. James Allan, FCA *1951;* Shorts, 6 Fairfield Road, CHESTERFIELD, DERBYSHIRE, S40 4TP.
BRIERLEY, Mr. Allen, FCA *1974;* 28 Hyde Road, Mottram, HYDE, SK14 6NG.
•BRIERLEY, Mr. Anthony Robert, BCom FCA *1978;* PM+M Solutions for Business LLP, Greenbank Technology Park, Challenge Way, BLACKBURN, BB1 5QB. See also PM & M Corporate Finance Limited
•ⒹBRIERLEY, Mr. Anthony William, MA FCA *1978;* Zolfo Cooper LLP, 10 Fleet Place, LONDON, EC4M 7RB.
BRIERLEY, Mr. Antony Edward, FCA *1963;* 2 Woodbine Terrace, ASHINGTON, NE63 8PP.
BRIERLEY, Mr. Christopher Andrew John, MChem ACA *2010;* with Sampson West, 34 Ely Place, LONDON, EC1N 6TD.
BRIERLEY, Mr. David Ian, BA ACA *1982;* 63a Belsize Lane, LONDON, NW3 5AU.
•BRIERLEY, Mr. David William, FCA *1971;* with RSM Tenon Limited, Cedar House, Sandbrook Business Park Sandbrook Way, ROCHDALE, LANCASHIRE, OL11 1LQ.
•BRIERLEY, Mrs. Elizabeth, BA FCA DChA *1992;* Saffery Champness, Midland House, 2 Poole Road, BOURNEMOUTH, DORSET, BH2 5QY.
BRIERLEY, Mr. Frank, BA FCA ATII *1971;* 82 Summerseat Lane, Ramsbottom, BURY, BL0 9RQ. (Life Member)
BRIERLEY, Mr. Graham, BA(Hons) ACA *2001;* Rydal Mount, 7 Stamford Road, Mossley, ASHTON-UNDER-LYNE, OL5 0BA.
BRIERLEY, Mr. Harold, FCA *1954;* 12 Thornlee Court, Grotton, OLDHAM, OL4 5RG.
BRIERLEY, Mr. James, BSc ACA *2007;* 58 Coppy Bridge Drive, ROCHDALE, OL16 3AR.
BRIERLEY, Mrs. Jeanette Alexia, BA FCA *1997;* (Tax Fac), with Ensors, Blyth House, Rendham Road, SAXMUNDHAM, IP17 1WA.
BRIERLEY, Mr. John Allan, MA BSc ACA *1989;* Sheffield University Management School, University Of Sheffield, 9 Mappin Street, SHEFFIELD, S1 4DT.
BRIERLEY, Mr. Jonathan, BSc ACA *1993;* Tresco, Fearn Close, East Horsley, LEATHERHEAD, KT24 6AE.
BRIERLEY, Mr. Jonathan Andrew, BSc(Hons) ACA *2004;* First Floor Flat, 151 Elsenham Street, LONDON, SW18 5NZ.
BRIERLEY, Mr. Kenneth James, FCA *1960;* 15 Padstow Drive, Bramhall, STOCKPORT, SK7 2HU.
BRIERLEY, Mr. Michael Charles, BA(Hons) FCA *1984;* Pine Cottage, Portland Towers, LEICESTER, LE2 2PG.
BRIERLEY, Mr. Nicholas James, BSc ACA *2003;* Ecclesiastical Insurance Office Plc, Beaufort House, Brunswick Road, GLOUCESTER, GL1 1JZ.
BRIERLEY, Mr. Peter, ACA *2011;* 5 Temple Square, Temple Street, LIVERPOOL, L2 5RH.
•BRIERLEY, Mr. Peter Michael, FCA *1975;* Hanby & Co, 209 High Street, NORTHALLERTON, DL7 8LW.
BRIERLEY, Mr. Simon Mark John, ACA *2007;* 32 Maes y Llech, Radyr, CARDIFF, CF15 8GL.
BRIERLEY, Mr. Stuart Alan, BA ACA *1983;* Springside House, Spring Lane, Lees, OLDHAM, OL4 5AJ.
BRIERLEY, Miss. Wendy June, BA ACA *1983;* 8 Farmleigh Grove, Hersham, WALTON-ON-THAMES, KT12 5BU.
BRIERLY, Mr. Andrew Stephen, BSc ACA *1999;* 2 Woodside Road, KINGSTON UPON THAMES, KT2 5AT.
BRIESE, Miss. Claire, ACA *2008;* Hazelwoods Staverton Court, Staverton, CHELTENHAM, GL51 0UX.
BRIEST, Mr. Michael Joseph, BA ACA *1997;* UBS Investment Bank, 1 Finsbury Avenue, LONDON, EC2M 2PP.
BRIGDEN, Miss. Charlotte Victoria, BSc ACA *2007;* ITV plc, 200 Gray's Inn Road, LONDON, WC1X 8HF.
BRIGDEN, Mr. Christopher Alan, BSc ACA *2006;* 2 Derwent Road, PRENTON, MERSEYSIDE, CH43 5SA.
BRIGDEN, Mr. Leonard Francis, FCA *1988;* P O Box 5525, CHRISTCHURCH 8542, NEW ZEALAND.
BRIGG, Mr. John Rodney Wilford, MA FCA *1951;* 23 Byron Court, Stockbridge Road, CHICHESTER, WEST SUSSEX, PO19 8ES. (Life Member)
BRIGGS, Mr. Alan Holland, FCA *1949;* Cromford, Braaid, Marown, ISLE OF MAN, IM4 2HW. (Life Member)
BRIGGS, Mr. Alec James William, BSc(Econ) FCA *1995;* 5 Teveray Drive, Penkridge, STAFFORD, STAFFORDSHIRE, ST19 5SW.
BRIGGS, Mr. Andrew David, BA(Hons) ACA *2000;* Ideal Stelrad Ltd, 69-75 Side, NEWCASTLE UPON TYNE, NE1 3JE.
BRIGGS, Mr. Andrew David, BSc ACA *1991;* 27 New Street, HENLEY-ON-THAMES, OXFORDSHIRE, RG9 2BP.
BRIGGS, Mr. Andrew James, ACA *2007;* Urenco Ltd, 18 Oxford Road, MARLOW, BUCKINGHAMSHIRE, SL7 2NL.
BRIGGS, Mr. Andrew John, BSc ACA *1989;* 9 Hazlemere Avenue, Melton Park, Gosforth, NEWCASTLE UPON TYNE, NE3 5QL.
BRIGGS, Miss. Catherine Jane, BA ACA *2004;* with Armstrong Watson, Fairview House, Victoria Place, CARLISLE, CA1 1HP.
BRIGGS, Mr. Christopher Charles, BA ACA *1984;* 5 Post Cottages, Crawley, WINCHESTER, SO21 2PT.
BRIGGS, Mr. Christopher James, FCA *1972;* Gleeds, Wilford House, 1 Clifton Lane, Wilford, NOTTINGHAM, NG11 7AT.
•BRIGGS, Mr. Christopher James, FCA *1979;* (Tax Fac), Thorne & Co (Ross-on-wye) Limited, 1 St. Marys Street, ROSS-ON-WYE, HEREFORDSHIRE, HR9 5HT.
BRIGGS, Mr. David, BA FCA *1971;* Blackwell Farm, CHESHAM, BUCKINGHAMSHIRE, HP5 1TN.
BRIGGS, Mr. David, FCA *1966;* 6 Scott Lane, Riddlesden, KEIGHLEY, WEST YORKSHIRE, BD20 5BT. (Life Member)
BRIGGS, Mr. David Rainford, MA FCA *1959;* Shortacre, 6 Macclesfield Road, Prestbury, MACCLESFIELD, SK10 4BN. (Life Member)
BRIGGS, Mr. Dennis, FCA *1964;* 9 Hazelwood Grove, WORKSOP, S80 3EW.
BRIGGS, Mr. Dominic Patrick, BSc ACA *1993;* 187 Clive Road, Dulwich, LONDON, SE21 8DG.
BRIGGS, Mr. Frederick Clifford, FCA *1956;* Albury House, 15b The Avenue, Branksome Park, POOLE, BH13 6HA. (Life Member)
•BRIGGS, Mr. George Anthony, FCA *1974;* G A Briggs FCA, Manor Farm, Farnham, KNARESBOROUGH, NORTH YORKSHIRE, HG5 9JE.
•BRIGGS, Mr. Graham, BA FCA *1971;* (Tax Fac), AIMS - Graham Biggs, Peak View, Stevens Cross, Sidford, SIDMOUTH, EX10 9QL.
•BRIGGS, Mr. Gregory Diarmid, BSc ACA CPA *1993;* PricewaterhouseCoopers LLP, The Atrium, 1 Harefield Road, UXBRIDGE, UB8 1EX. See also PricewaterhouseCoopers
BRIGGS, Mrs. Gwneth Barbara, FCA *1958;* Albury House, 15b The Avenue, Branksome Park, POOLE, BH13 6HA. (Life Member)
BRIGGS, Miss. Hayley Ann, ACA *2011;* 58 Grovewood Avenue, Eastwood, LEIGH-ON-SEA, ESSEX, SS9 5EG.
BRIGGS, Mrs. Helen Louise, BA ACA *2005;* WD40 Company Ltd, Brick Close, Kiln Farm, MILTON KEYNES, MK11 3LF.
BRIGGS, Mrs. Helena Maria, BA ACA *2004;* 38 Chart Lane, REIGATE, RH2 7DZ.
•BRIGGS, Mr. Henry Francis, BA FCA *1980;* HW Birmingham LLP, Sterling House, 71 Francis Road, BIRMINGHAM, WEST MIDLANDS, B16 8SP.
BRIGGS, Mrs. Hilary Elizabeth, BA ACA *1991;* 6 Rosedale, Pannal, HARROGATE, NORTH YORKSHIRE, HG3 1LB.
BRIGGS, Mr. Howard Julian, BCom FCA *1966;* Thorntree House, Hetton, SKIPTON, BD23 6LT.
BRIGGS, Mr. Hugh Alexander, MA ACA *1995;* C V C, 111 Strand, LONDON, WC2R 0AG.
BRIGGS, Mr. Iain Alexander Muir, BA ACA *2004;* 38 Chart Lane, REIGATE, RH2 7DZ.
BRIGGS, Mr. Iain Clifford Warburton, BSc ACA *1986;* 574 Grand Oaks Drive, BRENTWOOD, TN 37027, UNITED STATES.
BRIGGS, Mr. James Frodsham, FCA *1955;* 83 Queens Avenue, Finchley, LONDON, N3 2NN. (Life Member)
BRIGGS, Mr. James Harvey, ACA *1986;* 24 Tennyson Close, HORSHAM, RH12 5PN.
BRIGGS, Mr. James Rupert, BA ACA CFA *2001;* 29a Hampstead High Street, LONDON, NW3 1QA.
BRIGGS, Mr. James Stephen, ACA *2010;* 11 Kirklands Avenue, Baildon, SHIPLEY, BD17 6EQ.
BRIGGS, Ms. Janet Clare, BSc ACA *1990;* 384 Cooper Avenue, ELGIN, IL 60120, UNITED STATES.
•BRIGGS, Mr. John Charles, FCA *1962;* John C. Briggs, 54 Church Street, Warsop, MANSFIELD, NOTTINGHAMSHIRE, NG20 0AR.
•BRIGGS, Mr. John Howard, FCA MBA *1971;* Petersfield, High Street, Hook, GOOLE, DN14 5PJ.
BRIGGS, Mr. John Patrick, BSc FCA *1979;* Cathedral office, Christ Church, St. Aldates, OXFORD, OX1 1DP.
BRIGGS, Mr. John Stephen, BA FCA *1980;* 8 Hollin Gardens, Weetwood, LEEDS, LS16 5NL.
BRIGGS, Mr. Jonathan Mark, BCom FCA *1991;* Ashbourne, 85 Thievesdale Lane, WORKSOP, NOTTINGHAMSHIRE, S81 0PG.
•BRIGGS, Miss. Karen Sarah, BSc FCA *1990;* KPMG LLP, 15 Canada Square, LONDON, E14 5GL. See also KPMG Europe LLP
BRIGGS, Miss. Katie, ACA *2008;* JT Interntaional, 1 Rue de la Gabelle, 1211 GENEVA, SWITZERLAND.
BRIGGS, Mrs. Katrina Valerie, BA ACA *1992;* Ivy Cottage, Butlers Marston, WARWICK, CV35 0NG.
•BRIGGS, Mr. Kevin Edward, FCA *1971;* (Tax Fac), K.E. Briggs, Dukes Hagg Farmhouse, Moor Road, PRUDHOE, NE42 5PA.
BRIGGS, Miss. Lucy Jane, BSc ACA *1990;* Flagship Training Ltd, Shore House, Compass Road, PORTSMOUTH, PO6 4PR.
BRIGGS, Mr. Malcolm Ian, BSc FCA *1977;* Carbon Products Global Business, Rio Tinto Alcan, 725 Aristide Berges - BP7, 38341 VOREPPE, FRANCE.
•BRIGGS, Mr. Martin Stephen, ACA *1990;* (Tax Fac), Martin Briggs & Co, Banbury House, 121 Stonegrove, EDGWARE, MIDDLESEX, HA8 7TJ.
BRIGGS, Mr. Michael Denis, BA ACA *1979;* Low & Bonar Plc, Marble Arch Tower, 55 Bryanston Street, LONDON, W1H 7AA.
BRIGGS, Mr. Michael Dominic, BSc ACA *1987;* 11 Denham Road, EPSOM, SURREY, KT17 3AA.
•BRIGGS, Mr. Michael Edward, BA FCA *1998;* Lithgow Perkins LLP, Crown Chambers, Princes Street, HARROGATE, HG1 1NJ.
•BRIGGS, Mr. Michael John, BA ACA *1986;* Moore and Smalley LLP, Richard House, 9 Winckley Square, PRESTON, PR1 3HP.
BRIGGS, Miss. Michelle, BSc ACA *1995;* 17 Stokesay walk, WEST BRIDGFORD, NOTTINGHAMSHIRE, NG2 6TZ.
BRIGGS, Mr. Neil David, BSc ACA *1990;* Western Power Distribution, Lamby Way, Rumney, CARDIFF, CF3 2EQ.
BRIGGS, Mr. Nicholas Howard, BSc ACA *1995;* Hurricane Exploration Plc, 82 Anstey Road, ALTON, GU34 2RL.
BRIGGS, Mr. Nigel David, BSc FCA *1977;* Hogg Robinson Group Plc, Global House, Victoria Street, BASINGSTOKE, HAMPSHIRE, RG21 3BT.
BRIGGS, Mrs. Patricia, MA FCA *1983;* Place Farm, Balnakettle, Newmachar, ABERDEEN, AB21 0UP.
BRIGGS, Mr. Paul Andrew, BA ACA *1990;* Heathcote, Bridle Road, Hannington, NORTHAMPTON, NN6 9SY.
BRIGGS, Mr. Paul William, BSc ACA *1984;* (Tax Fac), Arkady Feed (UK) Ltd, 5 Hercules Way, Leavesden, WATFORD, WD25 7GS.
BRIGGS, Miss. Pauline Anne, BSc ACA *1983;* 182a Ashley Road, Hale, ALTRINCHAM, CHESHIRE, WA15 9SF.
BRIGGS, Mr. Peter William, BA ACA *1981;* 2 Bradgate Road, Cropston, LEICESTER, LE7 7GA.
BRIGGS, Mr. Peter William, FCA *1972;* Peak View Farm Bristol Road, Rooksbridge, AXBRIDGE, SOMERSET, BS26 2TQ.
BRIGGS, Mr. Philip George, FCA *1983;* 12 Hambling Drive, Molescroft Grange, BEVERLEY, HU17 9GD.
BRIGGS, Mr. Philip Neil, BA ACA *1986;* Deeley Freed, 7 Whiteladies Road, BRISTOL, BS8 1NN.
•BRIGGS, Mr. Philip Peter, FCA *1994;* 10 Halliford Road, SUNBURY-ON-THAMES, MIDDLESEX, TW16 6DR.
BRIGGS, Mr. Philip Richard Peter, BSc FCA *1992;* 44 Broxash Road, LONDON, SW11 6AB.
BRIGGS, Mrs. Rachel Clare, BSc(Hons) ACA *2001;* with Grant Thornton UK LLP, 4 Hardman Square, Spinningfields, MANCHESTER, M3 3EB.
BRIGGS, Mrs. Ruth, BA ACA *1995;* Nutfield, Hudnall Common, Little Gaddesden, BERKHAMSTED, HERTFORDSHIRE, HP4 1QN.
•BRIGGS, Mr. Stephen Richard James, BA ACA *1989;* Pembroke Consulting, Clive House, 12-18 Queens Road, WEYBRIDGE, SURREY, KT13 9XB.
•BRIGGS, Mr. Steven Trevor, FCA CTA *1991;* Windle & Bowker Limited, Croft House, Station Road, BARNOLDSWICK, LANCASHIRE, BB18 5NA.
BRIGGS, Mr. Thomas Charles William, BSc ACA *2005;* 14 Beechwood Road, HARTSDALE, NY 10530, UNITED STATES.
BRIGGS, Mr. William Anthony, FCA *1958;* Bolivia Beg, The Dhoor, Ramsey, ISLE OF MAN, IM7 4ED. (Life Member)
BRIGGS, Mr. William George, FCA *1972;* 32 Sebastian Avenue Shenfield, BRENTWOOD, ESSEX, CM15 8PN.
BRIGGS, Mr. William Roberts, FCA *1966;* William R. Briggs, Druels Lodge, Chinnor Road, Bledlow Ridge, HIGH WYCOMBE, BUCKINGHAMSHIRE HP14 4AA.
BRIGGS HARVEY, Mrs. Elizabeth Ann, BSc ACA *2003;* 61 Chester Road, NORTHWOOD, MIDDLESEX, HA6 1BG.
BRIGHAM, Mr. David, FCA *1974;* (Member of Council 2002 - 2005), The Old Granary, 19 Church Street, Elloughton, BROUGH, NORTH HUMBERSIDE, HU15 1HT.
•BRIGHAM, Mr. Peter John, BSc FCA *1987;* (Tax Fac), 208 avenue des Agaves, 06190 ROQUEBRUNE CAP MARTIN, FRANCE.
BRIGHOUSE, Mr. David John, BSc ACA *1994;* 1 Oak Drive, Burscough, ORMSKIRK, L40 5BQ.
BRIGHOUSE, Mr. David William, FCA *1965;* 6 Kirklake Bank, LIVERPOOL, L37 2YJ.
BRIGHOUSE, Mr. John Barrie, FCA *1959;* Stanhope House, Leashaw, Holloway, MATLOCK, DE4 5AT. (Life Member)
BRIGHOUSE, Nicholas Denison, Esq CBE FCA *1957;* 17 The Ridings, Cringleford, NORWICH, NR4 6UJ. (Life Member)
BRIGHT, Mr. Christopher Francis, FCA *1959;* 48 Cutenhoe Road, LUTON, LU1 3NE. (Life Member)
BRIGHT, Mr. Christopher John, MA FCA *1962;* 9 Woodspring Road, LONDON, SW19 6PL. (Life Member)
BRIGHT, Mrs. Gail, BA ACA *2000;* 1 Orchard Drive, Fairburn, KNOTTINGLEY, WEST YORKSHIRE, WF11 9NA.
•BRIGHT, Miss. Heather Jane, BA ACA *1999;* with Moore Thompson, Bank House, Broad Street, SPALDING, LINCOLNSHIRE, PE11 1TB.
BRIGHT, Mr. Ian, BSc ACA *1982;* Lyndhurst, Bere Court, Pangbourne, READING, RG8 8HT.
BRIGHT, Miss. Joanna Kathleen Mary, BSc ACA *1987;* 3998 Sweet Bottom Drive, DULUTH, GA 30096, UNITED STATES.
BRIGHT, Mr. John Ben, BA(Hons) ACA *2004;* 14 Blossoms Heights, NORTHWICH, CHESHIRE, CW8 4TF.
BRIGHT, Mrs. Kathryn Jane, BA ACA *1989;* Pound End, Cedar Drive, Cookham, MAIDENHEAD, SL6 9DZ.
BRIGHT, Mrs. Laura Kathryn, ACA *2007;* 234 Lancaster Road, Heath Farm, SHREWSBURY, SY1 3NT.
BRIGHT, Mr. Maurice, FCA *1959;* 16 Portland Drive, Pedmore, STOURBRIDGE, DY9 0SD. (Life Member)
BRIGHT, Mr. Neil Irvine, BSc ACA *1989;* H M V Media Group Plc, Shelley House, 2-4 York Road, MAIDENHEAD, BERKSHIRE, SL6 1SR.
BRIGHT, Mr. Nicholas Peter, BSc ACA *2004;* with BDO LLP, 55 Baker Street, LONDON, W1U 7EU.
BRIGHT, Mr. Oliver, ACA *2008;* 30 Fairwater Grove West, Llandaff, CARDIFF, CF5 2JQ.
BRIGHT, Mrs. Rebecca Ruth Diane, BSc(Hons) ACA CTA *2004;* 7 Wyndham Park, Orton Wistow, PETERBOROUGH, PE2 6YD.
•BRIGHT, Mr. Richard Steven, ACA MAAT *1997;* RSM Tenon Audit Limited, 2 Wellington Place, LEEDS, LS1 4AP.
BRIGHT, Mr. Richard Thomas, BEng ACA *2002;* 10 Queen Street, Rawdon, LEEDS, LS19 6BG.
BRIGHT, Mr. Sidney Lewis, FCA *1971;* 77 Rosedene Gardens, Clayhall, ILFORD, ESSEX, IG2 6YD.
•BRIGHT, Mr. Stephen John, MA FCA *1981;* (Tax Fac), Stephen J. Bright, 10 High Croft, Lower Argyll Road, EXETER, EX4 4JQ. See also Britac Limited
BRIGHT, Mr. Stephen Michael, FCA ATII MCT *1974;* The Ferns, Histons Hill, Codsall, WOLVERHAMPTON, WV8 2EY.
BRIGHT, Mr. Vivian David, FCA *1975;* Hogg Shain & Scheck, Suite 404, 2255 Sheppard Avenue East, WILLOWDALE M2J 4Y1, ON, CANADA.
•BRIGHTLING, Mrs. Nicola Lynn, BSc ACA *1996;* (Tax Fac), Brightling & Co, Vine Hall Farm, Bethersden, ASHFORD, KENT, TN26 3JY.
BRIGHTMAN, Mrs. Michelle Samantha, BA ACA *1993;* 74 Dickens Drive, Old Stratford, MILTON KEYNES, MK19 6NN.
BRIGHTMAN, Mrs. Stephanie Lorraine, ACA *2008;* 56 Durford Road, PETERSFIELD, HAMPSHIRE, GU31 4HA.

•**BRIGHTMORE, Mr. Andrew Robert Paul, BA(Hons) ACA** *2001;* (Tax Fac), ARP Brightmore Limited, Fairholme Bungalow, Hathersage Road, Bamford, HOPE VALLEY, DERBYSHIRE S33 0EB.
BRIGHTMORE, Miss. Catherine Sarah, BSc ACA *1998;* with Yorkshire Building Society, Yorkshire House, Yorkshire Drive, BRADFORD, WEST YORKSHIRE, BD5 8LJ.
BRIGHTMORE, Miss. Susan Anne, BSc(Hons) ACA *2003;* with KPMG LLP, Bureau 1500, 600 boul De Maisonneuve Ouest, MONTREAL H3A OA3, QUE, CANADA.
BRIGHTON, Mr. Alan, ACA *1991;* 25 Church Lane, Tilbrook, HUNTINGDON, CAMBRIDGESHIRE, PE28 0JS.
•**BRIGHTON, Mr. Richard Thomas, BA FCA** *1973;* (Tax Fac), R.T Brighton Ltd, 12 Wensleydale, DROITWICH, WR9 8PF.
BRIGHTWELL, Miss. Amy Clare, BSc ACA *2003;* Flat 5, 1 Meadow Road Harborne, BIRMINGHAM, B17 8DH.
BRIGHTWELL, Mr. Colin Roger, FCA *1973;* Courland Automotive Practice LLP, 25 Eccleston Square, LONDON, SW1V 1NS.
•**BRIGINSHAW, Mr. Steven Jon Goddard, ACA FMAAT** *2007;* SJB Accounting Ltd, 24 Elstow Avenue, Caversham, READING, RG4 6RX.
BRIGNALL, Miss. Elizabeth Jane, BA ACA *1994;* 30 Castletown Road, West Kensington, LONDON, W14 9HQ.
BRIGNELL, Miss. Sonia Victoria, MPhil MRes BSc(Hons) ACA *2009;* Flat 11 Thring House, Stockwell Road, LONDON, SW9 9EU.
•**BRIGSTOCKE, Mr. Christopher Julian, BA ACA** *1989;* Collards, 2 High Street, KINGSTON UPON THAMES, KT1 1EY.
BRIGSTOCKE, Mr. David Hugh Charles, MA MSc ACA *1979;* 270 Park Avenue, NEW YORK, NY 10017, UNITED STATES.
BRILEY, Mr. Colin John, BSc FCA *1983;* Bethgil Leasowes Lane, HALESOWEN, B62 8QE.
BRILEY, Mr. Stephen Andrew, BSc FCA *1992;* (Tax Fac), 34 Reynolds Place, Blackheath, LONDON, SE3 8SX.
BRILLIANT, Mr. Victor Edward, FCA *1964;* 25 Manor Hall Avenue, LONDON, NW4 1PA.
BRIMACOMBE, Mr. John Robert Paul, BSc FCA ATII *1977;* 14 Ladderbanks Lane, Baildon, SHIPLEY, WEST YORKSHIRE, BD17 6RX. (Life Member)
•**BRIMACOMBE, Mr. Kenneth Michael, FCA** *1979;* with Simpkins Edwards LLP, Michael House, Castle Street, EXETER, EX4 3LQ.
BRIMACOMBE, Mr. Michael William, LLB FCA FRSA *1968;* Temple View, Rue Des Marrettes, St Martin, JERSEY, JE3 6DS. (Life Member)
BRIMACOMBE, Mrs. Sheridan Kay, FCA *1965;* 2 Orchard Mews, West End, STREET, SOMERSET, BA16 0LU.
BRIMBLE, Mr. David Drury, BSc ACA *1995;* 85 Broomleaf Road, FARNHAM, GU9 8DH.
BRIMBLE, Mr. John, BSc ACA *2000;* 17 Silverwood Close, BECKENHAM, BR3 1RN.
BRIMBLE, Miss. Yvonne Sylvia, BA FCA *1985;* 96 Midland Road, OLNEY, BUCKINGHAMSHIRE, MK46 4BP.
BRIMBLECOMBE, Dr. Andrew Mark, PhD BSc ACA *2006;* 43 Meadowsweet, Eaton Ford, ST. NEOTS, CAMBRIDGESHIRE, PE19 7GR.
BRIMBLECOMBE, Mr. Kevin, BSc ACA *2000;* 63 The Ridings, BURGESS HILL, WEST SUSSEX, RH15 0PL.
BRIMELOW, Miss. Celia Ann, BA ACA *1997;* 68 South Drive, MANCHESTER, M21 8FB.
BRIMELOW, Mr. John Richard, BA ACA *1991;* Marshplatt Cottage Marsh Lane, Crowton, NORTHWICH, CHESHIRE, CW8 2RL.
BRIMELOW, Mr. Richard John, BSc ACA *1993;* 25 Gordondale Road, LONDON, SW19 8EN.
BRIMICOMBE, Mr. Ian Martin, BSc ACA CTA *1991;* Astra Zeneca Ltd, 2 Kingdom Street, LONDON, W2 6BD.
BRIMLEY, Mr. John Alan, FCA *1966;* 5 Washington Close, REIGATE, RH2 9LT. (Life Member)
BRIMLOW, Mr. James Edward, MSci BA ACA *2007;* Reed Elsevier Group Plc, 2nd Floor, 1-3 Strand, LONDON, WC2N 5JR.
•**BRIMMELL, Mr. Peter James, FCA** *1993;* (Tax Fac), with Colin Gray & Co Limited, 26 Lower Kings Road, BERKHAMSTED, HERTFORDSHIRE, HP4 2AE.
BRIMMER, Mr. Kenneth Edward, BA FCA *1957;* 6 Robsons Cl, ENFIELD, EN2 8PZ. (Life Member)
BRINAN, Mr. David George, BA ACA *1986;* (Tax Fac), 30 Cromwell Avenue, BROMLEY, BR2 9AQ.
BRIND, Mr. David Leonard, BA(Hons) FCA *2000;* M & M Value Ltd, Unit 10, Second Avenue, Tyne Tunnel Trading Estate, NORTH SHIELDS, TYNE AND WEAR NE29 7SY.
BRIND, Mr. Timothy John, ACA *2008;* 409 Whirlowdale Road, SHEFFIELD, S11 9NF.
BRINDLE, Mr. Andrew David, BSc ACA *2000;* 20 Stakers Court, Milton Road, HARPENDEN, HERTFORDSHIRE, AL5 5PA.
BRINDLE, Miss. Helen Marie, BA ACA *2010;* 61 Marsworth Road, Pitstone, LEIGHTON BUZZARD, BEDFORDSHIRE, LU7 9AX.
BRINDLE, Mr. Ian, BA FCA *1969;* (Member of Council 1994 - 1997), Milestones, Packhorse Road, Bessels Green, SEVENOAKS, TN13 2QP.
BRINDLE, Mr. Ralph Francis, BA ACA *1986;* 8 Curlys Way, Swallowfield, READING, RG7 1QZ.
BRINDLE, Mr. Thomas, BA ACA *2005;* Roundel Manufacturing Ltd Harton Centre, 52 Harton Lane, SOUTH SHIELDS, TYNE AND WEAR, NE34 0EE.
BRINDLEY, Mr. Adrian Charles Grosvenor, BSc(Hons) ACA *2004;* 37 Winterbourne Road, SOLIHULL, B91 1LX.
BRINDLEY, Mr. Alan Robert, BSc ACA *1992;* 160 Cyncoed Road, CARDIFF, CF23 6BP.
BRINDLEY, Mr. Andrew, BSc ACA *1993;* 14 Kirkdale Road, HARPENDEN, HERTFORDSHIRE, AL5 2PT.
BRINDLEY, Ms. Cecilia Rachel, BA ACA *1994;* Via Crocera 25, 21018 SESTO CALENDE, VA, ITALY.
BRINDLEY, Mr. Gordon Thomas, FCA *1962;* 2 Endwood Drive, SOLIHULL, B91 1NX.
BRINDLEY, Mr. Graham Martin, BSc ACA *1980;* 9 Yew Tree Close, Clayton le Dale, BLACKBURN, BB1 9HP.
BRINDLEY, Miss. Helen, ACA *2008;* 1 Paddock Close, Ackworth, PONTEFRACT, WEST YORKSHIRE, WF7 7RL.
•**BRINDLEY, Mr. Mark Geoffrey, MPhys ACA MInstP** *2008;* Business & Risk Solutions Limited, Forge House, Stodmarsh Road, CANTERBURY, KENT, CT3 4AG.
•**BRINDLEY, Mr. Maurice William, BSc FCA** *1976;* Brindley Millen Limited, 167 Turners Hill, Cheshunt, WALTHAM CROSS, HERTFORDSHIRE, EN8 9BH.
•①**BRINDLEY, Mr. Paul Ronald, FCA** *1985;* Midlands Business Recovery, Alpha House, Tipton Street, Sedgley, DUDLEY, WEST MIDLANDS DY3 1HE.
BRINDLEY, Mr. Peter Henry, FCA *1965;* 1 Albany Close, West Bergholt, COLCHESTER, CO6 3LE.
BRINDLEY, Mrs. Philippa Lucy, MSc BSc ACA *1999;* 2014 42nd Avenue SW, CALGARY T2T 2M7, AB, CANADA.
BRINE, Mrs. Jane Louise, BA ACA *1992;* Rockcliff House, Thorpe Lane, Fylingthorpe, WHITBY, NORTH YORKSHIRE, YO22 4TH.
•**BRINE, Mr. John, FCA** *1963;* Brine & Co, PO Box 6210, LEIGHTON BUZZARD, BEDFORDSHIRE, LU7 0ZN.
BRINE, Mr. Paul Andrew, BA ACA *1987;* H M C Ltd, 10 Howlett Way, THETFORD, NORFOLK, IP24 1HZ.
BRINGLOE, Mr. Mark Andrew, BA ACA *1998;* 31 Tanfield Drive, Radcliffe, MANCHESTER, M26 1GY.
BRINHAM, Mr. Edward, MA FCA *1964;* Shag Rock House, Lincombe Drive, TORQUAY, TQ1 2LP. (Life Member)
BRINING, Mr. Michael David, MA FCA MRPharmS *1961;* 44 Green Lane, Burnham, SLOUGH, SL1 8DX. (Life Member)
BRINKLEY, Mrs. Linda Anne, BSc FCA FCCA *1979;* 13 The Croft, DIDCOT, OXFORDSHIRE, OX11 8HS.
BRINKMAN, Miss. Claire Louise, MA MSc ACA *2003;* Frontier Economics Ltd, Mid City Place, 71 High Holborn, LONDON, WC1V 6DA.
BRINN, Mr. Nigel James, BSc FCA *1969;* 1A Oatlands Drive, HARROGATE, HG2 8JT. (Life Member)
BRINSDEN, Miss. Anna, BA ACA *2004;* 24 Langwith Valley Road, Collingham, WETHERBY, LS22 5DW.
BRINSMEAD, Mr. Peter Denis, FCA *1958;* 38 Oaktree Court, Portland Drive, Willen, MILTON KEYNES, MK15 9LP. (Life Member)
BRINTON, Mr. David Harry, BCom FCA *1979;* 7 Dene Lane, Lower Bourne, FARNHAM, GU10 3PW.
BRIODY, Mr. Thomas, FCA *1973;* Rolls-Royce Plc, PO Box 31, DERBY, DE24 8BJ.
BRISBANE, Mr. Kerry Thomas, BSc ACA *2007;* Barclays Capital, 10 South Colonnade, LONDON, E14 4PU.
BRISBIN, Mrs. Anne Catherine, BCom ACA AMCT *2002;* with PricewaterhouseCoopers LLP, 1 Embankment Place, LONDON, WC2N 6RH.
BRISBOURNE, Mr. Robert James, MA ACA *2001;* Brake Cottage, Bull Lane, Chalfont St. Peter, GERRARDS CROSS, BUCKINGHAMSHIRE, SL9 8RZ.
BRISCO, Mr. Stuart Alexander, BCom ACA *1991;* 1 The Kirklands, West Kirby, WIRRAL, CHESHIRE, CH48 7HW.
•**BRISCOE, Mr. David, FCA** *1970;* Stables Thompson & Briscoe Ltd, Lowther House, Lowther Street, KENDAL, CUMBRIA, LA9 4DX.
BRISCOE, Mrs. Fiona Margery, BSc ACA *1982;* Tormore, 27 Leigh Hill Rd, COBHAM, KT11 2HS.
BRISENDEN, Mr. Robert John, BSc FCA CTA *1981;* (Tax Fac), Solvay Interox Ltd, Baronet Road, WARRINGTON, CHESHIRE, WA4 6HA.
BRISKI, Mr. Andrew Michael, MA ACA *1988;* MARINA BAY TOWER #66-06, 2 MARINA BOIULEVARD, SINGAPORE 018987, SINGAPORE.
BRISLEY, Mr. Neil Kevin, MA FCA *1993;* 419 Winchester Drive, WATERLOO N2T 1H6, ON, CANADA.
•**BRISLEY, Mr. Roger Alan, BCom FCA** *1980;* (Tax Fac), Leonard Bye, 2 Romanby Court, NORTHALLERTON, NORTH YORKSHIRE, DL7 8PG.
•**BRISON, Mr. Stuart Alexander, BSc ACA** *1989;* Daishow Limited, Hirado 4-5-23, Totsuka-ku, YOKOHAMA, 244-0802 JAPAN.
BRISTER, Miss. Susan, LLB ACA *1998;* 21 Westhorpe Road, LONDON, SW15 1QH.
BRISTLEY, Mrs. Helen, BSc ACA *1992;* 9 Collings Place, NEWMARKET, Suffolk, CB8 0EX.
BRISTLIN, Mr. Anthony, ACA *2009;* 5 Smallwood Forge, Smallwood, SANDBACH, CHESHIRE, CW11 2UF.
•**BRISTOL, Mr. John Le Varrie, FCA** *1977;* Caleruega 61 11-A, 28033 MADRID, SPAIN.
BRISTON, Prof. Richard Jeremy, BSc FCA *1962;* Barrow House, Thornton Street, BARROW-UPON-HUMBER, SOUTH HUMBERSIDE, DN19 7DG. (Life Member)
•**BRISTOW, Mr. Alan Charles, BA ACA** *1985;* ICON Corporate Finance Limited, 53 Davies Street, LONDON, W1K 5JH.
BRISTOW, Mr. Alan Lindsay, FCA *1964;* Budds Oast, Mote Road, Shipbourne, TONBRIDGE, TN11 9QD.
BRISTOW, Mr. Alexander William, BSc ACA *1994;* Flat 1, 94 East Dulwich Road, LONDON, SE22 9AT.
BRISTOW, Mr. Andrew, BSc ACA *1988;* 22 Garden Road, BROMLEY, BR1 3LX.
•**BRISTOW, Mr. Anthony Norman, MA FCA** *1978;* Anthony N. Bristow, 84 Wisbech Road, Outwell, WISBECH, CAMBRIDGESHIRE, PE14 8PF.
BRISTOW, Mr. Christopher John, BA FCA *1978;* The Byre Coupass Cottages, Feckenham, REDDITCH, WORCESTERSHIRE, B96 6HW.
BRISTOW, Mrs. Claire Margaret, BSc ACA *1988;* (Tax Fac), 22 Garden Road, BROMLEY, BR1 3LX.
BRISTOW, Mr. David Edward, BA ACA *1992;* 9 Forest Close, North Baddesley, SOUTHAMPTON, SO52 9GW.
BRISTOW, Mr. Donald Edwin, FCA *1951;* 21 Withdean Court Avenue, BRIGHTON, BN1 6YF. (Life Member)
BRISTOW, Mr. Keith, FCA *1975;* 7 Rue du Lavoir, 85390 CHAVAGNES LES REDOUX, FRANCE.
BRISTOW, Mr. Matthew David, LLB ACA *2001;* BMW (Gb) Ltd, Ellesfield Avenue, BRACKNELL, RG12 8TA.
BRISTOW, Mrs. Michelle Susan, BSc ACA *1999;* 3 Bendeng Close, FLEET, HAMPSHIRE, GU51 1ET.
BRISTOW, Mr. Nicholas John, FCA *1971;* 5 Tuffnells Way, HARPENDEN, HERTFORDSHIRE, AL5 3HJ.
BRISTOW, Mr. Peter Lindsay, BA ACA *1998;* 3 Bendeng Close, FLEET, HAMPSHIRE, GU51 1ET.
BRISTOW, Mr. Richard Lawrence, BCom FCA *1953;* 11 Hampstead Way, LONDON, NW11 7JE. (Life Member)
•**BRISTOW, Mr. Roy Philip, FCA** *1975;* (Tax Fac), Williams Giles Limited, 12 Conqueror Court, SITTINGBOURNE, KENT, ME10 5BH.
BRITAIN, Mr. William Rossiter, BA FCA *1978;* 13 Bisham Gardens, Highgate, LONDON, N6 6DJ.
BRITCHFORD, Mr. Donald Edward, FCA *1953;* P.O. BOX N7505, NASSAU, BAHAMAS. (Life Member)
BRITLAND, Mr. James, BEng ACA *2010;* Flat 1, 859 Garratt Lane, LONDON, SW17 0LX.
BRITNELL, Miss. Louise, BSc ACA *2005;* 4 Rosedale Road, STOCKPORT, CHESHIRE, SK4 2QU.
BRITNELL, Mrs. Susan, BSc FCA *1994;* 11 Sun Crescent, Oakley, AYLESBURY, BUCKINGHAMSHIRE, HP18 9RF.
BRITNER, Mr. Adam, MA ACA *1998;* Imperial Tobacco Ltd, PO Box 244, BRISTOL, BS99 7UJ.
BRITO, Mr. Joseph Michael Suresh, LLB FCA MBA *1970;* Aitken Spence & Co, Vauxhall Towers, 305 Vauxhall Street, 2 COLOMBO, SRI LANKA.
BRITON, Mrs. Catherine, BEng ACA *1997;* 5 Belford Road, SUNDERLAND, SR2 7TJ.
BRITS, Mr. Barry Raymond, BSc ACA *1997;* International Power America Inc., 62 Forest Street Suite 102, MARLBOROUGH, MA 01752, UNITED STATES.
BRITT, Mr. Andrew John, BA ACA *1991;* 15 Lyminge Gardens, Wandsworth, LONDON, SW18 3JS.
•**BRITT, Mrs. Margaret, ACA** *1984;* Britt & Keehan, 33 Grimwade Avenue, CROYDON, CR0 5DJ. See also Westcliff Finance Limited
•**BRITT, Mr. Paul Eric, ACA** *1986;* Baker Britt Helm Ltd, Westcliff House, 106 Southlands Road, BROMLEY, BR2 9QY. See also Westcliff Finance Limited
BRITTAIN, Mr. Andrew Colin, BA FCA *1998;* with Ernst & Young LLP, Apex Plaza, Forbury Road, READING, RG1 1YE.
BRITTAIN, Mr. David Charles, FCA *1965;* 27 Bramley Way, Bidford-on-Avon, ALCESTER, WARWICKSHIRE, B50 4QG.
BRITTAIN, Mr. George Austin, BSc FCA *1975;* Rose Cottage, Spa Lane, Boston Spa, WETHERBY, LS23 6AG.
BRITTAIN, Mr. Henry William, FCA *1949;* 27 Dean Moor Road, Hazel Grove, STOCKPORT, CHESHIRE, SK7 5LW. (Life Member)
BRITTAIN, Mr. Jeremy Paul, BA FCA *1984;* Lynwood, Little Aston Park Road, Little Aston, SUTTON COLDFIELD, WEST MIDLANDS, B74 3BZ.
•**BRITTAIN, Mr. John Jeremy Mitchell, FCA** *1959;* (Tax Fac), Mitchell Brittain, 6 Lon Farchog, Upper Breeze Hill, Benllech, TYN-Y-GONGL, GWYNEDD LL74 8UL.
BRITTAIN, Mrs. Maura Elizabeth, BSc(Econ) ACA *1998;* 7 Duncan Drive, WOKINGHAM, RG40 2JX.
BRITTAIN, Mr. Michael Rodney, FCA *1976;* Stoney Cross Lodge, Ringwood Road, Stoney Cross, LYNDHURST, SO43 7GN.
BRITTAIN, Mr. Robert Alan, FCA *1960;* 143 Woodbury Road, HALESOWEN, B62 9AN.
BRITTAIN, Mr. Robert Anthony, BA FCA *1980;* 1 Vine Street, LONDON, W1J 0AH.
BRITTAIN, Mr. Robert William, BSc ACA *2005;* 11 Paget Close, Needham Market, IPSWICH, IP6 8XF.
BRITTAIN, Mr. Roger John, FCA *1963;* 14 The Paddock, Eaton Ford, ST. NEOTS, CAMBRIDGESHIRE, PE19 7SA. (Life Member)
BRITTAIN, Mr. Roy Martin, FCA *1969;* 7-41/ 43 Mount Street, Kingsview Apartments, PERTH, WA 6005, AUSTRALIA. (Life Member)
BRITTEN, Mr. Christopher Andrew, FCA *1975;* Nesfield, The Ballands South, Fetcham, LEATHERHEAD, SURREY, KT22 9EP.
BRITTEN, Mrs. Jayne Lesley, BA ACA *1983;* Rowan Preparatory School Rowan Hill, 6 Fitzalan Road Claygate, ESHER, KT10 0LX.
BRITTEN, Mrs. Joanna Claire, BA ACA *2002;* 28 Blackheath Grove, LONDON, SE3 0DH.
•**BRITTEN, Mrs. Kathryn Jane, BSc FCA** *1979;* KPMG LLP, 15 Canada Square, LONDON, E14 5GL. See also KPMG Europe LLP
BRITTEN, Mr. Matthew William, BSc ACA *2002;* HIGHLANDS, 2 TAMARISK HILL, SMITHS FL03, BERMUDA.
BRITTEN, Mr. Norman Walter, FCA *1975;* 19 College Gardens, Dulwich Village, LONDON, SE21 7BE.
BRITTEN, Mr. Richard Charles, BA ACA *1992;* Park House, Moor Park, Beckwithshaw, HARROGATE, NORTH YORKSHIRE, HG3 1QN.
•**BRITTER, Mrs. Helen Mary Harman, BA ACA** *1995;* Diverset Ltd, Canada House, 272 Field End Road, RUISLIP, MIDDLESEX, HA4 9NA.
•**BRITTER, Mr. Mark Christopher Harman, BSc ACA** *1995;* Diverset Ltd, Canada House, 272 Field End Road, RUISLIP, MIDDLESEX, HA4 9NA.
BRITTO, Mr. Alvee Thomas, BEng ACA *2010;* 21 Bergholt Crescent, LONDON, N16 5JE.
BRITTO, Mr. Keith Stuart, BSc ACA PMP *1999;* Bank of America Merrill Lynch, 10/F, Devon House, 979 King's Road, QUARRY BAY, HONG KONG ISLAND HONG KONG SAR.
BRITTO, Mr. Stephen, BEng ACA *2004;* Hilco UK Ltd, 80 New Bond Street, LONDON, W1S 1SB.
BRITTON, Mr. Adrian Mark, BSc FCA *1978;* Westerleigh Group plc, Chapel View, Westerleigh Road, Westerleigh, BRISTOL, BS37 8QP.
BRITTON, Miss. Andrea Louise, BSc(Hons) ACA *2002;* 22 Dale Close, HITCHIN, HERTFORDSHIRE, SG4 9AS.
BRITTON, Mr. Andrew Ronald, BSc FCA *1983;* Box 5058, WHANGAREI 0140, NEW ZEALAND.
•**BRITTON, Mrs. Angela Winifred, BA FCA** *1975;* (Tax Fac), Angela Britton Consulting, 22 Sennen Place, Port Solent, PORTSMOUTH, HAMPSHIRE, PO6 4SZ.
BRITTON, Mr. Anthony George, BA FCA *1960;* Bowstones, Linton, ROSS-ON-WYE, HR9 7RY. (Life Member)

•**BRITTON, Ms. Caroline Louise, MA ACA** *1992;* Deloitte LLP, Hill House, 1 Little New Street, LONDON, EC4A 3TR. See also Deloitte & Touche LLP
BRITTON, Mr. David James, BSc ACA *1999;* 16 Cambridge Square, Earlswood, REDHILL, RH1 6TG.
BRITTON, Mr. David John, FCA *1968;* 34 Windermere Drive, ALDERLEY EDGE, CHESHIRE, SK9 7UP.
•**BRITTON, Mr. Derek Oswald, FCA** *1955;* Britton & Co, 1 Chatsworth Manor, Ladybrook Road, Bramhall, STOCKPORT, CHESHIRE SK7 3NB.
BRITTON, Mrs. Heather Dawn, BSc ACA CTA *2001;* (Tax Fac), 7 Turnpike, Sampford Peverell, TIVERTON, DEVON, EX16 7BN.
BRITTON, Mr. James Martin, MA FCA *1980;* Limetrees, Dippenhall Street, Crondall, FARNHAM, SURREY, GU10 5NX.
BRITTON, Mr. James Simon Vaughan, MA(Hons) MSc ACA *2001;* 31 Bangalore Street, LONDON, SW15 1QD.
BRITTON, Mr. Jason Kevin, BA ACA *1997;* 6 Henson Close, Radcliffe-on-Trent, NOTTINGHAM, NG12 2JQ.
BRITTON, Mrs. Jean Catherine, FCA *1977;* KRF Ltd, 6 Bilton Road, RUGBY, WARWICKSHIRE, CV22 7AB.
BRITTON, Mr. John Derek, FCA *1976;* 3/1a Parliament Lane, GIBRALTAR, GIBRALTAR.
BRITTON, Mr. John Ernest Alan, BSc FCA *1977;* 432 Rochdale Old Road, BURY, LANCASHIRE, BL9 7TF.
BRITTON, Mr. Jonathan, BA ACA *1980;* Lloyds Banking Group, 2nd Floor, Alder Castle House, 10 Noble Street, LONDON, EC2V 7ED.
BRITTON, Mrs. Karen Mary, ACA *1990;* 54 Westwood Gardens, Chandler's Ford, EASTLEIGH, HAMPSHIRE, SO53 1FN.
BRITTON, Mrs. Linda Caroline Hunt, ACA *1984;* 58 Lillieshall Road, Clapham, LONDON, SW4 0LP.
BRITTON, Mrs. Nicola Jane, BSc ACA *2000;* 16 Cambridge Square, Royal Earlswood Park, REDHILL, RH1 6TG.
BRITTON, Mr. Nigel David, BA ACA *1992;* 32-34 Highgate Avenue, Fulwood, PRESTON, PR2 8LN.
BRITTON, Mr. Paul Jonathan, BA ACA *1991;* Next plc, Desford Road, Enderby, LEICESTER, LE19 4AT.
BRITTON, Mrs. Virginia Elspeth Vere, BA ACA *1988;* HBOS Plc, 10 Canons Way, BRISTOL, BS1 5LN.
BRITZE, Mr. Jens Christian, LLM ACA *2001;* Soevang 33, 2970 HOERSHOLM, DENMARK.
•**BRIZZOLARA, Mr. Martin John, BA FCA** *1982;* Bradley & Co, 18 Kingfisher Reach, Boroughbridge, YORK, YO51 9JS.
BROAD, Miss. Allison Susan, LLB FCA *1992;* with ICAEW, Metropolitan House, 321 Avebury Boulevard, MILTON KEYNES, MK9 2FZ.
BROAD, Mr. Andrew St John, BA ACA *1995;* 11 Foxleigh, Marlow Hill, HIGH WYCOMBE, BUCKINGHAMSHIRE, HP11 1QD.
BROAD, Mr. Donald Andrew Robertson, BA *1976;* Smiths Group plc, 2nd Floor, 80 Victoria Street, LONDON, SW1E 5JL.
BROAD, Mr. Gary Peter, FCA *1983;* (Tax Fac), Mallam House, 19 Castle Road, CAMBERLEY, GU15 2DS.
BROAD, Mr. Horace Wilfrid, FCA *1937;* 50 Ocean Heights, 22 Boscombe Cliff Road, BOURNEMOUTH, BH5 1LA. (Life Member)
BROAD, Mr. James, ACA *2011;* 244 Clarendon Park Road, LEICESTER, LE2 3AG.
BROAD, Mr. James Nicholas, BA(Hons) ACA *2001;* DEB Ltd, Denby Hall Way, Denby, RIPLEY, DERBYSHIRE, DE5 8JZ.
BROAD, Mrs. Jenny Lynn, ACA *1988;* Mallam House, Castle Road, CAMBERLEY, SURREY, GU15 2DS.
BROAD, Mrs. Lisa Jayne, BSc(Hons) ACA *2000;* Stoneycroft Clay Lake Endon, STOKE-ON-TRENT, STAFFORDSHIRE, ST9 9DD.
BROAD, Mrs. Melissa Ruth, BA ACA *1989;* Russet Glade, Little Sutton Lane, Langley, SLOUGH, SL3 8AN.
BROAD, Mr. Neil Anthony, BCom ACA *1979;* Elliott Group Ltd, Manor Drive, PETERBOROUGH, PE4 7AP.
BROAD, Mr. Nicholas Ian, BA FCA *1972;* 70 Westbourne Road, SOUTHPORT, PR8 2JB.
BROAD, Mr. Philip Henry, MEng ACA CF *2003;* 9 Marriott Lodge Close, ADDLESTONE, KT15 2XD.
BROAD, Mr. Robert, LLB ACA *2007;* Apartment 2905, 610 Granville Street, VANCOUVER V6C 3T3, BC, CANADA.
BROAD, Mr. Robert Thomas, FCA *1972;* 81 Milton Mount Avenue, CRAWLEY, RH10 3DP.
BROAD, Miss. Sarah Clare, BA ACA *2001;* S T A Travel Priory House, 6 Wrights Lane, LONDON, W8 6TA.
•**BROADBELT, Mr. Richard Derek, BA(Hons) ACA** *1996;* KPMG LLP, 15 Canada Square, LONDON, E14 5GL. See also KPMG Europe LLP
BROADBENT, Mr. Adam, BA(Hons) ACA *2010;* 22 Larch Road, Denton, MANCHESTER, M34 6DZ.
BROADBENT, Mrs. Alison Claire, BSc ACA *1990;* 6 Pinewood Road, CHELMSFORD, MA 01824, UNITED STATES.
BROADBENT, Mr. Andrew Benjamin, FCA *1972;* 20 Whitehall Road, Evington, LEICESTER, LE5 6GH.
BROADBENT, Mrs. Ann Sarah, MA ACA *1993;* 53 Albion Road, Pitstone, LEIGHTON BUZZARD, BEDFORDSHIRE, LU7 9AY.
BROADBENT, Mr. Bevan Winston, FCA *1961;* Rydal, Little Meadow Close, Prestbury, MACCLESFIELD, SK10 4HA.
BROADBENT, Mrs. Carole, FCA *1981;* 21 Elmfield Drive, Skelmanthorpe, HUDDERSFIELD, HD8 9BT.
BROADBENT, Mr. Darren Wayne, BSc(Hons) ACA ATT *2004;* (Tax Fac), Forrest Burlinson, 20 Owl Lane, Shawcross, DEWSBURY, WEST YORKSHIRE, WF12 7RQ.
BROADBENT, Mr. David, BSc FCA *1974;* 2 Fletsand Road, WILMSLOW, SK9 2AB. (Life Member)
BROADBENT, Mr. David Edward Spencer, BA ACA *1993;* Provident International Limited, 3 Leeds City Office Park, Meadow Lane, LEEDS, LS11 5BD.
BROADBENT, Mr. Frank Alan, FCA *1953;* 2 Kenway, Rainford, ST.HELENS, MERSEYSIDE, WA11 8AX. (Life Member)
BROADBENT, Mr. Gregory James Foster, BEng ACA *1991;* 49 Brodrick Road, Wandsworth, LONDON, SW17 7DX.
BROADBENT, Mrs. Helen Mary, BA ACA *1982;* with Peters Elworthy & Moore, Salisbury House, Station Road, CAMBRIDGE, CB1 2LA.
BROADBENT, Mr. Hugh Atherton, FCA *1958;* Friar Mere House, Rochdale Road, Denshaw, OLDHAM, OL3 5UE. (Life Member)
BROADBENT, Mrs. Jenny Lynne, FCA *1979;* 7 Mayfield Road, Girton, CAMBRIDGE, CB3 0PH.
BROADBENT, Mr. Mark, BSc ACA *1996;* The Cottage Stapleton Lane, Kirkby Mallory, LEICESTER, LE9 7QJ.
BROADBENT, Mr. Matthew Quintin, BA ACA *1991;* Sadler's Cottage, 96 North Street, Middle Barton, CHIPPING NORTON, OXFORDSHIRE, OX7 7BJ.
BROADBENT, Mr. Neil Webster, FCA *1965;* The Barn Nova Lane, Birstall, BATLEY, WEST YORKSHIRE, WF17 9LD.
BROADBENT, Mr. Peter James, BSc ACA *2009;* 90 Chartfield Avenue, LONDON, SW15 6HQ.
BROADBENT, Mrs. Rebecca Mary, BSc ACA *1991;* 27 Ash Close, WATLINGTON, OXFORDSHIRE, OX49 5LW.
BROADBENT, Mr. Richard Franklin, BSc ACA *1984;* 16 Lorraine Court, Camborne Road, SUTTON, SM2 6RE.
BROADBENT, Mr. Robert Michael, BSc ACA *2002;* 27 Goosehills Road, Burbage, HINCKLEY, LEICESTERSHIRE, LE10 2RY.
BROADBENT, Mr. Stephen Michael, BSc ACA *1982;* 3 Spinney Close, Boughton, NORTHAMPTON, NN2 8SD.
•**BROADBENT, Mr. Walter Louis Farndon, BSc ACA** *1988;* Louis Broadbent Limited, Cleevehead, Old Coach Road, Cross, AXBRIDGE, SOMERSET BS26 2EG.
BROADBERY, Miss. Joanne, ACA *2007;* 13 Greenfield Close, Westhoughton, BOLTON, BL5 3UU.
BROADBRIDGE, Mr. Desmond Anthony, FCA *1971;* 47 Cook Road, Tilgate, CRAWLEY, RH10 5DJ.
BROADBRIDGE, Mr. Michael, BSc ACA *2009;* 10 Byron Avenue, SUTTON, SM1 3RA.
BROADFIELD, Mr. Andrew David, BSc(Hons) ACA *2003;* Barclays Capital, 5 North Colonnade, LONDON, E14 4BB.
BROADFIELD, Mrs. Victoria Joy, BSc(Hons) ACA *2003;* 5 Addison Close, Petts Wood, ORPINGTON, KENT, BR5 1DS.
BROADFOOT, Mr. Andrew John, MA ACA *1980;* Bali View C7 No 11, Jl Cirendeu Raya 46, Ciputat, JAKARTA, 15419, INDONESIA.
BROADFOOT, Ms. Eleena Joy, ACA CA(AUS) *2010;* 25a Vera Road, LONDON, SW6 6QP.
BROADHEAD, Mr. George Warwick Buckley, FCA *1950;* Dormers, Stowey Bottom, Bishop Sutton, BRISTOL, BS39 5TL. (Life Member)
BROADHEAD, Mr. James Edward, FCA *1970;* (Tax Fac), Flat 2, Trinity Gate, 7 Wimborne Road, BOURNEMOUTH, BH2 6LU.
•**BROADHEAD, Mr. Mark, ACA CA(NZ)** *2010;* (Tax Fac), Tax 24-7.Com Limited, PO Box 47-118, LONDON, W6 0NX.
BROADHEAD, Mr. Michael Robinson, FCA *1968;* Apartment 24 The Weaving Hall, 48 Sharp Lane Almondbury, HUDDERSFIELD, HD4 6TJ. (Life Member)
BROADHEAD, Mr. Tymon Piers, MA ACA *1993;* Conifers, Burtons Lane, CHALFONT ST. GILES, BUCKINGHAMSHIRE, HP8 4BB.
BROADHURST, Mr. Anthony Mark, BSc(Econ) FCA *2000;* Barnett Waddingham Llp, Cheapside House, 138 Cheapside, LONDON, EC2V 6BW.
BROADHURST, Mr. Christopher John, FCA *1971;* 129 Harrowdene Gardens, TEDDINGTON, TW11 0DL.
BROADHURST, Mr. Clive Andrew, BSc ACA *1994;* 30 Teasel Way, Claines, WORCESTER, WR3 7LD.
BROADHURST, Mr. Colin, FCA *1969;* 5/F M Thai Tower, All Seasons Place, 87 Wireless Road, BANGKOK 10330, THAILAND.
BROADHURST, Mr. Daniel James, BA ACA *2010;* 26 Tarragon Close, LONDON, SE14 6DL.
BROADHURST, Mr. Iain James, BA ACA *1996;* 31 Talavera Road, Brockhill Village, Norton, WORCESTER, WR5 2SB.
BROADHURST, Mr. Ian Kevan Averill, FCA CTA *1962;* Langenfeld, 13 Meadow Way, Church Lawton, STOKE-ON-TRENT, ST7 3EW. (Life Member)
BROADHURST, Mr. James Reginald, BA FCA *1957;* 4 Altenbrook, 22 Harrop Road, Hale, ALTRINCHAM, CHESHIRE, WA15 9BZ. (Life Member)
BROADHURST, Mrs. Jane, BA ACA *1996;* 40 Elderberry Way, Almondsbury, BRISTOL, BS32 4FH.
BROADHURST, Mrs. Jillian Elizabeth, BSc ACA *1997;* Grant Thornton, Bradenham Manor, Bradenham, HIGH WYCOMBE, BUCKINGHAMSHIRE, HP14 4HF.
BROADHURST, Mr. John David, BSc ACA *1996;* 40 Elderberry Way, Almondsbury, BRISTOL, BS32 4FH.
BROADHURST, Mrs. Katherine Claire Thompson, ACA *2009;* 42 Cheriton Drive, Thornhill, CARDIFF, CF14 9DF.
BROADHURST, Mr. Norman Neill, FCA FCT *1965;* Hobroyd, Penny Bridge, ULVERSTON, LA12 7TD.
•**BROADHURST, Mr. Paul, FCA** *1965;* Paul Broadhurst & Co, 74-76 High Street, WINSFORD, CW7 2AP.
BROADHURST, Mr. Thomas Daniel, BA(Hons) ACA CFA *2001;* Flat 4 47 Chalcot Road, LONDON, NW1 8LS.
BROADLEY, Mrs. Gillian Elaine, BSc ACA *1987;* 5 Ernle Road, Wimbledon, LONDON, SW20 0HH.
•**BROADLEY, Mr. Ian Peter, BSc FCA** *1990;* PCLG Limited, Equinox House, Clifton Park Avenue, Clifton Park, Shipton Road, YORK YO30 5PA.
BROADLEY, Mr. James, BA(Hons) ACA *2011;* 28 Ballater Road, LONDON, SW2 5QR.
BROADLEY, Mr. James Roland, MSc BBA ACA *2010;* Doreen, 1 Orchard Street, CANTERBURY, CT2 8AP.
BROADLEY, Mr. John Maxwell, BA FCA *1983;* Downlands Liability Management LTD, DLM House, Downland Business Park, Lyons Way, WORTHING, WEST SUSSEX BN14 9RX.
BROADLEY, Mr. Jonathan Nicholas Venn, BSc ACA *2000;* with National Audit Office, 157-197 Buckingham Palace Road, Victoria, LONDON, SW1W 9SP.
BROADLEY, Mr. Philip Arthur John, MA FCA *1987;* Old Mutual Plc Millennium Bridge House, 2 Lambeth Hill, LONDON, EC4V 4GG.
BROADLEY, Mr. Robert, BSc ACA *1989;* Trelleborg Sealing Solutions, International Drive, Tewkesbury Business Park, TEWKESBURY, GLOUCESTERSHIRE, GL20 8UQ.
BROADWAY, Mr. Alan Keith, FCA *1965;* 83 Tilehouse Green Lane, Knowle, SOLIHULL, B93 9EU. (Life Member)
•**BROADWAY, Mr. Alistair Brice, FCA** *1967;* (Tax Fac), Broadway & Co, Nadder House, Lower Road, Bemerton, SALISBURY, SP2 9NB.
BROADWAY, Mr. Michael Ronald, FCA *1967;* Bay Tree House, Dacre Banks, HARROGATE, NORTH YORKSHIRE, HG3 4EN.
BROADWAY, Mr. Paul Nathan, MA ACA *1992;* 39 Maxwell Road, Charminster, BOURNEMOUTH, BH9 1DQ.
BROADWAY, Mr. Timothy Keith, BA(Hons) ACA *2000;* 11 St. Lawrence Close, Hedge End, SOUTHAMPTON, SO30 2TJ.
BROADWELL, Mr. Alan, FCA *1961;* 15 Dalby Avenue, Bushby, LEICESTER, LE7 9RE.
BROATCH, Mr. James Malcolm, FCA *1953;* 64 Gatton Rd., REIGATE, RH2 0HL. (Life Member)
BROCHWELL, Mrs. Deborah Jane, BEd ACA *1993;* Holly Cottage, Berries Road, Cookham, MAIDENHEAD, SL6 9SD.
BROCK, Mr. Aaron Justin James, BEng ACA *1997;* 6 Broadmead Crescent, Bishopston, SWANSEA, SA3 3BA.
BROCK, Mr. Alan Peter, BA ACA *1985;* 37 Newfield Lane, Dore, SHEFFIELD, S17 3DB.
BROCK, Miss. Alison Jane, BA ACA *1994;* 6th Floor, Deloitte & Touche, 2 New Street Square, LONDON, EC4A 3BZ.
BROCK, Mr. Colin Leslie, FCA *1960;* 53 Brownhill Road, Chandlers Ford, EASTLEIGH, SO53 2EH. (Life Member)
BROCK, Mr. Gareth Simon, BSc ACA *1997;* RCI Financial Services Ltd, Eagle House 78 St Albans Road, WATFORD, HERTFORDSHIRE, WD17 1AF.
BROCK, Mrs. Janet Claire, MA ACA *1982;* Flat 50, Hornby House, Clayton Street, LONDON, SE11 5DB.
BROCK, Mr. Jonathan Mark Carey, MA ACA *1995;* Flat 1, 33 Edith Road, LONDON, W14 0SU.
BROCK, Mr. Keith James, BA ACA *2000;* 267 Mallorca Way, SAN FRANCISCO, CA 94123, UNITED STATES.
BROCK, Miss. Lisa Mary, BSc ACA *1996;* 58 Alexander St, ALEXANDRIA, NSW 2015, AUSTRALIA.
BROCK, Ms. Sarah Jane, ACA CTA *2002;* (Tax Fac), 10 Claremont Road, Claygate, ESHER, KT10 0PL.
•**BROCK, Mrs. Sarah Louise, BA FCA** *1987;* Atkin Macredie & Co Ltd, Westbourne Place, 23 Westbourne Road, SHEFFIELD, S10 2QQ.
BROCK, Mr. Stratton James, BSc ACA *1998;* Molenberglaan 3, 3080 TERVUREN, BELGIUM.
BROCK, Miss. Vikki Catherine, BSc ACA *2002;* 50 Netley Road, ILFORD, IG2 7NR.
BROCK, Mr. William George, BSc FCA *1971;* Fernhall Cottage, Roding Lane South, Redbridge, ILFORD, ESSEX, IG4 5PR.
BROCKBANK, Mrs. Elizabeth, BSc ACA *1991;* 9 Blacklands Crescent, FOREST ROW, EAST SUSSEX, RH18 5NN.
BROCKBANK, Mrs. Fiona, BA ACA *2005;* 197 Wellbrook Way, Girton, CAMBRIDGE, CB3 0GL.
BROCKBANK, Mr. John Edward, FCA *1950;* Manesty, Hessle Drive, Heswall, WIRRAL, CH60 8PS. (Life Member)
BROCKBANK, Mr. Richard Daniel, MA ACA *2004;* 197 Wellbrook Way, Girton, CAMBRIDGE, CB3 0GL.
BROCKFIELD, Mr. Alan Harvey, BCom FCA *1979;* 14a Moorend Lane, THAME, OXFORDSHIRE, OX9 3BQ.
•**BROCKHURST, Mr. Anthony John, FCA** *1969;* (Tax Fac), AJB Consultancy, Ashby Pastures Farm, Great Dalby Road, Ashby Folville, MELTON MOWBRAY, LEICESTERSHIRE LE14 2TU.
•**BROCKHURST, Mrs. Nicola Hayley, ACA** *1987;* (Tax Fac), Brockhurst Davies Limited, 11 The Office Village, North Road, LOUGHBOROUGH, LEICESTERSHIRE, LE11 1QJ.
BROCKIES, Mr. John Charles, BA FCA *1982;* 148 Postman Rd, Dairy Flat, AUCKLAND 0794, NEW ZEALAND.
BROCKINGTON, Mr. Colin, FCA *1961;* Poppy Barn, 15 Fishpond Lane, Egginton, DERBY, DE65 6HJ. (Life Member)
BROCKINGTON, Mr. Matthew James, BA ACA *1987;* 49 Sir John's Road, Selly Park, BIRMINGHAM, B29 7EP.
BROCKINGTON, Mr. Raymond Bernard, BCom MSc FCA *1961;* 24 Lansdown Park, BATH, BA1 5TG. (Life Member)
BROCKLEBANK, Mr. Daniel Maurice, MA(Hons) ACA CFA *2002;* 9 Hansler Grove, EAST MOLESEY, SURREY, KT8 9JN.
BROCKLEBANK, Mrs. Helen Jane, BA ACA *2007;* with Baker Tilly Corporate Finance LLP, Festival Way, Festival Park, STOKE-ON-TRENT, ST1 5BB.
BROCKLEBANK, Mr. John Daniel, MA FCA *1970;* 9 Cleveland Road, LONDON, SW13 0AA.
BROCKLEBANK, Mr. Peter, FCA *1965;* 21 Dingle Road, St. Heliers, AUCKLAND 1071, NEW ZEALAND. (Life Member)
BROCKLEBANK, Mr. Quentin Mark, BSc ACA *1997;* Electric Word Plc, 33-41 Dallington Street, LONDON, EC1V 0BB.
BROCKLEBANK, Ms. Victoria Elizabeth Alice, BA ACA CTA *2003;* G 4 S Plc The Manor, Manor Royal, CRAWLEY, WEST SUSSEX, RH10 9UN.
•**BROCKLEHURST, Mr. Alan, BSc ACA** *1990;* Sadofskys, Princes House, Wright Street, HULL, HU2 8HX. See also Procuro Payroll Services Ltd
BROCKLEHURST, Mrs. Amy Hilary, BSc ACA *2005;* 127a Kennington Lane, LONDON, SE11 4HQ.
BROCKLEHURST, Miss. Amy Louise, ACA *2011;* 21 Rowden Street, PLYMOUTH, PL3 4NY.
BROCKLEHURST, Miss. Anna, ACA *2009;* 45 Roman Close, Barrow upon Soar, LOUGHBOROUGH, LE12 8XY.

BROCKLEHURST, Mr. Christopher, MA ACA *2003;* 55 Mendora Road, Fulham, LONDON, SW6 7ND.

BROCKLEHURST, Mr. David, BA FCA *1963;* Edge Cottage, Off Stoney Lane, Endon, STOKE-ON-TRENT, ST9 9BX.

BROCKLEHURST, Mrs. Diana Elizabeth, ACA *1984;* Mallard Hurn Farm, Donington, SPALDING, LINCOLNSHIRE, PE11 4XF.

BROCKLEHURST, Miss. Emma, MA ACA *2002;* 17 Rosewood Park, Mistley, MANNINGTREE, CO11 1UA.

•**BROCKLEHURST, Mrs. Jacqueline, ACA** *1982;* (Tax Fac), Jacqueline Brocklehurst, 21 Poulton Avenue, LYTHAM ST. ANNES, FY8 3JR.

BROCKLEHURST, Mrs. Jacqueline Elizabeth, BSc FCA *1981;* Rosewood Cottage, Coppice Brook, Brocton, STAFFORD, ST17 0TQ.

BROCKLEHURST, Mr. Jonathan Howard Maxwell, BSc ACA *1988;* 2 Peake Place, Curtin, CANBERRA, ACT 2605, AUSTRALIA.

BROCKLEHURST, Mr. Karl Jason, BSc(Hons) ACA *1997;* 31 Alford Road, West Bridgford, NOTTINGHAM, NG2 6GJ.

BROCKLEHURST, Mr. Paul, MBA BA ACA *1998;* 112 Studley Knapp, Walnut Tree, MILTON KEYNES, MK7 7NE.

BROCKLEHURST, Mr. Paul, BSc ACA *1991;* 35 Brookside Road, Breadsall, DERBY, DE21 5LF.

BROCKLEHURST, Mr. Richard Douglas, FCA *1971;* 16 Juniper Drive, Great Sutton, ELLESMERE PORT, CH66 2YW.

BROCKLEHURST, Mr. Richard Stanley, FCA *1965;* 26 Linwal Avenue, Houghton-on-the-Hill, LEICESTER, LE7 9HD.

•**BROCKLEHURST, Mr. Simon Enfield, FCA** *1969;* Gallagher & Brocklehurst, 4 Plantagenet Road, BARNET, EN5 5JQ.

•**BROCKLEHURST, Mr. Stephen Frederick, FCA** *1978;* S.F. Brocklehurst & Co., Forest Lodge, Forest Road, Pyrford, WOKING, SURREY GU22 8NA. See also Cobalt Accountancy Limited

BROCKLESBY, Mrs. Diane June, ACA *1995;* Broomy Husk, The Moor, Coleorton, COALVILLE, LEICESTERSHIRE, LE67 8GD.

•**BROCKLESBY, Mr. Donald Ian, FCA** *1972;* (Tax Fac), D.I. Brocklesby & Co, Kiln How, Rosthwaite, KESWICK, CUMBRIA, CA12 5XB.

BROCKLESBY, Mr. Graham, MA(Hons) ACA *2001;* Capita Life & Pensions Services (Ireland) Ltd, Montague House, Adelaide Road, DUBLIN, COUNTY DUBLIN, IRELAND.

BROCKLESBY, Miss. Laura, BA(Hons) ACA *2003;* 17 The Mount, LONDON, NW3 6SZ.

BROCKLESBY, Mr. Michael Graham, BSc ACA *1994;* Broomy Husk The Moor, Coleorton, COALVILLE, LEICESTERSHIRE, LE67 8GD.

BROCKLESBY, Mr. Richard Christopher Shearwood, BA(Hons) ACA *2002;* Nomura International Plc, 1 Angel Lane, LONDON, EC4R 3AB.

BROCKLEY, Miss. Rosemary Sonia, BA ACA *1986;* The Old Post Lodge, Whitchurch Road, Broomhall, NANTWICH, CHESHIRE, CW5 8BZ.

BROCKMAN, Mr. Daniel John, BSc(Hons) ACA *2001;* 88 Grosvenor Road, Harborne, BIRMINGHAM, B17 9AN.

BROCKMAN, Miss. Penelope, BSc FCA *1992;* 52 Woodyates Road, LONDON, SE12 9JG.

BROCKMAN, Mr. Stephen, FCA *1964;* St. John's Gate, Church Lane, Whitchurch, AYLESBURY, HP22 4JY.

BROCKSOM, Mr. David Graham, MA FCA *1987;* 7 York Road, HARROGATE, NORTH YORKSHIRE, HG1 2QA.

BROCKSOM, Mr. Michael Walter, LLB FCA *1952;* 16 Graeme Road, Sutton, PETERBOROUGH, PE5 7XF. (Life Member)

BROCKSOM, Mr. Richard Anthony, MA FCA *1986;* Greenbushes, 4 Greenbush Lane, CRANLEIGH, SURREY, GU6 8ED.

BROCKSOPP, Miss. Natalie Melanie, BSc ACA *1995;* 14 Hyndford Crescent, Ingress Park, GREENHITHE, DA9 9XB.

•**BROCKWAY, Mr. Gary, ACA FCCA** *2008;* Greenhalgh Business Services Ltd, The Lion Buildings, 8 Market Place, UTTOXETER, STAFFORDSHIRE, ST14 8HP.

•**BROCKWELL, Mr. Colin James, FCA** *1983;* (Tax Fac), Barker Hibbert & Co, 133 Cherry Orchard Road, CROYDON, CR0 6BE.

BROCKWELL, Mr. David Paul, ACA *1989;* Twin Ways, Spurlands End Road, Great Kingshill, HIGH WYCOMBE, BUCKINGHAMSHIRE, HP15 6HY.

•**BROCKWELL, Mr. Kenneth John, MA FCA** *1970;* Jones Fisher Downes, Corner House, 21 Coombe Road, Chiswick, LONDON, W4 2HR.

BROCKWELL, Mr. Peter Jonathon, BA ACA *1992;* 48 Brookmans Avenue, Brookmans Park, HATFIELD, HERTFORDSHIRE, AL9 7QJ.

BRODE, Mr. Andrew Stephen, BA FCA *1965;* Walkwood House, 65 Burkes Road, BEACONSFIELD, BUCKINGHAMSHIRE, HP9 1PW.

BRODER, Mr. Benjamin, BSc ACA CPA *1989;* 8 Harakefet street, 99504 BET SHEMESH, ISRAEL.

BRODER, Mr. Kevin, BA FCA *1980;* (Tax Fac), MacIntyre Hudson Llp, 30-34 New Bridge Street, LONDON, EC4V 6BJ.

BRODER, Mr. Michael Keith, BSc ACA *2008;* 61 Woodbrook Road, LONDON, SE2 0PE.

BRODERICK, Miss. Abigail Ruth, BA ACA *2004;* Birmingham & Solihull Mental Health NHS Foundation Trust, Unit 1 B1, 50 Summer Hill Road, BIRMINGHAM, B1 3RB.

BRODERICK, Mr. Aramyees Michael, ACA *2010;* 35 Chudleigh Road, LONDON, SE4 1JX.

BRODERICK, Mrs. Beverley Jeane, BA ACA *2000;* 29 Royal Park, Ramsey, ISLE OF MAN, IM8 3UF.

BRODERICK, Mr. David John, FCA *1961;* St. Christophers, Devon Road, SALCOMBE, DEVON, TQ8 8HQ. (Life Member)

BRODERICK, Mrs. Dawn, BA ACA *2001;* 16 Tom Blower Close, NOTTINGHAM, NG8 1JQ.

•**BRODERICK, Mr. Derek Nigel, FCA** *1966;* 87 Bawtry Road, DONCASTER, DN4 7AG.

•**BRODERICK, Mr. John Michael, FCA** *1962;* Brodericks, 1 Heslington Court, Heslington, YORK, YO10 5EX.

BRODERICK, Mrs. Julia, BA ACA *1994;* 35 Woodford Gardens, Didsbury, MANCHESTER, M20 2TF.

BRODERICK, Mrs. Suzanne Kim, BA ACA *1988;* 73 Colchester Road, West Mersea, COLCHESTER, CO5 8JZ.

BRODIE, Mr. Adam Ritchie, ACA *2009;* 1 Hunters Piece, Bourton, SWINDON, SN6 8JR.

BRODIE, Mrs. Christine Linda, BEd FCA *1994;* 31 Poplar Avenue, HOVE, BN3 8PX.

BRODIE, Mr. David Sidney, OBE BA BSc FCA *1980;* (Tax Fac), 58 Chatsworth Road, LONDON, NW2 4DD.

BRODIE, Mr. Eldred John Paterson, FCA *1959;* Highview House, Station Road, PULBOROUGH, WEST SUSSEX, RH20 1AH. (Life Member)

BRODIE, Mrs. Geraldine Susan, MA FCA *1983;* 50 Albert Court, Prince Consort Road, LONDON, SW7 2BH.

BRODIE, Miss. Gillian Margaret, BAcc ACA *2002;* 9 Chagford Close, BEDFORD, MK40 3AY.

BRODIE, Mr. James Alexander, BA ACA *2010;* Apartment 3 Centurion Building, 376 Queenstown Road, LONDON, SW8 4NW.

•**BRODIE, Mr. Jonathan David, ACA** *2007;* (Tax Fac), Lopian Gross Barnett & Co, 6th Floor, Cardinal House, 20 St. Marys Parsonage, MANCHESTER, M3 2LG.

BRODIE, Mr. Kenneth Grant, FCA *1965;* 41 New Street, Mawdesley, ORMSKIRK, L40 2QN.

•**BRODIE, Mr. Maurice Harvey, FCA** *1962;* The P M Partnership, 44 Allington Rd., LONDON, NW4 3DE.

BRODIE, Mrs. Moira Howell, MA FCA *1980;* Lydford, 1 Hunters Piece, Bourton, SWINDON, SN6 8JR.

BRODIE, Mrs. Rosanna Grace, BSc ACA *2001;* 61 Archway Street, LONDON, SW13 0AS.

BRODIGAN, Mr. Martin Peter, BSc ACA *1986;* 96 South Drive, TORONTO M4W 1R6, ON, CANADA.

BRODY, Mr. Mark Adrian, FCA *1967;* 9 Deanhill Road, LONDON, SW14 7DQ.

BRODY, Mr. Michael Howard, BSc FCA *1969;* Aboulafia Avital & Co, 15 Kanfei Nesharim Street, 95464 JERUSALEM, ISRAEL.

BROEKHUIZEN, Mr. Neil John, BSc ACA *1991;* Ironbridge, Level 39, 88 Phillip Street, SYDNEY, NSW 2000, AUSTRALIA.

BROERS, Mrs. Jacqueline, MA ACA *2006;* 49B Elsynge Road, LONDON, SW18 2HR.

•**BROERS, Mr. Jerome Adrian Paul, BA FCA** *1982;* (Tax Fac), Warrener Stewart Limited, Harwood House, 43 Harwood Road, LONDON, SW6 4QP.

BROGAN, Mr. Andrew Bernard, ACA *1980;* 8 Sheringham Close, Staplecross, ROBERTSBRIDGE, TN32 5PZ.

•**BROGAN, Mr. Andrew Robert, BSc ACA** *1990;* Ernst & Young LLP, 1 More London Place, LONDON, SE1 2AF. See also Ernst & Young Europe LLP

BROGAN, Mrs. Emily, ACA *2008;* 14 Sarek Park, West Hunsbury, NORTHAMPTON, NN4 9YA.

BROGAN, Mr. Michael, BSc ACA *2004;* 43 Enmore Gardens, LONDON, SW14 8RF.

BROGDEN, Mr. John Patrick Newton, FCA *1952;* Flat 2 Bramsden Court, 1 Eastern Parade, SOUTHSEA, HAMPSHIRE, PO4 9RA. (Life Member)

BROGDEN, Mr. Michael James, BSc ACA *1999;* Supertune Automotive Ltd, Coulton Close, Off Cromford Street, OLDHAM, OL1 4EB.

BROIDE, Mr. Henry, FCA *1956;* 11/25 Degal Reuven Street, PETACH TIKVA, 49402, ISRAEL. (Life Member)

BROJER, Mr. Nicholas Frederick, BSc FCA *1977;* 3 Port Lane, Brimscombe, STROUD, GL5 2QJ.

•**BROKE, Mr. Adam Vere Balfour, FCA** *1965;* (Tax Fac), The Old Stables Gracious Street, Selborne, ALTON, HAMPSHIRE, GU34 3JD.

•**BROKENSHIRE, Mr. Ian James, BEng FCA** *1992;* KPMG LLP, Plym House, 3 Longbridge Road, Marsh Mills, PLYMOUTH, PL6 8LT. See also KPMG Europe LLP

BROKER, Mr. Ali Reza, ACA *1993;* Ping An Bank, Ping AN Building, 1099 Shennan Road Central, SHENZHEN 518031, GUANGDONG PROVINCE, CHINA.

•**BROLLY, Mr. Martin, FCA** *1980;* (Tax Fac), John Alderdice & Son, 21 Sherburn Terrace, CONSETT, DH8 6ND.

BROLLY, Mr. Owen Gerard Matthew, BSc ACA *1995;* 27 Croydon Road, KESTON, BR2 6EA.

BROMAGE, Mr. Richard Malcolm, BSc FCA *1975;* Lane Cottage, Hempstead Lane, Potten end, BERKHAMSTED, HP4 2QJ.

BROMBERG, Mr. Jerzy George, BSc ACA *1979;* Cemex UK Cemex House, Evreux Way, RUGBY, CV21 2DT.

BROMBLEY, Mr. Graham Keith, BSc FCA *1981;* 21 Thistle Road, Hedge End, SOUTHAMPTON, SO30 4TS.

BROMELL, Mr. Anthony Martin, BA FCA *1983;* 3 Village Farm Close, West Leake, LOUGHBOROUGH, LE12 5RP.

BROMELL, Mrs. Julie Anne, BSc FCA *1983;* 3 Village Farm Close, West Leake, LOUGHBOROUGH, LE12 5RP.

BROMELL, Mr. Walter Mark, BA FCA *1980;* (Tax Fac), 7 Lyons Range Court, Bisazza Street, SLIEMA SLM 1640, MALTA.

•**BROMFIELD, Mr. John Robert, BSc FCA** *1980;* PricewaterhouseCoopers LLP, Hays Galleria, 1 Hays Lane, LONDON, SE1 2RD. See also PricewaterhouseCoopers

BROMFIELD, Mr. Mark Stephen, BSc ACA *2009;* 1 Fulmar Drive, KENDAL, CUMBRIA, LA9 7RN.

BROMFIELD, Mr. Reginald Neil, FCA *1953;* Chiltley House, Sopley, CHRISTCHURCH, BH23 7BB. (Life Member)

BROMHAM, Mrs. Susan Elizabeth, BA ACA *1991;* NVM private Equity Ltd, Northumberland House, Princess Square, NEWCASTLE UPON TYNE, NE1 8ER.

•**BROMHEAD, Mr. Alan Arthur, BA FCA** *1969;* A.A. Bromhead & Co, P.O. Box 709, ADDIS ABABA, ETHIOPIA.

BROMILEY, Mr. James, MA MBA ACA *1998;* 7 Dunottar Avenue, Eaglescliffe, STOCKTON-ON-TEES, CLEVELAND, TS16 0AB.

•**BROMILEY, Mr. Peter John, ACA** *1991;* AMS Accountancy Ltd, Delta 606, Welton Road, Delta Office Park, SWINDON, SN5 7XF.

BROMILEY, Mr. Robin, MA MBA ACA *1979;* Post Office Market Place, Uppingham, OAKHAM, LE15 9QH.

BROMILOW, Mr. David Bensley, FCA *1968;* 60 Sukumvit 62, BANGKOK, 10260, THAILAND.

BROMLEY, Mr. Alexander John, BSc ACA *1999;* 15 Parker Gardens, Stapleford, NOTTINGHAM, NG9 8QG.

BROMLEY, Mrs. Amy, BSc(Hons) ACA *2001;* 22 Southern Road, SALE, CHESHIRE, M33 6HQ.

BROMLEY, Miss. Amy Jade, BA(Hons) ACA *2010;* 9 Meadow Court Ballasalla, ISLE OF MAN, IM9 2DW.

BROMLEY, Mr. Andrew Michael James, BSc ACA *1995;* Russell & Bromley Ltd, 24-34 Farwig Lane, BROMLEY, BR1 3RB.

BROMLEY, Mrs. Diana Hilary, BSc FCA *1980;* Gatton Lodge, Gatton Park, REIGATE, RH2 0TW.

BROMLEY, Mr. Glynn, FCA *1966;* The Great House, Troutbeck, WINDERMERE, LA23 1PJ. (Life Member)

BROMLEY, Mr. Hugh Michael Charles, FCA *1976;* Le Juge Vent, Le Villocq Lane, Castel, GUERNSEY, GY5 7SE.

BROMLEY, Mrs. Joanna Louise, BSc ACA *2007;* with Armida Limited, Bell Walk House, High Street, UCKFIELD, TN22 5DQ.

•**BROMLEY, Mr. John Lannon, MA(Oxon) ACA** *2005;* King Morter Proud & Co, Kings Arms Vaults, The Watton, BRECON, LD3 7EF.

•**BROMLEY, Mrs. Katherine Margaret, BA ACA** *2004;* King Morter Proud & Co, Kings Arms Vaults, The Watton, BRECON, LD3 7EF.

BROMLEY, Mr. Paul Gerald, BSc FCA *1990;* 20 Moorgate, LONDON, EC2R 6DA.

BROMLEY, Mr. Robert Alan, FCA *1968;* Old Manor House, 16 Bath Street, Syston, LEICESTER, LE7 1GB. (Life Member)

BROMLEY, Mr. Robert John, FCA *1976;* Servigistics Ltd, Servigisitics House, Milbury Heath, WOTTON-UNDER-EDGE, GLOUCESTERSHIRE, GL12 8QH.

BROMLEY, Mrs. Ruth Kim, BA ACA *1999;* with PKF (UK) LLP, Pannell House, 6 Queen Street, LEEDS, LS1 2TW.

BROMLEY, Mr. Stuart, MBA BA ACA *1984;* 29 Rainshaw Street, Astley Bridge, BOLTON, BL1 8QZ.

•**BROMLEY, Mr. Stuart Richard Squire, FCA** *1984;* (Tax Fac), Bromley Clackett Limited, 76 Aldwick Road, BOGNOR REGIS, WEST SUSSEX, PO21 2PE.

BROMLEY-DAVENPORT, Mr. William Arthur, FCA *1966;* Capesthorne Hall, MACCLESFIELD, SK11 9JY. (Life Member)

BROMPTON, Mrs. Emma Louise, BSc ACA *2001;* H M Revenue & Customs Taxpayer District Office Leeds 2, Eleventh Floor Castle House 31 Lisbon Street, LEEDS, LS1 4SW.

BROMWICH, Mr. David Mervyn, FCA *1975;* 201 1000 - 9th Avenue SW, CALGARY T2P 2Y6, AB, CANADA.

•**BRONER-COHEN, Mr. Moshe, ACA** *2007;* Cohen Arnold, New Burlington House, 1075 Finchley Road, Temple Fortune, LONDON, NW11 0PU.

BRONIMANN, Mr. Alexander Marcus, MSc ACA *1996;* Fairview, 17 Milldown Road, Goring, READING, OXFORDSHIRE, RG8 0BA.

BRONKHORST, Mr. Martin David, FCA *1969;* 157 Albury Drive, PINNER, HA5 3RH. (Life Member)

BRONNERT, The Revd. John, FCA *1957;* Tyndale, 15 Craig Avenue, Urmston, MANCHESTER, M41 5RS. (Life Member)

BRONSON, Mr. Stuart Leigh, MA BSc ACA *2009;* Freyjugata 5, 101 REYKJAVIK, ICELAND.

•**BROOK, Mr. Adrian Geoffrey, BSc ACA** *1989;* Moore Stephens LLP, 150 Aldersgate Street, LONDON, EC1A 4AB.

•**BROOK, Mr. Andrew James, BA FCA** *1989;* Dorchester House, 7 Church Street West, PO Box HM1171, HAMILTON HM EX, BERMUDA.

BROOK, Mr. Andrew James, BA ACA *1991;* 17 Ormerod Road, BRISTOL, BS9 1BA.

BROOK, Mr. Andrew Stuart, BSc FCA *1996;* High Trees Barn, Silsden Road, Riddlesden, KEIGHLEY, BD20 5RA.

BROOK, Ms. Ann Caroline, BA ACA *1991;* Badminton School, Westbury Road, Westbury-on-Trym, BRISTOL, BS9 3BA.

BROOK, Mr. Anthony Donald, FCA *1960;* 20 Meadow Lane, Hamble, SOUTHAMPTON, SO31 4RD. (Life Member)

BROOK, Miss. Catherine, MA ACA *2002;* Pinecroft, Flat 8, 61 Westwood Road, SOUTHAMPTON, SO17 1DJ.

BROOK, Mr. Christopher John, MA BA ACA *1984;* Midhurst Wildwood Close, East Horsley, LEATHERHEAD, KT24 5EP.

•**BROOK, Mr. Clive Matthew, FCA CF** *1973;* 46 Brooklands Drive, Goostrey, CREWE, CW4 8JD.

BROOK, Mr. Geoffrey, FCA *1957;* 121 Brickhill Drive, BEDFORD, MK41 7QG. (Life Member)

BROOK, Miss. Jane Elizabeth, BSc ACA *1995;* 5 Lakis Close, Hampstead Village, LONDON, NW3 1JX.

BROOK, Mr. Jonathan Howard, BA(Hons) FCA *1993;* 6 Far Mead Croft, Burley in Wharfedale, ILKLEY, WEST YORKSHIRE, LS29 7RR.

•**BROOK, Mr. Lee Alan, BSc ACA** *2002;* Mazars LLP, The Atrium, Park Street West, LUTON, LU1 3BE.

BROOK, Mr. Mark Andrew, BSc ACA *1992;* 207 Earlham Road, NORWICH, NR2 3RQ.

BROOK, Mr. Martin Anthony, BSc ACA *1995;* 14 Harewood Road, Allestree, DERBY, DE22 2JN.

BROOK, Mr. Martin Clive, BA FCA ATII *1980;* Smith Group UK Ltd Calder House, St. Georges Park Kirkham, PRESTON, PR4 2DZ.

BROOK, Mr. Michael George, BA FCA *1975;* Latchetts, 6 Gorse Bank Road, Halebarns, ALTRINCHAM, WA15 0AL.

BROOK, Mr. Michael John, MSc FCA *1986;* 7a Ellington Street, Islington, LONDON, N7 8PP.

BROOK, Mr. Michael Joseph, BA ACA *1988;* 9a Leadhall Drive, HARROGATE, NORTH YORKSHIRE, HG2 9NL.

•**BROOK, Mr. Peter John, ACA** *1984;* Peter Brook, 15 Luxemburg Gardens, Brook Green, LONDON, W6 7EA. See also Longboat Tax Advisers LLP, Longboat Advisers Limited and Longboat VAT Advisers LLP

BROOK, Mr. Peter Raymond, BSc ACA *1995;* Beacon Cottage Aston Hill Aston Rowant, WATLINGTON, OXFORDSHIRE, OX49 5SD.

•**BROOK, Mr. Philip Dudley Anthony, BA ACA** *1991;* (Tax Fac), KPMG LLP, 15 Canada Square, LONDON, E14 5GL. See also KPMG Europe LLP

BROOK, Mr. Philip John, BEng ACA *1995;* 39 Hazelwood Avenue, Garforth, LEEDS, LS25 2AW.

BROOK, Miss. Rebecca Isabel, ACA DChA *2009;* 40 Upton Road, BRISTOL, BS3 1LX.

BROOK, Mr. Robert Anthony, FCA *1966;* Rosemount, 39A Nottingham Road, Ravenshead, NOTTINGHAM, NG15 9HG.
•**BROOK, Mr. Robert Paul, ACA CTA** *1987;* (Tax Fac), Broadhead Peel Rhodes Ltd, 27a Lidget Hill, PUDSEY, WEST YORKSHIRE, LS28 7LG.
BROOK, Mr. Roland Spencer, BA FCA CF *1984;* with Smith & Williamson Ltd, 25 Moorgate, LONDON, EC2R 6AY.
BROOK, Mrs. Rosaline Claire, BEng ACA *1999;* The Rectory, Orchard Close, Gislingham, EYE, SUFFOLK, IP23 8JW.
•**BROOK, Mrs. Rosemary Ann, FCA** *1977;* 49 Clifton Road, SUTTON COLDFIELD, B73 6EN.
BROOK, Mrs. Sarah Louise, BA ACA *2005;* 27 Butler Drive, Lidlington, BEDFORD, MK43 0UQ.
•**BROOK, Mr. Simon, BSc FCA** *1983;* SJB, Pleasant Place, The Street, Great Tey, COLCHESTER, CO6 1JS.
BROOK, Mr. Steven, BSc ACA *1988;* Calico Housing Ltd, Centenary Court, Croft Street, BURNLEY, LANCASHIRE, BB11 2ED.
BROOK, Mrs. Victoria Louisa, ACA *2009;* 14 Burke Avenue, BIRMINGHAM, B13 9XB.
BROOK, Mrs. Virginia Helen, BA ACA *1992;* 9 Glebe Field Close, WETHERBY, LS22 5RA.
BROOKE, Mr. Alan Michael, ACA CA(SA) *2008;* 11 Delaware Road, Maida Vale, LONDON, W9 2LH.
BROOKE, Mr. Andrew Edward, MA ACA *1997;* October House, Bayleys Hill, SEVENOAKS, TN14 6HS.
BROOKE, Mr. Brian Gordon, FCA *1970;* 115 Angelene Street, MISSISSAUGA L5G 1X1, ON, CANADA.
BROOKE, Mrs. Ceril Rees, BSc ACA *1999;* Charen, Lower Farm Road, Effingham, LEATHERHEAD, SURREY, KT24 5JJ.
BROOKE, Mr. David Leslie, ACA *1991;* with Mazars LLP, Mazars House, Gelderd Road, Gildersome, LEEDS, LS27 7JN.
BROOKE, Mr. David Newton, FCA *1956;* 43 Stretton Road, Great Glen, LEICESTER, LE8 9GN.
BROOKE, Mrs. Deborah Ann, ACA *1983;* 270 Lichfield Road, Rushall, WALSALL, WS4 1SA.
BROOKE, Mr. Graham Robert Charles, BA ACA *2000;* C V C, 111 Strand, LONDON, WC2R 0AG.
BROOKE, Miss. Harriet Jane, BA(Hons) ACA *2003;* Ernst & Young Kurumsal Finansman Danismanlik AS, Buyukdere Cad., Plaza No 22, Sisli, ISTANBUL 34381, TURKEY.
BROOKE, Mr. James Dominic, BA ACA *1997;* 13 Eglantine Road, Wandsworth, LONDON, SW18 2DE.
BROOKE, Mr. James Roger Barrington, BA(Hons) ACA *2002;* 44 Lingwell Road, LONDON, SW17 7NJ.
BROOKE, Mr. John Charles, FCA *1966;* Brandlehow, 73 Moorland Road, POULTON-LE-FYLDE, FY6 7ER.
BROOKE, Mr. John Hugo, FCA *1934;* St. Christophers Home, Abington Park Crescent, NORTHAMPTON, NN3 3AD. (Life Member)
BROOKE, Mr. Martin Charles, BA ACA *1989;* Talent 2 International Ltd, PO Box 1516, NORTH SYDNEY, NSW 2059, AUSTRALIA.
•**BROOKE, Mr. Martin Kingsley, FCA** *1969;* Holmes Beaumont & Holroyd, 15 Ropergate End, PONTEFRACT, WF8 1JT.
•**BROOKE, Mr. Michael Richard William, FCA** *1974;* (Tax Fac), Ross Brooke Limited, 2 Old Bath Road, NEWBURY, BERKSHIRE, RG14 1QL.
BROOKE, Mr. Michael Robert, BSc ACA *1996;* Charen Lower Farm Road, Effingham, LEATHERHEAD, SURREY, KT24 5JJ.
BROOKE, Mr. Nicholas George, BA ACA *1996;* 21 Shell Road, LONDON, SE13 7TW.
BROOKE, Mr. Patrick Thomas Joseph, FCA *1970;* 130 Albert Road, Pittville, CHELTENHAM, GL52 3JF.
BROOKE, Mrs. Rachael Elizabeth, BA ACA *1998;* 108 Long Lane, Honely, HOLMFIRTH, West Yorkshire, HD9 6EB.
BROOKE, Mr. Robert Barrington, FCA *1963;* Ford House, Ford Manor Road, Dormansland, LINGFIELD, RH7 6NZ.
BROOKE, Miss. Sarah, BSc ACA *1993;* Kings College London, Capital House, 42 Weston Street, LONDON, SE1 3QD.
BROOKE, Mr. Simon David, BA ACA *1985;* Merricks Farm, Park Lane, Huish Episcopi, LANGPORT, TA10 0NF.
BROOKE, Mr. Tom, FCA *1955;* 6 Balmoral Court, Hill Turrets Close, SHEFFIELD, S11 9RF. (Life Member)
•**BROOKE- TAYLOR, Mrs. Mary Elizabeth, ACA ACCA** *2005;* Graham Sunley & Co Limited, 52 Front Street, Acomb, YORK, YO24 3BX.
•**BROOKE-HOLLIDGE, Mr. Timothy Kenneth, FCA** *1977;* The Forge Lutterworth Road, Gilmorton, LUTTERWORTH, LEICESTERSHIRE, LE17 5PN.
BROOKE-WEBB, Mr. Michael Vernonn, FCA *1964;* Linfield House, Holcombe Rogus, WELLINGTON, SOMERSET, TA21 0PD. (Life Member)
BROOKER, Mr. Alan Bernard, JP DL FCA *1954;* Silkwater, East Hill, Evershot, DORCHESTER, DORSET, DT2 0LB. (Life Member)
BROOKER, Mr. Alan Walter, FCA *1961;* Wilbar Components Ltd, Martindale, Hawks Green, CANNOCK, WS11 2XN.
BROOKER, Mrs. Alison Claire, BSc ACA *2002;* 96 York Gardens, WALTON-ON-THAMES, SURREY, KT12 3EN.
•**BROOKER, Mrs. Alison Marie, BSc FCA** *1996;* Alison Brooker, 19 Calmore Crescent, Calmore, SOUTHAMPTON, SO40 2RJ.
BROOKER, Miss. Annette, BA(Hons) ACA *2000;* (Tax Fac), 42 Dean Way, Aston Clinton, AYLESBURY, BUCKINGHAMSHIRE, HP22 5GB.
BROOKER, Mr. Colin Peter, BA ACA AMCT *1990;* 45 Brooke End, Chequer Lane, Redbourn, ST. ALBANS, AL3 7GD.
BROOKER, Mr. Daniel Edward, BSc ACA *2009;* 24 Herbert Road, LONDON, SW19 3SH.
BROOKER, Mr. Derek William, FCA *1980;* Data Connection Limited, 100 Church Street, ENFIELD, EN2 6BQ.
•**BROOKER, Mrs. Fiona Margaret, BSc ACA** *1989;* PricewaterhouseCoopers LLP, The Atrium, 1 Harefield Road, UXBRIDGE, UB8 1EX. See also PricewaterhouseCoopers
•**BROOKER, Mr. Graham, JP FCA** *1969;* Graham Brooker FCA, River Hill Cottage, River Hill, Flamstead, ST. ALBANS, HERTFORDSHIRE AL3 8BY.
BROOKER, Mrs. Lorraine Theresa, FCA *1975;* C/O NN Snaith, Department TDD, Sakhalin Energy, Sakhalin Expat Mail, Shell Centre, 4-6 York Road LONDON SE1 7NA.
BROOKER, Mr. Martin Douglas, FCA *1972;* Brewfitt Ltd, International House, Penistone Road, Fenay Bridge, HUDDERSFIELD, HD8 0LE.
BROOKER, Miss. Nancy Merryn, BA ACA *2008;* 42 Walnut Tree Road, LONDON, SE10 9EU.
BROOKER, Mr. Richard Arthur, FCA CTA *1967;* 6 Farlington Avenue, HAYWARDS HEATH, WEST SUSSEX, RH16 3EY. (Life Member)
•**BROOKER, Mr. Simon Warren, BA FCA** *1985;* BDO LLP, Kings Wharf, 20-30 Kings Road, READING, RG1 3EX. See also BDO Stoy Hayward LLP
•**BROOKER, Mr. Stephen Michael, MA FCA** *1974;* stephen brooker consulting ltd, 3 Playles Yard, Bassingbourn, ROYSTON, HERTFORDSHIRE, SG8 5XW.
BROOKER, Mr. Thomas Paul, FCA *1958;* Wyndi, Brick Kiln Lane, HITCHIN, SG4 9BQ. (Life Member)
•**BROOKES, Mr. Alan, FCA** *1984;* (Tax Fac), Brookes O'Hara Limited, Old Hall Farmhouse, Barthomley, CREWE, CHESHIRE, CW2 5PE.
BROOKES, Mr. Alistair Daniel, LLB ACA *2002;* 17 Silverburn Close, BEDFORD, MK41 0GB.
BROOKES, Mr. Andrew Charles, BSc ACA *1995;* 20 The Street, Alburgh, HARLESTON, NORFOLK, IP20 0DF.
•**BROOKES, Mr. Andrew Warner, FCA CF** *1989;* Hazlewoods LLP, Windsor House, Bayshill Road, CHELTENHAM, GLOUCESTERSHIRE, GL50 3AT.
BROOKES, Mr. Anthony Joseph William, BA ACA *1980;* Alpine Trustees SA, 15 rue du Cendrier, PO Box 1057, 1211 GENEVA, SWITZERLAND.
•**BROOKES, Mr. Anthony Stephen, FCA** *1977;* A.S. Brookes & Co, 19 Claydon Road, Wall Heath, KINGSWINFORD, WEST MIDLANDS, DY6 0HR.
BROOKES, Mr. Christopher, BSc ACA *2010;* Flat 3 Astoria Court, 73 Middleton Road, LONDON, E8 4DW.
BROOKES, Mr. Clive Andrew, BSc ACA *1991;* South Boderwennack, Trevenen Bal, HELSTON, TR13 0PS.
BROOKES, Mr. Colin Richard, FCA *1967;* 3 Thornton Avenue, Warsash, SOUTHAMPTON, SO31 9FL.
BROOKES, Mr. Daniel, BA ACA CTA *1999;* with Ernst & Young LLP, 1 Bridgewater Place, Water Lane, LEEDS, LS11 5QR.
•**BROOKES, Mr. David, FCA** *1995;* (Tax Fac), BDO LLP, Kings Wharf, 20-30 Kings Road, READING, RG1 3EX. See also BDO Stoy Hayward LLP
BROOKES, Mr. David, BSc ACA *1992;* Home Farm, 37 Church Street, Coton-in-the-Elms, SWADLINCOTE, DERBYSHIRE, DE12 8EZ.
•**BROOKES, Mr. David Michael, BSc FCA** *1995;* Robinson Udale Limited, The Old Bank, 41 King Street, PENRITH, CUMBRIA, CA11 7AY.
•**BROOKES, Mr. David Russell, BA FCA** *1985;* (Tax Fac), with RSM Tenon Audit Limited, Highfield Court, Tollgate, Chandlers Ford, EASTLEIGH, SO53 3TY.
•**BROOKES, Mr. Gary Peter, BSc FCA** *1977;* G.P. Brookes, 24 Abbotsford Drive, DUDLEY, WEST MIDLANDS, DY1 2HD.
BROOKES, Mr. Graham Lindsay, BSc FCA *1975;* Priory House, The Green, MARKFIELD, LEICESTERSHIRE, LE67 9WD.
BROOKES, Mrs. Hazel Ann Heather, BA(Hons) ACA *2002;* 20 The Street, Alburgh, HARLESTON, NORFOLK, IP20 0DF.
BROOKES, Mr. Ian John, BA ACA *1988;* Stamford House, 39 Hurst Lane, Waingate Village, Rawtenstall, ROSSENDALE, LANCASHIRE BB4 7RE.
BROOKES, Mr. Jeffrey William, FCA *1961;* 15 Chessfield Park, Little Chalfont, AMERSHAM, HP6 6RU.
BROOKES, Miss. Jocelyn Elizabeth, BA ACA *1989;* Lieranta, Worcester Road, Great Witley, WORCESTER, WR6 6JT.
BROOKES, Mr. John Charles, BA FCA *1979;* The Old Stables, Church Road, North Waltham, BASINGSTOKE, RG25 2BL.
BROOKES, Mrs. Karina, BA ACA *1997;* with PricewaterhouseCoopers LLP, Pricewaterhousecoopers, 12 Plumtree Court, LONDON, EC4A 4HT.
BROOKES, Mr. Mark Jeremy, BSc ACA *1984;* 89 Hay Green Lane, Bournville, BIRMINGHAM, B30 1UP.
BROOKES, Mr. Matthew Tristan Alexander, BA ACA *1996;* Basement, 13 Stanlake Road, LONDON, W12 7HE.
•**BROOKES, Mr. Michael, BA FCA** *1977;* Michael Brookes & Co Ltd, Hampton House, Oldham Road, Middleton, MANCHESTER, M24 1GT.
BROOKES, Mr. Nicholas Kelvin, FCA *1973;* De la Rue Plc, Jays Close, Viables, BASINGSTOKE, HAMPSHIRE, RG22 4BS.
BROOKES, Miss. Nicola, BSc FCA *1977;* Amadeus, 26a Holloway Lane, Chesham Bois, AMERSHAM, BUCKINGHAMSHIRE, HP6 6DJ.
•**BROOKES, Mrs. Nicola Denise, ACA** *1999;* Nicola Brookes Limited, Mole End, Shorts Green Lane, Motcombe, SHAFTESBURY, DORSET SP7 9PA.
BROOKES, Mr. Paul, BA FCA *1987;* 22 Withnell Fold, Withnell, CHORLEY, PR6 8BA.
BROOKES, Mr. Peter Julyan, BA ACA *1993;* Knights BMW, Bede Road, STOKE-ON-TRENT, ST4 4GU.
BROOKES, Dr. Rachael Carolyn, PhD BSc ACA *2006;* Wellington House, Kemble Airfield Enterprise Park, Kemble, CIRENCESTER, GLOUCESTERSHIRE, GL7 6BQ.
BROOKES, Mr. Raymond, FCA *1955;* Bassett, Springfield Lane, Reading Road North, FLEET, GU51 4AH. (Life Member)
•**BROOKES, Mr. Richard Anthony, BA FCA** *1988;* TaxAssist Accountants, 173 Mill Road, CAMBRIDGE, CB1 3AN. See also RABrookes & Co
BROOKES, Mr. Richard Basil, BA ACA *1983;* 34 Oakhill Drive, WELWYN, AL6 9NW.
BROOKES, Mrs. Sara Elizabeth, BSc ACA *1980;* Blue Skies Holdings Ltd, Paddock View, Spring Hill Farm, Harborough Road, Pitsford, NORTHAMPTON NN6 9AA.
BROOKES, Mr. Timothy Alastair Edward, FCA *1972;* Bentley Court, Holt Heath, WORCESTER, WR6 6TX.
BROOKES, Mr. Toby Alexander John, BSc ACA *1989;* 1/4 Hyam St, BALMAIN, NSW 2041, AUSTRALIA.
BROOKES, Miss. Victoria Louise, ACA *2010;* Eurostar (UK) Ltd Times House, 5 Bravingtons Walk, LONDON, N1 9AW.
BROOKES, Ms. Zarena, BA ACA *2005;* T U I UK, Wigmore House, Wigmore Lane, LUTON, BEDFORDSHIRE, LU2 9TN.
BROOKFIELD, Mr. David, DPhil BA ACA *1986;* 50 Berwick Road, Little Sutton, ELLESMERE PORT, CH66 4PR.
•**BROOKFIELD, Mrs. Judith Anne, BCom ACA** *1985;* Brookfield & Co, 52 Church Road, Crystal Palace, LONDON, SE19 2EZ.
BROOKFIELD, Mr. Steven Joseph, BSc ACA *1990;* 33 Southport Road, Formby, LIVERPOOL, L37 7EN.
BROOKHOUSE, Mrs. Suzanne Alison Eaton, BSc FCA *1980;* The King's Lodging, SANDWICH, KENT, CT13 9EX.
BROOKING, Mr. Anthony Nigel Gordon, FCA *1972;* 31 Bis rue Barla, 06300 NICE, FRANCE. (Life Member)
BROOKING, Mr. Antony Clive, FCA *1957;* Hall Farm, Bentworth, ALTON, GU34 5JU. (Life Member)
BROOKING, Mrs. Mary Rose, BA ACA *2002;* 17 Hilly Fields Crescent, LONDON, SE4 1QA.
BROOKING, Mr. Paul James, MChem ACA *2003;* 17 Hilly Fields Crescent, LONDON, SE4 1QA.
BROOKINGS, Miss. Sarah Louise, ACA *1988;* 2 Waters Place, Danemere Street, Putney, LONDON, SW15 1LH.
BROOKLAND, Mr. Alan William, FCA *1948;* 4 Dulverton Road, New Eltham, LONDON, SE9 3RH. (Life Member)
BROOKLAND, Mr. David Anthony, BA FCA *1986;* Les Baux La Rue A Don, Grouville, JERSEY, JE3 9GB.
BROOKMAN, Mr. George David, FCA *1970;* 28 Mayfield Avenue, Formby, LIVERPOOL, L37 2FN. (Life Member)
•**BROOKMAN, Mr. Ian Charles, FCA DChA** *1982;* Ensors, Saxon House, Moseleys Farm, Business Centre, Fornham All Saints, BURY ST. EDMUNDS SUFFOLK IP28 6JY.
BROOKMAN, Mr. Paul Michael, BA(Hons) ACA *2000;* Flat 18, Thanet Court, Queens Drive, LONDON, W3 0HW.
•**BROOKS, Mr. Alan, FCA** *1975;* Morris Gregory, County End Business Centre, Jackson Street, Springhead, OLDHAM, OL4 4TZ. See also Morris Gregory Ltd
BROOKS, Mr. Alan James William, BSc ACA *2002;* 1 Greenacres, Little Melton, NORWICH, NR9 3QU.
BROOKS, Mr. Alan John, BSc FCA *1975;* Shell International Petroleum Co Ltd, Shell Centre, York Road, LONDON, SE1 7NA.
•**BROOKS, Mr. Alan Michael, FCA** *1974;* PO Box 31494, GEORGE TOWN, GRAND CAYMAN, KY1-1206, CAYMAN ISLANDS.
BROOKS, Mr. Alan Tempest, FCA *1967;* 7 Southgate Street, BURY ST. EDMUNDS, IP33 2AF.
BROOKS, Mr. Alastair David, BA ACA *2005;* 71 Maury Road, LONDON, N16 7BT.
BROOKS, Mrs. Amanda, BSc ACA AMCT *1991;* 4 Naseby Close, LONDON, NW6 4EY.
BROOKS, Mr. Andrew Clive, BSc FCA *1986;* Amex House, 154-155 Edward Street, BRIGHTON, BN88 1AH.
BROOKS, Mr. Andrew Jonathan, MA ACA CTA *1987;* 170 Farmers Close, WITNEY, OX28 1NS.
BROOKS, Mr. Anthony George, BSc FCA *1979;* Yeomans Limited, Yeomans House 33 Brougham Road, WORTHING, WEST SUSSEX, BN11 2NR.
BROOKS, Mrs. Barbara Mary, BSc ACA *1991;* The Coach House The Green, Chiddingfold, GODALMING, GU8 4TU.
BROOKS, Mr. Barry John, BSc ACA *1986;* Meridian Healthcare Ltd Enterprise House, Grange Road South, HYDE, CHESHIRE, SK14 5NU.
BROOKS, Mr. Brian, FCA *1968;* 86 Penshurst Gardens, EDGWARE, HA8 9TU.
BROOKS, Mr. Brian Norman, FCA *1956;* 66 Tom Lane, SHEFFIELD, S10 3PB. (Life Member)
BROOKS, Mr. Bryan Harrison, FCA *1959;* Flat 10, Beaulieu, 16 Leicester Road, Hale, ALTRINCHAM, CHESHIRE WA15 9QA. (Life Member)
BROOKS, Mr. Bryce Rowan Nicholas, BSc ACA *1991;* 5 Kingsbury Drive, WILMSLOW, CHESHIRE, SK9 2GU.
BROOKS, Mr. Charles David, BSc ACA *1988;* Planetrees, Wall, HEXHAM, NORTHUMBERLAND, NE46 4EQ.
BROOKS, Mr. Christopher James, ACA *1981;* Liverpool School of Tropical Medicine, Pembroke Place, LIVERPOOL, L3 5QA.
BROOKS, Mr. Christopher John, BA(Hons) FCA *2001;* 8 Green Way, Bookham, LEATHERHEAD, SURREY, KT23 3PA.
BROOKS, Mr. Christopher John, BA ACA *1990;* 34 Dukes Avenue, Chiswick, LONDON, W4 2AE.
•**BROOKS, Mr. Christopher John, FCA FCCA CTA** *1973;* 1 2 & 3 College Yard, WORCESTER, WR1 2LB.
BROOKS, Mr. Christopher Martin, BSc FCA *1989;* Musgrave House, Greatford, STAMFORD, LINCOLNSHIRE, PE9 4QA.
BROOKS, Mr. Christopher Michael, BA ACA *1997;* 21 Arterberry Road, LONDON, SW20 8AF.
BROOKS, Mr. Christopher Michael Charles, ACA *2008;* Flat 35 Saturday Bridge, Gas Street, BIRMINGHAM, B1 2JX.
BROOKS, Mr. Christopher Paul, BA ACA *1993;* Baines & Ernst Financial Management Ltd, Lloyds House, 18-22 Lloyd Street, MANCHESTER, M2 5BE.
BROOKS, Mr. Christopher Robert, FCA *1969;* 12 Dowry Walk, Ridge Lane, WATFORD, WD17 4TG. (Life Member)
BROOKS, Mr. Christopher Simon, BSc ACA *1990;* 128 Cumnor Hill, Cumnor, OXFORD, OX2 9PH.
BROOKS, Mrs. Claire Louise, MA ACA APFS *2002;* Little Thornby Nursery Close, WOKING, SURREY, GU21 4UQ.
BROOKS, Mrs. Claudia, BSc ACA *1999;* 21 Arterberry Road, LONDON, SW20 8AF.
BROOKS, Mr. Clive, FCA *1972;* Rua do Atlantico, Lote 3, Quinta da Marinha, 2750-006 CASCAIS, PORTUGAL.

BROOKS, Mr. Clive, BA ACA *1997;* 4 Hilda Vale Road, ORPINGTON, KENT, BR6 7AN.

BROOKS, Mr. Clive Percy, FCA *1971;* 50 Smitham Bottom Lane, PURLEY, SURREY, CR8 3DB.

BROOKS, Mr. David Nicholas, FCA CF *1972;* The Old Rectory, Harborough Road, Brampton Ash, MARKET HARBOROUGH, LEICESTERSHIRE, LE16 8PD.

BROOKS, Mr. David Read, BA FCA *1952;* Flat 2, The Hill, Parkfield Road, KNUTSFORD, CHESHIRE, WA16 8NP. (Life Member)

BROOKS, Mr. David Robert, BSocSc ACA *2003;* A S I G Ltd, 137-139 High Street, EGHAM, SURREY, TW20 9HL.

•BROOKS, Mr. David Stewart, CA FCA *1970;* 17 St. Helens Well, Tarleton, PRESTON, PR4 6NB.

BROOKS, Mr. David Stuart, BA ACA *1991;* European Bank for Reconstruction & Development, 1 Exchange Square, LONDON, EC2A 2JN.

BROOKS, Mrs. Deborah, BSc ACA *1990;* Marantomark Ltd, Northgate Lane Moorside, OLDHAM, OL1 4RU.

BROOKS, Mr. Edwin Linton, MA FCA *1965;* El Almendro, Goodacre Lane, Lacey Green, PRINCES RISBOROUGH, HP27 0QD. (Life Member)

BROOKS, Mrs. Fiona McMillan, BA ACA *1992;* 3 Maners Way, CAMBRIDGE, CB1 8SL.

BROOKS, Mr. Frank, FCA *1958;* 50 Fir Road, Bramhall, STOCKPORT, CHESHIRE, SK7 2JJ. (Life Member)

•BROOKS, Mr. George Marios, BSc FCA *1986;* BDO LLP, Prospect Place, 85 Great North Road, HATFIELD, HERTFORDSHIRE, AL9 5BS. See also BDO Stoy Hayward LLP

•BROOKS, Mr. Gerald Richard, FCA *1980;* (Tax Fac), Brooks & Co, 9A Leicester Road, Blaby, LEICESTER, LE8 4GR.

BROOKS, Mr. Hector Charles, BA FCA *1998;* with Strover Leader & Co, Barry House, 20/22 Worple Road, Wimbledon, LONDON, SW19 4DH.

•BROOKS, Mr. Hugh Stephen Arthur, BA FCA *1977;* Brewery House, Norton Canon, HEREFORD, HR4 7BG.

BROOKS, Mr. Ian Alastair, BA FCA *1982;* Mercer Inc, Suit 950, 200 South Biscayne Blvd, MIAMI, FL FL 33131, UNITED STATES.

BROOKS, Mr. Ian Charles, BA ACA *1986;* Milando, Portsmouth Road, Ripley, WOKING, SURREY, GU23 6EJ.

•BROOKS, Mr. Ian Ludlow, FCA *1978;* c/o Mutual Trust, 7 Heliopolis Street, Ayios Andreas, CY1101 NICOSIA, CYPRUS.

BROOKS, Mrs. Janet, FCA *1953;* 7 Wainwright Road, ALTRINCHAM, WA14 4BW. (Life Member)

BROOKS, Mr. Jeremy, BSc ACA *1987;* Chemin du Polny 12B, 1066 EPALINGES, SWITZERLAND.

BROOKS, Mr. Jermyn Paul, MA FCA *1966;* 26 Shouldham Street, LONDON, W1H 5FL. (Life Member)

BROOKS, Mr. John Howard, FCA *1968;* Native Land Ltd, Pollen House, 10-12 Cork Street, LONDON, W1S 3NP.

BROOKS, Mr. John Michael Arthur, FCA *1963;* 2 Lavender Cottages, Reigate Road, LEATHERHEAD, SURREY, KT22 8NA.

BROOKS, Mr. John Reginald, BSc FCA *1970;* 8 Amberslade Walk, Dibden Purlieu, SOUTHAMPTON, SO45 4NW.

BROOKS, Mr. Jonathan Peter Chilton, FCA *1977;* 59 Meadway, HARPENDEN, AL5 1JH.

BROOKS, Mr. Jonathan Robert, BSc ACA *1994;* Cunard House, 15 Regent Street, LONDON, SW1Y 4LR.

BROOKS, Mrs. Julie Anne, BSc ACA *1985;* Surrey NHS Primary Care Trust, Randalls Way, LEATHERHEAD, KT22 7TW.

BROOKS, Miss. Karen Maria, BA ACA *1991;* 930 Seena Avenue, LOS ALTOS, CA 94024, UNITED STATES.

BROOKS, Miss. Kathryn Ann, ACA *2009;* 58 Sherington Avenue, PINNER, MIDDLESEX, HA5 4DT.

BROOKS, Mr. Kenneth, FCA *1951;* 1 Dalguise Grove, Heworth Green, YORK, YO31 7SY. (Life Member)

BROOKS, Mr. Kenneth William, FCA *1973;* 40 Baldwin Avenue, EASTBOURNE, EAST SUSSEX, BN21 1UP.

BROOKS, Mr. Kyro Edward, ACA *2011;* Flat 2, 149 Brecknock Road, LONDON, N19 5AD.

BROOKS, Ms. Laura Jane, BA(Hons) ACA *2001;* 3 Furze Court, Ashburton Road, CROYDON, CR0 6AP.

BROOKS, Mr. Laurence John, BSc ACA CISA *1997;* 9 Wycombe Close, Derry Hill, CALNE, WILTSHIRE, SN11 9PB.

BROOKS, Mr. Malcolm Stuart, BSc ACA *1983;* Amsafe Bridport, The Court, The Court West Street, BRIDPORT, DORSET, DT6 3QU.

BROOKS, Mrs. Mandy Diane, BSc ACA *1992;* 8 Selwyn Drive, HATFIELD, HERTFORDSHIRE, AL10 9NJ.

BROOKS, Mrs. Marilyn Doris, FCA *1966;* 6 Arundel Wing Tortington Manor, Ford Lane, Tortington, ARUNDEL, WEST SUSSEX, BN18 0FG.

BROOKS, Mr. Mark David, BA ACA ACII *1995;* 12 The Footpath, Roehampton, LONDON, SW15 5AW.

BROOKS, Mr. Matthew Daniel, BA(Hons) ACA *1998;* Bayridge Upper, 22 Woodbourne Avenue, PEMBROKE HM 08, BERMUDA.

•BROOKS, Mr. Maurice Brian, BSc FCA *1977;* Brooks Johnson Consultancy Services Limited, Northumberland House, Drake Avenue, STAINES, MIDDLESEX, TW18 2AP. See also Johnson Smith & Co Ltd

BROOKS, Mr. Melvyn Paul, BSc ACA *2000;* 14 Goldfinch Close, ORPINGTON, BR6 6NF.

BROOKS, Mr. Michael Henry, ACA *1991;* Easterton House Easterton, DEVIZES, SN10 4PU.

•BROOKS, Mr. Michael James, BA ACA *1996;* MJ Brooks Consultancy Limited, 9 Waterside, Station Road, HARPENDEN, HERTFORDSHIRE, AL5 4US.

BROOKS, Mr. Michael James, BA FCA *1983;* 12 Princethorpe Road, Sydenham, LONDON, SE26 4PF.

BROOKS, Mr. Michael John, FCA *1976;* 7 Haig Avenue, SINGAPORE 438862, SINGAPORE.

•BROOKS, Mr. Michael Stephen, FCA *1984;* Bourner Bullock, Sovereign House, 212-224 Shaftesbury Avenue, LONDON, WC2H 8HQ.

BROOKS, Mr. Neil Edward Charles, BA ACA *2006;* 49 Byrne Road, LONDON, SW12 9HZ.

BROOKS, Mr. Neil James, ACA *2009;* 45 Priory Street, Bowdon, ALTRINCHAM, CHESHIRE, WA14 3BQ.

BROOKS, Mr. Neil Matthew, ACA *2008;* with PricewaterhouseCoopers, Level 21, PWC Tower, 188 Quay Street, Private Bag 92162, AUCKLAND 1142 NEW ZEALAND.

BROOKS, Mr. Niall, BSc ACA *1992;* P.O. Box 4441, ROAD TOWN, TORTOLA ISLAND, VG1110, VIRGIN ISLANDS (BRITISH).

•BROOKS, Mr. Nicholas, BA FCA *1975;* Nicholas Brooks BA FCA, 10 School Road, Elmswell, BURY ST. EDMUNDS, SUFFOLK, IP30 9EQ.

BROOKS, Mr. Nicholas John, BA ACA *1999;* 2-29-6 Okubo, Shinijuku, TOKYO, JAPAN.

•BROOKS, Mr. Nicholas St John, FCA DChA *1976;* Kingston Smith LLP, Devonshire House, 60 Goswell Road, LONDON, EC1M 7AD. See also Kingston Smith Limited Liability Partnership, Devonshire Corporate Services LLP, Kingston Smith Consulting LLP and Kingston Smith Services Limited

•BROOKS, Mrs. Nicola Marie, BA ACA *1998;* Brooks & Jeal, Eddystone Road, WADEBRIDGE, CORNWALL, PL27 7AL.

BROOKS, Mr. Nigel John, MA ACA *1983;* 31 St Lawrence Terrace, LONDON, W10 5SR.

BROOKS, Mr. Norman James, FCA *1958;* 20 Inglewood, Kemnal Road, CHISLEHURST, BR7 6NF. (Life Member)

BROOKS, Mr. Paul Martin, BSc ACA *2001;* 269 Mays Lane, BARNET, HERTFORDSHIRE, EN5 2LY.

BROOKS, Mr. Paul Timothy Coleman, MA ACA *1978;* Experian, 80 Victoria Street, LONDON, SW1E 5JL.

BROOKS, Mr. Peter Clive, FCA *1968;* 7 Pikes Pool Lane, Burcot, BROMSGROVE, B60 1LJ.

•BROOKS, Mr. Peter David, BSc FCA *1983;* (Tax Fac), 48 Wordsworth Street, PENRITH, CA11 7QY.

BROOKS, Mr. Richard John, BSc ACA *1993;* D T Z, One Curzon Street, LONDON, W1A 5PZ.

BROOKS, Mr. Richard John, BSc ACA *2006;* 28 Epperstone Road, West Bridgford, NOTTINGHAM, NG2 7QF.

BROOKS, Mr. Richard Simon, FCA *1954;* York House, Clifton Down Road, BRISTOL, BS8 4AG. (Life Member)

BROOKS, Mr. Robert Anthony, FCA *1957;* Hattingley Cottage, Medstead, ALTON, GU34 5NQ. (Life Member)

BROOKS, Miss. Rosalynd, BA(Hons) ACA *2011;* 1 Sussex Road, SOUTHSEA, HAMPSHIRE, PO5 3EX.

BROOKS, Mr. Roy Selwyn, FCA *1960;* Hedgerley Cottage, 152 Tilt Road, COBHAM, SURREY, KT11 3HR. (Life Member)

•BROOKS, Mr. Russel Alan, FCA *1980;* Kent Consultancy, PO Box 261, ST. NEOTS, PE19 9DE.

BROOKS, Miss. Sarah, ACA *2010;* Arla Foods Plc, 4 Savannah Way Leeds Valley Park, LEEDS, LS10 1AB.

BROOKS, Miss. Sarah Mary, BA ACA *2005;* AEG The Studio, The O2, Peninsula Square, LONDON, SE10 0DX.

BROOKS, Mr. Simon, ACA *1984;* 3 St. Marys Mead, Painswick, STROUD, GLOUCESTERSHIRE, GL6 6UQ.

BROOKS, Mr. Stephen John, BA ACA *1990;* Schroder Investment Management PLC, Garrard House, 31 Gresham Street, LONDON, EC2V 7QA.

BROOKS, Mr. Steven, ACA *2011;* Flat 504, Sheridan Court, 66 Mansfield Road, NOTTINGHAM, NG1 3GY.

BROOKS, Mr. Terence Charles, FCA *1961;* Forest Garden Cottage, Beechwood Lane, Burley, RINGWOOD, BH24 4AR.

BROOKS, Mr. Trevor Briarcliffe, FCA *1953;* Langside, Tattenham Crescent, EPSOM, KT18 5NR. (Life Member)

•BROOKS, Mr. Trevor David, FCA *1973;* T.D. Brooks & Co, Flat 8, The Ferns, 90 Golf Links Road, FERNDOWN, DORSET BH22 8BZ.

BROOKS, Mrs. Victoria Emma Louise, BA(Hons) ACA *2010;* 8 Birch Court, Leeswood, MOLD, CLWYD, CH7 4UF.

BROOKS, Mr. William Anthony, BA FCA *1982;* MEMBER OF COUNCIL, with Eximus Capital Limited, Warnford Court, 29 Throgmorton Street, LONDON, EC2N 2AT.

BROOKS, Mr. William Samuel Kennedy, BSc ACA *2006;* 608 President Street, Apartment 3A, BROOKLYN, NY 11215, UNITED STATES.

BROOKS-WOOD, Mrs. Fiona Samantha, BEng ACA *1991;* 29 Oberwyl Road, CAMBERWELL, VIC 3124, AUSTRALIA.

BROOKSBANK, Mr. David William, FCA *1971;* 61 Doneraile Street, LONDON, SW6 6EW.

BROOKSBANK, Mr. James Robert, BEng ACA *1999;* 18d Uxbridge Road, KINGSTON UPON THAMES, SURREY, KT1 2LL.

BROOKSBANK, Mr. Raymond Bernard, FCA *1968;* British Polythene Ind. PLL, 96 Port Glasgow Road, GREENOCK, RENFREWSHIRE, PA15 2UL.

BROOKSBANK, Mr. Robert James, BSc ACA *1994;* Carclo Plc, Springstone House, PO Box 88, 27 Dewsbury Road, OSSETT, WEST YORKSHIRE WF5 9WS.

BROOKSBANK, Mr. Stamp Godfrey, FCA *1950;* 3N Oak Lodge, Lythe Hill Park, HASLEMERE, GU27 3TF. (Life Member)

BROOKSON, Mr. Philip Howard, ACA *1981;* 6 Mayflower Close, CRAWLEY, WEST SUSSEX, RH10 7WH.

BROOKSON, Mr. Stephen Brice, BSc ACA *1980;* 39 Carlyle Court, Chelsea Harbour, LONDON, SW10 0UQ.

BROOKWELL, Mr. Christopher Mark, BSc ACA *1998;* PO Box 216, KINGSTON, TAS 7051, AUSTRALIA.

BROOKWELL, Miss. Kerri Ann, ACA *2008;* Apartment 45 The Wharf, Dock Head Road, CHATHAM, ME4 4ZN.

BROOM, Mr. Adam John, BA ACA *2007;* 18 Briardale Walk, ALTRINCHAM, CHESHIRE, WA14 5GU.

BROOM, Mr. Anthony Ernest John, FCA *1954;* 10 Monkseaton Road, SUTTON COLDFIELD, B72 1LB. (Life Member)

BROOM, Mr. David Thomas, BSc ACA *1994;* 3 Manor Road, LONDON, SW20 9AE.

BROOM, Ms. Deborah Jane, FCA *1991;* 84 Sandhill Road, CRADOC, TAS 7109, AUSTRALIA.

BROOM, Miss. Emily Louise, ACA *2008;* B & Q Plc Hampshire Corporate Park, Templars Way Chandler's Ford, EASTLEIGH, SO53 3YX.

•BROOM, Mr. John Anthony, FCA *1970;* (Tax Fac), Harper Broom, Aston House, York Road, Maidenhead, MAIDENHEAD, BERKSHIRE SL6 1SF.

BROOM, Mr. Jonathan William, ACA *2009;* Flat 5, 14 Furrow Lane, LONDON, E9 6JS.

BROOM, Mrs. Nichola Jane, BSc ACA *1987;* The Radionetwork of New Zealand Ltd, 54 Cook Street, Private Bag 92198, AUCKLAND, NEW ZEALAND.

BROOM, Mr. Paul George, BSc FCA *1992;* Thatch Cottage, 20 Reading Road, Eversley, HOOK, HAMPSHIRE, RG27 0RP.

BROOMAN, Mr. John Cresswell, FCA *1949;* Pembroke Lodge, 6 Brock Way, VIRGINIA WATER, GU25 4SD. (Life Member)

BROOMAN, Mr. Richard John, MA FCA *1984;* 27 Rivermead Court, Marlow Bridge Lane, MARLOW, SL7 1SJ.

BROOMBERG, Mr. Ashley Dan, MPhil ACA *1998;* Stoneycroft Barnet Lane, Elstree, BOREHAMWOOD, HERTFORDSHIRE, WD6 3RQ.

BROOME, Mr. Alan, BSc ACA *1990;* 26 High Street, Wicklewood, WYMONDHAM, NORFOLK, NR18 9QE.

•BROOME, Mr. Andrew Malcolm, BA ACA *1997;* haysmacintyre, Fairfax House, 15 Fulwood Place, LONDON, WC1V 6AY.

BROOME, Mr. David James Dudley, BA ACA *1993;* 25 Oakfield Road, Selly Park, BIRMINGHAM, B29 7HH.

BROOME, Mr. Nicholas, BA ACA *1994;* 85 Powisland Drive, Derriford, PLYMOUTH, PL6 6AE.

BROOME, Mr. Paul Alan, BA ACA *1990;* 3 Letcombe Place, Horndean, WATERLOOVILLE, HAMPSHIRE, PO8 0DE.

BROOME, Miss. Susannah Mary Jane, BSc ACA *2008;* Beazley, Floor 8, Plantation Place South, 60 Great Tower Street, LONDON, EC3R 5AD.

BROOME, Ms. Theresa Mary, BA FCA *1977;* International Transport Workers' Federation, Itf House, 49-60 Borough Road, LONDON, SE1 1DR.

BROOMFIELD, Miss. Alison Sian, BA(Hons) ACA *2001;* Hogg Robinson Plc Global House, Victoria Street, BASINGSTOKE, RG21 3BT.

BROOMFIELD, Mr. Ryan Haigh, BA ACA CTA *2003;* 21 Chesham Terrace, Ealing, LONDON, W13 9HX.

BROOMFIELD, Mr. Timothy Neil, BSc ACA *1992;* 29 Wakehurst Close, Maple Park, NUNEATON, CV11 4YF.

BROOMHALL, Mr. Jonathan, BA ACA *2011;* 75 Derwent Close, Alsager, STOKE-ON-TRENT, ST7 2EL.

BROOMHALL, Mrs. Juliette Louise, BA(Hons) ACA *2004;* 25 Malthouse Square, BEACONSFIELD, BUCKINGHAMSHIRE, HP9 2LD.

•BROOMHEAD, Mr. Andrew Thomas, MA FCA *1986;* Pacific Basin Shopping (HK) Ltd, 7/F Hutchison House, 10 Harcourt Road, CENTRAL, HONG KONG ISLAND, HONG KONG SAR.

BROOMHEAD, Mr. Jeremy Frank, BA FCA *1976;* 14/A Langham Mansions, Earl's Court Square, LONDON, SW5 9UH.

BROOMHEAD, Mr. Philip, FCA *1959;* The White House, 26 Crowlees Road, MIRFIELD, WF14 9PJ. (Life Member)

BROOMHEAD, Mr. Walter, FCA *1957;* 179 Wellington Hill West, Westbury On Trym, BRISTOL, BS9 4QW. (Life Member)

BROPHY, Miss. Jennifer Catherine, BA(Hons) FCA *2001;* 8 William Smith Close, CAMBRIDGE, CB1 3QF.

BROPHY, Mrs. Kathryn Emma, BA ACA *1992;* Elmvale Lodge, 7 Flag Lane, Heath Charnock, CHORLEY, PR6 9ED.

•BROPHY, Mr. Kieran Michael, BA ACA *1992;* R.P. Smith & Co, 28 St Thomas's Rd, CHORLEY, PR7 1HX. See also R P Smith & Co Ltd

BROPHY, Miss. Laura, MChem ACA *2011;* 34 Rowan Grove, Huyton, LIVERPOOL, L36 5XX.

•BROPHY, Mr. Thomas Martin, BA FCA *1980;* 32 Brooklands Drive, Kings Heath, BIRMINGHAM, B14 6EJ.

BROSINOVICH, Miss. Nicola Lara, BA FCA *1995;* 241 Grove End Gardens, Grove End Road, St Johns Wood, LONDON, NW8 9LU.

•BROSNAN, Mr. Adam John, BA(Hons) ACA *2001;* Brosnans Limited, Birkby House, Bailiff Bridge, BRIGHOUSE, WEST YORKSHIRE, HD6 4JJ.

•BROSNAN, Mr. Bernard Joseph, FCA *1973;* (Tax Fac), Brosnans Limited, Birkby House, Bailiff Bridge, BRIGHOUSE, WEST YORKSHIRE, HD6 4JJ.

BROSNAN, Miss. Caroline, BSc ACA *2010;* 7/24 Quinton Road, MANLY, NSW 2095, AUSTRALIA.

BROSNIHAN, Mr. Gerard, BA ACA *1998;* 127 Moor Lane, WILMSLOW, CHESHIRE, SK9 6BY.

BROSNIHAN, Mrs. Sarah Jayne, BA ACA *1996;* 127 Moor Lane, WILMSLOW, CHESHIRE, SK9 6BY.

BROSTER, Mr. David Arthur, BSc ACA *1992;* 53 Poplar Crescent, Norton, STOURBRIDGE, DY8 3BA.

BROSTER, Mrs. Eleanor Muriel Fenella, BA(Hons) ACA *2001;* 47 Grosvenor Avenue, LONDON, SW14 8BU.

BROSTER, Mr. James Anthony, FCA *1967;* 17 Saxmundham Road Framlingham, WOODBRIDGE, SUFFOLK, IP13 9BU.

BROSTER, Mr. Peter Charles Ramsay, BSc ACA *1993;* Eliasova 763/50, Bubenec, 16000 PRAGUE, CZECH REPUBLIC.

BROTHERSTON, Mrs. Jennie, BSc ACA *2006;* Flat 53, Cottrill Gardens, Marcon Place, LONDON, E8 1NY.

BROTHERTON, Miss. Emma, ACA *2007;* 179 Stroud Road, Shirley, SOLIHULL, B90 2LA.

BROTHERTON, Mr. James Edward, BSc ACA *1996;* 65 Buckingham Gate, LONDON, SW1E 6AS.

BROTHERTON, Mr. Peter James, BSc ACA *1994;* 25 Newton Terrace, YORK, YO1 6HE.

BROTHERTON, Mr. Simon Guy, MA ACA *1992;* Ernst & Young, P O Box 2146, AUCKLAND, NEW ZEALAND.

BROTHERTON, Mr. Stephen Robert, ACA *2008;* with Deloitte LLP, Global House, High Street, CRAWLEY, RH10 1DL.

BROUARD, Mr. Karl Peter, BEng ACA *2007;* Tamarisk, La Rue Des Escaliers, St Martin, GUERNSEY, GY4 6HZ.

BROUARD, Mr. Robert, BSc FCA *1959;* Whiteoaks, Parcq de L'oeillere, La Pulente St Brelade, JERSEY, JE3 8HF. (Life Member)

BROUDE, Mr. Leslie Paul, BA FCA *1979;* 17 Woodbank Avenue, GERRARDS CROSS, SL9 7PY.

•BROUGH, Mr. Christopher William, BA ACA *1988;* Deloitte LLP, 2 New Street Square, LONDON, EC4A 3BZ. See also Deloitte & Touche LLP

BROUGH, Mr. Colin Lupton, FCA *1969;* Little Sarsens, Mill Lane, West Hendred, WANTAGE, OXFORDSHIRE, OX12 8RJ.

BROUGH, Mr. Gary, BA FCA *1987;* KPMG, KPMG Building, The Village at Grace Bay, PROVIDENCIALES, TURKS AND CAICOS ISLANDS.

BROUGH, Mr. Graeme Michael, BA ACA CTA *2006;* 174 Biddlestone Road, NEWCASTLE UPON TYNE, NE6 5SP.

BROUGH, Ms. Joyce Marilyn, BSc ACA *1981;* 2 Peartree Cottage, Halmore, BERKELEY, GL13 9HL.

BROUGH, Mr. Nicholas, BSc ACA *1994;* Arawak Energy Ltd, Belgrave House, 76 Buckingham Palace Road, LONDON, SW1W 9TQ.

BROUGH, Mr. Paul Jeremy, BA ACA *1983;* KPMG, 8/F Prince's Building, 10 Chater Road, CENTRAL, HONG KONG ISLAND, HONG KONG SAR.

BROUGH, Mr. Richard Martin, BSc(Econ) ACA *1995;* The Hermitage, Back Lane, Hardingstone, NORTHAMPTON, NN4 6BY.

BROUGH, Mr. Robert Neil, BSc ACA *2011;* 152a London Road, SEVENOAKS, TN13 1DJ.

BROUGH, Mr. Samuel John, FCA *1956;* 3 Coppice Beck Court, Coppice Drive, HARROGATE, HG1 2LB. (Life Member)

BROUGH, Mrs. Sara Kirstine, BSc ACA *1998;* 10 Uplands Close, GERRARDS CROSS, BUCKINGHAMSHIRE, SL9 7JH.

BROUGH, Mr. Simon Timothy, FCA CTA *1968;* Oak Tree House, Oak Tree Lane, Dunsfold, GODALMING, GU8 4LE.

BROUGHALL, Mr. Barry, FCA *1974;* Ashtree House, Croft Road, Upton Snodsbury, WORCESTER, WR7 4NS.

BROUGHAM, Miss. Alexandra Mary, MA FCA *1992;* 101 Pepys Road, LONDON, SW20 8NW.

BROUGHAM, Mr. Max, BSc FCA *1982;* 6 Rookery Lane, Fellside Park, Whickham, NEWCASTLE UPON TYNE, NE16 5TX.

•BROUGHAM, Mr. Simon Brookes, ACA FCCA *1983;* Bramil Associates, Rex House, 354 Ballards Lane, North Finchley, LONDON, N12 0DD.

BROUGHTON, Mr. Alan, FCA *1965;* 3223 Country Club Pkwy, CASTLE ROCK, CO 80108-8300, UNITED STATES. (Life Member)

BROUGHTON, Mr. Edward William George, FCA *1968;* 56 Barrow Road, Burton-on-the-Wolds, LOUGHBOROUGH, LEICESTERSHIRE, LE12 5TB.

BROUGHTON, Mr. Gareth James, BA ACA *2005;* Pumpkin Patch, 439 East Tamaki Road, East Tamaki, MANUKAU 2013, NEW ZEALAND.

BROUGHTON, Mr. Graham John Lytton, MMath ACA *2003;* Chaucer Syndicates Ltd, Plantation Place, 30 Fenchurch Street, LONDON, EC3M 3AD.

BROUGHTON, Mr. Mark David, BSc ACA *2005;* 4 Hambledon Gardens, BLANDFORD FORUM, DORSET, DT11 7SE.

BROUGHTON, Sir Martin Faulkner, FCA *1969;* Rosemary House, Woodhurst Park, OXTED, RH8 9HA.

BROUGHTON, Mr. Paul, ACA *2010;* 34 Fords Avenue, Healing, GRIMSBY, SOUTH HUMBERSIDE, DN41 7RP.

BROUGHTON, Mr. Roger Harry, BA FCA *1992;* Monks Quarry Cottage, 53 Rose Close, Winterbourne Down, BRISTOL, BS36 1DA.

BROUGHTON, Miss. Sarah, BSc(Hons) ACA *2001;* 65 Green Lane, Bovingdon, HEMEL HEMPSTEAD, HERTFORDSHIRE, HP3 0LA.

BROUGHTON, Mr. Stewart John, FCA *1973;* 4 Oakfield, LYMINGTON, SO41 3AD.

•BROUGHTON, Miss. Susan Rosemary, BSc ACA *1991;* 47 Pinfold Hill, Shenstone, LICHFIELD, STAFFORDSHIRE, WS14 0JN.

BROUGHTON, Mrs. Suzanne, ACA *1991;* Standwell, Lower Street, Barford St. Michael, BANBURY, OX15 0RH.

BROW, Mr. John David Bromfield, FCA *1959;* Lea Bank, Westerfield Road, Westerfield, IPSWICH, IP6 9AJ. (Life Member)

BROWELL, Mr. Robert Harrison, MMath ACA *2006;* Pricewaterhousecoopers Donington Court Herald Way, East Midlands Airport Castle Donington, DERBY, DE74 2UZ.

BROWN, Mr. Adam Cem, BA(Hons) ACA *2011;* Smith & Williamson, 25 Moorgate, LONDON, EC2R 6AY.

BROWN, Mr. Adam David, BSc ACA *1991;* The Corner House, Kimpton Road, WELWYN, HERTFORDSHIRE, AL6 9NN.

•BROWN, Mr. Adam John Witherow, BSc ACA *1989;* Hitchin Practice Limited, Hemmings, Kings Walden, HITCHIN, HERTFORDSHIRE, SG4 8NW.

BROWN, Mr. Adrian Christopher, BSc ACA *1991;* 5 Highcrown Mews, SOUTHAMPTON, SO17 1PT.

•BROWN, Mr. Alan David, FCA *1979;* (Tax Fac), The Jamesons Partnership Limited, 92 Station Road, CLACTON-ON-SEA, CO15 1SG.

BROWN, Mr. Alan Francis, FCA *1968;* 1c Bickerton Road, SOUTHPORT, MERSEYSIDE, PR8 2DY.

BROWN, Mr. Alan Geoffrey, FCA MBA *1972;* The Doctor's Inn, 304 Trudeau Road, SARANAC LAKE, NY 12983, UNITED STATES.

BROWN, Mr. Alan Jeffrey, BSc ACA *1982;* 115 Francklyn Gardens, EDGWARE, HA8 8SB.

BROWN, Mr. Alan John, FCA *1973;* 27 Sylvania Drive, Sylvania Park, EXETER, EX4 5DT.

BROWN, Mr. Alastair, ACA *2008;* 26 Priory Road, NEWCASTLE, STAFFORDSHIRE, ST5 2EW.

BROWN, Mr. Alastair Colin Gillies, BSc(Econ) ACA *2002;* 257 Magdalen Road, LONDON, SW18 3PA.

•BROWN, Mrs. Alba Constance Ermida, BA(Hons) ACA *2001;* Guildway Bungalow, Radclive, BUCKINGHAM, MK18 4AB.

BROWN, Mr. Alec Charles, FCA *1953;* 22 Harwood Gardens, Old Windsor, WINDSOR, BERKSHIRE, SL4 2LJ. (Life Member)

BROWN, Mrs. Alexandra Louise Stafford, BSc FCA AMCT *1995;* Frogmore Farm, Back Lane, Bradfield, READING, RG7 6DS.

BROWN, Mrs. Alice Elizabeth, BSc ACA *1990;* The Old Waterboard House, Icknield Road, Goring, READING, RG8 0DE.

BROWN, Ms. Alisa Jane, BA ACA *1997;* 13 Vancouver Road, LONDON, SE23 2AG.

BROWN, Miss. Alison, BA FCA *1978;* High Mosser Gate, Mosser, COCKERMOUTH, CA13 0SR.

BROWN, Mrs. Alison Dawn, BA ACA *1992;* (Tax Fac), 15 Allanhurst Crescent, BRAMPTON L6P 1C6, ON, CANADA.

BROWN, Mrs. Alison Jane, BSc FCA *1984;* 168 Upper Woodcote Road, Caversham, READING, RG4 7LD.

BROWN, Mr. Alistair Mark, BSc ACA *1998;* Dublin Axis Group, 34 upper mount street, DUBLIN 2, COUNTY DUBLIN, IRELAND.

•BROWN, Mr. Allan Keith, FCA *1969;* (Tax Fac), Allan Brown Accountancy & Taxation Services Limited, 18/22 Church Street, MALVERN, WR14 2AY. See also Allan Brown & Co

BROWN, Mrs. Andrea Dawn, BA ACA *1994;* L S I Logic Europe Ltd Greenwood House, London Road, BRACKNELL, RG12 2UB.

BROWN, Mrs. Andrea Marie, BA ACA *1996;* Ryecroft, High Street, Upton, DIDCOT, OX11 9JE.

BROWN, Mr. Andrew, BA ACA *2006;* with PricewaterhouseCoopers, Mississauga Executive Centre, 1 Robert Speck Parkway, Suite 1100, MISSISSAUGA L4Z 3M3, ON CANADA.

BROWN, Mr. Andrew, BSc ACA *1994;* 12 Greenbrook Avenue, BARNET, HERTFORDSHIRE, EN4 0LS.

BROWN, Mr. Andrew, ACA *2009;* (Tax Fac), 68 Brynteg, CARDIFF, CF14 6TT.

BROWN, Mr. Andrew, ACA *2009;* 12 Parsonage Lane, ENFIELD, MIDDLESEX, EN2 0AJ.

•BROWN, Mr. Andrew Christopher, FCA *1974;* Sherwoods, 30 Addiscombe Grove, CROYDON, CR9 5AY. See also Twinemanda Limited

BROWN, Mr. Andrew David, ACA *1993;* 10 Wilkinson Way, SCUNTHORPE, SOUTH HUMBERSIDE, DN16 3NS.

BROWN, Mr. Andrew David Patrick, BA ACA *1994;* Amundi Private Equity Funds, 90 Boulevard Pasteur, CS 21564, 75015 PARIS, FRANCE.

BROWN, Mr. Andrew Denis, BA ACA *1993;* Bramley Cottage, 1 The Orchard, Rue De Jambart, ST CLEMENT, JE2 6LA.

BROWN, Mr. Andrew James, BSc FCA *1991;* 56 Southdown Crescent, Cheadle Hulme, CHEADLE, SK8 6HA.

BROWN, Mr. Andrew John, FCA *1970;* 15 Garden Fields, Stebbing, DUNMOW, CM6 3RG.

BROWN, Mr. Andrew Jonathan, FCA *1968;* Pilgrims, Ebbisham Lane, Walton-On-The-Hill, TADWORTH, KT20 5BT.

BROWN, Mr. Andrew Robert, BA ACA *2002;* Cello Group plc, 11-13 Charterhouse Buildings, LONDON, EC1M 7AP.

BROWN, Mr. Andrew Robin, BSc FCA *1992;* with Deloitte LLP, Athene Place, 66 Shoe Lane, LONDON, EC4A 3BQ.

BROWN, Mr. Andrew Wallis, BSc ACA *1994;* A T & T, Highfield House, Headless Cross Drive, REDDITCH, WORCESTERSHIRE, B97 5EQ.

BROWN, Mr. Angus Robert, FCA *1983;* 16 Bridgefield Road, SUTTON, SM1 2DG.

BROWN, Mrs. Ann Margaret, BA FCA *1995;* Clough & Co New Chartford House, Centurion Way, CLECKHEATON, WEST YORKSHIRE, BD19 3QB.

BROWN, Mrs. Anne Patricia, BA ACA *1995;* 85 Samrose Drive, NOVATO, CA 94945, UNITED STATES.

BROWN, Mrs. Annette Claire, MBA BSc FCA *1987;* The Old Mill House, Barkestone Lane, Redmile, NOTTINGHAM, NG13 0GR.

BROWN, Mr. Anthony, BA ACA *1999;* with Deloitte LLP, 1 City Square, LEEDS, WEST YORKSHIRE, LS1 2AL.

BROWN, Mr. Anthony Graeme, BSc FCA *1977;* 1395 Highgate Court, OAKVILLE L6H 2V4, ON, CANADA.

BROWN, Mr. Anthony James, BA ACA *1992;* 84 Lyncroft Mansions, Lyncroft Gardens, West Hampstead, LONDON, NW6 1JY.

•BROWN, Mr. Anthony John, FCA *1977;* A J Brown Limited, 91 Front Street, Acomb, YORK, YO24 3BU.

•BROWN, Mr. Anthony Stanley, FCA *1968;* Clayton & Co, 9 Lynton Close, KNUTSFORD, CHESHIRE, WA16 8BH.

BROWN, Mr. Anthony Stuart Edlund, FCA *1965;* Pantiles, Chapel Lane, Swallow, MARKET RASEN, LINCOLNSHIRE, LN7 6DE. (Life Member)

BROWN, Mr. Antony Richard, BSc ACA *1995;* 7 Rotterdam Drive, London Yard, LONDON, E14 3JA.

BROWN, Mr. Antony William, FCA *1987;* 41 Hazel Close, Colden Common, WINCHESTER, HAMPSHIRE, SO21 1DL.

BROWN, Mrs. Anya, MA BA(Hons) ACA *2002;* 172 Cromwell Road, CAMBRIDGE, CB1 3EQ.

BROWN, Mr. Arthur Ernest, FCA *1967;* 53 Woodside Road, Beaumont Park, HUDDERSFIELD, HD4 5JF. (Life Member)

BROWN, Mrs. Belinda Jane, BSc ACA *1994;* Suites 4&5 Oxford House, Oxford Road, MACCLESFIELD, CHESHIRE, SK11 8HS.

BROWN, Mr. Benjamin, BA ACA *2009;* 30 Jardine Close, STOURBRIDGE, DY8 4AT.

BROWN, Mr. Benjamin John, ACA *2008;* with Ernst & Young LLP, 1 More London Place, LONDON, SE1 2AF.

BROWN, Mr. Benn, ACA *2004;* 20 Millbrook Gardens, Blythe Bridge, STOKE-ON-TRENT, ST11 9JQ.

BROWN, Mr. Bernard Samuel, BSc FCA *1971;* 15 The Cloisters, Long Street, SHERBORNE, DORSET, DT9 3BS. (Life Member)

BROWN, Mr. Bryan William, FCA *1962;* 23 Rosehill Avenue, Horsell, WOKING, GU21 4SD. (Life Member)

BROWN, Mr. Carl Michael, MSc ACA *2000;* 3 Holly Close, Walmley, SUTTON COLDFIELD, B76 2PD.

BROWN, Mr. Carl Richard, BCom ACA *2003;* 1a Tenzing Road, HEMEL HEMPSTEAD, HERTFORDSHIRE, HP2 4HT.

BROWN, Mr. Carl Whitmore, BA ACA *1992;* L I B G Ltd, Wigham House, Wakering Road, BARKING, ESSEX, IG11 8PJ.

BROWN, Mr. Carlton Jeffrey, BSc(Econ) *1997;* Bradstones, 18 Heatherdale Road, CAMBERLEY, GU15 2LT.

BROWN, Mrs. Carol Jane, BA ACA *2000;* 30 Bramley Way, Bramley Green, Angmering, LITTLEHAMPTON, WEST SUSSEX, BN16 4GA.

BROWN, Miss. Carole Elisabeth, BA ACA *1995;* 49 Rosemoor Gardens, Appleton, WARRINGTON, WA4 5RF.

BROWN, Mrs. Carole Joanne, ACA *1993;* 60 Hartswood Close, Pewterspear, Appleton, WARRINGTON, WA4 5QZ.

BROWN, Miss. Caroline Louise, BA FCA *1985;* (Tax Fac), with Haines Watts (Lancashire) LLP, Northern Assurance Buildings, 9-21 Princess Street, MANCHESTER, M2 4DN.

•BROWN, Mrs. Catherine Lucy, BA ACA *1996;* Kate Brown BA ACA, The Annexe, Rectory Farm, Cranford Road, Great Addington, KETTERING NORTHAMPTONSHIRE NN14 4BH.

•BROWN, Mrs. Catherine Mary, BA FCA *1990;* Wright Connections Limited, Bedford Business Centre, 61-63 St. Peters Street, BEDFORD, MK40 2PR.

BROWN, Mrs. Cathryn Ruth, BSocSc ACA *2001;* 17 Woodside Close, AMERSHAM, BUCKINGHAMSHIRE, HP6 5EG.

BROWN, Mr. Charles Edwin, MA ACA *1979;* 64 High Street, Over, CAMBRIDGE, CB24 5ND.

BROWN, Mr. Charles Mcdermott, BA ACA *1980;* 12 Southdown Road, LONDON, SW20 8PT.

BROWN, Mr. Charles Michael, FCA *1954;* Millstream Cottage, Hamstead Mill, Hamstead Marshall, NEWBURY, RG20 0JD. (Life Member)

BROWN, Mr. Charles Peter, FCA *1963;* Duchy Cottage, 38a Duchy Road, HARROGATE, HG1 2ER.

BROWN, Miss. Charlotte Anna, BA(Hons) ACA *2000;* 61 Underlane, Plympton, PLYMOUTH, PL7 1QX.

BROWN, Miss. Charlotte Louise, BA ACA *1998;* 40 Naylors Terrace Belmont, BOLTON, BL7 8AP.

•BROWN, Mrs. Christine Amy, FCA *1977;* C.A. Brown, 24 Woodlands Road, HAYWARDS HEATH, RH16 3JU.

BROWN, Mrs. Christine Barbara, FCA *1974;* 27 Heol Tre Forys, PENARTH, SOUTH GLAMORGAN, CF64 3RE.

BROWN, Mrs. Christine Helen, ACA *1978;* with Kinnair & Company, Aston House, Redburn Road, NEWCASTLE UPON TYNE, NE5 1NB.

BROWN, Mr. Christopher, ACA *2008;* 33 Vanguard Chase, NORWICH, NR5 0UG.

BROWN, Mr. Christopher Campbell, FCA *1964;* Hilperton House, The Knap, Hilperton, TROWBRIDGE, WILTSHIRE, BA14 7RJ.

BROWN, Mr. Christopher Charles, BSc ACA *2001;* 111 Wright Way, Stapleton, BRISTOL, BS16 1WE.

BROWN, Mr. Christopher David, FCA *1969;* Badgers Croft, 17 Mountain Ash, Marlow Bottom, MARLOW, BUCKINGHAMSHIRE, SL7 3PB.

BROWN, Mr. Christopher David, BSc ACA *1992;* Badgers, Church Road, Sutton, SANDY, BEDFORDSHIRE, SG19 2NB.

BROWN, Mr. Christopher Frank, ACA *1989;* Centrebus Ltd, 37 Wenlock Way, LEICESTER, LE4 9HU.

BROWN, Mr. Christopher George, ACA *1979;* 34 Dykelands Road, SUNDERLAND, SR6 8EP.

•BROWN, Mr. Christopher Gerald, FCA *1969;* Too Much Tax Ltd, 9 Alburys, Wrington, BRISTOL, BS40 5NZ.

BROWN, Mr. Christopher James, ACA *2006;* 15 Durham Avenue, THORNTON-CLEVELEYS, LANCASHIRE, FY5 2DP.

BROWN, Mr. Christopher Lyndon, BSc ACA *1979;* 27 Heol Tre Forys, PENARTH, SOUTH GLAMORGAN, CF64 3RE.

•BROWN, Mr. Christopher Mark, FCA *1971;* (Tax Fac), Goldwyns (Bristol) Limited, 9 Portland Square, BRISTOL, BS2 8ST.

BROWN, Mr. Christopher Martin, BA ACA *1994;* Lloyds Banking Group, 10 Gresham Street, LONDON, EC2V 7AE.

BROWN, Mr. Christopher Martin Eastwood, FCA *1958;* Bracken Wood, Rake Hanger, Hill Brow, LISS, HAMPSHIRE, GU33 7NP. (Life Member)

BROWN, Mr. Christopher Paul, BA FCA *1982;* 18 Headley Road, BILLERICAY, ESSEX, CM11 1BJ.

•BROWN, Mr. Christopher Raymond, BA ACA *1988;* (Tax Fac), Christopher R. Brown Limited, 24 Albert Road, CLEVEDON, BS21 7RR.

BROWN, Mr. Christopher Robert, BEng FCA *1994;* 332a Straight Road, COLCHESTER, CO3 9DX.

BROWN, Mr. Christopher Scott, LLB ACA *2005;* 10 Compton Avenue, Top floor Flat, BRIGHTON, BN1 3PN.

•BROWN, Mr. Christopher Stuart, BA FCA *1978;* (Tax Fac), The cba Partnership, 72 Lairgate, BEVERLEY, HU17 8EU. See also CBA Financial Services Limited

BROWN, Mr. Christopher William Booth, FCA *1972;* 3250 Locke Lane, HOUSTON, TX 77019, UNITED STATES.

BROWN, Mrs. Claire, BSc ACA *1998;* 18 Broomfield Road, SEVENOAKS, KENT, TN13 3EL.

BROWN, Mrs. Claire, BA ACA *2006;* 25 Heath Road, Timperley, ALTRINCHAM, CHESHIRE, WA15 6BH.

BROWN, Mrs. Claire Anne, BA ACA *1985;* 4 Roberts Grove, WOKINGHAM, RG41 4WR.

BROWN, Miss. Claire Elizabeth Agnes, BSc ACA *2007;* 3 Peace Grove, WELWYN, AL6 0RS.

BROWN, Mrs. Claire Fiona, BA ACA *1993;* Kings Place & Events Kings Place, 90 York Way, LONDON, N1 9AG.

BROWN, Mrs. Clare, BA ACA *1992;* 2c Penn Avenue, CHESHAM, BUCKINGHAMSHIRE, HP5 2HT.

BROWN, Mr. Claude Brownlie, FCA *1959;* 140 Poulton Road, BLACKPOOL, FY3 7JL. (Life Member)

•BROWN, Mr. Clive Arne, BA FCA *1987;* 26 Ladymeade, ILMINSTER, SOMERSET, TA19 0EA.

BROWN, Mr. Clive Stuart, BSc ACA *1986;* Greenwood, The Green, Frant, TUNBRIDGE WELLS, TN3 9DR.

•**BROWN, Mr. Clive Thomas, BSc FCA** *1975;* Dunn & Ellis, St Davids Building, Lombard Street, PORTHMADOG, GWYNEDD, LL49 9AP.

BROWN, Miss. Colette, BSc BSc(Hons) ACA *2010;* Mazars Llp Regency House, 3 Grosvenor Square, SOUTHAMPTON, SO15 2BE.

BROWN, Mr. Colin, BSc FCA *1969;* 1 Cedar House, Warberry Park Gardens, TUNBRIDGE WELLS, KENT, TN4 8GF.

•**BROWN, Mr. Colin Charles, FCA** *1980;* 25 Carmarthen Avenue, East Cosham, PORTSMOUTH, PO6 2AG.

BROWN, Mr. Colin Ian, FCA *1956;* Yeddinges, Upper Court Road, Woldingham, CATERHAM, CR3 7BE. (Life Member)

BROWN, Mr. Colin Leslie, BA ACA *1991;* 4 Sovereign Court, LEEDS, LS17 7UT.

BROWN, Mr. Colin Ross, MA ACA *1991;* 3 Greenaway Villas, Old Exeter Road, NEWTON ABBOT, DEVON, TQ12 2NQ.

BROWN, Mr. Colin Vincent, ACA *1982;* Alliance Oil Group, 39 Sivtsev Vrazhek, 119002 MOSCOW, RUSSIAN FEDERATION.

BROWN, Mr. Craig Jonathan, BA ACA *1997;* Milton Point, Wildernesse Avenue, SEVENOAKS, TN15 0EA.

BROWN, Mr. Craig Robert, BSc ACA *1999;* 701 Millennium Apartments, 95 Newhall Street, BIRMINGHAM, B3 1BA.

BROWN, Mr. Cyril Frederick, FCA *1958;* 203 Eden Way, BECKENHAM, BR3 3DS. (Life Member)

BROWN, Mr. David, FCA *1964;* 11 Kruger Place, BOORAGOON, WA 6154, AUSTRALIA. (Life Member)

BROWN, Mr. David, FCA *1965;* The Manor House, 66 High Street, TARPORLEY, CW6 0AG.

BROWN, Mr. David, BSc FCA *1992;* PricewaterhouseCoopers, 20/F Princes Building, CENTRAL, Hong Kong Island, HONG KONG SAR.

BROWN, Mr. David, BSc ACA *1988;* Banbury House, 60 Church Way, Iffley, OXFORD, OX4 4EF.

BROWN, Mr. David, FCA *1974;* 2a Whitcliffe Grove, RIPON, NORTH YORKSHIRE, HG4 2JW.

BROWN, Mr. David Alexander, FCA *1980;* 7 Badgers Walk, PURLEY, SURREY, CR8 3PX.

BROWN, Mr. David Andrew, BA(Hons) ACA *2003;* 3 Abri Lane, PEMBROKE HM 02, BERMUDA.

•**BROWN, Mr. David Andrew, FCA** *1977;* Thomas David, 6-7 Castle Gate, Castle Street, HERTFORD, HERTFORDSHIRE, SG14 1HD.

BROWN, Mr. David Andrew, MA ACA *1979;* 26 Calonne Road, Wimbledon, LONDON, SW19 5HJ.

•**BROWN, Mr. David Andrew, MBA BSc FCA** *1983;* 168 Upper Woodcote Road, Caversham, READING, RG4 7LD.

BROWN, Mr. David Anthony, MA ACA AMCT *1997;* 1 Baycliffe Close, CAMBRIDGE, CB1 8EE.

•**BROWN, Mr. David Anthony, ACA** *1993;* Allchurch Bailey Limited, 93 High Street, EVESHAM, WORCESTERSHIRE, WR11 4DU.

BROWN, Mr. David Burdett, FCA *1968;* SolarEmpower Limited, 74-75 Brunner Road, LONDON, E17 7NW.

BROWN, Mr. David Charles, BSc ACA *1990;* Marathon Asset Management Ltd, 5 Upper St. Martin's Lane, LONDON, WC2H 9EA.

•**BROWN, Mr. David Christopher, FCA** *1973;* 3 Pinewood Drive, MANSFIELD, NG18 4PG.

BROWN, Mr. David Dean, FCA *1961;* 35 West Street, STRATFORD-UPON-AVON, WARWICKSHIRE, CV37 6DN. (Life Member)

BROWN, Mr. David Edward, BSc(Hons) ACA *2000;* 14 Valley Mill Court, Laneshawbridge, COLNE, LANCASHIRE, BB8 7ND.

•**BROWN, Mr. David Edward, BA ACA** *1994;* Deloitte LLP, Athene Place, 66 Shoe Lane, LONDON, EC4A 3BQ. See also Deloitte & Touche LLP

BROWN, Mr. David Howard, FCA *1972;* 2 Brookfield, Hopton Hall Lane, MIRFIELD, WF14 8HL.

BROWN, Mr. David John, BA FCA *1972;* Field End Cottage, Spade Oak Farm, Coldmoorholme Lane, BOURNE END, BUCKINGHAMSHIRE, SL8 5PS.

•**BROWN, Mr. David John, FCA** *1989;* DJB Accontancy Limited, Sandy Farm Business Centre, The Sands, FARNHAM, SURREY, GU10 1PX.

BROWN, Mr. David John, FCA *1973;* 9 Deepdale, Wilnecote, TAMWORTH, B77 4PD.

BROWN, Mr. David Jonathan, MSc BSc ACA *2006;* 6 Neville Drive, ROMSEY, SO51 7RP.

BROWN, Mr. David Michael, BSc ACA *1993;* Ofcom, 2a Southwark Bridge Road, LONDON, SE1 9HA.

BROWN, Mr. David Michael, FCA *1968;* 142 Ribchester Road, Clayton-Le-Dale, BLACKBURN, BB1 9EE.

BROWN, Mr. David Nicholas, BSc FCA *1989;* 13 Elstree Gardens, BLYTH, NE24 3RW.

BROWN, Mr. David Nicholas, BSc FCA *1998;* 84 Sistova Road, LONDON, SW12 9QS.

BROWN, Mr. David Nigel, BSc ACA *1986;* 116 Clarence Road, ST. ALBANS, HERTFORDSHIRE, AL1 4NW.

BROWN, Mr. David Thomas, BSc ACA *1998;* J C Bamford Excavators Ltd Lakeside Works, Denstone Road Rocester, UTTOXETER, STAFFORDSHIRE, ST14 5JP.

•**BROWN, Mr. David Trevor, FCA** *1977;* (Tax Fac), DB Associates Limited, 4th Floor, Imperial House, 15 Kingsway, LONDON, WC2B 6UN. See also DTB Associates LLP

BROWN, Mr. David Victor, MBA BSc FCA *1983;* Legal & General House, Bay 314, St. Monicas Road, Kingswood, TADWORTH, SURREY KT20 6EU.

BROWN, Mr. David Wall, FCA *1964;* with A1 Lifestyle Village Accounts, Executive Suite, Great North Road Little Paxton, ST. NEOTS, CAMBRIDGESHIRE, PE19 6EN.

BROWN, Mr. David Walter, BSc ACA *2003;* Prudential Plc Governors House, 5 Laurence Pountney Hill, LONDON, EC4R 0HH.

BROWN, Mr. David William, BA ACA *1984;* The Old Rectory South, The Street, Albury, GUILDFORD, SURREY, GU5 9AX.

•**BROWN, Mrs. Dawn Tracey, BSc ACA** *2004;* ABC North East Limited, 2 Auton Court, Bearpark, DURHAM, DH7 7AW.

BROWN, Miss. Deborah Caroline, BSc ACA *1986;* 66 Ambleside Gardens, SUTTON, SM2 5HN.

BROWN, Miss. Deborah Margaret, MBA BSc ACA *1995;* 14 Normanhurst, Hutton, BRENTWOOD, CM13 1BG.

BROWN, Mrs. Deborah Sophia, BSc ACA *1986;* Copthorne, Wix Hill, West Horsley, LEATHERHEAD, SURREY, KT24 6ED.

BROWN, Mr. Declan Linsay, BA ACA *1999;* 51 Well Lane, Stock, INGATESTONE, ESSEX, CM4 9LZ.

BROWN, Mr. Denis Cyril Houghton, FCA *1952;* 63 Barlaston Old Road, Trentham, STOKE-ON-TRENT, ST4 8HD. (Life Member)

BROWN, Ms. Denise, BCom ACA *1991;* 10 Charnley Close, SALE, CHESHIRE, M33 7LP.

BROWN, Mr. Derek Raymond, FCA *1961;* Beau Rivage, 8a Dee Banks, Great Boughton, CHESTER, CH3 5UX.

BROWN, Miss. Diane Elizabeth, BSc ACA *1996;* The Hollies, 12 Ridgemount Way, REDHILL, RH1 6JT.

•**BROWN, Miss. Diane Elizabeth, BSc ACA** *1989;* (Tax Fac), Antrams, 44-46 Old Steine, BRIGHTON, BN1 1NH.

BROWN, Mrs. Diane Marie, BSc ACA *1994;* 5 Malvern Road, AYLESBURY, BUCKINGHAMSHIRE, HP20 1QF.

BROWN, Miss. Dominique Anne, BA FCA *1993;* 15 Voltaire, Ennerdale Road, RICHMOND, SURREY, TW9 3PQ.

•**BROWN, Mr. Donald Mark, BA FCA** *1988;* Higginson & Co (UK) Ltd, 3 Kensworth Gate, 200-204 High Street South, DUNSTABLE, BEDFORDSHIRE, LU6 3HS.

•**BROWN, Mr. Douglas Clive, FCA** *1976;* D.C. Brown, 48 Airedale Avenue, Tickhill, DONCASTER, DN11 9UD.

BROWN, Mr. Douglas Frederick, FCA *1966;* Grovers Corners, 165 Pembroke Close, BANSTEAD, SM7 2BH.

•**BROWN, Mr. Douglas John, BA ACA** *1982;* (Tax Fac), DJB Tax Ltd, Gravel Hill, Chalfont St. Peter, GERRARDS CROSS, BUCKINGHAMSHIRE, SL9 9QP.

•**BROWN, Mr. Duncan John, BSc FCA** *1989;* PricewaterhouseCoopers LLP, Marlborough Court, 10 Bricket Road, ST. ALBANS, HERTFORDSHIRE, AL1 3JX.

BROWN, Mr. Duncan Neil, MA BSc ACA *2001;* Heatherley, Longdown, EXETER, EX6 7SR.

•**BROWN, Mr. Edwin Christopher, FCA** *1975;* Edwin C. Brown, 15 St Joseph, Carouge-GE, CH-1227 GENEVA, SWITZERLAND.

BROWN, Mrs. Elizabeth Kate, LLB ACA *2004;* (Tax Fac), A P Robinson & Co, 107 Cleethorpe Road, GRIMSBY, SOUTH HUMBERSIDE, DN31 3ER.

BROWN, Mrs. Emily Jane, ACA *2008;* Rogoff & Co, 167-169 Great Portland Street, LONDON, W1W 5PF.

BROWN, Mrs. Emma Jane, BA ACA *1998;* 9 Bowerleaze, Sea Mills, BRISTOL, BS9 2HJ.

BROWN, Miss. Emma Joy, BSc(Hons) ACA *2003;* with Royce Peeling Green Limited, The Copper Room, Deva Centre, Trinity Way, MANCHESTER, M3 7BG.

BROWN, Mrs. Emma Kate, ACA *2008;* 66 St. Barnabas Street, WELLINGBOROUGH, NORTHAMPTONSHIRE, NN8 3HB.

BROWN, Miss. Emma Lucy Jane, BA ACA *2000;* 11 Kidbrooke Gardens, Blackheath, LONDON, SE3 0PD.

BROWN, Mr. Eric Ormiston, FCA *1972;* 1571 Funf Kinder Road, FREDERICKSBURG, TX 78624, UNITED STATES. (Life Member)

BROWN, Mrs. Felicity Anne, MA ACA *1985;* The Merchant Venturers, Merchants Hall, The Promenade, BRISTOL, BS8 3NH.

BROWN, Mrs. Fiona Jane, BA(Hons) ACA *2001;* 26 Pilgrim's Mead, Bishopdown, SALISBURY, SP1 3GX.

BROWN, The Revd. Fiona Lesley, FCA *1974;* The Manse, 22 St. Michaels Close, Penkridge, STAFFORD, ST19 5AD.

BROWN, Mrs. Fiona Mary, MA ACA *1988;* Hillocks Farm, Kniveton, ASHBOURNE, DE6 1JH.

BROWN, Mr. Fraser James, BSc ACA *2006;* 69 Colomb Street, LONDON, SE10 9EZ.

BROWN, Mr. Fred, FCA *1959;* Brindlestones, New Ridley Road, New Ridley, STOCKSFIELD, NE43 7RQ. (Life Member)

BROWN, Mr. Frederick Hew Milne, FCA *1963;* Calle Los Eucaliptos 623 Apto. 301, Urbanizacion Country Club, San Isidro, LIMA, 27, PERU. (Life Member)

BROWN, Mr. Frederick James, BSc ACA *1992;* with Grant Thornton UK LLP, 11-13 Penhill Road, CARDIFF, CF11 9UP.

BROWN, Mr. Gareth Morgan, MSc ACA *1991;* Eastcott Hall, 4 Barry Place, Derry Hill, CALNE, SN11 9NX.

BROWN, Mr. Gary, MBA BA ACA *1992;* Holly Tree House, Main Street, Flecknoe, RUGBY, WARWICKSHIRE, CV23 8AT.

BROWN, Mr. Gary James, BA ACA *1994;* 3 Dewberry Fields, Upholland, SKELMERSDALE, WN8 0BQ.

BROWN, Mr. Gavin, BA(Hons) ACA *2006;* Kaplan Financial, 6th floor, St. James Buildings, 79 Oxford Street, MANCHESTER, M1 6FQ.

BROWN, Mr. Gavin Lee, FCA *1969;* 2 The Willows, Dogge Lane Croft, Acocks Green, BIRMINGHAM, B27 7XJ. (Life Member)

BROWN, Mr. Gavin Mackie, FCA *1977;* Jessamine Lodge, 77 Victoria Drive, BOGNOR REGIS, PO21 2TB.

BROWN, Mrs. Gaynor Rhiannon, BA ACA *1983;* 8 Lime Close, West Clandon, GUILDFORD, GU4 7UL.

•**BROWN, Mr. Geoffrey, MSc FCA** *1969;* IQ Accountants Limited, 1 Seamer Road Corner, SCARBOROUGH, NORTH YORKSHIRE, YO12 5BB.

BROWN, Mr. Geoffrey Harold, FCA *1949;* 53 Galton Road, WESTCLIFF-ON-SEA, ESSEX, SS0 8LA. (Life Member)

BROWN, Mr. Geoffrey Stuart, FCA *1973;* Rosemount Cottage, Longmire Yeat, Troutbeck, WINDERMERE, CUMBRIA, LA23 1PH.

BROWN, Mr. Geoffrey William Kingsley Moore, FCA *1975;* Spaltlaan 18, 3090 OVERIJSE, BELGIUM.

BROWN, Mr. George Spraggon, BSc FCA *1991;* 18 Manor Gardens, LONDON, W3 8JU.

BROWN, Mr. George Stuart Grindley, FCA *1966;* The Garden House, 51 Kippington Road, SEVENOAKS, KENT, TN13 2LL. (Life Member)

BROWN, Mr. Gerald, FCA *1960;* 56 Melbury Road, Woodthorpe, NOTTINGHAM, NG5 4PG. (Life Member)

BROWN, Miss. Gillian Kathryn, BSc ACA *1994;* 20 Danebank Mews, Windmill Lane, Denton, MANCHESTER, M34 2JN.

BROWN, Mr. Gordon Hamilton, MA FCA *1967;* Wharfemead, Wood Lane, Grassington, SKIPTON, BD23 5ND. (Life Member)

BROWN, Mr. Gordon Sanderson, BEng ACA *1984;* 55 Parkmore Road, Bentleigh East, MELBOURNE, VIC 3165, AUSTRALIA.

BROWN, Miss. Grace, BA(Hons) ACA *2003;* Pharmacybrands Limited, Millenium Centre, Level 2 Building C, 600 Great South Road, Ellerslie, AUCKLAND 1542 NEW ZEALAND.

BROWN, Mr. Graeme John, BSc ACA *1990;* Smith & Nephew Ltd, PO Box 81, HULL, HU3 2BN.

BROWN, Mr. Graham Anthony, BA ACA *1982;* 21 Holly Gardens, West End, SOUTHAMPTON, SO30 3RU.

BROWN, Mr. Graham Daniel, BSc ACA *1996;* Zeta House, Avonbury Business Park Howes Lane, BICESTER, OXFORDSHIRE, OX262UA.

•**BROWN, Mr. Graham Douglas, BSc ACA** *1979;* (Tax Fac), Thornhill Accountancy Services, 88 Thornhill Street, Calverley, PUDSEY, WEST YORKSHIRE, LS28 5PD.

BROWN, Mr. Graham Joseph, FCA *1952;* 3 Hartswood Close, Appleton, WARRINGTON, WA4 5QZ. (Life Member)

BROWN, Mr. Graham Marshall, FCA *1968;* Tudor Lodge, 14 Cressington Drive, Four Oaks Park, SUTTON COLDFIELD, B74 2SU.

BROWN, Mr. Graham Robert Logan, FCA *1958;* 17 Main Street, Farnhill, KEIGHLEY, BD20 9BJ. (Life Member)

BROWN, Mr. Graham Roger, BSc ACA *1987;* 22 Orchard Rise, RICHMOND, SURREY, TW10 5BX.

BROWN, Mr. Gregory Lawrence, MA ACA *2002;* with PricewaterhouseCoopers LLP, The Atrium, 1 Harefield Road, UXBRIDGE, UB8 1EX.

BROWN, Miss. Hannah Camilla Lester, ACA *2008;* Platts Farm Ughill, Bradfield, SHEFFIELD, S6 6HU.

BROWN, Mr. Harold, FCA *1965;* Flat 37, Frances & Dick James Court, 35 Langstone Way, LONDON, NW7 1GT.

BROWN, Mr. Harold Stuart, MA BSc FCA *1969;* Bradston House, 40A Mearse Lane, Barnt Green, BIRMINGHAM, B45 8HL. (Life Member)

BROWN, Miss. Helen Louise, BSc ACA *2005;* Cu Plas Supplies Ltd, 60-68 Durning Road, LIVERPOOL, L7 5NG.

BROWN, Mr. Henry Edward, ACA *2008;* 80 Pall Mall, LONDON, SW1Y 5ES.

BROWN, Mr. Howard Roger, FCA *1969;* Bocketts, 1 Downs Road, EPSOM, KT18 5HA. (Life Member)

BROWN, Mr. Hugh Taylor Mark, BA ACA *1988;* Langland House, 17 Park Road, Menston, ILKLEY, WEST YORKSHIRE, LS29 6LS.

BROWN, Mr. Huw James William, BA ACA *2005;* with KPMG LLP, 100 Temple Street, BRISTOL, BS1 6AG.

BROWN, Mr. Iain Michael, BSc ACA *1993;* 14 Royalston Avenue, WINCHESTER, MA 01890, UNITED STATES.

BROWN, Mr. Iain Mitchell, BSc ACA *1997;* 17 Woodside Close, AMERSHAM, BUCKINGHAMSHIRE, HP6 5EG.

•①**BROWN, Mr. Ian, FCA** *1982;* 9 Mitchell Avenue, Jesmond, NEWCASTLE UPON TYNE, NE2 3JY.

BROWN, Mr. Ian, ACA *1978;* 73 Hangleton Valley Drive, HOVE, BN3 8ED.

BROWN, Mr. Ian, FCA ATII *1990;* Globe OP Financial Servcies Ltd Grand Buildings, 1-3 Strand, LONDON, WC2N 5HR.

•**BROWN, Mr. Ian, BSc ACA** *1985;* Deloitte LLP, 2 New Street Square, LONDON, EC4A 3BZ. See also Deloitte & Touche LLP

BROWN, Mr. Ian James Palmer, MA ACA *1994;* 39 Kippington Road, SEVENOAKS, KENT, TN13 2LL.

BROWN, Mr. Ian Patrick, ACA *2005;* 32 Mitchelldean, PEACEHAVEN, EAST SUSSEX, BN10 8EF.

•**BROWN, Mr. Ian Stewart, FCA** *1982;* Churchills, 1st Floor, Shenstone Station, Station Road, Shenstone, LICHFIELD STAFFORDSHIRE WS14 0NW.

•**BROWN, Mr. Ian William, FCA** *1980;* (Tax Fac), Dodd & Co., Fifteen Rosehill, Montgomery Way, Rosehill Estate, CARLISLE, CA1 2RW.

BROWN, Mr. Ivor, MBA BA FCA *1966;* 4 Schwartz Street, RA'ANANA, ISRAEL. (Life Member)

•**BROWN, Mr. Ivor Garfield, FCA** *1973;* Nichol Goodwill Brown Ltd, 112 Whitley Road, WHITLEY BAY, TYNE AND WEAR, NE26 2NE.

BROWN, Miss. Jacqueline Ann, BSc ACA *1990;* 49 Clonmore Street, Southfields, LONDON, SW18 5ET.

BROWN, Mrs. Jacqueline Anne, PhD ACA *2003;* 9 Linden Drive, Chalfont St. Peter, GERRARDS CROSS, BUCKINGHAMSHIRE, SL9 9UP.

BROWN, Mrs. Jacqueline Helen, BSc ACA *1996;* 48 Moor Crescent, Gosforth, NEWCASTLE UPON TYNE, NE3 4AQ.

BROWN, Mr. James, BSc ACA *2007;* 79 Riverview Gardens, Barnes, LONDON, SW13 8RA.

•**BROWN, Mr. James Alan, MA ACA** *2001;* BRAL Limited, 12 York Gate, Regents Park, LONDON, NW1 4QS. See also Blick Rothenberg

BROWN, Mr. James Andrew, BSc ACA *1989;* with Deloitte & Touche, Deloitte & Touche House, Earlscourt Terrace, DUBLIN 2, COUNTY DUBLIN, IRELAND.

BROWN, Mr. James Anthony, BSc FCA *1969;* 9 The Rowans, Aughton, ORMSKIRK, LANCASHIRE, L39 6TD.

BROWN, Mr. James Christopher, BA(Hons) ACA *2001;* 33 Mimosa Street, LONDON, SW6 4DS.

BROWN, Mr. James Franklin, BSc ACA *1992;* 23 Landrock Road, LONDON, N8 9HR.

BROWN, Mr. James Frederick Spence, ACA *2008;* Everton Carr Farm, Everton, DONCASTER, SOUTH YORKSHIRE, DN10 5BZ.

•**BROWN, Mr. James Graham, FCA** *1962;* (Member of Council 1989 - 1995), (Tax Fac), Graham Brown & Co., 2 Bathwick Terrace, Bathwick Hill, BATH, BA2 4EL.

BROWN, Mr. James John, ACA *2009;* Bruggen La Route de la Hougue Du Pommier, Castel, GUERNSEY, GY5 7XX.

•**BROWN, Mr. James Lawrence Harrison, ACA** *1991;* Holly Lodge, Claverton Down Road, Claverton Down, BATH, BA2 7AP. See also BDO Stoy Hayward LLP

BROWN, Mr. James Peter Findlay, BA(Hons) ACA *2010;* Flat 3, 73 Queens Drive, LONDON, N4 2BG.

BROWN, Mr. James Richard, FCA ACOL *1964;* 2 Frant Cottages, High Street Ticehurst, WADHURST, TN5 7BG.

•**BROWN, Mr. James Robert, LLB ACA** *1994;* Grant Thornton UK LLP, Crown House, Crown Street, IPSWICH, IP1 3HS. See also Grant Thornton LLP

BROWN, Mr. James Vancourt, BCom ACA *1998;* 33 Curzon Avenue, HORSHAM, RH12 2LA.

BROWN, Mr. Jamie Peter, ACA *2007;* 17 Brambling Close, STOWMARKET, SUFFOLK, IP14 5UN.

BROWN, Mr. Jamie Robert, BA(Hons) ACA *2002;* Apartment 450, 1550 Bay Street, SAN FRANCISCO, CA 94123, UNITED STATES.

BROWN, Miss. Jane Catherine, BA ACA *1993;* D Brown & Sons Ltd, 2nd floor, 14 High Street, COWBRIDGE, SOUTH GLAMORGAN, CF71 7AG.

BROWN, Mrs. Jane Louise, BA ACA *1995;* 4 Melrose Avenue, SALE, CHESHIRE, M33 3AZ.

BROWN, Mr. Jason, BA ACA *1999;* 2a Shelgate Road, LONDON, SW11 1BE.

BROWN, Mr. Jason Conrad, BA ACA *2006;* 3 Winstanley Road, Little Neston, NESTON, CH64 0UZ.

BROWN, Mrs. Jay Marguerite, ACA *1995;* 17 Far Lane, Normanton on Soar, LOUGHBOROUGH, LEICESTERSHIRE, LE12 5HA.

•①**BROWN, Mrs. Jeanette, FCA** *1985;* Dodd & Co., Clint Mill, Cornmarket, PENRITH, CA11 7HW.

BROWN, Miss. Jeanette Marie, ACA CTA *2004;* 17 The Gallop, YATELEY, HAMPSHIRE, GU46 7SG.

BROWN, Mrs. Jeevanjot, BA ACA *1995;* Brambles, Old Mill Lane, Bray, MAIDENHEAD, SL6 2BG.

BROWN, Mr. Jeffrey Carl, FCA *1969;* 1 Fluder Hill, Kingskerswell, NEWTON ABBOT, DEVON, TQ12 5JD.

BROWN, Mr. Jeffrey Edmund, ACA *1995;* 109 Tudor Avenue, WORCESTER PARK, SURREY, KT4 8TU.

BROWN, Mrs. Jennifer Ann, FCA *1969;* 90 Gregories Road, BEACONSFIELD, HP9 1HL.

•**BROWN, Miss. Jennifer Margaret, BA ACA** *2003;* with Grant Thornton UK LLP, Grant Thornton House, 22 Melton Street, Euston Square, LONDON, NW1 2EP.

BROWN, Mr. Jeremy David, FCA *1967;* Implementation Ltd, 58 Hope Road, KINGSTON 6, JAMAICA.

BROWN, Mr. Jeremy Ivor, BSc ACA *1993;* 85 Samrose Drive, NOVATO, CA 94945, UNITED STATES.

BROWN, Mrs. Jill Linda, BA ACA *1981;* Aga Rangemaster plc, Juno Drive, LEAMINGTON SPA, CV31 3RG.

BROWN, Mr. Jim Dundas, ACA MBA *1995;* 4 Manor Court, Heighington Village, NEWTON AYCLIFFE, DL5 6TL.

BROWN, Mrs. Joan, BSc ACA *1992;* 15 Bootham Terrace, YORK, YO30 7DH.

BROWN, Mrs. Joanna Susan, BA ACA *2006;* 4 Wisdom Drive, HERTFORD, SG13 7RF.

BROWN, Mrs. Joanne Eileen, BSc ACA *1995;* La Chansonnette, La Verte Rue, St. Lawrence, JERSEY, JE3 1JH.

BROWN, Miss. Joanne Elizabeth Foord, MEng ACA ACCA MBA *1999;* Croft Chapel, HEXHAM, NE47 7EN.

•**BROWN, Mr. John, ACA** *1990;* (Tax Fac), Browns, 42 Greenhaugh, West Moor, NEWCASTLE UPON TYNE, NE12 7WA.

BROWN, Mr. John, FCA *1950;* 10 Riccarton Ave., CURRIE, EH14 5PQ. (Life Member)

BROWN, Mr. John Alisdair Speers, FCA *1967;* 87 Love Lane, PINNER, MIDDLESEX, HA5 3EY.

BROWN, Mr. John Craig, MA ACA CTA *1994;* (Tax Fac), Killingan Beg Churchtown, Ramsey, ISLE OF MAN, IM7 2AN.

BROWN, Mr. John David, FCA *1969;* 90 Gregories Road, BEACONSFIELD, BUCKINGHAMSHIRE, HP9 1HL.

BROWN, Mr. John David, FCA *1957;* Westerleigh, 4 Bucklands View, Nailsea, BRISTOL, BS48 4TZ. (Life Member)

BROWN, Mr. John David Fraser, FCA *1971;* Nottingham Ind. Cleaners Ltd, Elizabeth House, Wigman Road, Bilborough, NOTTINGHAM, NG8 3HY.

BROWN, Mr. John Forster, BA ACA *1979;* 7 Hurst Avenue, LONDON, N6 5TX.

BROWN, Mr. John Frederick, FCA *1949;* 27 Hillcrest Avenue, Nether Poppleton, YORK, YO26 6LD. (Life Member)

BROWN, Mr. John Graham, FCA *1965;* 77 Worden Lane, Leyland, PRESTON, PR25 3BD. (Life Member)

BROWN, Mr. John Granger, BA FCA *1964;* Rose Cottage, 32 West End, Costessey, NORWICH, NR8 5AG.

BROWN, Mr. John James, FCA *1963;* 10 Greenacre Close, Great Ayton, MIDDLESBROUGH, CLEVELAND, TS9 6PG.

BROWN, Mr. John Michael, FCA *1962;* 8 Wroxham Close, COLCHESTER, CO3 3RQ.

BROWN, John Neville, Esq CBE MA FCA *1964;* 22 Wykeham Way, Haddenham, AYLESBURY, HP17 8BX.

BROWN, Mr. John Osborne, LLB FCA *1958;* Boulters Barn Cottage, Churchill Road, CHIPPING NORTON, OXFORDSHIRE, OX7 5UT. (Life Member)

•**BROWN, Mr. John Robert, ACA** *1979;* J R Brown (Accountants) Ltd, Rose Cottage, 3 Pasture Land, Gaddesby, LEICESTER, LE7 4XB.

BROWN, Mr. John Robert David, BA(Hons) ACA *2011;* 52 Northbrook Road, Shirley, SOLIHULL, WEST MIDLANDS, B90 3NP.

BROWN, Mr. Jonathan, BA(Hons) ACA *2010;* 8 Andrews Reach, BOURNE END, BUCKINGHAMSHIRE, SL8 5GA.

BROWN, Mr. Jonathan David, BSc ACA *2001;* 14 Colliers Way, Haydon, RADSTOCK, BA3 3RE.

BROWN, Mr. Jonathan Paul, MA ACA *2004;* Monitor, 4 Matthew Parker Street, LONDON, SW1H 9NP.

BROWN, Mr. Jonathan William, BSc ACA *1987;* 66 Artarmon Road, ARTARMON, NSW 2064, AUSTRALIA.

•**BROWN, Mr. Joseph, BA ACA** *1980;* Joseph Brown, The Mount, Church Lane, Kingsbury, TAMWORTH, B78 2LR.

BROWN, Mr. Joseph Anthony, FCA ATII *1985;* 9 Carlisle Grove, BUXTON, DERBYSHIRE, SK17 6XP.

BROWN, Mr. Joseph Kellett, FCA *1960;* Ridge Cottage, Park Hill Rise, CROYDON, CR0 5JD. (Life Member)

BROWN, Mr. Josephus Peter, ACA MAAT *2011;* 15 Titchfield Road, ENFIELD, MIDDLESEX, EN3 6AZ.

BROWN, Mrs. Judith, BSc ACA *1986;* Langland House, 17 Park Road, Menston, ILKLEY, WEST YORKSHIRE, LS29 6LS.

BROWN, Mrs. Judith Anne, BSc FCA *1973;* 927 Warwick Road, SOLIHULL, B91 3EP.

BROWN, Dr. Julia, BSc ACA *2004;* 55 High Street, Collingtree, NORTHAMPTON, NN4 0NE.

BROWN, Mrs. Julia Catherine, BCom ACA *1993;* Longlac, White House Lane, Jacobs Well, GUILDFORD, GU4 7PT.

•**BROWN, Mrs. Julia Frances, BSc ACA** *2002;* Archangel Accounting Limited, Burnham House, Splash Lane, Wyton, HUNTINGDON, CAMBRIDGESHIRE PE28 2AF.

BROWN, Miss. Julie, BSc ACA *2006;* 5 Langley Close, NORWICH, NR4 6XW.

BROWN, Miss. Julie Alison, BSc ACA *1994;* 28 Brownlow Close, NEWCASTLE UPON TYNE, NE7 7FF.

BROWN, Miss. Julie Ann, BSc ACA *1996;* Pilkington Group Ltd, Hall Lane, Lathom, ORMSKIRK, L40 5UF.

BROWN, Mrs. Julie Ann, BA ACA *1989;* 4 Sovereign Court, LEEDS, LS17 7UT.

BROWN, Mrs. Julie Belita, BA FCA *1987;* 7320 Mindello Street, CORAL GABLES, FL 33143, UNITED STATES.

BROWN, Mrs. Julie Deborah, ACA *1992;* Old Orchard, Leat Road, LIFTON, DEVON, PL16 0EA.

BROWN, Mrs. June Harriette, MBS BCom ACA *1997;* 43 Houndean Rise, LEWES, EAST SUSSEX, BN7 1EQ.

BROWN, Ms. Karen Ruth, BSc ACA *1994;* 221 Croxted Road, Dulwich, LONDON, SE21 8NL.

BROWN, Mr. Karl Trevor, BSc ACA *1990;* Dawn Foods Ltd, Worcester Road, EVESHAM, WR11 4QU.

BROWN, Mrs. Kate Jane, BSc(Hons) ACA *2002;* C/o Prime Management Limited, Mechanic's Building, 12 Church Street, HAMILTON HM11, BERMUDA.

BROWN, Miss. Katherine, ACA *2011;* Flat A, 5 Darville Road, LONDON, N16 7PT.

•**BROWN, Mrs. Katherine Mary, ACA ATII** *1985;* Kate Brown Accountancy Ltd, 81 Gurney Court Road, ST. ALBANS, AL1 4QX.

BROWN, Mrs. Katrina Jane, BSc ACA *1994;* South Lodge, South Road, WEYBRIDGE, SURREY, KT13 9DZ.

BROWN, Mr. Keith Francis, BSc FCA *1977;* Haines Watts Sterling House, 97 Lichfield Street, TAMWORTH, STAFFORDSHIRE, B79 7QF.

BROWN, Mr. Keith Neville, BA ACA *1987;* Gloria Jeans Coffees, 11 Hoyle Avenue, CASTLE HILL, NSW 2153, AUSTRALIA.

BROWN, Mr. Keith Thompson, FCA *1966;* 11 Oak Hill, Main Street, Willerby, HULL, HU10 6DH. (Life Member)

•**BROWN, Mrs. Kelly, FCA** *1999;* 49 Garlichill Road, EPSOM, KT18 5TZ.

BROWN, Mr. Kenneth Allan Lindsay, BA ACA *1990;* Nomura International Plc, 1 Angel Lane, LONDON, EC4R 3AB.

BROWN, Mr. Kenneth Aubrey James, FCA *1951;* Henlis, 40A Coinagehall Street, HELSTON, TR13 8EQ. (Life Member)

BROWN, Mr. Kenneth Edward Lindsay, FCA *1965;* 65 St. Andrews Drive, GLASGOW, G41 4HP.

BROWN, Mr. Kenneth Frederick, FCA *1937;* 25 Westcliff Mansion, St. Johns Road, EASTBOURNE, BN20 7HR. (Life Member)

BROWN, Mr. Kenneth Frederick, FCA *1955;* Room 19, Ashwood Nursing Home, Heathfield Road, Burwash Common, ETCHINGHAM, EAST SUSSEX TN19 7LT. (Life Member)

BROWN, Mr. Kenneth Hazel, FCA *1960;* Flat 2, 27 Victoria Road, CLEVEDON, AVON, BS21 7RU. (Life Member)

BROWN, Mr. Kenneth Robert, FCA *1962;* Robin Cottage, East Common, HARPENDEN, HERTFORDSHIRE, AL5 1DA.

•**BROWN, Mr. Kerrie Paul, ACA** *1986;* Hawkins Scott, Wyvern House, 55-61 Frimley High Street, Frimley, CAMBERLEY, SURREY GU16 7HJ.

BROWN, Mrs. Kerry Elizabeth, BSc ACA DChA *1993;* 23 Summercourt Square, KINGSWINFORD, DY6 9QJ.

BROWN, Mr. Kevin James, BA ACA *1990;* Brackley House, Heyford Road, Kirtlington, KIDLINGTON, OX5 3HL.

BROWN, Mr. Kevin Michael, BSc ACA *2005;* 22 Comber Place, Hampton Gate, Johnsonville, WELLINGTON 6037, NEW ZEALAND.

•**BROWN, Mr. Kevin Neil, ACA MAAT** *2000;* Walter Wright, 89 High Street, Hadleigh, IPSWICH, IP7 5EA. See also Walter Wright Consultancy Ltd

•**BROWN, Mr. Kevin Nigel, BSc ARCS ACA** *1983;* 5 Croxton Close Fairfield, STOCKTON-ON-TEES, TS19 7SW.

•①**BROWN, Mr. Kevin Thomas, FCA MBA** *1983;* Marriots Recovery LLP, Allan House, 10 John Princes Street, LONDON, W1G 0AH. See also Marriots LLP

BROWN, Miss. Laura Anne, LLB(Hons) ACA *2009;* 4 Sopwith Road, EASTLEIGH, HAMPSHIRE, SO50 5GH.

BROWN, Miss. Laura Elizabeth, ACA *2011;* 17 Greenway, CHATHAM, KENT, ME5 9UY.

BROWN, Miss. Laura Ellen, ACA *2004;* 21 Sherbrooke Street, LINCOLN, LN2 5QA.

BROWN, Mrs. Laura Joanne, BSc ACA *2005;* Icera Inc, 2520 The Quadrant, Aztec West, Almondsbury, BRISTOL, BS32 4AQ.

BROWN, Mr. Lawrence Joseph, ACA *1983;* 11 Park Avenue, Dunston, GATESHEAD, NE11 9QE.

BROWN, Mr. Leo James, BA ACA *2001;* 1 Bridgewater Place, Water Lane, LEEDS, LS11 5QR.

•**BROWN, Mr. Leonard, FCA** *1961;* Leonard Brown Ltd, Thornbury House, 16 Woodlands, GERRARDS CROSS, SL9 8DD.

BROWN, Mr. Leonard Ernest, FCA *1941;* Lamont, 18 East Rise, Llanishen, CARDIFF, CF14 0RJ. (Life Member)

BROWN, Mr. Leslie, BCom FCA *1965;* 20 Wellacre Rd., Kenton, HARROW, HA3 0BN. (Life Member)

BROWN, Mr. Leslie, FCA *1969;* 2 Menlo Close, PRENTON, CH43 9YD.

BROWN, Mr. Leslie Kenneth, MA FCA *1970;* Flat 5, 4 Park Drive South, HUDDERSFIELD, HD1 4HT.

BROWN, Miss. Linzee Sarah Colchester, ACA *2009;* 16 Fowey Road, WESTON-SUPER-MARE, AVON, BS22 7ST.

BROWN, Miss. Lisa, BA ACA *2002;* 72 Chessel Street, BRISTOL, BS3 3DN.

BROWN, Mr. Louis Charles John, FCA *1952;* The Well House, 95 High Street, Lindfield, HAYWARDS HEATH, WEST SUSSEX, RH16 2HN. (Life Member)

BROWN, Miss. Louise, BSc ACA *2007;* 99 Calder Drive, Walmley, SUTTON COLDFIELD, B76 1GG.

BROWN, Miss. Louise, ACA *2009;* Arkle House, 31 Lonsdale Street, CARLISLE, CUMBRIA, CA1 1BJ.

BROWN, Miss. Louise Anne, ACA *2008;* Craegmoor Healthcare, Craegmoor House, Perdiswell Park, WORCESTER, WR3 7NW.

•**BROWN, Miss. Louise Elizabeth, BA ACA** *1991;* Browns Accountancy & Taxation Ltd, Rowan Cottage, 74 Hailey Road, WITNEY, OXFORDSHIRE, OX28 1HF.

BROWN, Miss. Lydia Marissa Helga, ACA *2008;* 5 Railton Avenue, MANCHESTER, M16 8AU.

BROWN, Mrs. Mai Ngoc, BSc ACA *1996;* 7 Rotterdam Drive, London Yard, LONDON, E14 3JA.

BROWN, Mr. Malcolm Stewart, FCA *1960;* 202 Woodlands Road, BATLEY, WEST YORKSHIRE, WF17 0RE.

•**BROWN, Mr. Malcolm Trevor, BSc FCA DChA** *1986;* Accounting & Financial Solutions (London) Ltd, 66 Norman Road, Wimbledon, LONDON, SW19 1BN. See also Waterman Brown Limited

BROWN, Mrs. Marcia Diane, BSc ACA *1993;* 8 Denshire Court, Baston, PETERBOROUGH, PE6 9QL.

BROWN, Mr. Mark Jonathan, BA FCA *1984;* 36 Chestnut Drive, Pennington, LEIGH, WN7 3JW.

BROWN, Mr. Mark Oliver, BA ACA *2002;* 19 Culverden Avenue, TUNBRIDGE WELLS, KENT, TN4 9RE.

•**BROWN, Mr. Mark Philip, BA FCA** *1986;* HW, Keepers Lane, The Wergs, WOLVERHAMPTON, WEST MIDLANDS, WV6 8UA. See also Haines Watts

BROWN, Mr. Martin, BA(Hons) ACA *2011;* 10 The Grove, North End, DURHAM, DH1 4LU.

BROWN, Mr. Martin Douglas, FCA *1971;* 3 Bury Hill View, Downend, BRISTOL, BS16 6PA.

BROWN, Mr. Martin Graham, FCA *1981;* Woodview, Nags Head Lane, Minchinhampton, STROUD, GL6 9AY.

BROWN, Mr. Martin Philip Lawrence, BA FCA *1992;* Meadowcroft, Gillhams Lane, HASLEMERE, SURREY, GU27 3ND.

BROWN, Mr. Martin Timothy, BA FCA *1981;* (Tax Fac), Asda Stores Ltd Asda House, Great Wilson Street, LEEDS, LS11 5AD.

BROWN, Mr. Martyn Francis, ACA *1982;* 5 Nicholls Court, Nicholls Lane, Winterbourne, BRISTOL, BS36 1NX.

BROWN, Mr. Matthew, ACA *2009;* with Cartwrights Audit Limited, Regency House, 33 Wood Street, BARNET, EN5 4BE.

BROWN, Mr. Matthew John Alexander, BSc ACA *1991;* 7 Birkhills, Burton Leonard, HARROGATE, NORTH YORKSHIRE, HG3 3SF.

BROWN, Mrs. Maxine, BA ACA *1997;* 25 Ravens Croft, East Hunsbury, NORTHAMPTON, NN4 0RL.

BROWN, Dr. Meredith, MA ACA *2006;* 9 Dawnay Gardens, Earlsfield, LONDON, SW18 3PW.

BROWN, Mr. Michael, BA ACA *1985;* Bratch Farm, Bratch Lane, Wombourne, WOLVERHAMPTON, WV5 9AD.

•**BROWN, Mr. Michael, BSc ACA** *1984;* Michael Brown, 36 Blackmile Lane, Grendon, NORTHAMPTON, NN7 1JR.

BROWN, Mr. Michael, BA FCA *1959;* Flat 5, 67 Castlebar Road, Ealing, LONDON, W5 2DA. (Life Member)

BROWN, Mr. Michael, BSc FCA *1974;* Box 508, FORESTVILLE, NSW 2087, AUSTRALIA.

•**BROWN, Mr. Michael Alan, BSc FCA** *1979;* 17-19 Church Road, Northfield, BIRMINGHAM, B31 2JZ.

•**BROWN, Mr. Michael Edward, MSc BA ACA** *1979;* Highview Management Services Limited, 35 Broad Meadows, NEWCASTLE UPON TYNE, NE3 4PZ.

BROWN, Mr. Michael Henry, FCA *1966;* Millers Cottage, High Callerton, Ponteland, NEWCASTLE UPON TYNE, NE20 9TT.

BROWN, Mr. Michael Howard, BA ACA *2010;* Flat 2 Chalford Court, 45-47 Putney Hill, LONDON, SW15 6QR.

BROWN, Mr. Michael James, ACA *2008;* Angley House, Goudhurst Road, CRANBROOK, KENT, TN17 2PR.

•**BROWN, Mr. Michael James, FCA** *1973;* MacIntyre Hudson LLP, Peterbridge House, The Lakes, NORTHAMPTON, NN4 7HB.

BROWN, Mr. Michael John, FCA *1971;* 20 Penny Lane, Guarlford, MALVERN, WR13 6PG.

BROWN, Mr. Michael John, FCA *1977;* Cheyne Walk Basses Capelles Road, St. Sampson, GUERNSEY, GY2 4WE.

BROWN, Mr. Michael John Raymond, FCA *1958;* 8913 E Fairway Blvd, SUN LAKES, AZ 85248, UNITED STATES. (Life Member)

BROWN, Mr. Michael Leslie, FCA *1971;* Rechov Hibner 31, 49400 PETACH TIKVA, ISRAEL.

BROWN, Mr. Michael Robert, FCA *1975;* 68 Harwich Road, Little Clacton, CLACTON-ON-SEA, CO16 9NE.

BROWN, Mr. Michael Stewart, BSc ACA *1988;* 17 Watergate, Audenshaw, MANCHESTER, M34 5QP.

•**BROWN, Mrs. Natalie Louise, ACA ACCA** *2011;* Alliott Wingham Limited, Kintyre House, 70 High Street, FAREHAM, HAMPSHIRE, PO16 7BB. See also Nolan Williams Ltd

BROWN, Mr. Nathan James, BA(Hons) ACA *2002;* Perry Capital UK LLP, 4 Grosvenor Place, LONDON, SW1X7HJ.

BROWN, Mr. Neil Andrew, MBA ACA *1983;* 12 Blatchford Court, YORK, YO30 5GW.

BROWN, Mr. Neil Antony, BSc ACA *1996;* with Deloitte Touche Tohmatsu, 505 Bourke Street, (P.O.Box 78B), MELBOURNE, VIC 3001, AUSTRALIA.

BROWN, Mr. Neil Douglas, BA FCA *1968;* Eshott, Heath Road, Horsell, WOKING, GU21 4DT.
BROWN, Mr. Neil Francis, BA ACA *1993;* Weidstrasse 2, 8808 PFAFFIKON, SWITZERLAND.
BROWN, Mr. Neil Graeme, BA ACA *1983;* Subito Partners, Staple Inn Buildings South, LONDON, WC1V 7PZ.
BROWN, Mr. Nicholas Andrew, BA(Hons) ACA *1991;* Willow Bank, Main Street, Kirkby Overblow, HARROGATE, HG3 1HD.
BROWN, Mr. Nicholas Edward, BA ACA *1983;* 21 Lenox Road, SUMMIT, NJ 07901, UNITED STATES.
BROWN, Mr. Nicholas Edward, BSc ACA *2003;* 52 Agraria Road, GUILDFORD, SURREY, GU2 4LF.
•**BROWN, Mr. Nicholas James, FCA** *1980;* N.J. Brown, 36 Kingsleigh Place, MITCHAM, CR4 4NU.
BROWN, Mr. Nicholas James Edward, ACA *2008;* 11 Silverton Road, LONDON, W6 9NY.
BROWN, Mr. Nicholas John, ACA *2009;* 5 Rydal Way, BIRMINGHAM, B28 9DA.
•**BROWN, Mr. Nicholas John Harlow, FCA DChA** *1983;* Plummer Parsons, 18 Hyde Gardens, EASTBOURNE, BN21 4PT. See also Plummer Parsons Accountants Ltd
BROWN, Mr. Nicholas Lawrence, MA FCA *1996;* 55 Eltisley Avenue, CAMBRIDGE, CB3 9JQ.
•**BROWN, Mr. Nicholas Martin, BEng ACA** *1992;* with Ernst & Young LLP, 1 More London Place, LONDON, SE1 2AF.
•**BROWN, Mr. Nicholas Maurice, FCA** *1974;* GSO Business Management, Suite 2100, 15260 Ventura Blvd, SHERMAN OAKS, CA CA 91403, UNITED STATES.
BROWN, Mr. Nicholas Maxwell, BA FCA *1983;* with The Rowleys Partnership LLP, 6 Dominus Way, Meridian Business Park, LEICESTER, LE19 1RP.
BROWN, Mr. Nicholas Record, FCA *1967;* Grove Cottage, Grove Lane, Hinton, CHIPPENHAM, WILTSHIRE, SN14 8HF.
BROWN, Mr. Nicholas Timothy, BA FCA *1991;* Pennridge, 2c Penn Avenue, CHESHAM, BUCKINGHAMSHIRE, HP5 2HT.
BROWN, Miss. Nicola Christina, MSc ACA *2007;* David A Henderson, Care of Qatar Shell Doha, Shell Centre, 4-6 York Road, LONDON, SE1 7NA.
BROWN, Mrs. Nicole Laraine, BA(Hons) ACA *2002;* 4 Albany Close, BUSHEY, HERTFORDSHIRE, WD23 4SG.
BROWN, Mr. Nigel, BSc ACA *1980;* 3 Garrod Approach, Melton, WOODBRIDGE, IP12 1TD.
BROWN, Mr. Nigel Denis Spence, FCA *1968;* The Old Rectory, Fulbeck, GRANTHAM, NG32 3JS.
BROWN, Mr. Nigel Paul, FCA *1976;* 29 Alfreda Road, Whitchurch, CARDIFF, CF14 2EH.
BROWN, Mr. Nigel Roy, FCA *1971;* The Birches, 17 Temple Garth, Copmanthorpe, YORK, YO23 3TF.
BROWN, Mr. Norman Clifford, BSc FCA *1981;* 56 Magnolia Dene, Hazelmere, HIGH WYCOMBE, HP15 7QE.
BROWN, Mr. Norman John, FCA *1955;* Tyne Reach, Redburn, HEXHAM, NE47 7EA. (Life Member)
BROWN, Mr. Norman John, BA ACA *1995;* 12-503 Yi An Hua Yuan, Hong Qiao Lu, NANTONG 226006, JIANGSU PROVINCE, CHINA.
BROWN, Mr. Oliver Charles, BSc ACA *2007;* Garden Flat, 23 Wellington Park, BRISTOL, BS8 2UW.
BROWN, Mrs. Pamela Jane, ACA *1990;* 42 Greenhaugh, West Moor, NEWCASTLE UPON TYNE, NE12 7WA.
•**BROWN, Mrs. Patricia Anne, BCom ACA** *1982;* P.A. Brown, 52 Northbrook Road, Shirley, SOLIHULL, B90 3NP.
BROWN, Mr. Patrick Beresford, FCA *1973;* BASF Malta Limited, The Mayfair Complex, St Georges Bay, ST JULIANS STJ 3311, MALTA.
BROWN, Mr. Paul, MBA BA FCA *1990;* 825 Bainbridge Drive, WEST CHESTER, PA 19382, UNITED STATES.
BROWN, Mr. Paul Alan, BA ACA *1988;* 13 Beverley Terrace, Cullercoats, NORTH SHIELDS, NE30 4NT.
BROWN, Mr. Paul Alexander, BSc ACA *1994;* South Lodge, South Road, WEYBRIDGE, SURREY, KT13 9DZ.
BROWN, Mr. Paul Anders, BSc ACA *2010;* Flat A-c, 73-75 Union Street, LONDON, SE1 1SG.
•**BROWN, Mr. Paul Anthony, FCA** *1987;* Brown & Co LLP, 2 Lords Court, Cricketers Way, BASILDON, ESSEX, SS13 1SS. See also Brown & Co Audit Ltd
BROWN, Mr. Paul Charles, MSc ACA *1996;* Thames Water, Clearwater Court, First East, Vastern Road, READING, RG1 8DB.
BROWN, Mr. Paul David, BA ACA *1999;* Suite 92, Mailboxes Etc, 272 Kensington High Street, LONDON, W8 6ND.
BROWN, Mr. Paul James, BSc ACA *2003;* 11 Elgar Road, READING, RG2 0BH.
BROWN, Mr. Paul Michael, BA ACA *1980;* 22 The Grove, Twyford, READING, RG10 9DU.
BROWN, Mr. Peter, FCA *1975;* Herdsman Rest, Green Lane, Middleton, TAMWORTH, B78 2BJ.
BROWN, Mr. Peter, BSc FCA *1975;* 189 Hoyles Lane, Cottam, PRESTON, PR4 0LD.
BROWN, Mr. Peter Cameron, LLB BA(Econ) FCA *1978;* 4 Tewkesbury Avenue, Hale, ALTRINCHAM, WA15 8PN.
BROWN, Mr. Peter Cedric Clifton, FCA *1963;* Ballinamona, Cashel, TIPPERARY, COUNTY TIPPERARY, IRELAND. (Life Member)
BROWN, Mr. Peter Dixon, FCA *1952;* 53 Powisland Drive, Derriford, PLYMOUTH, PL6 6AD. (Life Member)
BROWN, Mr. Peter Duncan, FCA *1963;* Le Moulin Du Poirot, 85230 ST URBAIN, FRANCE.
BROWN, Mr. Peter Harold Samuel, FCA *1965;* 4 Westminster Court, Barcote Park, Buckland, FARINGDON, OXFORDSHIRE, SN7 8PP.
BROWN, Mr. Peter Henry, FCA *1958;* 6601 Conifer Cove, AUSTIN, TX 78736, UNITED STATES. (Life Member)
BROWN, Mr. Peter James, BA FCA *1973;* Brown Westbury Consulting, Westbury, Church Hill, Horsell, WOKING, SURREY GU21 4QE.
BROWN, Mr. Peter Leonard, FCA *1976;* Cirencester Friendly Society Ltd, 5 Dyer Street, CIRENCESTER, GLOUCESTERSHIRE, GL7 2PP.
BROWN, Mr. Peter Michael, FCA *1960;* Synergy Holdings Ltd, 12 Hyde Park Place, LONDON, W2 2LH. (Life Member)
BROWN, Mr. Peter Richard, BSc FCA *1979;* Four Elms Blackstone Lane, Blackstone, HENFIELD, WEST SUSSEX, BN5 9TA.
•**BROWN, Mr. Peter Stuart, BSc FCA** *1978;* Ross Brooke Limited, 2 Old Bath Road, NEWBURY, BERKSHIRE, RG14 1QL.
BROWN, Mr. Philip, BSc FCA *1990;* Highbury West Lane, EAST GRINSTEAD, WEST SUSSEX, RH19 4HH.
•**BROWN, Mr. Philip Adrian, BSc FCA** *1994;* Taylor Viney & Marlow, 1422-4 London Road, LEIGH-ON-SEA, SS9 2UL.
BROWN, Mr. Philip Alan, ACA *2007;* 11 Goodwyns Place, DORKING, SURREY, RH4 2AW.
BROWN, Mr. Philip Andrew, BSc ACA *2006;* Apartment 43 Mere House, 62 Ellesmere Street, MANCHESTER, M15 4QR.
BROWN, Mr. Philip Anthony, PhD BSc ACA *1992;* M T I Technology Ltd Riverview House, Weyside Park Catteshall Lane, GODALMING, GU7 1XE.
BROWN, Mr. Philip Henry, BSc ACA *1993;* PO Box 31689, SEVEN MILE BEACH, GRAND CAYMAN, KY1-1207, CAYMAN ISLANDS.
BROWN, Mr. Philip Ian, MBA BA FCA *1984;* Tate & Lyle Plc, Sugar Quay, Lower Thames Street, LONDON, EC3R 6DQ.
BROWN, Mr. Philip Kenneth, MA BSc ACA *2001;* Apartment 19 Springbank, Springbank Avenue St. Helier, JERSEY, JE2 3TH.
BROWN, Mr. Philip Leslie, FCA *1986;* Farthings, Ullenhall, HENLEY-IN-ARDEN, WEST MIDLANDS, B95 5PB.
•**BROWN, Mr. Philip Michael, BA ACA** *1998;* P M Brown & Company Limited, 37 Haighton Drive, Fulwood, PRESTON, PR2 9LU.
•**BROWN, Mr. Philip Norman, BSc ACA** *1979;* (Tax Fac), Robert Miller & Company (Houghton) Limited, Kings Hall, Imperial Buildings, HOUGHTON LE SPRING, TYNE AND WEAR, DH4 4DJ. See also Robert Miller & Co
BROWN, Mr. Philip William Armstrong, BSc FCA *1970;* Church Cottage, 1 East Close, Matfen, NEWCASTLE UPON TYNE, NE20 0TF.
BROWN, Mr. Phillip Arthur Joseph, BSc FCA *1978;* 1 Hollybrook Gardens, Locks Heath, SOUTHAMPTON, SO31 6WH.
BROWN, Miss. Poppy Elizabeth Lewis, BA ACA *1999;* 2 Armstrong Street, SEAFORTH, NSW 2092, AUSTRALIA.
BROWN, Mrs. Rachel Claire, BA ACA *1999;* Holmcroft, Over Lane, Baslow, BAKEWELL, DERBYSHIRE DE45 1SA.
BROWN, Miss. Rachel Eleanor, ACA MAAT *2010;* 20 Drift Avenue, STAMFORD, LINCOLNSHIRE, PE9 1UY.
BROWN, Mrs. Rachel Kathryn, BSc(Hons) ACA *2000;* 41 New Road, Little Kingshill, GREAT MISSENDEN, BUCKINGHAMSHIRE, HP16 0EZ.
BROWN, Mrs. Rachel Rowntree, BA ACA *1991;* The Stone House, 2 Mill Street, Harbury, LEAMINGTON SPA, CV33 9HR.
BROWN, Mrs. Rebecca Louise, BA ACA *1993;* Cleaves Barn, Thirlby, THIRSK, YO7 2DQ.
BROWN, Mr. Rene Luke, BSc ACA *2007;* 22 Marbella Hill Club, Phase 2, 29600 MARBELLA, MALAGA, SPAIN.
BROWN, Mr. Reuben, FCA *1953;* Paddocks, 14 Collingwood Road, HORSHAM, RH12 2QW. (Life Member)
BROWN, Miss. Rhiann Clare, BA ACA *2007;* 16 Baytree Road, LONDON, SW2 5RP.
BROWN, Dr. Rhoda Mary, PhD BA FCA *1990;* Business School, Loughborough University, LOUGHBOROUGH, LE11 3TU.
•**BROWN, Mr. Richard, BSc ACA** *1997;* Ernst & Young LLP, 1 More London Place, LONDON, SE1 2AF. See also Ernst & Young Europe LLP
BROWN, Mr. Richard, MSc BA ACA *2003;* Pala Investments AG, Dammstrasse 19, 6300 ZUG, SWITZERLAND.
BROWN, Mr. Richard Edward, FCA *1961;* Birchwood, The Glade, Kingswood, TADWORTH, KT20 6LL.
•**BROWN, Mr. Richard Graham, BA ACA** *1988;* (Tax Fac), Swat UK Limited, Tor View House, Darklake View, Estover, PLYMOUTH, PL6 7TL.
BROWN, Mr. Richard James, BA ACA *1988;* with BDO LLP, 55 Baker Street, LONDON, W1U 7EU.
BROWN, Mr. Richard James, BSc ACA *2010;* Flat 1, Dartmouth House, 15 Catherine Grove, LONDON, SE10 8BG.
BROWN, Mr. Richard John, FCA *1969;* Ashlea, 9 Green Lane, HARROGATE, HG2 9JP.
BROWN, Mr. Richard Norman Mills, BSc(Hons) ACA *2001;* 48 Moor Crescent, NEWCASTLE UPON TYNE, NE3 4AQ.
BROWN, Mr. Richard Paul, ACA *1993;* Kincain, Copnor Close, Woolton Hill, NEWBURY, BERKSHIRE, RG20 9UR.
•**BROWN, Mr. Richard Seymour, BA FCA** *1991;* (Tax Fac), Highlands House, Holtye, Cowden, EDENBRIDGE, KENT, TN8 7ED.
•**BROWN, Mr. Richard Simon, BSc FCA** *1991;* Ernst & Young LLP, 1 More London Place, LONDON, SE1 2AF. See also Ernst & Young Europe LLP
•**BROWN, Mr. Richard Stewart Seymour, FCA** *1977;* Richard Brown & Co, 1 High Street, Roydon, HARLOW, CM19 5HJ. See also Brown Accountants Ltd
•**BROWN, Mr. Richard William James, ACA FCCA** *2006;* ERC Accountants & Business Advisers Limited, Suite 26, Century Building, Tower Street, Brunswick Business Park, LIVERPOOL L3 4BJ. See also Brunswick Trustees Limited and The Tax Place Solutions LLP
BROWN, Mr. Robbie, ACA *2010;* 524 Duffield Road, DERBY, DE22 2DL.
BROWN, Mr. Robert, FCA *1956;* Sherwood House, Burnthorne Lane, Dunley, STOURPORT-ON-SEVERN, DY13 0TN. (Life Member)
BROWN, Mr. Robert, FCA *1959;* 6 Ashgarth Court, Rossett Green, HARROGATE, HG2 9LE. (Life Member)
•**BROWN, Mr. Robert, FCA** *1981;* Robert Brown, 30 Thornbridge Close, RUSHDEN, NORTHAMPTONSHIRE, NN10 9NJ.
BROWN, Mr. Robert Adrian, BCom ACA *2004;* 3 Waterfield Cottages, Derby Road, LONDON, SW14 7DT.
BROWN, Mr. Robert Alan, BA FCA *1975;* 13 Lea Drive, NANTWICH, CHESHIRE, CW5 5JS.
•**BROWN, Mr. Robert Alan, BA ACA** *1981;* Crossley & Co, Star House, Star Hill, ROCHESTER, KENT, ME1 1UX. See also Fortisratio Limited, First Payroll & Accounting
BROWN, Mr. Robert Andrew, ACA *1982;* The Cottage, Le Coin Farm, Mont Cochon St Lawrence, JERSEY, JE3 1ND.
BROWN, Mr. Robert David, BSc ACA *1996;* 54 Mayfield Road, Wylde Green, SUTTON COLDFIELD, WEST MIDLANDS, B73 5QJ.
BROWN, Mr. Robert Henry, FCA *1963;* 7 Connaught Gardens West, CLACTON-ON-SEA, CO15 6HX.
•**BROWN, Mr. Robert Ian, ACA** *2008;* with DMC Partnership, Yew Tree House, Lewes Road, FOREST ROW, RH18 5AA.
BROWN, Mr. Robert James, BA ACA *2007;* Flat 2, 138 Barlow Moor Road, West Didsbury, MANCHESTER, M20 2PU.
BROWN, Mr. Robert James, LLB ACA *2004;* 35 Nursery Road, GODALMING, SURREY, GU7 3JU.
BROWN, Mr. Robert John, BSc FCA *1982;* 1 Recreation Road, STOWMARKET, IP14 1LA.
BROWN, Mr. Robert John, BA ACA *2010;* 62 High Street, Weston, BATH, BA1 4DB.
BROWN, Mr. Robert John Johnston, MA ACA *2003;* Garden flat, 8 Highland Road, LONDON, SE19 1DP.
•**BROWN, Mr. Robert Thomas, FCA** *1977;* (Tax Fac), Robert Brown & Co., Monarch House, 1 Smyth Road, BRISTOL, BS3 2BX.
•**BROWN, Mr. Robert Warburton, BSc FCA** *1992;* (Tax Fac), Landers Accountants Ltd, Church View Chambers, 38 Market Square, Toddington, DUNSTABLE, BEDFORDSHIRE LU5 6BS.
BROWN, Mr. Robert William, BCom ACA *1987;* Keter (UK) Ltd, Unit 12, Woodgate Business Park, Clapgate Lane, BIRMINGHAM, B32 3DB.
•**BROWN, Mr. Robert William, FCA** *1973;* RBC, 1 Victoria Square, BIRMINGHAM, B1 1BD.
•**BROWN, Mr. Robert William Ives, FCA** *1969;* Robert Brown & Co, 21 Westley Street, DUDLEY, DY1 1TS.
BROWN, Mr. Robin David, BSc ACA *2002;* PO Box 52162, V&A waterfront, CAPE TOWN, 8002, SOUTH AFRICA.
BROWN, Mr. Robin James Oglesby, BA ACA *1996;* Save the Children, 1 St. John's Lane, LONDON, EC1M 4AR.
•**BROWN, Mr. Robin Lindsay, BA FCA** *1981;* Davies Gimber Brown LLP, Ryebrook Studios, Woodcote Side, EPSOM, SURREY, KT18 7HD.
BROWN, Mr. Roger Anthony, BA ACA *1982;* 90 Morthen Road, Wickersley, ROTHERHAM, S66 1EG.
•**BROWN, Mr. Roger Garrett, FCA** *1970;* (Tax Fac), with Mercer & Hole, Gloucester House, 72 London Road, ST. ALBANS, HERTFORDSHIRE, AL1 1NS.
BROWN, Mr. Roger Godfrey, FCA *1969;* 1 Chancel Way, Charlton Kings, CHELTENHAM, GL53 7RR.
•①**BROWN, Mr. Roger Howard, BA FCA MSPI MABRP** *1969;* The Old Mill, Hampton Loade, BRIDGNORTH, SHROPSHIRE, WV15 6HD.
BROWN, Mr. Roland, FCA *1949;* 1 Perwick House, Perwick Bay, Port St. Mary, ISLE OF MAN, IM9 5PD. (Life Member)
BROWN, Mr. Ronald, FCA *1960;* Tinahely, Wyatts Green, BRENTWOOD, Essex, CM15 0PT. (Life Member)
BROWN, Mr. Ronald Andre Alfred, FCA *1953;* Carrer des Comte 10, 07369 BINIAMAR, MALLORCA, SPAIN. (Life Member)
BROWN, Mr. Ronald George Douglas, FCA *1951;* 142 Bellemoor Road, SOUTHAMPTON, SO15 7RA. (Life Member)
•**BROWN, Mrs. Rosalynd Jane Seymour, FCA** *1995;* Mrs R Brown, 18 Church Lane, Acklam, MIDDLESBROUGH, TS5 7EG.
•**BROWN, Mr. Roy David, FCA** *1962;* Roy D. Brown, 13 Mountain Road, Coppull, CHORLEY, PR7 5EL.
•**BROWN, Mr. Roy Spencer, BSc FCA MBA** *1977;* (Tax Fac), Business Equilibrium Solutions Limited, Business Equilibrium Ltd, 5 Straiton View, Straiton, LOANHEAD, MIDLOTHIAN EH20 9QZ.
BROWN, Mr. Russell, BA ACA *2007;* Flat 5 Heath View, 8 Windmill Drive, LONDON, SW4 9DE.
•**BROWN, Mr. Russell Mark, BSc ACA** *1994;* CMB Partnership, Chapel House, 1 Chapel Street, GUILDFORD, SURREY, GU1 3UH.
BROWN, Mr. Russell Milton, FRGS FCA *1951;* Flat 8, 284 Old Brompton Road, LONDON, SW5 9HR. (Life Member)
BROWN, Mr. Russell Peter, BA(Hons) ACA *2007;* 1062 Le Leman Lake Villas, Bai Xin Zhuang Cun, Dong Nan, Hou Sha Yu Xiang, Shun Yi District, BEIJING 101300 CHINA.
BROWN, Mrs. Ruth Louise, BSc ACA *2003;* 23 Woodland Close, VERWOOD, DORSET, BH31 7PN.
BROWN, Mr. Ryan, ACA MAAT *2011;* 19 Suttons Lane, WIDNES, CHESHIRE, WA8 7UF.
•**BROWN, Ms. Sally, BA FCA** *1989;* 2 Hollybrook Road, SOUTHPORT, MERSEYSIDE, PR8 2AA.
BROWN, Mrs. Sally Jane, BA ACA *2001;* with Bristol & West plc, PO Box 27, One Temple Quay, BRISTOL, BS99 7AX.
•**BROWN, Mrs. Sandra Kay, BA FCA** *1974;* (Tax Fac), Sandra Brown & Co, Sunnyside, Holyport Street, Holyport, MAIDENHEAD, BERKSHIRE SL6 2JR.
BROWN, Mrs. Sandra Patricia, BSc ACA *1994;* 287 Runley Road, LUTON, LU1 1TY.
BROWN, Miss. Sarah, ACA *2010;* 4 Bobbin Road, NORWICH, NR3 2AS.
BROWN, Mrs. Sarah Ann, LLB ACA *1991;* 34 Cedar Road, FARNBOROUGH, Hampshire, GU14 7AX.
BROWN, Mrs. Sarah Anne, BSc ACA *2006;* 11 Goose Green, HOOK, HAMPSHIRE, RG27 9QY.
BROWN, Miss. Sarah Elizabeth, BSc ACA *2006;* Invensys plc, 40 Grosvenor Place, LONDON, SW1X 7EN.
BROWN, Mrs. Sarah Helen, BA ACA *2006;* 4 Hannants Piece, Castle Acre, KING'S LYNN, NORFOLK, PE32 2FG.
BROWN, Miss. Sarah Helen Granger, ACA *1995;* 11 Hill Street, NORWICH, NR2 2DT.

BROWN, Mrs. Sarah Louise, BSc(Hons) ACA *2002;* 12 Thirlmere Road, CHESTER, CH2 2LS.
BROWN, Mr. Scott, BSc ACA *2002;* Amadeus Capital Partners, Mount Pleasant House, 2 Mount Pleasant, CAMBRIDGE, CB3 0RN.
BROWN, Mr. Scott James, ACA *2011;* 2/126 Wandsworth Bridge Road, LONDON, SW6 2UL.
BROWN, Miss. Serena Marie, BA(Hons) ACA *2001;* 5 Allenby Road, LONDON, SE23 2RQ.
BROWN, Mrs. Sharyn Juliet, FCA *1972;* 3 Manor Vale, Mosterton, BEAMINSTER, DORSET, DT8 3LF.
BROWN, Mr. Shaun Marcus, BSc ACA *1997;* with Ernst & Young LLP, 1 More London Place, LONDON, SE1 2AF.
BROWN, Mrs. Sheila, BSc ACA *1986;* 1 Barford Lane, Downton, SALISBURY, SP5 3PY.
BROWN, Mr. Simeon Thomas, BA ACA *1994;* H S B C Asset Management Ltd, 78 St. James's Street, LONDON, SW1A 1EJ.
BROWN, Mr. Simon, BA FCA *1984;* 19 Mill End Close, Eaton Bray, DUNSTABLE, BEDFORDSHIRE, LU6 2FH.
BROWN, Mr. Simon Christopher Zia, BA ACA *1984;* Ashcourt Rowan, 11 Tower View Kings Hill, WEST MALLING, ME19 4UN.
BROWN, Mr. Simon David, BA ACA *1988;* Cognetas LLP, Paternoster House, 65 St. Paul's Churchyard, LONDON, EC4M 8AB.
BROWN, Mr. Simon John, BSc ACA *1993;* Beck Brook Equestrian Centre, Oakington Road, Girton, CAMBRIDGE, CB3 0QH.
BROWN, Mr. Simon Michael John, BA ACA *2000;* Tait Walker Bulman House, Regent Centre Gosforth, NEWCASTLE UPON TYNE, NE3 3LS.
BROWN, Miss. Sophie Nina, BSc ACA *2003;* Tibthorpe Grange, Tibthorpe, DRIFFIELD, NORTH HUMBERSIDE, YO25 9LG.
BROWN, Miss. Stacey, BA(Hons) ACA *2001;* 49 Lake Avenue, RAINHAM, ESSEX, RM13 9SH.
•BROWN, Mr. Stephen, LLB ACA CTA *2001;* Deloitte LLP, Athene Place, 66 Shoe Lane, LONDON, EC4A 3BQ. See also Deloitte & Touche LLP
•BROWN, Mr. Stephen Andrew, BA FCA CF *1988;* R S M Tenon, Davidson House, The Forbury, READING, RG1 3EU.
BROWN, Mr. Stephen Andrew, BA FCA *1980;* Lower Cumery Barn, Aveton Gifford, KINGSBRIDGE, DEVON, TQ7 4NN.
BROWN, Mr. Stephen Gareth, BSc FCA *1992;* 2 Beech Walk, TADCASTER, NORTH YORKSHIRE, LS24 9TH.
BROWN, Mr. Stephen Graham, BA ACA *1986;* Ingeni Ingeni Building, 17 Broadwick Street, LONDON, W1F 0DJ.
BROWN, Mr. Stephen Gwynn Jones, LLB ACA *2002;* 98 Deakin Leas, TONBRIDGE, TN9 2JY.
BROWN, Mr. Stephen Irwin, BSc ACA *2005;* 72 Kingswood Avenue, BROMLEY, BR2 0NP.
BROWN, Mr. Stephen John Thursfield, FCA *1972;* 73 Exeter Gardens, STAMFORD, PE9 2SA.
•BROWN, Mr. Stephen Michael, BA ACA *1995;* Baker Tilly Tax & Advisory Services LLP, The Waterfront, Salts Mill Road, Saltaire, SHIPLEY, WEST YORKSHIRE BD17 7EZ.
BROWN, Mr. Stephen Paul, BSc FCA *1986;* (Tax Fac), with Baker Tilly Tax and Advisory Services LLP, 25 Farringdon Street, LONDON, EC4A 4AB.
•BROWN, Mr. Stephen Ray, BA FCA *1996;* Mazars LLP, The Pinnacle, 160 Midsummer Boulevard, MILTON KEYNES, MK9 1FF.
BROWN, Mr. Steven, MEng ACA *1997;* 41 Brand Street, LONDON, SE10 8SP.
•BROWN, Mr. Steven Allen John, BA ACA *2004;* (Tax Fac), Pointon Young, 33 Ludgate Hill, BIRMINGHAM, B3 1EH.
BROWN, Mr. Steven Andrew, BSc FCA *1987;* 36 St. Mary's Avenue, LONDON, N3 1SN.
BROWN, Mr. Steven David Russell, BA ACA *1993;* W C L S Group Ltd Eggington House, 25-28 Buckingham Gate, LONDON, SW1E 6LD.
BROWN, Mr. Steven John, BA(Econ) ACA *1995;* 7 Um Railand, Junglinster, L-6114 LUXEMBOURG, LUXEMBOURG.
BROWN, Mr. Steven John, BSc FCA *1978;* Thorn Knoll, 7 Broadwater Lane, Aston, STEVENAGE, SG2 7EN.
ⓘBROWN, Mr. Steven Joseph, BA ACA *2005;* Flat 29 Park Hall, The Cloisters, SUNDERLAND, SR2 7QB.
BROWN, Mr. Steven Paul, BA ACA *1993;* 17 Exeter Gardens, STAMFORD, LINCOLNSHIRE, PE9 2RN.
BROWN, Dr. Steven Richard, BSc ACA *1999;* Frogmore Farm Back Lane, Bradfield, READING, RG7 6DS.
BROWN, Mr. Stuart, BSc ACA *1999;* 41 New Road, Little Kingshill, GREAT MISSENDEN, BUCKINGHAMSHIRE, HP16 0EZ.
BROWN, Mr. Stuart Alexander, MSci ACA *2010;* 112 Maximus Road, North Hykeham, LINCOLN, LN6 8JU.
BROWN, Mr. Stuart Lawrence, BSc(Econ) ACA *1991;* Gartner, Level 12, 607 Bourke Street, MELBOURNE, VIC 3000, AUSTRALIA.
BROWN, Mr. Stuart Roger, ACA *2009;* Hanburys Chartered Accountants, 6b Parkway Porters Wood, ST. ALBANS, HERTFORDSHIRE, AL3 6PA.
BROWN, Mr. Stuart William, BA FCA *1971;* Church Farm, Ratley, BANBURY, OX15 6DS. (Life Member)
•BROWN, Miss. Susan Elizabeth, FCA *1979;* (Tax Fac), S.E. Brown, 2 Chancel Way, Charlton Kings, CHELTENHAM, GL53 7RR.
BROWN, Mrs. Susan Mary, BSc ACA *1994;* Woodpeckers, The Avenue, ASCOT, BERKSHIRE, SL5 7LY.
BROWN, Miss. Suzanne, BA(Hons) ACA *2010;* 110 Church Lane, Culcheth, WARRINGTON, WA3 5DJ.
BROWN, Miss. Suzanne Jacqueline, BSc ACA *1989;* 30 Oak Road, COBHAM, KT11 3BA.
BROWN, Mrs. Tanya Catrin, BA ACA *1996;* Sycamore View, 12 Kenyon Fold, ROCHDALE, OL11 5HP.
BROWN, Mr. Thomas Henry, BSc FCA *1990;* 52 Downing Street, Crofton Downs, WELLINGTON 6035, NEW ZEALAND.
•BROWN, Mr. Thomas James, MA ACA *1991;* KPMG LLP, 15 Canada Square, LONDON, E14 5GL. See also KPMG Europe LLP
•BROWN, Mr. Timothy David, BA ACA *1986;* (Tax Fac), T D Brown & Co, 50 The Ridings, SURBITON, SURREY, KT5 8HQ.
•BROWN, Mr. Timothy Michael, BSc FCA *1995;* Rosscot Assurance Limited, Thomas Edge House, Tunnell Street, St. Helier, JERSEY, JE2 4LU.
BROWN, Mr. Tom, BSc ACA *2003;* The Clapham House Group Plc, 1 Lindsey Street, LONDON, EC1A 9HP.
BROWN, Mrs. Tracey, BA ACA *1992;* 9 Lodge Road, Orrell, WIGAN, LANCASHIRE, WN5 7AT.
BROWN, Mrs. Tracy Claire, BSc ACA *2004;* 3 Mallard Close, Burnham, SLOUGH, SL1 7DT.
•BROWN, Mr. Trevor Alan, BSc ACA *1988;* (Tax Fac), Throgmorton UK Limited, 4th Floor, Reading Bridge House, Reading Bridge, George Street, READING RG1 8LS. See also Throgmorton
BROWN, Mr. Trevor David, FCA *1982;* Stanwix, 89B Sandpit Lane, ST. ALBANS, AL1 4BJ.
•BROWN, Mr. Trevor Frederick, BCom FCA *1973;* T.F. Brown & Co, West Farm, Eavestone, RIPON, HG4 3HD.
BROWN, Mr. Trevor Haward, FCA *1973;* TM Group (UK) Limited, 200 Delta Business Park, SWINDON, SN5 7XD.
BROWN, Mr. Trevor Ronald, FCA *1970;* 2218 Stratford Road, Hockley Heath, SOLIHULL, WEST MIDLANDS, B94 6NU.
BROWN, Miss. Trudy Louise, BEng ACA *1995;* 50 Ryarsh Lane, WEST MALLING, ME19 6QP.
BROWN, Ms. Valerie, BA ACA *1990;* (Tax Fac), Glen Dimplex Home Appliances Ltd, Stoney Lane, PRESCOT, MERSEYSIDE, L35 2XW.
BROWN, Miss. Victoria, BA(Hons) ACA *2011;* 138 Rodway Road, Tilehurst, READING, RG30 6DU.
BROWN, Mrs. Victoria Jane, BSc(Hons) ACA CTA *2003;* 14 The Sidings, Bristol Road, Erdington, BIRMINGHAM, WEST MIDLANDS, B23 6AX.
BROWN, Miss. Victoria Jane, BSc ACA *2006;* 3/33 Dumbarton Street, McMahons Point, SYDNEY, NSW 2060, AUSTRALIA.
BROWN, Miss. Victoria Lyndsey, BSc ACA *2003;* 9 Andover Place, WALLSEND, TYNE AND WEAR, NE28 9UD.
BROWN, Mr. Vivian Fox, FCA *1950;* 417 Rue des Glycines, Les Vergers D'Yvremont, 45160 OLIVET, FRANCE. (Life Member)
BROWN, Mrs. Wendy Jayne, BA(Hons) ACA *2000;* 20 Westmorland Road, MANCHESTER, M20 2TA.
BROWN, Mr. William Bruce Pringle, FCA *1963;* 16 Penryn Road, WALSALL, WS5 3EU.
BROWN, Mr. William Royles, FCA *1959;* 26 Longfellow Road, BANBURY, OX16 9LB. (Life Member)
BROWN, Mr. Willis Ian, FCA *1976;* A M F Bowling Focus, 31 Mark Road Hemel Hempstead Industrial Estate, HEMEL HEMPSTEAD, HERTFORDSHIRE, HP2 7BW.
BROWN, Mrs. Yvonne, ACA *1983;* 9 Deepdale, Wilnecote, TAMWORTH, B77 4PD.
BROWNE, Mr. Adrian, BA ACA *1987;* Halliards, 56 Burgess Wood Road South, BEACONSFIELD, BUCKINGHAMSHIRE, HP9 1EJ.
BROWNE, Mr. Alan Hume, BSc FCA *1992;* Scottish Enterprise, 17-19 Hill Street, KILMARNOCK, AYRSHIRE, KA3 1HA.
•BROWNE, Mr. Allan, FCA *1960;* Allan Browne, 34 Frankland Crescent, Parkstone, POOLE, BH14 9PX.
BROWNE, Mr. Anthony Patrick, BEng ACA *2000;* BRG (UK) Ltd, C P House, 97-107 Uxbridge Road, LONDON, W5 5TL.
BROWNE, Mr. Arthur Colin Bruce, BSc FCA *1975;* South Cobbaton Farm, Chittlehampton, UMBERLEIGH, DEVON, EX37 9RZ.
•BROWNE, Mr. Benjamin James, ACA CA(AUS) *2011;* Zolfo Coopers, 10 Fleet Place, LONDON, EC4M 7RB.
BROWNE, Ms. Cindy, ACA *2003;* 24 Reddington Way, BRENTWOOD, WA 6153, AUSTRALIA.
BROWNE, Mr. Clive Acteson, BSc ACA *1983;* (Tax Fac), 7 Drynham Park, WEYBRIDGE, SURREY, KT13 9RE.
•BROWNE, Mr. David Andrew, FCA CF *1985;* Cooper Parry LLP, 14 Park Row, NOTTINGHAM, NG1 6GR.
BROWNE, Mr. David James, FCA *1967;* 70 St. Ann Street, SALISBURY, SP1 2DX.
BROWNE, Mrs. Emily Rebecca, BA ACA *2002;* 8 Lemsford Road, ST. ALBANS, HERTFORDSHIRE, AL1 3PB.
BROWNE, Mr. Eric William, BSc ACA *1999;* 28 Normurra Avenue, TURRAMURRA, NSW 2074, AUSTRALIA.
BROWNE, Mr. Geoffrey John Paul, FCA *1964;* 44 Redland Court Road, BRISTOL, BS6 7EH. (Life Member)
BROWNE, Mr. Graham, FCA *1968;* 117 Foliejohn Way, MAIDENHEAD, BERKSHIRE, SL6 3XY. (Life Member)
BROWNE, Mrs. Jackie, BSc ACA CTA *1992;* Rashleigh Farm, Throwleigh, OKEHAMPTON, DEVON, EX20 2JF.
BROWNE, Mr. John Dunsmore, FCA *1956;* 4 Manor Gardens, SOUTH CROYDON, CR2 7BU. (Life Member)
BROWNE, Mr. John Patrick Paul, FCA *1989;* 2 Bromycroft Rd, Britwell Estate, SLOUGH, SL2 2BQ.
BROWNE, Mr. Kerry Michael, FCA *1966;* Grosvenor House, 105 Chalkwell Esplanade, WESTCLIFF-ON-SEA, ESSEX, SS0 8JJ.
BROWNE, Mr. Kevin Paul, BSc ACA *1987;* (Tax Fac), 10 Maes-Y-Dderwen, Mynach Farm, Creigiau, CARDIFF, MID GLAMORGAN, CF15 9JS.
BROWNE, Mr. Mark Alan, BA ACA *1989;* 14 Brocks Hill Drive, Oadby, LEICESTER, LE2 5RD.
•BROWNE, Mr. Nicholas Valentine, FCA ATII *1982;* (Tax Fac), Graybrowne Limited, The Counting House, Nelson Street, HULL, HU1 1XE.
BROWNE, Mr. Patrick Alexander Howe, BA ACA *1991;* (Tax Fac), Slade & Cooper Ltd, 6 Mount Street, MANCHESTER, M2 5NS.
•BROWNE, Mr. Peter Graham, BSc FCA *1973;* (Tax Fac), Chanter Browne & Curry, 1 Plato Place, 72-74 St Dionis Road, LONDON, SW6 4TU.
BROWNE, Mrs. Rosaline Alice, BA ACA *1989;* Halliards, 56 Burgess Wood Road South, BEACONSFIELD, BUCKINGHAMSHIRE, HP9 1EJ.
BROWNE, Mr. Shaun Dominick, BA ACA *1990;* McQueen Limited, 50 Pall Mall, 5th Floor, LONDON, SW1Y 5JH.
BROWNE, Mr. Stephen John Storey, FCA *1973;* 771 Upper East Coast Road, SINGAPORE 466625, SINGAPORE.
BROWNE, Mr. Steven, ACA *2009;* 35 Plymouth Wharf, LONDON, E14 3EL.
BROWNE, Mr. Terry Ernest, FCA *1969;* 31 Kingfisher Drive, REDHILL, RH1 2AD.
BROWNELL, Mr. Shaun David, BA ACA *2005;* Flat 2 The Grange, 25 Ashley Road, WALTON-ON-THAMES, KT12 1JB.
BROWNELL, Mr. Simon Paul, ACA *2009;* 11 North View Close, Twerton, BATH, BA2 1EH.
BROWNER, Mr. Keith James Anthony, ACA CA(SA) *2010;* 41 Knowle Park, COBHAM, SURREY, KT11 3AA.
BROWNHILL, Miss. Alison Mary, BSc ACA *1990;* (Tax Fac), Balderton Capital, 20 Balderton Street, LONDON, W1K 6TL.
BROWNHILL, Mr. Andrew John, ACA *1979;* 22 Reeds Close, Reedsholme, ROSSENDALE, BB4 8ND.
•BROWNHILL, Mr. Daniel James, ACA MAAT *2005;* Integra Advisers Limited Liability Partnership, The Cedars, Barnsley Road, Hemsworth, PONTEFRACT, WEST YORKSHIRE WF9 4PU.
BROWNHILL, Mr. John Roger, FCA *1959;* 4 Bramber Close, HAYWARDS HEATH, RH16 4AZ. (Life Member)
BROWNHILL, Mr. Keith John, ACA *1987;* brambles, Main Street, Chilthorne Domer, YEOVIL, BA22 8RD.
BROWNHILL, Miss. Sasha Elaine, BSc ACA *2010;* 36 Kingsley Road, PINNER, MIDDLESEX, HA5 5RB.
BROWNING, Mr. Allen John, BSc ACA *1994;* Mountwood, 6 The Drive, RICKMANSWORTH, HERTFORDSHIRE, WD3 4EB.
BROWNING, Mrs. Angela Jane, BA(Hons) ACA *2001;* 5 Caxmere Drive, Wollaton, NOTTINGHAM, NG8 1GG.
•BROWNING, Miss. Carol Elizabeth, BA FCA FCCA *1988;* Cox & Browning Limited, 35 Manor Road, Bladon, WOODSTOCK, OX20 1RU.
•BROWNING, Mr. Christopher Richard, FCA *1966;* Browning Hotchkiss & Partners, Buckhurst Chambers, Coppid Beech Hill, London Road, WOKINGHAM, RG40 1PD.
BROWNING, Mr. David George, FCA *1951;* 17 Sutherington Way, Anstey, LEICESTER, LE7 7TH. (Life Member)
BROWNING, Mr. Gary, BSc FCA *1987;* 15 Burywick, HARPENDEN, HERTFORDSHIRE, AL5 2AQ.
BROWNING, Mr. Gavin John, BSc(Hons) ACA CTA *1990;* Ashhurst House, Cedar Road, WOKING, SURREY, GU22 0JJ.
BROWNING, Mr. Jolyon, BSc FCA *1978;* The Cottage, Chapel Road, Boxted, COLCHESTER, CO4 5RS.
BROWNING, Mr. Mark George, ACA *2009;* Deloitte & Touche Abbots House, Abbey Street, READING, RG1 3BD.
BROWNING, Mr. Richard Compton, BSc FCA *1976;* 48 Lucastes Lane, HAYWARDS HEATH, RH16 1LF.
BROWNING, Mr. Robert John, FCA *1959;* Ladywood, 15 Bryce Close, WARE, SG12 0RH. (Life Member)
•BROWNING, Mr. Robin Nicholas, BA(Hons) ACA FCCA MAAT *2008;* (Tax Fac), R D Owen, 18A Queen Square, BATH, BA1 2HR. See also R D Owen Services Limited and Pethericks & Gillard Ltd
BROWNING, Mr. Scott Alan, ACA *2007;* 26 Vincent Square, Biggin Hill, WESTERHAM, KENT, TN16 3EL.
•BROWNING, Mr. Simon Jonathan, BA(Hons) ACA *2002;* PKF (UK) LLP, Regent House, Clinton Avenue, NOTTINGHAM, NG5 1AZ.
BROWNING, Mr. Timothy Edward, BA ACA *2000;* 43 Recreation Ground, STANSTED, ESSEX, CM24 8BD.
BROWNING, Mrs. Vikki Clare, BSc ACA *1999;* 20 Blythe Close, Enham Alamein, ANDOVER, HAMPSHIRE, SP11 6HX.
BROWNING, Mr. Walter Geoffrey, FCA *1961;* Beech Barn Slegaby Ride, Onchan, ISLE OF MAN, IM4 5BW.
•BROWNLEE, Mr. Charles, BA FCA CTA *1974;* (Tax Fac), Charles Brownlee, 11 Graffham Close, CHICHESTER, WEST SUSSEX, PO19 5AW.
BROWNLEE, Mr. Fergus Stuart, MA MBA FCA *1981;* Streatley House, High Street, Streatley, READING, RG8 9HY.
BROWNLEE, Mr. Ian Colin, FCA *1971;* Badgers Bend, Bradley, WHITCHURCH, SHROPSHIRE, SY13 4QY.
BROWNLEE, Mrs. Louise Jane, ACA *2000;* 7 Hatchlands, Cuckfield, HAYWARDS HEATH, WEST SUSSEX, RH17 5LS.
BROWNLEE, Mr. Neil Robert, BSc FCA *1976;* 2 Palmers Way, Newcastle Under-Lyme, NEWCASTLE, ST5 1HA.
BROWNLEE, Mr. William James, BA ACA *1999;* 7 Hatchlands, Cuckfield, HAYWARDS HEATH, WEST SUSSEX, RH17 5LS.
BROWNLESS, Mrs. Susan Michelle, BA FCA *1990;* 28 Grey Avenue, Southfield Green, CRAMLINGTON, NE23 6PR.
BROWNLEY, Mrs. Sharon Jane, BSc ACA *1991;* 11 Grove Crescent, Adlington, CHORLEY, PR6 9RJ.
BROWNLIE, Mr. Malcolm Philip, FCA *1968;* 5 Juniper Court, CHESTER, CH2 3EH.
BROWNLIE, Mr. Rodney Alan, BSc ACA *1978;* Red Wall House, 26 Sheering Road, Old, HARLOW, CM17 0LS.
BROWNLOW, Mr. Ian Michael, BA ACA *1988;* HSBC Private Bank (Suisse) SA, Rue de Lausanne 18-20, 1211 GENEVA, SWITZERLAND.
BROWNLOW, Mr. Ian Philip, BSc ACA *1984;* 330 Garfield Street, SANTA FE, NM 87501, UNITED STATES.
BROWNLOW, Mr. Robert David, BSc ACA *1982;* Chestnut House, North Lane, Wheldrake, YORK, YO19 6BB.
•BROWNLOW, Miss. Shelagh, BSc FCA *1992;* Brownlow Consulting Limited, 428 Preston Old Road, Cherry Tree, BLACKBURN, BB2 5LP.
BROWNLOW, Mr. Yinka, BA(Hons) ACA *1994;* 4 Acer Crescent, Almondsbury, BRISTOL, BS32 4FL.
BROWNRIDGE, Mr. Paul David, BSc(Econ) ACA *2000;* 372a New Hythe Lane, Larkfield, AYLESFORD, KENT, ME20 6RZ.
•BROWNRIGG, Mr. David Maurice Alexander, MA FCA *1970;* David Bowden & Co, 19 Den Avenue, BOGNOR REGIS, PO21 1HE.

BROWNRIGG-GLEESON, Miss. Annabel, BSc ACA *2010;* 48 Sutherland Grove, LONDON, SW18 5PU.

BROWNSCOMBE, Mr. Robert Alan, BSc FCA *1980;* Bosanneth, Restronguet Point, Feock, TRURO, CORNWALL, TR3 6RB.

BROWNSELL, Miss. Tracy Lorraine, BA(Hons) ACA *2003;* with BDO LLP, 55 Baker Street, LONDON, W1U 7EU.

•**BROWNSEY, Mr. Martin David, BSc ACA** *1995;* 137 High Street, BURTON-ON-TRENT, STAFFORDSHIRE, DE14 1JZ.

BROWNSMITH, Mrs. Michelle Theresa, BA ACA *2007;* 11 Spruce Road, AYLESBURY, BUCKINGHAMSHIRE, HP19 7AE.

BROWNSMITH, Mr. Shaun Kieran, BA ACA *2005;* 11 Spruce Road, AYLESBURY, BUCKINGHAMSHIRE, HP19 7AE.

•**BROWNSON, Mr. Henry Mark, BA FCA** *1989;* (Tax Fac), S.D. Woolf & Co, 113 Union Street, OLDHAM, OL1 1RY. See also Longden & Cook Dental Accountancy Practice

•**BROWNSON, Mr. Jonathan Selwyn, BA FCA** *1986;* (Tax Fac), Royce Peeling Green Limited, The Copper Room, Deva Centre, Trinity Way, MANCHESTER, M3 7BG. See also RPG Holdings Limited

BROWNSON, Mr. Keith McKee, FCA *1956;* chishlom & co (holdings) ltd, Centriforce Products Ltd, 14-16 Derby Road Kirkdale, LIVERPOOL, L20 8EE. (Life Member)

•**BROWNSTEIN, Mr. Ian Jeffrey, FCA** *1968;* I.J. Brownstein & Co, 59 Deacons Hill Road, Elstree, BOREHAMWOOD, WD6 3HZ.

BROWSE, Mr. Mark Richard, MA ACA *1988;* 48 Church Street, Warnham, HORSHAM, WEST SUSSEX, RH12 3QR.

BROXHAM, Mr. Norman Harold, FCA *1965;* Woodside, The leys, HORNSEA, HU18 1ET.

BROXUP, Mr. Ian Richard, BSc FCA MBA *1976;* Aylesford Newsprint Ltd Bellingham Way, AYLESFORD, KENT, ME20 7DL.

BROXUP, Mrs. Joanne Christina, BA ACA *1999;* 1 Rosetree Close, Prestwood, GREAT MISSENDEN, HP16 9EW.

BROYDEN, Mr. Nicholas John, BA ACA *1994;* 91 Honeywell Road, LONDON, SW11 6ED.

BRUCCIANI, Mr. Richard Louis, OBE FCA *1969;* Pal International Ltd, Bilton Way, LUTTERWORTH, LEICESTERSHIRE, LE17 4JA.

BRUCE, Mr. Adrian John, BSc ACA *1997;* Argos Ltd, 489-499 Avebury Boulevard, MILTON KEYNES, MK9 2NW.

BRUCE, Mr. Alastair Charles, BA ACA *1989;* Pantheon Ventures Ltd, Norfolk House, 32 St. James Square, LONDON, SW1Y 4JR.

BRUCE, Mr. Alastair James, FCA *1971;* PO Box 48027, Roosevelt Park, JOHANNESBURG, GAUTENG, 2129, SOUTH AFRICA.

BRUCE, Mr. Andrew, MEng ACA *2006;* Flat 35 Woodlands, 30 Lindsay Road, POOLE, DORSET, BH13 6BG.

BRUCE, Mr. Andrew Harvey, FCA *1973;* Churchmans House, Ospringe, FAVERSHAM, ME13 0HA.

BRUCE, Mr. Andrew Nicholas, MBA BA ACA *1990;* 6 Overdale Grange, SKIPTON, NORTH YORKSHIRE, BD23 6AG.

BRUCE, Mr. Anthony William, FCA *1956;* Oakwood, Nursery Lane, North Wootton, KING'S LYNN, PE30 3QB. (Life Member)

BRUCE, Mr. Christopher, BEng ACA *1993;* Ulica Lelewela 27, 05-420 JOZEFOW, POLAND.

BRUCE, Mr. Christopher Paul, MA(Oxon) ACA *2007;* 5 Madgeways Close, Great Amwell, WARE, HERTFORDSHIRE, SG12 9RU.

BRUCE, Mr. Clive, BSc FCA FRSA *1986;* The White House, High Street, Angmering, LITTLEHAMPTON, BN16 4AH.

BRUCE, Mr. David, ACA *2008;* K P M G Quayside House, 110 Quayside, NEWCASTLE UPON TYNE, NE1 3DX.

BRUCE, Mr. David Alan, ACA *2007;* 15 Rowcroft, HEMEL HEMPSTEAD, HERTFORDSHIRE, HP1 2JF.

BRUCE, Mr. David Ian Rehbinder, MA FCA *1972;* 5 Bolingbroke Grove, Wandsworth Common, LONDON, SW11 6ES.

BRUCE, Mr. David Jonathan, ACA *2008;* Veresen, Suite 440 Livingston Place, South Tower, 222-3rd Avenue SW, CALGARY T2P0B4, AB CANADA.

BRUCE, Mr. David Julian, BSc FCA *1990;* 22a Sunnybank, MARLOW, BUCKINGHAMSHIRE, SL7 3BL.

BRUCE, Mr. David Kevin, ACA *1987;* Keepers Cottage Suffield Lane, Puttenham, GUILDFORD, GU3 1BQ.

BRUCE, Mrs. Elizabeth Anne, BSc FCA *1977;* Linden, Crowborough Hill, CROWBOROUGH, TN6 2JA.

BRUCE, Miss. Elizabeth Louise, ACA *2008;* Unit 3, 35 Robert Street, Como, PERTH, WA 6152, AUSTRALIA.

BRUCE, Mrs. Frances Julia, BSc(Hons) ACA *2003;* 17 Village Garth, Wigginton, YORK, YO32 2QU.

BRUCE, Mr. Geoffrey Ian, BSc FCA *1985;* 31 Bristow Close, Great Sankey, WARRINGTON, WA5 5EU.

BRUCE, Mr. Geoffrey Scott, FCA *1972;* Maginnis & Carey LLP, 220 NW 2nd Avenue Suite 1000, PORTLAND, OR 97209-3971, UNITED STATES.

•①**BRUCE, Miss. Gillian Eleanor, LLB FCA** *1991;* with PricewaterhouseCoopers LLP, 1 East Parade, SHEFFIELD, S1 2ET.

BRUCE, Mr. Gordon Alexander, ACA *1982;* 26 Renfrew Drive, WOLLATONNotts, NOTTINGHAM, NG8 2FX.

•**BRUCE, Mrs. Helen Patricia, BA FCA** *1987;* (Tax Fac), Dyke Yaxley Limited, 1 Brassey Road, Old Potts Way, SHREWSBURY, SY3 7FA.

BRUCE, Mr. Iain Jack, LLB ACA *2010;* 2 Deacon Close, MARKET HARBOROUGH, LEICESTERSHIRE, LE16 7UT.

BRUCE, Mr. Ian Hamilton, CA ACA *1983;* 21 Coln St. Aldwyns, CIRENCESTER, GLOUCESTERSHIRE, GL7 5AA.

BRUCE, Mr. Ian Nigel, BA FCA *1979;* Grant Thornton UK LLP, 30 Finsbury Square, LONDON, EC2P 2YU.

BRUCE, Mr. James, BSc ACA *2003;* Ground Floor, 56 Rowallan Road, LONDON, SW6 6AG.

BRUCE, The Hon. James Henry Morys, FCA *1971;* Chalcot House, Dilton Marsh, WESTBURY, WILTSHIRE, BA13 4DF.

BRUCE, Miss. Jennifer Alice Fraser, MA ACA *1989;* Boston Cottage, 31 Lower Street, Quainton, AYLESBURY, BUCKINGHAMSHIRE, HP22 4BL.

BRUCE, Miss. Joanna Elizabeth, BA ACA *2005;* with KPMG LLP, 15 Canada Square, LONDON, E14 5GL.

BRUCE, Mr. John, FCA *1951;* Highfield, 29 Charlton Close, Hampton, EVESHAM, WR11 2QE. (Life Member)

BRUCE, Mrs. Julie Caroline, BA ACA *1994;* 51 Seymour Road, West Bridgford, NOTTINGHAM, NG2 5EE.

BRUCE, Mrs. Lara Jane, BSc ACA *1996;* 47 Carters Close, Sherington, NEWPORT PAGNELL, MK16 9NW.

BRUCE, Mr. Michael Alexander, FCA *1973;* Mont D'Or Petroleum Singapore Pte Ltd, Six Battery Road, #17 - 07, SINGAPORE 049909, SINGAPORE.

BRUCE, Mr. Michael Gordon, BSc FCA *1985;* Moore Stephens, 150 Aldersgate Street, LONDON, EC1A 4AB.

BRUCE, Mr. Murray Euan Fyvie, BA ACA *1998;* 51 Crystal Green Drive, OKOTOKS T1S 2N7, AB, CANADA.

BRUCE, Mr. Peveril John, FCA *1977;* Hampage House, Ovington, ALRESFORD, SO24 0HY.

BRUCE, Mr. Philip David, ACA *2007;* 6 Reighton Drive, YORK, YO30 5QH.

BRUCE, Mr. Richard Alfred Reginald, BSc FCA *1977;* Bewl Ridge House, Flimwell, WADHURST, TN5 7QG.

•**BRUCE, Mrs. Sabrina Marion Christine, FCA** *1978;* (Tax Fac), S.M.C Bruce, 28 Pheasants Way, RICKMANSWORTH, WD3 7ES.

•**BRUCE, Mr. Simon Charles, BSc FCA** *1982;* Virbix Ltd, North Lodge, South Horrington Village, WELLS, SOMERSET, BA5 3DZ.

BRUCE, Mrs. Susan Nicola, BA ACA *1991;* 19 Blenheim Close, SAWBRIDGEWORTH, CM21 0BE.

BRUCE-GARDYNE, Mr. Evan David, MA ACA *1995;* Middleton House, ARBROATH, DD11 4SD.

BRUCE-JONES, Mrs. Carolyn Louise, BSc ACA *1984;* Amoril House, 278 High Street, Batheaston, BATH, BA1 7RA.

BRUCE-MORGAN, Mr. Claes Owen Llewellyn, ACA *1988;* (Tax Fac), 15 Lady Margaret Road, Kentish Town, LONDON, NW5 2NG.

BRUCE-SMYTHE, Mr. Simon Carrington, FCA *1967;* Stone Cross Farmhouse, Ashurst, Groombridge, TUNBRIDGE WELLS, TN3 9SX.

•**BRUCH, Mr. David Ernst, FCA** *1974;* (Tax Fac), Bruch & Co Limited, 1 School Lane, WISBECH, CAMBRIDGESHIRE, PE13 1AW.

BRUCK, Mr. Jack Edward, ACA *2009;* 795 Garratt Lane, LONDON, SW17 0PF.

•**BRUCK, Mr. Steven Mark, MSc BSc(Hons) FCA** *1972;* Blick Rothenberg, 12 York Gate, Regent's Park, LONDON, NW1 4QS.

BRUDENELL, Mr. Mark Ian, BA FCA *1997;* 84 Rutland Avenue, SOUTHEND-ON-SEA, SS1 2XN.

BRUDNE, Mr. Leslie, FCA *1975;* 2647 Tavistock Court, STERLING HEIGHTS, MI 48310, UNITED STATES.

BRUELL, Mr. John Peter Hawley, BSc ACA *1990;* The Dower House, Aldsworth, EMSWORTH, HAMPSHIRE, PO10 8QT.

•**BRUETON, Mr. Trevor Paul, BA ACA** *1992;* Muras Baker Jones, Regent House, Bath Avenue, WOLVERHAMPTON, WV1 4EG. See also Muras Management Services Ltd

•**BRUFF, Mr. Peter Frederick James, FCA CTA** *1967;* Peter Bruff & Co, Cherry Court, 5 Cherry Orchard, Littlebourne, CANTERBURY, CT3 1QG.

BRUFFELL, Mr. Glyn, FCA *1968;* 38 Edenhurst Apartments, Manchester Road, Haslingden, ROSSENDALE, LANCASHIRE, BB4 6LJ.

•**BRUFORD, Mr. Alan George, FCA** *1982;* SB&P LLP, Oriel House, 2-8 Oriel Road, BOOTLE, MERSEYSIDE, L20 7EP. See also Satterthwaite Brooks & Pomfret LLP

BRUFORD, Mrs. Hannah Louise, BA ACA *2005;* Kautex Textron C V S Ltd 3 Alder Avenue, Dyffryn Business Park Ystrad Mynach, HENGOED, MID GLAMORGAN, CF82 7TW.

BRUFORD, Mr. Paul James, BSc ACA *1992;* 2 Silver Birch Court, Shadoxhurst, ASHFORD, KENT, TN26 1NR.

BRUFORD, Mr. Peter Jonathon Caisley, BSc FCA *1991;* Borough House, 99 The Borough, Downton, SALISBURY, SP5 3LX.

BRUFORD, Mr. Philip Alan, ACA *2010;* 6 Marldon Avenue, Crosby, LIVERPOOL, L23 0SL.

BRUGERE, Mr. Julien Gilles, ACA *1999;* Time Warner, Time Warner House, 44 Great Marlborough Street, LONDON, W1F 7JL.

BRULL, Mrs. Danielle Leoni, ACA *1992;* 12 Twineham Green, LONDON, N12 7EP.

BRUMBY, Mr. Mark Andrew, ACA *1984;* Langton House, Metcalfe Lane, Osbaldwick, YORK, YO19 5UR.

BRUMFITT, Mr. Gordon Lionel, FCA *1974;* Willowfield, Spring Lane, Eldwick, BINGLEY, WEST YORKSHIRE, BD16 3AU.

BRUMMER, Mr. Andrew Jonathan, BA ACA *2003;* 29 Windsor Avenue, EDGWARE, HA8 8SR.

BRUMWELL, Mr. James William, FCA *1974;* 23 Springbanks Way, Merefields East Hunsbury, NORTHAMPTON, NN4 0QA.

BRUNDELL, Mrs. Faye, BA(Hons) ACA *2000;* (Tax Fac), 1 Hertford Way, Knowle, SOLIHULL, B93 0PD.

BRUNDELL, Miss. Julia Lilian, BSc ACA *1992;* 11 Chalcroft Road, LONDON, SE13 5RE.

BRUNDELL, Mr. Paul James, BSc ACA *1986;* 7 The Cedars, Bushby, LEICESTER, LE7 9RZ.

BRUNDISH, Mr. David Keith, BSc ACA *1996;* Gidley Wood, Gidley Farm, Chieveley, NEWBURY, BERKSHIRE, RG20 8TX.

BRUNDLE, Mr. Thomas, BA ACA *2006;* 52 Main Street Scholes, LEEDS, LS15 4DH.

BRUNEL-COHEN, Mr. Edward Stuart, FCA *1975;* Maultway Lodge, 9 Copped Hall Drive, CAMBERLEY, GU15 1NN.

BRUNEL-COHEN, Miss. Jane, BA ACA *2010;* Flat 7, 9 Clifton Park, BRISTOL, BS8 3BU.

BRUNING, Mr. Christian Lewis, BSc ACA CF *1997;* Windmill Bank, Selsfield Common, EAST GRINSTEAD, RH19 4LW.

BRUNING, Mr. Michael Lewis, FCA *1969;* Chartstone, Tally Road, Limpsfield Chart, OXTED, RH8 0TG.

BRUNING, Miss. Tania, BA ACA *1998;* 27 Clifton Road, ISLEWORTH, MIDDLESEX, TW7 4HJ.

BRUNING GEN BRINKMANN, Ms. Gesa, ACA *2004;* Pearson Plc Shell Mex House, 80 Strand, LONDON, WC2R 0RL.

BRUNNEN, Mr. John Richard Lance, FCA *1974;* 24a St. Andrews Road, Caversham, READING, RG4 7PH.

BRUNNING, Mr. Edward Crawford, BA ACA *2002;* The Berkeley Partnership, 48-49 Chancery Lane, LONDON, WC2A 1JF.

BRUNNING, Mrs. Jennifer Elise, BA(Hons) ACA *2002;* Twin Valley, Brinkworth, CHIPPENHAM, WILTSHIRE, SN15 5BY.

BRUNNING, Mr. Mark, FCA *1987;* 11 South Parade, SOUTHSEA, HAMPSHIRE, PO5 2JB.

BRUNNING, Mr. Nigel Peter, BA FCA *1993;* 21 Trinity Road, RAYLEIGH, ESSEX, SS6 8QD.

BRUNNING, Mr. Simon David John, BA(Hons) ACA MCT *2000;* 4East155, Ernst & Young Llp, 1 More London Place, LONDON, SE1 2AF.

BRUNNING, Mrs. Tracy, BA ACA *1997;* 21 Trinity Road, RAYLEIGH, ESSEX, SS6 8QD.

BRUNO, Mr. Dominique Austin, ACA *2008;* GFF, 109 St. Thomas's Road, LONDON, N4 2QJ.

•**BRUNO, Mr. Maurice, BA FCA** *1988;* Maurice Bruno Ltd, Wyndham House, Sunning Avenue, ASCOT, BERKSHIRE, SL5 9PW.

BRUNSDEN, Mr. Paul Geoffrey, BSc ACA *1995;* 31 Napoleon Road, TWICKENHAM, TW1 3EW.

BRUNSDON, Miss. Sara Julie, BSc ACA *2009;* Lady Croft, Little Marcle, LEDBURY, HEREFORDSHIRE, HR8 2JX.

BRUNSKILL, Mr. Martin Stuart, BSc FCA *1989;* 12 Mount View Terrace, STOCKSFIELD, NE43 7HL.

BRUNSKILL, Mr. William Alan, FCA *1962;* 31 Post Office Lane, Kirmington, ULCEBY, SOUTH HUMBERSIDE, DN39 6YT.

BRUNSNES, Mr. Thomas, MA MSc ACA *2011;* 8c Fernwood Road, Jesmond, NEWCASTLE UPON TYNE, NE2 1TJ.

BRUNT, Mr. Antony John, FCA *1972;* 2 Church Street, CULLOMPTON, EX15 1JU.

BRUNT, Mrs. Belinda Ann, BA ACA *1985;* Afford Bond LLP, Enterprise House, 97 Alderley Road, WILMSLOW, CHESHIRE, SK9 1PT.

BRUNT, Mrs. Denise Elizabeth, BSc ACA *1991;* Lower Hollinhead Farm, Littledale Road, Littledale and Quernmore, LANCASTER, LA2 9ER.

•**BRUNT, Mr. Hedley Charles, BSc FCA FIPA FABRP** *1976;* HCB Solutions, Keys Cottage, Woodgate Road, Lower Bentley, BROMSGROVE, WORCESTERSHIRE B60 4HA.

BRUNT, Miss. Jennifer Louise, BA(Hons) ACA *2011;* 97 Radnor Drive, WIDNES, CHESHIRE, WA8 7PH.

BRUNT, Mr. Jonathan Peter, BSc ACA *1992;* 67 Avoncroft Road, Stoke Heath, BROMSGROVE, WORCESTERSHIRE, B60 4NG.

BRUNT, Mr. Paul Harvey John, BSc FCA *1989;* with Hillier Hopkins LLP, 64 Clarendon Road, WATFORD, WD17 1DA.

BRUNT, Miss. Sandra Helen, FCA MAAT *1996;* Josolyne & Co Silk House, Park Green, MACCLESFIELD, CHESHIRE, SK11 7QW.

BRUNT, Mrs. Sarah Dawn, BSc ACA *1992;* 67 Avoncroft Road, Stoke Heath, BROMSGROVE, WORCESTERSHIRE, B60 4NG.

BRUNT, Mrs. Sarah Elizabeth, BA ACA *2005;* 8 Oval Drive, DUKINFIELD, CHESHIRE, SK16 4XB.

BRUNT, Miss. Sarah Victoria, BSc ACA *2010;* 22 Northfield Road, Harborne, BIRMINGHAM, B17 0SU.

BRUNT, Mr. Simon Rogerson, BA FCA *1986;* 73 Beacon Way, RICKMANSWORTH, WD3 7PB.

BRUNT, Mr. Tom, ACA *2011;* 80 New Street, MATLOCK, DERBYSHIRE, DE4 3FH.

BRUNTON, Mrs. Erica Elizabeth Sylvia, BA ACA *1994;* 20 Haines Hill, TAUNTON, SOMERSET, TA1 4HW.

BRUNTON, Mr. Jeffrey, BA ACA *1983;* D1, BP International Ltd, Chertsey Road, SUNBURY-ON-THAMES, MIDDLESEX, TW16 7LN.

BRUNTON, Mrs. Kay, ACA *2009;* 11 Leigh Hill, Emerson Valley, MILTON KEYNES, MK4 2BJ.

•**BRUNTON, Mr. Mark Richard Cail, BSc FCA** *1991;* Tait Walker LLP, Bulman House, Regent Centre, Gosforth, NEWCASTLE UPON TYNE, NE3 3LS. See also Tait Walker Management Limited

•**BRUNTON, Mr. Peter Howard James, FCA** *1971;* (Tax Fac), P.H.J. Brunton & Co, 14 The Brackens, Locks Heath, SOUTHAMPTON, SO31 6TU.

BRUNTON, Mr. Timothy Dickinson, MA BPhil FCA *1973;* New Place, 8b Harberton Mead, Headington, OXFORD, OX3 0DB. (Life Member)

BRUSCHI, Mr. Paul Julian, FCA *1961;* The Lodge, Cookham Dene, Manor Park, CHISLEHURST, BR7 5QD.

BRUTEN, Ms. Claire Marie, MA ACA *1999;* BNP Paribas, 787 Seventh Avenue, 29th Floor, NEW YORK, NY 10019, UNITED STATES.

BRUTNALL, Mr. Ashley Stephen, BA(Hons) ACA *2001;* with Ernst & Young LLP, 1 More London Place, LONDON, SE1 2AF.

BRUTON, Miss. Anna Claire, BSc ACA *2001;* Puig UK Ltd Grafton House, 2-3 Golden Square, LONDON, W1F 9HR.

BRUTON, Mr. Dax Michael Thomas, BA ACA *1998;* PricewaterhouseCoopers Ltd, Abacus House, P O Box 63, PROVIDENCIALES, TURKS AND CAICOS ISLANDS.

BRUTON, Mr. John David, ACA *2010;* Lloyds Banking Group Plc, HBOS Plc, Harbourside 2 Zone A, 10 Canons Way, BRISTOL, BS1 5LF.

BRUTON, Mr. John Philip, MPhil ACA *1988;* Raglan Housing Association Wright House, Castle Street, POOLE, BH15 1BQ.

BRUTON, Mr. Roger Neil, FCA *1971;* 17 Hill Lane, Bassetts Pole, SUTTON COLDFIELD, B75 6LE.

BRUTON, Miss. Verity Rose, ACA *2010;* Francis Clark Chartered Accountants Sigma House, Oak View Close, TORQUAY, TQ2 7FF.

BRYAN, Mr. Albert Henry Patrick, FCA *1962;* 14 Stanmore Way, Goldings Manor, LOUGHTON, IG10 2SA.

BRYAN, Mr. Andrew David, BA(Hons) ACA *2001;* 70 Brunswick Street, READING, RG1 6NZ.

BRYAN, Mrs. Anne Louise, BA ACA *2007;* 169 Ravenscroft Road, BECKENHAM, BR3 4TN.

BRYAN, Mr. David, BSc ACA *2007;* Broadridge Financial Soluations Ltd, The ISIS Building, 193 Marsh Wall, LONDON, E14 9SG.
BRYAN, Mr. David Andrew, ACA *1983;* 23 Austin Friars, LONDON, EC2N 2QP.
BRYAN, Mr. David John, FCA *1969;* 8 Sea Pines, Victoria Road, Milford on Sea, LYMINGTON, HAMPSHIRE, SO41 0NQ. (Life Member)
BRYAN, Mr. Everton, BA ACA *1986;* 149a Green Dragon Lane, Winchmore Hill, LONDON, N21 1EU.
BRYAN, Mrs. Heidi Melanie, BSc ACA *2002;* 10 Haywards Villas Colwell Road, HAYWARDS HEATH, WEST SUSSEX, RH16 4HS.
BRYAN, Mr. John Donald, FCA *1958;* 9 Winds Ridge, Send, WOKING, SURREY, GU23 7HU. (Life Member)
BRYAN, Mr. John Richard, FCA *1963;* 80 Brompton Close, LUTON, LU3 3QT. (Life Member)
BRYAN, Mr. John William, FCA *1974;* 4 Berrington Gardens, TENBURY WELLS, WORCESTERSHIRE, WR15 8ET.
•BRYAN, Mr. Michael Ernest, FCA *1970;* M.E. Bryan, Croft House, Gt. Finborough, STOWMARKET, IP14 3BG.
BRYAN, Mr. Neil Peter, BSc ACA *1991;* (Tax Fac), 14 Montagus Harrier, GUISBOROUGH, CLEVELAND, TS14 8PB.
BRYAN, Mr. Nicholas, BSc ACA *2003;* 37 Chantry Avenue, Hartley, LONGFIELD, DA3 8DD.
BRYAN, Mr. Nicholas George, BA ACA *1991;* 8 The Breach, DEVIZES, SN10 5BJ.
BRYAN, Mr. Nicholas Martin, BA FCA *1979;* Innserve, The Old Maltings, TADCASTER, NORTH YORKSHIRE, LS24 9PZ.
BRYAN, Mr. Nigel David, BSc ACA *1998;* 5 Ilmington Close, Hatton Park, WARWICK, WARWICKSHIRE, CV35 7TL.
BRYAN, Mr. Peter Gerald, BA ACA *1989;* 51 Holt Way, Hook, HOOK, RG27 9LG.
BRYAN, Mr. Peter Nigel, BA ACA *1985;* Marlborough College, MARLBOROUGH, SN8 1PA.
•BRYAN, Mr. Philip Douglas, FCA *1966;* East Cottage, Roughwood Lane, CHALFONT ST. GILES, BUCKINGHAMSHIRE, HP8 4AA.
BRYAN, Mrs. Rachel Elizabeth, BSc(Hons) ACA *2009;* 86 Cleveland Gardens, LONDON, SW13 0AH.
BRYAN, Mr. Richard Andrew, BA FCA *1988;* Ross House, Macarthy & Stone Retirement Lifestyles Ltd Ross House, Binley Business Park Harry Weston Road, COVENTRY, CV3 2TR.
BRYAN, Mr. Richard David, BSc ACA *1992;* Inspectorate International Ltd, 2 Perry Road, WITHAM, ESSEX, CM8 3TU.
BRYAN, Mr. Roger Albert, FCA *1950;* 72 Dovehouse Lane, SOLIHULL, B91 2EG. (Life Member)
BRYAN, Mr. Simon Alan, BA ACA *1979;* Ferrers Farm, Woolmongers Lane, Blackmore, INGATESTONE, CM4 0JX.
BRYAN, Mr. Stephen David, BA ACA *2002;* 193 St. Barnabas Road, WOODFORD GREEN, ESSEX, IG8 7DG.
•BRYAN, Mr. Stephen Robert, BSc FCA CTA *1986;* Cooper Parry LLP, 14 Park Row, NOTTINGHAM, NG1 6GR.
BRYAN, Mr. Tafari, BSc ACA *2005;* 5 Thornhill Road, PLYMOUTH, PL3 5NF.
BRYAN, Mr. Thomas Patrick Nicholas, ACA *2008;* 86 Cleveland Gardens, LONDON, SW13 0AH.
BRYAN-BROWN, Miss. Jennifer Anne, MA ACA CTA *1990;* (Tax Fac), with PricewaterhouseCoopers LLP, 1 Embankment Place, LONDON, WC2N 6RH.
BRYAN-HARRIS, Mr. Paul Nicholas, BSc ACA *1998;* 11 Braemar Avenue, Wimbledon Park, LONDON, SW19 8AY.
BRYANS, Mr. Thomas David, BA ACA *2004;* avenue d'echallens 8, 1004 LAUSANNE, SWITZERLAND.
•BRYANT, Mr. Adrian Jeremy, BSc ACA *1987;* A & M Bryant Consulting Ltd, 6 Pheasants Way, RICKMANSWORTH, HERTFORDSHIRE, WD3 7ES. See also Margaret Bryant Consulting Limited
BRYANT, Mr. Andrew John, ACA *1993;* Expeditors International UK Ltd, 1 Ascot Road, Bedfont, FELTHAM, MIDDLESEX, TW14 8QH.
BRYANT, Mr. Andrew Robert, BSc ACA *1989;* Mountney Ltd, 6 Lombard Way, BANBURY, OXFORDSHIRE, OX16 4TJ.
BRYANT, Mr. Anthony Peter, BA FCA *1977;* Southgate, Hurstwood, SOUTH, ASCOT, SL5 9SP. (Life Member)
BRYANT, Mr. Ben Peter, BA FCA *1991;* 109 Leschenault Parade, Galway Green, BUNBURY, WA 6233, AUSTRALIA.
BRYANT, Miss. Carly Anne, ACA *2009;* 6 Ambra Vale South, BRISTOL, BS8 4RN.
BRYANT, Mr. Charles Malcolm, BA ACA *1983;* 18 Troutbeck Crescent, Bramcote, NOTTINGHAM, NG9 3BP.
BRYANT, Miss. Clare, BSc ACA *2008;* 12 Wealdhurst Park, St. Peters, BROADSTAIRS, CT10 2LD.
BRYANT, Mr. Darren, MEng FCA *1995;* The Orchards, Crag Lane, Huby, LEEDS, LS17 0BW.
•BRYANT, Mr. David John, FCA *1982;* Bryant & Co Limited, North Houghton Mill, North Houghton, STOCKBRIDGE, HAMPSHIRE, SO20 6LF.
BRYANT, Mr. David Walter, FCA *1959;* 5 Mansion House Close, Biddenden, ASHFORD, KENT, TN27 8DE. (Life Member)
•BRYANT, Mrs. Diane Joyce, FCA *1974;* Diane J. Bryant, Eversley, Gorse Way, Hartley, LONGFIELD, DA3 8AF.
BRYANT, Mr. Edward Henry, FCA *1964;* 6 Seaforth Gdns, Stoneleigh, EPSOM, KT19 0NR. (Life Member)
BRYANT, Miss. Elizabeth Sarah, BSc ACA *2010;* 4 Clay Street, Wymeswold, LOUGHBOROUGH, LEICESTERSHIRE, LE12 6TY.
BRYANT, Miss. Elsie Mary, FCA *1961;* 18 Bartholomew Close, Wandsworth, LONDON, SW18 1JQ. (Life Member)
BRYANT, Mr. Geoffrey James, BA ACA *2006;* 98 Earls Road, SOUTHAMPTON, SO14 6SE.
•BRYANT, Mr. George Robert, MA FCA *1964;* Bryant Mayl & Co, 24 South Street, VALLETTA VLT 1102, MALTA.
BRYANT, Mr. Ian Stuart Macdonald, FCA *1971;* 194 Woodlands Road, AYLESFORD, KENT, ME20 7QF.
BRYANT, Mr. James Gwyn, BSc ACA *2007;* 1 Bel Royal Gardens, La Route de St. Aubin, St. Lawrence, JERSEY, JE3 1JU.
BRYANT, Mr. James Richard Stansfeld, FCA *1965;* Drapers Farm House, Shaw Green, Rushden, BUNTINGFORD, SG9 0TB.
•BRYANT, Mrs. Janine Adonia, BA FCA ATII *1990;* with Moore Stephens, 12/13 Alma Square, SCARBOROUGH, YO11 1JU.
BRYANT, Mr. John Hartwell Alexander, LLB FCA *1980;* 5 Tauranga, 119 King George Road, Avondale, HARARE, 2824, ZIMBABWE.
BRYANT, Miss. Julie Catherine, MA FCA CTA *1995;* with HW, 30 Camp Road, FARNBOROUGH, HAMPSHIRE, GU14 6EW.
•BRYANT, Mr. Justin Adam, MA ACA *2001;* MacIntyre Hudson LLP, New Bridge Street House, 30-34 New Bridge Street, LONDON, EC4V 6BJ. See also Backfriars Tax Soluations LLP
BRYANT, Miss. Katherine Alexandra, ACA *2010;* 8 Balmain Close, LONDON, W5 5BY.
BRYANT, Mrs. Laura Jennifer, BSc ACA *2001;* Britvic Soft Drinks, Britvic House, Broomfield Road, CHELMSFORD, CM1 1TU.
•BRYANT, Mrs. Linda Marian, ACA *1984;* Bryant & Co, 3 Burcott Gardens, New Haw, ADDLESTONE, KT15 2DE.
BRYANT, Mr. Lysander Nicolo, ACA *2009;* Top floor flat, 11 Webb's Road, LONDON, SW11 1XJ.
BRYANT, Mr. Malcolm Kenneth, FCA *1974;* 291 Springfield Road, CHELMSFORD, CM1 7RB.
BRYANT, Mr. Mark Brinley, MA ACA *1979;* Ernst & Young, The Ernst & Young Building, 680 George Street, SYDNEY, NSW 2000, AUSTRALIA.
BRYANT, Mr. Michael Alec, BSc ACA *1986;* 36 Maes y Sarn, Pentyrch, CARDIFF, CF15 9QQ.
BRYANT, Mr. Michael Edward, BSc ACA *1992;* Interdelta, Citypoint, 1 Ropemaker Street, LONDON, EC2Y 9HT.
BRYANT, Mr. Michael John, FCA *1960;* Shalom, 44 Grange Park Avenue, Winchmore Hill, LONDON, N21 2LJ. (Life Member)
BRYANT, Mr. Neil Anthony, FCA *1971;* 3 Victoria Road, Meole Brace, SHREWSBURY, SY3 9HX.
BRYANT, Mr. Peter, BSc ACA *2009;* Drapers Farm House, Rushden, BUNTINGFORD, HERTFORDSHIRE, SG9 0TB.
BRYANT, Mr. Peter Anthony, BSc FCA *1977;* 16 Park Lane, FAREHAM, PO16 7JX.
•BRYANT, Mr. Peter George, FCA *1986;* (Tax Fac), Bryant & Co, 35 Ashurst Road, Ash Vale, ALDERSHOT, HAMPSHIRE, GU12 5AF.
BRYANT, Mr. Robert Frederick, FCA *1975;* 6 Fairfield Avenue, TWICKENHAM, TW2 6JY. (Life Member)
BRYANT, Mr. Robert Michael, FCA *1973;* (Member of Council 1993 - 2007), 29 Park Road, BROMLEY, BR1 3HJ.
•BRYANT, Mr. Roger Graham, MSc BSc(Econ) FCA FCCA *1973;* Roger Bryant MSc BSc (Econ) FCA FCCA, Linden House, Chapel Hill, Clayton West, HUDDERSFIELD, HD8 9NH.
BRYANT, Mr. Simon James, ACA *2009;* 6 Bateson Street, BRADFORD, BD10 0BE.
BRYANT, Mr. Thomas Buckland, PhD BEng ACA *2003;* QBE Insurance, Level 2, 82 Pitt Street, SYDNEY, NSW 2000, AUSTRALIA.
BRYANT, Miss. Vicki Ann, BSocSc ACA *2003;* 12 Andrew Street, SCARBOROUGH, WA 6019, AUSTRALIA.
BRYARS, Mr. David Andrew, LLB ACA *1991;* The Farm, Seaton Mill Mill Road, Seaton, OAKHAM, LE15 9HX.
•BRYARS, Mr. Martin Joel, MA FCA *1970;* Bryars & Co., Cloverfield, Houghton Down, STOCKBRIDGE, SO20 6JR.
BRYCE, Mr. Graham David, BCom ACA *1993;* 15 Dublin Street, EDINBURGH, MIDLOTHIAN, EH1 3PG.
BRYCE, Mr. Iain Ross, TD DL FCA *1959;* 76 Cardigan Road, BRIDLINGTON, YO15 3JT. (Life Member)
•BRYDEN, Mr. David John, FCA *1972;* Coulsons, 2 Belgrave Crescent, SCARBOROUGH, NORTH YORKSHIRE, YO11 1UB.
•BRYDEN, Mr. Kenneth Antony, ACA *1981;* (Tax Fac), Bryden & Co, 17 Mornington Road, SALE, M33 2DA.
BRYDEN, Mr. Neil Conway, ACA *1989;* Ballacottier House, The Dhoor, Lezayre, ISLE OF MAN, IM7 4ED.
BRYDEN-SMITH, Mr. Matthew Garfield, MA ACA *1997;* Adam Communication Systems International Ltd The Mission, Wellington Street, STOCKPORT, CHESHIRE, SK1 3AH.
BRYDGES, Mr. Peter Edward, ACA *2008;* 2 Eversleigh Road, LONDON, SW11 5UZ.
BRYDGES, Mr. Philip Richard, BSc ACA *1997;* 264 Ryebank Road, Chorlton Cum Hardy, MANCHESTER, M21 9LJ.
•BRYDONE, Mr. Christopher Malcolm, BA FCA *1985;* (Tax Fac), Brydone & Co, 65 Meersbrook Road, SHEFFIELD, S8 9HU.
BRYER, Mrs. Julie Caroline, ACA *1987;* Serco plc, Serco House, Bartley Way, HOOK, HAMPSHIRE, RG27 9XB.
BRYMER-GRIFFITH, Miss. Sian Elizabeth, ACA *2010;* Bryneira, Upper Dolfor Road, NEWTOWN, POWYS, SY16 3AB.
•BRYNING, Mr. Charles Frederick, FCA *1972;* Jones Harris Limited, 17 St. Peters Place, FLEETWOOD, LANCASHIRE, FY7 6EB.
BRYOIS, Mrs. Zoe, BSc ACA *1999;* 16 Garfield Road, Clapham, LONDON, SW11 5PN.
BRYON, Mr. Alan Charles Gurney, FCA *1982;* Le Grand Dixcart, Sark, GUERNSEY, GY9 0SD.
BRYON, Mr. Michael Charles, BSc(Hons) ACA *2009;* 112 Islingword Road, BRIGHTON, BN2 9SG.
BRYON, Mr. Paul Anthony Gurney, FCA *1970;* 1838 Baillie Glass lane, Orlando, ORLANDO, FL 32835, UNITED STATES.
•BRYSON, Mr. Graeme William Bruce, BA ACA CTA *1995;* (Tax Fac), William Duncan & CO, 30 Miller Road, AYR, AYRSHIRE, KA7 2AY.
BRYSON, Mr. Ian Lindsay, BA ACA *1982;* Philip Morris International, 107 avenue de Cour, 1001 LAUSANNE, SWITZERLAND.
BRYSON, Mr. Ian Robertson, MBA BSc FCA CIA *1982;* Selmattweg 17, CH 4246 WAHLEN, SWITZERLAND.
BRYSON, Mr. John Macdonald, FCA MBA *1969;* Nether Craigow, KINROSS, KY13 0RR.
BRYSON, Mrs. Mary Margaret, BA ACA *1980;* (Tax Fac), K P M G Llp, 10 Upper Bank Street, LONDON, E14 5GH.
BRYSON, Mrs. Nina, MA ACA *1993;* 15 Chartwell Place, EPSOM, SURREY, KT18 5JH.
BRYSON, Mr. Robert Andrew, BSc ACA *1979;* International Power Plc, Senator House, 85 Queen Victoria Street, LONDON, EC4V 4HQ.
BRZEZICKI, Miss. Natalie, MSc BSc ACA *2010;* Apartment 71, Stanton House, 620 Rotherhithe Street, LONDON, SE16 5DJ.
BRZEZICKI, Mr. Stefan Marian, BA FCA *1980;* 44 Wellington Road, Ealing, LONDON, W5 4UH.
BTESH, Mr. John Richard Mark, BA FCA CTA *1982;* Vale Cottage, Apsley Grove, Bowdon, ALTRINCHAM, WA14 3AH.
BUANG, Miss. Aileen, BSc ACA *1997;* Khazanah Nasional Berhad, Level 33 Tower 2, Petronas Twin Towers, KLCC, 50088 KUALA LUMPUR, FEDERAL TERRITORY MALAYSIA.
BUB, Mr. Julian Stanley, FCA *1968;* Flat 11 Burlington House, Wedderburn Road, LONDON, NW3 5QS.
•BUBB, Mr. Daren, FCA *1990;* Chase Reeves & Co Limited, Chase House, 90 Springbank Road, LONDON, SE13 6SX.
•BUBB, Mr. Michael, FCA *1980;* Perkins, The Albany, South Esplanade, St. Peter Port, GUERNSEY, GY1 1AE.
BUBB, Mrs. Sarah Louise, BEng ACA *1992;* 4 Royston Road, Bearsted, MAIDSTONE, ME15 8NS.
BUBBER, Mr. Arvinder Singh, FCA *1976;* A.S. Bubber & Associates Inc, 208-8120 128 Street, SURREY V3W 1R1, BC, CANADA.
BUCHAN, Mr. Daniel, BA ACA *2006;* with Baker Tilly Tax and Advisory Services LLP, 25 Farringdon Street, LONDON, EC4A 4AB.
BUCHAN, Mr. David, ACA *1980;* 21 Lawrence Road, HOVE, EAST SUSSEX, BN3 5QA.
BUCHAN, Mr. David John Graham, ACA CPFA *2010;* 7 Claremont Road, Redhill, SURREY, RH1 2JT.
BUCHAN, Mr. Edward Charles Walter Ralph, BSc FCA *1976;* LCF Edmond de Rothschild Securities Limited, Orion House, 5 Upper St Martin's Lane, LONDON, WC2H 9EA.
BUCHAN, Miss. Katherine Louise, BSc ACA *1997;* Holtes, Park Road, HASLEMERE, GU27 2NL.
BUCHAN, Mr. Mark James, BSc ACA *1992;* 16A JERVOIS LANE, #03-09 CLYDESVIEW, SINGAPORE 159192, SINGAPORE.
BUCHAN, Mr. Philip Giles, ACA MAAT *1996;* Sonnenallee 96, 12045 BERLIN, GERMANY.
BUCHAN, Mrs. Toni Elizabeth, BCom FCA *1972;* The Old Vicarage, West Down, ILFRACOMBE, EX34 8NF.
BUCHANAN, Miss. Alexandra Clare Merttens, BSc ACA *2010;* 61 Hazel Close, TWICKENHAM, TW2 7NP.
BUCHANAN, Mr. Alistair George, BA FCA *1986;* Englefield Green House, Middle Hill, Englefield Green, EGHAM, TW20 0JR.
BUCHANAN, Mrs. Andrea, ACA *1995;* UK Land & Property Nations House, Edmund Street, LIVERPOOL, L3 9NY.
BUCHANAN, Miss. Catherine Lindsay Jane, BSc ACA *1979;* Flat 4, Pinewood Gate, 28 Perrymount Road, HAYWARDS HEATH, WEST SUSSEX, RH16 3DN.
BUCHANAN, Miss. Dianne Elizabeth, MA ACA *1999;* 173 Trinity Road, LONDON, SW17 7HL.
BUCHANAN, Mr. Ian Elsworth, ACA *1978;* Harthover Place, 10 Campbell Road, Hanwell, LONDON, W7 3EA.
BUCHANAN, Mr. James, BSc ACA *1998;* News Ltd, Business Development, Level 5, 2 Holt Street, Surry Hills, SYDNEY NSW 2010 AUSTRALIA.
BUCHANAN, Mr. James Richard, BSc ACA *1979;* 7010 Dayton Avenue North, SEATTLE, WA 98103, UNITED STATES.
BUCHANAN, Miss. Katherine Jane, ACA *2008;* Unit 2, 10 The Grange, LONDON, SE1 3AG.
BUCHANAN, Mr. Keith Michael, BA ACA *1980;* 39A Lanchester Road, Highgate, LONDON, N6 4SX.
•BUCHANAN, Mr. Leslie William, FCA *1971;* Waugh Haines Rigby Limited, 18 Miller Court, Severn Drive, Tewkesbury Business Park, TEWKESBURY, GLOUCESTERSHIRE GL20 8DN.
BUCHANAN, Mrs. Muriel, ACA *2002;* 715 Balmoral Apartments, 2 Praed Street, LONDON, W2 1JN.
BUCHANAN, Mr. Nigel James Cubitt, FCA *1967;* Longwood, 16 Park Avenue South, HARPENDEN, AL5 2EA.
BUCHANAN, Mr. Paul, BA ACA *1992;* Dodleston Farm, Kinnerton Road, Dodleston, CHESTER, CH4 9LP.
BUCHANAN, Mr. Paul John, BA(Hons) ACA *2001;* 38 Winchester Road, TWICKENHAM, TW1 1LF.
BUCHANAN, Mr. Robert, FCA *1970;* ODD (Oxford) Ltd, Foxholes, Foscot, Kingham, CHIPPING NORTON, OXFORDSHIRE OX7 6RW.
BUCHANAN, Mr. Robin William Turnbull, FCA *1975;* 37 Blomfield Road, Little Venice, LONDON, W9 2PF.
BUCHANAN, Mrs. Sarah Ann, BA ACA *1981;* 39A Lanchester Road, Highgate, LONDON, N6 4SX.
•BUCHANAN, Mrs. Sharon Anne Veronica, BA FCA *1986;* S A V Buchanan, Heathfield, 49 Raglan Road, REIGATE, SURREY, RH2 0DY.
BUCHANAN, Mr. Stephen Paul, FCA *1976;* Helenswood Lower School, The Ridge, ST. LEONARDS-ON-SEA, EAST SUSSEX, TN37 7PS.
BUCHANAN, Mr. Stuart John, BSc FCA *1992;* 34 Grosvenor Road, RUGBY, CV21 3LF.
BUCHANAN-SMITH, Mrs. Brenda Kay, FCA *1960;* with Cooper Paul, 18 Forest Road, LOUGHTON, IG10 1DX.
•BUCHHOLZ, Mrs. Lynne Fiona, LLB FCA *1988;* (Tax Fac), Pearson Buchholz Limited, North House, Farmoor Court, Cumnor Road, Farmoor, OXFORD OX2 9LU.
BUCHLER, Mr. Adam Philip, BA(Hons) ACA *2003;* Stream Capital Limited, 12 Curzon Street, LONDON, W1J 5HL.

•**BUCHLER, Mr. David Julian, FCA** *1974;* Buchlers LLP, 6 Grosvenor Street, LONDON, W1K 4PZ.
BUCHNER, Mr. Philip, ACA CA(SA) *2010;* 9 Raffles Place Level 58 Republic Plaza, SINGAPORE 048619, SINGAPORE.
•**BUCHSBAUM, Mr. Abraham Jacob, ACA** *1991;* (Tax Fac), Wilds Limited, Lancaster House, 70-76 Blackburn Street, Radcliffe, MANCHESTER, M26 2JW.
BUCHSBAUM, Mr. Shlomo Perez, FCA *1977;* Sheshet Hayamim Street 44, 43223 RA'ANANA, ISRAEL.
BUCK, Mr. Adrian Thomas Francis, FCA *1970;* 1 Bec Close, WANTAGE, OX12 9EP.
BUCK, Mr. Ainsley, BSc ACA *1995;* GB Ingredients Ltd, Dock Road, FELIXSTOWE, SUFFOLK, IP11 3QW.
•**BUCK, Mr. Alan Howard, FCA** *1972;* The Prudential Assurance Co Ltd, 121 Kings Road, READING, BERKSHIRE, RG1 3ES.
BUCK, Mr. Alexander James, BSc ACA *2006;* 1a Dering Road, CROYDON, CR0 1DS.
BUCK, Mr. Anthony Michael George Kett, ACA *1980;* 71 Bullescroft Road, EDGWARE, HA8 8RN.
BUCK, Mr. Antony, BA ACA *1995;* 5 Riviera Court, ROCHDALE, OL12 7UB.
BUCK, Mr. Brian Edward, BA FCA *1976;* General Council of the Bar, 289 High Holborn, LONDON, WC1V 7HZ.
BUCK, Mr. Bryan, FCA CTA *1983;* Mountneys, The Belyars, ST. IVES, CORNWALL, TR26 2DD.
BUCK, Mrs. Carol Margaret, BSc ACA *1991;* 8 Harlescott Road, Nunhead, LONDON, SE15 3BZ.
BUCK, Miss. Charlotte, BSc ACA *2007;* Grant Thornton UK Llp Grant Thornton House, 22 Melton Street, LONDON, NW1 2EP.
•**BUCK, Mr. Christie Alexander, BA ACA** *2000;* Deloitte LLP, Abbots House, Abbey Street, READING, RG1 3BD. See also Deloitte & Touche LLP
BUCK, Mr. Colin, MSc BMet FCA *1977;* 8 Northumberland Road, LEAMINGTON SPA, CV32 6HA.
BUCK, Mr. David Howard, FCA DChA *1972;* 2 Riverside, Reedham, NORWICH, NR13 3TQ.
BUCK, Mr. Duncan James, BA(Econ) ACA *1996;* Lexicon Partners, 1 Paternoster Square, LONDON, EC4M 7DX.
BUCK, Mr. John Albert Charles, FCA *1958;* 4 De Grosmont Close, ABERGAVENNY, GWENT, NP7 9JN. (Life Member)
BUCK, Mrs. Katy Anne, LLB ACA *1999;* Ernst & Young Llp, 1 More London Place, LONDON, SE1 2AF.
BUCK, Mr. Keith Robert, BSc ACA *1992;* KPMG Level 32, Emirates Towers, Sheikh Zayed Road, Dubai, PO Box 3800, DUBAI UNITED ARAB EMIRATES.
BUCK, Mr. Kevin Charles, BA(Hons) FCA *2001;* 49a Abbots Lane, KENLEY, SURREY, CR8 5JB.
BUCK, Mr. Matthew Radley Grant, ACA *2009;* 26 Cornwallis Road, LONDON, N19 4LT.
•**BUCK, Mr. Peter, ACA FCCA DChA** *2008;* TLL Accountants Limited, 7-9 Station Road, Hesketh Bank, PRESTON, PR4 6SN.
•**BUCK, Mr. Richard Alan, BA ACA** *1990;* Deloitte LLP, 2 New Street Square, LONDON, EC4A 3BZ. See also Deloitte & Touche LLP
BUCK, Miss. Vanessa Louise, BSc ACA *2002;* 30 Lairum Rise, Clifford, WETHERBY, WEST YORKSHIRE, LS23 6HG.
BUCK, Mrs. Yvonne Margaret, FCA *1992;* Graybrowne Ltd, 13 Nelson Street, HULL, HU1 1XE.
•**BUCKBY, Mr. Richard James, ACA** *2008;* with Clifford Roberts, Pacioli House, 9 Brookfield, Duncan Close, Moulton Park, NORTHAMPTON NORTHAMPTONSHIRE NN3 6WL.
BUCKEL, Mr. Graham Duncan William, BA ACA *1991;* Random House Publishing Group, 20 Vauxhall Bridge Road, LONDON, SW1V 2SA.
•**BUCKELL, Mr. Graham John, MA FCA** *1981;* (Tax Fac), Bates Weston, The Mill, Canal Street, DERBY, DE1 2RJ. See also Bates Weston LLP
BUCKENHAM, Mr. Lindsay, BA ACA *2007;* 19 Jervis Crescent, SUTTON COLDFIELD, B74 4PW.
BUCKETT, Mr. Austin Craig, ACA *2000;* 630 Southpointe Court, Suite 200, COLORADO SPRINGS, CO 80906, UNITED STATES.
BUCKETT, Mr. Cecil John, FCA *1964;* Vectis House, 10 Cherry Hill Drive, Barnt Green, BIRMINGHAM, B45 8JY. (Life Member)
BUCKETT, Mr. Simon, BSc ACA *2005;* Worldtech Security Technologies, 1680-401 W Georgia Street, VANCOUVER V6B 5A1, BC, CANADA.
BUCKHURST, Mr. Andrew Stephen, BA ACA *1992;* 5 Michel Rodange, L-7248 BERELDANGE, LUXEMBOURG.
BUCKINGHAM, Mr. David, BSc ACA *1993;* 6 Malton Place, City Beach, PERTH, WA 6015, AUSTRALIA.
BUCKINGHAM, Mr. David William, FCA *1974;* 52 Aldwick Felds, BOGNOR REGIS, WEST SUSSEX, PO21 3TT.
BUCKINGHAM, Miss. Dawn, BSc(Hons) ACA *2003;* 5 Bridge Way, Ickenham, UXBRIDGE, MIDDLESEX, UB10 8QR.
BUCKINGHAM, Miss. Gemma, ACA *2011;* 48 Fennel Grove, SOUTH SHIELDS, TYNE AND WEAR, NE34 8TJ.
BUCKINGHAM, Mr. Graham Paul, BSc FCA *1987;* 25 Horseguards, EXETER, EX4 4UU.
BUCKINGHAM, Mr. Graham Richard, FCA *1974;* Flat 40 Hollier Court, French Horn Lane, HATFIELD, HERTFORDSHIRE, AL10 8BX.
BUCKINGHAM, Mr. John Alan, BSc FCA *1973;* Highcliffe House Townhead, Eyam, HOPE VALLEY, DERBYSHIRE, S32 5RE.
•**BUCKINGHAM, Mr. Matthew John, BSc ACA** *1999;* with KPMG LLP, St. Nicholas House, 31 Park Row, NOTTINGHAM, NG1 6FQ.
BUCKINGHAM, Mr. Maurice John, FCA *1978;* Great Lakes Reinsurance(UK)plc, Plantation Place, 30 Fenchurch Street, LONDON, EC3M 3BD.
BUCKINGHAM, Mr. Peter George, FCA *1972;* Westover, Blacksmiths Lane, STAINES, MIDDLESEX, TW18 1UB.
BUCKINGHAM, Mr. Simon Alexander, BA FCA *1982;* 2 Thirlmere Drive, ST. ALBANS, HERTFORDSHIRE, AL1 5QR.
BUCKINGHAM, Mr. Stephen Michael Charles, BSc ACA *1994;* Linden Lea Trevenna Cross, St. Mawgan, NEWQUAY, CORNWALL, TR8 4HB.
BUCKINGHAM, Mr. Stuart, BSc ACA *1992;* Lloyds TSB Bank Plc, 25 Gresham Street, LONDON, EC2V 7HN.
BUCKINGHAM, Mrs. Tania Loraine, BA ACA *1991;* Meadow Gate, Oakshade Road, Oxshott, LEATHERHEAD, SURREY, KT22 0JU.
BUCKLAND, Mr. Alan, BA ACA *2005;* 59 Melrose Avenue, Penylan, CARDIFF, CF23 9AT.
BUCKLAND, Mr. Clive Graham, BSc ACA *1990;* with Grant Thornton UK LLP, 1 Dorset Street, SOUTHAMPTON, SO15 2DP.
BUCKLAND, Mr. Daniel, BSc ACA *2011;* 13 Manor Gardens, HIGH WYCOMBE, BUCKINGHAMSHIRE, HP13 5HD.
BUCKLAND, Mrs. Hazel, BSc ACA *2004;* 127 The Grove, CHRISTCHURCH, BH23 2EZ.
•**BUCKLAND, Mr. John, BA FCA** *1970;* Greaves & Co, 41 North Seaton Rd, ASHINGTON, NE63 0AG.
•**BUCKLAND, Mr. Keith John Roger, BA FCA** *1975;* BSR Bespoke, Linden House, Linden Close, TUNBRIDGE WELLS, KENT, TN4 8HH.
•**BUCKLAND, Mr. Michael Edwin, FCA DChA** *1979;* David Owen & Co, 17 Market Place, DEVIZES, SN10 1BA.
•**BUCKLE, Mr. Alan Arthur, BA ACA** *1986;* KPMG LLP, 15 Canada Square, LONDON, E14 5GL. See also KPMG Europe LLP
•**BUCKLE, Mr. Alan Edric, FCA** *1974;* (Tax Fac), Alan E. Buckle, 39 The Croft, Haddenham, AYLESBURY, HP17 8AS.
BUCKLE, Miss. Clare Anne, BSc ACA CTA *1999;* Apartment 4307, 301 Deansgate, MANCHESTER, M3 4LX.
BUCKLE, Mrs. Clare Erica, BA ACA *1992;* 58 Dukes Avenue, LONDON, W4 2AF.
BUCKLE, Mr. Derek William, ACA *1987;* 18 Fircroft Road, IPSWICH, IP1 6AQ.
BUCKLE, Mr. Gavin Paul, ACA MAAT *2006;* 24 Soames Close, STOWMARKET, SUFFOLK, IP14 1PA.
BUCKLE, Mr. Ian David, ACA *1992;* c/o Pulman, Abbey Road, DURHAM, DH1 5HA.
BUCKLE, Mr. John Frederick, FCA *1961;* 38 Wood Lodge Lane, WEST WICKHAM, BR4 9LZ. (Life Member)
BUCKLE, Mr. Jonathan Mark, BA ACA *2004;* Retail Decisions The Clocktower, Cemetery Pales Brookwood, WOKING, SURREY, GU24 0BL.
BUCKLE, Mr. Mark, BA(Hons) ACA *2010;* 194 Kings Avenue, ELY, CAMBRIDGESHIRE, CB7 4PJ.
BUCKLE, Mr. Nicholas James, BA ACA *1992;* 85 Queens Road, RICHMOND, SURREY, TW10 6HJ.
BUCKLE, Mr. Peter Bryan, MA FCA *1980;* Buzon Serreta 370, Santa Gertrudis, Ibiza, 07814 BALEARES, SPAIN.
BUCKLE, Mr. Roger Nicholas, FCA *1966;* The Old Rectory, Denton, GRANTHAM, NG32 1JT. (Life Member)
BUCKLER, Mrs. Deborah Louise, BSc ACA *1997;* Shire House, 4 Long Street, Stoney Stanton, LEICESTER, LE9 4DQ.
BUCKLER, Mr. John, ACA *2011;* Deloitte LLP, 3 Rivergate, BRISTOL, BS16GD.
•**BUCKLER, Mr. John Mark, MA FCA** *1969;* (Tax Fac), Buckler Spencer Limited, Old Police Station, Church Street, SWADLINCOTE, DERBYSHIRE, DE11 8LN.
•**BUCKLER, Mr. Peter Robert, BSc ACA** *1989;* with Ernst & Young LLP, 1 Bridgewater Place, Water Lane, LEEDS, LS11 5QR.
BUCKLER, Mr. Philip Skelton, BSc FCA *1976;* 2 Marefield Close, Thurnby, LEICESTER, LE7 9US.
BUCKLEY, Prof. Adrian Arthur, PhD MSc BA FCA *1963;* 31 MacDonald Close, Chesham Bois, AMERSHAM, BUCKINGHAMSHIRE, HP6 5LX. (Life Member)
BUCKLEY, Mr. Aidan Robert, MSc BComm ACA *2009;* 15 Barons Keep, Gliddon Road, LONDON, W14 9AT.
•**BUCKLEY, Mrs. Alison Leigh, BA FCA** *2000;* Mitchell Charlesworth, Centurion House, 129 Deansgate, MANCHESTER, M3 3WR.
BUCKLEY, Mr. Andrew James, BSc FCA *1996;* 108 Pewterspear Green Road, Appleton, WARRINGTON, WA4 5FR.
BUCKLEY, Mr. Anthony James Joseph, FCA *1971;* Martindale, Church Lane, Upton Bishop, ROSS-ON-WYE, HR9 7UL.
BUCKLEY, Mr. Brian Bertrand, BCom FCA *1964;* Benfro, 8 Brundhurst Fold, Mellor, BLACKBURN, BB2 7JT.
BUCKLEY, Mr. Brian Thomas, FCA *1967;* Chegwidden & Co, Priestley House, Priestley Gardens, Chadwell Heath, ROMFORD, RM6 4SN.
BUCKLEY, Miss. Cathryn Ann, BSc ACA *1988;* 38 Calder Close, DROITWICH, WR9 8DU.
BUCKLEY, Mr. Charles David, ACA *1980;* Gore Browne Investment Management LLP, 39 Brown Street, SALISBURY, SP1 2AS.
BUCKLEY, Miss. Christine Ann, FCA *1981;* 315 Eastern Valley Cove, MIDDLE COVE, NSW 2068, AUSTRALIA.
BUCKLEY, Mr. Christopher Arthur Francis, BA ACA *1989;* Avanade 3rd Floor Abbey House, 18-24 Stoke Road, SLOUGH, SL2 5AG.
BUCKLEY, Mr. Christopher John, BA ACA *1985;* Glaxo Smithkline Plc, G S K House, 980 Great West Road, BRENTFORD, MIDDLESEX, TW8 9GS.
BUCKLEY, Mr. Christopher William, MSc BSc FCA *1975;* 29 Kensington Road, Coppice, OLDHAM, OL8 4BZ.
BUCKLEY, Mr. Craig John, MA MSc BA ACA *1999;* 307 Roselawn Avenue, TORONTO M4R 1G2, ON, CANADA.
BUCKLEY, Mr. Craig Stuart, BA ACA *1999;* with PricewaterhouseCoopers LLP, Benson House, 33 Wellington Street, LEEDS, LS1 4JP.
BUCKLEY, Mr. Darren Neale, BSc ACA *1992;* Citigroup Japan Holdings Corp., Shin Marunouchi Bldg., 1-5-1 Marunouchi, Chiyoda-Ku, TOKYO, 100-6520 JAPAN.
BUCKLEY, Mr. Denis Martin, BA ACA *1991;* Combs Hall Barn, Combs, STOWMARKET, IP14 2EH.
BUCKLEY, Mr. Denis Patrick, BCom ACA *1984;* Bellvue, Richmond Wood, GLANMIRE, COUNTY CORK, IRELAND.
BUCKLEY, Mr. Edward, BA FCA *1974;* Preston City Council Town Hall, Lancaster Road, PRESTON, PR1 2RL.
BUCKLEY, Mrs. Fiona Marie, BSc ACA *1991;* 14 Barry Rise, Bowdon, ALTRINCHAM, CHESHIRE, WA14 3JS.
BUCKLEY, Mrs. Heather Mary, BSc ACA *1992;* Deddington Lodge, Moor Lane, Beeston, NOTTINGHAM, NG9 3GE.
BUCKLEY, Miss. Helen Louise, BA(Hons) ACA *2010;* 41 Birchwood Gardens, Braithwell, ROTHERHAM, SOUTH YORKSHIRE, S66 7BT.
BUCKLEY, Mr. Ian Carysfort, BA ACA *1980;* 32 Christchurch Street, LONDON, SW3 4AR.
BUCKLEY, Mr. Ian Douglas, BA ACA *2006;* 6 Churchfields, Barnton, NORTHWICH, CHESHIRE, CW8 4UR.
BUCKLEY, Mr. Ian Michael, BSc FCA *1975;* Rathbone Brothers plc, 159 New Bond Street, LONDON, W1S 2UD.
BUCKLEY, Mr. Ian Philip, BA ACA *1989;* 6 Waingap View, Whitworth, ROCHDALE, OL12 8QD.
BUCKLEY, Mr. Ian Robert William, BSc ACA *1999;* Travelex UK Ltd, 65 Kingsway, LONDON, WC2B 6TD.
BUCKLEY, Mrs. Ingrid Caroline, BA ACA *1999;* The Vine House, 21 Hadlow Park, Hadlow, TONBRIDGE, TN11 0HY.
•**BUCKLEY, Mr. Jeremy John, ACA FCCA CTA** *2008;* Try Lunn & Co, Roland House, Princes Dock Street, HULL, HU1 2LD.
BUCKLEY, Mr. John Howard, LLB FCA MCT *1975;* Buckley Young Associates Ltd, Tregeseal House, Broadstone Lane, Hardington Mandeville, YEOVIL, SOMERSET BA22 9PR.
BUCKLEY, Miss. Julia Mary, BA ACA *1996;* 9 The Kingfishers, VERWOOD, DORSET, BH31 6NP.
BUCKLEY, Miss. Karen Louise, BSc ACA *2005;* 29 Mardle Road, Linslade, LEIGHTON BUZZARD, BEDFORDSHIRE, LU7 2UR.
BUCKLEY, Mrs. Kate Louise, BA ACA *1993;* Redthorn, Merrymans Lane, ALDERLEY EDGE, CHESHIRE, SK9 7TP.
BUCKLEY, Miss. Lianne Marie, BA ACA *2005;* 5 Maplers Drive, FLEET, GU51 1JW.
BUCKLEY, Miss. Lorna Mary, BSc(Hons) ACA *2001;* 6 Milngavie Road, Strathblane, GLASGOW, G63 9EH.
BUCKLEY, Miss. Lyndsey Caroline, BSc ACA *2010;* 3 Perth Grove, STOCKTON-ON-TEES, CLEVELAND, TS18 5BJ.
BUCKLEY, Mrs. Lynn, BSc ACA *1989;* 113 Polefield Road, Prestwich, MANCHESTER, M25 2QN.
•**BUCKLEY, Mrs. Marie-Therese, ACA** *1980;* (Tax Fac), M T Buckley & Co, 2 Beulah Walk, Woldingham, CATERHAM, SURREY, CR3 7LL.
BUCKLEY, Mr. Martin, BA ACA *1989;* 6b Eastfield, Henleaze, BRISTOL, BS9 4BQ.
BUCKLEY, Mr. Martin Howard, FCA *1969;* Ausbourne Grange, Linton Common, Linton, WETHERBY, LS22 4JD.
BUCKLEY, Mr. Michael William, ACA *2010;* with Grant Thornton, Currency House, Level 6, DIFC, PO Box 482017, DUBAI UNITED ARAB EMIRATES.
BUCKLEY, Mrs. Michelle Annette, LLB ACA *2001;* with Grant Thornton UK LLP, Enterprise House, 115 Edmund Street, BIRMINGHAM, B3 2HJ.
BUCKLEY, Mr. Paul Antony, FCA *1980;* Zwergenweg 8A, 70567 STUTTGART, GERMANY.
BUCKLEY, Mrs. Penelope Carol Jean, ACA *1982;* Cogent Heath Farm, Hampton Lane Meriden, COVENTRY, CV7 7LL.
BUCKLEY, Mr. Peter, BCom ACA *1993;* Meden Valley Making Places, 34 Sherwood Street, Warsop, MANSFIELD, NOTTINGHAMSHIRE, NG20 0JW.
•**BUCKLEY, Mr. Peter John, BA FCA** *1980;* Royce Peeling Green Limited, The Copper Room, Deva Centre, Trinity Way, MANCHESTER, M3 7BG. See also RPG Holdings Limited
•**BUCKLEY, Mr. Philip Leslie, FCA** *1974;* ABC 123 Limited, 41 Park Road, Freemantle, SOUTHAMPTON, SO15 3AW. See also AKP LTD
BUCKLEY, Mr. Richard Austen, BA FCA *1967;* 1 Lansdown Parade, CHELTENHAM, GL50 2LH. (Life Member)
BUCKLEY, Mr. Richard John, BA ACA *1993;* 25 Napoleon Road, TWICKENHAM, TW1 3EW.
BUCKLEY, Mr. Roger Michael, BSc FCA *1977;* 6 Sandlebridge Rise, ALDERLEY EDGE, CHESHIRE, SK9 7TE.
BUCKLEY, Miss. Sandra Jane, BSc ACA CPsychol *1992;* End Cottage, 7 Mill Street, CALNE, WILTSHIRE, SN11 8DP.
BUCKLEY, Dr. Sarah Louise, BSc(Hons) ACA *2004;* NG Bailey, Denton Hall, Denton, ILKLEY, WEST YORKSHIRE, LS29 0HH.
BUCKLEY, Mr. Stephen William, BA ACA *1991;* 13 Porth Crigyll, RHOSNEIGR, GWYNEDD, LL64 5RB.
•**BUCKLEY, Miss. Susan, ACA** *1989;* HBD Accountancy Services LLP, Gladstone House, 2 Church Road, Wavertree, LIVERPOOL, L15 9EG.
BUCKLEY, Mr. Thomas Richard, FCA *1969;* 27 St. Johns Avenue, BRENTWOOD, Essex, CM14 5DF.
BUCKLEY, Mr. William Howard, FCA *1965;* 18 Radnor Walk, LONDON, SW3 4BN. (Life Member)
BUCKLEY-MELLOR, Mr. Alan, FCA *1974;* 16 Templeton Drive, Fearnhead, WARRINGTON, WA2 0WR.
BUCKLEY-SHARP, Mr. Guy, BEng ACA *2003;* Milton End, Priory Lane, LYNEHAM, OXFORDSHIRE, OX7 6QL.
BUCKLOW, Mr. Peter Lawrence, BSc ACA *1982;* 7 Cambridge Road, Godmanchester, HUNTINGDON, PE29 2BW.
BUCKMAN, Ms. Bianca, ACA CA(AUS) *2011;* (Tax Fac), Flat 8, 23 Nightingale Lane, LONDON, SW4 9AH.
BUCKMAN, Mr. Keith Roy, FCA *1969;* Biolab UK Ltd Oriel Lodge, Oriel Road, CHELTENHAM, GL50 1NX.
BUCKMAN, Mr. Mike, BSc ACA *2000;* Top Floor Flat, 4 Leighton Crescent, LONDON, NW5 2QY.
BUCKNALL, Mr. Brian Neil, FCA *1953;* Meldon Heights, Meldon Hill, Chagford, NEWTON ABBOT, TQ13 8EG. (Life Member)
BUCKNALL, Mr. Clive, FCA *1970;* 23 Cherry Tree Lane, HALESOWEN, B63 1DU.
BUCKNALL, Mr. Clive Richard, MA ACA *1989;* HSBC 3F No 68 Nanjing E Road, Section 3, Zhongshan District, TAIPEI, TAIWAN.

BUCKNALL, Mr. Michael John, FCA *1958;* AP-3 Bayu Beach Resort, Batu 4 1/2 Jln Pantai, Sirusa, PORT DICKSON, NEGERI SEMBILAN, MALAYSIA. (Life Member)
BUCKNALL, Mrs. Sally Anne, ACA *1988;* The Old Rectory, High Street, Stoke Goldington, NEWPORT PAGNELL, MK16 8NP.
BUCKNELL, Mr. Andrew Thomas, BA FCA *1990;* South Lodge, Midgham Park, Bath Road, Midgham, READING, RG7 5XB.
BUCKNELL, Mrs. Nicola Jayne, BA ACA *1992;* Damory, Hurst Drive, Walton on the Hill, TADWORTH, SURREY, KT20 7QT.
BUCKNELL, Mr. Robert Ian Kenneth, FCA *1976;* 81 Harberton Road, LONDON, N19 3JT.
BUCKNELL, Mr. William Evan, BSc FCA *1979;* W E Bucknell & Co Ltd Pingemead House, Pingewood, READING, RG30 3UR.
BUCKNOLE, Mr. Simon, ACA *2011;* 1 Top House Flats, High Street Broughton, STOCKBRIDGE, SO20 8AD.
BUCKS, Mr. David, FCA *1957;* Paddock House, Sutton Montis, YEOVIL, BA22 7HG. (Life Member)
•**BUCKS, Mr. Michael, BSc ACA** *1989;* Kingswood Chase, Kingswood Lane, HINDHEAD, GU26 6DQ.
BUCKWELL, Mr. Edwin Richard, FCA *1952;* 4 Beechwood Close, BRIGHTON, BN1 8EP. (Life Member)
BUCKWORTH, Mr. Darren, ACA *2008;* 17 Royal Sovereign Crescent, Bradwell, GREAT YARMOUTH, NORFOLK, NR31 9GE.
•**BUCKWORTH, Mr. Edward William, FCA** *1965;* (Tax Fac), Weaver Buckworth & Partners, 18 Queens Road, COVENTRY, CV1 3EG.
BUCKWORTH, Mrs. Sara Louise, BSc ACA *2002;* 22 Levington Wynd, Nunthorpe, MIDDLESBROUGH, CLEVELAND, TS7 0QD.
BUCQUET, Mr. John Aubrey Lloyd, FCA *1968;* Flat 2, Warren Court, The Warren, Caversham, READING, RG4 7TF.
BUD, Mr. Martin, FCA *1942;* 9 Heathgate, LONDON, NW11 7AR. (Life Member)
BUDARKIEWICZ, Mrs. Anna Teresa, BSc ACA *1990;* 11 Devereux Drive, WATFORD, WD17 3DD.
BUDD, Mrs. Claire Elizabeth, BSc ACA *1997;* 10 Finlayson Place, LARBERT, STIRLINGSHIRE, FK5 4FX.
BUDD, Mrs. Colleen, BSc ACA *1979;* 21 Shaftesbury Avenue, Ashgate, CHESTERFIELD, S40 1HN.
BUDD, Mr. David Charles, FCA *1976;* Du Boulay Contracts Ltd Studio 7, Royal Victoria Patriotic Building John Archer Way, LONDON, SW18 3SX.
BUDD, Mrs. Heather Louise, BSc(Hons) ACA CTA *1994;* Bullockwoodburn Ltd Norfolk House, Hardwick Square North, BUXTON, DERBYSHIRE, SK17 6PU.
BUDD, Mr. Jason, BSc ACA *1997;* 10 Finlayson Place, Falkirk, LARBERT, STIRLINGSHIRE, FK5 4FX.
BUDD, Mr. John Derek, FCA *1960;* 16 St Matthews Avenue, SURBITON, KT6 6JJ. (Life Member)
BUDD, Mr. Jonathan William, BA ACA *1986;* 12 Foxley Close, LYMM, WA13 0BS.
•**BUDD, Mr. Julian Robert, BSc FCA** *1976;* Accede Financial Services Ltd, 7 Glentworth Road, Clifton, BRISTOL, BS8 4TB.
BUDD, Mrs. Katherine Louise, BSc ACA *2001;* 14 Beck Close Emersons Green, BRISTOL, BS16 7HD.
BUDD, Mrs. Lene, BA(Hons) ACA *2010;* 47 Collingwood Road, Goring-by-Sea, WORTHING, WEST SUSSEX, BN12 6HY.
BUDD, Mr. Matthew Jeffrey James, BSc ACA *2010;* with BDO Limited, PO Box 180, Place du Pre, Rue du Pre, St Peter Port, GUERNSEY GY1 3LL.
BUDD, Mr. Paul Walter, BA FCA *1982;* Speart House, Abbots Morton, WORCESTER, WR7 4LY.
BUDD, Ms. Sheila, BA ACA *1985;* Mill House, Field Lane, Hempnall, NORWICH, NR15 2PB.
BUDD, Mr. Stuart Edward, BA(Hons) ACA *2001;* 14 Beck Close Emersons Green, BRISTOL, BS16 7HD.
BUDD, Mr. Tony William Peter, FCA *1953;* Chestnuts, 31 The Avenue, TADWORTH, KT20 5AY. (Life Member)
BUDDEN, Mrs. Andrea Angela, ACA *1990;* 35 Lavant Street, PETERSFIELD, GU32 3EL.
BUDDEN, Mr. Derek Ernest Arthur, FCA *1956;* Kimberley, Burtons Way, CHALFONT ST.GILES, HP8 4BW. (Life Member)
BUDDEN, Mr. Ian Derek, BA ACA *1990;* 24 Crab Tree Close, Bloxham, BANBURY, OXFORDSHIRE, OX15 4SE.
BUDDEN, Mr. Martin, BA ACA ACMA *1984;* Newlands, 8 Thorner Lane, Scarcroft, LEEDS, LS14 3AR.
BUDDEN, Mr. Neil, MSc ACA *2008;* Flat 12, 23 Hulse Road, SOUTHAMPTON, SO15 2QZ.
BUDDEN, Mrs. Tara Louise, BA ACA *2000;* The Royal School, Farnham Lane, HASLEMERE, GU27 1HQ.
BUDDEN, Mr. Timothy Leslie, BSc ACA *1993;* 14 Copperkins Lane, AMERSHAM, BUCKINGHAMSHIRE, HP6 5QF.
BUDDHARAJU, Mr. Narasimharaju, FCA ACMA *1975;* 8-2-120/112/A/14 Road No 9, Jubilee Hills, HYDERABAD 500033, INDIA.
BUDDHDEV, Mr. Ketan, BSc ACA *1995;* 14 Lynton Road, Bucklands Beach, MANUKAU CITY 2012, AUCKLAND, NEW ZEALAND.
•**BUDDHDEV, Mr. Krutsnadeek Devjibhai, FCA** *1978;* (Tax Fac), Shelley & Partners, Brentmead House, Britannia Road, LONDON, N12 9RU.
BUDDIN, Mr. Paul Anthony, MPhys ACA *2006;* Hightrees, Kemsing Road, Wrotham, SEVENOAKS, KENT, TN15 7BS.
BUDDING, Mr. David Glyn, MSc ACA *2007;* 43 Lime Road, Southville, BRISTOL, BS3 1LS.
BUDGE, Mr. Andrew Thomas Peter, BA ACA *2001;* Meadows End, 7 Heathcote Place, Hursley, WINCHESTER, HAMPSHIRE, SO21 2LH.
BUDGE, Mr. Kevin John, BA FCA *1987;* Old Astwood Farm, Astwood Lane, Hanbury, BROMSGROVE, WORCESTERSHIRE, B60 4BL.
BUDGE, Mr. Michael Robert Bowen, BSc ACA *2007;* Clydesdale Bank, 5th Floor, 33 Gracechurch Street, LONDON, EC3V 0BT.
•**BUDHDEO, Mr. Jayprakash Lalitrai, ACA** *1982;* (Tax Fac), Clayton Stark & Co, 5th Floor Charles House, 108-110 Finchley Road, LONDON, NW3 5JJ.
BUDIBENT, Mr. John Barry, FCA *1969;* 88 Wickham Hill, Hurstpierpoint, HASSOCKS, BN6 9NR. (Life Member)
BUDIMIR, Mr. Dane, BA FCA *1989;* 24 Thurlstone Drive, Penn, WOLVERHAMPTON, WV4 5QL.
BUDLEIGH, Mr. Christopher John, MBA ACA *1986;* 2 Boxhill Station House, Westhumble Street, Westhumble, DORKING, SURREY, RH5 6BT.
•**BUDWORTH, Mr. Adam Thomas, BAcc FCA** *2000;* Mazars Channel Islands Limited, International House, 3rd Floor, 41 The Parade, St. Helier, JERSEY JE2 3QQ.
BUELS, Miss. Anna, BSc ACA *1999;* Level 32, H S B C, 8-16 Canada Square, LONDON, E14 5HQ.
BUERK, Mrs. Victoria May, BA ACA *2004;* 11 Kelmscott Close, Caversham, READING, RG4 7DG.
BUES, Mr. Michael, ACA *2009;* 22 Briar Road, SHEFFIELD, S7 1SA.
BUESNEL, Mr. Jonathan Mark, BA ACA *2000;* Moore Management Limited, P.O Box 1363, ST HELIER, JE2 3AT.
BUFF, Mr. Timothy Roy, BA FCA *1984;* Kyneton Park Lodge, Sweetwater Lane The Mumbleys, Thornbury, BRISTOL, BS35 3JX.
•**BUFFERY, Mr. Mark Charles, MA FCA** *1985;* (Tax Fac), Buffery & Co Ltd, 25 Hart Street, HENLEY-ON-THAMES, OXFORDSHIRE, RG9 2AR. See also Buffery Mark
BUFFERY, Mr. Mark Paul, BSocSc ACA *2001;* S S L International Plc, Venus, 1 Old Park Lane, MANCHESTER, M41 7HA.
BUFFEY, Ms. Sarah, BSc(Hons) ACA *2001;* Flat A, 31 Hornsey Lane Gardens, LONDON, N6 5NY.
BUFFHAM, Mr. Martyn, BA ACA *2010;* Flat 42, 100 Drayton Park, LONDON, N5 1NF.
BUFFIN, Mr. Anthony David, BA ACA *1998;* 7 Thatch Close off Duffield Rd, Darley Abbey, DERBY, DE22 1EA.
BUFFIN, Mr. Colin John, BA ACA *1983;* Palmetto Crest, Elbow Cay, HOPE TOWN, ABACO ISLANDS, BAHAMAS.
BUFTON, Miss. Claire, ACA *2011;* Donegal, Hougue Anthan, St. Pierre Du Bois, GUERNSEY, GY7 9BN.
BUFTON, Mr. David James, BSc ACA *2010;* 6 Willowbrook Gardens, Douglas, ISLE OF MAN, IM2 2QQ.
BUFTON, Mrs. Jodie Elizabeth, BSc(Hons) ACA *2010;* 6 Willowbrook Gardens, Douglas, ISLE OF MAN, IM2 2QQ.
BUFTON, Mr. Jonathan, ACA *2008;* 53 Wyngate Road, Cheadle Hulme, CHEADLE, CHESHIRE, SK8 6ER.
•**BUGDEN, Mr. Christopher Anthony, ACA** *1980;* (Tax Fac), Priestfield Farm, Henfield Road, Hurstpierpoint, HASSOCKS, BN6 9DE.
•**BUGDEN, Mr. James Edwin, FCA** *1971;* Red Acre, Hundred Acre Lane, Wivelsfield Green, HAYWARDS HEATH, RH17 7RU.
BUGG, Mrs. Amy, ACA *2007;* 3 Walnut Court Yard, Brook Street, Soham, ELY, CAMBRIDGESHIRE, CB7 5AE.
BUGG, Mr. Dennis Stephen, FCA *1979;* 33 Gippingstone Road, Bramford, IPSWICH, IP8 4DR.
BUGG, Mr. Kevin Gordon, BA ACA *1991;* 2 Wharton Drive Springfield, CHELMSFORD, CM1 6BF.
BUGGEY, Mr. Will, ACA *2010;* 54 Turberville Place, WARWICK, CV34 4JZ.
BUGGS, Miss. Deborah Ruth, BSc(Hons) ACA *1996;* Global Aerospace Underwriting Managers Ltd Fitzwilliam Hous, 10 St. Mary Axe, LONDON, EC3A 8EQ.
BUGLASS, Mr. Alan, FCA *1964;* 93 Dene Road, WYLAM, NORTHUMBERLAND, NE41 8HB.
BUGLER, Miss. Elisabeth Jane, BA ACA *2007;* Ground Floor Flat, 44 Guernsey Grove, LONDON, SE24 9DE.
•**BUGLER, Mr. Richard Gerald, BA ACA** *1996;* Albert Goodman CBH Limited, The Lupins Business Centre, 1-3 Greenhill, WEYMOUTH, DORSET, DT4 7SP.
•**BUHARIWALLA, Mr. Manek Savak, FCA** *1975;* M.S.Buhariwalla & Co, 35a Norton Road, WEMBLEY, HA0 4RG. See also Buhariwalla S.A.
BUHARIWALLA, Mr. Soli Aderji, FCA *1950;* Flat 203 Konark Classic, 85 Hill Road, Bandra, MUMBAI 400 050, INDIA. (Life Member)
BUI, Mrs. Hongkong, BSc ACA *2005;* 239 Rocky Lane, Perry Barr, BIRMINGHAM, B42 1QY.
BUIST, Mr. John Charles Seaton, BA ACA *1988;* The Coach House, Manor Lane, WOTTON-UNDER-EDGE, GL12 7LS.
BUIST, Mrs. Penny Anne, BA FCA *1979;* (Tax Fac), Cony Lodge, 24 Barleymow Close, Walderslade, CHATHAM, ME5 8JZ.
BUJAKOWSKI, Mr. Christopher Anthony, BSc ACA *1994;* Netsuite Inc, 1 Grenfell Road, MAIDENHEAD, BERKSHIRE, SL6 1HN.
BUKHARI, Mr. Syed, ACA *2008;* 10 Beaufort Drive, LONDON, NW11 6BU.
•**BUKHARI, Mr. Syed Fida Hussain, FCA** *1982;* Bukhari & Co, 389 Wilbraham Road, Chorlton Cum Hardy, MANCHESTER, M21 0UT.
BUKHARI, Mr. Syed Nazir Ahmad, FCA *1957;* 42F/1 Block VI, P.E.C.H.S., KARACHI, PAKISTAN. (Life Member)
BUKHARI, Mr. Zahid, BSc FCA *1999;* 26 Ringwood Way, Winchmore Hill, LONDON, N21 2QY.
BULBECK, Mr. Malcolm, BEng ACA *2005;* 54 Downs Road, COULSDON, CR5 1AA.
BULBULIAN, Mr. Ardem Puzant, FCA *1982;* PO Box 78, Bikfaya, BEIRUT, LEBANON.
•**BULCOCK, Mr. Michael John, FCA** *1982;* Bulcock & Co, 10 The Bull Ring, NORTHWICH, CW9 5BS.
BULFORD, Miss. Anne Christine, BA FCA *1985;* 211 Pierpoint, 16 Westferry Road, LONDON, E14 8NQ.
BULGIN, Mr. Duncan Robert Edward, MSc BA ACA *1999;* Newton Investment Management, Mellon Financial Centre, 160 Queen Victoria Street, LONDON, EC4V 4LA.
BULKELEY, Mr. Peter Francis, FCA *1987;* 18 Wellfield Gardens, CARSHALTON, SURREY, SM5 4EA.
BULKELEY, Mr. Russell, ACA *1984;* 63 Park Hall Road, WALSALL, WS5 3HL.
BULKELEY-JONES, Mr. David, FCA *1973;* Mill View Cottage, Fernhill Road, Sutton, NEWPORT, SHROPSHIRE, TF10 8DH. (Life Member)
BULL, Mr. Adam Richard, ACA *2008;* 48 Northen Grove, MANCHESTER, M20 2NW.
BULL, Mr. Adrien Michael, BA FCA *1992;* Kevandra House, Little Hallingbury, BISHOP'S STORTFORD, HERTFORDSHIRE, CM22 7PX.
BULL, Mrs. Alison Sarah, BA ACA *1990;* 1 Uplands Way, SEVENOAKS, TN13 3BN.
BULL, Mr. Barry Robert, FCA *1968;* 32 Haven Gardens, Crawley Down, CRAWLEY, WEST SUSSEX, RH10 4UD.
BULL, Mr. Brian James, FCA *1970;* 20 Sampsons Drive, Gribble Lane Oving, CHICHESTER, PO20 2AY.
BULL, Mr. Christopher, FCA *1962;* Kantara Reading Road North, FLEET, HAMPSHIRE, GU51 4AQ. (Life Member)
BULL, Mr. Christopher Allen, BA ACA *1991;* Integreon Managed Solutions Ltd, 92 Redcliff Street, BRISTOL, BS1 6LU.
BULL, Mr. Christopher John, BSc ACA *1999;* 14 Seymour Drive, CAMBERLEY, SURREY, GU15 1LE.
BULL, Mr. Christopher Robert Howard, MA FCA *1968;* T6B/21 Favray Court, Tigne Point, SLIEMA TP01, MALTA. (Life Member)
BULL, Mr. Christopher Ronald, BA ACA *2010;* 53 Beaumont Road, Flitwick, BEDFORD, MK45 1AL.
BULL, Mr. David Joseph, BSc(Hons) ACA *2002;* 27 Greenlaw Road, CRAMLINGTON, NORTHUMBERLAND, NE23 6NP.
BULL, Mr. David Richard, BSc ACA *1996;* Flat 3 Chesham Court, 148 Gordon Hill, ENFIELD, EN2 0QT.
BULL, Mrs. Denise Paula, BA ACA CTA *1988;* 8 Gardners Drive, Hullavington, CHIPPENHAM, SN14 6EL.
BULL, Mrs. Elizabeth Sarah, BA ACA *2006;* 35 Kent Avenue, West Wick, WESTON-SUPER-MARE, AVON, BS24 7FL.
•**BULL, Mr. Fraser, BSc ACA** *1995;* Mobb Cottage, 68 High Street, Stoke Goldington, NEWPORT PAGNELL, MK16 8NR.
BULL, Mr. Geoffrey Ronald, BCom FCA *1978;* 8 Highfields Close, ASHBY-DE-LA-ZOUCH, LE65 2FN.
BULL, Mr. George Sebastian Matthew, BA ACA *1985;* 39 Cholmeley Crescent, Highgate, LONDON, N6 5EX.
•**BULL, Mr. Gordon Richard, FCA** *1980;* (Tax Fac), BRYDEN JOHNSON, Kings Parade, Lower Coombe Street, CROYDON, CR0 1AA. See also Bryden Johnson Payroll Services Limited
BULL, Mrs. Helen Ruth, BSc ACA ATII *1993;* Hilltop Villa, Pale Green, Helions Bumpstead, HAVERHILL, CB9 7AF.
•**BULL, Mr. Howard Mark, BA ACA** *1992;* 33 Park Grove, EDGWARE, MIDDLESEX, HA8 7SH.
BULL, Mr. James, BA(Hons) ACA *2011;* Flat 6, 43 Devons Road, LONDON, E3 3DT.
BULL, Mrs. Jane Elizabeth, BSc FCA *1979;* Efg Offshore Ltd, PO Box 641, No 1 Seaton Place, St Helier, JERSEY, JE4 8YJ.
BULL, Miss. Julie Deborah Nicola, ACA *2009;* with PricewaterhouseCoopers LLP, Pricewaterhousecoopers, 12 Plumtree Court, LONDON, EC4A 4HT.
BULL, Mr. Kenneth Raymond, FCA *1973;* 3 Roedean Close, BEXHILL-ON-SEA, EAST SUSSEX, TN39 4HR.
•**BULL, Mrs. Kim, FCA ACCA CTA** *1999;* KB Accountancy, Croft House Farm, Biggin Lane, Little Fenton, LEEDS, LS24 6HQ.
BULL, Mr. Malcolm David, BA FCA *1959;* 11 Ernsford Close, Dorridge, SOLIHULL, WEST MIDLANDS, B93 8QT. (Life Member)
BULL, Mr. Martin Philip, BSc ACA *1986;* 1404 Warwick Road, Knowle, SOLIHULL, B93 9LG.
BULL, Miss. Melissa, BA ACA *2005;* Barclays Capital, 5 North Colonnade, LONDON, E14 4BB.
•**BULL, Mr. Michael Arnold Geoffrey, BSc FCA** *1976;* BPC Partners, 1 Rockfield Business Park, Old Station Drive, Leckhampton, CHELTENHAM, GLOUCESTERSHIRE GL53 0AN. See also BPC Partners Limited
BULL, Mr. Michael John, FCA *1966;* 53 Crosslands, Caddington, LUTON, LU1 4EP.
•**BULL, Mr. Neville Roy, FCA** *1970;* Neville R. Bull, 32 Well Lane, Stock, INGATESTONE, CM4 9LZ.
BULL, Mr. Nicholas James Douglas, BSc FCA *1976;* One Angel Court, LONDON, EC2R 7HJ.
BULL, Mr. Peter Alan, BSc ACA *1985;* 94 Attingham Drive, DUDLEY, WEST MIDLANDS, DY1 3HL.
BULL, Mr. Richard David, FCA *1977;* Domaine des Hautes Bruyeres, 48 chemin du Ru d'Avril, 95130 FRANCONVILLE, FRANCE.
BULL, Mr. Richard George, BA FCA CPA *1973;* 5 Finch Court, BERKELEY HEIGHTS, NJ 07922-2322, UNITED STATES.
•**BULL, Mr. Robert Austin, MSc FCA** *1969;* R. Bull, 4 Park Lodge, 80 Auckland Road, LONDON, SE19 2DF.
BULL, Mr. Robert Kendrick, BA(Hons) ACA *2004;* Financial Services Dept, Markham Stouffville Hospital, 381 Church Street, PO Box 1800, MARKHAM L3P 7P3, ON CANADA.
BULL, Mr. Simon Richard, BA(Hons) ACA *2002;* 21 Bryansglen Avenue, BANGOR, COUNTY DOWN, BT20 3RU.
BULL, Mr. Stephen John Antony, ACA *1984;* Le Marco Polo, 9-11 Avenue Albert 1er, 06230 VILLEFRANCHE-SUR-MER, FRANCE.
BULL, Mr. Stuart Alan, BSc ACA *1980;* Wingletang, Old Farm Road, HAMPTON, TW12 3RJ.
BULL, Mr. Stuart Martin, FCA *1973;* 24 Three Acre Road, NEWBURY, RG14 7AW.
BULL, Mr. Talika Maxwell, BSc ACA *2006;* with Future plc, 30 Monmouth Street, BATH, BA1 2BW.
BULL, Mrs. Thelma, FCA *1967;* 7 Brookfield Avenue, Syston, LEICESTER, LE7 2AB. (Life Member)
•**BULLARD, Mr. Andrew Stuart, BSc FCA** *1977;* (Tax Fac), Assured Accountancy, 14 Market Place, Pocklington, YORK, YO42 2AR. See also Independent Drivers Ltd and Andy Bullard
BULLARD, Mr. Jeremy James, BA ACA *1987;* 16 Fairmile Lane, COBHAM, KT11 2DJ.
BULLAS, Mr. Dermot Stanley, FCA *1948;* Edgeways, 54 Stone Lane, Kinver, STOURBRIDGE, DY7 6DY. (Life Member)
BULLAS, Mr. Julian Edward, BA ACA *1993;* 24 Parkwood Grove, Charlton Kings, CHELTENHAM, GL53 9JP.

•**BULLAS, Mr. Nigel Charles, FCA CF** *1984;* Clough & Company LLP, New Chartford House, Centurion Way, CLECKHEATON, WEST YORKSHIRE, BD19 3QB. See also Corporate Finance Services LLP, Clough Taxation Solutions LLP and Clough Management Services LLP
BULLATA, Mr. Jamil Yousif, FCA *1970;* 2 Castle Close, Parkside, Wimbledon, LONDON, SW19 5NH. (Life Member)
BULLEN, Mr. Alan Michael Ruari, BSc ACA *1986;* 17 Chepstow Road, LONDON, W2 5BP.
BULLEN, Mr. Clive, BSc ACA *1989;* 40 Queens Road, TWICKENHAM, TW1 4EX.
BULLEN, Mr. David Martin, BA ACA *2003;* 5 Higher Redannick, TRURO, CORNWALL, TR1 2DH.
BULLEN, Mrs. Karen Margaret Mary, BSc FCA CTA *1989;* (Tax Fac), 22 Old Broadway, Withington, MANCHESTER, M20 3DF.
•**BULLEN, Mr. Nicholas Peter Rhodes, FCA** *1979;* Whitley Stimpson LLP, Penrose House, 67 Hightown Road, BANBURY, OXFORDSHIRE, OX16 9BE.
BULLEN, Mr. Samuel David, BA ACA *2001;* British Petroleum Co Plc, 1 St. James's Square, LONDON, SW1Y 4PD.
BULLEN, Mrs. Suzanne Kim, BA ACA *2007;* 16 Bedford Avenue, Frimley Green, CAMBERLEY, SURREY, GU16 6HP.
BULLEN, Mr. Trevor William, ACA *1979;* 27 Manor Road, Mears Ashby, NORTHAMPTON, NN6 0DU.
BULLER, Mr. Alan, FCA *1951;* 17 Spencer Lane, Bamford, ROCHDALE, OL11 5PE. (Life Member)
BULLER, Mr. Andrew Peter, MA MSc ACA *2009;* 36 Castilla Place, BURTON-ON-TRENT, STAFFORDSHIRE, DE13 0SU.
•**BULLER, Mr. David John, FCA** *1985;* Lovewell Blake LLP, The Gables, Old Market Street, THETFORD, NORFOLK, IP24 2EN.
BULLER, Mr. David Michael, MChem ACA *2003;* Grant Thornton UK Llp Grant Thornton House, 22 Melton Street, LONDON, NW1 2EP.
BULLER, Mr. Thomas Michael, LLB ACA *2004;* Sunrise 10 Courtil Des Charmes, Les Grands Marais Vale, GUERNSEY, GY3 5DT.
BULLERS, Mr. Paul Andrew, BSc ACA *1991;* Heatherside, 11 Church View, Campsall, DONCASTER, SOUTH YORKSHIRE, DN6 9RA.
BULLETT, Mr. Michael Leonard Searchfield, BSc FCA *1971;* (Tax Fac), Mid Barn Ashcombe Priory, Chafford Lane, Fordcombe, TUNBRIDGE WELLS, KENT, TN3 0SP.
BULLEY, Mr. Alan Michael, FCA *1964;* 16 Elmgrove Drive, North Yate, BRISTOL, BS37 5BA.
BULLEY, Mr. Duncan, BA ACA *1992;* Hillside House, Heathend, WOTTON-UNDER-EDGE, GL12 8AX.
BULLEY, Mr. Ian, BSc ACA *1992;* Hollydale, Station Road, Bramley, GUILDFORD, SURREY, GU5 0DP.
•**BULLING, Mr. Stephen Francis Langlands, FCA** *1968;* (Tax Fac), Whitmill Prescott & Co, The Green Garages, Cambridge Road, Newport, SAFFRON WALDEN, ESSEX CB11 3TN.
BULLIVANT, Mr. Frank, FCA *1961;* 44 Station Road, Stallingborough, GRIMSBY, DN41 8AX. (Life Member)
BULLIVANT, Mr. Ian Michael, BA ACA *1993;* 2 Sunart Close, Wistaston, CREWE, CW2 6RT.
BULLIVANT, Miss. Jane Louise, BSc(Hons) ACA *2002;* 4 Woodside, Denby Dale, HUDDERSFIELD, HD8 8QX.
BULLIVANT, Miss. Jennifer Helen, LLB ACA *2003;* 58 Claude Road, MANCHESTER, M21 8UN.
BULLIVANT, Mr. Matthew, MA(Hons) ACA *2010;* Flat 7, 31 Trinity Church Square, LONDON, SE1 4HY.
BULLIVANT, Mr. Peter, BA ACA *1988;* 25 Nortoft Road, Chalfont St. Peter, GERRARDS CROSS, BUCKINGHAMSHIRE, SL9 0LA.
BULLIVANT, Miss. Sara Louise, ACA *2010;* Church View Main Street South, Aberford, LEEDS, LS25 3DA.
BULLIVANT, Mr. Timothy Wild, FCA *1961;* Rushetts, Grafham, Bramley, GUILDFORD, GU5 0LH.
BULLIVANT, Mrs. Zoe Rachel, BSc FCA *1992;* Brook Cottage, Moreton, THAME, OXFORDSHIRE, OX9 2HX.
BULLMAN, Mr. Antony George, MSc BSc FCA MCT *1990;* Wrotham Hill Manor, Wrotham Hill Road, Wrotham, SEVENOAKS, KENT, TN15 7PU.
BULLMAN, Mr. Paul, BSc ACA *2005;* 8 High Street, Wicken, ELY, CB7 5XR.
•**BULLMORE, Mr. George Theodore Lanyon, MA FCA** *1975;* KPMG, P O Box 493 Century Yard, Cricket Square, GEORGE TOWN, GRAND CAYMAN, KY1-1106 CAYMAN ISLANDS.
BULLOCH, Mr. Nicholas James, BSc ACA *2001;* 29 Fitzgerald Avenue, LONDON, SW14 8SZ.
BULLOCH, Mr. Nicholas Malcolm, FCA *1973;* 13 chemin Taponnet, 1291 Commugny, VAUD, SWITZERLAND.
BULLOCH, Mrs. Sabrina, ACA *2008;* 29 Fitzgerald Avenue, LONDON, SW14 8SZ.
•**BULLOCK, Mr. Anthony Robert, FCA** *1981;* Dutton Moore, 6 Silver Street, HULL, HU1 1JA.
BULLOCK, Mr. Anthony William Somerset, BSc FCA *1973;* Priory Farm House, Park Lane, REIGATE, RH2 8JX.
BULLOCK, Mrs. Elizabeth Ceri, BSc ACA *1999;* Westview House, 5 Commonside, STOURPORT-ON-SEVERN, WORCESTERSHIRE, DY13 0BE.
BULLOCK, Mr. Frederick Martin, FCA *1960;* Petroc, 7 Linden Avenue, NEWQUAY, TR7 2ES. (Life Member)
•**BULLOCK, Mr. Gavin James, BAcc ACA** *1997;* Deloitte LLP, Athene Place, 66 Shoe Lane, LONDON, EC4A 3BQ. See also Deloitte & Touche LLP
BULLOCK, Miss. Georgina Jane, BSc ACA *1996;* 8 Avenue Road, LEIGH-ON-SEA, SS9 1AX.
BULLOCK, Mr. Ian Peter, BA ACA *2001;* Flat 1, The Shubbery, 2 Lavender Gardens, LONDON, SW11 1DL.
BULLOCK, Mr. James, BA ACA *2000;* Water UK, 1 Queen Annes Gate, LONDON, SW1H 9BT.
BULLOCK, Mr. John, FCA *1954;* 62 Brackenfield Way, Thurmaston, LEICESTER, LE4 8GT. (Life Member)
BULLOCK, Mr. John, FCA *1956;* Gove House, 15 Clarendon Road, SEVENOAKS, KENT, TN13 1EU. (Life Member)
BULLOCK, Mr. John Michael, MA ACA *2004;* 69 Whitehill Place, VIRGINIA WATER, GU25 4DG.
BULLOCK, Mrs. Marcia Joan, BA ACA *2003;* Harrison House The Avenue, STRATFORD-UPON-AVON, WARWICKSHIRE, CV37 0RH.
•**BULLOCK, Mr. Mark, FCA** *1998;* Murphy Salisbury, 15 Warwick Road, STRATFORD-UPON-AVON, CV37 6YW.
BULLOCK, Mr. Michael David, FCA *1988;* NTR Plc, Burton Court, Burton Hall Road, Sandyford, DUBLIN 18, COUNTY DUBLIN IRELAND.
•**BULLOCK, Mr. Michael George, FCA** *1979;* Crossfields Limited, 85/87 High Street West, GLOSSOP, DERBYSHIRE, SK13 8AZ.
BULLOCK, Miss. Nicola Ann, ACA *2008;* 23 Penman Close, ST. ALBANS, HERTFORDSHIRE, AL2 3DJ.
BULLOCK, Mrs. Nicola Jane, BSc ACA *2001;* 1 Stokesay Drive, Cheadle, STOKE-ON-TRENT, ST10 1YU.
•**BULLOCK, Mr. Stephen Michael, BA FCA** *1988;* Crowe Clark Whitehill LLP, St Bride's House, 10 Salisbury Square, LONDON, EC4Y 8EH. See also Horwath Clark Whitehill LLP
BULLOCK, Mr. Stephen Robert, ACA *1983;* Lower Saltonstall, Wainstalls, HALIFAX, HX2 7TR.
BULLOCK, Mr. Thomas, BBA ACA *2010;* Deloitte, 5th Floor, Al Fattan Currency House, DIFC, DUBAI, 28256 UNITED ARAB EMIRATES.
BULLOCK, Mr. Timothy David, FCA *1984;* Bin Ghanem Tower, Hamdan Street, ABU DHABI, UNITED ARAB EMIRATES.
BULLON, Mr. Alun, FCA *1973;* Flat 22, Belvedere House, Churchfields Avenue, WEYBRIDGE, SURREY, KT13 9XY. (Life Member)
BULLOSS, Mr. James John, BSc ACA *2010;* 5 Summerhill Gardens, LEEDS, LS8 2EL.
BULLOUGH, Mr. Christopher, ACA *2011;* 31 Victoria Street, Chapel Allerton, LEEDS, LS7 4PA.
BULLOUGH, Mr. David Arthur, BCom ACA *1998;* 23 Oakwood Drive, LEIGH, LANCASHIRE, WN7 3LZ.
BULLOUGH, Mr. Ian John, FCA *1984;* Woodlands, 5 Moorwood Drive, SALE, M33 4QB.
BULLOUGH, Mr. John Mark, BSc ACA *2003;* Gleesom Homes, Sandringham House, 2 Little 66, Roach Bank Road, BURY, LANCASHIRE BL9 8RN.
BULLOUGH, Mr. Rodney Howard, BSc FCA *1968;* 2 Shenley Close, SOUTH CROYDON, CR2 0LT. (Life Member)
BULLWORTHY, Mr. Gerald Arthur, FCA *1972;* The Home Office Immigration Service Documentation Unit, Green Park House 29 Wellesley Road, CROYDON, CR0 2AJ.
BULMAN, Mr. Francis William, BA(Hons) ACA *2000;* 39 Woodside, LONDON, SW19 7AG.
BULMAN, Mrs. Pauline, FCA *1971;* Poppy's Place, Roundabout Lane, West Chiltington, PULBOROUGH, RH20 2RB.
BULMAN, Mr. Thomas Emmet, BCom FCA *1998;* (Tax Fac), 138 Apton Road, BISHOP'S STORTFORD, HERTFORDSHIRE, CM23 3SW.
BULMER, Mrs. Clare Sandra, BA FCA *1992;* 782 Glenmary Road, ENDERBY V0E 1V3, BC, CANADA.
•**BULMER, Mrs. Donna Marie, BA(Hons) ACA** *2000;* HW, Floor 11, Cale Cross House, 156 Pilgrim Street, NEWCASTLE UPON TYNE, NORTHUMBERLAND NE1 6SU. See also Haines Watts
BULMER, Mrs. Joanna Elizabeth, BA ACA *2005;* 26 Lockhart Avenue, Oxley Park, MILTON KEYNES, MK4 4TY.
BULMER, Mr. Patrick David, BA ACA *1982;* 33 St John's Wood Road, LONDON, NW8 8RA.
•**BULMER, Mrs. Yuen Man Anna, BA FCA** *1991;* (Tax Fac), Newman Peters, 19 Fitzroy Square, LONDON, W1T 6EQ.
BULPITT, Mrs. Deborah, BA ACA *1998;* 1500 Blackberry Ct, NAPERVILLE, IL 60565, UNITED STATES.
BULPITT, Mrs. Jayne Michelle, BSc ACA *1995;* 1 Old Park Road, LEEDS, LS8 1JT.
BULPITT, Mr. Nigel Peter, FCA *1970;* The Old School, Upper Froyle, ALTON, GU34 4LB.
BULSARA, Mrs. Archna K, BA ACA *2006;* Capet Management Services Limited, P O Box 60419 - 00200, NAIROBI, KENYA.
BULSARA, Mr. Mukesh Ratilal, BSc ACA *1997;* 47a Guilford Road, Stoneygate, LEICESTER, LE2 2RD.
BULSARA, Mr. Sorab, ACA *2010;* PO Box 3800, DUBAI, UNITED ARAB EMIRATES.
•**BULSTRODE, Mrs. Lynne Paula, BA(Hons) ACA** *1993;* Inspire Audit Ltd, 37 Commercial Road, POOLE, DORSET, BH14 0HU.
BULSTRODE, Mr. Marc Robert Andrew, BSc ACA *1994;* The Elms, 15 Stagswood, VERWOOD, BH31 6PX.
BUMBY, Miss. Christine Ann, BSc ACA *2007;* with Deloitte LLP, 2 New Street Square, LONDON, EC4A 3BZ.
BUMBY, Miss. Susan Mary, BSc ACA *1998;* Thornhill, Eilansgate, HEXHAM, NE46 3EJ.
BUMPSTEED, Mr. Clive Edward, MSc FCA *1979;* with Shareway Financial Services Limited, Penns Grange, 9 Netherdale Close, Wylde Green, SUTTON COLDFIELD, WEST MIDLANDS B72 1YW.
•**BUMPSTEED, Mrs. Susan, BSc FCA** *1983;* Shareway Financial Services Limited, Penns Grange, 9 Netherdale Close, Wylde Green, SUTTON COLDFIELD, WEST MIDLANDS B72 1YW.
BUMSTEAD, Mr. Eric Leonard, FCA *1962;* 4931 Bonita Bay Boulevard, Apartment 1001, BONITA SPRINGS, FL 34134, UNITED STATES. (Life Member)
BUMSTEAD, Mrs. Frances Kirstie, MA ACA *1998;* 15 Fletcher Drive, Bowdon, ALTRINCHAM, CHESHIRE, WA14 3FZ.
BUMSTEAD, Mr. Ivan Victor, BSc(Hons) ACA *2001;* Late Rooms Ltd, 2 Cheetham Hill Road, MANCHESTER, M4 4EW.
BUNBURY, Mr. Philip Graham, FCA *1971;* 12 Cresswick, Whitwell, HITCHIN, SG4 8HU.
BUNBURY, Mr. William Francis, ACA *2010;* Church Corner Cottage, Church Lane, Playford, IPSWICH, IP6 9DS.
BUNCE, Mr. David, BA ACA *1984;* KPMG Corporate Finance, Caixa Postal 2467, SAO PAULO, 01060-970, BRAZIL.
BUNCE, Mr. Stafford Malcolm, FCA *1974;* Real Asset Management Plc Central Court, 1b Knoll Rise, ORPINGTON, BR6 0JA.
•**BUNCE, Mr. Stephen William, FCA** *1968;* Ridley Marreco & Co Limited, Dove House, Mill Lane, Barford St. Michael, BANBURY, OXFORDSHIRE OX15 0RH.
BUNCH, Mr. Andrew James, BSc FCA *1991;* Bekeleigh, Private Road, CHELMSFORD, ESSEX, CM12 0FB.
BUNCH, Mr. Crawford, ACA *2009;* 250 Hurst Road, BEXLEY, DA5 3DY.
BUNCH, Mr. Marc Edward, BSc(Econ) ACA *1999;* Ernst & Young, 680 George Street, SYDNEY, NSW 2000, AUSTRALIA.
BUNDAY, Mr. Jeremy David Heaton, BSc ACA *1984;* 4 Sandrock Park, HASTINGS, EAST SUSSEX, TN34 2RQ.
BUNDEY, Mr. Roland Robert, FCA *1970;* 171 Wigton Lane, LEEDS, LS17 8SH.
•**BUNDHUN, Mr. Mohamed Iqbal, FCA** *1980;* M.I. Bundhun, Apartment 3, 15 Wedderburn Road, LONDON, NW3 5QS.
BUNDHUN, Mr. Ziyad Abdool Raouf, ACA *1991;* 66 Gentilly Estate, MOKA, MAURITIUS.
BUNDOCK, Mrs. Catharine Margaret, BSc ARCS FCA *1988;* The Rectory, West Raynham, FAKENHAM, NR21 7HH.
BUNDOCK, Mr. Richard John, BSc ACA *1991;* ABS Consulting, Suite 601 AL Jahra Building, Khaled Bin Waleed Street, DUBAI, UNITED ARAB EMIRATES.
BUNDY, Mr. Christopher, FCA *1970;* Bridge House Main Street, Elvington, YORK, YO41 4AA.
BUNDY, Mr. James Joseph, BA ACA *2010;* with Ernst & Young LLP, 1 Bridgewater Place, Water Lane, LEEDS, LS11 5QR.
•**BUNE, Mr. Michael John, FCA** *1985;* Michael Bune & Co, 16c South Street, WAREHAM, DORSET, BH20 4LT.
BUNGAR, Mr. Satvir, BSc ACA *1999;* 25 Pear Tree Drive, BIRMINGHAM, B43 6HR.
BUNGARD, Mr. Michael Norman, FCA *1963;* Stanwell House, 20 West Drive, Ferring, WORTHING, BN12 5QZ.
BUNGAY, Mr. Richard Edward, BSc ACA *1994;* Chroma Therapeutics Ltd, 93 Milton Park, ABINGDON, OXFORDSHIRE, OX14 4RY.
BUNGEY, Mr. Jeremy Peter, BSc ACA *1997;* 54 Woodlea Drive, SOLIHULL, WEST MIDLANDS, B91 1PQ.
•**BUNKELL, Mr. Keith William, FCA** *1977;* K.W. Bunkell & Co, The Counting House, 1A Furze Hill, PURLEY, CR8 3LB.
BUNKER, Ms. Abigail Catherine, BA(Hons) ACA *2001;* 5c Lion Court, Market Square, Potton, SANDY, BEDFORDSHIRE, SG19 2NP.
•**BUNKER, Mr. Charles Spencer, FCA** *1980;* 83 Baker Street, LONDON, W1U 6AG.
•**BUNKER, Mr. David Alan Langley, BA FCA** *1975;* David Bunker, Kings House, 14 Orchard Street, BRISTOL, BS1 5EH.
BUNKER, Mr. Jonathan Richard, BSc ACA *1999;* London Clubs International, 10 Brick Street, LONDON, W1J 7HQ.
BUNKER, Mr. Keith James, FCA *1958;* 4 Hazel Close, BRACKLEY, NN13 6PE. (Life Member)
BUNKER, Mr. Mark Philip Spencer, BSc(Hons) ARCS ACA *2001;* 2 Glenbrook Road, West Hampstead, LONDON, NW6 1TW.
BUNKER, Mr. Philip Mark, BSc FCA *1988;* LV, 69 Park Lane, CROYDON, CR9 1BG.
•**BUNKER, Mr. Richard William, FCA ATII** *1985;* Richard Bunker & Co Limited, Colkin House, 16 Oakfield Road, Clifton, BRISTOL, BS8 2AP. See also Whyatt Pakeman Partners
BUNKLE, Mr. Adam Russell, BSc(Hons) ACA *2002;* 8 West Street, North Creake, FAKENHAM, NR21 9LQ.
BUNKUM, Mr. James Taylor, BA FCA *1992;* Brookfield, The Green, Whimple, EXETER, DEVON, EX5 2UA.
•**BUNN, Mr. Alan Leslie, FCA** *1968;* (Tax Fac), Reynolds 2000 (Taxation Services) Ltd, Whitstone Farm, Bovey Tracey, NEWTON ABBOT, TQ13 9NA.
BUNN, Mr. Alan Stuart, FCA *1979;* 2 Westleigh Court, Newbold Back Lane, CHESTERFIELD, DERBYSHIRE, S40 4NY.
BUNN, Mr. Andrew Thomas, ACA *2009;* 51 Cleaver Square, LONDON, SE11 4EA.
BUNN, Mr. James Richard, BSc ACA *1998;* The Willow Tree Faygate Lane, Faygate, HORSHAM, WEST SUSSEX, RH12 4SN.
BUNN, Mr. Jonathan David, BA ACA *1992;* 158 Felsham Road, LONDON, SW15 1DP.
BUNN, Mr. Matthew James, MA ACA *1998;* Emmaus, 32 Droitwich Road, Barbourne, WORCESTER, WR3 7LH.
BUNN, Miss. Melissa Julie, BSc ACA *2002;* 123 Scott Road, Thorpe Park, NORWICH, NR1 1YL.
BUNN, Mr. Robert Henry, FCA *1974;* Azalea, 167 High Street South, Northchurch, BERKHAMSTED, HERTFORDSHIRE, HP4 3QT. (Life Member)
BUNN, Mr. Steven, ACA *2008;* Beggars Roost Clive Road, Pattingham, WOLVERHAMPTON, WV6 7EN.
BUNN, Ms. Susan, BSc FCA DChA *1988;* 9 St Marys Walk, Kennington, LONDON, SE11 4UA.
BUNNELL, Mr. John Andrew, FCA *1970;* Little Orchard, Goodshelter, East Portlemouth, SALCOMBE, TQ8 8PA. (Life Member)
BUNNETT, Mr. James, ACA *2009;* Flat 3, 1 Briset Street, LONDON, EC1M 5NR.
BUNNEY, Mr. George, FCA *1951;* Marston Croft, 24 Mitchell Walk, AMERSHAM, BUCKINGHAMSHIRE, HP6 6NW. (Life Member)
•**BUNNEY, Mr. Keith Wilson, FCA** *1972;* Cound & Co LLP, 104/106 Market Street, ASHBY-DE-LA-ZOUCH, LE65 1AP.
BUNNING, Mr. Christopher John, FCA *1976;* 147 Queens Road, Wimbledon, LONDON, SW19 8NS.
BUNNY, Mr. Dennis Clive, FCA *1952;* 1015-3010 Lawrence Avenue East, SCARBOROUGH M1P 4Y6, ON, CANADA. (Life Member)
BUNPOKKRONG, Miss. Chutima, BA(Hons) ACA *2010;* 8 Corran Pirragh, Reayrt Ny Cronk Peel, ISLE OF MAN, IM5 1GN.
•**BUNSTER, Mr. John, FCA** *1968;* J Bunster, 24 Hillway, Tranmere Park, Guiseley, LEEDS, LS20 8HB. See also John Bunster and Barker & Bunster
•**BUNSTON, Mr. Adrian Noel, FCA** *1976;* Princecroft Willis LLP, The George Business Centre, Christchurch Road, NEW MILTON, HAMPSHIRE, BH25 6QJ. See also PW Business Solutions

Members - Alphabetical BUNT - BURGESS

BUNT, Mr. Brian Stanley, FCA *1961;* The Dees, Vicarage Lane, Scaynes Hill, HAYWARDS HEATH, RH17 7PB.
BUNT, Mr. Christopher John, BA ACA *1982;* (Tax Fac), 2 St Marys Village, St Marys Village, St Mary, JERSEY, JE3 3BQ.
•**BUNT, Mr. Philip Alan, FCA** *1981;* 176 Whitchurch Lane, Canons Park, EDGWARE, HA8 6QJ.
BUNTAIN, Mr. Archibald Ian, MBA BSc FCA *1975;* 4 Tainui Drive, HAVELOCK NORTH 4130, HAWKES BAY, NEW ZEALAND.
•**BUNTER, Mr. Richard, FCA** *1984;* PricewaterhouseCoopers, Benson House, 33 Wellington Street, LEEDS, LS1 4JP. See also PricewaterhouseCoopers LLP
BUNTHON, Miss. Montha, ACA *2005;* 1 Hebbecastle Down, Warfield, BRACKNELL, BERKSHIRE, RG42 2QD.
BUNTING, Mr. Adam, LLM LLB(Hons) ACA *2011;* K P M G One Snowhill, Snow Hill Queensway, BIRMINGHAM, B4 6GH.
BUNTING, Mr. Alan John, BA ACA *1988;* The Old Vicarage, Stickford, BOSTON, PE22 8EP.
BUNTING, Mr. Bruce, FCA *1969;* Albury Cottage, 119A Westfield Road, Mayford, WOKING, GU22 9QR.
BUNTING, Miss. Christine Suzanne, BSc ACA *1996;* PO Box 655, GABORONE, BOTSWANA.
BUNTING, Mr. Colin William, FCA *1960;* 36 The Fields, Tacolneston, NORWICH, NR16 1DG. (Life Member)
•**BUNTING, Mr. David Arthur, FCA** *1964;* (Tax Fac), Bunting Accountants Limited, 5 Orchard Close, Wheatley, OXFORD, OX33 1US.
BUNTING, Mr. Derek Alleyn, FCA *1955;* 5 Fishermans Close, Formby, LIVERPOOL, L37 1XX. (Life Member)
BUNTING, Mr. Frank Thomas, BSc FCA *1958;* The Rylands, 2 Dovehouse Lane, Harbury, LEAMINGTON SPA, CV33 9HD. (Life Member)
•**BUNTING, Mr. Glyn, BA ACA** *1989;* Deloitte LLP, 2 New Street Square, LONDON, EC4A 3BZ. See also Deloitte & Touche LLP
BUNTING, Mr. Mark Bevan, ACA CA(SA) *2009;* PO Box 2819, PORT ALFRED, 6170, SOUTH AFRICA.
BUNTING, Mr. Martin Brian, FCA *1960;* The Long House, 41 High Street, Odiham, HOOK, RG29 1LF. (Life Member)
BUNTING, Mr. Michael, ACA *2009;* 81 Baron's Hill Avenue, LINLITHGOW, WEST LOTHIAN, EH49 7JQ.
BUNTING, Mrs. Silveta, ACA *2011;* 122 Lupin Drive, CHELMSFORD, CM1 6FJ.
BUNTING, Miss. Susan Elaine, ACA *2004;* 36 The Fields, Tacolneston, NORWICH, NR16 1DG.
BUNTING, Mr. William Keith, FCA *1972;* (Tax Fac), 147 St. Helens Road, Eccleston Park, PRESCOT, L34 2QB.
BUNTON, Mr. Ian, ACA *1993;* 2 Oriel Close, Walkington, BEVERLEY, HU17 8YD.
BUNYAN, Mr. David Keith, BA FCA *1985;* The Institution of Engineering & Technology, Michael Faraday House, Six Hills Way, STEVENAGE, HERTFORDSHIRE, SG1 2AY.
BUNYAN, Mr. Michael Robert, FCA *1965;* 30 Lodge Close, Coppins Road, CLACTON-ON-SEA, CO15 3HU.
BUNYAN, Mr. Paul Duncan, BSc ACA *1983;* Brookside House, Thruxton, ANDOVER, SP11 8LZ.
•**BUNYARD, Mr. Andrew Michael, BA FCA** *1977;* Field House, Somerset Place, TEWKESBURY, GLOUCESTERSHIRE, GL20 5HQ.
BUONTEMPO, Mr. Alan Godfrey, FCA *1970;* 7 Lambourn Avenue, Stone Cross, PEVENSEY, EAST SUSSEX, BN24 5PQ.
BURBEDGE, Mr. Matthew Ian, BSc ACA *1997;* 11 The Spinney, LONDON, N21 1LL.
BURBIDGE, Miss. Clare Elizabeth, ACA *2009;* Mazars, Unit 7/8, 2 New Fields Business Park, Stinsford Road, POOLE, DORSET BH17 0NF.
BURBIDGE, Mr. James Edward, BSc ACA *2000;* HCP Social Infrastructure (UK) Ltd, Unit 8 White Oak Square, London Road, SWANLEY, BR8 7AG.
BURBIDGE, Mr. John Alexander, FCA *1974;* P.O BOX 228, GEORGE, WESTERN CAPE PROVINCE, 6530, SOUTH AFRICA.
BURBIDGE, Mr. John Warwick, BA ACA *1984;* Tanners, Rectory Lane, Brasted, WESTERHAM, TN16 1NH.
BURBIDGE, Mrs. Lesley Anne, BSc ACA *1994;* 18 Morley Square, BRISTOL, BS7 9DW.
BURBIDGE, Mrs. Lynsey Joan, BSc ACA *2005;* 4 Norfolk Walk, LEEDS, LS7 4PS.
•**BURBIDGE, Mr. Nigel Ferrier, FCA** *1981;* BDO LLP, Emerald House, East Street, EPSOM, SURREY, KT17 1HS. See also BDO Stoy Hayward LLP
BURBIDGE, Mr. Peter William John, FCA *1974;* Berweg 30, 3941 RA DOORN, NETHERLANDS. (Life Member)
BURBIDGE, Mr. Richard James, BA ACA *1992;* 39 Sharmans Cross Road, SOLIHULL, WEST MIDLANDS, B91 1RQ.
BURBIDGE, Mr. Robert William, BA ACA *1999;* 4 Rose Close, Leyland, PRESTON, PR25 5TQ.
BURBIDGE, Mr. Wayne Ivor, ACA *1987;* The Cottage, The Bank, Shearsby, LUTTERWORTH, LE17 6PF.
BURBRIDGE, Mr. Neil, BSc ACA *2001;* 15 Granville Way, Willetton, PERTH, WA 6155, AUSTRALIA.
BURBRIDGE, Carmichael of Carmichael Richard John Newton, FCA *1971;* Carmichael Estate, Carmichael, BIGGAR, ML12 6PG.
BURBRIDGE, Mr. Simon Charles, BSc ACA *1999;* 11C Fairmile Avenue, LONDON, SW16 6AG.
BURBRIDGE-JAMES, Mr. Dominic, MA ACA *1985;* 11 Wooderson View, ALBANY, WA 6330, AUSTRALIA.
•**BURCH, Mr. Andrew Keith, BA(Hons) FCA** *1991;* Sayers Butterworth LLP, 3rd Floor, 12 Gough Square, LONDON, EC4A 3DW.
BURCH, The Revd Canon Peter John, FCA *1960;* 6 Jordans Close, Willersey, BROADWAY, WORCESTERSHIRE, WR12 7QD. (Life Member)
BURCH, Mr. Philip Alan, FCA *1971;* 38 Shirley Gardens, BARKING, ESSEX, IG11 9UZ. (Life Member)
BURCH, Mr. Quentin Slade, FCA *1969;* Southview Cottage, Southview Road, CROWBOROUGH, TN6 1HL.
BURCH, Mr. Steven James, MA MEng ACA *2001;* with KPMG LLP, 15 Canada Square, LONDON, E14 5GL.
BURCHALL, Mr. Andrew Jeremy, BSc ACA *1990;* Impellam Group Plc, 800 The Boulevard, Capability Green, LUTON, LU1 3BA.
•**BURCHELL, Mrs. Carolyn Jeanne, BA ACA** *1997;* Composure Accounting & Taxation, 9 Tennyson Close, HORSHAM, WEST SUSSEX, RH12 5PN.
BURCHELL, Mr. Jeremy Joseph Benjamin, FCA *1961;* 6 Mackenzie Lodge, 57 Maida Vale, LONDON, W9 1SD.
BURCHELL, Mr. Philip Raymond, FCA *1966;* Bulls Farm, Nuthampstead, ROYSTON, HERTFORDSHIRE, SG8 8NA. (Life Member)
BURCHELL, Mr. Russell Francis, ACA *1981;* Appledore, Camden Road, LINGFIELD, SURREY, RH7 6AF.
BURCHETT, Mr. Paul Igino, BSc ACA *1999;* with RSM Tenon Limited, York House, 20 York Street, MANCHESTER, M2 3BB.
BURCHILL, Mr. Kenneth Peter, FCA *1959;* Overbecks, 6 Sutton Park, Bishop Sutton, BRISTOL, BS39 5UQ. (Life Member)
BURCHILL, Ms. Kim Heather, BA ACA *1985;* Woodlands, 6 Ladylawn, Wild Oak Lane Trull, TAUNTON, TA3 7LR.
•**BURCHMORE, Mr. Martin Arthur, FCA** *1977;* Kingston Smith LLP, Devonshire House, 60 Goswell Road, LONDON, EC1M 7AD. See also Kingston Smith Limited Liability Partnership, Devonshire Corporate Services LLP, Kingston Smith Consulting LLP and Devonshire Corporate Finance Limited
BURDASS, Mr. James Edward Bradshaw, BSc ACA *1993;* (Tax Fac), 105 York Road, Haxby, YORK, YO32 3EN.
•**BURDASS, Mr. Stuart, BSc ACA** *1990;* KPMG LLP, St. James's Square, MANCHESTER, M2 6DS. See also KPMG Europe LLP
BURDEN, Mr. Arthur James, OBE FCA *1951;* Axholme, 288 Wilbraham Road, MANCHESTER, M16 8LT. (Life Member)
BURDEN, Mr. David Colin, FCA *1992;* Gaderill, 25 Water Lane, KINGS LANGLEY, WD4 8HP.
BURDEN, Mr. Edward Tregenna, FCA *1964;* Negremont, 46090 ESCLAUZELS, FRANCE.
•**BURDEN, Mrs. Elizabeth Jane, BSc ARCS FCA** *1982;* (Tax Fac), Elizabeth Burden, 254 Coggeshall Road, Little Tey, COLCHESTER, CO6 1HT.
BURDEN, Mr. Graham John, BA ACA *1995;* 160 E Chateau Place, WHITEFISH BAY, WI 53217, UNITED STATES.
BURDEN, Mr. Michael John, FCA *1971;* Redhouse, Penshurst Road, Speldhurst, TUNBRIDGE WELLS, TN3 0PB. (Life Member)
•**BURDEN, Mr. Mitchell Alan, ACA** *1992;* Bulley Davey & Co, 9/10 The Crescent, WISBECH, PE13 1EH. See also Bulley Davey
BURDEN, Mr. Peter David, BA ACA *2002;* 9 Bucklands Lane, Nailsea, BRISTOL, BS48 4PJ.
BURDEN, Mr. Robert James, ACA *2008;* Cooper Parry Llp, 14 Park Row, NOTTINGHAM, NG1 6GR.
BURDEN, Mr. Roderick John, BSc ACA *1979;* Warbank House, Westerham Road, KESTON, BR2 6AG.
BURDEN, Mr. Stephen Michael James, BSc FCA CF *1995;* with Deloitte LLP, Athene Place, 66 Shoe Lane, LONDON, EC4A 3BQ.
•**BURDEN, Ms. Susan Patricia, MA FCA** *1983;* (Tax Fac), Leach & Co, Ashley House, 136 Tolworth Broadway, SURBITON, SURREY, KT6 7LA.
BURDER, Mr. Stephen Basil, BSc FCA *1978;* (Tax Fac), 11 Daryngton Drive, Merrow, GUILDFORD, GU1 2QB.
BURDETT, Mr. Howard Francis, BSc ACA *1995;* Flat 2, 33 Wimpole Street, LONDON, W1G 8GU.
BURDETT, Mr. Ian Steven, BSc ACA *1985;* 151 Hillhurst Blvd., TORONTO M5N 1N7, ON, CANADA.
BURDETT, Miss. Jane Elizabeth, BA ACA *2002;* 84 Acorn Way, YORK, YO24 2RP.
BURDETT, Mr. John Coventry, BSc FCA *1970;* 11 Lawn Crescent, Kew, RICHMOND, TW9 3NR.
BURDETT, Mrs. Louisa, BSc ACA *1995;* Flat 2, 33 Wimpole Street, LONDON, W1G 8GU.
BURDETT, Mr. Paul Ian, BSc ACA *2006;* 30 The Avenue, Innwood, ENFIELD, COUNTY MEATH, IRELAND.
BURDETT, Mr. Thomas, LLB ACA *2011;* Larking Gowen, Kingstreet House, 15 Upper King Street, NORWICH, NR3 1RB.
BURDIN, Mr. Paul Boscoe Leo, BA(Hons) ACA *2003;* (Tax Fac), Touchnote Ltd, 17-19 Bonny Street, LONDON, NW1 9PE.
BURDOCK, Mr. Matthew, BA ACA *1998;* 26 Batford Road, HARPENDEN, HERTFORDSHIRE, AL5 5AT.
BURDON, Mr. Ian James, BA ACA *1991;* 9 Taylor Lane, HARRISON, NY 10528, UNITED STATES.
BURDON, Mr. Paul Raymond, MA ACA *1986;* 17 Mill Lane, BILLINGHAM, TS23 1HH.
BURDON-COOPER, Mr. John Richard Beverley, FCA *1965;* 12 The Grove, RADLETT, WD7 7NF.
BURDSEY, Miss. Anne Patricia, BSc FCA *1974;* Penrose, Milton Avenue, GERRARDS CROSS, SL9 8QN.
BURFOOT, Mrs. Hannah, ACA *2002;* 5 Village Close, Flint Mountain, FLINT, CLWYD, CH6 5WA.
BURFOOT, Mrs. Lucy, BSc ACA *2006;* with KPMG LLP, One Snowhill, Snow Hill Queensway, BIRMINGHAM, B4 6GN.
BURFOOT, Mr. Meyrick Arthur, FCA *1953;* 29 Katherine Drive, Beeston, NOTTINGHAM, NG9 6JB. (Life Member)
•**BURFORD, Mr. Bruce Warren, BA ACA** *1986;* Bruce Burford, 8 Beechfield Road, BROMLEY, BR1 3BU.
•ⓘ**BURFORD, Mr. Christopher Stuart, BA FCA** *1983;* Pathfinder Strategic Partners LLP, The Royd, 40 Duchy Road, HARROGATE, NORTH YORKSHIRE, HG1 2ER.
BURFORD, Mr. David Brian, ACA *2006;* 15 Beech Close, MARKFIELD, LEICESTERSHIRE, LE67 9RT.
BURFORD, Miss. Elizabeth Louise, BA(Hons) ACA *2010;* 7 Coombes Grove, ROCHFORD, ESSEX, SS4 1DX.
•**BURFORD, Mrs. Irene Monica, BA ACA** *1992;* S Foster (BOA) Ltd, The Courtyard, 33 Duke Street, TROWBRIDGE, WILTSHIRE, BA14 8EA.
BURFORD, Dr. Mark, MEng ACA *2010;* First Floor Flat, 262 Queenstown Road, LONDON, SW8 4LP.
BURFORD, Mr. Robert Brian, BEng ACA *1992;* 21 Wensley Gardens, EMSWORTH, HAMPSHIRE, PO10 7RA.
BURFORD, Mr. Ryan Robert, BA(Hons) ACA CTA *2003;* (Tax Fac), Flat 12 Jersey Court, Dairy Close, LONDON, SW6 4HB.
BURFORD, Mrs. Susan Patricia, BA ACA *1993;* 21 Wensley Gardens, EMSWORTH, HAMPSHIRE, PO10 7RA.
BURGE, Mr. Adam, ACA *2010;* Old Mutual Plc Millennium Bridge House, 2 Lambeth Hill, LONDON, EC4V 4GG.
BURGE, Mr. Anthony Proctor, ACA *2009;* 54 Elsley Road, LONDON, SW11 5LL.
BURGE, Mrs. Catherine Mary, BSc ACA *1992;* B & Q Plc, Portswood House, 1 Hampshire Corporate Park, Chandler's Ford, EASTLEIGH, HAMPSHIRE SO53 3YX.
BURGE, Mr. Julian Charles, BA(Hons) ACA *2001;* with KPMG LLP, Aquis Court, 31 Fishpool Street, ST. ALBANS, HERTFORDSHIRE, AL3 4RF.
BURGE, Miss. Kim Amanda, ACA *2009;* 7 Carnegie Road, WORTHING, WEST SUSSEX, BN14 7BD.
BURGE, Mrs. Laura, BA ACA *1999;* with KPMG, 1 Stokes Place, St. Stephen's Green, DUBLIN 2, COUNTY DUBLIN, IRELAND.
•**BURGE, Mr. Matthew James, BSc FCA** *1994;* Beavis Morgan Audit Limited, 82 St. John Street, LONDON, EC1M 4JN. See also Beavis Morgan LLP
BURGE, Mr. Nick James Harold, BA ACA *2011;* Apartment 6, Futura House, 169 Grange Road, LONDON, SE1 3BN.
•**BURGE, Mr. Nigel David Ritchie, BSc FCA** *1977;* (Tax Fac), Ritchie Burge & Co, 14 Earlish, Portree, ISLE OF SKYE, IV51 9XL.
•**BURGE, Mr. Nigel Martin, FCA** *1977;* (Tax Fac), Burge Accountancy Ltd, Whitecroft House, Hatton Hill, WINDLESHAM, SURREY, GU20 6AB.
BURGE, Miss. Sarah Louise, ACA *2002;* 11 Brickyard Cottages, NORTH FERRIBY, NORTH HUMBERSIDE, HU14 3AD.
BURGE, Mrs. Selena Jane, FCA *1975;* 32 Seymour Road, EAST MOLESEY, SURREY, KT8 0PB.
BURGE, Mr. Stephen Christopher, BSc ACA *1998;* with PricewaterhouseCoopers LLP, Cornwall Court, 19 Cornwall Street, BIRMINGHAM, B3 2DT.
BURGELL, Mr. John William, FCA *1950;* Pfalzstrasse 43, 40477 DUSSELDORF, GERMANY. (Life Member)
BURGER, Mr. John Michael, ACA *2009;* 7 Friars Court, Lenton Road The Park, NOTTINGHAM, NG7 1EW.
BURGER, Mrs. Lisa Jane, BMus ACA *1987;* Royal National Theatre, Upper Ground, LONDON, SE1 9PX.
BURGER, Mr. Philip Thomas Frederick, FCA *1959;* Bracon Ash, 49 Purley Bury Close, PURLEY, CR8 1HW.
BURGES, Mr. John Cecil, FCA *1956;* 13 South View, LETCHWORTH GARDEN CITY, SG6 3JH. (Life Member)
BURGESS, Mr. Andrew, BSc ACA *1989;* 11 Copper Rigg, BROUGHTON-IN-FURNESS, CUMBRIA, LA20 6AJ.
BURGESS, Mr. Andrew Peter Lloyd, BSc ACA *1995;* 6 Barshaw Gardens, Appleton, WARRINGTON, WA4 5FA.
BURGESS, Mr. Andrew Richard, BSc ACA *1990;* The Carlyle Group, 57 Berkeley Square, LONDON, W1J 6ER.
BURGESS, Mr. Andrew Scott, BSc ACA *1997;* DADCO, Hamilton House, St. Julians Avenue, St. Peter Port, GUERNSEY, GY1 1WA.
BURGESS, Mrs. Anna Katherine, BSc ACA *2006;* 20 Cranberry Rise, Loveclough, ROSSENDALE, BB4 8FB.
BURGESS, Miss. Anna Louise, BA FCA *1993;* 81a Rowell Avenue, CAMBERWELL, VIC 3124, AUSTRALIA.
BURGESS, Mr. Anthony Darren, BSc ACA *1998;* 212 Main Street, Thornton, COALVILLE, LE67 1AG.
BURGESS, Mr. Anthony Frederick, FCA *1963;* Ellerton Hall, Ellerton, NEWPORT, TF10 8AW.
BURGESS, Mr. Anthony John, BA ACA *1989;* 18 Sandford Park Place, CHELTENHAM, GL52 6HP.
BURGESS, Mr. Carl James Hugh, FCA *1963;* 41 Eton Hall, Eton College Road, LONDON, NW3 2DP. (Life Member)
BURGESS, Mrs. Caroline Melody, FCA *1977;* The Oxbyre, Lower Chedworth, Chedworth, CHELTENHAM, GLOUCESTERSHIRE, GL54 4AN.
BURGESS, Mr. Christian John, ACA CA(AUS) *2011;* 9a Strathray Gardens, LONDON, NW3 4PA.
BURGESS, Mr. Christopher John, FCA *1974;* 87 Valley Ridge Loop, COCKEYSVILLE, MD 21030, UNITED STATES.
•**BURGESS, Mr. Christopher Joseph, FCA** *1980;* with Plummer Parsons, 18 Hyde Gardens, EASTBOURNE, BN21 4PT.
BURGESS, Mrs. Claire Louise, BSc ACA *2000;* 24 Scarhouse Lane, Golcar, HUDDERSFIELD, HD7 4DX.
•**BURGESS, Mr. Daniel Richard, BA ACA** *1984;* KPMG LLP, 15 Canada Square, LONDON, E14 5GL. See also KPMG Europe LLP
BURGESS, Mr. David, BA FCA *1979;* Aviva Investors, 1 Poultry, LONDON, EC2R 8EJ.
BURGESS, Mr. David William Ashley, FCA *1995;* Glebe House, 7 Church Walk, Upton, PETERBOROUGH, PE6 7BD.
•**BURGESS, Mr. Geoffrey John, FCA** *1955;* G.J.Burgess & Co., 175 Jersey Road, Osterley, ISLEWORTH, TW7 4QJ.
BURGESS, Mrs. Gillian Karen, BA ACA *1999;* 37 Manor Road, RICHMOND, SURREY, TW9 1YA.
BURGESS, Mr. Graeme Stanley, BSc ACA *1995;* Bali Hai, Cudham Lane North, Cudham, SEVENOAKS, KENT, TN14 7RB.
BURGESS, Mrs. Hanah, BA(Hons) ACA *2001;* 9a Strathray Gardens, LONDON, NW3 4PA.
BURGESS, Mrs. Heather Jane, BSc ACA *1993;* 41 Burns Road, Battersea, LONDON, SW11 5GX.
BURGESS, Mrs. Helen Alice, MA ACA *2000;* Moss Construction, 96 Leckhampton Road, CHELTENHAM, GLOUCESTERSHIRE, GL53 0BP.
BURGESS, Mr. Ian Jeffrey, MA ACA *1987;* Flat 181 Cranmer Court, Whiteheads Grove, LONDON, SW3 3HG.

BURGESS, Mr. Ian Spencer, FCA AMCT *1995;* Strategic Finance 9th Floor, The Royal Bank of Scotland Plc, 280 Bishopsgate, LONDON, EC2M 4RB.

BURGESS, Mr. Ian Stuart, FCA *1981;* 58 Manor Wood Road, PURLEY, CR8 4LF.

BURGESS, Mrs. Jane Alison Claire, BA ACA *1989;* Prospect House, 29 Common Road, Dunnington, YORK, YO19 5NG.

BURGESS, Miss. Joanna Katie, BSc ACA *2006;* with Deloitte LLP, Hill House, 1 Little New Street, LONDON, EC4A 3TR.

BURGESS, Mr. John, FCA *1959;* 33 Richmond Lane, ROMSEY, SO51 7LB. (Life Member)

BURGESS, Mr. Julian Alexander, BSc ACA *2004;* 66 Turning Lane, SOUTHPORT, MERSEYSIDE, PR8 5HY.

BURGESS, Ms. Kate, ACA *2010;* Rockspring PIM LLP, 166 Sloane Street, LONDON, SW1X 9QF.

•**BURGESS, Mr. Keith, FCA** *1974;* KB Accountancy Services Ltd, Swan Meadow Cottage, Mere Lake Road, Talke, STOKE-ON-TRENT, ST7 1UE.

BURGESS, Mr. Laurence Edward, MA FCA *1983;* Monk Soham House The Green, Monk Soham, WOODBRIDGE, SUFFOLK, IP13 7ET.

•**BURGESS, Mr. Leslie, FCA** *1953;* Leslie Burgess, 87 Shirley Avenue, CROYDON, CR0 8SP.

BURGESS, Mrs. Marie Angele, FCA *1980;* Camp Wiehe, GRAND BAY, MAURITIUS.

BURGESS, Mr. Mark Geoffrey William, BA ACA *1983;* 10 Fairbairn Road, TOORAK, VIC 3142, AUSTRALIA.

•**BURGESS, Mr. Mark Lee, ACA ACCA** *2007;* Simpson Burgess Nash Ltd, Ground Floor, Maclaren House, Lancastrian Office Centre, Talbot Road, Old Trafford MANCHESTER M32 0FP. See also Dialmode (328) Limited

BURGESS, Mr. Martin Frank, BA ACA *1988;* Llwyndewi, Capel Dewi, CARMARTHEN, SA32 8AE.

BURGESS, Mr. Martin Simon, MA BA ACA *2002;* with National Audit Office, 157-197 Buckingham Palace Road, Victoria, LONDON, SW1W 9SP.

BURGESS, Mr. Matthew, MA(Cantab) BSc ACA *1996;* 148 Vinery Road, CAMBRIDGE, CB1 3DT.

BURGESS, Mr. Matthew Michael, BSc ACA *1992;* 4 Lawrence Close, Charlton Kings, CHELTENHAM, GL52 6NN.

BURGESS, Mr. Michael Alan, ACA *2008;* 54 Souldern Way, STOKE-ON-TRENT, ST3 1TN.

BURGESS, Mr. Michael John, ACA *1986;* Kemp Chatteris Deloitte, 7th. Floor, Raffles Tower, 19 Cybercity, EBENE, MAURITIUS.

BURGESS, Mr. Michael John, ACA *1980;* 63 Inkerman Drive, Hazlemere, HIGH WYCOMBE, HP15 7JJ.

BURGESS, Mr. Michael John Stephen, BA FCA *1974;* 36 Ham Street, RICHMOND, TW10 7HT.

BURGESS, Mr. Michael Stuart, FCA *1975;* The Old Stables Crugsillick, Ruan High Lanes, TRURO, CORNWALL, TR2 5LJ.

BURGESS, Mrs. Naina, BSc ACA *1993;* 20 Downfield Road, BRISTOL, BS8 2TJ.

BURGESS, Mr. Neil Jonathon, BSc ACA *1993;* 146 High Street, Wollaston, STOURBRIDGE, WEST MIDLANDS, DY8 4PE.

BURGESS, Mr. Nicholas Neil, LLB ACA *1989;* 31 Valley Road, West Bridgford, NOTTINGHAM, NG2 6HG.

BURGESS, Mrs. Penelope Suzanne, LLB ACA *1992;* 1 Georges Square, Bath Street, BRISTOL, BS1 6BA.

•**BURGESS, Mr. Peter John, FCA** *1982;* (Tax Fac), Peter J. Burgess, 113 High Street, Yelling, ST. NEOTS, PE19 6SB.

BURGESS, Ms. Rachel Anne, BMus ACA *2001;* 97 Finchampstead Road, WOKINGHAM, BERKSHIRE, RG41 2PE.

BURGESS, Mr. Richard Anthony, MA FCA *1978;* 27 Wicks Lane, LIVERPOOL, L37 3JF.

BURGESS, Mr. Richard Samuel, LLB ACA *1982;* 130 St. Vincent Street, GLASGOW, G2 5HF.

BURGESS, Mrs. Rima, BCom ACA *1997;* (Tax Fac), KBC House, K B C Process Technology Ltd, 42-50 Hersham Road, WALTON-ON-THAMES, SURREY, KT12 1RZ.

BURGESS, Mr. Robert Herbert Thomas, ED FCA *1937;* 23 Halyards, Topsham, EXETER, EX3 0JU. (Life Member)

BURGESS, Mr. Robert John, BSc ACA *1991;* Firs Cottage, Wells Way, Blackford, WEDMORE, BS28 4NE.

BURGESS, Mrs. Sian, ACA *2008;* 6 Third Avenue, Chadwell Heath, ROMFORD, RM6 5DB.

•**BURGESS, Mr. Steven, ACA** *1993;* S Burgess & Co, 11 Slayleigh Avenue, Fulwood, SHEFFIELD, S10 3RA.

BURGESS, Mr. Steven James, ACA *2009;* Unit 1 Claydon Business Park, Great Blakenham, IPSWICH, IP6 0NL.

BURGESS, Mrs. Susan, BA ACA *1988;* 15 Church Lane, Upton by Chester, CHESTER, CH2 1DJ.

BURGESS, Miss. Susan, ACA *1992;* 22 Tyburn Lane, Pulloxhill, BEDFORD, MK45 5HG.

•**BURGESS, Mr. Thomas Edward, MA ACA** *1983;* Tom Burgess, 27 Ellesmere Road, Uphill, WESTON-SUPER-MARE, AVON, BS23 4UT.

BURGESS, Mr. Trevor Herbert, FCA *1956;* The Barns, Clifton Court Clifton, Severn Stoke, WORCESTER, WR8 9JF. (Life Member)

BURGHALL, Miss. Catherine Elizabeth, BA ACA *2007;* 138 Causeway Head Road, SHEFFIELD, S17 3DZ.

BURGHAM, Mr. Tim, MEng ACA *2007;* Flat 2, Yarrell Mansions, Queen's Club Gardens, LONDON, W14 9TB.

BURGIN, Mr. Adrian Gwyn John, FCA *1973;* 5 Hall Farm Rise, Cawthorpe, BOURNE, LINCOLNSHIRE, PE10 0AW. (Life Member)

•**BURGIN, Mr. Alistair David, BSc ACA** *1985;* Burgin & Co, Artichoke House, 11 Swinegate, GRANTHAM, LINCOLNSHIRE, NG31 6RJ. See also D Burgin Limited

BURGIN, Mr. Andrew Philip, BA ACA *1991;* Unit B 16th Floor W Square 314-324 Hennessy Road, WAN CHAI, HONG KONG SAR.

BURGIN, Mr. Denis Albert, FCA *1953;* 1 Branston Close, Winthorpe, NEWARK, NG24 2PQ. (Life Member)

•**BURGIN, Mr. Kenneth Richard, FCA** *1964;* K.R. Burgin, 1 Nightjar Close, Ewshot, FARNHAM, SURREY, GU10 5TQ.

BURGIN, Miss. Marie Anne, BA ACA *2007;* 143C, Offord Road, LONDON, N1 1LR.

BURGIN, Miss. Michele Claudia, BSc ACA *1992;* (Tax Fac), 11 Colless Road, Seven Sisters, LONDON, N15 4NR.

BURGIN, Mr. Neil, BSc ACA *2000;* 9 Brethergate, Westwoodside, DONCASTER, SOUTH YORKSHIRE, DN9 2AU.

•**BURGIN, Mr. Neil Andrew, BA FCA** *1985;* Cobb Burgin & Co, 129a Middleton Boulevard, Wollaton Park, NOTTINGHAM, NG8 1FW.

BURGIN, Mrs. Rebecca Elizabeth, BA ACA *1984;* The Pike Lock House, Eastington, STONEHOUSE, GL10 3RT.

BURGOINE, Mr. John Keith, FCA *1963;* (Tax Fac), 6 Ashley Court, Shipston Road, STRATFORD-UPON-AVON, WARWICKSHIRE, CV37 7PY. (Life Member)

BURGON, Mr. James David, BA ACA *1995;* Exposure Promotions Ltd, 22-23 Little Portland Street, LONDON, W1W 8BU.

BURGON, Mrs. Jean, ACA *1992;* 10 Partridge Way, OAKHAM, LE15 6BX.

BURGOYNE, Mr. David George, BA FCA *1955;* 3 The Fort, The Esplanade, SIDMOUTH, DEVON, EX10 8NS. (Life Member)

BURGOYNE, Mr. Jack, FCA *1952;* 12 Tapton Crescent Road, SHEFFIELD, S10 5DA. (Life Member)

BURGOYNE, Miss. Jane Elizabeth, BA(Hons) ACA *2000;* 27 Hill Street Totterdown, BRISTOL, BS3 4TW.

BURGUM, Miss. Kathleen Joy, FCA *1968;* 56 Auburn Road, HEALESVILLE, VIC 3777, AUSTRALIA.

BURHAN, Mr. Eric B R, BSc ACA *1982;* Taman Permata Buana, JL Buana Biru Besar II/24, JAKARTA, 11610, INDONESIA.

•**BURIAN, Mr. Alastair Stephen, BA FCA** *1977;* Coachman's Cottage, 2 Old Wells Road, GLASTONBURY, BA6 8EB.

BURKE, Mr. Anthony Dominic, ACA *2007;* 13 Greenfield Close, Westhoughton, BOLTON, BL5 3UU.

•**BURKE, Mr. Brian Michael, BA FCA** *1984;* (Tax Fac), Ashleys (Hitchin) Limited, Invision House, Wilbury Way, HITCHIN, HERTFORDSHIRE, SG4 0TY. See also Ashleys

BURKE, Miss. Catherine Jane, BSc ACA *1993;* 39, Sterndale Road, LONDON, W14 0HT.

BURKE, Mr. Christopher Michael, MA FCA *1971;* 27 Trefonwys, BANGOR, GWYNEDD, LL57 2HU.

BURKE, Mr. Cian David, BSc ACA *1992;* Rosehill London Road, Cuckfield, HAYWARDS HEATH, WEST SUSSEX, RH17 5EU.

BURKE, Mr. Colin John, BSc ACA *1988;* 18 Rutlish Road, LONDON, SW19 3AL.

BURKE, Mr. Daniel, ACA *2011;* 13a North Villas, Camden, LONDON, NW1 9BJ.

BURKE, Mr. Daniel Edmund, BAcc ACA *2005;* with Robertshaw Myers, Number 3, Acorn Business Park, Keighley Road, SKIPTON, NORTH YORKSHIRE BD23 2UE.

•**BURKE, Mr. Daniel Shaun, BA(Hons) ACA** *2003;* BSG Valentine, Lynton House, 7/12 Tavistock Square, LONDON, WC1H 9BQ.

BURKE, Mr. Daniel Thomas, MSc FCA *1987;* 5 Wigmore Place, LONDON, W1U 2LR.

BURKE, Mr. David Anthony, BA ACA *1992;* 133 Laburnum, Sushant Lok 1, GURGAON 122002, HARYANA, INDIA.

BURKE, Mr. David James, BSc ACA *1985;* 18 Hill View Drive, WELLING, KENT, DA16 3RS.

BURKE, Mr. David Macduff, FCA *1972;* Dunford House, Guildford Road, Ottershaw, CHERTSEY, KT16 0QW.

BURKE, Mr. Denis Richard, BSc ACA *1997;* with BDO LLP, 1 Bridgewater Place, Water Lane, LEEDS, LS11 5RU.

BURKE, Mr. Edmond Noel, FCA *1973;* Alpenstrasse 5, Postfach 2114, 8600 DUBENDORF, SWITZERLAND.

BURKE, Mrs. Erica Lynne, BSc ACA *1994;* Novo Nordisk Ltd Broadfield Park, Brighton Road Pease Pottage, CRAWLEY, WEST SUSSEX, RH11 9RT.

BURKE, Mrs. Fiona Janet, BA ACA *1988;* 58 Lynwood Grove, ORPINGTON, BR6 0BH.

BURKE, Mr. Gerald John, FCA *1950;* The Pool House, 9 Oval Way, GERRARDS CROSS, SL9 8PY. (Life Member)

BURKE, Mr. Gerald Michael, BSc FCA *1976;* (Tax Fac), 2 Swans Court, Twyford, READING, RG10 0AZ.

BURKE, Miss. Geraldine, MSci ACA *2011;* 12 Sherwood Road, BIRMINGHAM, B28 0HB.

BURKE, Mr. Harold Max, FCA *1965;* Splugenstrasse 10, 8002 ZURICH, SWITZERLAND.

BURKE, Mr. James, MA ACA *2003;* 49 Silver Street, Ashwell, BALDOCK, HERTFORDSHIRE, SG7 5QL.

BURKE, Mr. Jeffrey, BA FCA *1955;* 10 Beacon Heights, Point Clear, CLACTON-ON-SEA, CO16 8JW. (Life Member)

BURKE, Mrs. Jennifer, ACA *1982;* 115 Torrington Park, Finchley, LONDON, N12 9PN.

BURKE, Mr. Kevin Aubrey Francis, FCA *1970;* Westland Farm, Foxhill, PETWORTH, GU28 9NU.

BURKE, Dr. Lisa Marie, BSc(Hons) ACA *2002;* 80 Norton Road, READING, RG1 3QJ.

•**BURKE, Mr. Malcolm Peter, FCA** *1980;* Ernst & Young LLP, 1 More London Place, LONDON, SE1 2AF. See also Ernst & Young Europe LLP

BURKE, Mrs. Meeka, BSc ACA *1982;* 11 Belvedere Grove, Wimbledon, LONDON, SW19 7RQ.

•**BURKE, Mr. Michael Joseph, BSc FCA** *1983;* Michael Burke & Company Limited, 12 Littleworth Road, ESHER, SURREY, KT10 9PD.

BURKE, Miss. Nicola, BA(Hons) ACA *2003;* 2 Hazelwood, DONABATE, COUNTY DUBLIN, IRELAND.

BURKE, Mr. Paul, BA ACA *2005;* 124 Max Road, LIVERPOOL, L14 4BJ.

BURKE, Mr. Peter Robert, BA ACA *1981;* 11 Belvedere Grove, Wimbledon, LONDON, SW19 7RQ.

BURKE, Miss. Rebecca, BSc ACA *2006;* Flat 7, Oak House, Manor Road, SIDCUP, KENT, DA15 7HX.

BURKE, Mr. Richard Rickard, FCA *1967;* Manulife Securities Inc., 463 Belleville Street, VICTORIA V8V 1X3, BC, CANADA.

BURKE, Mrs. Sarah Louise Jane, BSc(Hons) ACA *2002;* Manley Cottage 47 Manley Road, ILKLEY, WEST YORKSHIRE, LS29 8QP.

•**BURKE, Mr. Stephen John James, BSc FCA** *1989;* I M S Consulting Ltd, 3 Tenterden Street, LONDON, W1S 1TD.

BURKE, Mr. Stephen Martin Patrick, BA(Hons) ACA *2003;* Building 178, Honeywell Aerosoace, Bunford Lane, YEOVIL, SOMERSET, BA20 2YD.

BURKE, Mr. Stephen Pierre, BSc ACA *1987;* 18 Bridge Island, Shotley Bridge, CONSETT, COUNTY DURHAM, DH8 9TB.

BURKE, Mrs. Tara Dawn, BSc ACA *2004;* 3 Railway Terrace, KINGS LANGLEY, HERTFORDSHIRE, WD4 8JB.

BURKELL, Mrs. Catherine Celia, BSc ACA *1993;* ATB Financial, 5th Floor9888 Jasper Avenue, EDMONTON T5J 1P1, AB, CANADA.

BURKHILL, Miss. Laura Jennifer, MEng ACA *2003;* C S First Credit Suisse Financial Products, 1 Cabot Square, LONDON, E14 4QJ.

BURKILL, Mr. Jonathan, MA BSc ACA *2011;* 10c-10d Oakfield Road, Clifton, BRISTOL, BS8 2AW.

•**BURKIMSHER, Mr. Richard Mark, BA FCA** *1989;* Hawsons, Jubilee House, 32 Duncan Close, Moulton Park, NORTHAMPTON, NN3 6WL.

BURKINSHAW, Mrs. Lynda Jane, BA FCA CTA *1996;* (Tax Fac), 16 Salters Way, Penistone, SHEFFIELD, S36 6UE.

BURKINSHAW, Mrs. Marie Jane, BSc ACA *2004;* Finance Directorate, Sheffield Hallam University Registry, City Campus Howard Street, SHEFFIELD, S1 1WB.

BURKINSHAW, Mr. Norman Bloor, FCA *1952;* 33 Burnt Stones Drive, SHEFFIELD, S10 5TT. (Life Member)

•①**BURKINSHAW, Mr. Stephen John, FCA FABRP** *1975;* H R Harris & Partners (2010) Limited, 44 St. Helens Road, SWANSEA, SA1 4BB. See also H R Harris & Partners Ltd

•**BURKITT, Mr. Jason, ACA** *2007;* PricewaterhouseCoopers LLP, 1 Embankment Place, LONDON, WC2N 6RH. See also PricewaterhouseCoopers

BURKITT, Mrs. Tiffani Chow Nuan Yin, BSc ACA *2007;* Flat 41 Geneva Court, 2 Rookery Way, LONDON, NW9 6GA.

BURKS, Mr. Nicholas Ralph, MA ACA *1987;* Crumbleigh Corners 18 Bridge Street Great Harwood, BLACKBURN, BB6 7NQ.

BURLES, Mr. Victor, FCA *1965;* 6 Manor Court, Stoke Fleming, DARTMOUTH, TQ6 0PG. (Life Member)

BURLEY, Mr. Andrew Thomas, BA ACA *2008;* 10 Harwood Terrace, LONDON, SW6 2AB.

•**BURLEY, Mr. Anthony John, FCA** *1959;* 18 Markwells, Elsenham, BISHOP'S STORTFORD, HERTFORDSHIRE, CM22 6LT.

BURLEY, Mr. Brian Godfrey, FCA *1966;* Apartment 3 Wellingtonia House, Hellyer Close, NORTH FERRIBY, NORTH HUMBERSIDE, HU14 3JD.

BURLEY, Mr. Graham John, BA(Hons) ACA *2004;* 12 The Dell, Westbury-on-Trym, BRISTOL, BS9 3UD.

•**BURLEY, Mr. Ian Douglas, BSc FCA** *1989;* Cadwallader & Co Llp, Eagle House, 25 Severn Street, WELSHPOOL, POWYS, SY21 7AD.

BURLEY, Miss. Jane Elizabeth, BA ACA *1988;* 165 Bannerdale Road, SHEFFIELD, S7 2DS.

•**BURLEY, Mr. Philip Nigel, FCA** *1972;* (Tax Fac), with Philip Burley (Whitby) Limited, 28 Bagdale, WHITBY, YO21 1QL.

BURLEY, Mr. Simon John, ACA *1990;* Hugo de Vrieslaan 16, 2341 NT OEGSTGEEST, NETHERLANDS.

BURLING, Miss. Sandra Caroline, BA ACA *1986;* 27 Calonne Road, Wimbledon, LONDON, SW19 5HH.

BURLINGHAM, Mrs. Patricia Mary, MA FCA *1951;* Springbank, Fladbury, PERSHORE, WR10 2QA. (Life Member)

BURLINGTON, Mr. Nicholas Peter, ACA *2008;* Flat 28/A Cyril Mansions, Prince of Wales Drive, LONDON, SW11 4HP.

•**BURLISON, Mr. David John, BSc ACA ACCA** *1999;* KPMG Europe LLP, 15 Canada Square, LONDON, E14 5GL. See also KPMG LLP

BURLISON, Mr. Michael, MA ACA *1988;* (Tax Fac), Canadel Lodge, 12 Warwick Crescent, HARROGATE, HG2 8JA.

BURLISON, Mrs. Paula Jane, BA ACA *1989;* 12 Warwick Crescent, HARROGATE, NORTH YORKSHIRE, HG2 8JA.

BURLISTON, Mr. Paul William, BA(Hons) ACA *2003;* 23 Station Road, Heddon-on-the-Wall, NEWCASTLE UPON TYNE, NE15 0DY.

BURLTON, Mr. Christopher John, BSc ACA *1999;* 6 Grangeside, DARLINGTON, COUNTY DURHAM, DL3 8QJ.

BURMAN, Mr. Andrew Marc, BSc ACA MBA *2004;* (Tax Fac), 12 Cullera Close, NORTHWOOD, MIDDLESEX, HA6 3SE.

•**BURMAN, Mrs. Anna Elizabeth, BA ACA** *1995;* 9 Alfriston Road, LONDON, SW11 6NS.

•**BURMAN, Mr. Christopher Edward James, FCA** *1969;* Christopher E.J. Burman FCA, Ardmhor House, 3 The Paddocks, Ampfield, ROMSEY, HAMPSHIRE SO51 9BG.

BURMAN, Mr. Cyril, FCA *1955;* 4 Evanston Gardens, Redbridge, ILFORD, IG4 5AF. (Life Member)

•**BURMAN, Mr. David Richard, ACA** *1978;* Burman & Co, Brunswick Hse, Birmingham Rd, REDDITCH, B97 6DY.

BURMAN, Mr. Grahame Gary, FCA *1976;* Priority Protect Ltd, 4 Royal Mint Court, LONDON, EC3N 4HJ.

BURMAN, Mr. Jonathan Eliot, BSc(Econ) ACA *1999;* Volkswagen Group UK Ltd Yeomans Drive, Blakelands, MILTON KEYNES, MK14 5AN.

•**BURMAN, Mr. Nicholas William Edwin Selby, BSc FCA** *1979;* 4 Hawkshead Street, SOUTHPORT, MERSEYSIDE, PR9 9HF.

BURMAN, Mr. Paul Robert James, FCA *1972;* Trentham House 40-42 Red Lion Street Alvechurch, BIRMINGHAM, B48 7LF.

BURMAN, Mr. Robin Jonathan, BA ACA *1991;* RPM Ltd, The Old Treacle Factory, 24-40 Goodwin Road, LONDON, W12 9JW.

BURMAN, Mr. Roger James, FCA *1974;* 41 Lawfield Avenue, WEST KILBRIDE, AYRSHIRE, KA23 9DQ.

BURMAN, Mrs. Shan Tracy, BCom ACA *1997;* Atkins Ltd, Shared Services Ltd, 1 Kings Court Business Park, Charles Hastings Way, WORCESTER, WR5 1WS.

•**BURN, Mr. Andrew, BA ACA** *1980;* Denzel Paddocks, Crowcombe Heathfield, TAUNTON, TA4 4BS.

BURN, Mr. Andrew James Sebastian, BA(Hons) ACA *2000;* K P M G, St. James's Square, MANCHESTER, M2 6DW.
BURN, Mr. Anthony John, ACA *1982;* Larchwood, Gasden Copse, Witley, GODALMING, GU8 5QD.
BURN, Mr. Bryan Adrian Falconer, FCA *1968;* 13 Woodthorpe Road, Putney, LONDON, SW15 6UQ.
BURN, Miss. Charlotte Emma, BA ACA *2010;* 43 Perpetual House, Station Road, HENLEY-ON-THAMES, OXFORDSHIRE, RG9 1AT.
BURN, Mr. Christopher Charles, FCA *1964;* Old Joiners Shop, The Green, Skirling by Biggar, BIGGAR, LANARKSHIRE, ML12 6HD.
BURN, Miss. Claire Louise, BSc ACA *2010;* 7 Maypole Mews, Barwick in Elmet, LEEDS, LS15 4PE.
BURN, Mrs. Claire Melanie, BSc ACA ATII *1992;* 15 Cuxhaven Way, Saxonfields, ANDOVER, SP10 4LN.
•**BURN, Mr. David Jeffrey, BA ACA** *1985;* PricewaterhouseCoopers LLP, 101 Barbirolli Square, Lower Mosley Street, MANCHESTER, M2 3PW. See also PricewaterhouseCoopers
BURN, Mr. Geoffrey Robert, FCA *1973;* Hillview, Molesworth, HUNTINGDON, PE28 0QD.
BURN, Mrs. Gillian, BSc ACA *1989;* The Sycamores, Little Acre, BRIDGEND, MID GLAMORGAN, CF35 5BT.
BURN, Mrs. Joanna, BA ACA *1990;* Penny Moon, Goshen, ST. AGNES, CORNWALL, TR5 0QB.
BURN, Mr. Raymond John, FCA *1966;* Downwood, Dusthouse Lane, Finstall, BROMSGROVE, B60 3AE. (Life Member)
BURN, Mr. Richard Edward, FCA *1960;* St. Anthonys, High Street, Burwash, ETCHINGHAM, EAST SUSSEX, TN19 7EN.
BURNAL, Mr. Mark, BSc ACA *2003;* 91 South View Drive, South Woodford, LONDON, E18 1NR.
BURNAND, Miss. Nicola Jane, BA ACA *1995;* 34 Six Acres, Slinfold, HORSHAM, WEST SUSSEX, RH13 0TH.
•**BURNAND, Mr. Robert George, BA ACA CTA** *1986;* R. G. Burnand & Co, Suite 4, Thamesbourne Lodge, Station Road, BOURNE END, BUCKINGHAMSHIRE SL8 5QH.
•**BURNARD, Mr. Ivan Leslie, BSc ACA** *1989;* Francis Clark, North Quay House, Sutton Harbour, PLYMOUTH, PL4 0RA. See also Francis Clark LLP
BURNARD, Mrs. Karen Louise, ACA *1995;* Allweathers, Carkeel, SALTASH, CORNWALL, PL12 6PH.
•**BURNARD, Mr. Paul Martin, FCA** *1979;* BDO Limited, PO Box 180, Place du Pre, Rue du Pre, St Peter Port, GUERNSEY GY1 3LL.
BURNDRED, Mr. David John, BA FCA *1988;* 3 Braemar Close, GODALMING, GU7 1SA.
BURNDRED, Mr. George William, FCA *1960;* New Pools Cottage, Tirley, GLOUCESTER, GL19 4EU.
BURNE, Mr. Ross Alexander Houlihan, BA(Hons) ACA *2002;* 9/2 Munro Street, MCMAHONS POINT, NSW 2060, AUSTRALIA.
BURNELL, Miss. Alison Christie, ACA *1996;* Danecroft, School Road, Great Barton, BURY ST. EDMUNDS, IP31 2RJ.
BURNELL, Mr. Christopher William Edward, ACA *2009;* 14 Lancaster Mews, LONDON, SW18 1BA.
•**BURNELL, Mr. Mark Anthony, BSc ACA** *1989;* Pells, 1 Derby Road, Eastwood, NOTTINGHAM, NG16 3PA. See also T Wilford Pell & Company
BURNELL, Mrs. Naomi, ACA *2009;* 81 Graham Way, Cotford St. Luke, TAUNTON, SOMERSET, TA4 1JG.
BURNELL, Mr. Roger Douglas, BSc FCA *1974;* Marraway House, Heath End, Snitter Field, STRATFORD-UPON-AVON, CV37 0PL.
•**BURNELL, Mr. Stuart Willis, FCA** *1989;* Willis Burnell Ltd, Spectrum House, Bromells Road, LONDON, SW4 0BN.
BURNELL, Mrs. Susan, BA ACA *1992;* 18 Manor Park, TUNBRIDGE WELLS, TN4 8XP.
BURNET, Mr. Andrew Travers De Jersey, BSc ACA *1993;* Chococo, 21c Commercial Road, SWANAGE, BH19 1DF.
BURNET, Miss. Carla Jane, BA ACA *2010;* 6 The Bartletts, Hamble, SOUTHAMPTON, SO31 4RP.
BURNETT, Mr. Alistair Mark, BA ACA *1998;* 21 Willingham Way, Kirk Ella, HULL, HU10 7NL.
BURNETT, Mr. Andrew David, BA ACA *1990;* 25 Ennismore Green, Hedley Rise, LUTON, LU2 8UP.
•**BURNETT, Mr. Andrew Richard, BA ACA** *1992;* Royce Peeling Green Limited, The Copper Room, Deva Centre, Trinity Way, MANCHESTER, M3 7BG.
•**BURNETT, Mrs. Ann Kathleen, ACA** *1992;* Ann Burnett ACA, 23 Tanfield Drive, Burley in Wharfedale, ILKLEY, WEST YORKSHIRE, LS29 7RT.
BURNETT, Mr. Christopher James, BA ACA *1992;* 3 Fern Circuit, Warriewood, SYDNEY, NSW 2102, AUSTRALIA.
BURNETT, Mr. Clive Ashley, BA ACA *1998;* Briar Bank, 74 Whalley Road, Wilpshire, BLACKBURN, LANCASHIRE, BB1 9LF.
BURNETT, Mr. Darren Michael, BSc(Hons) ACA *2001;* 24 Albert Gardens, HARLOW, CM17 9QF.
BURNETT, Mrs. Eleanor Mary, LLB ACA *1999;* 43 Binswood Avenue Headington, OXFORD, OX3 8NY.
BURNETT, Mr. Ernest John, FCA CTA *1955;* Flat 21, 4 Grand Avenue, HOVE, EAST SUSSEX, BN3 2LD. (Life Member)
BURNETT, Mr. Graham George, BA ACA *2006;* Mazars Tower Bridge House, St. Katharines Way, LONDON, E1W 1DD.
BURNETT, Mr. Hugh Thomas, FCA *1966;* 36 Wilbury Villas, HOVE, BN3 6GD. (Life Member)
BURNETT, Mr. Ian, BSc ACA *1980;* 18 Heys Close, ROSSENDALE, LANCASHIRE, BB4 7LW.
•**BURNETT, Mr. James Angus, ACA** *1994;* Martin and Company, 25 St Thomas Street, WINCHESTER, SO23 9HJ. See also Martin and Company Accountants Limited
BURNETT, Mr. John Drew, BSc ACA *1987;* Universal Group Direct, 76 Oxford Street, LONDON, W1D 1BS.
•**BURNETT, Mr. Leslie Michael, BA FCA CTA** *1980;* Francis Clark LLP, Sigma House, Oak View Close, Edginswell Park, TORQUAY, TQ2 7FF. See also Francis Clark Tax Consultancy Ltd
BURNETT, Ms. Lorraine Margaret Elizabeth, BA(Hons) ACA *2000;* 5 Rosebrook, Dungiven, LONDONDERRY, BT47 4GA.
BURNETT, Mrs. Louisa Marie, BA(Hons) ACA *2003;* 22 Chilgrove Road, PORTSMOUTH, PO6 2ER.
•**BURNETT, Mr. Mark Peter, ACA** *1988;* Moore Stephens, 30 Gay Street, BATH, BA1 2PA.
BURNETT, Mr. Michael John, BA FCA *1979;* 7 Spinney Drive, Cheswick Green Shirley, SOLIHULL, B90 4HB.
BURNETT, Mr. Michael Peter, BSc FCA *1988;* 4 Jarombek Drive, TOWACO, NJ 07082, UNITED STATES.
BURNETT, Mr. Peter, FCA *1951;* Old Brook Cottage, Danehill, HAYWARDS HEATH, RH17 7HP. (Life Member)
BURNETT, Mr. Peter Frederic, FCA *1975;* Bramleys, Bath Road, Langford, BRISTOL, BS40 5DN.
BURNETT, Mr. Peter William, MA ACA *1989;* Flat 2/E, Grenville House, 1 Magazine Gap Road, MID LEVELS, HONG KONG SAR.
BURNETT, Dr. Richard David, BSc ACA MBA *1993;* Hill House, West Burton, LEYBURN, NORTH YORKSHIRE, DL8 4JN.
BURNETT, Mr. Robert Andrew, FCA *1965;* The Old Granary, 24 High Street, Odiham, HOOK, RG29 1LG. (Life Member)
BURNETT, Mr. Robert Kenneth, MA FCA *1973;* Flat 5, 86 Addison Road, LONDON, W14 8ED.
BURNETT, Mr. Robert Paul, FCA *1965;* Anstey, Chichester Road, West Wittering, CHICHESTER, PO20 8QA.
BURNETT, Mr. Stephen Andrew, BSc FCA *1986;* Hunters Lodge, Station Road, Claverdon, WARWICK, CV35 8PE.
BURNETT, Mr. Stuart Mathieson, FCA MBA *1970;* Braeside House, 13 Braeside Road, Green Point, CAPE TOWN, WESTERN CAPE PROVINCE, 8005 SOUTH AFRICA.
BURNETT, Mrs. Susan Verona, BA ACA *1991;* 25 Ennismore Green, Hedley Rise, LUTON, LU2 8UP.
BURNETT-HURST, Mr. Clive Robert, FCA *1958;* Hedgerows, Tanfield Nook, Parbold, WIGAN, LANCASHIRE, WN8 7DQ. (Life Member)
BURNEY, Mr. Sohail Anwar, ACA *1995;* 26 Abbotts Drive, WEMBLEY, HA0 3SD.
BURNEY, Mr. Syed Shahid Muzaffar, FCA *1974;* 14 Woodleigh Avenue, Friern Barnet, LONDON, N12 0LL.
BURNEY, Mr. William Hugh, FCA *1972;* 9 Emmanuel Road, SUTTON COLDFIELD, B73 5LY.
BURNFORD, Mr. Andrew Philip, MA ACA *1995;* Church Cottage Church Street, Kelvedon, COLCHESTER, CO5 9AL.
BURNFORD, Miss. Antonia, ACA *2008;* Flat 10, Belgravia Court, 33 Ebury Street, LONDON, SW1W 0NY.
BURNHAM, Mr. Andrew Carl, MEng ACA *1997;* 3 Cedar Green, SOUTHWELL, NOTTINGHAMSHIRE, NG25 0FJ.
•**BURNHAM, Mr. Andrew Ernest, FCA** *1986;* MacIntyre Hudson LLP, New Bridge Street House, 30-34 New Bridge Street, LONDON, EC4V 6BJ.
BURNHAM, Mr. David Gordon, BA FCA *1968;* Carleton Lodge, 48 Shorton Road, PAIGNTON, TQ3 1RG. (Life Member)
BURNHAM, Mrs. Deborah, BA ACA *1989;* Langdon West Williams, Curzon House, 24 High Street, BANSTEAD, SURREY, SM7 2LJ.
BURNHAM, Ms. Debra Kay, BSc ACA *1987;* Eichenstrasse 23, 61476 KRONBERG, GERMANY.
•**BURNHAM, Mr. Douglas Patrick, BSc ACA** *1994;* Ernst & Young S R O, Karlovo Namesti 10, 12000 PRAGUE, CZECH REPUBLIC. See also Ernst & Young Europe LLP
BURNHAM, Mrs. Elizabeth, BSc ACA *1978;* 5 Morven Close, POTTERS BAR, HERTFORDSHIRE, EN6 5HE.
•**BURNHAM, Mr. Graeme Michael, BA ACA** *1999;* (Tax Fac), Complete Tax Solutions, Second Floor, Cardiff House, Tilling Road, LONDON, NW2 1LJ. See also Complete Audit and Accounting Solutions Ltd
BURNHAM, Mr. Ian John, FCA *1976;* 47 Salisbury Road, ANDOVER, SP10 2JN.
BURNHAM, Mrs. Malin, ACA *2008;* Pricewaterhousecoopers Llp Marlborough Court, 10 Bricket Road, ST. ALBANS, HERTFORDSHIRE, AL1 3JX.
BURNHAM, Miss. Natalie Helen, BSc ARCS ACA *2005;* 55 Ripplevale Grove, LONDON, N1 1HS.
BURNHAM, Mr. Nigel John, MA ACA *1990;* 51 Kenilworth Avenue, Wimbledon, LONDON, SW19 7LP.
•**BURNHAM, Mrs. Patricia Ann, FCA** *1977;* (Tax Fac), Hillier Hopkins LLP, 64 Clarendon Road, WATFORD, WD17 1DA. See also HH Accounting & Tax Solutions Limited
BURNHAM, Mr. Peter Michael, BA FCA JDipMA *1959;* The Old Coach House Sheep Lane Midhurst, Old Coach House, Sheep Lane, MIDHURST, WEST SUSSEX, GU29 9NT. (Life Member)
BURNHAM, Mr. Stephen Paul, BSc(Hons) ACA *2001;* 22 Allen Avenue, Quorn, LOUGHBOROUGH, LEICESTERSHIRE, LE12 8TR.
BURNHOPE, Mr. Mark Edward, BCom ACA *1985;* Wallington House, 113 Stafford Road, WALSALL, WS3 3PG.
•**BURNHOPE, Mr. Stuart Derek, BSc ACA** *1997;* Deloitte LLP, Global House, High Street, CRAWLEY, RH10 1DL. See also Deloitte & Touche LLP
BURNIE, Mr. David, BA ACA *1981;* 107 Elibank Road, Eltham, LONDON, SE9 1QJ.
•**BURNIE, Mr. Joseph Robert, BSc ACA** *1985;* (Tax Fac), Baker Tilly Tax & Advisory Services LLP, The Clock House, 140 London Road, GUILDFORD, SURREY, GU1 1UW.
BURNLEY, Mr. Ian David, MA ACA *1988;* 1 The Paddocks, Blackmore Way Wheathampstead, ST. ALBANS, HERTFORDSHIRE, AL4 8HE.
BURNLEY, Mr. Martyn James, FCA *1985;* Flat 12, 14 Rectory Road, BECKENHAM, KENT, BR3 1HW.
BURNS, Mr. Alan, BA ACA *1996;* Reckitt Benckiser Plc, 103-105 Bath Road, SLOUGH, SL1 3UH.
BURNS, Mr. Alan George, BSc ACA *2000;* Glaxo Smithkline, G S K House, 980 Great West Road, BRENTFORD, MIDDLESEX, TW8 9GS.
BURNS, Mr. Alan Robert, BA FCA *1999;* 125 Stapleton Hall Road, LONDON, N4 4RB.
BURNS, Mrs. Amanda Jane, ACA *1991;* 22 Kingsend, RUISLIP, MIDDLESEX, HA4 7DA.
BURNS, Mr. Andrew Rae, BSc ACA *1989;* 11 Glebe Avenue, ENFIELD, EN2 8NZ.
BURNS, Mr. Brian Francis, MA FCA *1967;* Coldwell Brook, Shipton Road, Ascott-under-Wychwood, CHIPPING NORTON, OX7 6AG.
BURNS, Mr. Christopher, ACA *2011;* 128 Gunners Road, Shoeburyness, SOUTHEND-ON-SEA, SS3 9SB.
•**BURNS, Mr. Christopher John, BCom ACA** *1996;* PricewaterhouseCoopers LLP, 1 Embankment Place, LONDON, WC2N 6RH. See also PricewaterhouseCoopers
BURNS, Mr. Christopher Neil, BSc ACA *2010;* 2 Dartmouth Mews, Morley, LEEDS, LS27 0UA.
BURNS, Mr. Colin Ernest Brodie, FCA *1957;* 7 Wilderness Gardens, Northiam, RYE, EAST SUSSEX, TN31 6GB. (Life Member)
•**BURNS, Mr. Colin Robert, FCA CTA** *1981;* 8 Wellfields, LOUGHTON, IG10 1NX.
BURNS, Mr. Craig, BSc ACA *2001;* 3 Renishaw Avenue, ROTHERHAM, SOUTH YORKSHIRE, S60 3LW.
BURNS, Mr. David Anthony, BSc(Hons) FCA MIoD *1996;* Villa Rose, 2 Lacets St Leon, MC98000 MONACO, MONACO.
•**BURNS, Mr. David Steve, ACA** *1986;* Evolution Business and Tax Advisors LLP, 17-25 Scarborough Street, HARTLEPOOL, CLEVELAND, TS24 7DA.
BURNS, Mr. Dennis Arthur, FCA *1949;* Belmont Lodge, 392-396 Fencepiece Road, CHIGWELL, ESSEX, IG7 5DY. (Life Member)
BURNS, Mr. Dennis James, ACA *1992;* 8 Sharps Green, Horringer, BURY ST. EDMUNDS, SUFFOLK, IP29 5PP.
BURNS, Miss. Emma Joanne, ACA *2009;* 26 Etna Road, ST. ALBANS, HERTFORDSHIRE, AL3 5NJ.
BURNS, Mr. Fraser Mason, FCA *1947;* 48 Carlyle Road, CAMBRIDGE, CAMBRIDGESHIRE, CB4 3DH. (Life Member)
BURNS, Ms. Gillian, BSc ACA *1991;* Dell House, Broadhead Road, Edgworth, BOLTON, BL7 0BQ.
BURNS, Mr. Gordon MacGregor, BA ACA DChA *1992;* (Tax Fac), 4 Warren Court, Langdale Grange, ASHINGTON, NE63 8LL.
BURNS, Mrs. Hollie Nicola, ACA *2009;* Tradeweb Europe Ltd, 99 Gresham Street, LONDON, EC2V 7NG.
BURNS, Mr. Ian Adrian, BA ACA *1989;* Timbers, Hopgarden Lane, SEVENOAKS, KENT, TN13 1PX.
BURNS, Mr. Ian Hedley, BA ACA *1984;* Dray House Brassknocker Hill Monkton Combe, BATH, BA2 7JD.
•**BURNS, Mr. Ian Michael, FCA** *1983;* Via Executive Limited, PO Box 46, Envoy House, St Peter Port, GUERNSEY, GY1 4AY.
•**BURNS, Mr. Ian Thomas, BA FCA CF** *1977;* Smith & Williamson Ltd, 25 Moorgate, LONDON, EC2R 6AY. See also Nexia Audit Limited
BURNS, Mrs. Jacqueline Anne, BSc FCA *1983;* Hanger Park House, Hinton Parva, SWINDON, SN4 0DH.
BURNS, Miss. Jacqueline Anne, BSc ACA *1995;* 5 Hunters Way, Spencers Wood, READING, RG7 1HW.
BURNS, Mr. James Nigel, BSc FCA *1984;* Yuills Ltd, 104 Park Street, LONDON, W1K 6NF.
BURNS, Mrs. Jane Margaret, BSc ACA *2001;* 13 Norfolk Avenue, SOUTH CROYDON, SURREY, CR2 8BT.
BURNS, Miss. Joanna, BA ACA *2007;* with Baker Tilly, 12 Gleneagles Court, Brighton Road, CRAWLEY, WEST SUSSEX, RH10 6AD.
BURNS, Mr. John Derek, FCA *1976;* 37 Muirfield Drive, Astley Tyldesley, MANCHESTER, M29 7QJ.
BURNS, Mr. John Dominic, BCom ACA *1985;* Esentai Tower, 77/7 Al Farabi Avenue, 12th Floor, ALMATY 050040, KAZAKHSTAN.
BURNS, Mr. John Paul, BA ACA *2005;* The Evergreens, Mill Lane, Sindlesham, WOKINGHAM, BERKSHIRE, RG41 5DF.
BURNS, Mr. Jonathan Mark William Jude, BA ACA *2001;* 13 Norfolk Avenue, SOUTH CROYDON, SURREY, CR2 8BT.
BURNS, Miss. Karen Margaret, BSc ACA *1991;* 28 Station Road, Woolton, LIVERPOOL, L25 3PZ.
BURNS, Miss. Lauren Jean, ACA *2008;* Deloitte & Touche Llp, 66 Shoe Lane, LONDON, EC4A 3BQ.
BURNS, Mr. Louis Paul, BSc(Econ) ACA *2001;* 7 Floyd Grove, Balsall Common, COVENTRY, CV7 7RP.
BURNS, Mrs. Louise, BA ACA *1993;* 34 Queens Drive, Mossley Hill, LIVERPOOL, L18 0HE.
BURNS, Mr. Malcolm, BA ACA *1998;* 76 Cowleigh Road, MALVERN, WORCESTERSHIRE, WR14 1QN.
BURNS, Mr. Martin David, BA FCA *1983;* Westlands, Mount View Road, Claygate, ESHER, KT10 0UB.
BURNS, Mr. Matthew John, BSc ACA *2008;* 20 Trevelyan Place, St. Stephens Hill, ST. ALBANS, HERTFORDSHIRE, AL1 2DT.
BURNS, Mr. Matthew Patrick, BSc ACA *2010;* 5 Hele Close, BASINGSTOKE, RG21 3JF.
BURNS, Miss. Megan Elizabeth, ACA *2009;* Pricewaterhousecoopers, 1 Embankment Place, LONDON, WC2N 6RH.
BURNS, Mr. Michael Hamer, FCA *1972;* The Rookery, Hall Lane, Lathom, ORMSKIRK, LANCASHIRE, L40 5UG.
BURNS, Mr. Michael John, BA(Hons) ACA *2010;* 51 The Oaks, WEST BYFLEET, KT14 6RN.
BURNS, Mrs. Nicola, BA ACA *1996;* 14 Moorland Road, HARROGATE, HG2 7HD.
BURNS, Mrs. Nicola Jane, BA ACA *1999;* 7 Floyd Grove, Balsall Common, COVENTRY, CV7 7RP.
BURNS, Mr. Oliver Graham, MA ACA *1982;* 1 Purcell Close, Tewin, WELWYN, HERTFORDSHIRE, AL6 0NN.
BURNS, Mr. Paul Harold George, MA BEng ACA *2007;* with haysmacintyre, Fairfax House, 15 Fulwood Place, LONDON, WC1V 6AY.
•**BURNS, Mr. Paul Robert, BSc ACA** *2006;* Alexander Myerson & Co, Alexander House, 61 Rodney Street, LIVERPOOL, L1 9ER.

•**BURNS, Mr. Peter, FCA** *1976;* with Abrams Ecob Limited, 41 St. Thomas's Road, CHORLEY, LANCASHIRE, PR7 1JE.
BURNS, Mr. Philip, ACA *2011;* 29 Hawkroyd Bank Road, HUDDERSFIELD, HD4 7JP.
•**BURNS, Mr. Philip Julian, FCA CF** *1991;* Clearwater Corporate Finance LLP, 6th Floor, 9 Colmore Row, BIRMINGHAM, B3 2BJ.
BURNS, Mr. Richard Paul, FCA *1982;* 4 Cattle End, Silverstone, TOWCESTER, NN12 8UX.
BURNS, Mr. Robert Michael, FCA *1973;* 4 Century Close, CIRENCESTER, GLOUCESTERSHIRE, GL7 1FL.
•**BURNS, Mr. Roger, FCA** *1970;* Roger Burns, 125 Tamworth Road, Long Eaton, NOTTINGHAM, NG10 1BH.
BURNS, Mrs. Sarah, ACA *2010;* 2 Dartmouth Mews, Morley, LEEDS, LS27 0UA.
BURNS, Miss. Sarah Marie, ACA *2008;* 20 Swan Bank Court, Swan Bank Lane, HOLMFIRTH, HD9 2DS.
BURNS, Mr. Simon John, ACA *2006;* Churches Fire Security Ltd Fire House, Mayflower Close Chandler's Ford, EASTLEIGH, SO53 4AR.
•**BURNS, Mr. Stephen James, BSc ACA** *1991;* S.J. Burns & Co, Jubilee House, Suite 9A Altcar Road, Formby, LIVERPOOL, L37 8DL.
BURNS, Mr. Stephen Paul, MBA BSc ACA *1992;* Willow Cottage, Crowbrook Road, Askett, PRINCES RISBOROUGH, HP27 9LS.
BURNS, Mr. Steve Paul, MA FCA *1983;* Q B E European Operations, Plantation Place, 30 Fenchurch Street, LONDON, EC3M 3BD.
•**BURNS, Mr. Stuart, BSc FCA** *1980;* H W Fisher & Company, Acre House, 11-15 William Road, LONDON, NW1 3ER. See also H.W. Fisher & Company and H W Fisher & Company Limited
BURNS, Miss. Susan Clare, MA(Hons) ACA *2010;* 5 St. Lukes Court, 136 Falcon Road, LONDON, SW11 2LP.
BURNS-LUNT, Mrs. Louise Elsa, FCA *1996;* Canter Levin & Berg, 1 Temple Square, 24 Dale Street, LIVERPOOL, L2 5RU.
BURNSIDE, Mr. Sean Michael Patrick, BSc(Hons) ACA *2002;* with PricewaterhouseCoopers LLP, Abacus Court, 6 Minshull Street, MANCHESTER, M1 3ED.
•**BURNSIDE, Mr. Stephen Andrew, BA ACA** *1990;* Burnside (Bristol) Limited, 8 Pipe Lane, BRISTOL, BS1 5AJ.
BURNTON, Miss. Abigail Ruth, BA ACA *2000;* 5 Prospero Road, LONDON, N19 3QX.
BURR, Mr. Alexander Ford, FCA *1939;* 17 Chiltern Avenue, BUSHEY, WD23 4PY. (Life Member)
•**BURR, Mr. Christopher James, BSc ACA** *1993;* Broad Reach Partnership Limited, 49 High Street, West Mersea, COLCHESTER, CO5 8JE.
BURR, Mr. Christopher John, FCA *1972;* Ashmore House Evesham Road, Norton, EVESHAM, WORCESTERSHIRE, WR11 4TL.
BURR, Mr. Christopher Lewis, FCA *1966;* Quinta dos Cardos, Apt 291Luz-Lgs, Vila da Luz, 8600 LAGOS, PORTUGAL.
BURR, Mr. Clive Kingston, FCA *1968;* 26 Pear Tree Lane, Little Common, BEXHILL-ON-SEA, TN39 4PG.
BURR, Mrs. Emma, BA(Hons) ACA *2003;* MGN, FL 22, 1 Canada Square, LONDON, E14 5AP.
BURR, Mr. Graham Richard, BA ACA *2005;* Monarch Airlines, Prospect House, Prospect Way, London Luton Airport, LUTON, LU2 9NU.
BURR, Mr. Graham Shepheard, BA ACA *1981;* 36 Am Duerf, L-8289 KEHLEN, LUXEMBOURG.
BURR, Mr. Jonathan Charles, BA ACA *1986;* 15 Leicester Road, Hale, ALTRINCHAM, WA15 9QA.
BURR, Miss. Louise Georgina Mary, BA(Hons) ACA *2002;* Spring Cottage, Pyrford Road, WEST BYFLEET, SURREY, KT14 6RQ.
BURR, Mr. Stephen Mark, BA ACA *1991;* 57 Station Road, Cheadle Hulme, CHEADLE, CHESHIRE, SK8 7AA.
BURRAGE, Mr. Ian Robert, FCA *1968;* The Dell House, Green Lane, MALVERN, WR14 4HU. (Life Member)
BURRAGE, Mr. Kenneth Guy, FCA *1971;* The Forts, Ranmore Common, DORKING, RH5 6SP.
BURRAGE, Mr. Mark Anthony, BSc ACA DChA *2007;* 21 Embassy Gardens, BECKENHAM, KENT, BR3 1HE.
BURRAGE, Mr. Paul, BSc FCA *1978;* 85 Middle Mead, HOOK, HAMPSHIRE, RG27 9TE.
BURRAGE, Mr. Simon, BSc ACA *2000;* 7 Elmslie Close, EPSOM, SURREY, KT18 7JT.
BURRARD-LUCAS, Mr. Stephen Charles, BA ACA *1981;* 50 The Rise, SEVENOAKS, TN13 1RL.
BURRARD-LUCAS, Mr. William, MSci ACA *2010;* 9a Thornton Place, LONDON, W1H 1FG.
BURRELL, Mr. Alan Frederick, FCA *1949;* Kingsley, 18 Mayfield Road, WALTON-ON-THAMES, KT12 5PL. (Life Member)
BURRELL, Mrs. Diane Elisabeth, BSc ACA *2002;* 23 Avenue Road, KINGSTON UPON THAMES, SURREY, KT1 2RD.
BURRELL, Mrs. Frances Julie, BA FCA *1982;* Rundale House, Old Scriven, KNARESBOROUGH, NORTH YORKSHIRE, HG5 9DY.
BURRELL, Mr. Ian David, BA FCA *1982;* Rundale House, Old Scriven, KNARESBOROUGH, HG5 9DY.
BURRELL, Mr. Ian David, BSc ACA *2001;* 23 Avenue Road, KINGSTON UPON THAMES, SURREY, KT1 2RD.
BURRELL, Mr. James Alexander, BSc ACA *2000;* Permira Advisers Limited, 2806-07 28th Floor, One Exchange Square, CENTRAL, HONG KONG SAR.
BURRELL, Mr. John, FCA *1974;* 6 Tregaron Avenue, PORTSMOUTH, PO6 2JX.
BURRELL, Mr. John Edward, FCA *1964;* 23 Parker Avenue, PYMBLE, NSW 2073, AUSTRALIA.
BURRELL, Mr. John Leslie, FCA *1969;* Flat 4, High Cedars, 20 Wray Park Road, REIGATE, SURREY, RH2 0DD.
BURRELL, Miss. Kathryn Sarah, ACA *1996;* 6 Oak Close, NORTH WALSHAM, NR28 0BY.
BURRELL, Mr. Kenneth John, BA ACA *1994;* 111 West Hill Road, LONDON, SW18 5HR.
BURRELL, Mrs. Marion Jean, BA FCA *1976;* 6 Hilltop Road, Guilden Sutton, CHESTER, CH3 7HJ. (Life Member)
BURRELL, Mr. Peter Frederick, FCA *1966;* The Old Bakery, 17 Shaw Hill, Shaw, MELKSHAM, WILTSHIRE, SN12 8ET.
BURRELL, Mr. Peter Martin, FCA *1969;* 49 Common Road, Thorpe Salvin, WORKSOP, NOTTINGHAMSHIRE, S80 3JJ.
BURRELL, Mr. Richard Mitchell, BA FCA *1982;* 48 Audley Road, Hendon, LONDON, NW4 3EY.
BURRELL, Mr. Roger Geoffrey, FCA *1969;* 119 Parkanaur Avenue, SOUTHEND-ON-SEA, SS1 3JD.
BURRELL, Miss. Sarah Louisa, BSc ACA *2007;* 32 Northlands Road, SOUTHAMPTON, SO15 2LF.
•**BURRELL, Mr. Stephen John, FCA FCCA CTA(Fellow)** *1971;* Burrells Accountancy Limited, Jubilee House, Jubilee Court, Dersingham, KING'S LYNN, PE31 6HH.
•**BURRELLS, Mr. Terence, BSc FCA** *1975;* Terry Burrells, 33 Rectory Avenue, Corfe Mullen, WIMBORNE, BH21 3EZ.
BURRETT, Mr. James, ACA *2008;* 19 Grebe Court, CAMBRIDGE, CB5 8FR.
BURRIDGE, Ms. Charlene Ann, ACA *2009;* 5 Berryfield Park, Osbaston, MONMOUTH, GWENT, NP25 3DQ.
•**BURRIDGE, Mr. David Jeffrey, BA FCA** *1991;* 4 Croft Lane, LETCHWORTH GARDEN CITY, HERTFORDSHIRE, SG6 1AP.
BURRIDGE, Mr. Graham Paul, BSc ACA *1995;* 20 Summerfield Road, LONDON, W5 1ND.
BURRIDGE, Miss. Helen Jane, BSocSc FCA *2000;* 3 Powell House, 96 Wimbledon Hill Road, Wimbledon, LONDON, SW19 7GJ.
BURRIDGE, Mr. Ian David Cecil, FCA *1963;* Meadow Cottage, Twyford Road, Waltham St Lawrence, READING, RG10 0HG.
BURRIDGE, Mr. James George Thomas, BA ACA *1987;* 5 Julien Road, LONDON, W5 4XA.
BURRIDGE, Ms. Judith Deborah, BSc ACA *1980;* Portland House, Common Lane, Beer, SEATON, DEVON, EX12 3EY.
BURRIDGE, Mrs. Louise Anne, BA(Hons) ACA *2002;* Lime Pictures, Campus Manor, Childwall Abbey Road, Childwall, LIVERPOOL, L16 0JP.
BURRIDGE, Mr. Malcolm Stuart, BSc ACA *1994;* 2 Beech Hurst Close, HAYWARDS HEATH, RH16 4AE.
BURRIDGE, Mr. Paul Russell, BSc(Hons) ACA *2001;* 19 Sunnyside, BRISTOL, BS9 1BQ.
BURRIDGE, Mr. Roy Victor, FCA *1964;* West Haye Barn, Haye, CALLINGTON, PL17 7JW.
BURRIDGE, Miss. Shelagh Mary, BA FCA *1976;* 69 The Quarries, Boughton Monchelsea, MAIDSTONE, ME17 4NJ.
BURRIDGE, Mr. William Ranson, BA ACA *2002;* L M S Unit 3-4 The Oaks, Stanney Mill Lane Little Stanney, CHESTER, CH2 4HY.
BURRILL, Mr. Fraser Stuart, LLB FCA *1986;* (Tax Fac), Sony UK Ltd, The Heights, Brooklands, WEYBRIDGE, KT13 0XW.
BURRILL, Mr. Martin Henry, BSc ACA *1984;* Oakbank, 8 Regent Drive, Lostock, BOLTON, BL6 4DH.
BURRILL, Miss. Tabitha Sara, ACA *2010;* Stink, 1 Alfred Mews, LONDON, W1T 7AA.
BURRIS, Mrs. Elizabeth Mary, BSc ACA *1999;* 14 Milestone Close, St James Park, Heath, CARDIFF, CF14 4NQ.
BURRIS, Mr. Mathew William, BA ACA *1999;* T E S Aviation Group, Aviation House, Brocastle Avenue, Waterton Industrial Estate, BRIDGEND, MID GLAMORGAN CF31 3XR.
BURRLUCK, Miss. Helen Joan, BA FCA *1979;* Garden Flat, 193 Sutherland Avenue, LONDON, W9 1ET.
BURROUGH, Mr. James Hedley, MA ACA *2007;* 52 Collingsway, DARLINGTON, COUNTY DURHAM, DL2 2FD.
BURROUGH, Mr. Richard James Heathcliffe, BA ACA *1993;* 84a Riddlesdown Road, PURLEY, SURREY, CR8 1DD.
BURROUGHES, Mr. Robert Lindon, FCA MBA *1970;* Gryphon House, 14 Hamburg St., Merville Park, PARANAQUE 1709, METRO MANILA, PHILIPPINES.
BURROUGHS, Mr. Ian, ACA *1992;* 75 Braziers Quay, South Street, BISHOP'S STORTFORD, CM23 3YW.
BURROUGHS, Mr. Nicholas Jason, BSc ACA *1997;* 15 Augustus Gardens, CAMBERLEY, GU15 1HL.
BURROUGHS, Mr. Nicholas John, BSc ACA *1978;* 35 Redfern Close, CAMBRIDGE, CB4 2DT.
BURROUGHS, Mr. Nigel John, BSc FCA *1989;* (Tax Fac), 45 Farleigh Fields Orton Wistow, PETERBOROUGH, PE2 6YB.
BURROUGHS, Mr. Timothy Martin, MA BSc(Hons) FCA *1979;* 53-55 Cranbrook Road, BELLEVUE HILL, NSW 2023, AUSTRALIA.
BURROW, Mr. Gareth William, BSocSc ACA *2002;* with UHY Calvert Smith, 31 St Saviourgate, YORK, YO1 8NQ.
BURROW, Mr. Kim Christopher, BSc(Hons) ACA *2011;* 9 Rembrandt Way, WALTON-ON-THAMES, SURREY, KT12 3SH.
BURROW, Mr. Michael Wilfred, FCA *1968;* 15 Foss Avenue, WETHERBY, WEST YORKSHIRE, LS22 7YL.
BURROW, Mr. Peter William, FCA *1957;* 2 Meadow Walk, Colwall, MALVERN, WORCESTERSHIRE, WR13 6RH. (Life Member)
BURROW, Mr. Philip Charles, BA FCA *1990;* 17 Park Road, NANTWICH, CW5 7AQ.
BURROW, Mr. Simon Richard James, BSc ACA *1998;* The Royal Bank of Scotland Plc, 280 Bishopsgate, LONDON, EC2M 4RB.
BURROW, Mr. Thomas, FCA *1952;* 16 Hillary Court, Freshfield Road, Formby, LIVERPOOL, L37 3PS. (Life Member)
BURROWES, Mr. Colin James, FCA *1961;* 5 Harvest Fields Brewers End Takeley, BISHOP'S STORTFORD, HERTFORDSHIRE, CM22 6TS. (Life Member)
BURROWES, Mr. David William, BSc ACA CTA *1991;* (Tax Fac), 60 Westwater Way, DIDCOT, OX11 7TY.
•**BURROWES, Mr. Kevin James, ACA** *1986;* PricewaterhouseCoopers LLP, Hays Galleria, 1 Hays Lane, LONDON, SE1 2RD. See also PricewaterhouseCoopers
BURROWES, Mrs. Sarah Fiona, BSc ACA *1995;* Plumbe House, Hatchford Park, Ockham Lane, COBHAM, KT11 1LR.
BURROWS, Mr. Alan, BMet ACA *1979;* 3 Cornfield View, SLEAFORD, LINCOLNSHIRE, NG34 7WF.
BURROWS, Mr. Alex, ACA *2010;* 79 Welwyndale Road, SUTTON COLDFIELD, B72 1AN.
BURROWS, Miss. Alison Jane, BSc ACA *2002;* Flat 9 Ebenezer Court, North Road, HERTFORD, SG14 1LT.
BURROWS, Mrs. Amanda, BA ACA *1990;* 7 Honeysuckle Way, Abington Vale, NORTHAMPTON, NN3 3QE.
BURROWS, Mrs. Amanda Jane, BSc FCA *1992;* 37 Charlbury Road, Wollaton, NOTTINGHAM, NG8 1ND.
BURROWS, Mr. Andrew James, BSc ACA *1996;* 30 Penny Black Lane, BASINGSTOKE, RG24 9TG.
BURROWS, Mr. Anthony Hugh, FCA *1963;* 31 Shuttleworth Place, Manly, WHANGAPARAOA 0930, AUCKLAND, NEW ZEALAND.
BURROWS, Mr. Chris, BA ACA *2010;* 18 Sherborne Court, The Mount, GUILDFORD, SURREY, GU2 4HR.
BURROWS, Miss. Christine Dawn, ACA *1987;* 134 Kingsway, PETTS WOODKent, ORPINGTON, BR5 1PU.
•**BURROWS, Mr. Christopher Nigel, FCA** *1970;* (Tax Fac), Bertram Burrows, 10 Grange Road, West Kirby, WIRRAL, CH48 4HA.
BURROWS, Mr. Clive Peter, BCom FCA *1978;* Wessex Archaeology, Portway House, Old Sarum Park, SALISBURY, SP4 6EB.
BURROWS, Mr. Clive Edward, BA ACA *2010;* R G L Forensics, 8th Floor, Dashwood House, 69 Old Broad Street, LONDON, EC2M 1QS.
BURROWS, Mr. Darren Owen, LLB ACA *2001;* 15 Old Leicester Road, Wansford, PETERBOROUGH, PE8 6JR.
BURROWS, Mr. David, FCA *1990;* 20 Plasturton Gardens, Pontcanna, CARDIFF, CF11 9HF.
BURROWS, Mr. David Arthur, ACA *1981;* Royal Borough of Kensington & Chelsea, R123/A5 KensingtonTown Hall, Hornton Street, LONDON, W8 7NX.
•**BURROWS, Mr. David Howard, BSc ACA** *1986;* (Tax Fac), Castle Accountancy Limited, Parkfield House, Park Street, STAFFORD, ST17 4AL.
•**BURROWS, Mr. David John, FCA** *1979;* (Tax Fac), Worton Rock Limited, Churchfield House, 36 Vicar Street, DUDLEY, WEST MIDLANDS, DY2 8RG. See also Worth LLP
BURROWS, Mrs. Eilis Sarah, BA ACA *2005;* 8th Floor - Credit Risk Royal Bank of Scotland, 135 Bishopsgate, LONDON, EC2M 3UR.
•**BURROWS, Mrs. Emma Caroline, BA(Hons) ACA** *2000;* Affinity Accounting Ltd, Cherry Tree House, Lincoln Hill, Ironbridge, TELFORD, SHROPSHIRE TF8 7QA.
BURROWS, Gordon Edwin Charles, Esq OBE FCA *1961;* Via Cassia 1170, 00189 ROME, ITALY. (Life Member)
•**BURROWS, Mrs. Hilma Zoe, BSc FCA** *1993;* H & M Ltd, 1-5 Alma Terrace, Otley Street, SKIPTON, NORTH YORKSHIRE, BD23 1EJ.
BURROWS, Mr. Ian Bryan, MA ACA *2001;* Flat 55, Jessel House, Page Street, LONDON, SW1P 4BJ.
BURROWS, Mr. James Timothy, ACA *2009;* Flat 4 Old All Saints School, Fairview Road, CHELTENHAM, GLOUCESTERSHIRE, GL52 2EQ.
BURROWS, Mrs. Jessie Josephine, BA ACA *1995;* Lincoln Gate, Kelvedon Road, Wickham Bishops, WITHAM, ESSEX, CM8 3NA.
BURROWS, Mr. John Eric, FCA *1955;* (Member of Council 1975 - 1982), 18a High Street, Redbourn, ST. ALBANS, AL3 7LJ.
BURROWS, Mr. John Richard, BSc ACA *1988;* 35 Chiltern Park, Thornbury, BRISTOL, BS35 2HX.
BURROWS, Mr. Jonathan Charles, BA ACA *1992;* 57 Heather Close, Thurston, BURY ST. EDMUNDS, SUFFOLK, IP31 3PX.
BURROWS, Miss. Karen Nicola, BSc ACA *2002;* Toad Hall, The Butts, ILMINSTER, SOMERSET, TA19 0AX.
BURROWS, Mrs. Keziah Jane, BA ACA *1998;* 55 Brisbane Avenue, Wimbledon, LONDON, SW19 3AF.
BURROWS, Mr. Luke William, BSc ACA *2004;* Flat C, 376 Wandsworth Road, LONDON, SW8 4TE.
BURROWS, Mr. Mark John, BSc ACA *1994;* 11 Malting Close, Robin Hood, WAKEFIELD, WEST YORKSHIRE, WF3 3AN.
BURROWS, Mr. Mark Paul, BSc(Econ) ACA *1998;* 80 Ember Lane, ESHER, KT10 8EN.
•**BURROWS, Mr. Mark Stuart, FCA** *1993;* Morris Wheeler & Co Limited, 26 Church Street, BISHOP'S STORTFORD, HERTFORDSHIRE, CM23 2LY.
BURROWS, Mr. Martin Paul, BSc ACA *1999;* 46 Harvest Way, Broughton Astley, LEICESTER, LE9 6WL.
BURROWS, Mr. Matthew, ACA *2011;* 23 Albert Road, South Woodford, LONDON, E18 1LE.
BURROWS, Mr. Matthew Charles, BA ACA *1995;* c/o Amcor Bristol Central Services, Alcan Packaging Bristol, 83 Tower Road North, BRISTOL, BS30 8XP.
BURROWS, Mr. Michael George, BSc CA *1986; (CA Scotland 1976);* 2 Old Rectory Close, Thorpe St Andrews, NORWICH, NR7 0PY.
BURROWS, Mr. Michael John, FCA *1955;* Apartment 10, The Gables, Queen Parade, HARROGATE, NORTH YORKSHIRE, HG1 5QG. (Life Member)
BURROWS, Mr. Nicholas Edmund, BSc ACA *1999;* Triad Group Plc, Huxley House, Weyside Park, Catteshall Lane, GODALMING, SURREY GU7 1XE.
•**BURROWS, Mr. Nicholas John, BA FCA** *1989;* (Tax Fac), Burrows Scarborough Silk Limited, Sovereign House, 12 Warwick Street, Earlsdon, COVENTRY, CV5 6ET.
BURROWS, Mr. Nigel Derek, BA ACA *1982;* 45 Bunbury Way, Epsom Downs, EPSOM, KT17 4JP.
BURROWS, Mr. Patrick James, BSc ACA *1992;* Barn C Biggins Farm, Barwick High Cross, WARE, HERTFORDSHIRE, SG11 1DD.
BURROWS, Mr. Paul Ashley, MA FCA *1990;* 26 Lancaster Gardens, KINGSTON UPON THAMES, KT2 5NL.
•**BURROWS, Mr. Paul Vincent, FCA** *1981;* 1 Brington Drive, Barton Seagrave, KETTERING, NORTHAMPTONSHIRE, NN15 6UW.
BURROWS, Mr. Peter Anthony, FCA *1959;* 44 Highland Road, AMERSHAM, HP7 9AY. (Life Member)

•**BURROWS, Mr. Peter George, FCA** *1970;* (Tax Fac), 24 Templemere, Oatlands Drive, WEYBRIDGE, SURREY, KT13 9PB.
•**BURROWS, Mr. Peter Henry, FCA** *1973;* (Tax Fac), Peter Burrows, 11 Telford Close, Preston, WEYMOUTH, DT3 6PG.
BURROWS, Mr. Peter James, BA ACA *1994;* Home Owners Friendly Society, PO Box 94, HARROGATE, NORTH YORKSHIRE, HG2 8XE.
BURROWS, Mrs. Rebecca Jane, BA ACA *1999;* 20 Plasturton Gardens, Pontcanna, CARDIFF, CF11 9HF.
BURROWS, Mr. Richard Anthony, BSc ACA *1998;* Wolseley Private Equity, Level 4, 2 Bulletin Place, SYDNEY, NSW 2000, AUSTRALIA.
•**BURROWS, Mr. Richard John Freeman, FCA** *1972;* (Tax Fac), Mazars LLP, Tower Building, 22 Water Street, LIVERPOOL, L3 1PQ.
BURROWS, Mr. Simon Gordon, FCA *1981;* 18 Illingworth, WINDSOR, BERKSHIRE, SL4 4UP.
BURROWS, Mr. Simon Jonathan Mark, BSc CEng FCA CITP FBCS *1998;* 67 Sumatra Road, LONDON, NW6 1PT.
BURROWS, Mr. Simon Robert, BSc ACA *1986;* Micheldelving, Davey Lane, ALDERLEY EDGE, CHESHIRE, SK9 7NZ.
BURROWS, Mr. Stephen Albert Joseph, FCA *1976;* 118 Green Lane, Timperley, ALTRINCHAM, WA15 8QL.
BURROWS, Mr. Stephen Roy, MA ACA *1998;* 55 Brisbane Avenue, Wimbledon, LONDON, SW19 3AF.
BURROWS, Mrs. Suzanne Elizabeth, MA ACA *1998;* 80 Ember Lane, ESHER, SURREY, KT10 8EN.
BURROWS, Mrs. Suzi Jane Claire, BA(Econ) ACA *2002;* Clifford Chance, 10 Upper Bank Street, LONDON, E14 5JJ.
BURROWS, Mr. Timothy, ACA *2010;* 2 Lombardy Road, SUDBURY, SUFFOLK, CO10 1LQ.
BURROWS, Miss. Victoria Louise, BSc ACA *2010;* Flat 6 Richmond House, Hatfield Road, ST. ALBANS, HERTFORDSHIRE, AL1 4GL.
BURROWS, Mr. William Anthony, FCA *1963;* 8 Malkin Close, Blacko, NELSON, BB9 6LY.
•**BURSACK, Mr. Graeme Philip, BA MCMI FCA FRSA** *1983;* (Tax Fac), Goodman Jones LLP, 29-30 Fitzroy Square, LONDON, W1T 6LQ.
BURSEY, Miss. Philippa Mary, FCA *1973;* 35 South Hermitage, SHREWSBURY, SHROPSHIRE, SY3 7JS.
•**BURSEY, Mr. Robert James, BA FCA** *1979;* UHY Kent LLP, Thames House, Roman Square, SITTINGBOURNE, KENT, ME10 4BJ.
•**BURSTON, Mr. Ben, MA ACA** *2003;* with PricewaterhouseCoopers, 7 More London Riverside, LONDON, SE1 2RT.
BURSTON, Ms. Heather Claire, BA ACA *1993;* 39 Salisbury Road, Redland, BRISTOL, BS6 7AR.
BURSTON, Mr. John Richard, FCA *1954;* 4 Ferndown close, Albury Road, GUILDFORD, GU1 2DN. (Life Member)
BURT, Mr. Aaron Christian Clayton, BSc ACA *2006;* Flat 303 Sanctuary Court, Reardon Path, LONDON, E1W 2PP.
BURT, Mr. Alan David, FCA *1965;* Tree Tops, Hougue Du Moulin, Vale, GUERNSEY, GY3 5NH.
BURT, Miss. Alison Pollard, BSc(Hons) ACA *2011;* 28a Station Road, CORSHAM, WILTSHIRE, SN13 9EY.
•**BURT, Mr. Anthony James, FCA** *1982;* 11 The Spinney, SIDCUP, KENT, DA14 5NE.
BURT, Mr. Christopher John, FCA *1983;* with PricewaterhouseCoopers, Darling Park Tower 2, 201 Sussex Street, GPO Box 2650, SYDNEY, NSW 1171 AUSTRALIA.
•**BURT, Mr. Christopher John, MSc BA ACA** *1999;* Halex Business Risk Services Limited, 20 Fletcher Gate, NOTTINGHAM, NG1 2FZ.
BURT, Mr. Dennis Victor, FCA *1948;* 42 Stoke Road, COBHAM, KT11 3BD. (Life Member)
BURT, Mrs. Helen Margaret, BCom ACA *1987;* Drayseywood, Vann Lake Road, Ockley, DORKING, RH5 5NT.
BURT, Mr. James Lawson Macgregor, LLB FCA *1984;* Cannon Bridge House, 25 Dowgate Hill, LONDON, EC4R 2YA.
BURT, Miss. Katherine Louise, BSc ACA *1998;* Glaxo Smithkline Plc, GSK House, 980 Great West Road, BRENTFORD, MIDDLESEX, TW8 9GS.
•**BURT, Mr. Laurence Spears, BSc FCA** *1984;* Kay, 59/63 Station Road, NORTHWICH, CHESHIRE, CW9 5LT.
•**BURT, Mr. Michael John, BSc FCA CTA** *1988;* (Tax Fac), Grant Thornton UK LLP, Grant Thornton House, 202 Silbury Boulevard, MILTON KEYNES, BUCKINGHAMSHIRE, MK9 1LW. See also Grant Thornton LLP
BURT, Mrs. Rosemary Ethel, FCA *1975;* (Tax Fac), 34 Hawthorn Way, ROYSTON, HERTFORDSHIRE, SG8 7JS.
BURT, Mr. Ross Peter, BSc(Hons) ACA *2003;* 27 Radcliffe House, Rollason Way, BRENTWOOD, ESSEX, CM14 4DY.
BURT, Mr. Russell John, BSc ACA CFA *1998;* GLG Partners Services LP, The Waterfront Centre, P O Box 2427GT, GEORGE TOWN, GRAND CAYMAN, KY1-1105 CAYMAN ISLANDS.
BURT, Mr. Simon Derek, BSc ACA *1993;* 18 Longlands, WORTHING, WEST SUSSEX, BN14 9NN.
BURT, Mr. Stephen James, BA ACA *1994;* Wentloog Environmental Centre, Wentloog Avenue, CARDIFF, CF3 2EE.
BURT, Miss. Tessa Katy, ACA *2010;* 95 St. Philip Street, LONDON, SW8 3SS.
BURTENSHAW, Mr. James Henry, BA FCA *1979;* Isocom Ltd, 48 Hutton Close, Crowther, WASHINGTON, TYNE AND WEAR, NE38 0AH.
BURTOFT, Miss. Maren Clare Sidau, MA(Hons) ACA *2009;* Neuhofstraße 39, 60318 FRANKFURT AM MAIN, GERMANY.
BURTON, Mr. Adam Robert, BA(Econ) ACA *2001;* 19 Farmers Lane, #4 Lucky Hill, WARWICK WK04, BERMUDA.
BURTON, Mr. Alan Frank, FCA *1973;* Computer Science Corporation Manor Offices, Old Road, CHESTERFIELD, DERBYSHIRE, S40 3QT.
BURTON, Mrs. Alison Michelle Ker, BA ACA *1993;* Poylldooey House, Gardeners Lane, Ramsey, ISLE OF MAN, IM8 2TF.
BURTON, Miss. Amy Louise, BSc ACA CTA *2010;* 30 Leawood Road, Midway, SWADLINCOTE, DERBYSHIRE, DE11 7PN.
BURTON, Mrs. Andrea Louise, BSc ACA *1995;* 8 Hawthorn Drive, Balsall Common, COVENTRY, CV7 7BF.
BURTON, Mr. Andrew James Frederick, BSc ACA *2000;* 32 Beechtree Avenue, MARLOW, BUCKINGHAMSHIRE, SL7 3NJ.
BURTON, Mr. Andrew John, BSc ACA *1991;* 9 Willow Walk, Barton on Sea, NEW MILTON, HAMPSHIRE, BH25 7TL.
•**BURTON, Mr. Andrew John, BSc FCA** *1979;* A J Burton Ltd, 16 Lapwings, LONGFIELD, KENT, DA3 7NH.
BURTON, Mr. Andrew Taylor, FCA *1975;* Au Bourdieu, Cutxan, 32150 CAZAUBON, FRANCE.
BURTON, Mrs. Angela, BSc ACA *1991;* 9 Willow Walk, Barton on Sea, NEW MILTON, HAMPSHIRE, BH25 7TL.
BURTON, Mrs. Ann Elizabeth, BA FCA *1983;* (Tax Fac), 5 Argyll Square, OBAN, ARGYLL, PA34 4AZ.
BURTON, Mr. Anthony Stanley, BSc ACA *1994;* 6 Hotchkin Avenue, Saxilby, LINCOLN, LN1 2GU.
BURTON, Mr. Bernard Francis Clive, TD MA FCA *1957;* Oak House, Mottram Road, ALDERLEY EDGE, SK9 7JF. (Life Member)
•**BURTON, Mr. Brian Stuart, BA FCA** *1970;* Stuart Burton & Co, 18 Crosby Road North, Waterloo, LIVERPOOL, L22 4QF.
•**BURTON, Mr. Charles Peter, BA FCA** *1982;* 10 Madison Drive, Bawtry, DONCASTER, SOUTH YORKSHIRE, DN10 6SG.
•**BURTON, Mr. Charles William, BA FCA** *1977;* CW Burton & Co, 3 Meadowcroft, Draughton, SKIPTON, NORTH YORKSHIRE, BD23 6EG.
•**BURTON, Mr. Christopher, FCA MBA** *1986;* Intandem Business Services, c/o Fiduciaire Chavaz SA, Rue Jacques-Grosselin 8, Case Postale 1835, CH-1227 CAROUGE, SWITZERLAND.
BURTON, Mr. Christopher Alexander, BA FCA *1977;* 44 Esmond Road, Chiswick, LONDON, W4 1JQ.
•**BURTON, Mr. Christopher Charles, BA ACA** *1984;* Chris Burton, 13 Warren Way, Digswell, WELWYN, HERTFORDSHIRE, AL6 0DQ. See also AIMS - Chris Burton
BURTON, Mr. Christopher John Charles, BCom FCA CTA *1982;* (Tax Fac), 14 Redgrove House, Stonards Hill, EPPING, ESSEX, CM16 4QQ.
BURTON, Mr. Christopher Michael, BSc FCA *1973;* 122 Kippington Road, SEVENOAKS, KENT, TN13 2LN.
BURTON, The Revd. Christopher Paul, FCA *1964;* Damson Cottage, 69b London Road North, Poynton, STOCKPORT, CHESHIRE, SK12 1AG.
BURTON, Mrs. Claire Louise, BSc ACA *1998;* 10 Brook Rise, Oakdale, BLACKWOOD, GWENT, NP12 0ES.
BURTON, Miss. Clare, BSc ACA *1996;* 27 River Holme View, Brockholes, HOLMFIRTH, HD9 7BP.
BURTON, Mr. Colin William, FCA *1973;* The Old Dairy, 5 North Parade Avenue, OXFORD, OX2 6LX. (Life Member)
•**BURTON, Mr. Craig Myles, BSc ACA** *1998;* with Grant Thornton UK LLP, Unit 2, Broadfield Court, SHEFFIELD, S8 0XF.
•**BURTON, Mr. David, FCA** *1967;* Spencer Gardner Dickins Limited, 3 Coventry Innovation Village, Cheetah Road, COVENTRY, CV1 2TL.
BURTON, Mr. David Alan Harvey, BCom ACA *1998;* 46 Victoria Avenue, Cheadle Hulme, CHEADLE, CHESHIRE, SK8 5DL.
BURTON, Mr. David Arthur, MA FCA *1969;* Meadow Brook, Water Street, Somerton, BICESTER, OXFORDSHIRE, OX25 6NE. (Life Member)
•**BURTON, Mr. David Gowan, FCA** *1965;* D.G. Burton, 3 The Green, WOODFORD GREEN, IG8 0NF.
BURTON, Mr. David James, BSc ACA *2005;* 18 St. Julians Road, ST. ALBANS, HERTFORDSHIRE, AL1 2AZ.
BURTON, Mr. David James, BA ACA *1985;* 4th Floor, 18 Mansell Street, LONDON, E1 8AA.
•**BURTON, Mrs. Deborah Joanne, BA(Econ) FCA** *1996;* Christian Douglass LLP, 2 Jordan Street, Knott Mill, MANCHESTER, M15 4PY.
BURTON, Mr. Dennis Harry, FCA *1952;* 66 Cranmere Avenue, Tettenhall, WOLVERHAMPTON, WV6 8TS. (Life Member)
•**BURTON, Mr. Donald Gerard, FCA** *1962;* Connellys, Trident House, 222 Katherine Street, ASHTON-UNDER-LYNE, OL6 7AS.
•**BURTON, Mr. Gareth John, BEng FCA** *1995;* Ash Shaw LLP, 180 Piccadilly, LONDON, W1J 9HF.
BURTON, Mr. George Mark, FCA *1972;* Electrical Contractors Association, E C A Court, 24-26 South Park, SEVENOAKS, KENT, TN13 1DU.
BURTON, Mr. Gerald, FCA *1961;* Le Village, 31580 CAZARIL TAMBOURES, FRANCE. (Life Member)
BURTON, Mr. Gerald Morris, BSc FCA *1977;* 50 12th Street, North Ahmadi, AHMADI, 61008, KUWAIT.
BURTON, Mr. Graham Pearson, MSc FCA *1970;* Brook Cottage, North Lees, RIPON, NORTH YORKSHIRE, HG4 3HW. (Life Member)
BURTON, Mr. Gregory John, FCA *1974;* 3 Manor Crescent, Standlake, WITNEY, OX29 7RX. (Life Member)
BURTON, Mr. Grenville Clive, FCA *1964;* 95 High Street, Lavenham, SUDBURY, SUFFOLK, CO10 9PZ.
BURTON, Mr. Hamish Russell, FCA *1976;* Furnace House, Killinghurst Lane, HASLEMERE, SURREY, GU27 2EJ.
•**BURTON, Ms. Helen Anne, FCA** *1978;* (Tax Fac), H.A. Burton, 17 Hertford Avenue, East Sheen, LONDON, SW14 8EF.
BURTON, Mr. Hugh Alan, BA FCA *1979;* 821 North Euclid Avenue, OAK PARK, IL 60302, UNITED STATES.
•**BURTON, Mr. Ian Michael, MA FCA** *1983;* AIMS Accountants for Business - Ian Burton, 7 Dover Road, Birkdale, SOUTHPORT, MERSEYSIDE, PR8 4TF.
•**BURTON, Mr. Ian Nicholas, MEng ACA** *1998;* The Bullen Healthcare Group, 85-87 Kempston Street, LIVERPOOL, L3 8HE.
BURTON, Mr. Jamie Max, ACA *2010;* 49 Stockwell Road, LONDON, SW9 9QA.
BURTON, Mrs. Jean Irene, BA ACA *1981;* 23 Richmond Drive, LICHFIELD, STAFFORDSHIRE, WS14 9SZ.
BURTON, Mrs. Jennie Sheryl, BSc ACA *1998;* 13 Granville Road, ST. ALBANS, AL1 5BE.
BURTON, Mrs. Joanna, BA ACA *2000;* 27 Stanbury Close, Bosham, CHICHESTER, WEST SUSSEX, PO18 8NS.
BURTON, Mr. John Alan Thomas, FCA ATII *1963;* Garth Cottage, Middle Entrance, Drive Storrs Park, Bowness-On-Windermere, WINDERMERE, LA23 3JY.
BURTON, Mr. John Marcus, BSc ACA *2010;* Stockwell House, Lower Binton, STRATFORD-UPON-AVON, WARWICKSHIRE, CV37 9TQ.
•**BURTON, Mr. John Michael, BCom ACA** *1995;* 8 Hawthorn Drive, Balsall Common, COVENTRY, CV7 7BF.
BURTON, Mr. John Richard Spencer, BSc ACA MIM *1993;* Suilven, Wanborough Lane, CRANLEIGH, SURREY, GU6 7DS.
BURTON, Mr. Jonathan Robert, ACA *1993;* 4 Dovecote Close, CREWE, CW2 6TW.
BURTON, Ms. Julie Marion, BA FCA *1989;* (Tax Fac), with Reeves & Co LLP, Montague Place, Quayside, Chatham Maritime, CHATHAM, KENT ME4 4QU.
•**BURTON, Mrs. Kathryn Elizabeth, MSc BSc ACA DChA** *2004;* haysmacintyre, Fairfax House, 15 Fulwood Place, LONDON, WC1V 6AY.
BURTON, Mr. Kenneth Holmes, FCA *1953;* South Park, KESTON, BR2 6HB. (Life Member)
BURTON, Mr. Mark Andrew, BA ACA *1999;* (Tax Fac), Gate Gourmet Unit 9, Radius Park Faggs Road, FELTHAM, MIDDLESEX, TW14 0NG.
BURTON, Mr. Mark John, FCA *1992;* 57 Woodfield Avenue, PORTSMOUTH, PO6 1AN.
BURTON, Mr. Mark William, MChem ACA *2005;* 11 Birkhead Close, Kirkburton, HUDDERSFIELD, HD8 0GR.
BURTON, Mr. Matthew Charles, BSc ACA *1993;* 36 Avenue Road, ST. ALBANS, HERTFORDSHIRE, AL1 3QB.
BURTON, Mr. Matthew James, BSc(Hons) ACA *2009;* 5 Mundy Close, Burghfield, READING, RG30 3DQ.
BURTON, Mr. Matthew Patrick, LLB FCA *1981;* 10T Holdings plc Northern House, Moor Knoll Lane East Ardsley, WAKEFIELD, WF3 2EE.
BURTON, Mr. Matthew Simon, MA ACA *1996;* High Pines, Beech Grove, AMERSHAM, HP7 0AZ.
BURTON, Mr. Michael Charles, BSc ACA *2006;* 2 Ardmore Close, Tuffley, GLOUCESTER, GL4 0BL.
BURTON, Mr. Michael Charles Pearson, FCA *1956;* 8 Byron Court, Beech Grove, HARROGATE, HG2 0LL. (Life Member)
•**BURTON, Mr. Michael Richard John, BSocSc FCA** *1985;* Brebners, The Quadrangle, 180 Wardour Street, LONDON, W1F 8LB.
BURTON, Mr. Michael Trevor, BA ACA *1989;* Palram Industries Ltd, Unit 2, Doncaster Carr Ind Est, White Rose Way, DONCASTER, SOUTH YORKSHIRE DN4 5JH.
BURTON, Mr. Michael William, FCA *1969;* City of Leeds YMCA, Otley Old Road, LEEDS, LS16 6HQ. (Life Member)
BURTON, Miss. Nadine Elizabeth, BA ACA *2004;* 183 Healy Road, HAMILTON HILL, WA 6163, AUSTRALIA.
BURTON, Mr. Nicholas Edward, BSc ACA *2009;* 45 Hilltop Avenue, BUCKINGHAM, MK18 1YH.
BURTON, Mr. Nicholas Henry, FCA *1981;* Oakfield House, Friths Avenue, Hoghton, PRESTON, PR5 0DX.
BURTON, Mr. Oliver James, BSc ACA *2004;* 2 Laurel Cottages, Lower Road, Cookham, MAIDENHEAD, BERKSHIRE, SL6 9EU.
BURTON, Mrs. Patricia Louise, ACA *2003;* Brooke House, North Street, Charminster, DORCHESTER, DORSET, DT2 9QS.
BURTON, Mr. Paul Anthony, BA ACA *1986;* 65 Hartford Road, BEXLEY, KENT, DA5 1NL.
•**BURTON, Mr. Perry Stuart, BA ACA** *1999;* Grant Thornton UK LLP, 1-4 Atholl Crescent, EDINBURGH, EH3 8LQ. See also Grant Thornton LLP
BURTON, Mr. Peter, BSc FCA *1979;* 45 Hilltop Avenue, BUCKINGHAM, MK18 1YH.
BURTON, Mr. Peter Tom, FCA *1963;* 56 Arno Vale Road, Woodthorpe, NOTTINGHAM, NG5 4JJ.
BURTON, Mr. Peter William, FCA *1962;* 55 Barlavington Way, MIDHURST, GU29 9TG.
BURTON, Mr. Philip Brian, BA FCA *1989;* Belron, Milton Park, Stroude Road, EGHAM, TW20 9EL.
•**BURTON, Mr. Philip David, BSc ACA** *1992;* 88 Kings Crescent South, LETHBRIDGE T1K 5G5, AB, CANADA.
•**BURTON, Mr. Philip John, BSc FCA** *1995;* Bronsens, 6 Langdale Court, WITNEY, OXFORDSHIRE, OX28 6FG.
BURTON, Mr. Phillip John, ACA *1990;* Faldouet Farm, La Rue Du Ministre, St. Martin, JERSEY, JE3 6EN.
BURTON, Mr. Raymond Noel, BSS FCA *1974;* MEMBER OF COUNCIL, 12 Bannerdown Close, Batheaston, BATH, BA1 7JN.
BURTON, Mr. Richard Neil, BSc FCA *1979;* 1392 Malibou Terrace, MISSISSAUGA L5J 4B8, ON, CANADA.
BURTON, Mr. Richard Neil, BSc ACA *1998;* 14/73 Darley Road, MANLY, NSW 2095, AUSTRALIA.
•**BURTON, Mr. Richard Seagrave, FCA** *1968;* Richard S Burton Ltd, 48c Main Street, Meadow Lane, Burton Joyce, NOTTINGHAM, NG14 5EX.
•**BURTON, Mr. Richard Westell, BA FCA** *1990;* PricewaterhouseCoopers GmbH, Friedrich-Ebert-Anlage 35-37, 60327 FRANKFURT AM MAIN, GERMANY. See also PricewaterhouseCoopers LLP
BURTON, Mr. Robert James, BSc ACA *1998;* Marie-Curie Strasse 30, 60439 FRANKFURT AM MAIN, GERMANY.
BURTON, Mr. Robert James Stanley, BA ACA *1993;* Poylldooey House, Gardeners Lane, Ramsey, ISLE OF MAN, IM8 2TF.
BURTON, Mr. Robert Lloyd, BA ACA *2004;* with Mazars LLP, Mazars House, Gelderd Road, Gildersome, LEEDS, LS27 7JN.
BURTON, Mrs. Samantha Jane, BSc ACA *1996;* 218 Redlands Road, PENARTH, SOUTH GLAMORGAN, CF64 2QS.
•**BURTON, Mr. Stanley Philip James, FCA** *1968;* (Tax Fac), 6 Fernhill Walk, Hawley, CAMBERLEY, GU17 9HB.

BURTON, Mr. Stephen John, ACA *1992;* Brooke House, Middle Street, Nazeing, WALTHAM ABBEY, ESSEX, EN9 2LQ.
BURTON, Mr. Steven John, BSc ACA *1988;* 44 Streathbourne Road, LONDON, SW17 8QX.
BURTON, Mr. Steven John, BA ACA *1991;* 9 Southview, Woodley, STOCKPORT, SK6 1PD.
BURTON, Mr. Stuart Blakeway, FCA *1969;* Post Mill Cottage, Argos Hill, Rotherfield, CROWBOROUGH, EAST SUSSEX, TN6 3QF.
•**BURTON, Mr. Thomas, FCA** *1977;* T. Burton & Co, 178 Brownhill Rd, Catford, LONDON, SE6 2DJ.
BURTON, Mr. Thomas Bodley, MA FCA *1964;* Hawthorn Cottage, Elm Lane, BOURNE END, BUCKINGHAMSHIRE, SL8 5PF.
BURTON, Mr. Thomas Nelson, BSc ACA *1994;* Hamilton Recruitment (Bermuda) Limited, HAMILTON, BERMUDA.
BURTON, Mr. Thomas Richard, BA ACA *2010;* 79 Falcon Road, LONDON, SW11 2PF.
•**BURTON, Mr. Tony Lawrence, FCA** *1977;* (Tax Fac), T.L. Burton, Accountants Place, Heath Road, Linton, MAIDSTONE, ME17 4NU.
•**BURTON, Mrs. Tracy Lorraine, BSc FCA** *1997;* Blencowe & Partners Limited, 15 High Street, BRACKLEY, NORTHAMPTONSHIRE, NN13 7DH.
BURTON, Mrs. Wendy Nicola, BA(Hons) FCA *2000;* with Ernst & Young LLP, 100 Barbirolli Square, MANCHESTER, M2 3EY.
BURTON-BROWN, Mr. Christopher Andrew, BSc FCA *1988;* Stonedene, 3 Mylor Close, WOKING, GU21 4DD.
BURTON-PRATELEY, Sir Michael Peter, MPhil BA ACA *1988;* c/o View Systems Inc., 1550 Caton Center Drive, Suite E, BALTIMORE, MD 21227, UNITED STATES.
BURTON-THORNE, Mr. Andrew Barry, BSc ACA *1995;* 36 Penrose Way, Four Marks, ALTON, GU34 5BG.
BURTT-JONES, Mr. Richard Derek John, FCA *1969;* Malvern House, Coed Morgan, ABERGAVENNY, GWENT, NP7 9UD.
•**BURWOOD, Mr. John Charles, FCA** *1977;* MacIntyre Hudson LLP, New Bridge Street House, 30-34 New Bridge Street, LONDON, EC4V 6BJ.
•**BURWOOD, Mr. Michael Keith, BA ACA** *1987;* ASAP Accounting Services Ltd, The Old Cartlodge, Warrens Farm, Great Tey, COLCHESTER, CO6 1JG. See also Clacton Business Services Ltd
BURY, Miss. Clair, BSc ACA *2007;* 12 The Curlews, SHOREHAM-BY-SEA, WEST SUSSEX, BN43 5UQ.
BURY, Mr. David Gordon, FCA *1964;* The Viking Wing, Thurland Castle, Tunstall, CARNFORTH, LA6 2QR. (Life Member)
BURY, Mr. James Michael, BA ACA *1986;* Norton, Walpole Avenue, Chipstead, COULSDON, SURREY, CR5 3PQ.
•**BURY, Mr. Jerome Quentin James Patrick, BSc FCA** *1991;* Anderson Barrowcliff LLP, Waterloo House, Thornaby Place, Thornaby on Tees, STOCKTON-ON-TEES, CLEVELAND TS17 6SA. See also Anderson Barrowcliff
BURY, Miss. Karen, BSc ACA *1989;* 4 Barrow Road, KENILWORTH, WARWICKSHIRE, CV8 1EH.
•**BURY, Mr. Leslie, FCA** *1966;* (Tax Fac), Beever and Struthers, Central Buildings, Richmond Terrace, BLACKBURN, BB1 7AP.
BURY, Mrs. Sheila, FCA *1959;* 4 Riverside, SCARBOROUGH, NORTH YORKSHIRE, YO12 6UE. (Life Member)
BUSAIDY, Mr. Ghalib, BA ACA *1991;* P.O.Box 515, 116 MINA AL FAHAL, OMAN.
•**BUSBY, Mr. Alan George, FCA** *1968;* (Tax Fac), Elliott Mortlock Busby & Co, Abacus House, 7 Argent Court, Sylvan Way, Southfields Business Park, BASILDON ESSEX SS15 6TH.
BUSBY, Mrs. Alice Kate, BSc ACA *2003;* 71 Twilley Street, LONDON, SW18 4NU.
BUSBY, Mr. Andrew James, BA ACA *1997;* 194 Coombe Lane West, KINGSTON UPON THAMES, KT2 7EQ.
BUSBY, Miss. Caroline Lucy, BSc ACA *2001;* 44 Nutbourne Street, LONDON, W10 4HL.
BUSBY, Mr. Christopher, BA ACA *1998;* Latimer House, Water End Road, Potten End, BERKHAMSTED, HERTFORDSHIRE, HP4 2SH.
BUSBY, Mr. Christopher Rodney, FCA *1964;* Redbrook Farm Redbrook Street, Woodchurch, ASHFORD, KENT, TN26 3QS.
BUSBY, Mr. Colin Ronald William, FCA *1969;* 34 Duloe Road Eaton Socon, St. Neots, ST. NEOTS, PE19 4HW.
BUSBY, Mr. Michael John, BA ACA *1989;* 21 Tidmington Close, Hatton Park, WARWICK, CV35 7TE.
BUSBY, Mr. Michael Robert, ACA *1982;* 7 Parkway Court, Drakes Drive, ST. ALBANS, AL1 5AA.
BUSBY, Mr. Peter Geoffrey, BA ACA *1992;* Withinlee Hollow Withinlee Road, Prestbury, MACCLESFIELD, CHESHIRE, SK10 4AT.
BUSBY, Mr. Peter Stephen, FCA *1973;* 28 Hesketh Road, SOUTHPORT, MERSEYSIDE, PR9 9PD.
BUSBY, Mrs. Sarah Jane, BA ACA *1998;* Latimer House, Water End Road, Potten End, BERKHAMSTED, HERTFORDSHIRE, HP4 2SH.
•**BUSCH, Mr. Graham, BCom ACA CA(SA)** *2009;* Lawrence Grant, 2nd Floor, Hygeia House, 66 College Road, HARROW, MIDDLESEX HA1 1BE.
BUSCOMBE, Mr. Philip John, MA ACA *1979;* with Lyceum Capital Partners LLP, Burleigh House, 357 Strand, LONDON, WC2R 0HS.
•**BUSE, Mrs. Jennifer Louise, BA ACA** *2002;* Sam Rogoff & Co Limited, 2nd Floor, 167-169 Great Portland Street, LONDON, W1W 5PF.
•**BUSE, Mr. John Arthur, FCA** *1969;* John Buse & Co, Shears Farmhouse, Umborne, Shute, AXMINSTER, EX13 7QL.
BUSFIELD, Mr. Stephen James, FCA *1977;* Staalmeesterslaan 130, 1057 NN AMSTERDAM, NETHERLANDS.
•**BUSGEETH, Mr. Dharmraj, BSc FCA** *1981;* Moore Stephens Mauritius, 6th Floor, Newton Tower, Sir William Newton Steet, PORT LOUIS, MAURITIUS. See also Moore Stephens
BUSH, Mr. Alexander Murray, ACA *2008;* Flat 1, 21 Windsor Road Douglas, ISLE OF MAN, IM1 3LD.
BUSH, Miss. Alison Margaret, BSc ACA *1988;* 77 Erpingham Road, Putney, LONDON, SW15 1BH.
BUSH, Mr. Andrew Lindsay William, ACA *2008;* 7 The Croft, Shirland, ALFRETON, DERBYSHIRE, DE55 6EY.
BUSH, Mr. Anthony Edward Laurence, FCA *1964;* Lakeview House, Chedworth Road, Withington, CHELTENHAM, GL54 4BN. (Life Member)
BUSH, Mr. Brian Douglas, FCA *1978;* 23 Rte du Boham, Le Monteil, 24680 LAMONZIE ST MARTIN, FRANCE.
BUSH, Mr. Brian Stanton, FCA *1965;* Barn-Hey, Burghfield Common, READING, RG7 3EL. (Life Member)
BUSH, Mr. Cary Thomas, ACA *1979;* 11 Dunsford Place, Dunsford Place, BATH, BA2 6HF.
BUSH, Mrs. Cheryl, BA ACA *2005;* 80 Watkins Drive, Prestwich, MANCHESTER, M25 0DS.
BUSH, Mr. Christopher Gordon, FCA *1967;* St. Catherines Cottage, Whitwell Road, VENTNOR, ISLE OF WIGHT, PO38 1LJ. (Life Member)
•**BUSH, Mr. Christopher John, BA ACA** *1988;* Clarity, 2 Lancaster Close, Weston Heights, STEVENAGE, HERTFORDSHIRE, SG1 4RX.
•**BUSH, Mr. Christopher John, FCA** *1980;* (Tax Fac), Francis Clark LLP, Vantage Point, Woodwater Park, Pynes Hill, EXETER, EX2 5FD.
•**BUSH, Mr. Christopher John, BA FCA** *1986;* Berkeley Bate Limited, Cheviot House, 71 Castle Street, SALISBURY, WILTSHIRE, SP1 3SP.
BUSH, Mr. Clayton, BSc ACA *2001;* 51 Blandford Road, LONDON, W4 1EA.
BUSH, Mr. Daniel Alan, ACA *2008;* 23 Damaskfield, WORCESTER, WR4 0HY.
BUSH, Mr. David William, BCom ACA *1984;* The Shubbery, 2 The Chestnuts, Lea, MALMESBURY, WILTSHIRE, SN16 9PG.
BUSH, Mr. Duncan John, ACA *1999;* Accsys Business Consultants Ltd, 38 Roman Way, Higham Ferrers, RUSHDEN, NORTHAMPTONSHIRE, NN10 8NS.
•**BUSH, Mr. Gary Richard, LLB ACA** *1993;* Gary Bush, Badgers Hollow, 40 Badgers Hall Avenue, BENFLEET, ESSEX, SS7 1TN.
BUSH, Mr. Geoffrey Thomas, MSc FCA FRSA *1974;* Silverstone, Edburton Road, Fulking, HENFIELD, BN5 9LP.
BUSH, Mr. Graham Charles, FCA *1981;* 17 Bridle Way, ORPINGTON, BR6 7TJ.
BUSH, Mr. Hugo, ACA *2009;* Quaves Cottage Sutton Green Road, Sutton Green, GUILDFORD, GU4 7QD.
BUSH, Mr. Ian Phillip, BSc ACA *1998;* 68 Rotton Park Road, Edgbaston, BIRMINGHAM, B16 0LH.
BUSH, Mr. James Philip, MEng ACA *1992;* 17 St. Arvans Close, CROYDON, CR0 5UR.
BUSH, Mr. John Laccohee, FCA *1963;* 1 Hall Farm Close, Queniborough, LEICESTER, LE7 3TZ.
BUSH, Mr. Peter Alden, FCA *1958;* 67 Hampton Hill, Wellington, TELFORD, TF1 2ER. (Life Member)
BUSH, Miss. Rebecca Ann, BSc ACA *1992;* Chester House, PO Box 87, FARNBOROUGH, GU14 6YU.
BUSH, Miss. Sally Ann, ACA *2008;* (Tax Fac), B D O Stoy Hayward Llp 2 City Place, Beehive Ring Road London Gatwick Airport, GATWICK, WEST SUSSEX, RH6 0PA.
BUSH, Mrs. Susan, BEd ACA *1993;* Meadow Bank, 76 Church Street, Oughtibridge, SHEFFIELD, S35 0FW.
BUSH, Mr. Timothy, BSc FCA *1988;* (Member of Council 2004 - 2005), 5 Mustow Place, LONDON, SW6 4EL.
BUSH, Ms. Virginia Louise, BA ACA *1995;* 48 Holtwhites Hill, ENFIELD, MIDDLESEX, EN2 0RX.
BUSH, Ms. Vivienne Jane, FCA *1997;* 40 Cranesbill Drive, BURY ST. EDMUNDS, IP32 7JU.
•①**BUSHBY, Mr. Graham Paul, BA ACA** *1990;* Baker Tilly Tax & Advisory Services LLP, The Pinnacle, 170 Midsummer Boulevard, MILTON KEYNES, MK9 1BP. See also Baker Tilly Restructuring and Recovery LLP
BUSHBY, Mr. John Robert, BA FCA *1980;* 6 Wilton Road, FOLKESTONE, KENT, CT19 5HS.
BUSHBY, Mr. Jonathan Carlyle, BA ACA *1988;* Island House, SOUTH BRENT, DEVON, TQ10 9AJ.
BUSHBY, Mr. Mark Edward, BSc ACA *1997;* Alliance Boots, 2 The Heights Brooklands, WEYBRIDGE, KT13 0NY.
BUSHBY, Mr. Thomas Albert, FCA *1952;* Knockrobin, Rookery Way, Foxhill, HAYWARDS HEATH, RH16 4RE. (Life Member)
BUSHELL, Mr. Alan Gregory, BSc FCA *1981;* Hazel Cottage, Water Lane, Bisley, WOKING, GU24 9BA.
BUSHELL, Miss. Cara Jayne, ACA *2007;* 61 Eastbrook Road, Portslade, BRIGHTON, BN41 1LN.
BUSHELL, Mrs. Claire Louise, BSc ACA *1993;* 1 St. Peters Drive, Libanus Fields, BLACKWOOD, NP12 2ER.
BUSHELL, Mr. Cyril Anthony, FCA *1961;* 7 St. Judes Walk, CHELTENHAM, GLOUCESTERSHIRE, GL53 7RU. (Life Member)
BUSHELL, Mr. Damian Philip, FCA *1976;* 12 Coney Gree, SAWBRIDGEWORTH, CM21 0DA.
BUSHELL, Miss. Elizabeth Anne, BA FCA *1999;* The Arts Council, The Arts Council Of England, 14 Great Peter Street, LONDON, SW1P 3NQ.
BUSHELL, Miss. Heather, BA ACA *2005;* 158/9 Hin Lef Fai, HUA HIN, PRACHUAP KHIRI KHAN, THAILAND.
BUSHELL, Mr. Ian William, BA ACA *1992;* 70a Common Lane, Culcheth, WARRINGTON, WA3 4HD.
BUSHELL, Miss. Jane Sarah, MA ACA *1993;* Dunrobin, Feather Lane, Heswall, WIRRAL, CH60 4RL.
BUSHELL, Mr. John Hudson, FCA *1964;* Andorra, Wrens Hill, Oxshott, LEATHERHEAD, KT22 0HJ.
BUSHELL, Mr. Mark Christopher Cannings, BCom FCA *1980;* 5 Hartmann Place, TUCKAHOE, NY 10707, UNITED STATES.
•**BUSHELL, Mr. Michael Derek, FCA CTA** *1970;* with Wilkins Kennedy FKC Limited, Stourside Place, 35-41 Station Road, ASHFORD, KENT, TN23 1PP.
•**BUSHELL, Mr. Paul William, ACA** *1987;* Robert Alice Limited, 6 Victoria Avenue, HARROGATE, NORTH YORKSHIRE, HG1 1ED.
•**BUSHELL, Mr. Raymond Andrew, FCA** *1985;* Stafford Challis & Co, PO Box 344, Mont Crevelt House, Bulwer Avenue, St Sampson GUERNSEY GY1 3US. See also Stafford Challis & Co Limited
BUSHELL, Mr. Richard Scott, BA ACA *1992;* Trademade International Limited, 8 Archers Court, 48 Masons Hill, BROMLEY, BR2 9JG.
BUSHELL, Miss. Victoria Kathryn, BA ACA *2008;* Apartment 21, Velocity East, 4 City Walk, LEEDS, LS11 9BF.
BUSHILL, Mr. Tobias James Newsome, BA FCA *1985;* 13 Mill Street, Harbury, LEAMINGTON SPA, CV33 9HR.
BUSHNELL, Mr. James, ACA *2008;* 22 Mizen Close, COBHAM, KT11 2RJ.
BUSHNELL, Mr. Kenneth Edward, BSc FCA *1983;* 120 Melville Terrace, MANLY, QLD 4179, AUSTRALIA.
•**BUSHNELL, Mrs. Marsha Ann, FCA** *1976;* (Tax Fac), MB Accountancy Limited, Peacehaven, Coltstaple Lane, Newfoundout, HORSHAM, WEST SUSSEX RH13 9BB.
BUSHNELL, Mr. Michael David, MA(Cantab) ACA *2010;* 147 Albert Road, LONDON, N22 7AQ.
BUSHROD, Miss. Caroline Jane, BSc ACA *2000;* 111 Forest Road, Fishponds, BRISTOL, BS16 3ST.
BUSHROD, Mrs. Natalie, BSc ACA *2002;* Towergate House Eclipse Park, Sittingbourne Road, MAIDSTONE, ME14 3EN.
BUSK, Miss. Claire Janet, BSc ACA *1984;* 77 Burton Road, Kennington, ASHFORD, KENT, TN24 9DT.
BUSKELL, Mr. Simon Zachary, BA(Hons) ACA *2004;* Flat 44 Ranelagh House, 3-5 Elystan Place, LONDON, SW3 3LD.
•**BUSS, Mrs. Brenda Mary, BSc ACA** *1982;* HLM Resources Ltd, School House, Healaugh, TADCASTER, NORTH YORKSHIRE, LS24 8DB.
BUSS, Miss. Rachel, BSc ACA *2005;* Flat 1, 18 Christchurch Avenue, LONDON, NW6 7QN.
BUSS, Mr. Robin Julian, FCA *1973;* 22 Pine Brae Drive, SKILLMAN, NJ 08558, UNITED STATES.
BUSS, Mr. Timothy, BA ACA *2006;* 46 Gower Road, HAYWARDS HEATH, WEST SUSSEX, RH16 4PN.
BUSSANDRI, Mr. Adrian Peter John, MSc ACA *1990;* 23 Ellerby St, LONDON, SW6 6EX.
BUSSELL, Miss. Lorraine, BSc ACA *1990;* 18 Austin Street, FAIRLIGHT, NSW 2094, AUSTRALIA.
BUSSETIL, Mr. Emmanuel Leonard, FCA *1977;* (Tax Fac), Sete S.A., 3-5 Chemin Des Tuileries, 1293 Bellevue, GENEVA, SWITZERLAND.
BUSSEY, Mr. Anthony Brian Seaton, FCA *1971;* Cockrells Farm, Horkesley Road, Worming Ford, COLCHESTER, CO6 3AP.
BUSSEY, Miss. Clair Wendy, MA ACA *2002;* with PricewaterhouseCoopers LLP, 1 Embankment Place, LONDON, WC2N 6RH.
BUSSEY, Mr. Robin, BSc ACA *2010;* 2 Old Millbrook Terrace, CHELTENHAM, GL50 3RX.
•**BUSSEY, Mr. William Neale, MA ACA** *1992;* Mazars LLP, Tower Bridge House, St. Katharines Way, LONDON, E1W 1DD.
BUSST, Mr. Matthew Marvin, BSc ACA *1997;* 2-8-2 Emerald Condo, Jalan PJU 8/3, Damansara Perdana, 47820 PETALING JAYA, SELANGOR, MALAYSIA.
BUSSY, Mr. Paul Stephen, FCA *1971;* 23 Glentrammon Avenue, Green Street Green, ORPINGTON, BR6 6JY.
BUSSY, Mr. Roger Bernard, FCA *1968;* Flat 41, Shrewsbury House, 42 Cheyne Walk, LONDON, SW3 5LW.
BUSUTTIL, Mr. Paul Edgar, ACA *1981;* 5 Thornton Street, SLIEMA SLM3150, MALTA.
BUSUULWA, Mr. Robert Jack, LLB ACA ATT *2001;* BDO East Africa, DCDM House, PO Box 9113, Plot 22 Mbuya Road, Bugolobi, KAMPALA UGANDA.
BUSWELL, Miss. Gail Rebecca, MA(Hons) ACA *2001;* OCFI, New Road, OXFORD, OX1 1AY.
BUSWELL, Miss. Janice Mary, FCA *1962;* 1 Cottenham Drive, LONDON, SW20 0TD. (Life Member)
BUSWELL, Mr. Keith Malcolm, FCA *1962;* 21 Carmarthen Avenue, East Cosham, PORTSMOUTH, PO6 2AG. (Life Member)
BUSWELL, Miss. Sarah Louise, ACA MAAT *2003;* 47 Ruskin Road, NORTHAMPTON, NN2 7SY.
BUT, Ms. Wai Sze, ACA *2007;* Flat F 4/F Block 4, Palm Mansions, Whampoa Garden Site 4, HUNG HOM, HONG KONG SAR.
BUT, Mr. Yun Wai, ACA *2007;* But Do Yeung C.P.A. Limited, 3/F Kam Sang Building, 257 Des Voeux Road Central, CENTRAL, HONG KONG ISLAND, HONG KONG SAR.
BUTCHART, Miss. Anne Maria, LLB ACA *1992;* 1 Lyrical Way, HEMEL HEMPSTEAD, HP1 3HZ.
BUTCHART, Mr. Timothy Alexander, BA ACA *2004;* Flat 6, 34 Sisters Avenue, LONDON, SW11 5SQ.
BUTCHART, Mr. William, BSc ACA *1983;* 20 Oakfield Grove, Clifton, BRISTOL, BS8 2BN.
BUTCHER, Mr. Andrew Paul, ACA *1992;* The Stables, Station Road, ATTLEBOROUGH, NORFOLK, NR17 2AS.
BUTCHER, Mr. Anthony Osborne, FCA *1950;* 9 Cottesmore Court, Stanford Road, LONDON, W8 5QL. (Life Member)
BUTCHER, Mr. Antony William Frederick, BA ACA *2000;* Hale House Main Road, Sellindge, ASHFORD, TN25 6EQ.
BUTCHER, Mr. Charles Edward, BSc ACA *1993;* Woodhill, Hawkley, LISS, HAMPSHIRE, GU33 6LX.
BUTCHER, Mrs. Clare June, LLB ACA ATII *1991;* University of Durham, Old Shire Hall, DURHAM, DH1 3HP.
BUTCHER, Mr. Colin Edward, FCA *1984;* SG Hambros Bank Limited, Exchange House, Primrose Street, LONDON, EC2A2EF.
BUTCHER, Mr. Craig Nicholas, MBA BSc ACA *1990;* MCB Management Investment Ltd, Suite 204, Mailboxes Etc, 79 Friar Street, WORCESTER, WR1 2NT.
BUTCHER, Mr. David, BA ACA *1993;* 13 Shirley Street, SHIPLEY, BD18 4LY.
BUTCHER, Mr. David Brian, BSc ACA *2006;* 42 Thorne Road, Kelvedon, COLCHESTER, CO5 9JU.

BUTCHER, Mr. David Harry Loftus, BA FCA *1965;* 66 Galway Road, Parkview, JOHANNESBURG, 2193, SOUTH AFRICA.
BUTCHER, Mr. David James, FCA *1971;* Muehlgasse 22, 60486 FRANKFURT AM MAIN, GERMANY. (Life Member)
BUTCHER, Mr. David Keith, BA ACA *1991;* E C S United Kingdom Plc Eton House, 18-24 Paradise Road, RICHMOND, TW9 1SE.
BUTCHER, Mr. David Philip, FCA *1969;* 1/17 Kiteroa Terrace, Rothesay Bay, North Shore City, AUCKLAND, NEW ZEALAND.
•BUTCHER, Mr. Edward John, FCA *1968;* Butcher and Company, 3-7 Wyndham Street, ALDERSHOT, HAMPSHIRE, GU12 4NY.
BUTCHER, Miss. Hazel Anne, ACA *2008;* 42 Windsor Road, Polesworth, TAMWORTH, STAFFORDSHIRE, B78 1DA.
BUTCHER, Mr. Ian George, FCA *1973;* 134 & A Half, Abbey Road, LONDON, NW6 4SR.
BUTCHER, Mr. Ian Leonard, MEng ACA *2010;* Flat 35 Bramley Court, 19 Orchard Grove, ORPINGTON, BR6 0AT.
BUTCHER, Mr. Ian Philip, BSc FCA *1976;* Keldholme Priory Keldholme, Kirkbymoorside, YORK, YO62 6LZ.
BUTCHER, Mr. Jack Basil, FCA *1958;* PO Box BE 15, Belvedere, HARARE, ZIMBABWE. (Life Member)
BUTCHER, Miss. Jacqueline Ann, BA ACA *1988;* 52 Grange Road, BISHOPS STORTFORD, CM23 5NQ.
BUTCHER, Mr. James, BA ACA *2007;* Condor House, 10 St Paul's Churchyard, LONDON, EC4M 8AL.
•BUTCHER, Mr. James Richard, BA FCA *1993;* Ford Campbell Freedman LLP, 34 Park Cross Street, LEEDS, LS1 2QH.
BUTCHER, Mr. Jed, ACA *2008;* 58 Jessett Drive, Church Crookham, FLEET, GU52 0XB.
BUTCHER, Mr. John Charles, BA ACA *1990;* Nissan Motor Manufacturing (UK) Ltd, Washington Road, SUNDERLAND, SR5 3NS.
BUTCHER, Mr. John Thomas Philip, FCA *1976;* The Willows, Victoria Road, MACCLESFIELD, CHESHIRE, SK10 3JA.
BUTCHER, Mr. Keith, BSc ACA *1998;* Neovia/ Optimal Payments, 10 Albemarle Street, LONDON, W1.
•BUTCHER, Mr. Kenneth Leslie, FCA *1980;* Wheatley Pearce Limited, 11 Winchester Place, North Street, POOLE, DORSET, BH15 1NX.
BUTCHER, Mrs. Louise, ACA *2008;* 64 North Street, LONDON, SW4 0HE.
BUTCHER, Mrs. Marie, ACA *2008;* Hardy & Greys Ltd, Willowburn Trading Estate, ALNWICK, NORTHUMBERLAND, NE66 2PF.
BUTCHER, Mr. Michael Leonard, BA ACA *1987;* Talbot & Muir, 22-26 Clarendon Street, NOTTINGHAM, NG1 5HQ.
BUTCHER, Mr. Michael Zygmund, MA(Hons) MSc ACA *2010;* 110 Brunel Road, MAIDENHEAD, BERKSHIRE, SL6 2RN.
BUTCHER, Mr. Neil Martin, ACA *1992;* 11 Rookery Way, Old Newton, STOWMARKET, SUFFOLK, IP14 4ER.
BUTCHER, Mr. Paul Andrew, FCA *1971;* 25 Fairbank Avenue, ORPINGTON, BR6 8JY.
BUTCHER, Mr. Paul David, LLB ACA *1992;* 6 The Grange, STEVENAGE, HERTFORDSHIRE, SG1 3WA.
BUTCHER, Mr. Paul Russell, BSc ACA *1989;* 27 Gilroy Road, TURRAMURRA, NSW 2074, AUSTRALIA.
BUTCHER, Mrs. Rosemary, BSc ACA *1987;* Linwood, Tyndale Gardens, FELIXSTOWE, IP11 9UG.
BUTCHER, Miss. Sarah, MA CA ACA *1993;* 73 Millfield Road, YORK, YO23 1NH.
BUTCHER, Miss. Sarah Elaine Haworth, BA ACA *1985;* 10 Batavia Way, SALTER POINT, WA 6152, AUSTRALIA.
BUTCHER, Mr. Stephen John, ACA ACCA *2007;* with Deloitte LLP, Athene Place, 66 Shoe Lane, LONDON, EC4A 3BQ.
BUTCHER, Mr. Steven, BSc ACA *2005;* City & Guilds of London Institute, 1 Giltspur Street, LONDON, EC1A 9DD.
BUTCHER, Miss. Susan Emma, BSc(Hons) ACA *2004;* (Tax Fac), Barloworld Equipment Ltd, Ground Floor, Statesman House, Stafferton Way, MAIDENHEAD, BERKSHIRE SL6 1AD.
BUTCHER, Mr. Wayne Stephen, BSc(Hons) ACA *2010;* 27 Alderley Road, STOCKPORT, CHESHIRE, SK5 7NN.
BUTCHERS, Mr. Alan Raymond, BSc ACA *1982;* Fairfax House, 85 Castle Road, SALISBURY, SP1 3RW.
BUTCHERS, Mr. Andrew Mark, MA ACA *1987;* Residencia Cecilia Apartamento 31 B, Avenida 3ra, Esquina de 96A, Playa, HAVANA, CUBA.
BUTLAND, Mr. Andrew Rex, BSocSc ACA *1999;* 85 Brampton Way, Portishead, BRISTOL, BS20 6YT.
BUTLER, Mr. Aidan Edward, BSc ACA *1998;* 7 Grosvenor Mews, Rawdon, LEEDS, LS19 6SD.
•BUTLER, Mr. Alan Francis, FCA *1976;* (Tax Fac), Butler Cook Accountants Ltd, 30/32 High Street, Codnor, RIPLEY, DE5 9QB.
BUTLER, Mrs. Alison Jane, FCA *1994;* 50 Lynmouth Road, Hucclecote, GLOUCESTER, GL3 3JD.
BUTLER, Mrs. Alison Jane, BSc ACA *1991;* Taliesin, Pen y Waun, Pentyrch, CARDIFF, CF15 9SJ.
BUTLER, Mr. Alister Gordon James, BSc ACA *2004;* Flat 7, 406 St. John Street, LONDON, EC1V 4ND.
BUTLER, Mr. Andrew Marcus Curzon, BSc FCA *1997;* 1 Grove Road, Shawford, WINCHESTER, SO21 2DD.
BUTLER, Mr. Andrew Philip, BSc ACA *1989;* Taliesin Pen y Waun, Pentyrch, CARDIFF, CF15 9SJ.
BUTLER, Mrs. Angela Mary, BA ACA *1991;* Amber House, Lincombe Drive, TORQUAY, TQ1 2LP.
BUTLER, Mr. Anthony Edgar, ACA *1987;* G E A Pharma Systems Ltd, School Lane, Chandler's Ford, EASTLEIGH, HAMPSHIRE, SO53 4DG.
BUTLER, Mr. Anthony George, FCA *1965;* Flat 8, 12 St. Martins Lane, BECKENHAM, BR3 3XS. (Life Member)
BUTLER, Mr. Antony Rex, MA FCA *1970;* Buis Cottage, Wheeler End, HIGH WYCOMBE, HP14 3NF.
BUTLER, Mr. Benjamin James, MA(Cantab) MSc ACA *2009;* 18 Thornbury Green, Twyford, READING, RG10 9RH.
BUTLER, Mr. Brian Francis, ACA *2000;* James Brearley & Sons, PO Box 34, BLACKPOOL, FY4 4WX.
•BUTLER, Mrs. Carole Eileen, ACA *1989;* Butler Fancourt, Boon Court, Papyrus Road, Werrington, PETERBOROUGH, PE4 5HQ.
BUTLER, Mrs. Catherine, BA(Econ) ACA *1980;* Beechwood, 46 Kings Road, ILKLEY, LS29 9AT.
BUTLER, Mr. Charles Alistair Nielson, BSc ACA FPC *2000;* 54 Sistova Road, LONDON, SW12 9QS.
BUTLER, Mr. Charles Richard Peter, BA ACA *2005;* 3 Runnymede, La Rue de Samares, St. Clement, JERSEY, JE2 6LZ.
BUTLER, Mr. Christian, BSc ACA *1993;* Blandings, 63 Church Street, GREAT MISSENDEN, HP16 0AZ.
•BUTLER, Mr. Christopher Charles, MA ACA *1994;* PricewaterhouseCoopers UAB, Jasinskio 16B, VILNIUS LT-01112, LITHUANIA.
BUTLER, Mr. Christopher James, BSc ACA *2008;* 7 Convent Gardens, LONDON, W5 4UT.
BUTLER, Mr. Christopher Latour, ACA *2008;* Friends Provident Axa Centre Bristol, Brierly Furlong Stoke Gifford, BRISTOL, BS34 8SW.
BUTLER, Ms. Clare, BSc ACA *1993;* 77 Fernside Road, LONDON, SW12 8LH.
BUTLER, Mr. Colin Philip, BBS FCA *1975;* Locked Bag 18, SUBIACO, WA 6904, AUSTRALIA.
BUTLER, Mr. Darryl John, BA(Econ) ACA *1996;* Figart, Isle of Doagh, CLONMANY, COUNTY DONEGAL, IRELAND.
BUTLER, Mr. David, FCA *1954;* 9 Beaumont Crescent, CAMBRIDGE, CB1 8QA. (Life Member)
•BUTLER, Mr. David Alexander, ACA *2002;* Butler Accountancy Services Ltd, Suite 1 Telford House, Riverside, Warwick Road, CARLISLE, CA1 2BT.
BUTLER, Mr. David Arthur William, BA FCA *1979;* 44 Oakwood Drive, BILLERICAY, ESSEX, CM12 0SA.
•BUTLER, Mr. David George, BSc FCA *1981;* (Tax Fac), Clay Shaw Butler Ltd, 24 Lammas Street, CARMARTHEN, DYFED, SA31 3AL.
BUTLER, Mr. David John, BSc ACA MCT *1987;* Park House, 28 Eaton Road, NORWICH, NR4 6PZ.
BUTLER, Mr. David John, FCA *1968;* Barn Cottage, Common Wood, KINGS LANGLEY, HERTFORDSHIRE, WD4 9BB.
BUTLER, Mr. David Michael, BSc ACA *2000;* 89 Birchall Road, BRISTOL, BS6 7TT.
BUTLER, Ms. Deirdre Kathryn, MA ACA *1984;* 30C Tower 1, Scenic Heights, 58 Conduit Road, MID LEVELS, HONG KONG ISLAND, HONG KONG SAR.
•BUTLER, Mrs. Delia Marie, BSc ACA *1990;* (Tax Fac), Prospero, 12 Hockerley New Road, Whaley Bridge, HIGH PEAK, DERBYSHIRE, SK23 7GA.
•BUTLER, Miss. Elizabeth Jane, BSc FCA *1986;* (Tax Fac), E J Butler, Manor Road House, 42 Manor Road, BECKENHAM, BR3 5LE.
BUTLER, Mrs. Emma Louise, ACA *2008;* 19 Harwood Square, BRISTOL, BS7 8QN.
BUTLER, Mr. Ernest James, FCA *1961;* Humber Mill, Humber, TEIGNMOUTH, TQ14 9TD. (Life Member)
BUTLER, Miss. Frances Helen, LLB ACA *1981;* (Tax Fac), 6 Sunray Avenue, Herne Hill, LONDON, SE24 9PY.
•BUTLER, Mr. Geoffrey Robert, PhD BSc FCA CertPFS DChA *1982;* (Tax Fac), Geoffrey R Butler, The Mullions, New Road, Beer, SEATON, EX12 3EB.
•BUTLER, Mr. Geoffrey William, BA FCA *1987;* G.W Butler, 5 Rothsbury Drive, Valley Park, Chandlers Ford, EASTLEIGH, SO53 4QQ.
BUTLER, Mr. Graham Kenneth, FCA *1970;* Bel-Air, Sandy Lane, NORTHWOOD, HA6 3ES.
BUTLER, Mr. Graham Michael, BCom ACA *1988;* 3 Malthouse Close, Church Crookham, FLEET, HAMPSHIRE, GU52 6TB.
BUTLER, Mr. Guy Ross, BCom ACA *1981;* 6a Sunbird Crescent, BOAMBEE EAST, NSW 2452, AUSTRALIA.
BUTLER, Mr. Iain David, BA(Econ) ACA *1997;* 2305, 26TH STREET, VERNON V1T 4T3, BC, CANADA.
•BUTLER, Mr. Iain Hamish, BA FCA *1970;* I.H. Butler & Co, 25 Gainsborough Drive, Adel, LEEDS, LS16 7PF.
BUTLER, Mr. Ian Frederick, BCom FCA *1965;* Culverhayes, Colehill, WIMBORNE, BH21 2QR. (Life Member)
BUTLER, Mrs. Jacqueline Anne, BA ACA *2000;* 33 Judith Street, SEAFORTH, NSW 2092, AUSTRALIA.
BUTLER, Mr. James Edward, BSc(Hons) ACA *2001;* 10 Kilnsey Mews West Lane, Baildon, SHIPLEY, BD17 5TS.
BUTLER, Sir James James, CBE DL MA FCA *1955;* (Member of Council 1992 - 1994), Littleton House, Crawley, WINCHESTER, SO21 2QF. (Life Member)
BUTLER, Mrs. Jean, BSc FCA *1978;* 29 Darracott Road, BOURNEMOUTH, BH5 2AY.
BUTLER, Mr. Jeffrey Brian, MA ACA *1991;* 101 Wattleton Road, BEACONSFIELD, BUCKINGHAMSHIRE, HP9 1RW.
BUTLER, Mr. Jeremy Richard, BA ACA *1996;* 43 Primrose Road, WALTON-ON-THAMES, KT12 5JD.
BUTLER, Mr. John, FCA *1970;* 37A Crownhill Street, NEW PLYMOUTH 4310, NEW ZEALAND.
•BUTLER, Mr. John David, BSc FCA *1980;* Butlers, 4 Oakwood Gardens, Knaphill, WOKING, SURREY, GU21 2RX. See also Butlers Chartered Accountants
BUTLER, Mr. John Duncan, FCA *1965;* Little Orchard, Tidmarsh Lane, Tidmarsh, READING, RG8 8HA. (Life Member)
BUTLER, Mr. John Greer, FCA *1972;* Ikoyi Rickman Hill Road, Chipstead, COULSDON, CR5 3LD.
BUTLER, Mr. John Peter Neilson, BSc FCA *1972;* Milton Farm, Milton Rough, Acton Bridge, NORTHWICH, CW8 2RF.
•BUTLER, Mr. John William, BSc FCA *1974;* (Tax Fac), Butlers, Little Garth, Tirley Lane, Utkinton, TARPORLEY, CHESHIRE CW6 0JZ.
•BUTLER, Mr. John William, BA ACA MABRP *2006;* Redman Nichols Butler, Maclaren House, Skerne Road, DRIFFIELD, YO25 6PN.
BUTLER, Ms. Joy Anne, BA ACA *1987;* Hastings Direct, 32-34 Collington Avenue, BEXHILL-ON-SEA, EAST SUSSEX, TN39 3LW.
•BUTLER, Ms. Julie Elizabeth, BMus FCA *1984;* (Tax Fac), J E Butler & Co., 222 The Avenue, Highams Park, LONDON, E4 9SE.
•BUTLER, Mrs. Julie Marion, FCA *1980;* (Tax Fac), Butler & Co, Bennett House, The Dean, ALRESFORD, HAMPSHIRE, SO24 9BH. See also Butler & Co (Bishops Waltham) Ltd
BUTLER, Miss. Julie Suzanne, BA(Hons) ACA *2002;* 29 Clarinda House, Clovelly Place, GREENHITHE, DA9 9FB.
BUTLER, Miss. Justine Mary, BA ACA *1992;* 20 Paxton Gardens, WOKING, SURREY, GU21 5TR.
BUTLER, Mrs. Kate Alison, MSc ACA *2004;* 2 Mount Cottages, The Mount, Barley, ROYSTON, HERTFORDSHIRE, SG8 8JH.
BUTLER, Mrs. Katharine Mary, BSc ACA *1986;* Cherry Valley Farms Ltd, Villa Office Rothwell, MARKET RASEN, LINCOLNSHIRE, LN7 6BJ.
•BUTLER, Mr. Keith David, FCA *1983;* (Tax Fac), Butler & Co, 1 Manor Park, Arkendale, KNARESBOROUGH, HG5 0QH.
BUTLER, Mr. Keith Edmund, FCA *1961;* 2 Newlands Avenue, West Monkseaton, WHITLEY BAY, TYNE AND WEAR, NE25 9DU. (Life Member)
BUTLER, Mr. Keith Eric, BA ACA *1986;* 54 Picklers Hill, ABINGDON, OXFORDSHIRE, OX14 2BB.
BUTLER, Mr. Kelvin Richard, FCA *1973;* Meadow Cottage, Hutton, BERWICK-UPON-TWEED, BERWICKSHIRE, TD15 1TN.
BUTLER, Mr. Kevin George, BA FCA *1986;* 17 Knotts Road, TODMORDEN, LANCASHIRE, OL14 8JE.
BUTLER, Mrs. Kim Louise, BSc ACA *2009;* 71 Lumley Road, HORLEY, SURREY, RH6 7JF.
BUTLER, Miss. Kirstan Anna, BSc ACA *2004;* 52 Haigh Side Close, Rothwell, LEEDS, LS26 0UH.
•BUTLER, Miss. Laura, BSc ACA *2003;* Butlers, Little Garth, Tirley Lane, Utkinton, TARPORLEY, CHESHIRE CW6 0JZ.
BUTLER, Mr. Lewis James, ACA *2010;* 167 Northstand Apartments, Highbury Stadium Square, LONDON, N5 1FN.
•BUTLER, Mrs. Lorraine, FCA *1984;* KBDR, The Old Tannery, Hensington Road, WOODSTOCK, OXFORDSHIRE, OX20 1JL.
BUTLER, Mrs. Manon, LLB ACA ATII *1988;* Alliance BootsPlc, 2 The Heights, Brooklands, WEYBRIDGE, SURREY, KT13 0NY.
BUTLER, Mrs. Marie Anne, BA ACA *1999;* 23 Grange Hill, Coggeshall, COLCHESTER, CO6 1RE.
BUTLER, Mr. Mark Richard, BA ACA *1987;* 27 Grafton Square, LONDON, SW4 0DB.
BUTLER, Mr. Martin Keith, BA ACA *1999;* 3 Dunton Grove Hadleigh, IPSWICH, IP7 5HD.
BUTLER, Michael Howard, Esq OBE FCA *1958;* Banstead Down, Old Chorleywood Road, RICKMANSWORTH, HERTFORDSHIRE, WD3 4EH. (Life Member)
•BUTLER, Mr. Michael John, BSc ACA *1994;* Old Mill, Number One, Goldcroft, YEOVIL, SOMERSET, BA21 4DX. See also Old Mill Accountancy LLP and Old Mill Audit LLP
BUTLER, Mr. Michael John, FCA *1977;* 31 Stammers Place, MYAREE, WA 6154, AUSTRALIA.
•BUTLER, Mr. Michael John Christopher, ACA ATII *1979;* Moore Stephens LLP, 150 Aldersgate Street, LONDON, EC1A 4AB. See also Moore Stephens & Co
BUTLER, Mrs. Myra, FCA CTA *1981;* 1 Manor Park, Arkendale, KNARESBOROUGH, HG5 0QH.
BUTLER, Miss. Natalie Cassandra, ACA *2009;* Flat 14 Davoll Court, Marine Street, LONDON, SE16 4RJ.
BUTLER, Mr. Neil Jonathon, BA(Hons) FCA *2001;* 8 Leydene Park, Hyden Farm Lane, East Meon, PETERSFIELD, HAMPSHIRE, GU32 1HF.
BUTLER, Mr. Neil William, MA MSc ACA *1990;* Northorpe House, Northorpe, Donington, SPALDING, LINCOLNSHIRE, PE11 4XY.
•BUTLER, Mr. Norman Thomas, FCA *1951;* N.T.Butler, 26 Rose Lane, Melbourn, ROYSTON, SG8 6AD.
BUTLER, Mr. Paul, FCA *1985;* 6 Masefield View, ORPINGTON, BR6 8PH.
BUTLER, Mr. Paul, BSc ACA *2006;* with Francis Clark, Francis Clark LLP, Sigma House, Oak View Close, Edginswell Park, TORQUAY TQ2 7FF.
BUTLER, Mr. Paul Ian, BSc ACA *1995;* Stuart Darling Ltd, 3 Greenside Waterbeach, CAMBRIDGE, CB25 9HW.
BUTLER, Mr. Paul James, ACA *2004;* with BDO LLP, 2 City Place, Beehive Ring Road, GATWICK, WEST SUSSEX, RH6 0PA.
BUTLER, Mr. Paul James, ACA *2009;* 112 Rock Avenue, GILLINGHAM, KENT, ME7 5PS.
BUTLER, Mr. Paul William, BA ACA *1991;* 2 Church Hill, North Rigton, LEEDS, LS17 0DF.
BUTLER, Mr. Peter John, BA ACA *1992;* 14 Paterson Drive, Woodhouse Eaves, LOUGHBOROUGH, LE12 8RL.
BUTLER, Mr. Peter Mark, BSc ACA *1979;* Suite 2 Havannah House, Cuba Industrial Estate, Bolton Road North, Ramsbottom, BURY, LANCASHIRE BL0 0NE.
BUTLER, Mr. Peter Robert, BSc FCA *1973;* Governance for Owners LLP, 26 Throgmorton Street, LONDON, EC2N 2AN.
BUTLER, Mr. Piers Daniel, BSc ACA *1986;* 37 Lancaster Road, LONDON, SW19 5DF.
BUTLER, Miss. Rebecca Margaret, BA ACA *2002;* 167 Penwith Road, LONDON, SW18 4PZ.
BUTLER, Mr. Reginald Richard, FCA *1960;* 22 Heath Drive, South Sutton, SUTTON, SM2 5RP. (Life Member)
BUTLER, Mr. Richard, BA ACA *2004;* Church Farm House, Haddenham, AYLESBURY, BUCKINGHAMSHIRE, HP17 8AE.
BUTLER, Mr. Richard, FCA *1982;* 10 Bond Street, ARUNDEL, WEST SUSSEX, BN18 9BL.
BUTLER, Mr. Richard John, BSc ACA *1991;* Interserve IS Ltd, Intersection House, 110-120 Birmingham Road, WEST BROMWICH, WEST MIDLANDS, B70 6RP.
BUTLER, Sir Richard Pierce, Bt FCA *1963;* IT - Torri, Hondoq, Qala, GOZO, MALTA. (Life Member)

BUTLER, Mr. Robert Alan, BSc FCA *2009;* 173 Woodhall Road, Calverley, PUDSEY, WEST YORKSHIRE, LS28 5QT.
BUTLER, Mr. Robert Edward William, MPhil BA ACA *2007;* 80a Dunstan Street, ELY, CAMBRIDGESHIRE, CB6 3AQ.
BUTLER, Mr. Robert William, ACA *2009;* C/o PM Mexico Cigatam, Robert Butler, Manual Salazar No 132, Azcapotzalco, CP 02240 MEXICO CITY, MEXICO.
BUTLER, Mr. Robert John, ACA *2011;* 49 Browning Crescent, Bletchley, MILTON KEYNES, MK3 5AU.
BUTLER, Mr. Robin William, FCA *1956;* 47 Colin Avenue, TORONTO M5P 2B8, ON, CANADA. (Life Member)
BUTLER, Mr. Roger John, FCA *1969;* (Tax Fac), Riverslea, Glen Auldyn, Lezayre, ISLE OF MAN, IM7 2AQ.
•**BUTLER, Mrs. Rosemary Clare, FCA** *1980;* R.C. Butler, 83 Strathcona Avenue, Bookham, LEATHERHEAD, KT23 4HS.
BUTLER, Mr. Roy Joseph, FCA *1975;* Heydour, 24 Glebe Road, Purley on Thames, READING, RG8 8DP.
BUTLER, Mr. Sam, ACA *2011;* Hillcrest, Tower Road, Coleshill, AMERSHAM, BUCKINGHAMSHIRE, HP7 0LB.
•**BUTLER, Mrs. Sarah Anne, BA(Hons) FCA** *2001;* Infinity Asset Management LLP, 26th Floor, City Tower, Piccadilly Plaza, MANCHESTER, M1 4BD.
•**BUTLER, Miss. Sharon Dawn, BSc FCA ATII** *1984;* Wheat & Butler, 19 Holbrook Lane, CHISLEHURST, BR7 6PE. See also Maratea Limited
BUTLER, Mr. Shaun, BSc FCA *1980;* (Tax Fac), Woodpecker Cottage, Grubwood Lane, Cookham, MAIDENHEAD, BERKSHIRE, SL6 9UD.
BUTLER, Mr. Simon, BSc ACA *2008;* Muras Baker Jones Regent House, Bath Avenue, WOLVERHAMPTON, WV1 4EG.
BUTLER, Mr. Simon, BSc FCA MBA CPA *1995;* 29 The Highway, Croesyceiliog, CWMBRAN, GWENT, NP44 2BG.
BUTLER, Mr. Stephen Leslie, BSc ACA *1995;* (Tax Fac), 236 Gray's Inn Road, LONDON, WC1X 8HL.
BUTLER, Mr. Stephen Nicholas, FCA *1977;* Bryn Coed, 4 Woolton Park CLose, Woolton Park, LIVERPOOL, L25 6JZ.
•**BUTLER, Mr. Stephen Paul, BA FCA** *1993;* HW, Sterling House, 97 Lichfield Street, TAMWORTH, STAFFORDSHIRE, B79 7QF. See also HW Progress Accountants Ltd
BUTLER, Mr. Stephen William, ACA *1979;* 6 Somerset Close Long Eaton, NOTTINGHAM, NG10 2ET.
BUTLER, Mr. Steven James, ACA *2000;* 67 Green Street, SUNBURY-ON-THAMES, TW16 6RD.
BUTLER, Mr. Steven Jon, BA ACA *1992;* Rex House, 4-12 Regent St, LONDON, SW1Y 4PE.
BUTLER, Mr. Steven Robert, BA FCA *1981;* P.O.Box 1854, GEORGETOWN, GRAND CAYMAN, KY1 1110, CAYMAN ISLANDS.
BUTLER, Mrs. Susan, BA ACA *1993;* Barton Lodge, Beach, Bitton, BRISTOL, BS30 6NW.
BUTLER, Mrs. Susan Patricia, BSc FCA *1980;* with The TACS Partnership, Graylaw House, Mersey Square, STOCKPORT, CHESHIRE, SK1 1AL.
BUTLER, Mrs. Tracy Ann, BA ACA *1995;* 20 Millfield, NESTON, CH64 3TF.
BUTLER, Mrs. Victoria Jayne, ACA *2008;* 11 Harrogate Road, HOCKLEY, ESSEX, SS5 5HT.
BUTLER, Mr. Warrick, BSc FCA *1970;* 5 Manscombe Road, TORQUAY, TQ2 6SP. (Life Member)
BUTLER, Mrs. Wendy Elizabeth, BSc ACA *1991;* The Dingle, Greenlands Lane, Prestwood, GREAT MISSENDEN, HP16 9QX.
BUTLER-ADAMS, Mr. Richard, MA FCA *1969;* (Tax Fac), The Old Vicarage, Church Street, Upton Grey, BASINGSTOKE, RG25 2RB.
BUTLER-WHEELHOUSE, Mr. Duncan, ACA *2009;* 18 Eton Park, Eton Road, Sandhurst, JOHANNESBURG, 2196, SOUTH AFRICA.
BUTLIN, Mrs. Joanna Louise, BA ACA *1994;* Grange Meadow Alton Green, Lower Holbrook, IPSWICH, IP9 2RN.
BUTLIN, Mr. Phillip Charles, BA ACA *1988;* Main Camp Natural Extracts Pty Ltd, 25 Beach Street, COTTESLOE, WA 6011, AUSTRALIA.
•**BUTNICK, Mr. Alan Edward, FCA** *1964;* A. Butnick & Co, 18 Barn Crescent, STANMORE, HA7 2RY.
BUTONKEE, Mr. Twaleb, FCA ACCA *1997;* Kemp Chatteris Deloitte, 7th. Floor, Raffles Tower, 19 Cybercity, EBENE, MAURITIUS.
BUTSON, Mr. Malcolm Gordon, FCA *1959;* 47 Queensway, HORSHAM, RH13 5AP. (Life Member)
BUTSON, Mr. Reginald Keith, FCA *1957;* South View Farm, Bramshaw, LYNDHURST, HAMPSHIRE, SO43 7JL. (Life Member)
BUTT, Mr. Alexander, FCA *1984;* 18 Crockford Park Road, ADDLESTONE, SURREY, KT15 2ND.
•**BUTT, Mr. Brian Mervyn, FCA** *1962;* (Tax Fac), with Chalmers & Co (SW) Limited, 6 Linen Yard, South Street, CREWKERNE, SOMERSET, TA18 8AB.
BUTT, Mr. Christopher Edwin, ACA *2008;* Flat 1, Eton Court, 11 Allerton Park, LEEDS, WEST YORKSHIRE, LS7 4ND.
BUTT, Mr. Graham, LLB FCA *1979;* The Coach House, Barwell Close, LEAMINGTON SPA, WARWICKSHIRE, CV32 6QA.
•**BUTT, Mrs. Jacqueline Angela, BSc ACA** *1988;* Jeff Butt & Co, Broadacres, The Ridge, Woodfalls, SALISBURY, SP5 2LQ.
•**BUTT, Mr. Jeffrey Neil, BSc ACA** *1989;* (Tax Fac), Jeff Butt & Co, Broadacres, The Ridge, Woodfalls, SALISBURY, SP5 2LQ.
BUTT, Mr. Khayyam, BA(Econ) ACA *2009;* 18 Holly Drive, LONDON, E4 7NG.
•**BUTT, Mr. Mohammad Irfan-Ul-Haq, BCom FCA ATII** *1994;* 26 Lincoln Gardens, ILFORD, ESSEX, IG1 3NF.
BUTT, Mr. Mohammed Ashraf, BSc ACA *2006;* C S First Credit Suisse Financial Products, 1 Cabot Square, LONDON, E14 4QJ.
BUTT, Mr. Mudassir Amin, ACA *1996;* 359 Ormond Road Narre Warren South, MELBOURNE, VIC 3805, AUSTRALIA.
BUTT, Mr. Muhammad Aamir, ACA FCCA *2011;* AAMIR BUTT & CO, H# 11 NEW MILLAT COLONY NEAR WELCOME HOTEL COMMITTEE CHOWK, RAWALPINDI 46000, PAKISTAN.
BUTT, Mr. Munir Uddin, FCA *1970;* 27 Pebworth Road, HARROW, MIDDLESEX, HA1 3UD.
BUTT, Mr. Nadim, LLB ACA *1997;* 18 Cherry Avenue, SLOUGH, BERKSHIRE, SL3 7BT.
BUTT, Miss. Nicola Jane, BSc ACA *1998;* Old Dairy Barn, Cote, BAMPTON, OXFORDSHIRE, OX18 2EG.
•**BUTT, Mr. Nigel Bevan, BA FCA** *1975;* (Tax Fac), Butt Miller Limited, 92 Park Street, CAMBERLEY, GU15 3NY.
•**BUTT, Mr. Nisar Ahmed Fazal Elahi, FCA** *1973;* 109 Granville Road, LONDON, SW18 5SF.
BUTT, Mr. Philip Ronald, FCA *1965;* 39 Somerville Road, SUTTON COLDFIELD, B73 6HH.
BUTT, Mr. Rahim, ACA *2011;* Flat 22 Amber Court, High Street, ROMFORD, RM1 1AP.
BUTT, Mr. Sohail Ahmed, FCA *1979;* 3650 Kaneff Crescent, APT # 205, MISSISSAUGA L5A 4A1, ON, CANADA.
BUTT, Mr. Stephen Frederick, FCA *1978;* Hobbits, Victoria Road, North Common, Warmley, BRISTOL, BS30 5LA.
BUTT, Mr. Waqas Ahmed, BSc ACA *1999;* 13 Longnor Road, Heald Green, CHEADLE, CHESHIRE, SK8 3BW.
•**BUTTARS, Mrs. Sarah Louise, BSc FCA** *1993;* Sarah Buttars & Company, Brensham Cottage, Malting Lane, Aldbury, TRING, HERTFORDSHIRE HP23 5RH.
BUTTEN, Mr. Nigel Anthony, MA FCA *1969;* 18 Regents Place, EASTBOURNE, EAST SUSSEX, BN21 2XY.
•**BUTTER, Mr. Christian, BSc ACA** *1999;* PricewaterhouseCoopers LLP, Pricewaterhousecoopers, 12 Plumtree Court, LONDON, EC4A 4HT. See also PricewaterhouseCoopers
BUTTER, Mrs. Joanne Sarah, BA ACA *1999;* 7 Bangalore Street, Putney, LONDON, SW15 1QD.
BUTTER, Dr. Ruth Stafford, PhD BSc ACA *2001;* PO Box 32, PAHIATUA 4941, NEW ZEALAND.
BUTTER, Mr. Sebastian, BSc ACA *2007;* with Deloitte LLP, 2 New Street Square, LONDON, EC4A 3BZ.
BUTTERFIELD, Mr. Alan John William, BSc ACA *1990;* GE Capital, Level 13, 255 George Street, SYDNEY, NSW 2000, AUSTRALIA.
BUTTERFIELD, Mrs. Caroline Ann, BSc ACA *1982;* Craigmill House, Craigmill, STIRLING, FK9 5PP.
BUTTERFIELD, Mr. Christopher Alan, FCA *1978;* North Lodge Farm, Widmerpool Lane, Widmerpool, NOTTINGHAM, NG12 5QE.
BUTTERFIELD, Mr. Christopher John, MBA FCA *1969;* 6 Ashville Close, Green Lane, HARROGATE, HG2 9LZ. (Life Member)
BUTTERFIELD, Mr. Garry, ACA *1986;* 12 Highgate Avenue, WALSALL, WS1 3BH.
BUTTERFIELD, Mr. Ian Gordon, BSc ACA *1990;* Acres High, Tile Barn, Woolton Hill, NEWBURY, RG20 9UX.
BUTTERFIELD, Mr. John Anthony, FCA *1951;* 8 Southernhay Road, LEICESTER, LE2 3TJ. (Life Member)
BUTTERFIELD, Mrs. Margaret Anne, BA ACA *1987;* Mayflex, Excel House, Junction 6 Industrial Park, Electric Avenue, BIRMINGHAM, B6 7JJ.
BUTTERFIELD, Mr. Mark Benjamin, ACA *2008;* 3 Stonecross Lea, CHATHAM, KENT, ME5 0BL.
BUTTERFIELD, Mr. Nigel Robert Adamson, FCA *1969;* Bullrush Farm Hillgrove, Lurgashall, PETWORTH, WEST SUSSEX, GU28 9EP. (Life Member)
BUTTERFIELD, Mr. Paul, BSc ACA *1993;* 12 Rutland Street, COLNE, BB8 0QJ.
BUTTERFIELD, Mr. Paul Matthew, BSc ACA *1983;* 6 Meadowcroft, Barkisland, HALIFAX, HX4 0FB.
BUTTERFIELD, Mr. Peter Michael, FCA *1955;* Ringborough, Culmhead, Churchinford, TAUNTON, SOMERSET, TA3 7EB. (Life Member)
BUTTERFIELD, Mr. Richard Andrew Peter, BSc ACA *1980;* Woodlands, Lower Stone, BERKELEY, GL13 9DL.
•**BUTTERFIELD, Mr. Robert Steven, FCA MEWI** *1972;* Wilkins Kennedy, Greytown House, 221-227 High Street, ORPINGTON, BR6 0NZ. See also W K Finn-Kelcey & Chapman Limited
BUTTERFIELD, Miss. Selina Natasha, BSc ACA *2009;* Flat 7 Ralph Court, Queensway, LONDON, W2 5HT
BUTTERFIELD, Mr. Simon Percy, FCA *1971;* 9 Blunts Wood Road, HAYWARDS HEATH, RH16 1ND. (Life Member)
BUTTERICK, Mr. Peter Stephen, FCA *1956;* Openfields, Love Lane, KINGS LANGLEY, WD4 9HW. (Life Member)
BUTTERILL, Miss. Carol Ann, BA ACA *1990;* Compass, Langton House, 5 Priory Street, YORK, YO1 6ET.
BUTTERISS, Mrs. Amanda Jayne, BSc ACA *1997;* 11 Golden Oak Close, Farnham Common, SLOUGH, SL2 3SY.
•**BUTTERLEY, Miss. Diane Elizabeth, BA ACA** *2005;* (Tax Fac), Leigh Philip & Partners, 1/6 Clay Street, LONDON, W1U 6DA.
BUTTERS, Mr. Adrian Paul, BA ACA *1994;* 2 Pembroke Drive, Aston Lodge Park, STONE, ST15 8XE.
BUTTERS, Mr. Andrew Macneil, BCom FCA *1993;* Willow Hanye, Cottage Lane, Gayton, WIRRAL, MERSEYSIDE, CH60 8PB.
BUTTERS, Mr. Andrew Martin, MA ACA *1980;* 1 Eaton Road, Handbridge, CHESTER, CH4 7EN.
BUTTERS, Miss. Carol Alison, ACA MAAT *1998;* 112 rue Madame de Maintenon, 78120 RAMBOUILLET, FRANCE.
BUTTERS, Mr. Christopher Charles, FCA *1990;* Heathfield House, Creech Heathfield, TAUNTON, SOMERSET, TA3 5EG.
•①**BUTTERS, Mr. Daniel Francis, BA(Hons) ACA** *2000;* Deloitte LLP, 1 City Square, LEEDS, WEST YORKSHIRE, LS1 2AL. See also Deloitte & Touche LLP
•**BUTTERS, Mr. Jonathan Richard, FCA** *1991;* (Tax Fac), Butters Gates & Company, 107 Bell Street, LONDON, NW1 6TL.
•**BUTTERS, Mr. Laurence Bernard, FCA** *1956;* Laurence B Butters, 28 Elm Avenue, WATFORD, WD19 4BE.
•**BUTTERS, Mr. Peter Sydney, FCA** *1958;* Butters & Company, 129 High St, TEDDINGTON, TW11 8HJ.
BUTTERS, Mrs. Sonya, MA(Hons) ACA *2001;* 15 Priory Drive, REIGATE, SURREY, RH2 8AF.
BUTTERWORTH, Mr. Alan George, MSc FCA *1977;* 122 Kenwood Drive, BECKENHAM, BR3 6RB.
•**BUTTERWORTH, Mr. Alexander Robert, BA ACA** *1989;* Deloitte LLP, Abbots House, Abbey Street, READING, RG1 3BD. See also Deloitte & Touche LLP
BUTTERWORTH, Mr. Andrew Craig, BA ACA *1997;* 19 Springbank Gardens, LYMM, CHESHIRE, WA13 9GR.
BUTTERWORTH, Mr. Andrew James, BSc ACA *2005;* with Deloitte LLP, Athene Place, 66 Shoe Lane, LONDON, EC4A 3BQ.
BUTTERWORTH, Mr. Brian, FCA *1964;* Greystones, 5 Shawfield Avenue, HOLMFIRTH, West Yorkshire, HD9 2LZ. (Life Member)
BUTTERWORTH, Mr. Clifford, FCA *1951;* Castell, Worcester Road, PERSHORE, WR10 1HQ. (Life Member)
BUTTERWORTH, Mr. Colin, FCA *1969;* The Granary, Lowsdon Lane, Riseley, BEDFORD, MK44 1SN. (Life Member)
•**BUTTERWORTH, Mr. David Martin, FCA ATII** *1987;* (Tax Fac), Wheawill & Sudworth, P.O. Box B30, 35 Westgate, HUDDERSFIELD, HD1 1PA.
•**BUTTERWORTH, Mr. Gavin, ACA** *2002;* Butterworth Barlow, Prescot House, 3 High Street, PRESCOT, MERSEYSIDE, L34 3LD. See also Butterworth Barlow Limited
BUTTERWORTH, Mrs. Gayle Margaret, BA ACA *2007;* 29 Chervil, Coulby Newham, MIDDLESBROUGH, CLEVELAND, TS8 0GB.
BUTTERWORTH, Mr. Geoffrey, BA FCA *1952;* Eversley, 36 Leadhall Road, HARROGATE, HG2 9PE. (Life Member)
BUTTERWORTH, Mr. Geoffrey Frank, FCA *1958;* 7 Allee des Capucines, 78450 CHAVENAY, FRANCE. (Life Member)
BUTTERWORTH, Mr. George Edward, BA ACA *2005;* 46A Carminia Road, LONDON, SW17 8AH.
BUTTERWORTH, Miss. Gina Claire, ACA *1998;* 15 Common Lane, HARPENDEN, HERTFORDSHIRE, AL5 5BT.
BUTTERWORTH, Mr. Graeme John, ACA *1987;* with IBM, 76 Upper Ground, South Bank, LONDON, SE1 9PZ.
•**BUTTERWORTH, Mr. Guy Michael, ACA** *1992;* Lucraft Hodgson & Dawes, 2/4 Ash Lane, Rustington, LITTLEHAMPTON, BN16 3BZ.
BUTTERWORTH, Mrs. Jenny Fay, BSc ACA *2003;* 10 Pear Tree Drive, STOURBRIDGE, WEST MIDLANDS, DY8 2LB.
BUTTERWORTH, Mr. Jonathan Greg, BEng ACA ATII *1992;* 50 Tyron Way, SIDCUP, DA14 6AZ.
BUTTERWORTH, Mr. Jonathan Paul, BA(Hons) ACA *2002;* 10 Pear Tree Drive, Pedmore, STOURBRIDGE, WEST MIDLANDS, DY8 2LB.
•**BUTTERWORTH, Mr. Mark Bernard, BSc(Hons) FCA FCCA** *1992;* (Tax Fac), Mark Butterworth Limited, Windsor House, 26 Mostyn Avenue, LLANDUDNO, GWYNEDD, LL30 1YY. See also Butterworths Accountants Limited
BUTTERWORTH, Mr. Maurice Stewart, FCA *1962;* 19/322 Orrong Road, CAULFIELD NORTH, VIC 3161, AUSTRALIA. (Life Member)
BUTTERWORTH, Mr. Michael Guy, BA ACA *1987;* The Woodman, Howe Street, Great Waltham, CHELMSFORD, ESSEX, CM3 1BA.
BUTTERWORTH, Mr. Nicholas, FCA *1960;* Old Bruns Farm, St. Leonards, TRING, HERTFORDSHIRE, HP23 6NR. (Life Member)
BUTTERWORTH, Mr. Nicholas Mark, BSc ACA *2009;* Flat 2, 1 Kilmorey Road, TWICKENHAM, TW1 1PX.
BUTTERWORTH, Mrs. Nicola Jane, ACA *1997;* 2 The Straits, Astley, Tyldesley, MANCHESTER, M29 7RR.
BUTTERWORTH, Mr. Philip, BA FCA *1972;* PB Interim Financial Management Ltd, 4 Glebe Close, Long Ashton, BRISTOL, BS41 9DB.
•**BUTTERWORTH, Mr. Philip John, ACA** *1981;* (Tax Fac), Butterworth Jones, 7 Castle St, BRIDGWATER, SOMERSET, TA6 3DT.
•**BUTTERWORTH, Mr. Richard, FCA** *1968;* Samuel Slater & Sons, 11 Queen Street, OLDHAM, OL1 1RG.
BUTTERWORTH, Mr. Richard Anthony, BA ACA *1990;* 380 Mulgrave Place, WEST VANCOUVER V7S 1H1, BC, CANADA.
BUTTERWORTH, Mr. Richard James Thomas, MA ACA *1995;* DFID Burma, British Embassy, 80 Strand Road, YANGON, MYANMAR.
BUTTERWORTH, Mrs. Ruth Elizabeth, ACA *2009;* 41 Wesham Park Drive, Wesham, PRESTON, PR4 3EF.
BUTTERWORTH, Mr. Simon Henry, BSc ACA *1979;* Church Farm Cliffash Lane, Idridgehay, BELPER, DERBYSHIRE, DE56 2SJ.
BUTTERWORTH, Miss. Susan Mary, BA FCA *1975;* 79 Harberton Road, Archway, LONDON, N19 3JT.
BUTTERY, Mr. Michael John, BA(Hons) ACA *2000;* British Telecom Kelvin House, 123 Judd Street, LONDON, WC1H 9NP.
BUTTIGIEG, Miss. Judith, MA FCA *1995;* Aviva Plc, St Helens, 1 Undershaft, LONDON, EC3 3DQ.
BUTTINGER, Miss. Lydia Hannah, BSc ACA *2007;* Flat 2, 51 Shortlands Road, BROMLEY, BR2 0JJ.
BUTTLE, Mr. Sean Terry, BSc ACA *2004;* 29 High Street, PO Box 212, RANGIORA 7440, NEW ZEALAND.
BUTTLE, Miss. Sophie, ACA *2005;* Flat 5 Surridge Court Clapham Road, LONDON, SW9 9AG.
BUTTLER, Mr. Mark James, BSc ACA FSI *1997;* Key Capital Partners LLP, Princes Exchange, 2 Princes Square, LEEDS, LS1 4HY.
BUTTLER, Mrs. Rebecca Jane, LLB ACA *1999;* 1 Pennyfield Close, LEEDS, LS6 4NZ.
BUTTON, Mrs. Clare Dominica, BSc ACA *1988;* 3 Curzon Drive, Church Crookham, FLEET, GU52 6JL.
BUTTON, Mr. Graham Christopher, BSc FCA *1980;* 1 Harmston Park Avenue, Harmston, LINCOLN, LN5 9GF.
BUTTON, Miss. Janet Frances, BA ACA *1990;* 19 Amberlands Cl, Backwell, BRISTOL, BS48 3LW.
•**BUTTON, Mr. Keith Albert, BA ACA** *1984;* 17-19 Cudgerie Court, BURPENGARY, QLD 4505, AUSTRALIA.

BUTTON, Mr. Michael Hugh Norman, FCA *1962;* Pennllain Lodge, 8 Barbers Wood Close, HIGH WYCOMBE, BUCKINGHAMSHIRE, HP12 4EW. (Life Member)
BUTTON, Mr. Neville Patrick Charles, BSc ACA *1992;* 2 Barkshire Court, Hulse Road, SOUTHAMPTON, SO15 2PZ.
BUTTON, Mr. Peter Lowther, BA ACA *1981;* 24 Copper Ridge, Chalfont St. Peter, GERRARDS CROSS, SL9 0NF.
BUTTON, Mr. Ralph Frederick, BCom FCA *1945;* 30 Kingsway, Petts Wood, ORPINGTON, BR5 1PR. (Life Member)
BUTTON, Miss. Ruth, BSc ACA *2011;* 18 Pepper Street, Inkberrow, WORCESTER, WR7 4EJ.
BUTTON, Mrs. Sarah May, BSc ACA *1988;* 4025 Fechin Circle, PLANO, TX 75023, UNITED STATES.
BUTTON, Mrs. Tracy, BA ACA *2000;* 34 Meadowside Avenue, Clayton le Moors, ACCRINGTON, LANCASHIRE, BB5 5XF.
BUTTOO, Mr. Sumit Kumar, BSc ACA *2011;* 5 Centuria Walk, HUDDERSFIELD, HD3 3WP.
BUTTS, Mr. John Edward, FCA *1958;* 10 Acorn Grove, PERSHORE, WR10 1PQ. (Life Member)
BUXO, Mr. Paul Anthony, FCA *1968;* No. 10 Fairmount Townhouses, Fairways, Maraval, PORT OF SPAIN, TRINIDAD, TRINIDAD AND TOBAGO.
BUXTON, Mrs. Christine Ann, ACA *1994;* 8 Stumperlowe Hall Road, SHEFFIELD, S10 3QR.
BUXTON, Mr. Christopher Raymond, BSc ACA *1985;* 51 Brampton Avenue, MACCLESFIELD, SK10 3RH.
•BUXTON, Mr. David Charles, ACA *2008;* Baker Tilly Tax & Advisory Services LLP, 3 Hardman Street, MANCHESTER, M3 3HF. See also Baker Tilly Revas Limited
BUXTON, Mr. David John, BSc ACA *1991;* 77a High Street, Stanstead Abbotts, WARE, SG12 8AS.
•BUXTON, Mr. David Michael, BA FCA *1982;* H.L. Barnes & Sons, Barclays Bank Chambers, Bridge Street, STRATFORD-UPON-AVON, WARWICKSHIRE, CV37 6AH.
•BUXTON, Mr. David Vyvyan, ACA *1982;* Open Administration Systems Limited, Ampney House, Falcon Close, Quedgeley, GLOUCESTER, GL2 4LS. See also Solutions For Evolution Limited
•BUXTON, Mr. David William, BSc FCA *1999;* (Tax Fac), Buxton Accounting LLP, 98 Middlewich Road, NORTHWICH, CHESHIRE, CW9 7DA.
BUXTON, Mr. Gary Philip, BSc(Hons) ACA *2002;* 22 Cleveland Avenue, HAMPTON, MIDDLESEX, TW12 2RD.
BUXTON, Mr. Henry Gurney, ACA *1992;* Hopkins Architects Ltd, 27 Broadley Terrace, LONDON, NW1 6LG.
BUXTON, Mr. James Antony, BA ACA *2005;* 31 Green Courts, Bowdon, ALTRINCHAM, CHESHIRE, WA14 2SR.
BUXTON, Mr. Mark Christopher, BSc ACA *1996;* Optima Legal Arndale House, Charles Street, BRADFORD, WEST YORKSHIRE, BD1 1UN.
BUXTON, Mr. Michael, ACA *2006;* 46 Byrom Street, SOUTHPORT, MERSEYSIDE, PR9 7AD.
BUXTON, Mr. Michael Cecil, FCA *1957;* 2 Green Farm Barns, Little Snoring, FAKENHAM, NORFOLK, NR21 0JW. (Life Member)
•BUXTON, Mr. Michael John, MA ACA *1988;* Ernst & Young, 15/F Hutchison House, 10 Harcourt Road, CENTRAL, HONG KONG ISLAND, HONG KONG SAR. See also Ernst & Young Europe LLP and Ernst & Young LLP
BUXTON, Mr. Nicholas Fowell, BSc ACA *1992;* Manor House, Watersplace, WARE, SG12 7QQ.
•BUXTON, Mr. Nicholas James, MA ACA *1995;* PKF (UK) LLP, Cedar House, 105 Carrow Road, NORWICH, NORFOLK, NR1 1HP.
BUXTON, Mrs. Nicola, BA ACA *2005;* 31 Green Courts, Green Walk, Bowdon, ALTRINCHAM, CHESHIRE, WA14 2SR.
BUXTON, Mrs. Nicola Shirley, BA ACA *1986;* 8 Studley Road, HARROGATE, NORTH YORKSHIRE, HG1 5JU.
BUXTON, Mr. Nigel Peter, ACA *1979;* Aha Skupina d.o.o, Poljanski Nasip 6, 1104 LJUBLJANA, SLOVENIA.
BUXTON, Mr. Peter, FCA *1961;* 76 Hallam Grange Road, SHEFFIELD, S10 4BL. (Life Member)
•BUXTON, Mr. Peter, LLB FCA *1981;* Buxton & Co, Le Pallion, La Route Des Landes, St Ouen, JERSEY, JE3 2AA.
•BUXTON, Mrs. Priscilla Caroline, BA FCA *1984;* (Tax Fac), Cilla Watts FCA, Vectis House, Banbury Street, Kineton, WARWICK, WARWICKSHIRE CV35 0JS.
BUXTON, Mrs. Rachel Elise, BSc(Hons) ACA *2002;* Willis Group, 51 Lime Street, LONDON, EC3M 7DQ.
BUXTON, Miss. Sarah Ann, MA ACA *1985;* Flat 103 Drake House, Dolphin Square, LONDON, SW1V 3NN.
BUXTON, Mr. Stephen Timothy, BA ACA *1985;* Bond Bryan Architects Ltd, The Church Studio 400 Springvale Rd, SHEFFIELD, S10 1LP.
BUXTON, Mrs. Victoria Alexandra Louise, MA(Hons) ACA *2001;* 88 Elms Road, LONDON, SW4 9EW.
BUXTON, Mr. William David, FCA *1966;* Avenida Emidio Navarro, 505 Apt F, 2750 337 CASCAIS, PORTUGAL. (Life Member)
BUY, Mr. Edwin Arthur, FCA *1952;* 14 Quoyne Court, Station Road, ROMSEY, SO51 8AP. (Life Member)
BUY, Miss. Sandra Lyn, BSc ACA *1991;* 37 Southwold Close, SWINDON, SN25 2BD.
•BUYS, Mr. Marais, ACA CA(SA) *2008;* (Tax Fac), Marsh Accounting & Consulting Ltd, Suite 298, Kemp House, 152-160 City Road, LONDON, EC1V 2NX.
BUYSMAN, Mr. Robert Alexander, MSci ACA *2007;* 106 Rushdene, LONDON, SE2 9RU.
BUZZA, Mr. Ian Alistair Murray, FCA *1953;* 11 Horner Drive, OTTAWA K2H 5E6, ON, CANADA. (Life Member)
BUZZARD, Mr. Frank, FCA *1952;* 31 Beresford Drive, SUTTON COLDFIELD, B73 5QZ. (Life Member)
BUZZONI, Mr. Richard, BSc FCA CF *1985;* with Watersheds Ltd, 2nd Floor, The Old Granary, Cotton End, NORTHAMPTON, NN4 8HP.
BYAM-COOK, Mr. Charles Henry, MA FCA *1970;* Oakhanger House, Shefford Woodlands, HUNGERFORD, RG17 7AN.
BYAM-COOK, Mr. William Christian, MEng ACA *2010;* 38 Flaxley Road, MORDEN, SURREY, SM4 6LJ.
BYARS, Mr. Alexander George, BSc(Hons) ACA *2002;* 17a Gravel Lane, WILMSLOW, CHESHIRE, SK9 6LQ.
BYATT, Miss. Elizabeth, BA ACA *1989;* 660 Sheppard Avenue East, Unit 202, TORONTO M2K 3E5, ON, CANADA.
BYCRAFT, Miss. Michelle, ACA *2007;* South West Water Plc, Peninsula House, Rydon Lane, EXETER, EX2 7HR.
BYDAWELL, Mr. Richard David, MBA BEng FCA *1992;* 102 Alfriston Road, LONDON, SW11 6NW.
BYE, Mrs. Amanda Jane, BA ACA *1994;* 9 Barshaw Gardens, Appleton, WARRINGTON, WA4 5FA.
BYE, Mr. Ferris Charles, ACA *1979;* No 1601, 16F New World Tower 1, 18 Queens Road, CENTRAL, HONG KONG ISLAND, HONG KONG SAR.
BYE, Mr. James Patrick, ACA *2009;* K P M G, 1 Forest Gate, Tilgate Forest Business Centre, Brighton Road, CRAWLEY, WEST SUSSEX RH11 9PT.
BYE, Mr. Matthew Charles, BA ACA *1989;* 67 Knutsford Road, WILMSLOW, SK9 6JD.
BYE, Mr. Michael James, FCA *1970;* 81 Saxon Way, Bradley Stoke, BRISTOL, BS32 9AR.
BYE, Mr. Richard Alan Charles, MA FCA *1968;* Faceby House, Faceby, MIDDLESBROUGH, CLEVELAND, TS9 7BW.
BYER, Mr. Colin James, BA ACA *1991;* 16 Fineshade Close, Barton Seagrave, KETTERING, NORTHAMPTONSHIRE, NN15 6SL.
BYERLEY, Mr. Paul, BSc ACA *2007;* Flat 19 Kings Court, 25 Cox Street, BIRMINGHAM, B3 1RD.
BYERS, Mr. Andrew Brian, BSc FCA *1994;* Acclaim House, 12 Mount Havelock, Douglas, ISLE OF MAN, IM1 2QG.
BYERS, Mrs. Elizabeth Anne, BA ACA *1986;* 13423 Sundowner Drive, HOUSTON, TX 77041, UNITED STATES.
BYERS, Mr. James Robertson, FCA *1966;* 25 Hillview Drive, EDINBURGH, EH12 8QP.
•BYERS, Mr. Jeremy Richard, BSc FCA *1992;* (Tax Fac), Daniels & Co (Accountants) Limited, 111a Station Road, WEST WICKHAM, KENT, BR4 0PX.
BYERS, Mr. John Francis David, BA ACA *1979;* Rua Belgrado 19, Vila Sao Fernando, COTIA, 06709-245 SP, BRAZIL.
•BYERS, Mr. Mark Richard, FCA *1983;* Grant Thornton UK LLP, 30 Finsbury Square, LONDON, EC2P 2YU. See also Grant Thornton LLP
BYERS, Mr. William, MEng ACA *2007;* 1 Orchard Road East, MANCHESTER, M22 4FQ.
•BYETT, Mr. Paul, LLB ACA *2001;* Peacheys CA Limited, Lanyon House, Mission Court, NEWPORT, GWENT, NP20 2DW.
BYFIELD, Mrs. Frances, BSc ACA *2006;* Economist Intelligence Unit Ltd, 26 Red Lion Square, LONDON, WC1R 4HQ.
•BYFIELD, Mr. Nicholas Donald, BSc ACA *1992;* (Tax Fac), Donald Scott Associates Limited, PO Box 7785, HUNGERFORD, RG17 1DB.
BYFORD, Mr. Adam Peter, BSc ACA *1994;* Eli Lilly & Co Lilly House, Priestley Road, BASINGSTOKE, HAMPSHIRE, RG24 9NL.
•BYFORD, Mr. David Arthur, FCA *1979;* Waller & Byford, Clements House, 1279 London Road, LEIGH-ON-SEA, SS9 2AD.
BYFORD, Mr. Giles, MSci ACA *2005;* 29 Elmwood Road, LONDON, SE24 9NS.
•BYFORD, Mrs. Michele Roberta, FCA *1980;* Waller & Byford, Clements House, 1279 London Road, LEIGH-ON-SEA, SS9 2AD.
BYGATE, Mr. James, BSc(Hons) ACA *2011;* 47 Huntingdon Way, Sketty, SWANSEA, SA2 9HN.
BYGOTT, Mr. John James, LLB FCA *1969;* (Tax Fac), Haremere View, Lower Road, Harmer Hill, SHREWSBURY, SY4 3QX.
•BYGOTT, Mr. Stephen William, FCA *1974;* Bygott & Co, 1-3 Dudley Street, GRIMSBY, LINCOLNSHIRE, DN31 2AW. See also Pinfold Secretarial Services Limited
•BYGRAVE, Mr. Clifford, FCA ATII *1958;* (Member of Council 1980 - 2003), (Tax Fac), Clifford Bygrave, The Rustlings, Valley Close, Studham, DUNSTABLE, LU6 2QN.
BYGRAVE, Mr. David Charles, BA FCA *1995;* Foxhill End Brick Hill, Chobham, WOKING, SURREY, GU24 8TH.
•BYGRAVE, Miss. Heather Alison, BA(Hons) FCA *1997;* Deloitte LLP, 3 Victoria Square, Victoria Street, ST. ALBANS, HERTFORDSHIRE, AL1 3TF. See also Deloitte & Touche LLP
BYGRAVE, Mr. John Paul, BSc ACA *1994;* 3 Lucas Avenue, MALABAR, NSW 2036, AUSTRALIA.
BYGRAVE, Miss. Lisa Susannah, BSc ACA *1999;* West Devon Borough Council, Kilworthy Park, TAVISTOCK, DEVON, PL19 0BZ.
BYGRAVE, Mr. Robert John, BSc ACA *1996;* 12 Lincoln Close, Flitwick, BEDFORD, MK45 1UN.
BYGRAVE, Miss. Susan Jane, BA ACA *1991;* 2 The Mill, Hertingfordbury, HERTFORD, SG14 2SB.
BYLE, Dr. Philip Andrew Frank, PhD ACA *1992;* 20 Green Garth, Holme, CARNFORTH, LA6 1RF.
BYLES, Mrs. Marnie, MEng ACA *1999;* 12 Downs View, Bow Brickhill, MILTON KEYNES, MK17 9JS.
BYLETT, Mr. Brian John, BSc ACA *1979;* Cheynes, Barkway Road, ROYSTON, HERTFORDSHIRE, SG8 9EB.
BYLINA, Mrs. Susan Mary Croxford, BSc ACA *1980;* 4 Vicarage Gardens, Rastrick, BRIGHOUSE, HD6 3HD.
BYNG, Mr. Graham Godfrey, FCA *1962;* 2 Spadesbourne Road, Lickey End, BROMSGROVE, B60 1JP. (Life Member)
BYNG, Mr. Michael Laurence, BA ACA *1994;* 12 Berkeley Close, REDDITCH, WORCESTERSHIRE, B98 0QB.
BYNG, Mr. Thomas Michael, BSc(Hons) ACA CTA *2004;* 5 Talbot Street, HERTFORD, SG13 7BX.
BYNOE, Mr. Richard Michael, BSc FCA *1990;* PricewaterhouseCoopers, Financial Services Centre, Bishop's Court Hill, BRIDGETOWN, BARBADOS.
BYNOTH, Mr. Adam, ACA *2008;* 19 Tillie Street, GLASGOW, G20 6JA.
•BYRD, Mr. Russel Ian, ACA FCCA ACCA FMAAT *2007;* Randall & Payne LLP, 79 Promenade, CHELTENHAM, GLOUCESTERSHIRE, GL50 1PJ.
BYRNE, Mr. Adrian Peter, BSc ACA *1998;* Flat 4 Amber Court, 100 Richmond Road, LONDON, SW20 0PD.
BYRNE, Mr. Adrian Robert, MMath ACA *2006;* 5 Jessamine Avenue, LEEDS, LS11 7AD.
BYRNE, Mr. Alastair James, BA FCA CTA *1988;* Beech House, Tholthorpe, YORK, YO61 1SN.
BYRNE, Miss. Alice Mary, BCom ACA *1997;* 98 Grove Road, LONDON, E17 9BY.
BYRNE, Mrs. Andrea Joan, BSc ACA *1992;* Sandown House, Cedar Road, Hook Heath, WOKING, SURREY, GU22 0JJ.
BYRNE, Mr. Andrew Donaldson, MA ACA *2002;* Flat 56, Wendover Court, Chiltern Street, LONDON, W1U 7NU.
BYRNE, Ms. Angela Mary Jermyn, ACA *1999; (ACA Ireland 1988);* Flat E, 215 Elgin Avenue, Maida Vale, LONDON, W9 1NH.
BYRNE, Mr. Anthony John, BA ACA *1998;* 33 Homefield Road, LONDON, W4 2LW. (Life Member)
BYRNE, Mr. Brian, BA ACA *2002;* Vent-Axia Ltd, Fleming Way, CRAWLEY, WEST SUSSEX, RH10 9YX.
BYRNE, Mr. Christian, ACA *2008;* 112 Ickenham Road, RUISLIP, HA4 7DX.
BYRNE, Mr. Christopher Denis, BSc ACA *1997;* 181 Menlove Avenue, LIVERPOOL, MERSEYSIDE, L18 3JE.
BYRNE, Mr. Christopher John, FCA *1974;* Oxford Community Churches The Kings Centre, Osney Mead, OXFORD, OX2 0ES.
•BYRNE, Ms. Clare Elizabeth, BSc ACA *1995;* Medrus UK Limited, 43 Parkfields, Penyfai, BRIDGEND, MID GLAMORGAN, CF31 4NQ.
BYRNE, Mr. Conor Joseph, BA ACA *2011;* 18 Albert Street, Douglas, ISLE OF MAN, IM1 2QA.
BYRNE, Mr. Damian James, BSc ACA *2002;* 5 Callaway Close, Wollaton, NOTTINGHAM, NG8 2BT.
BYRNE, Mr. David, BA ACA *2001;* Flat D, 70 Highgate West Hill, LONDON, N6 6BU.
BYRNE, Mr. David Anthony, BSc ACA *2002;* Flat 8, 3 Lancaster Road, MANCHESTER, M20 2TY.
BYRNE, Mr. David Joseph, BA ACA *1990;* Sandown House, Cedar Road, Hook Heath, WOKING, SURREY, GU22 0JJ.
BYRNE, Miss. Edel Margaret, BA ACA *1994;* 44 Ringwood Avenue, LONDON, N2 9NS.
BYRNE, Mr. Eric Charles Sprague, BA ACA *1993;* U B S Asset Management, 21 Lombard Street, LONDON, EC3V 9AH.
BYRNE, Mr. Ian Matthew, ACA *1986;* 167 Vicarage Hill, BENFLEET, ESSEX, SS7 1PF.
BYRNE, Mr. Ian William, MA FCA *1981;* 17 Medland, Woughton Park, MILTON KEYNES, MK6 3BH.
BYRNE, Mr. John Douglas, BSc ACA *1997;* Chestnuts, Elkstone, CHELTENHAM, GLOUCESTERSHIRE, GL53 9PD.
BYRNE, Mr. John Francis, BSc ACA *1989;* 12 Pheasant Grove, Halewood Village, LIVERPOOL, L26 7WT.
•BYRNE, Mr. John Robert, FCA *1975;* Horscroft Turner Byrne & Co, 78 The Green, TWICKENHAM, TW2 5AG.
BYRNE, The Revd Canon John Victor, LTh FCA *1970;* 28 Western Road, POOLE, DORSET, BH13 7BP.
•BYRNE, Mr. Kevin Charlton, BSc FCA *1980;* Critchleys, Avalon House, Marcham Road, ABINGDON, OX14 1UD. See also Landtax LLP
BYRNE, Mr. Kevin Martin, BSc ACA *1985;* 15 Turnpike Way, Coven, WOLVERHAMPTON, WV9 5HY.
BYRNE, Mr. Laurence, BSc ACA *2000;* 29 Rue de la Cote, 92500 RUEIL MALMAISON, FRANCE.
BYRNE, Mr. Leigh Anthony, BA ACA PGCE *1999;* 11 Carlton Green, REDHILL, RH1 2DB.
•BYRNE, Mrs. Lesley Patricia, BA FCA *1984;* Apartment 11 The Gables, Queen Parade, HARROGATE, NORTH YORKSHIRE, HG1 5QG.
BYRNE, Mr. Mark Michael, MA ACA *2000;* 120 Kyrle Road, LONDON, SW11 6BA.
BYRNE, Mr. Matthew, ACA *2009;* Flat 102 Westfields, Railway Side, LONDON, SW13 0PL.
BYRNE, Mr. Matthew, *2010;* R F I B Group Ltd, 20 Gracechurch Street, LONDON, EC3V 0AF.
BYRNE, Mr. Matthew Stephen, BA ACA *1998;* Clay House Business Centre, 5 Horninglow Street, BURTON-ON-TRENT, STAFFORDSHIRE, DE14 1NG.
BYRNE, Mr. Matthew Thomas, BA(Hons) ACA *2003;* Ty Abbot, Llangeinor, BRIDGEND, MID GLAMORGAN, CF32 8RX.
BYRNE, Mr. Michael Francis, MA FCA *1961;* 3 Highbury Road, Wimbledon, LONDON, SW19 7PR. (Life Member)
•BYRNE, Mr. Michael Gabriel, BCL ACA *2002;* Bas de L'Epine, La Rue de L'Epine, Trinity, JERSEY, JE3 5AU.
•BYRNE, Mr. Michael Landon, MBE FCA MAE *1971;* Robert S. Boys, 28-30 Grange Road West, BIRKENHEAD, CH41 4DA.
BYRNE, Mr. Patrick James, BCom ACA *1987;* 1 Station Road, Rearsby, LEICESTER, LE7 4YX.
•BYRNE, Mr. Patrick Joseph, FCA *1975;* MacIntyre Hudson LLP, 31 Castle Street, HIGH WYCOMBE, BUCKINGHAMSHIRE, HP13 6RU.
BYRNE, Mr. Paul Allan, BA FCA *1995;* 8 Watkins Drive, Prestwich, MANCHESTER, M25 0DS.
•BYRNE, Mr. Paul Austin, BSc FCA *1981;* Baker Tilly UK Audit LLP, 2 Whitehall Quay, LEEDS, LS1 4HG. See also Baker Tilly Tax and Advisory Services LLP
BYRNE, Mr. Peter David, BSc FCA *1972;* SDA Logic System Ltd, 21 The Coda Centre, 189 Munster Road, LONDON, SW6 6AW.
•BYRNE, Mr. Peter Edward, FCA *1966;* (Tax Fac), Peter E. Byrne, 68 Lavender Avenue, Kingsbury, LONDON, NW9 8HE.
•BYRNE, Mr. Peter Joseph, BSc FCA *1978;* 26 Campion Grove, HALESOWEN, WEST MIDLANDS, B63 1HB.
BYRNE, Mr. Philip Geoffrey, BA ACA *1979;* U B S Wealth Management, 1 Curzon Street, LONDON, W1J 5UB.
BYRNE, Mr. Raymond John, MA ACA *1990;* 16 Woodstock Avenue, Ealing, LONDON, W13 9UG.

BYRNE, Mr. Sean Damian, BSc ACA 1994; 18 Bramwell Close, SUNBURY-ON-THAMES, TW16 5PU.
BYRNE, Mr. Simon Carl, BA ACA 2000; 54 Cambridge Road, TWICKENHAM, TW1 2HL.
BYRNE, Mr. Simon James, BSc FCA 1978; Sungard, Methuen Park, CHIPPENHAM, SN14 0TW.
BYRNE, Mr. Simon John, BA ACA 1993; 74 Whitmore Road, HARROW, HA1 4AH.
BYRNE, Mr. Simon Lees-Buckley, BA ACA 1992; 35 Burghley Road, St Andrews, BRISTOL, BS6 5BL.
BYRNE, Ms. Siobhan, ACA 2010; 8 De Vere Close, Hemingford Grey, HUNTINGDON, CAMBRIDGESHIRE, PE28 9BH.
BYRNE, Mr. Stephen David, BA ACA 2010; 34 Manorwood Drive, Whiston, PRESCOT, MERSEYSIDE, L35 3UH.
BYRNE, Mr. Stephen John, BSc ACA 1997; Avenue Giuseppe Motta 31-33, 1202 GENEVA, SWITZERLAND.
BYRNE, Mr. Thomas, FCA 1979; 46 Garran Na Coille, Shanaway Road, ENNIS, COUNTY CLARE, IRELAND.
•**BYRNE, Mr. Timothy Bernard, MA MSc ACA** 1995; Byrne and Co, Trenhaile Bungalow, St Newlyn East, NEWQUAY, TR8 5JL.
BYRNE, Mr. Timothy Russell, FCA 1984; The Management Alliance, The Stables, 24 Church Road, Mellor, STOCKPORT, CHESHIRE SK6 5LY.
BYRNE, Miss. Yvonne, BA(Econ) ACA 2002; C/O ASOD, PO Box 70556, Kyebando Central, KAMPALA, UGANDA.
BYRNES, Mr. Gerrard Anthony, FCA 1974; Alcatel Submarine Networks, Christchurch Way, LONDON, SE10 0AG.
BYROM, Mr. David Andrew, MSc ACA 1999; 14 Terrington Court, The Swallows, Strensall, YORK, YO32 5PA.
BYROM, Miss. Diane Janice, BSc ACA 1998; 28 Wisteria Way, Bold, ST. HELENS, MERSEYSIDE, WA9 4LN.
BYROM, Mrs. Estelle Claire Anna, BSc ACA 2000; 19a Lime Grove, NEW MALDEN, SURREY, KT3 3TW.
BYROM, Mr. Philip Martin, BSc ACA 1991; Lane End Cottage Aldersey Lane, Handley Tattenhall, CHESTER, CH3 9EQ.
BYRON, Mr. Alan Robert, FCA 1971; Haighlands, 46 Central Avenue, Eccleston Park, PRESCOT, L34 2QP.
BYRON, Mrs. Fiona Jane, BSc ACA 1998; 5 Elizabeth Close, BARNET, HERTFORDSHIRE, EN5 4DP.
BYRON, Mrs. Michelle Jane, ACA 2008; Lime Management Ltd, Park House, Manor Park Court, Manor Park Avenue, Manor Park, RUNCORN CHESHIRE WA7 1TN.
BYRON, Mr. Robert David, BSc ACA 1990; Manton House, 19 Knossington Road, Braunston, OAKHAM, LEICESTERSHIRE, LE15 8QX.
BYRON EVANS, Mr. Sam, ACA 2011; Flat E, 16 Vera Road, Fulham, LONDON, SW6 6RN.
BYRT, Mr. Douglas Hansford, FCA 1958; The Firs, 58 Bath Road, WELLS, BA5 3LQ. (Life Member)
BYTHELL, Mr. Peter, FCA 1972; The Cherries, 15 Hallows Drive, Kelsall, TARPORLEY, CHESHIRE, CW6 0QE. (Life Member)
BYWATER, Mrs. Claire, BA ACA 2005; 11 Youngs Orchard, Abbeymead, GLOUCESTER, GL4 4RR.
BYWATER, Mr. David, BSc ACA CTA 1995; (Tax Fac), 10 Radnor Park West, FOLKESTONE, KENT, CT19 5HJ.
BYWATER, Mr. John Patrick, BSc ACA 1997; 17 Chantry Grove, Royston, BARNSLEY, S71 4QR.
BYWATER, Mr. Richard Michael, FCA 1969; 6 Los Fresnos, Los Barrios, 11370 CADIZ, SPAIN. (Life Member)
BYWATER, Mr. Scott Richard, ACA 2009; 10 Oaklands, BUILTH WELLS, POWYS, LD2 3EN.
BYWATER, Mrs. Susannah Jane, BSc ACA 1998; Aspinalls Club Ltd, 29 Curzon Street, LONDON, W1J 7TJ.
BYWORTH, Mr. Peter John, FCA 1948; 47 Anchor Court, 2 Carey Place, LONDON, SW1V 2RT. (Life Member)
CABBAN, Mr. Randolph Anthony Kadwell, FCA 1965; Calle Gual 8, 03730 JAVEA, ALICANTE, SPAIN.
CABELL, Mrs. Helen Felicity, BA ACA 1994; The Limes, 115 Andover Road, NEWBURY, RG14 6JJ.
CABLE, Mr. Adam Richard, BSc ACA 2004; 44 Stockmore Street, OXFORD, OXFORDSHIRE, OX4 1JT.
CABLE, Mr. Alan James, FCA 1971; 31 Cambridge Drive, WISBECH, PE13 1SE.
CABLE, Mrs. Chantal Louise, BA ACA 1998; Howden Kitchens Ltd, Thorpe Road, Howden, GOOLE, NORTH HUMBERSIDE, DN14 7PA.
•**CABLE, Mr. Charles Hylton, BCom FCA** 1987; (Tax Fac), Rothman Pantall LLP, 229 West Street, FAREHAM, HAMPSHIRE, PO16 0HZ.
CABLE, Mr. James Derek, BEng ACA 1995; Kewill Bramley House The Guildway, Old Portsmouth Road Artington, GUILDFORD, GU3 1LR.
CABLE, Mr. James Seymour, BA FCA 1977; 37 Green Lane, Paddock Wood, TONBRIDGE, TN12 6BF.
•**CABLE, Ms. Jane Elizabeth, BA ACA MInstD** 1995; Cable Financial Directions Limited, 5 Downs Road, West Stoke, CHICHESTER, PO18 9BQ.
•**CABLE, Mr. Jonathan Clive, FCA ATT** 1972; Harwood Hutton Limited, 22 Wycombe End, BEACONSFIELD, BUCKINGHAMSHIRE, HP9 1NB. See also Harwood Hutton Tax Advisory LLP
CABLE, Mrs. Linda Frances, FCA 1975; P O Box 5, MARBLE HALL, 0450, SOUTH AFRICA.
CABLE, Dr. Martin John, BA ACA 1994; Loc. Cappella, 52, San Cassiano di Controne, Bagni Di Lucca, 55050 LUCCA, ITALY.
CABLE, Mr. Patrick Olaf, FCA 1970; Pennyhill House, Hyde, Chalford, STROUD, GLOUCESTERSHIRE, GL6 8NZ. (Life Member)
CABOCHE, Mrs. Caroline Emma, ACA 1993; 84 Thursday Street, SWINDON, SN25 1SR.
CABRAAL, Mr. Charith, ACA 2011; 34 Clarence Road, LONDON, SW19 8QE.
CABRERA, Mr. Julian Edward, BA ACA 1992; 2 Alexandra Terrace, EXETER, EX4 6SY.
CACHIA, Dr. Christopher, LLD ACA 2010; 'The Olives', Lourdes Lane, SWIEQI SWQ 3332, MALTA.
•**CACHO, Mr. Richard, ACA CA(AUS)** 2010; JackalAdvisory, Level 19, Portland House, Bressenden Place, LONDON, SW1E 5RS. See also Jackal Advisory Ltd
CADAMY, Mr. Daniel James, BSc ACA 2007; Ellan Vannin, Main Road, Ballaugh, ISLE OF MAN, IM7 5EF.
CADAMY, Mr. James Isaac, ACA 2009; Apartment 11 Rochester Court, 61 Loch Promenade Douglas, ISLE OF MAN, IM1 2NB.
CADBURY, Mr. Bruce Jeremy John, FCA 1976; 47 Lanark Road, Maida Vale, LONDON, W9 1DE.
CADBURY, Mrs. Caroline, LLB ACA 2003; 25 Grebe Road, BICESTER, OXFORDSHIRE, OX26 6WG.
CADBURY, Sir George Adrian Hayhurst, FCA(Honorary) Rising Sun House, Bakers Lane, Knowle, SOLIHULL, WEST MIDLANDS, B93 8PT.
•**CADBURY, Mrs. Pamela Kathleen, BA FCA** 1976; (Tax Fac), BPC Partners, 1 Rockfield Business Park, Old Station Drive, Leckhampton, CHELTENHAM, GLOUCESTERSHIRE GL53 0AN. See also BPC Partners Limited
CADBURY, Mr. Tim Luke Martin, BSc ACA 2009; Flat 4, 80-86 St. John's Road, LONDON, SW11 1PX.
CADBY, Ms. Hannah Louisa, BSc(Hons) ACA 2003; 1310 Saddle Rack Street, # 343, SAN JOSE, CA 95126, UNITED STATES.
CADBY, Mrs. Rachel Mary, FCA 1992; 8 Southwood Road, TROWBRIDGE, BA14 7BY.
CADD, Mr. Norman Harry, FCA 1961; 3 New Barns, Castle Farm, Eardisley, HEREFORD, HEREFORDSHIRE, HR3 6NT.
CADDICK, Mrs. Lisa Suzanne, ACA 2008; The Acorns, Beech Road, Tokers Green, READING, RG4 9EH.
CADDICK, Mrs. Lucy Jane, BA ACA 2007; 182 Walmley Road, SUTTON COLDFIELD, B76 2PY.
•**CADDOCK, Mr. Michael Richard, BA FCA** 1973; Tom Peck's House, Borley Green, Woolpit, BURY ST. EDMUNDS, IP30 9RW.
CADDY, Mr. David Henry Arnold Courtenay, FCA 1968; 79b Iverna Court, LONDON, W8 6TU.
CADDY, Mr. David Kenneth, BA ACA 1979; 94 Meols Drive, West Kirby, WIRRAL, CH48 5DD.
CADDY, Mr. Dominic Jon, BSc ACA 2004; 77 Ravenscliffe Road, Kidsgrove, STOKE-ON-TRENT, ST7 4HX.
CADDY, Mrs. Kim, ACA 2003; 20 Inman Road, LONDON, SW18 3BB.
CADDY, Mr. Lee John, BSc(Hons) ACA 2000; 309 Ash Bank Road, Werrington, STOKE-ON-TRENT, ST9 0JS.
CADDY, Mrs. Mary, BA ACA 1992; 35 Honister Gardens, STANMORE, HA7 2EH.
CADDY, Mr. Michael John, BA ACA 1979; House 6Coral Villas, 27 Horizon Drive, CHUNG HOM KOK, Hong Kong Island, HONG KONG SAR.
CADE, Mrs. Amanda Jayne, MSc BA ACA 2000; 51 Oakhall Park, Thornton, BRADFORD, BD13 3QW.
CADE, Mr. David Patrick Gordon, MA FCA 1967; Michaelmas House, 28 Tangier Road, GUILDFORD, GU1 2DF. (Life Member)
CADE, Mrs. Julia Hilary, BA ACA 1998; Windrush, 12 Cutbush Lane, Shinfield, READING, RG2 9AH.
CADE, Mr. Martin John, BSc ACA 1999; 51 Oakhall Park, Thornton, BRADFORD, BD13 3QW.
CADE, Mr. Richard John, FCA 1965; 30 High Oaks Road, WELWYN GARDEN CITY, AL8 7BH. (Life Member)
CADE, Miss. Sarah Frances, BSc ACA 1996; 8 Peters Close, STANMORE, HA7 4SE.
CADEDDU, Mr. Alessio, ACA 2010; BLK69 #02-78 Redhill Close, Singapore 150069, SINGAPORE 150069, SINGAPORE.
CADEN, Mrs. Joan Rose, FCA 1955; Old School House, Red Lane, OXTED, SURREY, RH8 0RS. (Life Member)
•**CADER, Mr. Dominic Simon, ACA** 2005; with Dickinsons, Enterprise House, Beesons Yard, Bury Lane, RICKMANSWORTH, HERTFORDSHIRE WD3 1DS.
CADIGAN, Mr. Denis Vincent, FCA 1975; 20 Abbotsmount St. Johns Road, St. Helier, JERSEY, JE2 3LA.
CADIGNAN, Miss. Isabelle Beatrice, ACA MBA 2001; New Asurion Europe Ltd, 272 Gunnersbury Avenue, LONDON, W4 5QB.
CADIZ, Mrs. Zoe Rachel, BSc ACA 2000; 253 Impasse Des Carrieres, 74140 SCIEZ, FRANCE.
•**CADLE, Mr. Peter, BA FCA** 1976; 16 Spring View Road, WARE, HERTFORDSHIRE, SG12 9LB.
•**CADMAN, Mr. Clive, FCA** 1974; Gleek Cadman Ross LLP, Credcoll House, 96 Marsh Lane, LEEDS, LS9 8SR. See also Gleek Cadman Ross Limited
CADMAN, Mr. John Ashley, MA ACA 1980; 2838 Leslie Park Circle, ANN ARBOR, MI, 48105, UNITED STATES.
CADMAN, Miss. Karen Ruth Zena, BSc ACA 1996; 94 Astonville Street, Southfields, LONDON, SW18 5AJ.
CADMAN, Mr. Peter Henry Broadbent, MA FCA 1960; 19 Tudor Hill, SUTTON COLDFIELD, B73 6BD. (Life Member)
CADOGAN, Mr. James, BSc ACA 1998; Colt Telecommunications, Beaufort House, 15 St. Botolph Street, LONDON, EC3A 7QN.
CADOUX-HUDSON, Mr. Humphrey Allen Edward, BSc BEng ACA 1988; 19 Pit Farm Road, GUILDFORD, SURREY, GU1 2JL.
CADWALLADER, Mr. Derek, FCA 1966; Gayford House, Keighley Road, COLNE, BB8 7HL.
CADWALLADER, Mr. John Stuart, FCA 1970; Spoonley Farm, MARKET DRAYTON, TF9 3SR.
•**CADWALLADER, Mr. Mark Jones, BSc ACA** 1987; Cadwallader & Co LLP, Eagle House, 25 Severn Street, WELSHPOOL, POWYS, SY21 7AD.
CADWALLADER, Mr. Robert James, BA ACA 2003; 11 Sovereign Close, Granborough, BUCKINGHAM, MK18 3DA.
CADWALLADER, Miss. Sarah Jane, BA ACA 2006; 3 The Green, Longwick, PRINCES RISBOROUGH, BUCKINGHAMSHIRE, HP27 9QY.
CADWALLADER-WEBB, Miss. Victoria Jayne, BSc ACA 2003; Flat 41, Riplingham, Arlington Avenue, LEAMINGTON SPA, WARWICKSHIRE, CV32 5UQ.
CADWELL, Mrs. Alison Jane, BA ACA 1991; Whitebrook Park, 68 Lower Cookham Road, MAIDENHEAD, SL6 8XY.
CADZOW, Mr. James, ACA 2008; 12 Oak Tree Close, LONDON, W5 2AQ.
CADZOW, Mrs. Nicola Anne, BSc ACA 2006; 12 Oak Tree Close, LONDON, W5 2AQ.
CAETHOVEN, Miss. Rachel Samantha, BA ACA 1998; Prendergast School Hilly Fields, Adelaide Avenue, LONDON, SE4 1LE.
CAFFERY, Miss. Gemma, BSc ACA 2008; 29 Redwood, Chadderton, OLDHAM, OL9 9TG.
CAFFREY, Miss. Joanne, BSc ACA 2003; 9 Hawtrey Road, WINDSOR, SL4 3AU.
CAFFREY, Mr. Matthew Peter, BA ACA 2000; with ISIS EP LLP, Bank House, 8 Cherry Street, BIRMINGHAM, B2 5AN.
CAFFYN, Mr. Robert James Morris, MA FCA 1961; 6 Holbrook Close, EASTBOURNE, EAST SUSSEX, BN20 7JT. (Life Member)
CAFFYN, Mrs. Rosalind Elizabeth, BSc ACA 1992; Brookside, High Street, Upton, DIDCOT, OX11 9JE.
CAFFYN, Miss. Victoria Lucy, BSc ACA 2007; Which?, 2 Marylebone Road, LONDON, NW1 4DF.
CAHILL, Miss. Claire Rosemary, BA ACA 1988; 10a Cross Lane Close, Orwell, ROYSTON, HERTFORDSHIRE, SG8 5QW.
•**CAHILL, Mr. Conor Dominique, MEng ACA** 1997; Deloitte LLP, Athene Place, 66 Shoe Lane, LONDON, EC4A 3BQ. See also Deloitte & Touche LLP
CAHILL, Mr. David John, BA ACA 1988; 16 Heritage Drive, Wellington Point, BRISBANE, QLD 4160, AUSTRALIA.
CAHILL, Mr. David Terrence Phillip, BA ACA 1984; 84 Lampton Road, HOUNSLOW, TW3 4DJ.
•**CAHILL, Mr. Kevin Richard, BSc ACA** 1991; K R Cahill & Co Ltd, The Old Granary, Lilbourne Road, Clifton upon Dunsmore, RUGBY, WARWICKSHIRE CV23 0BD.
CAHILL, Miss. Maura, BSc ACA 1998; Midfield, Ford, AYLESBURY, BUCKINGHAMSHIRE, HP17 8XH.
CAHILL, Mr. Michael James, ACA 2004; with Albert Goodman LLP, Mary Street House, Mary Street, TAUNTON, TA1 3NW.
CAHILL, Mr. Michael John Christopher, MA ACA 1988; Clarkson Plc, St. Magnus House, 3 Lower Thames Street, LONDON, EC3R 6HE.
CAHILL, Mr. Paul David, BSc FCA 1974; 5 Williton Road, KARRINYUP, WA 6018, AUSTRALIA.
CAHILLANE, Miss. Alex, BSc ACA 2010; 7a Theatre Street, LONDON, SW11 5NE.
CAHILLANE, Mr. John Dermot, BA FCA 1977; Inter American Development Bank, 1300 New York Avenue, NW, WASHINGTON, DC 20577, UNITED STATES.
CAHILLANE, Ms. Paula Mary, BA FCA 1978; 12 Brightfield Road, Lee Green, LONDON, SE12 8QF.
•**CAIDEN, Mr. Paul Martin, BSc ACA** 1980; St. Mellion Accounting Services, 1 Edwy Parade, GLOUCESTER, GL1 2QH.
•**CAIGER, Mrs. Angela Grace, FCA** 1983; Shaw Gibbs LLP, 264 Banbury Road, OXFORD, OX2 7DY.
CAIGER, Miss. Janet Christina, FCA 1981; 1 St. Austins Cottages, Frensham, FARNHAM, GU10 3EH.
CAIL, Mr. Ian, FCA 1967; 189 Coniscliffe Road, DARLINGTON, DL3 8DE. (Life Member)
CAIN, Miss. Alison Nicola, BSc ACA 1992; 2 Westerham Road, OXTED, SURREY, RH8 0ER.
CAIN, Mr. Andrew John, LLB ACA 1992; Malthouse Cottage, Ardens Grafton, ALCESTER, B49 6DS.
CAIN, Mr. Anthony Gerard, FCA 1965; 6 karda place, GYMEA, NSW 2227, AUSTRALIA.
CAIN, Mr. Christopher Barry, FCA 1969; 5 Kennedy Gardens, SEVENOAKS, TN13 3UG.
CAIN, Mr. Clive Peter, ACA CA(SA) 2010; 23 Oaklands Road, BROMLEY, BR1 3SJ.
CAIN, Mr. David Michael, ACA 1980; Venn Farm, Kings Nympton, UMBERLEIGH, DEVON, EX37 9TR.
CAIN, Mr. Gregg Andrew, BA ACA 2007; with KPMG LLP, 15 Canada Square, LONDON, E14 5GL.
CAIN, Miss. Helen, MA ACA 1992; 2 Harrow Road, FLEET, HAMPSHIRE, GU51 1JD.
•**CAIN, Miss. Helen, BA FCA** 1994; Mercer & Hole, 76 Shoe Lane, LONDON, EC4A 3JB.
CAIN, Miss. Helen Louise, BSc FCA 1993; 15 Cambridge Drive, Woodley, STOCKPORT, SK6 1HX.
CAIN, Mr. James Crookall, FCA 1953; Maughold, Alexander Drive, Douglas, ISLE OF MAN, IM2 3QX. (Life Member)
CAIN, Ms. Jaqueline Penelope, MA ACA 1987; Upper Maisonette, 29 St Peters Street, LONDON, N1 8JP.
•**CAIN, Mr. John David, BSc FCA** 1990; KPMG LLP, 15 Canada Square, LONDON, E14 5GL. See also KPMG Europe LLP
CAIN, Mr. Julian, MA ACA 1995; The Pines, Low Catton Road, Stamford Bridge, YORK, YO41 1DQ.
CAIN, Mr. Matthew, BSc ACA 2010; 14 Broxash Road, LONDON, SW11 6AB.
CAIN, Mr. Neil David, ACA 2002; 1 Close Cubbon, Peel, ISLE OF MAN, IM5 1NS.
CAIN, Mrs. Nora Marie, BSc ACA 1986; 2 Grosvenor Road, NORTHWOOD, HA6 3HJ.
CAIN, Mr. Paul Andrew, BSc ACA 1989; Holmcross, 28 Manor Drive, Farm Hill, ISLE OF MAN, IM2 2NS.
•①**CAIN, Mr. Roger Laurence, FCA** 1973; with Haslers, Old Station Road, LOUGHTON, ESSEX, IG10 4PL.
•**CAIN, Mrs. Sheryl Margaret, FCA** 1985; (Tax Fac), Sheryl Cain Limited, 237 Sheen Lane, LONDON, SW14 8LE.
CAIN, Mr. Simon Nicholas, BSc(Hons) ACA 2001; 13 The Hams, Ide, EXETER, DEVON, EX2 9RU.
CAIN, Mr. William John, BCom FCA 1964; 30 George Lane, Hayes, BROMLEY, BR2 7LQ.
CAINE, Ms. Amanda, MA BA ACA 1994; Enever Pound Lane, Little Rissington, CHELTENHAM, GLOUCESTERSHIRE, GL54 2NB.
CAINE, Mr. Frederick William, FCA 1950; Lawn Cottage, Darsham, SAXMUNDHAM, IP17 3PU. (Life Member)

CAINE, Mr. George Harold, FCA *1957;* 16 Waunci Crescent, Gorleston, GREAT YARMOUTH, NR31 6EB. (Life Member)

•CAINE, Mr. Philip Peter, MA FCA CTA *1992;* (Tax Fac), 32 Spencers Way, HARROGATE, NORTH YORKSHIRE, HG1 3DN.

CAINE, Mrs. Sarah Louise, BSc ACA *1999;* 1c Castle Street, FLEET, HAMPSHIRE, GU52 7ST.

CAINE, Mr. Shaun Michael, BSc(Econ) ACA *2002;* 38 Langley Avenue, Arnold, NOTTINGHAM, NG5 6NN.

CAINE, Miss. Shena Marie, LLB ACA *2000;* 200 Park Avenue, NEW YORK, NY 10166, UNITED STATES.

CAINE, Mr. Stephen Charles, BSc FCA *1986;* with Ernst & Young LLP, 1 More London Place, LONDON, SE1 2AF.

CAINE, Mr. Steven John, BA ACA *1989;* 92 Lockerbie Close, Cinnamon Brow, WARRINGTON, WA2 0LU.

CAINES, Mr. Andrew Morgan, BA ACA *2000;* 73 Bluecoat Pond, Christs Hospital, HORSHAM, WEST SUSSEX, RH13 0NW.

CAINES, Mr. Geoffrey Harold, FCA *1962;* Bindon, 48 Hartley Old Road, PURLEY, CR8 4HG. (Life Member)

CAINEY, Mr. Alan David, BA ACA *1987;* 18 Clive Street, ALPHINGTON, VIC 3078, AUSTRALIA.

•CAIRA, Mrs. Donna Louise, BSc FCA *1994;* (Tax Fac), Saffery Champness, Lion House, Red Lion Street, LONDON, WC1R 4GB.

CAIRNS, Mr. Adam Paul, BA(Hons) ACA *2004;* Ancon Ltd, President Way, President Park, SHEFFIELD, S4 7UR.

CAIRNS, Mr. Alexander Thomas, FCA *1966;* Bowmanhill Bungalow, MAYBOLE, AYRSHIRE, KA19 8JU. (Life Member)

CAIRNS, Mr. Anthony Joseph Alexander, BSc ACA *1996;* 17 Tilehurst Road, READING, RG1 7TP.

CAIRNS, Mrs. Barbara Zofia, BSc ACA *1988;* 14 Norman Court, Oadby, LEICESTER, LE2 4UD.

•①CAIRNS, Mr. Benjamin Thom, BSc ACA *1998;* Ernst & Young LLP, 1 More London Place, LONDON, SE1 2AF. See also Ernst & Young Europe LLP

•CAIRNS, Mr. Christopher Stuart, BSc FCA *1994;* Alliotts, Friary Court, 13-21 High Street, GUILDFORD, SURREY, GU1 3DL.

CAIRNS, Mrs. Clare Sara, ACA *1994;* Ruperts House, Bowers Hill, Badsey, EVESHAM, WORCESTERSHIRE, WR11 7HG.

•CAIRNS, Mr. David Howard, OBE MSc FCA *1969;* David Cairns, Bramblewood, Turville Heath, HENLEY-ON-THAMES, OXFORDSHIRE, RG9 6JY. See also Cairns David

CAIRNS, Mr. David James, MA FCA *1958;* Linwood, 22 The Mount, PONTEFRACT, WF8 1ND. (Life Member)

•CAIRNS, Mr. David Thomas, FCA CTA *1987;* Hawsons, Jubilee House, 32 Duncan Close, Moulton Park, NORTHAMPTON, NN3 6WL.

CAIRNS, Mr. Eric, FCA *1969;* 7 Callerton Court, Darras Hall, Ponteland, NEWCASTLE UPON TYNE, NE20 9EN. (Life Member)

CAIRNS, Mr. Gregory Keith, FCA *1968;* The Leaze, Milbury Heath, WOTTON-UNDER-EDGE, GL12 8QL.

•CAIRNS, Mr. James Cyril, BSc FCA *1976;* Cairns Bailey & Co, 3 Beacon Court, Birmingham Road, Great Barr, BIRMINGHAM, B43 6NN.

CAIRNS, Miss. Jennifer Louise, ACA *2008;* 17 Norton Close, NEWBURY, BERKSHIRE, RG14 6SR.

CAIRNS, Mr. John Warner, FCA *1950;* Dormers, West Marden, CHICHESTER, PO18 9ES. (Life Member)

CAIRNS, Mrs. Kerry Louise, ACA *2006;* with Reeves & Co LLP, 37 St. Margarets Street, CANTERBURY, KENT, CT1 2TU.

CAIRNS, Ms. Laura Elizabeth, BA ACA *1986;* 44 Lake Street, OXFORD, OX1 4RP.

•CAIRNS, Mrs. Margaret Ann, FCA *1975;* Cairns Bailey & Co, 3 Beacon Court, Birmingham Road, Great Barr, BIRMINGHAM, B43 6NN.

CAIRNS, Mr. Martin Stuart, MSci ACA *2002;* with AlixPartners Ltd, 20 North Audley Street, LONDON, W1K 6WE.

CAIRNS, Mr. Michael, BSc ACA *1991;* ROTANA Holding, Kingdom Tower 58th Floor, PO Box 2, RIYADH, 11321, SAUDI ARABIA.

CAIRNS, Mrs. Michelle Anne, ACA *1993;* No 30 Mang Kung Wo Village, SAI KUNG, SAR, HONG KONG SAR.

CAIRNS, Miss. Natalie Elizabeth, BSc ACA *2007;* 34d Marlborough Road, RICHMOND, TW10 6JR.

CAIRNS, Mr. Peter Christopher, BA ACA *1987;* Suite 6303, The Center, 99 Queen's Road, CENTRAL, HONG KONG ISLAND, HONG KONG SAR.

CAIRNS, Mr. Robert Mark, FCA *1973;* 11 Mcdonough Close, CHESSINGTON, KT9 1ER.

CAIRNS, Miss. Sarah Louise, BSc ACA *2010;* 6 Mors End, Stratford St. Mary, COLCHESTER, CO7 6YF.

CAIRNS, Mr. Stephen Thomas Matthew, ACA *1993;* 2451 Elm Street, MANCHESTER, NH 03104, UNITED STATES.

CAIRNS, Mr. Thomas James, BA ACA *1999;* Barclays Capital, 5 North Colonnade, LONDON, E14 4BB.

CAIRNS-TERRY, Mr. Henry Alexander, BA FCA *1985;* with Ernst & Young LLP, 1 Colmore Square, BIRMINGHAM, B4 6HQ.

•CAISLEY, Mr. Quentin, BA ACA *1991;* (Tax Fac), Quentin Caisley, Unit 6, Bearl, STOCKSFIELD, NORTHUMBERLAND, NE43 7AJ.

•CAISTER, Mr. Mark Stephen, BCom ACA *1989;* M.S. Caister & Co Ltd, Prosperity House, 121 Green Lane, DERBY, DE1 1RZ. See also Payacademy Ltd

•CAISTER, Mrs. Nicola Susan, BSS ACA *1994;* M.S. Caister & Co Ltd, Prosperity House, 121 Green Lane, DERBY, DE1 1RZ. See also Payacademy Ltd

CAISTOR, Mr. Richard Geoffrey, FCA *1970;* St Petrock Barns, Trevengenow, St Ervan, WADEBRIDGE, PL27 7SZ.

CAKE, Mr. Michael Walter James, FCA *1958;* 131 Chessfield Park, AMERSHAM, HP6 6RU. (Life Member)

CAKE, Mr. Philip John, BEng ACA *2004;* with Gibson Hewitt & Co, 5 Park Court, Pyrford Road, WEST BYFLEET, SURREY, KT14 6SD.

CAKEBREAD, Mr. David James, FCA *1952;* Lantana, 11 Fosters Close, East Preston, LITTLEHAMPTON, WEST SUSSEX, BN16 2TL. (Life Member)

CAKEBREAD, Mr. Norman Francis, FCA *1962;* 75 Dan-y-Bryn Avenue, Radyr, CARDIFF, CF15 8DQ. (Life Member)

CAKEBREAD, Mr. Stephen Robert, FCA *1971;* 17 Springfield Place, CHELMSFORD, CM1 7ZA.

CALANGLANG, Mrs. Jo Ann Marie, BSc ACA *1992;* A T Kearney Management Consultants, Lansdowne House, 57 Berkeley Square, LONDON, W1J 6ER.

CALCUTT, Mr. Alexander Charles George Denniss, BSc ACA *1995;* 28 Connaught Avenue, East Sheen, LONDON, SW14 7RH.

CALCUTT, Mr. David Patrick, FCA *1967;* Tan House, Penn Lane, Tanworth-in-Arden, SOLIHULL, B94 5HH. (Life Member)

CALCUTT, Mr. Martin Leonard, BSc(Hons) FCA FCCA CTA *1985;* (Tax Fac), Montpelier Tax Planning (Liverpool) Ltd, 17a Sweeting Street, LIVERPOOL, L2 4TE.

•CALCUTTEEA, Mr. Prashant, MSc BSc ACA *2005;* Calculus International Limited, 4 Manita House, Broad Avenue, Belle Rose, Quatre Bones, ROSE HILL MAURITIUS.

•CALDARA, Ms. Angela Jane, BSc FCA DipCII ACIS *1984;* (Tax Fac), A. Caldara, 10 Crossway, West Wimbledon, LONDON, SW20 9JA.

CALDECOTT, Mr. David Gareth, BSc ACA *1992;* Heath House Heath Drive, Walton on the Hill, TADWORTH, KT20 7QQ.

CALDER, Mr. Andrew, ACA *2009;* Benson House, Pricewaterhousecoopers, 33 Wellington Street, LEEDS, LS1 4JP.

CALDER, Mrs. Angela, ACA *1988;* 14 The Hop Kilns, Bishops Frome, WORCESTER, WR6 5BP.

CALDER, Ms. Beverley Joanne, BA ACA *2006;* with KPMG LLP, 100 Temple Street, BRISTOL, BS1 6AG.

CALDER, Mr. Desmond James, FCA *1959;* 12 Second Avenue, Felpham, BOGNOR REGIS, PO22 7LJ. (Life Member)

CALDER, Mr. Duncan Harvey, ACA *1987;* KPMG, 235 St George's Terrace, PERTH, WA 6000, AUSTRALIA.

CALDER, Mr. Gavin Edward, ACA *2009;* 20c, 20 Anson Road, LONDON, NW2 3UU.

•CALDER, Mrs. Helen Moyra, BA ACA *1979;* Helen Calder, Black Cat Cottage, Broadwell Road, Oddington, MORETON-IN-MARSH, GL56 0UX.

CALDER, Mr. John Murray, BSc ACA *2007;* 312-460 Buckland Avenue, KELOWNA V1Y 5Z4, BC, CANADA.

CALDER, Mrs. Katherine Rebecca, ACA *2008;* 12 Braddock Close, Lenton, NOTTINGHAM, NG7 2FN.

CALDER, Mr. Michael John, MA FCA *1959;* 42 Carson Road, LONDON, SE21 8HU. (Life Member)

CALDER, Mr. Neil, ACA *2008;* 12 Braddock Close, Lenton, NOTTINGHAM, NG7 2FN.

•CALDER, Mr. Timothy Christopher Philip, ACA *1986;* Kendall Wadley LLP, Merevale House, 27 Sansome Walk, WORCESTER, WR1 1NU.

CALDERAN, Mrs. Clare Elizabeth, BSc ACA *1996;* 22 Deanway, CHALFONT ST. GILES, BUCKINGHAMSHIRE, HP8 4JL.

CALDERBANK, Mr. Adam Patrick, BSc ACA *1991;* 10 Elswick Gardens, Mellor, BLACKBURN, BB2 7JD.

•CALDERBANK, Ms. Allison Margaret, BSc(Econ) ACA *1995;* (Tax Fac), Donnan Calderbank (Warrington) Ltd, 25 Sandmoor Place, LYMM, CHESHIRE, WA13 0LQ.

CALDERBANK, Mrs. Amanda, BA ACA *1996;* 10 Elswick Gardens, Mellor, BLACKBURN, BB2 7JD.

CALDERBANK, Mr. Andrew Charles, BA ACA *1993;* 3 Dewe Lane, Burghfield, READING, RG30 3SU.

CALDERBANK, Mr. Graham Robert, BA ACA *1984;* 57 Acorn Ridge, Walton, CHESTERFIELD, DERBYSHIRE, S42 7HF.

•CALDERBANK, Mr. Mark James, ACA *1982;* M J Calderbank Limited, Rustic Ridge, Benton Green Lane, Berkswell, COVENTRY, CV7 7DB.

CALDERBANK, Mr. Mark Jefferson, BA ACA *2004;* 18 Cholmley Drive, NEWTON-LE-WILLOWS, MERSEYSIDE, WA12 8EE.

CALDERBANK, Mrs. Patricia Anne, FCA *1960;* 15 The Butts, Aynho, BANBURY, OX17 3AN. (Life Member)

CALDERBANK, Mr. Peter Charles Edward, MA ACA *1992;* 46 Finsen Road, LONDON, SE5 9AW.

CALDERBANK, Ms. Victoria Anne, BSc ACA *2005;* Withinlee Hollow Withinlee Road, Prestbury, MACCLESFIELD, CHESHIRE, SK10 4AT.

CALDERON, Mr. Denis Alva, BCom FCA *1973;* 7 Minster Walk, Hurworth on Tees, DARLINGTON, DL2 2AR.

CALDERWOOD, Mr. Brian, FCA *1972;* 17 Birch Crescent, AYLESFORD, ME20 7QE.

CALDERWOOD, Mr. Philip Kenneth, BSc ACA *1979;* 700 NE 72nd St, BOCA RATON, FL 33487, UNITED STATES.

•CALDERWOOD, Mr. Richard Johnston, FCA *1970;* Burns Waring, Roper Yard, Roper Road, CANTERBURY, CT2 7EX. See also SME Payroll Services Limited, Waring & Partners. and Burns Waring & Partners Ltd

CALDON, Mr. Gary John, BA ACA *1996;* 140 Norsey Road, BILLERICAY, ESSEX, CM11 1BH.

CALDWELL, Mr. Alasdair David, FCA *1976;* 8 Maple Close, Petts Wood, ORPINGTON, BR5 1LP.

CALDWELL, Mr. Allan Graham, BSc FCA *1975;* 10 The Acorns, Radstock, BATH, BA3 5BT.

CALDWELL, Mrs. Amanda Frances Louise, BSc ACA *1998;* 7 Lyndhurst Grove Road, BRIGHOUSE, WEST YORKSHIRE, HD6 3SD.

CALDWELL, Mr. Andrew Lester, BSc ACA *1999;* 24 Crowborough Close, Lostock, BOLTON, BL6 4LZ.

•CALDWELL, Mr. Barry Martin, BBS ACA *1990;* Barry Caldwell & Co, 135 Hillside, GREYSTONES, COUNTY WICKLOW, IRELAND.

CALDWELL, Mr. David, ACA *1981;* 123 Lutterworth Road, NUNEATON, CV11 6QA.

CALDWELL, Mr. Gavin Beaton, BSc(Hons) ACA *2002;* 6 Acacia Close, Petts Wood, ORPINGTON, BR5 1LL.

CALDWELL, Mr. Gordon Stewart, FCA *1965;* Arran Lodge, 18 Wood Drive, CHISLEHURST, BR7 5EU.

CALDWELL, Mrs. Helen Tracy, BA ACA *1996;* Old Hall Farmhouse Broadway Lane, Waterfall Waterhouses, STOKE-ON-TRENT, ST10 3JB.

CALDWELL, Mrs. Hilary Louise, BA FCA *1993;* 6 Kingsmere Avenue, LYTHAM ST.ANNES, FY8 3AT.

CALDWELL, Mrs. Jacqueline G, BA ACA *1985;* 17 Chapel Street, WARMINSTER, BA12 8BZ.

CALDWELL, Mr. John Christopher, BA ACA *1984;* C S E Global (UK) Ltd, Rotherside Road, Eckington, SHEFFIELD, S21 4HL.

CALDWELL, Mr. John Christopher, ACA *2007;* 2 Meadowgate, WIGAN, WN6 7QN.

CALDWELL, Mr. John Michael, FCA *1965;* 12 Newfield Court, LYMM, CHESHIRE, WA13 9QU.

•CALDWELL, Mr. Jonathan Edward Murray, FCA *1968;* J.E.M. Caldwell, 105 Carrowreagh Road, Garvagh, COLERAINE, COUNTY LONDONDERRY, BT51 5LH.

CALDWELL, Ms. Kathryn, BSc ACA *2009;* 56 Aubrey Road, BRISTOL, BS3 3EX.

CALDWELL, Mrs. Laura Emma, BA(Hons) ACA *2003;* 6 Acacia Close, Petts Wood, ORPINGTON, KENT, BR5 1LL.

•CALDWELL, Miss. Nancy Christina, BSc FCA *1984;* 29 Marston Drive, Vinters Park, MAIDSTONE, ME14 5NB.

CALDWELL, Mr. Paul, BSc ACA *1983;* 90 Langham Road, TEDDINGTON, TW11 9HJ

CALDWELL, Mr. Paul Ambrose, MEng ACA *1996;* 621 Cassiar Road, KELOWNA V1V 1M8, BC, CANADA.

CALDWELL, Mr. Peter Vivian Benson, LLB FCA *1972;* 14/2 Shipley Street, SOUTH YARRA, VIC 3141, AUSTRALIA.

CALDWELL, Mr. Stephen Martin, BA FCA *1994;* 14 Relmar Road, TORONTO M5P 2Y5, ON, CANADA.

CALDWELL, Mr. Stuart Murdoch, BA ACA MCT *1998;* 7 Lyndhurst Grove Road, BRIGHOUSE, WEST YORKSHIRE, HD6 3SD.

CALDWELL, Mr. Thomas Forrest, FCA *1974;* Bracken Rise, Hutton Road, Ash Vale, ALDERSHOT, GU12 5EY.

CALDWELL, Mr. Wilfrid Moores, MA FCA *1963;* The Grange, Hesworth Lane, Fittleworth, PULBOROUGH, RH20 1EW. (Life Member)

CALE, Mr. Christopher James, BSc(Hons) ACA *2003;* 9 Barn Owl Road, CHIPPENHAM, SN14 6XL.

CALE, Mr. Daniel Robert, BSc ACA *1997;* 39 Dickins Road, WARWICK, WARWICKSHIRE, CV34 5NS.

CALE, Mr. David Clive, MA FCA *1974;* 6 Robinson Close, Backwell, BRISTOL, BS48 3BT.

CALE, Mr. John Douglas, FCA *1976;* Longley & Co, 81 Melton Road West Bridgford, NOTTINGHAM, NG2 6EN.

CALEY, Mrs. Alison Pauline, FCA CTA *1981;* with Ernst & Young LLP, Apex Plaza, Forbury Road, READING, RG1 1YE.

CALEY, Mr. Andrew Maitland, MA FCA CTA *1987;* (Tax Fac), 41 Chester Avenue, BEVERLEY, HU17 8UQ.

CALEY, Mr. Edward Russell, BSc(Econ) ACA *1996;* Via F. Marescalchi 9, 20133 MILAN, ITALY.

CALEY, Miss. Elizabeth, ACA *2011;* 86 Dorsey Drive, BEDFORD, MK42 9FP.

•CALEY, Mr. Richard Michael, BSc FCA *1977;* Richard Caley Ltd, Havenside, Trewent Hill, Freshwater East, PEMBROKE, SA71 5LJ.

CALEY, Mr. Roland Charles, BA ACA *1991;* 6 Cornel Court, Forest Town, MANSFIELD, NOTTINGHAMSHIRE, NG19 0NF.

CALEY, Mrs. Tracy, BA ACA *1990;* with Try Lunn & Co, Roland House, Princes Dock Street, HULL, HU1 2LD.

CALF, Miss. Rachel Angela, ACA *2009;* 26 King George Avenue, LOUGHBOROUGH, LEICESTERSHIRE, LE11 2NU.

CALFA, Mr. Antoine, FCA *1972;* Antoine S Calfa, 18 Crown Steel Drive, Suite 201, MARKHAM L3R 9X8, ON, CANADA.

CALHOUN, Mr. Martin James, FCA *1971;* Cromptons Healthcare Ltd Unit 2, Crockford Lane Chineham, BASINGSTOKE, RG24 8NA.

CALIERNO, Mrs. Amanda Mary, BEng ACA *1999;* 18 Falconer Street, BISHOP'S STORTFORD, HERTFORDSHIRE, CM23 4FE.

CALKIN, Mr. Lawrence Richard, FCA *1972;* Little Acre, 66B Hawthorn Bank, SPALDING, PE11 1JQ.

CALLAGHAN, Mrs. Andrea Michelle, BSc ACA *1997;* 1 Oakwood, Shootersway, BERKHAMSTED, HERTFORDSHIRE, HP4 3NQ.

CALLAGHAN, Miss. Angela Marie, ACA *2007;* 32 Thornbury Close, HARTLEPOOL, CLEVELAND, TS27 3RA.

•①CALLAGHAN, Mr. Brian Reginald Anthony, FCA *1970;* with Chantrey Vellacott DFK LLP, Russell Square House, 10-12 Russell Square, LONDON, WC1B 5LF.

CALLAGHAN, Mrs. Cynthia Valentine, FCA *1971;* 7 Hazel Close, WALTHAM CROSS, HERTFORDSHIRE, EN7 6NJ.

CALLAGHAN, Mr. Daniel, BSc ACA *2003;* 5 Bourke Street, COBURG, VIC 3058, AUSTRALIA.

CALLAGHAN, Mr. Daniel Patrick, BA ACA *1999;* 5 Nottingham Mansions, Nottingham Street, LONDON, W1U 5EN.

CALLAGHAN, Mr. David Peter John, BSc ACA *1992;* 9 Knoll Gardens, NEWBURY, BERKSHIRE, RG20 0NZ.

CALLAGHAN, Mr. Ian Robert, BA ACA *1997;* 1 Oakwood, Shootersway, BERKHAMSTED, HP4 3NQ.

CALLAGHAN, Mrs. Jennifer Laura, BSc ACA *1992;* 14 St. Barnabas Court, CAMBRIDGE, CB1 2BZ.

CALLAGHAN, Mr. John, BA ACA *1991;* 9 Kingfisher Close, Hamble, SOUTHAMPTON, SO31 4PE.

CALLAGHAN, Mrs. Kim, BSc ACA *1984;* 3 College Avenue, EGHAM, SURREY, TW20 8NR.

CALLAGHAN, Mr. Matthew, BA ACA *2010;* 22 Madison Apartments, Seymour Grove, MANCHESTER, M16 0NB.

CALLAGHAN, Mrs. Melanie Jane Cecile, BSc ACA *1989;* Greystone Cottage, Harewood Road, Collingham, WETHERBY, LS22 5BL.

CALLAGHAN, Mr. Michael, FCA *1974;* Caracas Pouch, PO Box 6046, SAN RAMON, CA 94583, UNITED STATES.

CALLAGHAN, Mr. Paul, BSc FCA *1993;* with KPMG, 4th Floor HSBC Building, Muttrah Business District, PO Box 641, 112 MUSCAT, OMAN.

CALLAGHAN, Mr. Peter John, FCA *1975;* Bildeston House High Street, Bildeston, IPSWICH, IP7 7EX.

CALLAGHAN, Mr. Philip John, BSc FCA *1978;* c/o Tatum, 350 Park Avenue, 22nd Floor, NEW YORK, NY 10022, UNITED STATES.
CALLAGHAN, Mr. Richard James, LLB ACA *1993;* 20 Hearnville Road, LONDON, SW12 8RR.
CALLAGHAN, Mr. Robert John, BSc ACA *1998;* 31 Queens Drive, PRENTON, MERSEYSIDE, CH43 0RR.
CALLAGHAN, Mr. Ronan, BSc(Hons) ACA *2011;* 22 Carden Crescent, BRIGHTON, BN1 8TQ.
CALLAGHAN, Mr. Sean, BA ACA *1992;* 14 St. Barnabas Court, St. Barnabas Road, CAMBRIDGE, CB1 2BZ.
•**CALLAGHAN, Mr. Sean Laurence, BA FCA** *1995;* Ernst & Young LLP, 1 More London Place, LONDON, SE1 2AF. See also Ernst & Young Europe LLP
CALLAGHAN, Mrs. Sharon Mary, BSc ACA *1987;* 23 Cairn Avenue, Guiseley, LEEDS, LS20 8QQ.
CALLAGHAN, Mr. Trevor, BSc FCA *1985;* Unit 1 Hanover Trading Estate, North Road, LONDON, N7 9HD.
CALLAHAN, Mr. Clive Stuart, FCA *1972;* Apartado 124, Valldoreix, 08197 BARCELONA, SPAIN.
CALLAN, Mr. Mark Adrian, BA ACA *1991;* PO Box 5538, Frankton, HAMILTON, NEW ZEALAND.
CALLAN, Mr. Robert John, BA ACA *1995;* Catlin Holdings Ltd, 3 Minster Court, LONDON, EC3R 7DD.
CALLAN, Mr. Ross, BA ACA *1998;* 28 Burnaby Mill, GREYSTONES, COUNTY WICKLOW, IRELAND.
CALLAND, Mr. Philip, BEng ACA *1998;* 13312 Edgetree Drive, PINEVILLE, NC 28134, UNITED STATES.
CALLAND, Mr. Stephen Richard, ACA *1985;* 37 Hook Road, Ampfield, ROMSEY, HAMPSHIRE, SO51 9DB.
CALLANDER, Mr. Alistair Alexander, BA ACA *2001;* 10 Lodge Hill Addingham, ILKLEY, WEST YORKSHIRE, LS29 0NG.
CALLAR, Ms. Susan Elizabeth, BSc ACA *1991;* 17 Caroline Buildings, Pulteney Road, BATH, BA2 4JH.
CALLARD, Mr. Richard John, BSc(Hons) ACA *2001;* Department for Business Innovation & Skills, 1 Victoria Street, LONDON, SW1H 0ET.
CALLAS, Mr. Peter John, BSc ACA *2006;* Flat 49 Aura Court, 163 Peckham Rye, LONDON, SE15 3GW.
CALLAWAY, Ms. Jacqueline Wynn, ACA CA(NZ) *2011;* 12 Chateau Valeuse, La Rue De La Valeuse, St Brelade, JERSEY, JE3 8EE.
CALLAWAY, Mr. Paul Robert, FCA *1975;* Orchard Cottage, Post Office Lane, Cleeve Hill, CHELTENHAM, GLOUCESTERSHIRE, GL52 3PS.
CALLCUT, Mrs. Michele Sara Frances, BEd ACA *1991;* The Lodge, Uplands Park, Park Lane, Brook, GODALMING, SURREY GU8 5LA.
CALLE, Mr. David Graeme, BA FCA *1992;* 2 Kinsbourne Close, HARPENDEN, HERTFORDSHIRE, AL5 3PB.
CALLEAR, Mr. David James, BSc FCA *1979;* Office 2 Office plc, St. Crispins House, Duke Street, NORWICH, NR3 1PD.
CALLEN, Mr. Andrew James, MA ACA *2003;* Lloyds Bank House, 5 Fore Street, CALSTOCK, CORNWALL, PL18 9RN.
•**CALLEN, Mr. Nicholas Edward, BSc(Hons) FCA CTA** *1990;* Callen Consultants Ltd, 146 Bath Road, Longwell Green, BRISTOL, BS30 9DB.
CALLEN, Mr. Stephen Gibson, BA ACA *1980;* 14 St Pauls Road, RICHMOND, TW9 2HH.
CALLENDER, Mr. Alexei Robert, ACA *2008;* Zeus Capital Ltd, 3 Ralli Courts, West Riverside, SALFORD, M3 5FT.
CALLER, Mr. Gareth Alexander, BA ACA *2001;* Flat 7, Wolsey House, Oseney Crescent, LONDON, NW5 2AX.
CALLEWAERT, Mr. William George, LLB ACA *2006;* with KPMG (BVI) Limited, PO Box 4467, 3rd Floor Benco Popular Building, Road Town, TORTOLA, VG-1110 VIRGIN ISLANDS (BRITISH).
•**CALLICOTT, Mr. Michael, BA ACA** *1986;* Callicott & Co, 46 Fairacres, Prestwood, GREAT MISSENDEN, HP16 0LE.
CALLIGEROS, Mr. Ronnie, BSc ACA *2010;* 524 Waterways P.O. box 1311, WEST BAY, KY1-1108, CAYMAN ISLANDS.
•**CALLIN, Mr. David Malcolm, FCA** *1981;* Callow Matthewman & Co., Atholl House, 29-31 Hope Street, Douglas, ISLE OF MAN, IM1 1AR.
CALLINAN, Miss. Elizabeth Emma, ACA *2008;* Bannatyne Fitness Ltd Powerhouse, Haughton Road, DARLINGTON, COUNTY DURHAM, DL1 1ST.
CALLINGHAM, Mr. Mark, MSc FCA *1972;* 2 Old Farm Close, North Poulner, RINGWOOD, BH24 3LH.
CALLINGHAM, Mr. Peter Harold, FCA *1970;* 5 Highfield Gardens, Hatch Lane, LISS, GU33 7NQ. (Life Member)
•**CALLINGHAM, Mr. Ray Michael, BA FCA** *1989;* Beeley Hawley & Co Ltd, 44 Nottingham Road, MANSFIELD, NOTTINGHAMSHIRE, NG18 1BL.
CALLIS, Mr. Gerard John, ACA *2009;* 43 De Bohun Avenue, LONDON, N14 4PU.
CALLIS, Mr. Richard John, ACA *1979;* 120 Warralong Avenue, GREENSBORO, VIC 3088, AUSTRALIA.
CALLIS, Mr. Sidney, BSc FCA *1958;* The Old School House, School Lane, BUCKINGHAM, MK18 1HB. (Life Member)
CALLISON, Mr. Ralph William, FCA *1971;* 78 Brian Avenue, CLEETHORPES, DN35 9DG.
•**CALLISS, Mr. Brian Leslie, FCA** *1983;* with Altwood Business & Accountancy Services Ltd, Chantecler, Altwood Bailey, MAIDENHEAD, BERKSHIRE, SL6 4PQ.
CALLISTER, Mrs. Alison, BSc ACA *1995;* Baltic House Baltic Road, Kirk Michael, ISLE OF MAN, IM6 1EF.
•**CALLISTER, Mr. Martin Richard, FCA** *1972;* Harding Lewis Limited, 34 Athol Street, Douglas, ISLE OF MAN, IM1 1JB.
CALLISTER, Mr. Peter, MA FCA *1970;* 29 Eccles Road, Chapel-en-le-Frith, HIGH PEAK, SK23 9RR.
CALLISTER, Mr. William Alexander George, BSc ACA *2008;* 1/81 Barkly Street, ST KILDA, VIC 3182, AUSTRALIA.
CALLMAN, Mrs. Sarah Miriam, BSc ACA *1996;* 12 Holne Chase, LONDON, N2 0QN.
•**CALLOW, Mr. Arthur Christopher, FCA** *1978;* McCabe Ford Williams, Market House, 17 Hart Street, MAIDSTONE, KENT, ME16 8RA.
CALLOW, Mrs. Dawn Rose, BA FCA *1992;* 29 Alexandra Drive, Yoxall, BURTON-ON-TRENT, DE13 8PL.
CALLOW, Mr. Donald Laurence, BSc ACA *1984;* 6 Holly Road, FARNBOROUGH, HAMPSHIRE, GU14 0DZ.
CALLOW, Mr. Peter John, BSc ACA *1988;* Visa International, CEMEA Region, PO Box 39662, LONDON, W2 6WH.
•**CALLOW, Mr. Phillip, BSc FCA** *1991;* Moore Stephens, P O Box 236, First Island House, Peter Street, St. Helier, JERSEY JE4 8SG.
CALLOW, Mr. Roy Stanley, BSc ACA TEP *1980;* (Tax Fac), with PKF (Isle of Man) LLC, PO Box 16, Analyst House, Douglas, ISLE OF MAN, IM99 1AP.
CALLOW, Mr. Steven John, MSc ACA *1993;* 72 Huckley Way, Bradley Stoke, BRISTOL, BS32 8AR.
CALLOW, Mr. Timothy Simon Henry, BA FCA *1989;* 26 Abbots Way, Abbotswood, Ballasalla, ISLE OF MAN, IM9 3EQ.
CALLWOOD, Mr. Richard Michael, BA ACA *1986;* 14 Kensington Gardens, Hale, ALTRINCHAM, CHESHIRE, WA15 9DP.
CALMAN, Mr. Adam, BSc ACA *1991;* High beeches, The Avenue, RADLETT, HERTFORDSHIRE, WD7 7DR.
•**CALNAN, Mr. Philip James Lawrence, BA FCA** *1981;* PricewaterhouseCoopers LLP, Hays Galleria, 1 Hays Lane, LONDON, SE1 2RD. See also PricewaterhouseCoopers
CALOGERO, Mrs. Laura Anne, BSc ACA *1997;* Fehrsen & Douglas, PO Box 521, HARTBEESPOORT, 0216, SOUTH AFRICA.
CALOUPIS, Mr. Dimitrios, FCA *1969;* 4 Agias Filotheis, Filothei, 15237 ATHENS, GREECE. (Life Member)
CALOW, Mrs. Amanda Clare, ACA *2007;* 9 Salmon Lane, LONDON, E14 7NA.
CALOW, Miss. Catherine, BCom ACA *1991;* 22c Vant Road, Tooting, LONDON, SW17 8TJ.
•**CALOW, Mr. John Anthony, FCA** *1976;* 2 Stamford Rise, Newtown Linford, LEICESTER, LE6 0PY.
CALOW, Mr. Paul Frederick, BA ACA *1979;* 15 Elmgrove Road, WEYBRIDGE, SURREY, KT13 8NZ.
CALOW, Mr. Timothy Hugh, BA ACA *1987;* 3 Laurel Close, Embsay, SKIPTON, BD23 6RS.
CALROW, Mr. Simon John, BA FCA *1983;* The Glyders, 6 The Highfields, Wightwick, WOLVERHAMPTON, WV6 8DW.
CALVELEY, Mr. Timothy Owen, MA ACA *1999;* PO BOX 780, WARWICK WK BX, BERMUDA.
CALVER, Mr. David Lester Daniel, MA ACA *1987;* Brambles, 31a Green End, Granborough, BUCKINGHAM, MK18 3NT.
CALVER, Mrs. Susan Mary, BSc FCA *1984;* 12 Bramley Gardens, Whimple, EXETER, EX5 2SJ.
CALVER-JONES, Mr. James, TD FCA *1954;* The Meads, Winstone, CIRENCESTER, GL7 7JU. (Life Member)
CALVERLEY, Mr. David Maxwell, FCA *1965;* The Four Winds Pitch Hill, Ewhurst, CRANLEIGH, GU6 7NL.
•①**CALVERLEY, Mr. Duncan James, BA ACA** *1996;* with AlixPartners Ltd, 20 North Audley Street, LONDON, W1K 6WE.
CALVERLEY, Mr. Peter, FCA *1969;* 8/4 Were Street, BRIGHTON, VIC 3186, AUSTRALIA. (Life Member)
CALVERT, Mr. Adam, BSc ACA *2000;* 116, Leeds Road, LIVERSEDGE, WF15 6AA.
CALVERT, Mr. Alastair Niall, BSc FCA *1992;* 8 Marlborough Avenue, Cheadle Hulme, CHEADLE, CHESHIRE, SK8 7AW.
CALVERT, Mrs. Alison Valerie, BA ACA *1989;* Moores Furniture Group Ltd Unit 350, Thorp Arch Estate, WETHERBY, LS23 7DD.
CALVERT, Mr. Andrew Richard John, MA FCA *1975;* PO Box 118392, DUBAI, UNITED ARAB EMIRATES.
CALVERT, Mrs. Caroline Mary, BA ACA *1988;* Tudor House, Bridge End, Newport, SAFFRON WALDEN, CB11 3TH.
CALVERT, Mr. Douglas Stuart, FCA *1951;* Holly Grove, Hugmore Lane, Llanypwll, WREXHAM, LL13 9YE. (Life Member)
CALVERT, Mr. Glyn, ACA *1984;* Car Care Plan Ltd Jubilee House, Mid Point Thornbury, BRADFORD, WEST YORKSHIRE, BD3 7AG.
CALVERT, Mr. James Richard, BSc FCA *1978;* Riemore, Bangors Road South, IVER, SL0 0AY.
CALVERT, Mr. John Michael, BSc ACA *1982;* Tudor House, Bridge End, Newport, SAFFRON WALDEN, CB11 3TH.
•**CALVERT, Miss. Lisa Jane, BA(Hons) ACA** *2004;* with Ford Campbell Freedman LLP, 34 Park Cross Street, LEEDS, LS1 2QH.
•**CALVERT, Mrs. Margaret Elizabeth, ACA** *1991;* 14 York Lane, York Village, Langho, BLACKBURN, BB6 8DT.
CALVERT, Mr. Mark Daniel, BSc(Hons) ACA *2004;* with PricewaterhouseCoopers, 18 CyberCity, EBENE, MAURITIUS.
•**CALVERT, Mr. Neil Malcolm, FCA** *1980;* Rushtons (NW) Limited, Shorrock House, 1 Faraday Court, Fulwood, PRESTON, PR2 9NB.
•**CALVERT, Mr. Paul Anthony, ACA** *1987;* (Tax Fac), Calvert Dawson LLP, 288 Oxford Road, Gomersal, CLECKHEATON, BD19 4PY. See also Calvert Dawson Limited
CALVERT, Mr. Peter Steven, MA BSc ACA *2009;* Flat 114, 3 Cornell Square, LONDON, SW8 2ES.
CALVERT, Mr. Philip Leslie, FCA *1977;* Lambson Ltd Unit 603, Avenue D Thorp Arch Estate, WETHERBY, LS23 7FS.
CALVERT, Mr. Roger Alfred, FCA *1950;* 16 Wedgewood Court, Roundhay, LEEDS, LS8 1DD. (Life Member)
CALVERT, Mrs. Samantha Abigail Louise, BSc ACA *2000;* 116 Leeds Road, LIVERSEDGE, WEST YORKSHIRE, WF15 6AA.
CALVERT, Mr. Simon Christopher, BA ACA *1999;* with PricewaterhouseCoopers, Rovuma Carlton Hotel, Centro de EscritoriosPiso 3, Sala 1 Rua de Se MAPUTO, 114, MOZAMBIQUE.
CALVERT, Mr. Timothy Lees, ACA *1979;* Hewlett Packard Ltd, Cain Road, BRACKNELL, BERKSHIRE, RG12 1HN.
CALVERT, Mrs. Yvonne Valerie, BA ACA *1990;* M B N A Europe Ltd, Phase 1, Chester Business Park, CHESTER, CH4 9FB.
•**CALVERT-DAVIES, Mr. Jonathan Robert, BA ACA** *1994;* PricewaterhouseCoopers LLP, Hays Galleria, 1 Hays Lane, LONDON, SE1 2RD. See also PricewaterhouseCoopers
CAMACHO, Mr. Julio Pereira, FCA *1974;* Via Montebello 17, 20012 Cuggiono, MILAN, ITALY. (Life Member)
CAMAMILE, Mr. Nevile James, BA FCA *1956;* 7 Lee Road, LINCOLN, LN2 4BJ. (Life Member)
CAMBELL, Mr. Michael John, BA ACA *1985;* Bergische Land Strasse 20, 51503 ROSRATH, GERMANY.
CAMBERG, Mr. Jeremy Gordon, BSc ACA *1993;* Jones Lang LaSalle, 22 Hanover Square, LONDON, W1A 2BN.
CAMBLE, Mr. Julian Mark, BSc ACA *1995;* STM Group plc, Montagu Pavilion, 8-10 Queensway, PO Box 575, GIBRALTAR, GIBRALTAR.
CAMBRAY, Mr. Norman John, FCA *1960;* Moorleaze House, Wanborough, SWINDON, SN4 0SW. (Life Member)
•**CAMBRAY, Mr. Philip Anthony, FCA** *1975;* (Tax Fac), Clarke & Co, Acorn House, 33 Churchfield Road, Acton, LONDON, W3 6AY. See also Datacount Limited
CAMBRIDGE, Mrs. Helena Tracy, BSc ACA *1991;* 69 Main Street, Mursley, MILTON KEYNES, MK17 0RT.
CAMBRIDGE, Mr. Martin Paul, FCA *1976;* Little Birchetts, Stockland Green Road, Speldhurst, TUNBRIDGE WELLS, TN3 0TY.
CAMBRIDGE, Mr. Michael Burnett, FCA *1964;* The Old Rectory East, Grundisburgh, WOODBRIDGE, SUFFOLK, IP13 6TB. (Life Member)
CAMBRIDGE, Ms. Susan, BA ACA *1986;* Associated Board of the Royal School of Music, 24 Portland Place, LONDON, W1B 1LU.
•**CAMBROOK, Mr. Richard Harold, BSc FCA** *1977;* Chiltern Accountancy Services Limited, 29 Highmoor, AMERSHAM, BUCKINGHAMSHIRE, HP7 9BU.
CAMBURN, Mr. Liam Alan Robert, BSc ACA *2003;* Broadhaven, Broadfields, EAST MOLESEY, KT8 0BW.
•**CAMDEN, Mr. Edward James, BA ACA** *1984;* (Tax Fac), E J Camden, 3 Trews Weir Court, Trews Weir Reach, EXETER, EX2 4JS.
CAMELI, Mr. Joseph, BSc(Hons) ACA *2010;* 1 Crossway, LEIGHTON BUZZARD, BEDFORDSHIRE, LU7 3ND.
CAMELIA, Miss. Codirla, ACA *2010;* 17B George Dimitrof Street, Pallouriotissa, 1048 NICOSIA, CYPRUS.
CAMERON, Mr. Alastair David, BA ACA *1994;* 46 Erpingham Road, LONDON, SW15 1BG.
•**CAMERON, Mr. Alastair Langdon Craig, FCA** *1969;* AIMS - Alastair Cameron, 48 Lowther Road, Barnes, LONDON, SW13 9NU.
CAMERON, Mr. Alexander James, ACA *2008;* 41 Chaucer Road, LONDON, SE24 0NY.
•**CAMERON, Mr. Alexander William Richard, FCA** *1973;* F. Church Ltd, 7 Deanes Close, Castle Street, Steventon, ABINGDON, OXFORDSHIRE OX13 6SZ.
CAMERON, Mr. Alisdair Charles John, BA ACA *1993;* Brooklands, Stadhampton Road, Little Milton, OXFORD, OXFORDSHIRE, OX44 7QD.
CAMERON, Mr. Andrew, BSc ACA *2001;* 21 Mona Road, West Bridgford, NOTTINGHAM, NG2 5BS.
CAMERON, Mr. Andrew Clark, BA(Hons) ACA *2002;* with Ryecroft Glenton, 32 Portland Terrace, Jesmond, NEWCASTLE UPON TYNE, NE2 1QP.
CAMERON, Mr. Andrew John, FCA *1961;* 5 Hill Rise, RICKMANSWORTH, WD3 7NY.
CAMERON, Mr. Archibald David, MBA BSc ACA *1982;* 465 Stoneridge Lane, BLOOMFIELD HILLS, MI 48302, UNITED STATES.
CAMERON, Mr. Brent John, BA ACA *1989;* 47 Granary Way, SALE, M33 4GF.
CAMERON, Mr. Brian Keith, FCA *1961;* Hamm Staithe, Hamm Court, WEYBRIDGE, KT13 8YG. (Life Member)
CAMERON, Mr. Bruce Stewart, BEng ACA *1994;* 53 Nunroyd Road, Moortown, LEEDS, LS17 6PH.
CAMERON, Mr. Charles Donald Ewen, BCom ACA *1983;* Oasis Dental Care Ltd Unit E1-E2 Vantage Office Park, Old Gloucester Road Hambrook, BRISTOL, BS16 1GW.
•**CAMERON, Mrs. Christa Ann, BA ACA** *2001;* C A Cameron ACA, Opera Close, 22b Court Street, HADDINGTON, EAST LOTHIAN, EH41 3JA.
CAMERON, Mrs. Clare Juliet, BMus ACA *2005;* 2 Midleton Cottage, Faversham Road, Boughton Lees, ASHFORD, KENT, TN25 4HP.
CAMERON, Mr. Daniel Stephen, MA ACA *1991;* 17 Heron Island, Caversham, READING, RG4 8DQ.
CAMERON, Miss. Dawn Louise, BSc ACA *1992;* 20 Enmore Road, LONDON, SW15 6LL.
CAMERON, Donald Angus, MA FCA *1972;* Achnacarry, Spean Bridge, INVERNESS, PH34 4EJ. (Life Member)
CAMERON, Mrs. Eleanor May, BSc ACA *2006;* 5 Laleham Abbey, Laleham Park, STAINES, TW18 1SZ.
CAMERON, Mrs. Fiona Catherine, BSc ACA *1987;* Upper Woodhill Farm, Woodhill Lane, Shamley Green, GUILDFORD, GU5 0SR.
CAMERON, Mr. Gordon Biggart, OBE MA ACA *1992;* Quotient Bioscience Limited, Newmarket Road, Fordham, ELY, CAMBRIDGESHIRE, CB7 5WW.
•**CAMERON, Mr. Graham Duncan, BA ACA** *1979;* 4 Ingle Close, PINNER, MIDDLESEX, HA5 3BJ.
CAMERON, Ms. Helen Mary, MA ACA *1984;* Rhumhor, Old Ferry Road, Onich, FORT WILLIAM, PH33 6SA.
CAMERON, Miss. Helen Owen, BA(Hons) ACA *2004;* Shell International Petroleum Co Ltd Shell Centre, York Road, LONDON, SE1 7NA.
CAMERON, Mr. Hugh, BA FCA *1977;* Brocklebank Cottage, Torver, CONISTON, LA21 8BS.
CAMERON, Mr. Ian Anthony, BA ACA *1996;* 7 Foxwell Close, Haslingden, ROSSENDALE, BB4 6TP.
•**CAMERON, Mr. Ian Lindsay, FCA** *1975;* Ian L. Cameron, 100 Northwood Lane, Darley Dale, MATLOCK, DERBYSHIRE, DE4 2HR.
CAMERON, Mr. Ian Sandifer, MA FCA *1979;* 60 Burnfoot Avenue, LONDON, SW6 5EA.
CAMERON, Mr. James David, BA ACA *2000;* 3, Tudor Oaks, Elston, NEWARK, NG23 5NW.
CAMERON, Mrs. Jane Louise, BA ACA *1990;* Dickins House, Cherington, SHIPSTON-ON-STOUR, CV36 5HS.

CAMERON, Mrs. Jennifer Estelle, ACA *2004;* 1 Moorfields Road, Canford Cliffs, POOLE, BH13 7HA.

CAMERON, Mr. Jonathan Ian Duncan, BAcc ACA *1999;* 1 Pavilion Way, CONGLETON, CHESHIRE, CW12 4EW.

CAMERON, Mrs. Julie Doreen, BSc ACA *1989;* Rose Lea, Congleton Road, Mow Cop, STOKE-ON-TRENT, ST7 3PL.

CAMERON, Mr. Keith Gordon, FCA *1970;* 83 Clemenceau Avenue, #10-05 UE Square, Shell House, SINGAPORE 239920, SINGAPORE.

CAMERON, Mrs. Machiko Nancy, ACA *1990;* Cound Mill, Cound, SHREWSBURY, SY5 6AP.

CAMERON, Mr. Michael Graeme Stuart, FCA *1971;* Cound Mill, Cound, SHREWSBURY, SY5 6AP. (Life Member)

CAMERON, Mr. Neil Stuart, BSc FCA *1986;* 6 Ashington Road, LONDON, SW6 3QJ.

CAMERON, Mr. Robert Craig, FCA *1971;* 101 The Tors, 3 Wulumay Close, Balmain Cove, ROZELLE, NSW 2039, AUSTRALIA. (Life Member)

•CAMERON, Mr. Roger Alan, ACA *1985;* (Tax Fac), Cameron Ferriby & Co, Bridge House, 41 Wincolmlee, HULL, HU2 8AG.

CAMERON, Mrs. Sarah Patricia Allard, BA FCA *1988;* Chadlington House 18 Cliddesden Court, BASINGSTOKE, HAMPSHIRE, RG21 3ES.

CAMERON, Ms. Shirley Faye, BA ACA AMCT *1992;* British Broadcasting Corporation, Broadcasting House, Portland Place, LONDON, W1A 1AA.

CAMERON, Miss. Susan Jane, BSc(Hons) ACA CTA *2002;* Flat 16, Yewdale, 196 Harborne Park Road, Harborne, BIRMINGHAM, B17 0BP.

•CAMERON-CLARKE, Mr. Robert, FCA *1974;* (Tax Fac), Thorne Lancaster Parker, 8th Floor, Aldwych House, 81 Aldwych, LONDON, WC2B 4HN.

CAMERON-DOE, Mrs. Julie Mireille, BA ACA *1995;* Hotel Club, Level 29, 680 George Street, SYDNEY, NSW 2001, AUSTRALIA.

CAMERON-MOWAT, Mr. David, ACA *2009;* Flat 72 Tyndale Mansions, Upper Street, LONDON, N1 2XG.

CAMERON-MOWAT, Mr. Rory, BSc(Hons) ACA *2009;* 5 Broomfield Ride Oxshott, LEATHERHEAD, KT22 0LR.

•CAMERON-SMITH, Mr. Jonathan Andrew, FCA *1991;* Overdale, Langfords Lane, Hallatrow, BRISTOL, BS39 6HE.

CAMERON-WILLIAMS, Mr. Richard Graham, ACA *2008;* First Floor, 29 Hoveden Road, LONDON, NW2 3XE.

•CAMFIELD, Mr. Alan James, FCA *1980;* Camfield Chapman Lowe Limited, 9 High Street, Woburn Sands, MILTON KEYNES, MK17 8RF.

CAMFIELD, Mrs. Ann, BSc ACA *1978;* 35 Durham Close, Flitwick, BEDFORD, MK45 1UR.

CAMFIELD, Mr. Guy Robert, FCA *1954;* 11 Redwood Court, Llanishen, CARDIFF, CF14 5RD. (Life Member)

CAMFIELD, Mr. Timothy Trevor, ACA *1983;* 6 Grindal Place, Cawston, RUGBY, WARWICKSHIRE, CV22 7TS.

CAMIAH, Mr. Vinesh, BSc ACA *2011;* Flat 85 Studley Court, 4 Jamestown Way, LONDON, E14 2DA.

CAMIDGE, Mr. Peter Neil, BSc FCA *1990;* DHL-Excel Supply Chain, 251 Midsummer Boulevard, MILTON KEYNES, MK9 1EQ.

CAMIER WRIGHT, Mr. David George, BA ACA *1989;* 27 Canonbury Place, LONDON, N1 2NY.

•CAMILLERI, Mr. Joseph, FIA FCA CPA *1986;* PricewaterhouseCoopers, 167 Merchants Street, VALLETTA VLT 1174, MALTA.

CAMILLERI, Mr. Kurt James, BA ACA *2000;* 61 Laitwood Road, LONDON, SW12 9QH.

•CAMISSAR, Mr. Brian Bentzien, FCA FCCA *1973;* (Tax Fac), Brian Ben Camissar & Co, 38 Hendon Lane, LONDON, N3 1TT.

CAMM, Mr. Andrew John, BCom ACA *1988;* 4 Habberley Croft, SOLIHULL, B91 3YR.

CAMM, Mrs. Barbara Jean, FCA *1963;* 106 Tickhill Road, Balby, DONCASTER, DN4 8QQ. (Life Member)

•CAMM, Miss. Jennifer, BA ACA *2005;* RNS, 50-54 Oswald Road, SCUNTHORPE, NORTH LINCOLNSHIRE, DN15 7PQ.

CAMM, Mr. Michael Haydon, FCA *1966;* Camm & co, PO Box 63, Karen, NAIROBI, 00502, KENYA.

CAMMACK, Mrs. Catherine Marie, BA(Hons) ACA *2004;* 297a High Road, Chilwell, Beeston, NOTTINGHAM, NG9 5DD.

CAMMACK, Mr. Ian, MA ACA *1991;* Newhouse Farm, Northington, ALRESFORD, SO24 9UB.

CAMMACK, Mr. Nicholas James, BA ACA *1999;* Saint-Gobain Pam UK Limited, Lows Lane, ILKESTON, DERBYSHIRE, DE74QU.

•CAMMACK, Mr. Timothy John, MSc BSc FCA CPA *1975;* PO Box 27116, Rhine Road, CAPE TOWN, 8050, SOUTH AFRICA.

CAMMEGH, Mrs. Patricia Mary, BA ACA *1984;* 5 Swan Lane, Marsh Gibbon, BICESTER, OX27 0HH.

CAMMEGH, Mr. Stephen John, BCom FCA *1983;* 5 Swan Lane, Marsh Gibbon, BICESTER, OX27 0HH.

CAMMELL, Mr. Howard Mark, MA FCA *1989;* 2 Temple Bar Business Park, Strettington, CHICHESTER, WEST SUSSEX, PO18 0TU.

CAMP, Mr. David Martin, ACA *2009;* 22 Millfields, Oundle, PETERBOROUGH, PE8 4LF.

CAMP, Mr. James, ACA *2009;* Flat 40, Marlow Court, 221 Willesden Lane, LONDON, NW6 7PS.

CAMP, Mr. Lee Michael Richard, ACA MAAT *2005;* 1 Blossom Close, DAGENHAM, ESSEX, RM9 6YE.

CAMP, Mr. Michael James, MA ACA *1985;* Heath Cottage, Marriotts Avenue, South Heath, GREAT MISSENDEN, HP16 9QW.

CAMP, Mr. Michael Kurt, MA ACA *1999;* 101 Woolacombe Avenue, Sutton Leach, ST. HELENS, WA9 4NH.

•CAMP, Mr. Paul David, FCA *1981;* Paul D. Camp, Jarrards, Church Hill, Radwinter, SAFFRON WALDEN, CB10 2SX.

CAMP, Mr. Peter John, BA(Hons) ACA *2000;* 3 Bodmin Grove, DARLINGTON, COUNTY DURHAM, DL3 0ZP.

•CAMPAGNA, Ms. Gianna, FCA *1982;* Campagna-Smith, Fernleigh House, 10 Uttoxeter Road, Mickleover, DERBY, DE3 0DA.

CAMPBELL, Mr. Adrian Clemont, BEng FCA *1994;* 16 Etna Road, ST. ALBANS, HERTFORDSHIRE, AL3 5NJ.

CAMPBELL, Mr. Alan Robert, FCA *1975;* Carsemill Lodge, Burnhead, Auldgirth, DUMFRIES, DG2 0RX.

CAMPBELL, Mr. Alastair, MMath ACA *2011;* Flat 7, 28 Warrington Crescent, LONDON, W9 1EL.

CAMPBELL, Mr. Alastair Bolton, BSc ACA *2000;* 3 Durban Way, Yatton, BRISTOL, BS49 4QZ.

•CAMPBELL, Mr. Alastair Hugh Forbes, FCA *1968;* Brantwood, Putney Heath Lane, LONDON, SW15 3JF.

CAMPBELL, Mr. Alastair John, BEng ACA *1997;* 7 Hollingbourne Gardens, LONDON, W13 8EN.

CAMPBELL, Mrs. Alison, BSc ACA *1992;* 51 High Street, BIGGAR, ML12 6DA.

CAMPBELL, Mrs. Alison Bryden, MA ACA *1989;* 20 Links Avenue, WHITLEY BAY, NE26 1TG.

CAMPBELL, Mr. Alistair Hugh, FCA *1974;* Garth House, Newby Wiske, NORTHALLERTON, DL7 9ET.

CAMPBELL, Mr. Allan Shaw, MA ACA *1990;* 3 Rue De l'eglise, 78160 MARLY LE ROI, FRANCE.

CAMPBELL, Mrs. Amanda Jayne, BSc ACA *2002;* PricewaterhouseCoopers, Freshwater Place, 2 Southbank Boulevard, SOUTHBANK, VIC 3006, AUSTRALIA.

CAMPBELL, Miss. Amie, BA(Hons) ACA *2011;* Flat 1, Lane End, 196 West Hill, Putney, LONDON, SW15 3SH.

CAMPBELL, Mr. Andrew Arthur, FCA *1949;* 62 Nayland Road, COLCHESTER, CO4 5EW. (Life Member)

CAMPBELL, Mr. Andrew Bolton Allan, FCA *1975;* 17 The Wood Kilns, Yatton, BRISTOL, BS49 4QF.

CAMPBELL, Mr. Andrew James, MMath ACA *2002;* 20 New Road, Formby, LIVERPOOL, L37 7EF.

CAMPBELL, Mr. Andrew Kenneth, BA ACA *2001;* Monarch Airlines, Prospect House, Prospect Way, London Luton Airport, LUTON, LU2 9NU.

•CAMPBELL, Mr. Andrew Stewart, ACA *1992;* Crowe Clark Whitehill LLP, Arkwright House, Parsonage Gardens, MANCHESTER, M3 2HP. See also Horwath Clark Whitehill LLP

•CAMPBELL, Mr. Anthony Stuart, BA ACA *1993;* Nortons Group, Highlands House, Basingstoke Road, Spencers Wood, READING, RG7 1NT.

CAMPBELL, Mr. Aodhan John, BA ACA *2007;* 34 Burren Road, Warrenpoint, NEWRY, COUNTY DOWN, BT34 3SA.

CAMPBELL, Mrs. Barbara Elizabeth, BSc ACA *1999;* 17 Headley Road, LIPHOOK, HAMPSHIRE, GU30 7NS.

•CAMPBELL, Mr. Barrie, FCA *1976;* (Tax Fac), Glover & Co, 50A Oswald Road, SCUNTHORPE, DN15 7PQ.

CAMPBELL, Mr. Brian David, FCA *1974;* 10 St Mary's Close, BATH, BA2 6BR.

CAMPBELL, Mr. Bruce Hugh, FCA *1955;* 6 Brendon Avenue, WESTON-SUPER-MARE, BS23 2TE. (Life Member)

CAMPBELL, Mrs. Carol Elizabeth, BA ACA *1989;* 45 Deloraine Avenue, TORONTO M5M 2A8, ON, CANADA.

CAMPBELL, Ms. Christina Margaret, ACA *2004;* Miranda Technologies P A Ltd Stanford House, Main Street Stanford on Soar, LOUGHBOROUGH, LE12 5PY.

CAMPBELL, Mr. Christopher, BA(Hons) ACA *2009;* Flat 8, Westfield Hall, Hagley Road, BIRMINGHAM, B16 9LG.

CAMPBELL, Christopher James, Esq CBE FCA *1958;* 19 Morpeth Mansions, Morpeth Terrace, LONDON, SW1P 1ER. (Life Member)

CAMPBELL, Mr. Colin, FCA *1951;* Flat 2C, 21 Conduit Road, MID LEVELS, HONG KONG ISLAND, HONG KONG SAR. (Life Member)

CAMPBELL, Mr. Colin, BSc FCA *1992;* Zouk Ventures Ltd, 140 Brompton Road, LONDON, SW3 1HY.

CAMPBELL, Mr. Colin Hugh, MA DPhil FCA *1978;* 18 Ferguson Close, BASINGSTOKE, RG21 3JA. (Life Member)

•CAMPBELL, Mr. Colin Peter, BSc FCA *1975;* CMB Partnership, Chapel House, 1 Chapel Street, GUILDFORD, SURREY, GU1 3UH.

CAMPBELL, Mr. Colin Vezey, FCA *1964;* PO Box 423, PINEGOWRIE, 2123, SOUTH AFRICA.

CAMPBELL, Mr. Darren Samuel, LLB ACA *2003;* Box 798, EDENVALE, 1610, SOUTH AFRICA.

CAMPBELL, Mr. David, FCA *1968;* Ingledene, Micklea Lane, Longsdon, STOKE-ON-TRENT, ST9 9QA.

•CAMPBELL, Mr. David, FCA *1962;* David Campbell & Co., 8 New Heys Way, Bradshaw, BOLTON, BL2 4AR.

CAMPBELL, Mr. David, BSc FCA ACII *1976;* 7-8 The Abbey Woods, Douglas, ISLE OF MAN, IM2 5PL.

CAMPBELL, Mr. David Gerard, BSc ACA *1984;* 1 Broadfield Close, SHEFFIELD, SOUTH YORKSHIRE, S8 0XN.

•CAMPBELL, Mr. David Ian Henderson, BA FCA *1985;* 19 Endcliffe Grove Avenue, SHEFFIELD, S10 3EJ.

•CAMPBELL, Mr. David Keith, BSc ACA *1999;* BDO LLP, 55 Baker Street, LONDON, W1U 7EU. See also BDO Stoy Hayward LLP

CAMPBELL, Mr. David Martin, FCA *1981;* 116 Woodstock Road, WITNEY, OXFORDSHIRE, OX28 1DY.

CAMPBELL, Mr. David Patrick, BA ACA *2005;* Stobart Group, Stretton Green Distribution Park, Langford Way, Appleton, WARRINGTON, WA4 4TZ.

CAMPBELL, Mrs. Denise Frances, BMus(Hons) ACA *2010;* Deloitte & Touche Llp, 2 Hardman Street, MANCHESTER, M3 3HF.

•CAMPBELL, Ms. Diane Ingrid, BSc FCA *1990;* BDO Canada LLP, 600 Cathedral Place, 925 West Georgia Street, VANCOUVER V6C 3L2, BC, CANADA.

CAMPBELL, Mr. Donald Ramsay, FCA *1970;* 33 Ludlow Road, SUNDERLAND, SR2 9HH.

CAMPBELL, Douglas Alexander, Esq OBE FCA *1972;* The Disability Resource Centre, Unit 1A Humphrys Road, DUNSTABLE, LU5 4TP.

•CAMPBELL, Mr. Duncan Ian James, BSc FCA *1987;* with Harper Broom, Aston House, York Road, Maidenhead, MAIDENHEAD, BERKSHIRE SL6 1SF.

CAMPBELL, Mr. Duncan James, BCom ACA *1989;* Flat 58, 1-6 Dufours Place, LONDON, W1F 7SH.

CAMPBELL, Mr. Duncan Stewart, FCA *1965;* 2 Olive Branch Cottages, Folly Road Inkpen, HUNGERFORD, RG17 9QB.

CAMPBELL, Mrs. Eleanor Jane, BA ACA *1993;* 12 St. Margarets Road, MAIDENHEAD, SL6 5DZ.

CAMPBELL, Mrs. Elisabeth Anne, BSc ACA *1988;* 22 Kettil'stoun Grove, LINLITHGOW, EH49 6PP.

CAMPBELL, Ms. Fiona Siobhan, MA ACA *1990;* Long Road Sixth Form College, Long Road, CAMBRIDGE, CB2 8PX.

CAMPBELL, Mr. Gary Brian, FCA *1992;* Flat 4, 4th floor, Block C, Dragon Court, 6 Dragon Terrace, TIN HAU HONG KONG ISLAND HONG KONG SAR.

CAMPBELL, Mr. Gordon Michael, MA FCA *1995;* 3 South Road, Impington, CAMBRIDGE, CB24 9PB.

CAMPBELL, Mr. Graeme Robert James, BSc ACA *2001;* 5 Grove Crescent South, Boston Spa, WETHERBY, WEST YORKSHIRE, LS23 6AY.

CAMPBELL, Mrs. Helen Elizabeth, BA ACA *1995;* 27 Park View, NEW MALDEN, SURREY, KT3 4AY.

CAMPBELL, Miss. Helen Jane, BSc(Hons) ACA *2000;* 27 Bull Street, Harborne, BIRMINGHAM, B17 0HH.

CAMPBELL, Mr. Iain, BSc ACA *1992;* Lloyds, 10 Gresham Street, LONDON, EC2V 7AE.

CAMPBELL, Mr. Iain, MA(Hons) ACA *2010;* 50 Oakwood Road, BRISTOL, BS9 4NT.

CAMPBELL, Mr. Ian, FCA *1968;* 63 Chapel Road, Dersingham, KING'S LYNN, PE31 6PJ.

CAMPBELL, Mr. Ian Foster, FCA *1952;* 54 Manor Road, Swanland, NORTH FERRIBY, HU14 3PB. (Life Member)

CAMPBELL, Mr. Ian George, BSc ACA *1989;* 2 Bernards, Cornsland, BRENTWOOD, CM14 4JL.

CAMPBELL, Mr. Ian James, FCA *1955;* The Old Byre, 5 Manor Farm Walk, Portsham, WEYMOUTH, DT3 4PH. (Life Member)

CAMPBELL, Mr. Ian Neil, FCA *1969;* Strathglass View, Mullardoch Road, Cannich, BEAULY, INVERNESS-SHIRE, IV4 7LX. (Life Member)

CAMPBELL, Mr. Ian Patrick, FCA *1982;* The Old School House, Ashcombe, DAWLISH, EX7 0PY.

CAMPBELL, Mrs. Isabelle Eleanor, BA ACA *2009;* Flat 18 Riverhope Mansions, Harlinger Street, LONDON, SE18 5SS.

CAMPBELL, Mr. James, BA ACA *2011;* 14 St. Leonards, Tickhill, DONCASTER, SOUTH YORKSHIRE, DN11 9HX.

CAMPBELL, Mr. James Hamilton, BSc ACA *2002;* Sunnyside, New Road, CRANBROOK, TN17 3LE.

CAMPBELL, Mr. James Michael Stuart, LLB ACA *2000;* 9 Brookside Close, Paulton, BRISTOL, BS39 7NN.

CAMPBELL, Mr. James Richard, BA ACA *2006;* 39 Cavendish Drive, BIRKENHEAD, MERSEYSIDE, CH42 6RG.

CAMPBELL, Mr. James William, BA ACA *1993;* Willis Risk Services (Ireland) Ltd, Grand Mill Quay, Barrow Street, DUBLIN 4, COUNTY DUBLIN, IRELAND.

CAMPBELL, Ms. Jane, BA ACA *1993;* Granite Villa, Fountain Road, GOLSPIE, SUTHERLAND, KW10 6TH.

CAMPBELL, Miss. Janice Elaine, BSc ACA *1991;* 343 Alexandra Park Road, LONDON, N22 7BP.

CAMPBELL, Mr. John, BSc FCA *1978;* 6 Montagu Way, WETHERBY, WEST YORKSHIRE, LS22 5PZ.

CAMPBELL, Mr. John Graham, PhD BSc FCA *1975;* 18 Eaglesfield, Hartford, NORTHWICH, CW8 1NQ.

CAMPBELL, Mr. John Joseph, BSc ACA *1991;* Brandhouse Beverges pty Ltd Black River Park North Fir Road Observatory, CAPE TOWN, 7925, SOUTH AFRICA.

CAMPBELL, Mr. John Nelson Robb, BA FCA CTA *1988;* Zurich Financial Services UK Life Centre, Station Road, SWINDON, SN1 1EL.

•CAMPBELL, Mr. John Oliver, FCA AIIT CA(SA) *1975;* (Tax Fac), DSC Accountants Limited, Tattersall House, East Parade, HARROGATE, NORTH YORKSHIRE, HG1 5LT. See also DSC Wealth Management LLP and DSC Accountants Limited

CAMPBELL, Mr. Jonathan Francis, BSc FCA *1997;* (Tax Fac), Gearbulk (UK) Limited, 5 The Heights, Brooklands, WEYBRIDGE, SURREY, KT13 0NY.

CAMPBELL, Mr. Jonathan Huw, BSc ACA *1990;* Wildacres Lodge, Farningham Hill Road, Farningham, DARTFORD, DA4 0JR.

CAMPBELL, Ms. Joyce Mckenzie, MA FCA *1977;* with Ernst & Young LLP, 1 More London Place, LONDON, SE1 2AF.

CAMPBELL, Mrs. Karen Jean, MA ACA ATII *1988;* The New Cottage, Orchard Close, SOUTHWELL, NOTTINGHAMSHIRE, NG25 0DY.

CAMPBELL, Mr. Laurence James, MA FCA *1977;* The Holt, Briestfield Road, Briestfield, DEWSBURY, WF12 0PA.

CAMPBELL, Mr. Malcolm, FCA *1963;* 26 St. Fimbarrus Road, FOWEY, PL23 1JJ.

CAMPBELL, Mr. Malcolm Hamilton, FCA *1978;* 32 Besford Court Estate, Besford, WORCESTER, WR8 9LZ.

CAMPBELL, Mr. Marcus Thomas, BSc ACA *1989;* Downview, 7 Hayes Close, Lavant, CHICHESTER, PO18 0DW.

CAMPBELL, Mr. Martin Conleth, BA FCA *1996;* Croda Europe, Cowick Hall, Snaith, GOOLE, NORTH HUMBERSIDE, DN14 9AA.

CAMPBELL, Mr. Matthew, ACA *2011;* Flat 108 Ovaltine Court, Ovaltine Drive, KINGS LANGLEY, HERTFORDSHIRE, WD4 8GY.

CAMPBELL, Mr. Matthew Eamon, BA ACA *1996;* The Barn Layters Green Lane, Chalfont St. Peter, GERRARDS CROSS, BUCKINGHAMSHIRE, SL9 8TH.

CAMPBELL, Mrs. Melanie Candice, ACA CA(SA) *2010;* 47 Florence Road, Wimbledon, LONDON, SW19 8TH.

CAMPBELL, Mr. Neil Andrew, MA ACA *1995;* Flat 15 Belgrave Houses, Stortford Hall Park, BISHOP'S STORTFORD, HERTFORDSHIRE, CM23 5AQ.

CAMPBELL, Mr. Neil James, BA FCA *1987;* 220 Buckhurst Way, BUCKHURST HILL, ESSEX, IG9 6JG.

CAMPBELL, Miss. Nicola Ann, BA ACA *1992;* 37935 Hungry Hill Road, SCIO, OR 97374, UNITED STATES.

CAMPBELL, Mr. Patrick James, FCA *1973;* (Tax Fac), Pentland Group Plc, 8 Manchester Square, LONDON, W1U 3PH.

CAMPBELL, Mr. Paul Adam, BA ACA *1989;* 49 Parliament Hill, LONDON, NW3 2TB.

CAMPBELL, Mr. Paul David, BA ACA *1994;* 121 Marshalswick Lane, ST. ALBANS, HERTFORDSHIRE, AL1 4UX.

CAMPBELL, Mr. Paul James Drelincourt, ACA *2008;* 309 Hodgeson House, 26 Christian Street, LONDON, E1 1AY.

•CAMPBELL, Mr. Peter Adrian, BA ACA *1995;* with Ernst & Young LLP, 1 More London Place, LONDON, SE1 2AF.

•CAMPBELL, Mr. Peter Elphinstone, FCA *1967;* Peter E Campbell & Co, Burnside Cottage, Strachur, CAIRNDOW, ARGYLL, PA27 8DG.

CAMPBELL, Mr. Peter Gordon Vere, FCA *1968;* Llwys Helyg, Ffordd Bedd Morys, NEWPORT, PEMBROKESHIRE, SA42 0QZ.

CAMPBELL, Mrs. Philippa Lisa, ACA *1993;* 6 Goulders Cottages Upper Culham Road, Cockpole Green Wargrave, READING, RG10 8NJ.

CAMPBELL, Mrs. Rachel Ann, BA ACA *2004;* 48 View Road, Rainhill, PRESCOT, MERSEYSIDE, L35 0LS.

•CAMPBELL, Ms. Rachel Mary, BA FCA *1994;* KPMG LLP, 15 Canada Square, LONDON, E14 5GL. See also KPMG Europe LLP

CAMPBELL, Mr. Richard, LLB FCA *1980;* Affinity Connect Limited, 8 Farleigh Court, Flax Bourton, BRISTOL, BS48 1UL.

•CAMPBELL, Mr. Richard, FCA *1977;* Hampton Management Resources Ltd, 37 Linden Road, HAMPTON, TW12 2JG.

CAMPBELL, Mr. Robert Anthony, BSc ACA *1984;* Measurements Group UK Ltd Unit 1, Cartel Business Centre Stroudley Road, BASINGSTOKE, RG24 8FW.

CAMPBELL, Mr. Robert George, FCA *1969;* Rua Povina Cavalcanti 153, Sao Conrado, RIO DE JANEIRO, 22610 080, BRAZIL.

CAMPBELL, Mr. Robert Ian, BCom ACA *2003;* KPMG Centre, 18 Viaduct Harbour Avenue, PO Box 1584, AUCKLAND 1140, NEW ZEALAND.

CAMPBELL, Mr. Robert John, MA ACA *1993;* Grote Halstraat 28, 2513 AX THE HAGUE, NETHERLANDS.

CAMPBELL, Mrs. Rosalind Ilona, BSc FCA *1987;* 6 Hawthorn Close, WATFORD, WD17 4SB.

•CAMPBELL, Mrs. Rosemary Ann, BSc ACA *1982;* (Tax Fac), Rosemary A Campbell, Butterscotch House, 32 Besford Court Estate, Besford, WORCESTER, WR8 9LZ.

CAMPBELL, Mr. Ross Stuart, MA BSc ACA *1999;* 69 Cholmley Gardens, Fortune Green Road, LONDON, NW6 1AJ.

CAMPBELL, Miss. Sally Victoria, BSc ACA *2002;* 10 Segrave Close, WEYBRIDGE, SURREY, KT13 0TD.

CAMPBELL, Mrs. Samantha Marjorie, ACA *1990;* Merrishaw Farm, Harley, SHREWSBURY, SY5 6PB.

CAMPBELL, Miss. Sandra Janice, BA ACA *2007;* 31 Elliot Street, Sacriston, DURHAM, DH7 6JH.

CAMPBELL, Miss. Sarah Ann, BSc ACA *1995;* (Tax Fac), Flat 609, Mountjoy House, Barbican, LONDON, EC2Y 8BP.

CAMPBELL, Miss. Sarah Jane, BSc ACA *1993;* The Old Cottage, 501 Waterside, CHESHAM, HP5 1QF.

CAMPBELL, Mrs. Sheila J, BSc ACA *1984;* 46 Rothwell Drive, SOLIHULL, B91 1HG.

CAMPBELL, Mr. St John Frederick Ludford, CA FCA *1983;* Caloundra Post Shop, PO Box 1052, CALOUNDRA, QLD 4551, AUSTRALIA.

CAMPBELL, Mr. Stephen, MA ACA *1997;* Standard Life Investments, Investment House, 1 George Street, EDINBURGH, EH2 2LL.

CAMPBELL, Mr. Stuart Victor Muir, BSc FCA *1978;* KPMG LLP, Three Chestnut Ridge Road, MONTVALE, NJ 07645, UNITED STATES.

CAMPBELL, Mrs. Susan Helen, ACA *1980;* 11 rue de Hassel, 5899 Syren, LUXEMBOURG, LUXEMBOURG.

CAMPBELL, Miss. Suzanne Francesca, BA(Hons) ACA *2002;* Xchanging, 13 Hanover Square, LONDON, W1S 1HN.

CAMPBELL, Ms. Tania, ACA *2008;* 75 Osprey Heights, 7 Bramlands Close, Clapham Junction, LONDON, SW11 2NP.

CAMPBELL, Mrs. Tessa Mary, MA ACA *1989;* Craig Rannoch, Grampian Terrace, Torphins, BANCHORY, AB31 4JS.

CAMPBELL, Mr. Trevor Hugh, ACA *2008;* 100 Spring Road, ABINGDON, OXFORDSHIRE, OX14 1AX.

•CAMPBELL, Mr. William John, FCA *1980;* (Tax Fac), Beever and Struthers, Central Buildings, Richmond Terrace, BLACKBURN, BB1 7AP.

CAMPBELL-ACE, Mr. Creag, BSc ACA *2010;* 34 Gardeners, CHELMSFORD, CM2 8YU.

CAMPBELL-BARNARD, Mr. William, BSc(Hons) ACA *2001;* Standard Bank Plc, 20 Gresham Street, LONDON, EC2V 7JE.

CAMPBELL-GRAY, Mrs. Jayne Margaret, BA ACA *1991;* Wall Farm House, Harkstead Road, Lower Holbrook, Holbrook, IPSWICH, IP9 2RQ.

CAMPBELL-HARRIS, Mr. James Neil, BSc ACA *1993;* Field House, Wormsley, WATLINGTON, OX49 5HX.

CAMPBELL-HART, Mr. Andrew James, BA FCA *1973;* 23 Rose Hill, DORKING, RH4 2EA.

CAMPBELL-KELLY, Mr. David John, ACA *1983;* Bridgemere House, Yew Tree Close, Willoughby Waterleys, LEICESTER, LE8 6BU.

•CAMPBELL-LAMBERT, Mr. Nicholas Alexander Vaughan, BA ACA *1998;* PricewaterhouseCoopers LLP, 1 Embankment Place, LONDON, WC2N 6RH. See also PricewaterhouseCoopers

CAMPBELL-WHITE, Mr. Paul Alexander, BSc ACA *2000;* ITV Studios, London Television Centre 58-72, Upper Ground, LONDON, SE1 9LT.

CAMPDEN, Mr. David John, BSc ACA *1990;* Bushboard Ltd, 9-29 Rixon Road, WELLINGBOROUGH, NORTHAMPTONSHIRE, NN8 4BA.

CAMPIN, Mrs. Linda Virginia, ACA *1984;* Summerhill, Woodland Rise, SEVENOAKS, TN15 0HZ.

CAMPIN, Mr. Richard Loxton, BA ACA MBA *1986;* Summerhill, Woodland Rise, SEVENOAKS, KENT, TN15 0HZ.

CAMPION, Mr. Alexander Davidson, FCA *1969;* 17 St. Edmunds Church Street, SALISBURY, WILTSHIRE, SP1 1EF. (Life Member)

CAMPION, Mr. Christopher John, BSc ACA *1993;* Tricor Services Limited, Level 28, Three Pacific Place, 1 Queens Road East, CENTRAL, HONG KONG ISLAND HONG KONG SAR.

CAMPION, Mr. Clive James, FCA *1965;* 7 Merrilyn Close, Claygate, ESHER, KT10 0EQ. (Life Member)

CAMPION, Mr. Harold Jacques Albert Paul, FCA *1965;* 22 Rue Beautreillis, 75001 PARIS, FRANCE. (Life Member)

CAMPION, Mr. Herbert Walter, ACA *1978;* Beckbury Hall, Beckbury, SHIFNAL, TF11 9DJ.

CAMPION, Mr. Paul Anthony, BA FCA *1982;* Ashvale, Kilquade, GREYSTONES, COUNTY WICKLOW, IRELAND.

CAMPION, Mr. Richard Charles, FCA *1975;* 524 Chemin du Chateau, 01220 DIVONNE-LES-BAINS, FRANCE.

CAMPION, Ms. Stephanie Ann, BA FCA *1972;* 142 Boulevard de Menilmontant, 75020 PARIS, FRANCE.

CAMPION, Mr. Stephen, MBChB ACA *1995;* 36 Cornmoor Road, Whickham, NEWCASTLE UPON TYNE, NE16 4PU.

CAMPION, Mr. Stephen Paul, FCA *1964;* Tudor House, Copthill Lane, TADWORTH, KT20 6HN.

CAMPION, Mr. William Ian, FCA *1963;* 11 Shireburn Road, Formby, LIVERPOOL, L37 1LR.

CAMPION-SMITH, Mrs. Jennifer, BA ACA *2007;* Lloyds TSB Bank Plc Canons House, Canons Way, BRISTOL, BS1 5LL.

CAMPKIN, Mr. David Frederick, BSc ACA *1990;* British Broadcasting Corporation White City, 201 Wood Lane, LONDON, W12 7TS.

•CAMPKIN, Mr. John Anthony, FCA *1968;* Ashleigh Norrington & Co, PO Box 816, HORSHAM, WEST SUSSEX, RH12 9EJ.

CAMPKIN, Miss. Sophie, BSc ACA *2010;* Flat 30, The Pryors, East Heath Road, LONDON, NW3 1BS.

•CAMPLEJOHN, Mr. Andrew Colin, ACA *1980;* A.C. Camplejohn, The Old Rectory, Main Street, Frolesworth, LUTTERWORTH, LE17 5EE.

CAMPLING, Ms. Elizabeth Anne, BA ACA *1994;* 60 Orchard Avenue, CHICHESTER, PO19 3BG.

CAMPLING, Mr. Kenneth Peter, BA ACA *1987;* Westbrook Cottage Baker Street, Appleton Wiske, NORTHALLERTON, NORTH YORKSHIRE, DL6 2AQ.

•CAMPLING, Mr. Nigel John, FCA *1981;* Campling & Co Ltd, 4 Burges Close, SOUTHEND-ON-SEA, SS1 3JW.

•CAMPLISSON, Ms. Joanne, BSc ACA *1995;* with Blue Spire South LLP, 201 Dyke Road, HOVE, EAST SUSSEX, BN3 1TL.

CAMPODONIC, Miss. Helen Marie, BSc ACA *2000;* 57 South Parade, BELFAST, BT7 2GN.

CANAVAN, Miss. Emma, BA ACA *2006;* Flat 5 Astoria Court, 73 Middleton Road, LONDON, E8 4DW.

•CANAVAN, Mr. Finbar Patrick, BSc ACA *1992;* 5 Ferrestone Road, Crouch End, LONDON, N8 7BX.

CANAVAN, Mr. Paul, BA ACA *1998;* 9 Adbert Drive, East Farleigh, MAIDSTONE, ME15 0DE.

CANBY, Mr. John Stuart, BA FCA *1972;* Richmond, West Ella Road, West Ella, HULL, HU10 7SD.

CANBY, Mr. Neil William, BA ACA *1994;* 363 Wellington Street, PERTH, WA 6008, AUSTRALIA.

CANDELOT, Mr. Nigel Allan, BSc FCA *1972;* 81 Alder Lodge, Stevenage Road, LONDON, SW6 6NR.

CANDERLE, Mr. Sebastien, ACA *1997;* Ground Floor Flat 116 Edith Road, LONDON, W14 9AP.

CANDEY, Mrs. Elizabeth Joanna, ACA *1998;* Pine Ridge, 12 Dean Close, Pyrford, WOKING, SURREY, GU22 8PA.

CANDISH, Mr. Keith Gerald, FCA *1963;* 1 Hillside Close, Swardeston, NORWICH, NR14 8DY.

CANDLER, Mr. Richard Anthony, ACA *2001;* 18 Goldlay Avenue, CHELMSFORD, CM2 0TL.

CANDY, Mr. Benjamin Charles, MChem ACA *2010;* 10/2 Oriental Terrace, Mount Vic, WELLINGTON 6011, NEW ZEALAND.

•CANDY, Mrs. Jennifer Angela Margaret, BSc ACA *2001;* with PricewaterhouseCoopers LLP, 1 Embankment Place, LONDON, WC2N 6RH.

CANDY, Mr. John Philip Dominic, FCA *1957;* Bracken Lair, 23 Chargate Close, WALTON-ON-THAMES, KT12 5DW. (Life Member)

CANDY, Mr. Robert Charles, FCA *1957;* 51 Bushey Way, BECKENHAM, BR3 6TH. (Life Member)

CANDY, Miss. Sara Catherine, BA ACA *1996;* 22 Parthenia Road, LONDON, SW6 4BE.

CANE, Mrs. Carol Ann, FCA *1985;* 7 Buckden Road, Edgerton, HUDDERSFIELD, HD3 3AX.

CANE, Mrs. Charlotte Kathryn Bourne, BA ACA *1993;* Weston House, 246 High Holborn, LONDON, WC1V 7EX.

CANE, Mr. Daniel James, ACA *2010;* 24 Magnolia Gardens, EDGWARE, MIDDLESEX, HA8 9GH.

•CANE, Mr. David Alexander, FCA *1971;* (Tax Fac), Business Assurance & Taxation Services Limited, 10 Sundial Court, Barnsbury Lane, SURBITON, SURREY, KT5 9RN.

CANE, Mr. David John, MA ACA *1989;* Cabinda Gulf Oil Company Ltd, 1 Westferry Circus, LONDON, E14 4HA.

CANE, Mrs. Deborah Hannah, BA(Hons) ACA *2004;* 12 Woburn Close, BUSHEY, WD23 4XA.

CANE, Mr. James Andrew, FCA *1977;* 26 Bellevue Road, Barnes, LONDON, SW13 0BJ.

CANE, Mr. Leon Richard, MA LLM ACA *1981;* 61 Salisbury Road, Redland, BRISTOL, BS6 7AS.

CANE, Miss. Marion Hazel, BA ACA *1984;* (Tax Fac), 91 Greenham Road, LONDON, N10 1LN.

CANE, Mr. Michael Geoffrey, BSc ACA *1992;* Dark Lane Cottage, Dark Lane, Longdon, RUGELEY, STAFFORDSHIRE, WS15 4QL.

CANE, Mr. Peter Charles, FCA *1971;* 8 Millers Close, CHIGWELL, ESSEX, IG7 6DF.

CANE, Mr. Simon James, BEng ACA *1998;* QGC, 275 George Street, BRISBANE, QLD 4000, AUSTRALIA.

CANE, Mr. Stuart John, BSc ACA *1994;* 15 Troed Y Garth, Pentyrch, CARDIFF, CF15 9AB.

CANE, Mr. William John, ACA *2007;* 23 Humbolt Road, LONDON, W6 8QH.

CANELL, Mrs. Katie Jennifer, MA ACA *2002;* 31 Boswell Drive, Ickleford, HITCHIN, HERTFORDSHIRE, SG5 3YB.

CANEPA-ANSON, Mr. Robert Nicholas, BA ACA *2004;* Newton BNY Mellon Financial Centre, 160 Queen Victoria Street, LONDON, EC4V 4LA.

CANFIELD, Mr. Barry, BA FCA *1983;* Entec UK Limited, Northumbria House, Regent Centre, Gosforth, NEWCASTLE UPON TYNE, NE3 3PX.

•CANFIELD, Mr. Gerald Thomas, FCA *1961;* (Tax Fac), Canfield & Co., Bankfield, 38 The Orchards, SAWBRIDGEWORTH, HERTFORDSHIRE, CM21 9BB.

CANHAM, Mr. Daniel Graham, BA ACA *1992;* 46 Eastcroft Road, GOSPORT, HAMPSHIRE, PO12 3LG.

CANHAM, Mrs. Helen Louise, BSc ACA *1993;* Martin Staithe, The Green, Stokesby, GREAT YARMOUTH, NORFOLK, NR29 3EX.

CANHAM, Mr. John Michael, FCA *1959;* 15 Eden Park Avenue, BECKENHAM, KENT, BR3 3HJ. (Life Member)

CANHAM, Mr. Philip, BA ACA *1985;* Incommunities Trust House, 5 New Augustus Street, BRADFORD, WEST YORKSHIRE, BD1 5LL.

CANI, Miss. Gabriella, BSc ACA *2004;* Tyne Cottage, Preston Road, Charnock Richard, CHORLEY, PR7 5JP.

CANK, Miss. Vivienne Elaine, ACA *1987;* with Baker Tilly Tax and Accounting Limited, 3rd Floor Preece House, Davigdor Road, HOVE, EAST SUSSEX, BN3 1RE.

CANKETT, Mr. Mark Christopher, MEng ACA *2006;* Deloitte & Touche Hill House, 1 Little New Street, LONDON, EC4A 3TR.

CANN, Mr. Adrian Godfrey, FCA *1968;* Cannon Asset Management Ltd, PO Box 393, St Peter Port, GUERNSEY, GY1 3FN.

•CANN, Mr. Allan Edward, FCA *1973;* 10 Cae Brynton Road, NEWPORT, GWENT, NP20 3FY.

CANN, Miss. Andrea Jane, BSc ACA *1991;* 5 Campion Way, WOKINGHAM, BERKSHIRE, RG40 5YG.

CANN, Mr. Andrew Calvert, BA ACA *1989;* 51 Meadowvale Road, Lickey End, BROMSGROVE, WORCESTERSHIRE, B60 1JY.

CANN, Mr. Andrew John, BSc FCA *1971;* Glenwood, St George's Avenue, Kings Stanley, STONEHOUSE, GL10 3HJ.

CANN, Mr. Andrew William, BA ACA *1998;* Offleys, East Hill, Charminster, DORCHESTER, DORSET, DT2 9QL.

CANN, Mr. Christopher Richard, FCA CTA *1959;* The Walled House, 87 Christchurch Road, LONDON, SW14 7AT. (Life Member)

CANN, Mr. Daniel, BA ACA *2001;* Folio Administrators Ltd, Folio Chambers, Road Town, P.O. Box 800, TORTOLA, VG 1110 VIRGIN ISLANDS (BRITISH).

•CANN, Mr. David Francis, BA FCA ATII CTA *1985;* (Tax Fac), David Cann, 22 Chartwell Place, EPSOM, SURREY, KT18 5JH.

•CANN, Mrs. Dawn Elizabeth, BCom ACA *1995;* Dawn Cann, 26 Dawley Road, Wall Heath, KINGSWINFORD, DY6 9BH. See also Dawn Cann Accounting Service

CANN, Mrs. Frances Anne, BA ACA *1987;* 4 Penrith Road, Boscombe Manor, BOURNEMOUTH, BH5 1LT.

CANN, Mr. Michael Neil, BA(Hons) ACA *2009;* with KPMG, Crown House, 4 Par-la-Ville Road, HAMILTON HM 08, BERMUDA.

CANN, Mrs. Penelope Jane, FCA *1973;* Glenwood, St. George's Avenue, King's Stanley, STONEHOUSE, GLOUCESTERSHIRE, GL10 3HJ.

CANN, Mr. Stephen James, BSc ACA *1990;* Bailey Court, Green Street, MACCLESFIELD, CHESHIRE, SK10 1JQ.

CANN, Miss. Susan Elizabeth, BSc ACA *1990;* (Tax Fac), 17 Claremont Gardens, MARLOW, BUCKINGHAMSHIRE, SL7 1BP.

CANNAN, Mr. Jonathan Michael, LLB FCA *1988;* (Tax Fac), Exchange Chambers, 7 Ralli Courts, West Riverside, SALFORD, M3 5FT.

CANNAN, Mr. Peter John, MBA BCom FCA *1984;* 7 William Emes Garden, Blockley, MORETON-IN-MARSH, GL56 9RL.

CANNEAUX, Mr. Anthony Bradley, FCA *1961;* Lis House, 11 Anscombe Close, WORTHING, WEST SUSSEX, BN11 5EW.

•CANNELL, Mr. John Hatcliffe, FCA *1977;* Hillcrest, Alexander Drive, Douglas, ISLE OF MAN, IM2 3QX.

CANNELL, Mr. Michael Dan Harry, FCA *1964;* 7 Carrs Hill Close, Old Costessey, NORWICH, NR8 5DW.

•CANNELL, Mr. Simon Nicholas Justin, FCA *1974;* Wordsworth, 35 Cambridge Road, CLEVEDON, BS21 7DW.

CANNEY, Mr. Duncan Inglis, BSc FCA *1979;* The Limes, 1 Alms Hill, Bourn, CAMBRIDGE, CB23 2SH.

CANNING, Miss. Fiona Margaret, BA(Oxon) ACA *2003;* 1 Savery Drive, Long Ditton, SURBITON, SURREY, KT6 5RD.

CANNING, Mr. John Daniel, MSci ACA MBA *2003;* 10 River Lane, Fetcham, LEATHERHEAD, KT22 9RP.

CANNING, Mrs. Judith Anne, MSc ACA *1987;* with PricewaterhouseCoopers, Strandvejen 44, P O Box 2709, Hellerup, DK 2900 COPENHAGEN, DENMARK.

CANNING, Mr. Philip James, BA ACA *1985;* Cobtree House, The Green, West Peckham, MAIDSTONE, ME18 5JW. (Life Member)

CANNING, Mrs. Susan Jane, ACA *1980;* Somerhill Charitable Trust Ltd, Somerhill, TONBRIDGE, KENT, TN11 0NJ.

CANNING JONES, Mr. Anthony David, FCA *1964;* Larchwood, Deadhearn Lane, CHALFONT ST.GILES, HP8 4HG. (Life Member)

•CANNING-JONES, Mr. David Gareth, BA ACA *1995;* Ernst & Young LLP, 1 More London Place, LONDON, SE1 2AF. See also Ernst & Young Europe LLP

CANNINGS, Mr. Andrew Bruce, ACA *1982;* 4a Front Street, Sedgefield, STOCKTON-ON-TEES, CLEVELAND, TS21 3AT.

CANNINGS, Mr. Barry John, FCA *1988;* Treetops, 9 Roundhill Way, COBHAM, KT11 2EX.

CANNINGS, Mr. Craig Robert, ACA *2008;* B Braun Medical Ltd, Unit 8, Thorncliffe Park Estate, Chapeltown, SHEFFIELD, S35 2PW.

CANNINGS, Mr. Paul Jonathan, BSc ACA *1990;* Pennymead, Three Pears Road, Merrow, GUILDFORD, GU1 2XU.
CANNINGS, Mr. Russell, BA ACA *1989;* Wildacre, Long Lane, Shaw, NEWBURY, BERKSHIRE, RG14 2TA.
CANNON, Mr. Andrew David, MBA BA ACA *1990;* The Breach, Main Road, Haunton, TAMWORTH, B79 9HJ.
CANNON, Mr. Anthony Stuart Douglas, BSc(Econ) FCA *1970;* 45 Valley Road, RICKMANSWORTH, WD3 4DT. (Life Member)
CANNON, Mr. Anthony William, FCA *1980;* Weightmans, India Buildings, Water Street, LIVERPOOL, L2 0GA.
•**CANNON, Mrs. Brenda Caroline, ACA** *1986;* Brenda Cannon, West House, West Street, HASLEMERE, SURREY, GU27 2AB.
CANNON, Miss. Claire Louise, BSc ACA *2010;* 176 Raeburn Avenue, SURBITON, SURREY, KT5 9ED.
CANNON, Miss. Clare Frances, BA ACA *2006;* 21 Ingleglen, Farnham Common, SLOUGH, SL2 3QA.
CANNON, Mr. David Oliver, BA ACA *1981;* 12 Ernle Road, LONDON, SW20 0HJ.
CANNON, Mr. Drw, BA(Hons) ACA *2003;* 15 Silver Street, Congresbury, BRISTOL, BS49 5EY.
CANNON, Mrs. Elizabeth Julia, BA ACA MBA *1997;* Treetops, 52 Sunnybank, EPSOM, KT18 7DX.
CANNON, Mrs. Fiona Anne, BA ACA ATII *1993;* Dent Company, Greengill, PENRITH, CUMBRIA, CA11 8SE.
•**CANNON, Mr. John Wayne, BSc FCA** *1980;* John Cannon & Co, The Gables, 47 Efflinch Lane, Barton-under-Needwood, BURTON-ON-TRENT, STAFFORDSHIRE DE13 8EU.
CANNON, Mrs. Martha Louise, MEng ACA *2005;* 47 High Street, Wicken, ELY, CAMBRIDGESHIRE, CB7 5XR.
CANNON, Mr. Matthew Lee, BA ACA *1999;* 9 Laurel Road, LONDON, SW13 0EE.
CANNON, Mr. Michael, BA ACA *1982;* Holly House, Coggeshall Road, Dedham, COLCHESTER, CO7 6ET.
•**CANNON, Mr. Michael John, FCA** *1969;* Chantrey Vellacott DFK LLP, Russell Square House, 10-12 Russell Square, LONDON, WC1B 5LF.
•**CANNON, Mr. Peter Harold, BSc FCA** *1976;* Cannon Moorcroft Limited, 3 Manor Courtyard, Hughenden Avenue, HIGH WYCOMBE, HP13 5RE.
CANNON, Mr. Richard Anthony, BA ACA *1997;* HM Revenue & Customs, Local Compliance London & Anglia, 17th Floor Euston Tower, 286 Euston Road, LONDON, NW1 3DP.
CANNON, Mrs. Sara Ann, BA ACA *1989;* Malthouse & Co America House, 8b Rumford Court Rumford Place, LIVERPOOL, L3 9DD.
CANNON, Miss. Stephanie Amy, BSc ACA *2010;* 39 Watercress Way, Broughton, MILTON KEYNES, MK10 7AJ.
CANNON, The Revd. Tony Arthur, FCA *1980;* St. Johns Vicarage, St. Johns Hill Road, WOKING, GU21 7RQ.
CANNON, Mrs. Victoria Claire, BA ACA *1993;* 4 Park Road, HARROGATE, NORTH YORKSHIRE, HG2 9AZ.
CANOVA, Mr. John, FCA *1969;* Kelvingrove, Worsted Lane, EAST GRINSTEAD, WEST SUSSEX, RH19 3UF.
CANOVA, Mr. Michael, FCA *1969;* Silverston House, 3 Fish Lane, BOGNOR REGIS, WEST SUSSEX, PO21 3AG. (Life Member)
•**CANSICK, Mr. Gary John, FCA** *1984;* Gary J. Cansick & Co, Janelle House, 6 Hartham Lane, HERTFORD, SG14 1QN.
CANSICK, Mr. Raymond, BA ACA *1987;* Flat 14, 27 William Road, LONDON, NW1 3EY.
CANSICK, Mr. Ross Kelvin, BSc ACA *2007;* 48 Fairlawn Avenue, LONDON, W4 5EF.
CANT, Ms. Amanda Jane, MA ACA *2003;* 1 Cromford Close, ORPINGTON, KENT, BR6 9QF.
CANT, Mr. Andrew Mark, BA(Hons) ACA *2001;* 304 Foundry House, 47 Morris Road, LONDON, E14 6NJ.
CANT, Mr. David Antony, BSc ACA *1980;* The Old Rectory, Church Road Thorrington, COLCHESTER, CO7 8HE.
CANT, Miss. Lucy, LLB ACA *2003;* Fitness First Health Club, Fleets Lane, POOLE, DORSET, BH15 3BT.
CANT, Mr. Nicholas James, FCA *1975;* 26 Greenfield Road, EASTBOURNE, BN21 1JJ.
CANT, Mrs. Poonam, BA ACA *1993;* Wharfside, 118 Skipton Road, ILKLEY, LS29 9HE.
CANT, Mr. Robert James, ACA *2011;* Flat 48, Caversham Place, Richfield Avenue, READING, RG1 8BY.
•**CANT, Mr. Robert Thomas, BSc(Econ) FCA** *1979;* with RSM Tenon Audit Limited, Stoughton House, Harborough Road, Oadby, LEICESTER, LE2 4LP.
CANT, Mrs. Sally Patricia, BSc FCA *1978;* 11 Franklin Way, Whetstone, LEICESTER, LE8 6QY.
CANT, Mr. Simon John, ACA *2009;* 58a Swaby Road, LONDON, SW18 3RA.
CANTEENWALA, Mr. Javid Soli, BCom ACA MBA *1998;* 15 The Warren Drive, Wanstead, LONDON, E11 2LR.
CANTELLOW, Mr. Ralph Steven, BSc FCA *1984;* 32 Airedale Avenue, Chiswick, LONDON, W4 2NW.
CANTELO, Mr. Alan Edward, FCA *1961;* 4a Alva Way, WATFORD, WD19 5ED.
CANTELO, Mr. Edward Peter, BA ACA *2006;* with PricewaterhouseCoopers LLP, 1 Embankment Place, LONDON, WC2N 6RH.
CANTLE, Mrs. Melanie, BA ACA *1998;* 1 Bramley Green Road, Bramley, TADLEY, HAMPSHIRE, RG26 5UE.
CANTLIN, Mr. Steven Graham, BSc ACA *2005;* 4 Stamford Green Road, EPSOM, KT18 7ST.
CANTOR, Mr. Gary Stuart, MBA FCA *1976;* 5 rue Louis Vuitton, Asnières-sur-Seine, 92600 PARIS, FRANCE.
CANTOR, Mr. Peter James, LLB ACA *1992;* 28 The Paddock, GODALMING, SURREY, GU7 1XD.
CANTOR, Mr. Richard Martin, FCA *1970;* B D O Stoy Hayward Kings Wharf, 20-30 Kings Road, READING, RG1 3EX.
CANTOR, Mrs. Susan Katherine, FCA *1973;* 12 Marlow Mill, Mill Road, MARLOW, SL7 1QD.
CANTRELL, Miss. Alison Mary, BSc ACA *1993;* 2b Park Mount, HARPENDEN, HERTFORDSHIRE, AL5 3AR.
CANTRELL, Mrs. Margaret Anne, BA FCA *1978;* Granada Material Handling Ltd Unit 5, Sherwood Industrial Park Queensway, ROCHDALE, OL11 2NU.
CANTRELL, Miss. Marian, BSc ACA *2007;* FTI Consulting, 322 High Holborn, LONDON, WC1V 7PB.
CANTRILL, Mr. Charles John, BSc FCA *1974;* 678 Abbey Lane, SHEFFIELD, S11 9NB.
CANTWELL, Mr. Christopher James, BA ACA *1985;* with ICAEW, Chartered Accountants' Hall, Moorgate Place, LONDON, EC2P 2BJ.
CANTWELL, Miss. Elizabeth Sarah, BA ACA *2005;* Adnams Plc, Sole Bay Bewery, East Green, SOUTHWOLD, IP18 6JW.
CANTWELL, Mr. Michael John, BSc ACA *2004;* 7 Baulkham Hills, HOUGHTON LE SPRING, TYNE AND WEAR, DH4 7RY.
CANTWELL, Mr. Richard Andrew, BA ACA *1991;* 24 Huxley Drive, ROMFORD, RM6 4RH.
CANTY, Mr. Michael John, FCA *1965;* Corner Barn, Foyle Hill, SHAFTESBURY, SP7 0AG. (Life Member)
•**CANTY, Mr. Roderic Neil, BA FCA** *1976;* 7 Blewfield, GODALMING, SURREY, GU7 1TR.
CANTY, Mr. Terence Douglas, FCA *1973;* India Cottage, School Lane, SWANLEY, BR8 7PJ.
CANVIN, Mr. Stuart Charles Ian, BA ACA *1996;* with PricewaterhouseCoopers, 11//F, PricewaterhouseCoopers Center, 2 Corporate Avenue, 202 Hu Bin Road, SHANGHAI 200021 CHINA.
CANVIN, Mr. Tony Michael, ACA *1981;* 33 Kingmere, South Terrace, LITTLEHAMPTON, WEST SUSSEX, BN17 5LD.
CAO, Miss. Shanshan, ACA *2010;* Flat 4, 22 Roberts Road, SOUTHAMPTON, SO15 5DE.
CAO, Mr. Vince, ACA CA(AUS) *2009;* Flat 2, 8 Muswell Avenue, Muswell Hill, LONDON, N10 2EG.
CAO, Mr. Xujun, ACA *2010;* Room 302, Building No.165, No.2688 Hunan Road, Nanhui District, SHANGHAI 201315, CHINA.
CAO, Miss. Yijun, MSc ACA *2009;* 18 Topmast Point, The Quarterdeck, LONDON, E14 8SL.
CAO, Mr. Zibo, BSc ACA *2009;* 8th Floor Tower E2 Oriental Plaza 1 East Chang An Avenue, BEIJING 100738, CHINA.
CAPEL, Mr. David, FCA *1976;* 1 Church Lane, Mildenhall, MARLBOROUGH, WILTSHIRE, SN8 2LU.
CAPEL, Mr. David Frederick, BSc FCA *1980;* 1 Tintern Gardens, Southgate, LONDON, N14 6AS.
CAPEL, Mr. Marcus William, BCom ACA *1983;* Glendale, 47 Wilson Road, CARDIFF, CF1 4LL.
CAPELL, Miss. Claire Frances, BA ACA *2007;* Thistle Hotels Ltd, PO Box 909, UXBRIDGE, MIDDLESEX, UB8 9FH.
CAPELL, Mr. Matthew, BSc(Hons) ACA *2010;* Hazlewoods Windsor House, Barnett Way Barnwood, GLOUCESTER, GL4 3RT.
CAPES, Mr. Ian Stewart, ACA *1983;* 8 The Granary, Stanstead St Margarets, WARE, SG12 8XH.
CAPES, Mrs. Marie Winifred, BSc ACA *1983;* Wyndcliffe, Shootersway Lane, BERKHAMSTED, HP4 3NW.
CAPES, Mr. Robert Geddes, FCA *1970;* 4 Church Farm Court, WIRRAL, MERSEYSIDE, CH60 0EU.
•**CAPES, Mr. Trevor, FCA** *1975;* Capes Gittins Limited, 28 Mount Grace Road, POTTERS BAR, HERTFORDSHIRE, EN6 1RD.
CAPES, Mrs. Wai Meng, FCA *1980;* 28 Mount Grace Road, POTTERS BAR, HERTFORDSHIRE, EN6 1RD.
CAPEWELL, Mrs. Ellen, ACA *2008;* 14 Horsefair Street, Charlton Kings, CHELTENHAM, GLOUCESTERSHIRE, GL53 8JE.
CAPEWELL, Mr. Eric, FCA ACII FCILA *1974;* Route de Duillier 18, 1270 TRELEX, SWITZERLAND.
•**CAPEWELL, Mr. Harry, BA FCA** *1992;* with RSM Tenon Limited, International House, 66 Chiltern Street, LONDON, W1U 4JT.
•**CAPEWELL, Mr. John Dennis, FCA** *1957;* John D Capewell, 47 Hockley Lane, Netherton, DUDLEY, DY2 0JW.
•**CAPEWELL, Mr. Paul Anthony, ACA** *1999;* The A9 Partnership (Highland) Ltd, Elm House, Cradlehall Business Park, INVERNESS, IV2 5GH.
CAPEZIO, Mr. Frank, BA ACA *2007;* 33 Shelsley Way, SOLIHULL, WEST MIDLANDS, B91 3UZ.
CAPINDALE, Miss. Laura, ACA MAAT *2010;* Duncan & Toplis Unit 4, Henley Way, LINCOLN, LN6 3QR.
CAPLAN, Mr. Adam, BSc(Hons) ACA *2010;* 31 Parksway, Prestwich, MANCHESTER, M25 0JB.
•**CAPLAN, Mr. Jack, FCA** *1954;* Caplan J. & Co, 39 Silverston Way, STANMORE, HA7 4HS.
•**CAPLAN, Mr. Philip Michael, FCA MCIM** *1982;* (Tax Fac), Caplan Associates, Cardinal Point, Park Road, RICKMANSWORTH, HERTFORDSHIRE, WD3 1RE.
CAPLAN, Mr. Robert Benjamin, ACA *2009;* Zerach Barnett 13/15, Har Nof, 95404 JERUSALEM, ISRAEL.
CAPLAN, Mr. Stuart Samuel, BA ACA *2005;* 155 Coleridge Way, BOREHAMWOOD, HERTFORDSHIRE, WD6 2AF.
CAPLAN, Mrs. Vicki Maria, BSc ACA *2006;* 155 Coleridge Way, Boreham Wood, BOREHAMWOOD, WD6 2AF.
CAPLAN, Mr. Woolf, BA FCA *1950;* 44 Heathdene Manor, Grandfield Avenue, WATFORD, WD17 4PZ. (Life Member)
CAPLE, Mr. Ian Alexander, BA ACA *2006;* 8 Denholm Gardens, GUILDFORD, GU4 7YU.
•**CAPLEN, Miss. Jane, FCA** *1974;* A & T Accounting Services Limited, The Office, Oaklands, La Rue Du Coin Varin, St. Peter, JERSEY JE3 7ZG.
CAPLEN, Mr. Stephen Gerard, BA ACA *1992;* 21 Saxon Road, WINCHESTER, HAMPSHIRE, SO23 7DJ.
CAPON, Mr. Andrew Charles, BA ACA *1989;* Unit 2201 Tower 2, Mega Hall, 1 Xiangheyuan Road, Dongzhimenwai, Dongcheng, BEIJING 100028 CHINA.
CAPON, Mrs. Claire Louise, MA ACA *2002;* 24 High Street, Whitwell, HITCHIN, HERTFORDSHIRE, SG4 8AG.
CAPON, Mr. David Jethro, FCA *1962;* The Cottage, Tawton Lane, South Zeal, OKEHAMPTON, DEVON, EX20 2LG.
CAPON, Mr. George Cecil Charles, FCA *1955;* 20 Chapel Lane, Hadleigh, BENFLEET, SS7 2PQ. (Life Member)
CAPON, Mr. Oliver, MEng BA ACA *1997;* 1er Sweelinckstraat 34, 2517GD THE HAGUE, NETHERLANDS.
•**CAPON, Miss. Rosemary Elizabeth, BA ACA** *1978;* Mercer & Hole Trustees Limited, Gloucester House, 72 London Road, ST. ALBANS, AL1 1NS.
CAPORN, Mr. David Richard, MA ACA *2003;* 17 Cransley Crescent, Henleaze, BRISTOL, BS9 4PH.
CAPPELLI, Miss. Sonia, ACA *1988;* Petrofac Ltd, Crystal Plaza, office Tower, Suite 1702, Buhairah Carniche, PO Box 23467 SHARJAH UNITED ARAB EMIRATES.
CAPPER, Mr. Anthony David, FCA *1961;* Strictly Private and Confidential, Seven Corners, 16 Mill Road, MARLOW, SL7 1PX. (Life Member)
CAPPER, Mrs. Caroline, BA(Hons) ACA *2003;* Wellstream Do Brasiz, Pkaca Alcides, Pereira 1, Parte KMA, Conceisao, Nitiroi RIO DE JANEIRO 24050-350 BRAZIL.
CAPPER, Mr. David John, FCA *1975;* Stand House, Racecourse Lane, Cotebrook, TARPORLEY, CW6 9EF.
CAPPER, Mrs. Gwendolen May, FCA *1975;* 12 Marlowe Close, Offmore Farm, KIDDERMINSTER, DY10 3QT.
•**CAPPER, Mr. John Anthony, BSc FCA** *1982;* John Capper & Co, 12 West Drive, Cheddleton, LEEK, STAFFORDSHIRE, ST13 7DW.
CAPPER, Mr. Jonathan, MBA BA ACA *1991;* Paragon Global Resources, Unit 1, College & Technology Business Park, Blanchardstown, DUBLIN 15, COUNTY DUBLIN IRELAND.
CAPPER, Mr. Richard Gerald, FCA *1967;* Garden Flat, 356 Albert Drive, Pollokshields, GLASGOW, G41 5PB.
CAPPER, Mr. Robert Ernest, FCA *1971;* P.O. Box 65143, Benmore, JOHANNESBURG, GAUTENG, SOUTH AFRICA.
CAPPER, Mr. Simon, BA ACA *1994;* 3 The Gowans, Sutton-on-the-Forest, YORK, YO61 1DL.
CAPPER, Miss. Stephanie Anne, BSc ACA *2011;* 68b Anglesey Road, West Kirby, WIRRAL, MERSEYSIDE, CH48 5EG.
CAPPER, Mr. Stephen Patrick, MA FCA *1984;* 42 Birchall Road, Redland, BRISTOL, BS6 7TS.
CAPPS, Mr. Keith Thompson, FCA *1963;* Hart Cottage, Hall Lane, Mobberley, KNUTSFORD, WA16 7AH.
CAPRARI, Mr. Giovanni, BSc ACA *1991;* 16 University Mansions, Lower Richmond Rd. Putney, LONDON, SW15 1EP.
CAPRARO, Mrs. Valerie Jacqueline, FCA *1963;* Via Trara Genoino 13, 84017 Positano, SALERNO, ITALY. (Life Member)
•**CAPSTICK, Mr. Geoffrey, FCA** *1961;* G Capstick & Co, Ashwood Lodge, Berry Hill Road, Adderbury, BANBURY, OXFORDSHIRE OX17 3HF.
CAPSTICK, Mr. Geoffrey, BSc ACA MBA *1999;* 18 Brunswick Court, 1 Darlaston Road, LONDON, SW19 4LF.
CAPSTICK, Mr. James, BSc ACA *2011;* 26 Gaydon Road, SALE, CHESHIRE, M33 5DY.
CAPSTICK, Mr. Malcolm Geoffrey, BSocSc ACA *1982;* 4 Fourstones Close, SOLIHULL, B91 3GF.
•**CAPTUR, Mr. Nicholas John, BSc FCA** *1993;* Deloitte & Touche, Deloitte Place, Mriehel Place, Mriehel Bypass, MRIEHEL BKR3000, MALTA.
•**CAPUTO, Mr. Michael William, FCA** *1973;* McLintocks, 2 Hilliards Court, Chester Business Park, CHESTER, CH4 9PX. See also McLintocks Ltd and McLintocks Partnership
CARA, Mr. Charles Mills, BA ACA *1994;* 23 Rocks Lane, Barnes, LONDON, SW13 0DB.
CARA, Mrs. Sarah, BSc ACA *1986;* 9 Beverley Close, Wrea Green, PRESTON, PR4 2NP.
CARABIN, Mr. Anthony, BA ACA *1991;* 8 Ellesmere Close, Wanstead, LONDON, E11 1PT.
CARAVATI, Dr. Marco, ACA *2010;* Via Monte Generoso 141, 21100 VARESE, ITALY.
•**CARAWAN, Mr. Mark John, PhD ACA** *1989;* Barclays Bank Plc, 1 Churchill Place, LONDON, E14 5HP.
CARBONELL, Mr. John William, BA ACA *1985;* 43 Whitehouse Way, Southgate, LONDON, N14 7LX.
CARBY, Mr. Michael John, FCA *1974;* Barley Meadow, Corkhill Lane, Normanton, SOUTHWELL, NG25 0PR.
CARBY, Mr. Richard Andrew, BEng ACA *1999;* Rochtron Ltd, Wessex House, Pixash Lane, Keynsham, BRISTOL, BS31 1TX.
CARCHRAE, Mr. John Anthony, FCA *1974;* Lowelstrasse 8, Top 16, 1010 VIENNA, AUSTRIA.
•**CARD, Mr. Alan Jeffrey, FCA** *1980;* Sevenstones, Pindale Road, Hope, HOPE VALLEY, S33 6RN.
CARD, Mr. Charles Rodger, FCA *1970;* Hewitt Card, 70-72 Nottingham Road, MANSFIELD, NOTTINGHAMSHIRE, NG18 1BN.
CARD, Miss. Emily Rebecca, ACA *2009;* 12 Jenison Close, School Aycliffe, NEWTON AYCLIFFE, COUNTY DURHAM, DL5 6QR.
•**CARD, Mr. John Alan, FCA** *1973;* Ensors, Cardinal House, 46 St Nicholas Street, IPSWICH, IP1 1TT.
CARD, Mr. Jonathan Martin, BA ACA *1981;* Imperial War Museum, Lambeth Road, LONDON, SE1 6HZ.
CARDALE, Mr. Dowglass Charles, BSc FCA *1972;* 82 Rosebank, Holyport Road, LONDON, SW6 6LJ.
CARDALE, Mr. William Tyndale, FCA *1973;* Cardale, West Lodge, Bradfield St. George, BURY ST. EDMUNDS, SUFFOLK, IP30 0DL. (Life Member)
CARDALL, Mr. Stephen David, BA ACA *1997;* 4 Birchway, Heswall, WIRRAL, MERSEYSIDE, CH60 3SX.
CARDALL, Mrs. Tanya, MSc BA(Hons) ACA *2001;* 15 Woodpecker Close, Great Barford, BEDFORD, MK44 3BG.
CARDELL, Miss. Anna-Louise, BSc ACA *2006;* Aviva plc, St. Helens, 1 Undershaft, LONDON, EC3P 3DQ.
CARDELL, Mr. Peter Julian Southwell, BA FCA *1975;* 75 Copers Cope Road, BECKENHAM, BR3 1NR.
CARDEN, Mr. Michael Bruce, MEng ACA *1995;* 14 Glebe Road, HARROGATE, HG2 0LZ.

•**CARDEN, Mr. Philippe O'Neill, MA FCA** *1975;* (Tax Fac), P.O'N. Carden, 1st Floor (Rear Suite), 56-58 High Street, Ewell, EPSOM, KT17 1RW.

•**CARDER, Miss. Esther Marie, BSc ACA** *1999;* Kingston Smith LLP, 141 Wardour Street, LONDON, W1F 0UT. See also Kingston Smith Limited Liability Partnership, Devonshire Corporate Services LLP and Kingston Smith Consulting LLP

CARDER, Mr. Frederick William, MBE TD FCA *1949;* Cleveland House Heath Road, Whitmore, NEWCASTLE, STAFFORDSHIRE, ST5 5HB. (Life Member)

CARDER, Mr. Philip James, BCom FCA *1975;* 1st Floor Ecumenical Centre, Northway, SKELMERSDALE, LANCASHIRE, WN8 6PN.

CARDER, Mr. Robert, MSci ACA *2006;* 6 Henrys Avenue, WOODFORD GREEN, ESSEX, IG8 9RA.

•**CARDER, Mr. Roger William, MA FCA** *1977;* (Tax Fac), with PricewaterhouseCoopers LLP, Cornwall Court, 19 Cornwall Street, BIRMINGHAM, B3 2DT.

•**CARDEW, Mr. Gordon, FCA** *1996;* McColm Cardew Ltd, 10 Main Street, Bilton, RUGBY, WARWICKSHIRE, CV22 7NB. See also Coleopterus Limited

CARDEW-HALL, Mrs. Denise, BSc FCA *1988;* 102 Perry Drive, CHAPMAN, ACT 2611, AUSTRALIA.

•**CARDIFF, Mr. Mark John, BSc(Hons) FCA** *2000;* Grant Thornton UK LLP, Grant Thornton House, 22 Melton Street, Euston Square, LONDON, NW1 2EP. See also Grant Thornton LLP

CARDLE, Miss. Dominique Ruth, LLB ACA *2004;* 10 Keppel Bay Drive, #04-12, SINGAPORE 098640, SINGAPORE.

CARDNELL, Mrs. Elena Bridget, BSc ACA *2007;* 33 Lockesfield Place, LONDON, E14 3AH.

•**CARDNELL, Mr. John Kenneth, BSc FCA** *1981;* F.W. Berringer & Co, Lygon House, 50 London Road, BROMLEY, BR1 3RA.

CARDNO, Miss. Susan Helen, BSc ACA *1996;* National Exhibition Centre Ltd, BIRMINGHAM, B40 1NT.

CARDOSA, Mr. John Peter, ACA *1982;* 110 Dedap Batik, Sierramas Sungai Buloh, 47000 SUNGAI BULOH, SELANGOR, MALAYSIA.

CARDOSI, Mr. Stephen James, BA(Hons) ACA *2009;* Roquetas, Trowley Bottom, Flamstead, ST. ALBANS, HERTFORDSHIRE, AL3 8DR.

CARDRICK, Ms. Helen Charlotte Lucy, BA ACA *1995;* 54 Elfindale Road, Herne Hill, LONDON, SE24 9NW.

CARDUS, Mr. Raymond James, BSc FCA *1975;* 29 Victoria Road, Farnham Common, SLOUGH, SL2 3NL.

CARDWELL, Mr. Andrew James, BA ACA *1994;* 15 Hilltop Rise, Douglas, ISLE OF MAN, IM2 2LE.

CARDWELL, Mr. James Frederick, MA FCA *1976;* 2721 La Cuesta Drive, LOS ANGELES, CA 90046, UNITED STATES.

CARDWELL, Miss. Paula, MA BSc ACA *2000;* Top Floor Flat, 57 Rotherwood Road, LONDON, SW15 1LA.

CARDWELL, Miss. Sarah Louise Elspeth, BA ACA *2006;* HBOS Plc, 10 Canons Way, BRISTOL, BS1 5LL.

•**CARDWELL, Mr. Stuart James Patrick, FCA** *1967;* Stuart Cardwell Ltd, 9a Alexandra Parade, WESTON-SUPER-MARE, AVON, BS23 1QT. See also Cardwell S.J.P

CARDY, Mr. Paul Mark, ACA *1991;* Allied Mills, Sunblest Flour Mill, Tilbury Docks, TILBURY, ESSEX, RM18 7JR.

CARDY, Mr. Roy William, FCA *1957;* 49 Alexandra Avenue, Craighall, JOHANNESBURG, 2196, SOUTH AFRICA. (Life Member)

CAREEM, Mr. Riz, ACA *2008;* 34 Lower Station Road, Staple Hill, BRISTOL, BS16 4LU.

CAREFULL, Mr. Robert Charles, FCA *1970;* 13 St Matthew's Avenue, SURBITON, SURREY, KT6 6JJ.

CARELESS, Mr. Robert Arthur, MA FCA *1978;* Flat 6, 147 George Street, LONDON, W1H 5LB.

CARELESS, Mr. Robert John Paget, FCA *1978;* 2196 Rochester Circle, OAKVILLE L6M 5E3, ON, CANADA.

•**CAREW, Mr. David Alun, FCA** *1976;* (Tax Fac), Alun Carew Limited, Cyder House, 11 Pilgrims Way, GUILDFORD, SURREY, GU4 8AD.

•**CAREW, Mr. John Stanley George, FCA** *1961;* John S.G. Carew, 20 Brunel Drive, Upton Grange, Upton, NORTHAMPTON, NN5 4AF.

CAREY, Mr. Adrian Richard, ACA *2010;* 75 Pendle Crescent, NOTTINGHAM, NG3 3DU.

CAREY, Mr. Alan Newman Richard, FCA *1966;* 36 Rue Albert Roussel, 94440 SANTENY, FRANCE. (Life Member)

CAREY, Ms. Alison Aithna, MA FCA CTA *1987;* (Tax Fac), with PricewaterhouseCoopers LLP, 101 Barbirolli Square, Lower Mosley Street, MANCHESTER, M2 3PW.

CAREY, Mr. Allan Robert, BSc FCA *1982;* Croudace Homes Group Ltd, Croudace House, CATERHAM, SURREY, CR3 6XQ.

•**CAREY, Mr. Anthony, MBA BSc FCA** *1981;* Mazars LLP, Tower Bridge House, St. Katharines Way, LONDON, E1W 1DD.

CAREY, Mr. David John, FCA *1968;* Evenden Oast House, Wrotham Road, Meopham, GRAVESEND, KENT, DA13 0JE. (Life Member)

CAREY, Mrs. Diane, BSc ACA *1993;* Wansdyke Cottage, Bourton, Bishops Cannings, DEVIZES, SN10 2LQ.

CAREY, Mr. Gary Jerry, MSc BSc ACA *1996;* 9 South Lodge Mews, South Road, BALDOCK, HERTFORDSHIRE, SG7 6FB.

CAREY, Mrs. Helen, LLB ACA *2001;* Flat 73 Wymering Mansions, Wymering Road, LONDON, W9 2NE.

CAREY, Mrs. Helen Elizabeth, BSc ACA *1989;* Hill Manor, Old Grantham Road, Whatton, NOTTINGHAM, NG13 9FR.

CAREY, Mr. John Francis, FCA *1971;* 57 Kingsfield Avenue, HARROW, HA2 6AQ.

CAREY, Mr. John Sidney, BA(Hons) ACA *2002;* Flat 73 Wymering Mansions, Wymering Road, LONDON, W9 2NE.

CAREY, Mr. Jonathan Hugh David, FCA *1975;* Weston Farm House, Weston, PETERSFIELD, GU32 3NN.

CAREY, Mrs. Julia Frances, ACA *2008;* 1 Stevens Drove, Houghton, STOCKBRIDGE, SO20 6LP.

•**CAREY, Mr. Kevin Ronald, BA FCA** *1996;* McDade Roberts Accountants Limited, 316 Blackpool Road, Fulwood, PRESTON, PR2 3AE.

•**CAREY, Mr. Lawrence Daniel, FCA FCCA** *1975;* The Walled Garden, Longhirst, MORPETH, NORTHUMBERLAND, NE61 3LJ.

CAREY, Mr. Mark Andrew, MA FCA *1993;* Manor Cottage South Street Blewbury, DIDCOT, OXFORDSHIRE, OX11 9PX.

CAREY, Mr. Martin Gerald, BSc ACA *1989;* 22 Alan Cobham Road, DEVIZES, WILTSHIRE, SN10 3GE.

CAREY, Mrs. Mary Margaret, BSc ACA *1982;* Oxford Brookes University Wheatley Campus, Wheatley, OXFORD, OX33 1HX.

•**CAREY, Mr. Michael David, FCA** *1968;* with PricewaterhouseCoopers LLP, 125 High Street, BOSTON, MA 02110, UNITED STATES.

CAREY, Mrs. Pamela Marie, ACA MAAT *1994;* 79 Park Lane, CONGLETON, CHESHIRE, CW12 3DD.

CAREY, Mr. Paul, BSc ACA *2005;* Flat 5 Central Place, Station Road, WILMSLOW, CHESHIRE, SK9 1BU.

CAREY, Mr. Peter Charles, FCA *1973;* 14 Melville Road, Barnes, LONDON, SW13 9RJ.

CAREY, Mr. Peter Damian, BSc ACA *1993;* Trinity Farmhouse, 21 Orwell Road, Barrington, CAMBRIDGE, CB22 7SE.

CAREY, Mr. Peter John, BSc FCA *1971;* Long View, Kettlewell, SKIPTON, NORTH YORKSHIRE, BD23 5RL.

CAREY, Mrs. Rebecca Sarah, BA ACA *2003;* 60 Penrose Avenue, WATFORD, WD19 5AB.

•**CAREY, Mr. Robin Frederick, FCA** *1970;* (Tax Fac), R.F. Carey, 5 Courtrai, Lansdown Castle Drive, CHELTENHAM, GL51 7AF.

CAREY, Mr. Ryan, ACA *2011;* Flat 1, 11 Moresby Road, Hackney, LONDON, E5 9LE.

CAREY, Mr. Sean, BA FCA *1984;* The Santon Group, 3rd Floor, Saunders House, 52-53 The Mall, LONDON, W5 3TA.

•**CAREY, Mr. Steven Howard, BA ACA CTA** *1989;* (Tax Fac), Steven Carey & Co, Countrywide House, 166 Fore Street, SALTASH, CORNWALL, PL12 6JR.

CAREY, Miss. Susan, BSc ACA *1995;* 13A Football, Yeadon, LEEDS, LS19 7QF.

CAREY, Mr. Timothy William, BSc ACA *1994;* (Tax Fac), Warley House, 79 Park Lane, CONGLETON, CW12 3DD.

CAREY-YARD, Mr. Timothy James, BA ACA *1994;* 6 Alsford Close, LIGHTWATER, GU18 5LF.

CARGILL, Mrs. Helen Lynda, BSc ACA *1992;* with RSM Tenon Audit Limited, Ground Floor, 33-35 Cathedral Road, CARDIFF, CF11 9HB.

CARGILL, Mr. Neil Russell, BSc ACA *1993;* 47 Dan-Y-Bryn Avenue, Radyr, CARDIFF, CF15 8DD.

CARIM, Mr. Joseph, BSc FCA *1994;* Flat A, 11 Rosary Gardens, LONDON, SW7 4NN.

CARLE, Mr. Christopher John, BA ACA *2006;* Flat 10, The Highbury, Atlantic Road, WESTON-SUPER-MARE, AVON, BS23 2DL.

CARLESS, Mr. Benjamin John, BA(Hons) ACA *2000;* Greystones, Church Street, Bloxham, BANBURY, OXFORDSHIRE, OX15 4ET.

•**CARLESS, Mr. Bruce, FCA** *1970;* Westfields, Leamington Road, Long Itchington, SOUTHAM, CV47 9PL.

•**CARLESS, Mrs. Jean Margaret, BA ACA** *1984;* (Tax Fac), Jean M. Carless, Tudor Cottage, Leamoor Common, Wistanstow, CRAVEN ARMS, SY7 8DN.

CARLETON, Mr. Ian Neil, BA ACA *1986;* 4 Folding Close, Stewkley, LEIGHTON BUZZARD, BEDFORDSHIRE, LU7 0XE.

CARLETON, Mrs. Rosemary, BA FCA *1986;* (Tax Fac), 4 Folding Close, Stewkley, LEIGHTON BUZZARD, LU7 0XE.

CARLETON, Mr. Stephen John, BSc ACA *1979;* 65A Harvest Road, FELTHAM, TW13 7JH.

•**CARLEY, Mr. Stewart Glasgow, FCA** *1973;* M. Proudlock & Co. Limited, Mazhar House, 48 Bradford Road, Stanningley, LEEDS, WEST YORKSHIRE LS28 6DF.

CARLILE, Mr. Robert, LLB ACA *2009;* 17a Seething Wells Lane, SURBITON, SURREY, KT6 5NR.

CARLIN, Mr. Charles, FCA *1963;* 31 Owler Lane, Chadderton, OLDHAM, OL9 9PA. (Life Member)

CARLIN, Miss. Donna Marie, BSc ACA *1995;* Cotswold Archaeology Building 11, Kemble Enterprise Park Kemble, CIRENCESTER, GLOUCESTERSHIRE, GL7 6BQ.

CARLIN, Mr. Hubert Arthur, FCA *1964;* 5 Palmer Crescent, Carlton, NOTTINGHAM, NG4 1ER. (Life Member)

•**CARLIN, Mr. Peter David, BSc FCA** *1984;* (Tax Fac), Thompson Jones LLP, 2 Heap Bridge, BURY, LANCASHIRE, BL9 7HR. See also Thompson Jones Business Solutions Limited

CARLIN, Miss. Wendy Louise, BSc ACA *2011;* 94 Black Horse Hill, WIRRAL, MERSEYSIDE, CH48 6DT.

CARLINE, Mr. Christopher George, FCA *1969;* House 14 Ham Tin San Tsuen, Pui O, LANTAU ISLAND, HONG KONG ISLAND, HONG KONG SAR. (Life Member)

CARLING, Mr. Charles Widdows, FCA *1965;* Kreuzmoos 42, 6094 AXAMS, AUSTRIA.

CARLING, Mr. Edward Charles, BA FCA *1997;* 24 Wheat Sheaf Close, Mill Quay, LONDON, E14 9UU.

CARLING, Mrs. Elena, ACA *1998;* Veolia Water East, Mill Hill, MANNINGTREE, CO11 2AZ.

•**CARLING, Mrs. Janette Scott, BSc ACA** *1981;* J S Carling Accountancy, 41 Knaith Close, YARM, CLEVELAND, TS15 9TL.

CARLING, Mr. Richard James, BA ACA *1998;* 63 Canford Lane, Westbury-on-Trym, BRISTOL, BS9 3NX.

CARLISLE, Mr. Edward Gareth Hugh, BA ACA *1991;* Allenbuild Limited, Unit 4B Interchange 25 Business Park, Bostocks Lane, Sandiacre, NOTTINGHAM, NG10 5QG.

CARLISLE, Miss. Helen, BA ACA *2005;* 12 Bunting Mews, Worsley, MANCHESTER, M28 7XG.

CARLISLE, Mr. Mark Andrew Russell, BSc(Hons) ACA *2004;* 34 Wilna Road, LONDON, SW18 3BA.

CARLISLE, Mr. Torquil James Jan, ACA *2008;* 1236 Chicago Avenue Apt 409, EVANSTON, IL 60202, UNITED STATES.

CARLSON, Mr. Brian Timothy, BA ACA *2003;* 2 Strides Court, Ottershaw, CHERTSEY, KT16 0GZ.

CARLSON, Mrs. Deborah Claire, BA ACA *1991;* 71 Queens Drive, TAUNTON, SOMERSET, TA1 4XD.

•**CARLSON, Mr. Ian James, BA ACA** *1995;* Old Mill Accountancy LLP, The Old Mill, Park Road, SHEPTON MALLET, SOMERSET, BA4 5BS. See also Old Mill Audit LLP

CARLSON, Miss. Katherine, BA ACA *1998;* Wash Cottage Church Lane, Hargrave, BURY ST. EDMUNDS, SUFFOLK, IP29 5HH.

CARLSON, Miss. Sarah Helen, BSc(Hons) ACA *2010;* 16 Robins Grove, WARWICK, CV34 6RF.

•**CARLTON, Miss. Anne Caroline, BMet FCA** *1979;* 5 Haslemere Gardens, Finchley, LONDON, N3 3EA.

CARLTON, Mr. Kevin Paul, MA ACA *1987;* EIM, 170 Piccadilly, LONDON, W1J 9EJ.

CARLTON, Mrs. Laura Ann, ACA *2004;* with Peters Elworthy & Moore, Salisbury House, Station Road, CAMBRIDGE, CB1 2LA.

CARLTON, Mr. Michael Gary, BA FCA *1988;* 23 Ragged Staff Wharf, Queensway Quay, GIBRALTAR, GIBRALTAR.

CARLTON JONES, Mr. Benjamin Thomas, BA ACA *2007;* with Ernst & Young, Ernst & Young Building, 8 Exhibition Street, MELBOURNE, VIC 3000, AUSTRALIA.

CARLYLE, Mr. Alexander, ACA *2008;* 17 Chiltern Close, Arnold, NOTTINGHAM, NG5 9PX.

CARLYLE, Mrs. Joyce Marian, ACA *1980;* Denplan Ltd, Denplan Court, Victoria Road, WINCHESTER, HAMPSHIRE, SO23 7RG.

•**CARLYLE, Miss. Julie May, LLM LLB ACA** *2001;* Ernst & Young LLP, 1 More London Place, LONDON, SE1 2AF. See also Ernst & Young Europe LLP

CARLYLE, Mr. Philip James, BSc ACA *2010;* 50 Westminster Drive, Burn Bridge, HARROGATE, NORTH YORKSHIRE, HG3 1LW.

CARLYON, Mrs. Catherine Joanne, BA ACA *1999;* 120 Murray Road, LONDON, W5 4DA.

CARLYON, Mr. John Clement, BSc FCA *1990;* 21 Queens Close, Sutton Benger, CHIPPENHAM, SN15 4SB.

CARMAN, Mr. David Martin, ACA *1987;* Sundown Common Lane, Rough Close, STOKE-ON-TRENT, ST3 7ND.

•①**CARMAN, Mr. Russell John, FCA** *1972;* Bates Weston LLP, The Mills, Canal Street, DERBY, DE1 2RJ. See also BW Business Services Limited

CARMEDY, Mr. Michael, BA ACA *1991;* 16 Upper Warren Avenue, Caversham, READING, BERKSHIRE, RG4 7EJ.

•**CARMEL, Mr. Barrie Alan, FCA** *1965;* (Tax Fac), Wilson Wright LLP, First Floor, Thavies Inn House, 3-4 Holborn Circus, LONDON, EC1N 2HA.

CARMEL, Mr. Jeremy Mark, BA FCA *1996;* The Associated Press, 450 West 33rd Street, NEW YORK, NY 10001, UNITED STATES.

CARMICHAEL, Mr. Alastair James Hugh, BSc BSc(Hons) ACA *2011;* 9 Modder Place, LONDON, SW15 1PA.

CARMICHAEL, Miss. Chloe Frances Alice, ACA *2008;* 75 Chasefield Road, LONDON, SW17 8LW.

CARMICHAEL, Mr. David John, BSc FCA *1974;* 33 Etheldene Avenue, LONDON, N10 3QG.

CARMICHAEL, Mrs. Dawn Linda, BSc FCA *1985;* Oakdown, Commonside, Great Bookham, LEATHERHEAD, KT23 3LA.

CARMICHAEL, Mr. Derek John, BCom FCA *1967;* 2 Boucher Road, BUDLEIGH SALTERTON, DEVON, EX9 6HG. (Life Member)

CARMICHAEL, Mr. Ian Stewart, BSc ACA *1979;* 10 Huxterstone Terrace, Kingswells, ABERDEEN, AB15 8UL.

•**CARMICHAEL, Keith Stanley, Esq CBE FCA** *1951;* (Tax Fac), K S Carmichael, 117 Newberries Avenue, RADLETT, WD7 7EN.

CARMICHAEL, Mr. Robert Neil Bruce, FCA *1969;* 82 Stanhope Mews East, South Kensington, LONDON, SW7 5QT.

CARMICHAEL, Mr. Thomas Roderick Iain, ACA *1980;* 6 Cambridge Road, West Wimbledon, LONDON, SW20 0SH.

CARMODY, Miss. Claire Antoinette, MA ACA *1998;* 8 Skelbrook Street, LONDON, SW18 4EY.

CARMODY, Miss. Katherine Anne, ACA *2011;* 64a Wimbledon Park Road, LONDON, SW18 5SH.

CARMONA, Mr. Oliver James, BSc ACA *1994;* 45 Manor Wood Road, PURLEY, CR8 4LJ.

CARMONT, Mr. John Mclaren, FCA *1960;* The Oaks, 1 Top Park, GERRARDS CROSS, SL9 7PP. (Life Member)

CARNALLY, Mr. Raymond, BSc FCA *1976;* 34 Old Barn Road, CHRISTCHURCH, DORSET, BH23 2QY.

CARNE, Mr. Bernard, FCA *1968;* 5 Meadowbanks, BARNET, HERTFORDSHIRE, EN5 3LY. (Life Member)

•**CARNE, Mr. Charles Nicholas, ACA** *1991;* (Tax Fac), Charlie Carne & Co, 49 Windmill Road, LONDON, W4 1RN.

CARNE, Miss. Gillian Margaret, BA ACA *1987;* Les Courtillets, Le Mont Durand, St Martins, GUERNSEY, GY4 6DL.

CARNE, Mr. Jason Lee Clayton, BSc FCA *1992;* KPMG, Crown House, 4 Par-la-Ville Road, HAMILTON HM 08, BERMUDA.

CARNE, Mr. Jeffrey, BA ACA *1995;* 54 Cwrt Y Carw, Coed Hirwaun, Margram Park Village, PORT TALBOT, SA13 2TS.

CARNE, Mr. Peter Geoffrey Camin, BA FCA *1972;* 37 Worthing Road, HORSHAM, WEST SUSSEX, RH12 1TD.

•**CARNE, Mr. Roger Percy, BA FCA** *1985;* Bush & Co, 2 Barnfield Crescent, EXETER, EX1 1QT. See also Westcountry Payroll Ltd

CARNE, Mr. Thomas Charles, CBE FCA *1969;* 42 Arlington Gardens, Harold Wood, ROMFORD, RM3 0EB. (Life Member)

CARNEGIE, Mr. James Webster, BA(Hons) ACA *2001;* 312 Bentley Lane, WALSALL, WEST MIDLANDS, WS2 8TW.

CARNEGIE, Mr. Simon Duthac, BA ACA *1999;* Woodstock Bishops Green, NEWBURY, BERKSHIRE, RG20 4HT.

CARNEGIE, Mr. Stuart Francis, FCA *1972;* La Clairiere, Havilland Road, St. Peter Port, GUERNSEY, GY1 1ER.

CARNEGIE-BROWN, Mr. Ian Donald, BA ACA *1987;* Campsie Hill, Guildtown, PERTH, PH2 6DP.

CARNEGY, Mr. Charles Alexander, MA ACA *2006;* 87b Marney Road, LONDON, SW11 5EW.

CARNEIRO, Miss. Rachel, ACA *2009;* Flat 16, 4 Moon Street, PLYMOUTH, PL4 0AL.

CARNELL, Mr. Christopher Mark Andrew, MA BSc ACA *2000;* Flat 74 Nelson Court, Brunel Road, LONDON, SE16 5GE.

•CARNELL, Mr. Damian John, BCom FCA *1983;* The Old Hall, Boley Hill, ROCHESTER, ME1 1TE.

CARNEY, Mr. Anthony Joseph, BSc ACA *1990;* 23 Redston Road, LONDON, N8 7HL.

CARNEY, Mrs. Antonia Louise, BEng ACA *1993;* 1459 Cherrydale Drive, SAN JOSE, CA 95125, UNITED STATES.

CARNEY, Mr. Brian, BA ACA *1982;* 81 Owler Park Road, ILKLEY, WEST YORKSHIRE, LS29 0BG.

CARNEY, Miss. Charlotte, ACA MAAT *2009;* 90 Murchison Avenue, BEXLEY, DA5 3LL.

CARNEY, Mr. Christopher, MA ACA *2000;* Taylor Wimpey South West Thames, Tyrell House, Challenge Court, Barnett Wood Lane, LEATHERHEAD, SURREY KT22 7LL.

CARNEY, Mr. Christopher, BA ACA *2009;* with Deloitte Middle East, Currency House, Building 1 Level 5, DIFC, PO Box 282056, DUBAI UNITED ARAB EMIRATES.

CARNEY, Mr. Christopher Eaton, BSc ACA *1993;* 1459 Cherrydale Drive, SAN JOSE, CA 95125, UNITED STATES.

CARNEY, Mr. David, BSc ACA *2004;* 15 Westfield Common, Hamble, SOUTHAMPTON, SO31 4LB.

CARNEY, Mr. Michael, FCA *1959;* 3 Hallgate Cl, Hartburn, STOCKTON-ON-TEES, TS18 5NT. (Life Member)

•CARNEY, Mr. Michael Anthony, FCA *1981;* UHY Hacker Young, 22 The Ropewalk, NOTTINGHAM, NG1 5DT. See also UHY Hacker Young LLP

CARNEY, Mr. Patrick Spencer, MA ACA *2001;* 14 Eversfield Road, REIGATE, SURREY, RH2 0PJ.

•CARNEY, Mr. Paul Francis, FCA *1978;* Ainsworths Limited, Charter House, Stansfield Street, NELSON, LANCASHIRE, BB9 9XY.

•CARNEY, Mr. Timothy John, FCA *1975;* AIMS - Tim Carney, Tudor House, The Green, Great Bentley, COLCHESTER, CO7 8PG.

•CARNIE, Mr. Nigel John, FCA *1965;* Trenchard Carnie Limited, 3 Rhododendron Close, CARDIFF, CF23 7HS. See also Trenchard Carnie

CARNWATH, Mrs. Alison Jane, BA ACA *1979;* The Old Dairy, Sidbury, SIDMOUTH, DEVON, EX10 0QR.

CARNWATH, Mr. Anthony Stewart, FCA *1984;* with KPMG LLP, 15 Canada Square, LONDON, E14 5GL.

CARNWATH, Mr. James Richard Alexander, BSc FCA *1978;* 20 Brooklands Avenue, CAMBRIDGE, CB2 2BB. (Life Member)

CARNWATH, Mr. Michael Stewart, FCA *1975;* Sunnyside Farm, Kimbolton Road, Stow Longa, HUNTINGDON, CAMBRIDGESHIRE, PE28 0TR. (Life Member)

CARNWATH, Mr. Peter Andrew, FCA *1971;* Electra Partners Inc, 708 Third Avenue, NEW YORK, NY 10017, UNITED STATES.

CARNWELL, Mrs. Susan Patricia, BA FCA *1992;* Bramley House, Kiddlestitch, UTTOXETER, ST14 5BD.

CAROE, Mr. Mark Frederick, BSc ACA *1987;* Eden Ventures (UK) Ltd, 1 Widcombe Crescent, BATH, BA2 6AH.

CAROLAN, Ms. Bernadette Mary, MA ACA *1993;* 27 Haydon Park Road, Wimbledon, LONDON, SW19 8JQ.

CAROLAN, Mr. Damien, ACA *2011;* Flat 40, Clarendon Court, Sidmouth Road, LONDON, NW2 5HB.

CAROLAN, Mr. Michael, BSc ACA *2006;* with KPMG LLP, 15 Canada Square, LONDON, E14 5GL.

CAROLAN, Miss. Renee Nichola, BSc ACA *2008;* 98 Rayleigh Road, Hutton, BRENTWOOD, ESSEX, CM13 1BH.

CARPEN, Mr. Krissan Jaye, BA(Hons) ACA *2001;* with KPMG LLP, 15 Canada Square, LONDON, E14 5GL.

CARPENDALE, Mr. Hugo Maxwell, BA ACA *1990;* 19 Woodstock Avenue, Redland, BRISTOL, BS6 6EW.

CARPENTER, Mr. Andrew, BSc FCA *1979;* 27 Ridge Park Avenue, PLYMOUTH, PL4 6QB.

CARPENTER, Mr. Andrew Charles, BSc ACA *2002;* with Baker Tilly Tax & Advisory Services LLP, The Clock House, 140 London Road, GUILDFORD, SURREY, GU1 1UW.

CARPENTER, Mr. Andrew Edwin, ACA *1986;* with Grant Thornton UK LLP, Enterprise House, 115 Edmund Street, BIRMINGHAM, B3 2HJ.

CARPENTER, Mrs. Angela Claire, BSc ACA *2005;* 27 Sandholme Drive, Burley in Wharfedale, ILKLEY, WEST YORKSHIRE, LS29 7RG.

CARPENTER, Mr. Charles Andrew, BA ACA *1987;* Flat C, 208 Croydon Road, BECKENHAM, BR3 4DE.

CARPENTER, Mr. David Nigel, ACA *1987;* 17 Porters Close, Petteridge LaneMatfield, TONBRIDGE, TN12 7LY.

•CARPENTER, Mr. David Philip, FCA *1977;* Beck Randall & Carpenter Limited, Aldwych House, Winchester Street, ANDOVER, HAMPSHIRE, SP10 2EA.

CARPENTER, Mr. David Ronald, BSc FCA *1960;* Cleeve Hill House, Cleeve Hill, CHELTENHAM, GL52 3QQ. (Life Member)

CARPENTER, Mr. Edward Jeffery, FCA *1975;* 11a High Street, Foxton, CAMBRIDGE, CB22 6SP.

•CARPENTER, Mrs. Fiona Frances, MSc BA ACA *2003;* Hemingford, Prey Heath Road, WOKING, GU22 0RN.

CARPENTER, Mr. Gary Boyd, BSc ACA *1983;* 20 Spencer Hill, LONDON, SW19 4NY.

CARPENTER, Mr. Geoffrey, BSc ACA *1999;* Abbey National Plc, 2-3 Triton Square, LONDON, NW1 3AN.

•CARPENTER, Mr. James Ernest, FCA *1982;* James Carpenter & Co, 73 Cricketers Lane, Herongate, BRENTWOOD, ESSEX, CM13 3QB.

•CARPENTER, Mr. James John, FCA *1959;* Jim Carpenter, 12 Juniper Road, Boreham, CHELMSFORD, CM3 3DB.

CARPENTER, Mr. John Allan, BSc ACA *1997;* with RSM Tenon Limited, Arkwright House, Parsonage Gardens, MANCHESTER, M3 2LF.

CARPENTER, Mr. John Andrew, BA ACA *1987;* 35 Rollscourt Avenue, LONDON, SE24 0EA.

CARPENTER, Ms. Kathleen May, BSc ACA *1986;* 5 Assheton Road, BEACONSFIELD, HP9 2NP.

CARPENTER, Mr. Kevin Michael, BA ACA *1986;* (Tax Fac), PricewaterhouseCoopers, First House, Corner Livingstone & Chilembwe Avenue, PO Box 1147, BLANTYRE MALAWI.

CARPENTER, Mr. Mark Gwilym, BA(Hons) ACA *2000;* The Acorns Station Road, Upper Broughton, MELTON MOWBRAY, LE14 3BQ.

CARPENTER, Mr. Michael Edward Arscott, MA FCA *1975;* 14 Dynevor Road, RICHMOND, TW10 6PF.

•CARPENTER, Mr. Michael William, MSc FCA *1984;* LAM, Oakwood, The Paddock, Melmerby, RIPON, NORTH YORKSHIRE HG4 5HW.

CARPENTER, Mr. Neil Edward, BSc ACA *1996;* 15 St Elizabeth Drive, EPSOM, KT18 7LA.

•CARPENTER, Mr. Nicholas Peter, ACA *1987;* Fisher Michael, Boundary House, 4 County Place, New London Road, CHELMSFORD, CM2 0RE.

CARPENTER, Mr. Peter John, FCA *1961;* 3 Rockside Drive, Henleaze, BRISTOL, BS9 4NW. (Life Member)

CARPENTER, Mr. Robert Paul, FCA *1955;* 4 Swan Court, South Chailey, LEWES, EAST SUSSEX, BN8 4BN. (Life Member)

CARPENTER, Mr. Robert Sherston, FCA FIoD FRSA *1991;* 2 Laurel Close, BURGESS HILL, WEST SUSSEX, RH15 0UG.

CARPENTER, Mr. Roger Stanley, BSS FCA *1977;* P.O. Box 9 Council House, Solihull Metropolitan Borough Council Director of Finance, PO Box 9, SOLIHULL, B91 9QR.

CARPENTER, Mr. Roland John, FCA *1956;* 18 Kingswood Close, SWANAGE, DORSET, BH19 2SP. (Life Member)

CARPENTER, Mr. Stephen Paul, BSc FCA *1989;* Day Smith & Hunter, Globe House, Eclipse Park, Sittingbourne Road, MAIDSTONE, KENT ME14 3EN.

•CARPENTER, Mr. Stuart David, MA FCA *1984;* (Tax Fac), Carpenter Keen LLP, Grand Prix House, 102-104 Sheen Road, RICHMOND, SURREY, TW9 1UF.

•CARPENTER, Mr. Terence Edwin, FCA *1967;* T.E. Carpenter, 362 Pickhurst Rise, WEST WICKHAM, BR4 0AY.

CARPENTER-LEITCH, Mr. Tom Gordon, MA ACA *1989;* Flat 3 Pair South, 8 Kings Bench Walk, LONDON, EC4Y 7DU.

CARR, Mrs. Adele Donna, BA ACA *1996;* The Rock, 1 Broomfields Road, Appleton, WARRINGTON, WA4 3AE.

CARR, Mrs. Adrienne Elizabeth Anne, MA ACA *1985;* Link HouseLink Hill Lane, Egerton ASHFORD, Kent, TN27 9BH.

CARR, Mr. Alan, MA ACA *1990;* The Old Vicarage Coed Masarnen, Colwinston, COWBRIDGE, SOUTH GLAMORGAN, CF71 7NG.

CARR, Mr. Alexander, ACA *2009;* 89 Bower Street, BEDFORD, MK40 3RB.

CARR, Mrs. Alexandra Katherine, MA ACA *2005;* Moss Cottage Hall Lane, Osbaston, NUNEATON, CV13 0BW.

CARR, Mr. Amnon, BA ACA *1990;* 954 Lexington Avenue 258, NEW YORK, NY 10021, UNITED STATES.

CARR, Mrs. Amy Victoria, ACA *2009;* 40 Oakfields, Burnopfield, NEWCASTLE UPON TYNE, NE16 6PQ.

CARR, Mr. Andrew Christopher, BSc ACA *1989;* Merlin Entertainments Group International Ltd, 3 Market Close, POOLE, DORSET, BH15 1NQ.

CARR, Mr. Andrew Hamilton, BSc ACA *1991;* Tylers, 59 Sheepcote Dell Road, Holmer Green, HIGH WYCOMBE, HP15 6TL.

CARR, Miss. Angela Marie, BA ACA *2004;* U B S AG, 100 Liverpool Street, LONDON, EC2M 2RH.

•CARR, Mrs. Angela Mary, BA FCA *1986;* Heaton Lumb Lisle, Thorpe House, 61 Richardshaw Lane, PUDSEY, LS28 7EL.

CARR, Mrs. Ann Jane, LLB ACA *1992;* Byewood, Bolney Road, Ansty, HAYWARDS HEATH, WEST SUSSEX, RH17 5AW.

CARR, Mrs. Beverley Ann, BSc ACA *1989;* 5556 Arbor Bay Drive, BRIGHTON, MI 48116, UNITED STATES.

CARR, Mr. Brendan Michael, FCA *1964;* Cudsdens Cottage, Chesham Road, GREAT MISSENDEN, HP16 0QT.

CARR, Mr. Brian Russell, BSc FCA *1972;* 56 Pembroke Road, Clifton, BRISTOL, BS8 3DT. (Life Member)

CARR, Mr. Charles Garnett, BSc ACA *1983;* Riverholme, 18 Sandy Lane, CHESTER, CH3 5UL.

•CARR, Mr. Christopher David, BSc FCA CF *1979;* Celarben Ventures Limited, 4 Whiteley Close, Dane End, WARE, HERTFORDSHIRE, SG12 0NB.

CARR, Mr. Christopher John, BA ACA *1990;* 1120 Avenue of Americas, 5th Floor, NEW YORK, NY 10036-6700, UNITED STATES.

CARR, Mr. Christopher McIntosh, ACA CTA *2003;* 10 The Nurseries, Linstock, CARLISLE, CA6 4RR.

CARR, Mr. Christopher Patrick, BSc ACA *1993;* Flat 307 Melrose Appts, 159 Hathersage Road, MANCHESTER, M13 0HX.

CARR, Mr. Daniel Paul, ACA MAAT *2009;* 37 Chadwell Road, LEICESTER, LE3 6LG.

CARR, Mr. David Antony, BA ACA *1996;* 6 Elborough Street, Southfields, LONDON, SW18 5DW.

CARR, Mr. David Francis, FCA *1959;* 11 Tudor Court, CHARD, SOMERSET, TA20 1LX. (Life Member)

CARR, Mr. David John, BSc(Econ) ACA *1995;* 25 Balmoral Road, Ash Vale, ALDERSHOT, HAMPSHIRE, GU12 5BB.

CARR, Mrs. Elisabeth Margaret, BSc ACA *2007;* 21 St. Georges Avenue, Timperley, ALTRINCHAM, CHESHIRE, WA15 6HF.

CARR, Mr. Frank, FCA *1959;* 1 Abernethy, Ouston, CHESTER LE STREET, COUNTY DURHAM, DH2 1RX. (Life Member)

CARR, Gordon Verner, Esq CBE FCA *1951;* 51 Oaklands, Gosforth, NEWCASTLE UPON TYNE, NE3 4YP. (Life Member)

CARR, Mr. Graham Douglas Quintin, FCA *1963;* The Spinney, The Green, Cuddington, AYLESBURY, HP18 0AN.

CARR, Mr. Graham Stuart, BA ACA *1999;* 11 Whartons Close, Ashurst, SOUTHAMPTON, SO40 7EE.

CARR, Mr. Greg Philip, BA ACA *2003;* 4 Mallinson Close, HARROGATE, HG2 9HW.

CARR, Mrs. Helen Louise, BSc ACA *1995;* 75 Hawthorne Way, Shelley, HUDDERSFIELD, HD8 8JX.

CARR, Mr. Hugh Jonathan, BA ACA *1987;* Dumfries & Galloway Housing Partnership Grierson House, The Crichton Bankend Road, DUMFRIES, DG1 4ZS.

•CARR, Mr. Ian Stewart, BA ACA *1985;* Grant Thornton UK LLP, 101 Cambridge Science Park, Milton Road, CAMBRIDGE, CB4 0FY. See also Grant Thornton LLP

CARR, Mr. James Ronald, DL MA FCA *1971;* Moorhouse Hall, Warwick on Eden, CARLISLE, CA4 8PA.

•CARR, Mrs. Janet Mary, BA FCA *1983;* (Tax Fac), Morris & Co (2011) Limited, Chester House, Lloyd Drive, Chesire Oaks Business Park, ELLESMERE PORT, CHESHIRE CH65 9HQ.

CARR, Miss. Jennifer, ACA *2008;* 47 Paxmead Close, COVENTRY, CV6 2NS.

•CARR, Mrs. Jennifer Rachel, BA FCA *1989;* with RSM Tenon Limited, Davidson House, Forbury Square, READING, RG1 3EU.

•CARR, Mr. Jeremy Peter, BA ACA *1993;* The Rock, Broomfields Road, Appleton, WARRINGTON, WA4 5BE.

CARR, Mrs. Joanne, BSc ACA *2005;* Barn 2, The Old Smithy, Portskewett, CHEPSTOW, GWENT, NP26 5SA.

CARR, Mrs. Joanne Allyson, BA ACA *2005;* 10 Sovereign Square, Bailiff Bridge, BRIGHOUSE, WEST YORKSHIRE, HD6 4DD.

CARR, Mr. John Anthony, ACA *1990;* Suite 4 Level 1, 1 Swann Road, TARINGA, QLD 4068, AUSTRALIA.

CARR, Mr. John David, BSc FCA *1962;* 16 Kestrel Close, Weston Favell, NORTHAMPTON, NN3 3JG. (Life Member)

CARR, Mr. John Gower, ACA *1997;* 762 Upper Lansdowne, WESTMOUNT H3Y 1J8, QUE, CANADA.

•CARR, Mr. John Granville, FCA *1979;* Schonhut Carr & Co, Thames House, Mayo Road, WALTON-ON-THAMES, SURREY, KT12 2QA.

CARR, Miss. Julia Rebecca, ACA *2005;* SIG Plc, Signet House, Europa View, Sheffield Business Park, SHEFFIELD, S9 1XH.

CARR, Mr. Julian Edward, LLB ACA *1990;* 23 Prebend Gardens, Chiswick, LONDON, W4 1TN.

CARR, Mr. Kenneth Edmund, FCA *1951;* Bridge House, Woodhill Road, Sandon, CHELMSFORD, CM2 7SG. (Life Member)

CARR, Mr. Kenneth Edmund, BA FCA FCT *1976;* Alliance Boots Mabagement Services Ltd, 2 The Heights, Brooklands, WEYBRIDGE, SURREY, KT13 0NY.

CARR, Mr. Kevin Raymond, FCA *1979;* Maple Farm Rosemary Lane, Alfold, CRANLEIGH, GU6 8EZ.

CARR, Mrs. Laura Elizabeth, BSc ACA *2000;* JTI-Macdonald Corp., 1 Robert Speck Parkway, Suite 1601, MISSISSAUGA L4Z 0A2, ON, CANADA.

CARR, Miss. Laura Jane, ACA *2010;* with Rickard Keen LLP, 7 Nelson Street, SOUTHEND-ON-SEA, SS1 1EH.

CARR, Mr. Mark Robert, BSc ACA *1991;* Associated Newspapers Ltd Northcliffe House, 2 Derry Street, LONDON, W8 5TT.

CARR, Mr. Martin, MA ACA *1980;* LHR1, 145 Faggs Road, FELTHAM, MIDDLESEX, TW14 0LZ.

CARR, Mr. Martin Leo, BA(Hons) ACA *2010;* 22 Ashbrook Mews, NEWRY, COUNTY DOWN, BT34 1SJ.

CARR, Mr. Neil Stanley, BSc ACA *1989;* Federal - Mogul Corporation, 26555 North Western Highway, SOUTHFIELD, MI 48034, UNITED STATES.

•CARR, Mr. Neville William, BSc FCA *1976;* Hall Livesey Brown, 68 High Street, TARPORLEY, CW6 0AT.

•①CARR, Mr. Nigel Edmund, BA FCA *1987;* with KPMG LLP, 15 Canada Square, LONDON, E14 5GL.

CARR, The Revd. Norman Ernest, FCA *1956;* 5 Stapes Garth, Grainthorpe, LOUTH, LINCOLNSHIRE, LN11 7FD. (Life Member)

CARR, Mrs. Patricia Rosa, FCA *1976;* Stewart and MacLochlainn, Portland House, LETTERKENNY, COUNTY DONEGAL, IRELAND.

•CARR, Mr. Paul Ernest, FCA *1977;* Redwood Wales Limited, Redwood Court, Tawe Business Village, Swansea Enterprise Park, SWANSEA, SA7 9LA.

CARR, Mr. Paul Wilfred, FCA *1979;* Hill View Grange, Ilketshall St. John, BECCLES, SUFFOLK, NR34 8JE.

CARR, Mrs. Pollyanna Mary, BA ACA *1993;* E Oppenheiher & Son (PTY) Ltd, 6 St Andrews Road, Parktown 2193, P O Box 61631, MARSHALLTOWN, 2107 SOUTH AFRICA.

CARR, Mr. Raymond Harold, FCA *1956;* 16 Claremont Heights, Crescent Road, ENFIELD, EN2 7RY. (Life Member)

CARR, Mr. Richard Coventry, FCA *1951;* 40 Cliff Road, PAIGNTON, TQ4 6DH. (Life Member)

CARR, Mr. Richard David, BSc ACA *1987;* 52 Pishiobury Drive, SAWBRIDGEWORTH, HERTFORDSHIRE, CM21 0AE.

CARR, Mr. Robin, FCA *1966;* Church House, Clyst St George, EXETER, EX3 0RE.

CARR, Miss. Samantha Jane, BA ACA *1996;* 6 Chatto Road, Battersea, LONDON, SW11 6LL.

CARR, Mrs. Sharon, ACA *2006;* 10 The Nurseries, Linstock, CARLISLE, CA6 4RR.

CARR, Mr. Simon, ACA *2008;* 31 Broadfields Avenue, EDGWARE, MIDDLESEX, HA8 8PF.

CARR, Mr. Simon Charles, MBA ACA *1987;* 6282 Via Trato, CARLSBAD, CA 92009, UNITED STATES.

CARR, Mr. Simon Timothy, BA ACA *1992;* 14 Wellington Close, Burbage, HINCKLEY, LE10 2GH.

CARR, Mr. Stephen John, BSc ACA *1995;* 46a Foxgrove Road, BECKENHAM, BR3 5DB.

CARR, Mr. Steven, BSc ACA *2004;* 1 Church Mews, Denton, MANCHESTER, M34 3GL.

•CARR, Mrs. Teresa, FCA *1978;* (Tax Fac), Schonhut Carr & Co, Thames House, Mayo Road, WALTON-ON-THAMES, SURREY, KT12 2QA.

CARR, Mr. Timothy Buxton, FCA *1965;* 607 Desert Oak Drive, PENSACOLA, FL 32514, UNITED STATES.

CARRADICE, Dr. Maria Terese, BSc(Hons) ACA CTA *2004;* 25 Langley Crescent, ST. ALBANS, AL3 5RR.

CARRADUS, Mr. Malcolm, BSc ACA *1988;* Informa Regional Business Services - Asia, 111 Somerset Road #10-06, TripleOne Somerset, SINGAPORE 238164, SINGAPORE.

CARRAHAR, Miss. Joanne, BA ACA *2001;* Gentoo Emperor House, 2 Emperor Way Doxford International Business Park, SUNDERLAND, SR3 3XR.

CARRATT, Mr. Mike, BA ACA *2011;* Flat 1, 22 Trinity Church Square, LONDON, SE1 4HY.

CARRATU, Mr. Anthony Domenic John, FCA *1960;* Pine Lodge, East Road, St Georges Hill, WEYBRIDGE, KT13 0LG. (Life Member)

CARRATU, Mr. Nicholas Francis Ralph, FCA *1964;* 11 The Riverside, Graburn Way, EAST MOLESEY, KT8 9BF.

CARRAZEDO, Mr. Zane, BSc(Hons) ACA *2011;* 52 Park Road, Duffield, BELPER, DERBYSHIRE, DE56 4GR.

CARRE, Mrs. Carole Laura Margaret, MBA BSc FCA *1988;* Ivy Cottage, Blennerhasset, WIGTON, CUMBRIA, CA7 3QR.

CARRE, Miss. Joanna, BSc(Hons) ACA *2001;* 62 Lombard Drive, CHESTER LE STREET, DH3 4BD.

CARRECK, Mr. John Raymond, FCA *1955;* 40 Deneside, East Dean, EASTBOURNE, BN20 0JG. (Life Member)

CARREL, Mr. Simon Timothy, BA FCA *1974;* 8 Hillview Road, MOUNT LAWLEY, WA 6050, AUSTRALIA.

CARRIBAN, Mr. Mark Coupland, BCom ACA *1986;* Unit 1501-07, 15/F Tower One, Times Square, CAUSEWAY BAY, HONG KONG SAR.

•**CARRICK, Mrs. Bethan Bowen, BSc ACA** *1981;* Carrick, 10 Oxford Street, MALMESBURY, SN16 9AZ.

CARRICK, Mr. Brian Robert Bullard, FCA *1973;* Orange House, 53 Malthouse Crescent, Heacham, KING'S LYNN, NORFOLK, PE31 7EG.

CARRICK, Miss. Caroline Louise, BA(Hons) ACA *2001;* Building 200, British Petroleum Co Plc, Chertsey Road, SUNBURY-ON-THAMES, MIDDLESEX, TW16 7LN.

CARRICK, Mr. Geoffrey Michael, FCA *1953;* Bolam Crofts, Whalton, MORPETH, NE61 3UA. (Life Member)

CARRICK, Mr. John David, FCA *1973;* 18 West Green, West Ella, HULL, HU10 7TW.

CARRICK, Miss. Julia Elizabeth, BSc ACA *2004;* 19 Charterhouse Apartments, 21 Eltringham Street, LONDON, SW18 1AU.

CARRICK, Mr. Neil Richard, FCA *1985;* 6A Church Hill, South Cave, BROUGH, HU15 2EU.

CARRICK, Miss. Tamara, BSc ACA *2003;* Flat 122a Highlands Heath, Portsmouth Road, LONDON, SW15 3TZ.

CARRICO DE AGUIAR, Miss. Yuki, ACA CA(SA) *2010;* 6 Longfield Gate, Orton Longueville, PETERBOROUGH, PE2 7BL.

CARRIGAN, Miss. Anne Kathleen, FCA *1980;* (Tax Fac), 46 St Matthews Road, BRISTOL, BS6 5TU.

CARRIGAN, Mr. Nigel Peter, BSc ACA *1986;* 5 Melbury Close, CHISLEHURST, BR7 5ET.

CARRIGAN, Mr. Philip Patrick, ACA *1980;* 37 East Acton Lane, LONDON, W3 7HD.

CARRINGTON, Mr. Andrew Howard, BSc ACA *2008;* C/o Mr and Mrs Carrington, 9 Harlington Road, Sharpenhoe, BEDFORD, MK45 4SG.

CARRINGTON, Mr. Charles David, BSc ACA CPA CIA *1997;* 314 Greenhill Road, WEST CHESTER, PA 19380, UNITED STATES.

CARRINGTON, Mr. David John, FCA *1967;* The Dairy, Manor Farm Court, Titchmarsh, KETTERING, NN14 3EJ.

•**CARRINGTON, Mr. Gary Douglas, BA ACA CTA** *1996;* Baker Tilly Tax & Advisory Services LLP, 1210 Centre Park Square, WARRINGTON, WA1 1RU.

•**CARRINGTON, Mr. Ian Michael, MA FCA** *1984;* Edwards & Keeping, Unity Chambers, 34 High East Street, DORCHESTER, DT1 1HA.

•**CARRINGTON, Mr. John Paul, LLB ACA** *1999;* Peter Simon & Co Limited, The Old Maids Head, 110 High Street, Stalham, NORWICH, NR12 9AU.

CARRINGTON, Mrs. Judith Lucy Elizabeth, BSc ACA *1995;* with PricewaterhouseCoopers LLP, Lennox House, 7 Beaufort Buildings, Spa Road, GLOUCESTER, GL1 1XD.

CARRINGTON, Miss. Marabeth Louise, BA(Hons) ACA *2009;* 96 Bridgewater Street, SALE, CHESHIRE, M33 7HB.

•**CARRINGTON, Mr. Nicholas David, BA ACA** *1992;* Deloitte LLP, Athene Place, 66 Shoe Lane, LONDON, EC4A 3BQ. See also Deloitte & Touche LLP

CARRINGTON, Mr. Robert Andrew, BSc ACA *1995;* Flat 1, 88 Fleet Road, LONDON, NW3 2QT.

•**CARRINGTON, Mr. Stuart James, BA FCA** *1992;* Thomas Westcott, Timberly, South Street, AXMINSTER, DEVON, EX13 5AD.

CARRIVICK, Mr. Luke, ACA *2008;* 4 Park Avenue, ENFIELD, MIDDLESEX, EN1 2HP.

CARROLL, Miss. Adelle Frances, BA ACA *2004;* 198 Kinson Road, BOURNEMOUTH, BH10 5EW.

•**CARROLL, Mr. Adrian, FCA** *1982;* Townends Chartered Accountants Carlisle Chambers, 8-14 Carlisle Street, GOOLE, NORTH HUMBERSIDE, DN14 5DX. See also Townends Accountants Limited and Townends

CARROLL, Mr. Alan Thomas, BA ACA *2007;* Pricewaterhousecoopers Cornwall Court, 19 Cornwall Street, BIRMINGHAM, B3 2DT.

CARROLL, Mrs. Amanda Joy, MA ACA *1986;* Rose House, High Street, Nawton, YORK, YO62 7TT.

•**CARROLL, Mr. Andrew John, FCA** *1981;* Carroll Business Consulting Limited, 335 Jockey Road, SUTTON COLDFIELD, WEST MIDLANDS, B73 5XE. See also Senn Payroll Limited

CARROLL, Mr. Barry Patrick Ambrose, BA ACA *1992;* Augentius Fund Administration Llp Two, London Bridge, LONDON, SE1 9RA.

CARROLL, Mr. Ben, BSc ACA *1999;* 181 Elsley Road, Battersea, LONDON, SW11 5LG.

•**CARROLL, Mr. Brian Charles, FCA** *1972;* (Tax Fac), Harold D. Pritchard & Co, Old Oak House, 49-51 Lammas Street, CARMARTHEN, DYFED, SA31 3AL.

•**CARROLL, Mr. Brian John, FCA** *1973;* (Tax Fac), Whiting & Partners, Eagle House, 108 High Street, Ramsey, HUNTINGDON, CAMBRIDGESHIRE PE26 1BS.

CARROLL, Mr. Brian Joseph, TD FCA *1953;* 26 Bower Road, Hale, ALTRINCHAM, WA15 9DR. (Life Member)

CARROLL, Mr. David Antony, BSc(Hons) ACA *2000;* Sony Computer Entertainment, 10 Great Marlborough Street, LONDON, W1F 7LP.

CARROLL, Mr. David John, FCA *1976;* 191 New Toronto Street, TORONTO M8V 2E7, ON, CANADA.

CARROLL, Mr. Dominic, BA(Hons) ACA *2002;* 15 Pentire Avenue, SOUTHAMPTON, SO15 7RR.

CARROLL, Miss. Emma, BSc(Hons) ACA *2011;* 115 Avon Drive, CONGLETON, CHESHIRE, CW12 3RG.

CARROLL, Mr. Gideon Isaac, BA ACA *2009;* 1 Hervey Court Hervey Close, LONDON, N3 2HE.

CARROLL, Mr. Glenn Anthony John, BA ACA *1980;* 1 Beechcroft, Compton Street Compton, WINCHESTER, SO21 2AS.

CARROLL, Mr. Gregory Michael, BA ACA *2010;* Flat 2, 1 Lower Vauvert, St. Peter Port, GUERNSEY, GY1 1LZ.

CARROLL, Mrs. Helen Lisa, BSc ACA *1992;* 4 Lonsdale Road, Barnes, LONDON, SW13 9EB.

•**CARROLL, Mrs. Jean Evelyn, BA FCA** *1991;* Armstrong Watson, Fairview House, Victoria Place, CARLISLE, CA1 1HP.

CARROLL, Mrs. Jill, BSc ACA *1997;* Intel (UK) Ltd, Pipers Way, SWINDON, SN3 1RJ.

CARROLL, Mr. John, BA ACA *2005;* 32 Claybank Drive, Tottington, BURY, BL8 4BU.

•**CARROLL, Mr. John Patrick, FCA** *1973;* Kybert Carroll Ltd, 52 Brighton Road, SURBITON, SURREY, KT6 5PL. See also J & B Carroll Limited

•**CARROLL, Mr. John Rodney, FCA** *1970;* J R Carroll, 8 Arthur Kennedy Close, Boughton, FAVERSHAM, ME13 9BQ.

•**CARROLL, Mr. Julian Markham, BSc FCA** *1976;* (Tax Fac), Carroll & Co, 6 Willow Drive, Twyford, READING, RG10 9DD.

CARROLL, Miss. Juliette Elizabeth, LLB ACA *2007;* Pump House Slugwash Lane, Wivelsfield Green, HAYWARDS HEATH, WEST SUSSEX, RH17 7RG.

CARROLL, Mr. Matthew, BBA ACA CTA *2006;* RWE NPower Plc, Trigonos Building, Windmill Hill Business Park, Whitehill Way, SWINDON, SN5 6PB.

•**CARROLL, Ms. Michelle, ACA** *2006;* Kinetic Partners, 1 London Wall, Level 10, LONDON, EC2Y 5HB. See also Kinetic Partners Audits LLP

CARROLL, Mrs. Nicola Jayne, BA(Hons) ACA *2001;* 43 Southlands, Kirkheaton, HUDDERSFIELD, HD5 0JU.

CARROLL, Mr. Paul Bryan, ACA MAAT *1993;* 8 Falkirk Avenue, High Grove, WIDNES, CHESHIRE, WA8 9DX.

CARROLL, Mr. Peter Michael, BSc ACA *1979;* Redbourn Group Ltd, Unit 2 Homefarm, Luton Hoo Estate, LUTON, BEDFORDSHIRE, LU1 3TD.

•**CARROLL, Mrs. Philippa Claire, BA ACA** *2006;* Parsons Royle & Co Ltd, Capital House, 2 Market Street, Atherton, MANCHESTER, M46 0DN.

CARROLL, Mr. Phillip, BMus ACA *2006;* 14 Rosehill Court, LIVERPOOL, L25 4TA.

CARROLL, Mrs. Rebecca Susan, BA ACA *1997;* SIG Ireland, Unit 42 O Casey Avenue, Parkhurst Industrial Estate, Nanger Road, DUBLIN 12, COUNTY DUBLIN IRELAND.

CARROLL, Mr. Redmond Anthony, FCA *1976;* Calobo Holdings Ltd, #5 - 665 Tranquille Rd, KAMLOOPS V2B 3H7, BC, CANADA.

CARROLL, Mr. Robert William, BSc FCA *1990;* 57 Washington Road, WORCESTER PARK, KT4 8JG.

CARROLL, Mr. Roger Edwin, FCA *1965;* 10 St. John's Avenue, CLEVEDON, BS21 7TQ. (Life Member)

CARROLL, Mrs. Sally Ann, BA FCA CTA *1987;* (Tax Fac), 5 Eastway, EPSOM, KT19 8SG.

CARROLL, Ms. Sara Amelia, ACA *1993;* 12 Sloane Street, NEWTOWN, NSW 2042, AUSTRALIA.

CARROLL, Mr. Shannon Patrick, BSc ACA *1992;* 43 Millbrook Close, Wheelton, CHORLEY, PR6 8JY.

CARROLL, Mr. Stephen Christopher, MA ACA *1984;* Rose House, High Street, Nawton, YORK, YO62 7TT.

CARROLL, Mr. Stephen John, BSc ACA *1981;* Ecolab Limited, Chancery House, St. Nicholas Way, SUTTON, SURREY, SM1 1JB.

CARROLL, Mr. Stuart, FIA ACA CA(SA) *2009;* 37a South Park Road, LONDON, SW19 8RS.

CARROLL, Mrs. Tanya Katrina, BSc ACA CTA *1994;* (Tax Fac), 3 Osborne Road, ALTRINCHAM, WA15 8EU.

CARROLL, Mr. Terence Patrick, BSc FCA FCT *1974;* 18 Skipton Road, ILKLEY, WEST YORKSHIRE, LS29 9EJ. (Life Member)

•**CARROLL, Mr. Thomas George, BA FCA** *1984;* Tom Carroll Associates Ltd, 166 Prescot Road, ST. HELENS, MERSEYSIDE, WA10 3TS.

CARROLL, Mr. William James, BSc ACA *2002;* Monmouthshire Bldg Soc, 13 John Frost Square, NEWPORT, GWENT, NP20 1PX.

•**CARROLL, Mr. William Michael Arthur, FCA** *1969;* W.M.A Carroll, 16 Ormonde Place, Old Avenue, WEYBRIDGE, KT13 0PE.

CARROLL, Mrs. Zoe Jane, BSc ACA *1987;* 31 Lattimore Close, West Haddon, NORTHAMPTON, NN6 7GL.

CARROTT, Ms. Lisa, ACA *2009;* Stockland, Level 23, 133 Castlereagh Street, SYDNEY, NSW 2000, AUSTRALIA.

•**CARRUTH, Mr. John Christian Claasen, FCA** *1978;* (Tax Fac), Parker Cavendish, 28 Church Road, STANMORE, HA7 4XR. See also Parker Cavendish Limited

CARRUTHERS, Mr. Andrew Bruce, BSc ACA *1992;* Spark Ventures, 33 Glasshouse Street, LONDON, W1B 5DG.

•**CARRUTHERS, Mr. Brian Stuart, FCA** *1973;* Thomas May & Co, Allen House, Newarke Street, LEICESTER, LE1 5SG.

CARRUTHERS, Mr. David Charles, FCA *1966;* 35 Trimingham Hill, PAGET PG 05, BERMUDA.

CARRUTHERS, Mr. Donald, FCA *1961;* 8 Harewood Close, BELPER, DE56 0FB. (Life Member)

•**CARRUTHERS, Miss. Elizabeth Helen, BA ACA CTA** *1996;* Ernst & Young LLP, 1 More London Place, LONDON, SE1 2AF. See also Ernst & Young Europe LLP

CARRUTHERS, Mrs. Emma-Lucy, BCom ACA *2004;* 11 The Grove, BURNTWOOD, WS7 1ZW.

CARRUTHERS, Mr. Gary, BA ACA *2006;* 21 Orchard Road, Fair Oak, EASTLEIGH, HAMPSHIRE, SO50 7AS.

CARRUTHERS, Mr. Ian Paul, BSc FCA CPFA *1988;* 15A The Terrace, Barnes, LONDON, SW13 0NP.

CARRUTHERS, Mrs. Nicola Mary, BCom ACA *1989;* Dudley & Co, 33 New Street, CARNFORTH, LANCASHIRE, LA5 9BX.

CARRUTHERS, Mr. Paul, BA ACA *1990;* Foleshill, Denne Park, HORSHAM, WEST SUSSEX, RH13 0AY.

CARRUTHERS, Mr. Paul Reid, BSc ACA *2005;* 93 Deer Way, HORSHAM, WEST SUSSEX, RH12 1PX.

CARRUTHERS, Mrs. Samantha Jane, BA FCA *2001;* 115 Upland Road, LONDON, SE22 0DF.

CARRUTHERS, Mrs. Sarah Ellen, BSc(Hons) ACA *2001;* 59 Burnside, Parbold, WIGAN, WN8 7PE.

CARRUTHERS, Mr. Simon Peter, BA FCA CF *1986;* with Grant Thornton UK LLP, 4 Hardman Square, Spinningfields, MANCHESTER, M3 3EB.

CARRUTHERS, Mrs. Suzanne Ruth, MA ACA *1988;* 15a, The Terrace, LONDON, SW13 0NP.

CARRUTHERS, Miss. Wendy Ann, BSc ACA *1991;* C G I Europe Ltd Broadlands House, Primett Road, STEVENAGE, HERTFORDSHIRE, SG1 3EE.

CARRUTHERS, Mr. William Douglas, FCA *1959;* 16 Candelan Way, The Belfry, High Legh, KNUTSFORD, CHESHIRE, WA16 6TP. (Life Member)

CARRUTHERS, Ms. Zena, BA FCA *1982;* 4036 Albert Drive, NASHVILLE, TN 37204, UNITED STATES.

CARSBERG, Sir Bryan Victor, MA MSc FCA *1960;* (Member of Council 1975 - 1979), 14 The Great Quarry, GUILDFORD, GU1 3XN.

•**CARSLAKE, Mr. John Alfred Lawrence, BA FCA** *1966;* (Tax Fac), John A.L.Carslake, 29 Beckett Road, WORCESTER, WR3 7NH.

CARSLAW, Mr. Charles Arthur Powell Nash, MA FCA *1975;* Department of Accounting and IS, MS 026, University of Nevada Reno, RENO, NV 89557, UNITED STATES.

CARSLEY, Mrs. Katherine Ann, BA ACA *1993;* 11 Pine Close Shottery, STRATFORD-UPON-AVON, WARWICKSHIRE, CV37 9FB.

•**CARSON, Mr. Anthony Roger, FCA** *1970;* Carson & Company, Unit 3, Dukes Court, Wellington Street, LUTON, LU1 5AF.

CARSON, Mr. Christopher Ian, BSc ACA *1993;* Bigbury Court Farmhouse, Bigbury, KINGSBRIDGE, DEVON, TQ7 4AP.

CARSON, Mr. David William, BSc ACA *1981;* Lanntair, Cowden, DOLLAR, FK14 7PJ.

CARSON, Mrs. Elisabeth Clare, BA(Hons) ACA *2002;* 77 Burwood Road, Hersham, WALTON-ON-THAMES, KT12 4AE.

•**CARSON, Mr. Geoffrey, BA FCA** *1969;* Geoffrey Carson, Twin Pines, Devenish Road, ASCOT, BERKSHIRE, SL5 9PH.

CARSON, Mr. John Seton Burrell, LLB FCA *1976;* Congalton House, NORTH BERWICK, EAST LOTHIAN, EH39 5JL.

CARSON, Mr. Michael, MA BA(Hons) ACA *1996;* Greater Manchester Police, Nexus House, Alexandria Drive, ASHTON-UNDER-LYNE, OL7 0QP.

•**CARSON, Mr. Paul John, BA FCA CTA** *1994;* (Tax Fac), Simpson Wood, Bank Chambers, Market Street, HUDDERSFIELD, HD1 2EW.

CARSON, Mr. Peter Richard, BSc ACA *1992;* 1 Angel Lane, LONDON, EC4R 3AB.

CARSON, Mr. Rory, BSc ACA *2003;* 3318 Ravens Roost, MISSOURI CITY, TX 77459, UNITED STATES.

CARSS, Mrs. Sarah Helen, BSc ACA CTA *1992;* Willow Tree Farmhouse, Minshull Lane, Church Minshull, NANTWICH, CHESHIRE, CW5 6EF.

CARSWELL, Mr. Adam Peter, BSc ACA *1993;* BIMM, 48-52 Brunswick Street West, HOVE, EAST SUSSEX, BN3 1EL.

CARSWELL, Mr. Benjamin Edward, BA ACA MBA *2000;* 36 Skelbrook Street, LONDON, SW18 4EZ.

CARSWELL, Mr. Richard Neil, BSc(Hons) ACA *2004;* Floor 5 Kings Place, Wolverine Europe Ltd Kings Place, 90 York Way, LONDON, N1 9AG.

CARSWELL, Mrs. Sarah Valerie Louise, BA ACA *1986;* Brentwood School, Ingrave Road, BRENTWOOD, CM15 8AS.

•**CARTE, Mr. Andrew John, FCA** *1974;* A.J. Carte, 215 Nanpantan Road, LOUGHBOROUGH, LE11 3YD.

CARTEN, Mr. Paul Louis, BA FCA *1992;* 57 Station Road, THAMES DITTON, SURREY, KT7 0PA.

CARTEN, Mrs. Suzanne Elizabeth, BSc ACA *1994;* 3 Powel Court, Bottoms Farm Lane, Doynton, BRISTOL, BS30 5TY.

•**CARTER, Mr. Alan John, FCA** *1968;* (Tax Fac), Alan J. Carter, Goddards, 46 Maltese Road, CHELMSFORD, CM1 2PA.

•**CARTER, Mr. Alan Leslie, BA FCA** *1984;* Leonard Jones & Co, 1 Printing House Yard, LONDON, E2 7PR.

CARTER, Mr. Alan Samuel, FCA *1964;* 74 Gleneagles Drive, Ainsdale, SOUTHPORT, PR8 3TH.

CARTER, Miss. Alison Jane, MSc BA FCA *1999;* with KPMG LLP, St. James's Square, MANCHESTER, M2 6DS.

CARTER, Mrs. Amanda Patricia, BSc FCA *1993;* Tata Motors, 4th Floor IARC Building, University of Warwick, Gibbet Hill Road, COVENTRY, CV4 7AL.

CARTER, Mr. Andrew Charles, BSc ACA *1999;* 1 Clifton Heights, Horsham Road, DORKING, RH4 2DS.

•**CARTER, Mr. Andrew Jeremy, BSc FCA** *1975;* Carter A.J. & Co, 22B High Street, WITNEY, OX28 6RB.

CARTER, Mr. Andrew Lawrence Kennedy, FCA *1969;* Brambles Stonham Road Mickfield, STOWMARKET, SUFFOLK, IP14 5LR. (Life Member)

•**CARTER, Mr. Andrew Paul, BA ACA** *2004;* ABT Services (UK) Limited, 50 Haygate Road, Wellington, TELFORD, SHROPSHIRE, TF1 1QN.

CARTER, Mr. Andrew William, BSc FCA *1974;* 5 Copper Wood, Cuddington, NORTHWICH, CHESHIRE, CW8 2UN.

CARTER, Mrs. Angela Joy, BSc ACA *1983;* Dherai Ramro, High Street, Naseby, NORTHAMPTON, NN6 6DD.

CARTER, Mrs. Anna Louise, ACA *2009;* 45 Ael-y-Bryn, Llanedeyrn, CARDIFF, CF23 9LG.

CARTER, Miss. Anne Elizabeth, BEng ACA *1992;* Grant Thornton Enterprise House, 115 Edmund Street, BIRMINGHAM, B3 2HJ.

CARTER, Mrs. Anne Margaret, BSc(Hons) ACA *2004;* 48 Foxbury Drive, Chelsfield, ORPINGTON, BR6 6EL.

CARTER, Mr. Anthony George, BA ACA *1992;* Momentum Activating Demand Limited, Stanley Court, Earl Road, Stanley Green Trading Estate, Handforth, WILMSLOW CHESHIRE SK9 3RL.

CARTER, Mr. Anthony Howard, FCA *1951;* 6 Byefields, Kempsey, WORCESTER, WR5 3NN. (Life Member)

CARTER, Mr. Anthony James, FCA *1972;* La Ferme Des Bordes, 77160 CHENOISE, FRANCE.

•CARTER, Mr. Barry Keith, BA FCA *1989;* KPMG LLP, 15 Canada Square, LONDON, E14 5GL. See also KPMG Europe LLP

CARTER, Mr. Benjamin Jake, BSc FCA *1999;* 15 Blackthorn Road, WYMONDHAM, NORFOLK, NR18 0PY.

CARTER, Mrs. Bree Louisa, BA ACA *2009;* Adam Cottage, Coffinswell, NEWTON ABBOT, DEVON, TQ12 4SW.

•CARTER, Mr. Brian, FCA *1975;* (Tax Fac), Brian Carter & Co, River House, 6 Firs Path, LEIGHTON BUZZARD, BEDFORDSHIRE, LU7 3JG.

•CARTER, Mr. Brian Edward Michael, FCA *1962;* B.E.M.Carter, Russetts, Coach and Horses Lane, Dane Hill, HAYWARDS HEATH, RH17 7JF.

•CARTER, Mr. Brian Edwin, FCA *1963;* with Reeves & Co LLP, Third Floor, 24 Chiswell Street, LONDON, EC1Y 4YX.

•CARTER, Mrs. Caroline, BA FCA *1993;* Baker & Co, Arran House, 42 Gravel Hill, LUDLOW, SHROPSHIRE, SY8 1QR.

CARTER, Mrs. Catherine Anne, BA ACA *1990;* 201 Marlow Bottom, MARLOW, BUCKINGHAMSHIRE, SL7 3PL.

CARTER, Miss. Catherine Patricia, BA ACA *2010;* 71 Chilkwell Street, GLASTONBURY, SOMERSET, BA6 8DD.

CARTER, Mr. Charles Ralph Ambrose, BA ACA *1992;* Le Vista Rue de la Folie, Torteval, GUERNSEY, GY8 0PL.

CARTER, Mrs. Charlotte Rebecca, BSc ACA *2004;* 3 Shortfield Close, Balsall Common, COVENTRY, CV7 7UN.

CARTER, Mr. Christopher Douglas, ACA *2009;* 23 Ebony House, Buckfast Street, LONDON, E2 6GJ.

CARTER, Mr. Christopher James, BSc ACA *1993;* 17 Hall Farm Road, Duffield, BELPER, DE56 4FS.

CARTER, Mr. Christopher John, BSc ACA *2005;* with Deloitte & Touche, Deloitte & Touche House, Earlscourt Terrace, DUBLIN 2, COUNTY DUBLIN, IRELAND.

CARTER, Mr. Christopher Michael David, MSc BSc ACA *2007;* 4 Beverley Gardens, WORCESTER PARK, KT4 8AG.

CARTER, Mr. Christopher Rufus, FCA *1973;* Drunkard's Ease, Dumbleton Lane, Eardiston, TENBURY WELLS, WR15 8JR.

•CARTER, Mrs. Claire Elizabeth, BSc FCA *1984;* CPL Audit Limited, 110 Viglen House, Alperton Lane, WEMBLEY, MIDDLESEX, HA0 1HD. See also GKP Partnership Ltd

CARTER, Mr. Colin Stanley, FCA *1957;* Flat 1 Budock Veane Flats, La Route Orange, St. Brelade, JERSEY, JE3 8GP.

CARTER, Mr. David, BA ACA *2007;* with Deloitte LLP, Stonecutter Court, 1 Stonecutter Street, LONDON, EC4A 4TR.

CARTER, Mr. David Alistair, BA FCA *1978;* Solihull School, 793 Warwick Road, SOLIHULL, WEST MIDLANDS, B91 3JJ.

CARTER, Mr. David Charles, BA(Hons) ACA *2002;* 37 Sandcross Lane, REIGATE, SURREY, RH2 8EX.

CARTER, Mr. David Charles, FCA *1978;* Lynhayes, Sticklepath, OKEHAMPTON, EX20 2NT.

CARTER, Mr. David Graham, BA ACA *1993;* Aon Corporation Briarcliff House, Kingsmead, FARNBOROUGH, GU14 7TE.

•CARTER, Mr. David Reeves, BSc ACA *1981;* (Tax Fac), D.R. Carter, Park Farm, Mileham, KING'S LYNN, PE32 2RD.

CARTER, Mr. David Robert, BA FCA *1977;* The Glade Brook Road, Sandhills Wormley, GODALMING, GU8 5UR.

CARTER, Mr. David Roger, BSc FCA *1973;* Flat 2, 65 Ladbroke Grove, LONDON, W11 2PD. (Life Member)

CARTER, Mr. David William, BSc FCA *1990;* 41 Wolfreton Garth, Kirk Ella, HULL, HU10 7AB.

CARTER, Mr. Derek Arnold, FCA *1949;* Room 28, Menwinnion Country House Residential Home, Lamorna Valley, PENZANCE, CORNWALL, TR19 6BJ. (Life Member)

CARTER, Mr. Derek Roy, FCA *1971;* 11 Maxstoke Lane, Coleshill, BIRMINGHAM, B46 3BA. (Life Member)

•CARTER, Mrs. Diane Mary, FCA *1980;* Tsavo Accounts Limited, Amador, Tower Road, St. Helier, JERSEY, JE2 3HR.

CARTER, Mr. Dominic Alan, BA(Hons) ACA *2002;* (Tax Fac), with Grant Thornton UK LLP, 4 Hardman Square, Spinningfields, MANCHESTER, M3 3EB.

CARTER, Mr. Dominic Julian Louis Toh, ACA *2008;* K P M G Salisbury Square House, 8 Salisbury Square, LONDON, EC4Y 8BB.

CARTER, Mr. Edgar George Shelton, BSc ACA *1992;* with KPMG LLP, 15 Canada Square, LONDON, E14 5GL.

CARTER, Mr. Edward George, BCom FCA *1972;* Sherwood Oaks, Broad Lane, Tanworth-in-Arden, SOLIHULL, B94 5HR.

CARTER, Mrs. Fiona, BSc ACA *1996;* 4 Miles's Buildings, George Street, BATH, BA1 2QS.

CARTER, Mrs. Frances Susan, BA(Hons) ACA *2003;* 3a Randolph Road, EPSOM, SURREY, KT17 4LA.

CARTER, Mr. Francis John, FCA *1958;* Lawnswood, 11 Whitburn Close, KIDDERMINSTER, WORCESTERSHIRE, DY11 6BH. (Life Member)

•CARTER, Mr. Frank Joseph Patrick, BA FCA CF *1989;* KPMG LLP, 15 Canada Square, LONDON, E14 5GL. See also KPMG Europe LLP

CARTER, Mrs. Gillian Elizabeth, ACA *2010;* 113 Pitt Crescent, LONDON, SW19 8HR.

CARTER, Ms. Gillian Mary, BSc ACA *1983;* Hanrahan Media, Unit 8, Grove Business Park, Atherstone on Stour, STRATFORD-UPON-AVON, WARWICKSHIRE CV37 8DX.

•CARTER, Mrs. Gillian Mary, MA ACA *1978;* (Tax Fac), Carter & Co, 7 Downs Road, Westbury-on-Trym, BRISTOL, BS9 3TX.

CARTER, Mr. Gordon Michael Charles, FCA *1964;* 106 Hogshill Lane, COBHAM, KT11 2AW.

•CARTER, Mr. Graham Nigel, FCA *1974;* The Wells Partnership The Old Rectory, Church Street, WEYBRIDGE, KT13 8DE.

•CARTER, Mr. Graham William Vincent, FCA *1971;* Graham Carter FCA, 20 Hardys Field, Kingsclere, NEWBURY, BERKSHIRE, RG20 5EU.

CARTER, Mr. Gregory Charles, FCA *1973;* 35 Warren Road, Gorleston, GREAT YARMOUTH, NR31 6JT.

CARTER, Miss. Hannah, BSc ACA *2005;* 16 Porthallow Close, ORPINGTON, KENT, BR6 9XU.

CARTER, Mrs. Helen, BA ACA *1994;* 30 Kewferry Road, NORTHWOOD, MIDDLESEX, HA6 2PB.

CARTER, Miss. Helen Anne, BA(Hons) ACA *2004;* 20 Montfort Road, ROMSEY, HAMPSHIRE, SO51 5SS.

CARTER, Ms. Helen Jane, MA ACA *1997;* Rathan, 84 Knowsley Road, Wilpshire, BLACKBURN, LANCASHIRE, BB1 9PN.

CARTER, Mrs. Helen Louise, BSc ACA *1997;* 8 Meadowfields, BLACKBURN, BB2 4JH.

•CARTER, Mr. Ian Alan, ACA *2002;* Gowers Limited, The Old School House, Bridge Road, Hunton Bridge, KINGS LANGLEY, HERTFORDSHIRE WD4 8SZ.

CARTER, Mr. Ian Oliver, MA ACA *1982;* The Global Fund to Fight AIDS Tuberculosis Malaria, Mevrouw Brantlaan 5, 5583 EA WAALRE, NETHERLANDS.

CARTER, Mr. James Marcus, BSc FCA *1973;* P.O. Box 97843, Petervale, JOHANNESBURG, GAUTENG, 2151, SOUTH AFRICA.

CARTER, Mr. James Sidney, FCA *1970;* James Carter Consulting Limited, 28 Lingarth Street, Remuera, AUCKLAND, NEW ZEALAND. (Life Member)

CARTER, Mr. Jamie, ACA *2010;* 10 Charlotte Close, BEXLEYHEATH, DA6 8JX.

CARTER, Miss. Jane, BSc(Hons) ACA *2004;* Merrill Lynch, 2 King Edward Street, LONDON, EC1A 1HQ.

CARTER, Miss. Jane Elizabeth, BSc ACA *1992;* 7 Marine Terrace, PENZANCE, CORNWALL, TR18 4DL.

CARTER, Mr. Jason Lee, BSc(Econ) ACA CTA *2001;* (Tax Fac), 42 Lordswood Close, Wootton, NORTHAMPTON, NN4 6BP.

CARTER, Mr. Jason Paul, BA ACA *1995;* 7 Lady Harewood Way, EPSOM, SURREY, KT19 7LE.

CARTER, Mr. Jeffery Archibald, FCA *1941;* 144 Derwen Fawr Road, Sketty, SWANSEA, SA2 8DP. (Life Member)

CARTER, Mrs. Jennifer Mary, BSc FCA *1997;* 17 Lakeside Grange, WEYBRIDGE, KT13 9ZE.

CARTER, Mr. Jeremy Bedell, BA FCA *1985;* with Capital Group, Business & Residential, west Wing, Buckstone Hall, Cliffe Drive, Rawdon LEEDS LS19 6LL.

CARTER, Mr. Jeremy Francis Fairlie, FCA *1965;* 76 Avenue de la Bourdonnais, 75007 PARIS, FRANCE. (Life Member)

•CARTER, Mrs. Joanne, BA FCA *1991;* with KPMG LLP, One Snowhill, Snow Hill Queensway, BIRMINGHAM, B4 6GN.

CARTER, Miss. Joanne Lauren, ACA *2010;* 20 Mount Road, Marsden, HUDDERSFIELD, HD7 6HP.

•CARTER, Mr. John Anthony, FCA *1965;* (Tax Fac), Raymond Carter & Co, 1b Haling Road, SOUTH CROYDON, Surrey, CR2 6HS.

CARTER, Mr. John Richard, FCA *1959;* Woodrow House, Holt Road, Cawston, NORWICH, NR10 4HS. (Life Member)

CARTER, Mr. John Richard, FCA MAE TEP *1972;* (Tax Fac), 17 Clan House, Sydney Road, BATH, BA2 6NS.

CARTER, Mr. John Robert Ernest, FCA *1963;* 20 Eyebrook Close, LOUGHBOROUGH, LEICESTERSHIRE, LE11 4PS. (Life Member)

CARTER, Mr. Jonathan David, BSc ACA *1993;* 77B Indian Harbor Drive, GREENWICH, CT 06830, UNITED STATES.

CARTER, Mr. Jonathan Patrick, BA ACA *1995;* 35 Vallis Way, Ealing, LONDON, W13 0DD.

CARTER, Mr. Jonathan Philip, BSc ACA *1992;* Upper Beanacre Barn, Beanacre, MELKSHAM, WILTSHIRE, SN12 7PY.

CARTER, Mr. Kerry, FCA *1972;* Amador, Tower Road, St. Helier, JERSEY, JE2 3HR. (Life Member)

CARTER, Mr. Kevin Joseph, FCA *1973;* 58 Sheldon Avenue, Standish, WIGAN, WN6 0LW.

CARTER, Mrs. Lisa Marie, ACA *1995;* Unit 2B, Swan Lane Business Park, Exning, NEWMARKET, CB8 7FN.

CARTER, Miss. Lucy Helen, ACA *2010;* W K Finn-Kelcey Stourside Place, 35-41 Station Road, ASHFORD, TN23 1PP.

CARTER, Miss. Lynn, BA ACA *2001;* 42 Greencourt Road, ORPINGTON, KENT, BR5 1QW.

CARTER, Miss. Maria Cristina, BSc ACA *2004;* 10 Cranmer Road, CROYDON, CR0 1SR.

CARTER, Ms. Marion Joan, LLB ACA *1989;* 16 Tavistock Road, WATFORD, WD24 4HL.

CARTER, Mr. Mark Aaran, BA ACA *1991;* Baker & McKenzie, 100 New Bridge Street, LONDON, EC4V 6JA.

CARTER, Mr. Mark Andrew, BSc ACA *1986;* Personnel Selection Pearl Assurance House, 28 High Street, WOKING, GU21 6BW.

CARTER, Mr. Mark Lawrence, FCA *1971;* 17 Rosehill Avenue, Whittington, OSWESTRY, SHROPSHIRE, SY11 4DX.

CARTER, Mr. Mark Patrick Antony, FCA *1973;* 48 Rectory Road, West Bridgford, NOTTINGHAM, NG2 6BG.

CARTER, Mr. Mark Robert, ACA *1997;* Quayside House, Canal Wharf, Holbeck, LEEDS, LS11 5PU.

•CARTER, Mr. Martin Arthur Charles, BSc ACA *1989;* (Tax Fac), Morris Palmer Limited, Barttelot Court, Barttelot Road, HORSHAM, WEST SUSSEX, RH12 1DQ. See also Jackson Green Carter Limited

•CARTER, Mr. Matthew John, BSc FCA *1992;* Ernst & Young LLP, 1 Colmore Square, BIRMINGHAM, B4 6HQ. See also Ernst & Young Europe LLP

•①CARTER, Mr. Melvyn Julian, BA FCA *1978;* Carter Backer Winter LLP, Enterprise House, 21 Buckle Street, LONDON, E1 8NN.

CARTER, Mr. Michael Alfred Frederick, FCA *1966;* 52 Golden Avenue, East Preston, LITTLEHAMPTON, BN16 1QX. (Life Member)

CARTER, Mr. Michael Gareth, BSc ACA *1990;* 2A Hampstead Hill Gardens, LONDON, NW3 2PL.

CARTER, Mr. Michael Shaun, BA ACA *1978;* 50 Margravine Gardens, LONDON, W6 8RJ.

CARTER, Mr. Miles Everitt, FCA *1975;* 30 Brook Street, Glemsford, SUDBURY, SUFFOLK, CO10 7PL.

CARTER, Miss. Miranda Louise, BA ACA *1994;* Independent Regulator of NHS Foundation Trusts, 4 Matthew Parker Street, LONDON, SW1H 9NL.

•CARTER, Mr. Neal David, ACA *1994;* Hillier Hopkins LLP, 2a Alton House Office Park, Gatehouse Way, AYLESBURY, BUCKINGHAMSHIRE, HP19 8YF. See also Neal Carter Limited

CARTER, Mr. Neil Allen, BA FCA *1992;* Brook House Station Road, North Cave, BROUGH, NORTH HUMBERSIDE, HU15 2LA.

CARTER, Mr. Neil Richard, BA ACA *1994;* 54 Chart Lane, REIGATE, SURREY, RH2 7DZ.

CARTER, Mr. Nicholas, BA(Hons) FCA *1968;* Auldearn, The Old Walled Garden, Compton Verney, WARWICK, CV35 9HJ.

CARTER, Mr. Nicholas Charles, BSc FCA *1990;* Antalis International S.A.S., 122 Rue Edouard Vaillant, 92300 LEVALLOIS-PERRET, FRANCE.

CARTER, Mr. Nicholas John, BA ACA *1993;* 120 Falling Water Drive, BRANDON, FL 33511, UNITED STATES.

CARTER, Mr. Nicholas Michael, BA ACA *1992;* Gondola Group Limited, 5th Floor 2 Balcombe Street, LONDON, NW1 6NW.

CARTER, Mr. Nicholas Richard Andrew, MSc ARCS ACA *2010;* Flat 6, Canonbury Heights West, 12 Dove Road, LONDON, N1 3GB.

CARTER, Mr. Nigel Alexander, BSc ACA MBCS MCT *1992;* 3 Port Laing Wynd, North Queensferry, INVERKEITHING, FIFE, KY11 1EW.

CARTER, Mr. Nigel John, FCA *1977;* Millets Farm, Garfond, ABINGDON, OX13 5PD.

CARTER, Mrs. Olga, BSc ACA MAAT *2011;* 20 Bridge View, Oundle, PETERBOROUGH, PE8 4DT.

CARTER, Mr. Patrick James, LLB FCA *1998;* Charteris Plc, 39-40 Bartholomew Close, LONDON, EC1A 7JN.

CARTER, Mr. Paul Anthony, BA ACA *1998;* Old School Cottage, School Lane, Medmenham, MARLOW, BUCKINGHAMSHIRE, SL7 2HJ.

•CARTER, Mr. Paul Edward, FCA FCCA *1982;* Stephenson Smart, 22-26 King Street, KING'S LYNN, NORFOLK, PE30 1HJ.

CARTER, Mr. Paul Mark, FCA *1971;* Castle Bernard, BANDON, COUNTY CORK, IRELAND.

CARTER, Mr. Paul Michael, BSc ACA *2003;* 37 Sunnybank Road, SUTTON COLDFIELD, B73 5RJ.

CARTER, Mr. Paul Townsend, FCA *1970;* 11 High Beeches, GERRARDS CROSS, BUCKINGHAMSHIRE, SL9 7HU.

CARTER, Mrs. Paula, BA(Hons) ACA *2003;* 37 Briarwood Way, Wollaston, WELLINGBOROUGH, NORTHAMPTONSHIRE, NN29 7QR.

CARTER, Mr. Peter, BA ACA *2004;* 55 Manor Way, GUILDFORD, SURREY, GU2 7RR.

CARTER, Mr. Peter James, MBA BA ACA *1995;* Cedar Lea, Hall Lane, Little Brington, NORTHAMPTON, NN7 4HX.

CARTER, Mr. Philip Arthur, BSc FCA *1976;* 3 Churn Hill, North Cerney, CIRENCESTER, GLOUCESTERSHIRE, GL7 7DN.

CARTER, Mr. Philip James Alexander, FCA *1971;* Old School House, Hankerton, MALMESBURY, WILTSHIRE, SN16 9LF.

CARTER, Mr. Philip Stephen, BSc ACA *1986;* St Nicholas House, St Nicholas Road, SUTTON, SM1 1EL.

CARTER, Mrs. Rachael Suzanne, ACA MAAT *2001;* 15 Blackthorn Road, WYMONDHAM, NORFOLK, NR18 0PY.

CARTER, Mr. Rex, FCA *1957;* 16 Cresta Drive, Bottesford, SCUNTHORPE, DN17 2SD. (Life Member)

CARTER, Mr. Richard David, BA FCA *1980;* PO Box 15243, Langata, NAIROBI, 00509, KENYA.

CARTER, Mr. Richard Graham, FCA *1971;* Mill House, Brenchley Road, Brenchley, TONBRIDGE, TN12 7NS.

CARTER, Mr. Richard Ian Gordon, BSc ACA *1994;* 18 Furzefield Road, LONDON, SE3 8TX.

CARTER, Mr. Richard Leigh, BEng BCom ACA *2003;* 3 Shortfield Close, Balsall Common, COVENTRY, CV7 7UN.

CARTER, Mr. Richard Matthew, BSc ACA *1997;* (Tax Fac), Isoft, Daventry Road, BANBURY, OXFORDSHIRE, OX16 3JT.

CARTER, Mr. Robert Frederick, BA FCA *1978;* Cornerways, 45 Wyedale Crescent, BAKEWELL, DERBYSHIRE, DE45 1BE.

•CARTER, Mr. Robert Jeffrey, BA(Econ) ACA *2000;* Pumphrey Dasalo Limited, 1 The Green, RICHMOND, SURREY, TW9 1PL.

CARTER, Mr. Robert John, BSc ACA *1982;* 40 Guildford Drive, Chandler's Ford, EASTLEIGH, SO53 3PT.

CARTER, Mr. Robert John, FCA *1973;* Gayton End, Gayton Farm Road, Heswall, WIRRAL, CH60 8NN.

CARTER, Mr. Roger Michael George, MA FCA *1963;* 2A Elcho Road, Bowdon, ALTRINCHAM, WA14 2TH. (Life Member)

CARTER, Mr. Ronald Gordon, FCA *1971;* Lansdowne, 32 Chiltley Way, LIPHOOK, HAMPSHIRE, GU30 7HQ.

CARTER, Miss. Rosalind Mary, FCA *1974;* 27 Alcester Drive, SUTTON COLDFIELD, WEST MIDLANDS, B73 6PZ.

CARTER, Miss. Rosamund Jane, BSc ACA *2003;* Flat 75 Goulden House, Bullen Street, LONDON, SW11 3HQ.

CARTER, Mrs. Sandra, BSc ACA *1992;* 280 Rosedale Road, RD2, UPPER MOUTERE 7175, NEW ZEALAND.

CARTER, Miss. Sarah Jane, BA ACA *2002;* 3 Fir Tree Lane, Claydon, IPSWICH, IP6 0RB.

CARTER, Mrs. Sarah Jane, BSc ACA *1998;* 7 Lady Harewood Way, EPSOM, SURREY, KT19 7LE.

CARTER, Mrs. Sarah Jayne, LLB ACA *2001;* 10 Munnion Road, Ardingly, HAYWARDS HEATH, WEST SUSSEX, RH17 6RP.

CARTER, Mr. Simon Geofferey, MA ACA *2001;* The British Land Co Plc, York House, 45 Seymour Street, LONDON, W1H 7LX.

CARTER, Mr. Simon John, BSc FCA CF *1993;* Barton Willmore, Beansheaf Farm House, Bourne Close, Calcot, READING, RG31 7BW.

CARTER, Mr. Simon Matthew, BA(Hons) ACA *2003;* 26 Medina Close, WOKINGHAM, BERKSHIRE, RG41 3TZ.
•**CARTER, Mr. Stephen, FCA** *1985;* Baker Tilly Tax & Advisory Services LLP, 3 Hardman Street, MANCHESTER, M3 3HF.
CARTER, Mr. Stephen Barham, BSc FCA *1978;* Hogwood Farmhouse, The Forestry Road, Plaistow, BILLINGSHURST, RH14 0PA.
CARTER, Mr. Stephen David, BSc ACA *2006;* 20 Porthill Road, Benson, WALLINGFORD, OXFORDSHIRE, OX10 6NF.
CARTER, Mr. Stewart Graham, BSc ACA *1994;* 34 Court Oak Road, Harborne, BIRMINGHAM, B17 9TJ.
CARTER, Mrs. Susan, BA ACA *1978;* 38 Langridge Street, MIDDLE PARK, VIC 3206, AUSTRALIA.
•**CARTER, Mrs. Susan Ann, FCA DChA** *1979;* with Moore Stephens, 30 Gay Street, BATH, BA1 2PA.
CARTER, Mrs. Susanne, BA ACA *1993;* The Royal Bank of Scotland, House F 1st Floor, Gogarburn, EDINBURGH, EH12 1HQ.
CARTER, Mr. Terence Charles, FCA *1965;* 39 Magdalen Road, Wandsworth Common, LONDON, SW18 3ND.
CARTER, Mr. Thomas Richard James, ACA *2007;* Greenstede, West Hill, EAST GRINSTEAD, WEST SUSSEX, RH19 4EP.
CARTER, Mr. Timothy William, FCA *1976;* 20 Lakeside, ENFIELD, MIDDLESEX, EN2 7NN.
CARTER, Mrs. Vivienne Joy, BA FCA *1992;* 17 Hall Farm Road, Duffield, BELPER, DE56 4FS.
•**CARTER, Mr. Walter Jonathan, FCA** *1977;* Jonathan Carter Ltd, 50-52 Aire Street, GOOLE, NORTH HUMBERSIDE, DN14 5QE.
CARTER, Mr. William David Antony, MA FCA *1964;* 9 Shardeloes, Missenden Road, AMERSHAM, BUCKINGHAMSHIRE, HP7 0RL.
CARTER, Mr. William George Key, CBE FCA *1957;* The Old Rectory, Elmley Lovett, DROITWICH, WR9 0PS. (Life Member)
CARTER-CLOUT, Miss. Angharad, BA ACA *2004;* 34 Inman Road, LONDON, SW18 3BB.
CARTER-CLOUT, Mr. Anthony Michael, FCA *1974;* 41 Furze Lane, PURLEY, CR8 3EJ.
CARTER-CLOUT, Mr. Daniel Christopher, BA(Hons) ACA *2003;* 34 Inman Road, LONDON, SW18 3BB.
CARTER-FERRIS, Mr. Richard James, BSc ACA *1989;* Whitwell House, Whitwell-on-the-hill, YORK, YO60 7JJ.
CARTER-FERRIS, Mrs. Susan Elizabeth, BA ACA *1987;* Townsend Harrison Ltd, 13 Yorkersgate, MALTON, YO17 7AA.
•**CARTER PEGG, Mr. Hallam, FCA** *1964;* Wandle House Associates, Wandle House, 47 Wandle Road, CROYDON, SURREY, CR0 1DF.
•**CARTER-PEGG, Mr. Nicholas Hallam, BA FCA** *1990;* BDO LLP, 55 Baker Street, LONDON, W1U 7EU. See also BDO Stoy Hayward LLP
CARTER SHAW, Mrs. Henrietta Davidson Jane, BSc ACA *2007;* 13 Felsham Road, LONDON, SW15 1AX.
CARTER SHAW, Mr. Nicholas Peter, BA ACA *1999;* 13 Felsham Road, LONDON, SW15 1AX.
CARTER SHAW, Mr. Robertt, MA FCA *1967;* Oak Cottage, The Avenue, Bucklebury, READING, RG7 6NS. (Life Member)
CARTERS, Mrs. Janet Isabel, BSc FCA *1977;* 40 Church Lane, Barton Mills, BURY ST.EDMUNDS, IP28 6AY.
•**CARTHIGESAN, Mr. Shakthidharan, FCA** *1983;* 3 Tillingbourne Gardens, LONDON, N3 3JJ.
CARTHY, Mr. Daniel Mark, BSc ACA *2006;* 18 Darbys Way, TIPTON, WEST MIDLANDS, DY4 7NY.
CARTLAND, Mr. Howard John, FCA *1979;* 19 The Close, Olton, SOLIHULL, B92 8AP.
CARTLEDGE, Mr. Gethin Rhys, ACA *2008;* Apartment 182, 51 Sherborne Street, BIRMINGHAM, B16 8FP.
CARTLEDGE, Mr. Matthew James, BSc(Hons) ACA *2002;* Flat 45 Arnhem Wharf, 2 Arnhem Place, LONDON, E14 3RU.
CARTLEDGE, Mr. Matthew Liam, BSc ACA *2002;* 2 Devonshire Close, SHEFFIELD, S17 3NX.
CARTLEDGE, Mr. Roger, BSc FCA *1975;* 17 Buxton Old Road, Disley, STOCKPORT, CHESHIRE, SK12 2BB.
•**CARTLEDGE, Mrs. Sally Jane, ACA CTA** *1983;* Sully & Co, 18-22 Angel Crescent, BRIDGWATER, SOMERSET, TA6 3AL.
•**CARTLIDGE, Mr. John William, FCA** *1974;* Cartlidge & Co Ltd, 137 Laughton Road, Dinnington, SHEFFIELD, S25 2PP.
CARTLIDGE, Mrs. Natalie Lois, BA ACA *1999;* with PricewaterhouseCoopers LLP, One Kingsway, CARDIFF, CF10 3PW.
CARTLIDGE, Mr. Richard John, FCA *1970;* 44 St. Georges Avenue, Tunstall, STOKE-ON-TRENT, ST6 7JR.
CARTLIDGE, Mr. Stephen John Anthony, BSc(Hons) ACA *2004;* 16 Kestrel Close, Mulbarton, NORWICH, NR14 8BD.
•**CARTMAN, Mr. Ashley, BSc(Hons) FCA** *2000;* (Tax Fac), Juniper Accountancy, The Yews, Sandy Lane, Lower Failand, BRISTOL, BS8 3SH.
•**CARTMELL, Mr. Cameron Grant, BA ACA** *1997;* Ernst & Young LLP, 1 More London Place, LONDON, SE1 2AF. See also Ernst & Young Europe LLP
CARTMELL, Mr. Gordon, FCA *1965;* Brooklyn House, Stainton, PENRITH, CUMBRIA, CA11 0EP.
CARTMELL, Mrs. Helena Catherine, BA ACA *2005;* with PricewaterhouseCoopers LLP, 101 Barbirolli Square, Lower Mosley Street, MANCHESTER, M2 3PW.
CARTMELL, Mr. Jonathan Peter Michael, BSc ACA *1986;* 9b Oldfield, Honley, HOLMFIRTH, HD9 6RL.
CARTMELL, Mr. Peter Anthony, MA FCA *1971;* 15 Longcroft Avenue, HARPENDEN, HERTFORDSHIRE, AL5 2RD.
•**CARTNER, Mrs. Ann Elizabeth, FCA** *1975;* Cartner & Co., 47 Sandy Lodge Way, NORTHWOOD, HA6 2AR.
CARTON, Mr. Mark Liam, BBLS ACA *2000;* 2 Ashley Gardens, Borris Road, PORTLAOISE, COUNTY LAOIS, IRELAND.
CARTON, Mr. Paul Anthony, FCA *1972;* 21 Richmond Way, Fetcham, LEATHERHEAD, KT22 9NP.
CARTON, Mr. Richard Paul, FCA *1972;* LUCN, RTS De Mauvverney 28, 1196, GLAND, SWITZERLAND.
CARTWRIGHT, Mr. Alan John, BA ACA *1984;* Interdean Limited, 15 Central Way, Park Royal, LONDON, NW10 7XW.
CARTWRIGHT, Mr. Andrew Mark, BA(Hons) ACA *2001;* 41 Quinton Close Hatton Park, WARWICK, CV35 7TN.
CARTWRIGHT, Mr. Anthony, FCA *1969;* Walton View, 45 Beecher Street, HALESOWEN, B63 2DP.
•**CARTWRIGHT, Mr. Anthony Robert John, FCA** *1963;* (Tax Fac), Anthony R.J. Cartwright, 16 Taleworth Park, ASHTEAD, SURREY, KT21 2NH. See also BSS Associates Limited
CARTWRIGHT, Mr. Christopher Egerton, FCA *1969;* Bellmans Green, Prettymans Lane, EDENBRIDGE, KENT, TN8 6LU.
CARTWRIGHT, Mr. Christopher Johnathan, BA ACA *1989;* Honeycombe Leaze Farm, Honeycombe Leaze, CIRENCESTER, GLOUCESTERSHIRE, GL7 5TA.
CARTWRIGHT, Mrs. Cielo Bicol, BSc ACA *1992;* 47 Grove Lane, Headingley, LEEDS, LS6 4EQ.
CARTWRIGHT, Mr. Clifford Keith, BA FCA *1988;* 42 Blakeman Way, LICHFIELD, STAFFORDSHIRE, WS13 8FH.
CARTWRIGHT, Mr. Clive Emile Gustav, FCA *1970;* 6 Lyrical Way, Gadesbridge Park, HEMEL HEMPSTEAD, HERTFORDSHIRE, HP1 3HZ.
•**CARTWRIGHT, Mr. David William, BSc FCA** *1976;* The Hedges, The Hedges Flacks Green, Terling, CHELMSFORD, CM3 2QS.
CARTWRIGHT, Mrs. Diane Elisabeth, FCA *1976;* North House, Thornton le Beans, NORTHALLERTON, NORTH YORKSHIRE, DL6 3SP.
CARTWRIGHT, Mr. Gordon Henry, FCA *1949;* 70 Longdown Lane North, EPSOM, KT17 3JG. (Life Member)
•**CARTWRIGHT, Mr. Graham Alan, BA FCA** *1976;* (Tax Fac), Chantrey Vellacott DFK LLP, 73-75 High Street, STEVENAGE, HERTFORDSHIRE, SG1 3HR.
CARTWRIGHT, Mr. Grant, BSc ACA CTA *2004;* JC Bamford Excavators Limited, Lakeside Works, Denstone Road, Rocester, UTTOXETER, STAFFORDSHIRE ST14 5JP.
•**CARTWRIGHT, Mr. Hugh Walter Matheson, FCA** *1969;* (Tax Fac), H.W.M. Cartwright LTD, 22 Shrewsbury Mews, Chepstow Road, LONDON, W2 5PN.
•**CARTWRIGHT, Mr. Ian Crossley, BCom FCA** *1975;* (Tax Fac), Hanby & Co, 209 High Street, NORTHALLERTON, DL7 8LW.
•**CARTWRIGHT, Mr. Ian Keith, FCA** *1966;* The Linhay, Netherton, Farway, COLYTON, DEVON, EX24 6EB.
CARTWRIGHT, Mrs. Jacqueline Anne, BA ACA *1985;* 53 Eynsham Road, Botley, OXFORD, OX2 9BS.
CARTWRIGHT, Mr. James Alexander, BA(Hons) ACA *2003;* Flat 5/A River View Heights, 27 Bermondsey Wall West, LONDON, SE16 4TN.
CARTWRIGHT, Miss. Janet Ann Florence, FCA *1960;* Shealing, Station Rd, Bramley, GUILDFORD, GU5 0AY. (Life Member)
CARTWRIGHT, Mr. John Ernest Charles, BA FCA *1964;* 6 Trewartha Terrace, PENZANCE, TR18 2HE. (Life Member)
CARTWRIGHT, Mr. John Martin, FCA *1953;* 1 Cooters Hill Barns, Cooters End Lane, HARPENDEN, HERTFORDSHIRE, AL5 3NR. (Life Member)
CARTWRIGHT, Mr. John Martyn, FCA *1962;* 10 Stubbs End Close, AMERSHAM, HP6 6EW.
CARTWRIGHT, Mr. Jonathan Harry, BSc FCA *1980;* Rectory Meadow, Hawthorn Place, Penn, HIGH WYCOMBE, BUCKINGHAMSHIRE, HP10 8EH.
•**CARTWRIGHT, Mr. Lee, LLB ACA** *1999;* Mazars LLP, 45 Church Street, BIRMINGHAM, B3 2RT.
CARTWRIGHT, Mr. Martin Andrew, FCA *1974;* 71 Storey's Way, CAMBRIDGE, CB3 0DR.
CARTWRIGHT, Mr. Michael, BSocSc ACA *1999;* 1 Nourse Close, CHELTENHAM, GLOUCESTERSHIRE, GL53 0NQ.
CARTWRIGHT, Mr. Michael Francis, FCA *1965;* The Spinney, Hill Brow Road, Hill Brow, LISS, GU33 7PS. (Life Member)
CARTWRIGHT, Mr. Michael John, BA FCA *1981;* Orchestra Group Ltd, Walk Mills, Kingswood, WOTTON-UNDER-EDGE, GLOUCESTERSHIRE, GL12 8JT.
CARTWRIGHT, Mr. Neil Richard, BA ACA *1994;* 129 Seven Star Road, SOLIHULL, WEST MIDLANDS, B91 2BN.
•**CARTWRIGHT, Mr. Nicholas John, BA ACA ATII** *1995;* (Tax Fac), Smith & Williamson Ltd, 25 Moorgate, LONDON, EC2R 6AY.
CARTWRIGHT, Miss. Pamela Ann, ACA *1992;* 121 Green Lanes, Wylde Green, SUTTON COLDFIELD, B73 5LT.
CARTWRIGHT, Mr. Paul, BSc ACA *2007;* 5 Pippin Grove, ROYSTON, HERTFORDSHIRE, SG8 5HP.
CARTWRIGHT, Mr. Paul Ian, BSc ACA *1987;* 11 Howitt Road, LONDON, NW3 4LT.
CARTWRIGHT, Mr. Paul Martin, MA FCA *1985;* 17 Hall Place Gardens, ST. ALBANS, HERTFORDSHIRE, AL1 3SB.
CARTWRIGHT, Mr. Peter Raymond, FCA *1967;* The Brook House, Himbleton, DROITWICH, WR9 7LQ. (Life Member)
CARTWRIGHT, Mr. Richard John, BA FCA *1980;* Devereux Chambers Queen Elizabeth Building, Temple, LONDON, EC4Y 9BS.
CARTWRIGHT, Mr. Robert Ian, FCA *1978;* Shanks Group plc, Dunedin House, Auckland Park, Mount Farm, MILTON KEYNES, BUCKINGHAMSHIRE MK1 1BU.
CARTWRIGHT, Mrs. Sarah Ann, BSc(Hons) ACA CTA *2000;* 292 Walsall Wood Road, WALSALL, WS9 8HH.
CARTWRIGHT, Mrs. Stacey Lee, BSc ACA *1988;* 34 Roedean Crescent, LONDON, SW15 5JU.
CARTWRIGHT, Mr. Stephen William, ACA *1981;* Walton Garden Buildings, The Old Great North Road, Sutton-on-Trent, NEWARK, NOTTINGHAMSHIRE, NG23 6QN.
•**CARTWRIGHT, Ms. Susan Margaret, BSc FCA** *1981;* Peter Bowers Optometrist, 63a High Street, STONE, STAFFORDSHIRE, ST15 8AD.
CARTWRIGHT, Mr. Thomas, MEng ACA *2002;* 9 De Burgh Park, BANSTEAD, SURREY, SM7 2PP.
CARTWRIGHT, Mr. Timothy John, ACA *2009;* 45 Stocking Way, LINCOLN, LN2 4FX.
CARTWRIGHT BAIN, Mr. Adrian Bryan, FCA FCILA *1989;* Nelson House, Vericlaim UK Nelson House, Park Road Timperley, ALTRINCHAM, CHESHIRE, WA14 5BZ.
•**CARTY, Mr. David, FCA** *1978;* (Tax Fac), David Carty & Co, 234 Manchester Road, WARRINGTON, WA1 3BD.
•**CARTY, Mr. Gary, BA FCA DChA** *1996;* Gibbons, Carleton House, 136 Gray Street, WORKINGTON, CUMBRIA, CA14 2LU. See also Gibbons & Company
•**CARTY, Mr. James, ACA FCCA MAAT** *2008;* Thomas & Young LLP, 240-244 Stratford Road, Shirley, SOLIHULL, WEST MIDLANDS, B90 3AE. See also Thomas & Young
CARTY, Mr. James Patrick, MA BSc FCA *1968;* 37 Abbotsmede Close, Strawberry Hill, TWICKENHAM, TW1 4RL. (Life Member)
CARTY, Mrs. Rachel Julia, BEng ACA *1990;* 1 Hyrst Grove, Heworth Green, YORK, YO31 7TD.
CARUANA, Mr. Anthony Constantine Carmel Joseph Emmanuel, FCA *1966;* 75 West Road, PETERHEAD, AB42 2AS. (Life Member)
•**CARUANA, Mr. Joseph Lewis, BSc ACA** *1988;* (Tax Fac), Deloitte Limited, PO Box 758, Merchant House, 22/24 John Mackintosh Square, GIBRALTAR, GIBRALTAR.
CARUANA, Mr. Paul Anthony, ACA BEng(Hons) *2008;* 61 Barrowell Green, LONDON, N21 3AS.
CARUANA, Mr. Saviour, BA ACA *1990;* Salvia, Triq L-Imdina, BALZAN, MALTA.
CARUS, Mr. Alexander Michael, FCA *1956;* 28 Windsor Road, CHORLEY, PR7 1LN. (Life Member)
CARUSO, Miss. Carmela, ACA *2010;* 179 Beatrice Street, SWINDON, SN2 1BD.
CARUTHERS-LITTLE, Mr. Robert John, BA ACA *1995;* New Light Hotels Ltd, 33 Eastfield Road Westbury-on-Trym, BRISTOL, BS9 4AE.
CARVALHO, Ms. Barbara Olivia, BSc ACA *2006;* Ernst & Young Llp, 1 More London Place, LONDON, SE1 2AF.
CARVEL, Mrs. Catherine Louise, ACA *2011;* 14 Matlock Avenue, Kenton, NEWCASTLE UPON TYNE, NE3 3GL.
CARVELEY, Mr. John Stanley, FCA *1971;* 328 Camp Road, ST. ALBANS, AL1 5PB.
CARVELL, Mr. Andrew Philip, BSc FRGS FCA *1992;* with IBM, 76 Upper Ground, South Bank, LONDON, SE1 9PZ.
CARVELL, Mr. Jeremy Charles Harold Finney, ACA *1981;* 35 Rusthall Avenue, LONDON, W4 1BW.
•**CARVELL, Mr. Paul, FCA** *1985;* (Tax Fac), Stewart Fletcher and Barrett, Manor Court Chambers, 126 Manor Court Road, NUNEATON, CV11 5HL. See also SFB Consultants Limited
CARVELL, Mr. Ronald Stanley, FCA *1955;* 36 Goldenacres, Springfield, CHELMSFORD, CM1 6YT. (Life Member)
•**CARVER, Mr. Andrew, BSc FCA** *1985;* Tearle & Carver, Chandos House, School Lane, BUCKINGHAM, MK18 1HD. See also Tearle & Carver Limited
CARVER, Mr. Andrew Kinnaird, FCA *1981;* 16 Hearne Road, LONDON, W4 3NJ. (Life Member)
CARVER, Mr. Bruce Kinnaird, BA FCA *1953;* 23 Shenden Way, SEVENOAKS, KENT, TN13 1SE. (Life Member)
CARVER, Mr. Clive Nathan, BSc FCA *1986;* FinnCap, 60 New Broad Street, LONDON, EC2M 1JJ.
•**CARVER, Mrs. Corinne Suzanne, BSc ACA** *1979;* (Tax Fac), Corinne S. Carver, Pippin Lodge, Church Road, Snitterfield, STRATFORD-UPON-AVON, CV37 0LF.
CARVER, Mr. James Jeremy Thomas, MA FCA *1972;* Mill House, Nayland, COLCHESTER, CO6 4HU. (Life Member)
CARVER, Mr. John Harding, FCA *1968;* Manor Farmhouse, Slawston, MARKET HARBOROUGH, LE16 7UF. (Life Member)
CARVER, Mr. John Philip, BSc ACA *2000;* 174 Windmill Lane, Kemble, CIRENCESTER, GLOUCESTERSHIRE, GL7 6AN.
CARVER, Mr. Jonathan Charles, MSc ACA *2004;* 299a Kingston Road, LONDON, SW20 8LB.
CARVER, Mrs. Margaret Sandra, FCA *1971;* 46 Sturges Road, WOKINGHAM, RG40 2HE.
CARVER, Mr. Michael James, BSc ACA *1979;* KPMG Phoomchai Audit Ltd, 48th Floor Empire Tower, 196 South Sathorn Road, BANGKOK 10120, THAILAND.
CARVER, Mr. Nicholas John, FCA *1971;* 47 East St. Helen Street, ABINGDON, OX14 5EE.
CARVER, Mr. Paul, ACA *2007;* Samil PricewaterhouseCoopers, 5th Floor LS Yongsan Tower, 191 Hangangno 2-Ga, Yongsan-Gu, SEOUL, 140-702 KOREA REPUBLIC OF.
CARVER, Mr. Peter Frederic Gunn, ACA *1981;* 23 Lavant Road, CHICHESTER, WEST SUSSEX, PO19 5RA.
CARVER, Mr. Philip David, FCA *1973;* 8 Wakes Close, Dunton Bassett, LUTTERWORTH, LEICESTERSHIRE, LE17 5LL.
CARVER, Mr. Richard Andrew, FCA *1974;* Plane Trees Farm, Coley Road, Lower Shelf, HALIFAX, WEST YORKSHIRE, HX3 7SA.
CARVER, Mr. Rowan Victor, BEng ACA *2000;* 15 Marmion Road, HENLEY-ON-THAMES, RG9 1DG.
CARVER, Mr. William James, BSc ACA *2002;* 36 Park Road, FARNHAM, SURREY, GU9 9QN.
CARVERHILL, Mr. John George, BSc ACA *1983;* 23 Argyle Drive, CHIPPENHAM, SN14 6RP.
CARVERHILL, Mrs. Susan Lynn, BA ACA *1983;* 23 Argyle Drive, CHIPPENHAM, SN14 6RP.
CARVETH, Mr. John Harris Alleyne, FCA *1947;* 4 Claire Court, 235 Lymington Road, Highcliffe, CHRISTCHURCH, DORSET, BH23 5DZ. (Life Member)
CARVILL, Mr. Mel Gerard, FCA CF *1985;* Generali Worldwide, PO Box 613, GUERNSEY, GY1 4PA.
CARVILLE, Mr. Colin Martin Oliver, BA ACA *1998;* Yew Tree Cottage, 11 Old Hill, Avening, TETBURY, GLOUCESTERSHIRE, GL8 8NR.
CARVILLE, Mr. David Gerard, BA ACA *1992;* SIHI Pumps (Asia)Pte Ltd, 25 International Business park, #01-02 German Centre, SINGAPORE 609916, SINGAPORE.
CARVILLE, Mrs. Dorinnia, LLB ACA *2003;* Northern Ireland Audit Office, 106 University Street, BELFAST, BT7 1EU.
CARVOSSO, Mr. Paul Buller, MA ACA *1979;* Royston Cottage, Chiltern Green, LUTON, LU2 9PW.

CARVOSSO, Mr. Tim, BSc ACA *2007;* Flat 2-02 The School House, Pages Walk, LONDON, SE1 4HG.

•CARY, Mr. David William, LLB FCA *1985;* (Tax Fac), Wilkins Kennedy, Anglo House, Bell Lane Office Village, Bell Lane, AMERSHAM, BUCKINGHAMSHIRE HP6 6FA.

CARY-ELWES, Mr. Charles Gervase Rundle, MA FCA *1979;* 122 Court Lane, Dulwich, LONDON, SE21 7EA.

CASBEN, Mr. Peter John, FCA *1963;* Freshfields, Milford Rd, Elstead, GODALMING, GU8 6HF.

•CASCIOLI, Mr. Michele, ACA *1978;* (Tax Fac), Austen & Co, 57 Upper Fant Road, MAIDSTONE, ME16 8BU.

CASDAGLI, Mr. Thomas Theodore, MSc ACA *2003;* 14 Barclay Road, LONDON, SW6 1EH.

•CASE, Mr. Brian Edward, BA FCA *1963;* Rimmer Case Partnership, Fir Tree House, Truemans Way, Hawarden, DEESIDE, CLWYD CH5 3LS.

•CASE, Mr. Edmund John, FCA *1972;* Teffant Magna, Salisbury Road, Tower Hill, HORSHAM, WEST SUSSEX, RH13 0AJ.

CASE, Mrs. Elizabeth, BSc(Hons) ACA *2003;* Sensient Colours UK Ltd, Oldmedow Road, Hardwick Industrial Est, KING'S LYNN, NORFOLK, PE30 4LA.

CASE, Miss. Emma Jane, ACA *2008;* Wagtails, West Woodlands, FROME, SOMERSET, BA11 5EP.

CASE, Mr. James Justin Godfray, LLB ACA *1994;* Baker Homeyard, Ingouville House, Ingouville Lane, St. Helier, JERSEY, JE2 4SG.

CASE, Mr. John Michael, BSc ACA *1993;* Argenta Syndicate Management Ltd, S O C Group, Fountain House, 130 Fenchurch Street, LONDON, EC3M 5DJ.

CASE, Mr. Nicholas Jocelyn, BSc FCA *1976;* Prama House, 267 Banbury Road, OXFORD, OX2 7HT.

CASE, Mr. Philip Lee Malim, FCA *1970;* Halls Farm, Silchester, READING, RG7 2NH. (Life Member)

CASE, Mr. Robert David, BSc ACA *1993;* 22b Worple Road, EPSOM, SURREY, KT18 5EF.

CASE, Mr. Robert Ian, BA ACA *2005;* with Randall & Payne LLP, 10 Wheatstone Court, Waterwells Business Park, Quedgeley, GLOUCESTER, GL2 2AQ.

•CASE, Mrs. Sarah, FCA DChA *1998;* Broomfield & Alexander Limited, Waters Lane Chambers, Water Lane, NEWPORT, GWENT, NP20 1LA. See also B & A Associates

CASE, Mr. Simon John, BA ACA *2003;* 29 Cross Way, HARPENDEN, HERTFORDSHIRE, AL5 4QU.

•CASE, Mr. Thomas Richard, BSc ACA *2003;* Case & Co, 20 Goodwood Way, Cepen Park South, CHIPPENHAM, WILTSHIRE, SN14 0SY.

CASEBY, Mr. Michael Ian, BA FCA *1983;* Bank Julius Baer - Guernsey Branch, PO Box 87, GUERNSEY, GY7 9RX.

•CASELDINE, Mr. David Charles, BA ACA *1998;* with PricewaterhouseCoopers, Benson House, 33 Wellington Street, LEEDS, LS1 4JP.

CASELDINE, Mrs. Honey Belinda, BSc ACA CTA *1995;* The Paddock, Lidgett Place, LEEDS, LS8 1HE.

CASELEY, Mrs. Claire Margaret, MSci ACA *2004;* 5 The Home Croft, Bramcote, NOTTINGHAM, NG9 3DQ.

CASELEY, Mr. John Paul, FCA *1976;* Landmark Management SAM, 17 Avenue de la Costa, B.P. 167, MC 98004 MONTE CARLO, MONACO.

CASELEY, Mr. Ronald, FCA *1962;* 9 Residence de L'Observatoire, 8 Rue Du Bel-Air, 92190 MEUDON, FRANCE. (Life Member)

CASELTON, Mr. Tom, FCA *1989;* 9 Crowtrees Lane, BRIGHOUSE, HD6 3LZ.

CASELY, Miss. Paula, MA(Hons) ACA *2003;* Tigh-Nan-Eun-Mara, Aberlady, LONGNIDDRY, EH32 0RD.

CASEY, Mr. Andrew, BSc ACA *2011;* Flat 5, 9 Clifton Park, Clifton, BRISTOL, BS8 3BU.

•CASEY, Mrs. Ann Elizabeth, MSc FCA *1981;* 4 St. Margarets Road, LONDON, E12 5DP.

CASEY, Miss. Caroline Mary, BA ACA *2007;* 34 Duntshill Road, LONDON, SW18 4QL.

CASEY, Mr. Charles, BA FCA *1975;* 136 Barnstaple Road, SOUTHEND-ON-SEA, SS1 3PW.

•CASEY, Mr. Christopher Michael, BA FCA *1981;* Bullpark Barn, Sopworth, CHIPPENHAM, WILTSHIRE, SN14 6PT.

CASEY, Mr. Darrel Austin, BSc ACA *1979;* Bayernstr. 27, D-91336 HEROLDSBACH, GERMANY.

CASEY, Mr. David William Pitt, MA FCA *1974;* 95 Bishops Mansions, Bishops Park Road, LONDON, SW6 6DY. (Life Member)

CASEY, Mrs. Elizabeth Ann Lesley, FCA *1986;* 1 Giffards Close, EAST GRINSTEAD, WEST SUSSEX, RH19 3YH.

CASEY, Mrs. Elspeth Jean Furmage, BSc ACA *1991;* 23 The Byeways, SURBITON, KT5 8HT.

CASEY, Miss. Frances Teresa, BSc ACA *1990;* UK I Partnerships, Royal Bank of Scotland Insurance, Business Projects, 3rd Floor, The Wharf, 1 Neville Street LEEDS LS1 4AZ.

CASEY, Mr. Gavin Frank, FCA *1969;* (Member of Council 2003 - 2005), 44 Eaton Terrace, LONDON, SW1W 8TY.

CASEY, Miss. Joanna-Marie, BSc(Hons) ACA *2009;* 4 Walton Close, LONDON, SW8 2UJ.

CASEY, Mr. John, FCA *1958;* Chenotrie, Noctorum Road, PRENTON, CH43 9WU. (Life Member)

•①CASEY, Mr. John Anthony Laurence, BA FCA MBA *1990;* J Casey & Co Ltd, Langstone Gate, Solent Road, HAVANT, HAMPSHIRE, PO9 1RL.

CASEY, Mr. John Christopher, BSc ACA *1981;* 9 The Cedars, Milford, GODALMING, SURREY, GU8 5DH.

CASEY, Mr. John Daniel, MSc BA ACA *1984;* 25 Craster Road, LONDON, SW2 2AT.

CASEY, Mr. John Trevor, BA FCA *1980;* 17 Tempest Road, Birstall, LEICESTER, LE4 3BD.

CASEY, Mrs. Julia Elizabeth, BEng ACA *2006;* 3 Semaphore 30 Stoke Road, COBHAM, SURREY, KT11 3BF.

CASEY, Mr. Kevin Lawrence, FCA *1974;* Apartado 679, Vale Do Loba, 8135-1034 ALMANCIL, PORTUGAL.

CASEY, Miss. Leigh Anne, MA MBA ACA FCIPD *1988;* Miller's Cottage, 23 Main Street, Sudborough, KETTERING, NORTHAMPTONSHIRE, NN14 3BX.

CASEY, Mrs. Melanie Jane, BA ACA *2007;* 64 Kingston Road, BRISTOL, BS3 1DP.

CASEY, Miss. Nia, MSc(Econ) BA(Hons) ACA *2011;* 41 Kings Road, Canton, CARDIFF, CF11 9DA.

CASEY, Mr. Nicholas Patrick Stephen, BSc ACA *1996;* 14 Maes Celyn, Northop, MOLD, FLINTSHIRE, CH7 6BA.

CASEY, Mr. Noel Gavin, BA ACA *2001;* 7 King's Bench Walk, Temple, LONDON, EC4Y 7DS.

CASEY, Mr. Patrick Joseph, BSc ACA *1993;* Sterigenics UK Ltd Cotes Park Lane, Somercotes, ALFRETON, DERBYSHIRE, DE55 4NJ.

CASEY, Mr. Paul Michael, ACA *2008;* 46 Lavister Avenue, MANCHESTER, M19 1RT.

CASEY, Mr. Peter Shigetoshi, ACA *2008;* 136 Barnstaple Road, Thorpe Bay, SOUTHEND-ON-SEA, ESSEX, SS1 3PW.

CASEY, Mr. Stephen, ACA *2007;* 7 Folkstone Close, CHIPPENHAM, WILTSHIRE, SN14 0XZ.

•CASEY, Mr. Stuart Norman, FCA *1979;* Caseys, Wild Acre, Old Green Lane, CAMBERLEY, SURREY, GU15 4LG.

CASEY, Ms. Victoria Anne, BA ACA *1995;* Carnagh East, Kiltoom, ATHLONE, COUNTY ROSCOMMON, IRELAND.

CASEY-MARTEN, Ms. Samantha Jane, BA ACA *1992;* 27 Shadwell Park Drive, LEEDS, LS17 8TT.

CASH, Mr. Peter Withiel Trevor, FCA *1962;* Berringer Pty Ltd, 11 Stirling Street, FOOTSCRAY, VIC 3011, AUSTRALIA.

•①CASH, Mr. Russell Stewart, BSc ACA *1992;* Baker Tilly Restructuring & Recovery LLP, 3 Hardman Street, MANCHESTER, M3 3HF. See also Baker Tilly Tax and Advisory Services LLP

CASH, Mr. Stephen Robert, MA ACA CTA *1986;* 17C Belsize Square, LONDON, NW3 4HT.

CASHIN, Mr. Peter James, FCA *1978;* 3 Grange Close, Denton, NORTHAMPTON, NN7 1EB.

CASHMAN, Mr. David Peter Charles, ACA *1989;* 6 Main Street, Thorpe Satchville, MELTON MOWBRAY, LEICESTERSHIRE, LE14 2DQ.

CASHMAN, Mr. James Timothy, BA FCA *1974;* 92 Northumberland Road, LEAMINGTON SPA, CV32 6HG. (Life Member)

CASHMAN, Mrs. Louise Suzanne, BA ACA *2000;* Boston Scientific Corporation, One Boston Scientific Place, NATICK, MA 01760, UNITED STATES.

CASHMAN, Mr. Michael Allan, FCA ACA CA(AUS) *2011;* (Tax Fac), 39 Milton Road, HARPENDEN, HERTFORDSHIRE, AL5 5LZ.

CASHMAN, Mr. Shaun, FCA *1964;* 71 Greybeaver Trail, SCARBOROUGH M1C 4N7, ON, CANADA. (Life Member)

CASHMAN, Mr. Simon Lee, BSc FCA *1989;* 635 Pine Point Drive, AKRON, OH 44333, UNITED STATES.

CASHMAN, Mr. Stuart, BSc ACA *1998;* 111 Bacon Street, NATICK, MA 01760, UNITED STATES.

•CASHMORE, Miss. Alison, BSc ACA *1997;* with PricewaterhouseCoopers LLP, The Atrium, 1 Harefield Road, UXBRIDGE, UB8 1EX.

CASHMORE, Mrs. Anita Mary, ACA *1989;* 13 Copthall Gardens, TWICKENHAM, TW1 4HH.

CASHMORE, Mr. Geoffrey Harold, FCA *1959;* Amelanchier, 2a Jasmine Road, Great Bridgeford, STAFFORD, ST18 9PT. (Life Member)

•CASHMORE, Mrs. Georgine Elizabeth, FCA *1951;* Mrs G.E.Cashmore, The Old Post Office, Edwalton, NOTTINGHAM, NG12 4AB.

CASHMORE, Mr. James Edward, BA FCA *1982;* The Hayloft, Cropwell Road, Radcliffe-on-Trent, NOTTINGHAM, NG12 2JJ.

•CASHMORE, Mr. Malcolm John, FCA *1974;* Cashmore & Co, Third Floor, The Robbins Building, Albert Street, RUGBY, CV21 2SD.

CASHMORE, Mr. Mark Daniel, mm ACA *2006;* Clement Keys, 39-40 Calthorpe Road, Edgbaston, BIRMINGHAM, B15 1TS.

CASHMORE, Mr. Richard, FCA *1960;* Meadow Rise, Squirrel Walk, Little Aston Pk, SUTTON COLDFIELD, B74 3AU. (Life Member)

CASHMORE, Mrs. Wendy Jane, BSc ACA *2001;* North Bristol NHS Trust, Southmead Hospital, Southmead Road, Westbury-On-Trym, BRISTOL, BS10 5NB.

CASIE CHETTY, Mr. Devindra Benedict Nilesh, MEng ACA *2002;* 23 Hunt Close, LONDON, W11 4JU.

•CASILLAS, Mrs. Terase Nora Anne, BSc ACA *1985;* (Tax Fac), T. Casillas & Co, 27 St Lawrence Drive, Eastcote, PINNER, HA5 2RL.

•CASIMO, Mrs. Julia, BSc(Hons) ACA *2004;* (Tax Fac), John Kerr, 369-375 Eaton Road, West Derby, LIVERPOOL, L12 2AH.

CASKEY, Mr. Neil Wilfred, BSc ACA *2005;* 14 Leighton Road, CHELTENHAM, GLOUCESTERSHIRE, GL52 6BD.

CASKEY, Mrs. Suzanne Clare, BSc ACA *2000;* Oakhurst, Canons Walk, Brasted, WESTERHAM, KENT, TN16 1NA.

CASLAKE, Mr. Philip, FCA *1954;* 220 Audley Court, Audley Road, SAFFRON WALDEN, CB11 3HX. (Life Member)

•CASLEY, Mr. Andrew John Lewis, BSc ACA *1991;* PricewaterhouseCoopers LLP, 1 Embankment Place, LONDON, WC2N 6RH. See also PricewaterhouseCoopers

CASLEY, Mrs. Lisa Cecilia, MA ACA *2000;* 89 Knatchbull Road, LONDON, SE5 9QU.

CASLIN, Mrs. Lesley Anne, MSc ACA *1989;* Po Box HM 337, HAMILTON HMBX, BERMUDA.

CASLING, Mrs. Kate, ACA *2008;* with Goldwyns (Bristol) Limited, 9 Portland Square, BRISTOL, BS2 8ST.

CASLING, Mr. Maurice George, TD FCA *1952;* 38 Oaklands, CIRENCESTER, GL7 1FA. (Life Member)

•CASLING, Mr. Richard Charles, FCA *1979;* London United Busways Ltd, Busways House, Wellington Road, TWICKENHAM, TW2 5NX.

•CASO, Mr. Nicholas John, BSc FCA *1984;* Riches & Company, 34 Anyards Road, COBHAM, SURREY, KT11 2LA.

CASON, Mrs. Melanie Anne, ACA *1993;* 4 Heron Gardens, Portishead, BRISTOL, BS20 7DH.

CASS, Miss. Gillian Barbara, BSc(Hons) ACA *2001;* with PricewaterhouseCoopers LLP, Hays Galleria, 1 Hays Lane, LONDON, SE1 2RD.

•CASS, Mr. Malcolm Leslie, FCA *1971;* 13 Arden Road, LONDON, N3 3AB.

CASS, Mrs. Marisa Elena, BSc ACA *1998;* with PricewaterhouseCoopers, One Kingsway, CARDIFF, CF10 3PW.

CASS, Mr. Michael Trevor, BA ACA *1985;* 29 Hillview Road, PINNER, MIDDLESEX, HA5 4PB.

CASS, Mr. Oliver James, MA(Hons) ACA *2003;* with Ernst & Young LLP, 1 More London Place, LONDON, SE1 2AF.

CASS, Mr. Peter Vernon Charles, PhD BSc ACA *1983;* 6 Dunstable Court, St Johns Park Blackheath, LONDON, SE3 7TN.

CASS, Mr. Stephen Edward, BA ACA *1989;* Oak Tree Barn, Isfield, UCKFIELD, EAST SUSSEX, TN22 5XG.

CASS, Mr. Stewart Laurence, FCA *1985;* 15 Augustus Close, STANMORE, MIDDLESEX, HA7 4PT.

CASSAR, Mr. Dean Michael, BSc ACA *1994;* 74 Vowler Road, BASILDON, SS16 6AQ.

CASSAR, Mr. Edward Mark, BSc ACA *1996;* Lexis Nexis International, Halsbury House, LONDON, WC2A 1EL.

CASSAR, Mrs. Melanie Jane, ACA *1994;* Melanie Casser Training Ltd, 39 The Wickets, BURGESS HILL, WEST SUSSEX, RH15 8TG.

CASSAR, Mr. Stefan John, BA ACA *1990;* 22 Hazlewell Road, LONDON, SW15 6LH.

CASSEGRAIN, Mrs. Bettina, MA ACA *2005;* 117 rue Jean Baffier, 18000 BOURGES, FRANCE.

CASSELL, Mr. Bernard Philip, FCA *1974;* 35 Chaucer Crescent, MELBOURNE, VIC 3126, AUSTRALIA.

•CASSELL, Mr. George, FCA *1973;* George Cassell, Old Abbey Farm House, Quarr Lane, RYDE, ISLE OF WIGHT, PO33 4ER.

•CASSELL, Mr. Jamie Robert, BA(Hons) ACA *2000;* with BDO LLP, Prospect Place, 85 Great North Road, HATFIELD, HERTFORDSHIRE, AL9 5BS.

CASSELL, Miss. Penelope Jane, BA ACA *1989;* 43 Deronda Road, LONDON, SE24 9BQ.

•①CASSELL, Miss. Penelope Millicent, BSc FCA *1992;* PKF (UK) LLP, Farringdon Place, 20 Farringdon Road, LONDON, EC1M 3AP.

CASSELL-WARD, Mrs. Anna, LLM BA(Hons) ACA *2010;* 33 Clover Way, SYSTON, LEICESTERSHIRE, LE7 2BR.

CASSELLA, Mrs. Emma, BSc(Hons) ACA *2000;* 236 Shaw Place, PARK RIDGE, NJ 07656, UNITED STATES.

CASSELLS, Mr. Brian Adrian, FCA *1975;* The Dhoon, Quintons Road, East Bergholt, COLCHESTER, CO7 6RB.

CASSELLS, Mr. Eric Walter, MA MBA FCA *1985;* 8 Kingfisher Close, ABINGDON, OX14 5NP. (Life Member)

CASSELS, Mr. Geoffrey Herbert, FCA *1966;* 14 Trout Beck Crescent, AMENIA, NY 12501-5806, UNITED STATES. (Life Member)

CASSELS, Mr. Robert Allan Sylvester, FCA *1963;* 20 Catterick Road, Essenwood, DURBAN, 4001, SOUTH AFRICA. (Life Member)

•CASSERLY, Mr. Ian Vincent James, ACA *1994;* (Tax Fac), Casserly Accounting Limited, 16 Tilsworth Road, BEACONSFIELD, BUCKINGHAMSHIRE, HP9 1TR.

•CASSEY, Dr. Susanna Marie, PhD BSc ACA *2003;* with Moore and Smalley LLP, Priory Close, St Mary's Gate, LANCASTER, LA1 1XB.

CASSIANO-SILVA, Mr. Daniel Lawrence, MSc BSc ACA *2005;* Highland African Mining Company Limitada, Rua de Mukumbura N° 386 R/C, MAPUTO, MOZAMBIQUE.

CASSIDY, Miss. Carys Michelle, BA FCA *1994;* 45 Thurleigh Road, LONDON, SW12 8TZ.

CASSIDY, Mr. Christopher Jonathan Fitzgerald, FCA *1977;* Brimstone, Beauchamp Lane, Callow End, WORCESTER, WORCESTERSHIRE, WR2 4UQ.

CASSIDY, Miss. Ellen Patricia, BA ACA *1994;* Agility Logistics Ltd, Nielsen Road, GOOLE, NORTH HUMBERSIDE, DN14 6XH.

CASSIDY, Mr. Gerard, BA(Hons) ACA *2010;* 29 Parc Gilbertson, Gelligron, Pontardawe, SWANSEA, SA8 4PT.

CASSIDY, Mr. John, FCA *1957;* 6 Huntly Chase, WILMSLOW, CHESHIRE, SK9 2AU. (Life Member)

CASSIDY, Mr. John, MA(Cantab) ACA *2011;* Top Floor Flat, 107 Bolingbroke Grove, LONDON, SW11 1DA.

•CASSIDY, Mr. John Bernard, BSc FCA *1991;* (Tax Fac), PKF (UK) LLP, Farringdon Place, 20 Farringdon Road, LONDON, EC1M 3AP.

CASSIDY, Mr. Joseph Marcus, BA ACA *2002;* R S A Leadenhall Court, 1 Leadenhall Street, LONDON, EC3V 1PP.

CASSIDY, Ms. Margaret Mary, BSc FCA *1989;* with PricewaterhouseCoopers LLP, 1 Embankment Place, LONDON, WC2N 6RH.

CASSIDY, Mrs. Maria Bernadette, MA(Hons) ACA *2001;* Beere Cottage, 61 Station Road, Smallford, ST. ALBANS, AL4 0HB.

•CASSIDY, Mr. Mark Stephen, FCA *1997;* Day Smith & Hunter, Batchworth House, Batchworth Place, Church Street, RICKMANSWORTH, HERTFORDSHIRE WD3 1JE.

CASSIDY, Miss. Nuala Ann, ACA *2008;* Head Office, Matalan Retail Ltd, Gillibrands Road, SKELMERSDALE, WN8 9TB.

CASSIDY, Mr. Paul Bernard, MA ACA *1989;* 39 Fanshawe Street, Bengeo, HERTFORD, SG14 3AT.

•CASSIDY, Mr. Peter George, FCA *1962;* Cassidy & Co., 1 Grasmere Avenue, Locksbottom, ORPINGTON, KENT, BR6 8HD.

CASSIDY, Mr. Richard Joseph, BA(Hons) ACA *2001;* 78 Stormont Road, LONDON, SW11 5EL.

CASSIDY, Mrs. Shirley Jane, BCom FCA *1992;* 53 Roydon Road, Stanstead Abbotts, WARE, SG12 8HQ.

CASSINELLI, Mrs. Hadeel Teresa, BSc ACA *2006;* 2 Ball Road, Llanrumney, CARDIFF, CF3 4BY.

CASSON, Mr. Howard Stanley, ACA *1980;* 209 Garstang Road, Fulwood, PRESTON, LANCASHIRE, PR2 8JP.

•CASSON, Mr. Jeremy, BSc FCA *1980;* Deloitte LLP, Hill House, 1 Little New Street, LONDON, EC4A 3TR. See also Deloitte & Touche LLP

CASSON, Mr. John Fraser, MA FCA MBA *1976;* 44 Hurlingham Road, LONDON, SW6 3RQ.

CASSON, Dr. Peter David, PhD MSc BTech FCA *1983;* 7 Archery Lane, WINCHESTER, SO23 8GG.

•CASSON, Mr. Randal Lewis, ACA *1998;* PricewaterhouseCoopers LLP, Benson House, 33 Wellington Street, LEEDS, LS1 4JP. See also PricewaterhouseCoopers

CASSONI, Miss. Maria-Luisa, BSc ACA *1979;* 125, Providence Square, LONDON, SE1 2ED.

CASSOOBHAI, Mr. Munawarali, ACA *1984;* 61-5255 Guildwood Way, MISSISSAUGA L5R 4A8, ON, CANADA.

CASSTLES, Mr. John Wallace, TD FCA *1960;* 28 Highview, PINNER, HA5 3PA. (Life Member)

•CASSTLES, Mr. Julian David, BA(Hons) ACA CF *2001;* TMG Corporate Finance LLP, 16 Oxford Court, MANCHESTER, M2 3WQ.

CASSWELL, Mr. Joshua James, ACA *2009;* Flat 24, King Edward Mansions, 629 Fulham Road, LONDON, SW6 5UH.

•CAST, Miss. Joanne Elizabeth, BA ACA *2001;* JML Business Services Ltd, 25 Church Street, GODALMING, SURREY, GU7 1EL.

CAST, Mr. Robert Henry, BSc ACA CFA *1994;* Chelsworth, Paddocks Way, ASHTEAD, KT21 2QY.

•CASTAGNETTI, Mr. Antonio Giuliano, BA FCA *1988;* with RSM Tenon Audit Limited, 66 Chiltern Street, LONDON, W1U 4JT.

CASTAGNETTI, Mrs. Coral, BA ACA *1992;* 121 Hookfield, EPSOM, KT19 8JH.

CASTELINO, Mr. Colin Xavier, BSc ACA *1987;* 7 Lammas Park Gardens, LONDON, W5 5HZ.

CASTELINO, Mrs. Katherine Ruth Mansell, BA ACA *1991;* Reed Exhibitions Ltd, 28 The Quadrant, RICHMOND, TW9 1DN.

CASTELINO PRABHU, Mr. Adrian Peter, ACA *2009;* Yonnosaka Townhouse 009, Nakai 2-19-1, Shinjuku-Ku, TOKYO, 161-0035 JAPAN.

CASTELL, Mr. Andrew Sean, MA ACA *1995;* The Old Stables Tomich, Cannich, BEAULY, INVERNESS-SHIRE, IV4 7LY.

•CASTELL, Mr. Benjamin Arthur, BSc ACA *1995;* Ernst & Young LLP, 1 More London Place, LONDON, SE1 2AF. See also Ernst & Young Europe LLP

CASTELL, Mr. Geoffrey Ernest, FCA *1952;* 22 Bowhayes, BRIDPORT, DORSET, DT6 4EB. (Life Member)

CASTELL, Mrs. Rhona, BSc ACA *2006;* with Deloitte LLP, 2 New Street Square, LONDON, EC4A 3BZ.

CASTELL, Sir William Martin, LVO FCA *1974;* Barton Hatch, Stoneswood Road, Limpsfield Chart, OXTED, RH8 0QY. (Life Member)

CASTELL, Mr. William Thomas, BA ACA *2006;* 4 Park Road, RICHMOND, TW10 6NS.

CASTELLANO, Ms. Simonetta, BSc(Hons) ACA *2002;* PricewaterhouseCoopers, Largo Angelo Fochetti 29, 00154 ROME, ITALY.

CASTELLAS, Mr. Martin Lee, MEng ACA *1998;* with Ernst & Young, Ernst & Young Building, 8 Exhibition Street, MELBOURNE, VIC 3000, AUSTRALIA.

CASTENSKIOLD, Mr. Erik Holten, BA ACA *1993;* Mitchell &Butlers, 73-77 Euston Road, LONDON, NW1 2QS.

CASTERTON, Mr. James, BA ACA *2000;* 26 Shaldon Close, NOTTINGHAM, NG5 5EN.

•CASTERTON, Miss. Penelope Mary, BA ACA *1985;* The MGroup Partnership, Cranbrook House, 287/291 Banbury Road, OXFORD, OX2 7JQ. See also The MGroup Corporate Finance LLP

CASTIGLIONE, Mr. Andrew James Luigi, BSc ACA *1996;* 100 Gloucester Road, BARNET, HERTFORDSHIRE, EN5 1NA.

CASTILLO-ALONSO, Miss. Emmanuelle, BSc ACA *2001;* 18 Springfield Close, Croxley Green, RICKMANSWORTH, HERTFORDSHIRE, WD3 3HQ.

CASTLE, Mr. Allan Campbell Diarmid, FCA *1970;* Manor Farmhouse, West Grimstead, SALISBURY, SP5 3RE.

•CASTLE, Mrs. Arlene, BA ACA *1991;* 31 Redcrest Gardens, CAMBERLEY, SURREY, GU15 2DU. See also Arlene Castle

CASTLE, Mr. David Mark Bathurst, MA FCA *1958;* 10 Barton Close, CAMBRIDGE, CB3 9LQ. (Life Member)

CASTLE, Mr. Gary Stephen, FCA *1974;* 15 Orange Drive, JERICHO, NY 11753, UNITED STATES.

CASTLE, Mrs. Helen, BA(Hons) ACA *2001;* 16 Alameda Road, Ampthill, BEDFORD, MK45 2LA.

•CASTLE, Ms. Janice, BCom FCA *1976;* Machan Gillan, Manaccan, HELSTON, CORNWALL, TR12 6HG.

CASTLE, Mrs. Jeanne Margaret, BSc FCA *1977;* Beverley Minster PCC Parish Office, 38 Highgate, BEVERLEY, NORTH HUMBERSIDE, HU17 0DN.

CASTLE, Mr. Joseph, ACA *2011;* Falcon House, Queen's Road, St. Helier, JERSEY, JE2 3GR.

CASTLE, Mr. Kevin Gareth, BA FCA *1972;* 13 Ashcombe Street, Fulham, LONDON, SW6 3AW.

CASTLE, Mr. Leonard H, FCA *1960;* 1 Kings Close, BEACONSFIELD, BUCKINGHAMSHIRE, HP9 1ED. (Life Member)

CASTLE, Mr. Matthew, BSc ACA *2005;* 186 Trinity Road, LONDON, SW17 7HR.

•CASTLE, Mr. Mitchell, BSc FCA *1984;* Mitch Castle, 30 Radway Close, Church Hill North, REDDITCH, B98 8RZ.

•CASTLE, Mr. Paul Richard, BA FCA *1986;* (Tax Fac), Harrison Hill Castle & Co., Melbury House, 34 Southborough Road, Bickley, BROMLEY, BR1 2EB.

•CASTLE, Mr. Peter John, FCA *1974;* Castle Johns, 1 Warwick Row, LONDON, SW1E 5ER.

CASTLE, Mr. Richard Jeremy, BA(Hons) ACA *2001;* Costain Group of Companies Plc Costain House, 111 Westminster Bridge Road, LONDON, SE1 7UE.

CASTLE, Mrs. Sharne Louise, ACA *2009;* 21 Barnwell Lane, Cromford, MATLOCK, DERBYSHIRE, DE4 3QY.

CASTLE, Mr. Stephen Victor, BSc FCA *1985;* LV=, 4TH FLOOR, 69 PARK LANE, CROYDON, CR9 1BG.

CASTLE, Miss. Victoria, ACA *2007;* Prince of Wales House, Gatley Read Accountants, 18-19 Salmon Fields Business Village Royton, OLDHAM, OL2 6HT.

CASTLE, Mr. William Edward, BSc ACA *2000;* Flat 2, 94-96 Melbury Gardens, LONDON, SW20 0DN.

CASTLEDEN, Mr. John Lewis, FCA *1934;* Little Norsey, 22 Princess Anne Place, WESTVILLE, KWAZULU NATAL, SOUTH AFRICA. (Life Member)

•CASTLEDINE, Mr. Alan Douglas, FCA *1969;* (Tax Fac), Blythe Squires Wilson, 1-2 Vernon Street, DERBY, DE1 1FR.

CASTLEDINE, Mr. Edward, BSc ACA *2004;* with Deloitte LLP, Athene Place, 66 Shoe Lane, LONDON, EC4A 3BQ.

CASTLEDINE, Mr. Ivan William, FCA *1975;* 59 Douglas Road, Long Eaton, NOTTINGHAM, NG10 4BH. (Life Member)

CASTLEDINE, Mrs. Katharine Lindsey, BA ACA CTA *1998;* 3 Wilmerhatch Lane, EPSOM, SURREY, KT18 7EQ.

CASTLEDINE, Mrs. Lauren Emma Felicity, ACA *2009;* 2 The Gables, GUILDFORD, GU2 9JR.

CASTLEDINE, Mr. Lee, BSc ACA *1998;* with RSM Tenon Limited, International House, 66 Chiltern Street, LONDON, W1U 4JT.

CASTLEDINE, Mr. Stuart Ian, BSc FCA *1978;* South Lodge, Fairwater Road, CARDIFF, CF5 2LD.

CASTLEDINE, Mr. Tom James, ACA *2008;* 151 Sumatra Road, LONDON, NW6 1PN.

CASTLEDINE, Mr. Trevor Vaughan, MA ACA *1995;* 22 Woodhayes Road, Wimbledon, LONDON, SW19 4RF.

•CASTLEMAN, Mr. Christopher John, FCA *1975;* (Tax Fac), Newby Castleman, West Walk Building, 110 Regent Road, LEICESTER, LE1 7LT.

•CASTLEMAN, Mr. Michael David, FCA *1983;* Newby Castleman, West Walk Building, 110 Regent Road, LEICESTER, LE1 7LT.

•CASTLEMAN, Mr. Stephen Derek, FCA *1977;* Newby Castleman, West Walk Building, 110 Regent Road, LEICESTER, LE1 7LT.

CASTLETON, Mr. Adam Robert, BA ACA *1989;* 12 Brockley Avenue, STANMORE, MIDDLESEX, HA7 4LX.

CASTLEY, Mr. David Roger, FCA *1961;* 5 Burford Lodge, London Road, DORKING, RH5 6BP. (Life Member)

CASTLING, Mrs. Andrea, LLB ACA *1990;* Audit Commission, The Heath Business & Technical Park, RUNCORN, CHESHIRE, WA7 4QF.

CASTLING, Mrs. Jill Patricia, BA ACA *1981;* Rock Farm, Llandenny, USK, GWENT, NP15 1DL.

CASTON, Ms. Karen Dawn, BSc ACA *1995;* 20 Wolsey Road, Moor Park, NORTHWOOD, MIDDLESEX, HA6 2EP.

•CASTON, Mr. Leslie Ernest, FCA *1975;* (Tax Fac), Leslie E. Caston, 8 Bower Close, Eaton Bray, DUNSTABLE, BEDFORDSHIRE, LU6 2DU.

CASTON, Mr. Richard Charles Austin, MA ACA *1991;* R J D Partners, 8-9 Well Court, LONDON, EC4M 9DN.

CASTOR, Miss. Jane Maria, BA ACA *1993;* Homes & Communities Agency St. Georges House, Kingsway Team Valley Trading Estate, GATESHEAD, TYNE AND WEAR, NE11 0NA.

•CASTREE, Mr. Michael, ACA ACMA *2010;* Dains LLP, St. Johns Court, Wiltell Road, LICHFIELD, STAFFORDSHIRE, WS14 9DS.

CASTREE, Mr. Stephen Mark, BA ACA *1999;* 'Soundings', 13 Doctors Lane, Access lemon Grove Road, HAMILTON CR01, BERMUDA.

CASTRO, Mr. Ashley John, BA ACA *1999;* 147 Dover Street, CREMORNE, VIC 3121, AUSTRALIA.

CASTRO, Mr. David Jesus, BSc ACA CISA *2000;* 51 Albemarle Link, Springfield, CHELMSFORD, CM1 6AH.

CASTRO, Mr. Louis Emmanuel, BSc BCom FCA *1986;* 25 Abbey Drive, Bexley Park, DARTFORD, KENT, DA2 7WP.

CASTRO, Mr. Nicholas, BA FCA *1975;* 18 Branscombe Gardens, LONDON, N21 3BN.

CASTRO, Mrs. Susan Jane, BSc ACA *2000;* 51 Albemarle Link, Springfield, CHELMSFORD, CM1 6AH.

CASWELL, Mr. James, BSc ACA *2002;* 21 Prince Consort Cottages, WINDSOR, SL4 1JB.

CASWELL, Ms. Katie, MBA BA ACA *1998;* 18 Panmuir Road, West Wimbledon, LONDON, SW20 0PZ.

CASWELL, Mr. Richard Kelvin, BSc ACA *1995;* Flat 1 Glen Andred, Colway Lane, LYME REGIS, DORSET, DT7 3HE.

CASWELL, Mr. Stephen Cleveland, ACA *1979;* Sapperton House, Lawbrook Lane, Peaslake, GUILDFORD, GU5 9QW.

CASWELL, Mr. Timothy James, BCom FCA *1983;* 8 Gilldown Place, Wheeleys RoadEdgbaston, BIRMINGHAM, B15 2LR.

CASWILL, Mr. Gregory Spencer, FCA *1975;* The Music Rooms, Tanbridge Park, HORSHAM, RH12 1SU.

CATCHPOLE, Mrs. Beverley Helen, BSc ACA *2002;* Flat 2, 25 Chartfield Avenue, LONDON, SW15 6DZ.

CATCHPOLE, Mr. Edward Scott, FCA *1964;* 1 Ashmead Drive, Gotherington, CHELTENHAM, GL52 9ES.

CATCHPOLE, Miss. Hellene Elizabeth, BSc ACA *1990;* 74 Walton Drive, HIGH WYCOMBE, BUCKINGHAMSHIRE, HP13 6TT.

CATCHPOLE, Mr. Martin Paul, BA ACA *2000;* 75 Hotham Road, LONDON, SW15 1QW.

CATCHPOLE, Ms. Susan Jane, MA ACA *1984;* H M Treasury, 1 Horse Guards Road, LONDON, SW1A 2HQ.

•CATEN, Mrs. Stephanie Jane, FCA CTA *1984;* Maynard Heady LLP, Matrix House, 12-16 Lionel Road, CANVEY ISLAND, ESSEX, SS8 9DE. See also Kiloview Ltd and Maynard Heady

CATER, Ms. Barbara Dawn, BA ACA *1987;* Unite Technologies, Willow House, Llanlayo Court, USK, GWENT, NP15 1HY.

CATER, Mrs. Fazia, BA ACA *1995;* Orchard House, 13 Hillier Road, GUILDFORD, GU1 2JG.

•CATER, Mr. James David, FCA *1983;* Whiting & Partners, Berol House, Oldmedow Road, KING'S LYNN, NORFOLK, PE30 4JJ.

CATER, Miss. Stephanie Jane, BSc ACA *1986;* (Tax Fac), 22 Maple Avenue, FARNBOROUGH, HAMPSHIRE, GU14 9UR.

•CATER, Mr. Stephen James, BA ACA *1995;* PricewaterhouseCoopers LLP, 7 More London Riverside, LONDON, SE1 2RT. See also PricewaterhouseCoopers

•CATER, Mrs. Suzanne Louise, BA ACA *1990;* (Tax Fac), S.L. Cater, 6 Terminal House, Station Approach, SHEPPERTON, TW17 8AS.

•CATES, Mr. Antony George, BSc FCA *1991;* KPMG LLP, 15 Canada Square, LONDON, E14 5GL. See also KPMG Europe LLP, KPMG Audit plc, KPMG Holding plc

•CATES, Mr. Dean Richard, BA ACA *2000;* (Tax Fac), Couch Bright King & Co, 91 Gower Street, LONDON, WC1E 6AB.

CATES, Mr. Martin John, ACA MAAT *2003;* 72 Turnstone Drive, BURY ST. EDMUNDS, SUFFOLK, IP32 7GT.

CATHCART, Ms. Catherine Wendy, LLB ACA *1989;* 52 Stokenchurch Street, LONDON, SW6 3TR.

CATHCART, The Earl Cathcart Charles Alan Andrew, ACA *1982;* 52 Pimlico Road, LONDON, SW1W 8LP.

CATHCART, Mr. Donald Ian, BA ACA *2000;* 15 Deben Road, COLCHESTER, CO4 3UZ.

CATHCART, Mr. Hugh Duncan, BSc FCA *1989;* Low Hall, Travers Farm Lane, La Route de Noirmont, St. Brelade, JERSEY, JE3 8LA.

CATHERALL, Mr. Marc James, BEng ACA *2000;* Bank of America, M B N A International Bank Ltd, Chester Business Park, CHESTER, CH4 9FB.

•CATHERALL, Mr. Paul Gareth, BSc ARCS ACA *1987;* Paul Catherall, Holm Oak, Mount Park Avenue, Harrow on the Hill, HARROW, HA1 3JN. See also Venture Alliance Corporate Finance Ltd

CATHERALL, Mr. Philip Neil, MA ACA *1992;* The Magnolias, Jacksons Meadow, Bidford-on-Avon, ALCESTER, B50 4HQ.

CATHERALL, Mrs. Rebecca Louise, BA(Hons) ACA *2010;* 14 Hankelow Close, CHESTER, CH2 2DZ.

CATHERWOOD, Sir Henry Frederick Ross, Kt CA *1951;* Flat 14, Meadow Croft House, Trumpington Road, CAMBRIDGE, CAMBRIDGESHIRE, CB2 8EX. (Life Member)

CATLEY, Mr. Nicholas, ACA *2008;* National Audit Office, 157-197 Buckingham Palace Road, LONDON, SW1W 9SP.

CATLEY, Mr. Simon William, BSc ACA *1991;* 2 Kingsley, Chesham Road Wigginton, TRING, HERTFORDSHIRE, HP23 6HJ.

CATLIN, Mr. Alan George, FCA *1955;* 86 Evesham Rd, Narborough Rd, LEICESTER, LE3 2BD. (Life Member)

•CATLIN, Mr. Morris John, FCA *1969;* Morris John Catlin, 209 High Town Road, LUTON, LU2 0BZ.

CATLIN-HALLETT, Mr. William, MSci ACA *2005;* Fulcrum Pharma plc Hemel One, Boundary Way, HEMEL HEMPSTEAD, HERTFORDSHIRE, HP2 7YU.

CATLOW, Mrs. Alison, FCA *1979;* 58 Princes Way, FLEETWOOD, FY7 8DB.

CATLOW, Mrs. Anne Geraldine Mary, MSc BA CertEd FCA *1979;* (Member of Council 1995 - 1995), 7 Wordsworth Road, LEICESTER, LE2 6EB.

CATO, Mr. Guy Howard, BA(Hons) ACA *2001;* 1 Old Warrens, The Street Great Tey, COLCHESTER, CO6 1JS.

CATO, Miss. Lisa, BA ACA *2006;* The Dees, Pound Lane, Mannings Heath, HORSHAM, WEST SUSSEX, RH13 6JJ.

CATO, Mr. Philip Roy, BA FCA *1977;* Nant y Bella Lodge, Tan y Gopa, ABERGELE, CLWYD, LL22 8DS.

CATOLICO, Mr. Michael, ACA *2008;* with Baker Tilly UK Audit LLP, 1st Floor, 46 Clarendon Road, WATFORD, WD17 1JJ.

•CATON, Mrs. Christine Ann, FCA *1967;* (Tax Fac), with Caton Fry & Co Limited, Essex House, 7-8 The Shrubberies, George Lane, LONDON, E18 1BD.

CATON, Mr. Dale Antony Valentine, MA ACA *1997;* Narvida Ltd, Hillend Industrial Park, DUNFERMLINE, FIFE, KY11 9JT.

•CATON, Mr. Edward Owen, FCA ATII ASFA *1967;* with Caton Fry & Co Limited, Essex House, 7-8 The Shrubberies, George Lane, LONDON, E18 1BD.

CATON, Mr. John Andrew, FCA *1973;* Bridge House, The Green, Blackmore, INGATESTONE, CM4 0RT.

•CATON, Mr. Jonathan Edward, ACA FCCA *2007;* Caton Fry & Co Limited, Essex House, 7-8 The Shrubberies, George Lane, LONDON, E18 1BD.

CATON, Mr. Matthew Laurence Victor, BA ACA *1997;* J P Morgan Chase, 125 London Wall, LONDON, EC2Y 5AJ.

•CATON, Mr. Nicholas Scott, BSc FCA *1991;* Mill Scott Ltd, 3a Market Hill, SAFFRON WALDEN, ESSEX, CB10 1HQ.

CATON, Mr. Simon David, BSc ACA *2003;* Ernst & Young, 5 Times Square, NEW YORK, NY 10023, UNITED STATES.

•CATOR, Mr. Marcus, ACA *2005;* A P Bemment & Co Limited, 101 Bridge Road, Oulton Broad, LOWESTOFT, SUFFOLK, NR32 3LN.

CATOVSKY, Mr. Michael David, ACA *2008;* 1 Greenford View, Higher Frome Vauchurch, DORCHESTER, DORSET, DT2 0AS.

CATT, Mr. Benson Franklyn, JP FCA *1951;* 44 Pickhurst Lane, Hayes, BROMLEY, BR2 7JF. (Life Member)

CATT, Mr. Clifford Richard, FCA *1965;* Park View, Camp Road, Woldingham, CATERHAM, CR3 7LH.

CATT, Miss. Nicola, ACA *2008;* with PricewaterhouseCoopers LLP, 1 Embankment Place, LONDON, WC2N 6RH.

•CATT, Mr. Timothy Charles, BA FCA *1977;* (Tax Fac), Gardiner Hunter & Catt, 13 Station Approach, ASHFORD, MIDDLESEX, TW15 2GH.

•CATTANEO, Mr. Charles Enea, MBA BCom FCA CF FSI *1987;* Cattaneo LLP, One Victoria Square, BIRMINGHAM, B1 1BD.

CATTEE, Mr. Matthew, BSc ACA *2002;* 36 Bucharest Road, LONDON, SW18 3AR.

•CATTELL, Mr. Ian James, ACA *1996;* (Tax Fac), Crombies Corfield Accountants Limited, 34 Waterloo Road, WOLVERHAMPTON, WV1 4DG. See also Crombies Accountants Limited

CATTELL, Mr. John, BA ACA *1989;* 95 Village Court, WHITLEY BAY, NE26 3QB.

CATTELL, Mr. John William, BA FCA *1970;* 7 Keats Road, Woodley, READING, RG5 3RJ.

CATTELL, Mr. Jonathan Danes, FCA *1965;* Flat 5, Edward House, Royal Earlswood Park, REDHILL, SURREY, RH1 6TL. (Life Member)

CATTELL, Mr. Michael Anthony Perrier, FCA *1962;* 2 Bouverie Close, Barton on Sea, NEW MILTON, BH25 7HB.

CATTELL, Mr. Nicholas James, BSc(Hons) ACA *2001;* 10 Northenden Road, Gatley, CHEADLE, SK8 4DN.
CATTELL, Mr. Roger, FCA *1960;* Cowley Farm, Cowley Lane, Holmesfield, DRONFIELD, S18 7SD. (Life Member)
•CATTELL, Mr. Ross Brett, MA FCA *1985;* Deloitte LLP, 20 route de Pre-Bois, ICC Building H, 1215 GENEVA, SWITZERLAND. See also Deloitte & Touche LLP
CATTERALL, Mr. Anthony Howard, FCA *1963;* Flat 1, 6 Westcliffe Road, Birkdale, SOUTHPORT, PR8 2BN.
CATTERALL, Miss. Fiona Lindsay, BSc ACA *2003;* Monkswood Woodside Green, Great Hallingbury, BISHOP'S STORTFORD, HERTFORDSHIRE, CM22 7UG.
CATTERALL, Ms. Jill Nicola, BCom FCA CTA *1985;* with Patricia J. Arnold & Co, Black House, Dipton Mill Road, HEXHAM, NE46 1RZ.
CATTERALL, Mr. Michael James James, BA(Hons) ACA *2001;* KPMG, 10 Shelley Street, SYDNEY, NSW 2000, AUSTRALIA.
CATTERALL, Miss. Nicola Jane, BA ACA *1986;* National Galleries of Scotland, 73 Belford Road, EDINBURGH, EH4 3DS.
CATTERALL, Mrs. Nicola Mary, BA ACA *1982;* Church House Barn, Mill Lane, Goosnargh, PRESTON, PR3 2BJ.
CATTERALL, Mr. Peter Francis, BA ACA *1996;* 52 Coverdale Drive, BLACKBURN, BB2 5ED.
CATTERALL, Mr. Peter John Rishton, BCom FCA *1967;* 20 Nassau Street, LONDON, W1W 1AG. (Life Member)
•CATTERALL, Mr. Stephen John Cliffe, MA FCA *1975;* (Tax Fac), Cliffe Catterall Limited, 21 Dick Place, EDINBURGH, EH9 2JU.
CATTERICK, Mr. William James, ACA *2009;* with BDO LLP, 125 Colmore Row, BIRMINGHAM, B3 3SD.
CATTERMOLE, Mrs. Angela Joy, MBA BSc FCA *1992;* 8 Colonel Grantham Avenue, AYLESBURY, BUCKINGHAMSHIRE, HP19 9AP.
CATTERMOLE, Mr. David John, MA ACA *1985;* with KPMG LLP, 15 Canada Square, LONDON, E14 5GL.
CATTERMOLE, Miss. Marguerite Clare, BSc ACA *1988;* (Tax Fac), South Lodge, Sandy Lane, GUILDFORD, SURREY, GU3 1HF.
•CATTERMOLE, Mr. Peter Alexander, BA ACA *2004;* (Tax Fac), Coyne Butterworth Reid Ltd, 48 High West Street, DORCHESTER, DORSET, DT1 1UT. See also Coyne Butterworth (Dorchester) Limited
CATTERMOLE, Mrs. Susan Jill, BA ACA *1991;* 116 Hemingford Road, LONDON, N1 1DE.
CATTERSON, Mr. Alan, BA ACA *1989;* Schlossstrasse 2, 8234 STETTEN, SWITZERLAND.
CATTLE, Mr. Robert Harry Spencer, FCA *1963;* Deneside, Ford End, Ivinghoe, LEIGHTON BUZZARD, LU7 9EA.
CATTO, Mr. Neil James, BEng FCA *1993;* Manor Farm, Cartridge Lane, Grappenhall, WARRINGTON, WA4 4SH.
CATTON, Mr. Dean, BEng ACA *1998;* Burnside, Alexander Lane, Shenfield, BRENTWOOD, ESSEX, CM13 1AG.
CATTON, Mr. Stephen Frank, BSc ACA *1984;* 25 Belmont Road, HARROGATE, NORTH YORKSHIRE, HG2 0LR.
CATTRALL, Mr. David Anthony, FCA *1975;* Incus Consultants Limited, PO Box 25-413, St Heliers, AUCKLAND 1741, NEW ZEALAND.
•CATTY, Mr. Jon, FCA *1962;* Jon Catty & Company, 12 Durham Road, LONDON, N2 9DN. See also Jon Catty Consultants Limited
CATTY, Miss. Ruth Frances, MA ACA *1993;* 8 Radnor Avenue, HARROW, HA1 1SB.
CAUFIELD, Mr. Timothy Charles, BA ACA *1988;* 49 Hermitage Road, Mannamead, PLYMOUTH, PL3 4RX.
•CAUKILL, Mr. David, BSc FCA *1979;* Garden House, Hawkley, LISS, HAMPSHIRE, GU33 6LU.
CAUL, Mr. Robert Scott, BEng ACA *1993;* Rose Cottage, Tockington Green, Tockington, BRISTOL, BS32 4LG.
CAUL, Mrs. Susan Anne, BA ACA *1994;* Rose Cottage, The Green Tockington, BRISTOL, BS32 4LG.
CAULFEILD, Mr. James Alexander Toby, MA FCA *1963;* Hookland, Redford, MIDHURST, WEST SUSSEX, GU29 0QF. (Life Member)
CAULFIELD, Mr. Derek, FCA *1959;* 79 Plymyard Avenue, Bromborough, WIRRAL, CH62 6BL. (Life Member)
CAULFIELD, Mr. Edward Charles, FCA *1966;* 74 Church Lane, Lowton, WARRINGTON, WA3 2PX. (Life Member)
CAULFIELD, Miss. Geraldine Mary, BSc FCA MSI *1974;* 2A Caversham Avenue, LONDON, N13 4LN.
CAULFIELD, Mrs. Louise Joanne, BA ACA *1995;* 35 The Grove Urmston, MANCHESTER, M41 6JH.
•CAULFIELD, Mr. Martin Patrick, FCA *1980;* M W Medical, 2 Westbury Mews, Westbury Hill, Westbury on Trym, BRISTOL, BS9 3QA.
CAULFIELD, Mr. Paul James, BA FCA *1991;* Corriegour, Botus Fleming, SALTASH, CORNWALL, PL12 6NJ.
CAULFIELD, Mrs. Penelope Elizabeth Carmel, BSc ACA *1993;* 74 Bedford Avenue, BARNET, EN5 2ER.
CAULFIELD, Mrs. Susan, ACA *2006;* 8 Beaumont Park, Danbury, CHELMSFORD, CM3 4DE.
CAULFIELD, Mr. Terence, BA ACA *1995;* with National Audit Office, 157-197 Buckingham Palace Road, Victoria, LONDON, SW1W 9SP.
CAULFIELD, Miss. Wendy Laura, BSc FCA *1991;* Little Canons Tanyard Lane, Chelwood Gate, HAYWARDS HEATH, WEST SUSSEX, RH17 7LX.
CAULTON, Mr. Adam, ACA *2011;* 60 Thames Way, Hilton, DERBY, DE65 5NB.
CAULTON, Mr. Eliot Robert Spencer, BSc(Econ) ACA *1999;* 5 Mapledene Crescent, NOTTINGHAM, NG8 2SS.
CAUNCE, Mrs. Ann Elizabeth, FCA *1976;* Becconsall, Hunters Lane, Tarleton, PRESTON, PR4 6JL.
CAUNCE, Mr. David Christopher, BSc ACA *1989;* Assystem Ltd Club Street, Bamber Bridge, PRESTON, PR5 6FN.
CAUNCE, Mr. Graham Thomas, BSc ACA *1982;* Rudd MacNamara Ltd, Island Works, Holyhead Road, Handsworth, BIRMINGHAM, B21 0BS.
CAUNCE, Mr. Stephen James, BSc ACA *1994;* The Gables, 88 Station Road, Croston, LEYLAND, PR26 9RP.
CAUNCE, Mr. William David, FCA *1977;* 26 The Sycamores, BALDOCK, HERTFORDSHIRE, SG7 5BJ.
CAUNHYE, Mr. Max, BSc ACA *2002;* 33 Rook Way, HORSHAM, WEST SUSSEX, RH12 5FR.
CAUNT, Mr. Ian Charles, FCA *1967;* 2453 Folkestone Way, WEST VANCOUVER V7S 3J1, BC, CANADA.
CAUNT, Mr. Peter Edward, FCA *1973;* Caunt and Lowbeer, PO Box 1575, CHATSWOOD, NSW 2057, AUSTRALIA.
CAUNTER, Mr. Clive Anthony, BSc ACA *1981;* Dunsaller, Thorverton, EXETER, EX5 5JR.
CAUSER, Mr. David John, FCA *1972;* Hampton Lodge, 15 North Road, Highgate, LONDON, N6 4BD.
CAUSER, Mr. Jason Keith, BA ACA *1996;* Friends Provident, Pixham End, DORKING, RH4 1QA.
•CAUSER, Mr. Lee Andrew, BSc ACA MABRP *2005;* Zolfo Cooper LLP, 10 Fleet Place, LONDON, EC4M 7RB.
CAUSER, Mr. Qasim Ebrahim, FCA *1977;* BDO Ebrahim & Co, 2nd Floor, Block C, Lakson Square Building No1, Sarwar Shahead Road, KARACHI 74200 PAKISTAN.
CAUSON, Mr. Wayne Anthony, BSc FCA *1991;* 75 Leicester Road, HINCKLEY, LEICESTERSHIRE, LE10 1LP.
CAUTER, Mrs. Kara Leigh, ACA *1998;* Chantecler, Pond Road, WOKING, GU22 0JT.
CAUTER, Mr. Michael Lee, BA ACA *1997;* Chantecler, Pond Road, WOKING, GU22 0JT.
CAVACIUTI, Mrs. Nikki, BA ACA *1998;* 1 Richmond Close, Littleover, DERBY, DE23 3UH.
CAVALE, Mrs. Gowri, BSc(Hons) ACA *2001;* 402 9th Street, Apt E5E, HOBOKEN, NJ 07030, UNITED STATES.
CAVALIERE, Mrs. Louise Jane, BA ACA *1994;* 11 Oaklands Avenue Adel, LEEDS, LS16 8NR.
CAVAN, Mr. Craig, BSc ACA *2006;* with Deloitte LLP, 1 Woodborough Road, NOTTINGHAM, NG1 3FG.
CAVANAGH, Mr. Daniel Joseph, BSc ACA *2000;* Brooklands, Skerries Road, LUSK, COUNTY DUBLIN, IRELAND.
CAVANAGH, Mrs. Julia Naomi, BSocSc ACA *1992;* 27 Langdon Park, TEDDINGTON, MIDDLESEX, TW11 9PR.
CAVANAGH, Mrs. Katie Victoria, ACA *1997;* Burberry Ltd Horseferry House, Horseferry Road, LONDON, SW1P 2AW.
CAVANAGH, Mrs. Patricia Anne, BSc FCA *1978;* 28 Portland Rise, Manor House, LONDON, N4 2PP.
CAVANAH, Mr. William Peter, FCA *1972;* 1 Riders Gate, BURY, BL9 7RD.
•CAVE, Mr. Andrew Jonathan, MA FCA *1979;* (Tax Fac), Wheelers, 16 North Street, WISBECH, CAMBRIDGESHIRE, PE13 1NE.
CAVE, Mr. Andrew Michael, BSc(Hons) ACA *2002;* 6 Campbell Drive, WAHROONGA, NSW 2076, AUSTRALIA.
CAVE, Mr. Anthony Robert, FCA *1958;* 22 Chemin Du Champ-carre, 1256, TROINEX, SWITZERLAND. (Life Member)
CAVE, Miss. Elizabeth Sian, ACA *1987;* 35 The Fairway, NORTHWOOD, HA6 3DZ.
CAVE, Mr. Jeremy Charles, BA ACA *1986;* 47 Park Mount, HARPENDEN, AL5 3AS.
CAVE, Miss. Joanna Louise, MA(Oxon) ACA *2001;* Aardman Animations Ltd, Gas Ferry Road, BRISTOL, BS1 6UN.
CAVE, Miss. Johanna Caroline, BSc ACA *2001;* Flat 5, 25 Sinclair Road, LONDON, W14 0NS.
CAVE, Mr. John Halliday, FCA *1961;* 82 St. Andrews Road, HENLEY-ON-THAMES, RG9 1JE. (Life Member)
CAVE, Mr. Jonathan Martin, BA ACA *2005;* 100/2-18 Buchanan Street, BALMAIN, NSW 2041, AUSTRALIA.
CAVE, Mrs. Julie Ann, BA FCA *1994;* with Morrell Middleton, 3 Cayley Court, George Cayley Drive, Clifton Moor, YORK, YO30 4WH.
CAVE, Mr. Matthew Leonard, BA ACA *2007;* 28 Falstaff Court, King Edward Close, CALNE, WILTSHIRE, SN11 9RG.
CAVE, Mr. Nicholas Edward, BSc ACA *1994;* (Tax Fac), The Flat, 5-7 High Street, WINCANTON, SOMERSET, BA9 9JN.
CAVE, Miss. Philippa Anne, MEng ACA CTA *2003;* Apartment 34, Citygate1, Blantyre Street, MANCHESTER, M15 4JT.
•CAVE, Mr. Robert Andrew, BSc FCA *1979;* R A Cave Limited, Yew tree, 13 Leeds Road, MIRFIELD, WEST YORKSHIRE, WF14 0BY.
CAVE, Mr. Ronald James, FCA *1965;* Flat 15, Henchard Court, The Grove, DORCHESTER, DT1 1XR. (Life Member)
CAVE, Miss. Solenn, ACA *2009;* 20 Valley Road, Sandgate, FOLKESTONE, CT20 3BT.
CAVE, Ms. Susan, BA ACA *1992;* 97 Wepham Green, Wepham, ARUNDEL, BN18 9RB.
CAVE, Mr. Timothy Andrew, BA ACA *1990;* Carleton Cottage, Wymondham Road, East Carleton, NORWICH, NR14 8HY.
CAVE SMITH, Miss. Clare Frances, BSc FCA *1982;* 19 Glebelands, Bidborough, TUNBRIDGE WELLS, TN3 0UQ.
•CAVELL, Mr. Roger Ian, BSc FCA *1978;* R.I. Cavell, 155 Reepham Road, Hellesdon, NORWICH, NR6 5PW.
CAVELL, Mr. Steven David, BSc ACA *1985;* 17 Cae Garw, Thornhill, CARDIFF, CF14 9DX.
CAVENAGH, Mr. Charles Michael, BA FCA *1978;* 17 Chepstow Road, LONDON, W7 2BG.
CAVENDISH, Mrs. Susan Elizabeth, MEng ACA *2001;* 4 Corsair Close, LEE-ON-THE-SOLENT, PO13 8GF.
CAVENDISH, Miss. Susanna Suki, BSc(Hons) ACA *2000;* 16 St. Johns Street, GODALMING, GU7 3EJ.
CAVENEY, Mr. Terence Austin, PhD BSc FCA *1976;* Bod Hyfryd, Ruthin Road, Cadole, MOLD, CH7 5LQ.
CAVES, Mr. John Edward, FCA *1975;* Home & Capital Trust Ltd, 31 Goldington Road, BEDFORD, MK40 3LH.
CAVET, Mr. David Mitchell, BSc ACA *1989;* Thomas Swan & Co Ltd, Rotary Way, CONSETT, COUNTY DURHAM, DH8 7ND.
CAVEY, Mr. Andrew, BA ACA *1991;* 136 Upper Road, Greenisland, CARRICKFERGUS, COUNTY ANTRIM, BT38 8RL.
•CAVEY, Mr. Martin Cameron, BA ACA *1999;* (Tax Fac), Cameron Cavey Consulting Limited, 3 Branksome Park House, Branksome Business Park, Bourne Valley Road, POOLE, DORSET BH12 1ED.
•CAVILL, Mr. Alan Robert, FCA *1974;* (Tax Fac), Malmesbury Accountancy Ltd, Gable House, 46 High Street, MALMESBURY, WILTSHIRE, SN16 9AT.
CAVILL, Mr. David Bryan, FCA *1972;* 49 West End Grove, Horsforth, LEEDS, LS18 5JJ.
CAWDELL, Mr. John Antony, FCA *1979;* 1 Gregg Hall Drive, LINCOLN, LN6 8AN.
CAWDRON, Mr. Andrew Michael, BSc FCA *1990;* Chilbury, Rumsam Road, BARNSTAPLE, EX32 9ER.
CAWDRON, Mr. Peter Edward Blackburn, FCA *1966;* The Old Bakery, Rectory Road, Great Haseley, OXFORD, OX44 7JG.
CAWDRON, Mr. Richard, BA ACA *1993;* 90 Wakehurst Road, LONDON, SW11 6BT.
CAWDRON, Mr. Richard Arthur, FCA *1968;* Sanderson Asset Management Ltd, Heathcoat House, 20 Savile Row, LONDON, W1S 3PR.
CAWDRY, Mr. Joseph, FCA *1953;* Hillmead, 65 Second Avenue, FRINTON-ON-SEA, CO13 9LY. (Life Member)
CAWKER, Mr. Richard Neil, BSc ACA *1991;* Sunnybank Dorking Road, Chilworth, GUILDFORD, GU4 8RR.
CAWLEY, Mr. Colin, FCA *1952;* Flat 12 Hanover Court, NEWCASTLE, STAFFORDSHIRE, ST5 1HE. (Life Member)
CAWLEY, Mrs. Deborah Anne, BA ACA *1994;* Coin Varin House, Le Mont de St. Anastase, St. Peter, JERSEY, JE3 7ES.
CAWLEY, Mr. Fergal, MSc ACA *2005;* 12 Trehern Road, LONDON, SW14 8PD.
CAWLEY, Mr. Hugh Charles Laurence, BA FCA *1984;* Red Roke, 137 Epsom Road, GUILDFORD, SURREY, GU1 2PP.
•CAWLEY, Mr. John Anthony, BA ACA *1982;* Michael A. Jarvis & Co, Edenthorpe, Grove Road, ROTHERHAM, S60 2ER.
CAWLEY, Mrs. Katherine Anne, BA(Hons) ACA *2003;* 12 Trehern Road, LONDON, SW14 8PD.
•CAWLEY, Mr. Martin, BA ACA *1984;* Bartfields Business Services LLP, Burley House, 12 Clarendon Road, LEEDS, LS2 9NF.
CAWLEY, Mr. Nicholas Blair, BSc FCA TEP *1993;* Bedell Trust Company limited, PO Box 75, JERSEY, JE4 8PP.
CAWLEY, Mr. Nigel Alexander, ACA *1982;* 19 rue des Genêts, 91430 IGNY, FRANCE.
CAWLEY, Mr. Stephen Ingleby, CVO MA FCA *1973;* Robin Post, Firle Road, SEAFORD, BN25 2HJ.
CAWLEY, Miss. Tayha, ACA *2011;* Flat 4, Novus House, 181 Hatfield Road, ST. ALBANS, HERTFORDSHIRE, AL1 4LG.
CAWOOD, Mr. Gregory Paul, BSc ACA *1992;* 17 WOLSELEY COURT, ANNANDALE, QLD 4814, AUSTRALIA.
CAWOOD, Mr. Laird, LLB ACA *2003;* 20 Albany Court, 18 Plumbers Row, Whitechapel, LONDON, E1 1EP.
CAWSER, Mr. George Owen, FCA *1952;* 31 Manor Road, SOLIHULL, WEST MIDLANDS, B91 2BH. (Life Member)
CAWSEY, Mr. Martin, BA ACA *1990;* 26B Lake Street, SOMERVILLE, MA 02143, UNITED STATES.
CAWTE, Mr. Iain Michael, BSc ACA *1997;* 7 Jervois Close, #03-14 One Jervois, SINGAPORE 249103, SG, SINGAPORE.
CAWTE, Mr. Thomas David, FCA *1967;* Shaws Corner House, 99 Reigate Road, REDHILL, RH1 6BA.
•CAWTHORN, Mr. Geoffrey, FCA *1977;* Ryecroft Glenton, 55 Newgate Street, MORPETH, NORTHUMBERLAND, NE61 1AY.
CAWTHORNE, Miss. Andrea Michelle, BSc ACA *1987;* with Deloitte LLP, Stonecutter Court, 1 Stonecutter Street, LONDON, EC4A 4TR.
CAWTHORNE, Mrs. Anna-Louise, BSc ACA CTA *2003;* 12 Palmerston Road, LONDON, SW19 1PQ.
CAWTHORNE, Mrs. Beverley Louise, BSc ACA *1992;* Vernon House, Main Street, Upton, RETFORD, DN22 0RA.
CAWTHORNE, Mr. David Alwyn, FCA *1970;* Threeways, Brick Kiln Lane, Limpsfield Common, OXTED, RH8 0QZ.
CAWTHORNE, Mr. John, BA FCA *1971;* Mayfield Fulwood Ltd, Belmayne House, 99 Clarkehouse Road, SHEFFIELD, S10 2LN.
CAWTHORNE, Mr. John Brian, BSc FCA *1975;* Deloitte & Touche LLP, 2 Queen Street East, Suite 1200, Maritime Tower, PO Box 8, TORONTO M5C 3G7 ON CANADA.
CAWTHORNE, Mr. Peter, BSc FCA *1975;* 3 Kingshill Drive, HARROW, HA3 8TE.
CAWTHRA, Mr. Maxwell, BA(Hons) ACA *2002;* 14 Birkdale Way, Alwoodley, LEEDS, LS17 7SY.
CAWTHRA, Mr. Richard Giles, LLB ACA *1996;* 41/F Cheung Kong Center, 1 Queen's Road Central, CENTRAL, HONG KONG SAR, HONG KONG SAR.
CAWTHRAY, Mr. Andrew, ACA *2009;* Flat 16 Hodge Hill Court Bromford Road, BIRMINGHAM, B36 8AN.
CAWTHRAY, Mr. Andrew Charles, ACA *2009;* 8 Wellfield Lane, Burley in Wharfedale, ILKLEY, LS29 7SX.
CAWTHRON, Mr. Andrew Richard, BSc ACA *2009;* Unit 501, 36-40 Burgundy Street, HEIDELBERG, VIC 3084, AUSTRALIA.
CAWTHROW, Mr. David Robert, BA ACA *1990;* Pictet Asset Management Ltd, Moorhouse - Level 11 120 London Wall, LONDON, EC2Y 5ET.
CAYEUX ROGERS, Mrs. Edwige Francoise, BSc ACA *1991;* 33 Hadley Gardens, LONDON, W4 4NU.
CAYGILL, Mr. Paul, ACA *2009;* 11 Warwick Drive, Endmoor, KENDAL, CUMBRIA, LA8 0EE.
CAYGILL, Mr. Robert Nicholas, BA ACA *1994;* Chartis Chile Compañía de Seguros Generales SA, Austinas 640 Piso 9, SANTIAGO, CHILE.
•CAYLESS, Mr. Martyn Howard, FCA *1972;* with MacIntyre Hudson LLP, New Bridge Street House, 30-34 New Bridge Street, LONDON, EC4V 6BJ.
CAYWOOD, Miss. Pauline, BSc(Hons) ACA *2000;* Flat 21 Duke Shore Wharf, 106 Narrow Street, LONDON, E14 8BU.
CAZALET, Mr. Charles Julian, MA FCA *1973;* 38 Norland Square, LONDON, W11 4PZ.
•CAZALET, Mrs. Valerie Elizabeth, LLB FCA *1989;* with RSM Tenon Audit Limited, 66 Chiltern Street, LONDON, W1U 4JT.

•**CAZEAUX, Mr. Daniel Sebastian, BA ACA** *2001;* KPMG LLP, 15 Canada Square, LONDON, E14 5GL. See also KPMG Europe LLP
CAZENOVE, Mr. James, BA ACA *2004;* 11 Heslop Road, LONDON, SW12 8EG.
CEARNS, Mrs. Alison Ruth, BA FCA *1983;* Bank House, 142 Barnston Road, Barnston, WIRRAL, CH61 1BY.
CEARNS, Mr. Anthony Steven, MSc FCA *1989;* Bank House, 142 Barnston Road, Heswall, WIRRAL, CH61 1BY.
CEARNS, Mrs. Kathryn, BA *1990;* Exchange House Rm 513, Primrose Street, LONDON, EC2A 2HS.
CEATON, Mr. David Alan, BSc FCA *1973;* 9 Branksome Towers, POOLE, DORSET, BH13 6JT. (Life Member)
•**CECIL, Mr. Anthony Robert, MA FCA** *1987;* KPMG LLP, 15 Canada Square, LONDON, E14 5GL. See also KPMG Europe LLP
CECIL, Mr. Robert, MMath ACA *2003;* 66 Wigmore Street, LONDON, W1U 2SB.
CECIL-WRIGHT, Mr. James Allann, FCA *1961;* Garden Cottage, Kitwalls Lane, Milford-on-Sea, LYMINGTON, SO41 0RJ.
CEDAR, Mr. Elliott Spencer, BA ACA *1997;* C/O Capital & Provident, 43-45 Dorset Street, LONDON, W1U 7NA.
CEDER, Miss. Ebba Ragna, MPhil BA ACA *2002;* with PricewaterhouseCoopers, Strandvejen 44, DK 2900 HELLERUP, DENMARK.
•**CEENEY, Mr. Michael Ernest, FCA** *1961;* Munro's, 1341 High Road, Whetstone, LONDON, N20 9HR. See also Munro's (Accounting Services) Limited and Munros
CEGIELSKI, Miss. Olivia, BSc ACA *2011;* 32 Charnwood Avenue, LONDON, SW19 3EJ.
CEGLOWSKI, Mrs. Jacqueline Rita, MA ACA *1979;* 71 Great Brownings, College Road Dulwich, LONDON, SE21 7HR.
CELASCHI, Mr. John Beato, FCA *1957;* Long Meadow, Llanvaches, CALDICOT, NP26 3AY. (Life Member)
CELERIER, Mr. Paul Alexander, FCA *1979;* 6th Floor, 80 Cannon Street, LONDON, EC4N 6HL.
•**CELIA, Mr. Roger, FCA** *1970;* (Tax Fac), Roger Celia, 23 Lodge Close, HERTFORD, SG14 3DH.
CENCI, Mr. Steven Raymond, ACA *2006;* 28 Coleridge Close, Twyford, READING, RG10 0XL.
CENTURY, Mr. Daniel Benjamin, ACA *2008;* 2 Ashley Court, Somerset Road, New Barnet, BARNET, HERTFORDSHIRE, EN5 1RQ.
CERVANTES-WATSON, Mr. Nicholas John, LLB FCA *1970;* Robins, The Green, Sarratt, RICKMANSWORTH, HERTFORDSHIRE, WD3 6BJ.
CERVO, Mrs. Louise Mary, BA ACA *1997;* 14, Blackcap Lane, BRACKNELL, RG12 8AA.
CH'NG, Mr. Desmond, BA ACA *1994;* 22 Jalan Terasek 7, Bangsar Baru, 59100 KUALA LUMPUR, FEDERAL TERRITORY, MALAYSIA.
CH'NG, Mr. Soo Keong, FCA *1977;* 56 Lengkok Zaaba, Taman Tun Dr.Ismail, 60000 KUALA LUMPUR, FEDERAL TERRITORY, MALAYSIA.
CHAANG, Miss. Wei Sum, BSc ACA *1991;* 15th Floor Citibank Tower, 3 Garden Road, CENTRAL, HONG KONG ISLAND, HONG KONG SAR
CHABLANI, Mr. Ashok, ACA *1982;* 36H Dunearn Road, No.08-47 Chancery Court, SINGAPORE 309433, SINGAPORE.
CHABOT, Mr. Simon Charles, FCA *1971;* 16 Norman Road, HOVE, BN3 4LS.
CHACKO, Mr. Adil, ACA *2002;* G-36 Sainik Farms, Forest Lane, Neb Sarai Ext, NEW DELHI 110068, INDIA.
CHADA, Mr. Davy, BEng ACA *2002;* 33 Little Roodee, Hawarden, DEESIDE, CLWYD, CH5 3PU.
•**CHADAWAY, Mr. Andrew Kevin, BSc FCA** *1985;* Burgis & Bullock, Gethin House, 36 Bond Street, NUNEATON, CV11 4DA.
CHADAWAY, Mr. David Michael, FCA *1979;* 120 St. Nicolas Park Drive, NUNEATON, CV11 6EE.
CHADBURN, Mr. Richard Fowkes, BA FCA *1976;* Highlands, Weem, ABERFELDY, PERTHSHIRE, PH15 2LD.
•**CHADDA, Mr. Parveen, FCA** *1983;* (Tax Fac), Kingston Smith LLP, Surrey House, 36-44 High Street, REDHILL, RH1 1RH. See also Kingston Smith Limited Liability Partnership, Devonshire Corporate Services LLP and Kingston Smith Consulting LLP
CHADDA, Mr. Sanjeet, BA(Hons) ACA AMCT *2003;* GE Oil & Gas, PII Limited, Atley Way, CRAMLINGTON, NORTHUMBERLAND, NE23 1WW.
CHADDA, Miss. Sarika, BSc(Hons) ACA *2010;* 26 Selborne Road, CROYDON, CR0 5JQ.
CHADDA, Mr. Surbjit Singh, BSc ACA *1997;* 3 Erleigh Court Drive, Earley, READING, RG6 1EB.
CHADDAER, Mrs. Jagdeep Kaur, BSc ACA *2009;* 33 Mappleborough Road, Shirley, SOLIHULL, B90 1AG.
CHADDER, Mr. Roger Vivyan James, MA FCA *1962;* 64 Church Road, Wimbledon, LONDON, SW19 5AA. (Life Member)
CHADDERTON, Miss. Dena, BSc ACA *2001;* Polar Capital Partners Ltd, 4 Matthew Parker Street, LONDON, SW1H 9NP.
CHADHA, Mr. Rajesh, BA ACA *1992;* Be Enterprises Ltd, Hedsor Road, BOURNE END, BUCKINGHAMSHIRE, SL8 5EE.
CHADHA, Mr. Sanjiv, BSc ACA *1992;* 85 Cranford Lane, HOUNSLOW, TW5 9HQ.
CHADHA, Mr. Sheetal, FCA *1980;* 2 Hayes Hill Road, BROMLEY, BR2 7HT.
CHADHA, Mr. Yash Pal, BSc ACA *1989;* 15 Seagry Road, Wanstead, LONDON, E11 2NG.
CHADNEY, Mr. Michael, BSc ACA *1989;* 12 Grand Union Walk, Kentish Town Road, LONDON, NW1 9LP.
CHADWICK, Mr. Allan, FCA *1963;* 32 Chamberlain Way, PINNER, HA5 2AX.
CHADWICK, Mr. Andrew John, BA ACA *1993;* Unit 2, Mile Oak Industrial Estate, Maesbury Road, OSWESTRY, SHROPSHIRE, SY10 8GA.
CHADWICK, Mr. Andrew Mark, ACA *1993;* Freedom Finance plc, Freedom House, Church Street, WILMSLOW, CHESHIRE, SK9 1AX.
CHADWICK, Miss. Beverley, BA ACA *2000;* 16 Glenside Drive, WILMSLOW, CHESHIRE, SK9 1EH.
•**CHADWICK, Mr. Bill, FCA** *1977;* Chadwicks Accountants Limited, 16a Menston Old Lane, Burley in Wharfedale, ILKLEY, WEST YORKSHIRE, LS29 7QQ.
•**CHADWICK, Mr. Carl Bruce, ACA** *1983;* Sunaxis Ltd, Checkpoint House, Unit 8 Checkpoint Court, Sadler Road, LINCOLN, LINCOLNSHIRE LN6 3PW. See also Mcgregors Corporate (Lincoln) Ltd and McGregors (Mansfield) Ltd
CHADWICK, Miss. Carolyn Jane, BA ACA *1990;* Zurich Financial Services UK Life Centre, Station Road, SWINDON, SN1 1EL.
CHADWICK, Mr. Christopher James, MA(Hons) ACA *2000;* Neugutstrasse 4, 8304 WALLISELLEN, SWITZERLAND.
CHADWICK, Mr. Christopher Robert, BA ACA *1998;* Flowserve Corporation, Burrell Road, HAYWARDS HEATH, WEST SUSSEX, RH16 1TL.
CHADWICK, Mr. Clive Frederick, FCA *1977;* 75 Gorselands, Wash Common, NEWBURY, RG14 6PU.
CHADWICK, Mrs. Deborah Jane, MA ACA ATII *1985;* 28 Queens Road, CHELTENHAM, GL50 2LT.
CHADWICK, Mr. Edward James, MA ACA *1996;* Villa Soledad, Route Royale, Upper Vale, Fond Du Sac, PAMPLEMOUSSES, MAURITIUS.
CHADWICK, Mrs. Emily, BSc ACA *2007;* 17 Cavendish Road, Hazel Grove, STOCKPORT, CHESHIRE, SK7 6HY.
CHADWICK, Mrs. Emma Victoria, BA ACA *2000;* 56 Bathford Hill, Bathford, BATH, BA1 7SN.
CHADWICK, Mr. Eric, FCA *1960;* 483 Marine Road East, MORECAMBE, LANCASHIRE, LA4 6AF.
CHADWICK, Mr. Francois Pascal, LLB ACA *1999;* 135 Beulah Street, SAN FRANCISCO, CA 94117, UNITED STATES.
CHADWICK, Mr. Gavin, BSc ACA *2005;* 17 Cavendish Road, Hazel Grove, STOCKPORT, CHESHIRE, SK7 6HY.
CHADWICK, Mr. Geoffrey Hugh, BA ACA *2006;* The Lodge, St. Giles Close, WINCHESTER, HAMPSHIRE, SO23 0JJ.
CHADWICK, Mrs. Gillian, BSc ACA *2005;* 36 Laurel Avenue, Spring Meadow, Darcy Lever, BOLTON, BL3 1AS.
CHADWICK, Miss. Isabel Mary, BA ACA *1993;* 4 Laurel Bank, Grappenhall, WARRINGTON, WA4 2SF.
CHADWICK, Mr. James Kenneth, BSc ACA *2005;* 36 Laurel Avenue, Spring Meadows, Darcy Lever, BOLTON, BL3 1AS.
CHADWICK, Mr. Jonathan Cooper, BSc ACA *1992;* 500 Kingsley Avenue, PALO ALTO, CA 94301, UNITED STATES.
CHADWICK, Mrs. Judith, BSc ACA *1996;* 18 Northleach Close, BURY, LANCASHIRE, BL8 1QD.
CHADWICK, Mrs. Karen, BA ACA *1993;* Bristol-Myers Squibb Unit 2, Sanderson Road, UXBRIDGE, MIDDLESEX, UB8 1DH.
CHADWICK, Mr. Leigh George, MBA BSc FCA *1981;* Jasmine Cottage, 16 Nursery Lane, SUTTON COLDFIELD, WEST MIDLANDS, B74 4TP.
CHADWICK, Mr. Marcus Alan, BSc ACA *1990;* The Bank, Foxwist Green, Whitegate, NORTHWICH, CW8 2BJ.
CHADWICK, Mr. Maurice William, FCA *1956;* 3 Carrock Close, KENDALL PARK, CUMBRIA, LA9 7HW. (Life Member)
•**CHADWICK, Mr. Michael, FCA FCCA** *1976;* (Tax Fac), Chadwick & Company, Capital House, 272 Manchester Road, Droylsden, MANCHESTER, M43 6PW. See also Chadwick & Co (Manchester) Ltd
CHADWICK, Mr. Michael Guy, BA ACA *1979;* National Grid Plc, N G T House, Warwick Technology Park, Gallows Hill, WARWICK, CV34 6DA.
CHADWICK, Mr. Michael John, ACA *1982;* Edale Manor Lea Road, Milford, GODALMING, GU8 5EF.
CHADWICK, Mr. Michael Leslie, FCA *1955;* 24 Chorley Drive, SHEFFIELD, S10 3RR. (Life Member)
•**CHADWICK, Mr. Neil, FCA** *1970;* 9 Sequoia Gardens, ORPINGTON, KENT, BR6 0TZ.
CHADWICK, Mr. Nigel, BSc ACA *1986;* 10 Beaver Street, EAST MALVERN, VIC 3145, AUSTRALIA.
CHADWICK, Mr. Nigel Andrew, BA ACA *1991;* Stream Communications, 2 La Belle Place, GLASGOW, G3 7LH.
CHADWICK, Mr. Paul Brian, MA ACA *2003;* Flat 22, Edge Hill Court, Edge Hill, LONDON, SW19 4LL.
CHADWICK, Mr. Paul William, BA(Hons) ACA *2004;* Thyme Romsey Road, Kings Somborne, STOCKBRIDGE, SO20 6PN.
CHADWICK, Mr. Peter Ian, FCA *1961;* 13 Fletchers Lane, LYMM, WA13 9PP. (Life Member)
CHADWICK, Mr. Philip, LLB ACA *1993;* C R H Fencing Ltd Herons Way, Balby, DONCASTER, SOUTH YORKSHIRE, DN4 8WA.
CHADWICK, Mr. Philip Roy, ACA *1979;* 39 Tavern Road, Hadfield, GLOSSOP, DERBYSHIRE, SK13 2RB.
CHADWICK, Miss. Rachel Jane, ACIB ACA *1996;* 42 Old Wool Lane, Cheadle Hulme, CHEADLE, CHESHIRE, SK8 5JA.
CHADWICK, Mr. Raymond Leslie, FCA *1956;* Cappanacush East, Greenane, KILLARNEY, COUNTY KERRY, IRELAND. (Life Member)
CHADWICK, Mr. Richard Andrew, FCA *1973;* 13 Castello Ave, LONDON, SW15 6EA.
CHADWICK, Mr. Richard Barrowclough, BSc ACA *1996;* 36 Pinewood Avenue, SEVENOAKS, TN14 5AF.
CHADWICK, Mr. Richard Charles, ACA *2008;* 13 Liberty Street, LONDON, SW9 0EE.
CHADWICK, Mr. Richard John, FCA *1966;* 1 Barrington Close, Headington, OXFORD, OX3 7AX. (Life Member)
CHADWICK, Mr. Richard Michael, BA ACA *1996;* 19 Princes Avenue, Finchley, LONDON, N3 2DA.
CHADWICK, Mr. Robin Leslie, MA FCA *1975;* 16 Ashford Road, Whitwick, COALVILLE, LEICESTERSHIRE, LE67 5DG.
•**CHADWICK, Mr. Roger Arthur Holden, FCA** *1973;* Roger Chadwick FCA, 11 Oakfield Court, 252 Pampisford Road, SOUTH CROYDON, SURREY, CR2 6DD.
CHADWICK, Miss. Sallyann Jane, BA ACA *1984;* 12 Hollingworth Close, WEST MOLESEY, KT8 2TW.
CHADWICK, Mrs. Sian Victoria, BSc ACA *1996;* 19 Princes Avenue, LONDON, N3 2DA.
CHADWICK, Mr. Stephen John, BSc ACA *1986;* The Limes, Church Walk, Harrold, BEDFORD, MK43 7DG.
•**CHADWICK, Mr. Stuart Neil, BA ACA** *1992;* Wyatt Morris Golland & Co, Park House, 200 Drake Street, ROCHDALE, OL16 1PJ.
CHADWICK, Mr. Thomas David, BSc ACA *1992;* Astrop Hill Farmhouse, Kings Sutton, BANBURY, OXFORDSHIRE, OX17 3DU.
•**CHADWICK, Mr. Wallace George, FCA** *1978;* (Tax Fac), W.G. Chadwick Ltd, 20 Colne Road, BARNOLDSWICK, LANCASHIRE, BB18 5QU.
CHADWICK, Mr. William Herbert, FCA *1955;* Hillside, 17 Queen Street, Hoddlesden, DARWEN, BB3 3LY. (Life Member)
CHAFFE, Mr. Graeme, ACA *2008;* AnaCap Financial Partners LLP (4th Floor), 25 Bedford Street, LONDON, WC2E 9ES.
CHAFFE, Mr. John Anthony, FCA *1962;* Narvik, 1b Parkwood Road, TAVISTOCK, DEVON, PL19 0HG.
CHAFFE, Mr. John Stephen, FCA *1973;* Parametric Investments Limited, 193 Harrow Road, NOTTINGHAM, NG8 1FL.
CHAFFER, Mrs. Caroline, BA ACA *1998;* 32 Bishopdale Drive, Collingham, WETHERBY, WEST YORKSHIRE, LS22 5LP.
CHAFFER, Mr. Daniel, ACA *2002;* 14 Beaumont Road, MANCHESTER, M21 8BR.
CHAFFEY, Mr. Robert Amyon John Templeman, MA BA ACA *2001;* c/o John Swire & Sons, 35/F Two Pacific place, 88 Queensway, ADMIRALTY, HONG KONG SAR.
•**CHAGANI, Mr. Aunali, FCA** *1977;* Chagani, 37 Kingfishers, Orton Wistow, PETERBOROUGH, PE2 6YH.
•**CHAGGAR, Mr. Raghbir Singh, FCA** *1972;* Garratts Wolverhampton Limited, 29 Waterloo Road, WOLVERHAMPTON, WV1 4DJ.
CHAGGER, Mr. Balbinder Singh, ACA MBA *1993;* 2 Marlow Gardens, HAYES, UB3 1QZ.
CHAGPAR, Mr. Latiff Mohamedali Abdulla, CA FCA MBA CPA *1981;* 465 E Union Street, Suite # 207, PASADENA, CA 91101-1720, UNITED STATES.
CHAHAL, Mr. Amarjyot, ACA *2011;* Post Office, 84-85 High Street Willington, CROOK, DL15 0PE.
CHAHAL, Mr. Dipinderpal Singh, BSc ACA *2011;* 23 Lincoln Road, LONDON, E7 8QN.
CHAHAL, Mr. Jaspreet, MSc BSc ACA *2005;* 2031 Redstone Crescent, OAKVILLE L6M 5B2, ON, CANADA.
•**CHAHAL, Mr. Makhan Singh, MA ACA** *1997;* Deloitte LLP, 2 New Street Square, LONDON, EC4A 3BZ. See also Deloitte & Touche LLP
CHAHAL, Dr. Nirmal Singh, PhD BSc ACA *1995;* Ridgefield, Winkfield Road, ASCOT, SL5 7EX.
CHAHEL, Mr. Jang Singh, BA ACA *1995;* 27 Reihana Street, Orakei, AUCKLAND 1071, NEW ZEALAND.
CHAI, Mr. Chi Man, ACA *2008;* Apex CPA Limited, Units 2205-07, 22/F China Merchants Building, 303-307 Des Voeux Road Central, SHEUNG WAN, HONG KONG SAR.
CHAI, Mr. Chung Wai, ACA *2005;* Flat A 2/F Block 5, Discovery Park, 398 Castle Peak Road, TSUEN WAN, NEW TERRITORIES, HONG KONG SAR.
CHAI, Mr. Jonathan Mark, BEng ACA *1995;* 11 Dryburgh Avenue, SINGAPORE 459454, SINGAPORE.
CHAI, Mr. Koh Chan, BA ACA *1985;* 503A Taman Melaka Raya, 75000 MALACCA CITY, MALACCA STATE, MALAYSIA.
CHAI, Miss. Pek Looi, FCA *1977;* 50 Saxton Street, BOX HILL, VIC 3129, AUSTRALIA.
CHAI, Ms. Valentina Wei Li, ACA *2008;* 24 Barrier Point Road, LONDON, E16 2SB.
CHAI, Miss. Way Cheng, BA ACA *1981;* No. 1 Jalan 5/33, 46000 PETALING JAYA, SELANGOR, MALAYSIA.
CHAI, Miss. Wei Mei, BCom ACA *2001;* 285 JOO CHIAT PLACE, EASTERN RESIDENCE, #01-02, SINGAPORE 427966, SINGAPORE.
CHAI, Miss. Yuen Peng, ACA *2008;* 39 Jalan SS 23/3, Fasa 12 Taman SEA, 47400 PETALING JAYA, SELANGOR, MALAYSIA.
CHAICHIAN, Mr. Mark, BSc ACA *2004;* 14 Ullswater Road, LONDON, SW13 9PJ.
CHAIT, Mr. Steven Jonathan, BA ACA *1992;* Burdale Financial Ltd Bow Bells House, 1 Bread Street, LONDON, EC4M 9BE.
CHAIT, Mr. Stuart Alan, BA FCA *1961;* 53 Cavendish Road, SALFORD, M7 4NQ. (Life Member)
CHAJET, Mr. Gary Alexander, BA ACA *2008;* Flat 2 Helvi Court, 41 Hendon Lane, LONDON, N3 1RY.
•**CHAJET, Mr. Neville David, FCA** *1975;* Harris Lipman LLP, 2 Mountview Court, 310 Friern Barnet Lane, LONDON, N20 0YZ.
CHAK, Mrs. Yin Han Naomi, BA LLB CA FCA *1986;* 48 Craigmont Drive, NORTH YORK M2H 1C9, ON, CANADA.
CHAK, Mr. Yiu Kwong Stoney, MBA BSc CA ACA *1980,* 40 Craigmont Drive, NORTH YORK M2H 1C9, ON, CANADA.
CHAKKAR, Miss. Sharon Sarinder, BSc ACA *2010;* Greenside, 2 Malwood Gardens, Totton, SOUTHAMPTON, SO40 8BX.
•**CHAKKO, Mr. Philip Francis, FCA** *1961;* with Haines Watts, Interwood House, Stafford Avenue, HORNCHURCH, RM11 2ER.
•**CHAKRABORTTI, Mr. Amal Chandra, FCA** *1957;* 22/2A Gora Chand Road, CALCUTTA 700 014, INDIA.
CHAKRABORTY, Mr. Dilip, ACA *1980;* 4 Brookpark Crescent, CALGARY T2W 2W5, AB, CANADA.
•**CHAKRABORTY, Mr. Dilip Kumar, FCA** *1973;* (Tax Fac), Chakraborty & Co, 19 Elmfield Road, East Finchley, LONDON, N2 8EB.
•**CHALCRAFT, Mrs. Deborah Mary, BA ACA CTA** *1992;* Draycott, Prescot Road, Hale, ALTRINCHAM, CHESHIRE, WA15 9PZ.
CHALCRAFT, Miss. Jennette Elisabeth, BA CA ACA *1999;* Deloitte & Touche LLP, PO Box 49279 Four Bentall Centre, 2800-1055 Dunsmuir Street, VANCOUVER V7X 1P4, BC, CANADA.
CHALCRAFT, Mr. Stuart Martin, BA(Hons) ACA *2000;* with Ernst & Young LLP, 1 More London Place, LONDON, SE1 2AF.
CHALFONT, Mr. Steven Philip, BSc ACA *1997;* 11 Trellis Drive, Lychpit, BASINGSTOKE, RG24 8YU.
CHALK, Ms. Annette, BSc ACA *1983;* The Willows, 20 Clifton Road, Ben Rhydding, ILKLEY, LS29 8TT.

CHALK, Mr. Clive Andrew, LLB FCA *1972;* 12 Rydon Mews, Wimbledon, LONDON, SW19 4RP. (Life Member)

CHALK, Mr. Harry Raymond, FCA *1958;* 16 Loxford Way, CATERHAM, CR3 6BX. (Life Member)

CHALK, Mr. John Leslie, FCA *1956;* 7 Estate Road, Hadleigh, BENFLEET, SS7 2EW. (Life Member)

CHALK, Miss. Karen Elizabeth, BA ACA *1991;* 5 St. Marks Road, LEAMINGTON SPA, WARWICKSHIRE, CV32 6DL.

•**CHALK, Mr. Kenneth Stephen, FCA** *1970;* Craigwest Consulting Ltd, Hilltop Meadow, Cuck Hill, Shipham, WINSCOMBE, AVON BS25 1RB.

•**CHALK, Mr. Paul Andrew, BA FCA** *1984;* 5 Temple Fortune Lane, LONDON, NW11 7UB.

CHALK, Mr. Peter Henry, FCA *1963;* 6 Brechin Place, LONDON, SW7 4QA.

CHALK, Mr. Richard Neil, BA ACA *1989;* 48 Aldwark, YORK, YO1 7BU.

•**CHALK, Mr. Rupert Alexander, FCA** *1974;* (Tax Fac), Teddington Tax Services Ltd, 6 Marina Way, TEDDINGTON, MIDDLESEX, TW11 9PN.

CHALK, Mr. Stephen Edward, ACA *2009;* (Tax Fac), Grant Thornton UK Llp Grant Thornton House, 22 Melton Street, LONDON, NW1 2EP.

CHALKER, Mr. Andrew Robert Paul, BSc ACA *1993;* 33 Corfe Way, BROADSTONE, BH18 9ND.

CHALKIOPOULOS, Mr. Dionisis, ACA *2007;* Amyklon 16, Chalandri, 15231 ATHENS, GREECE.

CHALKLEY, Mr. Martin John, BSc ACA *2000;* 8 Netherwood Close, SOLIHULL, B91 1DU.

CHALKLEY, Mr. Martyn, BEng ACA *2002;* 31 Forest End Road, SANDHURST, GU47 8JT.

CHALKLEY, Mr. Reginald Harrison, FCA *1959;* 15 Halmer Gate, SPALDING, PE11 2DS.

CHALKLY-MABER, Mr. Colin John William, BSc FCA *1983;* 28 Sandringham Road, Lower Parkstone, POOLE, BH14 8TH.

CHALKOWSKI, Mr. Frederick, FCA *1953;* Kibbutz Lavee, Mobile Post, LOWER GALILEE, 15267, ISRAEL. (Life Member)

CHALLACOMBE, Mr. Simon, BA(Hons) ACA *2004;* 4 Adstone Lane, Anchorage Park, PORTSMOUTH, HAMPSHIRE, PO3 5TE.

CHALLANDS, Mr. John Norman, FCA *1972;* 10 Abbey Hill Road, Allestree, DERBY, DE22 2PS. (Life Member)

CHALLEN, Mr. Edmund Francis, BSc FCA *1972;* Flat 7, 413A Upper Richmond Road, LONDON, SW15 5QX.

CHALLEN, Mr. Jeremy, LLB ACA *1986;* 399 Box Road, KAREELA, NSW 2232, AUSTRALIA.

CHALLEN, Mrs. Lydia Mary, BSc FCA *1995;* The Royal Bank of Scotland, 4th Floor, 1 Spinningfields Square, MANCHESTER, M3 3AP.

CHALLEN, Miss. Stacey, BA ACA *2011;* 2a Roman Road, Wheatley, OXFORD, OX33 1UU.

•**CHALLENGER, Mr. David Philip, FCA** *1976;* Watts Gregory LLP, Elfed House, Oak Tree Court, Mulberry Drive, Cardiff Gate Business Park Pontprennau, CARDIFF CF23 8RS.

CHALLENGER, Mr. Dean, BA ACA *2003;* 17 Ribston Close, BEDFORD, MK41 7FG.

CHALLENGER, Mr. Henry James, FCA *1957;* Carrick Du, Upper Castle Road, St. Mawes, TRURO, TR2 5BZ. (Life Member)

•**CHALLENOR, Mr. Paul Winston, FCA** *1971;* Light Fantastic (UK) Limited, 44 Lower Town Street, Bramley, LEEDS, LS13 2BW.

CHALLENOR, Mr. Thomas William, BSc FCA *1982;* 12 Florence Road, Ealing, LONDON, W5 3TX.

CHALLINGSWORTH, Mr. Gareth Ashley, BSc ACA *1991;* Old School House Langton Road, Langton Green, TUNBRIDGE WELLS, TN3 9SS.

CHALLINOR, Mr. Andrew Paul, MBA BA ACA *1996;* 4 The Rex, High Street, BERKHAMSTED, HERTFORDSHIRE, HP4 2BT.

CHALLINOR, Mr. David John, BA ACA *1988;* (Tax Fac), Blue Cross Farm, Mount Pleasant, Derrington, STAFFORD, ST18 9NB.

CHALLINOR, Mr. David John, BA FCA *1993;* C/O Doha Bank, PO Box 3818, DOHA, QATAR.

CHALLINOR, Miss. Deborah, MA ACA *1993;* 2 Prince Edward Circle Kingsford, SYDNEY, NSW 2032, AUSTRALIA.

CHALLINOR, Mr. Hugh Alan, FCA *1960;* Pear Tree Cottage, Forton, NEWPORT, TF10 8DA. (Life Member)

CHALLINOR, Mrs. Jane Alexandra, BSc ACA *2006;* 4a Circular Road, Didsbury, MANCHESTER, M20 3LP.

CHALLINOR, Mrs. Jayne Ellen Beatrice, BA ACA *1997;* 8 Berkeley Close, IPSWICH, IP4 2TS.

CHALLINOR, Mr. Paul, BA ACA *1987;* PricewaterhouseCoopers, 250 Howe Street, Suite 700, VANCOUVER V6C 3S7, BC, CANADA.

•**CHALLIS, Mr. Christopher Richard, MA FCA CMC** *1984;* Camwell Consulting, Arena 119, 5 High Street, MAIDENHEAD, BERKSHIRE, SL6 1JN.

CHALLIS, Mr. David Harry, BSc ACA *1992;* 6 Beechwood Drive, COBHAM, SURREY, KT11 2DX.

CHALLIS, Mrs. Joanne, ACA *2006;* 52 Albert Road, ROMFORD, RM1 2PP.

CHALLIS, Mr. John Alfred, ACA *1991;* 26 Lindisfarne Road, Newton Hall, DURHAM, DH1 5YQ.

•①**CHALLIS, Mr. Julian Simon, FCA** *1977;* H W Fisher & Company, Acre House, 11-15 William Road, LONDON, NW1 3ER. See also H W Fisher & Company Limited

CHALLIS, Mr. Mark James, BA ACA *2005;* 8 Buckingham Gate, Emmer Green, READING, RG4 8RT.

•**CHALLIS, Mr. Nigel Kenneth, MA FCA** *1975;* Lincoln House, 519 High Road, Harrow Weald, HARROW, MIDDLESEX, HA3 6HL.

CHALLIS, Mr. Richard, ACA *1982;* Kingsley Cottage, Hill Lane, Kingswood, TADWORTH, KT20 6DZ.

CHALLIS, Mr. Robin Edward, BA(Hons) ACA *2002;* RBS, One Raffles Quay, South Tower, SINGAPORE, SINGAPORE.

•**CHALLIS, Mr. Stafford Drake, FCA** *1965;* Roskelly, Brock Road, St. Peter Port, GUERNSEY, GY1 1RU.

CHALLONER, Mr. Richard David, ACA *2011;* Sunnybank Cottage, West Baldwin, ISLE OF MAN, IM4 5HD.

CHALMER, Mr. Jamie Rory Alexander, BSc ACA *1988;* Flat 55 Pelham Court, 145 Fulham Road, LONDON, SW3 6SH.

CHALMERS, Mr. Alistair Scott, BA(Hons) ACA *2002;* 129 Route de Choulex, Choulex, 1244 GENEVA, SWITZERLAND.

CHALMERS, Mrs. Ann, LLB ACA *1984;* Hunters Lodge, 241 Hillbury Road, WARLINGHAM, SURREY, CR6 9TL.

CHALMERS, Mr. Arthur Thomas, BSc ACA MCIM DipM *1990;* Moss Bridge Cottage, Moss Lane, SANDBACH, CHESHIRE, CW11 3PW.

CHALMERS, Ms. Caron Fiona, BA ACA *1991;* 333 Glasgow Road, Eaglesham, GLASGOW, G76 0ER.

CHALMERS, Mr. Douglas Michael, BSc ACA *1998;* 8 Egham Court, Grove Road, SURBITON, SURREY, KT6 4DW.

•**CHALMERS, Mr. Ian William, FCA** *1980;* Phillips Frith LLP, 9 Tegarne Terrace, ST. AUSTELL, CORNWALL, PL25 4DD.

•**CHALMERS, Mr. James William Pender, BA ACA** *1989;* PricewaterhouseCoopers LLP, 1 Embankment Place, LONDON, WC2N 6RH. See also PricewaterhouseCoopers

CHALMERS, Mrs. Janet, FCA *1977;* 44 New Endrick Road Killearn, GLASGOW, G63 9QT.

CHALMERS, Mr. John Gerald William, FCA *1967;* 7 Napier Avenue, LONDON, E14 3QB.

CHALMERS, Mr. Mark Jonathan, BSc ACA *1987;* 63 Elm Grove, Milton-under-Wychwood, CHIPPING NORTON, OX7 6EF.

CHALMERS, Mr. Norman Ashley, FCA *1964;* Brook House, Templewood Lane, Farnham Common, SLOUGH, SL2 3HW. (Life Member)

CHALMERS, Mrs. Philippa Alice, BA FCA *1986;* The Hazels, 12 Church Road, Cholsey, WALLINGFORD, OXFORDSHIRE, OX10 9PR.

CHALMERS, Mr. Roderick Edwin David, FCA *1970;* Devonshire House, Preca Street, LJA 1913, LIJA, MALTA.

•**CHALMERS, Miss. Samantha Jane, BSc(Hons) ACA CTA** *2005;* Williams Grant Ltd, 83 Liverpool Street, SOUTHAMPTON, SO14 6FU.

CHALMERS-MORRIS, Mr. Stephen Geoffrey, MA ACA *1991;* Dale House, Tiviot Dale, STOCKPORT, CHESHIRE, SK1 1TA.

CHALONER, Mr. Christopher Benjamin, MA ACA ATII *1982;* Man Group Plc Sugar Quay, Lower Thames Street, LONDON, EC3R 6DU.

CHAMBERLAIN, Mr. Alan Graham, BCom FCA *1968;* Island View, Chalbury, WIMBORNE, DORSET, BH21 7EZ.

CHAMBERLAIN, Mr. Alan John, FCA *1966;* 10 The Haven, Thorpeness, LEISTON, SUFFOLK, IP16 4NN.

CHAMBERLAIN, Mr. Andrew, BSc ACA *1991;* 47 Browning Road, Fetcham, LEATHERHEAD, KT22 9HN.

CHAMBERLAIN, Mrs. Anne Catherine, BA ACA *1991;* 24 Cartref Close, VERWOOD, DORSET, BH31 6UT.

CHAMBERLAIN, Ms. Catherine Mary, MSc ACA *1988;* 6 Wick Road, Ewenny, BRIDGEND, MID GLAMORGAN, CF35 5BL.

CHAMBERLAIN, Miss. Claire Madeline, BSc ACA *2002;* 5 Temple Road, EXETER, EX2 4HG.

CHAMBERLAIN, Mrs. Claire Maria, BA ACA *1990;* Bakkavor Logistics, Bakkavor Ltd, West Marsh Road, SPALDING, LINCOLNSHIRE, PE11 2BB.

•**CHAMBERLAIN, Mr. Clive Douglas, FCA** *1977;* (Tax Fac), 11a Hale Pit Road, Bookham, LEATHERHEAD, KT23 4BS.

CHAMBERLAIN, Miss. Debra, MMath ACA *2009;* 1 Parkway, STOCKPORT, CHESHIRE, SK3 0PX.

CHAMBERLAIN, Mr. Gareth, MSc BSc ACA *2009;* 5 Mornington Mansions, New Church Road, HOVE, EAST SUSSEX, BN3 4JS.

CHAMBERLAIN, Mrs. Helen, BSc ACA *1991;* 4, The Horseshoe, YORK, YO24 1LX.

CHAMBERLAIN, Mr. Ian Steven, BSc ACA CF *1985;* with Deloitte LLP, 3 Rivergate, Temple Quay, BRISTOL, BS1 6GD.

CHAMBERLAIN, Mrs. Jean Maud, FCA *1957;* Top House, St Mary's Square, Kelvedon, COLCHESTER, CO5 9AN. (Life Member)

CHAMBERLAIN, Mr. John, BA(Hons) ACA *2004;* Bunzl Plc York House, 45 Seymour Street, LONDON, W1H 7JT.

CHAMBERLAIN, Mr. John Ashley, FCA *1973;* 4 Cuffelle Close, Chineham, BASINGSTOKE, RG24 8RH.

•**CHAMBERLAIN, Mr. John Brian, BSc FCA** *1987;* Brebners, The Quadrangle, 180 Wardour Street, LONDON, W1F 8LB.

•**CHAMBERLAIN, Mr. John Robert, FCA** *1959;* (Tax Fac), John R Chamberlain, Westcott, 16 Western Road, HENLEY-ON-THAMES, RG9 1JL. See also Brebners Limited

CHAMBERLAIN, Miss. Justine Evette Victoria, BA ACA *1999;* 7a The Drive, Countesthorpe, LEICESTER, LE8 5PB.

CHAMBERLAIN, Mr. Kevin, BSc FCA *1987;* with KPMG, 10 Shelley Street, SYDNEY, NSW 2000, AUSTRALIA.

CHAMBERLAIN, Miss. Lesley Joy, BSc ACA *1991;* 10 Faircross Way, ST. ALBANS, HERTFORDSHIRE, AL1 4SD.

CHAMBERLAIN, Mrs. Linda Jennifer, MA ACA *1986;* 3 Burford Lea, Elstead, GODALMING, GU8 6HT.

CHAMBERLAIN, Mr. Michael, FCA *1961;* 31 Maidstone Drive, Wollaton, NOTTINGHAM, NG8 2RF.

•①**CHAMBERLAIN, Mr. Michael, BA ACA** *1990;* Michael Chamberlain & Co Limited, Aireside House, 24-26 Aire Street, LEEDS, LS1 4HT.

CHAMBERLAIN, Mr. Michael Aubrey, OBE LLD FCA *1963;* (President 1993 - 1994) (Member of Council 1982 - 1996), Willow End, 3 Spinney Nook, Main Street, Tugby, LEICESTER, LE7 9EY. (Life Member)

•**CHAMBERLAIN, Mr. Neil Howard, ACA** *1980;* (Tax Fac), Mosley & Co., 14 Market Place, Ramsbottom, BURY, BL0 9HT.

CHAMBERLAIN, Mr. Paul Anthony, BA(Hons) ACA *2001;* 3 Newlands Road, TUNBRIDGE WELLS, KENT, TN4 9AS.

CHAMBERLAIN, Mr. Paul Bernard Stanley, BSc FCA CTA *1994;* 78 Polwarth Road, Brunton Park, Gosforth, NEWCASTLE UPON TYNE, NE3 5NE.

•**CHAMBERLAIN, Mr. Paul Ivor, FCA** *1972;* 17 Priory Close, WALTON-ON-THAMES, KT12 1JR.

•**CHAMBERLAIN, Mr. Paul Jonathan, MA FCA DChA** *1986;* (Tax Fac), Chamberlains, 3 Burford Lea, Elstead, GODALMING, SURREY, GU8 6HT. See also FAI Audit Ltd

CHAMBERLAIN, Mr. Peter David, FCA *1970;* 24 Hillary Road, RUSHDEN, NORTHAMPTONSHIRE, NN10 9NZ.

CHAMBERLAIN, Mr. Philip Howard, FCA CF *1975;* 6 Blenheim Close, SAWBRIDGEWORTH, HERTFORDSHIRE, CM21 0BE.

CHAMBERLAIN, Mr. Richard, BA ACA *1999;* 42 Willow Road, Hampstead, LONDON, NW3 1TS.

CHAMBERLAIN, Mr. Richard Anthony, FCA *1965;* 3 Queens Crescent, RICHMOND, SURREY, TW10 6HG.

CHAMBERLAIN, Mr. Robert Anthony, FCA *1969;* 10 Brigg Road, FILEY, NORTH YORKSHIRE, YO14 0AF. (Life Member)

CHAMBERLAIN, Mr. Rupert Joseph, BA FCA *1996;* with KPMG, 8/F Prince's Building, 10 Chater Road, CENTRAL, HONG KONG ISLAND, HONG KONG SAR.

CHAMBERLAIN, Mr. Sam John, ACA *2008;* 72 York Road, IPSWICH, IP3 8BU.

CHAMBERLAIN, Miss. Sarah, ACA *2011;* 45 Alkrington Hall Road South, Middleton, MANCHESTER, M24 1NJ.

•**CHAMBERLAIN, Miss. Sarah Louise, ACA** *2008;* Kirk Hills, 5 Barnfield Crescent, EXETER, EX1 1QT. See also Kirk Hills Insolvency Ltd

CHAMBERLAIN, Mr. Simon John, BA FCA *1983;* (Tax Fac), MacIntyre Hudson Llp, 30-34 New Bridge Street, LONDON, EC4V 6BJ.

CHAMBERLAIN, Mr. Stephen Keith, MEng&Man ACA *1998;* Herewake, 17 High Street, Willingham, CAMBRIDGE, CB24 5ES.

CHAMBERLAIN-WEBBER, Mr. William James Elwyn, BSc ACA *1989;* Chamberlain Dunn Associates, Gothic House, 3 The Green, RICHMOND, SURREY, TW9 1PL.

CHAMBERLIN, Mr. Peter Arthur, BA FCA *1979;* 28 Windmill Avenue, Birstall, LEICESTER, LE4 4JJ.

CHAMBERS, Mr. Adam Paul, BA ACA *2003;* 3 Oakwood Gardens, Knaphill, WOKING, GU21 2RX.

CHAMBERS, Mr. Alan Keith, ACA CTA *1980;* Lake View, Sike Lane, Walton, WAKEFIELD, WEST YORKSHIRE, WF2 6PP.

CHAMBERS, Prof. Andrew David, BA CEng FCA FCCA FIIA FBCS FRSA *1968;* Management Audit, Moat Lane, Old Bolingbroke, SPILSBY, LINCOLNSHIRE, PE23 4ES.

CHAMBERS, Mr. Andrew John, BSc ACA *1996;* Bae Systems Plc Burwood House, 14-16 Caxton Street, LONDON, SW1H 0QT.

CHAMBERS, Mrs. Anita, BPharm ACA *1996;* 11 Henton Close, Coddington, NEWARK, NOTTINGHAMSHIRE, NG24 2TE.

CHAMBERS, Mr. Bernard Basil, FCA *1966;* 6 Chaucer Avenue, WEYBRIDGE, KT13 0SS. (Life Member)

CHAMBERS, Mr. Carl James, LLB ACA *1988;* The Old Farm House, 73 Breary Lane East, Bramhope, LEEDS, LS16 9EU.

•**CHAMBERS, Mrs. Caryl Anne, BSc FCA** *1983;* Caryl Chambers Limited, Kamara, 6a Church Street, Burton Latimer, KETTERING, NN15 5LU.

CHAMBERS, Miss. Christina Rose, BA ACA *2004;* 19 Hartford Road, Davenham, NORTHWICH, CHESHIRE, CW9 8JA.

CHAMBERS, Mr. Christopher John, FCA *1973;* 75a Main Street, SEDBERGH, CUMBRIA, LA10 5AB.

CHAMBERS, Ms. Claire, BA(Hons) ACA *2001;* 8 Cambanks, CAMBRIDGE, CB4 1PY.

CHAMBERS, Mr. Colin, FCA *1965;* 38 Hickings Lane, Stapleford, NOTTINGHAM, NG9 8PA. (Life Member)

CHAMBERS, Mr. Darryl John, ACA *1991;* Marshall Arts Ltd, Unit 6, Utopia Village, 7 Chalcot Road, LONDON, NW1 8LH.

CHAMBERS, Mr. David, FCA *1976;* Westmount, Ravenshayes, Silverton, EXETER, EX5 4DA.

CHAMBERS, Mr. David Cowan, BSc ACA *1992;* Jalna Firbank Lane, WOKING, SURREY, GU21 7QP.

CHAMBERS, Miss. Dora Alice, MA(Hons) ACA *2011;* Flat 67 Floor 5, Paddington Basin, North Wharf Road, LONDON, W2 1LF.

CHAMBERS, Mr. Edward Dillingham, FCA *1956;* Heathers, Brushes Lane, Lindfield, HAYWARDS HEATH, RH16 2JE. (Life Member)

CHAMBERS, Mrs. Elizabeth Dawn, BSc ACA ATII *1992;* Claremont, 14 Huia Street, DEVONPORT 0624, AUCKLAND, NEW ZEALAND.

CHAMBERS, Ms. Frances Clare, MSci ACA CFA *2007;* 6 Danemere Street, LONDON, SW15 1LT.

CHAMBERS, Mr. Frederick John Anthony, FCA DChA *1977;* 12 Kestrel Heights, Codnor Park, NOTTINGHAM, NG16 5PW.

CHAMBERS, Mr. Graeme George, BSc(Hons) ACA AMCT *2002;* 112 Berw Road, PONTYPRIDD, MID GLAMORGAN, CF37 2AB.

•**CHAMBERS, Mr. Graham Leonard, FCA** *1969;* (Tax Fac), Dixon Wilson, 22 Chancery Lane, LONDON, WC2A 1LS.

•**CHAMBERS, Miss. Helen, BSc FCA** *1979;* (Tax Fac), Warings, Bedford House, 60 Chorley New Road, BOLTON, BL1 4DA. See also Warings Business Advisers LLP

CHAMBERS, Mr. Hubert Neville, FCA *1957;* 28 Rectory Lane, Thurcaston, LEICESTER, LE7 7JQ. (Life Member)

CHAMBERS, Mr. Iain Matthew, MChem ACA *2006;* 32 Crimicar Drive, SHEFFIELD, S10 4EG.

•**CHAMBERS, Mr. Ian Grenville, MA FCA** *1975;* I.G. Chambers, Compass House, 15 West Meade, Milland, LIPHOOK, GU30 7NB.

•**CHAMBERS, Mr. Ian Robert, BSc FCA** *1991;* PricewaterhouseCoopers LLP, 1 Embankment Place, LONDON, WC2N 6RH. See also PricewaterhouseCoopers

CHAMBERS, Mr. James Martin, ACA *2010;* 55 Ashen Grove, LONDON, SW19 8BL.

CHAMBERS, Mrs. Jane Mary Clare, BSc FCA *1985;* with Grant Thornton UK LLP, Grant Thornton House, Kettering Parkway, Kettering Venture Park, KETTERING, NORTHAMPTONSHIRE NN15 6XR.

CHAMBERS, Miss. Jane Sarah, BSc ACA *1992;* 55 Beechwood Park Road, SOLIHULL, WEST MIDLANDS, B91 1ES.

CHAMBERS, Mrs. Jennifer Mary, BA FCA *1979;* (Tax Fac), The Hollies, 18 Harvey Lane, Thorpe St Andrew, NORWICH, NR7 0BN.

CHAMBERS, Mr. John, BCom FCA FCMI *1965;* Golden Square Films Ltd, Pinewood Studios, Pinewood Road, IVER, SL0 0NH.

CHAMBERS, Mr. Jolyon Ray, BSc ACA *1996;* 46 Oxberry Avenue, LONDON, SW6 5SS.

CHAMBERS, Mr. Jonathan George Michael, ACA *2008;* 20 Williams Grove, Long Ditton, SURBITON, KT6 5RN.

•CHAMBERS, Mr. Keith, FCA *1971;* Keith Chambers, 24 Westgate, SLEAFORD, NG34 7PN.

CHAMBERS, Mr. Kenneth William, FCA *1969;* 6 Kings Walk, HENLEY-ON-THAMES, OXFORDSHIRE, RG9 2DJ.

CHAMBERS, Mr. Lewis, FCA *1968;* 15 Rowan Court, FROME, SOMERSET, BA11 2SJ. (Life Member)

CHAMBERS, Mrs. Linda Ruth, BSc FCA *1975;* 10 Twining Brook Road, Cheadle Hulme, CHEADLE, SK8 5PU.

CHAMBERS, Mrs. Lisa Jane, BSc ACA *1992;* Wain Wood Edge, Hitchin Road, Preston, HITCHIN, SG4 7TZ.

CHAMBERS, Mr. Matthew, BSc ACA MAAT *2010;* 20b Cavendish Street, PETERBOROUGH, PE1 5EG.

CHAMBERS, Mr. Michael Robert, BSc ACA *2006;* The Cooperative Asset Management 22nd Floor, Miller Street, MANCHESTER, M60 0AL.

CHAMBERS, Mr. Neil Clifford, FCA *1972;* Computer Generated Packaging Ltd, 8-10 Outram House, Piccadilly Village, Great Ancoats Street, MANCHESTER, M4 7AA.

CHAMBERS, Mr. Oliver Edward, BA(Hons) ACA *2010;* Flat 2, 139 Holland Road, LONDON, W14 8AS.

CHAMBERS, Mr. Paul, BA(Hons) ACA *2002;* 8 Kew Gardens, Nuthall, NOTTINGHAM, NG16 1RG.

CHAMBERS, Mr. Paul, BA ACA *2006;* 15 Freshfield Road, Formby, LIVERPOOL, L37 3JA.

CHAMBERS, Mr. Paul Andrew, BSc ACA *2006;* Deloitte & Touche LLP, PO Box 49279 Four Bentall Centre, 2800 - 1500 Dunsmuir Street, VANCOUVER V7X 1P4, BC, CANADA.

CHAMBERS, Mr. Paul John, BSc ACA *1999;* 19 Kingland Drive, LEAMINGTON SPA, CV32 6BL.

CHAMBERS, Mr. Paul Jonathan, BCom FCA *1975;* 24 Constable Road, ILKLEY, WEST YORKSHIRE, LS29 8RW.

CHAMBERS, Mr. Paul Stuart, BCom ACA *1992;* 10 Burntwood Road, SEVENOAKS, TN13 1PT.

CHAMBERS, Mr. Paul Thomas, BSc FCA *1991;* 34 Anne Street, Wadestown, WELLINGTON 6012, NEW ZEALAND.

CHAMBERS, Mr. Raymond Walter, FCA *1966;* Brocks Way, Green Lane, Ilsington, NEWTON ABBOT, DEVON, TQ13 9RB.

CHAMBERS, Mr. Robert, BA FCA *1975;* Flat 1, 49 Cromwell Avenue, Highgate, LONDON, N6 5HP.

CHAMBERS, Mr. Robert Andrew, FCA *1977;* The Old School House, 38 Bramcote Lane, Wollaton, NOTTINGHAM, NG8 2ND.

CHAMBERS, Mr. Roy Duncan, BSc ACA *1989;* British American Tobacco UK, Oxford House, Oxford Road, AYLESBURY, BUCKINGHAMSHIRE, HP21 8SZ.

CHAMBERS, Mr. Russell David, LLB ACA *2003;* with PricewaterhouseCoopers, Darling Park Tower 2, 201 Sussex Street, GPO Box 2650, SYDNEY, NSW 1171 AUSTRALIA.

CHAMBERS, Mrs. Sally Jill, BSc FCA *1992;* 3 Phillipott Close, NEWARK, NOTTINGHAMSHIRE, NG24 2LT.

CHAMBERS, Mrs. Sarah Elizabeth, BSc ACA *1995;* Elderberry House, Dog Lane, Childrey, WANTAGE, OX12 9UW.

CHAMBERS, Mr. Sebastian George, BA ACA *1993;* CIL, The Cil Buildings, Corsley, WARMINSTER, BA12 7QE.

•CHAMBERS, Mr. Steven Michael, FCA *1980;* (Tax Fac), Phipps Henson McAllister, 22/24 Harborough Road, Kingsthorpe, NORTHAMPTON, NN2 7AZ.

•CHAMBERS, Mr. Stuart Malcolm, FCA *1966;* Chambers Cope & Partners Limited, 121 Smedley Street, MATLOCK, DE4 3JG.

CHAMBERS, Mr. Thomas William, BA FCA AMCT *1986;* 32 Montague Road, RICHMOND, SURREY, TW10 6QJ.

CHAMBERS, Mr. Timothy John Essex, MA ACA *1997;* Flat 4, 4 Rosslyn Hill, LONDON, NW3 1PH.

CHAMDAL, Miss. Sonika, BSc ACA *2011;* Bank of America Merrill Lynch, Warwick Court, 2 King Edward Street, LONDON, EC1A 1HQ.

CHAMDIA, Mr. Navid, BSc ACA *1997;* Qatar Investment Authority, 2nd Floor Corniche Road, PO BOX 23224, DOHA, QATAR.

CHAMI, Mr. Rostam, FCA *1975;* Rosen Villa, 2nd Floor, 81 Matarpakhdi Road, Mazagaon, MUMBAI 400-010, INDIA.

CHAMIER, Mr. Michael Edward Deschamps, FCA *1965;* 1 Rue De Limpach, L-4980 RECKANGE MESS, LUXEMBOURG.

CHAMINGS, Mr. Daniel Anthony, MA BA ACA *2006;* 53 Holywell Lane, LEEDS, LS17 8EY.

CHAMOUN, Mr. Charbel, BSc ACA *2007;* 25 Kolokotroni Street, Ayios Dometios, 2369 NICOSIA, CYPRUS.

CHAMP, Mrs. Jacqueline, FCA *1965;* Highcliffe, 2 Cherry Orchard, LICHFIELD, STAFFORDSHIRE, WS14 9AN.

•CHAMP, Mr. Nicholas John, BA FCA *1982;* Rianta Capital Zurich, Raemistrasse 6, 8001 ZURICH, SWITZERLAND.

CHAMPAGNON, Mr. Francois Jean-Pierre, ACA *2000;* Southview, 35 Old Heybeck Lane, Tingley, WAKEFIELD, WEST YORKSHIRE, WF3 1DW.

CHAMPION, Mr. Adrian Noel Bramble, BSc FCA AMCT *1977;* Ivy House, Ivy House Lane, BERKHAMSTED, HP4 2PP.

CHAMPION, Mr. Anthony Richard Coverley, BA ACA *1990;* 11 Grange Park Place, Wimbledon, LONDON, SW20 0EE.

CHAMPION, Mr. David, FCA *1947;* Ambassador Unit 24, 100 Esplanade, BURLEIGH HEADS, QLD 4220, AUSTRALIA. (Life Member)

CHAMPION, Mr. Hugh Board, MA FCA *1981;* Champion Processes Ltd., St.Georges, WESTON-SUPER-MARE, BS22 7XS.

•CHAMPION, Mr. John Rainer, FCA *1982;* McLean Reid, 1 Forstal Road, AYLESFORD, ME20 7AU.

CHAMPION, Mr. Malcolm John, FCA *1958;* Copperwood, The Spinney, Bonnington, ASHFORD, KENT, TN25 7BN. (Life Member)

CHAMPION, Mr. Mark Alistair, BA FCA *1999;* 65 Winslade Park Avenue, Clyst St Mary, EXETER, DEVON, EX5 1DB.

CHAMPION, Mr. Michael Roger, BSc ACA *1993;* Schroder, Garrard House, 31-45 Gresham Street, LONDON, EC2V 7QA.

CHAMPION, Mr. Simon Paul, BA ACA *1997;* 44 Rusholme Road, LONDON, SW15 3LG.

CHAMPION DE CRESPIGNY, Mr. Michael Anthony Peter, ACA *2010;* Flat 15, 35 Buckingham Gate, LONDON, SW1E 6PA.

CHAMPKEN, Mr. Graham Roy, BCom ACA *1989;* (Tax Fac), 147 Knightlow Road, Harborne, BIRMINGHAM, B17 8PY.

CHAMPKIN, Mrs. Gemma Elizabeth, BSc ACA *2004;* HCP Social Infrastructure (UK) Ltd, Unit 8 White Oak Square, London Road, SWANLEY, BR8 7AG.

CHAMPKINS, Mr. Tim Ross, MEng ACA *2006;* 189 Hawes Lane, WEST WICKHAM, BR4 9AG.

CHAMPNESS, Mr. Ronald Douglas, FCA *1955;* 30 Reynards Copse, COLCHESTER, CO4 9UR. (Life Member)

CHAMPSI, Mr. Amit, BSc ACA *1997;* Liberty Mutual Insurance Group, 16th Floor, 525 B Street, SAN DIEGO, CA 92101, UNITED STATES.

•CHAMPSI, Mr. Bhagwatsinh Shivji, FCA *1970;* Amchin Management Services Limited, 23 Northiam, LONDON, N12 7ET.

CHAN, Miss. Ai Tin, ACA *1982;* 7 Island View Terrace, HOWICK, AUCKLAND, NEW ZEALAND.

CHAN, Mr. Alan Tat Hung, ACA *2005;* 632 West Broadway, VANCOUVER V5Z 1G1, BC, CANADA.

CHAN, Mr. Alan Wai-Yiu, BSc(Hons) ACA *2010;* 122 Humberstone Drive, LEICESTER, LE5 0RD.

CHAN, Miss. Alice Suk Fun, BA ACA *1995;* Room 301, 3rd Floor BLK 78, Bamboo Grove, 78 Kennedy Road, WAN CHAI, HONG KONG ISLAND HONG KONG SAR.

CHAN, Mrs. Alison Yau Fun, BA ACA *1988;* Fleming House, 71 King Street, MAIDENHEAD, SL6 1DU.

CHAN, Mr. Allan Chai Kong, BSc FCA *1989;* Flat A2 Block A 21/F, Beverly Hill, 6 Broadwood Road, HAPPY VALLEY, HONG KONG ISLAND, HONG KONG SAR.

CHAN, Mr. Alvin Hon Biu, MBA ACA *1992;* Nair & Co Whitefriars, Lewins Mead, BRISTOL, BS1 2NT.

CHAN, Mr. Andrew Chun Wah, ACA *1984;* 3A Jalan Sayang, SINGAPORE 418624, SINGAPORE.

CHAN, Mr. Andrew Yik Hong, BA FCA *1992;* 239 Jalan 5/50, 46000 PETALING JAYA, SELANGOR, MALAYSIA.

CHAN, Miss. Anne Poh Ling, BSc ACA *2004;* Flat 41 Sail Court, 15 Newport Avenue, LONDON, E14 2DQ.

CHAN, Mr. Arthur Sung Lai, MSc BEng ACA *2000;* with PricewaterhouseCoopers, Prince's Building, 22/F, 10 Chater Road, CENTRAL, HONG KONG ISLAND HONG KONG SAR.

CHAN, Ms. Barbara Shih Wen, BSc ACA *1995;* 20 School Lane, Copmanthorpe, YORK, NORTH YORKSHIRE, YO23 3SG.

CHAN, Mr. Basil, BSc ACA *1982;* 77 West Coast Grove, SINGAPORE 127877, SINGAPORE.

CHAN, Miss. Becky Pik Yee, MSc BA ACA *1996;* SCG Hong Kong SAR Limited, 2/F No.1 Science Park East Avenue, Pak Shek Kok, SHA TIN, NEW TERRITORIES, HONG KONG SAR.

•CHAN, Ms. Belle, BSc ACA *1992;* Belle Chan, Flat 906 Block A, Peninsula Heights, 63 Broadcast Drive, KOWLOON TONG, KOWLOON HONG KONG SAR.

CHAN, Mrs. Benedicta Lan Mee, FCA *1975;* Beneton Properties Sdn Bhd, L18 Menara Chan, 138 Jalan Ampang, 50450 KUALA LUMPUR, FEDERAL TERRITORY, MALAYSIA.

CHAN, Mr. Bernard Kai Luen, ACA *1995;* 17 MERINO CRESCENT, SINGAPORE 149164, SINGAPORE.

CHAN, Mr. Billy Sheung Wai, ACA *2008;* 67 Ferry Street, LONDON, E14 3DT.

CHAN, Mr. Bing Kwong Henry, ACA *2008;* Flat F, 29/F, Block 9, Monte Vista, 9 Sha on Street, Ma on Shan SHA TIN NEW TERRITORIES HONG KONG SAR.

CHAN, Mrs. Brenda Margaret Wai Ming, BSc FCA *1988;* Flat B 25/F Kingsford Height, 17-19 Babington Path, MID LEVELS, HONG KONG ISLAND, HONG KONG SAR.

CHAN, Mr. Brian Yoon Kong, ACA CA(NZ) *2011;* Flat 5, The Carltons, 32 Carlton Drive, LONDON, SW15 2BL.

CHAN, Mr. Calvin Tai Wah, ACA *2008;* 2/F 19A Sands Street, WEST POINT, HONG KONG SAR.

CHAN, Mr. Chant Fai, ACA *2007;* C.F. Chan & Company, 28th Floor, Times Tower, 393 Jaffe Road, WAN CHAI, HONG KONG SAR.

CHAN, Mr. Charles Tit Hee, ACA *2006;* Flat F 10/F Block 6, Pokfulam Gardens, 180 Pokfulam Road, POK FU LAM, HONG KONG SAR.

CHAN, Mr. Che Sum Story, ACA *2007;* B7 Bayside Villa, No.1 Pik Sha Road, CLEARWATER BAY, HONG KONG SAR.

CHAN, Mr. Chee Beng, BA FCA *1981;* 3 JLN TR 6/1Tropicana Golf &, Country Resort PETALING JAYA, Selangor, MALAYSIA.

CHAN, Mr. Chee Hang, ACA *2008;* Flat D, 33/F, Block 17, South Horizons, AP LEI CHAU, HONG KONG SAR.

CHAN, Mr. Cheong Meng, BA ACA *1992;* 1-3A-07 Lanai Kiara Condo, No1 Jalan Kiara 3, Bukit Kiara, 50480 KUALA LUMPUR, FEDERAL TERRITORY, MALAYSIA.

CHAN, Mr. Cheow Tong Jeffery, FCA *1972;* 33 OXLEY RISE #05-03, VISION CREST, SINGAPORE 238710, SINGAPORE.

CHAN, Miss. Cheryl Wing-Han, BSc ACA *1999;* EDF Energy, 5th Floor 80 Victoria Street, LONDON, SW1e 5JL.

CHAN, Mr. Cheuk Chi, ACA *2006;* World Link CPA Limited, 5/F Far East Consortium Building, 121 Des Voeux Road, CENTRAL, HONG KONG ISLAND, HONG KONG SAR.

CHAN, Mr. Chi Bor, ACA *2007;* Chan Li Law & Co, Unit 402, 4/F Malaysia Building, 50 Gloucester Road, WAN CHAI, HONG KONG ISLAND HONG KONG SAR.

CHAN, Mr. Chi Wai, ACA *2007;* with Ernst & Young, Level 16, Tower E3, Oriental Plaza, No 1 East Chang Avenue, Dong Cheng Street BEIJING CHINA.

CHAN, Mr. Chi Yuen, BSc ACA *2000;* Hermes Sourcecap, Hermes Pensions Management Ltd Lloyds Chambers, 1 Portsoken Street, LONDON, E1 8HZ.

CHAN, Mr. Chi Yuen, ACA *2007;* 31A Tower 8, The Palazzo, SHA TIN, NEW TERRITORIES, HONG KONG SAR.

CHAN, Mr. Chi Cheong, ACA *2007;* 2/F, 147 Argyle Street, MONG KOK, KOWLOON, HONG KONG SAR.

CHAN, Mr. Chi Chung, ACA *2007;* 24/F, CDW Bldg, 388 Castle Peak Road, TSEUNG KWAN O, NEW TERRITORIES, HONG KONG SAR.

CHAN, Mr. Chi Keung, ACA *2008;* Room 16, Block C 7/F, Fontana Gardens, Tai Hang Road, CAUSEWAY BAY, HONG KONG SAR.

CHAN, Mr. Chi Kong, ACA *2010;* (Tax Fac), 52D Tower 1, The Victoria Towers, 188 Canton Road, TSIM SHA TSUI, KOWLOON, HONG KONG SAR.

CHAN, Mr. Chi Kong Morison, ACA *2007;* 1/F, House 12, Monte Villas, 6 Monte Path, Kau To Shan, SHA TIN NEW TERRITORIES HONG KONG SAR.

CHAN, Mr. Chi Leung Ambrose, ACA *2006;* Unit 411 Austin Tower, 22-26 Austin Avenue, TSIM SHA TSIU, KOWLOON, HONG KONG SAR.

CHAN, Mr. Chi Pan, ACA *2005;* Flat B 19/F Block 12a, Provident Centre, 45 Wharf Road, NORTH POINT, HONG KONG ISLAND, HONG KONG SAR.

CHAN, Mr. Chi Po Andy, ACA *2008;* Flat B, 29/F, Block 26, South Horizons, AP LEI CHAU, HONG KONG SAR.

CHAN, Miss. Chiao Lin, BSc ACA *2003;* 48 Tingkat Besi, 11600 GEORGE TOWN, PULAU PINANG, MALAYSIA.

CHAN, Mrs. Chiew Tiap, FCA *1986;* 3 Hillcrest Court, Hillcrest, BRIGHTON, BN1 5FR.

CHAN, Mr. Chik Fai, ACA *2004;* Flat B 18/F Block 3, The Grand Panorama, 10 Robinson Road, MID LEVELS, HONG KONG ISLAND, HONG KONG SAR.

CHAN, Mr. Chin Kwan Tommy, ACA *2005;* 46 Sherwood Hill NW, CALGARY T3R 1P4, AB, CANADA.

CHAN, Mr. Ching Pang, ACA *2011;* Flat C, 34/F Tower 2, Bauhinia Garden, 11 Tong Chun Street, TSEUNG KWAN O, NEW TERRITORIES HONG KONG SAR.

CHAN, Ms. Ching-Chu, ACA *2007;* PricewaterhouseCoopers, Prince's Building, 22/F, 10 Chater Road, CENTRAL, HONG KONG ISLAND HONG KONG SAR.

CHAN, Mr. Chit Ming Joeie, ACA *2008;* Flat B, 6/F, Block 19, Chi Fu Fa Yuen, POK FU LAM, HONG KONG SAR.

CHAN, Mr. Chiu Hung Alex, ACA *2007;* Flat J, 4/F 43 Ma Tau Wai Road, HUNG HOM, KOWLOON, HONG KONG SAR.

CHAN, Miss. Chiu Ying Connie, BA ACA *1985;* Flat 1304, Block B, Villa Rocha, 10 Broadwood Road, HAPPY VALLEY, HONG KONG ISLAND HONG KONG SAR.

CHAN, Mr. Cho Hing, ACA *2008;* with Ernst & Young Tax Services Ltd, 18/F, Two IFC, 8 Finance Street, CENTRAL, HONG KONG ISLAND HONG KONG SAR.

CHAN, Mr. Chong Kei, ACA *2006;* Flat C 13/F Seaview Building, 2-8 Wharf Road, NORTH POINT, HONG KONG SAR.

CHAN, Mr. Chong Yan, BSc ACA *1997;* 905/187 Kent Street, SYDNEY, NSW 2000, AUSTRALIA.

CHAN, Mr. Choong Fai, MEng ACA *1992;* 49 Atwood Avenue, RICHMOND, TW9 4HF.

CHAN, Mr. Choong Yoo Bernard, ACA *1983;* 12 Kimberley Road, CARLINGFORD, NSW 2118, AUSTRALIA.

CHAN, Mr. Chor Hung, ACA *2008;* Chan Chor Hung & Co, Room 1801A, Sunbeam Commercial Building, 469-474 Nathan Road, YAU MA TEI, KOWLOON HONG KONG SAR.

CHAN, Mr. Chor Kwong Aldous, ACA *2008;* Flat 17D, Block 22, Baguio Villa, 555 Victoria Road, POK FU LAM, HONG KONG SAR.

CHAN, Mr. Chow Hong, MSc ACA *1987;* D-19-1, One Menerung, 1 Jalan Menerung, 59100 KUALA LUMPUR, FEDERAL TERRITORY, MALAYSIA.

CHAN, Mr. Chrispian Chiaw Huan, FCA *1976;* 43 Cameron Court, Willetton, PERTH, WA 6155, AUSTRALIA. (Life Member)

CHAN, Mrs. Christine Wai-Yee, MBA FCA CTA *1992;* 9 Kenilworth Road, Blundellsands, Crosby, LIVERPOOL, L23 3AD.

CHAN, Mr. Christopher Wing Kin, ACA *1981;* 15 A Sunlight Garden, 2 Man Wan Road, HO MAN TIN, Kowloon, HONG KONG SAR.

CHAN, Ms. Chui Mei Mary, ACA *2007;* Flat B1, 11 F Paterson Building, 7 Great George Street, CAUSEWAY BAY, HONG KONG ISLAND, HONG KONG SAR.

CHAN, Mr. Chuk Cheung Ivan, ACA *2007;* P.O.Box 7547, General Post Office, CENTRAL, HONG KONG ISLAND, HONG KONG SAR.

CHAN, Mr. Chun Hoi, ACA *2006;* Flat F 37/F Block 5, Kingsford Terrace, No.8 King Tung Street, WONG TAI SIN, KOWLOON, HONG KONG SAR.

CHAN, Mr. Chun Kit Ivan, CA ACA *2010;* (Tax Fac), Room 1804 Block A, Cheung Wo Court, 277 Hip Wo Street, KWUN TONG, KOWLOON, HONG KONG SAR.

CHAN, Mr. Chun Kwong, ACA *2008;* Chan Chun Kwong & Co, 904 Wellborne Commercial Centre, 8 Java Road, NORTH POINT, HONG KONG SAR.

CHAN, Mr. Chun Sing, ACA *2008;* 9/F, Flat A, Block 2, Skylodge, 8 Yin Ping Road, KOWLOON TONG KOWLOON HONG KONG SAR.

CHAN, Mr. Chun Wai, ACA *2005;* Flat A 15/F Campion Court, 20 Cheung Wah Street, CHEUNG SHA WAN, KOWLOON, HONG KONG SAR.

CHAN, Mr. Chun Ying, ACA *2008;* C Y Chan & Co, Room B, 5/F, Kiu Yin Com Building, 361-363 Lockhart Road, WAN CHAI HONG KONG SAR.

Members - Alphabetical CHAN - CHAN

CHAN, Mr. Chung Wah Clement, ACA *2004;* Clement C. W. Chan & Co., 3/F & 5/F, Heng Shan Centre, 145 Queen's Road East, WAN CHAI, HONG KONG ISLAND HONG KONG SAR.
CHAN, Mr. Clement Kai Leung, MBA ACA *1992;* Flat A 18/F Block 6, Cavendish Heights, 33 Perkins Road, JARDINE'S LOOKOUT, HONG KONG SAR.
CHAN, Mr. Colin, MEng ACA *2004;* OneTeam 8th NLA Tower, 12-16 Addiscombe Road, CROYDON, CR9 6DS.
CHAN, Miss. Cynthia Sze Wan, ACA *1999;* Fitch Ratings, Fimalac, 30 North Colonnade, LONDON, E14 5GN.
CHAN, Mr. David Ming To, ACA *2007;* Room 8, 19th Floor, Block C, Fanling Centre, FANLING, NEW TERRITORIES HONG KONG SAR.
CHAN, Mr. David Wing Yun, BSc ACA *1988;* Flat 11, 25th Floor, Block D, Villa Lotto, 18 Broadwood Road, HAPPY VALLEY HONG KONG ISLAND HONG KONG SAR.
CHAN, Mr. David Yik Keung, BSc ACA *1981;* 27E Block B, Ning Yeung Terrace, 78 Bonham Road, SHEUNG WAN, HONG KONG ISLAND, HONG KONG SAR.
CHAN, Ms. Denise Valerie, ACA *2010;* Flat 5, 90 Greencroft Gardens, LONDON, NW6 3PH.
CHAN, Miss. Diana Pui Tse, BSc(Hons) ACA *2004;* 37 Kimberley Road, 2nd Floor 'C' Block, TSIM SHA TSUI, KOWLOON, HONG KONG SAR.
CHAN, Mr. Dominic, BA(Hons) ACA *2011;* 16 Red Lodge Road, BEXLEY, KENT, DA5 2JW.
CHAN, Mr. Dominic Chim Ming, ACA *2005;* Flat B 31/F Block 3, Victoria Centre, 15 Watson Road, NORTH POINT, HONG KONG ISLAND, HONG KONG SAR.
CHAN, Mr. Eddie Kin Man, ACA *2007;* Suites 1201-4, Tower 2 The Gateway, 25-27 Canton Road, TSIM SHA TSUI, KOWLOON, HONG KONG SAR.
CHAN, Miss. Edith, BA ACA *2007;* 3B Brilliant Court, 8 Kennedy Street, WAN CHAI, HONG KONG ISLAND, HONG KONG SAR.
CHAN, Ms. Edith Wai Wa, ACA *2007;* Flat A, 11/F, Block 7, Provident Centre, NORTH POINT, HONG KONG SAR.
CHAN, Mr. Edwin Chun Kit, BA(Hons) ACA *2003;* Lacrosse Global Fund Services UK Ltd Munro House, Portsmouth Road, COBHAM, KT11 1TF.
CHAN, Ms. Elaine Su Yi, MA ACA *2002;* Cadbury Enterprises Pte Ltd, 346 Jalan Boon Lay, SINGAPORE 619528, SINGAPORE.
CHAN, Miss. Emily Ngar Kay, BSc(Econ) ACA *1997;* 21/F Flat A Claymore Lodge, 33 Village Road, HAPPY VALLEY, HONG KONG ISLAND, HONG KONG SAR.
CHAN, Miss. Eng Pheng, BSc ACA *1993;* P.O. Box 297, BANDAR SERI BEGAWAN, BS 8670, BRUNEI DARUSSALAM.
CHAN, Mr. Eugene Nga Ching, MSc BEng ACA *2000;* 29 Howard Street, GATESHEAD, TYNE AND WEAR, NE8 3QD.
CHAN, Miss. Fiona Chor Wei, ACA *2008;* Flat 16, Ashworth Mansions, Elgin Avenue, LONDON, W9 1JL.
CHAN, Mr. Francis Sing Chuen, ACA *2007;* 236-252, 2/F Shopping Centre, Belvedere Garden Phase 2, 620 Castle Peak Road, TSUEN WAN, NEW TERRITORIES HONG KONG SAR.
•**CHAN, Mr. Frederick Hoi Kit, BSc FCA** *1986;* Flat 23A Block 19 Baguio Villa, 555 Victoria Road, POK FU LAM, HONG KONG ISLAND, HONG KONG SAR.
CHAN, Ms. Fung Kuen Dorothy, ACA *2008;* 5th Floor, 409 Shanghai Street, MONG KOK, HONG KONG SAR.
CHAN, Mr. Graham Ho Yin, ACA *2006;* Graham H Y Chan & Co, Unit 1, 15/F The Center, 99 Queens Road, CENTRAL, HONG KONG ISLAND HONG KONG SAR.
CHAN, Mr. Gregory Tak Shing, BSc ACA *1983;* 66 Lyttelton Court, Lyttelton Road, LONDON, N2 0ED.
CHAN, Mr. Harold Hoi Sing, MA FCA *1995;* 31E - 2 Robinson Place, 70 Robinson Road, MID LEVELS, HONG KONG ISLAND, HONG KONG SAR.
CHAN, Miss. Helen Hoi Yee, BA ACA *1987;* Flat H, 8th Floor Block 17, Laguna City, LAM TIN, KOWLOON, HONG KONG SAR.
CHAN, Mr. Hermann Karl, BA ACA *1990;* University of Hong Kong, Estates Office, 17/F Kennedy Town Centre, 23 Belcher Street, KENNEDY TOWN, HONG KONG SAR.
CHAN, Miss. Hill Man, BSc ACA CTA *2003;* Level 24, Barclays Bank Plc, 1 Churchill Place, LONDON, E14 5HP.
CHAN, Mr. Hin Fun, ACA *2007;* Flat E 16/F, Scholastic Garden, 48 Lyttelton Road, MID LEVELS, HONG KONG ISLAND, HONG KONG SAR.
CHAN, Mr. Ho Leung, ACA *2008;* with PricewaterhouseCoopers, 33/F Cheung Kong Center, 2 Queen's Road, CENTRAL, HONG KONG ISLAND, HONG KONG SAR.
CHAN, Mr. Hoi Jack, ACA *2005;* with Ernst & Young, 18/F, Two International Finance Centre, 8 Finance Street, CENTRAL, HONG KONG ISLAND HONG KONG SAR.
CHAN, Miss. Holly Se-Ho, BSc ACA *2011;* 47 Church Road, Formby, LIVERPOOL, L37 3NA.
CHAN, Mr. Hon Chung Johnny Pollux, ACA *2008;* Flat D 36 Floor, Block 5 Kenswood Court, Kingswood Villas, TIN SHUI WAI, NEW TERRITORIES, HONG KONG SAR.
CHAN, Mr. Hon Hung, ACA *2008;* Flat H 33/F, Tower 10 Ocean Shores, 88 O King Road, TSEUNG KWAN O, NEW TERRITORIES, HONG KONG SAR.
CHAN, Mr. Hooi Wah, FCA *1974;* 13 Jalan Tualang, Bukit Bandaraya, 59100 KUALA LUMPUR, FEDERAL TERRITORY, MALAYSIA.
CHAN, Ms. Huahui, ACA *2008;* 38 Roundhouse Crescent, PEACEHAVEN, EAST SUSSEX, BN10 8GL.
CHAN, Mr. Ivor Yee Tim, ACA *2005;* 25 Langtry Place, THORNHILL L4J 8K8, ON, CANADA.
CHAN, Mr. Jo Sing, LLB ACA *2010;* Flat 12, Cabot Court, Worgan Street, LONDON, SE16 7WE.
CHAN, Mr. John Ka Cheong, BSc ACA *1993;* 32 Machon Bank Road, SHEFFIELD, S7 1PG.
CHAN, Mr. John Keen Weng, ACA *2010;* 12 Jalan 5/153A, Taman Angkasa, Off Jalan Puchong, 58200 KUALA LUMPUR, FEDERAL TERRITORY, MALAYSIA.
CHAN, Mr. John Sing Chong, BA ACA *1999;* 14B Hale Road, MOSMAN, NSW 2088, AUSTRALIA.
CHAN, Mr. Joseph Kam Fui, FCA *1977;* 28 Belleview Drive, 14/Floor, REPULSE BAY, HONG KONG SAR.
CHAN, Mr. Joseph Shuen Chuen, ACA *2007;* 10F, 40 Nullah Road, MONG KOK, KOWLOON, HONG KONG SAR.
•**CHAN, Ms. Josephine Yin-On, BSc FCA ATII MBA** *1990;* (Tax Fac), CAP, 6 Holly Road, High Lane, STOCKPORT, CHESHIRE, SK6 8HW. See also CAP Accountancy Limited
CHAN, Mr. Jun Hwa, BA ACA *2010;* No. 119 Jalan S2 K7, Vision Homes, Seremban 2, 70300 SEREMBAN, NEGERI SEMBILAN, MALAYSIA.
CHAN, Ms. Ka Yee, ACA *2008;* with PricewaterhouseCoopers, Prince's Building, 22/F, 10 Chater Road, CENTRAL, HONG KONG ISLAND HONG KONG SAR.
CHAN, Mr. Ka Kit Benny, ACA *2011;* China E Learning GRP Ltd, Unit 3306 West Tower, Shun Tak Centre, 200 Connaught Road, CENTRAL, HONG KONG SAR.
CHAN, Ms. Ka Lam, ACA *2008;* Flat B 22/F In House, 307 To Kwa Wan Road, TO KWA WAN, KOWLOON, HONG KONG SAR.
CHAN, Mr. Kah Peng, FCA *1976;* Department of Transport, GPO Box C102, PERTH, WA 6839, AUSTRALIA.
CHAN, Mr. Kai Chi Kenneth, ACA *2007;* Apartment A, 14th Floor, Skyscraper Mansion, 132 Tin Hau Temple Road, NORTH POINT, HONG KONG ISLAND HONG KONG SAR.
CHAN, Mr. Kam Hung Derek, BA ACA *1991;* 9C Tung Shan Mansion, TAIKOO SHING, HONG KONG ISLAND, HONG KONG SAR.
CHAN, Mr. Kam Loon Philip, BSc ACA *1987;* 25 Duchess Road, SINGAPORE 268995, SINGAPORE.
CHAN, Mr. Kam Wah, ACA *2008;* Flat C, 12/F Block 4, Greenwood Terrace, CHAI WAN, HONG KONG SAR.
CHAN, Mr. Kam Wing Clement, ACA *2004;* 25/F, Wing On Centre, 111 Connaught Road, CENTRAL, HONG KONG ISLAND, HONG KONG SAR.
CHAN, Mr. Kam Yiu, ACA *2008;* Flat E 28 Floor Block 15, Sceneway Garden, LAM TIN, KOWLOON, HONG KONG SAR.
CHAN, Mr. Kee Chiu Kingsley, ACA *2008;* 7c Block 11, Sceneway Garden, LAM TIN, KOWLOON, HONG KONG SAR.
CHAN, Mr. Kee Huen Michael, ACA *2004;* 501 Block B, The Dahfuldy, 21 Ho Man Tin Hill Road, HO MAN TIN, KOWLOON, HONG KONG SAR.
CHAN, Mr. Kenneth Chi-Yun, BA ACA *2008;* 10 Harwood Terrace, LONDON, SW6 2AB.
CHAN, Mr. Kenneth Chun-Chung, ACA *1979;* 11 Glengarry Drive, Woodforde, ADELAIDE, SA 5072, AUSTRALIA.
CHAN, Mr. Kenneth See Yuen, MSc(Econ) BEng ACA *1998;* 5 Broad Reach, SHOREHAM-BY-SEA, WEST SUSSEX, BN43 5EY.
CHAN, Mr. Kim Chee, ACA *2007;* F.S. Li & Co, Room 1001, Admiralty Centre, Tower 1, 18 Harcourt Road, ADMIRALTY HONG KONG SAR.
CHAN, Mr. Kim Wan Nicholas, ACA *2007;* Ernst & Young Tax Services Ltd, 18/F, Two IFC, 8 Finance Street, CENTRAL, HONG KONG ISLAND HONG KONG SAR.
CHAN, Mr. Kin Wai, ACA *2007;* Flat 32J, Block 6, Tsui Ning Garden, TUEN MUN, NEW TERRITORIES, HONG KONG SAR.
CHAN, Mr. Kin Wa, ACA *2008;* Flat E 15/F, Tower 6, Nan Fung Plaza, 8 Pui Shing Road, TSEUNG KWAN O, HONG KONG SAR.
CHAN, Mr. Kin Yip, ACA *2008;* Room 1105 Shek Fai House Chun Shek Est, SHA TIN, HONG KONG SAR.
CHAN, Mr. King Shu, ACA *2007;* Leung & Chan, Room 1203 Valley Centre, 80-82 Morrison Hill Road, WAN CHAI, HONG KONG SAR.
CHAN, Miss. King Chu, ACA *2006;* Flat H 18/F. Tower 8, Island Harbourview, No.11 Hoi Fai Road, TAI KOK TSUI, KOWLOON, HONG KONG SAR.
CHAN, Mr. Kit Meng, MBA BSc ACA *1982;* 36 Lorong Rahim Kajai 2, Taman Tun Dr Ismail, 60000 KUALA LUMPUR, FEDERAL TERRITORY, MALAYSIA.
CHAN, Mr. Kit Ming, ACA *2006;* K.M.Chan & Company, Room 1702, One Peking, 1 Peking Road, TSIM SHA TSUI, KOWLOON HONG KONG SAR.
CHAN, Mrs. Kit Sin, FCA *1974;* 1 Carramar Avenue, CAMBERWELL, VIC 3124, AUSTRALIA.
CHAN, Mr. Kit Kwong, ACA *2010;* Iceland Wharf, Flat 13, 1 Yeoman Street, LONDON, SE8 5DP.
CHAN, Mr. Kit Wang, ACA *2007;* (Tax Fac), Rooms 604-7, Dominion Centre, 43-59 Queen's Road East, WAN CHAI, HONG KONG SAR.
CHAN, Mr. Kok Chun, BSc ACA *2009;* Flat 23, 105 Hallam Street, LONDON, W1W 5HD.
CHAN, Mr. Koon Lum Alan, ACA *2008;* Flat 2C University Court, 169 Boundary Street, KOWLOON TONG, KOWLOON, HONG KONG SAR.
CHAN, Mr. Ku Kin Thomas, ACA *2008;* Chu and Chu, Suite 1801-5 18/F, Tower 2, China HONG KONG SAR City, 33 Canton Road, TSIM SHA TSUI KOWLOON HONG KONG SAR.
CHAN, Mr. Kuen Hoong, BA ACA *1986;* P O Box 138, KEW EAST, VIC 3102, AUSTRALIA.
CHAN, Mr. Kum Leong, ACA *1984;* 5 Cardiff Grove, SINGAPORE 558872, SINGAPORE.
CHAN, Mr. Kuok Kun, ACA *2008;* KTC Partners CPA Limited, Unit 501502 &508, 5/F, Mirror Tower, 61 Mody Road, TSIM SHA TSUI KOWLOON HONG KONG SAR. See also KTC CPA Limited
CHAN, Ms. Kwai Ping, ACA *2008;* Chu and Chu, Suite 1801-5 18/F, Tower 2, China HONG KONG SAR City, 33 Canton Road, TSIM SHA TSUI KOWLOON HONG KONG SAR.
CHAN, Mr. Kwan Kong, ACA *2008;* 8D, Tower 5, Aegean Coast, 2 Kwun Tsing Road, TUEN MUN, NEW TERRITORIES HONG KONG SAR.
CHAN, Mr. Kwok Hoi, ACA *2008;* Land Registry, Queensway Government Offices 28th Floor, 66 Queensway, CENTRAL, HONG KONG ISLAND, HONG KONG SAR.
CHAN, Mr. Kwok Yuen Elvis, ACA *2007;* Room 903, 9th Floor, Tak Yat House, Yat Tung Estate, TUNG CHUNG, NEW TERRITORIES HONG KONG SAR.
CHAN, Mr. Kwong Loi, ACA *2006;* Flat D, 27th Floor, Block 5, Sceneway Garden, LAM TIN, KOWLOON HONG KONG SAR.
CHAN, Miss. Lai Wah Maggie, BSc FCA *1982;* 15665 102B AVENUE, SURREY V4N 2M1, BC, CANADA.
CHAN, Mr. Lai Pong Thomas, ACA *2007;* Flat B 41/F Block 1, The Grandiose, 9 Tong chun Street, Tseung Kwan O, TSEUNG KWAN O, KOWLOON HONG KONG SAR.
CHAN, Ms. Lan Chi, ACA *2007;* Flat E 7/F Block 5, Highland Park, 11 Lai Kong Street, KWAI CHUNG, NEW TERRITORIES, HONG KONG SAR.
CHAN, Mr. Lap Hong Frederick, ACA *2008;* Navigant Consulting, Suites 2901-2904, Dah Sing Financial Centre, 108 Gloucester Road, WAN CHAI, HONG KONG ISLAND HONG KONG SAR.
CHAN, Mrs. Laura Mei-Wah, BEng ACA *1995;* 19 Oxford Avenue, LONDON, N14 5AF.
CHAN, Mr. Laurence, ACA *2008;* 1 Holly Drive, Grantstown Village, WATERFORD, COUNTY WATERFORD, IRELAND.
CHAN, Mr. Laurence Shung Yip, FCA *1976;* 12 Third Avenue, SINGAPORE 266585, SINGAPORE. (Life Member)
CHAN, Ms. Linda, BA ACA *1998;* 9 Stable Close, KINGSTON UPON THAMES, KT2 5PJ.
CHAN, Miss. Linda Mee-Yi, BA(Hons) ACA *2000;* 27a Stanton Road, LONDON, SW20 8RW.
CHAN, Miss. Lorraine, ACA *2009;* Flat 2, 25 Symphony Close, EDGWARE, HA8 0AR.
CHAN, Miss. Lydia, BSc ACA *2007;* Flat 2, Gainsborough House, Frognal Rise, Hampstead, LONDON, NW3 6PZ.
CHAN, Mr. Man Ko, ACA *2007;* China Taiping Insurance Holdings Company Limited, 12/F China Taiping Tower Phase II Sunning Road, CAUSEWAY BAY, HONG KONG SAR.
CHAN, Mr. Man Pong, ACA *2008;* Flat F 20/F Blk 8, Sea Crest Villa, 18 Castle Peak Road, TSUEN WAN, NEW TERRITORIES, HONG KONG SAR.
CHAN, Mr. Man Wa, ACA *2009;* Room 2406, Kam Tin House, Kam Tai Court, Ma On Shan, SHA TIN, NEW TERRITORIES HONG KONG SAR.
CHAN, Mr. Man Yin, ACA *2005;* Room 312-318 3/F, China Insurance Group Building, 141 Des Voeux Road, CENTRAL, HONG KONG ISLAND, HONG KONG SAR.
CHAN, Miss. Man-Tsz, BA ACA *1997;* 9 Campden Grove, LONDON, W8 4JG.
•**CHAN, Ms. Mandy Man-Fong, BA ACA** *1997;* (Tax Fac), TBW, E3 The Premier Centre, Abbey Park, ROMSEY, SO51 9DG.
CHAN, Miss. Mei Yin, BSc ACA *1998;* 17 Rogers Walk, Holden Road North Finchley, LONDON, N12 7DA.
CHAN, Miss. Mei Ying, ACA *2008;* 54 Hertford Road, LONDON, N1 5AE.
CHAN, Ms. Mei Bo Mabel, ACA *2008;* Mabel Chan & Co, Suite 2208-11, 22/F Tower One, Times Square, 1 Matheson Street, CAUSEWAY BAY HONG KONG SAR.
CHAN, Ms. Mei Fong, ACA *2004;* Flat G 17/F, Tower 2 Academic Terrace, 101 Pokfulam Road, POK FU LAM, HONG KONG ISLAND, HONG KONG SAR.
CHAN, Ms. Mei Mei, ACA *2008;* Canny CPA & Co, Rm 1603, Tung Chiu Commercial Centre, 193 Lockhart Road, WAN CHAI, HONG KONG SAR.
CHAN, Ms. Mei Yan, ACA *2008;* Flat C, 28/F, Tower 10, South Horizons, AP LEI CHAU, HONG KONG SAR.
CHAN, Ms. Mi Ling, ACA *2005;* Soluteck Holdings Limited, Room 1104, SUP Tower, 75-83 King's Road, NORTH POINT, HONG KONG ISLAND HONG KONG SAR.
CHAN, Mr. Michael Moon Kee, FCA *1983;* Unit A1 3/F Hillgrove, 18 Cape Drive, CHUNG HOM KOK, HONG KONG ISLAND, HONG KONG SAR.
CHAN, Mr. Michael Wai Kwong, ACA *1979;* B14/F Greenville Gardens, 15 Shiu Fai Terrace, WAN CHAI, HONG KONG ISLAND, 852, HONG KONG SAR.
CHAN, Mr. Michael Man Chung, ACA *2007;* Michael M.C. Chan & Co, Room 2401, 24/F, 280 Portland Street Commercial Building, 276-280 Portland Street, MONG KOK KOWLOON HONG KONG SAR.
CHAN, Miss. Mimi Chi Min, BA ACA CTA *2007;* 85 Brampton Grove, Kenton, HARROW, HA3 8LE.
CHAN, Miss. Mimosa Ka-Lai, BA FCA *1992;* with Ernst & Young, 18/F, Two International Finance Centre, 8 Finance Street, CENTRAL, HONG KONG ISLAND HONG KONG SAR.
CHAN, Mr. Ming Cho Joe, ACA *2008;* Flat 23D, Ka Shing Lau, Ka Wai Chuen, HUNG HOM, KOWLOON, HONG KONG SAR.
CHAN, Mr. Ming Yeung, ACA *2008;* 3/F, 37 Ming Yuen Street West, NORTH POINT, HONG KONG SAR.
CHAN, Ms. Miu Ping, ACA *2008;* Jardine Matheson & Co Ltd, Group Finance Dept, 25/F Devon House, Taikoo Place, 979 Kings Road, QUARRY BAY HONG KONG SAR.
CHAN, Ms. Nap Shan, ACA *2008;* 8C Block 2, The Floridian, 18 Sai Wan Terrace, QUARRY BAY, HONG KONG ISLAND, HONG KONG SAR.
•**CHAN, Mr. Nelson Chi Fai, BSc FCA** *1987;* 6 Woodville Road, LONDON, W5 2SF.
CHAN, Mr. Nelson Tsang-Wing, FCA *1981;* Dickson Concepts Int, 4/F East Ocean Centre, E98 Granville Road, TSIM SHA TSUI, KOWLOON, HONG KONG SAR.
CHAN, Mr. Neville Chi Lick, BSc ACA *1994;* 45D Tower 3 Les Saisons, 28 Tai On Street, SAI WAN HO, HONG KONG SAR.
CHAN, Miss. Ngar Yan, BSc(Econ) ACA *2000;* 59 Cranley Gardens, LONDON, N10 3AB.
CHAN, Mr. Norbert Siu-Tuen, BA FCA *1993;* Flat 4, 27th Floor Block L, Sunshine City, Ma On Shan, SHA TIN, NEW TERRITORIES HONG KONG SAR.
CHAN, Mr. Oi Man, ACA *2005;* Suite 1326-31, Ocean Centre, Harbour City, TSIM SHA TSIU, KOWLOON, HONG KONG SAR.
CHAN, Mr. Oy, ACA *1980;* Flat E 2/F Block 2, Juniper MansionWhampoa Garden, Site 1 HUNG HOM, Kowloon, HONG KONG SAR.

CHAN, Mr. Pak Kwong Joseph, ACA *2005;* 12a Blk 10 Botania Villa, TUEN MUN,, NEW TERRITORIES, HONG KONG SAR.
CHAN, Mr. Pak Shing, ACA *2008;* 17D, Block 36, Laguna City, LAM TIN, KOWLOON, HONG KONG SAR.
CHAN, Mr. Paul Anthony, BSc ACA *1991;* 38 Mayfield Avenue, LONDON, W13 9UR.
CHAN, Ms. Peck-Yoke, BSc ACA *1992;* 104 Jalan Langgar Bedok, SINGAPORE 468556, SINGAPORE.
CHAN, Mr. Pei Cheong Andy, ACA *2007;* Lixin CPA Limited, Unit 1602, Malaysia Building, 50 Gloucester Road, WAN CHAI, HONG KONG SAR.
•**CHAN, Mr. Peter Wing Kai, BA ACA** *1987;* (Tax Fac), PC & Chan Limited, 14 The Village Square, Netherne on the Hill, COULSDON, SURREY, CR5 1LZ.
CHAN, Mr. Petrus Dor Cheong, ACA *2007;* 8A Right Mansion, 29 Robinson Road, CENTRAL, HONG KONG ISLAND, HONG KONG SAR.
CHAN, Mrs. Phaik Choo, FCA *1983;* 3 JALAN TR6/1, TROPICANA GOLF & COUNTRY RESORT, 47410 PETALING JAYA, MALAYSIA.
CHAN, Mr. Philip Timothy Kin Chung, ACA *2008;* Flat 41, Peel House, 105 Regency Street, LONDON, SW1P 4EF.
CHAN, Miss. Phyllis Chui Yee, BA ACA *1989;* Flat 1, 4-8 Creechurch Lane, LONDON, EC3A 5AY.
CHAN, Mr. Po Cheung, ACA *2005;* Flat G 25/F Block H19, Chi Fu Fa Yuen, POK FU LAM, HONG KONG ISLAND, HONG KONG SAR.
CHAN, Dr. Po Fun Peter, ACA *2009;* Peter Chan (CPA) Limited, 2nd Floor, Caltex House, 258 Hennessy Road, WAN CHAI, HONG KONG SAR.
CHAN, Ms. Po Lam, ACA *2009;* Flat 2 8/F Siu Fai House, Siu Hong Court, TUEN MUN, NT, HONG KONG SAR.
CHAN, Miss. Po Yi, BSc ACA *2011;* 39 Avenue Road, Harold Wood, ROMFORD, RM3 0SS.
CHAN, Ms. Poh Geok, BSc FCA *1989;* 41E Lorong L, Telok Kurau, SINGAPORE 425458, SINGAPORE.
CHAN, Ms. Pui Fan, ACA *2008;* Flat 6 23/F, Block B Pearl Court, No 13 Belchers Street, KENNEDY TOWN, HONG KONG SAR.
CHAN, Mr. Pui Chung Stephen, ACA *2005;* 120 Serangoon Ave 3, Amaranda Gardens #04-08, SINGAPORE 554774, SINGAPORE.
CHAN, Ms. Pun Hing, ACA *2007;* 2608, Chung Wa House, Tin Chung Court, TIN SHUI WAI, NEW TERRITORIES, HONG KONG SAR.
CHAN, Mr. Raymond Wing Shing, MA FCA *1989;* 1D Shelford Road, 04-22, NEWTON 286889, SINGAPORE.
CHAN, Miss. Rosemary Chung Yan, BSc(Hons) ACA CTA *2002;* (Tax Fac), Marks & Spencer Plc, Waterside House, 35 North Wharf Road, LONDON, W2 1NW.
CHAN, Miss. Ruby Soon Hong, FCA *1964;* 41 Sixth Crescent, SINGAPORE 276448, SINGAPORE. (Life Member)
CHAN, Mr. Sai Hung, ACA *2008;* Flat 606 6/F, Block M, Kornhill, QUARRY BAY, HONG KONG SAR.
CHAN, Miss. Samantha Lok-Yi, ACA *2008;* Flat B 20/F Block B, 17 Wylie Path, Wylie Road, HO MAN TIN, KOWLOON, HONG KONG SAR.
CHAN, Mr. Samuel Wing Sun, BA FCA *1973;* 4/F 22 Tai Yau Street, SAN PO KONG, Kowloon, HONG KONG SAR.
CHAN, Mr. Sandy Chai Yan, FCA *1972;* 63 Repulse Bay Road, 6A Manhattan Tower, REPULSE BAY, HONG KONG ISLAND, HONG KONG SAR. (Life Member)
CHAN, Mr. See Chuen, MA FCA *1971;* 42 Margoliouth Road, SINGAPORE 258567, SINGAPORE.
CHAN, Mr. Seng Chow, FCA *1973;* 1 Carramar Avenue, CAMBERWELL, VIC 3124, AUSTRALIA.
CHAN, Miss. Seow Cheng, BA ACA *1986;* 9 Jalan SS 1/26, 47300 PETALING JAYA, Selangor, MALAYSIA.
CHAN, Mr. Shek Yee Lawrence, ACA *2005;* Chan & Man, 1603 16/F Island Place Tower, 510 King's Road North Point, WAN CHAI, HONG KONG SAR.
CHAN, Miss. Shiao-Mae, LLB ACA *2002;* Redgrave Partners Llp, 165 Fleet Street, LONDON, EC4A 2DY.
CHAN, Miss. Shook-Yuen Janett, BA FCA *1976;* c/o Penthouse, Menara Chan, 138 Jalan Ampang, 50450 KUALA LUMPUR, FEDERAL TERRITORY, MALAYSIA.
CHAN, Mr. Shu Kin, ACA *2006;* Ting Ho Kwan & Chan, 9th Floor Tung Ning Bldg, 249-253 Des Voeux Road C, CENTRAL, HONG KONG ISLAND, HONG KONG SAR.
CHAN, Ms. Shui Lan Hildy, ACA *2005;* Unit 2512A, Immigration Tower, WAN CHAI, HONG KONG ISLAND, HONG KONG SAR.
CHAN, Miss. Siang Geck, ACA *1990;* 95a Siglap Road, SINGAPORE 454967, SINGAPORE.
CHAN, Miss. Siew Fong, BSc ACA *1986;* 5 Lorong PJU 3/28B, Sunway Damansara, 47810 PETALING JAYA, SELANGOR, MALAYSIA.
CHAN, Ms. Sim Kwan, ACA *2008;* S K Chan & Co, Flat D 8th Floor, Tak Lee Commercial Building, 113-117 Wanchai Road, WAN CHAI, HONG KONG SAR.
CHAN, Mr. Sin Keung Richard, ACA *2006;* Richard S K Chan & Co, Room 1601, Yu Sung Boon Building, 107 Des Vouex Road C, CENTRAL, HONG KONG ISLAND HONG KONG SAR. See also Graham H Y Chan & Co
CHAN, Ms. Sin Yee, ACA *2008;* Warnaco Asia Limited, 20/F Two Harbour Front, 22 Tak Fung Street, HUNG HOM, KOWLOON, HONG KONG SAR.
CHAN, Mr. Siu Pang, ACA *2007;* 26 Forester Crescent, MARKHAM L6C 1R2, ON, CANADA.
CHAN, Mr. Siu Tak, ACA *2007;* with Ernst & Young, 18/F, Two International Finance Centre, 8 Finance Street, CENTRAL, HONG KONG ISLAND HONG KONG SAR.
CHAN, Miss. Siu Tsang, ACA *2007;* Room B6, 25th Floor, Midland Centre, 328 Queen's Road, CENTRAL, HONG KONG ISLAND HONG KONG SAR.
CHAN, Ms. Siu Man Winnie, ACA *2008;* Flat B, 31/F, Tower 1, Hampton Place, 11 Hoi Fan Road, TAI KOK TSUI HONG KONG SAR.
CHAN, Mr. Siu Ting Joseph, ACA *2008;* Wong Chan Lau C.P.A. Ltd, Rooms 805 - 6, 8/F, Tai Yau Building, 181 Johnston Road, WAN CHAI HONG KONG SAR.
CHAN, Ms. So King Tina, ACA *2008;* 2 Warwick Street, SYDNEY, NSW 2071, AUSTRALIA.
CHAN, Miss. Sonia, ACA *2009;* Flat D 22/F, Tower 2, Serenade, 11 Tai Hang Road, TAI HANG, HONG KONG SAR.
CHAN, Ms. Soo Wah, FCA *1977;* 27 Jalan Menerung 4, Taman SA, 59000 KUALA LUMPUR, FEDERAL TERRITORY, MALAYSIA.
CHAN, Miss. Stella Yee Yaeng, BSc(Hons) FCA MCT *1993;* Apartment 26, Globe View, 10 High Timber Street, LONDON, EC4V 3PL.
CHAN, Mr. Stephen Siu Lun, BCom FCA *1986;* BDO Limited CPA, 25TH Floor Wing On Centre, 111 Connaught Road, CENTRAL, HONG KONG ISLAND, HONG KONG SAR.
CHAN, Mr. Stephen Wing Bun, ACA *2007;* LED International Holding Limited, Suite 911 9/F Exchange Tower, 33 Wang Chiu Road, KOWLOON BAY, KOWLOON, HONG KONG SAR.
CHAN, Mr. Steven Sze-Wing, BCom ACA *1992;* 118B, West Street, CARSHALTON, SM5 2NR.
CHAN, Ms. Sui Wa, ACA *2005;* Flat G, 18/F, Block 29, Laguna City, Cha Kwo Ling Road, KWUN TONG KOWLOON HONG KONG SAR.
CHAN, Ms. Suk Yin, ACA *2007;* Room 1309, Sau Man House, Choi Wan Estate, WAN CHAI, KOWLOON, HONG KONG SAR.
CHAN, Ms. Suk King, ACA *2008;* Graham H Y Chan & Co, Unit 1, 15/F, The Center, 99 Queen's Road Central, CENTRAL HONG KONG SAR.
CHAN, Ms. Sun Yi, ACA *2007;* Flat 8, 3/F, Chung Sing Bing, Chung Wui St, TAI KOK TSUI, KOWLOON HONG KONG SAR.
CHAN, Mr. Sun Kwong Ken, ACA *2007;* Ken Chan & Co, Office No. 1818, 18/F, Beverley Commercial Centre, 87-105 Chatham Road South, TSIM SHA TSUI KOWLOON HONG KONG SAR.
CHAN, Miss. Sylvaine, MSc ACA *2011;* 12 Queen's Gate, LONDON, SW7 5EL.
CHAN, Mr. Sze Chun, ACA *2011;* 2/F Block 19, Galore Garden, 100 Tin Ha Road, YUEN LONG, HONG KONG SAR.
CHAN, Ms. Sze Wan Dawn, ACA *2006;* Flat A 3/F., 73 Sing Woo Road, HAPPY VALLEY, HONG KONG SAR.
CHAN, Mr. Tak Kwong, ACA *2007;* with Deloitte Touche Tohmatsu, 8-F Tower W2, The Towers, Oriental Plaza, 1 East Chang An Avenue, BEIJING 100738 CHINA.
CHAN, Mr. Tak Hing Kenji, ACA *2005;* Unit 2708, 27/F Billion Plaza, 8 Cheung Yue Street, CHEUNG SHA WAN, KOWLOON, HONG KONG SAR.
CHAN, Mr. Tak Ming, ACA *2005;* Flat A 10/F, Block 14 City Garden, 233 Electric Road, NORTH POINT, HONG KONG SAR.
CHAN, Mr. Tak Pun, ACA *2008;* Flat B 13/F Cornwall Court, 54 King's Road, NORTH POINT, HONG KONG ISLAND, HONG KONG SAR.
CHAN, Mr. Tak Wai, ACA *2007;* TW Chan & Co, Unit 2203, 22/F Malaysia Building, 50 Gloucester Road, WAN CHAI, HONG KONG ISLAND HONG KONG SAR.
CHAN, Mr. Tak Yin Daniel, ACA *2007;* Andrew Corporation, Room 1901, Cosco Tower, 183 Queens Road, CENTRAL, HONG KONG ISLAND HONG KONG SAR.
CHAN, Mr. Tat Man, ACA *2005;* Flat C 20th Floor, Wah Shan Mansion, 17 Taikoo Shing Road, TAIKOO SHING, HONG KONG ISLAND, HONG KONG SAR.
CHAN, Mr. Terence Chun Wing, FCA *1977;* 5A Block 5 Julimount Gardens, 1-5 Hin Tin Street, SHA TIN, New Territories, HONG KONG SAR.
CHAN, Miss. Teri Ngan Ming, BSc ACA *1995;* 35 Schooner Close, LONDON, E14 3GG.
CHAN, Mr. Tin Wai David, ACA *2004;* 25/F CITIC Telecom Tower, 93 Kwai Fuk Road, KWAI CHUNG, KOWLOON, HONG KONG SAR.
CHAN, Mr. Tony Siu-Chung, BSc ACA *2006;* 21 Hurst Hill Crescent, ASHTON-UNDER-LYNE, OL6 9NJ.
CHAN, Mr. Tsan Fai Lawrence, ACA *2008;* Lawrence Chan & Co, Suite 601A, Fourseas Building, 208 - 212 Nathan Road, TSIM SHA TSUI, KOWLOON HONG KONG SAR.
CHAN, Mrs. Tsui Ling Brenda, ACA *2005;* STA(MS)3, 1509B15/F, Wu Chung House, 213 Queens Road East, WAN CHAI, HONG KONG ISLAND HONG KONG SAR.
CHAN, Miss. Vicky, BSc ACA *2007;* 10/C Tower 1, Elegant Terrace, 36 Conduit Road, MID LEVELS, HONG KONG ISLAND, HONG KONG SAR.
•**CHAN, Miss. Vicky Chung Sze, BA ACA** *1993;* Flat 12 A, Tower4, Beverly Villas 16 La Salle Road, KOWLOON CITY, KOWLOON, HONG KONG SAR.
CHAN, Mr. Victor, MEng BA ACA *2006;* 7 Chancellors Walk, CAMBRIDGE, CB4 3JG.
CHAN, Miss. Victoria Pui Yee, BA ACA *2010;* 12 Artesian Grove, BARNET, HERTFORDSHIRE, EN5 5HU.
CHAN, Mr. Wai, ACA *2007;* Flat A, 16/F Kam Fung Mansion, 59 - 61 Bonham Road, MID LEVELS, HONG KONG ISLAND, HONG KONG SAR.
CHAN, Mr. Wai Chung, BA FCA *1991;* (Tax Fac), Marks Bloom, 60/62 Old London Road, KINGSTON UPON THAMES, SURREY, KT2 6QZ.
CHAN, Mr. Wai Kit, ACA *2006;* Kanter Casias Ltd, Room 1106 11/F Haleson Building, CENTRAL, HONG KONG SAR.
CHAN, Ms. Wai Ling, ACA *2007;* 19D 19/F Glen Haven, 117 Argyle Street, KOWLOON CITY, KOWLOON, HONG KONG SAR.
CHAN, Mr. Wai Man, ACA *2007;* 107 Lockhart Road, 19/F. Beverly House, WAN CHAI, HONG KONG ISLAND, HONG KONG SAR.
CHAN, Mr. Wai Wah David, BA(Hons) ACA *2002;* 23 Rimsdale Drive, MANCHESTER, M40 0GN.
CHAN, Mr. Wai Yip, ACA FCCA *2001;* 73 Chelmsford Road, Southgate, LONDON, N14 5PY.
CHAN, Ms. Wai Han Tammy, ACA *2007;* Flat 32 E, No 1 Star Street, WAN CHAI, HONG KONG SAR.
CHAN, Mr. Wai Hei, ACA *2004;* Li Tang Chen & Co., 10/F Sun Hung Kai Centre, 30 Harbour Road, WAN CHAI, HONG KONG ISLAND, HONG KONG SAR.
CHAN, Ms. Wai Hing, ACA *2008;* with Mazars CPA Limited, 42nd Floor, Central Plaza, 18 Harbour Road, WAN CHAI, HONG KONG ISLAND HONG KONG SAR.
CHAN, Mr. Wai Kan, MBA BSc FCA *1988;* 18A Cumine Court, 52 King's Road, NORTH POINT, HONG KONG SAR.
CHAN, Mr. Wai Kee Phileo, ACA *2007;* Tony Kwok Tung NG & Co, Rooms 201-205, 2/F Alliance Building, 130-136 Connalight Road, CENTRAL, HONG KONG SAR.
CHAN, Mr. Wai Kwong Joel, ACA *2008;* Flat A 1/F. Tower 11, Parc Royale, 8 Hin Tai Street, SHA TIN, NEW TERRITORIES, HONG KONG SAR.
CHAN, Miss. Wai Leng Audrey, ACA *2011;* BDO International, 12th Floor Menara Uni. Asia, Jalan sultan Ismail, 1008 KUALA LUMPUR, FEDERAL TERRITORY, MALAYSIA.
CHAN, Mr. Wai Lok Lok, ACA *2007;* Flat K 30th Floor, Block 4 Aldrich Garden, 2 Oi Lai Street, Aldrich Bay, SHAU KEI WAN, HONG KONG ISLAND HONG KONG SAR.
CHAN, Ms. Wai Man, ACA *2007;* But Do Yeung C.P.A. Limited, Rooms 1801-05, 18th Floor, Hua Qin International Building, 340 Queen's Road Central, CENTRAL HONG KONG ISLAND HONG KONG SAR.
CHAN, Mr. Wai Ming, ACA *2005;* 202 Kwan Ming House, Yuk Ming Court, TSEUNG KWAN O, NEW TERRITORIES, HONG KONG SAR.
CHAN, Mr. Wai Ming, ACA *1981;* 28a Dallwood Avenue, EPPING, NSW 2121, AUSTRALIA.
CHAN, Ms. Wai Mun Cindy, ACA *2008;* Flat E, 35/F Tower 8, AP Lei Chan, SOUTH HORIZONS, HONG KONG SAR.
CHAN, Ms. Wai Shan Karen, ACA *2005;* Flat B 23rd Floor, Tower 2 Aquamarine, 8 Sham Shing Road, CHEUNG SHA WAN, KOWLOON, HONG KONG SAR.
CHAN, Mr. Wai Sum, ACA *2007;* Flat H 6/F., Block 1 Scenic View, No.63 Fung Shing Street, Ngau Chi Wan, WONG TAI SIN, KOWLOON HONG KONG SAR.
CHAN, Mr. Wai Tong Christopher, ACA *2005;* PricewaterhouseCoopers, 22/F Prince's Building, CENTRAL, HONG KONG ISLAND, HONG KONG SAR.
CHAN, Mr. Wai Yip, ACA *2007;* Flat D, 30/F Tower II, Scenecliff, 33-35 Conduit Road, MID LEVELS, HONG KONG ISLAND HONG KONG SAR.
CHAN, Mr. Wai-Ming Raymond, ACA *2005;* 11B Block 2, Maritime Bay, TSEUNG KWAN O, NEW TERRITORIES, HONG KONG SAR.
CHAN, Mr. Wallace Tat Yuen, ACA *2006;* 3A Block 6, Cavendish Heights, 33 Perkins Road, JARDINE'S LOOKOUT, HONG KONG ISLAND, HONG KONG SAR.
CHAN, Mr. Wan Po, ACA *2005;* 23D Tower 6, The Belcher's, 89 Pokfulam Road, POK FU LAM, HONG KONG ISLAND, HONG KONG SAR.
CHAN, Mr. Wang Kei Christopher, ACA *2011;* Flat C, 14 Floor, Ying Piu Mansion, 1 Breezy Path, MID LEVELS, HONG KONG SAR.
CHAN, Mr. Warren Kwing-Choi, ACA *2007;* P.O.Box 98149, Tsim Sha Tsui Post Office, TSIM SHA TSUI, KOWLOON, HONG KONG SAR.
CHAN, Mr. Way Sin, BA(Hons) ACA *2001;* Exide Technologies Canada Corporation, 6950 Creditview Road, MISSISSAUGA L5N 0A6, ON, CANADA.
CHAN, Mr. Wei Beng, ACA *1992;* Units 2&3, 26th Floor Tower 2, China Central Place, No 79 Jianguo Road, Chaoyang District, BEIJING 100025 CHINA.
CHAN, Miss. Wendy Wing Sze, BA(Econ) ACA *2002;* 35 Sandywarps, Irlam, MANCHESTER, M44 6RF.
CHAN, Mr. Weng Keong, ACA *2011;* with Deloitte Touche Tohmatsu, 35/F One Pacific Place, 88 Queensway, CENTRAL, HONG KONG ISLAND, HONG KONG SAR.
CHAN, Mr. William Kam Wing, BSc FCA *1993;* (Tax Fac), 20th Floor Sunning Plaza, 10 Hysan Avenue, CAUSEWAY BAY, HONG KONG SAR.
•**CHAN, Mr. Wilson, FCA** *1972;* Chan Chee Hong & Co, No. 6 & 8 Jalan Gereja, 2nd Floor, Bangunan Keng, 50100 KUALA LUMPUR, FEDERAL TERRITORY MALAYSIA.
CHAN, Ms. Wing, ACA *2010;* Flat D, 22/f Tower 2, Sky Tower, 38 Sung Wong Toi Road, TO KWA WAN, KOWLOON HONG KONG SAR.
CHAN, Mr. Wing Kin Kevin, MSc ACA *1993;* 12A Block 15, One Beaconhill, 1 Beaconhill Road, KOWLOON TONG, KOWLOON, HONG KONG SAR.
CHAN, Miss. Wing Mun Anita, ACA *1986;* 11D Butler Towers, 3 Boyce Road, JARDINE'S LOOKOUT, HONG KONG ISLAND, HONG KONG SAR.
CHAN, Mr. Wing Chung, ACA *2008;* Flat D 25/F Tower, 10 Ocean Shores, 88 O King Road, TIU KENG LENG, KOWLOON, HONG KONG SAR.
CHAN, Mr. Wing Fai, ACA *2005;* 26/H Tower 2 The Sea Creast, 1 Hang Kwai Street, TUEN MUN, NEW TERRITORIES, HONG KONG SAR.
CHAN, Mr. Wing Fai, ACA *2008;* Flat 2, 16/F Block M, Kornhill, QUARRY BAY, HONG KONG SAR.
CHAN, Mr. Wing Fai Ronald, ACA *2008;* Ronald W. F. Chan & Co., Room 1901, 19/F Henan Building, 90-92 Jaffe Road, WAN CHAI, HONG KONG SAR.
CHAN, Mr. Wing Kan Archie, ACA *2007;* Room 401, 4/F, St George's Building, 2 Ice House Street, CENTRAL, HONG KONG SAR.
CHAN, Ms. Wing Ki, ACA *2008;* 56A Upper Montagu Street, Baker Street, LONDON, W1H 1SN.

CHAN, Mr. Wing Kwong Bobby, ACA *2008;* Flat 9B, Block 3, Oscar by the Sea, 8 Pung Loi Road, TSEUNG KWAN O, NEW TERRITORIES HONG KONG SAR.

CHAN, Mr. Wing Ming Joseph, ACA *2007;* Deloitte Touche Tohmatsu, 30th Floor, Bund Centre, 222 Yan An Road East, SHANGHAI 20002, CHINA.

CHAN, Mr. Yat Hei, ACA *2009;* 7D Block 9 Woodland Crest, SHEUNG SHUI, NEW TERRITORIES, HONG KONG SAR.

CHAN, Mr. Yat Tai T, ACA *2008;* Flat F, 21 Floor, Tang Kung Mansion, 31 Taikoo Shing Road, TAIKOO SHING, HONG KONG SAR.

CHAN, Dr. Yat-Po, ACA CA(NZ) *2009;* Flat F 21 Floor, Tang Kung Mansion, 31 Taikoo Shing Road, TAIKOO SHING, HONG KONG ISLAND, HONG KONG SAR.

CHAN, Mr. Yau Leung Joseph, ACA *2008;* Falt D 1/F Block 9 Villa Esplanada, 8 Nga Ying Chau Street, TSING YI, HONG KONG SAR.

CHAN, Ms. Yee Lin Elaine, ACA *2008;* Flat F 7/F, Corona Tower, 91-93 Caine Road, CENTRAL, HONG KONG ISLAND, HONG KONG SAR.

CHAN, Ms. Yee Wah Eva, ACA *2008;* Unit A, 21/F, Manu Life Tower, 169 Electric Road, NORTH POINT, HONG KONG SAR.

•CHAN, Mr. Yeuk Wai, FCA *1982;* Pang Chan & Co., Unit A 13th Floor, E.I.B. Centre, 40-44 Bonham Strand, SHEUNG WAN, HONG KONG ISLAND HONG KONG SAR.

CHAN, Mr. Yick Hung, BSc ACA *1980;* Julius Baer (Hong Kong) Ltd 18th Floor, Two Exchange Square, 8 Connaught Place, CENTRAL, HONG KONG ISLAND, HONG KONG SAR.

CHAN, Ms. Yim, ACA *2008;* 6/F, New Henry House, 10 Ice House Street, CENTRAL, HONG KONG SAR.

CHAN, Ms. Yin Lin, ACA *2008;* Flat H21/ FBlock 13, Laguna City, Cha Kwo Ling, KWUN TONG, KOWLOON, HONG KONG SAR.

CHAN, Ms. Yin Ling Alice, ACA *2009;* 22 Kapok Path, Palm Springs, YUEN LONG, NEW TERRITORIES, HONG KONG SAR.

CHAN, Mrs. Yin Shan, ACA *2007;* Flat 3 28/F. Block B, Sun Kwai Hing Gardens, 163 Tai Wo Hau Road, KWAI CHUNG, KOWLOON, HONG KONG SAR.

CHAN, Mr. Yip Keung, ACA *2007;* Chan Yip Keung & Co, Unit 1702-03, 17/F Skyline Commercial Centre, 71-77 Wing Lok Street, SHEUNG WAN, HONG KONG ISLAND HONG KONG SAR. See also Chan Yip Keung

CHAN, Mr. Yiu Tong Jerry, ACA *2007;* Flat B3 1/F Wah Lai Mansion 24 Yuet Wah Street, KWUN TONG, HONG KONG SAR.

CHAN, Miss. Yong Yong, MSc ACA *1981;* No. 4 Jalan Rendang, SINGAPORE 428343, SINGAPORE.

CHAN, Mr. Yu Lun Gary, ACA *2007;* Flat D 13/F Block 6 Sea Crest Villa Phase 2 18 Castle Peak Road, TSING LUNG TAU, HONG KONG SAR.

CHAN, Mr. Yuen Tao, ACA *2008;* Ernst & Young, 18/F, Two International Finance Centre, 8 Finance Street, CENTRAL, HONG KONG ISLAND HONG KONG SAR.

CHAN, Ms. Yuen Yee Jenny, ACA *2004;* c/o KPMG, 8/F Prince's Building, 10 Chater Road, CENTRAL, HONG KONG ISLAND, HONG KONG SAR.

CHAN, Mr. Yum Man Dennis, ACA *2005;* 25/F Block A1, Fairway Garden, 3-7 Liberty Avenue, HO MAN TIN, KOWLOON, HONG KONG SAR.

CHAN, Mr. Yun Choi, ACA *2005;* Flat 25G Block 2, Felicity Garden, SHAU KEI WAN, HONG KONG ISLAND, HONG KONG SAR.

CHAN, Miss. Yvette Yu Ting, ACA *2008;* Flat 2912, Block B, Kornhill, Hong King Street, QUARRY BAY, HONG KONG ISLAND HONG KONG SAR.

CHAN-A-SUE, Mr. Paul Augustus, FCA *1967;* Lot 25 Bel Air Avenue, Lamaha Gardens, GEORGETOWN, GUYANA.

CHAN FOOK TIN, Miss. Maggy, BA(Hons) ACA *2002;* 77 Sugden Road, LONDON, SW11 5ED.

CHAN SUI-HING, Miss. Jessica, BA(Hons) ACA *2003;* B Z W, 10 South Colonnade, LONDON, E14 4PU.

CHAN SUI KO, Mr. Didier Thomas, BSc(Hons) ACA *2009;* 14 King Edward Road, LONDON, E10 6LE.

CHAN-WALKER, Mrs. Janet Yuen Shan, BSc ACA *1994;* 17 Hurstbourne Gardens, BARKING, IG11 9UY.

CHAN YAM, Mr. Paul, ACA *1986;* 151 Village Gate Drive, MARKHAM L6C 1W5, ON, CANADA.

•CHAN YIN, Mr. Li How Foong, FCA *1991;* with KPMG Audit, 9 Allee Scheffer, 2520 LUXEMBOURG, LUXEMBOURG.

CHAN YOU FEE, Mr. Lim Kee Sen, BSc FCA *1990;* 113 Boundary Road, LONDON, E17 8NQ.

CHANA, Mr. Amardeep, BSc ACA *2007;* 4 Thornhill Road, NORTHWOOD, MIDDLESEX, HA6 2LN.

CHANA, Mr. Basant Singh, BSc(Hons) ACA *2011;* 20 Acacia Avenue, HAYES, MIDDLESEX, UB3 2ND.

CHANA, Mr. Jasvinder Singh, BSc ACA *1992;* 47 Elgood Avenue, NORTHWOOD, MIDDLESEX, HA6 3QT.

CHANA, Miss. Manisha, ACA *2010;* Flat 17, Oldfield House, Devonshire Road, LONDON, W4 2AP.

CHANA, Mr. Rajhvir, BSc ACA *2011;* 59 Acfold Road, BIRMINGHAM, B20 1HG.

CHANA, Mr. Rickie Diljeet Singh, BSc ACA *2006;* 102 Lambourne Road, Chigwell Row, CHIGWELL, IG7 6EJ.

CHANA, Mr. Surjinder Singh, BSc FCA *1991;* 38 Copthall Lane, Chalfont St. Peter, GERRARDS CROSS, BUCKINGHAMSHIRE, SL9 0DG.

CHANAN, Miss. Geeta, BSc ACA *2007;* 2 Macarthur Terrace, Charlton Park Road, LONDON, SE7 8HZ.

CHANCE, Mr. Brian, FCA *1951;* 78 Mosslea Road, WHYTELEAFE, CR3 0DQ.

CHANCE, Mr. James Frederick, FCA *1963;* 460 Old Bedford Road, LUTON, BEDFORDSHIRE, LU2 7BN. (Life Member)

•CHANCE, Mr. Martin John, BA FCA *1982;* Glover Stanbury & Co, 27 Bridgeland Street, BIDEFORD, EX39 2PZ.

CHANCE, Mr. Myles Geoffrey, FCA *1971;* 21 Eyebrook Road, Bowdon, ALTRINCHAM, WA14 3LH.

•CHANCELLOR, Mr. Brian Leslie, FCA *1963;* B L Chancellor, 29 rue des Petits Champs, 75001 PARIS, FRANCE.

CHANCELLOR, Mr. Russell Edwin, FCA *1953;* Institute of Chartered Accountants, 399 Silbury Boulevard, MILTON KEYNES, MK9 2HL. (Life Member)

CHAND, Mrs. Poonam, BSc ACA *1993;* 22 Pemberley Avenue, BEDFORD, MK40 2LQ.

•CHANDA, Mr. Ranabir, MSc FCA *1969;* Chanda Associates, 23 King Edward Walk, LONDON, SE1 7PR.

CHANDA, Mr. Uday Kumar, FCA *1979;* Flat 1, Elm Quay Court, Nine Elms Lane, LONDON, SW8 5DE. (Life Member)

CHANDAN, Mr. Amandeep, BSc(Econ) ACA *1995;* 46 Yeading Gardens, HAYES, UB4 0DW.

CHANDAN, Mr. Anmol, ACA *1996;* 1399 Park Garden Lane, RESTON, VA 20194, UNITED STATES.

CHANDAN, Miss. Anukriti, BSc ACA *2008;* 160 Blackberry Lane, Four Oaks, SUTTON COLDFIELD, B74 4JJ.

CHANDANI, Mr. Tarun D, BCom ACA *2005;* with BDO LLP, 55 Baker Street, LONDON, W1U 7EU.

CHANDAR, Mr. Ravijot, ACA *2011;* 34 Gledwood Avenue, HAYES, MIDDLESEX, UB4 0AN.

•CHANDARANA, Mr. Bhanulal Pragjibhai, FCA *1975;* BPC Chandarana & Co Ltd, Prebend House, 72 London Road, LEICESTER, LE2 0QR.

CHANDARANA, Mr. Kashyap Pravin, BSc ACA *1996;* 47 St. James Close, Prince Albert Road, LONDON, NW8 7LQ.

CHANDARANA, Mr. Neel, ACA *2009;* 7 St. Michaels Close, WORCESTER PARK, SURREY, KT4 7NA.

CHANDARANA, Mr. Pritesh, BSc ACA *2011;* 72 Swithland Lane, Rothley, LEICESTER, LE7 7SE.

CHANDARANA, Mr. Rish Rajendra, ACA *2009;* 5 Galton Close, BIRMINGHAM, B24 0QH.

•CHANDARANA, Mr. Rishi, BSc(Hons) ACA *2003;* BPC Chandarana & Co Ltd, Prebend House, 72 London Road, LEICESTER, LE2 0QR.

CHANDARIA, Mr. Dilip Khetshi, FCA *1971;* P.O. Box 18087, NAIROBI, KENYA.

CHANDARIA, Mr. Jai, BSc ACA *2003;* Comcraft Services Ltd, 49 Queens Gardens, LONDON, W2 3AA.

CHANDARIA, Mr. Nyalchand Nathalal, FCA *1970;* Petroplastics & Chemicals Ltd, Unit 18, Silicon Business Centre, 28 Wadsworth Road, PERIVALE MIDDLESEX UB6 7JZ.

CHANDARIA, Ms. Priya, ACA *2011;* PricewaterhouseCoopers Services Pty Ltd, Darling Park Tower 2, 201 Sussex Street, SYDNEY, NSW 2000, AUSTRALIA.

•CHANDE, Mr. Anuj Jayantilal, FCA CF *1983;* Grant Thornton UK LLP, 30 Finsbury Square, LONDON, EC2P 2YU. See also Grant Thornton LLP

CHANDE, Mr. Manish Jayantilal, ACA *1980;* Clarebell House, 6 Cork Street, LONDON, W1S 3NX.

CHANDER, Miss. Sarita, BSc ACA *2002;* 31 Knights Place, St. Leonards Road, WINDSOR, SL4 3LE.

CHANDI, Mrs. Premkunver, BSc ACA *1991;* MWAKILINGO STREET, P. O. BOX 80638, MOMBASA, 80100, KENYA.

CHANDI, Mr. Sanjay Pravinlal Prabhudas, BSc ACA *1991;* MWAKILINGO STREET, P. O. BOX 80638, MOMBASA, 80100, KENYA.

CHANDIOK, Mr. Arvind, MCom FCA *1968;* 64 L'Estrange Street, GLENSIDE, SA 5065, AUSTRALIA. (Life Member)

•CHANDIOK, Mr. Vishesh, MSc ACA *2000;* Grant Thornton, L41 Connaught Circus, NEW DELHI 110001, INDIA.

CHANDIRAMANI, Miss. Leena, LLB ACA *1999;* 30 Queens Court, Queens Road, RICHMOND, SURREY, TW10 6LA.

CHANDLER, Mr. Albert John William, FCA *1956;* 6 Downsway Close, TADWORTH, KT20 5DR. (Life Member)

•CHANDLER, Mr. Andrew Philip, BA FCA *1981;* APC Interim Solutions Ltd, 30 Parkhurst Road, BEXLEY, DA5 1AR.

CHANDLER, Mr. Antony James, FCA *1974;* 18 Lingfield Road, LONDON, SW19 4QD.

CHANDLER, Mr. Brian Ronald, MBA FCA *1966;* 6 The Meadows, Hale House Lane, Churt, FARNHAM, SURREY, GU10 2JR.

CHANDLER, Miss. Carol Victoria, BSc ACA *1981;* Westenhanger, Leaves Green Common, KESTON, BR2 6DS.

CHANDLER, Mr. Charles, ACA *2007;* 5 Trinity Street, TAUNTON, SOMERSET, TA1 3JG.

CHANDLER, Mr. Christopher Philip, FCA *1977;* 14 rue Cadoudal, 56230 QUESTEMBERT, FRANCE.

•CHANDLER, Mr. Clifford Roy, BSc FCA *1981;* (Tax Fac), Applegarth, 41 Forge Lane, Higham, ROCHESTER, ME3 7AJ. See also Goatcher Chandler Limited

CHANDLER, Mr. David Paul, BA ACA *2002;* 1 Lime Close, REIGATE, RH2 8AP.

CHANDLER, Miss. Deborah, BSc ACA *2011;* 17 Shearwater, Whitburn, SUNDERLAND, SR6 7SF.

CHANDLER, Mrs. Deborah Carmel, BA ACA *1997;* 12 Hoodcote Gardens, Winchmore Hill, LONDON, N21 2NE.

CHANDLER, Mr. Edward Charles, BA(Hons) ACA *2004;* Barn Farm, Winsford Road, WINSFORD, CHESHIRE, CW7 4DR.

CHANDLER, Mr. Gareth John, ACA *2008;* 150 Merrivale Road, SMETHWICK, WEST MIDLANDS, B66 4EB.

CHANDLER, Mr. Gary Wyndham, BA ACA ATII *1995;* Heavi Tree, Moulsham Street, CHELMSFORD, CM2 0JJ.

•CHANDLER, Mr. Ian James, FCA *1975;* Hedges Chandler (Sudbury) Ltd, Hamlet House, 366-368 London Road, WESTCLIFF-ON-SEA, ESSEX, SS0 7HZ. See also Hedges Chandler (Westcliff) Limited

CHANDLER, Mr. James Edward, ACA *2000;* 18 Walkers Road, Longwick, PRINCES RISBOROUGH, BUCKINGHAMSHIRE, HP27 9SS.

CHANDLER, Mr. John Geoffrey, FCA *1974;* (Tax Fac), 1 West View, Seamill Lane, ST. BEES, CA27 0BD.

CHANDLER, Mr. John George, BSc ACA *1983;* 22 Weetwood Avenue, LEEDS, LS16 5NF.

CHANDLER, Mr. John Gordon, FCA *1959;* 459 Bath Road, Saltford, BRISTOL, BS31 3AZ. (Life Member)

CHANDLER, Mrs. Karen Louise, BSc ACA *1998;* The Laurels Heath Ride, Finchampstead, WOKINGHAM, BERKSHIRE, RG40 3QN.

CHANDLER, Mr. Kevin, ACA *2009;* 18 Bitterne Drive, Goldsworth Park, WOKING, SURREY, GU21 3JU.

CHANDLER, Mr. Laurence George, JP FCA *1961;* 25 Church Meadow, SURBITON, KT6 5EP.

CHANDLER, Mrs. Lauri Ann, BSc ACA *1990;* 5 North Ridge, Red House Farm, WHITLEY BAY, NE25 9XT.

CHANDLER, Mrs. Louise, BA ACA *1989;* 16 Sarum Close, WINCHESTER, HAMPSHIRE, SO22 5LY.

CHANDLER, Miss. Lynn Angharad, BA ACA *1986;* 32 Wingate Rd, Hammersmith, LONDON, W6 0UR.

CHANDLER, Mr. Mark Bradley, BA FCA *1998;* 66 Barn Hey Crescent, Meols, WIRRAL, MERSEYSIDE, CH47 9RR.

CHANDLER, Mr. Martin Andrew, BSc ACA *1998;* Abbots Wood Bramley Road, Pamber End, TADLEY, RG26 5QP.

CHANDLER, Mr. Matthew, BA ACA *1993;* Lloyd's Of London, 1 Lime Street, LONDON, EC3M 7HA.

CHANDLER, Mr. Matthew, BA(Hons) ACA *2011;* 31 Elleray Road, SALFORD, M6 7RA.

CHANDLER, Mr. Matthew Jon, BSc(Hons) ACA *2000;* 2 Waldo Close, LONDON, SW4 9EY.

CHANDLER, Mr. Miles Jonathan Lewis, BSc FCA *1980;* Firethorn, Rattlesden Road, Drinkstone, BURY ST. EDMUNDS, IP30 9TL.

•CHANDLER, Mr. Nicholas, BA ACA *1994;* KPMG LLP, 15 Canada Square, LONDON, E14 5GL. See also KPMG Europe LLP

•CHANDLER, Mrs. Nicola Sally, ACA *2006;* Goodwin Shaw, 39 Market Place, CHIPPENHAM, SN15 3HT.

CHANDLER, Dr. Robert, ACA *2009;* 61 Bloomfield Road, BROMLEY, BR2 9RY.

CHANDLER, Mr. Robert Alun, BA ACA *1996;* 86 Effra Road, LONDON, SW19 8PR.

CHANDLER, Mr. Robert Charles, FCA *1971;* Grange Farm House, Brockhampton, CHELTENHAM, GLOUCESTERSHIRE, GL54 5XQ.

CHANDLER, Mr. Robert Ian, BSc ACA *1992;* 2 Mill Steps, Winterbourne Down, BRISTOL, BS36 1BT.

CHANDLER, Mr. Robert John, BSc FCA *1988;* with Ernst & Young, P.O. Box 140, MANAMA, BAHRAIN.

CHANDLER, Prof. Roy Anthony, BSc FCA *1981;* 6 Kelvin Road, Roath Park, CARDIFF, CF23 5ET.

•CHANDLER, Mr. Roy John, BSc FCA *1991;* Michael Welfare & Company Ltd, 100 High Road, Byfleet, WEST BYFLEET, SURREY, KT14 7QT. See also MW & Co LLP

CHANDLER, Miss. Sarah Joanne, BA(Hons) ACA *2010;* Flat B, 29 Webb's Road, LONDON, SW11 6RU.

CHANDLER, Mr. Stephen, ACA *1990;* 215 The Street, Kirtling, NEWMARKET, Suffolk, CB8 9PD.

CHANDLER, Mr. Stephen Charles, BA ACA *1995;* Message Labs Group, 1240 Lansdowne Court, Gloucester Business Park, Brockworth, GLOUCESTER, GL3 4AB.

CHANDLER, Mr. Stephen John, BSc ACA *1987;* Mainline Communications Group Plc, Century Court, First Avenue, Centrum 100, BURTON-ON-TRENT, STAFFORDSHIRE DE14 2GR.

CHANDLER, Mr. Stephen Paul, ACA *1992;* N Power Communication Ltd, Windmill Hill Business Park, Whitehill Way, SWINDON, SN5 6PB.

•CHANDLER, Mr. Vincent Paul, ACA FCCA *2010;* Moore Green, 22 Friars Street, SUDBURY, SUFFOLK, CO10 2AA.

•CHANDLEY, Miss. Anna Maria, BEng ACA CTA *2002;* (Tax Fac), Lewis Curtis Limited, 10 Durham Avenue, Gidea Park, ROMFORD, RM2 6JS.

CHANDLEY, Mr. Charles William Duncan, FCA *1962;* (Tax Fac), 14 Avondale Avenue, Hazel Grove, STOCKPORT, SK7 4PZ.

•CHANDLEY, Mr. Nigel John, BA ACA *1986;* Chandley Robinson Ltd, 33 Church Road, Gatley, CHEADLE, CHESHIRE, SK8 4NG.

CHANDOO, Ms. Malika, BA(Hons) ACA *2000;* c/o Safder Jaffer - Milliman, PO BOX506784, Grosvenor Business Tower, Sheikh Zayed Road, (Near Crowne Plaza Hotel), DUBAI UNITED ARAB EMIRATES.

CHANDRA, Mrs. Abigayil, BA ACA *2004;* with Deloitte LLP, Stonecutter Court, 1 Stonecutter Street, LONDON, EC4A 4TR.

CHANDRA, Mr. Debansu David, MA(Hons) ACA *2001;* Constantin Ltd, 25 Hosier Lane, LONDON, EC1A 9LQ.

•CHANDRAN, Mr. Ruban, BA ACA *2000;* 5 Campden Hill Gardens, LONDON, W8 7AX.

CHANDRAN, Mr. Vikranth, BSc ACA *2003;* 227 Carlton Avenue East, WEMBLEY, MIDDLESEX, HA9 8QB.

CHANDRASENA, Mr. Bhevan Ravinesh, MA ACA *2003;* 136 rue charles quint, 1000 BRUSSELS, BELGIUM.

CHANDRASHEKHAR, Mr. Panchami, ACA *2008;* International Power Senator House, 85 Queen Victoria Street, LONDON, EC4V 4DP.

CHANDRU, Miss. Shalini, MSc BA ACA *2006;* Flat C, 190 Ashmore Road, LONDON, W9 3DE.

CHANETSA-MAZARURA, Mr. Given, ACA *2011;* Fairview No 4, 12 Allez Street, St Peter Port, GUERNSEY, GY1 1NG.

CHANEY, Mr. Alan Robert, FCA *1966;* 2 North Lodge, Little Offley, HITCHIN, SG5 3BS.

CHANEY, Mr. Alex, ACA *2009;* 43a California Avenue, Scratby, GREAT YARMOUTH, NORFOLK, NR29 3NS.

CHANG, Mr. Da Ko, BSc FCA *1974;* 4th Floor, 1A Forfar Road, KOWLOON CITY, KOWLOON, HONG KONG SAR. (Life Member)

CHANG, Ms. Jeanette Shu Lei, ACA *1996;* 18 Springleaf Lane, SINGAPORE 788063, SINGAPORE.

CHANG, Mr. Kon Sang, FCA *1978;* House No 2Lorong Bestari 2, Taman Bestari, 88300 KOTA KINABALUSabah, MALAYSIA.

CHANG, Mr. Kwok Ting, ACA *2007;* 14/F Shanghai Industrial Investment Building, 48 Henessy Road, WAN CHAI, HONG KONG SAR.

CHANG, Miss. Li Ling, BEng ACA *2009;* Flat 6, Derwent Court, Eleanor Close, LONDON, SE16 6PS.

CHANG, Mrs. Linda Kah Eng, BSc ACA *1993;* Anz Bank Lll, 100 Queen Street, MELBOURNE, VIC 3000, AUSTRALIA.

CHANG, Mr. Lip Kee David, BA FCA *1993;* 7 Coniston Grove, Serangoon Garden Estate, SINGAPORE 558303, SINGAPORE.
CHANG, Miss. Lona I Yien, BA ACA *1991;* 14B Celeste Court, 12 Fung Fai Terrace, HAPPY VALLEY, HONG KONG SAR.
CHANG, Mr. Man Ho Peter, ACA *2007;* Flat E 9th Floor, Tower 1, The Sparkle, 500 Tung Chau Street, TAI KOK TSUI, KOWLOON HONG KONG SAR.
CHANG, Mr. Peter, BSc ACA *1982;* Cheng Kwok & Chang, 5/F, Wah Kit Commercial Centre, 302 Des Voeux Road, CENTRAL, HONG KONG ISLAND HONG KONG SAR.
•**CHANG, Mr. Simon Hao Lin, MSc ACA** *1991;* ATC Accountants, 5 Castle Court, 1 Brewhouse Lane, LONDON, SW15 2JJ.
CHANG, Mr. Stephen Francis Wen Kai, FCA *1973;* Rosemullion, Woodlands Road, Bickley, BROMLEY, BR1 2AP.
CHANG, Mr. Stephen Tso Tung, BSc FCA *1977;* Flat C3 Shouson Garden, 6A Shouson Hill Road, SHOUSON HILL, HONG KONG ISLAND, HONG KONG SAR.
CHANG, Mr. Terrance Gene, FCA *1965;* Terrance G. Chang, PO Box 3037, Tragarete Road Post Office, PORT OF SPAIN, TRINIDAD AND TOBAGO.
CHANG, Mr. Wai Kwan Vincent, ACA *2007;* #1608, 16th Floor, Block B, 25-27 Hong Shing Street, Kornhill, QUARRY BAY HONG KONG SAR.
CHANG, Mr. Wei Kong, ACA *2006;* Flat A 20/F, Block 5 Mountain Shore, 8 Yuk Tai Street, Ma On Shan, SHA TIN, NEW TERRITORIES HONG KONG SAR.
CHANG, Mr. Wei Ming, ACA *1979;* 60 Bayshore Road, # 05-05 Jade Tower, Bayshore Park, SINGAPORE 469982, SINGAPORE.
CHANG, Ms. Win Yin Anita, ACA *2011;* (Tax Fac), Room 2001, 20th Floor, Hung Fai House, Hung Hom Est, HUNG HOM, KLN HONG KONG SAR.
CHANG, Miss. Yixin, MA BSc ACA *2009;* Flat 15 Adriatic Building, 51 Narrow Street, LONDON, E14 8DN.
CHANG, Mr. Yu Wai, BSc ACA *1986;* VTech Holdings Limited, 23/F Tai Ping Industrial Ctr, Block 1, 57 Ting Kok Road, TAI PO, NEW TERRITORIES HONG KONG SAR.
CHANG, Ms. Yue Rong, ACA CA(SA) *2009;* 38 Braemar House, 135 Maida Vale, LONDON, W9 1UT.
CHANG, Ms. Yuet Kwan, ACA *2008;* Flat J, 3rd Floor Block 7, Chevalser Garden, SHA TIN, NEW TERRITORIES, HONG KONG SAR.
CHANG, Mr. Yuk Fung Lawrence, ACA *2010;* Flat F 12/F Block 17, On Ming Mansion, Lei King Wan, QUARRY BAY, HONG KONG ISLAND, HONG KONG SAR.
CHANG, Mr. Zhewei, BA ACA *2007;* 5 Urban Mews, Hermitage Road, LONDON, N4 1AH.
CHANMUGAM, Mr. Jerome Roshanth, FCA *1984;* 184 Elvitigala Mawatha, 8 COLOMBO, SRI LANKA.
•**CHANNA, Mrs. Gurpreet, LLB ACA** *2002;* with Clifford Towers (Accountants) Limited, 1st Floor Suites, Units 8-9, Webb Ellis Business Park, RUGBY, CV21 2NP.
CHANNA, Miss. Kirandeep Kaur, MSc BSc ACA *2006,* 47 Bromley Gardens, BROMLEY, BR2 0ES.
CHANNA, Mrs. Nirmaljit Kaur, BA FCA *1985;* Woodbridge, 138 Purley Oaks Road, SOUTH CROYDON, Surrey, CR2 0NS.
•**CHANNA, Mr. Pritpal Singh, BA ACA** *1988;* (Tax Fac), Abacus & Co, 416 Green Lane, ILFORD, IG3 9JX.
•**CHANNER, Mr. Colin Patrick, BA FCA** *1974;* (Tax Fac), Colin Channer T/A Cojac Training, 17 St. Peters in The Field, BRAINTREE, ESSEX, CM7 9AR.
CHANNING, Mr. Antony John, BA ACA *1981;* Patchetts, 118 The Street, Puttenham, GUILDFORD, SURREY, GU3 1AU.
CHANNING, Mr. Peter Brian, BA ACA *1992;* Eurostar International Ltd, Times House, 5 Bravingtons Walk, LONDON, N1 9AW.
CHANNO, Mr. Jamil Ishaq, FCA *1973;* 1 Carrer de Josep Carner, Alella Park, Alella, BARCELONA, SPAIN. (Life Member)
CHANNON, Mr. Philip David, BA ACA *1990;* Edelman, 701 Central Plaza, 18 Harbour Road, WAN CHAI, HONG KONG ISLAND, HONG KONG SAR.
•**CHANNON, Mr. Rodney Owen, BSc ACA** *1984;* Channon & Co, The Mill, Balls Corner, Kingsteignton Road, NEWTON ABBOT, DEVON TQ12 2QA.
CHANT, Mr. Andrew John, BSc(Econ) ACA *1995;* 17 Laurel Gardens, KENDAL, CUMBRIA, LA9 6FE.
CHANT, Mr. John Reginald, FCA *1956;* 6310 45A Avenue, DELTA V4K 4T5, BC, CANADA. (Life Member)
•**CHANT, Mr. Peter John, FCA** *1965;* (Tax Fac), Peter Chant, 22 Cottage Offices, Latimer Park, Latimer Road, CHESHAM, BUCKINGHAMSHIRE HP5 1TU.
CHANT, Mr. Richard, FCA CTA *1979;* (Tax Fac), 7 Campkin Road, WELLS, SOMERSET, BA5 2DG.
•**CHANTER, Mr. David John, MA FCA** *1961;* (Tax Fac), Chanter Browne & Curry, PO Box 6, DELABOLE, CORNWALL, PL33 9ET.
CHANTER, Mr. David Wolferstan, FCA *1952;* The Vine House, 54A Church Road, Abbots Leigh, BRISTOL, BS8 3QU. (Life Member)
CHANTER, Mr. Keith, BA FCA *1984;* The Pines, Burnhams Road, Bookham, LEATHERHEAD, KT23 3BB.
CHANTER, Mrs. Susan Caroline, BCom ACA *1983;* The Pines, Burnhams Road, Bookham, LEATHERHEAD, KT23 3BB.
CHANTER, Mr. Timothy Robert, BA ACA *1980;* Investec Bank plc, 2 Gresham Street, LONDON, EC2V 7QP.
CHANTLER, Mr. Brian Edward Charles, FCA *1975;* 48 Oaks Road, CROYDON, CR0 5HL.
CHANTLER, Mr. Daniel James, BSc(Hons) ACA *2002;* 14 Rhapsody Crescent, Warley, BRENTWOOD, CM14 5GD.
CHANTLER, Miss. Hannah, BA ACA *2006;* 1 Springthorpe Road, BIRMINGHAM, B24 0PL.
CHANTLER, Mr. Jonathan David, BSc ACA *2003;* 30 Dean Road, HOUNSLOW, MIDDLESEX, TW3 2EZ.
CHANTLER, Mr. Peter Donald, FCA *1966;* Westhaven, 148 West Bay Road, BRIDPORT, DT6 4AZ. (Life Member)
CHANTREY, Mr. Justin Nigel, MA ACA *2001;* The Old Farmhouse, The Green, Chearsley, AYLESBURY, BUCKINGHAMSHIRE, HP18 0DJ.
CHANTREY, Mr. Philip Simon, FCA *1969;* Hockering House, 11 Ashwood Place, Ashwood Road, WOKING, SURREY, GU22 7JR.
CHANTRILL, Mr. Steven Paul, BSocSc ACA *1998;* 29 Lockington Lane, Hemington, DERBY, DE74 2RF.
CHANTRY, Miss. Ruth Lillian, LLB ACA *1993;* 41 Oak Road, OLDBURY, WEST MIDLANDS, B68 0BH.
CHAO, Mr. Man Keung, ACA *2006;* Flat B, 2F, Pak Hoi Mansion, TAIKOO SHING, HONG KONG SAR.
CHAPCHAL, Mr. Daniel Robert, FCA *1973;* Varykino, 9 Ridgelands, Fetcham, LEATHERHEAD, KT22 9DB.
CHAPELL, Mrs. Nicola Jane, ACA *1993;* 9 East Hill, TENTERDEN, KENT, TN30 6RL.
CHAPLIN, Mr. Benjamin, BA ACA *2000;* 3 School Crescent, Broughton Astley, LEICESTER, LE9 6ST.
CHAPLIN, Mrs. Claire Mary, ACA *2008;* 6 Belmont Hill, Newport, SAFFRON WALDEN, CB11 3RF.
CHAPLIN, Mr. David John Harold, BSc ACA *1991;* Office 10, Neath Farm Business Park, Church End, CAMBRIDGE, CB1 3LD.
CHAPLIN, Mrs. Deborah, BA FCA *1995;* (Tax Fac), with ICAEW, Chartered Accountants' Hall, Moorgate Place, LONDON, EC2P 2BJ.
CHAPLIN, Miss. Deborah Jane, MA ACA *1988;* 33 Agates Lane, ASHTEAD, KT21 2ND.
CHAPLIN, Mr. Jeremy McDowell, BSc ACA *1997;* Maxxium UK, Maxxium House, The Castle Business Park, STIRLING, FK9 4RT.
CHAPLIN, Mr. John Richard, FCA *1963;* 50 Storey's Way, CAMBRIDGE, CB3 0DX.
CHAPLIN, Mr. Mark Douglas Lekay, BSc FCA *1989;* (Tax Fac), 11 Roundmoor Drive, Cheshunt, WALTHAM CROSS, EN8 9HZ.
•**CHAPLIN, Mr. Mark Peter, ACA** *1982;* (Tax Fac), Altorfer Financial Management Ltd, 5 Regent Gate, WALTHAM CROSS, HERTFORDSHIRE, EN8 7AF.
CHAPLIN, Mr. Michael Roger, MA FCA *1977;* Chaplin & Co, 1110 Finch Ave W, Ste 710, NORTH YORK M3J 2T2, ON, CANADA.
CHAPLIN, Ms. Nicole Fay, ACA *2008;* 14 Laurel Street, LONDON, E8 3AY.
CHAPLIN, Mrs. Norah Patricia, FCA *1955;* 30 Westbeech Road, Pattingham, WOLVERHAMPTON, WV6 7AQ. (Life Member)
CHAPLIN, Mr. Richard James, MA ACA *1979;* (Member of Council 1997 - 2001), Practice Management International Llp Salisbury House, London Wall, LONDON, EC2M 5QQ.
CHAPLIN, Mr. Richard Jeremy, BA ACA *1992;* 29 Hawthorn Drive Hollywood, BIRMINGHAM, B47 5QT.
CHAPLIN, Mr. Richard John, ACA *1994;* 11811 Willows Road NE, PO Box 97006, REDMOND, WA 98073, UNITED STATES.
•**CHAPLIN, Mr. Richard John, BTech FCA** *1980;* Grant Thornton UK LLP, Crown House, Crown Street, IPSWICH, IP1 3HS. See also Grant Thornton LLP
CHAPLIN, Mr. Russell Ian, ACA *1982;* (Tax Fac), 13 Chestnut Avenue, EDGWARE, HA8 7RA.
CHAPLIN, Mr. Stanley Frederick, FCA *1953;* (Tax Fac), The Croft, 30 Westbeech Road, Pattingham, WOLVERHAMPTON, WV6 7AQ. (Life Member)
CHAPLIN, Mr. Steven Thomas, BSocSc ACA *2004;* 71 Belfry Drive, Wollaston, STOURBRIDGE, DY8 3SE.
CHAPLING, Miss. Veronica Ruth, BA ACA *1990;* (Tax Fac), 70A Highgate Hill, LONDON, N19 5NQ.
•**CHAPLOW, Mr. Christopher, ACA** *1981;* C. Chaplow, 32 Granville Road, ACCRINGTON, BB5 2LA.
CHAPMAN, Mr. Alan Bernard, FCA *1964;* Maison De La Vieille Fontaine, Place De La Vieille Fontaine, Freinet, 83680 LA GARDE-FREINET, FRANCE.
CHAPMAN, Mr. Alexander Neil, BSc(Hons) ACA *2003;* Apex Fund Services (Canada) Ltd., 175 Bloor St East, Suite 807 South Tower, TORONTO M4W 3R8, ON, CANADA.
CHAPMAN, Mrs. Andrea Louise, BA(Hons) ACA MSI *2001;* 13 Browning Road, HARPENDEN, HERTFORDSHIRE, AL5 4TS.
•**CHAPMAN, Mr. Andrew, BSc FCA** *1987;* (Tax Fac), Leonard Gold, 24 Landport Terrace, PORTSMOUTH, PO1 2RG. See also Carter Gold Ltd
CHAPMAN, Mrs. Angela Patricia, BSc ACA *1980;* 10 Priest Hill Gardens, WETHERBY, WEST YORKSHIRE, LS22 7UD.
•**CHAPMAN, Mrs. Anna Mary, BSc FCA** *1993;* Chapman Worth Limited, 6 Newbury Street, WANTAGE, OXFORDSHIRE, OX12 8BS.
CHAPMAN, Miss. Anna Ruth, BA(Hons) ACA *2011;* 29 Church Road, Chavey Down, ASCOT, BERKSHIRE, SL5 8RR.
CHAPMAN, Miss. Anne, BSc FCA *1991;* Suite 86, Private Bag X1, MELKBOSSTRAND, WESTERN CAPE PROVINCE, 7437, SOUTH AFRICA.
CHAPMAN, Mrs. Anne Stephanie, FCA *1985;* 5 The Hayfields, Mytholmes Lane, Haworth, KEIGHLEY, WEST YORKSHIRE, BD22 8HU.
CHAPMAN, Miss. Annette Louise, BSc ACA *1984;* (Tax Fac), 91 Humber Road, Greenwich, LONDON, SE3 7LR.
CHAPMAN, Mr. Anthony, FCA *1975;* 47 Queen Street, Weedon, NORTHAMPTON, NN7 4RA.
•**CHAPMAN, Mr. Anthony, BSc ACA** *1989;* Baker Tilly Tax & Advisory Services LLP, 2 Whitehall Quay, LEEDS, LS1 4HG. See also Baker Tilly Restructuring and Recovery LLP
CHAPMAN, Mr. Anthony James, BSc ACA *1982;* 1, International Insurance Co of Hannover Novell House, 1 Arlington Square Downshire Way, BRACKNELL, RG12 1WA.
CHAPMAN, Mr. Anthony John, BCom ACA *1987;* Seraphina, 20 Main Street, Bagworth, COALVILLE, LE67 1DN.
CHAPMAN, Mr. Anthony Neil, BA ACA *1982;* Leeds Teaching Hospitals, NHS Trust, Trust Headquarters, Beckett Street, LEEDS, LS9 7TF.
CHAPMAN, Mr. Antony Charles, BA ACA *1987;* 4051 E DESERT CREST DR, PARADISE VALLEY, AZ 85018-3942, UNITED STATES.
CHAPMAN, Mr. Barry David, FCA *1961;* Bridge Farm Cottage, Lower Road, Grundisburgh, WOODBRIDGE, SUFFOLK, IP13 6UQ. (Life Member)
CHAPMAN, Mr. Benedict Anthony, BA ACA *1993;* 27 Old Gloucester Street, LONDON, WC1N 3XX.
CHAPMAN, Mrs. Brenda Elizabeth, BSc ACA *1995;* 9 Nursery Close, PERSHORE, WR10 1NE.
CHAPMAN, Mr. Brian, MEng ACA *2003;* 94 Rushams Road, HORSHAM, WEST SUSSEX, RH12 2NZ.
CHAPMAN, Mr. Brian Roy, BSc ACA *1979;* Spring Acre, Lower Washwell Lane, Painswick, STROUD, GLOUCESTERSHIRE, GL6 6XW.
•**CHAPMAN, Mr. Bruce William, BSc FCA CTA** *1999;* Roger Lugg & Co, 12/14 High Street, CATERHAM, CR3 5UA. See also Roger Lugg & Co Limited
CHAPMAN, Mr. Bryan Leslie, FCA *1966;* 92 Sandy Lane, Middlestown, WAKEFIELD, WF4 4PP.
•**CHAPMAN, Miss. Cara, BA(Hons) ACA** *2003;* (Tax Fac), Cara Chapman, 6 Wingfield Close, Ewelme, WALLINGFORD, OXFORDSHIRE, OX10 6JY.
CHAPMAN, Mrs. Carly Teresa, BSc ACA CTA *2005;* 22 Chesterton Drive, Merstham, REDHILL, RH1 3NZ.
CHAPMAN, Ms. Carol Ann, BA ACA DChA *1989;* 16 Rydal Road, LANCASTER, LA1 3HA.
•**CHAPMAN, Mrs. Caroline Rosemary Jane, FCA** *1982;* Chapman & Chapman, Satley House, Satley, BISHOP AUCKLAND, COUNTY DURHAM, DL13 4HU.
CHAPMAN, Mrs. Carolyn Jane, BA ACA *1994;* Isles Farm, East Coker, YEOVIL, SOMERSET, BA22 9JF.
CHAPMAN, Mr. Christopher Joseph, FCA *1971;* 4 Humberdale Close, Tranby Lane Swanland, NORTH FERRIBY, HU14 3NS.
•**CHAPMAN, Mr. Christopher Stanley, FCA** *1972;* (Tax Fac), with RSM Tenon Limited, Park House, Church Place, SWINDON, SN1 5ED.
CHAPMAN, Mr. Clive Richard, MSc FCA *1971;* 36A Oakley Street, LONDON, SW3 5NT.
CHAPMAN, Mr. Colin James, BSc ACA *1980;* Little Acorns, Boyneswood Road, Medstead, ALTON, HAMPSHIRE, GU34 5EA.
CHAPMAN, Mr. Craig Daniel, ACA *2009;* 41 Summerhouse Drive, BEXLEY, DA5 2EB.
CHAPMAN, Mr. Daryl Alan, BA ACA *1999;* 27 Kalmia Green, Gorleston, GREAT YARMOUTH, NORFOLK, NR31 8LS.
CHAPMAN, Mr. David, BA ACA *1985;* 59 Peascroft Road, HEMEL HEMPSTEAD, HP3 8ER.
•**CHAPMAN, Mr. David George, BSc ACA** *1981;* Mazars LLP, 45 Church Street, BIRMINGHAM, B3 2RT.
CHAPMAN, Mr. David Henry, FCA *1976;* Alean, Greengate Farm Estate, Coedpoeth, WREXHAM, LL11 3PJ.
•**CHAPMAN, Mr. David John, BA FCA** *1987;* Chapman Pugh, 4 Tregarne Terrace, ST. AUSTELL, CORNWALL, PL25 4BE.
CHAPMAN, Mr. David Leslie, FCA *1968;* Conrad Corporate Finance Ltd, 6 The Thicket, Hainault Road, Foxrock, DUBLIN 18, COUNTY DUBLIN IRELAND.
•**CHAPMAN, Mr. David Lindsay, BA FCA** *1977;* (Tax Fac), David Chapman Accountancy Limited, 18 Stoneleigh Avenue, SALE, M33 5FF.
CHAPMAN, Mr. David Peter, BA FCA DChA *1980;* with PricewaterhouseCoopers LLP, One Kingsway, CARDIFF, CF10 3PW.
CHAPMAN, Mr. David Philip, BTech ACA *1988;* Midway House, 19 Grooms Lane, Kemberton, SHIFNAL, SHROPSHIRE, TF11 9LS.
CHAPMAN, Miss. Deanne, BA ACA *1995;* Flat 42, 86 Wapping Lane, LONDON, E1W 2RX.
CHAPMAN, Mr. Derek James, FCA *1968;* The Cottage, Badgemore, HENLEY-ON-THAMES, RG9 4NR.
CHAPMAN, Mr. Douglas Harold Victor, FCA *1951;* Badgers Brake, One Pin Lane, Farnham Common, SLOUGH, SL2 3RA. (Life Member)
CHAPMAN, Mr. Douglas Patrick, MA FCA *1976;* 93 Teddington Park Road, TEDDINGTON, TW11 8NG.
CHAPMAN, Mr. Edward, BA ACA *1989;* 4 Brundon Avenue, WHITLEY BAY, NE26 1SE.
CHAPMAN, Mr. Edward Brian, ACA *1987;* Eastbrook, Gooseham, BUDE, CORNWALL, EX23 9PG.
•**CHAPMAN, Ms. Elizabeth Ann, BSc ACA CTA** *1992;* E.Chapman Limited, Clearways, Colley Way, REIGATE, SURREY, RH2 9JH.
CHAPMAN, Mr. Francis David, FCA *1955;* The Institute Of Plant Engineers Benevolent Fund, 22 Greencoat Place, LONDON, SW1P 1PR. (Life Member)
CHAPMAN, Mr. Frank, BA ACA *1978;* 223 Kempshott Lane, BASINGSTOKE, HAMPSHIRE, RG22 5NB.
CHAPMAN, Mr. Gary Ivan, BSc(Hons) ACA *2000;* 162 Windsor Drive, ORPINGTON, KENT, BR6 6HQ.
•**CHAPMAN, Mr. Gary John, BSc FCA** *1994;* Warrener Stewart Limited, Harwood House, 43 Harwood Road, LONDON, SW6 4QP.
CHAPMAN, Mr. Gavin John, BSc ACA *1995;* Barclays Capital, 5 North Colonnade, LONDON, E14 4BB.
CHAPMAN, Mrs. Geetha, LLM LLB ACA *2004;* 15 Hermitage Woods Crescent, WOKING, SURREY, GU21 8UE.
CHAPMAN, Mr. George William, BEng ACA *1994;* Stanton Consultancy Ltd Pavilion House, 6-7 Old Steine, BRIGHTON, BN1 1EJ.
CHAPMAN, Mr. Geraint John, FCA *1970;* Lydstep, 19 Fields Park Avenue, NEWPORT, GWENT, NP20 5BG.
CHAPMAN, Mr. Graham Stanley, BA ACA *1996;* The Bank of New York Mellon Centre, 160 Queen Victoria Street, LONDON, EC4V 4LA.
CHAPMAN, Mr. Haywood Trefor, BSc ACA *2000;* Marden Hill House Marden Hill, HERTFORD, SG14 2NE.
CHAPMAN, Miss. Helen Louise, MSc ACA *2006;* 705 Antonine Heights, City Walk, LONDON, SE1 3DF.
CHAPMAN, Mr. Howard George, FCA *1968;* 89 Dartington Road, Platt Bridge, WIGAN, LANCASHIRE, WN2 5BA. (Life Member)
CHAPMAN, Mr. Howard John, MA BA(Hons) ACA *2004;* Murdoch Building 1st Floor, B G Group Plc, 100 Thames Valley Park Drive, READING, RG6 1PT.

CHAPMAN, Mr. Ian Ernest, BSc FCA *1971;* Orchard Cottage, Old Barnstaple Road, BIDEFORD, EX39 4ND.
CHAPMAN, Mr. Ian Marcus, BA ACA *1992;* 64 Old Kiln Lane, Grotton, OLDHAM, OL4 5RZ.
CHAPMAN, Mr. Ian Nigel, BA FCA *1987;* Altran Praxis, 20 Manvers Street, BATH, BA1 1PX.
CHAPMAN, Mr. Ian William, BSc ACA *2004;* 65 Brambletye Park Road, Earlswood, REDHILL, RH1 6EN.
CHAPMAN, Mrs. Jacqueline Ann, MA FCA *1989;* 4 Brundon Avenue, WHITLEY BAY, NE26 1SE.
•**CHAPMAN, Mrs. Jane Elizabeth, ACA** *1979;* with Derek Field & Co, 2nd Floor, Crown House, 37 High Street, EAST GRINSTEAD, RH19 3AF.
CHAPMAN, Miss. Janet Patricia, MA FCA *1989;* Union Bank, 7th floor, 400 California Street, SAN FRANCISCO, CA 94104, UNITED STATES.
•**CHAPMAN, Mr. Jeffrey Michael, FCA** *1967;* J.M. Chapman, 22 St. Albans Road, Codicote, HITCHIN, SG4 8UT.
•**CHAPMAN, Mr. Jeremy Stephen, ACA FCCA ATII** *2008;* Chapman Nash LLP, Unit 4, Barford Exchange, Wellesbourne Road, Barford, WARWICK CV35 8AQ.
CHAPMAN, Mrs. Joanne, ACA *2009;* 2 Cross Lane, North Hykeham, LINCOLN, LN6 9QY.
CHAPMAN, Mr. John, FCA *1958;* Foxes Lodge, 33 Little Marlow Rd, MARLOW, SL7 1HA. (Life Member)
CHAPMAN, Mr. John Andrew, FCA *1991;* with Nigel Webster & Co Ltd, 129 North Hill, PLYMOUTH, PL4 8JY.
•**CHAPMAN, Mr. John Christopher, FCA** *1973;* Baker Tilly & Co Limited, 25 Farringdon Street, LONDON, EC4A 4AB.
CHAPMAN, Mr. John Howard, FCA *1956;* 31 Hawthorndene Road, Hayes, BROMLEY, BR2 7DY. (Life Member)
CHAPMAN, Mr. John Huw, FCA *1982;* 1 Brewery House, Longden Coleham, SHREWSBURY, SY3 7JD.
CHAPMAN, Mr. John Lionel, FCA *1971;* New York Cottage, Rochdale Road, Ripponden, SOWERBY BRIDGE, HX6 4JU.
CHAPMAN, Mr. John Robert, BA FCA *1972;* 14 Croft End, WETHERBY, LS22 6XA. (Life Member)
CHAPMAN, Mr. Jonathan Paul, ACA *1979;* 12 Havelock Road, HAWTHORN EAST, VIC 3123, AUSTRALIA.
CHAPMAN, Miss. Julia Ann, BSc ACA *1999;* 10 Warbler Drive, Lower Earley, READING, RG6 4HD.
CHAPMAN, Mrs. Julia Anne, BA ACA *1998;* Homebase Ltd, Argos Ltd, 489-499 Avebury Boulevard, MILTON KEYNES, MK9 2NW.
CHAPMAN, Ms. Julia Jacquetta Caroline, ACA *1983;* Riverlea, Moor End, Acaster Malbis, YORK, YO23 2UH.
CHAPMAN, Mr. Julian Paul, ACA *1992;* 389 Elder Lane, WINNETKA, IL 60093, UNITED STATES.
CHAPMAN, Mr. Keith Howard, BSc ACA *1982;* Selham Ltd, 91 Raymouth Road, LONDON, SE16 2DA.
•**CHAPMAN, Mr. Keith John, BA FCA** *1971;* (Tax Fac), Crouch Chapman, 62 Wilson Street, LONDON, EC2A 2BU.
•**CHAPMAN, Mr. Keith Sidney, ACA** *1985;* Keith S Chapman, 37 Church Row, BURY ST. EDMUNDS, SUFFOLK, IP33 1NT.
CHAPMAN, Mr. Kenneth, FCA *1962;* 31 Sutherland Boulevard, LEIGH-ON-SEA, SS9 3PT. (Life Member)
•**CHAPMAN, Mr. Kevin Rodney, BSc FCA** *1988;* 6 Corrie Gardens, VIRGINIA WATER, SURREY, GU25 4JH.
CHAPMAN, Miss. Laurenne Claire, ACA *2010;* 20 Thorncliffe Drive, DARWEN, LANCASHIRE, BB3 3QA.
CHAPMAN, Mr. Lawrence Ian, BA ACA *2000;* Riverhill Partners Limited, Amadeus House, Floral Street, LONDON, WC2E 9DP.
CHAPMAN, Mr. Leonard, FCA *1949;* 3 Westway, Eldwick, BINGLEY, BD16 3LZ. (Life Member)
CHAPMAN, Mrs. Lesley Margaret, BSc ACA *1979;* 10, St Georges Yard, FARNHAM, SURREY, GU9 7LW.
CHAPMAN, Mr. Lloyd Crendon, FCA *1968;* 27 Kings Road, Great Totham, MALDON, CM9 8DJ.
CHAPMAN, Mrs. Lorraine Diana Margaret, ACA *2008;* Garden Flat, 11 Beaufort Road Clifton, BRISTOL, BS8 2JU.
•**CHAPMAN, Mr. Malcolm Saul, FCA** *1965;* Chapman & Co, 39 Ferndene Road, Whitefield, MANCHESTER, M45 6RB.
CHAPMAN, Mr. Marcus Timothy, MA ACA *2003;* Flat A, 3 White Hart Lane, LONDON, SW13 0PX.
CHAPMAN, Mr. Mark Christopher, BA ACA *1995;* 3 Haven Lane, DIAMOND CREEK, VIC 3089, AUSTRALIA.
CHAPMAN, Mr. Mark Godson, BCom(Hons) ACA CA(SA) *2009;* Ferry Cottage, Sutton Road, Cookham, MAIDENHEAD, BERKSHIRE, SL6 9SN.
•**CHAPMAN, Mr. Mark Iain Sorby, BSc FCA** *1982;* Deloitte & Touche, James Frett Building, Wickhams Cay 1, P O Box 3083, ROAD TOWN, TORTOLA ISLAND VIRGIN ISLANDS (BRITISH).
CHAPMAN, Mr. Mark Sutherland, BSc ACA *2004;* Mountrose Ltd Allen House Ashton Road, Bredbury Park Industrial Estate Bredbury, STOCKPORT, SK6 2QN.
CHAPMAN, Mr. Martin, BSc ACA *2007;* 3 St. Pauls Court, Water Orton, BIRMINGHAM, B46 1SQ.
CHAPMAN, Mr. Martin Joseph, ACA *2010;* Apartment 115, Viva, 10 Commercial Street, BIRMINGHAM, B1 1RR.
CHAPMAN, Mr. Martyn Richard, FCA *1975;* Orca Book Services Ltd Unit A3, Fleets Corner, POOLE, DORSET, BH17 0HL.
•**CHAPMAN, Mr. Matthew, BCom FCA** *2000;* (Tax Fac), Chapman Worth Limited, 6 Newbury Street, WANTAGE, OXFORDSHIRE, OX12 8BS.
CHAPMAN, Mr. Matthew Allott, BSc ACA *1994;* Furzewood, Fox Hill Village, HAYWARDS HEATH, RH16 4QZ.
CHAPMAN, Mr. Michael Christopher, FCA *1973;* 8 Mountain View, Borrowdale, KESWICK, CA12 5XH.
CHAPMAN, Mr. Michael David, BSc ACA CTA *1989;* 89 Vicarage Road, Old Town, EASTBOURNE, EAST SUSSEX, BN20 8AH.
CHAPMAN, Mr. Michael Howard, FCA *1970;* 15 Bucks Lane, Sutton Bonnington, LOUGHBOROUGH, LE12 5PB.
CHAPMAN, Mr. Michael Thomas, BSc ACA *2010;* 22 Taw Drive, Chandler's Ford, EASTLEIGH, HAMPSHIRE, SO53 4SL.
CHAPMAN, Mrs. Natalie D, ACA MAAT *2005;* 97a Woodplumpton Road, Ashton-on-Ribble, PRESTON, PR2 2LQ.
•**CHAPMAN, Mr. Neil Scott, BSc ACA** *2004;* with Dutton Moore, 6 Silver Street, HULL, HU1 1JA.
CHAPMAN, Mr. Neil Spencer, BA FCA *1980;* Endeavour Holdings Ltd, Victoria Road, Portslade, BRIGHTON, BN41 1WY.
CHAPMAN, Mr. Nicholas Antony Ingram, BA FCA *1958;* Winchmore, Barcombe, LEWES, BN8 5TJ. (Life Member)
CHAPMAN, Mr. Nicholas David, BSc(Hons) ACA *2002;* Holly House 4 Glemsford Drive, HARPENDEN, HERTFORDSHIRE, AL5 5RB.
CHAPMAN, Mr. Nicholas James, BA FCA *1994;* 27 Rennets Close, LONDON, SE9 2NQ.
•**CHAPMAN, Mr. Nigel Peter, FCA** *1974;* Rosemergy Farm, Chapel Porth, ST. AGNES, CORNWALL, TR5 0NR.
CHAPMAN, Mr. Oliver Paul, BSc ACA *2004;* Plan International UK, 5-7 Cranwood Street, LONDON, EC1V 9LH.
CHAPMAN, Mr. Paul Antony, BSc ACA *1996;* Luscombe House, Morchard Bishop, CREDITON, DEVON, EX17 6NW.
•**CHAPMAN, Mr. Paul Graham, FCA** *1970;* (Tax Fac), MAGI Associates, Holly Cottage, Berden, BISHOP'S STORTFORD, HERTFORDSHIRE, CM23 1AE.
•**CHAPMAN, Mr. Paul Robert, BSc FCA** *1989;* McCranors Limited, Clifford House, 38-44 Binley Road, COVENTRY, CV3 1JA. See also McCranor Kirby Smale Limited
•**CHAPMAN, Mr. Paul Robert, FCA** *1980;* Peters Elworthy & Moore, Salisbury House, Station Road, CAMBRIDGE, CB1 2LA. See also PEM VAT Services LLP, PEM Corporate Finance LLP
CHAPMAN, Miss. Pauline Alison, BA ACA *1988;* Rendezvous Chez Moi, Barras Lane, Vale, GUERNSEY, GY6 8EB.
CHAPMAN, Mrs. Penny Dawn, BA(Hons) ACA *2002;* (Tax Fac), Holly House, 4 Glemsford Drive, HARPENDEN, HERTFORDSHIRE, AL5 5RB.
CHAPMAN, Mr. Peter Anthony, BA ACA *1987;* Ambleside, Oakhanger, BORDON, GU35 9JN.
•**CHAPMAN, Mr. Peter James, BSc(Hons) FCA** *2000;* with Buzzacott LLP, 130 Wood Street, LONDON, EC2V 6DL.
•**CHAPMAN, Mr. Peter Jeremy, BA ACA** *1986;* with Ernst & Young LLP, 100 Barbirolli Square, MANCHESTER, M2 3EY.
CHAPMAN, Mr. Peter John, BSc CA ACA *2000;* George Weston Foods, Building A Level 1, 11 Talavera Road, NORTH RYDE, NSW 2113, AUSTRALIA.
CHAPMAN, Mr. Peter Lawton, BCom FCA *1966;* 6 Old Town Square, STRATFORD-UPON-AVON, WARWICKSHIRE, CV37 6DY. (Life Member)
•**CHAPMAN, Mr. Peter Nixon, BA FCA** *1979;* Chapman & Chapman, Satley House, Satley, BISHOP AUCKLAND, COUNTY DURHAM, DL13 4HU.
CHAPMAN, Mr. Peter Reginald, FCA *1953;* 9 Lilac Avenue, Willerby, HULL, HU10 6AE. (Life Member)
CHAPMAN, Mr. Peter Richard, FCA DChA *1964;* 3 Downs Way, TADWORTH, KT20 5DH.
CHAPMAN, Mr. Philip John, FCA *1973;* Spinnaker, Horsell Park, WOKING, SURREY, GU21 4LY.
CHAPMAN, Mr. Richard Antony, MA ACA *1997;* 13 Browning Road, HARPENDEN, HERTFORDSHIRE, AL5 4TS.
CHAPMAN, Mr. Richard John, FCA *1969;* Hillberry, Greenways, Lambourn, HUNGERFORD, RG17 7LD.
CHAPMAN, Mr. Richard Kenneth, FCA *1963;* Residence 'Le Calme', Bat. Charlotte - 13 D, 7 avenue Marcel Proust, 14360 TROUVILLE SUR MER, FRANCE. (Life Member)
CHAPMAN, Mr. Richard Owen, FCA *1971;* 2 Knightsbridge Court, NOTTINGHAM, NG5 2HY.
CHAPMAN, Mr. Robin Gregory, BSc FCA *1975;* 2 Bagby Grange Cottages Bagby, THIRSK, NORTH YORKSHIRE, YO7 2AE.
•**CHAPMAN, Mr. Robin Nigel, LLB FCA** *1971;* Langdon Gray LLP, 39 St James Street, LONDON, SW1X 8ED.
CHAPMAN, Mr. Roger Paul, BCom ACA *1992;* 9 Nursery Close, PERSHORE, WR10 1NE.
CHAPMAN, Roger Stanley, Esq MBE MA FCA *1955;* Larchfield, Farm Lane, EPSOM, KT18 6BS. (Life Member)
CHAPMAN, Mr. Ronald Walter, FCA *1959;* The Brooms, Green Lane, Farnham Common, SLOUGH, SL2 3SR. (Life Member)
CHAPMAN, Mr. Roy John, MA FCA *1961;* 9 Chislehurst Road, Bickley, BROMLEY, BR1 2NN.
CHAPMAN, Mr. Russell John, FCA *1978;* Grant Thornton Grant Thornton House, Kettering Parkway Kettering Venture Park, KETTERING, NORTHAMPTONSHIRE, NN15 6XR.
CHAPMAN, Mrs. Sally Ruth, MA ACA *2001;* Highland Cottage, 4 Park Road, CLEVEDON, AVON, BS21 7JG.
CHAPMAN, Mrs. Samantha Jane, BSc(Hons) ACA *2000;* MBNA Europe Bank Ltd, Chester Business Park, CHESTER, CH4 9FB.
CHAPMAN, Mr. Samuel, MSci ACA *2005;* The Offices, Avenals Farm Water Lane, Angmering, LITTLEHAMPTON, WEST SUSSEX, BN16 4EP.
CHAPMAN, Mr. Samuel William Linsan, ACA *2011;* 12 Ketcher Green, Binfield, BRACKNELL, BERKSHIRE, RG42 5TA.
CHAPMAN, Miss. Sandrine Laura, BSc ACA *2010;* 18 Triggs Close, WOKING, GU22 0EJ.
CHAPMAN, Miss. Sarah, BSc ACA *2011;* 14 Leiros Parc Drive, Rhyddings, Bryncoch, NEATH, WEST GLAMORGAN, SA10 7EW.
CHAPMAN, Mrs. Sarah Jane, BSc ACA *1992;* 39 Seymour Road, West Hill, Southfields, LONDON, SW18 5JB.
CHAPMAN, Mr. Simon Edward, LLB ACA *1999;* 9 Clare Wood Drive, East Malling, WEST MALLING, KENT, ME19 6PA.
CHAPMAN, Mr. Simon Huntingdon, MA MBA ACA *1991;* 41 Davenant Road, OXFORD, OX2 8BU.
•**CHAPMAN, Mr. Simon John, BSc FCA** *1979;* Regil Farm, The Street, Regil, Winford, BRISTOL, BS40 8BB.
•**CHAPMAN, Mr. Simon John, BA ACA CF** *1993;* Burgis & Bullock, 2 Chapel Court, Holly Walk, LEAMINGTON SPA, CV32 4YS. See also Burgis & Bullock Corporate Finance Ltd
CHAPMAN, Mr. Stephen, BA ACA MSI *1991;* 81 Manchuria Road, LONDON, SW11 6AF.
CHAPMAN, Mr. Stuart, ACA *2010;* 7 Sullivan Close, CANTERBURY, KENT, CT1 3TF.
CHAPMAN, Miss. Susan Jane, BA ACA *1981;* 31 Penn Meadow, Stoke Poges, SLOUGH, SL2 4EB.
CHAPMAN, Mr. Terence David, FCA *1961;* 16 Belper Close, Oadby, LEICESTER, LE2 5WB. (Life Member)
CHAPMAN, Mrs. Teresa May, BSc(Hons) ACA *2003;* 92 Lyndhurst Drive, HORNCHURCH, RM11 1JZ.
CHAPMAN, Mr. Timothy, BA ACA *2009;* 46 Cumberland Mills Square, LONDON, E14 3BJ.
CHAPMAN, Mr. Timothy William, BSc ACA *1991;* 53 Cranley Road, GUILDFORD, GU1 2JW.
CHAPMAN, Mrs. Tracy, BA FCA CTA *1998;* Horwath Clark Whitehill, Oakland House, 38-42 Victoria Road, HARTLEPOOL, CLEVELAND, TS26 8DD.
CHAPMAN, Mrs. Tracy Helen, BSc ACA *1991;* 94 Sherburn Street, Cawood, SELBY, NORTH YORKSHIRE, YO8 3SS.
CHAPMAN, Miss. Tracy Louise, BA ACA *1996;* Pringle of Scotland Ltd, Glebe Mill, Noble Place, HAWICK, ROXBURGHSHIRE, TD9 9QE.
•**CHAPMAN, Mr. Trevor, ACA** *2000;* Berry & Warren Ltd, 54 Thorpe Road, NORWICH, NR1 1RY.
CHAPMAN, Mr. Wayne, BSc ACA *2011;* 5 Stoke Road, LEIGHTON BUZZARD, BEDFORDSHIRE, LU7 2SW.
CHAPMAN, Mr. William Cook, FCA *1973;* 47 South Hill Park, Hampstead, LONDON, NW3 2SS.
CHAPMAN, Mr. William Harold, FCA *1967;* Chapman Associates, PO Box R1605, Royal Exchange, SYDNEY, NSW 1225, AUSTRALIA.
CHAPMAN, Mr. William Robert, FCA *1970;* The Old Malt House, 5 The Nook, Great Glen, LEICESTER, LE8 9GQ.
•**CHAPPELL, Mr. Andrew David, FCA** *1980;* (Tax Fac), Chappell Associates limited, Westfield House, Bratton Road, WESTBURY, WILTSHIRE, BA13 3EP. See also Bridge Accountancy Ltd
CHAPPELL, Mr. Andrew John, FCA *1989;* 30 Pomeroy Crescent, WATFORD, WD24 6RZ.
CHAPPELL, Mr. David James, BSc ACA *1989;* Cumbria County Council, c/o Cumbria Fire & Rescue Service HQ, Station Road, COCKERMOUTH, CUMBRIA, CA13 9PR.
CHAPPELL, Mr. Edmund, BEng ACA *2003;* with Crowe Clark Whitehill, Aquis House, 49-51 Blagrave Street, READING, RG1 1PL.
•**CHAPPELL, Mr. Geoffrey George, BA ACA** *1983;* Chappell & Co, Baysfield House, Silfield Road, WYMONDHAM, NR18 9AZ.
•**CHAPPELL, Mr. Graham Michael, FCA** *1986;* D. Stoker & Co, Abacus House, 367 Blandford Road, BECKENHAM, BR3 4NW.
CHAPPELL, Mr. Ian Stanley, BSc FCA *1982;* 5 Keiths Wood, KNEBWORTH, SG3 6PU.
CHAPPELL, Mr. James George Andrews, BA ACA *1997;* 56 Ridgway Place, LONDON, SW19 4SW.
CHAPPELL, Miss. Jane, BSc ACA *1997;* 5 The Croft, Collingham, WETHERBY, WEST YORKSHIRE, LS22 5LG.
CHAPPELL, Mr. Mark Stephen, BA ACA *1998;* 1 Cloister Garth, BERKHAMSTED, HERTFORDSHIRE, HP4 2DU.
•**CHAPPELL, Mr. Paul Robert, BA FCA** *1983;* Astracon Limited, 2 The Firs, Moorfield Road, Duxford, CAMBRIDGE, CB2 4PY. See also Chappell Paul
CHAPPELL, Mr. Peter Brian, ACA *1988;* Nordea Bank Plc, City Place House, 55 Basinghall Street, LONDON, EC2V 5NB.
CHAPPELL, Mrs. Rachel Mary, BA(Hons) ACA *2004;* (Tax Fac), 36 Oldbury Court Road, BRISTOL, BS16 2JG.
CHAPPELL, Mr. William John, BSc ACA *1987;* PO Box 6009, DUBAI, UNITED ARAB EMIRATES.
CHAPPELL, Mrs. Yvonne Marie, ACA CTA MAAT *1995;* (Tax Fac), with Grant Thornton UK LLP, Grant Thornton House, 202 Silbury Boulevard, MILTON KEYNES, BUCKINGHAMSHIRE, MK9 1LW.
•**CHAPPELLE, Mr. John Bennet, BSc FCA** *1993;* Duncan & Toplis, 27 Lumley Avenue, SKEGNESS, LINCOLNSHIRE, PE25 2AT.
CHAPPIN, Mr. Andrew James, BA(Hons) ACA *2001;* T N S UK Ltd, 6 More London Place, LONDON, SE1 2QY.
CHAPPLE, Mr. Andrew George, BSc ACA *1991;* Mole Valley Farmers Ltd, Station Road, SOUTH MOLTON, EX36 3BH.
•**CHAPPLE, Mr. Andrew Graham, ACA** *1981;* (Tax Fac), Collins Chapple & Co. Limited, Van Gaver House, 48 Bridgford Rd, West Bridgford, NOTTINGHAM, NG2 6AP.
CHAPPLE, Mr. Bryan Gee, FCA *1961;* Lane End, 30 The Avenue, Claygate, ESHER, KT10 0RY. (Life Member)
CHAPPLE, Mr. Christopher David, MA BA ACA *1999;* with BDO LLP, 55 Baker Street, LONDON, W1U 7EU.
CHAPPLE, Mr. Dean, ACA *2002;* 179 Bideford Green, LINSLADE, BEDFORDSHIRE, LU7 2TS.
CHAPPLE, Mrs. Elizabeth Claire, BA ACA *1994;* Badbury House, Shelfield, ALCESTER, B49 6JN.
•**CHAPPLE, Mr. Jonathan Richard, BA ACA** *2008;* (Tax Fac), Chapple Accounting Services Ltd, 77 Chapel Street, BILLERICAY, ESSEX, CM12 9LR.
CHAPPLE, The Revd. Richard Hubert, FCA *1973;* 9 Marwin Close, MARTOCK, SOMERSET, TA12 6HF.
•**CHAPPLE, Mr. Timothy Jonathan, BA FCA** *1983;* Tim Chapple, 10 St. Mellion Close, Monkton Park, CHIPPENHAM, WILTSHIRE, SN15 3XN.
CHAR KEE CHUNG, Mr. Robert Yeong Kwong, ACA *1993;* 9 Steel Street, SYDNEY, NSW 2010, AUSTRALIA.
CHAR KEE CHUNG, Mr. Roland, BCom FCA *1989;* 6 Australia Street, HURSTVILLE, NSW 2220, AUSTRALIA.
CHARALAMBIDES, Mr. Andreas, MBA BSc ACA *2004;* 5 Nafpactou Street, Strovolos, 2060 NICOSIA, CYPRUS.
CHARALAMBIDES, Mr. Christos, BA(Econ) ACA *2004;* Filotheou 32, 2036 Strovolos, NICOSIA, CYPRUS.

CHARALAMBIDES, Mr. George, BSc ACA *1995;* Philippou Litsa 31, HALANDRI, 15232 ATHENS, GREECE.

CHARALAMBIDES, Mr. Kyriacos, ACA *2011;* Vasilis Michaelides 25, Ayia Zoni 3026 Limassol, P.O.Box 51916, 3509 LIMASSOL, CYPRUS.

•**CHARALAMBIDES, Mr. Leon Bernard, BA FCA** *1989;* Leon Charles Ltd, 247 Gray's Inn Road, LONDON, WC1X 8QZ.

CHARALAMBIDES, Mr. Marios, BSc ACA *2006;* 9 Trikallon street, Lakatameia, 2313 NICOSIA, CYPRUS.

CHARALAMBIDOU, Ms. Maria, ACA *2003;* Sminagou Michali Shiakalli 12A Strovolos, 2045 NICOSIA, CYPRUS.

•**CHARALAMBOS, Mrs. Claire Louise, ACA** *1992;* (Tax Fac), Claire Charalambos, 59 Northaw Road East, Cuffley, POTTERS BAR, HERTFORDSHIRE, EN6 4LY.

•**CHARALAMBOU, Mr. Harry, BA FCA** *1980;* Georgiades Charalambou & Co LLP, 283 Green Lanes, LONDON, N13 4XS.

•**CHARALAMBOUS, Mr. Alexandros, ACA** *1981;* Alexandros Charalambous, 3 Prokopiou street, 2000 STROVOLOS, CYPRUS.

CHARALAMBOUS, Miss. Christiana, MSc ACA *2004;* P.O.Box 51870, 3509 LIMASSOL, CYPRUS.

CHARALAMBOUS, Miss. Christiana, ACA *2010;* 3 Iacovou Patatsou Street, Empa, 8250 PAPHOS, CYPRUS.

CHARALAMBOUS, Mr. Christos, BSc(Hons) ACA *2002;* 34A DIOGENOUS STREET, AGLANTZIA, 2122 NICOSIA, CYPRUS.

CHARALAMBOUS, Mr. Christos Yiannaki, BSc ACA CF *1995;* Lanitis Development, EuroHouse, 82 Spyrou Kyprianoy Street, 1st Floor, Yermasoyia, 4043 LIMASSOL CYPRUS.

•**CHARALAMBOUS, Miss. Effie, BA FCA** *1992;* (Tax Fac), CC Panayi & Co LLP, 2nd Floor, 44-46 Whitfield Street, LONDON, W1T 2RJ.

•**CHARALAMBOUS, Mr. Efthymios, BA FCA** *1978;* Lambous & Co, 327 Bowes Road, LONDON, N11 1BA.

CHARALAMBOUS, Ms. Fotoulla, BSc ACA *1992;* Citigroup Centre, 33 Canada Square, LONDON, E14 5LB.

CHARALAMBOUS, Mr. George Nicos, BA ACA *1999;* 112 Archibishop Kyprianou Street, CY6015 LARNACA, CYPRUS.

•**CHARALAMBOUS, Mr. John, BA FCA** *1992;* Post Office Box 41027, 6308 LARNACA, CYPRUS.

CHARALAMBOUS, Ms. Maria, BSc ACA *2010;* 11 Nafpaktou Street, 2221 NICOSIA, CYPRUS.

CHARALAMBOUS, Mr. Marios Telemachou, BSc ACA *1992;* 50 Acropolis Avenue, Strovolos, 2012 NICOSIA, CYPRUS.

CHARALAMBOUS, Mr. Michael, ACA *2011;* Apartment 363, Metro Central Heights, 119 Newington Causeway, LONDON, SE1 6DQ.

CHARALAMBOUS, Mr. Minos, BA FCA *1987;* Erechthiou 28, Agliantzia, 2121 NICOSIA, CYPRUS.

CHARALAMBOUS, Ms. Natasa, BA ACA *2006;* 5 Anthemidos str, Flat 21 Panthea Court, Mesa Yitonia, 4007 LIMASSOL, CYPRUS.

CHARALAMBOUS, Mr. Panicos, BA ACA *2007;* 14A Gropius Street, 3076 LIMASSOL, CYPRUS.

CHARAMELI HERAS, Mrs. Helen Margaret, BA ACA *1999;* 1556 Calle Caceres, El Coto El Casar, 19170 GUADALAJARA, SPAIN.

CHARD, Mr. Ian Clive, FCA *1975;* Spinningwebs Ltd, Kenilworth, Farther Commons, Hillbrow, LISS, HAMPSHIRE GU33 7QQ.

CHARD, Mr. Martin Leslie, BA ACA *1992;* 10 Comfrey Close, WOKINGHAM, BERKSHIRE, RG40 5YN.

CHARD, Mr. Peregrine Dominic Gill, BSc FCA *1995;* Elm Gables Parkway Drive, Sonning, READING, RG4 6XG.

CHARD, Mr. Philip John Robson, BSc ACA *1997;* 68 Bowen Street, CAMPERDOWN, VIC 3260, AUSTRALIA.

CHARDIN, Mr. John Christopher Robert, FCA *1936;* 208 Elizabeth House, 314 Rayleigh Road, LEIGH-ON-SEA, SS9 5PZ. (Life Member)

CHARE, Mr. Mark Francis, BSc ACA *1995;* 31 Hallam Road, GODALMING, SURREY, GU7 3HW.

•**CHARGE, Mrs. Jacqueline Anne, ACA** *1981;* LC & JA Charge, 6 Hawk Close, WALTHAM ABBEY, ESSEX, EN9 3NE.

•**CHARGE, Mr. Philip, FCA** *1981;* (Tax Fac), Richardson Watson & Co, Mint House, 6 Stanley Park Road, WALLINGTON, SM6 0HA.

CHARGE, Mr. Stephen Philip, MA FCA *1988;* Apartment 3101, 26 Hertsmere Road, LONDON, E14 4EG.

CHARGE, Mr. Timothy Philip Brian, MA FCA *1978;* Dower House, Croft Lane, Newton Kyme, TADCASTER, NORTH YORKSHIRE, LS24 9LR.

CHARIDEMOU, Miss. Christina, BSc ACA *2010;* Flat D168, Parliament View Apartments, 1 Albert Embankment, LONDON, SE1 7XQ.

CHARIE, Mr. Paul Anthony, FCA FSI LRPS *1969;* 10 Thirlmere Rise, BROMLEY, BR1 4HY.

•**CHARIK, Mr. Anthony Joseph, FCA** *1975;* A.J. Charik & Co, 24 Churchill Crescent, Headley, BORDON, GU35 8ND.

•**CHARILAOU, Mr. George Homer, FCA** *1990;* George & Co, Thornhill House, 26 Fisher Street, MAIDSTONE, ME14 2SU. See also George & Co (audit) Limited

CHARILAOU, Ms. Niki, BSc ACA *1997;* 6 Troias Street, Kato Lakatamia, 2322 NICOSIA, CYPRUS.

CHARIN, Mr. John Neil, BSc FCA *1960;* 'Sherwood', Mill Ridge, EDGWARE, MIDDLESEX, HA8 7PE. (Life Member)

•**CHARING, Mr. Simon Lawrence, FCA** *1971;* (Tax Fac), Charing & Company, 6 Sewardstone Road, WALTHAM ABBEY, EN9 1NA.

CHARITY, Mr. William Brian, FCA *1958;* The Deans, Newton Green, SUDBURY, CO10 0QS. (Life Member)

•**CHARLES, Mr. Alan Paul, ACA** *1992;* Charles Associates, 32 Coleraine Road, LONDON, N8 0QL.

CHARLES, Miss. Alice, BA ACA *2006;* Flat 4 Greenhill, Prince Arthur Road, LONDON, NW3 5UB.

•**CHARLES, Mr. Andrew Stewart, BSc FCA** *1985;* Sochall Smith Limited, 3 Park Square, LEEDS, LS1 2NE.

CHARLES, Mr. Barrie Joseph, FCA *1967;* 54 Laurel Close, North Warnborough, HOOK, RG29 1BH. (Life Member)

CHARLES, Mrs. Catherine Mary, LLB ACA *1991;* Westfield, Gipsy Lane, WOKINGHAM, BERKSHIRE, RG40 2HP.

CHARLES, Mr. Christopher Audley, FCA *1974;* 12 North Road, WELLS, BA5 2TJ.

CHARLES, Mr. Christopher David Albert, BA FCA *1980;* East Thames Group, 29-35 West Ham Lane, LONDON, E15 4PH.

CHARLES, Mr. Colin David, BSc ACA *1984;* The Holt, 48 Woodcote Avenue, WALLINGTON, SM6 0QY.

CHARLES, Mr. Darren Lee, MSc ACA *2001;* Franmar House Temple Street, Brill, AYLESBURY, BUCKINGHAMSHIRE, HP18 9SU.

CHARLES, Mr. David John Bolton, FCA *1963;* Eathorne Manor, Eathorne, Constantine, FALMOUTH, TR11 5PJ.

•**CHARLES, Mr. David Lawrence, BSc FCA** *1992;* PricewaterhouseCoopers LLP, 31 Great George Street, BRISTOL, BS1 5QD. See also PricewaterhouseCoopers

CHARLES, Mr. Dominic Alexander, BA(Hons) ACA *2009;* Twenty Two, Colomberie, ST HELIER, JE1 4XA.

CHARLES, Mr. Dominic Peter, BSc ACA *1989;* Letchmore Lodge Farm, Station Road, Plumpton Green, LEWES, EAST SUSSEX, BN7 3DF.

CHARLES, Mr. Eric Arnold, FCA *1955;* 38 Chester Close North, Regents Park, LONDON, NW1 4JE.

CHARLES, Mr. Fraser Mark Stafford, MA FCA *1985;* R. Stafford Charles & Son, Queens House, 55/56 Lincoln's Inn Fields, LONDON, WC2A 3NB.

CHARLES, Mr. Gareth John, BSc ACA *1992;* Oakridge Direct Ltd, Maerdy Industrial Estate, Rhymney, TREDEGAR, GWENT, NP22 5YD.

CHARLES, Mr. Gavin, BA ACA *1992;* Air Partner Plc Platinum House, Gatwick Road, CRAWLEY, WEST SUSSEX, RH10 9RP.

CHARLES, Mrs. Geraldine, BSc ACA *2003;* 1 Knottocks Close, BEACONSFIELD, BUCKINGHAMSHIRE, HP9 2AL.

•**CHARLES, Dr. Gillian Susan, BSc FCA** *1992;* Gillian Charles, 29 Aldbourne Avenue, Earley, READING, RG6 7DB.

CHARLES, Mr. Graham Lewis, MA ACA *2004;* 2 Armstrong Close, BROMLEY, BR1 2QT.

•**CHARLES, Mr. Henry Martin, BA FCA** *1985;* Citroen Wells, Devonshire House, 1 Devonshire Street, LONDON, W1W 5DR.

CHARLES, Mr. Ian David, BSc ACA *1992;* Bozedown Windmill Bozedown Drive, Whitchurch Hill, READING, RG8 7PE.

CHARLES, Mr. Ian Reginald, BSc FCA *1981;* 8 Cooper Close, CHIPPING NORTON, OX7 5BQ.

CHARLES, Mr. Jeremy Douglas, BA ACA *1982;* Thames River Capital (UK) Ltd, 51 Berkeley Square, LONDON, W1J 5BB.

CHARLES, Mr. John Harold, FCA *1974;* 5 Brookhouse Dell, Thurcroft, ROTHERHAM, SOUTH YORKSHIRE, S66 9JX.

CHARLES, Mr. John Philip, LLB ACA *2004;* 12 Lynmouty Road, READING, RG1 8DD.

CHARLES, Miss. Kimberley, ACA *2009;* 33 Sennen Place, Port Solent, PORTSMOUTH, PO6 4SZ.

CHARLES, Miss. Laila Kirsty, BA(Hons) ACA *2009;* 37 Le May Avenue, LONDON, SE12 9SU.

CHARLES, Mr. Luke Daniel, BEng ACA *2005;* 18 Albany Terrace, WORCESTER, WR1 3DU.

CHARLES, Miss. Nicola, BSc ACA *2011;* 40 Keats Lane, Wincham, NORTHWICH, CHESHIRE, CW9 6PP.

•**CHARLES, Mr. Peter, BSc FCA** *1992;* RL Charles Limited, Fernwood House, Fernwood Road, Jesmond, NEWCASTLE UPON TYNE, NE2 1TJ.

•**CHARLES, Mr. Philip David, BEng ACA** *1994;* KPMG LLP, St. Nicholas House, 31 Park Row, NOTTINGHAM, NG1 6FQ. See also KPMG Europe LLP

CHARLES, Mr. Stephen Andrew, BSc ACA *2000;* 11 Hardwick Crescent, SHEFFIELD, S11 8WB.

CHARLES, Miss. Tess, BSc(Hons) ACA *2011;* 146 Edmund Road, HASTINGS, EAST SUSSEX, TN35 5LQ.

CHARLES-ROBERTS, Mr. Anthony Owen, FCA *1972;* 1455 Hillgrove Rd, NORTH SAANICH V8L 5K6, BC, CANADA.

CHARLESON, Mr. Christopher John, BSc ACA *1991;* 6 Prior Avenue, Cremorne Point, SYDNEY, NSW 2090, AUSTRALIA.

CHARLESON, Mr. Mark Boleslaw Robert, FCA *1972;* PO Box 779-00502, Langata, NAIROBI, KENYA.

CHARLESON, Mr. Matthew Ben, BA ACA *2007;* 3 Cedars, 15 Trinity Church Road, HAMILTON CR04, BERMUDA.

CHARLESTON, Mr. Ian, BA ACA *1987;* Alpha Hospitals, Buller Street, off Bolton Road, BURY, LANCASHIRE, BL8 2BS.

CHARLESWORTH, Mr. Adam Michael, ACA *2008;* Flat 1, 11a Hackney Road, LONDON, E2 7NX.

CHARLESWORTH, Mr. Alan Lindsay, BA ACA *1987;* IPS Group Limited, Suite 7b 80 Mosley Street, MANCHESTER, M2 3FX.

CHARLESWORTH, Mrs. Jeanne, ACA *1980;* 4 Bond End, Yoxall, BURTON-ON-TRENT, STAFFORDSHIRE, DE13 8NH.

CHARLESWORTH, Mr. John Barrie, BSc(Econ) FCA *1971;* 196 Eastwood Road, RAYLEIGH, ESSEX, SS6 7LY.

CHARLESWORTH, Mr. Joseph, BSc ACA *2010;* Flat 6, Aintree House, Park Court, Lawrie Park Road, LONDON, SE26 6EW.

CHARLESWORTH, Miss. Lynsey Marie, BSc ACA *2000;* 77 Coniston Road, WOLVERHAMPTON, WV6 9DT.

CHARLESWORTH, Mr. Martin Lester, FCA *1978;* 8 Treston Close, DAWLISH, DEVON, EX7 0DH.

CHARLESWORTH, Mr. Robert, BSc FCA *1981;* 37 Gordon Avenue, Highams Park, LONDON, E4 9QT.

CHARLESWORTH, Mr. Robert William, BA FCA *1995;* 510 Cypress Court, BRIDGEVILLE, PA 15017, UNITED STATES.

CHARLESWORTH, Mr. Roger Vivian, FCA *1970;* 8 St. Smithwick Way, FALMOUTH, CORNWALL, TR11 3XU.

CHARLESWORTH, Mrs. Sally, MMath ACA *2007;* 10 Tarongo Drive, ASPENDALE, VIC 3195, AUSTRALIA.

CHARLESWORTH, Mr. Stephen Michael, BA ACA *1993;* 143 Parkway, WELWYN GARDEN CITY, HERTFORDSHIRE, AL8 6JB.

CHARLESWORTH, Miss. Terri Christine, ACA *2011;* 87 Newlands Grove, Intake, SHEFFIELD, S12 2FU.

CHARLESWORTH, Mrs. Victoria Margaret Linda, BA ACA *2008;* 1 Coles Green, Leigh Sinton, MALVERN, WORCESTERSHIRE, WR13 5DW.

CHARLETT, Miss. Deborah Jane, BEng ACA *1992;* Flat 5, Nightingales, 5 Milner Road, BOURNEMOUTH, BH4 8AD.

CHARLICK, Mrs. Barbara Melanie, BA FCA *1977;* Curscombe, 227 Court Road, Mottingham, LONDON, SE9 4TG.

CHARLICK, Mr. Douglas John, BA FCA *1972;* 4 Amblecote, COBHAM, SURREY, KT11 2JP.

CHARLICK, Mr. Simon Robert, BSc FCA *1978;* National Housing Federation Lion Court, 25 Procter Street, LONDON, WC1V 6NY.

CHARLICK, Mr. Steven Robert Richard, BSc ACA *1993;* 11 Princetown Avenue, BANGOR, COUNTY DOWN, BT20 3BD.

CHARLTON, Mr. Alan, FCA *1960;* 1 The Paddock, Meadowfield Road, STOCKSFIELD, NE43 7PH. (Life Member)

CHARLTON, Mrs. Alison, BSc ACA *1985;* Washington Road, Nissan Motor Manufacturing (UK) Ltd, Washington Road, SUNDERLAND, SR5 3NS.

CHARLTON, Mr. Andrew, BA FCA *1977;* 23 The Runnells, ST. NEOTS, CAMBRIDGESHIRE, PE19 6AN.

CHARLTON, Mr. Andrew Kenneth, MA ACA *1989;* 25 Broad Walk, WILMSLOW, CHESHIRE, SK9 5PJ.

CHARLTON, Ms. Angela Mary, BSc ACA *1994;* 2 Main Street, Wilsford, GRANTHAM, LINCOLNSHIRE, NG32 3NP.

CHARLTON, Mr. Anthony, BA FCA *1997;* 6 ave Franklin D Roosevelt, 75008 PARIS, FRANCE.

•**CHARLTON, Miss. Cecilia Claire, FCA ATII TEP** *1994;* (Tax Fac), Ryecroft Glenton, 32 Portland Terrace, Jesmond, NEWCASTLE UPON TYNE, NE2 1QP.

CHARLTON, Mrs. Chaing Suan, FCA *1974;* Monobuoy, 22 Boulevard Princesse Charlotte, MC 98000 MONTE CARLO, MONACO.

•**CHARLTON, Mr. Christopher, FCA** *1975;* Chris Charlton Ltd, 38 Middlehill Road, Colehill, WIMBORNE, DORSET, BH21 2SE.

CHARLTON, Mr. Christopher Stewart, BA(Hons) ACA *2002;* 42 Ewald Road, LONDON, SW6 3ND.

•**CHARLTON, Mr. David, FCA** *1975;* The Charlton Williamson Partnership LLP, 77 Osborne Road, Jesmond, NEWCASTLE UPON TYNE, NE2 2AN.

CHARLTON, Mr. David Hugh, FCA *1962;* Conifer Hill, 8 Birches Nook Road, STOCKSFIELD, NE43 7PA. (Life Member)

CHARLTON, Mr. David Neil, BA(Hons) ACA *2003;* Houston Casualty Company, Walsingham House, 35 Seething Lane, LONDON, EC3N 4AH.

•**CHARLTON, Mr. David William, BSc FCA** *1980;* (Tax Fac), Barber Harrison & Platt, 2 Rutland Park, SHEFFIELD, S10 2PD. See also Charlton D.W.

CHARLTON, Mr. Derek Raymond, BSc ACA *1991;* 19 Sandecotes Road, Lower Parkstones, POOLE, BH14 8NT.

•**CHARLTON, Mr. George, FCA** *1975;* George Charlton, 11 Stoneleigh Court, Woodham Village, NEWTON AYCLIFFE, DL5 4TL.

•**CHARLTON, Mr. James Robert, BSc ACA** *1996;* Ernst & Young LLP, 1 More London Place, LONDON, SE1 2AF. See also Ernst & Young Europe LLP

CHARLTON, Mrs. Janet Catherine, BA ACA *1999;* Bostockwhite Ltd Unit 1 Cabourn House, Station Street Bingham, NOTTINGHAM, NG13 8AQ.

CHARLTON, Mr. John, ACA *2011;* 17 Lanhill Road, LONDON, W9 2BS.

CHARLTON, Mr. John Bland, MA MBA ACA *1987;* Bleach Green Farm, New Brancepeth, DURHAM, DH7 7JP.

•**CHARLTON, Mr. John William, BEng ACA** *1999;* Deloitte LLP, 2 New Street Square, LONDON, EC4A 3BZ. See also Deloitte & Touche LLP

CHARLTON, Mrs. Kate Louise, BA ACA *2007;* 7 Royal Crescent, HARROGATE, NORTH YORKSHIRE, HG2 8AB.

CHARLTON, Mr. Keith Smith, MSc ACA *1991;* 2 King Johns Court, Ponteland, NEWCASTLE UPON TYNE, NE20 9AR.

•**CHARLTON, Mr. Kenneth Reginald, FCA** *1950;* (Tax Fac), K.R. Charlton, 17 Butt Lane, Laceby, GRIMSBY, SOUTH HUMBERSIDE, DN37 7BB.

CHARLTON, Mr. Kevin John, ACA *1987;* U B S Asset Management, 21 Lombard Street, LONDON, EC3V 9AH.

CHARLTON, Miss. Lara Elizabeth Jane, BSc ACA *2000;* Trent Farm House, Main Street, Fiskerton, SOUTHWELL, NOTTINGHAMSHIRE, NG25 0UL.

CHARLTON, Miss. Lucy Claire, ACA *2008;* 28 Radlet Drive, Timperley, ALTRINCHAM, CHESHIRE, WA15 6DE.

•**CHARLTON, Mr. Mark, FCA** *1981;* (Tax Fac), Charlton & Co, Saville Chambers, 4 Saville Street, SOUTH SHIELDS, NE33 2PR.

•**CHARLTON, Mrs. Mhairi Fiona, MSc ACA CTA** *1990;* 2 King Johns Court, Ponteland, NEWCASTLE UPON TYNE, NE20 9AR.

•**CHARLTON, Mr. Michael, FCA** *1968;* Michael Charlton, 19 Lodge Road, Fleckney, LEICESTER, LE8 8BX.

CHARLTON, Mr. Michael Gerard, BSc ACA *1991;* 49 Trinity Church Road, LONDON, SW13 8EN.

CHARLTON, Mr. Michael Robert, FCA *1975;* Le Beau Rivage, 9 ave. d'Ostende, 98000 MONTE CARLO, MONACO.

CHARLTON, Mr. Murray Anthony, FCA *1953;* 1 Brook View, South Street, Letcombe Regis, WANTAGE, OXFORDSHIRE, OX12 9RG. (Life Member)

CHARLTON, Mrs. Naomi Sarah, MA ACA *1997;* 73 Kingswell, MORPETH, NE61 2TY.

•**CHARLTON, Mr. Paul, FCA** *1980;* Ryecroft Glenton, 32 Portland Terrace, Jesmond, NEWCASTLE UPON TYNE, NE2 1QP.

CHARLTON, Mr. Paul Alan Edwin, MSc BSc FCA *1981;* 1 Temperance Row, Tisbury, SALISBURY, SP3 6HW.

CHARLTON, Mr. Peter Bennett, FCA *1957;* Camino De Los Mesoncillos 18, La Moraleja, Alcobendas, 28109 MADRID, SPAIN. (Life Member)

CHARLTON, Mr. Peter James, FCA *1977;* A.J. Charlton & Sons Ltd, Sawmills, Buckland Down, FROME, BA11 2RH.

Members - Alphabetical CHARLTON - CHAU

CHARLTON, Mr. Peter John, FCA *1963;* Corvedale House, Bridge Road, Potter Heigham, GREAT YARMOUTH, NORFOLK, NR29 5JB.
CHARLTON, Mrs. Rachel Clare, BA(Hons) ACA *2009;* 61 Ashley Common Road, NEW MILTON, HAMPSHIRE, BH25 5AN.
CHARLTON, Mrs. Renee Claire, BA ACA *1997;* 1 Longcroft Avenue, HARPENDEN, HERTFORDSHIRE, AL5 2QY.
CHARLTON, Mr. Rex Victor, FCA *1974;* 5 The Breach, DEVIZES, WILTSHIRE, SN10 5BJ.
CHARLTON, Mr. Richard, MA MSt ACA *2011;* 108 Station Road, LONDON, SW13 0NB.
CHARLTON, Mr. Richard Lovell Gregory, FCA *1977;* 10 Orchard Road, BARNET, HERTFORDSHIRE, EN5 2HL.
CHARLTON, Mr. Robert Joseph, BA(Com) FCA *1957;* 43 Pit Lane, Hough, CREWE, CW2 5JH. (Life Member)
CHARLTON, Miss. Sarah Julie, BA(Hons) ACA *2010;* Flat 11, 28 Bartholomew Close, LONDON, EC1A 7ES.
CHARLTON, Mr. Simon Andrew, BSc ACA *1992;* with Deloitte Middle East, Currency House, Building 1 Level 5, DIFC, PO Box 282056, DUBAI UNITED ARAB EMIRATES.
CHARLTON, Mr. Stephen, BA ACA *1986;* Trehurst House, 4 Milbourne Lane, ESHER, KT10 9DX.
•**CHARLTON, Mr. Stephen Gordon, FCA** *1984;* (Tax Fac), Stokoe Rodger, St Matthews House, Haugh Lane, HEXHAM, NORTHUMBERLAND, NE46 3PU.
CHARLTON, Mr. Stuart Edward, BA(Hons) ACA *2002;* Unit 23, 5-17 High Street, MANLY, NSW 2095, AUSTRALIA.
CHARLTON, Miss. Susan Elaine, ACA *2008;* Pricewaterhousecoopers, 89 Sandyford Road, NEWCASTLE UPON TYNE, NE1 8HW.
CHARLTON, Mrs. Victoria Elizabeth, BA ACA *1999;* 10 Chadwick Park Thistle Hill, KNARESBOROUGH, NORTH YORKSHIRE, HG5 8QD.
CHARLWOOD, Miss. Alice Clare Madhu, BSc ACA *2007;* Flat 3 Keats House, 34 Faraday Road, LONDON, W10 5RS.
•**CHARLWOOD, Mr. Jeffrey Allan John, BA ACA** *1998;* JAC Accountancy, Flat 6, 62 Woodbury Park Road, TUNBRIDGE WELLS, KENT, TN4 9NG.
CHARLWOOD, Mr. Michael, FCA *1976;* Cheale Meats Ltd, Orchard Farm, Little Warley, BRENTWOOD, ESSEX, CM13 3EN.
CHARLWOOD, Mr. Toby David Stephen, FCA *1985;* 64 Eastern Road, HAYWARDS HEATH, RH16 3NL.
CHARMAN, Mr. Howard John, BA *1968;* Elm Cottage, Graffham, PETWORTH, WEST SUSSEX, GU28 0NS.
CHARMAN, Ms. Judith Anne, BA ACA *1994;* 10 Queen Marys Avenue, WATFORD, WD18 7JP.
•**CHARMAN, Mr. Nicholas James, FCA** *1975;* N J Charman, The Coppice, 184 Medstead Road, Beech, ALTON, HAMPSHIRE GU34 4AJ.
CHARMAN, Mr. Robert Kevin, BSc(Hons) ACA *2011;* 24 Chains Drive, CORBRIDGE, NORTHUMBERLAND, NE45 5BP.
CHARMAN, Miss. Sarah Jane, ACA *2009;* Roger Lugg & Co, 12-14 High Street, CATERHAM, CR3 5UA.
CHARMAN, Mrs. Susan Elizabeth, BA ACA *1986;* 20 Stourpaine Road, POOLE, BH17 9AT.
CHARNAUD, Mr. Christopher Adam, MA FCA *1964;* 10 Frilsham Home, Farm Yattendon, READING, RG18 0XT.
CHARNAUD, Mr. Giles Sebastian, BSc ACA *1991;* Rowcroft House Foundation Ltd, Rowcroft Hospice, Avenue Road, TORQUAY, TQ2 5LS.
CHARNLEY, Mrs. Alison Rose, BA ACA *1996;* 22A Broadhinton Road, Clapham, LONDON, SW4 0LU.
CHARNLEY, Miss. Ellen Sarah, BSc ACA *1995;* 7940 Castle Pines Ave, LAS VEGAS, NV 89113, UNITED STATES.
CHARNLEY, Mr. John William, BSc ACA *1995;* 22a Broadhinton Road, Clapham, LONDON, SW4 0LU.
CHARNLEY, Mr. Shaun, BA BCom ACA *2011;* 71 Mariners Wharf, Quayside, NEWCASTLE UPON TYNE, NE1 2BJ.
CHARNOCK, Mrs. Claire Elaine, BA ACA *1996;* Ctra a Piedades de Sta Ana, Del Rest. Bar Motor Psychos, 500m en Condo. Oro Sol, Casa 50-4, SANTA ANA, COSTA RICA.
CHARNOCK, Mr. David, FCA *1977;* 28 St. Andrews Close, Fearnhead, WARRINGTON, WA2 0EJ.
•**CHARNOCK, Ms. Helen, BA FCA** *1990;* Garlands, Clifford, HEREFORD, HR3 5HF.
CHARNOCK, Mr. Ian, BSc ACA *1992;* BK04007017, 41-43 Brook Street, LONDON, W1K 4HJ.
CHARNOCK, Mr. Ian Graeme Lloyd, BA FCA *1987;* Woodcote, Holly Bank Drive, HALIFAX, HX3 8PA.
CHARNOCK, Mr. Robert Edward, BSc(Hons) ACA *2004;* Apartment 2 Romulus House, Olympian Court, YORK, YO10 3UG.
CHARNOCK, Mrs. Ruth Fiona, BA ACA *1994;* 23 Aintree Drive, Balby, DONCASTER, SOUTH YORKSHIRE, DN4 8TU.
CHARNOCK, Mr. Steven Richard, BA ACA *1986;* Cenkos Fund Managers Ltd, 12 The Parks, NEWTON-LE-WILLOWS, MERSEYSIDE, WA12 0JQ.
CHARRINGTON, Mr. Eric Bernard, FCA *1972;* 3B Champion Court, 67 Wongneichong Road, HAPPY VALLEY, HONG KONG SAR.
CHARRINGTON, Mr. Simon Leonard Mowbray, FCA *1981;* 19 Oaklands Avenue, ESHER, KT10 8HX.
CHARTER, Mr. Andrew Alan, BSc FCA *1993;* Gambit Corporate Finance, 3 Assembly Square Britannia Quay, CARDIFF, CF10 4PL.
CHARTERS, Mr. Andrew Ian, ACA *2009;* 60 Clapton Square, LONDON, E5 8HE.
CHARTERS, Miss. Annaka Laura, LLB ACA *2011;* 71, Hemming way, NORWICH, NORFOLK, NR3 2AF.
•**CHARTERS, Mr. John Alan, FCA** *1969;* (Tax Fac), J A Charters & Co Ltd, 1 Chapel Street North, COLCHESTER, CO2 7AT.
CHARTERS, Mr. Martin Alexander, BA FCA *1972;* The Pines, The Roundway, Rustington, LITTLEHAMPTON, BN16 2BW.
CHARTERS, Mr. Martin James, LLB ACA *1992;* Brooklands, Bishops Frome, WORCESTER, WR6 5BT.
CHARTERS, Mr. Philip Arthur, FCA *1955;* Four Winds, Church Lane, Ashbury, SWINDON, SN6 8LZ. (Life Member)
CHARTRES, Mrs. Caroline Wendy, MA ACA *1997;* 22 Blake Road, West Bridgford, NOTTINGHAM, NG2 5JL.
CHARTRES, Mr. John Henry Auchinleck, MA ACA *1982;* c/o Goldman Sachs, 30 Hudson Street - 16th Floor, JERSEY CITY, NJ 07303-4699, UNITED STATES.
CHARTRES, Mr. Jon, BSc ACA *2009;* 31 Moor Park Road, HEREFORD, HR4 0RR.
•**CHARTRES, Michael Duncan, Esq OBE FCA** *1966;* (Tax Fac), 25 D'Abernon Drive, Stoke D'Abernon, COBHAM, SURREY, KT11 3JE.
CHARVILL, Ms. Hannah Lucy, BA(Hons) ACA *2003;* Sheepcote Cottage, Lower Road, Great Amwell, WARE, HERTFORDSHIRE, SG12 9SY.
CHARVILL, Mrs. Vivienne, BCom ACA *1990;* The Route Development Group Ltd, 113-115 Portland Street, MANCHESTER, LANCASHIRE, M1 6DW.
CHASE, Miss. Jennifer Marianne Alison, BSc ACA *2005;* 96 Plimsoll Road, LONDON, N4 2ED.
CHASE, Mr. Nicholas John, FCA *1971;* North Lodge, Minstead, LYNDHURST, SO43 7FY.
CHASE, Mr. Norman Harold, DFC FCA *1948;* 88 Ridge Lane, WATFORD, WD17 4TA. (Life Member)
CHASE, Mr. Robert Henry Armitage, FCA *1969;* Garden Cottage The Street, Upper Farringdon, ALTON, GU34 3DT.
CHASE GARDENER, Mr. Paul Simon, BA ACA *1982;* Kings Acre, 27 Prince Consort Drive, ASCOT, SL5 8AW.
CHASE-RAHMAN, Ms. Leanne Catharine, BSc ACA *1995;* 117 Lichfield Grove, Finchley, LONDON, N3 2JL.
CHASEMORE, Mrs. Christine Jane, BA ACA *1988;* Heathcote, Darlington Road, BATH, BA2 6NL.
CHASEMORE, Mr. David Lyndon, BSc FCA *1989;* with Richardson Swift Ltd, 11 Laura Place, BATH, BA2 4BL.
CHASHMAWALA, Mr. Abdulla, FCA *1973;* Flat 11 Glyn Court, 199 Leigham Court Road, LONDON, SW16 2SF.
CHASNEY, Mr. Paul Charles, BA FCA *1978;* Wilstrop Hall, Wilstrop, Green Hammerton, YORK, YO26 8HA.
CHASSER, Mr. Brian Armstrong, FCA *1972;* 2 Manor Drive, Cuckfield, HAYWARDS HEATH, RH17 5BT.
CHASTELL, Mrs. Emily, BSc ACA *2003;* 97 Drakes Drive, STEVENAGE, SG2 0HA.
CHASTELL, Mr. Philip John, BSc(Hons) ACA *2002;* 97 Drakes Drive, STEVENAGE, SG2 0HA.
CHASTELL, Mr. Stephen Michael, BSc ACA *1990;* 8 Burnet Avenue, GUILDFORD, GU1 1YD.
CHASTNEY, Mr. John Garner, MA FCA *1973;* Beech House, 4 Benslow Rise, HITCHIN, SG4 9QX.
CHASTON, Mr. David Carl Anthony, ACA *1978;* (Tax Fac), McNicholas Construction Services Ltd Elstree Road, Elstree, BOREHAMWOOD, HERTFORDSHIRE, WD6 3EA.
CHASTON, Mr. Peter Harding, FCA *1956;* 27 Red House Close, Lower Earley, READING, RG6 4XB. (Life Member)
CHASTY, Mr. Christopher Jack, FCA *1975;* 18 West Common Way, HARPENDEN, HERTFORDSHIRE, AL5 2LF.
CHASTY, Mrs. Mei Lee, ACA *1980;* Cabot Square Capital LLP, 1-3 Connaught Place, LONDON, W2 2ET.
•**CHATBURN, Mr. Edward Andrew, FCA** *1979;* Deloitte West & Central Africa, 235 Ikorodu Road, Llupeeju, PO Box 965, Marina, LAGOS NIGERIA.
CHATBURN, Mr. John Herbert, FCA *1948;* Hammerwood, 5a Appleton Drive, Whitmore, NEWCASTLE, ST5 5BT. (Life Member)
CHATBURN, Mr. John Norman, FCA *1957;* Honister, 28 Hough Lane, WILMSLOW, SK9 2LQ. (Life Member)
CHATBURN, Mrs. Susan Pamela, MSc ACA *1983;* 49 Charlcombe Rise, Portishead, BRISTOL, BS20 8ND.
CHATBURN, Miss. Victoria Louise, ACA *2008;* 14 Runnymede Road, Whickham, NEWCASTLE UPON TYNE, NE16 4LD.
CHATELLIER, Miss. Juliette Kate, ACA *2010;* Flat 9, Russell Court, Woburn Place, LONDON, WC1H 0LL.
CHATER, Mr. Alan Malcolm, BSc FCA *1980;* Hadleigh House, Hinksey Hill, OXFORD, OX1 5BE.
CHATER, Mr. Christopher Thomas, FCA *1957;* 33 Church Street, Isham, KETTERING, NN14 1HD. (Life Member)
•**CHATER, Mr. Colin, BA FCA** *1991;* Rowlands, Rowlands House, Portobello Road, Birtley, CHESTER LE STREET, COUNTY DURHAM DH3 2RY.
CHATER, Mr. David Maxwell, FCA *1973;* The Oak House, High Street, Hinxton, SAFFRON WALDEN, ESSEX, CB10 1RF. (Life Member)
CHATER, Miss. Dawn, BA(Hons) ACA *2011;* Pricewaterhousecoopers Abacus House, Castle Park, CAMBRIDGE, CB3 0AN.
CHATER, Mr. Nicholas Vernon, BA ACA *1981;* 570 Valley Hall Drive, ATLANTA, GA 30350, UNITED STATES.
CHATER, Mrs. Vivienne Tina, BSc ACA *1987;* 5 Upper Highway, Hunton Bridge, KINGS LANGLEY, WD4 8PP.
CHATFIELD, Mr. Carl Anthony, MA ACA CIOT *1991;* 145 North Deeside Road, MILLTIMBER, AB13 0JS.
CHATFIELD, Mr. Daniel, BA ACA *2007;* 6a Hartfield Road, Saltdean, BRIGHTON, BN2 8RE.
CHATFIELD, Mr. Ralph Frederick, BSc ACA *1991;* with Grant Thornton UK LLP, Hartwell House, 55-61 Victoria Street, BRISTOL, BS1 6FT.
CHATFIELD, Mr. Roy Charles, MA FCA *1971;* 22 Old Winton Road, ANDOVER, HAMPSHIRE, SP10 2DA.
CHATFIELD, Mr. Sidney, FCA *1949;* P O Box 44, FONTAINEBLEAU, GAUTENG, 2032, SOUTH AFRICA. (Life Member)
CHATFIELD, Ms. Teresa Magdalen, BSc ACA *1982;* M.E.F.Enterprises Ltd, P.O. Box HM 994, HAMILTON HM DX, BERMUDA.
CHATHA, Mr. Theovinder Singh, ACA *2008;* Durleigh Croft, Poplar Avenue, SOUTHALL, MIDDLESEX, UB2 4PN.
CHATHAM, Mr. Alfred, FCA *1963;* 12 Sycamore Lane, Leeming, NORTHALLERTON, DL7 9SU. (Life Member)
CHATHAM, Mrs. Margaret Helen, ACA *1987;* Times & Chronicle Goole, 102 Boothferry Road, GOOLE, NORTH HUMBERSIDE, DN14 6AE.
CHATIZA, Mr. Admire, ACA *2007;* Flat 7 Warwick House, 106-112 Ladbroke Road, REDHILL, RH1 1LB.
•**CHATOO, Mr. Shabbir Abdulhusein, FCA** *1983;* (Tax Fac), Chatoo & Co, 22 Sherington Ave, Hatch End, PINNER, HA5 4DT.
CHATRATH, Mr. Jagat Mohan, FCA *1974;* 19b Brampton Road, ST. ALBANS, HERTFORDSHIRE, AL1 4PP.
CHATRATH, Mr. Shyam Sundar, FCA *1958;* 8 Cissbury Ring North, LONDON, N12 7AN. (Life Member)
CHATT, Mr. James, ACA *2010;* 14b Clarence Avenue, LONDON, SW4 8HU.
•**CHATTEN, Mr. Brian Walter, FCA** *1963;* B W Chatten LLP, Room 44, Millfield Business Centre, Ashwells Road, BRENTWOOD, ESSEX CM15 9ST.
•**CHATTEN, Mr. Martin Andrew, BA FCA** *1993;* Royce Peeling Green Limited, The Copper Room, Deva Centre, Trinity Way, MANCHESTER, M3 7BG.
CHATTERIS, Mr. Simon James, ACA *2008;* Apartment 25, 24 Point Pleasant, LONDON, SW18 1GG.
CHATTERJEA, Mr. Sunil Kumar, FCA *1960;* 7-1 Ballygunge Park, CALCUTTA 19, INDIA. (Life Member)
CHATTERJEE, Mr. Aroop, ACA *2010;* 98 Barnfield Avenue, KINGSTON UPON THAMES, KT2 5RF.
CHATTERJEE, Mr. Atanu, FCA *1976;* D. Basu & Co, 10 Old Post Office Street, CALCUTTA 700001, INDIA.
CHATTERJEE, Mr. Atanu, ACA *1980;* 3 Greenwood Gardens, LONDON, N13 5RT.
CHATTERJEE, Mr. Barun Prasad, FCA *1969;* 3332 Monarch Lane, ANNANDALE, VA 22003, UNITED STATES.
CHATTERJEE, Mr. Bhaswar, BA ACA *1998;* 60 Wall Street, NEW YORK, NY 10005, UNITED STATES.
CHATTERJEE, Mr. James Khlebnikov, BA ACA *2010;* Imperial Tobacco Ltd, Upton Road, BRISTOL, BS3 1QZ.
CHATTERJEE, Dr. Robin Abhijit, MPhil BSc ACA *1999;* 2 Bury Hall Villas, Edmonton, LONDON, N9 9LE.
CHATTERJEE, Mr. Satyajit, BSc ACA *1994;* 8B Horizon, 11A pali Hill, Bandra, MUMBAI 400050, INDIA.
CHATTERJEE, Miss. Vengalil Kalyani, BA ACA *1989;* 23637 Black Oak Way, CUPERTINO, CA 95014, UNITED STATES.
CHATTERS, Ms. Bethan Louisa, BA(Hons) ACA *2003;* Herbert Smith Llp Exchange House, 12 Primrose Street, LONDON, EC2A 2HS.
CHATTERTON, Miss. Catherine, BSc(Econ) ACA *2001;* Flat 5 Briar Patch, 11 Salisbury Road, FARNBOROUGH, GU14 7AN.
CHATTERTON, Mr. Denis Lionel, BSc ACA *1980;* Moorcroft, 2 Avenue Road, EPSOM, KT18 7QT.
•**CHATTERTON, Ms. Elaine, BSc(Hons) ACA ATT CTA** *1990;* Elaine Chatterton, 5 Heathbank Avenue, WALLASEY, CH44 3AS.
CHATTERTON, Mr. Grant Justin, MA BSc ACA *2004;* Flat 1, 112 Wandsworth Bridge Road, Fulham, LONDON, SW6 2TF.
•**CHATTERTON, Mr. Mark Henry, BSc FCA** *1992;* Duncan & Toplis, 14 London Road, NEWARK, NG24 1TW.
CHATTERTON, Mr. Peter James, FCA *1963;* 6048E Harvard Street, SCOTTSDALE, AZ 85257, UNITED STATES. (Life Member)
CHATTERTON, Mr. Philip Leigh, BEng ACA *1996;* Royal Bank of Scotland, RBS Tower, 88 Phillip Street, SYDNEY, NSW 2000, AUSTRALIA.
CHATTO, Mrs. Gillian, BA ACA *1997;* Guide Post House, Nether Heage, BELPER, DE56 2AQ.
CHATTOCK, Mrs. Jennifer Anne, BA ACA *1995;* D14 Green Villas 700 Biyun Road, SHANGHAI 201206, CHINA.
CHATTOCK, Mr. John Paul, BEng FCA *1994;* KPMG, 8/F Prince's Building, 10 Chater Road, CENTRAL, HONG KONG ISLAND, HONG KONG SAR.
CHATUR, Mr. Liaquatali Rahimtula, FCA *1977;* Chatur L. Ali, 601 1088 - 6 Avenue SW, CALGARY T2P 5N3, AB, CANADA.
CHATUR, Mr. Mahebub Alam, FCA *1975;* Hamdan Building, Rigga Road Deira, DUBAI, 49830, UNITED ARAB EMIRATES.
CHATWAL, Mr. Arbinder Singh, BSc ACA *2005;* 41 Wychwood Grove, SOUTHAMPTON, SO53 1FQ.
CHATWANI, Mrs. Hansa Satish, FCA *1981;* (Tax Fac), Kanta House, Victoria Road, RUISLIP, MIDDLESEX, HA4 0JQ.
•**CHATWANI, Mr. Jay Prakash, BSc FCA** *1982;* Lawrence & Co, 132/134 College Road, HARROW, HA1 1BQ.
CHATWANI, Mr. Satish Jamnadas, FCA *1976;* Kanta House, Victoria Road, RUISLIP, MIDDLESEX, HA4 0JQ.
CHATWANI, Mr. Vidyadhar Popatlal, FCA *1957;* 139/1/3 Ottakringer Strasse, A-1160 VIENNA, AUSTRIA. (Life Member)
CHATWIN, Mr. Brian, BCom FCA *1958;* 7 Green Hollow Close, FAREHAM, PO16 7XP. (Life Member)
•**CHATWIN, Mr. Charles Richard David, BSc FCA** *1987;* with Ernst & Young LLP, Apex Plaza, Forbury Road, READING, RG1 1YE.
CHATWIN, Mr. John Ernest, FCA FCMA *1970;* 48 Leach Heath Lane, Rubery, Rednal, BIRMINGHAM, B45 9DF.
CHATWIN, Mrs. Lucy, BA ACA *1997;* Dunscombe Cottage, Salcombe Regis, SIDMOUTH, DEVON, EX10 0PN.
CHATWIN, Mr. Robert Claus, BSc ACA *1998;* Alameda Colibri 124, Morada dos Passaros, SAO PAULO, 06428-120, BRAZIL.
CHATWOOD, Mr. Christopher David, BA ACA *1988;* 32 Middlewood Close, Eccleston, CHORLEY, LANCASHIRE, PR7 5QG.
CHATWOOD, Mrs. Jacqueline Ann, BA ACA *1992;* 23 Chaucer Close, Eccleston, CHORLEY, PR7 5UJ.
CHATZIVASILIOU, Mrs. Dimitra, BSc ACA *2009;* Militiadou 14, N. Ionia 142 31, ATHENS, GREECE.
CHAU, Ms. Belinda King Yee, ACA FCCA CPA FTIHK *2006;* with Thomas C.I. Leung & Co., Room 1301-1302, Kowloon Building, 555 Nathan Road, MONG KOK, KOWLOON HONG KONG SAR.
CHAU, Miss. Catherine Mo-Wah, FCA *1990;* Flat 20A, Tower 3, 37 Repulse Bay Road, REPULSE BAY, HONG KONG ISLAND, HONG KONG SAR.
CHAU, Mr. Chi Yin, ACA *2006;* 24/F Flat F, Oak Mansion, 20 Taikoo Wan Road, TAIKOO SHING, HONG KONG ISLAND, HONG KONG SAR.

CHAU, Ms. Eloise Man Fung, BSc ACA *1992;* Flat 3b, 23 Broadcast Drive, KOWLOON TONG, KOWLOON, HONG KONG SAR.
CHAU, Miss. Emilie Shuk-Man, BSc ACA *1993;* House E Villa Corniche, 21 South Bay Road, REPULSE BAY, HONG KONG SAR.
CHAU, Mr. Ka Hong Alfred, ACA *2008;* Flat J 19/F Tower C, Clague Garden Estate, 30 Hoi Shing Road, TSUEN WAN, HONG KONG SAR.
CHAU, Mr. Kwok Wah Edward, ACA *2007;* 29 Warrington Way, MARKHAM L6C 0B9, ON, CANADA.
CHAU, Mr. Pak Ki, BEng FCA *1994;* Room 405 Lai Tak House, Lai On Estate, SHAM SHUI PO, KOWLOON, HONG KONG SAR.
•**CHAU, Mr. Peter, ACA FCCA** *2009;* J.V. Banks, Banks House, 3 Paradise Street, RHYL, CLWYD, LL18 3LW.
CHAU, Mr. Shing Yim David, BSc ACA CF *1992;* 5/F ST. JOHN'S BUILDING, 33 GARDEN ROAD, CENTRAL, CENTRAL, 00852, HONG KONG SAR.
CHAU, Ms. Tsz Ling Florence, ACA *2005;* 1-33-104, Omaru, Tsuzuki-Ku, YOKOHAMA, KANAGAWA, 224-0061 JAPAN.
CHAU, Mr. Wai Tong, BSc(Econ) ACA *2002;* 26D Tower 6, Harbour Place, 8 Oi King Street, HUNG HOM, KOWLOON, HONG KONG SAR.
CHAU, Ms. Wun Yi, ACA *2008;* 12/F. Novel Industrial Building, 850-870 Lai Chi Kok Road, CHEUNG SHA WAN, KOWLOON, HONG KONG SAR.
CHAU, Mr. Yiu Kay Danny, ACA *2008;* Flat B, 23rd Floor, Wah Lai Court, Wah Yuen Chuen, 12 Wah King Hill Road, KWAI CHUNG NEW TERRITORIES HONG KONG SAR.
CHAUBERT, Mrs. Louisa Sue, ACA *1991;* Chemin de la Chavanne, 4 bis, 1196 GLAND, SWITZERLAND.
CHAUDARY, Mr. Waleed, BSc ACA *2009;* 124 Hoylake Crescent, UXBRIDGE, MIDDLESEX, UB10 8JG.
CHAUDHARI, Mr. Sohail, ACA *1997;* 55 Starfield Road, Shepherds Bush, LONDON, W12 9SN.
•**CHAUDHARY, Mr. Anwar Ul Haq, FCA** *1979;* Anwar Chaudhary & Co, 9 Littleton Road, HARROW, MIDDLESEX, HA1 3SY.
CHAUDHARY, Miss. Mariam, BComm BCom ACA *2007;* 828D New Providence Wharf, 1 Fairmont Avenue, LONDON, E14 9PL.
•**CHAUDHARY, Mr. Nadeem Taj, ACA** *1984;* BC & C Ltd, 50 Mansfield Road, ILFORD, ESSEX, IG1 3BD.
CHAUDHARY, Mr. Ravendra Kumar, ACA *1979;* 58 Clarinda Drive, TORONTO M2K 2W3, ON, CANADA.
CHAUDHARY, Mr. Vijay, BSc ACA *1981;* British Petroleum Co Plc, 20 Canada Square, LONDON, E14 5NJ.
CHAUDHRI, Mr. Abdul Majeed, FCA *1969;* c/o Hameed Chaudhri & Co, 5th Floor, Karachi Chambers, Hasrat Mohani Road, KARACHI, PAKISTAN.
CHAUDHRI, Mr. Abid Aslam, ACA *2008;* 310 Hodgeson House, 26 Christian Street, LONDON, E1 1AY.
CHAUDHRI, Mr. Assad Haq, BA ACA *2004;* with KPMG, P O Box 3800, Level 32, Emirates Towers, Sheikh Zayed Road, DUBAI UNITED ARAB EMIRATES.
CHAUDHRI, Mr. Fazal Haq, BSc ACA *2007;* 10 Pound Place, Binfield, BRACKNELL, BERKSHIRE, RG42 5HY.
CHAUDHRI, Mr. Harsh Vardhan, ACA *1982;* Flat No.5, S-457 Greater Kailash-2, NEW DELHI 110048, INDIA.
•**CHAUDHRI, Mr. Muhammad Aslam, BA LLB FCA** *1972;* (Tax Fac), Chaudhri & Chaudhri, 47 Hodder Drive, Perivale, GREENFORD, UB6 8LL.
CHAUDHRI, Mr. Najmul Islam, FCA *1969;* 10/2 Eight Zamzama Street, Clifton, KARACHI 75600, PAKISTAN. (Life Member)
CHAUDHRY, Mr. Devender Kumar, FCA *1962;* 238B A.J.C. BOSE RD, FLAT C3, KOLKATA 700020, WEST BENGAL, INDIA. (Life Member)
CHAUDHRY, Mr. Faisal Abbas, ACA *2006;* Qatar Investment Authority, Q-tel Tower, West Bay, P.O.Box 23224, DOHA, QATAR.
CHAUDHRY, Mr. Gulistan Ahmad, BSc ACA *1998;* 8 Sterne Street, LONDON, W12 8AD.
CHAUDHRY, Mr. Irfan Ahmad, BSc ACA *2007;* 68 Westway, Raynes Park, LONDON, SW20 9LU.
CHAUDHRY, Mr. Jamal, BA ACA *1998;* 44 Cunnington Street, Chiswick, LONDON, W4 5EN.
•**CHAUDHRY, Mr. Javed Iqbal, FCA** *1971;* Grow Capital LLC, PO Box 211530, DUBAI, UNITED ARAB EMIRATES.
CHAUDHRY, Mr. Mohammad Sharif, FCA *1975;* 158 Styal Road, Heald Green, CHEADLE, SK8 3TG.
CHAUDHRY, Mr. Muhammad Aamer, CA FCA *1995;* House No. 26, Street No. 52, MPCHS, Sector E 11/3, ISLAMABAD, ISLAMABAD CAPITAL TERRITORY PAKISTAN.
CHAUDHRY, Mrs. Nabela, BSc ACA *1999;* 8 Teasville Road, Allerton, LIVERPOOL, L18 3EP.
CHAUDHRY, Mr. Omer Ahmad, ACA *2008;* 41/1 - J, Phase 1, Defence Housing Authority, LAHORE, PAKISTAN.
CHAUDHRY, Mr. Osman, BSc ACA *2004;* 3 Holt Park Close, LEEDS, LS16 7QA.
CHAUDHRY, Mr. Shallin, BSc ACA *1980;* 69 Imperial Road, WINDSOR, SL4 3RU. (Life Member)
•**CHAUDHRY, Mr. Sohail, BA ACA** *2003;* Blandfords and Co Limited, 284 Station Road, HARROW, MIDDLESEX, HA1 2EA.
•**CHAUDHURI, Mr. Alan, BSc ACA** *1999;* Deloitte LLP, Hill House, 1 Little New Street, LONDON, EC4A 3TR. See also Deloitte & Touche LLP
CHAUDHURI, Mrs. Rhiannon, BSc ACA *2003;* 75 Disraeli Road, Putney, LONDON, SW15 2DR.
CHAUDHURI, Mr. Samir Kumar, FCA *1974;* Alter Seeweg 2a, CH 8124 MAUR, SWITZERLAND.
CHAUDHURY, Mr. Ajit Kumar, FCA *1960;* 765 Upper Belmont Avenue, Westmount, MONTREAL H3Y 1K3, QUE, CANADA. (Life Member)
CHAUDHURY, Mr. Akhter Matin, FCA *1977;* Nuvista Pharma Ltd., Mascot Plaza (8th Floor), 107/A Sonargaon Janapath, DHAKA 1230, BANGLADESH.
CHAUDRY, Mr. Sikandar Aziz, ACA *2010;* 132 Westwood Road, ILFORD, ESSEX, IG3 8SA.
CHAUHAN, Mr. Anish, BSc ACA *2003;* Westworld, River Island Clothing Co Chelsea House, West Gate, LONDON, W5 1DR.
•**CHAUHAN, Mr. Ashok Uttamlal, ACA** *1982;* (Tax Fac), A U Chauhan Limited, 5 Theobald Court, Theobald Street, ELSTREE, WD6 4RN.
CHAUHAN, Mr. Chandrakant, ACA *1993;* Sefalana Holding Company Limited, Private Bag 0080, GABORONE, BOTSWANA.
CHAUHAN, Miss. Deena, ACA *2008;* 8 Percival Road, BIRMINGHAM, B16 9SX.
CHAUHAN, Mr. Kailas Parbhu Dayal, FCA *1969;* Lewis Simler, 83 Baker Street, LONDON, W1U 6AG.
CHAUHAN, Mr. Rakesh, BA ACA *1997;* Southernwood House, Grayshott Road, Headley Down, BORDON, HAMPSHIRE, GU35 8JQ.
•**CHAUHAN, Mr. Sarbjit Singh, BSc FCA** *1997;* (Tax Fac), Sarbacco Limited, 18 Coldershaw Road, LONDON, W13 9DX.
CHAUHAN, Miss. Tina, BSc ACA *2005;* 16 Dobree Avenue, LONDON, NW10 2AE.
CHAULAGAIN, Mr. Nirmal, BSc ACA *2007;* 112 Pole Hill Road, UXBRIDGE, MIDDLESEX, UB10 0QE.
CHAUMETON, Mrs. Doramy Elizabeth, BA ACA *1985;* Keep Cottage, 17 Lancaster Avenue, FARNHAM, GU9 8JY.
CHAUMOO, Mr. Haiderally, BSc(Econ) ACA *1997;* 86 Fir Tree Road, BANSTEAD, SM7 1NQ.
CHAUNCY, Mr. James Benjamin Edward, MA ACA *1995;* 4 Fir Tree Road, GUILDFORD, GU1 1JJ.
CHAVASSE, Mrs. Margaret Anne Howard, BSc ACA *1985;* Northwood Farmhouse, Northwood, SHREWSBURY, SY4 5NN.
CHAVASSE, Mr. Peter Marcus Grant, MA FCA *1986;* EPM Consulting Limited, 64 Church Road, TEDDINGTON, MIDDLESEX, TW11 8EY.
CHAVDA, Mr. Anil, BSc ACA *1995;* 3 Bardolph Street, LEICESTER, LE4 6EH.
•**CHAVE, Mr. Philip Thomas, FCA** *1975;* (Tax Fac), Philip T. Chave & Co, Belfry House, Bell Lane, HERTFORD, SG14 1BP.
CHAVENTRE, Mr. Robin Cyril, FCA *1960;* Mill House, Garden Reach, CHALFONT ST. GILES, BUCKINGHAMSHIRE, HP8 4BE. (Life Member)
CHAVES, Mr. Stephen Louis, ACA *2008;* 65 Downs Court Road, PURLEY, CR8 1BG.
CHAWATAMA, Mr. Michael, ACA *2010;* Basement Flat, 13 St. Marks Road St. Helier, JERSEY, JE2 4LD.
CHAWLA, Mr. Dilraj Singh, ACA *1992;* 8 Laurel Lane, SEYMOUR, CT 06483, UNITED STATES.
CHAWLA, Mr. Karan, BA ACA *2002;* H S B C, 8-14 Canada Square, LONDON, E14 5HQ.
CHAWLA, Mr. Madhu Sudan, FCA *1977;* A 65 A Nizamuddin East, NEW DELHI 110 013, INDIA.
CHAWNER, Mr. Brian John, BCom ACA CTA *1991;* 53 Lodge Crescent, Hagley, STOURBRIDGE, WEST MIDLANDS, DY9 0ND.
CHAWNER, Mr. Martin Andrew, MA FCA *1959;* 40 Stamford Drive, Groby, LEICESTER, LE6 0YD. (Life Member)
•**CHAYTOR, Mr. Jonathan, FCA** *1966;* Jonathan Chaytor, The Old Vicarage, Lord Sefton Way, Great Altcar, LIVERPOOL, L37 5AA.
CHAYTOW, Mr. Stephen Ian, BSc ACA *1984;* 3 Tithe Meadows, VIRGINIA WATER, SURREY, GU25 4EU.
CHAZELLE, Mrs. Laure-Aglae, BSc ACA *2006;* Murphy West Africa Ltd, Immeuble les Manguiers 4eme etage, POINTE NOIRE, BP 4264, CONGO People's Republic of.
CHE ABAS, Mr. Hassan Bin, BA ACA *1979;* Peremba (Malaysia) Sdn Bhd, 11th Fl Bangunan A Peremba Sq, Saujana Resort Seksyen U2, 40150 SHAH ALAM, Selangor, MALAYSIA.
CHE ANI, Mr. Muhammad Azman, BSc(Econ) ACA *2001;* 16 JALAN SEPAH PUTERI 5/8, SERI UTAMA, KOTA DAMANSARA, 47810 PETALING JAYA, SELANGOR, MALAYSIA.
CHE MOKHTAR, Miss. Marina, ACA *2009;* No. 7 PJU 1A/33B, Ara Damansara, 47301 PETALING JAYA, MALAYSIA.
•**CHEADLE, Mr. Anthony Peter, BA ACA** *1997;* (Tax Fac), KPMG LLP, 15 Canada Square, LONDON, E14 5GL. See also KPMG Europe LLP
•**CHEADLE, Mr. Martin Richard, BA FCA** *1977;* (Tax Fac), Cheadles, Telegraph House, 59 Wolverhampton Road, STAFFORD, ST17 4AW. See also Cheadle Business Services Ltd
CHEAH, Mr. Allan Siew Weng, BA ACA *1984;* No. 29B Jalan SS22/19, Damansara Jaya, 47400 PETALING JAYA, MALAYSIA.
CHEAH, Miss. Choo Hong, FCA *1956;* 7 Tingkat Bendahara, 31650 IPOH, PERAK, MALAYSIA. (Life Member)
CHEAH, Mr. Christopher, BSc ACA *2003;* 6 Shrubbery Road, Streatham, LONDON, SW16 2AT.
CHEAH, Mr. Edmond Swee Leng, BA ACA *1982;* 8 Jalan Setiamurni 12, Bukit Damansara, 50490 KUALA LUMPUR, FEDERAL TERRITORY, MALAYSIA.
CHEAH, Mr. Hoong Kwun, BSc ACA *2003;* 54 Genas Close, ILFORD, ESSEX, IG6 2PL.
CHEAH, Ms. Laurena Su-Lynn, BEng ACA *1992;* 6 Lorong Batai, Damansara Heights, 50490 KUALA LUMPUR, FEDERAL TERRITORY, MALAYSIA.
CHEAH, Mr. Michael Choy Chin, BCom FCA *1993;* 33B Tower 6, Larvotto, 8 Ap Lei Chau Praya Road, AP LEI CHAU, HONG KONG ISLAND, HONG KONG SAR.
CHEAH, Miss. Nicola, ACA *2008;* 05-01 vogx, 109 Dorset road, SINGAPORE 219498, SINGAPORE.
CHEAH, Mr. Shu Kheem Andy, BSc(Econ) ACA *1998;* 15 Jalan Desa Residen, Levenue Desa Parkcity, 52200 KUALA LUMPUR, FEDERAL TERRITORY, MALAYSIA.
CHEAH, Mr. Theam Khim, BA FCA *1964;* 1042 Eyremount Drive, VANCOUVER V7S 2B3, BC, CANADA.
CHEAL, Mr. David Geoffrey Alexander, FCA *1970;* 2e Grange Road, COLERAINE, COUNTY LONDONDERRY, BT52 1NG.
•**CHEAL, Mrs. Kay Elizabeth, BSc ACA** *1991;* Kay Cheal, 4 Chilcomb, BURGESS HILL, WEST SUSSEX, RH15 0DJ.
CHEAL, Mr. Simon James, MSc ACA *2007;* 138 Church Parade, CANVEY ISLAND, SS8 9RD.
CHEALE, Mr. John Desmond, FCA *1953;* 17 Cantelupe Road, Haslingfield, CAMBRIDGE, CB3 7LU. (Life Member)
CHEALES, Mr. Maxwell Bellingham, MA FCA *1955;* Blewburton Hall, Aston Upthorpe, DIDCOT, OX11 9EE. (Life Member)
CHEANG, Miss. Chin Neo, FCA *1974;* 10 Richards Avenue, SINGAPORE 546406, SINGAPORE.
•**CHEASON, Mr. Allan, BA ACA** *1986;* Barnes Roffe LLP, Leytonstone House, Leytonstone, LONDON, E11 1GA.
•**CHEATHAM, Mr. Adrian Paul, BSc ACA** *1999;* Cooper Parry LLP, 3 Centro Place, Pride Park, DERBY, DE24 8RF.
CHEATHAM, Mrs. Helen Laura, BSc ACA *2003;* with Cooper Parry LLP, 3 Centro Place, Pride Park, DERBY, DE24 8RF.
CHEATHAM, Mrs. Katherine, BSc ACA *1998;* 80 Otter Street, DERBY, DE1 3FB.
CHEATLE, Mr. Duncan Mackenzie, BSc FCA *1995;* Loft 1, 19-20 Dufferin Street, LONDON, EC1Y 8PD.
•**CHEATLEY, Ms. Karen May, BA ACA ATII** *1988;* Cheatley and Co, 90 West Street, Oundle, PETERBOROUGH, PE8 4EF.
CHECK, Mr. Nicholas Howard, BSc ACA *1993;* 4 Honiton Gardens, LONDON, NW7 1GF.
CHECK, Mrs. Samantha Mary, BA ACA *1997;* 7 Sheppard Close, CHIPPENHAM, SN15 3FD.
CHECKETTS, Mr. Peter Guy, BSc ACA *1985;* 22 East Esplanade, Manly, SYDNEY, NSW 2095, AUSTRALIA.
CHECKLEY, Mr. Dean Vivian, BA(Hons) ACA *2004;* Apartment 11, Kondanska 23/559, Praha 10, PRAGUE, CZECH REPUBLIC.
CHECKLEY, Mr. Robert Jack, BSc ACA *2000;* 4F Grant Thornton UK, 30 Finsbury Square, LONDON, EC2P 2YU.
•**CHECKLEY, Mrs. Vivienne Jane, MA FCA** *1984;* Bunting Accountants Limited, 5 Orchard Close, Wheatley, OXFORD, OX33 1US.
CHEDGEY, Mr. James, BCom ACA *2004;* Pear Tree Cottage Aldermaston Road, Pamber End, TADLEY, RG26 5QN.
CHEDZOY, Mr. David Robert, FCA *1969;* Foxes Mead, 47 Saxon Close, Oake, TAUNTON, TA4 1JA. (Life Member)
CHEDZOY, Mr. John Hann, FCA *1948;* Reynards Wood, Blueberry Hill. Hampers Lane, Storrington, PULBOROUGH, RH20 3HZ. (Life Member)
CHEE, Mr. Chwee Cheong, BSc ACA *2000;* 140 Pinggir Zaaba, Taman Tun Dr Ismail, 60000 KUALA LUMPUR, FEDERAL TERRITORY, MALAYSIA.
CHEE, Miss. Le Anne, LLB ACA *2002;* 40 Sennett Place, SINGAPORE 466868, SINGAPORE.
CHEE, Miss. May Yeu, BA ACA *1984;* 64 JALAN SS24/1, TAMAN MEGAH, 47301 PETALING JAYA, SELANGOR, MALAYSIA.
CHEE, Ms. Su-Ann, ACA *2008;* 55 Meyer Road, #24-01, SINGAPORE 437978, SINGAPORE.
CHEE, Mr. Su-En, ACA *1979;* 52 Mojave Crescent, RICHMOND HILL L4S 1R7, ON, CANADA.
CHEE, Miss. Yuen Eng, BA ACA *1986;* 19 Jalan Meranti, Melodies Gardens, 80250 JOHOR BAHRU, Johor, MALAYSIA.
CHEEK, Mr. Giles Ashley, BA BSc ACA *1993;* Fairmead, Simone Close, Bickley, BROMLEY, BR1 2PY.
CHEEK, Mrs. Sharon Louise, BSc ACA *1993;* Fairmead, Simone Close, BICKLEY, BR1 2PY.
CHEEMA, Mr. Daljeet, ACA *2009;* 11 Peerage Way, HORNCHURCH, ESSEX, RM11 3BE.
•**CHEEMA, Mr. Darbara Singh, FCA** *1978;* (Tax Fac), Cheema Goffe & Co, 26 Plashet Grove, East Ham, LONDON, E6 1AE.
CHEEMA, Mr. Kanwaljeet, ACA *2007;* Ormes Lodge, 2 Ormes Lane, Tettenhall Wood, WOLVERHAMPTON, WV6 8LL.
CHEEMA, Mr. Parmjit, ACA *2008;* 101 Bathurst Walk, IVER, BUCKINGHAMSHIRE, SL0 9EF.
CHEEMA, Mr. Rupinder Singh, BSc ACA *2000;* 57 Rosemary Hill Road, SUTTON COLDFIELD, WEST MIDLANDS, B74 4HJ.
CHEESBROUGH, Mr. David Stephen, FCA *1970;* Flat 3, 12a Northfield Lane, Horbury, WAKEFIELD, WEST YORKSHIRE, WF4 5DL.
CHEESBROUGH, Mr. Peter Hilton, FCA *1974;* 5424 South Emporia Court, GREENWOOD VILLAGE, CO 80111-3634, UNITED STATES.
CHEESE, Mr. Karl David, BSc ACA *1994;* Harcourt Building, Harcourt Street, DUBLIN 2, COUNTY DUBLIN, IRELAND.
CHEESEBROUGH, Mr. Frederick William, FCA *1961;* Green Pastures, Pleasington Lane, Pleasington, BLACKBURN, BB2 5JH.
CHEESEBROUGH, Mr. William Graham, BA FCA *1989;* 1 Park View Crescent, LEEDS, LS8 2ES.
CHEESEMAN, Mr. Alan Richard, FCA *1954;* 15224 Blue Verde Drive West, SUN CITY WEST, AZ 85375, UNITED STATES. (Life Member)
CHEESEMAN, Mr. Gareth, BSc ACA *2003;* 6th Floor MidCity Place, Westfield Shopping Towns Ltd, 71 High Holborn, LONDON, WC1V 6EA.
CHEESEMAN, Mrs. Janet Mary, FCA *1974;* #38 3115 - 119 Street, EDMONTON T6J 5N5, AB, CANADA.
CHEESEMAN, Ms. Jennifer, FCA *1974;* 11228-70 Avenue, EDMONTON T6H 2H1, AB, CANADA. (Life Member)
CHEESEMAN, Mr. John Jeffrey, FCA *1973;* 24 Starts Hill Road, ORPINGTON, BR6 7AP.
•**CHEESEMAN, Mrs. Karen, FCA** *1986;* Grugeon Reynolds Limited, Rutland House, 44 Masons Hill, BROMLEY, BR2 9JG.
CHEESEWRIGHT, Mr. Andrew, BSc FCA *1989;* Lanes Wood Hazel Grove, Ashurst, SOUTHAMPTON, SO40 7AJ.
CHEESEWRIGHT, Mr. James, BSc FCA *1989;* Eurostar (UK) Ltd Times House, 5 Bravingtons Walk, LONDON, N1 9AW.
CHEESEWRIGHT, Mr. Nicolas William, BA FCA *1976;* 151 Compton Road, WOLVERHAMPTON, WV3 9JT.
CHEESLEY, Mr. Adrian Christopher, BA ACA *1990;* EMI Music Arabia, PO Box 61003, Jebel Ali, DUBAI, UNITED ARAB EMIRATES.
CHEESLEY, Mr. Roger Gwynne, FCA *1965;* Wysh House, Amberley, ARUNDEL, WEST SUSSEX, BN18 9LT. (Life Member)

•**CHEESMAN, Miss. Carol Ann, BSc FCA** *1975;* (Tax Fac), Cheesmans, 4 Aztec Row, Berners Road, LONDON, N1 0PW.

CHEESMAN, Mr. Christopher, FCA *1970;* Copper Beeches, Ox Lane, St Michaels, TENTERDEN, TN30 6PE.

CHEESMAN, Mr. Frederick Kenneth John, FCA *1957;* 15 Lyndhurst Avenue, SURBITON, KT5 9LN. (Life Member)

CHEESMAN, Mrs. Heather, ACA *2003;* MEMBER OF COUNCIL, Spofforths, 9 Donnington Park, 85 Birdham Road, CHICHESTER, WEST SUSSEX, PO20 7AJ.

•**CHEESMAN, Mr. Jason, ACA** *2004;* Mitchells, Suite 4, Parsons House, Parsons Road, WASHINGTON, TYNE AND WEAR NE37 1EZ.

CHEESMAN, Mr. Nicholas Andrew, BA ACA *1992;* Holly Cottage, Kingfield Road, WOKING, GU22 9DZ.

CHEESMAN, The Revd. Peter, FCA *1965;* Frampton Court The Green, Frampton on Severn, GLOUCESTER, GL2 7EX.

CHEESMAN, Mr. Stuart Andrew, FCA *1966;* 211 Old Lodge Lane, PURLEY, CR8 4AY.

•**CHEESMAN, Mr. Trevor John, FCA** *1977;* St James Accounting Limited, 53 Manor Way, Deeping St. James, PETERBOROUGH, PE6 8PS.

CHEETHAM, Mr. Andrew Geoffrey, FCA *1976;* Spinney Cottage, Kempnough Hall Road, Worsley, MANCHESTER, M28 2QP.

CHEETHAM, Mr. Andrew James, BA FCA *1976;* Essilor Ltd East Wing St. Lukes House, Emerson Way Emersons Green, BRISTOL, BS16 7AR.

CHEETHAM, Mr. Barrington, FCA *1962;* 3 The Covert, Thorpe Road, PETERBOROUGH, PE3 6HT.

CHEETHAM, Mr. Christopher Andrew, MA FCA *1990;* Scisys Plc, Methuen Park, CHIPPENHAM, WILTSHIRE, SN14 0GB.

CHEETHAM, Mr. Christopher John, BSc ACA *1987;* Forge House, Kemble, CIRENCESTER, GLOUCESTERSHIRE, GL7 6AD.

•**CHEETHAM, Mr. David Anthony, BEng ACA** *2000;* Ford Campbell Corporate Finance LLP, Bass Warehouse, 4 Castle Street, Castlefield, MANCHESTER, M3 4LZ. See also Ford Campbell Corporate Finance Ltd

•**CHEETHAM, Mr. David John Cannell, FCA** *1977;* Cheetham & Co, Holmlea House, Quarrier's Village, BRIDGE OF WEIR, RENFREWSHIRE, PA11 3SX.

CHEETHAM, Mr. Derek Leslie, FCA *1951;* 9 Flanchford Road, REIGATE, RH2 8AB. (Life Member)

CHEETHAM, Mr. Jack, FCA *1952;* Three Ways, Chapel Chorlton, NEWCASTLE, ST5 5JL. (Life Member)

CHEETHAM, Mr. Jeremy David, BA ACA *1992;* 5 Seahill Road, HOLYWOOD, COUNTY DOWN, BT18 0DA.

CHEETHAM, Mr. John Alistair, MA ACA *1980;* 44 Hillier Road, LONDON, SW11 6AU.

•**CHEETHAM, Mr. John Buchanan, FCA** *1963;* (Tax Fac), Cheetham Allen, 17 Wright St., HULL, HU2 8HU.

CHEETHAM, Mr. John Francis, FCA *1960;* 16237 Coco Hammock Way #201, FORT MYERS, FL 33908, UNITED STATES. (Life Member)

CHEETHAM, Mr. Malcolm Barry, BSc FCA *1977;* Sommerhaldenweg 3, CH 4410 LIESTAL, SWITZERLAND.

CHEETHAM, Mr. Martin Richard, MA ACA *1993;* Mill House, Field Lane, Hempnall, NORWICH, NR15 2PB.

CHEETHAM, Mr. Matthew Richard, BSc(Hons) FCA *2001;* 238 Kings Road, KINGSTON UPON THAMES, SURREY, KT2 5HX.

CHEETHAM, Mr. Michael David James, BCom FCA *1991;* 27 Severn Drive, ESHER, SURREY, KT10 0AJ.

•**CHEETHAM, Mr. Peter James, FCA** *1974;* Fairhurst, Douglas Bank House, Wigan Lane, WIGAN, WN1 2TB.

CHEETHAM, Mrs. Sonia Michelle, BSc ACA *1993;* (Tax Fac), 5 Seahill Road, HOLYWOOD, COUNTY DOWN, BT18 0DA.

CHEIM, Mr. Robert Dau Meng, FCA *1976;* CIMB Investment Bank Berhad, P O Box 12362, 50776 KUALA LUMPUR, FEDERAL TERRITORY, MALAYSIA.

CHELK, Mr. Michael Laszlo, MA FCA *1965;* 105 Hatfield Road, IPSWICH, IP3 9AG.

CHELL, Mr. Steven John, ACA *1996;* 36 Croft Avenue, Porthill, NEWCASTLE, ST5 8EY.

CHELLAM, Mrs. Claire, BSc ACA *1999;* D L A Piper, 1 St. Pauls Place, SHEFFIELD, S1 2JX.

CHELLAM, Mr. Krishnan, FCA *1975;* PO Box 3663, SARATOGA, CA 95070, UNITED STATES.

CHELLAM, Mr. Vaidyanathan Venkata, BSc(Econ) ACA *1995;* 1 Alexandra Gardens, Brincliffe, SHEFFIELD, S11 9DQ.

CHELLEW, Mrs. Elaine Susan, MA ACA *1991;* 10 Collylinn Road, Bearsden, GLASGOW, G61 4PN.

CHELLIAH, Mr. Ruban, FCA *1979;* The Anexxe, 7 LORONG 5/19C, 46000 PETALING JAYA, SELANGOR, MALAYSIA.

CHELLIAH, Mr. Sathya Seelan, FCA FTII CPA *1974;* 2 Jalan 5/41, 46000 PETALING JAYA, SELANGOR, MALAYSIA.

CHELLINGSWORTH, Mr. David Robert, FCA *1973;* UK Biobank Ltd Unit 1-2, Spectrum Way, STOCKPORT, CHESHIRE, SK3 0SA.

CHELVATHURAI, Mrs. Christine Inpamalar, ACA *1990;* 11 Newton Street, Surrey Hills, VICTORIA, VIC 3127, AUSTRALIA.

CHEN, Mr. Bin, ACA CA(AUS) *2010;* 13FChina Resources Building5001 Shennan Road East, SHENZHEN 518010, CHINA.

CHEN, Mr. Charlie Chu Cheng, BSc ACA *1999;* 33 The Grove, LONDON, NW11 9SJ.

CHEN, Miss. Denise Jiun Jing, BSc ACA *2003;* Flat 3A 1st Floor, 3-3A Shouson Hill Rd, DEEP WATER BAY, HONG KONG SAR.

CHEN, Miss. Hui, ACA *2011;* Flat 11 Susan Constant Court, 14 Newport Avenue, LONDON, E14 2DL.

CHEN, Mr. Jia Jer, ACA *2010;* 2 Barbara Avenue, GLEN WAVERLEY, VIC 3150, AUSTRALIA.

CHEN, Ms. Jian, ACA *2009;* Room 1704 No.88, Lane 569, Xinhua Road, SHANGHAI 200052, CHINA.

CHEN, Mr. Kai, ACA *2011;* Flat 204, Building No.5, Jinxiu Jiayuan, Yuanzhou Road, ZHEJIANG 317000, CHINA.

CHEN, Mr. Kai Yen, ACA *2008;* 11 Toh Tuck Road, High Oak Condominium, #02-44, SINGAPORE S(596290), SINGAPORE.

CHEN, Miss. Kok Chien, FCA *1982;* 10 Hickory Street, LOWER TEMPLESTOWE, VIC 3107, AUSTRALIA.

CHEN, Mr. Kok Peng, ACA *2008;* 8 Jalan Bunga Rampai, Taman P Ramlee, Setapak, 53000 KUALA LUMPUR, FEDERAL TERRITORY, MALAYSIA.

CHEN, Miss. Li Sian, ACA *2008;* 67 Ferry Street, LONDON, E14 3DT.

CHEN, Ms. Lirong, MEng ACA *2011;* Flat 26, The Oxygen, 18 Western Gateway, LONDON, E16 1BL.

CHEN, Ms. Man Wai Molly, ACA *2005;* A1 16/F Maiden Court, 46 Cloud View Road, NORTH POINT, HONG KONG SAR.

CHEN, Ms. Mun Yu, ACA *2006;* 11/F East, Savoy Court, 101 Robinson Road, MID LEVELS, HONG KONG ISLAND, HONG KONG SAR.

CHEN, Ms. Pui Yin, BSc ACA CTA *2002;* 1 Winkfield Road, ASCOT, BERKSHIRE, SL5 7LX.

CHEN, Mr. Terng Bhing, BA FCA *1991;* 30 Brittany Crescent, MARKHAM L3R 0R1, ON, CANADA.

CHEN, Ms. Ting Man Lorraine, ACA *2006;* Flat 413, 4/F, Block B, Kornhill, QUARRY BAY, HONG KONG SAR.

CHEN, Miss. Xi, MSc BSc ACA *2006;* 74 Settlers Court, 17 Newport Avenue, Poplar, LONDON, E14 2DG.

CHEN, Miss. Xiaoyin, ACA *2009;* Block 345 #08-94, Clementi, SINGAPORE 120345, SINGAPORE.

CHEN, Ms. Yanni, ACA *2011;* Flat 310 Naylor Building West, 1 Assam Street, LONDON, E1 7QL.

CHEN, Miss. Yao, ACA *2008;* Flat 11, Susan Constant Court, 14 Newport Avenue, LONDON, E14 2DL.

CHEN, Mr. Yeow Sin, BSc FCA *1990;* with LTC & Associates, 1 Raffles Place, 20-02 OUB Centre, SINGAPORE 048616, SINGAPORE.

CHEN, Mr. Zongyin, ACA *2010;* Room 14BB 3 Zhaonan Flat, 23 Yanjiang 3 West Road, HAIKOU CITY 570208, CHINA.

CHENERY, Mr. David Thomas, FCA *1965;* 10 Cranleigh Rise, NORWICH, NR4 6PQ. (Life Member)

•**CHENERY, Mr. John Richard, BSc FCA** *1999;* Plushcourt Estates Limited, 2 The Estate Yard, Ixworth, BURY ST. EDMUNDS, SUFFOLK, IP31 2HE.

CHENERY, Mr. Peter John, FCA *1959;* Hazelwood Park Warren Road, Hazelwood Park Dawlish Warren, DAWLISH, DEVON, EX7 0PF. (Life Member)

•**CHENERY, Mr. Trevor John, FCA** *1971;* Chenery & Company, 36 Palliser Road, CHALFONT ST. GILES, HP8 4DL.

CHENEY, Mr. Andrew John, BCom ACA *1984;* 15 Fellows Way, RUGBY, CV21 4JP.

CHENEY, Mrs. Carolyn, BSc ACA *2004;* Building 2 floor 3, Microsoft Ltd, Microsoft Campus, READING, RG6 1WG.

•**CHENEY, Mr. Francis Peter, FCA** *1974;* (Tax Fac), Spain Brothers & Co, 29 Manor Road, FOLKESTONE, KENT, CT20 2SE.

CHENEY, Mr. Paul William, FCA *1970;* 46 Thorburn Road, Weston Favell, NORTHAMPTON, NN3 3DA.

CHENEY, Mr. Peter, BSc ACA *2011;* 20 Ulverston Avenue, Chadderton, OLDHAM, OL9 9DP.

CHENG, Mr. Albert Chi Leung, BSc ACA *1988;* 26C Tower 1, Robinson Place, 70 Robinson Road, MID LEVELS, HONG KONG ISLAND, HONG KONG SAR.

CHENG, Miss. Alice, BSc(Hons) ACA *2011;* 62 Hampton Park, BRISTOL, BS6 6LJ.

CHENG, Miss. Alice Wai Ching, BSc FCA *1991;* 1/F 82 Fo Tan Village, SHA TIN, NEW TERRITORIES, HONG KONG SAR.

CHENG, Mr. Andersen Yuk Fai, MSc FCA *1990;* 1C Queens Grove, St Johns Wood, LONDON, NW8 6EL.

CHENG, Mr. Anthony Kai-Chiu, BSc ACA *1988;* 34 Repulse Bay Road, REPULSE BAY, HONG KONG ISLAND, HONG KONG SAR.

CHENG, Mr. Bing Kin Alain, ACA *2006;* PO Box 2677, General Post Office, CENTRAL, HONG KONG ISLAND, HONG KONG SAR.

CHENG, Mr. Chi Man, ACA *2007;* Flat F, 30th Floor, Block 7, Full View Garden, CHAI WAN, HONG KONG SAR.

CHENG, Mr. Chi Tao, ACA *2007;* Room 1302 ICAC Building, 303 Java Road, NORTH POINT, HONG KONG SAR.

CHENG, Dr. Chi Hung Edward, ACA *2008;* Flat D 50/F. Tower 3, The Habourside, 1 Austin Road West, TSIM SHA TSUI, KOWLOON, HONG KONG SAR.

CHENG, Mr. Chi Pang, ACA *2006;* Flat A 22/F Glory Heights, 52 Lyttleton Road, MID LEVELS, HONG KONG ISLAND, HONG KONG SAR.

CHENG, Mr. Chi Wai W, ACA *2007;* Flat G5/F, Block 10, Royal Ascot, SHA TIN, NEW TERRITORIES, HONG KONG SAR.

CHENG, Mr. Chong Ching Thomas, ACA *2008;* Thomas Cheng & Co, Units 803-4, 8/F, Nan Fung Tower, 173 Des Voeux Road, CENTRAL HONG KONG SAR.

CHENG, Mr. Chun Fun, BSc ACA *1988;* The Moat House, Church Road, Warboys, HUNTINGDON, PE28 2RJ.

CHENG, Mr. Chun Shing, ACA *2008;* BDO, 6th Floor, Nexus Building, 41 Conaught Road, CENTRAL, HONG KONG ISLAND HONG KONG SAR.

CHENG, Mr. Chung Por Gordon, ACA *2005;* Wong Brothers & Co, 19th Fl Mass Mutual Tower, 38 Gloucester Road, WAN CHAI, HONG KONG ISLAND, HONG KONG SAR.

CHENG, Mr. Crispin Ka-Shing, BA ACA *1981;* Apt 17-01 Horizon Tower, 15 Leonie Hill Road, SINGAPORE 0923, SINGAPORE.

CHENG, Mr. Damien Hung Sun, MBA BA FCA *1979;* 258 Hamptons Terrace NW, CALGARY T3A 5R5, AB, CANADA.

•**CHENG, Mr. David Kwok Wai, FCA** *1969;* 4 Mount Davis Road, 8th Floor Flat D, POK FU LAM, HONG KONG ISLAND, HONG KONG SAR.

CHENG, Mr. Dennis Ko Sheng, BSc ACA *2010;* Flat 5, Cotterell Court, Hop Street, LONDON, SE10 0QR.

CHENG, Ms. Edwina Hwei Fung, LLB ACA MRSS LCA *1997;* 70 Cambridge Drive, LONDON, SE12 8AJ.

CHENG, Miss. Elaine, BSc ACA *2010;* 8 Helder Grove, LONDON, SE12 0RB.

CHENG, Mr. Erik Yuk Wo, MSc BA FCA *1987;* Flat C, 3/F 59 Nga Tsin Wai Road, KOWLOON CITY, KOWLOON, HONG KONG SAR.

CHENG, Mr. Ho Beng, BSc ACA *1993;* 75 Seabee Lane, DISCOVERY BAY, NEW TERRITORIES, HONG KONG SAR.

CHENG, Mr. Ho See, ACA *1979;* Flat 30 c, Tower One, Ocean Shores, 88 O King Road, TSEUNG KWAN O, NEW TERRITORIES HONG KONG SAR.

CHENG, Mr. Iue Seng, FCA *1987;* 22 Fernwood Terrace, #06-01, SINGAPORE 458553, SINGAPORE.

CHENG, Mr. Jan-Wei, BSc ACA *1994;* with Ernst & Young LLP, 1 More London Place, LONDON, SE1 2AF.

CHENG, Mr. Kai Tai Allen, ACA *2005;* Chan Chee Cheng & Co, 19/F Beverly House, 93-107 Lockhart Road, WAN CHAI, HONG KONG ISLAND, HONG KONG SAR.

CHENG, Mr. Kam Nam, ACA *2007;* No 1 Breezy Path, 7C Ying Piu Mansion, MID LEVELS, HONG KONG ISLAND, HONG KONG SAR.

CHENG, Mr. Kam Por, ACA *2008;* KP Cheng & Co, Room 2707, 27/F, Shui On Centre, 6-8 Harbour Road, WAN CHAI HONG KONG SAR.

CHENG, Mr. Kim Sing, ACA *2006;* Flat E, 5th Floor, Block 3, Phase I Chelsea Heights, No.1 Shek Pai Tau Path, TUEN MUN NEW TERRITORIES HONG KONG SAR.

CHENG, Mr. Kin Hung, ACA *2007;* Hong Kong Land Limited, 5/F One Exchange Square, CENTRAL, HONG KONG SAR.

CHENG, Mr. Kin Chung, ACA *2005;* 2405 Windsor House, 311 Gloucester Road, CAUSEWAY BAY, HONG KONG SAR.

CHENG, Mr. Kwok Kit Edwin, ACA *2005;* Room 1406, 14/F Nan Fung Tower, No 173 Des Voeux Road, CENTRAL, HONG KONG SAR.

CHENG, Mr. Kwok Shing Anthony, ACA *2004;* Flat G 12th Floor, Tower 3 Sorrento, 1 Austin Road West, TSIM SHA TSUI, KOWLOON, HONG KONG SAR.

CHENG, Mr. Man Jimmie, ACA *2008;* Flat 4 15/F, Block G, Sunshine City, Ma On Shan, SHA TIN, NEW TERRITORIES HONG KONG SAR.

CHENG, Ms. Mei Kuen, ACA *2007;* 9B Ficus Garden, 11 Lok King Street, Fotan, SHA TIN, NT, HONG KONG SAR.

CHENG, Mr. Ming Hong Morning, ACA *2007;* 38 B, Tower 3, The Waterfront, 1 Austin Road West, TSIM SHA TSUI, HONG KONG SAR.

CHENG, Dr. Nam Sang, PhD MSc BSc FCA *1993;* 61 Lorong Sarhad, #04-11, SINGAPORE 119174, SINGAPORE.

•**CHENG, Mr. Paul Kwok Kin, FCA** *1976;* Mitsubishi UFJ Securities, 11th Floor, AIA Central, 1 Connaught Road, CENTRAL, HONG KONG ISLAND HONG KONG SAR.

CHENG, Mr. Paul Wyman, BSc FCA *1981;* 5A Monmouth Place, 9L Kennedy Road, MID LEVELS, HONG KONG ISLAND, HONG KONG SAR.

CHENG, Ms. Pik Luen, ACA *2007;* Room C 14/F. Tower 2, Prosperity Court, 168 Lai Chi Kok Road, SHAM SHUI PO, HONG KONG SAR.

CHENG, Mr. Po Yuen, ACA *2006;* Unit 318, Shui On Centre, 6-8 Habour Road, WAN CHAI, HONG KONG ISLAND, HONG KONG SAR.

CHENG, Mr. Raymond Chung Ching, BSc(Econ) FCA CPA *1995;* HLB Hodgson Impey Cheng, 31/F Gloucester Tower, The Landmark, 11 Pedder Street, CENTRAL, HONG KONG ISLAND HONG KONG SAR.

CHENG, Mr. Ronie Yun Chung, BSc ACA *1999;* Flat C. 16/F Ho King View, 2 Breamer Hill Road, NORTH POINT, HONG KONG SAR.

CHENG, Miss. Sau San, MSc ACA *1980;* JALAN AMAN 8, MAMPANG PRAPATAN, JAKARTA, 12790, INDONESIA.

CHENG, Ms. Sau Man, ACA *2008;* Flat G 57/F., No.8 Clear Water Bay Road, Choi Hung, NGAU CHI WAN, KOWLOON, HONG KONG SAR.

CHENG, Mr. Shu Kai, ACA *2008;* Flat E 15/F, Block 3, Marina Garden, 280 Wuchui Road, TUEN MUN, NEW TERRITORIES HONG KONG SAR.

CHENG, Mr. Shun Cheong Henric, ACA *2004;* 2701 Jardine House, 1 Connaught Place, CENTRAL, HONG KONG ISLAND, HONG KONG SAR.

CHENG, Mr. Siew Hon, BA ACA *1994;* 985 Bukit Timah Road #05-14 Maplewoods, SINGAPORE 589627, SINGAPORE.

CHENG, Ms. Silvana Yu-Har, BA FCA *1990;* Flat A 18/F Princess Court, 9 King Tak Street, HO MAN TIN, KOWLOON, HONG KONG SAR.

CHENG, Mr. Sin Kwong Stephen, FCA *1973;* 1575 Acadia Road, VANCOUVER V6T 1P8, BC, CANADA. (Life Member)

CHENG, Mr. Stephen Ho Fee, ACA *1980;* 17A Park Garden, 6 Tai Hang Drive, JARDINE'S LOOKOUT, HONG KONG SAR.

CHENG, Ms. Suet Fei Sophia, ACA *2007;* Flat D, 4th Floor, 44 FA Po Street, Village Garden, YAU YAT TSUEN, HONG KONG SAR.

CHENG, Mr. Sum, ACA *2005;* Cheng Yeung & Co. CPA, Room 1001-2, 10th Floor, Chow Tai Fook Centre, No 580 A-F Nathan Road, MONG KOK KOWLOON HONG KONG SAR.

CHENG, Miss. Ting Yan Amanda, ACA *2008;* Flat 14, Tollhouse Point, London Road, ST. ALBANS, AL1 1NU.

CHENG, Mr. Toon Wah, FCA *1974;* Mazars LLP, 133 Cecil Street, Apt.15-02 Keck Seng Tower, SINGAPORE 048545, SINGAPORE. (Life Member)

CHENG, Mr. Wai Hung, ACA *2005;* Suite 1326-31, Ocean Centre, Harbour City, TSIM SHA TSUI, KOWLOON, HONG KONG SAR.

CHENG, Ms. Wai Ling Annie, ACA *2008;* 2nd Floor, Wah Kit Commercial Centre, 302 Des Voeux Road, CENTRAL, HONG KONG ISLAND, HONG KONG SAR.

CHENG, Mr. Wai Ming Vincent, ACA *2007;* 26E Block 22 Park Island, MA WAN, NEW TERRITORIES, HONG KONG SAR.

CHENG, Mr. Wai Po Samuel, ACA *2005;* c/o Citybus Limited, 8 Chong Fu Road, CHAI WAN, HONG KONG ISLAND, HONG KONG SAR.

CHENG, Mr. William Chuk Man, BCom FCA *1987;* Flat B 4/F. Hawthorn Garden, 70 - 70A Sing Woo Road, HAPPY VALLEY, HONG KONG SAR.

CHENG, Miss. Wincy Yat Sai, BSc ACA *1996;* Flat 2B, Brewin Court, 5-7 Brewin Path, MID LEVELS, HONG KONG ISLAND, HONG KONG SAR.
CHENG, Mr. Wing Ming, ACA *2007;* 2 Floor, 43A Ngau Pei Sha Village, Siu Lek Yuen, SHA TIN, NEW TERRITORIES, HONG KONG SAR.
CHENG, Mr. Wing Hong, ACA *2007;* Flat 1707 17/F, Hung Chak House, Hung Fuk Court, Tin Wan, ABERDEEN, HONG KONG SAR.
CHENG, Mr. Woon Yin Michael, BSc ACA *1990;* with PricewaterhouseCoopers, Prince's Building, 22/F, 10 Chater Road, CENTRAL, HONG KONG ISLAND HONG KONG SAR.
CHENG, Mr. Woon Hung, ACA *2010;* Phase 1 Block 1, Flat 25a Carribbean Coast, TUNG CHUNG, NEW TERRITORIES, HONG KONG SAR.
CHENG, Mr. Yanhua, ACA *2009;* 21/FBlock BScience&Technology Building, Science ParkNo 1 Zhongguancun East Road, Haidian District, BEIJING 100084, CHINA.
CHENG, Mr. Yiu Hung, ACA *2008;* Flat F, 33/F, Tower 7, South Horizons, AP LEI CHAU, HONG KONG SAR.
CHENG, Miss. Yiying, ACA *2011;* No 13 Lane 535 Middle Yan'an Road, SHANGHAI 200020, CHINA.
CHENG, Ms. Yuen-Ching Jennifer, ACA *2008;* 10/F Devon House, Taikoo Place, 979 King's Road, QUARRY BAY, HONG KONG ISLAND, HONG KONG SAR. See also Cheng Yuen Ching Jennifer & Associates CPA Limited
CHENG, Mr. Yuk Keung Marco, ACA *2008;* Flat 4B, Faber Court, 31 Tai Tam Road, TAI TAM, HONG KONG SAR.
CHENG KAI ON, Mrs. Sien Yin, FCA *1977;* Hi Tec (Laboratories) Ltd, 430 Bath Road, SLOUGH, SL1 6BB.
CHENG WHITEHEAD, Mr. Stephen Andrew, BSc ACA *1994;* Palmers Cottage Starrock Lane Chipstead, COULSDON, SURREY, CR5 3QD.
CHENGA-REDDY, Mr. Richard, BSc ACA *1993;* Foxcote, 77d Tolmers Road, Cuffley, POTTERS BAR, HERTFORDSHIRE, EN6 4JJ.
CHENNELL, Mr. David John, BSc ACA *2007;* 15 Wilderness Court, Wilderness Road, GUILDFORD, SURREY, GU2 7QS.
CHENNELL, Mrs. Natalie Barbara, BA(Hons) ACA *2009;* 15 Wilderness Court, Wilderness Road, GUILDFORD, SURREY, GU2 7QS.
CHENU, Mr. Donatien, BSc ACA *2006;* with Deloitte & Touche, 185 avenue Charles de Gaulle, 92524 NEUILLY-SUR-SEINE, FRANCE.
CHEONG, Ms. Choon Yeen, ACA *2004;* 15B-20-3 Everett Tower, Mont Kiara Pines, Jalan Kiara, Mont Kiara, 50480 KUALA LUMPUR, FEDERAL TERRITORY MALAYSIA.
CHEONG, Mr. Eugene, BSc ACA *1993;* 26 Bredon Ave, WEST PENNANT HILLS, NSW, AUSTRALIA.
CHEONG, Mr. Fook Seng Anthony, ACA *1982;* 479 River Valley Road #20-01, Valley Park, SINGAPORE 248364, SINGAPORE.
CHEONG, Miss. I-Ning, BSc ACA *1998;* Clariden Leu Ltd, 80 Raffles Place, #27-01, UOB Plaza 1, SINGAPORE 048624, SINGAPORE.
CHEONG, Miss. Joanna, BSc ACA *2008;* Flat 25 Alban House, 5 Sumpter Close, LONDON, NW3 5JR.
CHEONG, Mr. Kok Hooi, ACA *1987;* 19 Jalan Tanjung 3, Seksyen BS 2, Bukit Sentosa, 48300 RAWANG, SELANGOR, MALAYSIA.
CHEONG, Miss. Phak Peng, BSc(Hons) ACA *2004;* c/o Ashish Dave, Abraaj Capital, Level 7 Emirates Towers offices, PO Box 504905, DUBAI, UNITED ARAB EMIRATES.
CHEONG, Mr. Yoong Weng, ACA *1994;* 265 Bishan Street 24, #06-124, SINGAPORE 570265, SINGAPORE.
CHEONG, Mr. Yue Choe, ACA *2009;* Flat 17, Toronto House, Surrey Quays Road, LONDON, SE16 7AJ.
CHEONG, Mr. Yue Kuan, FCA *1975;* #58-01 UOB PLAZA 1, 80 RAFFLES PLACE, sINGAPORE 048624, SINGAPORE, SINGAPORE.
CHEONG, Mr. Yuk Kee, BSc ACA *1993;* No.2 Jalan Daun Inai 11, Sunway SPK Damansara, 52200 KUALA LUMPUR, FEDERAL TERRITORY, MALAYSIA.
CHEONG YOUNE, Mr. Eng Keung, FCA *1977;* Cheong Youne E.K., 7 Remy Ollier Street, BEAU BASSIN, MAURITIUS.
CHEQUER, Mrs. Sharon Denise, ACA *1996;* D E Beers UK Ltd, 17 Charterhouse Street, LONDON, EC1N 6RA.
CHER, Miss. Lucy Soon Eng, ACA *1993;* 15 Jalan Usaha, SINGAPORE 537155, SINGAPORE.
CHERA, Miss. Surinder Kaur, BSc ACA *1994;* 12 Broadway, WILMSLOW, CHESHIRE, SK9 1NB.
CHERIAN, Mr. Poothicote Oommen, BA FCA *1953;* 5500 Friendship Boulevard, No. 823N, CHEVY CHASE, MD 20815, UNITED STATES. (Life Member)
CHERK, Mr. Kwok Sing, ACA *2005;* Room 2809, Hong Keung Court, LOK FU, KOWLOON, HONG KONG SAR.
CHERNICK, Mr. Laurence, BCom FCA *1973;* 2 Richmond Hill Road, CHEADLE, CHESHIRE, SK8 1QG.
•**CHERNOFF, Mr. Barry Grant, BA FCA FCCA** *1986;* (Tax Fac), Davis Grant LLP, Treviot House, 186-192 High Road, ILFORD, ESSEX, IG1 1LR.
CHERNOUSENKO, Mr. Anton, BSc ACA *2010;* Flat 3, 23 Philbeach Gardens, LONDON, SW5 9DY.
CHERRETT, Mr. Paul John, FCA *1977;* 7 King Richard Drive, Bearwood, BOURNEMOUTH, BH11 9UA.
CHERRETT, Mr. Richard Michael, MSc ACA *2006;* with Deloitte LLP, 2 New Street Square, LONDON, EC4A 3BZ.
CHERRIMAN, Mr. Andrew, BSc ACA *1998;* 38 Queens Road, SINGAPORE 266751, SINGAPORE.
CHERRINGTON, Mrs. Linda Mary, ACIB ACA *2001;* St Andrews Healthcare, The Braye Centre, Cliftonville Centre, Cliftonville Road, NORTHAMPTON, NN1 5BW.
CHERRY, Miss. Amanda Louise, BA(Hons) ACA *2003;* Higher Swineherd Lowe Farm, Cob Castle Road, Haslingden, ROSSENDALE, LANCASHIRE, BB4 5TS.
CHERRY, Mr. Andrew, BSc FCA *1993;* 49 Wrentham Avenue, LONDON, NW10 3HN.
•**CHERRY, Mr. Anthony Ian, BA FCA MAE MCIArb** *1982;* MEMBER OF COUNCIL, A I Cherry Limited, 26 Winckley Square, PRESTON, PR1 3JJ.
CHERRY, Mr. Christopher John, FCA *1980;* TWIN OAKS, 1 Hitherside, Dickens Heath, SOLIHULL, WEST MIDLANDS, B90 1RT.
CHERRY, Mr. Eric Harold, FCA *1955;* 4 East Dale Drive Kirton Lindsey, GAINSBOROUGH, DN21 4BN. (Life Member)
CHERRY, Mr. Ian, BA ACA *1996;* 19 Hollin Gardens, Far Headingley, LEEDS, LS16 5NL.
CHERRY, Mr. John Loraine, MA FCA *1967;* Mill House, Iping, MIDHURST, GU29 OPF.
CHERRY, Mr. John Roy, FCA *1969;* Dell Cottage, Rock Road, Storrington, PULBOROUGH, RH20 3AG.
CHERRY, Mrs. Katherine Anne, MA ACA *1995;* 12 Highfield Drive, Claydon, IPSWICH, IP6 0EY.
CHERRY, Mr. Keith, BA FCA *1957;* 4 Meadow Park Irwell Vale, Ramsbottom, BURY, BL0 0QB. (Life Member)
CHERRY, Mrs. Lorna Ann, ACA *2005;* with BDO LLP, Prospect Place, 85 Great North Road, HATFIELD, HERTFORDSHIRE, AL9 5BS.
CHERRY, Mr. Malcolm, FCA *1975;* 19 Lake Road, TUNBRIDGE WELLS, KENT, TN4 8XT.
CHERRY, Mr. Michael Colin, BA FCA *1982;* 16 London Road, Harston, CAMBRIDGE, CB22 7QH.
CHERRY, Dr. Michael John, MA ACA *1999;* 12 Highfield Drive, Claydon, IPSWICH, IP6 0EY.
CHERRY, Mr. Paul Francis, BA ACA *2003;* 104b Caversham Avenue, Palmers Green, LONDON, N13 4LN.
CHERRY, Mr. Richard John, FCA *1975;* Primrose Cottage, North Newton, BRIDGWATER, SOMERSET, TA7 0BQ.
CHERRY, Mr. Robert Ian, MEng ACA *2000;* 47, Park Road, BATH, BA1 3EE.
CHERRY, Mrs. Ruth Frances, BA ACA *1993;* Yorkshire Bank Aquisition Finance, 4 Victoria Place, Holbeck, LEEDS, LS11 5AE.
CHERRY, Mr. Simon John, BSc ACA *1992;* 27 Wickery Dene, Wootton, NORTHAMPTON, NN4 6BE.
CHERRY, Mr. Stephen Michael, ACA *2010;* 57 Georges Wood Road, Brookmans Park, HATFIELD, HERTFORDSHIRE, AL9 7BX.
CHESCULESCU, Mr. Ernesto, MA ACA *2006;* 34 Forge Place, LONDON, NW1 8DQ.
CHESHIRE, Mr. Alan, FCA *1973;* Polar Speed Distribution, 8 Chartmoor Road, LEIGHTON BUZZARD, BEDFORDSHIRE, LU7 4WG.
CHESHIRE, Mr. Brian Leonard Edward, FCA *1962;* 63 Brownleaf Road, BRIGHTON, BN2 6LD.
CHESHIRE, Mrs. Caroline Elizabeth, BSc ACA *1996;* 8 Hadrians Walk, Emersons Green, BRISTOL, BS16 7HE.
CHESHIRE, Mrs. Deborah Janet, BSc ACA *1988;* Servigistics Ltd, Servigisitics House, Milbury Heath, WOTTON-UNDER-EDGE, GLOUCESTERSHIRE, GL12 8QH.
CHESHIRE, Mr. Joseph Paul, BA(Hons) ACA CTA *2002;* N F U Mutual Insurance Society Ltd, Tiddington Road, STRATFORD-UPON-AVON, WARWICKSHIRE, CV37 7BJ.
CHESHIRE, Mr. Keith Clyde, BSc ACA *1993;* 22 Rydons Mews, LONDON, SW19 4RP.
CHESHIRE, Mrs. Mumtaz, ACA *1981;* Polar Speed Distribution Ltd, Unit 8, Chartmoor Road, LEIGHTON BUZZARD, BEDFORDSHIRE, LU7 4WG.
CHESHIRE, Mr. Ross David, BA ACA *1984;* High Bank House, 32 Station Road, Blackwell, BROMSGROVE, WORCESTERSHIRE, B60 1PZ.
•**CHESLIN, Mr. Michael Walter, FCA** *1968;* 47 Farmer Ward Road, KENILWORTH, WARWICKSHIRE, CV8 2DJ.
CHESNAY, Mr. Francois, MSc ACA *2004;* Sunhaven 6 Millais Park, Mont Millais St. Helier, JERSEY, JE2 4RU.
CHESNEY, Mrs. Ellen Carol Tredway, BA FCA *1989;* Halma p.l.c., Misbourne Court Rectory Way, AMERSHAM, HP7 0DE.
CHESSELL, Mr. Shaun Anthony, MA ACA *1993;* 1 Highview Close, TADWORTH, KT20 5GR.
CHESSELLS, Sir Arthur David Tim, Kt FCA *1965;* Oakleigh, Catts Hill, Mark Cross, CROWBOROUGH, TN6 3NQ.
CHESSER, Mr. David, BSc ACA *1979;* Dunkirk House, Watling Street, CORBRIDGE, NORTHUMBERLAND, NE45 5AQ.
CHESSHER, Mr. Mark Christopher, BA FCA *1986;* A O N Ltd, 8 Devonshire Square, LONDON, EC2M 4PL.
CHESSHIRE, Mr. David Harvey, FCA *1974;* 49 Hartington Way, Mickleover, DERBY, DE3 9BH.
CHESTER, Mr. Christopher Frank, BSc FCA *1972;* 36 Tower Lane, Fulwood, PRESTON, PR2 9HP.
CHESTER, Mr. David Samuel, FCA *1963;* 2nd Floor, 25/26 Albemarle Street, LONDON, W1S 4HX.
CHESTER, Ms. Isobel Kathryn, BA ACA *2001;* 137a Denmark Road, LONDON, SE5 9LB.
CHESTER, Mr. Jonathan Roger, MBA ACA *1991;* Carillion Plc Pendeford House Overstrand, Pendeford Business Park Pendeford, WOLVERHAMPTON, WV9 5AP.
•**CHESTER, Miss. Katherine Joan, BSc FCA** *1976;* John Ellis & Co, The Barn, 173 Church Road, Northfield, BIRMINGHAM, B31 2LX.
CHESTER, Mr. Kevin Wayne, FCA *1973;* 61 South Park Road, Wimbledon, LONDON, SW19 8RT.
CHESTER, Miss. Lesley Ann, BA FCA AMCT *1983;* 1 Hill End Lane, ST. ALBANS, HERTFORDSHIRE, AL4 0TX.
CHESTER, Mr. Paul Jeremy, BA ACA *1982;* Caynham Court, Caynham, LUDLOW, SHROPSHIRE, SY8 3BJ.
CHESTER, Mrs. Renata Angela Karolina, BSc ACA *1995;* 153 Princes Street, IPSWICH, IP1 1QJ.
CHESTER, Miss. Rona Elizabeth, BSc FCA *1985;* Dale Cottage, Church Path, Merton Park, LONDON, SW19 3HL.
CHESTER, Mr. Ross Steven, BSc FCA *1993;* 19 Oaklands, LYMINGTON, SO41 3TH.
CHESTER, Mr. Timothy Andrew, MSc ACA *2004;* Larkfield Warfield Lane, Cowthorpe, WETHERBY, WEST YORKSHIRE, LS22 5EU.
CHESTERFIELD, Mr. Benjamin, BA ACA *1984;* 1 Coverdale Road, Brondesbury Park, LONDON, NW2 4DB.
CHESTERFIELD, Mr. John Desborough, FCA *1961;* 23 Downs View Road, HASSOCKS, WEST SUSSEX, BN6 8HJ. (Life Member)
CHESTERMAN, Mr. Harvey Alan, FCA *1956;* P.O. Box 2157, JERUSALEM, 91021, ISRAEL. (Life Member)
CHESTERS, Mr. Jeffrey Whitaker, BA FCA *1977;* 6 Rue du Carpon, 56920 ST GONNERY, FRANCE.
CHESTERS, Mr. Philip, FCA *1975;* 2 Columbine Cl, Deeside Pk, Huntington, CHESTER, CH3 5BH.
•**CHESTERTON, Miss. Lynne Mary, FCA** *1979;* (Tax Fac), King & Taylor, 10-12 Wrotham Road, GRAVESEND, DA11 0PE.
•①**CHESTERTON, Mr. Neil Douglas, ACA CA(SA)** *2010;* The MacDonald Partnership plc, Level 25, Tower 42, 25 Old Broad Street, LONDON, EC2N 1HQ.
CHESTNUTT, Mr. David Moore Alexander, FCA *1974;* 23 Park Avenue, Crosby, LIVERPOOL, L23 2SP.
CHESTNUTT, Mrs. Susan Jean, BA ACA *1992;* Peel Ports Ltd, Maritime Centre, Port of Liverpool, LIVERPOOL, L21 1LA.
CHESWORTH, Mr. Andrew, BSc(Hons) ACA *2003;* (Tax Fac), 54 Mabledon Road, TONBRIDGE, KENT, TN9 2TG.
CHESWORTH, Mr. Christopher Frank, BSc FCA *1977;* 6 Singleton Road, Heaton Moor, STOCKPORT, SK4 4PW.
CHESWORTH, Miss. Deborah Jayne, BA ACA *1986;* Financial Services Authority, 25 North Colonnade, LONDON, E14 5HS.
CHESWORTH, Mr. John, FCA *1964;* Oulton Farm, Rushton Spencer, MACCLESFIELD, CHESHIRE, SK11 0RS. (Life Member)
•**CHESWORTH, Mr. Philip Leonard, BA FCA** *1976;* (Tax Fac), 12 Cape Street, Hanley, STOKE-ON-TRENT, ST1 5AZ.
•**CHETHAM, Mr. William Humphrey, FCA** *1954;* William H. Chetham, 10 Arnesby Avenue, SALE, CHESHIRE, M33 2WJ.
CHETNIK, Mrs. Louisa, ACA *2007;* Francis Clark, Vantage Point, Pynes Hill, EXETER, EX2 5FD.
CHETTLE, Mr. Nathan Richard, ACA MAAT *2010;* 46 Hidcote Way, DAVENTRY, NN11 8AE.
CHETTLE, Mrs. Rachel, BSc ACA *2006;* 73 Upper Queen Street, RUSHDEN, NORTHAMPTONSHIRE, NN10 0BS.
CHETTY, Mr. Magashlin, BSc ACA *2007;* 66-68 Crediton Hill, LONDON, NW6 1HR.
CHETWODE, Mr. Joshua Lariston Knightley, BA ACA *1994;* C/o The Jardine Engineering Corporation, Limited, 5/F Tower A Manulife Financial Centre, 223-231 Wai Yip Street, KWUN TONG, KOWLOON HONG KONG SAR.
•**CHETWOOD, Mrs. Caroline Margaret Denise, BA ACA CTA** *1980;* (Tax Fac), Caroline Chetwood, Banacle Field, Church Lane, Brook, GODALMING, SURREY GU8 5UQ.
CHETWOOD, Mr. Peter John, FCA *1975;* 145 Mills Street, Middle Park, MELBOURNE, VIC 3206, AUSTRALIA.
CHETWOOD, Mr. William Henry, LLB ACA *2002;* 137 Brookwood Road, LONDON, SW18 5BD.
CHETWYND, Mrs. Lesley Ann, BA ACA *1990;* 8 Four Lanes Way, Norden, ROCHDALE, OL11 5TL.
CHETWYND, Mr. Mark Richard, BA ACA *1998;* 65 Grosvenor Street, LONDON, W1K 3JH.
CHEUK, Mr. Wa Pang Raymond, ACA *2008;* 7C, Tower 6, Park Avenue, 18 Hoi Ting Road, YAU MA TEI, KOWLOON HONG KONG SAR.
CHEUNG, Miss. Alexandra Shui-Wah, BA ACA *1991;* 20 Avondale Road, Mortlake, LONDON, SW14 8PT.
CHEUNG, Mr. Allan, BSc ACA *2011;* 18 Cuckoo Dene, Hanwell, LONDON, W7 3DP.
CHEUNG, Miss. Amy Yee Ling, BA(Hons) ACA *2011;* 137 Casterton Road, STAMFORD, LINCOLNSHIRE, PE9 2UG.
CHEUNG, Miss. Anna Po King, BSc ACA *1988;* Flat F 11/F Laguna City, Block 26, LAM TIN, KOWLOON, HONG KONG SAR.
CHEUNG, Ms. Annie, BSc(Hons) ACA *2000;* 29 Savery Drive, Long Ditton, SURBITON, SURREY, KT6 5RJ.
CHEUNG, Mr. Anthony Yam-Tong, BCom ACA *1987;* 46 Melva Crescent, SCARBOROUGH M1V 1A3, ON, CANADA.
CHEUNG, Mr. Benny Shu Kin, BA ACA *1991;* Flat 7D Tower1, Hillsborough Court, 18 Old Peak Road, MID LEVELS, HONG KONG ISLAND, HONG KONG SAR.
CHEUNG, Mrs. Cecilia Wun Se, BSc ACA *1993;* 27B Visalia Garden, 48 Macdonnell Road, MID LEVELS, HONG KONG ISLAND, HONG KONG SAR.
CHEUNG, Ms. Cham Lo Chanel, ACA *2010;* 1B Pokfulam Court, 94 Pokfulam Road, POK FU LAM, HONG KONG ISLAND, HONG KONG SAR.
CHEUNG, Ms. Chau Yee, ACA *2008;* Room 1925, On Tao House, Cheung On Estate, TSING YI, NEW TERRITORIES, HONG KONG SAR.
CHEUNG, Mr. Chi Hoi Jimmy, ACA *2007;* Jimmy C H Cheung & Co, 1607 Dominion Centre, 43 Queen's Road East, WAN CHAI, HONG KONG SAR.
CHEUNG, Mr. Chi Keung Kany, MBA ACA FCCA FCPA *2007;* 2304 W Miners Drive, DUNLAP, IL 61525, UNITED STATES.
CHEUNG, Mr. Chiu Fan, ACA *2008;* CF Cheung, 19th Floor, Cameron Commercial Centre, 468 Hennessy Road, CAUSEWAY BAY, HONG KONG SAR.
CHEUNG, Mr. Chris, BA(Hons) ACA *2010;* 24 Adler Way, LIVERPOOL, L3 4FX.
•**CHEUNG, Mr. Dominic Chee, FCA** *1973;* Cheung & Co, 342 Windmill Road, LONDON, W5 4UR.
CHEUNG, Mrs. Donna Yan Ting, ACA *2011;* 8 Borrowdale Close, Gamston, NOTTINGHAM, NG2 6PD.
CHEUNG, Mr. Edwin Ho-Ming, BEng FCA *1993;* Unit H 21/F Block 5 Tanner Garden, 18 Tanner Road, NORTH POINT, HONG KONG ISLAND, HONG KONG SAR.
CHEUNG, Mr. Hon Wing, BSc ACA *1987;* 168 Robinson Road, 33-01 Capital Tower, SINGAPORE 068912, SINGAPORE.
CHEUNG, Mr. Humbert Kam Hung, BSc ACA *1993;* 47 St Vincent Road, WALTON-ON-THAMES, KT12 1PA.
CHEUNG, Mr. Jason Wai Ming, BEng ACA *1992;* 89 Ennismore Avenue, Greenford, GREENFORD, UB6 0LQ.
CHEUNG, Mr. Jaspar Jan-Pang, ACA *2011;* 18 The Ridings, Whittle-le-Woods, CHORLEY, LANCASHIRE, PR6 7QH.

CHEUNG, Mr. Jeffrey Chun Kit, BSc ACA *2010;* 19 Hazelwood Close, HARROW, MIDDLESEX, HA2 6HD.
CHEUNG, Miss. Jennifer Hok Yan, BSc(Econ) ACA *2001;* Flat 23B Kennedy Heights, 10-18 Kennedy Road, Central, MID LEVELS, HONG KONG ISLAND, HONG KONG SAR.
CHEUNG, Mr. Jimmy Dak-Kin, BSc ACA *1999;* Flat F2 9/F, Evergreen Villa, 43 Stubbs Road, HAPPY VALLEY, HONG KONG ISLAND, HONG KONG SAR.
CHEUNG, Mr. John Chung-Wai, BSc ACA *1997;* 83 Chadwick Place, Long Ditton, SURBITON, KT6 5RG.
CHEUNG, Ms. Ka Huen Emerald, ACA *2008;* Flat A 7/F, Harrison Court IV, 9 Man Wan Road, HO MAN TIN, KOWLOON, HONG KONG SAR.
CHEUNG, Mr. Ka Yue, ACA *2007;* CCIF CPA Limited, 20/F Sunning Plaza, 10 Hysan Avenue, CAUSEWAY BAY, HONG KONG ISLAND, HONG KONG SAR.
CHEUNG, Mr. Kang Fai Alexander, ACA *2008;* Cheung Lee Ng & Co, Room 1208, Two Grand Tower, 625 Nathan Road, MONG KOK, KOWLOON HONG KONG SAR.
CHEUNG, Miss. Katy Wai Ki, MSci ACA *2010;* 2 Wark Court, NEWCASTLE UPON TYNE, NE3 1YR.
CHEUNG, Mr. Ken, BA ACA *2006;* 30 Lexington Walk, Boston Boulevard Great Sankey, WARRINGTON, WA5 8GE.
CHEUNG, Mr. Kevin Yusaku, ACA *2010;* 30 St. Johns Avenue, HARLOW, ESSEX, CM17 0BB.
CHEUNG, Mr. Ki Fai Edwin, ACA *2008;* Edwin Cheung & Siu, Room A, 7/F, China Overseas Building, 139 Hennessy Road, WAN CHAI HONG KONG ISLAND HONG KONG SAR.
CHEUNG, Mr. Kin Bong Sherman, BEng ACA *1993;* with PricewaterhouseCoopers, 33/F Cheung Kong Center, 2 Queen's Road, CENTRAL, HONG KONG ISLAND, HONG KONG SAR.
CHEUNG, Mr. Kin Man Clement, MSc FCA *1992;* P K F Accountants & Business Advisors Farringdon Place, 20 Farringdon Road, LONDON, EC1M 3AP.
CHEUNG, Mr. Kin Piu Valiant, FCA *1971;* Flat 14A No 2 Conduit Road, Yukon Court, MID LEVELS, HONG KONG ISLAND, HONG KONG SAR.
CHEUNG, Mr. Kin Yip, ACA *2007;* Tower 2, Flat C 55/F, Residence Oasis, TSEUNG KWAN O, NEW TERRITORIES, HONG KONG SAR.
CHEUNG, Mr. Kin Wing Edwin, ACA *2005;* Sunplex Consultants Ltd, Unit 9C, Wing Hang Insurance Building, 11 Wing Kut Street, CENTRAL, HONG KONG SAR.
CHEUNG, Mr. King Fu, ACA *2007;* Flat E, 3/F Wing Cheong Court, Fortune Plaza, TAI PO, NEW TERRITORIES, NT HONG KONG SAR.
CHEUNG, Mr. Kwan Hoi, MSc ACA *1992;* Hutchison Whampoa Limited, 22nd Floor, Hutchison House, 10 Harcourt Road, CENTRAL, HONG KONG ISLAND HONG KONG SAR.
CHEUNG, Mr. Kwok Cheung, ACA FCCA *2008;* Flat 8, 18 Hilldrop Crescent, LONDON, N7 0JF.
CHEUNG, Mr. Kwok Man, ACA *2008;* FL Tang & Company, 12/F, Yat Chau Building, 262 Des Voeux Road Central, CENTRAL, HONG KONG SAR.
CHEUNG, Mr. Kwok Yan Wilfred, ACA *2009;* 5A Kiu Fu Commercial Building, 300 Lockhart Road, WAN CHAI, HONG KONG ISLAND, HONG KONG SAR.
CHEUNG, Mr. Lap Yin, MSc FCA *1989;* 10D Prosperous Height, 62 Conduit Road, MID LEVELS, HONG KONG ISLAND, HONG KONG SAR.
•**CHEUNG, Mrs. Linda Mary, BSc FCA** *1984;* Mall & Co, PO Box 433, MANCHESTER, M28 8AT.
CHEUNG, Mr. Man Ki, BSc ACA *1992;* Flat 8-E 37 Broadcast Drive, KOWLOON TONG, KOWLOON, HONG KONG SAR.
CHEUNG, Mr. Man Wai, ACA *2008;* Flat 15, 34/F, Chun Fei House, Tin Ma Court, WONG TAI SIN, KOWLOON HONG KONG SAR.
CHEUNG, Ms. Mariana, ACA *2010;* Flat L 40/F, Block 1 The Grandiose, 9 Tong Chun Street, TSEUNG KWAN O, HONG KONG SAR.
CHEUNG, Mr. Marvin Kin Tung, FCA *1969;* Flat 23B Kennedy Heights, 10-18 Kennedy Road, MID LEVELS, HONG KONG ISLAND, HONG KONG SAR.
CHEUNG, Mr. Michael, ACA *2010;* 39 Parham Drive, ILFORD, ESSEX, IG2 6NB.
CHEUNG, Mr. Michael Wai Hung, BA ACA AMCT *1988;* BP Plc, 20 Canada Square, LONDON, E14 5NJ.
CHEUNG, Mr. Pak Yin, ACA *2008;* Flat D, 23/F Caine Mansion, 80-88 Caine Road, SAR, HONG KONG SAR.
CHEUNG, Mr. Peter Kwok Wai, MSc ACA *1991;* 8 Bellrock Drive, SCARBOROUGH M1V 2V9, ON, CANADA.
CHEUNG, Mr. Pui Chung, ACA *2008;* Cheung Pui Chung & Co, Office A, 21/F, Crawford Tower, 99 Jervois Street, SHEUNG WAN HONG KONG SAR.
CHEUNG, Mr. Pui Hung Steven, ACA *2008;* Kam & Cheung, Room 401 4th Floor, Wah Yuen Building, 149 Queen's Road, CENTRAL, HONG KONG SAR.
CHEUNG, Mr. Richard, BSc ACA *2006;* with Ernst & Young LLP, 1 More London Place, LONDON, SE1 2AF.
CHEUNG, Mr. Ricky Lap Kei, BA ACA *1994;* Level 30, Three Pacific Place, 1 Queen's Road East, ADMIRALTY, HONG KONG ISLAND, HONG KONG SAR.
CHEUNG, Miss. Rosalind Yik-Ha, BSc ACA *1996;* Flat F 33/F Block 1, Illumination Terrace, 5 Tai Hang Road, TAI HANG, HONG KONG ISLAND, HONG KONG SAR.
CHEUNG, Mr. Sai Fun, ACA *2005;* S. F. Cheung & Co., Room 704 Belgian Bank Building, 721-725 Nathan Road, TSIM SHA TSUI, KOWLOON, HONG KONG SAR.
CHEUNG, Miss. Sandra Mun Yee, BSc ACA *2005;* Flat A 8/F Block 1, The Sparkle, 500 Tung Chau Street, CHEUNG SHA WAN, KOWLOON, HONG KONG SAR.
•**CHEUNG, Mr. Simon Kam Loi, BA FCA** *1986;* (Tax Fac), with Cheung & Co, St. Vincent House, 15 Oldham Road, MANCHESTER, M4 5EQ.
CHEUNG, Mr. Sing Kuen, ACA *2007;* Lawrence Cheung C P A Company Limited, 20th Floor, Euro Trade Centre, 21-23 Des Voeux Road, CENTRAL, HONG KONG SAR.
CHEUNG, Mr. Sing Wah, ACA *2005;* 2/F. Dah Sing Life Building, 99 Des Voeux Road, CENTRAL, HONG KONG ISLAND, HONG KONG SAR.
CHEUNG, Ms. Siu Chun, ACA *2008;* Rm A 5/F, No.100 Broadway, Stage 8, Mei Foo Sun Chuen, KOWLOON CITY, HONG KONG ISLAND HONG KONG SAR.
CHEUNG, Mr. Siu Hung, ACA *2008;* Flat C, 16/F Man King Bldg, 3 Hing Wo Street, ABERDEEN, HONG KONG SAR.
CHEUNG, Mr. Siu Yiu, ACA *2004;* Room 1004, 10th Floor, Wing On Plaza, 62 Mody Road, TSIM SHA TSUI, KOWLOON HONG KONG SAR.
CHEUNG, Miss. Siu-Yee, BA ACA *2002;* 28 Transom Square, LONDON, E14 3AQ.
CHEUNG, Mr. Stephen Man, FCA *1971;* Dynasty Court, Flat 9A Tower One, 23 Old Peak Road, MID LEVELS, HONG KONG ISLAND, HONG KONG SAR. (Life Member)
CHEUNG, Miss. Sui-Lai, ACA *1987;* 1 Oaklands Drive, ASCOT, SL5 7NE.
CHEUNG, Miss. Suzanna, ACA *2009;* with BDO LLP, 55 Baker Street, LONDON, W1U 7EU.
CHEUNG, Mr. Ting Pong, ACA *2010;* (Tax Fac), Flat 1901 Block F, Ching Tai Court, TSING YI, NEW TERRITORIES, HONG KONG SAR.
CHEUNG, Mr. Tsang Fai, ACA *2008;* KPMG Huazhen, 38th Floor, Teem Tower, 208 Tianhe Road, GUANGZHOU 510620, CHINA. See also KPMG
CHEUNG, Miss. Tung, BA ACA *2011;* Flat C 4th Floor Block 35 Parc Versailles II, TAI PO, HONG KONG SAR.
•**CHEUNG, Mr. Tung Kwong, BA ACA** *1984;* (Tax Fac), Chadsworth Limited, Unit 3A Wing Yip Centre, 278 Thimble Mill Lane, Nechells, BIRMINGHAM, B7 5HD.
CHEUNG, Miss. Vivian Wai-Yan, BEng ACA *1994;* Flat B 7/F Block 5, Tropicana, Dynasty Heights, 2 Yin Ping Road, BEACON HILL, KOWLOON HONG KONG SAR.
CHEUNG, Mr. Wai Keung, ACA *2005;* Flat A 17/F Block 4, Royal Peninsula, HUNG HOM BAY, KOWLOON, HONG KONG SAR.
CHEUNG, Mr. Wai Shing, ACA *2008;* Room 2912 29/F., West Tower Shun Tak Centre, 168-200 Connaught Road Central, SHEUNG WAN, HONG KONG SAR.
CHEUNG, Ms. Wai Yan Winnie, ACA *2008;* Flat 12, 1/F Block M, Kornhill, QUARRY BAY, HONG KONG SAR.
CHEUNG, Mr. Wai Yin, ACA *2008;* Unit 2001 20 Floor Block G Kornhill, QUARRY BAY, HONG KONG SAR.
CHEUNG, Mr. Wai-Ching, BSc ACA *2004;* PCA, 13/F, One IFC, 1 Harbour View St, CENTRAL, HONG KONG SAR.
CHEUNG, Mr. Wang Kei, ACA *2010;* Flat G 55th Floor, Tower 1 Hampton Place, 11 Foi Fan Road, TAI KOK TSUI, KOWLOON, HONG KONG SAR.
CHEUNG, Mr. Wang Ngai, ACA *2005;* Suite 2909, Two Exchange Square, 8 Connaught Place, CENTRAL, HONG KONG ISLAND, HONG KONG SAR.
CHEUNG, Mr. Wen Ping, LLB ACA FSI Bar(NP) *1997;* 108 Hollywood Road, Tower 2 35C, CENTRAL, HONG KONG ISLAND, HONG KONG SAR.
CHEUNG, Mr. William, ACA *2007;* Flat 30, Meridian Court, 7 East Lane, LONDON, SE16 4UF.
CHEUNG, Mr. Wing Hong, ACA *2006;* Flat F, 25/Floor Block 7, Sceneway Garden, LAM TIN, KOWLOON, HONG KONG SAR.
CHEUNG, Mr. Wing Kong, ACA *2006;* TS1F 3rd Floor, House 1, Forest Hill, 31 Lo Fai Road, TAI PO, NEW TERRITORIES HONG KONG SAR.
CHEUNG, Ms. Wing Yee, BSc ACA *1995;* 78 Park Hill Road, Harborne, BIRMINGHAM, B17 9HJ.
CHEUNG, Ms. Wing Chi Ellison, ACA *2008;* No 9, 7th Street, Section F, Fairview Park, YUEN LONG, HONG KONG SAR.
CHEUNG, Ms. Wing Han Miranda, ACA *2005;* G/F Sanitarian Apts 24 Green Lane, HAPPY VALLEY, HONG KONG SAR.
CHEUNG, Mr. Wing Kin Leslie, ACA *2011;* with Deloitte Touche Tohmatsu, 35/F One Pacific Place, 88 Queensway, CENTRAL, HONG KONG ISLAND, HONG KONG SAR.
CHEUNG, Mr. Wing Tung Peter, ACA *2008;* Unit 3H Tower 1, High Prosperity Terrace, 188 Kwai Shing Circuit, KWAI CHUNG, KOWLOON, HONG KONG SAR.
CHEUNG, Mr. Wing Yuen Dominic, ACA *2007;* Dominic Cheung and Company, Room 1502, 15/F, Harcourt House, No.39, Gloucester Road WAN CHAI HONG KONG SAR.
CHEUNG, Ms. Winnie Chi-Woon, BA FCA *1984;* 10E Greenview Gardens, 125 Robinson Road, MID LEVELS, HONG KONG ISLAND, HONG KONG SAR.
CHEUNG, Mr. Yan Yung Gabriel, BSc ACA *1986;* Moon Fair Mansion, 11 Shiu Fai Terrace, Flat 9E Stubbs Road, WAN CHAI, HONG KONG ISLAND, HONG KONG SAR.
CHEUNG, Ms. Yan Chi Banita, ACA *2008;* Flat C, 5/F, Tower 1, 2 Kin Tung Road, Caribbean Coast, TUNG CHUNG HONG KONG SAR.
CHEUNG, Mr. Yat Ming, ACA *2007;* 18/F Block 41, Baluio Villa, 550 Victoria Road, POK FU LAM, HONG KONG ISLAND, HONG KONG SAR.
CHEUNG, Dr. Yee Wah, BA ACA *2002;* 1b Friars Avenue Shenfield, BRENTWOOD, ESSEX, CM15 8HY.
CHEUNG, Mr. Ying-Wah Gerry, ACA *1985;* 23 Whistlers Avenue, LONDON, SW11 3TS.
CHEUNG, Mr. Yuk Ching, ACA *2005;* Unit 1701 President Comm CTR, 608 Nathan Road, MONG KOK, KOWLOON, HONG KONG SAR.
CHEUNG, Ms. Yuk Chun Crissie, ACA *2008;* 30th FloorWorld Trade Centre, 280 Gloucester Road, CAUSEWAY BAY, HONG KONG SAR.
CHEUNG, Mr. Yuk Lam, ACA *2005;* with Deloitte & Touche, 35/F One Pacific Place, 88 Queensway, CENTRAL, HONG KONG ISLAND, HONG KONG SAR.
CHEUNG, Mr. Yuk Ming, ACA *2008;* Lau Cheung Fung & Chan, 1707, Chinachem Plaza, 338 King's Road, NORTH POINT, HONG KONG SAR.
CHEUNG CHUN WAH, Mr. Gnee Tai, BSc ACA *1994;* 1 Lings Coppice, West Dulwich, LONDON, SE21 8SY.
CHEUNG SHAN YUEN, Mr. Jean Alain, BSc ACA *2000;* Flat 104, Rossmore Court, Park Road, LONDON, NW1 6XZ.
CHEUNG WOO, Mr. Chong Chun Hing, ACA *1980;* RT Knits Ltd, Peupliers Avenue, SLDC New Industrial Park, La Tour Koenig, POINTE AUX SABLES, MAURITIUS.
CHEVALIER, Miss. Karine Maryvonne, MA ACA *1997;* 36 Holmes Road, TWICKENHAM, TW1 4RE.
CHEVELEY, Mrs. Anna, BA ACA *1993;* 78 Edith Road, LONDON, W14 9AR.
•**CHEVERN, Mr. Stephen, FCA** *1971;* (Tax Fac), Passer Chevern & Co, 5 Spring Villa Road, EDGWARE, MIDDLESEX, HA8 7EB.
CHEVERTON, Mr. Peter James, FCA *1973;* Prior Estates Ltd, County House, 221-241 Beckenham Road, BECKENHAM, KENT, BR3 4UF.
CHEVIN-HALL, Mr. Nigel Clive, ACA *1986;* Longridge House, Church Lane, Church Brampton, NORTHAMPTON, NN6 8AT.
CHEVREAU, Mrs. Anna Elizabeth, BSc ACA *2007;* 26 Moss Lane, Middleton, MANCHESTER, M24 1WX.
CHEW, Mr. Anthony Ian, FCA *1974;* 38 Overcombe Drive, WEYMOUTH, DT3 6QF.
•**CHEW, Ms. Bee Lean, MSc BA(Hons) FCA** *2001;* Wilder Coe LLP, 233-237 Old Marylebone Road, LONDON, NW1 5QT. See also Wilder Coe
CHEW, Mr. Chin Choong, BSc ACA *1995;* 46 Jalan Bintang, Sunrise Garden, 31400 IPOH, PERAK, MALAYSIA.
CHEW, Mr. David Leonard, LLB ACA *1990;* 47 Denmark Road, TWICKENHAM, TW2 5EN.
•**CHEW, Mr. David Robert, MA ACA** *2000;* DRC Accountancy Services Ltd, Hafotty Bach, Cyffylliog, RUTHIN, CLWYD, LL15 2DY.
CHEW, Mr. En-Lai Dickie, BA ACA *1983;* 10 Neram Crescent, SINGAPORE 807816, SINGAPORE.
CHEW, Mr. Eng Chai, FCA *1975;* 85 Jalan SS15/6A, Subang Jaya, 47500 PETALING JAYA, SELANGOR, MALAYSIA.
CHEW, Mr. Eng Kee, BSc ACA *1991;* KENANGA INVESTMENT BANK BERHAD, 8TH FLOOR KENANGA INTERNATIONAL, JALAN SULTAN ISMAIL, 50250 KUALA LUMPUR, FEDERAL TERRITORY, MALAYSIA.
CHEW, Mr. Fook Aun, BSc FCA *1987;* (Tax Fac), 8A Mandarin Villa, 10 Shiu Fai Terrace, WAN CHAI, HONG KONG ISLAND, HONG KONG SAR.
CHEW, Miss. Gek Hiang, ACA *1991;* 42 Cairnhill Road, 02-01, SINGAPORE 229661, SINGAPORE.
CHEW, Mr. Ka Twang, MSc ACA ACMA *1982;* 3351 Springthorne Crescent, RICHMOND V7E1Z8, BC, CANADA.
CHEW, Mr. Kean Sin, LLB FCA *1993;* 14 Jalan Batu Laut, Taman Bukit Seputeh, 58000 KUALA LUMPUR, FEDERAL TERRITORY, MALAYSIA.
CHEW, Mr. Keat Seng, BSc ACA *1988;* 19 Bramley Crescent, WHEELERS HILL, VIC 3150, AUSTRALIA.
CHEW, Mr. Keat Teong, ACA *1980;* D 206 Block D, Kelana Square, No. 17 Jalan SS 7 / 26 Kelana Jaya, 47301 PETALING JAYA, SELANGOR, MALAYSIA.
CHEW, Mr. Kong Seng, FCA *1970;* 12-1 Seri Duta II Condominium, 11 Jalan Langgak Duta, 50480 KUALA LUMPUR, FEDERAL TERRITORY, MALAYSIA.
CHEW, Mr. Lawrence Richard, FCA *1955;* 20 Potters Place, HORSHAM, WEST SUSSEX, RH12 2PL. (Life Member)
•**CHEW, Mr. Nee Tong, ACA** *1980;* T Chew & Co Limited, Second Floor, Cathay Building, 86 Holloway Head, BIRMINGHAM, B1 1NB. See also N T Chew
CHEW, Mr. Nyen Aun, LLB ACA *1993;* 8A Mandarin Villa, 10 Shiu Fai Terrace, HAPPY VALLEY, HONG KONG ISLAND, HONG KONG SAR.
CHEW, Mr. Seng Chen, FCA *1981;* 16 Jalan Sri Hartamas 13, Taman Sri Hartamas, 50480 KUALA LUMPUR, FEDERAL TERRITORY, MALAYSIA.
CHEW, Mr. Seong Aun, BSc ACA *1991;* 93A Jalan Dedap Batik, Sierramas, 47000 SUNGAI BULOH, SELANGOR, MALAYSIA.
CHEW, Miss. Shee Ghee, ACA *2009;* 10 Jalan SS 2/4, 47300 PETALING JAYA, SELANGOR, MALAYSIA.
CHEW, Ms. Shiao Hua, ACA *2011;* 56, Jalan Cempaka, Bangi Golf Resort, Bandar Boru Bangi, 43650 BANDAR BARU BANGI, SELANGOR MALAYSIA.
•**CHEWTER, Mr. Paul Robert, ACA** *2008;* BSR Bespoke Limited, Hilden Park House, 79 Tonbridge Road, Hildenborough, TONBRIDGE, KENT TN11 9BH.
CHEWTER, Miss. Rebecca Suzanne, BSc ACA *2008;* C R A International UK, 99 Bishopsgate, LONDON, EC2M 3XD.
CHEWTER, Mr. Stephen Michael, BSc ACA *2004;* Pricewaterhousecoopers Llp, 1 Hays Lane, LONDON, SE1 2RD.
CHEYETTE, Mr. Allen Neal, MA ACA *1986;* Jalan Raya, Seminyak 56, kuta, BALI, 80361, INDONESIA.
•**CHEYETTE, Mr. Keith Leonard, FCA** *1956;* Cheyettes Ltd, 167 London Road, LEICESTER, LE2 1EG.
CHEYNE, Mr. John David, FCA *1959;* 6728 Hillpark Drive, Suite 407, LOS ANGELES, CA 90068, UNITED STATES.
CHEYNE, Mr. Mark Rider, BSc FCA *1965;* 38d Whistlers Avenue, Morgan's Walk, LONDON, SW11 3TS. (Life Member)
CHEYNE, Miss. Rachael, ACA *2011;* Bluebell Cottage, 5 Church Alley, Blofield, NORWICH, NR13 4JJ.
CHEYNE, Mr. William Gerald, BA FCA *1981;* Gerald Cheyne & Co Ltd, 32 Ringmer Avenue, LONDON, SW6 5LW.
CHHABRA, Mr. Rajan Kumar, FCA *1974;* Food and Agriculture Organization of the United Nations, PO Box 142654, AMMAN, 11844, JORDAN.
CHHABRA, Mr. Rakesh Charles, MA ACA *1992;* Knight Equity Markets International Ltd, Guildhall House, 81-87 Gresham Street, LONDON, EC2V 7NQ.

CHHABRA, Mr. Raoul Joseph, BSc(Econ) ACA *1997;* Byt c. 73, Rezidence Riegrovy Sady, Italska 2564/57, Vinohrady, 120 00 PRAGUE, CZECH REPUBLIC.
CHHATRALIA, Mr. Dipesh, BSc ACA *2010;* 168c Pinner Road, HARROW, HA1 4JP.
CHHAYA, Mr. Jaymin, BCom ACA *2011;* 33 Earls Lane, SLOUGH, SL1 5DJ.
CHHEDA, Mr. Veenay Surendra, BA ACA *1997;* 61 Redhill Drive, EDGWARE, HA8 5JL.
CHHITA, Miss. Priya, ACA *2008;* 16 Webb Ellis Road, RUGBY, CV22 7AU.
CHHOA, Mr. Philip Chao Yang, BSc ACA *1984;* 47 Lorong Iramanis 2, Taman IramanisOff Jalan Linta, KOTA KINABALU, Sabah, MALAYSIA.
CHHOKAR, Mr. Harpal Singh, BSc ACA *2010;* Heusden House, Heusden Way, GERRARDS CROSS, BUCKINGHAMSHIRE, SL9 7BD.
CHHOKAR, Mr. Randip Singh, BSc ACA *2002;* 57 Woodward Close, Winnersh, WOKINGHAM, BERKSHIRE, RG41 5NW.
CHHOKER, Miss. Narinder, BSc ACA *2009;* 106 The Glade, ILFORD, IG5 0NL.
CHI, Miss. Vivian Wai-Yin, MSc ACA *1992;* House 6 Royal Bay, 82 Chung Hom Kok Road, CHUNG HOM KOK, HONG KONG ISLAND, HONG KONG SAR.
CHIA, Mr. Alexander Hock Lon, BA ACA *1992;* 148 Jalan Desa Mesra, Taman Desa, 58100 KUALA LUMPUR, FEDERAL TERRITORY, MALAYSIA.
CHIA, Miss. Debbie Pei San, BCom(Hons) ACA *2011;* 255 Kim Keat Avenue, #07-138, SINGAPORE 310255, SINGAPORE.
CHIA, Mr. Eric Meng Huat, FCA *1994;* Ernst & Young, 18th Floor Two International Finance Centre, 8 Finance Street, CENTRAL, HONG KONG ISLAND, HONG KONG SAR.
CHIA, Ms. Irene Ai Ling, ACA *2003;* 52 Hartismere Road, LONDON, SW6 7UD.
CHIA, Mr. Jin Sian, ACA *1981;* 20 Jalan Rebung 9/KS6, Bandar Batanic, 41200 KLANG, SELANGOR, MALAYSIA.
CHIA, Mr. Lawrence Kee Loong, BCom FCA CF *1982;* 3rd Floor, 27 Happy View Terrace, HAPPY VALLEY, HONG KONG ISLAND, HONG KONG SAR.
CHIA, Mr. Seng Yen, ACA *2008;* Grant Thornton UK Llp, 4 Hardman Square, MANCHESTER, M3 3EB.
CHIA, Ms. Siew Chin, ACA *1979;* SC Yong Chia & Co, P O Box 20858, Luyang, 88765 KOTA KINABALU, Sabah, MALAYSIA.
CHIA, Mr. Sin Cheng, ACA *1981;* 51 Tuas South Street 5, SINGAPORE 808044, SINGAPORE.
CHIA, Mr. Soo Hien, FCA *1986;* BDO LLP, 21 Merchant Road, 05-01 Royal Merukh, S.E.A Building, SINGAPORE 058267, SINGAPORE.
CHIAM, Miss. Chin-Yee, BSc ACA *1992;* Blk 111 #08-40 Sunset Way Clementi Street 13, SINGAPORE 120111, SINGAPORE.
CHIAM, Miss. EE Lin, BEng ACA *2010;* Flat 17 Wilkie House, Cureton Street, LONDON, SW1P 4EH.
CHIANG, Mr. Alexander Jong-Luan, MA ACA *1986;* (Tax Fac), 40 Sutherland Chase, ASCOT, BERKSHIRE, SL5 8TF.
CHIANG, Mr. Eu Sheng, ACA *2008;* Flat 8 Gladstone Court, 97 Regency Street, LONDON, SW1P 4AL.
CHIANG, Mr. Gary, MChem ACA *2009;* 184 Broughton Lane, SALFORD, M7 1UF.
CHIANG, Miss. Josephine Aizhen, BA(Hons) ACA *2011;* Flat 5, 134 Elgin Avenue, Maida Vale, LONDON, W9 2NS.
CHIANG, Mr. Mark Avery, BA ACA *2003;* Prudential Plc Governors House, 5 Laurence Pountney Hill, LONDON, EC4R 0HH.
CHIANG, Miss. Natalie, MEng ACA *2001;* The Oast House Powder Mills, Leigh, TONBRIDGE, TN11 9AR.
CHIANG, Mr. Sham Lam Anthony, ACA *2007;* (Tax Fac), St George's Building, Suite 1908 19/F, No 2 Ice House Street, CENTRAL, HONG KONG SAR.
CHIANG, Mrs. Sin Mei Cindy, ACA *2008;* Flat E 10/F, Block 5, Central Park, 18 Hoi Ting Road, West Kowloon, CENTRAL HONG KONG SAR.
CHIANG, Ms. Siu Mei Emily, ACA *2008;* Flat H 28/F, Tsuen Fung Centre, 168 Sai Lau Kok Road, TSUEN WAN, NEW TERRITORIES, HONG KONG SAR.
CHIANG, Mr. Wai Kwong Eric, ACA *2005;* c/o Algorithmics, Room 1903 PICC Building, 2 Jianguomenwai Street, Chaoyang District, BEIJING 100022, CHINA.
CHIANG, Mr. Yiu Keung Victor, ACA *2005;* Block F 31/F Royal Court, 9M Kennedy Road, WAN CHAI, HONG KONG ISLAND, HONG KONG SAR.
CHIAPPE, Mr. Jeremy Peter, BA ACA *1992;* The Old Chapel, Aspley Hill, Woburn Sands, MILTON KEYNES, MK17 8NH.
CHIBA, Mr. Khozaim Eban, FCA *1972;* PO Box 29281, DUBAI, UNITED ARAB EMIRATES.
CHIBBETT, Mr. Geoffrey John, BCom FCA *1953;* 3 Kings View, Coronation Road, Hoylake, WIRRAL, CH47 1JL. (Life Member)
CHIC, Mr. Yun Sang, ACA *2007;* 10/F, 169 Electric Road, NORTH POINT, HONG KONG ISLAND, HONG KONG SAR.
CHICHON, Mr. Christian Paul, BSc ACA *2004;* Willis Management (Gibraltar) Limited, Suite 827, Europort PO Box 708, GIBRALTAR, GIBRALTAR.
CHICK, Mr. Alvar James, FCA *1967;* Beech View, The Old Orchard, Burwash, ETCHINGHAM, EAST SUSSEX, TN19 7BF.
CHICK, Mr. David James, BSc ACA *2010;* 21 King Henry Mews, HARROW, MIDDLESEX, HA2 0JF.
CHICK, Mr. Derek Michael, BSc ACA *1979;* (Tax Fac), Totemic Group Ltd, Kempton House, Dysart Road, GRANTHAM, NG31 7LE.
CHICK, Mr. Raymond Lindsey, FCA *1974;* Highcroft, Stane Street, Adversane, BILLINGSHURST, RH14 9JR.
CHICK, Miss. Suzannah Kate, BSc ACA *2006;* Flat 11, The Chocolate Studios, 7 Shepherdess Place, LONDON, N1 7LJ.
•**CHICKEN, Mrs. Rosemary Jane, FCA** *1975;* (Tax Fac), SWC4Limited, 11 Moor Street, CHEPSTOW, GWENT, NP16 5DD.
•**CHICKSAND, Mr. Stanley Barry, BSc FCA ATII** *1971;* (Tax Fac), Chicksand Gordon Avis Limited, 12 Northfields Prospect, Putney Bridge Road, LONDON, SW18 1PE.
CHICOOREE, Mr. Youdish, BA(Hons) ACA *2011;* Flat 83, Studley Court, 4 Jamestown Way, LONDON, E14 2DA.
•**CHIDGEY, Mr. Peter Charles Joseph, BSc FCA** *1975;* BDO LLP, 55 Baker Street, LONDON, W1U 7EU. See also BDO Stoy Hayward LLP
•**CHIDLEY, Mr. David Anthony, BSc(Econ) ACA CTA** *1997;* W.J. Matthews & Son, 11 - 15 Bridge Street, CAERNARFON, LL55 1AB.
CHIDLEY, Mr. Jonathan, ACA *2007;* Ernst & Young, Bleicherweg 21, CH-8022 ZURICH, SWITZERLAND.
CHIDLOW, Ms. Megan Ruth, BA(Hons) ACA *2001;* 45 Avondale Road, LONDON, N3 2EU.
CHIDLOW, Mr. Robert, BSc ACA *2011;* 136 Apedale Road, Wood Lane, STOKE-ON-TRENT, ST7 8PH.
CHIDOTHE, Dr. Fungayi Michael, MD ACA *2009;* 10 Chisbury Close, BRACKNELL, BERKSHIRE, RG12 0TX.
CHIDSON, Mr. Jeremy John, FCA *1975;* 6 Unwin Mansions, Queen's Club Gardens, LONDON, W14 9TH.
CHIDWICK, Mr. Anthony James, BSS ACA *1997;* 4 Radnor Close, HENLEY-ON-THAMES, OXFORDSHIRE, RG9 2DA.
CHIDWICK, Mr. Grahame Leonard, BSc ACA *1991;* 10 Arran Way, Rothwell, LEEDS, LS26 0WB.
CHIEN, Mr. Hoe Yong, LLB ACA *1992;* 23/F Yue Thai Commercial Building, 128 Connaught Road, CENTRAL, HONG KONG ISLAND, HONG KONG SAR.
•**CHIENG, Mr. Ing Mui, FCA** *1972;* Peter I M Chieng & Co, A-5-4A 5th Floor, Northpoint Office, Northpoint Mid Valley City, No 1 Medan Syed Putra Utara, 59200 KUALA LUMPUR FEDERAL TERRITORY MALAYSIA.
CHIENG, Mr. James Kai Seng, BA(Hons) ACA *2001;* D4-G3 Scot Pine Condo, Persiaran SG Long 1, Bandar SG Long, 43000 KAJANG, SELANGOR, MALAYSIA.
CHIESE, Mr. Ross Anthony Norman, FCA *1974;* Aeromet International Plc, Unit 6, Eurolink Industrial Centre, Castle Road, SITTINGBOURNE, KENT ME10 3RN.
CHIESMAN, Mr. David Walter Rennie, MA FCA *1961;* Flat 1, 99 Blackheath Park, LONDON, SE3 0EU. (Life Member)
CHIEW, Mr. Jaime, BSc(Hons) ACA *2003;* 135 Sunset Way, 09-07 Clementi Park, SINGAPORE 597158, SINGAPORE.
CHIEW, Mr. Lik Hing Anthony, BA ACA *1987;* EMP plc, EMP House, 2 Pembroke Road, Muswell Hill, LONDON, N10 2HR.
CHIEW, Mr. Sin Cheok, MSc ACA *1989;* Jardine Cycle & Carriage Limited, 239 Alexandra Road, SINGAPORE 159930, SINGAPORE.
CHIEW, Mr. Sin Weng, FCA *1969;* 505 - 455 Beach Crescent, VANCOUVER V6Z 3E5, BC, CANADA. (Life Member)
CHIGBU, Miss. Chinenye, LLB ACA *2002;* 32 Buckland Road, LONDON, E10 6QS.
CHIGIROV, Mr. Timur, ACA *2010;* 7 Vauxhall Grove, LONDON, SW8 1TD.
CHIK, Mr. Sung, BSc ACA *1997;* Flat A, 51 Quicks Road, Wimbledon, LONDON, SW19 1EY.
CHIKETA, Mr. Valentine, ACA *2006;* 7 William Olders Road, Angmering, LITTLEHAMPTON, WEST SUSSEX, BN16 4FD.
CHIKHALIKAR, Miss. Shrutisha, BSc ACA *2006;* 16 Sandmoor Place, LYMM, WA13 0LQ.
CHIKOORE, Mr. Tawanda, ACA *2011;* Flat 10 Ozanne Court, Cordier Hill, St. Peter Port, GUERNSEY, GY1 1JJ.
CHILCOTT, Mr. Edwin Henry, FCA *1954;* 28 Fairways Road, SEAFORD, BN25 4EN. (Life Member)
CHILCOTT, Mr. John Bowering, FCA *1950;* C/O Ms Sarah Chilcott, 3 Durleigh Close, BRIDGWATER, SOMERSET, TA6 7HT. (Life Member)
CHILCOTT, Mr. Keith Trevor, ACA *1983;* 11 Blenheim Drive, Willand, CULLOMPTON, EX15 2TB.
CHILD, Miss. Alexandra, BA(Hons) ACA *2009;* Coors Brewers Ltd, 137 High Street, BURTON-ON-TRENT, STAFFORDSHIRE, DE14 1JZ.
CHILD, Mr. Andrew Leonard, BA FCA *1983;* Castlewood, Waltham Road, Ruscombe, READING, RG10 0HB.
•**CHILD, Mrs. Anne Elizabeth, BA FCA** *1977;* Child & Co, 20 Kirkgate, Sherburn In Elmet, LEEDS, LS25 6BL.
•**CHILD, Mrs. Anne Elizabeth Mary, BBS FCA** *1975;* (Tax Fac), Rouse Partners LLP, 55 Station Road, BEACONSFIELD, BUCKINGHAMSHIRE, HP9 1QL.
CHILD, Mrs. Beverly, BA ACA *1981;* Waterside House, Worthy Road, Headbourne Worthy, WINCHESTER, HAMPSHIRE, SO23 7JR.
CHILD, Mr. Colin, FCA *1972;* Leonora, 209 Ilchester Road, YEOVIL, BA21 3BQ.
CHILD, Mr. Colin Charles, BSc FCA *1982;* Waterside House, Worthy Road, Headbourne Worthy, WINCHESTER, HAMPSHIRE, SO23 7JR.
CHILD, Mr. David, FCA *1957;* 20 Dene Bank, Lady Lane, BINGLEY, BD16 4AR. (Life Member)
CHILD, Mr. Eric James, BSc ACA *1992;* 18 West Lea Crescent, Yeadon, LEEDS, LS19 7EE.
CHILD, Mr. Francis John, BSc ACA *1986;* 76 Bridge Street, Lane Cove, SYDNEY, NSW 2066, AUSTRALIA.
CHILD, Mr. Hugh, FCA *1969;* Plas y Coed, Bonvilston, Vale of Glamorgan, CARDIFF, CF5 6TR.
•**CHILD, Mr. Ian Douglas, BA ACA** *1992;* I D Child ACA, 68 Cherry Garden Road, MALDON, ESSEX, CM9 6ET.
CHILD, Mr. Ian Lester, FCA *1970;* South Wood, Pachesham Drive, LEATHERHEAD, KT22 0DF.
CHILD, Mr. Ian Phillip, FCA *1975;* 12 Harestone Drive, CATERHAM, CR3 6HX.
•**CHILD, Mr. John, FCA** *1969;* (Tax Fac), Child & Child Accountants Limited, 49 Somerset Street, ABERTILLERY, GWENT, NP13 1DL. See also Child & Child
•**CHILD, Mr. Michael James, ACA** *2008;* Child & Co, 20 Kirkgate, Sherburn In Elmet, LEEDS, LS25 6BL.
CHILD, Miss. Pauline Therese, FCA *1950;* Meadow Cottage, 1 Commonside, KESTON, BR2 6BP. (Life Member)
•**CHILD, Mr. Peter Francis, BA FCA** *1973;* with PFC Associates Limited, 34 College Road, MAIDENHEAD, BERKSHIRE, SL6 6AT.
•**CHILD, Miss. Rachel Jane, BSc ACA** *2001;* Child & Child Accountants Limited, 49 Somerset Street, ABERTILLERY, GWENT, NP13 1DL. See also Child & Child
•**CHILD, Mr. Roger, BSc FCA** *1974;* (Tax Fac), Child & Co, 20 Kirkgate, Sherburn In Elmet, LEEDS, LS25 6BL.
CHILD, Mr. Simon David Lipsett, BA ACA *2006;* 17c Kingsgate Road, LONDON, NW6 4TD.
•**CHILD, Mr. Simon Jonathan, FCA** *1991;* Jon Child & Co, 107 Oldham Street, MANCHESTER, M4 1LW.
CHILD, Mr. Stephen Alan, BA ACA *1997;* 27 Streathbourne Road, LONDON, SW17 8QZ.
CHILD, Mr. Tony Frank, BSc FCA *1970;* 2 Cherry Tree Close, High Salvington, WORTHING, BN13 3QJ.
CHILDE, Mr. Andrew Joseph, ACA *2008;* 68 Church Road, LIVERSEDGE, WEST YORKSHIRE, WF15 7LP.
CHILDERLEY, Mr. Jonathan Scott, FCA *1974;* 405 Toni Lane, MAMARONECK, NY 10543, UNITED STATES.
CHILDERS, Mr. Anthony Deniol, MBA BSc ACA *1992;* Eduardo Mondlane 177, LUANDA, ANGOLA.
CHILDERS, Miss. Helen Mary, MA ACA *1995;* Easter Hall, Bromley, Standon, WARE, SG11 1NX.
CHILDERSTONE, Mr. Jeremy Martin, BSc ACA *1991;* Cleenol Group Ltd, Neville House, Beaumont Road, BANBURY, OXFORDSHIRE, OX16 1RB.
CHILDS, Mr. Andrew Dominic William, BA ACA *1992;* HOK International Ltd. Qube, 90 Whitfield Street, LONDON, W1T 4EZ.
•**CHILDS, Mr. Andrew John, ACA** *2002;* Larkings Ltd, 180 Upper Pemberton, Eureka Business Park, ASHFORD, KENT, TN25 4AZ.
CHILDS, Mr. Barry, FCA *1977;* 2 Eastbrook Avenue, Radcliffe, MANCHESTER, M26 2RT.
CHILDS, Mr. Christopher Michael, ACA *1980;* Angloco Ltd, Upper Station Road, BATLEY, WEST YORKSHIRE, WF17 5TA.
CHILDS, Mr. David Andrew, BSc ACA *1987;* 35D Birkbeck Road, Acton, LONDON, W3 6BQ.
•**CHILDS, Mr. Duncan Philip, FCA** *1982;* Meadows & Co, 1 Kings Court, Kettering Parkway, KETTERING, NORTHAMPTONSHIRE, NN15 6WJ.
•**CHILDS, Mrs. Jaqueline Irene, BSc FCA** *1991;* Williamson Morton Thornton LLP, 47 Holywell Hill, ST. ALBANS, HERTFORDSHIRE, AL1 1HD.
CHILDS, Mr. Jeffrey, BA ACA *1983;* Morris Material Handling Ltd, P O Box 7, North Road, LOUGHBOROUGH, LE11 1RL.
CHILDS, Mrs. Joanna Ruth, ACA *1982;* 31 St. Leonards Road, LONDON, SW14 7LY.
CHILDS, Mr. John Cecil, FCA *1965;* 4 Oakwood Hall, Eyhurst Park, Outwood Lane, Kingswood, TADWORTH, SURREY KT20 6JP. (Life Member)
CHILDS, Miss. Julie, ACA *2001;* 12 Hamilton Close, Bricket Wood, ST. ALBANS, AL2 3NA.
CHILDS, Mr. Lee David, BA ACA *2000;* 282 Spendmore Lane, Coppull, CHORLEY, LANCASHIRE, PR7 5DE.
CHILDS, Ms. Lisbeth Ann, PhD ACA *1991;* Flat 3, 9 Cavendish Place, BATH, BA1 2UB.
CHILDS, Mrs. Lynne Mary, ACA *1981;* 1 Victoria Mills, HOLMFIRTH, HD9 2TP.
CHILDS, Mr. Mark Lucien, FCA *1987;* EMG Ventures, Dockland Offices, 23 Castalia Square, LONDON, E14 3NG.
CHILDS, Mr. Mervyn Peter, FCA *1968;* The White House, 19 Church Road, Stretton, BURTON-ON-TRENT, STAFFORDSHIRE, DE13 0HD.
CHILDS, Miss. Morag Ruth, BSc ACA *1992;* 49 Main Street, Swannington, COALVILLE, LE67 8QL.
•**CHILDS, Mr. Nicholas John, FCA** *1987;* (Tax Fac), Mapperson Price, 286a High Street, DORKING, RH4 1QT.
CHILDS, Mr. Patrick Carthew Fuller, FCA *1957;* 5 The Boundary, Langton Green, TUNBRIDGE WELLS, TN3 0YA. (Life Member)
CHILDS, Mr. Peter Alexander, BSc ACA *2005;* with PricewaterhouseCoopers LLP, Marlborough Court, 10 Bricket Road, ST. ALBANS, HERTFORDSHIRE, AL1 3JX.
CHILDS, Mr. Peter Barry, BSc ACA *1981;* 30 Ridge Avenue, HARPENDEN, HERTFORDSHIRE, AL5 3LT.
CHILDS, Mr. Peter Michael, FCA *1966;* 9 Ray Park Road, MAIDENHEAD, SL6 8PZ.
CHILDS, Mr. Raymond, BA ACA *1992;* 31 Hazeldene Court, NORTH SHIELDS, NE30 4AD.
CHILDS, Mr. Robin Francis, ACA *1980;* 50 Larkhill Road, Wollaston, STOURBRIDGE, DY8 3LN.
•**CHILDS, Mr. Stephen, BSc(Econ) FCA** *1977;* Easterbrook Eaton Limited, Cosmopolitan House, Old Fore Street, SIDMOUTH, DEVON, EX10 8LS.
•**CHILDS, Mrs. Suzanne, ACA MAAT** *2006;* Taxbak Limited, Park House, 91 Garstang Road, PRESTON, PR1 1LD.
CHILDS, Mr. Timothy David, BA ACA *1992;* KPMG AG, Badenerstrasse 172, CH 8004 ZURICH, SWITZERLAND.
CHILDS, Mr. Warren Goldsmith, FCA *1963;* 26 Banbury Park, TORQUAY, TQ2 7HN. (Life Member)
CHILDS-CLARKE, Mr. James Michael, ACA *2009;* 41 Deacon Crescent, SOUTHAMPTON, SO19 7BS.
CHILKA, Mr. Swapnil, BA(Hons) ACA *2003;* 32 Mount Street, DERBY, DE1 2HH.
CHILLERY, Mr. Scott Alexander, BSc ACA *1996;* 31 Craneford Way, TWICKENHAM, TW2 7SB.
CHILMAN, Mr. John David, MA ACA *1992;* First Group Plc, 395 King Street, ABERDEEN, AB24 5RP.
CHILTON, Mrs. Joanne Louisa, FCA *1995;* 30 Sunnyhill, HINCKLEY, LEICESTERSHIRE, LE10 2SB.
CHILTON, Mr. Joseph, FCA *1952;* 14 Oak Lodge Close, Dennis Lane, STANMORE, HA7 4QB. (Life Member)
CHILTON, Mr. Michael Barry, BSc ACA *1989;* 29 Bancroft Avenue, LONDON, N2 0AR.
CHILTON, Mr. Stephen John, BA ACA *1995;* 30 Sunnyhill, Burbage, HINCKLEY, LEICESTERSHIRE, LE10 2SB.
•**CHILTON, Mrs. Susan Margaret, FCA** *1977;* Davis & Company, Room 11, 1-5 Warstone Lane, Hockley, BIRMINGHAM, B18 6JE.
CHILVER, Mr. David Robert, BA ACA *1990;* 2/F, No 28 First Street, Sok Kwu Wan, LAMMA ISLAND, NEW TERRITORIES, HONG KONG SAR.

CHILVER, Mr. Ian Charles William, BA ACA *1992;* 103 Brook Gardens, EMSWORTH, HAMPSHIRE, PO10 7LB.
•**CHILVER, Mr. Martin James, BSc ACA** *2004;* The Chartwell Practice, Chartwell House, 4 St. Pauls Square, BURTON-ON-TRENT, STAFFORDSHIRE, DE14 2EF. See also The PayCompany Ltd
CHILVERS, Mr. Alex, ACA *2011;* 39d Bentley Lane, LEEDS, LS6 4AJ.
CHILVERS, Mr. Angus Donald, BA ACA *1993;* Epsilon Partners LLP, 60 Pembroke Road, LONDON, W8 6NX.
CHILVERS, Mr. Antony Robert, MSc BA ACA *2010;* Flat 11 Galaxy Building, 5 Crews Street, LONDON, E14 3SP.
CHILVERS, Mr. Donald Richard, FCA *1952;* Chilvers, Glebe Farm, Brightwell Baldwin, WATLINGTON, OXFORDSHIRE, OX49 5NP. (Life Member)
•**CHILVERS, Mr. Julian David John, BA FCA** *1982;* (Tax Fac), Julian Chilvers, 72 Cavendish Avenue, CAMBRIDGE, CB1 7UT.
CHILVERS, Mrs. Lynne Margaret, BSc ACA *1982;* Regis Mutual Management Ltd Unit A-b the Winery, Lamberhurst Vineyard Furnace Lane Lamberhurst, TUNBRIDGE WELLS, TN3 8EW.
•**CHILVERS, Mr. Martyn Leslie, MA ACA** *1981;* (Tax Fac), Martyn Chilvers & Co, Long Lane Studios, 142-152 Long Lane, LONDON, SE1 4BS.
•**CHILVERS, Mr. Michael David, FCA** *1975;* Carter Nicholls Consultants Ltd, 415 Limpsfield Road, WARLINGHAM, SURREY, CR6 9HA.
CHILVERS, Mr. Neal David, FCA *1975;* 45 Newland Park, Cottingham Road, HULL, HU5 2DN.
CHIM, Mr. Edwin, MA ACA *2010;* 26 Timberling Gardens, SOUTH CROYDON, SURREY, CR2 0AW.
CHIM, Miss. Elaine, BAcc ACA *2006;* Flat 22, 199-205 Old Marylebone Road, LONDON, NW1 5QR.
CHIM, Miss. Foong Heng, BSc ACA *1992;* 7F Central Tower, Cathay Pacific City, 8 Scenic Road, LANTAU ISLAND, HONG KONG SAR.
•**CHIMARIDES, Mr. Nicos, BSc ACA** *1994;* PricewaterhouseCoopers Limited, Julia House, 3 Themistocles Dervis Street, CY-1066 NICOSIA, CYPRUS.
CHIMCHIRIAN, Mr. Haig Peter, FCA *1968;* Clos de la Fontaine 5A, 1410 WATERLOO, BELGIUM. (Life Member)
CHIMCHOME, Mr. Natasek, FCA *1972;* 69 Lan Luang Road, Wat Soemmanus Sub District, Pomprabasattruphai District, BANGKOK, 10100, THAILAND.
CHIN, Mr. Aik Han, ACA CA(NZ) *2011;* 69 Octavia House, 213 Townmead Road, Imperial Wharf, LONDON, SW6 2FH.
CHIN, Miss. Anne Siew Kim, BA ACA *1991;* 9 Bedford Road, South Woodford, LONDON, E18 2AQ.
CHIN, Miss. August Emily, ACA *2009;* 34 Torrington Place, LONDON, E1W 2UY.
CHIN, Miss. Betty Yee Fun, FCA *1973;* 15A Caddy Avenue, West Leederville, PERTH, WA 6007, AUSTRALIA. (Life Member)
CHIN, Mr. Christopher, BA ACA *1982;* 53 White Moss Avenue, Chorlton-cum-Hardy, MANCHESTER, M21 0XS.
CHIN, Mr. David Mui Yee, FCA *1975;* 29 Stonefield Crescent, TORONTO M1E 4J4, ON, CANADA.
•**CHIN, Mr. Feng Tak, FCA** *1977;* Newman & Co, Regent House, 1 Pratt Mews, LONDON, NW1 0AD.
CHIN, Mr. Fook Kheong, ACA *2008;* GHL Systems Berhad, Unit L8C-G-15 Block C, Jalan Dataran SD1, Dataran SD PJU9, Banvar Sri Damansara, 52200 KUALA LUMPUR FEDERAL TERRITORY MALAYSIA.
CHIN, Ms. Hooi Tien, BSc ACA *1990;* 28 Bellamy Close, UXBRIDGE, MIDDLESEX, UB10 8SJ.
CHIN, Miss. Jee May, MSc LLB ACA *2003;* 12 Dollis Park, LONDON, N3 1HG.
CHIN, Mr. Jon Wei, ACA *2010;* Block 49-3-4, Bangsar Puteri, Jalan MeDang Seral, Bukit bandaraya, 59100 KUALA LUMPUR, FEDERAL TERRITORY MALAYSIA.
CHIN, Mr. Jude Gerald, BSc FCA *1982;* The Fields Glemham Road, Sweffling, SAXMUNDHAM, SUFFOLK, IP17 2BQ.
CHIN, Mrs. Judy Caroline, BSc ACA *1990;* 1 Cambrian Street, Churton Park, WELLINGTON 6037, NEW ZEALAND.
CHIN, Miss. Kar Yin, MSc ACA *2003;* 57 Wrottesley Road, LONDON, SE18 3EW.
CHIN, Miss. Karen Wei Sim, ACA *2009;* 21 Thame Road, LONDON, SE16 6AR.
CHIN, Mr. Kean Cheang, BA ACA *1991;* 15 Pempath Place, Hazelwood Grove Carlton Ave, WEMBLEY, HA9 8QW.
CHIN, Mr. Kian-Hoong, ACA ACCA *2008;* B1105 Perdana Exclusive Condo, No 15 Jalan PJU 8/1, Damansara Perdana, 47820 PETALING JAYA, SELANGOR, MALAYSIA.
CHIN, Mr. Kon Kah, FCA *1973;* Jaschin Mgmt Consultants Sdn Bhd, No 25-5 Block H Jalan Pju 1/37, Dataran Prima, 47301 PETALING JAYA, SELANGOR, MALAYSIA.
CHIN, Mr. Kwai Fatt, BSc FCA *1981;* PricewaterhouseCoopers, P.O.Box 10192, Level 10 1 Sentral, Jalan Travers, 50470 KUALA LUMPUR, FEDERAL TERRITORY MALAYSIA.
CHIN, Mr. Kwai Yoong, FCA *1974;* Lot 3690 Jalan Ukay 2, 68000 AMPANG, MALAYSIA.
CHIN, Mr. Kwok-Keung, BCom ACA *1982;* Count Ten CPA Limited, 17/F Shing Lee Commerical Building, 6-12 Wing Kut Street, CENTRAL, HONG KONG ISLAND, HONG KONG SAR.
CHIN, Miss. Louise Yen Theng, BSc ACA *2007;* Flat 17 The Clock Tower, Kings Road, WOKING, SURREY, GU21 5HU.
CHIN, Mr. Michael Andrew, FCA *1974;* Residenza Quadrifoglio 2, Via Liberazione 27/6, 20068 Peschiera Borromeo, MILAN, ITALY.
CHIN, Mr. Michael Yoon Kheong, ACA *1984;* 26 St. Edyths Road, Sea Mills, BRISTOL, BS9 2ES.
CHIN, Mr. Patrick Yoke Chung, FCA *1971;* unit 165-18, Sri Wangsaria Condominium, Jalan Ara, Bangsar, 59100 KUALA LUMPUR, FEDERAL TERRITORY MALAYSIA.
CHIN, Miss. Pei Sze, BSc ACA *2001;* 3 Lorong Kingfisher Sulaman 2A Taman Kingfisher Sulaman, 88450 KOTA KINABALU, SABAH, MALAYSIA.
CHIN, Mr. Peng Koon, BEng ACA *1985;* 1 Lorong 16/3A, 46350 PETALING JAYA, Selangor, MALAYSIA.
CHIN, Mr. Peter Cheen Kee, FCA *1980;* 12 Jalan Aminuddin Baki, Seremban, 70100 SEREMBAN, NEGERI SEMBILAN, MALAYSIA.
CHIN, Miss. Pow Siew, BSc ACA *1989;* Capgemini Building, Xiaxi International Business Zone, Nanhai District, FOSHAN 5282000, CHINA.
•**CHIN, Dr. Robert Kick Chong, FCA** *1974;* Robert Chin Lee & Associates, 2nd Floor, Lot 15 Bl.B Lintus Sq, Jalan Lintus, 88300 KOTA KINABALUSabah, MALAYSIA.
CHIN, Mr. Sek Peng, BA FCA *1983;* 23 Jalan Raja Udang, No. 07-07 The Arte, SINGAPORE 329216, SINGAPORE.
CHIN, Miss. Sew Ying Joy, FCA *1984;* 69 Jalan Keruing, Bukit Bandara ya, 59100 KUALA LUMPUR, FEDERAL TERRITORY, MALAYSIA.
CHIN, Miss. Sheau Yuan, MA ACA CTA *2004;* 57 Vicarage Road, LONDON, E15 4HD.
•**CHIN, Mr. Sin Beng, FCA** *1984;* Foo Kon Tan Grant Thornton LLP, 47 Hill Street, 5th Fl. Unit 01, Chinese Chamber of Comm & Industry Bldg, SINGAPORE 179365, SINGAPORE.
CHIN, Mr. Stanley En Leong, MSc(Econ) ACA *1999;* 19C Block 3, Grand Promenade, 38 Tai Hong Street, SAI WAN HO, HONG KONG ISLAND, HONG KONG SAR.
CHIN, Mr. Tian Hsi, ACA *2007;* 20D La Rossa B, Coastal Skyline, 12 Tung Chung Waterfront Road, LANTAU ISLAND, NEW TERRITORIES, HONG KONG SAR.
CHIN, Mr. Voon Loong, BSc FCA *1984;* Carlsberg Brewery Malaysia Berhad, 55 Persiaran Selangor, Section 15, SHAH ALAM, SELANGOR, MALAYSIA.
CHIN, Mr. Winston Wei Chern, BSc ACA *2005;* Invista Real Estate, Unit 820 8 Floor, Two Exchange Square, 8 Connaught Place, CENTRAL, HONG KONG ISLAND HONG KONG SAR.
CHIN, Mr. Yean Choon, FCA *1977;* 50 Lengkok Sungai Emas 1, Batu Feringghi, 11100 PENANG, PULAU PINANG, MALAYSIA.
CHIN, Mr. Yoke Choong Bobby, ACA *1979;* 7 Maple Lane, SINGAPORE 277551, SINGAPORE.
CHIN, Miss. Yoke Ping, FCA *1985;* 2 Houghton Court, The Green, Houghton Regis, DUNSTABLE, LU5 5DY.
•**CHIN, Dr. Yoong Kheong, FCA ATII CF CPA** *1982;* KPMG, Level 10, KPMG Tower, 8 First Avenue, Bandar Utama, 47800 PETALING JAYA SELANGOR MALAYSIA.
CHIN-LI, Ms. Cheryl Choo, ACA CA(NZ) *2011;* 43 Friars Mead, LONDON, E14 3JY.
CHIN PO KOI, Mr. Chung Ching Chow, FCA *1976;* 15 Allstate Parkway, Suite 600, MARKHAM L3R 5B4, ON, CANADA.
CHIN PO KOI, Mr. Chung Yung Chow, FCA *1973;* 21 Carlisle Way, Tooting, LONDON, SW17 9NZ.
CHINCHANWALA, Mr. Rashid Peter, BSc ACA *1989;* 6a Davenham Avenue, NORTHWOOD, MIDDLESEX, HA6 3HN.
CHIND, Mr. Amanpreet Singh, BSc ACA *1998;* 49 Westbury Road, NORTHWOOD, MIDDLESEX, HA6 3DB.
CHINDULURI, Mrs. Clare, ACA *2010;* Flat 16 Ocean Wharf, 60 Westferry Road, LONDON, E14 8LN.
CHINERY, Mr. Peter Frank, FCA *1951;* The Cottage, 2 Linden Drive, Old Swinford, STOURBRIDGE, DY8 2LF. (Life Member)
CHING, Mr. Chun Chung, ACA *2008;* CC Ching & Co, Rooms 801-2, The Centre Mark, 287-299 Queen's Road Central, CENTRAL, HONG KONG SAR.
CHING, Miss. Chung Yi, BSc ACA *2010;* Flat 4 11/F, Ting On House, Siu On Court, TUEN MUN, NEW TERRITORIES, HONG KONG SAR.
CHING, Mr. Gavin Chin-Ngai, BA ACA *1992;* (Tax Fac), 6/F Flat A, Glen Circuit, 41 Cloudview Road, NORTH POINT, HONG KONG SAR.
CHING, Mr. Hock Chuan, BA FCA *1984;* 101 Eley Road, BOX HILL SOUTH, VIC 3128, AUSTRALIA.
CHING, Mr. Kai Ming, ACA *2007;* 18/F AIA Building, No. 1 Stubbs Road, HAPPY VALLEY, HONG KONG ISLAND, HONG KONG SAR.
CHING, Mr. Neng Shyan, FCA *1981;* Kennedy Burkill & Co Bhd, 1st Floor, Standard Chartered Bank, Chambers, Beach Street, 10300 PENANG MALAYSIA.
CHING, Miss. Nicola Clair, BSc FCA ACII *1994;* Flat C306, 16 Hertsmere Road, LONDON, E14 4AX.
CHING, Mrs. Sarah Elizabeth, BSc ACA *1996;* Fairlight, 132 Bluehouse Lane, Limpsfield, OXTED, SURREY, RH8 0AR.
CHING, Mr. Shun Fu, ACA *2005;* Ching Shun Fu & Company, Block B 14/F, Hillier Commercial Building, 89-91 Wing Lok Street, SHEUNG WAN, HONG KONG ISLAND HONG KONG SAR.
CHING, Mr. William Pik Fai, BEng ACA *1994;* Flat A, 24th floor, Yukon Court, 2 Conduit Road, CENTRAL, HONG KONG SAR.
CHING-A-SUE, Miss. Phyllis Eunice Mary, ACA *1989;* 23 Woodhatch Spinney, COULSDON, CR5 2SU.
CHINN, Mrs. Carolyn Jane, BSc FCA *1996;* 8 Stubfield, HORSHAM, WEST SUSSEX, RH12 2AJ.
CHINN, Mr. Christopher Martin, MSc BA ACA *1993;* 4 Windsor Walk, WEYBRIDGE, SURREY, KT13 9AP.
CHINN, Mr. John Nicholas Mark, BSc ACA *1998;* 3a Hartlepool Court, LONDON, E16 2RL.
•**CHINN-SHAW, Mrs. Deborah Patricia, BA(Hons) ACA** *1997;* Michael F Keevil, Park House, 10 Osborne Road, POTTERS BAR, EN6 1RZ.
CHINNECK, Mr. Oliver James, BSc ACA *2009;* with BDO LLP, Prospect Place, 85 Great North Road, HATFIELD, HERTFORDSHIRE, AL9 5BS.
CHINNERY, Dr. Nicholas John, PhD BSc ACA *2006;* Shoon Ltd, Southover, WELLS, SOMERSET, BA5 1UH.
CHINOY, Mr. Farouk Mohammedhusain, FCA *1963;* Meher Buildings 3rd Floor, Dadyseth Road, Chowpatty, MUMBAI 400007, INDIA.
CHINOY, Mr. Rutton Buji, ACA *1981;* Dina Lodge, Garden Road, MUMBAI 400039, MAHARASHTRA, INDIA.
CHINOY, Mr. Salim, ACA *1981;* Ernst & Young Ford Rhodes Sidat Hyder, 601 Progressive Plaza, Beaumont Road, KARACHI 75530, SINDH, PAKISTAN.
CHINYEMBA, Mrs. Kudzanai, ACA *2011;* 19 Vale Close, HARPENDEN, HERTFORDSHIRE, AL5 3LX.
•**CHIOTIS, Mr. Alexis, BA ACA** *1992;* Adema Associates Ltd, 100 Pall Mall, St. James, LONDON, SW1Y 5NQ. See also Adema Associates and Penta Associates Limited
CHIPCHASE, Mr. Graham Andrew, MA FCA *1989;* Shallows Cottage, Pilley Hill, Pilley, LYMINGTON, HAMPSHIRE, SO41 5QF.
CHIPCHASE, Mr. John Michael, FCA *1959;* 72 Eastern Way Darras Hall, Ponteland, NEWCASTLE UPON TYNE, NE20 9RE. (Life Member)
CHIPCHASE, Mr. Michael John, FCA *1972;* 141 Woodhouse Lane, BISHOP AUCKLAND, COUNTY DURHAM, DL14 6JT. (Life Member)
CHIPMAN, Mr. Stephen Mark, ACA *1985;* 1050 Forest Avenue, WILMETTE, IL 60091, UNITED STATES.
•**CHIPP, Mr. George Morton, BA FCA** *1977;* GMC Accountancy Limited, 18 North End, BEDALE, NORTH YORKSHIRE, DL8 1AB.
CHIPP, Mr. Glen, BSc ACA *1986;* Woodlands, Oakley Close, EAST GRINSTEAD, RH19 3UG.
CHIPPENDALE, Mr. Keith, BSc ACA *1980;* 18 Friesian Close, FLEET, GU51 2TP.
CHIPPENDALE, Mr. Peter John Selwyn, BSc ACA *1997;* 5 rue des Crières, 78420 CARRIERES SUR SEINE, FRANCE.
CHIPPENDALE, Mr. Ryan Lee, LLB ACA *2000;* Flat 1, 25 Copers Cope Road, BECKENHAM, BR3 1NE.
CHIPPENDALE, Mr. Simon Robert, BA ACA *1992;* 2 Forge Cottages, Beenham, READING, RG7 5NX.
•**CHIPPENDALE, Mr. Thomas, FCA** *1970;* Thomas Chippendale, 39 Market Place, CHIPPENHAM, SN15 3HT.
CHIPPERFIELD, Mr. Paul Stephen, ACA *1991;* with Price Bailey LLP, The Quorum, Barnwell Road, CAMBRIDGE, CB5 8RE.
CHIPPINDALE, Mr. Stewart Ian, BA ACA *1991;* Flat 5, 77 Hamilton Terrace, LONDON, NW8 9QX.
CHIPPING, Mr. Stephen Richard, BA ACA *1983;* The Glebe House Ewehurst Lane, Speldhurst, TUNBRIDGE WELLS, TN3 0JX.
CHIPPINGTON, Mr. John Michael, FCA *1965;* 18 Purbeck Court, De Moulham Road, SWANAGE, DORSET, BH19 1PA. (Life Member)
•**CHIRUME, Mr. Malvern Tapfumaneyi, ACA** *2003;* Maltey Limited, 57 Waylands, SWANLEY, KENT, BR8 8TN.
CHISHICK, Mr. Jonathan Paul Harry, MA FCA *1975;* Conyers Green, Tidmarsh, Pangbourne, READING, RG8 8ES.
CHISHOLM, Miss. Aileen Louise, LLB ACA *2002;* 5/1 Savile Place, EDINBURGH, EH9 3EB.
CHISHOLM, Mr. Alan, FCA *1961;* 51 Greenbank Drive, South Hylton, SUNDERLAND, SR4 0JX. (Life Member)
CHISHOLM, Mr. Ashley Mackellaz, BA ACA *2006;* 33 Cologne Road, LONDON, SW11 2AH.
CHISHOLM, Mr. Brian Rodney, FCA *1969;* 19 Davenant Road, OXFORD, OX2 8BT.
CHISHOLM, Mr. Dean, BSc FCA *1987;* INVESCO Asset Management Pacific Limited, 32/F Three Pacific Place, 1 Queens Road East, WAN CHAI, HONG KONG ISLAND, HONG KONG SAR.
CHISHOLM, Miss. Fiona Louise, ACA *2009;* 11 Aire Close, ELLESMERE PORT, CH65 3DW.
CHISHOLM, Mr. James Alexander, BSc ACA *1992;* La Maladreme, Av Georges Coupois, Saillans, 26340 DROME, FRANCE.
CHISHOLM, Mrs. Joelie, MA(Hons) FCA *2001;* 90 MacPherson Street, BRONTE, NSW 2024, AUSTRALIA.
CHISHOLM, Mr. John Archibald, FCA *1972;* 32 Nightingale Road, RICKMANSWORTH, HERTFORDSHIRE, WD3 7DF. (Life Member)
CHISHOLM, Mr. Julian Roderick, MA BA FCA *1974;* 20 Arthur Road, WINCHESTER, SO23 7EA.
CHISHOLM, Mr. Keith, BSc ACA *1991;* 48 Sandington Drive, Cuddington, NORTHWICH, CHESHIRE, CW8 2ZD.
CHISHOLM, Mr. Martin, BSc ACA *1990;* 11 Farnell Place, Gulf Harbour, Whangaparoa, AUCKLAND 1463, NEW ZEALAND.
CHISHOLM, Mrs. Norma Margaret, ACA *1993;* (Tax Fac), 25 West Farm Avenue, ASHTEAD, SURREY, KT21 2LD.
CHISHOLM, Mr. Simon, BSc(Hons) ACA *2003;* 20 Woodland Drive, ST. ALBANS, HERTFORDSHIRE, AL4 0EU.
CHISHOLM, Mr. Simon Roy, BA ACA *1997;* Berenberg Bank, 60 Threadneedle Street, LONDON, EC2R 8HP.
CHISHOLM, Ms. Susan Patricia, BA ACA *1980;* Hartsholme, City Lane, Colmworth, BEDFORD, MK44 2LE.
CHISHOLM, Mr. Thomas Ellison, FCA *1947;* 15 Wykeham Gate, Haddenham, AYLESBURY, HP17 8DF. (Life Member)
CHISHTI, Mr. Aftab Ahmad, MA ACA *1980;* 11 ALI BLOCK, NEW GARDEN TOWN, LAHORE, PAKISTAN.
CHISLETT, Mr. David Colin, MSc ACA *2009;* 40 Roseville Street, St. Helier, JERSEY, JE2 4PJ.
•**CHISM, Mr. Nicholas James, MA FCA** *1994;* KPMG LLP, 15 Canada Square, LONDON, E14 5GL. See also KPMG Europe LLP
CHISM, Mr. Nigel William Michael Goddard, FCA *1979;* Flat 11 Sailmakers Court, William Morris Way, LONDON, SW6 2UX.
•**CHISNALL, Mr. Clive Antony, BA FCA** *1987;* (Tax Fac), Ryans, 67 Chorley Old Road, BOLTON, BL1 3AJ.
•**CHISNALL, Mr. Colin Haworth, FCA** *1977;* Chisnall & Co, 17 Stowell Close, ASHFORD, KENT, TN23 5HS.
CHISNALL, Mr. David Campbell, FCA *1964;* S T L Agencies Ltd, 48 Mount Street, LONDON, W1K 2SB.
CHISNALL, Mrs. Hilary Frances, FCA *1972;* 41 Overmead, SHOREHAM-BY-SEA, WEST SUSSEX, BN43 5NS. (Life Member)
CHISNELL, Mr. Paul Rowland Robert Kenneth, BSc ACA *1988;* The Poplars, 20 Stonyhurst Crescent, Culcheth, WARRINGTON, WA3 4DS.
CHISSELL, Miss. Nicola Jane, BA ACA *2000;* Flat 7, 118 Palace Road, Tulse Hill, LONDON, SW2 3JZ.
CHISSICK, Mr. Alan, FCA *1971;* 8 Redbridge Lane East, ILFORD, IG4 5ES.
•**CHITRODA, Mr. Jayanti Mandan, FCA FCCA** *1975;* Jay & Co London Limited, 15 Alexandria Road, Ealing, LONDON, W13 0NP.

CHITTENDEN, Dr. Stella Jane Rebecca, ACA *1990;* (Tax Fac), 1 Ivy Chase, PUDSEY, LS28 9LG.
CHITTLEBOROUGH, Mr. Christopher, BA(Hons) ACA *2011;* 44 Cuckoo Hill Drive, PINNER, MIDDLESEX, HA5 3PJ.
•**CHITTOCK, Mr. John Philip, FCA** *1969;* The Surrey Practice Limited, Tara, Tite Hill, Englefield Green, EGHAM, TW20 0NH.
CHITTY, Mr. Bernard Anthony, BA FCA *1977;* 30 Masons Rise, BROADSTAIRS, KENT, CT10 1AZ.
•**CHITTY, Mr. David William Kirkham, BA FCA** *1990;* MEMBER OF COUNCIL, Crowe Clark Whitehill LLP, St Bride's House, 10 Salisbury Square, LONDON, EC4Y 8EH. See also Horwath Clark Whitehill LLP and Crowe Clark Whitehill
CHITTY, Mr. Jonathan, LLB ACA *2001;* Unipart Group of Companies Unipart House, Garsington Road Cowley, OXFORD, OX4 2PG.
CHITTY, Mr. Jonathan Lees, BA ACA *1992;* 42 Linden Road, SMETHWICK, B66 4DY.
CHITTY, Mr. Julian, FCA *1961;* Kimberley, Water Lane, Speen, PRINCES RISBOROUGH, BUCKINGHAMSHIRE, HP27 0SW. (Life Member)
CHIU, Mr. Adolphus Kin Yan, ACA *2007;* 2421 Coppersmith Court, MISSISSAUGA L5L 3B5, ON, CANADA.
CHIU, Mr. Bing Fu Henry, ACA *2008;* Flat 4, 22/F, Mei Kwong Court, Aberdeen Centre, ABERDEEN, HONG KONG SAR.
CHIU, Ms. Chai Wing Grace, ACA *2008;* Sun Hing Group of Companies, 10/F, United Centre, 95 Queensway, ADMIRALTY, HONG KONG SAR.
CHIU, Mr. Ching Wai, ACA *2005;* Flat F13/ FBlock 2, Greenview Terrace, 6 Castle Peak Road, Ting Kau, TSEUNG KWAN O, NEW TERRITORIES HONG KONG SAR.
•**CHIU, Mr. Christopher Wan-Tuo, MA FCA** *1982;* Chew & Chiu, Level 7, 60 York Street, SYDNEY, NSW 2000, AUSTRALIA.
CHIU, Mr. Chun Hay, ACA *2007;* Flat H 18/F, Block 32, South Horizons, AP LEI CHAU, HONG KONG SAR.
CHIU, Mr. Chung Hoi, ACA *2007;* Room 2403 China Insurance Group Building, 141 Des Voeux Road Central, CENTRAL, HONG KONG SAR.
CHIU, Mr. David Chun Leong, LLB ACA *1989;* Chung Yuen Electrical Co Ltd, 4/F Acme Building, 22 Nanking Street, YAU MA TEI, KOWLOON, HONG KONG SAR.
CHIU, Miss. Elaine Man Yee, BA ACA *1983;* Suite 1109, 28 Empress Avenue, NORTH YORK M2N 6Z7, ON, CANADA.
CHIU, Mr. Fan Wa, ACA *2006;* Room 1001 Tower One, Admiralty Centre, 18 Harcourt Road, ADMIRALTY, HONG KONG ISLAND, HONG KONG SAR.
CHIU, Ms. Hau Yee Paulina, ACA *2008;* 36A Tower 2, Tierra Verde, TSING YI, HONG KONG SAR.
CHIU, Miss. Janice Mei Yung, MSc BA ACA CISA CIA *1993;* Flat 14A Wah Cheong Court, Fortune Plaza, On Chee Road, TAI PO, NEW TERRITORIES, HONG KONG SAR.
CHIU, Dr. Jessica, DPhil MChem ACA *2011;* Flat 4, 2 The Terrace, 136 Richmond Hill, RICHMOND, TW10 6RN.
CHIU, Mr. Ka Kui Kenneth, ACA *2005;* Flat F 18/F Block 2, Ronsdale Garden, 25 Tai Hang Drive, TAI HANG, HONG KONG ISLAND, HONG KONG SAR.
CHIU, Mr. Kenneth Yat Ting, ACA *2007;* Orient Overseas International Ltd, 33/F Harbour Centre, 25 Harbour Road, WAN CHAI, HONG KONG ISLAND, HONG KONG SAR.
CHIU, Mr. Kevin Kwok Yeung, MSc BSc ACA *2010;* Flat 20D Block 7, Villa Oceania, 8 On Chun Street, Ma On Shan, SHA TIN, NEW TERRITORIES HONG KONG SAR.
CHIU, Mr. Kim Boo, MA FCA *1976;* 177-18 Jalan Sarjana, Taman Connaught Cheras, 56000 KUALA LUMPUR, FEDERAL TERRITORY, MALAYSIA.
CHIU, Mr. Kwok Kit, ACA *2007;* (Tax Fac), 14/F Revenue Tower, 5 Gloucester Road, WAN CHAI, HONG KONG ISLAND, HONG KONG SAR.
CHIU, Ms. Lai Chun Rhoda, ACA *2007;* Flat 1105, On Tung House, Tung Tau Estate, KOWLOON TONG, HONG KONG SAR.
CHIU, Miss. Lai Kuen Susanna, BA ACA *1986;* 22B Fu Bon Court, Fortress Garden, 32 Fortress Hill Road, NORTH POINT, HONG KONG ISLAND, HONG KONG SAR.
CHIU, Mr. Man Kin, BSc ACA *1993;* 2903 Block A, Kornhill, QUARRY BAY, HONG KONG SAR.
CHIU, Ms. Man Yi Teresa, ACA *2008;* Flat C. 40/F Tower 9, Park Avenue, 18 Hoi Ting Road, TAI KOK TSUI, KOWLOON, HONG KONG SAR.
CHIU, Miss. Matilda Yik-Tze, BA ACA *1991;* 16B Block 4, Cavendish Heights, 33 Perkins Road, JARDINE'S LOOKOUT, HONG KONG ISLAND, HONG KONG SAR.
CHIU, Mr. Ming Chung Joe, ACA *2007;* Unit F 23/F., Tower 25, Laguna Verde, HUNG HOM, KOWLOON, HONG KONG SAR.
CHIU, Mr. Ngar Wing, ACA *2005;* 13/F Amber Commercial Building, 10 Morrison Hill Road, WAN CHAI, HONG KONG ISLAND, HONG KONG SAR.
CHIU, Mr. Pak Hei William, ACA *2010;* (Tax Fac), Flat 13B, Fortune Mansion, 28-36 Apliu Street, SHAM SHUI PO, KOWLOON, 852 HONG KONG SAR.
CHIU, Mr. Patrick Tsun-Ngai, ACA *2008;* 23 Oakhurst Close, ILFORD, IG6 2LT.
CHIU, Mr. Ping Chun, ACA *2008;* P. C. Chiu & Co, Room 1303, Cameron Commercial Centre, 458-468 Hennessy Road, CAUSEWAY BAY, HONG KONG SAR.
CHIU, Mr. Sebastien Say Phi, LLB ACA *2011;* 17 Whitehall Road, Handsworth, BIRMINGHAM, B21 9AY.
CHIU, Mr. Si Hon, ACA *1982;* First Floor, 163 Wong Nai Chung Road, HAPPY VALLEY, Hong Kong Island, HONG KONG SAR.
CHIU, Mr. Sin Keung Eddie, ACA *2008;* with Deloitte Touche Tohmatsu, 8-F Tower W2, The Towers, Oriental Plaza, 1 East Chang An Avenue, BEIJING 100738 CHINA.
CHIU, Mr. Sit Kit Elton, ACA *2005;* 160316/ FIsland Place Tower, 510 King's Road, NORTH POINT, HONG KONG ISLAND, HONG KONG SAR.
CHIU, Mrs. Soon Eng, ACA *1979;* P.O. Box 481, SIBU, Sarawak, MALAYSIA.
CHIU, Mr. Stanley Cheuk Chung, ACA *2009;* Flat 5 4/F, Ming Hoi House, Ming Nga Court, TAI PO, HONG KONG SAR.
CHIU, Mr. Sui Cheung, ACA *2006;* 18/F Taikang International Tower, 2 Wudinghou Street Xicheng District, BEIJING 100033, CHINA.
CHIU, Mr. Sze Kei, ACA *2007;* Deloitte Touche Tohmatsu, 8-F Tower W2, The Towers, Oriental Plaza, 1 East Chang An Avenue, BEIJING 100738 CHINA.
CHIU, Mr. Vincent Shung Wai, BA ACA *1993;* 4/F. 9-11 Lock Road, TSIM SHA TSUI, KOWLOON, HONG KONG SAR.
CHIU, Mr. Wing Ning, ACA *2008;* Unit G, 15/ F, Tower 3, The Belchers, 89 Pokfulam Road, POK FU LAM HONG KONG ISLAND HONG KONG SAR.
CHIU, Miss. Yvonne Sok Hua, ACA *1998;* Block 21 #15-05 Jalan Raja Udang The Arte@Thomson, SINGAPORE 329215, SINGAPORE.
CHIVA, Miss. Emma Louise, BSc ACA *2005;* 72 Sandringham Road, BRISTOL, BS4 3PP.
CHIVERS, Mrs. Alicia Daphne, BA ACA DChA *2004;* with Kingston Smith & Partners LLP, Devonshire House, 60 Goswell Road, LONDON, EC1M 7AD.
•**CHIVERS, Mrs. Amanda Jane, BSc ACA** *1997;* Certax Accounting (Chelmsford) Ltd, 44 Oak Lodge Tye, Springfield, CHELMSFORD, CM1 6GZ.
CHIVERS, Mr. Andrew Paul, BA(Hons) ACA *2005;* 9 Cottes Way, FAREHAM, PO14 3NB.
CHIVERS, Mr. Brian Arthur Calne, FCA *1972;* 25 Cambridge Avenue, NEW MALDEN, SURREY, KT3 4LD.
CHIVERS, Miss. Caroline Sophie, BSc(Hons) ACA *2005;* Skandia House, Skandia Life Assurance Co Ltd, PO Box 37, SOUTHAMPTON, SO14 7AY.
CHIVERS, Miss. Gemma May Meadley, ACA *2007;* MML Capital Partners, Grand Buildings, 1-3 Strand, LONDON, WC2N 5HR.
CHIVERS, Mr. Graham John, FCA *1974;* 42 Meadow Park, Bathford, BATH, BA1 7PY.
CHIVERS, Mr. Graham John, BSc ACA *2009;* 3 Thrower Place, DORKING, RH5 4GD.
•**CHIVERS, Mr. Jeremy Charles Alistair, BSc ACA FCCA CIOT MIMgt** *2007;* (Tax Fac), Chivers & Co, 15 St. James Road, LONDON, E15 1RL. See also Tuson & Partners Limited
CHIVERS, Mrs. Karyn Julie, BA ACA *1998;* 93b Brook Street, Soham, ELY, CAMBRIDGESHIRE, CB7 5AE.
•**CHIVERS, Mr. Nicholas James, FCA** *1982;* (Tax Fac), Sully Partnership, 8 Unity Street, College Green, BRISTOL, BS1 5HH. See also Sully Partnership Limited
CHIVERS, Mr. Paul, FCA *1965;* Pendowrie Manor, Upton Cross, LISKEARD, CORNWALL, PL14 5AA. (Life Member)
CHIVERS, Mr. Peter Michael, FCA *1975;* London Metropolitan University, 166-220 Holloway Road, LONDON, N7 8DB.
CHIVERS, Ms. Sarah, BSc ACA *1996;* Flat 17 Blue Building, Gunwharf Quays, PORTSMOUTH, PO1 3ET.
CHIVERTON, Mr. David, BA ACA *1982;* 7 Crossfield Avenue, LYMM, WA13 0JL.
•**CHIZANA, Ms. Thandiwe Fadzai, ACA** *2007;* Number Solutions Limited, Rolling Woods, Walpole Drive, Ramsey, ISLE OF MAN, IM8 1LX.
CHLADEK, Mrs. Joanne Lesley, BA ACA *1998;* 23 Alma Road, REIGATE, SURREY, RH2 0DH.
CHLADEK, Mr. Mark Peter, BSc ACA *1998;* 23 Alma Road, REIGATE, SURREY, RH2 0DH.
CHMIELEWSKI, Mr. Michal, ACA *2011;* Flat 5 1 Windsor Terrace, 37 St. Marks Road St. Helier, JERSEY, JE2 4LD.
CHNG, Ms. Lu Ling, BA(Hons) ACA *2003;* Swiss RE Properties Ltd, 30 St. Mary Axe, LONDON, EC3A 8EP.
CHNG, Mr. Seh Chong, ACA *1981;* 2C Dunbar Walk, SINGAPORE 459269, SINGAPORE.
CHO, Mr. Choo Meng, ACA *1982;* PricewaterhouseCoopers, 16th Floor Bangunan KWSP, Jalan Sultan Ahmad Shah, PO Box 856, 10810 PULAU PINANG, MALAYSIA.
CHO, Ms. Cynthia Wing Shan, MBS BSc ACA CTA *2009;* 34 Melrose Gardens, EDGWARE, MIDDLESEX, HA8 5LN.
CHO, Mr. Kui Keung Gilbert, ACA *2011;* (Tax Fac), Flat A 19/F Block 14, Chengtu House, 92 Tsuen King Circuit, Tsuen Wan Centre, TSUEN WAN, NT HONG KONG SAR.
CHO, Ms. Suet Man Mikado, ACA *2009;* Flat D, 20/F Block 9 Ocean Shores, TSEUNG KWAN O, NEW TERRITORIES, HONG KONG SAR.
CHOATE, Mr. Stephen Lawrence, PhD BSc ACA *1988;* 33a West Hill Avenue, EPSOM, KT19 8LE.
•**CHOCKALINGAM, Mr. Ramasamy, FCA** *1995;* JURONG EAST STREET 21, BLOCK 287 B # 12 - 342, SINGAPORE 602287, SINGAPORE.
CHOE, Mr. Christopher Keat, BA FCA *1988;* 9A Berrima Road, SINGAPORE 299924, SINGAPORE.
•**CHOHAN, Miss. Neela Narshi, FCA** *1975;* Balfour Sanson, 17 Bourne Court, Southend Road, WOODFORD GREEN, ESSEX, IG8 8HD.
CHOHAN, Miss. Nina, BA ACA *2007;* with PKF (UK) LLP, Pannell House, 159 Charles Street, LEICESTER, LE1 1LD.
CHOHAN, Mr. Sandeep Singh, ACA *2008;* 87 Oakwood Crescent, GREENFORD, MIDDLESEX, UB6 0RG.
CHOHAN, Mr. Shushilkumar, BSc ACA *1994;* MUSIC MARKETING SERVICES LTD, UNIT 1 92 LOTS ROAD, LONDON, SW10 0QD.
CHOHAN, Mrs. Trishna, BSc ACA *1985;* 41 Guinea Crescent, Westwood Heath, COVENTRY, CV4 8HW.
CHOI, Ms. Bik Hok, ACA *2005;* 22C Block 4, Provident Centre, 27 Wharf Road, NORTH POINT, HONG KONG SAR.
CHOI, Mr. Chi Leong Ivan, ACA *2007;* Sumitomo Mitsui Banking Corporation, 7/F One International Finance Centre, 1 Harbour View Street, CENTRAL, HONG KONG SAR.
CHOI, Mr. Fan Wai, ACA *2007;* Elmore Capital Limited, 3603 The Centre, 99 Queen's Road, CENTRAL, HONG KONG ISLAND, HONG KONG SAR.
CHOI, Ms. Gina, ACA *2005;* Sims Asia Holdings Ltd, Room 5501-03, 55/F Hopewell Centre, 183 Queens Road East, WAN CHAI, HONG KONG ISLAND HONG KONG SAR.
CHOI, Mr. Jonathan Doun, BSc(Hons) ACA *2011;* 28 Middle Road, HARROW, MIDDLESEX, HA2 0HL.
CHOI, Mr. Kam Chong Joseph, ACA *1980;* 7 The Witheys, Grange Park, NORTHAMPTON, NN4 5BR.
CHOI, Miss. Kit Yi, BA ACA *1991;* 30E Tower 2, Les Saisons 28 Tai On Street, SAI WAN HO, HONG KONG ISLAND, HONG KONG SAR.
CHOI, Mr. Kwok Yui, ACA *2005;* K. L. Young & Co., 20th Floor Capitol Centre, 5-19 Jardine's Bazaar, CAUSEWAY BAY, HONG KONG ISLAND, HONG KONG SAR.
CHOI, Mr. Kwong Yu, ACA *2008;* Baker Tilly Hong Kong Limited, 2nd Floor, 625 Kings Road, NORTH POINT, HONG KONG SAR.
CHOI, Mr. Man Ban, ACA *1979;* 23 Parsborough Court, SCARBOROUGH M1B 4Y2, ON, CANADA.
CHOI, Mr. Man On, BSc FCA *1986;* 25/F Wing On Centre, 111 Connaught Road, CENTRAL, HONG KONG SAR.
CHOI, Mr. Man Kwong, ACA *2007;* 9A Manrich Court, 33 St Francis Street, WAN CHAI, HONG KONG SAR.
CHOI, Mr. Michael Man-Chau, FCA *1982;* Credence and Partners CPA, 12/F Kam Sang Building, 255-257 Des Vouex Road, CENTRAL, HONG KONG SAR. See also NCN CPA Limited
CHOI, Miss. Minna Jung Min, ACA CA(NZ) *2009;* 38 Shipwright Road, LONDON, SE16 6QA.
CHOI, Mr. Onward, ACA *2004;* 28/F SP Tower D Tsinghua Science Park, No. 1 Zhongguancun East Road, Haidian District, BEIJING 100084, CHINA.
CHOI, Mr. Pang Lin Philip, ACA *2008;* Philip P L Choi & Co, 2702-6 Lucky Commercial Centre, 103-9 Des Voeux Road West, CENTRAL, HONG KONG SAR.
CHOI, Ms. Po Yee Alice, ACA *2008;* 29 Thomson Road, 2/F, Flat D, WAN CHAI, HONG KONG SAR.
CHOI, Miss. Pui Fong, BSocSc FCA *1984;* 6a Jonsim Place, 228 Queen's Road East, WAN CHAI, Hong Kong Island, HONG KONG SAR.
CHOI, Miss. Sarah, ACA *2010;* 4 Mayfair House, Piccadilly, YORK, YO1 9QJ.
CHOI, Ms. Sau Chu, ACA *2008;* 31A, Block 6, La Cite Noble, 1 Ngan O Road, TSEUNG KWAN O, NEW TERRITORIES HONG KONG SAR.
CHOI, Ms. Shuen Kuen Erica, ACA *2008;* K H Law & Company, Block A, 4/F, Hillier Commercial Building, 65-67 Bonham Strand East, CENTRAL HONG KONG SAR.
CHOI, Ms. Shuet Chun, ACA *2007;* Flat B, 10F, On Ping Mansion, No. 62, Lei King Road, LEI KING WAN HONG KONG SAR.
CHOI, Mr. Tze Kit Sammy, ACA *2005;* YWC & Partners, 15th Floor, Empire Land Commercial Centre, 81-85 Lockhart Road, WAN CHAI, HONG KONG ISLAND HONG KONG SAR.
CHOI, Mr. Wai Hong Clifford, ACA *2008;* Flat 27B Tower 4, South Horizons, AP LEI CHAU, HONG KONG SAR.
CHOI, Miss. Yee Ling, BA ACA *2010;* 12 Harmsworth Drive, STOCKPORT, CHESHIRE, SK4 4RP.
CHOI, Ms. Yee May, ACA *2008;* Flat F13 Floor, King Tien Mansion, Horizon Garden, 18D Taikoo Shing Road, TAIKOO SHING, HONG KONG ISLAND HONG KONG SAR.
CHOI, Mr. Yi Kwong, ACA *2007;* Flat 1 30/F Block A, Galaxia, 3 Lung Poon Street, DIAMOND HILL, KOWLOON, HONG KONG SAR.
CHOISY, Mrs. Amanda Mary, BSc ACA *1998;* Home Farm Lodge, 12 Kettering Road, Stanion, KETTERING, NORTHAMPTONSHIRE, NN14 1DH.
CHOITRAM, Miss. Kavita Lalchand, BA ACA *2006;* Flat 9, 24 Nevern Place, LONDON, SW5 9PR.
CHOKRA, Mr. Akhil, ACA *1996;* Honeywell House, Arlington Business Park, Downshire Way, BRACKNELL, BERKSHIRE, RG12 1EB.
CHOKSHI, Mr. Krishna, ACA *2009;* 119 Providence Square, LONDON, SE1 2ED.
CHOKSHI, Miss. Radhika, ACA *2011;* 119 Providence Square, LONDON, SE1 2ED.
CHOKSHI, Mr. Rajeev, ACA *2010;* 34 Newbury Road, ILFORD, ESSEX, IG2 7HD.
•**CHOKSY, Mr. Haji Arif, FCA** *1977;* Choksy Associates, PO Box 11529, DUBAI, 75500, UNITED ARAB EMIRATES.
CHOLERTON, Mr. Simon David, BEng ACA *2006;* 85 Oaklands, South Godstone, GODSTONE, RH9 8HX.
CHOLMELEY, Mr. John Montague, FCA *1964;* Banca March, Miguel de Cervantes 6, 07730 ALAIOR, MENORCA, SPAIN. (Life Member)
CHOLMONDELEY-CLARKE, Mr. Edward Stanhope Kyle, BA ACA *1978;* 7 Adie Road, LONDON, W6 0PW.
CHOMOKO, Mrs. Latifa, ACA *2009;* 19 Swan Island, Strawberry Vale, TWICKENHAM, TW1 4RP.
CHONG, Mr. Chiew Yin, FCA *1974;* Vy Aux Vergnes 4, 1295 MIES, SWITZERLAND.
CHONG, Mr. Cho Kheen, ACA *1982;* 38 Wareemba Avenue, THORNLEIGH, NSW 2120, AUSTRALIA.
CHONG, Mr. Chung Yik Jimmy, FCA *1972;* 23 Stanley Street, Nedlands, PERTH, WA 6009, AUSTRALIA. (Life Member)
CHONG, Mr. Clarence Ho Yin, BSc FCA *1991;* FLAT 32 E, NO. 1 STAR STREET, WAN CHAI, HONG KONG ISLAND, HONG KONG SAR.
CHONG, Mr. David Eng-Tee, BCom ACA *1991;* Kuala Lumpur Kepong Berhad, Level 8 Menara Batu Kawan, No. 1 Jalan PJU 7/6, Mutiara Damansara, 47810 PETALING JAYA, MALAYSIA.
CHONG, Mr. Fong Fatt, FCA *1982;* E1 01 4, Pantai Hillpark Phase I, 59200 KUALA LUMPUR, FEDERAL TERRITORY, MALAYSIA.
CHONG, Miss. Gillian Valerie Tze Yen, BSc CA ACA ACCA *2009;* with Peter Chong & Co, 51 Changkat Bukit Bintang, 50200 KUALA LUMPUR, FEDERAL TERRITORY, MALAYSIA.
•**CHONG, Mr. Gregory Chong Khiat, BSc ACA** *1979;* UHY Hacker Young LLP, Quadrant House, 4 Thomas More Square, LONDON, E1W 1YW.

CHONG, Mr. Hai Heong, FCA *1974;* 2 Jalan SS 22A/5, Damansara Jaya, 47400 PETALING JAYA, SELANGOR, MALAYSIA.
CHONG, Ms. Heather Jane, BSc ACA *1983;* Qew Orchards, PO Box 182, RICHMOND, TAS 7025, AUSTRALIA.
CHONG, Mr. James Ki Woi, BSc ACA *1993;* 19 LINGKUNGAN DESA TAMAN DESA, 58100 KUALA LUMPUR, MALAYSIA.
CHONG, Mr. Jason, BA ACA *2006;* 169 Oulton Road, LOWESTOFT, SUFFOLK, NR32 4QT.
CHONG, Miss. Jennifer Margaret, ACA *2004;* 10 Howitt Close, Howitt Road, LONDON, NW3 4LX.
CHONG, Ms. Kar Wui, BSc ACA *1991;* 125 Arthur Road Apt 10-02, Arthur Mansions, SINGAPORE 439829, SINGAPORE.
CHONG, Mr. Ki Fung, ACA *2005;* Flat A 8/F, May Bong Mansion, 221 Sai Yeung Choi Street North, SHAM SHUI PO, KOWLOON, HONG KONG SAR.
CHONG, Mr. Kim Tong, BSc FCA *1991;* 55/F, Two International Finance Centre, 8 Finance Street, CENTRAL, HONG KONG ISLAND, HONG KONG SAR.
CHONG, Mr. Koh Ying, FCA *1977;* 9 Packham Crescent, GLEN WAVERLEY, VIC 3150, AUSTRALIA.
CHONG, Mr. Kok Hoong, BA ACA *2005;* 2611 Twin Oaks Court #136, DECATUR, IL 62526, UNITED STATES.
CHONG, Mr. Kwok Shing, ACA *2008;* Flat C, 5/F, Block 1, King's Park Villa, 1 King's Park Rise, HO MAN TIN KOWLOON HONG KONG SAR.
CHONG, Miss. Lisa Pei-Ting, BSc ACA *2010;* Caxton FX Ltd, 4-5 Grosvenor Place, LONDON, SW1X 7HJ.
CHONG, Mr. Martin, MEng ACA *2009;* 23 Arundel Court, Duppas Road, CROYDON, CR0 4BP.
CHONG, Mr. Min Lai Nikki, ACA *2008;* Flat G, 15/F, Block 7, The Sherwood, 8 Fuk Hang Tsuen Road, TUEN MUN NEW TERRITORIES HONG KONG SAR.
CHONG, Mr. Pak Wei, BA ACA *1986;* Flat G 42/F Tower 6, Park Central, 9 Tong Tak Street, TSEUNG KWAN O, NEW TERRITORIES, HONG KONG SAR.
CHONG, Mr. Paul Choong Leong, MBA LLB FCA *1992;* 12B Riviera Mansion, 59-65 Paterson Street, CAUSEWAY BAY, HONG KONG ISLAND, HONG KONG SAR.
CHONG, Miss. Pei Kian, ACA *2008;* Blk 657 Choa Chu Kang Crescent No12-41, SINGAPORE 680657, SINGAPORE.
CHONG, Mr. Peng Oon, FCA *1975;* Flat B 45/ Floor Block 2, Seaview Crescent, TUNG CHUNG, NEW TERRITORIES, HONG KONG SAR.
•**CHONG, Mr. Peter Ton Nen, FCA** *1973;* Peter Chong & Co, 51 Changkat Bukit Bintang, 50200 KUALA LUMPUR, FEDERAL TERRITORY, MALAYSIA.
•**CHONG, Mr. Shun, BA(Hons) ACA** *2001;* J V Wilson & Co, 41a Chambers Street, HERTFORD, SG14 1PL.
CHONG, Ms. Siew Shiam Polly, BSc ACA *1983;* 3 Lochee Place, STIRLING, ACT 2611, AUSTRALIA.
CHONG, Mr. Sin Fong, ACA *1980;* 72 Newnham Way, HARROW, HA3 9NT.
CHONG, Miss. Sok Yuen, BA ACA *1992;* Trane Air Conditioning Co. Ltd., 10/F Raffles City, 268 Xi Zang Road Central, SHANGHAI 200001, CHINA.
CHONG, Miss. Stephanie Kar Cheng, BSc ACA *2009;* Flat 100, 46 Palmers Road, LONDON, E2 0TD.
CHONG, Mr. Stephen Frederick, MBA ACA *1980;* Unit 17/215 Pacific Highway, HORNSBY, NSW 2077, AUSTRALIA.
CHONG, Ms. Sue Ching, BSc(Econ) ACA *2001;* 19C Tower 3, Grand Promenade, 38 Tai Hong Street, SAI WAN HO, HONG KONG ISLAND, HONG KONG SAR.
CHONG, Mr. Tam Chee, ACA *1988;* Deloitte & Touche, 6 Shenton Way, 32-00, DBS Building Tower Two, SINGAPORE 068809, SINGAPORE.
CHONG, Mr. Tet On, FCA *1971;* Moore Stephens, 8A Jalan Sri Semantan Satu, Damansara Heights, 50490 KUALA LUMPUR, FEDERAL TERRITORY, MALAYSIA.
CHONG, Ms. Theresa Choon-Ngor, FCA *1971;* N2 Na Hale O Keauhou, 78-6833 Alii Drive, KAILUA, HI 96740, UNITED STATES.
CHONG, Mr. Vincent Tao Boon, BSc ACA *1986;* 10/F, Flat D, Hilltop Mansion, 60 Cloud View Road, NORTH POINT, HONG KONG ISLAND HONG KONG SAR.
CHONG, Miss. Wai Hong, ACA *2008;* Flat 130 Holly Court, Greenroof Way, LONDON, SE10 0BP.
CHONG, Mr. Wei Man Wilman, ACA *2008;* 32/F, The Lee Gardens, 33 Hysan Avenue, CAUSEWAY BAY, HONG KONG SAR.
CHONG, Miss. Wui Jean, BSc ACA *2010;* No 2 Jalan SS22A/5, Damansara Jayla, PETALING JAYA, SELANGOR, MALAYSIA.
CHONG, Mr. Yee Cheung, ACA *2008;* Flat B 48/F, Block 5 Liberte, 833 Lai Chi Kok Road, SHAM SHUI PO, KOWLOON, HONG KONG SAR.
CHONG, Miss. Yen Ting, ACA *2010;* 8 Jalan Helang 3, Bandar Puchong Jaya, 47100 PETALING JAYA, SELANGOR, MALAYSIA.
CHONG, Mr. Yiu Kan Sherman, ACA *2008;* Sherman Chong & Co, Suite 902, 9th Floor, Parkes Commercial Centre, No. 2-8 Parkes Street, TSIM SHA TSUI KOWLOON HONG KONG SAR.
CHONG, Mr. Yoon Hor, BA ACA *2001;* 175 West 93rd Street, Apartment 7C, NEW YORK, NY 10025, UNITED STATES.
CHONG, Mr. Yoon Khian, FCA *1977;* 88 Thurlow Park Road, West Dulwich, LONDON, SE21 8HY.
CHOO, Mr. Chee Fatt, ACA *1981;* 299 Whitchurch Lane, EDGWARE, HA8 6RA.
CHOO, Miss. Serena Sien Huei, BSc(Econ) ACA *2002;* #06-03 tanglin park 5A ridley park, SINGAPORE 248477, SINGAPORE.
CHOO, Miss. Sook Yean, BSc(Econ) ACA *1999;* Apartment 368 Metro Central Heights, 119 Newington Causeway, LONDON, SE1 6DX.
CHOO, Mr. Teck Song, FCA *1975;* Largo Cav.di Vittorio Veneto 4, 05010 PORANO, ITALY. (Life Member)
CHOO, Mr. Vincent, ACA ACMA *2009;* Mapletree Vietnam Management Consultancy Co.Ltd, 18 L2 - 1 Tao Luc 5 Street (VSIP II), Singapore Industrial Park II, Binh Duong Industry, THU DAU MOT, BING DUONG PROVINCE VIETNAM.
CHOO, Mr. Weng-Choong, FCA *1973;* Railway Cottage, 94 Stow Road, Magdalen, KING'S LYNN, NORFOLK, PE34 3BB.
•**CHOO KIM PIN, Mr. Chau Shyan, BSc ACA AMCT** *1998;* CKP, 141 Queen Anne Avenue, BROMLEY, BR2 0SH.
CHOOI, Mr. Alvin, LLB ACA *2003;* 16A Jervois Lane, #02-06 Clydesview, SINGAPORE 159192, SINGAPORE.
CHOOLUN, Miss. Annika Roma, BA ACA *2011;* 16 Hadley Avenue, WORTHING, WEST SUSSEX, BN14 9HB.
CHOOLUN, Miss. Gyanisha, ACA *2011;* 5 Cotterell Gardens, Twyford, READING, RG10 0XP.
CHOON, Ms. Cheng Cheng, ACA *2011;* 41 Lorong Burung Bayan 2, Taman Bukit Maluri, Kepong, 52100 KUALA LUMPUR, FEDERAL TERRITORY, MALAYSIA.
CHOON, Miss. Siew Wah, BA ACA *1980;* Apt No A-G-1, Sutera Bukit Tunku Condo, 20A Jalan Tun Ismail, 50480 KUALA LUMPUR, FEDERAL TERRITORY, MALAYSIA.
CHOONG, Miss. Anne-Marie, BSc ACA *2011;* 10 Moorfield Road, UXBRIDGE, MIDDLESEX, UB8 3SL.
CHOONG, Ms. Grace, ACA *2011;* Flat 5 Selsey Court, Fairfield Street, LONDON, SW18 1DS.
CHOONG, Mr. Khuat Leok Lionel, BA FCA CF *1989;* Zenith Professionals Limited, Room 4304 43rd Floor, China Resources Bldg, 26 Harbour Road, WAN CHAI, HONG KONG ISLAND HONG KONG SAR.
CHOONG, Miss. Nai Kang, BSc ACA *2000;* 115 Jalan Pokok Sakat, 41100 KLANG, SELANGOR, MALAYSIA.
CHOONG, Mr. Sek Wai, ACA *1988;* 116 Tinakori Road, Thorndon, WELLINGTON 6011, NEW ZEALAND.
CHOONG, Mr. Show Tong, ACA *1982;* 7 Jalan Bukit Segar 6, Taman Bukit Segar, Cheras, 56100 KUALA LUMPUR, FEDERAL TERRITORY, MALAYSIA.
CHOONG, Mr. Sin Kheong, ACA *1983;* Blk 31 Bedok, South Avenue 2, 18 - 305, SINGAPORE 460031, SINGAPORE.
•**CHOONG, Mr. Thean Yew, FCA** *1979;* Nexus Capital Finance LLP, Greener House, 66-68 Haymarket, LONDON, SW1Y 4RF.
CHOONG, Mr. Wei Yih, ACA *2009;* 33 JALAN PJU 1A/29, ARA DAMANSARA, PJ, 47301 PETALING JAYA, SELANGOR, MALAYSIA.
CHOPPING, Mr. Clive David, BA ACA *1985;* Fairholme High Street, Gislingham, EYE, SUFFOLK, IP23 8JD.
•**CHOPPING, Mr. David Michael, BA ACA** *1989;* Moore Stephens LLP, 150 Aldersgate Street, LONDON, EC1A 4AB. See also Moore Stephens & Co
CHOPRA, Mr. Ashoke, BSc ACA *1998;* 5 The Croft, Collingham, WETHERBY, WEST YORKSHIRE, LS22 5LG.
•**CHOPRA, Mrs. Kamal Jit, FCA** *1979;* Kamal J. Chopra, 46 Drake Road, CHESSINGTON, SURREY, KT9 1LW.
CHOPRA, Mr. Peter David, LLB ACA CF *1992;* 5 Walpole Avenue, RICHMOND, TW9 2DJ.
CHOPRA, Miss. Poonam, ACA *2010;* 2 Tintern Close, SLOUGH, SL1 2TB.
CHOPRA, Mr. Rahul, BA ACA *2007;* 46 Drake Road, CHESSINGTON, KT9 1LW.
•**CHOPRA, Mr. Rajeev Kishore, BSc ACA** *1986;* Deloitte LLP, Athene Place, 66 Shoe Lane, LONDON, EC4A 3BQ. See also Deloitte & Touche LLP
CHOPRA, Mr. Robin Krishnan, BSc ACA *1992;* Littlewood House, Mile Path, WOKING, SURREY, GU22 0DY.
CHOPRA, Mr. Sanjeev, FCA *1974;* C-1 Panchsheel Enclave, NEW DELHI 110017, CAPITAL TERRITORY OF DELHI, INDIA.
CHOPRA, Mr. Sanjeev Kumar, BSc FCA *1999;* 10 St Barnabas Road, SUTTON, SM1 4NL.
CHOPRA, Mr. Subhash, BA ACA *1979;* 21 Hill Barn, SOUTH CROYDON, Surrey, CR2 0RU. (Life Member)
•**CHOPRA, Mr. Sunil, ACA** *1992;* (Tax Fac), Brackman Chopra LLP, 8 Fairfax Mansions, Finchley Road Swiss Cottage, LONDON, NW3 6JY.
CHOPRA, Mr. Tribhawan Kumar, FCA *1975;* 4 Marble Faun Lane, WINDSOR, CT 06095, UNITED STATES.
CHORLEY, Mr. Adrian Neill, ACA *1986;* 2nd Floor, 8 - 10 Old Jewry, LONDON, EC2R 8Dn.
CHORLEY, Mr. Christopher Robert Hopkinson, BSc ACA *1993;* Aviva International Insurance Ltd St. Helens, 1 Undershaft, LONDON, EC3P 3DQ.
CHORLEY, Mrs. Katie, LLB ACA *2003;* 37 Bolton Road, WINDSOR, BERKSHIRE, SL4 3JX.
CHORLEY, Lord Roger Richard Edward, BA FCA *1958;* 9 Melbourne House, 50 Kensington Place, LONDON, W8 7PW. (Life Member)
CHORLTON, Mrs. Angela Helen, BSc ACA *2003;* 2 Woodlands Road, STALYBRIDGE, CHESHIRE, SK15 2SQ.
CHORMOVITIS, Mr. Panagiotis, BSc ACA *2010;* Kalamos Attikis, Stylianou Margeta Str 1, 19017 ATHENS, GREECE.
CHOTAI, Mr. Anish, ACA *2009;* 55 Cranleigh Drive, Brooklands, SALE, CHESHIRE, M33 3PN.
CHOTAI, Mrs. Anita, MA ACA *1996;* 2 Gloucester Road, LONDON, SW7 4RB.
•**CHOTAI, Mr. Jashvant Jagjivan, BSc FCA** *1976;* 48 Harrowes Meade, EDGWARE, MIDDLESEX, HA8 8RP.
•**CHOTAI, Mr. Manish Manish, FCA** *1986;* Chotai & Co, 3 Ambassador House, Wolseley Road, HARROW, HA3 5RT.
CHOTAI, Mr. Nishit Gokaldas, BSc ACA *1993;* 20 Lyon Meade, STANMORE, MIDDLESEX, HA7 1JA.
•**CHOTAI, Mr. Piyoosh Kamarshibhai, ACA** *1979;* Waremoss Ltd, 6 Bolton Close, Bellbrook Business Park, UCKFIELD, EAST SUSSEX, TN22 1PH.
CHOTAI, Mr. Prakash, BSc(Econ) ACA *2010;* 23 Leaver Gardens, Western Avenue, GREENFORD, MIDDLESEX, UB6 8EW.
•**CHOTHANI, Mr. Devshi, BSc FCA** *1990;* (Tax Fac), DBF Associates, South Cheetham Business Centre, 10 Park Place, MANCHESTER, M4 4EY.
CHOU, Mr. Andrew Wei Yew, BSc ACA *1995;* No 2, SS 1/30, 47300 PETALING JAYA, SELANGOR, MALAYSIA.
CHOU, Ms. Sonia Yan-Yan, BA ACA *2000;* AT & T, 4th Floor, Cardinal Place, 80 Victoria Street, LONDON, SW1E 5JL.
CHOU, Mr. William Kam Cheong, ACA *2007;* Deloitte Touche Tohmatsu, 8-F Tower W2, The Towers, Oriental Plaza, 1 East Chang An Avenue, BEIJING 100738 CHINA.
CHOUDHARI, Mr. Udit, ACA *2009;* Flat 3 Waterford Court, 18 Daventry Street, LONDON, NW1 6TD.
•**CHOUDHARY, Mr. Noor Ullah, ACA** *2010;* Capshire Consulting Limited, 15 Heath Mead, Wimbledon, LONDON, SW19 5JP.
CHOUDHARY, Dr. Saad, ACA *2009;* KPMG, Salisbury Square, LONDON, EC478BB.
CHOUDHRI, Mrs. Nicola Marion, BA ACA *1999;* Diageo plc, 801 Main Avenue, NORWALK, CT 06851, UNITED STATES.
CHOUDHRY, Mr. Adeel, ACA *2010;* 20 Sutherland Drive, Moseley, BIRMINGHAM, B13 8AY.
CHOUDHRY, Mr. Mohamed Pervaze, ACA *1980;* P.O. Box 212118, DUBAI, UNITED ARAB EMIRATES.
CHOUDHRY, Mr. Obaid, BA ACA *2011;* 13 Golds Hill Road, BIRMINGHAM, B21 9DG.
CHOUDHRY, Mr. Sohail, MSc BSc ACA *2007;* Flat 6 Connaught Court, LONDON, W2 2AJ.
CHOUDHURI, Mr. Avik, BSc ACA *2006;* Royal Bank of Scotland, 135 Bishopsgate, LONDON, EC2M 3UR.
CHOUDHURY, Mr. Abdul Hafiz, FCA *1966;* House No. 34, Road No. 1 Block J, Banani, DHAKA, BANGLADESH.
CHOUDHURY, Miss. Angela, BA ACA *1997;* Queen Mary University of London, 327 Mile End Road, LONDON, E1 4NS.
CHOUDHURY, Mr. Fayezul Haque, MA FCA *1978;* 5121 Fairglen lane, CHEVY CHASE, MD 20815, UNITED STATES.
CHOUDHURY, Mr. Jahurul Islam, BSc(Hons) ACA *2010;* Flat 14, Redmond House, Barnsbury Estate, LONDON, N1 0TN.
CHOUDHURY, Miss. Jasmin, BSc(Hons) ACA *2003;* 11 Burrow Road, LONDON, SE22 8DU.
•**CHOUDHURY, Mr. Kamran Idris, FCA** *1981;* A Qasem & Co, Gulshan Pink City, Suites 01-03 Level 7, Plot No. 15 Road No. 103, Gulshan Avenue, DHAKA 1212 BANGLADESH.
CHOUDHURY, Mr. Mansoor Ali Asghar, BSc ACA *2008;* with Myers Clark Limited, Iveco House, Station Road, WATFORD, WD17 1DL.
•**CHOUDHURY, Mr. Mohammad Asghar, FCA** *1972;* Nazman, Rutland House, 114-116 Manningham Lane, BRADFORD, WEST YORKSHIRE, BD8 7JF. See also Bradford Accountancy Services
•**CHOUDHURY, Dr. Mohammed Sanawar Islam, PhD BA(Hons) FCA** *1993;* RCi Audit and Assurance Services Limited, 3rd Floor, 2-12 Victoria Street, LUTON, BEDFORDSHIRE, LU1 2UA. See also RCi (Luton) Limited
CHOUDHURY, Mr. Nathan, BA ACA *2011;* Apartment 18 Globe View, 10 High Timber Street, LONDON, EC4V 3PL.
CHOUDHURY, Mr. Robin, BSc ACA *1988;* 51 Winsham Grove, Clapham, LONDON, SW11 6NB.
CHOUDHURY, Mr. Sandip, BSc ACA *2006;* 177 Colney Hatch Lane, LONDON, N10 1EY.
CHOUDHURY, Mr. Shafiques Samad, MSc ACA *1995;* 7 Ridgemead Close, LONDON, N14 6NW.
CHOUDHURY, Mr. Sultan Ahmed, BA ACA *1998;* 15 Clarence Road Moseley, BIRMINGHAM, B13 9SX.
CHOUDREE, Mr. Dinesh, ACA CA(SA) *2010;* 4 Hyde Place, Summertown, OXFORD, OX2 7JB.
CHOUDREY, Mr. Mohammed Zaheer, BA ACA *1995;* 10 Rowdon Avenue, LONDON, NW10 2AL.
CHOUDREY, Mr. Zameer Mohammed, BA FCA *1985;* 2 Rowdon Avenue, LONDON, NW10 2AL.
CHOUDRI, Mr. Naveed, BSocSc ACA *1996;* 315 West 36th Street, Apartment 12C, NEW YORK, NY 10018, UNITED STATES.
CHOUDRIE, Mr. Kiran Roy, BA(Hons) ACA *2002;* 31 Batford Road, HARPENDEN, HERTFORDSHIRE, AL5 5AT.
CHOUDRIE, Mr. Paramjeet Kumar, FCA *1970;* Sarnen House, Moreton Paddox, Moreton Morrell, WARWICK, CV35 9BT. (Life Member)
CHOUHAN, Mrs. Sushmadevi, LLM LLB ACA *2004;* (Tax Fac), 82 Broadway North, WALSALL, WS1 2QF.
CHOUHAN, Mrs. Usha, BA ACA *2007;* 29 Elm Tree Avenue, Glenfield, LEICESTER, LE3 8QA.
CHOUKSEY, Mr. Nikhil, MA BSc ACA *2009;* 3 Ebner Street, LONDON, SW18 1BT.
CHOULS, Miss. Bonnie, ACA *2009;* with Ernst & Young LLP, 1 More London Place, LONDON, SE1 2AF.
•**CHOURDAKIS, Mr. Michael, MSc ACA** *2000;* Ernst & Young, 11 KLM National Road, Athens Lamia, Metamorphosi, PC 14451 ATHENS, GREECE. See also Ernst & Young Europe LLP
CHOURRES, Mr. Onisiforos, MSc BSc ACA *2009;* Flat 2, 145 George Street, LONDON, W1H 5LB.
CHOUX, Mr. Nicholas John, BSc ACA *1994;* Threadneedle Asset Management Holbrook House, Station Road, SWINDON, SN1 1HH.
CHOVIL, Mr. Edward Roger Clive, FCA *1969;* Field House, 8 Danes Way, Oxshott, LEATHERHEAD, KT22 0LX.
CHOW, Mr. Andrew, BSc ACA *1993;* 229 Washway Road, SALE, CHESHIRE, M33 4AL.
CHOW, Mr. Chee Yan, ACA *1981;* 6 Jalan SS21\48, Damansara Utama, PETALING JAYA, SELANGOR, 47400, MALAYSIA.
CHOW, Mr. Chi Tong, ACA *2006;* Ting Ho Kwan & Chan, 9th Floor Tung Ning Bldg, 249-253 Des Voeux Road C, CENTRAL, HONG KONG ISLAND, HONG KONG SAR.
CHOW, Mr. Chi Leung, ACA *2007;* Flat D, 30/F, Tower 5, Ocean Shores, TSEUNG KWAN O, NEW TERRITORIES HONG KONG SAR.
CHOW, Ms. Ching Winnie, ACA *2007;* Flat F 39/F, Tower 5 Harbour Green, 8 Sham Mong Road, TAI KOK TSUI, KOWLOON, HONG KONG SAR.
CHOW, Mr. Chuen Wei, ACA *1987;* 1 Sophia Road, 07-09 Peace Centre, SINGAPORE 228149, SINGAPORE.

CHOW, Mr. Chun Hong Ernest, ACA *2004;* Flat B 50/F, Block 6 Aquamarine, No. 8 Sham Shing Road, LAI CHI KOK, KOWLOON, HONG KONG SAR.
CHOW, Mr. Chun Keung, ACA *2005;* Kinson CPA & Co., Room 901, Hang Seng Castle Peak Road Building, 339 Castle Peak Road, CHEUNG SHA WAN, KOWLOON HONG KONG SAR.
CHOW, Mr. Clement, BSc ACA *1990;* 2 Wong Chuk Hang San Wai, WONG CHUK HANG, HONG KONG ISLAND, HONG KONG SAR.
•CHOW, Mr. Dennis Chi In, BCom FCA *1989;* Dennis Chi In Chow, 35th Floor, One Pacific Place, 88 Queensway, CENTRAL, HONG KONG ISLAND HONG KONG SAR.
CHOW, Mr. Derek Hong Shing, BSc FCA *1986;* with Ernst & Young Hua Ming Shanghai Branch, 50th Floor, Shanghai World Financial Center, 100 Century Avenue, Pudong New Area, SHANGHAI 200120 CHINA.
CHOW, Mr. Edward Kwong Fai, BA FCA *1978;* MEMBER OF COUNCIL, 2909A Bank of America Tower, 12 Harcourt Road, CENTRAL, HONG KONG SAR
CHOW, Miss. Fiona, BA(Econ) ACA *2004;* 7 Leinster Mews, LONDON, W2 3EY.
CHOW, Mr. Hok Lim, ACA *2007;* 2803 Block B, Kornhill, QUARRY BAY, HONG KONG ISLAND, HONG KONG SAR.
CHOW, Mrs. Hooi Juan, BSc ACA *1997;* 67 Ravensbourne Road, BROMLEY, BR1 1HW.
CHOW, Mr. Jason Kong Ting, BSc ACA *2001;* Hutchison Whampoa Limited, 22nd Floor Hutchison House, 10 Harcourt Road, CENTRAL, HONG KONG ISLAND, HONG KONG SAR.
CHOW, Mr. Jonathan Edward Chun-Chung, ACA *2010;* 32 Belleview Drive, 9/F Repulse Bay Garden, REPULSE BAY, HONG KONG ISLAND, HONG KONG SAR.
CHOW, Mr. Kai Cheong Isaac, ACA *2008;* 15th Floor Flat C, Palatial Crest, 3 Seymour Road, MID LEVELS, HONG KONG ISLAND, HONG KONG SAR.
CHOW, Miss. Karen Ka Yi, BSc ACA *1992;* 13N Breamar Terrace, 1 Pak Fuk Road, NORTH POINT, HONG KONG ISLAND, HONG KONG SAR.
CHOW, Mr. Kek Tong, ACA *1983;* 1C Ridley Park, 03-04 Tanglin Park, SINGAPORE 248469, SINGAPORE.
CHOW, Mr. Khee Meow, BSc ACA *2003;* 22 Coriander Crescent, GUILDFORD, GU2 9YU.
CHOW, Mr. Kin Fai, ACA *2006;* Flat C 19/F, Block 11 Villa Esplanada, 8 Nga Ying Chau Street, TSING YI, NEW TERRITORIES, HONG KONG SAR.
CHOW, Ms. Kit Man Clarissa, ACA *2008;* Flat C, 6/F, Tower 7, Laguna Verde, HUNG HOM, KOWLOON HONG KONG SAR.
CHOW, Mr. Kwan Yin Henry, ACA *2007;* Flat D, 9/F lunar Building, 28-30 Leighton Road, CAUSEWAY BAY, HONG KONG ISLAND, HONG KONG SAR.
CHOW, Mr. Kwok Wah, FCA *1978;* 33 Torrens Street, MATRAVILLE, NSW 2036, AUSTRALIA.
CHOW, Miss. Lai Shan Regina, MBA ACA FCCA FCPA *2005;* Regina L.S. Chow, 5/F, Dahsing Life Building, 99 -105 Des Voeux Road, CENTRAL, HONG KONG SAR.
CHOW, Mr. Man Wai Sam, ACA *2005;* Flat D 23/F Block 10, Park Avenue, 18 Hoi Ting Road, TAI KOK TSUI, KOWLOON, HONG KONG SAR.
CHOW, Miss. Margot Yan Tse, BSc(Econ) ACA *2000;* Flat 4B, Wealthy Heights, 35-37 MacDonnell Road, CENTRAL, HONG KONG ISLAND, HONG KONG SAR.
CHOW, Mr. Martin Paul, MA ACA CTA *2002;* Building B, BP Group, Chertsey Road, SUNBURY-ON-THAMES, TW16 7BP.
CHOW, Miss. Mei Mei, BA ACA *1993;* Sime Darby Motor Div S/B, 1st Floor Lot 33, Jalan Pelukis U1/46, Temasya Industrial Park, Seksyen U1, 40150 SHAH ALAM SELANGOR MALAYSIA.
CHOW, Miss. Michelle King-Chi, BSc(Hons) ACA *2004;* 70 Carlton Mansions, 203 Randolph Avenue, LONDON, W9 1NS.
CHOW, Miss. Poh Mei, FCA *1983;* 24 Prince of Wales Avenue, MILL PARK, VIC 3082, AUSTRALIA.
CHOW, Mr. Seng Hee, FCA *1968;* 73 Beauchamp Road, Upper Norwood, LONDON, SE19 3BZ. (Life Member)
CHOW, Mrs. Sook Yin, FCA *1983;* 2A Lorong PJU 3/28H, Sunway Damansara, 47810 PETALING JAYA, SELANGOR, MALAYSIA.
CHOW, Mr. Tak Sing, BSc ACA *2004;* Flat 27 Osprey Heights, 7 Bramlands Close, LONDON, SW11 2NP.
CHOW, Mr. Tak Sing Peter, ACA *2008;* BDO McCabe Lo Ltd, 25th Floor, Wing On Centre, 111 Connaught Road, CENTRAL, HONG KONG SAR.
CHOW, Mr. Teck Boo, FCA *1975;* C/O Al Meera Consumer Goods Co. (Q.S.C.), P.O. Box 3371, DOHA, QATAR.
CHOW, The Revd. Wai Meng, MA BA BSc ACA *1993;* 29 Carillon Court, Oxford Road, LONDON, W5 3SX.
CHOW, Mr. Wan Hoi Paul, BA ACA *1983;* 12D Block 27 Baguio Villa, 555 Victoria Road, KENNEDY TOWN, HONG KONG ISLAND, HONG KONG SAR.
CHOW, Mr. Wilson, BSc ACA *1986;* 20/E Block 8, Chi Fu Fa Yuen, POK FU LAM, HONG KONG ISLAND, HONG KONG SAR.
CHOW, Mr. Wing Hong, ACA *2008;* A Chow & Partners, 17/F, Amtel Building, 144-148 Des Voeux Road Central, CENTRAL, HONG KONG SAR.
CHOW, Mr. Wing Pong Calvin, ACA *2006;* Room 707, 7th floor Wing Lok House, Fuk Loi Estate, TSUEN WAN, NEW TERRITORIES, HONG KONG SAR.
CHOW, Miss. Wing Shuen Venetia, BSc ACA *2009;* 18A MacDonnell House, 8 MacDonnell Road, MID LEVELS, HONG KONG ISLAND, HONG KONG SAR.
CHOW, Mr. Yiu Wah Joseph, ACA *2006,* Room 501 5/F., Mirror Tower, 61 Mody Road, TSIM SHA TSUI, KOWLOON, HONG KONG SAR.
CHOW, Miss. Yuen-Yee, MSc LLB ACA *1988;* China International Capital Corporation (Hong Kong) Limited, 29/F One International Finance Centre, 1 Harbour View Street, CENTRAL, HONG KONG ISLAND, HONG KONG SAR.
CHOW, Mr. Yui Cheung Justin Cheung Justin, MSc ACA *2002;* Flat2C Skyline Mansion, 51 Conduit Road, MID LEVELS, HONG KONG ISLAND, HONG KONG SAR.
CHOW KOK MENG, Mr. Bernard, BSc ACA *2001;* Flat 21/A Alexandra Mansions, 347 West End Lane, LONDON, NW6 1LU.
•CHOW YICK CHEUNG, Mr. Philippe Chow Quang Chong, ACA *1984;* Maurice & Co, 71 Coldershaw Road, Ealing, LONDON, W13 9DU.
CHOWDHARY, Mr. Awais Muhammad, ACA *2008;* Seef Tower, Level 6, Road 2825 Block 428, Seef, MANAMA, 31594 BAHRAIN.
•CHOWDHARY, Mr. Bhupindar Singh, FCA *1975;* (Tax Fac), Chowdhary & Co., 46 Syon Lane, Osterley, ISLEWORTH, TW7 5NQ. See also Chowdhary & Co (Morden) Ltd
CHOWDHARY, Mr. Shamim Anver Shermohamad, FCA *1968;* 4 Annand Road, Upper Mall, LAHORE 54000, PAKISTAN.
CHOWDHARY, Mr. Shamsul Haq, FCA *1974;* 50 Hollybush Hill, Wanstead, LONDON, E11 1PX.
CHOWDHAY, Mr. Kevin John, BA ACA *1991;* 33G Netherwood Road, Hammersmith, LONDON, W14 0BL.
CHOWDHERY, Mr. Saleem Anwar, BSc ARCS ACA *1995;* Wm Morrison Supermarkets Plc, Hillmore House, 71 Gain Lane, BRADFORD, WEST YORKSHIRE, BD3 7DL.
CHOWDHURY, Mr. Anisuz Zaman, FCA *1965;* Apartment No.5, House No.3, Road No.16, Gulshan-1, DHAKA 1212, BANGLADESH.
CHOWDHURY, Mr. Barik Amanat, BSc(Econ) ACA *2001;* 4 Amberwood Close, WALLINGTON, SM6 8QH.
CHOWDHURY, Mr. Ekram, ACA *2011;* Springboard Urban, 643 Fulham Road, LONDON, SW6 5PU.
CHOWDHURY, Mr. Golam Mowla, FCA *1966;* 13 Langdale Avenue, Holdbrooks, COVENTRY, CV6 4LU.
CHOWDHURY, Mr. M Anwarul Islam, FCA *1984;* Chowdhury and Company, 37 Curtin Crescent, MAROUBRA, NSW 2035, AUSTRALIA.
•CHOWDHURY, Mr. Mohammad Karimul Huq, ACA *1982;* M.K. Chowdhury & Co, 250 Bethnal Green Road, LONDON, E2 0AA.
CHOWDHURY, Dr. Mohammed Abdul Mobin, BA ACA *1998;* PO Box 30092, BUDAIYA, BAHRAIN.
CHOWDHURY, Mr. Mohammed Abdul Muiz, BSc ACA *1993;* Arcapita Bank, PO Box 1406, MANAMA, BAHRAIN.
CHOWDHURY, Mr. Mohammed Anwar Golam Quddus, FCA *1969;* Transcom Beverages Ltd, Gulshan Tower 10th Floor, Plot 31, Road 53, Gulshan North, DHAKA 1212 BANGLADESH.
CHOWDHURY, Mr. Mohan Aleem, BA ACA *1986;* 29 The Maltings, Hunton Bridge, KINGS LANGLEY, HERTFORDSHIRE, WD4 8QL.
CHOWDHURY, Mr. Muraheb Malik, ACA *2010;* Flat-B3 House-32 Road-9/A, Dhanmondi, DHAKA, BANGLADESH.
CHOWDHURY, Mr. Osman Kaiser, ACA *1981;* Beximco group, 17 Dhanmondi R.A., Road No 2, DHAKA 1205, BANGLADESH.
CHOWDHURY, Mr. Pervaze Mahmoud, BSc ACA *2010;* 94 Merryhills Drive, Oakwood, ENFIELD, MIDDLESEX, EN2 7PQ.
CHOWDHURY, Mr. Rathindra Nath, FCA *1980;* 28 Harvard Drive, Woodbury., NEW YORK, NY 11797, UNITED STATES.
CHOWDHURY, Mrs. Rebecca, MA BA ACA CTA *1993;* 227 Mather Avenue, LIVERPOOL, L18 9UB.
CHOWDHURY, Mr. Shahriar Mahmud, ACA *2008;* Deloitte & Touche, Po Box 1475, HAMILTON, BERMUDA.
•CHOWDHURY, Mr. Shamsuddoha, FCA *1973;* S Chowdhury & Co Ltd, 17 Midholm, Wembley Park, WEMBLEY, MIDDLESEX, HA9 9LJ.
CHOWDHURY, Miss. Shimona, ACA *2008;* 15 Beacon Close, UXBRIDGE, MIDDLESEX, UB8 1PX.
CHOWDHURY, Mrs. Zakia Rashid, BA(Hons) ACA *2009;* 15 Weld Place, LONDON, N11 1QZ.
CHOWDRY, Mr. Neil, BSc ACA *2009;* Marlowes, Oxhey Lane, PINNER, MIDDLESEX, HA5 4AL.
CHOWDRY, Mr. Rahoul, ACA *1982;* with PricewaterhouseCoopers, Darling Park Tower 2, 201 Sussex Street, GPO Box 2650, SYDNEY, NSW 1171 AUSTRALIA.
CHOWEN, Mr. Matthew Jonathan, MSc(Econ) FCA ATII *2000;* (Tax Fac), Barclays Bank Plc, 1 Churchill Place, LONDON, E14 5HP.
CHOWINGS, Mr. Kevin Stephen, BEng ACA *2001;* 9TH FLOOR, 135 Bishopsgate, LONDON, EC2M 3UR.
•CHOWN, Mr. Ian Jack, BCom FCA *1983;* (Tax Fac), Smith Hodge & Baxter, Thorpe House, 93 Headlands, KETTERING, NN15 6BL.
•CHOWN, Mr. John Beresford, BSc FCA *1977;* (Tax Fac), Williams Ross Ltd, 4 Ynys Bridge Court, Gwaelod Y Garth, CARDIFF, CF15 9SS. See also Epiphany Business Solutions Limited
CHOWN, Mr. Mark John Hardwick, BA ACA *1984;* La Poudretterie, La Route Des Pelles, St Martin, JERSEY, JE3 6BR.
CHOWN, Mr. Michael Percy, FCA *1960;* 2 Clevelands, ABINGDON, OXFORDSHIRE, OX14 2EG. (Life Member)
•CHOWNEY, Mr. Christopher John, FCA *1976;* Menzies LLP, Woking Office, Midas House, 62 Goldsworth Road, WOKING, SURREY GU21 6LQ.
CHOY, Mr. Alex Yuen Wo, BEng ACA *1992;* RM 601-603 6/F, Mass Mutual Tower, 38 Gloucester Road, WAN CHAI, HONG KONG ISLAND, HONG KONG SAR.
CHOY, Mr. Chak Wa Peter, ACA *2007;* Flat B3 3/F, 150Tai Hang Road, CENTRAL, HONG KONG ISLAND, HONG KONG SAR.
CHOY, Mr. Chung-Yuen, BA FCA *1971;* Rhine Court, Block B 14th Fl. Flat B2, 80 Bonham Road MID LEVELS, Hong Kong Island, HONG KONG SAR. (Life Member)
CHOY, Mr. Hon Chuen Johnny, ACA *2005;* 23 Blue Ridge Road, TORONTO M2K 1R6, ON, CANADA.
CHOY, Mr. Kai Sing, ACA *2007;* Room 1919, Tsui Yung House, Tsui Ping Road, KWUN TONG, KOWLOON, HONG KONG SAR.
CHOY, Ms. Lily Tse Kwan, MA ACA *1993;* 1st & 2nd Floor Maisonette, 14 Abercorn Place, St John's Wood, LONDON, NW8 9XP.
CHOY, Mr. Man Yick Simon, ACA *2008;* 12th Floor, V. Heun Building, No 138 Queen's Road, CENTRAL, HONG KONG SAR.
CHOY, Ms. Mei Yuk, ACA *2008;* Flat A, 27/F, Tower 7, Ocean Shores, TSEUNG KWAN O, HONG KONG SAR.
CHOY, Ms. Pei Ling, BSc(Hons) ACA *2001;* 21H Kota Sri Mutiara, Jalan Sultan Yahya Petra, 15200 KOTA BHARU, KELANTAN, MALAYSIA.
CHOY, Ms. Po Fong, ACA *2008;* KLC Kennic Lui & Co, 5/F, Ho Lee Commercial Building, 38 - 44 D' Aguilar Street, CENTRAL, HONG KONG SAR. See also Kennic L H Lui & Co Ltd
CHOY, Mr. Wah Tak, MA ACA *2000;* 28 Walden Avenue, CHISLEHURST, BR7 6EN.
CHOY, Dr. Wai Cho Petrus, ACA *2006;* 9C Tower 2, Neptune Terrace, CHAI WAN, HONG KONG ISLAND, HONG KONG SAR.
CHRIMES, Mr. Patrick, FCA *1971;* The Beeches, Oakway, Chesham Bois, AMERSHAM, HP6 5PQ.
CHRIMES, Mr. Paul Andrew, BSc FCA MCT *1981;* Sun Court, E Trade Securities Ltd, 66-67 Cornhill, LONDON, EC3V 3NB.
CHRIS, Mr. Ben Edward, BSc(Hons) ACA *2002;* 3 Lord Palmerston Apartments, 45 Hewlett Road, LONDON, E3 5JR.
CHRIS, Mr. Robert Graham, BSc FCA *1971;* Romanoff Lodge, Castle Road, TUNBRIDGE WELLS, TN4 8BY.
•CHRISFIELD, Mr. Lawrence John, FCA CTA *1963;* (Tax Fac), L.J. Chrisfield, 29 The Meadow, CHISLEHURST, KENT, BR7 6AA.
CHRISMAS, Mr. Trevor Martin, BSc FCA *1987;* Europ Assistance Holdings Ltd Sussex House, Perrymount Road, HAYWARDS HEATH, RH16 1DN.
CHRISP, Mr. Peter David Calvert, FCA *1964;* 9 Barrow Road, Denham, BURY ST. EDMUNDS, SUFFOLK, IP29 5EQ.
CHRISPIN, Mrs. Elizabeth Sophie, BSc ACA *1989;* with Deloitte LLP, Hill House, 1 Little New Street, LONDON, EC4A 3TR.
CHRISPIN, Mrs. Sally Jayne, BSc ACA CTA *1993;* Electrolux PLC, Addington Way, LUTON, BEDFORDSHIRE, LU4 9QQ.
CHRISPIN, Mr. Simon Jonathan, BSc ACA *1989;* 41 Claygate Avenue, HARPENDEN, AL5 2HE.
CHRIST, Miss. Anne-Sophie, ACA *2010;* American International Underwriters, American International Building 2-8 Altyre Road, CROYDON, CR9 2LG.
CHRISTELOW, Miss. Julia Caroline, BSc ACA *1993;* West View House, 15 Church Lane, Old Sodbury, BRISTOL, BS37 6NB.
CHRISTENSEN, Mr. Matthew James, BA(Hons) ACA *2010;* Woodlands Court La Route Des Cotils, Grouville, JERSEY, JE3 9AP.
CHRISTENSEN, Dr. Richard Oliver, FCA *1989;* 1 Castle View, Westmount Road, St. Helier, JERSEY, JE2 3LP.
•CHRISTER, Mr. Ian Richard, FCA *1979;* Stokoe Rodger, St Matthews House, Haugh Lane, HEXHAM, NORTHUMBERLAND, NE46 3PU.
CHRISTIAN, Mr. Gary, BA ACA *2006;* 3 Albany Road, Peel, ISLE OF MAN, IM5 1JS.
CHRISTIAN, Mr. Graham, BSc ACA *2005;* Jing'an District, 90 Maoming Bei Lu, Building 10, Room 504, SHANGHAI 200041, CHINA.
CHRISTIAN, Mrs. Helen Joanne, BA ACA *1998;* 14 Farmhill Gardens, Douglas, ISLE OF MAN, IM2 2EG.
•CHRISTIAN, Mr. James Stephen, ACA *1990;* Gas Works Media Ltd, 3rd Floor Murdoch Chambers, South Quay, Douglas, ISLE OF MAN, IM1 5PA.
CHRISTIAN, Mr. John Edmund, FCA *1956;* 10 Church Drive, Ravenshead, NOTTINGHAM, NG15 9FF. (Life Member)
CHRISTIAN, Mr. John Nigel, BA ACA *1989;* 44 Cluny Gardens, EDINBURGH, EH10 6BN.
CHRISTIAN, Mr. Kevin, BSc(Econ) FCA *1979;* 12 Close Quane, Peel, ISLE OF MAN, IM5 1PY.
CHRISTIAN, Mr. Michael Peter, BA ACA *1981;* 6 Harvey Road, CONGLETON, CW12 2BU.
•CHRISTIAN, Mr. Neil Howard George, FCA *1967;* Christian & Co Ltd, 26 High Street, HOLYWELL, FLINTSHIRE, CH8 7LH.
•CHRISTIAN, Mr. Nicholas Edward, BSc(Hons) ACA FCCA *2003;* Christian & Co Ltd, 26 High Street, HOLYWELL, FLINTSHIRE, CH8 7LH.
CHRISTIAN, Mrs. Patricia Frances, BSc ACA *1990;* 5 Deans Farm, The Causeway, Caversham, READING, RG4 5JZ.
•CHRISTIAN, Mr. Paul, BEng FCA *1985;* 41 Croxteth Drive, Rainford, ST.HELENS, MERSEYSIDE, WA11 8JZ.
CHRISTIAN, Mr. Perry, BA FCA *1990;* 80 Fairfax Road, TEDDINGTON, MIDDLESEX, TW11 9BX.
CHRISTIAN, Mr. Stuart, BSc ACA *2005;* 1 Beaumont Road, Ramsey, ISLE OF MAN, IM8 2HN.
CHRISTIANSEN, Mr. Nils Paul Holm, BA ACA *1993;* Lane Side Guildown Avenue, GUILDFORD, SURREY, GU2 4HB.
CHRISTIE, Mr. Andrew Martin, BSc FCA *1969;* 51 Greenway, Totteridge, LONDON, N20 8ET. (Life Member)
CHRISTIE, Mr. Andrew S, ACA *2008;* 62 Garvel Road, Milngavie, GLASGOW, G62 7JD.
CHRISTIE, Ms. Anne Margaret, BA ACA *1993;* 133 Norfolk Avenue, LONDON, N13 6AL.
CHRISTIE, Mr. Colin Gordon, LLB ACA *1993;* Hawkpoint Partners Ltd, 41 Lothbury, LONDON, EC2R 7AE.
CHRISTIE, Miss. Diane, BSc ACA *1991;* 12 B Old Church House High Street Bowmore, ISLE OF ISLAY, PA43 7JE.
CHRISTIE, Mrs. Fiona Mary, MA ACA *1991;* 69 Crawford Road, Houston, JOHNSTONE, RENFREWSHIRE, PA6 7DA.
CHRISTIE, Mr. Guy Charles, BA ACA *1989;* 44 Radnor Walk, LONDON, SW3 4BN.
•CHRISTIE, Mr. Hamish Alexander, FCA *1971;* H.A. Christie & Co, 36 Robinson Road, 14-03, City House, SINGAPORE 068877, SINGAPORE.
CHRISTIE, Mr. Ian Michael Napier, BA FCA *1994;* 56 Florence Road, Wimbledon, LONDON, SW19 8TJ.
CHRISTIE, Mr. James Rupert Alexander, MA ACA *1986;* Canrrion Goverment Services, Westlink House Great West Road, LONDON, TW8 9DN.

CHRISTIE, Miss. Jane Suzanne, MA MSc ACA CTA *2003;* Via della Casa 20/3, 16146 GENOA, ITALY.

•**CHRISTIE, Mr. John Campbell, BSc FCA** *1992;* (Tax Fac), C & S Christie Ltd, 1 Nalton Close, Copmanthorpe, YORK, NORTH YORKSHIRE, YO23 3YY.

CHRISTIE, Mr. John Nicholas, MA FCA *1967;* Chandlers Cottage, Bishop's Cannings, DEVIZES, WILTSHIRE, SN10 2LW.

CHRISTIE, Mr. John Raymond, FCA *1951;* Riverside, Anderton's Lane, SHIPSTON-ON-STOUR, CV36 4AY. (Life Member)

CHRISTIE, Mr. Jonathan David, FCA *1976;* Energy Alloys UK Ltd Poplar Way, Catcliffe, ROTHERHAM, SOUTH YORKSHIRE, S60 5TR.

CHRISTIE, Mr. Jonathan George, BA FCA *1977;* Berner House, Hasketon, WOODBRIDGE, SUFFOLK, IP13 6JA.

•**CHRISTIE, Mr. Jonathan Peter, FCA FCCA** *1974;* 52 Woodgrange Avenue, LONDON, N12 0PS.

CHRISTIE, Ms. Karen, BSc ACA *1996;* Ernst & Young, 5 Times Square, NEW YORK, NY, UNITED STATES.

CHRISTIE, Miss. Kate, BA(Hons) ACA *2011;* 6 Lavender Flats, Meadowsweet Road, HARTLEPOOL, CLEVELAND, TS26 0QS.

CHRISTIE, Miss. Lauren Nicola, ACA *2009;* KPMG, Cricket Square, Century Yard, GEORGETOWN, GRAND CAYMAN, KY1 1106 CAYMAN ISLANDS.

•**CHRISTIE, Mrs. Lorna Bisset, MA ACA** *1980;* (Tax Fac), Christie Proud Thompson, 64 Duke Street, DARLINGTON, DL3 7AN.

CHRISTIE, Mrs. Mary Clare, BA ACA *1987;* 3 Timmins Close, SOLIHULL, B91 2SW.

•**CHRISTIE, Mr. Michael James, ACA** *2005;* J V Wilson & Co, 41a Chambers Street, HERTFORD, SG14 1PL.

CHRISTIE, Mr. Neil, LLB ACA *2003;* Flat 122 Vanguard Building, 18 Westferry Road, LONDON, E14 8LZ.

CHRISTIE, Mr. Neil, BSc ACA *2010;* 26 Cornec Avenue, LEIGH-ON-SEA, ESSEX, SS9 5EN.

CHRISTIE, Mr. Robert Stephen, BSc ACA *1988;* Bull Information Systems Ltd, A1 Formwell Garden, 46-48 Blue Pool Rd, HAPPY VALLEY, HONG KONG ISLAND, HONG KONG SAR.

CHRISTIE, Miss. Samantha Emma, BSc FCA *2001;* with PricewaterhouseCoopers LLP, 1 Embankment Place, LONDON, WC2N 6RH.

CHRISTIE, Mr. Scott Somervaille, MA ACA *1992;* Intense Ltd, 4 Stanley Boulevard, Hamilton Intnl Technology Park, Blantyre, GLASGOW, G72 0BN.

CHRISTIE, Mrs. Susan Jane, ACA *1996;* with Rushtons (NW) Limited, Shorrock House, 1 Faraday Court, Fulwood, PRESTON, PR2 9NB.

•**CHRISTIE-BROWN, Mr. Dominic James, BSc FCA MABRP** *1997;* Greengage Finance Ltd, 28 Portland Street, LEAMINGTON SPA, CV32 5EY.

CHRISTIE-TAYLOR, Mr. David Ransome, FCA *1955;* Cluster Box 6584, Le Domaine, HILLCREST, KWAZULU NATAL, 3626, SOUTH AFRICA. (Life Member)

CHRISTISON, Mr. Mark Andrew, BSc ACA *1998;* 9 Victoria Avenue, MARKET HARBOROUGH, LEICESTERSHIRE, LE16 7BQ.

CHRISTISON FARRELLY, Mrs. Nichola Anne, MRes BA(Hons) ACA *2002;* 61 Lhon Vane Close, Onchan, ISLE OF MAN, IM3 3BA.

CHRISTMAS, Mr. Colin Roy George, FCA *1957;* 4 College Place, Alfred Road, FARNHAM, SURREY, GU9 8JE. (Life Member)

CHRISTMAS, Mr. Jamie Graham, BSc ACA *2007;* CBRE Investors, 21 Bryanston Street, LONDON, W1H 7PR.

CHRISTMAS, Miss. Joanne, BSc ACA *1995;* 76 Othello Drive, ROLLESTON 7614, NEW ZEALAND.

CHRISTMAS, Mr. John Leslie, BSc ACA *1979;* Innerdown, Langton Road, Langton Green, TUNBRIDGE WELLS, TN3 0BA.

CHRISTMAS, Mr. Paul Julian, BA ACA *1998;* 14 Whittonditch Road, Ramsbury, MARLBOROUGH, WILTSHIRE, SN8 2PY.

•**CHRISTMAS, Mr. Philip Anthony, BA FCA** *1987;* Milcap Media Group S.L.U., Marina 16-18, Floor 18 Suite D, 08005 BARCELONA, CATALONIA, SPAIN. See also Christmas & Co

CHRISTMAS, Mr. Richard, BMus FCA MCT *1993;* 15 Madrid Road, GUILDFORD, GU2 5NU.

CHRISTODOULIDES, Mr. Anthimos Christodoulou, BA(Hons) ACA ACCA *2007;* Messinias 14, Potamos Yermasoyias, 4040 LIMASSOL, CYPRUS.

CHRISTODOULIDES, Mr. Antonis, BSc ACA *2002;* 15 Dositheou Street, Dasoupolis, 2028 NICOSIA, CYPRUS.

CHRISTODOULIDES, Mr. Georgios, BSc FCA *1980;* Alvanikou Epous 1A, 6041 LARNACA, CYPRUS.

CHRISTODOULIDES, Mr. Kleanthis, ACA *2009;* 7A Thespion Street, Ayia Fyla, 3110 LIMASSOL, CYPRUS.

CHRISTODOULIDES, Mr. Stelios, BSc ACA *2009;* 19D Tefkrou Anthia Street, Tseri, 2480 NICOSIA, CYPRUS.

CHRISTODOULIDOU, Ms. Marilena, BA ACA *2009;* 12 Fthiotidos street, Flat 4, CY 8035 PAFOS, CYPRUS.

•**CHRISTODOULOU, Mr. Christodoulos, BA ACA** *2008;* CFA, 10 Patron Street, 6051 LARNACA, CYPRUS.

CHRISTODOULOU, Mr. Christodoulos, BSc ACA *1995;* 134 Odyssea Eliti, Ilioypoli, Dhali 2546, NICOSIA, CYPRUS.

CHRISTODOULOU, Mr. Christodoulos, MA BA ACA *2010;* 3 Pavlos Kouppas Street, Neo Chorio, 8852 PAFOS, CYPRUS.

CHRISTODOULOU, Mr. Christodoulos, BSc ACA *2006;* Faneromenis 8, Kato Defetera, 2450 NICOSIA, CYPRUS.

CHRISTODOULOU, Mr. Christos, BSc(Hons) ACA *2004;* National Bank of Greece SA, 5th Floor, 6-10 Charilaou Trikoupi Street, 10679 ATHENS, GREECE.

CHRISTODOULOU, Mr. Constantinos, BA ACA *2006;* 9 Athanasiou Diakou, Egkomi, 2415 NICOSIA, CYPRUS.

CHRISTODOULOU, Mr. Demetrios, BA ACA *2007;* 27 Griva Digeni, Mesa Geitonia, 4002 LIMASSOL, CYPRUS.

CHRISTODOULOU, Miss. Eftychia, BA(Econ) ACA *1999;* 71A Arch. Makariou C', Lakatamia, 2323 NICOSIA, CYPRUS.

CHRISTODOULOU, Ms. Elena, BSc ACA *2005;* 9A Argostoliou Street, Agia Filaxi, 3117 LIMASSOL, CYPRUS.

CHRISTODOULOU, Miss. Evgenia Panayiotis, BSc ACA *1994;* 6 Iasiou Street, Pallouriotissa, 1046 NICOSIA, CYPRUS.

CHRISTODOULOU, Mr. Georgios, BSc(Hons) ACA *2000;* TRANTER LTD, OFFICE 5A TONIA COURT II, CORNER KOUMANDARIAS & SPYROU ARAOUZOU STREET, CY - 3036 LIMASSOL, CYPRUS.

CHRISTODOULOU, Miss. Ira, ACA *2005;* 10 Char. Mouskov, Pano Deftera, 2460 NICOSIA, CYPRUS.

CHRISTODOULOU, Mrs. Katerina, BSc ACA *2003;* Halifax Bank of Scotland, 10 Canons Way, BRISTOL, BS1 5LF.

CHRISTODOULOU, Mr. Michael, BA ACA *1992;* Sky Broadband S.A., Centre Helfent, 1 Rue Pletzer, L 8080 BERTRANGE, LUXEMBOURG.

CHRISTODOULOU, Miss. Myrto Emiliou, BA FCA *1992;* 5 Larissa Street, Ayios Dhometios, 2360 NICOSIA, CYPRUS.

CHRISTODOULOU, Mr. Nicholas John, BA ACA *1988;* Enterprise Care, Unit 2 4th Floor, Universal Square Devonshire St, MANCHESTER, M12 6JH.

CHRISTODOULOU, Miss. Pamela, ACA *2009;* 145 Athinon, Stovolos, 2035 NICOSIA, CYPRUS.

CHRISTODOULOU, Mr. Panayiotis, BA ACA *1998;* 1 KYVELIS, AGIOS VASILIOS, STROVOLOS, 2052 NICOSIA, CYPRUS.

CHRISTODOULOU, Mr. Savvas, BSc ACA *1978;* 26 Heath Drive, Gidea Park, ROMFORD, RM2 5QJ.

CHRISTODOULOU, Mr. Sozos, MSc ACA *2010;* 10 Ithakis Street, 8028 PAPHOS, CYPRUS.

CHRISTODOULOU, Mr. Stelios, ACA *2011;* Flat D168, Parliament View Apartments, 1 Albert Embankment, LONDON, SE1 7XQ.

CHRISTODOULOU, Mr. Stelios T, BA ACA *1982;* P O Box 22404, 1521 NICOSIA, CYPRUS.

CHRISTODOULOU, Mr. Themis, BSc ACA *2004;* 41 Kyrenia Street, Ypsonas, 4180 LIMASSOL, CYPRUS.

CHRISTODOULOU, Miss. Vevey, BA ACA *2003;* 7 Agaristis Street, 4154 LIMASSOL, CYPRUS.

CHRISTOFI, Mr. Christakis, BSc ACA *1993;* 10 Litchfield Way, Hampstead Garden Suburb, LONDON, NW11 6NJ.

•**CHRISTOFI, Mr. Christofis, BSc ACA** *2007;* A & C Christofi Ltd, 37 Nicou and Despinas Pattichi Avenue, Evi Court, 3rd Floor, Offices 302-303, CY-3071 LIMASSOL CYPRUS.

CHRISTOFI, Mrs. Clare Teresa, BSc ACA *1993;* 10 Litchfield Way, LONDON, NW11 6NJ.

CHRISTOFI, Mr. Efstathios, BA ACA *2002;* Tweede Jan Van der Heijdenstraat 107 I-II, 1074 XT AMSTERDAM, NETHERLANDS.

•**CHRISTOFIDES, Mr. Andreas Kyprou, FCA CF** *1979;* KPMG, 14 Esperidon Street, 1087 NICOSIA, CYPRUS. See also KPMG Metaxas Loizides Syrimis

CHRISTOFIDES, Miss. Artemis, BA ACA *1995;* 6 Crowther Close, Fulham, LONDON, SW6 7EY.

CHRISTOFIDES, Mr. Christoforos, MA BSc ACA *2005;* 11 Michalakis Parides Street, 3091 LIMASSOL, CYPRUS.

CHRISTOFIDES, Mr. Constantinos Andrea, FCA *1970;* 28 Byzantium Street, STROVOLOS, CY 2064, CYPRUS.

CHRISTOFIDES, Mr. Costas, BA ACA *2008;* 7 Kefalinias Street, Kiti, 7550 LARNACA, CYPRUS.

CHRISTOFIDES, Mr. Georgios Constantinos, BSc ACA *2008;* 28 Byzantium Street, Strovolos, CY 2064 NICOSIA, CYPRUS.

CHRISTOFIDES, Mr. Harris, MSc ACA *2009;* Flat 10, Sandover House, 124 Spa Road, LONDON, SE16 3FD.

CHRISTOFIDES, Mr. Ioannis, BSc ACA *2008;* 2 Marias Singlitikis Street, 4001 LIMASSOL, CYPRUS.

CHRISTOFIDOU, Ms. Eleonora, ACA *2009;* 20 Economou Panayidi, Anna Maria Court, Flat 202, Neapolis, 3101 LIMASSOL, CYPRUS.

CHRISTOFIDOU, Miss. Maria, BSc FCA *1992;* Three Larissis Street, Agios Dhometios, 2360, NICOSIA, CYPRUS.

CHRISTOFIDOU, Miss. Maria, ACA *2003;* 5 Patmos Street, Strovolos, 2062 NICOSIA, CYPRUS.

CHRISTOFIDOU, Miss. Vicky, ACA *2010;* 7 Andrea Strouthidi Street, Dasoupoli, 2015 NICOSIA, CYPRUS.

CHRISTOFIS, Mr. Alexander Peter Stavros, ACA *2009;* 1/F, 16/B Sheung Sze Wan Road, CLEARWATER BAY, HONG KONG SAR.

CHRISTOFOROU, Miss. Christiana Maria, ACA *2004;* 38 Calder Avenue, Brookmans Park, HATFIELD, HERTFORDSHIRE, AL9 7AG.

•**CHRISTOFOROU, Mr. Christis Michael, BA FCA** *1986;* Deloitte Limited, 24 Spyrou Kyprianou Avenue, P.O.Box 21675 CY-1512, 1075 NICOSIA, CYPRUS.

CHRISTOFOROU, Mr. Christoforos Ioannou, ACA *1980;* Flat 302, 16 Petraki Yialourou Street, 1077 NICOSIA, CYPRUS.

CHRISTOFOROU, Mr. Constantinos, BSc ACA *2004;* 3 Chloridos, Panthea Heights, Flat 31, 4007 LIMASSOL, CYPRUS.

CHRISTOFOROU, Mr. Constantinos, BA ACA *2006;* P.O.Box 60032, 8100 PAFOS, CYPRUS.

CHRISTOFOROU, Ms. Eleni, BSc ACA *2008;* 10 Evrou Street, Flat 21 Acropolis, CY 2004 NICOSIA, CYPRUS.

CHRISTOFOROU, Mr. Michalis, MEng ACA *2009;* Charalambou Pettemeride 8, 2220 LATSIA, CYPRUS.

CHRISTOPHER, Mr. Brian George, BA ACA *1981;* 118 Osborne Street, WILLIAMSTOWN, VIC 3016, AUSTRALIA.

CHRISTOPHER, Mr. Colin Michael, FCA *1961;* 100 Redway Drive, Whitton, TWICKENHAM, TW2 7NW. (Life Member)

CHRISTOPHER, Mr. David John, BA ACA *1981;* Orgeris Villa, Les Rouvets, Vale, GUERNSEY, GY6 8NH.

•**CHRISTOPHER, Mr. Gary David, BSc FCA** *1983;* Horner Christopher, First House, Altrincham Road, Styal, WILMSLOW, SK9 4JE.

CHRISTOPHER, Mrs. Helen Mary, BA ACA *1996;* 37 St. Peters Road, DUNSTABLE, BEDFORDSHIRE, LU5 4HY.

CHRISTOPHER, Miss. Lucy Emma, BSc ACA *2010;* PricewaterhouseCoopers, 188 Quay Street, Private Bag 92162, AUCKLAND 1142, NEW ZEALAND.

CHRISTOPHER, Mrs. Melissa Jane, BA ACA *1995;* (Tax Fac), 43 Regency Gardens, WALTON-ON-THAMES, SURREY, KT12 2BE.

•**CHRISTOPHER, Mr. Nicholas, BSc FCA** *1979;* (Tax Fac), Christopher & Co, 51A Anson Road, LONDON, N7 0AR.

•**CHRISTOPHER, Mr. Simon John, BA FCA CTA** *1991;* (Tax Fac), Simon John Christopher Ltd, First Floor Suite, Drapers House, Market Place, STURMINSTER NEWTON, DORSET DT10 1AS.

CHRISTOPHER, Mr. Thomas Aleks, ACA *2008;* Flat 3, 32 Shepherds Hill, LONDON, N6 5AH.

CHRISTOPHERS, Mr. Sidney John, FCA *1960;* 12 Killerton Park Drive, West Bridgford, NOTTINGHAM, NG2 7SB.

CHRISTOPHI, Mr. Costas, ACA *1998;* Amathountos Avenue, Periyiali Gardens 4, 4534 LIMASSOL, CYPRUS.

CHRISTOPHIDES, Mr. Alexis, BSc ACA *2007;* 7 Apostolos Varnavas, 2059 STROVOLOS, CYPRUS.

CHRISTOPHOROU, Miss. Michelle, ACA *2008;* 58c Lawford Road, LONDON, NW5 2LN.

•**CHRISTOU, Mr. Achilleas, FCA** *1975;* (Tax Fac), Christou & Co, 132 Salmon Street, LONDON, NW9 8NT.

CHRISTOU, Mr. Alexis, BA(Hons) ACA *2002;* 25 Riverside Drive, RICHMOND, TW10 7QA.

CHRISTOU, Mr. Charalambos, BA(Hons) ACA *2010;* Atlantis 2, PO Box 20290, 2150 Aglantzia, 2150 NICOSIA, CYPRUS.

CHRISTOU, Mr. Christakis, BSc ACA *2005;* Vyronos 5, Akaki, 2720 NICOSIA, CYPRUS.

CHRISTOU, Ms. Christina, BSc ACA *2001;* 15 Ayias Phaneromenis Str, Archangelos, 2334 NICOSIA, CYPRUS.

CHRISTOU, Mr. Christopher Stelios, FCA *1973;* PO Box 508, ARTARMON, NSW 1570, AUSTRALIA.

CHRISTOU, Mr. Christos Philippou, BSc ACA *1996;* 19 Arsakiou, Stovolos, 2045 NICOSIA, CYPRUS.

•**CHRISTOU, Mr. George, BA ACA** *1995;* CK Partnership Limited, 1 Old Court Mews, 311a Chase Road, LONDON, N14 6JS.

CHRISTOU, Mr. Giannis, ACA *2011;* 34 Seychellon Street, Apostolos Andreas, 3065 LIMASSOL, CYPRUS.

CHRISTOU, Mr. Soteris, ACA *1980;* Emonos 4 & Mytilinis Str, 14569 ANIXI, ATTIKI, GREECE.

CHRISTY, Mr. Colin William, BSc FCA *1984;* Hinxton Hall Ltd, Wellcome Trust Genome Campus, Hinxton, SAFFRON WALDEN, ESSEX, CB10 1RQ.

CHRISTY, Miss. Hazel, BSc ACA *2010;* Flat 3, 34 Nightingale Lane, LONDON, SW12 8TD.

CHRISTY, Mr. Martin John, BSc ACA *2010;* 16 Goodeve Park, Hazelwood Road, BRISTOL, BS9 1PZ.

•**CHRISTY, Mrs. Morisha Kim, FCA** *1991;* (Tax Fac), Greenback Alan LLP, 11 Raven Wharf, Lafone Street, LONDON, SE1 2LR.

•**CHRISTY, Mr. Norman David, FCA** *1959;* (Tax Fac), George Hay & Company, 83 Cambridge Street, Pimlico, LONDON, SW1V 4PS.

CHRISTY, Mr. Stuart Norman, MSc BA ACA *2007;* 15 Hunnels Close, Church Crookham, FLEET, HAMPSHIRE, GU52 6YR.

•**CHRYSANTHOU, Mr. Achilleas, FCA** *1984;* 2 Aristomenous Street, 2045 STROVOLOS, CYPRUS.

CHRYSANTHOU, Miss. Chrysanthi, BSc ACA *2010;* 8 Apostolou Melachrinou, Flat 202, Strovolos, 2049 NICOSIA, CYPRUS.

CHRYSANTHOU, Mr. Harris, BA ACA *1987;* N D Properties Ltd, 42-44 Makarius Avenue, P O Box 40525, 6305 LARNACA, CYPRUS.

CHRYSAPHIADES, Mr. Alexander, ACA *2008;* 31 Greenway, LONDON, N20 8EH.

CHRYSOSPATHI, Ms. Marianna, ACA *2008;* Flat 201, 17 Odysseos Street, Strovolos, 2040 NICOSIA, CYPRUS.

•**CHRYSOSTOMOU, Mr. Alex, BSc ACA** *2008;* Premier Accountants Limited, Suite 1A 3rd Floor, Hillside House, 2-6 Friern Park, LONDON, N12 9BT.

CHRYSOSTOMOU, Mr. Dimitris, BSc ACA *2010;* 4 Pilea Street, Strovolos, 2023 NICOSIA, CYPRUS.

•**CHRYSOSTOMOU, Mr. Kyriacos, FCA** *1975;* Chrysostomou & Co Ltd, 407 Green Lanes, Palmers Green, LONDON, N13 4JD.

CHRYSOSTOMOU, Miss. Panayiota, BSc ACA *2010;* Archiepiscopou Makariou No 3, Arediou, 2614 NICOSIA, CYPRUS.

•**CHRYSOSTOMOU, Mr. Vassos, MSc BA ACA** *2003;* Thomas Alexander & Company Ltd, 590 Green Lanes, LONDON, N13 5RY.

CHRYSOSTOMOU, Miss. Victoria, BA ACA *2009;* Flat 203, 22 Thoukididou Street, Acropolis, NICOSIA, CYPRUS.

CHRYSSAPHES, Mr. Harry, MBA BA FCA *1978;* Chryssaphes Associates, 23 Berkeley Square, LONDON, W1J 6HA.

CHRYSTIE, Mr. Ian Peter, BSc FCA *1984;* 26 Hurst View Road, CROYDON, SURREY, CR2 7AG.

CHRYSTIUK, Ms. Tamara, BA ACA *1990;* 2 Warwick Place, Ealing, LONDON, W5 5PS.

CHU, Mr. Alan Cuong Chan, BA(Hons) ACA *2003;* Apartment 6, Wood Wharf Apartments, Horseferry Place, LONDON, SE10 9BB.

CHU, Mr. Alexander Kin Chung, FCA *1983;* Room 605 6th Floor, Eastern Commercial Centre, 397 Hennessy Road, WAN CHAI, HONG KONG SAR.

CHU, Mr. Andrew Chi Onn, MA ACA *2000;* Deutsche Bank AG London 4th Floor, 99 Bishopsgate, LONDON, EC2M 3XD.

CHU, Miss. Ching Chen, MA ACA *2002;* Flat 69, 4th Floor, Marathon House, 200 Marylebone Road, LONDON, NW1 5PL.

CHU, Mr. Hon Kit, ACA *2005;* Foremost Worldwide Co Ltd, Flat B 4/F, Carbo mansion, 325 Queens Road, CENTRAL, HONG KONG ISLAND HONG KONG SAR.

CHU, Mr. Jason Yau Wing, BSc FCA *1989;* Flat 902 9/F Block J, Kornhill, QUARRY BAY, HONG KONG ISLAND, HONG KONG SAR.

CHU, Miss. Jessica Fung Yi, MA ACA *2006;* Flat 177, 41 Millharbour, LONDON, E14 9ND.

CHU, Mr. John Siew Wah, BA ACA *1989;* 1 Clementi Crescent, SINGAPORE 599504, SINGAPORE.
CHU, Mr. John Sun Yue, BA FCA *1965;* 13D Green Valley Mansion, 51 Wong Nai Chung Road, HAPPY VALLEY, HONG KONG ISLAND, HONG KONG SAR.
CHU, Mrs. Judy Peck Lan, ACA *1983;* Maxis Broadband SDN BHD, Level 13, Menara Maxis, Kuala Lumpur City Centre, 50088 KUALA LUMPUR, FEDERAL TERRITORY MALAYSIA.
CHU, Mr. Ka Kun Vincent, LLB FCA *1968;* Flat A, 30/F Tower 1, 29 Lyttelton Road, Lyttelton Garden, MID LEVELS, HONG KONG ISLAND HONG KONG SAR.
CHU, Ms. Ka Yee, ACA *2006;* Flat A, 2/F Tower 2, One Beacon Hill, 1 Beacon Hill Road, KOWLOON TONG, KOWLOON HONG KONG SAR.
CHU, Mr. Kai Wah, ACA *2008;* Flat E 17th Floor, Tower 1 Park Towers, 1 King's Road, NORTH POINT, HONG KONG ISLAND, HONG KONG SAR.
CHU, Mr. Kevin Patrick Francis, BSc ACA *1990;* Flat C 21/F Tower 8, The Belcher's, 89 Pok Fu Lam Road, POK FU LAM, HONG KONG ISLAND, HONG KONG SAR.
CHU, Mr. Kin Chung Alex, ACA *2008;* Flat 42H, Block 3, Park Central, 9 Tong Tak Street, TSEUNG KWAN O, HONG KONG SAR.
CHU, Mr. Kiu Fat, ACA *2006;* Flat E 25/F Block 6, Saddle Ridge Garden, Ma On Shan, SHA TIN, NEW TERRITORIES, HONG KONG SAR.
CHU, Miss. Kwan Ying, ACA *2005;* Flat C 27/F Block 29, Park Island, MA WAN, NEW TERRITORIES, HONG KONG SAR.
CHU, Ms. Linda Tze Ning, ACA *2006;* with PricewaterhouseCoopers LLP, 1 Embankment Place, LONDON, WC2N 6RH.
CHU, Miss. Lisa Li San, BA(Hons) ACA *2001;* 82 Empire Square East, Empire Square, LONDON, SE1 4NB.
CHU, Mr. Lung Hai Jimmy, ACA *2008;* Flat F, 18/F, Tower 4, Jubilant Place, 99 Pau Chung Street, MA TAU WAI KOWLOON HONG KONG SAR.
CHU, Ms. Mei Man, ACA *2008;* Hang Lung Properties Ltd, 28/F, 4 Des Voeux Road, CENTRAL, HONG KONG ISLAND, HONG KONG SAR.
CHU, Ms. Mei Yue Michelle, ACA *2008;* Flat 24A Rowen Court, 25 Babington Path, MID LEVELS, HONG KONG ISLAND, HONG KONG SAR.
CHU, Ms. Pik Yee, ACA *2008;* Flat C, 11/F Tsuen Lok Building, Tsuen Lok Street, TSUEN WAN, NT, HONG KONG SAR.
CHU, Mr. Po Choi, BA ACA *1988;* 73 Zetland Street, LONDON, E14 6PR.
CHU, Mr. Tin Ngai, ACA *2007;* Flat K, 33/F, Block 2, Broadview Court, 11 Sham Wan Road, ABERDEEN HONG KONG ISLAND HONG KONG SAR.
CHU, Mr. Wai Kei, ACA *2008;* 13B Talon Tower, 38 Connaught Road West, SHEUNG WAN, HONG KONG ISLAND, HONG KONG SAR.
CHU, Mr. Wai Keung Edmund, ACA *2008;* Flat A 15/F Block 4 City Garden, NORTH POINT, HONG KONG SAR.
CHU, Mr. Wai Kok, ACA *2005;* RSM Nelson Wheeler, 29th Floor Caroline Centre, Lee Gardens Two, 28 Yun Ping Road, CAUSEWAY BAY, HONG KONG ISLAND HONG KONG SAR.
CHU, Ms. Wen Jin Winnie, ACA *2008;* Flat E 25/Floor, Block 34 Laguna City, 3 South Laguna Street, Cha Kwo Ling, KWUN TONG, KOWLOON HONG KONG SAR.
CHU, Miss. Wenlan, BSc ACA *2010;* BDO Shanghai CPA Ltd, East Yan An Road 550, Ocean Tower 12F, SHANGHAI 20001, CHINA.
CHU, Mr. Wing Kin Ricky, ACA *2008;* Flat 22D Tower 3, The Belchers, 89 Pok Fu Lam Road, POK FU LAM, HONG KONG ISLAND, HONG KONG SAR.
CHU, Ms. Yaoyao, MSc BSc ACA *2009;* 67 St. Lawrence Quay, SALFORD, M50 3XT.
CHU, Mr. Yin Kam, ACA *2006;* 28B Block 1 Scenic Garden 9 Kotewall Road, MID LEVELS, HONG KONG ISLAND, HONG KONG SAR.
CHU, Mr. Yin Man, ACA *2008;* Flat F 10/F, Block 10 Royal Ascot, Fo Tan, SHA TIN, HONG KONG SAR.
CHU, Ms. Yin Yin Georgina, ACA *2008;* Room 1512, Block H, Lok Man Sun Chuzn, TO KWA WAN, KOWLOON, HONG KONG SAR.
•**CHU, Miss. Yuen Mei Amanda, BSc ACA** *1995;* Espira Limited, 74 Castleton Road, Lightwood, STOKE-ON-TRENT, ST3 7TD.
CHU, Mr. Yum Leung, ACA *2007;* FlatT G, 15th Floor Block A, Hollywood Terrace, 268 Queens Road, Central, SHEUNG WAN HONG KONG ISLAND HONG KONG SAR.
CHU CHUNG KEE, Miss. Mary Jane, MSci ACA *2006;* 37 Elliscombe Road, LONDON, SE7 7PF.
CHU-FONG, Mrs. Fiona, BSc ACA *1992;* 9 Abilene Crescent, Churton Park, WELLINGTON 6037, NEW ZEALAND.
CHU SIN CHUNG, Mr. Philip Kiong Kiang, FCA *1976;* 1 Sente des Marnieres Palus, 78740 EVECQUEMONT, FRANCE.
CHU TSANG KWAN, Mr. Andy, BSc(Hons) ACA *2009;* with Hazlems Fenton LLP, Palladium House, 1-4 Argyll Street, LONDON, W1F 7LD.
CHUA, Miss. Al Ling, ACA *2010;* No.15 Jalan Kasturi, Tanamera, UEP Subang Jaya, 47630 SUBANG, SELANGOR, MALAYSIA.
CHUA, Mr. Billy Kuan Yang, ACA *2007;* 20 Jalan Naung, SINGAPORE 537684, SINGAPORE.
CHUA, Mr. Chee Seng, ACA *2004;* BLK 691A #04-36, Choa Chu Kang Crescent, SINGAPORE 681691, SINGAPORE.
CHUA, Mr. Christopher Chong Xun, MPhil BSc ACA *2003;* Credit Suisse, 45/F Two Exchange Square, 8 Connaught Place, CENTRAL, HONG KONG SAR.
CHUA, Mr. Chuan Teong, FCA *1969;* Suite 301 3rd Floor, Wisma Hong Bee, 50-J Pengkalan Weld, 10300 PENANG, MALAYSIA.
CHUA, Mr. Chun Kit Frankie, ACA *2007;* Block 924, Tampines Street 91, #05 - 269, SINGAPORE 520924, SINGAPORE.
CHUA, Mr. Foon Cheng, ACA FCCA *2010;* 298B Compassvale Street, #14 - 170, SINGAPORE 542298, SINGAPORE.
CHUA, Madam Guat Beng, FCA *1974;* 12D Jalan Dungun, Damansara Heights, 50490 KUALA LUMPUR, FEDERAL TERRITORY, MALAYSIA.
CHUA, Mr. Han Seng, ACA *2008;* 608-613 Level 6 HSBC Building Shanghai IFC 8 Century Avenue Pudong New Area, SHANGHAI 200120, CHINA.
CHUA, Mr. Hong Pong, ACA *1980;* 1 Jalan SS21/36, Damansara Utama, 47400 PETALING JAYA, Selangor, MALAYSIA.
CHUA, Mr. Huan Sang, BSc FCA *1983;* unit 29, 51 Grand Parade, PARREARRA, QLD 4575, AUSTRALIA.
CHUA, Miss. Ik Hwa, FCA *1979;* 39 HINDHEDE WALK, #08-03, SINGAPORE 587971, SINGAPORE. (Life Member)
CHUA, Mr. James Hua Seng, BSc ACA *1985;* 61 Medway Drive, SINGAPORE 556561, SINGAPORE.
CHUA, Miss. Mei Lee, ACA *1983;* 15 JALAN KEMUNING BAYU 33/32H, KEMUNING UTAMA, 40400 SHAH ALAM, MALAYSIA.
CHUA, Mr. Sidney Siang Loong, FCA FCCA *1992;* 8 Glasgow Road, SINGAPORE 549306, SINGAPORE.
CHUA, Mr. Song Kuey, FCA *1973;* 44-02 Jalan Titiwangsa 3, Taman Tampoi Indah, 81200 JOHOR BAHRU, JOHOR, MALAYSIA.
CHUA, Ms. Suk Lin Ivy, MBA ACA CPA *2007;* PCP CPA Limited, 34/F The Lee Gardens, 33 Hysan Avenue, CAUSEWAY BAY, HONG KONG SAR.
CHUA, Miss. Suzanie May Li, LLB FCA *1994;* 15 Carraway Priv., OTTAWA K1S 5S3, ON, CANADA.
CHUA, Miss. Teck Cheng, BSc ACA *1989;* 2 Teesdale Close, Great Sankey, WARRINGTON, WA5 3BL.
•**CHUA, Mr. Teck Hwee, BCom FCA** *1984;* T.H. Chua & Co., No 5-2 1st Floor, Jalan Othman, 84000 MUAR, JOHOR, MALAYSIA.
CHUA, Miss. Wee-Kim, BA ACA *2000;* 28 Carlisle Road, LONDON, NW6 6TS.
CHUA, Mr. Wye Man, BSc ACA *1990;* Suite B-7-2, Megan Avenue 1, P.O. Box 10189, 189 Jalan Tun Razak, 50706 KUALA LUMPUR, FEDERAL TERRITORY MALAYSIA.
CHUAH, Mr. Kay Kian, BA ACA *1992;* 26 Leboh Chateau, Chateau Garden, IPOH, PERAK, MALAYSIA.
CHUAH, Miss. Lay Gnoh, FCA *1990;* The Coca Cola Company, P.O. Box 1734, ATLANTA, GA 30301, UNITED STATES.
CHUAH, Mr. Seong Phaik, FCA *1975;* PAUL CHUAH & CO., NO. 17 JALAN IPOH KECIL, 50350 KUALA LUMPUR, FEDERAL TERRITORY, MALAYSIA.
CHUAH, Miss. Sue Yin, BSc ACA *1997;* Paul Chuah & Co, No. 17 Jalan Ipoh Kecil, 50350 KUALA LUMPUR, FEDERAL TERRITORY, MALAYSIA.
CHUANG, Mr. Tze Cheung Christopher, BSc ACA CPA *1997;* Unit 809, Millennium City II, 378 Kwun Tong, KWUN TONG, KOWLOON, HONG KONG SAR.
CHUBB, Mr. Anthony Gerald Trelawny, FCA *1951;* 11 Hartopp Rd, Four Oaks, SUTTON COLDFIELD, B74 2RQ. (Life Member)
CHUBB, Mr. Daniel Campos, MEng ACA *2006;* 42 Prior Street, Greenwich, LONDON, SE10 8SF.
CHUBB, Mrs. Louise Jane, BSc ACA *2004;* 24 Beacon Road, SUTTON COLDFIELD, B73 5ST.
CHUBB, Mr. Paul Alan, BSc ACA *1985;* FSML 4th Floor 1 Minster Court, Mincing Lane, LONDON, EC3R 7AA.
CHUBB, Mr. Peter William Brown, FCA *1956;* 53 Higham Lane, TONBRIDGE, TN10 4BN. (Life Member)
CHUBB, Mr. Richard Stewart, BA(Hons) ACA *2001;* International SOS PT ASIH EKA ABADI, Jl. Puri Sakti No 10, Cipete, Jakarta Selatan, JAKARTA, 12410 INDONESIA.
CHUDASAMA, Mr. Sureshchandra Maganlal, ACA *1979;* 7 Miller Close, LEICESTER, LE4 7TU. (Life Member)
CHUDLEY, Miss. Lynda, BSc ACA *2000;* 3 Tern Close, Kelvedon, COLCHESTER, CO5 9NQ.
CHUGANI, Mr. Neil, MA FCA *1995;* Shine Group Primrose Studios, 109 Regents Park Road, LONDON, NW1 8UR.
CHUGG, Mr. Gerald Alfred, FCA *1950;* 147 Pantmawr Road, Rhiwbina, CARDIFF, CF4 6US. (Life Member)
CHUGHTAI, Miss. Shazia Jamshed, ACA *2008;* 101 Wellesley Road, ILFORD, ESSEX, IG1 4LJ.
•**CHUHAN, Mr. Abdul Majeed, FCA** *1968;* (Tax Fac), Chuhan & Singh Partnership Limited, 81 Borough Road, MIDDLESBROUGH, TS1 3AA.
CHUHAN, Mr. John, BA ACA *1999;* BMW Financial Services, Lodderstraat 16, 2880 Bornem, BORNEM, BELGIUM.
CHUI, Mr. Bruce, MEng ACA *2010;* 5A Serene Court, 26 College Road, KOWLOON TONG, KOWLOON, HONG KONG SAR.
•**CHUI, Mr. Chee Keung, BA FCA** *1967;* C.K. Chui & Co., 1st Floor, 2 Waterloo Street, MANCHESTER, M1 6HX.
•**CHUI, Mr. Chi Tak, BA ACA** *1988;* Chui & Kwok, Room 705 & 706, 7th Floor, China Insurance Group Building, No 141 Des Voeux Road Central, CENTRAL HONG KONG ISLAND HONG KONG SAR.
CHUI, Mr. Chi Wai, ACA *2008;* Flat 5, 17th Floor, Block M, Kornhill, QUARRY BAY, HONG KONG SAR.
CHUI, Miss. Edith Wai Yan, ACA *2010;* Flat 131 Ralph Court, Queensway, LONDON, W2 5HU.
CHUI, Mr. Henry Chee-Hung, FCA MBA *1975;* 5C 26-28 College Road, KOWLOON TONG, KOWLOON, HONG KONG SAR.
CHUI, Mr. Ka Hing, BSc ACA *1990;* Cl Springfield Garden, 5 Shouson Hill Road West, WONG CHUK HANG, HONG KONG ISLAND, HONG KONG SAR.
CHUI, Miss. Karen Mun Yi, BA ACA *2006;* 2-1-6 Villa Setia, Jalan Setiakasih 8, Bukit Damansara, 50490 KUALA LUMPUR, FEDERAL TERRITORY, MALAYSIA.
CHUI, Mr. Kin Ming, ACA *2007;* Flat B, 12th Floor, Block 1, Scenic Garden, 9 Kotewall Road, CENTRAL HONG KONG ISLAND HONG KONG SAR.
CHUI, Ms. Kit Ha, ACA *2008;* Flat A 1/F. Tower 11, Parc Royale, 8 Hin Tai Street, Tai Wai, SHA TIN, NEW TERRITORIES HONG KONG SAR.
CHUI, Ms. Kit Lin, ACA *2007;* Flat 6, 5/F Hoi Chun Court, Aberdeen Centre, ABERDEEN, HONG KONG SAR.
CHUI, Ms. Mabel, LLB ACA *2006;* Flat 27 Robin House, Barrow Hill Estate, LONDON, NW8 7AD.
CHUI, Mr. Man Lung Everett, ACA *2008;* Cen-1 Partners Ltd., 2104 A Tower 1, Admiralty Centre, 18 Hardcourt Road, CENTRAL, HONG KONG ISLAND HONG KONG SAR.
CHUI, Ms. Siu Fong Evelyn, BA ACA *1993;* 6a Eastbury Avenue, NORTHWOOD, MIDDLESEX, HA6 3LG.
CHUI, Mr. Vincent Xinghua, BEng ACA *2009;* Flat 8 College House, 52 Putney Hill, LONDON, SW15 6BF.
CHUI, Mr. Wai Shing, ACA *2008;* Wai S Chui, 100 Lafayette Circle, Suite 204, LAFAYETTE, CA 94549, UNITED STATES.
CHUI, Ms. Yue Chue, ACA *2007;* 25 Tai Hang Drive, Flat A 24th Floor, Ronsdale Garden (Block 2), CAUSEWAY BAY, HONG KONG SAR.
CHUI, Ms. Yuet Man Gloris, ACA *2008;* Rear Flat, 6/F Gartin Court, 11A Ho Man Tin Street, HO MAN TIN, KOWLOON, HONG KONG SAR.
CHUI YEW CHEONG, Mrs. Nita, FCA *1978;* 19 Oriole Drive, KIRKLAND H9H 4S2, QUE, CANADA.
CHUK, Ms. Hiu Yin, ACA *2009;* Flat D 43/F, Block 10, Royal Ascot, SHA TIN, NEW TERRITORIES, HONG KONG SAR.
CHUKWU, Miss. Ncheta, BSc ACA *2005;* TBWA UK Group, 76-80 Whitfield Street, LONDON, W1T 4EZ.
CHULANI, Mr. Arun, MSc ACA *2002;* 85 Dorset House, Gloucester Place, LONDON, NW1 5AF.
•**CHUMBER, Mr. Satnam Chand, BA FCA** *1997;* Brindleys Limited, 2 Wheeleys Road, Edgbaston, BIRMINGHAM, B15 2LD.
CHUMILLAS, Mr. Jesus Alberto, MSci ACA *2002;* St Minver Limited, Suite 812, Europort, GIBRALTAR, GIBRALTAR.
CHUMMUN, Mr. Dipak, BSc ACA *1993;* 55 Meyer Road, Flat 07-06, Seafront on Meyer, SINGAPORE 437978, SINGAPORE.
CHUMROO, Mrs. Preeya, ACA *2003;* 462 La Visitation, VACOAS, MAURITIUS.
CHUN, Mr. Ho, MA ACA *2011;* 3 Wincanton Way, WATERLOOVILLE, HAMPSHIRE, PO7 8NJ.
•**CHUNDRIGAR, Mr. Nadeem Yusuf, MSc BSc ACA** *2006;* nyc, 36 Birkbeck Road, LONDON, N12 8DZ. See also nyc & co
CHUNDYDYAL, Mr. Pechal, MSc BSc(Hons) ACA *2010;* 75 Tynemouth Road, MITCHAM, CR4 2BR.
CHUNG, Mr. Adrian, ACA *2009;* 20 Huson Close, LONDON, NW3 3JW.
CHUNG, Mr. Andrew Wing Leung, BA ACA *1994;* Compass Offices, 10/F Central Building, 1-3 Pedder Street, CENTRAL, HONG KONG SAR.
CHUNG, Mr. Antony Lee, ACA *2009;* Flat 69 Medland House, 11 Branch Road, LONDON, E14 7JT.
CHUNG, Mr. Brian Christopher, MBA BSc FCA *1991;* 242 Powell Street, CLARENDON HILLS, IL 60514, UNITED STATES.
CHUNG, Miss. Carmen, LLB ACA *2004;* 11 Brookland Close, LONDON, NW11 6DJ.
CHUNG, Ms. Chau Yu Catherine, ACA *2007;* Flat A 16/F, Block 3 Monte Vista, Sha on Street, SHA TIN, NEW TERRITORIES, HONG KONG SAR.
CHUNG, Mr. Chin Keung, ACA *2008;* Flat B 6F Block 17, Sereno Verde Phas 3, 99 Tai Tong Road, YUEN LONG, NEW TERRITORIES, HONG KONG SAR.
CHUNG, Mr. Chuen On Dennis, ACA *2007;* CWCC, Suites 1201-4, Tower 2, THe Gateway, TSIM SHA TSUI, KOWLOON HONG KONG SAR.
CHUNG, Miss. Cindy Sin-Ting, ACA *2008;* 8 Hurst Road, BUCKHURST HILL, IG9 6AB.
CHUNG, Mr. Cliff, BA ACA *2011;* 2 Sullom View, Garstang, PRESTON, PR3 1QF.
CHUNG, Mr. Edmund, BSc ACA *2005;* 59 Brindley Close, WEMBLEY, MIDDLESEX, HA0 1BS.
CHUNG, Ms. Elaine, ACA *2008;* HKICPA, 37th Floor, Wu Chung House, 213 Queens Road East, WAN CHAI, HONG KONG ISLAND HONG KONG SAR.
CHUNG, Miss. Florence, BSc ACA *2011;* 15 Heath Court, Park Road, UXBRIDGE, MIDDLESEX, UB8 1NU.
CHUNG, Mr. Freddie, ACA CA(AUS) *2009;* c/o The Hong Kong Jockey Club, One Sports Road, HAPPY VALLEY, HONG KONG SAR.
CHUNG, Mr. Hoi Tong, BSc ACA *1980;* 55 JALAN SARMUKH, TAMAN CHATEAU, 30250 IPOH, PERAK, MALAYSIA.
CHUNG, Miss. Imelda Lim Tung, BSc ACA *2010;* Flat 63 Fondant Court, 2 Taylor Place Payne Road, LONDON, E3 2PJ.
CHUNG, Mr. Ka Po, ACA *2007;* Flat 37B Tower 7, Island Resort, 28 Siu Sai Wan Road, SIU SAI WAN, HONG KONG ISLAND, HONG KONG SAR.
CHUNG, Mr. Kenneth Patrick, BA ACA *1984;* Red Hill Park House 14, 12 Pak Pat Shan Road, Redhill, TAI TAM, HONG KONG ISLAND, HONG KONG SAR.
CHUNG, Mr. King Cheung, ACA *2008;* Flat 907, Block Q, Telford Gardens, KOWLOON BAY, KOWLOON, HONG KONG SAR.
CHUNG, Mr. King Fung Tony, ACA *2007;* 19 Whiteman Ave, BELLA VISTA, NSW 2153, AUSTRALIA.
CHUNG, Ms. Kit Yee Katty, ACA *2008;* Flat C 16/F Tower 8, Metro Town, 8 King Ling Road, TIU KENG LENG, NEW TERRITORIES, HONG KONG SAR.
CHUNG, Mr. Koon Shing Patrick, ACA *2007;* Chung & Yeung, Room 1001, Centre Point, 181-185 Gloucester Road, WAN CHAI, HONG KONG SAR.
CHUNG, Mr. Koon Yan, ACA *2004;* Chiu Choy & Chung CPA Ltd, Unit A 5/F Yu Fung Commercial Centre, 289-295 Hennesey Road, WAN CHAI, HONG KONG ISLAND, HONG KONG SAR.
CHUNG, Ms. Kwai Hing, ACA *2006;* Suite 2212 22/F, Tower 1 The Gateway, 25 Canton Road, TSIM SHA TSUI, KOWLOON, HONG KONG SAR.
CHUNG, Miss. Laura, MA BA ACA *2009;* Bolt Sussex House, 143 Long Acre, LONDON, WC2E 9AD.
CHUNG, Miss. Lee-Jan, BA ACA *2005;* with KPMG, 10 Shelley Street, SYDNEY, NSW 2000, AUSTRALIA.
CHUNG, Miss. Mandy, BSc ACA *2007;* 9 Stanley Drive, NEWCASTLE, STAFFORDSHIRE, ST5 7TW.
CHUNG, Miss. Mei Ha, BSc ACA *1985;* 3156 Camino Avenue, HACIENDA HEIGHTS, CA 91745, UNITED STATES.

CHUNG, Mr. Min Chik, MEng ACA CFA FRM *2001;* Flat G, 3rd Floor, Block 6, Site 12, Whampoa Garden, HUNG HOM KOWLOON HONG KONG SAR.

CHUNG, Miss. Pauline, BSc ACA *2003;* 3 Chatbrook Close, Aigburth, LIVERPOOL, L17 6EU.

CHUNG, Mr. Ping Sum, ACA *2007;* Flat B, 28/F Block 6, Monte Vista, Ma on shan, SHA TIN, NEW TERRITORIES HONG KONG SAR.

CHUNG, Mr. Sai Ho, ACA *2008;* Room 12, 14 Floor Chung May House, Chung Ngo Court, TAI PO, HONG KONG SAR.

CHUNG, Miss. Sarah Kin-Yee, BA(Hons) ACA *2011;* Ocean King Fish Bar, 313 Forton Road, GOSPORT, PO12 3HF.

CHUNG, Mr. Siu Wa, ACA *2008;* 608, Block 4, Heng Fa Chuen, CHAI WAN, HONG KONG SAR.

CHUNG, Miss. Siu-Ping Stella, BA FCA *1989;* Flat E 3/F Eastbourne Court, 7 Eastbourne Road, KOWLOON TONG, KOWLOON, HONG KONG SAR.

CHUNG, Mr. Stephen Nicholas, BSc ACA *1990;* 11 Maycock Grove, NORTHWOOD, MIDDLESEX, HA6 3PU.

CHUNG, Ms. Suk Fung Alice, ACA *2007;* Chan Yip Keung & Co, Unit 1702-0317/F, Skyline Commercial Centre, 71-77 Wing Lok Street, SHEUNG WAN, HONG KONG ISLAND HONG KONG SAR.

CHUNG, Mr. Sum Tin Abraham, ACA *2007;* HKR International Ltd, 23/F China Merchants Tower, Shun Tak Centre, 168 Connaught Road, CENTRAL, HONG KONG SAR.

CHUNG, Miss. Susan, ACA *2011;* Apartment 229, Block 5 Spectrum, Blackfriars Road, SALFORD, M3 7BT.

CHUNG, Mr. Victor, ACA *2009;* 9 Briscoe Road, Colliers Wood, LONDON, SW19 2AH.

CHUNG, Mr. Wai Ming, ACA *2008;* CIG CPA Limited, Unit 702 7th Floor, Tung Hip Commercial Building, 244 Des Voeux Road, CENTRAL, HONG KONG SAR.

CHUNG, Mr. Wai Yip Wilson, ACA *2006;* Flat G 5/F. Tower 2 Miami Beach Tower 268 Wu Chui Road, TUEN MUN, NEW TERRITORIES, HONG KONG SAR.

CHUNG, Miss. Wendy Wun Man, BSc ACA *2004;* Flat 66 Robin House, Barrow Hill Estate, LONDON, NW8 7AD.

CHUNG, Mr. William, BCom FCA *1983;* Sino Qualitex Inc, 450 Seventh Avenue, 10th Floor, NEW YORK, NY 10123, UNITED STATES.

CHUNG, Mr. Wing Yin, ACA *2007;* with Deloitte & Touche, 35/F One Pacific Place, 88 Queensway, CENTRAL, HONG KONG ISLAND, HONG KONG SAR.

CHUNG, Dr. Yau Yan Sammy, ACA *2004;* Chung & Partners Limited, Room 2408, 24/F Hopewell Centre, 183 Queens Road East, WAN CHAI, HONG KONG SAR.

CHUNG, Mr. Yu To, BCom FCA *1961;* B31 Po Shan Mansions, 12 Po Shan Road, MID LEVELS, Hong Kong Island, HONG KONG SAR. (Life Member)

CHUNG, Mr. Yuk Lun, ACA *2007;* Flat A, 11/F, Block 15, Villa Rhapsody, 533 Sai Sha Road, SAI KUNG NEW TERRITORIES HONG KONG SAR.

CHUNG, Mr. Yuk Man Clarence, ACA *2008;* Suite 30B, Tower 3, Tregunter, 14 Tregunter Path, MID LEVELS, HONG KONG SAR.

CHUNG-CHUN-LAM, Mr. Nian Kiam, ACA *1980;* QEWC, Finance Manager, Box 22046, DOHA, QATAR.

CHUNG CHUNG WAI, Mr. John, BSc ACA *1995;* KPMG, KPMG Centre, 30 St George Street, PORT LOUIS, MAURITIUS.

CHUNG NIEN CHIN, Mr. William, ACA *1980;* (Tax Fac), Kemp Chatteris Deloitte, 7th. Floor, Raffles Tower, 19 Cybercity, EBENE, MAURITIUS.

CHUNG SHUI, Mr. Andre Chung Siong Fan, BSc FCA *1991;* 62 Morc Gentilly, MOKA, 8888, MAURITIUS.

CHUNG TICK KAN, Ms. Julie, ACA *2009;* Dookun Lane, Mare Gravier, BEAU BASSIN, MAURITIUS.

CHUNG WONG TSANG, Miss. Jenifer, BA(Hons) ACA *2003;* with PricewaterhouseCoopers LLP, 1 Embankment Place, LONDON, WC2N 6RH.

CHURCH, Mr. David Andrew, MA ACA *1991;* 38 The Close, HENLEY-ON-THAMES, RG9 1SR.

CHURCH, Mrs. Diana Claire, BSc ACA *1993;* Spires Consultancy Ltd 3 Chapel Road, EPPING, ESSEX, CM16 5DS.

CHURCH, Miss. Emma, MA MEng ACA *2003;* 97 Dukes Avenue, NEW MALDEN, KT3 4HR.

CHURCH, Mr. James Jonathan, BSc ACA *1997;* Barclays Bank Plc, Barclays Treasury, 9th Floor, 1 Churchill Place, LONDON, E14 5HP.

CHURCH, Mr. John Andrew, FCA *1976;* The Shires, Old Grantham Road, Whatton, NOTTINGHAM, NG13 9FR.

CHURCH, Mr. John George, CBE FCA *1959;* The Old Rectory, Farthingstone, TOWCESTER, NN12 8EZ.

CHURCH, Miss. Kristina, BA ACA *2007;* 04-20 Equity Research, Citigroup Centre, 33 Canada Square, LONDON, E14 5LB.

CHURCH, Ms. Linda Maureen, BSc ACA CTA *1991;* 20 Braeworth Close, YARM, CLEVELAND, TS15 9SB.

CHURCH, Miss. Louise, BA FCA *1988;* 1 Rosery Close, BRISTOL, BS9 3HF.

•CHURCH, Mr. Michael John, FCA *1969;* Coulthards Mackenzie, 17 Park Street, CAMBERLEY, GU15 3PQ.

•CHURCH, Mr. Paul Alexander, FCA *1971;* Church & Partners SL, El Rosario 143, 29600 MARBELLA, MALAGA, SPAIN. See also Church P A

CHURCH, Mr. Richard James, BA ACA *2000;* 3 Church Stile Cottages, Woodbury, EXETER, EX5 1HP.

CHURCH, Mr. Robert John, BA ACA *1992;* Somer Community Housing Trust The Maltings, River Place Lower Bristol Road, BATH, BA2 1EP.

CHURCH, Miss. Sarah Louise May, ACA *2005;* Hanson UK Hanson House, 14 Castle Hill, MAIDENHEAD, SL6 4JJ.

•CHURCH, Mr. Sebastian Alexander, BSc FCA *1995;* Church & Co, 1st Floor, Burleigh House, 357 Strand, LONDON, WC2R 0HS.

•CHURCH, Mrs. Susan Julia, BTech ACA *1986;* Susan Church Accountancy Services, 8 Dandridge Drive, BOURNE END, SL8 5UW.

CHURCH, Miss. Tamsind Melissa, BSc(Hons) ACA *2002;* 51 Cyprian Rust Way, Soham, ELY, CAMBRIDGESHIRE, CB7 5ZE.

CHURCH, Mr. Timothy John Edward, BSc FCA *1982;* with McKinsey & Co, 1 Jermyn Street, LONDON, SW1Y 4UH.

CHURCH, Mr. William David, FCA *1966;* Middle Barn, Grit Lane, MALVERN, WR14 1UR.

•CHURCH, Mr. William Edward, MA FCA *1969;* (Tax Fac), Church & Young, 11 Station Road, Headcorn, ASHFORD, Kent, TN27 9SB.

CHURCHARD, Mr. Alan John Barrington, FCA *1980;* 50 Perne Avenue, CAMBRIDGE, CB1 3SA.

•CHURCHER, Mr. David Bruce, BA FCA *1982;* PricewaterhouseCoopers, Sixty Circular Road, Douglas, ISLE OF MAN, IM1 1SA.

CHURCHER, Mr. Ian Michael, BA ACA *1992;* Spiral Healthcare, Regents Gate, 25-41 Crown Street, READING, RG1 2SE.

CHURCHER, Mr. Peter Walton, BA FCA *1976;* 2 Sparrowgrove, Otterbourne, WINCHESTER, SO21 2DL.

CHURCHHOUSE, Mr. Robert Andrew Joseph, BSc ACA *1982;* PO Box 3600, ABU DHABI, UNITED ARAB EMIRATES.

CHURCHILL, Mr. Adrian Francis, BSocSc ACA *1993;* (Tax Fac), No 7, Rue Jean Du Bellay, 75004 PARIS, FRANCE.

CHURCHILL, Mr. Andrew Hayward, FCA *1971;* 28 Hiron Street, ST LUCIA, QLD 4067, AUSTRALIA.

CHURCHILL, Mr. Andrew Philip, BSc ACA *1983;* 2 Leasway, WICKFORD, SS12 0HF.

CHURCHILL, Mr. Brian Alwyn, FCA *1956;* 19 Daneshill, REDHILL, RH1 2DW. (Life Member)

•CHURCHILL, Mrs. Carolyn Joan, FCA *1984;* Solent Accountancy Services Limited, 7 Captains Parade, EAST COWES, ISLE OF WIGHT, PO32 6GU.

CHURCHILL, Mr. Cyril Robert William, FCA *1962;* 5 Angel Yard, North Street, MIDHURST, WEST SUSSEX, GU29 9FN. (Life Member)

CHURCHILL, Mr. Ian, BA ACA *1993;* Chestnut House, Paines Hill, Steeple Aston, BICESTER, OXFORDSHIRE, OX25 4SQ.

CHURCHILL, Mr. Jonathan, BSc ACA *2006;* Bonlea, 32 Chequers Lane, Wychbold, WORCESTER, WR9 7PH.

CHURCHILL, Mr. Martin, BSc FCA *1972;* 35 The Park, LONDON, NW11 7ST.

•CHURCHILL, Mr. Martin John, FCA *1976;* (Tax Fac), M.J. Churchill, 5 Bracken Dell, RAYLEIGH, ESSEX, SS6 8LP.

CHURCHILL, Mr. Peter James, MMath ACA *2006;* Pricewaterhousecoopers Llp, 1 Hays Lane, LONDON, SE1 2RD.

CHURCHILL, Mr. Peter Robert, FCA *1974;* Quince Cottage, Windsor Road, Chobham, WOKING, GU24 8LE. (Life Member)

CHURCHILL, Mr. Randolph Leonard Spencer, BSc ACA *1995;* Rathbones Investment Management, 159 New Bond Street, LONDON, W1S 2UD.

CHURCHILL, Miss. Rhiannon, BSc FCA *1995;* (Tax Fac), 40 Old Road, East Peckham, TONBRIDGE, TN12 5ET.

•CHURCHILL, Mr. Richard William Roger, BSc(Hons) ACA *2004;* Shelley Stock Hutter LLP, 7-10 Chandos Street, LONDON, W1G 9DQ.

CHURCHILL, Miss. Samantha Jane, ACA *2003;* 17 Cowley Avenue, GREENHITHE, KENT, DA9 9QA.

CHURCHILL, Miss. Suzanne Nicole, MA LLB ACA *2005;* 77 Leathermarket Court, LONDON, SE1 3HS.

•CHURCHILL STONE, Mr. Andrew, FCA DChA *1991;* Mercer Lewin Ltd, 41 Cornmarket Street, OXFORD, OX1 3HA.

CHURCHMAN, Miss. Allison Jayne, BSc ACA *1995;* 24B Ka Fu Building, 19 Bonham Road, MID LEVELS, HONG KONG SAR.

CHURCHMAN, Mr. Andrew David, BEng ACA *1992;* Warren House, Nightingales Lane, CHALFONT ST. GILES, BUCKINGHAMSHIRE, HP8 4SH.

CHURCHMAN, Mrs. Caroline Margaret, BSc ACA *1988;* 23 Waldegrave Gardens, Strawberry Hill, TWICKENHAM, TW1 4PQ.

CHURCHMAN, Mr. Keith Howard, BA FCA *1982;* Holly Lodge, 8 Templemore Close, CAMBRIDGE, CB1 7TH.

CHURCHMAN, Mr. Michael John, BA ACA *1996;* 53/331 Miller Street, CAMMERAY, NSW 2062, AUSTRALIA.

CHURCHMAN, Mr. Tony Frank, FCA *1957;* 6B Moreton End Lane, HARPENDEN, AL5 2EX. (Life Member)

CHURCHOUSE, Mr. Robin James, BA ACA *1992;* Low Wood House, Smelthouses, HARROGATE, HG3 4DL.

CHURCHUS, Mr. Peter John, FCA *1977;* The Grove, 3 Eastfield Road, ROSS-ON-WYE, HR9 5AN.

CHURCHWARD, Miss. Linda Mary, BCom ACA *1995;* 11 Meadow Court, BERRINGS, COUNTY CORK, IRELAND.

CHURCHYARD, Ms. Julie, BSc ACA ATII *1999;* Eastholme, Station Road, Ashwell, BALDOCK, HERTFORDSHIRE, SG7 5RJ.

CHURLEY, Miss. Sara Louise, BA ACA *1993;* 120 Falling Water Drive, BRANDON, FL 33511, UNITED STATES.

CHURMS, Mr. Kenneth John, FCA JDipMA *1957;* The Willows, 10a Peulwys Lane, Old Colwyn, COLWYN BAY, CLWYD, LL29 8YD. (Life Member)

CHURN, Miss. Hui Ping, BSc(Hons) ACA *2003;* 150-4-4 Villa Flora Condominium, Jalan Burhanuddin Helmi, Taman Tun Dr Ismail, 60000 KUALA LUMPUR, FEDERAL TERRITORY, MALAYSIA.

CHURTON, Mrs. Sarah Florence, MMath ACA *2002;* with Ernst & Young LLP, 1 More London Place, LONDON, SE1 2AF.

CHURTON, Mr. Thomas Edward Harding, BA ACA *1999;* 5 Rodyk Street, #3-22 Watermark @ Robertson Quay, SINGAPORE 238214, SINGAPORE.

CHUTE, Mr. Peter Nicholas, FCA *1975;* Brook Birmingham, 59-65 John Bright Street, BIRMINGHAM, B1 1BL.

CHUTER, Mr. Michael David, FCA *1973;* 167 Mottingham Road, Mottingham, LONDON, SE9 4SS.

CHUTOO, Miss. Hushna, BSc ACA *2010;* 7 Pickering Road, WOLVERHAMPTON, WV11 3RA.

CHYB, Mr. Steven, BSc(Hons) ACA *2009;* Byways, Uplands Way, SEVENOAKS, TN13 3BN.

CHYLINSKI, Mr. Mark, BA ACA *2005;* 62 Broadwells Crescent, COVENTRY, CV4 8JD.

CIAMPA, Mr. Alfredo Francesco Giuseppe, BA FCA *1976;* 4 Cholmeley Park, LONDON, N6 5EU.

CIANCHI, Mrs. Anne Elizabeth, ACA *1988;* Bycross Bungalow, Bycross, Moccas, HEREFORD, HR2 9LJ.

CIANCI, Miss. Helena Maria, BSc ACA *1992;* Temenos, 18 Place des Philosophes, 1205 GENEVA, SWITZERLAND.

•CICCONE, Mr. Peter Vincent, FCA *1984;* (Tax Fac), CPP, 81 Essex Road, Islington, LONDON, N1 2SF.

CICHOCKI, Mr. Adam George, ACA *2007;* with Deloitte LLP, Hill House, 1 Little New Street, LONDON, EC4A 3TR.

CICHOCKI, Mr. Daniel Anthony, BA ACA *2004;* with Hall Liddy Ltd, 12 St. John Street, MANCHESTER, M3 4DY.

CIECHAN, Miss. Emma Marie, BA(Hons) ACA *2001;* 551 Finchley Road, LONDON, NW3 7BJ.

•CIENTANNI, Mr. Mario Phillip, BSc FCA *1984;* Barnes Roffe LLP, 16-19 Copperfields, Spital Street, DARTFORD, DA1 2DE.

CIESLA, Mr. Peter, ACA *2011;* 68 Barons Mead, SOUTHAMPTON, SO16 9TD.

CILLIERS, Mr. LeRoux, ACA CA(SA) *2010;* 1 Down End Road, PORTSMOUTH, PO6 1HT.

CIMA, Mr. Nicholas David, BA ACA *2009;* 11 Sowbury Park, Chieveley, NEWBURY, BERKSHIRE, RG20 8TZ.

CINESI, Mr. Mirco, ACA *2005;* 51 Taeping Street, LONDON, E14 9UT.

•CINI, Mr. Jonathan Anthony, FCA *1973;* (Tax Fac), J A Cini, 6 Birnam Close, Ripley, WOKING, SURREY, GU23 6JH.

CINNAMON, Mr. Allan, FCA *1957;* (Tax Fac), with BDO LLP, 55 Baker Street, LONDON, W1U 7EU.

CINQUEMANI, Mr. Giovanni, BSc(Hons) ACA *2003;* 114 Clifford Gardens, LONDON, NW10 5JB.

CITROEN, Mr. Michael Robert Charles, BSc FCA *1987;* C/O HBS Finance Ltd, 20 Shire Lane, Chorleywood, RICKMANSWORTH, HERTFORDSHIRE, WD3 5NQ.

CITRON, Prof. David Bernard, MA FCA *1970;* 13 Bruria Street, 93184 JERUSALEM, ISRAEL.

CITRON, Mr. Marcus Benjamin, ACA *1988;* c/o Mr T J Maguire, Flat 2, 17 Cambridge Park, TWICKENHAM, TW1 2JE.

•CITRON, Mr. Richard Jonathan, MA FCA FTII MAE TEP *1977;* (Tax Fac), BDO LLP, 55 Baker Street, LONDON, W1U 7EU. See also BDO Stoy Hayward LLP

CITRON, Mr. Robert Joshua, BSc FCA CPA *1984;* 12 Ben Azai Street, 93505 JERUSALEM, ISRAEL.

CIUFFARDI, Miss. Nina Roberta, BA ACA *1998;* 34 The Glen, NORTHWOOD, MIDDLESEX, HA6 2UR.

CLAASSEN, Mr. Bruce Vaughan, ACA *2002;* 47 Shaftesbury Way, TWICKENHAM, TW2 5RW.

CLAASSEN, Mrs. Jane Wendy, BSc(Hons) ACA CTA *2002;* 47 Shaftesbury Way, Strawberry Hill, TWICKENHAM, TW2 5RW.

CLABER, Miss. Karen Pamela, BA ACA *1992;* 2a Bankside Avenue, Radcliffe, MANCHESTER, M26 2QH.

CLACK, Mr. Michael, BSc ACA *1993;* Flat 7, 20-21 Bartholomew Square, LONDON, EC1V 3QT.

CLACK, Mrs. Stacey Marie, ACA *2006;* 29 Chandler Close, BAMPTON, OX18 2NW.

•CLACKETT, Mr. Lee David, ACA FCCA *2009;* Bromley Clackett Limited, 76 Aldwick Road, BOGNOR REGIS, WEST SUSSEX, PO21 2PE.

CLACKETT, Mr. Timothy James, BA ACA *1985;* 23812 Crosson Drive, WOODLAND HILLS, CA 91367, UNITED STATES.

CLACKSON, Mrs. Charlotte Fiona Stewart, MA ACA *1991;* 26 Montague Road, RICHMOND, SURREY, TW10 6QJ.

CLACKSON, Mr. Patrick Andrew, BSc ACA *1990;* 26 Montague Road, RICHMOND, SURREY, TW10 6QJ.

•CLACY, Mr. John Gilmour, BSc FCA *1994;* Deloitte LLP, PO Box 137, Regency Court, Glategny Esplanade, St Peter Port, GUERNSEY GY1 3HW. See also Deloitte & Touche LLP

•CLADD, Mr. Roger John, FCA *1970;* (Tax Fac), R.J. Cladd, Suite 134, Milton Keynes Business Centre, Foxhunter Drive, Linford Wood, MILTON KEYNES MK14 6GD.

CLAFF, Mr. Michael Norman, FCA *1961;* Flat 48, Ferrydale Lodge, 48 Church Road, LONDON, NW4 4EW.

CLAGUE, Mrs. Deborah, BA ACA *2005;* 61 Ard Reayrt, Ramsey Road, Laxey, ISLE OF MAN, IM4 7QQ.

CLAGUE, Mrs. Deborah Ann, BSc ACA *1992;* Glendown House, Truggan Road, Port St. Mary, ISLE OF MAN, IM9 5LD.

•CLAGUE, Mr. Ian Graham, BSc FCA *1990;* PricewaterhouseCoopers, Sixty Circular Road, Douglas, ISLE OF MAN, IM1 1SA.

CLAGUE, Mr. James Joseph, BA ACA *2005;* 16 Burston Drive, Park Street, ST. ALBANS, HERTFORDSHIRE, AL2 2HR.

CLAGUE, Miss. Joanne, BA FCA *1995;* (Tax Fac), 18 Rose Hill, Delph, OLDHAM, OL3 5ED.

CLAGUE, Mrs. Joanne Louise, BA(Hons) ACA *2002;* 15 Dee Park Road, WIRRAL, MERSEYSIDE, CH60 3RG.

CLAGUE, Mr. Simon Frank, MEng ACA *2000;* 3 Cleiy Rhennee, Kirk Michael, ISLE OF MAN, IM6 1HT.

CLAIDEN, Mr. Richard John, MA BSc FCA *1977;* 10 Beechwood Road, BRONXVILLE, NY 10708, UNITED STATES.

•CLAISSE, Mrs. Paula Irena, BSc ACA ATII *1987;* (Tax Fac), KPMG LLP, Dukes Keep, Marsh Lane, SOUTHAMPTON, HAMPSHIRE, SO14 3EX. See also KPMG Europe LLP

CLAISSE, Miss. Simone Leonie, ACA *2011;* 21 Copperfield Street, LONDON, SE1 0EP.

CLAKE, Miss. Verity Laura, BA ACA CTA *2007;* 2 Hyde Farm Mews, LONDON, SW12 0QB.

•CLAMP, Mr. David, FCA *1972;* D. Clamp & Co, Park Farm, Church Road, Ashton Hayes, CHESTER, CH3 8AB.

CLAMP, Mr. David John, BA LLB FCA *1975;* 12 Calverley Lane, Horsforth, LEEDS, LS18 4DZ.

CLAMP, Mr. James Jolyon Robert Da Silva, BSc ACA *2002;* 57 Highland Avenue, JERSEY CITY, NJ 07306, UNITED STATES.

CLAMP, Mrs. Louise, BSc ACA *2006;* 45 Charlotte Road, Edgbaston, BIRMINGHAM, B15 2NH.
CLAMP, Mr. Philip John, ACA *2009;* 1a Retreat Road, RICHMOND, TW9 1NN.
CLAMP, Ms. Ruth Anna, BSc ACA *1993;* Thomson Reuters (Markets) SA, 153 Route de Thonon, 1245 COLLONGE BELLERIVE, SWITZERLAND.
CLAMP, Mr. Thomas, BSc ACA *2006;* 45 Charlotte Road, Edgbaston, BIRMINGHAM, B15 2NH.
CLAMP, Mr. Thomas Michael, BA FCA *1974;* (Tax Fac), with PricewaterhouseCoopers LLP, 31 Great George Street, BRISTOL, BS1 5QD.
CLAMPIN, Mr. Michael Edward Barrington, FCA *1963;* 8 Marlborough Place, WIMBORNE, BH21 1HW.
CLANCY, Mr. Edward John, BBS FCA *1979;* 160 Eastcote Road, RUISLIP, MIDDLESEX, HA4 8DX.
CLANCY, Mr. Hugh Patrick, BSc ACA *1992;* Homeground Farm, 15 The Chantry, ROOKSBRIDGE, SOMERSET, BS26 2JR.
CLANCY, Mr. Martin Bernard, BSc ACA *1989;* 9209 Olmstead Drive, Lake Worth, PALM BEACH, FL, 33467, UNITED STATES.
CLANCY, Mr. Paul Fabian, MBA BA ACA *1989;* Muller Dairies UK Ltd, Tern Valley Business Park, MARKET DRAYTON, SHROPSHIRE, TF9 3SQ.
CLANCY, Mr. Sean Aidan, BSc ACA *1993;* PO Box 23479, DOHA, QATAR.
•**CLANCY, Mr. Stephen Gerard, BA FCA FABRP** *1990;* MCR, The Chancery, 58 Spring Gardens, MANCHESTER, M2 1EW.
CLANCY, Mr. Thomas, FCA *1968;* 2 Lees Field, SOUTHWELL, NG25 0LJ.
CLANNACHAN, Mr. Mark Paul, MA ACA *1996;* Linchmere House, Linchmere, HASLEMERE, GU27 3NG.
CLAPCOTT, Mr. John Peter, BA FCA *1973;* 109 Nether Hall Avenue, BIRMINGHAM, B43 7ET.
CLAPHAM, Mr. Barry Royston, FCA *1967;* Flat 18, Warnham Manor, Ends Place, Byfleets Lane, Warnham, HORSHAM WEST SUSSEX RH12 3RN.
•**CLAPHAM, Mr. David Austin, FCA** *1974;* 28 Avenue Franklin D Roosevelt, 75008 PARIS, FRANCE.
CLAPHAM, Mr. Malcolm David, FCA *1963;* M22, 38 Westacre Cres, WOLVERHAMPTON, WV3 9AX. (Life Member)
CLAPHAM, Mrs. Valda Mary, BSc FCA *1976;* Well Cottage, 12 Deanshanger Road, Wicken, MILTON KEYNES, MK19 6BS.
CLAPIS, Ms. Ilaria, ACA *2008;* A, 173 Harvist Road, LONDON, NW6 6HB.
CLAPP, Mr. Andrew David, BEng ACA *2003;* Barclays Private Equity Condor House, 5-10 St. Paul's Churchyard, LONDON, EC4M 8AL.
CLAPP, Mr. Cedric Marsden, FCA *1973;* Chelwood House, Chelvey Batch, Backwell, BRISTOL, BS48 3BZ.
CLAPP, Mr. David, BSc ACA *2005;* 303 Calmore Road, Calmore, SOUTHAMPTON, SO40 2RF.
•**CLAPP, Mr. David George, FCA** *1973;* Simpkins Edwards LLP, 21 Boutport Street, BARNSTAPLE, DEVON, EX31 1RP.
CLAPPE, Mr. Michael Norman, FCA CA(SA) *1956;* 10 Marston Close, Fairfax Road, LONDON, NW6 4EU. (Life Member)
CLAPPERTON, Mr. Martin John, BSocSc ACA *1992;* 17 Mount Pleasant, Edgworth, BOLTON, BL7 0AG.
CLAPPISON, Mr. Grant, FCA *1973;* 4 West Ella Road, Kirk Ella, HULL, HU10 7QE.
•**CLAPSHAW, Mr. Russell Ernest Aquila, BA FCA** *1967;* (Tax Fac), R. Clapshaw, Norney Grange, Shackleford, GODALMING, GU8 6AY.
•**CLAPSON, Mr. Martin William Herbert, FCA** *1992;* Price Bailey LLP, The Quorum, Barnwell Road, CAMBRIDGE, CB5 8RE. See also Price Bailey Private Client LLP and Colin Pickard & Company Limited
•**CLAPTON, Mr. Eric, BA FCA** *1981;* (Tax Fac), Reeves & Co LLP, Third Floor, 24 Chiswell Street, LONDON, EC1Y 4YX. See also F W Stephens Taxation Limited
CLARANCE, Mr. Alan Angus, BA ACA *1990;* 19-4 Deer Path, MAYNARD, MA 01754, UNITED STATES.
CLARANCE, Mr. Leon Alexander, MA ACA *2001;* (Tax Fac), Octopus Investments Limited, 20 Old Bailey, LONDON, EC4M 7AN.
CLARE, Mrs. Anne Margaret, ACA *1992;* Court Mill, Lower Street, MERRIOTT, SOMERSET, TA16 5NL.
CLARE, Mr. Anthony, BSc FCA *1992;* Swinton Group Ltd, 6-8 Great Marlborough Street, MANCHESTER, M1 5SW.
•**CLARE, Mr. Brian Edwin, FCA** *1980;* Thorne & Co (Ross-on-wye) Limited, 1 St. Marys Street, ROSS-ON-WYE, HEREFORDSHIRE, HR9 5HT.
CLARE, Mr. Franklin Stevens, BA ACA *1997;* 9 Renwick Lane, Cardrona, PEEBLES, EH45 9LU.
CLARE, Ms. Gemma Catherine, MA(Hons) ACA *2001;* 12 Ashley Avenue, BATH, BA1 3DS.
CLARE, Mr. Harry George, FCA *1969;* PO Box 7107, CRESTA, 2118, SOUTH AFRICA. (Life Member)
•**CLARE, Mrs. Julie, BSc FCA** *1987;* Clare & Co, Bannisters, Chorley Road, Withnell, CHORLEY, LANCASHIRE PR6 8BG.
CLARE, Mrs. Julie Anne, FCA *1982;* 9 Blacksmiths Close, Great Amwell, WARE, SG12 9TH.
CLARE, Mr. Leonard, FCA *1949;* 35 Pound Meadow, LEDBURY, HR8 2EU. (Life Member)
CLARE, Miss. Maria, MA ACA *2011;* Flat 3, 24 Park Hill, Ealing, LONDON, W5 2JN.
CLARE, Mr. Steven Gerard, BA ACA *1999;* Fenner Plc, Hesslewood Country Office Park, HESSLE, NORTH HUMBERSIDE, HU13 0PW.
CLAREMONT, Mr. Mark Claude, BA ACA *1981;* Everycare (MK & Beds) Ltd, Suite L G A Oak House, Breckland, Linford Wood, MILTON KEYNES, MK14 6EY.
CLARET, Mr. Jake, FCA *1959;* 39 Morpeth Mansions, Morpeth Mansions, Morpeth Terrace, LONDON, SW1P 1ET. (Life Member)
CLAREY, Mr. Andrew Lindsey, FCA *1968;* 1 Royal Farm Mews, Edgewell Lane, Eaton, TARPORLEY, CHESHIRE, CW6 9XE.
CLAREY, Mr. Richard Jonathan, ACA *2007;* 97 Gracefield Gardens, LONDON, SW16 2TU.
CLARGO, Mrs. Andrea Michelle, BSc ACA *1995;* 22 Highfields Drive, LOUGHBOROUGH, LE11 3JT.
CLARIDGE, Miss. Hazel, BSc ACA *2011;* 3 Richmond Road, PLYMOUTH, PL6 5EE.
CLARIDGE, Mr. Jonathan Peter, ACA *2009;* Pserimos, The Reddings, CHELTENHAM, GLOUCESTERSHIRE, GL51 6RL.
CLARIDGE, Mr. Matthew James, ACA *2002;* Anchor Aweigh, P.O. Box HS 81, HARRINGTON SOUND HS BX, BERMUDA.
CLARIDGE, Mr. Ronald Arthur, FCA *1957;* The Lilacs, 6 Mere Lane, Queniborough, LEICESTER, LE7 3DE. (Life Member)
CLARK, Mr. Aden Brian, FCA *1969;* Oakleigh, Guelles Road, St. Peter Port, GUERNSEY, GY1 2DB.
CLARK, Mr. Adrian Spencer, BSc ACA *1992;* 81a Cambridge Road, Milton, CAMBRIDGE, CB24 6AW.
•**CLARK, Mr. Alan Douglas, FCA** *1979;* Greaves Grindle, Victoria House, Bondgate Within, ALNWICK, NE66 1TA.
•①**CLARK, Mr. Alan John, BA ACA** *1990;* Carter Clark, Meridian House, 62 Station Road, North Chingford, LONDON, E4 7BA.
CLARK, Mr. Alastair George, FCA *1964;* The Copse, Mile Path, Hook Heath, WOKING, GU22 0JL.
CLARK, Mr. Albert Neville, FCA *1977;* 1 Mow Barton, Yate, BRISTOL, BS37 5NF.
CLARK, Mr. Albert Roy, FCA *1956;* 2 Pyne Gardens, Upton Pyne, EXETER, EX5 5JE. (Life Member)
CLARK, Mr. Alexander David, ACA *2008;* Apartment 18, 33 Osiers Road, LONDON, SW18 1NL.
CLARK, Mr. Alexander Ross, LLB ACA *2003;* 1 Derby Villas, Derby Road Caversham, READING, RG4 5DP.
CLARK, Miss. Alison Irene Joyce, BA(Hons) ACA *2002;* 11a Howard Park, Greystoke, PENRITH, CUMBRIA, CA11 0TU.
CLARK, Miss. Alison Jane, BSc ACA ACCA *1995;* Bridge End Barn, Ullock, WORKINGTON, CUMBRIA, CA14 4TP.
CLARK, Mr. Allan John, MBA BSc FCA *1980;* 6 Snaith Crescent, Loughton, MILTON KEYNES, MK5 8HG.
•**CLARK, Mr. Allan Leonard, FCA** *1974;* (Tax Fac), C.H. Jefferson & Co, 108 Oswald Road, SCUNTHORPE, SOUTH HUMBERSIDE, DN15 7PA.
•**CLARK, Mr. Alun, BSc FCA** *1976;* (Tax Fac), Clark & Co, 4 Broad Street, BUILTH WELLS, LD2 3DT.
CLARK, Ms. Amanda Jane, ACA *2003;* 2 Barrett Road, Fetcham, LEATHERHEAD, SURREY, KT22 9HL.
CLARK, Miss. Amanda Jane, ACA *2007;* 9 Fettes Road, CRANLEIGH, SURREY, GU6 7EU.
•**CLARK, Mrs. Amelia-Jane, ACA** *2008;* Clark Accounting Services, 18 Homevale Cottages, Main Road, Knockholt, SEVENOAKS, KENT TN14 7JE.
CLARK, Mr. Andrew, BA(Hons) ACA *2009;* Flat 2, 74 Loveridge Road, LONDON, NW6 2DT.
CLARK, Mr. Andrew, BA ACA *1985;* 96 Aldenham Road, GUISBOROUGH, TS14 8LD.
CLARK, Mr. Andrew, FCA *1973;* 9 Rochford Grove, Barns Park, CRAMLINGTON, NE23 7XQ.
•**CLARK, Mr. Andrew Aidan, BSc FCA** *1986;* (Tax Fac), Carter & Coley, 3 Durrant Road, BOURNEMOUTH, BH2 6NE.
CLARK, Mr. Andrew David, BA ACA *1990;* 101 Bower Road, Crookes, SHEFFIELD, S10 1ER.
CLARK, Mr. Andrew Gilbert, ACA *1985;* 10 Walnut Grove, Crick, CALDICOT, NP26 5UX.
CLARK, Mr. Andrew James, BA ACA AMCT *2003;* 27 Station Road, Cheddington, LEIGHTON BUZZARD, BEDFORDSHIRE, LU7 0SG.
CLARK, Mr. Andrew James, BA ACA *2006;* Flat B, 78 Birnam Road, LONDON, N4 3LQ.
CLARK, Mr. Andrew John, BSc ACA CTA *1985;* Verdant, Greenwood Road, Tilehurst, READING, RG30 4JG.
CLARK, Mr. Andrew John Francis, BA ACA *2006;* 10 Fairlands Road, BURY, BL9 6QA.
CLARK, Mr. Andrew Keith, BA(Hons) ACA *2001;* 41 Warwick Road, COULSDON, SURREY, CR5 2EF.
CLARK, Mr. Andrew Michael, BA ACA *1994;* 1 Bellingham Mount, Wigan Lane, WIGAN, LANCASHIRE, WN1 2NJ.
CLARK, Mr. Andrew Nicholas, BA ACA *1998;* 6 Crud Yr Awel, Pen Y Fai, BRIDGEND, Mid Glamorgan, CF31 4GH.
CLARK, Mr. Andrew Paul, BSc ACA *1990;* ANNFIELD, 41 Rosebank, CARLUKE, LANARKSHIRE, ML8 5QB.
•**CLARK, Mr. Andrew Peter, BSc ACA** *1991;* PricewaterhouseCoopers LLP, Pricewaterhousecoopers, 12 Plumtree Court, LONDON, EC4A 4HT. See also PricewaterhouseCoopers
•**CLARK, Mr. Andrew Peter, BA FCA** *1991;* Deloitte LLP, 2 New Street Square, LONDON, EC4A 3BZ. See also Deloitte & Touche LLP
CLARK, Mr. Andrew Philip, BA ACA *1990;* 71 High Street, Linton, CAMBRIDGE, CB21 4HS.
CLARK, Mrs. Anne Rosemary, BSc ACA *1991;* Hyder Consulting (UK) Ltd, The Pithay, BRISTOL, BS1 2NL.
CLARK, Mr. Anson Frazer, MA ACA *2000;* Flat 1, 11 Dean Bank Lane, EDINBURGH, EH3 5BS.
CLARK, Mr. Anthony David, FCA *1962;* Porch House, Peasmarsh, ILMINSTER, SOMERSET, TA19 0SG.
•**CLARK, Mr. Anthony Ernest, FCA** *1952;* Ernest Clark & Co, 26 St.Catherines Close, LONDON, SW17 7UA.
CLARK, Mr. Anthony Lewis Russell, FCA *1968;* The Water Gardens, Birchley Road, Battledown, CHELTENHAM, GL52 6NY.
CLARK, Mr. Anthony Maurice, FCA *1964;* 114 Conway Road, FALMOUTH, CORNWALL, TR11 4LJ.
•**CLARK, Mr. Antony John, FCA** *1965;* AJ Clark, 14 Cricket Lawns, OAKHAM, LEICESTERSHIRE, LE15 6HT.
CLARK, Miss. Barbara Lesley, MA ACA *2005;* with Deloitte LLP, 2 New Street Square, LONDON, EC4A 3BZ.
CLARK, Mr. Barry, BSc FCA *1977;* 23 Freshfield Drive, MACCLESFIELD, SK10 2TU.
CLARK, Mr. Barry Philip, FCA *1973;* Seascapes, Redlap Lane, Stoke Fleming, DARTMOUTH, TQ6 0QU.
CLARK, Mr. Bernard, FCA *1951;* 40 Damson Road, Thorngumbald, HULL, HU12 9QL. (Life Member)
CLARK, Mr. Bernard Colin, FCA *1966;* Mill Hatch, Dunmow Road, Thaxted, DUNMOW, CM6 2LU. (Life Member)
CLARK, Mr. Bernard James, FCA *1965;* 33 Marylands Avenue, HOCKLEY, ESSEX, SS5 5AH.
CLARK, Mr. Brian John Thompson, FCA *1959;* 1 Pauls Place, ASHTEAD, SURREY, KT21 1HN. (Life Member)
•**CLARK, Mr. Brian Leslie, BSc ACA** *1989;* PricewaterhouseCoopers LLP, 101 Barbirolli Square, Lower Mosley Street, MANCHESTER, M2 3PW. See also PricewaterhouseCoopers
CLARK, Mr. Brian Michael, BCom ACA *1981;* 30 Oliver Road, South Ascot, ASCOT, SL5 9DZ.
CLARK, Mr. Bryan David, FCA *1953;* 6 Cavendish Place, BOURNEMOUTH, BH1 1RQ. (Life Member)
•**CLARK, Mr. Bryce Roger, ACA** *1989;* CKA Consultancy Limited, Pen Afon, Maunsel Road, North Newton, BRIDGWATER, SOMERSET TA7 0BS.
•**CLARK, Mr. Cameron Mccallum, BSc FCA** *1981;* (Tax Fac), Cameron Clark, Prinlaws House, 12 Walkerton Drive, Leslie, GLENROTHES, FIFE KY6 3BT.
CLARK, Miss. Catherine Louise, BA(Hons) ACA *2001;* (Tax Fac), Flat 2 Lyne House, Rusper Road Capel, DORKING, SURREY, RH5 5HQ.
CLARK, Mrs. Catherine Mary, BA ACA *1986;* Stoddah, Penruddock, PENRITH, CUMBRIA, CA11 0RY.
CLARK, Mr. Charles Edwin Lincoln, BA FCA *1989;* KPMG LLP, 500 East Middlefield Road, MOUNTAIN VIEW, CA 94043, UNITED STATES.
•**CLARK, Mrs. Christine Margaret, BSc ACA** *1981;* Christine Clark Accountants Ltd, 43 Poplar Avenue, WETHERBY, WEST YORKSHIRE, LS22 7RA.
•**CLARK, Mr. Christopher David, BA ACA CF** *1996;* BDO LLP, 55 Baker Street, LONDON, W1U 7EU. See also BDO Stoy Hayward LLP
CLARK, Mr. Christopher John, FCA *1969;* 4 Richards Close, Court DriveHillingdon, UXBRIDGE, UB10 0BT.
CLARK, Mr. Christopher John, BA ACA *1998;* 946 West 20th Avenue, VANCOUVER V5Z 1Y5, BC, CANADA.
CLARK, Mr. Christopher Owen Paul, BA ACA *2002;* Flat 9 Weirside Place, Old Mill Close, EXETER, EX2 4BW.
CLARK, Mrs. Claire Elizabeth, BA(Hons) ACA *2000;* 41 Warwick Road, COULSDON, SURREY, CR5 2EF.
CLARK, Mr. Clive Henry, FCA *1963;* Wreeds, Parsonage Downs, DUNMOW, ESSEX, CM6 2AT.
•**CLARK, Mr. Colin, MA BSc FCA** *1985;* University House, University of Warwick, Gibbet Hill Road, COVENTRY, CV4 7AL.
CLARK, Mr. Colin David, BSc FCA *1960;* Briar Cottage, The Green, Shamley Green, GUILDFORD, GU5 0UA. (Life Member)
•**CLARK, Mr. Colin David, FCA** *1965;* Colin D Clark, Riverside House, Off Glen Road, Laxey, ISLE OF MAN, IM4 7AT.
CLARK, Mr. Daniel, FCA *1951;* Charlewood, 20 Vicarage Street, Woburn Sands, MILTON KEYNES, MK17 8RE. (Life Member)
CLARK, Mr. Daniel Adam, MPhil BA(Hons) FCA *1998;* Chatsworth House, 6 Chatsworth Gardens, SHREWSBURY, SHROPSHIRE, SY3 7BG.
CLARK, Mr. Daniel Charles, BA ACA *1997;* K P M G Llp, 15 Canada Square, LONDON, E14 5GL.
CLARK, Mr. Daniel James Macaulay, ACA *1987;* Netherfield, 241 Barton Road, Comberton, CAMBRIDGE, CB3 7BU.
CLARK, Mr. Darren Paul, MA ACA *1996;* SWG Sales Operations Department, IBM United Kingdom Ltd, 1-6 New Square, FELTHAM, TW14 8HB.
CLARK, Mr. Darren Wayne, BSc ACA *2005;* Wellington House, 3 Exhims Mews, Darrs Lane Northchurch, BERKHAMSTED, HERTFORDSHIRE, HP4 3RA.
CLARK, Mr. David, FCA *1970;* (Member of Council 1992 - 1993), 2 Meadow Rise, Littleton, WINCHESTER, HAMPSHIRE, SO22 6NH. (Life Member)
CLARK, Mr. David, ACA *1978;* Avenue De La Gare 49, Case Postale 2067, CH-2001 NEUCHATEL, SWITZERLAND.
•**CLARK, Mr. David Anthony, FCA** *1966;* (Tax Fac), D A Clark & Co Limited, 4 Peel House, Barttelot Road, HORSHAM, WEST SUSSEX, RH12 1DE.
CLARK, Mr. David Barry, FCA *1966;* Flat 55, St. Leonards Court, St. Leonards Road, East Sheen, LONDON, SW14 7LS. (Life Member)
CLARK, Mr. David Charles, BA ACA *1989;* Colliers, 1-41 Sutton Road, BIRMINGHAM, B23 6QH.
CLARK, Mr. David Clarence, FCA *1959;* 22 Bayham Road, SEVENOAKS, KENT, TN13 3XD. (Life Member)
CLARK, Mr. David Digby Mullin, FCA *1947;* 171 Heathwood Road, Heath, CARDIFF, CF14 4BN. (Life Member)
CLARK, Mr. David Henry, FCA *1969;* 46a East Borough, WIMBORNE, DORSET, BH21 1PL.
CLARK, Mr. David James, MA MPhil ACA *1992;* 35 Thistle Street, GALASHIELS, SELKIRKSHIRE, TD1 1LX.
•**CLARK, Mr. David James, BA FCA DChA** *1984;* David Clark, 1st Floor, Church House, 61 College Road, BROMLEY, BR1 3QG.
CLARK, Mr. David John, BA ACA *1993;* 24 Dorothy Road, LONDON, SW11 2JP.
CLARK, Mr. David John Charles, BA ACA *1994;* 73 Gurney Court Road, ST. ALBANS, HERTFORDSHIRE, AL1 4QX.
CLARK, Mr. David Kenneth, BCom ACA *1986;* 6b Kings Gardens, BIRMINGHAM, B30 1DZ.
CLARK, Mr. David Michael, BSc FCA *1988;* Valparaiso, Ave du Manoir Ville Au Roi, St Peter Port, GUERNSEY, GY1 1PE.
CLARK, Mr. David Richard, FCA *1968;* 17 Hazeldene, SEAFORD, BN25 4NQ. (Life Member)

•**CLARK, Mr. David Samuel, BA FCA** *1993;* Baker Tilly Tax and Advisory Services LLP, 25 Farringdon Street, LONDON, EC4A 4AB. See also Baker Tilly UK Audit LLP
CLARK, The Hon. David William, FCA *1971;* 7-9 Rua Dr.Franciso Fernandes Lopes, 8700-228 OLHAO, ALGARVE, PORTUGAL.
CLARK, Mrs. Deborah, BSc ACA *1984;* Yewtree House, High Street, Hunsdon, WARE, SG12 8NT.
•**CLARK, Mrs. Debra, FCA** *1998;* Debra Clark & Co, 128 Rawreth Lane, RAYLEIGH, SS6 9RR.
•**CLARK, Mr. Derek, FCA** *1977;* (Tax Fac), Clark & Co, 22 Leaman Close, Chipping Sodbury, BRISTOL, BS37 6HA.
CLARK, Mrs. Diane Josephine, ACA *1986;* 8 Cypress Drive, Puriton, BRIDGWATER, SOMERSET, TA7 8AQ.
CLARK, Mr. Edward Gene, BA FCA *1985;* 58 Broadwalk, WILMSLOW, SK9 5PN.
CLARK, Mr. Edward William Herbert, FCA *1963;* 13 Warners Avenue, HODDESDON, EN11 8LP. (Life Member)
•**CLARK, Miss. Elaine Carole, BSc(Hons) ACA** *1989;* All on the Web Limited, 51 Hambledon Drive, WIRRAL, MERSEYSIDE, CH49 2QH.
•**CLARK, Mrs. Elizabeth, BA(Hons) ACA** *1996;* Liz Clark, 32 Sandhurst Avenue, West Didsbury, MANCHESTER, M20 1ED. See also Liz Elliott
CLARK, Miss. Emily, BA(Hons) ACA *2002;* with BDO LLP, 55 Baker Street, LONDON, W1U 7EU.
CLARK, Miss. Emma Jane, BSc(Hons) ACA *2010;* 19 Church Crescent, Sproughton, IPSWICH, IP8 3BJ.
CLARK, Mr. Eric Maurice, BA ACA *1980;* Kalah Consulting Ltd, Kalah, Puddletown, Haselbury Plucknett, CREWKERNE, SOMERSET TA18 7NZ.
CLARK, Mrs. Fiona Grace, BA ACA *1987;* Windyridge, 58 Stanley Hill Avenue, AMERSHAM, HP7 9BA.
•**CLARK, Mrs. Frances Helen, MA ACA** *2002;* (Tax Fac), Keswick Accountants Limited, Bracken Hue, Millbeck, KESWICK, CUMBRIA, CA12 4PS.
CLARK, Mr. Fraser Jeremy Austin, BA ACA *1995;* 4 Sunways, MIRFIELD, WF14 9TN.
CLARK, Dr. Frazer Stephen, MA DPhil ACA *2005;* with National Audit Office, 157-197 Buckingham Palace Road, Victoria, LONDON, SW1W 9SP.
CLARK, Mr. Gary, BEng ACA *1990;* La Folie St Brelades Park, La Route de Noirmont, St Brelade, JERSEY, JE3 8AN.
CLARK, Mr. Gary David, BA ACA *1990;* 5 Curlys Way, Swallowfield, READING, RG7 1QZ.
CLARK, Mr. Gary James, BA FCA *1999;* 22 The Close, RADLETT, HERTFORDSHIRE, WD7 8HA.
•**CLARK, Miss. Gemma Louise, BSc ACA** *2005;* 8 Stumps Close, WAKEFIELD, WEST YORKSHIRE, WF1 3RA.
CLARK, Mr. Geoffrey David, FCA *1966;* 16 The Downlands, WARMINSTER, WILTSHIRE, BA12 0BD.
CLARK, Mr. Geoffrey Ian, BA ACA *1996;* UNIT4A, Gateway Business ParkBeancross Road, GRANGEMOUTH, FK3 8WX.
CLARK, Mrs. Gillian, BA ACA *1987;* 137 Blenheim Crescent, LONDON, W11 2EQ.
CLARK, Mr. Glen John, BCom ACA *1992;* 50 High Street, Wicken, ELY, CAMBRIDGESHIRE, CB7 5XR.
CLARK, Mr. Gordon Martin, BSc FCA *1981;* 550 East Flat 10, Triq San Geraldu, ST PAULS BAY SPB 3315, MALTA.
CLARK, Mr. Graeme Charles, ACA *1978;* Whitefield Cottage, Frieth, HENLEY-ON-THAMES, RG9 6NP.
CLARK, Mr. Graham, FCA *1963;* 32/33 Beverley Road, STEVENAGE, HERTFORDSHIRE, SG1 4PR.
CLARK, Mr. Graham, BSc ACA *2011;* 23b Queen Street, NEWCASTLE UPON TYNE, NE1 3UG.
CLARK, Mr. Graham Andrew, BSc ACA *1979;* Hollycroft, 52 Green Lane, HARROGATE, NORTH YORKSHIRE, HG2 9LP.
CLARK, Mr. Graham James, FCA *1969;* P.O. Box CB 11219, NASSAU, NEW PROVIDENCE, BAHAMAS.
CLARK, Mr. Hamish Gerrard, LLB ACA *2010;* 74b The Chase, LONDON, SW4 0NG.
CLARK, Miss. Hayley, ACA *2010;* 1 Billings Close, HAVERHILL, SUFFOLK, CB9 9SA.
CLARK, Mrs. Hazel, ACA *1987;* 3 Miramar, Bradley Manor, HUDDERSFIELD, HD2 1NA.
CLARK, Miss. Heather Simone, ACA *2008;* Flat 27, Kings Oak Court, Queens Road, READING, RG1 4PX.
CLARK, Mr. Hedley Stuart, BA FCA *1987;* Long Acre, Blackhall Lane, SEVENOAKS, KENT, TN15 0HN.
•**CLARK, Mrs. Helen, MA ACA CTA** *1995;* (Tax Fac), Dixon Wilson, 22 Chancery Lane, LONDON, WC2A 1LS.
CLARK, Mrs. Helen Mary, BA ACA *1987;* 7 Glenshiel Road, LONDON, SE9 1AQ.
CLARK, Mrs. Helen Stasia, BA ACA *1992;* The Cottage, High Street, Twyford, WINCHESTER, HAMPSHIRE, SO21 1NP.
CLARK, Mr. Henry Walker, FCA *1947;* 45 Manor Farm Court, Manor Farm Lane, EGHAM, SURREY, TW20 9JR. (Life Member)
CLARK, Mr. Hugh Alan, FCA *1965;* 56 Alexandra Avenue, LUTON, LU3 1HG.
CLARK, Mr. Ian, BA ACA ATII *1992;* (Tax Fac), 13 Abbots Avenue, BRISTOL, BS15 3PL.
CLARK, Mr. Ian Arthur, ACA *1981;* 3509 Commodore Court, OAK HILL, VA 20171, UNITED STATES.
•**CLARK, Mr. Ian Edward, FCA** *1983;* Deloitte LLP, Athene Place, 66 Shoe Lane, LONDON, EC4A 3BQ. See also Deloitte & Touche LLP
CLARK, Mr. Ian Robert, FCA *1977;* 21 Atkins Avenue, RUSSELL LEA, NSW 2046, AUSTRALIA.
CLARK, Mr. Iayn G, BSc ACA *1983;* 44 Sylvester Road, LONDON, N2 8HN.
CLARK, Ms. Isabelle Anne, BA ACA *1997;* 15 South Ealing Road, LONDON, W5 4QT.
CLARK, Mrs. Jacqueline Maria, BSc ACA *1991;* 88 Twyford Avenue, Acton, LONDON, W3 9QF.
CLARK, Mr. James Antony Corbett, MA ACA *1996;* 38 Derwent Drive, LEEDS, LS16 8JD.
CLARK, Mr. James Charles Leslie, BSc ACA *1980;* 1451 Warren Drive, OAKVILLE L6J 5T7, ON, CANADA.
CLARK, Mr. James Daniel, CA ACA CF *1997;* with RSM Tenon Limited, International House, 66 Chiltern Street, LONDON, W1U 4JT.
CLARK, Mr. James Douglas, BA(Hons) ACA *2009;* 15 The Priory, Epsom Road, CROYDON, CR0 4NT.
CLARK, Mr. James John, BA ACA *2000;* 41 Annie Besant Close, LONDON, E3 2ER.
CLARK, Mr. James Richard, MA(Oxon) ACA MABRP *2005;* Grove House, Soothill Lane, BATLEY, WEST YORKSHIRE, WF17 5SS.
CLARK, Mr. Jamie, BSc ACA *2005;* Merrill Lynch Financial Centre, 2 King Edward Street, LONDON, EC1A 1HQ.
•**CLARK, Mrs. Jane Clare Hattersley, BSc FCA** *1985;* Hattersley Clark, Copthall Bridge House, Station Bridge, HARROGATE, NORTH YORKSHIRE, HG1 1SP.
CLARK, Mr. Jason Lee, BA FCA *1997;* Tringonos, Windmill Hill Business Park, SWINDON, SN5 6PB.
•**CLARK, Mr. Jeremy Francis, BSc ACA** *1986;* (Tax Fac), AIMS - Jeremy Clark ACA, The Moat House, Sallow Lane, Wacton, NORWICH, NR15 2UL.
CLARK, Mrs. Jill, BA ACA *1987;* 43 Loxley Road, Wandsworth Common, LONDON, SW18 3LL.
CLARK, Miss. Joanne, BSc ACA *2006;* M G Kailis Pty Ltd, 50 Mews Road, FREMANTLE, WA 6160, AUSTRALIA.
CLARK, Mrs. Johanna Maria, BA ACA *2005;* 8 Dovehouse Close, ELY, CAMBRIDGESHIRE, CB7 4BY.
•**CLARK, Mr. John, ACA ACCA** *2009;* Philip Barnes & Co Ltd, The Old Council Chambers, Halford Street, TAMWORTH, B79 7RB.
CLARK, Mr. John, ACA *2008;* with Credit Suisse, One Cabot Square, LONDON, E14 4QJ.
CLARK, Mr. John, FCA *1953;* 17 Orchard Way, SOUTHAM, WARWICKSHIRE, CV47 1EG. (Life Member)
CLARK, Mr. John, BA ACA *1980;* Fair View, Lower Road, Soudley, CINDERFORD, GL14 2TZ.
CLARK, Mr. John Cameron, FCA *1967;* 55 Skeena Hill, LONDON, SW18 5PW.
CLARK, Mr. John Charles Travers, FCA *1952;* Manor Cottage, Woodhurst Lane, OXTED, RH8 9HJ. (Life Member)
CLARK, Mr. John Ogden, FCA *1957;* 8 Town Wells Drive, Calverley, PUDSEY, LS28 5NN. (Life Member)
CLARK, Mr. John Robert Morton, BSc FCA *1982;* Play Direst Limited, 1 Esplanade, St. Helier, JERSEY, JE2 3QA.
CLARK, Mr. John Vincent Michael Gordon, FCA *1956;* Hillfield, 8 Little Warren Close, GUILDFORD, GU4 8PW. (Life Member)
CLARK, Mr. John Webb, BA FCA *1965;* Orchard Priors, Battledown Close, CHELTENHAM, GL52 6RD.
CLARK, Mr. John William, FCA *1965;* Flat 24 Nelson Court, Glen View, GRAVESEND, DA12 1PL.
CLARK, Mr. Jonathan, BSocSc ACA *2003;* 68 Lightwoods Hill, SMETHWICK, B67 5EB.
CLARK, Mr. Jonathan Charles, ACA *1996;* 121 Redriff Road, LONDON, SE16 7PS.
CLARK, Mr. Jonathan Dudley, BA ACA *1983;* 203 Derby Road, Beeston, NOTTINGHAM, NG9 3AP.
CLARK, Mr. Jonathan Mark, BSc ACA CF *2000;* 47 St. Martins Drive, Eynsford, DARTFORD, DA4 0EY.
CLARK, Mrs. Judith, BSc ACA *1986;* Mawcroft Cottage, Mawcroft Grange Drive, Rawdon, LEEDS, LS19 6DJ.
CLARK, Mrs. Judith, ACA CTA *1992;* 108 Lowry Hill Road, CARLISLE, CA3 0DH.
CLARK, Miss. Julie-Anne, BSc ACA *2010;* 9 North Street, Downend, BRISTOL, BS16 5SY.
CLARK, Miss. Karen, ACA *1995;* West Reidford, Drumoak, BANCHORY, KINCARDINESHIRE, AB31 5AU.
•**CLARK, Mrs. Karen Frances, MA ACA CTA** *1990;* (Tax Fac), Baker Tilly Tax and Advisory Services LLP, 25 Farringdon Street, LONDON, EC4A 4AB.
CLARK, Mrs. Kathryn Mary, MA ACA *1984;* First Floor, International Accounting Standards Board, 30 Cannon Street, LONDON, EC4M 6XH.
CLARK, Mr. Kenneth Gerald, FCA *1962;* Quinta Souto do Paco Reriz, 3600-598 CASTO DAIRE, PORTUGAL. (Life Member)
CLARK, Mr. Kenneth William, BA ACA *1991;* 15 Dunnillow Field, Stapeley, NANTWICH, CW5 7GX.
CLARK, Mr. Kevin James Thomas, MEng ACA *1999;* 6 Eastwood Lane South, WESTCLIFF-ON-SEA, SS0 9XJ.
CLARK, Mr. Kevin Neil, BCom ACA *1986;* 12 Wedderburn Court, Inveresk, MUSSELBURGH, MIDLOTHIAN, EH21 7TU.
•**CLARK, Mr. Kevin Roy, BSc ACA** *1987;* with KPMG LLP, 15 Canada Square, LONDON, E14 5GL.
•**CLARK, Mrs. Kim Louise, BA ACA** *2003;* Cambridge Financial Partners LLP, St. Johns Innovation Park, Cowley Road, CAMBRIDGE, CB4 0WS.
CLARK, Miss. Kirsty Jolanta, BSc ACA *2005;* Flat 6 Exchange Building, 132 Commercial Street, LONDON, E1 6NG.
CLARK, Mr. Leonard, FCA *1961;* 39 Windermere Crescent, Ainsdale, SOUTHPORT, PR8 3QS.
•**CLARK, Mrs. Lesley Mary, FCA** *1980;* Lesley Clark, The Beeches, Manor Court, Carlton-le-Moorland, LINCOLN, LN5 9JJ.
CLARK, Mr. Lessel James Martin, FCA *1975;* 14 Lanes End, Heath & Reach, LEIGHTON BUZZARD, LU7 0AE.
CLARK, Ms. Linda Mary, ACA CA(NZ) *2010;* 151 Cholmley Gardens, Mill Lane, LONDON, NW6 1AD.
CLARK, Miss. Louise, BA ACA *1999;* with Deloitte LLP, 2 New Street Square, LONDON, EC4A 3BZ.
CLARK, Mr. Malcolm Graham, BA FCA *1979;* 12 Mitchell Avenue, WHITLEY BAY, NE25 8NH.
•**CLARK, Mr. Malcolm Ian, FCA** *1975;* (Tax Fac), Malcolm Clark & Co, 39 Grange Road, DARLINGTON, COUNTY DURHAM, DL1 5NB. See also Mollart & Co
•**CLARK, Mr. Malcolm Laurence, FCA** *1981;* ECL Howard Watson Smith LLP, E C L House, Lake Street, LEIGHTON BUZZARD, BEDFORDSHIRE, LU7 1RT.
CLARK, Mr. Marcelo Arthur Adam, BSc ACA *1992;* 19 Cambridge Road, Moseley, BIRMINGHAM, B13 9UE.
CLARK, Mrs. Maria Naomi, BA(Hons) ACA *2003;* 22 Gloucester Road, Ealing, LONDON, W5 4JA.
CLARK, Mr. Martin Grant, ACA CA(NZ) *2009;* 34 Hazel Road, LONDON, NW10 5PP.
•**CLARK, Mr. Michael Anthony, FCA** *1990;* Clarkson Hyde LLP, 3rd Floor, Chancery House, St. Nicholas Way, SUTTON, SURREY SM1 1JB. See also Business Matters (UK) Ltd
CLARK, Mr. Michael Colin, FCA *1983;* Shrimpton Cottage, Selling Road, Old Wives Lees, CANTERBURY, CT4 8BE.
CLARK, Mr. Michael Eldred, BEng ACA *1998;* 46 Oldfield Road, HAMPTON, MIDDLESEX, TW12 2AE.
CLARK, Mr. Michael Gerard, BA(Hons) ACA *2001;* 14 Kirkwick Avenue, HARPENDEN, HERTFORDSHIRE, AL5 2QN.
CLARK, Mr. Michael Philip, BSc(Econ) ACA *2001;* 7 Cawthorn Close, DRIFFIELD, NORTH HUMBERSIDE, YO25 5PG.
CLARK, Mr. Michael Ralph, BA ACA CF *1992;* Medve utca 4-14, H-1995 BUDAPEST, HUNGARY.
CLARK, Mr. Michael Robert, BSc FCA *1982;* Ranfurly, Normanstead, Greys Hill, HENLEY-ON-THAMES, RG9 1SW.
CLARK, Mr. Michael Roger, FCA *1967;* Farthings, Roman Road, Little Aston Park, SUTTON COLDFIELD, B74 3AR. (Life Member)
•**CLARK, Mr. Michael Stuart, MSc BA ACA** *1986;* (Tax Fac), Francis Clark LLP, Vantage Point, Woodwater Park, Pynes Hill, EXETER, EX2 5FD. See also Francis Clark Tax Consultancy Ltd
CLARK, Mr. Neil Peter, BSc ACA *1987;* Northolt, 394 Goldington Road, BEDFORD, MK41 9NT.
CLARK, Mr. Neil Robert, BSc ACA *1992;* 15 Holland Street, CAMBRIDGE, CB4 3DL.
CLARK, Mr. Niall, BA(Hons) ACA *2003;* 22 Gloucester Road, LONDON, W5 4JA.
CLARK, Mr. Nicholas Jackson, FCA *1965;* Abbeylands Farm, Wineham Lane, Wineham, HENFIELD, WEST SUSSEX, BN5 9AQ.
CLARK, Ms. Nicola, BA ACA *2004;* A J Bennewith & Co Hitherbury House, 97 Portsmouth Road, GUILDFORD, GU2 4YF.
CLARK, Mr. Nigel Graham, BSc FCA *1980;* CML Microsystems Ltd, Oval Park, Hatfield Road, Langford, MALDON, ESSEX CM9 6WG.
CLARK, Mr. Nigel Ian Kynoch, MA FCA *1966;* 26 Boreham Holt, Elstree, BOREHAMWOOD, WD6 3QF. (Life Member)
CLARK, Mr. Oliver Ian David, BA ACA *2007;* Flat 3 Mercia Court, Highwood Close, LONDON, SE22 8NN.
CLARK, Mrs. Pamela Grace, BA BSc ACIB ACA *2001;* 67 Highfield Avenue, HARPENDEN, HERTFORDSHIRE, AL5 5TZ.
•**CLARK, Mr. Paul, BSc FCA** *1979;* 21 Queensway, Darras Hall, NEWCASTLE UPON TYNE, NE20 9RZ.
•**CLARK, Mr. Paul Andrew, BSc ACA** *1987;* Moore Stephens LLP, 150 Aldersgate Street, LONDON, EC1A 4AB. See also Moore Stephens & Co
CLARK, Mr. Paul Andrew, BEng ACA *2002;* 121 Longhurst Road, LONDON, SE13 5NA.
CLARK, Mr. Paul Andrew, BA ACA *1984;* Virgin Homes Ltd, 6 Half Moon St, LONDON, W1S 7DA.
CLARK, Mr. Paul Gerard Andrew, BSc ACA *1991;* Emery Down, 13 Bolters Lane, BANSTEAD, SURREY, SM7 2AU.
CLARK, Mr. Paul Jonathan, MA ACA *1979;* Family Matters Institute, Moggerhanger Park Ltd The Park, Park Road Moggerhanger, BEDFORD, MK44 3RW.
CLARK, Mr. Paul Nicholas, BEng ACA *1997;* with Ernst & Young, The Ernst & Young Building, 680 George Street, SYDNEY, NSW 2000, AUSTRALIA.
CLARK, Mr. Peter David, BSc ACA *1993;* 2 Cedar Road, TEDDINGTON, TW11 9AL.
CLARK, Mr. Peter Donald, FCA *1980;* 84 Elloughton Road, BROUGH, NORTH HUMBERSIDE, HU15 1AL.
CLARK, Mr. Peter Edmondson Drummond, BA ACA *1982;* 10015 Tesla Road, LIVERMORE, CA 94550, UNITED STATES.
CLARK, Mr. Peter Fergusson, ACA *1979;* 2 Didsbury Court, Wilmslow Road, MANCHESTER, M20 6AD.
CLARK, Mr. Peter Gerald Badger, FCA *1971;* 21 Vicarage Meadow, FOWEY, CORNWALL, PL23 1DZ. (Life Member)
•**CLARK, Mr. Peter John, FCA FCMI** *1974;* Peter Clark, Milestones, 98 Woodside Road, AMERSHAM, BUCKINGHAMSHIRE, HP6 6AP.
•**CLARK, Mr. Peter Morten, FCA** *1975;* (Tax Fac), Welbeck Associates Limited, 31 Harley Street, LONDON, W1G 9QS.
CLARK, Mr. Peter Nicholas, FCA *1977;* 23 Abbeydale Garth, LEEDS, LS5 3RQ.
CLARK, Mr. Peter Norman, MA ACA *1985;* International Accounting Standards Board, 30 Cannon Street, LONDON, EC4M 6XH.
CLARK, Mr. Peter Stephen, FCA *1966;* 11 Broad Oak, Corseley Road, TUNBRIDGE WELLS, TN3 9SD. (Life Member)
CLARK, Mr. Peter William, ACA MAAT *2004;* 320 Kempshott Lane, BASINGSTOKE, RG22 5LT.
•**CLARK, Mr. Philip Antony, BA FCA** *1990;* Chantrey Vellacott DFK LLP, 23-28 Great Russell Street, LONDON, WC1B 3NG.
CLARK, Miss. Rachel Anne, BSc ACA *1989;* Ridings, New York Lane, Rawdon, LEEDS, LS19 6JJ.
CLARK, Mr. Raymond Albert, BA FCA MIBC *1980;* 17 Oak End Way, GERRARDS CROSS, BUCKINGHAMSHIRE, SL9 8DA.
CLARK, Mr. Reginald George, FCA *1946;* 2 Tower Close, HORSHAM, RH13 0AF. (Life Member)
CLARK, Mr. Richard, ACA *2011;* 16 Moor Allerton Hall, Lidgett Lane, LEEDS, LS8 1SG.
CLARK, Mr. Richard James, BSc ACA CTA *1998;* (Tax Fac), Marks & Spencer Plc Waterside House, 35 North Wharf Road, LONDON, W2 1NW.
CLARK, Mr. Richard Jason, BSc ACA *1999;* Liz Earle Beauty Co Limited, The Green House, Ryde Business Park, Nicholson Road, RYDE, ISLE OF WIGHT PO33 1BD.
CLARK, Mr. Richard John, FCA *1966;* 4 Bayside Drive, LAUDERDALE, TAS 7021, AUSTRALIA. (Life Member)
CLARK, Mr. Richard Jonathan, BSc ACA *1989;* 46 Hillcrest, HATFIELD, AL10 8HG.

CLARK, Mr. Richard Joseph John, BSc FCA CISA CISM *1994;* National Audit Office, 157-197 Buckingham Palace Road, LONDON, SW1W 9SP.
CLARK, Mr. Robert Alan, FCA *1970;* 22 Kennet Way, Oakley, BASINGSTOKE, RG23 7AN. (Life Member)
CLARK, Mr. Robert Andrew, BSc ACA *1987;* 2, Hollybank Drive, Lostock, BOLTON, BL6 4DD.
CLARK, Mr. Robert Edmund, FCA *1968;* 50 Motspur Park, NEW MALDEN, KT3 6PL.
CLARK, Mr. Robert James, MA ACA *1993;* Northampton House, Aysgarth, LEYBURN, NORTH YORKSHIRE, DL8 3AH.
CLARK, Mr. Robert James, BSc ACA *1992;* Westbrook House, 3 Lower End, Piddington, BICESTER, OXFORDSHIRE, OX25 1QD.
CLARK, Mr. Robert Neil George, BSc ACA *2003;* 18 Bemish Road, LONDON, SW15 1DG.
CLARK, Mr. Robert Norman Edward, FCA *1965;* Fairlawn, Byways, Gravel Path, BERKHAMSTED, HP4 2PJ.
CLARK, Mr. Robin, FCA *1963;* Dugdales Farm, Compton Bassett, CALNE, SN11 8SW.
CLARK, Mr. Robin Douglas, BSc ACA *1982;* Somerden Barn, Tonbridge Road, Bough Beech, EDENBRIDGE, TN8 7AJ.
•**CLARK, Mr. Roger Geoffrey, FCA PIIA** *1971;* R G Clark FCA, Brunel House, Ediva Road, Meopham, GRAVESEND, KENT DA13 0ND.
CLARK, Mr. Roger Jackson, MA FCA *1960;* 53 Bedford Gardens, LONDON, W8 7EF. (Life Member)
•**CLARK, Mr. Roland Graham, BA FCA DChA** *1979;* Baker Tilly UK Audit LLP, The Waterfront, Salts Mill Road, Saltaire, SHIPLEY, WEST YORKSHIRE BD17 7EZ. See also Baker Tilly Tax and Advisory Services LLP
CLARK, Mr. Ronald James, MSc FCA *1951;* 22A Quarry High Street, Headington, OXFORD, OX3 8JT. (Life Member)
•**CLARK, Mr. Roy John, MA ACA** *1986;* PricewaterhouseCoopers LLP, Hays Galleria, 1 Hays Lane, LONDON, SE1 2RD. See also PricewaterhouseCoopers
CLARK, Mrs. Ruth, BA ACA *1999;* 7 Cawthorn Close, DRIFFIELD, NORTH HUMBERSIDE, YO25 5PG.
CLARK, Miss. Ruth Margaret, FCA *1975;* 41 St. Johns Road, Great Wakering, SOUTHEND-ON-SEA, SS3 0AL.
CLARK, Miss. Samantha Rachel, ACA *2004;* Morris Owen, 43-45 Devizes Road, SWINDON, WILTSHIRE, SN1 4BG.
CLARK, Miss. Sara, BSc ACA *1990;* 2 Tranquil Passage, LONDON, SE3 0BJ.
CLARK, Ms. Sarah Lucy, BSc ACA CTA *1998;* Little Wanden Wanden Lane, Egerton, ASHFORD, TN27 9DB.
•**CLARK, Mr. Sean Richard, BSc ACA** *1995;* Southwell Tyrrell & Co, 9 Newbury Street, LONDON, EC1A 7HU.
CLARK, Mrs. Sharon, BA ACA *1994;* Lincoln City Council City Hall, Beaumont Fee, LINCOLN, LN1 1DD.
CLARK, Mrs. Sharon Carla, BA ACA *1999;* 10 Poppylands, Bure Park, BICESTER, OX26 3ZP.
CLARK, Mrs. Sharon Joanne, ACA *1990;* 108-75 Songhees Road, Mariners Landing, British Columbia, VICTORIA V9A 7M5, BC, CANADA.
CLARK, Mr. Simon, BEng ACA *1992;* ACPI Investments Limited, 56 Conduit Street, LONDON, W1S 2YZ.
•**CLARK, Mr. Simon, BA(Hons) ACA** *2001;* with KPMG LLP, One Snowhill, Snow Hill Queensway, BIRMINGHAM, B4 6GN.
CLARK, Mr. Simon James, MA ACA *1991;* Fidelity Investments Ltd, 25 Cannon Street, LONDON, EC4M 5TA.
CLARK, Mr. Simon Phillip, BSc FCA *1986;* 33 Gubyon Avenue, Herne Hill, LONDON, SE24 0DU.
•**CLARK, Mr. Simon Timothy, BSc ACA** *2004;* Kingston Smith LLP, Devonshire House, 60 Goswell Road, LONDON, EC1M 7AD. See also Devonshire Corporate Services LLP and Kingston Smith Consulting LLP
CLARK, Mr. Simon Timothy, BA ACA *1993;* 14 Hemingford Gardens, YARM, CLEVELAND, TS15 9ST.
CLARK, Miss. Sophie Camilla, ACA *2010;* High Barn, Field Court, Duns Tew, BICESTER, OXFORDSHIRE, OX25 6LD.
CLARK, Mr. Stanley, FCA *1961;* 105 Sea Road, WESTGATE-ON-SEA, CT8 8QE. (Life Member)
CLARK, Mr. Stephen, ACA *2009;* 53 Limpton Gate, YARM, CLEVELAND, TS15 9JA.
•**CLARK, Mr. Stephen Austen, BA FCA** *1985;* Aylmore Limited, 6 Long Mark Road, LONDON, E16 3TH.
•**CLARK, Mr. Stephen Richard, ACA** *2008;* with KPMG Audit plc, 15 Canada Square, LONDON, E14 5GL.
CLARK, Mr. Steven, BA ACA *2003;* 14 Sorrel Close, WOKINGHAM, BERKSHIRE, RG40 5YA.
CLARK, Mr. Steven Anthony, ACA *2008;* with Harold Smith, Unit 32, Llys Edmund Prys, St. Asaph Business Park, ST. ASAPH, LL17 0JA.
CLARK, Mr. Stuart Brian, BA ACA *1984;* 6 Cherry Hill Park, Roos, HULL, HU12 0HF.
CLARK, Mr. Stuart Clifford, BA FCA *1967;* 23 Barracks Lane, Ravensmoor, NANTWICH, CW5 8PR. (Life Member)
CLARK, Mr. Stuart William, BA ACA *1995;* Oakhatch, 11 Heath Ridge Green, COBHAM, SURREY, KT11 2QL.
CLARK, Mrs. Susan, BA ACA *1990;* Labrey Cottage, 14 Victoria Gardens, SAFFRON WALDEN, ESSEX, CB11 3AF.
CLARK, Mrs. Susan Jane, BSc ACA *1983;* (Tax Fac), 11 Northumberland Avenue, READING, RG2 7PS.
CLARK, Mrs. Susan Margaret, ACA *2008;* Apartment 18, 33 Osiers Road, LONDON, SW18 1NL.
CLARK, Miss. Susannah, BSc ACA *2002;* 2nd Floor Flat, 195 Upper Richmond Road, Putney, LONDON, SW15 6SG.
CLARK, Miss. Suzanne Elisabeth, BEng FCA *1996;* 18 Queens Crescent, RICHMOND, SURREY, TW10 6HG.
CLARK, Mrs. Suzanne Elizabeth, BA ACA *1987;* 809 Creekside Drive, MOUNT PLEASANT, SC 29464, UNITED STATES.
•**CLARK, Mr. Terence Charles, FCA** *1965;* Levett Charles & Co, Abacus House, 70-72 High Street, BEXLEY, DA5 1AJ.
CLARK, Mr. Thomas John, MSc BA ACA *2006;* 67 Chaveney Road, Quorn, LOUGHBOROUGH, LE12 8AB.
CLARK, Mr. Tim, BA ACA *2005;* Sierra, Grange Road, ELLESMERE, SHROPSHIRE, SY12 9DJ.
CLARK, Mr. Timothy, BA ACA *1985;* 3 Furrow Close, Rothley, LEICESTER, LE7 7RQ.
CLARK, Mr. Timothy Charles Mullin, BSc ACA *2002;* 5 Beaufort Place, Frenchay, BRISTOL, BS16 1PE.
CLARK, Mr. Timothy Keats Urling, BSocSc ACA *1997;* Haygarth Group, 28-31 High Street, Wimbledon Village, LONDON, SW19 5BY.
CLARK, Mr. Timothy Moger, FCA *1964;* 12 Squirrels Way, Earley, READING, RG6 5QT. (Life Member)
CLARK, Mr. Trevor John, BA FCA *1980;* 17 Miranda Drive, Heathcote, WARWICK, CV34 6FE.
CLARK, Mrs. Trudi, BA ACA *1986;* Valparisso, Avenue Du Manoir, Ville Au Roi, St. Peter Port, GUERNSEY, GY1 1PE.
CLARK, Miss. Victoria Ann, ACA *2008;* 37 Marlowe Road, Larkfield, AYLESFORD, KENT, ME20 6TW.
CLARK, Miss. Victoria Lucy De Launay, BSc ACA *2009;* Garden Flat 2, 6 Linden Park Road, TUNBRIDGE WELLS, KENT, TN2 5QL.
CLARK, Mr. Vivian Charles, BA(Hons) ACA *1992;* Lambourne House, 7 Abraham Close, GRANTHAM, LINCOLNSHIRE, NG31 8PS.
CLARK, Mr. Walter, FCA *1966;* 18 Woodend Park, COBHAM, KT11 3BX.
CLARK, Mr. William Arthur, BA ACA *1993;* High Tor, 28 Gayton Road, Lower Heswall, WIRRAL, MERSEYSIDE, CH60 8PZ.
CLARK, Mr. William David, FCA *1965;* 45 Penrhyn Beach East, Penrhyn Bay, LLANDUDNO, GWYNEDD, LL30 3NY. (Life Member)
CLARK, Mr. William David Boland, BA ACA *1999;* 3 Grange Croft, LEEDS, LS17 7TZ.
CLARK, Mr. William Michael, LLB ACA *1984;* 38 Blythwood Road, LONDON, N4 4EU.
•**CLARK-WILSON, Mr. Alistair John, ACA** *1980;* Shimmin Wilson & Co, 13-15 Hope Street, Douglas, ISLE OF MAN, IM1 1AQ.
CLARKE, Mr. Adam, BSc ACA *2011;* 167 Hamilton Avenue, HALESOWEN, B62 8UB.
CLARKE, Mrs. Adrienne Elizabeth Lea, BA ACA *1989;* Birch House Back Lane, Wickham Bishops, WITHAM, CM8 3LU.
CLARKE, Mr. Alan, FCA *1956;* 19 Windmill Close, Gillway Lane, TAMWORTH, STAFFORDSHIRE, B79 8PH. (Life Member)
•**CLARKE, Mr. Alan, FCA** *1974;* Alan Clarke FCA, Heawood House, Congleton Road, Nether, Alderley, MACCLESFIELD SK10 4TN. See also Downham Mayer Clarke Limited and Clarke Alan
CLARKE, Mr. Alan Leslie, FCA *1957;* Ceilidh, 8 Granville Avenue, NEWPORT, TF10 7DX. (Life Member)
CLARKE, Mr. Albert Edward, FCA *1955;* 77 Maple Drive, Nuthall, NOTTINGHAM, NG16 1EJ. (Life Member)
CLARKE, Mr. Alistair James Roger, BA ACA *2000;* 19 Highfield Park, MARLOW, BUCKINGHAMSHIRE, SL7 2DE.
CLARKE, Mr. Alister, BA ACA *2007;* Unit 11, 197 Birrell Street, WAVERLEY, NSW 2024, AUSTRALIA.
CLARKE, Miss. Amy Frances, ACA MAAT *2003;* Washers Barn, West Fitzhead, TAUNTON, TA4 3LA.
CLARKE, Mr. Andrew Charles, BSc(Hons) ACA *2004;* Altium Capital Ltd, 12 Booth Street, MANCHESTER, M2 4AW.
•**CLARKE, Mr. Andrew Charles Simon, FCA** *1975;* (Tax Fac), Morris Cook, 6 Salop Road, OSWESTRY, SHROPSHIRE, SY11 2NU.
•**CLARKE, Mr. Andrew David, ACA** *2003;* Andy Clarke Motor Limited, 23 Brownlow Road, CAMBRIDGE, CB4 3NG.
CLARKE, Mr. Andrew David, BEng ACA *1994;* 78 The Hall, Blackheath, LONDON, SE3 9BG.
CLARKE, Mr. Andrew Edward, BSc ACA *1999;* 170 Rayleigh Road, LEIGH-ON-SEA, ESSEX, SS9 5XQ.
CLARKE, Mr. Andrew George, BSc ACA *1991;* with RSM Tenon Audit Limited, Chapel House, Westmead Drive, Westlea, SWINDON, SN5 7UN.
CLARKE, Mr. Andrew James, MSc FCA MBA *1982;* 16 Abbots Way, Horningsea, CAMBRIDGE, CB25 9JN.
•**CLARKE, Mr. Andrew John, ACA** *1983;* CKS Accountancy Limited, 1 Church Hill, LEIGH-ON-SEA, ESSEX, SS9 2DE.
CLARKE, Mr. Andrew Kenneth, BA FCA *1976;* 35 Efflinch Lane, Barton-under-Needwood, BURTON ON TRENT, DE13 8EU.
CLARKE, Mr. Andrew Murray, MA ACA *2001;* Swire Pacific Offshore Operations, 300 Beach Road #12-01 The Concourse, SINGAPORE 199555, SINGAPORE.
•**CLARKE, Mr. Andrew Paul, MA FCA FITI** *1975;* Andrew Clarke MA FCA FITI, 15 Palmerston Road, Rathmines, DUBLIN 6, COUNTY DUBLIN, IRELAND.
CLARKE, Mrs. Angela Michelle, ACA *1992;* 18 Meadway, WESTCLIFF-ON-SEA, SS0 8PJ.
•**CLARKE, Ms. Anna Theresa, BA FCA** *1989;* Sheridan Clarke Ltd, Bridge House, 25-27 The Bridge, Wealdstone, HARROW, MIDDLESEX HA3 5AB.
CLARKE, Mr. Anthony, BA ACA *1988;* 103 Barugh Green Road, Barugh Green, BARNSLEY, SOUTH YORKSHIRE, S75 1JX.
CLARKE, Mr. Anthony, FCA *1965;* 728 West Buckingham Place, CHICAGO, IL 60657, UNITED STATES.
CLARKE, Mr. Anthony John, FCA *1969;* Badgers End, Ouston Lane, TADCASTER, NORTH YORKSHIRE, LS24 8DP. (Life Member)
CLARKE, Mr. Anthony Richard, ACA *1980;* Angel Capital Group Limited, 100 Pall Mall, St James, LONDON, SW1Y 5NQ.
•**CLARKE, Mr. Ashley Richard Nicholas, BCom FCA** *1999;* KPMG, Naberezhnaya Tower Complex, Block C, 10 Presnenskaya Naberezhnaya, 123317 MOSCOW, RUSSIAN FEDERATION. See also KPMG Europe LLP
CLARKE, Mr. Barry James, FCA *1967;* 8 Barringer Way, ST. NEOTS, CAMBRIDGESHIRE, PE19 1LW. (Life Member)
CLARKE, Mr. Barry Peter, FCA *1968;* Edgmond, Boughmore Road, SIDMOUTH, DEVON, EX10 8SJ.
CLARKE, Mr. Brad, BSc ACA *2010;* 20b Severus Road, LONDON, SW11 1PL.
•**CLARKE, Mr. Brian, BA FCA** *1981;* Brian Clarke, 5 Downsway, ORPINGTON, BR6 9NU.
CLARKE, Mr. Brian Reginald, FCA *1959;* 87 Riverside Park, OTLEY, WEST YORKSHIRE, LS21 2RW. (Life Member)
CLARKE, Mr. Bruce Charles Brandon, FCA *1973;* 84 Langham Way, IVYBRIDGE, DEVON, PL21 9BY.
CLARKE, Mr. Bryan Hardwick, FCA *1956;* 50 Clockhouse Avenue, BURNLEY, LANCASHIRE, BB10 2SU. (Life Member)
CLARKE, Mrs. Carol, ACA *1991;* G S S Support Services Ltd Unit 1, Holwood Business Centre Blunts, SALTASH, CORNWALL, PL12 5DW.
CLARKE, Mrs. Carole Leslie, ACA *1982;* (Tax Fac), 148a Sywell Road, Overstone, NORTHAMPTON, NN6 0AG.
CLARKE, Miss. Caroline Emma, ACA *2004;* 29 Francklin Road, Lowdham, NOTTINGHAM, NG14 7BG.
CLARKE, Mrs. Caroline June, BA(Hons) ACA *1990;* (Tax Fac), 84 Bellevue Road, Ealing, LONDON, W13 8DE.
•**CLARKE, Mrs. Carolyn Sarah, BA(Hons) ACA** *2000;* PricewaterhouseCoopers LLP, 1 Embankment Place, LONDON, WC2N 6RH. See also PricewaterhouseCoopers
CLARKE, Mrs. Catherine Margaret, MChem ACA *2006;* Medela, 9 Huntsman Drive Irlam, MANCHESTER, M44 5EG.
CLARKE, Mr. Christopher George, FCA *1968;* The Old Mill House, Preston Crowmarsh, WALLINGFORD, OX10 6SL.
CLARKE, Mr. Christopher John, BA ACA *2004;* 12 Lavender Walk, BEVERLEY, NORTH HUMBERSIDE, HU17 8WE.
•**CLARKE, Mr. Christopher Michael, FCA** *1971;* Roberts & Co, 136 Kensington Church Street, LONDON, W8 4BH.
•**CLARKE, Mr. Christopher Raymond, FCA** *1971;* Christopher R. Clarke, 26 Elm Court, Highburton, HUDDERSFIELD, HD8 0TB.
CLARKE, Mr. Clive Houghton, FCA *1955;* Lower Park, Station Lane, Milford, GODALMING, SURREY, GU8 5HS. (Life Member)
•**CLARKE, Mr. Colin Harcourt Norman, FCA** *1965;* 6 Cobbold Avenue, EASTBOURNE, EAST SUSSEX, BN21 1XA.
•**CLARKE, Mr. Colin Nigel, ACA** *1985;* C.J. Driscoll, The Old Surgery, 19 Mengham Lane, HAYLING ISLAND, PO11 9JT.
CLARKE, Mr. Craig, BSc DipEd ACA ATII *1992;* 78 Dalkeith Road, EDINBURGH, EH16 5AF.
CLARKE, Mr. Craig Malcolm, BA FCA *1966;* 9 Dymchurch Close, Clayhall, ILFORD, IG5 0LB. (Life Member)
CLARKE, Mr. Daniel Iain, BSc(Hons) ACA *2001;* Cardy Construction, Maynard Road, Wincheap Industrial Estate, CANTERBURY, KENT, CT1 3RH.
CLARKE, Mr. Daniel William, BSc ACA *2004;* 12 Millersdale Road, LIVERPOOL, L18 5HQ.
CLARKE, Mr. Darren, ACA *2006;* M G I Rickard Keen Llp, 7-13 Nelson Street, SOUTHEND-ON-SEA, SS1 1EH.
CLARKE, Mr. Darryl John, BA ACA *2000;* 88 Towncourt Crescent, Petts Wood, ORPINGTON, BR5 1PJ.
CLARKE, Mr. David, BA ACA *2002;* Orchard Cottage, Beech Knapp, Burleigh, STROUD, GLOUCESTERSHIRE, GL5 2PS.
CLARKE, Mr. David, MSc BSc ACA *2002;* (Tax Fac), 31 Choseley Road, Knowl Hill, READING, RG10 9YS.
•**CLARKE, Mr. David Alan, BA FCA** *1968;* 13 Howard Drive, CHELMSFORD, CM2 6PE.
•**CLARKE, Mr. David Andrew, BSc FCA** *1983;* David A. Clarke, 20 Longhill Drive, SALISBURY, SP2 8TD.
•**CLARKE, Mr. David Antony, BA FCA** *1984;* DAC Accountancy Services, 8 Vernon Crescent, Galgate, LANCASTER, LA2 0LX.
•**CLARKE, Mr. David Brownlow Marshal, BA ACA** *1981;* R & B Ltd, Meteor House, Whittle Road, SALISBURY, SP2 7YW.
CLARKE, Mr. David Elton, BSc FCA *1982;* 12 Poplar Drive, Hutton Poplars, BRENTWOOD, Essex, CM13 1YU.
CLARKE, Mr. David Graham, BA FCA *1985;* 3 Woodside Road, NEW MALDEN, KT3 3AH.
•**CLARKE, Mr. David Howard, BSc FCA** *1977;* Rhodes Clarke & Co, 42 Market Street, Eckington, SHEFFIELD, S21 4JH. See also RCC Processing Limited
CLARKE, Mr. David Hurley Larche, FCA *1960;* Beech Cottage, 39 Crabtree Lane, Bookham, LEATHERHEAD, KT23 4PJ. (Life Member)
CLARKE, Mr. David John, BSc ACA *1992;* 31 Le May Avenue, LONDON, SE12 9SU.
CLARKE, Mr. David John, BA ACA *2005;* 13 Radnor Park Road, FOLKESTONE, CT19 5BW.
CLARKE, Mr. David Narborough, FCA *1975;* 70 Pier Road, ERITH, DA8 1BA.
CLARKE, Mr. David Nicholas Rogotta, ACA *2008;* 38 Ellen Street, LONDON, E1 1PE.
CLARKE, Mr. David Philip, FCA *1968;* Heather Bank, 10 Moorland Close, Heswall, WIRRAL, CH60 0EL.
CLARKE, Mr. Dermot Patrick, BA FCA AITI *1974;* The Hall, Killiney Hill Road, Killiney, DUBLIN, COUNTY DUBLIN, IRELAND.
CLARKE, Mr. Desmond Gooding, FCA *1950;* 5 Northfield Court, ALDEBURGH, IP15 5LU. (Life Member)
CLARKE, Mr. Dominic Rupert, LLB ACA *1999;* 3 Curzon Road, WEYBRIDGE, SURREY, KT13 8UW.
CLARKE, Mr. Dominique, ACA *2009;* Apartment 408 Holden Mill, Blackburn Road, BOLTON, BL1 7QJ.
CLARKE, Mr. Duncan James, BSc ACA *2004;* with RSM Tenon Limited, 1 Bede Island Road, Bede Island Business Park, LEICESTER, LE2 7EA.
CLARKE, Mrs. Emma Jane, ACA *2004;* 15 Parkside Halstead, SEVENOAKS, KENT, TN14 7HA.
•**CLARKE, Miss. Faye Nicola, ACA** *2007;* (Tax Fac), Hilary Adams Ltd, 158 High Street, HERNE BAY, KENT, CT6 5NP. See also Adams Hilary Ltd
CLARKE, Mrs. Felicity Jane, BSc BM ACA *1990;* 21 route de la cascade, 78110 LE VESINET, FRANCE.
CLARKE, Mr. Garry Paul, MEng ACA *2002;* with Ernst & Young, 41 Shortland Street, PO Box2146, AUCKLAND 1140, NEW ZEALAND.
CLARKE, Mr. Gary David, ACA *1989;* M4 Systems Ltd Tredomen Innovation & Technology Centre, Tredomen Park Ystrad Mynach, HENGOED, MID GLAMORGAN, CF82 7FQ.
CLARKE, Mr. Geoffrey Brian, FCA *1961;* 19 Sunningdale Mount, SHEFFIELD, S11 9HA. (Life Member)

CLARKE, Mr. Geoffrey Edward Jeremy, FCA *1973;* GENEDON ASSET MANAGEMENT S.A., 8 BOULEVARD JAMES-FAZY, 1201 GENEVA, SWITZERLAND.
CLARKE, Mr. Geoffrey Ernest, FCA *1951;* Willowbrook, 23 Myrtle Grove, Willowhayne, East Preston, LITTLEHAMPTON, WEST SUSSEX BN16 2SW. (Life Member)
CLARKE, Mr. Geoffrey Francis, FCA *1970;* 17 Oaken Coppice, ASHTEAD, KT21 1DL. (Life Member)
CLARKE, Mr. Geoffrey Robert, FCA *1953;* 6 The Knolls, EPSOM, KT17 3ND. (Life Member)
CLARKE, Mr. George William Herbert, BSc ACA *1979;* 56 Stockwell Park Road, LONDON, SW9 0DA.
•CLARKE, Mr. Gerard Joseph John, BSc FCA *1989;* (Tax Fac), 61 Stanley Road Limited, 61 Stanley Road, BOOTLE, MERSEYSIDE, L20 7BZ.
CLARKE, Mr. Godfrey Walter, FCA *1958;* 8 Lindisfarne Drive, KETTERING, NN15 5JD.
•CLARKE, Mr. Graham, FCA *1968;* Clarke Nicklin LLP, Clarke Nicklin House, Brooks Drive, Cheadle Royal Business Park, CHEADLE, CHESHIRE SK8 3TD.
CLARKE, Mr. Graham Staward, TD MA FCA FRSA *1964;* Bourn Investments Ltd, 9 Montrose Gardens, Oxshott, LEATHERHEAD, KT22 0UU.
•CLARKE, Mr. Grahame Anthony, BSc FCA *1962;* William Evans & Partners, 20 Harcourt Street, LONDON, W1H 4HG.
CLARKE, Miss. Hannah, ACA *2007;* 15 Queen Street, Stony Stratford, MILTON KEYNES, MK11 1EG.
•CLARKE, Miss. Hannah Louise, ACA *2009;* Transparent Accountancy Limited, 48 Dean Park Road, BOURNEMOUTH, BH1 1QA.
CLARKE, Mr. Harold Stuart, BA FCA *1977;* Laynards, Mayfield Park, WADHURST, TN5 6DH.
•CLARKE, Miss. Helen Charity, ACA *2002;* Crowe Clark Whitehill LLP, St Bride's House, 10 Salisbury Square, LONDON, EC4Y 8EH. See also Horwath Clark Whitehill LLP
CLARKE, Miss. Helen Elizabeth, BA ACA *1993;* 3 Norris Close, BISHOP'S STORTFORD, HERTFORDSHIRE, CM23 5RE.
CLARKE, Mrs. Helen Sarah, BSc ACA *1990;* Sussex Cottage, 82 Bluehouse Lane, OXTED, RH8 0AD.
CLARKE, Mrs. Helen Tracey, BA ACA *1987;* 103 Westcar Lane, WALTON-ON-THAMES, KT12 5ES.
CLARKE, Miss. Holly, BSc(Hons) ACA *2009;* 70 Chapel Lane, LICHFIELD, STAFFORDSHIRE, WS14 9BQ.
•CLARKE, Mr. Iain Christopher, BA FCA *1984;* (Tax Fac), Downham Mayer Clarke Limited, 41 Greek Street, STOCKPORT, CHESHIRE, SK3 8AX.
CLARKE, Mr. Iain Kenneth John, BSc ACA *1996;* (Tax Fac), Beech Cottage, High Street, Brinkley, NEWMARKET, SUFFOLK, CB8 0SE.
CLARKE, Mr. Ian, BSc ACA *1991;* Flat 2301, East Tower, 3 Pan Peninsula Square, LONDON, E14 9HQ.
•CLARKE, Mr. Ian Michael, BSc ACA *1989;* with PricewaterhouseCoopers LLP, Llys Tawe, Kings Road, SA1 Swansea Waterfront, SWANSEA, SA1 8PG.
CLARKE, Mr. Ian Michael, BSc FCA *1989;* (Tax Fac), 132 Lovelace Drive, Pyrford, WOKING, SURREY, GU22 8RZ.
CLARKE, Mrs. Irene Ann, BA FCA *1985;* PO Box 218, MOUNT HAWTHORN, WA 6915, AUSTRALIA.
CLARKE, Mr. James, FCA *1970;* 124 New Adel Lane, LEEDS, LS16 6BB.
CLARKE, Mr. James, BSc ACA *1994;* 6 Ramillies Street, LONDON, W1F 7TY.
CLARKE, Mr. James Edmund Bruce, BSc ACA *1992;* Ground Floor Lector Court, 151-153 Farringdon Road, LONDON, EC1R 3AF.
CLARKE, Mr. James Francis, BSc ACA *1999;* with Ernst & Young LLP, Apex Plaza, Forbury Road, READING, RG1 1YE.
CLARKE, James Frederick Emlyn, Esq MBE FCA *1977;* Newport, Chedworth, CHELTENHAM, GLOUCESTERSHIRE, GL54 4NU. (Life Member)
CLARKE, Mr. James Ian, BSc ACA *2000;* Mitie Group Plc 8 Monarch Court, The Brooms Emersons Green, BRISTOL, BS16 7FH.
CLARKE, Mr. James John, BA FCA *1998;* St Clements House, St Clements Road, POOLE, DORSET, BH12 4GP.
CLARKE, Mr. James Lorton, BSc FCA *1984;* 2 Clare Road, CAMBRIDGE, CB3 9HN.
CLARKE, Mr. James Maxwell, BA FCA *1962;* Lower Veddw, Devauden, CHEPSTOW, NP16 6PH.
CLARKE, Mr. James Peter Wilthew, FCA *1972;* Rocklands North Corner, Coverack, HELSTON, CORNWALL, TR12 6TQ.
CLARKE, Ms. Jane Carol, BSc ACA *1990;* Creative New Zealand, PO Box 3806, WELLINGTON 6140, NEW ZEALAND.
CLARKE, Mrs. Janet, BSc ACA *1989;* 9 Ossmere Close, SANDBACH, CHESHIRE, CW11 1FB.
•CLARKE, Mr. Jason, BSc ACA *1995;* PricewaterhouseCoopers LLP, One Kingsway, CARDIFF, CF10 3PW. See also PricewaterhouseCoopers
CLARKE, Dr. Jason Richard Lee, MSc BA ACA *1999;* Strategic Value Partners (UK) LLP, 5 Savile Row, LONDON, W1S 3PD.
CLARKE, Mrs. Jennifer Anne, BA FCA *1982;* 12 Rockland Park, LARGS, AYRSHIRE, KA30 8HB.
CLARKE, Miss. Joanne Margaret, BA(Hons) ACA *2010;* 21a Chearsley Road, Long Crendon, AYLESBURY, BUCKINGHAMSHIRE, HP18 9BS.
CLARKE, Mrs. Joanne Michelle, BSc ACA *1997;* The Thomas Cook Group, Coningsby Road, Bretton, PETERBOROUGH, PE3 8SB.
CLARKE, Mr. John, BSc ACA *2010;* Pricewaterhousecoopers, 7 More London Riverside, LONDON, SE1 2RT.
CLARKE, Mr. John Adrian, BSc ACA *1991;* Quintox, Sherfield English Road, Landford, SALISBURY, SP5 2BD.
CLARKE, Mr. John Alan, FCA *1981;* P O Box 2238, LAE, 411, PAPUA NEW GUINEA.
CLARKE, Mr. John Brian, BA FCA *1975;* Coal Pension Trustees Services Ltd, Ventana House, 2 Concourse Way, Sheaf Street, SHEFFIELD, S1 2BJ.
•CLARKE, Mr. John David, FCA *1974;* John Clarke & Co, 22 Hope Street, Douglas, ISLE OF MAN, IM1 1AP.
CLARKE, Mr. John Edward, MBA FCA *1969;* Millbrook Cottage, 27 Clint Lane, Navenby, LINCOLN, LN5 0EX. (Life Member)
CLARKE, Mr. John Elton, BA FCA *1973;* 98 East Sheen Avenue, LONDON, SW14 8AU.
•CLARKE, Mr. John Evelyn, FCA *1961;* Folly Cottage, 21 Ledborough Lane, BEACONSFIELD, BUCKINGHAMSHIRE, HP9 2PZ.
CLARKE, Mr. John Gale, FCA *1960;* Cotswold, Humfrey Lane, Boughton, NORTHAMPTON, NN2 8RN.
CLARKE, Mr. John Graham, FCA *1968;* The Red Lodge, Parkgate Road, Mollington, CHESTER, CH1 6NE.
CLARKE, Mr. John James, MSc FCA *1992;* AMEC E&E, 10706 Sikes Place, Suite 250, CHARLOTTE, NC 28277, UNITED STATES.
•CLARKE, Mr. John Leonard, FCA *1972;* (Tax Fac), Clarke & Co, 59 Curzon Road, Muswell Hill, LONDON, N10 2RB.
CLARKE, Mr. John Neil, LLB FCA *1959;* High Willows, 18 Park Avenue, Farnborough Park, ORPINGTON, BR6 8LL. (Life Member)
CLARKE, Mr. John Peter, FCA *1969;* PO Box 1695, ROZELLE, NSW 2039, AUSTRALIA.
CLARKE, Mr. John Richard, FCA *1979;* 104 Silhill Hall Road, SOLIHULL, B91 1JS.
•CLARKE, Mr. John Stephen, LLB ACA *1987;* HBAS Limited, Amwell House, 19 Amwell Street, HODDESDON, HERTFORDSHIRE, EN11 8TS. See also Hardcastles Limited
CLARKE, Mr. John Trevor, FCA *1960;* The Coppins, Kidderminster Road, BEWDLEY, DY12 1LW. (Life Member)
CLARKE, Mr. Johnpaul, BSc ACA *2006;* with Clearwater Corporate Finance LLP, 7th Floor, Chancery Place, 50 Brown Street, MANCHESTER, M2 2JT.
CLARKE, Mr. Jonathan, MEng ACA *2007;* 10/6 Stafford Street, DOUBLE BAY, NSW 2028, AUSTRALIA.
CLARKE, Mr. Jonathan Anthony, BA(Hons) ACA *2000;* 1 Kendal Way, Chorlton, CREWE, CW2 5SA.
CLARKE, Mr. Jonathan George Gough, MA FCA *1985;* Logmore Place, Logmore Lane, DORKING, RH4 3JN.
CLARKE, Mr. Jonathan Paul, BA ACA *1995;* 25 Lower Sand Hills, SURBITON, SURREY, KT6 6RP.
CLARKE, Mr. Jonathan Paul, BSc(Hons) ACA *2011;* 53 Springfield Road, WINDSOR, SL4 3PP.
CLARKE, Mr. Joseph Alan, FCA *1963;* 74 Mountbatten Avenue, Sandal, WAKEFIELD, WF2 6HE.
CLARKE, Miss. Julia, BA ACA *1993;* 42 Ivy Bank Lane, Hawarth, KEIGHLEY, BD22 8PD.
CLARKE, Mr. Julian, BSc ACA *1991;* 22 Cranes Drive, SURBITON, SURREY, KT5 8AL.
CLARKE, Mr. Julian, BA ACA *1989;* Ramon Lee & Partners, Kemp House, 152-160 City Road, LONDON, EC1V 2DW.
CLARKE, Miss. Juliet, MA ACA *2011;* 80A Granville Road, LONDON, SW18 5SG.
CLARKE, Mrs. Karen Jane, BA ACA *1985;* 33 Princess Street, NEWCASTLE, STAFFORDSHIRE, ST5 1DD.
CLARKE, Mrs. Karen Jane, BSc ACA *1986;* 62 Constable Road, FELIXSTOWE, IP11 7HN.
CLARKE, Miss. Karen Jardine, BA ACA *1985;* Seedammstrasse 3, CH 8808 PFAFFIKON, SWITZERLAND.
CLARKE, Mrs. Kate Elizabeth Rachael, BSc ACA *2000;* Oakleigh, 1 Chestnut Springs, Mission Road, Iron Acton, BRISTOL, BS37 9XR.
CLARKE, Miss. Katherine Ann, ACA *2010;* Flat 6, 89 Ribston Street, MANCHESTER, M15 5RJ.
CLARKE, Mrs. Katie Ann, ACA *2008;* 20 Channing Way, Ellistown, COALVILLE, LEICESTERSHIRE, LE67 1HA.
•CLARKE, Mr. Kenneth Edwin, FCA *1976;* (Tax Fac), Pugh Clarke & Co, 175 Manor Road, CHIGWELL, IG7 5QB.
CLARKE, Mr. Kenneth Michael, FCA *1971;* 7 Thorpe Bay Gardens, SOUTHEND-ON-SEA, SS1 3NS.
CLARKE, Mr. Kenneth Robert, FCA *1968;* 9-223 Rebecca Street, OAKVILLE L6K 3YZ, ON, CANADA.
CLARKE, Mrs. Kerrie Anne, MSci ACA *2010;* 2 New Links Avenue, Ingol, PRESTON, PR2 7EX.
CLARKE, Mrs. Laura Jane, BA ACA *2006;* 28 Waterfield Road, Cropston, LEICESTER, LE7 7HN.
CLARKE, Miss. Laura Jayne, ACA *2011;* 6 Budworth Park, Kingswood, HULL, HU7 3JW.
•CLARKE, Mr. Lee, ACA *2003;* with PricewaterhouseCoopers LLP, 1 Embankment Place, LONDON, WC2N 6RH.
CLARKE, Mrs. Leigh Monica, BA ACA *2002;* 26 The Ridings, SURBITON, KT5 8HQ.
CLARKE, Mrs. Lesley Catherine, BA FCA *1986;* with ICAEW, Metropolitan House, 321 Avebury Boulevard, MILTON KEYNES, MK9 2FZ.
CLARKE, Miss. Lisa Annette, FCA *1995;* 14 Warren House Walk, Walmley, SUTTON COLDFIELD, WEST MIDLANDS, B76 1TS.
CLARKE, Miss. Lisa Sarah, BA FCA *1998;* 5 The Stables Rufford New Hall, Rufford Park Lane Rufford, ORMSKIRK, L40 1XE.
CLARKE, Mr. Malcolm Raymond, ACA *1984;* Chemin des Feuillus 11, 1217 MEYRIN, SWITZERLAND.
CLARKE, Mr. Mark Galbraith, BA FCA *1979;* 49 Hemingford Road, LONDON, N1 1BY.
CLARKE, Mr. Mark Owen, BA ACA *1985;* Yew Tree Cottage, 12 Calcutt Street, Cricklade, SWINDON, SN6 6BD.
CLARKE, Mr. Mark Raymond, BA ACA *1989;* Woodside Cottage Rectory Road, Chipstead, COULSDON, CR5 3SY.
CLARKE, Mr. Martin Courtenay, MA FCA *1966;* 91 Bedford Gardens, Kensington, LONDON, W8 7EQ.
CLARKE, Mrs. Mary Adam, BSc ACA *1996;* 6 Gaiastowe, LICHFIELD, WS13 7LY.
CLARKE, Mrs. Mary Carolyn, BCom FCA *1967;* 16 Court Lane Gardens, LONDON, SE21 7DZ.
CLARKE, Mr. Matthew, BA CertITM ACA *2007;* 162 Redesdale Gardens, LEEDS, LS16 6AX.
CLARKE, Mr. Matthew David, BSc ACA *2001;* Eddy's Dream, 1 Upper Unit, 21 Music Heights, SOUTHAMPTON SN 03, BERMUDA.
CLARKE, Mr. Matthew James, BCom ACA *2001;* 4 Quarndon View, Allestree, DERBY, DE22 2XJ.
CLARKE, Mr. Matthew James, MA ACA *2002;* 35 Betenson Avenue, SEVENOAKS, KENT, TN13 3EP.
CLARKE, Mr. Matthew James Stanhope, MA ACA *1992;* Windmill Bungalow, Holwell, SHERBORNE, DORSET, DT9 5LN.
CLARKE, Miss. Melanie, BA(Hons) ACA *2004;* 18 Westwood Road, Tilehurst, READING, RG31 5PW.
CLARKE, Mr. Michael, BA ACA *2011;* Flat 10, Gardenhurst, 45 Cardigan Road, LEEDS, LS6 1WD.
CLARKE, Mr. Michael Andrew, BA(Hons) ACA *2010;* 8 Cranley Drive, Codsall, WOLVERHAMPTON, WV8 1AS.
CLARKE, Mr. Michael Frederick, BA ACA *1979;* 4827 Thornwood Drive, ACWORTH, GA 30102, UNITED STATES.
CLARKE, Mr. Michael John, BCom ACA *1981;* Time To Do It, 1 The Nurseries, Asselby, GOOLE, NORTH HUMBERSIDE, DN14 7GB.
CLARKE, Mr. Michael John, BA ACA *1995;* 77 Second Avenue, STANFORD-LE-HOPE, SS17 8DS.
CLARKE, Mr. Michael John Owen, BSc FCA *1992;* 4 Sezincote Close, Eastcombe, STROUD, GLOUCESTERSHIRE, GL6 7EQ.
•CLARKE, Mr. Michael Richard Neil, BA FCA *1971;* with PricewaterhouseCoopers, Woluwe Garden, Woluwedal 18, Sint-Stevens-Woluwe, B-1932 BRUSSELS, BELGIUM.
CLARKE, Mrs. Natasha Marielle, BSc(Hons) ACA CTA *2000;* with BDO LLP, 55 Baker Street, LONDON, W1U 7EU.
CLARKE, Mr. Neil, BA(Hons) ACA *2001;* 3 Ravenswood Drive, SOLIHULL, WEST MIDLANDS, B91 3NL.
•CLARKE, Mr. Nicholas John, BSc ACA *2003;* Hawkins Scott, Wyvern House, 55-61 Frimley High Street, Frimley, CAMBERLEY, SURREY GU16 7HJ.
CLARKE, Mr. Nicholas Roy Kenneth, BSc ACA *1988;* Corus, PO Box 1, SCUNTHORPE, SOUTH HUMBERSIDE, DN16 1BP.
CLARKE, Mrs. Nina, BSc ACA *2003;* 29 Bronte Farm Road, Shirley, SOLIHULL, WEST MIDLANDS, B90 3DE.
CLARKE, Mr. Norman Victor Granville, FCA *1960;* c/o Casilla 17-17-1485, QUITO, ECUADOR. (Life Member)
CLARKE, Mr. Oliver Frederick, BSc FCA *1969;* The Gleaner Co Ltd, Box 40, 7 North Street, KINGSTON, JAMAICA.
•CLARKE, Miss. Pamela Mary, BSc FCA *1982;* Clarkes, First Floor, 5 Walker Terrace, GATESHEAD, NE8 1EB.
CLARKE, Mr. Paul, BSc FCA *1999;* PIP Asset Management LLP, 92 New Cavendish Street, LONDON, W1W 6XJ.
CLARKE, Mr. Paul Anthony, BSc FCA *1971;* Little Warren, Seven Hills Road, COBHAM, KT11 1ER.
CLARKE, Mr. Paul Charles, BSc ACA *1993;* Flat 9, 16 Ravenscroft Road, Chiswick, LONDON, W4 5EQ.
•CLARKE, Mr. Paul Eric Cameron, FCA *1986;* PricewaterhouseCoopers LLP, Hays Galleria, 1 Hays Lane, LONDON, SE1 2RD. See also PricewaterhouseCoopers
CLARKE, Mr. Paul James, BSc ACA *2002;* 5 Oakhill, Claygate, ESHER, KT10 0TG.
CLARKE, Mr. Paul John, BSc ACA *1981;* 151 Maldon Road, Tiptree, COLCHESTER, CO5 0PN.
CLARKE, Mr. Paul Lee, BA FCA *1992;* The Willows, Went Edge Road, Kirk Smeaton, PONTEFRACT, WEST YORKSHIRE, WF8 3JS.
•CLARKE, Mr. Paul Mervyn, BA FCA *1980;* (Tax Fac), PKF (UK) LLP, Pannell House, 6 Queen Street, LEEDS, LS1 2TW.
CLARKE, Mr. Paul Steven Gay, MA FCA *1984;* 203 Barnard Street, WELLINGTON 6012, NEW ZEALAND.
CLARKE, Mr. Peter, MSc ACA *2009;* Rastrick Lodge, Field Lane, BRIGHOUSE, WEST YORKSHIRE, HD6 3NY.
CLARKE, Mr. Peter Beverley, FCA *1959;* 11 Oakhurst Avenue, HARPENDEN, AL5 2NB. (Life Member)
•CLARKE, Mr. Peter John, FCA *1972;* Clarkes, Shaw House, 54 Bramhall Lane South, Bramhall, STOCKPORT, CHESHIRE SK7 1AH.
CLARKE, Mr. Peter John Frederick, FCA *1964;* 38 Lake View Road, COVENTRY, CV5 8JY.
•CLARKE, Mr. Philip, FCA *1970;* P Clarke FCA, 48 Dorothy Avenue, Glen Parva, LEICESTER, LE2 9JD.
CLARKE, Mr. Phillip Adrian, BA ACA *1984;* BP International Ltd, Chertsey Road, SUNBURY-ON-THAMES, MIDDLESEX, TW16 7LN.
CLARKE, Mr. Pierre Alexis, BSc ACA *1998;* 10 Lower Grosvenor Place, LONDON, SW1W 0EN.
CLARKE, Miss. Rachael, ACA *2008;* Deloitte & Touche Hill House, 1 Little New Street, LONDON, EC4A 3TR.
CLARKE, Mrs. Rachel Louise, BCom ACA *2000;* (Tax Fac), 19 Forge Avenue, BROMSGROVE, WORCESTERSHIRE, B60 3GG.
CLARKE, Mrs. Rachel Margaret, MA ACA *1992;* 125 South Park Road, Wimbledon, LONDON, SW19 8RX.
CLARKE, Mrs. Rebecca Louise, ACA *2011;* 7 Ashby Square, LEEDS, LS13 3BQ.
CLARKE, Mrs. Rhian, BA ACA *1999;* with Deloitte Middle East, Currency House, Building 1 Level 5, DIFC, PO Box 282056, DUBAI UNITED ARAB EMIRATES.
CLARKE, Mr. Richard Alan, BSc FCA *1981;* 23 Milehouse Road, PLYMOUTH, PL3 4AD.
CLARKE, Mr. Richard Anthony, FCA *1970;* Snowdenham House, Bramley, GUILDFORD, GU5 0DB.
CLARKE, Mr. Richard Brian, BA FCA *1977;* (Tax Fac), 53 Eastwood Road, LEIGH-ON-SEA, SS9 3AH.
•CLARKE, Mr. Richard David, MA FCA DChA *1981;* (Tax Fac), 7 Chapter Road, LONDON, SE17 3ES.
•CLARKE, Mr. Richard Frank, BSc(Hons) ACA *2004;* Harris & Clarke LLP, 7 Billing Road, NORTHAMPTON, NN1 5AN.
CLARKE, Mr. Richard John, ACA *2008;* Flat 3, 15 Monza Street, LONDON, E1W 3TL.
CLARKE, Mr. Richard John, BA ACA *1994;* Veolia Water, Three Valleys Water, Tamblin Way, HATFIELD, HERTFORDSHIRE, AL10 9EZ.
CLARKE, Mr. Richard John George, MBA BSc FCA *1980;* Dage Holdings Limited, 25 Faraday Road, Rabans Lane Industrial Area, AYLESBURY, HP19 8RY.

•CLARKE, Mr. Richard Jonathan, BSc FCA 1991; (CA Scotland KPMG LLP, 15 Canada Square, LONDON, E14 5GL. See also KPMG Europe LLP
CLARKE, Mr. Richard Owen, BA BCom ACA 2001; 4 The Royd, Deepcar, SHEFFIELD, S36 2SS.
•CLARKE, Mr. Richard Stephen, FCA 1991; Barker Hibbert & Co, 133 Cherry Orchard Road, CROYDON, CR0 6BE.
CLARKE, Mr. Robert, BSc ACA 1986; 21 Arthur Road, LONDON, SW19 7DL.
•CLARKE, Mr. Robert Adam Paul, BA FCA 1986; Mitten Clarke Limited, Festival Way, Festival Park, STOKE-ON-TRENT, ST1 5TQ.
CLARKE, Mr. Robert Charles, FCA 1967; Hudnall Farm, Little Gaddesden, BERKHAMSTED, HP4 1QN.
•CLARKE, Mr. Robert David Farnham, FCA 1978; The Hunters Wood Partnership Ltd, Hunters Wood, Heath Ride, Finchampstead, WOKINGHAM, BERKSHIRE RG40 3QJ.
CLARKE, Mr. Robert Edwards, MSc BSc ACA 1981; High Down, 9 Little Warren Close, GUILDFORD, GU4 8PW.
CLARKE, Mr. Robert John, FCA FCCA 1978; 157 Hempstead Road, GILLINGHAM, KENT, ME7 3QG. (Life Member)
CLARKE, Mr. Roderick Hugh, BA FCA 1977; 64d Fore Street, HERTFORD, SG14 1BY.
CLARKE, Mr. Rodger Kenneth, LLB FCA 1996; PO Box 476117, DUBAI, UNITED ARAB EMIRATES.
CLARKE, Mr. Roger Arthur, BA FCA 1981; 21 Whiteley Croft Rise, OTLEY, LS21 3NR.
CLARKE, Mr. Roger John, FCA 1968; Spindlewood, Hillcrest Road, HYTHE, KENT, CT21 5EX.
CLARKE, Mr. Roger John, MA FCA 1973; 7 Trym Road, Westbury On Trym, BRISTOL, BS9 3EN.
CLARKE, Mrs. Rosalind Maureen, BEng ACA 1993; 2 Hornbeam Avenue, Great Sutton, ELLESMERE PORT, CH66 2US.
CLARKE, Miss. Ruth Elizabeth, BSc ACA 2010; Flat 16 Balfour Court, Station Road, HARPENDEN, HERTFORDSHIRE, AL5 4XS.
CLARKE, Mr. Ryan, ACA 2010; 17 Mercia Close, Quarrington, SLEAFORD, LINCOLNSHIRE, NG34 8WP.
CLARKE, Miss. Sally, ACA 2008; 10 Moorland Close, WIRRAL, MERSEYSIDE, CH60 0EL.
CLARKE, Miss. Samantha Elizabeth, ACA 2011; 37 Harper Drive, Maidenbower, CRAWLEY, WEST SUSSEX, RH10 7LD.
CLARKE, Mr. Samuel Christopher Godwin, BSc FCA 1984; with BDO LLP, Arcadia House, Maritime Walk, Ocean Village, SOUTHAMPTON, SO14 3TL.
•CLARKE, Mr. Samuel David, BA FCA DChA 1989; The Gallagher Partnership LLP, PO Box 698, 2nd Floor, Titchfield House, 69/85 Tabernacle Street, LONDON EC2A 4RR.
CLARKE, Miss. Sandra, BA(Hons) ACA 2000; 2 The Courtyard, Aston, BAMPTON, OX18 2NY.
CLARKE, Mrs. Sarah Elizabeth, BSc ACA 1995; The Willows, Went Edge Road, Kirk Smeaton, PONTEFRACT, WEST YORKSHIRE, WF8 3JS.
CLARKE, Miss. Sarah Louise, BA(Hons) ACA 2001; Odeon Cinemas Ltd, Lee House, 90 Great Bridgewater Street, MANCHESTER, M1 5JW.
•CLARKE, Mr. Seamus Padraig, ACA 1979; AIMS - Seamus Clarke ACA, Unit X1, European House, Rudford Industrial Estate, Ford Arundel, ARUNDEL WEST SUSSEX BN18 0BF.
CLARKE, Mr. Sean John, MBA ACA 1993; Wal-Mart Canada Corp, 1940 Argentia Road, Mississauga, ONTARIO L5N IP9, ON, CANADA.
CLARKE, Mr. Sean Thomas, BA ACA 1988; 59 Collingwood Crescent, GUILDFORD, GU1 2NU.
•CLARKE, Miss. Shelly Nicola, BA(Hons) ACA 2001; Rostrons, St Peter's House, Cattle Market Street, NORWICH, NR1 3DY. See also Rostron & Partners
CLARKE, Mr. Simon John, LLB ACA 1999; Cherry Gardens, Bonnington, ASHFORD, KENT, TN25 7AZ.
•CLARKE, Mr. Simon Liddiard, ACA 1998; 2 Howard Close, Holystone, NEWCASTLE UPON TYNE, NE27 0UU.
CLARKE, Mrs. Sophie Rebecca, BSc ACA 2004; Flat 2, 26 Rathen Road, MANCHESTER, M20 4GH.
CLARKE, Mr. Stephen Andrew, MA ACA 1979; 6 Esmond Road, Chiswick, LONDON, W4 1JQ.
CLARKE, Mr. Stephen Arthur, FCA 1977; Magpie Cottage, High Street, Welford-on-avon, STRATFORD-UPON-AVON, CV37 8EF.
CLARKE, Mr. Stephen John, FCA 1960; 48 The Orchard, KINGS LANGLEY, WD4 8JR. (Life Member)
CLARKE, Mr. Stephen John, BSc(Econ) FCA 1997; 36 Atridge Chase, BILLERICAY, CM12 0HR.
CLARKE, Mr. Stephen Kenneth, FCA CPA 1977; 5130 North Central Avenue, PHOENIX, AZ 85012, UNITED STATES.
CLARKE, Mr. Stephen Paul, MA ACA 1992; 125 South Park Road, Wimbledon, LONDON, SW19 8RX.
•CLARKE, Mr. Stephen Peter, FCA 1982; DTZ, 1 Curzon Street, LONDON, W1A 5PZ. See also DTZ Pieda Consulting
CLARKE, Mr. Stephen Robert, FCA 1984; 3 Castleton Court, MARLOW, BUCKINGHAMSHIRE, SL7 3HW.
CLARKE, Mr. Stephen Sheridan, FCA 1963; Forge House, Taynton, BURFORD, OXFORDSHIRE, OX18 4UH.
CLARKE, Mr. Stephen Thomas, FCA 1987; 1 Culm Valley Way, Uffculme, CULLOMPTON, DEVON, EX15 3XZ.
•CLARKE, Mr. Stephen Timothy, FCA 1973; (Tax Fac), Stephen T. Clarke Limited, 23 Rolleston Crescent, Watnall, NOTTINGHAM, NG16 1JU.
CLARKE, Mr. Steven Robert, FCA 1979; Eden House, 23 Grange Road, Wickham Bishops, WITHAM, CM8 3LT.
CLARKE, Mr. Stuart, ACA 1981; 592 Van Beuren Road, Harding Township, MORRISTOWN, NJ 07960, UNITED STATES.
CLARKE, Mr. Stuart Andrew, FCA 1971; 1 Rosebriars, Majors Green, Shirley, SOLIHULL, B90 1EG.
CLARKE, Mr. Stuart David, BSc ACA 1995; White Lodge, 1 Anderson Lane, Southgate, SWANSEA, SA3 2BX.
CLARKE, Mr. Stuart Michael, BSc ACA ACMA 1991; 45 Hartington Road, St Margarets, TWICKENHAM, TW1 3EL.
CLARKE, Ms. Susan Alice, BA ACA 1993; Southgate, The Precinct, ROCHESTER, KENT, ME1 1SR.
CLARKE, Mr. Thomas Michael, BCom ACA 2006; 3 Wessex Close, Newbury Park, ILFORD, IG3 8JT.
CLARKE, Mr. Timothy, BA ACA 1984; Grant Thornton Hartwell House, 55-61 Victoria Street, BRISTOL, BS1 6FT.
CLARKE, Mr. Timothy James, MSc BSc ACA 2006; 22 Hall Grove, Hyde Park, LEEDS, LS6 1NT.
CLARKE, Mr. Timothy James, BA ACA 1986; Wildacre, Browns Lane, Effingham, LEATHERHEAD, SURREY, KT24 5NL.
CLARKE, Mr. Timothy Michael, BA ACA 1986; 13 Kirkstall Road, LONDON, SW2 4HD.
•CLARKE, Mr. Timothy Paul, BA ACA 1990; BDO LLP, 1 Bridgewater Place, Water Lane, LEEDS, LS11 5RU. See also BDO Stoy Hayward LLP
CLARKE, Mr. Timothy Ruthven, ACA 1993; Fernleigh, Cargreen, SALTASH, PL12 6PA.
CLARKE, Mrs. Vanessa Elizabeth, ACA 1991; 11 Ridgemount, WEYBRIDGE, SURREY, KT13 9JD.
CLARKE, Miss. Victoria, BA FCA 2000; 1a Minerva Road, KINGSTON UPON THAMES, SURREY, KT1 2QA.
CLARKE, Miss. Victoria, BA(Hons) ACA 2010; 70 Shevington Grove, Marton-in-Cleveland, MIDDLESBROUGH, CLEVELAND, TS7 8PY.
CLARKE, Mrs. Victoria Ellen, BSc FCA 1994; 16632 NE 46th Street, REDMOND, WA 98052, UNITED STATES.
•CLARKE, Mr. William, FCA 1965; 78 Seel Street, LIVERPOOL, L1 4BH.
CLARKE, Mr. William Barry, FCA 1955; Longwood, Park Road, ASHTEAD, KT21 2QR. (Life Member)
CLARKE, Mr. William Joseph, LLB FCA 1971; 11 The Bowmans, Victoria Road, MACCLESFIELD, CHESHIRE, SK10 3JA. (Life Member)
•CLARKE-MCCULLAGH, Mr. Geoffrey Frederick, FCA 1969; with Prager and Fenton LLP, 8th Floor, Imperial House, 15-19 Kingsway, LONDON, WC2B 6UN.
CLARKE-WALKER, Mr. Marcus Alex, BA ACA 2002; 5 Badger Close, Portslade, BRIGHTON, BN41 2EQ.
•CLARKE-WILLIAMS, Mr. Timothy David, FCA 1973; 23 Ecton Avenue, MACCLESFIELD, CHESHIRE, SK10 1QS.
CLARKIN, Mr. Paul Thomas, MA BSc ACA 1999; 25 Wyncairn Road, LARNE, COUNTY ANTRIM, BT40 2DY.
CLARKSON, Mr. Alexander James, BSocSc ACA CF MSI 1999; 68 Leigh Road, Hale, ALTRINCHAM, CHESHIRE, WA15 9BD.
CLARKSON, Mrs. Allyson Joan, BA ACA 1993; Hillcrest, Holme Street, Tarvin, CHESTER, CH3 8EQ.
CLARKSON, Mr. Ashley Mark Edward, BSc ACA 1996; (Tax Fac), 9 Heath Way, Burton Latimer, KETTERING, NORTHAMPTONSHIRE, NN15 5YF.
•CLARKSON, Mrs. Chrysoulla Louise, BSc(Hons) ACA 2004; (Tax Fac), Soulla Clarkson, Rowgate, Thorpe Bassett, MALTON, NORTH YORKSHIRE, YO17 8LU.
CLARKSON, Mr. David Andrew, BA FCA 1979; 44 Brompton Road, KENSINGTON, NSW 2033, AUSTRALIA.
CLARKSON, Mr. David Anthony, BSc ACA 1996; Credit Suisse, Uetlibergstr 231, 8070 ZURICH, SWITZERLAND.
CLARKSON, Mr. Donald, FCA 1955; 223 Beckfield Lane, Acomb, YORK, YO26 5PH. (Life Member)
CLARKSON, Miss. Emilie, ACA 2008; RBS PLC, 135 Bishopsgate, LONDON, EC2M 3UR.
CLARKSON, Mrs. Fiona Jane, BSc ACA 1995; (Tax Fac), 2 Hillbeck Grove, Middleton, MILTON KEYNES, MK10 9JJ.
CLARKSON, Mr. Gary Charles, BSc ACA 2004; 34 Black Acre Close, AMERSHAM, BUCKINGHAMSHIRE, HP7 9EW.
CLARKSON, Miss. Hannah Ruth, ACA 2009; 34a Montpellier Spa Road, CHELTENHAM, GLOUCESTERSHIRE, GL50 1UL.
CLARKSON, Miss. Helen Louisa, BA ACA 1999; 109 Cambridge Road, TEDDINGTON, MIDDLESEX, TW11 8DF.
CLARKSON, Mr. Iain Geoffrey, BSc ACA 1993; 68 Hill Top Avenue, Cheadle Hulme, CHEADLE, SK8 7JA.
CLARKSON, Mr. James Norman, BSc ACA 1998; 12 Honey Head Lane, Honley, HOLMFIRTH, HD9 6RW.
CLARKSON, Mr. Jeremy David, BA ACA 1987; 179 Queens Road, WEYBRIDGE, KT13 0AH.
CLARKSON, Miss. Joanna, ACA 2008; The Hepworth Wakefield, Gallery Walk, WAKEFIELD, WF1 5AW.
•CLARKSON, Mrs. Joanne Frances, BSc ACA 2000; JF Clarkson, 16 Ffynone Drive, SWANSEA, SA1 6DD.
CLARKSON, Miss. Joanne Lois, BA ACA 1992; Yew Tree House Bowers, Standon, STAFFORD, ST21 6RW.
CLARKSON, Mr. Martin, MA FCA 1995; 14 Woodland Rise, Birkby, HUDDERSFIELD, HD2 2SZ.
CLARKSON, Mr. Nicholas Luke, ACA 2007; American Express Europe Ltd, Sussex House, Civic Way, BURGESS HILL, WEST SUSSEX, RH15 9AQ.
CLARKSON, Mr. Peter David, BA ACA 1991; LMS Group Holdings Ltd, LMS House, Lloyd Drive, ELLESMERE PORT, CHESHIRE, CH65 9HQ.
•CLARKSON, Mr. Robert Hollings, FCA 1980; (Tax Fac), Clarkson & Co, Centre of Excellence, Hope Park, Trevor Foster Way, BRADFORD, WEST YORKSHIRE BD5 8HH.
CLARKSON, Mr. Roy Edward, FCA 1966; 32 Yarmouth Road, Great Sankey, WARRINGTON, WA5 3EJ.
CLARKSON, Mrs. Sally-Ann, BA(Hons) FCA 1994; 8 Ashbourne Road, Ealing, LONDON, W5 3ED.
CLARKSON, Mr. Samuel Thomas, ACA 2010; 57 Oakmead Road, LONDON, SW12 9SH.
•CLARKSON, Mrs. Sarah Jane, BA ACA 1992; Clarkson Cleaver & Bowes Ltd, 8A Wingbury Courtyard Business Village, Wingrave, AYLESBURY, BUCKINGHAMSHIRE, HP22 4LW.
•CLARKSON, Mrs. Sarah Virginia, BSc ACA 1992; (Tax Fac), Craggs & Co Ltd, Hollydene, 58 Otley Road, LEEDS, LS6 4DL. See also Craggs & Co
CLARKSON, Dr. Steven Gary, BSc ACA 2002; 35 Hampton Court Road, Harborne, BIRMINGHAM, WEST MIDLANDS, B17 9AF.
CLARKSON, Mr. Stuart, BA ACA 1995; 150 Park Hill Road, Harborne, BIRMINGHAM, B17 9HD.
CLARKSON, Mrs. Susan Elaine, BA ACA 1996; PPG Industries Europe Sarl, Route de Gilly 32, 1180 ROLLE, SWITZERLAND.
CLARKSON, Mrs. Susan Gail, BA ACA 1987; 17 Oakridge, WETHERBY, LS22 6GT.
CLARKSON, Mr. William Ernest, FCA 1957; 7 Manor Drive, SUTTON COLDFIELD, WEST MIDLANDS, B73 6ER. (Life Member)
CLARKSON WEBB, Michael Robert, Esq OBE FCA 1952; Apple Tree Cottage, Thursley Road, Elstead, GODALMING, GU8 6DG. (Life Member)
CLARSON, Dr. Benjamin, DPhil MChem ACA 2011; Apartment 90, Cutlass Court, 28 Granville Street, BIRMINGHAM, B1 2LJ.
CLARSON, Mr. David Stephen, BA FCA 1974; 1A Clumber Road East, The Park, NOTTINGHAM, NG7 1BD.
CLARSON, Mr. Peter, BA(Hons) ACA 2011; 29 Marnham Drive, NOTTINGHAM, NG3 5HG.
CLARY, Mr. Andrew Paul, BSc ACA 1996; 1 Northall Road, BEXLEYHEATH, DA7 6JF.
CLARY, Mr. Thomas, BSc ACA 2011; 58 The Drive, BECKENHAM, KENT, BR3 1EQ.
CLASEN, Mr. Andrew Bernard Patrick, FCA 1964; 60 Bridge Street, PERSHORE, WR10 1AX.
CLASEN, Mrs. Caroline Susan, BA ACA 1984; Camron Public Relations, 7 Floral Street, LONDON, WC2E 9DH.
CLATWORTHY, Mr. Barrie James, FCA 1967; Felly Lodge Front Street, Pebworth, STRATFORD-UPON-AVON, CV37 8XQ.
•CLATWORTHY, Mr. Michael Jason, BEng ACA 1997; Deloitte LLP, Athene Place, 66 Shoe Lane, LONDON, EC4A 3BQ. See also Deloitte & Touche LLP
CLATWORTHY, Mr. Philip Thomas P, FCA 1971; PO Box 130873, BRYANSTON, GAUTENG, 2021, SOUTH AFRICA. (Life Member)
CLAUSEN-THUE, Mr. David, BA ACA 1981; with Deloitte LLP, Athene Place, 66 Shoe Lane, LONDON, EC4A 3BQ.
•CLAVANE, Mr. Martin, BSc ACA 1990; (Tax Fac), Clavane & Company, 6 Trans Walk, Church Fenton, TADCASTER, LS24 9RR.
•CLAVELL, Mr. Anthony Roger, FCA 1977; (Tax Fac), A.R. Clavell, 2 Whitbred Road, SALISBURY, SP2 9PE.
•CLAVERING, Mr. Robert John, BA FCA 1976; Clavering & Co, Crew-yard House, Water Lane, Stainby, GRANTHAM, LINCOLNSHIRE NG33 5QZ.
CLAXTON, Mr. Benjamin, BSc(Econ) ACA 2010; 27 Canal Road, NEWTOWN, POWYS, SY16 2JN.
•CLAXTON, Mr. Brian Douglas, FCA 1975; HBAS Limited, Amwell House, 19 Amwell Street, HODDESDON, HERTFORDSHIRE, EN11 8TS. See also Hardcastles Limited
CLAXTON, Mrs. Claire Elizabeth, BSc(Hons) ACA 2001; 7 Maple Way, DUNMOW, ESSEX, CM6 1WZ.
•CLAXTON, Mr. David Neal, BSc ACA 1985; Deloitte LLP, Lomond House, 9 George Square, GLASGOW, G2 1QQ. See also Deloitte & Touche LLP
•CLAXTON, Mrs. Elizabeth Jane, ACA FCCA 2007; (Tax Fac), Rostrons, St Peter's House, Cattle Market Street, NORWICH, NR1 3DY. See also Rostron & Partners
CLAXTON, Miss. Louise Elizabeth, BSocSc ACA 2002; 28 Isis Street, LONDON, SW18 3QN.
CLAXTON, Mr. Neil Darren, BSc ACA 1988; 4 Coneycroft, Dunnington, YORK, YO19 5RL.
•CLAXTON, Mr. Roger John, FCA 1980; Roger Claxton, 7 Indigo Yard, NORWICH, NR3 3QZ.
CLAXTON-INGHAM, Owen Christopher, BSc ACA 1990; with PricewaterhouseCoopers LLP, Benson House, 33 Wellington Street, LEEDS, LS1 4JP.
CLAY, Mr. Bryan Lewis, FCA 1952; Cock House, Langcliffe, SETTLE, BD24 9LY. (Life Member)
CLAY, Mrs. Clare Louise Ann, ACA 2005; Eston House, 65 Chester Road, Audley, STOKE-ON-TRENT, STAFFORDSHIRE, ST7 8JF.
CLAY, Mr. David, ACA 2008; 105 Shire Road, Morley, LEEDS, LS27 0SN.
CLAY, Mr. Ian Robert, BSc FCA 1980; PricewaterhouseCoopers - Qatar LLC, 3rd Floor, Al Amadi Business Centre, P O Box 6689, DOHA, QATAR.
CLAY, Mr. Jared Seth, BA ACA 2006; 2870 South Rock Street, GILBERT, AZ 85295, UNITED STATES.
CLAY, Mr. John Charles Olsen, FCA 1981; Apartado de Correos 03006, PTDA Figuerals 21C, 03729 LLIBER, ALICANTE, SPAIN.
•CLAY, Mr. John Neil, BA FCA 1981; Willow Brook, Bairstow Lane, SOWERBY BRIDGE, WEST YORKSHIRE, HX6 2SY.
•CLAY, Mr. Keith Sidney, FCA 1981; Parkhurst Hill Limited, Torrington Chambers, 58 North Road East, PLYMOUTH, DEVON, PL4 6AJ. See also Parkhurst Hill
CLAY, Mr. Kenneth John, FCA 1952; 48 Barleycorn Way, Emerson Park, HORNCHURCH, RM11 3JJ. (Life Member)
CLAY, Mrs. Louise, BA ACA 2005; with HW, 30 Camp Road, FARNBOROUGH, HAMPSHIRE, GU14 6EW.
CLAY, Mr. Martin John, FCA 1969; 61 Bourton Road, SOLIHULL, WEST MIDLANDS, B92 8AZ. (Life Member)
CLAY, Mr. Martin Richard Debreaux, BA ACA 1988; 4 Great Bounds Drive, TUNBRIDGE WELLS, TN4 0TP.
CLAY, Mr. Michael John, FCA 1957; Llwynhelig House, Llwynhelig, COWBRIDGE, SOUTH GLAMORGAN, CF71 7FF. (Life Member)
CLAY, Mr. Nicholas Charles Cameron, BSc ACA 1988; 34 Lucastes Avenue, HAYWARDS HEATH, RH16 1JX.
CLAY, Mrs. Olivia Helen, BA(Hons) ACA 2001; 92 New Lane, Croft, WARRINGTON, WA3 7JL.
CLAY, Mr. Paul Timothy Joseph, ACA 2008; Basement flat, 46 Overstone Road, LONDON, W6 0AB.
•CLAY, Mr. Peter, FCA 1984; (Tax Fac), Dawkins Lewis & Soar, 4 Cowdown Business Park, Micheldever, WINCHESTER, SO21 3DN. See also DLS Accounting Services Ltd

CLAY, Mr. Richard Henry, FCA *1966;* The Copse, Shiplate Road, Bleadon, WESTON-SUPER-MARE, BS24 0NX. (Life Member)
CLAY, Mr. Richard Henry Arden, BA ACA *2003;* 13 Melrose Gardens, LONDON, W6 7RN.
CLAY, Mr. Richard William, ACA *2002;* 65 Chester Road, Audley, STOKE-ON-TRENT, ST7 8JF.
•**CLAY, Mrs. Tina Theresa, BA FCA** *1982;* Foot Davson, 17 Church Road, TUNBRIDGE WELLS, TN1 1LG.
•**CLAYDEN, Mr. Anthony Louis, BSc FCA MSI** *1994;* (Tax Fac), Strategic Finance Director Limited, 18 Roughgrove Copse, Binfield, BRACKNELL, BERKSHIRE, RG42 4EZ.
CLAYDEN, Mrs. Antonia Helen Victoria, MSc ACA *1997;* 76 Hill Top, Hampstead Garden Suburb, LONDON, NW11 6EE.
CLAYDEN, Mr. Christopher Howard John, BA ACA *1989;* Burson Marsteller, 24-28 Bloomsbury Way, LONDON, WC1A 2PX.
•**CLAYDEN, Mr. Ian, BA(Hons) ACA** *2000;* with BDO LLP, 55 Baker Street, LONDON, W1U 7EU.
CLAYDEN, Mr. Jack, FCA *1951;* Rose Cottage, 9 Longdown Road, Lower Bourne, FARNHAM, SURREY, GU10 3JT. (Life Member)
CLAYDEN, Miss. Joanne Michelle, BSc ACA *2006;* 24 Broadlands Way, Rushmere St. Andrew, IPSWICH, IP4 5SU.
CLAYDEN, Mr. Joseph, FCA *1949;* No. 126, 1770, 128th Street, WHITE ROCK V4A 8V2, BC, CANADA. (Life Member)
CLAYDEN, Mr. Paul Francis, BSc ACA *1994;* A O N Ltd, 8 Devonshire Square, LONDON, EC2M 4PL.
CLAYDEN, Mr. Robert Brian Frederick, FCA *1957;* Flat 53, Vivary House, Kinglake Drive, TAUNTON, TA1 3RR. (Life Member)
•**CLAYDON, Mrs. Elizabeth Ann, BSc ACA** *1995;* KPMG LLP, 15 Canada Square, LONDON, E14 5GL. See also KPMG Europe LLP
CLAYDON, Mrs. Emma Christine, BSc ACA *1996;* 43 Evelegh Road, Farlington, PORTSMOUTH, PO6 1DJ.
CLAYDON, Mr. Gary James, BA ACA *1989;* 10137 Miguelita Road, SAN JOSE, CA 95127, UNITED STATES.
CLAYDON, Miss. Lorraine Iris, BA FCA *1991;* 59 Ennerdale Drive, CONGLETON, CW12 4FJ.
CLAYDON, Mr. Paul Victor, BSc ACA *1992;* 43 Evelegh Road, Farlington, PORTSMOUTH, PO6 1DJ.
CLAYDON, Mr. Shaun, BA ACA *1996;* 54 Cloudesdale Road, LONDON, SW17 8EU.
CLAYDON-BUTLER, Mrs. Christine Anne, BSc ACA *1992;* 6 Hardwick Close, Bradley Fold, Radcliffe, MANCHESTER, M26 3XF.
CLAYMAN, Mr. Arnold Michael, FCA *1953;* Casa Das Figueiras, Alfanzina, 8400-550 CARVOEIRO, PORTUGAL. (Life Member)
CLAYS, Mr. Malcolm John, BSocSc ACA *1992;* 9 Llewellyn Park, Twyford, READING, RG10 9NB.
CLAYS, Mrs. Pauline Anne, BEng ACA *2000;* 6 Hornbeam Close, Paddock Wood, TONBRIDGE, KENT, TN12 6LL.
CLAYSON, Mrs. Hazel Carolyn, BSc FCA *1988;* 4 Neasham Court, Stokesley, MIDDLESBROUGH, CLEVELAND, TS9 5PJ.
CLAYSON, Mrs. Sally Rowena, MA FCA *1987;* Selwyn College, Grange Road, CAMBRIDGE, CB3 9DQ.
CLAYTON, Mr. Adam James, BSc ACA *2006;* 60 The Royal, Wilton Place, SALFORD, M3 6WP.
CLAYTON, Mr. Andrew David Griswolde, ACA CA(SA) *2011;* 11 Murfett Close, Wimbledon, LONDON, SW19 6QB.
•**CLAYTON, Mr. Andrew John, ACA** *2004;* (Tax Fac), RNS, 50-54 Oswald Road, SCUNTHORPE, NORTH LINCOLNSHIRE, DN15 7PQ.
CLAYTON, Mr. Andrew John Pensam, BSc ACA *1986;* Duggans House, Blackhouse Lane, Suckley, WORCESTER, WR6 5DP.
CLAYTON, Mr. Ben, BSc ACA *2005;* Apartment 211 Westgate Apartments, 14 Western Gateway, LONDON, E16 1BP.
CLAYTON, Mrs. Catherine, BA ACA CTA *1994;* 64 Mill Bank Road, Meltham, HOLMFIRTH, HD9 4AX.
CLAYTON, Mr. Christopher John, FCA *1968;* 17 Brookside, Bicton, SHREWSBURY, SY3 8EP.
CLAYTON, Mr. Christopher John Moffat, FCA *1970;* Flat 27, Creed Court, 1 Outram Road, CROYDON, CR0 6XG. (Life Member)
CLAYTON, Mr. Daniel Mark, BA ACA *1996;* 706 Rossetti Place, 2 Lower Byrom Street, MANCHESTER, M3 4AN.
CLAYTON, Mr. David, FCA *1951;* Flat 310, 138 Hanassi Street, 46399 HERZLIA PETUACH, ISRAEL. (Life Member)
CLAYTON, Mr. David Harry, FCA *1971;* 4 Old Farm Road, Silverhurst, Main Road, Constantia, CAPE TOWN, 7806 SOUTH AFRICA.
CLAYTON, Mr. David Ian, FCA *1969;* 7B Hunts Close, Broughton, BRIGG, SOUTH HUMBERSIDE, DN20 0SF. (Life Member)
CLAYTON, Mr. Dean, BSc FCA *1976;* 63 Peaslands Road, SIDMOUTH, DEVON, EX10 8XD.
•**CLAYTON, Mr. Dennis James, FCA** *1965;* 19 Moss Lane, Broadbottom, HYDE, SK14 6BD.
CLAYTON, Mr. Donald Eric, FCA *1951;* The Firs, 44 Hall Rise, Bramhope, LEEDS, LS16 9JG. (Life Member)
CLAYTON, Miss. Elizabeth Rose, ACA *2010;* 26 Scotland Road, BUCKHURST HILL, ESSEX, IG9 5NR.
CLAYTON, Mr. Graham, BSc FCA *1980;* Brookside, Woodcourt Road, Harbertonford, TOTNES, TQ9 7TY.
CLAYTON, Mr. Graham David, BA ACA *1980;* 13018 Mossy Ridge Cove, HOUSTON, TX 77041, UNITED STATES.
CLAYTON, Mr. Graham Robert, BSc ACA *1990;* McArdles Solicitors, 26 Frederick Street, SUNDERLAND, SR1 1LT.
CLAYTON, Miss. Helen Louise, BSc ACA *1999;* 6 Stormer Hill Fold, Tottington, BURY, BL8 4AU.
•**CLAYTON, Mr. Iain, ACA FCCA** *2007;* CG Lee Ltd, Ingram House, Meridian Way, NORWICH, NR7 0TA.
•**CLAYTON, Mrs. Jane Elizabeth, BSc FCA** *1978;* Jane E. Clayton, Dolgoy House, 49 West Cross Lane, West Cross, SWANSEA, SA3 5LS.
CLAYTON, Mrs. Jenny Natasha, BA(Hons) ACA *2000;* Garden Flat, 3 South Villas, LONDON, NW1 9BS.
•**CLAYTON, Miss. Jessica Sarah, BSocSc ACA** *2001;* Ernst & Young LLP, 1 More London Place, LONDON, SE1 2AF. See also Ernst & Young Europe LLP
CLAYTON, Mrs. Joanna Elizabeth, BA ACA *1996;* Alliance Boots, 2 The Heights Brooklands, WEYBRIDGE, KT13 0NY.
CLAYTON, Mr. John David, BA FCA *1977;* Unipart Rail Ltd Icon, Firstpoint Balby Carr Bank, DONCASTER, SOUTH YORKSHIRE, DN4 5JQ.
CLAYTON, Mr. John Jardine, FCA *1938;* 8 Ocean Heights, 22 Boscombe Cliff Road, Boscombe, BOURNEMOUTH, BH5 1LA. (Life Member)
CLAYTON, Mr. Jonathan Mark, BSc ACA *2000;* Briar House, Spinfield Lane, MARLOW, BUCKINGHAMSHIRE, SL7 2JT.
CLAYTON, Mrs. Katrina Elise, BA ACA *1991;* Cold Norton Priory, Priory Road, Heythrop, CHIPPING NORTON, OX7 5TA.
CLAYTON, Mr. Keith Edward Boyd, FCA *1965;* Little Orchard, Pedlars Lane, Therfield, ROYSTON, HERTFORDSHIRE, SG8 9PX.
CLAYTON, Mr. Keith Edwin, BCom FCA *1978;* 67 Grundale, Kirk Ella, HULL, HU10 7LB.
CLAYTON, Mr. Kevin James, BA ACA *1983;* 2317 Marine Drive, WEST VANCOUVER V7V 1K9, BC, CANADA.
CLAYTON, Mr. Landon Robert, FCA *1963;* 84a Warwick Avenue, LONDON, W9 2PU.
CLAYTON, Mrs. Lynn Hazel, ACA *1990;* 5 Swan Lane, Sellindge, ASHFORD, TN25 6EP.
CLAYTON, Mr. Neil William Harold, BA ACA *1989;* Cold Norton Priory, 1 Priory Road, CHIPPING NORTON, OX7 5TA.
CLAYTON, Mr. Nicholas David, ACA *1985;* Flat 35 Dundee Wharf, 100 Three Colt Street, LONDON, E14 8AX.
•**CLAYTON, Mr. Nicholas Edward, MEng ACA** *2002;* (Tax Fac), Nick Clayton Ltd, 44 Drewitt House, 865 Ringwood Road, BOURNEMOUTH, DORSET, BH11 8LW. See also Claytons
CLAYTON, Mr. Nicholas Simon, MA ACA *2003;* 42A Broxash Road, LONDON, SW11 6AB.
•**CLAYTON, Ms. Nicola Jane, LLB ACA** *1985;* Quantico, Nottingham Castle Marina, Marina Road, Castle Marina Park, NOTTINGHAM, NG7 1TN.
CLAYTON, Mr. Nigel, BSc ACA *1992;* 20 High Fieldside, Grasmere, AMBLESIDE, LA22 9QQ.
CLAYTON, Mr. Paul Andrew, BSc ACA *1995;* Trinity Protection Systems Ltd, Unit 5, Little Bridge Business Park, Oil Mill Lane, Clyst St. Mary, EXETER EX5 1AU.
CLAYTON, Mr. Peter Grattan, FCA *1964;* Muirbeck, 17 Coltbridge Gardens, EDINBURGH, EH12 6AQ.
•**CLAYTON, Mr. Peter Harold, MA FCA CF** *1971;* Ellacotts LLP, Countrywide House, 23 West Bar Street, BANBURY, OXFORDSHIRE, OX16 9SA.
CLAYTON, Mrs. Philippa, ACA *2011;* 33 Alder Hill Grove, LEEDS, LS7 2PT.
CLAYTON, Mr. Quinton Donald, FCA *1952;* 23 Norfolk Road, BURY ST.EDMUNDS, IP32 6AY. (Life Member)
CLAYTON, Miss. Rebecca, BA ACA *2011;* 18 Simmons Field, THATCHAM, RG18 4ET.
CLAYTON, Mr. Richard Alexander, FCA *1962;* Crosbies Cottage, Brookside, Buxworth, HIGH PEAK, SK23 7NE.
CLAYTON, Mr. Richard Michael, BSc ACA *1987;* Bramley House, Hall Lane, KETTERING, NN15 7LH.
CLAYTON, Mr. Sean, BA ACA *2007;* 16 The Cobbles, Meltham, HOLMFIRTH, HD9 5QG.
CLAYTON, Mr. Simon Anthony, BA ACA *1982;* Dunas Lifestyle Lda, 5 Quinta Shopping, Quinta do Lago, 8135 862 ALMANCIL, PORTUGAL.
CLAYTON, Mr. Stefan Arthur, BA FCA *1983;* Woudbury, 64 Grange Gardens, PINNER, MIDDLESEX, HA5 5QF.
CLAYTON, Mr. Stephen Frederick, FCA *1975;* 268 Bramhall Lane, STOCKPORT, CHESHIRE, SK3 8TR.
CLAYTON, Mrs. Susan, BSc ACA *1991;* 24 Iris Drive, Kings Heath, BIRMINGHAM, B14 5AG.
CLAYTON-JONES, Mr. Christopher Edmund, BA ACA *1998;* Christies, 213 Oxford Street, LONDON, W1D 2LG.
CLAYTON-JONES, Mrs. Lisa Maria, BA ACA *1998;* 39 Thornash Road, Horsell, WOKING, SURREY, GU21 4UW.
•**CLAYWORTH, Mr. Graham Charles, BSc FCA** *1988;* BDO LLP, 125 Colmore Row, BIRMINGHAM, B3 3SD. See also BDO Stoy Hayward LLP
CLEAK, Mr. Andrew John, BSc FCA *1982;* SI.T.A., 26 Chemin De Joinville, Case Postale 31, Cointrin, 1216 GENEVA, SWITZERLAND.
CLEAL, Mr. Andrew Leslie, BA ACA *2005;* 22 Ivygreen Road, MANCHESTER, M21 9ET.
CLEANTHOUS, Mr. Yiannis, BSc ACA *2007;* Flat 202, 10 Elia Venezi, CY - 1076 NICOSIA, CYPRUS.
CLEAR, Mr. Charles Jeremy, FCA *1974;* Camozzi Pneumatics Ltd The Fluid Power Centre, Watling Street, NUNEATON, CV11 6BQ.
•**CLEAR, Mr. Sam James, FCA** *1976;* Bell & Company, 64 Harpur Street, BEDFORD, MK40 2ST.
CLEARY, Mr. David James, BSc FCA *1988;* Deluxe Laboratories Ltd North Orbital Road, Denham, UXBRIDGE, MIDDLESEX, UB9 5HQ.
CLEARY, Mr. Douglas Michael, BSc FCA *1989;* 88 Merton Way, WEST MOLESEY, SURREY, KT8 1PQ.
CLEARY, Miss. Helen Marie, BSc ACA *2005;* 23 Hollington Drive, Pontprennau, CARDIFF, CF23 8PG.
CLEARY, Miss. Joan Ann, LLB ACA *1989;* 6 Dillon Street, PADDINGTON, NSW 2021, AUSTRALIA.
CLEARY, Mr. John Gerard, BA ACA *1987;* Rest Harrow London Road, DORKING, SURREY, RH4 1JE.
CLEARY, Mr. Matthew Thomas, BCom FCA *1976;* 2 Didbrook Fields Cottages, Didbrook Fields Toddington, CHELTENHAM, GLOUCESTERSHIRE, GL54 5PE.
CLEARY, Mr. Michael, BSc ACA *1999;* Barratt Homes, 4 Brindley Road, MANCHESTER, M16 9HQ.
CLEARY, Mr. Michael John, BSc FCA *1975;* Yew Tree House, Hensting Lane, Owslebury, WINCHESTER, HAMPSHIRE, SO21 1LE. (Life Member)
CLEARY, Mr. Michael John, ACA *1988;* Pendrells, Blackgate Lane, HENFIELD, WEST SUSSEX, BN5 9HA.
CLEARY, Mr. Peter James, FCA *1975;* 80 Courtlands Avenue, LONDON, SE12 8JA.
CLEASBY, Mrs. Joanne Mary, BA ACA *1998;* 39 The Wynd Kenton, NEWCASTLE UPON TYNE, NE3 4LA.
CLEASBY, Miss. Nicola Jane, BSc ACA *1989;* Cortijo Almiarejo, Ctra Murtas - Turon, 18490 Murtas, GRANADA, SPAIN.
•**CLEATON-ROBERTS, Mrs. Hannah Lucia, BA ACA** *1999;* (Tax Fac), Ernst & Young LLP, 1 More London Place, LONDON, SE1 2AF. See also Ernst & Young Europe LLP
CLEAVER, Mr. Adrian Robert, BSc ACA *1979;* 39 Vivary Road, TAUNTON, SOMERSET, TA1 3JW.
CLEAVER, Miss. Amanda Jayne, MA(Oxon) ACA *2001;* with BDO LLP, 2 City Place, Beehive Ring Road, GATWICK, WEST SUSSEX, RH6 0PA.
•①**CLEAVER, Mr. Barry Keith, FCA** *1980;* (Tax Fac), Gardiners Limited, Hutton House, Dale Road, Sheriff Hutton, YORK, YO60 6RZ.
CLEAVER, Mrs. Clare Janine, BCom ACA *1993;* (Tax Fac), Riding School House Bulls Lane, Wishaw, SUTTON COLDFIELD, B76 9QW.
•**CLEAVER, Mr. David Charles, FCA FInstD** *1966;* (Tax Fac), David C Cleaver, Blackden Heath Farm, Blackden Lane, Holmes Chapel, CREWE, CW4 8DG.
•**CLEAVER, Mr. David Kenneth, FCA** *1970;* David Cleaver & Co, 25 Heycroft, COVENTRY, CV4 7HE.
CLEAVER, Ms. Deborah Ann, BSc(Hons) ACA *2003;* Predvoje 30, 16200 PRAGUE, CZECH REPUBLIC.
•**CLEAVER, Mr. Gary Arthur, BSc FCA** *1992;* Geo Little Sebire & Co, Oliver House, 19-23 Windmill Hill, ENFIELD, MIDDLESEX, EN2 7AB.
CLEAVER, Mr. Gary Lloyd, BA ACA *1990;* 14 Avenue du Prince, d'Orange, Uccle, 1180 BRUSSELS, BELGIUM.
•**CLEAVER, Mr. Goronwy James, FCA** *1971;* PO Box 1102, 4th Floor Building 3, Cayman Financial Centre, GEORGE TOWN, GRAND CAYMAN, KY1-1102 CAYMAN ISLANDS.
CLEAVER, Mr. Hugh Richard, BA ACA *1980;* Hampden Agencies Ltd, 85 Gracechurch Street, LONDON, EC3V 0AA.
•**CLEAVER, Mr. Ian, FCA** *1982;* Bristow Still, 39 Sackville Road, HOVE, BN3 3WD.
CLEAVER, Mr. James Edward Robert, FCA *1955;* 6 Branksome Grange, 1 Lakeside Road, POOLE, DORSET, BH13 6LR. (Life Member)
CLEAVES, Mr. Colin Geoffrey, BA FCA *1975;* with KPMG LLP, Management Services Centre, 58 Clarendon Road, WATFORD, WD17 1DE.
•**CLEDEN, Mr. John Lloyd, BSc FCA** *1980;* (Tax Fac), Cleden Howard and Company Limited, 121 Albert Street, FLEET, HAMPSHIRE, GU51 3SR.
CLEE, Mrs. Alexandra Mary, BSc ACA *1992;* Willow Cottage, 36 Berwick Road, MARLOW, SL7 3AT.
CLEE, Mr. Jonathan Peter, BA(Hons) ACA *2001;* The Eden Collection Ltd Seasons House, Lakeside Business Village St. Davids Park Ewloe, DEESIDE, CLWYD, CH5 3YE.
CLEE, Mr. Peter William, FCA *1951;* 160 Lake Road East, Roath Park, CARDIFF, CF23 5NQ. (Life Member)
CLEE, Mr. Simon Martin, BA ACA *1993;* 13 Tangmere Grove, KINGSTON-UPON-THAMES, KT2 5GT.
CLEERE, Mr. Edward George, FCA *1953;* 42 Dudsbury Avenue, FERNDOWN, BH22 8DU. (Life Member)
CLEEVE, Mr. Marc William, BA ACA *2006;* Deloitte & Touche, Lord Coutanche House, 66-68 Esplanade, St Helier, JERSEY, JE4 8WA.
CLEEVELY, Mrs. Nicola Kate, LLB ACA *2002;* 16 Taylor Drive, Bramley, TADLEY, HAMPSHIRE, RG26 5XP.
CLEGG, Mr. Aidan Charles Barwick, MA ACA *1992;* Blackmoor Farm, Ockham Lane, COBHAM, SURREY, KT11 1LZ.
CLEGG, Mr. Andrew Carl, MEng ACA *2002;* 4 Stratford Park Drive, TERRIGAL, NSW 2260, AUSTRALIA.
CLEGG, Mr. Andrew David, BSc ACA *1997;* with KPMG LLP, 1 Forest Gate, Brighton Road, CRAWLEY, WEST SUSSEX, RH11 9PT.
•**CLEGG, Mr. Anthony Paul, FCA** *1966;* Hillingdale Ltd, 24 Sellerdale Avenue, Wyke, BRADFORD, BD12 9LJ.
•**CLEGG, Mr. Brian, FCA** *1975;* (Tax Fac), Hewitts, 11 Venture One Business Park, Long Acre Close, SHEFFIELD, S20 3FR.
CLEGG, Mr. Charles Ian, FCA *1959;* Tolcarne, Whalley Lane, Uplyme, LYME REGIS, DT7 3UR. (Life Member)
CLEGG, Mr. Christopher Charles Darby, BA(Hons) ACA *2000;* 28 Shire Road, Morley, LEEDS, LS27 0QL.
CLEGG, Mr. Christopher John Southwell, LLB FCA *1974;* 50 Abingdon Villas, LONDON, W8 6XD.
CLEGG, Mr. Daniel Peter, BSc ACA *2007;* 29 Kyle Crescent, CARDIFF, CF14 1ST.
•**CLEGG, Mr. David Luke, ACA** *2008;* Sedulo Business Services Limited, 42-44 Chorley New Road, BOLTON, BL1 4AP. See also Ascendis Audit Limited
CLEGG, Mr. Finlay Brian, BA ACA *1995;* Saga Group Ltd Enbrook Park, Sandgate High Street Sandgate, FOLKESTONE, CT20 3SE.
CLEGG, Mrs. Hannah, BSc ACA *2009;* 2 Groveside Road, LONDON, E4 6JD.
CLEGG, Miss. Helen, MEng ACA *2006;* (Tax Fac), Astrazeneca Plc, G48 Alderley House, Alderley Park, MACCLESFIELD, CHESHIRE, SK10 4TF.
CLEGG, Mr. James Joseph Norris, ACA *2000;* Warren Hill Farm Hulfords Lane, Hartley Wintney, HOOK, RG27 8AG.
CLEGG, Mr. John Neville, FCA *1951;* Haighfield Nursing Home, 241 Wigan Road, Standish, WIGAN, LANCASHIRE, WN1 2RF. (Life Member)
CLEGG, Mr. John Ormerod, FCA *1967;* 6 Brentwood Close, Smithy Bridge, LITTLEBOROUGH, OL15 0ND. (Life Member)
•**CLEGG, Mrs. Mary Clare, BA FCA** *1975;* (Tax Fac), Merganser Limited, 51 Priestnall Road, STOCKPORT, CHESHIRE, SK4 3HW.
CLEGG, Mr. Michael David, MA BA FCA *1975;* Cregg, Rosses Point, SLIGO, COUNTY SLIGO, IRELAND.

CLEGG, Mr. Nicholas William, BSc ACA *1982;* Porter Dodson, Central House, Church Path, YEOVIL, SOMERSET, BA20 1HH.
•**CLEGG, Mr. Nigel Stephen, BA ACA** *1984;* 18 Highwood Road, Appleton, WARRINGTON, WA4 5AJ.
•**CLEGG, Mr. Paul, FCA** *1969;* (Tax Fac), Paul Clegg & Company, Riverside Offices, Second Floor, 26 St Georges Quay, LANCASTER, LA1 1RD.
•**CLEGG, Mr. Peter Dixon, BSc FCA** *1981;* (Tax Fac), Westlake Clark, 7 Lynwood Court, Priestlands Place, LYMINGTON, HAMPSHIRE, SO41 9GA.
CLEGG, Mr. Philip David, MSc BSc ACA *2005;* Pala Investments AG, Dammstrasse 19, 6300 ZUG, SWITZERLAND.
CLEGG, Mr. Richard Hilton, MBA FCA *1973;* Church Farmhouse, Braceby, SLEAFORD, NG34 0TA.
CLEGG, Mr. Ross Jonathan, MPhys ACA *2007;* Lloyds TSB, 10 Gresham Street, LONDON, EC2V 7AE.
CLEGG, Mr. Rupert Mark Roland, BA BSc ACA *1992;* 37 Nalya Road, NARRAWEENA, NSW 2099, AUSTRALIA.
CLEGG, Mr. Simon David, ACA *2008;* 50 Longridge Avenue, NEWCASTLE UPON TYNE, NE7 7LB.
CLEGG, Mr. Stephen Charles, FCA *1976;* 9 South Drive, Timperley, ALTRINCHAM, WA15 6QJ.
CLEGHORN, Mr. Alasdair John Cameron, MA ACA *1984;* 18 Woodlands Road, VALSAYN, TRINIDAD AND TOBAGO.
CLEGHORN, Mr. Matthew Paul, BSc(Hons) ACA *2010;* 53 Pulborough Road, Storrington, PULBOROUGH, WEST SUSSEX, RH20 4HJ.
CLEIN, Mr. Ian Stanley, FCA *1990;* Flat 48 Belsize Court, Wedderburn Road, LONDON, NW3 5QH.
CLELAND, Mrs. Emma Jane, ACA *2001;* 5 Park Road West, CHESTER, CH4 8BQ.
CLELAND, Miss. Rachel Louise, ACA *2007;* Flannigan Edmonds Bannon, Pearl Assurance House, 2 Donegall Square East, BELFAST, BT1 5HB.
CLELFORD, Mr. Donald Peter, BA FCA *1986;* Larkings, 31 St. Georges Place, CANTERBURY, CT1 1XD.
CLELLAND, Mr. Jonathan Charles, BA ACA *1985;* 13 The Hermitage, RICHMOND, TW10 6SH.
•**CLEMAS, Mr. Vincent Edward, FCA DChA** *1966;* (Tax Fac), Vincent Clemas LLP, Cornerways House, School Lane, RINGWOOD, HAMPSHIRE, BH24 1LG.
CLEMENCE, Mr. Alexander James Raoul, BSc ACA *2001;* 36 Dunkeld Road, BOURNEMOUTH, BH3 7EW.
CLEMENCE, Mr. James Alexander, ACA *1995;* with PricewaterhouseCoopers LLP, 17-00 PWC Building, 8 Cross Street, SINGAPORE 048424, SINGAPORE.
CLEMENCE, John Alistair, Esq CBE TD FCA *1964;* Bassetts, Mill Lane, Hildenborough, TONBRIDGE, TN11 9LX.
CLEMENS, Mr. Neil, BA(Hons) ACA ACII *1984;* S I G C O, Ascot House, 28 Queen Street, P O Box H M3398, HAMILTON HMPX, BERMUDA.
CLEMENT, Mr. Alexander, BA(Hons) ACA *2000;* 7 Pitters Piece, Long Crendon, AYLESBURY, BUCKINGHAMSHIRE, HP18 9PP.
CLEMENT, Mrs. Alison, BA ACA *1987;* Dene Farm Cottage, Dean Oak Lane, Leigh, REIGATE, SURREY, RH2 8PY.
CLEMENT, Mr. Charles Edwin, MPhil ACA *1989;* Keyland Developments Ltd, Western House, Western Way, Buttershaw, BRADFORD, WEST YORKSHIRE BD6 2SZ.
CLEMENT, Mr. Craig Darren, BA ACA *1999;* 34 Oaklands Avenue, Adel, LEEDS, LS16 8NR.
•**CLEMENT, Mr. Jeremy James, BA FCA** *1981;* (Tax Fac), J.J. Clement, 57 Boulevard, WESTON-SUPER-MARE, AVON, BS23 1PG.
CLEMENT, Mrs. Jodie Day, BSc ACA *2002;* with KPMG LLP, Aquis Court, 31 Fishpool Street, ST. ALBANS, HERTFORDSHIRE, AL3 4RF.
CLEMENT, Miss. Laura Jayne, MSc BA ACA *2009;* 1961 Filbert Street, Apt 204, SAN FRANCISCO, CA 94123, UNITED STATES.
CLEMENT, Ms. Lisa Jane, BA ACA *1995;* 70 Bolingbroke Road, LONDON, W14 0AH.
CLEMENT, Mr. Mark Rowland, BSc FCA *1987;* 45 Abbotswood, GUILDFORD, GU1 1UY.
CLEMENT, Mr. Richard Mark, BSc ACA *1988;* 36 High Street, Naseby, NORTHAMPTON, NN6 6DD.
•**CLEMENT, Mr. Roger John, FCA** *1964;* PB Associates, 2 Castle Business Village, Station Road, HAMPTON, MIDDLESEX, TW12 2BX.
CLEMENTS, Mrs. Alexandra Susan, BSc ACA *2002;* (Tax Fac), 38 Hyde Street, WINCHESTER, HAMPSHIRE, SO23 7DX.
CLEMENTS, Mr. Andrew, BA ACA *2007;* Grant Thornton LLP, 2010 Corporate Ridge, Suite 400, MCLEAN, VA 22102, UNITED STATES.
•**CLEMENTS, Mr. Andrew Vernon, ACA** *1979;* Andrew Clements, 19 Page Furlong, Dorchester-on-Thames, WALLINGFORD, OX10 7PU.
CLEMENTS, Mr. Carl John, BA ACA *2006;* 6 Sea View Rise, Hopton, GREAT YARMOUTH, NORFOLK, NR31 9SE.
CLEMENTS, Ms. Catherine Elizabeth, BA ACA *1992;* 85 Acredales, LINLITHGOW, WEST LOTHIAN, EH49 6JA.
CLEMENTS, Mrs. Catherine Mary, BA ACA *2003;* Valentines, Stocks Lane, Newland, MALVERN, WORCESTERSHIRE, WR13 5AZ.
CLEMENTS, Miss. Christine, BSc ACA *2002;* 144 Donnybrook Street, BELFAST, BT9 7DG.
CLEMENTS, Mr. Christopher Charles, BSc(Hons) ACA *2010;* Flint Oaks, Nacton Road, Levington, IPSWICH, IP10 0LE.
•**CLEMENTS, Mr. Christopher Michael St John, BA FCA** *1996;* Grant Thornton UK LLP, 1 Whitehall Riverside, Whitehall Road, LEEDS, WEST YORKSHIRE, LS1 4BN. See also Grant Thornton LLP
CLEMENTS, Mrs. Clare Susan, BSc(Hons) ACA *2001;* 34 Addison Road, TEDDINGTON, MIDDLESEX, TW11 9EX.
CLEMENTS, Mr. David Robert, BA FCA *1975;* 15 Meadow Park, Irwell Vale, Ramsbottom, BURY, BL0 0QB.
CLEMENTS, Mrs. Deborah Rachel Kamiel, BSc ACA *1999;* 44 Beechwood Avenue, LONDON, N3 3AX.
CLEMENTS, Mrs. Elaine Susan, BA ACA ATII *1989;* 29 Pynne Close, Stockwood, BRISTOL, BS14 8QW.
CLEMENTS, Mrs. Emma Janet, BSc ACA *1998;* Hill House, Carlton-in-Cleveland, STOKESLEY, NORTH YORKSHIRE, TS9 7DP.
CLEMENTS, Mrs. Felicity, BSc(Hons) ACA *2009;* 30 Northampton Close, BRACKNELL, BERKSHIRE, RG12 9EF.
CLEMENTS, Mr. Geoffrey James, BA FCA *1968;* 41 Canynge Square, Clifton, BRISTOL, BS8 3LB.
CLEMENTS, Miss. Helen Louise, BSc ACA *2002;* 86 Main Road, Hursley, WINCHESTER, SO21 2JY.
•**CLEMENTS, Mr. Ian Robson, FCA** *1972;* Clements & Co, 2 Eslington Terrace, Jesmond, NEWCASTLE UPON TYNE, NE2 4RJ.
•**CLEMENTS, Mrs. Jennifer Susan, BSc FCA** *1978;* Clements Jones Limited, 1 Picton Lane, SWANSEA, SA1 4AF.
CLEMENTS, Mr. John Francis, FCA *1966;* (Member of Council 1999 - 2007), 4 Church Meadows, Henley, IPSWICH, IP6 0RP. (Life Member)
CLEMENTS, Mr. John Rodney, BA FCA *1973;* People & Planet, 51 Union Street, OXFORD, OX4 1JP.
CLEMENTS, Mr. John William, ACA *1980;* (Tax Fac), 6 Hampton Way, EAST GRINSTEAD, RH19 4SG.
CLEMENTS, Mr. Jonathan Paul, BSc ACA *1990;* 5 Royal Park Mews, Vyvyan Rd, BRISTOL, BS8 3AD.
CLEMENTS, Mr. Jonathan Samuel, BMus ACA CTA *2003;* Valentines, Stocks Lane, Newland, MALVERN, WORCESTERSHIRE, WR13 5AZ.
CLEMENTS, Mr. Julian James, LLB FCA *2000;* 38 Hyde Street, WINCHESTER, HAMPSHIRE, SO23 7DX.
CLEMENTS, Mr. Leslie Craig, BA FCA CPA *1969;* 6 Woodbury Park Road, LONDON, W13 8DB.
CLEMENTS, Mr. Luke Nicolas, LLB ACA *2005;* 26 Wingate Square, LONDON, SW4 0AF.
CLEMENTS, Mr. Martin James, BSc ACA *1988;* 27 Park Place, CHELTENHAM, GL50 2QU.
CLEMENTS, Mr. Matthew Paul, ACA *2007;* Flat 22 Holst House, Du Cane Road, LONDON, W12 0EB.
CLEMENTS, Mr. Nicholas William Simon, BSc ACA *1988;* 10 Charlbury Close, WELLINGBOROUGH, NN8 2NS.
CLEMENTS, Mrs. Pamela Dawn, BA ACA *1989;* 10 Charlbury Close, WELLINGBOROUGH, NN8 2NS.
CLEMENTS, Mr. Paul Leonard, BSc ACA *1999;* 17 Cairns Close, ST. ALBANS, HERTFORDSHIRE, AL4 0EA.
CLEMENTS, Mr. Peter Hamilton Campbell, LLB FCA *1964;* West Calflea, Greenhill, LOCKERBIE, DUMFRIESSHIRE, DG11 1JB.
•**CLEMENTS, Mr. Peter Reginald, FCA** *1970;* Maurice J. Bushell & Co, Curzon House, 64 Clifton Street, LONDON, EC2A 4HB. See also C.M.G. Associates
CLEMENTS, Mr. Ralph William, FCA *1958;* 31 Fern Avenue, Oulton Broad North, LOWESTOFT, SUFFOLK, NR32 3JF. (Life Member)
CLEMENTS, Mr. Richard Alexander, ACA *2008;* 31 Wansbeck Close, STEVENAGE, HERTFORDSHIRE, SG1 6AA.
CLEMENTS, Mr. Robert Charles, BSc FCA *1994;* Nahshon 6, 43259 RA'ANANA, ISRAEL.
CLEMENTS, Mr. Ronald James, BSc FCA *1972;* 3707 Nottingham, HOUSTON, TX 77005-2025, UNITED STATES.
CLEMENTS, Mrs. Sandra, BSc ACA *1987;* (Tax Fac), 7 Walnutgarth, SLEAFORD, NG34 7FL.
CLEMENTS, Mr. Simon Robert, BSc ACA *1999;* Merchant Securities Limited, 51-55 Gresham Street, LONDON, EC2V 7HQ.
CLEMENTS, Mr. Timothy, BA ACA *1991;* 51 Hampton Road, BRISTOL, BS6 6HZ.
•**CLEMENTS, Mr. Timothy John, BSc FCA** *1977;* Clements Jones, 1 Picton Lane, SWANSEA, SA1 4AF. See also Clements Jones Limited
CLEMENTS, Mr. Victor Henry James, FCA *1957;* Foxwood, Aubrey Lane, Redbourn, ST. ALBANS, AL3 7AN. (Life Member)
CLEMENTS, Miss. Zoe, BSc(Econ) ACA *1998;* Flat 56 Sir John Lyon House, 8 High Timber Street, LONDON, EC4V 3PA.
CLEMENTSON, Mr. Rex Alexander, BA ACA *1985;* PricewaterhouseCoopers, 33/F Cheung Kong Center, 2 Queen's Road, CENTRAL, HONG KONG ISLAND, HONG KONG SAR.
CLEMES, Mr. John William Willis, BSc(Econ) FCA *1950;* (Member of Council 1983 - 1989), 8 Upper Hall, Worcester Road, LEDBURY, HR8 1JA. (Life Member)
CLEMETT, Mr. Graham Colin, BA ACA *1987;* Chester House Kennington Park, 1-3 Brixton Road, LONDON, SW9 6DE.
CLEMETT, Mrs. Paula Hazel, BA ACA *1985;* Flat 53, Gallery Lofts, 69 Hopton Street, LONDON, SE1 9LF.
•**CLEMINSON, Mrs. Sarah, BSc ACA** *1989;* Sarah Cleminson Consultancy, Island Chase, Steep, PETERSFIELD, HAMPSHIRE, GU32 1AE.
CLEMMENCE, Mr. Ian, BA ACA *2005;* Flat 3, 48 Geraldine Road, LONDON, SW18 2NT.
•**CLEMMENCE, Mr. John William, FCA CTA** *1970;* Clemmence & Co., Linton, Rawdon Hall Drive, Rawdon, LEEDS, LS19 6HD.
CLEMMET, Miss. Lauren Ruth, BA ACA *2010;* 342 Stainbeck Road, LEEDS, LS7 3PP.
CLEMMEY, Mr. Kenneth Lionel Martin, MA MBA FCA *1986;* Old Coach House Cound Hall, Cound, SHREWSBURY, SY5 6AH.
CLEMMEY, Mrs. Melanie Sue, MA ACA *1993;* Old Coach House Cound Hall, Cound, SHREWSBURY, SY5 6AH.
CLEMMITT, Miss. Ruan, MBA BSc ACA *2000;* 11 Thomas Bland Road, STRATFORD-UPON-AVON, WARWICKSHIRE, CV37 0TX.
CLEMO, Mr. John Michael, BSc FCA *1970;* 226 Winchmore Hill Road, LONDON, N21 1QR.
•**CLEMONS, Mr. George Nigel John, MA MBA FCA** *1993;* La Clemonie, Route de St Cergue 41, 1273 ARZIER, SWITZERLAND.
CLEMONS, Mr. George Richard Henry, FCA JDipMA *1960;* Forton House, Saltergate Lane, Bamford, HOPE VALLEY, S33 0BE. (Life Member)
CLEMOW, Mr. Matthew James, ACA *2008;* 22 Bicton Street, EXMOUTH, DEVON, EX8 2RU.
CLENCH, Miss. Victoria, BSc ACA *2003;* 40e Woodstock Road, LONDON, W4 1UF.
CLENNELL, Mr. Andrew James, BSc ACA *2003;* 56 Friern Road, LONDON, SE22 0AX.
•**CLENNELL, Mr. Philip John, BSc FCA** *1994;* Stewart & Co, Knoll House, Knoll Road, CAMBERLEY, GU15 3SY. See also Stewart & Co Accountancy Services Ltd
CLENNELL, Mrs. Sarah Louise, BEng ACA *1995;* Stewart & Co Accountancy Services Ltd, Knoll House, Knoll Road, CAMBERLEY, SURREY, GU15 3SY.
CLENNETT, Mr. John, FCA *1965;* Couelle Cottage, Le Coin, ST OUEN, JERSEY, JE3 2LJ. (Life Member)
•**CLENNETT, Mr. John, MA FCA** *1985;* Deloitte LLP, Abbots House, Abbey Street, READING, RG1 3BD. See also Deloitte & Touche LLP
CLEPHAN, Mrs. Claire Joanne, BSc ACA *1999;* 628 Fulwood Road, SHEFFIELD, S10 3QJ.
CLEPHAN, Mr. Mark William, BA ACA *2000;* 628 Fulwood Road, SHEFFIELD, S10 3QJ.
•**CLEREY, Mr. Richard Albert, FCA** *1970;* Richard Clerey & Co, 18 Brenkley Way, Blezard Business Park, Seaton Burn, NEWCASTLE UPON TYNE, NE13 6DS.
CLERIDES, Mr. Zacharias, ACA *2008;* P.O.Box 25072, 1306 NICOSIA, CYPRUS.
CLERMONT, Mr. David Charles, BSc ACA *1992;* 48 Kingsfield Drive, MANCHESTER, M20 6HX.
•**CLEVELAND, Mr. Simon Lionel, BEng BCom FCA** *1999;* Deloitte LLP, 3 Rivergate, Temple Quay, BRISTOL, BS1 6GD. See also Deloitte & Touche LLP
CLEVELEY, Mr. John, FCA *1970;* 28 Ridgmont Croft, Quinton, BIRMINGHAM, B32 2PT.
•**CLEVERDON, Mr. Jonathan James, FCA** *1995;* (Tax Fac), J Cleverdons Limited, 7 The Broadway, BROADSTAIRS, KENT, CT10 2AD.
CLEVERDON, Mrs. Karen, ACA *1992;* 48 Broadstairs Road, BROADSTAIRS, KENT, CT10 2RJ.
CLEVERDON, Mr. Michael Philip, BA(Hons) ACA *2001;* 1 Low Row Cottages, Steadman's Lane, DURHAM, DH7 9EG.
CLEVERDON, Mr. Philip Henry, FCA *1973;* 1 Scots Pine Avenue, Nailsea, BRISTOL, BS48 1QL. (Life Member)
CLEVERLEY, Mr. Alastair John, BA ACA *1992;* Hannoversche Strasse 22, 04157 LEIPZIG, GERMANY.
CLEVERLY, Mr. Philip Edward, BSc FCA *1969;* 24 Hardenhuish Avenue, CHIPPENHAM, SN15 1NW.
CLEVERLY, Mr. Thomas William James, BA ACA *2005;* Kayson Green Ltd, 3 Clough Road Severalls Industrial Park, COLCHESTER, CO4 9QS.
•**CLEWER, Mr. Andrew Stephen, BSc FCA** *1991;* Ernst & Young LLP, 400 Capability Green, LUTON, LU1 3LU. See also Ernst & Young Europe LLP
CLEWES, Mrs. Emma Jane, MSc ACA *2004;* (Tax Fac), with KPMG LLP, One Snowhill, Snow Hill Queensway, BIRMINGHAM, B4 6GN.
CLEWES, Mr. Michael, FCA *1974;* Cote House, Burley Road, Menston, ILKLEY, WEST YORKSHIRE, LS29 6NP.
•**CLEWES, Mr. Tony, FCA** *1990;* Haines Watts (East Midlands) Limited, 10 Stadium Business Court, Millennium Way, Pride Park, DERBY, DE24 8HP.
CLEWETT, Mr. Charles James, FCA *1969;* (Tax Fac), Seafield, North Cliffe, TENBY, SA70 8AT.
CLEWLOW, Mr. Simon, BSc ACA CF *1998;* 15 Cherry Hill Avenue, Barnt Green, BIRMINGHAM, B45 8LA.
CLEWS, Mrs. Louise Anne, ACA *1990;* 10 Ambergate Close, Little Bloxwich, WALSALL, WS3 3RH.
CLEWS, Mr. Michael John, BA ACA *1981;* Church View, Furzeway, Burgate, DISS, NORFOLK, IP22 1QF.
CLEWS, Mr. Robert James, BSc ACA CF *1993;* Old Forge Cottage, Seal Chart, SEVENOAKS, TN15 0EU.
CLEWS, Mr. Stephen Geoffrey, BSc FCA *1993;* 29 Stockley Crescent, Shirley, SOLIHULL, B90 3SW.
CLEWS, Mr. Steven John, BSc FCA *1988;* Pointon York S I P P Solutions Ltd Pointon York House Unit, Welland Industrial Estate Valley Way, MARKET HARBOROUGH, LE16 7PS.
CLIBBENS, Mr. Nigel, MSc BA ACA MABRP *1995;* 2 Broomhall Avenue, Wrenthorpe, WAKEFIELD, WEST YORKSHIRE, WF1 2BB.
CLIBBENS, Mr. Nigel Timothy John, BSc ACA *1985;* 40a Pennington Road, Southborough, TUNBRIDGE WELLS, KENT, TN4 0SL.
CLIFF, Mr. Alistair John, BEng FCA *1991;* with Deloitte LLP, 1 Woodborough Road, NOTTINGHAM, NG1 3FG.
CLIFF, Mr. Dennis William, FCA *1960;* 4 Maxwell Road, ASHFORD, MIDDLESEX, TW15 1RN. (Life Member)
CLIFF, Mr. Geoffrey Norman, ACA *2004;* 36 Johnson Drive, HEANOR, DERBYSHIRE, DE75 7SR.
CLIFF, Mr. Grahame John, FCA *1968;* 245 Eglinton Ave. E., Suite 410, TORONTO M4P 3J1, ON, CANADA.
CLIFF, Mr. Guy Hamilton, FCA *1957;* 12 Carlton Croft, Sandal, WAKEFIELD, WF2 6DA. (Life Member)
CLIFF, Mr. James Stuart, FCA *1953;* 15 Sussex Square, LONDON, W2 2SL. (Life Member)
CLIFF, Mr. Mark Alistair, ACA *1984;* Rotherbridge Farm, Rotherbridge Lane, Tillington, PETWORTH, GU28 0LL.
•**CLIFF, Mr. Peter Brian Maurice, FCA** *1974;* (Tax Fac), Francis Clark, Francis Clark LLP, Sigma House, Oak View Close, Edginswell Park, TORQUAY TQ2 7FF. See also Francis Clark LLP
CLIFF, Mrs. Samantha Joy, BA ACA *1999;* 8 Woodside Road, SEVENOAKS, KENT, TN13 3HB.
CLIFF, Mrs. Sophie Joanna, BA ACA *1992;* 19 Dovedale Road, West Bridgford, NOTTINGHAM, NG2 6JB.
CLIFF, Mr. Stephen, BSc FCA ATII *1994;* La Roche, La Route de Sausmarez, St. Martin, GUERNSEY, GY4 6SQ.
CLIFF, Mr. Steven Peter, BSc(Hons) ACA *2004;* Avon House, The Green, Ripley, WOKING, SURREY, GU23 6AR.
•**CLIFFE, Mr. Andrew, ACA** *1980;* Appleton Dale Limited, Orchard House, 347c Wakefield Road, Denby Dale, HUDDERSFIELD, HD8 8RT.

•CLIFFE, Mr. Andrew Nicholas, MA FCA *1986;* Nicholas Cliffe & Co Limited, Mill House, Mill Court, Great Shelford, CAMBRIDGE, CB22 5LD. See also ABLC Cambridge Limited
•CLIFFE, Mr. Giles David Thomas, BA FCA *1990;* Simpson Wood, Bank Chambers, Market Street, HUDDERSFIELD, HD1 2EW.
CLIFFE, Mr. Ian David, BA ACA *1997;* The Sands Sandpit Hall Road, Chobham, WOKING, GU24 8AN.
•CLIFFE, Mr. Ian James Richard, BSc ACA CF *1996;* haysmacintyre, Fairfax House, 15 Fulwood Place, LONDON, WC1V 6AY.
CLIFFE, Mrs. Kathryn Margaret, BA ACA *1997;* The Sands Sandpit Hall Road, Chobham, WOKING, GU24 8AN.
CLIFFE, Mr. Malcolm, BSc ACA *1983;* Haines Watts Chartered Accountants Bridge House, 157a Ashley Road Hale, ALTRINCHAM, CHESHIRE, WA14 2UT.
CLIFFE, Mr. Michael, FCA *1969;* 7 Springfield, Littleover, DERBY, DE23 6EZ.
•CLIFFE, Mr. Michael Leslie, FCA *1951;* M L Cliffe, 7 Lime Tree Road, NORWICH, NR2 2NF.
CLIFFE, Mr. Nicholas James, BA ACA *1993;* 10 Blackstone Close, REDHILL, SURREY, RH1 6BG.
CLIFFE, Mr. Paul Grenville, FCA *1958;* 31 Ullswater Road, BUCKLEY, CH7 3LE. (Life Member)
•CLIFFE, Mrs. Penelope Jane, BCom FCA *1977;* Appleton Dale Limited, Orchard House, 347c Wakefield Road, Denby Dale, HUDDERSFIELD, HD8 8RT.
CLIFFE, Miss. Sarah Elizabeth, BSc ACA *2006;* Clair Val Cottage, La Grande Route de Faldouet, St. Martin, JERSEY, JE3 6UE.
CLIFFE, Mr. Stephen Charles, BA ACA *1986;* Barn One, Lydes Farm, Stowey, BRISTOL, BS39 4DW.
CLIFFE, Mr. Stephen Nicholas, BA FCA *1974;* 5 Primrose Cottages, Lower North Dean, HIGH WYCOMBE, HP14 4NQ.
CLIFFE, Mrs. Suzanne Wendy, LLB ACA *1993;* 10 Blackstone Close, REDHILL, SURREY, RH1 6BG.
CLIFFORD, Mrs. Alison Frances, BSc ACA *1992;* 79 Durham Road, BROMLEY, BR2 0SP.
CLIFFORD, Mr. Andrew Francis James, BSc ACA *1995;* The Baxters, Station Road, Bransford, WORCESTER, WR6 5JH.
•①CLIFFORD, Mr. Andrew James, MSc FCA ATII CF DChA MEWI MABRP *1985;* Baker Tilly Tax & Advisory Services LLP, 1st Floor, 46 Clarendon Road, WATFORD, WD17 1JJ. See also Baker Tilly Corporate Finance LLP
CLIFFORD, Mr. Andrew Martin, BSc ACA *2004;* DNG Dove Naish, Eagle House, 28 Billing Road, NORTHAMPTON, NN1 5AJ.
CLIFFORD, Mr. Andrew Martin, BA FCA *1988;* Glencoin, 129 Bramhall Lane South, Bramhall, STOCKPORT, SK7 2PP.
•CLIFFORD, Mr. Anthony Robin Edward, MA FCA *1986;* Ernst & Young LLP, 1 More London Place, LONDON, SE1 2AF. See also Ernst & Young Europe LLP
•CLIFFORD, Mrs. Audrey Elizabeth, FCA *1978;* (Tax Fac), R.L. Vaughan & Co, Mortimer House, 40 Chatsworth Parade, Queensway, Petts Wood, ORPINGTON KENT BR5 1DE.
CLIFFORD, Mr. Brian, BSc ACA *2006;* 39 Nansen Road, LONDON, SW11 5NS.
CLIFFORD, Mr. Brian Robert, BA ACA *1992;* 8 Ranmore Avenue, CROYDON, CR0 5QA.
CLIFFORD, Mr. Carl Stephen, FCA *1955;* Beechdale, Shady Lane, SOUTHWELL, NG25 0HX. (Life Member)
•CLIFFORD, Mr. Daniel Sean Patrick, BA ACA CTA *1994;* (Tax Fac), Ensors, Cardinal House, 46 St Nicholas Street, IPSWICH, IP1 1TT.
CLIFFORD, Mr. David Phillimore, BSc FCA *1978;* 14 The Crescent, Barnes, LONDON, SW13 0NN.
•CLIFFORD, Mr. Glenn, BA ACA *1999;* with CLB Coopers, Fleet House, New Road, LANCASTER, LA1 1EZ.
CLIFFORD, Mrs. Jacqueline Margaret Claire, MA FCA *1989;* D T E Business Advisory Services Ltd, Hollins Mount, BURY, LANCASHIRE, BL9 8AT.
CLIFFORD, Miss. Jayne Frances, MA CA *2006; (CA Scotland* Martin Aitken & Co, Caledonia House, 89 Seaward Street, GLASGOW, G41 1HJ.
CLIFFORD, Mr. John, BSc ACA *1998;* 31 Barnard Hill, LONDON, N10 2HB.
CLIFFORD, Mr. John Patrick, BSc ACA *1990;* 512 State Street, ANNAPOLIS, MD 21403, UNITED STATES.
•CLIFFORD, Mrs. Lynn Diane, BSc FCA *1983;* (Tax Fac), Clifford & Co, 11 Manor Farm Drive, Hinstock, MARKET DRAYTON, SHROPSHIRE, TF9 2SN.
CLIFFORD, Mr. Paul David, BA ACA *1999;* with Ernst & Young, Ernst & Young Building, 8 Exhibition Street, MELBOURNE, VIC 3000, AUSTRALIA.
CLIFFORD, Mr. Paul Leighton, FCA *1975;* Lidco Cardiac Sensor Systems, 16 Orsman Road, LONDON, N1 5QJ.
CLIFFORD, Mr. Paul Michael, BEng ACA *2001;* 34 Muncaster Road, LONDON, SW11 6NU.
CLIFFORD, Mr. Paul Richard, BCom FCA CPFA *1975;* The Manse, 22 Madeley Road, Ironbridge, TELFORD, TF8 7QZ.
CLIFFORD, Mr. Peter, FCA *1966;* Stables End, 17b Guildown Road, GUILDFORD, GU2 4ET. (Life Member)
•CLIFFORD, Mrs. Sarah Elizabeth, BA ACA *1986;* Ernst & Young LLP, 1 More London Place, LONDON, SE1 2AF. See also Ernst & Young Europe LLP
CLIFFORD, Mr. Simon Chalcot, FCA *1968;* 91 Woodcote Drive, ORPINGTON, KENT, BR6 8DT.
CLIFFORD, Mrs. Susan Margaret, BSc ACA *1984;* Sanbrook House, High Street, Colnbrook, SLOUGH, SL3 0LX.
CLIFFORD, Mrs. Valerie Ann Margaret, BCom FCA *1993;* Pricewaterhousecoopers, PO Box 1331I GPO, MELBOURNE, VIC 3001, AUSTRALIA.
CLIFFORD-JONES, Mr. Neville Leoo, FCA *1953;* Shoes Farm, Ockley, DORKING, RH5 5PN. (Life Member)
•CLIFFORD-KING, Mrs. Alison Jane, BSc FCA *1991;* AJCK Limited, 29 Eghams Wood Road, BEACONSFIELD, BUCKINGHAMSHIRE, HP9 1JU.
•CLIFFORD-KING, Mr. Martin Keith, BSc ACA *1989;* Lordsbury Consulting Ltd, 29 Eghams Wood Road, BEACONSFIELD, BUCKINGHAMSHIRE, HP9 1JU.
CLIFT, Miss. Adrienne, ACA *2003;* 1738 Larchwood Green, BURLINGTON L7P 2X7, ON, CANADA.
•CLIFT, Mrs. Claire Elizabeth, BSc FCA *1996;* Davies Mayers Barnett LLP, Pillar House, 113-115 Bath Road, CHELTENHAM, GLOUCESTERSHIRE, GL53 7LS. See also Barnett DM Limited
•CLIFT, Mr. David Richard, BA FCA *1990;* CLB Coopers, Ship Canal House, 98 King Street, MANCHESTER, M2 4WU.
•CLIFT, Mr. David Scott, BA FCA CTA *1998;* (Tax Fac), Hazlewoods LLP, Staverton Court, Staverton, CHELTENHAM, GLOUCESTERSHIRE, GL51 0UX.
CLIFT, Mr. Harold Eric, FCA *1938;* Marcelo T. De Alvear, 1531 10A, BUENOS AIRES, ARGENTINA. (Life Member)
CLIFT, Mr. Malcolm John, FCA *1967;* 60 Sir Thomas Mitchell Drive, DAVIDSON, NSW 2085, AUSTRALIA.
CLIFT, Mr. Peter, BSc ACA *2000;* 79 Agraria Road, GUILDFORD, GU2 4LG.
•CLIFT-MATTHEWS, Mr. Michael Francis, FCA *1969;* Michael F. Clift-Matthews Limited, 21 Clarence Street, PENZANCE, TR18 2NZ.
•CLIFTLANDS, Mr. Philip Damon, BA(Hons) ACA *2002;* with PricewaterhouseCoopers LLP, 1 Embankment Place, LONDON, WC2N 6RH.
CLIFTON, Mr. Adam Henry, BA ACA *1994;* Kirkwood, Borwick Road, CARNFORTH, LANCASHIRE, LA6 1BG.
CLIFTON, Mr. Alan John, BA FCA *1981;* 30 Wellstead Gardens, WESTCLIFF-ON-SEA, SS0 0AY.
CLIFTON, Mr. Andrew John, BSc ACA *1990;* 9 Wilton Road, HORNSEA, HU18 1EU.
CLIFTON, Mr. Cheston Russell Patrick, FCA *1957;* 42 Hill Brow, HOVE, BN3 6QH. (Life Member)
•CLIFTON, Mr. David Sylvester, FCA *1983;* Trewardreva Mill, Constantine, FALMOUTH, CORNWALL, TR11 5QD.
•CLIFTON, Mr. Ian Paul James, FCA *1969;* Clifton Page Wood, 36a West Hill Road, BRIGHTON, EAST SUSSEX, BN1 3RT.
CLIFTON, Mr. James Andrew, BSc ACA AMCT *1990;* 2 Cheviot Close, EASTBOURNE, EAST SUSSEX, BN23 8ET.
CLIFTON, Mr. Jeremy Peter, BA ACA *1999;* with Grant Thornton UK LLP, 1 Dorset Street, SOUTHAMPTON, SO15 2DP.
CLIFTON, Miss. Maria Nicole, BA ACA *2010;* Ernst & Young, PO Box 510, GEORGE TOWN, GRAND CAYMAN, KY1- 1106, CAYMAN ISLANDS.
CLIFTON, Mr. Mark Richard, MA FCA *1993;* with PricewaterhouseCoopers LLP, 1 Embankment Place, LONDON, WC2N 6RH.
CLIFTON, Mr. Martin David, BA ACA *1994;* 71 Langsett Avenue, SHEFFIELD, S6 4AB.
CLIFTON, Mr. Michael, BSc FCA *1957;* 1 Willowcroft Lodge, 127 Aldermans Hill, LONDON, N13 4QB. (Life Member)
CLIFTON, Mr. Nicholas James, BSocSc ACA *2004;* 49 Lavender Way, Bradley Stoke, BRISTOL, BS32 0LR.
CLIFTON, Mr. Paul Spencer, BSc ACA *1989;* Ty Blaidd Skenfrith, ABERGAVENNY, GWENT, NP7 8UF.
CLIFTON, Mr. William, BA ACA MBA *2000;* IPF Plc, 3 Leeds City Office Park, Holbeck, LEEDS, LS11 5BD.
CLIFTON-CRICK, Mr. Ernest Lawrence, FCA *1965;* Orchard Cottage, Main Street, Wick, PERSHORE, WORCESTERSHIRE, WR10 3NZ.
CLIMPSON, Mr. James Anthony Ernest, FCA *1954;* Dorian, 109 Anderson Avenue, Earley, READING, RG6 1HA. (Life Member)
•CLIMPSON, Mr. Trevor Sidney, FCA *1966;* (Tax Fac), King & Taylor, 10-12 Wrotham Road, GRAVESEND, DA11 0PE.
CLINCH, Mr. Antony John, BSc FCA *1988;* Treetops, 14 Lucastes Lane, HAYWARDS HEATH, RH16 1LD.
CLINCH, Mr. Charles Guy, FCA *1975;* 12 Rowan Way, Angmering, LITTLEHAMPTON, WEST SUSSEX, BN16 4FW.
CLINCH, Mr. Mark Julian Lister, BSc FCA *1987;* Hadley House, Romford Road, Pembury, TUNBRIDGE WELLS, KENT, TN2 4BB.
CLINCH, Mr. Robert Anthony, FCA *1967;* Winter Thoughts, Cakeham Road, West Wittering, CHICHESTER, PO20 8EB.
CLINE, Mr. Philip, MA FCA *1959;* 10 Oakdene Close, Cyncoed, CARDIFF, CF23 6HJ. (Life Member)
CLINT, Dr. Oswald Conan, BSc ACA *2005;* Sanford Bernstein, Devonshire House, 1 Mayfair Place, LONDON, W1J 8SB.
CLINTON, Mr. Arthur Gilbert, BA FCA *1953;* Suites 2&3 Gibraltar Heights, 215 Main Street, GIBRALTAR, GIBRALTAR. (Life Member)
•CLINTON, Mr. Dennis Michael, BA(Hons) ACA *1979;* D.M. Clinton, 116 Rosia Plaza, P O Box 677, GIBRALTAR, GIBRALTAR.
CLINTON, Mr. Ian Louis, BEd ACA *1993;* (Tax Fac), 3 Churchill Close, Hartley Wintney, HOOK, RG27 8RA.
CLINTON, Mr. John Michael, BSc(Hons) ACA *2004;* with KPMG, 10 Shelley Street, SYDNEY, NSW 2000, AUSTRALIA.
•CLINTON, Miss. Katherine Helen, BSc(Hons) ACA *2004;* with KPMG LLP, 15 Canada Square, LONDON, E14 5GL.
CLINTON, Mr. Nicholas Paul, ACA *1982;* 703 Bankside Lofts, 65 Hopton Street, LONDON, SE1 9GZ.
•CLINTON, Mr. Roy Mark, BCom FCIB FCA AMCT *1994;* 13 Barley Hill House, 35/45 Prince Edward's Road, GIBRALTAR, GIBRALTAR.
CLINTON, Mr. Simon Arthur, MA ACA *2000;* 16 Albany Road, WINDSOR, SL4 1HL.
CLINTON, Mr. Walter Burnham, BA FCA *1959;* Cricketer's Cottage, The Green, Pirbright, WOKING, GU24 0JT. (Life Member)
CLINTON-TARESTAD, Mr. Gregory, BSc ACA CISA *2011;* Dominikanerbastei 21/46, 1010 VIENNA, AUSTRIA.
CLINTON-TARESTAD, Mr. Kieran Ingemar Philip, ACA *2008;* Flat 2, 4 Stannary Street, LONDON, SE11 4AA.
CLINTON-TARESTAD, Mr. Piers Bjorn Anthony, BSc *2004;* with Deloitte LLP, 4 Brindley Place, BIRMINGHAM, B1 2HZ.
•CLIPPERTON, Mrs. Sharon Kennelly, BA FCA *1990;* Winn & Co (Yorkshire) Limited, 62/63 Westborough, SCARBOROUGH, YO11 1TS.
CLIPSHAM, Mr. Andrew James, BA(Hons) ACA *2001;* Sony (UK) Ltd The Heights, Brooklands, WEYBRIDGE, SURREY, KT13 0XW.
•CLIPSHAM, Mr. Gordon Jack, BA FCA *1988;* Asia Pacific, 42nd Floor Central Plaza, 18 Harbour Road, WAN CHAI, HONG KONG ISLAND, HONG KONG SAR.
CLIPSHAM, Mr. John Nigel, BA ACA *1979;* 205 Catherine Street Suite 200, OTTAWA K2P 1C3, ON, CANADA.
CLIPSTON, Mr. Daniel Charles, ACA *1991;* 48 Prospect Street, Caversham, READING, RG4 8JL.
•CLIPSTON, Mrs. Karen Jane, ACA *1996;* Weald Accountancy & Bookkeeping Services Limited, 1 Brook Farm Cottages, Bowzell Road, Weald, SEVENOAKS, KENT TN14 6NE.
CLISSET, Mr. John, FCA *1954;* 11 Alston Avenue, SALE, M33 4AS. (Life Member)
•CLITHEROE, Mr. Alan James, BA ACA *1986;* (Tax Fac), C./Los Cipreses 100, Urb El Rosario, 29604 MARBELLA, MALAGA, SPAIN.
CLITHEROE, Mr. David Maurice, BA ACA *1981;* 3 Norman Court, Oadby, LEICESTER, LE2 4UD.
CLITHEROW, Mr. Adam, BA FCA AMCT *1988;* Selesk House, Spring Lane, Aston Tirrold, DIDCOT, OX11 9EJ.
CLITHEROW, Mr. Christopher, FCA *1962;* 19 Girdwood Road, LONDON, SW18 5QR. (Life Member)
CLIVAZ, Mr. Jeremy Gordon, BA ACA *1991;* O D L Securities Ltd The Northern & Shell Building, 10 Lower Thames Street, LONDON, EC3R 6AD.
•CLIVE, Mr. Kregar Burgess Jerome, FCA *1973;* KC Partners, 1st Floor, 76 New Bond Street, LONDON, W1S 1RX.
•CLIXBY, Mr. Paul Arthur, BSc FCA *1979;* Paul Clixby, 27 Hornyold Road, MALVERN, WORCESTERSHIRE, WR14 1QQ.
CLOAKE, Mr. Adrian Richard, BA ACA *2001;* Link Financial Ltd Camelford House, 87-90 Albert Embankment, LONDON, SE1 7TP.
•CLOAKE, Mr. Roger Sidney, BSc FCA *1981;* (Tax Fac), Till & Cloake, 70 South Street, LANCING, WEST SUSSEX, BN15 8AJ.
CLODE, Mrs. Carolyn Mary, BA ACA *1988;* Lawhill Farm, DOLLAR, CLACKMANNANSHIRE, FK14 7PN.
CLOHERTY, Mr. John Henry, BA FCA *1994;* 18 Woodham Close, Hartford, NORTHWICH, CHESHIRE, CW8 1SG.
CLOHESSY, Miss. Maria Patricia, BSc ACA *1990;* 23 Cambridge Avenue, NEW MALDEN, SURREY, KT3 4LD.
CLOKE, Mr. Andrew Mark, BSc ACA *1987;* Station Farm, Station Road, Pilning, BRISTOL, BS35 4JW.
CLOKE, Mr. Andrew Martin, BA ACA *2000;* 72 A Curban Street, Balgowlah, Heights, SIDNEY, NSW 2093, AUSTRALIA.
CLOKE, Miss. Gillian Sheila, BSc ACA *1990;* 36 Plymouth Road, Barnt Green, BIRMINGHAM, B45 8JD.
•CLOKE, Mr. Ian Frank, ACA *1980;* (Tax Fac), D.B. Lye & Co, 34 Cheriton Gardens, FOLKESTONE, CT20 2AX.
•CLOKE, Mr. Jeffrey Alan, BSc FCA *1973;* Gable Cottage, 18 Letchmore Road, RADLETT, HERTFORDSHIRE, WD7 8HT.
CLOKE, Mr. Richard Charles, BSc FCA *1987;* Abbots Barn, High Street, HEMINGFORD ABBOTS, CAMBRIDGESHIRE, PE28 9AH.
CLOKE, Mr. Robert Andrew, MSc ACA *2010;* with Buzzacott LLP, 12 New Fetter Lane, LONDON, EC4A 1AG.
•CLOKEY, Mr. Peter James, MA FCA CF *1979;* Long Holt, Vines Lane, Hildenborough, TONBRIDGE, KENT, TN11 9LT.
CLORAN, Mr. Kevin David, FCA *1958;* Balmacara, The Avenue, Farnham Common, SLOUGH, SL2 3JX. (Life Member)
CLORLEY, Mrs. Helen Louise, ACA *2003;* (Tax Fac), 2 Marlowe Road, NORTHWICH, CHESHIRE, CW9 7GA.
CLOSE, Mrs. Alison Joanne, BA ACA *2000;* 11 Pennington Drive, NEWTON-LE-WILLOWS, WA12 8BA.
CLOSE, Mr. Donald, FCA *1962;* 18 Wychwood Close, BOGNOR REGIS, WEST SUSSEX, PO21 4DW. (Life Member)
CLOSE, Miss. Jacqui, BSc ACA *2010;* 126a East Dulwich Road, LONDON, SE22 9AT.
•CLOSE, Mr. James Dominic Edward, BSc ACA *1993;* Ernst & Young LLP, 1 More London Place, LONDON, SE1 2AF. See also Ernst & Young Europe LLP
CLOSE, Mrs. Karen, BSc FCA *1979;* 8 Hibiscus Place, CHERRYBROOK, NSW 2126, AUSTRALIA.
CLOSE, Mrs. Kate, LLB ACA *2002;* 50 Church Walk, THAMES DITTON, SURREY, KT7 0NW.
CLOSE, Miss. Katie Helen, BA ACA *1999;* Sabmiller Plc, 1-2 Stanhope Gate, LONDON, W1K 1AF.
•CLOSE, Mr. Martin Michael, BSc ACA *1987;* 15 The Dell, Sandpit Lane, ST. ALBANS, AL1 4DY.
CLOSE, Miss. Meriel Lillian, ACA *2009;* Second Floor Flat, 37b Grove Vale, LONDON, SE22 8EQ.
•CLOSE, Mr. Simon Michael, FCA *1989;* Censis, Exchange Building, 66 Church Street, HARTLEPOOL, TS24 7DN.
•①CLOSE, Mr. Timothy Alexander, BA ACA *1986;* Milsted Langdon LLP, Winchester House, Deane Gate Avenue, TAUNTON, SOMERSET, TA1 2UH.
CLOTWORTHY, Mrs. Dominique Christina, ACA *2009;* with Grant Thornton, PO Box 307, 3rd Floor, Exchange House, 54-58 Athor Street, Douglas ISLE OF MAN IM99 2BE.
CLOUGH, Mr. Charles Richard, MA ACA *2000;* with Ernst & Young LLP, 1 More London Place, LONDON, SE1 2AF.
•CLOUGH, Mrs. Claire Victoria, BA ACA *2003;* with PricewaterhouseCoopers LLP, 1 Embankment Place, LONDON, WC2N 6RH.
•CLOUGH, Mr. David, FCA *1968;* Tanglewood, Church Lane, Sarratt, RICKMANSWORTH, WD3 6HL.
CLOUGH, Mr. Geoffrey Edmund, BSc FCA *1974;* 46 Laurel Drive, Southmoor, ABINGDON, OX13 5DJ.
CLOUGH, Mr. Gerald, MA FCA *1980;* Catalyst International Limited, Flat A 27/F South Tower 5, Residence Bel-Air, 38 Bel-Air Avenue, POK FU LAM, HONG KONG SAR.
CLOUGH, Mr. Harry Watson, FCA *1947;* The Cottage, 9 Richmond Mews, Moorhead Lane, SHIPLEY, BD18 4TA. (Life Member)
CLOUGH, Mr. Ian David, BA ACA *1991;* 1210 South Pine Island Road, 4th Floor, PLANTATION, FL 33324, UNITED STATES.

CLOUGH, Mr. James George, LLB ACA *1992;* ITS TESTING SERVICES (UK) LTD, Academy Place 1-9 Brook Street, BRENTWOOD, CM14 5NQ.
CLOUGH, Mr. John, FCA *1959;* Dukes, Main Road, Danbury, CHELMSFORD, CM3 4DT. (Life Member)
•CLOUGH, Mr. John Dufton, FCA *1970;* Moore Stephens, 6 Ridge House, Ridge House Drive, STOKE-ON-TRENT, ST1 5TL.
CLOUGH, Mr. John Stephen, FCA *1970;* 37 Ravensdowne, BERWICK-UPON-TWEED, TD15 1DQ.
CLOUGH, Mr. Jonathan Nicholas, BSc ACA *1992;* Cooper Controls Ltd, 20 Greenhill Crescent, WATFORD, WD18 8JA.
•CLOUGH, Mr. Julian Simon, BA FCA *1985;* with RSM Tenon Limited, The Poynt Building, 45 Wollaton Street, NOTTINGHAM, NG1 5FW.
CLOUGH, Mr. Michael Anthony, FCA *1978;* 5 Furlong Parade, STOKE-ON-TRENT, ST6 3AX.
CLOUGH, Miss. Nicola Jane, BSc ACA *2003;* Aegis Group PLC, 180 Great Portland Street, LONDON, W1W 5QZ.
CLOUGH, Mrs. Nicola Jane, BSS ACA *1991;* 27 Rayleigh Road, LONDON, SW19 3RE.
CLOUGH, Mrs. Patricia Anne, ACA *1980;* Reliance Medical Ltd, The Radnor Building, Radnor Park Trading Estate, CONGLETON, CHESHIRE, CW12 4XP.
CLOUGH, Mr. Paul James, MA ACA *1996;* Oxfam House, Oxfam, 2700 John Smith Drive Oxford Business Park South, OXFORD, OX4 2JY.
CLOUGH, Mr. Richard Stanley, FCA *1968;* Healthcare Homes Ltd, Lodge House, Lodge Lane, Langham, COLCHESTER, ESSEX CO4 5NE.
CLOUGH, Mr. Stephen Anthony, BSc ACA *1988;* 16 The Cloisters, Ampthill, BEDFORD, MK45 2UJ.
CLOUGH, Mr. Stephen John, BSc ACA *1986;* Cransley East Downs Road, Bowdon, ALTRINCHAM, CHESHIRE, WA14 2LQ.
CLOUGH, Mr. Wilfred, FCA *1951;* Highmoor, 19 Beechfield, Grasscroft, OLDHAM, OL4 4EN. (Life Member)
CLOUGH, Mrs. Yvonne, LLB ACA *1994;* 128 Grange Loan, EDINBURGH, EH9 2EF.
CLOUGHTON, Miss. Karen Teresa, BA ACA CTA *1990;* (Tax Fac), 159 The Greenway, EPSOM, KT18 7JD.
CLOUGHTON, Mr. Robert Barrie, BSc ACA *1987;* ORD Minnett Limited, PO Box 2613, SYDNEY, NSW 2001, AUSTRALIA.
CLOUSTON, Ms. Susan Rachel, BEng ACA ATII *1991;* WPP Plc, 27 Farm Street, LONDON, W1X 6RD.
CLOUSTON-JONES, Mrs. Emma Jayne, BA(Hons) ACA *2000;* 6 Brook Street, Wymeswold, LOUGHBOROUGH, LE12 6TU.
CLOUT, Mr. Richard John, MA BA FCA *1978;* 145 Marlborough Crescent, SEVENOAKS, KENT, TN13 2HW.
•CLOUTER, Mr. Richard John, BSc FCA *1993;* Critical Path Solutions, The Mews, Canaan Lane, EDINBURGH, EH10 4SG.
CLOUTING, Miss. Deborah Mary, BSc ACA *1987;* The Grange, 18 Guys Cliffe Avenue, LEAMINGTON SPA, CV32 6LY.
CLOVER, Mr. Colin Manning, FCA *1952;* Flat 1, 130 Kew Road, RICHMOND, TW9 2AU. (Life Member)
CLOVER, Mr. Dean James, MMath ACA *2009;* 11 Little Norsey Road, BILLERICAY, ESSEX, CM11 1BL.
CLOVER-BROWN, Mr. Robert John, MA FCA *1972;* 4336 SHENANDOAH STREET, DALLAS, TX 75205, UNITED STATES.
CLOW, Mr. Bernard John, FCA *1964;* 14 Richmond Crescent, Islington, LONDON, N1 0LZ. (Life Member)
CLOW, Mr. Graham Raymond, BSc FCA *1974;* 7420 Airport Road, No 205, MISSISSAUGA L4T 4E5, ON, CANADA.
CLOW, Mr. John, BSc ACA *1983;* Ferndown House, 186 Preston Road, CHORLEY, PR6 7AZ.
CLOW, Mr. Leonard Roger, FCA *1965;* Glebelands, Pilgrims Lane, Titsey, OXTED, RH8 0SE.
CLOW, Mr. Peter Jon, FCA *1961;* Suite 94, Private Bag X11, HONEYDEW, 2040, SOUTH AFRICA.
•CLOW, Mr. Robert Christopher, FCA *1973;* (Tax Fac), Robert Clow & Co Ltd, 40-44 High Street, NORTHWOOD, MIDDLESEX, HA6 1BN.
•CLOW, Mr. Roger Heber, FCA *1976;* (Tax Fac), Friend-James Ltd, 169 Preston Road, BRIGHTON, BN1 6AG.
CLOWES, Mr. Charles Richard, FCA *1965;* 701 Lightwood Road, Lightwood, STOKE-ON-TRENT, ST3 7HD.
CLOWES, Mrs. Emily Elizabeth, BSc ACA *2005;* A A H Pharmaceuticals Ltd Sapphire Court, Paradise Way Coventry Walsgrave Triangle, COVENTRY, CV2 2TX.
CLOWES, Mr. Paul John, BSc ACA *1985;* Woodlands Ladylawn, Wild Oak Lane, Trull, TAUNTON, TA3 7LR.
CLOWES, Mr. Stephen Bernard, BCom ACA *1986;* Hartsridge, Hartslane, South Godstone, GODSTONE, RH9 8LZ.
CLOWSER, Mr. Stuart, BSc ACA *2007;* Heartford, Greville Park Road, ASHTEAD, KT21 2QT.
CLUBB, Mr. Justin Stuart, ACA *1996;* Upper Farm Barn Penthorne Close, Grimscote, TOWCESTER, NORTHAMPTONSHIRE, NN12 8LL.
CLUBB, Mr. Martin, BSc ACA *1993;* Martin Clubb Development Limited, Flat 13 Wellesley House, Churchway, LONDON, NW1 1LL.
CLUBB, Mr. Thomas James, BSc ACA *2009;* (Tax Fac), 47 Milton Road, Broughton, MILTON KEYNES, MK10 9RA.
CLUBBS, Mr. Simon James, BA ACA *2002;* 110 Kingsway, Petts Wood, ORPINGTON, KENT, BR5 1PU.
CLUBE, Mr. Benedict James Murray, BSc ACA *1993;* 50 Monk Street, KENSINGTON, WA 6151, AUSTRALIA.
CLUBE, Mrs. Joanne Elizabeth, BSc ACA *1992;* with Aviva PLC, St. Helens, 1 Undershaft, LONDON, EC3P 3DQ.
CLUBLEY, Mrs. Alison Jane, BA(Hons) ACA *2003;* with BDO LLP, 55 Baker Street, LONDON, W1U 7EU.
CLUEIT, Mr. David William, BA FCA *1993;* 5 Torside Drive, POULTON-LE-FYLDE, FY6 7FS.
CLUEIT, Mr. William Kenneth, FCA *1966;* Samron, Copthurst Lane, Whittle-Le-Woods, CHORLEY, PR6 8LR. (Life Member)
•CLUER, Miss. Bronya Joy, FCA *1982;* (Tax Fac), Pacific Ltd, 1st Floor Woburn House, 84 St. Benedicts Street, NORWICH, NR2 4AB. See also Pacific
CLUFF, Mr. Peter Charles, BA ACA *1990;* Warwicks Mead, Warwicks Bench Lane, GUILDFORD, SURREY, GU1 3TP.
CLULEY, Mr. Michael Jonathan Wigg, BCom ACA *1993;* 7 Massingberd Way, LONDON, SW17 6AA.
CLULEY, Mr. Robert Allan, BA ACA *1996;* 34 Torridon Way, HINCKLEY, LE10 0UH.
CLUNIE, Miss. Elizabeth Anne, BSc(Hons) ACA *2003;* 311 Lonsdale Road, Barnes, LONDON, SW13 9PY.
•CLUNIE, Mr. Tim Alexander, FCA *1972;* S.G.Banister & Co, 40 Great James Street, LONDON, WC1N 3HB.
CLUTTERBUCK, Mrs. Jane, LLB FCA *1987;* Flat 32, Chiswick Green Studios, 1 Evershed Walk, Chiswick, LONDON, W4 5BW.
CLUTTERBUCK, Mr. John, FCA *1968;* 3 Shermanbury Grange, Brighton Road, Shermanbury, HORSHAM, WEST SUSSEX, RH13 8HN.
CLUTTERBUCK, Mr. Troy Adam, ACA CA(AUS) *2011;* JLT Benefit Solutions, 6 Crutched Friars, LONDON, EC3N 2PH.
CLUTTON, Mr. John Russell, BSc ACA *1999;* 102 Folly Lane, ST. ALBANS, AL3 5JH.
CLUTTON, Mr. Robin Ian David, BEng ACA *1989;* 5 Walcote House, Sandy Lane, Blackdown, LEAMINGTON SPA, WARWICKSHIRE, CV32 6QS.
CLUTTON, Mr. Steven, BSc ACA *1989;* Shepley Lodge, Horsell Rise, WOKING, SURREY, GU21 4AY.
CLYBURN, Mr. Martin Anthony, BSc(Hons) ACA *2007;* 11 Shaftesbury Road, MIDDLESBROUGH, CLEVELAND, TS6 9BE.
CLYDE, Mr. Michael Patrick, FCA *1971;* Olde Stocks, Holyport Road, Bray, MAIDENHEAD, BERKSHIRE, SL6 2HD.
CLYNE, Mrs. Emma Victoria, ACA *2004;* Melrow Salads, Rydings Lane, SOUTHPORT, MERSEYSIDE, PR9 8EB.
•CLYNE, Mr. Gordon Roger, FCA *1972;* (Tax Fac), Clyne & Co Ltd, 3 Mountain Road, CAERPHILLY, MID GLAMORGAN, CF83 1HG.
CLYNES, Miss. Hilary Susan, BSc FCA *1978;* 43 Gloucester Court, Kew Road, RICHMOND, TW9 3EA.
CO, Mr. Beng Yu, ACA *2006;* Rm 1427 Blk D, Ming Yuen Mansion, Peacock Road, NORTH POINT, HONG KONG ISLAND, HONG KONG SAR.
COAD, Mr. Frederick Roy, FCA *1948;* 11 Hazler Orchard, CHURCH STRETTON, SY6 7AL. (Life Member)
COAD, Mr. Gregory Daniel, ACA *2004;* 194 Hercules Road, LONDON, SE1 7LD.
COAD, Mr. Jocelyn Charles, FCA *1973;* Structured Finance Management Ltd, 35 Great St. Helen's, LONDON, EC3A 6AP.
COAD, Mr. Richard Louis, FCA *1966;* The Glebe, Thorpe, Wycliffe, BARNARD CASTLE, COUNTY DURHAM, DL12 9TU.
COAKER, Miss. Rachel Elizabeth, BSc ACA *2005;* 32 Lodge Mill Lane, Edenfield, BURY, LANCASHIRE, BL0 0RW.
COAKER, Mr. Tristan, MSci ACA *2006;* 56 Stamford Park Road, Hale, ALTRINCHAM, CHESHIRE, WA15 9EP.
COAKES, Mr. Raymond John, FCA *1964;* 10 Berkley Avenue, West Parley, FERNDOWN, DORSET, BH22 8QJ.
•COAKLEY, Mrs. Anne Barbara, FCA *1981;* (Tax Fac), Coakley & Co, West House, Milford Road, Elstead, GODALMING, SURREY GU8 6HF.
•ⒹCOAKLEY, Mr. Dermot Brendan, FCA *1982;* MBI Coakley Ltd, Second Floor, Tunsgate Square, 98-110 High Street, GUILDFORD, SURREY GU1 3HE. See also Coakley & Co
COAKLEY, Miss. Laura Jane, BCom ACA *2004;* 1 Eton Road, ORPINGTON, BR6 9HD.
COAPES, Miss. Claire, ACA *2009;* 23 Houghton Avenue, NORTH SHIELDS, TYNE AND WEAR, NE30 3NQ.
COAR, Mr. Anthony, BSc FCA *1986;* T C Harrison Group Ltd, Milford House, Mill Street, BAKEWELL, DERBYSHIRE, DE45 1HH.
COASE, Mr. Charles Dawson, MA ACA *1987;* Diageo Plc, Lakeside Drive, Park Royal, LONDON, NW10 7HQ.
COATES, Mr. Adam John, BSocSc FCA *1993;* National Cradle Maintenance Ltd, 13 Flemming Court, CASTLEFORD, WF10 5HW.
COATES, Mr. Alan, FCA *1977;* 17 Newdigate Road, Falcon Lodge, SUTTON COLDFIELD, B75 7ER.
COATES, Mrs. Alexa Jane, BSc ACA *1995;* 6 Keildon Road, LONDON, SW11 1XH.
COATES, Mr. Andrew, ACA *2011;* 36 Sandilands, CROYDON, CR0 5DB.
COATES, Mr. Andrew Edmund, ACA CA(SA) *2009;* 27 Yorkshire Place, Warfield, BRACKNELL, RG42 3XE.
•COATES, Mr. Andrew Mark, BA FCA *1989;* Strategic Corporate Finance Transactions Ltd, 27 Gander Lane, Napier Court, Barlborough, CHESTERFIELD, DERBYSHIRE S43 4PZ. See also Strategic Corporate Finance Partners LLP
•COATES, Mr. Anthony, FCA *1979;* (Tax Fac), Tony Coates & Co Limited, 2 Fairhope Avenue, Bare, MORECAMBE, LA4 6JZ.
COATES, Mr. Anthony Patrick Richard, BSc FCA *1972;* Orchards, Chilbolton, STOCKBRIDGE, HAMPSHIRE, SO20 6BA.
•COATES, Mr. Anthony William, BSc FCA *1975;* Stephenson Coates, Asama Court, West 2, Newcastle Business Park, NEWCASTLE UPON TYNE, NE4 7YD.
COATES, Mr. Christopher George, BA FCA *1978;* Denbrae, Tower Hill, DORKING, SURREY, RH4 2AR.
COATES, Mr. Colin James, FCA *1972;* 36 Sandilands, CROYDON, CR0 5DB.
COATES, Mr. Colin John Unett, FCA *1965;* 18 Lincolns Mead, LINGFIELD, SURREY, RH7 6TA.
COATES, Mr. Damian Paul, ACA *2004;* Windermere Marina Village The Marina, Bowness-on-Windermere, WINDERMERE, CUMBRIA, LA23 3JQ.
•COATES, Mr. David, FCA *1974;* 9 Enderby Drive, HEXHAM, NORTHUMBERLAND, NE46 2PA.
COATES, Mr. David John, BSc FCA *1974;* 4 Donigers Dell, Swanmore, SOUTHAMPTON, SO32 2TL.
COATES, Mr. Donald William, BSc ACA *1987;* Flat 70 North Contemporis, 20 Merchants Road Clifton, BRISTOL, BS8 4HH.
COATES, Ms. Elaine Helen, BSc ACA *1994;* 1 Mile End Lane, Mile End, STOCKPORT, SK2 6BN.
COATES, Mrs. Elizabeth Jane, FCA *1982;* Pemberley House, Church Farm Lane, Willoughby Waterleys, LEICESTER, LE8 6UD.
COATES, Miss. Emily Anne, BSc FCA *1998;* Ground Floor Maisonette, 14 Comeragh Road, West Kensington, LONDON, W14 9HP.
COATES, Mr. Giles Richard, BSc ACA *1985;* 5356 29th Street NW, WASHINGTON, DC 20015, UNITED STATES.
COATES, Mr. Graham Carlton, FCA *1964;* 4 Toll Down Way, Burton, CHIPPENHAM, SN14 7PD. (Life Member)
COATES, Mr. Graham John, BA FCA *1975;* Johnson Matthey Plc, 25 Farringdon Street, LONDON, EC4A 4AB.
COATES, Mr. Ian, BSc(Econ) ACA *1997;* Department of Transport, Great Minster House, 76 Marsham Street, LONDON, SW1P 4DR.
COATES, Mr. Ian Nigel, BSc ACA *1998;* 24 Trehern Road, Sheen, LONDON, SW14 8PD.
COATES, Mr. James Robert Giles, BSc ACA *1992;* Sussex End, Coombe Road, Hillbrow, LISS, GU33 7NU.
COATES, Miss. Jennifer Louise, ACA *2008;* Penmon, Dalton Lane, Halsham, HULL, HU12 0DG.
COATES, Mr. Jeremy William, ACA *1979;* 62 The Grove, BEDFORD, MK40 3JN.
COATES, Mr. John James Digby, FCA *1955;* 37 Causeway Head Road, SHEFFIELD, S17 3DS. (Life Member)
COATES, Mr. John Reginald, FCA *1963;* 38 Linwood Crescent, Ravenshead, NOTTINGHAM, NG15 9FZ.
COATES, Mr. John Richard, BSc FCA *1976;* Green Bank, Stirton, SKIPTON, NORTH YORKSHIRE, BD23 3LH.
•COATES, Mr. John Robert, BSc FCA *2001;* with PricewaterhouseCoopers LLP, Cornwall Court, 19 Cornwall Street, BIRMINGHAM, B3 2DT.
COATES, Mr. Jonathan Peter, ACA *2008;* 102 Scotland Road, Stanwix, CARLISLE, CA3 9EX.
COATES, Mrs. Julie Sandra, BA CA ACA *1992;* with PricewaterhouseCoopers LLP, Hays Galleria, 1 Hays Lane, LONDON, SE1 2RD.
•COATES, Mr. Kevin James, BEng ACA MABRP *2001;* with Zolfo Cooper Ltd, 10 Fleet Place, LONDON, EC4M 7RB.
COATES, Mr. Leslie Frederick, BSc ACA *1998;* 2 Tromode Green, Onchan, ISLE OF MAN, IM2 5NT.
COATES, Mrs. Lynne Sharman, BSc FCA *1974;* 4 Donigers Dell, Swanmore, SOUTHAMPTON, SO32 2TL.
COATES, Mr. Mathew, BA(Hons) ACA *2009;* 5 Somerfield Road, LONDON, N4 2JN.
COATES, Mr. Matthew John, ACA *2008;* with Kingston Smith LLP, Devonshire House, 60 Goswell Road, LONDON, EC1M 7AD.
COATES, Mr. Michael James, FCA *1966;* 404 Stenson Road, DERBY, DE23 1HD.
COATES, Mr. Michael Timothy, BSc FCA *1979;* 73A Mayow Road, Sydenham, LONDON, SE26 4AA.
COATES, Mrs. Michelle Joanne, BSc ACA *2003;* 3 Constable Close, STOKE-ON-TRENT, ST3 7GG.
COATES, Mr. Nicholas Aaron, BSc ACA *1991;* 4 Clifton Wood Road, Cliftonwood, BRISTOL, BS8 4TA.
COATES, Mr. Nicholas Andrew, BSc FCA *1983;* High Acre, 23 Stonehouse Lane, BATH, BA2 5DW.
•COATES, Mr. Nicholas Russell John, FCA *1979;* Nicholas Coates, Fawley House, 4A Station Approach, Somersham, HUNTINGDON, CAMBRIDGESHIRE PE28 3JD.
COATES, Mr. Paul Antony, ACA CFA *2000;* Camelia House Crossways Road, Grayshott, HINDHEAD, GU26 6HE.
COATES, Mr. Paul Christopher, BSc ACA *1984;* 10 High Court Way, Hampton Vale, PETERBOROUGH, PE7 8ER.
COATES, Mr. Paul Michael, BSc(Hons) ACA *2001;* Deutsche Bank, Deutsche Bank Place, Level 11, 126 Phillip Street, SYDNEY, NSW 2000 AUSTRALIA.
COATES, Mr. Peter Gavin, BA FCA *1974;* 50 Moor Crescent, Gosforth, NEWCASTLE UPON TYNE, NE3 4AQ.
COATES, Mr. Peter John, FCA *1966;* Orchard View, 1 Huish Cottages, South Huish, KINGSBRIDGE, DEVON, TQ7 3EJ.
COATES, Mr. Peter Terry, BSc FCA *1978;* 1270 Spoonbill Landings Circle, BRADENTON, FL 34209, UNITED STATES.
COATES, Mr. Peter Timothy, BSc ACA *1988;* West Midlands Travels Limited, 51 Bordesley Green, BIRMINGHAM, B9 4BZ.
COATES, Mr. Ralph, ACA CA(SA) *2010;* 6 Keildon Road, Battersea, LONDON, SW11 1XH.
COATES, Mr. Richard John, BA ACA *1991;* 7 Spinfield Lane West, MARLOW, BUCKINGHAMSHIRE, SL7 2DB.
•COATES, Mr. Richard Jonathan, BSc ACA *1998;* Baker Tilly Tax and Advisory Services LLP, 25 Farringdon Street, LONDON, EC4A 4AB. See also Baker Tilly UK Audit LLP
COATES, Mr. Richard Warren, FCA *1978;* 191/54 Soi Sawasdee, Sukhumvit 31, BANGKOK, 10110, THAILAND.
COATES, Mr. Robert, ACA *2009;* Apartment 9 Terracotta Court, 167 Tower Bridge Road, LONDON, SE1 3LN.
•COATES, Mr. Robert Edward, FCA *1977;* R.E. Coates, 48 Countess Wear Road, EXETER, EX2 6LR.
COATES, Mr. Roger John, MA FCA *1979;* (Tax Fac), White Steps, 34 Low Road, Manthorpe, GRANTHAM, NG31 8NQ.
•COATES, Mr. Ron Alan, BSc FCA *1979;* Ron Coates & Co Limited, 374 Cowbridge Rd East, CARDIFF, CF5 1JJ.
•COATES, Mr. Roy, FCA *1983;* Day Smith & Hunter, Globe House, Eclipse Park, Sittingbourne Road, MAIDSTONE, KENT ME14 3EN.
COATES, Mr. Simon Ross, BSc ACA *1988;* Credit Suisse, Investment Banking, IB Finance VHEC 4, Uetlibergstrasse 231, 8070 ZURICH, SWITZERLAND.
COATES, Mr. Stephen John, MA ACA *1990;* Lantern House, 14 Burgess Wood Road, BEACONSFIELD, BUCKINGHAMSHIRE, HP9 1EQ.

•**COATES, Mr. Steven Richard, BSc ACA CTA** *1997;* (Tax Fac), Coates Franklin Ltd, Accountancy House, Station Road, Upper Broughton, MELTON MOWBRAY, LEICESTERSHIRE LE14 3BQ.
•**COATES, Mrs. Susan, FCA** *1989;* (Tax Fac), Larkings Ltd, 180 Upper Pemberton, Eureka Business Park, ASHFORD, KENT, TN25 4AZ.
•**COATES, Mrs. Susan Margaret, FCA** *1975;* Pryor Begent Fry & Co., 97 Meneage Street, HELSTON, TR13 8RE.
COATES, Miss. Susan Mary, BA ACA *1989;* Nissan Motor Manufacturing (UK) Ltd, Washington Road, SUNDERLAND, SR5 3NS.
COATES, Mr. Terence John, BSc ACA *1993;* Standard Brands(UK) Ltd, 4 Cleeve Court, Cleeve Road, LEATHERHEAD, SURREY, KT22 7SD.
COATH, Mr. Michael, BA ACA *1992;* (Tax Fac), James Taylor Construction Ltd, 4 Maple Park, HODDESDON, HERTFORDSHIRE, EN11 0EX.
COATHAM, Mrs. Susan Claire, BSc ACA *1986;* Paul Murray Plc, School Lane, Chandler's Ford, EASTLEIGH, HAMPSHIRE, SO53 4YN.
•**COATS, Mr. Dominic Peter, BSc ACA** *1989;* Ernst & Young, Bleicherweg 21, P.O. Box 5272, CH-8022 ZURICH, SWITZERLAND. See also Ernst & Young Europe LLP
COBAN, Mrs. Elizabeth Anne, ACA *1992;* 15 Haytor Grove, NEWTON ABBOT, DEVON, TQ12 4DS.
COBB, Mr. Adrian Noel Walter, BA FCA *1975;* TMK IPSCO, 2650 Warrenville Road (7th Floor), DOWNERS GROVE, IL 60515, UNITED STATES.
•**COBB, Mr. Alan Arthur, FCA** *1971;* 21 Caraway Gate, STIRLING, WA 6021, AUSTRALIA.
COBB, Mrs. Amanda Jean Orr, MA ACA *1994;* 23 Nether Auchendrane, Alloway, AYR, KA7 4EE.
•**COBB, Mr. Christopher Paul, BCom FCA** *1979;* (Tax Fac), Cobb Burgin & Co, 129a Middleton Boulevard, Wollaton Park, NOTTINGHAM, NG8 1FW.
•**COBB, Mr. David Fraser, BSc ACA** *1990;* Deloitte LLP, 2 New Street Square, LONDON, EC4A 3BZ. See also Deloitte & Touche LLP
•**COBB, Mr. Edward Gilbert, FCA** *1973;* E C C Limited, 73 Chapel Lane, Hale Barns, ALTRINCHAM, CHESHIRE, WA15 0BN.
COBB, Mrs. Gillian Elizabeth, BSc FCA *1999;* Simmons & Simmons, Citypoint, 1 Ropemaker Street, LONDON, EC2Y 9SS.
COBB, Miss. Harriet, BA(Hons) ACA *2011;* 76 Reform Street, LONDON, SW11 5AJ.
COBB, Mr. James Robert, BSc ACA *1995;* 12 The Deerings, HARPENDEN, AL5 2PE.
COBB, Mr. John Stewart, FCA *1957;* Pond Cottage, Castle Grove Road, Chobham, WOKING, GU24 8EE. (Life Member)
COBB, Mr. John Timothy, BSc ACA *1992;* 14 Cyprus Park, BELFAST, BT5 6EA.
COBB, Mr. Jonathan Richard Lees, BSc ACA *2004;* with KPMG LLP, 15 Canada Square, LONDON, E14 5GL.
COBB, Mr. Michael, ACA *2008;* 5 Blue Anchor Court, NEWCASTLE UPON TYNE, NE1 3HB.
COBB, Mr. Michael John, BSc ACA *1984;* Stukeley House, 9 Barn Hill, STAMFORD, LINCOLNSHIRE, PE9 2AE.
COBB, Mr. Neville James, MA FCA *1994;* 23 Nether Auchendrane, By Alloway, AYR, KA7 4EE.
•**COBB, Mr. Patrick John, FCA** *1977;* Byrne Palmer & Co, 14 Queens Road, Hersham, WALTON-ON-THAMES, KT12 5LS.
COBB, Mr. Roger Charles, MSc FCA *1974;* 127 Buxton Lane, CATERHAM, CR3 5HN.
COBB, Mr. Simon Alexander, MA ACA *2000;* Nailbourne Cottage, Bonny Bush Hill, Kingston, CANTERBURY, KENT, CT4 6HT.
COBB, Mrs. Stephanie Elaine, BA ACA *1996;* The Stocks, 12 Woodside Hill Close, Horsforth, LEEDS, LS18 4HW.
COBB, Miss. Suzanne, BCom ACA *2011;* 117a Parkland Drive, LEEDS, LS6 4PT.
COBBAN, Mr. David Alexander, BSc ACA *1995;* 1825 NW 24th Ave, PORTLAND, OR 97210, UNITED STATES.
COBBETT, Mr. Andrew Stephen, BSc ACA *1982;* 36 Burford Road, WORCESTER PARK, SURREY, KT4 7SU.
•**COBBIN, Mr. Simon, FCA** *1978;* S Cobbin & Co Limited, The Old Surgery, 15a Station Road, EPPING, ESSEX, CM16 4HG.
COBBOLD, Mr. Timothy Russell, BSc FCA *1988;* Yendor House, Hundredsteddle Lane, Birdham, CHICHESTER, PO20 7BL.
•**COBDEN, Mr. Ian Howard, FCA** *1985;* (Tax Fac), Ian Cobden & Co, Rowlandson House, 289-293 Ballards Lane, LONDON, N12 8NP.
COBDEN, Mr. Paul Charles, BA ACA *1986;* 272 Edgecliff Road, WOOLLAHRA, NSW 2025, AUSTRALIA.
•**COBDEN, Mr. Philip Malcolm, BSc ACA** *1978;* (Tax Fac), Hicks & Co, 53 Lampton Road, HOUNSLOW, TW3 1LY.
COBERSY, Mr. Shimon, BSc ACA *1994;* 24 Aintree Avenue, Savoy Estate, JOHANNESBURG, 2090, SOUTH AFRICA.
COBHAM, Miss. Louise Claire, BSc ACA *2006;* Holly Cottage Black Dykes Lane, Upper Poppleton, YORK, YO26 6PT.
•**COBLEY, Mr. Bryan Anthony, FCA** *1962;* Oakwood Accountancy Limited, 26 Beechwood Avenue, MELTON MOWBRAY, LEICESTERSHIRE, LE13 1RT.
•**COBLEY, Mr. Eric Michael, FCA** *1966;* Eric M. Cobley, Great Dalby House, Great Dalby, MELTON MOWBRAY, LEICESTERSHIRE, LE14 2EY.
COBLEY, Miss. Gail, BA ACA *1996;* 18 Henfield Road, LONDON, SW19 3HU.
COBLEY, Mr. Kenneth, FCA *1964;* 6 Windy Ridge Close, LONDON, SW19 5HB. (Life Member)
COBLEY, Mr. Peter Richard, MA FCA *1994;* 25 Camphill Avenue, WORCESTER, WR5 2HQ.
COBLEY, Mrs. Rachel Jayne, BSc ACA *1994;* 46 Horsham Road, Owlsmoor, Sandhurst, SANDHURST, GU47 0YZ.
COBURN, Mr. Mark Christopher, ACA *2004;* St. Joseph's Health Centre, 100 Westmount Road, GUELPH N1H 5H8, ON, CANADA.
COBURN, Mrs. Mary Siobhain, ACA *1994;* Cargill Plc, Knowle Hill Park, Fairmile Lane, COBHAM, KT11 2PD.
COBURN, Mr. Paul Michael, BA ACA *1991;* Old pines, 103 Oldfield Drive, Heswall, WIRRAL, MERSEYSIDE, CH60 9LQ.
COCCONI, Miss. Elena, BA ACA *2005;* 4a Petrarchi Street, Neaolis, 3107 LIMASSOL, CYPRUS.
COCCONIS, Mr. Michael, BA ACA *2005;* 4A Petrarhi Street, Neapolis, 3107 LIMASSOL, CYPRUS.
COCHRAM, Mr. Alan, BEng ACA MAAT *2009;* Hillmore, Station Road, Wakes Colne, COLCHESTER, CO6 2DS.
COCHRAN, Mr. Alastair Edward, BA ACA *1995;* Little Coopers, Coopers Hill, Eversley, HOOK, HAMPSHIRE, RG27 0QA.
•**COCHRAN, Mr. Gerald Charles, BSc FCA** *1974;* Cube Partners Limited, 5 Giffard Court, Millbrook Close, NORTHAMPTON, NN5 5JF.
COCHRANE, Mrs. Catherine Margaret, BA ACA *1994;* 13 Southern Road, LONDON, N2 9LH.
COCHRANE, Mr. Charles Frank James, BSc ACA *1993;* 278 Kings Road, KINGSTON UPON THAMES, SURREY, KT2 5JL.
COCHRANE, Mr. David George, OBE FCA *1943;* 18 Weald Rise, Fox Hill, HAYWARDS HEATH, RH16 4RB. (Life Member)
COCHRANE, Mr. David Haslop, BA FCA *1972;* 5-6 Gibbs Lane, Appledore, BIDEFORD, DEVON, EX39 1PR.
•**COCHRANE, Ms. Elizabeth Jane, MA ACA** *1986;* (Tax Fac), Jane Cochrane, 35 Thornton Hill, EXETER, EX4 4NN.
COCHRANE, Mr. Francis Michael, MA FCA *1982;* with RSM Tenon Limited, Sumner House, St Thomas's Rd, CHORLEY, PR7 1HP.
COCHRANE, Mr. Gordon Douglas, BA FCA *1990;* Pooh Corner, 42 Richardsons Road, East Bergholt, COLCHESTER, CO7 6RR.
•**COCHRANE, Mr. Hugh James, BSc ACA** *1979;* Hugh Cochrane and Co, 26B High Street, SAXMUNDHAM, SUFFOLK, IP17 1AJ.
COCHRANE, Mr. Ian Andrew, BSc FCA CF *1976;* Woolton House, Oval Way, GERRARDS CROSS, SL9 8QD.
COCHRANE, Mrs. Jane, BSc ACA *1999;* PO Box 911490, Victoria Street West, AUCKLAND 1124, NEW ZEALAND.
•**COCHRANE, Mrs. Joanne Louise, BSc FCA** *1997;* Cochrane & Co Accountants Limited, 38 Kings Road, LEE-ON-THE-SOLENT, HAMPSHIRE, PO13 9NU.
COCHRANE, Mr. John Alexander, BA FCA *1964;* Fairspear House, Leafield, WITNEY, OX29 9NY.
COCHRANE, Mr. Justin Malcolm Brian, MEng ACA *2001;* with Clear Channel Outdoor, 33 Golden Square, LONDON, W1F 9JT.
COCHRANE, Mr. Mark Ernest, MSc ACA *1998;* 147 Campbell Road, OXFORD, OX4 3NX.
COCHRANE, Mr. Stephen Robert, BA ACA *1988;* 17 Bolton Gardens, TEDDINGTON, TW11 9AX.
COCHRANE, Mrs. Susan Elizabeth, BSc ACA *2005;* 2 Violet Cottages Cores End Road, BOURNE END, BUCKINGHAMSHIRE, SL8 5HP.
•**COCHRANE, Mr. Thomas Paul, BA FCA DChA** *1987;* McEwan Wallace, 68 Argyle Street, Birkenhead, WIRRAL, CH41 6AF.
COCHRANE, Mr. Timothy John Samuel, FCA *1972;* 9 Grove Court, Drayton Gardens, LONDON, SW10 9QY.
•**COCHRANE-DYET, Mr. Duncan George, BSc FCA** *1999;* Day Smith & Hunter, Globe House, Eclipse Park, Sittingbourne Road, MAIDSTONE, KENT ME14 3EN.
COCK, Mr. Matthew John, BSc ACA *2000;* 18 Blue Leaves Avenue, Netherne-on-the-Hill, COULSDON, SURREY, CR5 1NU.
COCKBAIN, Mr. David Gordon Phillip, ACA *2008;* 7 Radnor Court, Linkfield Street, REDHILL, RH1 6BZ.
COCKBILL, Miss. Lynne Patricia, MBA MSc FCA *1986;* Canada Life Ltd, Canada Life Place, High Street, POTTERS BAR, HERTFORDSHIRE, EN6 5BA.
COCKBURN, Mr. Ian, BA ACA MBA *1980;* 16 Strathmore Road, LONDON, SW19 8DB.
COCKBURN, Mr. Ian, MEng ACA *2010;* 57 Beacon Way, RICKMANSWORTH, HERTFORDSHIRE, WD3 7PB.
COCKBURN, Mr. James, ACA CA(NZ) *2010;* 5 Kings Road, LONDON, SW14 8PF.
COCKBURN, Miss. Marie Claire, BA ACA *1996;* 2 Ivanhoe Place, Felpham, BOGNOR REGIS, WEST SUSSEX, PO22 7QN.
COCKBURN, Mrs. Vivienne Marie, MSc BA ACA *1992;* 77 Redford Loan, Colinton, EDINBURGH, EH13 0AU.
COCKBURN-PRICE, Mr. David Charles, MA FCA *1992;* Hey Royd, Skipton Old Road, COLNE, LANCASHIRE, BB8 7AD.
COCKCROFT, Mr. Graham Christopher, BA FCA *1987;* 33 Stones Drive Ripponden, SOWERBY BRIDGE, WEST YORKSHIRE, HX6 4NY.
COCKCROFT, Mr. Kevin, BA(Hons) ACA *2011;* 24 Chapelhill Road, Moreton, WIRRAL, MERSEYSIDE, CH46 9QN.
COCKCROFT, Mr. Michael Jon, BSc ACA *2001;* IHG, Suite 2201, Festival Tower, Dubai Festival City, Al Rebbat Street, PO Box 58191 DUBAI UNITED ARAB EMIRATES.
•①**COCKCROFT, Mr. Timothy Simon, BA(Econ) ACA** *1983;* Timothy S Cockcroft, Vale Cottage, 16 Watsons Lane, Harby, MELTON MOWBRAY, LE14 4DD.
COCKER, Mr. Christopher John, MA FCA *1976;* 6 St. Joseph's Close, BLACKPOOL, FY3 8LU.
COCKER, Mr. Frank, BSc ACA *1980;* Acton House, Acton, NEWCASTLE, STAFFORDSHIRE, ST5 4EQ.
COCKER, Miss. Hilary Margaret, BSc ACA *1983;* 5 The Rise, Caversham, READING, RG4 8NZ.
COCKER, Mrs. Jennifer Elizabeth, LLB ACA *1999;* Corporate Finance Department, South Yorkshire Police HQ, Snig Hill, SHEFFIELD, S3 8LY.
COCKER, Mr. John Anthony, FCA *1966;* 19 Wentworth Drive, LICHFIELD, STAFFORDSHIRE, WS14 9HN.
COCKER, Mr. Martin Robert, BSc ACA *1985;* Bliss Developments Limited, Vale da Areia, Apartado 52, 8401-906 FERRAGUDO, PORTUGAL.
COCKER, Mr. Paul, BSc ACA *2004;* Flat 1, 22 Cavendish Road, LONDON, NW6 7XP.
COCKER, Mr. Peter Douglas, BSc(Hons) ACA *2002;* 15 Alanbrooke Road, COLCHESTER, CO2 8EG.
COCKER, Mr. Robert Alfred, BA FCA *1961;* 31 Hollybush Hill, Wanstead, LONDON, E11 1PS.
•**COCKER, Mr. Ross Andrew, ACA** *1995;* Clement Keys, 39/40 Calthorpe Road, Edgbaston, BIRMINGHAM, B15 1TS.
COCKER, Mr. Simon William, BSc ACA *1989;* 42 Stathern Lane, Harby, MELTON MOWBRAY, LE14 4DA.
COCKER, Mrs. Zosia Celina, BSc ACA *1986;* 42 Stathern Lane, Harby, MELTON MOWBRAY, LE14 4DA.
COCKERAM, Mrs. Carolyn, BSc ACA *1984;* 43 Potterton Lane, Barwick in Elmet, LEEDS, LS15 4DU.
COCKERAM, Mr. Howard Michael, FCA *1973;* Watson Prickard, 1 Union Court, LIVERPOOL, L2 4SJ.
COCKERELL, Miss. Eliza, ACA *2011;* 49 Netherwood Road, LONDON, W14 0BL.
COCKERHAM, Mr. Alan Stuart, BSc ACA *1996;* 7 South Dene, Stoke Bishop, BRISTOL, BS9 2BW.
COCKERHAM, Mrs. Lesley, BA ACA *1986;* 23 St. Simon's Close, SUTTON COLDFIELD, B75 7ST.
COCKERILL, Mr. Glenn, MA ACA *2003;* 95 Britannia Avenue, Basford, NOTTINGHAM, NG6 0EA.
COCKERILL, Mr. Ian Peter, BA ACA *1982;* 2 Moorfield Avenue, Scholes, CLECKHEATON, BD19 6PG.
COCKERILL, Mr. John Peter, BSc FCA *1975;* 26 Lowther Road, Barnes, LONDON, SW13 9ND.
COCKERTON, Mr. Roger William Rhys, BSc FCA *1980;* 23 High Street, Debenham, STOWMARKET, IP14 6QL.
•**COCKETT, Mr. Lee David, ACA MAAT** *2005;* Cockett & Co Limited, 2e Rainbow Street, LEOMINSTER, HEREFORDSHIRE, HR6 8DQ.
COCKIN, Mrs. Anna Margaret, BA ACA *1992;* Rikan Farm Wilkins Road, Emneth, WISBECH, CAMBRIDGESHIRE, PE14 8DQ.
COCKIN, Mrs. Bryony Caroline, BSc ACA *1991;* c/o Cooperheat Middle East, PO Box 16921, Jebel Ali, DUBAI, UNITED ARAB EMIRATES.
COCKING, Mr. David, BA ACA *1985;* Hachette Australia PTY Ltd, Level 17, 207 Kent Street, SYDNEY, NSW 2000, AUSTRALIA.
COCKINGS, Mr. Peter George, FCA *1950;* Apartment H, Hanover House, St. Stephens Road, CHELTENHAM, GLOUCESTERSHIRE, GL51 3BG. (Life Member)
COCKINGS, Mr. Simon Arthur Leyshon, BSc ACA *2011;* 2 Cound Terrace, PORT TALBOT, WEST GLAMORGAN, SA13 1PP.
COCKMAN, Mr. Brian David, FCA *1968;* Copsewood, 26 Rambling Way, Potten End, BERKHAMSTED, HERTFORDSHIRE, HP4 2SF.
COCKMAN, Mr. Derrick Harry, FCA *1953;* Tower House, 1 Temple Gardens, BRIGHTON, BN1 3AE. (Life Member)
COCKMAN, Mr. Ian Francis, FCA *1970;* (Tax Fac), 88 Eastwood Rd., LEIGH-ON-SEA, SS9 3AD.
COCKRAM, Mr. John Phillip, FCA *1970;* 1 Damer Terrace, LONDON, SW10 0NZ.
COCKRAM, Mr. Keith Henry, FCA *1978;* 4 Loxley Green, Wyton, HUNTINGDON, PE28 2JN.
COCKRAM, Mr. Michael James, BSc ACA *1988;* Melvill, Knowle Grove, VIRGINIA WATER, GU25 4JD.
COCKRELL, Ms. Alison Elisabeth, BSc FCA *1991;* Westpac, L19, 275 Kent Street, SYDNEY, NSW 2000, AUSTRALIA.
COCKRELL, Mr. David, ACA FCCA *2011;* with Moore Stephens LLP, 150 Aldersgate Street, LONDON, EC1A 4AB.
COCKRELL, Mr. Stephen John, BSc FCA *1977;* Home Farm House, Weston, TOWCESTER, NN12 8PU.
COCKREM, Mr. Anthony Philip, FCA *1970;* 45 West End Grove, Horsforth, LEEDS, LS18 5JJ. (Life Member)
COCKREM, Mrs. Denise Patricia, MA FCA *1987;* 21 Pointers Hill, Westcott, DORKING, SURREY, RH4 3PF.
COCKREM, Mr. Michael, BSc ACA *2005;* Level 1, Building 7, Botanicca Corporate Park, RICHMOND, VIC 3121, AUSTRALIA.
•**COCKREM, Mr. Raymond John, BSc ACA** *1995;* Ray Cockrem ACA, 38 Elmgate Drive, Littledown, BOURNEMOUTH, BH7 7EG.
COCKROFT, Mr. John David, FCA *1958;* 58 Hare Close, BUCKINGHAM, MK18 7EW. (Life Member)
COCKS, Mr. Andrew John, BSc ACA *1992;* Willowbrook, 40 Beckford Road, Alderton, TEWKESBURY, GL20 8NL.
COCKS, Mrs. Christine Mary, BSc FCA *1978;* 40 Bournehall Avenue, BUSHEY, WD23 3AX.
•**COCKS, Mr. Christopher Stephen, FCA** *1965;* C.S. Cocks, 45 Rannoch Drive, Lakeside, CARDIFF, CF23 6LP.
COCKS, Mr. Daniel, BA ACA *1988;* 4A Devon Road, BEDFORD, MK40 3DF.
COCKS, Mr. Jeremy Mark, BSc FCA *1987;* 2 Eaton Gate, Mill Lane, Keswick, NORWICH, NR4 6TP.
COCKS, Mr. Richard Charles, FCA *1966;* Baywell Cottage, Fawler Road, Charlbury, CHIPPING NORTON, OXFORDSHIRE, OX7 3AD. (Life Member)
COCKS, Mr. Robert Antony, BSc ACA *2005;* 5 Beauchamp Drive, Amesbury, SALISBURY, SP4 7TT.
COCKS, Mr. Robert Stuart, BA ACA *1986;* Equality Training Ltd, 10-12 Water Street, NEWCASTLE, STAFFORDSHIRE, ST5 1HP.
COCKS, Mrs. Sharon Mary, ACA *1990;* Hilltops, Skew Road, FAREHAM, HAMPSHIRE, PO17 6AP.
COCKSHAW, Mr. William Robert, FCA *1966;* 2 Grange Avenue, Garforth, LEEDS, LS25 1HQ.
COCKSHOTT, William David, Esq MBE FCA *1951;* Apartamento B-51, Casas do Gandarinha, Avenida Rei Humberto de Italia, 2750-641 CASCAIS, PORTUGAL. (Life Member)
COCKSHUTT, Miss. Paula Marie, BSc ACA *1997;* 88 Old Lansdowne Road, MANCHESTER, M20 2WX.
COCKTON, Mr. Richard Edward, MA FCA *1978;* 17 Greystoke House, 150 Brunswick Road, LONDON, W5 1AW.
•**COCKWELL, Mr. Mark Julian, LLB FCA ATII** *1991;* (Tax Fac), KPMG LLP, 100 Temple Street, BRISTOL, BS1 6AG. See also KPMG Europe LLP

•COCORACCHIO, Mr. Robert Francis, FCA 1975; Cranfields, Suite 2, 3rd Floor, Leon House, 233 High Street, CROYDON CR0 9XT.
COCORACCHIO, Mr. Stephen Peter, MSc BSc ACA 2006; Flat 38, Astoria Court, 116 High Street, PURLEY, SURREY, CR8 2XT.
CODA, Mr. John, BSc ACA 1986; Stirling Cottage, Sweethaws Lane, CROWBOROUGH, TN6 3SS.
CODA, Mrs. Melanie Jane, BCom ACA 1990; 6 Carlton Gardens, LONDON, W5 2AN.
CODD, Miss. Zoe Margaret Laura, MA ACA 1995; Portland House, Sibthorpe, NEWARK, NG23 5PN.
CODE, Miss. Paula, BA ACA 1992; 40 Bickershaw Drive, Worsley, MANCHESTER, M28 0GG.
CODLING, Mrs. Amanda Jane, ACA 1993; 44 Broadacres, LUTON, LU2 7YF.
CODLING, Mr. David Knowles, BSc(Econ) FCA 1963; 51 Steepleton Rd, BROADSTONE, BH18 8LH.
CODLING, Mr. Mark, BSc ACA 2001; 18 Orient Close, ST. ALBANS, HERTFORDSHIRE, AL1 1AJ.
CODLING, Mr. Michael John, BSc ACA 1987; PricewaterhouseCoopers, Darling Park Tower 2, 201 Sussex Street, GPO Box 2650, SYDNEY, NSW 1171 AUSTRALIA.
CODRINGTON, Mr. Simon Humphrey John, BA FCA 1972; 23 Bellevue Road, Barnes, LONDON, SW13 0BJ.
CODY, Miss. Elizabeth Jane Kingsborough, ACA 1984; 13 Michigan Close, Kesgrave, IPSWICH, IP5 1HG.
CODY, Ms. Gabrielle Mary Jude, BA ACA 1996; 14 Adrian Place, Balgowlah Heights, SYDNEY, NSW 2093, AUSTRALIA.
CODY, Mr. Mark Vincent, BA ACA 1986; 40 Selwyn Avenue, RICHMOND, SURREY, TW9 2HA.
CODY, Mr. Paul Frank, LLB ACA 1988; Brown Shipley & Co Ltd, Founders Court, Lothbury, LONDON, EC2R 7HE.
COE, Mr. Albert Henry, FCA 1967; Finvara, Wilmslow Road, Mottram St. Andrew, MACCLESFIELD, SK10 4QT. (Life Member)
COE, Mr. Daniel John, BSc ACA 1994; 17 Napoleon Road, TWICKENHAM, TW1 3EW.
COE, Mr. David James, FCA 1964; 11 Freshfields Avenue, UPMINSTER, ESSEX, RM14 2BY.
COE, Mr. Derek Ian, BA FCA 1982; Foxmeadow Croft, Main Street, Sutton on Derwent, YORK, YO41 4BT.
COE, Miss. Fiona Jane, BSc ACA 1992; P.O. Box 6139, French Forest Delivery Centre, FRENCHS FOREST, NSW 1640, AUSTRALIA.
COE, Mr. Greville Ashley Alexander, BA ACA 1998; 17a East St. Helen Street, ABINGDON, OXFORDSHIRE, OX14 5EE.
COE, Miss. Jennifer, BSc ACA 1992; 10 The Heythrop, INGATESTONE, ESSEX, CM4 9HG.
COE, Mr. Julian Richard Thomas, LLB ACA 1995; Farm View Manor, Horsebridge Road, MINSTERLEY, SHROPSHIRE, S75 0AE.
COE, Mrs. Martene Andrea, BA(Hons) ACA 2002; 3 Tuffnell Close, Willen, MILTON KEYNES, MK15 9LB.
COE, Mr. Matthew Charles, BA FCA DChA 1998; 10 The Verlands, COWBRIDGE, SOUTH GLAMORGAN, CF71 7BY.
COE, Mr. Michael Charles, BSc ACA 1993; Withyhurst, Riverside, BANWELL, BS29 6EH.
COE, Mr. Nigel Edward, BSc FCA CFA 1997; 3 Woods Way, LARCHMONT, NY 10538, UNITED STATES.
COE, Mr. Peter, PhD BA ACA CTA 2003; with Deloitte LLP, Abbots House, Abbey Street, READING, RG1 3BD.
COE, Mr. Phillip, BA ACA 2006; 3 Tuffnell Close, Willen, MILTON KEYNES, MK15 9LB.
COE, Mr. Richard John, BSc ACA 1983; Travis Perkins Plc, Ryehill House, Ryehill Close, Lodge Way, NORTHAMPTON, NN5 7UA.
•COE, Mr. Robert Michael, BA FCA 1971; Wilder Coe LLP, 233-237 Old Marylebone Road, LONDON, NW1 5QT. See also Addison, Beyer, Green & Co and Wilder Coe
COE, Mr. Roger Stanley, BCom FCA 1971; Norville Group Ltd, Magdala Road, GLOUCESTER, GL1 4DG.
COE, Mr. Scott Christopher, BA(Hons) ACA 2001; with Jacob Cavenagh & Skeet, 5 Robin Hood Lane, SUTTON, SURREY, SM1 2SW.
COE, Mr. Stephen Charles, BSc FCA 1990; 7 New Street, St. Peter Port, GUERNSEY, GY1 2PF.
COE, Mr. Stephen John, MA ACA 1986; Coe & Co, 63 Mayow Road, LONDON, SE23 2XH.
COE, Mr. Stuart, BA ACIB ACA MBA 1999; Co-operativeFinancial Services, 13th Floor, Miller Street, MANCHESTER, M60 0AL.
COELHO, Mr. David Michael, FCA 1983; 16 The Grove, CAMBERWELL, VIC 3124, AUSTRALIA.
COELLN, Miss. Julia, BSc ACA 2010; Flat 3, 46 Harrington Gardens, LONDON, SW7 4LT.
COEN, Ms. Anna, BSc FCA MBA 1983; AC Integration, 2 Church Lane, Shepreth, ROYSTON, HERTFORDSHIRE, SG8 6RG.
COEN, Mr. Rael Trevor, BSc ACA 2001; PartnerRe Ltd, 90 Pitts Bay Road, PEMBROKE HM08, BERMUDA.
•COESHALL, Miss. Elizabeth Jane, BSc FCA 1979; (Tax Fac), Jaynes & Co, 20 New Street, BRAINTREE, CM7 1ES.
COESHOTT, Mrs. Melanie Jane Tamsyn, BSc(Hons) ACA 2001; 12 Northern Avenue, HENLOW, BEDFORDSHIRE, SG16 6ET.
COETZEE, Mr. Jacques, ACA CA(SA) 2008; Die Wilgers, PO Box 70981, PRETORIA, GAUTENG, 0041, SOUTH AFRICA.
COEY, Mr. James Edward Colin, MA FCA 1953; 15 Bramley Grange, Horsham Road, Bramley, GUILDFORD, SURREY, GU5 0ES. (Life Member)
COFF, Miss. Tanya Louise, ACA CA(AUS) 2009; 10 Burnaby Street, LONDON, SW10 0PH.
COFFEE, Mr. Alan Mark Stuart Jackson, BA ACA 1994; 38 Riverdale Drive, LONDON, SW18 4UR.
COFFER, Mr. Raymond Charles, FCA 1967; 5 The Lake, Bushey Heath, BUSHEY, WD23 1HS.
COFFEY, Mr. Alexander James, BSc ACA 2003; 8 Salcombe Gardens, Clapham Common North Side, LONDON, SW4 9RY.
•COFFEY, Mr. Charles Edward, FCA 1968; (Tax Fac), Charles E. Coffey & Co, Unicredit House, Irwell Street Entrance, 16 Paley Road, BRADFORD, BD4 7EJ.
COFFEY, Mr. John Gareth, ACA 2011; 4 Mikardo Court, 260 Poplar High Street, LONDON, E14 0BQ.
COFFEY, Dr. Paul Anthony, PhD BSc ACA 1998; 9A Rothbury Drive, ASHINGTON, NORTHUMBERLAND, NE63 8TJ.
COFFEY, Mr. Peter William, BA FCA 1985; Department of Transport Great Minster House, 76 Marsham Street, LONDON, SW1P 4DR.
COFFEY, Mr. Stephen Joseph, BEng FCA 1995; 40 Nomond Avenue, La Pouquelaye, St. Helier, JERSEY, JE2 3FW.
•COFFEY, Mr. William Patrick, FCA 1981; 6 Ryland Road, Erdington, BIRMINGHAM, B24 8JH.
COFFIN, Mrs. Jacqueline Angela, BA ACA 1998; Drymen House, Horn Lane, East Hendred, WANTAGE, OXFORDSHIRE, OX12 8LD.
COFFIN, Mr. Malcolm, BA ACA 2006; 24 Syddal Road, Bramhall, STOCKPORT, CHESHIRE, SK7 1AD.
COFFIN, Dr. Malcolm Andrew, BSc ACA 1996; Drymen House, Horn Lane, East Hendred, WANTAGE, OXFORDSHIRE, OX12 8LD.
•COFFIN, Mr. Michael Robert, BA(Econ) FCA 1984; 30 The Ridgeway, FAREHAM, PO16 8RE.
COFFIN, Mrs. Rosemary Ann, MA ACA 1983; Wimborne Junior School, Wimborne Road, SOUTHSEA, PO4 8DE.
COFFMAN, Mr. David Leslie, BA ACA 1996; 31 Lyndhurst Gardens, LONDON, N3 1TA.
COFIE, Mr. Alfred Quao-Ashie, FCA 1966; P O Box KB 112, Korle BU, ACCRA, GHANA. (Life Member)
COFIE, Mr. Robert Frederick, BA ACA 1992; 39 Claygate Road, LONDON, W13 9XG.
COFMAN-NICORESLI, Mr. Timothy, BA ACA 1978; 106 Greenfield Road, Harborne, BIRMINGHAM, B17 0EF.
COGAN, Miss. Heather Dawn, ACA 2009; (Tax Fac), 66 Aspen Park Road, WESTON-SUPER-MARE, AVON, BS22 8ER.
COGAN, Mr. Paul Murray, BA FCA 1994; 22 Stretton Avenue, Meanwood, LEEDS, LS6 4QU.
COGGAN, Mr. Ben, MEng ACA 2006; 63 Goldsworthy Road, Flixton, MANCHESTER, M41 8TP.
COGGAN, Mrs. Imogen Frances, BEng ACA 1999; 72 Griffiths Road, LONDON, SW19 1ST.
COGGINS, Mr. David John, FCA 1983; 37 Baron Grove, MITCHAM, SURREY, CR4 4EH.
COGGINS, Mrs. Elizabeth Rose, BSc ACA 2003; 3 Westfield Drive, PENARTH, SOUTH GLAMORGAN, CF64 3NT.
COGGINS, Mrs. Lynda Anne, BSc ACA CFA FRM 1989; Flat 21A The Albany, One Albany Road, MID LEVELS, HONG KONG ISLAND, HONG KONG SAR.
COGGINS, Mr. Mark Stuart, BSc ACA 1991; 21a The Albany, One Albany Road, MID LEVELS, HONG KONG ISLAND, HONG KONG SAR.
COGGINS, Mrs. Mary Ruth, MA ACA 1984; 37 Baron Grove, MITCHAM, CR4 4EH.
COGGINS, Mr. Michael John, FCA 1981; 7 Green Trees, EPPING, CM16 4QT.
COGGINS, Mr. Ronald, FCA 1966; Warren Croft, Warren Lane, Stain Cross, BARNSLEY, S75 5BQ.
COGGINS, Mr. William Henry, ACA 1982; 26 Springwood Drive, Aston Lodge Park, STONE, ST15 8TU.
COGHILL, Mrs. Alexandra Frances, MA(Cantab) ACA 2009; 16 Down Wood Road, Blandford Camp, BLANDFORD FORUM, DORSET, DT11 8AH.
COGHILL, Mr. Anthony Edward, FCA 1960; 86 Waterlea, Furnace Green, CRAWLEY, RH10 6SP. (Life Member)
COGHILL, Mr. Nicholas Mark, BSc ACA 1997; The Small House, Hawthorn Lane, Farnham Common, SLOUGH, SL2 3SW.
COGHILL, Mr. Nigel Victor Ashton, FCA 1971; 5 Congreve Close, Walton on the Hill, STAFFORD, ST17 0LN.
COGHLAN, Mr. Anthony James Granville, BA FCA 1983; Pipers Corner, Snowdenham Links Road, Bramley, GUILDFORD, GU5 0BX.
COGHLAN, Mr. Anthony John, BA FCA 1975; 1 Alpine Lodge Barn, Rowney Green Lane, Alvechurch, BIRMINGHAM, B48 7QZ.
COGHLAN, Mr. Bryan John, FCA 1974; 379 Crewe Road, Wistaston, NANTWICH, CW5 6NW.
COGHLAN, Mr. Christopher Austin Francis, BA ACA 2006; 24b Lupus Street, LONDON, SW1V 3DZ.
COGHLAN, Mr. John Bernard, BCom ACA ATII 1982; Southview, Warren Park, KINGSTON UPON THAMES, SURREY, KT2 7HX.
COGHLAN, Mr. Timothy Julian Peter, BA FCA 1973; Braunston Marina Limited, Braunston, DAVENTRY, NN11 7JH.
COGMAN, Mr. Rowland Andrew, BSc ACA 1981; Timbers, 55 Kingswood Avenue, Taverham, NORWICH, NR8 6UW.
COGSWELL, Mrs. Pamela, BA FCA 1971; 11 Courtwood Close, SALISBURY, SP1 2RX.
COGSWELL, Mr. Stephen, BEng ACA 1991; 23 Bankfield Road, SHIPLEY, WEST YORKSHIRE, BD18 4AJ.
COHEN, Mr. Adam George Joseph, BA ACA 2010; (Tax Fac), Harvey Smith & Co, 2 High Street, BURNHAM-ON-CROUCH, ESSEX, CM0 8AA.
COHEN, Mr. Adam Hayden, BA ACA 1989; Baram, 64 Galley Lane, Arkley, BARNET, EN5 4AL.
COHEN, Mr. Adam Paul, BA ACA 2000; 10 Bancroft Avenue, LONDON, N2 0AS.
•COHEN, Mr. Adrian Arnold, FCA 1971; Sterlings Ltd, Lawford House, Albert Place, LONDON, N3 1QA.
COHEN, Mr. Alan Abraham, FCA 1959; Alan A Cohen, 31 Camlet Way, Hadley Wood, BARNET, EN4 0LJ. (Life Member)
•COHEN, Mr. Alan Ivan, FCA 1966; (Tax Fac), A I Cohen & Associates Ltd, 61 Crowstone Road, WESTCLIFF-ON-SEA, ESSEX, SS0 8BG.
•COHEN, Mr. Alan Jon, BSc FCA 1974; Alan Jon Cohen, 2 Ganton Avenue, Whitefield, MANCHESTER, M45 7LT.
COHEN, Mr. Alan Peter, FCA 1962; Alan Cohen & Co, 4 Westbrae Road, Newton Mearns, GLASGOW, G77 6EQ.
COHEN, Mr. Alan Solomon, FCA 1952; 34 Farthing Court, Langstone Way, Mill Hill, LONDON, NW7 1GQ. (Life Member)
COHEN, Miss. Amanda Ruth, BA ACA 1984; (Tax Fac), 27 Collingwood Avenue, LONDON, N10 3EH.
COHEN, Mr. Andrew Jonathan Simon, BA FCA 1993; Flat 66 Sailmakers Court, William Morris Way, LONDON, SW6 2UX.
COHEN, Mr. Andrew Selwyn, FCA 1987; 34 Highfield Gardens, LONDON, NW11 9HB.
•COHEN, Mr. Andrew Simon Reisler, BSocSc ACA 2002; (Tax Fac), Freedman Frankl & Taylor, Reedham House, 31 King Street West, MANCHESTER, M3 2PJ.
COHEN, Mr. Andrew Trevor, MA ACA 1982; (Tax Fac), 10 Gurney Drive, East Finchley, LONDON, N2 0DG.
•COHEN, Mr. Anthony, FCA 1969; Donald Jacobs & Partners, Suite 2 1st Floor, Fountain House, 1a Elm Park, STANMORE, HA7 4AU.
•COHEN, Mr. Anthony Jeremy, BA FCA 1991; (Tax Fac), with FSPG, 21 Bedford Square, LONDON, WC1B 3HH.
•COHEN, Mr. Anthony Joseph Henry, BA FCA 1971; (Tax Fac), Monahans, 38-42 Newport Street, SWINDON, SN1 3DR.
COHEN, Mr. Anthony Steven, BA ACA 1982; 65 Forest Side, North Chingford, LONDON, E4 6BA.
•COHEN, Mr. Arnold Judah, FCA 1962; Cohen Arnold, New Burlington House, 1075 Finchley Road, Temple Fortune, LONDON, NW11 0PU. See also Cohen Arnold & Co
•COHEN, Mr. Brian Jonathan, BA ACA 1992; Brian Cohen, 88 Camden Road, LONDON, NW1 9EA.
COHEN, Mr. Bruce James Rodney, MA LLM FCA 1964; 32 Abbotsbury Close, Kensington, LONDON, W14 8EG. (Life Member)
COHEN, Mr. Christopher Ben, MEng ACA 2005; Mitie Group PLC, Unit 1, Harlequin Office Park, Fieldfare, Emersons Green, BRISTOL BS16 7FN.
COHEN, Mr. Cyril, BA FCA 1966; Flat 32, Hilton Lodge, Hilton Lane, Prestwich, MANCHESTER, M25 9SA.
COHEN, Mr. Daniel Charles, BSc FCA 1973; 25 Berwyn Road, RICHMOND, TW10 5BP.
COHEN, Mr. David Elliot, BA FCA 1976; (Tax Fac), 12 Avenue Road, PINNER, MIDDLESEX, HA5 3HA.
COHEN, Mr. David Harvey, FCA 1971; 59 Rue Rouelle, 75015 PARIS, FRANCE. (Life Member)
COHEN, Mr. David Meyer, FCA 1958; 48 Gurney Drive, LONDON, N2 0DE. (Life Member)
COHEN, Mr. David Michael, FCA 1967; (Tax Fac), 43 Bodley Road, NEW MALDEN, SURREY, KT3 5QD.
COHEN, Mr. David Mordecai, FCA 1964; 16 Dorset Square, LONDON, NW1 6QB. (Life Member)
•COHEN, Miss. Deborah Barbara, BSc FCA 1986; 52 Harvist Road, Queens Park, LONDON, NW6 6SH.
•COHEN, Mr. Des, FCA 1995; Baginsky Cohen, 930 High Road, North Finchley, LONDON, N12 9RT.
COHEN, Mr. Edward Sassoon, FCA 1964; 5 Rehov Elroi, 92108 JERUSALEM, ISRAEL. (Life Member)
•COHEN, Mr. Elliot Victor, FCA 1974; SCB (Accountants) Limited, 31 Sackville Street, MANCHESTER, M1 3LZ. See also Shacter Cohen & Bor LLP
•COHEN, Mr. Errol Frederick, BSc ACA 1981; (Tax Fac), E F Cohen & Co, 21A Russell Gardens, LONDON, NW11 9NJ.
•COHEN, Mr. Ezra Hayim, FCA 1969; E.H. Cohen & Co, 58 Anthony Road, BOREHAMWOOD, HERTFORDSHIRE, WD6 4NG.
COHEN, Mr. Gary Stephen, BA ACA 1999; 3 Tate Gardens, BUSHEY, WD23 4GS.
COHEN, Mr. George Nigel, FCA 1983; Chalkpit Nurseries, Chalk Pit Lane, Burnham, SLOUGH, SL1 8NH.
COHEN, Mr. Gerald Ray, FCA 1966; 41 Southover, Woodside Park, LONDON, N12 7JG.
•COHEN, Mr. Gerard Philip, BSc FCA 1983; Clive House, 2 Old Brewery Mews, LONDON, NW3 1PZ.
•COHEN, Mr. Giles, BA FCA FCCA 1988; Numera Partners LLP, 6th Floor, Charles House, 108-110 Finchley Road, LONDON, NW3 5JJ.
•COHEN, Mr. Graham, BSc FCA 1973; Graham Cohen & Co Limited, 16 South End, CROYDON, SURREY, CR0 1DN. See also Croydon Business Centre Limited and Aynesley Walters Cohen Ltd
COHEN, Mr. Hal, ACA 2009; 159b East End Road, LONDON, N2 0LY.
COHEN, Mr. Harvey, FCA 1955; 97 Rehov Kaplan, 46606 HERZLIA PETUACH, ISRAEL. (Life Member)
COHEN, Miss. Hilary Susanne, BSc ACA 1990; 11 Willow Close, Unsworth, BURY, BL9 8NU.
•COHEN, Mr. Howard John, FCA 1972; Howard Cohen, Tall Trees, 15a Dean Park Road, BOURNEMOUTH, BH1 1HU.
•COHEN, Mr. Ian Michael, FCA 1969; (Tax Fac), Cohen Davidson Limited, 7 Marlborough Place, BRIGHTON-LE-SANDS, BN1 1UB.
•COHEN, Mr. Ian Richard, FCA 1974; UHY Hacker Young LLP, Quadrant House, 4 Thomas More Square, LONDON, E1W 1YW.
COHEN, Mr. Ilan Louis, BSc(Hons) ACA 2008; 32 The Drive, EDGWARE, MIDDLESEX, HA8 8PT.
COHEN, Mr. Ilan Wayne, ACA 2008; 5 Grange Close, EDGWARE, MIDDLESEX, HA8 9PQ.
COHEN, Mr. Irvin Milton, LLB FCA MABRP 1990; with Begbies Traynor, 32 Cornhill, LONDON, EC3V 3BT.
COHEN, Mr. Ivor, ACA 1981; 44 Briar Road, HARROW, MIDDLESEX, HA3 0DR.
COHEN, Mr. Ivor Malcolm, FCA 1951; 29 Dalkeith Grove, STANMORE, HA7 4SQ. (Life Member)
COHEN, Mr. Jason, BA ACA 1995; Tudor House, Park Avenue, RADLETT, HERTFORDSHIRE, WD7 7DZ.
COHEN, Mr. Jason Jonathan, BSc ACA 2000; 21 Marion Road, Furnace Green, CRAWLEY, RH10 6QQ.
COHEN, Mr. John Robert, FCA 1969; Dandara Holdings Ltd, Dadara Group Head office, Isle of Man Business Park, Douglas, ISLE OF MAN, IM2 2SA.

COHEN, Mr. Jonathan, TD MA FCA *1971;* Dancing Hill High Street, East Hendred, WANTAGE, OXFORDSHIRE, OX12 8JY.
COHEN, Mr. Jonathan, ACA *2008;* 168 Bethune Road, LONDON, N16 5DS.
COHEN, Mr. Jonathan, BA(Hons) ACA *2011;* 24A Dartmouth Park Avenue, LONDON, NW5 1JN.
COHEN, Mr. Jonathan, ACA *2011;* Flat 29 Fairacres, 164 East End Road, LONDON, N2 0RR.
•COHEN, Mr. Jonathan Brett, FCA *1984;* (Tax Fac), Brett Adams, 25 Manchester Square, LONDON, W1U 3PY.
COHEN, Mr. Jonathan Mark, BSc(Hons) FCA *2001;* with Virgin Management Limited, The School House, 50 Brook Green, LONDON, W6 7RR.
COHEN, Mr. Jonathan Michael, BA(Hons) FCA *1995;* 14 Clandon Road, Allerton, LIVERPOOL, L18 9UL.
COHEN, Mr. Josef Baruch, BSc FCA *1957;* Suite 3600, 60 Broad Street, NEW YORK, NY 10004, UNITED STATES.
COHEN, Mr. Julian Gavril, BSc ACA *1986;* ELCY Ltd, 5 Spring Villa Park, EDGWARE, MIDDLESEX, HA8 7EB.
COHEN, Miss. Lauren, ACA *2009;* 81 Bishops Road, Prestwich, MANCHESTER, M25 0AS.
COHEN, Mr. Laurence, FCA *1955;* 1 Carlisle Lodge, 82 Hendon Lane, LONDON, N3 1RR. (Life Member)
•COHEN, Mr. Laurence Anthony, FCA *1969;* Laurence A Cohen, 25 Hartfield Avenue, Elstree, BOREHAMWOOD, WD6 3JB.
•COHEN, Mr. Laurence David, BSc FCA *1977;* Ballards Newman (Finchley) Limited, Apex House, Grand Arcade, Tally Ho Corner, LONDON, N12 0EH.
•COHEN, Mr. Laurence Sydney, FCA *1968;* Gordon Down & Partners, 275 Cowbridge Road East, CARDIFF, CF5 1JB. See also Able Consulting Services Limited
COHEN, Mr. Leslie Harold, FCA *1953;* 5 Westchester Court, Westchester Drive, LONDON, NW4 1RB. (Life Member)
•①COHEN, Mr. Malcolm, BSc FCA *1982;* BDO LLP, 55 Baker Street, LONDON, W1U 7EU. See also BDO Stoy Hayward LLP
COHEN, Mr. Mark Harvey Saxe, FCA *1977;* 11 The Maples, ROSLYN ESTATES, NY 11576, UNITED STATES.
COHEN, Mr. Martin Benjamin, FCA *1963;* Flat 38, Free Trade Wharf, 340 The Highway, LONDON, E1W 3ES. (Life Member)
COHEN, Mr. Max, FCA *1966;* Great Oaks House, Puttenden Road, Shipbourne, TONBRIDGE, KENT, TN11 9RX.
•COHEN, Mr. Michael, FCA *1972;* with Freedman Frankl & Taylor, Reedham House, 31 King Street West, MANCHESTER, M3 2PJ.
COHEN, Mr. Michael George, BSc ACA *1990;* 8 Hadley Close, Elstree, BOREHAMWOOD, WD6 3LB.
COHEN, Mr. Neil Matthew, ACA *2011;* 11 Barn Crescent, STANMORE, MIDDLESEX, HA7 2RY.
COHEN, Mr. Norman Alan, BA FCA *1955;* 69 Holmleigh Road, LONDON, N16 5QG. (Life Member)
COHEN, Mr. Paul Anthony, FCA *1959;* 14 Brampton Grove, LONDON, NW4 4AG. (Life Member)
COHEN, Mr. Ralph, BSc ACA *1990;* 124 Barking Road, LONDON, E16 1EN.
COHEN, Mr. Ralph Leslie, FCA *1970;* Fire Testing Technology Ltd Unit 19, Charlwoods Road, EAST GRINSTEAD, WEST SUSSEX, RH19 2HL.
COHEN, Mr. Raymond Francis, FCA *1979;* 25 A Santos Street cor R Avancena, Phase 2 BF Homes, PARANAQUE 1718, METRO MANILA, PHILIPPINES.
•COHEN, Mr. Richard Lawrence, FCA *1975;* 36 Broadhurst Avenue, EDGWARE, MIDDLESEX, HA8 8TS.
COHEN, Rabbi Richard Solomon, ACA *1986;* 73 Avne Hahoshen Street, Har Shmuel, 90917 GIVAT ZEEV, ISRAEL.
COHEN, Mr. Robert Paul, BSocSc ACA *2003;* Enterprise House, 21 Buckle Street, LONDON, E1 8NN.
•COHEN, Mr. Samuel David, FCA *1973;* (Tax Fac), SL Accountancy Limited, Lear House, 259 Cranbrook Road, ILFORD, ESSEX, IG1 4TG. See also Deanbrook Accounting Services Ltd
•COHEN, Mr. Samuel Vidal Moses, BA FCA *1995;* 21 Engineer Lane, GIBRALTAR, GX11 1AA, GIBRALTAR. See also Benady Cohen & Co
COHEN, Mr. Shai, ACA *2008;* 27 Gyles Park, STANMORE, MIDDLESEX, HA7 1AN.
COHEN, Mr. Simon Antony, BSc ACA *1991;* 15 The Mead, BECKENHAM, BR3 5PE.
•①COHEN, Mr. Solomon, FCA *1965;* Pitman Cohen Recoveries LLP, Great Central House, Great Central Avenue, RUISLIP, MIDDLESEX, HA4 6TS.
COHEN, Mrs. Susan Eva Gottlieb, BA ACA DChA *1993;* 2 Broadway, CHEADLE, CHESHIRE, SK8 1NQ.
COHEN, Mrs. Susan Yvonne, FCA *1985;* 14 Broadfields Avenue, EDGWARE, HA8 8PG.
COHEN, Mrs. Talia, BA(Hons) ACA *2009;* 32 Johns Avenue, LONDON, NW4 4EN.
COHEN, Mr. Timothy Peter Reginald, FCA *1986;* Chalkpit Nurseries, Chalk Pit Lane, Burnham, SLOUGH, SL1 8NH.
COHEN, Mr. Toby, BSc ACA *2001;* 144 Tranmere Road, LONDON, SW18 3QU.
•COHEN, Mr. Vivian Marcel, BSc FCA *1981;* with Frenkels Forensics, Churchill House, 137 Brent Street, LONDON, NW4 4DJ.
COHEN, Mr. Warren Harvey, BA ACA *1995;* 40 Southway, LONDON, NW11 6SA.
COHEN, Mr. Warwick Gilden, FCA *1970;* 84 Old Church Lane, STANMORE, HA7 2RR.
COHN, Mr. Anthony Michael Hardy, BA ACA *1997;* The Stables, Lodge Hill Road, Lower Bourne, FARNHAM, SURREY, GU10 3RD.
COHN, Mr. Michael Herbert, FCA *1973;* 48 Santa Catalina Drive, RANCHO PALOS VERDES, CA 90275, UNITED STATES. (Life Member)
COHN, Mr. Ronald Peter Hardy, BSc FCA *1971;* 5 Mountway, POTTERS BAR, HERTFORDSHIRE, EN6 1ER.
COILEY, Mr. Jonathan Charles Adrian, BEng FCA *1999;* The Gable House Yattendon Road, Hermitage, THATCHAM, RG18 9RG.
•COISH, Mrs. Janet Ann, FCA *1969;* (Tax Fac), Janet Coish, 2 Paradise Square, BEVERLEY, HU17 0HG.
COKE, Mr. Iain Douglas, MPhil LLB ACA *2002;* with ICAEW, Chartered Accountants' Hall, Moorgate Place, LONDON, EC2P 2BJ.
COKE, Mr. John Charles, BA FCA *1983;* Wickens Birch Grove Horsted Keynes, HAYWARDS HEATH, WEST SUSSEX, RH17 7BT.
COKE, Miss. Stephanie, ACA *2009;* 79 Beulah Grove, CROYDON, CR0 2QW.
•COKE, Mr. Stephen John, ACA FRSA *1986;* (Tax Fac), C.B. Heslop & Co, 1 High Street, THATCHAM, RG19 3JG.
•COKE-WALLIS, Mr. Piers Ross, BA FCA *1989;* Le Florestan, 35 Boulevard du Larvotto, M9800 MONTE CARLO, MONACO.
COKELL, Miss. Sian Elizabeth, BSc ACA *2009;* 51 Eastern Arterial Road, ST. IVES, NSW 2075, AUSTRALIA.
COKER, Mr. Andrew, BSc ACA *1993;* Studio Lambert Limited, 2nd Floor 42 Beak Street, LONDON, W1F 9RH.
COKER, Bryan Sydney, Esq MBE FCA *1953;* 14 College Avenue, GRAYS, RM17 5UW. (Life Member)
COKER, Mr. Christopher, BSc ACA *1993;* 80 Clarendon Drive, Putney, LONDON, SW15 1AH.
COKER, Miss. Eugenia Aderonke, BSc ACA *2011;* Flat 24, Spencer Court, 208 Woodcote Road, WALLINGTON, SURREY, SM6 0PJ.
COKER, Mr. John Edwin, FCA *1969;* 3 Somersall Willows, CHESTERFIELD, S40 3SR. (Life Member)
COKER, Mr. Nicholas Andrew, ACA MAAT *2003;* Unit 1, 23 Dalleys Road, NAREMBURN, NSW 2065, AUSTRALIA.
COKER, Ms. Oluwatoyin Olufemi, BA ACA *1990;* Mockbeggar Oast, Collier Street, TONBRIDGE, TN12 9RJ.
COKER, Mr. Stephen William, ACA *1986;* 26 West Drive, SUTTON, SURREY, SM2 7NA.
COKER, Mr. William Joseph, BSc ACA *1993;* 8 Westville Road, THAMES DITTON, SURREY, KT7 0UJ.
•COLACO, Mr. Nelson Rosario, FCA *1983;* (Tax Fac), BSG Valentine, Lynton House, 7/12 Tavistock Square, LONDON, WC1H 9BQ.
COLADANGELO, Mr. Carmine Aurelio, BSc(Econ) ACA *1998;* 4 Coopers Close, Biddenham, BEDFORD, MK40 4DH.
COLADANGELO, Mrs. Michelina, BA ACA *1997;* Holly Tree House, 4 Cooper Close, Biddenham, BEDFORD, MK40 4DH.
COLAH, Mr. Homi Rustamji, ACA *1980;* 66 Belsize Park, LONDON, NW3 4EH.
COLAM, Mrs. Rachel Anne, BCom ACA *1988;* ISCA, Court Wood, NEWTON FERRERS, PLYMOUTH, PL8 1BW.
COLANGELI, Mr. Matteo, MSc BA ACA *2002;* 16 Nemyrovycha-Danchenka Street, 01133 KIEV, UKRAINE.
COLATO, Mr. Michael Andrew, BSc ACA *1990;* Cinven Services Ltd Warwick Court, 5 Paternoster Square, LONDON, EC4M 7AG.
COLBEAR, Mr. Jonathan, BSc ACA *2004;* Neuberger Berman Lansdowne House, 57 Berkeley Square, LONDON, W1J 6ER.
•COLBECK, Mr. Andrew, FCA *1975;* (Tax Fac), Andrew Colbeck, 313a Ipswich Road, COLCHESTER, CO4 0HN.
COLBECK, Mr. Stephen Mark, BSc ACA *2006;* Landis & Gyr Pty Ltd, 60 O'Riordan Street, SYDNEY, NSW 2015, AUSTRALIA.
COLBERT, Mrs. Deborah Louise, BA FCA *1996;* B D O Stoy Hayward Llp Kreston House, 66 Broomfield Road, CHELMSFORD, CM1 1SW.
COLBERT, Mr. Denzil Lewis, FCA *1967;* 65 Shelford Road, CAMBRIDGE, CB2 9LZ. (Life Member)
COLBERT, Mr. Graham Peter, BSc ACA *1989;* Astra Zeneca Ltd, 2 Kingdom Street, LONDON, W2 6BD.
COLBORN, Mr. Timothy Michael, MA ACA *1982;* KFC GB Ltd, 32 Goldsworth Road, WOKING, SURREY, GU21 6JT.
COLBORNE-BABER, Mrs. Clare Louise, BSc(Hons) ACA *2002;* Nandina 10 Bowes Road, WALTON-ON-THAMES, SURREY, KT12 3HS.
•COLBORNE-BABER, Mr. Julian Peter, BSc ACA *2001;* Deloitte LLP, Athene Place, 66 Shoe Lane, LONDON, EC4A 3BQ. See also Deloitte & Touche LLP
COLBOURNE, Mr. Colin James, FCA *1966;* 3 Woodstock Road, Burton, CHRISTCHURCH, DORSET, BH23 7HY.
COLBOURNE, Miss. Emily Jane, BA ACA *2006;* 16 Perrycroft, WINDSOR, SL4 4HJ.
COLBOURNE, Miss. Jennifer Anne, BSc ACA *1992;* UK Home Office, Costco Wholesale (UK) Ltd, Hartspring Lane, WATFORD, WD25 8JS.
COLBOURNE, Mr. Martin James, BA(Hons) ACA *2002;* with PricewaterhouseCoopers LLP, The Atrium, St. Georges Street, NORWICH, NR3 1AG.
COLBOURNE, Mrs. Sally Elizabeth, BSc ACA *1990;* 125 Meadow Road, MALVERN, WR14 2SA.
COLBRAN, Mr. Trevor Keith, BSc ACA *1983;* Kent County Council, Brenchley House, Week Street, MAIDSTONE, KENT, ME14 1RF.
COLBY, Mr. Derrick Andrew, BA ACA *1988;* Via Fiume 16, Riva del Garda, 38066 TRENTO, ITALY.
COLCHESTER, Mr. Giles Sparrow, BSc FCA *1978;* 38 Myddelton Square, LONDON, EC1R 1YB.
COLCLOUGH, Mr. David Anthony, BSc ACA *1989;* 6 Nevada Close, Great Sankey, WARRINGTON, WA5 5WW.
•COLCLOUGH, Mr. James Samuel, FCA *1976;* Flat 24 La Mondine Apartments, Greve D'azette, St. Clement, JERSEY, JE2 6TZ.
COLCLOUGH, Mr. Mark, ACA *2009;* Flat 1 Cygnus Court, 850 Brighton Road, PURLEY, CR8 2FB.
•COLCLOUGH, Mrs. Michelle, BSc ACA *2001;* Bright Grahame Murray, 131 Edgware Road, LONDON, W2 2AP.
COLCOMB, Mr. Mark, BSc FCA *1992;* 68 Lanelay Road, Talbot Green, PONTYCLUN, MID GLAMORGAN, CF72 8HY.
COLCOMBE, Mr. Paul Andrew, BA ACA *1998;* Scotch Firs, Longney, GLOUCESTER, GL2 3SW.
COLDERICK, Mr. Malcolm Stuart, BSc FCA *1984;* PricewaterhouseCoopers, Darling Park Tower 2, 201 Sussex Street, GPO Box 2650, SYDNEY, NSW 1171 AUSTRALIA.
COLDHAM, Mrs. Frances Clare, BSc(Hons) ACA *2004;* with PricewaterhouseCoopers LLP, Donington Court, Pegasus Business Park, Castle Donington, DERBY, DE74 2UZ.
COLDRAKE, Mr. Robert, BA ACA *2003;* 18 Sunderland Grove, WATFORD, WD25 7GL.
•COLDWELL, Mr. Andrew Keith, BA FCA *1987;* Moore Stephens (South) LLP, 33 The Clarendon Centre, Salisbury Business Park, Dairy Meadow Lane, SALISBURY, SP1 2TJ. See also Moore Secretaries Limited
COLDWELL, Mr. David John, FCA *1966;* South Lodge, Wade Lane, HAVANT, PO9 2TB. (Life Member)
COLDWELL, Mr. Richard James, BA ACA *1996;* 18 Blenheim Mews, SHEFFIELD, S11 9PR.
COLDWELL, Mr. Stafford Reginald, FCA *1948;* Flat 1 Meadowbank, Eversley Park Road, Winchmore Hill, LONDON, N21 1JE. (Life Member)
COLE, Mr. Alan Edward, BSc FCA *1982;* P.O.Box N-9934, NASSAU, BAHAMAS.
•COLE, Mr. Alistair Bernard, FCA *1978;* with Menzies, 1st floor Midas House, 62 Goldsworth Road, WOKING, SURREY GU21 6LQ.
•COLE, Miss. Andrea Jane Merrill, BA ACA *2001;* KPMG LLP, 15 Canada Square, LONDON, E14 5GL. See also KPMG Audit plc
•COLE, Mr. Andrew Albert, MA FCA *1977;* (Tax Fac), Cole & Co, 15 Emperor Close, BERKHAMSTED, HP4 1TD.
•COLE, Mr. Andrew Francis, MBA BSc ACA *2000;* with KPMG LLP, 15 Canada Square, LONDON, E14 5GL.
COLE, Mr. Andrew Kevin, FCA *1985;* 23 Townsend Lane, HARPENDEN, AL5 2PY.
COLE, Mr. Andrew Lewis, MSci ACA *2010;* Flat 6, 406 St. John Street, LONDON, EC1V 4ND.
COLE, Mr. Andrew Stephen, BSc ACA *1988;* (Tax Fac), Euro Hair Fashion UK Ltd, PO BOX 144, HAILSHAM, EAST SUSSEX, BN27 3YT.
COLE, Mr. Anthony Bernard, BSc FCA *1975;* 61 Du Cros Drive, STANMORE, MIDDLESEX, HA7 4TL.
COLE, Mr. Anthony Jack, FCA *1964;* Fairways, Neb Lane, OXTED, RH8 9JN.
•COLE, Mr. Anthony Maurice, FCA CTA *1979;* Tony Cole & Co, 227 London Road, North End, PORTSMOUTH, PO2 9AJ.
COLE, Mr. Antony Edward, FCA *1962;* Janton Lodge, 3 Argyle Road, CLEVEDON, AVON, BS21 7BP.
COLE, Mr. Basil Harold, FCA *1950;* 6 The Spinney, Grange Lane, Thurnby, LEICESTER, LE7 9QS. (Life Member)
COLE, Mrs. Carol Jane, FCA *1975;* Cavarcou, 13 Sycamore Avenue, Chandlers Ford, EASTLEIGH, SO53 5RJ.
COLE, Mrs. Catherine, BA *1999;* with Warings Business Advisers LLP, Bedford House, 60 Chorley New Road, BOLTON, BL1 4DA.
COLE, Mr. Christopher Michael, BA ACA *1993;* 30 Lucas Avenue, HARROW, MIDDLESEX, HA2 9UJ.
•COLE, Mr. Daniel John, BA FCA *1999;* Hale & Company LLP, Ground Floor, Belmont Place, Belmont Road, MAIDENHEAD, BERKSHIRE SL6 6TB. See also Hale & Company
COLE, Mr. Daniel Paul, BA(Hons) ACA *2003;* Free Hill Farm Free Hill, Westbury sub Mendip, WELLS, SOMERSET, BA5 1HR.
•COLE, Mr. David Anthony, FCA *1987;* (Tax Fac), LBCA Limited, 8 Waterside, Station Road, HARPENDEN, HERTFORDSHIRE, AL5 4US.
COLE, Mr. David Douglas, BSc ACA *1987;* 10 Manston Way, ST. ALBANS, AL4 0AG.
COLE, Mr. David Geoffrey, BA ACA *1981;* 2 Salisbury Place, Tytherington, MACCLESFIELD, SK10 2HP.
COLE, Mr. David Gordon, FCA *1966;* 24 Old Sneed Rd, Stoke Bishop, BRISTOL, BS9 1ET.
COLE, Mr. David John, BSc ACA *1992;* The Old School House, North Lane, Weston-On-The-Green, BICESTER, OXFORDSHIRE, OX25 3RG.
COLE, Mrs. Dawn Nicola, BA ACA *1995;* 97 St. Werburghs Road, Chorlton Cum Hardy, MANCHESTER, M21 8UJ.
COLE, Mr. Denis Oliver, OBE FCA *1963;* Bay Willow Cottage, 8 Darvells Yard, Chorleywood, RICKMANSWORTH, HERTFORDSHIRE, WD3 5QG.
•COLE, Mr. Denys Lucien Hubert, FCA *1972;* Blease Lloyd Associates, Banholzsirasse 16, Box 381, FL 9490 VADUZ, LIECHTENSTEIN.
COLE, Mrs. Elizabeth Ann, BSc ACA *2004;* 7 Prospect Drive, CARDIFF, CF5 2HL.
•COLE, Miss. Elizabeth-Anne, BA ACA *1989;* (Tax Fac), French Associates, The Swan Centre, Fishers Lane, Chiswick, LONDON, W4 1RX.
COLE, Miss. Emily Margaret, BA ACA *2006;* 25 Windmill Street, TUNBRIDGE WELLS, TN2 4UU.
COLE, Mrs. Fiona Jane, BTech ACA *1986;* c/o Mr A Julian Cole, JPMorgan Chase Bank, 168 Robinson Road, 17th Fl Capital Tower, SINGAPORE 068912, SINGAPORE.
•COLE, Mr. Gary Peter, FCA *1973;* G.P. Cole & Co, Suite 2 Ground Floor, 5 Hercules Way, Leavesden, WATFORD, WD25 7GS.
•COLE, Mr. Geoffrey Harry, FCA *1985;* Burton Sweet Limited, Exhibition House, 23 Spa Road, GLOUCESTER, GL1 1UY. See also Burton Sweet
•COLE, Mr. Geoffrey Stanley John, FCA *1973;* (Tax Fac), Geoffrey Cole & Co Ltd, 4 Reading Road, Pangbourne, READING, RG8 7LY.
COLE, Mr. George Barry Daniel, FCA *1960;* Phillips Farm, Stockerston, OAKHAM, RUTLAND, LE15 9JF. (Life Member)
COLE, Mr. Graham, BA FCA *1971;* The Old Farm House Cricklade Street, Poulton, CIRENCESTER, GLOUCESTERSHIRE, GL7 5HS.
COLE, Mr. Graham Alan Jocelyn, BA ACA *1993;* Ramblers Cottage, Layters Green Lane, Chalfont St. Peter, GERRARDS CROSS, BUCKINGHAMSHIRE, SL9 8TH.
•COLE, Mr. Graham Laurence, BA FCA *1990;* Wenn Townsend, 30 St Giles', OXFORD, OX1 3LE. See also Wenn Townsend Accountants Limited
COLE, Mrs. Helen Iris, ACA *1980;* 5 Raad-ny-Gabbil, Castletown, ISLE OF MAN, IM9 1HH.
•COLE, Mr. Ian Malcolm, ACA FCCA *2010;* Miller Davies, Unit A3, Broomsleigh Business Park, Worsley Bridge Road, LONDON, SE26 5BN.
COLE, Mr. Ian Michael, BSc(Econ) ACA *1997;* 12 New Road, Gellinudd, Pontardawe, SWANSEA, SA8 3DY.

COLE, Mr. Ian Michael Russell, BSc ACA *1979;* 10 Glenure Road, Eltham, LONDON, SE9 1UF.

COLE, Mr. Ian Robert, BSc FCA *1979;* Ridgemead House, 143 Amblecote Road, BRIERLEY HILL, DY5 2YD.

COLE, Mr. Ian Roy, BSc FCA *1986;* 103 Wodeland Avenue, GUILDFORD, GU2 4LD.

COLE, Mr. Ian William, FCA *1975;* 10 Cromwell Avenue, Penyuern, NEATH, SA10 8DW.

COLE, Mrs. Jennifer Ann Medina, BSc(Hons) ACA *2002;* Tangara, Ashley, Box, CORSHAM, WILTSHIRE, SN13 8AQ.

•**COLE, Mrs. Jennifer Dawn, BSc ACA** *2003;* Jennifer Cole, The Rookery, Burton Hill, MALMESBURY, WILTSHIRE, SN16 0EL.

•**COLE, Mr. Jeremy Benjamin, BA FCA CF** *1985;* Cole Associates Corporate Finance, 19 Spring Gardens, MANCHESTER, M2 1FB.

COLE, Mrs. Joanna Blanche, BSc(Hons) ACA *2001;* 38A College Road South, RIVERVIEW, NSW 2066, AUSTRALIA.

COLE, Ms. Joanna Renata Katherine, BSc ACA *1992;* C/o Cargill Srl, Via girardo Patecchio 4, 20141 MILAN, ITALY.

COLE, Mrs. Joanne Carolyn, BA ACA *1993;* 205 The Homend, LEDBURY, HR8 1BS.

COLE, Miss. Joanne Lesley, BA(Hons) ACA *2001;* 1 Highcrest Avenue, Gatley, CHEADLE, CHESHIRE, SK8 4HD.

COLE, Mr. John David Merrill, BA FCA *1973;* Longdown House, 4 Sunnydale Road, SWANAGE, BH19 2JA. (Life Member)

•**COLE, Mr. John Granville, BSc ACA** *1979;* Ernst & Young LLP, 1 More London Place, LONDON, SE1 2AF. See also Ernst & Young Europe LLP

COLE, Mr. John Metcalfe, FCA *1951;* 12 Wheatfield Road, HARPENDEN, AL5 2NY. (Life Member)

COLE, The Revd. John Spensley, MA FCA *1965;* 11 Long Meadow, Farnsfield, NEWARK, NOTTINGHAMSHIRE, NG22 8DR.

COLE, Mr. Jonathan Robert, FCA *1971;* World Fuel Services Europe Ltd, Portland House, Bressenden Place, LONDON, SW1E 5BH.

COLE, Mrs. Judy Dianne, ACA *1988;* Launceston Medical Centre, Landlake Road, LAUNCESTON, CORNWALL, PL15 9HH.

COLE, Mr. Justin Mark, BCom ACA *1993;* Castlewood, Llanfair Disgoed, CHEPSTOW, NP16 6LX.

COLE, Mr. Kenneth Brian, FCA *1951;* 19 Town Road, Quarrington, SLEAFORD, LINCOLNSHIRE, NG34 8RT. (Life Member)

COLE, Mr. Kevin James, BSc ACA *1993;* 23 Tamorisk Drive, Totton, SOUTHAMPTON, SO40 8UD.

•**COLE, Mr. Leslie Ronald, FCA** *1956;* (Tax Fac), Cole & Co, 400 Harrow Rd, LONDON, W9 2HU.

COLE, Miss. Madeline Jane, BA(Hons) ACA *2001;* 64 Porteous Crescent, Chandler's Ford, EASTLEIGH, HAMPSHIRE, SO53 2DH.

COLE, Mrs. Marilyn Dawn, BSc FCA *1979;* Hole Farm, Farnham Lane, Langton Green, TUNBRIDGE WELLS, TN3 0JS.

COLE, Mr. Mark Andrew, ACA *2008;* with Beever and Struthers, 3rd Floor, Alperton House, Bridgewater Road, WEMBLEY, MIDDLESEX HA0 1EH.

•**COLE, Mr. Mark Christopher Nicholas, BA FCA** *1984;* (Tax Fac), Bright Grahame Murray, 131 Edgware Road, LONDON, W2 2AP.

COLE, Mr. Mark Daniel, BA(Hons) ACA *2000;* 10745 Maple Chase Drive, BOCA RATON, FL 33498, UNITED STATES.

COLE, Mr. Matthew, BSocSc ACA *1996;* 43b Trentino Road, TURRAMURRA, NSW 2074, AUSTRALIA.

COLE, Mr. Maurice George, FCA *1968;* Dormer House, Banbury Lane, Thorpe Mandeville, BANBURY, OX17 2HR. (Life Member)

COLE, Mr. Michael Eric, FCA *1975;* (Tax Fac), 7 Blackbrook Park Avenue, FAREHAM, HAMPSHIRE, PO15 5JJ.

•**COLE, Mr. Michael John, FCA** *1975;* PRB Accountants LLP, Kingfisher House, Hurstwood Grange, Hurstwood Lane, HAYWARDS HEATH, WEST SUSSEX RH17 7QX. See also PRB Martin Pollins LLP

•**COLE, Mr. Michael Maurice, FCA** *1967;* Michael Cole & Co, 10 Cecil Road, LONDON, N14 5RJ.

COLE, Mr. Michael William, FCA *1956;* Nansawsan House, Ladock, TRURO, TR2 4PW.

COLE, Mr. Nathan Brynley, BA ACA *1999;* 12 Laurel Way, Bottesford, NOTTINGHAM, NG13 0FP.

COLE, Mr. Neil William, ACA *2005;* with KPMG LLP, One Snowhill, Snow Hill Queensway, BIRMINGHAM, B4 6GN.

COLE, Mr. Nicholas David, FCA *1982;* Apartment 6 Magnolia Villa, La Route de St. Aubin St. Lawrence, JERSEY, JE3 1LW.

COLE, Mr. Nigel William, BSc ACA *1980;* Kidde Products Limited, Station Road, High Bentham, LANCASTER, LANCASHIRE, LA2 7NA.

COLE, Miss. Patricia, MBT MBA BA FCA CPA CFA *1974;* 101 Lombard Street, Apt. 415 East, SAN FRANCISCO, CA 94111, UNITED STATES. (Life Member)

•**COLE, Mr. Peter, FCA** *1983;* CTC, 13 Portland Terrace, Jesmond, NEWCASTLE UPON TYNE, NE2 1SN. See also Rowlands Newcastle

•**COLE, Mr. Philip Andrew Reginald, FCA** *1983;* Sproull & Co, 31-33 College Road, HARROW, MIDDLESEX, HA1 1EJ.

COLE, Mr. Philip Neal, BA ACA *1992;* 15 St. Marys Grove, Chiswick, LONDON, W4 3LL.

COLE, Mrs. Rachel Elizabeth, ACA *1993;* 15 Margaret Road, Headington, OXFORD, OX3 8NJ.

COLE, Mr. Richard John, BSc ACA *1995;* 16 Breton Close, Upton, CHESTER, CH2 1HY.

COLE, Mr. Richard Thomas, ACA *2008;* 13 Leicester Road, SALE, CHESHIRE, M33 7DU.

COLE, Mr. Robert Alan, FCA *1959;* 7 Lordell Place, West Side Common, LONDON, SW19 4UY. (Life Member)

COLE, Mr. Robert Maurice, FCA *1974;* 3 Oaks Crescent, Chapel Ash, WOLVERHAMPTON, WV3 9SA.

COLE, Mr. Roy Charles, FCA *1959;* 14 Tyrrells Road, BILLERICAY, CM11 2QE. (Life Member)

COLE, Mr. Rupert Ellison, BA ACA *1984;* Burford House, Woodland Way, Kingswood, TADWORTH, KT20 6NW.

COLE, Miss. Samantha Jane, ACA *2010;* 206 Manor Way, Risca, NEWPORT, GWENT, NP11 6AE.

COLE, Mrs. Sandra, BSc ACA *1988;* Charter Central Services, 322 High Holborn, LONDON, WC1V 7PB.

COLE, Mrs. Sarah Jane, BSc ACA *1995;* 10 Lime Road, Walton Cardiff, TEWKESBURY, GL20 7RJ.

•**COLE, Mr. Sheldon Andrew, BA FCA CTA** *1997;* (Tax Fac), Albert Goodman LLP, Mary Street House, Mary Street, TAUNTON, TA1 3NW.

COLE, Mr. Simon Richard, BSc ACA *1982;* 7 rues des Alpes, PO Box 1380, CH-1211 GENEVA, SWITZERLAND.

COLE, Mr. Stanley Ernest Diwaniyah, FCA *1952;* 4 Fernhill Lane, FARNHAM, SURREY, GU9 0JJ. (Life Member)

COLE, Mr. Stephen Anthony, BA FCA *1976;* 604 City Pavilion, 33 Britton Street, LONDON, EC1M 5UG.

COLE, Mr. Stuart, FCA CTA *1980;* Maisons Marques Et Domaines, 4 College Mews, LONDON, SW18 2SJ.

COLE, Mr. Stuart Paul, BSocSc ACA ATII *1998;* 13 Hazelhurst, BECKENHAM, BR3 5TL.

COLE, Mrs. Tanya, BA ACA *1997;* 211 Rye Street, BISHOP'S STORTFORD, HERTFORDSHIRE, CM23 2HE.

COLE, Mrs. Theresa Bridget, LLB ACA *2005;* 1 Grenadier Close, North Brickhill, BEDFORD, MK41 7GG.

COLE, Mr. Timothy Phillip, ACA MAAT *2002;* 1 Beech Tree Road, COALVILLE, LE67 4JN.

COLE, Mrs. Tracey Michelle, BSc ACA *1993;* (Tax Fac), 25 Melville Road, Barnes, LONDON, SW13 9RH.

COLE, Miss. Victoria Clare, BEng ACA *1999;* Pound Farm, Sheffield Green, Sheffield Park, UCKFIELD, EAST SUSSEX, TN22 3RB.

COLE, Mr. Vivian Jerome, BSc ACA *1998;* 53 Greenways, HAYWARDS HEATH, WEST SUSSEX, RH16 2DT.

COLE, Mr. Vivyan Anthony, FCA *1973;* 51 Kersey Drive, SOUTH CROYDON, SURREY, CR2 8SX.

COLE, Mr. William Charles, FCA *1970;* 38 Buckingham Close, Petts Wood, ORPINGTON, KENT, BR5 1SA.

COLEBOURN, Mr. Michael Ian, BSc(Hons) ACA *2006;* 9 Seaton Close, West End, SOUTHAMPTON, SO18 3NT.

COLEBOURNE, Mr. Paul Christopher, BSc FCA CMC FRSA *1978;* 41 Bedford Square, LONDON, WC1B 3HX.

COLEBROOK, Mr. Simon John, BSc ACA *1994;* 131 Walmer Road, PORTSMOUTH, PO1 5AT.

COLEBY, Mr. Michael Edward, BA FCA *1994;* 74 Station Road, HARPENDEN, HERTFORDSHIRE, AL5 4TZ.

COLEGATE, Mr. Adrian Tracey, BA FCA *1968;* September Cottage, Courtlands Hill, Pangbourne On Thames, READING, RG8 7BE. (Life Member)

COLEMAN, Mr. Adrian Harris, FCA *1953;* 28 Shaftesbury Avenue, Kenton, HARROW, MIDDLESEX, HA3 0QX. (Life Member)

COLEMAN, Mr. Adrian Michael, BA ACA *1995;* Rose Cottage, Netherwood Lane, Crowle, WORCESTER, WR7 4AB.

COLEMAN, Mr. Aidan, ACA *2009;* 22 Goodsmoor Road, Littleover, DERBY, DE23 1NH.

COLEMAN, Mr. Andrew Marcus, BSc FCA *1975;* 104 Richmond Hill, RICHMOND, TW10 6RJ. (Life Member)

•**COLEMAN, Miss. Ann Georgina, FCA** *1989;* (Tax Fac), Ann Coleman Accountancy Ltd, Ground Floor, 5c Parkway, Valley Road, Porters Wood, ST. ALBANS HERTFORDSHIRE AL3 6PA.

COLEMAN, Mrs. Ann Katherine, ACA *1996;* 2 Foxcroft, ST. ALBANS, AL1 5SN.

COLEMAN, Mr. Anthony, BA ACA *1998;* 2 Foxcroft, ST. ALBANS, AL1 5SN.

COLEMAN, Mr. Anthony Patrick, MA MSci ACA *2004;* Flat B, 3 Kingscroft Road, LONDON, NW2 3QE.

•**COLEMAN, Mr. Barry Russell, FCA** *1963;* Barry.R. Coleman, 28 Dufferin Street, CAMPBELLTON E3N 2N2, NB, CANADA.

COLEMAN, Mr. Christopher John, FCA *1975;* Shirebrook Investments Ltd, Carter Lane Shirebrook, MANSFIELD, NOTTINGHAMSHIRE, NG20 8AH.

COLEMAN, Mr. Christopher John, BA ACA *1979;* 11 Lypiatt Street, Tivoli, CHELTENHAM, GL50 2UA.

COLEMAN, Mrs. Claire Louise, BSc ACA *2005;* with Deloitte LLP, Hill House, 1 Little New Street, LONDON, EC4A 3TR.

COLEMAN, Mr. Clive Thomas, BSc FCA *1977;* Yellowmead Farm, Sheepstor, YELVERTON, DEVON, PL20 6PF.

•**COLEMAN, Mr. Dale, ACA** *2006;* with Ford Campbell Freedman LLP, 34 Park Cross Street, LEEDS, LS1 2QH.

COLEMAN, Mr. David, BA ACA *1986;* Kareol, Mines Avenue, LIVERPOOL, L17 6AL.

COLEMAN, Mr. David Jeremy Robert, BA ACA *1989;* with PricewaterhouseCoopers LLP, 1 Embankment Place, LONDON, WC2N 6RH.

•**COLEMAN, Mr. David John, FCA** *1972;* D.J. Coleman, 2 Redcar Street, ROCHDALE, OL12 0PU.

COLEMAN, Mrs. Elizabeth Sally, FCA *1977;* Grove Meadow, Jordans Way, Jordans, BEACONSFIELD, HP9 2SP.

COLEMAN, Mr. Eric, BSc ACA *2008;* Latitude, Flat 219, 130 Clapham Common South Side, LONDON, SW4 9DX.

•**COLEMAN, Miss. Fiona Gay, BA ACA** *1994;* Nether Haresceugh, Renwick, PENRITH, CUMBRIA, CA10 1JE.

COLEMAN, Mr. Gary Paul, BA FCA *1993;* 42 Warren Walk, FERNDOWN, BH22 9LY.

COLEMAN, Mr. Gary Richard, BSc ACA *2005;* L X B Grafton House, 2-3 Golden Square, LONDON, W1F 9HR.

•**COLEMAN, Mr. George William, ACA** *1982;* Honey Barrett Limited, 48 St. Leonards Road, BEXHILL-ON-SEA, EAST SUSSEX, TN40 1JB.

COLEMAN, Mr. Gerald David Weston, FCA *1975;* Hawksbill, 22 Stag Lane, BUCKHURST HILL, IG9 5TD.

COLEMAN, Mrs. Gillian Mary, BSc ACA *1981;* 32 Burlingham Avenue, WIRRAL, CH48 8AP.

COLEMAN, Mr. Gregory John, BA ACA *1986;* Experian, 80 Victoria Street, LONDON, SW1E 5JL.

COLEMAN, Mr. James Anthony, BA ACA *1985;* Swallows, Upper Street, Stanstead, SUDBURY, SUFFOLK, CO10 9AT.

COLEMAN, Mr. James Richard, ACA *2006;* 21 Chatsworth Road, LONDON, NW2 4BJ.

COLEMAN, Mrs. Janet Elizabeth, BSc ACA *1995;* Rose Cottage, Netherwood Lane, Crowle, WORCESTER, WR7 4AB.

COLEMAN, Mr. John, FCA *1965;* Apartment 5, The White House, Suffolk Road, ALTRINCHAM, CHESHIRE, WA14 4QX. (Life Member)

•**COLEMAN, Mr. John Donald, FCA** *1971;* John D. Coleman, Howards, Middle Street, Nazeing, WALTHAM ABBEY, EN9 2LH.

COLEMAN, Mr. Jonathan Charles, BA ACA *1992;* 7 Rydal Grove, CHESTER, CH4 8HJ.

COLEMAN, Mr. Jonathon Paul, BSc(Hons) ACA *2001;* Island Heritage Insurance Company Ltd., P O Box 32155 SMB, GEORGE TOWN, GRAND CAYMAN, CAYMAN ISLANDS.

•**COLEMAN, Mr. Laurence Ronald, FCA** *1972;* 53 Littlefield Crescent, Chandler's Ford, EASTLEIGH, HAMPSHIRE, SO53 4PB.

COLEMAN, Mr. Lee Fraser, BA ACA *2002;* NES Global Limited, 08-02/03 Commerce Point, 3 Philip Street, SINGAPORE 048693, SINGAPORE.

COLEMAN, Mr. Liam Patrick Joseph, BA ACA *1979;* 7 Rock Court, Blackrock, DUNDALK, COUNTY LOUTH, IRELAND.

COLEMAN, Mrs. Louise, BA(Hons) ACA *2010;* Apartment 1 Hampton Court, Wilmslow Road Handforth, WILMSLOW, CHESHIRE, SK9 3GA.

COLEMAN, Miss. Lynne, ACA *1996;* with Ernst & Young LLP, 400 Capability Green, LUTON, LU1 3LU.

COLEMAN, Mr. Malcolm Jerry, FCA *1961;* 37 Springfield Road, LONDON, NW8 0QJ.

COLEMAN, Mrs. Margaret Louise, BSc ACA *2001;* Kaplan Financial, 179-191 Borough High Street, LONDON, SE1 1HR.

COLEMAN, Mr. Mark Robert, FCA DChA *1983;* Briar Cottage, Honeysuckle Close, HORLEY, RH6 9AD.

•**COLEMAN, Mr. Martin Anthony, FCA** *1971;* (Tax Fac), Greenberg 17/16, 69379 TEL AVIV, ISRAEL.

COLEMAN, Mr. Marvin Harvey, BA ACA *1996;* 6 Cromer Road, BEAUMARIS, VIC 3193, AUSTRALIA.

COLEMAN, Mrs. Michelle, BA ACA *1992;* (Tax Fac), K M C Electronics Unit 5 Farcroft, Doley Gate Gnosall, STAFFORD, ST20 0EH.

COLEMAN, Mr. Neal, BA ACA *2006;* UBS Fund Services(Cayman) Ltd, UBS House 227 Elgin Avenue, PO BOX 852GT, Grand Cayman, GEORGE TOWN, CAYMAN ISLANDS.

COLEMAN, Mr. Nicholas Charles, BA FCA *1981;* Commercialbank of Qatar, Commercialbank Plaza, P.O. Box 3232, DOHA, QATAR.

COLEMAN, Mr. Nicholas Ian, BA ACA *1992;* 177 Valley Road, IPSWICH, IP1 4PJ.

•**COLEMAN, Mr. Nicholas John, FCA** *1962;* Coleman & Co., 57 West End Lane, PINNER, HA5 1AH.

COLEMAN, Mr. Nicholas Robert, BA ACA *1998;* S V Life Sciences Advisers Llp International Buildings, 71 Kingsway, LONDON, WC2B 6ST.

•**COLEMAN, Mr. Paul David, BA ACA** *1989;* (Tax Fac), Coleman & Company, 8A Alfred Square, DEAL, CT14 6LU.

COLEMAN, Mr. Paul James, FCA *1974;* Grove Meadow, Jordans Way, Jordans, BEACONSFIELD, HP9 2SP.

COLEMAN, Mr. Paul Simon, BA ACA *1990;* PricewaterhouseCoopers (Vietnam) Ltd, 4th Floor Saigon Tower, 29 Le Duan Boulevard, District 1, HO CHI MINH CITY, VIETNAM.

COLEMAN, Mr. Paul Wilford, ACA *2009;* 9 Prospect Place, Osborne Road, WINDSOR, BERKSHIRE, SL4 3JA.

COLEMAN, Mr. Peter Brian, BSc FCA *1999;* 26 Old Sneed Avenue, Stoke Bishop, BRISTOL, BS9 1SE.

•**COLEMAN, Mr. Philip David, FCA** *1984;* RSM Tenon Audit Limited, 66 Chiltern Street, LONDON, W1U 4JT. See also Tenon Audit Limited

COLEMAN, Mrs. Rachel, BA(Hons) ACA *2000;* (Tax Fac), with PricewaterhouseCoopers LLP, Cornwall Court, 19 Cornwall Street, BIRMINGHAM, B3 2DT.

COLEMAN, Mr. Richard Alexander, BSc(Hons) ACA *2010;* Eden Square West - Apartment 2, 12 Cheapside, LIVERPOOL, MERSEYSIDE, L2 2DQ.

COLEMAN, Mr. Richard Edward Lovell, FCA *1969;* 41 Theberton Street, LONDON, N1 0QY.

COLEMAN, Mr. Richard Henry, FCA *1974;* Old School House, Abbots Worthy, WINCHESTER, SO21 1DR.

•**COLEMAN, Mr. Richard Hugh, BA ACA** *1986;* Richard Coleman, 3 Pentland Drive, Warren Wood Arnold, NOTTINGHAM, NG5 9PZ.

COLEMAN, Mr. Richard John, FCA *1973;* 2 Middle Street, Scotton, GAINSBOROUGH, LINCOLNSHIRE, DN21 3RA.

COLEMAN, Mr. Robert, FCA *1971;* 19 Roberts Wood Drive, GERRARDS CROSS, SL9 0NH. (Life Member)

COLEMAN, Mr. Robert Grant, MA BCom FCA *1940;* Abbeyfield, 4 Market Hill, WOODBRIDGE, SUFFOLK, IP12 4LU. (Life Member)

COLEMAN, Mr. Robert Ian, BSc FCA *1968;* 38 Cranbourne Road, LONDON, N10 2BT.

COLEMAN, Mr. Robin Bernard, FCA *1968;* 381 Woodridge Avenue, FAIRFIELD, CT 06825, UNITED STATES.

COLEMAN, Mr. Rooney James Selfe, BSocSc ACA *1995;* 27 Scudder Road, WESTFIELD, NJ 07090, UNITED STATES.

COLEMAN, Mr. Stephen Melvin, FCA *1970;* 28 The Avenue, PINNER, MIDDLESEX, HA5 4ER.

•**COLEMAN, Mr. Stephen Paul, BA(Hons) ACA** *2000;* Gerald Edelman, 25 Harley Street, LONDON, W1G 9BR. See also Stephen Coleman LLP

COLEMAN, Miss. Susannah, ACA *2009;* 30 Ancastle Green, HENLEY-ON-THAMES, OXFORDSHIRE, RG9 1TR.

COLEMAN, Mr. Sydney John, FCA *1966;* PO Box 1111, Boundary Hall, Cricket Square, GEORGE TOWN, GRAND CAYMAN, KY1-1102 CAYMAN ISLANDS.

COLEMAN, Mr. William Cyril, FCA *1947;* 3A Lovers Walk, WELLS, BA5 2QL. (Life Member)

COLEMAN, Mr. William Frederick, FCA *1975;* 34 Norbreck Close, Great Sankey, WARRINGTON, WA5 2SX.

COLEMAN-SMITH, Mr. Alan, BSc FCA *1976;* N P I A Bramshill House, Bramshill, HOOK, RG27 0JW.
COLENUTT, Mr. Roy Maurice, BSc ACA *1980;* 23 Lon y Fro, Pentyrch, CARDIFF, CF15 9TE.
COLES, Mr. Adam, BSc ACA *1985;* 45 Tanfield Lane, Rushmere Road, NORTHAMPTON, NN1 5RN.
COLES, Mr. Andrew, FCA *1980;* Evergreen, Rugby Road, Weston under Wetherley, LEAMINGTON SPA, WARWICKSHIRE, CV33 9BY.
•COLES, Mr. Andrew Gordon, ACA *1980;* TaxAssist Accountants, 3 Boldmere Road, SUTTON COLDFIELD, WEST MIDLANDS, B73 5UY.
COLES, Mr. Andrew Stewart, BSc ACA *1979;* 15 Hotchin Way, KARDINYA, WA 6163, AUSTRALIA.
COLES, Miss. Barbara Elizabeth, FCA *1961;* The Coach House, Fords Barn, Chaldon Herring, DORCHESTER, DT2 8DN.
COLES, Mr. Charles Graham, BSc FCA *1977;* Willow Cottage, Chalfont Lane, Chorleywood, RICKMANSWORTH, WD3 5PP.
COLES, Mr. Daren Neil, BSocSc ACA *1999;* 52 Benett Drive, HOVE, EAST SUSSEX, BN3 6UQ.
COLES, Mr. David Paul, BSc(Econ) ACA *1999;* Omega Underwriting Holdings Ltd New London House, 6 London Street, LONDON, EC3R 7LP.
COLES, Mr. David Roderick, BA ACA *1993;* 2 Waltham Road, MAIDENHEAD, BERKSHIRE, SL6 3NH.
COLES, Mr. David William, MA ACA *1989;* 26 Avenue Georges Clemenceau, 11160 RIEUX MINERVOIS, FRANCE.
COLES, Mrs. Denise Evelyn, BSc ACA *1990;* 152 Rosemary Hill Road, Little Aston, SUTTON COLDFIELD, B74 4HN.
COLES, Mr. Dominic Peter, BA ACA *1991;* British Broadcasting Corporation, Room 5090, TVC, Wood Lane, LONDON, W12 7RJ.
COLES, Mr. Edward John, BSc ACA *2010;* 45a Plover Way, LONDON, SE16 7TS.
COLES, Mr. Geoffrey, BA FCA *1973;* 11 Silver Sands, Lancaster Road, GORDONS BAY, WESTERN CAPE PROVINCE, 7140, SOUTH AFRICA.
COLES, Ms. Gillian Susan, BA FCA *1985;* 27 Quaggy Walk, Blackheath, LONDON, SE3 9EJ.
COLES, Mr. Jess, BEng ACA *2000;* 17 Cherrywood Drive, LONDON, SW15 6DS.
COLES, Mr. John Michael, BBS ACA *1986;* Old Change House, 128 Queen Victoria Street, LONDON, EC4V 4BJ.
COLES, Mr. John Raymond, ACA *2010;* 14 Werfa Close, ABERDARE, MID GLAMORGAN, CF44 0YT.
COLES, Mrs. Julie Ann, BSc ACA *2000;* 52 Benett Drive, HOVE, EAST SUSSEX, BN3 6UQ.
COLES, Mr. Justin Simon, MA(Hons) ACA *2001;* Mansion House, Manchester Road, ALTRINCHAM, WA14 4RW.
COLES, Mr. Mark Gregory, ACA *1994;* Flat 1, 32 Emperors Gate, South Kensington, LONDON, SW7 4JA.
COLES, Mr. Mark Richard, ACA *1995;* 65 Marlborough Street, No.4, BOSTON, MA 02116, UNITED STATES.
•COLES, Mr. Neil Owen, BSc FCA ATII *1990;* Deloitte LLP, 2 New Street Square, LONDON, EC4A 3BZ. See also Deloitte & Touche LLP
COLES, Mrs. Nicola Jane, LLB ACA *2002;* Alix Partners Ltd, 20 North Audley Street, LONDON, W1K 6WE.
COLES, Mr. Peter Andrew, FCA ATII *1974;* with Cooper Parry LLP, 14 Park Row, NOTTINGHAM, NG1 6GR. (Life Member)
COLES, Mr. Richard, MSc ACA *2002;* 32 Freshford Street, LONDON, SW18 3TF.
COLES, Mr. Richard, BCom FCA *1975;* 8 Woodlands Walk, SKIPTON, BD23 1TZ.
COLES, Mr. Richard James, BA(Hons) ACA *2004;* Alcontrol Laboratories Unit 7-8, Hawarden Industrial Park Hawarden, DEESIDE, CLWYD, CH5 3US.
COLES, Mr. Robert Barton, FCA *1962;* Goodtrees, Colts Hill, Pembury, TUNBRIDGE WELLS, KENT, TN2 4AL. (Life Member)
COLES, Mrs. Sarah Jane, BSc ACA *1999;* 9 Owens Road, WINCHESTER, HAMPSHIRE, SO22 6RU.
•COLES, Mr. Simon Graham, FCA *1981;* Simon Coles Limited, P O Box 600, LONDON, WC1H 0XB.
COLES, Mr. Stephen James, BA FCA *1976;* 48 Ardmore Lane, BUCKHURST HILL, IG9 5SA.
COLES, Mr. Stephen John Hamilton, FCA *1973;* Hollanden Park Barn, Riding Lane, Hildenborough, TONBRIDGE, TN11 9LH.
COLES, Mr. Stephen Ralph, FCA *1975;* 10 Bannerman Road, PETERSFIELD, HAMPSHIRE, GU32 2HQ.
COLES, Miss. Tamsin Clare, BSc ACA *2003;* with PricewaterhouseCoopers LLP, Cornwall Court, 19 Cornwall Street, BIRMINGHAM, B3 2DT.
COLES, Mr. Thomas, BA ACA *2007;* 4 Sunningdale Gardens, LONDON, W8 6PX.
COLES, Mr. Victor Ashley, FCA *1981;* Valhalla, Firbank Lane, WOKING, SURREY, GU21 7QS.
COLETTA, Mr. Jonathan David, BA FCA ATII *1987;* 106 The Stray, South Cave, BROUGH, HU15 2AL.
COLETTA, Miss. Tonya Adele, BA FCA *1996;* XL House, X L Insurance, 70 Gracechurch Street, LONDON, EC3V 0XL.
COLEY, Mr. Andrew, ACA *2011;* The Cottage, Craig Street, St. Helier, JERSEY, JE2 4TS.
COLEY, Mr. Andrew Stephen, BA ACA *1992;* 30 Siviters Lane, ROWLEY REGIS, WEST MIDLANDS, B65 8DS.
COLEY, Ms. Ann Elizabeth, BA ACA *1990;* 35 Danby Street, LONDON, SE15 4BS.
COLEY, Mr. Benn Edward, BSc ACA *1999;* Houtsak Ina, 14 Rue Alfred Longuefosse, 40350 POUILLON, FRANCE.
COLEY, Mr. David Bruce, BSocSc ACA *1992;* 65 Lady Byron Lane, Knowle, SOLIHULL, B93 9AX.
COLEY, Mr. Gregg Russell, BSocSc ACA *1985;* 27 Hillcrest Road, Romsley, HALESOWEN, B62 0PB.
COLEY, Mrs. Helen Andrea, BA ACA *1995;* 65 Lady Byron Lane, Knowle, SOLIHULL, B93 9AX.
COLEY, Mrs. Josephine Ann, ACA *1987;* 13 Blake Walk, Higham Ferrers, RUSHDEN, NN10 8DB.
COLEY, Miss. Laura, BSc ACA *2007;* 133 Sellywood Road, BIRMINGHAM, B30 1XA.
COLEY, Mr. Neil Simon, BSc(Hons) ACA *2010;* 5 Rochford Court, Shirley, SOLIHULL, B90 4XJ.
COLEY, Mr. Paul Murray, FCA *1973;* 12 Darfield Road, GUILDFORD, GU4 7YY.
COLEY, Mr. Simon John, ACA *1984;* 4th Floor Lancaster House, 67 Newhall Street, BIRMINGHAM, b3 1ng.
COLEY, Mr. Stephen John, FCA *1978;* 13 Blake Walk, Higham Ferrers, RUSHDEN, NN10 8DB.
COLEY, Mrs. Susan Gaynor, BSc ACA *1988;* Foundation Building, Eden Project, Bodelva, PAR, CORNWALL, PL24 2SG.
COLEY, Mr. William Barbour Maitland, MA ACA *1994;* New House Farm, Mamble, KIDDERMINSTER, DY14 9JP.
COLEYSHAW, Mr. Lee, BSc ACA *1996;* 4 Greenwood Place, Bonehill, TAMWORTH, B78 3BL.
COLFER, Mrs. Sarah, BA ACA *1998;* 3 Glendale Avenue, Garforth, LEEDS, LS25 1LB.
COLGAN, Miss. Aisling, BSc ACA *2011;* 228 Ballygawley Road, DUNGANNON, COUNTY TYRONE, BT70 1TF.
COLGAN, Mr. Ian Michael, FCA *1969;* 5 The Green, Cheadle Hulme, CHEADLE, SK8 6JB.
COLGAN, Dr. Joanne Elizabeth, PhD MChem ACA *2006;* 5 Nightingale Way, ROYSTON, HERTFORDSHIRE, SG8 7XZ.
COLGAN, Miss. Julie, MA(Hons) ACA *2000;* Top Floor Flat, 52 St. Johns Park, LONDON, SE3 7JP.
COLGAN, Mrs. Karen Ann, BSc ACA *1992;* Colgan Expert services Ltd, 17 Lisson Grove, Hale, ALTRINCHAM, CHESHIRE, WA15 9AE.
COLGAN, Mrs. Lisa, BA(Hons) ACA *2002;* with Ernst & Young LLP, 1 Bridgewater Place, Water Lane, LEEDS, LS11 5QR.
COLGAN, Mr. Neale, BSc ACA *1989;* 22 School Walk, Yate, BRISTOL, BS37 5PS.
COLGRAVE, Mr. Ben Anthony, BA ACA *2010;* Apartment 5, 121 Abbey Street, HULL, HU9 1LE.
COLGRAVE, Miss. Wendy Elizabeth, BA FCA *1990;* 1 Alloway Road, Bow, LONDON, E3 5AS.
COLIN, Mr. Michael, FCA *1968;* MEMBER OF COUNCIL, 4 Vine Court, Clifton, BRIGHOUSE, WEST YORKSHIRE, HD6 4JT.
COLIN, Mr. Pierre Louis, ACA *2009;* Fat Face Clothing Ltd, 1-3 Ridgway, HAVANT, PO9 1QJ.
COLIN-MORGAN, Mrs. Celine Valerie Anne, BA ACA *1990;* 5 rue H Lebas, 75009 PARIS, FRANCE.
•COLINSWOOD, Mrs. Carol Rosemary Ethel, FCA *1974;* (Tax Fac), Carol Colinswood & Co, Ground Floor, Dorchester House, 15 Dorchester Place, THAME, OXFORDSHIRE OX9 2DL.
COLL, Mr. Andrew, BSc ACA *1997;* Flat 48, Hillfield Court, Belsize Avenue, LONDON, NW3 4BG.
COLL, Mr. Brendan, BSc ACA *1990;* Via Cimarosa 43, 2272vb VOORBURG, NETHERLANDS.
•COLL, Miss. Margaret Mary, MA ACA *1990;* Ernst & Young, 5 Times Square, NEW YORK, NY 10036, UNITED STATES.
COLL, Mr. Martin John, ACA *2009;* 22 Acre Road, LONDON, SW19 2AJ.
COLL, Mrs. Nicole, ACA CA(SA) *2010;* 5 Downsview Road, SEVENOAKS, KENT, TN13 2JT.
COLL, Mr. Plinio Nicholas Rosendo, BSc ACA *1980;* Lomas de Carrasco (178), Camino de los Horneros 220, CIUDAD DE LA COSTA, 15006, URUGUAY.
•COLLACOTT, Mr. James Robert, ACA ATII *1991;* Flat 3, 2 St. James's Road, Hampton Hill, HAMPTON, MIDDLESEX, TW12 1DQ.
COLLACOTT, Mr. Peter Barrie, FCA *1968;* Chart Cottage, Seal Chart, SEVENOAKS, TN15 0ES.
COLLAR, Mr. Michael Charles, BA ACA *2000;* Quilon, Hillcrest Waye, GERRARDS CROSS, BUCKINGHAMSHIRE, SL9 8DN.
COLLARD, Mr. Jamie, BA FCA *1997;* Hess Corporation, The Adelphi, 1-11 John Adam Street, LONDON, WC2N 6AG.
COLLARD, Mr. Jeffrey John, FCA *1972;* 36 Barton Road, Market Bosworth, NUNEATON, WARWICKSHIRE, CV13 0LQ.
COLLARD, Mrs. Jennifer Anne, ACA *1984;* 6 Heathervale, West Bridgford, NOTTINGHAM, NG2 7ST.
•COLLARD, Mr. Jonathan Giles, FCA *1969;* Collard Associates Limited, 26 Orleans Road, TWICKENHAM, TW1 3BL.
COLLARD, Mr. Nicholas William, LLB ACA *1984;* 6 Heathervale, West Bridgford, NOTTINGHAM, NG2 7ST.
COLLARD, Mr. Paul, BSc FCA *1993;* 74 Tring Avenue, LONDON, W5 3QB.
COLLARD, Mr. Philip David, ACA *2009;* 66a St. Marys Road, WEYBRIDGE, SURREY, KT13 9QA.
COLLARD, Mr. Richard David, FCA *1965;* Glebe View, The Long Croft, Wisborough Green, BILLINGSHURST, WEST SUSSEX, RH14 0DP. (Life Member)
COLLARD, Mr. Samuel William Peter, BA(Hons) ACA *2001;* 4 The Haven, Hale, ALTRINCHAM, CHESHIRE, WA15 8SA.
COLLARD, Mr. Simon John, BSc ACA *1989;* 1st Floor Flat, 75 Woodside, LONDON, SW19 7QL.
COLLAS, Mrs. Christine Margaret, FCA *1976;* Henley Park, HENLEY-ON-THAMES, RG9 6HY.
COLLECOTT, Mr. Matthew John, BSc FCA *1995;* Tottenham Hotspur plc, 748 High Road, Tottenham, LONDON, N17 0AP.
COLLEDGE, Mr. Adrian Charles, ACA *1987;* 4 High Ridge, HARPENDEN, AL5 3LL.
COLLEDGE, Mr. David James Wearmouth, FCA *1967;* Chemin De La Gatillarde 8, 1295 TANNAY, SWITZERLAND.
COLLEDGE, Miss. Lauren Mary, BSc(Hons) ACA *2010;* 63 Dunkerry Road, BRISTOL, BS3 4LD.
•COLLEDGE, Mr. Matthew Peter, LLB(Hons) ACA *2004;* MPC Financial Consulting Ltd, 16 Conaglen Road, Aylestone, LEICESTER, LE2 8LD.
COLLEDGE, Mr. Peter, MSc BSc FCA *1977;* with Cooper Parry LLP, 3 Centro Place, Pride Park, DERBY, DE24 8RF.
COLLEDGE, Mr. Peter Duncan, BSc(Hons) ACA *2010;* Flat 5 Icon Apartments, 15 Cluny Place, LONDON, SE1 4QS.
COLLEDGE, Mr. Peter John, FCA *1963;* 16 Conaglen Road, Aylestone, LEICESTER, LE2 8LD.
COLLEDGE, Mr. William John Baker, FCA *1962;* Somerton House, 2 St Johns Avenue, FILEY, YO14 9AZ.
COLLENETTE, Mr. Andrew Mark, BSc ACA *2000;* Chichester Solar Ltd, 16a The Wren Centre, EMSWORTH, PO10 7SU.
COLLENETTE, Mr. Colin David, BEng ACA *2006;* Retour-Du-Tertre Rue Du Tertre, St. Andrew, GUERNSEY, GY6 8SG.
•COLLENETTE, Mr. Jonathan Peter, BSc FCA *1996;* Collenette Jones Limited, Crossways Centre, Braye Road, Vale, GUERNSEY, GY3 5PH.
COLLENETTE, Mrs. Louise Jayne, BSc(Econ) ACA *1998;* The Elms, Pleinheaume Lane, St. Sampson, GUERNSEY, GY2 4XH.
•COLLENETTE, Mr. Michael James, MSc BA(Oxon) FCA *1999;* Collenette Jones Limited, Crossways Centre, Braye Road, Vale, GUERNSEY, GY3 5PH.
COLLENETTE, Mr. Richard Alan, BA(Hons) ACA *2003;* La Hanniere Barras Lane, Vale, GUERNSEY, GY6 8EN.
COLLENETTE, Mrs. Zoe Francesca, BA(Hons) ACA *2004;* La Haniere, Barras Lane, Vale, GUERNSEY, GY6 8EN.
COLLERTON, Mrs. Mary Elizabeth, BA ACA *1991;* 58 Chestnut Grove, LONDON, SW12 8JJ.
•COLLERTON, Mr. Timothy Edwin Albert, ACA FCCA CTA *2010;* (Tax Fac), Wilkins Kennedy, Anglo House, Bell Lane Office Village, Bell Lane, AMERSHAM, BUCKINGHAMSHIRE HP6 6FA.
COLLET, Mr. Robert Thomson, MA FCA *1966;* The School House, Wimble Hill, Crondall, FARNHAM, SURREY, GU10 5HL. (Life Member)
•COLLETT, Mr. Alan, BSc CA FCA *1989;* (Tax Fac), Go Matilda (Accounting and Tax) Pty Limited, L27 Rialto South Tower, 525 Collins Street, MELBOURNE, VIC 3000, AUSTRALIA. See also Collett & Co
COLLETT, Mr. Angus Christopher Calvert, MA FCA *1991;* 33 Rostrevor Road, LONDON, SW6 5AX.
COLLETT, Ms. Anne, ACA *2009;* 30 Mulberry Drive, BIRMINGHAM, B13 9PL.
COLLETT, Mr. Anthony Michael, BA FCA *1966;* Old Stoke, Stoke Charity, WINCHESTER, SO21 3PL.
•COLLETT, Mr. Aubrey James, FCA *1971;* (Tax Fac), Collett Hulance LLP, 40 Kimbolton Road, BEDFORD, MK40 2NR.
COLLETT, Mr. Benedict Thomas, BSc ACA *1994;* 33 Main Street, Higham-On-The-Hill, NUNEATON, CV13 6AH.
COLLETT, Mr. Christopher, FCA *1953;* Barrowby Lodge, Barrowby, GRANTHAM, NG32 1DE. (Life Member)
COLLETT, Sir Christopher, GBE MA FCA *1958;* Altnaharrie, Lodsworth, PETWORTH, WEST SUSSEX, GU28 9DG. (Life Member)
COLLETT, Mr. Christopher David, ACA *2011;* 19 Gosden Road, West End, WOKING, SURREY, GU24 9LH.
COLLETT, Miss. Claire Joanne, BA ACA *2007;* 22 Park Close, HATFIELD, HERTFORDSHIRE, AL9 5AY.
•COLLETT, Mr. David John, FCA *1973;* Rigbey Harrison, 4 Church Green East, REDDITCH, B98 8BT.
COLLETT, Mr. David John, FCA *1969;* Manor Farm House, Village Green, Hampsthwaite, HARROGATE, HG3 2HA.
COLLETT, Mr. Edward James, MSc LLB ACA *2007;* First Floor, 29 Steerforth Street, LONDON, SW18 4HF.
COLLETT, Ms. Gail Christine, BA ACA *1991;* 4 Heatherside Close, Little Bookham, LEATHERHEAD, SURREY, KT23 3AE.
•COLLETT, Mr. Graham Aubrey, FCA *1972;* Crane & Partners, Leonard House, 5-7 Newman Road, BROMLEY, BR1 1RJ.
COLLETT, Mr. Henry Alexander, FCA *1969;* Chariaud, 16210 ST ROMAIN, FRANCE. (Life Member)
COLLETT, Mr. Iain, BSc ACA *2001;* 43 Eynsford Rise, Eynsford, DARTFORD, DA4 0HS.
•COLLETT, Mr. John Charles, BSc ACA *1994;* FD OnBoard, 36 Amherst Road, SEVENOAKS, KENT, TN13 3LS.
•COLLETT, Mr. Kevin Mark, BSc ACA AMCT *2003;* 3 Hatfield Road, LONDON, W13 9DG.
COLLETT, Mr. Mark Jeremy Gordon, BSc ACA *1985;* 19 Bow Grove, Sherfield-on-Loddon, HOOK, HAMPSHIRE, RG27 0DY.
COLLETT, Mr. Martyn Stephen, FCA *1981;* 37 Seaview Street, BALGOWLAH HEIGHTS, NSW 2093, AUSTRALIA.
COLLETT, Mr. Michael Royston, BA FCA *1973;* Close Cottage, High Street, Iron Acton, BRISTOL, BS37 9UG.
COLLETT, Mr. Nigel John David, BEng ACA *1989;* JP Morgan Chase Thames Court, 1 Queenhithe, LONDON, EC4V 3DX.
COLLETT, Mrs. Sarah Margaret, BSc ACA *2000;* 59 Kelston Road, CARDIFF, CF14 2AH.
COLLETT-NAIDOO, Mrs. Emma Melissa, ACA *2010;* 71 Pursers Cross Road, LONDON, SW6 4QZ.
•COLLETTS, Mr. Ian Michael, BSc FCA *1988;* 23 Purcells Avenue, EDGWARE, HA8 8DP.
COLLEY, Mr. Derek Alan Singer, FCA MCT *1972;* Maywood Farmhouse, Woodchurch, ASHFORD, KENT, TN26 3QZ. (Life Member)
COLLEY, Mr. Edward, ACA *2008;* Tri Centre One, Zurich Financial Services The Tri Centre, New Bridge Square, SWINDON, SN1 1HN.
COLLEY, Mrs. Elizabeth Rachel, BSc ACA *1993;* 6 Greenrigg Close, Standish, WIGAN, LANCASHIRE, WN6 0UH.
COLLEY, Mrs. Helen, BA ACA *1994;* 49 Manor Drive South, YORK, YO26 5SB.
COLLEY, Mr. James Edward, FCA *1959;* Thistledown, Huckshott, Compton, CHICHESTER, PO18 9NS. (Life Member)
COLLEY, Miss. Jessica Louise, BA ACA *2010;* 12 Hillbury Road, LONDON, SW17 8JT.
COLLEY, Mr. Michael, BSc ACA *1991;* 19 Richmond Crescent, BILLINGHAM, TS23 2JP.
•COLLEY, Mr. Michael Anthony, FCA *1974;* (Tax Fac), Michael A Colley, Leicester House, 6 Hamilton Terrace, Main Street, PEMBROKE, SA71 4DE.
COLLEY, Mr. Richard Gwyn, ACA *1981;* 20 Church Street, Wellesbourne, WARWICK, CV35 9LS.

COLLEY, Mr. Robert Peter, ACA CA(SA) *2010;* 27 Sullivan Way, Elstree, BOREHAMWOOD, HERTFORDSHIRE, WD6 3DG.

COLLIE, Mr. Marcus Anthony, BBS FCA *1975;* Feltrim Lodge, Streamstown Lane, Malahide, DUBLIN, COUNTY DUBLIN, IRELAND. (Life Member)

COLLIE, Mr. Richard Angus, ACA *1993;* The Honkkong & Shanghai Banking Corp Ltd, Western India, Mumbai Main Office, 52-60 Mahatma Gandhi Road, Fort, MUMBAI 400001 INDIA.

•**COLLIER, Mr. Adrian Paul, BSc ACA** *2000;* with KPMG LLP, 15 Canada Square, LONDON, E14 5GL.

COLLIER, Mrs. Alison Debra, BSc ACA CTA AMCT *1993;* Edgcumbe, 4 Rue de la Ree, La Grande Rue, St. Saviour, GUERNSEY, GY7 9PW.

COLLIER, Mrs. Amanda Louise, BA ACA *1997;* with PricewaterhouseCoopers LLP, 1 Embankment Place, LONDON, WC2N 6RH.

COLLIER, Mr. Andrew, MA ACA *1990;* 25 Daisy Road, BRIGHOUSE, HD6 3SY.

COLLIER, Mr. Andrew Paul, BA ACA *1990;* R 5 M International, 11 Old Jewry, LONDON, EC2R 8DU.

COLLIER, Mr. Anthony Paul, BSc ACA *2006;* 133b Liverpool Road, MANCHESTER, M3 4JN.

•**COLLIER, Mr. Christopher John, FCA** *1972;* Rawlinsons, Ruthlyn House, 90 Lincoln Road, PETERBOROUGH, PE1 2SP.

•**COLLIER, Mr. Douglas Alexander, BSc FCA CTA** *1992;* 42 Central Avenue, PINNER, MIDDLESEX, HA5 5BS.

COLLIER, Mr. Edward John, ACA *2008;* 6 Kingsmead Road North, PRENTON, MERSEYSIDE, CH43 6TB.

COLLIER, Mrs. Elizabeth Jane, BSc ACA *1980;* Langdon West Williams Plc, Curzon House, 2nd Floor, 24 High Street, BANSTEAD, SURREY SM7 2LJ.

COLLIER, Mr. Graham James, FCA *1974;* Australia & New Zealand Banking Group Ltd, 9A/833 Collins Street, DOCKLANDS, VIC 3008, AUSTRALIA.

COLLIER, Miss. Helen Mary, ACA *2008;* Flat 36, 11 Tarves Way, LONDON, SE10 9JP.

COLLIER, Mr. Hugh, BSc ACA *2000;* 21 Messaline Avenue, Acton, LONDON, W3 6JX.

COLLIER, Mr. Ivor Goodwin, FCA *1955;* 20 South Meade, Timperley, ALTRINCHAM, WA15 6QL. (Life Member)

COLLIER, Mr. James Jack, BA ACA *2005;* 90 Springfield Road, SHEFFIELD, S7 2GF.

COLLIER, Miss. Jane Ann, MA ACA ATII *1989;* (Tax Fac), Lynwood, Hoober, Nr Wentworth, ROTHERHAM, S62 7SA.

•**COLLIER, Mr. Jeffrey Steven, ACA** *1980;* (Tax Fac), Collier & Co, PO Box 3450, BARNET, HERTFORDSHIRE, EN5 9GD.

COLLIER, Mr. John Desmond, BA FCA *1980;* 17 Horseshoe Lane West, Merrow, GUILDFORD, GU1 2SX.

COLLIER, Mr. John Hibbert George, BA FCA *1975;* The Willows, 23a Howbeck Road, PRENTON, CH43 6TD. (Life Member)

COLLIER, Mr. John Spencer, BA FCA *1973;* (Member of Council 1991 - 1997 2003 - 2011), Clive & Stokes Ltd, 63 Catherine Place, LONDON, SW1E 6DY

•**COLLIER, Mr. Michael Andrew, ACA** *1981;* (Tax Fac), Levicks, Station Gates, 3 Lloyd Road, BROADSTAIRS, CT10 1HY. See also Somerfield Consultants Limited

COLLIER, Miss. Naomi Lawson, LLB ACA *1986;* 4 Kemp Street, BRIGHTON, WEST SUSSEX, BN1 4EF.

COLLIER, Mr. Neal John, FCA *1965;* Chemin De Varmey 12, 1299 CRANS, SWITZERLAND.

COLLIER, Mr. Nicholas Dudley, BA ACA *1985;* 15 Cleveland Road, Barnes, LONDON, SW13 0AA.

COLLIER, Mr. Nicholas Michael, FCA *1962;* Flat 2 Grange House, Highbury Grange, LONDON, N5 2QD.

COLLIER, Mr. Nigel James, BSc ACA *1993;* Flat 20 Da Vinci House, 44 Saffron Hill, LONDON, EC1N 8FH.

COLLIER, Prof. Paul Arnold, PhD BSc FCA *1974;* 27 Hampshire Close, St. Thomas, EXETER, EX4 1NA.

COLLIER, Mr. Peter, FCA *1958;* Oakwood, 26 High Street, Spaldwick, HUNTINGDON, CAMBRIDGESHIRE, PE28 0TD. (Life Member)

COLLIER, Mr. Peter Charles, FCA *1978;* Brown Shipley & Co Ltd, Founders Court, Lothbury, LONDON, EC2R 7HE.

•**COLLIER, Mr. Philip Edward, FCA** *1974;* Allens Accountants Limited, 123 Wellington Road South, STOCKPORT, SK1 3TH.

COLLIER, Mr. Philip John, FCA *1960;* 58 Eden Strret, CARLISLE, CA3 9LH. (Life Member)

COLLIER, Mr. Reginald John, FCA *1970;* 27A Talbot Road, Highgate, LONDON, N6 4QS.

COLLIER, Mr. Richard John, FCA *1978;* 12 Carriage Close, Northpark, AUCKLAND 2013, NEW ZEALAND.

•**COLLIER, Mr. Richard Stuart, LLM BA ACA** *1988;* PricewaterhouseCoopers LLP, Hays Galleria, 1 Hays Lane, LONDON, SE1 2RD. See also PricewaterhouseCoopers

COLLIER, Mr. Robert Charles, BA ACA *1985;* 10 Holly Hill Drive, BANSTEAD, SM7 2BD.

COLLIER, Mrs. Rosemary Leah, BSc ACA *2002;* 50 Chadworth Avenue, Dorridge, SOLIHULL, B93 8SX.

COLLIER, Miss. Sarah, MA ACA *2011;* 14 Fair Lea Close, Long Eaton, NOTTINGHAM, NG10 1EJ.

COLLIER, Miss. Shan, BA ACA *1987;* 52/8 Water Street, BIRCHGROVE, NSW 2041, AUSTRALIA.

COLLIER, Mr. Simon, FCA *1966;* 17 Hazel Way, Crawley Down, CRAWLEY, RH10 4JS. (Life Member)

COLLIER, Mrs. Stephanie Anne, BA ACA *1990;* Crudens Farm The Village, Ashleworth, GLOUCESTER, GL19 4HT.

•**COLLIER, Mr. Stephen Francis, FCA** *1977;* (Tax Fac), Horsfield-Smith Limited, Tower House, 269 Walmersley Road, BURY, LANCASHIRE, BL9 6NX.

COLLIER, Mr. Stephen Howard, FCA *1972;* Lindum, The Green, Adderbury, BANBURY, OX17 3NE.

•**COLLIER, Mr. Stewart Cyril, FCA** *1979;* (Tax Fac), Mark J Rees, Granville Hall, Granville Road, LEICESTER, LE1 7RU.

COLLIER, Mr. Timothy David, BA ACA *1999;* 29 Salisbury Road, Weston Park, STAFFORD, ST16 3SE.

•**COLLIER-KEYWOOD, Mr. Richard David, LLB FCA** *1986;* PricewaterhouseCoopers LLP, 1 Embankment Place, LONDON, WC2N 6RH. See also PricewaterhouseCoopers

COLLIER-MARSH, Mrs. Janette Mary, BA ACA *2006;* Old Coach House Seagry Road, Sutton Benger, CHIPPENHAM, SN15 4RX.

COLLIER-MARSH, Mr. Peter James, BA ACA *2004;* RWE Supply & Trading, Windmill Hill Business Park Whitehill Way, SWINDON, SN5 6PB.

COLLIEU, Miss. Sophia Jane, MA ACA *1994;* 7 Cedar Rock Meadows, EAST GREENWICH, RI 02818, UNITED STATES.

COLLIGAN, Mrs. Annabelle Clare, BA ACA *1992;* 130 Rusthall Avenue, Chiswick, LONDON, W4 1BS.

•**COLLIGHAN, Mr. Justin Thomas, BCom ACA** *1993;* Justin Collighan ACA, 5 Farm House Close, Whittle-le-Woods, CHORLEY, LANCASHIRE, PR6 7QN.

COLLIN, Mr. Nigel Kenneth Benno Sippel, MA FCA *1975;* 77 Gilhams Avenue, BANSTEAD, SURREY, SM7 1QW.

COLLIN, Mr. Paul Henry, FCA *1971;* 28 Highview Avenue, EDGWARE, MIDDLESEX, HA8 9TZ.

COLLING, Mr. Andrew Robert, MA ACA *1996;* 2 The Old Warehouse, Summerbridge, HARROGATE, NORTH YORKSHIRE, HG3 4BG.

COLLING, Miss. Dorothy Sarah, LLB ACA *1989;* 12 Sebastian Street, LONDON, EC1V 0JA.

COLLING, Mr. John, FCA *1967;* Kinda Cool, Wycombe Road, Stokenchurch, HIGH WYCOMBE, BUCKINGHAMSHIRE, HP14 3RR. (Life Member)

COLLING, Mr. Mark, BSc ACA *1998;* with Baker Tilly Tax & Advisory Services LLP, Hartwell House, 55-61 Victoria Street, BRISTOL, BS1 6AD.

COLLING, Mr. Michael Leonard, BSc ACA *1987;* 16 Beeston Road, SALE, CHESHIRE, M33 5AG.

COLLING, Mr. Richard Aubrey, FCA *1977;* 16 Martindale Gr, Eaglescliffe, STOCKTON-ON-TEES, TS16 9DL.

COLLING, Mrs. Ruth Mary, BSc(Hons) ACA *2000;* 121 Abbey Road, BRISTOL, BS9 3QJ.

COLLINGE, Mrs. Clare Elizabeth, BSc ACA *1996;* The Tile House, 34 Bakehouse Lane, Ockbrook, DERBY, DE72 3RH.

COLLINGE, Mr. David Arthur, BSc ACA *2003;* 3 Heron Way, ROYSTON, HERTFORDSHIRE, SG8 7XH.

COLLINGE, Mrs. Jodi, BA(Hons) ACA CTA *2003;* 21 Lucknow Road, HAVELOCK NORTH 4130, NEW ZEALAND.

COLLINGE, Mr. Mark Peter, MSc ACA *2002;* 4417 N Damen Ave, CHICAGO, IL 60625, UNITED STATES.

COLLINGE, Mr. Roger Arnold, FCA *1966;* Laneside, Staveley, KENDAL, CUMBRIA, LA8 9QZ.

COLLINGE, Mr. Thomas, BSc ACA *2010;* 4 The Chapel, Scammonden, HUDDERSFIELD, HD3 3FW.

COLLINGRIDGE, Mr. Neil Angus, BSc ACA *1991;* Headmaster's House, 41 The Lycee, 1 Stannary Street, LONDON, SE11 4AD.

COLLINGS, Mr. Andrew Christopher, BSc ACA *1999;* 21 Warham Road, Otford, SEVENOAKS, KENT, TN14 5PF.

COLLINGS, Mr. Glynn Martin, BSc ACA *1985;* 187 Baldock Road, LETCHWORTH GARDEN CITY, SG6 2EJ.

COLLINGS, Mr. John Davison, BSc FCA *1978;* 5 The Pickerings, Humber Road, NORTH FERRIBY, HU14 3EJ.

COLLINGS, Mr. Justin Stuart, MA BA ACA *2002;* 21 Desmond Avenue, CAMBRIDGE, CB1 9JS.

•**COLLINGS, Mr. Patrick Nigel, FCA** *1965;* (Tax Fac), Collings & Co, Treen, Perranwell, Goonhavern, TRURO, TR4 9PD.

•**COLLINGS, Mr. Paul Andrew, MSc ACA CTA** *2002;* Francis Clark LLP, Sigma House, Oak View Close, Edginswell Park, TORQUAY, TQ2 7FF. See also Francis Clark Tax Consultancy Ltd

COLLINGS, Mr. Peter Glydon, FCA CF *1966;* Wellesley Consulting, Green Cottage, Woodgate Green, Knighton-on-Teme, TENBURY WELLS, WORCESTERSHIRE WR15 8LX.

COLLINGS, Mr. Peter Richard, BSc ACA *1987;* (Tax Fac), with PricewaterhouseCoopers LLP, 31 Great George Street, BRISTOL, BS1 5QD.

COLLINGS, Mr. Simon David, BSc FCA *1981;* 9 Lundy Walk, HAILSHAM, EAST SUSSEX, BN27 3BJ.

COLLINGS, Mr. Stuart Gordon, FCA *1956;* Woodstock, Park Road, Combs, STOWMARKET, IP14 2JS. (Life Member)

COLLINGWOOD, Mr. Andrew Vinden, LLB ACA *2000;* 6 Fair View, ALRESFORD, SO24 9PR.

COLLINGWOOD, Mr. Craig Lee, BA(Hons) ACA *2001;* 4 Apollo Close, Oakhurst, SWINDON, SN25 2JB.

COLLINGWOOD, Mr. Keith John, FCA *1972;* The Grange, Sutton Cum Granby, NOTTINGHAM, NOTTINGHAMSHIRE, NG13 9QA.

COLLINGWOOD, Mr. Matthew, ACA *2008;* 16 Victory Road, LONDON, SW19 1HN.

COLLINGWOOD, Mr. Nigel Ronald, FCA *1968;* 55 Croftdown Road, Harborne, BIRMINGHAM, B17 8RE. (Life Member)

•**COLLINGWOOD, Mr. Paul, FCA** *1982;* HW, Sterling House, 22 St. Cuthberts Way, DARLINGTON, COUNTY DURHAM, DL1 1GB. See also Haines Watts

COLLINGWOOD, Mr. Roland Frank, BA FCA ATT CTA *1970;* (Tax Fac), HMG Law LLP, 126 High Street, OXFORD, OX1 4DG.

COLLINGWOOD, Dr. Sophia, PhD BA ACA *2002;* Flat A, 90 Kingscourt Road, LONDON, SW16 1JB.

COLLINI, Mr Mark Paul, BA ACA *1981;* 26 Eastcastle Street, LONDON, W1W 8DQ.

COLLINI, Mr. Peter Mark, MA ACA *1993;* Wellingtonia, Linden Chase Road, SEVENOAKS, KENT, TN13 3JU.

•**COLLINI, Mr. Roy Michael Daniel, FCA** *1975;* DeVines Accountants Limited, DeVine House, 1299-1301 London Road, LEIGH-ON-SEA, ESSEX, SS9 2AD. See also De Vines

COLLINS, Mr. Adam, BEng ACA *1997;* 8 Oates Way, Ramsey, HUNTINGDON, CAMBRIDGESHIRE, PE26 1UX.

COLLINS, Mr. Alexander John Howard, MA ACA *1998;* 135 Bishopsgate, LONDON, EC2M 3UR.

COLLINS, Ms. Alexis Deborah, ACA *1994;* 1 Linnet Grove, GUILDFORD, GU4 7DT.

COLLINS, Mrs. Alison Elizabeth Clare, BA ACA *1986;* 20 Carlingford Road, Hampstead, LONDON, NW3 1RX.

COLLINS, Miss. Alison Kate, MA ACA *2001;* Experian, 1271 Avenue of the Americas, 45th Floor, NEW YORK, NY 10020, UNITED STATES.

COLLINS, Mrs. Alison Louise, BSc ACA *2002;* 7 Lavender Close, off Highlands Road, LEATHERHEAD, KT22 8LZ.

COLLINS, Mr. Allan, BA ACA CTA *1987;* 29 St. Johns Green, CHELMSFORD, CM1 3DZ.

COLLINS, Mrs. Amy, ACA *2008;* (Tax Fac), Grant Thornton Enterprise House, 115 Edmund Street, BIRMINGHAM, B3 2HJ.

COLLINS, Mr. Andrew David, BSc FCA *1977;* 25 Haldon Avenue, TEIGNMOUTH, TQ14 8LA.

COLLINS, Mr. Andrew John, BSc ACA *1984;* 84 Stanlake Road, LONDON, W12 7HJ.

COLLINS, Mr. Andrew Richard, FCA *1974;* Suite 394, 48 Par La Ville Road, HAMILTON HM 11, BERMUDA.

COLLINS, Mr. Andrew Richard Purnell, BSc(Hons) ACA *2001;* 3 Middle Grass, Irthlingborough, WELLINGBOROUGH, NORTHAMPTONSHIRE, NN9 5TW.

COLLINS, Ms. Anna, ACA *2010;* 96 Playford Road, LONDON, N4 3NL.

COLLINS, Mr. Anthony, ARCS ACA *1978;* 43 Beatrice Avenue, Norbury, LONDON, SW16 4UW.

COLLINS, Mr. Anthony Brian, BSc FCA *1990;* Plummer Parsons, 4 Frederick Terrace, Frederick Place, BRIGHTON, EAST SUSSEX, BN1 1AX.

COLLINS, Mr. Anthony David, FCA *1975;* 64 Watkins Road, DALKEITH, WA 6009, AUSTRALIA.

COLLINS, Mr. Benedict John, ACA *2008;* Konall Culture Exchange, No. 88 Huai An Xi Lu, Zhuo Da Mei Gui Yuan, 24-2-301, SHIJIAZHUANG 050091, HEBEI PROVINCE CHINA.

COLLINS, Mr. Benjamin Leigh, MMath ACA *2010;* 1 St. Anthony's Close, LONDON, E1W 1LT.

COLLINS, Mr. Bernard, FCA *1954;* Flat 11, The Watergardens, Elrington Road, WOODFORD GREEN, ESSEX, IG8 0GD. (Life Member)

•**COLLINS, Mr. Bernard Michael, FCA** *1955;* Munro's, 1341 High Road, Whetstone, LONDON, N20 9HR. See also Munro's (Accounting Services) Limited and Munros

COLLINS, Mr. Brian, FCA *1963;* 1 Meadow Drive, The DriveChestfield, WHITSTABLE, CT5 3NR.

COLLINS, Mr. Brian Arthur, FCA *1955;* 54 The Park, YEOVIL, BA20 1DF. (Life Member)

COLLINS, Mr. Bryan John, BSc ACA *1995;* Schlossberg 3d, 6343 RISCH, SWITZERLAND.

•**COLLINS, Mrs. Caroline Mary, BA ACA** *1989;* 44 Bradmore Way, COULSDON, CR5 1PA.

•**COLLINS, Mrs. Carolyn Amanda, BSc ACA** *1993;* Ledgers Accountancy Services Limited, 15 Sedgmoor Close, Flackwell Heath, HIGH WYCOMBE, BUCKINGHAMSHIRE, HP10 9BH.

COLLINS, Mr. Chris, BA ACA *1991;* Cornerstone Private Equity, 29 Farm Street, LONDON, W1J 5RL.

COLLINS, Mr. Christopher Andrew, FCA *1973;* 27 The Paddocks, WITHAM, ESSEX, CM8 2DR.

COLLINS, Mr. Christopher John, BSc ACA *2003;* G K N Plc, Ipsley House, Ipsley Church Lane, REDDITCH, WORCESTERSHIRE, B98 0TL.

COLLINS, Mr. Christopher Peter, BSc ACA *1995;* 9 Pound Close, Long Ditton, SURBITON, KT6 5JW.

COLLINS, Mr. Christopher Richard, BA ACA *1993;* Pension Protection Fund, Knollys House, 17 Addiscombe Road, CROYDON, CR0 6SR.

COLLINS, Mrs. Chulanapa, MSci ACA *2010;* Hall floor flat, 10 Alma Road, Clifton, BRISTOL, BS8 2BY.

COLLINS, Mrs. Claire Mary, ACA *1999;* 1 The Arbour, Hurtmore, GODALMING, GU7 2RU.

COLLINS, Mr. Daniel Paul, BSc(Hons) ACA *2004;* 4 Tony Webb Close, COLCHESTER, ESSEX, CO4 9ST.

COLLINS, Mr. David Alan, FCA *1968;* 4 Cedar Close, Lillington, LEAMINGTON SPA, CV32 7DD.

COLLINS, Mr. David Alford, BA ACA *1980;* 3 Malkin Drive, BEACONSFIELD, HP9 1JN.

COLLINS, Mr. David Alistair, ACA *2010;* 7 Pasture View, Sherburn in Elmet, LEEDS, LS25 6LZ.

COLLINS, Mr. David Andrew, BSc ACA *2003;* Flat 5, 4 Mercier Road, LONDON, SW15 2AT.

COLLINS, Mr. David Anthony, MBA MEng ACA MIET *1993;* 42 Derwent Street, MENTONE, VIC 3194, AUSTRALIA.

COLLINS, Mr. David George, FCA *1973;* 9 Westfield Drive, Skelmanthorpe, HUDDERSFIELD, HD8 9AN. (Life Member)

COLLINS, Mr. David Harold, FCA *1965;* c/o M S H, 784 Memorial Drive, CAMBRIDGE, MA 02139, UNITED STATES.

COLLINS, Mr. David Jeremy, BA FCA *1985;* KPMG, 8/F Prince's Building, 10 Chater Road, CENTRAL, HONG KONG ISLAND, HONG KONG SAR.

COLLINS, Mr. David John, ACA CA(AUS) *2008;* PO Box 108, BRISBANE, QLD 4000, AUSTRALIA.

COLLINS, Mr. David Michael, BA ACA *2003;* with Halpern and Co, 20 Berkeley Street, LONDON, W1J 8EE.

COLLINS, Mr. David Richard, FCA *1970;* Wynstay, Widmerpool Road, Wysall, NOTTINGHAM, NG12 5QW.

COLLINS, Mr. Donald Eric, BA FCA *1972;* Barn House Wierton Hill, Boughton Monchelsea, MAIDSTONE, ME17 4JS.

COLLINS, Mr. Edward Patrick, BSc ACA *1998;* 1 Brookvale Drive, #04-19 Bowland Block, Sunset Way, SINGAPORE 599968, SINGAPORE.

COLLINS, Mrs. Elisabeth Mary, BA ACA *1996;* Church Farm, Church Lane, Lower Failand, BRISTOL, BS8 3SW.

COLLINS, Mrs. Elizabeth Alice Leonie, BSc(Hons) ACA *2001;* Fourways Littleford Lane, Blackheath, GUILDFORD, GU4 8QY.

COLLINS, Miss. Elizabeth Anne, ACA CTA *1993;* 1 Thirlmere Avenue, Litherland, LIVERPOOL, L21 5HP.

COLLINS, Mrs. Elizabeth Mary, ACA CA(SA) *2009;* 40 Leeward Gardens, Wimbledon, LONDON, SW19 7QR.
COLLINS, Mr. Elliot, BSc ACA *2001;* Sunnyside, Chinnor Road, Bledlow Ridge, HIGH WYCOMBE, BUCKINGHAMSHIRE, HP14 4AB.
COLLINS, Mr. Eric James, ACA *1979;* 14 Winds Point, Hagley, STOURBRIDGE, WEST MIDLANDS, DY9 0PN.
COLLINS, Mr. Francis Peter, FCA *1969;* Barnabas Associates, The Hope Centre, Western Avenue, CHESTER, CH1 5PP.
COLLINS, Mr. Francis Philip, FCA *1940;* Chez Mme Nicole Jacquet, La Blonniere, 74230 DINGY ST CLAIR, FRANCE. (Life Member)
COLLINS, Mr. Fraser Reid, BSc ACA *1988;* The Old Forge, Oulston, YORK, YO61 3PX.
COLLINS, Mr. Frederick Donald, FCA *1954;* 79 The Esplanade, FRENCHS FOREST, NSW 2086, AUSTRALIA. (Life Member)
COLLINS, Mr. Gary, BSc ACA *2010;* 35 Abberley Wood, Great Shelford, CAMBRIDGE, CB22 5EF.
•COLLINS, Mr. Gary Milo, MA FCA CTA *1986;* (Tax Fac), KPMG LLP, One Snowhill, Snow Hill Queensway, BIRMINGHAM, B4 6GN. See also KPMG Europe LLP
•COLLINS, Mr. Geoffrey, MA FCA CTA *1979;* (Tax Fac), Geoffrey Collins Ltd, Parallel House, 32 London Road, GUILDFORD, SURREY, GU1 2AB.
COLLINS, Mr. Geoffrey Andrew, BSc FCA *1993;* 68 Manor Farm Road, SOUTHAMPTON, SO18 1NQ.
COLLINS, Mr. Geoffrey James, BSc FCA *1976;* La Casuarina Ave Opalo, Buzon 221, Mijas La Nueva 30, Mijas Pueblo, 29650 MIJAS, SPAIN.
COLLINS, Mr. Gerald Peter Leslie, ACA *1986;* Bidwells LLP, Trumpington Road, Trumpington, CAMBRIDGE, CB2 9LD.
COLLINS, Mrs. Gillian Mary, BSc ACA *1996;* 27 Park Road, Hagley, STOURBRIDGE, DY9 0NS.
•COLLINS, Mr. Graham Edward, BA FCA *1991;* M T Manley & Co Ltd, 696 Yardley Wood Road, Billesley, BIRMINGHAM, B13 0HY.
COLLINS, Mr. Grant John, BA FCA *1999;* Capita, 12 Castle Street, St. Helier, JERSEY, JE2 3RT.
COLLINS, Mrs. Hayley Kathryn, BA(Hons) ACA *2002;* 16 Frankfield Rise, TUNBRIDGE WELLS, KENT, TN2 5LF.
COLLINS, Mr. Iain Alistair, MA MBA FCA CTA *1995;* (Tax Fac), 11 Ramsdale Road, Bramhall, STOCKPORT, CHESHIRE, SK7 2PZ.
COLLINS, Mr. Ian Richard, BA ACA *1993;* 11a Harrington Road, BRIGHTON, BN1 6RE.
COLLINS, Mr. Ian Roger, FCA *1959;* The Holme, Green Lane, DRONFIELD, S18 2FG. (Life Member)
COLLINS, Mrs. Jackie Louise, BSc ACA *1987;* 29 St. Johns Green, CHELMSFORD, CM1 3DZ.
•COLLINS, Miss. Jacqueline Brenda, FCA *1971;* (Tax Fac), Le Menage Farm, Les Petites Rues, St. Lawrence, JERSEY, JE3 1FD.
COLLINS, Mr. James, BEng ACA *2005;* 12 David's Close, Skidby, COTTINGHAM, NORTH HUMBERSIDE, HU16 5UD.
COLLINS, Mr. James Francis, BSc ACA *2010;* 9 Dulverton Drive, Sully, PENARTH, SOUTH GLAMORGAN, CF64 5EW.
COLLINS, Mrs. Jane Elizabeth, ACA *1995;* Keim Mineral Paints Ltd, Santok Building, Deer Park Way, Donnington Wood, TELFORD, SHROPSHIRE TF2 7NA.
COLLINS, Mrs. Jenice Clare, MA ACA *2000;* 69 Felsham Road, LONDON, SW15 1AZ.
COLLINS, Mrs. Joanne Elizabeth, BA ACA *1995;* Schlossberg 3d, 6343 RISCH, SWITZERLAND.
COLLINS, Mr. John Alford Kingswell, FCA *1948;* Blackwater Mill, Blackwater Road, NEWPORT, ISLE OF WIGHT, PO30 3BE. (Life Member)
COLLINS, Mr. John Anthony, MA FCA *1967;* 22 rue Etienne-Dumont, CH-1204 GENEVA, SWITZERLAND. (Life Member)
•COLLINS, Mr. John David, FCA *1964;* 17 Ashley Close, WALTON-ON-THAMES, KT12 1BJ.
COLLINS, Mr. John Geoffrey, BCom FCA *1956;* Flat 11 Carnegie Court, 17 Springs Lane, ILKLEY, WEST YORKSHIRE, LS29 8SN. (Life Member)
COLLINS, Mr. John Joseph, MA ACA *1983;* 48 Shaftesbury Road, Earlsdon, COVENTRY, CV5 6FN.
COLLINS, Mr. John William, BA ACA *1978;* 62a Richmond Road, LONDON, SW20 0PQ.
COLLINS, Mr. John William Martin, BA(Hons) ACA *2011;* 38 Hertford Way, Knowle, SOLIHULL, WEST MIDLANDS, B93 0PD.
COLLINS, Mr. Jonathan, MA(Hons) ACA *2011;* Leyside, 2 Marks Orchard, Granborough, BUCKINGHAM, MK18 3QS.
COLLINS, Mr. Jonathan, BA ACA *2008;* Fauchier Partners, 72 Welbeck Street, LONDON, W1G 0AY.
COLLINS, Mr. Jonathan Mark, BSc ACA *1996;* Manor Park, Storwood, YORK, YO42 4TD.
COLLINS, Mr. Jonathan Philip, ACA *2010;* 65 Copthorne Road, LEATHERHEAD, SURREY, KT22 7EE.
COLLINS, Mrs. Julia Ann, MA ACA *1981;* Whinbush Farm, Walthams Cross, Great Bardfield, BRAINTREE, ESSEX, CM7 4QJ.
COLLINS, Miss. Julia Downing, MA(Hons) ACA *2003;* 30 Woodfall Street, LONDON, SW3 4DJ.
COLLINS, Mrs. Julie Ann, BSc ACA *1993;* Delves, Newland Street, Eynsham, WITNEY, OXFORDSHIRE, OX29 4LD.
COLLINS, Mrs. Karen Anne, BA ACA *1997;* Queen Anne House, 4-6 New Street, LEICESTER, LE1 5NR.
COLLINS, Mr. Leslie John, BSc ACA *1985;* 2 The Finches, Greet, CHELTENHAM, GLOUCESTERSHIRE, GL54 5NR.
COLLINS, Miss. Lucie Jessica, ACA *2005;* Zurlindenstrasse 9, 8003 ZURICH, SWITZERLAND.
COLLINS, Ms. Maebh, LLB ACA *2002;* ARDCULLEN, OMEATH, COUNTY LOUTH, IRELAND.
COLLINS, Mr. Mark, BSc(Hons) ACA *1999;* 32 Park Road, WITNEY, OX28 6EN.
•COLLINS, Mr. Mark David, BA FCA *1998;* 20 Roslyn Close, BROXBOURNE, HERTFORDSHIRE, EN10 7DA.
•COLLINS, Mr. Mark William Gerard, FCA *1977;* Whitelow House Farm, Whitelow Lane, SHEFFIELD, S17 3AG.
COLLINS, Mr. Martin Charles, ACA *1980;* Kundalila, Rance Pitch, Upton St. Leonards, GLOUCESTER, GL4 8AE.
COLLINS, Mr. Matthew Thomas, ACA *1986;* PO Box 133300, Eastridge, AUCKLAND 1146, NEW ZEALAND.
COLLINS, Mr. Michael Anthony Mclaughlin, BA ACA *1979;* 19 Fulford Road, EPSOM, KT19 9QZ.
COLLINS, Mr. Michael Benedict, FCA *1975;* Derryvella, Glengoole, THURLES, COUNTY TIPPERARY, IRELAND.
•COLLINS, Mr. Michael Brian, FCA *1969;* Les Adams Farm, Rue Des Adams, St. Pierre Du Bois, GUERNSEY, GY7 9LH.
COLLINS, Mr. Michael Gregory, BSc ACA *1994;* 1a Onslow Road, HOVE, EAST SUSSEX, BN3 6TA.
COLLINS, Mr. Michael James, BSc FCA *1973;* Rambler Cottage, Chapel Drove, Horton Heath, EASTLEIGH, SO50 7DL.
•COLLINS, Mr. Michael Nathan, FCA *1971;* (Tax Fac), Collins & Company, 2nd Floor, 116 College Road, HARROW, HA1 1BQ.
COLLINS, Mr. Miles Eric, LLB ACA *1991;* SSP Group Limited, 1 The Heights, Brooklands, WEYBRIDGE, SURREY, KT13 0NY.
COLLINS, Mr. Nathaniel James, BSc ACA *2001;* 16 Frankfield Rise, TUNBRIDGE WELLS, KENT, TN2 5LF.
COLLINS, Mr. Neville Vernon, FCA *1948;* Le Menage Farm, Les Petites Rues, St Lawrence, JERSEY, JE3 1FD. (Life Member)
COLLINS, Mr. Nicholas, BA ACA *1997;* 15 Farmleigh Close, Farmleighwoods, Castleknock, DUBLIN 15, COUNTY DUBLIN, IRELAND.
COLLINS, Mr. Nicholas Charles Elliot, BSc(Econ) ACA *2001;* 30 Dewey Street, LONDON, SW17 8TQ.
COLLINS, Mr. Nicholas Marshall, MPhys ACA AMCT *2006;* 2 St. Marys Walk, Hambleton, SELBY, NORTH YORKSHIRE, YO8 9GH.
•COLLINS, Mr. Nigel John, FCA *1983;* Collins Hart, Victoria House, 437 Birmingham Road, SUTTON COLDFIELD, B72 1AX.
COLLINS, Miss. Pamela Jane, BSc ACA *1984;* Threestacks Cottage, Twyning Road, Upper Strensham, WORCESTER, WR8 9LH.
COLLINS, Mr. Patrick Hugh, BA FCA *1977;* (Tax Fac), 39 Julian Road, Chelsfield, ORPINGTON, KENT, BR6 6HT.
COLLINS, Mr. Patrick John, BA ACA *1982;* 102 Woodberry Avenue, Winchmore Hill, LONDON, N21 3LB.
COLLINS, Mr. Paul, FCA *1969;* 402 East 90 Street, Apt 3A, NEW YORK, NY 10128, UNITED STATES.
COLLINS, Mr. Paul Andrew, BA ACA *1993;* 1st Floor Flat 50 Harley Street, LONDON, W1G 9PX.
COLLINS, Mr. Paul Edward, FCA *1978;* Daniels, 14-14a Station Field Industrial Estate, KIDLINGTON, OXFORDSHIRE, OX5 1JD.
•COLLINS, Mr. Paul Jeffrey, FCA *1984;* Collins & Co, 73a New Court Way, Ormskirk Business Park, ORMSKIRK, L39 2YT. See also Collins, Williams & Co
COLLINS, Mr. Paul Jonathan, BSc ACA *1987;* 31 Dickinson Square, Croxley Green, RICKMANSWORTH, WD3 3HA.
•COLLINS, Mr. Paul Leslie, BSc(Econ) ACA *1982;* 89 Canford Cliffs Road, POOLE, DORSET, BH13 7EW.
COLLINS, Mr. Paul Simon, BSc ACA *1984;* 5 Weare Close, Billesdon, LEICESTER, LE7 9DY.
COLLINS, Mr. Peter Graham, FCA *1960;* 17 Guillards Oak, MIDHURST, GU29 9JZ. (Life Member)
COLLINS, Mr. Peter James, BSc ACA *2007;* with KPMG LLP, One Snowhill, Snow Hill Queensway, BIRMINGHAM, B4 6GN.
COLLINS, Mr. Peter John, MEng ACA *1997;* 40B Lower Kirklington Road, SOUTHWELL, NOTTINGHAMSHIRE, NG25 0DN.
COLLINS, Mr. Peter John, FCA *1960;* Dragon Waters, 56 Barolin Esplanade, CORAL COVE, QLD 4670, AUSTRALIA. (Life Member)
COLLINS, Mr. Peter Martin, BSc ACA *1984;* P.O. Box F-40444, FREEPORT, BAHAMAS.
•COLLINS, Mr. Peter Richard, FCA *1990;* (Tax Fac), Hartley Fowler LLP, 44 Springfield Road, HORSHAM, WEST SUSSEX, RH12 2PD.
COLLINS, Mr. Peter William, MBA BSc FCA *1978;* 4 Barkhart Close, WOKINGHAM, BERKSHIRE, RG40 1PN.
COLLINS, Mr. Philip, BSc FCA *1975;* Castle Hill House, Castle Hill, Nether Stowey, BRIDGWATER, SOMERSET, TA5 1NA. (Life Member)
•COLLINS, Mr. Philip, BSc ACA CTA *1991;* Philip Collins, 37 Carmarthen Road, Up Hatherley, CHELTENHAM, GLOUCESTERSHIRE, GL51 3JZ.
COLLINS, Mr. Philip John, MSc FCA *1991;* Facilities Department, House of Commons, LONDON, SW1A 0AA.
•COLLINS, Mr. Phillip, FCA *1983;* Hillier Hopkins LLP, 64 Clarendon Road, WATFORD, WD17 1DA.
COLLINS, Mr. Phillip Ross, BA(Hons) ACA *2004;* 8 Witches Lane, SEVENOAKS, TN13 2AU.
COLLINS, Mr. Raymond Herbert, FCA *1970;* 24 Normandie Close, LUDLOW, SY8 1UJ.
COLLINS, Mr. Richard Alexander, BSc FCA *1978;* 41 Thickthorn Close, KENILWORTH, CV8 2AF.
COLLINS, Mr. Richard Anthony, MA FCA *1984;* Wood Macenzie Ltd Milbank House, 1 Finsbury Square, LONDON, EC2A 1AE.
•COLLINS, Mr. Richard Howard, FCA *1970;* Collins Davies Ltd, 371 Exeter Road, EXMOUTH, DEVON, EX8 3NS.
COLLINS, Mr. Richard Leycester, MA FCA CF *1996;* Granville House, 132 Sloane Street, LONDON, SW1X 9AX.
COLLINS, Mr. Robert James Walter, BA ACA *1993;* c/o Expat Strategies Limited, Rm 207 2/f. St. George's Building, 2 Ice House Street, CENTRAL, HONG KONG SAR.
COLLINS, Mr. Robert Michael, MA MPhil ACA *2002;* 21 Chatsworth Road, BRIGHTON, BN1 5DB.
COLLINS, Mr. Robert Simon, BSc ACA *2002;* Pricewaterhousecoopers Llp Central Business Exchange, Midsummer Boulevard, MILTON KEYNES, MK9 2DF.
COLLINS, Mr. Robert Stewart, BA ACA ACCA *1998;* Evolution Securities Ltd, 100 Wood Street, LONDON, EC2V 7AN.
COLLINS, Mr. Robin Peter, BSc FCA *1977;* 9 King Johns Place, Egham Hill, EGHAM, SURREY, TW20 0AP.
COLLINS, Mr. Roderic, FCA *1975;* Calleva, 32 Lark Hill Rise, Badger Farm, WINCHESTER, SO22 4LX.
COLLINS, Mr. Ronald Michael, FCA *1953;* Apartment 1, 7 The Springs, Bowdon, ALTRINCHAM, CHESHIRE, WA14 3JH. (Life Member)
COLLINS, Mr. Roy Edwin, FCA *1973;* 39 Nelson Street, OAKVILLE L6L 3H5, ON, CANADA.
•COLLINS, Mr. Russell Peter, MA FCA *1982;* Deloitte LLP, Hill House, 1 Little New Street, LONDON, EC4A 3TR. See also Deloitte & Touche LLP
COLLINS, Mrs. Samantha Angharad, BEng ACA *2004;* 53 Sackville Road, SOUTHEND-ON-SEA, SS2 4UG.
COLLINS, Miss. Samantha Louise, ACA *2009;* (Tax Fac), Victoria Suite, Balmoral Executive Apartments, 8 Clarendon Road, St. Helier, JERSEY, JE2 3YW.
COLLINS, Mrs. Samantha Louise, BA ACA *2007;* 2 Burnet Close, Pinewood, IPSWICH, IP8 3TN.
COLLINS, Mrs. Sarah Elizabeth, BA ACA *2006;* 3 Mead Close, Peasemore, NEWBURY, BERKSHIRE, RG20 7JD.
COLLINS, Mr. Sean Anthony, MA FCA *1975;* 7 Shortheath Road, FARNHAM, SURREY, GU9 8SR.
COLLINS, Mrs. Sharon Louise, BSc ACA *2003;* with Livesey Spottiswood Limited, 17 George Street, ST.HELENS, WA10 1DB.
COLLINS, Mr. Shaun Anthony, BSc FCA *1993;* Delves, Newland Street, Eynsham, WITNEY, OXFORDSHIRE, OX29 4LD.
•COLLINS, Mr. Simon Jeremy, BA ACA *1986;* KPMG LLP, 15 Canada Square, LONDON, E14 5GL. See also KPMG Europe LLP
COLLINS, Mr. Simon Jonathan, BA ACA *1987;* 23 Harbour Street, MOSMAN, NSW 2088, AUSTRALIA.
COLLINS, Mrs. Stacey, ACA *2009;* 27 Little Weighton Road, Skidby, COTTINGHAM, NORTH HUMBERSIDE, HU16 5TW.
COLLINS, Mr. Stanley Simon, FCA *1960;* Tepesmede, High Road, CHIPSTEAD, SURREY, CR5 3QP. (Life Member)
COLLINS, Ms. Stephanie Margaret, CA ACA *1994;* Apartment 816, 2261 Lakeshore Boulevard West, TORONTO M8V 3X1, ON, CANADA.
COLLINS, Mr. Stephen Andrew, BSc ACA *2000;* 26 Ashcourt Drive, Woodfield Plantation, DONCASTER, DN4 8SZ.
COLLINS, Mr. Stephen Nicholas, BSc(Hons) ACA *2000;* c/o Ernst & Young Terco, Avenida Nações Unidas 12.995, Brooklin Paulista, SAO PAULO, 04578-000, BRAZIL.
COLLINS, Mr. Stephen Philip, BSc ACA *1992;* 11 Chelford Drive, Kingsmead, NORTHWICH, CW9 8XP.
COLLINS, Mr. Stephen Richard, BCom FCA *1993;* 27 Park Road, Hagley, STOURBRIDGE, DY9 0NS.
•COLLINS, Mr. Stephen Robert, BA FCA *1985;* Saffery Champness, Stuart House, City Road, PETERBOROUGH, PE1 1QF.
•COLLINS, Mr. Steven, BSc ACA *1978;* The Vine Cottage, Railway Street, BRIDGNORTH, SHROPSHIRE, WV16 4AT.
COLLINS, Mr. Steven, BSc ACA *2005;* C Czarnikow Sugar Ltd, 24 Chiswell Street, LONDON, EC1Y 4SG.
COLLINS, Mr. Steven Ian, BSc(Hons) ACA *2003;* BDO USA LLP, 3200 Bristol Street, Suite 400, COSTA MESA, CA 92602, UNITED STATES.
COLLINS, Mr. Stuart, BEng ACA *1995;* Holmecroft, Park Road, Scotby, CARLISLE, CA4 8AR.
•COLLINS, Mr. Stuart Charles, MA FCA ATII *1995;* PKF (UK) LLP, Pannell House, Park Street, GUILDFORD, SURREY, GU1 4HN.
COLLINS, Mr. William, FCA *1967;* Copper Beeches, Beacon Hill, Wickham Bishops, WITHAM, ESSEX, CM8 3EA.
COLLINS, Mr. William Rupert, BA ACA *1998;* 51 Shakespeare Road, LONDON, W3 6SD.
COLLINS, Mr. William Sidney, FCA *1953;* 49 Droylesdon Park Road, Finham, COVENTRY, CV3 6EQ. (Life Member)
•COLLINS-DRYER, Mr. Simon John, BA FCA *1982;* S. Collins-Dryer, 23 Millpond Court, ADDLESTONE, SURREY, KT15 2JY.
•COLLINS-HALL, Mrs. Louise, ACA *2009;* with Stopford Associates Limited, Synergy House, 7 Acorn Business Park, Commercial Gate, MANSFIELD, NOTTINGHAMSHIRE NG18 1EX.
COLLINS-TAYLOR, Mr. James Desmond, BA ACA *1983;* Lannhall, Tynron, THORNHILL, DUMFRIESSHIRE, DG3 4LB.
COLLINSON, Mr. Adam Richard, BSc ACA *1996;* 16 Judson Avenue, Stapleford, NOTTINGHAM, NG9 7FH.
COLLINSON, Mr. Alexander George, BSc ACA *2004;* 14 Rangers Avenue, MOSMAN, NSW 2088, AUSTRALIA.
COLLINSON, Mrs. Amanda Jane, ACA *1980;* Oleander, 12a Farleigh Road, Backwell, BRISTOL, BS48 3PA.
COLLINSON, Mrs. Amanda Sarah, ACA *2009;* with Deloitte & Touche LLP, Two World Financial Center, NEW YORK, NY 10281-1414, UNITED STATES.
COLLINSON, Mr. Andrew John, BSc FCA *1978;* 7 Norris Road, SALE, M33 3QW.
•COLLINSON, Mr. Anthony John Urquhart, FCA *1968;* (Tax Fac), 9 West Green Close, Edgbaston, BIRMINGHAM, B15 2LA.
COLLINSON, Mr. Antony Charles, BSc FCA *1978;* 19 Clare Road, BEDFORD, MK41 8QX.
•COLLINSON, Mr. Charles Robert, MBA FCA *1967;* Allery Scotts Ltd, 118 Piccadilly, LONDON, W1J 7NW.
COLLINSON, Mr. David Leo, BSc FCA *1980;* 66 Parish Ghyll Drive, ILKLEY, LS29 9PR.
COLLINSON, Mrs. Diane Margaret Eileen, BSc ACA *1997;* 2 Doulton Close, WINSFORD, CHESHIRE, CW7 3JS.
COLLINSON, Mr. Frank Arthur, FCA *1950;* 24 West Street, Corfe Castle, WAREHAM, BH20 5HD. (Life Member)
COLLINSON, Mr. Harold Hugh, FCA *1966;* Raaes Wyke, Longlands Road, WINDERMERE, CUMBRIA, LA23 1DL. (Life Member)
•COLLINSON, Mr. Ian Paul, BSc FCA *1986;* Baker Tilly (Gibraltar) Limited, Regal House, Queensway, PO Box 191, GIBRALTAR, GIBRALTAR.
COLLINSON, Miss. Joanne Linsey, BA ACA *1991;* Stroud & Swindon Building Society, Rowcroft, STROUD, GLOUCESTERSHIRE, GL5 3BG.
COLLINSON, Mr. John Arthur, FCA *1960;* 7 Hawthornden Drive, BELFAST, BT4 2HG. (Life Member)

COLLINSON, Mr. John David, FCA *1969;* 42 Dinorben Close, FLEET, GU52 7SL.
COLLINSON, Mrs. Joy Margaret, BSc ACA *1997;* 16 Judson Avenue, Stapleford, NOTTINGHAM, NG9 7FH.
•**COLLINSON, Mrs. Judith Irene, BSc ACA** *1983;* (Tax Fac), J.I.Collinson, 12 Windsor Place, Mangotsfield, BRISTOL, BS16 9DD.
COLLINSON, Mr. Martin, BSc ACA *2000;* QGC, Level 29, 275 George Street, BRISBANE, QLD 4000, AUSTRALIA.
COLLINSON, Mrs. Nina Elizabeth, BA ACA *2003;* 14 Rangers Avenue, MOSMAN, NSW 2088, AUSTRALIA.
COLLINSON, Mr. Peter Anthony, BA FCA *1962;* Langbank Business Services, Langbank, 115 Culduthel Road, INVERNESS, IV2 4EE.
COLLINSON, Mr. Philip John, MA FCA *1978;* Oleander, 12A Farleigh Road, Backwell, BRISTOL, BS48 3PA.
COLLINSON, Mrs. Rebecca, BSc FCA *1993;* 59 Broom Field, LIGHTWATER, SURREY, GU18 5QW.
COLLINSON, Mr. Richard Justin, BA ACA *1995;* 13 2, North Park Road, LEEDS, LS8 1JD.
COLLINSON, Miss. Sally Jane, BSc ACA *2001;* 8 Sandpiper Court, Calder Grove, WAKEFIELD, WEST YORKSHIRE, WF4 3FF.
•**COLLINSON, Mr. Stephen, BSc FCA** *1971;* (Tax Fac), 17 Redcliffe Road, SWANAGE, DORSET, BH19 1LZ.
COLLIS, Mr. Andrew Neil, BSc ACA *2005;* 18 Paddock Way, Higher Kinnerton, CHESTER, CH4 9BA.
COLLIS, Mrs. Angela Margaret, ACA *1979;* The Beren Hatchgate Farm Hatchgate Lane, Cockpole Green Wargrave, READING, RG10 8NE.
COLLIS, Mrs. Camilla Louise, LLB ACA *2003;* with PricewaterhouseCoopers LLP, 1 Embankment Place, LONDON, WC2N 6RH.
COLLIS, Mr. David Anthony, ACA *2009;* 24 Chewter Lane, WINDLESHAM, SURREY, GU20 6JP.
COLLIS, Mr. David John, FCA *1954;* 145 Blackbridge Lane, HORSHAM, WEST SUSSEX, RH12 1SD. (Life Member)
COLLIS, Mr. Douglas Patrick, BA ACA *1984;* 1 Penryhn Close, KENILWORTH, CV8 2PT.
COLLIS, Mr. Edward Terence, FCA *1958;* 6 Oaken Drive, SOLIHULL, B91 1RJ. (Life Member)
COLLIS, Mr. Edward Worsley Gurney, BSc ACA MCT *1994;* Glebe Cottage Church Lane, Bury, PULBOROUGH, WEST SUSSEX, RH20 1PB.
COLLIS, Mrs. Hannah Ruth, MA ACA *2003;* 8 Mitchley Avenue, PURLEY, SURREY, CR8 1EA.
COLLIS, Mr. Harvey Jack, FCA *1962;* 18 Blandford Close, LONDON, N2 0DH.
COLLIS, Mr. John, BA ACA *1992;* Easyhotel House, 80 Old Street, LONDON, EC1V 9AZ.
COLLIS, Mr. John Matthew Leigh, BA FCA *1994;* 10 Sunnyside Road, Ealing, LONDON, W5 5HU.
COLLIS, Mr. Julian James, BSc ACA *1999;* 11 Coltsfoot Way, Broughton Astley, LEICESTER, LE9 6YX.
COLLIS, Miss. Juliet, BA ACA *1987;* Mill House, Coarsewell, Ugborough, IVYBRIDGE, DEVON, PL21 0HP.
COLLIS, Mrs. Katherine Lisa, BSc(Hons) ACA *2000;* 20 Sherwood Avenue, ST. ALBANS, HERTFORDSHIRE, AL4 9QL.
COLLIS, Mr. Mark Russell, FCA *1998;* First Floor Davidson House, Forbury Square, READING, BERKSHIRE, RG1 3EU.
COLLIS, Mr. Michael Christopher, BA ACA *1992;* 145 Holme Road, West Bridgford, NOTTINGHAM, NG2 5AG.
COLLIS, Mr. Nigel Leigh, BCom FCA *1967;* 1 Coles Green, Leigh Sinton, MALVERN, WR13 5DW. (Life Member)
COLLIS, Mr. Noel, BA ACA *1989;* 3510 York Road, WINSTON-SALEM, NC 27104, UNITED STATES.
•**COLLIS, Mr. Richard John, BSc ACA** *2003;* Saffery Champness, Lion House, Red Lion Street, LONDON, WC1R 4GB.
COLLIS, Mr. Ronald Stephen Paul, ACA *1982;* (Tax Fac), Hunters Lodge, Old Lane, Brown Edge, STOKE-ON-TRENT, ST6 8TG.
COLLIS, Mrs. Sally Gilian, BA ACA *1984;* 2 The Crescent, FARNBOROUGH, HAMPSHIRE, GU14 7AH.
COLLISHAW, Mr. Donald Frederick, FCA *1968;* 77 Hartfield Road, FOREST ROW, RH18 5BZ.
COLLISON, Mr. Brian, FCA *1965;* Flat 2, 13 Holbeck Road, SCARBOROUGH, YO11 2XF. (Life Member)
COLLISON, Miss. Chantal Evelyn Kordei, BSc ACA *2005;* 49 Byrne Road, LONDON, SW12 9HZ.
COLLISON, Mr. David, MA FCA *1975;* Nestor Healthcare Group Plc Beaconsfield Court, Beaconsfield Road, HATFIELD, HERTFORDSHIRE, AL10 8HU.
•**COLLISON, Mr. David William, BSc FCA CTA AKC TEP** *1982;* (Tax Fac), David Collison Ltd, Toby Churchill House, 25 Norman Way Industrial Estate, Norman Way, Over, CAMBRIDGE CAMBRIDGESHIRE CB24 5QE.
COLLISON, Mr. Mark Andrew, MEng ACA *1997;* 5 Harris Street, MARBLEHEAD, MA 01945, UNITED STATES.
•**COLLISTER, Mr. Adrian James, FCA TEP** *1977;* (Tax Fac), Baker Tilly Bennett Roy, 2a Lord Street, Douglas, ISLE OF MAN, IM1 2BD. See also Baker Tilly Bennett Roy LLC
COLLISTER, Mrs. Ann, BSc ACA *1987;* Cooil Veg, 18 High Street, Finstock, CHIPPING NORTON, OX7 3BY.
•**COLLISTER, Mr. Carlton Keith Kinrade, BSc FCA** *1988;* (Tax Fac), landtax LLP, Mitre House, Lodge Road, Long Hanborough, Business Park, WITNEY OXFORDSHIRE OX29 8SS.
COLLIVER, Mr. Joseph Tregonning, BSc ACA *2008;* Flat 67, Belvedere Court, 372 374 Upper Richmond Road, LONDON, SW15 6HZ.
COLLOBY, Mrs. Sophie, BSc ACA *2002;* with Ernst & Young LLP, City Gate West, Toll House Hill, NOTTINGHAM, NG1 5FY.
COLLOFF, Mr. Clive Edward, BSc ACA *1995;* 1 Springfield Cottages, 25 High Street, West End, WOKING, GU24 9PL.
COLLS, Mr. Andrew John, BSc ACA *1988;* 31 Tulyar Court, BINGLEY, WEST YORKSHIRE, BD16 3ND.
COLLYER, Mr. Anthony David, BSc ACA *1981;* East Week, CHULMLEIGH, EX18 7EE.
COLLYER, Mr. Brian Percy, FCA *1961;* 144 Lambley Lane, Burton Joyce, NOTTINGHAM, NG14 5BN.
COLLYER, Mrs. Katie Elizabeth, BSc ACA *1999;* Rickstones, Fox Lane, Lower Chaddesley, KIDDERMINSTER, WORCESTERSHIRE, DY10 4QR.
COLLYER, Mr. Richard John, BSc ACA *1999;* 22 Penrith Close, VERWOOD, BH31 6XE.
•**COLLYER, Mr. Russell Charles, ACA** *1981;* Collyer & Co, 17A Fairacres, RUISLIP, HA4 8AN.
COLLYER, Mr. Simon Aron, ACA CTA *1999;* (Tax Fac), 7 Millers Green Close, ENFIELD, EN2 7BD.
COLLYER, Mr. Stephen Peter, MA ACA *1982;* Diocesan Office, Old Alresford Place, Old Alresford, ALRESFORD, HAMPSHIRE, SO24 9DH.
COLLYNS, Mr. Harry Napier Law, BA FCA *1985;* 462 Warner Avenue, LOS ANGELES, CA 90024, UNITED STATES.
COLMAN, Mr. Adrian Maxwell, BA ACA *1995;* Flat 2 Chiswick Green Studios 1 Evershed Walk, LONDON, W4 5BW.
COLMAN, Mr. Andrew James, BSc FCA *1987;* 46a Whyteleafe Road, CATERHAM, CR3 5EF.
•**COLMAN, Mr. David John, BSc FCA** *1986;* Triesse Ltd, Lancaster Close, Sherburn in Elmet, LEEDS, LS25 6NS.
COLMAN, Mr. Edward Richard Morgan, BSc ACA *2001;* Glebe Barn Rectory Lane, Yardley Hastings, NORTHAMPTON, NN7 1EW.
COLMAN, Mr. George Robert Hill, BA ACA *1986;* 85 Wrottesley Road, WOLVERHAMPTON, WV6 8SQ.
•**COLMAN, Mrs. Hannah Elizabeth, BSc ACA** *1988;* Cuckoo Cottage, Moor Road, Burley-in-Wharfedale, ILKLEY, LS29 7BE.
COLMAN, Mr. Motti, BSc(Hons) ACA *2010;* 19 Russell Gardens, Golders Green, LONDON, NW11 9NJ.
COLMAN, Mr. Paul Michael, BA ACA *2002;* 2 Old Bath Road, NEWBURY, RG14 1QL.
COLMAN, Mr. Paul Ronald, BSc ACA *1985;* Merkurweg 6, CH 9470 BUCHS, SWITZERLAND.
COLMAN, Mr. Peter Charles Alderson, LLB FCA *1975;* 12 Bruthen Road, HIGHTON, VIC 3216, AUSTRALIA.
COLMAN, Miss. Victoria Louise, BSc ACA *2009;* 80c Sandy Lane, Hucknall, NOTTINGHAM, NG15 7GP.
•**COLMER, Mr. Douglas John, FCA** *1976;* (Tax Fac), Douglas Colmer & Co, Orwell Lodge, 13 Lesney Park Road, ERITH, DA8 3DQ.
COLMER, Mr. Phillip, ACA *1984;* 3 Darlington Gardens, Upper Shirley, SOUTHAMPTON, SO15 5HH.
COLMER, Mr. Robin David, FCA *1981;* 30 St. Pauls Road West, DORKING, SURREY, RH4 2HU.
•**COLOM, Mr. David James, FCA** *1981;* DJ Colom & Co Ltd, Hillside House, 2-6 Friern Park, North Finchley, LONDON, N12 9BT.
COLQUHOUN, Mr. Andrew Talbot, ACA *1989;* 59 Oakington Avenue, AMERSHAM, HP6 6SX.
COLQUHOUN, Mr. James Arthur, BA ACA *2003;* Yew Tree Cottage, North Oakley, TADLEY, RG26 5TS.
COLQUHOUN, Mr. Kenneth, FCA *1951;* 6 Nightingale Gardens, Orton Road, MANCHESTER, M23 0NY. (Life Member)
COLQUHOUN, Mr. Patric David, FCA *1970;* c/o Deloitte & Touche, PO Box 4254, DUBAI, UNITED ARAB EMIRATES.
COLQUHOUN, Mrs. Sarah Jane, BSc ACA PGCE *1994;* 16 Cottesmore Gardens, LEIGH-ON-SEA, SS9 2TG.
COLQUITT, Mr. Ronald, FCA *1968;* 13 Westminster Drive, Burn Bridge, HARROGATE, HG3 1LW.
COLSON, Mr. Darren John, BSc ACA *1994;* (Tax Fac), with PricewaterhouseCoopers LLP, Pricewaterhousecoopers, 12 Plumtree Court, LONDON, EC4A 4HT.
•**COLSON, Mr. David John, FCA** *1969;* Burford and Partners LLP, Suite 75, London Fruit Exchange, Brushfield Street, LONDON, E1 6EP. See also Colson D.J.
COLSON, Mr. Jeremy Richard, FCA *1970;* Church Green Bickleigh, TIVERTON, EX16 8RH.
COLSON, Mrs. Marie Suzanne, BCom ACA *2000;* 10 Whitmore Road, HARROW, MIDDLESEX, HA1 4AB.
COLSTON, Mr. Peter James, ACA *2009;* 125 Newdigate Road, BEDWORTH, WARWICKSHIRE, CV12 8DE.
COLTART, Mrs. Claire Jayne, MChem ACA *2004;* 6 Goldsworthy Drive, BUDE, CORNWALL, EX23 8EX.
COLTHORPE, Mr. Robert Charles Lumsden, BSc ACA *1988;* Europa Partners, 33 St. James's Square, LONDON, SW1Y 4JS.
COLTMAN, Mr. David James, FCA *1969;* 16 Parklands Close, Loddington, KETTERING, NN14 1LG.
COLTMAN, Mrs. Emily Josephine, MA *2003;* Lorien, Tree Road, BRAMPTON, CUMBRIA, CA8 1UA.
•**COLTMAN, Mr. Jonathan David, BA ACA** *1999;* KPMG LLP, 15 Canada Square, LONDON, E14 5GL.
COLTMAN, Mr. Stephen, MA ACA *1985;* Flat 3, 35 Priory Road, LONDON, NW6 4NN.
COLTON, Mr. Charles Hugo, FCA *1971;* 28 Greenlands, Flackwell Heath, HIGH WYCOMBE, HP10 9PL.
•**COLTON, Mrs. Jane Elizabeth, BA ACA** *1992;* Colton & Co, Honeysuckle House, 17 Field Lane, LETCHWORTH GARDEN CITY, HERTFORDSHIRE, SG6 3LF.
COLTON, Mr. Matthew Paul, BA(Hons) ACA *2000;* 29 Chicago Place, Great Sankey, WARRINGTON, WA5 3SH.
COLTON, Mrs. Natalie May, BSc ACA *1997;* 23 Anglesey Gardens, WICKFORD, SS12 9GT.
COLUMBINE, Miss. Julie Suzanne, BSc FCA *1990;* Moss Cottage, Macclesfield Road, Holmes Chapel, CREWE, CW4 8AH.
COLUZZI, Mr. Steve, ACA *2009;* Ernst & Young Ltd., 3 Bermudiana Road, HAMILTON HM 11, BERMUDA.
COLVER, Miss. Jennie Louise, BA ACA *2005;* 25B Monarch Avenue, HILLCREST 0627, NEW ZEALAND.
•**COLVER, Mr. Mark Andrew, FCA** *1984;* Grant Thornton Ltd, PO Box 31, Lefebvre House, Lefebvre Street, St Peter Port, GUERNSEY GY1 3TF.
COLVERD, Mr. Christopher John, FCA *1967;* Po Box 461, SABIE, MPUMULANGA PROVINCE, 1260, SOUTH AFRICA.
•**COLVERD, Ms. Tracey Ann, BA ACA ATII** *1985;* Antrams Taxation, 44-46 Old Steine, BRIGHTON, BN1 1NH.
COLVILL, Mr. Martin Arthur, FCA *1965;* Bell & Colvill (Horsley) Ltd, Head Office, Epsom Road, West Horsley, LEATHERHEAD, SURREY KT24 6DG.
COLVILLE, Mr. David Hulton, MA FCA *1973;* (Tax Fac), Pearson plc, 80 Strand, LONDON, WC2R 0RL.
•**COLVILLE, Mr. Derek Sinclair Walter, FCA** *1971;* Colville & Co, Rhoscwm, BUILTH WELLS, POWYS, LD2 3PT.
COLVILLE, Mr. George Beal, MA ACA *1995;* Chester Diocesan Board of Finance, Church House, Lower Lane, Aldford, CHESTER CH3 6HP.
COLVILLE, Dr. John Robert, MA DPhil FCA CTA TEP *1981;* (Tax Fac), 22 Ellington Road, Muswell Hill, LONDON, N10 3DG.
COLVILLE, Mr. Michael John, FCA *1971;* Inglenook, 33 Stewart Road, HARPENDEN, AL5 4QE.
COLVILLE, Mr. Philip John, MSc FCA *1977;* Persie, East Mey, THURSO, CAITHNESS, KW14 8XL.
COLVILLE, Mr. Thomas Sinclair, BA ACA *2000;* Camusfearna, Chapel Road, Keeston, HAVERFORDWEST, DYFED, SA62 6HL.
COLVILLE, Mrs. Wendy, BA FCA *1983;* Time Products Ltd, 34 Dover Street, LONDON, W1S 4NG.
•**COLVIN, Mrs. Anne Letitia, BSc FCA** *1987;* Anne Colvin, Hollendene, Goodrich, ROSS-ON-WYE, HR9 6JA.
COLVIN, Mrs. Caroline Ruth, BSc ACA *2007;* 31 AES, 32 Engineers Regiment, Campbell Baracks, BFPO, 30.
COLVIN, Miss. Jennifer Ann, ACA *2009;* 627 Rochester Way, LONDON, SE9 1RJ.
COLVIN, Mr. Paul James, BSc ACA *1992;* with Bird & Bird, 15 Fetter Lane, LONDON, EC4A 1JP.
COLVIN, Mr. Roger Graham, FCA *1975;* Belwood Cottage, Emery Down, LYNDHURST, HAMPSHIRE, SO43 7FH.
COLVIN, Mr. Steven, BA ACA *2010;* 56 Badger Lane, BOURNE, LINCOLNSHIRE, PE10 0FT.
COLVIN, Mr. Stuart Martin, ACA *1996;* 55 Rutland Gardens, HOVE, EAST SUSSEX, BN3 5PD.
COLVIN, Mr. William Thomas, BSc ACA *1989;* 22 Stewart Street, ORMOND, VIC 3204, AUSTRALIA.
COLWELL, Mr. Charles John, BA ACA *1992;* 37 Linden Grove, WALTON-ON-THAMES, SURREY, KT12 1EY.
COLWELL, Mrs. Jennifer Ann, BSc ACA *2001;* 56 Hamelin Road, GILLINGHAM, KENT, ME7 3EX.
COLWELL, Mrs. Sarah Louise, BA ACA *1992;* 37 Linden Grove, WALTON-ON-THAMES, SURREY, KT12 1EY.
COLWELL, Mr. Simon Richard, BSc ACA *1996;* Mere Cottage, The Street, Mereworth, MAIDSTONE, ME18 5NA.
COLWELL, Mr. Thomas, BSc ACA *2010;* Ernst & Young Llp, 1 More London Place, LONDON, SE1 2AF.
COLWILL, Mr. Matthew Henry, BSc(Hons) ACA *2002;* West Winds Tredragon Road, Mawgan Porth, NEWQUAY, CORNWALL, TR8 4DH.
COLWILL, Mr. Nicholas Foster, BA ACA *1990;* 100 Portland Road, REMUERA 1005, AUCKLAND, NEW ZEALAND.
COLWILL, Mr. Ross Spencer, FCA *1966;* 7 The Croft, Bishopstone, SALISBURY, SP5 4DF. (Life Member)
COLWYN-THOMAS, Mr. Anthony, BSc FCA *1981;* (Member of Council 1995 - 1998), 8 Achilleos Street, 176074 KALLITHEA, GREECE.
COLWYN-THOMAS, Miss. Janet Kaye, FCA *1982;* 102 Gabalfa Road, Sketty, SWANSEA, SA2 8NA.
COLYER, Mr. Ben Edward Oliver, BSc ACA *2009;* 16 Fern Drive, MALVERN, WORCESTERSHIRE, WR14 1BN.
COLYER, Miss. Helen Jane, BSc ACA *1984;* 5 Mill Hill Road, NORWICH, NR2 3DP.
COLYER, Mr. Martin Stanley, FCA *1975;* IFonline Limted, 2nd Floor, Octagon House, 81-83 Fulham High Street, LONDON, SW6 3JW.
COLYER, Mr. Michael Andrew James, MA MBA FCA *1999;* The Old Sawmill, Allerston, PICKERING, YO18 7PJ.
COLYER, Mrs. Sarah Elizabeth, BA ACA *1997;* Brynavon, 32 Lodway, Easton-in-Gordano, BRISTOL, BS20 0JB.
COMBA, Mr. Alexander Michael, BSc ACA *1981;* 15 Cleveland Walk, BATH, BA2 6JP.
•**COMBE, Mr. Brian Francis, FCA** *1971;* (Tax Fac), TaxAssist Accountants, 41 High Street, EAST GRINSTEAD, WEST SUSSEX, RH19 3AF.
COMBE, Mr. Charles Henry Charlton, MA ACA *2005;* 25 Afghan Road, LONDON, SW11 2QD.
COMBE, Mrs. Martine Louise, ACA *2008;* National Audit Office, 157-197 Buckingham Palace Road, LONDON, SW1W 9SP.
COMBEN, Mrs. Sally Claire, BSc(Hons) ACA *2010;* 118 Place Road, COWES, ISLE OF WIGHT, PO31 7AE.
COMBER, Mr. Andrew Wandesford Pater, FCA *1977;* 25 High Street, Sunninghill, ASCOT, BERKSHIRE, SL5 9NG.
COMBER, Mr. Christopher Alan, ACA *1983;* Poets Corner, 35 Spencer Road, BIRCHINGTON, KENT, CT7 9EY.
COMBER, Mr. David Alan, BSc ACA *1994;* 11 Longleat Drive, Tilehurst, READING, RG31 6YY.
COMBER, Mr. Jonathan Patrick, BA ACA *1993;* 1 The Stables, Southcott Village, LEIGHTON BUZZARD, BEDFORDSHIRE, LU7 2PR.
COMBES, Mrs. Barbara Elizabeth, BA ACA *1992;* 99 London Road, Twyford, READING, RG10 9EL.
COMBES, Mrs. Claire Francoise, BSc ACA *1993;* Capital Shopping Centres Plc 40 Broadway, LONDON, SW1H 0BT.
COMBES, Mr. Graham Alan, FCA ACII *1980;* 1A Rye Walk, INGATESTONE, CM4 9AL.
COMBES, Mr. John Alfred, FCA *1970;* 7 Copsehill, Leybourne, WEST MALLING, KENT, ME19 5QR.
COMBES, Mrs. Rebecca Jane, BSc ACA *1999;* Smith & Williamson, 21 Chipper Lane, SALISBURY, SP1 1BG.

COMBES, Mr. Richard George, FCA *1967;* The Grange, Church Road, Westoning, BEDFORD, MK45 5JW.
COMBES, Mr. Timothy St John, BSc ACA *1990;* 2 Manor Close, Hanslope, MILTON KEYNES, MK19 7PE.
COMBI, Mr. Stefano Alessandro, BA ACA *2001;* H S B C, 8 Canada Square, LONDON, E14 5HQ.
COMBRINK, Mr. Wienand, ACA CA(SA) *2011;* 41A Bedok Ria Crescent, 04-40 Stratford Court Condo, SINGAPORE 489929, SINGAPORE.
COMBS, Mr. John Adrian, FCA *1975;* 4 Sollars Close, Whitecross Road, HEREFORD, HR4 0LX.
COMEAU, Mr. Michael Paul, BA ACA *1982;* 21 Ullswater Road, LONDON, N14 7BL.
•COMENS, Mr. Martin John, FCA *1969;* (Tax Fac), M.J. Comens, Maritime House, Basin Road North, HOVE, EAST SUSSEX, BN41 1WR.
COMER, Mrs. Carol, BA ACA *1990;* 50 St James Road, TUNBRIDGE WELLS, TN1 2LB.
COMER, Mr. Dudley David Swan, BA FCA *1964;* The Oast House, Breakstones, Langton Green, TUNBRIDGE WELLS, TN3 0JL.
COMER, Mr. Geoffrey Stephen, BSc FCA FCT *1974;* Box 161, Ctra Cabo de la Nao (Pla) 124-6, 03730 JAVEA, ALICANTE, SPAIN.
COMER, Mr. James Anthony, MEng ACA *2010;* National Audit Office, 157-197 Buckingham Palace Road, LONDON, SW1W 9SP.
COMER, Mrs. Jennifer Jeanne, ACA *1998;* 64 Innovation Way, Lynch Wood, PETERBOROUGH, PE2 6FL.
COMER, Mr. Murray, BSc ACA *2001;* Optiver Pty Ltd, 39 Hunter Street, SYDNEY, NSW 2000, AUSTRALIA.
COMER, Mr. Philip Allen, FCA *1951;* Berrycroft, 27 Tuffley Crescent, GLOUCESTER, GL1 5ND. (Life Member)
COMER, Mr. Sean, BA ACA *1989;* Barclays Capital, 5 North Colonnade, Canary Wharf, LONDON, E14 4BB.
COMER, Mr. Simon, BSc ACA *2007;* 7 Denham Green Place, EDINBURGH, EH5 3PA.
COMER, Mr. William Bevis, MPhil BSc ACA *1990;* Flat, 1 Queen Street, BATH, BA1 1HE.
COMERY, Mr. David Royce, FCA *1989;* with Brown Butler, Leigh House, 28-32 St Paul's Street, LEEDS, LS1 2JT.
COMERY, Mr. James Antony, BSc ACA *1995;* Greenacre, Green Lane, Aspley Guise, MILTON KEYNES, BEDFORDSHIRE, MK17 8EN.
COMFORT, Miss. Amy Leah, ACA *2008;* 2 Fernden Cottages, Merrow Lane, GUILDFORD, GU4 7BW.
COMFORT, Mr. Philip Arthur, MA ACA *1989;* 120 Pickford Road, Markyate, ST. ALBANS, AL3 8RL.
COMISKEY, Mr. Mark, BSc ACA *1993;* 4 Royston Road, ST. ALBANS, AL1 5NG.
COMLEY, Mr. Adrian Seymour, BA ACA *1993;* 20 Oaklands Avenue, ESHER, SURREY, KT10 8HX.
COMLEY, Mr. Mark Maxwell, BA ACA *1998;* 79 Lodge Road, Writtle, CHELMSFORD, CM1 3HZ.
•COMLEY, Ms. Paula Annette, BA(Hons) ACA MAAT *2001;* Paula Comley, Ingles Manor, Castle Hill Avenue, FOLKESTONE, KENT, CT20 2RD.
COMLEY, Miss. Sally Anne, ACA *2009;* 68 Melrose Close, MAIDSTONE, ME15 6ZE.
•COMMON, Miss. Rachel, ACA FCCA *2011;* 45 Pope Iron Road, WORCESTER, WR1 3FF.
COMMONS, Mr. Anthony John, BCom ACA *1998;* 134 Effra Road, LONDON, SW19 8PR.
COMMONS, Mr. Paul, BA(Hons) ACA *2010;* 17 Abington Avenue, SUTTON-IN-ASHFIELD, NOTTINGHAMSHIRE, NG17 4NH.
COMNINOS, Mr. Gregory James, BCom FCA *1973;* Holdsworth, Cross Oak Road, BERKHAMSTED, HP4 3NA. (Life Member)
COMPSON, Mr. Christopher John, FCA *1966;* St Helens House, St. Helens Way, THETFORD, NORFOLK, IP24 1HG.
COMPSON, Miss. Sarah Jane, MEng ACA *2006;* 32 Aphelion Way, READING, BERKSHIRE, RG2 9FR.
COMPSON, Mr. Stephen Edwin John, FCA *1977;* Fernside Place, 179 Queens Road, WEYBRIDGE, KT13 0AH.
COMPTON, Mr. Aidan Patrick, BA ACA *2005;* 5 Yarmouth Road, POOLE, DORSET, BH12 1HD.
•COMPTON, Mr. Barry Charles Chittenden, ACA *1980;* Barry Compton & Co, 14 Hallsland Way, OXTED, SURREY, RH8 9AL.
COMPTON, Mr. Christopher James, BEng ACA *2001;* 279 Weston Road, STOKE-ON-TRENT, ST3 6HA.
COMPTON, Mr. David Gregory, BA FCA *1972;* The Old Beer House, Laylands Green, Kintbury, HUNGERFORD, BERKSHIRE, RG17 9UD.
COMPTON, Mr. David Horace, FCA *1964;* 13 Hillbrow, HOVE, BN3 6QG.
COMPTON, Mr. Desmond Glen, BSc ACA *2005;* 18 Palmer Street, SALE, CHESHIRE, M33 7TH.
COMPTON, Mr. Gerald Stephen, FCA *1971;* 9 Kimber Road, BOURNEMOUTH, BH11 8HN.
COMPTON, Miss. Hannah, BA ACA *2011;* 70 Heritage Court, 15 Warstone Lane, BIRMINGHAM, B18 6HU.
COMPTON, Mrs. Jennifer Anne, BSc ACA *2006;* 50 Angerton Avenue, Shiremoor, NEWCASTLE UPON TYNE, NE27 0TU.
COMPTON, Mr. Jonathan Charles, BA(Hons) ACA *2003;* with BDO LLP, 55 Baker Street, LONDON, W1U 7EU.
COMPTON, Miss. Lindsay, ACA *2009;* 30 Queen Elizabeth Road, CIRENCESTER, GLOUCESTERSHIRE, GL7 1DJ.
•COMPTON, Mrs. Lisa Helen, FCA *1990;* Liric Accountants Ltd, Wyndmere House, Ashwell Road, Steeple Morden, ROYSTON, HERTFORDSHIRE SG8 0NZ. See also Compton Business Services Ltd
COMPTON, Mr. Mark Andrew, BSc ACA *1988;* 15a Scotland Lane, Houghton-on-the-Hill, LEICESTER, LE7 9GH.
COMPTON, Mr. Nicholas, BCom ACA *2004;* Flat 1, 21 Wray Crescent, LONDON, N4 3LN.
COMPTON, Mr. Peter John, BA ACA *1995;* 17 rue de Pauillac, 33200 BORDEAUX, FRANCE.
COMPTON, Mrs. Sharon, ACA FCCA *2011;* 17 Hillside, Sawston, CAMBRIDGE, CB22 3BL.
COMPTON-WILLIAMS, Miss. Charlotte Elizabeth, ACA *2008;* 38b Downleaze, Stoke Bishop, BRISTOL, BS9 1LY.
COMRAS, Mr. Michael David, ACA *1978;* Bedlam Assets Management Plc, 20 Abchurch Lane, LONDON, EC4N 7BB.
COMRAS, Mr. Richard Alexander, BA ACA *2010;* Top Floor (Flat C), 1 Hambalt Road, LONDON, SW4 9EA.
COMRIE, Mr. Cosmo, BA ACA *2011;* 7 Lingwood Close, SOUTHAMPTON, SO16 7GB.
COMRIE, Mrs. Hazel, FCA CTA *1981;* Dickinson Dees LLP, One Trinity Gardens, Broad Chare, NEWCASTLE UPON TYNE, NE1 2HF.
COMRIE, Mr. Richard Lascelles, FCA *1978;* 12 Briar Close, Shiney Row, HOUGHTON LE SPRING, TYNE AND WEAR, DH4 4PY.
COMYN, Mr. Darra Martin, ACA *1987;* Gautier Design, 79 Redston Road, LONDON, N8 7HL.
COMYN, Mr. James, ACA *2011;* 86 Claxton Grove, LONDON, W6 8HE.
COMYN, Mr. Paul Fergus, ACA *1982;* Rookery Close, Woodhouse Lane, Holmbury St. Mary, DORKING, SURREY, RH5 6NN.
•COMYN, Mr. Roderic Patrick, BBS FCA *1976;* CCMG, 7 Fairview Strand, Fairview 3, DUBLIN 3, COUNTY DUBLIN, IRELAND.
COMYN, Mr. William Andrew, FCA *1966;* 37 Lawrence Road, ST. AGNES, CORNWALL, TR5 0XQ.
CONAGHAN, Mr. Daniel Patrick, BA(Econ) ACA *2006;* 74 Hillbury Road, LONDON, SW17 8JT.
CONAGHAN, Mr. Neil Francis, BSc ACA *1998;* X L N Telecom, Bondway Commercial Centre 69-71, Bondway, LONDON, SW8 1SQ.
•CONBOY, Mr. Mark, BA FCA CF *1983;* 1 Gleneagles Drive, Brockhall Village, Old Langho, BLACKBURN, LANCASHIRE, BB6 8BF.
CONCANON, Mr. Brian Anthony Ross, FCA *1967;* (Tax Fac), 11 Cavell Court, BISHOPS STORTFORD, HERTFORDSHIRE, CM23 5PR.
COND, Mr. David Anthony, FCA *1988;* 7 Cranmer Grove, Heathcote, WARWICK, CV34 6EP.
CONDER, Miss. Caroline Elizabeth, BSc ACA *2002;* 36 Beechwood Road, Sanderstead, SOUTH CROYDON, SURREY, CR2 0AA.
CONDER, Miss. Elizabeth Joan, MA ACA CTA *2004;* (Member of Council 2005 - 2008), (Tax Fac), with 3i Group plc, 16 Palace Street, LONDON, SW1E 5JD.
CONDER, Ms. Julie Wendy, MA ACA *1986;* 1 Chantry Close, Church Lane Kingston, CAMBRIDGE, CB23 2NG.
CONDER, Mr. Martin Philip, BA ACA *1986;* 63 Bute Gardens, LONDON, W6 7DX.
CONDON, Mr. Anthony Kevin, BSc ACA *1985;* 59 Henleaze Park Drive, Henleaze, BRISTOL, BS9 4LN.
CONDON, Mr. Benjamin James, ACA *2004;* Flat 22, 1 Angel Lane, LONDON, E15 1BL.
CONDON, Mr. Bruce Andrew, BA ACA *1996;* 39 St Catharines Way, Houghton on the Hill, LEICESTER, LE7 9HE.
CONDON, Mr. Nicholas Edward, BSc(Hons) ACA *2003;* 4 Wymersley Close, Great Houghton, NORTHAMPTON, NN4 7PT.
CONDON, Mr. Patrick Albert, BCom FCA *1974;* 11 Catherine Street, WATERFORD, COUNTY WATERFORD, IRELAND.
CONDON, Mr. Peter Gerald, MA FCA *1965;* The Old Rectory, Playley Green, Redmarley, GLOUCESTER, GL19 3NB. (Life Member)
•CONDON, Mr. Richard Simon, BA FCA *1991;* (Tax Fac), Broadside Business Services Limited, Hawkstone House, Portland Mews, Portland Street, LEAMINGTON SPA, WARWICKSHIRE CV32 5HD. See also Infocus Business Services Ltd
CONDON, Mr. Rory Martin, MEng ACA *2001;* 61A Synge St, PORTOBELLO, COUNTY DUBLIN, IRELAND.
CONDON, Mr. Toby, BSc ACA *2011;* Flat 3, 2 Caroline Street, READING, RG1 7DD.
CONDREN, Mrs. Samantha, BEng ACA *1995;* Hillside House, Anick Village, HEXHAM, NE46 4LW.
CONDRON, Mr. Darrell James, BA ACA *2010;* 27 Manor Way, BANSTEAD, SM7 3PN.
CONDRON, Mrs. Fiona Jane, BA FCA *1998;* with BDO LLP, 2 City Place, Beehive Ring Road, GATWICK, WEST SUSSEX, RH6 0PA.
CONEY, Mr. Richard Ian, BA ACA *2000;* 37 Hendford Road, BOURNEMOUTH, BH10 5AU.
CONEYBEARE, Mrs. Alison Louise, BA ACA *1995;* 8 Greystoke Road Caversham, READING, RG4 5EL.
CONEYBEARE, Mr. Duncan James, MA MPhil ACA *1997;* 8 Greystoke Road, Caversham, READING, RG4 5EL.
CONEYS, Mr. Michael Lawrence De Vere, BA FCA *1969;* 14 Argyll Mansions, 303/323 Kings Road, Chelsea, LONDON, SW3 5ER. (Life Member)
CONGDON, Mr. Philip John, MA ACA *1984;* 43 Morley Road, TWICKENHAM, TW1 2HG.
CONGDON, Mr. Richard John, MA ACA CPFA *1987;* Flat 188, Chiltern Court, Baker Street, LONDON, NW1 5SD.
CONGLETON, Mr. Ian, FCA *1991;* 5 Ashton Close, Abbey Grange North Walbottle, NEWCASTLE UPON TYNE, NE5 1QU.
CONGRAVE, Mr. James Thomas, FCA *1968;* 20 Willmore End, Merton, LONDON, SW19 3DF.
•①CONIBEAR, Mr. James, BA ACA MABRP *1979;* 3 Stannington Rise, SHEFFIELD, S6 5HH.
CONINX, Mr. Jonathan Roger, BA FCA *1979;* 30 Hanger Way, PETERSFIELD, GU31 4QE.
CONISBY, Miss. Meryl Mei Lea, BA ACA *2010;* 1 Pembroke Close, MERTHYR TYDFIL, MID GLAMORGAN, CF48 1JF.
CONLAN, Mr. Andrew James, FCA *1980;* 10 Redstart Road, CHARD, SOMERSET, TA20 1SD.
CONLAN, Mr. James, ACA *2006;* 43a Shirley Drive, HOVE, EAST SUSSEX, BN3 6UA.
•CONLAN, Mr. John James William, FCA DChA *1974;* (Tax Fac), Baker Tillly Tax & Advisory Services LLP, St Philips Point, Temple Row, BIRMINGHAM, B2 5AF.
CONLEY, Miss. Anna Louise, BSc ACA *1995;* 9 St. Marys Close, BARNARD CASTLE, COUNTY DURHAM, DL12 8NS.
CONLEY, Mrs. Barbara Jane, FCA *1989;* 34 Relton Way, HARTLEPOOL, CLEVELAND, TS26 0BB.
CONLEY, Ms. Deborah Jane, BA ACA *1993;* 54 Arden Road, LONDON, N3 3AE.
CONLEY, Mr. Jeffrey Reginald, MSci ACA AMCT *2001;* 600 Washington Blvd, STAMFORD, CT 06901, UNITED STATES.
CONLEY, Mr. Philip, FCA *1969;* 28 Abbots Road South, LEICESTER, LE5 1DB.
CONLEY, Mrs. Susan Anne, FCA *1963;* Southlands Farm, Moretonhampstead, NEWTON ABBOT, TQ13 8QU.
CONLIN, Mr. Owen, BA ACA *1995;* 6 Katnook Place, WEST PENNANT HILLS, NSW 2125, AUSTRALIA.
CONLON, Miss. Anne Marie, BA FCA *1975;* (Tax Fac), 6 Park Drive, Acton, LONDON, W3 8NA.
CONLON, Mr. Bernard Aiden, BA ACA *1987;* 15 Ghyll Wood, ILKLEY, LS29 9NR.
CONLON, Mr. David George, LLB ACA *2004;* 10 Elia Street, LONDON, N1 8DE.
CONLON, Mrs. Joanna, BSc ACA *2005;* 10 Honeydon Avenue, Eaton Socon, ST. NEOTS, CAMBRIDGESHIRE, PE19 8PJ.
CONLON, Mr. Kieran Joseph, BA FCA *1959;* 2 Ranfurly Avenue, DUNGANNON, COUNTY TYRONE, BT71 6PJ. (Life Member)
CONLON, Mr. Michael, BSc ACA *1993;* James Burden Ltd, 40 West Market Building London Central Markets, LONDON, EC1A 9PS.
CONLON, Mrs. Patricia Beverly, BA ACA *1992;* 41a Aughton Road, Birkdale, SOUTHPORT, PR8 2AJ.
CONLON, Mr. Stephen John, FCA *1980;* Little Orchard, 10 Gullet Lane, Kirby Muxloe, LEICESTER, LE9 2BL.
CONLON, Mrs. Zaida Bibi, BA(Hons) ACA *2002;* Semperian Group, St Martins House, 1 Gresham Street, LONDON, EC2V 7BX.
CONLONG, Mr. George Francis, FCA *1957;* Oakley, 10 Diamond Ridge, Barlaston, STOKE-ON-TRENT, ST12 9DT. (Life Member)
CONN, Mr. Alastair Macbeth, MA FCA *1980;* Old Appletree House, Clifton Terrace, ALNWICK, NORTHUMBERLAND, NE66 1XF.
CONN, Mrs. Danielle Liza, BA ACA ACCA *1994;* 11 Meadway, LONDON, NW11 7JR.
CONN, Mr. Rowan, BSc ACA *1996;* 30 Oakley Avenue, LONDON, W5 3SD.
•CONN, Mr. Stephen Leonard, FCA FIPA *1969;* Begbies Traynor, 340 Deansgate, MANCHESTER, M3 4LY. See also Begbies Traynor Limited
CONNAH, Mr. Glyn, BA(Hons) ACA *2010;* 2 Lockeaflash Gardens, Lockeaflash Crescent, BARNSLEY, SOUTH YORKSHIRE, S70 3NZ.
CONNAH, Mr. Michael Terence, FCA *1964;* 28 Fairmead Avenue, Daws Heath, BENFLEET, ESSEX, SS7 2UQ.
CONNAUGHTON, Miss. Naomi Louise, BSc ACA *2011;* 18 Keyfield, ST. ALBANS, HERTFORDSHIRE, AL1 1QH.
•CONNAUGHTON, Mr. Vincent Peter, BA ACA *2004;* Lewis Alexander & Connaughton, Second Floor, Boulton House, 17-21 Chorlton Street, MANCHESTER, M1 3HY. See also Lewis Alexander & Collins
CONNEALLY, Miss. Sarah-Jane, ACA *2009;* with Deloitte LLP, 2 New Street Square, LONDON, EC4A 3BZ.
•CONNEELY, Mrs. Anne Marie, BSc ACA *1980;* Anne Conneely & Co, 199 Friern Barnet Lane, Whetstone, LONDON, N20 0NN.
CONNEELY, Dr. Dawn, BSc ACA *1996;* 27 Ryelands Close, MARKET HARBOROUGH, LE16 7XE.
•CONNEELY, Mr. Joseph Michael, BA FCA CTA *1975;* 26 Queen Annes Grove, LONDON, W4 1HN.
•CONNEELY, Miss. Laura-Jayne, ACA *2009;* 11 Ivy Walk, Midsomer Norton, RADSTOCK, BA3 2EE.
CONNELL, Mr. Adrian Paul, BSc ACA *1989;* 123 Doeford Close, Culcheth, WARRINGTON, WA3 4DP.
CONNELL, Mr. Andrew Martin, BA ACA *1997;* South Winds, The Common, Potten End, BERKHAMSTED, HERTFORDSHIRE, HP4 2QF.
CONNELL, Mrs. Caroline Anne, BA ACA *1993;* (Tax Fac), 2 Balmoral Close, Greenmount, BURY, LANCASHIRE, BL8 4DL.
CONNELL, Mr. Christopher William, BA ACA *2010;* Flat 32, Harvey House, Aylesford Street, Pimlico, LONDON, SW1V 3RU.
•CONNELL, Mrs. Claire Elizabeth, MA ACA CTA *2001;* (Tax Fac), Claire Connell, 195 Silverdale Road, Earley, READING, RG6 7NY.
CONNELL, Mr. Edward Weston, BA ACA *2003;* 22 Huntington Crescent, Headingley, LEEDS, LS16 5RT.
CONNELL, Mr. Ian, BA ACA *1993;* 56 Strawberry Mead, Fair Oak, EASTLEIGH, SO50 8RG.
CONNELL, Mr. Jeffrey Graham, BSc ACA *1998;* Shell International Petroleum Co Ltd Shell Centre, York Road, LONDON, SE1 7NA.
CONNELL, Mr. Matthew, BA ACA *2003;* 103/ 7 Wills Avenue, BRONTE, NSW 2024, AUSTRALIA.
CONNELL, Mr. Michael Joseph, ACA *1981;* Black Country Housing, 134 High Street, BLACKHEATH, WEST MIDLANDS, B65 0EE.
CONNELL, Mrs. Naomi Anne, BSocSc ACA *1992;* 22 Eardley Road, LONDON, SW16 6BP.
CONNELL, Mr. Peter, BSc FCA *1985;* 20 Compton Drive, EASTBOURNE, EAST SUSSEX, BN20 8BX.
CONNELL, Mr. Richard Andrew, MA FCA *1980;* Lower Roundhurst Farm, Tennyson's Lane, Roundhurst, HASLEMERE, WEST SUSSEX, GU27 3BN.
CONNELL, Mr. Stewart James, BA FCA *1980;* Fox Hall Common Road, Weston Colville, CAMBRIDGE, CB21 5NS.
CONNELL, Mrs. Vanessa, BSc ACA *1991;* 1 Greenfield Road, SOUTHPORT, PR8 5LX.
CONNELL, Mr. William Selby Temple, BSc ACA *1985;* Windrush, Widmoor, Wooburn Green, HIGH WYCOMBE, HP10 0JG.
•CONNELLAN, Mr. Steven Robert, LLB ACA *1989;* S.R. Connellan & Co, Our Shell, Hempnall Road, Bedingham, BUNGAY, SUFFOLK NR35 2NW.

CONNELLY, Mrs. Annette Elizabeth, BA(Hons) FCA *2000;* with Francis Clark LLP, Sigma House, Oak View Close, Edginswell Park, TORQUAY, TQ2 7FF.
CONNELLY, Mr. Derek Alexander, BSc ACA *1990;* 43 Scotts Avenue, SUNBURY-ON-THAMES, MIDDLESEX, TW16 7HY.
CONNELLY, Dr. Liam John, PhD BSc ACA *1993;* 9 Kensington Gardens, Lostock Hall, PRESTON, PR5 5TW.
CONNELLY, Dr. Paul Martin, PhD BSc(Hons) ACA *2003;* 8 Rue des Rossignols, 68220 HESINGUE, FRANCE.
CONNELLY, Mrs. Shirley Ann, ACA *2008;* 4 The Bye Way, HARROW, MIDDLESEX, HA3 7EF.
CONNELLY, Mr. Stephen Thomas, BA FCA CF *1991;* Oakland House, 21 Hope Carr Road, LEIGH, LANCASHIRE, WN7 3ET.
CONNELLY, Mrs. Tracey Michelle, BA ACA *1992;* 168 Saber Creek Dr, MONUMENT, CO 80132, UNITED STATES.
CONNER, Mr. Anthony Paul, BSc FPFS FCA *1994;* Balmesh Farm, Glenluce, NEWTON STEWART, WIGTOWNSHIRE, DG8 0AG.
•**CONNER, Mr. David, BCom FCA** *1974;* (Tax Fac), A. David Conner, 19 Lower Elms, St. Minver, WADEBRIDGE, CORNWALL, PL27 6QB.
CONNER, Mrs. Judith, BA FCA *1992;* 47 The Broadway, NORTH SHIELDS, TYNE AND WEAR, NE30 2LL.
CONNER, Mr. Robert Alexander, MA(Hons) ACA *2001;* Edinburgh International Festival, The Hub, Castlehill, EDINBURGH, EH1 2NE.
CONNER, Miss. Sarah, ACA *2006;* T T R Barnes, 3-5 Grange Terrace, SUNDERLAND, SR2 7DG.
CONNERY, Mr. John Frederick, FCA *1974;* Thornfield Hall Farm, Arundel Street, ASHTON-UNDER-LYNE, OL6 6RH. (Life Member)
CONNERY, Mrs. Sarah Jane, BA ACA *2002;* 7 Cranbourne Chase, North Hykeham, LINCOLN, LN6 9TX.
CONNETT, Mr. Edwin Alan, FCA *1960;* Yew Tree House, Chapel Lane, Farnsfield, NEWARK, NOTTINGHAMSHIRE, NG22 8JP. (Life Member)
CONNETT, Mr. Richard, FCA *1964;* Twickers, 11 Penzer Street, KINGSWINFORD, WEST MIDLANDS, DY6 7AA. (Life Member)
CONNICK, Mr. David Roy Neil, BA FCA *1972;* 1320 21st Street N.W., Apt 102, WASHINGTON, DC, 20036, UNITED STATES.
CONNICK, Mr. Michael, BSc FCA *1981;* 32 Hermitage Road, KENLEY, CR8 5EB.
CONNING, Mr. Francis Henry, VRD FCA *1951;* 45 Saxon Way, SAFFRON WALDEN, CB11 4EQ. (Life Member)
CONNOCK, Mr. Geoffrey, FCA *1977;* Gullivers Truck Hire Ltd, Swift House, Albert Crescent, St Philips, BRISTOL, BS2 0UD.
CONNOLD, Mr. Robert David, BSc ACA *2006;* with Deloitte LLP, Athene Place, 66 Shoe Lane, LONDON, EC4A 3BQ.
CONNOLE, Mrs. Elizabeth Kathryn, MSc BSc ACA *1992;* 10 Chestnut Place, Leckhampton, CHELTENHAM, GL53 0QE.
CONNOLLEY, Mr. Dominic, BSc ACA *1993;* 39 Fairlawn Road, LONDON, SW19 3QR.
CONNOLLEY, Mr. Mark Richard, BEng ACA *2002;* 65 Lombard Street, GLEBE, NSW 2037, AUSTRALIA.
CONNOLLY, Mr. Adrian Joseph, MSc BA ACA *2005;* Alemdag Cad, Yanyol Sok, No 10/9, Uskudar, ISTANBUL, TURKEY.
CONNOLLY, Miss. Anne, BA ACA *2003;* 37 Swarland Avenue, NEWCASTLE UPON TYNE, NE7 7TE.
•**CONNOLLY, Mr. Brendan Stephen, MSc FCA DChA** *1974;* Service Industry Support Limited, Covertside, Kings Mill Lane, South Nutfield, REDHILL, RH1 5JX.
CONNOLLY, Mrs. Carol, MSc ACA *1998;* 5 Marlow Way, Whickham, NEWCASTLE UPON TYNE, NE16 5RH.
CONNOLLY, Mr. Christopher James, BA ACA *2002;* Promethean Ltd Promethean House, Lower Philips Road Whitebirk Industrial Estate, BLACKBURN, BB1 5TH.
CONNOLLY, Mr. Christopher Thomas, BSc ACA *2006;* Flat 32, Lupin Point, Abbey Street, LONDON, SE1 2DW.
CONNOLLY, Mr. David Michael, BA ACA *1998;* 248 Liverpool Road South, Burscough, ORMSKIRK, L40 7RF.
CONNOLLY, Mrs. Debra Gillian, ACA *1988;* 35 Cavendish Road, Heaton Mersey, STOCKPORT, CHESHIRE, SK4 3DN.
•**CONNOLLY, Mr. Edward Francis, FCA** *1996;* Ed Connolly & Co, 126 Bassett Avenue, SOUTHAMPTON, SO16 7EZ.
CONNOLLY, Mr. Felix, MSc BA ACA *2007;* with Grant Thornton UK LLP, 101 Cambridge Science Park, Milton Road, CAMBRIDGE, CB4 0FY.
CONNOLLY, Miss. Fiona Margaret, BA ACA *2009;* P N Connolly Building Contractors Ltd Glandore, 61 Stopford Road St. Helier, JERSEY, JE2 4LB.
CONNOLLY, Mrs. Joanne Catherine, ACA *1999;* with KPMG LLP, 15 Canada Square, LONDON, E14 5GL.
CONNOLLY, Mr. John, BSc FCA *1987;* 61 Swanpool Lane, Aughton, ORMSKIRK, LANCASHIRE, L39 5AY.
CONNOLLY, Mr. John, BA FCA *1987;* 9 The Chantry, Calveley, TARPORLEY, CW6 9JU.
•**CONNOLLY, Mr. John Patrick, FCA** *1971;* Upper House, Westburton, PULBOROUGH, WEST SUSSEX, RH20 1HD.
CONNOLLY, Mr. Joseph Adam, MA ACA *2004;* 1a Ware Road, Tonwell, WARE, HERTFORDSHIRE, SG12 0HN.
CONNOLLY, Mr. Joseph Philip, BSc ACA *1981;* PricewaterhouseCoopers Ltd, Abacus House, P O Box 63, PROVIDENCIALES, TURKS AND CAICOS ISLANDS.
CONNOLLY, Mr. Joseph Timothy James, MA FCA *1978;* 32 Brambledown Road, WALLINGTON, SURREY, SM6 0TF.
•**CONNOLLY, Mrs. Juliet Gay, BA ACA CTA** *1992;* (Tax Fac), UK Expat Pty Ltd, 5/491 Nicholson Street, Carlton North, MELBOURNE, VIC 3054, AUSTRALIA.
CONNOLLY, Miss. Karen Anne, BE ACA *2009;* 119 Malpas Road, NORTHWICH, CHESHIRE, CW9 7BJ.
•**CONNOLLY, Miss. Linda Ann, BA ACA** *1995;* 24 Courtfield Avenue, HARROW, HA1 2JX.
•**CONNOLLY, Mrs. Margaret Mary, MA FCA ATII** *1986;* (Tax Fac), Reeves & Co LLP, 37 St. Margarets Street, CANTERBURY, KENT, CT1 2TU.
CONNOLLY, Mr. Maurice Brendan, BSc ACA *1983;* Flat 113, Albert Palace Mansions, Lurline Gardens, LONDON, SW11 4DH.
CONNOLLY, Mr. Michael, FCA *1964;* 4 Warblers Way, Constantia, CAPE TOWN, 7806, SOUTH AFRICA. (Life Member)
CONNOLLY, Mr. Michael, ACA *2011;* Flat 4 Hampton Court, 12a Branksome Wood Road, BOURNEMOUTH, BH2 6BZ.
CONNOLLY, Mr. Michael John Bader, FCA *1970;* Wheatley, Martinsend Lane, GREAT MISSENDEN, HP16 9BH.
CONNOLLY, Miss. Noa, BA ACA *2004;* E M I Music Crown House, 72 Hammersmith Road, LONDON, W14 8UD.
CONNOLLY, Mr. Patrick Edward Geoffrey Gunnell, FCA *1969;* Connolly Frames, 7 Southwick Street, Southwick, BRIGHTON, BN42 4AD.
CONNOLLY, Mr. Patrick Joseph, MBA BA FCA *1962;* 51 Avondale Lawn, BLACKROCK, COUNTY DUBLIN, IRELAND. (Life Member)
CONNOLLY, Mr. Patrick William Giles, BSc ACA *2007;* Kaplan Financial, 10-14 White Lion Street, LONDON, N1 9PD.
CONNOLLY, Mr. Peter, FCA *1986;* (Tax Fac), with Haines Watts, Sterling House, 177-181 Farnham Road, SLOUGH, BERKSHIRE, SL1 4XP.
CONNOLLY, Mr. Peter James, BA ACA *1989;* Topshaw, 79 Kingswood Way, Selsdon, SOUTH CROYDON, SURREY, CR2 8QN.
CONNOLLY, Miss. Sian Marissa, ACA *2008;* Chapel House, 129 Church Street, LOUTH, LINCOLNSHIRE, LN11 9DE.
CONNOLLY, Mrs. Stacy Jane, MA ACA ATII *1995;* 1 Crosbie Road, Harborne, BIRMINGHAM, B17 9BG.
CONNOLLY, Mr. Steven Ronald, FCA *1983;* 11017 JENKINS COURT, SAN ANTONIO, FL 33576-7806, UNITED STATES.
CONNOLLY, Mr. Terence Ralph, FCA *1966;* Windward Cottage, Ashprington, TOTNES, TQ9 7UW.
CONNON, Ms. Anne Sylvia, MA FCA *1980;* Australian Tax Office, 2 Lonsdale St, MELBOURNE, VIC 3000, AUSTRALIA.
CONNON, Mr. Anthony Vincent, BA FCA FAICD *1976;* Australian Unity Limited, 114 Albert Road, SOUTH MELBOURNE, VIC 3205, AUSTRALIA.
CONNON, Mr. Ian Grant, MA FCA *1980;* with PKF (UK) LLP, Farringdon Place, 20 Farringdon Road, LONDON, EC1M 3AP.
CONNOP, Mr. Kenneth Charles, FCA *1970;* Birney Grange, Stamfordham Road, NEWCASTLE UPON TYNE, NE15 9RB.
CONNOP, Mr. Thomas, ACA *2008;* Flat 1, 6 Ringers Road, BROMLEY, BR1 1HR.
CONNOR, Mr. Adam Michael, BA(Hons) ACA *2004;* 21 Pavilion Square, LONDON, SW17 7DN.
CONNOR, Miss. Alison Suzanne Elizabeth, BA ACA *1992;* Merrieleas, Arrowsmith Lane, WIMBORNE, BH21 3AJ.
CONNOR, Mr. Carl Francis, BSc ACA *1989;* 97 Trimingham Drive, BURY, LANCASHIRE, BL8 1EL.
CONNOR, Miss. Carolyne, ACA *2004;* PO Box 2828, GEORGETOWN, KY1-1112, CAYMAN ISLANDS.
CONNOR, Mr. Christopher, BA FCA *1975;* 3 Dales Drive, Guiseley, LEEDS, LS20 8HR.
CONNOR, Mrs. Deborah Louise, BSc ACA *1992;* Digswell Water Lodge, Digswell Lane, WELWYN, AL6 OSN.
•**CONNOR, Mr. Grahame Henry, BA FCA DChA** *1978;* Connor Warin Limited, Trinity House, Sewardstone Road, WALTHAM ABBEY, ESSEX, EN9 1PH.
CONNOR, Miss. Helen Elizabeth, BSc ACA *2010;* K P M G, St. James's Square, MANCHESTER, M2 6DS.
•**CONNOR, Mr. Howard Arthur, FCA** *1960;* (Tax Fac), G.H. Attenborough & Co. Limited, 1 Tower House, Tower Centre, HODDESDON, HERTFORDSHIRE, EN11 8UR.
CONNOR, Mr. Ian Graham, MEng BEng ACA *2006;* with PricewaterhouseCoopers LLP, 9 Greyfriars Road, READING, RG1 1JG.
•**CONNOR, Mr. Ian Richard Marcel, LLB ACA** *1987;* (Tax Fac), Connor Richardson, Victoria Buildings, 9 Silver Street, BURY, BL9 0EU.
CONNOR, Mr. Jason Christopher, BSc ACA *1994;* Priv. San Juan 916-19, Col Comercial Gomez Morin, San Pedro, Garza Garcia, 66220 MONTERREY, NUEVO LEON MEXICO.
CONNOR, Mr. John, BSc ACA *1987;* A-One Business Centre, ZA Vers La Piece 10, CH-1180 ROLLE, SWITZERLAND.
CONNOR, Mr. Kevin David, ACA *2010;* 22 Admiralty Street, Keyham, PLYMOUTH, PL2 2BP.
CONNOR, Miss. Larissa Naomi, MA ACA *1995;* with Ernst & Young LLP, 1 More London Place, LONDON, SE1 2AF.
CONNOR, Mrs. Louisa Helen, BA ACA *2006;* 22 Meadowdown Close, Hempstead, GILLINGHAM, KENT, ME7 3SU.
CONNOR, Mr. Neil Alexander, BSc ACA *1993;* 24 Jocelyn Road, RICHMOND, TW9 2TH.
CONNOR, Mr. Norman, FCA *1965;* Flat 13, Henrietta Court, Bathwick Street, BATH, BA2 6PG.
CONNOR, Mr. Paul, MMath ACA *2004;* Flat 214 Harwood Court, Upper Richmond Road, LONDON, SW15 6JG.
CONNOR, Mr. Paul Anthony, ACA *2010;* 14 Yarmouth Road, Great Sankey, WARRINGTON, WA5 3EJ.
CONNOR, Mr. Robert Crothers, FCA *1960;* 35 Moss Road, BALLYNAHINCH, COUNTY DOWN, BT24 8EG. (Life Member)
CONNOR, Mr. Roger Gerard, MEng ACA *1996;* 104 Lower Road, Chalfont St. Peter, GERRARDS CROSS, BUCKINGHAMSHIRE, SL9 8LB.
CONNOR, Mrs. Sarah Maria, BSc ACA *1994;* 17 Butterley Close, DUKINFIELD, SK16 5QX.
CONNOR, Mrs. Susan Grace, BCom ACA *1993;* 24 Jocelyn Road, RICHMOND, TW9 2TH.
•**CONNOR, Mrs. Suzanne, ACA FCCA** *2011;* 63 Willow Lea, TONBRIDGE, KENT, TN10 3RE.
•**CONNOR, Mrs. Tracey, BSc FCA** *1988;* with Chadwick & Company (Manchester) Ltd, Capital House, 272 Manchester Road, Droylsden, MANCHESTER, M43 6PW.
CONNORS, Mrs. Diane Elizabeth, BSc ACA *1987;* 9 Watters Close, Coalpit Heath, BRISTOL, BS36 2LZ.
•**CONNORS, Mr. Maurice Patrick, LLB FCA** *1988;* Integer, Highview, Latimer Road, GODALMING, SURREY, GU7 1BW.
CONNORS, Miss. Melanie Claire, BA ACA CTA *2002;* with Deloitte LLP, 5 Callaghan Square, CARDIFF, CF10 5BT.
CONOBOY, Miss. Sally, BA ACA *2006;* 29 Trout Road, HASLEMERE, SURREY, GU27 1RD.
CONOLEY, Mr. Simon Nicholas, ACA *2008;* 23 Barford Drive, WILMSLOW, CHESHIRE, SK9 2GB.
CONOLLY, Mrs. Claire Helen, BSc(Hons) ACA *2000;* Sage UK Ltd, North Park, Great Park, NEWCASTLE UPON TYNE, NE13 9AA.
CONOLLY, Mr. Kenneth John, FCA *1972;* 10th Floor Walker House, Exchange Flags, LIVERPOOL, L2 3YL.
•**CONQUEST, Mr. Andrew David, FCA** *1976;* The Lodge, Upper Green, Felsham, BURY ST. EDMUNDS, IP30 0PL.
CONRAD, Mr. Stephen, ACA *2008;* (Tax Fac), Ove Arup & Partners, 13 Fitzroy Street, LONDON, W1T 4BQ.
CONRAD-PICKLES, Mr. Jeremy Philip, BSc ACA *1995;* 2 Luche Du Crot, Route De Messery, 74140 NERNIER, FRANCE.
•**CONRADI, Mr. Paul Hammond, FCA** *1975;* (Tax Fac), Conradi Morrison & Co, 4 Summerhill Road, DARTFORD, DA1 2LP. See also Ace Associates
CONRADI, Miss. Zoe Helen, ACA *2009;* Flat 16 Hillcrest Court, Shoot up Hill, LONDON, NW2 3PG.
CONRATHE, Mr. Michael Roy, FCA *1967;* Beaconsfield Farm, Ingham Road, Hickling, NORWICH, NR12 0BB.
•**CONRICH, Mr. Laurence Murray, FCA** *1974;* Conrich & Co, 65 Castellan Avenue, Gidea Park, ROMFORD, RM2 6EB. See also Conrich & Associates
•**CONRON, Mr. Paul Anthony, FCA** *1969;* Paul Conron, 4 Robin Hood Lane, Wrightington, WIGAN, WN6 9QG. See also Conron P.A.
CONROY, Mr. Andrew Peter, BSc(Hons) ACA *2001;* 10 Hall Meadow, Hagley, STOURBRIDGE, WEST MIDLANDS, DY9 9LE.
CONROY, Mr. Arnold, FCA *1960;* 27 Beaumont Avenue, ST. ALBANS, HERTFORDSHIRE, AL1 4TL. (Life Member)
CONROY, Ms. Claire Louise, BA ACA *2008;* South Manchester University Hospitals N H S Trust, Wythenshawe Hospital Southmoor Road, MANCHESTER, M23 9LT.
CONROY, Mr. David James, BSc FCA *1980;* 14 Stanley Court, Alsager, STOKE-ON-TRENT, ST7 2BH.
CONROY, Mr. Graham Leslie, FCA *1981;* Lime House, Harmston Park Avenue, Harmston, LINCOLN, LN5 9GF.
CONROY, Miss. Jane Elizabeth, BCom FCA *1994;* 708 Longboat Quay South, Hanover Quay, DUBLIN, COUNTY DUBLIN, IRELAND.
CONROY, Mr. Mark John, BA ACA *1997;* 29 Cove Street, BIRCHGROVE, NSW 2041, AUSTRALIA.
•**CONROY, Mr. Melvyn, FCA** *1963;* M. & B. J. Conroy, Fishponds House, 700 Wellingborough Road, Billing Park, NORTHAMPTON, NN3 9BQ.
CONROY, Mr. Peter David, LLB ACA *1985;* 93 Silverdale Avenue, WALTON-ON-THAMES, KT12 1EJ.
CONROY, Mr. Peter Mark, BA ACA *1988;* Appartment 5C, The Savoy, 200 61st Street, Upper East Side, Manhattan, NEW YORK NY 10065 UNITED STATES.
CONROY, Mr. Simon Thomas, BA ACA *1999;* Madgex, Suite 1, Clarence House, 30-31 North Street, BRIGHTON, BN1 1EB.
•**CONSIDINE, Mr. Joseph Patrick, BSc FCA** *1977;* Cork Gully Restructuring LLP, 52 Brook Street, LONDON, W1K 5DS.
CONSIDINE, Mr. Stephen Thomas, BSc ACA *2004;* Flat 10 Perry Court, 1 Maritime Quay, LONDON, E14 3QE.
CONSTABLE, Mr. Andrew Stephen, ACA *2007;* (Tax Fac), with Kingston Smith LLP, Devonshire House, 60 Goswell Road, LONDON, EC1M 7AD.
CONSTABLE, Mr. James, MPhil(Cantab) BA ACA *2010;* Flat 8, 2a Clare Road, CAMBRIDGE, CB3 9BT.
CONSTABLE, Miss. Kathryn Diana, BSc FCA *1977;* 268 Fowler Road, ILLAWONG, NSW 2234, AUSTRALIA.
CONSTABLE, Mr. Stanley Ernest, FCA *1958;* Broomfield Farm, Easton Piercy, Kington St. Michael, CHIPPENHAM, SN14 6JU. (Life Member)
CONSTANCE, Mr. Jonathan Paul, MMath ACA *2003;* 17 Hallmark Apartments, 34 Newhall Hill, BIRMINGHAM, B1 3JP.
CONSTANDA, Mr. Dan, DCS BSc ACA *1996;* Flat 28, Warwick Mansions, Cromwell Crescent, LONDON, SW5 9QR.
CONSTANDINOU, Miss. Katerina Andrea, ACA *2009;* Kifissou 1, 8028 PAPHOS, CYPRUS.
CONSTANT, Mr. Denis Michael, BA FCA *1950;* 11 Avondale Road, HOVE, BN3 6ER. (Life Member)
CONSTANT, Mr. Mark, BSc ACA *2010;* 11 Lydon Road, LONDON, SW4 0HP.
CONSTANT, Mr. Simon, BSc ACA *2006;* (Tax Fac), Barclays Capital, 5 The North Colonnade, Canary Wharf, LONDON, E14 4BB.
•**CONSTANT, Mr. Stephen Michael, OBE BCom FCA** *1976;* PricewaterhouseCoopers DA, Bjørvika, Postboks 748, Sentrum, NO-0106 OSLO, NORWAY. See also PricewaterhouseCoopers AS
CONSTANTINE, Mr. Andrew James, MA FCA *1981;* Inverdart Castle Road, Kingswear, DARTMOUTH, DEVON, TQ6 0BT.
•**CONSTANTINE, Miss. Bernice Elizabeth, BA FCA** *1986;* Riley, 51 North Hill, PLYMOUTH, PL4 8HZ.
CONSTANTINE, Mr. Clement, MSc ACA *1989;* 17 Homefield Road, RADLETT, WD7 8PX.
CONSTANTINE, Mr. John Lupton, BSc(Econ) FCA *1974;* 7 Westhay Gardens, East Sheen, LONDON, SW14 7RU. (Life Member)
CONSTANTINE, Mr. Michael Denis, FCA *1962;* 601 Watergardens, PO Box 1325, GIBRALTAR, GIBRALTAR.
CONSTANTINE, Mr. Neil Andrew, BA FCA *1992;* 53 Overhill Drive, BRIGHTON, BN1 8WG.
CONSTANTINE, Mr. Nigel Loudon, BSc ACA *1981;* Constantine Craven House, Station Road, GODALMING, GU7 1EX.

CONSTANTINE, Mrs. Rose Aylmer, MA ACA *1986;* Otsuka Pharmaceuticals UK Ltd, 3 Furzeground Way Stockley Park, UXBRIDGE, MIDDLESEX, UB11 1EZ.

CONSTANTINE, The Hon. Roy, FCA *1959;* 11 Grove Park Terrace, Chiswick, LONDON, W4 3QG. (Life Member)

CONSTANTINE, Mr. Simon John, MA ACA *1984;* Lower Farmhouse, Ibworth, TADLEY, RG26 5TJ.

CONSTANTINE-COLES, Mrs. Diane, BSc FCA *1981;* Higher Heights Farm, Heights Lane, Eldwick, BINGLEY, BD16 3AH.

CONSTANTINIDES, Mr. Andreas Michael, BSc FCA *2000;* 14 Ippokratous Street Flat 301, Strovolos, 2006 NICOSIA, CYPRUS.

•**CONSTANTINIDES, Mr. Andreas Theodoulou, BA FCA** *1984;* PricewaterhouseCoopers Limited, Julia House, 3 Themistocles Dervis Street, CY-1066 NICOSIA, CYPRUS.

CONSTANTINIDES, Mr. Charalambos Socrates, MSc ACA *1990;* c/o International Fund for Agricultural Development, Via Paolo di Dono 44, 00142 ROME, ITALY.

CONSTANTINIDES, Mr. Costas, BSc ACA *2005;* 3a rue d'Athenes, L-8224 MAMER, LUXEMBOURG.

CONSTANTINIDES, Mr. Dimitris, ACA *2008;* 24 Tillou, Kaimakli, 1036 NICOSIA, CYPRUS.

CONSTANTINIDES, Mr. George Ioannis, BA(Hons) ACA *2002;* (Tax Fac), 23 Nafpliou Street, Parissinos, Strovolos, 2066 NICOSIA, CYPRUS.

CONSTANTINIDES, Miss. Irene, BA ACA *2008;* 85 Andreas Avraamides Street, CY2024 NICOSIA, CYPRUS.

CONSTANTINIDES, Miss. Lilian, BA ACA *2005;* 5 Chalkidos Street, Potamos Yermasoyias, 4042 LIMASSOL, CYPRUS.

CONSTANTINIDES, Mr. Michael, ACA *2009;* 3 Ellados, Erimi Gardens, 4630 LIMASSOL, CYPRUS.

CONSTANTINIDES, Dr. Michael, ACA *1987;* 18 Theophilos Georgiades Str, Aglantzia, 2123 NICOSIA, CYPRUS.

CONSTANTINIDES, Mr. Michael Ioannis, BSc ACA *2003;* (Tax Fac), 23 Nafpliou Street, 2066 Strovolos, 2066 NICOSIA, CYPRUS.

CONSTANTINIDES, Mr. Sotos, BSc ACA *1991;* Mereway Limited, Redfern Park Way, Tysley, BIRMINGHAM, B11 2BF.

CONSTANTINIDES, Mr. Vasilakis Costa, BSc ACA *1979;* 13A Kalli Sakka, 2066 NICOSIA, CYPRUS.

CONSTANTINIDI, Mr. Antony George, FCA *1977;* Wallmead Farm, Lippiatt Lane, Timsbury, BATH, BA2 0GE.

CONSTANTINIDOU, Miss. Andrea, ACA *2009;* 11 Nikou Xylouri, 4106 AYIOS ATHANASIOS, CYPRUS.

CONSTANTINOU, Mr. Andreas Kyriakou, MBA ACA ACCA *2007;* 6 Oneirou Street, 2035 Strovolos, NICOSIA, CYPRUS.

CONSTANTINOU, Mr. Christophoros, BSc ACA *2001;* DFK Demetriou Trapezaris Ltd, 59-61 Acropolis Avenue, 3rd Floor, 2012 NICOSIA, CYPRUS.

CONSTANTINOU, Mr. Chrysanthos, ACA CC *2011;* P.O Box 20274, 2150 NICOSIA, CYPRUS.

•**CONSTANTINOU, Mr. Constantinos, BSc ACA** *1993;* PricewaterhouseCoopers Limited, Julia House, 3 Themistocles Dervis Street, CY-1066 NICOSIA, CYPRUS.

•**CONSTANTINOU, Mr. Constantinos, FCA** *1982;* Constant & Co Accountancy Services Ltd, 344 Croydon Road, BECKENHAM, KENT, BR3 4EX.

CONSTANTINOU, Mr. Constantinos, BSc ACA *2008;* 28 PERA EKKLISIAS, LOUVARAS, 4560 LIMASSOL, CYPRUS.

CONSTANTINOU, Mr. Constantinos Savva, BSc ACA *1991;* 9 Panteli Michanikou, Engomi, 2412 NICOSIA, CYPRUS.

CONSTANTINOU, Mr. Costas, BA ACA *2008;* 12 Ithakis Street, Tseri, 2480 NICOSIA, CYPRUS.

•**CONSTANTINOU, Mr. Costas, BSc FCA** *1995;* Moore Stephens, (P.O.Box No. 80 132), 93 Akti Miaouli, GR-185 38, PIRAEUS, GREECE.

•**CONSTANTINOU, Mr. Damianos, FCA** *1963;* Moore Stephens, (P.O.Box No. 80 132), 93 Akti Miaouli, GR-185 38, PIRAEUS, GREECE. See also Moore Stephens OOD

CONSTANTINOU, Mr. Demetris, ACA *2010;* 8 Alkinoou, Kapsalos, 3087 LIMASSOL, CYPRUS.

CONSTANTINOU, Miss. Eleni Kyprou, BSc ACA *2004;* 3 COSTA LOIZOU, 2222 LATSIA, CYPRUS.

CONSTANTINOU, Mrs. Eleonora, LLB ACA *1992;* 9 Panteli Michanikou, Engomi, 2412 NICOSIA, CYPRUS.

CONSTANTINOU, Mr. George, ACA *1980;* 12 S. Orfanou Street, CY-7700 Pano Lefkara, LARNACA, CYPRUS.

CONSTANTINOU, Mr. Georgios, MSc BSc ACA *2009;* 106 Hermes Street, 6022 LARNACA, CYPRUS.

CONSTANTINOU, Miss. Maria, BSc ACA *2009;* 23 Iroon Street, Strovolos, 2034 NICOSIA, CYPRUS.

•**CONSTANTINOU, Mr. Nicos, FCA** *1982;* N Constantinou & Co Audit Ltd, Limassol Centre PO Box 54039, Block B. Office 508, Rega Fereou St., 3720 LIMASSOL, CYPRUS.

CONSTANTINOU, Mr. Paul, BA ACA *2010;* 379 Nottingham Road, Newthorpe, NOTTINGHAM, NG16 2EB.

CONSTANTINOU, Mr. Phivos, ACA *2011;* Kamelias 18a, Gkali, 3110 LIMASSOL, CYPRUS.

•**CONSTANTINOU, Mr. Stelios Charalambou, BSc FCA** *1991;* PricewaterhouseCoopers Limited, City House, 6 Karaiskakis Street, CY-3032 LIMASSOL, CYPRUS.

CONSTANTINOU, Mr. Vass, BA(Hons) ACA *2010;* 379 Nottingham Road, Newthorpe, NOTTINGHAM, NG16 2EB.

CONSTERDINE, Mr. David Andrew, BA ACA *1985;* 27 Westfields, ST. ALBANS, HERTFORDSHIRE, AL3 4LR.

•**CONTE, Mr. Louis Bartholomew, FCA** *1976;* Conte Davies & Co Ltd, 60 Walter Road, SWANSEA, SA1 5PZ.

•**CONTE, Mr. Michael Anthony, FCA** *1967;* 4 Locking Stumps Lane, Locking Stumps, WARRINGTON, WA3 7LZ.

CONTI, Mr. Andrew John William, BEng FCA *1994;* with Baker Tilly Restructuring And Recovery LLP, 25 Farringdon Street, LONDON, EC4A 4AB.

CONTI, Mr. Daniel Timothy, BSc ACA *2005;* with BDO LLP, 55 Baker Street, LONDON, W1U 7EU.

CONTI, Mrs. Susan Rosemary, BA ACA *1986;* 25a Tarn Moor Crescent, SKIPTON, NORTH YORKSHIRE, BD23 1LT.

CONTRACTOR, Mr. Histasp Aspi, BSc ACA *1987;* Flat 8, 30 Thurlow Road, Hampstead, LONDON, NW3 5PH.

CONTRACTOR, Mr. Hunaid, ACA *2008;* 23 Floor One NBAD Tower Khalifa Street, P.O. Box 4, ABU DHABI, UNITED ARAB EMIRATES.

CONTRACTOR, Mr. Luckman Jacky, FCA *1973;* 123-B Shabbirabad, off Tippu Sultan Road, KARACHI 8, PAKISTAN.

CONTRERAS, Mrs. Jayne, BA ACA *1992;* Applegarth, 9 Thorp Arch Park, Thorp Arch, WETHERBY, LS23 7AP.

CONTRERAS, Mr. Robert Leonard, BA ACA *1988;* Applegarth, 9 Thorp Arch Park, Thorp Arch, WETHERBY, LS23 7AP.

CONVERY, Mr. Roy Anthony, BSc ACA *2007;* 16 Wheelers Orchard, Chalfont St Peter, GERRARDS CROSS, SL9 0HL.

CONVEY, Mr. Peter Daniel, BSc ACA *1983;* KCA DEUTAG DRILLING GMBH - LIBYA BRANCH OFFICE, TRIPOLI, LIBYAN ARAB JAMAHIRIYA.

•**CONVISSER, Mr. David Albert, FCA** *1986;* 9 Sylvia Avenue, PINNER, HA5 5QY.

CONWAY, Ms. Alison Charlotte, BA(Hons) ACA *2003;* 5th Floor, 25 Farringdon Street, LONDON, EC4A 4AB.

CONWAY, Mr. Allan Brian, BA ACA *1983;* Upper Milton Barn, Upper Milton, Milton-under-Wychwood, CHIPPING NORTON, OXFORDSHIRE, OX7 6EX.

•**CONWAY, Mr. Anthony Liam, BA ACA** *1991;* TF & Partners Limited, New Maxdov House, 130 Bury New Road, Prestwich, MANCHESTER, M25 0AA.

CONWAY, Mr. Arthur Noel, FCA FTII *1972;* (Tax Fac), The Willows, CORBRIDGE, NE45 5AU.

•**CONWAY, Mr. Barry Michael, FCA** *1974;* Cooper Paul, Abacus House, 14-18 Forest Road, LOUGHTON, IG10 1DX.

CONWAY, Mr. Christopher James, BSc(Hons) ACA *2011;* 32 Clacton Road, LONDON, E17 8AR.

CONWAY, Mr. Daniel Simon, BA ACA *2001;* with BDO LLP, 55 Baker Street, LONDON, W1U 7EU.

CONWAY, Mr. David, FCA *1956;* 247 Chase Side, Southgate, LONDON, N14 5LD. (Life Member)

•**CONWAY, Mr. David Isaac, FCA** *1951;* Harvey Marcus & Conway, 30 Dene Gardens, STANMORE, MIDDLESEX, HA7 4TD.

•**CONWAY, Mr. David Jeffrey, FCA** *1973;* (Tax Fac), Trafalgar Associates Limited, Unit 24, Bury Business Centre, Kay Street, BURY, LANCASHIRE BL9 6BU.

CONWAY, Mr. David Michael, FCA *1975;* 1 Beech Lane, Prestwood, GREAT MISSENDEN, HP16 9DP.

CONWAY, Mr. Deane Dominic, ACA *2005;* 14 Hardie Street, DARLINGHURST, NSW 2010, AUSTRALIA.

CONWAY, Ms. Erica Sian Rees, BA ACA *1994;* 107 Station Road, Wylde Green, SUTTON COLDFIELD, WEST MIDLANDS, B73 5LA.

CONWAY, Mrs. Felicity Claire, BA ACA *1994;* Mizbrooks House, Cleavers Lane, Cuckfield, HAYWARDS HEATH, WEST SUSSEX, RH17 5HZ.

CONWAY, Miss. Fiona Diane, LLB ACA *1987;* Copyright Licensing Agency Ltd, 6-10 Kirby Street, LONDON, EC1N 8TS.

•**CONWAY, Mr. George, BSc FCA** *1971;* (Tax Fac), Conway Davis Ltd, Greenfield, The Causeway, Undy, CALDICOT, GWENT NP26 3DP. See also ZDP Limited

CONWAY, Mr. Gerard Patrick Adriaan McCleester, MA ACA *1995;* Mizbrooks House, Cleavers Lane, Cuckfield, HAYWARDS HEATH, WEST SUSSEX, RH17 5HZ.

•**CONWAY, Mr. Ian Frank, FCA CTA** *1978;* Ian F Conway & Co, 6 Blue Water Drive, Elborough Village, WESTON-SUPER-MARE, AVON, BS24 8PF.

•**CONWAY, Mr. James Edward, FCA** *1968;* James E. Conway, 12 Marchant Road, WOLVERHAMPTON, WV3 9QG.

CONWAY, Mr. James William, FCA *1973;* Short Heath Farm, CHESHAM, BUCKINGHAMSHIRE, HP5 3PA.

CONWAY, Mr. Liam Richard Vincent, BA ACA *2003;* 138 Penwith Road, Earlsfield, Wandsworth, LONDON, SW18 4QB.

CONWAY, Mr. Marc Solomon, BA FCA *1997;* 1 Degas Close, SALFORD, M7 3BG.

CONWAY, Miss. Maresa Ellen Rita, BSc ACA *1997;* 55 Lysia Street, LONDON, SW6 6NF.

CONWAY, Mr. Michael, FCA *1966;* 11 The Crescent, NORTH SHIELDS, NE30 2LZ.

CONWAY, Mr. Michael John, MA ACA *1979;* 8 Friars Gate Close, WOODFORD GREEN, IG8 0SG.

CONWAY, Mrs. Monica Ursula, BA ACA *1996;* Hicklin Slade & Partners Ltd Bewlay House, 2 Swallow Place, LONDON, W1B 2AE.

CONWAY, Ms. Natasha Louise, ACA *2001;* 7 Moor Drive, Headingley, LEEDS, LS6 4BY.

•**CONWAY, Mr. Paul Gregory, FCA** *1972;* Conway Fielden Gough Limited, Colne House, Guithavon Street, WITHAM, CM8 1BL.

CONWAY, Mr. Paul Richard, BA FCA *1995;* 22 Birkdale Place, Little Ees Lane, SALE, CHESHIRE, M33 5BR.

CONWAY, Mrs. Penelope Ann, BSc ACA *1987;* 191 West End, Costessey, NORWICH, NR8 5AW.

CONWAY, Mr. Peter, FCA *1964;* Magpies, 2 Sycamore Close, Sibford Gower, BANBURY, OXFORDSHIRE, OX15 5SB.

CONWAY, Mr. Philip James, LLB ACA *1998;* 20 Tower Street, CIRENCESTER, GLOUCESTERSHIRE, GL7 1EF.

CONWAY, Mrs. Rachel Louise, ACA *2009;* with Michael Greenhalgh & Co Ltd, Elland House, 22 High Street, Burgh le Marsh, SKEGNESS, LINCOLNSHIRE PE24 5JT.

CONWAY, Mr. Robert John, BSc FCA *1977;* Primavera, Goodworth Clatford, ANDOVER, SP11 7QX.

CONWAY, Mr. Ronald Harvey, FCA *1957;* 5 London Road, STANMORE, MIDDLESEX, HA7 4PA. (Life Member)

•**CONWAY, Mrs. Samantha Louise, ACA FMAAT** *2003;* SLD Accountants, 30 Wyatt Place, Strood, ROCHESTER, KENT, ME2 2DQ.

CONWAY, Mr. Simon Alexander Malcolm, BSc ACA *1994;* Matterhorn Capital Ltd, 10 Gloucester Place, LONDON, W1U 8EZ.

①**CONWAY, Mr. Simon Richard, BCom ACA** *2002;* PO Box 258, Strathvale House, GEORGETOWN, GRAND CAYMAN, KY1-1104, CAYMAN ISLANDS.

•**CONWAY, Mr. Steven John, FCA** *1976;* Boardman Conway, 23A High Street, Weaverham, NORTHWICH, CHESHIRE, CW8 3HA.

CONWAY, Mr. Terence Joseph, FCA *1960;* 8 Scalby Close, NEWCASTLE UPON TYNE, NE3 5LJ. (Life Member)

CONWAY-CRAGG, Mr. John, FCA *1958;* 27 Eugene Marais Avenue, CONSTANTIA, C.P., 7806, SOUTH AFRICA. (Life Member)

•**CONWAY-HUGHES, Mr. David Anthony, FCA** *1971;* Bay Tree House, 82 Crescent Road, READING, RG1 5SP.

CONWELL, Miss. Elaine, BSc ACA *1998;* 69 Mayfield Road, Crouch End, LONDON, N8 9LN.

CONYBEARE, Mrs. Nicola Dawn, BSc ACA *1991;* with Huw J Edmund Limited, Garth House, Unit 7, Ty-Nant Court, Morganstown, CARDIFF CF15 8LW.

CONYBEARE-CROSS, Mr. James Thomas, BA ACA *1988;* 100 Hurlingham Road, LONDON, SW6 3NR.

CONYERS, Mr. Brian, FCA *1961;* Jalna, 58 Dinerth Road, Rhos-on-Sea, COLWYN BAY, LL28 4YG.

•**CONYERS, Ms. Carol Yvonne, BSc FCA** *1992;* 3 Fairwood Road, HEXHAM, NE46 1LG.

CONYERS, Mr. Harold Lionel, FCA *1970;* The Red House, 23 St Marys Walk, MIRFIELD, WF14 0QB.

COOCH, Mr. Matthew Handley, BSc ACA *1998;* 90 Coombe Rise, Oadby, LEICESTER, LE2 5TW.

COOCH, Mr. Robin Nicolas, BA(Hons) ACA *2002;* Enfield Farm, Elkstone, CHELTENHAM, GLOUCESTERSHIRE, GL53 9PB.

COOGANS, Ms. Karma Kristin Sorcha, BSc(Hons) ACA *2010;* Flat 3, Penfields House, York Way Estate, LONDON, N7 9PZ.

COOK, Miss. Abigail Jane, ACA *2008;* 82a Haverhill Road, LONDON, SW12 0HB.

COOK, Mr. Adrian, BEng ACA *2010;* Flat 1 Lane End, 196 West Hill, LONDON, SW15 3SH.

COOK, Mr. Adrian Barry, FCA *1973;* Roalco Ltd, Ardleigh House, Dedham Road, Ardleigh, COLCHESTER, ESSEX CO7 7QA.

COOK, Mr. Adrian Robert, ACA *2004;* 17 Norfolk Way, CANVEY ISLAND, SS8 9TJ.

COOK, Mr. Alan Hugh, FCA *1971;* 27 Rover Road, Lordswood, CHATHAM, ME5 8SN.

COOK, Miss. Alicia Louise, BA(Hons) ACA *2001;* Ernst & Young Llp, 1 More London Place, LONDON, SE1 2AF.

•**COOK, Ms. Alison Joyce, BSc FCA** *1992;* AJC Accountancy Services, Basepoint Business Centre, 110 Butterfield, LUTON, LU2 8DL.

COOK, Mr. Allan Cameron, BSc ACA *1999;* 72 Lavenham Road, LONDON, SW18 5HE.

COOK, Mr. Allan Charles, FCA *1964;* 55 Philip Gardens, Eynesbury, ST. NEOTS, PE19 2QJ. (Life Member)

COOK, Allan Vincent Cannon, Esq CBE BSc FCA *1964;* 5 Lissant Close, Lovelace Road, Long Ditton, SURBITON, SURREY, KT6 6SA.

COOK, Mr. Andrew, BSc ACA *1989;* 1 The Cedars, Milford, GODALMING, SURREY, GU8 5DH.

•**COOK, Mr. Andrew Cameron, BA ACA CF** *1979;* MacIntyre Hudson LLP, 31 Castle Street, HIGH WYCOMBE, BUCKINGHAMSHIRE, HP13 6RU. See also MacIntyre Hudson Corporate Finance Ltd

COOK, Mr. Andrew James, FCA *1985;* Bosch Rexroth SL, The Drive & Control Company, C I Santiga Obradors 14-16, 08130 SANTA PERPETUA DE MOGODA, SPAIN.

•**COOK, Mr. Andrew James, FCA** *1990;* Menzies LLP, 3rd Floor Kings House, 12-42 Wood Street, KINGSTON UPON THAMES, SURREY, KT1 1TG.

COOK, Mr. Andrew John, BA ACA *1998;* 1 Dartons Yard, Church Street, BALDOCK, HERTFORDSHIRE, SG7 5AF.

COOK, Mr. Andrew Martin, BSc FCA *1977;* 7 Malcolm Drive, Langley Avenue, SURBITON, KT6 6QS.

COOK, Mr. Andrew Richard, BTech FCA CTA *1984;* (Tax Fac), Filtrona plc, Avebury House, 201-249 Avebury Boulevard, MILTON KEYNES, MK9 1AU.

•**COOK, Mr. Andrew Robert, ACA** *1981;* 29 Whittington Way, Bream, LYDNEY, GL15 6AW.

COOK, Miss. Anne Margaret, FCA *1974;* 8 Hill Road, PRENTON, CH43 8TL.

COOK, Mr. Anthony Alexander, FCA *1970;* 78 Bargate, GRIMSBY, DN34 4SR. (Life Member)

COOK, Mr. Arthur John, FCA *1975;* 7 New Cottages, Frog Lane, Great Somerford, CHIPPENHAM, SN15 5JA.

COOK, Mr. Arthur William, FCA *1951;* 18 Agricola Way, THATCHAM, BERKSHIRE, RG19 4GB. (Life Member)

COOK, Mr. Bradley Stephen, BAcc ACA *2000;* 16 Chandlers Ridge, Nunthorpe, MIDDLESBROUGH, CLEVELAND, TS7 0JL.

COOK, Mr. Brian George, FCA *1976;* 10 Boyton Close, BENFLEET, SS7 3BJ.

COOK, Mr. Brian Robert, FCA *1972;* Wereldhave Property Management Co Ltd, 39 Sloane Street, LONDON, SW1X 9WR.

•**COOK, Mr. Brian Thomas, BSc FCA** *1976;* Brian Cook Associates, Marine House, 151 Western Road, HAYWARDS HEATH, WEST SUSSEX, RH16 3LH.

COOK, Mrs. Caroline Jayne, MA ACA *2001;* with PricewaterhouseCoopers LLP, 1 Embankment Place, LONDON, WC2N 6RH.

COOK, Mrs. Catherine Reid, ACA *1995;* Forge Cottage, 35 Banbury Road, Litchborough, TOWCESTER, NORTHAMPTONSHIRE, NN12 8JF.

COOK, Mrs. Christine Margaret Alice, MA ACA *1992;* 43 Victoria Road, COLCHESTER, CO3 3NU.

COOK, Mr. Christopher Gaines, BSc ACA *2010;* 6 Salix Gardens, Twyford, READING, RG10 9AU.

COOK, Mr. Christopher Ian, BSc ACA *1999;* 36 Edinburgh Gardens, WINDSOR, BERKSHIRE, SL4 2AW.

•**COOK, Mr. Christopher Ian, BA ACA** *1992;* Brown & Co Audit Ltd, Brown & Co House, 4 High Street, Brasted, WESTERHAM, KENT TN16 1JA. See also Brown & Co LLP

•**COOK, Mr. Christopher John, MA FCA** *1974;* (Tax Fac), C.J. Cook & Co, 24A Suffolk Road, Barnes, LONDON, SW13 9NB.

•**COOK, Mr. Christopher Robert William, FCA** *1970;* 68 Stevenson Drive, Binfield, BRACKNELL, RG42 5TD.

•**COOK, Mr. Christopher Royston, FCA** *1980;* Nicklin LLP, Church Court, Stourbridge Road, HALESOWEN, WEST MIDLANDS, B63 3TT. See also Nicklin Management Services Limited and HSP Nicklin

COOK, Mrs. Claire Louise, BSc ACA *1995;* 149 Bower Lane, RUGELEY, WS15 2TS.

COOK, Mrs. Claire Nicola, BSc ACA *2000;* 48 Hillside, HORSHAM, WEST SUSSEX, RH12 1NG.

COOK, Mr. Colin Ian Steele, BA ACA *1979;* Dower House, Maugersbury, CHELTENHAM, GL54 1HR.

COOK, Mr. David James, BA(Hons) ACA *2001;* 9 Rutland Road, MAIDENHEAD, SL6 4HZ.

COOK, Mr. David Jeremy Matheson, BA ACA *1983;* with Ernst & Young LLP, 1 More London Place, LONDON, SE1 2AF.

COOK, Mr. David John, BA FCA *1994;* 100 High Street, Tetsworth, THAME, OX9 7AE.

•**COOK, Mr. David Jonathan, BA ACA** *1995;* The Cook Partnership Ltd, Suites 11 &12, Akeman Business Park, Akeman Street, TRING, HERTFORDSHIRE HP23 6AF. See also Ivinghoe Accountancy Services Ltd

COOK, Mr. David Laurence, BA ACA *1995;* 30 Hargreaves Close, Morley, LEEDS, LS27 9TE.

COOK, Mr. David Robert, BA ACA *1992;* 33 St. Paul Street, Islington, LONDON, N1 7DJ.

•**COOK, Mr. David Ronald, FCA** *1966;* DRC Forensics Limited, Kestrel Court, Harbour Road, PORTISHEAD, BS20 7AN.

•**COOK, Mr. Dean Spencer, MA FCA** *1999;* Deloitte LLP, 2 New Street Square, LONDON, EC4A 3BZ. See also Deloitte & Touche LLP

COOK, Mrs. Denise Gaynor, FCA *1992;* Fish Partnership Llp The Mill House, Boundary Road Loudwater, HIGH WYCOMBE, BUCKINGHAMSHIRE, HP10 9QN.

COOK, Mrs. Diana Katherine, BSc ACA *1996;* 81 Abbott Street, SANDRINGHAM, VIC 3191, AUSTRALIA.

COOK, Mr. Dominic Paul, BSc ACA *1993;* 90 Brabourne Rise, BECKENHAM, KENT, BR3 6SH.

COOK, Mr. Edward Giles Bradford, BEng ACA *2002;* 1 Heytesbury Court, Pembroke Lane, Ballabridge, DUBLIN 4, COUNTY DUBLIN, IRELAND.

COOK, Mr. Edward John Nicholas, BCom ACA *1988;* Heathview, Oaksend Close, Copsem Lane, Oxshott, LEATHERHEAD, SURREY KT22 0NX.

COOK, Mr. Eric, MA FCA *1980;* 15 Chevet Lane, WAKEFIELD, WEST YORKSHIRE, WF2 6HN.

COOK, Mr. Francis Walker, FCA *1959;* The Paddocks, Philpots Lane, Hildenborough, TONBRIDGE, TN11 8PB. (Life Member)

COOK, Mr. Frederick Anthony, FCA *1971;* 170 Hawthorne Road, HAWTHORNE, QLD 4171, AUSTRALIA.

COOK, Mr. Garry Stephen, BSc ACA *1991;* 14 Hunts Close, Colden Common, WINCHESTER, SO21 1FX.

•**COOK, Mr. Gary, BA ACA** *1989;* Booth Ainsworth LLP, Alpha House, 4 Greek Street, STOCKPORT, CHESHIRE, SK3 8AB.

COOK, Mr. Gary Richard, FCA *1978;* 2 Bickham Cottage, Timberscombe, MINEHEAD, SOMERSET, TA24 7UA.

COOK, Mr. Geoffrey Alan, FCA *1973;* 11 Cedars Gardens, BRIGHTON, BN1 6YD.

COOK, Mr. Geoffrey Allan, FCA *1964;* 10 Pine Dean, Bookham, LEATHERHEAD, KT23 4BT. (Life Member)

•**COOK, Mr. George Stewart, BTech ACA** *1981;* G.S. Cook, 2 Hall Orchards Avenue, WETHERBY, WEST YORKSHIRE, LS22 6SN.

•**COOK, Miss. Gillian May, BA ACA** *1984;* Hamstead View, Park Lane, Hamstead Marshall, NEWBURY, RG20 0HL.

COOK, Mr. Graham, BA(Hons) ACA *2001;* HBOS Plc, Trinity Road, HALIFAX, WEST YORKSHIRE, HX1 2RG.

•**COOK, Mr. Graham Irvin, ACA FCMA CertPFS** *2007;* (Tax Fac), Godfrey Mansell & Co LLP, Hales Court, Stourbridge Road, HALESOWEN, WEST MIDLANDS, B63 3TT. See also Godfrey Mansell & Co Ltd

COOK, Mr. Graham John, MBA BSc ACA *1996;* Apartment 9 The Pinnacle, 23 Granville Road, SEVENOAKS, TN13 1DQ.

COOK, Mr. Graham Mansell, FCA *1976;* 1 Pipers Ash, WINSFORD, CHESHIRE, CW7 2TN.

COOK, Mr. Graham Thomas, ACA *2001;* 50 Elm Grove, Hildenborough, TONBRIDGE, KENT, TN11 9HF.

COOK, Mr. Grahame David, MA ACA *1982;* 9 Alleyn Road, Dulwich, LONDON, SE21 8AB.

COOK, Mr. Greg, MEng ACA *2002;* 8 Aran Close, HARPENDEN, HERTFORDSHIRE, AL5 1SW.

COOK, Miss. Hannah Beata, BA(Hons) ACA *2010;* 4 Barossa Place, BRISTOL, BS1 6SU.

•**COOK, Mr. Ian Andrew, MA MPhil FCA** *1999;* Greystone LLC, 18 Athol Street, Douglas, ISLE OF MAN, IM1 1JA.

COOK, Mr. Ian Neil, BSc ACA *2009;* 11 Taunton Road, WESTON-SUPER-MARE, AVON, BS22 7DU.

COOK, Mrs. Jacalyn Mary, MA FCA *1986;* La Bleure, Dilay, 79160 ARDIN, FRANCE.

COOK, Mr. Jack Douglas, FCA *1954;* 16 Lynwood Grove, ORPINGTON, BR6 0BG. (Life Member)

COOK, Mr. James Alexander, BSc ACA *2007;* Flat 95 Kenilworth Court, Lower Richmond Road, LONDON, SW15 1HA.

COOK, Mr. James Colquhoun, MA FCA *1968;* The Cottage, Powdermill Lane, Leigh, TONBRIDGE, TN11 8PZ. (Life Member)

COOK, Mr. James Elliott, BA(Hons) ACA *2002;* 42 The Avenue, SUTTON, SM2 7QE.

COOK, Mr. James Mitchell, FCA *1959;* 8 Felden Drive, HEMEL HEMPSTEAD, HP3 0BD. (Life Member)

COOK, Mr. James William, FCA *1967;* The Cottage, Rushlake Green, HEATHFIELD, TN21 9QH.

COOK, Dr. Jeanette Claire, DPhil BSc ACA *2003;* (Tax Fac), 74 West Avenue, BATH, BA2 3QD.

COOK, Mrs. Jennie Margaret, MA ACA CTA *1996;* (Tax Fac), Rose Cottage, Pound Lane, Ampfield, ROMSEY, HAMPSHIRE, SO51 9BL.

COOK, Miss. Jennifer, MA(Hons) ACA *2011;* 27 Mervan Road, LONDON, SW2 1DP.

•**COOK, Mr. Jeremy Guy, BA ACA** *1984;* Peter Hunt & Co Limited, Argon House, Argon Mews, Fulham Broadway, LONDON, SW6 1BJ.

•**COOK, Mr. Jeremy John, FCA** *1976;* J J Cook & Co, 50-51 Albemarle Crescent, SCARBOROUGH, NORTH YORKSHIRE, YO11 1XX. See also Wyatt Husler Cook(Accountants) Limited

COOK, Mr. Jeremy Richard, BSc ACA *1993;* FE Associates, 1 High Street, TAUNTON, SOMERSET, TA1 3PG.

COOK, Mrs. Joanne Clare, ACA MAAT *1996;* 73 Lucas Close, Maidenbower, CRAWLEY, WEST SUSSEX, RH10 7EY.

COOK, Mrs. Joanne Serena, MBA BA ACA *1992;* 15 North Claremont Street, GLASGOW, G3 7NR.

COOK, Mr. John, FCA *1975;* with McKenzies, 14-16 Station Road West, OXTED, SURREY, RH8 9EP.

COOK, Mr. John Andrew Fletcher, FCA *1973;* Deloitte & Touche LLP, 2 Queen Street East, Suite 1200, Maritime Tower, PO Box 8, TORONTO M5C 3G7 ON CANADA.

COOK, Mr. John Arthur, MA ACA CFA *1981;* 74 Valetta Road, Acton, LONDON, W3 7TW.

COOK, Mr. John Charles, FCA *1966;* (Tax Fac), Ladygrove Farm, School Lane, Preston, HITCHIN, SG4 7UE.

COOK, Mr. John David, FCA *1993;* Maynard Heady Matrix House, 12-16 Lionel Road, CANVEY ISLAND, SS8 9DE.

COOK, Mr. John Francis, MSc FCA *1961;* 81 Foxley Lane, PURLEY, CR8 3HP.

•**COOK, Mr. John Kenneth Halesworth, MBA FCA** *1969;* Cooks, 61 Thurstaston Road, Heswall, WIRRAL, CH60 6SA.

COOK, Mr. John Malcolm, FCA *1968;* Dingleberry Cottage, Ossetts Hole Lane, Claverdon, WARWICK, CV35 8HN. (Life Member)

COOK, Mr. John Paul, BSc ACA *2000;* Macquarie Bank, 125 West 55th Street, NEW YORK, NY 10019, UNITED STATES.

COOK, Mr. John Robert Lonsdale, FCA *1975;* The Skinners Company, 8 Dowgate Hill, LONDON, EC4R 2SP.

COOK, Mr. Jonathan Bramley, BA ACA *1987;* 49 The Avenue, DURHAM, DH1 4ED.

COOK, Mr. Jonathan Charles, MA ACA *1986;* SLR Management Ltd, 7 Wornal Park, Worminghall, AYLESBURY, BUCKINGHAMSHIRE, HP18 9PH.

COOK, Mr. Jonathan David, BA ACA *2000;* 1 Dean Swift Green, Glasnevin, DUBLIN, COUNTY DUBLIN, IRELAND.

COOK, Mr. Jonathan Mark, BSc ACA *1993;* 27 Lime Trees, Staplehurst, TONBRIDGE, TN12 0SS.

COOK, Mrs. Judith, BSc ACA MCT *1999;* 7 Argyle Place, EDINBURGH, EH9 1JU.

COOK, Mrs. Karen, BSc ACA *1996;* with KPMG LLP, 100 Temple Street, BRISTOL, BS1 6AG.

COOK, Ms. Karon Isabell, MA BA ACA *1994;* 1 Therapia Road, LONDON, SE22 0SF.

COOK, Mr. Kenneth Alan, FCA FCIS *1968;* 27 Glendower Road, East Sheen, LONDON, SW14 8NY.

COOK, Mr. Kenneth Anthony, FCA CTA FCIS FABRP *1963;* Newnham Court, Sittingbourne Road, Detling, MAIDSTONE, ME14 3ER. (Life Member)

•**COOK, Mr. Kenneth Clifford, OBE FCA** *1939;* K. Clifford Cook, Kingsmead, Upton Road, PRENTON, CH43 7QQ. (Life Member)

COOK, Mr. Kenneth John, FCA *1973;* I M L Labels & Systems Ltd, 441 Brightside Lane, SHEFFIELD, S9 2RS.

•**COOK, Mr. Kenneth John Charles, BA FCA** *1959;* (Tax Fac), K.J.C. Cook, Cuckoo Cottage, Cuckoo Lane, TONBRIDGE, TN11 0AG.

COOK, Mr. Kevin, BSc FCA *1977;* Riversdale, Kentrigg, KENDAL, CUMBRIA, LA9 6EE. (Life Member)

•**COOK, Mr. Kevin Richard, BA FCA** *1984;* (Tax Fac), BDO LLP, Emerald House, East Street, EPSOM, SURREY, KT17 1HS. See also BDO Stoy Hayward LLP

COOK, Mrs. Kirstie Louise, BSc ACA *2004;* 3 Baldwins Place, MAIDENHEAD, BERKSHIRE, SL6 5BP.

COOK, Miss. Kristie Lauren, LLB ACA *2005;* Apartment 910, 747 Anzac Parade, Maroubra, SYDNEY, NSW 2035, AUSTRALIA.

COOK, Miss. Laura Jane, ACA *2008;* 34 Field Bank, HORLEY, RH6 9EH.

COOK, Miss. Lindsey Jane, BSc ACA *2003;* 11 Ridge Street, WATFORD, WD24 6BL.

•**COOK, Mr. Malcolm Roderick Grant, BSc FCA CF** *1980;* PKF (UK) LLP, New Guild House, 45 Great Charles Street, BIRMINGHAM, B3 2LX.

COOK, Mrs. Marion Louise, BSc ACA *2001;* 104 Church Road, Wheatley, OXFORD, OX33 1LU.

COOK, Mr. Mark Nicholas, BA ACA *2004;* with KPMG LLP, 15 Canada Square, LONDON, E14 5GL.

COOK, Mr. Mark Steven, ACA *1985;* 9 Little Catherells, HEMEL HEMPSTEAD, HP1 3QB.

COOK, Mr. Martin, BA ACA *1988;* 16 Hanningtons Way, Burghfield Common, READING, RG7 3BE.

COOK, Mr. Martin, ACA *2011;* 27 Hoctun Close, CASTLEFORD, WEST YORKSHIRE, WF10 4TF.

COOK, Mr. Martin Anthony, FCA *1982;* Medway Galvanising Co Ltd, Unit 9 Castle Road, Eurolink Industrial Centre, SITTINGBOURNE, KENT ME10 3RN.

•**COOK, Mr. Martin Charles, FCA** *1970;* Martin C Cook & Co Limited, 19 The Fairways, Cold Norton, CHELMSFORD, CM3 6JJ.

COOK, Mr. Martin David, BA FCA *1978;* The Farriers, Charlton St Peter, PEWSEY, SN9 6EU.

COOK, Mr. Martin John, BSc ACA *1989;* Biddles Air Systems Ltd, St. Marys Road, NUNEATON, CV11 5AU.

COOK, Mr. Matthew Adrian, BA ACA *1989;* Via Scornetta 31, 40068 San Lazzaro di Savena, BOLOGNA, ITALY.

COOK, Mr. Matthew Alexander, BA(Hons) ACA *1998;* Seddon Group Ltd, Manor House, Manor Lane, Holmes Chapel, CREWE, CW4 8AF.

COOK, Mr. Matthew William, MMath ACA *2004;* with Goodman Jones LLP, 29-30 Fitzroy Square, LONDON, W1T 6LQ.

•**COOK, Mr. Maurice John, FCA** *1970;* M.J.Cook & Co, Sutton House, 4 Coles Lane, SUTTON COLDFIELD, B72 1NE.

COOK, Mr. Michael, FCA *1971;* Stoney Mead, Townsend, Curry Rivel, LANGPORT, TA10 0HW.

COOK, Mr. Michael Frank Benjamin, BA(Hons) ACA *2000;* 10 Blackthorn Grove, MENSTRIE, CLACKMANNANSHIRE, FK11 7DX.

COOK, Mr. Michael Frederick, FCA *1968;* Cracknut Hill House, Haye Lane, Mappleborough Green, STUDLEY, WARWICKSHIRE, B80 7DS. (Life Member)

•**COOK, Mr. Michael George, FCA** *1975;* Cook & Partners Limited, Manufactory House, Bell Lane, HERTFORD, SG14 1BP. See also Cook & Partners

•**COOK, Mr. Michael Ian, BSc FCA** *1995;* Joseph Miller & Co, Floor A, Milburn House, Dean Street, NEWCASTLE UPON TYNE, NE1 1LE.

•**COOK, Mr. Michael John, BA(Hons) ACA** *2000;* Reeves & Co LLP, Third Floor, 24 Chiswell Street, LONDON, EC1Y 4YX.

COOK, Mr. Michael John, LLB ACA *1999;* 59 Woodburn Square, Whitley Lodge, WHITLEY BAY, NE26 3JD.

COOK, Mr. Morgan David, BA ACA *1992;* 14 Kotara Dive, SALISBURY HEIGHTS, SA 5109, AUSTRALIA.

COOK, Mr. Neil, BA(Hons) ACA *2001;* with PricewaterhouseCoopers LLP, 1 Embankment Place, LONDON, WC2N 6RH.

COOK, Dr. Neil Robert, PhD BSc(Hons) ACA *2009;* 48 Prospect Road, Bradway, SHEFFIELD, S17 4JD.

COOK, Mr. Nicholas, BSc ACA *2004;* with PricewaterhouseCoopers LLP, 1 East Parade, SHEFFIELD, S1 2ET.

COOK, Mr. Nicholas Paul, ACA *2009;* 3 Hasted Close, GREENHITHE, KENT, DA9 9HS.

COOK, Miss. Nicola Michelle, MChem ACA *2010;* 20 Spinney Rise, Beeston, NOTTINGHAM, NG9 6JN.

COOK, Mr. Nigel Anthony, BSc ACA *1992;* 4 Radnor Road, LONDON, NW6 6TT.

COOK, Mrs. Pamela Jane, ACA ATII *1995;* with The Cook Partnership Ltd, Suites 11 &12, Akeman Business Park, Akeman Street, TRING, HERTFORDSHIRE HP23 6AF.

•**COOK, Mrs. Patricia Elizabeth, FCA** *1975;* Patricia Cook, 1 Rib Vale, Bengeo, HERTFORD, SG14 3LE.

COOK, Mr. Paul, ACA *2009;* 9 Bowl Hill, Kingscourt, STROUD, GLOUCESTERSHIRE, GL5 5DS.

COOK, Mr. Paul, BSc ACA *2002;* National Probation Service, 185 Dyke Road, HOVE, EAST SUSSEX, BN3 1TL.

COOK, Mr. Paul David, BSc(Hons) FCA *1990;* 10 St. Denis View, Pailton, RUGBY, CV23 0QS.

COOK, Mr. Paul Edward Cannon, BSc ACA *2002;* English Glass Co Ltd, Scudamore Road, LEICESTER, LE3 1UG.

•**COOK, Mr. Peter Alexander Raymond, BA FCA** *1977;* Amyas Limited, 32 Argyll Road, EXETER, EX4 4RY.

•**COOK, Mr. Peter Austin, FCA** *1972;* P A Cook & Co (Oxford) Ltd, Crown House, London Road, Loudwater, HIGH WYCOMBE, BUCKINGHAMSHIRE HP10 9TJ.

COOK, Mr. Peter Charles Henry, FCA *1958;* Waulkmill Farm, Ingersley Vale, Bollington, MACCLESFIELD, CHESHIRE, SK10 5BP. (Life Member)

•**COOK, Mr. Peter David, FCA** *1978;* BDO Audiberia, Rafael Calvo 18, 28010 MADRID, SPAIN. See also BDO International

COOK, Mr. Peter George, BA ACA *1980;* The Crown House, Kings Walden, HITCHIN, SG4 8LT.

COOK, Mr. Peter Hartley, FCA *1960;* Forest Cottage, 4 Briscoe Lane, Woodhouse, LOUGHBOROUGH, LEICESTERSHIRE, LE12 8UF.

COOK, Mr. Peter John, FCA *1955;* The Old Post Office, 44 London Road, SANDY, BEDFORDSHIRE, SG19 1HA. (Life Member)

•**COOK, Mr. Peter Marshall, BCom FCA** *1986;* PM Cook & Co Ltd, 2 Hunters Buildings, Bowesfield Lane, STOCKTON-ON-TEES, CLEVELAND, TS18 3QZ.

COOK, Mr. Philip Anthony, ACA *1980;* A.H. Warren Trust Ltd, Coombe Farm, CREWKERNE, SOMERSET, TA18 8RR.

COOK, Mr. Philip Graham, FCA *1973;* Curland House, Curland, TAUNTON, SOMERSET, TA3 5SG. (Life Member)

•**COOK, Mr. Philip Thomas, FCA** *1979;* (Tax Fac), Clement Keys, 39/40 Calthorpe Road, Edgbaston, BIRMINGHAM, B15 1TS.

COOK, Mr. Richard, BCom ACA *2006;* with BDO LLP, 2 City Place, Beehive Ring Road, GATWICK, WEST SUSSEX, RH6 0PA.

COOK, Mr. Richard Charles, FCA *1954;* 15 Tensing Gardens, BILLERICAY, CM12 9JX. (Life Member)

•**COOK, Mr. Richard Charles, FCA** *1979;* Harwood Lane & Co, 1-4 Crossley Farm Business Centre, Swan Lane, Winterbourne, BRISTOL, BS36 1RH.

COOK, Mr. Richard Lee, BSc ACA *1990;* Ernst & Young, 400 Capability Green, LUTON, LU1 3LU.

COOK, Mr. Robert, BSc ACA *2001;* 11 Warwick Drive, Urmston, MANCHESTER, M41 7AY.

COOK, Mr. Robert Derek, BSc ACA *1997;* 4 Dagnan Road, Clapham, LONDON, SW12 9LQ.

COOK, Mr. Robert Ian, ACA MAAT *2010;* 15 High Peak, GUISBOROUGH, CLEVELAND, TS14 7NG.

COOK, Mr. Robin James, BSc ACA *2010;* Deloitte Touche Tohmatsu, Level 8, 550 Bourke Street, MELBOURNE, VIC 3000, AUSTRALIA.

COOK, Mr. Rodney Nicholas, FCA *1980;* 3 Swancombe, Clapton in Gordano, BRISTOL, BS20 7RR.

COOK, Mr. Roger Daniel, FCA *1970;* 54 Pebblemoor Edlesborough, DUNSTABLE, BEDFORDSHIRE, LU6 2HZ.

COOK, Mr. Roger Norman, FCA *1978;* 11 Woodlands, Welshwood Park, COLCHESTER, CO4 3JA.

COOK, Mr. Russell John, BA ACA *1993;* 81 Abbott Street, SANDRINGHAM, VIC 3191, AUSTRALIA.

COOK, Mrs. Ruth Marian, BSc ACA *1984;* with PricewaterhouseCoopers LLP, 1 Embankment Place, LONDON, WC2N 6RH.

COOK, Ms. Ruth Marion, BA ACA *1990;* 27 Monellan Crescent, Caldecotte, MILTON KEYNES, MK7 8NA.

COOK, Mrs. Sally Louise, BA ACA *1999;* 2 Church Row, Poole Keynes, CIRENCESTER, GL7 6EG.
COOK, Mr. Sam, BSc ACA *2011;* 30 Relko Gardens, Sutton Grove, SUTTON, SM14TJ.
COOK, Miss. Samantha Jane, ACA *2001;* 17 Windward Road, The Willows, TORQUAY, DEVON, TQ2 7GA.
COOK, Mr. Samuel James, ACA *2008;* The Garden Flat, 127 Tufnell Park Road, LONDON, N7 0PU.
COOK, Mr. Samuel James, BA(Hons) ACA *2001;* 16 Home Field Close, Emersons Green, BRISTOL, BS16 7BH.
COOK, Mrs. Sarah Jane, BSc(Hons) ACA *2000;* 26 Lathom Avenue, Parbold, WIGAN, LANCASHIRE, WN8 7NT.
COOK, Miss. Sarah Louise, BA ACA *1992;* Suite 133, 12 Church Street, HAMILTON HM11, BERMUDA.
COOK, Miss. Sasha, ACA *2007;* 99 Prices Court, Cotton Row, Battersea, LONDON, SW11 3WY.
COOK, Ms. Seonaid Louise, BA(Hons) ACA *2001;* 103/8 Montgomery Street, EDINBURGH, EH7 5EX.
COOK, Mr. Simon James, BSc ACA *2011;* 7 Kingsdowne Court, The Common, LONDON, W5 3TT.
COOK, Mr. Simon John, MSc MSocSc BA ACA *2003;* BDO, 38 Station Street, SUBIACO, WA 6008, AUSTRALIA.
COOK, Miss. Sophie Emma, BSc ACA *2006;* 29/5-17 Queen Street, NEWTOWN, NSW 2042, AUSTRALIA.
•COOK, Mr. Stephen James, MA FCA *1987;* David Roberton & Co, 84 Whiting Street, BURY ST. EDMUNDS, IP33 1NZ.
COOK, Mr. Stephen John, ACA *1981;* 8 Friars Avenue, YEOVIL, SOMERSET, BA21 3HY.
COOK, Mr. Steven James, BSc ACA *1990;* Sparrowes Nest Farm, Henley Road, IPSWICH, IP1 6TB.
COOK, Mr. Stuart Donald, LLB ACA *1989;* (Tax Fac), 86 Church Road, RICHMOND, TW10 6LW.
COOK, Mr. Stuart James, BEng ACA *2004;* (Tax Fac), 48 Hillside, HORSHAM, WEST SUSSEX, RH12 1NG.
•COOK, Mrs. Suzanne Louise, BSc ACA *1989;* S Cook Bookkeeping Services, Kinta Cottage, Edwin Road, West Horsley, LEATHERHEAD, SURREY KT24 6LN. See also Bookkeeping & Beyond Limited
COOK, Mr. Terence Vernon, MA ACA *1989;* 24 Highfield Avenue, HARPENDEN, HERTFORDSHIRE, AL5 5UA.
COOK, Mr. Thomas Eric, BSc FCA *1975;* 403 Denby Lane, Grange Moor, WAKEFIELD, WF4 4BJ.
COOK, Mr. Timothy Martin, BA(Hons) ACA *2010;* 15 Cornwell Close, WILMSLOW, CHESHIRE, SK9 2QH.
COOK, Mrs. Tracey Pamela, BSc ACA *1989;* 7 Enid Close, Bricket Wood, ST. ALBANS, HERTFORDSHIRE, AL2 3EL.
•COOK, Mr. Trevor, FCA *1980;* (Tax Fac), Baines Jewitt, Barrington House, 41-45 Yarm Lane, STOCKTON-ON-TEES, CLEVELAND, TS18 3EA. See also Barrington House Solutions Limited
COOK, Miss. Vicki Ann, MA ACA *1985;* House 3, No 3 Consort Rise, POK FU LAM, HONG KONG ISLAND, HONG KONG SAR.
COOK, Miss. Victoria, BSc ACA *2011;* 5 Longcroft, Astley, Tyldesley, MANCHESTER, M29 7EN.
COOK, Mrs. Victoria Jane, ACA MAAT *2003;* 15 Invicta Court, BILLERICAY, CM12 0LR.
COOK, Mr. William Russell, BA ACA *1988;* 7 Castlerigg Close, West Bridgford, NOTTINGHAM, NG2 6RN.
COOK ROBBINS, Mrs. Janice Susan, BSc ACA *1989;* Les Cedres, Chemin Des Cornillons 90, Chambesy, 1292 GENEVA, SWITZERLAND.
COOKE, Mr. Aaron, ACA *2010;* 1 Haddon Close, West Hallam, ILKESTON, DERBYSHIRE, DE7 6NY.
COOKE, Mr. Alan Douglas, FCA *1967;* 17 Brackens Way, Off Old Orchards, LYMINGTON, SO41 3TL.
COOKE, Mrs. Andrea Claire, MA ACA *1991;* Siamsa, The Drive, SUTTON, SURREY, SM2 7DP.
COOKE, Mr. Andrew Mark, BSc(Hons) ACA *2000;* 6 The Staddles, Little Hallingbury, BISHOP'S STORTFORD, HERTFORDSHIRE, CM22 7SW.
COOKE, Mr. Andrew Martin, BA ACA *1994;* 72 The Mount, Wrenthorpe, WAKEFIELD, WEST YORKSHIRE, WF2 0BY.
COOKE, Mr. Andrew Robert, MA FCA *1979;* 4 Powys Avenue, Oadby, LEICESTER, LE2 2DP. (Life Member)
COOKE, Mrs. Ann Ruth, MA ACA *1979;* Vencap International Plc, King Charles House, Park End Street, OXFORD, OX1 1JD.
COOKE, Mrs. Anne-Marie, BA ACA *1987;* 103 High Street, Lindfield, HAYWARDS HEATH, RH16 2HR.
COOKE, Mr. Anthony John, FCA *1962;* 228, Rectory Road, SUTTON COLDFIELD, B75 7RX.
COOKE, Mr. Anthony Paul, MA FCA MBA *1996;* Prestbury Investment Holdings, 18 Cavendish Square, LONDON, W1G 0PJ.
•COOKE, Mr. Anthony Richard, FCA *1981;* (Tax Fac), Carter & Coley, 3 Durrant Road, BOURNEMOUTH, BH2 6NE.
COOKE, Mr. Anthony Roderick Chichester Bancroft, MSc FCA *1964;* Poland Court, Odiham, HOOK, HAMPSHIRE, RG29 1JL.
COOKE, Miss. Antoinette, BA ACA *2005;* 45 Wilkie Road, WELLINGBOROUGH, NORTHAMPTONSHIRE, NN8 4SZ.
COOKE, Mr. Barry John, FCA *1973;* Make Ltd, 55-65 Whitfield Street, LONDON, W1T 4HE.
COOKE, Mr. Basil Vosper, FCA *1951;* 445 Caesar Avenue, OAKVILLE L6J 3Z1, ON, CANADA. (Life Member)
COOKE, Mr. Benjamin Nicolas Stephen, BA FCA *1995;* Dominion Fiduciary Services Group, PO Box 603, JERSEY, JE4 0WH.
COOKE, Mr. Bernard, MBA FCA *1970;* 14 Hillview Terrace, EDINBURGH, EH12 8RA. (Life Member)
COOKE, Miss. Caroline Sarah Louise, MA(Hons) ACA *2003;* Mood Media Forest Lodge, Westerham Road, KESTON, BR2 6HE.
COOKE, Mr. Charles, BSc ACA *1986;* 2 Dorset Road, LONDON, SW19 3HA.
•COOKE, Mr. Christopher George, FCA *1978;* (Tax Fac), Francis Clark, Vantage Point, Woodwater Park, Pynes Hill, EXETER, EX2 5FD. See also Francis Clark LLP
COOKE, Mr. Christopher John, FCA *1977;* 29 3rd Poselkovy St, 344033 ROSTOV-ON-DON, RUSSIAN FEDERATION.
•COOKE, Mr. Christopher Michael, FCA *1980;* 2Cookes Limited, 1 Cranesfield, Sherborne St. John, BASINGSTOKE, RG24 9LN.
COOKE, Mr. Cyril Norman, FCA *1947;* Swans Down, Chapel Lane, Wyre Piddle, PERSHORE, WR10 2JA. (Life Member)
•COOKE, Mr. David Charles Samuel, MA FCA *1986;* David Cooke & Co, 6 Seacourt Road, Botley, OXFORD, OX2 9LD.
COOKE, Mr. David George, FCA *1973;* Le Faurat, 24410 ST AULAYE, FRANCE. (Life Member)
COOKE, Mr. David John, FCA *1966;* Mill Craggs, Bampton, PENRITH, CA10 2RQ.
COOKE, Mr. David John, FCA *1974;* 2 Kinleside Way, Angmering, LITTLEHAMPTON, WEST SUSSEX, BN16 4FE.
COOKE, Mr. David John, BA ACA *1992;* 3 Foxhanger Gardens, WOKING, GU22 7BQ.
•COOKE, Mr. David John Hayward, BA ACA *1979;* PricewaterhouseCoopers LLP, The Atrium, 1 Harefield Road, UXBRIDGE, UB8 1EX. See also PricewaterhouseCoopers
COOKE, Mr. David Joseph, ACA *1980;* 30 Osborn Road, FAREHAM, PO16 7DS.
COOKE, Mr. David Thomas, BA FCA *1964;* 34 Cromwell Road, HENLEY-ON-THAMES, RG9 1JH.
COOKE, Mr. Dean Christopher, BA ACA *1998;* 14 Erleigh Drive, CHIPPENHAM, WILTSHIRE, SN15 2NQ.
COOKE, Mr. Derek Leonard, FCA *1959;* Fairhurst, 5 Meadway, Prestbury, MACCLESFIELD, CHESHIRE, SK10 4DF. (Life Member)
•COOKE, Mrs. Elizabeth, BSc FCA *1977;* Cookes, 4 Powys Avenue, Oadby, LEICESTER, LE2 2DP.
COOKE, Miss. Emma Louise, BA ACA *2010;* 5 Aveley House, Iliffe Close, READING, RG1 2QF.
COOKE, Eric Raymond, Esq OBE FCA *1950;* Flat 5 Oaklands, 14 Esplanade, SCARBOROUGH, YO11 2AF. (Life Member)
COOKE, Dr. Fay, PhD(Cantab) MA(Cantab) ACA *2011;* 18 Gibbs Court, CORSHAM, WILTSHIRE, SN13 9GR.
•COOKE, Mr. Francis Joseph, BA FCA *1977;* 117 Congleton Road, SANDBACH, CW11 1DW.
COOKE, Mr. Geoffrey Albert, FCA *1958;* 273 Cairncroft Road, OAKVILLE L6J 4M5, ON, CANADA. (Life Member)
COOKE, Mr. George Arthur, FCA *1951;* 11 Jennifer Close, EXETER, EX2 4RB. (Life Member)
COOKE, Mr. George Grattan, FCA *1972;* Linwood, 6 Lower Linden Road, CLEVEDON, BS21 7SU.
COOKE, Mr. Gerald Alan, FCA *1968;* with Hawsons, Pegasus House, 463a Glossop Road, SHEFFIELD, S10 2QD.
COOKE, Mr. Glenn, ACA *2008;* Informa UK Ltd, Sheepen Place, COLCHESTER, CO3 3LP.
COOKE, Mr. Gordon, FCA *1964;* 396 Ings Road, Sutton, HULL, HU7 4UZ. (Life Member)
COOKE, Mr. Graham Evans, BA ACA *1999;* 7 Besthorpe Close, Oakwood, DERBY, DE21 4RQ.
COOKE, Mrs. Helen, BA ACA *1994;* 72 The Mount, Wrenthorpe, WAKEFIELD, WF2 0BY.
COOKE, Miss. Helen Yvonne, BSocSc ACA *1992;* 9 Elson Road, Formby, LIVERPOOL, L37 2EG.
COOKE, Miss. Helena Mary, BSc ACA *1984;* Tab House, Tilford Road, HINDHEAD, SURREY, GU26 6RA.
COOKE, Ms. Henrietta Louise, BA ACA *2000;* 10b Digby Crescent, LONDON, N4 2HR.
COOKE, Mr. Howard Mark, ACA *1992;* with Deloitte LLP, Abbots House, Abbey Street, READING, RG1 3BD.
COOKE, Mr. Ian Nicholas, MBA BSc(Hons) ACA *1990;* 10 Gresham Street, LONDON, EC2V 7JD.
•COOKE, Mr. Ian Peter, ACA *2007;* Crowthers Accountants Limited, 10 The Southend, LEDBURY, HEREFORDSHIRE, HR8 2EY.
COOKE, Mr. James, BSc ACA *1991;* 63065 NE 18th Street, BEND, OR 97701, UNITED STATES.
•COOKE, Mrs. Jean Margaret, BSc(Hons) ACA *2002;* JMC Accountants Limited, The Old Bell, Bell Lane, Nuthampstead, ROYSTON, HERTFORDSHIRE SG8 8ND.
•COOKE, Mrs. Jennifer Mary, FCA *1978;* 2Cookes Limited, 1 Cranesfield, Sherborne St. John, BASINGSTOKE, RG24 9LN.
COOKE, Mr. John, FCA *1975;* 17 Loughborough Avenue, SUNDERLAND, SR2 9AS.
COOKE, Mr. John Caister, FCA *1972;* 15 Nevill Court, WEST MALLING, KENT, ME19 6HZ.
•COOKE, Mr. Jonathan Barry, FCA *1976;* (Tax Fac), J.B. Cooke & Co, 2nd Floor, Hillside House, 2-6 Friern Park, North Finchley, LONDON N12 9BT.
COOKE, Mr. Jonathan James, ACA *2008;* 47a Silvester Road, LONDON, SE22 9PB.
COOKE, Mr. Jonathon Kimbal, BSc FCA *1992;* Flat 2 Kimber Court, 219 Long Lane, LONDON, SE1 4PB.
•COOKE, Mr. Keith Felix, FCA *1966;* (Tax Fac), 7 Iron Bridge Walk, Pedmore, STOURBRIDGE, DY9 0SF.
COOKE, Ms. Laura, ACA *2011;* 12 Fisher's Close, Streatham, LONDON, SW16 1JN.
COOKE, Miss. Laura, BA ACA *2007;* Make, Asta House, 55 Whitfield Street, LONDON, W1T 4HE.
COOKE, Ms. Laura, BA(Econ) ACA *2002;* 115 Florence Road, LONDON, SW19 8TL.
COOKE, Mr. Laurence David, FCA *1973;* 8 Kirkstall Close, Poynton, STOCKPORT, CHESHIRE, SK12 1QL.
COOKE, Mr. Leonard Stanley, BA ACA *1982;* 2 Sunnymede Avenue, CHESHAM, BUCKINGHAMSHIRE, HP5 3LE.
COOKE, Mrs. Louise Susanne, BSc FCA *1989;* (Tax Fac), 36 Stevenage Road, KNEBWORTH, HERTFORDSHIRE, SG3 6NN.
COOKE, Mr. Mark Anthony, BSc ACA *1984;* Big Lottery Fund, 1 Plough Place, LONDON, EC4A 1DE.
COOKE, Mr. Mark William, BSc ACA *1993;* Barclays Bank Plc, Barclays Wealth, 1 Churchill Place, Canary Wharf, LONDON, E14 5HP.
COOKE, Mr. Martin James Paul, FCA *1969;* Lion House, Tattenhall Road, Tattenhall, CHESTER, CH3 9QH.
•COOKE, Mr. Martin Paul, FCA *1974;* MC-CA, 19 Kendrick Close, SOLIHULL, B92 0QD. See also Cooke Martin
COOKE, Mr. Myles John Dunne, FCA *1948;* 4225 Reeves Road, OJAI, CA 93023, UNITED STATES. (Life Member)
COOKE, Mr. Nicholas Vandeleur, MA ACA *1989;* Meadow Grange, 4 Poplar Farm Close, Bassingbourn, ROYSTON, HERTFORDSHIRE, SG8 5NA.
COOKE, Miss. Nicola Louise, MA ACA *2003;* 6 Durham House, Scholars Park, DARLINGTON, COUNTY DURHAM, DL3 7FD.
•COOKE, Mr. Nigel Hamilton, FCA *1976;* Sandisons Limited, Badger House, Salisbury Road, BLANDFORD FORUM, DORSET, DT11 7QD.
COOKE, Mr. Nigel John, BSc ACA *1994;* with Deloitte LLP, 1 Woodborough Road, NOTTINGHAM, NG1 3FG.
COOKE, Mr. Oliver Charles, ACA *1979;* Exchequer Court, Exchequer House, Thruxton, HEREFORD, HR2 9AX.
COOKE, Mr. Patrick Charles, BCom ACA *1991;* Abbey National Plc, 2-3 Triton Square, LONDON, NW1 3AN.
COOKE, Mr. Patrick Vincent, BSc ACA *1989;* 3 Park Edge, Hathersage, HOPE VALLEY, DERBYSHIRE, S32 1BS.
COOKE, Mr. Paul Francis, MSc ACA *2001;* 10 Paton Grove, BIRMINGHAM, B13 9TG.
COOKE, Mr. Paul Roger, BA(Hons) ACA *2001;* 4 Oak Manor View, Great Leighs, CHELMSFORD, CM3 1GZ.
COOKE, Mr. Peter David, FCA *1989;* IAIS, c/o BIS, Centralbahnplatz 2, 4002 BASEL, SWITZERLAND.
COOKE, Mr. Peter John, FCA *1970;* The Coach House, Macclesfield Road, ALDERLEY EDGE, SK9 7BH.
COOKE, Mr. Peter John, FCA *1972;* Heathcote, 29 Bowes Hill, ROWLAND'S CASTLE, PO9 6BP. (Life Member)
COOKE, Mr. Peter Noel David Mackillop, BSc ACA *1992;* 27 Hermitage Gardens, EDINBURGH, EH10 6AZ.
COOKE, Mr. Peter William Taggart, BSc ACA *1992;* Caldicote, 103 High Street, Lindfield, HAYWARDS HEATH, RH16 2HR.
COOKE, Mr. Philip John, FCA *1956;* Hollyoak, 1 White House Drive, Barnt Green, BIRMINGHAM, B45 8HF. (Life Member)
COOKE, Miss. Rebecca, BSc ACA *2011;* 24 Foxholes Hill, EXMOUTH, DEVON, EX8 2DQ.
COOKE, Mrs. Rebecca Karen, BSc ACA *1995;* 18 Tythebarn Lane, Shirley, SOLIHULL, B90 1RW.
COOKE, Mr. Richard Anthony, FCA *1980;* 33 Worsboom Street, Weltevreden Park, ROODEPOORT, GAUTENG, 1709, SOUTH AFRICA.
COOKE, Mr. Richard Michael, BSc ACA *1993;* 18 Tythebarn Lane, Shirley, SOLIHULL, B90 1RW.
COOKE, Mr. Robert David Upton, BSc ACA *1985;* The Old Bakery 106 Brook Drive, LONDON, SE11 4TS.
COOKE, Mr. Robert Michael, BA FCA *1982;* Rainenweg 102, CH-4153 REINACH, SWITZERLAND.
•COOKE, Mr. Robin Nicholas, BA FCA *1981;* Robins, Leonard House, 12-14 Silver Street, TAMWORTH, STAFFORDSHIRE, B79 7NH.
COOKE, Miss. Robin Pamela Haruko, BSc ACA *2006;* 224 Southfield Road, LONDON, W4 5LD.
COOKE, Mr. Roger Malcolm, FCA *1968;* Madoreen, Larch Avenue, Sunninghill, ASCOT, SL5 0AP. (Life Member)
COOKE, Mr. Russell Michael, BA ACA *1994;* Neubaugasse 53 / 36, A-1070 WIEN, AUSTRIA.
COOKE, Mrs. Ruth Margaret, BA ACA *2000;* 4 Upper Washwell, Painswick, STROUD, GLOUCESTERSHIRE, GL6 6QY.
COOKE, Mrs. Sarah Frances, ACA *1989;* 33 Hoveden Road, LONDON, NW2 3XE.
COOKE, Mrs. Sarah Joanne, BA ACA *1999;* 6 Victoria Mews, LONDON, SW18 3PY.
COOKE, Miss. Sharon Julie, ACA *2002;* (Tax Fac), The Smithy, Cardinham, BODMIN, CORNWALL, PL30 4BN.
COOKE, Mr. Simon, BA ACA *2011;* Flat 7, Regent Court, 1240 High Road, LONDON, N20 0LR.
COOKE, Mr. Stephen, BSc FCA *1977;* High Oaks, East Paddock Hockett Lane, Cookham, MAIDENHEAD, SL6 9UP.
COOKE, Mr. Stephen Andrew, MA ACA *1992;* LSL Property Services PLC, 1/3 Sun Street, LONDON, EC2A 2EP.
•COOKE, Mr. Stephen John, ACA *1981;* (Tax Fac), S.J. Cooke & Company, Stone Farm, Borough Lane, Great Finborough, STOWMARKET, IP14 3AS.
•COOKE, Mr. Stuart, BEng ACA *2001;* with RSM Tenon Audit Limited, 3 Hollinswood Court, Stafford Park, TELFORD, TF3 3BD.
COOKE, Mrs. Susanna Hope, ACA *2008;* (Tax Fac), 205 Frederick Street, Apartment 507, TORONTO M5A 4V2, ON, CANADA.
COOKE, Prof. Terence Edward, FCA *1977;* Kingfishers, Higher Marley Road, EXMOUTH, EX8 5DT.
COOKE, Mr. Thomas, FCA *1952;* 16 Maybourne Grange, Turnpike Link, CROYDON, CR0 5NH. (Life Member)
COOKE, Mr. Thomas Ian, ACA *2009;* 57 Brithdir Street, CARDIFF, CF24 4LF.
•COOKE, Mr. Thomas John Mary, FCA *1982;* Thomas Cooke, 1 Kilmarsh Road, LONDON, W6 0PL.
COOKE, Mr. Timothy Hugh, FCA *1966;* Barn Cottage, Chapel Street, Welford on Avon, STRATFORD-UPON-AVON, WARWICKSHIRE, CV37 8QE.
COOKE-HURLE, Mr. Charles Frederick, FCA *1975;* Whitehall, Beaulieu, BROCKENHURST, SO42 7YA.
COOKES, Mr. Howard Neville, MA(Oxon) FCA AMCT *1983;* Higher Greenhill, Burgmanns Hill, Lympstone, EXMOUTH, EX8 5HP.
COOKLIN, Mr. Henry, FCA *1957;* 2 Glebe Gardens, LEICESTER, LE2 2LQ. (Life Member)
COOKLIN, Mr. Jonathan Laurence, MA ACA CTA *1989;* (Tax Fac), 14 Middleway, LONDON, NW11 6SP.

COOKLIN, Mr. Steven, ACA CF ASI *1991;* 2 St. Michaels Green, BEACONSFIELD, BUCKINGHAMSHIRE, HP9 2BW.

COOKMAN, Mr. Benjamin Adam, BA ACA *2006;* Cottage Farm High Street, Stillington, YORK, YO61 1LG.

COOKMAN, Mr. Richard James, BSc(Hons) ACA *2003;* 63 Malham Drive, KETTERING, NORTHAMPTONSHIRE, NN16 9FS.

COOKSEY, Mr. Andrew Paul, BCom ACA *1986;* 7 Craddocks Close, ASHTEAD, KT21 1AF.

•**COOKSEY, Mr. Christopher John, FCA** *1974;* Cooksey Perry & Co, Wayside, Old Horsham Road, Beare Green, DORKING, RH5 4RB.

COOKSEY, Mr. Gary Stephen, LLB FCA ACA *1983;* Priory School Sir Harrys Road, Edgbaston, BIRMINGHAM, B15 2UR.

COOKSEY, Mr. Hugh, FCA *1971;* Container Investment Services Ltd, 9th Floor, C I Tower, St. Georges Square, NEW MALDEN, SURREY KT3 4TE.

COOKSEY, Mr. James Edward, BSc ACA *1995;* The Hollies, Long Hedge Lane, Anslow, BURTON-ON-TRENT, DE13 9QR.

COOKSEY, Mrs. Karen Elizabeth, BA ACA *1996;* The Hollies, Long Hedge Lane, Anslow, BURTON-ON-TRENT, DE13 9QR.

COOKSON, Mr. Andrew Frank, MA MBA FCA *1973;* 4 Villa Gallieni, 93250 VILLEMOMBLE, FRANCE.

COOKSON, Mr. Andrew John, BSc ACA *1979;* Riverdale, Grimley, WORCESTER, WR2 6LU.

COOKSON, Ms. Caroline, BA ACA *2006;* Flat 29, Stephen Sanders Court, Salcott Road, LONDON, SW11 6DD.

COOKSON, Mr. David Michael, BA ACA *2003;* 69 Union Road, LONDON, SW4 6JF.

COOKSON, Mr. Elmer Arthur, FCA *1950;* Chaturanga, Cutnall Green, DROITWICH, WR9 0PH. (Life Member)

COOKSON, Mrs. Gillian Louise, ACA *2003;* (Tax Fac), 13 The Meadows, Elswick, PRESTON, PR4 3US.

COOKSON, Mr. Gordon John, FCA *1967;* 15 Craven Avenue, Ealing, LONDON, W5 2SY. (Life Member)

COOKSON, Mr. Henry Brian, FCA *1945;* Heathlands, Station Road, PERSHORE, WORCESTERSHIRE, WR10 1NG. (Life Member)

COOKSON, Mr. James, ACA *2008;* 36 Evelegh Road, PORTSMOUTH, PO6 1DL.

•**COOKSON, Mr. John Joseph, FCA** *1975;* Ainley Cookson & Co, 102 Market Street, Hoylake, WIRRAL, MERSEYSIDE, CH47 3BE.

•**COOKSON, Mr. Michael Andrew, BA ACA** *1980;* with Dyke Yaxley Limited, 1 Brassey Road, Old Potts Way, SHREWSBURY, SY3 7FA.

COOKSON, Mr. Michael Dean, FCA *1965;* Bankside Farm, Winsford Road, Wettenhall, WINSFORD, CW7 4DL. (Life Member)

COOKSON, Mr. Michael Jeremy, BSc ACA *1985;* 87 Haydon Park Road, Wimbledon, LONDON, SW19 8JH.

•**COOKSON, Mr. Michael John Edwin, FCA** *1972;* (Tax Fac), Feeley & Co, 11 Glenpark Drive, Hesketh Bank, PRESTON, PR4 6TA.

COOKSON, Mr. Paul, BSc(Econ) ACA *1997;* Le Petit Menage La Rue de la Maitrerie, St Martin, JERSEY, JE3 6HZ.

COOKSON, Mr. Peter John, FCA *1969;* (Tax Fac), 18 Whalley Road, Hale, ALTRINCHAM, CHESHIRE, WA15 9DF.

COOKSON, Mr. Roger Paul, LLB FCA FCCA FAIA ACIL *1982;* 10 Freshfields, Heald Green, CHEADLE, CHESHIRE, SK8 3EH.

COOKSON, Miss. Sarah, ACA *2007;* 6 Greenmount Drive, Greenmount, BURY, BL8 4HA.

COOKSON, Mr. Thomas Joseph, BA ACA *2010;* Flat C, 52 Caversham Road, LONDON, NW5 2DS.

COOLE, Mr. Christopher John, FCA *1969;* Larkfield, South Lane, Thornton Dale, PICKERING, NORTH YORKSHIRE, YO18 7QU. (Life Member)

COOLE, Mr. Roger Nicholas, FCA *1951;* 10 Oakhurst, 4 Hayes Lane, KENLEY, SURREY, CR8 5GZ. (Life Member)

•**COOLEY, Mr. Christopher Martin, MA ACA** *1981;* (Tax Fac), Cooley & Co, Sampuran House, 3a Chislehurst Road, ORPINGTON, BR6 0DF.

COOLEY, Mr. Colin, FCA *1975;* 22 Stonechat, AYLESBURY, BUCKINGHAMSHIRE, HP19 0WD.

COOLEY, Miss. Nicola Ann, BSc ACA *2005;* 172 b Mitcham Lane, LONDON, SW16 6NS.

•**COOLING, Mr. Grahame Ashley, BCom FCA** *1975;* 2 High Acres, Billesdon, LEICESTER, LE7 9FB.

COOMBE, Mr. Adrian Geoffrey, BA ACA *2009;* 22 Gronau Close, HONITON, DEVON, EX14 2YT.

COOMBE, Mr. Andrew Jackson, FCA *1969;* 45 Stumperlowe Crescent Road, SHEFFIELD, S10 3PR.

COOMBE, Mr. Christopher John, BA ACA *1983;* Attn Ms Hadeel Al Ansari, Mubadala Services Ventures Unit, PO Box 45005, ABU DHABI, UNITED ARAB EMIRATES.

COOMBE, Mr. John David, BSc FCA *1970;* Langdon, Burtons Way, LITTLE CHALFONT, BUCKINGHAMSHIRE, HP8 4BW.

COOMBE, Mr. John Robert, FCA *1958;* 15 Milton Court, Ickenham, UXBRIDGE, UB10 8NB. (Life Member)

COOMBE, Miss. Kathryn Beryl, BSc ACA *1995;* 22 Quoitings Drive, MARLOW, BUCKINGHAMSHIRE, SL7 2PE.

COOMBE, Mrs. Margaret, MA FCA *1977;* 124 Home Park Road, Wimbledon, LONDON, SW19 7HU.

COOMBE, Mr. Peter Francis, BA ACA *1998;* Unit 2, 27 Argyle Street, West Footscray, MELBOURNE, VIC 3012, AUSTRALIA.

COOMBE, Mr. Stephen Neil, BA ACA *1983;* Kemfine UK Limited, Earls Road, GRANGEMOUTH, FK3 8XG.

•**COOMBE, Mr. Steven David, FCA** *1990;* with Burnside (Bristol) Limited, 8 Pipe Lane, BRISTOL, BS1 5AJ.

•**COOMBER, Mr. Alan Thomas, FCA** *1976;* CW & G Partnership LLP, 68 Great Portland Street, LONDON, W1W 7NG.

COOMBER, Mr. Anthony John, FCA *1959;* Cherry Tree Cottage, 45 East End Lane, Ditchling, HASSOCKS, BN6 8UP.

COOMBER, Mr. Daniel, ACA *2011;* 37 Lynton Estate, Lynton Road, LONDON, SE1 5QU.

COOMBER, Mrs. Elizabeth Helen, ACA *1988;* UM (A Trading Division UK Mediabrand Ltd), 42-47 St Johns Square, LONDON, EC4M 4EA.

•**COOMBER, Mr. Malcolm Edwin, FCA CF** *1972;* Clarkson Hyde LLP, 2nd Floor, Mutual House, 70 Conduit Street, LONDON, W1S 2GF.

•**COOMBER, Mr. Neil Christopher, BA ACA** *1999;* PricewaterhouseCoopers LLP, 1 Embankment Place, LONDON, WC2N 6RH. See also PricewaterhouseCoopers

COOMBER, Mr. Peter David, BSc ACA *1981;* Infor, 1 Lakeside Road, FARNBOROUGH, HAMPSHIRE, GU14 6XP.

COOMBER, Mr. Stephen John, BA ACA *1984;* National Grid Plc N G T House Warwick Technology Park Gallows Hill, WARWICK, CV34 6DA.

COOMBES, Mr. Alan Warren, BSc FCA *1980;* 8a Collins Street, MERIMBULA, NSW 2548, AUSTRALIA.

COOMBES, Mr. Alexander John, BCom ACA *2001;* 1 Harlequin Office Park, Fieldfare, Emersons Green, BRISTOL, BS16 7FN.

COOMBES, Mr. Barry Patrick, FCA *1974;* Roserrow Golf & Country Club, St. Minver, WADEBRIDGE, PL27 6QT.

•**COOMBES, Mr. David John, MA FCA** *1988;* Coombes Corporate Finance LLP, Adamson House, Towers Business Park, Wilmslow Road, MANCHESTER, M20 2YY.

COOMBES, Mr. Duncan, BA(Hons) ACA *2004;* 48 Asgard Drive, BEDFORD, MK41 0US.

COOMBES, Mr. Eric Edward, FCA *1972;* 27 Eton Court, Heath, CARDIFF, CF14 4HZ.

COOMBES, Mr. John, FCA *1965;* Brainshaugh House, Acklington, MORPETH, NORTHUMBERLAND, NE65 9AE. (Life Member)

COOMBES, Mr. John Frederick, BSc ACA *1992;* 4 Occupation Road, Lindley, HUDDERSFIELD, HD3 3AZ.

COOMBES, Mrs. Judith Christine, BA FCA *1974;* 15 Lamcote Gardens, Radcliffe-on-Trent, NOTTINGHAM, NG12 2BS.

COOMBES, Mr. Julian Andres Dalmedo, FCA *1970;* 3 King Georges Lodge, Monro Drive, GUILDFORD, SURREY, GU2 9PF.

COOMBES, Mr. Michael John, BSc ACA *1991;* Cordison Hall, Yarningale Lane, Claverdon, WARWICK, CV35 8HW.

COOMBES, Mr. Nicholas Laurence, BSc FCA *1995;* 2192 Marselina, TUSTIN, CA 92782, UNITED STATES.

COOMBES, Mr. Nicholas Patrick, FCA *1969;* Conybury Heights, Mogador, TADWORTH, KT20 7HU.

•**COOMBES, Mr. Paul David, BSc ACA** *2002;* Action Tax Consulting Limited, Unit 5, Radcliffe Court, Radcliffe Road, SOUTHAMPTON, SO14 0PH.

COOMBES, Mr. Robert Henry, FCA *1945;* Robert Coombes Ltd, 6 Smith Barry Circus, Upper Rissington, CHELTENHAM, GL54 2NQ.

COOMBES, Mr. Stephen Mark, MA ACA *1985;* 7 Brokes Road, REIGATE, SURREY, RH2 9LJ.

COOMBEY, Mr. Ian David Andrew, BSc ACA *1987;* 22 Alma Avenue, HORNCHURCH, RM12 6SR.

COOMBS, Miss. Alexandra Louise Ann, BSc ACA *1995;* Blackdown Cottage, Forest Road, WOKING, SURREY, GU22 8LU.

COOMBS, Mrs. Andrea Marie, BSc ACA *1997;* 3 Swift Close, KENILWORTH, CV8 1QT.

COOMBS, Mr. Andrew Peter, BEng ACA *1998;* 27 Arundel Road, TUNBRIDGE WELLS, KENT, TN1 1TB.

COOMBS, Mrs. Cheryl Dorothy, BA ACA *1998;* 27 Arundel Road, TUNBRIDGE WELLS, KENT, TN1 1TB.

COOMBS, Mr. David Andrew, MA FCA *1990;* 34 Grove Way, ESHER, KT10 8HL.

COOMBS, Mr. David Malcolm, MA FCA *1965;* Flat 22, Pemberton House, 6 East Harding Street, LONDON, EC4A 3AS.

COOMBS, Mr. Derrick Hugh Jamieson, FCA *1961;* 1707-2170 Marine Drive, OAKVILLE L6L 5V1, ON, CANADA. (Life Member)

COOMBS, Mr. Edmund Joseph, BA FCA *1978;* Story World Wide Ltd, 15b St. Georges Mews, LONDON, NW1 8XE.

COOMBS, Mr. Ian Courtenay, FCA JDipMA *1949;* 13 Greys Park Close, KESTON, KENT, BR2 6BD. (Life Member)

•**COOMBS, Mr. John Leslie, MA FCA** *1984;* (Tax Fac), Simpkins Edwards LLP, Michael House, Castle Street, EXETER, EX4 3LQ.

COOMBS, Mrs. Julie Elizabeth, MA ACA *1990;* 4 Church Court, Bolton le Sands, CARNFORTH, LA5 8EB.

COOMBS, Mrs. Juliet Fiona, MEng ACA CTA *2003;* with Deloitte LLP, 2 New Street Square, LONDON, EC4A 3BZ.

COOMBS, Mrs. Linda May, BSc ACA *1983;* Pembury Lodge, 28 Icklingham Road, COBHAM, KT11 2NH.

COOMBS, Mr. Martin Edmund, BSc ACA *1993;* 3 Swift Close, KENILWORTH, CV8 1QT.

COOMBS, Mr. Meredith Maxwell, MA FCA *1976;* 31c Bedford Road, NORTHWOOD, MIDDLESEX, HA6 2AY.

•**COOMBS, Mr. Michael John, FCA** *1965;* Michael J. Coombs, 27 Ty Nant, Rotcombe Lane, High Littleton, BRISTOL, BS39 6JP.

COOMBS, Mr. Michael Vincent Arthue Eugene, BSc FCA *1974;* 10 Maxwell Road, BOURNEMOUTH, BH9 1DJ.

COOMBS, Mr. Philip John Morgan, FCA *1975;* 11 Southover High Street, LEWES, EAST SUSSEX, BN7 1HT.

•**COOMBS, Mr. Richard Adam, BA ACA** *1997;* Premier Strategies Limited, The Poynt, 45 Wollaton Street, NOTTINGHAM, NG1 5FW.

•**COOMBS, Mr. Richard Christopher Philemon, FCA** *1975;* (Tax Fac), Harris Coombs & Company, 5 Jaggard Way, LONDON, SW12 8SG.

•**COOMBS, Mr. Roger Alan, FCA** *1974;* (Tax Fac), Thakrar Coombs & Co, The Dairy House, Moneyrow Green, Holyport, MAIDENHEAD, SL6 2ND.

COOMBS, Mr. Simon George Robert, BSc ACA *1983;* 28 Icklingham Road, COBHAM, KT11 2NH.

COOMBS, Mrs. Susan Elizabeth, BSc ACA *1979;* The Outlook, Olive Grove, STOURPORT-ON-SEVERN, DY13 8XY.

COOMBS-PROLE, Mr. Reginald, FCA *1972;* AIHA Ltd, 206 Lordship Road, LONDON, N16 5ES.

COOMER, Mr. Edward Alan, FCA *1974;* (Tax Fac), 84 Queenhythe Road, Jacob's Well, GUILDFORD, SURREY, GU4 7NX.

•**COOMER, Mr. Timothy, FCA** *1988;* Timothy Coomer, 3 Greenfields, Dunhills Lane, Enham Alamein, ANDOVER, HAMPSHIRE SP11 6RB.

COOMES, Mrs. Sarah, BA ACA *2003;* 1 Kings Mead, South Nutfield, REDHILL, RH1 5NN.

COON, Mr. Peter, FCA *1965;* 113 Edgcumbe Green, ST AUSTELL, CORNWALL, PL25 5EE.

COON, Mr. Richard Adrian, MBA BA FCA *1974;* 8 Twin Wharf Road, Herald Island, AUCKLAND, NEW ZEALAND.

•**COONEY, Mr. Anthony J, ACA ACCA** *2007;* Ashworth Treasure Limited, 17-19 Park Street, LYTHAM ST. ANNES, LANCASHIRE, FY8 5LU.

COONEY, Mr. David Edward, BA ACA *1989;* QBE Insurance (Europe), Plantation Place, 30 Fenchurch Street, LONDON, EC3M 3BD.

COONEY, Mr. James Christopher, BA FCA *1978;* 7 The Mount, Lisvane, CARDIFF, CF14 0FJ.

•**COONEY, Mr. Peter John, FCA** *1955;* Peter J Cooney, 42 London Road, Oadby, LEICESTER, LE2 5DH.

COONEY, Mr. Stephen James, ACA *1981;* Paddocks, School Lane, Hamble, SOUTHAMPTON, SO31 4JD.

COONEY, Mrs. Susan, FCA *1974;* 7 The Mount, Lisvane, CARDIFF, CF14 0FJ.

•**COONEY, Mrs. Tanuja Rohini, ACA** *1995;* TRC Accountancy Ltd, 26 Coopers Row, LYTHAM ST. ANNES, LANCASHIRE, FY8 4UD.

COOP, Mr. Geoffrey Brian, MA FCA *1959;* The Old Barn, 45 Bath Road, EMSWORTH, PO10 7ER. (Life Member)

•**COOP, Mr. Raymond Clifford, FCA** *1981;* Batchelor Coop Ltd, The New Barn, Mill Lane, Eastry, SANDWICH, CT13 0JW.

COOPE, Mrs. Sian Annette, BSc ACA *1989;* 2 Gableson Avenue, BRIGHTON, BN1 5FG.

COOPE, Mr. Timothy John, BA ACA *1989;* 2 Gableson Avenue, BRIGHTON, BN1 5FG.

•**COOPER, Mr. Adam, ACA** *2003;* (Tax Fac), Townends, Carlisle Chambers, Carlisle Street, GOOLE, DN14 5DX.

COOPER, Mr. Adam, BA ACA *2010;* 11 Lindisfarne Close, MORPETH, NORTHUMBERLAND, NE61 2UG.

COOPER, Mr. Adam Charles, BA FCA *1997;* 10 Richmond Road, LONDON, SW20 0PQ.

•**COOPER, Mr. Alan Albert, FCA** *1957;* (Tax Fac), Alan Cooper Saunders Angel, Kenton House, 666 Kenton Road, HARROW, HA3 9QN.

COOPER, Mr. Alan Charles, FCA *1976;* Harkaway House, Corse Lawn, GLOUCESTER, GL19 4LT.

COOPER, Mr. Alan John, FCA *1974;* 17 Windsor Close, NEWTON AYCLIFFE, DL5 4YF.

COOPER, Mr. Alan William, BSc ACA *2010;* Top Flat, 28 Bond Road, SOUTHAMPTON, SO18 1LQ.

COOPER, Mr. Alastair James, MEng ACA *1993;* 8 Mansfield Road, Burley in Wharfedale, ILKLEY, WEST YORKSHIRE, LS29 7LQ.

COOPER, Mrs. Alice Susannah, BSc(Hons) ACA *2002;* 21 Church Gardens, Ravensthorpe, NORTHAMPTON, NN6 8EY.

COOPER, Mrs. Alison Ann, BSc ACA *1989;* (Tax Fac), 919 Pershore Road, Selly Park, BIRMINGHAM, B29 7PS.

COOPER, Mrs. Alison Jane, BSc ACA *1992;* Imperial Tobacco Ltd, PO Box 244, Upton Road, Southville, BRISTOL, BS99 7UJ.

COOPER, Mr. Alistair, MSc ACA *2011;* 24 Latium Close, Holywell Hill, ST. ALBANS, HERTFORDSHIRE, AL1 1XU.

COOPER, Mr. Allan John, BCom FCA *1976;* 33 Station Road, BUDLEIGH SALTERTON, DEVON, EX9 6RR.

COOPER, Mr. Andrew, BA ACA *1992;* Aviva UK Life, Wellington Row, YORK, YO90 1WR.

•**COOPER, Mr. Andrew, BSc ACA** *1993;* (Tax Fac), Andrew Cooper & Company Accountants Limited, 650 Anlaby Road, HULL, HU3 6UU. See also Andrew Cooper & Company Limited

COOPER, Mr. Andrew, BSc ACA *1999;* 9 Randall Drive, Orsett, GRAYS, ESSEX, RM16 3GT.

•**COOPER, Mr. Andrew David, BA FCA** *2000;* UHY Kent LLP, Thames House, Roman Square, SITTINGBOURNE, KENT, ME10 4BJ.

COOPER, Mr. Andrew George, MA BCom ACA MCIM *1995;* Flat 4, 26 Medway Street, Westminster, LONDON, SW1P 2BD.

COOPER, Mr. Andrew Lee, BA ACA *2007;* with McIntosh (Ilkeston) Limited, 20 Burns Street, ILKESTON, DERBYSHIRE, DE7 8AA.

COOPER, Mr. Andrew Michael, BA ACA *1989;* Brent Lodge, Doctors Commons Road, BERKHAMSTED, HERTFORDSHIRE, HP4 3DW.

COOPER, Mrs. Anna Elizabeth, BSc ACA *2004;* 13 Morton Road, EAST GRINSTEAD, WEST SUSSEX, RH19 4AF.

COOPER, Mr. Anthony Geoffrey, FCA *1963;* Beechland, Churn Lane, Horsmonden, TONBRIDGE, KENT, TN12 8HW. (Life Member)

COOPER, Mr. Anthony Paul, FCA *1974;* (Member of Council 2001 - 2009), 59 Snaithing Lane, SHEFFIELD, S10 3LF.

COOPER, Mr. Arthur Richard, FCA *1953;* The Cross, Congleton Road, ALDERLEY EDGE, SK9 7AD. (Life Member)

COOPER, Mr. Ashley James, BSc(Hons) ACA *2003;* 1 The Meads, Valley Park, Chandler's Ford, EASTLEIGH, HAMPSHIRE, SO53 4QL.

•**COOPER, Mr. Barry James, FCA** *1969;* (Tax Fac), Walker Sutcliffe & Cooper, 4 The Square, Aspley Guise, MILTON KEYNES, MK17 8DF.

COOPER, Mr. Bryan Clark, ACA *1994;* 9 Llysfaen Road, Old Colwyn, COLWYN BAY, CLWYD, LL29 9EU.

COOPER, Mr. Byron Lloyd, BA ACA *1999;* Frank Roberts & Sons Ltd School Road, Rudheath, NORTHWICH, CHESHIRE, CW9 7RQ.

•**COOPER, Mr. Carlton George, BSc FCA** *1985;* Cassons, St Crispin House, St. Crispin Way, Haslingden, ROSSENDALE, LANCASHIRE BB4 4PW.

COOPER, Miss. Caroline Lesley, BSc ACA *2001;* Flat 8, The Fountains, 2 Lafone Street, LONDON, SE1 2LT.

COOPER, Miss. Catherine Margaret, PhD MSc FCA MCT *1983;* Sirius International, London Underwriting centre, Minster Court, 3 Mincing Lane, LONDON, EC3R 7DD.

COOPER, Mr. Charles Mark, BA FCA *1985;* 73008 VAMOS, CRETE, GREECE.

COOPER, Mrs. Chloe Charlotte Frances, BSocSc ACA *2001;* 5th Floor, 6 Front Street, HAMILTON HM NX, BERMUDA.
COOPER, Mrs. Christine Anne, BSc ACA *1982;* St. Vincents Housing Association Metropolitan House, 20 Brindley Road, MANCHESTER, M16 9HQ.
COOPER, Mrs. Christine Jane, BA ACA *1990;* 7 St. Peters Close, Speen, PRINCES RISBOROUGH, HP27 0SS.
•COOPER, Mr. Christopher, ACA FCCA *2008;* (Tax Fac), Price Pearson, 6 Church Street, KIDDERMINSTER, WORCESTERSHIRE, DY10 2AD. See also Price Pearson Ltd
•COOPER, Mr. Christopher Andrew, FCA *1974;* Cooper & Co, 18 Magdalen Grove, ORPINGTON, KENT, BR6 9WE.
COOPER, Mr. Christopher James, MBA ACA *1982;* 26 Lowfields, Little Eversden, CAMBRIDGE, CB3 7HJ.
COOPER, Mr. Christopher John, BA FCA *1990;* 31 Engler Street, Booragoon, PERTH, WA 6154, AUSTRALIA.
•COOPER, Mr. Christopher Selwyn, FCA *1972;* Ockhams, Shernden Lane, Marsh Green, EDENBRIDGE, TN8 5PS.
COOPER, Miss. Claire Louise, BSc ACA *2005;* 44 School Avenue, BASILDON, SS15 6GJ.
COOPER, Mrs. Clare Jennifer, BA ACA *1991;* Walnut Trees, Chapel Lane, Sissinghurst, CRANBROOK, TN17 2JN.
•COOPER, Mr. Clifford Robert, FCA *1980;* Buzzacott LLP, 130 Wood Street, LONDON, EC2V 6DL.
•COOPER, Mr. Colin, FCA *1970;* C. Cooper, 24 Haughgate Close, WOODBRIDGE, IP12 1LQ.
COOPER, Mr. Colin Anthony, FCA *1974;* 5 Molescroft Drive, BEVERLEY, HU17 7JH.
COOPER, Mr. Colin Thompson, BA ACA *1983;* Palmer & Harvey McLane Ltd P & H House, Davigdor Road, HOVE, EAST SUSSEX, BN3 1RE.
COOPER, Mr. Craig John, MBA ACA *1992;* Orchard End, Benover Road, Yalding, MAIDSTONE, ME18 6AS.
COOPER, Mr. Damian Christopher Grey, BSc ACA *2007;* Saddlebole, Mottram Road, ALDERLEY EDGE, CHESHIRE, SK9 7JF.
COOPER, Mr. Daniel John, ACA MAAT *2011;* 22 Shaws Close, Norby, THIRSK, NORTH YORKSHIRE, YO7 1TP.
•COOPER, Mr. Daniel Paul, BA(Hons) ACA *2002;* Ernst & Young LLP, 1 More London Place, LONDON, SE1 2AF. See also Ernst & Young Europe LLP
•COOPER, Mr. Darren Clark, BA(Hons) ACA CTA *2000;* A Allen & Son Limited, 45 Union Road, New Mills, HIGH PEAK, DERBYSHIRE, SK22 3EL.
COOPER, Mr. Darren Ian, BA(Hons) ACA *1995;* 42 Kirkwood Way, LEEDS, LS16 7EX.
COOPER, Mr. David, MA(Hons) ACA *2000;* 2a Dovercourt Road, LONDON, SE22 8ST.
•COOPER, Mr. David Alan Irwin, ACA *1991;* C H London Limited, The Ground Floor, Suite G1, Buckingham Court, 78 Buckingham Gate, LONDON SW1E 6PE.
COOPER, Mr. David Andrew, BSc ACA *1987;* 5209 Hammock Circle, SAINT CLOUD, FL 34771, UNITED STATES.
COOPER, Mr. David Arthur, MBA FCA *1963;* Offham House, Offham, ARUNDEL, WEST SUSSEX, BN18 9PD.
•COOPER, Mr. David Charles, BCom FCA *1995;* Cooper Adams Limited, 12 Payton Street, STRATFORD-UPON-AVON, WARWICKSHIRE, CV37 6UA.
COOPER, Mr. David Charles Gamble, FCA *1969;* Old Vicarage, Tuttington, NORWICH, NR11 6TE.
COOPER, Mr. David Charles Tyas, BA FCA *1982;* 9 Ash Lawns, BOLTON, BL1 4PD.
COOPER, Mr. David Christopher, FCA *1982;* 102 Redwood Drive, HUDDERSFIELD, HD2 1PW.
COOPER, Mr. David Edward Alexander, MSc FCA CPsychol *1992;* 23 Wheatley Lane, Ben Rhydding, ILKLEY, WEST YORKSHIRE, LS29 8BW.
COOPER, Mr. David Ernest, FCA *1963;* Pitcott House, Winsford, MINEHEAD, SOMERSET, TA24 7JE. (Life Member)
•COOPER, Mr. David George, ACA FCCA *2007;* Hamlyns LLP, Sundial House, 98 High Street, Horsell, WOKING, SURREY GU21 4SU.
COOPER, Mr. David James, BSc ACA *1999;* Kilsby & Williams Cedar House, Hazell Drive, NEWPORT, GWENT, NP10 8FY.
COOPER, Mr. David Jeffrey, BA ACA FSI *1988;* 8 Great Oaks, Hutton, BRENTWOOD, CM13 1AZ.
COOPER, Mr. David John Michael, FCA *1967;* 24 Clover Way, Killinghall, HARROGATE, NORTH YORKSHIRE, HG3 2WE. (Life Member)
COOPER, Mr. David Laurence, FCA *1976;* Coney Hill House, Upper Winchendon, AYLESBURY, BUCKINGHAMSHIRE, HP18 0ET.
COOPER, Mr. David Norman, MA ACA *1979;* 19 East Castle Street, BRIDGNORTH, SHROPSHIRE, WV16 4AN.
COOPER, Mr. David William Elliott, FCA *1966;* Windmill Cottage, Eastcombe, STROUD, GL6 7DR. (Life Member)
COOPER, Mr. Dean Michael, BA ACA *1999;* 1 The Sycamores, South Milford, LEEDS, NORTH YORKSHIRE, LS25 5FE.
COOPER, Mrs. Deborah Joy, BSc(Econ) ACA *2000;* Rose Cottage, The Causeway, Furneux Pelham, BUNTINGFORD, HERTFORDSHIRE, SG9 0LN.
•COOPER, Ms. Debra Louise, BSc FCA *1989;* Harding Lewis Limited, 34 Athol Street, Douglas, ISLE OF MAN, IM1 1JB.
COOPER, Mr. Derek, FCA *1971;* Fernside Frog Lane, Pickmere, KNUTSFORD, CHESHIRE, WA16 0LJ.
COOPER, Mr. Dinyar Behram, FCA *1976;* 40 Valley Drive, Kingsbury, LONDON, NW9 9NR.
COOPER, Mr. Duncan Charles, BA ACA *1985;* Adia, PO Box 3600, ABU DHABI, UNITED ARAB EMIRATES.
COOPER, Mr. Duncan John, BSc ACA *2005;* Sainsburys Supermarkets Ltd, 33 Holborn, LONDON, EC1N 2HT.
COOPER, Mr. Duncan Ronald Ward, FCA *1966;* Tuckers Cottage, Maidensgrove Common, HENLEY-ON-THAMES, OXFORDSHIRE, RG9 6EX.
COOPER, Mr. Edward Horace Enoch, FCA *1957;* Gresham House, Dereham Road, Colkirk, FAKENHAM, NR21 7NH. (Life Member)
COOPER, Mr. Edward James Ashley, MSc ACA *1994;* (Tax Fac), 18 St. Lukes Road, BOURNEMOUTH, BH3 7LT.
•COOPER, Miss. Ella Frances, ACA MAAT *2006;* Ella Cooper, Owl Cottage, 6 Knox Lane, HARROGATE, NORTH YORKSHIRE, HG1 3AP.
COOPER, Mrs. Emma Claire, BA(Hons) ACA *2004;* 72 Links Drive, SOLIHULL, WEST MIDLANDS, B91 2DL.
COOPER, Miss. Emma Louise, BSc ACA *2007;* Flat 1, Waterfront House, 20 Lombard Road, Battersea, LONDON, SW11 3RU.
COOPER, Mrs. Fiona Luisa, BA FCA *1999;* Apax Partners Ltd, 33 Jermyn Street, LONDON, SW1Y 6DN.
•COOPER, Miss. Frances, ACA *2007;* Flat 13 St. Michaels Court, Priory Close, SOUTHAMPTON, SO17 2FR.
COOPER, Mr. Geoffrey Clifford, FCA *1954;* 5 Fairway, Trentham, STOKE-ON-TRENT, ST4 8AS. (Life Member)
COOPER, Mr. Geoffrey Wilfrid, FCA *1964;* 2890 9th Line Beckwith, CARLETON PLACE K7C 3P2, ON, CANADA.
COOPER, Mr. George, BA ACA *2003;* Ernst & Young Llp, 1 More London Place, LONDON, SE1 2AF.
COOPER, Mr. George Vernon, FCA *1973;* 221 Hazebrouck Road, FAVERSHAM, KENT, ME13 7QZ.
COOPER, Mr. Giles Robert Nasmyth, BSc ACA *1991;* York House, 58 Leicester Road, Uppingham, OAKHAM, LEICESTERSHIRE, LE15 9SD.
COOPER, Mr. Gordon, FCA *1957;* 61 Fallowfield Road, Hasbury, HALESOWEN, B63 1BZ. (Life Member)
COOPER, Mr. Gordon Neville, BSc ACA *1992;* 6 Stoke Paddock Road, BRISTOL, BS9 2DJ.
COOPER, Prof. Gordon Stewart, BSc AM FCA *1975;* Cooper & Co, Level 15, Lumley House, 309 Kent Street, SYDNEY, NSW 2000 AUSTRALIA.
COOPER, Mr. Graeme Francis, MA ACA *1987;* c/o Coopers & Coopers Limited, Suite 601-2, Wing On House, 71 Des Voeux Road, CENTRAL, HONG KONG SAR.
•COOPER, Mr. Graham Michael, FCA *1956;* Graham M. Cooper & Co, Peek Building, George St., P.O. Box N8160, NASSAU, BAHAMAS.
COOPER, Mr. Grant William, BA ACA *2001;* 24 Siskin Gardens, Paddock Wood, TONBRIDGE, TN12 6XP.
COOPER, Mr. Gregory, BSc ACA *2004;* 16 The Crescent, BLACKBURN, BB2 5NE.
COOPER, Mr. Gyles Penry, MA FCA *1968;* 88 Woodside Avenue, LONDON, N10 3HY. (Life Member)
COOPER, Mr. Harold Frank, FCA *1954;* Lingmoor, Holt End, Beoley, REDDITCH, B98 9AW. (Life Member)
COOPER, Mrs. Hayley Clark, BA ACA *1997;* 39 Darkie Meadow, Bunbury, TARPORLEY, CHESHIRE, CW6 9RB.
•COOPER, Mrs. Hazel Clare, BEng ACA *1987;* 3 Edyvean Close, RUGBY, WARWICKSHIRE, CV22 6LD.
COOPER, Miss. Helen Denise, BA ACA *2006;* 41 St. Francis Court, SHEFFORD, BEDFORDSHIRE, SG17 5RU.
COOPER, Mrs. Helen Marie, BSc ACA *2000;* 1 The Sycamores, South Milford, LEEDS, NORTH YORKSHIRE, LS25 5FE.
COOPER, Mr. Iain Edmund, ACA *1998;* 98 Basevi Way, Millenium Quay, LONDON, SE8 3JT.
COOPER, Mr. Iain James, BA(Hons) ACA *2005;* 350 West 37th Street, Apartment 27E, NEW YORK, NY 10018, UNITED STATES.
COOPER, Mr. Ian, ACA *2009;* Flat 103 Tequila Wharf, 681 Commercial Road, LONDON, E14 7LH.
COOPER, Mr. Ian Anderson, FCA *1970;* Ramblers Ferry Lane, North Muskham, NEWARK, NOTTINGHAMSHIRE, NG23 6HB.
COOPER, Mr. Ian Andrew, BSc ACA *1989;* 22 Wollaton Vale, Wollaton, NOTTINGHAM, NG8 2NR.
COOPER, Mr. Ian Charles, BSc ACA *1994;* 122 Carbery Avenue, BOURNEMOUTH, BH6 3LH.
COOPER, The Revd. Ian Clive, MTh FCA *1970;* Preshute Vicarage, 7 Golding Avenue, MARLBOROUGH, WILTSHIRE, SN8 1TH.
COOPER, Mr. Ian Douglas, FCA *1972;* 4 Blakeway Hollow, MUCH WENLOCK, TF13 6AR.
COOPER, Mr. Ian Francis, BSc ACA *1998;* 99 Rodenhurst Road, LONDON, SW4 8AF.
•COOPER, Mr. Ian Paul, BA ACA *1991;* BDO LLP, 55 Baker Street, LONDON, W1U 7EU. See also BDO Stoy Hayward LLP
COOPER, Mr. Ian Richard, BSc ACA *1991;* The Cottage, Beavers Hill, Crondall Lane, FARNHAM, GU9 7DF.
•COOPER, Mr. Ian Stuart, BA FCA *1985;* Smith & Williamson (Bristol) LLP, Portwall Place, Portwall Lane, BRISTOL, BS1 6NA. See also Smith & Williamson Ltd and Nexia Audit Limited
COOPER, Mr. James, BA(Hons) ACA *2001;* 72 Links Drive, SOLIHULL, WEST MIDLANDS, B91 2DL.
COOPER, Mr. James, BSc ACA *2009;* 34 Moffats Lane, Brookmans Park, HATFIELD, HERTFORDSHIRE, AL9 7RU.
COOPER, Mr. James Maxwell Downham, FCA *1978;* DCAL, Ashcroft, Somerton, BICESTER, OXFORDSHIRE, OX25 6LL.
COOPER, Mr. James Philip Alexander, BA ACA *2008;* 18 Collingwood Crescent, GUILDFORD, SURREY, GU1 2NS.
COOPER, Mr. James Richard, BA ACA *1999;* 38 Park Drive, WICKFORD, SS12 9DJ.
COOPER, Mr. James Sidney William, MA FCA *1977;* Deers Leap Hampton Lane, Meriden, COVENTRY, CV7 7JR.
•COOPER, Mr. Jeffrey Michael, FCA *1982;* Cooper Murray, Fifth Floor, Tennyson House, 159-165 Great Portland Street, LONDON, W1W 5PA.
•COOPER, Mr. Jeffrey Stanton, ACA *1980;* (Tax Fac), Stanton & Co, 6 Princes Park Avenue, LONDON, NW11 0JP. See also Truequest Limited
•COOPER, Mr. Jeremy Stephen, FCA *1991;* Crowe Clark Whitehill LLP, Aquis House, 49-51 Blagrave Street, READING, RG1 1PL. See also Horwath Clark Whitehill LLP and Crowe Clark Whitehill
COOPER, Mr. John, MBA FCA *1974;* Gardener's Cottage, Chilton Road, Chearsley, AYLESBURY, HP18 0DN.
COOPER, Mr. John Anthony, BA FCA *1969;* (Tax Fac), 13 Highgate Close, LONDON, N6 4SD.
COOPER, Mr. John Anthony, FCA *1957;* Croft Cottage, 7 Spinney Close, Boughton, NORTHAMPTON, NN2 8SD. (Life Member)
COOPER, Mr. John Arthur, FCA ATII *1970;* 5 Abington Court, Hall Lane, UPMINSTER, ESSEX, RM14 1BA.
COOPER, Mr. John Douglas, FCA *1968;* 19A Alderbrook Road, SOLIHULL, B91 1NN.
COOPER, Mr. John Edward Norman, ACA *1983;* 16 Skinner Street, WORCESTER, WR2 4JD.
COOPER, Mr. John Lester, BA ACA *1984;* 266 Helmshore Road, Haslingden, ROSSENDALE, BB4 4DJ.
COOPER, Mr. John Malcolm Peter, FCA *1961;* 12 Shepherds Hill, BRACKNELL, BERKSHIRE, RG12 2LS.
COOPER, Mr. John Martin, BA ACA *1987;* 15 Bunbury Gardens, Kings Norton, BIRMINGHAM, B30 1BA.
COOPER, Mr. John Mervyn, FCA *1967;* Minnis Mount, Minnis Lane, DOVER, CT17 0PT.
COOPER, Mr. John Neville, FCA *1962;* 8 Long Perry, Capel St. Mary, IPSWICH, IP9 2XD.
COOPER, Mr. John Philip, ACA *1994;* 9 Corfield Close, Finchampstead, WOKINGHAM, RG40 4PA.
COOPER, Mr. John Vincent, FCA *1970;* Louise-Bohm-Weg 13, 28357 BREMEN, GERMANY.
COOPER, Mr. Jon, ACA *2011;* 188 Canal Lane, Stanley, WAKEFIELD, WEST YORKSHIRE, WF3 4QF.
COOPER, Mr. Jonathan Edward, MA ACA *2005;* 1 West Garden Place, Kendal Street, LONDON, W2 2AQ.
•COOPER, Mr. Jonathan Edward, BSc ACA *1994;* PricewaterhouseCoopers LLP, 101 Barbirolli Square, Lower Mosley Street, MANCHESTER, M2 3PW. See also PricewaterhouseCoopers
COOPER, Mr. Jonathan Nigel Rex, BSc ACA *1990;* 67 Orchard Avenue, POOLE, BH14 8AH.
COOPER, Mr. Jonathan Robert, BSc ACA *2004;* 7 Harvey Court, Sandy Mead, EPSOM, KT19 7NH.
COOPER, Dr. Jonathan Robert, BEng FCA *1997;* 69 Grandison Road, LONDON, SW11 6LT.
COOPER, Mr. Jonathan Wellesly, BA FCA *1987;* 85 Newmarket Road, NORWICH, NR2 2HP.
COOPER, Mr. Jordan Arron, BSc(Hons) ACA *2007;* 19 Apollo Avenue, BURY, BL9 8HG.
COOPER, Mrs. Julia Karin, ACA *2008;* with PricewaterhouseCoopers, Darling Park Tower 2, 201 Sussex Street, GPO Box 2650, SYDNEY, NSW 1171 AUSTRALIA.
•COOPER, Mr. Julian Edward Peregrine, MA ACA *1990;* MMC Partners LLP, Albemarle House, 1 Albemarle Street, LONDON, W1S 4HA.
COOPER, Mr. Julian Mark Culmer, MA FCA *1982;* Adbury Holt House, Adbury Holt, Burghclere, NEWBURY, RG20 9BW.
COOPER, Miss. Karen, ACA *2010;* 14 Hill View, Uffington, FARINGDON, OXFORDSHIRE, SN7 7RZ.
COOPER, Mrs. Kate, BSc(Hons) ACA CTA *2001;* 57 Leyfield, WORCESTER PARK, KT4 7LP.
COOPER, Mrs. Kate Louise, BSc ACA *2005;* Tryst, 41 Crete Road Dibden Purlieu, SOUTHAMPTON, SO45 4JX.
COOPER, Mrs. Katharine Megan, MA ACA *2007;* with BDO LLP, 2 City Place, Beehive Ring Road, GATWICK, WEST SUSSEX, RH6 0PA.
COOPER, Mrs. Katie, ACA MAAT *1998;* The Cooper Group, 16 Finchley Road, LONDON, NW8 6EB.
COOPER, Mr. Kenneth Graham, BA FCA *1976;* Trevarth St. Johns Gardens Flushing, FALMOUTH, CORNWALL, TR11 5TU.
•COOPER, Mr. Kenneth James, FCA *1974;* Kenneth J Cooper FCA, Griffin Dene, 16 Kimberley Road, Nuthall, NOTTINGHAM, NG16 1DF.
COOPER, Mr. Kenneth Michael, FCA *1966;* 74 Hookfield, EPSOM, KT19 8JG.
COOPER, Mr. Kevin Paul, BSc(Hons) FCA FCILA *1990;* VRS Vericlaim UK Limited Suite 306, 1 Alie Street, LONDON, E1 8DE.
•COOPER, Mr. Kevin Robert, BA ACA DChA *1992;* Moore Stephens (South) LLP, 9 St. Johns Place, NEWPORT, ISLE OF WIGHT, PO30 1LH. See also Moore Secretaries Limited
COOPER, Mr. Kieran David, BA FCA *1996;* Arrow ECS Nidderdale House, Otley Road Beckwith Knowle, HARROGATE, NORTH YORKSHIRE, HG3 1SA.
•COOPER, Mr. Kieren John, BSc(Hons) ACA *2003;* with KPMG Audit plc, 1 The Embankment, Neville Street, LEEDS, LS1 4DW.
COOPER, Miss. Laura Jane, ACA *2008;* Unit 6A, Harewood Yard Harewood, LEEDS, WEST YORKSHIRE, LS17 9LF.
•COOPER, Mrs. Lesley Ann, FCA *1968;* (Tax Fac), Lesley Ann Cooper, 160 Whitmore Road, HARROW, HA1 4AQ. See also Cooper Lesley
•COOPER, Mr. Lewis, BA FCA *1997;* with Rostrons, St Peter's House, Cattle Market Street, NORWICH, NR1 3DY.
•COOPER, Mrs. Linda Marjorie, BA FCA *1988;* PKF (UK) LLP, Pannell House, 6 Queen Street, LEEDS, LS1 2TW.
COOPER, Mrs. Lindsay Jane, BA ACA *1990;* Uppingham School, Hawley, 20-24 High Street West, Uppingham, RUTLAND, LE15 9QB.
•①COOPER, Miss. Lindsey Jane, BSc FCA *1993;* Baker Tilly Tax & Advisory Services LLP, 3 Hardman Street, MANCHESTER, M3 3HF. See also Baker Tilly Restructuring and Recovery LLP
COOPER, Mr. Lionel Martin, FCA *1963;* 4 Ridge Lane, WATFORD, WD17 4TD. (Life Member)
COOPER, Mrs. Lorraine Susan, ACA *1985;* Leighs Paints Tower Works, Kestor Street, BOLTON, BL2 2AL.
•COOPER, Mr. Louis Melvin, BEd FCA *1984;* Crowe Clark Whitehill LLP, St Bride's House, 10 Salisbury Square, LONDON, EC4Y 8EH. See also Horwath Clark Whitehill LLP and Crowe Clark Whitehill
COOPER, Mrs. Louise, BA(Hons) ACA *2001;* 2 Hopwass Close, Averham, NEWARK, NOTTINGHAMSHIRE, NG23 5UA.
COOPER, Mrs. Lynda Caroline, BA ACA *1992;* Grangewood, 75 Grove Road, TRING, HERTFORDSHIRE, HP23 5PB.

COOPER, Mr. Malcolm Howard, BSc ACA *1986;* 24 Malthouse Close, Church Crookham, FLEET, GU52 6TB.
COOPER, Mr. Mark, BA ACA *1980;* 52 Carrwood Road, WILMSLOW, CHESHIRE, SK9 5DN.
COOPER, Mr. Mark Andrew, BSc ACA *1990;* (Tax Fac), with Grant Thornton UK LLP, Unit 2, Broadfield Court, SHEFFIELD, S8 0XF.
•**COOPER, Mr. Mark Anthony, FCA** *1988;* (Tax Fac), CWM, 1a High Street, EPSOM, KT19 8DA. See also Pristine Data Limited
COOPER, Mr. Mark Christopher, BSc ACA *1991;* Westcot, 109 Western Road, Hurstpierpoint, HASSOCKS, WEST SUSSEX, BN6 9SY.
COOPER, Mr. Mark David, BA(Hons) ACA *2000;* 21 Longhope Drive, Wrecclesham, FARNHAM, SURREY, GU10 4SN.
COOPER, Mr. Martin, FCA *1991;* 398 Kallang Road, #27-03 The Riverine by the Park, SINGAPORE 339098, SINGAPORE.
COOPER, Mr. Martin Howard, MA ACA *1986;* (Tax Fac), 42 Bourne Street, LONDON, SW1W 8JA.
COOPER, Mr. Martin Luke, BA(Hons) ACA ATII *2001;* 2 Hopwass Close, Averham, NEWARK, NOTTINGHAMSHIRE, NG23 5UA.
•**COOPER, Mr. Martin Raymond, BA FCA** *1981;* M.R Cooper, 1 Cheddar Close, Nailsea, BRISTOL, BS48 4YA.
COOPER, Mr. Martin Richard, BSc FCA *1977;* 1 Old Rectory Meadow, London Road Denver, DOWNHAM MARKET, PE38 0DF.
COOPER, Mr. Martin William, BA ACA *1992;* 1 The Hawthorns, EAST BOLDON, NE36 0DP.
COOPER, Mr. Matthew John, MMath ACA AMCT *2003;* 90 Wargrave Road, Twyford, READING, RG10 9PJ.
COOPER, Mr. Matthew Peter Nolan, BSc ACA *1993;* Kilderkin Lea Road Blackfield, SOUTHAMPTON, SO45 1YW.
•**COOPER, Mr. Michael, FCA** *1974;* (Tax Fac), M Cooper & Co, 18 Habankim Street, 33265 HAIFA, ISRAEL.
COOPER, Mr. Michael David, BSc FCA *1983;* Seven Limited, 35-37 St. Peters Street, IPSWICH, IP1 1XF.
•**COOPER, Mr. Michael Francis Robert, BSc ACA CTA** *1989;* (Tax Fac), Chantrey Vellacott DFK LLP, Russell Square House, 10-12 Russell Square, LONDON, WC1B 5LF.
COOPER, Mr. Michael Justin, LLB ACA *2003;* with PricewaterhouseCoopers LLP, 1 Embankment Place, LONDON, WC2N 6RH.
•**COOPER, Mr. Michael Vaughan, MA FCA FRSA MCIArb** *1990;* Northcote Lea, Elm Road, Tokers Green, READING, RG4 9EG.
COOPER, Mr. Montague, FCA *1940;* Flat 11, Sherborne Court, Ludlow Road, MAIDENHEAD, BERKSHIRE, SL6 2RS. (Life Member)
COOPER, Mr. Neil, BA ACA *1996;* 49 Millfield Road, Barningham, BURY ST. EDMUNDS, SUFFOLK, IP31 1DX.
COOPER, Mr. Neil Antony, BSc ACA *2005;* 13 Morton Road, EAST GRINSTEAD, WEST SUSSEX, RH19 4AF.
•**COOPER, Mr. Nicholas Brian, FCA** *1980;* Barringtons Limited, 570 572 Etruria Road, NEWCASTLE, ST5 0SU. See also Barringtons Corporate Recovery Limited, Barringtons Corporate Recovery (NW) LLP
COOPER, Mr. Nicholas David, ACA *1986;* 37 Killerton Park Drive, West Bridgford, NOTTINGHAM, NG2 7SB.
COOPER, Mr. Nicholas George, FCA *1973;* Sterling Insurance Group Ltd Ambassador House, Paradise Road, RICHMOND, TW9 1SQ.
COOPER, Mr. Nicholas James, BCom ACA *2009;* Attn Nicholas Cooper, Al Nahdha Investment, PO BOX 3497, ABU DHABI, UNITED ARAB EMIRATES.
COOPER, Mr. Nicholas John, BSc FCA *1974;* 1621 West Coast Rd, RD 1, CHRISTCHURCH 7671, NEW ZEALAND. (Life Member)
COOPER, Mr. Nicholas Pellew, FCA *1967;* Wychwood, 13 Colney Lane, NORWICH, NR4 7RE. (Life Member)
COOPER, Miss. Nicola, BSc(Hons) ACA *2010;* Apartment 9, 152 Withington Road, MANCHESTER, M16 8FB.
COOPER, Miss. Nicola Ann, BSc ACA CTA *1992;* (Tax Fac), 170 Dukes Avenue, RICHMOND, TW10 7YJ.
COOPER, Mrs. Nicola Jane, BA ACA *2006;* 100 Brownswall Road, DUDLEY, DY3 3NT.
COOPER, Mr. Nigel John, BA ACA *1985;* 320 West Grand Avenue, Suite 200, WISCONSIN RAPIDS, WI 54495, UNITED STATES.
COOPER, Mr. Nigel Robin, FCA *1971;* Gravell Cottage, Cranham, GLOUCESTER, GL4 8HP.
COOPER, Mr. Nigel William, BA FCA *1975;* 35 Richmond Hill, RICHMOND, SURREY, TW10 6RE.
COOPER, Mr. Oliver Paul, BSc ACA *2010;* 5 Downs View Lodge, Amhurst Road, LONDON, E8 2AY.
COOPER, Mr. Paul, BA FCA *1980;* Dellow, Beehive Road, Binfield, BRACKNELL, BERKSHIRE, RG12 8TR.
COOPER, Mr. Paul, BSc ACA *2007;* 6 Dunster Gardens, Willsbridge, BRISTOL, BS30 6UR.
COOPER, Mr. Paul, MA FCA *1990;* with Hazlems Fenton LLP, Palladium House, 1-4 Argyll Street, LONDON, W1F 7LD.
COOPER, Mr. Paul, BA ACA *2010;* 2 Stagwell Road, Great Cambourne, CAMBRIDGE, CB23 5DU.
•**COOPER, Mr. Paul Alexander, BSc FCA ATII AMCT** *1997;* Grant Thornton UK LLP, 30 Finsbury Square, LONDON, EC2P 2YU. See also Grant Thornton LLP
COOPER, Mr. Paul Andrew, BA ACA *1993;* Copse Edge, 3 Sampford Gardens, Horrabridge, YELVERTON, DEVON, PL20 7QZ.
COOPER, Mr. Paul Andrew, ACA *1995;* 7 Merthen Grove, Tattenhoe, MILTON KEYNES, MK4 3AX.
COOPER, Mr. Paul Anthony, BA ACA *1990;* 73 Duncan Terrace, Kilbirnie, WELLINGTON 6003, NEW ZEALAND.
COOPER, Mr. Paul Anthony, BA FCA *1976;* 18 Hallam Road, Moorgate, ROTHERHAM, S60 3DA.
COOPER, Mr. Paul Anthony, MEng ACA *1999;* 90 Long Acre, LONDON, WC2E 9RA.
COOPER, Mr. Paul Douglas, BA FCA *1977;* Centek Ltd, Forde Road Brunel Industrial Estate, NEWTON ABBOT, DEVON, TQ12 4AE.
COOPER, Mr. Paul Graeme, BSc ACA *1978;* Experian Finance plc, Universal Square Suite 3.1.4 Devonshire Street, MANCHESTER, M12 6JH.
•**COOPER, Mr. Paul John, FCA** *1979;* Paul J Cooper, Crumps Cottage, Harlow Common, HARLOW, ESSEX, CM17 9NE.
COOPER, Mr. Paul Michael, BA ACA *1991;* 17 Latton Close, Chilton, DIDCOT, OXFORDSHIRE, OX11 0SU.
COOPER, Mr. Paul Stephen Ian, BA FCA ATII *1999;* 137 Oldham Street, Latchford, WARRINGTON, WA4 1EX.
COOPER, Mr. Paul Steven, BSc ACA *1994;* 95 Uphill Road, LONDON, NW7 4QD.
COOPER, Mr. Peter Arthur, FCA *1971;* 6 Croft Meadows, Cheddington, LEIGHTON BUZZARD, BEDFORDSHIRE, LU7 0XH.
•**COOPER, Mr. Peter Graham, ACA** *1996;* Baker Tilly Tax and Advisory Services LLP, 25 Farringdon Street, LONDON, EC4A 4AB. See also Baker Tilly Restructuring and Recovery LLP
COOPER, Mr. Peter Graham, FCA *1968;* 24 Pelham Road, Clavering, SAFFRON WALDEN, CB11 4PQ.
COOPER, Mr. Peter James, BSc FCA *1976;* 9 Kara Court, Hammonds Plains, HALIFAX B4B 1L4, NS, CANADA.
•**COOPER, Mr. Peter John, FCA** *1978;* HPT (Luton) Limited, Unit F21, Basepoint Business & Innovation Centre, 110 Butterfield, Great Marlings, LUTON LU2 8DL.
COOPER, Mr. Peter Ronald, FCA *1967;* PricewaterhouseCoopers, PO Box 569, MBABANE, SWAZILAND.
COOPER, Mr. Philip, PhD MA MBA FCA CTA *1984;* School of Management, University of Bath, The Avenue, Claverton Down, BATH, BA2 7AY.
COOPER, Mr. Philip Richard, ACA *1979;* 14 Grange Knowe, LINLITHGOW, WEST LOTHIAN, EH49 7HX.
•**COOPER, Mr. Phillip, FCA** *1975;* Phillip Cooper & Co, 9 Dock Street, HULL, HU1 3DL.
COOPER, Miss. Rachel Alexandra, MSc ACA *2001;* Orchard House, Thurlaston, RUGBY, CV23 9LB.
COOPER, Mr. Raymond, FCA *1966;* 108 Northall Road, BEXLEYHEATH, DA7 6JE.
COOPER, Mr. Raymond Francis, FCA *1969;* 6 Roehampton Wick, 401 Upper Richmond Road, LONDON, SW15 5QW.
COOPER, Mrs. Rebecca Louise, BA ACA *2006;* 49 Lindley Drive, Parbold, WIGAN, WN8 7ED.
•**COOPER, Mr. Richard James, FCA** *1960;* Cooper Dawn Jerrom Limited, Units SCF 1 & 2, Western International Market, Hayes Road, SOUTHALL, MIDDLESEX UB2 5XJ. See also Goodhaven Limited
COOPER, Mr. Richard John, BSc FCA *1989;* 46 Kent Rd, LITTLEHAMPTON, BN17 6LQ.
COOPER, Mr. Richard Mark David, BA ACA *2005;* 111 Stevens Street, LOWELL, MA 01851, UNITED STATES.
COOPER, Mr. Richard Quentin Mortimer, BA ACA *1985;* 27 Caithness Road, Redcliffe Gardens, LONDON, W14 0JA.
COOPER, Mr. Robert, BSc ACA *2007;* Flat 5, 7 Highfield Close, LONDON, SE13 6UT.
COOPER, Mr. Robert, BSc ACA *2007;* 12 Gleneagles Court, Brighton Road, CRAWLEY, WEST SUSSEX, RH10 6AD.
•**COOPER, Mr. Robert, FCA** *1979;* (Tax Fac), Coopers, Apex House, Grand Arcade, Tally Ho Corner, LONDON, N12 0EH.
COOPER, Mr. Robert, BA ACA *2004;* Garland Cottage, New Road, Cookham, MAIDENHEAD, BERKSHIRE, SL6 9HD.
COOPER, Mr. Robert George, FCA *1972;* 1 Blythe Way, SOLIHULL, B91 3EY.
COOPER, Mr. Robert Hamilton, FCA *1970;* Great Yews, Lubbock Road, CHISLEHURST, BR7 5LA.
COOPER, Mr. Robert Hayward, FCA *1969;* Olympus, The Avenue, SHERBORNE, DT9 3AJ.
•**COOPER, Mr. Robert James, BA FCA** *1990;* Willis Cooper Limited, Unit 6, Derby Road, BELPER, DERBYSHIRE, DE56 1SW. See also Easy Accounts Ltd
COOPER, Mr. Robert Michael, FCA *1969;* 2 Somerlea, Court Road, MAIDENHEAD, SL6 8LH. (Life Member)
COOPER, Mr. Roger Euan Barham, FCA *1964;* 15 Bourne Close, Fishbourne, CHICHESTER, PO19 3QJ.
COOPER, Mr. Roger Henry Edward, FCA *1967;* 2 Wolsey Road, Moor Park, NORTHWOOD, MIDDLESEX, HA6 2HS.
COOPER, Mr. Ronald Frederick, BSc ACA *1986;* 6 Royal Court, Barnsley Road, Barugh Green, BARNSLEY, S75 1LS.
COOPER, Miss. Rosemary, BSc(Hons) ACA *2004;* Flat 12 Challoner Mansions, Challoner Street, LONDON, W14 9LD.
COOPER, Mr. Roy, FCA *1961;* 8/5 Ehud Manor, Eir Yamim, 42664 NETANYA, ISRAEL. (Life Member)
COOPER, Mr. Rustom Cavasjee, FCA *1948;* 22 Pier House, 31 Cheyne Walk, LONDON, SW3 5HG. (Life Member)
COOPER, Miss. Sally, BSc(Hons) ACA *2000;* 12 St. Helens Way, LEEDS, LS16 8LP.
COOPER, Ms. Sally-Ann, ACA CA(AUS) *2009;* 8 Beaconsfield Road, St Margarets, TWICKENHAM, TW1 3HU.
COOPER, Mr. Sam, ACA *2009;* La Piece Barn, Route Des Capelles, St. Sampson, GUERNSEY, GY2 4UN.
COOPER, Mrs. Samantha Jane, BA(Hons) ACA *2000;* Aviva Health, Chilworth House, Hampshire Corporate Park, Templars Way, Chandler's Ford, EASTLEIGH HAMPSHIRE SO53 3RY.
COOPER, Ms. Sarah Corrina, BA ACA *2001;* Thomson Reuters Ltd Aldgate House, 33 Aldgate High Street, LONDON, EC3N 1DL.
COOPER, Mr. Scott, BA ACA *1990;* 77 Wentworth Road, Vaucluse, SYDNEY, NSW 2030, AUSTRALIA.
COOPER, Mrs. Sharon Denise, BSc ACA *2003;* Oakdene, Pangbourne Road, Upper Basildon, READING, RG8 8LN.
COOPER, Mr. Simon, MA ACA *2001;* 128 Tressillian Road, LONDON, SE4 1XX.
COOPER, Mr. Simon Ernest, ACA *1995;* with RSM Tenon Limited, The Poynt Building, 45 Wollaton Street, NOTTINGHAM, NG1 5FW.
COOPER, Mr. Simon Henry Giles, ACA *2008;* 140 Heeley Road, BIRMINGHAM, B29 6EZ.
COOPER, Mr. Simon John, BCom FCA *1992;* with Deloitte LLP, Athene Place, 66 Shoe Lane, LONDON, EC4A 3BQ.
COOPER, Mr. Simon John, ACA *1980;* The Lodge Deaks Lane, Cuckfield, HAYWARDS HEATH, WEST SUSSEX, RH17 5JB.
COOPER, Mr. Simon John, BA ACA *1991;* 24 Hawthorn Way, ST. ALBANS, AL2 3BH.
COOPER, Mr. Simon John Waldron Scott, MSc FCA *1965;* 49 Pittville Lawn, CHELTENHAM, GL52 2BH.
•**COOPER, Mr. Simon Mark, BA FCA** *1997;* Monahans, 16 Forest Gate, Pewsham, CHIPPENHAM, WILTSHIRE, SN15 3RS.
COOPER, Miss. Stella, BA ACA *2006;* 68 Swan Avenue, BINGLEY, WEST YORKSHIRE, BD16 3PA.
COOPER, Mrs. Stephanie Jayne, ACA *1993;* 12 Poplar Lane, CANNOCK, STAFFORDSHIRE, WS11 1NQ.
COOPER, Mr. Stephen Donald, BA FCA *1976;* Flat 1, 11 Park Road, HARROGATE, HG2 9BH.
•**COOPER, Mr. Stephen John, LLB ACA** *1991;* KPMG LLP, 15 Canada Square, LONDON, E14 5GL. See also KPMG Europe LLP
COOPER, Mr. Stephen Mark, BA FCA *1979;* 76 Mainway, Middleton, MANCHESTER, M24 1PP.
COOPER, Mr. Stephen Richard, BSc ACA *1992;* The Firs, 2 Winterbourne, HORSHAM, RH12 5JW.
COOPER, Mr. Steven Joseph, BSc ACA *1991;* 78 Banastre Drive, NEWTON-LE-WILLOWS, WA12 8BE.
COOPER, Mr. Steven Leslie, FCA *1977;* Hylands, Hylands Close, West Hill, OTTERY ST.MARY, EX11 1XJ.
COOPER, Mr. Stuart Edward, FCA *1964;* 2 Roe Close, Stotfold, HITCHIN, SG5 4HX. (Life Member)
COOPER, Mr. Stuart Martin, PhD BA ACA *1995;* 78 Willow Avenue, Edgbaston, BIRMINGHAM, B17 8HE.
COOPER, Mrs. Sukhvinder Kaur, BSc ACA *2005;* 43 Boscombe Road, BIRMINGHAM, B11 3RH.
COOPER, Mrs. Susan Jane, BSc ACA CTA *1992;* 3 Brown Avenue, Quorn, LOUGHBOROUGH, LE12 8RH.
COOPER, Mr. Thomas Knut Glenn, BA ACA *1988;* Tanglewood Hall, Luton Road, Markyate, ST ALBANS, AL3 8PZ.
COOPER, Mr. Timothy Alan, BA ACA *1989;* Brookfield Global Relocation Services, 1 Finsbury Market, LONDON, EC2A 2BN.
COOPER, Mr. Timothy Charles, BA ACA *1992;* 15 The Daedings, Deddington, BANBURY, OXFORDSHIRE, OX15 0RT.
COOPER, Mr. Timothy William Downey, FCA *1980;* 29 Lockwood Street, DRIFFIELD, YO25 6RU.
COOPER, Mr. Toby James, BA FCA *1986;* RPC Group Plc, Sapphire House, Crown Way, RUSHDEN, NORTHAMPTONSHIRE, NN10 6FB.
COOPER, Mr. Trevor, BSc FCA FIIA *1975;* Old Orchard Costa Row, Long Bennington, NEWARK, NOTTINGHAMSHIRE, NG23 5DY.
COOPER, Miss. Vanessa Amelia, ACA *1990;* 81 The Waterfront, HERTFORD, SG14 1SD.
COOPER, Mrs. Venetia Lois, BSc ACA *1999;* The Old School House, Pillerton Road, Butlers Marston, WARWICK, WARWICKSHIRE, CV35 0NH.
COOPER, Mrs. Victoria Jane, LLB ACA *2004;* 119 Cramptons Road, SEVENOAKS, KENT, TN14 5DU.
COOPER, Mrs. Virginia Teresa Louise, ACA *2002;* Hawthorne House Radburn Brow, Clayton-le-Woods, CHORLEY, PR6 7RA.
COOPER, Mr. William Alec, FCA *1956;* 2 Burlington Glen, Dore, SHEFFIELD, S17 3PL. (Life Member)
COOPER, Mr. William James, BCom ACA *1999;* D T Z Group, 125 Old Broad Street, LONDON, EC2N 2BQ.
COOPER, Mr. William Paul, FCA *1978;* Pennygum, PO Box 315, UNDERBERG, KWAZULU NATAL, SOUTH AFRICA.
COOPER, Mrs. Zoe Caroline, BA ACA *1992;* 24 St. Leonards Road, HARROGATE, NORTH YORKSHIRE, HG2 8NX.
COOPER BAILEY, Mr. William John, MA FCA *1971;* 20 Burnsall Street, LONDON, SW3 3ST.
COOPER-HOLMES, Mrs. Katherine Louise, ACA *2008;* 15 Victoria Road, West Bridgford, NOTTINGHAM, NG2 7JW.
COOPERMAN, Mrs. Amanda, ACA *2002;* 26 Penshurst Gardens, EDGWARE, MIDDLESEX, HA8 9TP.
COOPERMAN, Mr. Malcolm, ACA *2000;* 26 Penshurst Gardens, EDGWARE, MIDDLESEX, HA8 9TP.
COOPEY, Mr. Graham Stephen, FCA *1980;* Swallow Barn, Berryfields Gated Road, Quarrendon, AYLESBURY, BUCKINGHAMSHIRE, HP22 4AA.
COOPS, Mrs. Louise Yvonne, ACA *1998;* with Ernst & Young, 100 Barbirolli Square, MANCHESTER, M2 3EY.
COORAY, Mr. Christian Peter, BSc(Hons) FCA *1999;* Flat 14, 5 Kendra Hall Road, SOUTH CROYDON, SURREY, CR2 6DT.
COOTE, Mrs. Hazel Ann, BA ACA *1994;* 23 Vicarage Lane, Upper Hale, FARNHAM, GU9 0PG.
COOVADIA, Mr. Danyal Hoosen, MA ACA *1995;* 2 Melville Avenue, LONDON, SW20 0NS.
COPAS, Mr. Hans-Frederick Ronald, BSc ACA *1994;* 6 Tweedale Close, Mursley, MILTON KEYNES, MK17 0SB.
COPE, Mr. Alan Howard, FCA *1952;* Sunnymeade, Lezayre Road, Ramsey, ISLE OF MAN, IM8 2TD. (Life Member)
COPE, Miss. Amy Louise, BA(Hons) ACA *2002;* 9 Rendel Grove, Whitebridge Manor, STONE, ST15 8ZN.
COPE, Mr. Andrew Julian Bailye, BEng FCA *1991;* with PricewaterhouseCoopers LLP, 1 Embankment Place, LONDON, WC2N 6RH.
COPE, Mr. Anthony, FCA *1966;* 66 Hill View, Henleaze, BRISTOL, BS9 4PU. (Life Member)
COPE, Mr. Anthony James, ACA *2008;* Elmwood Farm, Le Mont Cambrai, St. Lawrence, JERSEY, JE3 1JN.
COPE, Mr. Barry Edwards, BA ACA *2006;* 2 Wyrescourt Road, West Derby, LIVERPOOL, L12 9EP.
COPE, Mrs. Brenda Christine, BA ACA *1985;* Rio Tinto, 2 Eastbourne Terrace, LONDON, W2 6LG.
COPE, Mr. Cecil Edward, FCA *1968;* The Coach House, Bakewell Road, MATLOCK, DERBYSHIRE, DE4 3BN.

COPE, Mrs. Christine Helen, BSc ACA *2004;* 1 Blunts Hall Farm Cottages, Blunts Hall Road, WITHAM, ESSEX, CM8 1LX.
COPE, Mr. David Graham, BCom FCA *1966;* 7 Upton Avenue, Cheadle Hulme, CHEADLE, SK8 7HX.
COPE, Mr. David Walter, MSc FCA *1971;* 5 Lynch Hill Park, WHITCHURCH, Hampshire, RG28 7NF.
•COPE, Miss. Emma Jane, BSc FCA *1995;* (Tax Fac), Cope Consulting, 15 One End Lane, Benson, WALLINGFORD, OXFORDSHIRE, OX10 6PA.
COPE, Miss. Fionnuala Charity, ACA *2008;* Elmwood Farm Le Mont Cambrai, St. Lawrence, JERSEY, JE3 1JN.
COPE, Mr. Gareth Howard, BSc ACA *1989;* 18 Iluka Road, CLIFTON GARDENS, NSW, 2088, AUSTRALIA.
COPE, Miss. Holly Elizabeth, BSc ACA *2009;* Holly Cottage, Main Street, Gunthorpe, NOTTINGHAM, NG14 7EU.
COPE, Mr. James, BSc(Hons) ACA *2011;* Bishops Court, Onslow Road, ASCOT, BERKSHIRE, SL5 0HW.
COPE, Miss. Jennifer Elizabeth, BA ACA *1986;* 4 Helford Close, RUISLIP, HA4 7EN.
•COPE, Mr. Jeremy Albert, BSc FCA *1984;* Smith Cooper, Livery Place, 35 Livery Street, BIRMINGHAM, WEST MIDLANDS, B3 2PB. See also Smith Cooper LLP
COPE, Mr. Jeremy Simon, BA FCA *1998;* 87 Kingsfield Road, WATFORD, WD19 4TP.
COPE, Mrs. Joanne, LLB ACA *2003;* 6 Hill Top Road, LYMM, CHESHIRE, WA13 0EA.
COPE, Mr. John, FCA *1965;* 20 Lidget, Oakworth, KEIGHLEY, BD22 7HH. (Life Member)
COPE, Lord John Ambrose, FCA *1963;* 27 Daniel Street, BATH, BA2 6ND. (Life Member)
COPE, Mr. Jonathan Sinclair David, BSc FCA DChA *1980;* 232 Hatch Road, Pilgrims Hatch, BRENTWOOD, ESSEX, CM15 9QR.
COPE, Mrs. Kathryn Louise, BA ACA *2007;* Sunnyside House West Edge, Marsh Gibbon, BICESTER, OXFORDSHIRE, OX27 0HA.
COPE, Mr. Kenneth, FCA *1958;* 4 Manor Cottage Mews, Wetherby Road, Scarcroft, LEEDS, LS14 3HN. (Life Member)
COPE, Mr. Kenneth Robert, FCA *1969;* 9 Amber Heights, RIPLEY, DERBYSHIRE, DE5 3SP.
COPE, Ms. Marie Anne, BA FCA *1999;* Bell Mount, Valley Road, Ffrith, WREXHAM, CLWYD, LL11 5LP.
•COPE, Mr. Michael Francis Gordon, FCA *1969;* Michael F.G. Cope, 21 Godfrey Avenue, Whitton, TWICKENHAM, TW2 7PE.
•COPE, Mr. Michael Hugh, MA FCA *1992;* (Tax Fac), Duncan & Toplis, 27 Lumley Avenue, SKEGNESS, LINCOLNSHIRE, PE25 2AT.
COPE, Mr. Michael Joseph, FCA *1973;* 1 Trinity View, Ketley Bank, TELFORD, SHROPSHIRE, TF2 0DX.
COPE, Mr. Roland, FCA *1958;* Sytten Lodge, 15 Windsor Road, NEWARK, NOTTINGHAMSHIRE, NG24 4HS. (Life Member)
COPE, Mr. Ronald William, FCA *1948;* 26 Daimler Close, Rectory Farm, NORTHAMPTON, NN3 5JT. (Life Member)
COPE, Mr. Simon Jeffrey, MA ACA *2004;* Sunnyside House, Marsh Gibbon, BICESTER, OXFORDSHIRE, OX27 0HA.
COPE, Mr. Simon Michael, BA FCA *1991;* UNICEF, DFAM, 24th Floor, 633 3rd Avenue, NEW YORK, NY 10017 UNITED STATES.
COPE, Mr. Stephen Francis, BD ACA *1980;* St. Anthonys Hospital, London Road, SUTTON, SM3 9DW.
COPE, Mr. Steven David, FCA *1976;* 2 New Hall Avenue, SALFORD, M7 4JU.
COPE-THOMPSON, Mr. Simon Daniel, BA ACA *1994;* 5 Hill Top, LONDON, NW11 6EH.
COPELAND, Miss. Alexandra, BSc ACA *2005;* Turf Lea Farm, The Ridge, Marple, STOCKPORT, CHESHIRE, SK6 7EZ.
COPELAND, Mr. Colin William, ACA *1988;* 580 Thornton Road, RD4, WHAKATANE, NEW ZEALAND.
COPELAND, Mr. Dennis, BA FCA *1959;* 48 West End Avenue, PINNER, MIDDLESEX, HA5 1BW. (Life Member)
COPELAND, Miss. Felicity, BSc(Hons) ACA *2011;* 132 Mid Street, South Nutfield, REDHILL, RH1 4JH.
COPELAND, Mr. Graham Peter, BA ACA *1987;* Athene Place, 66 Shoe Lane, LONDON, EC4A 3BQ.
•COPELAND, Mr. Ian Trevor, FCA *1978;* I.T. Copeland, 4 Heather Close, Werrington, STOKE-ON-TRENT, ST9 0LB.
COPELAND, Mr. James, BSc(Hons) ACA *2010;* Flat 4, 120 Gowers Walk, LONDON, E1 8GG.
COPELAND, Mr. James Fergus, FCA *1974;* Fairhaven, 5 The Byres, Todenham, MORETON-IN-MARSH, GLOUCESTERSHIRE, GL56 9NG.
COPELAND, Mr. John Chilton, FCA *1960;* 28 Rue Des Iris, 76840 ST MARTIN DE BOSCHERVILLE, FRANCE. (Life Member)
COPELAND, Mr. Peter John, BA ACA *2008;* 8 Copse Road, COBHAM, SURREY, KT11 2TN.
COPELAND, Mr. Philip Robert, BCom ACA CTA *1984;* Crofton, Sheldon Road, Ickford, AYLESBURY, HP18 9HY.
COPELAND, Mr. Robert Nigel, FCA *1966;* Cherry Tree Cottage, Hearns Lane, Gallows Tree Common, READING, RG4 9DE.
COPELIN, Mr. John Ernest, FCA *1958;* 30 Litle Forest Road, Talbot Woods, BOURNEMOUTH, BH4 9NW. (Life Member)
COPEMAN, Miss. Clare Elizabeth, MA FCA CF *1998;* 25a Abbeville Road, LONDON, SW4 9LA.
COPEMAN, Mr. Michael Richard, ACA *1984;* 139 Newmarket Road, NORWICH, NORFOLK, NR4 6SY.
COPEMAN, Mr. Sam, ACA BEng(Hons) *2004;* Alexander House, 7 - 13 Rose Lane, NORWICH, NR1 1PL.
COPESTAKE, Mrs. Pauline Mary, FCA *1968;* 3 Hambleden Mill, Mill End Hambleden, HENLEY-ON-THAMES, RG9 3AF.
COPLAND, Mr. Christopher John, ACA *2009;* with Deloitte LLP, 4 Brindley Place, BIRMINGHAM, B1 2HZ.
COPLAND, Mr. Kelvin Alexander, FCA *1974;* Salt Cottage, West End, MARAZION, CORNWALL, TR17 0EL.
COPLAND, Mr. Stewart James, BSc(Hons) FCA CMC FSI FIBC *1985;* Flat 16D, Lee Wing Building, 158 Hennessy Road, WAN CHAI, HONG KONG SAR.
•COPLESTON, Mr. Alan John, BA FCA *1981;* The HHC Partnership, Suite 2, 9 West End, Kemsing, SEVENOAKS, KENT TN15 6PX.
•COPLEY, Mr. David Martin, FCA CF MAAT *1994;* with RSM Tenon Limited, Highfield Court, Tollgate, Chandler's Ford, EASTLEIGH, HAMPSHIRE SO53 3TY.
COPLEY, Mr. Gerald Francis, BA FCA *1993;* 12 Valmont Road, Sherwood, NOTTINGHAM, NG5 1GA.
COPLEY, Miss. Jenna Charlotte, BSc ACA *2008;* Harvest Barn Farm, Aldsworth, CHELTENHAM, GL54 3QR.
COPLEY, Mrs. Linzi Andra, BSc ACA *1997;* Craigland House, 48 Back Lane, Bilbrough, YORK, YO23 3PL.
COPLEY, Mr. Martin, MA FCA *1966;* Australian Wildlife Conservancy, PO Box 8070, SUBIACO, WA 6008, AUSTRALIA. (Life Member)
•COPLEY, Mr. Matthew John, MA ACA *1998;* BDO LLP, 1 Bridgewater Place, Water Lane, LEEDS, LS11 5RU. See also BDO Stoy Hayward LLP
COPLEY, Mr. Nicholas Brent, MA ACA *1988;* 117 Prospect Street, NEWTON, MA 02465, UNITED STATES.
•①COPLEY, Mr. Paul David, BA(Hons) ACA *2000;* PricewaterhouseCoopers LLP, Pricewaterhousecoopers, 12 Plumtree Court, LONDON, EC4A 4HT. See also PricewaterhouseCoopers
COPLEY, Mr. Simon Charles, BSc FCA *1989;* PricewaterhouseCoopers, 33/F Cheung Kong Center, 2 Queen's Road, CENTRAL, HONG KONG ISLAND, HONG KONG SAR.
COPLEY, Mr. Steven Paul, BSc ACA *1999;* 14 Kensington Ave, Balmoral, AUCKLAND 1024, NEW ZEALAND.
•COPLEY, Mr. Wilfred Brian, FCA *1962;* W. Brian Copley, Barn Cottage, 5 Crossland Gardens, Tickhill, DONCASTER, SOUTH YORKSHIRE DN11 9QS.
COPLOWE, Mr. Eric, FCA *1952;* 81 Waterloo Road, SOUTHPORT, PR8 2NW. (Life Member)
COPLOWE, Mrs. Judith, BA FCA DChA *1983;* with Peters Elworthy & Moore, Salisbury House, Station Road, CAMBRIDGE, CB1 2LA.
COPNELL, Mr. Timothy, BSc FCA *1991;* 67 High Street, BERKHAMSTED, HERTFORDSHIRE, HP4 2DE.
COPP, Mrs. Deirdre Pamela Susan, FCA *1982;* Le Theil, 19300 SOUDEILLES, FRANCE.
•COPP, Mr. Peter Richard, FCA *1971;* Peter Copp, Mawenzi, Muir of Fowlis, ALFORD, ABERDEENSHIRE, AB33 8JX.
•COPPARD, Mr. David John, FCA *1980;* (Tax Fac), MacIntyre Hudson LLP, New Bridge Street House, 30-34 New Bridge Street, LONDON, EC4V 6BJ.
•COPPARD, Mr. Kevin Andrew, FCA *1981;* (Tax Fac), James Todd & Co Limited, Nos 1 & 2 The Barn, Oldwick, West Stoke Road, Lavant, CHICHESTER WEST SUSSEX PO18 9AA.
COPPARD, Mr. Timothy James, BA FCA *1986;* Servite Houses Ltd, 2 Bridge Avenue, LONDON, W6 9JP.
COPPEL, Mr. Andrew Maxwell, CBE LLB FCA *1976;* De Vere Group, 1 West Garden Place Kendal Street, LONDON, W2 2AQ.
COPPEL, Mr. Edwin Philip, LLB FCA *1969;* Whiffen Spit, 1a Holyrood, BELFAST, BT9 5DA. (Life Member)
COPPELMAN, Mr. Harold, FCA *1959;* Flat 2 Coppice House, Award Road Church Crookham, FLEET, HAMPSHIRE, GU52 6ER. (Life Member)
•COPPEN, Miss. Penelope Elizabeth, BSc ACA *1989;* with KPMG LLP, 15 Canada Square, LONDON, E14 5GL.
COPPERTHWAITE, Mr. David John, FCA *1960;* 2514 Shore Drive, ST AUGUSTINE, FL 32086, UNITED STATES. (Life Member)
•COPPERWHEAT, Mr. David Anthony, FCA *1977;* Coppers & Co, Green End Farmhouse, 22 Green End, Granborough, BUCKINGHAM, MK18 3NT.
COPPIN, Mr. Glen, MSc BSc ACA *2010;* 32 Lansdowne Road, Shepshed, LOUGHBOROUGH, LEICESTERSHIRE, LE12 9RS.
COPPIN, Mr. Mark Ian, BSc ACA *1995;* Three Gables Earlswood Common, Earlswood, SOLIHULL, B94 5SQ.
COPPIN, Mr. Raymond, ACA *1982;* Lilac Cottage, 9 Lee Lane, MAIDENHEAD, BERKSHIRE, SL6 6NU.
•COPPING, Mr. Andrew Charles, BA FCA *1988;* Harold Sharp, Holland House, 1-5 Oakfield, SALE, M33 6TT.
COPPING, Mr. Francis James Bertram, FCA *1966;* 10 Macpherson Avenue, TORONTO M5R 1W8, ON, CANADA. (Life Member)
COPPING, Mr. Francis John, FCA *1970;* 21 Tabors Avenue, Great Baddow, CHELMSFORD, CM2 7ES.
COPPING, Miss. Lynsey Claire, BSc ACA *2003;* PO Box 504902, DUBAI, UNITED ARAB EMIRATES.
COPPING, Mrs. Tracey Marie, BSc ACA *1999;* 52, Wilshire Avenue, Springfield, CHELMSFORD, CM2 6QW.
COPPOCK, Mr. Kenneth Francis, FCA *1971;* The Duke of Edinburghs Award, Gulliver House, Madeira Walk, WINDSOR, BERKSHIRE, SL4 1EU.
•COPPOCK, Mr. Lawrence Patrick, FCA *1974;* Lawrence P. Coppock, The Close, Church Lane, Braishfield, ROMSEY, SO51 0QH.
•COPPOCK, Mr. Richard John, FCA *1984;* Richard Coppock Associates Limited, 80 Beulah Road, CARDIFF, CF14 6LZ.
COPSEY, Mr. David Russell, MA ACA *1988;* (Tax Fac), Maritime Cargo Processing plc, The Chapel, Maybush Lane, FELIXSTOWE, SUFFOLK, IP11 7LL.
COPSEY, Miss. Emily, ACA *2009;* Flat 1, 10 Alexandra Road, LONDON, SW19 7JZ.
COPSON, Ms. Alison Katrina, BSc ACA *1989;* 16 Beechcrest View, HOOK, RG27 9RF.
COPSON, Mrs. Sarah Louise, BA ACA *1997;* 16 Snowdrop Close, Bedworth, NUNEATON, WARWICKSHIRE, CV12 0GN.
•COPSON, Mr. Stephen Roy, BSc FCA *1992;* Copson Grandfield Ltd, 30-31 St James Place, Mangotsfield, BRISTOL, BS16 9JB.
COPUS, Mrs. Maggie, BA ACA *1985;* Chadlington House, Chapel Road, Chadlington, CHIPPING NORTON, OXFORDSHIRE, OX7 3LZ.
COPUS, Mr. Roy Bernard, MA ACA *1984;* Thompson Investments, Chadlington House, Chapel Road, Chadlington, CHIPPING NORTON, OXFORDSHIRE OX7 3LZ.
CORAL, Mrs. Lynda Sharon, FCA *1985;* Apartado 3657, EC Almancil, 8136-908 ALMANCIL, PORTUGAL.
CORB, Mr. Maurice, FCA *1966;* Mevo Timna 4, JERUSALEM, 97753, ISRAEL.
CORBALLY, Mrs. Kathryn Elsie, BA ACA *1989;* 21 Cob Drive, WESTPORT, CT 06880, UNITED STATES.
CORBEN, Mr. Darcy John, BA ACA *1993;* 68 Victoria Road, POOLE, DORSET, BH12 3AE.
CORBEN, Miss. Kathryn Norma, FCA *1979;* 15 Abbotsbury Close, Rise Park, NOTTINGHAM, NG5 5AL.
CORBEN, Mr. Mark Edward Macleod, BA ACA *1997;* 33 Coalecroft Road, LONDON, SW15 6LW.
CORBERSMITH, Mrs. Leanne Genette, BA ACA *2008;* 2 Grasmere Gardens Kirby Cross, FRINTON-ON-SEA, ESSEX, CO13 0SX.
CORBET, Mr. Richard, MSc LLB ACA *2010;* Preston Hall, Preston Brockhurst, SHREWSBURY, SY4 5QA.
CORBETT, Mr. Adam Robert, ACA *2008;* with Deloitte LLP, Athene Place, 66 Shoe Lane, LONDON, EC4A 3BQ.
•CORBETT, Mr. Alan, FCA *1976;* Alan Corbett, 45 Rooker Avenue, Parkfields, WOLVERHAMPTON, WV2 2DT.
CORBETT, Mr. Barry John, ACA *1992;* 21 Newstead Way, LONDON, SW19 5HR.
CORBETT, Mrs. Briony Lamorna, FCA *1968;* T M B Patterns Ltd, 24 Brue Avenue, BRIDGWATER, SOMERSET, TA6 5LT.
CORBETT, Miss. Eimhear Hannah, ACA *2009;* Arsenal Football Club, 75 Drayton Park, LONDON, N5 1BU.
•CORBETT, Mr. Gary Kenneth, BA FCA MCIM FRSA *1976;* Boundary Accounting Limited, Bank Farm, Leigh, WORCESTER, WR6 5LA. See also Boundary Accounting
CORBETT, Miss. Irene, BA ACA *2006;* 235 Croxted Road, LONDON, SE21 8NL.
CORBETT, Mr. Isambard, BA ACA *2005;* 56a Claverton Street, LONDON, SW1V 3AX.
CORBETT, Mrs. Jennifer Jane, BSc ACA *1989;* Gable Cottage, Blakehouse Farm, Thurstonland, HUDDERSFIELD, HD4 6XD.
CORBETT, Miss. Joanne, BA ACA *1995;* 42 Bowes Road, Wivenhoe, COLCHESTER, CO7 9RE.
CORBETT, Mr. John Edmund, FCA *1962;* PO Box 1, BEQUIA, SAINT VINCENT AND THE GRENADINES. (Life Member)
CORBETT, Mr. John James, FCA *1968;* 18 Carlisle Mansions, Carlisle Place, LONDON, SW1P 1HX. (Life Member)
CORBETT, Mr. Jonathan James Mortimer, MA FCA *1988;* Regmmind Inc, 300 Frank H. Ogalia Plaza, Suite 650, OAKLAND, CA 94612, UNITED STATES.
CORBETT, Mrs. Julia Anne, BSc ACA *1978;* Nelm Development Trust, 51 Ivy Road, NORWICH, NR5 8BF.
CORBETT, Mrs. Kathleen Horwood, BSc ACA *1990;* 98 Thames Avenue, GUISBOROUGH, TS14 8AJ.
•CORBETT, Mrs. Kathleen Sarah, BSc FCA *1992;* Kathleen Corbett, 44a Barclay Road, LONDON, SW6 1EH.
CORBETT, Mr. Martin Alan, BSc ACA DChA *1987;* with PricewaterhouseCoopers LLP, 31 Great George Street, BRISTOL, BS1 5QD.
CORBETT, Mr. Michael, MA ACA *1995;* Health Service Executive, Stewart House, Lonsdale Road, Plassey Technology Park, LIMERICK, COUNTY LIMERICK IRELAND.
CORBETT, Mr. Nicholas, FCA CTA *1984;* Santander Corporate Banking, 298 Deansgate, MANCHESTER, M3 4HH.
CORBETT, Mrs. Nicola Louise, BA ACA *2005;* Co-operative Financial Serives, Miller Street, MANCHESTER, M60 0AL.
CORBETT, Mr. Oliver Roebling Panton, BSc FCA *1990;* 13 Jubilee Place, LONDON, SW3 3TD.
CORBETT, Mr. Paul Graham, FCA *1980;* 98 Culver Way, Yaverland, SANDOWN, PO36 8QL.
CORBETT, Mr. Peter Graham, CBE FCA *1957;* 95 Coleherne Court, Old Brompton Road, LONDON, SW5 0ED. (Life Member)
CORBETT, Mr. Peter James, BA ACA *2007;* 16 Dovedale Close, Crofton, WAKEFIELD, WEST YORKSHIRE, WF4 1SS.
CORBETT, Mr. Peter Michael, MA FCA *1983;* 13 Kestrel Close, EPSOM, SURREY, KT19 7EJ.
CORBETT, Mr. Richard, BA FCA *1996;* 19 Brows Lane, LIVERPOOL, L37 3HY.
CORBETT, Mr. Stephen John, FCA *1975;* 25 Wycombe Road, Holmer Green, HIGH WYCOMBE, BUCKINGHAMSHIRE, HP15 6RX.
CORBIN, Mrs. Anne Yvonne, FCA *1986;* 2a Bridge End, Earith, HUNTINGDON, PE28 3PT.
CORBIN, Mr. Ian James, BA ACA *1984;* 3 DAWS ROAD, DONCASTER EAST, VIC 3109, AUSTRALIA.
•CORBIN, Mr. Matthew John, BA(Hons) FCA *2000;* BDO Alto Limited, Windward House, La Route de la Liberation, St Helier, JERSEY, JE1 1BG.
•CORBIN, Mr. Phillip Andrew, FCA *1978;* (Tax Fac), Phillip Corbin & Associates, Trym Lodge, 1 Henbury Road, Westbury-on-Trym, BRISTOL, BS9 3HQ.
CORBIN, Mr. Tony John, ACA *2009;* Pricewaterhousecoopers, PO Box 321, GUERNSEY, GY1 4ND.
CORBISHLEY, Mr. Francis John, BA(Hons) ACA *2003;* 97 Old London Road, ST. ALBANS, HERTFORDSHIRE, AL1 1QD.
•CORBISHLEY, Mr. John, BA ACA *1984;* Grant Thornton UK LLP, Grant Thornton House, 202 Silbury Boulevard, MILTON KEYNES, BUCKINGHAMSHIRE, MK9 1LW. See also Grant Thornton LLP
CORBITT, Mr. David Gavin, ACA *2008;* 52 Clearbrook Close, HIGH WYCOMBE, BUCKINGHAMSHIRE, HP13 7BP.
•CORBITT, Miss. Margaret Anne, BSc FCA *1989;* (Tax Fac), Anderson Neal Limited, 1 The Mews, 6 Putney Common, LONDON, SW15 1HL.
CORBOY, Mr. John Mark, BA(Hons) ACA *2002;* 20 The Mall, BRISTOL, BS8 4DR.
CORBRIDGE, Mr. Ian, FCA *1984;* 65 Wittenbury Road, Heaton Norris, STOCKPORT, SK4 3LY.

CORBRIDGE, Miss. Janet, BA(Hons) ACA *2011;* Fairview, Eshton Road, Gargrave, SKIPTON, NORTH YORKSHIRE, BD23 3PN.
CORBY, Mrs. Cynthia Petro, ACA FCCA CA(SA) *2011;* Deloitte & Touche (M.E), 1001 City Tower 2, Sheikh Zayed Rod, PO Box 4254, DUBAI, UNITED ARAB EMIRATES.
CORBY, Mr. David Charles, BSc ACA *1980;* 30 Chiltern Avenue, Cosby, LEICESTER, LE9 1UF.
•CORBY, Mr. Derek George, BSc FCA *1984;* 35 Linton Rise, Alwoodley, LEEDS, LS17 8QW.
CORBY, Mrs. Emma Louise, BSc ACA *2000;* 199b Nine Mile Ride, Finchampstead, WOKINGHAM, RG40 4JD.
•CORBY, Mr. Giles Matthew, BSc ACA *2002;* Merlin Accountancy Services Ltd, 4 Charnley Avenue, Redhills, EXETER, EX4 1RE.
CORBY, Mr. James Richard, BSc ACA *2005;* Digicel Bermuda, Washington Mall Phase II, 22 Church Street, HAMILTON HM11, BERMUDA.
CORBY, Mr. Michael, BA(Econ) ACA *2001;* 199b Nine Mile Ride, Finchampstead, WOKINGHAM, BERKSHIRE, RG40 4JD.
CORBY, Mrs. Nicola Susan, BSc ACA *1997;* 5 Elm Avenue, ASHBY-DE-LA-ZOUCH, LEICESTERSHIRE, LE65 1SS.
CORBYN, Miss. Judith Naomi, MSc BA ACA *1998;* C A A, 45-59 Kingsway, LONDON, WC2B 6TP.
CORCORAN, Mr. Brian Christopher, BA ACA *1986;* 16 Carrwood Road, Bramhall, STOCKPORT, CHESHIRE, SK7 3EL.
CORCORAN, Miss. Georgia-Ann, BSc(Hons) ACA *2002;* 3 Goodbody Road, Larkhill, SALISBURY, SP4 8QL.
CORCORAN, Miss. Gillian, ACA *2008;* 21 Airedale Gardens, LEEDS, LS13 1DN.
CORCORAN, Mr. James, BA ACA *2011;* 6 Dunwich Place, Great Barton, BURY ST. EDMUNDS, SUFFOLK, IP31 2TJ.
CORCORAN, Ms. Janet Susan, BA ACA *1986;* Tennings House, Sutton Place, Abinger Hammer, DORKING, RH5 6RP.
CORCORAN, Mr. Kevin Anthony, BSc FCA *1981;* Tennings House, Sutton Place, Abinger Hammer, DORKING, SURREY, RH5 6RP.
•CORCORAN, Mrs. Melva Jane, MBA BA FCA CTA *1984;* (Tax Fac), Back Office People Ltd, 66 Pwllmelin Road, CARDIFF, CF5 2NH.
•CORCORAN, Mr. Michael Gerard, BSc ACA *1990;* 49 Naseby Road, SOLIHULL, B91 2DR.
CORCORAN, Mr. Michael John, MA FCA *1987;* Franklin Templeton, One Franklin Parkway, 970 Park Place3rd Floor, SAN MATEOCA 94403-1906, UNITED STATES.
CORCORAN, Mr. Peter Noel, MSc BA ACA *2006;* 77/11 Soi chamchan Thonglor Soi 20 sukhumvit 55 Wattana, BANGKOK 10110, THAILAND.
CORCORAN, Mr. Simon Paul, ACA *1996;* 41 Windmill Avenue, ST. ALBANS, HERTFORDSHIRE, AL4 9SJ.
•CORCORAN, Mr. Stephen Albert Martin, MA(Oxon) FCA FTII *1989;* (Tax Fac), Achilles Accountancy Ltd, 7 Radbroke Close, SANDBACH, CW11 1YT.
CORDAS, Mr. Peter, FCA *1979;* 5 Court Way, LONDON, W3 0PY.
•CORDEIRO, Mr. Kenneth Anthony, FCA *1967;* Kenneth Cordeiro, 26 Baronsmere Road, LONDON, N2 9QE.
CORDELL, Mrs. Elizabeth Clare, MA ACA CTA *2005;* 24 Gladeside, CAMBRIDGE, CB4 1GA.
CORDELL, Mrs. Mary Claire, BA ACA *1996;* 27 Cleaver Square, LONDON, SE11 4EA.
CORDELL, Mr. Mathew James, MA ACA *2009;* 24 Gladeside, CAMBRIDGE, CB4 1GA.
CORDELL, Mr. Michael, FCA *1981;* 3 The Paddocks, Frederick Road, BIRMINGHAM, B15 1JB.
•CORDEN, Mr. Nicholas John, BSc ACA *1986;* (Tax Fac), Summers Morgan, Sheraton House, Lower Road, Chorleywood, RICKMANSWORTH, WD3 5LH.
CORDERO LEDO, Miss. Celia, ACA *2002;* 23 Prospect St Paddington, SYDNEY, NSW 2021, AUSTRALIA.
CORDERY, Mr. Antony John, BA FCA *1975;* C J Wildbird Foods Ltd, The Rea, Upton Magna, SHREWSBURY, SY4 4UR.
CORDERY, Mr. Jason James, ACA *2000;* 30 Lower Farlington Road, PORTSMOUTH, PO6 1JH.
•CORDERY, Mr. Julian, ACA FCCA *2009;* Gibson McKerrell Brown LLP, 14 Rutland Square, EDINBURGH, EH1 2BD.
CORDERY, Mrs. Sarah Margaret, BSc ACA *2006;* 3 Madhuran Court, London Road, ROCHESTER, ME2 3HS.
CORDEY, Mr. Neil Arthur, BA ACA *1979;* Shell Inernational B.V., PO Box 162, 2501 AN THE HAGUE, NETHERLANDS.
CORDINER, Mr. Brian Robert, BSc FCA *1975;* Flat 7, The Elms, Elmfield Road, Gosforth, NEWCASTLE UPON TYNE, NE3 4BD.
CORDINER, Mr. John Alexander, MBA FCA *1967;* Flat 4, Beachline Appartments, Tower Street, ST.PAULS BAY, MALTA.
CORDINER, Mr. Steven Robert, ACA MAAT *2004;* with KPMG LLP, 15 Canada Square, LONDON, E14 5GL.
CORDINGLEY, Mrs. Alison, BSc ACA *2006;* 407 Transport House, 1 The Cresent, SALFORD, M5 4JN.
CORDINGLEY, Miss. Susan Jane, BA ACA *1991;* 1 Sharon Road, LONDON, W4 4PD.
•CORDLE, Mrs. Nicola Louise, ACA MAAT *2004;* Foreshore Accountancy, Balmoral, Shotley Road, Chelmondiston, IPSWICH, IP9 1EE.
CORDLE, Miss. Sarah Joy, MA ACA *1999;* 27 Bucknell Avenue, Pangbourne, READING, RG8 7JU.
CORDOCK, Mr. Robert, BA ACA *2011;* Ground Floor Flat, 46a Leathwaite Road, LONDON, SW11 6RS.
CORDRAN, Mr. John Peter Robert, FCA *1969;* 10 Woodlands, Welshwood Park, COLCHESTER, CO4 3JA.
CORDREY, Mr. Peter Graham, MSc FCA *1971;* Ockham End, Old Lane, COBHAM, KT11 1NF. (Life Member)
CORDWELL, Mr. Geoffrey, BSc ACA *1985;* 63 Hughenden Lane, GLASGOW, G12 9XN.
CORDWELL, Miss. Helen Louise, BA ACA *1998;* 24 Park Avenue, Hawarden, DEESIDE, FLINTSHIRE, CH5 3HZ.
CORDWELL, Mr. Ian Derek, BA FCA *1988;* Keepers Cottage, Hanford, BLANDFORD FORUM, DORSET, DT11 8PS.
CORDY, Miss. Fiona Maria, BA ACA *1991;* 55 Knightwood Crescent, NEW MALDEN, KT3 5JP.
CORDY, Mr. Martin David, BSc ACA *2004;* Flat 2, 53 Holmdale, SIDMOUTH, DEVON, EX10 8DN.
CORDY, Miss. Michelle Louise, BA ACA *2007;* 153 Longfleet Road, POOLE, BH15 2HS.
CORDY, Miss. Sarah, ACA *2009;* 25 Montacute Way, WIMBORNE, DORSET, BH21 1UB.
CORE, Mr. Roland William, BSc FCA *1988;* 7 Anshaw Close, Belmont, BOLTON, BL7 8BS.
COREN, Mr. Clive Simon, ACA *2011;* 54 The Avenue, Muswell Hill, LONDON, N10 2QL.
CORERA, Miss. Vanessa Mary Natasha, BSc ACA *2007;* 45 boulevard carl vogt, 1205 GENEVA, SWITZERLAND.
CORFIELD, Mr. Alasdair Macleod, BA ACA *1992;* 26 Princes Road, Gosforth, NEWCASTLE UPON TYNE, NE3 5AL.
•CORFIELD, Mrs. Anne Helen, ACA *1988;* Anne Corfield, 15 Curzon Way, Chelmer Village, CHELMSFORD, CM2 6PF.
CORFIELD, Mr. Christopher Andrew, BSc ACA *1992;* 5 Tarragon Close, BRACKNELL, RG12 2BZ.
CORFIELD, Mr. Graham John, BSc ACA *1993;* Greencroft House, Bunstrux, TRING, HERTFORDSHIRE, HP23 4HT.
•ⓘCORFIELD, Mr. Ian James, ACA *1997;* with KPMG LLP, 15 Canada Square, LONDON, E14 5GL.
•CORFIELD, Miss. Melanie Rosalind, ACA ACMA *2010;* Morgan Griffiths LLP, Cross Chambers, 9 High Street, NEWTOWN, POWYS, SY16 2NY.
CORFIELD, Mr. Philip David, BSc ACA *1998;* (Tax Fac), 70 Highfields Road, Chasetown, BURNTWOOD, STAFFORDSHIRE, WS7 4QU.
CORFIELD, Ms. Samantha Jayne, LLB ACA *2001;* 28 The Lorne, Bookham, LEATHERHEAD, SURREY, KT23 4JZ.
•ⓘCORFIELD, Mr. Timothy Frank, LLB FCA FABRP *1984;* Griffin & King Limited, 26/28 Goodall Street, WALSALL, WS1 1QL. See also Griffin & King
CORIN, Mr. Anthony Hugo, MA FCA *1973;* Brook Farm, Wet Lane, Boxted, COLCHESTER, CO4 5TN.
•ⓘCORK, Mr. David Jenner, FCA *1973;* (Tax Fac), McCabe Ford Williams, 2 The Links, HERNE BAY, KENT, CT6 7GQ.
CORK, Miss. Naomi, ACA *2009;* 7 Woodview Crescent, Hildenborough, TONBRIDGE, KENT, TN11 9HD.
CORK, Mr. Philip, BA FCA *1977;* 1185 Landings Run, WEST PALM BEACH, FL 33413, UNITED STATES.
CORK, Mr. Stephen Richard, BSc FCA *1972;* 1 Sandringham Close, Barrowford, NELSON, LANCASHIRE, BB9 6PT. (Life Member)
CORKE, Mr. Alexander, ACA *1997;* 59 Highview Gardens, POTTERS BAR, HERTFORDSHIRE, EN6 5PL.
CORKE, Mr. David Arthur, FCA *1967;* 40 Maplehurst Road, CHICHESTER, WEST SUSSEX, PO19 6RP.
CORKE, Mr. Derek Anthony, FCA *1966;* 7 Watergate Road, NEWPORT, ISLE OF WIGHT, PO30 1XN. (Life Member)
CORKE, Mr. James William, BSc ACA *1982;* Level 1, 2 Willis Street, WELLINGTON, NEW ZEALAND.
CORKE, Mrs. Jennifer, BA(Hons) ACA *2003;* Bupa Care Services, Outwood Lane, Horsforth, LEEDS, LS18 4UP.
CORKE, Mr. Richard Dudley, BA FCA *1967;* 12 Edgehill Road, CLEVEDON, AVON, BS21 7BZ.
CORKER, Mr. Eric, BA FCA *1962;* Silver Birch, 3 Wentworth Road, Four Oaks, SUTTON COLDFIELD, B74 2SG.
CORKER, Mr. James Ashley, BA ACA *1996;* The Crescent, 30 Crescent Road, Locks Heath, SOUTHAMPTON, SO31 6PF.
CORKER, Mr. John Richard Nicholas, BA ACA *1992;* 112 Selby Road, NOTTINGHAM, NG2 7BA.
CORKER, Mr. Matthew Nicholas, BA ACA *1999;* Seven Trent Plc, Seven Trent Centre, PO Box 5309, COVENTRY, CV3 9FJ.
•CORKERY, Mr. Edward Frank, ACA *1991;* Cohen Corkery Limited, 30 Chertsey Road, WOKING, SURREY, GU21 5AJ. See also Cohen Corkery
CORKETT, Mr. Jonathan Michael Richard, MChem ACA *2009;* 98 St. Johns Road, EPPING, ESSEX, CM16 5DP.
CORKETT, Mr. Richard Arthur John, BA FCA *1973;* Trimmings By Design Ltd, Gresham Road, DERBY, DE24 8AW.
CORKILL, Mr. Robert Keith, BSc ACA *1994;* Chamberlain Fund Services Ltd, 3rd Floor Exchange House, 54-62 Athol Street, Douglas, ISLE OF MAN, IM1 1JD.
CORKIN, Mrs. Julie Louise, ACA *2007;* Pharm Research Associates International Pacific House, Imperial Way, READING, RG2 0TD.
CORKING, Mr. Brian Martin, BSc ACA *2006;* (Tax Fac), 120 Wraysbury Drive, WEST DRAYTON, MIDDLESEX, UB7 7FR.
CORKISH, Mr. Alan Edward, ACA *1993;* PO Box 11772, GEORGETOWN, GRAND CAYMAN, KY1-1009, CAYMAN ISLANDS.
CORKISH, Ms. Julie Margaret, BA ACA *1993;* BPP Professional Education Ground Floor, 401 Grafton Gate, MILTON KEYNES, MK9 1AQ.
CORLESS, Mr. Alexander, MSc BA FCA *1976;* 90 Old Lane, Rainford, ST.HELENS, MERSEYSIDE, WA11 8JJ. (Life Member)
CORLESS, Mrs. Christine, BSc FCA *1984;* 1 Eddies Lane, Elford, TAMWORTH, B79 9BW.
CORLESS, Mr. Michael John, BA ACA *1986;* North Heath, Carmelstead Close, Frankton Avenue, HAYWARDS HEATH, RH16 3AT.
CORLESS, Mr. Stephen David, BA ACA *1987;* 86 Kelham Hall Drive, Wheatley, OXFORD, OX33 1YB.
CORLESS, Mr. William Richard, BSc ACA *1984;* 8 Dawson Road, Heald Green, CHEADLE, SK8 3AE.
CORLETT, Mr. Alan Stephen, FCA *1984;* Firstrand Trustees Ltd, PO Box 602, GUERNSEY, GY1 4NL.
CORLETT, Mr. Colin Graham Fynlo, BSc FCA *1981;* 3 Rose Paddock, Heads Nook, BRAMPTON, CA8 9AN.
CORLETT, Mr. Daniel, ACA *2010;* 12 Elia Street, LONDON, N1 8DE.
•CORLETT, Mr. George James Brian, FCA *1971;* (Tax Fac), Rothman Pantall LLP, 114 Christchurch Road, RINGWOOD, HAMPSHIRE, BH24 1DP.
•CORLETT, Mr. John Kenneth, ACA *1984;* (Tax Fac), Corlett & Co Ltd, Ellan Vannin, Baldrine, ISLE OF MAN, IM4 6HA.
CORLETT, Mr. Ronald William, FCA *1951;* Grenaby, 1 Links Close, Peel, ISLE OF MAN, IM5 1DG. (Life Member)
CORLETT, Mr. Steven, ACA *1982;* Moss Cottage, Macclesfield Road, Holmes Chapel, CREWE, CW4 8AH.
CORLEY, Mr. Dominic Anthony Thomas, BA ACA CPA *2000;* MAXIMUS INC, 11419 Sunset Hills Road, RESTON, VA 20190, UNITED STATES.
CORLEY, Mr. Kevin Patrick, LLB ACA *1995;* U P S Ltd, 22 Changi South Ave 2, SINGAPORE, SINGAPORE.
CORLEY, Mr. Peter Francis Macintyre, FCA *1967;* 142 North Road, HERTFORD, SG14 2BZ.
CORLEY, Mr. Raymond Peter, MA ACA *1989;* 141 Ridgewood Drive, Pensby, WIRRAL, CH61 8SE.
CORLEY, Mr. Simon Arthur, BSc ACA *1991;* Orchard House, Cowfold Lane, Rotherwick, HOOK, RG27 9BP.
CORMACK, Mr. Alistair, ACA *2000;* Dawson & Sanderson Accounts, Ridley Place, NEWCASTLE UPON TYNE, NE1 8JW.
CORMACK, Mr. Andrew, BA ACA *1995;* Genworth Financial Building 11 Chiswick Park, 566 Chiswick High Road, LONDON, W4 5XR.
CORMACK, Mr. Andrew, BSc ACA *2000;* Flat D, 132 Elgin Avenue, LONDON, W9 2NS.
•CORMACK, Mr. Andrew Stephen, FCA *1974;* Royd House Farm, Sharp Lane, Almondbury, HUDDERSFIELD, HD4 6SX.
CORMACK, Mrs. Samantha Jane, BA ACA *2000;* High Lees Farm, Sheffield Road, Hathersage, HOPE VALLEY, DERBYSHIRE, S32 1DA.
•CORMACK, Mr. Scott Roger, ACA *1979;* KPMG LLP, 15 Canada Square, LONDON, E14 5GL. See also KPMG Europe LLP
•CORMACK, Mr. Thomas Christopher, BA FCA *1997;* MaxAim LLP, United Business Centre, 1 Mariner Court, Calder Park, WAKEFIELD, WEST YORKSHIRE WF4 3FL.
CORMANO, Mr. Antonio, BSc ACA *2006;* 43 Church End, Biddenham, BEDFORD, MK40 4AS.
CORMIE, Miss. Linsey, ACA *2008;* Lynemouth Smelter, Alcan Smelting & Power UK, ASHINGTON, NORTHUMBERLAND, NE63 9YH.
CORNABY, Mr. Jonathon James, BA ACA *1996;* Flat 2, 88 Cromwell Avenue, Highgate, LONDON, N6 5HQ.
CORNALL, Mr. Robert James, BA FCA *1990;* Dunstan Steads Farmhouse, Dunstan Steads, Embleton, ALNWICK, NORTHUMBERLAND, NE66 3DT.
•CORNE, Mr. Stephen, BSc ACA *1981;* (Tax Fac), March:Engenus, 5B The Stables, Newby Hall, Ripon, KNARESBOROUGH, NORTH YORKSHIRE HG4 5AE.
CORNEA, Miss. Anca-Maria, ACA *2008;* 16 Weightman House, 124A Spa Road, LONDON, SE16 3FG.
CORNECK, The Revd. Warrington Graham, FCA *1960;* 42 Nadine Street, LONDON, SE7 7PG.
CORNELIUS, Mr. Anthony John, FCA *1964;* Flat 1, Broomhill Court, Esher Close, ESHER, SURREY, KT10 9LL. (Life Member)
CORNELIUS, Mr. George Charles Caswell, FCA *1963;* 11 Loddington Hall, Main Street, Loddington, KETTERING, NORTHAMPTONSHIRE, NN14 1PP. (Life Member)
•CORNELIUS, Mr. Ian, BSc ACA *1992;* Cashability Limited, The Office, 4 Shaw Green Lane, Prestbury, CHELTENHAM, GLOUCESTERSHIRE GL52 3BP. See also Ambitious Minds Limited
CORNELIUS, Mr. Keith Melville, FCA *1971;* 65 High Beeches, BANSTEAD, SM7 1NW. (Life Member)
CORNELIUS, Miss. Mandy, BSc ACA *2006;* 26 Fox Road, Lower Bourne, FARNHAM, SURREY, GU10 3NZ.
CORNELIUS, Mr. Michael, MA FCA *1960;* 7 Leaside Court, MANCHESTER, MO 63011-4029, UNITED STATES. (Life Member)
CORNELIUS, Mr. Paul Anthony, BA ACA *1986;* (Tax Fac), Pricewaterhousecoopers Singapore, PWC Building, 8 Cross Street, #17-00, SINGAPORE 048424, SINGAPORE.
CORNELL, Mr. Andrew Robert, MSc ACA *1996;* Newcroft, Horcott Road, FAIRFORD, GLOUCESTERSHIRE, GL7 4DD.
CORNELL, Mr. Gerald Charles John, FCA *1968;* 5 Cheviot Close, Astley Cross, STOURPORT-ON-SEVERN, WORCESTERSHIRE, DY13 0NX.
CORNELL, Mrs. Kathleen, BA ACA *2006;* 31 Turners Close, Southwater, HORSHAM, WEST SUSSEX, RH13 9LJ.
CORNELL, Mrs. Miranda, BA ACA *1992;* Cornwall & Isles of Scilly Pct, Sedgemoor Centre, Priory Road, ST. AUSTELL, CORNWALL, PL25 5AS.
CORNER, Mr. Alexander, FCA *1963;* 31 Cardinals Walk, HAMPTON, TW12 2TR.
CORNER, Mrs. Alison Margaret, BA ACA *1985;* 57 Mayfield Avenue, ORPINGTON, BR6 0AJ.
CORNER, Mr. Andrew Scott, BSc ACA *1998;* 51 Gordon Street, MANLY VALE, NSW 2093, AUSTRALIA.
•CORNER, Miss. Christine Elizabeth, BSc FCA *1986;* Grant Thornton UK LLP, Grant Thornton House, 22 Melton Street, Euston Square, LONDON, NW1 2EP. See also Grant Thornton LLP
•CORNER, Mr. Iain, BA FCA *1986;* with RSM Tenon Audit Limited, Tenon House, Ferryboat Lane, SUNDERLAND, SR5 3JN.
CORNER, Mr. Ian John, BA ACA *2000;* 40 Snowshill Close, REDDITCH, WORCESTERSHIRE, B98 8RG.
CORNER, Mr. Ian Stuart, BSc ACA *1988;* 1600 Arlington Business Park, Theale, READING, RG7 4SA.
CORNER, Mr. Julian Nicholas, BA ACA *1998;* 6 Church View, Sunderland Road, LONDON, SE23 2PJ.
•CORNER, Mr. Stephen Ashley, LLB FCA *1987;* (Tax Fac), Barnes Roffe LLP, 35 Great Marlborough Street, LONDON, W1F 7JF.
CORNER, Mr. Stephen Donald, BSc FCA *1984;* 57 Mayfield Avenue, ORPINGTON, BR6 0AJ.
CORNER, Mrs. Wendy Jayne, LLB(Hons) ACA *2001;* Astrazeneca Alderley House, Alderley Park, MACCLESFIELD, CHESHIRE, SK10 4TF.

CORNES, Mrs. Alison, ACA *2003;* 9 Levengreave Close, Belvedere Farm, Hindley, WIGAN, LANCASHIRE, WN2 4GG.

CORNES, Mr. Andrew David, BSc FCA *1995;* with KPMG, Cairns Corporate Tower, Level 13, 15 Lake Street, P.O. Box 7200, CAIRNS QLD 4870 AUSTRALIA.

CORNES, Mr. Daniel Andrew, BSc ACA *2003;* with Grant Thornton UK LLP, 4 Hardman Square, Spinningfields, MANCHESTER, M3 3EB.

CORNES, Miss. Dianne Ruth Hambleton, BSc ACA *1988;* 3 Laurence Court, 36 Lansdowne Road, LONDON, W11 2LX.

CORNES, Mr. Ian Richard, BA ACA *1991;* 20 Celandine Close, Thornbury, BRISTOL, BS35 1UB.

CORNES, Mrs. Jacqueline Anne, BSc ACA *1979;* White Cottage, Pinchinthorpe, GUISBOROUGH, TS14 8HE.

CORNES, Miss. Jennifer Lilian, BA ACA *1994;* 154 Camberwell New Road, LONDON, SE5 0RR.

CORNES, Mr. Michael Henry, FCA *1972;* Study Group UK Limited, Voyager House, 1 Billinton Way, BRIGHTON, BN1 4LF.

•**CORNES, Mr. Roger Langford, FCA** *1970;* with PM+M Solutions for Business LLP, Greenbank Technology Park, Challenge Way, BLACKBURN, BB1 5QB.

CORNEY, Mr. Alan, FCA *1973;* Apartment 21, Wells House, Brodrick Drive, ILKLEY, WEST YORKSHIRE, LS29 9SP.

CORNEY, Mr. Andrew Derrick, BA ACA *1989;* Custompac Ltd, Delta Works, 27 Methley Road, CASTLEFORD, WEST YORKSHIRE, WF10 1PA.

CORNEY, Mr. Darryl John, ACA CA(AUS) *2010;* Inexus, Ocean Park House, East Tyndall Street, CARDIFF, CF24 5GT.

•**CORNEY, Mr. David Charles Masse, FCA** *1954;* 3819 Maplecrest Road, Woodmere Village, CLEVELAND, OH 44122-4415, UNITED STATES.

CORNEY, Mr. David John, FCA *1964;* Wayside Cottage, Chessetts Wood Road, Lapworth, SOLIHULL, B94 6EL.

•**CORNEY, Mr. Graham Charles, FCA FCCA** *1974;* Harwood Hutton Limited, 22 Wycombe End, BEACONSFIELD, BUCKINGHAMSHIRE, HP9 1NB. See also Harwood Hutton Tax Advisory LLP

CORNEY, Mr. Hugo Frederick William, BA(Hons) ACA MBA *2002;* 16 Badgerdale Way, Littleover, DERBY, DE23 3ZA.

CORNEY, Mr. James Benedict, ACA *2008;* 56 Yester Road, CHISLEHURST, KENT, BR7 5HR.

CORNEY, Mr. John William, BSc ACA *1993;* 26 Brayton Park, KILCOCK, COUNTY KILDARE, IRELAND.

CORNEY, Mr. Patrick, FCA *1962;* Sunset House, 3 The Glebe, Sudbury Road, Lavenham, SUDBURY, SUFFOLK CO10 9SN. (Life Member)

CORNEY, Mrs. Sarah, BSc(Hons) ACA *2003;* Rest Harrow, 3 Heathfield, CHISLEHURST, BR7 6AF.

CORNFIELD, Mr. Andrew Tresham, BEng ACA *1996;* BHP Billiton Iron Ore, 225 St Georges Terrace, PERTH, WA 6000, AUSTRALIA.

CORNFIELD, Mr. Graham Hugh, FCA *1968;* 8 Beausale Drive, Knowle, SOLIHULL, B93 0NS.

CORNFIELD, Mr. Roger William, FCA *1964;* 94 Lower Road, Fetcham, LEATHERHEAD, KT22 9NG. (Life Member)

CORNFORD, Miss. Christine Anne, BSc(Hons) ACA *2000;* 8 Nursery Hill, St. Andrews Place, HITCHIN, HERTFORDSHIRE, SG4 9GD.

CORNFORD, Mr. Jeremy Richard, BA FCA *1973;* Barbers Cottage, High Street, Rotherfield, CROWBOROUGH, TN6 3LJ.

CORNFORTH, Mr. Graham Robert, BA(Hons) ACA *2004;* 7 Trevithick Close, Eaglescliffe, STOCKTON-ON-TEES, CLEVELAND, TS16 0RY.

CORNFORTH, Mr. Harold Edward, FCA *1975;* Unit 8, Hockliffe Business Centre, Watling Street, Hockliffe, LEIGHTON BUZZARD, BEDFORDSHIRE LU7 9NB.

CORNFORTH, Miss. Lynn Janice, BSc ACA *1990;* Antler-Ridge, Willisham, IPSWICH, IP8 4SP.

CORNICK, Miss. Natasha Liane, BSc ACA *1992;* 9 Croft Road, THAME, OXFORDSHIRE, OX9 3JE.

CORNICK, Mr. Roy John, BA ACA *1994;* 2 Manor Farm Close, Lower Blandford St. Mary, BLANDFORD FORUM, DORSET, DT11 9ND.

CORNICK, Miss. Sarah Hilary, BA(Hons) ACA *2003;* 5 Kingsmead Close, TEDDINGTON, TW11 9EP.

•**CORNISH, Mr. Alan David, ACA** *1988;* Berry & Co, 7 Clarendon Place, King Street, MAIDSTONE, ME14 1BQ.

CORNISH, Mr. Daniel Lee, ACA *2008;* 47 Tudor Road, NEWTON ABBOT, DEVON, TQ12 1HT.

•**CORNISH, Mr. David Alan, FCA** *1972;* David Cornish, Marlins, Back Lane, CHALFONT ST. GILES, HP8 4PF.

CORNISH, Mr. Eric John, FCA *1958;* The Oaks, Stoke Poges Lane, Stoke Poges, SLOUGH, SL2 4NP. (Life Member)

CORNISH, Miss. Jennifer Lynn, ACA *2007;* Flat 12, Kinnear Apartments, Chadwell Lane, LONDON, N8 7RB.

CORNISH, Mr. John Essex, BSc FCA *1967;* Oakwood, Quarry Road, OXTED, RH8 9HF. (Life Member)

CORNISH, Mr. Keith Graham, BA FCA *1975;* 24 Blenheim Mews, SHEFFIELD, S11 9PR.

CORNISH, Mr. Malcolm Peter Ralph, BSc FCA *1978;* Wattletree, 18 Oakwood Road, WINDLESHAM, GU20 6JD.

CORNISH, Mr. Mark Conrad, BSc FCA *1997;* 7-9 Rickett Street, LONDON, SW6 1RU.

CORNISH, Mr. Michael, BA ACA *1986;* 80 Seven Bridges Road, CHAPPAQUA, NY 10514, UNITED STATES.

CORNISH, Mr. Michael Bruce, FCA *1970;* Ravenstone Lodge, Bassenthwaite, KESWICK, CUMBRIA, CA12 4QG.

CORNISH, Mr. Neil Roy, BA ACA *1998;* 10 Clover Way, Paddock Wood, TONBRIDGE, KENT, TN12 6BQ.

•**CORNISH, Mrs. Patricia Susan, FCA CTA** *1986;* Birchway Tax Ltd, Birchway Farm, Mundham, NORWICH, NR14 6HE.

CORNISH, Mr. Paul Radford, BSc FCA *1982;* 11 Cambria Rd, DEVONPORT 0624, NEW ZEALAND.

CORNISH, Mr. Peter, BSc ACA *1989;* 3 Meadow Way, Stockton Lane, YORK, YO31 1EQ.

CORNISH, Mr. Philip James, BA ACA *1986;* 16 Aragon Street, INDOOROOPILLY, QLD 4068, AUSTRALIA.

•**CORNISH, Mr. Philip Richard, BSc ACA** *1992;* P Cornish, 4 Deacon Close, Bowdon, ALTRINCHAM, CHESHIRE, WA14 3ND.

•**CORNISH, Mr. Roger Frederick, FCA** *1966;* R F Cornish, 22 Bayview Road, WHITSTABLE, KENT, CT5 4NP.

CORNISH, Mr. Roland David, MA *1984;* Beaumont Cornish Ltd, 29 Wilson Street, LONDON, EC2M 2SJ.

CORNISH, Mr. Roy Alan, ACA *1980;* SABMiller PLC, Po Box 6335, JOHANNESBURG, 2000, SOUTH AFRICA.

CORNISH, Mr. Samuel Roy, ACA *2009;* 96 St. Ann's Hill, LONDON, SW18 2RR.

CORNISH, Miss. Victoria Michelle, BSc(Hons) ACA *2006;* Flat 2, 103 Shooters Hill Road, LONDON, SE3 7HU.

CORNMELL, Mr. Paul John, BA ACA *2007;* Flat 2, 10 Archer Road, PENARTH, SOUTH GLAMORGAN, CF64 3LS.

•**CORNMELL, Mr. Steven Joseph, BA FCA** *1990;* Grant Thornton UK LLP, 30 Finsbury Square, LONDON, EC2P 2YU. See also Grant Thornton LLP

CORNTHWAITE, Mr. Christopher John, BSc FCA *1984;* Mulberry House, Chart Lane, Brasted Chart, WESTERHAM, KENT, TN16 1LU.

CORNTHWAITE, Mr. James Cottam, ACA *2009;* Moors Farm, Mill Lane, Hambleton, POULTON-LE-FYLDE, LANCASHIRE, FY6 9DE.

CORNTHWAITE, Mrs. Lucy Caroline, BSc ACA *2007;* 14 Portman Street, Calverley, PUDSEY, WEST YORKSHIRE, LS28 5PG.

CORNTHWAITE, Mr. Paul Alexander, BSc ACA *2008;* No.1 Godwin Street, BRADFORD, BD1 2SU.

CORNTHWAITE, Mr. Peter John, BA ACA *1986;* Blackpool Pleasure Beach Ltd, Ocean Boulevard, BLACKPOOL, FY4 1EZ.

CORNWALL, Mr. Christopher Philip, FCA *1970;* 24 Acorn Grove, Ditton, AYLESFORD, ME20 6EW. (Life Member)

CORNWALL, Miss. Claire Louise, BA ACA *2000;* 552 Milverton Boulevard, TORONTO M4C1X5, ON, CANADA.

CORNWALL, Mr. Douglas Charles, FCA *1957;* Domaine De La Roche, Le Bigard, Forest, GUERNSEY, GY8 0HT. (Life Member)

CORNWALL, Mr. Ian Sinclair, BA ACA *1981;* Vine Cottage The Street, West Clandon, GUILDFORD, SURREY, GU4 7TJ.

CORNWALL, Mrs. Katherine Anne, BA ACA *1981;* Vine Cottage, The Street, West Clandon, GUILDFORD, SURREY, GU4 7TJ.

CORNWALL, Mr. Stephen Barrie, MA FCA *1996;* F.Hinds Ltd, 24 Park Road, UXBRIDGE, UB8 1NH.

CORNWALL-LEGH, Mrs. Ann Helen, BA ACA *2003;* Mill House South, West Lane, High Legh, KNUTSFORD, CHESHIRE, WA16 6LS.

CORNWELL, Mr. Anthony Bruce, FCA *1968;* 134 London Road, BAGSHOT, GU19 5BZ.

CORNWELL, Mrs. Charlotte Ann, ACA *2008;* 161 Carter Street, Fordham, ELY, CAMBRIDGESHIRE, CB7 5JU.

CORNWELL, Mr. Richard John, FCA *1966;* 226 Stanley Park Road, CARSHALTON, SM5 3JP.

CORNWELL, Mr. Roger Franklin, FCA *1959;* DP World, PO Box 17000, DUBAI, UNITED ARAB EMIRATES. (Life Member)

CORNWELL, Mr. Tom, ACA *2008;* 48 West Street, STOURBRIDGE, WEST MIDLANDS, DY8 1XN.

CORP, Mr. Lester Desmond, BSc(Econ) FCA FCMI *1970;* 3 Sunte Avenue, Lindfield, HAYWARDS HEATH, WEST SUSSEX, RH16 2AB.

•**CORP, Ms. Nicola Catherine, BA ACA** *1986;* PricewaterhouseCoopers LLP, 1 Embankment Place, LONDON, WC2N 6RH. See also PricewaterhouseCoopers

CORPES, Mr. Karl Edward, ACA *1993;* 76 Addison Road, GUILDFORD, GU1 3QF.

CORPS, Mr. Robin Terry, BSc ACA *2002;* 10 Deanhead Grove, YORK, YO30 4UH.

CORPUZ, Miss. June Adeline, BA ACA *1984;* 4 Glenilla Road, LONDON, NW3 4AW.

CORR, Mr. Alan Joseph Arthur, BBS ACA *1990;* Unit 41D, Tower 3, Tregunter, 14 Tregunter Path, MID LEVELS, HONG KONG ISLAND HONG KONG SAR.

CORR, Mr. Gareth Richard, BEng ACA *1997;* 2 Marlow Road, ARTARMON, NSW 2064, AUSTRALIA.

CORRADI, Miss. Daniela, ACA *2009;* Mandeville Lodge, 50 Village Road, ENFIELD, MIDDLESEX, EN1 2ET.

CORRALL, Mr. Gareth Luke, ACA *2003;* with Moore Stephens (South) LLP, 9 St. Johns Place, NEWPORT, ISLE OF WIGHT, PO30 1LH.

CORRAN, Mrs. Caroline Elizabeth, BA ACA *2002;* 369 Luton Road, HARPENDEN, HERTFORDSHIRE, AL5 3LZ.

CORRAN, Mr. Stephen Paul, BSc ACA *2006;* Bridgewaters, 26 Victoria Street, Douglas, ISLE OF MAN, IM1 2LE.

CORRE, Mr. John Howard Abraham, FCA *1966;* Flat 342 Derech Bet Lechem, 93504 JERUSALEM, ISRAEL.

CORRIE, Mr. Alistair George, BA FCA *1994;* Cheriton, Basingstoke Road, Riseley, READING, RG7 1QL.

CORRIE, Miss. Frances Elaine, MA ACA *1986;* Taxaid, Unit 304-305, 164-180 Union Street, LONDON, SE1 0LH.

CORRIE, Miss. Hannah Mary, BA(Hons) ACA *2004;* 5 Sommerville Mews, Pudsey, LEEDS, LS28 6PN.

CORRIE, Mr. John Roy, MA FCA *1971;* Lugar Paserra, Covas, Villa Nova De Cerveira, 4920 OLR OPORTO, PORTUGAL. (Life Member)

•**CORRIE, Mr. Martin Francis, BSc FCA** *1979;* Hicks and Company, Vaughan Chambers, Vaughan Road, HARPENDEN, AL5 4EE.

CORRIGAN, Miss. Caroline Patricia, BA ACA *1989;* 24 Hookfield, EPSOM, KT19 8JG.

•**CORRIGAN, Mr. Colin Nicholas, ACA ACCA** *2008;* Cooper Paul, Abacus House, 14-18 Forest Road, LOUGHTON, IG10 1DX.

CORRIGAN, Mr. Edward Charles, FCA *1972;* Cornercroft, 24 Ferndale Avenue, CHERTSEY, KT16 9RB.

•**CORRIGAN, Mr. Edward John, BA FCA** *1987;* Corrigan Associates Bristol LLP, Venturers House, King Street, BRISTOL, BS1 4PB.

CORRIGAN, Mr. Francis, MA ACA *2004;* Tower Bridge Court, The West of England Ship Owners Insurance Services Ltd, 224-226 Tower Bridge Road, LONDON, SE1 2UP.

CORRIGAN, Mr. John Joseph, FCA *1970;* 3 The Lindens, Beechwood Park, HEMEL HEMPSTEAD, HP3 0DD.

CORRIN, Miss. Elizabeth Jane, BSc FCA *1990;* H M Treasury, 1 Horse Guards Road, LONDON, SW1A 2HQ.

CORRIN, John Richard, Esq CBE FCA *1961;* (Member of Council 1991 - 2001), High Stead, Ben Rhydding Drive, ILKLEY, WEST YORKSHIRE, LS29 8BQ.

CORRIN, Mr. Stephen George Houghton, MA ACA CTA *1983;* with Baker Tilly Corporate Finance LLP, 25 Farringdon Street, LONDON, EC4A 4AB.

CORRY, Mrs. Claire Louise, BEng ACA *1999;* 14 Ailsa Road, HOLYWOOD, COUNTY DOWN, BT18 0AS.

CORRY, Mr. Michael Robert, ACA *1984;* 32 Seaton Street, GLEN IRIS, Vic 3146, AUSTRALIA.

CORRY, Mr. Robert John, BA FCA *1978;* London & Associated Properties, 22a St. James's Square, LONDON, SW1Y 4JH.

CORRY, Mr. Stephen David, MA FCA *1963;* Flat 204, Av Vieira Souto 366, RIO DE JANEIRO, 22 420 000, BRAZIL. (Life Member)

CORSAN, Mr. Robert John, BA ACA *1980;* 59 Magdalen Road, LONDON, SW18 3ND.

CORSAN, Mr. Sidney John David, FCA *1951;* Orchard House, Orchard Lane, CHICHESTER, PO20 7AD. (Life Member)

CORSER, Mr. Patrick John Bidlake, FCA *1966;* Flat 2, 16 Upper Brook Street, LONDON, W1K 7PT. (Life Member)

CORSON, Mr. John Roger, MA FCA *1964;* Guardian Managment SL, Club Tarahal, Calle Acevino 49, Urbanizacion La Paz, Puerto De La Cruz, 38400 TENERIFE CANARY ISLANDS SPAIN.

•**CORSON, Mr. Myles Jonathan David, BA ACA** *2000;* Ernst & Young LLP, 1 More London Place, LONDON, SE1 2AF. See also Ernst & Young Europe LLP

CORT, Mr. Roger, BSc FCA *1969;* 1 Church Road, Seal, SEVENOAKS, TN15 0AU.

CORTACANS, Mr. Mark David, BSc ACA *1990;* 94 Nelson Road, LONDON, N8 9RT. (Life Member)

CORTE, Mr. James Roger, BSc ACA *2003;* 17 Chestnut Avenue Littleton, WINCHESTER, HAMPSHIRE, SO22 6PL.

CORTEEN, Mr. John Christopher, FCA *1986;* 5 Copperfield Close, Worsthorne, BURNLEY, BB10 3RT.

CORTI, Mr. Andrew David, BSc ACA *1997;* 7 St. Stephens Road, LONDON, E3 5JD.

CORTI, Miss. Lisa Ann, BA(Hons) ACA *2003;* 54 Massingberd Way, LONDON, SW17 6AD.

CORTIS, Mr. Mark Patrick, BSc ACA *1987;* 1 Crane Close, Little Cransley, KETTERING, NORTHAMPTONSHIRE, NN14 1QN.

CORTIS, Mr. Roger James, MA FCA *1967;* Keepers Cottage, Stoke Road, Dunston, NORWICH, NR14 8PE.

•**CORY, Mr. Andrew Timothy, BSc ACA** *1988;* AC Accounting Limited, Glencoe, 3A Springfield, BUCKFASTLEIGH, DEVON, TQ11 0LL.

CORY, Mrs. Catriona Mary Hellen, MA FCA *1990;* 55 Bayside Drive, Browns Bay, AUCKLAND 0630, NEW ZEALAND.

CORY, Mr. Charles Lempriere, BSc FCA *1972;* 7 Keelson Lane, SAVANNAH, GA 31411, UNITED STATES.

CORY, Mr. David John, FCA *1968;* The Outspan, Wilden, STOURPORT-ON-SEVERN, WORCESTERSHIRE, DY13 9JF.

CORY, Mrs. Elizabeth Sheila, FCA *1968;* Cob Cottage, Garth Hill, Pentyrch, CARDIFF, CF15 9NS. (Life Member)

CORY, Mr. John Philip Francis, FCA *1967;* Cob Cottage, Garth Hill, Pentyrch, CARDIFF, CF15 9NS. (Life Member)

CORY, Mr. Nicholas David, BEng ACA *1991;* 55 Bayside Drive, Browns Bay, AUCKLAND 0630, NEW ZEALAND.

CORY, Mr. Rupert William Michael, BSc FCA *1998;* Flat 1, Alexandra Mansions, 347 West End Lane, LONDON, NW6 1LU.

CORY, Mr. Simon Jonathan James, BSc ACA *1996;* Nationwide House, Pipers Way, SWINDON, WILTSHIRE, SN38 3LN.

•**CORY-WRIGHT, Mr. Anthony Johnathan, MA FCA** *1975;* KPMG Moscow 82, IPS Suite 2F9, Heathrow Cube, 9 Arkwright Road, Colnbrook, SLOUGH BERKSHIRE SL3 0HJ.

CORY-WRIGHT, Mrs. Jill, BSc ACA *1992;* Orchard Cottage, Cranleigh Road, Wonersh, GUILDFORD, SURREY, GU5 0QZ.

COSAITIS, Mrs. Caroline, BSc ACA *1995;* 18 Lyford Road, LONDON, SW18 3LG.

COSAITIS, Mr. Mark Anthony, BSc ACA *1994;* 18 Lyford Road, LONDON, SW18 3LG.

COSBY, Mr. Michael Patrick Richard, BA FCA *1991;* Ashleigh, Bowden Hill, Yealmpton, PLYMOUTH, PL8 2JX.

COSE, Mr. John David, FCA *1969;* 16 Phillips Hatch, Wonersh, GUILDFORD, SURREY, GU5 0PX.

COSGROVE, Mrs. Fiona Louise, BA ACA *1992;* 151 Grove Lane, Hale, ALTRINCHAM, WA15 8LR.

•**COSGROVE, Mr. Gerard, FCA** *1981;* Champion Accountants LLP, 1 Worsley Court, High Street, Worsley, MANCHESTER, M28 3NJ. See also Champion Business Solutions Limited, Champion Allwoods Limited, Champion Consulting Ltd, Champion Business Advisors Limited and Champion Howarth Moore Limited

COSGROVE, Mr. Hayden Arthur, LLB FCA *1955;* 44 Baring Avenue, BRADFORD, WEST YORKSHIRE, BD3 7ET. (Life Member)

COSGROVE, Miss. Kathryn, ACA *2008;* 90 Leyburn Road, DARLINGTON, COUNTY DURHAM, DL1 2ES.

COSGROVE, Mr. Peter Robert, FCA *1972;* 28 Mulgrave Road, WHITBY, NORTH YORKSHIRE, YO21 3JS.

•**COSGROVE, Ms. Sally, ACA** *2007;* PricewaterhouseCoopers, 7 More London Riverside, LONDON, SE1 2RT. See also PricewaterhouseCoopers LLP

COSGROVE, Mr. Sean James, BSc(Hons) ACA CTA *2000;* Vodafone Investments Luxembourg Sarl, 15 rue Edward Steichen, L-2540 KIRCHBERG, LUXEMBOURG.

COSGROVE, Mrs. Stephanie Anne, BA ACA *1998;* Stable Cottage, Ashampstead, READING, RG8 8RT.

COSH, Mr. Nicholas John, MA FCA *1972;* 61 Leopold Road, Wimbledon, LONDON, SW19 7JG.

COSHAM, Mr. Andrew Philip, BA(Hons) FCA CA(NZ) *1987;* P O Box 128 139, REMUERA 1541, AUCKLAND, NEW ZEALAND.
COSHAM, Mrs. Fiona Patricia, BA ACA *1987;* 42 Brookville Road, LONDON, SW6 7BJ.
COSHOTT, Mr. Michael David, BA ACA *1998;* 116 Harestock Road, WINCHESTER, HAMPSHIRE, SO22 6NY.
COSKUN, Mr. Timur, MSc ACA *1991;* 21 Park Road, Limpsfield, OXTED, RH8 0AN.
COSMA, Mr. Marios, MA BA(Hons) ACA *2001;* (Tax Fac), K Treppides & Co, Treppides Tower, 9 Kafkasou Street, PO BOX 27142, CY-1642 NICOSIA, CYPRUS.
COSSEY, Miss. Louise Mary, BA FCA *1996;* with KPMG S.A., 1 Cours Valmy, Paris La Défense Cedex, 92923 PARIS LA DÉFENSE, FRANCE.
COSSEY, Mr. Neil James, BSc ACA *1996;* 1 Queens Close, Heaton Mersey, STOCKPORT, CHESHIRE, SK4 3JL.
COSSEY, Mr. Robert John, BA FCA *1981;* 2 Blyth's Wharf, Narrow Street, Limehouse, LONDON, E14 8BF.
COSSINS, Mr. Christopher James, BEng ACA *1991;* 9 Warwick Road, COULSDON, CR5 2EF.
•**COSSINS, Mr. John Christopher, BSc FCA** *1972;* John Cossins & Co, Mulberry House, 11 Oxfield Close, BERKHAMSTED, HP4 3NE.
COSSINS, Mr. Nicholas Scott, BSc ACA *2007;* 27a Midmoor Road, LONDON, SW12 0EW.
COSSINS, Mr. Stephen Peter, FCA *1974;* Maplewood, Park Grove, CHALFONT ST.GILES, HP8 4BG.
COSSLETT, Mr. Edward Peter, FCA *1951;* 1 The Willows, Luston, LEOMINSTER, HEREFORDSHIRE, HR6 0DF. (Life Member)
COSSLETT, Mrs. Kim, BSc ACA CTA *1991;* (Tax Fac), 12 Heol Peredur, Thornhill, CARDIFF, CF14 9HP.
COSSON, Ms. Charlotte, BA(Hons) ACA *2002;* Blackrock, 33 King William Street, LONDON, EC4R 9AS.
COSSON, Mr. Simon Christopher, BCom ACA *1994;* E on UK Plc, Westwood Way, Westwood Business Park, COVENTRY, CV4 8LG.
COSSTICK, Mr. Andrew, ACA *2011;* Flat 5, 12 Gleneldon Road, LONDON, SW16 2AY.
COSSTICK, Mr. Christopher John, FCA *1969;* 22 Shakespeare Road, Hanwell, LONDON, W7 1LR.
•**COSTA, Mr. Amilios Christodoulos, BSc FCA** *1995;* (Tax Fac), KCAS LLP, 3rd Floor, Brook Point, 1412-1420 High Road, LONDON, N20 9BH. See also KCBS LLP
•**COSTA, Mr. David, BSc(Econ) FCA** *1977;* (Tax Fac), Latham Lees Costa, 12 Park St, Lytham, LYTHAM ST. ANNES, FY8 5LU.
COSTA, Mr. Erotokritos, BSc ACA *2009;* 4 Andreas Zakos Street, Engomi, NICOSIA, CYPRUS.
COSTA, Miss. Eve, BSc ACA *1995;* 26 Hamilton Road, Cockfosters, BARNET, EN4 9HE.
COSTA, Miss. Maria, BSc ACA *1998;* Flat J, Rose Court, 11 Mattock Lane, LONDON, W5 5BG.
COSTA, Miss. Victoria Elizabeth, BSc ACA *2001;* 31 Great Eastern Road, Warley, BRENTWOOD, ESSEX, CM14 5EH.
•**COSTA CORREA, Mr. Michael Francis, FCA** *1974;* Michael Costa Correa & Co., 7 Windermere Road, WEST WICKHAM, BR4 9AN.
COSTABILE, Mr. Michael John, BSc ACA *1994;* 6 Thresher Close, LUTON, LU4 0TX.
COSTAIN, Mr. John Andrew, BSc ACA *1991;* Tankers UK agencies Ltd, Moreau House, 116 Brompton Road, LONDON, SW3 1JJ.
COSTAIN, Miss. Laura Mary, BSc ACA *2011;* 17 Chantry Rise, OLNEY, BUCKINGHAMSHIRE, MK46 5FE.
COSTAIN, Mr. Peter John, FCA *1961;* Heronden, Smallhythe Road, TENTERDEN, TN30 7LN.
COSTANZA, Mr. Filippo, BA ACA *1992;* Comet Plc Comet House, Homestead Road, RICKMANSWORTH, HERTFORDSHIRE, WD3 1FX.
COSTARA, Mr. Peter, ACA *1992;* 8 Causeyware Road, Edmonton, LONDON, N9 8BS.
•**COSTAS, Mr. Eraklis, FCA** *1984;* (Tax Fac), Easebay Limited, Unit 3, Gateway Mews, Ringway, LONDON, N11 2UT.
COSTELLA, Mr. Stefano, ACA *1999;* Cisco Systems, 9-11 New Square, FELTHAM, MIDDLESEX, TW14 8HA.
COSTELLO, Mr. David Anthony, FCA *1966;* Ringers, Upper Street, Leeds, MAIDSTONE, KENT, ME17 1SL.
COSTELLO, Ms. Helen Anne, BEd ACA *1992;* Was Tor Chapel, Lydford Station, Lydford, OKEHAMPTON, DEVON, EX20 4BW.
•**COSTELLO, Mr. John Joseph, BA FCA** *1988;* KPMG LLP, St. James's Square, MANCHESTER, M2 6DS. See also KPMG Europe LLP
COSTELLO, Mr. Mark Stephen, ACA BEng(Hons) *2010;* 11 Milne Court, WISHAW, LANARKSHIRE, ML2 8ND.
COSTELLO, Mr. Michael James, BSc ACA *1979;* 11 Shrewsbury Lane, LONDON, SE18 3JE.
COSTELLO, Miss. Michaela Ann, LLB ACA *2002;* 39 St Ann's Hill, Wandsworth, LONDON, SW18 2EZ.
COSTELLO, Ms. Rachel, BA ACA *2010;* with PricewaterhouseCoopers, Mariano Escobedo No 573, Col Polanco Chapultecpec, MEXICO CITY CP 11560, MEXICO.
COSTELLO, Mrs. Rebecca Louise, BA ACA *2005;* 21 Tarvin Avenue, STOCKPORT, CHESHIRE, SK4 5LG.
COSTELLO, Miss. Sarah, BA ACA *2004;* with KPMG LLP, 303 East Wacker Drive, CHICAGO, IL 60601-5255, UNITED STATES.
COSTELLO, Mr. Steven John, BSc ACA *2006;* 30 Bridle Crescent Chapeltown, SHEFFIELD, S35 2QX.
COSTELLO, Mrs. Theresa Mary, BA ACA *1990;* 11 Martlet Close, Wootton, NORTHAMPTON, NN4 6EX.
•**COSTELLO-BYRNE, Mrs. Sarah Elizabeth, ACA FCCA** *2009;* Crowther Beard LLP, 1a Church Street, TEWKESBURY, GLOUCESTERSHIRE, GL20 5PA.
COSTELLOE, Mr. David Michael, FCA *1977;* 25 Sambrook Crescent, MARKET DRAYTON, SHROPSHIRE, TF9 1NG.
COSTELLOE, Mrs. Sian, BSc ACA *2006;* 304 Belvedere Road, BURTON-ON-TRENT, STAFFORDSHIRE, DE13 0RD.
COSTEN, Mr. Matthew John, MEng ACA *2010;* Crowbush, Hadspen, CASTLE CARY, SOMERSET, BA7 7LY.
COSTER, Mr. Graham David, BA FCA *1986;* 50 Clerkenwell Place, Springfield, MILTON KEYNES, MK6 3HF.
COSTER, Mrs. Jane Elizabeth, FCA *1975;* Lye Green House, Lye Green, CROWBOROUGH, EAST SUSSEX, TN6 1UU.
•**COSTER, Mr. Stephen William, FCA** *1975;* (Tax Fac), Unit 275B, The Wenta Business Centre, Colne Way, WATFORD, HERTFORDSHIRE, WD24 7NE.
COSTIGAN, Miss. Anna Frances, BSc ACA *2006;* K P M G Salisbury Square House, 8 Salisbury Square, LONDON, EC4Y 8BB.
COSTIGAN, Miss. Jennifer Anne, BA ACA *2007;* 10 Barn Owl Close, Humberston, GRIMSBY, SOUTH HUMBERSIDE, DN36 4SH.
COSTIGAN, Mrs. Pascale, BSc ACA *2004;* 40 rue des Apennins, 75017 PARIS, FRANCE.
COSTIGAN, Mr. Patrick Michael, BA ACA *2003;* 40 rue des Apennins, 75017 PARIS, FRANCE.
COSTIGAN, Mr. William Patrick, BA ACA *1996;* 2 Downes Close, MACCLESFIELD, CHESHIRE, SK10 3DW.
COSTIGANE, Dr. Helen Bernadette, PhD MA ACA *1986;* 10 Holland Park Avenue, LONDON, W11 3QU.
COSTIN, Mr. James Anthony, BSc(Hons) ACA *2002;* Flat 5 Chloe Court, 79 Worple Road, LONDON, SW19 4LS.
COSTIN, Mr. John Edward, LLB ACA *2003;* 4004a Lake Terrace, Jumeirah Lake Towers, PO Box 116902, DUBAI, AB, UNITED ARAB EMIRATES.
COSTIN, Mr. Ronald Alan Stuart, FCA *1965;* Woodview, Redland End, Speen, PRINCES RISBOROUGH, HP27 0RW. (Life Member)
COSTLEY, Mrs. Jennifer Susan, BA ACA *1996;* The Farmhouse Village Farm Main Road Easter Compton, BRISTOL, BS35 5QX.
COSTLEY, Miss. Sharron Julie, BA ACA *1987;* 19 Darlington Place, BATH, BA2 6BX.
•①**COSTLEY-WOOD, Mr. David James, BA ACA** *1992;* KPMG LLP, St. James's Square, MANCHESTER, M2 6DS. See also KPMG Europe LLP
COTES, Mr. Peter Charles, BSc FCA *1975;* Finchams Farm, Lower Stow Bedon, ATTLEBOROUGH, NR17 1EL.
COTGROVE, Mr. Peter Leonard George, FCA *1971;* 21 Cages Way Melton, WOODBRIDGE, SUFFOLK, IP12 1TE.
COTICELLI, Mr. Andrew James, LLB ACA *2004;* 23 Harewood Mews, Harewood, LEEDS, LS17 9LY.
COTILLARD, Mr. Christopher Billot, ACA *2009;* (Tax Fac), Alex Picot & Co, 95-97 Halkett Place, St Helier, JERSEY, JE1 1BX.
COTILLARD, Mrs. Mary Louise, BA FCA *1985;* 2 Hill Street, Lgl Trustees Ltd, PO Box 167, JERSEY, JE4 8RY.
COTONET, Mrs. Tatiana, ACA *2009;* 11 Queen Marys House, 1 Holford Way, LONDON, SW15 5DH.
COTTA, Mr. Julien, BSc ACA *1993;* Well House, The Barns, Shackleford, GODALMING, GU8 6BU.
COTTAM, Mr. Adam, BSc(Hons) ACA *2011;* 10 Milton Road, COLNE, LANCASHIRE, BB8 9RN.
COTTAM, Miss. Anita Jane, MMath ACA *2003;* with Grant Thornton UK LLP, 30 Finsbury Square, LONDON, EC2P 2YU.
COTTAM, Mr. Anthony George Joseph, MA FCA *1952;* Longbarn, Temple Grafton, ALCESTER, WARWICKSHIRE, B49 6NU. (Life Member)
•**COTTAM, Mr. Anthony James Leslie, BSc FCA** *1980;* KPMG LLP, Arlington Business Park, Theale, READING, RG7 4SD. See also KPMG Europe LLP
COTTAM, Mr. Charles Robert Edward, BA ACA *1995;* 5 Cambridge Place, LONDON, W8 5PB.
COTTAM, Mr. David, BSc ACA *1991;* 11 Kingscroft Close, Streetly, SUTTON COLDFIELD, B74 2HJ.
COTTAM, Mr. David George, FCA *1975;* 21 Silksworth Hall Drive, Silksworth, SUNDERLAND, SR3 2PG.
•**COTTAM, Mr. David Michael, BSc ACA** *1980;* 40 Gilderdale Close, Birchwood, WARRINGTON, WA3 6TH. See also AIMS - David Cottam
COTTAM, Mr. Graeme Robin, LLB FCA *1983;* Parsons Farm Warren Corner, Froxfield, PETERSFIELD, HAMPSHIRE, GU32 1BJ.
COTTAM, Mr. Harold, FCA *1960;* Pentwyn, Dorstone, HEREFORD, HR3 6AD. (Life Member)
COTTAM, Mr. John-Joe, BSc ACA *2004;* Gardiners Nursing Agency, 10 Church Street, Caversham, READING, RG4 8DZ.
COTTAM, Mrs. Mary Fiona, BSc ACA *1991;* Xoserve Ltd, 31 Homer Road, SOLIHULL, WEST MIDLANDS, B91 3LT.
COTTAM, Mr. Matthew Neil, BSc ACA *1995;* Duresta Upholstery Ltd Fields Farm Road, Long Eaton, NOTTINGHAM, NG10 3FZ.
COTTAM, Mr. Michael David, BA ACA *1987;* Barn House Oxford Street, Lee Common, GREAT MISSENDEN, BUCKINGHAMSHIRE, HP16 9JP.
COTTAM, Mr. Philip, FCA JDipMA *1957;* 7 The Grange, Shepherds Lane, Caversham, READING, RG4 7HZ. (Life Member)
COTTAM, Mr. Roger Denis, MA ACA *1979;* 1 Minerva Close, STEVENAGE, HERTFORDSHIRE, SG2 7RA.
COTTAM, Miss. Sarah Jayne, BSc(Hons) ACA *2004;* (Tax Fac), 140 Maney Hill Road, SUTTON COLDFIELD, B72 1JU.
COTTAM, Mrs. Sarah Louise, BSc(Hons) ACA *2002;* 20 Royds Close, Tottington, BURY, LANCASHIRE, BL8 3QD.
COTTEE, Mr. John William, FCA *1972;* 14 Church Street, BALDOCK, HERTFORDSHIRE, SG7 5AE.
COTTEE, Mrs. Julie, BA ACA *2001;* South End House Church Lane, Whitburn, SUNDERLAND, SR6 7JL.
COTTEE, Mr. Michael, FCA *1956;* Parke Paddock, Radwell, BEDFORD, MK43 7HS.
•**COTTEE, Mr. Stuart John, BSc ACA** *1997;* Deloitte LLP, One Trinity Gardens, Broad Chare, NEWCASTLE UPON TYNE, NE1 2HF. See also Deloitte & Touche LLP
COTTEE, Miss. Susan Kim, BA ACA *1988;* 216 Clinton Avenue, OAK PARK, IL 60302, UNITED STATES.
COTTELL, Miss. Tessa Louise, MA ACA *1990;* Via Peleatti 7, 30026 PORTOGRUARO, ITALY.
•**COTTER, Mr. Donal Paul, BCom ACA** *1994;* Kevin O'Connell & Co, 1A Time Square, Ballincollig, CORK, COUNTY CORK, IRELAND.
COTTER, Mr. Ewan David, BA ACA *2007;* Flat, 182 Chiswick High Road, LONDON, W4 1PP.
COTTER, Mr. John Francis, FCA *1967;* 25 Onward Walk, St Helen's, Portmarnock, DUBLIN 13, COUNTY DUBLIN, IRELAND.
COTTER, Mr. Michael George, BEd ACA *1993;* 3 Priory Close, Whitchurch, TAVISTOCK, PL19 9DH.
COTTER, Mr. Terence Edward, FCA *1957;* 9 Burlington House, 30 Burlington Place, EASTBOURNE, EAST SUSSEX, BN21 4AR. (Life Member)
•**COTTERELL, Mr. John David, FCA** *1963;* with Cotterell Partnership Limited, The Curve, 83 Tempest Street, WOLVERHAMPTON, WV2 1AA.
COTTERELL, Mr. Thomas Aidan, BA(Hons) ACA *2002;* 20 Trafalgar Road, LONDON, SW19 1HR.
COTTERILL, Miss. Elizabeth, MMath ACA *2009;* Flat 23 Jagger House, Rosenau Road, LONDON, SW11 4QY.
COTTERILL, Mrs. Heather Jean, LLB ACA *2001;* 34 Station Road, Alvechurch, BIRMINGHAM, WORCESTERSHIRE, B48 7SD.
COTTERILL, Mr. John David, FCA *1970;* 34 Rockcliffe, SOUTH SHIELDS, TYNE AND WEAR, NE33 3JH.
COTTERILL, Mr. John Stuart, BA ACA *1990;* 82 Grosvenor Road, LONDON, N10 2DS.
COTTERILL, Mr. Keith, MA(Oxon) ACA *1988;* PO Box 1089, MENLO PARK, CA 94026-1089, UNITED STATES.
•**COTTERILL, Dr. Linda Ann, PhD FCA** *1990;* (Tax Fac), LCCA Limited, Hopton Corner House, Alfrick, WORCESTER, WR6 5HP.
COTTERILL, Mr. Michael David, BSc ACA *1988;* 70 Tabors Avenue, Great Baddow, CHELMSFORD, CM2 7EJ.
COTTERILL, Mr. Simon Philip, BA FCA ACT *1984;* 7 Clarendon Gardens, TUNBRIDGE WELLS, KENT, TN2 5LA.
COTTERILL, Mr. William Henry, FCA *1949;* 12 Brookside Way, Blakedown, KIDDERMINSTER, DY10 3NE. (Life Member)
COTTERRELL, Mr. Ian, ACA *2008;* 27 Lexington Avenue, MAIDENHEAD, SL6 4HL.
COTTEY, Mr. Graham Edward, BSc ACA *1992;* Tearfund, 100 Church Road, TEDDINGTON, TW11 8QE.
COTTEY, Mrs. Jacqueline Clare, BA ACA *1992;* CYPD Finance Team B3, Somerset County Council, County Hall, TAUNTON, SOMERSET, TA1 4DY.
COTTEY, Mr. Kenneth Francis, FCA *1951;* 25 Silver Drive, ALDEBURGH, IP15 5JZ. (Life Member)
•**COTTIER, Mr. Timothy Robin, FCA** *1977;* Kinloch Corporate Finance Ltd, 1 Whitehall, 1 Whitehall Road, LEEDS, LS1 4HR.
COTTINGHAM, Mr. Barrie, FCA *1955;* Waterstones, 2 Beckside, Off Tivy Dale Close, Cawthorne, BARNSLEY, SOUTH YORKSHIRE S75 4EP. (Life Member)
COTTINGHAM, Mr. Clive Douglas, MBA BA ACA *1984;* J W T, 1 Knightsbridge Green, LONDON, SW1X 7NW.
•**COTTINGHAM, Mr. Dudley Reginald, FCA** *1975;* Arthur Morris & Co, P.O. Box HM 1806, Century House, 16 Par La Ville Road, HAMILTON HM HX, BERMUDA. See also Morris Snelling & Co. and Morris, Cottingham & Co
•**COTTINGHAM, Mr. Stephen Richard, FCA** *1974;* (Tax Fac), Stoner Cottingham, 42 London Rd, HORSHAM, RH12 1AY.
COTTINGHAM, Mrs. Susan Claire, BA ACA *1985;* Corinthian Brands (CBL) Ltd Copthall Bridge House, Station Bridge, HARROGATE, HG1 1SP.
COTTINGTON, Miss. Emma, ACA *2007;* 41 Barkway Road, ROYSTON, SG8 9EA.
•**COTTIS, Miss. Ann Doreen, BSc ACA** *1979;* PricewaterhouseCoopers LLP, 1 Embankment Place, LONDON, WC2N 6RH. See also PricewaterhouseCoopers
COTTIS, Ms. Georgia, BA bsc ACA *2003;* 5 Evripidou Street, Pelecanos Court, Flat 102, Acroplis, 2007 STROVOLOS, CYPRUS.
COTTIS, Mr. Robert Clifford, BA ACA *2005;* 52 Malting Villas road, ROCHFORD, SS4 1RU.
•**COTTLE, Mr. Andrew Vaughan, BA FCA** *1989;* BDO LLP, 55 Baker Street, LONDON, W1U 7EU. See also BDO Stoy Hayward LLP
COTTLE, Mr. Martin David, BSc ACA *1995;* Pricewaterhousecoopers Cornwall Court, 19 Cornwall Street, BIRMINGHAM, B3 2DT.
COTTLE, Mr. Richard John, BA ACA *1981;* Bray Cottage, The Old Orchard, Calcot, READING, RG31 7RF.
COTTLE, Mr. William Waterson, BA FCA *1981;* Unicef UK, Unicef House, 30a Great Sutton Street, LONDON, EC1V 0DU.
COTTOM, Mr. Joseph, FCA *1947;* 2250 South Millway Apt 325, MISSISSAUGA L5L 3J6, ON, CANADA. (Life Member)
COTTON, Mrs. Alison, BA(Hons) ACA *2001;* Kellogg Co of GB Ltd, The Kellogg Building, Talbot Road, Old Trafford, MANCHESTER, M16 0PU.
COTTON, Miss. Alix Joanne, BA ACA *2002;* 27 Amante Crescent, Mairangi Bay, AUCKLAND 0630, NEW ZEALAND.
COTTON, Mr. Andrew, MA ACA CPA *1988;* Ernst & Young, 560 Mission Street, Suite 1600, SAN FRANCISCO, CA 94105-2907, UNITED STATES.
COTTON, Mr. Anthony Charles, BSc FCA *1979;* 55 Yew Tree Lane, Wergs, WOLVERHAMPTON, WV6 8UQ.
COTTON, Mr. Anthony Ross, FCA *1966;* Woodlands Colmore Lane Kingwood, HENLEY-ON-THAMES, OXFORDSHIRE, RG9 5NA. (Life Member)
COTTON, Mr. Brian John Powell, FCA *1958;* Hardwycke House, Knott Park, Oxshott, LEATHERHEAD, KT22 0HZ. (Life Member)
•**COTTON, Mr. Christopher Bernard, MSc ACA** *1980;* Mortons, 7A Brooklands Avenue, SHEFFIELD, S10 4GA.
COTTON, Mr. Christopher Philip, FCA *1974;* 13 Aireville Close, Utley, KEIGHLEY, WEST YORKSHIRE, BD20 6EG.
COTTON, Miss. Clare Helen, BA ACA *1988;* 16 Palace Street, LONDON, SW1E 5JD.
COTTON, Mr. David John, FCA *1969;* 7 Fairfield Close, KINGSBRIDGE, TQ7 1JS.
COTTON, Miss. Emma Jane, BA ACA *1986;* Ernst & Young Llp, 1 More London Place, LONDON, SE1 2AF.

COTTON, Mr. James Ross, BA ACA *1999;* 49 Waldergrave Gardens, Strawberry Hill, Middlesex, TWICKENHAM, TW1 4PH.
COTTON, Mr. John, BA FCA FIIA *1963;* 2 Shotwood Close, Rolleston-on-Dove, BURTON-ON-TRENT, DE13 9BN.
COTTON, Mr. John Raymond, MSc ACA MBA *1998;* 15 Regent Close, Bramhall, STOCKPORT, CHESHIRE, SK7 1JA.
COTTON, Ms. Louise Angela, MA FCA *1989;* Plan WARO, Amitie II 4023, BP 21121, Dakar Ponty, DAKAR, SENEGAL.
COTTON, Mr. Michael Joseph, FCA *1956;* 39 Dartmouth Avenue, Almondbury, HUDDERSFIELD, HD5 8UP. (Life Member)
COTTON, Mrs. Nicola Jane, MA ACA CTA *2002;* with Dixon Wilson, 22 Chancery Lane, LONDON, WC2A 1LS.
COTTON, Mr. Nigel Roy, ACA *2009;* Weathervane Lodge, Potash Road, BILLERICAY, ESSEX, CM11 1HG.
•**COTTON, Mr. Philip James, BSocSc FCA** *1985;* KPMG LLP, 100 Temple Street, BRISTOL, BS1 6AG. See also KPMG Europe LLP
COTTON, Mr. Raymond Peter, BCom FCA *1954;* Court Barn, Churt, FARNHAM, GU10 2NX. (Life Member)
COTTON, Mr. Robert Francis Charles, BA ACA *1991;* N C C Group Plc, Manchester Technology Centre, Oxford Road, MANCHESTER, M1 7EF.
COTTON, Mrs. Sarah Louise, BSc ACA *1996;* Greenhaven, 23 Hillside, Abbotts Ann, ANDOVER, HAMPSHIRE, SP11 7DF.
COTTON, Mr. Simon John, BA ACA *1983;* 67 Penrhyn Crescent, Chilwell, NOTTINGHAM, NG9 5PA.
COTTON, Mrs. Susan Veronica, FCA *1967;* 50 Broadgate, Beeston, NOTTINGHAM, NG9 2FW. (Life Member)
•**COTTON, Mr. Wilson Peter, BA FCA** *1981;* (Tax Fac), Smith & Williamson Ltd, 25 Moorgate, LONDON, EC2R 6AY.
COTTRELL, Mr. Adrian Peter, BSc ACA *1992;* Canterbury College, New Dover Road, CANTERBURY, CT1 3AJ.
COTTRELL, Dr. Andrew Charles, ACA *2009;* 3 Corn Avill Close, ABINGDON, OXFORDSHIRE, OX14 2ND.
COTTRELL, Mr. Andrew Graeme, MA ACA *1995;* 106 Moselle Avenue, Wood Green, LONDON, N22 6ET.
COTTRELL, Mr. Anthony Jason, BSc ACA *1997;* 6 Texas Lane, Malahide, DUBLIN, COUNTY DUBLIN, IRELAND.
COTTRELL, Mr. Christopher Mark, ACA *1981;* Selsfield Place, Selsfield Common, EAST GRINSTEAD, RH19 4LW.
COTTRELL, Mr. Christopher Noel, MBA ACA *2006;* 31 Eastmearn Road, LONDON, SE21 8HA.
•**COTTRELL, Mr. David, BA FCA** *1971;* (Tax Fac), David Cottrell & Company, The Old Bakery, 11a Canford Lane, Westbury-on-Trym, BRISTOL, BS9 3DE.
COTTRELL, Mr. David Charles, BSc FCA *1974;* Grove Cottage, Hillwood Grove, BRENTWOOD, Essex, CM13 2PF. (Life Member)
COTTRELL, Mr. Gareth David, BSc ACA *2007;* 3 Bittern Close, BASINGSTOKE, HAMPSHIRE, RG22 5JA.
COTTRELL, Mr. Geoffrey Morley, FCA *1972;* 810/250 St Kilda Road, SOUTHBANK, VIC 3006, AUSTRALIA. (Life Member)
COTTRELL, Mr. James Andrew, BA ACA *2007;* Computer Science Corporation Royal Pavilion, Wellesley Road, ALDERSHOT, GU11 1PZ.
COTTRELL, Mr. James Harvey, ACA *2007;* Deloitte & Touche LLP, 555 12th Street NW, Suite 500, WASHINGTON, DC 20004, UNITED STATES.
COTTRELL, Dr. John, MA FCA *1965;* 90 Redland Road, Redland, BRISTOL, BS6 6QZ. (Life Member)
COTTRELL, Miss. Judith, BSc ACA *1997;* Hillcrest, Field Assarts, WITNEY, OXFORDSHIRE, OX29 9NQ.
COTTRELL, Ms. Liliana, BA ACA *2005;* 15 Dorchester Road, BRISTOL, BS7 0LA.
COTTRELL, Mr. Paul Alan, FCA *1979;* 16 Goldcrest Drive, Ridgewood, UCKFIELD, EAST SUSSEX, TN22 5QG.
COTTRELL, Mr. Richard, ACA *2008;* 26 Wises Firs, Sulhamstead, READING, RG7 4EH.
COTTRELL, Mr. Richard Grey, FCA *1967;* Flat 112, Dunkeld Square, 15 North Road, Dunkeld West, JOHANNESBURG, 2196 SOUTH AFRICA.
COTTRELL, Mrs. Sally Ann, BSc ACA *1989;* 25 Poplar Lane, CANNOCK, WS11 1NQ.
COTTRELL, Mr. Stephen Roger, BSc ACA *1991;* 400 S. El Camino Real, SAN MATEO, CA 94402, UNITED STATES.
COTTRELL, Mr. Thomas, MA ACA *2011;* 94 Greenhow Street, SHEFFIELD, S6 3TP.
COTTRELL, Mr. William George Ernest, FCA *1951;* 47 Greenway, LONDON, N20 8ET. (Life Member)
•**COTTRILL, Mr. Nicholas Michael, BSc(Hons) ACA** *2001;* Nick Cottrill, 73 Burley Lane, Quarndon, DERBY, DE22 5JR. See also Accountancy Services
COUCH, Mr. David Paul, BEng ACA MSI *1994;* Arjent Ltd, 25 Christopher Street, LONDON, EC2A 2BS.
COUCH, Mr. Mark Andrew, MEng ACA CTA *1999;* (Tax Fac), 9 Dark Lane, Romsley, HALESOWEN, B62 0PW.
COUCH, Mr. Matthew Charles Anthony, BSc ACA *2004;* Flat 12, Dartmouth House, Dartmouth Row, LONDON, SE10 8BF.
COUCH, Mrs. Melanie Susan, BSc ACA *1999;* Quadnetics Group plc, Haydon House, 5 Alcester Road, STUDLEY, WARWICKSHIRE, B80 7AN.
•**COUCH, Mr. Stephen John, LLB ACA** *1989;* (Tax Fac), PricewaterhouseCoopers LLP, The Atrium, 1 Harefield Road, UXBRIDGE, UB8 1EX. See also PricewaterhouseCoopers
COUCHMAN, Mr. Ernest Henry, FCA *1963;* 4 Stapleton Road, STUDLEY, B80 7RH.
COUCHMAN, Mr. Terence John, FCA *1971;* Croft House, Technical Filtration Systems Ltd Croft House, Sandbeck Way, WETHERBY, WEST YORKSHIRE, LS22 7DP.
•**COUDOUNARIS CHATTALAS, Mrs. Frederiki, BSc FCA** *1982;* Coudounari & Elisseou, PO Box 50103, 3601 LIMASSOL, CYPRUS.
COUGHLAN, Mr. Anthony Gerard, BCom ACA *1981;* 21 Little Warren Close, GUILDFORD, SURREY, GU4 8PW.
COUGHLAN, Mr. Ian David, ACA *1990;* 1st Floor, 6 Crutched Friars, LONDON, EC3N 2PH.
COUGHLAN, Mr. Paul Terence, BA ACA *1997;* Dell Inc, One Dell Way, MS RR1-35, ROUND ROCK, TX 78682, UNITED STATES.
COUGHLAN, Mrs. Sally Ann, BA ACA *1993;* (Tax Fac), QMH Limited, Queens Court, 9-17 Eastern Road, ROMFORD, ESSEX, RM1 3NG.
•**COUGHLAN, Miss. Terri, BBS ACA** *2000;* with PricewaterhouseCoopers, 1 Embankment Place, LONDON, WC2N 6RH.
COUGHLIN, Mr. Nathan, BSc ACA *2002;* 51 Coleman Drive, PLYMOUTH, PL9 9UN.
•**COUGHTREY, Mr. Michael Thomas, FCA** *1984;* (Tax Fac), KPMG Audit plc, Aquis Court, 31 Fishpool Street, ST. ALBANS, AL3 4RF. See also KPMG Europe LLP and KPMG LLP
COUGILL, Miss. Diane, BA ACA *1990;* 1 Edenhurst Close, 403 Unthank Road, NORWICH, NR4 7QG.
COUKHAM, Mrs. Juliet Anne, BA ACA *1997;* 27 Ullswater Drive, WETHERBY, LS22 6YF.
COUKHAM, Mr. Richard Antony, BSc ACA *1991;* 39 West Park Road, LEEDS, LS8 2HA.
COULBECK, Mr. Christopher Francis, BSc ACA *2005;* 21 Pendrell Road, LONDON, SE4 2PB.
COULBORN, Mrs. Helen, BSc ACA ACCA *1996;* Woodgate Farm, Crawley Lane, Kings Bromley, BURTON-ON-TRENT, STAFFORDSHIRE, DE13 7JF.
COULCHER, Mr. Christopher, FCA *1968;* 28 Chapel Side, Moscow Road, LONDON, W2 4LL.
•**COULDERY, Mr. Frederick Alan James, FCA** *1952;* Fredk A.J. Couldery, 81 Hove Park Road, HOVE, BN3 6LN.
COULDERY, Mrs. Susan Jane, BSc ACA *1989;* The Spinney, Beechway, GUILDFORD, GU1 2TA.
•**COULDREY, Mr. Philip Peter, FCA** *1965;* Philip P. Couldrey, 93 Avenue Besme, 1190 BRUSSELS, BELGIUM.
•**COULDWELL, Mr. Leslie Stewart, FCA** *1974;* Mitchells (Knaresborough) Limited, 37 High Street, KNARESBOROUGH, NORTH YORKSHIRE, HG5 0HB.
COULING, Mrs. Elizabeth Mary, BSc ACA *1981;* 8 The Dell, SCUNTHORPE, DN17 2XB.
COULING, Mr. Paul William, FCA *1956;* Blundells Barn, Risborough Road, Little Kimble, AYLESBURY, HP17 0UE. (Life Member)
COULL, Ms. Alexandra, BA ACA *2003;* 65 First Avenue, Mortlake, LONDON, SW14 8SP.
COULL, Mr. Duncan Hunter, FCA *1975;* Lloyds (Animal) Feeds Limited, The Mill, Morton, OSWESTRY, SY10 8BH.
COULL, Mrs. Trudy Isabel, MA(Hons) ACA *2001;* 11 Brighouse Park Gardens, EDINBURGH, EH4 6GY.
COULLING, Mr. Richard Peter Charles, BSc ACA *2005;* Flat 52, Shearwater Court, Star Place, LONDON, E1W 1AD.
COULSON, Mr. Andrew Robert, BA ACA *1992;* Apperley House, 30 Hunters Close, Medomsley, CONSETT, COUNTY DURHAM, DH8 6SP.
•**COULSON, Mr. Andrew Scott, MBA FCA** *1994;* Dolfinblue Business Advisory Services Limited, 6 Marlborough Place, LUTTERWORTH, LEICESTERSHIRE, LE17 4DE.
COULSON, Mr. Anthony Brett, FCA *1970;* M&A International SA, Dreve Richelle 159, B-1410 WATERLOO, BELGIUM.
COULSON, Mrs. April Helen, BA FCA *1994;* 51 Guildford Road, Frimley Green, CAMBERLEY, GU16 6NW.
COULSON, Mr. David, BSc FCA *1976;* 17 York Close, Westwood Grange, CRAMLINGTON, NE23 1TN.
COULSON, Mr. David John, BA ACA *1993;* 51 Guildford Road, Frimley Green, CAMBERLEY, GU16 6NW.
COULSON, Mr. David John, MA ACA *1978;* 74 South Eden Park Road, BECKENHAM, BR3 3BD.
COULSON, Miss. Jennifer, BSc ACA *2007;* 5 Bromley Grove, BROMLEY, BR2 0LP.
COULSON, Mr. John Arthur, FCA *1954;* 21 Cannon Hill Road, COVENTRY, CV4 7AZ. (Life Member)
•**COULSON, Mr. John Colin, FCA** *1968;* Macleod & Tonkin, 54 Coinagehall Street, HELSTON, CORNWALL, TR13 8EL.
COULSON, Mrs. Karen Ka Wai, BSc ACA *2010;* 188 Withington Road, MANCHESTER, M16 8WJ.
•**COULSON, Mr. Keith Douglas, FCA** *1969;* Keith Coulson & Co Ltd, Benvenut, 61 Norfield Road, DARTFORD, DA2 7NY. See also AArdvark Taxation Services Ltd
COULSON, Mr. Leslie, FCA *1977;* Commercial Services, Kent County Council Commercial Services, Gibson Drive Kings Hill, WEST MALLING, ME19 4QG.
•**COULSON, Mrs. Lisa, BSc FCA** *2000;* SME Accounting Services Ltd, 24 Speen Lane, Speen, NEWBURY, BERKSHIRE, RG14 1RN.
COULSON, Mr. Martin, BA(Hons) ACA *2003;* Flat 15 King Edward Mansions, 629 Fulham Road, LONDON, SW6 5UH.
COULSON, Mrs. Mary, BA ACA *1993;* 169 Sheen Lane, East Sheen, LONDON, SW14 8NA.
•**COULSON, Mr. Matthew, BA ACA** *1999;* with Deloitte LLP, Global House, High Street, CRAWLEY, RH10 1DL.
•**COULSON, Mr. Neil Anthony, BA ACA** *1986;* Littlejohn LLP, 1 Westferry Circus, Canary Wharf, LONDON, E14 4HD.
•**COULSON, Mr. Paul Thomas, ACA** *1990;* Sheen Consulting Services Ltd, 169 Sheen Lane, LONDON, SW14 8NA.
•**COULSON, Mr. Richard Allen, FCA** *1973;* with Ashby Berry & Co, 48/49 Albemarle Crescent, SCARBOROUGH, YO11 1XU.
•**COULSON, Mr. Thomas, FCA** *1973;* Horne Brooke Shenton, 21 Caunce Street, BLACKPOOL, FY1 3LA.
COULSON, Mr. William Andrew, MBA BSc FCA *1983;* 40 Holly Avenue, Jesmond, NEWCASTLE UPON TYNE, NE2 2PY.
COULSON-THOMAS, Prof. Colin Joseph, FCA *1973;* Mill Reach, Mill Lane, WATER NEWTON, PETERBOROUGH, CAMBRIDGESHIRE, PE8 6LY.
COULTAS, Mr. James Alan, ACA *2007;* Nuffield Health, Derby Hospital, Rykneld Road, Littleover, DERBY, DE23 4SN.
COULTAS, Mrs. Katy Anna, BSc ACA *2007;* 19 Eltham Road, West Bridgford, NOTTINGHAM, NG2 5JP.
COULTEN, Mr. William, MA ACA *2007;* 56 Dickens Street, Elwood, MELBOURNE, VIC 3184, AUSTRALIA.
COULTER, Mr. Julian George Berrisford, BA ACA *2010;* 12 Sweetcroft Lane, UXBRIDGE, MIDDLESEX, UB10 9LD.
COULTER, Mr. Keiron Edward, MEng ACA *2008;* 3/6 Holgate Road, Kohimarama, AUCKLAND 1071, NEW ZEALAND.
•**COULTER, Mrs. Louise Elizabeth, BA ACA** *1996;* Pollards Accountancy Services Limited, 54 Ebury Road, RICKMANSWORTH, HERTFORDSHIRE, WD3 1BN.
COULTER, Mrs. Louise Helen, BSc ACA *2002;* 8 New Walk, BEVERLEY, NORTH HUMBERSIDE, HU17 7AD.
COULTER, Mrs. Madeline Rose, MSc BA FCA *1973;* 31 Rampark, Lurgan, CRAIGAVON, BT66 7JH.
•**COULTER, Mr. Michael Ian, ACA** *1987;* Coulter & Co, 1st Floor, 4 Sherrard Street, MELTON MOWBRAY, LE13 1XJ. See also C & C Accountants
COULTER, Mr. Nicholas David, BSc ACA *1997;* 16 Cambridge Road, Barnes, LONDON, SW13 0PG.
COULTER, Mr. Peter Robert, BEng ACA *1998;* with Bristol & West plc, PO Box 27, One Temple Quay, BRISTOL, BS99 7AX.
COULTER, Miss. Sandra Lynne, ACA *2009;* Marland House, 13 Huddersfield Road, BARNSLEY, SOUTH YORKSHIRE, S70 2LW.
COULTHARD, Mr. Brian Dawson, FCA *1962;* 4 The Chancery, Bramcote, NOTTINGHAM, NG9 3AJ. (Life Member)
COULTHARD, Mr. David Andrew, BEng ACA MCT *2003;* 3 Shondean Street, Catford, LONDON, SE12 8RU.
COULTHARD, Mr. George, FCA *1969;* Kassandra, Dean, WORKINGTON, CUMBRIA, CA14 4TJ.
COULTHARD, Mr. Graeme, BSc ACA *1993;* 39 St. James's Drive, LONDON, SW17 7RN.
COULTHARD, Miss. Natalie, BA ACA *2006;* Group Finance, Sage (UK) Ltd, North Park Avenue, NEWCASTLE UPON TYNE, NE13 9AA.
•**COULTHARD, Mr. Neil Irving, FCA** *1973;* Coulthard Adams Majeed Ltd, 145 Albert Road, MIDDLESBROUGH, CLEVELAND, TS1 2PP.
•**COULTHARD, Mr. Richard Ian, BA FCA** *1994;* Robert S. Boys, 28-30 Grange Road West, BIRKENHEAD, CH41 4DA.
COULTHWAITE, Mr. Richard Edwin, BSc FCA *1990;* Brit Insurance Plc, 55 Bishopsgate, LONDON, EC2N 3AS.
COULTON, Mr. Anthony Thomas Trevena, MMath ACA *2009;* 262a King Street, LONDON, W6 0SP.
COULTON, Mr. Christopher Martin, BEng ACA *2005;* 30 Wollaton Vale, NOTTINGHAM, NG8 2NR.
COULTON, Mrs. Helen, BSc ACA *1983;* The Channings, Scale Hall Lane, Newton, PRESTON, PR4 3TL.
COULTON, Mr. Jack, FCA *1937;* 5 Monkswood Avenue, MORECAMBE, LANCASHIRE, LA4 6TW. (Life Member)
COULTON, Mrs. Linda June, BSc ACA *1991;* Primula Grange, Brompton On Swale, RICHMOND, DL10 7HL.
COULTON, Mr. Richard Robert Trevena, FCA *1967;* 10 Le Haras au Bois, 60500 CHANTILLY, FRANCE. (Life Member)
COULTON, Ms. Teresa, FCA *1962;* 1200 South Idalia Street, unit C, AURORA, CO 80017, UNITED STATES.
COULTRUP, Mr. Edward James, BEng ACA *2004;* with KPMG, 8/F Prince's Building, 10 Chater Road, CENTRAL, HONG KONG ISLAND, HONG KONG SAR.
COULTRUP, Mr. Timothy Jon, BA ACA ATII *1988;* (Tax Fac), 13 North Court, HASSOCKS, BN6 8JS.
COUMAS, Mr. Paul, BA ACA *2007;* 707 Lincoln Gate, 39 Red Bank, MANCHESTER, M4 4AD.
COUMIDIS, Mrs. Patricia Anne, BSc FCA *1991;* 26 Coval Gardens, East Sheen, LONDON, SW14 7DG.
COUND, Mr. David Mansell Aubrey, FCA *1956;* 5 The Birches, Grimes Gates, Diseworth, DERBY, DE74 2PU. (Life Member)
COUNDLEY, Mr. Paul Leonard, BSc(Hons) ACA TEP *2002;* Flat 1 Fountain Court, Roseville Street St. Helier, JERSEY, JE2 4PJ.
•**COUNSELL, Mrs. Alison Judy, FCA** *1980;* (Tax Fac), Alison J Counsell, Meadow House, 2 Chapel Close, Empingham, OAKHAM, RUTLAND LE15 8BX.
•**COUNSELL, Mr. David John, FCA** *1979;* (Tax Fac), Counsells, Smithbrook Kilns, CRANLEIGH, GU6 8JJ.
•**COUNSELL, Mr. David William, FCA** *1980;* (Tax Fac), DC Accounting Solutions Ltd, Heron House, 39 - 41 Higher Bents Lane, Bredbury, STOCKPORT, SK6 1EE. See also DC Payroll Solutions Limited
COUNSELL, Mr. James Charles, BSc FCA *1983;* 4 Blacksmiths Close, The Green, Thrussington, LEICESTER, LE7 4UJ.
COUNSELL, Mr. Matthew, ACA *2009;* 8 Durham Close, DUKINFIELD, CHESHIRE, SK16 5JR.
COUNSELL, Miss. Nicola Louise, ACA *2008;* 7 Newlyn Avenue, CONGLETON, CHESHIRE, CW12 3AX.
•**COUNSELL, Mr. Peter Marcus, BSc ACA CF** *1992;* Meta Corporate Finance Limited, Hop House, Lower Green Road, Pembury, TUNBRIDGE WELLS, TN2 4HS.
COUNSELL, Mr. Robert Elgar, MA FCA *1956;* 1 Parkfields, Pen-y-fai, BRIDGEND, CF31 4NQ. (Life Member)
COUNSELL, Mrs. Rosemary Frances, FCA *1987;* Blacksmiths Close, Thrussington, LEICESTER, LE7 4UJ.
COUNSELL, Mr. Simon Thomas, BSc ACA *1993;* 42 Duddingston Road West, EDINBURGH, EH15 3PS.
•**COUNSELL, Mr. Stuart Robin, FCA CF** *1973;* Grange Barn, Carr Lane, Thorner, LEEDS, LS14 3HG.
COUNSELL MCCAY, Mrs. Amanda, BA ACA *1987;* 26 Appleby Road, Gatley, CHEADLE, SK8 4QD.
COUNTE, Mr. Ronald David, BSc ACA *1984;* 5 Dunmore Road, MARKET HARBOROUGH, LEICESTERSHIRE, LE16 8AZ.
COUNTER, Mr. Simon Russell Mark, BA ACA *2004;* 44 Lambourne Crescent, WOKING, SURREY, GU21 5RQ.

COUPAR, Miss. Alison Jane, BSc ACA *1995;* 4 Strands Farm Court, Hornby, LANCASTER, LA2 8JF.
COUPAR, Mr. John Mcdonald, FCA *1958;* 3 Spinney Brow, Ribbleton, PRESTON, PR2 6YG. (Life Member)
COUPE, Mrs. Alison Jane, MA ACA *1996;* 9 Albert Street, GLADESVILLE, NSW 2111, AUSTRALIA.
COUPE, Mr. Neil Anthony, BA ACA *1994;* 50 Easthampstead Road, WOKINGHAM, RG40 2EF.
COUPE, Mr. Nicholas Peter, BEng ACA *2002;* Flat 42, 57 Stamford Street, LONDON, SE1 9DJ.
COUPE, Mr. Trevor John, FCA *1987;* Paul Hartmann Ltd P2, Parklands Heywood Distribution Park, HEYWOOD, LANCASHIRE, OL10 2TT.
•**COUPEE, Mr. David Harry, FCA** *1967;* (Tax Fac), D H Coupee, Holmes House, The Green, Sedlescombe, BATTLE, TN33 0QA.
COUPER, Mr. Andrew John, BSc ACA *2002;* Barnfield Construction Ltd, 8 Kenyon Road Brierfield, NELSON, LANCASHIRE, BB9 5SP.
COUPER, Miss. Gayle, LLB ACA *2009;* 12 Hill Bank Road, BIRMINGHAM, B38 9AN.
COUPER, Mrs. Jennifer Jane, BA(Hons) ACA *2001;* Bramalea, 1 High Knoll Lane, SMITHS HS01, BERMUDA.
COUPES, Mr. Dominic, BA ACA *1996;* 1 Homer Drive, Marple Bridge, STOCKPORT, CHESHIRE, SK6 5DR.
COUPLAND, Mr. Adam, MEng ACA *2011;* Flat 1 Elm Court, Elm Lane, BRISTOL, BS6 6UF.
COUPLAND, Mrs. Alison Jane, BA ACA *1991;* 7 Chipstone Close, SOLIHULL, B91 3YS.
•**COUPLAND, Mr. Neil, FCA DChA** *1987;* RWB CA Limited, Northgate House, North Gate, Basford, NOTTINGHAM, NG7 7BE.
COUPLAND, Mr. Paul David, BA ACA *1992;* 7 Chadkirk Road, Romiley, STOCKPORT, CHESHIRE, SK6 3JY.
COUPLAND, Mr. Robert William, BCom ACA CTA *1981;* with Baker Tilly UK Audit LLP, 12 Gleneagles Court, Brighton Road, CRAWLEY, WEST SUSSEX, RH10 6AD.
•**COUPLAND, Mr. William David, FCA** *1964;* (Tax Fac), PPK Accountants Limited, Evolution House, 2-6 Easthampstead Road, WOKINGHAM, BERKSHIRE, RG40 2EG. See also PPK Professional Services LLP and PPK Professional Services Limited
COUPS, Mrs. Alix, MEng BA ACA *1998;* 60 Faraday Road, LONDON, SW19 8PD.
•**COUPS, Mr. Ashley David, BA FCA** *1998;* Ernst & Young LLP, 1 More London Place, LONDON, SE1 2AF. See also Ernst & Young Europe LLP
COURIARD, Mr. Marc Lucien, BSc ACA *1995;* Four Seasons La Rue de la Rosiere, St. Mary, JERSEY, JE3 3DH.
COURNANE, Mrs. Fenella Clare, BA ACA *1990;* The Old Carpenters' Shop, Whiligh, WADHURST, TN5 7JU.
COURT, Mr. Andrew Philip Alden, BA ACA *1990;* British Broadcasting Corporation Broadcast Centre, 201 Wood Lane, LONDON, W12 7TP.
COURT, Mr. Anthony Neville, ACA *1980;* 110 Church Street, WITHAM, ESSEX, CM8 2JH.
COURT, Mr. Benjamin, BSc ACA *2003;* 23 Melford Drive, MAIDSTONE, ME16 0UN.
COURT, Mr. Charlie, BSc ACA *2011;* Travelex UK Ltd, 65 Kingsway, LONDON, WC2B 6TD.
COURT, Mrs. Elizabeth Mary, MA FCA *1974;* 8 Beconsfield Close, Dorridge, SOLIHULL, B93 8QZ. (Life Member)
COURT, Miss. Gemma Claire, BSc ACA *2010;* A C Mole & Sons Stafford House, Blackbrook Park Avenue, TAUNTON, SOMERSET, TA1 2PX.
•**COURT, Mrs. Helen Louise, BSc(Hons) ACA** *2001;* Diamond Accounting Services, 23 Melford Drive, MAIDSTONE, KENT, ME16 0UN.
COURT, Mr. James Mark, BSc ACA *1995;* Rentokil Initial Services Ltd, Bridge House, Mathisen Way, Colnbrook, SLOUGH, SL3 0HH.
•**COURT, Mrs. Jane Elizabeth, BSc ACA** *1988;* (Tax Fac), Barn Owl Enterprises Ltd, Beechwood, Perrys Lane, Cawston, NORWICH, NR10 4HJ.
COURT, Mr. John Henry, FCA *1940;* Villa Karamoja, 91 Bullara Street, XAGHRA, XRA 102, MALTA. (Life Member)
COURT, Mr. John Michael, BA FCA *1967;* 5 Cleave Prior, Chipstead, COULSDON, CR5 3YF.
COURT, Mrs. Julie Sharon, BA ACA *1997;* Henry Doubleday Research Association Ryton Organic Gardens, Wolston Lane Ryton on Dunsmore, COVENTRY, CV8 3LG.
COURT, Mr. Justin Southworth, BSc FCA *1973;* Flat 11 CARDINAL MANSIONS, CARLISLE PLACE, LONDON, SW1P 1EY.
•**COURT, Mr. Matthew Jon, BA ACA** *1999;* 38 Haswell Road, HALESOWEN, WEST MIDLANDS, B63 1DA.
COURT, Mr. Peter Jan, MA FCA *1975;* 8 Beconsfield Close, Dorridge, SOLIHULL, B93 8QZ.
COURT, Mr. Richard Jeremy, BSc ACA *2007;* R J D Partners Ltd, 8-9 Well Court, LONDON, EC4M 9DN.
COURT, Mrs. Samantha Jane, ACA *2000;* 4 Ward Close, Barwell, LEICESTER, LE9 8ND.
COURTENAY, Mr. Roger Ian, FCA *1967;* 93 Claughton Avenue, LEYLAND, PR25 5TP. (Life Member)
COURTENAY, Mrs. Wendy Fiona, BA FCA *1992;* United Bible Societies, Zurich House, East Park, Southgate, CRAWLEY, WEST SUSSEX RH10 6AS.
COURTIER, Mr. Martin Peter, FCA *1977;* 7 Brook Office Park, Emersons Green, BRISTOL, BS16 7FL.
COURTIOUR, Mr. John Bartlett, FCA *1955;* 16 The Oaks, Bovey Tracey, NEWTON ABBOT, TQ13 9QX. (Life Member)
COURTIS, Miss. Catherine Mary, LLB ACA *2000;* 15 Higher Drive, BANSTEAD, SURREY, SM7 1PL.
COURTIS, Mr. John, FCA MCIPD *1959;* Oaklands House, Blackwater Covert, Reydon, SOUTHWOLD, SUFFOLK, IP18 6RD. (Life Member)
COURTMAN, Mr. David Christopher, FCA *1968;* Gill House, Alne Road, Tollerton, YORK, YO61 1QA.
COURTMAN, Mr. Dominic Michael James, BSc ACA *1997;* 4 Legard Road, LONDON, N5 1DE.
•①**COURTMAN, Mr. Tyrone Shaun, FCA** *1986;* Cooper Parry LLP, 1 Colton Square, LEICESTER, LE1 1QH.
COURTMAN-STOCK, Mrs. Eleanor Margaret, BSc(Hons) ACA *2001;* 2 Sedgegarth, Thorner, LEEDS, LS14 3LB.
COURTMAN-STOCK, Mr. Matthew Andrew, BA(Hons) ACA *2001;* The Orchard Butts Garth, Thorner, LEEDS, LS14 3DA.
COURTNEY, Mr. Aidan Benedict, BA ACA *1990;* The Roslin Institute, ROSLIN, MIDLOTHIAN, EH25 9PS.
COURTNEY, Mr. Denis Anthony, FCA *1956;* The Grove, Hudswell, RICHMOND, DL11 6BW. (Life Member)
COURTNEY, Mr. Douglas James, FCA *1951;* 11/69 Maesbury Street, KENSINGTON, SA 5068, AUSTRALIA. (Life Member)
COURTNEY, Mr. Julian Morgan, FCA *1984;* Gorse Cottage, Gorse Lane, Chobham, WOKING, SURREY, GU24 8RB.
COURTNEY, Mr. Mark Andrew, BSc FCA *1994;* 1 St. Hughes Close, DAVENTRY, NORTHAMPTONSHIRE, NN11 4TX.
•**COURTNEY, Mr. Martin Ralph, BSc ACA** *1985;* Smith & Williamson Ltd, 25 Moorgate, LONDON, EC2R 6AY.
COURTNEY, Mr. Peter Harvey, FCA *1956;* 11 Carysfort Close, Elton, PETERBOROUGH, PE8 6RW. (Life Member)
COURTNEY, Mr. Philip George, BSc ACA *1988;* (Tax Fac), with Clifford Chance LLP, 10 Upper Bank Street, LONDON, E14 5JJ.
•**COURTNEY, Mr. Stephen, BA ACA** *1995;* KPMG LLP, 15 Canada Square, LONDON, E14 5GL. See also KPMG Europe LLP
COURTNEY, Miss. Victoria Louise, BSc(Hons) ACA *2001;* 44 Uxbridge Road, RICKMANSWORTH, HERTFORDSHIRE, WD3 7AR.
COURTS, Mr. Benjamin David, BSc ACA *2004;* with Chantrey Vellacott DFK LLP, Russell Square House, 10-12 Russell Square, LONDON, WC1B 5LF.
COURTS, Mr. Ian Andrew, BSc ACA *2000;* Lowe and Partners Singapore Pte Ltd, 150 Cantonment Road, Blk A Cantonment Centre #03-00, SINGAPORE 089762, SINGAPORE.
COURTS, Mrs. Jennifer Marie, BSc ACA *1996;* Meads Gloucester Road, Pitchcombe, STROUD, GL6 6LP.
COURTS, Mrs. Jill Marion, BA(Hons) ACA *2001;* (Tax Fac), Noble Courts Unit 11, Mildmay House Foundry Lane, BURNHAM-ON-CROUCH, CM0 8BL.
COURTS, Mr. Joel Anthony, BSc ACA *2010;* 22 Harrowes Meade, EDGWARE, MIDDLESEX, HA8 8RP.
•**COURTS, Mr. Leonard David, FCA** *1968;* Apple Leonard Limited, PO Box 928, ST. ALBANS, HERTFORDSHIRE, AL1 9GB.
COURTS, Mr. Stephen John, BA ACA *1996;* Credit Suisse, 1 Cabot Square, LONDON, E14 4QJ.
COUSANS, Miss. Sarah, BA ACA *1996;* 72 Birkbeck Road, Mill Hill, LONDON, NW7 4AY.
COUSE, Mr. Philip Edward, FCA *1961;* (President 1989 - 1990) (Member of Council 1978 - 1987 1990 - 1992), 23 Frederick Road, Edgbaston, BIRMINGHAM, B15 1JN. (Life Member)
COUSEN, Mr. Matthew George, MEng ACA *2009;* Flat 1, 35 Tremadoc Road, LONDON, SW4 7NF.
•**COUSEN, Mrs. Sharon, BSc FCA** *1990;* Peel Walker, 11 Victoria Rd, ELLAND, HX5 0AE.
•**COUSENS, Mr. Derek Adrian, ACA** *2004;* Derek Cousens Ltd, 58 Kestell Parc, BODMIN, CORNWALL, PL31 1HP.
COUSENS, Miss. Polly Clare Balfour, MA(Hons) ACA *2001;* The Old Ostlers House, 87 Monkton Deverill, WARMINSTER, BA12 7EX.
•**COUSIN, Mr. Douglas James, FCA** *1978;* Hartington Accountancy Services Ltd, Upper Floor, Holme Court, Matlock Street, BAKEWELL, DERBYSHIRE DE45 1GQ.
•**COUSINS, Mr. Alan Richard, BSc FCA** *1990;* Cousins & Co Limited, The Vanguard Suite, Broadcasting House, Newport Road, MIDDLESBROUGH, TS1 5JA. See also Cousins & Co
COUSINS, Mr. Andrew Graham, MA ACA *2000;* 2 The Mill House, 198 Wandle Road, MORDEN, SM4 6AU.
COUSINS, Mr. Andrew Mark, ACA *1992;* Peter Jones (China) Ltd, Punit B, Kirkgate Business Centre, WAKEFIELD, WEST YORKSHIRE, WF1 5DL.
•**COUSINS, Mr. Andrew Neil, BSc FCA** *1983;* (Tax Fac), Stewart & Co, Knoll House, Knoll Road, CAMBERLEY, GU15 3SY. See also Stewart & Co Accountancy Services Ltd
COUSINS, Miss. Bethan, LLB ACA *2002;* Ty Blaidd Leckwith Road, Llandough, PENARTH, SOUTH GLAMORGAN, CF64 2LY.
COUSINS, Mr. David, ACA *2009;* 12 Houlgrave Road, LIVERPOOL, L5 9RQ.
COUSINS, Mr. H Leslie, FCA *1965;* Fludyers, West Clandon, GUILDFORD, GU4 7SX.
COUSINS, Miss. Jane Elizabeth, BSc ACA *1984;* 14 Settrington Road, LONDON, SW6 3BA.
COUSINS, Miss. Jenny, BSc ACA *2009;* 8 Earsdon Terrace, West Allotment, NEWCASTLE UPON TYNE, NE27 0DY.
•**COUSINS, Mr. John Edward, FCA** *1966;* Cousins Brett, 20 Bulstrode Street, LONDON, W1U 2JW.
COUSINS, Mr. Kenneth John, FCA *1963;* Flat 17, 2 Corscombe Close, WEYMOUTH, DORSET, DT4 0UG. (Life Member)
COUSINS, Mr. Malcolm Charles, FCA *1960;* 117 Arbour Lane, CHELMSFORD, CM1 7SB. (Life Member)
•**COUSINS, Mr. Mark Stephen, BA ACA** *2001;* Holmes Widlake Chartered Accountants, 3 Sharrow Lane, SHEFFIELD, S11 8AE.
COUSINS, Mr. Peter Colin, FCA *1970;* 4th floor Provincialate, St. Wilfrids Convent, 29 Tite Street, LONDON, SW3 4JX.
•**COUSINS WOODROW, Mrs. Judith Isabel, BA(Hons) ACA** *2002;* Alco Audit Limited, 12-14 Percy Street, ROTHERHAM, SOUTH YORKSHIRE, S65 1ED. See also Terence Houghton & Co Ltd
•**COUSSENS, Mr. Michael Charles, FCA** *1984;* (Tax Fac), Coussens, Chimneys, Boughton Hall Avenue, Send, WOKING, GU23 7DD.
COUSTAI, Miss. Martha Solomoni, MA BA ACA *2009;* Flat 501, 13 Prevezis Street, 1056 NICOSIA, CYPRUS.
COUSTAN, Mr. Roderick, FCA *1968;* 1 New Road, BUCKFASTLEIGH, DEVON, TQ11 0AJ. (Life Member)
•**COUTANCHE, Mr. Brian John, MBA FCA CISA** *1987;* Brian J Coutanche, Egret House, Mount Bingham, St. Helier, JERSEY, JE2 4XY.
COUTIE, Miss. Helen Elizabeth, BSc ACA *1993;* 3 Airedale Drive, Horsforth, LEEDS, LS18 5ED.
COUTINHO, Mr. Jason, BSc ACA *2010;* (Tax Fac), Flat 58, Osprey Heights, 7 Bramlands Close, LONDON, SW11 2NP.
•**COUTINHO, Mr. John Baptist, FCA** *1973;* (Tax Fac), J.B. Coutinho & Co, 46 Eleanor Road, LONDON, N11 2QS.
COUTINHO, Mr. Keith, BA ACA *2010;* 26 Eton Road, HAYES, MIDDLESEX, UB3 5HR.
COUTINHO, Miss. Lucy Anne, BA ACA *2010;* 42 Preston Road, Grimsargh, PRESTON, PR2 5SD.
COUTTIE, Mr. Stephen, BA ACA *1985;* RAB Capital, 1 Adam Street, LONDON, WC2N 6LE.
COUTTS, Miss. Amy, ACA *2011;* Flat 11, Tufnell Mansions, 73 Anson Road, LONDON, N7 0AT.
COUTTS, Mr. David Michael James, BA FCA *1983;* The Hawthorns, Reading Road, Streatley, READING, RG8 9JJ.
COUTTS, Mr. Graham, ACA *2009;* 66a Bottrells Lane, CHALFONT ST. GILES, BUCKINGHAMSHIRE, HP8 4EJ.
COUTTS, Mr. Kevin Andrew Michael, MA FCA *1990;* Pino House, Lea, MALMESBURY, WILTSHIRE, SN16 9PA.
COUTTS, Mr. Robert, MSc BA ACA *2011;* 48 Coborn Road, LONDON, E3 2DG.
COUTTS-WOOD, Mr. Charles Ian Farquharson, BSc ACA *2004;* 32b Dalberg Road, LONDON, SW2 1AN.
COUTTS-WOOD, Mr. Ian Robert, FCA *1974;* Ropemaker Place, Bank of Tokyo Mitsubishi U F J Ltd Ropemaker Place, 25 Ropemaker Street, LONDON, EC2Y 9AN.
COUTURE, Mr. Peter John, FCA *1967;* 51 Linden Road, BAIE D'URFE H9X 3K4, QUE, CANADA. (Life Member)
COUTURIER, Mr. Graeme, BSc ACA *2007;* 26 Cresswell Grove, MANCHESTER, M20 2NH.
COUVARAS, Miss. Athena, ACA *2011;* 7 Maplewood Gardens, BEACONSFIELD, BUCKINGHAMSHIRE, HP9 1BU.
•**COUZENS, Mr. Brian John, BA ACA** *1987;* Band 4 Brown Communications, 57 Jamestown Road, LONDON, NW1 7DB. See also Jackson Birch Limited
•**COUZENS, Mr. Ian, BSc ACA** *1979;* Ian Couzens Limited, 4 Denbigh Road, NORWICH, NR2 3AA.
COUZENS, Mr. Michael William, BA(Hons) ACA *2002;* Environmental Education Centre, Sustainability Way, LEYLAND, PR26 6TB.
COUZENS, Mrs. Nicola Jane, BA ACA *1998;* Tamarisk, Ridgeway Close, Oxshott, LEATHERHEAD, SURREY, KT22 0LQ.
COUZENS, Mr. Richard George Armitt, BA ACA *1998;* Green Lane Cottage Green Lane, Chieveley, NEWBURY, BERKSHIRE, RG20 8XB.
•**COUZENS, Mr. William Hugh, MSc FCA** *1960;* (Tax Fac), Bill Couzens, 40 Digswell Road, WELWYN GARDEN CITY, AL8 7PA.
COUZINS, Mrs. Susan, ACA *1992;* 11 Bullsland Lane, Chorleywood, RICKMANSWORTH, HERTFORDSHIRE, WD3 5BD.
•**COVA, Miss. Alison Jane, ACA** *1992;* Cova & Co, Pedlars March, 4 Meadway, Oxshott, LEATHERHEAD, SURREY KT22 0LZ.
COVE, Mr. Mark Andrew, BA ACA *2005;* 8 Somersby Drive, Bromley Cross, BOLTON, BL7 9PX.
COVE, Miss. Nicola Jane, BSc(Hons) ACA *2001;* 9 Foxwood Gardens, PLYMOUTH, PL9 9HX.
•**COVE, Mrs. Susan Davidson, BSc ACA** *1992;* The JRW Group, Riverside House, Ladhope Vale, GALASHIELS, SELKIRKSHIRE, TD1 1BT. See also James Rosie Partnership
COVELL, Mr. Beverley Michael, FCA ATII TEP *1977;* (Tax Fac), The Manor House, Buckland Newton, DORCHESTER, DORSET, DT2 7BX.
COVELL, Mr. John Charles, BA FCA MBA CIA *1974;* General Growth Properties INC, 110 North Wacker Drive, CHICAGO, IL 60606, UNITED STATES.
COVENEY, Mr. Andrew, ACA *1992;* Yew Cottage, Wolferstan Drive, Bishopdown, SALISBURY, SP1 3XZ.
•**COVENEY, Mr. Andrew Hilbre, BSc ACA** *1992;* The Old Vicarage, Knutsford Road, Antrobus, NORTHWICH, CHESHIRE, CW9 6JW.
COVENEY, Mr. Dale Austen, BSc ACA *1999;* 139 Robin Hood Lane, CHATHAM, KENT, ME5 9NL.
COVENEY, Mr. Peter Nigel, FCA *1976;* The Old Vicarage, Lower Road, East Farleigh, MAIDSTONE, KENT, ME15 0JW.
COVENEY, Mr. Raymond Hilbre, FCA *1964;* 380 Station Road, Dorridge, SOLIHULL, B93 8ES. (Life Member)
COVENTRY, Mr. David, BSc ACA *1991;* 35 Melbourne Street, YORK, YO10 5AQ.
COVENTRY, Mr. Edward Reginald, FCA *1959;* Avda Del Prado 60, Esq Con Calle Milan, Las Brisas N Andalucia, 29660 MARBELLA, SPAIN. (Life Member)
COVENTRY, Mr. Neill Farquharson, BA FCA *1983;* Autumn Wood, Pheasants Nest, Weston Underwood, OLNEY, MK46 5LA.
COVENTRY, Mr. Richard Andrew, BA ACA *2005;* 29 Beachcroft Road, WIRRAL, MERSEYSIDE, CH47 6BD.
COVENTRY, Miss. Sarah Elizabeth, BSc ACA *1999;* 47 Rolleston Avenue, Petts Wood, ORPINGTON, BR5 1AJ.
COVENTRY, Mr. Stuart James, MSc ACA *1998;* 38 Broomwood Road, Clapham, LONDON, SW11 6HT.
COVERDALE, Mr. Andrew James, ACA ACMA *2007;* 40 Stirling Road, NORWICH, NR6 6GF.
•**COVERDALE, Mr. John Edwin, BSc FCA** *1990;* MacIntyre Hudson LLP, New Bridge Street House, 30-34 New Bridge Street, LONDON, EC4V 6BJ.
COVERLEY, Mr. Mark David Sanderson, BA ACA *1993;* Redcats (UK) Plc, Holdsworth Street, BRADFORD, WEST YORKSHIRE, BD1 4AH.
COVERLEY, Mr. Richard Andrew Faura, FCA *1966;* 20 Delphene Avenue, THORNTON-CLEVELEYS, FY5 1RY.
COVERLEY, Mr. Roger Bernard, FCA *1971;* 12 Laywood Close, BURY ST.EDMUNDS, IP32 7JD.

COVIELLO, Mr. Edward David Henry, MA FCA *1973;* 8 Wallace Road, BROADSTONE, DORSET, BH18 8NG.
COVILLE, Mr. Peter Simon John, MA(Hons) ACA *2001;* Ground floor Building B, British Petroleum Co Plc, Chertsey Road, SUNBURY-ON-THAMES, MIDDLESEX, TW16 7LN.
COW, Mrs. Philippa Merrielle, BA(Hons) ACA *2000;* 6 Fox Leigh, Marlow Hill, HIGH WYCOMBE, HP11 1QD.
COWAN, Mr. Alexander Menzies, BSc ACA *2009;* 123 Merchants Quay, East Street, LEEDS, LS9 8BB.
COWAN, Mr. Andrew Simon, BA ACA *1986;* 8 Fisher Close, Duxford, CAMBRIDGE, CB22 4XU.
COWAN, Mr. Anthony, BSc ACA *2011;* 12 Brownlow Road, BOREHAMWOOD, HERTFORDSHIRE, WD6 2DE.
COWAN, Ms. Caroline Rachel, BA ACA *2000;* PARKER HANNIFIN EUROPE SARL, EUROPEAN HEADQUARTERS, LA TUILERE 6, CH 1163 ETOY, VAUD, SWITZERLAND.
COWAN, Mrs. Dawn, BSc ACA *2002;* 1 Lingfield Walk, Catshill, BROMSGROVE, WORCESTERSHIRE, B61 0LJ.
COWAN, Miss. Elizabeth McLean, ACA *1993;* 7 Brooklynn Close, Waltham Chase, SOUTHAMPTON, HAMPSHIRE, SO32 2RY.
COWAN, Miss. Emma Joy, BSc ACA *2006;* The Garden Flat, 12 Grosvenor Place, BATH, BA1 6AX.
COWAN, Mr. Guy Michael, BSc FCA *1976;* 20 Broadwater Street, RUNAWAY BAY, QLD 4216, AUSTRALIA.
•**COWAN, Mr. Ian Michael, BSc ACA** *1986;* Littlejohn LLP, 1 Westferry Circus, Canary Wharf, LONDON, E14 4HD.
COWAN, Mr. James, BA(Hons) ACA *2009;* 5 Manor Court, Huntington, YORK, YO32 9QY.
•**COWAN, Mr. John Andrew, BA FCA TEP** *1984;* (Tax Fac), Crowe Clark Whitehill Audit LLC, 6th Floor, Victory House, Prospect Hill, Douglas, ISLE OF MAN IM1 1EQ. See also Horwath Clark Whitehill Audit LLC and Horwath Clark Whitehill LLC
COWAN, Mr. Jonathan Brandon, FCA *1975;* 17 Murieston Road, Hale, ALTRINCHAM, CHESHIRE, WA15 9SU.
•**COWAN, Mr. Justin David Alexander, BA(Hons) ACA** *2001;* Albeck Limited, 112 Green Lane, EDGWARE, MIDDLESEX, HA8 8EJ.
•**COWAN, Mr. Laurence, FCA** *1968;* Laurie Cowan, 4 Chase Side, ENFIELD, EN2 6NF.
•**COWAN, Mr. Michael Russell, BA FCA** *1985;* PricewaterhouseCoopers LLP, 80 Strand, LONDON, WC2R 0AF. See also PricewaterhouseCoopers
COWAN, Mr. Neil John, FCA *1972;* Roughway Converters Ltd Roughway Mill, Dunks Green, TONBRIDGE, TN11 9SG.
COWAN, Mr. Nigel Ian, FCA *1974;* (Tax Fac), Turner Ferguson Cowan Shelton & Sager PC, 4001 E 42nd Street Suite 310, ODESSA, TX 79762, UNITED STATES.
•①**COWAN, Mr. Norman, FCA FABRP** *1967;* Wilder Coe LLP, Oxford House, Campus 6, Caxton Way, STEVENAGE, HERTFORDSHIRE SG1 2XD. See also Wilder Coe
COWAN, Mr. Peter, FCA *1948;* 304-442 Maple Avenue, BURLINGTON L7S 2L7, ON, CANADA. (Life Member)
COWAN, Mr. Peter John, FCA *1959;* Casablanca, Wild Cherry Drive, LUTON, LU1 3UH. (Life Member)
COWAN, Mr. Philip James, BSc FCA CF *1990;* V.Ships plc, Bank of India Ormond House, 63 Queen Victoria Street, LONDON, EC4N 4UA.
COWAN, Miss. Rebecca Louise, BSc ACA *2007;* 25 Wilderness Road, Earley, READING, RG6 7RU.
COWAN, Mrs. Sally Ann, BA ACA ATII *1986;* (Tax Fac), British Land Co Plc, York House, 45 Seymour Street, LONDON, W1H 7JT.
COWAN, Mr. Simon Bernard, BA(Hons) ACA *2001;* 53, Coppetts Road, LONDON, N10 1JH.
•**COWAN, Mr. Stanley, FCA** *1967;* (Tax Fac), Benjamin Taylor & Co, 201 Great Portland Street, LONDON, W1W 5AB. See also Compubook Services Ltd and Wigmore Registrars Ltd
COWAN, Mr. Stanley Samuel, FCA *1952;* 47 Southwood Lane, LONDON, N6 5ED. (Life Member)
•**COWAN, Mr. Wayne Alexander Mckim, FCA** *1982;* P.O.Box 1159, GEORGE TOWN, GRAND CAYMAN, KY1-1102, CAYMAN ISLANDS.
COWARD, Mrs. Caroline Ellen, BSc ACA *2010;* 2 Houghtons Court, Kirkham, PRESTON, PR4 2TN.
COWARD, Mr. Iain Kendal, BSc(Hons) ACA *2001;* Rational Entertainment Enterprises Ltd Douglas Bay Complex, King Edward Road Onchan, ISLE OF MAN, IM3 1DZ.
•**COWARD, Mr. James Alexander, BSc ACA** *2006;* James Coward ACA, 4 Fairview, North Brewham, BRUTON, SOMERSET, BA10 0JT.
•**COWARD, Mrs. Janet Kathleen Ann, FCA** *1973;* Sutcliffe & Co Ltd, Old Bank House, STURMINSTER NEWTON, DT10 1AN.
COWARD, Mrs. Joanna Mary, BA ACA *1991;* The Cottage Station Road, Bishops Itchington, SOUTHAM, CV47 2QB.
COWARD, Mr. John Michael, FCA *1961;* Quinta, 27 The Parkway, Rustington, LITTLEHAMPTON, WEST SUSSEX, BN16 2BT. (Life Member)
COWARD, Mr. Lee Thomas, BSc ACA *2010;* Broad View, Holme Lane, Allithwaite, GRANGE-OVER-SANDS, CUMBRIA, LA11 7QD.
COWARD, Mr. Mark David, BSc ACA *2005;* Level 5, 55 Clarence Street, SYDNEY, NSW 2000, AUSTRALIA.
•**COWARD, Mr. Mervyn Roderic, FCA** *1973;* The Lindens, Nooklands, Fulwood, PRESTON, PR2 8XN.
•**COWARD, Mr. Peter John, BA ACA** *1981;* PricewaterhouseCoopers LLP, 89 Sandyford Road, NEWCASTLE UPON TYNE, NE1 8HW. See also PricewaterhouseCoopers
COWARD, Mr. Richard Stanley, BA ACA *1999;* 17 Cromer Road Overstrand, CROMER, NR27 0NT.
•**COWARD, Mr. Robert Ernest, FCA** *1961;* Valentine Ellis & Co, Preacher's Court, The Charterhouse, Charterhouse Square, LONDON, EC1M 6AS.
COWARD, Mr. Robert James, BSc ACA *1992;* 7 Woodland Avenue, NORTHAMPTON, NN3 2BY.
COWARD, Mr. Simon Douglas, MA ACA *1986;* The Oaks, 16 Broadwater Close, Burwood Park, WALTON-ON-THAMES, KT12 5DD.
•**COWARD, Mr. William George Allen, BSc FCA** *1983;* George Allen & Co, 6 Lakeside View, Rawdon, LEEDS, LS19 6RN.
COWBURN, Mrs. Barbara Louise, MA FCA *1991;* Topping Partnership, 8 Exchange Quay, SALFORD, M5 3EJ.
COWBURN, Mr. John Heatley, FCA *1979;* John Cowburn Ltd, Oakwood, Cheddleton Road, LEEK, STAFFORDSHIRE, ST13 5QZ.
COWBURN, Miss. Lucille Mary, BA ACA *1994;* 64 Church Road, Uppermill, OLDHAM, OL3 6EH.
COWDALL, Mr. Andrew John, BSc ACA *1996;* The Pound House, Aston Rogers, Westbury, SHREWSBURY, SHROPSHIRE, SY5 9HQ.
COWDELL, Mrs. Ailsa Ann, MA ACA *1993;* West Dean, 37 Hooton Road, Willaston, NESTON, CH64 1SF.
COWDELL, Mr. John Bartholomew, BA ACA *1989;* Field House, Fyfield, ABINGDON, OX13 5LN.
COWDELL, Mr. Jonathan Nigel Edward, BSc ACA *1992;* West Dean, 37 Hooton Road, Willaston, NESTON, CH64 1SF.
COWDREY, Mr. Alan Paul, FCA *1973;* P C Partnership Ltd, 9 Firbarn Close, Firgrove, ROCHDALE, LANCASHIRE, OL16 3BF.
•**COWDREY, Mr. Michael Robin, FCA** *1969;* M.R. Cowdrey & Co, 125 Nottingham Road, Stapleford, NOTTINGHAM, NG9 8AT.
COWDRILL, Mr. Gary Terence, FCA *1981;* The Orchard, High Street, Belbroughton, STOURBRIDGE, DY9 9ST.
•**COWDY, Mr. Peter Edward Mason, MA MSc FCA** *1988;* (Tax Fac), P E M Cowdy Limited, Belmont House, Shrewsbury Business Park, SHREWSBURY, SY2 6LG.
COWDY, Mr. Philip Grenville, BSc ACA *1992;* 30 Veronica Road, LONDON, SW17 8QL.
COWE, Mr. Ian Duncan McNab, BSc(Hons) ACA *2003;* c/o Bata Brands SA, Rue Haldimand 4, 1003 LAUSANNE, VAUD, SWITZERLAND.
COWE, Mr. Peter, FCA *1965;* The Byre Muirton of Clunes, Kirkhill, INVERNESS, IV5 7PN.
COWELL, Miss. Allison, BA ACA *2005;* with Duncan & Toplis, 5 Resolution Close, Endeavour Park, BOSTON, LINCOLNSHIRE, PE21 7TT.
COWELL, Mrs. Alyson Jane, BA ACA *1992;* 16 Lache Lane, CHESTER, CH4 7LR.
COWELL, Mr. Andrew Stephen, BSc(Hons) ACA *2000;* 57 Claremont Avenue, NEW MALDEN, KT3 6QN.
COWELL, Mr. Anthony John, BSc ACA *1999;* with KPMG, P O Box 493 Century Yard, Cricket Square, GEORGE TOWN, GRAND CAYMAN, KY1-1106 CAYMAN ISLANDS.
COWELL, Mr. Benjamin Dominic Roland, BSc ACA *2005;* 2 Wellington Place, LEEDS, WEST YORKSHIRE, LS1 4AP.
COWELL, Mrs. Diana Jean, ACA *1981;* 7 Beechcroft, Chesham Road, BERKHAMSTED, HP4 3BT.
COWELL, Mrs. Jane Louise, BA ACA *1991;* Beechwood House, 2 Copse Lane, Hamble, SOUTHAMPTON, SO31 4QH.
COWELL, Mrs. Joanne, BSc ACA *1994;* House 5A UN Road, Floor 4, Baridhara, DHAKA, BANGLADESH.
COWELL, Mr. Peter Harry, FCA *1973;* Elmfield Hook Green Road, Southfleet, GRAVESEND, DA13 9NQ.
COWELL, Mr. Richard Stainsby, BA FCA *1971;* Les Arbres, Priory Road, Sunningdale, ASCOT, BERKSHIRE, SL5 9RH.
COWELL, Mrs. Sarah Louise, BSc ACA *1998;* P.O. BOX 10603, GEORGE TOWN, KY1-1006, CAYMAN ISLANDS.
•**COWELL, Mr. William James, FCA** *1958;* W.J. Cowell, 7 Spinney Close, Douglas, ISLE OF MAN, IM2 1NF.
COWELL, Mr. William Richard Forbes, BA(Hons) ACA *2002;* Anglesea Capital 0 LLP, 11 Hill Street, LONDON, W1J 5LF.
COWEN, Mr. Anthony Michael, FCA *1969;* 11 Milton Road, PEWSEY, SN9 5JJ. (Life Member)
COWEN, Mrs. Claire, MA ACA CTA DChA *1999;* (Tax Fac), 89 Estoril Avenue, WIGSTON, LEICESTERSHIRE, LE18 3RE.
COWEN, Mr. David John, BSc FCA *1988;* Molins Plc, Rockingham Drive, Lindford Wood East, MILTON KEYNES, MK14 6LY.
COWEN, Mr. Gavin, FCA *1970;* City Cottage, Preston Capes, DAVENTRY, NN11 3TE.
•**COWEN, Mrs. Julie Dawn, BA ACA** *1989;* (Tax Fac), Rowland Cowen & Co, 1 Holders Meadows, Holders Green, Lindsell, DUNMOW, ESSEX CM6 3QQ.
COWEN, Mr. Mark Phillip, BA ACA *1989;* Claverton Court, Claverton Road, Roundthorn Industrial Estate, MANCHESTER, M23 9NE.
COWEN, Mrs. Michele Christine, BA ACA *1988;* 33 Belfry Lane, Collingtree Park, NORTHAMPTON, NN4 0PB.
•**COWEN, Mr. Nicholas Stuart, BSc FCA** *1985;* Francis Clark, North Quay House, Sutton Harbour, PLYMOUTH, PL4 0RA. See also Francis Clark LLP
COWEN, Mrs. Paula Jane, BA ACA *1993;* The Chalet, 3 Hawthorn Drive, West Kirby, WIRRAL, MERSEYSIDE, CH48 9XJ.
•**COWEN, Mr. Richard Nathan, BA(Hons) ACA** *2001;* CWC Resources, Regus Euston Road Division, 338 Euston Road, LONDON, NW1 3BT.
COWEN, Mr. Robert Ian, BA ACA *1981;* PWS Distributors Ltd, PO Box 20, Aycliffe Industrial Park, NEWTON AYCLIFFE, DL5 6XJ.
COWEN, Mr. Simon, BA ACA *1987;* CLSA (UK), 12th Floor Moor House, 120 London Wall, LONDON, EC2Y 5ET.
COWEN, Mr. Stuart, FCA *1967;* Stuart Cowen Prof Corp'n, 11148-81 Avenue, EDMONTON T6G 0S5, AB, CANADA. (Life Member)
COWENS, Mr. James Robert, ACA *2010;* Flat 23, Hermitage Court, Knighten Street, LONDON, E1W 1PW.
COWEY, Mr. John Edwin, BSc FCA *1993;* 2 Neville's Cross Villas, Neville's Cross, DURHAM, DH1 4JR.
COWGILL, Mr. Andrew Anthony, BSc ACA *1988;* (Tax Fac), 24 Hawkhead Crescent, EDINBURGH, EH16 6LR.
COWGILL, Mr. Ben, ACA *2009;* 4 Reeceton Gardens, BOLTON, BL1 5BG.
•**COWGILL, Mrs. Carole Mary, BSc ACA** *1990;* Mrs C M Cowgill ACA, 4 Penny Meadow, Capel St. Mary, IPSWICH, IP9 2UU.
COWGILL, Ms. Karen Patricia, BSc ACA *1998;* Cross House, Main Street, Staveley, KENDAL, CUMBRIA, LA8 9LN.
•**COWGILL, Mr. Peter Alan, BSc FCA** *1981;* Cowgill Holloway LLP, Regency House, 45-51 Chorley New Road, BOLTON, BL1 4QR. See also Cowgill Holloway & Co
•**COWHAM, Mr. Paul Michael, MA ACA DChA** *2006;* Slade & Cooper Limited, 6 Mount Street, MANCHESTER, M2 5NS.
COWHIG, Mr. Neil Eltin, BSc ACA *1993;* 18 Millway, REIGATE, RH2 0RH.
COWHIG, Mr. Timothy Joseph, BSc ACA *1983;* 45 Carbery Avenue, Southbourne, BOURNEMOUTH, BH6 3LN.
COWIE, Mr. Andrew Jonathan Scott, BSc ACA *2007;* 26 Bantock Close, Browns Wood, MILTON KEYNES, MK7 8DS.
COWIE, Mr. Bruce Murdoch, MA FCA *1985;* Hill House, Handforth Road, WILMSLOW, SK9 2LU.
COWIE, Miss. Clare, ACA *2011;* 35 Harton House Road, SOUTH SHIELDS, TYNE AND WEAR, NE34 6EE.
COWIE, Mr. David Edward, BSc FCA *1977;* Manchester Building Society, Beaver House, 125 Portland Street, MANCHESTER, M1 4QD.
COWIE, Miss. Elaine, MA ACA *1993;* 77 Long Lane, Ickenham, UXBRIDGE, UB10 8QS.
COWIE, Mr. Ewen Ross, FCA *1977;* Thornleigh, 145 Maldon Road, COLCHESTER, CO3 3BJ.
COWIE, Mr. John Randall Lorn, BA FCA CF *1992;* Seymour Pierce Limited, 20 Old Bailey, LONDON, EC4M 7EN.
COWIE, Mr. Kevin Neil, BA FCA *1984;* Holborn Cottage, 38 Feckenham Road, Headless Cross, REDDITCH, B97 5AR.
•**COWIE, Mr. Martin Alexander, ACA** *2007;* with PricewaterhouseCoopers LLP, Erskine House, 68-73 Queen Street, EDINBURGH, EH2 4NH.
•**COWIE, Mr. Robert Richard, FCA** *1976;* Winter Rule LLP, Lowin House, Tregolls Road, TRURO, CORNWALL, TR1 2NA. See also Francis Clark LLP
COWIN, Mr. Andrew John, BSc ACA *1979;* 27 Causley Drive, Barrs CourtWarmley, BRISTOL, BS30 7BA.
COWIN, Mr. Christopher Barry Philip, BA ACA *1999;* 70 Victor Road, TEDDINGTON, MIDDLESEX, TW11 8SR.
COWIN, Mr. Ian Harold, ACA *1982;* 39 The Elms, HERTFORD, SG13 7UY.
COWIN, Mr. Peter Kevin, BA ACA *1992;* 16 Third Avenue, Douglas, ISLE OF MAN, IM2 6AL.
•**COWIN, Mr. Robert Andrew, BA FCA** *1989;* 3 Brockwell Place, HILLARYS, WA 6025, AUSTRALIA.
COWIN, Mr. Robert William, FCA *1960;* 9 Howstrake Drive, Onchan, ISLE OF MAN, IM3 1BP. (Life Member)
COWL, Miss. Joanne, ACA *2002;* Communisis Plc, Wakefield Road, LEEDS, LS10 1DU.
COWLAND, Mr. Daniel James, FCA *1998;* 19 Woodhurst Lane, OXTED, SURREY, RH8 9HN.
COWLAND, Mr. Mark James, BA ACA *1998;* (Tax Fac), with KPMG LLP, 1 Forest Gate, Brighton Road, CRAWLEY, WEST SUSSEX, RH11 9PT.
COWLE, Mr. Robert Edward, BA FCA MSI *1997;* 141 Cassiobury Drive, WATFORD, WD17 3AH.
COWLES, Mr. Jonathan Robert, BSc ACA *1998;* 11 Glyncastle Caversham, READING, RG4 7XF.
COWLES, Mrs. Ruth Ann, BA ACA *1984;* 6 Moorland Rise, Haslingden, ROSSENDALE, BB4 6UA.
COWLEY, Mrs. Amanda Julie, ACA *1992;* 3 Nash Place, Penn, HIGH WYCOMBE, BUCKINGHAMSHIRE, HP10 8ES.
•**COWLEY, Mrs. Anne Louise, BA FCA** *1993;* Baines Jewitt, Barrington House, 41-45 Yarm Lane, STOCKTON-ON-TEES, CLEVELAND, TS18 3EA. See also Barrington House Solutions Limited
•**COWLEY, Mrs. Annette Maria, BA FCA** *1982;* (Tax Fac), Cowley & Co, 73 Arthur Road, LONDON, SW19 7DP.
•**COWLEY, Mr. Barry David, FCA** *1984;* (Tax Fac), Cowley Holmes Accountants LLP, 9 Goldington Road, BEDFORD, MK40 3JY.
COWLEY, Mr. Ben, BSc ACA *2010;* with PricewaterhouseCoopers LLP, 1 Embankment Place, LONDON, WC2N 6RH.
COWLEY, Mr. Brian Maurice, FCA *1971;* 85 Theydon Park Road, Theydon Bois, EPPING, CM16 7LS.
COWLEY, Mr. David Benjamin, BA ACA *2005;* 61 Park Road, STOURBRIDGE, WEST MIDLANDS, DY8 3QX.
COWLEY, Ms. Georgina Marie, BSc ACA *1993;* 33 Moorlands Avenue, KENILWORTH, CV8 1RZ.
COWLEY, Mrs. Helen Ruth, ACA *2007;* 16 Green Bank, Harwood, BOLTON, BL2 3NG.
•**COWLEY, Mr. John, ACA** *1980;* (Tax Fac), John Cowley, Bramleys, Bath Road, STURMINSTER NEWTON, DORSET, DT10 1EB.
COWLEY, Mr. John Neil, MA BA ACA *2004;* with PricewaterhouseCoopers, Sixty Circular Road, Douglas, ISLE OF MAN, IM1 1SA.
COWLEY, Mr. Keith Frank, BA ACA *1995;* Flat 10 Charleville Mansions, Charleville Road, LONDON, W14 9JB.
•**COWLEY, Dr. Kevin Michael, BSc ACA** *1999;* PricewaterhouseCoopers LLC, Sixty Circular Road, Circular Road, Douglas, ISLE OF MAN, IM1 1SA.
COWLEY, Mr. Nicholas Robert John, MA MSc ACA *1991;* Hakkasan Ltd, 151-153 Wardour Street, LONDON, W1F 8WE.
COWLEY, Mr. Patrick Louis, FCA *1957;* 53 Hillcrest, Withdean, BRIGHTON, BN1 5FP. (Life Member)
COWLEY, Mr. Paul Alexander, BA ACA *1994;* GHG, 4 Thameside Centre, Kew Bridge Road, BRENTFORD, MIDDLESEX, TW8 0HF.
COWLEY, Mr. Phillip Geoffrey, BSc ACA *1984;* NHS Derby City Cardinal Square, 10 Nottingham Road, DERBY, DE1 3QT.
COWLEY, Mrs. Rachel Anne, ACA *2009;* Hall Floor Flat, 9 Osborne Road, Clifton, BRISTOL, BS8 2HA.

COWLEY, Mr. Richard James Lewry, MSc BA ACA *1997;* Flint Cottage, 28 Straight Bit, Flackwell Heath, HIGH WYCOMBE, HP10 9LT.

COWLEY, Mr. Robin Frederick, FCA *1967;* The Willows, Sunnyside Lane, Balsall Common, COVENTRY, CV7 7FY.

COWLEY, Mr. Simon, BSc ACA *2011;* 7 Thames Eyot, Cross Deep, TWICKENHAM, TW1 4QL.

•**COWLEY, Mr. Simon Charles, FCA** *1973;* Simon Cowley, 73 Arthur Road, LONDON, SW19 7DP.

COWLEY, Mrs. Stephanie Louise, BSc ACA *2001;* Leicester Rugby Football Club, Aylestone Road, LEICESTER, LE2 7TR.

COWLEY, Mr. Victor Herbert, FCA *1981;* 226 Leigh Hunt Drive, Southgate, LONDON, N14 6DS.

COWLEY, Miss. Victoria Claire, BA(Hons) ACA *2004;* 16 Ravenslea Road, LONDON, SW12 8RY.

COWLEY, Mr. William Terence, BA FCA *1969;* Streamside Cottage, Alton Pancras, DORCHESTER, DT2 7RS. (Life Member)

•**COWLING, Mrs. Christabel Helen Herod, LLB ACA** *1994;* Ernst & Young LLP, 1 Colmore Square, BIRMINGHAM, B4 6HQ. See also Ernst & Young Europe LLP

COWLING, Mr. David Wren, BA ACA *1998;* Cinven, Warwick Court, Paternoster Square, LONDON, EC4M 7AG.

COWLING, Miss. Deborah Jane, ACA *1995;* 639 Bradford Road, Birkenshaw, BRADFORD, BD11 2AU.

COWLING, Mr. John Anthony, FCA *1964;* 6 St. Stephens Close, ST. ALBANS, AL3 4AB. (Life Member)

•**COWLING, Mr. John Hugh, BA ACA** *1987;* (Tax Fac), John Cowling & Co, 1 Britten Close, Great Berry, Langdon Hills, BASILDON, ESSEX SS16 6TB.

•**COWLING, Mr. John Steven, BA ACA** *1980;* PricewaterhouseCoopers LLP, 1 East Parade, SHEFFIELD, S1 2ET. See also PricewaterhouseCoopers

COWLING, Mr. Malcolm John, BSc ACA *1986;* Highwood House, 6 Beech Road, Purley On Thames, READING, RG8 8DS.

COWLING, Mr. Martin Anderson, BA ACA *1984;* 36 Holden Lane, Baildon, SHIPLEY, WEST YORKSHIRE, BD17 6HZ.

COWLING, Mr. Maurice John Kenneth, FCA *1964;* Ravenshaw, Main Road, Wigtoft, BOSTON, LINCOLNSHIRE, PE20 2NX.

COWLING, Mrs. Nicola Ann, BA ACA *1987;* Old Orchard House, Two Mile Oak, NEWTON ABBOT, DEVON, TQ12 6DD.

COWLING, Mr. Robert John, BA ACA *1991;* Old Orchard House, Two Mile Oak, NEWTON ABBOT, DEVON, TQ12 6DD.

•**COWLING, Mr. Robert Kenneth, BSc FCA** *1982;* T Rawlinson & Co Limited, 127 Cleethorpe Road, GRIMSBY, SOUTH HUMBERSIDE, DN31 3EW.

COWLING, Miss. Sally Ann, BSc ACA *1988;* Nottinghamshire Police, Force Headquarters, Sherwood Lodge, Arnold, NOTTINGHAM, NG5 8PP.

COWLING, Miss. Shirley May, BA FCA *1976;* SHIRAL STAR PTY LTD, 544 Dandenong Road, CAULFIELD NORTH, VIC 3161, AUSTRALIA.

•**COWLING, Mr. Vincent Edward, FCA** *1989;* Woodward Hale, 38 Dollar Street, CIRENCESTER, GL7 2AN. See also Woodward Hale Limited

COWLISHAW, Mr. Alan, FCA *1958;* Warriors, Millfield Lane, St. Ippolyts, HITCHIN, SG4 7NH. (Life Member)

COWLISHAW, Mr. John, ACA *1987;* 5 Portland Place, Hertford Heath, HERTFORD, SG13 7RR.

COWLISHAW, Mrs. Marion Ernestein, BA ACA *1980;* 254 Stanton Road, Stapenhill, BURTON-ON-TRENT, DE15 9SG.

•①**COWLISHAW, Mr. Matthew James, BA ACA** *1999;* Deloitte LLP, 4 Brindley Place, BIRMINGHAM, B1 2HZ. See also Deloitte & Touche LLP

•**COWMAN, Mr. Simon Nicholas, FCA** *1971;* Simon N. Cowman, Mayfield, 8 Brooksby Road, Hoby, MELTON MOWBRAY, LEICESTERSHIRE LE14 3EA.

COWNEY, Mr. Nicholas Edward, BA ACA *1994;* 99 Hargrave Street, PADDINGTON, NSW 2021, AUSTRALIA.

COWNIE, Mrs. Sarah Josephine, BSc ACA *1981;* 178-180 Hotwell Road, BRISTOL, BS8 4RP.

COWOOD, Mr. Stephen Michael, BSc ACA *1991;* Flat 405 Adana Building, Conington Road, LONDON, SE13 7FB.

COWPE, Mrs. Joanna Ruth, MA BA ACA *2006;* 31 Victoria Road, BERKHAMSTED, HERTFORDSHIRE, HP4 2JT.

COWPER, Mr. Christopher Roland, FCA *1967;* 5 Carson Street, PYMBLE, NSW 2073, AUSTRALIA.

COWPER, Mr. Jeremy Glen, BA ACA PIIA PMP *1984;* Huber Engineered Woods LLC, 10925 David Taylor Drive, One Resource Square, Suite 300, CHARLOTTE, NC 28262 UNITED STATES.

COWPER, Mr. Mark, BA(Hons) ACA *2004;* 8 Plane Avenue, Northfleet, GRAVESEND, KENT, DA11 9QB.

COWPER, Mrs. Sharon Elizabeth, BA ACA *1993;* Miedera, Wood Lane, Kidmore End, READING, RG4 9BE.

COWPER, Mr. Stephen Paul, BSc ACA *2006;* Flat 61 Moore House, Cassilis Road, LONDON, E14 9LN.

COWPER, Mr. Timothy, BA ACA *1990;* Miedera, Wood Lane, Kidmore End, READING, RG4 9BE.

COWPERTHWAITE, Mr. Andrew Neill, BA ACA *2009;* 11 Elizabeth Court, The Square Glenfield, LEICESTER, LE3 8DQ.

COWPERTHWAITE, Mr. John Lawrence, FCA *1964;* 823 Mariner Way, PARKSVILLE V9P 1S3, BC, CANADA.

COWPERTHWAITE, Miss. Samantha, ACA *2011;* Hollin Hall, Crook, KENDAL, CUMBRIA, LA8 9HP.

COWPERTWAIT, Mr. Colin James, BA(Hons) ACA *2001;* Bindman & Partners, 275 Gray's Inn Road, LONDON, WC1X 8QB.

COWPLAND, Mr. Geoffrey William Ronald, FCA *1963;* Cockerswood, Horam, HEATHFIELD, EAST SUSSEX, TN21 0JN. (Life Member)

COWSILL, Mr. Iain Gordon, MEng BSc ACA *1996;* 7 Pierrepoint Road, LONDON, W3 9JJ.

COWX, Mr. Clive James, BA ACA *1980;* 47 Valley Way, KNUTSFORD, WA16 9AY.

COX, Sir Alan George, CBE FCA FCMA *1959;* PO BOX 27, CHEPSTOW, NP16 6EY.

COX, Mr. Alan Robert, FCA *1962;* Chapel House, All Saints Road, BATH, BA1 5HE. (Life Member)

COX, Mr. Alan William Lockhart, BSc FCA *1973;* Frank Buttle Trust, 13 Palace Street, LONDON, SW1E 5HX.

COX, Mr. Allister Russell, ACA *1986;* The Small House, Mynthurst, Leigh, REIGATE, RH2 8RJ.

COX, Mrs. Amy Katherine, BSc ACA *2004;* Greenleas Stokes Mead, Woodbury, EXETER, EX5 1DZ.

COX, Mrs. Amy Marie, BSc ACA *2004;* 9 Stirling Close, CONGLETON, CHESHIRE, CW12 4US.

COX, Mr. Andrew Benjamin, BA ACA *2005;* with Deloitte LLP, Athene Place, 66 Shoe Lane, LONDON, EC4A 3BQ.

COX, Mr. Andrew Charles, FCA *1981;* 5 Sheraton Grange, Norton, STOURBRIDGE, DY8 2BE.

COX, Mr. Andrew Dalway, BCom ACA *2002;* 21 Ruskin Avenue, Kew, RICHMOND, SURREY, TW9 4DR.

COX, Mr. Andrew David, BSc ACA ATII *1999;* (Tax Fac), 45 Nightingale Road, Petts Wood, ORPINGTON, BR5 1BH.

•**COX, Mr. Andrew Francis, BA FCA** *1995;* KPMG LLP, 15 Canada Square, LONDON, E14 5GL. See also KPMG Europe LLP

COX, Mr. Andrew John, BSc FCA *1982;* 19 Croft Road, BROMLEY, BR1 4DR.

•**COX, Mr. Andrew Joseph, BA FCA CTA** *1990;* Rawlinsons, Ruthlyn House, 90 Lincoln Road, PETERBOROUGH, PE1 2SP.

COX, Mr. Anthony Christopher, BSc ACA *1998;* Droogbak 6c, 1013 GE AMSTERDAM, NETHERLANDS.

COX, Mr. Anthony John, BSc ACA *1999;* Malden, 17 Lyndale Avenue, Wilpshire, BLACKBURN, LANCASHIRE, BB1 9LP.

COX, Mr. Anthony Leigh, FCA *1974;* 91 Glenforest Road, TORONTO M4N 2A1, ON, CANADA.

COX, Mr. Anthony Neil, BA(Hons) ACA *2000;* 282 Hardhorn Road, POULTON-LE-FYLDE, FY6 8DW.

COX, Mr. Anthony Norman, FCA *1967;* Blesswell Farm, The Bostel, Upper Beeding, STEYNING, WEST SUSSEX, BN44 3TA. (Life Member)

COX, Mr. Antony Paul, FCA MCT *1984;* 16 Linden Road, Muswell Hill, LONDON, N10 3DH.

COX, Mr. Ashley Paul, BSc ACA *2005;* KPMG, 10 Shelley Street, SYDNEY, NSW 2000, AUSTRALIA.

COX, Mr. Bradley Dwight, BA(Hons) ACA *2010;* Flat 14, 102 Great Titchfield Street, LONDON, W1W 6SL.

COX, Mr. Brian, ACA *1993;* 11 Dover Close, RUSHDEN, NN10 0RQ.

•**COX, Mr. Brian Alfred, FCA** *1963;* 4 Blenheim Mews, Beavers Road, FARNHAM, GU9 7FY.

•**COX, Mr. Brian John, FCA** *1968;* (Tax Fac), Brian Cox & Co, Crown Buildings, 18 Market Hill, CHATTERIS, PE16 6BA.

COX, Mr. Bryan Beeching, FCA *1956;* 41 Hazelmere Road, Petts Wood, ORPINGTON, BR5 1PA. (Life Member)

•**COX, Mrs. Carolyn Susan, FCA** *1981;* 22 The Timbers, FAREHAM, PO15 5NB. See also Rothman Pantall LLP

•**COX, Mrs. Catherine Ann, FCA CTA DChA** *1985;* C.A. Cox, 18 Chambers Close, MARKFIELD, LE67 9NB.

•**COX, Mr. Charles, FCA** *1972;* PKF (UK) LLP, Farringdon Place, 20 Farringdon Road, LONDON, EC1M 3AP.

COX, Mr. Christopher Paul, BA ACA *2003;* Greenleas Stokes Mead, Woodbury, EXETER, EX5 1DZ.

COX, Mr. Craig Rhys William, BA ACA *2006;* 22 Hafan yr Heli, Kinmel Bay, RHYL, CLWYD, LL18 5JQ.

COX, Mr. Darran, BEng FCA *1991;* 86 Woodland Avenue, HOVE, BN3 6BN.

COX, Mr. David, ACA *2007;* (Tax Fac), 127 Watermarque, 100 Browning Street, BIRMINGHAM, B16 8GZ.

•**COX, Mr. David, BSc ACA** *2002;* haysmacintyre, Fairfax House, 15 Fulwood Place, LONDON, WC1V 6AY.

•**COX, Mr. David Andrew, BA FCA FCCA** *1987;* Cox & Co (Accountancy) Limited, The Granary, High Street, Turvey, BEDFORD, MK43 8DB. See also Cox & Co(Management Consultancy) Ltd

COX, Mr. David Burgess, FCA *1974;* 18 Amante Crescent, Mairangi Bay, AUCKLAND 10, NEW ZEALAND.

•**COX, Mr. David Charles, FCA** *1978;* (Tax Fac), Harwood Lane & Co, 1-4 Crossley Farm Business Centre, Swan Lane, Winterbourne, BRISTOL, BS36 1RH.

COX, Mr. David Charles, BA ACA *1991;* The Economist Group, The Economist Building, 750 3rd Ave, NEW YORK, NY 10017, UNITED STATES.

•**COX, Mr. David John, FCA** *1968;* (Tax Fac), David J Cox (Midlands) Limited, 45 The Ridgeway, STOURPORT-ON-SEVERN, DY13 8XT.

•**COX, Mr. David Leslie James, FCA** *1973;* Roebuck, Hermitage, THATCHAM, RG18 9RZ.

•**COX, Mr. David Nigel, BSc FCA** *1986;* (Tax Fac), Metherell Gard Ltd, Burn View, BUDE, CORNWALL, EX23 8BX. See also M G Trustees Ltd

COX, Mr. David Norman, BSc ACA *2003;* Moss House Farm, Brandside, BUXTON, DERBYSHIRE, SK17 0SF.

COX, Mr. David Peter, BSc ACA *1992;* 54 Treguddock Drive, WADEBRIDGE, CORNWALL, PL27 6BQ.

COX, Mr. Dennis William, BSc FCA FSI *1981;* MEMBER OF COUNCIL, Risk Reward Limited, 60 Moorgate, LONDON, EC2R 6EL.

•**COX, Mr. Duncan John, BA ACA** *1998;* PricewaterhouseCoopers LLP, 7 More London Riverside, LONDON, SE1 2RT. See also PricewaterhouseCoopers

COX, Mr. Edward John Machell, MA FCA *1961;* 13 St Ann's Villas, LONDON, W11 4RT.

•**COX, Mrs. Eleana, BA(Hons) ACA** *2002;* (Tax Fac), Cox, PO Box 1241, BLACKPOOL, FY1 9FD.

COX, Mrs. Elizabeth A, BA ACA *2006;* Sainsburys Plc, 33 Holborn, LONDON, EC1N 2HT.

COX, Mrs. Elizabeth Ann, BA ACA *1995;* Willow House, Combe Lane, Wormley, GODALMING, SURREY, GU8 5TE.

COX, Miss. Elizabeth Louise, BSc ACA *2007;* Flat 52 Ionian Building, 45 Narrow Street, LONDON, E14 8DW.

COX, Mrs. Elizabeth Susan, MA ACA *1988;* British Geriatrics Society, Marjory Warren House, 31 St. John's Square, LONDON, EC1M 4DN.

•**COX, Miss. Emma Helen Louise, MA ACA** *1993;* PricewaterhouseCoopers LLP, 1 Embankment Place, LONDON, WC2N 6RH. See also PricewaterhouseCoopers

•**COX, Mrs. Emma June, BA ACA** *1997;* Deloitte LLP, 2 New Street Square, LONDON, EC4A 3BZ. See also Deloitte & Touche LLP

COX, Mr. Fletcher Richard Tregony, BSc ACA *2001;* 5 Holmwood Cottages, Bentley, FARNHAM, SURREY, GU10 5NF.

•**COX, Mr. Frank Arthur, BSc FCA** *1983;* (Tax Fac), Sandy Ridge, Beach Road, NEWQUAY, TR8 5RN.

•**COX, Mrs. Freda Madeleine, FCA** *1973;* Grays Accountants Limited, Kings Works, Kings Road, TEDDINGTON, MIDDLESEX, TW11 0QB.

COX, Mr. Garth Michael, BSc ACA *1996;* 123 Orphanage Road, BIRMINGHAM, B24 0AJ.

COX, Mr. Geoffrey Michael, FCA *1960;* 45 Manchester Road, Wollaston, WELLINGBOROUGH, NORTHAMPTONSHIRE, NN29 7SR. (Life Member)

•**COX, Mr. Geoffrey Robert, BA ACA** *1998;* Dafferns LLP, 1 Eastwood, Harry Weston Road, Binley Business Park, COVENTRY, CV3 2UB. See also Dafferns Resource LLP and Geoffrey Cox Limited

COX, Mr. Graeme Anthony, BA ACA *1995;* Dole Thailand Limited, 10th Floor Panjathani Tower, 127/11 Nonsee Road, Yannawa, BANGKOK, 10120 THAILAND.

COX, Mr. Graham Stewart, BA ACA *1991;* Parallel Private Equity, 49 St Jame's Street, LONDON, SW1A 1JT.

COX, Mr. Gregory Philip, LLB ACA *1998;* 30 Cooper Road, BRISTOL, BS9 3RA.

COX, Miss. Hannah Lucy, BSc ACA *2008;* 27 Frankston Avenue, Stony Stratford, MILTON KEYNES, MK11 1DR.

COX, Ms. Harriet Emily Wilson, BSc ACA *2011;* 16 Lansdowne Circus, LEAMINGTON SPA, WARWICKSHIRE, CV32 4SW.

COX, Miss. Hazel Lesley, BSc ACA *2004;* 14 Brooklands Avenue, ROSSENDALE, BB4 4EU.

COX, Mrs. Heather Elizabeth, BSc ACA *1985;* The Inches, Holyport Road, MAIDENHEAD, SL6 2HD.

COX, Mrs. Helen, BA ACA *2006;* 13 Carleton Rise, WELWYN, HERTFORDSHIRE, AL6 9RP.

COX, Miss. Helen Ann McKay, BSc ACA *1999;* with PricewaterhouseCoopers, Darling Park Tower 2, 201 Sussex Street, GPO Box 2650, SYDNEY, NSW 1171 AUSTRALIA.

COX, Mr. Homersham Martin, FCA *1966;* Littlewood Park View, Buxted, UCKFIELD, TN22 4LS. (Life Member)

COX, Mr. Humphrey James, FCA ACMA *1949;* 2 Margaret Close, BOGNOR REGIS, WEST SUSSEX, PO21 3AA. (Life Member)

COX, Mr. Ian Barry, BA FCA *1992;* Old Bullingstone, Bullingstone Lane, Speldhurst, TUNBRIDGE WELLS, TN3 0JY.

COX, Mr. James Edward Charles, ACA *1997;* 16 Boley Drive, CLACTON-ON-SEA, CO15 6LB.

COX, Mr. James Nicholas Marshall, BSc ACA *1994;* 6 Mill Road, Sturry, CANTERBURY, CT2 0AD.

•**COX, Mrs. Janet Elizabeth, BSc FCA** *1983;* with Whitakers, Bryndon House, 5-7 Berry Road, NEWQUAY, TR7 1AD.

COX, Mr. Jason, MEng ACA *2004;* I N G Bank NV, 60 London Wall, LONDON, EC2M 5TQ.

COX, Mr. Jeffrey Peter, BSc FCA *1993;* 102 The Grove, SIDCUP, DA14 5NQ.

COX, Dr. Jennifer Margaret, PhD ACA *1994;* South Holland House, Spendlas Lane, Long Sutton, SPALDING, LINCOLNSHIRE, PE12 9AP.

COX, Mr. Jeremy Edward, BA ACA *1995;* 11 CLAREMONT LODGE, 15 The Downs, LONDON, SW20 8UA.

COX, Mr. Jeremy James Homersham, BCom FCA *1998;* 5 Rock Mill Lane, LEAMINGTON SPA, CV32 6AP.

COX, Mr. John, FCA *1971;* (Tax Fac), The Rickyard, Orleton, LUDLOW, SHROPSHIRE, SY8 4HR.

•**COX, Mr. John Adrian, FCA** *1959;* Whitehouse Risdale, 26 Birmingham Road, WALSALL, WS1 2LZ.

COX, Mr. John Andrew, BA FCA *1989;* Landau Forte College, Fox Street, DERBY, DE1 2LF.

COX, Mr. John Anthony Sayers, FCA *1970;* Glebe House, School Lane, Skeyton, NORWICH, NR10 5BA.

COX, Mr. John Duncan Stewart, FCA *1973;* Maple Business Consultants Limited, 7 Danebury Gardens, Chandler's Ford, EASTLEIGH, SO53 4NQ.

•**COX, Mr. John Frederick, MA ACA** *1995;* Deloitte LLP, Athene Place, 66 Shoe Lane, LONDON, EC4A 3BQ. See also Deloitte & Touche LLP

COX, Mr. John Herbert, FCA *1952;* 4 Fernwood Close, SUTTON COLDFIELD, B73 5BH. (Life Member)

COX, Mr. John Luscombe, FCA *1958;* 52 Blenheim Road, ORPINGTON, BR6 9BH. (Life Member)

COX, Mr. John William, FCA *1963;* Whitethorn Lodge, New Road, Belton, GREAT YARMOUTH, NR31 9JW. (Life Member)

COX, Mr. Jonathan, BSc ACA *1992;* 3 Crosshills, Stony Stratford, MILTON KEYNES, MK11 1HD.

COX, Mr. Jonathan Francis, BA ACA *1987;* 11 Church Close, Alveston, STRATFORD-UPON-AVON, WARWICKSHIRE, CV37 7QG.

COX, Mr. Jonathan Hale, FCA *1977;* Railway Enginemens Assurance Society Ltd, 727 Washwood Heath Road, BIRMINGHAM, B8 2LE.

COX, Mr. Jonathan James, BSc ACA *1988;* 89 Station Road, Glenfield, LEICESTER, LE3 8GS.

COX, Mr. Jonathan James, BSc ACA *2010;* 7a Webb's Road, LONDON, SW11 1XJ.

•**COX, Mr. Jonathan Thirkell, MBA BA FCA** *1979;* Jonathan T Cox, 26 Anagh Coar Close, Douglas, ISLE OF MAN, IM2 2BG.

COX, Mrs. Julia Amanda, BSc ACA *2003;* 1 Annaleigh Place, Rydens Grove, WALTON-ON-THAMES, SURREY, KT12 5RW.

COX, Mr. Julian William, BSc ACA *1991;* D S Smith Plc Whitebrook Park, Lower Cookham Road, MAIDENHEAD, SL6 8XY.

COX, Mr. Kenneth Frederick, FCA *1972;* 2 Chaucer Drive, BURNTWOOD, STAFFORDSHIRE, WS7 2HT.

COX, Mrs. Kerry, BSc ACA CTA *2005;* Apartment 187, 51 Sherborne Street, BIRMINGHAM, B16 8FP.

•**COX, Mr. Kevin Alan, MA FCA** *1980;* Craig McIntyre & Peacock, 33 Lewis Street, STRANRAER, DG9 7LB.

COX, Mr. Laurence William, FCA *1982;* Robert Cort Ltd, Elgar Road South, READING, BERKSHIRE, RG2 0DL.

•**COX, Mr. Leslie Denis, ACA FCCA** *2008;* Brooking Ruse & Co Limited, 3 Beaconsfield Road, WESTON-SUPER-MARE, SOMERSET, BS23 1YE.

•**COX, Mr. Leslie James, FCA** *1976;* (Tax Fac), R.E.Jones & Co, 132 Burnt Ash Road, Lee, LONDON, SE12 8PU.

COX, Mrs. Lisa Suzanne, BSc ACA *1998;* 45 Nightingale Road, Petts Wood, ORPINGTON, BR5 1BH.

•**COX, Mrs. Lorna Elizabeth, ACA FCCA** *2010;* Mitchams Accountants Limited, 1 Cornhill, ILMINSTER, SOMERSET, TA19 0AD.

COX, Miss. Madeleine Norma, BSc ACA *1986;* Fir Tree House, 26 Woodlands Ride, South Ascot, ASCOT, SL5 9HN.

COX, Dr. Mark, MSc BSc ACA *2005;* 28 Ember Gardens, THAMES DITTON, KT7 0LN.

•**COX, Mr. Martin Christopher, FCA** *1986;* (Tax Fac), MCA Breslins Leamington Ltd, 5-7 Newbold Street, LEAMINGTON SPA, WARWICKSHIRE, CV32 4HN. See also Breslin Banbury Limited and Breslins Leamington Limited

COX, Mr. Martin Jonathan, BA ACA *1992;* 8 Oak Lane, WOKING, GU22 8BX.

COX, Mr. Martyn John, BA ACA *1990;* 27 The Shrubbery, Fields End, HEMEL HEMPSTEAD, HP1 2TG.

COX, Mr. Matthew, BA(Hons) ACA CFA *2000;* S G Hambros Bank Ltd Norfolk House, 31 St. James's Square, LONDON, SW1Y 4JR.

COX, Mr. Matthew, MSc BSc ACA *2007;* Deloitte & Touche Hill House, 1 Little New Street, LONDON, EC4A 3TR.

COX, Mr. Matthew James, MA(Hons) ACA *2002;* Rio Tinto, 2 Eastbourne Terrace, LONDON, W2 6LG.

COX, Mr. Matthew Victor Thomas, MSc BSc ACA *1996;* with Grant Thornton UK LLP, Grant Thornton House, 22 Melton Street, Euston Square, LONDON, NW1 2EP.

COX, Mr. Michael David, BA FCA *1972;* Delmonden, Springfield Road, Bickley, BROMLEY, BR1 2LJ.

COX, Mr. Michael David, LLB ACA *2001;* U B S AG, 100 Liverpool Street, LONDON, EC2M 2RH.

•**COX, Mr. Michael David, ACA** *1986;* Michael Cox Accounting Services Limited, 13b Westfield Road, BARTON-UPON-HUMBER, SOUTH HUMBERSIDE, DN18 5AA.

COX, Mr. Michael David, BA ACA *2009;* 49 Carisbrooke Avenue, HIGH WYCOMBE, BUCKINGHAMSHIRE, HP12 4NL.

•**COX, Mr. Michael Dexter, FCA** *1970;* Michael D. Cox, Rostrevor, Vicarage Lane, Water Orton, BIRMINGHAM, B46 1RX.

•**COX, Mr. Michael Francis, BSc FCA** *1985;* Cox Costello & Horne Limited, Langwood House, 63-81 High Street, RICKMANSWORTH, HERTFORDSHIRE, WD3 1EQ. See also Cox Costello & Horne Partners LLP

•**COX, Mr. Michael George, FCA** *1969;* 33 Storeton Road, PRENTON, CH43 5TN.

COX, Mr. Michael John, MBA BSc ACA *1983;* Hopkins Homes Ltd, Melton Park House, 4 Scott Lane, Melton, WOODBRIDGE, SUFFOLK IP12 1TJ.

•**COX, Mr. Michael John, FCA** *1967;* (Tax Fac), Baldwin Cox & Co., 15-17 Foster Avenue, Beeston, NOTTINGHAM, NG9 1AE.

•**COX, Mr. Michael Neill, ACA** *1980;* Price Firman, Prince Consort House, Albert Embankment, LONDON, SE1 7TJ.

COX, Mr. Michael William, FCA *1969;* 22 Wilson Gardens, Gosforth, NEWCASTLE UPON TYNE, NE3 4JA.

COX, Miss. Nicola Ruth, BA(Hons) ACA *2001;* Flat 1, Archfield Court, Archfield Road, BRISTOL, BS6 6BX.

COX, Mr. Nigel Robert, BSc ACA *1986;* Rowan Garth, 71 Bell Hill, PETERSFIELD, GU32 2EA.

COX, Mrs. Patricia, BA ACA *1991;* Espaliers, 8a Clifton Road, AMERSHAM, BUCKINGHAMSHIRE, HP6 5PU.

COX, Mr. Patrick Charles, FCA *1974;* Glovers Meadow, Glovers Road, Charlwood, HORLEY, RH6 0EG.

COX, Mr. Paul, BSc ACA *2006;* 2 Tagg Way, Rackheath, NORWICH, NR13 6SQ.

COX, Mr. Paul James, ACA *2008;* Apartment 187, 51 Sherborne Street, BIRMINGHAM, B16 8FP.

COX, Mr. Paul Raymond, BA FCA *1986;* Shelland House, Shelland, STOWMARKET, SUFFOLK, IP14 3JG.

COX, Mr. Paul Richard, BSc ACA *1997;* 43 Delamere Road, LONDON, W5 3JL.

COX, Miss. Penelope, BA ACA *1983;* 12 Beaumaris Grove, Shenley CHurch End, MILTON KEYNES, MK5 6EN.

COX, Mr. Peter Geoffrey, BA ACA *1991;* Oak House, Fiskerton, LINCOLN, LN3 4HD.

COX, Mr. Peter Robert, FCA *1959;* 4 Jewell Place, HIGHTON, VIC 3216, AUSTRALIA. (Life Member)

•**COX, Mr. Peter Ross, FCA** *1968;* Thomas Cox & Co, 4 Home farm, Luton Hoo Estate, LUTON, BEDFORDSHIRE, LU1 3TD.

COX, Mr. Peter William, BA ACA *1985;* Anerley House The Crescent, West Bergholt, COLCHESTER, CO6 3DA.

•**COX, Mr. Philip Edward Owen, BSc ACA** *1997;* Cotham Practice Management Limited, 17a Cotham Park, BRISTOL, BS6 6BZ.

COX, Mr. Philip Gotsall, MA FCA *1977;* Thatch Cottage, Collinswood Road, Farnham Common, SLOUGH, SL2 3LH.

COX, Miss. Rachel, ACA *2008;* B D O Stoy Hayward, 55 Baker Street, LONDON, W1U 7EU.

COX, Mrs. Rachel Anne, BA ACA *1992;* NG Bailey, Denton Hall, ILKLEY, WEST YORKSHIRE, LS290HH.

COX, Mr. Raymond Brian, FCA *1964;* 99 Ashurst Road, TADWORTH, KT20 5EY.

COX, Miss. Rebecca Marie, ACA CTA MAAT *2005;* (Tax Fac), 38 Avill Crescent, TAUNTON, SOMERSET, TA1 2PL.

COX, Miss. Rhianne, BSc ACA *2006;* with Ernst & Young LLP, The Paragon, Counterslip, BRISTOL, BS1 6BX.

COX, Mr. Richard Charles Alan, BSc FCA *2000;* Radiocode Clocks Ltd Trevarno Manor Trevarno Sithney, HELSTON, CORNWALL, TR13 0RU.

COX, Mr. Richard Wainwright, MA FCA *1996;* 6 Garden House Drive, Acomb, HEXHAM, NE46 4RZ.

COX, Mr. Robert James, BSc FCA *1974;* 4 North Drive, High Legh, KNUTSFORD, CHESHIRE, WA16 6LX.

COX, Mr. Robert James Howie, BA ACA *2000;* 47 Popes Grove, TWICKENHAM, TW1 4JZ.

COX, Mr. Robert Peter, BSc FCA *1989;* Audit New Zealand, PO Box 99, WELLINGTON 6140, NEW ZEALAND.

•**COX, Mr. Roger Arthur, FCA** *2000;* Miller & Co, 2 Victoria Road, HARPENDEN, HERTFORDSHIRE, AL5 4EA. See also M & CCA Limited and Miller & Co.

COX, Mr. Roy Arthur, CBE FCA FCMA JDipMA *1954;* 13 Park Lane, RICHMOND, SURREY, TW9 2RA. (Life Member)

COX, Mrs. Sally Jane, BCom ACA *1993;* Russell & Co, 125 Church Street, MALVERN, WORCESTERSHIRE, WR14 2AH.

COX, Ms. Sarah Geraldine Lynne, FCA *1990;* Clinton Cards Plc, The Crystal Building, Langston Road, LOUGHTON, ESSEX, IG10 3TH.

COX, Mr. Simon, MA ACA *1981;* 26 Gerard Road, LONDON, SW13 9RG.

•**COX, Mr. Simon, ACA** *1979;* Simon Cox (Norfolk) Ltd, 134 Norwich Road, Stoke Holy Cross, NORWICH, NR14 8QJ.

COX, Mr. Simon Edward, BSc ACA ATII *1999;* 66 Arundell, ELY, CAMBRIDGESHIRE, CB6 1BQ.

COX, Mr. Simon Gregory, ACA *2009;* 28 Hemp Walk, LONDON, SE17 1PF.

COX, Mr. Simon Guy, BSc ACA CF *2001;* 10 Leconfield Garth, Follifoot, HARROGATE, NORTH YORKSHIRE, HG3 1NF.

COX, Mrs. Sophie Clare, BSc ACA *2001;* 30 Cooper Road, Westbury-on-Trym, BRISTOL, BS9 3RA.

•**COX, Mr. Stephen Francis, ACA** *1989;* Hayvenhursts Limited, Fairway House, Links Business Park, St. Mellons, CARDIFF, CF3 0LT. See also Hayvenhursts

COX, Mr. Stephen Martin Patrick, BSc ACA *1991;* 21 Church Ponds Close, Ratby, LEICESTER, LE6 0QS.

COX, Mr. Stephen Richard Alexander, BA(Hons) FCA *1987;* 8 Cooks Green, Burnt Mills, BASILDON, SS13 1RL.

COX, Mr. Stuart Alan, BSc ACA *1985;* Morgan Crucible, The Quadrant, 55-57 High Street, WINDSOR, BERKSHIRE, SL4 1LP.

COX, Mr. Stuart Allison, BSc FCA *1956;* Rivendell, Cosheston, PEMBROKE DOCK, SA72 4UW. (Life Member)

COX, Mrs. Susan Anne, BA ACA *1983;* (Tax Fac), 7 Clint Hill Drive, Stoney Stanton, LEICESTER, LE9 4DB.

COX, Mrs. Susheila Kumari, BSc FCA *1994;* 4 North Drive, High legh, KNUTSFORD, CHESHIRE, WA16 6LX.

COX, Mr. Thomas Michael, MA(Cantab) ACA *2010;* 14 Westville Road, THAMES DITTON, KT7 0UJ.

COX, Mr. Timothy Michael, BSc FCA *1975;* Five Acres, St John's Road, Oakley, BASINGSTOKE, RG23 7DX. (Life Member)

COX, Mr. Tom Owen, ACA *2007;* Flat 25, Mulready House, Marsham Street, LONDON, SW1P 4JL.

COX, Mr. Tony Craig, BA ACA *2001;* Linvatec UK Ltd, 73-74 Shrivenham Hundred Business Park, Majors Road, Watchfield, SWINDON, SN6 8TY.

COX, Mr. Trevor, FCA *1960;* 3 Greenleas, Lostock, BOLTON, BL6 4PL. (Life Member)

COX, Mrs. Victoria Ann, BA ACA *1997;* 17a Cotham Park, BRISTOL, BS6 6BZ.

COX, Mr. Walter Trevor, FCA *1968;* Sant Antonio, Kentish Lane, HATFIELD, HERTFORDSHIRE, AL9 6NH. (Life Member)

•**COX, Mr. Wayne Russell, BA FCA** *1989;* KPMG LLP, St. Nicholas House, 31 Park Row, NOTTINGHAM, NG1 6FQ. See also KPMG Europe LLP

COX, Mr. William Michael, FCA *1976;* Cowpers Lodge, High Street, Weston Underwood, OLNEY, BUCKINGHAMSHIRE, MK46 5JS.

COX-HORTON, Miss. Sara Lorraine, BA(Hons) ACA *2002;* 7 Rogate Road, WORTHING, WEST SUSSEX, BN13 2DS.

COXAH, Mr. Stephen William, BSc ACA *1987;* 33 Van Dyck Road, COLCHESTER, CO3 4QE.

•**COXE, Mr. Clifford Arthur Michael, FCA** *1961;* (Tax Fac), Clifford Coxe, Greensted Hall, ONGAR, CM5 9LD.

COXELL, Mr. Martin Kenneth, BEng FCA ACA *2000;* Unit 5, 58 Park Street, ERSKINEVILLE, NSW 2043, AUSTRALIA.

•**COXEY, Mr. Michael David, FCA** *1968;* M D Coxey & Co Limited, 25 Grosvenor Road, WREXHAM, CLWYD, LL11 1BT.

COXHEAD, Mrs. Ann, BSc ACA *1982;* Norderstedt House, James Carter Road, MILDENHALL, SUFFOLK, IP28 7RQ.

COXHEAD, Mr. Peter David, BA ACA *1979;* Forden House, Timbercombe Lane, Charlton Kings, CHELTENHAM, GL53 8EE.

COXHILL, Mr. Colin Selwood, BA FCA *1974;* 103 Wallalong Crescent, PYMBLE, NSW 2073, AUSTRALIA.

COXON, Mr. Alan, MSc BA FCA *1984;* 4 Bellingham Court, BEDLINGTON, NE22 5QS.

COXON, Mr. Barrie Lee, ACA *2006;* 26 Shipman Road, Market Weighton, YORK, YO43 3RB.

COXON, Mr. Basil, FCA *1960;* 19 Spire View Road, LOUTH, LINCOLNSHIRE, LN11 8SL.

COXON, Mr. Christopher Andrew, BA ACA *1985;* Arun Estate Agencies Ltd, St Leonards House, North Street, HORSHAM, RH12 1RJ.

COXON, Mr. Colin John, BA ACA *1999;* 11 Brambling Crescent, Mickleover Country Park, DERBY, DE3 0UT.

•**COXON, Mr. John, BSc FCA AMCT** *1979;* Alpha Bank London Ltd, 66 Cannon Street, LONDON, EC4N 6EP.

COXON, Mr. Keith Nigel, BA FCA *1976;* 74 Melton Gardens, Edwalton, NOTTINGHAM, NG12 4BJ.

COXON, Ms. Lisa Marie, BComm ACA *2010;* (Tax Fac), 92 Westcombe Hill, LONDON, SE3 7DT.

COXON, Miss. Mandy Pamela, BSc ACA *1984;* Stock House, Stock Lane, BERKELEY, GLOUCESTERSHIRE, GL13 9BY.

COXON, Mr. Paul Daryl, BA ACA *1992;* C V S (UK) Ltd, 1 Vinces Road, DISS, NORFOLK, IP22 4AY.

COXON, Mr. Paul John, BA FCA *1985;* Don Amott Caravans Egginton Road, Hilton, DERBY, DE65 5FJ.

COXON, Mr. Peter James Edward, FCA *1962;* 18 Old Millmeads, HORSHAM, WEST SUSSEX, RH12 2LZ. (Life Member)

COXON, Mr. Robert Harold, BA ACA *1986;* Old Mutual Plc Millennium Bridge House, 2 Lambeth Hill, LONDON, EC4V 4GG.

COXON, Miss. Stephanie Claire, ACA *2009;* Apartment 34 Marina Court, Glategny Esplanade St. Peter Port, GUERNSEY, GY1 1WP.

•**COXSHALL, Mr. Andrew David, FCA** *1991;* 3rd Floor Besiki Business Centre, 4 Besiki Street, TBILISI, 0108, GEORGIA. See also KPMG Europe LLP

COXSON, Mr. Paul Anthony, BSc FCA *1976;* 46 Heyes Lane, ALDERLEY EDGE, CHESHIRE, SK9 7JY.

COY, Mr. Glyn, LLB FCA *1999;* 4 Sussex Walk, Hilperton, TROWBRIDGE, WILTSHIRE, BA14 7GT.

•**COY, Mr. Julian Richard Lee, FCA CF** *1985;* CHA Business Advisors Limited, Great Clough House, Goodshaw Fold Close, Loveclough, ROSSENDALE, LANCASHIRE BB4 8PZ.

COY, Mr. Lee, ACA *2011;* 35 Dexter Way, Winnersh, WOKINGHAM, RG41 5GR.

•**COYLE, Mr. Bryan Melvyn Edward, FCA** *1960;* 3 Via Marcello, 117 St. Helens Road, HASTINGS, EAST SUSSEX, TN34 2EL.

COYLE, Mr. Christopher Davis, BA FCA *1972;* 27 Seymour Road, BATH, BA1 6DZ.

COYLE, Mr. John Patrick, BSc FCA *1975;* 44 Ampthill Road, Maulden, BEDFORD, MK45 2DH.

COYLE, Mr. Jonathan Michael, BSc ARCS ACA *2010;* 22 Hunt Close, LONDON, W11 4JU.

•**COYLE, Mr. Nigel Edward, BSc ACA** *2009;* Nigel Coyle & Co Limited, 25 Hall Walk, COTTINGHAM, NORTH HUMBERSIDE, HU16 4RL.

COYLE, Mr. Nigel Kevin, FCA *1966;* 20 Silver Street, Stony Stratford, MILTON KEYNES, MK11 1JR.

COYLE, Mr. Patrick, BA ACA *1999;* 4 Creamer Avenue, Takapuna, AUCKLAND, NEW ZEALAND.

COYLE, Mr. Richard, BSc ACA *2010;* Littlejohn, 1 Westferry Circus, LONDON, E14 4HD.

COYLE, Mr. Robert Charles, BA FCA *1990;* Glendale, Deepdene Park Road, DORKING, SURREY, RH5 4AW.

COYLE, Mrs. Sarah Louise, BA(Hons) ACA *2001;* 22 Pimlico Avenue, Bramcote, NOTTINGHAM, NG9 3JJ.

COYLE, Mr. Timothy Joseph, PhD ACA *1982;* (Tax Fac), 24 Owen Grove, Henleaze, BRISTOL, BS9 4EH.

COYNE, Mrs. Diane, BSc ACA *1984;* The Worshipful Company of Brewers Brewers Hall, Aldermanbury Square, LONDON, EC2V 7HR.

COYNE, Mr. Julian Andrew, BA ACA *1998;* British Pipeline Agency Ltd, 5-7 Alexandra Road, HEMEL HEMPSTEAD, HERTFORDSHIRE, HP2 5BS.

COYNE, Miss. Julie Ann, BSc FCA *1988;* 23 Park Homer Drive, WIMBORNE, DORSET, BH21 2SR.

COYNE, Mrs. Karen Bernadette, BSc ACA *1995;* 16 Essex Avenue, Didsbury, MANCHESTER, M20 6AN.

•①**COYNE, Mr. Martin Thomas, FCA** *1982;* Poppleton and Appleby, 35 Ludgate Hill, BIRMINGHAM, B3 1EH.

COYNE, Mr. Raymond, ACA *1981;* Confederation of Passenger Transport Drury House, 34-43 Russell Street, LONDON, WC2B 5HA.

COYNE, Mr. Robert Padraig, BSc ACA *1984;* Level 28, Barclays Bank Plc, 1 Churchill Place, LONDON, E14 5HP.

COZENS, Mrs. Dorothy Jean, BA FCA *1973;* (Tax Fac), Penshurst Otford Lane, Halstead, SEVENOAKS, TN14 7EE.

COZENS, Mr. Ernest James, FCA *1953;* 37 Madsen Crescent, MARKHAM L3R 4P2, ON, CANADA. (Life Member)

CRABB, Mr. Dominic Edward, BA ACA *1999;* C S First Credit Suisse Financial Products, 1 Cabot Square, LONDON, E14 4QJ.

CRABB, Mr. Ian Denis, MA ACA *1983;* Quadriga Worldwide Ltd, Forum One, Station Road, Theale, READING, RG7 4RA.

CRABB, Mr. Julian George Michael, BA ACA *1990;* 34 Orchard Lane, Harrold, BEDFORD, MK43 7BP.

CRABB, Mr. Nigel Edwin, MBA BSc ACA *1979;* CNR International (UK) Limited, St. Magnus House, Guild Street, ABERDEEN, AB11 6NJ.

CRABB, Mr. Peter William, MA ACA *2001;* 20 Alkira Circuit, Narraweena, SYDNEY, NSW 2099, AUSTRALIA.

CRABB, Mr. Stephen John, BA FCA *1984;* 4 Abbotswood, Speen, PRINCES RISBOROUGH, BUCKINGHAMSHIRE, HP27 0SR.

CRABBE, Mr. Anthony John Travers, MA FCA *1964;* Fetterlocks Farmhouse, Fetterlocks Lane, Shelsley Beauchamp, WORCESTER, WR6 6QS. (Life Member)

CRABBE, Mrs. Patricia Jean, FCA *1962;* Fetterlocks Farmhouse, Fetterlocks Lane, Shelsley Beauchamp, WORCESTER, WR6 6QS. (Life Member)

CRABBE, Mr. Patrick David, FCA *1966;* Consumet Ltd, 50 Ringmer Avenue, LONDON, SW6 5LW.

CRABTREE, Mr. Alan Charles, FCA *1969;* Braeside, 6 Scott Park Road, BURNLEY, BB11 4JN.

CRABTREE, Mr. Andrew I'anson, FCA *1975;* Glusburn Holdings Ltd, Hayfield, Colne Road, Glusburn, KEIGHLEY, BD20 8QP.

CRABTREE, Mrs. Anna Victoria, BA ACA *2007;* Horseracing Betting Levy Board, Parnell House, 25 Wilton Road, LONDON, SW1V 1LW.

CRABTREE, Mr. David Wadsworth, FCA *1950;* Longreach, Ripon Road, Killinghall, HARROGATE, HG3 2AY. (Life Member)
CRABTREE, The Revd. Eric, BA FCA *1955;* Garden Flat A, St. Katharines House, Ormond Road, WANTAGE, OXFORDSHIRE, OX12 8EA. (Life Member)
CRABTREE, Mr. Geoffrey, BA FCA *1966;* 64 Ballagarey Road, Glen Vine, ISLE OF MAN, IM4 4EF. (Life Member)
CRABTREE, Mr. Ian David, BA ACA *1995;* 3332 Keenland Road, MARIETTA, GA 30062, UNITED STATES.
CRABTREE, Mr. Ian John, BA ACA *1998;* Nomura, 25 Bank street, LONDON, E14 5LE.
CRABTREE, Mr. Ian Michael, BA FCA *1979;* Woodlands, 34 Towers Road, Poynton, STOCKPORT, CHESHIRE, SK12 1DD.
CRABTREE, Mr. Jason Richard, BSc ACA *2003;* 40 Upper Ridings, Plympton, PLYMOUTH, PL7 5LD.
•**CRABTREE, Miss. Jessica Lynn, BSc FCA** *1987;* F E Metcalfe & Co, 40A Market Place, RIPON, NORTH YORKSHIRE, HG4 1BZ.
CRABTREE, Mr. John Gathorne, BA ACA *1981;* 11 Old Park Road, CLEVEDON, BS21 7JH.
CRABTREE, Mr. Martin Raymond, ACA *1979;* Ministry of Defence Defence Mail Centre, Ensleigh Granville Road, BATH, BA1 5AB.
CRABTREE, Mr. Paul Wilson, BA FCA *1972;* Storrs Hall, Storrs Lame, Stannington, SHEFFIELD, S6 6GY.
CRABTREE, Mr. Peter Farnell, BSc ACA *1988;* 10 Meadows Close, Leyton, LONDON, E10 7DH.
CRABTREE, Mrs. Sarah Elizabeth, BA ACA *1999;* 48 Odessa Road, LONDON, E7 9BH.
CRABTREE, Mr. Thomas Edward, FCA *1963;* 45 Beechwood Court, Queens Road, HARROGATE, HG2 0HD.
CRABTREE, Ms. Vanessa Jill, BA ACA *1992;* Deutsche Bank Private Wealth Management, Royal Liver Building, Pier Head, LIVERPOOL, L3 1NY.
•**CRACE, Mr. Raymond, ACA** *1990;* Edmund Carr LLP, 146 New London Road, CHELMSFORD, CM2 0AW. See also EC (Management Services) Ltd
•**CRACKETT, Mr. David, BSc FCA** *1974;* (Tax Fac), David Crackett, Viale Coni Zugna 17, 20144 MILAN, ITALY.
CRACKNELL, Mrs. Amanda Louise, BSc ACA *1992;* Weavers Cottage, The Hill, Freshford, BATH, BA2 7WG.
CRACKNELL, Mrs. Andrea Clare, BSc ACA *1993;* 28 Meadow Way, Rowledge, FARNHAM, GU10 4DY.
CRACKNELL, Mr. Bernard John, FCA *1959;* Fairway, Maer Road, EXMOUTH, EX8 2DA. (Life Member)
CRACKNELL, Mr. David Paul, BA ACA *1995;* Tesla Engineering Ltd Water Lane, Storrington, PULBOROUGH, WEST SUSSEX, RH20 3EA.
CRACKNELL, Mr. Greg, BSc(Hons) ACA *2006;* 3 Fox Road, HASLEMERE, GU27 1RG.
•**CRACKNELL, Mr. John David, FCA** *1967;* John Cracknell, Mark House, Aviary Road, Pyrford, WOKING, GU22 8TH.
CRACKNELL, Mr. Kevin Philip, BEng ACA *1991;* 4/5 Western Harbour Place, EDINBURGH, EH6 6NG.
CRACKNELL, Ms. Lucinda Marianne, BA ACA *1999;* 59 Mercers Row, ST. ALBANS, HERTFORDSHIRE, AL1 2QT.
CRACKNELL, Mr. Mark Ian, BSc ACA *1992;* 1 Monarch Way, Pinewood, IPSWICH, IP8 3TA.
CRACKNELL, Miss. Stephanie, BSc ACA *2011;* Apartment 19 Shaw Lodge, Lodge Street Wardle, ROCHDALE, OL12 9JQ.
•**CRACKNELL, Mr. Stephen James, FCA** *1988;* ESW Limited, 162-164 High Street, RAYLEIGH, ESSEX, SS6 7BS.
•**CRACROFT-BRENNAN, Mr. Stephen Patrick, FCA** *1974;* Bambury & Co, Flat 4, Goodwood House, Park Court, Lawrie Park Road, LONDON SE26 6EQ.
•**CRADDOCK, Mr. Alan Peter, FCA** *1992;* Kingston Smith & Partners LLP, Devonshire House, 60 Goswell Road, LONDON, EC1M 7AD. See also Kingston Smith Limited Liability Partnership, Kingston Smith LLP, Devonshire Corporate Services LLP and Kingston Smith Consulting LLP
CRADDOCK, Mr. Christopher David, ACA *2010;* 53 Lullingstone Lane, LONDON, SE13 6UH.
CRADDOCK, Mr. David John, BSc ACA *2004;* with Baker Tilly Corporate Finance LLP, 25 Farringdon Street, LONDON, EC4A 4AB.
CRADDOCK, Mr. Edward, MA ACA *2006;* 59a Klea Avenue, LONDON, SW4 9HY.
CRADDOCK, Mr. Gareth James, MA ACA *2001;* Pricewaterhousecoopers, 7 More London Riverside, LONDON, SE1 2RT.
CRADDOCK, Mrs. Helen Mhairi, MSc(Econ) BA(Hons) ACA *2001;* 11 Earlesfield, Nailsea, BRISTOL, BS48 4SF.
CRADDOCK, Mr. James Peter, BSc ACA *1999;* 10 Ambleside Walk, WETHERBY, WEST YORKSHIRE, LS22 6DP.
CRADDOCK, Mr. Martin Keith Robert, FCA *1967;* Court House Cottage School Lane, Nutley, UCKFIELD, EAST SUSSEX, TN22 3PG.
CRADDOCK, Mr. Oliver James, BA ACA *2007;* 99 Rogersfield, Langho, BLACKBURN, BB6 8HD.
CRADDOCK, Mrs. Sandra June, BA(Hons) FCA *1989;* Forest Lodge, Andover Down, ANDOVER, SP11 6LJ.
CRADDUCK, Mr. Neil John, BA FCA *1976;* 75 Pinkneys Rd, MAIDENHEAD, SL6 5DT.
•**CRADOCK-WATSON, Mr. Tom Michael, BCom FCA** *1980;* Ernst & Young, 19a Khreschatyk Street, 01001 KYIV, UKRAINE. See also Ernst & Young Europe LLP
•**CRAFT, Mr. David Charles, BSc FCA** *1973;* Charles & Company Accountancy Ltd, 1st Floor, 16 Massetts Road, HORLEY, SURREY, RH6 7DE. See also Charles & Company(Services) Ltd and Charles & Company
CRAFT, Miss. Kelly Louise, BA ACA *2004;* 33 Bedmond Road, Leverstock Green, HEMEL HEMPSTEAD, HP3 8LL.
CRAFT, Mrs. Tracey, LLB ACA *2002;* Linden, 3 St. James Close, RIDING MILL, NORTHUMBERLAND, NE44 6BS.
CRAFTER, Mr. Peter Kenneth, LLB CA FCA MCT MBA FAICD *1981;* 94 Stillwells Deviation, AVONSLEIGH, VIC 3782, AUSTRALIA.
CRAFTER, Mr. William David, MA CA FCA *1988;* 7 Branksome Hall, 13 Burton Road, POOLE, BH13 6DT.
CRAGG, Mr. Alan Howard, BSc FCA *1974;* 3 Field Gardens, Steventon, ABINGDON, OX13 6TE.
CRAGG, Mr. Bernard Anthony, BSc ACA *1979;* Big Park Manor House, New Hutton, KENDAL, CUMBRIA, LA8 0AY.
CRAGG, Mr. David, BSc ACA *2003;* Shorts Industries Ltd, PO Box 258, BRADFORD, WEST YORKSHIRE, BD2 1QR.
CRAGG, Mr. Ian Gordon, BSc ACA *1988;* Nationwide Building Society, Kings Park Road, Moulton Park, NORTHAMPTON, NN3 6NW.
•**CRAGG, Mr. Mark Stephen, BSc FCA** *1986;* (Tax Fac), Venthams Limited, The Old Tannery, Oakdene Road, REDHILL, RH1 6BT.
CRAGG, Mr. Mervyn Russell, BSc FCA *1986;* Flat B 21st Floor Tower 5, Residence Bel Air 1, 28 Bel Air Avenue, POK FU LAM, HONG KONG ISLAND, HONG KONG SAR.
•**CRAGG, Mr. Paul Roger, BA ACA** *1988;* PricewaterhouseCoopers LLP, 1 Embankment Place, LONDON, WC2N 6RH. See also PricewaterhouseCoopers
CRAGGS, Mrs. Alison Petra, BA(Hons) ACA *2001;* 11 Wheatley Grove, ILKLEY, WEST YORKSHIRE, LS29 8SA.
CRAGGS, Miss. Christine Sarah, BA FCA *1990;* 1 Coronation Cottages, The Common, Downley, HIGH WYCOMBE, HP13 5YQ.
•**CRAGGS, Mr. Christopher Paul, BA FCA** *1985;* Baker Watkin, Middlesex House, Rutherford Close, STEVENAGE, SG1 2EF.
CRAGGS, Mr. Dennis Foxton, BA FCA *1977;* Shurgard Storage Centres, 2 A C Court High Street, THAMES DITTON, KT7 0SR.
CRAGGS, Mr. Geoffrey Thomas, FCA *1955;* 15 Broom Hall, Oxshott, LEATHERHEAD, SURREY, KT22 0JZ. (Life Member)
CRAGGS, Mr. Gerald, BA ACA *1983;* 75 Dacre Park, Lewisham, LONDON, SE13 5BX.
CRAGGS, Mr. Ian, BSc(Hons) ACA *2003;* 29 Stuart Court, NEWCASTLE UPON TYNE, NE3 2QF.
CRAGGS, Mr. Ian Arthur, BSc ACA *1997;* (Tax Fac), Compass Group Plc Compass House, Guildford Street, CHERTSEY, SURREY, KT16 9BQ.
CRAGGS, Mrs. Janet Elizabeth, BSc ACA *1999;* High Swainston, Wynyard, BILLINGHAM, TS22 5NW.
CRAGGS, Mr. Michael Edward, BA FCA *1974;* Ystwm Gwadnaeth, Llanfachreth, DOLGELLAU, LL40 2DT.
CRAGGS, Mr. Robert Paul, MEng ACA *1998;* 8 Mole Close, Stone Cross, PEVENSEY, BN24 5QB.
CRAGGS, Mrs. Yvonne Mary, BSc FCA *1976;* 35 Barley Croft, Westbury-on-Trym, BRISTOL, BS9 3TG.
CRAIG, Mr. Adam Jerome, BA FCA *1997;* Partygaming Plc, Regal House, GIBRALTAR, 11111, GIBRALTAR.
CRAIG, Mr. Alastair John Gilchrist, FCA *1979;* Tierce Acre, High Street, Charlton On Otmoor, KIDLINGTON, OX5 2UG.
CRAIG, Mr. Andrew, FCA *1973;* The Sanctuary, 21 Matham Road, EAST MOLESEY, KT8 0SX.
CRAIG, Mr. Andrew John, BA FCA *1992;* 7 Kelvedon Road, Coggeshall, COLCHESTER, CO6 1RG.
CRAIG, Mr. Andrew Robert, BEng ACA *1992;* Moley Place New Road, Pamber Green, TADLEY, HAMPSHIRE, RG26 3AG.
CRAIG, Mr. Andrew Roger, BA FCA *1982;* 40 Barkers Lane, SALE, CHESHIRE, M33 6RG.
CRAIG, Mr. Benedict, BSc ACA *1993;* Deutsche Bank, 23 Great Winchester Street, LONDON, EC2P 2AX.
CRAIG, Mr. Brendan, ACA CA(AUS) *2010;* 19 Hamilton Avenue, HENLEY-ON-THAMES, OXFORDSHIRE, RG9 1SH.
CRAIG, Ms. Celia Jane, LLB ACA *1991;* St. Briavels, Nedderton, BEDLINGTON, NE22 6AT.
CRAIG, Mrs. Claire Joanne, BSc ACA CTA *1993;* CIS Healthcare Ltd, 55 Wimpole Street, LONDON, W1G 8YL.
CRAIG, Mr. David Alexander, MA ACA *1982;* 57 Claremont Drive, HARTLEPOOL, TS26 9PE.
CRAIG, Mr. Edward George, BA ACA *2000;* DTE Business Advisory Services Ltd, D T E House, Hollins Lane, BURY, LANCASHIRE, BL9 8AT.
CRAIG, Ms. Frances Ann, BA ACA *1985;* 10 Faroe Road, LONDON, W14 0EP.
CRAIG, Mr. Giles Cameron, BSc FCA *1986;* 5 The Barbette, Castlecrag, SYDNEY, NSW 2068, AUSTRALIA.
•①**CRAIG, Mr. Gordon, BA FCA** *1983;* Refresh Business Group, West Lancashire Investment Centre, Maple View, White Moss Business Park, SKELMERSDALE, LANCASHIRE WN8 9TG. See also Cresswell Associates Limited
CRAIG, Mr. Guy Franklin, BCom ACA *1994;* 114 Furniss Avenue, Dore, SHEFFIELD, S17 3QP.
CRAIG, Mr. Jason, BSc ACA *1996;* with Deloitte LLP, Abbots House, Abbey Street, READING, RG1 3BD.
•**CRAIG, Mr. John, FCA CF** *1980;* Brebners, The Quadrangle, 180 Wardour Street, LONDON, W1F 8LB. See also Brebner, Allen & Trapp Assoc. Serv. Ltd
CRAIG, Mr. John Andrew Duncan, BA FCA *1983;* 62 Wensley Road, Woodthorpe, NOTTINGHAM, NG5 4JT.
CRAIG, Mr. John Gordon, FCA *1955;* Rockbourne, FORDINGBRIDGE, SP6 3NA. (Life Member)
CRAIG, Mr. John Guy Robert, FCA *1973;* Craig Associates, Rosedene Cottage, Great Fencote, NORTHALLERTON, DL7 0RX.
CRAIG, Mrs. Keely Jill, BA(Hons) ACA *2001;* 2 Prince Henrys Court, OTLEY, WEST YORKSHIRE, LS21 2BF.
CRAIG, Mr. Malcolm, FCA *1975;* Wesley House, Cana Lane, Marton Le Moor, RIPON, NORTH YORKSHIRE, HG4 5AT.
CRAIG, Mr. Mark Skimming, MA ACA *1999;* 44 Old Church Street, LONDON, SW3 5BY.
CRAIG, Mr. Martin, BA ACA *1981;* 6 Burlington Road, Muswell Hill, LONDON, N10 1NJ.
CRAIG, Mrs. Mary, BSc ACA *1993;* 49 Bloomfield Road, HARPENDEN, HERTFORDSHIRE, AL5 4DD.
CRAIG, Mr. Michael David, BSc ACA *1979;* The Picotte, Harborough Hall Lane, Messing, COLCHESTER, ESSEX, CO5 9UA.
•**CRAIG, Ms. Pamela Mary, FCA DChA** *1988;* Sayer Vincent, 8 Angel Gate, City Road, LONDON, EC1V 2SJ.
CRAIG, Mrs. Patricia Moira, BSc ACA *1980;* The Picotte, Messing, COLCHESTER, CO5 9UA.
•**CRAIG, Mr. Peter Charles, FCA** *1994;* PricewaterhouseCoopers, Sixty Circular Road, Douglas, ISLE OF MAN, IM1 1SA. See also PricewaterhouseCoopers LLC
•**CRAIG, Mr. Peter Ross, BA FCA** *1980;* (Tax Fac), J.N Straughan & Co, Fram Well House, Framwelgate, DURHAM, DH1 5SU.
CRAIG, Mr. Philip Ian Dickson, BA ACA *1985;* M and G Investments Management Ltd, Laurence Pountney Hill, LONDON, EC4R 0HH.
CRAIG, Mrs. Rachel Helen, BSc ACA *2002;* 7 Yukon Road, LONDON, SW12 9PZ.
CRAIG, Mr. Robert Peter, BA FCA *1976;* 7 The Grove, Monkseaton, WHITLEY BAY, NE25 8BH.
CRAIG, Mr. Roderick John Morgan, BA ACA *1996;* The Culvert Brockencote Chaddesley Corbett, KIDDERMINSTER, WORCESTERSHIRE, DY10 4PY.
CRAIG, Mrs. Sheila Margaret, BA FCA *1983;* 15 Aldwych Close, Thornhill, CARDIFF, CF14 9DR.
CRAIG, Mr. Stephen James, ACA *2009;* 4 Pine Mansions, Gondar Gardens, LONDON, NW6 1HD.
CRAIG, Mr. Stephen John, BSc ACA *1993;* 49 Bloomfield Road, HARPENDEN, HERTFORDSHIRE, AL5 4DD.
CRAIG, Mr. Stephen Robert, ACA *2007;* 114 Fincairn Road, Drumahoe, LONDONDERRY, BT47 3LE.
CRAIG, Mr. Stuart Bowen, LLB FCA IMC MCSI ASIP *1969;* Little Spinney, Caenshill Road, WEYBRIDGE, KT13 0SW.
CRAIG, Mrs. Susan Elizabeth, BA FCA *1988;* 40 Barkers Lane, SALE, M33 6RG.
•**CRAIG, Mrs. Suzanne Louise, BA(Hons) ACA** *2002;* Knill James, One Bell Lane, LEWES, EAST SUSSEX, BN7 1JU.
CRAIG, Mr. Timothy James Austin, BSc ACA *1992;* 8 Hillbrow, NEW MALDEN, SURREY, KT3 4HT.
CRAIG, Mrs. Victoria, BSc ACA *1999;* 8 Hillbrow, NEW MALDEN, KT3 4HT.
CRAIG, Mr. Vivian Simon, FCA *1949;* Flat 3, 58 Carlton Hill, St Johns Wood, LONDON, NW8 0ES. (Life Member)
CRAIG, Mr. Wilfred Charles, LLB FCA FTII *1950;* 71 Heworth Green, YORK, YO31 7TL. (Life Member)
CRAIG, Mr. William Gordon, MA FCA CFE FRM *1990;* 3i Group, 16 Palace Street, LONDON, SW1E 5JD.
•**CRAIG WALLER, Mr. Gregory Mark, FCA** *1976;* Baker Tilly Tax and Advisory Services LLP, 25 Farringdon Street, LONDON, EC4A 4AB. See also Baker Tilly UK Audit LLP
CRAIGAVON, Viscount Janric Fraser, BA BSc FCA *1969;* House of Lords, Westminster, LONDON, SW1A 0PW.
CRAIGEN, Mr. Mark Andrew, BSc(Hons) ACA *2004;* 60 Pascal Drive, Medbourne, MILTON KEYNES, MK5 6LS.
CRAIGEN, Mr. Stephen, ACA *2010;* 26 Hedley Street, Gosforth, NEWCASTLE UPON TYNE, NE3 1DL.
CRAIGHAN, Mr. Peter John, FCA *1968;* 1 Broseley Avenue, Culcheth, WARRINGTON, WA3 4HH.
CRAIGHEAD, Mrs. Alexandra Fiona, BEng ACA *1999;* 23 Short Avenue, Allestree, DERBY, DE22 2EH.
CRAIGHEAD, Mr. Raghnall Macdonald, BA FCA *1976;* White Gates, Spring Road, Kinsbourne Green, HARPENDEN, AL5 3PP.
CRAIGHILL, Mr. Brian, FCA *1963;* 15 Knights Way, ALTON, GU34 1PJ.
CRAIGHILL, Mr. Ian David, BA ACA *1997;* 1 Leinster Avenue, KILLARNEY HEIGHTS, NSW 2087, AUSTRALIA.
CRAIGHILL, Mrs. Louise Mackinnon, ACA *1999;* 1 Leinster Avenue, KILLARNEY HEIGHTS, NSW 2087, AUSTRALIA.
CRAIGIE, Mr. Robert William Addison, BA ACA *1981;* 93 Northwood Avenue, PURLEY, CR8 2ES.
CRAIK, Mrs. Diane Marie, BSc ACA *2004;* Arkwright Room - Rolls Royce Computer Block, Moor Lane, DERBY, DE24 9HY.
CRAIK, Miss. Fiona Lesley, BA ACA *1986;* 11 Southridge Place, The Downs Wimbledon, LONDON, SW20 8JQ.
CRAIK, Mrs. Helen Mary, BSc ACA *1993;* Sapphire House, Crown Way, RUSHDEN, NORTHAMPTONSHIRE, NN10 6FB.
•**CRAIK, Mr. Joseph Patrick Paul, BSc ACA ATII** *1992;* Paul Craik, 51 Mead Way, BROMLEY, BR2 9ER. See also George Hay & Company
•**CRAIK, Mr. Stephen Harvey, BA FCA** *1985;* KPMG LLP, One Snowhill, Snow Hill Queensway, BIRMINGHAM, B4 6GN. See also KPMG Europe LLP
CRAILSHEIMER, Mr. George Henry, BSc FCA *1976;* Schwaketenstrasse 18, 78467 KONSTANZ, GERMANY.
•**CRAINE, Mr. David Peter, FCA** *1981;* Browne Craine Associates Limited, Burleigh Manor, Peel Road, Douglas, ISLE OF MAN, IM1 5EP.
CRAINE, Mr. George Henry, FCA *1973;* 17 Faaie Ny Cabbal, Kirk Michael, ISLE OF MAN, IM6 2HS.
CRAINE, Mr. Philip Richard, MSc BCom ACA *1983;* 11 Hilary Road, Douglas, ISLE OF MAN, IM2 3EG.
CRAINE, Mr. Richard John, BA ACA *1999;* 2 Oakfield Court Road, TUNBRIDGE WELLS, KENT, TN2 4TL.
•**CRAKER, Miss. Danielle Louise, BSc ACA** *2006;* Craker Business Solutions, 7A Ventnor Villas, HOVE, EAST SUSSEX, BN3 3DD.
•**CRAMB, Mr. Andrew Paul Duncan, BSc ACA** *1983;* (Tax Fac), Andrew PD Cramb BSc, 26/7 Eildon Terrace, EDINBURGH, EH3 5LU.
CRAMB, Mr. Peter Michael, BSc FCA *1978;* 29 Baxendale, LONDON, N20 0EG.
•**CRAMER, Mr. Adam Paul, FCA** *1988;* Wilson Wright LLP, First Floor, Thavies Inn House, 3-4 Holborn Circus, LONDON, EC1N 2HA.
•**CRAMER, Mr. David Marc, BA FCA** *1987;* Blinkhorns, 27 Mortimer Street, LONDON, W1T 3BL.
CRAMER, Mrs. Natalie Desiree, BA ACA *1997;* 1 Sunnyfield, LONDON, NW7 4RD.
CRAMER, Mr. Simon Anthony, BA ACA *1990;* 51 Carlton Place, Hazel Grove, STOCKPORT, SK7 6AG.
•**CRAMER, Mr. Stephen John, BSc ACA** *1994;* Financial Professional Support Services LLP, The Old Church, Quicks Road, Wimbledon, LONDON, SW19 1EX. See also FPSS Ltd

•**CRAMMER, Mr. David John, BSc FCA** *1975;* David Crammer & Co, 20 Courtland Drive, CHIGWELL, IG7 6PW.
•**CRAMP, Mr. David William, BSc ACA** *1993;* (Tax Fac), Cramp & Harding Ltd, 192D Huddersfield Road, MIRFIELD, WEST YORKSHIRE, WF14 8AU. See also TaxAssist Direct
CRAMP, Mr. Malcolm William, FCA *1981;* 12 Ventnor Road, Stoneygate, LEICESTER, LE2 3RL.
CRAMP, Miss. Stephanie Helen, BCom ACA *2001;* 124 Murray Avenue, BROMLEY, BR1 3DT.
•**CRAMPTON, Mr. Adrian Duncan, MA FCA** *1987;* Deloitte & Touche GmbH, Schwannstrasse 6, 40476 DUSSELDORF, GERMANY.
CRAMPTON, Mrs. Caroline Diana, BA ACA *2007;* K P M G Llp, 15 Canada Square, LONDON, E14 5GL.
•**CRAMPTON, Mr. John Richard, FCA** *1966;* Cramptons, Delgrae House, 25A St Matthews Road, Chelston, TORQUAY, TQ2 6JA.
CRAMPTON, Mr. Matthew David, BSc FCA *1997;* 71 Woodrow Crescent, Knowle, SOLIHULL, B93 9EQ.
CRAMPTON, Mrs. Nicole Joanne, MA ACA *1997;* 71 Woodrow Crescent, Knowle, SOLIHULL, B93 9EQ.
CRAMPTON, Mr. Phillip, MEng ACA *2003;* Northfield House, 263 Selly Oak Road, BIRMINGHAM, B30 1HR.
CRAMSIE, Mr. Marcus James Lendrum, MA FCA *1975;* 20 Lyford Road, LONDON, SW18 3LG.
CRAN, Mr. Iain George, MMath ACA *2004;* 266 Boundary Road, LONDON, N22 6AJ.
CRANAGE, Mr. Richard Anthony, BSc(Hons) ACA *2009;* Flat 3, 116 Whetstone Lane, BIRKENHEAD, MERSEYSIDE, CH41 2TQ.
CRANDON GILL, Mrs. Sally Helen, ACA *1990;* 60 Rosemont Road, RICHMOND, TW10 6QL.
•**CRANE, Mr. Barry William James, FCA** *1970;* B.W.J. Crane, 24 Korimako Street, St. Leonards, DUNEDIN 9022, NEW ZEALAND.
CRANE, Mr. David, FCA *1990;* Barber Harrison & Platt, 57-59 Saltergate, CHESTERFIELD, DERBYSHIRE, S40 1UL.
CRANE, Mr. Derek William, FCA *1954;* Woodlands, 4 Netherby Park, Queens Road, WEYBRIDGE, SURREY, KT13 0AE. (Life Member)
CRANE, Mr. Geoffrey, FCA *1971;* Glendare, Valley Road, Hughenden Valley, HIGH WYCOMBE, HP14 4PP.
CRANE, Mrs. Gillian Carol, BA ACA *1993;* The Old Forge, Bentley, FARNHAM, SURREY, GU10 5NF.
CRANE, Ms. Jacqueline Sarah, MA BA ACA *2007;* 6b Boot Alley, Chequer Street, ST. ALBANS, HERTFORDSHIRE, AL1 3YJ.
CRANE, Mr. James Alexander, BCom ACA *2004;* 7/51 Holmes Road, MOONEE PONDS, VIC 3039, AUSTRALIA.
CRANE, Mrs. Jane Alison, BSc ACA *1991;* The Valleys, School Road, Grayshott, HINDHEAD, GU26 6LR.
CRANE, Miss. Jemma, BSc ACA *2009;* (Tax Fac), with The Moore Scarrott Partnership LLP, Calyx House, South Road, TAUNTON, SOMERSET, TA1 3DY.
CRANE, Mr. John William, FCA *1973;* N R F (United Kingdom) Ltd Lamport Drive, Heartlands Business Park, DAVENTRY, NORTHAMPTONSHIRE, NN11 8YH.
CRANE, Mr. Julian Roger, BA ACA *1996;* Northgate Information Solutions Peoplebuilding Estate, Maylands Avenue Hemel Hempstead Industrial Estate, HEMEL HEMPSTEAD, HERTFORDSHIRE, HP2 4NW.
CRANE, Mrs. Linda Jane, BA ACA *1992;* 7 Lavender Gate, Steels Lane, Oxshott, LEATHERHEAD, SURREY, KT22 0RD.
CRANE, Mr. Martin, ACA *2011;* 20 Sidwell Avenue, BENFLEET, ESSEX, SS7 1LF.
CRANE, Mr. Martin John, MA MSc FCA *1977;* with KPMG LLP, Management Services Centre, 58 Clarendon Road, WATFORD, WD17 1DE.
CRANE, Mr. Martin Trevor, FCA *1958;* 9 Lindridge Park, Lindridge, TEIGNMOUTH, TQ14 9TF. (Life Member)
CRANE, Mr. Matthew John, BA ACA *2008;* 6/617 New South Head Road, ROSE BAY, NSW 2029, AUSTRALIA.
•**CRANE, Mr. Michael Reginald, FCA** *1969;* Crane Cox & Co, Hele Farmhouse, Hele Road, Marhamchurch, BUDE, EX23 0JB.
CRANE, Miss. Nikki Ann, BSc ACA *2008;* Wilson Wright & Co Thavies Inn House, 3-4 Holborn Circus, LONDON, EC1N 2HA.
•**CRANE, Mr. Peter Alan, FCA** *1974;* (Tax Fac), Crane & Johnston Limited, 11 Alverton Terrace, PENZANCE, TR18 4JH. See also Peter Crane & Co Ltd
CRANE, Mr. Peter Edward, FCA *1955;* 88 Lake Rise, ROMFORD, RM1 4EE. (Life Member)
•**CRANE, Mr. Ralph Clifford, BA FCA** *1983;* Fiducio Limited, Gable House, 18-24 Turnham Green Terrace, LONDON, W4 1QP.
CRANE, Mr. Robert Ewart Montague, FCA *1956;* Edgewood, 4 Mavelstone Close, BROMLEY, BR1 2PJ. (Life Member)
•**CRANE, Mr. Roger Alan, FCA** *1966;* with Steele Robertson Goddard, 28 Ely Place, LONDON, EC1N 6AA.
CRANE, Miss. Sheila Hazel, BA ACA *1997;* 26 Station Road, Claygate, ESHER, KT10 9DH.
CRANE, Mr. Stephen George, FCA *1971;* Pinsauron, 37120 RAZINES, FRANCE.
•**CRANE, Mr. William Richard Thomas, BSc ACA** *1990;* Deloitte LLP, City House, 126-130 Hills Road, CAMBRIDGE, CB2 1RY. See also Deloitte & Touche LLP
•**CRANENBURGH, Mr. Peter Joseph, FCA** *1991;* Cranenburgh Limited, 88 College Road, HARROW, MIDDLESEX, HA1 1BQ.
CRANER, Mrs. Ann, BA(Hons) ACA *2002;* with Deloitte LLP, 4 Brindley Place, BIRMINGHAM, B1 2HZ.
CRANER, Mr. James Marcus, BA ACA *1993;* 26 Bury Hill View, Downend, BRISTOL, BS16 6PA.
CRANER, Mr. John Martyn, MSocSc FCA FRSA *1972;* Old Forge, Wimpstone, STRATFORD-UPON-AVON, CV37 8NS.
•**CRANER, Mrs. Joy Elizabeth, FCA** *1990;* Craner & Co, PO Box 5196, STRATFORD-UPON-AVON, WARWICKSHIRE, CV37 1JJ.
CRANFIELD, Mr. Malcolm, BSc FCA *1973;* 8 Foxcover Road, Heswall, WIRRAL, MERSEYSIDE, CH60 1YB.
CRANFIELD, Mr. Stephen, BSc ACA *2006;* Sorrento House, 1 Ezel Court, Heol Glan Rheidol, CARDIFF, CF10 5NS.
CRANGLE, Mr. Peter Simon, BSc ACA *1991;* 21 Woodkind Hey, Spital, WIRRAL, MERSEYSIDE, CH63 9JY.
CRANKSHAW, Mr. Philip Michael, BA ACA *1993;* 49 School Road, THORNTON-CLEVELEYS, LANCASHIRE, FY5 5AW.
•**CRANLEIGH-SWASH, Mr. Philip Anthony, MA FCA** *1964;* (Tax Fac), Cranleigh-Swash & Co, Greenford Business Centre, I C G House, Station Approach, Oldfield Lane North, GREENFORD MIDDLESEX UB6 0AL.
CRANLEY, Mrs. Jane Victoria, BA ACA *1992;* 52 Station Road, Burley in Wharfedale, ILKLEY, WEST YORKSHIRE, LS29 7NG.
CRANMER, Mr. Andrew Graham, BA FCA *1990;* with FRP Advisory LLP, 10 Furnival Street, LONDON, EC4A 1YH.
CRANMER, Mr. Carl Hubert, FCA *1977;* 15 The Old Saw Mill, Long Mill Lane, Platt, SEVENOAKS, KENT, TN15 8QJ.
CRANMER, Mr. Charles David, BA ACA *1979;* Woodgate, 24a Hill Top, Hale, ALTRINCHAM, WA15 0NN.
CRANMER, Miss. Eleanor, BA FCA *1986;* 127 Dora Road, LONDON, SW19 7JT.
CRANMORE, Mr. Richard Simon, ACA *1979;* 97 Ombersley Road, WORCESTER, WR3 7BT.
CRANN, Mr. Oliver, ACA *2011;* 75 Oxford Road, Moseley, BIRMINGHAM, B13 9SG.
•**CRANNESS, Mr. David John, FCA** *1975;* (Tax Fac), Moore & Co, Belvoir House, 1 Rous Road, NEWMARKET, SUFFOLK, CB8 8DH.
•**CRANSTON, Mr. George Robertson, BA FCA CF** *1980;* Crowe Clark Whitehill LLP, St Bride's House, 10 Salisbury Square, LONDON, EC4Y 8EH. See also Horwath Clark Whitehill LLP and Crowe Clark Whitehill
CRANSTON, Mr. Ian James, FCA *1979;* 1 Bankside Close, Northwick, WORCESTER, WR3 7BG.
CRANSTON, Mr. John Malcolm, FCA *1967;* Harwood, 15 West Perry, Perry, HUNTINGDON, PE28 0BX.
CRANSTON, Mr. Robert Ian, BA FCA *1971;* Commandree, Gaston Street, East Bergholt, COLCHESTER, CO7 6SE.
CRANSWICK-SMITH, Mr. Alastair, ACA *2008;* RPS Group, PO Box 237, BRISBANE, QLD 4006, AUSTRALIA.
CRANTON, Miss. Catherine Ann, MEng ACA *2003;* 43 Fletton Avenue, Fletton, PETERBOROUGH, PE2 8AX.
CRANVILLE, Mrs. Kelly Ann, BSc ACA *2006;* 29 Dodsells Well, WOKINGHAM, RG40 4YE.
CRANVILLE, Mr. Robert Matthew, BSc ACA *2006;* 29 Dodsells Well, WOKINGHAM, RG40 4YE.
CRAPNELL, Mr. Anthony Jack, FCA *1955;* 30 Friar Road, BRIGHTON, BN1 6NG. (Life Member)
CRAPP, Mr. Leslie Rufus, FCA *1960;* Belle Etoile, 1 Le Clos Des Mielles, St. Brelade, JERSEY, JE3 8JF. (Life Member)
CRAPP, Mr. Nicholas Paul Le Cuirot, FCA *1989;* Goldman Sachs International, 133 Fleet Street, LONDON, EC4A 2BB.
CRASSAS, Mr. Alexie, ACA *2009;* 20 Kent Road, LONDON, N21 2JR.
CRATES, Mr. Alan John, FCA *1963;* Wickhurst Wood, Lamberhurst, TUNBRIDGE WELLS, KENT, TN3 8BJ.
•**CRAUGHWELL, Mr. John, FCA** *1974;* (Tax Fac), Craughwell & Co Limited, Brookwood House, 84 Brookwood Road, LONDON, SW18 5BY.
CRAVEN, Mr. Andrew James, BA ACA *1994;* 399 Park Avenue, 10th Floor, NEW YORK, NY 10022, UNITED STATES.
CRAVEN, Mr. Andrew John Cyril, BMus ACA *2003;* 24 Cyncoed Road, CARDIFF, CF23 5SG.
•**CRAVEN, Mr. Brian, FCA** *1975;* (Tax Fac), 9 Gernhill Avenue, Fixby, HUDDERSFIELD, HD2 2HR.
CRAVEN, Mr. Caspar James, BSc ACA *1997;* Unit 218, West Block, Westminster Business Square, Durham Street, LONDON, SE11 5JH.
CRAVEN, Mr. David, BSc FCA *1970;* 8 Osborne Court, Park View Road, Ealing, LONDON, W5 2JE. (Life Member)
CRAVEN, Mr. David Martin, MA FCA *1982;* Aarhus Karlshamn, King George Dock, HULL, HU9 5PX.
CRAVEN, Mr. Denis, BSc ACA *2011;* 334 West Point, Wellington Street, LEEDS, LS1 4JU.
CRAVEN, Mr. Edward, MPhys(Hons) ACA *2007;* 28 Conisboro Avenue, Caversham, READING, RG4 7JB.
CRAVEN, Mr. Giles Bernard Geoffrey, MBA BA FCA *1975;* 20 Court Lane Gardens, Dulwich, LONDON, SE21 7DZ.
CRAVEN, Mrs. Heather Ann, BA ACA *1987;* 6 Norwood, Tumbling Hill, Carleton, PONTEFRACT, WF8 3SD.
CRAVEN, Mr. Iain Scott, BA ACA *1997;* 4 Newlands Road, Stockton Heath, WARRINGTON, WA4 2DS.
CRAVEN, Mr. James, MA ACA *2005;* 22a Westbourne Gardens, LONDON, W2 5PU.
CRAVEN, Mrs. Joanna Ruth, LLB ACA MCIM *1990;* 24 The Street, Burgh, NORWICH, NR11 6TP.
CRAVEN, Mrs. Louisa Claire Renata, LLB ACA *2001;* Willow House, 24a Hook, SWINDON, SN4 8EA.
CRAVEN, Miss. Nicola Louise, ACA *2008;* 41 St. Marys Avenue, Hemingbrough, SELBY, NORTH YORKSHIRE, YO8 6YZ.
CRAVEN, Miss. Penelope Louise, BSc ACA *1999;* with KPMG, 10 Shelley Street, SYDNEY, NSW 2000, AUSTRALIA.
CRAVEN, Mr. Peter Cameron, MCMI FCA *1968;* 326 Barnsley Road, Sandal, WAKEFIELD, WF2 6BB.
CRAVEN, Mr. Robert Nicholas, BA ACA *1997;* 26 Far Moss, Alwoodley, LEEDS, LS17 7NR.
CRAVEN, Mr. Steven John, BA(Hons) ACA *2010;* 2 Sprucewood View, Foxdale, ISLE OF MAN, IM4 3HA.
CRAVEN, Mrs. Victoria Caroline, BAcc ACA *2001;* 9 Silverwood Grange, OSSETT, WEST YORKSHIRE, WF5 8NZ.
CRAVOS, Mr. Charles Sydney, BA ACA *1981;* 54 Manor Road, SOLIHULL, B91 2BL.
CRAVOS, Mrs. Jacqueline Marie, FCA *1971;* The Old Rectory, Naunton Beauchamp, PERSHORE, WR10 2LQ.
CRAVOS, Mr. Patrick Timothy, FCA *1968;* Ampleforth, Main Road, Gwaelod-Y-Garth, CARDIFF, CF15 9HH.
CRAW, Mr. Colin Iain James, BA ACA *1983;* Quai du Cheval-Blanc 20, Les Acacias, 1227 GENEVA, SWITZERLAND.
CRAWFORD, Mr. Adam John Sharman, BSc ACA *1992;* Apt 3C The Carmina, 7-9 Deepwater Bay Drive, SHOUSON HILL, HONG KONG SAR.
CRAWFORD, Mr. Alan Cameron Stewart, FCA *1984;* 19 Lyndhurst Road, BRISTOL, BS9 3QY.
•**CRAWFORD, Mr. Alan Michael, FCA** *1975;* (Tax Fac), Alan M Crawford & Co Limited, 10 Frankscroft, PEEBLES, EH45 9DX.
•**CRAWFORD, Mr. Alastair Colin, FCA** *1982;* Williams Giles Limited, 12 Conqueror Court, SITTINGBOURNE, KENT, ME10 5BH.
CRAWFORD, Mr. Alexander Mervyn Colville, BA FCA *1993;* Pall Mall Capital Ltd, 18a St. James's Place, LONDON, SW1A 1NH.
CRAWFORD, Mr. Andrew, BA FCA *1997;* Castle Heights, La Rue Jutize, Grouville, JERSEY, JE3 9UQ.
CRAWFORD, Mr. Andrew James McKinlay, BSc ACA *1993;* New England Seafood International Ltd, 48 Cox Lane, CHESSINGTON, SURREY, KT9 1TW.
CRAWFORD, Mr. Andrew Paul, BSc ARCS ACA *1988;* Threadneedle Asset Management Ltd, St. Mary Axe House, 60 St. Mary Axe, LONDON, EC3A 8JQ.
CRAWFORD, Mrs. Ann, FCA *1976;* 22 Winton Grove, Fairmilehead, EDINBURGH, EH10 7AS.
CRAWFORD, Mrs. Ann Melanie, ACA *1993;* 20 Martin Close, BICESTER, OX26 6XA.
CRAWFORD, Ms. Anna Victoria, BA ACA *1991;* with Deloitte Touche Tohmatsu, Grosvenor Place, 225 George Street, P.O. Box N 250, SYDNEY, NSW 2000 AUSTRALIA.
CRAWFORD, Mr. Brian Victor, FCA *1965;* Broadsword Group, P O Box 4185 B.C, LOGANHOLME, QLD 4129, AUSTRALIA. (Life Member)
CRAWFORD, Mrs. Cathryn Rhian, BA ACA *1997;* 1 Brynhyfryd Penllergaer, SWANSEA, SA4 9JJ.
CRAWFORD, Mr. Colin Charles Owen, BA ACA *1981;* 137 Geldert Drive, TIBURON, CA 94920, UNITED STATES.
•**CRAWFORD, Mr. Daniel Dundas Euing, MA ACA** *1993;* (Tax Fac), F.W. Smith Riches & Co, 15 Whitehall, LONDON, SW1A 2DD.
•**CRAWFORD, Mr. David Roger, BA FCA** *1991;* Clearwater Accountancy Ltd, 10 Worsley Place, Theale, READING, RG7 5QP. See also Crawford & Co
CRAWFORD, Mr. Donald Percival, FCA *1948;* 22 Elizabeth Crescent, Queens Park, CHESTER, CH4 7AZ. (Life Member)
CRAWFORD, Mr. Douglas, ACA *2006;* 24 Smithall Road, BEVERLEY, NORTH HUMBERSIDE, HU17 9GU.
•**CRAWFORD, Mr. Gavin, BA ACA** *1993;* PricewaterhouseCoopers LLP, 9 Greyfriars Road, READING, RG1 1JG. See also PricewaterhouseCoopers
CRAWFORD, Mr. George Edward James, BSc ACA *2002;* PO Box 5346, AUCKLAND 1141, NEW ZEALAND.
CRAWFORD, Mr. Gilles Mark, BA ACA *1993;* Foray 1255 Ltd, Long Marston Grounds, Station Road, Long Marston, STRATFORD-UPON-AVON, CV37 8RP.
CRAWFORD, Mr. Guy Mervyn Archdall, BA FCA *1967;* St. Blanes, High Street, DUNBLANE, PERTHSHIRE, FK15 0ER.
CRAWFORD, Mr. Iain Gregor, LLB ACA CTA *1991;* The Royal Bank of Scotland Plc, Business House F Gogarburn, PO Box 1000, EDINBURGH, EH12 1HQ.
CRAWFORD, Mr. Iain Philip Paul, BA ACA *1992;* Apartment 96, Britannic Park, 15 Yew Tree Road, Moseley, BIRMINGHAM, B13 8NQ.
CRAWFORD, Mr. Ian, FCA *1965;* Elmtree House, Smithy Farm, Askwith, OTLEY, LS21 2HX. (Life Member)
CRAWFORD, Mr. Ian Stephen, BA ACA *2006;* 18 The Meridian, Kenavon Drive, READING, RG1 3DG.
CRAWFORD, Miss. Isabel Mary, BA ACA *1979;* AT21, Royal Mail Rowland Hill House, Boythorpe Road, CHESTERFIELD, DERBYSHIRE, S49 1HQ.
CRAWFORD, Mr. James Andrew, BA ACA *1989;* 4 Derwent Road, LONDON, N13 4PU.
CRAWFORD, Mr. James Bernard, ACA *1989;* 31 Baatrice Road, DALKEITH, WA 6009, AUSTRALIA.
CRAWFORD, Mr. James Duncan, BA FCA *1982;* (Tax Fac), Rainford Solutions Ltd, Rainford House, Mill Lane, Rainford Industrial Estate, Rainford, ST. HELENS MERSEYSIDE WA11 8LS.
CRAWFORD, Mr. James Oswald, FCA *1952;* 25 Beechwood Court, Newfield Road, LISS, GU33 7TZ. (Life Member)
CRAWFORD, Mr. John Andrew, BA ACA *1993;* John Crawford, 4 Cooters Hill Barns, Cooters End Lane, HARPENDEN, HERTFORDSHIRE, AL5 3NR.
•**CRAWFORD, Ms. Karen Louise, BSc ACA** *1996;* Karen Crawford Limited, 2 Highbank, Slaughterford, CHIPPENHAM, SN14 8RG.
CRAWFORD, Mr. Keith Alan John, FCA *1968;* K B C Peel Hunt, 111 Old Broad Street, LONDON, EC2N 1AP.
CRAWFORD, Mr. Kevin David, BA FCA *1988;* Handelskade 15e, 5211 TH DEN BOSCH, NETHERLANDS.
CRAWFORD, Mr. Michael Grove, MA FCA *1951;* Paddock Lodge, Mark Lane, Kirk Deighton, WETHERBY, LS22 4EF. (Life Member)
CRAWFORD, Mr. Michael Iain, FCA *1971;* 24 Sheraton Avenue, Hatch Warren, BASINGSTOKE, RG22 4TS. (Life Member)
CRAWFORD, Mr. Michael Nigel Harman, BSc FCA MBA FSI *1990;* Great Meadow Lane End, Hambledon, GODALMING, GU8 4HE.
CRAWFORD, Mr. Nicholas James, ACA *1985;* 8 Jessica Gardens, ST. IVES, NSW 2075, AUSTRALIA.
CRAWFORD, Miss. Patricia Mary, BEd ACA *1983;* 25 Blaizefield Close, Woore, CREWE, CW3 9SU.
CRAWFORD, Mr. Paul Adrian, BSc ACA *2002;* 31 Hamilton Gardens, LONDON, NW8 9PU.
CRAWFORD, Mr. Philip Forrest, FCA *1964;* 5342 Monte Bre Cres, WEST VANCOUVER V7W 3A6, BC, CANADA. (Life Member)
CRAWFORD, Mr. Philip William Gowers, BA ACA *1978;* Flat 73, Lauderdale Tower, Barbican, LONDON, EC2Y 8BY.

CRAWFORD, Miss. Rachel Margaret, MSc ACA *1993;* 22 Bracken Hill, Moortown, LEEDS, WEST YORKSHIRE, LS17 6AD.

CRAWFORD, Mr. Robert, MA ACA *1987;* 24 Prince's Meadow, Gosforth, NEWCASTLE UPON TYNE, NE3 4RZ.

CRAWFORD, Mr. Robert Andrew Hunt, PhD BSc ACA *1986;* 5 Biton Close, Victoria RoadHarborne, BIRMINGHAM, B17 0AL.

CRAWFORD, Mrs. Sarah Kate Mary, BSc ACA *1993;* (Tax Fac), Newcastle Bldg Soc, Portland House, New Bridge Street West, NEWCASTLE UPON TYNE, NE1 8AL.

CRAWFORD, Mr. Stanley Derek, FCA *1953;* High Meadow, Bucklow View Park Road, Bowdon, ALTRINCHAM, WA14 3JP. (Life Member)

CRAWFORD, Miss. Victoria Ann, BA ACA *1997;* 8 Bedford Road, LONDON, N8 8HL.

•**CRAWFORD, Mr. William, FCA** *1974;* W. Crawford, 38 Oak Avenue, BINGLEY, WEST YORKSHIRE, BD16 1ES.

CRAWFORD, Mr. William Richard, BSc FCA *1989;* Stoke Cottage, Broom Way, WEYBRIDGE, KT13 9TG.

•**CRAWFORD-INGLE, Mrs. Angela Doreen, BSc FCA** *1977;* Muspatts Farm, Churchfield Road, Tewin, WELWYN, HERTFORDSHIRE, AL6 0JN.

CRAWHALL, Mr. John Michael, FCA *1962;* Pebblewater, Thorns Beach, Beaulieu, BROCKENHURST, HAMPSHIRE, SO42 7XN.

CRAWLEY, Mr. Andrew Stephen, BSc ACA *1984;* (Tax Fac), 3 Lyndhurst Way, SUTTON, SM2 6QA.

•**CRAWLEY, Mr. Anthony Leslie, FCA** *1983;* Tait Walker LLP, Bulman House, Regent Centre, Gosforth, NEWCASTLE UPON TYNE, NE3 3LS. See also Tait Walker Management Limited

CRAWLEY, Mr. Dennis Charles, FCA *1961;* Church Park House, Diptford, TOTNES, DEVON, TQ9 7NY. (Life Member)

CRAWLEY, Mr. Ian Alastair James, FCA *1967;* Urb. La Noria 64A, Nerja, 29780 MALAGA, SPAIN. (Life Member)

•**CRAWLEY, Miss. Jill, BSc FCA** *1985;* (Tax Fac), Crawley & Co, 47 Newton Street, MANCHESTER, M1 1FT.

CRAWLEY, Mr. John Arthur, FCA *1965;* Flat 3, 60 Warrior Square, ST. LEONARDS-ON-SEA, EAST SUSSEX, TN37 6BS. (Life Member)

•**CRAWLEY, Mr. John David, FCA** *1969;* (Tax Fac), Crawley, 23 Keswick Avenue, Gatley, CHEADLE, SK8 4LE. See also Ewing Commercial Brokers Ltd

•**CRAWLEY, Mr. Martyn Andrew, FCA TEP** *1976;* (Tax Fac), Chavereys, Mall House, The Mall, FAVERSHAM, KENT, ME13 8JL.

CRAWLEY, Mr. Matthew Edward, ACA *2006;* 22 Neptune Court, Trafalgar Square, Poringland, NORWICH, NR14 7WQ.

CRAWLEY, Mr. Matthew Phillip, BSc ACA *2006;* 5 Colony Mews, LONDON, N1 4RB.

CRAWLEY, Mr. Paul Francis, ACA *1986;* 9 Partridge Court, NOVATO, CA 94945, UNITED STATES.

CRAWLEY, Mr. Richard Christopher Anthony, BSc ACA *1985;* Mount Batten, 20 Ridgeway, Hutton, BRENTWOOD, CM13 2LP.

•**CRAWLEY, Mr. Richard John, FCA** *1978;* Geo Little Sebire & Co, Oliver House, 19-23 Windmill Hill, ENFIELD, MIDDLESEX, EN2 7AB.

CRAWLEY, Miss. Siobhan, BEng ACA *1993;* 44 Emmerson Avenue, STRATFORD-UPON-AVON, WARWICKSHIRE, CV37 9DX.

CRAWLEY, Mrs. Victoria Cheryl, BSc ACA *1982;* Tigh na Failte, Crathes, BANCHORY, AB31 5JJ.

CRAWLEY, Mr. William Alan Terence, BSc FCA *1966;* Alan Crawley Enterprises Ltd, 1006 Shing Chuen Indl Building, 25-27 Shing Wan Road, Tai Wai, SHA TIN, NEW TERRITORIES HONG KONG SAR. (Life Member)

CRAWLEY-BOEVEY, Miss. Julia, BSc(Hons) ACA *2010;* Ground floor flat, 196 Amesbury Avenue, LONDON, SW2 3BL.

CRAWSHAW, Mr. Andrew Julian, MA ACA *1992;* 44 Amyand Park Road, TWICKENHAM, MIDDLESEX, TW1 3HE.

•①**CRAWSHAW, Mr. David John, BSc(Hons) FCA** *1990;* KPMG Europe LLP, 15 Canada Square, LONDON, E14 5GL. See also KPMG LLP

CRAWSHAW, Miss. Marie Claire, ACA *2008;* 7 Robert Street, NORTHWICH, CHESHIRE, CW8 1DN.

CRAWSHAW, Mr. Peter Geoffrey, BA FCA *1978;* Woodlands, 18 Ringley Park Avenue, REIGATE, RH2 7EU.

CRAWSHAW, Mr. Richard Charles, ACA *1987;* PO Box 10763 APO, Grand Cayman, GEORGETOWN, KY1-1007, CAYMAN ISLANDS.

CRAWSHAW, Mr. Richard Hugh, BA FCA *1961;* Micklegate, Tarrington, HEREFORD, HR1 4EX. (Life Member)

CRAWSHAWE, Miss. Deborah, BSc ACA *1997;* Financial Reporting Council Aldwych House, 71-91 Aldwych, LONDON, WC2B 4HN.

CRAWTE, Mr. Antony Mitchell, BA ACA *1992;* (Tax Fac), 20 Hamhaugh Island, SHEPPERTON, MIDDLESEX, TW17 9LP.

CRAWTE, Mr. Darren James, LLB(Hons) ACA *2006;* 51 Lombardy Street, Woodlands, PERTH, WA 6018, AUSTRALIA.

CRAY, Mr. Jonathan Malcolm, BSc ACA *1989;* 60 Starbold Crescent, Knowle, SOLIHULL, B93 9JX.

CRAY, Mr. Nicholas Braydon, BA ACA *1982;* Hogan Lovells International LLP, Atlantic House, 50 Holborn Viaduct, LONDON, EC1A 2FG.

CRAYFORD, Mr. Philip Keith, BA ACA *1985;* 120 The Street, Boughton under Blean, FAVERSHAM, ME13 9AP.

CRAYFORD, Mr. Stephen Gerard, FCA *1982;* 2 Melrose Court, Redland bay, BRISBANE, QLD 4165, AUSTRALIA. (Life Member)

CRAYTON, Mr. Richard Martin, BA ACA *1987;* 10 Eastwick Drive, Bookham, LEATHERHEAD, SURREY, KT23 3PP.

CREABY, Mr. Garry, ACA *2008;* Pricewaterhousecoopers, 31 Great George Street, BRISTOL, BS1 5QD.

CREAK, Mr. Walter Michael, FCA *1969;* The Hollies, 1 Wallace Place, Bethlehem, TAURANGA 3110, BAY OF PLENTY, NEW ZEALAND.

CREAK, Mr. William Henry, BSc ACA *1989;* Winthorpe, Akeman Street, Combe, WITNEY, OX29 8NX.

•**CREAL, Mr. David Alexander, FCA** *1973;* (Tax Fac), D.A. Creal, Peterkin House, 76 Botley Road, Swanwick, SOUTHAMPTON, SO31 7BA.

CREAMER, Mr. James Arthur, BSc(Econ) ACA *1996;* 21b York Road, LONDON, N11 2TH.

CREAN, Mr. Dermot Anthony, BCom ACA *1989;* Acanthus Advisers Limited, 10-12 Blandford Street, LONDON, W1U 4AZ.

CREAN, Mr. Paul Martin, MA ACA *1996;* Flat 13, 35 Furnival Street, LONDON, EC4A 1JQ.

CREARY, Miss. Shirley May, ACA *1987;* 55 Rosewood Avenue, Elm Park, HORNCHURCH, RM12 5LH.

CREASER, Mrs. Katrina Helen, ACA *2010;* 36 Coltman Close, LICHFIELD, STAFFORDSHIRE, WS14 9YS.

•**CREASEY, Mr. Anthony Philip, FCA** *1971;* (Tax Fac), Creasey Alexander & Co, Parkgate House, 33A Pratt St, LONDON, NW1 0BG.

CREASEY, Mr. Frederick Alfred, FCA *1973;* 3233 Shoreline Drive, OAKVILLE L6L 5Z1, ON, CANADA.

CREASEY, Mr. Ian Phillip, BSc FCA *1989;* A A F Ltd, Bassington Industrial Estate, CRAMLINGTON, NORTHUMBERLAND, NE23 8AF.

CREASEY, Mr. John Stanley, FCA *1962;* Aldersyde, 2 Wellcross, St. Mary's, ISLES OF SCILLY, TR21 0PU.

CREASEY, Mr. Jonathan Anthony, BSc ACA *2005;* Cornerways, Richmond Avenue, St Peter Port, GUERNSEY, GY1 1QQ.

CREASEY, Mr. Martin Wright, BA FCA *1976;* 30 Anne Boleyns Walk, SUTTON, SM3 8DF.

•**CREASEY, Mr. Paul Andrew, BA FCA** *1990;* with Grant Thornton UK LLP, 1-4 Atholl Crescent, EDINBURGH, EH3 8LQ.

CREASEY, Mr. Paul Stuart, FCA *1968;* 9 Falcon Coppice, Woolton Hill, NEWBURY, RG20 9UE.

CREASEY, Mr. Timothy James, ACA *2008;* Cornerways, Richmond Avenue, St. Peter Port, GUERNSEY, GY1 1QQ.

•**CREASEY, Mr. William Eric, FCA** *1972;* 29 Birch Grove, SPALDING, PE11 2HL.

CREASY, Ms. Charlotte Jane, BSc ACA *1997;* 2 Plateia Latsi, Kalo Chorio, NICOSIA, CYPRUS.

•**CREASY, Mr. Paul, FCA** *1971;* (Tax Fac), Paul Creasy, St. Davids, Meavy Bourne, YELVERTON, DEVON, PL20 6AR.

CREASY, Mr. Steven, ACA FCCA *2009;* with KPMG LLP, 15 Canada Square, LONDON, E14 5GL.

CREATON, Mr. Michael, BSc ACA *1994;* University Hospital Birmingham, Foundation Trust, Finance, PO Box 881, Selly Oak, BIRMINGHAM B29 6JS.

CREAVEN, Ms. Mary Brigid, BSc ACA *1992;* 53 Blackmores Grove, TEDDINGTON, TW11 9AE.

CREBBIN, Mr. Simon Richard Lawrence, BSc ACA *1998;* 6 Newby Court, Menston, ILKLEY, WEST YORKSHIRE, LS29 6QS.

CREDALI, Mr. Giuseppe Antonio, BA ACA *1990;* (Tax Fac), 3 Richmond Gardens, Wombourne, WOLVERHAMPTON, WV5 0LQ.

CREE, Mr. David Mckendrick, FCA *1978;* 4 Pagoda Avenue, RICHMOND, TW9 2HF.

•**CREE, Mr. Geoffrey Stuart, FCA** *1968;* Page Kirk LLP, Sherwood House, 7 Gregory Boulevard, NOTTINGHAM, NG7 6LB.

CREE, Mr. Philip Robin, BA ACA *1985;* Chestnut Cottage, 1 Church Close, Hose, MELTON MOWBRAY, LEICESTERSHIRE, LE14 4JJ.

CREE, Mr. Tom, ACA *2008;* Flat G Floor 46 Merton tower 2, 38 New Praya St, KENNEDY TOWN, HONG KONG SAR.

CREECH, Miss. Anna Victoria, BA ACA *1992;* 19 The Avenue, Claygate, ESHER, SURREY, KT10 0RX.

CREED, Mr. Andrew, ACA *2011;* Flat 25, Anderson Heights, 1260 London Road, LONDON, SW16 4EH.

CREED, Mr. Brian Geoffrey, FCA *1950;* Milestone, 64 Seven Star Road, SOLIHULL, B91 2BY. (Life Member)

CREED, Mr. Colum, MBA BA FCA CPA *1982;* 30 Otterson Road, LONDONDERRY, NH 03053, UNITED STATES.

•**CREED, Mr. Humphrey Richard, BSc FCA** *1975;* 17 Slave Hill, Haddenham, AYLESBURY, HP17 8AY.

CREED, Mr. John Michael, FCA *1961;* 21 Uppingham Drive, Woodley, READING, RG5 4TH. (Life Member)

CREED, Mr. Julian Edward, BSc ACA *1989;* Yewtree Cottage, Luston, LEOMINSTER, HEREFORDSHIRE, HR6 0EB.

CREED, Mr. Tom, BA ACA *2004;* 28 Victoria Grove, SOUTHSEA, PO5 1NF.

CREED, Ms. Victoria Anne, BA FCA *2000;* 25 Dinsdale Road, Blackheath, LONDON, SE3 7RJ.

CREEDON, Mr. Aidan Patrick Michael, BA ACA *1981;* Tripp Ltd, 2 St. John's Square, LONDON, EC1M 4DE.

CREEDON, Ms. Andrea Jane, BSc FCA *1988;* 10 Sussex Avenue, Didsbury, MANCHESTER, M20 6AQ.

CREEDON, Miss. Samantha, BA ACA *1995;* 8 Stamford Green Road, EPSOM, SURREY, KT18 7ST.

CREEDY, Mr. Anthony James, BSc ACA *2003;* 20 Caythorpe Rise, NOTTINGHAM, NG5 3DJ.

CREEDY, Mr. William, BSc ACA *2005;* 12 Sandhurst Court, HARPENDEN, AL5 1SZ.

CREEDY SMITH, Mr. Simon Charles, BA ACA *1984;* Stocks House, Webbs Lane, Beenham, READING, RG7 5LH.

CREELEY, Mr. Stuart Michael, MSc ACA *1989;* Damartex UK Ltd Bowling Green Mills, Lime Street, BINGLEY, WEST YORKSHIRE, BD97 1AD.

CREELEY, Mrs. Susannah Linda, BA ACA *1988;* 21 Rossett Beck, HARROGATE, NORTH YORKSHIRE, HG2 9NT.

CREERY, Mr. John Michael, FCA *1971;* 2255 Graduation Place, VICTORIA V8N 6N3, BC, CANADA.

CREES, Mr. Martyn Paul, BA(Econ) FCA *1999;* Rabobank International, Thames Court, 1 Queenhithe, LONDON, EC4V 3RL.

CREES, Mr. Neil Edwin, BA ACA *1991;* 1 Primrose Way, STAMFORD, LINCOLNSHIRE, PE9 4BU.

•**CREES, Mr. Timothy David Merlin, FCA** *1969;* T D M Crees, 29 Summerdown Lane, East Dean, EASTBOURNE, BN20 0LE.

CREES-MORRIS, Mr. Martin Robert, BSc ACA *1982;* Po Box 72, BEACONSFIELD, TAS 7270, AUSTRALIA.

CREESE, Mr. Darren, BSc ACA *1999;* 72 The Glebe, TENBY, DYFED, SA70 8HB.

CREESE, Miss. Jayne Elizabeth, BA(Hons) ACA *2004;* 50 Beaumont Park Road, HUDDERSFIELD, HD4 5JP.

CREESE, Mrs. Marian Elaine, BSc ACA *1986;* Culver Lea, Rareridge Lane, Bishops Waltham, SOUTHAMPTON, SO32 1DX.

CREESE, Mrs. Olga, ACA *2003;* 16 Pine Close, Fernwood, NEWARK, NOTTINGHAMSHIRE, NG24 3FR.

CREESE, Mr. Oliver, BSc(Hons) ACA *2011;* 4 Navy Street, LONDON, SW4 6EZ.

CREETH, Mr. Richard Francis, BSc FCA *1976;* 250 Catalpa Road, WILTON, CT 06897, UNITED STATES.

CREEVY, Mr. Matthew John Bamborough, MA BA ACA *2005;* (Tax Fac), 18 Hampson Way, Bearsted, MAIDSTONE, ME14 4AP.

CREFFIELD, Mr. Graeme Peter, BA ACA *1987;* 54 Walnut Grove, HEMEL HEMPSTEAD, HERTFORDSHIRE, HP2 4AP.

CREFFIELD, Mr. Simon Henry Martin, FCA *1971;* 6 Linden Close, NEWBURY, RG14 1QA.

CREGAN, Mrs. Jane Elizabeth, BA ACA *1991;* 21 The Oaks, WEST BYFLEET, KT14 6RN.

CREGEEN, Mrs. Alison Lynne, MA ACA *1999;* Pricewaterhousecoopers Sixty Circular Road, Circular Road Douglas, ISLE OF MAN, IM1 1SA.

CREGEEN, Miss. Julia Ann, BSc ACA *1990;* Sunnycroft Mansion, Laxey, ISLE OF MAN, IM4 7PD.

CREGEEN, Mr. Martin Ryan, BSc ACA *1998;* Hillcrest 35 Ballagale Avenue, Surby Port Erin, ISLE OF MAN, IM9 6QJ.

CREGEEN, Mr. Roger James, BSc ACA *1995;* Unit D, No.47 Newton Terrace, CHRISTCHURCH, BARBADOS.

•**CREHAN, Mr. Stephen Charles, FCA** *1992;* Charles Crehan Ltd, 51 Victor Road, TEDDINGTON, MIDDLESEX, TW11 8SP.

CREIGHTON, Mrs. Alanna, BA ACA *2003;* 23 Church Road, REIGATE, RH2 8HY.

CREIGHTON, Mr. Anthony John, FCA *1969;* 32 Chapel Lane, Zeals, WARMINSTER, BA12 6NS.

CREIGHTON, Mr. Brian Leonard, BSc FCA *1983;* with BDO LLP, 55 Baker Street, LONDON, W1U 7EU.

CREIGHTON, Mr. Luke Taylor, BSc ACA *2007;* Flat 9, 11 Robsart Street, LONDON, SW9 0AE.

CREIGHTON, Mrs. Moira Evelyn, BA FCA *1988;* Rathbone Cottage, 63 Oakridge Avenue, RADLETT, WD7 8HB.

CREIGHTON, Mr. Richard Andrew, MA FCA *1987;* 10a St Martins Business Centre, BEDFORD, BEDFORDSHIRE, MK42 0LF.

CREIGHTON, Mr. Richard William, BSc ACA *1992;* 22 Wheatcroft Way, DEREHAM, NORFOLK, NR20 3SS.

CRELLIN, Mrs. Alison Helen, BSc ACA *1991;* 4 Hutchinson Villas, Douglas, ISLE OF MAN, IM2 4HR.

CRELLIN, Mr. David, FCA *1962;* 2 Pansington Farm Barns, Titton, STOURPORT-ON-SEVERN, WORCESTERSHIRE, DY13 9QX. (Life Member)

CRELLIN, Miss. Kate Susan, ACA *2008;* Mill House Glen Wyllin, Kirk Michael, ISLE OF MAN, IM6 1AW.

CRELLIN, Mr. Michael Vincent, BEng ACA *1991;* 4 Hutchinson Villas, Douglas, ISLE OF MAN, IM2 4HR.

CRELLIN, Mr. Samuel, BSc(Hons) ACA *2004;* Monkslea, Earlsmead, WITHAM, CM8 2EH.

CREME, Mrs. Danielle Simone, BA ACA *2001;* 3 Robin Close, LONDON, NW7 3AF.

CREMIN, Mr. Denis James Paul, FCA *1967;* (Tax Fac), Chambery, Gordon Avenue, Foxrock, DUBLIN 18, COUNTY DUBLIN, IRELAND.

CREMIN, Mr. Michael Jonathan, BA(Econ) ACA *1995;* 74 Moss Lane, ALTRINCHAM, WA15 8HW.

CRENOL, Mr. Bryan Norman, BSc ACA *1986;* Unit 11 Acton Park Estate, The Vale, LONDON, W3 7QE.

CRESPI, Miss. Laura Claire, MA BSc ACA *2010;* Deloitte & Touche, 3 Victoria Square Victoria Street, ST. ALBANS, HERTFORDSHIRE, AL1 3TF.

CRESSALL, Ms. Jane, BSc FCA *1990;* PricewaterhouseCoopers LLP, 2001 Ross Avenue, DALLAS, TX 75201, UNITED STATES.

CRESSEY, Dr. Jonathan Tony, PhD BSc ACA *2001;* (Tax Fac), 4 Kings Road, ST. ALBANS, HERTFORDSHIRE, AL3 4TG.

CRESSEY, Miss. Rachael, ACA *2009;* 14 Ridgely Drive, LEIGHTON BUZZARD, BEDFORDSHIRE, LU7 4UR.

CRESSEY, Mr. Robert William, BA ACA *1989;* Prometric Ltd, 6th Floor, 1 Exchange Quay, Salford Quays, SALFORD, M5 3EA.

CRESSMAN, Mr. David Edward, BSc ACA *2005;* 22 Buckridge Lane, Shirley, SOLIHULL, WEST MIDLANDS, B90 1TF.

•**CRESSWELL, Mrs. Barbara, BSc FCA** *1977;* (Tax Fac), Barbara Cresswell, 7 Baillieswells Grove, Bieldside, ABERDEEN, AB15 9BH.

CRESSWELL, Mr. David Amos, BA ACA *2009;* 23 Hawley Manor, BARNSTAPLE, DEVON, EX32 8AP.

•**CRESSWELL, Mrs. Fiona Jean, BA FCA CTA** *1993;* (Tax Fac), Haines Watts (Lancashire) LLP, Northern Assurance Buildings, 9-21 Princess Street, MANCHESTER, M2 4DN.

CRESSWELL, Mr. Gary, BA(Hons) ACA *2004;* 7 Burnt House Lane, FAREHAM, PO14 2LF.

CRESSWELL, Mr. John Harold, BA ACA *1986;* Rosslyn House, 8 Park Road, WINCHESTER, SO22 6AA.

•**CRESSWELL, Mr. John Robert, FCA** *1982;* (Tax Fac), Jones & Partners, Fifth Floor, 26-28 Great Portland Street, LONDON, W1W 8AS.

CRESSWELL, Mr. Michael Ian, FCA *1976;* (Tax Fac), Cardinal Shopfitting & Systems Ltd Systems House, Ives Street, SHIPLEY, WEST YORKSHIRE, BD17 7DZ.

CRESSWELL, Mr. Nicholas, BSc ACA *2009;* with Grant Thornton UK LLP, 4 Hardman Square, Spinningfields, MANCHESTER, M3 3EB.

CRESSWELL, Miss. Rachel Maria, LLB ACA *2000;* 16 Lipscomb Close, Hermitage, THATCHAM, RG18 9SZ.

CRESSWELL, Mr. Robert John, FCA *1986;* 75 KING WILLIAM STREET, LONDON, EC4N 7BE.

CRESSWELL, Mr. Roger Alan, MA FCA *1961;* Winsley, 37 Hightree Drive, Henbury, MACCLESFIELD, SK11 9PD. (Life Member)

CRESSWELL, Mrs. Sharon Louise Knight, BA ACA *1996;* PricewaterhouseCoopers, PO Box 191, HAMILTON 3240, NEW ZEALAND.

CRESSWELL, Mr. Stephen, BSc ACA *1992;* Mede House St. Judes Road, Englefield Green, EGHAM, SURREY, TW20 0DH.
•**CRESSWELL, Mr. Stephen Amos, BA FCA DChA** *1981;* (Tax Fac), Thomas Westcott, 96 High Street, ILFRACOMBE, DEVON, EX34 9NH.
CRESSWELL, Mr. Thomas Robert, BSc ACA *2008;* Flat 5, 23 St. Georges Square, LONDON, SW1V 2HX.
•**CRESSWELL, Mrs. Vanessa, BA ACA** *1992;* Three Kings Accounting Ltd, Mede House, St. Judes Road, Englefield Green, EGHAM, SURREY TW20 0DH. See also CCM Accountancy Limited
CRESWELL, Mr. Keith Peter, FCA *1970;* 2 Starwood Close, WEST BYFLEET, KT14 6QB.
CRESWELL, Mr. Robert Andrew, BSc FCA *1989;* Via Merano 191, Infernetto, 00124 ROME, ITALY.
CRESWICK, Mr. Graham Michael, FCA *1977;* Fairview Farmhouse, Brackenthwaite Lane, Pannal, HARROGATE, HG3 1PL.
•**CRESWICK, Mrs. Suvi Helena, ACA** *2005;* with Dickinsons, Enterprise House, Beesons Yard, Bury Lane, RICKMANSWORTH, HERTFORDSHIRE WD3 1DS.
CRETNEY, Mr. Jonathan Paul, BA ACA *2003;* 51 Cronk Drean, Douglas, ISLE OF MAN, IM2 6AT.
•**CREW, Mr. Robert Paul, FCA** *1973;* (Tax Fac), Crew & Hammond, 13 Park Hill Road, TORQUAY, DEVON, TQ1 2AL. See also Jordans International Limited
•**CREW, Mrs. Susan Wadie, BA FCA** *1996;* SWC, Hollywood, Furze Vale Road, Headley Down, BORDON, HAMPSHIRE GU35 8EP.
CREWE, Mrs. Amanda Jane, BSc ACA *1994;* 157 Cranbrook Road, Redland, BRISTOL, BS6 7DE.
•**CREWE, Mrs. Christine Leslie, ACA** *1990;* Parry & Co, Unit 1, Temple House Estate, 6 West Road, HARLOW, ESSEX CM20 2DU.
CREWE, Mrs. Dariya, ACA *2003;* 47 Glebe Road, Thringstone, COALVILLE, LEICESTERSHIRE, LE67 8NU.
•**CREWE, Mr. John Edward, FCA** *1967;* 9 Frankland Crescent, Parkstone, POOLE, DORSET, BH14 9PX.
CREWE, Mr. Matthew Austin, BA ACA *2000;* 20 Primrose Lane, Kirkburton, HUDDERSFIELD, HD8 0QY.
CREWS, Mrs. Charlotte Lisa, BSc ACA *1997;* 34 Old Sneed Park, Stoke Bishop, BRISTOL, BS9 1RF.
CREWS, Mr. Robert Tyrone Davy, BSc ACA *1996;* Momentum Corporate Finance LLP, Venturers House, King Street, BRISTOL, BS1 4PB.
•**CRIBB, Mr. Andrew Robert, FCA** *1988;* Smith Craven, Kelham House, Kelham Street, DONCASTER, DN1 3RE.
CRIBB, Mr. Derek Wayne, BSc ACA *1993;* Craigmore, Hockering Road, WOKING, SURREY, GU22 7HJ.
•**CRIBB, Mr. Nigel Andrew, BA ACA** *1985;* with B M Howarth, West House, King Cross Road, HALIFAX, HX1 1EB.
CRIBBIN, Miss. Colette, BCom ACA *1993;* 2 Tudor City Place, Apt 9B South, NEW YORK, NY 10017, UNITED STATES.
CRICHARD, Mrs. Dawn Ann, BA ACA *1989;* Bas Du Marais, La Route Du Marais, St. Ouen, JERSEY, JE3 2GX.
CRICHARD, Mr. Jonathan Paul, BEng ACA *1990;* 2e2 Jersey Limited, La Rue A la Dame, St. Saviour, JERSEY, JE2 7NH.
•**CRICHARD, Mr. Julian Robert, BSc FCA** *1972;* J.R. Crichard & Co, 23 Pennyford Court, Henderson Drive, LONDON, NW8 8UF.
CRICHARD, Miss. Rachael Claire, BA ACA *1992;* 41 Abbotsbury Road, EASTLEIGH, SO50 8NZ.
CRICHTON, Mr. Andrew David Denzil, FCA *1972;* (Tax Fac), 42 Rue du 31-Decembre, PO Box 6193, 1211 6 GENEVA, SWITZERLAND.
CRICHTON, Mr. David Ferguson, BA ACA *1992;* GL 23 Polwarth Street, Hyndland, GLASGOW, G12 9UD.
CRICHTON, Miss. Henrietta Catherine Louise, BA ACA *2010;* 49 Franche Court Road, LONDON, SW17 0JX.
CRICHTON, Mrs. Janet Catherine Elizabeth, MA MSc ACA *1981;* 2 Kersley Street, Battersea, LONDON, SW11 4PT.
CRICHTON, Mr. Robert Nigel, FCA *1967;* 5 Trevor Square, LONDON, SW7 1DT. (Life Member)
CRICHTON, Mr. Robin James, MA BA ACA *1999;* 17 Parsonage Way, CHEADLE, CHESHIRE, SK8 2JS.
CRICHTON, Mr. Ronald James, FCA *1966;* Woodstock, New Platt Lane, Goostrey, CREWE, CW4 8NJ. (Life Member)
CRICHTON-BAKER, Mr. Nigel, FCA *1970;* 56 Orchard Road, Tewin, WELWYN, HERTFORDSHIRE, AL6 0HN.
CRICK, Mr. Brian Patrick, BA FCA *1981;* Insurance Management Ltd., P.O. Box SS 6283, NASSAU, BAHAMAS.
CRICK, Mr. Daniel, BSc ACA *2010;* 407 Chapelier House, Eastfields Avenue, LONDON, SW18 1LR.
•**CRICK, Mr. David William, FCA** *1971;* Crick & Co, 15a Silver Street, BARNSTAPLE, EX32 8HR.
CRICK, Mr. Gavin Philip, BSc FCA *1983;* The Old Miners Arms, Snape Lane, WADHURST, TN5 6NS.
•**CRICK, Mr. Justin, BA(Hons) ACA ACIArb** *2002;* RGL LLP, 8th Floor, Dashwood, 69 Old Broad Street, LONDON, EC2M 1QS.
CRICK, Mr. Peter Hamish, BSc FCA *1973;* Ridley House, 4 Garford Lane, Easton on the Hill, STAMFORD, LINCOLNSHIRE, PE9 3NY.
CRICK, Mr. Richard William, MA FCA *1970;* 2 Craven Hill Mews, LONDON, W2 3DY.
CRICKMAR, Mr. Alex, BA ACA *2009;* Apartment 41, Waterloo Court, 17 Hunslet Road, LEEDS, LS10 1QN.
CRICKMORE, Mr. Gavin Paul, LLB ACA *1986;* Diageo Plc Lakeside Drive, Park Royal, LONDON, NW10 7HQ.
CRIDDLE, Mr. Mark Edward, ACA *2009;* 12 Lime Drive, FLEET, HAMPSHIRE, GU51 2XJ.
CRIDDLE, Mr. Maurice William, FCA *1955;* 2 Hillside Close, TEIGNMOUTH, TQ14 9XE. (Life Member)
CRIDDLE, Mr. Stephen Melville, MA ACA *1986;* 107 Gras Lawn, EXETER, EX2 4ST.
CRIDLAN, Mr. Richard John, BA FCA *1972;* 253 Kennington Road, LONDON, SE11 6BY.
CRIDLAND, Mr. Alastair Ryan, FCA *1967;* Quarry House, 34 Hoyle Ing, Linthwaite, HUDDERSFIELD, HD7 5RX.
CRIDLAND, Mr. John Henry James, FCA *1973;* Mill Cottage Long Street, Croscombe, WELLS, SOMERSET, BA5 3QJ.
CRIDLAND, Mr. Jonathan Michael Edward, FCA *1981;* Home Farm House, Lilford, PETERBOROUGH, PE8 5SG.
CRIDLAND, Mr. Kenneth Stephen, BSc FCA *1978;* 23 Towncourt Crescent, ORPINGTON, BR5 1PG.
•**CRIDLAND, Mrs. Manuela, FCA** *1982;* M Cridland & Associates, Home Farm, Lilford, Oundle, PETERBOROUGH, PE8 5SG.
•**CRIDLAND, Mr. Marcus James, BA FCA** *1998;* (Tax Fac), Scott Vevers Ltd, 65 East Street, BRIDPORT, DORSET, DT6 3LB.
•**CRIDLAND, Mr. Paul, BSc FCA** *1990;* Elliott Bunker Ltd, 3-8 Redcliffe Parade West, BRISTOL, BS1 6SP.
CRIDLAND, Mr. Paul Christopher, BSc ACA *1991;* 10 Maes Morrison, Pontarddulais, SWANSEA, SA4 8EB.
CRIDLAND, Mr. Robin James Scott, MA ACA *1992;* The Fairways, 12 Prestwick Close, Tytherington, MACCLESFIELD, CHESHIRE, SK10 2TH.
CRIDLAND, Mr. Simon John, BSc ACA *1989;* Box 101, Agusta Westland, Lysander Road, YEOVIL, SOMERSET, BA20 2YB.
CRIGHTON, Mr. Daniel Stuart, MEng ACA *2004;* 12 Cunliffe Walk, WREXHAM, CLWYD, LL11 2SR.
CRIGHTON, Miss. Laura Mary, MSci ACA *2007;* with Grant Thornton UK LLP, Grant Thornton House, 22 Melton Street, Euston Square, LONDON, NW1 2EP.
CRIGHTON, Mrs. Melanie Anne, BA ACA *1991;* 7 Westfield, REIGATE, SURREY, RH2 0DZ.
CRIGHTON, Miss. Suzanne Elizabeth, BSc ACA *1992;* Flat 2 Holmewood, 40 Gregories Road, BEACONSFIELD, BUCKINGHAMSHIRE, HP9 1GE.
CRILLEY, Mr. Stephen John, FCA *1981;* with Champion Haworth Moore Limited, 54 Caunce Street, BLACKPOOL, LANCASHIRE, FY1 3LJ.
•**CRILLY, Mr. Aidan Joseph, BA FCA** *1980;* (Tax Fac), Crilly & Co, Wyvern House, 1 Church Road, Bookham, LEATHERHEAD, SURREY KT23 3PD.
•**CRIMMIN, Mr. Michael Patrick, FCA** *1969;* Manser Hunot, Highland House, Albert Drive, BURGESS HILL, RH15 9TN.
CRIMMINS, Mr. Eric, FCA *1975;* 100 Knotts Lane, COLNE, BB8 8AE.
CRIMP, Mr. Graham Edwin, FCA *1956;* P.O. Box 23018, CLAREMONT, C.P., 7735, SOUTH AFRICA. (Life Member)
CRINGLE, Mr. Peter Stuart, BSc FCA *1974;* 362 Jean-Louis-Boudreau, GRANBY J2H 0A3, QC, CANADA.
CRINKS, Mr. Francis William, FCA *1965;* Uplands, 27 Hillcrest Rd, Saltwood, HYTHE, CT21 5EU. (Life Member)
CRIPPS, Mr. Albert Terence, FCA *1963;* 2 Le Brun Road, EASTBOURNE, BN21 2HY. (Life Member)
CRIPPS, Mr. Andrew Graham, BA ACA *1983;* 66 Forest Road, LONDON, E8 3BT.
•**CRIPPS, Mr. Andrew Paul, BA FCA** *1994;* APC Accountants Limited, 7 St. John Street, MANSFIELD, NOTTINGHAMSHIRE, NG18 1QH.
•**CRIPPS, Mr. Anthony Charles, FCA** *1957;* A.C.Cripps, 5 Kingcup Drive, Bisley, WOKING, SURREY, GU24 9HH.
•**CRIPPS, Mr. Brian Edward, FCA** *1960;* (Tax Fac), Cripps Dransfield, 206 Upper Richmond Road West, LONDON, SW14 8AH.
CRIPPS, Mr. Brian Ernest, FCA *1964;* 18 Birch Avenue, MACCLESFIELD, SK10 3NU.
CRIPPS, Mrs. Catherine Gail, MA ACA *1990;* 10 Coulson Street, LONDON, SW3 3NG.
CRIPPS, Charles Hugh, Esq FCA *1969;* Barn in Wood, Shogmoor Lane, Frieth, HENLEY-ON-THAMES, OXFORDSHIRE, RG9 6TB.
CRIPPS, Mr. David Malcolm, FCA *1967;* Hillingdon House, New Road, Stokenchurch, HIGH WYCOMBE, HP14 3RT.
CRIPPS, The Hon. Jeremy George Anthony, FCA CPA *1967;* PO Box 27, TIFFIN, OH 44883, UNITED STATES.
•**CRIPPS, Mr. Nigel John, FCA** *1981;* Lakin Clark, 1 Union Crescent, MARGATE, CT9 1NR. See also Lakin Clark Limited
CRIPPS, Mr. Paul Anthony, BSc ACA *1996;* 1 Turnstone Close, Winnersh, WOKINGHAM, BERKSHIRE, RG41 5LQ.
CRIPPS, Mr. Paul James, BSc ACA *1999;* with Ernst & Young LLP, 1 More London Place, LONDON, SE1 2AF.
•**CRIPPS, Mr. Paul Robin Sydney, FCA** *1972;* Cripps & Co, 8-10 Heronsgate Road, Chorleywood, RICKMANSWORTH, HERTFORDSHIRE, WD3 5BW.
CRIPPS, Mr. Stephen, BA(Hons) ACA *2009;* 2 Old Forge Road, Church Crookham, FLEET, GU52 0RL.
CRISAFI, Mr. Giuseppe, ACA *2009;* 57 Felden Street, LONDON, SW6 5AE.
CRISELL, Mr. Jeffrey Joseph, BSc FCA *1982;* with PKF (UK) LLP, Farringdon Place, 20 Farringdon Road, LONDON, EC1M 3AP.
CRISELL, Mr. Nicholas Damien, FCA *1974;* Hedgerow Cottage, Water Lane, Enton, GODALMING, SURREY, GU8 5AG.
•**CRISOP, Mr. Richard Ian, BSc FCA** *1993;* Needham Chipchase Manners & Co, 30b Market Place, RICHMOND, DL10 4QG.
CRISP, Miss. Catherine Mary, ACA *2009;* 33 Valley Road, Tasburgh, NORWICH, NR15 1NG.
CRISP, Mr. Edward John Henry, ACA *1982;* 46 Spooners Drive, Park Street, ST. ALBANS, AL2 2HL.
CRISP, Mr. George Charles Bromege, BA ACA *1984;* Charles Crisp Associates Limited, 3 Ashton Close, MAIDENHEAD, BERKSHIRE, SL6 4TA.
CRISP, Miss. Georgette Alicia, BSc ACA *2010;* 28 Hornsey Lane Gardens, LONDON, N6 5PB.
CRISP, Mr. John Michael, FCA *1977;* Grimme Butcher Jones Limited, New Loom House, 101 Back Church Lane, LONDON, E1 1LU.
•**CRISP, Mr. Matthew Jon, MSc BA(Hons) ACA** *2001;* Sigma 2002 LLP, 45-47 Cornhill, LONDON, EC3V 3PF.
CRISP, Mr. Richard Russell, BA ACA *1997;* 15 Blackheath Vale, LONDON, SE3 0TX.
CRISP, Mr. Stuart John, BSc ACA *2002;* with Baker Tilly UK Audit LLP, Hartwell House, 55-61 Victoria Street, BRISTOL, BS1 6AD.
•**CRISP, Mr. Tony Graham, FCA** *1987;* (Tax Fac), Giess Wallis Crisp LLP, 10-12 Mulberry Green, HARLOW, ESSEX, CM17 0ET.
CRISPE, Mr. Robert Nicholas, MA FCA *1959;* Field House, Nether Wallop, STOCKBRIDGE, SO20 8EP. (Life Member)
CRISPIN, Mr. Thomas Leonard, FCA *1937;* 4C Woodlands Court, Congleton Road, ALDERLEY EDGE, SK9 7AB. (Life Member)
CRISPINI, Mr. Dario Marcello, MSc ACA *1999;* Financial Services Authority, 25 North Colonnade, LONDON, E14 5HS.
CRIST, Mr. Bernard Henry, FCA *1960;* 142 Argyle Road, Ealing, LONDON, W13 8ER. (Life Member)
CRITCHLEY, Mr. Andrew Mark, BSc ACA *1988;* Global Aerospace Underwriting Managers L, Fitzwilliam House, 10 St. Mary Axe, LONDON, EC3A 8EQ.
CRITCHLEY, Mr. Andrew Mark, BA FCA *2001;* 38 The Bryceway, LIVERPOOL, L12 3HJ.
CRITCHLEY, Mr. Colin, BSocSc FCA *1996;* 20 Bracken Close, LICHFIELD, STAFFORDSHIRE, WS14 9RU.
CRITCHLEY, Mr. David James, BA ACA *2010;* 3A Harmsworth Street, LONDON, SE17 3TJ.
CRITCHLEY, Mr. David John, BSc ACA *1988;* 67 Bramley Road, BOLTON, BL1 7RN.
CRITCHLEY, Mr. Dominic Brian, BA ACA *1994;* Blackrock, 6d Route De Treves, Sennnegerberg, L 2449 LUXEMBOURG, LUXEMBOURG.
CRITCHLEY, Mr. Ian Douglas, BA ACA *1984;* Bradford & Bingley Group, 21-27 Lambs Conduit Street, LONDON, WC1N 3BD.
CRITCHLEY, Mr. James Alexander, MSc BSc ACA *2010;* 47 Agecroft Road East, Prestwich, MANCHESTER, M25 9RQ.
CRITCHLEY, Mr. John Phillip, BA ACA *2009;* 25 Balfour Road, BRISTOL, BS3 2AF.
CRITCHLEY, Mr. Jonathan Timothy, BA ACA *2009;* 58 Larkfield Road, LIVERPOOL, L17 9PU.
CRITCHLEY, Mr. Mark, BA FCA *1996;* 32 Wentworth Close Thorpe Hesley, ROTHERHAM, SOUTH YORKSHIRE, S61 2QT.
•**CRITCHLEY, Mr. Maurice Mortimer, ACA** *1979;* Critchley Cole & Co., 20 Lansdown, STROUD, GL5 1BG.
CRITCHLEY, Mr. Stephen Philip, BSc FCA *1994;* with KPMG LLP, 8 Princes Parade, LIVERPOOL, L3 1QH.
CRITCHLEY, Mr. Stephen Richard, MA DPhil FCA *1979;* Transport For London, Windsor House, 50 Victoria Street, LONDON, SW1H 0TL.
CRITCHLOW, Mr. Christopher Hugh, BSc FCA *1974;* Mark Warner Ltd, 20 Kensington Church Street, LONDON, W8 4EP.
CRITCHLOW, Mr. James Harold, FCA *1948;* 17 Downing Road, Greendale North, HARARE, ZIMBABWE. (Life Member)
CRITCHLOW, Mr. Norman James, BSc FCA *1972;* 19 Danehurst Close, EGHAM, SURREY, TW20 9PX.
CRITCHLOW, Mr. Simon Peter, BSc ACA *1982;* 36 Rue Du Nord, L-7242 HELMSANGE, LUXEMBOURG.
CRITOPH, Mr. Stephen Mark Anthony, BSc ACA *1986;* 42 Becmead Avenue, LONDON, SW16 1UQ.
CRITTEN, Mr. Shaun Keith, ACA *1996;* 4 Hardy Close, LONDON, SE16 6RT.
CRITTENDEN, Mr. Daniel John, BSc ACA *2004;* with HSBC Holdings plc, 8-16 Canada Square, LONDON, E14 5HQ.
CROAD, Mrs. Joanne Elizabeth, ACA CTA *1990;* 18 Hazel Close, Chandler's Ford, EASTLEIGH, HAMPSHIRE, SO53 5RF.
CROAD, Mr. Paul David, MEng ACA *2001;* 152 Amelia Street, LONDON, SE17 3AS.
CROAK, Miss. Louise, BA(Hons) ACA *2009;* Flat 35, Parkside, 193 Hart Road, MANCHESTER, M14 7BA.
CROALL, Mr. James Rae, MA ACA *1985;* Smith & Williamson, 206 St. Vincent Street, GLASGOW, G2 5SG.
CROALL, Mr. Robert George, FCA *1969;* South Laws House, Swinton, DUNS, TD11 3HZ.
CROASDALE, Miss. Gillian Anne, BA FCA *1986;* 391 Stroud Rd, GLOUCESTER, GL4 0DB.
CROCE, Mr. Massimo Corrado, BA ACA *1999;* 1 Tutnall Grange, Tutnall, BROMSGROVE, WORCESTERSHIRE, B60 1NN.
CROCI, Mr. Remo, BA FCA *1988;* European Commission, rue de la loi 200, SPA 2 (JII 00/111), B 1049 BRUSSELS, BELGIUM.
CROCKART, Miss. Michelle Louise, BSc ACA *1996;* 157 Ruden Way, EPSOM, KT17 3LW.
CROCKER, Mr. Arthur Rupert, BSc ACA *1988;* 35 Palmerston Rd, Wimbledon, LONDON, SW19 1PG.
CROCKER, Dr. Glenn, BSc ACA *1997;* Biocity Nottingham Ltd, Pennyfoot Street, NOTTINGHAM, NG1 1GF.
CROCKER, Mr. John, FCA *1967;* 16 Hartington Road, High Lane, STOCKPORT, CHESHIRE, SK6 8BY.
CROCKER, Mr. Matthew Alan, BA ACA *2005;* Beaumont Seymour & Co, 47 Butt Road, COLCHESTER, CO3 3BZ.
CROCKER, Miss. Melanie Jane, BSc ACA *1991;* Capari, Les Issues, St. Pierre Du Bois, GUERNSEY, GY7 9HT.
•**CROCKER, Mr. Neil Jesse, FCA** *1972;* (Tax Fac), Sous Les Arbres, La Rue Du Hamel, Castel, GUERNSEY, GY5 7QJ.
CROCKER, Mr. Paul David, BA ACA CF *1995;* 132 Pennsylvania Road, EXETER, EX4 6DW.
•**CROCKER, Mr. Richard Anthony, FCA** *1971;* (Tax Fac), Richard A. Crocker, 181 Chester Road, Hazel Grove, STOCKPORT, CHESHIRE, SK7 6EN. See also Richard A Crocker Ltd
CROCKER, Mr. Toby Nicholas Richard, BA(Hons) ACA *2001;* 19 Cranbrook Court, FLEET, HAMPSHIRE, GU51 4PY.
CROCKER, Mr. William Richard, BEng ACA FRSA *1996;* Lantoon Quarry, Dobwalls, LISKEARD, CORNWALL, PL14 4LR.
CROCKER, Mr. William Richard, MA ACA *1992;* 7 Winthrop Park, PRENTON, MERSEYSIDE, CH43 6XQ.
CROCKETT, Mr. David Thomas, BA ACA *2009;* 35 Freshwater Road, LONDON, SW17 9TH.
•**CROCKETT, Mrs. Eileen Louise, ACA** *1993;* Eileen Crockett ACA, The Cottage, Preston Lane, Lydeard St. Lawrence, TAUNTON, SOMERSET TA4 3QQ.
CROCKETT, Ms. Siobhan Camilla, BA ACA *1995;* 85 Calbourne Road, LONDON, SW12 8LS.

CROCKFORD, Mr. Alistair Martin, ACA *2009;* 1 Belle Vue, CHELMSFORD, CM2 0BD.
CROCKFORD, Mr. David Edward, BA ACA *1998;* 6 Paddock Road, Burpham, GUILDFORD, SURREY, GU4 7LL.
CROCKFORD, Mr. George William, BA ACA *2010;* 11 Edwards Gardens, SWANLEY, BR8 8HP.
CROCKFORD, Mrs. Hannelore, ACA *2008;* 34 West View Road, ST. ALBANS, HERTFORDSHIRE, AL3 5JX.
CROCKFORD, Ms. Jacqueline Anne, BA ACA *2005;* with KPMG LLP, 15 Canada Square, LONDON, E14 5GL.
CROCKFORD, Mr. James Noel, BSc(Econ) ACA *2003;* 23/F Princes Building, CENTRAL, HONG KONG ISLAND, HONG KONG SAR.
CROCKFORD, Mr. John Graham, FCA *1977;* 57 West Down Road, Beacon Park, PLYMOUTH, PL2 3HF.
CROCKFORD, Mrs. Karen Elizabeth, BA ACA *1992;* 7 Grangewood Court, Outwood, WAKEFIELD, WEST YORKSHIRE, WF1 3SL.
CROCKFORD, Mrs. Lara Jane, BA ACA *1993;* 52 Avocet Parade, PEREGIAN BEACH, QLD 4573, AUSTRALIA.
CROCKFORD, Miss. Lisa Gemma, ACA *2008;* with Haines Watts Exeter LLP, 3 Southernhay West, EXETER, EX1 1JG.
CROCKFORD, Mr. Michael Anthony, BSc ACA *1992;* 25 Glen Abby Avenue, PEREGIAN SPRINGS, QLD 4573, AUSTRALIA.
CROCKFORD, Mr. Nigel Leslie, BA FCA *1974;* The Old Vicarage, Screveton Road, Car Colston, NOTTINGHAM, NG13 8JG.
•**CROCKFORD, Miss. Shirley Anne, ACA** *1980;* with Barter Durgan & Muir Limited, 35 Lavant Street, PETERSFIELD, HAMPSHIRE, GU32 3EL.
CROCKFORD, Mr. Simon Peter, BA ACA *1991;* 7 Grangewood Court, Outwood, WAKEFIELD, WEST YORKSHIRE, WF1 3SL.
CROCKFORD, Mr. Thomas Leslie, MChem ACA *2007;* 34 West View Road, ST. ALBANS, HERTFORDSHIRE, AL3 5JX.
CROCKFORD, Mr. Timothy Mark, BEng ACA *2000;* 1 Vale View Cottages, Vale View Terrace, Batheaston, BATH, BA1 7RJ.
CROFT, Mr. Adrian Neil, BSc ACA *1996;* Liberty International Holdings Plc, 40 Broadway, LONDON, SW1H 0BT.
CROFT, Mr. Albert Henry, FCA *1956;* 126 Kimbolton Road, BEDFORD, MK41 9DN. (Life Member)
CROFT, Mr. Andrew, BA ACA *1992;* with Deloitte LLP, One Trinity Gardens, Broad Chare, NEWCASTLE UPON TYNE, NE1 2HF.
CROFT, Mr. Andrew, BA ACA *2005;* 80 Yarborough Crescent, LINCOLN, LN1 3LX.
•**CROFT, Mr. Andrew John, FCA** *1981;* Priory Checkpoint Limited, 6 Bull Ring, MUCH WENLOCK, SHROPSHIRE, TF13 6HS.
CROFT, Mr. Andrew Martin, BSc FCA *1988;* St. James's Place Wealth Management Plc, St. James's Place House 1 Tetbury Road, CIRENCESTER, GL7 1FP.
CROFT, Mrs. Annabel Heather, BSocSc ACA *1993;* The Priory, Bull Ring, MUCH WENLOCK, TF13 6HS.
CROFT, Mr. Anthony Paul, FCA *1973;* 2 Melfort Glen, SHEFFIELD, S10 5SU.
CROFT, Mr. Frederick, FCA *1955;* 38 Trinity Drive, Holme, CARNFORTH, LA6 1QL. (Life Member)
•**CROFT, Mr. Geoffrey, FCA** *1976;* Geoff Croft, 28 Hollins Road, Hindley, WIGAN, WN2 4JZ.
CROFT, Miss. Jacqueline, ACA *1998;* Traidcraft, Kingsway, Team Valley, GATESHEAD, TYNE AND WEAR, NE11 0NE.
CROFT, Mr. James Edward John, BA ACA *1999;* 259 Four Ashes Road, Dorridge, SOLIHULL, WEST MIDLANDS, B93 8NR.
CROFT, Mr. Jeffrey John, FCA *1965;* 23 Raddington Drive, Olton, SOLIHULL, WEST MIDLANDS, B92 7DU. (Life Member)
CROFT, Miss. Jennifer Jo, BA ACA *1992;* 22 Adelaide Square, WINDSOR, SL4 2AQ.
CROFT, Miss. Joanne Susan, BSc ACA *1992;* 16 Agatha Gardens, Fernhill Heath, WORCESTER, WR3 8PB.
CROFT, Miss. Laura Suzanne, BA ACA *1997;* 20 Melody Road, LONDON, SW18 2QF.
CROFT, Mr. Mark, BA ACA *1994;* 16 Carey Avenue, WIRRAL, CH63 8LU.
CROFT, Mr. Michael Colin, ACA *1994;* 7 Ashcroft Park, COBHAM, KT11 2DN.
CROFT, Miss. Nichola Jayne, BA(Hons) ACA *2009;* Harris & Co, Marland House, 13 Huddersfield Road, BARNSLEY, SOUTH YORKSHIRE, S70 2LW.
CROFT, Mr. Peter, FCA *1972;* 17 The Avenue, Horsforth, LEEDS, LS18 5JW.
CROFT, Miss. Rachel Jacqueline, BSc(Hons) ACA *2002;* 75 Woolley Street, BRADFORD-ON-AVON, WILTSHIRE, BA15 1AL.
CROFT, Mr. Richard David, BA ACA *1993;* European Commission, Rue De La Loi 200, 1049 BRUSSELS, BELGIUM.
CROFT, Mr. Robart John, FCA *1964;* Reedville, 34 Nepcote Lane, Findon, WORTHING, WEST SUSSEX, BN14 0SG.
CROFT, Mr. Robert Geoffrey Edward, BCom ACA *1980;* 1 Hamilton Close, PURLEY, CR8 1AW.
CROFT, Mr. Robert William, ACA *1982;* 8 Church Road, Oldswinford, STOURBRIDGE, DY8 2HQ.
CROFT, Mr. Roger, FCA *1966;* Oatcroft, 1B Moorside Walk, Drighlington, BRADFORD, BD11 1HL.
CROFT, Dr. Stuart, PhD BSc ACA *2009;* 51 Woodstock Road, Loxley, SHEFFIELD, S6 6TG.
CROFT, Mrs. Susan Patricia, MA ACA *1994;* 4 Lindum Road, TEDDINGTON, TW11 9DR.
CROFT, Mrs. Taposhi Sarah, BSc ACA *1997;* 259 Four Ashes Road, Dorridge, SOLIHULL, WEST MIDLANDS, B93 8NR.
CROFT, Mr. Timothy Gordon, BSc ACA *1990;* 8 Churchill Way Long Hanborough, WITNEY, OXFORDSHIRE, OX29 8JH.
•**CROFT, Mr. Timothy James, FCA** *1989;* P R Hornsby & Company Limited, 5 Yeomans Court, Ware Road, HERTFORD, SG13 7HJ.
CROFT-BAKER, Mr. Stephen, FCA *1970;* 8 Brassey Drive, Holtwood, AYLESFORD, ME20 7QL.
CROFTON, Mrs. Gillian, BSc ACA *2006;* with Revell Ward LLP, 7th Floor, 30 Market Street, HUDDERSFIELD, HD1 2HG.
CROFTON, Mr. Richard, BSc ACA *2004;* 35 Castle Lodge Way Rothwell, LEEDS, LS26 0ZH.
CROFTON MARTIN, Mr. Kenneth Graham, BA FCA *1973;* Woodlands, Bilsington, ASHFORD, TN25 7JR. (Life Member)
CROFTS, Mr. Alan Francis, BSc FCA *1975;* 26 Rock Lane, Stoke Gifford, BRISTOL, BS34 8PF.
CROFTS, Mr. Barrie Hugh, FCA *1959;* Vine Cottage, Main Street, Caythorpe, NOTTINGHAM, NG14 7ED. (Life Member)
CROFTS, Mr. Colin Graham, BCom FCA *1983;* Southampton University Hospital NHS Trust, Tremona Road, SOUTHAMPTON, SO16 6YD.
•**CROFTS, Mr. David John, BSc FCA CTA** *1981;* Porticum Limited, 7 Orestes Court, 39 Woodford Road, South Woodford, LONDON, E18 2EF.
CROFTS, Miss. Helen Claire, BA(Hons) ACA *2002;* 16 Walberton Park, The Street Walberton, ARUNDEL, WEST SUSSEX, BN18 0PJ.
CROFTS, Mr. Ian Michael, BA ACA *2008;* 34 Pleasant Drive, BILLERICAY, CM12 0JL.
CROFTS, Mrs. Lucy Claire Stratford, BSc ACA *1994;* 5 Water Lane, Greenham, THATCHAM, RG19 8SS.
CROFTS, Mr. Simon John, ACA *1979;* (Tax Fac), with Matthews Mist & Co, Westbury House, 14 Bellevue Road, SOUTHAMPTON, SO15 2AY.
CROFTS-BOLSTER, Mr. Raymond Godfrey Robert, FCA *1957;* The White House, 6 Silver Street, MALDON, CM9 4QE. (Life Member)
CROGHAN, Mr. Mark Arnold, BA ACA *1991;* 58 Woodland Rise, LONDON, N10 3UJ.
CROKE, Mrs. Alison Karen, BA ACA *2004;* with Deloitte LLP, Hill House, 1 Little New Street, LONDON, EC4A 3TR.
CROKER, Mr. Andrew Peter, FCA *1978;* Hanover House, Plane Tree Crescent, LONDON, TW13 7JJ.
CROKER, Mr. David Geoffrey, FCA *1977;* 5, Willow Close, BRAMPTON, CAMBRIDGESHIRE, pe284rj.
CROKER, Mr. Giles Michael Roger, BA ACA *1989;* 83 Wattle Valley Road, CANTERBURY, VIC 3126, AUSTRALIA.
CROKER, Mr. Michael Howard, BSc ACA *1986;* St Lawrence House, 29-31 Broad Street, BRISTOL, BS1 2HF.
CROKER, Mr. Patrick John Beresford, BSc FCA *1980;* Colonsay, 17 Upper Street, Quainton, AYLESBURY, BUCKINGHAMSHIRE, HP22 4AY.
CROKER, Mrs. Susie, BSc ACA *2001;* 604 New North Road, ILFORD, ESSEX, IG6 3TG.
CROKER, Mr. Timothy Thomas, MA ACA *2003;* Flat 206 Dakota Building, Deals Gateway, LONDON, SE13 7QE.
CROLL, Mr. Andrew, ACA *2011;* Flat 8/1, 15 Castlebank Place, GLASGOW, G11 6BJ.
CROLL, Mr. Michael John, FCA *1957;* 10 Strathearn Road, NORTH BERWICK, EAST LOTHIAN, EH39 5BZ. (Life Member)
CROLL, Mr. Paul Alexander James, BSc ACA *1998;* 9 Martins Rise, Whiteparish, SALISBURY, SP5 2EX.
CROMACK, Mr. Andrew Michael, BA ACA *1983;* 23 Knole Road, Lords Wood, CHATHAM, ME5 8PJ.
CROMAR, Mr. Roderick Nicholson, MA BSc ACA *2001;* Royal Mail, Rowland Hill House, Boythorpe Road, CHESTERFIELD, DERBYSHIRE, S49 1HQ.
•**CROMAR, Mr. Ronald James, BSc ACA** *1986;* RJ Cromar Ltd, 7 Kinnaird Avenue, Newton Mearns, GLASGOW, G77 5EL.
•**CROMBIE, Mr. Alastair Charles Macdonald, MA MBA FCA** *1977;* A C M Crombie, 20 Sandfield Road, Headington, OXFORD, OX3 7RQ.
•**CROMBIE, Mr. David John, BA FCA** *1991;* (Tax Fac), JAD Audit Ltd, 4 Bloors Lane, Rainham, GILLINGHAM, KENT, ME8 7EG. See also JAD Associates Ltd
CROMBIE, Mr. Richard Andrew, BA ACA *2000;* J P Morgan Asset Management, Finsbury Dials, 20 Finsbury Street, LONDON, EC2Y 9AQ.
CROMBIE, Mr. Roger Andrew, FCA *1972;* 16 Heron House, St John's Wood, LONDON, NW8 7AJ.
CROME, Mr. Bernard John, FCA *1958;* 2 West Farm Drive, ASHTEAD, SURREY, KT21 2LB. (Life Member)
CROME, Mr. Dennis Victor, FCA *1955;* 22 Heath Road, Thorpe End, NORWICH, NR13 5BQ. (Life Member)
CROMPTON, Mrs. Alexandra Jennie, BSc(Hons) ACA *2000;* Dell Cottage, Chartridge, CHESHAM, BUCKINGHAMSHIRE, HP5 2TS.
CROMPTON, Miss. Ann Elizabeth, ACA *2005;* 89 Queensway, Heald Green, CHEADLE, CHESHIRE, SK8 3HG.
CROMPTON, Mrs. Clare Victoria, BA ACA *2002;* 3 Wellington Gardens, Bradfield Southend, READING, RG7 6EJ.
CROMPTON, Miss. Hollie Jayne, ACA MAAT *2009;* Crowther Laithe Farm, Carrs Road, Marsden, HUDDERSFIELD, HD7 6JG.
CROMPTON, Mr. James Paul, BA ACA *1994;* Bowden Dibble & Hayes Ltd Parklands, 825a Wilmslow Road, MANCHESTER, M20 2RE.
•**CROMPTON, Mr. John Stewart, BA FCA** *1978;* (Tax Fac), Caldwell Crompton, Alderley, 35 Whitehall Road, SALE, CHESHIRE, M33 3NL.
CROMPTON, Mr. Kenneth Braithwaite, FCA *1947;* Briar Close, Hosey Hill, WESTERHAM, TN16 1TA. (Life Member)
CROMPTON, Miss. Linda, BSc ACA *2001;* 11 Watson Way, Marston Moretaine, BEDFORD, MK43 0RG.
CROMPTON, Mr. Nicholas William, BA ACA *2000;* Dell Cottage, Chartridge, CHESHAM, BUCKINGHAMSHIRE, HP5 2TS.
CROMPTON, Mr. Paul, BA FCA *1985;* Osborne House, Castlewood, RINGWOOD, BH24 2AX.
CROMPTON, Mr. Peter Anthony, BA ACA *1985;* 1 Howe Road, Onchan, ISLE OF MAN, IM3 2AP.
CROMPTON, Mr. Robert Morton, FCA *1976;* The Gables, 66 Eatock Way, Westhoughton, BOLTON, BL5 2RR.
CROMWELL, Mr. Alistair John, BA ACA *1992;* Old Manor House, 9 Stocks Road Aldbury, TRING, HERTFORDSHIRE, HP23 5RT.
•**CROMWELL, Mrs. Clare Elizabeth, BA ACA** *1992;* (Tax Fac), Saffery Champness, Lion House, Red Lion Street, LONDON, WC1R 4GB.
CROMWELL, Mr. Keith Lawrence, BSc ACA *1986;* 11 Bramshall Drive, Dorridge, SOLIHULL, B93 8TG.
CRONE, Mr. Charles Edward Straker, BA(Hons) ACA *2002;* 21 Trevor Road, LONDON, SW19 3PW.
CRONEY, Mr. Adam, ACA *2008;* 4 Bridgenhall Road, ENFIELD, MIDDLESEX, EN1 4AY.
CRONIN, Mr. Gerald Francis, MA FCA *1960;* 16 Chalfont Drive, HOVE, BN3 6QR. (Life Member)
CRONIN, Mrs. Joanne, BA ACA *1991;* 10 The Pipers, Heswall, WIRRAL, MERSEYSIDE, CH60 9LL.
•**CRONIN, Mr. Peter John Edmund, BSc FCA** *1986;* (Tax Fac), Clarkes, First Floor, 5 Walker Terrace, GATESHEAD, NE8 1EB.
CRONIN, Mr. Richard Wyndham, BSc ACA *1994;* Edelweiss, Poundfold, Croscombe, WELLS, BA5 3QY.
•**CRONIN, Mr. Ronald Brian, FCA** *1965;* Ronald B. Cronin, 2 Holly Hill Drive, BANSTEAD, SM7 2BD.
CRONIN, Mr. Timothy James, BA ACA *1983;* Home Farm, Newton Kyme, TADCASTER, LS24 9LS.
CRONIN, Ms. Vera Mary, BCom ACA *1993;* 22 Obelisk Avenue, BLACKROCK, COUNTY DUBLIN, IRELAND.
CRONIN-COLTSMANN, Mr. John Francis, BSc ACA *1991;* 78 Felsham Road, LONDON, SW15 1DQ.
•**CRONK, Mrs. Janet Sheila, BSc FCA** *1984;* (Tax Fac), CKLG Ltd, 9 Quy Court, Colliers Lane, Stow-cum-Quy, CAMBRIDGE, CB25 9AU.
CRONK, Mrs. Michele, ACA CA(SA) *2010;* BP Plc, Group Internal Audit, Building B, Chertsey Road, SUNBURY-ON-THAMES, MIDDLESEX TW16 7LN.
CRONK, Mrs. Naomi Ruth, ACA *2009;* with Old Mill Accountancy LLP, Leeward House, Fitzroy Road, Exeter Business Park, EXETER, EX1 3LJ.
•**CRONSHAW, Mr. Michael William, MBA LLB ACA** *1986;* Whitehead & Howarth, 327 Clifton Drive South, LYTHAM ST. ANNES, FY8 1HN.
•**CROOK, Mr. Andrew James, BA ACA** *1993;* Mercer & Hole, 76 Shoe Lane, LONDON, EC4A 3JB.
CROOK, Mr. Andrew James, BSc ACA *1986;* 14 Montgomery Avenue, ESHER, SURREY, KT10 9BB.
CROOK, Mr. Andrew John, BSc ACA *1983;* Perkin Elmer Ltd, Chalfont Road, Seer Green, BEACONSFIELD, HP9 2FX.
CROOK, Mr. Andrew Jonathan, BA ACA *1995;* 1 Ford Lodge, Ford Lane, Didsbury, MANCHESTER, M20 2RU.
CROOK, Mr. Anthony Peter, MA(Cantab) FCA CTA *2000;* Liberty Syndicate Management Ltd, 60 Great Tower Street, LONDON, EC3R 5AZ.
CROOK, Mr. Barry Freeman, FCA *1955;* 22 Turker Lane, NORTHALLERTON, NORTH YORKSHIRE, DL6 1PX. (Life Member)
•**CROOK, Mr. David Ford, MSc FCA** *1965;* (Tax Fac), David Crook & Co., 6 Martineau Close, BOGNOR REGIS, WEST SUSSEX, PO21 4BT.
CROOK, Mr. David John, BSc ACA *1998;* Team Simoco Ltd Field House, Uttoxeter Old Road, DERBY, DE1 1NH.
CROOK, Miss. Elizabeth, ACA *2010;* Arley View Farm Hobbs Hill Lane, High Legh, KNUTSFORD, CHESHIRE, WA16 0QZ.
•**CROOK, Ms. Elizabeth Anne, BA ACA MBA** *1995;* Andrews Orme & Hinton Limited, 4 Darwin Court, Oxon Business Park, SHREWSBURY, SY3 5AL.
CROOK, Miss. Emma, ACA MAAT *2010;* 24 White Hart Road, Fair Oak, EASTLEIGH, HAMPSHIRE, SO50 7JR.
CROOK, Mr. Geoffrey Peter, BSc FCA *1995;* 23A Third Avenue, SEMAPHORE PARK, SA 5019, AUSTRALIA.
•**CROOK, Mr. Jeremy Peter, FCA** *1971;* J P Crook & Co, 11a Austin Street, STAMFORD, LINCOLNSHIRE, PE9 2QR.
•**CROOK, Mr. John, FCA** *1968;* (Tax Fac), Crook & Co (Accounts) Ltd, Pencoed, Sheets Heath Lane, Brookwood, WOKING, GU24 0EL.
CROOK, Mr. John Arthur, FCA *1961;* 32 Langton Road, Great Bowden, MARKET HARBOROUGH, LEICESTERSHIRE, LE16 7EZ. (Life Member)
•**CROOK, Mr. Jonathan Charles, BA ACA** *1997;* Myers Clark Limited, Iveco House, Station Road, WATFORD, WD17 1DL. See also Bluedome Finance Limited
CROOK, Mrs. Judith Ann, BSc ACA *1978;* 50 Broadway, 4th Floor, NEW YORK, NY 10004, UNITED STATES.
CROOK, Mrs. Katherine Anne, ACA *1996;* 30 Fellbrigg Road, LONDON, SE22 9HH.
CROOK, Miss. Katherine Frances, BSc ACA *2010;* 38 Corve Dale Walk, West Bridgford, NOTTINGHAM, NG2 6TY.
CROOK, Mrs. Marisa, BSc ACA DChA *2005;* The Barn, 46 The Highway, Great Staughton, ST. NEOTS, CAMBRIDGESHIRE, PE19 5DA.
CROOK, Mr. Mark James, MEng ACA BEng(Hons) *2011;* Flat 34, Auckland Court, Auckland Road, CAMBRIDGE, CB5 8DS.
•**CROOK, Mr. Peter Allan, FCA** *1981;* 25 Mount House Road, Freshfield, LIVERPOOL, L37 3LA.
CROOK, Mr. Peter Stuart, MBA BSc ACA *1989;* Provident Financial plc, No. 1 Godwin Street, BRADFORD, BD1 2SU.
•**CROOK, Mr. Philip Howard, BSc FCA** *1972;* Bradavon Financial Services Limited, Bradavon, 45 The Dales, COTTINGHAM, HU16 5JS. See also Crook P.H.
•**CROOK, Mr. Stuart Peter, BSc ACA** *2000;* (Tax Fac), Wellers, Millweye Court, 73 Southern Road, THAME, OX9 2ED.
CROOKE, Mr. Robert John, MBA BA FCA *1974;* 24 Faroe Road, Brook Green, LONDON, W14 0EP.
CROOKENDEN, Mrs. Lucinda Jane, BSc ACA *1989;* Newnhams Rough, Horsted Keynes, HAYWARDS HEATH, RH17 7BT.
CROOKES, Mr. Anthony David, BA ACA *1988;* 9 St. Johns Road, Petts Wood, ORPINGTON, BR5 1HS.
CROOKES, Mrs. Jacqueline Mary, BSocSc ACA *1987;* Branching Out Two Limited, Sunrise House, Hulley Road, MACCLESFIELD, CHESHIRE, SK10 2LP.
•**CROOKES, Mrs. Janet Elizabeth, BA FCA** *1984;* with Grant Thornton UK LLP, Grant Thornton House, 22 Melton Street, Euston Square, LONDON, NW1 2EP.

CROOKES, Mr. John Brian, FCA *1961;* 3 Winston Close, Marple, STOCKPORT, SK6 6HW. (Life Member)

•**CROOKES, Mr. Ronald Michael, BA ACA** *1986;* Walker Moyle, Alverton Pavilion, Trewithen Road, PENZANCE, CORNWALL, TR18 4LS.

CROOKES, Mrs. Rowan Louise, BSc ACA *1995;* 2 Tangmere Close, Bowerhill, MELKSHAM, SN12 6XW.

CROOKS, Mr. Andrew Peter, BSc ACA *1993;* 1 Clifton High Grove, Stoke Bishop, BRISTOL, BS9 1TU.

CROOKS, Mrs. Emma Jayne, ACA *2008;* 4 Dale Court, Kilburn, BELPER, DERBYSHIRE, DE56 0JL.

CROOKS, Mr. Gareth James, ACA *2008;* Deloitte & Touche Hill House, 1 Little New Street, LONDON, EC4A 3TR.

CROOKS, Mr. James, ACA *2002;* Translinc Ltd, Jarvis House, 157 Sadler Road, LINCOLN, LN6 3RS.

CROOKS, Mr. James Broumpton, MA ACA *1983;* The Old Longhouse, Portworthy, Lee Moor, PLYMOUTH, PL7 5JT.

CROOKS, Mrs. Janet Elaine, BSc ACA *1993;* 39 Manor Drive, Horspath, OXFORD, OX33 1RW.

•**CROOKS, Mrs. Melanie Jane, BA ACA** *1995;* with RSM Tenon Audit Limited, Charterhouse, Legge Street, BIRMINGHAM, B4 7EU.

CROOKS, Mr. Michael Clive, BA ACA *1987;* The Stadium Group, Welton Grange, Welton, BROUGH, HU15 1NB.

•**CROOKS, Mr. Philip James, FCA** *1983;* Grant Thornton UK LLP, Grant Thornton House, 202 Silbury Boulevard, MILTON KEYNES, BUCKINGHAMSHIRE, MK9 1LW. See also Grant Thornton LLP

CROOKS, Dr. Richard James, BSc ACA *2001;* with Legal & General Group, Group Financial Control, 1 Coleman Street, LONDON, EC2R 5AA.

CROOKS, Mr. Roger Anthony, FCA *1974;* 12 Woodlands Park, LEIGH-ON-SEA, SS9 3TY.

CROOKS, Mr. Shane Michael, BSc ACA *1997;* 60 Vaughan Williams Way, Warley, BRENTWOOD, ESSEX, CM14 5WQ.

CROOKS, Mr. Toby Lloyd, ACA *2008;* (Tax Fac), Rawlinson & Hunter The Lower Mill, Kingston Road, EPSOM, KT17 2AE.

CROOKSTON, Mr. David Malcolm, BA FCA *1985;* 11 Elliswick Road, HARPENDEN, HERTFORDSHIRE, AL5 4TP.

CROOKSTON, Mr. Simon James, BA(Hons) ACA *1998;* 5 Ruglys Way, Charing, ASHFORD, KENT, TN27 0GZ.

CROOM, Mrs. Janis Elizabeth, BSc FCA ATII *1976;* New Hall School, Boreham, CHELMSFORD, CM3 3HS.

CROOM, Mr. Peter Geoffrey, BSc FCA *1999;* 22 New House Farm Drive, Bournville Park, Northfield, BIRMINGHAM, B31 2FN.

CROOM, Mr. Timothy Llewellyn, BSc ACA *2007;* 3 Smallhythe Close, Bearsted, MAIDSTONE, ME15 8JJ.

•**CROOMBS, Mr. Paul David, ACA** *2003;* (Tax Fac), Croombs C.A. Limited, Ilex House, The Green, Upper Clatford, ANDOVER, HAMPSHIRE SP11 7PS.

CROOME, Mr. Brian John, FCA *1961;* 55 Rothesay Drive Highcliffe, CHRISTCHURCH, BH23 4LD.

CROOT, Mr. Antony John, FCA *1971;* 316 Bunyan Court, Barbican, LONDON, EC2Y 8DH.

CROPLEY, Miss. Victoria Anne, BA(Hons) ACA *2009;* Flat 2 Clare Lodge, First Drift, Wothorpe, STAMFORD, LINCOLNSHIRE, PE9 3JL.

CROPP, Mr. Howard Reginald, FCA *1961;* 1c Elmoor Avenue, WELWYN, HERTFORDSHIRE, AL6 9PG.

CROPPER, Mr. Alan Richard, FCA *1966;* The Old Vicarage, Cassington, WITNEY, OX29 4DW.

CROPPER, Mr. Alan Trevor, FCA *1963;* 4 The Cloisters, Barnacres Road, HEMEL HEMPSTEAD, HERTFORDSHIRE, HP3 8JU.

CROPPER, Mrs. Ann, FCA *1968;* with AGP, 1st Floor, 2 City Road, CHESTER, CH1 3AE.

CROPPER, Mr. Brian, FCA *1961;* 11 The Greens Cowm Park, Whitworth, ROCHDALE, OL12 8AQ.

CROPPER, Mr. James Anthony, BA FCA *1966;* Tolson Hall, KENDAL, LA9 5SE.

•**CROPPER, Mr. Mark Nicholas, BSc ACA** *1998;* Zolfo Cooper, 10 Fleet Place, LONDON, EC4M 7RB.

CROPPER, Mr. Martin John, MA ACA *1991;* Shrewsbury School, The Alington Hall, Kingsland, SHREWSBURY, SY3 7BA.

CROPPER, Mr. Robert Henry, BCom FCA *1953;* 26 Park Drive East, MIRFIELD, WF14 9NH. (Life Member)

CROPPER, Mrs. Susan Maria, BSc ACA *1999;* 7 Holmwood Close, Ashton-In-Makerfield, WIGAN, WN4 9SJ.

CROSBIE, Mr. Mark John, BA ACA *1986;* white waltham house, White Waltham House Waltham Road, White Waltham, MAIDENHEAD, BERKSHIRE, SL6 3SH.

CROSBIE, Mr. Stanley, BCom FCA *1963;* 31 Tongdean Road, HOVE, BN3 6QE.

CROSBIE, Mr. Terence Marley, FCA *1958;* Seaville House, Tramore, WATERFORD, COUNTY WATERFORD, IRELAND. (Life Member)

CROSBIE-JONES, Mr. Adrian, BSc FCA *1976;* The Private Trust Corporation Ltd., Charlotte House, Charlotte Street, NASSAU, POB N-65, BAHAMAS.

CROSBY, Mrs. Belinda, BA ACA FSI *1998;* Schroder Property Managers (Jersey) Limited, 2-6 Church Street, St Helier, JERSEY, JE4 9WB.

CROSBY, Mr. Bernard Austin, FCA *1973;* Oaklodge, 32 Norfolk Road, LYTHAM ST. ANNES, LANCASHIRE, FY8 4JG.

CROSBY, Mr. David Graham, FCA *1973;* 5 Gorse Lane, West Kirby, WIRRAL, MERSEYSIDE, CH48 8BE. (Life Member)

CROSBY, Mr. David Keith, BSc FCA *1978;* Flowtech, Pimbo Road, SKELMERSDALE, LANCASHIRE, WN8 9RB.

CROSBY, Mr. David Patrick John, BSc ACA *1992;* Genus Plc, Belvedere House, Basing View, BASINGSTOKE, HAMPSHIRE, RG21 4HG.

CROSBY, Miss. Hayley, BA ACA *2011;* 47 Stanmore Crescent, LEEDS, LS4 2RY.

•**CROSBY, Miss. Heather Jane, BSc ACA** *1993;* 22 Spring Meadows, DARWEN, LANCASHIRE, BB3 3JS.

CROSBY, Mr. Jan Travers, BSc FCA FSI *1998;* 25 Kymer Gardens, HASSOCKS, WEST SUSSEX, BN6 8QZ.

CROSBY, Miss. Jane, ACA *2011;* Sage (UK) Ltd, North Park Avenue, NEWCASTLE UPON TYNE, NE13 9AA.

CROSBY, Mr. John, MEng ACA *2002;* Phoenix House, Kingfisher Way, Silverlink Business Park, WALLSEND, TYNE AND WEAR, NE28 9NX.

CROSBY, Mr. Martin, BA ACA *1997;* 20 Mount Drive, Alwoodley, LEEDS, LS17 7QW.

CROSBY, Mr. Matthew Lawrence, BSc(Hons) ACA *2010;* 24 Palmerston Road, LONDON, SW19 1PQ.

CROSBY, Ms. Nerys Eluned, BA ACA CISA *2002;* 47 Longacres, ST. ALBANS, HERTFORDSHIRE, AL4 0SL.

CROSBY, Mr. Peter, FCA *1959;* 11 Old House Court, Church Lane, Wexham, SLOUGH, SL3 6LN. (Life Member)

•**CROSBY, Mr. Philip James, BA(Hons) FCA** *2001;* Reads & Co Limited, PO Box 179, 40 Esplanade, St Helier, JERSEY, JE4 9RJ. See also Reads & Co. Group Limited and Reads (Audit) Limited

•**CROSBY, Mr. Richard William Villiers, FCA** *1969;* (Tax Fac), Richard Crosby, Shrublands Farmhouse, Barston Lane, Barston, SOLIHULL, B92 0JU.

•**CROSBY, Mr. Roy, FCA** *1963;* (Tax Fac), Austral Crosby, 20 Norgetts Lane, Melbourn, ROYSTON, SG8 6HS.

CROSBY, Mr. Stephen John, BA ACA *1979;* Bridleworth, Church Road, CRAWLEY, RH10 7RT.

CROSBY, Mr. Stephen Percival, BA ACA CTA *1985;* Standard Chartered, 1 Basinghall Avenue, LONDON, EC2V 5DD.

CROSBY-ATKINSON, Ms. Alison May, BSc ACA AMCT MICA *1991;* 74 Popes Grove, Strawberry Hill, TWICKENHAM, TW1 4JX.

•**CROSHAW, Mr. Neil John, BA ACA** *2006;* Croshaw & Co, 19 Windmill Road, ATHERSTONE, WARWICKSHIRE, CV9 1HP.

CROSIER, Mrs. Elizabeth, BA ACA *2008;* The Sage Group plc, Sage (UK) Ltd, North Park Avenue, NEWCASTLE UPON TYNE, NE13 9AA.

CROSLAND, Mr. John Michael Cowen, FCA *1962;* 7 Springfield Mews, Springfield Gardens, Stokesley, MIDDLESBROUGH, CLEVELAND, TS9 5GJ. (Life Member)

CROSLAND, Mr. Peter John, BA ACA *2003;* 3 The Croft, Swales Moor Road, HALIFAX, WEST YORKSHIRE, HX3 6UF.

CROSLAND, Mr. Richard Andrew, BSc FCA *1989;* 14 Lavery Close, OSSETT, WEST YORKSHIRE, WF5 8ES.

CROSLAND, Mr. Richard Bryan, FCA *1970;* 36 Rawson Avenue, Skircoat Green, HALIFAX, HX3 0LR.

CROSS, Mr. Alan Mervin, FCA *1969;* 5a Berrells Road, TETBURY, GL8 8ED.

CROSS, Miss. Alison Hellen, BA(Hons) ACA *2001;* 4 Cranbourne Court, Cranbourne Lane, BASINGSTOKE, RG21 3NW.

CROSS, Mr. Andrew Cecil, BA FCA *1992;* Credit Suisse Securities (Europe) Limited, One Cabot Square, LONDON, E14 4QJ.

•**CROSS, Mr. Andrew Colin, FCA** *1969;* Andrew Cross & Co, The Plaza Building, Lee High Road, Lewisham, LONDON, SE13 5PT.

CROSS, Mr. Andrew James, BA ACA *1985;* Dompfaffstr. 140, 91056 ERLANGEN, GERMANY.

CROSS, Mr. Andrew Nevill Alan, BSc FCA *1992;* Ul Baluckiego 12, Stary Mokotow, 02-604 WARSAW, POLAND.

CROSS, Mrs. Angela Anna, BA ACA FSI *1996;* 19 Claremont Drive, Headingley, LEEDS, LS9 4ED.

CROSS, Mr. Anthony John, MA FCA *1970;* 5 Saxon Close, STRATFORD-UPON-AVON, CV37 7DX.

CROSS, Mr. Anthony Michael, ACA *2002;* 3 Blackmore Road, Blackmore, INGATESTONE, CM4 0QX.

CROSS, Mr. Anthony Stimson, BA FCA *1974;* Technology in Action Group ltd, Thames Court 1 Victoria Street, WINDSOR, SL4 1YB.

CROSS, Mr. Charles John, MBA BSc FCA *1974;* 3560 Jackson Street, SAN FRANCISCO, CA 94118, UNITED STATES.

CROSS, Mr. Colin Paul, BSc ACA *1987;* 3 Hall Close, Maids Moreton, BUCKINGHAM, MK18 1RH.

CROSS, Mr. David, BA ACA *1991;* 28 Park Copse, Hall Lane Horsforth, LEEDS, LS18 5UN.

CROSS, Mr. David Alan, FCA *1963;* 4 The Hollies, Willerby, HULL, HU10 6HZ. (Life Member)

CROSS, Mr. David Andrew, BA FCA *1976;* Aurora Energy Ltd, The Old Rectory, Hinton-on-the-Green, EVESHAM, WORCESTERSHIRE, WR11 2QU.

CROSS, Mr. David Spencer, FCA *1963;* Highlands, 22 Whitehill Road, KIDDERMINSTER, DY11 6JJ. (Life Member)

•**CROSS, Mr. Denis, FCA** *1977;* (Tax Fac), Brown Butler, Leigh House, 28-32 St Paul's Street, LEEDS, LS1 2JT.

CROSS, Mr. Dennis, BA FCA *1965;* P O Box EE 16668, NASSAU, BAHAMAS.

CROSS, Mr. Edward, BA ACA *2008;* Horseferry House, Horseferry Road, LONDON, SW1P 2AW.

CROSS, Mrs. Erica Jeanne, BSc ACA *2007;* 5 Freston Park, LONDON, N3 1UP.

•**CROSS, Ms. Fiona Jane, BSc FCA ATII AIIT** *1992;* Chantrey Vellacott DFK LLP, Russell Square House, 10-12 Russell Square, LONDON, WC1B 5LF.

CROSS, Mr. Frank William, FCA *1960;* Foxglove Cottage, Red Hill Road, Hadleigh, IPSWICH, IP7 6BU. (Life Member)

•**CROSS, Mr. Geoffrey William, FCA** *1971;* Shoesmiths, Suites 1 & 2, Ground Floor, 54 Hagley Road, Edgbaston, BIRMINGHAM B16 8PE.

CROSS, Mrs. Helen Marie, BSc FCA *1975;* (Tax Fac), 73 Royalty Lane, New Longton, PRESTON, PR4 4JE.

CROSS, Mr. Ian Alexander Robertson, BSc ACA *2004;* (Tax Fac), 1a New Road, Digswell, WELWYN, HERTFORDSHIRE, AL6 0AE.

CROSS, Mr. Ian Fredrick Albert, FCA *1970;* Villa 1, 22 Earls Court, KINGSTON 8, JAMAICA.

CROSS, Mr. Ian Lewis, FCA *1982;* 28 Arlington Gardens, Harold Wood, ROMFORD, RM3 0EA.

CROSS, Ms. Jacqueline Anne, LLB ACA *1987;* LloydsTSB Australia Branch, 25/45 Clarence Street, SYDNEY, NSW 2000, AUSTRALIA.

CROSS, Mr. James Mark, BA ACA *1986;* (Tax Fac), 155 Rosendale Road, West Dulwich, LONDON, SE21 8HE.

CROSS, Mr. James Stephen, BA FCA *1976;* 44 Romney Drive, BROMLEY, BR1 2TE. (Life Member)

•**CROSS, Mr. James Thomas Laidlaw, BA FCA DChA** *1988;* Kingston Smith LLP, Devonshire House, 60 Goswell Road, LONDON, EC1M 7AD. See also Kingston Smith Limited Liability Partnership, Devonshire Corporate Services LLP and Kingston Smith Consulting LLP

CROSS, Mr. James William, FCA *1966;* Cherry House, Lyneal, ELLESMERE, SHROPSHIRE, SY12 0QG.

•**CROSS, Mrs. Jannine Linda, BA FCA** *1985;* 14 Wollescote Drive, SOLIHULL, B91 3YN.

CROSS, Mrs. Jennifer Ann, ACA *1982;* 34 Hinton Avenue, Alvechurch, BIRMINGHAM, B48 7LY.

CROSS, Mr. Jeremy David, BA ACA *1993;* 19 Claremont Drive, LEEDS, LS6 4ED.

CROSS, Mr. John, MMath ACA *2009;* 78 Stafford Place, HORLEY, RH6 9GY.

•**CROSS, Mr. John Dennis, FCA** *1958;* Dennis Cross, Sycamore House, 5 Vine Close, Stapleford, CAMBRIDGE, CB22 5BZ.

CROSS, Mr. John Michael, FCA *1959;* Michael Cross, Cherry Trees, 50 Wergs Road, WOLVERHAMPTON, WV6 8TD. (Life Member)

•**CROSS, Mr. John Morris, BSc FCA** *1963;* Cross & Company Business Development and Support, Grove End, Upper Brailes, BANBURY, OXFORDSHIRE, OX15 5BA.

•**CROSS, Mr. Jonathan Nicholas, FCA** *1980;* (Tax Fac), Everett & Son, 35 Paul Street, LONDON, EC2A 4UQ. See also Everett Horder Limited

CROSS, Mr. Jonathan Paul, BSc ACA *1995;* Ask Property Developments, The Old School House George Leigh Street, MANCHESTER, M4 6AF.

CROSS, Mrs. Julie Benita, BSc ACA *1993;* The Barn, 11 Durlings Orchard, Ightham, SEVENOAKS, KENT, TN15 9HW.

•**CROSS, Mr. Kevin Douglas, ACA** *1979;* The SS Partnership Limited, Barclays Bank Chambers, 9a Market Place, BRIGG, SOUTH HUMBERSIDE, DN20 8ES.

CROSS, Mr. Lee Adam, ACA *2008;* Deloitte & Touche Llp Horton House, Exchange Flags, LIVERPOOL, L2 3PG.

CROSS, Mr. Lewis Alexander, BSc ACA *2010;* 3 Warford Avenue, Poynton, STOCKPORT, CHESHIRE, SK12 1SY.

CROSS, Mrs. Louise Mary, BA ACA *1994;* 38 Pen-y-groes, Oakdale, BLACKWOOD, NP12 0ER.

CROSS, Mr. Malcolm Harold, BA FCA *1969;* 7 Hind Close, Pengam Green, CARDIFF, CF24 2EF.

CROSS, Mr. Mark Jason Blount, MEng ACA *2001;* 4 The Oaklands, Chandlers Ford, EASTLEIGH, HAMPSHIRE, SO53 3RP.

CROSS, Dr. Martin McLeod, PhD BSc ACA *2007;* 1 Horsley Terrace, NORTH SHIELDS, TYNE AND WEAR, NE30 2RT.

CROSS, Mrs. Mary Jane, BSc FCA ALCM *1990;* 31 Grosvenor Way, DROITWICH, WR9 7SR.

CROSS, Mr. Matthew, ACA *2005;* 21 Aston Chase, STONE, STAFFORDSHIRE, ST15 8SD.

•**CROSS, Mr. Matthew Miles, BSc ACA** *1993;* PricewaterhouseCoopers LLP, First Point, Buckingham Gate, London Gatwick Airport, GATWICK, WEST SUSSEX RH6 0NT. See also PricewaterhouseCoopers

CROSS, Mr. Neil, BA(Hons) ACA *2006;* Muar Lodge Station Road, Cotton, STOWMARKET, SUFFOLK, IP14 4NQ.

CROSS, Mr. Nicholas John, MA MSc FCA *1971;* Lashford House, Dry Sandford, ABINGDON, OX13 6JP.

CROSS, Mrs. Patricia, ACA *1989;* 10 Holland Road, ABINGDON, OX14 1PH.

•**CROSS, Mr. Peter, BSc FCA** *1978;* Barber Harrison & Platt, 2 Rutland Park, SHEFFIELD, S10 2PD.

CROSS, Mrs. Rachel Elizabeth, ACA *2008;* Mercer & Hole, 300 Pavilion Drive, NORTHAMPTON, NN4 7YE.

CROSS, Mr. Richard Andrew, BSc(Econ) ACA *1997;* 2197 S. Juniper St, LAKEWOOD, CO 80228, UNITED STATES.

CROSS, Mr. Robert Kingsley, FCA *1967;* 18 Ridgeway, Guiseley, LEEDS, LS20 8JA.

CROSS, Mr. Ronald Nelson, FCA *1975;* 40a Berry Lane, Wootton, NORTHAMPTON, NN4 6JX.

CROSS, Mrs. Ruth Kristina, BA(Hons) ACA *2002;* 16 Borrowdale Avenue, IPSWICH, IP4 2TN.

CROSS, Mrs. Sara Charlotte, BSc FCA *1988;* Spratt Endicott, 52-54 The Green, BANBURY, OXFORDSHIRE, OX16 9AB.

CROSS, Mrs. Sarah Lucille, BA(Hons) ACA *2001;* Rothman Pantall & Co, 10 St Ann Street, SALISBURY, SP1 2DN.

CROSS, Mr. Simon David, BSc ACA *2000;* 21 Bulkeley Road, Handforth, WILMSLOW, CHESHIRE, SK9 3DJ.

•**CROSS, Mr. Simon Gerrard, BA FCA** *1989;* (Tax Fac), Simon Cross, 34 Church Avenue, Swillington, LEEDS, LS26 8QH.

CROSS, Mr. Simon James, BEng ACA *2002;* 17 Devereux Road, LONDON, SW11 6JR.

CROSS, Mr. Stephen, BA ACA *1983;* Caraway Cottage, 2 Breach Cottages, Breach Lane, Upchurch, SITTINGBOURNE, KENT ME9 7PE.

CROSS, Mr. Steven Gordon, BA ACA *1991;* 32 Burridge Road, Burridge, SOUTHAMPTON, SO31 1BT.

CROSS, Mr. Stuart Andrew, MBA BA ACA *1991;* Morgan Cross Consulting, 3 Elston Hall, Top Street, Elston, NEWARK, NG23 5NP.

CROSS, Mrs. Vicki Claire, BA(Hons) ACA CTA *2002;* 183 Maybank Road, South Woodford, LONDON, E18 1EP.

CROSS, Mrs. Vivien Margaret, BA ACA *1997;* 22 Low Meadow, Whaley Bridge, HIGH PEAK, DERBYSHIRE, SK23 7AY.

CROSS, Mr. William Richard Jason Blount, FCA *1970;* Kings Keep, 1 Archery Fields, Odiham, HOOK, RG29 1AE. (Life Member)

CROSSE, Mr. Horace Hale, FCA *1956;* 18 Church Road, HAYLING ISLAND, PO11 0NT. (Life Member)

CROSSE, Mr. Peter Leonard Hale, FCA *1961;* Parkwood, 8b Park Road, HAYLING ISLAND, HAMPSHIRE, PO11 0HU.

CROSSEY, Mr. Robert Allison, FCA *1959;* Ashcroft, Riddings Lane Curbar, Calver, HOPE VALLEY, S32 3YN. (Life Member)

CROSSFIELD, Mr. Jonathan James, BA ACA *1999;* 11 Martindale, LONDON, SW14 7AL.
•CROSSGROVE, Mr. David John, BA FCA *1983;* The Crossgrove Partnership Ltd, 40 Belmont Road, Bramhall, STOCKPORT, SK7 1LE.
CROSSINGHAM, Ms. Jennifer Lynn, ACA *1994;* 166 Broomfield Road, CHELMSFORD, CM1 4HF.
CROSSLAND, Mr. Andrew Ashton, BA ACA *1998;* High Waterhouses Farm, Russell Street, Waterhouses, DURHAM, DH7 9AR.
CROSSLAND, Mr. Anthony Philip James, BA ACA *1992;* The Co-operative Group, New Century House, MANCHESTER, M60 4ES.
CROSSLAND, Mr. Dean, ACA *2011;* 1 Bardsey Place, NEWCASTLE UPON TYNE, NE12 8NU.
CROSSLAND, Mr. Donald Congreve, FCA *1952;* 2 Parkwood Drive, SKIPTON, BD23 1NG. (Life Member)
CROSSLAND, Mrs. Gaynor Leanne, BA ACA *2005;* 9 Port Way, Bisley, WOKING, GU24 9AJ.
CROSSLAND, Mr. Geoffrey Peter, ACA *2008;* 27 Hunter Hill Road, SHEFFIELD, S11 8UD.
CROSSLAND, Mr. Hugh Nicholas, BA(Hons) ACA *2001;* 84 Ramsden Road, LONDON, SW12 8QZ.
•CROSSLAND, Mrs. Lindsey Claire, BSc ACA *2001;* with KPMG LLP, 1 The Embankment, Neville Street, LEEDS, LS1 4DW.
CROSSLAND, Mr. Mathew, ACA *2009;* 6 Birch Close, CHEDDAR, SOMERSET, BS27 3JS.
•ⓘCROSSLAND, Mr. Thomas Lloyd, MA FCA *1989;* with Financial Services Authority, 25 The North Colonnade, Canary Wharf, LONDON, E14 5HS.
CROSSLAND, Mr. Thomas William, BA ACA *2004;* with PricewaterhouseCoopers LLP, Pricewaterhousecoopers, 12 Plumtree Court, LONDON, EC4A 4HT.
•CROSSLAND-HINCHLIFFE, Mr. Neil, FCA *1969;* AIMS - Neil Crossland Hinchliffe, 16 Devonshire Road, Eastcote, PINNER, HA5 1TX.
CROSSLEY, Mr. Adam Johnathan Shepherd, BSc(Hons) ACA *2006;* 23 Latimer Drive, HORNCHURCH, ESSEX, RM12 6TN.
CROSSLEY, Miss. Ailsa, BA ACA *1990;* 19 Primrose Bank Road, EDINBURGH, EH5 3JQ.
CROSSLEY, Mr. Andrew Charles, FCA *1972;* 23 Berystede, KINGSTON UPON THAMES, SURREY, KT2 7PQ.
CROSSLEY, Mr. Andrew Graham, MBA BSc ACA *1995;* 3 Wighill Lane, Walton, WETHERBY, LS23 7BN.
CROSSLEY, Mr. Andrew Michael, MPhil BSc FCA *1984;* Beaufort Cottage, Claremont Road, MARLOW, SL7 1BW.
•CROSSLEY, Mr. Andrew Philip, BA FCA *1997;* Baldwin Cox Limited, 15 Foster Avenue, Beeston, NOTTINGHAM, NG9 1AE.
CROSSLEY, Mrs. Catherine Rosemary, FCA *1973;* 20 Kendal Green, KENDAL, LA9 5PN.
CROSSLEY, Mrs. Cecilia Hooper, BA ACA DChA *2005;* 27 Alwyne Villas, LONDON, N1 2HG.
CROSSLEY, Mrs. Elizabeth Margaret, BA(Hons) ACA *2000;* 65 Atheldene Road, LONDON, SW18 3BN.
CROSSLEY, Miss. Gillea Ruth, BA ACA *1990;* 43 Graylands, Theydon Bois, EPPING, CM16 7LB.
CROSSLEY, Mr. Gregory John, BA ACA *1995;* 19 Shelley Court, HARROGATE, NORTH YORKSHIRE, HG1 3LR.
CROSSLEY, Mr. James Anthony George, BSc ACA *1993;* B P Investment Management Ltd, 20 Canada Square, LONDON, E14 5NJ.
•CROSSLEY, Miss. Jane Sally, BA(Hons) FCA CTA *1990;* Jolliffe Cork LLP, 33 George Street, WAKEFIELD, WEST YORKSHIRE, WF1 1LX. See also Jolliffe Cork Consulting Limited
CROSSLEY, Mrs. Jessica Lyn, BSc ACA *1988;* 61 Mitton Road, Whalley, CLITHEROE, LANCASHIRE, BB7 9RY.
CROSSLEY, Mr. Keith, FCA *1967;* 6 Huntsmill, Fulbourn, CAMBRIDGE, CB21 5RH.
•CROSSLEY, Mr. Kenneth Norman, FCA *1967;* 6 Glendene Avenue, Bramhall, STOCKPORT, SK7 1BH.
•CROSSLEY, Mrs. Lynda Jane, BSc ACA *1985;* 8 Silver Street, Thorverton, EXETER, EX5 5LT.
CROSSLEY, Mr. Mark Andrew, BSc ACA *1996;* 48 Castle Grove Avenue, Headingley, LEEDS, LS6 4BS.
CROSSLEY, Mr. Peter Charles, BA FCA *1996;* Thie Noa, Droghadfayle Park, Port Erin, ISLE OF MAN, IM9 6EP.
CROSSLEY, Mr. Peter Graham, MA BSc FCA *1977;* Haldime Limited, 62 Church Hill, LOUGHTON, IG10 1LB.
CROSSLEY, Mr. Robert Iain, MA FCA *1981;* Manor Top Burwardsley Road, Burwardsley, CHESTER, CH3 9PH.
CROSSLEY, Mr. Samuel Neil Thomas, BSc(Hons) FCA *2000;* Weir Minerals, Wilkinson House, Galway Road, Blackbush Business Park, YATELEY, HAMPSHIRE GU46 6GE.
CROSSLEY, Mr. Simon Gregory, BEng ACA *1999;* 33 Chaveney Walk, Quorn, LOUGHBOROUGH, LE12 8FH.
•CROSSLEY, Mr. Steven David, ACA *1987;* (Tax Fac), PPI Accounting Ltd, Horley Green House, Horley Green Road, Claremount, HALIFAX, WEST YORKSHIRE HX3 6AS.
•CROSSLEY, Mr. Terence Arnold, FCA *1973;* R.F. Miller & Co, Bellevue, Princes Street, ULVERSTON, LA12 7NB.
CROSSLEY, Mr. William Oliver, FCA *1951;* Wavecrest, The Beach, Laxey, ISLE OF MAN, IM4 7DF. (Life Member)
CROSSLEY-SMITH, Mr. James Andrew, BSc ACA *1995;* Abbeycrest Thailand Limited, Bangkok Gem & Jewelry Tower, 322/20-21 Surawong Road, Bangrak, BANGKOK 10500, THAILAND.
CROSSLING, Mr. Steven Ian, BA ACA *2001;* 19 Sherwood Avenue, OSSINING, NY 10562, UNITED STATES.
CROSSMAN, Mr. Andrew James, BSc ACA *1994;* 9 Locks Cross, Neston, CORSHAM, WILTSHIRE, SN13 9TB.
CROSSMAN, Mr. Andrew Mark, BSc ACA *2009;* 37 Sunnyside Road, EPPING, CM16 4JW.
CROSSMAN, Mrs. Deborah Helen, BSc ACA *1990;* 8 Oakhurst, Grayshott, HINDHEAD, SURREY, GU26 6JW.
CROSSMAN, Mr. Steven Guy, BSc ACA FCCA CTA *1991;* 31a Church Lane, Nailsea, BRISTOL, BS48 4NG.
•CROSSTHWAITE, Miss. Kaley Dawn, BA(Hons) ACA *2002;* BDO LLP, 55 Baker Street, LONDON, W1U 7EU. See also BDO Stoy Hayward LLP
CROSSWELL, Mr. Neil, BSc ACA *1993;* 4 Copse Close, PETERSFIELD, HAMPSHIRE, GU31 4DL.
CROSTHWAITE, Mr. David John Orme, FCA *1954;* 21 Peverell Avenue East, Poundbury, DORCHESTER, DORSET, DT1 3RH. (Life Member)
CROSTON, Mr. David Charles, BSc FCA *1980;* 201 Albury Drive, PINNER, HA5 3RH.
•CROSTON, Mr. Michael Joseph, FCA *1979;* Michael Croston, 33 Black Bull Lane, Fulwood, PRESTON, PR2 3PX.
CROSTON, Mr. Richard Andrew, BSc ACA *1993;* Manor Cottage, South Newbald, YORK, YO43 4SU.
•CROSTON, Mr. Sean Kenneth, BSc FCA *1990;* Grant Thornton UK LLP, 30 Finsbury Square, LONDON, EC2P 2YU. See also Grant Thornton LLP
CROTHERS, Mr. William, BSc FCA *1985;* Flint House The Ridge, Woldingham, CATERHAM, SURREY, CR3 7AN.
CROTON, Mr. Gary Joseph, ACA *1996;* 60 Evesham Road, LONDON, N11 2RN.
CROTTY, Alan, Esq OBE FCA *1950;* 2 Flaming Roseway, WILLOWDALE M2N 5W8, ON, CANADA. (Life Member)
CROTTY, Miss. Jane, BA ACA *1991;* (Tax Fac), Nymet Cottage, Nymet Rowland, CREDITON, DEVON, EX17 6AW.
CROTTY, Mr. Kevin James, BCom ACA *2002;* 80 Fairholme Road, MANCHESTER, M20 4SB.
CROUCAMP, Mrs. Alison Jane, BA(Hons) ACA *2001;* 17 Dyers Lane, LONDON, SW15 6JR.
CROUCH, Miss. Anita Lorraine, BA ACA ATII *1994;* 1 St. Andrews Road, Farlington, PORTSMOUTH, PO6 1AD.
CROUCH, Mrs. Helen Jane, BA ACA *2007;* 12 Vicarage Close, Menheniot, LISKEARD, CORNWALL, PL14 3QG.
•CROUCH, Mrs. Jayashree Srinivasan, FCA *1981;* J.Srinivasan Crouch & Co, 40A Rutland Gardens, HOVE, BN3 5PB.
CROUCH, Miss. Jennifer Louise, BA(Hons) ACA *2001;* 12 Welbeck Drive, BURGESS HILL, RH15 0BB.
CROUCH, Mr. John Bertram, BSc ACA *1997;* B G Group Plc, 100 Thames Valley Park Drive, READING, RG6 1PT.
CROUCH, Mr. Martin, BSc FCA *1974;* Flat 23, Mildenhall, 23-25 West Cliff Road, BOURNEMOUTH, BH4 8AX.
CROUCH, Mr. Martyn James, BSc ACA *1993;* Primrose Cottage, The Derry, Ashton Keynes, SWINDON, SN6 6PW.
CROUCH, Mr. Matt, BSc ACA *2006;* 10 St. Winifreds Avenue, HARROGATE, NORTH YORKSHIRE, HG2 8LT.
CROUCH, Mr. Michael Henry, FCA *1970;* Stepaside Cottage, Aldingbourne, CHICHESTER, PO20 3UB.
CROUCH, Mr. Neil Andrew, LLB ACA *1996;* Morgan Stanley, 55 Douglas Street, GLASGOW, G2 7NP.
CROUCH, Mr. Nigel William, FCA *1980;* 44 Heritage Hill Rd, NEW CANAAN, CT 06840-4604, UNITED STATES.
•CROUCH, Mr. Peter James Crosby, FCA *1973;* Newby Crouch, Ember House, 35-37 Creek Road, EAST MOLESEY, KT8 9BE.
CROUCH, Mr. Peter John, BA ACA *1987;* EEA Fund Management, 22 Billiter Street, LONDON, EC3M 2RY.
CROUCH, Mr. Peter William, FCA *1985;* 150 Princes Avenue, LONDON, W3 8LU.
CROUCH, Mr. Roland Paul, BA FCA *1985;* (Tax Fac), Suite 711, Citi Plaza 3, 14 Tai Woo Wan Road, TAIKOO SHING, HONG KONG SAR.
CROUCH, Mr. Simon David, MEng BEng ACA *2000;* Weitblick 7, Gisikon, 6038 LUCERNE, SWITZERLAND.
CROUCH, Mr. Stephen James, BA ACA *1999;* Vaughans, Wellington College, CROWTHORNE, RG45 7PT.
CROUCH, Mrs. Tsarina Elyasali, MChem ACA *2001;* Weitblick 7, 6038 GISIKON, CANTON OF LUCERNE, SWITZERLAND.
CROUCHER, Mr. Derek James, FCA *1958;* The Old Hall, Low Street, Collingham, NEWARK, NG23 7NL. (Life Member)
CROUCHER, Miss. Gemma, BA(Hons) ACA *2011;* Casson Beckman, Murrills House, 48 East Street, Portchester, FAREHAM, HAMPSHIRE PO16 9XS.
CROUCHER, Mr. John William, FCA *1972;* 31 Cecil Avenue, GILLINGHAM, ME8 6EH.
CROUCHER, Miss. Kelly, ACA MAAT *2010;* 340 Hythe Road, Willesborough, ASHFORD, KENT, TN24 0QH.
CROUCHER, Mr. Roger Henry Harley, FCA *1972;* 10 Rusthall Park, TUNBRIDGE WELLS, TN4 8NP.
CROUCHER, Mr. Trevor, ACA *1981;* 19 Pembury Way, Rainham, GILLINGHAM, Kent, ME8 7DL.
CROUDSON, Mr. David, BCom FCA *1955;* 228 Lidgett Lane, LEEDS, LS17 6QH. (Life Member)
CROUDSON, Mr. Roger, FCA *1961;* Flat 4, Oak Lodge, 64 Cold Bath Road, HARROGATE, HG2 0HW.
CROUTHERS, Mr. Thomas Arthur, FCA *1972;* Chestnut Close, 4 Smithies Lane, BARNSLEY, S75 1BH.
CROUZET, Mrs. Sian, BA ACA *1999;* 2454 Route de Rive de Gier, Les Granges, 69560 ST ROMAN EN GAL, FRANCE.
CROW, Miss. Alexandra Elizabeth Emily, BSc(Hons) ACA *2004;* 69 Saxifrage Drive, STONE, STAFFORDSHIRE, ST15 8XY.
CROW, Mr. Andrew Frank, MBA BSc FCA *1984;* 61 Palace Road, LONDON, SW2 3LB.
CROW, Mrs. Christina Margaret, BSc FCA DChA *1979;* Mencap Cymru Unit 31 Cardiff Business Park, Lambourne Crescent Llanishen, CARDIFF, CF14 5GF.
CROW, Mrs. Deborah Jane, BA ACA *1983;* 33 Menzies Close, Frankston South, VICTORIA, VIC 3199, AUSTRALIA.
CROW, Mr. Eric, FCA *1936;* 1 Windmill Close, BRIXHAM, TQ5 9SQ. (Life Member)
CROW, Mr. Raymond Felix, FCA *1950;* 22 Wharncliffe Road, Highcliffe-on-Sea, CHRISTCHURCH, BH23 5DE. (Life Member)
CROW, Mr. Rhys William, BA ACA *2005;* St Jamess Place, 1 Tetbury Road, CIRENCESTER, GLOUCESTERSHIRE, GL7 1FP.
CROW, Mr. Robert Hartley, BSc FCA *1972;* Peel House, The Glebe, Naphill, HIGH WYCOMBE, HP14 4QE.
CROW, Mr. William, ACA *2011;* 23 Ladbroke Crescent, LONDON, W11 1PS.
CROWDEN, Miss. Rosemary Anne, BSc ACA *2005;* 14 New Horton Manor, Dawn Redwood Close, Horton, SLOUGH, SL3 9QR.
CROWDER, Miss. Anne, BSc ACA *2003;* 16 Cambridge Road, Urmston, MANCHESTER, M41 6HH.
•CROWDER, Mrs. Rachael Mary, BA ACA *1999;* RM Crowder Ltd, Rest Haven, North Kelsey Road, Caistor, MARKET RASEN, LINCOLNSHIRE LN7 6SF.
CROWDY, Mr. Colin Alfred, FCA *1974;* Harris Lamb Ltd, 75-76 Francis Road Edgbaston, BIRMINGHAM, B16 8SP.
CROWDY, Mr. Martin Hugh, BSc FCA *1979;* 10 Bathwick Hill, BATH, BA2 6EW.
CROWDY, Mr. Ronald Alan, FCA *1974;* 18 Wellington Grove, SOLIHULL, B91 1EA.
CROWE, Mr. Andrew James, BA ACA *1999;* 21 Wellington Road, POOLE, DORSET, BH14 9LF.
CROWE, Mr. Anthony George, BSc ACA *1997;* Comedy Central - 3rd floor, M T V Europe United Kingdom House, 180 Oxford Street, LONDON, W1D 1DS.
CROWE, Mr. Brian John, BA ACA *1982;* Middle Blakebank, Broom Lane, Underbarrow, KENDAL, CUMBRIA, LA8 8HP.
CROWE, Mr. Christopher Neil, ACA *2007;* 51 Dalkeith Road, HARTLEPOOL, CLEVELAND, TS25 4EH.
CROWE, Mr. David Nicholas, BA ACA *1992;* 86a Widney Road, Bentley Heath, SOLIHULL, WEST MIDLANDS, B93 9BN.
CROWE, Mr. Edwin Peter, FCA *1955;* 1 Clarendon Place, Clarendon Road, SEVENOAKS, KENT, TN13 1DT. (Life Member)
CROWE, Mr. Gareth James, BA ACA *2001;* with PricewaterhouseCoopers, 31 Great George Street, BRISTOL, BS1 5QD.
CROWE, Mr. Geoffrey Michael, FCA *1970;* Bowdon House, 13 Manor Park, Onchan, ISLE OF MAN, IM3 2EW.
CROWE, Mr. George, BA ACA *2010;* Hay's Galleria, Pricewaterhousecoopers Llp, 1 Hays Lane, LONDON, SE1 2RD.
CROWE, Mr. Graham, BSc ACA *2002;* 13 Westhorpe Road, LONDON, SW15 1QH.
CROWE, Miss. Helen Rosemary, ACA *2003;* Court Cottage, The Green, Iron Acton, BRISTOL, BS37 9TQ.
CROWE, Mr. Jason Paul, BSc ACA *1999;* 5 Armiger Way, WITHAM, ESSEX, CM8 2UY.
•CROWE, Mr. John, FCA *1959;* (Tax Fac), Robert J. Crowe & Co, 93 Jesmond Park West, High Heaton, NEWCASTLE UPON TYNE, NE7 7BY.
CROWE, Mr. Kieran John, BA ACA *2002;* 232 Sovereign Road, COVENTRY, CV5 6LU.
•CROWE, Miss. Margaret Anne, FCA *1978;* (Tax Fac), Burrow & Crowe Limited, 8-9 Feast Field, Horsforth, LEEDS, LS18 4TJ.
CROWE, Mr. Michael Andrew, BA FCA *1976;* 3 Malibres Rd, Chandlers Ford, EASTLEIGH, SO53 5DS.
•CROWE, Mr. Michael Frank Gordon, FCA *1973;* Crowe Morgan, 8 St. George's Street, Douglas, ISLE OF MAN, IM1 1AH.
•CROWE, Mr. Michael Howard, BSc FCA *1994;* PKF (Isle of Man) LLC, PO Box 16, Analyst House, Douglas, ISLE OF MAN, IM99 1AP.
CROWE, Mr. Michael Ian, BSc ACA *2005;* Recycling Live Centre, 1a Essex Street, PRESTON, PR1 1QE.
CROWE, Mr. Neil, ACA *2008;* with Deloitte & Touche, The Old Courthouse, PO Box 250, Athol Street, Douglas, ISLE OF MAN IM99 1XJ.
CROWE, Mr. Peter Alan, BA ACA *1991;* 3 Church Lane, NEWCASTLE UPON TYNE, NE3 1AR.
CROWE, Mr. Peter Edwin, FCA *1948;* 2 Whittons Farm, High Street, Waterbeach, CAMBRIDGE, CB5 9JY. (Life Member)
CROWE, Mr. Philip Gerard, BA FCA *1987;* 307 Crimicar Lane, Fulwood, SHEFFIELD, S10 4EN.
CROWE, Mr. Reginald Michael, FCA *1959;* South Corner, Darcy Close, Hutton, BRENTWOOD, ESSEX, CM13 2PY. (Life Member)
CROWE, Mr. Russell James, BSc ACA *2009;* Cyril le Marquand House, The Parade, St. Helier, JERSEY, JE4 8QT.
CROWE, Mr. Stephen Paul, BA ACA *1983;* Chartered Institute of Internal Auditors, 88 Clapham Park Road, LONDON, SW4 7BX.
CROWE, Mr. Steven, BA(Hons) ACA *2000;* Norwich Union, PO Box 6, Surrey Street, NORWICH, NR1 3NS.
CROWE, Mr. Trevor John, FCA *1970;* 16 St. James Road, Little Paxton, HUNTINGDON, PE19 6QW.
CROWE, Mr. William Neil, FCA *1963;* The Orchard, Clifton Road North, Port St. Mary, ISLE OF MAN, IM9 5HB.
CROWELL, Miss. Nicola Faye, BA ACA *2004;* 21 Ville Vautier, La Rue Des Cosnets, St. Ouen, JERSEY, JE3 2WF.
•CROWFOOT, Mr. Anthony, FCA *1973;* Crowfoot and Company Limited, Lonsdale House, High Street, LUTTERWORTH, LEICESTERSHIRE, LE17 4AD.
CROWFOOT, Mr. Martyn Christopher, BA FCA CF *1994;* Thistle green, Barton Road, Welford on Avon, STRATFORD-UPON-AVON, WARWICKSHIRE, CV37 8HG.
CROWHURST, Mr. John Hanslip, BA FCA *1963;* 11 Queens Road, Belmont, SUTTON, SM2 6BZ. (Life Member)
CROWHURST, Mrs. Sarah Joanna, BA(Hons) ACA *2000;* 9 Manor Drive, AYLESBURY, BUCKINGHAMSHIRE, HP20 1EW.
CROWLE, Mr. Melvyn George, FCA *1969;* 20/B Skyscraper, 132 Tin Hau Temple Road, NORTH POINT, HONG KONG ISLAND, HONG KONG SAR. (Life Member)
CROWLEY, Mrs. Amanda Jane, BSc ACA CPA CIA *1993;* 5264 Jacobs Creek Place, HAYMARKET, VA 20169, UNITED STATES.
•CROWLEY, Mr. Colin John, FCA *1988;* (Tax Fac), Rawlinsons, Ruthlyn House, 90 Lincoln Road, PETERBOROUGH, PE1 2SP. See also Rawlinsons Payroll and HR Limited
CROWLEY, Mr. Dennis Trevor, FCA *1950;* Penina, 35 Old Park Road, CLEVEDON, BS21 7JN. (Life Member)
CROWLEY, Miss. Jacqueline, BA ACA *1985;* Solefield School, Solefields Road, SEVENOAKS, KENT, TN13 1PH.

•CROWLEY, Mr. Justin Phillip, BSc(Econ) ACA DChA *2002;* BDO Chartered Accountants & Advisors, 305 Al Futtaim Tower, Al Maktoum Street, Deira, PO Box 1961, DUBAI UNITED ARAB EMIRATES. See also BDO International
•CROWLEY, Mr. Paul James, BSc ACA *1984;* (Tax Fac), Derrick Newman Limited, 29 Bath Road, Old Town, SWINDON, SN1 4AS.
CROWLEY, Mrs. Pauline Lynette, BSc ACA *2004;* 10 Walnut Tree Close, BOURNE END, BUCKINGHAMSHIRE, SL8 5DS.
CROWLEY, Mr. Philip Andrew, FCA *1995;* 37 Baring Road, LONDON, SE12 0JP.
CROWLEY, Mr. Robert William, BSc ACA *2006;* Flat 18 Breezers Court 20 The Highway, LONDON, E1W 2BE.
CROWLEY, Mrs. Samantha Louise, ACA *2001;* 4 Kellett Road, SOUTHAMPTON, SO15 7PR.
CROWLEY, Mr. Stuart Watson, BA(Hons) ACA *2002;* Rose Villa Rue Au Page, St. Saviour, GUERNSEY, GY7 9UB.
CROWLEY, Mr. Trevor Patrick, FCA *1971;* 10 Woodridings Avenue, PINNER, MIDDLESEX, HA5 4NQ.
CROWN, Mr. Clifford, FCA *1981;* Smartodds Ltd, Unit 530, Highgate Studios, 53-79 Highgate Road, LONDON, NW5 1TL.
•CROWN, Mr. Irvin Russell, FCA *1983;* (Tax Fac), Crown & Co Accountants Limited, Apex House, Wonaston Road, MONMOUTH, MONMOUTHSHIRE, NP25 5JB.
CROWN, Mr. John Michael, FCA *1979;* 10 The Copse, BILLERICAY, CM12 0NR.
CROWN, Mr. Jonathan, BA ACA *1991;* Jonathan Crown Limited, Oak House, 13 North Grove, Highgate, LONDON, N6 4SH.
CROWNE, Mr. Peter Charles, BSc FCA *1990;* 38 Fitzroy Road, FLEET, GU51 4JW.
CROWNSHAW, Mr. John Langley, FCA *1974;* Bond Pearce LLP, Ballard House, West Hoe Road, PLYMOUTH, DEVON, PL1 3AE.
CROWNSHAW, Mr. Stephen, LLB ACA *1986;* 6311 Red Maple Drive, CHARLOTTE, NC 28277, UNITED STATES.
CROWSON, Mr. James Michael, BSc ACA *1997;* 4 Newry Road, TWICKENHAM, TW1 1PL.
CROWSON, Mr. Michael James, ACA *2008;* 47 Churchfield Road, WALTON-ON-THAMES, SURREY, KT12 2TX.
CROWTER, Mr. Mark Nicholas, BSc ACA *2011;* 1 Brunswick Mews, HOVE, EAST SUSSEX, BN3 1HD.
•CROWTHER, Mrs. Amanda Geraldine, BSc FCA CTA *1982;* (Tax Fac), Howard Matthews Partnership, Queensgate House, 23 North Park Road, HARROGATE, HG1 5PD.
CROWTHER, Miss. Anne Linda, BSc ACA *1983;* A la Carte Business Services Ltd Mount Street, New Basford, NOTTINGHAM, NG7 7HX.
CROWTHER, Mr. Christopher Brian, BA(Hons) ACA *2001;* 5 Clive Road, Eston, MIDDLESBROUGH, TS6 0RT.
CROWTHER, Mr. Daniel Bryan Elon, MA ACA CTA *1997;* (Tax Fac), with KPMG LLP, 15 Canada Square, LONDON, E14 5GL.
CROWTHER, Mr. David, MA ACA *2000;* 101 Trentham Street, Southfields, LONDON, SW18 5DH.
CROWTHER, Mr. David Alan, BSc FCA *1977;* Hawthorne Cottage, 135 Lime Lane, WALSALL, WS3 5AN.
•CROWTHER, Mr. David Arthur, FCA *1973;* Clough Tomblin & Co, Nat.Westminster Bank Chmbrs, The Grove, ILKLEY, LS29 9LS.
CROWTHER, Mr. David Stoner, FCA *1968;* Sunte House, Birchen Lane, HAYWARDS HEATH, WEST SUSSEX, RH16 1RZ.
CROWTHER, Mr. Domininc, BSc ACA *2007;* 76 Stonefall Avenue, HARROGATE, NORTH YORKSHIRE, HG2 7NP.
CROWTHER, Mr. Douglas John, BA FCA *1975;* London Gateway Port Ltd, The Manorway, STANFORD-LE-HOPE, ESSEX, SS17 9PD.
•CROWTHER, Mr. George Anthony, BA ACA *1983;* haysmacintyre, Fairfax House, 15 Fulwood Place, LONDON, WC1V 6AY.
CROWTHER, Mr. James Anthony, FCA *1967;* 6 Old Pheasant Court, Brookside, CHESTERFIELD, DERBYSHIRE, S40 3GY. (Life Member)
CROWTHER, Mr. John Nicholas, MA FCA DChA *1975;* (Tax Fac), 15 Goldfinch Close, Chelsfield, ORPINGTON, BR6 6NF.
CROWTHER, Mr. Jonathan Douglas, MA FCA ATII *1976;* (Tax Fac), Le Carre La Rue de la Pointe, St. Ouen, JERSEY, JE3 2AF.
•CROWTHER, Mr. Jonathan James, BSc FCA *1982;* (Tax Fac), Crowthers Accountants Limited, The Courtyard, 19 High Street, PERSHORE, WORCESTERSHIRE, WR10 1AA.
CROWTHER, Mr. Jonathan Michael, BA ACA *1987;* 11 Wheatley Rise, Ben Rhydding, ILKLEY, LS29 8SQ.
•CROWTHER, Mr. Justin Philip Ross, BA ACA CF *1999;* Catalyst Corporate Finance LLP, 21 The Triangle, NG2 Business Park, NOTTINGHAM, NG2 1AE.
CROWTHER, Mrs. Lynsey Elizabeth, ACA *2006;* Castle View, 220 Bridge End Road, GRANTHAM, NG31 7HD.
CROWTHER, Mr. Michael Graeme, BEng ACA *1996;* Butlins, Bourne Leisure, 1 Park Lane, HEMEL HEMPSTEAD, HERTFORDSHIRE, HP2 4YL.
CROWTHER, Mrs. Naomi Emma, BSc ACA *1996;* 53 Sugden Road, THAMES DITTON, SURREY, KT7 0AD.
CROWTHER, Mr. Nicholas John Edward, BA ACA *1986;* 9 The Park, Christleton, CHESTER, CHESHIRE, CH3 7AR.
CROWTHER, Mrs. Nicola Jane, BA ACA *1997;* 18 Jennings Road, ST. ALBANS, HERTFORDSHIRE, AL1 4NT.
•CROWTHER, Mr. Peter Lindsay, FCA *1974;* Peter Crowther & Co, 17 Springwood Drive, Skircoat Green, HALIFAX, WEST YORKSHIRE, HX3 0TQ.
CROWTHER, Mr. Richard Anthony, BA ACA *1988;* 19 Lorton Close, Fulwood, PRESTON, PR2 8YS.
CROWTHER, Mr. Ronald, FCA *1952;* 17 Glebe Road, Ampthill, BEDFORD, MK45 2TH. (Life Member)
CROWTHER, Mr. Ronald Peter Morrison, FCA *1959;* Holly, Heathway, East Horsley, LEATHERHEAD, KT24 5ET. (Life Member)
CROWTHER, Miss. Sara, LLB ACA *2007;* 24 Selkirk Street, CHELTENHAM, GLOUCESTERSHIRE, GL52 2HH.
CROWTHER, Mr. Stephen John, BSc ACA *1981;* 27 Fishery Road, Boxmoor, HEMEL HEMPSTEAD, HP1 1NB.
•CROWTHER, Mr. Steven Andrew, ACA *1986;* S. Crowther & Co, 19 Fieldhouse Drive, Slaithwaite, HUDDERSFIELD, HD7 5BY.
CROWTHER, Mr. Steven Arthur, MA ACA *1983;* 10147 Stancil Lane, FRISCO, TX 75035, UNITED STATES.
•CROWTHER, Mr. Steven Paul, FCA *1992;* S P Crowther & Co Limited, Woodland View House, 675 Leeds Road, HUDDERSFIELD, HD2 1YY.
CROWTHER, Mr. William Mark, BA(Hons) ACA *2002;* Intermediate Capital Group Plc, 20 Old Broad Street, LONDON, EC2N 1DP.
CROWTHER-GREEN, Mrs. Jayne, BA ACA *1989;* 14 Wolsey Grange, Cawood, SELBY, NORTH YORKSHIRE, YO8 3SB.
CROWTHER-GREEN, Mr. Richard, BSc ACA *1990;* 14 Wolsey Grange, Cawood, SELBY, NORTH YORKSHIRE, YO8 3SB.
CROXALL, Mr. Michael John, FCA *1977;* 42 Malvern Avenue, NUNEATON, WARWICKSHIRE, CV10 8ND.
CROXEN, Mrs. Anna Louise, BSc ACA *1999;* with KPMG LLP, Management Services Centre, 58 Clarendon Road, WATFORD, WD17 1DE.
CROXEN, Mr. James Martin, ACA *2008;* Lorent House Rein Road, Horsforth, LEEDS, LS18 4TA.
CROXEN, Mr. Martin, LLB FCA *1979;* Sterling Capitol Plc, 1 Lisbon Square, LEEDS, LS1 4LY.
•ⒹCROXEN, Mr. Robert Andrew, BA ACA *1999;* with KPMG LLP, 15 Canada Square, LONDON, E14 5GL.
CROXFORD, Mr. David, FCA *1962;* La Chaumiere, College Hill, St. Helier, JERSEY, JE2 4RE.
CROXON, Miss. Alison Mary, BA ACA ATII *1992;* Windsor House, 56 Harcourt Road, Dorney Reach, MAIDENHEAD, BERKSHIRE, SL6 0DU.
CROXSON, Mr. Andrew James, MPhil BA ACA *2000;* 6a Woodland Grove, WEYBRIDGE, SURREY, KT13 9EF.
CROXSON, Mrs. Louise, BA(Hons) ACA *2002;* 24 Albert Street, WINDSOR, BERKSHIRE, SL4 5BU.
CROXSON, Mr. Neil Michael, BSc ACA *1993;* 24 Priory Street, YORK, NORTH YORKSHIRE, YO1 6EX.
CROXTON, Mr. Frederick Wyndham, FCA *1964;* 8 Honeysuckle Close, Prestbury, CHELTENHAM, GL52 5LN.
CROXTON, Mr. Geoffrey Richard, BCom FCA *1962;* 58 Pembroke Street, BICTON, WA 6157, AUSTRALIA. (Life Member)
CROYDON, Mr. Richard John, BSc ACA *1985;* Timber Cove Ltd, PO Box 1309, Leisure Island Business Centre, Suite 2-9 2nd Floor, 23 Ocean Village Promenade, GIBRALTAR GIBRALTAR.
CROZIER, Mrs. Ann-Marie, BA ACA *1991;* 8 Jedburgh Close, The Priorys, NORTH SHIELDS, NE29 9NU.
CROZIER, Mrs. Elise, ACA *2006;* 8 Glamorgan Road, KINGSTON UPON THAMES, KT1 4HP.
CROZIER, Miss. Fiona Jane, MA ACA *1990;* Woodlands, Bates Hill, Ightham, SEVENOAKS, TN15 9BG.
CROZIER, Mr. Gavin Hugh, MEng ACA *1998;* (Tax Fac), 55 Cranbrook Road, LONDON, W4 2LJ.
•CROZIER, Mrs. Janice Elizabeth, BSc FCA *1986;* Crozier Kemp Ltd, 7 Ball Grove Drive, COLNE, LANCASHIRE, BB8 7HY.
CROZIER, Mr. John David William, BSc ACA *1999;* 22 Grosvenor Road, Caversham, READING, RG4 5EJ.
•CROZIER, Mr. Michael Shaun, MA ACA *1987;* (Tax Fac), Crozier Jones & Co, 9/13 Thorne Road, DONCASTER, SOUTH YORKSHIRE, DN1 2HJ.
•CROZIER, Mr. Paul Derek, BSc ACA *1989;* 12 Ashurst Place, DORKING, SURREY, RH4 1QY.
CROZIER, Mr. Philip Matthew Timothy, BA(Hons) ACA *2000;* with Ernst & Young LLP, Wessex House, 19 Threefield Lane, SOUTHAMPTON, SO14 3QB.
CROZIER, Mr. Stephen Mark, BA ACA *1990;* 8 Jedburgh Close, The Priorys, NORTH SHIELDS, NE29 9NU.
CRUDDIS, Mrs. Karen Ann, BA ACA *1998;* 22 Wandle Beck, DIDCOT, OX11 7XB.
•CRUDEN, Mr. David Alexander, BSc FCA *1981;* 99 Elmbridge Avenue, SURBITON, SURREY, KT5 9HB.
CRUDGE, Mr. Julian Paul, BA ACA *1990;* 4 Durrington Avenue, LONDON, SW20 8NT.
CRUDGINGTON-HIGHAM, Mrs. Lisa-Jane, BSc ACA *1999;* 186 Reculver Road, HERNE BAY, KENT, CT6 6QR.
CRUICKSHANK, Mr. David John Ogilvie, BCom CA *1989; (CA Scotland 1982);* Deloitte LLP, 2 New Street Square, LONDON, EC4A 3BZ. See also Deloitte & Touche LLP
•CRUICKSHANK, Mr. Graham David, BA FCA *1979;* Graham Cruickshank BA FCA, 35 Whittingstall Road, LONDON, SW6 4EA.
•CRUICKSHANK, Mr. James William Alexander, FCA ATT CTA *1985;* (Tax Fac), James W A Cruickshank Business Services Limited, Inglewood, Wreay, CARLISLE, CA4 0RL.
CRUICKSHANK, Mr. Jonathan Mark, ACA *2008;* 50 Friezewood Road, BRISTOL, BS3 2AB.
CRUICKSHANK, Mr. Kevin, ACA *2008;* Numis Securities Ltd, 10 Paternoster Square, LONDON, EC4M 7LT.
CRUICKSHANK, Mrs. Lynne Josephine, BA ACA *1999;* 9 Octavia Road, SOUTHAMPTON, SO18 2LX.
CRUICKSHANK, Miss. Mhairi Margaret, MA ACA *2004;* Flat 3F2, 90/3 Marchmont Road, EDINBURGH, EH9 1HR.
CRUICKSHANK, Mr. Sam, BSc ACA *2011;* BDO (PTY) Limited, Level 19, 2 Market Street, SYDNEY, NSW 2000, AUSTRALIA.
•CRUICKSHANKS, Mr. Neil Stewart, LLB FCA *1990;* Deloitte LLP, 1 Woodborough Road, NOTTINGHAM, NG1 3FG. See also Deloitte & Touche LLP
CRUIKSHANKS, Mr. Peter, BSc ACA *1991;* 62 Storrs Hill Road, OSSETT, WEST YORKSHIRE, WF5 0DQ.
CRUISE, Mr. Gavin, BA(Hons) ACA *2011;* 8 St. Bedes Way, Langley Moor, DURHAM, DH7 8YB.
CRUISE, Mr. Jonathan, ACA *2010;* 17 Cloverdale, 60 South Road, HAMILTON FL 05, BERMUDA.
CRUISE, Mrs. Nicola, BSc ACA *2001;* 67 Haldon Road, LONDON, SW18 1QF.
CRUISE, Miss. Rebecca Hope, BA ACA *2004;* 443 The Ridgeway, ST. ALBANS, HERTFORDSHIRE, AL4 9TY.
•CRUISE, Miss. Sarah, ACA ACCA *2008;* with Bird Luckin limited, Aquila House, Waterloo Lane, CHELMSFORD, CM1 1BN.
CRUM, Mr. John Robert, FCA *1954;* 9 The Rolle, 2 Fore Street, BUDLEIGH SALTERTON, EX9 6NG. (Life Member)
CRUMBIE, Mrs. Nicola Shirley, BSc ACA *2005;* 4 Nightingale Place, Grayswood Road, HASLEMERE, SURREY, GU27 2ER.
CRUMBIE, Mr. William John Milton, BA ACA *2005;* 4 Nightingale Place, Grayswood Road, HASLEMERE, SURREY, GU27 2ER.
CRUMMETT, Mr. Stephen Paul, BA ACA *1991;* Avebury House, Filtrona Plc, 201-249 Avebury Boulevard, MILTON KEYNES, MK9 1AU.
CRUMP, Mr. Adrian Charles Nicholas, MA ACA *1990;* Fairfield Houlston Lane, Myddle, SHREWSBURY, SY4 3RD. (Life Member)
CRUMP, Miss. Alison Elizabeth, BCom ACA *1982;* Windward House, Beachley Road, Tutshill, CHEPSTOW, NP16 7EQ.
CRUMP, Mr. David John, ACA *1978;* 73 Palmerston Road, BUCKHURST HILL, IG9 5NS.
CRUMP, Mr. Deryk Patrick, MSocSc FCA *1955;* 54 Rodborough Road, Dorridge, SOLIHULL, B93 8EF. (Life Member)
CRUMP, Miss. Harriet Frances, BSc ACA *1994;* 5 Sheepdown Close, PETWORTH, WEST SUSSEX, GU28 0BP.
CRUMP, Mr. Jeremy Graham, BSc ACA *2002;* FLTCE, Spitalgasse 2, 3011 BERNE, SWITZERLAND.
CRUMP, Mr. Jonathan William Michael, FCA *1973;* St. Annes Cottage, High Street, Sonning, READING, RG4 6UP.
CRUMP, Mr. Mark Leslie, BA FCA *1988;* 9 Birch Grove, Kingswood, TADWORTH, SURREY, KT20 6QU.
CRUMP, Mrs. Mary-Jane, BA(Hons) ACA *2001;* Buristrasse 55, 3006 BERNE, SWITZERLAND.
CRUMP, Mr. Matthew Peter Norman, BSc ACA *1987;* 91 Chalkdown, Chells Manor, STEVENAGE, SG2 7BN.
•CRUMP, Mr. Ralph, FCA *1976;* (Tax Fac), Ralph Crump Accountants Limited, 14 Bakers Drove, Rownhams, SOUTHAMPTON, SO16 8AD.
CRUMPLER, Mr. Russell Grant, BA(Hons) ACA *2004;* with KPMG LLP, 1 The Embankment, Neville Street, LEEDS, LS1 4DW.
•CRUMPTON, Mr. Neville David, FCA *1960;* Crumpton & Co Limited, 682 Anlaby Road, HULL, HU3 6UZ.
•CRUMPTON, Mr. Paul Kenneth, FCA *1974;* Business Interface Ltd, 7 Garden Court, Wheathampstead, ST.ALBANS, AL4 8RE.
CRUMPTON-TAYLOR, Mrs. Jane Elizabeth, BSc FCA *1974;* Pot Kilns, Pot Kiln Chase, Gestingthorpe, HALSTEAD, ESSEX, CO9 3BH.
•CRUSE, Mr. Ian Francis, FCA *1970;* (Tax Fac), Baker Tilly Tax & Advisory Services LLP, Marlborough House, Victoria Road South, CHELMSFORD, CM1 1LN.
CRUSE, Mr. Martyn Robert, BA FCA *1973;* 8 Newport Close, Portishead, BRISTOL, BS20 8DD. (Life Member)
CRUSE, Mr. Neal Alexander, BA ACA *1993;* 4 Pinckneys Way Durrington, SALISBURY, SP4 8BU.
CRUSE, Mr. Stafford Rorke Davis, BSc ACA *1998;* Church Mission Society, CMS House, Watlington Road, OXFORD, OX4 6BZ.
CRUSE, Mr. Stephen Edward, ACA *2008;* Pricewaterhousecoopers Llp, 1 Hays Lane, LONDON, SE1 2RD.
CRUSH, Mr. John Anthony, FCA *1964;* 46 Evelyn Drive, PINNER, HA5 4RS. (Life Member)
CRUSH, Mrs. Maisha Yvonne, BA ACA *2000;* 117 Longland Drive, LONDON, N20 8HN.
•CRUTCHFIELD, Mr. Donovan Ashley, ACA CA(SA) *2008;* (Tax Fac), Donovan Crutchfield, 34 Lower Richmond Road, LONDON, SW15 1JP.
•CRUTCHLEY, Mr. Clement Melvin, FCA *1966;* with Littlejohn LLP, 1 Westferry Circus, Canary Wharf, LONDON, E14 4HD.
CRUTCHLEY, Mr. Keith, BA ACA *1989;* 61 Peak CLose, Armitage, RUGELEY, WS15 4TY.
CRUTCHLEY, Miss. Lisa Jane, BA ACA *2003;* 3 Forest Road, Piddington, NORTHAMPTON, NN7 2DA.
CRUTCHLEY, Mr. Stephen Robert, FCA *1969;* 13 Baswich Lane, Weeping Cross, STAFFORD, ST17 0BH.
•CRUTTENDEN, Mr. Eric James, FCA *1976;* (Tax Fac), A R Raymond & Co Limited, 67 London Road, ST. LEONARDS-ON-SEA, EAST SUSSEX, TN37 6AR.
CRUWYS, Miss. Vanessa Elaine, BSc ACA *1986;* Garban-Intercapital Plc, 2 Broadgate, LONDON, EC2M 7UR.
CRUXTON, Mr. Anthony Michael, BA ACA *1992;* 1 Helsfell Hall, Windermere Road, KENDAL, CUMBRIA, LA9 5SH.
CRUXTON, Mrs. Sarah, BA ACA *1993;* 1 Helsfell Hall, Windermere Road, KENDAL, CUMBRIA, LA9 5SH.
CRUZ, Mr. Dale, BA(Hons) ACA *2004;* Baker Tilly (Gibraltar) Limited, Third Floor, Regal House, Queensway, GIBRALTAR, GIBRALTAR.
CRYER, Mr. Charles Nicholas, BSc ACA *1998;* Perrymans Dedham Road, Boxted, COLCHESTER, CO4 5SL.
CRYER, Mr. Dennis William, FCA *1974;* Oakhill House, 16 Smitham Bridge Road, HUNGERFORD, BERKSHIRE, RG17 0QP.
CRYER, Mr. Frank Mayo, FCA *1956;* 61 Osmaston Road, BIRKENHEAD, CH42 8LR. (Life Member)
•CRYER, Mr. Graham John, FCA *1973;* Graham J. Cryer, 3 Humpty Dumpty Meadow, St. Thomas Hill, CANTERBURY, CT2 8HN.
•CRYER, Mr. James Marshall, FCA *1977;* PKF (Isle of Man) LLC, PO Box 16, Analyst House, Douglas, ISLE OF MAN, IM99 1AP. See also Northwest Trust Company Limited
CRYER, Miss. Jennifer Susan, ACA *2008;* 6 Morell Close, BARNET, HERTFORDSHIRE, EN5 5JU.
CRYER, Mr. John Peter, FCA *1939;* 155 Percy Road, Whitton, TWICKENHAM, TW2 6JE. (Life Member)

•**CRYER, Mr. Jonathan David, BA FCA** *1992;* Cryer Sandham Limited, Epping House, 55 Russell Street, READING, RG1 7XG. See also Cryer & Co

CRYER, Mr. Martyn Christopher, ACA *2008;* Flat 75, Elm Quay Court, 30 Nine Elms Lane, LONDON, SW8 5DF.

CRYER, Mr. Richard Anthony, MA FCA *1974;* 295 Kings Road, KINGSTON UPON THAMES, KT2 5JJ.

CRYER, Mr. Roland, LLB FCA *1972;* 30 Hawes Lane, WEST WICKHAM, KENT, BR4 0DB. (Life Member)

•**CRYER, Mr. Simon John, FCA** *1972;* with Brebners Limited, The Quadrangle, 2nd Floor, 180 Wardour Street, LONDON, W1F 8LB.

•**CRYSTOL, Mr. Bryan Martin, FCA ACMA** *1968;* AIMS - Bryan Crystol, 13 Walham Court, 111 Haverstock Hill, LONDON, NW3 4SD.

CSOKA, Miss. Claire, BA ACA *2001;* 23 High Street, PORTSMOUTH, PO1 2LS.

CUADRA, Mr. Adam Joseph, BA(Hons) ACA *2001;* 20 Dales Road, WESTBURY, WILTSHIRE, BA13 3GE.

CUBBAGE, Mr. Paul Vincent, BA ACA *1995;* 21, Lingwell Nook Lane, Lofthouse Gate, WAKEFIELD, WF3 3HZ.

•**CUBBAGE, Mr. Robert, BA FCA** *1978;* Ernst & Young LLP, 1 More London Place, LONDON, SE1 2AF. See also Ernst & Young Europe LLP

CUBBIN, Mr. Alastair James, BSc(Hons) ACA *2002;* Muse Developments Ltd, 1 Anchorage Quay, SALFORD, M50 3YJ.

CUBBON, Mr. Charles Andrew John, BSc ACA *1998;* 27 Bradmore Park Road, LONDON, W6 0DT.

CUBBON, Mr. Martin, BA ACA *1984;* 64/F One Island East, 18 Westlands Road, QUARRY BAY, HONG KONG ISLAND, HONG KONG SAR.

CUBBON, Mr. Peter, MSc BA(Hons) ACA *2011;* 15 Lenhurst Avenue, LEEDS, LS12 2RE.

CUBITT, Mr. Brian Thomas, FCA *1965;* 38 Old Farleigh Road, SOUTH CROYDON, Surrey, CR2 8PE. (Life Member)

CUBITT, Mr. Cecil Charles, FCA *1959;* 15 Malus Drive, ADDLESTONE, KT15 1EP. (Life Member)

CUBITT, Mr. Jonathan Guy, BA ACA *1989;* 44 Elm Grove Road, LONDON, SW13 0BT.

CUBITT, Mrs. Mandy, BSc ACA *2005;* 6 Manor School View, Overseal, SWADLINCOTE, DERBYSHIRE, DE12 6LN.

CUBITT, Miss. Melissa Dawn, ACA *2005;* with Roger Hopkins, 18 Princes Street, NORWICH, NR3 1AE.

CUBITT, Mr. Michael Harry, BA FCA *1974;* Fox Glen, Court Green Heights, WOKING, GU22 0DS.

CUBITT, Mrs. Susannah Jane, BSc ACA *2005;* with Roger Lugg & Co, 12/14 High Street, CATERHAM, CR3 5UA.

CUBY, Mr. Solomon Sydney, FCA *1968;* Berkeley Seymour Property Finance Ltd, 40 George Street, LONDON, W1U 7DT.

CUCKSEY, Mr. John Davenport, FCA *1958;* Pinewood, Saxlingham Road, Blakeney, HOLT, NR25 7PB. (Life Member)

CUDDIHY, Mrs. Michelle Elizabeth, BSc ACA *2006;* Flat 4, 33-35 Baylis Road, LONDON, SE1 7AY.

CUDDIHY, Mr. Paul, MSc ACA *2000;* 68 Crescent Gardens, RUISLIP, MIDDLESEX, HA4 8TA.

CUDDINGTON, Mr. Ben, BA ACA *2004;* 9 Grove Road, MAIDSTONE, KENT, ME15 9AR.

CUDDY, Mr. Philip David, BA(Hons) ACA *2007;* 18 Green Hill Crescent, LEEDS, LS12 4HB.

CUDDY, Ms. Rachel, BA ACA *2007;* 42 Turnberry Avenue, Onchan, ISLE OF MAN, IM3 2JX.

CUDIA, Mrs. Emma Victoria Clare, BA ACA *1999;* Sothebys, PO Box 2AA, LONDON, W1A 2AA.

CUDLIP, Mrs. Sandra, ACA *2008;* 17 Yellow Brook Close, Aspull, WIGAN, WN2 1ZH.

CUDLIPP, Mr. Jonathan William James, BA ACA *2001;* 37 Candler Mews, Amyand Park Road, TWICKENHAM, TW1 3JF.

•**CUDMORE, Mr. Nicholas Peter, FCA** *1982;* (Member of Council 2003 - 2011), Duncan & Toplis, 15 Chequergate, LOUTH, LINCOLNSHIRE, LN11 0LJ.

CUDMORE, Mr. Paul Keith Carrington, ACA *1981;* 17 Jennings, Stantonbury, MILTON KEYNES, MK14 6AN.

•**CUDWORTH, Mr. Philip Stephen, ACA** *1986;* McGregors Corporate (Nottingham) Ltd, 13-15 Regent Street, NOTTINGHAM, NG1 5BS. See also McGregors Audt Services Ltd and McGregors Business Network Ltd

•**CUE, Mr. Bernard Godfrey, FCA MABRP** *1966;* (Tax Fac), Bond Partners LLP, 201 Newbridge Road, BATH, BA1 3HH. See also Cue & Co Ltd

CUENI, Mr. Charles Oliver, ACA *2010;* Broennerstrasse 21, 60313 FRANKFURT AM MAIN, HESSEN, GERMANY.

CUERDEN, Mr. Alan, FCA *1962;* apartment, 23 Lower Mill Lane, HOLMFIRTH, HD9 2JB.

•**CUERDEN, Mr. Simon Derek, BA ACA** *1991;* Deloitte LLP, PO Box 500, 2 Hardman Street, MANCHESTER, M60 2AT. See also Deloitte & Touche LLP

CUFF, Miss. Jemma, ACA *2010;* 33 High Street, Sproughton, IPSWICH, IP8 3AF.

CUFF, Mr. Thomas Anstice, FCA *1968;* The Manor House, Little Missenden, AMERSHAM, BUCKINGHAMSHIRE, HP7 0RA.

CUFFLIN, Mr. David Robert Palmer, FCA *1956;* 32 Nursery Hollow, ILKESTON, DERBYSHIRE, DE7 4LQ. (Life Member)

CUFLEY, Miss. Gillian Margaret, ACA *1981;* 6 Knole Way, SEVENOAKS, TN13 3RS.

CUFLEY, Mr. Sean Dominic Hardy, BA FCA *1984;* Medina Cottage, Medina Place, HOVE, EAST SUSSEX, BN3 2RF.

CUHLS, Mr. Matthew Hilmar, MEng ACA *1999;* Windsor Life Assurance Co Ltd Windsor House, Ironmasters Way Town Centre, TELFORD, SHROPSHIRE, TF3 4NB.

CUI, Mrs. Frances Ruth, MA FCA *1978;* 3 Place de la Pyramide, La Défense 9, 92800 PUTEAUX, FRANCE.

CUI, Ms. Yansong, ACA *2008;* 44 Varsity Drive, TWICKENHAM, TW1 1AG.

CULBERT, Miss. Antoinette, ACA *2010;* 29 Cumber Lane, WILMSLOW, CHESHIRE, SK9 6DX.

CULCHETH, Miss. Helen Selena, BSc ACA *2001;* 14 The Longlands, MARKET HARBOROUGH, LEICESTERSHIRE, LE16 7XZ.

CULHAM, Mr. Paul, ACA *2011;* 15 Waterloo Road, LEIGHTON BUZZARD, BEDFORDSHIRE, LU7 2NR.

CULHANE, Ms. Angela Mary Siobhan, BA FCA *1991;* Care UK Plc Connaught House, 850 The Crescent Colchester Business Park, COLCHESTER, CO4 9QB.

CULHANE, Mr. Julian Charles Desmond, BSc ACA *1993;* 13 Dewhurst Road, LONDON, W14 0ET.

CULL, Mr. Alan, FCA *1972;* 12 Duffield Road, Walton-on-the-Hill, TADWORTH, KT20 7UQ.

CULL, Mr. Jonathan Peter, MBA BSc FCA *1982;* 31 Hill Drive, Whaley Bridge, HIGH PEAK, DERBYSHIRE, SK23 7BH.

CULL, Miss. Rachel Elizabeth, BA ACA *1993;* 20 Stallcourt Avenue, CARDIFF, CF23 5AN.

CULL, Mrs. Sultana Begum, FCA *1974;* Meadows End, Lower Green Lane, Chearsley, AYLESBURY, HP18 0BZ.

CULL, Mr. Vernon, FCA *1949;* 30 Smith Square, LONDON, SW1P 3HF. (Life Member)

CULLEN, Mr. Adam Peter, MEng BEng ACA *2002;* Barclays Capital, B Z W, 10 South Colonnade, LONDON, E14 4PU.

CULLEN, Mr. Adrian Hugh, FCA *1969;* 2 Arno Vale Gardens, Woodthorpe, NOTTINGHAM, NG5 4JL.

CULLEN, Mr. Andrew Arthur, ACA *1997;* 19 Fitzhardinge Cresent, EVATT, ACT 2617, AUSTRALIA.

CULLEN, Mrs. Carolyn, BA(Hons) ACA *2001;* 5 Hawthorn Avenue, Eccles, MANCHESTER, M30 9NE.

CULLEN, Mr. David Anthony, BA ACA *2001;* Flat 12 Boothroyd, 281 Washway Road, SALE, CHESHIRE, M33 4BP.

CULLEN, Mr. David Richard, ACA CA(SA) *2010;* 9 Albion Close, Maiden Bower, CRAWLEY, WEST SUSSEX, RH10 7WJ.

•**CULLEN, Mr. Gary Peter, BA ACA** *1984;* 100 Princes Boulevard, Bebington, WIRRAL, CH63 5LP.

CULLEN, Mr. Gerald, BA ACA *1986;* Cap Gemini UK Plc, Cap Gemini House, 77-79 Cross Street, SALE, CHESHIRE, M33 7HG.

•**CULLEN, Mr. Gordon Jonathan, BSc ACA** *1996;* 13 Middleton Road, LONDON, NW11 7NR.

CULLEN, Mr. James Stephen, FCA *1968;* Barclays Bank Chambers, High Street, Yeadon, LEEDS, LS19 7PP.

CULLEN, Mr. James Stredwick, FCA *1963;* 6c Park Lane Court, Park Lane, Whitefield, MANCHESTER, M45 7PU. (Life Member)

CULLEN, Mr. John Charles, BSc FCA *1990;* A O N Ltd, 8 Devonshire Square, LONDON, EC2M 4PL.

CULLEN, Mrs. Lauren Rachel, ACA MAAT *2005;* 52 Ravensfield Gardens, Stoneleigh, EPSOM, SURREY, KT19 0SR.

CULLEN, Miss. Louise Victoria, MEng ACA *2009;* 61/5 Ashley Terrace, EDINBURGH, EH11 1RX.

CULLEN, Mr. Michael John, ACA *2003;* 34 Delamere Street, WARRINGTON, WA5 1PD.

CULLEN, Mr. Nicholas, ACA *2009;* 3 Back Lane, Drighlington, BRADFORD, BD11 1LS.

•**CULLEN, Mr. Paul Mario, ACA** *1991;* Citycas Limited, Fifth Floor, Linen Hall, 162-168 Regents Street, LONDON, W1B 5TF.

CULLEN, Mr. Raymond Thomas, MA ACA *1981;* 16 Hurst Road, EAST MOLESEY, SURREY, KT8 9AF.

CULLEN, Mr. Roderick Leonard Dunlop, BA ACA *1985;* Sherwood, 8 Heath Drive, SUTTON, SM2 5RP.

CULLEN, Dr. Sarah, BA ACA *1998;* Nokia (UK) Ltd, Summit Avenue, FARNBOROUGH, HAMPSHIRE, GU14 0NG.

CULLEN, Mr. Steven Peter, ACA *1995;* Record Currency Management Ltd Morgan House, Madeira Walk, WINDSOR, BERKSHIRE, SL4 1EP.

•**CULLEN-CRONSHAW, Mrs. Josephine Mary, FCA** *1980;* Parc Saint Roman, Les terrasses - Appt 405, 7 ave Saint Roman, MONTE CARLO, 98000, MONACO.

CULLENS, Mr. Alan Russell, BSc ACA *1993;* Flat 11 Highfield Manor, Highfield Lane Tyttenhanger, ST. ALBANS, HERTFORDSHIRE, AL4 0AN.

CULLEY, Mr. Derick Denis, BSc FCA *1967;* Kingslee House, Ridley Hill, Kingswear, DARTMOUTH, TQ6 0BY. (Life Member)

CULLEY, Mr. Frank Andrew, BA FCA *1991;* 11 Pheasant Rise, Bowdon, ALTRINCHAM, CHESHIRE, WA14 3HL.

CULLEY, Miss. Katharine Julia, BA ACA *1995;* (Tax Fac), Pricewaterhousecoopers, Princess Court, 23 Princess Street, PLYMOUTH, PL1 2EX.

CULLIFORD, Mrs. Janet, BSc FCA CTA *1986;* AGI World Ltd, A G I Media Services Ltd Unit 1-3, Slough Interchange Industrial Estate Whittenham Close, SLOUGH, SL2 5EP.

CULLIFORD, Mr. John David, BA FCA *1973;* 7 Cheveridge Close, SOLIHULL, WEST MIDLANDS, B91 3TT.

•**CULLIGAN, Miss. Anne-Marie, LLB ACA** *2000;* with PricewaterhouseCoopers Ltd, Abacus House, P O Box 63, PROVIDENCIALES, TURKS AND CAICOS ISLANDS.

•**CULLINANE, Mr. John Patrick, MA FCA CTA** *1990;* Deloitte LLP, 2 New Street Square, LONDON, EC4A 3BZ. See also Deloitte & Touche LLP

CULLINANE, Mr. Peter Michael, BA FCA *1975;* (Tax Fac), 12 Staunton Road, HAVANT, HAMPSHIRE, PO9 1NH.

CULLING, Mr. David Arthur, FCA *1962;* 3 Penn Close, Chorleywood, RICKMANSWORTH, HERTFORDSHIRE, WD3 5HG. (Life Member)

CULLING, Mr. Philip Gordon, MEng ACA *2010;* 55 Tasman Road, LONDON, SW9 9LZ.

CULLINGFORD, Mr. Paul Andrew, BSc ACA *1989;* Bibby Distribution, 105 Duke Street, LIVERPOOL, L1 5JQ.

CULLINGHAM, Mr. James David Herbert, MA FCA *1962;* 143 Boundary Road, WALLINGTON, SM6 0TE. (Life Member)

CULLINGHAM, Mr. James Mackay, MA ACA *1993;* 155 Ashbourne Road, Turnditch, BELPER, DERBYSHIRE, DE56 2LH.

CULLINGTON, Mr. David Graham, BA ACA *2000;* Hewitt Associates, 6 More London Place, LONDON, SE1 2DA.

CULLINGTON, Mr. John Frederic, BA ACA *1982;* with PricewaterhouseCoopers LLP, 1 Embankment Place, LONDON, WC2N 6RH.

CULLINGTON, Mr. Paul Andrew, BA FCA *1973;* 17 Colebrooke Place, LONDON, N1 8HZ. (Life Member)

CULLINGTON, Mrs. Sarah Joanne, BA ACA *2000;* 8 Rowfant Road, LONDON, SW17 7AS.

•**CULLINGWORTH, Mr. Robert, BSc FCA** *1983;* (Tax Fac), Cullingworth & Co, 96 High Street, HENLEY-IN-ARDEN, WARWICKSHIRE, B95 5BY.

CULLIS, Mr. Jack, BA ACA *2008;* 1 Pulteney Avenue, Widcombe, BATH, BA2 4HH.

CULLUM, Mr. David Andrew, BSc ACA *2004;* Cheval Properties Ltd, 8-10 North Audley Street, LONDON, W1K 6ZD.

CULLUM, Miss. Denise Ann, FCA *1993;* Pink Cottage The Turnpike, Bunwell, NORWICH, NR16 1SP.

CULLUM, Mr. Mark, ACA *2011;* 30 Hollow Lane, Draycott-in-the-Clay, ASHBOURNE, DERBYSHIRE, DE6 5HQ.

•**CULLUM, Mr. Neil Robert, BSc ACA** *1993;* with Ernst & Young LLP, 1 More London Place, LONDON, SE1 2AF.

•**CULLUM, Mr. Philip James, FCA** *1984;* (Tax Fac), Cullum and Co, 24 Home Field Close, Emersons Green, BRISTOL, BS16 7BH.

CULLUM, Mr. Rob, ACA *2006;* 2 Priors Acre, Boxgrove, CHICHESTER, PO18 0ER.

CULLUM, Miss. Susan, BA ACA *1982;* 53 Honey Close, DAGENHAM, ESSEX, RM10 8TF.

CULLUP, Mr. Robin John, FCA *1968;* 93 Blandford Avenue, KETTERING, NN16 9AS.

CULMER, Mrs. Barbara, BA ACA *1989;* Little Cranford House, Bridge Lane, Shawford, WINCHESTER, SO21 2BL.

•**CULMER, Mr. George Clifford, FCA** *1966;* BDO, P.O. Box N10144, East Street, NASSAU, BAHAMAS.

CULMER, Mr. Mark George, BA ACA *1989;* Little Cranford House, Bridge Lane, Shawford, WINCHESTER, SO21 2BL.

CULPAN, Mr. David James, BSc ACA *1997;* 53 Cresswell Road, TWICKENHAM, TW1 2EA.

CULPIN, Mr. Ian John, BSc ACA *1996;* 82 Sidney Road, WALTON-ON-THAMES, SURREY, KT12 2LX.

CULPIN, Mrs. Tina Anne, BCom ACA *1995;* 82 Sidney Road, WALTON-ON-THAMES, KT12 2LX.

CULPITT, Miss. Julia Eaton, BSc ACA *1991;* 32 Olola Avenue, Vaucluse, SYDNEY, NSW 2030, AUSTRALIA.

CULSHAW, Mr. Geoffrey, FCA *1953;* 23 Whitehill Lane, Sharples, BOLTON, BL1 7DL. (Life Member)

•**CULSHAW, Mr. Gregory, BA ACA** *1990;* Deloitte LLP, Abbots House, Abbey Street, READING, RG1 3BD. See also Deloitte & Touche LLP

CULSHAW, Mrs. Julia, BSc ACA *1993;* 10 Kew Gardens Road, RICHMOND, TW9 3HL.

•**CULSHAW, Mr. Martin John, ACA CTA** *1996;* (Tax Fac), 64 Mildred Avenue, WATFORD, WD18 7DX.

CULSHAW, Mr. Timothy Alexander, ACA *2009;* Lindengut 15, 8803 RUSCHLIKON, SWITZERLAND.

CULVER, Mr. Brian James, ACA *1987;* 28 Wheatfields, Lords Wood, CHATHAM, ME5 8HW.

CULVER, Mr. Peter Charles Leonard, MA ACA *1988;* 10 Linkswood Road, Burnham, SLOUGH, SL1 8AT.

CULVER, Mr. Peter James, FCA *1979;* (Tax Fac), 27 Highview, SUTTON, SM2 7DZ.

•**CULVER, Mr. Robert, FCA** *1972;* (Tax Fac), Robert Culver Limited, Field House, Brackley Avenue, Hartley Wintney, HOOK, HAMPSHIRE RG27 8QU.

•**CULVERHOUSE, Mr. John Robert, FCA** *1968;* (Tax Fac), Culverhouse & Co Ltd, 7 High Street, Farnborough, ORPINGTON, KENT, BR6 7BQ.

CULVERHOUSE, Mr. Mark Stephen, ACA *2009;* 24 Malvern Avenue, FAREHAM, HAMPSHIRE, PO14 1QB.

CULWICK, Mrs. Elaine, BSc(Hons) ACA CTA *2003;* (Tax Fac), Upper Shepley Farmhouse, Dale Lane, Lickey End, BROMSGROVE, WORCESTERSHIRE, B60 1GZ.

•**CULWICK, Mr. John Spencer, FCA** *1976;* John S Culwick, 9 Uplands Road, HOCKLEY, ESSEX, SS5 4DL. See also Culwick Consultancy Services Limited

CULWICK, Mr. Mark David, BSc FCA *2000;* Upper Shepley Farmhouse, Dale Lane, Lickey End, BROMSGROVE, WORCESTERSHIRE, B60 1GZ.

CUMARASAMY, Mr. Sanmugam, BA FCA *1948;* 148 Vauxhall Street, 2 COLOMBO, SRI LANKA. (Life Member)

CUMBERBATCH, Mr. Ian, FCA *1955;* 6 Petworth Road, Ainsdale, SOUTHPORT, PR8 2QL. (Life Member)

CUMBERBATCH, Mr. Stewart Neil, BSc ACA *2005;* Apartment 139, 50 Sherborne Street, BIRMINGHAM, B16 8FN.

CUMBERLAND, Mr. Iain McDonald, ACA *1990;* 28 Moorfield Road, ILKLEY, WEST YORKSHIRE, LS29 8BL.

•**CUMBERLAND, Mr. Stuart Richard, BSc ACA** *1995;* Olivine Capital Partners Ltd, 1 Grosvenor Crescent, LONDON, SW1X 7EF.

CUMBO, Mrs. Annette Muriel Couturier, BSc(Hons) ACA *2003;* 3 Boddington Drive, Grappenhall, WARRINGTON, WA4 3HB.

CUMBO, Mr. Mark Antony, BA ACA *2003;* 3 Boddington Drive, Grappenhall, WARRINGTON, WA4 3HB.

CUMING, Mrs. Deborah Jane, BA ACA *1994;* Micro Metalsmiths Ltd, Kirkdale Road, Kirkbymoorside, YORK, YO62 6PX.

CUMISKEY, Mr. Carl William, BA FCA *1989;* 13 Group Ltd, 52 Eggbridge Lane, Waverton, CHESTER, CH3 7PE.

CUMISKEY, Mrs. Jane Elizabeth, BA ACA *1995;* 5 Garstang Road West, POULTON-LE-FYLDE, FY6 8AA.

CUMMANE, Mr. David, MEng ACA *2002;* 10 King Edward Bay Apartments, Sea Cliff Road Onchan, ISLE OF MAN, IM3 2JE.

CUMMING, Mrs. Elizabeth Ann, BSc ACA *1987;* 41 The Nook, Whissendine, OAKHAM, LEICESTERSHIRE, LE15 7EZ.

CUMMING, Mr. Glenn Charles, ACA *2008;* Melodies, Wannock Road, POLEGATE, EAST SUSSEX, BN26 5PH.

CUMMING, Mr. Graeme Alexander, ACA *1993;* 19 Willowtree Way, BANCHORY, KINCARDINESHIRE, AB31 5JQ.

CUMMING, Mr. James Andrew, MSci ACA *2003;* B P P Professional Education, B P P House, Grove Avenue, Queen Square, BRISTOL, BS1 4QY.
CUMMING, Mr. James Andrew, BSc ACA *2006;* Ares Ltd Milbank House, 1 Finsbury Square, LONDON, EC2A 1AE.
CUMMING, Mr. Neil Tait, FCA *1961;* 8 Main Street, Repton, DERBY, DE65 6EZ.
•CUMMING, Mr. Paul Jonathan, FCA *1975;* Paul Cumming, Warwick House, Church Lane, Little Witley, WORCESTER, WR6 6LP. See also Woodbury Accounting Ltd
CUMMING, Mr. Peter, FCA *1967;* 14 Rosedale Rise, Boston Spa, WETHERBY, WEST YORKSHIRE, LS23 6PZ.
CUMMING, Miss. Sarah Elizabeth, MA ACA *1989;* with BDO LLP, 6th Floor, 3 Hardman Street, Spinningfields, MANCHESTER, M3 3AT.
CUMMINGS, Mr. Alan John, BA FCA *1985;* Ferry Cottage, Little Stoke, WALLINGFORD, OX10 6AX.
CUMMINGS, Mrs. Alice Sarah Louise, BEng FCA *1990;* (Tax Fac), Flowers Hill Farmhouse, Flowers Hill, Pangbourne, READING, RG8 7BD.
CUMMINGS, Mr. Edward William, FCA *1966;* 5 Hill Rise, Ramsbottom, BURY, LANCASHIRE, BL0 9QS. (Life Member)
CUMMINGS, Mr. Gordon, BAcc ACA *1993;* 2606 Lonsdale Avenue, NORTH VANCOUVER V7N 3H9, BC, CANADA.
CUMMINGS, Miss. Helen Elizabeth, BA ACA *2003;* PM+M Solutions For Business LLP, Greenbank Technology Park Challenge Way, BLACKBURN, BB1 5QB.
•CUMMINGS, Mr. Iain Alexander, BSc FCA *1987;* KPMG LLP, 15 Canada Square, LONDON, E14 5GL. See also KPMG Europe LLP
•CUMMINGS, Mr. Ian Charles, BA FCA *1976;* Ian C Cummings, 9 Parkland Drive, ST. ALBANS, HERTFORDSHIRE, AL3 4AH.
CUMMINGS, Mr. John Allan, BSc FCA *1981;* The Rosary, Long Marston, STRATFORD-UPON-AVON, CV37 8RG.
CUMMINGS, Mr. Mark David, BA ACA *1999;* with KPMG LLP, 1 The Embankment, Neville Street, LEEDS, LS1 4DW.
CUMMINGS, Mrs. Marzenna Franciszka Elzbieta, MA FCA *1983;* 2 Nightingale Square, LONDON, SW12 8QN.
CUMMINGS, Mr. Michael, MSc FCA *1975;* 777 Brickell Avenue Suite 1114, MIAMI, FL 33131, UNITED STATES.
CUMMINGS, Mr. Michael John, BSc ACA *2001;* 19 Macefin Avenue, MANCHESTER, M21 7QQ.
CUMMINGS, Mrs. Rhiannon, BSc ACA *1995;* 2606 Lonsdale Avenue, NORTH VANCOUVER V7N 3H9, BC, CANADA.
CUMMINGS, Mr. Rohan August, ACA CA(SA) *2008;* 135 Percheron Drive, Knaphill, WOKING, SURREY, GU21 2QZ.
CUMMINGS, Mr. Stanley William James, FCA *1968;* 3 Oakfield Lane, KESTON, BR2 6BY.
•CUMMINGS, Mr. Stephen Leslie, BSc FCA *1988;* 141 Adelaide Street West, Suite 770, TORONTO M5H 3L5, ON, CANADA.
CUMMINGS, Miss. Tracey Jean, BA FCA *1995;* Dial House, Chislehurst Road, BICKLEY, KENT, BR1 2NJ.
CUMMINS, Miss. Catherine Maria, BCom ACA *1988; (ACA Ireland 1985);* 99 Bryan Avenue, Willesden, LONDON, NW10 2AS.
CUMMINS, Mr. Christopher David, BA ACA *1982;* 96 Knightlow Road, Harborne, BIRMINGHAM, B17 8QA.
CUMMINS, Mr. Denis Gerard, BA ACA *1978;* 15 Cowley Way, Kilsby, RUGBY, CV23 8XB.
CUMMINS, Mrs. Fiona Christine, BSc ACA *1993;* 15, Provost Smith Crescent, INVERNESS, IV2 3TG.
CUMMINS, Mr. George Irving, FCA *1971;* Eco-Bat Technologies Plc, Cowley Lodge, South Darley, MATLOCK, DERBYSHIRE, DE4 2LE.
CUMMINS, Mr. Gordon, ACA *2006;* 42 Effingham Road, LONDON, N8 0AB.
•CUMMINS, Mrs. Jane, BSocSc FCA CTA *1986;* (Tax Fac), Cummins Young Ltd, 39 Westgate, THIRSK, NORTH YORKSHIRE, YO7 1QR.
CUMMINS, Miss. Julia, BA ACA *1997;* Toyota Financial Services (UK), plc, Great Burgh, Burgh Heath, EPSOM, KT18 5UZ.
CUMMINS, Mr. Julian, BSc ACA *1996;* Empire World Trade Ltd, Enterprise Way, Pinchbeck, SPALDING, LINCOLNSHIRE, PE11 3YR.
•CUMMINS, Miss. Moira Ann, FCA *1991;* 3 Barrards Way, Seer Green, BEACONSFIELD, BUCKINGHAMSHIRE, HP9 2YZ.
CUMMINS, Mr. Nicholas, BA(Hons) ACA *2011;* 136 Vartry Road, LONDON, N15 6HA.
CUMMINS, Mr. Paul Alexander, BSc ACA *1987;* Camelot, Chillies Lane, CROWBOROUGH, EAST SUSSEX, TN6 3TB.
CUMMINS, Mr. Paul David, BA ACA *1989;* 21/F Shun Feng International Centre, 182 Queen's Road East, WAN CHAI, HONG KONG ISLAND, HONG KONG SAR.
CUMMINS, Mr. Peter Ronald, FCA *1967;* Oak Grove, 184 Totaramahonga Road, DANNEVIRKE 4972, NEW ZEALAND.
CUMMINS, Mr. Sean Vincent, BSc ACA *1988;* 15 Brooke Gardens Dunmow Road, BISHOP'S STORTFORD, CM23 5JF.
CUMOW, Mrs. Julie Petrina, BA(Hons) ACA *1992;* 205 Crystal Brook Road, WATTLE GROVE, WA 6107, AUSTRALIA.
CUMPSON, Mr. Craig, FCA CTA *1996;* 51 Lesbury Close, CHESTER LE STREET, DH2 3SS.
CUNDALE, Mr. Neil, BSc ACA *2007;* 35 Dunston Hill, TRING, HERTFORDSHIRE, HP23 4AT.
CUNDIFF, Mr. Andrew Lionel, FCA *1980;* 30 Mill Close, Bookham, LEATHERHEAD, SURREY, KT23 3JX.
CUNDY, Mr. Albert Barrie, FCA *1953;* 26 Chestnut Court, Chestnut Road, Charlton Down, DORCHESTER, DORSET, DT2 9FN. (Life Member)
CUNDY, Mrs. Caroline Anne, BA(Hons) ACA CTA *1992;* with Cundy Solutions Limited, Birch Hollow, Netherhope Lane, Tidenham, CHEPSTOW, NP16 7JE.
CUNDY, Mr. Christopher John, BSc ACA *1986;* 74 Downscroft Gardens, Hedge End, SOUTHAMPTON, SO30 4RS.
•CUNDY, Mr. David, FCA *1986;* Cundy Solutions Limited, Birch Hollow, Netherhope Lane, Tidenham, CHEPSTOW, NP16 7JE.
CUNDY, Mr. Mark Christopher, BSc FCA *1985;* Flat 3 The Mansion House, Lees Court Sheldwich Lees, FAVERSHAM, ME13 0NQ.
CUNDY, Mr. Michael, ACA *1979;* 14 Park Road North, MIDDLESBROUGH, CLEVELAND, TS1 3LF.
CUNDY, Mrs. Sara Jane, BSc ACA *1996;* 10 Parfitt Drive, Farnsfield, NEWARK, NG22 8FA.
CUNDY, Ms. Sarah, BSc ACA *2002;* 31, Clifton Road, LONDON, N3 2AS.
CUNDY, Mr. Timothy Edward, ACA *2009;* 338 Durnsford Road, LONDON, SW19 8DX.
•CUNDY, Mr. Vincent Gregory, FCA *1977;* V.G. Cundy & Co, 175 Ladybank Road, Mickleover, DERBY, DE3 0QF.
CUNDY, Mr. William Brian, FCA *1956;* 4 The Coppice, 25 Douglas Road, HARPENDEN, HERTFORDSHIRE, AL5 2ER. (Life Member)
CUNLIFFE, Mr. Barry Stuart, BA ACA *1995;* ITM Power plc, 22 Atlas Way, SHEFFIELD, S4 7QQ.
CUNLIFFE, Mr. Darren Anthony, BSc(Hons) ACA *2003;* Unit 3, 56 - 58 Mount Street, WEST PERTH, WA 6005, AUSTRALIA.
CUNLIFFE, Mr. Gordon Kenneth, FCA *1977;* P.O. Box 3092, DAINFERN, 2055, SOUTH AFRICA.
CUNLIFFE, Mr. Graham, FCA *1955;* 5 Oaks Gate, Oaks Road, TENTERDEN, KENT, TN30 6RF. (Life Member)
CUNLIFFE, Mr. James, BA(Hons) ACA *2011;* 131 Bury Road, Radcliffe, MANCHESTER, M26 2UT.
CUNLIFFE, Mr. Jeffrey Paul, BEng ACA *1999;* 9 Golf Links Avenue, HINDHEAD, GU26 6PQ.
CUNLIFFE, Miss. Jemma, ACA *2009;* 229 Ormskirk Road, Rainford, ST. HELENS, MERSEYSIDE, WA11 8SB.
CUNLIFFE, Mr. Mark Raymond, ACA *2009;* 4 Daresbury Close, WILMSLOW, CHESHIRE, SK9 2GR.
•CUNLIFFE, Mr. Neil Stephen, BSc FCA *1993;* Gibbons Mannington & Phipps, 82 High Street, TENTERDEN, KENT, TN30 6JG.
CUNLIFFE, Mr. Peter Robin, BCom ACA *1983;* 23 Arley Road, SOLIHULL, WEST MIDLANDS, B91 1NJ.
CUNLIFFE, Mr. Steven Paul, BA ACA *1993;* Sportech Plc Walton House, Charnock Road, LIVERPOOL, MERSEYSIDE, L67 1AA.
CUNNELL, Miss. Samantha Jane, BSc ACA *2010;* 1 Wheatfield Way, Long Stratton, NORWICH, NR15 2WG.
CUNNELLY, Mr. Carl Edward, FCA *1960;* 2 Chew Vale, DUKINFIELD, SK16 5QT. (Life Member)
CUNNIFFE, Mr. James Tudor, BA ACA *2000;* 127 Broomwood Road, LONDON, SW11 6JU.
•CUNNINGHAM, Mr. Adrian Thomas, LLB ACA *1980;* Adrian Cunningham, 12 Cornwall Crescent, DiggleSaddleworth, OLDHAM, OL3 5PW.
•CUNNINGHAM, Mr. Alan Stewart, BSc FCA CTA *1985;* Haines Watts Wales LLP, Pagefield House, 24 Gold Tops, NEWPORT, GWENT, NP20 4PG.
CUNNINGHAM, Mr. Andrew Edward Tarrant, FCA *1969;* Flat 29, River Court, Upper Ground, LONDON, SE1 9PE.
CUNNINGHAM, Mr. Andrew Robert, MA ACA *2003;* Macquarie Group Limited, Level 9, 125 W 55th Street, NEW YORK, NY 10019, UNITED STATES.
CUNNINGHAM, Mr. Andrew Rolland, MA FCA *1981;* High Wray, 35 Montagu Avenue, NEWCASTLE UPON TYNE, NE3 4JH.
CUNNINGHAM, Mr. Andrew Roy, FCA *1981;* Northern Rock (Asset Management) Plc, Prudhoe Building, Regent Centre, Gosforth, NEWCASTLE UPON TYNE, NE3 4AW.
CUNNINGHAM, Mr. Anthony Gerald, FCA *1972;* Cleeve House, 7 Weathercock Lane, Woburn Sands, MILTON KEYNES, MK17 8NP.
CUNNINGHAM, Mr. Benjamin John, BSc(Hons) ACA *2001;* 4 Grange Close, Bletchingley, REDHILL, RH1 4LW.
CUNNINGHAM, Miss. Carol Ann, BA(Hons) ACA *2004;* 21/546 Flinders Street, MELBOURNE, VIC 3000, AUSTRALIA.
CUNNINGHAM, Miss. Charlene Maria, ACA *2010;* 3 Brooks Road, STREET, SOMERSET, BA16 0PN.
•CUNNINGHAM, Mrs. Christina Jane, BSc ACA *1990;* Chris Cunningham, The Wheelwrights, Silver Street, Abthorpe, TOWCESTER, NORTHAMPTONSHIRE NN12 8QR.
CUNNINGHAM, Mr. Christopher, BA(Hons) ACA *2009;* Level 10, PKF Chartered Accountants, 1 Margaret Street, SYDNEY, NSW 2000, AUSTRALIA.
CUNNINGHAM, Mrs. Clare, MA ACA *2003;* 64 Chantry Lane, London Colney, ST. ALBANS, HERTFORDSHIRE, AL2 1JU.
CUNNINGHAM, Mr. Colin Richard, BA(Hons) ACA *2001;* Lyndhurst, Charvil House Road, Charvil, READING, BERKSHIRE, RG10 9RD.
CUNNINGHAM, Mrs. Corinne Lisa, BA ACA *1990;* 115 Broomwood Road, LONDON, SW11 6JU.
CUNNINGHAM, Mr. Damian Christopher Michael, BSc ACA AMCT *2000;* 110 Coventry Road, Burbage, HINCKLEY, LE10 2HR.
CUNNINGHAM, Mr. Daniel William, BSc ACA *1994;* 87 James Street, LEICHHARDT, NSW 2040, AUSTRALIA.
CUNNINGHAM, Mr. David Jonathan, FCA *1975;* Falloden, Gasden Copse, Witley, GODALMING, GU8 5QD.
•CUNNINGHAM, Mr. David Maxwell, BSc ACA *1989;* Dave Cunningham, The Wheelwrights, Silver Street, Abthorpe, TOWCESTER, NORTHAMPTONSHIRE NN12 8QR. See also Kusa Limited
CUNNINGHAM, Mr. David William, ACA *2005;* 39 St. Helena Way, Horsford, NORWICH, NR10 3EA.
•CUNNINGHAM, Mr. Declan Thomas, BSc FCA *1985;* (Tax Fac), Cameron Cunningham LLP, 145 High Street, SEVENOAKS, KENT, TN13 1XJ. See also CC Secretaries Limited
CUNNINGHAM, Mr. Derek Peter, FCA *1977;* Coca-Cola CCEAG, Friedrichstrasse 68, 10117 BERLIN, GERMANY.
CUNNINGHAM, Mr. Geoffrey, FCA *1961;* 31 Station Road, Alresford, COLCHESTER, CO7 8BU. (Life Member)
CUNNINGHAM, Mrs. Gillian Margaret, BCom ACA *1988;* Leventis Overseas Ltd, West Africa House, Hanger Lane, Ealing, LONDON, W5 3QR.
CUNNINGHAM, Mrs. Harriet, MSci ACA CTA *2003;* Kingfisher Plc, 3 Sheldon Square, LONDON, W2 6PX.
•CUNNINGHAM, Mrs. Heather Ruth, MA FCA *1988;* Harold Sharp, Holland House, 1-5 Oakfield, SALE, M33 6TT.
CUNNINGHAM, Mr. Ian Richard, BSc ACA *1998;* Gala Coral Group Ltd New Castle House, Castle Boulevard, NOTTINGHAM, NG7 1FT.
CUNNINGHAM, Mrs. Jacqueline Elizabeth, BSc FCA *1990;* Engineering Employers Federation Broadway House, Tothill Street, LONDON, SW1H 9NQ.
CUNNINGHAM, Mr. James, ACA *2011;* 222 The Fairway, New Moston, MANCHESTER, M40 3NJ.
CUNNINGHAM, Mr. James Charles, BSc ACA *2001;* May Cottage, The Green, Great Milton, OXFORD, OX44 7NT.
CUNNINGHAM, Miss. Joan Elizabeth, MBA BA FCA *1976;* 78 Albany Mansions, Albert Bridge Road, LONDON, SW11 4PQ.
CUNNINGHAM, Mr. John Keiller, MSc BSc FCA *1975;* 1 Loudens Close, ST ANDREWS, FIFE, KY16 9EN.
CUNNINGHAM, Mr. John Leslie, ACA *2007;* (Tax Fac), with Grant Thornton UK LLP, Bradenham Manor, Bradenham, HIGH WYCOMBE, BUCKINGHAMSHIRE, HP14 4HF.
CUNNINGHAM, Mr. John Michael, BA ACA *1990;* Tyddyn Pen Y Gaer, Llandre, BOW STREET, SY24 5NX.
•CUNNINGHAM, Mr. Josias Stephen Charles, BSc ACA *1992;* Stephen Cunningham & Co, Silversprings, 140 The Burn Road, Templepatrick, BALLYCLARE, COUNTY ANTRIM BT39 0DQ.
CUNNINGHAM, Mr. Karl Scott, BA(Hons) ACA *2001;* 10 Kings Pool Walk, YORK, YO1 7NA.
CUNNINGHAM, Mr. Kevin Robert William, ACA *2003;* 105-21 66th Ave, Apt 2B, FOREST HILLS, NY 11375, UNITED STATES.
CUNNINGHAM, Mr. Luke, ACA CA(AUS) *2008;* 16 Bramwell Road, Noranda, PERTH, WA 6062, AUSTRALIA.
CUNNINGHAM, Mr. Malcolm Alfred Edwin, FCA *1947;* 5 Warren Close, Humberstone, LEICESTER, LE5 1BB. (Life Member)
CUNNINGHAM, Miss. Maria Shelagh, BA ACA *1990;* 150 Eastham Village Road, Eastham, WIRRAL, CH62 0AE.
CUNNINGHAM, Mr. Mark Andrew, ACA *1991;* office2office plc, St. Crispins House, Duke Street, NORWICH, NR3 1PD.
CUNNINGHAM, Mr. Mark Henry Michael, BSc ACA *1994;* Hill & Knowlton International, 118 Avenue de Corlenbergh, 1000 BRUSSELS, BELGIUM.
CUNNINGHAM, Mr. Martin Andrew, BSc ACA *1989;* 2 Walnut Tree Close, CHISLEHURST, BR7 5PF.
CUNNINGHAM, Miss. Melissa, BA(Hons) ACA *2011;* 21 Hawthorn Gardens, Clayton le Moors, ACCRINGTON, LANCASHIRE, BB5 5WL.
CUNNINGHAM, Mr. Michael Charles, BA ACA *1989;* 46 West Farm Avenue, ASHTEAD, KT21 2JY.
CUNNINGHAM, Mr. Michael Robert, ACA *1981;* (Tax Fac), 21 Grosvenor Road, SOUTH, BENFLEET, SS7 1NP.
CUNNINGHAM, Mr. Neil, FCA *1974;* 49 Dexter Way, Warmington, PETERBOROUGH, PE8 6WH.
CUNNINGHAM, Mr. Neil Gillies, LLB DipLP ACA *1990;* 11 Douglas Muir Gardens, Milngavie, GLASGOW, G62 7RZ.
•CUNNINGHAM, Mr. Paul Andrew, BSc FCA *1991;* PricewaterhouseCoopers, BusinessCommunityCenter, Katerinska 40/466, 120 00 PRAGUE, CZECH REPUBLIC.
CUNNINGHAM, Mr. Paul Gerard, BSc ACA *1990;* Prosperous Farm, Hurstbourne Tarrant, ANDOVER, SP11 0DJ.
CUNNINGHAM, Mr. Paul Massey, FCA *1961;* 5 Main Street, HILLSBOROUGH, COUNTY DOWN, BT26 6AE.
CUNNINGHAM, Mr. Peter Lloyd, BA ACA *1992;* 14 Mount Pleasant, WEYBRIDGE, KT13 8EP.
•CUNNINGHAM, Mr. Peter Nisbet Bruce, FCA *1971;* DMC Partnership, Yew Tree House, Lewes Road, FOREST ROW, RH18 5AA.
CUNNINGHAM, Mr. Philip James, BA ACA *2002;* 7 Willow Vale, Newport, SAFFRON WALDEN, CB11 3DD.
CUNNINGHAM, Mrs. Rachael Naomi, BSc ACA *1998;* 79 West Cross Avenue, West Cross, SWANSEA, WEST GLAMORGAN, SA3 5TX.
•CUNNINGHAM, Mr. Richard Leslie, BL ACA *2006;* (Tax Fac), Wellington Guscott Limited, No.1 Booths Hall, Chelford Road, KNUTSFORD, CHESHIRE, WA16 8QZ.
CUNNINGHAM, Mr. Richard Thomas, ACA *2002;* Siemens Limited, Corporate Controlling Department, 7 Wangjing Zhonghuan Nanlu, Chaoyang District, BEIJING 100102, CHINA.
CUNNINGHAM, Mr. Robert Stephen, MA ACA *1989;* 74 Belmont Hill, LONDON, SE13 5DN.
CUNNINGHAM, Mr. Simon Richard, BA ACA *2006;* 15 Fairthorn Close, TRING, HERTFORDSHIRE, HP23 4DT.
CUNNINGHAM, Mr. Simon Robert, BSc ACA *2002;* 6 Reapers Close, HORSHAM, WEST SUSSEX, RH12 5TG.
CUNNINGHAM, Dr. Stephen, BSc FCA ASIP *1993;* 2 Old Orchards, Church Road, Worth, CRAWLEY, WEST SUSSEX, RH10 7QA.
CUNNINGHAM, Mr. Stephen Robert, BA ACA *1987;* 51 Walumetta Drive, Wollstone Craft, SYDNEY, NSW 2065, AUSTRALIA.
CUNNINGTON, Mr. David Charles, BSc FCA *1999;* Cordea Savills LLP, Landsdowne House, 57 Berkeley Square, LONDON, W1J 6ER.
CUNNINGTON, Miss. Deborah, ACA *2011;* 20 St. Tibba Way, Ryhall, STAMFORD, LINCOLNSHIRE, PE9 4EN.
•CUNNINGTON, Mr. James Philip, FCA *1959;* James P Cunnington, Highcroft Cottage, 33 Berridges Lane, Husbands Bosworth, LUTTERWORTH, LEICESTERSHIRE LE17 6LE.
•CUNYNGHAME, Sir Andrew David Francis, Bt FCA *1966;* (Tax Fac), Milncraig Ltd, 12 Vicarage Gardens, LONDON, W8 4AH.

CUPIT, Mr. Dwight Nicholas, ACA CA(AUS) *2009;* Bregal Capital Llp Michelin House, 81 Fulham Road, LONDON, SW3 6RD.

CUPPLES, Mrs. Louise, BSc ACA *2007;* 2 The Dell, WOKING, GU21 7PF.

CURAS-THOMPSON, Mr. David Keith, ACA *1981;* P.O. Box A531, Avondale, HARARE, ZIMBABWE.

CURD, Mr. Charles Michael, BA ACA *1991;* 61 The Hopmarket, WORCESTER, WR1 1DD.

CURD, Mr. Graham, ACA MAAT *2007;* 22 Cuckoo Dene, Hanwell, LONDON, W7 3DP.

CURD, Mr. Jeremy Kenneth Edward, BSc ACA *1996;* (Tax Fac), 19 Manor Road, Sherborne St. John, BASINGSTOKE, HAMPSHIRE, RG24 9JJ.

CURD, Mr. Liam Giles, MEng ACA *2008;* 73 Wickenden Road, SEVENOAKS, KENT, TN13 3PN.

CURETON, Mrs. Amanda Julie, BSc ACA *1987;* Avon Water House, Barrows Lane, Sway, LYMINGTON, SO41 6DD.

CURL, Mrs. Carmel Ann, BA ACA *1989;* 137 Beresford Avenue, Berrylands, SURBITON, KT5 9LR.

CURL, Mr. Nigel Robert, BA ACA *1992;* 42 Tamarind Court, 18 Gainsford Street, LONDON, SE1 2NE.

CURLE, Mrs. Gillian Alisan, MSci ACA *2003;* Corsebank, 6 Devonburn Road, Lesmahagow, LANARK, ML11 9PX.

CURLE, Mr. Michael Guy Lister, BA ACA *1979;* Flat 1, 75 Cumberland Street, LONDON, SW1V 4NB.

CURLE, Mr. Nicholas Timothy, BSc ACA *1995;* with Barclays plc, 1 Churchill Place, Canary Wharf, LONDON, E14 5HP.

CURLE, Mrs. Tolla Joanne, MA(Cantab) ACA *2001;* Northern Foods Trinity Park House, Fox Way, WAKEFIELD, WEST YORKSHIRE, WF2 8EE.

CURLEY, Mr. John Gilbert, BA FCA *1977;* 44 Queens Road, Caversham, READING, RG4 8DL.

CURLEY, Mr. Paul Anthony, BA ACA *1999;* 23 St. Josephs Vale, LONDON, SE3 0XF.

CURLING, Mr. Tom, MEng ACA *2006;* with Target Consulting Limited, Lawrence House, Lower Bristol Road, BATH, BA2 9ET.

•CURMI, Mr. Christopher Robert, BA FCA *1986;* Deloitte & Touche, Deloitte Place, Mriehel Place, Mriehel Bypass, MRIEHEL BKR3000, MALTA.

CURNOCK, Mrs. Rebecca Kate, BA(Hons) ACA *2003;* 6 Kingsbury Square OFF Kingsbury Street, MARLBOROUGH, WILTSHIRE, SN8 1JF.

CURNOCK, Miss. Xandra Denise, ACA *2010;* 41 Marram Close, Stanway, COLCHESTER, CO3 0PJ.

CURNOW, Mrs. Jennifer Marie, BSc ACA *1993;* Debenhams Plc, Bedford House, Park Street, TAUNTON, TA1 4DB.

CURNOW, Mrs. Kate, BSc(Hons) ACA CTA *2000;* 22 Gingells Farm Road, Charvil, READING, RG10 9DJ.

CURNOW, Mrs. Mary Clare, BSc ACA *1993;* 86 Wellington Road, Timperley, ALTRINCHAM, WA15 7RJ.

CURNOW, Mr. Peter Douglas, FCA *1974;* Flat 5, Theydon Gate, Station Approach, Theydon Bois, EPPING, ESSEX CM16 7HS.

CURNUCK, Mr. Julian Peter, BSc ACA *1995;* Sandown, 11 Wolseley Place, Withington, MANCHESTER, M20 3LR.

CURR, Miss. Lesley Anne, LLB ACA *1997;* Jobsite UK & Worldwide Ltd Langstone Technology Park 2b, Langstone Road, HAVANT, PO9 1SA.

CURRALL, Mr. Duncan James Steel, FCA *1974;* West Country Publications Ltd, 17 Brest Road, Derriford Business Park, PLYMOUTH, DEVON, PL6 5AA.

CURRALL, Mr. Quentin Edmund Hugh, MA ACA *1985;* PO Box 440, WHANGAPARAOA 0943, NEW ZEALAND.

CURRAN, Ms. Ailbhe Grace, BCom ACA *1998;* 189 New Church Road, HOVE, EAST SUSSEX, BN3 4DA.

CURRAN, Mr. Brian William, BSc ACA *1986;* Diversified Agency Services, 437 Madison Avenue, NEW YORK, NY 10022, UNITED STATES.

CURRAN, Ms. Elizabeth Anne, BSc ACA *1988;* 64 Evershot Road, LONDON, N4 3BB.

•CURRAN, Mrs. Helen Christina, BSc ACA *1992;* Helen Curran, 35 Hawthorn Avenue, WILMSLOW, CHESHIRE, SK9 5BR.

CURRAN, Mrs. Jillian, BA ACA *1993;* 48 Armstrong Quay, LIVERPOOL, L3 4EF.

CURRAN, Mr. John Bertram, OBE FCA *1955;* 2 Cote House Lane, Stoke Bishop, BRISTOL, BS9 3UW. (Life Member)

CURRAN, Mr. John Paul, BA FCA *1977;* 29 Courthill, Bearsden, GLASGOW, G61 3SN.

CURRAN, Miss. Louise Anne, ACA *2011;* 5 Mercers Road, LONDON, N19 4PH.

•CURRAN, Mrs. Margaret Elizabeth, LLB FCA *1990;* Curran Tax Consultants Limited, The Cottage, Donkey Lane, Bradmore, NOTTINGHAM, NG11 6PG.

CURRAN, Mr. Mark James, MA ACA *1994;* 84 Knowsley Road Wilpshire, BLACKBURN, BB1 9PN.

CURRAN, Mr. Michael James, FCA *1982;* 6 Houlton Court, BAGSHOT, GU19 5QQ.

CURRAN, Mr. Philip Andrew, BA ACA ATII *1999;* 21 Siding Lane, Rainford, ST.HELENS, WA11 7SR.

CURRAN, Mr. Phillip David, BSc ACA *2001;* Crimond Croasdale Drive, Parbold, WIGAN, LANCASHIRE, WN8 7HR.

CURRAN, Mr. Raymond Derek, LLB FCA *1981;* 7 Sandbrier Close, Walnut Tree, MILTON KEYNES, MK7 7DU.

CURRAN, Mr. Sean Martin, BEng ACA *1996;* Inventive Leisure Ltd, 21 Old Street, ASHTON-UNDER-LYNE, OL6 6LA.

CURRAN, Mr. Stuart Valentine, BA ACA *1991;* 48 Armstrong Quay, Riverside Drive, LIVERPOOL, L3 4EF.

CURREEM, Ms. Zarina Abdul, BA ACA *1993;* Flat A2 14th Floor Nicholson Tower, 8 Wong Nai Chung, Gap Road, WAN CHAI, HONG KONG ISLAND, HONG KONG SAR.

CURRELL, Mr. James Robert, BSc ACA *1996;* Top Floor Flat, 101 Talbot Road, LONDON, W11 2AT.

CURREY, Miss. Joanna, BSc(Hons) ACA *2001;* with BDO LLP, 55 Baker Street, LONDON, W1U 7EU.

CURRIE, Mr. Adrian James, MBA BSc FCA *1991;* 46 Waiwetu Street, Fendalton, CHRISTCHURCH 8052, NEW ZEALAND.

CURRIE, Mr. Alistair Mitchell, BA ACA *1981;* Travelex UK Ltd, 65 Kingsway, LONDON, WC2B 6TD.

CURRIE, Mr. Andrew John, BSc ACA *1992;* 9 Bradshaw Hall Fold, Bradshaw Road, BOLTON, BL2 4JH.

CURRIE, Mr. Anthony Clifton, MBA BA FCA *1978;* 11 Brisson Close, West End, ESHER, KT10 8JZ.

CURRIE, Mr. Brian Murdoch, MA FCA *1963;* (President 1996 - 1997) (Member of Council 1988 - 1998), Westbrook House, Bampton, TIVERTON, EX16 9HU. (Life Member)

CURRIE, Mrs. Caroline Jane, BA ACA *1996;* 35 Brueton Avenue, SOLIHULL, B91 3EN.

CURRIE, Miss. Diane, ACA *2009;* 40a Cranston Road, LONDON, SE23 2HB.

•CURRIE, Ms. Elizabeth Claire, BA ACA *2001;* DNB Accounting Limited, 33 Luccombe Road, SOUTHAMPTON, SO15 7RJ.

•CURRIE, Miss. Fiona Alexandra, FCA *1981;* (Tax Fac), Price & Co, 30-32 Gildredge Road, EASTBOURNE, EAST SUSSEX, BN21 4SH.

CURRIE, Mr. Gordon Andrew Stuart, FCA *1959;* Greenstar Hotels plc, The Great House, Thames Street, Sonning On Thames, READING, RG4 6UT.

CURRIE, Mr. Gordon William, FCA *1953;* 59 Wicks Green, Formby, LIVERPOOL, L37 1PP. (Life Member)

CURRIE, Mrs. Helen Elisabeth, BSc ACA *2004;* 2 The Pavilion, Swalwell, NEWCASTLE UPON TYNE, NE16 3BZ.

CURRIE, Mr. Ian, BA ACA *2005;* 18/27 McGregor Street, Embleton, PERTH, WA 6162, AUSTRALIA.

CURRIE, Mr. Ian Dennis, BSc ACA *1988;* Royal & Sunalliance, PO Box 40, LIVERPOOL, L69 3SD.

CURRIE, Mr. Ian Hamilton, FCA *1970;* 72 Hill Road, Portchester, FAREHAM, PO16 8JY.

CURRIE, Mr. Ian Mark, LLB ACA *1990;* Waterworks Cottage South Meadow Lane Milton, DERBY, DE65 6PL.

CURRIE, Mr. Ian William, BA ACA *1987;* Crabtree House, Hillhouse Lane, Brindle, CHORLEY, PR6 8NR.

•CURRIE, Mrs. Isobel Jane, BSc FCA *1982;* (Tax Fac), Currie Accountancy Limited, 13a High Street, EDENBRIDGE, KENT, TN8 5AB.

•CURRIE, Mr. James Andrew, BA ACA CF *1992;* Catalyst Corporate Finance LLP, 9th Floor, Bank House, 8 Cherry Street, BIRMINGHAM, B2 5AL.

CURRIE, Mr. James Grierson, BSc ACA *2005;* Barclays Capital, Floor 8, 5 North Colonnade, Canary Wharf, LONDON, E14 4BB.

CURRIE, Miss. Josephine Anne, BSc(Hons) ACA *2000;* Debenhams Plc Bedford House, Park Street, TAUNTON, SOMERSET, TA1 4DB.

CURRIE, Mr. Mark Andrew, LLB FCA *1988;* Heathcote Fairoak Lane, Oxshott, LEATHERHEAD, SURREY, KT22 0TP.

CURRIE, Mr. Michael John, BSc(Hons) ACA *2001;* Opsec Security Ltd, 40 Phoenix Road, WASHINGTON, TYNE AND WEAR, NE38 0AD.

•CURRIE, Mr. Neill, FCA *1983;* Jerroms LLP, The Exchange, 26 Haslucks Green Road, Shirley, SOLIHULL, WEST MIDLANDS B90 2EL.

CURRIE, Mr. Oliver Humphrey Raphael, MPhil BA ACA CTA *2003;* (Tax Fac), Gregorciceva 11, 1000 LJUBLJANA, SLOVENIA.

CURRIE, Mr. Peter Jacob, ACA *2003;* Apartment 1, 60 Verdmont Road, SMITHS FL06, BERMUDA.

CURRIE, Mr. Philip Andrew James, FCA *1972;* Lansdowne House, Grayswood Road, HASLEMERE, SURREY, GU27 2BW.

CURRIE, Mr. Raymond Frank, BA FCA *1970;* (Member of Council 1994 - 2001), 160 Western Road, Mickleover, DERBY, DE3 9GT.

CURRIE, Mr. Simon Matthew, BSc ACA *1998;* 1 Orchard Avenue, NEW MALDEN, SURREY, KT3 4JU.

•CURRIE, Mr. Stephen Paul, BA ACA CF *1996;* Catalyst Corporate Finance LLP, 5th Floor, 12-18 Grosvenor Gardens, LONDON, SW1W 0DH.

CURRIE, Mr. Vernon Jeffrey, BA FCA *1973;* 45 Lynwood Avenue, Wall Heath, KINGSWINFORD, WEST MIDLANDS, DY6 9AL.

CURRIE, Mr. William Rognvald, ACA *1980;* 13 Kelsick Park, WORKINGTON, CUMBRIA, CA14 1PY.

CURRIER, Mr. John Simon, BSc ACA *1985;* Flat 3-10, 84 Parkhill Road, LONDON, NW3 2YT.

CURRIER, Mr. Michael Edward, BSc(Hons) ACA *2002;* 14 Ffordd Camlas, Rogerstone, NEWPORT, GWENT, NP10 9LW.

CURRIGAN, Miss. Elaine Mary, BSc ACA *2003;* Lindbergh-Allee 1, 8152 GLATTBRUGG, SWITZERLAND.

CURRIGAN, Mr. Stephen Jeffrey, MBA BSc ACA *1982;* 298 Liverpool Road South, LIVERPOOL, L31 7DJ.

CURRIMBHOY, Mr. Amyn, ACA *1986;* 41-A 19th Street, Off Khayaban-e-Mujahid, Phase V Defence Housing Auth, KARACHI, PAKISTAN.

CURRIMBHOY, Mr. Nazir Gulamali, FCA *1965;* 38 Broughton Avenue, LONDON, N3 3EN.

CURRIMBHOY, Miss. Salimah, LLB ACA *1999;* 38 Broughton Avenue, LONDON, N3 3EN.

•CURRIN, Mrs. Sally Anne, BA ACA *1982;* Sally Currin Ltd, 33 Lower Blackfriars Crescent, St. Marys Water Lane, SHREWSBURY, SY1 2BA.

CURRISTAN, Mr. Anthony, FCA *1981;* McCranor Kirby Hill Chartered Accountants, Clifford House, 38-44 Binley Road, COVENTRY, CV3 1JA.

CURROR, Mr. John Munro, FCA *1974;* Asset Care, Challenge House, 616 Mitcham Road, CROYDON, CR0 3AA.

CURRY, Mr. David Anthony, BSc ACA *1998;* 4 Wallace Parade, LINDFIELD, NSW 2070, AUSTRALIA.

CURRY, Mr. David Robert, ACA *1994;* 97 Route de Peney, 1214 VERNIER, SWITZERLAND.

•CURRY, Miss. Fiona Alexandra, ACA *1979;* (Tax Fac), Fiona Curry & Co, 9 Crookfur Road, Newton Mearns, GLASGOW, G77 6DY.

CURRY, Miss. Georgina Emma, ACA *2009;* First Floor Flat, 6 Scholars Road, LONDON, SW12 0PG.

CURRY, Mr. James Crispin Michael, BSc ACA *1990;* 17 Leven Road, YARM, CLEVELAND, TS15 9EY.

CURRY, Mr. Jason Michael Robert, BSc ACA *1994;* Adjug Limited, Variety Club House, 93 Bayham Street, LONDON, NW1 0AG.

CURRY, Mr. John Arthur Hugh, CBE MA MBA FCA *1964;* Stokewood Park House, Sheardley Lane, Droxford, SOUTHAMPTON, SO32 3QY.

CURRY, Mr. Jonathan Peter Stockwell, BSocSc FCA *1992;* Arcum Ltd, Unit 3, TealeTechnology Centre, Theale, READING, BERKSHIRE RG7 4XX.

CURRY, Mrs. Judith Penelope, BA ACA *1982;* Commonwealth Education Trust, New Zealand House, 80 Haymarket, LONDON, SW1Y 4TE.

CURRY, Miss. Lauren, BEng ACA *2010;* 10 Sedgwick Street, CAMBRIDGE, CB1 3AJ.

CURRY, Miss. Lucy Frances Victorine, BA(Hons) ACA *2002;* Moorstones Ruebury Lane, Osmotherley, NORTHALLERTON, NORTH YORKSHIRE, DL6 3BG.

•CURRY, Mr. Mark Andrew, BSc ACA *1994;* (Tax Fac), Milton Accounting, 10 Lawn Farm Close, Milton Lilbourne, PEWSEY, WILTSHIRE, SN9 5QA.

CURRY, Mr. Martin, BSc ACA *1993;* 18 Hambalt Road, Clapham, LONDON, SW4 9EF.

CURRY, Mr. Michael, BA ACA MBA *1999;* 96 Radnor Road, TWICKENHAM, MIDDLESEX, TW1 4ND.

CURRY, Ms. Natalie, MA BA(Hons) ACA *2002;* Apt 301 Oikothea Building, 12 Olympou Street, 2108 NICOSIA, CYPRUS.

CURRY, Mr. Patrick, BSc ACA CTA *2006;* Garden Flat, 29 Cotham Vale, BRISTOL, BS6 6HS.

CURRY, Mrs. Penelope Jane, BSc ACA *1990;* 17 Leven Road, YARM, TS15 9EY.

CURRY, Mr. Peter Jonathan, BSc ACA *2003;* (Tax Fac), Flat 16 Fairlawns, Putney Hill, LONDON, SW15 6BD.

CURRY, Mr. Philip Andrew, BSc ACA *1990;* 36 Fotheringham Road, ENFIELD, EN1 1QG.

CURRY, Mr. Sean William, BA ACA *1995;* 17 Cowper Street, BRIGHTON, VIC 3186, AUSTRALIA.

CURRY, Mr. Simon John, BSc(Hons) ACA *2001;* 49 Ashlea, HOOK, HAMPSHIRE, RG27 9RQ.

CURRY, Mr. Thomas Mark Jonathan, FCA *1972;* 56 Mill Green, CONGLETON, CHESHIRE, CW12 1JG.

•CURRY, Mr. Timothy John Anderson, MA FCA *1975;* 8 Mount Ararat Road, RICHMOND, SURREY, TW10 6PA.

CURRY, Mr. Timothy Perran, BA ACA *1999;* Locked Bag A3940, SYDNEY, NSW 1235, AUSTRALIA.

CURRY, Mr. William Roy, BCom FCA *1951;* 56 Valley Drive, GATESHEAD, NE9 5DH. (Life Member)

CURSLEY, Ms. Anne, BSc ACA *1986;* 33 Fairmile Lane, COBHAM, KT11 2DL.

CURSON, Miss. Clare Anne, BA ACA *1992;* An der Grenze 18, 1140 VIENNA, AUSTRIA.

CURTEIS, Mr. John Mascall Darby, FCA *1966;* The Cottage, St Hilary, COWBRIDGE, CF71 7DP.

CURTHOYS, Mr. Lee Richard, BSc ACA *2010;* (Tax Fac), 3 Emmanual Flats, 12 Garden Lane St. Helier, JERSEY, JE2 3YE.

CURTIES, Mr. Joshua, BA(Hons) ACA *2011;* 46 Farm Holt, New Ash Green, LONGFIELD, KENT, DA3 8QB.

CURTIN, Mr. Nicholas Simon, BSc ACA *2000;* 32 Grove Road, Church Crookham, FLEET, HAMPSHIRE, GU52 6DX.

CURTIN, Mr. Paul Rodney, BSc FCA *1982;* Park House, Wilsons Road, Headley Down, BORDON, HAMPSHIRE, GU35 8JG.

CURTIN, Miss. Rachel Emma, BSc ACA *1996;* Flat 32 Elgin Mansions, Elgin Avenue, LONDON, W9 1JG.

CURTIN, Mrs. Sarah Jane, BSc(Econ) ACA *2000;* 32 Grove Road, Church Crookham, FLEET, HAMPSHIRE, GU52 6DX.

CURTIS, Miss. Andrea Clare, BA ACA *1997;* 17 West Common Drive, Lindfield, HAYWARDS HEATH, WEST SUSSEX, RH16 2AN.

CURTIS, Mr. Andrew, MA ACA *1995;* 37 Kelsey Way, BECKENHAM, BR3 3LP.

CURTIS, Mrs. Anna Samantha Elizabeth, BA ACA *1991;* 9 South Park Road, Wimbledon, LONDON, SW19 8RR.

CURTIS, Mr. Arthur Charles, FCA *1963;* 10 The Beeches, CHATHAM, KENT, ME5 0NS.

CURTIS, Mr. Barry Dean, BSc(Econ) ACA *2010;* 9 Stainer Close, SOUTHAMPTON, SO19 0JA.

CURTIS, Mr. Chris, BSc ACA *2007;* 2 Acris Court, Acris Street, LONDON, SW18 2QS.

CURTIS, Mr. Christopher Ian, BSc ACA *2004;* 4 Tavern Walk, CORBY, NORTHAMPTONSHIRE, NN18 0TD.

CURTIS, Mrs. Coral Jane, BSc ACA *1999;* 34 Blakes Farm Road, Southwater, HORSHAM, WEST SUSSEX, RH13 9GJ.

CURTIS, Mr. Cyril, FCA *1968;* 63 The Ridgeway, RUISLIP, MIDDLESEX, HA4 8QQ. (Life Member)

CURTIS, Mr. Darren, BSc ACA *1997;* 41 Oakleigh Avenue, LONDON, N20 9JE.

CURTIS, Mr. David Michael, BA ACA *1987;* MacDermid Autotype Ltd, Grove Road, WANTAGE, OXFORDSHIRE, OX12 7BZ.

CURTIS, Mr. David Michael Timothy, BA ACA *1991;* 15 Eliot Place, Blackheath, LONDON, SE3 0QL.

CURTIS, Mr. David Phillip, BSc ACA *2002;* Mears Group Plc Unit 1390 Montpellier Court, Gloucester Business Park Brockworth, GLOUCESTER, GL3 4AH.

•CURTIS, Mr. Dean Michael, ACA *1992;* Maynard Heady LLP, 40-42 High Street, MALDON, ESSEX, CM9 5PN. See also Maynard Heady

•CURTIS, Mr. Derek Reginald, FCA *1973;* (Tax Fac), The Curtis Partnership, 1 Tape Street, Cheadle, STOKE-ON-TRENT, ST10 1BB. See also Curtis Partnership The and Tax Returns Nationwide Ltd

CURTIS, Mr. Douglas McLeod, BA ACA *2000;* 13 Galbraith Crescent, LARBERT, STIRLINGSHIRE, FK5 4GZ.

•CURTIS, Mr. Edmund Vincent, FCA *1985;* Quest Duthoit Limited, 19 Farncombe Road, WORTHING, BN11 2AY.

CURTIS, Mrs. Fiona, BSc ACA *1991;* East Toutley Hall, WOKINGHAM, RG41 1JA.

CURTIS, Mrs. Fiona Stephanie, BSc ACA *1999;* 4 Lodgelands Close, RAYLEIGH, SS6 8TN.
•**CURTIS, Mr. Gavin George, FCA** *1973;* Gavin G. Curtis, 24 Ashley Gardens, Green Street Green, ORPINGTON, BR6 9NH.
CURTIS, Mr. Greg, MA ACA *1993;* Sun Group, Paveletskaya Ploschad 2, Bld 1 Floor 9, 115054 MOSCOW, RUSSIAN FEDERATION.
•**CURTIS, Mr. Henry, FCA** *1973;* Curtis & Co, Bank Chambers, 1-3 Woodford Avenue, Gants Hill, ILFORD, IG2 6UF. See also Kingsleybusiness Online Limited
CURTIS, Mr. Henry Farquharson, FCA *1976;* (Tax Fac), 17 Lower Addison Gardens, LONDON, W14 8BG.
CURTIS, Mr. Howard Stanley, FCA *1972;* with Barker Hibbert & Co, 133 Cherry Orchard Road, CROYDON, CR0 6BE.
CURTIS, Mr. Ian, BA ACA *1994;* HPC plc, Victoria Gardens, BURGESS HILL, WEST SUSSEX, RH15 9RQ.
•**CURTIS, Mr. Ian James, BA ACA** *1989;* 8 Pembridge Road, Dorridge, SOLIHULL, B93 8SA.
CURTIS, Mrs. Ines Therese, BSc ACA *1985;* 45 Arundel Drive West, Saltdean, BRIGHTON, BN2 8SJ.
CURTIS, Mr. Ivor Thomas Chaytor, FCA *1949;* 3 South Crescent, Sowerby, THIRSK, YO7 1QZ. (Life Member)
CURTIS, Mr. James Paul, BA ACA *2004;* E & S J Walpole Ltd, Greens Road, DEREHAM, NORFOLK, NR20 3TG.
CURTIS, Mr. James Richard, FCA *1969;* 28 Amersham Hill Drive, HIGH WYCOMBE, HP13 6QY.
CURTIS, Mr. Jeremy Nigel, FCA *1981;* Meller House, 42 Chagford Street, LONDON, NW1 6EB.
CURTIS, Mrs. Jill Elizabeth, BA ACA *1989;* 8 Pembridge Road, Dorridge, SOLIHULL, B93 8SA.
CURTIS, Miss. Joanne, BA ACA *1997;* Morgan Stanley, Level 46, International Commerce Centre, 1 Austin Road West, TSIM SHA TSUI, KOWLOON HONG KONG SAR.
CURTIS, Mr. John Charles, BSc ACA *1992;* Eucalyptus, Hardingham Road, Hingham, NORWICH, NR9 4LX.
•**CURTIS, Mr. John Edward, FCA** *1976;* 106 Bois Lane, Chesham Bois, AMERSHAM, BUCKINGHAMSHIRE, HP6 6DE.
CURTIS, Mr. John Ernest, FCA *1958;* 250 Queen Street, WITHERNSEA, HU19 2NX. (Life Member)
CURTIS, Mr. John Nicholas Buller, BSc ACA *1988;* 78 Elms Road, LONDON, SW4 9EW.
CURTIS, Mr. John William Gerald, BSc ACA *1991;* 26 Vicarage Drive, LONDON, SW14 8RX.
CURTIS, Mrs. Julia, BSc ACA *1992;* Norwich Cathedral, 12 The Close, NORWICH, NR1 4DH.
CURTIS, Mr. Julian Laver, BSc ACA *1995;* 26 Crabtree Lane, HARPENDEN, AL5 5TE.
CURTIS, Mr. Julian Richard Alan, BSc ACA *1990;* Flat 11 43 Great Titchfield Street, LONDON, W1W 7PQ.
CURTIS, Mrs. Julie Marie, BSc ACA *2008;* Knowles Warwick, 183-185 Fraser Road, SHEFFIELD, S8 0JP.
CURTIS, Mrs. Katherine Lavinia, BSc(Hons) ACA *2004;* Travel Port Unit 1, Hurricane Way, SLOUGH, SL3 8AG.
CURTIS, Mrs. Katy Annabel, BSc ACA *1999;* with KPMG LLP, 15 Canada Square, LONDON, E14 5GL.
CURTIS, Mr. Kenneth Douglas, BA ACA *1989;* 9 South Park Road, Wimbledon, LONDON, SW19 8RR.
•**CURTIS, Mr. Lee, BA FCA** *1995;* (Tax Fac), Bromhead, Harscombe House, 1 Darklake View, Estover, PLYMOUTH, PL6 7TL. See also Bromhead Limited
CURTIS, Mr. Lee Graham, BA ACA *2002;* Ernst & Young Llp, 1 More London Place, LONDON, SE1 2AF.
CURTIS, Mr. Leonard Cyril, FCA *1946;* 12 Woodruff Avenue, HOVE, EAST SUSSEX, BN3 6PG. (Life Member)
•**CURTIS, Mr. Martin Philip, LLB FCA** *1977;* M.P. Curtis, New Barn Farm, Lindsell, DUNMOW, CM6 3QH.
CURTIS, Mr. Matthew, MA ACA *1985;* 152 Granville Road, LONDON, NW2 2LD.
•**CURTIS, Mr. Michael John, FCA** *1976;* M.J. Curtis & Co, 222 Broadgate House, Broadgate, COVENTRY, CV1 1NG.
CURTIS, Mr. Michael Peter John, BA FCA *1995;* 65 Chamberlain Way, PINNER, MIDDLESEX, HA5 2AT.
•**CURTIS, Mr. Neil McLean, BSc FCA** *1986;* Eacotts Limited, Grenville Court, Britwell Road, Burnham, SLOUGH, SL1 8DF. See also Eacotts
•**CURTIS, Mr. Neil Ralph, BSc FCA** *1980;* Thompson Jenner LLP, 28 Alexandra Terrace, EXMOUTH, DEVON, EX8 1BD.
CURTIS, Mr. Nicholas John, BSc FCA *1978;* Whitehouse Farm, Dwelly Lane, EDENBRIDGE, TN8 6QG.
CURTIS, Mr. Nicholas Simon, BSc ACA *1992;* 2 St Barnabas Villas, Stockwell, LONDON, SW8 2EH.
CURTIS, Dr. Nicola, BSc ACA *1999;* The Homestead, 27 Wicken Road, Newport, SAFFRON WALDEN, ESSEX, CB11 3QF.
•**CURTIS, Mrs. Patricia, FCA** *1975;* The Curtis Partnership, 1 Tape Street, Cheadle, STOKE-ON-TRENT, ST10 1BB. See also Curtis Partnership The and Tax Returns Nationwide Ltd
CURTIS, Mr. Paul Bernard, BSc ACA *1987;* 26 Regent Street, BRIGHTON EAST, VIC 3187, AUSTRALIA.
CURTIS, Mr. Paul James, MSc ACA *2004;* 9 Bruntwood Avenue, Heald Green, CHEADLE, SK8 3RT.
•**CURTIS, Mr. Paul James, FCA** *1983;* (Tax Fac), Cleethorpes Accountancy Limited, 3 Wardall Street, CLEETHORPES, DN35 8HA.
CURTIS, Mr. Paul Michael, BA ACA *2003;* 54 Ridgeway, Wargrave, READING, RG10 8AS.
CURTIS, Mr. Peter Howard, BA(Econ) FCA *1978;* 20 St. Hilda's Wharf, 160 Wapping High Street, LONDON, E1W 3PG.
•**CURTIS, Mr. Peter John, FCA** *1989;* (Tax Fac), Curtis & Co, 14 Crossfell Road, HEMEL HEMPSTEAD, HERTFORDSHIRE, HP3 8RF.
CURTIS, Mr. Peter John, FCA *1964;* 32 Marina Avenue, Motspur Park, NEW MALDEN, KT3 6NQ.
CURTIS, Mrs. Philippa, BSc ACA *1989;* Rock House Rock House Lane, Runfold, FARNHAM, SURREY, GU10 1NR.
CURTIS, Mrs. Philippa Mary, BSc ACA *1989;* Flat 20, 160 Wapping High Street, LONDON, E1W 3PG.
CURTIS, Mr. Richard John, BSc ACA *2001;* 504 Groveley Lane, Cofton Hackett, BIRMINGHAM, B45 8UB.
•**CURTIS, Mr. Richard Simon, FCA** *1974;* Alliotts, Congress House, 14 Lyon Road, HARROW, MIDDLESEX, HA1 2EN.
CURTIS, Mr. Robert Cyril, FCA *1952;* 12 Churchill Avenue, Kenton, HARROW, HA3 0AY. (Life Member)
•**CURTIS, Mr. Roger William Holbrook, FCA** *1973;* (Tax Fac), Holbrook Curtis Ltd, 1 Imperial Square, CHELTENHAM, GLOUCESTERSHIRE, GL50 1QB.
•**CURTIS, Mr. Ronald Frank, FCA** *1972;* (Tax Fac), Curtis & Co, 16 Middlefield, Bardsley, OLDHAM, OL8 2TP.
CURTIS, Mr. Simon Christopher, MA FCA *1989;* 36 Woodlands Road, EAST LINDFIELD, NSW 2070, AUSTRALIA.
CURTIS, Mr. Simon Peter, BSc ACA *1995;* Flat 20, 57a Chalk Farm Road, LONDON, NW1 8AN.
CURTIS, Mr. Stephen John, BSc FCA *1979;* Louis Group (IOM) Ltd, Louis Building, 29 Bucks Road, Douglas, ISLE OF MAN, IM1 3DE.
CURTIS, Mr. Stuart, FCA *1961;* 176 Ffordd y Parc, BRIDGEND, MID GLAMORGAN, CF31 1RA.
CURTIS, Mr. Thomas, MA MEng ACA ATII *1999;* Oxford Instruments Group Plc, Tubney Wood, ABINGDON, OXFORDSHIRE, OX13 5QX.
CURTIS, Mr. William Joseph, FCA *1962;* 27 Lynton Street, DOUBLEVIEW, WA 6018, AUSTRALIA. (Life Member)
CURTIS-LEWIS, Miss. Eleanor, ACA *2011;* 62 Lavernock Road, PENARTH, SOUTH GLAMORGAN, CF64 3PA.
CURTIS-POWELL, Mr. Stephen, BSc ACA *2001;* 1 Hazelbank Finchampstead, WOKINGHAM, RG40 4XD.
CURTIS-SMITH, Mrs. Aiko, BA ACA *2003;* 77 Lower Cookham Road, MAIDENHEAD, BERKSHIRE, SL6 8JY.
•**CURWEN, Mrs. Caroline, BMus FCA** *1998;* Curwen & Co Limited, 44 Queens Drive, Heaton Mersey, STOCKPORT, CHESHIRE, SK4 3JW.
•**CURWEN, Mr. John Andrew, BSc FCA** *1984;* The Coach House, Rectory Lane, Etton, PETERBOROUGH, PE6 7DB.
•**CURWEN, Mr. Jonathan Gregory, BA(Hons) ACA** *2002;* Afford Bond LLP, 31 Wellington Road, NANTWICH, CHESHIRE, CW5 7ED. See also Afford Astbury Bond LLP
CURWEN, Mr. Philip James, BSc ACA *1998;* Shelley Oak Ltd Wesley House, Bull Hill, LEATHERHEAD, KT22 7AH.
CURWEN, Mr. Stewart Robert, FCA *1949;* 22 Ellingham Close, ALRESFORD, SO24 9EY. (Life Member)
CURZON, Mrs. Avril, FCA *1971;* 32 Gleneagles, off Gordon Avenue, STANMORE, MIDDLESEX, HA7 3QG.
CURZON, Mr. Malcolm Samuel, FCA *1968;* 52 Chiltern Avenue, BUSHEY, WD23 4RG.
•**CURZON, Mr. Terence Stuart, FCA** *1970;* (Tax Fac), The KBSP Partnership, Harben House, Harben Parade, Finchley Road, LONDON, NW3 6LH. See also Stardata Business Services Limited
CURZON-TOMPSON, Mr. Roger Howard Lawrence, FCA *1958;* 22 Green Hill Road, CAMBERLEY, GU15 1PE. (Life Member)
CUSACK, Mr. Andrew Iain, LLB ACA *2005;* 40 Claremont Road, TUNBRIDGE WELLS, KENT, TN1 1TA.
CUSACK, Mrs. Fenella Jane Sara, BSc ACA *2004;* 40 Claremont Road, Royal Tunbridge Wells, TUNBRIDGE WELLS, KENT, TN1 1TA.
CUSACK, Miss. Fiona Louise, BSc ACA *2006;* 61, 102 Miller Street, Pyrmont, SYDNEY, NSW 2009, AUSTRALIA.
CUSACK, Mr. Julian Michael, PhD BSc ACA *1980;* 115 Providence Square, LONDON, SE1 2ED.
CUSACK, Mr. Mark Paul John, MA FCA ACA *1984; (ACA Ireland 1982);* Malvern House, 6 St. Mary's Road, Wimbledon, LONDON, SW19 7BW.
CUSDEN, Mr. Ian Vincent, BA ACA *1982;* 20 Pasture Road, LETCHWORTH GARDEN CITY, HERTFORDSHIRE, SG6 3LP.
CUSENS, Mr. Jeffrey, ACA *2003;* Betfair International Limited, Kappilan Mifsud Street, SANTA VENERA SVR1851, MALTA.
CUSHING, Miss. Claire May, BSc ACA *2001;* Cararra 0, Island Site, Surrey Street, NORWICH, NR1 3NX.
CUSHING, Mr. Jonathan Edward, ACA *2009;* 8 Waterloo Court, Dinnington, SHEFFIELD, S25 3RT.
CUSHING, Mr. Martin Keith, BA ACA *1993;* PO BOX 5171, HUNTER REGION MC, NSW 2310, AUSTRALIA.
CUSHING, Mrs. Susan Margaret, ACA *1984;* Gargrave Cottage, Woodseaves, MARKET DRAYTON, TF9 2AT.
CUSHION, Mr. Graham John, FCA *1959;* 67 Stanley Street, NEDLANDS, WA 6009, AUSTRALIA. (Life Member)
CUSHION, Mr. Peter, BA(Hons) ACA *2000;* 4 Shipton Close, LIVERPOOL, L19 7PG.
CUSHION, Mrs. Tracy, BA ACA *1990;* Barnes Roffe Llp, Leytonstone House, Hanbury Drive, LONDON, E11 1GA.
CUSHNAHAN, Mr. Paul Stephen, BA ACA *2000;* Paul Cushnahan, 2 Ballinclea Woods, KILLINEY, COUNTY DUBLIN, IRELAND.
CUSHNIR, Mr. Alan Maurice, FCA *1961;* 33 Caldecote Gardens, BUSHEY, HERTFORDSHIRE, WD23 4GP.
•**CUSICK, Ms. Laura Joanne, MA ACA** *1997;* Laura Cusick, 27 Midholm, LONDON, NW11 6LL.
CUSICK, Mr. Nicholas Jonathan Paul, BA ACA *1988;* 8 Pennington Drive, CARLISLE, CA3 0PF.
CUSK, Mr. Anthony Nigel John, BSc ACA *1988;* 3 Paper Mille Drive, REDDITCH, B98 8QJ.
CUSS, Mr. David Hilary Alexander, BA FCA *1982;* 43 Shakespeare Road, Hanwell, LONDON, W7 1LT.
CUSSONS, Mr. Andrew Michael, BA ACA *1984;* 2 Parish Ghyll Road, ILKLEY, WEST YORKSHIRE, LS29 9NE.
CUSSONS, Mr. Benjamin Frederick, ACA *2010;* 31 Bartrums Mews, DISS, NORFOLK, IP22 4RL.
CUSSONS, Mr. Christopher Loughlin, FCA *1975;* 67 Morland Close, HAMPTON, TW12 3YY.
•**CUSSONS, Mr. Peter Cousland, MA ACA** *1979;* PricewaterhouseCoopers LLP, 1 Embankment Place, LONDON, WC2N 6RH. See also PricewaterhouseCoopers
CUSSONS, Mr. Simon Hamish, FCA *1966;* 7 Earlston Court, Dee Hills Park, CHESTER, CH3 5BQ. (Life Member)
•①**CUSTANCE, Mr. Arthur Charles, FCA** *1972;* Arthur C Custance, Tigh na Bruaich, Garbhein Road, KINLOCHLEVEN, ARGYLL, PH50 4SE.
CUSTIS, Mr. Patrick James, CBE FCA JDipMA *1951;* (Member of Council 1979 - 1985), 18 Richmond Village, Stroud Road, Painswick, GLOUCESTER, GLOUCESTERSHIRE, GL6 6UH. (Life Member)
CUSWORTH, Mr. James Bruce, BA FCA *1975;* 155 Middle Drive, Darras Hall, NEWCASTLE UPON TYNE, NE20 9DU.
CUTCLIFFE, Mr. Norman Gwilym, FCA *1968;* 528 Dalmeny Hill, CALGARY T3A 1T6, AB, CANADA.
CUTHBERT, Mr. Austin Derrick, BSc ACA *1996;* Shell UK Oil Products Ltd Rowlandsway House, Rowlandsway, MANCHESTER, M22 5SB.
CUTHBERT, Mr. Barry Gordon, FCA *1978;* The Ramblers Furze Lane, Stock, INGATESTONE, ESSEX, CM4 9RW.
CUTHBERT, Mr. Christopher Mark, BA ACA *1989;* PricewaterhouseCoopers, Darling Park Tower 2, 201 Sussex Street, GPO Box 2650, SYDNEY, NSW 1171 AUSTRALIA.
CUTHBERT, Mr. Ian, BSc ACA *1994;* 27 Dorchester Court, Liebenrood Road, READING, RG30 2DS.
CUTHBERT, Mr. John, MA ACA *1979;* 26 Whitmore Road, HARROW, HA1 4AB.
CUTHBERT, Mr. John Arthur, OBE DL BSc ACA *1979;* 9 Larwood Court, CHESTER LE STREET, COUNTY DURHAM, DH3 3QQ.
CUTHBERT, Mr. Michael William, BA ACA *1981;* Gold Crest Holidays Holiday House, Valley Drive, ILKLEY, WEST YORKSHIRE, LS29 8PB.
CUTHBERT, Mr. Nathan, BSc ACA *2010;* 22 Edward Street, Southborough, TUNBRIDGE WELLS, KENT, TN4 0HA.
•**CUTHBERT, Mr. Philip, ACA FCCA** *2008;* M. Wasley Chapman & Co, 3 Victoria Square, WHITBY, NORTH YORKSHIRE, YO21 1EA.
CUTHBERT, Mr. Robert, BSc ACA *1988;* 15 BAYNARDS LANE, RICHMOND HILL L4C 9B2, ON, CANADA.
CUTHBERT, Miss. Sarah Louise, ACA *2008;* Flat 3, 8 St. Marys Walk, HARROGATE, NORTH YORKSHIRE, HG2 0LW.
CUTHBERT, Mr. Stephen Colin, CBE FCA *1968;* Long Meadow, 61 Burkes Road, BEACONSFIELD, HP9 1PW. (Life Member)
CUTHBERT, Ms. Wendy, ACA *1992;* 6 Braid Drive, Cardross, DUMBARTON, G82 5QD.
CUTHBERT, Mr. William John, FCA *1972;* White Lodge, Upper Bullington, Sutton Scotney, WINCHESTER, SO21 3RB.
CUTHBERT-SMITH, Mr. Peter Lawrence, BA FCA *1962;* Holly Tree Cottage, Botany Bay, Tintern, CHEPSTOW, NP16 6NJ. (Life Member)
CUTHBERTSON, Mr. Boyd, ACA *1983;* 6 Hillbury Gardens, WARLINGHAM, CR6 9TQ.
CUTHBERTSON, Mr. Christopher John, BSc FCA *1980;* 17 Wheatsheaf Wharf, Wheatsheaf Lane, LONDON, SW6 6LS.
•**CUTHBERTSON, Mr. Colin, MA FCA** *1985;* Cuthbertson Hewitt Limited, 5 Hill Gardens, MARKET HARBOROUGH, LE16 9EB.
CUTHBERTSON, Mr. Douglas, FCA *1977;* Isos Housing Limited, No 5, Gosforth Park Avenue, Gosforth Business Park, NEWCASTLE UPON TYNE, NE12 8EG.
CUTHBERTSON, Mr. John William, MA FCA *1978;* A1 Business Park, Great North Road, KNOTTINGLEY, WEST YORKSHIRE, WF11 0BS.
CUTHBERTSON, Mr. Robert Ian, FCA *1970;* 14 Ffriddoedd Road, BANGOR, GWYNEDD, LL57 2EH.
CUTHBERTSON, Mr. Simon Alexander, MEng ACA *1996;* (Tax Fac), 78 Cranley Gardens, Muswell Hill, LONDON, N10 3AJ.
CUTHBERTSON, Mr. Simon Mark, ACA *1979;* Orpheus Corporate Finance LLP, The Old Coach House Lodge Road, Sharnbrook, BEDFORD, MK44 1JP.
CUTHELL, Mrs. Elizabeth Anne, BSc ACA *2001;* 38A Corrie Road, NORTH MANLY, NSW 2100, AUSTRALIA.
CUTHILL, Mr. Colin Neil, BCom ACA AMCT *1993;* Lucite International UK, Cassel Works, New Road, PO Box 8, BILLINGHAM, CLEVELAND TS23 1LE.
CUTLER, Mr. Adam Ephraim, MA FCA *1998;* with Deloitte LLP, 2 New Street Square, LONDON, EC4A 3BZ.
CUTLER, Mr. Alan Charles John, BA ACA *1985;* 33 Tennyson Road, HARPENDEN, HERTFORDSHIRE, AL5 4BD.
CUTLER, Mrs. Barbara Nerys Cromwell, FCA *1982;* Ormsary Estate Office, Ormsary Farmers, Ormsary, LOCHGILPHEAD, ARGYLL, PA31 8PE.
CUTLER, Mr. Clive Richmond, FCA *1972;* 24 Woodbourne, Augustus Road, BIRMINGHAM, B15 3PH.
CUTLER, Mr. David John Colin, MA MBA FCA CTA CPA *1982;* Cutler & Co PC, 2460 West 26th Avenue, Suite 380C, DENVER, CO 80211, UNITED STATES.
CUTLER, Mr. David Richard, FCA *1966;* Alterian plc, Spectrum House, Bond Street, BRISTOL, BS1 3LG.
•**CUTLER, Mr. Gordon, FCA** *1966;* (Tax Fac), Gordon Cutler & Co Limited, The Maybird Suite, The Maybird Centre, Birmingham Road, STRATFORD-UPON-AVON, WARWICKSHIRE CV37 0HZ.
CUTLER, Mrs. Jennifer Louise, BSocSc ACA *2004;* 35 Walsall Road, Little Aston, SUTTON COLDFIELD, WEST MIDLANDS, B74 3BA.
•**CUTLER, Mr. John Ernest, BSc FCA** *1977;* (Tax Fac), Adje Limited, Orchard Lea, High Street, Tisbury, SALISBURY, SP3 6HF.
CUTLER, Mr. John Graham, BA FCA *1984;* Wedmans Lodge, Wedmans Lane, Rotherwick, HOOK, RG27 9BN.
CUTLER, Mrs. Kirstene, BA ACA *1995;* 33 Tennyson Road, HARPENDEN, HERTFORDSHIRE, AL5 4BD.
CUTLER, Mrs. Linda Anne, BSc ACA CTA *1999;* Cadbury Schweppes Plc, 25 Berkeley Square, LONDON, W1J 6HB.
CUTLER, Mr. Martin James, ACA *1987;* PO Box 5286, STAFFORD HEIGHTS, QLD 4053, AUSTRALIA.
CUTLER, Mr. Michael, FCA *1960;* Birnam, The Street, West Clandon, GUILDFORD, GU4 7ST. (Life Member)

CUTLER, Mr. Peter John Lewis, FCA *1978;* 8 Culley View, ALRESFORD, SO24 9PD.
CUTLER, Mr. Richard Stephen, FCA *1959;* Four Winds, Edenvale, Dormans Park, EAST GRINSTEAD, RH19 2LT.
CUTLER, Mr. Robert Stewart Martin, BA ACA *1997;* 18 Aslett Street, LONDON, SW18 2BN.
•CUTLER, Mrs. Shona Mary, BSc FCA *1983;* (Tax Fac), Clement Keys, 39/40 Calthorpe Road, Edgbaston, BIRMINGHAM, B15 1TS.
CUTLER, Mr. Stephen Joseph, MA FCA DChA CDir *1976;* 8 Larch Close, CAMBERLEY, GU15 4DB.
•CUTLER, Mr. Timothy Charles, BSc(Hons) ACA *2001;* with KPMG LLP, St. James's Square, MANCHESTER, M2 6DS.
CUTMORE, Mr. Martin James, BA FCA *1989;* 43 Broadhurst Drive, Kennington, ASHFORD, KENT, TN24 9RQ.
CUTMORE-SCOTT, Mr. Sam, BA ACA *2010;* 52 Eaton Mews North, LONDON, SW1X 8LL.
CUTNER, Mr. John, FCA *1955;* Great Dairy Farm, Dauntsey, CHIPPENHAM, SN15 4JA. (Life Member)
CUTNER, Mr. Maurice, FCA *1953;* Flat 16, Rossetti House, 106-110 Hallam Street, LONDON, W1W 5HG. (Life Member)
CUTRESS, Mr. Jonathan Peter George, BA ACA *1984;* Manor Farmhouse, Great Moulton, NORWICH, NR15 2JZ.
CUTRI, Mrs. Kirsty Elizabeth, FCA *1997;* The Old Barns, Leicester Road, Husbands Bosworth, LUTTERWORTH, LEICESTERSHIRE, LE17 6NW.
CUTTER, Mr. David John, BA ACA *1987;* Prospect House, High Bradley Lane, Bradley, KEIGHLEY, BD20 9EX.
CUTTER, Mrs. Kathryn Sian, BA(Hons) ACA *2004;* 19 West Ridge, Frampton Cotterell, BRISTOL, BS36 2JA.
CUTTER, Mr. Martyn David, BA(Hons) ACA *2004;* RWE UK IT, Mistral Westlea Campus Chelmsford Road, SWINDON, SN5 7EZ.
•CUTTER, Mr. Paul James, BA(Hons) ACA *2003;* (Tax Fac), David Cutter & Co, 2 Lyttleton Court, Birmingham Street, HALESOWEN, WEST MIDLANDS, B63 3HN. See also Cutter & Co Limited
CUTTERIDGE, Mr. Simon Nicholas Ralph, FCA *1973;* 23 Bedfordbury, LONDON, WC2N 4BN.
CUTTIFORD, Mr. Nicholas, BSc FCA *1979;* Bay Grove, La Vallee de St. Pierre, St. Lawrence, JERSEY, JE3 1EU.
•CUTTING, Miss. Hannah Claire, BA ACA *2005;* (Tax Fac), R.A. Leslie & Co LLP, Gowran House, 56 Broad Street, Chipping Sodbury, BRISTOL, BS37 6AG. See also R.A. Leslie & Co
CUTTING, Mrs. Helen, ACA *2008;* Candlewick Cottage, 1 Knutsford Road, Chelford, MACCLESFIELD, CHESHIRE, SK11 9AS.
CUTTING, Mrs. Kerry June, BA(Hons) ACA *2002;* (Tax Fac), 58 Beeleigh Link, CHELMSFORD, CM2 6RG.
CUTTING, Mr. Michael Edward, BSc FCA *1982;* Garden Flat, 4B Belsize Lane, LONDON, NW3 5AB.
CUTTING, Mr. Neil Graham, BSc FCA MBA *1996;* 5 Mount Beacon Row, Richmond Lane, Lansdown, BATH, BA1 5QH.
CUTTING, Mrs. Patricia Elaine, BA(Hons) ACA *2003;* 89 Kipling Way, STOWMARKET, SUFFOLK, IP14 1TS.
CUTTING, Mr. Phillip James, BSc ACA *1989;* 515 Burdick Street, LIBERTYVILLE, IL 60048, UNITED STATES.
•CUTTING, Mrs. Samantha Jane, BA ACA *1996;* (Tax Fac), Samantha Cutting ACA, 7 Beechwood Close, Whitfield, DOVER, KENT, CT16 3JZ.
CUTTING, Mr. Tim, ACA *2008;* with Deloitte LLP, PO Box 500, 2 Hardman Street, MANCHESTER, M60 2AT.
•CUTTS, Dr. Alison, PhD BSc ACA MBA *1998;* Blueface Consulting Limited, Mill Farm, Allendale, HEXHAM, NORTHUMBERLAND, NE47 9EQ.
CUTTS, Mr. Brian Albert, BSc FCA *1967;* 55 St. Peters Avenue, Caversham, READING, RG4 7DP. (Life Member)
CUTTS, Mr. Jacob Alexander, BSc ACA *2000;* 2 School Lane Cottages, School Lane, Shipbourne, TONBRIDGE, KENT, TN11 9RT.
CUTTS, Mr. James Arthur, FCA *1954;* The Pastures, Keddington, LOUTH, LN11 7HQ. (Life Member)
•CUTTS, Miss. Kathryn Margaret, BSc FCA *1999;* Vale & West, Victoria House, 26 Queen Victoria Street, READING, RG1 1TG.
CUTTS, Mrs. Margaret Ann, FCA *1970;* 55 St. Peters Avenue, Caversham, READING, BERKSHIRE, RG4 7DP. (Life Member)
CUTTS, Mr. Philip Martin, BSc ACA *1980;* 65 Cole Park Road, TWICKENHAM, TW1 1HT.
CUTTS, Miss. Sally, BA ACA *1994;* 22 Rolling Wood Drive, STAMFORD, CT 06905, UNITED STATES.
•CUTTS, Mr. Stephen John, BSc ACA *1990;* with BDO LLP, 1 Bridgewater Place, Water Lane, LEEDS, LS11 5RU.
CUTTS, Mr. William Noel, FCA *1952;* 16 Old Manor Close, Woodborough, NOTTINGHAM, NG14 6DJ. (Life Member)
CYBULSKI, Mr. Jan, ACA *2011;* Apartment 56, Cutlass Court, 28 Granville Street, BIRMINGHAM, B1 2LS.
•CYMERMAN, Mr. Selwyn, FCA ATII *1987;* (Tax Fac), Harold Everett Wreford LLP, 1st Floor, 44-46 Whitfield Street, LONDON, W1T 2RJ.
CYPHER, Mr. James Benedict, BCom ACA *2001;* 1 Bridge Meadow Drive, Knowle, SOLIHULL, B93 9QG.
•CYPHER, Mrs. Yvonne, BSc(Hons) ACA *2001;* (Tax Fac), PricewaterhouseCoopers LLP, Cornwall Court, 19 Cornwall Street, BIRMINGHAM, B3 2DT. See also PricewaterhouseCoopers
•CYROOS, Miss. Narges, BSc ACA *1988;* MZ Accountants, 51 Creighton Road, Ealing, LONDON, W5 4SH.
•CYSARZ, Mr. Richard Michael Gilbert, BSc FCA *1991;* KPMG Audyt Sp. z o.o, ul. Chlodna 51, XVI Floor, WARSAW, 00-867, POLAND.
CZARNIECKA, Miss. Anna Antonina, LLB FCA *1971;* 1 Fieldsway House, Fieldway Crescent, LONDON, N5 1QA.
CZASZNICKI, Mr. Jerzy Wojciech, BA ACA *1982;* The Minstrels, 58 Green Lane, Burnham, SLOUGH, SL1 8EB.
CZEKIRDA, Mr. Peter, BSc ACA *1995;* SCA Personal Care, Terminal Stcasse Mitte 18, Munich Airport, 85356 MUNICH, GERMANY.
CZERNIAWSKI, Mr. Jan Kazimierz, MA FCA *1978;* UL. Czerwonego Krzyza 6/18, 00 377 Warszawa, WARSAW, POLAND.
•CZERWONKA, Mr. John Joseph, BSc ACA *1980;* Redmayne & Co, The Old Bank House, Harris Court, Wellgate, CLITHEROE, BB7 2DP.
•CZORNYJ, Mr. Steven Andrew, FCA *1982;* Forrester Boyd, Waynflete House, 139 Eastgate, LOUTH, LN11 9QQ.
CZURA, Mrs. Lucy Patricia, BA ACA *1996;* 8 Southampton Road, FAREHAM, HAMPSHIRE, PO16 7DY.
CZURA, Mr. Peter, ACA *1996;* Comrie, 8 Southampton Road, FAREHAM, HAMPSHIRE, PO16 7DY.
CZYZOWICZ, Miss. Maria, BSc ACA *1992;* 36 Effra Road, Wimbledon, LONDON, SW19 8PP.
D'ABBRACCIO, Ms. Maria Louisa, BSc ACA *1997;* PO Box 1739, CHRISTCHURCH, NEW ZEALAND.
D'ABREO, Mr. John Alfred James, FCA *1960;* 32 Navarino Road, WORTHING, BN11 2NF. (Life Member)
D'ABRERA, Ms. Romaine Mary Caryll, FCA *1973;* PO Box 279, WINSTON HILLS, NSW 2153, AUSTRALIA.
D'ALEWYN, Mr. Steven Bernard, BA ACA *1985;* PO Box CB 13232, NASSAU, BAHAMAS.
D'ANGELO, Mr. Enrico, BSc ACA *1992;* Lea Meadow Jumps Road, Churt, FARNHAM, GU10 2JZ.
D'APOLITO, Mr. Arcangelo, ACA *2009;* 88 Longfield Avenue, LONDON, NW7 2SA.
D'ARCY, Mrs. Ann Marie, BA(Hons) ACA *2002;* 4 Farm Mount, Netherton, WAKEFIELD, WF4 4TS.
•D'ARCY, Mr. Anthony Richard Hugh, FCA *1981;* Anthony D'Arcy FCA, Bourne House, 10 Sandrock Hill Road, Wrecclesham, FARNHAM, SURREY GU10 4NS.
D'ARCY, Mr. Gareth John, MA(Hons) ACA *2002;* 32 Hermitage Gardens, CHESTER LE STREET, COUNTY DURHAM, DH2 3UD.
D'ARCY, Mr. Mark Robert, BSc(Hons) ACA *2000;* 10 Cooper Close, Mossley Hill, LIVERPOOL, L19 3PP.
•D'ARCY, Mr. Paul James, ACA *1992;* Ernst & Young LLP, 1 More London Place, LONDON, SE1 2AF. See also Ernst & Young Europe LLP
D'ARCY, Mr. Paul James, BEng ACA *1998;* Morgan Stanley, 20 Cabot Square, Canary Wharf, LONDON, E14 4QW.
D'ARCY, Mr. Simon Hunter, BSc ACA *2005;* 5 Hastings Street, LONDON, SE18 6SY.
D'ARCY-IRVINE, Miss. Alexandra, BA ACA *2000;* Upper Flat, 87 Stephendale Road, LONDON, SW6 2LT.
D'ARCY ORDERS, Mr. Derek Clive, MBE LLM MA FCA *1945;* 21 Gretton Court, Girton, CAMBRIDGE, CB3 0QN. (Life Member)
D'AUBNEY, Mr. Alistair John, BCom FCA *1992;* 20 Oaklands Road, SUTTON COLDFIELD, WEST MIDLANDS, B74 2TB.
D'AUBYN, Mrs. Emma Louise, ACA *2008;* Garden Apartment, 4 Manor Villas, BATH, BA1 3PF.
D'BRASS, Mrs. Lucy Jane, BSc ACA *1999;* 50 Soldiers Avenue, HARBORD, NSW 2096, AUSTRALIA.
D'COSTA, Mrs. Carolyn Ann, BA(Hons) ACA *2002;* 42 Southampton Street, FARNBOROUGH, HAMPSHIRE, GU14 6BG.
D'CRUZ, Mr. Christopher Michael, ACA *1981;* 7 Wainwright Avenue, RICHMOND HILL L4C 5R4, ON, CANADA.
D'CRUZ, Mrs. Kay, BSc ACA *2003;* 36 Lancaster Road, HARROW, MIDDLESEX, HA2 7NL.
D'CRUZ, Mrs. Marie Therese, ACA *1991;* 5 Forrest Aveneue, WAHROONGA, NSW 2076, AUSTRALIA.
D'CRUZ, Mr. Simon Nicholas, BSc ACA *2001;* 36 Lancaster Road, HARROW, MIDDLESEX, HA2 7NL.
D'CRUZ, Mr. Trevlyn Raphaell, FCA *1961;* 9 Allfarthing Lane, LONDON, SW18 2PG.
•D'CRUZ, Mr. Vincent Colin, FCA *1980;* D'Cruz & Co., 21 Hanworth Road, REDHILL, RH1 5HS.
D'EATH, Mr. James Terence, FCA *1957;* 1 Stephenson Road, CANTERBURY, CT2 7LA. (Life Member)
•D'ERLANGER, Mr. Robin Gerard, FCA *1968;* Hensleigh Cottage, Hensleigh, TIVERTON, DEVON, EX16 5NH.
D'INVERNO, Mrs. Isobel Jane, MA ACA ATII *1984;* (Tax Fac), Brodies LLP, 15 Atholl Crescent, EDINBURGH, EH3 8HA.
D'JANOEFF, Mr. Alexander Constatine Basil, FCA *1977;* Flat 11, Cadogan Court, Draycott Avenue, LONDON, SW3 3BX.
D'LIMA, Mr. Garth Augustine Marshall Benedict, FCA *1975;* 24 Wedderburn Road, LONDON, NW3 5QG.
D'MELLO, Mr. Joseph, BSc FCA *1992;* 5 Oscar Close, PURLEY, SURREY, CR8 2LU.
D'NETTO, Mr. David, BSc(Hons) ACA *2011;* 9 Dacre Street, MORPETH, NORTHUMBERLAND, NE61 1HW.
D'OFFAY, Mr. Jean-Paul, MSc ACA *2001;* 6 Dancer Road, RICHMOND, SURREY, TW9 4LA.
•D'SILVA, Mr. Alan Joseph Savio, FCA *1984;* PricewaterhouseCoopers, Paseo de la Castellana 53, 28046 MADRID, SPAIN. See also Alan D'Silva & Co
•D'SILVA, Mr. Gordon Patrick, BSc ACA *1985;* Gordons Knight & Co Ltd, Pendragon House, 170 Merton High Street, LONDON, SW19 1AY. See also Success Story Builder LLP
•D'SILVA, Dr. Kenneth Edgar Joseph, PhD MSc FCA *1971;* 4A Rutland Park Gardens, LONDON, NW2 4RG.
D'SOUZA, Mr. Adrian, ACA *2010;* 4 Holness Road, LONDON, E15 4EN.
D'SOUZA, Mr. Andrew Dominic Joseph, MEng ACA *2003;* 22 Segrave Close, WEYBRIDGE, SURREY, KT13 0TD.
D'SOUZA, Mr. Anthony Francis, MEng ACA *1999;* Lexicon Partners, 1 Paternoster Square, LONDON, EC4M 7DX.
D'SOUZA, Miss. Cymbeline Cecelia, ACA *1984;* Margaret House, 23 Manor Street, Ardwick, MANCHESTER, M12 6HE.
D'SOUZA, Mr. Deonne, BSc ACA *1994;* UBS AG, Level 32 Two Exchange Square, 8 Connaught Road, CENTRAL, HONG KONG SAR.
D'SOUZA, Mrs. Helen, BA ACA *2003;* National Audit Office, 157-197 Buckingham Palace Road, LONDON, SW1W 9SP.
D'SOUZA, Mr. Jeral Sylvester, BA ACA *1984;* Cargill Asia Pacific Ltd, 300 Beach Road 23-01, The Concourse, SINGAPORE 199555, SINGAPORE.
D'SOUZA, Mr. Josh Lawrence, BCom ACA *2010;* 7 Waycross Road, UPMINSTER, RM14 1LZ.
D'SOUZA, Mr. Merwyn, ACA *2008;* 28 Belmont Avenue, NEW MALDEN, KT3 6QD.
D'SOUZA, Miss. Nicola, BA ACA *2002;* with Ernst & Young LLP, 1 More London Place, LONDON, SE1 2AF.
•D'SOUZA, Mr. Oscar Crispino Philip, FCA *1975;* 20 Midway, SUTTON, SURREY, SM3 9EL.
DA COSTA, Ms. Claudia Anusta Pinguelo Coutinho, ACA CA(SA) *2009;* PO Box 2084, Glenvista, JOHANNESBURG, 2058, SOUTH AFRICA.
DA COSTA, Mr. John Anthony Walker, BSc FCA *1965;* 17 The Street, Brettenham, IPSWICH, IP7 7QP. (Life Member)
DA COSTA, Mr. Niall Alex, BEng ACA *2000;* Flat C, 16 South Island Place, LONDON, SW9 0DX.
•DA COSTA, Mr. Peter Michael Walker, FCA *1971;* Peter da Costa & Co, 56 Richmond Park Road, KINGSTON UPON THAMES, SURREY, KT2 6AJ.
DA COSTA, Mr. Stephen, FCA *1966;* 5 Keysham Court, Preston Road, WEMBLEY, HA9 8LD.
DA CRUZ, Mrs. Katie Louise, BA ACA *2004;* 6 Cairns Walk, Ripponden, SOWERBY BRIDGE, WEST YORKSHIRE, HX6 4JR.
DA CRUZ, Mr. Nicholas Rodney Ignatius, BSc ACA *1999;* 68 Gipsy Lane, LEICESTER, LE4 6RE.
DA CUNHA, Mr. David Anthony, FCA *1969;* Lower Riversdale, Royden Lane, Boldre, LYMINGTON, SO41 8PE.
DA ROZA, Mr. Mark Anthony, BSc FCA ATII *1984;* (Tax Fac), ConocoPhillips International Trading Pte Ltd., One Temasek Avenue No. 40-01, Millenia Tower, SINGAPORE 039192, SINGAPORE.
DA ROZA, Mrs. Suzanne Louise, BA FCA *1984;* ConocoPhillips International Trading, One Temasek Avenue 40-01, Millenia Tower, SINGAPORE 039192, SINGAPORE.
•DA SILVA, Mr. Howard David, BSc FCA *1993;* Deloitte LLP, General Guisan-Quai 38, PO Box 2232, 8022 ZURICH, SWITZERLAND. See also Deloitte & Touche LLP
DA SILVA, Mr. Leonel Maria Gomes, FCA *1951;* 8204 E Phillips Place, ENGLEWOOD, CO 80112, UNITED STATES. (Life Member)
DA SILVA, Mr. Ryan Cormack, ACA *2007;* 85 Otter Close, Stratford, LONDON, E15 2PT.
DA VALL, Mr. Anthony John, FCA *1976;* 2 Vallance Court, Hove Street, HOVE, EAST SUSSEX, BN3 2DE.
DABBS, Mr. Andrew Stephen, BSc ACA *1987;* 21 Ashby Road, DAVENTRY, NORTHAMPTONSHIRE, NN11 9QD.
•DABBS, Mrs. Tracy Ann, BSc ACA *1992;* TAD Consultancy, 41 Valentines Lea, Northchapel, PETWORTH, WEST SUSSEX, GU28 9HY.
•DABBY, Mr. Stephen Alan, FCA *1988;* Greenback Alan LLP, 11 Raven Wharf, Lafone Street, LONDON, SE1 2LR.
DABEE, Mr. Nirvan, ACA CFA *2009;* Athene Place, 66 Shoe Lane, LONDON, EC4A 3BQ.
DABEK, Mr. Bohdan, ACA *2002;* Kappelirainweg 29, 4147 AESCH, SWITZERLAND.
•DABEK, Mr. Julian Richard, FCA *1982;* (Tax Fac), Westbury, 145/157 St John Street, LONDON, EC1V 4PY.
DABHI, Mrs. Naina, BSc ACA *2005;* 63 Humberstone Road, LUTON, LU4 9SR.
DABIR-ALAI, Mr. Khosrow, FCA *1972;* 63 Campden Hill Court, Campden Hill Road, Kensington, LONDON, W8 7HL.
DABKE, Mrs. Madhvi, ACA *2010;* Flat 7 The Oaks, 84-86 Wimbledon Hill Road, LONDON, SW19 7PB.
•DABOO, Mr. Jimmy, MA FCA *1988;* MEMBER OF COUNCIL, KPMG LLP, 15 Canada Square, LONDON, E14 5GL. See also KPMG Europe LLP
DABOO, Mrs. Sally Margaret, MA ACA ATII *1989;* The Burrows, Dedswell Drive, West Clandon, GUILDFORD, SURREY, GU4 7TQ.
DABORN, Mr. Gordon Michael, FCA *1967;* Corner Cottage, The Street, Effingham, LEATHERHEAD, SURREY, KT24 5LP. (Life Member)
DABROWSKI, Mr. Stanislaus Eugeniusz, ACA CA(NZ) *2011;* Ulica Grenady 9/12, 01-154 WARSAW, POLAND.
DABSKI - NERLICH, Mr. Alexander Jason Paul, BA(Hons) ACA *2001;* 3 Windmill Rise, KINGSTON UPON THAMES, SURREY, KT2 7TU.
DABSON, Mr. Russell Alexander John, BSc ACA *2007;* 5 Denby Close, WOKINGHAM, RG41 2AL.
DABSON, Mr. Simon James, ACA *1993;* 1 Queens Crescent, Putnoe, BEDFORD, MK41 9BN.
DABYDIN, Mr. Didier, BA(Hons) ACA *2003;* 10 Higginson Street, BEAU BASSIN, MAURITIUS.
DACCUS, Mr. Paul David, BAcc ACA *1998;* 1st Floor, 2 Park Street, LONDON, W1K2XA.
DACEY, Mr. Alun Penrose, MA FCA *1979;* 90 Manor Road, Manselton, SWANSEA, SA5 9PN.
•DACHS, Mr. Martin, BCom FCA *1992;* 25 Sweetings Road, Godmanchester, HUNTINGDON, CAMBRIDGESHIRE, PE29 2JS.
DACHS, Mrs. Sheryl, BA ACA *1992;* 25, Sweetings Road, Godmanchester, HUNTINGDON, PE29 2JS.
DACK, Mr. Derek, FCA *1962;* 9 Chestnut Crescent, MARCH, PE15 9TG.
•DACK, Ms. Elizabeth, ACA FCCA *2011;* Harrison Black Limited, Pyle House, 137 Pyle Street, NEWPORT, ISLE OF WIGHT, PO30 1JW.
•DACK, Mr. Michael John, ACA *1987;* (Tax Fac), Michael Dack & Company, 75 Great George Street, LEEDS, LS1 3BR.
DACK, Mr. Paul Mark, BA ACA *1985;* Joseph Rowntree Foundation, The Homestead, 40 Water End, Clifton, YORK, YO30 6WP.
DACOMBE, Mr. David William, BSc FCA *1977;* (Tax Fac), 5 Glentworth Road, Redland, BRISTOL, BS6 7EG.

DACOMBE, Mr. John Ralph, BA FCA *1974;* 101 Heather Road, Atholl, JOHANNESBURG, GAUTENG, 2196, SOUTH AFRICA.
•①**DACRE, Miss. Rebecca Jane, BSc ACA MABRP** *2004;* with BRI (UK) Limited, Suite 1c, Oak House, Woodlands Business Park, Linford Wood West, MILTON KEYNES MK14 6EY.
DADA, Miss. Annette, BSc ACA *1991;* 17 White Road, Stratford, LONDON, E15 4HA.
•**DADA, Mr. Feeroze Ahmad, FCA** *1977;* MEMBER OF COUNCIL, (Tax Fac), Freeman and Partners Limited, 30 St James's Street, LONDON, SW1A 1HB.
DADA, Mrs. Olutobi Olubukola, BSc ACA *2011;* Deloitte & Touche Hill House, 1 Little New Street, LONDON, EC4A 3TR.
•**DADABHOY, Mr. Kavas Ratan, ACA** *1982;* Dadabhoy & Co., 7 Darbhanga Mansions, 12 Carmichael Road, MUMBAI 400026, MAHARASHTRA, INDIA.
•**DADD, Mrs. Marianne, ACA** *1998;* Marianne Dadd ACA, PO Box 856, Yalding, MAIDSTONE, KENT, ME18 6WE.
DADE, Mr. Richard Blackmore, BA(Hons) ACA *2002;* with Hazlewoods LLP, Windsor House, Bayshill Road, CHELTENHAM, GLOUCESTERSHIRE, GL50 3AT.
•**DADFARMA, Mr. Kianoush, BSc ACA** *1985;* Kian & Co, 23 Mountside, STANMORE, MIDDLESEX, HA7 2DS. See also Audit Network Limited
DADHANIA, Mrs. Hasmita Jayendra, BA ACA *1983;* 112 Uxbridge Road, HARROW, MIDDLESEX, HA3 6TR.
DADISETH, Mr. Keki Bomi, FCA *1973;* 8-A Manek, L.D. Ruparel Marg, Malabar Hill, MUMBAI 400 006, INDIA.
DADLANI, Mrs. Sonia, BSc ACA *1996;* 35/2 Jersey Street, Turramurra, SYDNEY, NSW 2074, AUSTRALIA.
DADLEY, Mr. Richard John, BSc ACA *1982;* Liverpool Victoria Friendly Society, Frizzell House, County Gates, BOURNEMOUTH, BH1 2NF.
DADRESSAN, Miss. Mahasti, FCA MBA *1999;* Flat 27, Hamilton House, 1 Hall Road, LONDON, NW8 9PN.
DADSWELL, Mr. Colin James, BA(Hons) ACA DChA *2004;* with Plummer Parsons, 18 Hyde Gardens, EASTBOURNE, BN21 4PT.
DADSWELL, Miss. Laura, ACA *2010;* 3 Ellicott Road, BRISTOL, BS7 9PT.
DADZIE, Miss. Vanessa Natalie, BSc ACA *2003;* 1 Immerstrase, 40474 DUSSELDORF, GERMANY.
DAECHE, Mr. William Leslie, FCA *1963;* Lindens, Chantry Lane, HATFIELD, HERTFORDSHIRE, AL10 9PH. (Life Member)
DAEL, Mr. Richard David, BSc ACA *1996;* 86 Darley Street, MONA VALE, NSW 2103, AUSTRALIA.
DAEMI, Mr. Vahid, BSc ACA *1983;* (Tax Fac), Fourwinds, Woodland Way, Kingswood, TADWORTH, KT20 6NX.
DAFF, Dr. Paul Jamieson, PhD BA ACA *2004;* B G Group Plc, Thames Valley Park, READING, BERKSHIRE, RG6 1PT.
DAFFERN, Mrs. Elizabeth Anne, BA(Hons) ACA *2002;* Psion PLC, 48 Charlotte Street, LONDON, W1T 2NS.
DAFFERN, Mr. Paul, BSc ACA *1990;* West Midlands Enterprise Ltd, Wellington House, 31-34 Waterloo Street, BIRMINGHAM, B2 5TJ.
DAFFRON, Mrs. Joanne Elizabeth, BSc ACA *1993;* 17 Hawthorn Crescent, Burbage, HINCKLEY, LEICESTERSHIRE, LE10 2JP.
DAFFURN, Mr. John Stephen, FCA *1971;* 2 Rock Terrace, Scotgate, STAMFORD, LINCOLNSHIRE, PE9 2YJ.
•**DAFFURN, Mr. Paul Roger, MSc FCA** *1980;* Daffurn & Co Ltd, 132 Parkwood Road, BOURNEMOUTH, BH5 2BN.
DAFFURN, Mr. Timothy Roger James, FCA *1986;* FRC Packaging Ltd, Paradise Mill Bell Street, OLDHAM, OL1 3PY.
DAFINONE, Miss. Daphne Oterie, BA FCA *1990;* Horwath Dafinone, Ceddi Towers 16 Wharf Road, Apapa PO Box 2151, Marina, LAGOS, NIGERIA.
•**DAFINONE, Mr. David Omueya, BSc FCA** *1963;* Horwath Dafinone, Ceddi Towers 16 Wharf Road, Apapa PO Box 2151, Marina, LAGOS, NIGERIA.
•**DAFINONE, Mr. Duvie Omueya, BA FCA** *1989;* Horwath Dafinone, Ceddi Towers 16 Wharf Road, Apapa PO Box 2151, Marina, LAGOS, NIGERIA.
DAFINONE, Mr. Ede Omueya, MA FCA *1989;* Horwath Dafinone, Ceddi Towers 16 Wharf Road, Apapa PO Box 2151, Marina, LAGOS, NIGERIA.
DAFINONE, Mr. Igho Omueya, MA FCA *1986;* (Tax Fac), Horwath Dafinone, Ceddi Towers 16 Wharf Road, Apapa PO Box 2151, Marina, LAGOS, NIGERIA.
DAFINONE, Miss. Joy Ufuoma, BSc ACA *1999;* 20 Ikorodu Road, Jibowu, Yaba, LAGOS, NIGERIA.
DAFT, Mr. Richard Hamilton, BSc ACA *2005;* Flat 57, Longstone Court, 22 Great Dover Street, LONDON, SE1 4LB.
DAGA, Mr. Ashok, ACA *1978;* Ausserhalb 10, 63329 EGELSBACH, HESSEN, GERMANY.
•**DAGG, Mrs. Charlotte Amy, BA(Hons) ACA** *2001;* (Tax Fac), Charlotte Dagg Financial Services Ltd, 14 Haverhill Road, LONDON, SW12 0HA.
DAGGAR, Mr. Rishi, ACA *2010;* 35 Melbourne Avenue, SLOUGH, SL1 3ED.
•**DAGGATT, Mr. Joseph, FCA** *1963;* Daggatt & Co, 21 Conchar Road, SUTTON COLDFIELD, B72 1LW.
DAGGE, Mr. Robert Brian, MA ACA *1991;* with PricewaterhouseCoopers Ltd, Building 8-B, 7th & 8th Floors, DLF Cyber City, GURGAON 122002, HARYANA INDIA.
DAGGER, Mr. John Michael Wilkinson, FCA *1974;* Clayhill Farmhouse The Common, Lavenham, SUDBURY, SUFFOLK, CO10 9PG.
DAGGETT, Mr. Paul Daniel Seymour, BEng ACA CFA *2000;* 3615 Greenbrier Drive, DALLAS, TX 75225, UNITED STATES.
•**DAGGETT, Mr. Timothy Michael, BA FCA** *1982;* Daggett and Company, 516 Wilmslow Road, Withington, MANCHESTER, M20 4BS.
•**DAGLESS, Mr. Andrew Edward, ACA** *1982;* (Tax Fac), Wags LLP, Richmond House, Walkern Road, STEVENAGE, HERTFORDSHIRE, SG1 3QP.
DAGLISH, Mr. Brian Calvert, FCA *1954;* 7 Torkington Road, Gatley, CHEADLE, CHESHIRE, SK8 4PR. (Life Member)
DAGNELL, Mr. Michael Peter, FCA *1955;* 22 Friths Drive, REIGATE, SURREY, RH2 0DS. (Life Member)
DAGUL, Mr. Lee Cyril, ACA *2009;* Dancastle Ltd 1 Dancastle Court, 14 Arcadia Avenue, LONDON, N3 2JU.
DAHABIYEH, Mr. Hassan Ahmad Ellayyan, FCA *1975;* HD Associates, Office 513, Radisson IAS Plaza, Deira Creek, PO Box 8811, DUBAI UNITED ARAB EMIRATES.
DAHABIYEH, Mr. Ussama, ACA *2007;* Al Mamoura B, Mouroor Street, Intersection 4th and 15th, ABU DHABI, 45005, UNITED ARAB EMIRATES.
DAHAN, Mr. Rafic Antoine, MSc ACA *1988;* 16618 Flying Jib Road, CORNELIUS, NC 28031, UNITED STATES.
DAHANAYAKE, Mr. Sunil Jayathunga, ACA CA(AUS) *2011;* 136 Herring Road, NORTH RYDE, NSW 2113, AUSTRALIA.
DAHL DAVIES, Mrs. Marianne, BA ACA *2004;* 19 Forest Close, CHISLEHURST, KENT, BR7 5QS.
DAHLAN, Mr. Abdul Halim Bin Haji, FCA *1968;* 9 Heron Court, 63 Lancaster Gate, LONDON, W2 3NJ.
DAHYA, Mrs. Sobhna Jitendra, BA ACA *1994;* 26 Eastern Road, Bounds Green, LONDON, N22 7DD.
DAI, Miss. Yilan, MSc ACA *2010;* B4 2302No.860Dong Feng Dong Road, Glorious City Garden, GUANGZHOU 510600, GUANGDONG PROVINCE, CHINA.
DAILEY, Mr. David Alex, BA ACA *2007;* 81 Stanley Hill, AMERSHAM, BUCKINGHAMSHIRE, HP7 9HH.
DAIN, Mr. John Stewart, FCA *1962;* 32 Captains Lane, Barton under Needwood, BURTON-ON-TRENT, STAFFORDSHIRE, DE13 8EZ. (Life Member)
DAINTITH, Mr. Brian John, BA ACA *1992;* 27 Stetchworth Road, Walton, WARRINGTON, WA4 6JE.
DAINTITH, Mr. Stephen Wayne, BA FCA *1989;* Associated Newspapers Ltd Northcliffe House, 2 Derry Street, LONDON, W8 5TT.
DAINTITH, Mrs. Victoria Lucy, MA ACA *1994;* Wychwood, Bagshot Road, ASCOT, SL5 9JN.
DAINTON, Mr. Gary Richard, BSc FCA *1992;* 19 Birkley Road, MANLY, NSW 2095, AUSTRALIA.
DAINTREE, Mr. Philip Gordon, BA ACA *1989;* 34 Marram Way, Peka Peka, RD1, WAIKANAE 5391, NEW ZEALAND.
DAINTY, Mr. Brian Ronald, FCA *1966;* 4 Wynchcombe Avenue, Penn, WOLVERHAMPTON, WV4 4JQ.
DAINTY, Miss. Elizabeth, BA ACA *2003;* DLA Piper UK Llp, 1 St. Pauls Place, SHEFFIELD, S1 2JX.
DAINTY, Mrs. Elizabeth Rose, BA ACA *2002;* 5 Wellington Grove, SOLIHULL, B91 1EA.
DAINTY, Mr. James Rowland, FCA *1962;* Apt 16 Thornhill Grange, Ryknild Drive, SUTTON COLDFIELD, WEST MIDLANDS, B74 2AZ.
•**DAINTY, Mr. Leonard, FCA** *1968;* Len Dainty & Co, 10 Glastonbury Close, STAFFORD, ST17 0PB.
DAINTY, Mr. Mark Joseph, ACA *2007;* Flat 53 Gainsborough Studios South, 1 Poole Street, LONDON, N1 5EE.
DAINTY, Mr. Steven Michael, BSocSc ACA *1999;* G K N Driveline, Ipsley House, Ipsley Church Lane, REDDITCH, WORCESTERSHIRE, B98 0TL.
DAKERS, Mr. Christopher Hugh, BCom FCA *1968;* Senson Do Ltd, The Cedars, Upper Butts, BRENTFORD, TW8 8DA. (Life Member)
DAKHAN, Mr. Muhammad Hassan, BSc ACA *2003;* Goldman Sachs, 10 Newgate Street, LONDON, EC1A 7HD.
DAKIN, Mrs. Jennifer Mary, BDS FCA *1989;* (Tax Fac), 5 Springfield Crescent, POOLE, DORSET, BH14 0LL.
•**DAKIN, Mr. John, BSc FCA** *1999;* Cresswells Accountants LLP, Barclays Bank Chambers, 12 Market Street, HEBDEN BRIDGE, WEST YORKSHIRE, HX7 6AA.
DAKIN, Mr. Kenneth Alec, FCA *1960;* 52 Appleton Drive, Ormesby St Margaret, GREAT YARMOUTH, NR29 3RL. (Life Member)
DAKIN, Mr. Mark Richard Ainley, MA ACA *1986;* 33 Clarendon Road, SHEFFIELD, S10 3TQ.
DAKIN, Mr. Tony John, FCA *1961;* Edgell House, Carlingcott, Peasedown St. John, BATH, BA2 8AP. (Life Member)
DAKOVIC, Mr. Peter Zeljko, BA FCA *1996;* 16 Talfourd Avenue, READING, RG6 7BP.
DAL, Mr. Kailash Kanubhai, BSc ACA *1979;* Prem Kutir, 7 Stanmore Close, Nuthall, NOTTINGHAM, NG16 1QY.
DALAL, Mr. Anup Nirmal, BCom ACA *1983;* Summerhill, 97 Alleyn Park, LONDON, SE21 8AA.
DALAL, Mr. Firoz Sultanali, FCA *1970;* 28 Wolsey Road, Moor Park, NORTHWOOD, HA6 2EW. (Life Member)
•**DALAL, Mr. Gautam Shashichandra, FCA** *1978;* with KPMG LLP, 15 Canada Square, LONDON, E14 5GL.
DALAL, Mr. Moez Firoz, BSc ACA *1999;* 28 Wolsey Road, NORTHWOOD, HA6 2EW.
DALAL, Miss. Perizad V, FCA *1986;* with Baker Tilly UK Audit LLP, 25 Farringdon Street, LONDON, EC4A 4AB.
DALBOTH, Mr. Robert James, BA ACA *1999;* 7 Cob Place, WESTBURY, WILTSHIRE, BA13 3GS.
•**DALBY, Mr. Anthony Hedley Burkitt, TD FCA** *1980;* (Tax Fac), Sykes Dalby & Truelove, 63 High Street, Hurstpierpoint, HASSOCKS, WEST SUSSEX, BN6 9RE.
•**DALBY, Mr. Brian, FCA** *1968;* (Tax Fac), R.N. Store & Co, 26 Hickman Street, GAINSBOROUGH, DN21 2DZ.
•**DALBY, Mr. Christopher Michael, FCA** *1968;* C.M. Dalby, 18 Merstow Green, EVESHAM, WR11 4BD.
DALBY, Mr. Simon Richard, BSc(Hons) FCA *1990;* 19 Temple Wood Drive, REDHILL, RH1 2QD.
DALDORPH, Mrs. Susan, BSc ACA *1987;* 67 Oakerthorpe Road, Wirksworth, MATLOCK, DE4 4GP.
DALE, Mr. Adam Stuart, BSc ACA *2003;* 20 Castle Road, ST. ALBANS, HERTFORDSHIRE, AL1 5DL.
DALE, Mr. Ajmere Singh, MEng ACA *1997;* Solar City Construction, 393 Vintage Park Drive, STE 140, FOSTER CITY, CA 94404, UNITED STATES.
DALE, Mr. Alan Christopher, BA ACA *1987;* The Oaks, Drift Road, Winkfield, WINDSOR, BERKSHIRE, SL4 4QQ.
DALE, Mr. Alan James, FCA *1960;* 10 Cralves Mead, TENBURY WELLS, WORCESTERSHIRE, WR15 8EX. (Life Member)
DALE, Mrs. Alison Jane, BSc ACA *1991;* 28 Shetland Way, Countesthorpe, LEICESTER, LE8 5PU.
•**DALE, Mr. Andrew John, BA(Hons) ACA** *2001;* PricewaterhouseCoopers LLP, Cornwall Court, 19 Cornwall Street, BIRMINGHAM, B3 2DT.
DALE, Mr. Anthony Charles Hughes, FCA *1957;* 20 Henry Street, RINGWOOD, VIC 3134, AUSTRALIA. (Life Member)
DALE, Mr. Barry Gordon, FCA *1960;* Tanglewood, Spinney Lane, KNUTSFORD, WA16 0NQ. (Life Member)
DALE, Mr. Barry James, FCA *1963;* Whitehill, Old School Lane, Hampton-on-the-Hill, WARWICK, CV35 8QS.
DALE, Miss. Caroline Frances, MA(Cantab) ACA *2010;* FS Audit 4th Floor, K P M G, 1 The Embankment, LEEDS, LS1 4DW.
DALE, Mrs. Catherine Louise, MA(Oxon) ACA CTA *1990;* BPP Professional Education, 401 Grafton Gate, MILTON KEYNES, MK9 1AQ.
•**DALE, Mr. Charles Edward Maxwell, MSc FCA** *1977;* Kempster & Dale Partnership, Prospect House, 20 High Street, WESTERHAM, KENT, TN16 1RG.
DALE, Mr. Christopher James, ACA CA(NZ) *2009;* (Tax Fac), 49 Midhurst Avenue, LONDON, N10 3EP.
DALE, Mr. Christopher Peter, BA ACA *2003;* 27 Dale Close, Fforestfach, SWANSEA, SA5 4NX.
DALE, Mrs. Cressida Mary May, LLB ACA *2003;* 18 Monarchs Gate, 74 Yew Tree Lane, SOLIHULL, WEST MIDLANDS, B91 2PS.
DALE, Mr. Daniel George, BSc ACA *1996;* c/o WHK, 53 Tamar Street, BALLINA, NSW 2478, AUSTRALIA.
DALE, Mr. Derek Newlyn, FCA *1963;* Emerson Group Emerson House, Heyes Lane, ALDERLEY EDGE, CHESHIRE, SK9 7LF.
•**DALE, Mr. Douglas Brian, MA FCA** *1977;* (Tax Fac), Ballard Dale Syree Watson LLP, Oakmoore Court, Kingswood Road, Hampton Lovett, DROITWICH, WORCESTERSHIRE WR9 0QH.
DALE, Mr. Grahame Jeffray Gosnay, FCA *1960;* Lane End, 2 Jackson's Lane, Thornhill, DEWSBURY, WEST YORKSHIRE, WF12 0NS. (Life Member)
DALE, Mr. Gregory James, BSc ACA *2005;* 1 Bestwick Close, ILKESTON, DERBYSHIRE, DE7 4QZ.
DALE, Mr. Ian Michael, ACA *1982;* 14 Harding Grove, STONE, STAFFORDSHIRE, ST15 8GT.
DALE, Mrs. Jacqueline Louise, BSc ACA *2000;* 25 Swan Street, Alvechurch, BIRMINGHAM, B48 7RR.
DALE, Mr. James Hall, FCA *1963;* Bradda Brae, Bradda East, Port Erin, ISLE OF MAN, IM9 6QB.
DALE, Mr. James William, ACA *2009;* 1 Craven Mews, LONDON, SW11 5PW.
DALE, Miss. Jane Elizabeth, BSc ACA *1985;* Apartment 403 Mandel House, Eastfields Avenue, LONDON, SW18 1JU.
DALE, Mrs. Jill Margaret, FCA *1961;* 18 Rotterdam Drive, CHRISTCHURCH, BH23 1HB.
•**DALE, Mr. John, FCA** *1971;* 23 Plane Tree Croft, LEEDS, LS17 8UQ.
•**DALE, Mr. John Bernard, FCA** *1972;* J.B. Dale, The Black Cottage, Bell Common, EPPING, ESSEX, CM16 4DZ.
DALE, Mr. John Malcolm, FCA *1958;* Field End, 7 Wellfield Close, Tugby, LEICESTER, LE7 9WF. (Life Member)
DALE, Mr. John Michael, FCA *1968;* Aberdour, Oak Tree Lane, Sambourne, REDDITCH, WORCESTERSHIRE, B96 6EY.
•**DALE, Mr. Jonathon Peter, BA(Hons) ACA** *2004;* Independent Auditors LLP, Emstrey House, Sitka Drive, Shrewsbury Business Park, SHREWSBURY, SY2 6LG.
DALE, Mrs. Josephine Catherine, BA ACA *1981;* Omersa & Company Ltd, Coldham Road, Coningsby, LINCOLN, LN4 4SE.
DALE, Miss. Laura, BSc(Hons) ACA *2011;* 144 Hollyhedge Road, WEST BROMWICH, WEST MIDLANDS, B71 3AL.
•**DALE, Mrs. Lorraine Stephanie, BCom FCA** *1989;* (Tax Fac), Rightway Accounting Services Ltd, 39 Finchley Avenue, CHELMSFORD, CM2 9BX.
•**DALE, Mrs. Louise Carmel, BA ACA** *1989;* 6 Speedwell Drive, Balsall Common, COVENTRY, CV7 7AU.
DALE, Mrs. Louise Elizabeth, ACA *2010;* Maize Cottage, Bruton Road, Evercreech, SHEPTON MALLET, SOMERSET, BA4 6HY.
DALE, Mr. Luke, BA ACA *2007;* Capita Financial Group, 51 New North Road, EXETER, EX4 4EP.
•**DALE, Mr. Maurice William, FCA** *1963;* M.W. Dale, 10 Hillfort Close, DORCHESTER, DT1 2QT.
DALE, Mr. Michael Philip, FCA *1969;* 26 Osborne Road, Hartshill, STOKE-ON-TRENT, ST4 7PF.
DALE, Mr. Nicholas Robin, LLB ACA *1982;* 19 Roseacre Lane, Bearsted, MAIDSTONE, ME14 4HZ.
DALE, Miss. Patricia Marguerite, FCA *1974;* Adas (Pvt) Ltd, PO Box 348, CHEGUTU, ZIMBABWE.
DALE, Mr. Peter David Sandwith, FCA *1965;* High Trees, Church Lane, Worplesdon, GUILDFORD, SURREY, GU3 3RU. (Life Member)
DALE, Miss. Rebecca, BSc(Hons) ACA MBA *2004;* 13 Nursery Gardens, WINCHESTER, HAMPSHIRE, SO22 5DT.
DALE, Mr. Robert Rigby, FCA *1963;* Flat 1, Bolsover Court, 19 Bolsover Road, EASTBOURNE, EAST SUSSEX, BN20 7JG. (Life Member)
DALE, Mr. Roger Ernest, FCA *1967;* The Old Presbytery, Minsteracres, Kiln Pit Hill, CONSETT, DH8 9RU. (Life Member)
DALE, Mr. Sam, BSc ACA *2001;* with Monahans, 38-42 Newport Street, SWINDON, SN1 3DR.
DALE, Mr. Scott, BA(Hons) ACA *2000;* Flat 18 Monarchs Gate, 74 Yew Tree Lane, SOLIHULL, B91 2PS.
•**DALE, Mr. Stephen Hugh, BA FCA** *1980;* PricewaterhouseCoopers LLP, 1 Embankment Place, LONDON, WC2N 6RH. See also PricewaterhouseCoopers

DALE, Mr. Steven Glyn, BA ACA *1992;* 6 St. Peters Way, Chorleywood, RICKMANSWORTH, HERTFORDSHIRE, WD3 5QE.

•DALE, Mr. Steven Mark, FCA *1992;* Rice & Co, Harance House, Rumer Hill Business Estate, Rumer Hill Road, CANNOCK, STAFFORDSHIRE WS11 0ET.

DALE, Mr. Thomas, ACA *2011;* 7 Dancer Road, LONDON, SW6 4DU.

DALE, Mr. Timothy Roger, BA(Hons) ACA *2001;* 22 Knutsford Road, ALDERLEY EDGE, CHESHIRE, SK9 7SD.

•DALE, Mr. William Ian Carrick, FCA *1976;* Crowe Clark Whitehill LLP, Aquis House, 49-51 Blagrave Street, READING, RG1 1PL. See also Horwath Clark Whitehill LLP and Crowe Clark Whitehill

DALES, Mr. Alistair Robert Harry, FCA *1972;* Apartment 1, Fosseway House, Stow on the Wold, CHELTENHAM, GLOUCESTERSHIRE, GL54 1DN.

DALES, Mr. John Handsley, FCA *1958;* 87 Billingbauk Drive, LEEDS, LS13 4RX. (Life Member)

DALEY, Mr. Andrew Gareth, MA LLM ACA *1993;* 16 Glenure Road, Eltham, LONDON, SE9 1UF.

•DALEY, Ms. Frances Margaret Catherine, MA FCA *1983;* 1 Frank Dixon Way, Dulwich, LONDON, SE21 7BB.

DALEY, Mr. Matthew, BA ACA *2011;* 28 Greenacres, South Cornelly, BRIDGEND, MID GLAMORGAN, CF33 4SE.

DALEY, Miss. Michelle, ACA *2011;* 9 Dunleary Court, Westcote Road, READING, RG30 2DJ.

DALEY, Mr. Nicholas, BA FCA *1978;* PO Box 641, Riverclub 2149, JOHANNESBURG, GAUTENG, SOUTH AFRICA.

DALEYMOUNT, Miss. Tamara, BSc(Hons) ACA *2011;* Flat 3, 12 Worcester Terrace, BRISTOL, BS8 3JW.

DALFEN, Mr. Nicholas Roger, BSc ACA *1998;* 63 Glenside, Appley Bridge, WIGAN, LANCASHIRE, WN6 9EG.

DALGARNO-PLATT, Mr. Christopher Nicholas, MA(Hons) ACA *2002;* 4 Mount Pleasant, Manse Brae, LOCHGILPHEAD, PA31 8RA.

DALGAS, Mrs. Pamela, BSc ACA *1998;* with Deloitte LLP, The Pinnacle, 150 Midsummer Boulevard, MILTON KEYNES, MK9 1FD.

DALGAS, Mr. Steen Pierce, BSc ACA *1995;* 8 Hall Park, BERKHAMSTED, HERTFORDSHIRE, HP4 2NU.

DALGLEISH, Mr. Andrew, BSc FCA *1974;* 8000 Decarie Blvd. # 500, MONTREAL H4P 2S4, QUE, CANADA.

DALGLEISH, Mr. Duncan George, BA ACA *1986;* 484 Hurst Road, BEXLEY, DA5 3JN.

DALGLEISH, Mr. Grant Louis, BSc ACA *1989;* Allied International Holdings, 10451 Gulf Boulevard, TREASURE ISLAND, FL 33706, UNITED STATES.

DALGLEISH, Mr. James Martin, MA MBA FCA *1970;* Dunbar Mill, PO Box 484, CHARLESTOWN, SAINT KITTS AND NEVIS. (Life Member)

•DALGLEISH, Mr. Robert Henry, BA FCA *1988;* (Tax Fac), Greaves West & Ayre, 1-3 Sandgate, BERWICK-UPON-TWEED, TD15 1EW.

DALL, Mr. Andrew James Gifford, ACA *2002;* 86 Charles Street, Sileby, LOUGHBOROUGH, LE12 7SJ.

DALL, Mrs. Serena Louise, BSc ACA *2002;* 48 Brendon Road, NOTTINGHAM, NG8 1HZ.

•DALLAL, Mr. Samy, FCA *1975;* with RSM Tenon Audit Limited, 66 Chiltern Street, LONDON, W1U 4JT.

DALLAMORE, Mr. Neil James, BSc ACA *2005;* Trelleborg Sealing Solutions Czechowice, ul. Legionow 255, 43-502 CZECHOWICE-DZIEDZICE, POLAND.

DALLAS, Miss. Collette Ann, BA ACA DChA *1994;* The Message Trust, Lancaster House, Harper Road, Sharston, MANCHESTER, M22 4RG.

DALLAS, Mr. Edward, BSc ACA *2011;* The Old Mill, Ramsbury, MARLBOROUGH, WILTSHIRE, SN8 2PN.

DALLAS, Mr. Grant Michael Mackintosh, FCA *1975;* 5524 St Patrick Street, No. 330, MONTREAL H4E 1A8, QC, CANADA.

DALLAS, Mrs. Joanna Victoria, BSc FCA *1997;* (Tax Fac), 80 Mill Lane, BUCKLEY, CLWYD, CH7 3HE.

DALLAS, Mr. Mark, BA ACA *2002;* 11 Telford Grove, EDINBURGH, EH4 2UL.

DALLAWAY, Mr. Mark Robert, BA ACA *1993;* Relcross Ltd Unit 11, Prince Maurice Court Hambleton Avenue, DEVIZES, SN10 2RT.

DALLAWAY, Mrs. Tean Elizabeth, BSc ACA *1993;* 15 St. Georges Place, Semington, TROWBRIDGE, WILTSHIRE, BA14 6GB.

DALLENDER, Mr. Craig, ACA *2011;* 52 Shrublands Avenue, BERKHAMSTED, HERTFORDSHIRE, HP4 3JQ.

DALLEY, Mr. John Chapman, BSc ACA *1989;* Scottish Midland Co-Op Society Ltd, Hillwood House, 2 Harvest Drive, NEWBRIDGE, MIDLOTHIAN, EH28 8QJ.

DALLEY, Mr. Robert James, BSc ACA *2004;* 30 Horseshoe Crescent, BEACONSFIELD, BUCKINGHAMSHIRE, HP9 1LL.

DALLI, Mr. Dominic Stefan, BA ACA *1998;* Templeton, 274a Kew Road, RICHMOND, SURREY, TW9 3EE.

DALLIMORE, Mr. Geoffrey, BSc ACA CTA *1993;* Afortis Limited, 2 Pennyblack Court, Barton Road, Worsley, MANCHESTER, M28 2PD.

DALLIMORE, Miss. Katie Beth, ACA *2011;* 114 Kirby Drive, Bramley, TADLEY, HAMPSHIRE, RG26 5FN.

DALLING, Miss. Kerri, BSc ACA *2011;* 45 Waldeck Street, READING, RG1 2RF.

DALLISON, Mr. Adrian John, BA FCA *1991;* 41 Common Hill, Steeple Ashton, TROWBRIDGE, BA14 6EE.

DALLISON, Mr. John Peter, FCA CTA FIMgt *1960;* (Member of Council 1984 - 1999), Holmrook, 120 Moor Hall Drive, SUTTON COLDFIELD, WEST MIDLANDS, B75 6LS. (Life Member)

•DALLMANN, Mrs. Stephney Joan, BSc(Hons) ARCS ACA *2001;* with PricewaterhouseCoopers LLP, 1 Embankment Place, LONDON, WC2N 6RH.

DALLOW, Mr. Arthur Thomas, FCA *1962;* Capri, 1 Glengarry Gardens, WOLVERHAMPTON, WV3 9HX. (Life Member)

DALLOW, Mr. Jonathan, BSc ACA *1998;* One Stop Stores Ltd, Apex Road, Brownhills, WALSALL, WS8 7TS.

DALLY, Mr. David James Michael, BA ACA *1989;* Merlion Pharmaceuticals Pte Ltd, 1 Science Park Road, The Capricorn, Apt 05-01, Singapore Science Park II, SINGAPORE 117528 SINGAPORE.

DALLY, Mr. Jonathan, BEng ACA *1999;* 8 Latimer Road, GODALMING, SURREY, GU7 1BL.

DALLYN, Miss. Emma Christine, BCom ACA *2004;* Cobblers, Kirdford, BILLINGSHURST, WEST SUSSEX, RH14 0LX.

DALMAN, Mr. Robert Alistair, BA ACA *1986;* (Tax Fac), Canon (UK) Ltd, Woodhatch, Cockshot Hill, REIGATE, SURREY, RH2 8BF.

DALRYMPLE, Mr. Hamish Hew, ACA *2009;* Flat D, 2 Nevern Square, LONDON, SW5 9NN.

•DALRYMPLE, Mr. Jocelyn Hew, MA FCA *1989;* Smith & Williamson Ltd, 25 Moorgate, LONDON, EC2R 6AY.

DALRYMPLE, Miss. Susan, BA ACA *2004;* H B O S Plc, Ettrick House, 37 South Gyle Crescent, South Gyle, EDINBURGH, EH12 9DS.

DALSANIA, Mr. Ameet, BSc ACA *1994;* 24 Crabtree Lane, HARPENDEN, HERTFORDSHIRE, AL5 5TE.

DALTON, Ms. Alison Jayne, FCA *1999;* 4 Dutch Yard House, 177 Wandsworth High Street, LONDON, SW18 4JE.

DALTON, Mrs. Anne, BSc ACA *1986;* Vale & West, 26 Queen Victoria Street, READING, RG1 1TG.

DALTON, Mr. Christopher James, BA ACA *2010;* 40 Dukesfield, Shiremoor, NEWCASTLE UPON TYNE, NE27 0EZ.

•DALTON, Mr. Colin Brian William, FCA *1987;* Colin Datlon, Hillside, 3 Tinacre Hill, West Midlands, WOLVERHAMPTON, WV6 8DB.

DALTON, Miss. Eileen Caroline, BA ACA *1994;* Stamford House Stoke Row Road, Peppard Common, HENLEY-ON-THAMES, OXFORDSHIRE, RG9 5JD.

DALTON, Mr. Geoffrey Horace, FCA *1958;* The Notch, Little Julians Hill, SEVENOAKS, TN13 1QB. (Life Member)

DALTON, Mrs. Helen Barbara, FCA ATII MAAT *1998;* 9 St George's Gate, Middleton St George, DARLINGTON, DL2 1FD.

DALTON, Irwin, Esq CBE FCA *1962;* 7 Aultmore Court, Kingswood Road, TUNBRIDGE WELLS, KENT, TN2 4UF. (Life Member)

DALTON, Mr. Jesse, ACA CA(NZ) *2009;* (Tax Fac), 121 Dulwich Road, LONDON, SE24 0NG.

DALTON, Mr. John Alan Greaves, BA FCA *1975;* Fulford House, 9 Burlington Grove, Dore, SHEFFIELD, S17 3PH.

•DALTON, Mr. John Leslie, FCA *1980;* (Tax Fac), John L Dalton & Co Ltd, 47 St. Pauls Close, Farington Moss, LEYLAND, PR26 6RT.

•DALTON, Miss. Katherine Jill, BA FCA *1985;* K.J. Dalton, Long Lane Farm, Ickenham, UXBRIDGE, UB10 8QT.

DALTON, Miss. Lindsay Jane, BSc ACA *2006;* Flat 7, 17 Lewin Road, LONDON, SW16 6JZ.

•DALTON, Mr. Mark John, BA ACA *2005;* Montpelier Professional (Leeds) Limited, Sanderson House, Station Road, Horsforth, LEEDS, LS18 5NT.

DALTON, Dr. Michael, BSc ACA CTA *1998;* (Tax Fac), 84 Camberton Road, LEIGHTON BUZZARD, BEDFORDSHIRE, LU7 2UP.

DALTON, Mr. Michael John, MA ACA *1983;* 29 Manor Crescent, Pool In Wharfedale, OTLEY, LS21 1ND.

DALTON, Mr. Pedro James, BA ACA *2009;* Flat 1, 19a Clapham Common South Side, LONDON, SW4 7AB.

DALTON, Mrs. Rachel Anne, BSc ACA *2001;* 29 Farm Street, LONDON, W1J 5RL.

DALTON, Mrs. Samantha Jane, BA ACA *1992;* 58 Shirley Road, DUDLEY, DY2 7HZ.

DALTON, Mr. William John Harling, BA ACA *1987;* Glenwood, Onslow Road, SUNNINGDALE, BERKSHIRE, SL5 0HW.

DALWOOD, Mr. Keith Lionel, BSc FCA *1959;* 39 Links Side, ENFIELD, EN2 7QZ. (Life Member)

DALY, Mrs. Angela Mary, BA ACA *1983;* 10 Pavilion Place, BILLERICAY, CM12 0ET.

DALY, Mr. Brendan Laurence, BSc ACA *1993;* Dunvegan, Birchall Lane, LEEK, STAFFORDSHIRE, ST13 5RA.

DALY, Mrs. Catherine Mary, MA ACA *1985;* 50 West Common, HARPENDEN, AL5 2JW.

DALY, Mr. Derek Keith, FCA *1958;* 45 Brookfield Drive, Rhos-on-Sea, COLWYN BAY, LL28 4SW. (Life Member)

•DALY, Miss. Elisabeth Anne, FCA *1997;* Griffith Williams & Co, 36 Stryd Fawr, PWLLHELI, LL53 5RT.

DALY, Mr. Fergus Gerard, BA ACA *1994;* 2 Black Swan Court, BROOKFIELD, CT 06804, UNITED STATES.

DALY, Mr. Gerard Peter, BA FCA MBA *1981;* 5 Wingfield Court, BINGLEY, WEST YORKSHIRE, BD16 4TE.

DALY, Miss. Gillian Frances, BSc ACA *2003;* 50 Coppice Green, Westbrook, WARRINGTON, WA5 7WA.

DALY, Mr. Glen, BSc(Hons) ACA *2002;* with HSBC Holdings plc, 8-16 Canada Square, LONDON, E14 5HQ.

DALY, Miss. Holly, ACA *2010;* 29 Ryle Road, FARNHAM, GU9 8RN.

DALY, Mr. Ian, BSc ACA *1989;* Asmec Management Associates Merlin House Commerce Park, Brunel Road Theale, READING, RG7 4AB.

•DALY, Mr. John, BA FCA *1983;* Orchard House, Cockhill Close, Bawtry, DONCASTER, SOUTH YORKSHIRE, DN10 6LU.

DALY, Mr. John, BSc ACA *1982;* Avinguda Paral.lel ent 1a, 08015 BARCELONA, SPAIN.

DALY, Mr. John Anthony, BA ACA *1992;* 39 Grove Street, LEAMINGTON SPA, WARWICKSHIRE, CV32 5AQ.

DALY, Mr. John Anthony, BSc FCA CF *1989;* with RSM Tenon Limited, Sumner House, St Thomas's Rd, CHORLEY, PR7 1HP.

DALY, Mr. John James, FCA *1964;* 78 Kiln Way, Polesworth, TAMWORTH, STAFFORDSHIRE, B78 1JE.

DALY, Mr. John Malachy, BEng FCA *1972;* Ladywood House, Mill Hill, EDENBRIDGE, TN8 5DA.

DALY, Mr. John Paul, ACA *2009;* Apartment 3, Burns Court, Bamford, ROCHDALE, LANCASHIRE, OL11 5AR.

DALY, Mr. Joseph Denis Anthony, BA FCA *1994;* 32 Palm Street, Rows Bay, TOWNSVILLE, QLD 4810, AUSTRALIA.

DALY, Mr. Julian Francis, BA FCA *1985;* 50 West Common, HARPENDEN, AL5 2JW.

•DALY, Miss. Kerry Ann, ACA *2007;* with Compass Accountants Ltd, Venture House, The Tanneries, East Street, Titchfield, FAREHAM HAMPSHIRE PO14 4AR.

DALY, Mrs. Linda Mary, BA ACA *1988;* Bell Meadow, Old Warwick Road, WARWICK, CV35 7BS.

DALY, Mrs. Lisa Kathleen, BSc ACA *1995;* Trade Winds, Send Marsh Road, Ripley, WOKING, GU23 6JR.

•DALY, Mr. Marcus Hugh Paul, FCA *1984;* Michael Kay & Company, 2 Water Court, Water Street, BIRMINGHAM, B3 1HP.

DALY, Mr. Mark William, ACA *2006;* 15 Eggars Field, Bentley, FARNHAM, GU10 5LD.

•DALY, Mr. Michael Owen, BSc ACA *1991;* 46 Kent Avenue, Ealing, LONDON, W13 8BH.

DALY, Mr. Niall Joseph, BA ACA *1986;* 18 Lapins Lane, WEST MALLING, ME19 4LA.

DALY, Mr. Norman Brian, FCA *1951;* 11 Evelyn Road, RICHMOND, TW9 2TF. (Life Member)

DALY, Mr. Paul Anthony, BA ACA *1987;* P Q Corporation, 4 Liverpool Road, WARRINGTON, WA5 1AQ.

•DALY, Mr. Paul Christopher, BEng ACA *1999;* ASE Audit LLP, Rowan Court, Concord Business Park, MANCHESTER, M22 0RR.

DALY, Mr. Peter Albert, FCA *1962;* The Great Bear, 4 Chichester Avenue, RUISLIP, HA4 7EH.

•DALY, Mr. Philip Malachy, LLB ACA *1992;* Daly & Co, The Portergate, Ecclesall Road, SHEFFIELD, S11 8NX.

DALY, Ms. Rachel Fiona, ACA *2004;* with Clement Keys, 39/40 Calthorpe Road, Edgbaston, BIRMINGHAM, B15 1TS.

DALY, Mrs. Rebecca Debbie, BSc ACA *2007;* West 1, Deerswood Farnham Road, Ewshot, FARNHAM, GU10 5AY.

DALY, Miss. Serena Melody, ACA MAAT *2011;* 3 Joy Clucas House, Apprentice Drive, COLCHESTER, CO4 5TY.

DALY, Mrs. Sharon Anne Mary, BA ACA *1994;* 46 Kent Avenue, Ealing, LONDON, W13 8BH.

DALY, Mr. Terence Patrick, JP FCA *1953;* Lucastes, Hacketts Lane, Pyrford, WOKING, GU22 8PJ. (Life Member)

DALY, Mrs. Victoria Jane, BA ACA *2005;* Bank of Scotland, 40 Spring Gardens, MANCHESTER, M2 1EN.

•DALZELL, Mr. Ian Robert, MA FCA *1971;* (Tax Fac), Ian Dalzell Ltd, Broughton Lodge Mews, Field Broughton, GRANGE-OVER-SANDS, CUMBRIA, LA11 6HL.

DALZELL, Mrs. Jacquelyn Amanda, BA ACA *1987;* Summer Trees, 40 Egerton Road, Ashton-On-Ribble, PRESTON, PR2 1AL.

DALZELL, Mr. Richard Arthur, FCA *1963;* 14 Perrymead Street, LONDON, SW6 3SP. (Life Member)

DALZIEL, Mr. Andrew James, MA FCA *1986;* (Tax Fac), 38 Filellinon Street, Strovolos, 2039 NICOSIA, CYPRUS.

DALZIEL, Mr. Colin Robert, FCA *1962;* 18 Oaklands Avenue, ESHER, SURREY, KT10 8HX. (Life Member)

DALZIEL, Mr. Gregory James, BSc ACA *2010;* 2 Hardman Street, Deloitte & Touche, PO Box 500, MANCHESTER, M60 2AT.

DALZIEL, Mr. Samuel, BSc ACA *2011;* Flat 5, Balloon Court, Cave Street, BRISTOL, BS2 8AG.

DAMALOU, Miss. Maria Georgiou, BSc FCA *1984;* Telecommunications Street P.O.Box 24929, CY1396 NICOSIA, CYPRUS.

DAMAN, Mrs. Josephine Linda, BA ACA *1985;* Sheeplands House Wargrave Road, Wargrave, READING, RG10 8DJ.

DAMAN, Mr. Michael James, BA ACA *1983;* Sheeplands House, Wargrave Road, Wargrave, READING, RG10 8DJ.

DAMANI, Mr. Mustak, BSc ACA *1979;* P.O. Box 1009, HASSOCKS, BN6 8RR.

DAMANI, Mr. Prajesh Anupchand, ACA *1987;* 87 Kingshill Avenue, HARROW, MIDDLESEX, HA3 8LA.

DAMANIA, Mr. Deepak, BSc ACA *1999;* Praca Getulio Vargas 134, Guaruja, SAO PAULO, 11421-250, BRAZIL.

DAMANT, Mr. Frederick Michael, FCA *1961;* 113B Superior Street, VICTORIA V8V 1T2, BC, CANADA. (Life Member)

DAMANT, Mr. Ian Reginald, BA ACA *1987;* 10 Grosvenor Gardens, SOUTHAMPTON, SO17 1RS.

•DAMARELL, Mr. Ian Robert, BA FCA *1986;* BDO Limited, PO Box 180, Place du Pre, Rue du Pre, St Peter Port, GUERNSEY GY1 3LL.

•DAMER, Mr. Anthony Joseph Charles, MA ACA *1987;* (Tax Fac), Ian Murray & Co, 40 Stockwell Street, LONDON, SE10 8EY.

DAMER, Mr. Justin Dawson, BSc ACA *1997;* Heather Cottage, Lansdown, BATH, BA1 9BL.

DAMERY, Mr. Aynsley Norman, BComm FCA *2004;* Ireland (Tax Fac), Tayabali-Tomlin Limited, Kenton House, Oxford Street, MORETON-IN-MARSH, GLOUCESTERSHIRE, GL56 0LA.

DAMIANI, Mr. Piero Jeann, FCA *1982;* Sapien Consulting Middle East, PO Box 31579, JANABYA, BAHRAIN.

DAMIANOU, Mr. Christos, BSc ACA *2007;* Arsakiou 13, Strovolos, 2045 NICOSIA, CYPRUS.

DAMIANOU, Mr. Costas, BA ACA *2006;* 5 Ypatis Street, Agios Athanasios, 4108 LIMASSOL, CYPRUS.

DAMIANOU, Mr. Panayiotis, BA(Hons) ACA *2009;* 9 Andrea Georgiou Street, Anarita, 8502 PAPHOS, CYPRUS.

DAMJI, Mr. Altaaf Tajdin Hussein, FCA *1980;* 343 Hawkcliff Way N.W., CALGARY T3G 2W7, AB, CANADA.

DAMJI, Mr. Salim Kahn, FCA *1979;* 9647 NW 67th Pl, Parkland, POMPANO BEACH, FL 33076, UNITED STATES.

DAMMERMANN, Mr. Peter Mills, FCA *1973;* Robindale, Honiley, KENILWORTH, WARWICKSHIRE, CV8 1NP.

DAMPIER, Mr. Alexander Paul, BA ACA *2003;* Flat 73, Pinehurst Court, 1-3 Colville Gardens, LONDON, W11 2BJ.

DAMPIER, Mr. James Denis, BA ACA *1993;* Dove Cottage, The Green, Ockley, DORKING, RH5 5SS.

•DAMYON, Mr. Andre Edward, FCA 1977; J R Bowls Shop, 52 Field Street, UPPER MOUNT GRAVATT, QLD 4122, AUSTRALIA.
DANAHER, Mr. Alan, ACA 2006; Flat 3 Goldington House, Evesham Road, CHELTENHAM, GLOUCESTERSHIRE, GL52 3AB.
DANAHER, Mr. Stephen Paul, BSc FCA 1977; (Tax Fac), 32 Lower Manor Lane, BURNLEY, BB12 0EB.
DANAN, Mr. Jonathan, ACA 2005; JD Accountants, Katzenelbogen, St. 48/1, 93871 JERUSALEM, ISRAEL.
DANBY, Mr. Michael Alan, BA ACA 1992; 12 Grange Road, LONDON, W5 5BX.
DANBY, Mr. Nicholas Gregory, BSc ACA 1990; Jersey Heritage Trust, The Weighbridge, St Helier, JERSEY, JE2 3NF.
DANBY, Miss. Stephanie, ACA 2008; with Nicholsons, Newland House, The Point, Weaver Road, LINCOLN, LN6 3QN.
DANBY, Mr. Stephen Paul, BSc ACA 1988; 7 Aspen Close, Walmley, SUTTON COLDFIELD, B76 2PA.
DANCASTER, Mr. David Patrick, BA ACA 1986; 1 Kenilworth Avenue, Wimbledon, LONDON, SW19 7LN.
DANCE, Mr. Alistair Charles Henzell, BSc ACA 1991; 9/78a Old Pittwater Road, BROOKVALE, NSW 2100, AUSTRALIA.
DANCE, Mr. Andrew Kevin, BSc ACA ATII 1987; (Tax Fac), Damhsa, Church Lane, Goodworth Clatford, ANDOVER, HAMPSHIRE, SP11 7HL.
DANCE, Mr. George Henry, ACA 1980; Haggerston Flowers, Haggerston, BERWICK-UPON-TWEED, TD15 2NZ.
DANCE, Mr. James, BSc ACA 2010; Flat 7, Ketley House, 65 Garratt Lane, LONDON, SW18 4GR.
DANCE, Mr. Michael Graham, ACA CA(SA) 2009; 5 St. Marys Grove, LONDON, W4 3LL.
DANCE, Mr. Samuel Christopher, BSc ACA 2007; 13 St. Marys Road, REIGATE, RH2 7JH.
DANCE, Mr. Stephen Gary, BA FCA 1977; 191 High Street, WINCHESTER, MA 01890-3364, UNITED STATES.
DANCE, Mr. Timothy Mark, BSc FCA 1996; 1st Floor S&C Dept., Royal Mail, 35-50 Rathbone Place, LONDON, W1T 1HQ.
DANCER, Mr. Paul William Albert, BA ACA 1986; 51 Hundred Acres Lane, AMERSHAM, BUCKINGHAMSHIRE, HP7 9EA.
DANCER, Ms. Sharon Faye, BSc ACA 1993; 55 Hickmans Close, GODSTONE, RH9 8EB.
DANCEY, Mr. Clive Robert, BA ACA 1984; 39 Montrose Avenue, TWICKENHAM, TW2 6HE.
DANCEY, Mr. Jonathan Peter, FCA 1983; with Geldards LLP, The Finance Department, Dumfries House, Dumfries Place, CARDIFF, CF10 3ZF.
DANCEY, Mrs. Linda Elizabeth, BA ACA 1984; 39 Montrose Avenue, Whitton, TWICKENHAM, TW2 6HE.
DANCIGER, Mr. Paul Anthony, FCA 1966; 51 Preston Road, Wembley Park, WEMBLEY, HA9 8JZ.
DANCOURT-CAVANAGH, Mr. Jonathan Jeremy Aidan, MA ACA 1995; Council of the European Union, Rue de la Loi 175, B 1048 BRUSSELS, BELGIUM.
DANCY, Mr. David Alan, FCA 1958; 6 Orde Close, Pound Hill, CRAWLEY, RH10 3NG. (Life Member)
DANDO, Mrs. Andrea, BSc ACA 1997; The Manor House, 53 Main Street, Long Whatton, LOUGHBOROUGH, LE12 5DF.
DANDO, Mr. Brian Harry, FCA 1959; Cobb Webbs, 30 South Street, Hatherleigh, OKEHAMPTON, DEVON, EX20 3JB. (Life Member)
DANDO, Mr. John Michael, MA FCA 1977; 10 Henley Gardens, PINNER, HA5 2DE.
•DANDO, Mr. Neil Adrian, FCA 1988; Wormald & Partners, Redland House, 157 Redland Road, BRISTOL, BS6 6YE.
DANDO, Mr. Stephen Peter, BSc ACA 1997; The Manor House, 53 Main Street, Long Whatton, LOUGHBOROUGH, LE12 5DF.
DANDRIDGE, Mr. John Presland, FCA 1950; 113A South Avenue, Athol Sandton, JOHANNESBURG, GAUTENG, 2196, SOUTH AFRICA. (Life Member)
DANDY, Mr. John, FCA 1964; 10 Jacksons Orchard, Long Marston, STRATFORD, WARWICKSHIRE, CV37 8RU. (Life Member)
•DANDY, Mrs. Sharla Jane, BA(Hons) ACA CTA 2001; Painswick Accounting & Taxation Services Ltd, Green Ridges, Cotswold Mead, Painswick, STROUD, GLOUCESTERSHIRE GL6 6XB.
DANE, Mr. Clifford Victor, MA ACA 1980; Snapper Music Plc, 1 Star Street, LONDON, W2 1QD.
DANE, Mr. David Avenell Spencer, FCA 1962; Roselen, 18 Egerton Road, PADSTOW, PL28 8DJ.
DANE, Mr. Ian Richard, BA FCA 1988; British American Tobacco Plc, Globe House, 4 Temple Place, LONDON, WC2R 2PG.
DANE, Miss. Janice Elizabeth, BSc ACA 1994; 20 Swaffham Road, Mundford, THETFORD, IP26 5HR.
DANE, Mr. Michael William Spencer, FCA 1957; Two Oaks, 22 Ashley Park Avenue, WALTON-ON-THAMES, KT12 1ER. (Life Member)
DANE, Mr. Thomas Andrew, MSc ACA 2007; Pricewaterhousecoopers, 7 More London Riverside, LONDON, SE1 2RT.
DANEE, Mrs. Richa, BSc ACA 2006; 2 HELICONIA TURN, STIRLING, WA 6021, AUSTRALIA.
DANENBERGS, Mr. Robert, BA(Hons) ACA 2001; ALSTOM Switzerland Ltd, Brown Boveri Strasse 8, 5401 BADEN, SWITZERLAND.
•DANES, Mr. Desmond Hector John, BA FCA 1984; (Tax Fac), Wheelers (2020) Limited, 6 Providence Court, Pynes Hill, EXETER, EX2 5JL.
DANES, Mr. Jack, BA ACA 2006; 4 Kings Moor, Southglade Park, NOTTINGHAM, NG5 9RE.
•DANESHZADEH, Miss. Nassim, LLB ACA 2003; 154 Oakwood Court, Abbotsbury Road, Holland Park, LONDON, W14 8JT.
DANFORTH, Mr. David Stuart, BSc FCA 1982; Image Data Group Ltd, Grange Park Lane, Willerby, HULL, HU10 6EB.
DANG, Miss. Anh, ACA 2011; Flat 2, 50 Sutherland Avenue, LONDON, W9 2QU.
DANG, Mr. Man Gon Edmund, ACA FCPA 2004; with Ernst & Young, 18/F, Two International Finance Centre, 8 Finance Street, CENTRAL, HONG KONG ISLAND HONG KONG SAR.
DANGERFIELD, Mrs. Carol Jessie, BSc ACA 1985; 61 Meadway, HARPENDEN, AL5 1JH.
•DANGERFIELD, Mr. Gary, BSc ACA 1994; 2 Finstock Heath, Witney Road, Finstock, CHIPPING NORTON, OXFORDSHIRE, OX7 3DF.
DANGERFIELD, Mrs. Holly Felicity, MA ACA 2000; Martens Oast Lower Ensden Farm, Lower Ensden Road Old Wives Lees, CANTERBURY, CT4 8BA.
DANGERFIELD, Mr. John Michael, FCA 1972; 24 Harvest House, Cobbold Road, FELIXSTOWE, SUFFOLK, IP11 7SP. (Life Member)
DANGERFIELD, Mr. Kevin Jeremy, BSc ACA 1995; 51 Longdown Lane North, EPSOM, KT17 3JB.
•DANGOOR, Mr. Robert Philip, FCA 1985; Dangoor & Company, 36 Chester Close North, Regents Park, LONDON, NW1 4JE.
DANIEL, Mr. Alan, FCA 1976; Techni-Build (Northern) Ltd Bent Ley Road, Meltham, HOLMFIRTH, HD9 4AP.
DANIEL, Mr. Bradley John, BSc FCA 1996; Moosbachweg 17, 6300 ZUG, SWITZERLAND.
DANIEL, Miss. Caroline Jane, BA ACA 2001; 1 Vine Farm Road, Talbot Village, POOLE, DORSET, BH12 5EN.
DANIEL, Mrs. Elanor Kate, BA ACA 2003; 29 Hamptons Lane, SOUTHAMPTON SN02, BERMUDA.
DANIEL, Mrs. Elizabeth Marion, FCA 1981; The Grange Centre The Grange, Rectory Lane Bookham, LEATHERHEAD, KT23 4DZ.
DANIEL, Miss. Emma Louise, ACA 2008; 14b Lausanne Road, LONDON, SE15 2HU.
DANIEL, Mr. Geoffrey, BA ACA 1983; with Deloitte LLP, 1 City Square, LEEDS, WEST YORKSHIRE, LS1 2AL.
DANIEL, Mr. Graeme Trevor, MBA BA ACA 1980; 30b Daleham Gardens, Hampstead, LONDON, NW3 5DD.
•DANIEL, Mr. Harry Jonathan, BA FCA 1988; (Tax Fac), Pinnick Lewis, Handel House, 95 High Street, EDGWARE, HA8 7DB.
DANIEL, Mrs. Jacqueline Mary, BA ACA 1985; 19 Benhall Mill Road, TUNBRIDGE WELLS, TN2 5JH.
DANIEL, Mr. Jonathan James, BA ACA 2004; 107 Farnsworth Court, West Parkside, GREENWICH, SE10 0RU.
DANIEL, Mr. Laurance James, BSc(Hons) ACA 2001; CastlePoint Reinsurance Company, 6th Floor Victoria Hall, 11 Victoria Street, HAMILTON HM11, BERMUDA.
DANIEL, Ms. Lynne, BA ACA 1981; 66 Boltons Lane, Pyrford, WOKING, GU22 8TN.
DANIEL, Mr. Martin, BA ACA 2001; with Moore Stephens LLP, 150 Aldersgate Street, LONDON, EC1A 4AB.
•DANIEL, Mr. Michael Neil, FCA 1963; Michael N. Daniel & Co, 4 Mill Street, CRICKHOWELL, POWYS, NP8 1BA.
•DANIEL, Mr. Peter Francis, MSc FCA CFE 1990; Fairlead Forensic Accounting, Roseleigh, New Street, BANBURY, OX15 0SP.
DANIEL, Mr. Peter George, FCA ATII 1948; 28 Bushell Way, Frinton Gates, FRINTON-ON-SEA, CO13 0TW. (Life Member)
•DANIEL, Mr. Peter Roger, FCA 1978; (Tax Fac), Murray Smith LLP, Darland House, 44 Winnington Hill, NORTHWICH, CHESHIRE, CW8 1AU.
DANIEL, Mr. Richard, FCA 1972; 20 Egglestone Square, Boston Spa, WETHERBY, LS23 6RX.
DANIEL, Mr. Richard, MA ACA CTA 2003; 98 Yoxall Road, Shirley, SOLIHULL, B90 3RP.
DANIEL, Mr. Richard Paul, BA(Hons) ACA 2000; Foreign Language Institute, Yeungnam University, Dae-dong 214-1, GYEONGSAN, 712-749, KOREA REPUBLIC OF.
DANIEL, Ms. Rio, BA ACA 2007; Solomon R. Guggenheim Museum, 12th Floor, 345 Hudson Street, NEW YORK, NY 10014, UNITED STATES.
DANIEL, Mr. Roy, BA FCA 1977; 20 Bittern Close, Kempshott, BASINGSTOKE, RG22 5JA.
DANIEL, Mr. Simon Charles, BSc ACA 2006; 53 Strode Road, LONDON, SW6 6BL.
DANIEL, Mr. Simon William, LLB ACA 1991; Serious Fraud Office, Elm House, 10-16 Elm Street, LONDON, WC1X 0BJ.
DANIEL-TAGISADE, Mrs. Dilys Elizabeth, BSc ACA ACT 1982; Mozarstrasse 7c, 61250 USINGEN, GERMANY.
•DANIELL, Mr. James Andrew, FCA 1981; Craufurd Hale Audit Services Ltd, Ground Floor, Belmont Place, Belmont Road, MAIDENHEAD, BERKSHIRE SL6 6TB.
DANIELL, Miss. Jessica Charlotte, BSc ACA 2010; RNRMC Building 29, H M S Excellent, Whale Island, PORTSMOUTH, PO2 8ER.
DANIELL, Mr. John Paul, BSc ACA 2009; Flat 12, 55 Tanner Street, LONDON, SE1 3PN.
DANIELL, Mr. Neil, BA ACA 2007; 6 Victory Way, Canada Water, LONDON, SE16 6QH.
DANIELL, Miss. Rebecca Jane, ACA 2008; 14 Graham Road, REDRUTH, CORNWALL, TR15 2HG.
DANIELLS, Mr. Paul Anthony, BA ACA 2009; Flat 10 The Towers, Lower Mortlake Road, RICHMOND, TW9 2JR.
•DANIELS, Mrs. Alison Joyce, FCA 1977; Hughes Waddell Limited, Hughes Waddell, 2 Meadrow, GODALMING, SURREY, GU7 3HN.
DANIELS, Mr. Andrew John Spencer, FCA 1978; Emil-Ruetti-Weg 2, 8050 ZURICH, SWITZERLAND.
DANIELS, Miss. Anne Elizabeth, BSc FCA 1992; with BDO LLP, 55 Baker Street, LONDON, W1U 7EU.
DANIELS, Mr. Anthony Patrick, FCA 1970; Derwent, 26 Sydenham Road North, CHELTENHAM, GLOUCESTERSHIRE, GL52 6EA.
DANIELS, Mr. Christopher Charles, BSc FCA 1975; 3 Bradbeers, Staplehay, TAUNTON, TA3 7JQ. (Life Member)
DANIELS, Mr. Christopher David, BSc ACA 1992; 1, Goodwood Close, CONSETT, DH8 0UF.
•DANIELS, Mr. Daniel, FCA 1973; (Tax Fac), Davis Bonley, Northside House, Mount Pleasant, BARNET, EN4 9EE.
DANIELS, Mr. David Twyning James, BSc ACA MCT 1993; InterContinental Hotels Group PLC, 1 First Avenue, Centrum One Hundred, BURTON-ON-TRENT, STAFFORDSHIRE, DE14 2WB.
DANIELS, Mrs. Deborah Jolene, BA(Hons) ACA 2002; 3 Brunswick Gardens, HAVANT, HAMPSHIRE, PO9 3HZ.
DANIELS, Mr. Frank Albert, FCA 1957; 59 Lodge Road, WALSALL, WS5 3LA. (Life Member)
DANIELS, Mr. George James Brian, BA ACA 1980; Bents Garden Centre Ltd, Warrington Road, Leigh End, Glazebury, WARRINGTON, CHESHIRE WA3 5NT.
DANIELS, Mrs. Georgina Mary, BSc ACA 1995; Greatworth Manor, Brackley Road, Greatworth, BANBURY, OXFORDSHIRE, OX17 2DX.
DANIELS, Mrs. Helen Julie, ACA MIIA 1999; 1 Edgehill Way, ASHBY-DE-LA-ZOUCH, LEICESTERSHIRE, LE65 1LH.
DANIELS, Mrs. Helen Louise, LLB ACA 2003; 8 Beechwood Park, Bailiff Bridge, BRIGHOUSE, WEST YORKSHIRE, HD6 4FD.
DANIELS, Mr. Herbert Norman, FCA 1953; The Laurels, 35 Highfield Street, Anstey, LEICESTER, LE7 7DU. (Life Member)
DANIELS, Mr. Ian, ACA 2006; HCP, Unit 8 White Oak Square, London Road, SWANLEY, BR8 7AG.
•DANIELS, Mr. Ian Alan, BSc FCA 1989; haysmacintyre, Fairfax House, 15 Fulwood Place, LONDON, WC1V 6AY.
DANIELS, Mr. Jeffrey Mark, ACA 2011; Flat 2b, 2a-2c Lydford Road, LONDON, NW2 5SA.
•DANIELS, Mr. John Arthur, FCA 1976; J Daniels & Co Ltd, 10 Wallers Hoppet, LOUGHTON, ESSEX, IG10 1SP.
DANIELS, Mr. John Ward Lyle, FCA 1955; Unit 140, Great brak river, GROENKLOOF, CAPE 6525, SOUTH AFRICA. (Life Member)
DANIELS, Mrs. Katherine Anna, BSc ACA 2007; 2 Leverton Gardens Naldertown, WANTAGE, OXFORDSHIRE, OX12 9NY.
•DANIELS, Mr. Keith Barry, FCA 1967; (Tax Fac), Daniels & Co, 111a Station Road, WEST WICKHAM, BR4 0PX.
DANIELS, Mr. Kenneth James, FCA 1974; 26 Lane End Road, Spinney Field, ROTHERHAM, SOUTH YORKSHIRE, S60 3HR.
DANIELS, Mrs. Kirsty, BSc(Hons) ACA 2001; 3 Marlgrove Court, Marlbrook, BROMSGROVE, WORCESTERSHIRE, B61 0HE.
DANIELS, Mrs. Lisa, BSc ACA 1998; with Larking Gowen, King Street House, 15 Upper King Street, NORWICH, NR3 1RB.
DANIELS, Mr. Matthew, ACA 2008; 2 Leverton Gardens, WANTAGE, OXFORDSHIRE, OX12 9NY.
DANIELS, Mr. Matthew James, PhD MSc ACA 1996; James W Shenton Ltd, Tinsley Street, Great Bridge, TIPTON, WEST MIDLANDS, DY4 7LQ.
DANIELS, Mr. Michael, FCA 1960; 8 Dalkeith Grove, STANMORE, HA7 4SG. (Life Member)
•DANIELS, Ms. Michelle Joanne, FCA 1997; James Todd & Co Limited, Nos 1 & 2 The Barn, Oldwick, West Stoke Road, Lavant, CHICHESTER WEST SUSSEX PO18 9AA.
DANIELS, Mr. Neville, BSc ACA 1994; Future Australia, PO Box 1077, Mount street, SYDNEY, NSW 2059, AUSTRALIA.
•DANIELS, Mr. Neville Cyril, FCA 1973; Wrigley Partington, Sterling House, 501 Middleton Road, Chadderton, OLDHAM, OL9 9LY.
•DANIELS, Mrs. Samantha Jane, FCA 1996; Pearson Buchholz Limited, North House, Farmoor Court, Cumnor Road, Farmoor, OXFORD OX2 9LU.
DANIELS, Mr. Simon, ACA 2009; Aminadav 3, 67067 TEL AVIV, ISRAEL.
•DANIELS, Mr. Stephen, BA FCA 1980; (Tax Fac), Practical Accounting Limited, 50 Ashby Road, TAMWORTH, STAFFORDSHIRE, B79 8AD.
DANIELS, Mr. Steven Henry, MSc BEng ACA 2002; 188 Picket Post Lane, PHOENIXVILLE, PA 19460, UNITED STATES.
DANIELS, Mr. Timothy John, MA ACA 1997; 3 Claremont Road, LONDON, N6 5DA.
•DANIELS, Mr. William Roger, BSc FCA 1972; (Tax Fac), Daniels Accounts LLP, Unit B1 Laser Quay, Culpeper Close, Medway City Estate, ROCHESTER, ME2 4HU. See also Daniels & Co LLP
DANIELSON, Mr. John Martin, MA BSc ACA 1999; 71 Derby Square, Douglas, ISLE OF MAN, IM1 3LR.
DANILATOS, Mr. Dimosthenis, BSc ACA 2008; 15 Kefallinias Street, 15126 MAROUSI, GREECE.
DANINO, Mr. Andrew Morgan, BSc FCA 1979; 22 Rue Villedieu, 33000 BORDEAUX, FRANCE.
DANKER, Mr. Maximillian John, BA FCA 1983; 29 Eppalong Street, The Gap, BRISBANE, QLD 4061, AUSTRALIA.
DANKS, Mr. Leigh Richard, MSci ACA 2004; 6 Buttermere Close, BRIERLEY HILL, DY5 3SD.
•DANKS, Mr. Nicholas Charles, FCA 1972; dhjh LLP, Springhill House, 94-98 Kidderminster Road, BEWDLEY, WORCESTERSHIRE, DY12 1DQ.
DANKS, Mrs. Patricia Dilys, BSc ACA 1979; 47 Willow Park Drive, Oldswinford, STOURBRIDGE, DY8 2HL.
DANKS, Mr. Trevor Anthony, BA(Hons)Oxon ACA CTA 2006; Crofters, 96 Station Road, AMERSHAM, BUCKINGHAMSHIRE, HP7 0AS.
DANKS, Mr. Walter Leslie, FCA 1950; 11 Dingle Road, STOURBRIDGE, DY9 0RS. (Life Member)
DANKWA, Miss. Christiana Angela, BA ACA FRSA 2007; 52 Abbots Road, EDGWARE, MIDDLESEX, HA8 0RE.
DANN, Mr. Adam Peter, BSc ACA 2006; 98 Rosary Road, NORWICH, NR1 4DA.
•DANN, Mr. Andrew Jonathan, FCA 1987; Ernst & Young LLP, Liberation House, Castle Street, St Helier, JERSEY, JE1 1EY. See also Ernst & Young Europe LLP
DANN, Mr. Nickolas Graeme Peter, BSc ACA 1987; Dan y Coed, LLANFYLLIN, POWYS, SY22 5LZ.
DANN, Mr. Peter, FCA 1968; Copse Hill, Fishers Lane, Cold Ash, THATCHAM, RG18 9NG.
•DANN, Mr. Peter Charles, BSc FCA 1974; Clifton-Crick Sharp & Co, 40 High Street, PERSHORE, WORCESTERSHIRE, WR10 1DP.

•**DANN, Mr. Phillip Andrew, BA ACA** *1988;* (Tax Fac), Dean Statham LLP, 29 King Street, NEWCASTLE, STAFFORDSHIRE, ST5 1ER.

•**DANN, Mr. William Edward, FCA** *1974;* (Tax Fac), William Dann & Co, 30-32 Norwich Street, DEREHAM, NR19 1BX.

DANNAN, Mr. Edward, BA(Hons) ACA *2001;* T-Mobile (UK) Ltd Unit 1, Mosquito Way, HATFIELD, HERTFORDSHIRE, AL10 9BW.

DANNATT, Mr. Gary John, BSc ACA *1995;* 13 College Ride, BAGSHOT, GU19 5EW.

DANNELL, Mr. Geoffrey Brian, BSc FCA *1963;* 28-30 Main Street, Woodnewton, PETERBOROUGH, PE8 5EB. (Life Member)

DANNHAUSER, Mr. David Stephen, MA FCA *1979;* 8 Marsworth Avenue, PINNER, MIDDLESEX, HA5 4UB.

DANOU, Ms. Irene, BA FCA *1987;* 26 Thessalonikis Street, 2122 NICOSIA, CYPRUS.

DANQUAH, Mr. Kenneth, ACA *2009;* Universal Pictures International Entertainment Ltd, Prospect House 80-110 New Oxford Street, LONDON, WC1A 1HB.

DANSER, Mr. Anthony Jack, FCA *1958;* A J Danger, Suite 2, 17 Elliott House, Allington Street, LONDON, SW1E 5EH.

DANSEY, Mrs. Lisa Sarah, BSc ACA *2000;* 28 Mareshall Avenue, Warfield, BRACKNELL, RG42 2QU.

DANSIE, Mr. Kenneth John, FCA *1971;* Burr Pilger & Mayer LLP, 110 Stony Point Road, Suite 210, SANTA ROSA, CA 95401, UNITED STATES.

•**DANSON, Mr. John Stuart, FCA** *1967;* John S Danson & Co, 35 Salisbury Road, DRONFIELD, DERBYSHIRE, S18 1UG.

DANT, Mr. Christopher James, MPhil BA ACA *1995;* Hallam Meat Company Ltd, Cheveley Park Stud, Duchess Drive, NEWMARKET, SUFFOLK, CB8 9DD.

DANT, Mrs. Elizabeth Karen, BSc ACA *1999;* 5 Barrow Road, CAMBRIDGE, CB2 8AP.

DANTON, Mr. Mark Paul, BSc ACA *1982;* (Tax Fac), 3214 Bonnebridge Way Blvd, HOUSTON, TX 77082, UNITED STATES.

DANVERS, Mrs. Gillian Mary, BA ACA *1989;* (Tax Fac), Unilever Plc Unilever House, 100 Victoria Embankment, LONDON, EC4Y 0DY.

•**DANZIG, Mr. John Jacob, BSc FCA** *1978;* Danzig & Co, 8-12 Torphichen Street, EDINBURGH, EH3 8JQ.

DAO, Mr. Tung Thanh, ACA FCCA ACCA *2007;* Ernst & Young Centre, 680 George Street, SYDNEY, NSW 2000, AUSTRALIA.

DAPLYN, Mrs. Claire Louise, BA ACA *1999;* 10 Vicarage Hill, FARNHAM, SURREY, GU9 8HJ.

DAPP, Mr. Nicholas Andrew Lancaster, BSc ACA *1995;* 22 Kingswood Close, Lapworth, SOLIHULL, B94 6JQ.

DAR, Mr. Ahmed Jamal, MSc BA ACA *2005;* 68 Leamington Avenue, MORDEN, SM4 4DN.

DAR, Senator Mohammad Ishaq, FCA *1974;* P.O.Box 487036, DUBAI, UNITED ARAB EMIRATES. (Life Member)

DAR, Mr. Mohit, BSc(Hons) ACA FCCA MBA *2010;* 21 Speedwell Road, Edgbaston, BIRMINGHAM, WEST MIDLANDS, B5 7QA.

DAR, Miss. Naddiah Amin, BSc ACA *2003;* 20 Meadow Hill, NEW MALDEN, KT3 5RQ.

DARA, Mr. Alireza, BSc FCA *1981;* 23 Lynwood Road, LONDON, W5 1JQ.

DARBAZ, Mr. Levent, BSc(Hons) ACA *2003;* Frogmore Property Company Limited, 11-15 Wigmore Street, LONDON, W1A 2JZ.

DARBISHIRE, Mr. William Anthony Peat, FCA *1975;* PO Box 847, LUTWYCHE, QLD 4030, AUSTRALIA.

DARBOURNE, Mr. Graham, BSc ACA *2005;* with Ryecroft Glenton, 32 Portland Terrace, Jesmond, NEWCASTLE UPON TYNE, NE2 1QP.

DARBY, Miss. Amabel Victoria Louise, BA(Hons) ACA *2003;* 29 A Limes Grove, LEWISHAM, SE13 6DD.

DARBY, Mr. Andrew Hamish, MA ACA *1990;* Oak House, 9a Oatlands Chase, WEYBRIDGE, SURREY, KT13 9RF.

•**DARBY, Mr. Andrew Thomas, BA FCA** *1986;* (Tax Fac), Gorman Darby & Co Limited, 74 Chancery Lane, LONDON, WC2A 1AD.

DARBY, Mrs. Barbara Joan, BSc FCA *1973;* (Tax Fac), Regnum House, 40 Lyndhurst Road, CHICHESTER, PO19 7PE.

DARBY, Mr. Barry James Arthur, FCA *1968;* 21 Russell Drive, East Budleigh, BUDLEIGH SALTERTON, DEVON, EX9 7EJ.

DARBY, Miss. Catherine, ACA *2009;* 58 Kay Road, LONDON, SW9 9DE.

•**DARBY, Mr. Christopher Thomas, MA ACA** *1993;* AIMS - CD 68 Enterprises Limited, 18 Kinnoul Road, LONDON, W6 8NQ.

DARBY, Mr. David Peter, BA FCA *1976;* 5 Torland Drive, Oxshott, LEATHERHEAD, KT22 0SA.

DARBY, Mrs. Elaine Sone, BA FCA *1999;* Hill View The Coombe, Streatley, READING, RG8 9QL.

DARBY, Miss. Elizabeth Claire, BA ACA *2004;* BG Group Plc, Thames Valley Park, READING, RG6 1PT.

DARBY, Mr. Jarrod Baden, BSc ACA *1993;* 18 Florence Park, Westbury Park, BRISTOL, BS6 7LP.

DARBY, Mr. John Oliver Robertson, FCA *1953;* The Tithe Barn High Street Headley, BORDON, HAMPSHIRE, GU35 8PW. (Life Member)

DARBY, Mr. John Trevor Hudson, FCA *1960;* 10 Chantry Road, Stourton, STOURBRIDGE, DY7 6SA.

DARBY, Mr. Lee Thomas, BA ACA *1992;* 5 Dean Close, Priorslee, TELFORD, SHROPSHIRE, TF2 9SN.

•**DARBY, Mrs. Lisa Jane, ACA** *1995;* Lisa Darby ACA, 18 Church Road, BUCKHURST HILL, ESSEX, IG9 5RU.

①**DARBY, Mr. Mark William, MA FCA FABRP** *1983;* 81 Thorkhill Road, THAMES DITTON, SURREY, KT7 0UQ.

DARBY, Mr. Michael Dieter, JP DL FCA *1960;* 20 Paddock Drive, Wood Lane, Parkgate, NESTON, CH64 6TQ. (Life Member)

DARBY, Mr. Neil John, BSc FCA *1993;* Lloyds Banking Group plc, 25 Gresham Street, LONDON, EC2V 7HN.

DARBY, Mr. Neil Sidney, BA FCA *1983;* 5 Martingale Close, BILLERICAY, CM11 1SQ.

DARBY, Mr. Ralph Simon, BA ACA *1982;* 733 Liquidamber Place, DANVILLE, CA 94506, UNITED STATES.

•**DARBY, Mr. Raymond, FCA** *1977;* (Tax Fac), Warings Business Advisers LLP, Bedford House, 60 Chorley New Road, BOLTON, BL1 4DA.

•**DARBY, Mr. Roger Michael, FCA** *1971;* Roger M Darby Limited, 85 High Street, Kinver, STOURBRIDGE, WEST MIDLANDS, DY7 6HD.

DARBY, Mrs. Sarah, BSc ACA *1993;* 18 Florence Park, Westbury Park, BRISTOL, BS6 7LP.

•**DARBY, Miss. Teresa Mary, BA FCA** *1996;* with BDO LLP, 125 Colmore Row, BIRMINGHAM, B3 3SD.

DARBYSHIRE, Mr. Andrew, MMath ACA *2011;* 26 Low Street, Leeming Bar, NORTHALLERTON, NORTH YORKSHIRE, DL7 9BN.

DARBYSHIRE, Mr. Brent Alfred, FCA *1974;* Egan Reid Stationary Co Ltd, Horsfield Way, Bredbury Business Park, STOCKPORT, CHESHIRE, SK6 2SU. (Life Member)

DARBYSHIRE, Mr. Colin George, FCA *1954;* Miguel Aljovin 115, Departamento 404, Miraflores, LIMA, 18, PERU. (Life Member)

DARBYSHIRE, Mr. David Stewart, MA FCA *1970;* Hutton Mount, Hutton Bank, RIPON, HG4 5DR. (Life Member)

•**DARBYSHIRE, Mr. John, BA FCA** *1960;* J. Darbyshire, 31 York Road, Grappenhall, WARRINGTON, WA4 2EH.

DARBYSHIRE, Mr. Mathew, BSc(Econ) ACA *2002;* 38 MacDowall Road, GUILDFORD, SURREY, GU2 9LD.

•**DARBYSHIRE, Mr. Robin Vivian, BSc FCA** *1979;* (Tax Fac), Robin Darbyshire FCA, 43 Ethelbert Road, Wimbledon, LONDON, SW20 8QE.

DARBYSHIRE, Mr. Timothy, BA ACA *1989;* 14 The Hawthorns, Wilpshire, BLACKBURN, BB1 9JW.

DARCEY, Mr. Roy, FCA *1974;* 25 Knightsbridge Court, Skircoat Green Road, HALIFAX, WEST YORKSHIRE, HX3 0DD.

•**DARCH, Mr. Robin Adrian, FCA** *1978;* 84 Main Road, Kempsey, WORCESTER, WR5 3JY.

DARCH, Mr. Trevor Anthony, BA ACA *1983;* Barford Farm House, Common Hill, Medstead, ALTON, GU34 5LZ.

DARCY, Mr. Eliot Mark, ACA *2008;* 7a Elmore Street, LONDON, N1 3AW.

DARCY, Mrs. Pui-Wan, BCom ACA *2001;* 6 Maurice Way, MARLBOROUGH, SN8 3LG.

DARCY, Mr. Stephen Joseph Christopher, BSc ACA *1993;* 211 Heath Road, HOUNSLOW, TW3 2NU.

DARDIS, Mr. Ian Michael, BSc FCA *1985;* 48 Prince Albert Street, MOSMAN, NSW 2088, AUSTRALIA.

DARE, Mr. Andrew Gordon, FCA *1967;* 7 The Beeches, BRIGHTON, BN1 5LS.

DARE, Mr. Barry Stanton, BSc FCA CCMI *1961;* Mill Dene, Blockley, MORETON-IN-MARSH, GLOUCESTERSHIRE, GL56 9HU.

•**DARE, Mr. John Bruce Reginald, FCA** *1968;* 38 Compton Avenue, Lower Parkstone, POOLE, DORSET, BH14 8PY.

DARE, Mr. Paul Alexander, MSc FCA FCT ASIP *1968;* 23 Cumberland Road, Barnes, LONDON, SW13 9LY. (Life Member)

DARE, Mr. Robin John, BA ACA *1984;* 1 Pennryn, Stoppers Hill, Brinkworth, CHIPPENHAM, WILTSHIRE, SN15 5AW.

DARGAN, Mr. Barry Patrick, BSc FCA *1984;* 7A The Avenue, LONDON, N3 2LB.

•①**DARGAN, Mr. Nicholas James, BA FCA** *1986;* 1 Long Lane, Attenborough Beeston, NOTTINGHAM, NG9 6BG.

DARGIE, Mr. Alastair, BA ACA *2010;* with Deloitte LLP, 1 City Square, LEEDS, WEST YORKSHIRE, LS1 2AL.

DARGIE, Mr. James Bruce, BSc ACA *1994;* 31 Kimberley Road, BENFLEET, SS7 5NG.

DARGIE, Mr. Jonathan William, MA ACA *2001;* The Garden House, Main Street, East Farndon, MARKET HARBOROUGH, LEICESTERSHIRE, LE16 9SJ.

DARGUE, Mrs. Joanna Margaret, BSc(Hons) ACA *2001;* Ledco Ltd, Kingswick House, Kingswick Drive, SUNNINGHILL, SL57BH.

DARGUE, Mr. Michael James, BSc ACA *2010;* 69 Lancaster Avenue, BARNET, HERTFORDSHIRE, EN4 0ER.

DARGUE, Mr. Robert, BSc ACA *2001;* 4 Manor Way, EGHAM, SURREY, TW20 9NG.

DARGUE, Mr. Robert Charles, BA ACA *1990;* 96 Queen Victoria Road, SHEFFIELD, S17 4HU.

DARGUE, Mr. Roger Thomas, BSc FCA *1967;* (Tax Fac), with Begbies Chettle Agar, Epworth House, 25 City Road, LONDON, EC1Y 1AR.

DARGUE, Mr. Stephen John, BA FCA *1993;* 10 Sylvias Close, Amble, MORPETH, NE65 0GB.

DARJI, Mr. Bhupendra Shankerlal, FCA CPA *1975;* 6121 Oakbroof PKWY, Norcross, ATLANTA, GA 30093, UNITED STATES.

DARJI, Miss. Darshana Hazel, BSc(Hons) ACA *2001;* 321 Brownhill Road, LONDON, SE6 1AL.

DARJI, Ms. Jyoti, BSc(Econ) ACA *1998;* 12 Dowding Way, Leavesden, WATFORD, WD25 7GA.

DARK, Mr. Ronald Charles, BA ACA *1981;* D'Acre House, Waterworks Road, Sheet, PETERSFIELD, GU32 2AT.

DARK, Mr. Walter John, FCA *1940;* 35 Outwoods Road, LOUGHBOROUGH, LE11 3LX. (Life Member)

DARKE, Mr. Dominic Robert, ACA *2002;* 14 Morris Drive, BANBURY, OX16 1DA.

DARKE, Miss. Jessica, BSc(Hons) ACA *2010;* The Climb, Welton le Wold, LOUTH, LINCOLNSHIRE, LN11 0QT.

DARKE, Mr. Kenneth George, MA FCA *1934;* 15 Lister Court, Dale Road, PURLEY, CR8 2EA. (Life Member)

DARKE, Miss. Zoe Kathleen, ACA *2004;* with David Turner & Co, Studio 701, 17 Princess Street, HULL, HU2 8BJ.

DARKIN, Miss. Heather Mary, BA ACA *1991;* H C A Lateral, 8 City Walk, LEEDS, LS11 9AT.

DARKIN, Mr. Philip Edwin, BSc ACA *1987;* 24 West Way, CARSHALTON, SURREY, SM5 4EW.

DARKIN, Miss. Rosie, LLB(Hons) ACA *2003;* West Dorset District Council, Stratton House, High West Street, DORCHESTER, DORSET, DT1 1UZ.

DARKINS, Miss. Frances, BSc ACA *2010;* 406/22 Fisher-Point Drive, St Mary's Bay, AUCKLAND 1011, NEW ZEALAND.

DARKINS, Mrs. Sarah Elizabeth, ACA FCCA *2001;* 1 Skippon Way, Thorpe St Andrew, NORWICH, NR7 0RU.

DARKO, Miss. Gloria Korleki, BA FCA *1992;* 18 Crovens Close, Governors Hill, Douglas, ISLE OF MAN, IM2 7AH.

DARKO, Mr. Samuel Wilberforce Awuku, FCA *1957;* P.O. Box 51, G P O, ACCRA, GHANA. (Life Member)

DARLASTON, Mr. Lance Michael, ACA *1981;* 25 Cyprus Road, Maperley Park, NOTTINGHAM, NG3 5EB.

•**DARLASTON, Mr. Russell David, BSc FCA** *1995;* Crowe Clark Whitehill LLP, Black Country House, Rounds Green Road, OLDBURY, WEST MIDLANDS, B69 2DG. See also Horwath Clark Whitehill LLP and Crowe Clark Whitehill

DARLEY, Mr. James, ACA *2007;* 24 Kingswood Road, NOTTINGHAM, NG8 1LD.

DARLEY, Miss. Monica Mary, BA BPhil ACA *1981;* Churchtown Cottage, West Anstey, SOUTH MOLTON, EX36 3PE.

DARLEY, Mr. William West, MA ACA *1988;* Harkaway, George Road, Milford on Sea, LYMINGTON, HAMPSHIRE, SO41 0RS.

DARLING, Mr. Adrian Egerton, BSc FCA *1978;* Joiners Cottage, Melbourne Road, Staunton Harold, ASHBY-DE-LA-ZOUCH, LEICESTERSHIRE, LE65 1RU.

DARLING, Ms. Gill, BA ACA *1992;* City South Manchester Housing Trust Turing House, Archway, MANCHESTER, M15 5RL.

DARLING, Mr. Jonathan Peter, BA(Econ) ACA *2003;* Npower Ltd Oak House, Bridgwater Road, WORCESTER, WR4 9FP.

DARLING, Mr. Lee Andrew, BSc(Hons) ACA *2002;* Wyvern House 33 Willow Lane Milton, ABINGDON, OX14 4EG.

DARLING, Mr. Paul Edwin, BA ACA *1986;* Leapfrog Online, 807 Greenwood Street, Evanston, EVANSTON, IL 60201, UNITED STATES.

DARLING, Mr. Paul Thornton, MSc BSc ACA MSI *1991;* 73 Wavendon Avenue, Chiswick, LONDON, W4 4NT.

DARLING, Ms. Sally Marina, BSc ACA *1995;* GE Capital, 201 Merritt 7, 3rd Floor, NORWALK, CT 06851, UNITED STATES.

DARLING, Mr. Simon Mark, LLB ACA *1988;* Ashton House, Old Park, DEVIZES, WILTSHIRE, SN10 5JR.

DARLING, Mr. Stuart, ACA *1988;* 10 Cossington Close, Cottenham, CAMBRIDGE, CB24 8US.

DARLING, Mrs. Susan Frances Turl, BSc ACA *1991;* 73 Wavendon, Chiswick, LONDON, W4 4NT.

•**DARLINGTON, Mr. Christopher Alan, BA FCA** *1990;* with RSM Tenon Limited, 1 Bede Island Road, Bede Island Business Park, LEICESTER, LE2 7EA.

•**DARLINGTON, Mr. David, FCA** *1977;* Mitchell Charlesworth, Victoria House, 488 Knutsford Road, WARRINGTON, WA4 1DX.

DARLINGTON, Mr. John, BCom FCA *1984;* KPMG, 8 Salisbury Square, LONDON, EC7 4BB.

DARLINGTON, Mr. Patrick Robert Cranstone, FCA *1973;* Wisteria House, The Street, Whiteparish, SALISBURY, SP5 2SG.

DARLINGTON, Mr. Robert William, BSc FCA TEP *1991;* Chemin Du Perreret 5, 1270 Trelex, VAUD, SWITZERLAND.

DARLINGTON, Mr. Stephen Jeffrey, BSc ACA *1987;* Millwood House Church Road, Snitterfield, STRATFORD-UPON-AVON, CV37 0LE.

DARLINGTON, Mr. Stephen Ross, BA ACA *2004;* B P D, 2 Brooklands Road, SALE, CHESHIRE, M33 3SS.

DARLINGTON, Mr. Steve David, BA ACA *1987;* Howe & Co Craven House, 40-44 Uxbridge Road, LONDON, W5 2BS.

DARLINGTON, Mrs. Zoe, BSc ACA *1992;* Chemin Du Perreret 5, 1270 TRELEX, SWITZERLAND.

DARLINGTON-CRAMOND, Mr. Simon Peter, FCA *1981;* Braunton Farm, Kiln Lane, Isfield, UCKFIELD, EAST SUSSEX, TN22 5UE.

DARLISON, Mrs. Sandra Kathryn, BA ACA *1990;* Scarborough Group, Tower Court Business Centre, Oakdale Road, YORK, YO30 4XL.

DARMON, Mr. James Christopher, BA ACA *1984;* with The TACS Partnership, Graylaw House, Mersey Square, STOCKPORT, CHESHIRE, SK1 1AL.

•**DARNBROUGH, Mr. John Alister, MA FCA** *1984;* (Tax Fac), Darnbrough & Co Ltd, 8 York Place, KNARESBOROUGH, NORTH YORKSHIRE, HG5 0AA.

DARNELL, Mr. Edward Peter George, FCA *1960;* St Raphael, 33 Welcomes Road, KENLEY, CR8 5HA. (Life Member)

DARNELL, Mr. John Raymond, FCA *1949;* 11 Derncleugh Gardens, Holcombe, DAWLISH, EX7 0JG. (Life Member)

DARNELL, Miss. Nicola, BA ACA *1997;* 2 Mossgiel Street, FAIRLIGHT, NSW 2094, AUSTRALIA.

DARNELL, Mr. Paul, MA FCA *1978;* Flat 427, Students Residence William Goodenough House, 35-42 Mecklenburgh Square, LONDON, WC1N 2AN.

DARNELL, Mr. Peter Watson, FCA *1948;* Tanglewood, 132 Whittingham Lane, Broughton, PRESTON, PR3 5DD. (Life Member)

DARNELL, Mr. Stephen, BSc FCA *1984;* Maybank, 2 Wychwood Paddocks, Charlbury, CHIPPING NORTON, OX7 3RW.

DARNTON, Mr. Stephen Frederick, FCA *1972;* The Old Cottage, Studridge Lane, Speen, PRINCES RISBOROUGH, HP27 0SA. (Life Member)

DAROS, Miss. Aloysia Mame, BA(Hons) ACA *2009;* Smith & Williamson, 21 Chipper Lane, SALISBURY, SP1 1BG.

DARRACOTT, Mr. Simon John, BA ACA *1999;* 261 Stoughton Road, GUILDFORD, SURREY, GU2 9PQ.

DARRAH, Mr. Gerald Roger, BA FCA *1963;* 19 Syddal Green, Bramhall, STOCKPORT, CHESHIRE, SK7 1HP.

•**DARRAH, Mr. Robert James, BA ACA** *1997;* 50 Courtmoor Avenue, FLEET, HAMPSHIRE, GU52 7UE.

DARRINGTON, Mr. Bruce Edmund Philip, BSc ACA *1985;* Shibuya Cross Tower 13F, 2-15-1 Shibuya, Shibuya-ku, Mazars Japan, TOKYO, 150-002 JAPAN.

DARRINGTON, Mr. Charles Edward, BA ACIB ACA *1990;* Lane Cottage, Purley Lane, Purley On Thames, READING, BERKSHIRE, RG8 8AT.

Members - Alphabetical DARRINGTON - DAVE

DARRINGTON, Mrs. Eva Margaret, BSc ACA *1986;* Lane Cottage, Purley Lane, Purley on Thames, READING, RG8 8AT.

DARRINGTON, Sir Michael John, FCA *1965;* Middle Grange, Slaley, HEXHAM, NE47 0AA.

DARRINGTON, Mr. Stuart, BA ACA *2005;* 5 Browns Hedge, Pitstone, LEIGHTON BUZZARD, BEDFORDSHIRE, LU7 9GH.

DARROCH, Mr. David Jeremy, BSc ACA *1987;* Tangley, West Road, WEYBRIDGE, SURREY, KT13 0LZ.

DARROCH, Mr. John Fagan, FCA *1966;* Furness Grange, Furness Road, EASTBOURNE, BN21 4EX. (Life Member)

DARROCH, Mr. Joseph Burnie Campbell, FCA *1951;* StoneRidge, Quarry Hill, SEVENOAKS, TN15 0HH. (Life Member)

DARROCH, Mr. Ross, BSc ACA *2009;* 2 Rhodes Street, Padfield, GLOSSOP, DERBYSHIRE, SK13 1EQ.

DARSHAN, Mrs. Emma Louise, BA(Hons) ACA *1997;* Maes Y Dderwyn Gardens, Off Tudor Street, Ystradgynlais, SWANSEA, SA9 1AN.

DARSLEY, Mr. Graham Robert, FCA *1977;* 44 Goldsmith Way, CROWTHORNE, BERKSHIRE, RG45 7QP.

DART, Mr. Gary, BA ACA *2010;* Estillo Apartments, Flat 11, 5 Wenlock Road, LONDON, N1 7SL.

DART, Mr. Geoffrey Court, CBE FCA CCMI FRSA *1971;* 63 Lyncombe Hill, BATH, BA2 4PH.

DART, Miss. Hannah Sally, BSc ACA *2004;* 9 Hornbeam Drive, Poringland, NORWICH, NR14 7WE.

DART, Mr. Jonathan Embling, BA FCA *1986;* Oaklands, Ewell Road, Cheam, SUTTON, SM3 8AA.

DART, Mr. Lindsay Roger, BA ACA *1987;* Deutsche Bank AG London, Winchester House, 1 Great Winchester Street, LONDON, EC2N 2DB.

DART, Mrs. Natasha Claudia, BA ACA *1996;* 5 Links Close, Churston Ferrers, BRIXHAM, TQ5 0JF.

DART, Mr. Paul Philip, BA FCA *1982;* 8 Birches Close, EPSOM, SURREY, KT18 5JG.

•①**DARTNAILL, Mr. Danny Nicolaus William, BSc ACA** *2001;* BDO LLP, 55 Baker Street, LONDON, W1U 7EU. See also BDO Stoy Hayward LLP

DARTON, Mr. Bruce Richard Francis, BA FCA *1997;* The Bank of New York Mellon Centre, 160 Queen Victoria Street, LONDON, EC4V 4LA.

DARTON, Mrs. Katherine Ann, BSc(Hons) ACA *2000;* 4 Belvedere Road, Earlsdon, COVENTRY, CV5 6PF.

DARTS, Miss. Rebecca Louise, BA ACA *2001;* Jersey Trust Co, PO Box 1075, Elizabeth House, 9 Castle Street, St. Hellier, JERSEY JE4 2QP.

DARU, Ms. Lopa, MBA BSc ACA *1978;* 89 Linden Gardens, LONDON, W2 4EX.

DARUGAR, Mr. Inaam Ali, FCA *1969;* Plot No.60/II, 30th St, Off Khayabani Mujahid, Phase V (Ext) D.H.A, KARACHI, PAKISTAN. (Life Member)

DARUKHANAWALA, Mrs. Selina Percy, MA ACA *1999;* (Tax Fac), 48 Durand Gardens, LONDON, SW9 0PP.

DARUTY, Mr. Sebastien, ACA *2011;* Flat 17 Finlay Court, Commonwealth Drive, CRAWLEY, WEST SUSSEX, RH10 1AJ.

DARUVALLA, Mr. Mark Neville, BA ACA *1987;* Wood Cottage, Barras Moor, Perranarworthal, TRURO, CORNWALL, TR3 7PE.

DARUWALA, Miss. Jenaz Sam, ACA *1996;* 15 The Warren Drive, LONDON, E11 2LR.

DARUWALA, Mr. Sarosh, BSc ACA *2000;* 41 Fulwood Avenue, WEMBLEY, HA0 1LS.

DARUWALA, Mr. Sham Tehmurasp Byramji, FCA *1953;* Rubans Apartments, 30 Nepean Sea Road, MUMBAI 40036, MAHARASHTRA, INDIA. (Life Member)

DARUWALLA, Mr. Cyrus Kersy, ACA *2008;* 3 Chamberlain House, 126 Westminster Bridge Road, LONDON, SE1 7UR.

•**DARUWALLA, Mr. Paurus Cawas, ACA** *1989;* (Tax Fac), P. C. Daruwalla & Co, 4 Raisins Hill, PINNER, HA5 2BS.

DARUWALLA, Mr. Yazdi Pesi, FCA *1974;* 63 Foxleys, Carpenders Park, WATFORD, WD19 5DE.

DARVALL, Mr. Robin John, BSc FCA AMCT *1987;* 10 Bideford Way, Cottam, PRESTON, PR4 0LX.

DARVELL, Mr. Malcolm Lawton, BSc ACA *1986;* (Tax Fac), 4TEUS Solutions Limited, Regus Second Floor, Berkeley Square House Berkeley Square, LONDON, W1J 6BD.

DARVELL, Mr. Michael John, MA BA ACA *2004;* 18D Haringey Park, Crouch End, LONDON, N8 9HY.

•**DARVELL, Mr. Michael John, MA(Cantab) ACA CTA** *2003;* (Tax Fac), 38 Rustat Avenue, CAMBRIDGE, CB1 3PF.

DARVILL, Mr. Keith, FCA *1971;* 5 Butlers Yard, Peppard Common, HENLEY-ON-THAMES, OXFORDSHIRE, RG9 5EL.

•**DARWIN, Mr. Christopher James, BSc ACA** *1996;* Thomas Coombs & Son, Century House, 29 Clarendon Road, LEEDS, LS2 9PG.

DARWIN, Mr. Richard James, BA ACA *1994;* Essenden Plc, 3rd Floor, 2-4 St. Georges Road, Wimbledon, LONDON, SW19 4DP.

DARWISH, Miss. Dahlia, ACA *2009;* 39 Sneath Avenue, LONDON, NW11 9AJ.

DARWOOD, Mr. Michael Barry, FCA *1968;* 15 Idris Villas, TYWYN, GWYNEDD, LL36 9AW.

DARYANANI, Mr. Anil Moolchand, ACA *2008;* 6C Block 4, Bamboo Mansions, Site 12 Whampoa Garden, Hung Hom, HUNG HOM, KOWLOON HONG KONG SAR.

DARYANANI, Mr. Haresh Ravi, BA ACA *1996;* 52 Beechcroft Road, BUSHEY, HERTFORDSHIRE, WD23 2JU.

DARYANANI, Mr. Jay, BSc ACA *2005;* 11 Windsor House, Pynnacles Close, STANMORE, MIDDLESEX, HA7 4FE.

DARYANANI, Mr. Khushi, BSc ACA *2009;* Flat 3 Emberton Court, 15-17 Eastbury Avenue, NORTHWOOD, HA6 3FJ.

DAS, Mr. Biswajit, BSc FCA *1970;* 35 Lullington Garth, LONDON, N12 7LT. (Life Member)

DAS, Miss. Devjani, BSc(Hons) ACA *2001;* 21 St. Andrews Place Shenfield, BRENTWOOD, ESSEX, CM15 8HH.

•**DAS, Mr. Ganesh Chandra, FCA** *1974;* G.C. Das & Co., 57 Icknield Drive, Gants Hill, ILFORD, IG2 6SE.

DAS, Mr. Malay, FCA *1974;* 91 McBryan Drive, HAY RIVER X0E 0R3, NT, CANADA.

DAS, Miss. Ranjana Lala, BSc ACA *2000;* Holman Fenwick Willan Friary Court, 65 Crutched Friars, LONDON, EC3N 2AE.

DAS, Mr. Sandeep, BSc ACA *2004;* 124 Bower Way, SLOUGH, SL1 5JG.

DAS, Mr. Saurabh, BA ACA *2003;* 41 Downs Hill, BECKENHAM, KENT, BR3 5ET.

DAS, Mr. Sugata Kumar, FCA *1962;* Flat 302 Middleton Court, 4/2 Middleton Street, CALCUTTA 700071, INDIA. (Life Member)

•**DAS GUPTA, Mr. Debajyoti, FCA** *1971;* Financial Accounts Limited, 88 Howberry Road, EDGWARE, MIDDLESEX, HA8 6SY. See also Gupta D. & Co

•**DAS GUPTA, Miss. Debarati, BSc ACA** *1995;* 2915 Rubino Circle, SAN JOSE, CA 95125, UNITED STATES.

DASANI, Mr. Pradip, BSc FCA *1983;* 36 Bourne End Road, NORTHWOOD, HA6 3BS.

DASANI, Mr. Shatish Damodar, BA ACA *1987;* 60 Eastbury Road, NORTHWOOD, MIDDLESEX, HA6 3AW.

DASCOMBE, Mr. Geoffrey Jon, BA FCA *1966;* 13 Canynge Square, Clifton, BRISTOL, BS8 3LA.

DASEY, Mr. David Francis, BSc FCA *1976;* Blue Cedar, Sutton Place, Abinger Hammer, DORKING, SURREY, RH5 6RL.

DASGUPTA, Mr. Kumarkanti, ACA *1994;* PricewaterhouseCoopers Ltd, 252 Veer Savarkar Marg, Shivaji Park Dadr, MUMBAI 400028, MAHARASHTRA, INDIA.

DASGUPTA, Mr. Ron, BA ACA *2007;* 49 Drayton Park, LONDON, N5 1NT.

DASGUPTA, Mr. Sandeep, ACA *2011;* 88 Howberry Road, EDGWARE, MIDDLESEX, HA8 6SY.

DASGUPTA, Mr. Sudip, BA ACA *1999;* National Audit Office, 157-197 Buckingham Palace Road, LONDON, SW1W 9SP.

DASH, Mr. Amar, BA ACA *1989;* Blabaerskogen 1, 1412 SOFIEMYR, NORWAY.

DASHANI, Mr. Ronak Jayprakash, ACA *2009;* 30 Kingsley Street, LONDON, SW11 5LE.

•**DASHFIELD, Mr. Mark Simon, BSc FCA** *1982;* Alexander Partnership, Barclays Bank Chambers, 18 High Street, TENBY, PEMBROKESHIRE, SA70 7HD.

DASHWOOD, Mr. Cyril Francis, FCA *1950;* Ruthwell, Oakway, Chesham Bois, AMERSHAM, HP6 5PQ. (Life Member)

DASHWOOD, Mr. James Hammond, FCA *1970;* 536 Mowbray Road, LANE COVE, NSW 2066, AUSTRALIA.

•**DASHWOOD, Mr. John Derek, BSc(Hons) ACA** *2001;* with PricewaterhouseCoopers, 1 Embankment Place, LONDON, WC2N 6RH.

DASHWOOD, Mr. William Robert, BA ACA *1994;* Outerfield, Tilford Road, HINDHEAD, SURREY, GU26 6SF.

DASILVA, Mr. Matthew, MSc BA(Hons) ACA *2006;* 57 Glendevon Way, Chellaston, DERBY, DE73 5AG.

DASKALAKIS, Mr. Markos, MEng ACA CISA ACGI CIA *2010;* Thaleias 18, Holargos, 15561 ATHENS, GREECE.

DASS, Mr. Harish Kumar, BA(Hons) ACA *2004;* 1 Waller Road, BEACONSFIELD, BUCKINGHAMSHIRE, HP9 2HD.

DASS, Mr. Pradip Kumar, ACA *1979;* 77 Whalley Drive, Bletchley, MILTON KEYNES, MK3 6HX.

DASS, Mr. Rajit, BSc ACA *2006;* Flat 18 Delaware Mansions, Delaware Road, LONDON, W9 2LH.

DASSARATH, Miss. Maha Lakshmi, ACA *2011;* 45 Corporation Street, LONDON, E15 3HB.

DASSENAIKE, Mr. Dilani, BSc FCA *1996;* with BDO LLP, 55 Baker Street, LONDON, W1U 7EU.

DASSI, Mr. Alessandro, BA ACA *2007;* 122 Ravensbury Road, Earlsfield, LONDON, SW18 4RU.

DASTOOR, Mr. Meheryar Kaikhushrao, ACA *1992;* 10560 Dr Luther Martin King Jr, ST PETERSBURG, FL 33716, UNITED STATES.

DASTOOR, Mr. Neville, MSc BA ACA *1998;* 44 Hall Royd Lane, Silkstone Common, BARNSLEY, SOUTH YORKSHIRE, S75 4PP.

DASTOOR, Mr. Vistasp Kaikhushroo, FCA CTA *1962;* 42 Knoll Rise, ORPINGTON, BR6 0DD.

DASTUR, Mr. Phiroze Dinshaw, FCA *1968;* 8 Brookside Lane, BEDMINSTER, NJ 07921, UNITED STATES.

•**DASTUR, Mr. William Charles Mason, MA FCA** *1977;* Marshall of Cambridge, (Holdings) Limited, The Airport, CAMBRIDGE, CB5 8RX.

DASZKIEWICZ, Mr. Richard Andrew, BA FCA *1986;* Claremont House, 5 Berrys Avenue, KNARESBOROUGH, NORTH YORKSHIRE, HG5 0EP.

•**DATE, Mr. Sachin Madhav, ACA** *1991;* 21 Cautley Avenue, LONDON, SW4 9HX. See also Ernst & Young Europe LLP and Ernst & Young LLP

DATE, Mr. Stephen Charles, BA FCA *1970;* 14 Grange Avenue, Sticklepath, BARNSTAPLE, DEVON, EX31 2DS. (Life Member)

DATHI, Mr. Riyaz, BSc ACA *1998;* Pernod Ricard UK Ltd Central House, 3 Lampton Road, HOUNSLOW, TW3 1HY.

•**DATLEN, Mr. Stuart Edmund, ACA** *1989;* Moore Stephens (South) LLP, The French Quarter, 114 High Street, SOUTHAMPTON, HAMPSHIRE, SO14 2AA.

DATO, Mr. Antonello Salvatore, BSc ACA *2009;* Basement Flat, 70 Pembroke Road, LONDON, W8 6NX.

•**DATOO, Mr. Mustafa Aunali Lalji, FCA** *1980;* (Tax Fac), Mustafa A Datoo Ltd, 144 Dorset Road, Merton Park, LONDON, SW19 3EF. See also Mustafa A. Datoo

DATOO, Mr. Zakirali Gulamali, BA FCA *1968;* P.O. Box 87227 - 80100, MOMBASA, KENYA.

•**DATSON, Mr. David, FCA** *1979;* Maynard Heady LLP, Matrix House, 12-16 Lionel Road, CANVEY ISLAND, ESSEX, SS8 9DE. See also Maynard Heady

•**DATTA, Mr. Gour Sadhan, FCA** *1973;* (Tax Fac), Datta & Co, 58 Whittington Road, LONDON, N22 8YF.

DATTA, Mr. Suvojyoti, ACA *2009;* Flat 3, Muylinda House, 121 Oxford Road, READING, RG1 7UH.

•①**DATTANI, Mr. Dilipkumar K, BA FCA** *1986;* with RSM Tenon Limited, 1 Bede Island Road, Bede Island Business Park, LEICESTER, LE2 7EA.

DATTANI, Mr. Dineshkumar, FCA *1973;* Hardy Oil & Gas plc, 137-143 Hammersmith Road, LONDON, W14 0QL.

DATTANI, Mr. Kaushik Mulji, FCA *1976;* Dattani & Co, 2218 Lombard Street, SAN FRANCISCO, CA 94123, UNITED STATES.

DATTANI, Mr. Madhusudan Harjiwan, FCA *1974;* Flat B1 2Nd Floor, Tirupati Apartments, Warden Road, MUMBAI 400 026, MAHARASHTRA, INDIA.

DATTANI, Mr. Manekshkumar, BSc ACA *1988;* Europa Partners, 33 St. James's Square, LONDON, SW1Y 4JS.

DATTANI, Mr. Mangaldas Gordhandas, BSc FCA *1972;* 48 Beaufort Gardens, ASCOT, BERKSHIRE, SL5 8PG.

•**DATTANI, Mr. Nitin, BA FCA** *1994;* (Tax Fac), Dattani, Scottish Provident House, 76-80 College Road, HARROW, MIDDLESEX, HA1 1BQ. See also Dattani Chartered Accountants

DATTANI, Mr. Pritesh, BCom FCA *2001;* 2 Emmer Green, LUTON, LU2 8UH.

DATTANI, Mr. Pritesh Amritlal, BA ACA *2001;* 8 Five Fields Close, WATFORD, WD19 5BZ.

DATTANI, Mrs. Rashmi, BA ACA *1985;* 12 Downage, Hendon, LONDON, NW4 1AH.

DATTANI, Mr. Rishi, ACA *2010;* 57 Merrion Avenue, STANMORE, MIDDLESEX, HA7 4RY.

DATTANI, Mrs. Ritu, BA(Hons) ACA *2001;* 18 Monarch Drive, Shinfield, READING, RG2 9EW.

DATTANI, Mr. Sunil, BA ACA *1985;* 19 Parkthorne Drive, HARROW, HA2 7BU.

DATTANI, Mrs. Urvashi, BA ACA *1989;* 18 Outwoods Road, LOUGHBOROUGH, LE11 3LY.

DATTANI, Mr. Vasant Gopaldas, BA ACA *1985;* Conifers, 12 Downage, LONDON, NW4 1AH.

•**DATTANI, Mr. Vijaykumar, BSc ACA** *1983;* (Tax Fac), Dattani & Co., 47 Hill Road, PINNER, HA5 1LB.

•**DAUBENEY, Mr. Henry James, BSc ACA** *1990;* PricewaterhouseCoopers LLP, Hays Galleria, 1 Hays Lane, LONDON, SE1 2RD. See also PricewaterhouseCoopers

DAUBENY, Mr. Charles Niel, FCA *1964;* Ewers, 1 Church Lane, Lodsworth, PETWORTH, WEST SUSSEX, GU28 9DD.

DAUBNEY, Mr. Georges Michel, ACA *2011;* 2 Holkar Meadows, Chapel Town Road, Bromley Cross, BOLTON, BL7 9NA.

DAUBNEY, Mr. Paul John, BSc ACA *1993;* Flat 5, Nightingales, 5 Milner Road, BOURNEMOUTH, BH4 8AD.

DAUD, Mr. Mahomed Iqbal, FCA *1979;* Casa Clare, Apt 3738, 8135-909 ALMANCIL, ALGARVE, PORTUGAL.

DAUD, Mr. Muhammad Affan, BA(Hons) ACA *2002;* No. 20 Jalan Sepah Puteri 5/22, PJU 5 Damansara Emas, Kota Damansara, 47810 PETALING JAYA, MALAYSIA.

DAUD, Mr. Raheez, BA ACA *1991;* 157 Stanford Road, Norbury, LONDON, SW16 4QD.

DAUDA, Mr. Kehinde, MSci ACA *2002;* 94 Brookmill Road, LONDON, SE8 4JJ.

DAUDA, Mr. Mayowa, ACA *2010;* 19 City Walk Apartments, 31 Perry Vale, LONDON, SE23 2AR.

DAUDIA, Mr. Vishal, BSc ACA *2005;* K P M G Llp, 15 Canada Square, LONDON, E14 5GL.

DAUDJEE, Mr. Hatimali Tayabali, FCA *1959;* 2 Bramham Court, Sandy Lodge Way, NORTHWOOD, HA6 2AL. (Life Member)

DAUGHERTY, Mr. James Robert, BEng ACA *2007;* Level 19, 2 Market Street, SYDNEY, NSW 2000, AUSTRALIA.

DAUGHNEY, Mr. David John, BSc ACA *1992;* 25 Crossfield Grove, Woodsmoor, STOCKPORT, SK2 7EQ.

DAUGHTRY, Mr. John Conway, FCA *1976;* 21 Woodside Avenue, AMERSHAM, BUCKINGHAMSHIRE, HP6 6BG.

DAUKES, Mr. Anthony Clendon, MA(Hons) ACA *2003;* Citigroup, 33 Canada Square, Canary Wharf, LONDON, E14 5LB.

DAULLXHIU, Miss. Gresa, BSc ACA *2011;* 34 Sherman Road, READING, RG1 2PJ.

DAULTREY, Ms. Laraine, BA FCA ATII *1992;* 30 Tile House Lane, Great Horkesley, COLCHESTER, CO6 4EA.

•**DAUNCEY, Mr. John Anthony, FCA** *1969;* (Tax Fac), John Dauncey FCA, New Farm, Colesden, BEDFORD, MK44 3DB.

DAUNT, Mr. Andrew, BSc ACA *1992;* 22a Stoney Road, BRACKNELL, RG42 1XX.

DAUNT, Mr. Timothy, BSc ACA *1995;* R N L I, West Quay Road, POOLE, BH15 1HZ.

•**DAUPPE, Mrs. Fiona Caroline, BSc ACA** *1979;* Payne Allen, 45 Whitelands Avenue, Chorleywood, RICKMANSWORTH, HERTFORDSHIRE, WD3 5RE.

•**DAUPPE, Mr. Victor Andre Francois, BSc FCA CTA AIIT TEP** *1978;* (Tax Fac), Arram Berlyn Gardner, 30 City Road, LONDON, EC1Y 2AB. See also MacIntyre Hudson LLP

DAVAR, Mr. Mohit, ACA *1993;* 12 Crespigny Road, LONDON, NW4 3DY.

DAVDA, Miss. Anokhee, ACA *2008;* 25 Mountview, NORTHWOOD, MIDDLESEX, HA6 3NZ.

DAVDA, Miss. Gira Prafulchandra, BSc ACA *2000;* 3 Anley Road, LONDON, W14 0BY.

•**DAVDA, Mr. Piyushkumar Dayalji, FCA** *1974;* Ableman Shaw & Co, Mercury House, 1 Heather Park Drive, WEMBLEY, HA0 1SX. See also Castle Ryce

DAVDA, Mr. Prafulchandra Dayalji, FCA *1963;* 5 Claremont End, ESHER, KT10 9LZ.

DAVDA, Miss. Sona, BSc ACA *2009;* 91 Woodlands, HARROW, MIDDLESEX, HA2 6EN.

DAVDA, Miss. Tejal, ACA *2009;* 5 Farrer Road, HARROW, MIDDLESEX, HA3 9LR.

•**DAVE, Mr. Anil, BSc ACA** *1980;* (Tax Fac), Dave & Co, 18 Fitzhardinge Street, Manchester Square, LONDON, W1H 6EQ. See also Regent Consultancy Limited

DAVE, Mr. Ashish Bhrugu, ACA *1998;* MEMBER OF COUNCIL, ABRAAJ Capital Limited, Dubai International Financial Centre, Gate Village, Building 8 3rd Floor, PO Box 504905, DUBAI UNITED ARAB EMIRATES.

•**DAVE, Mr. Atul, BA FCA** *1991;* Alexander & Associates, 76 Belmont Avenue, BARNET, HERTFORDSHIRE, EN4 9LA. See also Alexander Dave

DAVE, Mr. Bhaskarray Dayaram, FCA *1974;* # 208 520 57 Avenue SW, CALGARY T2V 0H2, AB, CANADA.

•**DAVE, Mr. Dineshchandra Jatashanker Bhavani Shanker, FCA** *1974;* (Tax Fac), D. Dave & Co., 60 Kenwyn Drive, LONDON, NW2 7NT.

DAVE, Mr. Nilesh Tuljashanker, ACA ACMA *1992;* P O Box 46414, NAIROBI, KENYA.

DAVE, Mr. Sagar, BCom ACA *1994;* Oxfam, Oxfam House, 2700 John Smith Drive, Oxford Business Park South, OXFORD, OX4 2JY.
DAVENEY, Miss. Louise Margot, BSc(Econ) ACA *2010;* 50 Purdom Road, WELWYN GARDEN CITY, HERTFORDSHIRE, AL7 4FH.
DAVENHILL, Mr. Christopher Richard, BA ACA *1984;* Hinton Perry & Davenhill Ltd, Dreadnought Road, Pensnett, BRIERLEY HILL, DY5 4TH.
DAVENPORT, Mr. Alan James, FCA *1965;* Apartado 583, Vale do Lobo, 8135 034 ALMANCIL, PORTUGAL. (Life Member)
DAVENPORT, Miss. Anne Margaret, BSc ACA *1980;* La Cache, Rue Des Maltieres, GROUVILLE, JERSEY, JE3 9EB.
DAVENPORT, Mr. Anthony Henry, MA ACA *1981;* (Tax Fac), 28 Bladon Crescent, Alsager, STOKE-ON-TRENT, ST7 2BG.
DAVENPORT, Mr. Anthony John, BSc FCA *1970;* 3 Dickinson Court, 15 Brewhouse Yard, LONDON, EC1V 4JX.
DAVENPORT, Mr. Antony Shane, BSc ACA *1989;* 573 Manchester Road, Crosspool, SHEFFIELD, S10 5PP.
DAVENPORT, Mrs. Carol Elaine, BSc ACA *1997;* Orchard End, North Down Lane, Shipham, WINSCOMBE, BS25 1SL.
DAVENPORT, Mr. Guy David Orme, FCA *1972;* Hill Farm Lodge, Camelsdale Road, HASLEMERE, GU27 3SG.
DAVENPORT, Mr. James, BSc(Hons) ACA *2003;* Innocent Drinks, Fruit Towers, 3 The Goldhawk Estate Brackenbury Road, LONDON, W6 0BA.
•DAVENPORT, Mrs. Julie Mary, BSc FCA *1992;* Crossley Lomas LLP, 25 Ryecroft, Manor Park Road, GLOSSOP, DERBYSHIRE, SK13 7SQ.
DAVENPORT, Mr. Keith, BSc ACA *1980;* The Laird Group Plc, 100 Pall Mall, LONDON, SW1Y 5NQ.
DAVENPORT, Mr. Leigh, BSc ACA *2002;* (Tax Fac), 44 St. Margarets Road Horsforth, LEEDS, LS18 5BG.
DAVENPORT, Mrs. Maxine Anne, BSc ACA *1995;* Go South Coast Ltd, Towngate House 2-8 Parkstone Road, POOLE, DORSET, BH15 2PR.
DAVENPORT, Mr. Michael Graham, BA ACA *1992;* Alfred Bagnall & Sons Ltd, 6 Manor Lane, SHIPLEY, WEST YORKSHIRE, BD18 3RD.
DAVENPORT, Mr. Michael Telford, FCA *1965;* 119 Gravel Lane, WILMSLOW, SK9 6EG. (Life Member)
DAVENPORT, Mr. Nicholas, MSc ACA *2011;* 68 Langleys Road, Selley Oak, BIRMINGHAM, B29 6HP.
DAVENPORT, Mrs. Nicola Mary, BA ACA *1992;* Unit 6, Davenport Business Centre, 8 Mill View, HINCKLEY, LEICESTERSHIRE, LE10 1XD.
•DAVENPORT, Mr. Nigel, BSc FCA ATII *1991;* (Tax Fac), Baker Tilly Tax & Advisory Services LLP, 1210 Centre Park Square, WARRINGTON, WA1 1RU.
DAVENPORT, Mr. Paul Daniel, BSc ACA *2005;* 94 Haberdasher Street, LONDON, N1 6EJ.
DAVENPORT, Mr. Paul Jonathan, ACA *1993;* 28, Laburnum Way, RAYLEIGH, SS6 9GN.
DAVENPORT, Mr. Robert Simpson, FCA *1963;* The Braemer Association, 46 Berwyn Road, RICHMOND, TW10 5BS. (Life Member)
DAVENPORT, Mr. Steven, BSc ACA *2011;* 9 Derwent Avenue, Chorlton, MANCHESTER, M21 7QP.
DAVENPORT, Mr. Timothy Joe, BEng ACA *2003;* 15 Cromford Road, LONDON, SW18 1NZ.
DAVENPORT-BROWN, Mr. Alan Paul, BSc FCA *1982;* Grayland House, 43 Strines Road, Marple, STOCKPORT, SK6 7DT.
DAVERAN, Mr. Leigh Garner, BA(Hons) ACA CF *2001;* 42 Kings Stand, Berry Hill Park, MANSFIELD, NG18 4AY.
•DAVERN, Mr. Fergal Gerard John, ACA *2008;* (Tax Fac), J B Davern & Co Ltd, 149-151 Sparrows Herne, BUSHEY, WD23 1AQ. See also J B Davern & Co
DAVEY, Mr. Alastair John Warley, BSc ACA *1993;* 5 Crown Point, Turton, BOLTON, BL7 0BD.
DAVEY, Mrs. Amanda Jane, BSc ACA *2000;* 41 Kewstoke Road, BRISTOL, BS9 1HE.
DAVEY, Mr. Anthony Charles, PhD MSc BA FCA *1977;* Strategy & Technology Limited, 1 Benjamin Street, LONDON, EC1M 5QY.
DAVEY, Mr. Arthur Michael, BA FCA *1972;* 3 Springhill Road, SAFFRON WALDEN, CB11 4AH.
DAVEY, Mr. Brian Charles, FCA *1962;* 1 Knoll Park, TRURO, CORNWALL, TR1 1FF. (Life Member)
DAVEY, Mr. Brian James, BSc ACA *2000;* Abbotts Wood, Frith End, BORDON, GU35 0QS.
DAVEY, Mr. Brian John, BCom FCA MEI *1982;* K B R, Hill Park Court, Springfield Drive, LEATHERHEAD, SURREY, KT22 7NL.
•DAVEY, Mr. Christopher John, FCA *1974;* Waltons Clark Whitehill LLP, Oakland House, 40 Victoria Road, HARTLEPOOL, CLEVELAND, TS26 8DD. See also Horwath Clark Whitehill (North East) LLP
DAVEY, Mr. Christopher Julian, BSc FCA *1978;* 49 Hosack Road, LONDON, SW17 7QW.
DAVEY, Mr. Christopher Wesley, BA ACA *1979;* Fairoaks, Lyncombe Vale Road, BATH, BA2 4LP.
DAVEY, Mrs. Deborah Claire, BA ACA *1995;* Gorse Bank, Church Lane, Church Brampton, NORTHAMPTON, NN6 8AT.
DAVEY, Mr. Edward Alfred Jonathan, BA(Econ) ACA *1998;* Albion, North Road, Chorleywood, RICKMANSWORTH, WD3 5LE.
DAVEY, Mr. Gavin Dennis, BA ACA *1995;* Bank Farm, North Bank, Thorney, PETERBOROUGH, PE6 0RW.
DAVEY, Mr. Gavin William, BSc ACA *1994;* Taintona, Court Street, Moretonhampstead, NEWTON ABBOT, DEVON, TQ13 8LG.
DAVEY, Mrs. Graham John, BSc ACA *1991;* British Council, 10 Spring Gardens, LONDON, SW1A 2BN.
DAVEY, Mr. Ian Harding, FCA *1960;* T P Dibdin Ltd Progress House, Cupola Way, SCUNTHORPE, SOUTH HUMBERSIDE, DN15 9YJ.
DAVEY, Mr. James Alexander, FCA *1963;* Flat 40, 4 Grand Avenue, HOVE, EAST SUSSEX, BN3 2LE. (Life Member)
DAVEY, Mr. James William Barlow, ACA *2008;* Flat 4, 92 High Street Colliers Wood, LONDON, SW19 2BT.
DAVEY, Mrs. Jane Karen, BSc FCA *1977;* 1 Fairsford Place, CAMBRIDGE, CB1 2QS.
DAVEY, Mrs. Jenifer, BSc ACA *2004;* Cranswick Plc, Helsinki Road, HULL, HU7 0YW.
DAVEY, Miss. Johann Lesley, MA ACA *1986;* Apartment B41 Montevetro, 100 Battersea Church Road, LONDON, SW11 3YL.
•DAVEY, Mr. John Lester, BSc FCA *1975;* (Tax Fac), Groves Davey Limited, 34 Wellfield Road, CARDIFF, CF24 3PB.
DAVEY, Mr. John Samuel, FCA *1961;* Windles, Runsell Green, Danbury, CHELMSFORD, CM3 4QZ. (Life Member)
•DAVEY, Miss. Julia, BA ACA *1998;* Julia Davey, 60 Fen Road, Timberland, LINCOLN, LN4 3SD.
•DAVEY, Miss. Laura, ACA *2002;* Laura Davey Bookkeeping Business Services, 6 Lime Grove, Elton, CHESTER, CH2 4PX. See also Laura Davey Bookkeeping & Business Services
DAVEY, Mrs. Lisa Elaine, BA(Hons) ACA *2004;* 3 St. Martins Close, Broadmayne, DORCHESTER, DORSET, DT2 8DG.
DAVEY, Mr. Martin Everett, MA FCA *1981;* 17 Merlin Street, Roseville, SYDNEY, NSW 2069, AUSTRALIA.
DAVEY, Mr. Martin Robert, BA ACA *2006;* 166 Acaster Lane, Bishopthorpe, YORK, YO23 2TD.
DAVEY, Mr. Martin Thomas Peter, FCA *1978;* Pantiles, 30 West End, Walkington, BEVERLEY, HU17 8SX.
DAVEY, Mr. Matthew John, ACA *2006;* 2 Rowans Way, Leavenheath, COLCHESTER, CO6 4UU.
DAVEY, Mr. Michael Edward, BSc ACA *1990;* Lilacs, 129 Mill Road, BURGESS HILL, RH15 8AY.
DAVEY, Mr. Michael Graham, BSc FCA CTA *1989;* (Tax Fac), with Grant Thornton UK LLP, Grant Thornton House, Kettering Parkway, Kettering Venture Park, KETTERING, NORTHAMPTONSHIRE NN15 6XR.
DAVEY, Mr. Michael John, BA FCA *1973;* 225 Sheen Lane, East Sheen, LONDON, SW14 8LE.
DAVEY, Mr. Neil William, FCA *1972;* 16 Craig Yr Haul Drive, Castleton, CARDIFF, CF3 2SA.
DAVEY, Mr. Nigel Thomas, MA FCA FTII *1972;* Longwood Lodge, Whites Hill, Stock, INGATESTONE, ESSEX, CM4 9QB. (Life Member)
DAVEY, Mr. Norman Clifford Andre, FCA *1947;* Kibworth Knoll Residential Home, 12 Fleckney Road, Kibworth, LEICESTER, LE8 0HE. (Life Member)
DAVEY, Mr. Peter Allen, MA ACA *1984;* Chestnuts Burnham Road, Althorne, CHELMSFORD, CM3 6BU.
DAVEY, Mr. Peter Simon, BA FCA *1979;* 19 The Ridgeway, Fetcham, LEATHERHEAD, KT22 9BB.
•DAVEY, Mr. Richard John Chatterton, FCA *1964;* (Tax Fac), R.J.C. Davey, 124 Old Park Ridings, Grange Park, LONDON, N21 2EP.
DAVEY, Mr. Richard Michael Edward, FCA *1976;* Birchwood House, Biddenden, ASHFORD, TN27 8DY.
•DAVEY, Mr. Robert Graham, FCA *1988;* Bishop Fleming, Cobourg House, Mayflower Street, PLYMOUTH, PL1 1LG.
DAVEY, Mr. Roger Stuart, BSc FCA *1976;* 412 Gray Horse Circle, WOODLAND PARK, CO 80863, UNITED STATES.
DAVEY, Mr. Sean Leslie, ACA *1990;* 2 Pilton Mews, Pilton Street, BARNSTAPLE, DEVON, EX31 1PJ.
DAVEY-EVANS, Ms. Susan Mary, BA ACA PGCE *1987;* 14 Gifford Close, FAREHAM, PO15 6PJ.
DAVID, Mr. Anthony, BSc ACA *2007;* 20 Parc Gellifaelog, TONYPANDY, MID GLAMORGAN, CF40 1BF.
DAVID, Mrs. Clare Anne, MA ACA *1991;* Uplands, Old Haslemere Road, HASLEMERE, GU27 2NN.
•DAVID, Mr. David William Patrick, BSc FCA *1974;* Dai David Ltd, Greyfriars Court, Paradise Square, OXFORD, OX1 1BE.
DAVID, Ms. Eirian Mair, MEng ACA *2006;* 11 Barleyfield Way, WITNEY, OXFORDSHIRE, OX28 1AA.
DAVID, Miss. Eleanor, ACA *2011;* 19 Narbonne Avenue, Clapham South, LONDON, SW4 9JR.
DAVID, Mrs. Elizabeth Jane, BA(Hons) ACIB ACA *2001;* The Chalet, 5 South Side, GERRARDS CROSS, BUCKINGHAMSHIRE, SL9 8NQ.
DAVID, Mr. Gareth, LLB ACA *2001;* 138 Wingate Square, LONDON, SW4 0AN.
DAVID, Mr. Irving Stephen, FCA *1971;* 4862 Matilija Avenue, SHERMAN OAKS, CA 91423, UNITED STATES.
DAVID, Mrs. Isabelle Mary, BSocSc ACA *1993;* 60 Woodlands Avenue, WEST BYFLEET, KT14 6AW.
DAVID, Mr. Jason Haroon, ACA *2009;* with RSM Tenon Limited, Highfield Court, Tollgate, Chandler's Ford, EASTLEIGH, HAMPSHIRE SO53 3TY.
DAVID, Mr. Jonathan Peter, ACA *1990;* 16 Gosden Road, West End, WOKING, GU24 9LH.
DAVID, Mr. Neville Graham, LLB ACA *1992;* 98 Star Street, Paddington, LONDON, W2 1QF.
DAVID, Mr. Peter Clive, FCA *1970;* Firs House, Ramsdell, Nr.Basingstoke, TADLEY, HAMPSHIRE, RG26 5SJ.
DAVID, Mr. Thomas Morgan, BA ACA *2010;* Harrow Cottage, Old London Road, Knockholt, SEVENOAKS, KENT, TN14 7JW.
DAVID, Mr. William Nigel, MA FCA *1978;* Harrow Cottage, Old London Road, Knockholt, SEVENOAKS, TN14 7JW.
DAVIDGE, Mr. Michael Richard, BA FCA *1981;* United Kingdom Debt Management Office, Eastcheap Court, 11 Philpot Lane, LONDON, EC3M 8UD.
DAVIDS, Mrs. Joanne Louise, BA ACA *1995;* 187a Gatley Road, Gatley, CHEADLE, CHESHIRE, SK8 4BB.
DAVIDSEN, Ms. Elizabeth Bulow, BA ACA *1999;* (Tax Fac), with Grant Thornton UK LLP, 30 Finsbury Square, LONDON, EC2P 2YU.
•DAVIDSON, Mr. Alan, BSc ACA *1993;* Pentins, Lullingstone House, 5 Castle Street, CANTERBURY, CT1 2FG. See also Pentins Business Advisers Limited
DAVIDSON, Mr. Alan, ACA *1980;* Greater Manchester Police, Finance Branch, Chester House, Boyer Street, MANCHESTER, M16 0RE.
DAVIDSON, Mr. Alan, BA FCA *1974;* Cobalt Business Exchange, Cobalt park Way, NEWCASTLE UPON TYNE, NE28 9nz.
DAVIDSON, Mr. Alan Neil Ramsay, FCA *1979;* Waterside, Curlew Drive, West Charleton, KINGSBRIDGE, DEVON, TQ7 2AA.
DAVIDSON, Mr. Alan Robert, BA ACA *1994;* 16 Ormeley Road, LONDON, SW12 9QE.
DAVIDSON, Mr. Alastair Richard, BA ACA *1990;* 23 Rectory Road, Barnes, LONDON, SW13 0DU.
DAVIDSON, Mrs. Alison Clare, BA ACA *1991;* The Royal Bank of Scotland Plc, PO Box 1000, EDINBURGH, EH12 1HQ.
DAVIDSON, Mr. Alistaire Mackenzie, BSc ACA *2005;* Invensys plc, 3rd Floor 40 Grosvenor Place, LONDON, SW1X 7AW.
•DAVIDSON, Dr. Allan George Hamilton, PhD BSc FCA *1975;* PricewaterhouseCoopers, 34 Al - Farabi Ave, Building A, 4th Floor, ALMATY 050059, KAZAKHSTAN.
DAVIDSON, Mrs. Allison Jane, BSc(Hons) ACA *2000;* 8 Moorfield, LIFTON, DEVON, PL16 0DX.
DAVIDSON, Mrs. Amy Jennifer, ACA MAAT *2004;* 1 Fitzwilliam Avenue, Hill Head, FAREHAM, HAMPSHIRE, PO14 3SD.
DAVIDSON, Mr. Andrew Charles Rutherford, BSc ACA MCT *1993;* Numis Securities Ltd, 10 Paternoster Square, LONDON, EC4M 7LT.
DAVIDSON, Mr. Angus Alexander, LLB ACA *2001;* Chemin des Plantaz 39, 1260 NYON, SWITZERLAND.
DAVIDSON, Ms. Ann Lloyd, MA FCA *1981;* (Tax Fac), Ballavilley, Arragon Lane, Santon, ISLE OF MAN, IM4 1HH.
DAVIDSON, Mrs. Anne Margaret, ACA *1982;* 5 Welborn Court, Main Street Flixton, SCARBOROUGH, NORTH YORKSHIRE, YO11 3XA.
•DAVIDSON, Mr. Barry, ACA FCCA *2008;* Webb & Co Limited, 1 New Street, WELLS, SOMERSET, BA5 2LA.
•DAVIDSON, Mr. Brian James, FCA *1968;* Davidson & Company, Anchor's Rest, Barnlake Point, Burton, MILFORD HAVEN, DYFED SA73 1PF.
•DAVIDSON, Mr. Calum Muir, LLB ACA *1988;* with PricewaterhouseCoopers, Prince's Building, 22/F, 10 Chater Road, CENTRAL, HONG KONG ISLAND HONG KONG SAR.
DAVIDSON, Miss. Carole Gillian, BSc FCA *1986;* Widgeons Home Close, West Runton, CROMER, NORFOLK, NR27 9QF.
DAVIDSON, Mrs. Catherine Jane, BSc ACA *1993;* Oaklea House, Old Shaw Lane, Shaw, SWINDON, SN5 5PA.
DAVIDSON, Mrs. Christina Laura, ACA ACCA *2009;* with Rostrons, St Peter's House, Cattle Market Street, NORWICH, NR1 3DY.
DAVIDSON, Mr. Christopher, ACA *2010;* 3 Church Court, HOLYWOOD, COUNTY DOWN, BT18 9FP.
•DAVIDSON, Mr. Clifford Edward, BSc FCA *1989;* CED Accountancy Services Limited, Unit 1, Lucas Bridge Business Park, 1 Old Greens Norton Road, TOWCESTER, NORTHAMPTONSHIRE NN12 8AX.
DAVIDSON, Mr. Colin John, BA FCA *1993;* 27 Shadforth Street, MOSMAN, NSW 2088, AUSTRALIA.
DAVIDSON, Mr. David Frederick Alan, FCA *1954;* The Sycamores, 19 North Road, LONDON, N6 4BD. (Life Member)
DAVIDSON, Mrs. Fiona Christine, BA FCA *1990;* (Tax Fac), Sedona, 7 Isla Place, FORFAR, DD8 3RG.
DAVIDSON, Mr. Gary Andrew, BSc ACA *1991;* Punter Southall & Co, 126 Jermyn Street, LONDON, SW1Y 4UJ.
DAVIDSON, Mr. Gavin Lindsay, ACA *1985;* Source Software Ltd, Drake House, Plymouth Road, PENARTH, SOUTH GLAMORGAN, CF64 3TP.
DAVIDSON, Mr. Grant Gordon, BSc ACA *2001;* with Lyceum Capital Partners LLP, Burleigh House, 357 Strand, LONDON, WC2R 0HS.
DAVIDSON, Miss. Helena, BA(Hons) ACA *2002;* Marketaxess Europe Ltd, 71 Fenchurch Street, LONDON, EC3M 4BS.
DAVIDSON, Mr. Ian, BA ACA *1989;* Gable End, 190 Station Road, Knowle, SOLIHULL, B93 0ER.
DAVIDSON, Prof. Ian Roderick, PhD FCA ACMA *1976;* (Member of Council 1993 - 1997), Trent Farm, Tenter Close, Long Eaton, NOTTINGHAM, NG10 1HX.
•①DAVIDSON, Mrs. Imogen Claire Maria, BSc(Hons) ACA *2001;* with Baines & Ernst Corporate Limited, 2nd Floor, 18-22 Lloyds House, Lloyd Street, MANCHESTER, M2 5BE.
•DAVIDSON, Ms. Jacqueline Roxane, MA FCA ATII *1991;* Jacqueline Davidson, 17 Wykeham Road, LONDON, NW4 2TB.
DAVIDSON, Mr. James Gresham Robert, ACA *2010;* 43 Southwood Gardens, NEWCASTLE UPON TYNE, NE3 3BX.
DAVIDSON, Miss. Jean Elizabeth, FCA *1966;* 208 Chapelier House, Eastfields Avenue, LONDON, SW18 1LR.
•DAVIDSON, Mr. Jeffrey Everard Charles, MA FCA *1988;* Crowe Clark Whitehill LLP, St Bride's House, 10 Salisbury Square, LONDON, EC4Y 8EH. See also Horwath Clark Whitehill LLP and Crowe Clark Whitehill
DAVIDSON, Mr. Jeffri Salim, BSc ACA *1990;* 23 Jalan Limau Purut, Bangsar Park, 59000 KUALA LUMPUR, FEDERAL TERRITORY, MALAYSIA.
DAVIDSON, Mr. Jeremy Paul, BSc ACA CTA *2004;* 48 Fox Dene, GODALMING, GU7 1YQ.
DAVIDSON, Ms. Jill, BA ACA *1989;* 3002 Copperfield Circle, Winfield, LAREDO, TX 78045, UNITED STATES.
DAVIDSON, Mr. John Robert, MBA FCA *1974;* Baysham Court, Sellack, ROSS-ON-WYE, HR9 6QR.
DAVIDSON, Mr. John Robert, BA FCA *1978;* 10 Windmill Rise, Aberford, LEEDS, LS25 3EW.
DAVIDSON, Mrs. Kelly Ann, BSc(Hons) ACA CTA *2001;* 48 Fox Dene, GODALMING, GU7 1YQ.
DAVIDSON, Mrs. Kristin Ai Ching, BSc ACA *1983;* 15B Cameron Tower, Essensa East Forbes Condominium, 21st Drive Corner 5 Avenue, TAGUIG CITY 1634, PHILIPPINES.

DAVIDSON, Mr. Lee Alan, BA ACA *1999;* 1 Hillside Fell Bank Birtley, CHESTER LE STREET, DH3 1RP.
DAVIDSON, Mr. Louis Cameron, FCA *1976;* 7 Roughlands, Pyrford, WOKING, SURREY, GU22 8PT.
DAVIDSON, Mrs. Louise, BA FCA *1988;* 27 Shadforth Street, MOSMAN, NSW 2088, AUSTRALIA.
DAVIDSON, Miss. Lynda Andrea, BA ACA *1985;* Suite 314, 48 Par La Ville Road, HAMILTON HM 11, BERMUDA.
DAVIDSON, Mr. Malcolm Stuart, FCA *1968;* The Steadings, Easter Myeriggs, COUPAR ANGUS, PERTHSHIRE, PH13 9HS. (Life Member)
DAVIDSON, Miss. Mandy Louise, BCom ACA *1994;* 40 Winterbrook Road, LONDON, SE24 9JA.
DAVIDSON, Mr. Mark Joseph, BSc ACA *2002;* Majdanske 556, 91903 HORNE ORESANY, SLOVAK REPUBLIC.
DAVIDSON, Dr. Mark Murison, BSc ACA *1999;* 2 Mayfield Road, Mobberley, KNUTSFORD, CHESHIRE, WA16 7PX.
DAVIDSON, Mr. Martin Stuart, BSc ACA *1997;* 52 Wolseley Avenue, LONDON, SW19 8BQ.
DAVIDSON, Mr. Michael James, ACA *2008;* 52 The Drive, Kippax, LEEDS, LS25 7NQ.
DAVIDSON, Miss. Michelle Dominique, BA ACA *1983;* 41 Athena Ave, St Ives, SYDNEY, NSW 2075, AUSTRALIA.
DAVIDSON, Mr. Nathan James, BSc(Hons) ACA *2010;* 38 Burmester Road, LONDON, SW17 0JN.
DAVIDSON, Mr. Neil Godwin, BA(Hons) ACA *2007;* 81 Romano Crescent, ILUKA, WA 6028, AUSTRALIA.
DAVIDSON, Mr. Nicholas Arthur, BSc ACA *1992;* Informa Group Plc Informa House, 30-32 Mortimer Street, LONDON, W1W 7RE.
DAVIDSON, Mrs. Nicola, BA ACA *1995;* 42 Ashley Way, MARKET HARBOROUGH, LEICESTERSHIRE, LE16 7XD.
•DAVIDSON, Mr. Oliver, BSc ACA *2000;* Ernst & Young LLP, 1 More London Place, LONDON, SE1 2AF. See also Ernst & Young Europe LLP
DAVIDSON, Mr. Paul John, BA ACA *2004;* Ordnance House, B D L Blackhill Road West, Holton Heath Trading Park, POOLE, DORSET, BH16 6LW.
DAVIDSON, Mr. Peter George, BSc ACA *1982;* 15B Cameron Tower, Essensa East Forbes Condominium, 21st Drive Corner 5th Avenue, Bonifacia Global City, TAQUIG CITY 1634, METRO MANILA PHILIPPINES.
•DAVIDSON, Mr. Philip Michael, BSc ACA *1989;* KPMG LLP, 15 Canada Square, LONDON, E14 5GL. See also KPMG Europe LLP
•DAVIDSON, Mr. Raymond Saul, BA FCA MAE *1983;* Bartfields (UK) Limited, Burley House, 12 Clarendon Road, LEEDS, LS2 9NF. See also Bartfields Business Services LLP
DAVIDSON, Mr. Reginald Terence James, BSc ACA *1986;* 97 Junction Road, WAHROONGA, NSW 2076, AUSTRALIA.
DAVIDSON, Mr. Robert, BSc ACA *1996;* 30 Amberhill Way, Worsley, MANCHESTER, M28 1YJ.
DAVIDSON, Mr. Robert, MA FCA *2001;* Monitor, 4 Matthew Parker Street, LONDON, SW1H 9NP.
DAVIDSON, Mr. Robert William, FCA *1972;* R.W. Davidson, 47 Squire Bakers Lane, MARKHAM L3P 3G8, ON, CANADA.
DAVIDSON, Mr. Robert William, BA ACA *1995;* P.O Box 24856, Karen, NAIROBI, 00502, KENYA.
DAVIDSON, Mr. Robin Neil, BA ACA *1994;* Lorica General Insurance Ltd, Hemel One Boundary Way, HEMEL HEMPSTEAD, HERTFORDSHIRE, HP2 7YU.
•DAVIDSON, Mr. Ronald Edward, ACA *2002;* Ronnie Davidson Accountancy & Taxation Services, 17 Murray Crescent, PINNER, MIDDLESEX, HA5 3QF.
DAVIDSON, Mr. Russell, BSc FCA *1988;* Flat 14B Kennedy Heights, 18 Kennedy Road, MID LEVELS, HONG KONG ISLAND, HONG KONG SAR.
•DAVIDSON, Mrs. Sandra, FCA *1986;* Davidsons, 23 Comfrey Close, FARNBOROUGH, HAMPSHIRE, GU14 9XX.
DAVIDSON, Miss. Shelley Ann, BA(Hons) ACA *2001;* 28 West Park Drive, PLYMOUTH, PL7 2GZ.
DAVIDSON, Mr. Simon, MA ACA *2006;* Garden House, Stonegate, Whixley, YORK, YO26 8AS.
•DAVIDSON, Mr. Steven, BA FCA *1984;* Brett Adams, 25 Manchester Square, LONDON, W1U 3PY.
DAVIDSON, Miss. Susanne, ACA *2010;* 100 City Road, Tilehurst, READING, RG31 5SB.
DAVIDSON, Miss. Suzanne Simpson, LLB ACA *2002;* Ernst & Young, 10 George Street, EDINBURGH, EH2 2DZ.
DAVIDSON, Mr. Terence Jude, FCA *1961;* Sonnhangstrasse 44, 6205 EICH, SWITZERLAND. (Life Member)
•DAVIDSON, Miss. Tessa Louise, ACA CTA *1995;* Tessa Davidson Limited, The Ashridge Business Centre, 121 High Street, BERKHAMSTED, HERTFORDSHIRE, HP4 2DJ. See also Davidson Tessa
DAVIDSON, Mr. Thomas Charles Ramsay, BSc ACA *2010;* 10 Horder Road, LONDON, SW6 5EE.
DAVIDSON, Mr. Thomas Henry, BA ACA *2007;* Flat 2, 98 Fawe Park Road, LONDON, SW15 2EA.
DAVIDSON-GAY, Mrs. Belinda Anne, BSc ACA *1992;* Atyrau Business Centre, 23 Kulmanov Street, ATYRAU 060011, KAZAKHSTAN.
DAVIDSON-JENKINS, Mrs. Nicola Susan, BSc ACA *2000;* 70 Edgemoor Drive Crosby, LIVERPOOL, L23 9UQ.
DAVIDSON-WRIGHT, Mr. Marcus John, BSc ACA *1994;* Cleardown, 29 Weybridge Park, WEYBRIDGE, SURREY, KT13 8SQ.
DAVIE, Mr. Alexander James Robert, BSc ACA *2007;* 37 Garfield Road, LONDON, SW11 5PL.
DAVIE, Mr. James Richard, BSc ACA *1987;* Rhodelland, 4 Thornsett Grove, Shirley, SOLIHULL, B90 3SU.
DAVIE, Mr. Jonathan Richard, FCA *1970;* 80 Addison Road, LONDON, W14 8ED.
DAVIE, Mr. Peter Albert Lethbridge, FCA *1950;* 21 Mill Hill Cottages, Mill Hill, TAVISTOCK, PL19 8NW. (Life Member)
DAVIE, Mrs. Rachel Jane, BSc ACA *2002;* 8 Birchwood Close, Gonerby Hill Foot, GRANTHAM, LINCOLNSHIRE, NG31 8GP.
DAVIE, Miss. Sarah Letitia, BSc ACA *2004;* with KPMG LLP, Box 10426 Pacific Centre, 777 Dunsmuir Street, VANCOUVER V7Y 1K3, BC, CANADA.
DAVIE, Mr. Stephen Howard, BSc FCA *1980;* 3 Bramble Close, BECKENHAM, BR3 3XE.
DAVIE-MARTIN, Miss. Paula, ACA *2007;* 7 Halsey Drive, HITCHIN, HERTFORDSHIRE, SG4 9QH.
DAVIES, Mrs. Abigail Victoria, BSc ACA *2003;* LMG Ltd, 80 The Strand, LONDON, WC2R 0NN.
DAVIES, Mr. Adam Edward, BA ACA *2007;* O2, 260 Bath Road, SLOUGH, SL1 4DX.
DAVIES, Mr. Adrian James, FCA *1969;* Le Vieux Chene, Le Haut de Viette, Chemin de l'Oree, 14140 SAINTE MARGUERITE DE VIETTE, FRANCE. (Life Member)
DAVIES, Mr. Adrian Kenneth, BA ACA CTA *2002;* 2 Whitelea Avenue, KILMACOLM, RENFREWSHIRE, PA13 4JR.
DAVIES, Mr. Alan James, MSc FCA *1970;* 37 Hotson Road, SOUTHWOLD, SUFFOLK, IP18 6BP. (Life Member)
DAVIES, Mr. Alan John, BSc ACA *2004;* with Hopper Williams & Bell Limited, Highland House, Mayflower Close, Chandler's Ford, SOUTHAMPTON, HAMPSHIRE SO53 4AR.
DAVIES, Mr. Alan John, BSc FCA *1979;* Meadow House, Darenth Way, Shoreham, SEVENOAKS, TN14 7SE.
DAVIES, Mr. Alan Martin, BA ACA *1988;* Pibydd y Traeth, Bro Nant Cellan, Clarach, ABERYSTWYTH, SY23 3PH.
•DAVIES, Mr. Alan Paul, FCA *1979;* Dyke Yaxley Limited, 1 Brassey Road, Old Potts Way, SHREWSBURY, SY3 7FA.
DAVIES, Mr. Alan Peter, BA ACA AMCT *1979;* GE Intelligent Platforms Holdings PLC, Tove Valley Business Park, TOWCESTER, NORTHAMPTONSHIRE, NN12 6PF.
DAVIES, Mr. Alan Price, FCA *1970;* A.P Davies, 17 Ravensdale Avenue, LONDON, N12 9HP.
•DAVIES, Mr. Alan Wilfred, FCA *1976;* Anderson Griffin Limited, Rotunda Buildings, Montpellier Exchange, CHELTENHAM, GLOUCESTERSHIRE, GL50 1SX.
DAVIES, Ms. Alison Clare, BA(Hons) ACA *2010;* Flat 217, Compass House, Smugglers Way, LONDON, SW18 1DQ.
DAVIES, Mrs. Alison Elizabeth, BSc ACA *1992;* 736 Thomas Court, LIBERTYVILLE, IL 60048, UNITED STATES.
DAVIES, Miss. Alison Lyn, BA ACA *2007;* 15 Radley Court, LONDON, SE16 6AJ.
DAVIES, Mr. Alistair, ACA *2011;* 28 Fieldview, LONDON, SW18 3HG.
DAVIES, Mr. Alistair Clive, BSc ACA *1986;* 210 Heol Hir, Thornhill, CARDIFF, CF14 9LA.
DAVIES, Mr. Alun Protheroe, BSc ACA ACCA *2008;* 1 Chapel Lane, Clipston, MARKET HARBOROUGH, LE16 9RL.
DAVIES, Miss. Amy, LLB ACA *2007;* Yew Trees Plough Lane, Harefield, UXBRIDGE, MIDDLESEX, UB9 6PF.
DAVIES, Mrs. Andrea Christine, BSc ACA *1990;* 21 Ploughmans Lane, Haxby, YORK, YO32 2WR.
•DAVIES, Mrs. Andrea Louise, BSc ACA *1992;* Arian Accountants Limited, 19 Sundew Close, Radyr Cheyne, CARDIFF, CF5 2SE.
•DAVIES, Mr. Andrew, ACA *1984;* F.A. Magee & Co., Wimborne House, 4-6 Pump Lane, HAYES, MIDDLESEX, UB3 3NB.
DAVIES, Mr. Andrew, BA ACA *1992;* 102 Chaveney Road, Quorn, LOUGHBOROUGH, LEICESTERSHIRE, LE12 8AD.
DAVIES, Mr. Andrew, LLB FCA *1987;* 1 Stockdale Farm, Moor Lane Flookburgh, GRANGE-OVER-SANDS, CUMBRIA, LA11 7LR.
DAVIES, Mr. Andrew, BSc ACA *2011;* 156 Iverson Road, West Hampstead, LONDON, NW6 2HH.
DAVIES, Mr. Andrew David, BA ACA *2000;* Bristol & West Plc, 1 Temple Back East, BRISTOL, BS1 6DX.
•DAVIES, Mr. Andrew David, MA FCA *2000;* Ernst & Young LLP, 1 More London Place, LONDON, SE1 2AF. See also Ernst & Young Europe LLP
DAVIES, Mr. Andrew Ernest, MA FCA *1982;* The Corner House, 25 Townsend Close, BRUTON, SOMERSET, BA10 0HD.
DAVIES, Mr. Andrew Frederick, MA ACA *1992;* Via Pieve di Campo 46, Ponte San Giovanni, PG06135 PERUGIA, ITALY.
DAVIES, Mr. Andrew Giles Pedder, BA ACA AIMC *1994;* Conservation Capital, PO Box 294, NANYUKI, 10400, KENYA.
•DAVIES, Mr. Andrew James, FCA *1990;* K M Business Solutions Limited, 4-6 Grimshaw Street, BURNLEY, LANCASHIRE, BB11 2AZ.
DAVIES, Mr. Andrew James, BA ACA *1999;* 59 Northampton Road, WELLINGBOROUGH, NORTHAMPTONSHIRE, NN8 3LS.
DAVIES, Mr. Andrew John, BSc ACA *1992;* Warley House, Morestead, WINCHESTER, HAMPSHIRE, SO21 1LF.
DAVIES, Mr. Andrew John, BA ACA *1996;* Keayn Reayrt, Croit-Quill Road, Lonan, ISLE OF MAN, IM4 7JD.
DAVIES, Mr. Andrew Mark, BSc ACA *1993;* Verizon Wireless, One Verizon Way, VC 43E 029, BASKING RIDGE, NJ 07920, UNITED STATES.
DAVIES, Mr. Andrew Michael, MA BSc FCA MBA *1992;* The Glen, Pennington Road, TUNBRIDGE WELLS, KENT, TN4 0SX.
DAVIES, Mr. Andrew Michael, BEng FCA *1989;* with KPMG LLP, 15 Canada Square, LONDON, E14 5GL.
•DAVIES, Mr. Andrew Norman, ACA *1981;* (Tax Fac), Creasey Son & Wickenden, Hearts of Oak House, 4 Pembroke Road, SEVENOAKS, TN13 1XR.
DAVIES, Mr. Andrew Paul, BSc ACA *1999;* Lennox Paton, Fort Nassau Centre, Marlborough Street, P O Box N-4875, NASSAU, BAHAMAS.
DAVIES, Mr. Andrew Peter, ACA *1993;* Chemring Group Plc Chemring House, 1500 Parkway Whiteley, FAREHAM, PO15 7AF.
DAVIES, Mr. Andrew Robert, BSc FCA *1989;* JN Bentley Ltd, Keighley Road, SKIPTON, NORTH YORKSHIRE, BD23 5QR.
DAVIES, Miss. Angela Lynne, BSc ACA *1981;* 30 Clapham Mansions, Nightingale LaneClapham, LONDON, SW4 9AQ.
•DAVIES, Miss. Ann Mckeeman, BSc FCA *1979;* The Moat House, Mill La, Tanners Grn Wythall, BIRMINGHAM, B47 6BJ.
DAVIES, Miss. Anna, BSc ACA *2005;* 9 Burns Street, North Fremantle, PERTH, WA 6159, AUSTRALIA.
DAVIES, Mrs. Anne, BSc ACA *1989;* Blendons, Highcotts Lane, West Clandon, GUILDFORD, GU4 7XA.
DAVIES, Mrs. Anne Tracey, BA ACA *1991;* 12 Vicarage Gardens, Flamstead, ST. ALBANS, HERTFORDSHIRE, AL3 8EF.
DAVIES, Miss. Anne-Marie Kathryn, BA ACA *1991;* 22 Birmingham Road, ALCESTER, B49 5ES.
DAVIES, Mr. Anthony Ambrose, FCA *1964;* 15 Despenser Avenue, Llantrisant, PONTYCLUN, CF72 8QA.
DAVIES, Mr. Anthony Charles Gwynne, BA FCA *1974;* PO BOX 287, NANNUP, WA 6275, AUSTRALIA.
DAVIES, Mr. Anthony Clive, BSc FCA *1981;* Ramot, Broom Hill, Stapleton, BRISTOL, BS16 1DN.
•DAVIES, Mr. Anthony Desmond, FCA *1972;* (Tax Fac), ADD Accounting Services, 107 Elm Low Road, WISBECH, CAMBRIDGESHIRE, PE14 0DF. See also T & I (Wisbech) Ltd
DAVIES, Mr. Anthony Ernest, FCA *1960;* 57 Manor Rd., SOLIHULL, B91 2BL. (Life Member)
DAVIES, Mr. Anthony John, MA ACA *1986;* 2 St. Lukes Terrace, East Morton, KEIGHLEY, WEST YORKSHIRE, BD20 5RX.
DAVIES, Mr. Anthony Paul, BSc ACA CTA *2007;* (Tax Fac), Flat 5, 366 Upper Richmond Road, LONDON, SW15 6TS.
DAVIES, Mr. Anthony Warren, FCA *1962;* Hesworth Barn, Hesworth Common, Fittleworth, PULBOROUGH, RH20 1EW. (Life Member)
DAVIES, Mr. Ben John, ACA *2008;* 13 Curness Street, LONDON, SE13 6JY.
DAVIES, Dr. Benjamin John, PhD BA ACA *2003;* Athene Place, 66 Shoe Lane, LONDON, EC4A 3BQ.
DAVIES, Mr. Benjamin Thomas, BA ACA *1981;* Cembre Ltd, Dunton Park, Kingsbury Road, Curdworth, SUTTON COLDFIELD, B76 9EE.
DAVIES, Mr. Bernard Colson, FCA *1955;* 94 Epping Way, WITHAM, ESSEX, CM8 1NQ. (Life Member)
DAVIES, Mr. Brian, BSc ACA *1988;* 25 Harness Close, CHELMSFORD, CM1 6UU.
DAVIES, Mr. Brian David, FCA *1974;* 10 Longfield Road, Capel St.Mary, IPSWICH, IP9 2UA.
DAVIES, Mr. Brian George, BSc FCA *1976;* 50 Cockshot Road, MALVERN, WR14 2TT.
DAVIES, Mr. Brian Richard, FCA *1959;* 3 Cil Fedw, Radyr, CARDIFF, CF15 8AR. (Life Member)
DAVIES, Mr. Bruce, FCA *1951;* 6 The Verlands, COWBRIDGE, CF71 7BY. (Life Member)
DAVIES, Mr. Bruce Boyden, FCA *1973;* Haw Lane Cottage, Haw Lane, Tockington, BRISTOL, BS32 4PD.
DAVIES, Mrs. Candida Jane, BSc ACA *1999;* Eli Lilly Export SA, PO Box 580, 16 Chemin des Coquelicots, 1214 VERNIER, SWITZERLAND.
DAVIES, Miss. Cari Fflur, BA(Hons) ACA *2010;* Flat 2, Livorno House, Ffordd Garthorne, CARDIFF, CF10 4DE.
DAVIES, Mrs. Caroline, BA ACA *1997;* 56 London Road, BERKHAMSTED, HERTFORDSHIRE, HP4 2NF.
DAVIES, Mrs. Caroline Annabel, BSc(Hons) ACA *2000;* 8 Ballinger Court, Upper Ashlyns Road, BERKHAMSTED, HERTFORDSHIRE, HP4 3BX.
DAVIES, Mrs. Caroline Jean, BMus ACA *2000;* 29 Gwyndy Road, Undy, CALDICOT, GWENT, NP26 3QE.
DAVIES, Ms. Caroline Margaret, BA FCA *1985;* (Tax Fac), 10 Waterside Mill, Denholme Road, Oxenhope, KEIGHLEY, BD22 9NP.
DAVIES, Mrs. Carolyn Margaret, MA ACA *1991;* Grange Farm, 14 Owston Road, Knossington, OAKHAM, LEICESTERSHIRE, LE15 8LX.
•DAVIES, Miss. Catherine Elaine, LLB ACA CTA *1993;* (Tax Fac), J.V. Banks, Banks House, Paradise Street, RHYL, LL18 3LW.
DAVIES, Miss. Catherine Linda, BSc ACA *2004;* 2 Brook Walk, SOUTHWELL, NOTTINGHAMSHIRE, NG25 0FN.
DAVIES, Miss. Cerian Sian, ACA *2008;* 8 Eton Court, CARDIFF, CF14 4HZ.
DAVIES, Mr. Charles Edward Kent, FCA *1974;* 1 Tai Cae Bryn, Groeswen, CARDIFF, CF15 7UQ.
DAVIES, Mr. Charles Meredydd, ACA *2008;* Granary Cottage, The Street, Dalham, NEWMARKET, SUFFOLK, CB8 8TF.
DAVIES, Mr. Charles William, BA ACA *1991;* 156 Abbeville Road, LONDON, SW4 9LP.
DAVIES, Mrs. Charlotte, DPhil MChem ACA *2010;* Francis Clark Vantage Point, Pynes Hill, EXETER, EX2 5FD.
DAVIES, Mr. Chris John, BA ACA *1995;* Flat 2A, 9 Possession Street, SHEUNG WAN, HONG KONG ISLAND, HONG KONG SAR.
DAVIES, Mr. Christopher, BA ACA *2011;* Flat 171 City House, 420 London Road, CROYDON, CR0 2NU.
DAVIES, Mr. Christopher James Gibson, BSc FCA *1985;* 13 Llwyn-Y-Grant-Road, Penylan, CARDIFF, CF23 9ET.
DAVIES, Mr. Christopher John, BSc(Hons) ACA CTA *2001;* 457 West Barnes Lane, NEW MALDEN, SURREY, KT3 6PA.
DAVIES, Mr. Christopher Morgan, BSc ACA *1984;* 12 The Lawns, Blackheath, LONDON, SE3 9TB.
DAVIES, Mr. Christopher Peter, MA ACA *1988;* The Old White Horse, Sparrows Herne, BUSHEY, WD23 1FU.
DAVIES, Mr. Christopher Roy, BSc ACA *1982;* Richardson Whitby Smith Ltd, 53 High Street, Keynsham, BRISTOL, BS31 1DS.
DAVIES, Mr. Christopher Simon, MPhil BSc ACA *2005;* 42 Marjoram Place, Bradley Stoke, BRISTOL, BS32 0DQ.
DAVIES, Mr. Christopher Stephen, ACA *1981;* 15 Lorong Jelutong Kanan, Damansara Heights, 50490 KUALA LUMPUR, MALAYSIA.
DAVIES, Mrs. Claire, MEng ACA *2007;* 744 Warrington Road, Risley, WARRINGTON, WA3 6AH.
DAVIES, Mrs. Claire Joanna, MEng ACA *2001;* 18 Linden Road, LONDON, N10 3DH.

DAVIES, Mrs. Clare Emma, BA ACA *1999;* Hamptworth New Road, Littleton, WINCHESTER, SO22 6QR.

DAVIES, Mr. Clement John, FCA *1970;* Renton Howard Wood Levin Llp, Ivory House, East Smithfield, LONDON, E1W 1AT.

DAVIES, Mr. Colin, BSc ACA *1990;* Vectair Systems Limited, Unit 3 Trident Centre, Armstrong Road, BASINGSTOKE, HAMPSHIRE, RG24 8NU.

DAVIES, Mr. Colin Michael, FCA *1959;* Hollands, Holland Road, STEYNING, BN44 3GJ. (Life Member)

DAVIES, Mr. Conrad Thomas, BA ACA *1996;* Morgan Guaranty Ltd, 60 Victoria Embankment, LONDON, EC4Y 0JP.

•DAVIES, Mr. Craig, ACA *1997;* Davies Tracey Ltd, 3rd Floor, Newport House, Thornaby Place Thornaby, STOCKTON-ON-TEES, CLEVELAND TS17 6SE.

DAVIES, Mr. Curtis Miles, BSc ACA *1990;* Qantas Airways Limited, 203 Coward Street, MASCOT, NSW 2020, AUSTRALIA.

•DAVIES, Mr. Daniel Ivor, FCA *1975;* (Tax Fac), D I Davies FCA, 3 Gwynfan, Nantycaws, CARMARTHEN, DYFED, SA32 8HF.

DAVIES, Mrs. Danielle Hazel, BA(Hons) ACA *2003;* Matalan Retail Ltd, Gillibrands Road, SKELMERSDALE, LANCASHIRE, WN8 9TB.

DAVIES, Mr. Darryl James, MA ACA *1999;* 3 Leverton Street, LONDON, NW5 2PH.

DAVIES, Mr. David, BA FCA *1963;* 157 Plymouth Road, PENARTH, SOUTH GLAMORGAN, CF64 5DG. (Life Member)

DAVIES, Mr. David Anthony, FCA *1961;* 17 Riverside, CHELMSFORD, CM2 6LL. (Life Member)

DAVIES, Mr. David Charles, MBA BA FCA *1981;* OMV AG, Trabrennstrasse 6-8, A 1020 VIENNA, AUSTRIA.

•DAVIES, Mr. David Craig, ACA CTA *2002;* (Tax Fac), Rawlinson & Hunter, Lower Mill, Kingston Road, Ewell, EPSOM, KT17 2AE.

DAVIES, Mr. David Gareth Lloyd, BSc ACA *2002;* 116 Henke Court, Atlantic Wharf, CARDIFF, CF10 4EJ.

DAVIES, Mr. David Hatfield, FCA *1967;* (Tax Fac), Little Britain Cottage, Kimbolton, LEOMINSTER, HR6 0HQ.

DAVIES, Mr. David Huw, MBA BA FCA *1984;* Little Croft, Blackmoor, Langford, BRISTOL, BS40 5HJ.

•DAVIES, Mr. David Huw, BSc FCA *1976;* Collins Davies, 19 Bettysmead, EXETER, EX4 8LN. See also Collins Davies Ltd

DAVIES, Mr. David Huw Frederick, BA ACA *1979;* 4 High Trees, Tulse Hill, LONDON, SW2 3PU.

DAVIES, Mr. David Llewellyn, FCA *1965;* 53 Brighton Road, HORSHAM, RH13 6EZ.

•DAVIES, Mr. David Michael Barry, ACA *1980;* (Tax Fac), DMB Davies Ltd, Broyan House, Priory Street, CARDIGAN, DYFED, SA43 1BU. See also E W Owen Limited

DAVIES, Mr. David Morris, BA FCA *1959;* 92 Wattleton Road, BEACONSFIELD, HP9 1RS. (Life Member)

DAVIES, Mr. David Nigel, BTech ACA *1985;* 1006 Constitution Ave NE, WASHINGTON, DC 20002, UNITED STATES.

DAVIES, Mr. David Peter Lloyd, DL FCA *1961;* 27 Anderson Lane, Southgate, SWANSEA, SA3 2BX.

DAVIES, Mr. David Thomas, MA MBA FCA *1974;* 4 Hayfell Grove, Hest Bank, LANCASTER, LA2 6DT.

DAVIES, Mr. Delme Terence, BSc ACA *1997;* 78 Ynys y Gored, Velindre, PORT TALBOT, WEST GLAMORGAN, SA13 2EB.

DAVIES, Mr. Dennis James, FCA *1964;* Fairfield, Goodwood Gardens, Runcton, CHICHESTER, WEST SUSSEX, PO20 1SP.

DAVIES, Mr. Derek Esmond, MSc BSc FCA *1975;* Goldcrest, Neyland Road, Steynton, MILFORD HAVEN, SA73 1HH.

DAVIES, Mrs. Diana Carol, BSc ACA *1987;* Riflemans Cottage, Shirvells Hill, Goring Heath, READING, RG8 7SP.

DAVIES, Dr. Dorothy Mary, ACA *1990;* 59 Hampton Park Road, HEREFORD, HR1 1TJ.

DAVIES, Mr. Douglas James, FCA *1975;* with Barron & Barron, Bathurst House, 86 Micklegate, YORK, YO1 6LQ.

DAVIES, Mr. Duncan Philip, BA ACA *1999;* Technology Services Group Ltd, 1 Gosforth Park Way, Gosforth Business Park, NEWCASTLE UPON TYNE, NE12 8ET.

DAVIES, Mr. Dyke Ian, LLB ACA *1992;* 10 Providence Ct, NEWTOWN, PA 18940, UNITED STATES.

DAVIES, Mr. Edward John, LLB ACA *2004;* Nepia, Baltic Place, South Shore Road, GATESHEAD, TYNE AND WEAR, NE8 3BA.

DAVIES, Mr. Edwin, ACA *2011;* 29a Over Lane, Almondsbury, BRISTOL, BS32 4BL.

DAVIES, Ms. Elizabeth Ann, BSc ACA *1990;* 16 Canonbury Grove, LONDON, N1 2HR.

DAVIES, Mrs. Elizabeth Mary, ACA *1996;* 7 Clinton Close, Grange Park, SWINDON, SN5 6BP.

DAVIES, Miss. Emma Jane, ACA *2009;* 281 Wellington Road North, STOCKPORT, CHESHIRE, SK4 5BP.

DAVIES, Miss. Emma Louise Besant, ACA *2003;* 160 Ashley Gardens, Emery Hill Street, LONDON, SW1P 1PD.

DAVIES, Mrs. Emma Sian Owen, BSc ACA *2007;* 20 Poets Way, Llanharan, PONTYCLUN, MID GLAMORGAN, CF72 9UZ.

•DAVIES, Mr. Eric, BSc FCA *1970;* DRP & Co, 6 St. Johns Court, Upper forest Way, SWANSEA, SA6 8QQ.

DAVIES, Mr. Eric Charles, FCA *1955;* 15 Nimrod Close, ST. ALBANS, HERTFORDSHIRE, AL4 9XY. (Life Member)

DAVIES, Mr. Eric Oswald, FCA JDipMA *1951;* 57a Furlong Lane, Alrewas, BURTON-ON-TRENT, STAFFORDSHIRE, DE13 7EE. (Life Member)

DAVIES, Mrs. Estelle Jane, BSc ACA *1995;* 6 Summerfield Road, Ealing, LONDON, W5 1ND.

DAVIES, Mr. Evan Goronwy, FCA *1951;* 410 Cyncoed Road, CARDIFF, CF23 6SB. (Life Member)

DAVIES, Miss. Fenella Dawn Howard, BEng ACA *1995;* 26 Ottways Lane, ASHTEAD, SURREY, KT21 2NZ.

•DAVIES, Mrs. Fiona Jean, BSc(Econ) FCA FCCA FABRP *1984;* Houghton Stone De Cymru Limited, The Executive Centre, Temple Court, Cathedral Road, CARDIFF, CF11 9HA.

DAVIES, Ms. Fiona Mary, BSc ACA *1989;* 43 Ashford Drive, Appleton, WARRINGTON, CHESHIRE, WA4 5GG.

DAVIES, Mr. Gareth, CBE FCA *1956;* 4 Beechgate, Roman Road, Little Aston Park, SUTTON COLDFIELD, B74 3AR. (Life Member)

DAVIES, Mr. Gareth Andrew, BSc ACA *2004;* 3 Clovelly Lodge, 2 Popes Grove, TWICKENHAM, TW2 5TA.

•DAVIES, Mr. Gareth Anthony, BSc FCA *1982;* Gareth A Davies Limited, Spec House, 83 Elm Road, LEIGH-ON-SEA, ESSEX, SS9 1SP. See also Gareth A. Davies Services Limited

DAVIES, Mr. Gareth Huw, BSc FCA *1996;* (Tax Fac), Tithe Barn, Main Street, Chackmore, BUCKINGHAM, BUCKINGHAMSHIRE, MK18 5JF.

•DAVIES, Mr. Gareth James, BA ACA *1986;* PricewaterhouseCoopers, Thomas R. Malthusstraat 5, P O Box 90351, 1006 BJ AMSTERDAM, NETHERLANDS.

•DAVIES, Mr. Gareth James Garfield, FCA *1988;* Keen Dicey Grover, Bathurst House, 50 Bathurst Walk, IVER, SL0 9BH.

DAVIES, Mr. Gareth John, BSc FCA *1991;* (Tax Fac), 63 Sterndale Road, LONDON, W14 0HU.

DAVIES, Mr. Gareth John, BSc ACA *1998;* 18 Linden Road, LONDON, N10 3DH.

•DAVIES, Mr. Gareth Maldwyn, BSc FCA *1976;* PricewaterhouseCoopers LLP, Pricewaterhousecoopers, 12 Plumtree Court, LONDON, EC4A 4HT. See also PricewaterhouseCoopers

DAVIES, Mr. Gareth Matthew, BA ACA *2007;* 24 Mercia Drive, SHEFFIELD, S17 3QF.

DAVIES, Mr. Gareth Michael, ACA *2010;* The Coppice, 46 South Downs Road, Hale, ALTRINCHAM, CHESHIRE, WA14 3HN.

DAVIES, Mr. Gareth Paul, ACA *2008;* 15 Harbledown Road, LONDON, SW6 5TW.

DAVIES, Mr. Gareth Rhys, BA ACA *2000;* 56 Grandison Road, Clapham, LONDON, SW11 6LN.

DAVIES, Mr. Gareth Wyn, BA ACA *1989;* Creskeld Valley House, 43 Hall Drive, Bramhope, LEEDS, LS16 9JF.

DAVIES, Mr. Gary Christopher, BSc ACA *2002;* Alix Partners Ltd, 20 North Audley Street, LONDON, W1K 6WE.

DAVIES, Mr. Gary Paul, BSc ACA *1997;* JBM International Limited, Kingsilver Refinery, Hixon, STAFFORD, ST18 0PY.

•DAVIES, Mr. Geoffrey, FCA *1973;* (Tax Fac), UHY Hacker Young, 168 Church Road, HOVE, BN3 2DL.

•DAVIES, Mr. Geoffrey Brian, FCA *1972;* (Tax Fac), Landau Morley LLP, Lanmor House, 370-386 High Road, WEMBLEY, MIDDLESEX, HA9 6AX.

DAVIES, Mr. Geoffrey Clive, LLB ACA *1986;* 14 Yr Arglawdd, Heathwood Road, CARDIFF, CF14 4GH.

•DAVIES, Mr. Geoffrey Martin, MA FCA *1975;* Geoff Davies Associates Ltd, 27 Main Street, PEMBROKE, DYFED, SA71 4JS.

DAVIES, Mr. Geoffrey Walter, BSc FCA *1961;* Southern Cross, 5 Thornton Grove, Hatch End, PINNER, HA5 4HG. (Life Member)

•DAVIES, Mr. Geraint Charles Boyens, BSc ACA *1982;* Ernst & Young LLP, Liberation House, Castle Street, St Helier, JERSEY, JE1 1EY. See also Ernst & Young Europe LLP

DAVIES, Mr. Geraint Cooper, BSc ACA *1992;* 51 Stamford Road, Bowdon, ALTRINCHAM, CHESHIRE, WA14 2JN.

•DAVIES, Mr. Geraint Evan, BA ACA *1979;* Millener Davies, Southfield House, Southfield Road, Westbury On Trym, BRISTOL, BS9 3BH.

•DAVIES, Mr. Geraint Vaughan, ACA *1981;* (Tax Fac), Davies & Associates Limited, Sherwood House, 2 Albert Road, TAMWORTH, B79 7JN. See also Tomkinson Teal Limited

DAVIES, Mr. Gerald David, FCA *1973;* Thosbys Trehysbys, Rhodiad, St. Davids, HAVERFORDWEST, DYFED, SA62 6PN.

DAVIES, Mr. Gethin Rhodri, BSc ACA *2003;* 22 Tyn-y-Pwll Road, CARDIFF, CF14 1AS.

DAVIES, Ms. Gillian, BA ACA *1992;* 4 Imprint Group Plc, 7-8 Market Place, LONDON, W1W 8AG.

DAVIES, Mrs. Gillian Margaret, FCA *1962;* Dunan Cottage, Clehonger, HEREFORD, HR2 9SF.

DAVIES, Mr. Glen, BSc FCA *1971;* Nordene, 10 The Spinney, Arnside, CARNFORTH, LANCASHIRE, LA5 0EX. (Life Member)

DAVIES, Mr. Glen Russell, FCA *1977;* 26 Hither Green Lane, Abbey Park, REDDITCH, B98 9BW. (Life Member)

•DAVIES, Mr. Glyn John, BSc FCA *1980;* 58 Bowham Avenue, BRIDGEND, MID GLAMORGAN, CF31 3PA.

DAVIES, Mr. Glynn Gareth, BSc FCA *1968;* 727 Race Passage Close, SOOKE V9Z 1C5, BC, CANADA.

DAVIES, Mr. Godfrey Vaughan, BA ACA *1978;* C D C Group Plc, 80 Victoria Street, LONDON, SW1E 5JL.

DAVIES, Mr. Graeme Racine, BA ACA *1994;* Ipswich Haven Marina, New Cut East, IPSWICH, IP3 0EA.

•DAVIES, Mr. Graham Arthur, BA ACA *1987;* Davies McLennon, 93 Wellington Road North, STOCKPORT, SK4 2LR.

DAVIES, Mr. Graham Lloyd, BSc ACA *1992;* The Royal Bank of Scotland Plc, 280 Bishopsgate, LONDON, EC2M 4RB.

DAVIES, Mr. Guy, BSc ACA *1990;* WestBridge Fund Managers Ltd, First Floor, The Gatehouse, Melrose Hall, Cypress Drive, St. Mellons CARDIFF CF3 0EG.

DAVIES, Mr. Guy Hanbury, BSc ACA *1990;* Lakeswood House, 25 Parkside, Wimbledon, LONDON, SW19 5NA.

DAVIES, Mr. Guy Malcolm, BSc ACA *1991;* with Dean Statham, Bank Passage, STAFFORD, ST16 2JS.

DAVIES, Miss. Haf Lisa, BA(Hons) ACA *2010;* 32 Birkdale Avenue, BUCKLEY, CLWYD, CH7 2NB.

DAVIES, Mrs. Hannah Jayne, MChem ACA *2006;* 24 Bayfield Wood Close, CHEPSTOW, GWENT, NP16 6FB.

DAVIES, Mrs. Hannah Michelle, BSc ACA *2007;* 17 Cefn Carnau Road, CARDIFF, CF14 4LZ.

DAVIES, Mr. Haydn John, MA FCA *1963;* Ryecroft, 9 Red Road, BOREHAMWOOD, HERTFORDSHIRE, WD6 4SR. (Life Member)

DAVIES, Mrs. Hazel Gillian, BSc ACA *2007;* 6 The Croft, Loughor, SWANSEA, SA4 6TB.

DAVIES, Mr. Hefin Lewis, BSc ACA *1995;* (Tax Fac), 11a Trosserch Road, Llangennech, LLANELLI, DYFED, SA14 8AQ.

DAVIES, Mrs. Helen, BSc ACA *1989;* 23 Sawyers, Elmsett, IPSWICH, IP7 6QH.

DAVIES, Ms. Helen, BSc ACA *1991;* 14 Cae Haf, Northop Hall, MOLD, CH7 6GB.

DAVIES, Mrs. Helen Clare, BA(Econ) ACA *2001;* 29 PARK RD, SALFORD, M6 8JP.

DAVIES, Mrs. Helen Pamela, BSc ACA *2007;* Just Retirement Ltd Vale House, Roebuck Close Bancroft Road, REIGATE, SURREY, RH2 7RU.

DAVIES, Mr. Henry Jonathan, BA ACA *1994;* 7 Briar Lane, CARSHALTON, SM5 4PX.

DAVIES, Mr. Hereward Scott, FCA *1958;* 11 Greenacre Close, Hadley Highstone, BARNET, HERTFORDSHIRE, EN5 4QB. (Life Member)

•DAVIES, Mr. Howard John, BEng ACA *1999;* Deloitte LLP, Stonecutter Court, 1 Stonecutter Street, LONDON, EC4A 4TR. See also Deloitte & Touche LLP

DAVIES, Mr. Hugh Anthony, FCA *1960;* 25 Middlemarsh, LEOMINSTER, HEREFORDSHIRE, HR6 8UP. (Life Member)

•DAVIES, Mr. Hugh William, ACA *1982;* Hugh Davies & Co Limited, 35 Chequers Court, Brown Street, SALISBURY, SP1 2AS.

DAVIES, Mr. Huw Gittins, FCA *1973;* 2 Vicarage Crescent, NEWCASTLE, STAFFORDSHIRE, ST5 1NJ.

DAVIES, Mr. Huw James, BA FCA *1999;* 6 The Croft, Loughor, SWANSEA, SA4 6TB.

DAVIES, Mr. Huw Owen, BSc ACA *1984;* Welsh Assembly Government, Cathays Park, CARDIFF, CF10 3NQ.

DAVIES, Mr. Iain Robert, BA ACA *1995;* Perstorp UK Ltd, Baronet Way, WARRINGTON, CHESHIRE, WA4 6HA.

•DAVIES, Mr. Ian, BA FCA *1979;* Tranter Lowe Bank House, 66 High Street Dawley, TELFORD, SHROPSHIRE, TF4 2HD. See also Tranter Lowe (D&W) LLP

•DAVIES, Mr. Ian, FCA *1980;* Alliotts, Congress House, 14 Lyon Road, HARROW, MIDDLESEX, HA1 2EN.

•DAVIES, Mr. Ian Arthur, FCA *1972;* with HSP Nicklin, Church Court, Stourbridge Road, HALESOWEN, WEST MIDLANDS, B63 3TT.

•DAVIES, Mr. Ian Frank, BSc FCA *1971;* I F Davies, 1 Ellesmere Drive, SHREWSBURY, SY1 2QU.

DAVIES, Mr. Ian Gareth, BA(Hons) ACA *2000;* Hamptworth New Road, Littleton, WINCHESTER, SO22 6QR.

DAVIES, Mr. Ian Gerard, BSc ACA *1991;* Brocklebank Butts Lane, Woodmancote, CHELTENHAM, GL52 9QH.

DAVIES, Dr. Ian John, BSc ACA *1996;* 30 Brynderwen Road, NEWPORT, GWENT, NP19 8LQ.

DAVIES, Mr. Ian Robert, MBA FCA CF *1981;* MEMBER OF COUNCIL, The Independent Director Limited, Estate Office, Cowesfield House Farm, Romsey Road, Whiteparish, SALISBURY SP5 2QY.

DAVIES, Mr. Ifan Richard, BSc ACA *1979;* 20 Archer Road, PENARTH, CF64 3HW.

DAVIES, Mr. Ioan Rhys, BA ACA *2009;* Envases UK Ltd Unit 1, Christchurch Road Baglan Industrial Park, PORT TALBOT, WEST GLAMORGAN, SA12 7BZ.

DAVIES, Mrs. Irina Michelle, ACA *1999;* J P Morgan Chase Manhatten Bank N A, 1 Chaseside, BOURNEMOUTH, BH7 7DA.

•DAVIES, Mr. Jack, FCA CTA *1960;* (Tax Fac), J. Davies, 9 Dunes House, 1 Fairhaven Road, LYTHAM ST. ANNES, LANCASHIRE, FY8 1NN.

DAVIES, Mr. James, ACA *2008;* Suffolk House, Bath Road, Knowl Hill, READING, RG10 9UT.

DAVIES, Mr. James Edwin, BA BCL ACA *2001;* 23 Beaumont Street, OXFORD, OX1 2NP.

DAVIES, Mr. James Rhys, ACA *2000;* 2 Convamore Lane, Panmure, AUCKLAND 1060, NEW ZEALAND.

DAVIES, Mr. James Vaughan, FCA *1970;* 51 Hendre Park, Llangennech, LLANELLI, SA14 8UP. (Life Member)

DAVIES, Mr. James Wallace, FCA *1951;* 13 Coniston Way, REIGATE, RH2 0LN. (Life Member)

DAVIES, Mrs. Jane, BA ACA *1992;* 180 Saron Road, Saron, AMMANFORD, SA18 3LN.

•DAVIES, Mrs. Jane Elizabeth, ACA *1994;* Brockhurst Davies Limited, 11 The Office Village, North Road, LOUGHBOROUGH, LEICESTERSHIRE, LE11 1QJ.

DAVIES, Mrs. Janet, FCA *1973;* 23 Albany Road, SALISBURY, SP1 3YQ.

DAVIES, Mr. Jared Scott, BSc ACA *1999;* 2 North View, Govilon, ABERGAVENNY, GWENT, NP7 9PW.

•DAVIES, Mr. Jason, BA ACA *1999;* Deloitte LLP, Abbots House, Abbey Street, READING, RG1 3BD. See also Deloitte & Touche LLP

•DAVIES, Mr. Jeffrey, FCA *1977;* Davies Associates, 77 Rue Charlemagne, L-1328 LUXEMBOURG, LUXEMBOURG.

DAVIES, Mr. Jeffrey Clive, FCA *1969;* 108 Pendwyallt Road, Whitchurch, CARDIFF, CF14 7EH. (Life Member)

•DAVIES, Mrs. Jennifer Ann, BSc FCA *1997;* Revell Ward LLP, 7th Floor, 30 Market Street, HUDDERSFIELD, HD1 2HG.

DAVIES, Miss. Jennifer Louise, BA(Hons) ACA *2009;* 13 Hutchinson Square, Douglas, ISLE OF MAN, IM2 4HT.

DAVIES, Miss. Jennifer Sian, BSc ACA *2003;* 16 Cranborne Avenue, HITCHIN, HERTFORDSHIRE, SG5 2BS.

DAVIES, Mr. Jeremy Mark, BA ACA *1985;* 16 Old Queen Street, LONDON, SW1H 9HP.

DAVIES, Mr. Jeremy Robin, FCA *1965;* 36 Cinnamon Lane, RANCHO PALOS VERDES, CA 90275, UNITED STATES.

DAVIES, Mrs. Jillian Margaret, BSc ACA *1980;* Lion Cottage, Chapel Lane, Blockley, MORETON-IN-MARSH, GLOUCESTERSHIRE, GL56 9BG.

DAVIES, Mrs. Joanna Marie, BSc ACA *2009;* Ground Floor Flat, 63 Devonshire Road, Westbury Park, BRISTOL, BS6 7NQ.

DAVIES, Miss. Joanne, BSc ACA *1996;* 20 Rue du Bois, L-1245 SENNINGERBERG, LUXEMBOURG.

DAVIES, Miss. Joanne Elizabeth, BA ACA *1995;* The Old Dairy, Grove Farm, Cherington, TETBURY, GL8 8SH.

DAVIES, Mrs. Johanna Maxted, BA FCA *1978;* Cotchet Barn, Blackdown, HASLEMERE, GU27 3BS.

DAVIES, Mr. John, FCA *1975;* Little Foxes, Pine Walk, Chilworth, SOUTHAMPTON, SO16 7HP.

•DAVIES, Mr. John, FCA *1960;* J Davies FCA, 96 Belgrave Road, Gorseinon, SWANSEA, SA4 6RE.

•DAVIES, Mr. John Alan, BSc FCA *1992;* (Tax Fac), The Ollis Partnership Limited, 2 Hamilton Terrace, Holly Walk, LEAMINGTON SPA, WARWICKSHIRE, CV32 4LY.

•**DAVIES, Mr. John Edward Vaughan, FCA** *1963;* 32 Harwood Avenue, Branston, BURTON-ON-TRENT, DE14 3JD.
DAVIES, Mr. John Elwyn, BSc ACA *1986;* 2 Hollowgate, Swinton, MANCHESTER, M27 0AD.
DAVIES, Mr. John Geoffrey, BSc FCA *1974;* Hunters Moon, La Rue de la Trappe, St. Ouen, JERSEY, JE3 2AL.
•**DAVIES, Mr. John Geraint, BA FCA** *1979;* Grant Thornton UK LLP, 11-13 Penhill Road, CARDIFF, CF11 9UP. See also Grant Thornton LLP
DAVIES, Mr. John Gwynne Martin, FCA *1965;* 4 Aldridge Road, FERNDOWN, BH22 8LT. (Life Member)
•**DAVIES, Mr. John Howard, LLB FCA JDipMA** *1960;* Jake Davies & Company, Haleswood, 2 The Crescent, St Stephens, CANTERBURY, CT2 7AG.
DAVIES, Mr. John Hurle, FCA *1948;* 8 Princes Road, FELIXSTOWE, IP11 7QY. (Life Member)
DAVIES, Mr. John Hywel, FCA *1970;* 655c Gower Road, Upper Killay, SWANSEA, SA2 7HE. (Life Member)
DAVIES, Dr. John Keith, ACA *1989;* Rifelman Cottage, Shirvell's Hill, Goring Heath, READING, RG8 7SP.
•**DAVIES, Mr. John Leslie, FCA** *1969;* John L Davies, 24 Thirlestane Close, KENILWORTH, CV8 2PW.
DAVIES, Mr. John Llewelyn, BA FCA *1975;* 8 Chestnut Court, Chestnut Lane, AMERSHAM, HP6 6ED.
DAVIES, Mr. John Martin, FCA *1971;* 7 Calle del Tejo, El Pinar de Campoverde, Pilar de la Horadada, CP 03191 ALICANTE, SPAIN.
•**DAVIES, Mr. John Peter, FCA** *1975;* (Tax Fac), Davies Downs & Co., Kemmel House, 6 Red Lane, Appleton, WARRINGTON, WA4 5AD.
DAVIES, Mr. John Quantrill, MA ACA *1999;* 42 West 11th Avenue, VANCOUVER V5Y 1S5, BC, CANADA.
DAVIES, Mr. John Richard, BSc ACA *1995;* SailTime South Wales Limited, Edenholme Hungerford Lane, Bradfield Southend, READING, RG7 6JJ.
•**DAVIES, Mr. John Richard Gordon, FCA** *1973;* Kings Barton, Caswell Bay, SWANSEA, SA3 3BU.
DAVIES, Mr. John Robert, FCA *1966;* Forest Farm, Chester High Road, NESTON, CH64 3TH.
DAVIES, Mr. John Robert, BA ACA *1991;* 15 Churchfields, LOUGHTON, ESSEX, IG10 1AG.
DAVIES, Mr. John Robert Collis, FCA *1977;* 26 Naseby Road, SOLIHULL, WEST MIDLANDS, B91 2DR.
DAVIES, Mr. John Spencer, BSc FCA *1973;* The Parsonage, 29 Chapel Lane, Rode Heath, STOKE-ON-TRENT, ST7 3SD.
DAVIES, Mr. John Trustram, FCA *1969;* 23 Bridgeview Road, TORONTO M6S 4M9, ON, CANADA. (Life Member)
DAVIES, Mr. John William, BSc ACA *2007;* 3 Cranleigh Drive, Astley Tyldesley, MANCHESTER, M29 7PW.
DAVIES, Mr. John Wyn, BSc FCA *1977;* Marl Cottage, Marl Lane, LLANDUDNO JUNCTION, LL31 9JA.
•**DAVIES, Mr. Jon Melvyn, BTech FCA** *1981;* Melvyn Davies & Co, 9 Limes Road, BECKENHAM, BR3 6NS.
•**DAVIES, Mr. Jonathan Ashley, BSc(Hons) ACA** *2000;* MJF Accountancy, 59a Booker Avenue, Mossley Hill, LIVERPOOL, L18 4QZ.
DAVIES, Mr. Jonathan Charles, MA FCA *1978;* Bank Cottage, Little Worthen, SHREWSBURY, SY5 9HL.
DAVIES, Mr. Jonathan David, MA ACA *1979;* First Floor, Bairstow Eves Countrywide, 2 High Street, BRENTWOOD, CM14 4AB.
DAVIES, Mr. Jonathan Edward, BSc FCA *1991;* (Tax Fac), 4 Briar Hill, Woolpit, BURY ST. EDMUNDS, IP30 9SD.
DAVIES, Mr. Jonathan Mark, BSc ACA *1990;* 83 Old Farm Road, WESTON, CT 06883, UNITED STATES.
DAVIES, Mr. Jonathan Peter James, ACA *1989;* 29 Bullimore Grove, KENILWORTH, WARWICKSHIRE, CV8 2QF.
DAVIES, Mr. Jonathan Rhys, BSc ACA *1992;* 40 Elm Road, BISHOP'S STORTFORD, CM23 2SS.
DAVIES, Mr. Jonathan Walter, BA ACA *1996;* 59 Longfield Drive, AMERSHAM, BUCKINGHAMSHIRE, HP6 5HE.
DAVIES, Mr. Jonathan William, BSc ARCS ACA CFA *1996;* Apt 47, 13 Herbert Street, St Leonards, SYDNEY, NSW 2065, AUSTRALIA.
DAVIES, Mr. Jonathan William Edward, BSc ACA *1988;* (Tax Fac), 6 Cherry Drive, CANTERBURY, CT2 8HF.
DAVIES, Mrs. Josephine Siu-Wai, BSc ACA *1990;* 156 Abbeville Road, LONDON, SW4 9LP.
DAVIES, Mrs. Judith Mary Bolan, BCom ACA *2001;* B B I Unit 18-19, Ffrwdgrech Industrial Estate, BRECON, POWYS, LD3 8LA.
DAVIES, Mrs. Judith Sarah, BA ACA CTA *1999;* 4 Douglas Drive, Shevington, WIGAN, WN6 8EJ.
DAVIES, Mrs. Julia Clare, BSc FCA ATII *1985;* Willowbrook House, Draycott, MORETON-IN-MARSH, GL56 9LF.
DAVIES, Mr. Julian Charles Wyndham, MA(Hons) ACA *2004;* Kynaston House Kynaston, Kinnerley, OSWESTRY, SHROPSHIRE, SY10 8EF.
DAVIES, Mr. Julian Lyndon, ACA *1987;* West Bush House, Hailey Lane, In Hailey, HERTFORD, SG13 7NY.
DAVIES, Mr. Julian Penry, FCA *1961;* Tarnside Barn, Lupton, CARNFORTH, LANCASHIRE, LA6 2PP. (Life Member)
DAVIES, Miss. Julie May, BSc ACA *1983;* 23 Lon Cwmgwyn, Sketty, SWANSEA, SA2 0TY.
DAVIES, Miss. Kate, ACA *2011;* Meadow House, Darenth Way, Shoreham, SEVENOAKS, KENT, TN14 7SE.
•**DAVIES, Mrs. Kate Elizabeth, ACA CTA** *2003;* Rickard Keen LLP, Glenny House, Fenton Way, Southfields Business Park, BASILDON, ESSEX SS15 6TD. See also MGI Rickard Keen LLP
•**DAVIES, Mrs. Kathryn, BA(Hons) ACA DChA** *2002;* KPD Business Services Limited, The Old Shippon, Bradley, FRODSHAM, CHESHIRE, WA6 7EP.
•**DAVIES, Miss. Kathryn Anne, BA ACA** *1985;* Aims Accountants for Business, PO Box 6419, Earl Shilton, LEICESTER, LE9 7ZJ.
DAVIES, Miss. Katy Alexandra, MA ACA *2007;* 174 High Street, Yelling, ST. NEOTS, CAMBRIDGESHIRE, PE19 6SD.
DAVIES, Mr. Keith, FCA *1974;* 85 Newton Road, Knowle, SOLIHULL, B93 9HN.
DAVIES, Mr. Keith, PhD BA FCA *1979;* 198 Mallinson Street, ALLENDALE, NJ 07401, UNITED STATES.
DAVIES, Mr. Keith Ernest, FCA *1960;* 30 Peache Road, Downend, BRISTOL, BS16 5RW. (Life Member)
DAVIES, Mr. Keith John, BA FCA *1973;* 10 Foxcombe Lane, Horsington, TEMPLECOMBE, SOMERSET, BA8 0DS.
DAVIES, Mr. Kenneth, FCA *1954;* 3 Brookwood Close, Shortlands, BROMLEY, BR2 0RP. (Life Member)
DAVIES, Mr. Kenneth Harold, ACA *1980;* 20 Ferndown, Claremont Road, SURBITON, SURREY, KT6 4RY.
DAVIES, Miss. Kerry Jane, BA ACA *1992;* Phoenix Contact Ltd, Halesfield 13, TELFORD, SHROPSHIRE, TF7 4PG.
•**DAVIES, Mr. Kevin, BSc FCA** *1984;* Griffiths Green Arnold, 11 New Street, Pontnewydd, CWMBRAN, NP44 1EE.
DAVIES, Mr. Kevin Maurice, BA ACA *2006;* Barber Harrison & Platt, 2 Rutland Park, SHEFFIELD, S10 2PD.
DAVIES, Mr. Kevin Robert, ACA *2010;* Ground Floor Flat, 63 Devonshire Road, BRISTOL, BS6 7NQ.
DAVIES, Miss. Kirsten Lisbet, ACA *2011;* 21 Pershore Drive, Branston, BURTON-ON-TRENT, STAFFORDSHIRE, DE14 3TY.
DAVIES, Mr. Langley John, BSc ACA *1983;* 3 Llandennis Avenue, Cyncoed, CARDIFF, CF23 6JD.
DAVIES, Miss. Laura Joanne, BA ACA *2006;* Flat 3, 92 Sunningfields Road, LONDON, NW4 4RH.
DAVIES, Miss. Lauren Vere, BA FCA *1998;* Redprairie Ltd Beacon House, Ibstone Road Stokenchurch, HIGH WYCOMBE, BUCKINGHAMSHIRE, HP14 3AQ.
DAVIES, Mr. Lee, ACA *2000;* 75 Galfrid Road, Bilton, HULL, HU11 4HQ.
DAVIES, Mr. Leighton Wynne, BSc ACA *1993;* 64 Cornerswell Road, PENARTH, CF64 2WA.
DAVIES, Mrs. Lesley Jane, ACA *1985;* 39 Heol Cefn Onn, Lisvane, CARDIFF, CF14 0TQ.
•**DAVIES, Mr. Leslie Edward, FCA** *1970;* (Tax Fac), Davies & Co, 136 Bridge Street, LEDBURY, HR8 2AS. See also Ledbury Business Services
DAVIES, Mr. Leslie Rees, FCA *1975;* Tryfan, Cadnant Park, CONWY, ll328pe.
•**DAVIES, Mr. Leslie William, FCA** *1973;* Haines Watts, Sterling House, 11 Omega Court, 350 Cemetery Road, SHEFFIELD, SOUTH YORKSHIRE S11 8FT.
•**DAVIES, Mr. Lionel, BSc FCA** *1972;* Station House, Brancepeth, DURHAM, DH7 8DL.
DAVIES, Mrs. Lisa Jane, BSc ACA *1993;* University of Glamorgan, Treforest, PONTYPRIDD, MID GLAMORGAN, CF37 1DL.
DAVIES, Mr. Lloyd Sean, BSc FCA *1991;* 611 TERESI LN, LOS ALTOS, CA 94024, UNITED STATES.
DAVIES, Miss. Lorna Catherine, BA ACA *2003;* Flat 17, Boundary House, 224-226 St. Margarets Road, TWICKENHAM, TW1 1NW.
•**DAVIES, Mrs. Lorraine Karen, BA ACA** *1989;* LK Davies Limited, 3 The Courtyard, Shapwick, BRIDGWATER, SOMERSET, TA7 9LQ.
DAVIES, Mrs. Louisa Mary, BSc ACA *1994;* Ludchurch Farms Ltd, Ludchurch Farm, Ludchurch, NARBERTH, DYFED, SA67 8JE.
DAVIES, Miss. Louise Ann, MEng ACA *2003;* Ashdene, Trafford Road, ALDERLEY EDGE, CHESHIRE, SK9 7DN.
DAVIES, Mrs. Louise Elizabeth, BSc ACA DChA *1993;* 19 Church Road, Whitchurch, CARDIFF, CF14 2DX.
DAVIES, Mrs. Louise Elizabeth, MA ACA *1999;* 8 Woodview Road, LIVERPOOL, L25 6HZ.
DAVIES, Mrs. Lucy Mary, BA ACA *1980;* Christopher Little Literary Agency Unit 10, 125 Moore Park Road, LONDON, SW6 4PS.
DAVIES, Mrs. Luned Margaret, BSc ACA *1999;* Ty Rhoslyn, Heol yr Gglwys, LLANGADOG, SA19 9AA.
DAVIES, Mr. Lyndon, BSc(Econ) FCA ATII *1981;* 76 Tremains Court, Brackla, BRIDGEND, CF31 2SS.
DAVIES, Mr. Malcolm John, FCA *1978;* 2 New Town Close, Kibworth, LEICESTER, LE8 0JR.
DAVIES, Mr. Marc Peter, MSc BA ACA *2006;* 24 Bayfield Wood Close, CHEPSTOW, GWENT, NP16 6FB.
DAVIES, Mr. Mark Anthony Philip, BA ACA *2000;* The Shippen, Great Haywards, Amberley Close, HAYWARDS HEATH, WEST SUSSEX, RH16 4AU.
DAVIES, Mr. Mark Clive, BA ACA *1999;* with Grant Thornton UK LLP, Enterprise House, 115 Edmund Street, BIRMINGHAM, B3 2HJ.
DAVIES, Mr. Mark David, ACA *2005;* 59 Beresford Street, BAYSWATER 0622, NEW ZEALAND.
DAVIES, Mr. Mark John, BSc FCA *1992;* 76 Doubling Road, GREENWICH, CT 06830, UNITED STATES.
DAVIES, Mr. Mark Redfern, BSc ACA *1980;* Level 4 179 Grey Street, SOUTH BRISBANE, QLD 4101, AUSTRALIA.
DAVIES, Mr. Mark Thomas Russell, BA ACA *1991;* Corrpro Companies Europe Ltd, Adam Street, Bowesfield Lane, STOCKTON-ON-TEES, CLEVELAND, TS18 3HQ.
DAVIES, Mr. Martin, FCA *1961;* 8 Beagle Close, FELTHAM, MIDDLESEX, TW13 7DG.
•**DAVIES, Mr. Martin John, BA ACA** *1986;* (Tax Fac), Davies Gimber Brown LLP, Ryebrook Studios, Woodcote Side, EPSOM, SURREY, KT18 7HD.
DAVIES, Mr. Martin Paul, BA ACA *1992;* 54 Wheatsheaf Drive, WARE, SG12 0XS.
•**DAVIES, Mr. Martin Richard, BSc FCA** *1976;* Miller Davies, Unit A3, Broomsleigh Business Park, Worsley Bridge Road, LONDON, SE26 5BN.
DAVIES, Mr. Martin Roy, ACA *1987;* Dolfach, Chapel Street, CAERSWS, SY17 5ED.
DAVIES, Mr. Martin William, BSc ACA *1993;* 11 Lombardy Close, HEMEL HEMPSTEAD, HERTFORDSHIRE, HP2 4NG.
DAVIES, Mr. Matthew, BA ACA *2002;* Summerhill Guildford Road, Ottershaw, CHERTSEY, KT16 0QS.
DAVIES, Mr. Matthew, BSc(Hons) ACA *2009;* Upper South Side Appartment, 102 Cobbs Hill Road, WARWICK WK10, BERMUDA.
DAVIES, Mr. Matthew John, ACA *2008;* 34 Tower Square, NORTHAMPTON, NN5 5FH.
•**DAVIES, Mr. Matthew Justin, BSc ACA** *1997;* with KPMG LLP, 15 Canada Square, LONDON, E14 5GL.
•**DAVIES, Mr. Matthew Lloyd, BA ACA** *1992;* MND Training & Consultancy, 2 Hillgrove Gardens, KIDDERMINSTER, WORCESTERSHIRE, DY10 3AN.
DAVIES, Mr. Maurice Beresford Tomkinson, FCA *1935;* 2112 Vista Dorado, NEWPORT BEACH, CA 92660, UNITED STATES. (Life Member)
DAVIES, Mr. Mervyn Goronwy, ACA *1981;* Berystede, Runnymede Road, STANFORD-LE-HOPE, SS17 0JY.
•**DAVIES, Mr. Mervyn Neil, BA ACA** *1991;* (Tax Fac), 4 Chapel Crescent, Hadnall, SHREWSBURY, SY4 4EQ.
DAVIES, Mr. Michael, BSc ACA *2004;* 52 Brogh Wyllin, Kirk Michael, ISLE OF MAN, IM6 1HU.
•**DAVIES, Mr. Michael Colin, BA ACA** *2001;* with KPMG LLP, St. James's Square, MANCHESTER, M2 6DS.
DAVIES, Mr. Michael Edward Owen, BA ACA *1992;* 48 Wolseley Parade, KENSINGTON, VIC 3031, AUSTRALIA.
DAVIES, Mr. Michael Francis, FCA *1960;* 57 Grafton Road, WORTHING, BN11 1QY. (Life Member)
DAVIES, Mr. Michael Howard, BA ACA *1992;* Hereford House, 24-26 Hereford Square, LONDON, SW7 4TS.
DAVIES, Mrs. Miriam Eileen, BA ACA *2005;* 2 Queen Victoria Road, BRISTOL, BS6 7PD.
•**DAVIES, Mr. Morgan Neil, ACA** *1998;* Prime Accountants & Business Advisers Limited, Marlborough House, 679 Warwick Road, SOLIHULL, WEST MIDLANDS, B91 3DA. See also Prime Pilleys, Prime Accountants Group Limited and Prime Coventry Ltd
DAVIES, Mr. Mustafa, BSc FCA *1998;* Finance Department, VIVA, Olympia Building, Salem Al Mubarak Street, PO Box 181, SALMIYA 22002 KUWAIT.
•**DAVIES, Mr. Neil, FCA** *1993;* (Tax Fac), Neil Davies Associates, Bude Business Centre, Kings Hill Industrial Estate, BUDE, CORNWALL, EX23 8QN.
DAVIES, Mr. Neil, BSc ACA *2001;* 25 Westminster Crescent, CARDIFF, CF23 6SE.
DAVIES, Mr. Neil, BSc ACA *2007;* 58 Dirac Road, BRISTOL, BS7 9LP.
DAVIES, Mr. Neil, BCom ACA *1985;* 2 Copperfields, Baldock Road, ROYSTON, SG8 5BH.
•**DAVIES, Mr. Neil Gordon Sturton, BSc ACA** *1987;* KPMG LLP, 15 Canada Square, LONDON, E14 5GL. See also KPMG Europe LLP
DAVIES, Mr. Neil Kendall, ACA *2007;* 2 Queen Victoria Road, BRISTOL, BS6 7PD.
DAVIES, Mr. Neil Trevor, MA FCA *1992;* 8 Brockley Court, Langley Road, SURBITON, KT6 6LL.
DAVIES, Mrs. Nia Sian, BSc ACA *1998;* 78 Ynys y Gored, PORT TALBOT, WEST GLAMORGAN, SA13 2EB.
DAVIES, Mr. Nicholas, BSc ACA *1990;* Alan Baxter & Associates, 75 Cowcross Street, LONDON, EC1M 6EL.
DAVIES, Mr. Nicholas James, BSc ACA *2010;* Flat 1, 49 Lewin Road, LONDON, SW16 6JZ.
DAVIES, Mr. Nicholas John, BA ACA *1992;* (Tax Fac), Thimble Cottage, Black Horse Lane, Shedfield, SOUTHAMPTON, SO32 2HT.
DAVIES, Mr. Nicholas Martin, ACA *1989;* 130 School Road, Hockley Heath, SOLIHULL, B94 6RB.
DAVIES, Mr. Nicholas Parry, MA FCA *1988;* 24 Cathedral Road, CARDIFF, CF11 9LJ.
DAVIES, Mr. Nicholas Philip, MA ACA *1991;* Financial Reporting Friends Centre, Sun Life Assurance Society Plc Axa Centre Bristol, Brierly Furlong Stoke Gifford, BRISTOL, BS34 8SW.
•**DAVIES, Mr. Nicholas Vernon, BA(Econ) ACA** *1999;* with RSM Tenon Audit Limited, 66 Chiltern Street, LONDON, W1U 4JT.
DAVIES, Miss. Nicola Faye, MSc BSc ACA *2002;* The University of Manchester Room 3.50b Simon Building, Brunswick Street, MANCHESTER, M13 9PL.
DAVIES, Mrs. Nicola Jane, BSc ACA CTA *1988;* Richardsons, 30 Upper High Street, THAME, OXFORDSHIRE, OX9 3EZ.
DAVIES, Miss. Nicola Jayne, ACA *1990;* Tudor Cottage Braintree Road, Felsted, DUNMOW, CM6 3DS.
DAVIES, Miss. Nicola Leanne, BA ACA *2006;* 5 Eastcote Avenue Lawley Village, TELFORD, SHROPSHIRE, TF4 2FR.
DAVIES, Miss. Nicola Louise, BSc ACA AMCT *2000;* InterContinental Hotel Group plc, 1 First Avenue, Centrum 100, BURTON-ON-TRENT, STAFFORDSHIRE, DE14 2WB.
•**DAVIES, Mrs. Nicola Ruth, BA ACA** *1993;* MND Training & Consultancy, 2 Hillgrove Gardens, KIDDERMINSTER, WORCESTERSHIRE, DY10 3AN.
•**DAVIES, Mr. Nigel Anthony, ACA** *1988;* with Grant Thornton UK LLP, 30 Finsbury Square, LONDON, EC2P 2YU.
DAVIES, Mr. Nigel Brian, BSc ACA *1989;* Henderson Global Investors 201 Bishopsgate LONDON EC2M 3AE, Henderson Global Investors, 201 Bishopsgate, LONDON, EC2M 3AE.
DAVIES, Mr. Nigel David Lyndon, MA ACA *1982;* Hermes Pensions Management Ltd, Lloyds Chambers, 1 Portsoken Street, LONDON, E1 8HZ.
DAVIES, Mr. Nigel Richard, BA ACA *1986;* Shelley Close, Lowmoor Business Park, Kirkby-in-Ashfield, NOTTINGHAM, NG17 7JZ.
DAVIES, Mr. Norman Anthony, BCom FCA *1969;* Callow Cottage, Cuck Hill, Shipham, WINSCOMBE, BS25 1RD. (Life Member)
DAVIES, Mr. Norman Rodney, FCA *1964;* 16 Rosemoor Gardens, Appleton, WARRINGTON, WA4 5RG.
DAVIES, Mr. Oliver Hylton, FCA *1964;* 191 Feltham Hill Road, ASHFORD, MIDDLESEX, TW15 1HJ.
DAVIES, Mr. Oliver Madoc, ACA *2008;* 60 Eaton Drive, KINGSTON UPON THAMES, SURREY, KT2 7QX.

•DAVIES, Mr. Owain Cooper, BEng ACA *1995;* ISCA Accountancy Services, 40 Ballymartin Road, Killinchy, NEWTOWNARDS, COUNTY DOWN, BT23 6QR.
DAVIES, Mr. Owen, FCA *1971;* Fourwynds, Coast Road, Berrow, BURNHAM-ON-SEA, SOMERSET, TA8 2QR.
DAVIES, Miss. Patricia Anne, BSc ACA *1981;* Genesis Housing Group Ltd, Capital House, 25 Chapel Street, LONDON, NW1 5DT.
DAVIES, Mrs. Patricia Ellen, BA ACA *1987;* Cobwebs, 39/40 Old Portmouth Road, Artington, GUILDFORD, GU3 1LN.
DAVIES, Mr. Paul, BA ACA *1986;* Cambrian Alliance Ltd, M N G House Unit 5A, Greenmeadow Springs Business Village, Village Way, Tongwynlais, CARDIFF CF15 7NE.
•DAVIES, Mr. Paul Duffield, FCA *1986;* Tudor John, Nightingale House, 46/48 East Street, EPSOM, KT17 1HQ.
DAVIES, Mr. Paul John, MEng ACA *2000;* 10 Constance Street, BLACKBURN SOUTH, VIC 3130, AUSTRALIA.
DAVIES, Mr. Paul Jonathan, ACA *1982;* 24 Arundel Gardens, LONDON, W11 2LB.
•DAVIES, Mr. Paul Richard, BSc ACA *2000;* BDO LLP, 1 Bridgewater Place, Water Lane, LEEDS, LS11 5RU. See also BDO Stoy Hayward LLP
DAVIES, Mr. Paul Trentham, BA(Hons) ACA *1993;* 4 Beck Road, Madeley, CREWE, CW3 9JF.
•DAVIES, Mr. Paul Tudor, BSc FCA *1973;* P T Davies & Co Limited, Hazeldene Lodge, Thame Road, Longwick, PRINCES RISBOROUGH, BUCKINGHAMSHIRE HP27 9SW. See also PT Davies & Co
DAVIES, Mr. Paul Walton, MA ACA *1993;* (Tax Fac), 3 Percy Terrace, Gosforth, NEWCASTLE UPON TYNE, NE3 1RS.
DAVIES, Mr. Paul William, BA(Hons) ACA *2002;* Brighthouse, 5 Hercules Way Leavesden, WATFORD, WD25 7GS.
DAVIES, Miss. Pauline, BSc FCA *1989;* Flat 3, Westbrooke Court, Cumberland Close, BRISTOL, BS1 6XE.
DAVIES, Mr. Peter Anfield, BSc FCA *1972;* 19 Glasfryn, Brackla, BRIDGEND, Mid Glamorgan, CF31 2JN.
DAVIES, Mr. Peter Bowen, MPhil BSc ACA *2010;* 56 Ynys y Mond Road, Alltwen, Pontardawe, SWANSEA, SA8 3BA.
•DAVIES, Mr. Peter Gwynne, FCA *1973;* Sunrise, Chapel Lane, Hermitage, THATCHAM, RG18 9RL.
DAVIES, Mr. Peter James, BSc ACA *1992;* The Old Vicarage Leek Road, Wetley Rocks, STOKE-ON-TRENT, ST9 0AP.
•DAVIES, Mr. Peter James, BSc FCA *1978;* CK, No 4 Castle Court 2, Castlegate Way, DUDLEY, WEST MIDLANDS, DY1 4RH.
DAVIES, Mr. Peter John, FCA *1969;* 5 Sandridge Road, ST. ALBANS, HERTFORDSHIRE, AL1 4AB.
DAVIES, Mr. Peter Martin, BA FCA *1985;* M J Maillis (UK) Ltd Monarch House, Chrysalis Way Eastwood, NOTTINGHAM, NG16 3RY.
DAVIES, Mr. Peter Richard, BA ACA *1985;* Argentum, 510 Bristol Business Park, BRISTOL, BS16 1EJ.
DAVIES, Mr. Peter Thomas, FCA *1955;* 16 Elm Tree Road, LYMM, WA13 0NB. (Life Member)
DAVIES, Mr. Peter Walters, MA ACA *1991;* (Tax Fac), Slade Farm, Southerndown, BRIDGEND, MID GLAMORGAN, CF32 0RP.
DAVIES, Mr. Peter William, ACA *2011;* WeiserMazars LLP, 14th Floor, 135 West 50th Street, NEW YORK, NY 10020, UNITED STATES.
DAVIES, Mr. Philip, MA ACA *1991;* Capita Group Plc, 71 Victoria Street, LONDON, SW1H 0XA.
DAVIES, Mr. Philip Antony, FCA *1971;* 31 Cotswold Avenue, Lisvane, CARDIFF, CF14 0TA. (Life Member)
DAVIES, Mr. Philip James, BSc ACA *1996;* 10 Redlands Road, SEVENOAKS, KENT, TN13 2JY.
DAVIES, Mr. Philip John, MBA BSc FCA *1986;* Hohlenbaumstrasse 56, CH-8200 SCHAFFHAUSEN, SWITZERLAND.
•DAVIES, Mr. Philip John, FCA *1985;* Philip Davies, 3 Park Hall Crescent, Castle Bromwich, BIRMINGHAM, B36 9SN.
DAVIES, Mr. Philip John, FCA *1977;* 27 Inchford Road, SOLIHULL, B92 9QD.
DAVIES, Mr. Philip John, BSocSc ACA *1995;* 3 Barton Common Lane, Barton on Sea, NEW MILTON, BH25 5PS.
DAVIES, Ms. Philippa Jane, BA ACA *1985;* Felmersham, 65 Bottrells Lane, CHALFONT ST. GILES, BUCKINGHAMSHIRE, HP8 4EJ.
DAVIES, Mr. Phillip Glyn, ACA *1979;* Oakleigh, Park Lane, Marchwood, SOUTHAMPTON, SO40 4WL.
DAVIES, Mr. Phillip Mark, BA ACA *1995;* 220 Creighton Avenue, LONDON, N2 9BD.
DAVIES, Miss. Polly Elizabeth, BSc ACA *2005;* 103 Vauxhall Street, PLYMOUTH, PL4 0HB.
DAVIES, Mrs. Rachel, BA(Hons) ACA *2001;* 25 Westminster Crescent, CARDIFF, CF23 6SE.
DAVIES, Miss. Rachel, BSc ACA *2011;* 8 Farthings, Knaphill, WOKING, SURREY, GU21 2JS.
DAVIES, Miss. Rachel Anne, BSc ACA *1992;* A H Pharmaceuticals Ltd Sapphire Court, Paradise Way Coventry Walsgrave Triangle, COVENTRY, CV2 2TX.
DAVIES, Mrs. Rachel Jane, BSc ACA *2006;* 92 Mowbray Street, NEWCASTLE UPON TYNE, NE6 5NL.
DAVIES, Miss. Rachel Rebekah, BA ACA *1989;* Compton Verney House Trust, Compton Verney House, Compton Verney, WARWICK, CV35 9HZ.
DAVIES, Mr. Raymond Alan, BSc FCA FCIS *1985;* 2 Winding Wood Drive, CAMBERLEY, SURREY, GU15 1EP.
•DAVIES, Mr. Raymond Melbourne, FCA *1977;* 21 Chartham Road, LONDON, SE25 4HN.
DAVIES, Mr. Raymund Michael, FCA *1963;* Hadley Cottage, Beatlands Road, SIDMOUTH, DEVON, EX10 8JH.
DAVIES, Miss. Rebecca, BA(Hons)Oxon ACA *2011;* Merrivale, Allensmore, HEREFORD, HR2 9AS.
DAVIES, Miss. Rebecca Suzanne, ACA *2009;* October Cottage La Sente Des Fonds, Grouville, JERSEY, JE3 9AS.
DAVIES, Miss. Rhian, BSc ACA *1990;* 25 Tennyson Road, NEWPORT, GWENT, NP19 8HN.
DAVIES, Mr. Rhodri, BSc ACA *2010;* 29 Clos Cradog, PENARTH, SOUTH GLAMORGAN, CF64 3RJ.
DAVIES, Mr. Rhys Catasime, BEng ACA *2004;* 25 Claughbane Drive, Ramsey, ISLE OF MAN, IM8 2AY.
DAVIES, Mr. Richard, FCA *1972;* 319 Howard Avenue, FAIR LAWN, NJ 07410, UNITED STATES.
•DAVIES, Mr. Richard, FCA CTA *1971;* 7 Cornelia Crescent, SHREWSBURY, SHROPSHIRE, SY2 5LZ.
•DAVIES, Mr. Richard, MA FCA *1976;* M R Salvage Limited, 7-8 Eghams Court, Boston Drive, BOURNE END, BUCKINGHAMSHIRE, SL8 5YS.
DAVIES, Mr. Richard, BA ACA *2011;* 164 Roberts Wharf, Neptune Street, LEEDS, LS9 8DW.
DAVIES, Mr. Richard Bernard, BSc ACA *1992;* 20 Bunratty Street, THE GAP, QLD 4061, AUSTRALIA.
DAVIES, Mr. Richard Gerald, BSc ACA *1994;* 7 Broadacre Place, ALDERLEY EDGE, CHESHIRE, SK9 7GR.
DAVIES, Mr. Richard Gerald, FCA *1978;* 57 Caeglas, Cross Hands, LLANELLI, SA14 6NH.
DAVIES, Mr. Richard Ian, BSc ACA *1994;* 16 Palace Road, Llandaf, CARDIFF, CF5 2AF.
DAVIES, Mr. Richard James, MSc ACA *2004;* 29 Asquith Avenue, Morley, LEEDS, LS27 9QA.
DAVIES, Mr. Richard James, BA(Hons) ACA *2010;* 17 Melstock Road, BIRMINGHAM, B14 7ND.
DAVIES, Mr. Richard James Meredith, BSc(Econ) ACA *2000;* First Floor Flat, 10 Miles Road, Clifton, BRISTOL, BS8 2JN.
DAVIES, Mr. Richard John, ACA *1993;* Pine Ridge, Woodhead Road, GLOSSOP, SK13 7RH.
DAVIES, Mr. Richard John, FCA *1977;* Prater Ltd Perrywood Business Park, Honeycrock Lane, REDHILL, RH1 5JQ.
DAVIES, Mr. Richard Lloyd, BSc ACA *2004;* Flat 16 Ashley Apartments, 63 Ashley Hill, BRISTOL, BS7 9EA.
DAVIES, Mr. Richard Mark, BSc FCA *1990;* 19 Ennerdale Close, CYNCOED, CARDIFF, CF23 5NZ.
DAVIES, Mr. Richard Owen, ACA *1989;* 38 York Avenue, LONDON, W7 3HU.
DAVIES, Mr. Richard Paul Brian, BEng ACA *2007;* 35 Engadine Close, CROYDON, CR0 5UU.
DAVIES, Mr. Richard Robert, FCA *1978;* 9 Goirle Avenue, CANVEY ISLAND, SS8 8BJ.
DAVIES, Mr. Richard Tyrone, BSc ACA *1990;* 8 Maes-Y-Celyn, Three Crosses, SWANSEA, SA4 3PA.
•DAVIES, Mr. Richard William, BSc ACA FCCA *2011;* Davies and Co(Accountants) Limited, 15 Rhyd-Y-Defaid Drive, Sketty, SWANSEA, SA2 8AH.
DAVIES, Mr. Robert, MSc BSc ACA *2010;* 91a Rukutai Street, ORAKEI 1071, NEW ZEALAND.
DAVIES, Mr. Robert Andrew, FCA *1978;* Abbey Garth, 28 Abbey Road, KNARESBOROUGH, NORTH YORKSHIRE, HG5 8HX.
DAVIES, Mr. Robert Geoffrey, BA FCA *1972;* 6 Goodwood Drive, SUTTON COLDFIELD, B74 2JG.
•DAVIES, Mr. Robert Goyne, BSc ACA *1985;* (Tax Fac), Robert Davies & Co, Marche Manor, Halfway House, SHREWSBURY, SY5 9DE.
DAVIES, Mr. Robert James, BA ACA *1987;* 10 Brookland Road, Hagley, STOURBRIDGE, DY9 0JZ.
DAVIES, Mr. Robert John, BSc ACA *1992;* 114 Clive Road, Pontcanna, CARDIFF, CF5 1GN.
DAVIES, Mr. Robert John, BSc FCA *1979;* 1002 Europlaza, Block 4 Europlaza, GIBRALTAR, GIBRALTAR.
•DAVIES, Mr. Robert Leonard, BSc FCA *1992;* Mitchell Charlesworth, Glebe Business Park, Lunts Heath Road, WIDNES, CHESHIRE, WA8 5SQ.
•DAVIES, Mr. Robert Ludford, FCA *1974;* RD Accountancy Solutions Ltd, 18 Poplar Road, NEWTOWN, POWYS, SY16 2AQ.
•DAVIES, Mr. Robert Owain, MChem ACA CTA *2008;* Advantage Accountancy & Advisory LLP, Sophia House, 28 Cathedral Road, CARDIFF, CF11 9LJ.
DAVIES, Mr. Robert Richard, FCA MBA *1969;* Pinetops Reach, 64 Yealm Road, Newton Ferrers, PLYMOUTH, PL8 1BQ.
DAVIES, Mr. Robert Stephen, FCA *1969;* Merecombe, Kemerton, TEWKESBURY, GL20 7JW.
•DAVIES, Mr. Robert William, FCA *1967;* (Tax Fac), Davies Edwards & Co, West Lodge, Rainbow Street, LEOMINSTER, HR6 8DQ. See also Tax Advice Shop Limited
DAVIES, Mr. Robert Wyn, BSc ACA *2004;* 31 Edward Street, OSWESTRY, SHROPSHIRE, SY11 2BN.
DAVIES, Mr. Robin Eric, FCA *1961;* 9 The Maltings, Dormington, HEREFORD, HR1 4FA. (Life Member)
•DAVIES, Mr. Roger Franklyn, FCA *1965;* Franklyn & Co, 9 Elm Close, Wheatley, OXFORD, OXFORDSHIRE, OX33 1UW.
•DAVIES, Mr. Roger Morris, BA FCA DChA *1979;* Baker Tilly Tax & Advisory Services LLP, Steam Mill, Steam Mill Street, CHESTER, CH3 5AN. See also Baker Tilly UK Audit LLP
DAVIES, Mr. Roger William, FCA *1961;* 3 Clive Road, ESHER, KT10 8PS.
DAVIES, Mr. Roy Ernest, BSc FCA *1974;* 14 Woodfield Road, Middleton, MANCHESTER, M24 1NF.
DAVIES, Mr. Roy Kenneth, FCA *1956;* 30 St John's Road, LOUGHTON, IG10 1RZ. (Life Member)
DAVIES, Mr. Russell Christopher, BSc ACA *1992;* 13 Meadowside, Sully, PENARTH, CF64 3JX.
DAVIES, Mr. Russell Glyn, FCA *1967;* 17 Westport Avenue, Mayals, SWANSEA, SA3 5EA.
DAVIES, Mr. Ryan, ACA *2010;* 41 Valley Road, HENLEY-ON-THAMES, OXFORDSHIRE, RG9 1RL.
DAVIES, Miss. Sally Ann, BSc ACA *2003;* with Scrutton Bland, Sanderson House, Museum Street, IPSWICH, IP1 1HE.
DAVIES, Mrs. Sally Anne, BA ACA *1995;* 7 Briar Lane, CARSHALTON, SURREY, SM5 4PX.
DAVIES, Miss. Samantha Jane, BSc ACA *1996;* International Power, Senator House, 85 Queen Victoria Street, LONDON, EC4V 4DP.
DAVIES, Mr. Samuel, BSc ACA *2011;* 5 St. Georges Court, TUNBRIDGE WELLS, TN4 9GX.
DAVIES, Mr. Samuel Patrick, ACA *2009;* Risk and Audit, Card Protection Plan Holgate Park, Holgate Road, YORK, YO26 4GA.
•DAVIES, Ms. Sarah, BA ACA *2000;* Peter Simon & Co Limited, The Old Maids Head, 110 High Street, Stalham, NORWICH, NR12 9AU.
DAVIES, Mrs. Sarah Claire, BA(Hons) ACA *2001;* Osborn House, 80 Middlesex Street, LONDON, E1 7EZ.
DAVIES, Miss. Sarah Jane, BA(Hons) ACA *2002;* Walden Phildraw Road Ballasalla, ISLE OF MAN, IM9 3EG.
DAVIES, Mrs. Sarah Margaret, BA ACA *1998;* 48 Eastway, SALE, CHESHIRE, M33 4DU.
DAVIES, Mr. Sean Martin, LLB ACA *2001;* 29 Park Road, SALFORD, M6 8JP.
DAVIES, Mrs. Sharon Elizabeth, ACA *2007;* Ty Nantcribba, Forden, WELSHPOOL, SY21 8NA.
DAVIES, Ms. Sheena Elizabeth, MA ACA *1993;* (Tax Fac), 37 Foxham Road, LONDON, N19 4RR.
DAVIES, Miss. Sheena Elizabeth, BA ACA *1981;* 18 Amberley Road, Palmers Green, LONDON, N13 4BJ.
DAVIES, Mrs. Shelley Brenda, BSc ACA *1992;* The Cottage, 40 Elm Road, BISHOP'S STORTFORD, CM23 2SS.
DAVIES, Mrs. Sheona Margaret, BA ACA *1990;* 91 Sandy Lane, SUTTON, SM2 7EP.
DAVIES, Mrs. Sian, BSc(Econ) ACA *2003;* 7 Ynysddu, PONTYCLUN, MID GLAMORGAN, CF72 9UA.
DAVIES, Ms. Sian, BA *2011;* 1 Albany Gardens, Emmer Green, READING, RG4 8PZ.
DAVIES, Mrs. Sian, BA ACA *1990;* 62 Main Road, Bryncoch, NEATH, WEST GLAMORGAN, SA10 7TL.
DAVIES, Mr. Simon, MMath ACA *2003;* 17 Heathfield Park, Middleton St. George, DARLINGTON, COUNTY DURHAM, DL2 1LN.
DAVIES, Mr. Simon, BA ACA *1985;* 5 Wooburn Manor Park, Wooburn Green, HIGH WYCOMBE, HP10 0ET.
DAVIES, Mr. Simon David Austin, MEng ACA *2006;* The Blackstone Group, 40 Berkeley Square, LONDON, W1J 5AL.
DAVIES, Mr. Simon James, BA(Hons) ACA CTA *1996;* Central Buildings, Richmond Terrace, BLACKBURN, BB1 7AP.
DAVIES, Mr. Simon Jeremy Guy, BA ACA *1993;* 290 Cave Run Circle, VERSAILLES, KY 40383, UNITED STATES.
DAVIES, Mr. Simon John, BSc ACA *1984;* Long Pipers, Little Hollis, GREAT MISSENDEN, HP16 9HZ.
DAVIES, Mr. Simon John Treharne, BA ACA *1980;* 26 Bushby Avenue, Rustington, LITTLEHAMPTON, WEST SUSSEX, BN16 2BY.
•DAVIES, Mr. Simon Nicholas, FCA *1980;* 2 Seamount Cottages, Seamount Road, MALAHIDE, COUNTY DUBLIN, IRELAND.
DAVIES, Mr. Simon Paul, BSc ACIB ACA CF *1989;* One Forbury Square, Forbury Square, READING, RG1 3BB.
•DAVIES, Mr. Simon Peter, FCA MAAT *1996;* Gowards, 102 Burnmill Road, MARKET HARBOROUGH, LEICESTERSHIRE, LE16 7JG. See also Hayles & Partners Limited
DAVIES, Mr. Simon Timothy Tudor, ACA *1986;* Abraaj Capital, PO Box 504905, DUBAI, UNITED ARAB EMIRATES.
•DAVIES, Mr. Solomon, ACA *1980;* (Tax Fac), S. Davies & Co, 148 Bury New Road, Whitefield, MANCHESTER, M45 6AD.
DAVIES, Mr. Stephen, BA FCA *1982;* Goldman Sachs Peterborough Court, 133 Fleet Street, LONDON, EC4A 2BB.
DAVIES, Mr. Stephen Arthur James, BSc ACA *1987;* Blendons, Highcotts Lane, West Clandon, GUILDFORD, GU4 7XA.
DAVIES, Mr. Stephen George Tristan, FCA *1964;* 30 Westdown House, Hartington Place, EASTBOURNE, BN21 3BW.
DAVIES, Mr. Stephen Gethyn, BSc ACA *1988;* 3d Riverdale Gardens, TWICKENHAM, TW1 2BX.
DAVIES, Mr. Stephen Hugh, FCA *1974;* 33 Borthwick Park, Orton Wistow, PETERBOROUGH, PE2 6YY.
DAVIES, Mr. Stephen James, BA ACA ATII *1997;* GE Capital Corporation (Funding) Ltd The Ark 7th Floor, 201 Talgarth Road, LONDON, W6 8BJ.
DAVIES, Mr. Stephen John, BSc ACA *1987;* Newlands, Exbury Road, BEAULIEU, HAMPSHIRE, SO427YS.
DAVIES, Mr. Stephen Matthew, BSc ACA *2005;* 81 Heol y Cadno, Thornhill, CARDIFF, CF14 9EW.
•DAVIES, Mr. Stephen Morris, BSc FCA *1991;* Davies Financial Management Ltd, 29 Solva Avenue, Llanishen, CARDIFF, CF14 0NP.
DAVIES, Mr. Stephen Wayne, BA ACA *1987;* 16 Bramford Drive, DUDLEY, DY1 4JU.
DAVIES, Mr. Stephen William, BA FCA *1973;* 8 Whitewell Road, ACCRINGTON, BB5 6DA.
•DAVIES, Mr. Steven, BSc FCA *1986;* Mazars LLP, Mazars House, Gelderd Road, Gildersome, LEEDS, LS27 7JN.
DAVIES, Mr. Steven, BSc ACA *1997;* 8 Graigwen Park, Graigwen, PONTYPRIDD, CF37 2EQ.
DAVIES, Mr. Steven Andrew, BSc ACA *1998;* OOO Moore Stephens, 4th Floor, 38 Stremyanny Perelok, MOSCOW, RUSSIAN FEDERATION.
DAVIES, Mr. Steven Daniel, BSc ACA *2000;* 7 Ynysddu, PONTYCLUN, MID GLAMORGAN, CF72 9UA.
•DAVIES, Mr. Steven Michael, ACA *1993;* (Tax Fac), Temple West Limited, PO Box 454, WEST BYFLEET, SURREY, KT14 9BD.
DAVIES, Mr. Steven Richard, BA ACA *1996;* 4 Fidgeon Close, BICKLEY, KENT, BR1 2FG.
•DAVIES, Mr. Steven Trevor, BA ACA *1994;* PricewaterhouseCoopers LLP, Erskine House, 68-73 Queen Street, EDINBURGH, EH2 4NH. See also PricewaterhouseCoopers
DAVIES, Mr. Stewart Edmund, FCA *1967;* Plot 19, Park Lane, Groesfaen, PONTYCLUN, CF72 8PB.
•DAVIES, Mr. Stuart James, BCom FCA *1974;* (Tax Fac), Flat 13, Duke Shore Wharf, 106 Narrow Street, LONDON, E14 8BU.
DAVIES, Mr. Stuart Robert, BA ACA *1993;* 41 Blackheath Park, LONDON, SE3 9RW.
•DAVIES, Miss. Susan Jayne, BA ACA *1993;* Susan Davies ACA, 26 Sion Court, Sion Road, TWICKENHAM, TW1 3DD.

DAVIES, Mrs. Susan Margaret, BSc ACA *1997;* 114 Clive Road, Canton, CARDIFF, CF5 1GN.
DAVIES, Mrs. Susanne, BA ACA *1990;* 10 Brookland Road, Hagley, STOURBRIDGE, DY9 0JZ.
DAVIES, Mrs. Suzanna Jane, BA(Hons) ACA ASI *2001;* 19 All Saints Avenue, MAIDENHEAD, BERKSHIRE, SL6 6EL.
DAVIES, Ms. Tania Ann, BA ACA *1987;* 3 Reece Mews, LONDON, SW7 3HE.
DAVIES, Mr. Thomas, FCA *1958;* Hunters Moon, Breinton, HEREFORD, HR4 7PB. (Life Member)
DAVIES, Mr. Thomas, ACA *2009;* 5 Forest Drive, BIRMINGHAM, B17 9HW.
DAVIES, Mr. Thomas Aubrey Pierce, FCA *1968;* (Member of Council 2001 - 2005), Bryn Derw, Trefonen Road, OSWESTRY, SHROPSHIRE, SY11 2TW.
DAVIES, Mr. Thomas Parry, ACA DChA *2008;* Lutterburn Cottage, Lutterburn Street, Ugborough, IVYBRIDGE, DEVON, PL21 0NG.
DAVIES, Mr. Timothy Bevan, BA ACA *1990;* Whitworth Bros Ltd, Victoria Mills, London Road, WELLINGBOROUGH, NORTHAMPTONSHIRE, NN8 2DT.
•**DAVIES, Mr. Timothy Grenville, LLB FCA ATII CTA** *1982;* (Tax Fac), Davies Mayers Barnett LLP, Pillar House, 113-115 Bath Road, CHELTENHAM, GLOUCESTERSHIRE, GL53 7LS. See also Barnett DM Limited
DAVIES, Mr. Timothy John, BA ACA *1990;* Dixcart International Ltd, Hillbrow House, Hillbrow Road, ESHER, SURREY KT10 9NW.
DAVIES, Mr. Timothy Lloyd, FCA *1970;* 112 Hillspoint Road, WESTPORT, CT 06880, UNITED STATES.
DAVIES, Mr. Timothy Paul, ACA *1982;* 5 Kings Lane, Yelvertoft, NORTHAMPTON, NN6 6LX.
DAVIES, Miss. Tracey Michelle, BSc FCA *1993;* 3 Garth Close, Eastcote, RUISLIP, MIDDLESEX, HA4 9PT.
DAVIES, Mr. Trevor, FCA *1972;* Woodside, 51a Chaldon Common Road, Chaldon, CATERHAM, CR3 5DH.
DAVIES, Mr. Trevor Anthony, FCA *1972;* 6 Amherst Road, HASTINGS, TN34 1TT.
•**DAVIES, Mr. Trevor Charles, FCA** *1972;* (Tax Fac), Trevor C. Davies, Brent Cottage, Hilltop, Cley-next-the-Sea, HOLT, NR25 7SD.
DAVIES, Mr. Trevor Paul, BA ACA *1996;* 6 Summerfield Road, Ealing, LONDON, W5 1ND.
DAVIES, Mr. Tudor John, FCA *1962;* Lochinver, Chapel Road, TADWORTH, KT20 5SD. (Life Member)
DAVIES, Mrs. Valerie Lorraine, FCA *1981;* The Old Rectory, Aberyscir, BRECON, POWYS, LD3 9NP.
DAVIES, Mr. Vaughan Thomas, LLB ACA *1986;* Turbo Systems Ltd, 1 Gillett Street, HULL, HU3 4JA.
DAVIES, Mrs. Veronica Kim, LLB ACA *2001;* 194 Radford Road, LEAMINGTON SPA, WARWICKSHIRE, CV31 1LQ.
DAVIES, Mr. Victor Albert, FCA *1968;* 55 Old Bisley Road, Frimley, CAMBERLEY, GU16 9RE. (Life Member)
DAVIES, Mrs. Victoria Shields, BA ACA *1999;* 3 Robert Burns Drive, Bearsden, GLASGOW, G61 3DD.
DAVIES, Mr. Vincent Edward, FCA *1966;* Lagern, Vineyards Road, Northaw, POTTERS BAR, EN6 4PH. (Life Member)
DAVIES, Miss. Vivien Elizabeth, FCA *1981;* Glandwr Close, Pandy, ABERGAVENNY, GWENT, NP7 8DW.
•**DAVIES, Mrs. Wendy Jane, BA ACA** *1991;* CK, No 4 Castle Court 2, Castlegate Way, DUDLEY, WEST MIDLANDS, DY1 4RH.
•**DAVIES, Mrs. Wendy Susan, BSc FCA** *1985;* (Tax Fac), F.A. Magee & Co., Wimborne House, 4-6 Pump Lane, HAYES, MIDDLESEX, UB3 3NB.
•**DAVIES, Mr. Wilfrid Mark Richard, BA ACA** *1989;* 23 Sawyers, Elmsett, IPSWICH, IP7 6QH.
DAVIES, Mr. William Adrian, BA ACA *1995;* 2 Long Close Lane, Shepley, HUDDERSFIELD, HD8 8BT.
•**DAVIES, Mr. William Howell Wyndham, BSc FCA** *1992;* Grant Thornton UK LLP, 11-13 Penhill Road, CARDIFF, CF11 9UP. See also Grant Thornton LLP
DAVIES, Mr. William Peter John, BSc(Hons) ACA *2000;* 8 Ballinger Court, Upper Ashlyns Road, BERKHAMSTED, HERTFORDSHIRE, HP4 3BX.
DAVIES, Mr. Wyn Meredith, FCA *1978;* 64 Popham Close, TIVERTON, DEVON, EX16 4GA.
DAVIES, Miss. Zoe Lovatt, MA FCA *1991;* 5 Robinsland Drive, WEST LINTON, PEEBLESSHIRE, EH46 7JD.
DAVIES-BROWN, Mrs. Julie Anne, ACA *1992;* with RSM Tenon Limited, Sumner House, St Thomas's Rd, CHORLEY, PR7 1HP.
DAVIES-EVANS, Mr. Huw, BSc ACA *1995;* 16 rue du Chateau, 21590 SANTENAY, FRANCE.
DAVIES-EVANS, Mrs. Jane Eleanor, LLB(Hons) ACA *1999;* Freshfields Bruckhaus Deringer, The Makeen Building, Office 202, PO Box 129817, ABU DHABI, UNITED ARAB EMIRATES.
DAVIES-JONES, Mr. John Henry, FCA *1963;* 9 Uppingham Close, LEICESTER, LE5 6HT. (Life Member)
DAVIES-KNAPP, Mr. Gethin, BA ACA AKC *2011;* Flat 1, 32 Maberley Road, LONDON, SE19 2JA.
DAVILA, Mrs. Justine Renee, MA ACA *1992;* 49 Ferndale Road, BURGESS HILL, WEST SUSSEX, RH15 0EZ.
DAVIS, Mr. Adam Colin, MA(Hons) ACA *2006;* Sodexo, 1 Southampton Row, LONDON, WC1B 5HA.
DAVIS, Mr. Adrian Denis, BA ACA *2003;* 8 Priors Close, Hertford Heath, HERTFORD, SG13 7QN.
DAVIS, Mr. Alan, FCA *1963;* 72 Fairfax Avenue, Ewell, EPSOM, SURREY, KT17 2QQ. (Life Member)
•**DAVIS, Mr. Alan Raymond, FCA** *1975;* Ward Davis, 10 Fusilier Way, Weedon, NORTHAMPTON, NN7 4TH. See also Acctem Management Limited
DAVIS, Mr. Alex, MA ACA *2003;* Flight Centre NZ Limited, Level 4 124 Vincent Street, AUCKLAND 1010, NEW ZEALAND.
DAVIS, Mr. Andrew, ACA *2010;* 10 Oathills, CORSHAM, WILTSHIRE, SN13 9NL.
DAVIS, Mr. Andrew Guy, BMus ACA *1995;* 50 Somerset Grove, ROCHDALE, OL11 5YS.
DAVIS, Mr. Andrew John, FCA *1959;* Monksfield, Pednor Bottom, CHESHAM, HP5 2SS. (Life Member)
DAVIS, Mr. Andrew John, BSc ACA *1994;* 30 Rottingdean Road, Camps Bay, CAPE TOWN, 8005, SOUTH AFRICA.
•**DAVIS, Mr. Andrew Simon, FCA** *1983;* Davis Bonley, Northside House, Mount Pleasant, BARNET, EN4 9EE.
DAVIS, Mr. Andrew Spencer, BSc ACA *1995;* 171 Starkey Street, Killarney Heights, SYDNEY, NSW 2087, AUSTRALIA.
DAVIS, Mr. Angus James Cummings, BSc ACA *1993;* 6 Choats Wood, Fordham Heath, COLCHESTER, CO3 9UY.
DAVIS, Miss. Anna Georgina, ACA *2008;* Global Crossing Telecommunications (UK) Ltd Crockford Lane, Chineham, BASINGSTOKE, HAMPSHIRE, RG24 8NA.
DAVIS, Mrs. Anne Julia, MA FCA *1993;* with ICAEW, Metropolitan House, 321 Avebury Boulevard, MILTON KEYNES, MK9 2FZ.
DAVIS, Mr. Anthony, ACA *2011;* 33 Dominion House, The Avenue, LONDON, W13 8JR.
•**DAVIS, Mr. Anthony Brian, BSc ACA** *1991;* Catalyst Corporate Finance LLP, 9th Floor, Bank House, 8 Cherry Street, BIRMINGHAM, B2 5AL.
DAVIS, Mr. Anthony John, BSc ACA *1998;* 69 Elm Road, WINDSOR, BERKSHIRE, SL4 3NB.
DAVIS, Mr. Anthony Lee, BA ACA *1997;* Black Rock, 33 King William Street, LONDON, EC4R 9AS.
DAVIS, Mr. Anthony Richard, FCA *1977;* Wynngreen, Marsh Lane, Taplow, MAIDENHEAD, SL6 0DE.
DAVIS, Mr. Antony Stephen, BA ACA *1987;* Flat B, 82 Barrow Road, LONDON, SW16 5PG.
DAVIS, Mr. Barry Charles, FCA *1975;* 62 Greenways, Ovingdean, BRIGHTON, BN2 7BL.
DAVIS, Mr. Bernard David, FCA *1951;* Suite A, 15 Portman Square, LONDON, W1H 6LJ. (Life Member)
DAVIS, Mr. Bertram Murlis, FCA *1937;* P.O.Box 3015, Northcliff, JOHANNESBURG, GAUTENG, 2115, SOUTH AFRICA. (Life Member)
•**DAVIS, Mr. Bretton Barrie, BA FCA** *1991;* Townends Accountants Limited, Fulford Lodge, 1 Heslington Lane, YORK, YO10 4HW.
DAVIS, Mr. Brian Stuart, BA FCA *1987;* 16 St Brannocks Road, Chorlton Cum Hardy, MANCHESTER, M21 0UP.
DAVIS, Miss. Carla Jayne, ACA *2010;* 55 Sandy Acres Drive, Waterthorpe, SHEFFIELD, S20 7LS.
DAVIS, Mrs. Carol Elizabeth, BA ACA *1991;* 46 Priory Close, Combe Down, BATH, BA2 5AN.
DAVIS, Mrs. Caroline Elizabeth, BSc FCA *1977;* 144 Kenilworth Street, OTTAWA K1Y 3Z7, ON, CANADA.
DAVIS, Mrs. Carolyn Clare, BSc ACA *1997;* Building B, British Petroleum Co Plc, Chertsey Road, SUNBURY-ON-THAMES, TW16 7LN.
DAVIS, Miss. Catherine, BA ACA *2010;* 5 Norton Road, WOKINGHAM, RG40 2BD.
DAVIS, Mr. Charles Derek, FCA *1950;* 38 Orchard Court, Arches Lane, MALMESBURY, WILTSHIRE, SN16 0ED. (Life Member)
DAVIS, Mr. Christopher John, FCA *1969;* 7 Madeley Close, AMERSHAM, HP6 6ET. (Life Member)
•**DAVIS, Mr. Christopher Michael, BA(Hons) ACA** *2003;* Command Accountancy Limited, 7 Tennyson Avenue, Gedling, NOTTINGHAM, NG4 3HJ.
DAVIS, Mr. Christopher Peter, FCA *1989;* 30 The Avenue, SALE, M33 4PD.
DAVIS, Mr. Christopher Peter, BSc ACA *2008;* 32a Jennings Road, ST. ALBANS, HERTFORDSHIRE, AL1 4PD.
•**DAVIS, Mr. Christopher Philip, FCA** *1964;* (Tax Fac), The Four Pages Limited, Canada House, 272 Field End Road, RUISLIP, HA4 9NA.
DAVIS, Mr. Christopher Richard, FCA *1978;* 5 Rushford Avenue, Wombourne, WOLVERHAMPTON, WV5 0HZ.
DAVIS, Mr. Christopher Thomas Hampson, FCA *1967;* 30 West View Grove, Whitefield, MANCHESTER, M45 7NQ.
DAVIS, Mrs. Claire Emma, BA(Hons) ACA *2002;* with Grant Thornton UK LLP, 1 Whitehall Riverside, Whitehall Road, LEEDS, WEST YORKSHIRE, LS1 4BN.
DAVIS, Mrs. Claire Gail Diane, BA ACA *1998;* 8 Willett Way, Petts Wood, ORPINGTON, KENT, BR5 1QD.
DAVIS, Mrs. Claire Maria, BA ACA *1990;* 11/82 Bergin Road, FERNY GROVE, QLD 4055, AUSTRALIA.
DAVIS, Mr. Clive Clayton, FCA *1973;* Overy House, Overy, Dorchester-on-Thames, WALLINGFORD, OXFORDSHIRE, OX10 7JU.
DAVIS, Miss. Colette Alana, ACA *2007;* 116 Bradmore Way, COULSDON, SURREY, CR5 1PB.
DAVIS, Mr. Colin, BSc(Hons) ACA *2009;* Flat 9 Chesterfield House, 120 Chesterfield Road St. Andrews, BRISTOL, BS6 5DU.
DAVIS, Mr. Colin Ernest, BA FCA *1975;* 90 Chartfield Avenue, LONDON, SW15 6HQ.
DAVIS, Mr. Colin George, MA FCA *1973;* 18 Wieland Road, NORTHWOOD, HA6 3QU.
DAVIS, Mr. Colin Malcolm, BSc ACA *1998;* Waters Ltd, Lea Valley Road, Chingford, LONDON, E4 7PX.
•**DAVIS, Mr. David, FCA** *1969;* Sugarwhite Associates, 5 Windus Road, LONDON, N16 6UT.
DAVIS, Mr. David, BSc FCA *1961;* Flat 6, 9 Amhurst Park, LONDON, N16 5DH. (Life Member)
•**DAVIS, Mr. David John, FCA** *1965;* John Davis & Associates, 24 Pentwyn Isaf, Energlyn, CAERPHILLY, MID GLAMORGAN, CF83 2NR.
DAVIS, Mr. David Kenneth, BA ACA *1992;* 19 Gibbs Green, EDGWARE, HA8 9RS.
•**DAVIS, Mr. David Paul, BA ACA** *1988;* (Tax Fac), Cameron Baum Davis LLP, 88 Crawford Street, LONDON, W1H 2EJ.
DAVIS, Mr. David Thomas, FCA *1963;* 9 Connaught Drive, LONDON, NW11 6BL.
DAVIS, Mr. David Thomas, BSc(Econ) FCA ATII *1963;* Benton House, Bratton Fleming, BARNSTAPLE, EX32 7LG. (Life Member)
DAVIS, Mr. David William, FCA *1966;* Blue Hills, Ibstone, HIGH WYCOMBE, HP14 3XT. (Life Member)
DAVIS, Mrs. Deborah Ann, BSc ACA *1982;* 22 Barmstedt Drive, OAKHAM, LE15 6RG.
DAVIS, Mr. Donald Conway, FCA *1955;* Austenwood Austenwood Lane, Chalfont St. Peter, GERRARDS CROSS, BUCKINGHAMSHIRE, SL9 8NL.
DAVIS, Mr. Donald Fuller, BA ACA *1992;* Argos Ltd, 489-499 Avebury Boulevard, MILTON KEYNES, MK9 2NW.
DAVIS, Mr. Edwin Paul, ACA *1993;* KPMG, 10 Shelley Street, SYDNEY, NSW 2000, AUSTRALIA.
DAVIS, Miss. Emma Christine, BA ACA *2002;* 59 Duke Street, WINDSOR, BERKSHIRE, SL4 1SJ.
DAVIS, Miss. Fiona Lesley, BCom ACA *1987;* 63 Spylaw Bank Road, EDINBURGH, EH13 0JB.
DAVIS, Mr. Frederick Arthur William, FCA *1957;* 211 Pershore Road, EVESHAM, WR11 2NB. (Life Member)
DAVIS, Mr. Gareth Owen, ACA *2010;* Fitzgerald & Law, 8 Lincoln's Inn Fields, LONDON, WC2A 3BP.
DAVIS, Mr. Gary Andrew, BA ACA *1989;* 10b Sunningfields Crescent, Hendon, LONDON, NW4 4RD.
DAVIS, Mr. Geoffrey Frederick, FCA CTA *1959;* 30 Bonny Wood Road, HASSOCKS, WEST SUSSEX, BN6 8HR. (Life Member)
DAVIS, Mr. Geoffrey Joseph, BA FCA *1981;* 17 Lintzford Road, Hamsterley Mill, ROWLANDS GILL, TYNE AND WEAR, NE39 1HA.
DAVIS, Mr. Geoffrey Michael, FCA *1966;* Chasmere, 8 Catherines Walk, Abbotts Inn, ANDOVER, HAMPSHIRE, SP11 7AS.
DAVIS, Mr. George Herbert, FCA *1948;* 7 Ladram Road, Thorpe BayESSEX, SOUTHEND-ON-SEA, SS1 3PX. (Life Member)
DAVIS, Mr. George Morris, FCA *1963;* 5 Salts Avenue, Loose, MAIDSTONE, ME15 0AY.
•①**DAVIS, Mr. Gerald Frederick, FCA** *1964;* with Chantrey Vellacott DFK LLP, Russell Square House, 10-12 Russell Square, LONDON, WC1B 5LF.
•**DAVIS, Mr. Glen Charles, BA(Hons) ACA** *2009;* Glen C Davis BA ACA, 22 High Road, Essendon, HATFIELD, HERTFORDSHIRE, AL9 6HW. See also Wilson Stevens LLP
DAVIS, Mr. Glen Howard, BSc ACA *1989;* 6 Penn Road, Speen, NEWBURY, RG14 1UU.
DAVIS, Mr. Godfrey Pawle, FCA *1972;* Mulberry Group Plc, The Rookery, Chilcompton, RADSTOCK, SOMERSET, BA3 4EH.
•**DAVIS, Mr. Graeme Andrew, BA FCA ATII** *1989;* Graeme Bruce & Partners, 911 Green Lanes, LONDON, N21 2QP.
•**DAVIS, Mr. Gregory Paul, BSc ACA** *1992;* 55b Riddell Rd, GLENDOWIE 1071, AUCKLAND, NEW ZEALAND.
DAVIS, Mr. Gregory Richard, BA(Hons) ACA *2004;* PO Box 202231, GABORONE, BOTSWANA.
DAVIS, Miss. Hannah, ACA *2011;* 25 Ebony House, Buckfast Street, LONDON, E2 6GJ.
DAVIS, Mrs. Helen Mary, FCA *1983;* Colt Group Ltd, New Lane, HAVANT, HAMPSHIRE, PO9 2LY.
•**DAVIS, Mr. Howard, BA FCA** *1992;* Price Davis Limited, The Old Baptist Chapel, New Street, Painswick, STROUD, GL6 6XH.
•**DAVIS, Mr. Ian Frank, ACA** *1988;* PricewaterhouseCoopers LLP, Hays Galleria, 1 Hays Lane, LONDON, SE1 2RD. See also PricewaterhouseCoopers
DAVIS, Mr. Ian Matthew, ACA *2007;* Flat 11 Harvest Court, 61 Park Road, BECKENHAM, KENT, BR3 1QG.
DAVIS, Mr. Ian Peter, BA(Hons) ACA *2002;* Department of Transport Great Minster House, 76 Marsham Street, LONDON, SW1P 4DR.
DAVIS, Mr. Ian Richard, BA ACA *1985;* Paddock Lodge, All Stretton, CHURCH STRETTON, SHROPSHIRE, SY6 6HG.
DAVIS, Mr. Ivor Stephen, BSc ACA *1988;* Unit 5A, Herald Industrial Estate, Hedge End, SOUTHAMPTON, SO30 2JW.
DAVIS, Mrs. Jacqueline Anne, BEng ACA *1999;* 3 Kinnaird Avenue, BROMLEY, BR1 4HG.
DAVIS, Miss. Jacqueline Victoria, BSc ACA *2003;* No. 256, 10 Market Street, GEORGE TOWN, GRAND CAYMAN, KY1-9006, CAYMAN ISLANDS.
DAVIS, Mr. James Alexander Blair, BA ACA *1999;* 2 Putney Park Avenue, LONDON, SW15 5QN.
DAVIS, Mr. James Edward Coleman, FCA *1989;* 12 Parkgate Gardens, LONDON, SW14 8BQ.
DAVIS, Mr. James Robert, BA ACA *1998;* 8 Blackwood Close, WEST BYFLEET, SURREY, KT14 6PW.
DAVIS, Mr. James Robert, MA ACA *1999;* 27 Corinium Gate, ST. ALBANS, HERTFORDSHIRE, AL3 4HY.
DAVIS, Mr. Jason Mark, BSc ACA *1998;* Holly Tree House, Bromsgrove Road, Clent, STOURBRIDGE, WEST MIDLANDS, DY9 9PY.
DAVIS, Mr. Jeffrey Frank, BSc ACA *1981;* 37 Lower Canes, YATELEY, GU46 6PY.
DAVIS, Miss. Joanne, ACA *2008;* 9 Manor Gardens, Desford, LEICESTER, LE9 9QB.
DAVIS, Miss. Jodee Samantha, BA ACA *2007;* PricewaterhouseCoopers, 113-119 The Terrace, PO Box 243, WELLINGTON 6140, NEW ZEALAND.
DAVIS, Mr. John, FCA *1969;* Tracey, Bow, CREDITON, DEVON, EX17 6EP.
DAVIS, Mr. John Alexander, BA ACA *1991;* 9 Walton Crescent, OXFORD, OX1 2JG.
DAVIS, Mr. John Anthony, FCA *1975;* 358 Heath Road South, Northfield, BIRMINGHAM, B31 2BH.
DAVIS, Mr. John Barry, FCA *1958;* 31 Mirfield Road, SOLIHULL, WEST MIDLANDS, B91 1JH. (Life Member)
DAVIS, Mr. John Basil, FCA *1974;* Hemingford House, Wood End, Little Horwood, MILTON KEYNES, MK17 0PE.
•**DAVIS, Mr. John Chapman, BSc FCA** *1976;* Chapman Davis LLP, 2 Chapel Court, LONDON, SE1 1HH.
DAVIS, Mr. John Charles, FCA *1971;* Ipsen Biopharm Limited, 190 Bath Road, SLOUGH, SL1 3XE.
DAVIS, Mr. John Christopher, FCA *1967;* 2 Meadow View, High Street Burbage, MARLBOROUGH, SN8 3AF.

•**DAVIS, Mr. John Ernest, BA FCA** *1983;* Bakers, Arbor House, Broadway North, WALSALL, WS1 2AN. See also Baker (Midlands) Limited
DAVIS, Mr. John Gilbert Mourton, FCA *1964;* Birchams, 5 Angeline Close, Highcliffe, CHRISTCHURCH, DORSET, BH23 5BS.
DAVIS, Mr. John Gordon, BA ACA *1987;* 24 Yeomans Row, LONDON, SW3 2AH.
DAVIS, Mr. John Gordon, FCA *1952;* 8036 Lilly Stone Drive, BETHESDA, MD 20037, UNITED STATES. (Life Member)
DAVIS, Mr. John Lawrence, BA FCA *1963;* 119 Valley Road, KENLEY, SURREY, CR8 5BY. (Life Member)
DAVIS, Mr. John Michael Gronow, FCA *1962;* 26 rue de la Taillade, 33430 BAZAS, FRANCE.
DAVIS, Mr. John Paul, BA(Hons) ACA *2002;* 19 Circular Road, MANCHESTER, M20 3LB.
DAVIS, Mr. John Philip Clements, FCA *1949;* 37 The Lawns, Collingham, NEWARK, NG23 7NT. (Life Member)
DAVIS, Mr. Jonathan, BSc ACA *2003;* with RSM Tenon Audit Limited, 2 Wellington Place, LEEDS, LS1 4AP.
DAVIS, Mr. Jonathan David, ACA *1994;* Cooper Parry LLP, 14 Park Row, NOTTINGHAM, NG1 6GR.
DAVIS, Mr. Jonathan Mark, BSc ACA *1992;* 46 Priory Close, Combe Down, BATH, BA2 5AN.
DAVIS, Mr. Julian Nigel, BEng ACA *2000;* 16 Longwood Crescent, Alwoodley, LEEDS, LS17 8SR.
DAVIS, Mr. Julian Pearce, FCA *1969;* 3214 Huntleigh Crescent, NORTH VANCOUVER V7H 1E1, BC, CANADA.
DAVIS, Mrs. Karen Gayle, ACA *2001;* Riviere House, Phillack, HAYLE, CORNWALL, TR27 5AB.
DAVIS, Mrs. Karen Marie, BSc ACA *1981;* Manyons, Church Lane, Barkway, ROYSTON, SG8 8EJ.
DAVIS, Mrs. Kate Victoria, BSc(Hons) ACA *2010;* 3 Pinewood Gardens, FERNDOWN, DORSET, BH22 9TT.
DAVIS, Mrs. Kathryn Alison, BA ACA *1993;* Wren Cottage, Rushers Cross, MAYFIELD, EAST SUSSEX, TN20 6PX.
DAVIS, Mrs. Kaye, BA(Hons) ACA *2000;* with ICAEW, Metropolitan House, 321 Avebury Boulevard, MILTON KEYNES, MK9 2FZ.
DAVIS, Mr. Keith, BCom ACA *1986;* 24 Wood Mount, Overton, WAKEFIELD, WF4 4SB.
•**DAVIS, Dr. Keith Donald, ACA** *1985;* Mayfield Business Services Ltd, 3 Crimicar Lane, SHEFFIELD, S10 4FA.
DAVIS, Mr. Kenneth, BA FCA *1953;* 7 Greenslade Road, Parkhall, WALSALL, WS5 3QH. (Life Member)
DAVIS, Mr. Kenneth George, FCA *1952;* 25 Oyster Bend, PAIGNTON, DEVON, TQ4 6NL. (Life Member)
DAVIS, Miss. Kim Louise, ACA *2008;* Old Mill Accountancy Llp, Number One Goldcroft, YEOVIL, SOMERSET, BA21 4DX.
DAVIS, Mr. Lee Karl, BEng ACA *1997;* 181 Hospital Bridge Road, Whitton, TWICKENHAM, TW2 6LE.
DAVIS, Mr. Leopold, FCA *1953;* 26 Uphill Road, Mill Hill, LONDON, NW7 4RB. (Life Member)
•**DAVIS, Ms. Lesley Ann, ACA** *1983;* Markley Davis, 31 Edinburgh Avenue, Sawston, CAMBRIDGE, CB22 3DW.
DAVIS, Miss. Lesley Ann, BA ACA *1997;* 22 West Street, REIGATE, RH2 9BS.
DAVIS, Miss. Lindsay Jane, MSc BSc ACA *2010;* 26 Vernon Avenue, LONDON, SW20 8BW.
DAVIS, Mrs. Lindsey Elizabeth, BA ACA *1997;* 171 Starkey Street, Killarney Heights, SYDNEY, NSW 2087, AUSTRALIA.
DAVIS, Mrs. Lisa Ann, BA ACA *1994;* Cobweb Cottage, 2 Red Lion Street, Kings Sutton, BANBURY, OXFORDSHIRE, OX17 3RH.
DAVIS, Miss. Lisa Jane, BSc ACA *1990;* Long Cottage, Compton Road, East Ilsley, NEWBURY, RG20 7LH.
DAVIS, Mrs. Lisa Natalie, BSc ACA *1995;* Tythe Lodge, Church Gate, High Street, Edlesborough, DUNSTABLE, BEDFORDSHIRE LU6 2LE.
•**DAVIS, Mr. Malcolm, FCA** *1981;* The Solutions Centre Limited, 218 Malvern Road, BOURNEMOUTH, BH9 3BX.
DAVIS, Dr. Margaret Gail, BDS ACA *2002;* Harbridge Hardimead, Lamerton, TAVISTOCK, DEVON, PL19 8SE.
DAVIS, Mrs. Maria, ACA *2009;* 28 Priory Street, Bowdon, ALTRINCHAM, CHESHIRE, WA14 3BQ.
DAVIS, Mrs. Marianne Elizabeth, ACA *2008;* St. James's Place, 1 Tetbury Road, CIRENCESTER, GLOUCESTERSHIRE, GL7 1FP.
DAVIS, Miss. Mariette Catherine, BSc FCA *1983;* (Tax Fac), 51 Hemingford Road, LONDON, N1 1BY.
DAVIS, Mr. Mark Christopher, ACA *2009;* Towy Castle Residential Home, Uplands, CARMARTHEN, DYFED, SA32 8DY.
•**DAVIS, Mr. Mark Edward, ACA** *1988;* Davis & Co, 66 Garner Drive, East Malling, WEST MALLING, ME19 6NF.
DAVIS, Mr. Mark James, BSc(Hons) ACA *2002;* 7 Spire Court, 11 Crescent Road, BECKENHAM, KENT, BR3 6NF.
DAVIS, Mr. Mark William George, BA ACA *1986;* 15 Calverley Park, TUNBRIDGE WELLS, TN1 2SH.
DAVIS, Miss. Marni, BA ACA *1998;* 93C Victoria Road, Queens Park, LONDON, NW6 6TD.
DAVIS, Mr. Martin James, FCA *1972;* 17 Pyne Point, CLEVEDON, BS21 7RL.
DAVIS, Mrs. Mary Elizabeth, BA ACA *1991;* 41 Hogback Wood Road, Knotty Green, BEACONSFIELD, HP9 1JT.
DAVIS, Mr. Matthew, BA(Hons) ACA *2003;* RBS Tower, 88 Phillip Street, GPO Box 4675, SYDNEY, NSW 2000, AUSTRALIA.
DAVIS, Mr. Matthew, BA ACA *2007;* Centrica plc Millstream West, Maidenhead Road, WINDSOR, SL4 5GD.
•**DAVIS, Mr. Matthew Christopher, BSc ACA** *2003;* Brebners, The Quadrangle, 180 Wardour Street, LONDON, W1F 8LB.
DAVIS, Mr. Matthew James, BA ACA *1996;* 7 Chisholm Road, RICHMOND, SURREY, TW10 6JH.
DAVIS, Mr. Matthew Jonathan, BA ACA *2004;* with Ernst & Young LLP, 1 More London Place, LONDON, SE1 2AF.
DAVIS, Mr. Matthew Spencer, BEng ACA *2001;* Bluewave Accountancy Ltd, Wistaria Cottage, Church Street, Blagdon, BRISTOL, BS40 7RY.
DAVIS, Mr. Maxwell Edmund, FCA *1959;* 52 Lee Crescent, Edgbaston, BIRMINGHAM, B15 2BJ. (Life Member)
DAVIS, Ms. Melanie Sara, MA ACA *2002;* 26 Roughdown Avenue, HEMEL HEMPSTEAD, HERTFORDSHIRE, HP3 9BH.
DAVIS, Mr. Michael, FCA *1964;* 16 Scoggins Way, Heckington, SLEAFORD, NG34 9UU.
•①**DAVIS, Mr. Michael Barry, FCA** *1977;* H W Fisher & Company, Acre House, 11-15 William Road, LONDON, NW1 3ER. See also FisherEase Limited, and H W Fisher & Company Limited
DAVIS, Mr. Michael Christopher, BSc ACA *1987;* 26 Avenue de la Foretaille, 1292 CHAMBESY, SWITZERLAND.
•**DAVIS, Mr. Michael Gerald, ACA FCCA** *2009;* George Hay & Company, 83 Cambridge Street, Pimlico, LONDON, SW1V 4PS.
DAVIS, Mr. Michael Gerard, FCA *1951;* Whitewalls, 30 Granville Road, St. Margarets Bay, DOVER, KENT, CT15 6DR. (Life Member)
DAVIS, Mr. Michael John, FCA *1955;* 23 Dunchurch Hall, Southam Road Dunchurch, RUGBY, CV22 6PD. (Life Member)
DAVIS, Mr. Michael Lawrence, ACA CA(SA) *2009;* Xstrata Plc, 4th Floor Panton House, 25 Haymarket, LONDON, SW1Y 4EN.
DAVIS, Mr. Miles, MA ACA *1999;* 16 Durham Road, LONDON, N2 9DN.
•**DAVIS, Mr. Neil Christopher, BSc(Hons) ACA** *2003;* Price Pearson Ltd, Finch House, 28-30 Wolverhampton Street, DUDLEY, DY1 1DB. See also Finch House Properties Limited
DAVIS, Mr. Neil Laurence, ACA *1979;* Piazza M. Bossi 3, 20121 MILAN, ITALY.
DAVIS, Mr. Neville, BA FCA *1979;* Manyons, Church Lane, Barkway, ROYSTON, HERTFORDSHIRE, SG8 8EJ.
DAVIS, Mr. Nicholas James, ACA *2007;* Threadneedle Asset Management Ltd St. Mary Axe House, 60 St. Mary Axe, LONDON, EC3A 8JQ.
DAVIS, Mr. Nicholas Jeremy, BSc ACA *2001;* 10 Pank Avenue, BARNET, EN5 1NF.
DAVIS, Mr. Nicholas John, BSc(Hons) ACA *2003;* 19 Outwoods Road, LOUGHBOROUGH, LE11 3LX.
DAVIS, Mr. Nicholas John Stratton, MBA BA ACA *1985;* Frontier Plastics Ltd, Newbridge Rd Ind Estate, BLACKWOOD, NP12 2YN.
DAVIS, Mr. Nicholas Mark, ACA FCCA *2008;* 88 Heath Road, SALISBURY, WILTSHIRE, SP2 9JX.
DAVIS, Miss. Nicola Anne, BSc ACA *2005;* BPP, Third Floor, Canterbury House, 83-85 Newhall Street, BIRMINGHAM, B3 1LH.
DAVIS, Mr. Nicolas Edward, MA ACA *2003;* Apartments Higashiyama 105, 2-5-12 Higashiyama, Meguro-ku, TOKYO, 153-0043 JAPAN.
DAVIS, Mr. Nigel Graham, BSc ACA *1992;* 380 Queenstown Road, LONDON, SW8 4PE.
DAVIS, Mr. Nigel Philip Anthony, BSc ACA *1992;* c/o Mrs Lindsay Wyles, 29 Brantwood Road, LONDON, SE24 0DH.
DAVIS, Mrs. Pamela Beverley, FCA *1992;* 4 Kingham Drive, CARTERTON, OX18 3HU.
DAVIS, Mr. Patrick, FCA *1970;* Clonshire Mills, Croagh, RATHKEALE, COUNTY LIMERICK, IRELAND.
•**DAVIS, Mr. Paul Anthony, BA FCA** *1979;* Keens Shay Keens MK, Sovereign Court, 230 Upper Fifth Street, MILTON KEYNES, MK9 2HR.
•**DAVIS, Mr. Paul Anthony, FCA** *1970;* (Tax Fac), Paul Davis, 27 Hill Road, Oakley, BASINGSTOKE, RG23 7HS.
DAVIS, Mr. Paul Charles Harding, BSc ACA *1992;* Belvedere, 18 Butts Batch, Wrington, BRISTOL, BS40 5LN.
•**DAVIS, Mr. Paul Corrin, FCA** *1979;* Paul Davis, 57 Chiltern Road, Quedgeley, GLOUCESTER, GL2 4TU.
DAVIS, Mr. Paul David, FCA *1958;* 5 Sheridan Walk, LONDON, NW11 7UF. (Life Member)
•**DAVIS, Mr. Paul Graham, BA FCA CTA** *1984;* 112 Broom Road, ROTHERHAM, SOUTH YORKSHIRE, S60 2SU. See also Davis & Co (Management Consultants) Ltd
DAVIS, Mr. Paul Malcolm, FCA *1975;* 3 Church Close, RADLETT, HERTFORDSHIRE, WD7 8BJ.
•①**DAVIS, Mr. Paul Michael, FCA** *1983;* MacIntyre Hudson LLP, New Bridge Street House, 30-34 New Bridge Street, LONDON, EC4V 6BJ.
DAVIS, Mr. Paul Richard, FCA *1976;* Ashbourne House, Meadow Lane, Houghton, HUNTINGDON, CAMBRIDGESHIRE, PE28 2BP.
DAVIS, Mr. Paul Richard Gillman, BSc(Hons) ACA *2003;* 5 Mill Farm Road, HORSHAM, WEST SUSSEX, RH13 6SL.
DAVIS, Mr. Paul Thomas, BSc ACA *1998;* 55 Emberton Way, Amington, TAMWORTH, STAFFORDSHIRE, B77 3QQ.
DAVIS, Mr. Paul Vivian, FCA *1958;* The Woodlands, 65 Hall Lane, Drayton, NORWICH, NORFOLK, NR8 6DP. (Life Member)
DAVIS, Mr. Peter Anthony, BA FCA CMC FIMC *1972;* 5 Randolph Crescent, LONDON, W9 1DP.
DAVIS, Mr. Peter Anthony, MA FCA *1967;* (Member of Council 1990 - 1995), 29 Arthur Road, Wimbledon, LONDON, SW19 7DN.
DAVIS, Mr. Peter James Bromiley, ACA CA(SA) *2011;* 119 Valley Road, KENLEY, SURREY, CR8 5BY.
DAVIS, Mr. Peter James Douglas, FCA *1950;* 33 Mayplace Road East, Barnehurst, BEXLEYHEATH, KENT, DA7 6EA. (Life Member)
DAVIS, Mr. Peter John, FCA *1967;* 4 Meadow View, WITNEY, OX28 3TY. (Life Member)
DAVIS, Mr. Peter Martin, MA ACA *1983;* R M D Kwikform, Brickyard Road, Aldridge, WALSALL, WS9 8BW.
DAVIS, Mr. Peter Michael, BSc ACA *1995;* 114 Station Road, Ystradgynlais, SWANSEA, SA9 1PL.
DAVIS, Mr. Peter Nicholas, BA FCA *1983;* 35 Chatsworth Road, Eccles, MANCHESTER, M30 9DZ.
DAVIS, Mr. Philip Ernest, BA ACA *1979;* Williams Refrigeration, Bryggen Road, KING'S LYNN, NORFOLK, PE30 2HZ.
DAVIS, Mr. Philip John, FCA *1971;* 19 Magna Close, HARPENDEN, HERTFORDSHIRE, AL5 1RH.
DAVIS, Miss. Philippa Jane, BA(Hons) ACA *2002;* First Floor Flat, 14 Thorndean Street, LONDON, SW18 4HE.
•**DAVIS, Mr. Phillip James, BA FCA** *1980;* P.J. Davis, 2 Essenden Court, Stony Stratford, MILTON KEYNES, MK11 1NW.
DAVIS, Miss. Rachel, BA ACA *2007;* 6 Meadow Croft Gardens, Hucknall, NOTTINGHAM, NG15 6UN.
•**DAVIS, Mrs. Rachel Ann, BA FCA** *1994;* Just Audit Limited, Unit 14, Riverside Business Centre, Foundry Lane, Milford, BELPER DERBYSHIRE DE56 0RN.
•**DAVIS, Mr. Ray Alan, BA ACA CTA** *1998;* (Tax Fac), Davis Lombard (UK) Limited, Whittington House, 64 High Street, FAREHAM, HAMPSHIRE, PO16 7BG. See also Davis Lombard (UK) Ltd and Davis Lombard
DAVIS, Mrs. Rebecca Jane, MMath ACA *2002;* Carrington Carr Home Finance Ltd, 37-39 Welford Road, LEICESTER, LE2 7AD.
DAVIS, Miss. Rhiannon Sarah, MA FCA *2000;* 90 The Hawthorns, Cyncoed, CARDIFF, CF23 7AR.
DAVIS, Mr. Richard, LLB ACA CTA *2002;* 7 Low Green, Copmanthorpe, YORK, YO23 3SD.
DAVIS, Mr. Richard Alan, BSc FCA CISA *1992;* Deutsche Bank Winchester House, 1 Great Winchester Street, LONDON, EC2N 2DB.
DAVIS, Mr. Richard David, ACA *1993;* Garden Cottage, Kiln Road, Redlynch, SALISBURY, SP5 2HT.
•**DAVIS, Mr. Richard James, FCA TEP** *1974;* (Tax Fac), Chavereys, Mall House, The Mall, FAVERSHAM, KENT, ME13 8JL.
DAVIS, Mr. Richard Jonathan, BA(Hons) ACA *2004;* 16 Sandringham Road, Golders Green, LONDON, NW11 9DP.
DAVIS, Mr. Richard William, BA FCA *1974;* 30 Grange Lane, Mountsorrel, LOUGHBOROUGH, LE12 7HY.
DAVIS, Mr. Robert Ian, BSc ACA *1997;* Hatton Cottage, Hatton, CHURCH STRETTON, SHROPSHIRE, SY6 6QP.
DAVIS, Mr. Robert Martin, MA ACA *1992;* Wren Cottage, Rushers Cross, MAYFIELD, EAST SUSSEX, TN20 6PX.
DAVIS, Mr. Robert William, BSocSc ACA *1984;* High Garth Farm West End, Witton le Wear, BISHOP AUCKLAND, COUNTY DURHAM, DL14 0BL.
DAVIS, Mr. Robin Christopher, ACA *2009;* 52 Fairview Way, Baswich, STAFFORD, ST17 0AX.
•①**DAVIS, Mr. Robin Hamilton, BA FCA** *1988;* Carter Backer Winter LLP, Enterprise House, 21 Buckle Street, LONDON, E1 8NN.
DAVIS, Mr. Robin Michael, FCA *1964;* 60 Winterbourne Road, SOLIHULL, B91 1LX. (Life Member)
DAVIS, Mr. Robin Scott, BSc ACA *2001;* 81 Thorndale Courts, Whitycombe Way, EXETER, EX4 2NY.
DAVIS, Mr. Roger David, FCA *1972;* 14 Camelia Way, WOKINGHAM, RG41 3NB.
DAVIS, Mr. Roger John, MA ACA *1979;* E S C Amiens, 18 Place St Michel, 80000 AMIENS, FRANCE.
DAVIS, Mr. Roger O'Byrne, FCA *1966;* Crafers North Street, Langham, HOLT, NORFOLK, NR25 7DG.
DAVIS, Mr. Roger Stuart, FCA *1965;* 14 Glyndon Court, BRIGHOUSE, HD6 3UB.
DAVIS, Mr. Roger William, FCA *1965;* 31 Dorchester Road, SOLIHULL, WEST MIDLANDS, B91 1LW.
•**DAVIS, Mr. Roy Byron, FCA** *1981;* with HW Lee Associates LLP, New Derwent House, 69-73 Theobalds Road, LONDON, WC1X 8TA.
DAVIS, Mr. Roy Mcalpin, FCA *1954;* 15 Links View, WALLASEY, CH45 0NQ. (Life Member)
•**DAVIS, Mr. Russell Stewart, LLB FCA** *1999;* Deloitte LLP, Hill House, 1 Little New Street, LONDON, EC4A 3TR. See also Deloitte & Touche LLP
DAVIS, Miss. Sally, ACA *1989;* 20 Vicarage Park, Redlynch, SALISBURY, SP5 2JZ.
DAVIS, Miss. Sarah, ACA *2003;* 6 The Hawthorns, Marchwood, SOUTHAMPTON, SO40 4SU.
DAVIS, Miss. Sarah Jeanne, BSc ACA *1996;* Newhaven Oldhill Wood, Studham, DUNSTABLE, BEDFORDSHIRE, LU6 2NE.
DAVIS, Miss. Sharon Marie, ACA *2000;* The Brandon Trust Olympus House, Britannia Road Patchway, BRISTOL, BS34 5TA.
•**DAVIS, Miss. Sheryl Marie, ACA** *1996;* Barnes Roffe LLP, 3 Brook Business Centre, Cowley Mill Road, Cowley, UXBRIDGE, MIDDLESEX UB8 2FX.
DAVIS, Mr. Simon, BSc ACA *2006;* with KPMG LLP, 55 Second Street, Suite 1400, SAN FRANCISCO, CA 94105, UNITED STATES.
DAVIS, Mr. Simon Anthony John, BA FCA *1990;* Berrington Farm Berrington, SHREWSBURY, SY5 6HB.
DAVIS, Mr. Simon James, BSc FCA *1977;* 144 Kenilworth Street, OTTAWA K1Y 3Z7, ON, CANADA.
DAVIS, Mr. Simon Jeremy Heyworth, FCA *1975;* 275 Sylvan Boulevard, WINTER PARK, FL 32789, UNITED STATES.
DAVIS, Mr. Simon John, BA ACA *1989;* Pricewaterhousecoopers Llp, 80 Strand, LONDON, WC2R 0AF.
DAVIS, Mr. Spencer Michael, BSc ACA *1991;* Larkswood Eardington, BRIDGNORTH, SHROPSHIRE, WV16 5JT.
DAVIS, Mr. Stephen David John, BA FCA *1986;* 34 Belsize Avenue, LONDON, NW3 4AH.
DAVIS, Mr. Stephen Mark, ACA *1997;* 33 Icen Road, Radipole, WEYMOUTH, DORSET, DT3 5JL.
DAVIS, Mr. Steven Jeffrey, BSc ACA *1986;* The Grainstore, 1 Main Street, Stonesby, MELTON MOWBRAY, LEICESTERSHIRE, LE14 4QX.
DAVIS, Mr. Steven Richard, BSc ACA *1994;* Smith Bilbrough & Co Ltd, 77 Gracechurch Street, LONDON, EC3V 0AG.
•**DAVIS, Mr. Stuart David, ACA FCCA** *2009;* Starplayer Limited, 510 Centennial Park, Centennial Avenue, Elstree, BOREHAMWOOD, HERTFORDSHIRE WD6 3FG.
DAVIS, Mrs. Susanne, ACA *2009;* 10 Warton Drive, Woodmansey, BEVERLEY, NORTH HUMBERSIDE, HU17 0FB.

DAVIS, Mr. Sydney, FCA *1970;* 34 The Bowls, Vicarage Lane, CHIGWELL, IG7 6NB.
DAVIS, Mr. Thomas Russell, BSc ACA *2009;* 60a Kingsley Grove, REIGATE, SURREY, RH2 8DX.
DAVIS, Mr. Timothy Andreas, BA ACA *2005;* DFS Furniture Co Ltd, Redhouse Interchange, Adwick-le-Street, DONCASTER, SOUTH YORKSHIRE, DN6 7NA.
DAVIS, Mr. Timothy Cummings, FCA *1955;* Gingjoy, 140 Mill Road, Stock, INGATESTONE, CM4 9LR. (Life Member)
•DAVIS, Mr. Timothy Robert, LLB ACA *1988;* Deloitte LLP, Abbots House, Abbey Street, READING, RG1 3BD. See also Deloitte & Touche LLP
DAVIS, Mr. Trevor Edmond, BA ACA *1990;* 33A Mount Pleasant, Hertford Heath, HERTFORD, SG13 7QU.
DAVIS, Mrs. Vanessa Anne, BA(Hons) ACA CTA *2002;* with Ernst & Young LLP, Compass House, 80 Newmarket Road, CAMBRIDGE, CB5 8DZ.
•DAVIS, Mr. Victor Edward, JP FCA *1952;* Victor Davis & Co, Horning Reach, Royston Park Road, Hatch End, PINNER, HA5 4AD.
DAVIS, Mrs. Victoria Rachael, BA ACA *2005;* National Audit Office, 157-197 Buckingham Palace Road, LONDON, SW1W 9SP.
DAVIS, Mrs. Victoria Susan, MBA BA FCA *1976;* 16 Prospect Close, Drayton Parslow, MILTON KEYNES, MK17 0JB. (Life Member)
DAVIS, Mrs. Wendy Carol, BSc FCA CTA *1993;* with Price Davis Limited, The Old Baptist Chapel, New Street, Painswick, STROUD, GL6 6XH.
DAVIS, Mr. William, ACA *2011;* 28a, Kensington Church Street, LONDON, W8 4EP.
DAVIS, Mr. William Edward, FCA *1961;* 22 Blackberry Lane, Four Marks, ALTON, GU34 5BP. (Life Member)
DAVIS-MAXWELL, Miss. Nicola Antonia, BA ACA *2006;* 6 Hitches Lane, Crookham Village, FLEET, GU51 5SW.
DAVIS MAXWELL, Miss. Paula Davinia, MA(Oxon) ACA *2003;* Fairfield, Dorchester Road, HOOK, HAMPSHIRE, RG27 9DW.
DAVISON, Mr. Adrian Bower, BA ACA *1993;* Crowthorne, 12 Vesey Road, SUTTON COLDFIELD, B73 5NZ.
•DAVISON, Mrs. Amanda Jane, BSc ACA *1999;* AJD Accounting, 17 Apperley Avenue, High Shincliffe, DURHAM, DH1 2TY.
•DAVISON, Mr. Andrew, BA ACA *1997;* with Ernst & Young LLP, 1 More London Place, LONDON, SE1 2AF.
DAVISON, Mr. Andrew John, FCA *1968;* 11 Shawfield Street, LONDON, SW3 4BA.
DAVISON, Mr. Barry George, FCA *1958;* 1 Fairways, 1240 Warwick Road, Knowle, SOLIHULL, WEST MIDLANDS, B93 9LL. (Life Member)
DAVISON, Mr. Christopher Michael, MA(Cantab) ACA *2006;* 29 Sorrel Close, Wootton, NORTHAMPTON, NN4 6EY.
DAVISON, Mrs. Claire Nicola, MA ACA *1997;* 32 Marlborough Crescent, SEVENOAKS, KENT, TN13 2HP.
•DAVISON, Mr. Colin Andrew, BSc ACA *1999;* (Tax Fac), Cranleys Consulting Limited, Winton House, Winton Square, BASINGSTOKE, HAMPSHIRE, RG21 8EN.
DAVISON, Mr. Colin Trevor, BSc ACA *1990;* 6 Windermere Avenue, ST. ALBANS, HERTFORDSHIRE, AL1 5QW.
DAVISON, Mrs. Dawn Karen, BEng ACA *1992;* Hugh Aston 3.32, De Montfort University, The Gateway, LEICESTER, LE1 9BH.
DAVISON, Mr. Edward, ACA *2011;* 1-4 Crewe Close, Albany, NORTH SHORE CITY 0632, NEW ZEALAND.
DAVISON, Miss. Esther, ACA *2008;* First Floor, 45 Wilberforce Road, LONDON, NW9 6AT.
DAVISON, Mr. Gary Michael, BA ACA *1990;* Sanford C Bernstein Ltd, Devonshire House, 1 Mayfair Place, LONDON, W1J 8SB.
DAVISON, Mr. Guy Bryce, MA ACA *1982;* Cinven Services Ltd Warwick Court, 5 Paternoster Square, LONDON, EC4M 7AG.
DAVISON, Ian Frederic Hay, Esq CBE BSc FCA *1956;* (Member of Council 1975 - 1999), 13 Catharine Place, BATH, BA1 2PR. (Life Member)
DAVISON, Mrs. Jacqueline Ann, LLB ACA *1997;* 28 Rosedew Road, LONDON, W6 9ET.
DAVISON, Dr. Jane Elizabeth, PhD MA BA FCA *1983;* 121 Esmond Road, Chiswick, LONDON, W4 1JE.
•DAVISON, Mr. Jeremy Robert, LLB ACA *1985;* The Mill Consultancy Limited, The Mill, Village Road, Christow, EXETER, EX6 7LX. See also The Mill Accountancy
DAVISON, Mrs. Joanna Peggy, BSc ACA *1991;* S & G Advisory Ltd St. Martins House, 1 Lyric Square, LONDON, W6 0NB.
DAVISON, Mr. John Andrew, FCA *1969;* 39 Jalan 17/21, 46400 PETALING JAYA, MALAYSIA.
DAVISON, Mr. John Barry, BSc FCA *1959;* 4 The Corbetts, Leigh Sinton, MALVERN, WR13 5HQ. (Life Member)
DAVISON, Mr. John Dexter, FCA *1951;* Waynside, Humshaugh, HEXHAM, NE46 4AA. (Life Member)
DAVISON, Mr. John Greener, FCA *1956;* Windward, 58 Painshawfield Road, STOCKSFIELD, NE43 7QY. (Life Member)
•DAVISON, Mr. John James, BSc FCA *1977;* J. Davison & Co, The Firs, Cold Newton, LEICESTER, LE7 9DA.
DAVISON, Mr. John Julian, BA ACA *1987;* with 3i Group plc, 16 Palace Street, LONDON, SW1E 5JD.
DAVISON, Mr. John Ward, BEng ACA ATII *1995;* Cooper Gay & Co Ltd, 52 Leadenhall Street, LONDON, EC3A 2EB.
DAVISON, Mrs. Julie, BA ACA *1993;* 6 Verney Close, Lighthorne, WARWICK, CV35 0AZ.
•DAVISON, Mr. Lawrence Geoffrey, BSc FCA *1992;* Lawrence Davison FCA, Rushwyck House, Old Road, Herstmonceux, HAILSHAM, EAST SUSSEX BN27 1PU.
•DAVISON, Ms. Lesley Jayne, BA ACA *1989;* L&J Accounting Services Ltd, 22 The Grove, Benton, NEWCASTLE UPON TYNE, NE12 9PE.
DAVISON, Mr. Lindon Mark, BA ACA *1996;* 30 Larchdale Close, Broadmeadows, South Normanton, ALFRETON, DERBYSHIRE, DE55 3NZ.
•DAVISON, Mr. Mark Joseph, BSc FCA *1988;* Mark J Davison, PO Box 7150, CHRISTCHURCH, BH23 9FZ.
DAVISON, Mr. Matthew St John, BSc ACA *1998;* 7 Lansdowne Road, Frimley, CAMBERLEY, SURREY, GU16 9UW.
DAVISON, Mr. Nicholas Ross, MA ACA *2001;* Ernst & Young ShinNihon LLC, Hibiya Kokusai Building, 2-2-3 Uchisaiwai-cho, Chiyoda-ku, TOKYO, 100-0011 JAPAN.
DAVISON, Mrs. Pamela Mary, BSc FCA *1979;* Sheraton Park, Blackwell, DARLINGTON, DL3 8QY.
DAVISON, Mr. Paul Matthew, ACA *2009;* 73 Bracken Road, BRIGHOUSE, WEST YORKSHIRE, HD6 2HX.
DAVISON, Mr. Peter Jeffrey, BA FCA *1980;* Sheraton Park, Blackwell, DARLINGTON, DL3 8QY.
DAVISON, Mr. Peter John, MEng ACA *2003;* Basement Flat, 24 Aldebert Terrace, LONDON, SW8 1BJ.
DAVISON, Mr. Richard Alistair, MA ACA *1989;* La Cheneau 6, 1276 GINGINS, SWITZERLAND.
DAVISON, Mr. Richard Andrew, MA ACA *1994;* 2 The Woodlands, ESHER, KT10 8DB.
•DAVISON, Mr. Richard Leslie, BSc FCA *1975;* Richard Davison Associates, Studio 320, Highgate Studios, 53-79 Highgate Road, LONDON, NW5 1TL.
DAVISON, Mr. Richard Merryn, FCA *1971;* Residence Boree B, 248 Bd de Provence, 06700 ST LAURENT DU VAR, FRANCE.
DAVISON, Mr. Robert Frankland, BSc ACA *2002;* flat 10, 3 Pelling Street, LONDON, E14 7EN.
•DAVISON, Mr. Roger, BA ACA *1979;* Davison & Shingleton, Boundary House, 91-93 Charterhouse Street, LONDON, EC1M 6HR.
DAVISON, Miss. Sandra Jane, BSc ACA *1989;* 7 Westmead, MAIDENHEAD, SL6 7HQ.
DAVISON, Mrs. Sheila, BSc ACA *1990;* 8 Oakham Drive, Carrville, DURHAM, DH1 1NB.
DAVISON, Mr. Simon, BA ACA *1993;* with Crowe Clark Whitehill LLP, St Bride's House, 10 Salisbury Square, LONDON, EC4Y 8EH.
DAVISON, Mr. Simon John, BA(Hons) ACA *2000;* Sewell Group Plc, Geneva Way, Leads Road, HULL, HU7 0DG.
DAVISON, Mr. Stafford Ivan, FCA *1967;* L'Orme Creux, 29 rue de l'Orme Creux, 91410 CORBREUSE, FRANCE.
•DAVISON, Mr. Thomas Noel, MA ACA *1988;* Ernst & Young LLP, 1 More London Place, LONDON, SE1 2AF. See also Ernst & Young Europe LLP
DAVISON, Mr. Wayne, BSc(Hons) ACA *2010;* Fairbank Canal Lane, West Stockwith, DONCASTER, SOUTH YORKSHIRE, DN10 4ET.
DAVISON, Mr. William Gordon, FCA *1959;* 2 Old Drovers Way, Stratton, BUDE, CORNWALL, EX23 9DZ. (Life Member)
DAVISON, Mr. William Leslie Egner, FCA *1958;* Green Valleys, Goodleigh, BARNSTAPLE, DEVON, EX32 7JT. (Life Member)
DAVITT, Mr. Martin, BA ACA *1995;* with Deloitte LLP, Athene Place, 66 Shoe Lane, LONDON, EC4A 3BQ.
DAVITT, Mrs. Sally Louise, MPhys ACA *2007;* 17/201 Sydney Road, FAIRLIGHT, NSW 2094, AUSTRALIA.
DAVSON, Mr. Noel George, FCA *1947;* 41 The Dell, Sandpit Lane, ST. ALBANS, AL1 4HF. (Life Member)
DAVY, Mr. Alexander Stuart, BSc ACA *1982;* DKSH Management PTE Ltd, 101 Thomson Road, #17-05 United Square, SINGAPORE 307591, SINGAPORE.
DAVY, Mr. Andrew William John, BA ACA *1994;* 37 Meadow Way, Yarnton, KIDLINGTON, OX5 1TA.
DAVY, Mr. Anthony Tallents, ACA *1981;* The Chaise House, West Street, Alfriston, POLEGATE, BN26 5UX.
DAVY, Mr. Christopher, BA ACA *1979;* 15 Blundering Lane, STALYBRIDGE, SK15 2ST.
DAVY, Mrs. Claire Louise, BSc ACA *1999;* 104 Downhall Park Way, RAYLEIGH, SS6 9QZ.
•DAVY, Mr. Martyn George, BA FCA *1976;* (Tax Fac), Martyn Davy, North Pole, Gorsley, ROSS-ON-WYE, HR9 7BJ.
DAVY, Mr. Robert Geoffrey, MA ACA *1986;* 43 Flood Street, LONDON, SW3 5ST.
DAVY, Miss. Sharon Louise, PhD BSc ACA *2004;* 314 Magpie Hall Road, CHATHAM, KENT, ME4 5XG.
DAVY, Mr. Stewart James, ACA *2007;* 11 Rosa Close, Spixworth, NORWICH, NR10 3NZ.
•DAVY, Mrs. Susan Jane, BSc ACA *1996;* Cedar Lodge, Ridgeway Mead, SIDMOUTH, DEVON, EX10 9DT.
DAVY, Mr. Terence Humphrey, FCA *1962;* Little Mistletoe Cottage, Graffham, PETWORTH, WEST SUSSEX, GU28 0NS. (Life Member)
DAVY, Mr. Timothy William, FCA *1981;* The Croft, Water Street, Somerton, BICESTER, OXFORDSHIRE, OX25 6NE.
DAVY-SMITH, Mr. Richard David, BA ACA *2002;* Prudential, 121 Kings Road, 4CN, READING, RG1 3ES.
DAVYS, Mr. Barry, FCA *1960;* 6 Winterton Cl, Arnold, NOTTINGHAM, NG5 6PZ.
DAW, Mr. Andrew Mark, BSc FCA *1988;* 7 Sidney Place, Beaulieu Park, CHELMSFORD, CM1 6BE.
DAW, Mr. Andrew St John Ian, BSc FCA *1981;* Andrew Daw, 1 Woodland View, Studridge Lane, Speen, PRINCES RISBOROUGH, BUCKINGHAMSHIRE HP27 0SG.
DAW, Mr. David Scott, BSc ACA *1995;* The White Barn, Longwood House, Beggar Bush Lane Failand, BRISTOL, BS8 3TJ.
DAW, Mr. John Jeffreys, BSc FCA *1991;* Grange Farm, Pembury Road, TUNBRIDGE WELLS, TN2 4ND.
DAW, Miss. Louisa, BA ACA *2004;* 58 Vernon Avenue, Raynes Park, LONDON, SW20 8BW.
•DAW, Mr. Philip, FCA *1982;* Daw White Murrall, 1 George Street, WOLVERHAMPTON, WV2 4DG.
DAW, Mrs. Sara, MBA BA ACA *1996;* 1 Woodlands View, Studridge Lane Speen, PRINCES RISBOROUGH, HP27 0SG.
DAW, Mrs. Sharon Lisa, BA ACA *1995;* The White Barn, Longwood House, Beggar Bush Lane Failand, BRISTOL, BS8 3TJ.
DAW, Miss. Susanna Kalo Catherine, BA ACA *1992;* Flat 2, 10 Northwick Terrace, St John's Wood, LONDON, NW8 8JE.
DAWADI, Mr. Shubhaj, ACA *2008;* Flat 201 Michigan Building, 2 Biscayne Avenue, LONDON, E14 9QT.
DAWAF, Miss. Karen Miriam, BSc ACA *2011;* 125 Tentelow Lane, SOUTHALL, MIDDLESEX, UB2 4LW.
DAWBER, Mr. Andrew Joseph, ACA *1989;* 1 Woodhall Avenue, Dulwich, LONDON, SE21 7HL.
DAWBER, Mr. Graham Derek, FCA *1970;* Seatoller, Weston Road, WILMSLOW, CHESHIRE, SK9 2AN.
DAWBER, Mr. James Eric, ACA *2009;* 77 Virginia Gardens, Great Sankey, WARRINGTON, WA5 8WN.
DAWBER, Mr. Matthew, ACA *2010;* 26 Coppice Close, Lostock, BOLTON, BL6 4GE.
DAWBORN, Mr. Richard Myles, FCA *1959;* Treloen, Rusper Road, Ifield, CRAWLEY, RH11 0LN. (Life Member)
DAWDA, Mr. Rajesh Gordhandas, BSc ACA *1997;* 3 Carew Way, WATFORD, WD19 5BG.
DAWDA, Mr. Rakesh, BSc(Hons) ACA *2002;* 28 Berry Hill, STANMORE, HA7 4XS.
DAWDA, Mr. Raoul, ACA *2008;* Flat 17, Hyndman House, Brecknock Road Estate, Brecknock Road, LONDON, N19 5AX.
DAWE, Mr. Adrian, ACA *2008;* 80 Boulton Close, Wyke Regis, WEYMOUTH, DORSET, DT4 9UY.
DAWE, Mr. Alexander James, BA ACA *2005;* Flat 34 Building 49, Argyll Road, LONDON, SE18 6XB.
DAWE, Mr. Crispin, BSc ACA *1986;* 1 St. Marys Field, Meysey Hampton, CIRENCESTER, GLOUCESTERSHIRE, GL7 5HE.
DAWE, Mr. Edward William, BSc ACA *1980;* Elm House, Spridlington, MARKET RASEN, LN8 2DE.
DAWE, Mr. Jonathan Leonard, BA ACA *1987;* RAASAY, Willingham Green Road, Brinkley, NEWMARKET, Suffolk, CB8 0SW.
DAWE, Mr. Kenneth Reginald, FCA *1950;* 37b Poplar Court, BRIELLE, NJ 08730, UNITED STATES. (Life Member)
DAWE, Mr. Mark Richard, MA ACA *1993;* 13 Vine Close, Stapleford, CAMBRIDGE, CB22 5BZ.
•DAWE, Mr. Michael John, FCA CF *1980;* Menzies LLP, Wentworth House, 4400 Parkway, Whiteley, FAREHAM, HAMPSHIRE PO15 7FJ.
DAWE, Mr. Nicholas David, BA(Econ) ACA *1996;* 12108 Capitol Saddlery, AUSTIN, TX 78732, UNITED STATES.
DAWE, Mr. Richard Arthur, BSc ACA *1996;* P O Box 860, MOUNT ELIZA, VIC 3930, AUSTRALIA.
DAWE, Mr. Stuart Edward, BSc FCA *1975;* 2 Humphries Drive, BRACKLEY, NN13 6NW.
DAWES, Mr. Adrian Keith, FCA *1970;* 28 Aldsworth Avenue, Goring-by-Sea, WORTHING, BN12 4XQ. (Life Member)
DAWES, Mr. Alan Lancelot, BSc ACA *1985;* 3 Newport Road, Barnes, LONDON, SW13 9PE.
DAWES, Mr. Alexander Mark, BA ACA AMCT *1995;* Live Nation Ltd, Regent Arcade House, 19-25 Argyll Street, LONDON, W1F 7TS.
DAWES, Mr. Anthony John Francis, BA ACA *1981;* PricewaterhouseCoopers, Avenida Andres Bello 2711, Torre Costanera Piso 5, SANTIAGO, CHILE.
•DAWES, Mr. Ashley Graham, FCA *1983;* Ashley Dawes FCA, 8 Cleland Court, Manor Road, Bishopsteignton, TEIGNMOUTH, DEVON TQ14 9SX.
DAWES, Mr. Brian Richard, FCA *1971;* 11 Kingsley Avenue, CAMBERLEY, SURREY, GU15 2NA.
DAWES, Miss. Elizabeth, BA ACA *2007;* Flat 24 Cheriton Lodge, 38 Pembroke Road, RUISLIP, HA4 8FB.
•DAWES, Mr. Graham Keith, FCA *1967;* Graham Dawes, 117 Nottingham Road, Kimberley, NOTTINGHAM, NG16 2ND.
•DAWES, Mr. Greyham Reginald Allen, FCA DChA *1966;* with Crowe Clark Whitehill LLP, St Bride's House, 10 Salisbury Square, LONDON, EC4Y 8EH.
DAWES, Mr. Howard Anthony Leigh, FCA *1960;* Craycombe House, Near Fladbury, PERSHORE, WR10 2QS. (Life Member)
DAWES, Mr. Jeremy Lees, MA ACA *1992;* 5 Manor Park, Froxfield, MARLBOROUGH, WILTSHIRE, SN8 3LF.
DAWES, Mr. Lee Alan, BA(Hons) ACA *2000;* Poly Pipe Terrain Ltd, New Hythe Business Park, College Road, AYLESFORD, KENT, ME20 7PJ.
DAWES, Ms. Margaret Mary, BSc ACA *1978;* 31 Myddelton Square, Islington, LONDON, EC1R 1YB.
DAWES, Mrs. Margaret Mercer, BSc ACA *1984;* PO Box 130651, BRYANSTON, GAUTENG, 2021, SOUTH AFRICA.
DAWES, Miss. Mary Elizabeth, BA ACA *1980;* Allotts Chartered Accountants, Sidings Court, DONCASTER, SOUTH YORKSHIRE, DN4 5NU.
•DAWES, Mr. Maurice Stephen George, FCA *1962;* Maurice Dawes, Glen View, Boughton Hall Avenue, Send, WOKING, SURREY GU23 7DF.
DAWES, Mr. Michael Charles Lawrence, BA ACA *1989;* Atrium Software Ltd, Lawes house, 66-68 Bristol Road, Portishead, BRISTOL, BS20 6QG.
•DAWES, Mr. Michael Harvey, FCA *1975;* (Tax Fac), The Old Rectory, Church Street, WEYBRIDGE, KT13 8DE.
•DAWES, Mr. Nicholas James, MA ACA *2001;* Ernst & Young LLP, 1 More London Place, LONDON, SE1 2AF. See also Ernst & Young Europe LLP
DAWES, Mr. Nigel David, ACA *1979;* 18 Beaver Way, Woodley, READING, RG5 4UD.
•DAWES, Miss. Pamela Louise, BSc FCA ATII *1989;* Mazars LLP, The Lexicon, Mount Street, MANCHESTER, M2 5NT.
DAWES, Mrs. Rachel Claire, BSc(Econ) ACA *2000;* 49 Fifth Cross Road, TWICKENHAM, TW2 5LJ.
DAWES, Mr. Richard Michael Martindale, BA ACA *1980;* 3 rue Albert de Lapparent, 75007 PARIS, FRANCE.
•DAWES, Mr. Robert Andrew, FCA *1968;* 7 Kenton Mews, BRISTOL, BS9 4LT.
DAWES, Mr. Robert James, BSc ACA *2006;* 9 Celestine Close, CHATHAM, ME5 9NG.

DAWES, Miss. Samantha, BA ACA *1998;* with Linklaters, 1 Silk Street, LONDON, EC2Y 8HQ.
DAWES, Mr. Stuart, MA ACA *1998;* with ACE European Group, ACE Building, 100 Leadenhall Street, LONDON, EC3A 3BP.
DAWES, Mrs. Vanessa Louise, BSc ACA *1995;* 31 Monkswell Road, MONMOUTH, GWENT, NP25 3PF.
DAWKES, Mr. Matthew, BSc ACA *2003;* 49 Alfred Road, BUCKHURST HILL, ESSEX, IG9 6DW.
DAWKINS, Mrs. Anna, MA(Hons) ACA *2001;* 42 Middlesex Road, DARIEN, CT 06820, UNITED STATES.
DAWKINS, Miss. Arabella, BA ACA *1987;* 16, Thompson Road, LONDON, SE22 9JR.
DAWKINS, Mr. Bryan George, FCA *1960;* Long Acres, West Broyle, CHICHESTER, PO19 3PR. (Life Member)
DAWKINS, Mrs. Catherine Mary, MSc ACA *2004;* 26 Vanbrugh Court, Wincott Street, LONDON, SE11 4NS.
DAWKINS, Mrs. Christine Jane, FCA *1977;* 294 Hills Road, CAMBRIDGE, CB2 2QG.
DAWKINS, Mrs. Helen Elizabeth, MA(Hons) ACA *2003;* 4 Eton Square, Eton, WINDSOR, SL4 6BG.
DAWKINS, Mr. Ian Christopher, BA ACA *1993;* 50 Berkeley Street, LONDON, W1J 8HA.
•DAWKINS, Mr. Jeremy Stephen, MA FCA *1973;* (Tax Fac), Dawkins Lewis & Soar, 4 Cowdown Business Park, Micheldever, WINCHESTER, SO21 3DN. See also DLS Accounting Services Ltd
DAWKINS, Mr. John Bruce, FCA *1965;* 6 Dale View, COCKERMOUTH, CA13 9EN.
DAWKINS, Mr. Richard William, MA ACA *2001;* Flat 2, 33 Ilminster Gardens, LONDON, SW11 1PJ.
DAWKINS, Mr. Robert Victor Michael, FCA *1974;* 294 Hills Road, CAMBRIDGE, CB2 2QG.
DAWKINS, Mr. Ross, MSc ACA *1992;* 83 Mallinson Road, LONDON, SW11 1BL.
DAWKINS, Mr. Simon Charles, BSc ACA *1989;* 21 Fold Crescent, Carrbrook, STALYBRIDGE, SK15 3NB.
DAWKINS, Mr. Thomas Edward, BSc FCA *1974;* The Old Stables, 44 High Street, Sydling St. Nicholas, DORCHESTER, DORSET, DT2 9PD.
DAWKINS, Mr. Tom Peter James, BA ACA *2001;* 42 Middlesex Road, DARIEN, CT 06820, UNITED STATES.
DAWNAY, Mr. Edward William, FCA *1973;* Hillington Hall, KING'S LYNN, PE31 6BW.
DAWNAY, The Hon. Richard Henry, BSc FCA *1992;* 20 Dingwall Road, LONDON, SW18 3AZ.
DAWOOD, Ms. Shamima, BA ACA *2000;* 80 Ventnor Drive, Totteridge, LONDON, N20 8BS.
DAWOODBHAI, Mr. Ali asger Hatimali, ACA *2009;* Flat 3, 60 Brighton Road, CRAWLEY, WEST SUSSEX, RH10 6SX.
•DAWOODBHAI, Mr. Enayet Ebrahimjee, ACA *1980;* E. Dawood & Co, 27 Wilbury Avenue, Cheam, SUTTON, SM2 7DU.
DAWOODBHAI, Mr. Mufaddal Sajjad, LLB ACA *2001;* Salehbhai Glass Industries Limited, PO Box 40917, Aggrey Street, DAR ES SALAAM, TANZANIA.
•DAWOODKHAN, Mr. Fakhrudin Abbas, FCA *1970;* F.A. Dawoodkhan & Co, 3 Wildacres, NORTHWOOD, HA6 3JD.
DAWS, Mr. Christopher William, MA FCA CTA MCT *1972;* Coombe Crab Mill Lane, Lea, MALMESBURY, SN16 9NF.
DAWS, Miss. Judith Frances, BSc ACA *2010;* alwyns LLP, 151 High Road, LOUGHTON, IG104LG.
DAWS, Mr. Peter William, BSc FCA *1979;* 19 Hillcrest Avenue, Spinney Hill, NORTHAMPTON, NN3 2AB.
DAWSON, Mr. Adrian Leo Erwin, BA ACA *1983;* 17 Tower Lane, Bearsted, MAIDSTONE, ME14 4JH.
DAWSON, Ms. Alice Louisa Damer, BSc ACA *1991;* Flat 5, 31 Cleveland Square, LONDON, W2 6DD.
DAWSON, Mr. Andrew Christopher, BSc ACA *1998;* Bank of Scotland, New Uberior House, 11 Earl Grey Street, EDINBURGH, EH3 9BN.
DAWSON, Mr. Andrew Howard, BSc FCA *1994;* 21 Croft Way, SEVENOAKS, TN13 2JU.
DAWSON, Mr. Andrew Mark, BA ACA *2001;* Mitchells (UK) Limited St. Michaels Mews, 20-22 St. Michaels Road, LEEDS, LS6 3AW.
DAWSON, Mr. Andrew Robert Anthony, BA ACA *2004;* 17 Nelson Close, Hethersett, NORWICH, NR9 3JZ.
DAWSON, Mr. Andrew William, BA ACA *1989;* 134 Tanjong Rhu Road, 01-03 Pebble Bay, SINGAPORE 436920, SINGAPORE.
DAWSON, Mrs. Anna Kate, BA ACA *1996;* with Deloitte LLP, 1 City Square, LEEDS, WEST YORKSHIRE, LS1 2AL.
DAWSON, Mr. Anthony David, FCA *1965;* 21 Hillbrow, Richmond Hill, RICHMOND, TW10 6BH.
DAWSON, Mr. Anthony James, MA FCA *1987;* 16 Ingleside Road, NORTH SHIELDS, NE29 9PB.
DAWSON, Mr. Anthony Robert, FCA *1972;* Huntington, Whiteleaf, PRINCES RISBOROUGH, HP27 0LL.
•DAWSON, Mr. Barry, FCA *1976;* Calvert Dawson LLP, 288 Oxford Road, Gomersal, CLECKHEATON, BD19 4PY. See also Calvert Dawson Limited
DAWSON, Mr. Benjamin Mark, BA ACA *2005;* 34 Priory Road, West Bridgford, NOTTINGHAM, NG2 5HU.
DAWSON, Bruce Errington, Esq OBE FCA *1965;* Garland Laidley SGPS SA, Travessa Do Corpo Santo 10, 2o Andar, 1200 LISBON, PORTUGAL.
DAWSON, Miss. Carolyn Susan, BA ACA *1989;* 40 Q RUE DES URSULINES, 78100 ST GERMAIN-EN-LAYE, FRANCE.
DAWSON, Mrs. Catherine, BSc ACA *1993;* Rushmoor House Chesham Road, Ashley Green, CHESHAM, BUCKINGHAMSHIRE, HP5 3PQ.
DAWSON, Mr. Charles Paul, FCA *1974;* North Farm, Blackobar Road, Roughlee, NELSON, BB9 6NL.
DAWSON, Mr. Charles William, FCA *1956;* The Lodge, 2 Park Green, Bookham, LEATHERHEAD, KT23 3NL. (Life Member)
DAWSON, Miss. Claire, ACA *2011;* 10 Thacker Drive, LICHFIELD, STAFFORDSHIRE, WS13 6NS.
DAWSON, Mr. David Andrew, FCA *1971;* (Tax Fac), 60 Hull Road, COTTINGHAM, NORTH HUMBERSIDE, HU16 4PU.
DAWSON, Mr. David Antony, BSc ACA *1994;* 85 San Mateo Court, CLONBINANE, VIC 3658, AUSTRALIA.
DAWSON, Mr. David Henry Milner, FCA *1961;* 5 Wakefield Croft, ILKESTON, DE7 9LG. (Life Member)
DAWSON, Mr. David James, FCA *1965;* 39 Walsall Road, Little Aston, SUTTON COLDFIELD, B74 3BA.
DAWSON, Mr. David John, ACA *1982;* 5/136 Hoffmans Road, ESSENDON, VIC 3040, AUSTRALIA.
DAWSON, Mr. David Robert, ACA *2010;* 22 Elspeth Road, LONDON, SW11 1DS.
DAWSON, Mr. Derek John, FCA *1963;* Southbrook Group Ltd, 8th Floor, 17 Old Park Lane, LONDON, W1K 1QT.
DAWSON, Miss. Gemma Louise, BSc ACA *2004;* 38 Sandy Lane, SUTTON, SM2 7PQ.
DAWSON, Mr. Geoffrey Eric, FCA *1985;* 4 Manor Orchard, Brixworth, NORTHAMPTON, NN6 9BX.
DAWSON, Mr. Geoffrey William, FCA *1952;* Avoca, 49 Laneside Road, GRANGE-OVER-SANDS, CUMBRIA, LA11 7BX. (Life Member)
DAWSON, Mr. Gerald Sean, BSc FCA *1992;* Long Tall Sally, 380 Brunel Road, MISSISSAUGA L4Z 2C2, ON, CANADA.
•DAWSON, Mr. Graham Neal, BA ACA *1996;* Blow Abbott Ltd, 36 High Street, CLEETHORPES, SOUTH HUMBERSIDE, DN35 8JN.
DAWSON, Mr. Henry Derek Webster, FCA *1975;* Woodwater House, Michelmores, Pynes Hill, EXETER, EX2 5WR.
DAWSON, Mr. Iain Norman, MA ACA AMCT *1988;* Dawson Commercial & Asset Finance Ltd, 17 Mayfield Close, Ramsbottom, BURY, BL0 9TL.
DAWSON, Mr. Ian Morley, MA ACA *1995;* with KPMG LLP, St. James's Square, MANCHESTER, M2 6DS.
DAWSON, Mr. Ian Richard, BSc ACA *1997;* 7 Priors Road, WINDSOR, SL4 4PD.
•DAWSON, Mr. Ingle Philip, BA ACA *1982;* Inspirational Development Group, 57a Catherine Place, LONDON, SW1E 6DY.
DAWSON, Mr. James Ronald, MA ACA *1988;* Nycomed International Management GmbH, Thurgauerstrasse 130, 8152 GLATTPARK-OPFIKON, SWITZERLAND.
•DAWSON, Mr. Jeremy Alan Courtenay, FCA *1992;* (Tax Fac), 84 Hillfield Road, LONDON, NW6 1QA.
DAWSON, Mr. John Andrew, BSc ACA *1987;* Arbour House, 13 The Mount, Fetcham, LEATHERHEAD, KT22 9EB.
DAWSON, Mr. John Anthony, BA ACA *1980;* Gunthorpe Consulting Ltd, 9d Sunnyside, Wimbledon, LONDON, SW19 4SH.
•DAWSON, Mr. John Anthony, FCA *1967;* J.A. Dawson, Old Post Office Chambers, St. Michaels Way, MIDDLEWICH, CHESHIRE, CW10 9QN.
DAWSON, Mr. John Hennessey, FCA *1968;* The Lawn Woodlands Road, Harpsden, HENLEY-ON-THAMES, OXFORDSHIRE, RG9 4AA. (Life Member)
DAWSON, Mr. John Michael, FCA *1948;* 294 Lorraine Drive, BAIE D'URFE H9X 2R1, QUE, CANADA. (Life Member)
DAWSON, Mr. John Nigel, BA ACA *1993;* HMC Group, Keelrow 12, The Watermark, Metro Riverside, GATESHEAD, NE11 9SZ.
•DAWSON, Mr. John Stephen, BA FCA *1975;* Child & Co, 20 Kirkgate, Sherburn In Elmet, LEEDS, LS25 6BL.
•DAWSON, Mr. Jonathan Michael, BEng ACA *2005;* Kingston Smith LLP, Devonshire House, 60 Goswell Road, LONDON, EC1M 7AD. See also Devonshire Corporate Services LLP and Kingston Smith Consulting LLP
•DAWSON, Mr. Jonathan Neil, BA FCA *1983;* Jon Dawson and Company, Midland Works, Station Road, Carlton, NOTTINGHAM, NG4 3AT. See also JND Accounting
DAWSON, Mrs. Kate Mary Elizabeth, MA ACA *2005;* 15 Bushwood Road, RICHMOND, SURREY, TW9 3BG.
DAWSON, Mr. Lance Christopher, MA ACA *1990;* 145 Earlham Road, NORWICH, NR2 3RG.
DAWSON, Miss. Linda Ann, BSc ACA *2002;* 31 Featherstone Close, NUNEATON, WARWICKSHIRE, CV10 7BP.
DAWSON, Mrs. Louisa Ann, MA ACA *2004;* 25 Fenton Avenue, SWINDON, SN25 2EB.
•DAWSON, Mr. Mark John, MSc BA FCA *1990;* PricewaterhouseCoopers LLP, 7 More London Riverside, LONDON, SE1 2RT. See also PricewaterhouseCoopers
DAWSON, Mr. Mark Jonathan, BA ACA *2000;* with KPMG LLP, One Snowhill, Snow Hill Queensway, BIRMINGHAM, B4 6GN.
DAWSON, Mr. Mark Simon, BA(Hons) ACA *2002;* 10 Sun Gardens, 216 Smit Street, Fairland, JOHANNESBURG, SOUTH AFRICA.
•DAWSON, Mr. Martin Christian, BSc ACA CTA *1992;* Aquarius Tax Consultancy Ltd, Atria Building, Spa Road, BOLTON, BL1 4AG.
DAWSON, Miss. Mary Louise, BSc ACA *1990;* 5 Franconia Road, LONDON, SW4 9NB.
DAWSON, Mr. Michael David, BSc ACA *1992;* 40 Withdean Crescent, BRIGHTON, BN1 6WH.
•DAWSON, Mr. Michael Forbes, MA FCA *1981;* (Tax Fac), BDO LLP, 6th Floor, 3 Hardman Street, Spinningfields, MANCHESTER, M3 3AT. See also BDO Stoy Hayward LLP
DAWSON, Mr. Michael Joseph, MSc ACA *2001;* 16 Green Bower Drive, BROMSGROVE, B61 0UN.
DAWSON, Mr. Michael Walter, FCA *1958;* Key Lodge, Hook Heath Road, WOKING, GU22 0LE. (Life Member)
DAWSON, Mr. Neil, BSc ACA *2011;* Citigroup Centre, 33 Canada Square, LONDON, E14 5LB.
DAWSON, Mr. Neil Andrew, BSc ACA *1999;* 22 Wentworth Way, Edwalton, NOTTINGHAM, NG12 4DJ.
DAWSON, Mr. Neil Matthew, BSc ACA *2001;* Brindleholm, 3a Barkfield Lane, Formby, LIVERPOOL, L37 3JW.
DAWSON, Mr. Nicholas Goodhugh, FCA *1981;* Fiddlers Green, 28 Avenue du Canigou, 66480 MAUREILLAS-LAS-ILLAS, FRANCE.
DAWSON, Mr. Nicholas Mowbray, BSc FCA *1975;* 38 Gilbert Road, Kennington, LONDON, SE11 4NL.
DAWSON, Miss. Nicola Honey, BA ACA *2006;* 37 Angel Road, THAMES DITTON, KT7 0AZ.
DAWSON, Mr. Patrick, BSc ACA *2001;* Genus Plc, Belvedere House, Basing View, BASINGSTOKE, HAMPSHIRE, RG21 4HG.
•DAWSON, Mr. Paul, FCA *1980;* Hart Shaw LLP, Europa Link, Sheffield Business Park, SHEFFIELD, S9 1XU.
DAWSON, Mr. Paul David, BSc FCA *1996;* 16 Viburnum Road, Almondsbury, BRISTOL, BS32 4DH.
•DAWSON, Mr. Paul Hugo, FCA *1972;* Paul H. Dawson, 104 Clarence Road, Four Oaks, SUTTON COLDFIELD, B74 4AS.
DAWSON, Mr. Peter Edward, FCA *1959;* Chestnut Cottage, South Harting, PETERSFIELD, GU31 5LR. (Life Member)
DAWSON, Mr. Peter Frederick, FCA *1959;* Ladderfarm Hall, Groton, SUDBURY, CO10 5EG. (Life Member)
•DAWSON, Mr. Peter Joseph, ACA *1979;* (Tax Fac), Rothman Pantall LLP, Avebury House, 6 St. Peter Street, WINCHESTER, HAMPSHIRE, SO23 8BN.
•DAWSON, Mr. Peter Michael, BSc ACA *1996;* Grant Thornton UK LLP, 30 Finsbury Square, LONDON, EC2P 2YU. See also Grant Thornton LLP
DAWSON, Mr. Philip Graham Donald, MA FCA *1973;* High House, Wakerley Road, Barrowden, OAKHAM, LE15 8EP.
DAWSON, Mr. Richard David Neil, BA ACA *1996;* Dorset Cottage, 34 Manor Road, WALTON-ON-THAMES, SURREY, KT12 2PF.
DAWSON, Mr. Richard Douglas James, MA(Hons) ACA *2001;* with PricewaterhouseCoopers, Sumitomo Fudosan Shiodome Hamarikyu Bldg, 8-21-1 Ginza, Chuo-ku, TOKYO, 104-0061 JAPAN.
•DAWSON, Mr. Richard Godfrey, FCA *1972;* (Tax Fac), Allens Accountants Limited, 123 Wellington Road South, STOCKPORT, SK1 3TH.
DAWSON, Mr. Richard William, BA ACA *1994;* Moores Management & Finance Ltd Mitre House, North Park Road, HARROGATE, NORTH YORKSHIRE, HG1 5RX.
DAWSON, Mr. Robin Charles Alfred, LLB ACA *1985;* Poupart Ltd, Turnford Place, Great Cambridge Road, Turnford, BROXBOURNE, HERTFORDSHIRE EN10 6NH.
DAWSON, Mr. Rodney John, FCA *1971;* 39 Curly Hill, ILKLEY, WEST YORKSHIRE, LS29 0AY.
DAWSON, Mr. Rupert Palliser, BSc FCA *1974;* 7 Carters Close, Sherington, NEWPORT PAGNELL, MK16 9NW.
DAWSON, Mrs. Sarah Elizabeth, ACA *1989;* 42 Hazel Grove, Mapperley, NOTTINGHAM, NG3 6DN.
DAWSON, Mrs. Sarah Joy, ACA *2002;* 16 Anglers Reach, Grove Road, SURBITON, KT6 4EU.
DAWSON, Mr. Simon, BSc ACA *2000;* Group Auto Union UK & Ireland Ltd Roydsdale House, Roydsdale Way Euroway Industrial Estate, BRADFORD, WEST YORKSHIRE, BD4 6SE.
DAWSON, Mr. Stephen, BA ACA *1992;* (Tax Fac), with Reeves & Co LLP, 37 St. Margarets Street, CANTERBURY, KENT, CT1 2TU.
•DAWSON, Mr. Stephen Patrick, BSc ACA *1992;* 5 Burncross Drive, Chapeltown, SHEFFIELD, S35 1DJ.
•DAWSON, Mr. Stephen Robert, BA FCA *1974;* S.R. Dawson, 37 Adelaide Road, SHEFFIELD, S7 1SQ.
DAWSON, Mr. Stephen Robin, BSc ACA *1989;* Malita, Rickman Hill Road, COULSDON, SURREY, CR5 3LA.
DAWSON, Mr. Steven Andrew, BA ACA *1997;* 10A Mount Sophia, #08-11, 8 @ Mount Sophia, SINGAPORE 228462, SINGAPORE.
DAWSON, Mr. Stuart, BSc ACA *1992;* 58 Grove Road, Sonning Common, READING, RG4 9RL.
DAWSON, Miss. Suzanne, BA ACA *2003;* 622 Chorley Road, Westhoughton, BOLTON, BL5 3NJ.
DAWSON, Mr. Terence Arthur, FCA *1972;* 20 Redwood Court, 52 Christchurch Avenue, LONDON, NW6 7BH.
DAWSON, Mr. Thomas Philip, MA MEng ACA *2010;* 69 Ketts Hill, NORWICH, NR1 4EX.
DAWSON, Mr. Thomas Rodney, ACA *2010;* 39 Curly Hill, ILKLEY, WEST YORKSHIRE, LS29 0AY.
DAWSON, Mr. Timothy Francis, MA ACA *1985;* Helvea S A, 5 Rue de Jargonnant, PO Box 6507, 1211 GENEVA, SWITZERLAND.
DAWSON, Mr. Timothy Michael, BSc FCA *1977;* 7 Druids Way, Shortlands, BROMLEY, BR2 0NQ.
DAWSON, Mr. Trevor, FCA *1952;* 6 Swarthmore Road, Weoley Hill, BIRMINGHAM, B29 4JR. (Life Member)
DAWSON, Mr. Trevor Graham, BA FCA *1984;* 91 Hampden Way, LONDON, N14 5AU.
DAWSON, Mr. Trevor James, FCA *1976;* T.J. Dawson & Co, The Limes, Comfort Road, Mylor Bridge, FALMOUTH, CORNWALL TR11 5SE.
DAWSON, Mr. William Bruce, FCA *1960;* Hucklesbrook Cottage, South Gorley, FORDINGBRIDGE, SP6 2PN. (Life Member)
•①DAWSON, Mr. William Kenneth, BA ACA *1990;* Deloitte LLP, PO Box 500, 2 Hardman Street, MANCHESTER, M60 2AT. See also Deloitte & Touche LLP
DAWSON, Mr. William Mark, FCA *1977;* 29 Geraldine Road, LONDON, SW18 2NR.
DAWTRY, Mrs. Julie Helen, BA(Hons) ACA *2002;* Sarclad Ltd, Broombank Park, CHESTERFIELD, DERBYSHIRE, S41 9RT.
•DAY, Mr. Alan Arthur, BA(Hons) ACA *1989;* Alan Day BA (Hons) ACA, 55 Bournside Road, CHELTENHAM, GLOUCESTERSHIRE, GL51 3AL.
DAY, Mrs. Alison Jane, FCA CTA *1995;* 12 Bishops Court Gardens, CHELMSFORD, CM2 6AZ.
•DAY, Mr. Andrew, FCA *1977;* (Tax Fac), Wakelin & Day, 9 Pound Lane, GODALMING, GU7 1BX.
DAY, Mr. Andrew, ACA *2009;* 4 Hythe Way, Broughton, MILTON KEYNES, MK10 7AW.
DAY, Mr. Andrew Bernard, MA ACA *1985;* Tanners, Laughton Road, Ringmer, LEWES, BN8 5NH.

DAY, Mr. Andrew George, MEng ACA *2003;* B G Group Plc, 100 Thames Valley Park Drive, READING, RG6 1PT.
DAY, Mr. Andrew John, FCA *1972;* 21 Scotts Crescent, Hilton, HUNTINGDON, PE28 9PG.
•**DAY, Mr. Andrew Neal, BA ACA** *1992;* Walkers Accountants Limited, 16-18 Devonshire Street, KEIGHLEY, WEST YORKSHIRE, BD21 2DG.
DAY, Mrs. Angela, BA ACA ATII *1993;* Beavis Morgan Llp, 82 St. John Street, LONDON, EC1M 4JN.
DAY, Ms. Anita Annabelle Dora, BSc ACA *1988;* IBM UK Ltd, Wayside House, Bedford Road, Ravensden, BEDFORD, MK44 2RA.
DAY, Miss. Annabelle Jane, BSc(Hons) ACA *2009;* 52 Golding Thoroughfare, Chelmer Village, CHELMSFORD, CM2 6TU.
DAY, Mrs. Anne Elizabeth, BSc ACA *1994;* Pharmaq Ltd Unit 14-15 Sandleheath Industrial Estate, Old Brickyard Road Sandleheath, FORDINGBRIDGE, HAMPSHIRE, SP6 1PA.
DAY, Mr. Anthony, FCA *1967;* 33 Appledore Road, TENTERDEN, TN30 7AY.
DAY, Mr. Anthony Michael, FCA *1971;* Cartone House, 3 River Close, Four Marks, ALTON, HAMPSHIRE, GU34 5XB.
DAY, Miss. Barbara Ingrid, FCA *1971;* 13 Cromwell Park, Over, CAMBRIDGE, CB24 5PX. (Life Member)
DAY, Mr. Barry David, BSc ACA *1989;* The Old Rectory, Hatton Green, Hatton, WARWICK, WARWICKSHIRE, CV35 7LA.
DAY, Mrs. Carolyn Patricia, ACA *1984;* 47 Hurn Way, CHRISTCHURCH, DORSET, BH23 2NX.
DAY, Miss. Catherine Anne, BA ACA *1994;* 15 Meadowcroft Way, Kirby Cross, FRINTON-ON-SEA, ESSEX, CO13 0TF.
DAY, Mr. Charles Rickard, FCA *1974;* High Rise La Haute Ferme, Mont A L'Abbe Manor, St Helier, JERSEY, JE2 3GJ.
DAY, Mr. Christopher, BSc ACA *2001;* 75 Clarence Road, Harborne, BIRMINGHAM, B17 9JY.
DAY, Mr. Christopher Alexander Coryton, BA ACA *1998;* 4 Stafford Square, WEYBRIDGE, KT13 9NG.
DAY, Mr. Christopher John, BSc ACA *1990;* Hill Top Farmhouse, Shrawley, WORCESTER, WR6 6TQ.
DAY, Mr. Christopher John, BSc ACA *1982;* Southfield Office, Main Road, Redbourne, GAINSBOROUGH, LINCOLNSHIRE, DN21 4QR.
•**DAY, Mr. Christopher Michael, BSc FCA** *1987;* Creative FD Limited, 6 Pigott Drive, Shenley Church End, MILTON KEYNES, MK5 6BY.
•**DAY, Mr. Clifford, FCA** *1966;* (Tax Fac), Clifford Day, 21 Pinfold, South Cave, BROUGH, HU15 2HE.
DAY, Mr. Clifford Charles, FCA *1958;* Timberlawn, Manor Road, Goring On Thames, READING, RG8 9EH. (Life Member)
DAY, Mr. Daniel Ian, MA ACA *2011;* 25 Heath Close, HARPENDEN, HERTFORDSHIRE, AL5 1QN.
DAY, Mr. David, BSc ACA *1982;* Sovereign House, Miles Gray Road, BASILDON, SS14 3FR.
DAY, Mr. David Clapham, FCA *1958;* 11 Royal Avenue, LONDON, SW3 4QE. (Life Member)
DAY, Mr. David Oliver, FCA *1959;* Gawthrop Villa, Gawthrop, Dent, SEDBERGH, LA10 5TA.
DAY, Mr. Derek William, BSc(Econ) FCA *1963;* 20 Wood Street, PENARTH, SOUTH GLAMORGAN, CF64 2NH. (Life Member)
DAY, Mr. Donald Alistair Reginald, FCA *1967;* Kyffhaeuserstr 11, 85579 NEUBIBERG, GERMANY. (Life Member)
DAY, Mr. Donald Austin, FCA *1954;* 28 Woodlands Park, LEIGH-ON-SEA, SS9 3TY. (Life Member)
DAY, Mr. Edward, BSc ACA *1978;* Pipistrelles' Barn, Pond Hall Road, Hadleigh, IPSWICH, IP7 5PQ.
DAY, Miss. Elizabeth Claire, BSc ACA *2009;* 2 Downs Wood, Vigo, GRAVESEND, KENT, DA13 0SQ.
DAY, Mr. Eric Frank, FCA *1969;* Marsh Ltd, Tower Place East, Lower Thames Street, LONDON, EC3R 5BU.
DAY, Mr. Frederick George, FCA *1965;* 22, Glebe Avenue, MITCHAM, CR4 3DY.
•**DAY, Mr. Geoffrey Allan, FCA** *1970;* (Tax Fac), Day & Company, 23 Park Road, GLOUCESTER, GL1 1LH.
DAY, Mr. Geoffrey Frank, FCA *1963;* The Crow's Nest, Marine Parade, Instow, BIDEFORD, EX39 4JN.
DAY, Mr. Graham Manton, FCA *1968;* Hazel Lodge, 91 Murton Lane, Newton, SWANSEA, SA3 3AA.
•**DAY, Mr. Graham Michael David, FCA DChA** *1974;* Chater Allan LLP, Beech House, 4a Newmarket Road, CAMBRIDGE, CB5 8DT.
DAY, Mrs. Guinevere Rosamunde, BA ACA *1998;* Lloyds Banking Group Alder Castle House, 10 Noble Street, LONDON, EC2V 7ED.
•**DAY, Mrs. Heather Kathryn, FCA** *1984;* (Tax Fac), 18 Leith View, North Holmwood, DORKING, SURREY, RH5 4TG. See also Day H.K. & co
DAY, Mr. Herbert James, FCA *1972;* 174 Bannings Vale, Saltdean, BRIGHTON, BN2 8DJ.
•**DAY, Mr. Howard Ian, BSc ACA DChA** *1990;* Howard I. Day, 75 Barton Road, Headington, OXFORD, OX3 9JE.
DAY, Mrs. Isla Elizabeth, BSc ACA *1986;* Essex Business School, University of Essex, Wivenhoe Park, COLCHESTER, CO4 3SQ.
DAY, Mrs. Janette, BSc ACA *2000;* 55 Sandhills Lane, Barnt Green, BIRMINGHAM, B45 8NU.
DAY, Mrs. Jennifer Jane, ACA *1984;* 131 Lower Glen Road, ST LEONARDS-ON-SEA, EAST SUSSEX, TN37 7AR.
DAY, Miss. Jenny, BSc ACA *1991;* 99 St. Marks Road, HENLEY-ON-THAMES, OXFORDSHIRE, RG9 1LP.
DAY, Dr. Joanne Marie, BSc(Hons) ACA *2001;* 7 Southbourne Close, Selly Park, BIRMINGHAM, B29 7LU.
DAY, Mr. John Campbell Lacy, MA FCA *1967;* Monks Post, 8/9 Mount Street, Bishops Lydeard, TAUNTON, TA4 3AN.
DAY, Mr. John Frederick Felix, FCA *1957;* 14 Ralph Swingler Place, Sollershott East, LETCHWORTH GARDEN CITY, HERTFORDSHIRE, SG6 3GZ. (Life Member)
DAY, Mr. John Gentle, BSc FCA *1975;* 67 oxford court, RAMSEY, NJ 07446, UNITED STATES.
DAY, Mr. John Leeson, BCom ACA *1983;* 5 Orchard Farm Road, PORT WASHINGTON, NY 11050, UNITED STATES.
•**DAY, Mr. Jonathan, BA(Hons) ACA** *2002;* Streets, 87 Park Road, PETERBOROUGH, PE1 2TN. See also Streets Whitmarsh Sterland
•**DAY, Mr. Jonathan, BA ACA** *1997;* 8 Mahara Apartments, Upper Kings Cliff, ST HELIER, JE2 3GP.
DAY, Mr. Jonathan Richard, BSc ACA *2001;* 4 Stafford Avenue, SHIFNAL, SHROPSHIRE, TF11 9AL.
DAY, Mr. Jonathan Stuart, BA ACA *1999;* 8 East Common, HARPENDEN, HERTFORDSHIRE, AL5 1BJ.
DAY, Mrs. Judith Gaye, BA ACA *1984;* Mill View Church Path Terrace, Lympstone, EXMOUTH, DEVON, EX8 5HJ.
DAY, Prof. Judy Frances Sara, MSc BSc(Econ) FCA *1979;* Hillside, Coppice Lane, Disley, STOCKPORT, CHESHIRE, SK12 2LT.
DAY, Mr. Julian, BSc ACA *2003;* 24 Lichfield Drive, CHELTENHAM, GLOUCESTERSHIRE, GL51 3DH.
DAY, Mr. Julian Michael, MA ACA AMCT *1990;* Flat 18, Spectrum House, 59 St. John's Square, LONDON, EC1V 4JF.
DAY, Miss. Katherine Anne, BA(Hons) ACA *2011;* 9 Parkgate Mews, LONDON, N6 5NB.
DAY, Miss. Kimberley Ann, BSc ACA *2008;* 10 Oriel Close, Wolverton, MILTON KEYNES, MK12 5FE.
DAY, Mr. Leonard Henry, FCA *1960;* La Carriere, Le Hocq, St Clement, JERSEY, JE2 6FQ.
DAY, Mrs. Linda Gail, BSc ACA *1989;* 67 Felstead Road, ORPINGTON, BR6 9AD.
•**DAY, Mrs. Marie, FCA** *1990;* Bennett Brooks & Co Ltd, First Floor Offices, 42 High Street, MOLD, FLINTSHIRE, CH7 1BH.
DAY, Mr. Mark, BA FCA *1991;* Welton Hill, Kidd Lane, Welton, BROUGH, NORTH HUMBERSIDE, HU15 1PH.
DAY, Mr. Mark Russell, BSc ACA *1989;* 29 Carlisle Road, Birkdale, SOUTHPORT, MERSEYSIDE, PR8 4DJ.
•**DAY, Mr. Martin Paul, BA ACA** *1985;* M.P. Day Accounting Services, 19 Orchard Lane, Brampton, HUNTINGDON, PE28 4TF.
DAY, Mr. Michael Charles Hamilton, BSc ACA *2005;* 4 Stanley Street, Berhampore, WELLINGTON, NEW ZEALAND.
DAY, Mr. Michael John, FCA *1956;* Little Woodlands, North Road, BATH, BA2 6HB. (Life Member)
DAY, Mr. Michael John, BCom FCA *1964;* Barn House, Great Comberton, PERSHORE, WORCESTERSHIRE, WR10 3DP.
DAY, Mr. Michael Robert, BA ACA *2003;* 10 Gainsborough Crescent, Knowle, SOLIHULL, B93 9EX.
DAY, Mr. Michael Stephen, BA FCA *1977;* 8 Moss Lane, ALDERLEY EDGE, SK9 7HN.
DAY, Mr. Neil Gary, ACA *2008;* 3 Walcher Grove, GATESHEAD, TYNE AND WEAR, NE8 3FJ.
DAY, Mr. Nicholas James, BSc(Hons) ACA *2001;* Methods Consulting, 125 Shaftesbury Avenue, LONDON, WC2H 8AD.
•**DAY, Mr. Oliver John, BSc ACA** *1997;* Day & Co (High Peak) Ltd, 1 Hunters Green Close, Chinley, HIGH PEAK, DERBYSHIRE, SK23 6DF. See also Day & Co
DAY, Mr. Paul Edward, MA ACA *1997;* 51 Crabtree Lane, LONDON, SW6 6LP.
DAY, Mr. Paul Simon, ACA BEng(Hons) *2004;* 74 Hartford Road, BEXLEY, DA5 1NF.
DAY, Mr. Peter Richard, MSc ACA *1992;* Cumberland House Sleaford Road, Wellingore, LINCOLN, LN5 0HR.
DAY, Mr. Philip Michael, BSc ACA *2000;* 36 West Towers, PINNER, MIDDLESEX, HA5 1UA.
DAY, Mr. Phillip, FCA *1970;* (Member of Council 1999 - 2002), Buzon 02024, Ctra De Gata 18, 03729 LLIBER, ALICANTE, SPAIN.
DAY, Mrs. Rachel Alice, BA ACA *1995;* 12 Cranmer Road, SEVENOAKS, TN13 2AT.
DAY, Ms. Rachel Laurence, BA ACA *1982;* CCRC South, 101 NE 3rd Ave., Suite 400, FORT LAUDERDALE, FL 33301, UNITED STATES.
DAY, Miss. Rachel Louise, BA ACA *2001;* 5, Chancery Lane, LONDON, EC4A 1BL.
DAY, Mr. Richard John, BSc ACA *2006;* 11 Coppice Place, Wormley, GODALMING, GU8 5TY.
DAY, Mr. Richard Lyddon, FCA *1956;* The Old Vicarage, Church Lane, Mickleton, CHIPPING CAMPDEN, GLOUCESTERSHIRE, GL55 6RZ. (Life Member)
DAY, Mr. Richard Newington, ACA *2008;* Little Inholms, 2 Frog Grove Lane, Wood Street Village, GUILDFORD, GU3 3EX.
•**DAY, Mr. Roger Edwin, FCA** *1968;* Chhaya Hare Wilson Limited, Redmead House, Uxbridge Road, Hillingdon Heath, UXBRIDGE, MIDDLESEX UB10 0LT.
DAY, Mr. Roger John Douglas, BA ACA *1995;* E M C Computer Systems (UK) Ltd, E M C Tower, Great West Road, BRENTFORD, MIDDLESEX, TW8 9AN.
•**DAY, Mr. Rohan, ACA FCCA** *2009;* Robertshaw Myers, Number 3, Acorn Business Park, Keighley Road, SKIPTON, NORTH YORKSHIRE BD23 2UE. See also Robertshaw & Myers
DAY, Mr. Rupert Michael, BSc ACA *1987;* Mindshare, 101 St. Martin's Lane, LONDON, WC2N 4DB.
DAY, Miss. Sara Jane, BSc ACA *2003;* 4 Camden Terrace, LONDON, NW1 9BP.
DAY, Mrs. Sarah Louise, BA(Hons) ACA *2000;* (Tax Fac), 35 Moat End, Thorner, LEEDS, LS14 3EU.
DAY, Mrs. Sheila Grant, BSc ACA *1988;* Hysons Chartered Accountant, 14 London Street, ANDOVER, HAMPSHIRE, SP10 2PA.
•**DAY, Mr. Simon, BSc FCA** *1979;* Simon Day Limited, Unit 2, Uffcott Farm, Uffcott, SWINDON, SN4 9NB. See also Simon Day & Co
DAY, Mr. Simon Charles, FCA *1994;* 20 Taylor Drive, Bramley, TADLEY, HAMPSHIRE, RG26 5XP.
DAY, Mr. Simon James, BSc ACA *2011;* Flat C, 68 Stroud Green Road, Finsbury Park, LONDON, N4 3ER.
DAY, Mr. Stephen Charles, BSc ACA *1979;* Arndtstr 34, 53113 BONN, GERMANY.
DAY, Miss. Susan Jane, BSc ACA CTA *1988;* 10 Rockleaze Road, Sneyd Park, BRISTOL, BS9 1NF.
DAY, Miss. Susan Margaret, BA ACA *2000;* 38 Pelham Road, LONDON, E18 1PX.
•**DAY, Mr. Thomas Henry Burton, BA FCA** *1977;* Tom Day, Ashleigh, Barton Blount, Church Broughton, DERBY, DE65 5AP.
DAY, Mr. Thomas Simon, BSc ACA *1998;* with PricewaterhouseCoopers LLP, 80 Strand, LONDON, WC2R 0AF.
•**DAY, Mr. Trevor John, FCA** *1986;* Burgis & Bullock, Unit 7B, Davy Court, Castle Mount, RUGBY, WARWICKSHIRE CV23 0UZ.
•**DAY, Mr. Trevor John, FCA** *1972;* J S Bethell & Co, 70 Clarkehouse Road, SHEFFIELD, S10 2LJ.
•**DAY, Mr. Trevor Joseph Frederick, FCA** *1971;* Trevor JF Day, 13 Heythrop Close, Oadby, LEICESTER, LE2 4SL.
DAY, Mrs. Vivienne, ACA *1982;* 9 Beech Close, Thruxton, ANDOVER, SP11 8NB.
DAY, Mr. William Joshua, BSc FCA *2000;* 44 Humber Street, Hilton, DERBY, DE65 5NW.
DAY, Mr. William Peter, LLB FCA *1975;* GPO BOX 1189, SURREY HILLS NORTH, VIC 3127, AUSTRALIA.
DAY, Mr. William Adrian, MEng ACA *1999;* 85 Middlebrook Street, WINCHESTER, HAMPSHIRE, SO23 8DQ.
•**DAYA, Mr. Ahmed Abdulhusein, ACA** *1979;* (Tax Fac), 101 Deacons Hill Road, Elstree, BOREHAMWOOD, HERTFORDSHIRE, WD6 3JF.
DAYA, Mr. Altaf Hussein, MEng ACA *2010;* 101 Deacons Hill Road, Elstree, BOREHAMWOOD, HERTFORDSHIRE, WD6 3JF.
DAYA, Ms. Jacqueline Anne, FCA *1979;* Apt 74, Church Court, 492 Beacon Street, BOSTON, MA 02115, UNITED STATES.
DAYAL, Mr. Vinit, FCA *1980;* 2nd Floor, 5 Southern Avenue, Maharani Bagh, NEW DELHI 110065, INDIA.
DAYE, Mr. Ian Edward, FCA *1974;* 2 Higham Cottages, Higham Gobion, HITCHIN, SG5 3HN.
•**DAYE, Mrs. Susan Ann, BSc ACA CTA** *1996;* (Tax Fac), Crowe Clark Whitehill LLP, Carrick House, Lypiatt Road, CHELTENHAM, GLOUCESTERSHIRE, GL50 2QJ. See also Horwath Clark Whitehill LLP
DAYER, Mr. Frederick George, FCA *1948;* 9 Beaufort Road, Frampton Cotterell, BRISTOL, BS36 2AD. (Life Member)
DAYER, John Arnold, Esq MBE FCA *1954;* 16 The Oaklands, DROITWICH, WR9 8AD. (Life Member)
DAYER, Mr. Philip John, LLB FCA *1976;* West Bradfield House, Bradfield, CULLOMPTON, DEVON, EX15 2QY.
DAYKIN, Mr. Clive Martin, BA FCA *1997;* 21 Larnach Road, LONDON, W6 9NX.
DAYKIN, Dr. Judith Margaret Katharine, BEng ACA CTA *2002;* 18 Shrublands Drive, LIGHTWATER, GU18 5QS.
DAYKIN, Mr. Michael Richard, MEng FCA *1995;* 94 Weydon Hill Road, FARNHAM, SURREY, GU9 8NZ.
DAYKIN, Mr. Peter Geoffrey, BA ACA *1979;* The Halflings, 3 Mill Road, Bintree, DEREHAM, NORFOLK, NR20 5NL.
•**DAYKIN, Mr. Philip James, BSc FCA** *1992;* Daykins, 6 Abergavenny Road, USK, MONMOUTHSHIRE, NP15 1SB. See also Philip Daykin
DAYKIN, Mr. Stephen David Paul, BSc ACA *1982;* Watermead House, Warnicombe Lane, TIVERTON, DEVON, EX16 4NE.
DAYMOND, Mr. Andrew Michael, BA ACA *1995;* Fieldhurst, 31 Highlands Road, Seer Green, BEACONSFIELD, BUCKINGHAMSHIRE, HP9 2XL.
DAYSON, Mr. Jonathan Martyn, FCA *1973;* 57 Heol Hir, Llanishen, CARDIFF, CF14 5AA. (Life Member)
DE, Mr. Amit Kumar, FCA *1970;* 10 Webb Hill Road, Great Neck, NEW YORK, NY 11020, UNITED STATES. (Life Member)
•**DE, Mr. Debaprasad, FCA** *1970;* (Tax Fac), De Susman & Co, 9th Floor, Hyde House, Edgware Road Hendon, LONDON, NW9 6LH.
DE, Mr. Sukamal, FCA *1972;* South Mao Ming Road 169, Apt 12 101, SHANGHAI 200020, CHINA.
•**DE, Mr. Thomas Gopala, FCA CF** *1995;* 5 Heath Road, Little Heath, POTTERS BAR, HERTFORDSHIRE, EN6 1LQ.
DE'ATH, Mr. Peter, BEng ACA *1999;* 30 Tunbridge Way, Emersons Green, BRISTOL, BS16 7EX.
DE ALWIS, Mr. Leslie Alan Winston, BSc FCA *1954;* 9 Queens Avenue, 3 COLOMBO, SRI LANKA. (Life Member)
DE ALWIS JAYASINGHE, Miss. Hiranya, ACA *2007;* 3 Pottery Lane, CHELMSFORD, CM1 4HH.
DE ANGELI, Mr. Frank, BCom FCA *1952;* PO Box 215, 3 Loch Maree Place, VAUCLUSE, NSW 2030, AUSTRALIA. (Life Member)
DE ARAUJO, Miss. Deidre Annabelle, BAcc ACA *1997;* 61 Sutton Lane South, LONDON, W4 3JT.
DE ARCANGELIS, Mrs. Nicola Sarah, BSc ACA *2006;* 27 Abbey Gardens, Upper Woolhampton, READING, RG7 5TZ.
DE AROSTEGUI, Miss. Clare Louise, MA ACA *2001;* Northern Foods Plc, 2180 Century Way, Thorpe Park, LEEDS, LS15 8ZB.
DE BAAT, Mrs. Julia Alice, BSc(Econ) ACA *2002;* 3 West Park Avenue, RICHMOND, SURREY, TW9 4AN.
DE BACKER, Mr. Damian Paul, BA ACA *1991;* (Tax Fac), with PricewaterhouseCoopers, Plot No 211 Second Sector, City Center, PO Box 170, CAIRO, 11835 EGYPT.
DE BACQ ROSE, Mr. Malcolm, BA FCA *1973;* (Tax Fac), PO Box 99, ABERYSTWYTH, DYFED, SY23 2XD.
DE BARR, Mr. Richard Jeremy, BSc FCA *1972;* (Tax Fac), Compco Holdings Limited, 10 Upper Berkeley Street, LONDON, W1H 7PE.
DE BARROS, Mr. Miguel Antonio Roosevelt, FCA *1966;* 4 Belafonte Street, MCDOWALL, QLD 4053, AUSTRALIA.
DE BEAUFORT-SUCHLICK, Mr. Anthony John, ACA *1980;* Ashcroft Estates Management Ltd, 1 Ashurst Court London Road Wheatley, OXFORD, OX33 1ER.
DE BEER, Mrs. Caroline, ACA CA(SA) *2011;* 247 Worplesdon Rd, GUILDFORD, SURREY, GU2 9XN.

DE-BEGER, Mr. Timothy, BSc ACA *2011;* 84c Edgeley Road, LONDON, SW4 6HB.
DE BELL, Mrs. Sarah Jennifer, BA ACA *1985;* 7 Berridge Mews, LONDON, NW6 1RF.
DE BIASI, Miss. Kylie, BSc ACA *2011;* Westview, Mayfield Avenue, St. Brelade, JERSEY, JE3 8FT.
DE BIEVRE, Ms. Susannah, BA FCA *1989;* Po Box 180, TAUPO, NEW ZEALAND.
DE BLOCQ VAN KUFFELER, Mr. John Philip, MA FCA *1973;* Park House, Chrishall, ROYSTON, SG8 8QT.
DE BOER, Mr. Christopher Michael, BA FCA *1971;* P.O. Box 128-055, Remuera, AUCKLAND, NEW ZEALAND.
DE BOER, Mr. Leks, ACA *2008;* Tegetthoffstrasse 1/7, 1010 VIENNA, AUSTRIA.
DE BOHUN, Mr. Richard Gregory, BA ACA *1997;* Willow Barn, London Road, Thorley, BISHOP'S STORTFORD, HERTFORDSHIRE, CM23 4AT.
DE BOO, Mr. Shaun Vernon, FCA *1982;* 40 Sebastian Avenue, Shenfield, BRENTWOOD, CM15 8PW.
DE BORDE, Mr. Timothy John, BA ACA *1992;* Easterton, 50 Ellesborough Road, Wendover, AYLESBURY, BUCKINGHAMSHIRE, HP22 6EL.
DE BOSDARI, Mr. Benedict David Edmeades, ACA *2010;* Flat B, 6 Knights Hill, West Norwood, LONDON, SE27 0HY.
DE BRAEKELEER, Mr. Alain, ACA *2008;* K P M G, 1 The Embankment, LEEDS, LS1 4DW.
DE BRULE, Mr. Douglas James, BA FCA *1972;* Laurel House, 13 Main Street, Adlestrop, MORETON-IN-MARSH, GL56 0UN.
DE BRUYN, Mr. Christiaan Leonard, ACA *1999;* (Tax Fac), Third Floor-1, No.50 Lane 269, Lin-sen East Road, CHIAYI, 600, TAIWAN.
DE CARLINI, Mrs. Colette Dominique, BSc ACA *2003;* Top Flat, 189 Queens Road, LONDON, SW19 8NX.
DE CAUX, Ms. Lisa, MA(Hons) ACA *2003;* 1st Floor, The Co-operative Group (C W S) Ltd Old Bank Building, Hanover Street, MANCHESTER, M60 0AB.
DE CHASTEAUNEUF, Mr. Louis Jean Jerome, BSc ACA *1992;* 62Domaine De Bon Espoir, PITON, MAURITIUS.
DE CHASTEIGNER DU MEE, Mr. Jacques Paul Rene, BA ACA *1986;* Kemp Chatteris Deloitte, 7th. Floor, Raffles Tower, 19 Cybercity, EBENE, MAURITIUS.
DE CHASTEIGNER DU MEE, Mr. Paul Rene, FCA *1951;* Angus Road, VACOAS, MAURITIUS. (Life Member)
DE CHAZAL, Mr. Alexander David, FCA *1971;* The Old Rectory, Coulston, WESTBURY, WILTSHIRE, BA13 4NY.
DE CHAZAL, Mr. Bertrand Denis Richard, FCA *1969;* Coastal Road, CALODYNE, MAURITIUS. (Life Member)
DE CHAZAL, Mrs. Deborah Susan, FCA *1974;* Chemin Campement, FLOREAL, MAURITIUS.
•**DE CHAZAL, Mr. Jean-Paul, FCA** *1974;* Societe Roger de Chazal, Sixth Floor, Cerne House, Chaussee, PORT LOUIS, MAURITIUS.
DE CHAZAL, Mr. Louis Jacques Roger, FCA *1949;* Chemin Campement, FLOREAL, MAURITIUS. (Life Member)
DE CHAZAL, Mr. Paul Richard Raymond, FCA *1971;* 11 Rue Desbordes-Valmore, 75116 PARIS, FRANCE.
DE CHAZAL, Mr. Roger, BA(Hons) ACA *2002;* Ernst & Young, 9th floor, NeXTeracom Tower 1, EBENE, MAURITIUS.
DE CHENU, Mr. Nicholas Roger, BSc FCA *1975;* 11 Babraham Road, CAMBRIDGE, CB2 0RB.
DE CHOISY, Mr. Simon John, BA ACA *1996;* Home Farm Lodge, 12 Kettering Road, Stanion, KETTERING, NN14 1DH.
DE CINTRA, Mrs. Catherine Mary, BA ACA *1988;* St. Benedicts School, 54 Eaton Rise, LONDON, W5 2ES.
DE COGAN, Mr. Dominic, ACA *2008;* Downing College, Regents Street, CAMBRIDGE, CB2 1DQ.
DE CONDAPPA, Mr. Gilles Jean Francois, MEng ACA *2006;* Apt 306, 618 Abbott Street, VANCOUVER V6B 0C1, BC, CANADA.
DE COURCY-BOWER, Mrs. Sarah Alexandra Louise, BSc ACA *1989;* Captain's Field, Peldon Road, Abberton, COLCHESTER, CO5 7PB.
DE CRUZ, Mr. Adrian Paul, BSc ACA *1993;* 5 Egdean Walk, SEVENOAKS, KENT, TN13 3UQ.
•**DE CRUZ, Mr. Benjamin, BA FCA** *1989;* Haines Watts Exeter LLP, 3 Southernhay West, EXETER, EX1 1JG. See also Haines Watts North Devon LLP
•**DE CRUZ, Mr. Hermando, ACA** *2009;* H Decruz Limited, 26 Oakleigh Avenue, EDGWARE, MIDDLESEX, HA8 5DT.
DE DOMBAL, Dr. Richard Francis, MA FCA *1996;* (Tax Fac), Arcadia Group Ltd, Hudson Road, LEEDS, LS9 7DN.
DE FEO, Mr. Francesco, ACA *2011;* 58 Bassein Park Road, LONDON, W12 9RZ.
•**DE FIGUEIREDO, Mr. Michael David, BSc FCA** *1985;* Le Vieux Menage La Rue Du Vieux Menage, St. Saviour, JERSEY, JE2 7XG.
DE FIGUEIREDO, Mr. Philip Eric, BA ACA *1980;* Flat 3 Links Court, La Rue A Don, Grouville, JERSEY, JE3 9DZ.
DE FOREST-BROWN, Mr. Martin Edward, MA FCA *1987;* 79 Lancaster Avenue, GUILDFORD, GU1 3JR.
•**DE FREITAS, Mrs. Ann Elizabeth, BSc ACA** *1984;* de Freitas & Co, 39 Berwyn Road, RICHMOND, SURREY, TW10 5BU. See also de Freitas & Co. Accountants Limited
DE FREITAS, Mr. Douglas Lorn, ACA CA(SA) *2008;* 11 Downing Close, BURY ST. EDMUNDS, SUFFOLK, IP32 7HU.
DE FREITAS, Mrs. Elizabeth Ann, BSc FCA *1992;* 11 Downing Close, BURY ST. EDMUNDS, IP32 7HU.
•**DE FRIAS, Mr. Philip Russell, BSc FCA** *1984;* James de Frias Limited, Llanover House, Llanover Road, PONTYPRIDD, CF37 4DY.
DE FRIEND, Mr. Simon Richard, BA ACA *1992;* 83 Parkside Drive, WATFORD, WD17 3AU.
DE FRIEZ, Mr. Alistair Norman Campbell, MA FCA *1977;* 6 Ridgway Gardens, Wimbledon, LONDON, SW19 4SZ.
DE FRINSE, Ms. Meabh Margaret, BA ACA *2005;* 105 Duane Street, Apt 32B, NEW YORK, NY 10007, UNITED STATES.
DE GALE, Mr. William Hervey, BA FCA CFA *1991;* Black Rock, 33 King William Street, LONDON, EC4R 9AS.
DE GIORGIO, Mr. Michael John, BSc FCA *1983;* 18 Clarendon Road, LONDON, W11 3AB.
•**DE GOUVEIA, Mr. Vasco Gonsalves, ACA CA(SA)** *2008;* Vasco de Gouveia Limited, 10 Lindens Close, Effingham, LEATHERHEAD, SURREY, KT24 5NZ.
DE GRAFT-HAYFORD, Mr. Alexander James, BA ACA *2010;* 23 Arncliffe Crescent, Morley, LEEDS, LS27 9DU.
DE GROOT, Mr. Andrew James, BA ACA *1999;* 55 Heathfield Road, LONDON, SW18 2PH.
DE GUINGAND, Mr. Anthony Paul, FCA *1970;* Playfoots, Bramble Reed Lane, Matfield, TONBRIDGE, TN12 7ET.
DE HAAN, Mr. Julian Jan Ivor, FCA *1972;* Southfield House, Forthampton, GLOUCESTER, GL19 4RA.
DE HAAST, Mr. Mark Richard Liddle, ACA *2006;* Level 7, Transpower House, 96 The Terrace, PO Box 1021, WELLINGTON, NEW ZEALAND.
DE JAGER, Mr. Gary Vigne, ACA CA(SA) *2011;* (Tax Fac), 1723 Freedom Avenue, Riverside, KITWE, ZAMBIA.
DE JAGER, Mr. Jonathan Geoffrey, BSc ACA *2006;* 6 Halsey Street, LONDON, SW3 2QH.
•**DE JERSEY, Mr. Steven Brian, ACA** *1997;* Ogier Fiduciary Services (Guernsey) Limited, Ogier Ogier House, St. Julians Avenue St. Peter Port, GUERNSEY, GY1 1WA.
DE JONGE, Mr. Gerald Ashley, MA FCA *1974;* 5 Judge Walk, Claygate, ESHER, SURREY, KT10 0RP.
DE KERSAINT GIRAUDEAU, Mr. Pierre Coetnempren Guy, OBE FCA *1954;* Rua Marechal Deodoro 135, Edificio Cisne Branco 52, Granja Julieta, SAO PAULO, 04738000, BRAZIL. (Life Member)
DE KEYSER, Mr. Jonathan David, BSc ACA *2010;* 55 Wrexham Road, LONDON, E3 2TJ.
•**DE KEYSER, Dr. Paul David, BSc MBBS ACA** *1989;* Paul de Keyser, 2 Constable Close, LONDON, NW11 6TY.
DE KEYSER, Mr. Theodore Robert Anthony, BSc ACA *1978;* Fashion R Ltd, 23 Old Bond Street, LONDON, W1S 4PZ.
DE LA HARPE, Mrs. Sara Ann, BSc ACA *1996;* 3 Wood End, FARNBOROUGH, HAMPSHIRE, GU14 7BA.
DE LA HAYE, Mr. Andrew Mark, BSc ACA *1996;* Cartref, Links Estate, La Rue A Don, Grouville, JERSEY, JE3 9DB.
DE LA HAYE, Mr. Joseph Michael William, MChem ACA *2010;* 7 Willow Tree Road, ALTRINCHAM, CHESHIRE, WA14 2EQ.
DE LA HAYE, Mrs. Katherine, ACA *2008;* 7 Willow Tree Road, ALTRINCHAM, CHESHIRE, WA14 2EQ.
DE LA MARE, Mr. Robert Guy, BA FCA *1975;* Ebro 2740 Oficina 805, Las Condes, SANTIAGO, CHILE.
DE LA PAZ, Mr. Edward Joseph, FCA *1970;* Calle Los Olivios, La Huerta, ALICANTE, SPAIN.
DE LA PAZ JAGGERS, Mrs. Maria Cristina Sofia, BA ACA *1992;* 765 Allen Lake Lane, SUWANEE, GA 30024, UNITED STATES.
DE LA RUE, Mr. Donald Cecil, FCA *1954;* P O Box F42583, FREEPORT, BAHAMAS. (Life Member)
DE LA RUE, Mr. Richard Paul, BA ACA *2002;* 22 Springfield Road, TEDDINGTON, TW11 9AP.
DE LA TOUCHE, Mr. Adrian, BA ACA *1995;* One, Bow Churchyard, LONDON, EC4M9DQ.
DE LA WYCHE, Mr. Peter Roylance, BA FCA *1974;* 16 Lindow Fold Drive, WILMSLOW, CHESHIRE, SK9 6DT.
•**DE LACEY, Mr. Anthony, BA FCA** *1976;* Buzzacott LLP, 130 Wood Street, LONDON, EC2V 6DL. See also Fiscal Solutions Ltd
•**DE-LACY ADAMS, Mr. Simon Downing, BA FCA** *1986;* (Tax Fac), Lovewell Blake LLP, Sixty Six, North Quay, GREAT YARMOUTH, NORFOLK, NR30 1HE.
•**DE LANDE LONG, Mr. Jonathan, FCA** *1974;* 425 East 58 Street, Apt 38E, NEW YORK, NY 10022, UNITED STATES.
DE LANGE, Mrs. Madele, ACA CA(SA) *2010;* (Tax Fac), 17 Pond Lane, Drayton, NORWICH, NR8 6PP.
DE LANGE, Mr. Matthew Felix, MA FCA *1979;* 11 St Germans Place, Blackheath, LONDON, SE3 0NN.
DE LANGE, Mr. Rudolf, ACA *2011;* 138 Cherry Hinton Road, CAMBRIDGE, CB1 7AJ.
DE LASZLO, Mr. Robert, BSc ACA *2003;* 6 Rossdale Road, LONDON, SW15 1AD.
DE LEUR, Miss. Tanne Maartje, ACA *2010;* 56a Harleyford Road, LONDON, SE11 5AY.
DE LISLE, Mr. Daniel Andros De Garis, BSc(Econ) ACA *2001;* Ruthschild Trust Guernsey Ltd, Po Box 472, St. Peter's House, Le Bordage, GUERNSEY, GY1 6AX.
DE LISSER, Mr. Ferdinand George, BA ACA *1994;* The Baltic Exchange Ltd The Baltic Exchange, 38 St. Mary Axe, LONDON, EC3A 8BH.
•**DE LONGA, Mr. Peter Charles, ACA** *1979;* de Longa & Company, Ffordd Celyn, Lon Parcwr Business Park, RUTHIN, CLWYD, LL15 1NJ.
•**DE LONGA, Mrs. Rachel Howell, BSc ACA** *1979;* de Longa & Company, Ffordd Celyn, Lon Parcwr Business Park, RUTHIN, CLWYD, LL15 1NJ.
•**DE LOOPER, Mrs. Valeriee, FCA** *1976;* 11 Montague Drive, CATERHAM, SURREY, CR3 5BY.
DE LOOZE, Miss. Emily, ACA *2011;* Flat 2/B, 2 Walton Street, ST. ALBANS, HERTFORDSHIRE, AL1 4DQ.
•**DE LORD, Mrs. Sandra Jean, BA FCA DChA** *1986;* Kingston Smith LLP, Devonshire House, 60 Goswell Road, LONDON, EC1M 7AD. See also Kingston Smith Limited Liability Partnership, Devonshire Corporate Services LLP and Kingston Smith Consulting LLP
DE LORENZO, Mr. Domenic John, ACA CA(SA) *2011;* Sabmiller House, Church Street West, WOKING, SURREY, GU21 6HS.
DE LUC, Mr. Anton Leon, BA FCA *1988;* 11D Ao Marama Place, R D 1, KERIKERI 0294, NEW ZEALAND.
DE LUCCHI, Mr. Ben, BSc(Hons) ACA *2004;* with KPMG LLP, St. Nicholas House, 31 Park Row, NOTTINGHAM, NG1 6FQ.
DE LUCCHI, Mrs. Louise Mary, BSc ACA *2005;* 6 Cromford Road, West Bridgford, NOTTINGHAM, NG2 6ES.
DE MAIO, Mrs. Kathryn Marion, BSc ACA *1993;* 23 Sheridan Way, WOKINGHAM, BERKSHIRE, RG41 3AP.
DE MALEPRADE, Mrs. Aude, ACA *2010;* Gloria Hotel Dubai, Apartment 2322, P.O. Box 502222, DUBAI, UNITED ARAB EMIRATES.
DE MARASSE ENOUF, Mr. Fabien, BCom ACA *2004;* with PricewaterhouseCoopers, 18 CyberCity, EBENE, MAURITIUS.
DE MARCO, Mr. Robert, ACA *1994;* Seaspray 12 Antonio Nani Street, TA' XBIEX XBX1084, MALTA.
DE MARGARY, Mr. Thomas George Bertram, ACA *2010;* Flat 33, Bartholomew Court, 163 Old Street, LONDON, EC1V 9NH.
DE MARTINO, Mr. John Frank, BSc FCA *1971;* 32 Roundhill Road, Hurworth, DARLINGTON, DL2 2EF.
DE MATTOS, Mr. Brian Henry, BSc FCA *1977;* 154 Bridgewater Road, BERKHAMSTED, HP4 1EE.
DE MAULEY, Lord Rupert Charles, TD FCA *1980;* Canford, Little Faringdon, LECHLADE, GLOUCESTERSHIRE, GL7 3QJ.
DE MEL, Mr. Dharshana Ruwan Harindra, BSc ACA *1982;* Thel Gobal Fund, Ch. de Blandonnet 8, 1214 Vernier, GENEVA, SWITZERLAND.
DE MEL, Mrs. Gwendalynne, BA ACA *1987;* Caversham SA, PO Box 6193, 1211 GENEVA, SWITZERLAND.
DE MEL, Mr. Nissanka Arjuna, BSc ACA *1980;* 19-3 Empire Tower, Braybrook Place, 2 COLOMBO, SRI LANKA.
•**DE MELLO, Mr. Rodney Hugh, FCA** *1968;* (Tax Fac), Rodney H. de Mello, The Orangery, 12a Lawn Road, Milford-on-Sea, LYMINGTON, HAMPSHIRE SO41 0QZ.
DE MENEZES, Mr. Anthony Michael, BSc ACA *1991;* 67 Endlesham Road, LONDON, SW12 8JY.
•**DE MERIS, Mr. Georges Hugo Constant, ACA** *1995;* Ernst & Young, Antonio Vivaldistraat 150, 1083 HP AMSTERDAM, NETHERLANDS. See also Ernst & Young Europe LLP
DE MEZA, Mrs. Karen Iris, BSc FCA *1991;* 4 Whitson Close, The Beeches High Legh, KNUTSFORD, WA16 6UD.
DE MEZA, Mr. Mark, BA ACA *1991;* 4 Whitson Close, The Beeches High Legh, KNUTSFORD, WA16 6UD.
DE MONTFORT, Mr. Roger James Harman, BA FCA *1990;* 85 MacNabb Place, OTTAWA K1L 8J5, ON, CANADA.
DE MORGAN, Miss. Dawn, BA ACA *1993;* 26 San Shek Wan, LANTAU ISLAND, HONG KONG SAR.
DE MORGAN, John Egerton Claridge, Esq OBE FCA *1956;* 17 Lady Cooper Court, Benningfield Gardens, Castle Village, BERKHAMSTED, HERTFORDSHIRE, HP4 2GY. (Life Member)
DE MORGAN, Mr. Robin Arthur, FCA *1959;* 10 Mayorfield House, Queens Road, MARLOW, BUCKINGHAMSHIRE, SL7 2PU. (Life Member)
DE MOUILPIED, Mrs. Marina Louise, ACA *1992;* Langdale Rue Cauchez, St. Martin, GUERNSEY, GY4 6NT.
DE MUNNIK, Mr. Hans, FCA *1977;* Balijeweg 4, 6874AJ WOLFHEZE, NETHERLANDS. (Life Member)
•**DE NAHLIK, Mr. Philip Adam Charles Tom Andrew Christo, BSc ACA** *1979;* Butlers Folly, Butlers Lane, Semley, SHAFTESBURY, DORSET, SP7 9AF.
DE NAZARETH, Mr. Anthony Agnelo Paul, MBA FCA AMCT *1977;* EC Capital Ltd, 7 Cork Street, LONDON, W1S 3LJ.
DE PALMA, Miss. Maria Rosa, ACA *2009;* (Tax Fac), 25 Redcliffe Close, Old Brompton Road, LONDON, SW5 9HX.
DE PAULA, Mr. Frederic Clive, CBE TD FCA JDipMA *1940;* 11 Motcombe, 62 Palace Road, EAST MOLESEY, KT8 9DW. (Life Member)
DE PAULA, Mr. Julian Frederick Jervis, FCA *1969;* Smallbrook Old Farm, Newton St Cyres, EXETER, EX5 5AZ.
DE PELET, Mr. Hubert Patrick Wentworth, BA ACA *1997;* Flat 1, 34 Victoria Road, LONDON, W8 5RG.
•**DE PEYRECAVE, Mr. Roger Francois, BSc ACA** *1984;* PricewaterhouseCoopers LLP, The Atrium, 1 Harefield Road, UXBRIDGE, UB8 1EX. See also PricewaterhouseCoopers
DE PIAN, Mr. Marcus Richard, ACA *2008;* Pricewaterhousecoopers, 1 Embankment Place, LONDON, WC2N 6RH.
DE POERCK, Mr. Bruno Daniel Martin, BSc ACA *2004;* 55 Baker Street, LONDON, W1U 8EW.
DE POERCK, Mrs. Lisa Jane, BA ACA *2004;* 10 Gravel Road, TWICKENHAM, TW2 6RH.
DE PUTRON, Mr. Ronald Anthonyy, FCA *1962;* Le Sapin, Calais, St. Martin, GUERNSEY, GY4 6AU. (Life Member)
DE QUIDT, Mr. Simon Mark Ridsdale, MA FCA *1985;* 7 Great Goodwin Drive, Merrow, GUILDFORD, GU1 2TX.
DE QUINCEY ADAMS, Mrs. Lucinda Clare, MA ACA *2001;* Vokins Barn, West Challow, WANTAGE, OXFORDSHIRE, OX12 9TN.
DE RENNES, Mr. Robert James, MSc BA ACA *1997;* 187 Douglas Road, SURBITON, KT6 7SE.
DE RENZO, Mrs. Novella, ACA *2000;* (Tax Fac), Willow House, 53 Willow Road, LONDON, NW3 1TP.
DE-RHUNE, Mr. Michael Anthony, BA ACA *1993;* (Tax Fac), 4 Stevens Lane, Claygate, ESHER, SURREY, KT10 0TE.
DE RIDDER, Ms. Jessica Diane, ACA CA(AUS) *2010;* 3/23 Glenluce Road, Blackheath, LONDON, SE3 7SD.
DE RIDDER, Mr. Robert Huibb, FCA *1977;* 5348 Windjammer Road, DELTA V4K 5A6, BC, CANADA.
DE RITIS, Miss. Joanne, BA(Hons) ACA *2011;* 86 Apartments, La Charroterie Mills, La Charroterie, St. Peter Port, GUERNSEY, GY1 1DR.
DE RIVAZ, Mr. Anthony Chevalley, MA ACA *1982;* 13 Hall Place Gardens, ST. ALBANS, AL1 3SB.
DE RIVAZ, Mr. Paul Chevalley, MA FCA *1973;* 64 Woodsford Square, LONDON, W14 8DS.
DE ROHAN, Mr. Charles Raoul, BSc ACA *1989;* The Binding Site Group Ltd, PO Box 11712, BIRMINGHAM, B14 4ZB.

DE ROZARIEUX, Mr. Mark Ian, BSc ACA *1995;* Ladywell House, Bar Road, Baslow, BAKEWELL, DERBYSHIRE, DE45 1SF.
DE RYCKMAN DE BETZ, Mr. Frederic Lj, BSc(Hons) ACA *2003;* Attic Self Storage Limited, 1 Maverton Road, Bow, LONDON, E3 2JE.
DE SACADURA, Mr. Jose Miguel Cabral Alexander, BSc(Hons) ACA *2001;* 11 Harvey Place, Cherrybrook, SYDNEY, NSW 2126, AUSTRALIA.
DE SALIS, Mr. James Edward Fane, BA ACA *1993;* Newfoundout East Reeds Lane, Southwater, HORSHAM, WEST SUSSEX, RH13 9DQ.
DE SALIS, Mr. Nicholas Charles Fane, BA FCA *1986;* 54 Foxbourne Road, LONDON, SW17 8EW.
DE SANTOS, Miss. Alison Victoria, BA ACA *1997;* Garden Flat, 217 Elgin Avenue, Maida Vale, LONDON, W9 1NH.
DE SARAM, Mr. Rex Stanley, FCA *1957;* 11 Langton Place, LONDON, SW18 5AZ. (Life Member)
DE SAXE, Mr. David Antony, FCA *1957;* Ivy Cottage, Axford, MARLBOROUGH, WILTSHIRE, SN8 2HA. (Life Member)
DE SELINCOURT, Mr. Derek Robin, FCA *1954;* The Old Farm House, West Tisted, ALRESFORD, SO24 0HJ. (Life Member)
DE SILVA, Mr. Ashok Prasanna, BSc ACA *1993;* with ICAEW, Metropolitan House, 321 Avebury Boulevard, MILTON KEYNES, MK9 2FZ.
DE SILVA, Mr. Chandana Lal, BSc FCA *1983;* 26 Anderson Road, Havelock Town, COL 05 COLOMBO, SRI LANKA.
DE SILVA, Mr. Christian Andrzej, BSc ACA *1984;* Pear Tree Cottage, High Street, Pavenham, BEDFORD, MK43 7NJ.
DE SILVA, Mr. Clive Raymond, BSc ACA *2005;* 7 Newlyn Gardens, Rayners Lane, London, HARROW, HA2 9TA.
DE SILVA, Mr. Denis Antoninuss, FCA *1972;* 37 Watling Street, ST. ALBANS, HERTFORDSHIRE, AL1 2PY. (Life Member)
DE SILVA, Mr. Dharshana Mahinda, BSc ACA *1994;* Flat 9, 46 Queens Gardens, LONDON, W2 3AA.
DE SILVA, Mr. Diresh Joseph, BSc ACA *1992;* 34 Pebworth Road, HARROW, HA1 3UD.
DE SILVA, Mr. Galappathige Priyalal Maithri, BCom ACA *1983;* 38 Greengate Road, KILLARA, NSW 2071, AUSTRALIA.
DE SILVA, Mr. Hembapura Tharanga, ACA *2002;* Barclays Internal Audit - UK Banking, Level 10, 1 Churchill Place, LONDON, E14 5HP.
•**DE SILVA, Mr. Ian, BA ACA** *2007;* Thinkfine Limited, 158 Buckingham Palace Road, LONDON, SW1W 9TR.
DE SILVA, Mr. Nalin, ACA *2008;* 6119 North Hoyne Avenue, CHICAGO, IL 60659, UNITED STATES.
DE SILVA, Mr. Romesh Charitha, BSc FCA *1994;* 107 Old Road, 10100 NAWALA, SRI LANKA.
DE SILVA, Mr. Thusitha Dharmapala, ACA *2010;* 194A High Road, Leyton, LONDON, E10 5PS.
DE SILVA, Mr. Udage Kankanamge Buddhi Sanjaya, BSc ACA *1993;* 19 Tai Hwan Close, SINGAPORE 555654, SINGAPORE.
DE SILVA WIJEYERATNE, Mr. Alphonsus John Gehan, BSc ACA *1992;* 155 Model Farm Road, 8 COLOMBO, SRI LANKA.
DE SILVA WIJEYERATNE, Mr. Anthony Lawrence Suraj, ACA *1988;* 56 Fox Valley Road, WAHROONGA, NSW 2076, AUSTRALIA.
DE SOMOGYI, Mr. Stephen Erik, MA FCA *1983;* 21 Bangalore Street, Putney, LONDON, SW15 1QD.
DE SOUSA, Mr. Ian Mario Joseph, BSc FCA *1994;* 16 Timberling Gardens, SOUTH CROYDON, Surrey, CR2 0AW.
DE SOUZA, Mr. Barrington Harold, BSc ACA *1994;* 11 Carysfort Road, LONDON, N16 9AA.
DE SOUZA, Mr. David, BA ACA *2004;* 7 Regent Close, BEDFORD, MK41 7XG.
DE SOUZA, Miss. Lindsey Penelope, LLB ACA *2002;* 4 Nigel Fisher Way, CHESSINGTON, SURREY, KT9 2SN.
DE SOUZA, Mr. Mark Jude, BA ACA *1994;* West Aish Farm, Morchard Bishop, CREDITON, DEVON, EX17 6RX.
DE SOUZA, Mr. Neville Newton, FCA *1972;* 4 Nigel Fisher Way, CHESSINGTON, SURREY, KT9 2SN.
DE SOUZA, Mr. Olegario Frederico Marino, ACA *1981;* 5 Wenlock Street, BRIGHTON, SA 5048, AUSTRALIA.
•**DE SOUZA, Mr. Ralph Albert, BCom FCA** *1974;* Leigh Carr, 72 New Cavendish Street, LONDON, W1G 8AU.
DE SOUZA, Mr. Tyson, BA ACA *2010;* Flat C, 38 Lanhill Road, LONDON, W9 2BS.
DE SOUZA, Mr. Victor Anthony Willibrord, FCA *1976;* 45 Somerset Avenue, LUTON, LU2 0PL.
DE SOYSA, Miss. Natasha, MA MPhys ACA *2006;* 3 Drake Court, 12 Swan Street, LONDON, SE1 1BH.
•**DE STE CROIX, Mr. Danny, BSc ACA** *1978;* B9 Maison Victor Hugo, Greve D'Azette, St. Clement, JERSEY, JE2 6PW.
DE STEIGER, Mr. Anthony Michael, FCA *1972;* Claypits Farm, Chuck hatch Lane, Colemans Hatch, HARTFIELD, EAST SUSSEX, TN7 4EN.
DE THAME, Mr. Michael Johnn, FCA *1972;* 116 Ernest Street, CROWS NEST, NSW 2065, AUSTRALIA.
DE VAL, Mr. Michael Thomas, BSc FCA *1973;* Hythe House, 200 Shepherds Bush Road, LONDON, W6 7NL.
DE VERE GOULD, Mr. Peter David, FCA *1966;* 3 Hillcrest Road, PURLEY, CR8 2JF.
DE VERE GOULD, Mr. William Peter, BSc(Hons) ACA *2003;* 3 Hillcrest Road, PURLEY, SURREY, CR8 2JF.
DE VEULLE, Mr. James Amice, BSc ACA *2001;* with PricewaterhouseCoopers CI LLP, Twenty Two Colomberie, St Helier, JERSEY, JE1 4XA.
DE VEULLE, Mrs. Nicola Ann, MEng ACA *2001;* La Chenaie des Bois, La Rue de Guilleaume Et D'Anneville, St. Martin, JERSEY, JE3 6DP.
DE VEULLE, Mr. Philip John, OBE MA FCA *1966;* La Vregie, Le Mont de la Guerande, St Martin, JERSEY, JE3 6DZ. (Life Member)
DE VILLIERS, Mr. John Lindsay Max, FCA CA(SA) *1965;* 29 Fourteenth Street, Parkmore, SANDTON, 2196, SOUTH AFRICA. (Life Member)
DE VILLIERS, Ms. Melanie, ACA CA(SA) *2010;* Flat 10 Sonning Court, 38 Outram Road, CROYDON, CR0 6XE.
DE VILLIERS, Mr. Tielman Francois, ACA CA(SA) *2009;* 22 Montague Street, Broughty Ferry, DUNDEE, DD5 2RD.
DE VINE, Miss. Alice, BA ACA *2003;* 1 The Grange, Brooklyn Avenue Urmston, MANCHESTER, M41 6PF.
DE VOIL, Mrs. Nina Claire, BA ACA *1989;* 90 Thornbury Road, ISLEWORTH, TW7 4LN.
DE VOIL, Mr. Philip Morley, BA FCA *1994;* with Deloitte LLP, 2 New Street Square, LONDON, EC4A 3BZ.
DE VRIES ROBBE, Mr. Alexander, MA FCA AMCT *1998;* Barclays Bank Plc, 1 Churchill Place, LONDON, E14 5HP.
DE VROOME, Mr. Peter John, MA FCA *1976;* 39A Avenue Gardens, Mill Hill Park, Acton, LONDON, W3 8HB.
DE WET, Mrs. Diane Maureen, ACA CA(SA) *2010;* 59 Floral Farm, Canford Magna, WIMBORNE, DORSET, BH21 3AT.
DE WHALLEY, Mr. Graham Claree, FCA *1950;* Grove House, Castle Lane, STEYNING, BN44 3GA. (Life Member)
DE WILDE, Mr. Phillipe James, MBA BCom ACA *1996;* Tumblers Chase, St. Hilary, COWBRIDGE, SOUTH GLAMORGAN, CF71 7DP.
DE WILDE, Mrs. Rachel Lloyd, BA ACA *1996;* Tumblers Chase, St. Hilary, COWBRIDGE, SOUTH GLAMORGAN, CF71 7DP.
DE WILDE, Mr. Thomas Charles, FCA *1964;* Willow Farm, Dereham Road, Garvestone, NORWICH, NR9 4QT.
DE WILTON, Mr. Jonathan, BSc ACA *1993;* (Tax Fac), Grant Thornton Hartwell House, 55-61 Victoria Street, BRISTOL, BS1 6FT.
DE WINTER, Mrs. Antonia, BA ACA *1995;* Haagwinde 121, 1391 ABCOUDE, NETHERLANDS.
•**DE WINTER, Mrs. Michelle Anna, BSc ACA** *1992;* De Winter Smith LLP, 22 The Green, Flore, NORTHAMPTON, NN7 4LG.
DE WINTON, Mr. Francis William Peter, FCA *1971;* 52 Montrose Avenue, Whitton, TWICKENHAM, TW2 6HB.
DE WIT, Mr. Francois Maree, ACA CA(SA) *2010;* The British Land Co Ltd, York House, 45 Seymour Street, LONDON, W1H 7LX.
•**DE WIT, Mr. Terence Peterr, FCA** *1975;* de Wit & Co, Audit House, Oakwellgate West, GATESHEAD, NE8 2AU.
•**DE YOUNG, Mr. Simon Louis, MPhil BA ACA** *2003;* PricewaterhouseCoopers LLP, 1 Embankment Place, LONDON, WC2N 6RH. See also PricewaterhouseCoopers
DE ZOETE, Mr. Charles Miles Fulton, BCom ACA CTA MBA *2002;* GPO Box 1, CENTRAL, HONG KONG ISLAND, HONG KONG SAR.
DE ZOUCHE, Mr. Richard Bearder, OBE FCA *1955;* Corran, Hinderton Lane, Neston, NESTON, CH64 9QA. (Life Member)
DE ZOUCHE, Miss. Victoria Mary, BA BSc ACA *2002;* 14 Crystal Glen, Llanishen, CARDIFF, CF14 5QJ.
DE ZOYSA, Mr. Salinda, BSc ACA *2005;* 8 Penn Close, UXBRIDGE, MIDDLESEX, UB8 3AW.
DE ZOYSA, Mr. Thishan Sudeshna, BA(Hons) ACA *2002;* with MCR, 43-45 Portman Square, LONDON, W1H 6LY.
DEACON, Mr. Andrew Robert, FCA *1972;* 25 Holland Park Avenue, LONDON, W11 3RW.
DEACON, Mr. Anthony Kenneth Victor, FCA *1963;* 32 Hardwicke Road, Narborough, LEICESTER, LE19 3LU. (Life Member)
DEACON, Mr. Benjamin Nigel, MEng ACA *2007;* 22 Drybridge Hill, WOODBRIDGE, SUFFOLK, IP12 4HB.
DEACON, Ms. Clare Rachel, BSc FCA *1991;* 2 Fernlea Cottage, Pindale Road, Castleton, HOPE VALLEY, S33 8WU.
DEACON, Mr. Daniel, BSc ACA *2010;* 8a Harrison Rd, SOUTHAMPTON, HAMPSHIRE, SO17 3TJ.
DEACON, Mr. David Ian, BSc FCA *1992;* Elmbank House, 2 Church Lane, Bardsey, LEEDS, LS17 9DH.
DEACON, Mr. David John, FCA *1974;* Veterinary Laboratories Agency, New Haw, ADDLESTONE, KT15 3NB.
DEACON, Miss. Fenella Mary, BSc ACA *1998;* Wellers Farm, Marringdean Road, BILLINGSHURST, WEST SUSSEX, RH14 9EJ.
•**DEACON, Mr. Graham Albert, FCA** *1975;* Deacon Jewell Limited, 7 West Street, LISKEARD, CORNWALL, PL14 6BW.
•**DEACON, Mr. Graham Arthur, FCA** *1969;* McCabe Ford Williams, Market House, 17 Hart Street, MAIDSTONE, KENT, ME16 8RA.
•**DEACON, Mr. Ian, FCA** *1975;* 1 Belmont, Pencoed, BRIDGEND, MID GLAMORGAN, CF35 6PF.
DEACON, Miss. Jennifer Louise, BSc ACA *2008;* Georgenstrasse 13, 80799 MUNICH, GERMANY.
DEACON, Mrs. Joanne, ACA *1993;* Mellanoweth House, Gweek, HELSTON, CORNWALL, TR12 6TX.
•**DEACON, Mr. Jonathan Roger, FCA** *1980;* Buckfast Abbey Trust, Buckfast Abbey, Buckfast, BUCKFASTLEIGH, DEVON, TQ11 0EE.
DEACON, Mr. Jonathan Spencer, BA ACA *1993;* The Bungalow, Langford Lane, Langford, BRISTOL, BS40 5DF.
DEACON, Mr. Joseph Clifford, BCom FCA *1954;* Apartment 22, Castle Keep, Scott Lane, WETHERBY, WEST YORKSHIRE, LS22 6NY. (Life Member)
DEACON, Mr. Michael John, BEng FCA *1995;* 52 Camellia Avenue, Rogerstone, NEWPORT, NP10 9JA.
DEACON, Mr. Michael Vernon, FCA *1966;* 706 Doonside, Leicester RdBedford Gardens, BEDFORDVIEW, GAUTENG, 2007, SOUTH AFRICA. (Life Member)
DEACON, Mr. Nicholas Charles, FCA *1978;* Caulcott House, 28 South Street, Caulcott, BICESTER, OXFORDSHIRE, OX25 4NE.
DEACON, Mr. Oliver James Joseph, MSci ACA *2007;* 63 Eccles Road, LONDON, SW11 1LX.
DEACON, Mr. Richard William, FCA *1960;* Blackmoor Paddock, Green Lane, Shamley Green, GUILDFORD, GU5 0RD. (Life Member)
DEACON, Mr. Robert William, FCA *1954;* 11 Redbrook Way, Adlington, MACCLESFIELD, SK10 4NF. (Life Member)
•**DEACON, Mrs. Sandra Karen, FCA** *1985;* (Tax Fac), Deacon's, The Stables, Shipton Bridge Farm, Widdington, SAFFRON WALDEN, ESSEX CB11 3SU.
DEACON, Mr. Stuart James, BSc ACA *1999;* with Ernst & Young LLP, 1 More London Place, LONDON, SE1 2AF.
DEADMAN, Mr. Brian Christopher, BSc FCA *1983;* 19 Jones Close, BRACKLEY, NORTHAMPTONSHIRE, NN13 6JD.
DEADMAN, Mrs. Jane Elizabeth, BSc FCA *1986;* Oakfield Cottage, 32 Stocks Lane, East Wittering, CHICHESTER, PO20 8NJ.
DEADMAN, Mr. Julian Russell, BA ACA *1997;* 17 The Oaks, WEST BYFLEET, KT14 6RN.
DEAK, Miss. Kathleen Monica, BA ACA *2010;* 57 Arundel Road, PEACEHAVEN, EAST SUSSEX, BN10 8RP.
DEAKIN, Mr. Alan, FCA *1968;* Greenacre, 1 Kingsway, Huncoat, ACCRINGTON, BB5 6LA.
DEAKIN, Mrs. Alice Gail, LLB ACA *2000;* Deloitte & Touche Saltire Court, 20 Castle Terrace, EDINBURGH, EH1 2DB.
DEAKIN, Mr. Andrew David, BA ACA *1999;* Phoenix Equity Partners, 33 Glasshouse Street, LONDON, W1B 5DG.
•**DEAKIN, Mrs. Anne Catherine, FCA** *1971;* (Tax Fac), ADH Consulting, 28 Tilmore Road, PETERSFIELD, HAMPSHIRE, GU32 2HH.
DEAKIN, Mrs. Anne Marie, BSc ACA *1982;* (Tax Fac), Wordsworth House, 10 Laureates Walk, Ladywood Rd. Four Oaks Est, SUTTON COLDFIELD, B74 2QF.
DEAKIN, Dr. Anthony Grayham, PhD MA MSc ACA *1980;* 3 Utkinton Close, Oxton, PRENTON, CH43 2GP.
•**DEAKIN, Mr. Ashley Martin, MBA BA ACA** *1990;* 1st Contact Accounting, Castlewood House, 77-91 New Oxford Street, LONDON, WC1A 1DG. See also 1st Contact Accountants Limited
DEAKIN, Miss. Catherine Rosemary, BSc FCA *1977;* White House Farm, Church Lane, Kenton, STOWMARKET, IP14 6JH.
DEAKIN, Mr. James Michael, BA FCA *1966;* 3 The Pavilions, Magazine Road, Shoeburyness, SOUTHEND-ON-SEA, SS3 9QA.
DEAKIN, Mr. John Alexander, FCA *1957;* PO Box 380, BEDFORDVIEW, GAUTENG, 2008, SOUTH AFRICA. (Life Member)
DEAKIN, Mr. John Frederick, FCA *1966;* Dorset House, Meadow Gate, Prestwood, GREAT MISSENDEN, HP16 0JN. (Life Member)
DEAKIN, Mr. Julian, BEng ACA *1986;* 22 Douglas Road, HALESOWEN, B62 9HR.
DEAKIN, Mrs. Lydia, BA ACA *2008;* Studio 1, 20 Albert Street, LONDON, NW1 7NU.
DEAKIN, Mr. Matthew John, ACA *1988;* HSBC Building, No25 Bongrae-Dong, Shung-Ku, SEOUL, KOREA REPUBLIC OF.
DEAKIN, Mr. Michael John, BSc FCA *1983;* Southlands, 472 Leeds Road, Idle, BRADFORD, BD10 9AA.
DEAKIN, Mr. Nicholas Peter, BSc ACA *1992;* Mole Hill, 20 Howard Road, REIGATE, SURREY, RH2 7JE.
DEAKIN, Mr. Norman Harry, FCA *1963;* 199 Melton Road, Edwalton, NOTTINGHAM, NG12 4BU.
DEAKIN, Mr. Philip, BA ACA *2002;* Exact Mortgage Experts, 2 Charter Court Broadlands, WOLVERHAMPTON, WV10 6TD.
DEAKIN, Mr. Philip James, BA ACA *2007;* 1 Norbury Grove, SOLIHULL, B92 8TT.
DEAKIN, Mr. Philip James, MPhil BA FCA *1999;* 41 Bickerton Road, Headington, OXFORD, OX3 7LT.
DEAKIN, Mr. Philip Matthew, BAcc ACA *2000;* 12 Wellington Court, Spencers Wood, READING, RG7 1BN.
DEAKIN, Mr. Simon Lloyd, BSc ACA *1998;* 23 Churchill Crescent, ALLAMBIE HEIGHTS, NSW 2100, AUSTRALIA.
•**DEAKIN, Mr. Terence Gordon, FCA** *1981;* T.G. Deakin, 36 Berkeley, LETCHWORTH GARDEN CITY, HERTFORDSHIRE, SG6 2HA.
•**DEAKIN WRAY, Mrs. Susan, BSc ACA FCCA** *1987;* Wray & Company, 36 Berkeley, LETCHWORTH GARDEN CITY, HERTFORDSHIRE, SG6 2HA.
DEAL, Mr. Peter Alexander, FCA *1965;* Sunny Cottage, Bishopstone, SWINDON, SN6 8PW. (Life Member)
DEAL, Ms. Sophie Karen, BA ACA *1993;* Flat 5, 41 Clapham Common North Side, LONDON, SW4 0AA.
DEALTRY, Miss. Sarah Lee, BSc ACA *2008;* 25 The Gardens, Radford Semele, LEAMINGTON SPA, WARWICKSHIRE, CV31 1TH.
DEALY, Mr. Nigel Derrick, BSc FCA *1980;* FLAT 46C, Tower 1 Robinson Place, 70 Robinson Road, MID LEVELS, HONG KONG SAR.
DEAMER, Mr. Kevin Joseph, ACA *1981;* 18 Richmond Close, Frimley, CAMBERLEY, GU16 8NR.
DEAN, Mr. Andrew, BA(Hons) ACA *2011;* 102 Heath Road, WIRRAL, MERSEYSIDE, CH63 2HE.
DEAN, Mr. Andrew David, BA(Hons) FCA *1994;* 9 Shoreswood Way, Greenside, Newcastle Great Park, NEWCASTLE UPON TYNE, NE13 9AE.
DEAN, Mr. Andrew Paul, BSc ACA *2008;* Craegmoor Group, Craegmoor House, Perdiswell Park, WORCESTER, WR3 7NW.
DEAN, Mr. Anthony Gordon, BSc ACA *1982;* Paddock House, Manor Road, Penn, HIGH WYCOMBE, HP10 8JA.
DEAN, Mr. Anthony Michael, BSc FCA CF *1984;* 9 Ridgway Road, FARNHAM, SURREY, GU9 8NN.
DEAN, Mr. Anthony Richard, BA(Hons) ACA *2005;* Aviva Plc, 5th Floor, Wellington Row, YORK, YO90 1WR.
DEAN, Mr. Barry Malcolm, FCA *1973;* Sandpit Cottage, 4 High Street, Ditchling, HASSOCKS, BN6 8TA.
DEAN, Mr. Barry Simon, BSc FCA *1990;* 11 Whetstone Lane, WALSALL, WS9 8PB.
DEAN, Mr. Benjamin Christopher Jacob, BSc(Hons) ACA *2006;* 44a High Street, THAMES DITTON, KT7 0SA.
DEAN, Miss. Carolyn Louise, BSc ACA *1999;* 15 Langley Crescent, LONDON, E11 2LZ.
DEAN, Mrs. Carys Elizabeth Meryl, ACA *2005;* 167 Central Avenue, CANVEY ISLAND, ESSEX, SS8 9QP.
DEAN, Mr. Cedric Peter, FCA *1951;* 9 Park Field, Menston, ILKLEY, LS29 6LP. (Life Member)

•DEAN, Mr. Charles Robert, BSc ACA *1979;* (Tax Fac), Charles R. Dean BSc ACA, Limbers Mead, Old Barn Lane, South Chailey, LEWES, BN8 4AS.
DEAN, Mr. Christian Richard, BSc ACA *2005;* 209 Beaumanor Road, LEICESTER, LE4 5QE.
•DEAN, Mr. Christopher Neil, BSc FCA *1983;* Christopher Dean & Co, Ivy Cottage, Bakers Lane, Tadmarton, BANBURY, OX15 5TB.
DEAN, Ms. Claire Elizabeth, BSc FCA *1995;* The Lodge, 120 Bolingbroke Grove, LONDON, SW11 1DA.
DEAN, Mr. Colin John, FCA *1969;* Mortimer House, The Street, Shurlock Row, READING, BERKSHIRE, RG10 0PR.
•DEAN, Mr. David John, FCA *1972;* D J Dean, 62 Reservoir Road, Elburton, PLYMOUTH, PL9 8NJ.
•DEAN, Mrs. Deborah Marie, BA(Hons) ACA CTA *2002;* Deborah Dean, 30 Postern Road, Tatenhill, BURTON-ON-TRENT, STAFFORDSHIRE, DE13 9SJ.
DEAN, Mr. Douglas Terence, BSc FCA *1988;* Flat A5 Trinity Gate, Epsom Road, GUILDFORD, GU1 3PJ.
•DEAN, Miss. Elizabeth Rose, BA FCA *1983;* ERD Services Limited, West Lodge, Hall Court, Bishops Frome, WORCESTER, HEREFORDSHIRE WR6 5BY. See also Elizabeth R Dean
DEAN, Mrs. Gail Louise, BSc ACA *1998;* with Audit Inspection Unit, Financial Reporting Council, 5th Floor, Aldwych House, 71-91 Aldwych, LONDON WC2B 4HN.
DEAN, Mrs. Georgina Louise, BA(Hons) ACA *2001;* 216 Walmley Road, SUTTON COLDFIELD, WEST MIDLANDS, B76 2PR.
DEAN, Mr. Gordon Douglas, MA FCA *1963;* 10 Honeywood House, 28 Alington Road, Canford Cliffs, POOLE, BH14 8LZ. (Life Member)
DEAN, Mr. Haider Omar, BA(Hons) ACA *2001;* 110 Bodley Road, NEW MALDEN, KT3 5QH.
DEAN, Mr. Ian Alasdair Barry, BA ACA *1993;* 20643 Hannington Lane, KATY, TX 77450-5034, UNITED STATES.
DEAN, Mr. Ian Alexander, ACA *2008;* 2 Rangers Square, LONDON, SE10 8HR.
DEAN, Mr. James Nicholas Anthony, MMath(Hons) BSc(Hons) ACA FCCA ATII *1996;* 11 Albert Park Mews, Albert Park Road, MALVERN, WR14 1HN.
•DEAN, Mr. James William, BA FCA *1983;* Ernst & Young LLP, 1 More London Place, LONDON, SE1 2AF. See also Ernst & Young Europe LLP
DEAN, Mrs. Jane, BSc ACA *2007;* 37 Lock Road, Broadheath, ALTRINCHAM, CHESHIRE, WA14 4HB.
DEAN, Mrs. Jennifer Clare, BA ACA *2001;* 9 Talisman Street, HITCHIN, HERTFORDSHIRE, SG4 0EZ.
DEAN, Mrs. Jennifer Elizabeth, MSc ACA *2006;* 25 Maybury Avenue, Durkar, WAKEFIELD, WEST YORKSHIRE, WF4 3PW.
DEAN, Mrs. Jennifer Sarah, BA ACA *2010;* 24 Ellis Road, CROWTHORNE, RG45 6PU.
DEAN, Mrs. Joanne, BSc ACIB ACA *1997;* Leabridge House, Farrs Lane, East Hyde, LUTON, LU2 9PY.
DEAN, Mr. John Robert, FCA *1976;* 7 Syresham Gardens, HAYWARDS HEATH, WEST SUSSEX, RH16 3LB.
DEAN, Mr. John Ronald, FCA *1963;* Marden House, 2 West Ridings, East Preston, LITTLEHAMPTON, BN16 2TD. (Life Member)
DEAN, Mrs. Judy Gillian, BSc ACA *1983;* Paddock House, Manor Road, HIGH WYCOMBE, HP10 8JA.
DEAN, Mr. Julian Mark, BA ACA *1992;* 24 Ottawa Drive, LIPHOOK, GU30 7TR.
DEAN, Mr. Kenneth, FCA *1969;* Pinebrook, Bouth, ULVERSTON, LA12 8JB.
DEAN, Mrs. Kimberley, BA ACA *1989;* 7 Woodbine Close, LISAROW, NSW 2250, AUSTRALIA.
DEAN, Mr. Marcus Edward, FCA *1972;* 8 Mayfield Road, Timperley, ALTRINCHAM, WA15 7SZ.
DEAN, Mr. Martin John, BA ACA *1988;* 22 Townley Street, ST LUCIA, QLD 4067, AUSTRALIA.
DEAN, Mr. Michael John, BSc ACA *1989;* Melli-Beese-Str. 10, FRANKFURT AM MAIN, GERMANY.
DEAN, Mr. Michael Matthew, BA ACA *1998;* Tembi, Knipp Hill, COBHAM, KT11 2PE.
DEAN, Miss. Natalie Anne, BA ACA *2005;* Flat 22, 2 Stanley Road, LONDON, SW19 8RL.
DEAN, Mr. Neville Arthur, FCA *1957;* 26 The Oval, Scartho, GRIMSBY, DN33 3NN. (Life Member)
DEAN, Mr. Nicholas William, BA ACA *2009;* 37 Lock Road, ALTRINCHAM, CHESHIRE, WA14 4HB.
DEAN, Mr. Nigel Robert, BA ACA *1990;* 9 Chieveley Drive, TUNBRIDGE WELLS, TN2 5HF.
DEAN, Mr. Paul Anthony, FCA *1976;* with Glover Stanbury & Co, 27 Bridgeland Street, BIDEFORD, EX39 2PZ.
ⒹDEAN, Mr. Peter Christopher, CA *2003; (CA Scotland 1981);* Carrington Dean Group Limited, 135 Buchanan Street, GLASGOW, G1 2JA.
DEAN, Mr. Peter Robert, BA ACA *1993;* 23 Field Lane, Willersey, BROADWAY, WORCESTERSHIRE, WR12 7QB.
DEAN, Mr. Philip Graham, BSocSc ACA *1995;* Stonehage SA, Rue du Puits-Godet 12, PO Box 763, 2002 NEUCHATEL, SWITZERLAND.
DEAN, Mr. Philip Kenneth, BCom ACA *1980;* avenue Henri Pirard 5, 1350 ORP LE GRAND, BELGIUM.
•DEAN, Mr. Philip Nicholas, BA FCA *1992;* Hicks and Company, Vaughan Chambers, Vaughan Road, HARPENDEN, AL5 4EE.
DEAN, Mrs. Rachel Louise, BA(Hons) ACA CTA *2005;* 13 Elmgrove Road, WEYBRIDGE, SURREY, KT13 8NZ.
DEAN, Mrs. Rayna, MA FCA *1975;* Moss Farm Moss Lane Over Tabley, KNUTSFORD, CHESHIRE, WA16 0PH.
DEAN, Mr. Richard James, BSc ACA *1987;* 123 Aveling Close, PURLEY, CR8 4DY.
DEAN, Mr. Richard John, FCA *1996;* 21 Treesdale Road, HARROGATE, NORTH YORKSHIRE, HG2 0LX.
DEAN, Mr. Rob, LLB ACA *2005;* 13 Elmgrove Road, WEYBRIDGE, KT13 8NZ.
DEAN, Mr. Robert Malcolm, BSc ACA *1996;* 4 Bittell Lane, Barnt Green, BIRMINGHAM, B45 8NS.
DEAN, Miss. Sarah, ACA *2011;* 6 Long Plough, Aston Clinton, AYLESBURY, BUCKINGHAMSHIRE, HP22 5HA.
DEAN, Mrs. Sharon Julie, BSc ACA *1996;* Walkers Snack Foods Ltd, 1530 Arlington Business Park Theale, READING, RG7 4SA.
DEAN, Mr. Simon Nicholas, BA ACA *1988;* U B S AG, 100 Liverpool Street, LONDON, EC2M 2RH.
DEAN, Mr. Stephen Andrew, BA ACA *2005;* Glover Stanbury & Co, 30 Bear Street, BARNSTAPLE, DEVON, EX32 7DD.
DEAN, Mr. Stephen Michael, BA ACA *1992;* 19 The Byfrons, Boundary Road, FARNBOROUGH, Hampshire, GU14 6SE.
•DEAN, Mr. Stephen Tregellas, BA(Hons) ACA DChA *2004;* with Baker Tilly UK Audit LLP, 1st Floor, 46 Clarendon Road, WATFORD, WD17 1JJ.
DEAN, Mrs. Susan Caroline, BA(Hons) ACA CTA *2001;* with KPMG LLP, 15 Canada Square, LONDON, E14 5GL.
DEAN, Mr. Sydney, FCA *1957;* 118 Buckstone Avenue, LEEDS, LS17 5ET. (Life Member)
DEAN, Mrs. Theresa, ACA *2009;* Hamlin Electronics Europe Limited, Lakeside, 200 Old Chapel Way Broadland Business Park, NORWICH, NR7 0WG.
DEAN, Mr. Timothy James, MA ACA *1988;* La Longue Maison Rue Des Bailleuls, St. Andrew, GUERNSEY, GY6 8XB.
DEANE, Mr. Alexander, BA ACA *2006;* Flat 4, 130-132 Knollys Road, LONDON, SW16 2JU.
DEANE, Mr. Anthony David, BA FCA *1992;* Flat 6, 344 London Road, LEICESTER, LE2 2PJ.
•DEANE, Mr. Carl, BSc FCA *1994;* Smith & Williamson Ltd, Portwall Place, Portwall Lane, BRISTOL, BS1 6NA. See also Nexia Audit Limited
DEANE, Mr. David John, BA ACA *2009;* Reliance Security Services Ltd Boundary House, Cricket Field Road, UXBRIDGE, MIDDLESEX, UB8 1QG.
DEANE, Mrs. Frances Mary, BSc ACA *1992;* 1764 Autumn Crescent, PICKERING L1V 6X2, ON, CANADA.
DEANE, Mr. Geoffrey Richard, ACA *2008;* 42 Osborne Road, LONDON, N4 3SD.
DEANE, Mr. James Andrew, MA ACA *1997;* Chancerygate Group Ltd The Old Barn, Fulford Farm Culworth, BANBURY, OXFORDSHIRE, OX17 2HL.
DEANE, Mr. Jean-Pierre, FCA *1968;* 2 Hatherley Road, Kew Gardens, RICHMOND, TW9 3LH.
DEANE, Mr. John Ernest, BA FCA *1964;* 19a Woodside Road, LONDON, SE25 5DP.
DEANE, Mr. Joseph, BSc ACA *1995;* 61 Cleveland Avenue, DARLINGTON, DL3 7HF.
DEANE, Mrs. Julie Patricia, MA ACA *1992;* 24 Green End, Fen Ditton, CAMBRIDGE, CB5 8SX.
DEANE, Mr. Martin Constantine, BSc ACA *1989;* 30 Whitefield Road, Stockton Heath, WARRINGTON, WA4 6LZ.
DEANE, Mr. Patrick Joseph, BA ACA *1990;* 19 Karori Crescent, ORAKEI, AUCKLAND, NEW ZEALAND.
•DEANE, Mr. Peter Michael, FCA *1970;* (Tax Fac), Peter Deane & Co, 21 Guildford Drive, Chandlers Ford, EASTLEIGH, SO53 3PR.
•DEANE, Mr. Richard John, BSc FCA *1990;* Richard Deane FCA, 58 Oldfields Close, LEOMINSTER, HEREFORDSHIRE, HR6 8TL.
DEANE, Mr. Simon Nicholas Newenham, BA FCA *1981;* Accountancy Plus Gordon Court, 4 Craigie Drive, PLYMOUTH, PL1 3JB.
DEANE, Mr. Thomas Gerald, BSc ACA *1991;* 12 Nottingham Road, Bottesford, NOTTINGHAM, NG13 0AP.
DEANEY, Mr. David Michael, BSc ACA *1991;* 200 West Street, NEW YORK, NY 10282, UNITED STATES.
DEANS, Mr. Andrew Mark, BCom ACA CTA *1990;* 32 Courtmount Grove, PORTSMOUTH, PO6 2BN.
DEANS, Mr. Matthew David, MA(Hons) ACA *2001;* 34 Crown Street, HARROW, HA2 0HR.
DEANS, Mrs. Nicola Jane, BA ACA *1995;* 1 Slim Road, Royal Military Academy, CAMBERLEY, GU15 4NL.
DEANS, Mr. Robin William Lauder, LLB ACA *1994;* (Tax Fac), Carderry Orpington by Pass, Badgers Mount, SEVENOAKS, TN14 7AG.
DEANS, Mrs. Sarah Elizabeth Naomi, BA ACA *1997;* Citigroup Centre, 33 Canada Square, LONDON, E14 5LB.
DEAR, Mr. Anthony James, ACA *2009;* Berkeley First, Berkeley House, 19 Portsmouth Road, COBHAM, SURREY, KT11 1JG.
•DEAR, Mr. David Michael, ACA *1980;* (Tax Fac), Haines Watts, Airport House, Purley Way, CROYDON, CR0 0XZ.
DEAR, Mr. John David Robert, BSc FCA *1980;* 127 Marlborough Crescent, Montreal Park, SEVENOAKS, TN13 2HN.
DEAR, Mr. Martin John, BSc ACA *1986;* 1 Long Acres Close, Coombe Dingle, BRISTOL, BS9 2RF.
DEAR, Mr. Paul Joseph, MSc ACA *2004;* 10 Mulberry Close, TUNBRIDGE WELLS, KENT, TN4 9XR.
DEAR, Mrs. Rosemary Mabel, BA FCA *1975;* 14 Pavilion House, Copers Cope Road, BECKENHAM, BR3 1DS.
DEAR, Miss. Sally, BA ACA *1991;* 12 Mount Pleasant, Nangreaves, BURY, BL9 6SP.
•DEARDEN, Mr. Antony Vincent, FCA *1968;* Eastbury House, Penn Lane, Stathern, MELTON MOWBRAY, LE14 4JA.
DEARDEN, Mrs. Helen Clare, BA ACA *1989;* (Tax Fac), Quarry Cottage, Stannage Lane, Churton, CHESTER, CH3 6LE.
DEARDEN, Mrs. Marianne Lee Shon, ACA *1993;* 5 Worcester Villas, HOVE, EAST SUSSEX, BN3 5TA.
DEARDEN, Mr. Mark Stephen, BA FCA *1999;* 31 Whiteway Close, Whimple, EXETER, EX5 2TL.
DEARDEN, Mr. Martyn James, FCA *1975;* Lychgate, Easebourne Lane, MIDHURST, GU29 9BN.
•DEARDEN, Mr. Phillip Edward, BA FCA ATII *1988;* (Tax Fac), PKF (Isle of Man) LLC, PO Box 16, Analyst House, Douglas, ISLE OF MAN, IM99 1AP. See also Northwest Trust Company Limited
DEARDS, Mrs. Amanda, BSc ACA *1987;* 54 Rose Crescent, PERTH, PH1 1NT.
DEARDS, Mr. David Alun, BA ACA *1987;* Hollybrook, 29 Wilson Street, PERTH, PH2 0EX.
DEARDS, Mr. Michael James Campbell, BSc ACA *1997;* Ericsson Canada Inc., 5255 Satellite Drive, MISSISSAUGA L4W 5E3, ON, CANADA.
DEARING, Mr. Adrian Spencer, BEng ACA *1993;* 128 Mere Road, WIGSTON, LEICESTERSHIRE, LE18 3RL.
DEARING, Mrs. Elizabeth Dawn, BA ACA *1988;* Unicorn Administration Ltd, 2nd Floor MKA House, 36 King Street, MAIDENHEAD, BERKSHIRE, SL6 1NA.
DEARING, Mr. Graham John, ACA *1998;* 13 Parkway, CRAWLEY, WEST SUSSEX, RH10 3BP.
•DEARING, Mr. James John, BA ACA *2002;* Mojo Financial Services Limited, Brookland Cottage, Birchgrove Road, Glais, SWANSEA, SA7 9ER.
DEARING, Mrs. Julie, BSc ACA *1992;* 18 Cobblestones, Hempstead, GILLINGHAM, KENT, ME7 3NT.
DEARING, Mrs. Kathryn Margaret, BSc FCA *1989;* (Tax Fac), Prichard & Co, 74 High Street, FISHGUARD, DYFED, SA65 9AU.
•DEARING, Mrs. Kelly Ann, LLB ACA *2002;* Mojo Financial Services Limited, Brookland Cottage, Birchgrove Road, Glais, SWANSEA, SA7 9ER.
DEARING, Mr. Philip, MA FCA *1974;* Lindale, Doncaster Road, Thrybergh, ROTHERHAM, S65 4NU.
DEARING, Mr. Richard Andrew, BSc FCA *1992;* 18 Cobblestones, Hempstead, GILLINGHAM, KENT, ME7 3NT.
•DEARING, Mr. Robert, BEng FCA *2000;* Chancery (UK) LLP, Chancery Pavilion, Boycott Avenue, Oldbrook, MILTON KEYNES, MK6 2TA. See also Chancery Hopkins LLP
•DEARING, Mr. Robert Stanley, FCA *1969;* Robert S. Dearing, Meadowbank, Parsonage Lane, Farnham Common, SLOUGH, SL2 3PA.
•DEARLE, Mr. Robin John Henry, BA ACA *1987;* Nicolaou Dearle (Audit) LLP, Unit 13, Highpoint Business Village, Henwood, ASHFORD, KENT TN24 8DH. See also Nicolaou Dearle & Co (2005) Ltd
DEARLOVE, Mr. John Steven, ACA *1982;* 2 Overdale, ASHTEAD, KT21 1PW.
•DEARMAN, Mr. David Mark, BA FCA *1996;* PKF (UK) LLP, Farringdon Place, 20 Farringdon Road, LONDON, EC1M 3AP.
DEARMAN, Mr. James Michael, MSc BA ACA *2008;* 145 Uxendon Hill, WEMBLEY, MIDDLESEX, HA9 9SH.
DEARMAN, Mr. John Charles, FCA *1954;* 649 Beverley High Road, HULL, HU6 7JJ. (Life Member)
•DEARN, Mr. Kenneth Raymond, FCA *1975;* Avanti Fitted Kitchens Ltd Avanti House, Hayes Lane, STOURBRIDGE, DY9 8RD.
DEARN, Mr. Matthew, BA ACA *2005;* 28 Blenheim Way, MORETON-IN-MARSH, GL56 9NA.
DEARNLEY, Mr. John Nigel, BSc ACA *1989;* North British Trust Hotels Ltd, 1 Queen Charlotte Lane, EDINBURGH, EH6 6BL.
DEARNS, Mr. Bill, FCA *1965;* Appletree Cottage, Little Preston, DAVENTRY, NORTHAMPTONSHIRE, NN11 3TF. (Life Member)
DEARSLEY, Mr. Arthur Mark, BA ACA *1986;* 66 Camden Park Road, CHISLEHURST, KENT, BR7 5HF.
DEARSLEY, Mrs. Helen Veronica, BSc ACA *1988;* 9 Denmark Avenue, Wimbledon, LONDON, SW19 4HF.
DEARSLEY, Mr. Trevor Anthony, ACA FCCA *2009;* Yali, La Grande Route Des Sablons, Grouville, JERSEY, JE3 9FR.
DEARTH, Miss. Sara, BA ACA *2000;* Calle de Cuestablanca 138, 28108 ALCOBENDAS, SPAIN.
DEARY, Mr. Mark Damien, ACA *1988;* 133 Boulevard National, 92500 RUEIL MALMAISON, FRANCE.
DEAS, Mr. Gordon David, MA(Hons) ACA CTA *2001;* 23 Onedin Point, 22 Ensign Street, LONDON, E1 8JT.
DEASEY, Mr. Anthony Paul, FCA *1972;* 458 Brickworks Lane, SEVERNA PARK, MD 21146, UNITED STATES.
DEASEY, Mr. Stephen Gregory, FCA *1974;* 74 King Edward Road, BARNET, EN5 5AU.
DEASY, Mr. Timothy, BSc ACA *1990;* GLOBAL INVESTMENT MARKETING SA, 27 RUE DE LA CROIX-D-OR, 1204 GENEVA, SWITZERLAND.
DEAVILLE, Mr. David Mark, BSc ACA *1996;* Pelham Farm, Bottom House, LEEK, ST13 7QJ.
DEAVILLE, Mr. Steven Barrie, BSc ACA *1988;* Manchester Football Club Ltd Old Trafford, Sir Matt Busby Way, MANCHESTER, M16 0RA.
DEAVILLE-POWNER, Miss. Jennifer, ACA *2011;* 19 Whytings, Mannings Heath, HORSHAM, WEST SUSSEX, RH13 6JZ.
DEAVILLE-POWNER, Mr. Matthew Charles, ACA *2008;* 5 Thornbury Avenue, LEEDS, WEST YORKSHIRE, LS16 5RN.
•DEAVIN, Mr. Hugh, FCA *1975;* Deavin & Co, 3 Russell-Cotes Road, BOURNEMOUTH, BH1 3AB.
DEAY, Mr. Iain, ACA *2007;* 1 Maritime Square #10-33A/B Harbourfront Centre, SINGAPORE 099253, SINGAPORE.
DEAZELEY, Mr. Brian James, BSc FCA *1971;* 2172 Dunvegan Avenue, OAKVILLE L6J 6P1, ON, CANADA.
DEB, Mr. Aaron Romano, BSc ACA *2009;* Flat 3, Fairwood Court, 33 Fairlop Road, Leytonstone, LONDON, E11 1BJ.
DEBATTISTA, Mr. Darren James, MA ACA *1994;* 57 Porthamal Road, CARDIFF, CF14 6AQ.
DEBATTISTA, Mr. Desmond Anthony Joseph, FCA *1992;* 31 Peto Avenue, COLCHESTER, CO4 5WH.
DEBATTISTA, Mrs. Elizabeth Jane, BSocSc ACA *2002;* 1 Curtyn Close, ABINGDON, OXFORDSHIRE, OX14 1SE.
DEBEERST, Miss. Lieve Maria Monique, ACA *2009;* 104 Douglas Road, ESHER, KT10 8BG.
•DEBELL, Mr. Anthony Mark, BA FCA *1986;* PricewaterhouseCoopers LLP, 10-18 Union Street, LONDON, SE1 1SZ. See also PricewaterhouseCoopers
DEBENHAM, Mr. Bruce Francis, BSc ACA *1993;* 71 Cheltenham Street, MALVERN, SA 5061, AUSTRALIA.
DEBENHAM, Mr. Malcolm John, FCA *1973;* 9 Beacon Avenue, DUNSTABLE, LU6 2AD.

Members - Alphabetical **DEBENHAM - DELL**

DEBENHAM, Mr. Nicholas James, FCA *1958;* Heybridge House, Roman Road, INGATESTONE, ESSEX, CM4 9AE. (Life Member)

DEBENHAM, Mr. Robin John Nelson, MBA BSc FCA *1982;* Debenham & Co, 5 Elouera Road, AVALON, NSW 2107, AUSTRALIA.

DEBNAM, Mrs. Helen Denise, BA ACA *1998;* 24 Turnham Green, NORWICH, NORFOLK, NR7 0TU.

•DEBNAM, Mr. Jack Wellesley, FCA *1970;* Redington, 13 Green Lane, WATFORD, WD19 4NL.

•DEBNAM, Mr. Nicholas James, BSc FCA *1990;* KPMG, 8/F Prince's Building, 10 Chater Road, CENTRAL, HONG KONG ISLAND, HONG KONG SAR.

DEBNEY, Ms. Ruth Kristeen, BA ACA *1992;* 16 Poppleton Hall Gardens, Nether Poppleton, YORK, YO26 6LE.

DEBONO, Mr. David George, FCA *1974;* 259 St Paul Street, VALLETTA VLT 1213, MALTA.

DEBRAY, Miss. Asoka, FCA *2000;* Flat 2, 10b Manor Park, LONDON, SE13 5RN.

•DEBSON, Mr. Jon Godfrey, FCA *1976;* (Tax Fac), Debson & Co., Galley House, Second Floor, Moon Lane, BARNET, HERTFORDSHIRE EN5 5YL.

DEBSON, Mr. Spencer William, BA ACA *1989;* 9 Rowan Walk, LONDON, N2 0QJ.

DEBUR, Mrs. Rita Ramanlal, ACA *1996;* 28 Washington Park, MAPLEWOOD, NJ 07040, UNITED STATES.

DECAEN, Mr. Laurent Jacques Raymond, ACA *2008;* MAZARS, 10A rue Henri M. Schnadt, L-2530 LUXEMBOURG, LUXEMBOURG.

DECHAINE, Mr. Kevin Stuart, ACA *2006;* 94 Linden Road, Coxheath, MAIDSTONE, KENT, ME17 4RA.

DECHAMPS, Mr. Alexander, ACA *2008;* 69 Faringford Road, LONDON, E15 4DP.

•DECKER, Mr. Paul John, BA FCA *1985;* Nyman Libson Paul, Regina House, 124 Finchley Road, LONDON, NW3 5JS.

DECOSTER, Mr. Peter Jules, FCA *1977;* Newman DeCoster & Co LLP, 111 Broadway, Suite 1504, NEW YORK, NY 10006-1924, UNITED STATES.

DECRUZ-YOUNG, Mr. John Peter, BA(Hons) ACA *2009;* Flat 5, 23 Balham Hill, LONDON, SW12 9DY.

•DEDAT, Mr. Akbar, ACA *1984;* Crystal Business Services Limited, 264 Stoney Stanton Road, COVENTRY, CV1 4FP.

DEDAT, Mr. Mohammed, ACA *1986;* 50 Wellesley Road, ILFORD, IG1 4JZ.

•DEDAT, Mr. Yusuf, FCA *1992;* Clay Ratnage Strevens & Hills, Suite D, The Business Centre, Faringdon Avenue, ROMFORD, RM3 8EN. See also Clay Ratnage Daffin & Co Ltd

DEDHAR, Mr. Diamond Abdulaziz Moosa, FCA *1975;* 76 Nestow Drive, Nepean, OTTAWA K2G 4L8, ON, CANADA.

DEDMAN, Miss. Alexandra Louise, BSc ACA *1993;* Kent Business School University of Kent at Canterbury, Parkwood Road, CANTERBURY, CT2 7PE.

•DEDMAN, Mr. Christopher George, FCA *1971;* HW, 117-119 Cleethorpe Road, GRIMSBY, LINCOLNSHIRE, DN31 3ET. See also Walker, Smyth & Marshall

DEDMAN, Mr. Christopher William, MChem ACA *2010;* 2nd floor flat, 23 St. John's Grove, LONDON, N19 5RW.

DEDMAN, Mr. Denis George, FCA *1965;* 23 Uphill Road, Mill Hill, LONDON, NW7 4RA. (Life Member)

DEDMAN, Mr. Jamie Paul Lewis, ACA *2009;* 9 Ploughmans Close, LONDON, NW1 0XH.

DEDMAN, Mrs. Jennifer Ruth, FCA *1988;* The Pollards, Cramptons, Wellhouse Road Beech, ALTON, GU34 4AY.

DEDMAN, Mr. John Arnold, BSc FCA *1976;* D'Icart, Sark, GUERNSEY, GY9 0SB.

DEDMAN, Miss. Katrina, ACA *2003;* Superdrug Stores Plc, 118 Beddington Lane, CROYDON, CR0 4TB.

DEE, Mr. Alan Trond, BA ACA *1993;* 6 Belle Vue Road, WARE, HERTFORDSHIRE, SG12 7BD.

DEE, Mr. Alexander, BA ACA *1995;* Flat C, 2 Strathray Gardens, LONDON, NW3 4NY.

DEE, Mr. David Thomas, FCA *1956;* 10 Baldwin Way, Swindon, DUDLEY, DY3 4PF. (Life Member)

DEE, Mr. Derek Adrian, BCom ACA *1986;* 53 Brook Court, Monkstown, DUBLIN, COUNTY DUBLIN, IRELAND.

DEE, Mr. John Robert Land, FCA *1963;* Shepherd's Cottage, Marsh Lane, Curridge, THATCHAM, RG18 9EB.

DEE, Mr. Jonathan Philip, BA ACA *1993;* 77 Hanover Terrace, BRIGHTON, BN2 9SP.

DEE, Miss. Katherine Louise, BSc ACA DChA *2002;* with Begbies Chettle Agar, Epworth House, 25 City Road, LONDON, EC1Y 1AR.

DEE, Mr. Neil Andrew, BA ACA *1993;* Combined Property Control, 66 Waterpark Road, SALFORD, M7 4JL.

DEE, Mr. Nicholas Charles, BA FCA *1976;* (Tax Fac), Blanefield, 2A Bois Avenue, AMERSHAM, BUCKINGHAMSHIRE, HP6 5NS.

•DEE, Mr. Nicholas Francis, BSc ACA *1992;* Hazlewoods LLP, Staverton Court, Staverton, CHELTENHAM, GLOUCESTERSHIRE, GL51 0UX.

DEE, Mr. Robert Leslie, BA FCA *1994;* with Deloitte LLP, Athene Place, 66 Shoe Lane, LONDON, EC4A 3BQ.

DEE, Mr. Stephen Hugh Minett, FCA *1974;* 13 Blunts Wood Road, HAYWARDS HEATH, RH16 1ND.

DEE, Mr. Stuart Craig, BSc ACA *1997;* 45 Milliners Way, BISHOP'S STORTFORD, HERTFORDSHIRE, CM23 4GG.

DEEBLE, Ms. Helen, ACA *1986;* P & O Ferries Ltd Channel House, Channel View Road, DOVER, KENT, CT17 9TJ.

DEED, Mr. Robert John, MA(Oxon) ACA *1996;* Deed Consulting Limited, 40 Arden Grove, Ladywood, BIRMINGHAM, B16 8HQ.

•DEEGAN, Mr. Anthony Peter, PhD FCA *1985;* Anthony Peter Deegan, Via Verdi 64, 27058 VOGHERA, ITALY.

DEEGAN, Ms. Catherine Mary, BSc ACA *1993;* 121 Discovery Drive, Kings Hill, WEST MALLING, ME19 4DS.

DEEGAN, Ms. Claire Lindsay, BA ACA *1999;* 35 Hollytree Road, Woolton, LIVERPOOL, L25 5PB.

DEEGAN, Ms. Fiona, ACA *2009;* 205 Wykeham Road, READING, RG6 1PL.

DEEHAN, Mr. James Patrick, BA FCA *1970;* 16 Alexandra Road, Clifton, BRISTOL, BS8 2DD. (Life Member)

DEEHAN, Mr. Paul Gerard, BA ACA *1992;* 8 Woodlea, ALTRINCHAM, CHESHIRE, WA15 8WH.

DEEKS, Mrs. Christine Elizabeth, BSc ACA *1982;* with Geoffrey Hodge, 30 Market Place, HITCHIN, SG5 1DY.

•DEEKS, Mr. Douglas John Arthur, FCA *1961;* The Hatters, 60 St Helens Wood Road, HASTINGS, TN34 2QR.

DEEKS, Mr. Jeremy Spencer, BSc(Hons) ACA ARCM *1995;* 29 Matthews Chase, Binfield, BRACKNELL, RG42 4UR.

DEEKS, Mr. Robert, BSc ACA *2005;* 19 Albion Road, CHRISTCHURCH, DORSET, BH23 2JQ.

DEEKS, Ms. Sarah Elizabeth, LLB FCA *1986;* 31 Hollybush Way, Linton, CAMBRIDGE, CB21 4XH.

DEELEY, Miss. Jennifer Caroline, BA(Hons) ACA *2011;* Flat 1, Nirvana Place, 384 Winchester Road, SOUTHAMPTON, SO16 7BB.

DEELEY, Mr. Kevin, BSc FCA *1994;* 5 Greenbury Close, Chorleywood, RICKMANSWORTH, WD3 5QT.

DEELEY, Mr. Martin John, FCA *1974;* 316 Blacksmith Way, PETERBOROUGH K9L 0B5, ON, CANADA.

DEELEY, Mr. Max Howard, BA ACA *2005;* 89 Gloucester Avenue, LONDON, NW1 8LB.

DEELEY, Mr. Richard Allen Barnett, BA FCA *1993;* 2 Kirkland Drive, Chilwell, NOTTINGHAM, NG9 6LX.

DEELEY, Miss. Samantha, ACA *2010;* with B&P Accounting Limited, Kingsley House, Church Lane, Shurdington, CHELTENHAM, GL51 5TQ.

DEELEY, Mr. Stephen, BA ACA *2007;* 114 Cyprus Street, LONDON, E2 0NN.

DEELEY, Mr. Terence Francis, BEd FCA *1974;* 50 Ridgeway, Guiseley, LEEDS, LS20 8JA.

•DEEMING, Mrs. Mary Jane, BA ACA *1986;* Mary Deeming, 34 Queensway, Sawston, CAMBRIDGE, CB22 3DJ.

DEEMING, Mr. Paul Jonathan, BA ACA *1993;* 22 Old Brompton Road, LONDON, SW7 3DL.

DEEN, Mr. Abdullatif Khalid Abdullatif Mohammed, ACA *2003;* PO Box 18687, MANAMA, BAHRAIN.

DEENA, Mr. Ashvin, BSc ACA *2009;* 37 Milliners Court, Lattimore Road, ST. ALBANS, HERTFORDSHIRE, AL1 3XT.

DEENEY, Mr. Paul Mark, BA ACA *1995;* Al Motahedoon LLC, PO Box 81577, Zawia Street, TRIPOLI, LIBYAN ARAB JAMAHIRIYA.

DEENY, Mr. James, BA ACA *1986;* 24 The Roystons, Berrylands, SURBITON, KT5 8HH.

DEENY, Mr. Michael Eunan Maclarnon, MA FCA *1970;* 60 Bedwin Street, SALISBURY, SP1 3UW.

DEERING, Mr. Jeremy Robert John, MA ACA *1989;* Roscarrack Vean, Roscarrack Road, Maen Valley, Goldenbank, FALMOUTH, CORNWALL TR11 5BL.

DEERING, Mr. Julian Malcolm St John, BSc ACA *1997;* 7th Floor, 7 Birchin Lane, LONDON, EC3V 9BW.

DEERING, Mr. Mathew William, LLB ACA *2002;* 30 West Park Avenue, LEEDS, LS8 2EB.

DEERING, Mr. Stephen, BA ACA *2002;* 36 Half Acre Road, Hanwell, LONDON, W7 3JJ.

DEERING, Miss. Tamara, ACA *2010;* 41 Wibbersley Park, Urmston, MANCHESTER, M41 6JG.

DEESON, Ms. Nicola Jane, BA ACA *1992;* 45 St Georges Road, FARNHAM, SURREY, GU9 8NA.

DEETH, Mr. Adam John, ACA *1995;* 14 Field Close, Blythe Bridge, STOKE-ON-TRENT, ST11 9LD.

DEETHER, Mr. John Frederick Charles, FCA *1967;* 37 Chadwell, WARE, SG12 9LD.

DEEX, Miss. Amanda Louise, BSc ACA *2000;* 22 Blackmore Way, Wheathampstead, ST. ALBANS, HERTFORDSHIRE, AL4 8LJ.

DEFREYNE, Mr. Colin Stephen, BSc ACA *1987;* 5 Nihill Crescent, Mission Bay, AUCKLAND, NEW ZEALAND.

•DEFRIES, Mr. Gerald Michael, FCA CF *1972;* Defries Weiss (Accountants) Limited, 311 Ballards Lane, North Finchley, LONDON, N12 8LY.

DEFRIEZ, Mrs. Linda Mavis, BSc ACA *1978;* 6 Ridgway Gardens, Wimbledon, LONDON, SW19 4SZ. (Life Member)

•DEFROAND, Mr. David Martin, FCA *1984;* KPMG LLP, 15 Canada Square, LONDON, E14 5GL. See also KPMG Europe LLP

DEFTERAS, Mr. Nicholas Ioannis, BSc(Econ) ACA *2003;* 8 Santorinis Street, Psimolofou, 2630 NICOSIA, CYPRUS.

DEFTY, Mrs. Emma Louise, BSc ACA *2006;* Arkells Brewery Ltd Kingsdown, Hyde Road, SWINDON, SN2 7RU.

•①DEFTY, Mr. Ian Mark, ACA FCCA *2007;* Kingston Smith & Partners LLP, 105 St. Peters Street, ST. ALBANS, HERTFORDSHIRE, AL1 3EJ. See also Kingston Smith Limited Liability Partnership

DEGENHARDT, Miss. Clare, BA ACA *1989;* 22 Clare Mead, Rowlegde, FARNHAM, GU10 4BJ.

DEGNAN, Dr. Ian Alan, PhD BSc ACA *1995;* Singel 436E, 1017AV AMSTERDAM, NETHERLANDS.

DEGNAN, Miss. Josephine, ACA *2004;* Punch Taverns Ltd Jubilee House, Second Avenue Centrum One Hundred, BURTON-ON-TRENT, STAFFORDSHIRE, DE14 2WF.

DEGRAFT-JOHNSON, Miss. Anne Marie, ACA *2008;* Newnham North Apartment, 4A Admiral Walk, SOUTHAMPTON SN01, BERMUDA.

DEGRAVES, Mrs. Caroline, BA(Hons) ACA *2002;* 43 Amersham Hill Drive, HIGH WYCOMBE, BUCKINGHAMSHIRE, HP13 6QX.

DEGROOT, Mrs. Annabelle, BA ACA *1999;* Post.Net 177, P Bag E835, LUSAKA, ZAMBIA.

DEGROVE, Mrs. Helen Jennifer, ACA *1991;* 24 Scrub Rise, BILLERICAY, CM12 9PG.

DEGROVE, Mr. Matthew Kennedy, BSc ACA AMCT *1998;* BP International Ltd, 20 Canada Square, LONDON, E14 5NJ.

DEHAYEN, Mr. Alexander George, BA ACA *2006;* Flat 15 Swinburne House, Roman Road, LONDON, E2 0HJ.

DEHGAMIA, Mr. Zuber, BA ACA *2003;* Al Sufouh Road, DUBAI, BOX 73137, UNITED ARAB EMIRATES.

DEHIRI, Mr. Arun, BA ACA *1995;* Rajvilas, Kewferry Drive, NORTHWOOD, MIDDLESEX, HA6 2NT.

•DEIGHAN, Mr. Alan William, BSc ACA *1983;* Deighan Perkins LLP, 6th Floor, Newbury House, 890-900 Eastern Avenue, ILFORD, ESSEX IG2 7HH.

DEIGHAN, Mr. Colm, ACA ACMA *2009;* 1A Tower Point, Tower Road, Strawberry Hill, LONDON, TW1 4PG.

DEIGHTON, Mrs. Carolyn Mairi, MA ACA *1993;* 8 Boswall Road, EDINBURGH, EH5 3RH. (Life Member)

DEIGHTON, Mr. David Raymond, FCA *1968;* 38 Holly Gardens, West End, SOUTHAMPTON, SO30 3RW.

DEIGHTON, Mr. Douglas William, BSc ACA *1989;* 26 Evelyn Avenue, TORONTO M6P 2Y9, ON, CANADA.

DEIGHTON, Miss. Eleanor Jane, MA ACA CTA *2001;* 46 Trelleck Road, READING, RG1 6EN.

DEKKER, Mr. John Charles, FCA *1957;* 63 Eriswell Road, Lakenheath, BRANDON, IP27 9AH. (Life Member)

DEL MAR, Mr. Sam Richard, BA(Hons) ACA *2001;* The Octagon, Middleborough, COLCHESTER, ESSEX, CO1 1TG.

DELACAVE, Mr. Bruno Daniel Geoffrey, ACA *1988;* Norwich School, 71a The Close, NORWICH, NR1 4DD.

DELAHAYE, Mr. Terence Donald, FCA *1962;* 49 Iron Walls Lane, Tutbury, BURTON-ON-TRENT, STAFFORDSHIRE, DE13 9NH. (Life Member)

•DELAHUNT, Mr. Anthony Henry, FCA *1963;* A H Delahunt, Wembury, 4A Green Lane, PURLEY, CR8 3PG.

•DELAHUNTY, Mr. John Joseph, FCA *1971;* (Tax Fac), Delahunty & Co, 4 Eagle Terrace, DUNDRUM 14, COUNTY DUBLIN, IRELAND.

DELALOYE, Mrs. Jacqueline Ann, BSc ACA *2000;* 27 Dyer Road, WOKINGHAM, BERKSHIRE, RG40 5PG.

DELALOYE, Mr. Marc Charles, MA ACA *2000;* 27 Dyer Road, WOKINGHAM, BERKSHIRE, RG40 5PG.

•DELAMERE, Miss. Louise Anne, BSc ACA *1990;* (Tax Fac), Bright Grahame Murray, 131 Edgware Road, LONDON, W2 2AP.

DELANEY, Mr. Adam, MA ACA *2007;* 8 Victoria Terrace, MUSSELBURGH, MIDLOTHIAN, EH21 7LW.

DELANEY, Mrs. Anna Clare, BSc ACA *2005;* KPMG LLP One Snowhill, Snow Hill Queensway, BIRMINGHAM, B4 6GH.

DELANEY, Mr. Arnold Thomas, FIHT FCA *1968;* 120 rue de Courcelles, 75017 PARIS, FRANCE.

DELANEY, Mr. Barry Hubert, FCA *1969;* Le Millefiori, 1 Rue Des Genets, MC 98000 MONTE CARLO, MONACO.

DELANEY, Mr. Denis Michael, FCA *1955;* Caixa Postal 118, Ubatuba, SAO PAULO, 11680-970, BRAZIL. (Life Member)

•DELANEY, Mr. James Stephen, BSc ACA *2003;* 64 Webster Avenue, KENILWORTH, WARWICKSHIRE, CV8 2EJ.

DELANEY, Miss. Jeanette, MSc ACA *2003;* Roselands, Mayfield Lane, WADHURST, TN5 6HX.

•DELANEY, Mr. John Joseph, FCA *1983;* Bourne & Co, 3 Charnwood Street, DERBY, DE1 2GY.

DELANEY, Mr. John Michael, BA ACA *2005;* Sainsbury's Supermarkets Ltd, North View, Walsgrave Triangle, COVENTRY, CV2 2SJ.

•DELANEY, Mrs. Julia Catherine, BA FCA *1994;* with PricewaterhouseCoopers, 1 East Parade, SHEFFIELD, S1 2ET.

DELANEY, Mr. Nicholas John, BA FCA *1994;* Lyons Davidson, 51 Victoria Street, BRISTOL, BS1 6AD.

•DELANEY, Mr. Peter John, FCA CTA *1970;* Deeks Evans, 3 Boyne Park, TUNBRIDGE WELLS, TN4 8EN.

DELANEY, Mr. Stephen Edward, BA ACA *1979;* 21 Holland Avenue, Knowle, SOLIHULL, B93 9DW.

DELANGLE, Mr. Eric, BA ACA *1993;* 16 Wool Road, LONDON, SW20 0HW.

•DELANY, Mr. Ian Richard, BA ACA *1997;* Hayton Accounts, 20 Hayton Close, Bramingham, LUTON, LU3 4HD.

DELAP, Mrs. Joanne Mary, BSc ACA *1993;* 130 Old Woolwich Road, LONDON, SE10 9PR.

•DELAUNAY, Mr. Francis Paul, FCA *1958;* F.P. Delaunay, 49 Beggarmans Lane, KNUTSFORD, WA16 9BA.

DELBAERE, Mr. Francois, ACA *2009;* Unit 9 Park Plaza, Battlefield Enterprise Park, SHREWSBURY, SY1 3AF.

DELBRIDGE, Mr. Martin Trevor, MSc BA FCA FRSA *1977;* Oak Trees, Roundwood Lane, Lindfield, HAYWARDS HEATH, WEST SUSSEX, RH16 1SJ.

DELBRIDGE, Mr. Richard, MBA BSc FCA *1966;* 48 Downshire Hill, LONDON, NW3 1NX.

DELDERFIELD, Mr. Gordon Basil, FCA *1959;* 68 Holywell Drive, LOUGHBOROUGH, LE11 3JZ. (Life Member)

DELDERFIELD, Mr. Nigel William, FCA *1974;* Berridale, 140 Harnath's Lane, TABOR, VIC 3289, AUSTRALIA.

DELEAY, Mr. Martin Roy, BA ACA *1992;* 7th Floor St Vincent House, 30 Orange Street, LONDON, WC2H 7HH.

DELEAY, Mrs. Sarah, BA ACA *1992;* Qinetiq, Cody Technology Park, Old Ively Road, FARNBOROUGH, HAMPSHIRE, GU14 0LX.

DELEHANTY, Mr. Barry Michael, BCom ACA *1997;* Lavender Cottage, Finchampstead, WOKINGHAM, RG40 4JR.

DELEHANTY, Mrs. Victoria, MEng ACA *1997;* Lavender Cottage, Finchampstead, WOKINGHAM, RG40 4JR.

DELF, Mr. Michael John, BA ACA *2005;* 6 Sunflower Close, ST. HELENS, MERSEYSIDE, WA9 4ZT.

•DELF, Mr. Peter James, BA FCA *1973;* (Tax Fac), Corporate Management Services Limited, 16 Park View, Winchmore Hill, LONDON, N21 1QX.

•DELGADO, Mr. Daniel, MA ACA *2002;* Deloitte Limited, PO Box 758, Merchant House, 22-24 John Mackintosh Square, GIBRALTAR, GIBRALTAR.

•DELICATA, Miss. Claire, BSc ACA *2000;* Cadham & Carter Limited, 7 Lethbridge Road, SWINDON, SN1 4BY.

•DELIGIANNIS, Mr. Christos, ACA *2005;* with Deloitte Hadjipavlou Sofianos & Cambanis S.A, 3a Fragoklissias & Granikou Str, Maroussi, 15125 ATHENS, GREECE.

DELL, Mr. Anthony Michael, BSc FCA *1986;* 1 Park Lodge, Bishops Down Park Road, TUNBRIDGE WELLS, KENT, TN4 8XR.

DELL, Mr. Graeme John, MA ACA *1992;* 72 Mount Ararat Road, RICHMOND, SURREY, TW10 6PN.

•**DELL, Mrs. Hillary Janice, FCA** *1984;* B2B, 82/84 High Street, Stony Stratford, MILTON KEYNES, MK11 1AH.

•**DELL, Mr. Paul, FCA** *1990;* Alexander Ash & Co Ltd, 1st Floor, Bristol & West House, 100 Crossbrook Street, Cheshunt, WALTHAM CROSS HERTFORDSHIRE EN8 8JJ.

DELL, Mr. Richard Frederick, BSc ACA *1988;* Lukannon, Broadview Road, LOWESTOFT, SUFFOLK, NR32 3PL.

DELL'ERA, Mr. Efrem, MSc ACA *2010;* PricewaterhousCoopers SA, Via della Posta 7, 6900 Lugano, LUGANO, SWITZERLAND.

DELLA, Mr. Martin James, BSc ACA *1999;* 12 Longfield Road Fair Oak, EASTLEIGH, HAMPSHIRE, SO50 7LX.

DELLA-PORTA, Mr. Gerald Barry, FCA *1959;* 21b Abercromby Place, EDINBURGH, EH3 6QE. (Life Member)

•**DELLAL, Mr. David, FCA** *1959;* Dellal & Co., 5 Park Drive, LONDON, SW14 8RB.

DELLAL, Mr. Ronald, FCA *1972;* 22a Rosemont Road, LONDON, NW3 6NE.

DELLAR, Mrs. Angela Marie, BA ACA *1995;* 12 Brook Close, Great Totham, MALDON, CM9 8PE.

DELLAR, Mr. John Howard, FCA *1970;* 25 Fairmead Avenue, HARPENDEN, AL5 5UD.

DELLAR, Mr. Paul George, BSocSc ACA *1992;* 12 Brook Close, Great Totham, MALDON, ESSEX, CM9 8PE.

DELLAR, Mr. Peter George, FCA *1967;* 515 BD Des Horizons, Vallauris, 06220 CANNES, FRANCE.

DELLER, Mr. Adam, ACA *2009;* 3 Bellflower Close, WIDNES, CHESHIRE, WA8 9EB.

DELLER, Mr. Adrian Francis, BSc ACA *2003;* ACS Business Process Solutions Limited, 160 Queen Victoria Street, LONDON, EC4V 4AN.

DELLER, Mr. David Andrew, BA FCA *1990;* 52a Prince of Wales Drive, LONDON, SW11 4SF.

DELLER, Miss. Diane Frances, BCom FCA *1986;* (Tax Fac), with Larking Gowen, King Street House, 15 Upper King Street, NORWICH, NR3 1RB.

DELLIERE, Mr. John Peter, FCA *1968;* The White House Ltd, Unit B36, Barwell Business Park, Leatherhead Road, CHESSINGTON, SURREY KT9 2NY.

DELLIS, Ms. Anna Louise, BA ACA *2002;* 3i Investments plc, 16 Palace Street, LONDON, SW1E 5JD.

DELLIS, Mr. Jeremy Andrew James, BA ACA *1999;* 39 Manchuria Road, LONDON, SW11 6AF.

DELLOW, Mrs. Jennifer Claire, BA ACA *1999;* 32 Barley Hills, BISHOP'S STORTFORD, HERTFORDSHIRE, CM23 4DS.

DELMAN, Mr. Ivor Jeremy, FCA *1952;* 48 Murray Crescent, PINNER, MIDDLESEX, HA5 3QE. (Life Member)

DELMAR, Mr. John Conning, BA ACA *1984;* XL Services UK Ltd, XL House, 70 Gracechurch Street, LONDON, EC3V 0XL.

DELMEGE, Mr. Antony David, FCA *1961;* 15 Mulberry Avenue, Cosham, PORTSMOUTH, PO6 2QX.

•**DELMEGE, Mr. Stuart, ACA** *2001;* SPD Accountants Limited, First Floor, Hampshire House, 169 High Street, SOUTHAMPTON, SO14 2BY. See also Hayhursts

DELMONTE, Mr. Harry, FCA *1956;* 13 Temple Mead Close, STANMORE, HA7 3RG. (Life Member)

DELVART, Miss. Lydie Beatrice, ACA *2001;* 36 chemin des Bleds, Watterdel, 62380 SENINGHEM, FRANCE.

•**DELVE, Mr. Andrew Richard, BA ACA** *1985;* Smith Cooper, Wilmot House, St James Court, Friar Gate, DERBY, DE1 1BT. See also F B 40 Limited

DELVE, Mrs. Christine, BA(Hons) ACA *2011;* 4 Jibbs Meadow, Bramley, TADLEY, RG26 5DZ.

•**DELVE, Mr. David Eifion, BSc FCA** *1981;* Bollands, Minerva Mill, Station Road, ALCESTER, WARWICKSHIRE, B49 5ET.

DELVE, Mrs. Elizabeth Jill, BA ACA *1985;* Smith Cooper, Bermuda House, Crown Square, First Avenue, BURTON-ON-TRENT, STAFFORDSHIRE DE14 2TB.

DELVE, Mrs. Emily Anne, ACA *2004;* 31 Robert Davy Road, EXETER, EX2 7AX.

DELVE, Mr. Martin Christopher, BA ACA *1992;* Alliance Boots, 2 The Heights, Brooklands, WEYBRIDGE, SURREY, KT13 0NY.

DELVIG, Mr. Pavel, MA ACA *2007;* Flat 3, 44 St. John's Grove, LONDON, N19 5RP.

DEMACK, Mr. John Geoffrey, FCA *1968;* 10 Pendlebury Close, Longton, PRESTON, LANCASHIRE, PR4 5YT.

DEMAIN, Mr. Mark, ACA *2008;* 27 Catherine Drive, SUTTON COLDFIELD, B73 6AX.

DEMAIN, Mr. Terry, BA(Hons) ACA *2001;* 5 Howard Avenue, Grove, WANTAGE, OX12 7PS.

DEMAINE, Mr. John George, BA ACA *1986;* Rookery Farm, Balchins Lane, Westcott, DORKING, SURREY, RH4 3LL.

DEMAN, Mr. Nicholas Alexander, BSc ACA *1998;* 69 Alexandra Road, THAMES DITTON, KT7 0QS.

DEMBY, Mrs. Nicola Anne, BSc ACA *1989;* 59 Church Road, RICHMOND, SURREY, TW10 6LX.

DEMBY, Mr. Paul David, BA ACA *1982;* 41 Woodside Park Road, LONDON, N12 8RT.

DEME, Mr. Mark, FCA *1980;* County Gate Properties, The Tannery, Crossgoats, Beacon Road, Ditchling, HASSOCKS WEST SUSSEX BN6 8XB.

DEMENIS, Mr. Alexander John, ACA *2009;* The Holt, Lower Aisholt, BRIDGWATER, SOMERSET, TA5 1AS.

DEMET, Mr. Paul, BA ACA *1979;* 119 London Road, Raunds, WELLINGBOROUGH, NN9 6DB.

DEMETRIADES, Mr. Andreas, BSc ACA *1988;* 3 Ezekias Papaioannou street, Flat 41, 1075 NICOSIA, CYPRUS.

DEMETRIADES, Mr. Christoforos Savva, BSc ACA *1990;* 6 Epias Avenue, Engomi, 2411 NICOSIA, CYPRUS.

DEMETRIADES, Mr. Marios, BSc ACA CFA *1996;* 14 Apostolou Varnava Yeri, 2200 NICOSIA, CYPRUS.

DEMETRIADES, Mr. Marios Ph, ACA *2008;* Patraikou No 27 Str, Palouriotisa, 1048 NICOSIA, CYPRUS.

DEMETRIADOU, Miss. Katerina Photi, ACA *2003;* 8 Nikiforou Foka street, Latsia, 2236 NICOSIA, CYPRUS.

DEMETRIADOU, Miss. Maria Ioannou, BA FCA *1987;* 28 Erechthiou Street, 2121 Aclanzia, NICOSIA, CYPRUS.

DEMETRIOU, Mr. Agisilaos Evangelou, FCA *1974;* Agisilaos E. Demetriou FCA, 9 Marathovounou Str, P.O. Box 53159, 3071 LIMASSOL, CYPRUS.

DEMETRIOU, Mr. Alexis, BSc ACA *2006;* 3 Mesogiou Street, Strovolos, 2060 NICOSIA, CYPRUS.

•**DEMETRIOU, Mr. Andreas, ACA** *1980;* Ernst & Young Cyprus Limited, Nicosia Tower Centre, 36 Byron Avenue, P.O Box 21656, 1511 NICOSIA, CYPRUS. See also Ernst & Young Europe LLP

DEMETRIOU, Miss. Christina, ACA *2010;* 14 Thiras Street, Ayios Dometios, 2360 NICOSIA, CYPRUS.

DEMETRIOU, Mr. Constantinos, BA ACA *2007;* (Tax Fac), 11 Makedonitissis Street, Makedonitissa, 2417 NICOSIA, CYPRUS.

DEMETRIOU, Mr. Costas, BSc ACA *2010;* 45 Ebrington Road, HARROW, MIDDLESEX, HA3 0LS.

DEMETRIOU, Miss. Demetra, BSc ACA *2011;* 2 Digeni Akrita, Psevdas, 7649 LARNACA, CYPRUS.

•**DEMETRIOU, Mr. Dimitrakis George, FCA** *1984;* (Tax Fac), Haines Watts, 2nd Floor, Argyll House, 23 Brook Street, KINGSTON UPON THAMES, SURREY KT1 2BN. See also Haines Watts Wimbledon LLP

DEMETRIOU, Ms. Elena, ACA *2011;* 19 Kritonos Street, Strovolos, 2028 NICOSIA, CYPRUS.

DEMETRIOU, Mr. George Kyriakou, BSc ACA CF *1987;* 21 Ipparchou Street, 3027 LIMASSOL, CYPRUS.

DEMETRIOU, Ms. Joanna, ACA *2011;* 2Parodos Litous, Ayia Phyla, 3116 LIMASSOL, CYPRUS.

DEMETRIOU, Mr. Louis, FCA *1954;* Flat 302 20 Lefconos, 2064 Strovolos, 2064 NICOSIA, CYPRUS. (Life Member)

•**DEMETRIOU, Ms. Margarita, BA FCA** *1988;* (Tax Fac), Vittis & Co, 21 Hillfield Park, Winchmore Hill, LONDON, N21 3QJ.

DEMETRIOU, Mr. Michale Sotiris, FCA *1965;* Waggoners, Hayes Lane, East Budleigh, BUDLEIGH SALTERTON, EX9 7DA.

•**DEMETRIOU, Mr. Photis, BSc ACA** *1983;* 8 Loggou, Strovolos, 2027 NICOSIA, CYPRUS.

DEMETRIOU, Mr. Stelios, BSc(Econ) ACA CF *2001;* 8 Grevenon street, 2112 NICOSIA, CYPRUS.

DEMETRIOU, Mr. Stelios, BSc ACA *2008;* 32 Vrisides Street, Kapsalos, 3087 LIMASSOL, CYPRUS.

DEMETRIOU, Mr. Theodoros, BA ACA *2005;* 9A Argostoliou Street, Agia Fyla, Lefkothea, 3117 LIMASSOL, CYPRUS.

DEMETRIOU, Miss. Theodosia, BSc ACA CTA *2001;* with KPMG LLP, 15 Canada Square, LONDON, E14 5GL.

DEMETRIOU, Mr. Yiangos C, BSc ACA *1983;* Central Bank of Cyprus, P. O. Box 25529, 1395 NICOSIA, CYPRUS.

DEMETZ, Miss. Esther Mary, BSc ACA *1996;* 6 Oak Tree Gardens, BROMLEY, BR1 5BH.

•**DEMEZA, Miss. Kirsty Lisa, ACA** *2009;* 21 Salisbury Road, Chingford, LONDON, E4 6TA.

DEMOSTHENOUS, Mr. Andreas, BA ACA *1999;* 22 Ravenstone Road, LONDON, N8 0JT.

DEMOSTHENOUS, Mr. Demos, BA ACA *2004;* FLAT 201, NEARCHOU COURT 8, 7A MESIMVRIAS STREET, AGIOS ATHANASIOS, 4100 LIMASSOL, CYPRUS.

DEMOSTHENOUS, Mr. George, BSc ACA *2011;* 43 Panikou Haraki &, Fillyras Street, Panthea, Ayios Athanasios, 4105 LIMASSOL, CYPRUS.

DEMOSTHENOUS, Mr. Michalis, MSc BSc ACA *2006;* 14A Charalambou Mouskou, Kaimakli, 1026 NICOSIA, CYPRUS.

DEMPSEY, Mr. Conall, BSc ACA CPA *1997;* PricewaterhouseCoopers, 2 Commerce Square Suite 1700, 2001 Market Street, PHILADELPHIA, PA 19103-7042, UNITED STATES. See also PricewaterhouseCoopers LLP

DEMPSEY, Mrs. Cornelia Elsie, ACA *2008;* 8 Sopwith Close, Biggin Hill, WESTERHAM, TN16 3UW.

DEMPSEY, Mr. Desmond Gerard, BA FCA *1975;* kings house, 4 Bridle Way, Grantchester, CAMBRIDGE, CB3 9NY.

DEMPSEY, Mr. Ian Michael, BA ACA *1994;* University of Salford, Faraday House, 43 Crescent, SALFORD, M5 4WT.

DEMPSEY, Mrs. Marilyn, FCA *1977;* 9 Battle Road, Upwood Ramsey, HUNTINGDON, CAMBRIDGESHIRE, PE26 2PT.

DEMPSEY, Mr. Mark Russell, ACA *1991;* Bronte House North Farm, Holywell Dene Road, Holywell, WHITLEY BAY, NORTHUMBERLAND, NE25 0LL.

DEMPSEY, Mr. Neil, BA ACA *1980;* Im Rehwechsel 39, CH-4102 BINNINGEN, SWITZERLAND.

DEMPSEY, Mr. Paul, BA ACA AMCT *1992;* Tradition (UK) Ltd Beaufort House, 15 St. Botolph Street, LONDON, EC3A 7QX.

DEMPSEY, Mr. Paul Michael, BSc ACA *2011;* Flat 24 Elbourne House, Lumley Road, HORLEY, SURREY, RH67LB.

DEMPSEY, Miss. Tara, BA ACA *2005;* with KPMG LLP, Dukes Keep, Marsh Lane, SOUTHAMPTON, HAMPSHIRE, SO14 3EX.

DEMPSEY, Mrs. Tara Thu Quynh, BA ACA *2005;* Bank of America, 5 Canada Square, LONDON, E14 5AQ.

DEMPSIE, Mr. John Newlands Hamilton, FCA *1976;* Semperit Industrial Products Ltd Unit 25, Cottesbrooke Park Heartlands Business Park, DAVENTRY, NORTHAMPTONSHIRE, NN11 8YL.

DEMPSTER, Mr. Edward, BSc ACA CTA *2005;* 94 Kirby Drive, Bramley, TADLEY, RG26 5FN.

DEMPSTER, Mr. Rodney William, BSc ACA *1994;* Blighline Ltd, Unit 5-10, Sparrow Way, Lakesview International Business Park, Hersden, CANTERBURY CT3 4JQ.

DEMPSTER, Mr. Stuart, BA ACA *1985;* 1 Malwood Court, Highvale, Samford Valley, BRISBANE, QLD 4520, AUSTRALIA.

DEMPSTER, Ms. Tara Helen, MA ACA *1998;* 38 Normanton Avenue, LONDON, SW19 8BB.

•**DEMUTH, Ms. Helen Veronica, MA FCA** *1981;* (Tax Fac), Smith & Williamson (Bristol) LLP, Portwall Place, Portwall Lane, BRISTOL, BS1 6NA. See also Smith & Williamson Ltd

DENARO, Mr. Alex, BSc ACA *2010;* with PricewaterhouseCoopers CI LLP, Twenty Two Colomberie, St Helier, JERSEY, JE1 4XA.

DENBURY, Mr. Stephen Michael, BA ACA *1997;* with Pearson May, 37 Great Pulteney Street, BATH, BA2 4DA.

DENBY, Mr. Crispian Humphrey, MA FCA *1980;* 33 Silver Crescent, LONDON, W4 5SF.

DENBY, Mr. Douglas Roy, FCA *1963;* 90 Darcey Road, CASTLE HILL, NSW 2154, AUSTRALIA.

DENBY, Mr. Nigel Anthony, ACA *1979;* 4 Woodlands House Woodlands, Roundwood Road Baildon, SHIPLEY, WEST YORKSHIRE, BD17 6SP.

•**DENBY, Mr. Paul Antony, BSc FCA** *1976;* Denby & Associates, Ravensbourne Business Centre, Westerham Road, KESTON, KENT, BR2 6HE.

DENBY, Mr. Paul Justin, LLB FCA *1995;* (Tax Fac), 17 Berkeley Close, Elstree, BOREHAMWOOD, WD6 3JN.

DENBY, Mr. Richard Philip, BSc ACA *1992;* 3 Alice Holt Cottages, Gravel Hill Road, Holt Pound, FARNHAM, GU10 4LG.

•**DENCH, Mr. Anthony George, LLB ACA** *1996;* 270/1 St Heliers Bay Road, St Heliers, AUCKLAND, NEW ZEALAND.

DENCH, Mr. Marcus Simon, BSc ACA *1997;* 46 Meadway, HARPENDEN, HERTFORDSHIRE, AL5 1JL.

DENCHER, Mr. John Stanley, BCom FCA FTII *1978;* (Tax Fac), 1 Heathy Close, Barton on Sea, NEW MILTON, BH25 7JP.

DENCHFIELD, Mr. Michael David, FCA *1961;* Flat 91, Bedford Court Mansions, Bedford Avenue, LONDON, WC1B 3AE.

DENDLE, Mr. Mark Vincent, FCA *1994;* 11527 Rosser Road, DALLAS, TX 75229, UNITED STATES.

DENDY, Miss. Fiona Charlotte, BSc ACA *2000;* with BDO LLP, 55 Baker Street, LONDON, W1U 7EU.

DENDY, Mr. Terence Arthur Grenville, FCA *1958;* Clune, Mill Green Road, Mill Green, INGATESTONE, ESSEX, CM4 0PT. (Life Member)

DENEKAMP, Mr. Johan Harmanus, BSc FCA *1983;* 7 Tower Walk, St katharines Way, St Katharines Dock, LONDON, E1W 1LP.

DENG, Mr. Heng Teck, CA ACMA MBA *1989; (CA Scotland 1984);* 57 Lorong Nikmat 8 (Jalan 3/128A), Happy Garden, Off Jalan Kuchai Lama, 58200 KUALA LUMPUR, FEDERAL TERRITORY, MALAYSIA.

DENG, Miss. Xuan, ACA *2011;* Unit 1314, 1 Sergeants Lane, ST LEONARDS, NSW 2065, AUSTRALIA.

DENG, Mr. Yu Hui, ACA *2008;* Rm 501 Block B Zhong Xin Jun Ting, Bin Jiang East Road, GUANGZHOU 51000, CHINA.

•**DENHAM, Mr. Alan Wilfred, FCA** *1957;* Alan W. Denham, Glen Lea, 25 Manor Close, Edwalton, NOTTINGHAM, NG12 4BH.

•①**DENHAM, Mr. Antony, BSc ACA** *1996;* DL Partnership LLP, Suite 5, 90 New North Road, HUDDERSFIELD, HD1 5NE.

DENHAM, Mr. Christopher Paul Fisher, BA FCA *1991;* 1 Peartree Cottage, Paddock Hill, Mobberley, KNUTSFORD, CHESHIRE, WA16 7DG.

•**DENHAM, Mr. Kevin, BA FCA CF** *1991;* Baker Tilly Corporate Finance LLP, 25 Farringdon Street, LONDON, EC4A 4AB. See also Baker Tilly Tax and Advisory Services LLP

DENHAM, Miss. Lucy Mary, MSc ACA *2004;* 4 Orchard Gate, ESHER, KT10 8HY.

DENHAM, Mr. Timothy Maurice, FCA *1971;* Flat 201 The Hawley, 31 Kentish Town Road, LONDON, NW1 8NL.

DENHART, Mr. Martin Howard, MA FCA *1977;* 52 Ormond Crescent, HAMPTON, TW12 2TH.

•**DENHOLM, Mr. Brian Trevor, FCA** *1973;* Braham Noble Denholm & Co., York House, Empire Way, WEMBLEY, HA9 0PA. See also BND Audits Limited

DENHOLM, Mr. John Neil, FCA MCT *1975;* No 1 Lloyds TSB Commercial Finance, Brookhill Way, BANBURY, OXFORDSHIRE, OX16 3EL.

DENINSON, Mrs. Helen Elizabeth, BA ACA *1989;* The Severals, Twitchells Lane, Jordans, BEACONSFIELD, HP9 2RE.

DENIS, Mr. Carl, BSc BCom ACA *1979;* Aylsham Manor, Norwich Road, Aylsham, NORWICH, NR11 6BN.

DENISON, Mrs. Charlotte Yvonne, BA(Hons) ACA *2002;* 9 rue Roli, 75014 PARIS, FRANCE.

DENISON, Mr. Michael John, LLB ACA *1990;* (Tax Fac), Abbey Business Centres Abbey House, Wellington Way, WEYBRIDGE, SURREY, KT13 0TT.

•**DENISON, Mr. Stephen John, BSc FCA** *1989;* PricewaterhouseCoopers LLP, Benson House, 33 Wellington Street, LEEDS, LS1 4JP. See also PricewaterhouseCoopers

DENISON, Mr. William Austen Raymond, FCA *1932;* 3 Berners Close, Kents Bank Road, GRANGE-OVER-SANDS, LA11 7DQ. (Life Member)

•**DENIZ, Mr. Dervish Kemal, BA FCA** *1981;* D.K. Deniz & Co, 2 Memduh Asaf Sokak, LEFKOSA, CYPRUS. See also Deniz D.K and Deniz-Gumus & Co

•**DENLEY, Mr. Andrew John, FCA** *1983;* (Tax Fac), Menzies LLP, 3rd Floor Kings House, 12-42 Wood Street, KINGSTON UPON THAMES, SURREY, KT1 1TG.

DENLEY, Mr. Christopher John, FCA *1981;* Whitbread Plc, Whitbread Court, Porz Avenue, Houghton Hall Park, Houghton Regis, DUNSTABLE BEDFORDSHIRE LU5 5XE.

DENLEY, Mrs. Clare Rachel, BA ACA *2001;* Horwath Clark Whitehill LLP, Aquis House, 49-51 Blagrave Street, READING, BERKSHIRE, RG1 1PL.

DENMAN, Miss. Chi Li Li, BSc ACA *1989;* HASMA Capital Advisors (UK) ltd, 11 Stanhope Gate, LONDON, W1K1AN.

DENMAN, Mr. Douglas Frederick, FCA *1968;* Homemead Farm, Woolmongers Lane, INGATESTONE, ESSEX, CM4 0JX. (Life Member)

DENMAN, Mr. Henry Nicholas, BEng ACA *1992;* Smooth Hill, 69 Fairmile Lane, COBHAM, KT11 2DG.

DENMAN, Mr. John Malcolm, BSc FCA *1977;* 3 Manor Farm, Church Street, Whittington, CARNFORTH, LANCASHIRE, LA6 2NU.

DENMAN, Mr. Philip Graham, BSc FCA *1990;* La Haina, Pamington, TEWKESBURY, GL20 8LX.

DENMAN, Mr. Thomas, BSc ACA *2000;* 20 Chartwell Drive, Lisvane, CARDIFF, CF14 0EZ.

DENMEAD, Mr. Christopher Julien, BAcc ACA *1997;* 1 Livingstone Walk, HEMEL HEMPSTEAD, HERTFORDSHIRE, HP2 6AH.
DENMEAD, Miss. Madeline Kendall, BSc ACA *1988;* Flat 3-7, 71 Holland Park, LONDON, W11 3SL.
•DENNARD, Mr. Roger Frederick, BA FCA *1982;* (Tax Fac), Manningtons, 39 High Street, BATTLE, EAST SUSSEX, TN33 0EE.
DENNE, Mr. Philip Allan, FCA *1957;* Chemin des Roches 18, 1803 CHARDONNE, SWITZERLAND. (Life Member)
DENNEHEY, Mr. Andrew, BEng ACA *2000;* 17 Miller Close, Redbourn, ST. ALBANS, HERTFORDSHIRE, AL3 7BG.
DENNEHY, Mr. Brian Joseph, BSc ACA *2005;* 15 Langland Crescent, STANMORE, HA7 1NE.
DENNES, Mr. Peter Warren, FCA *1957;* 32 Ryll Grove, EXMOUTH, DEVON, EX8 1TT. (Life Member)
DENNESS, Mr. Andrew Thomas, BSc ACA *1998;* 61 St. Marys Road, Adderbury, BANBURY, OXFORDSHIRE, OX17 3HA.
DENNETT, Mr. Anthony Michael, FCA *1969;* 319 Coniscliffe Road, DARLINGTON, DL3 8AH.
•DENNETT, Mr. Daniel Anthony, BA ACA *2004;* with PricewaterhouseCoopers LLP, 9 Greyfriars Road, READING, RG1 1JG.
DENNETT, Mr. David Edward, FCA *1962;* Apt 23 King Edward Bay, Sea Cliff Road, Onchan, ISLE OF MAN, IM3 2JF. (Life Member)
DENNETT, Miss. Kirsty Louise, BSc ACA *2001;* 47 Mayfair Gardens, SOUTHAMPTON, SO15 2TW.
DENNETT, Mr. Michael Charles, BSc ACA AMCT *1994;* Lodderstraat 16, Industriepark 'De Vliet', B - 2880 BORNEM, BELGIUM.
DENNEY, Mr. Andrew James William, MA(Hons) ACA *2002;* with National Audit Office, 157-197 Buckingham Palace Road, Victoria, LONDON, SW1W 9SP.
•DENNEY, Mrs. Elaine, BSc ACA *1992;* Denney & Co Accountants Ltd, Fox Farm Hatfield, Norton, WORCESTER, WR5 2QA.
DENNEY, Mr. Gordon Herbert, FCA *1956;* 15 Nicholas Gardens, Pyrford, WOKING, GU22 8SD. (Life Member)
DENNEY, Mr. John Warner, FCA *1970;* 35 Laurel Road, Blaby, LEICESTER, LE8 4DL.
DENNEY, Mr. Julian Spencer, MA ACA *1986;* Ivy Lodge, 48 Cannon Park Road, COVENTRY, CV4 7AY.
DENNEY, Mr. Peter John, FCA *1989;* Meadow View, Botley Road, Horton Heath, EASTLEIGH, HAMPSHIRE, SO50 7DT.
DENNEY, Mr. Peter John, BA ACA *1990;* 11 Park Glen, Park Gate, SOUTHAMPTON, SO31 6BZ.
DENNIE, Mrs. Andrea Lesley, ACA *1987;* R N Store & Co The Poplars, Bridge Street, BRIGG, SOUTH HUMBERSIDE, DN20 8NQ.
DENNING, Mr. Clive Graham, BSc ACA *1990;* 2 Cesson Close, St Johns Way, Chipping Sodbury, BRISTOL, BS37 6NJ.
DENNING, Mrs. Maria Ann, BA ACA *2002;* 7 Llys Coed, Coed Y Cwm, PONTYPRIDD, CF37 3JB.
DENNING, Mr. Michael Paul, BA ACA *1998;* Tabernacle Court, 16-28 Tabernacle Street, LONDON, EC2A 4DD.
DENNING, Mr. Thomas Mark, BA(Hons) ACA *2002;* with KPMG LLP, 15 Canada Square, LONDON, E14 5GL.
DENNIS, Mr. Aidan Charles Parfitt, BA ACA *1988;* Little Bradley, Weston Green Road, THAMES DITTON, KT7 0HX.
DENNIS, Mr. Allan Rory, BSc ACA *1997;* Hearn Farm, Dulford, CULLOMPTON, DEVON, EX15 2DE.
DENNIS, Mr. Andrew, BA ACA *1981;* Spring House, School Lane, Lower Ufford, WOODBRIDGE, IP13 6DX.
DENNIS, Mr. Andrew Michael, ACA *1998;* Calor Gas Ltd Athena House, Athena Drive Tachbrook Park, WARWICK, CV34 6RL.
DENNIS, Mrs. Emma Louise, BA ACA *1996;* c/o Brigg P Dennis 516586, BMM, SANG, BFPO, 5421, SAUDI ARABIA.
DENNIS, Mr. Geoffrey Alan, BSc ACA *1996;* 7 Fourth Avenue, BRIDLINGTON, NORTH HUMBERSIDE, YO15 2LN.
DENNIS, Mr. Geoffrey Anthony, FCA *1970;* 4 Dynevor Terrace, Coronation Street, FAIRFORD, GLOUCESTERSHIRE, GL7 4JD.
DENNIS, Mr. Gordon Frank, BCom ACA *1984;* (Tax Fac), Conoco Ltd Conocophillips Centre, 2 Kingmaker Court Warwick Technology Park Gallows Hill, WARWICK, CV34 6DB.
DENNIS, Mr. Ian, BA ACA *1991;* European Commission, Eurostat, L-2920 LUXEMBOURG, LUXEMBOURG.
DENNIS, Dr. Ian David, MA BPhil ACA *1982;* Spring Cottage, Haseley Road, Little Milton, OXFORD, OX44 7PP.
•DENNIS, Mrs. Jane, BA(Hons) FCA *1990;* (Tax Fac), Fairhurst, Douglas Bank House, Wigan Lane, WIGAN, WN1 2TB.
DENNIS, Mr. John Philip Stanley, FCA *1978;* 2 Heyford Hill Lane, Littlemore, OXFORD, OX4 4YG.
•DENNIS, Mr. John Richard Pollard, FCA *1963;* 106/ Flat 4, Triq Sir Adrian Dingli, SLIEMA, MALTA.
DENNIS, Mr. Jonathan Charles, BA ACA *2001;* 23 Greenacres, Woolton Hill, NEWBURY, BERKSHIRE, RG20 9TA.
DENNIS, Mr. Jonathan Robert, BSc ACA *2009;* 16 Cheltenham Drive, CHIPPENHAM, SN14 0SE.
DENNIS, Mrs. Karen Louise, BSc(Econ) ACA *1995;* Eichenhofsiedlung 35, 8047 Kainbach b Graz, GRAZ, AUSTRIA.
DENNIS, Miss. Kim, BSc(Hons) ACA *2011;* 114 Mount View Road, SHEFFIELD, S8 8PL.
DENNIS, Mr. Michael Kenneth, ACA *2009;* 102b Nyetimber Lane, BOGNOR REGIS, WEST SUSSEX, PO21 3HL.
DENNIS, Mr. Michael Robin, BSc ACA *1997;* 1 Arundel Crescent, SOLIHULL, B92 8RQ.
DENNIS, Mrs. Michelle Alexandra, LLB ACA *1995;* (Tax Fac), with KPMG LLP, 1 Waterloo Way, LEICESTER, LE1 6LP.
•DENNIS, Mr. Neal Leslie, BA ACA *1978;* Dennis & Turnbull Limited, Swatton Barn, Badbury, SWINDON, SN4 0EU.
DENNIS, Mr. Neil, BSc ACA *2011;* Flat 17, Masters Lodge, Johnson Street, LONDON, E1 0BE.
DENNIS, Mr. Nicholas John Stewart, BSc ACA *1992;* UHY Hacker Young, 168 Church Road, HOVE, EAST SUSSEX, BN3 2DL.
DENNIS, Miss. Nicola Jane, BSc ACA *1994;* B U P A BUPA House, 15-19 Bloomsbury Way, LONDON, WC1A 2BA.
•DENNIS, Mr. Paul James, BSc ACA *2005;* (Tax Fac), Ellis Dennis Warwick LLP, 59 Berks Hill, Chorleywood, RICKMANSWORTH, HERTFORDSHIRE, WD3 5AJ.
DENNIS, Mr. Peter Charles, FCA *1947;* 30 Spinfield Lane, MARLOW, SL7 2JT. (Life Member)
•DENNIS, Mr. Peter Richard, FCA *1972;* Peter R. Dennis, 37 Saxonbury Road, Southbourne, BOURNEMOUTH, BH6 5NB.
DENNIS, Mr. Philip, MA FCA *1988;* 17 High Wood, ILKLEY, LS29 8SB.
DENNIS, Mr. Philip Andrew, BA ACA *1985;* The Cedars, Cricket Way, WEYBRIDGE, KT13 9LP.
•DENNIS, Mr. Philip Gavril, FCA *1967;* (Tax Fac), DFC, First Floor Unit 4C, Village Way, GreenMeadow Springs Business Park, CARDIFF, CF15 7NE. See also Dennis, Freedman, Clayton & Co
•DENNIS, Mr. Richard John, FCA *1966;* R.J. Dennis, Kerian, Corkscrew Lane, Woolston, YEOVIL, BA22 7BP.
DENNIS, Ms. Samantha Ephesa Helena, BSc ACA *1996;* PO Box 313, FORESTVILLE, NSW 2087, AUSTRALIA.
DENNIS, Mr. Spencer Paul, ACA MAAT *1997;* Manches LLP, Aldwych House, 81 Aldwych, LONDON, WC2B 4RP.
DENNIS, Mr. Timothy, MA ACA *2001;* (Tax Fac), Granard Limited, 34 South Molton Street, LONDON, W1K 5RG.
DENNIS-BROWNE, Mr. Bernard James, FCA *1960;* The Redwoods, 5 Charlton Kings, WEYBRIDGE, SURREY, KT13 9QW. (Life Member)
DENNISON, Mr. Alexander Simon, BSc ACA *1980;* 2262 Paradise Avenue, COQUITLAM V3K 6H3, BC, CANADA.
DENNISON, Mr. Andrew, MMath ACA *2007;* 12 Chepstow Gardens, BEDFORD, MK41 8PQ.
DENNISON, Mr. Cameron Haigh, BEng ACA *1996;* 35 Port Hill Drive, SHREWSBURY, SHROPSHIRE, SY3 8RS.
DENNISON, Mr. David Brook, JP FCA *1966;* 1 Blue Dragon Yard, BEACONSFIELD, BUCKINGHAMSHIRE, HP9 1GW. (Life Member)
DENNISON, Mrs. Deborah, BA ACA *1985;* 46 Lordsfield Gardens, Overton, BASINGSTOKE, RG25 3EW.
DENNISON, Mr. Iain William, LLB ACA *1987;* Credit Suisse, Uetlibergstrasse 231, CH 8070 ZURICH, SWITZERLAND.
•DENNISON, Mr. John Michael, FCA *1975;* BDO LLP, 55 Baker Street, LONDON, W1U 7EU. See also BDO Stoy Hayward LLP
DENNISON, Mr. John Patrick Edmund, BSc FCA *1974;* 21 Linton Avenue, SOLIHULL, B91 3NN.
DENNISON, Mr. Richard James, FCA *1963;* 26 Albion Square, LONDON, E8 4ES. (Life Member)
DENNISON, Mr. Rodney Keith, FCA *1967;* Richmond House, High Street, FRESHWATER, PO40 9JX. (Life Member)
DENNISON, Mr. Stephen Edward, BTech FCA *1974;* 34 Rue Winston Churchill, 86500 MONTMORILLON, FRANCE. (Life Member)
DENNISON, Mr. Steven Christopher, BSc ACA *1992;* N F T Distribution Ltd, Azalea Close, Clover Nook Industrial Estate, Somercotes, ALFRETON, DERBYSHIRE DE55 4QX.
•DENNISS, Mr. Neil Michael, FCA *1983;* (Tax Fac), Bespoke Tax Accountants LLP, Westmoreland House, 80-86 Bath Road, CHELTENHAM, GLOUCESTERSHIRE, GL53 7JT.
DENNISTON, Mr. Nicholas Geoffrey Alastair, MA ACA *1982;* 40a, ladbroke square, LONDON, w11 3nd.
DENNY, Mr. Adam Thomas, BA ACA *2006;* Suite 2400 - 4720 Kingsway, Metrotower II, BURNABY V5H 4N2, BC, CANADA.
DENNY, Mr. Andrew Haig, BSc FCA *1994;* Newman House, Northgate Avenue, BURY ST.EDMUNDS, IP32 6BB.
•DENNY, Mr. Anthony William, FCA *1989;* Denny Sullivan & Associates LLP, Blackwell House, Guildhall Yard, LONDON, EC2V 5AE.
DENNY, Mr. Clive Andrew, FCA *1974;* 166 Harborne Park Road, BIRMINGHAM, B17 0BP.
DENNY, Mr. Greg, BSc ACA *2002;* Service Stream Limited, Level 12, 555 Lonsdale Street, MELBOURNE, VIC 3000, AUSTRALIA.
•DENNY, Mr. Martin Howard, BSc FCA DChA *1979;* MD Accounting Ltd, 53 Irwin Road, BEDFORD, MK40 3UN.
DENNY, Mrs. Michelle Stacey, BA ACA *2007;* 35 Shelley Road, CHELMSFORD, CM2 6ER.
DENNY, Mr. Robert William, FCA *1970;* C/- KBSA LTD, PO Box 27, KIMBE, WEST NEW BRITAIN, PAPUA NEW GUINEA.
DENNY, Mr. Russell John, BA(Hons) ACA *2008;* 35 Shelley Road, CHELMSFORD, CM2 6ER.
•DENNY, Mr. Trevor J, FCA *1979;* Upper Shortlands, Mudgley Road, WEDMORE, BS28 4DE.
DENSEM, Mr. Robert Gordon, FCA *1967;* Old Hall Cottage, Chelford Road, Henbury, MACCLESFIELD, CHESHIRE, SK10 4RS.
DENSEM, Mr. Timothy Robert, BSc ACA *1999;* White Cottage, School Lane, Ollerton, KNUTSFORD, CHESHIRE, WA16 8SQ.
DENSHAM, Mr. Edward Henry David, MA FCA *1997;* Lukoil Accounting & Finance Ltd, Rotunda Point, 11 Hartfield Crescent, LONDON, SW19 3RL.
DENSHAM, Mr. Michael Paul, BSc ACA *1993;* 80 Glenburnie Road, LONDON, SW17 7NF.
DENSHAM, Mr. Peter Ryan Cridland, FCA *1971;* Rhodyate Lodge, Congresbury, BRISTOL, BS49 5AQ.
•DENSLEY, Miss. Elizabeth Helen, FCA *1976;* Honey Barrett Limited, 48 St. Leonards Road, BEXHILL-ON-SEA, EAST SUSSEX, TN40 1JB.
DENSLEY, Mrs. Joanne Elizabeth, ACA *2009;* 28 Ned Ludd Close, Anstey, LEICESTER, LE7 7AQ.
DENSLOW, Mrs. Anne-Marie, BSc ACA *2008;* Five Pennies, Beaconsfield Road, Chelwood Gate, HAYWARDS HEATH, WEST SUSSEX, RH17 7LF.
DENT, Mr. Alastair Bruce, BSc ACA *1991;* Ernst & Young, PO Box 261, BRIDGETOWN, BARBADOS.
DENT, Mr. Angus, BA ACA *1987;* Grove Cottage, Yopps Green, Plaxtol, SEVENOAKS, TN15 0PY.
DENT, Mr. Barry Michael, FCA *1967;* 1 Cherry Paddock, Haxby, YORK, YO32 3DQ.
DENT, Mrs. Caroline Sarah, BSc ACA *2004;* 17 Southcote Farm Lane, READING, RG30 3DX.
DENT, Mr. Christopher Henry, MA ACA *1985;* 4 St. Ediths Court, St. Ediths Road, Kemsing, SEVENOAKS, KENT, TN15 6JQ.
•DENT, Mr. Christopher John, BA ACA *1986;* Graham Dent & Co, Compton House, 104 Scotland Road, PENRITH, CUMBRIA, CA11 7NR.
DENT, Mr. Christopher John, BSocSc FCA *1993;* 83 Grosvenor Avenue, Streetly, SUTTON COLDFIELD, WEST MIDLANDS, B74 3PE.
•DENT, Miss. Elizabeth Ann, FCA *1970;* (Tax Fac), Dent & Co, Beacon House, 1 Willow Walk, Woodley Park, SKELMERSDALE, WN8 6UR.
DENT, Mr. Geoffrey, BA ACA *1982;* 73 Skippers Lane, Normanby, MIDDLESBROUGH, CLEVELAND, TS6 0JE.
DENT, Mrs. Georgina Alma, BSc ACA *2002;* 80 Russell Road, WALTON-ON-THAMES, SURREY, KT12 2LA.
•DENT, Mr. Ian, BSc FCA FCCA *1988;* PO Box 266, KHARTOUM, 11111, SUDAN.
DENT, Mr. James, FCA *1960;* 46 Cleadon Lea, Cleadon, SUNDERLAND, SR6 7TQ. (Life Member)
DENT, Mr. Jeremy Alan, BSc ACA *1994;* 36 Main Street, North Rauceby, SLEAFORD, LINCOLNSHIRE, NG34 8QP.
DENT, Mr. Jeremy Francis, BSc FCA *1978;* 560 Hamilton House, 6 St. George Wharf, LONDON, SW8 2JE.
DENT, Mr. John, BA ACA *1986;* 5 Seymour Road, ALCESTER, B49 6JY.
DENT, Mr. John Christopher, BA ACA *2006;* 19 Mermaid Court, Lawrence Wharf, Rotherthithe Street, LONDON, SE16 6UB.
•DENT, Mr. John Warring, FCA *1979;* Crowe Clark Whitehill LLP, Jaeger House, 5 Clanricarde Gardens, TUNBRIDGE WELLS, KENT, TN1 1PE. See also Horwath Clark Whitehill LLP
DENT, Mr. Julian Evelyn Robert, MA ACA *1991;* Shell International, C16 412A, Carel van Bylandtlaan, 2596HR DEN HAAG, NETHERLANDS.
DENT, Mr. Julian Simon Ewart, BA FCA *1981;* Via International Ltd, Building 3, Chiswick Park, 566 Chiswick High Road, LONDON, W4 5YA.
DENT, Mrs. Karen, BA ACA *2009;* 7 Claypit Close, SOUTH SHIELDS, TYNE AND WEAR, NE33 1TH.
DENT, Miss. Karen Rosina, BSc ACA *1992;* with Harold Sharp, Holland House, 1-5 Oakfield, SALE, M33 6TT.
DENT, Mr. Kenneth William, FCA *1967;* Bracken House, Reigate Heath, REIGATE, SURREY, RH2 8QR.
DENT, Mr. Michael, BA ACA *1994;* Old Church Farm, 89 Main Street, Whissendine, OAKHAM, LEICESTERSHIRE, LE15 7ES.
DENT, Mr. Nicholas Daniel, BA ACA *2003;* 80 Russell Road, WALTON-ON-THAMES, SURREY, KT12 2LA.
DENT, Mr. Nicholas Michael, BSc ACA *1991;* (Tax Fac), 4 Acacia Road, STAINES, TW18 1BY.
DENT, Mr. Nicholas Peter, BSc ACA *1998;* 9 Oak Road, CHIPPENHAM, WILTSHIRE, SN14 0XJ.
DENT, Mr. Paul Benjamin, MMath ACA *2010;* 17 Southcote Farm Lane, READING, RG30 3DX.
DENT, Mr. Robert, FCA *1959;* Cherrywood, Grubwood Lane, Cookham Dean, MAIDENHEAD, BERKSHIRE, SL6 9UD.
DENT, Ms. Samantha, BA(Hons) ACA *2002;* 15 Searle Way, Eight Ash Green, COLCHESTER, CO6 3QS.
DENT, Mrs. Sara, BA(Hons) ACA *2004;* 64 Edinburgh Drive, BEDLINGTON, NORTHUMBERLAND, NE22 6NY.
•DENT, Mr. Simon Jeffrey Michael, ACA *1987;* (Tax Fac), S.J.M. Dent, 22a Bradmore Park Road, LONDON, W6 0DT.
DENT, Mr. Stanley Joseph, FCA *1939;* 61 Lanchester Road, Highgate, LONDON, N6 4SX. (Life Member)
DENT, Mr. Stephen Peter, DPhil BSc FCA *1975;* Greenacres, Annables Lane, Kinsbourne Green, HARPENDEN, AL5 3PL. (Life Member)
DENTON, Mr. Adrian Alexander, BSocSc ACA *1996;* Building B Ground Floor (Internal Audit), British Petroleum Co Plc, Chertsey Road, SUNBURY-ON-THAMES, MIDDLESEX, TW16 7LN.
•DENTON, Mr. Alasdair Keith, BSc ACA *1987;* Baldhu Consulting, 20 Pantbach Road, Birchgrove, CARDIFF, CF14 1UA.
•DENTON, Mr. Alistair James, BA ACA *1998;* Ernst & Young LLP, 1 Bridgewater Place, Water Lane, LEEDS, LS11 5QR. See also Ernst & Young Europe LLP
DENTON, Mrs. Annie Camille, FCA *1976;* 10 Rosemary Drive, Little Aston Park, SUTTON COLDFIELD, B74 3AG.
DENTON, Miss. Celia, LLB FCA *1977;* 54 Markham Street, Chelsea, LONDON, SW3 3NR.
DENTON, Mrs. Charlotte Ann, BA ACA TEP *1999;* Northern Trust Management Services, 50 Bank Street, LONDON, E14 5NT.
DENTON, Mr. David, FCA *1951;* 20 East Mead, Aughton, ORMSKIRK, L39 5ES. (Life Member)
DENTON, Mr. David John, ACA *1983;* 3 Old School Close, Nailsworth, STROUD, GLOUCESTERSHIRE, GL6 0NY.
DENTON, Ms. Laurie Lesley, ACA *1983;* (Tax Fac), Garrick Theatre, 2 Charing Cross Road, LONDON, WC2H 0HH.
DENTON, Mr. Mark Edward, MA ACA *1995;* 11 Rodney Way, GUILDFORD, GU1 2NY.
DENTON, Mr. Mark James, MA ACA *2001;* Flat 7, 16 Somers Road, REIGATE, SURREY, RH2 9DU.
•DENTON, Mr. Michael Wilson, ACA *1981;* MW Denton Limited, 29 Devonshire Street, KEIGHLEY, WEST YORKSHIRE, BD21 2BH.
DENTON, Mr. Norman George, FCA *1972;* 8 Cornfield, Mottram Rise, STALYBRIDGE, SK15 2UA.
•DENTON, Mr. Peter Raymond, BSc FCA *1978;* Williams Denton Cyf, San Remo, 13 Trinity Square, LLANDUDNO, LL30 2RB.
DENTON, Mr. Peter-Robert, BSc ACA *1998;* Bnp Paribas, 10 Harewood Avenue, LONDON, NW1 6AA.

DENTON, Mr. Robert William, BA ACA *1981;* Telham Cottage, Cottesmore Road, Ashwell, OAKHAM, LE15 7LJ.

•**DENTON, Mr. Roger, FCA** *1974;* (Tax Fac), Roger Denton, 8A Church Street, RUSHDEN, NN10 9YT.

DENTON, Mrs. Rosalind Mary, BA ACA *2000;* 5 Ryestone Drive, Ripponden, SOWERBY BRIDGE, WEST YORKSHIRE, HX6 4JW.

•**DENTON, Mr. Simon Mark, BSc ACA** *1995;* (Tax Fac), Milsted Langdon LLP, Winchester House, Deane Gate Avenue, TAUNTON, SOMERSET, TA1 2UH.

DENTON, Mr. Timothy Andrew James, BSc ARCS ACA *1996;* 23 St. Peter's Street, Islington, LONDON, N1 8JP.

DENVERS, Mrs. Gillian, BSc ACA *1984;* 8 Ullswater Avenue, DEWSBURY, WF12 7PJ.

•**DENYE, Mr. Simon Antony, BSc(Hons) ACA** *2002;* (Tax Fac), McDade Roberts Accountants Limited, 316 Blackpool Road, Fulwood, PRESTON, PR2 3AE.

DENYER, Mr. Brian Harold Vincent, FCA *1953;* 4949 San Pedro Drive NE, Apartment 85, ALBUQUERQUE, NM 87109-2583, UNITED STATES. (Life Member)

DENYER, Mr. John Alan McGilvray, FCA *1990;* 40a Granville Road, SEVENOAKS, TN13 1EZ.

DENYER, Mrs. Katie Amanda, ACA *2002;* William Jackson Food Group Limited, The Riverside Building, Livingstone Road, HESSLE, NORTH HUMBERSIDE, HU13 0DZ.

DENYER, Miss. Kirsty Lindsay Reoch, MA(Hons) ACA *2011;* Flat 67, Elmhurst Mansions, Edgeley Road, LONDON, SW4 6EU.

•**DENYER, Mr. Raymond Philip, FCA** *1967;* R.P. Denyer, 11 Stuarts Green, STOURBRIDGE, WEST MIDLANDS, DY9 0XR.

DENYER, Mr. Simon Timothy, BEng ACA *1992;* Lower Ground Floor, 445 Chiswick High Road, Chiswick, LONDON, W4 4AU.

DENYS, Mr. Peter, MA BA(Hons) ACA *2009;* 59 Oxford Street, Caversham, READING, RG4 8HN.

DENZA, Mr. John, MA FCA *1956;* (Tax Fac), 85 Redington Road, LONDON, NW3 7RR. (Life Member)

DEOCHAND, Mr. Shan, ACA *2008;* 11690 N.W. 105th Street, MIAMI, FL 33178-1103, UNITED STATES.

DEOL, Miss. Gurnarinder Kaur, MSc ACA *1991;* Flat 26, Kensington Mansions, Trebovir Road, LONDON, SW5 9TQ.

DEOL, Miss. Karandeep Kaur, ACA *2008;* 7 Herons Place, Court Road, MAIDENHEAD, SL6 8LA.

DEOL, Miss. Manjinder, BSc ACA *2009;* 244 Madison Avenue, Apt 12G, NEW YORK, NY 10016, UNITED STATES.

DEPALA, Mr. Rakesh, BSc ACA *2008;* 7 Granville Place, High Road, LONDON, N12 0AU.

DEPLEDGE, Mr. Adam James, ACA *2009;* 35 Prospect Street, Farsley, PUDSEY, WEST YORKSHIRE, LS28 5ER.

DEPLEDGE, Mr. Timothy Robert, BA(Hons) ACA *2002;* UK-Expat-TNK-Moscow, BP International Ltd, Chertsey Road, SUNBURY-ON-THAMES, MIDDLESEX, TW16 7LN.

•**DEPPER, Mr. Nigel Geoffrey, BA FCA** *1986;* Harrisons, 4 Brackley Close, South East Sector, Bournemouth International Airport, CHRISTCHURCH, DORSET BH23 6SE. See also Dorset Business Services Ltd

DER-KRIKORIAN, Mr. Miltos, BA ACA *1991;* 55 Marathonos Street, Voula, 16673 ATHENS, GREECE.

•**DERBY, Mr. Alan James, FCA** *1966;* (Tax Fac), Derby & Co, 52 Hickmans Close, GODSTONE, RH9 8EB.

•**DERBY, Mrs. Polly Elizabeth, BA FCA** *1996;* (Tax Fac), Ryedale Accountancy, Bridge Farm, Station Road, Gilling East, YORK, YO62 4JW.

DERBY, Mr. William John Patten, BSc FCA *1996;* York Race Course Knavesmire LLP, The Racecourse, Knavesmire Road, YORK, YO23 1EX.

•**DERBYSHIRE, Mr. David Robert, LLB ACA** *2001;* with KPMG LLP, 15 Canada Square, LONDON, E14 5GL.

DERBYSHIRE, Dr. Ian David, PhD MA ACA *1996;* 5 Tennyson Road, BEDFORD, MK40 3SB.

•**DERBYSHIRE, Mr. James Edward, FCA** *1974;* Livesey Spottiswood Holding Ltd, 17 George Street, ST. HELENS, MERSEYSIDE, WA10 1DB. See also Livesey Spottiswood Limited

DERBYSHIRE, Mr. Matthew Robert, BSc(Hons) ACA *2000;* 33 Lauderdale Road, Hunton Bridge, KINGS LANGLEY, HERTFORDSHIRE, WD4 8QA.

DERBYSHIRE, Mr. Peter, FCA *1973;* Higher Farm, West Bradley, GLASTONBURY, BA6 8LT.

DERBYSHIRE, Mr. Philip, BA ACA *2005;* 9 Brooke Hall Close, Saintfield Road, BELFAST, BT8 6WF.

DERBYSHIRE, Mr. Richard, BSc(Hons) ACA *2002;* 9 Proclamation Avenue, ROTHWELL, NORTHAMPTONSHIRE, NN14 6GY.

DERBYSHIRE, Mr. Richard Peter, BSc(Hons) ACA *2001;* 7 Woodlands Way, SOUTHAMPTON, SO15 2TJ.

DERGES, Mr. Samuel Derek, FCA *1955;* 7 Coleridge Close, EXMOUTH, EX8 5SP. (Life Member)

DERGIMAN, Mr. Mark Witold Kazimierz, FCA *1971;* FACTS, P.O. Box BW 1947, Borrowdale Brooke, HARARE, ZIMBABWE.

DERHAM, Mrs. Jessica Louise, BA(Hons) ACA *2009;* with Levicks, West Hill, 61 London Road, MAIDSTONE, ME16 8TX.

DERHAM, Mr. John Percival Maurice, FCA *1972;* 26 Crosslands, Fringford, BICESTER, OX27 8DF.

DERI, Mrs. Jane Elizabeth, BSc ACA *1989;* The Old Vicarage, Main Street, Boynton, BRIDLINGTON, NORTH HUMBERSIDE, YO16 4XJ.

•**DERI, Mr. Robert George, BA ACA** *1988;* Deri Consultants Limited, The Old Vicarage, Main Street, Boynton, BRIDLINGTON, NORTH HUMBERSIDE YO16 4XJ.

DERING, Miss. Alexandra Jacqueline, BA ACA *2005;* with KPMG Audit plc, Aquis Court, 31 Fishpool Street, ST. ALBANS, AL3 4RF.

DERMODY, Mr. Ian Joseph, BSc ACA *1983;* Pride Laffan House, Shoe Lane, ALDERSHOT, HAMPSHIRE, GU11 2ER.

DERMOTT, Mr. Alan Cresswell, FCA *1952;* 6/ 32-34 Nicholson Parade, CRONULLA, NSW 2230, AUSTRALIA. (Life Member)

DERNIE, Mrs. Fenella Garrett, BSc ACA *1990;* Crosslanes Farm House Crosslanes Purton Stoke, SWINDON, SN5 4JN.

DERRETT, Mr. Robert Julian, BA ACA *1993;* with PricewaterhouseCoopers, 26/F Office Tower A, Beijing Fortune Plaza, 23 Dongsanhuan North Road, Chaoyang District, BEIJING 100020 CHINA.

DERRICK, Mr. David Andrew, BA ACA *1993;* 4a Crescent Road, WOKINGHAM, RG40 2DB.

DERRICK, Mr. Julian Linford, BSc ACA *1999;* 124 Denison Road, DULWICH HILL, NSW 2203, AUSTRALIA.

DERRICK, Miss. Kirstine Ann, BSc(Hons) ACA *2002;* 8 Manor Road, Cheadle Hulme, CHEADLE, CHESHIRE, SK8 7DQ.

DERRICK, Miss. Lucy Jane, BSc ACA *2009;* TFF, 94 Pembroke Road, Clifton, BRISTOL, BS8 3EG.

DERRINGTON, Mr. Andrew David, BSc ACA *1999;* 11 Blue Dragon Yard, BEACONSFIELD, BUCKINGHAMSHIRE, HP9 1GW.

DERRY, Mr. Andrew Ironmonger, FCA *1974;* 6 Foxhall Close, Norwell, NEWARK, NG23 6GZ.

DERRY, Mrs. Charlotte Susannah, MEng ACA *1999;* Institute of Chartered Accountants in England & Wales, Metropolitan House, 4 Rillaton Walk, MILTON KEYNES, MK9 2FZ.

DERRY, Mr. Giles Thomas Bradley, BSc ACA *1997;* with Dunedin Capital Partners Limited, Dukes Court, 32 Duke Street, St James's, LONDON, SW1Y 6DF.

DERVIN, Mr. James, BA(Hons) ACA *2004;* with Deloitte LLP, Athene Place, 66 Shoe Lane, LONDON, EC4A 3BQ.

DERVISH, Mr. Alper Osman, BA ACA *2004;* 435 Bromsgrove Road, Hunnington, HALESOWEN, B62 0JJ.

•**DERVLEY, Mr. Jean-Paul, BSc FCA** *1984;* with Ernst & Young LLP, 400 Capability Green, LUTON, LU1 3LU.

DERWENT, Mr. Richard Austin, MSc BA FCA *1977;* Flat 7, Foxlea, 70 Northlands Road, SOUTHAMPTON, SO15 2LH.

DERWENT, Mr. Roger, FCA *1965;* The Croft, Barston, SOLIHULL, B92 0JU.

DERWIN, Mr. Garry Anthony, BSc ACA *1989;* Belmont, Belmont Road, Hale, ALTRINCHAM, CHESHIRE, WA15 9PT.

DES FORGES, Mr. Peter Michael, ACA *1989;* 19 Spindlewood, Elloughton, BROUGH, NORTH HUMBERSIDE, HU15 1LL.

DES FORGES, Ms. Samantha, MA(Hons) BSc(Hons) ACA *2001;* 3 Les Parquets, La Grande Route de St Martin, ST MARTIN, JE3 6UP.

DESAI, Mr. Akshit, ACA *2009;* Flat 1 Clementine Court, 65 Northwick Avenue, HARROW, HA3 0DG.

DESAI, Mrs. Alpa, BSc ACA CTA *2003;* 208 Edgwarebury Lane, EDGWARE, MIDDLESEX, HA8 8QW.

DESAI, Mr. Bhavik, ACA *2009;* Flat 29 Priory Heights, 2a Wynford Road, LONDON, N1 9SL.

DESAI, Mr. Bijal, BSocSc ACA *1995;* 12 Bishops Avenue, NORTHWOOD, MIDDLESEX, HA6 3DG.

DESAI, Mr. Bimal, BA ACA *1992;* 28 Highfield Lane, MAIDENHEAD, SL6 3AP.

DESAI, Mr. Biram Kikubhai, BEng ACA *1996;* 11a Little Preston Street, BRIGHTON, BN1 2HQ.

DESAI, Mr. Dilip, ACA *1986;* 14 Arnos Grove, Nuthall, NOTTINGHAM, NG16 1QA.

•**DESAI, Mr. Dineshchandra Kalidas, FCA** *1975;* (Tax Fac), Dinesh Desai, 31 Ennerdale Avenue, STANMORE, MIDDLESEX, HA7 2LB. See also Dinesh Desai & Co

DESAI, Mr. Dollar Ray, FCA *1965;* D1/44 Khiranagar, Swami Vivekanand Road, Santa-Cruz (West), MUMBAI 400 054, MAHARASHTRA, INDIA. (Life Member)

DESAI, Mrs. Gina, BSc ACA *1998;* with KPMG LLP, 15 Canada Square, LONDON, E14 5GL.

DESAI, Mr. Haresh, BA ACA ACT *1986;* Renault UK Ltd, The Rivers Office Park, Denham Way, Maple Cross, RICKMANSWORTH, HERTFORDSHIRE WD3 9YS.

DESAI, Mr. Jayanti, BSc ACA *1991;* (Tax Fac), Trinity Alderhithe Grove, SUTTON COLDFIELD, B74 3BN.

DESAI, Mrs. Kalpana, BSc ACA *1991;* House A, 90 Peak Road, THE PEAK, HONG KONG SAR.

DESAI, Mr. Kantilal Gopalji, FCA *1961;* 6 Park Lane, The Vine, SEVENOAKS, TN13 3UP. (Life Member)

•**DESAI, Mr. Kaushik Jayantilal Sunderlal, MSc FCA ATII** *1971;* (Tax Fac), Chown Dewhurst LLP, 51 Lafone Street, LONDON, SE1 2LX. See also K.J. Desai & Co

•**DESAI, Mr. Manoharlal Ratilal, FCA** *1973;* M.R.Desai, Suite 201-5990 Fraser Street, VANCOUVER V5W 2Z7, BC, CANADA.

DESAI, Mr. Mehul Mahendrakumar, BA ACA *1988;* 7 Moor Place, WINDLESHAM, GU20 6JS.

DESAI, Mr. Mirav, BSc ACA *2010;* 6 Casel Court, Brightwen Grove, STANMORE, MIDDLESEX, HA7 4ZB.

•**DESAI, Mr. Mukesh Sumant, MBA BSc FCA** *1989;* Butler & Co LLP, 3rd Floor, 126-134 Baker Street, LONDON, W1U 6UE. See also Butler & Co

•**DESAI, Mr. Narendra Kumar Dhirajlal, FCA** *1979;* (Tax Fac), Andrew Murray & Co, 144-146 Kings Cross Road, LONDON, WC1X 9DU. See also PS Accounting Services (UK) Ltd, PS2 (UK) Limited

•**DESAI, Mr. Naresh Nanubhai, ACA** *1979;* Desai & Co., 1 Tanjong Rhu Road, 05-01, SINGAPORE 436879, SINGAPORE.

DESAI, Mr. Nareshchandra Thakorlal, FCA *1966;* 201-5990 Fraesr Streer, VANCOUVER V5W 2Z7, BC, CANADA.

DESAI, Mrs. Neena, BSc ACA *1980;* 5 Peters Close, STANMORE, HA7 4SB.

DESAI, Mr. Nilesh, BSc ACA *2000;* 48 Derwent Road, HARPENDEN, HERTFORDSHIRE, AL5 3NX.

DESAI, Mr. Praveen Pratap, BSc ACA *1995;* 15 Frank Edinger Close, Kennington, ASHFORD, KENT, TN24 9RB.

DESAI, Mr. Purvez Minoo, FCA *1978;* 29 Bourne End Road, NORTHWOOD, HA6 3BP.

DESAI, Ms. Raakhee, BSc ACA *2000;* 30 Shaftesbury Avenue, Kenton, HARROW, MIDDLESEX, HA3 0QX.

DESAI, Mr. Rohit Kumar Ishverlal, BSc ACA *1982;* 5 Peters Close, STANMORE, HA7 4SB.

DESAI, Mr. Sameer, ACA *2011;* 36 Cedars Road, MORDEN, SURREY, SM4 5AB.

DESAI, Mr. Satish Kumar Natwerlal, BCom ACA *1982;* 14th Floor, P.O. Box 3555, JEDDAH, SAUDI ARABIA.

DESAI, Miss. Sonal, BSc(Hons) ACA *2011;* 105 Elm Avenue, RUISLIP, MIDDLESEX, HA4 8PG.

DESAI, Mr. Sureshchandra Ratilal, FCA *1967;* 201-5990 Fraser Street, VANCOUVER V5W 2Z7, BC, CANADA.

DESAI, Mr. Vinodrai Kikubhai, FCA ACMA *1963;* (Tax Fac), 299 Beulah Hill, Upper Norwood, LONDON, SE19 3UZ.

DESAI, Mr. Viral, BSc FCA *1993;* Littlebrook, Green Lane, CROWBOROUGH, TN6 2XB.

DESCHAMPSNEUFS, Mr. Hugo Bernard, FCA *1968;* Foresters, Station Road, Over Wallop, STOCKBRIDGE, SO20 8JA.

DESCROIZILLES, Mr. Marie Joseph Marcel Vivian, FCA *1973;* Coast Road, POINTE AUX CANONNIERS, MAURITIUS.

DESFORGES, Mr. Matthew John Gerard, ACA *1999;* Rocque Noire Sandy Lane, St. Sampson, GUERNSEY, GY2 4RW.

DESHAZO, Mrs. Lucy Gabrielle Barton, MA CA ACA *1991;* 7314 Bennington Drive, DALLAS, TX 75214, UNITED STATES.

DESHPANDE, Mr. Aneil Paul, BA FCA *1982;* Ark Syndicate Management Ltd, St. Helens, 1 Undershaft, LONDON, EC3A 8EE.

DESKEY, Mrs. Veronica Newson, BA FCA *1957;* PO Box 5011 PMB 115, FERNDALE, WA 98248, UNITED STATES. (Life Member)

•**DESLER, Mr. Gerald, FCA** *1968;* Stonebridge House, Chelmsford Road, Hatfield Heath, BISHOP'S STORTFORD, HERTFORDSHIRE, CM22 7BD.

DESMIER, Mr. Peter Kenneth, FCA *1981;* 36 Salisbury Avenue, HEYWOOD, LANCASHIRE, OL10 2NY.

DESMOND, Mr. James Terence Brian, FCA *1953;* 49 Ludlow Road, GUILDFORD, SURREY, GU2 7NR. (Life Member)

DESMOND, Mr. Kevin John, BSc FCA *1986;* The Homestead, Rectory Lane, Bentley, FARNHAM, SURREY, GU10 5JS.

DESMOND, Mr. Peter, MA MBA FCA *1980;* with Growth International Limited, 11 Manor Road, TWICKENHAM, TW2 5DF.

DESORH, Mr. Jagjeevan Lal, BA ACA *1993;* 7 St. Andrews Way, SLOUGH, SL1 5NH.

DESOURDY, Miss. Charlotte Mary Louise, BSc ACA *2010;* 91 Church Lane, Bessacarr, DONCASTER, SOUTH YORKSHIRE, DN4 6QG.

DESOUZA, Miss. Delyse Frances, BSc ACA *1993;* 727 Clarence Street, WESTFIELD, NJ 07090, UNITED STATES.

DESOUZA, Mr. Querobino Leo, BSc ACA *1989;* (Tax Fac), 4400 Britley Lane, HARRISBURG, NC 28075, UNITED STATES.

DESPARD, Mr. Richard Anthony, FCA *1975;* 2 Redcliffe Mews, LONDON, SW10 9JU.

DESPORT, Mrs. Rebekah Kate, ACA *2001;* Finance Department, University of York, Heslington, YORK, YO10 5DD.

DESSAIN, Mr. Giles William Charles, BA FCA *1975;* Heath Farmhouse, Hanwell, BANBURY, OX17 1HN.

DESSAIN, Mr. Paul Mark, BSc FCA *1977;* (Tax Fac), Unipart Group of Companies Unipart House, Garsington Road Cowley, OXFORD, OX4 2PG.

•**DESSE, Mrs. Maxine Carolyn, BA(Econ) FCA** *1994;* Additions Accountants Limited, Ground Floor, 24 Queen Avenue, Queen Insurance Buildings, Dale Street, LIVERPOOL L2 4TZ.

DESVAUX DE MARIGNY, Mr. Jean-Francois, FCA *1980;* 14th floor MCB Centre, 9-15Sir William Newton Street, PORT LOUIS, MAURITIUS.

DESVAUX DE MARIGNY, Mr. Renaud Jacques, FCA *1976;* Renaud Desvaux De Marigny, 29 Brown Sequard Street, CUREPIPE, MAURITIUS.

DETHERIDGE, Mrs. Heather Amanda, BSc ACA *2002;* 57 Covert Crescent, Radcliffe-on-Trent, NOTTINGHAM, NG12 2HN.

•**DETHERIDGE, Mr. John, BSc FCA** *1992;* (Tax Fac), Menzies LLP, Victoria House, 50-58 Victoria Road, FARNBOROUGH, HAMPSHIRE, GU14 7PG.

DETKO, Mr. Stephen Tadeusz, ACA *1982;* Football League Ltd, Edward VII Quay, Navigation Way, Ashton-on-Ribble, PRESTON, PR2 2YF.

DETRE, Mrs. Helen Marie, BA ACA *2003;* 16 Deans Yard, LONDON, SW1P 3PA.

DETTMAN, Mrs. Emma, ACA *2008;* Baker Tilly, 2 Humber Quays, Wellington Street West, HULL, HU1 2BN.

DETTMAR, Mrs. Kerry Leigh, ACA *2001;* 5 Marjoram Close, FARNBOROUGH, HAMPSHIRE, GU14 9XB.

DETTMER, Mr. Simon John, ACA *1979;* Mornington House Speltham Hill, Hambledon, WATERLOOVILLE, PO7 4RU.

•**DEUCHAR, Mrs. Gabrielle Jane, BA ACA** *1984;* Ernst & Young LLP, 1 More London Place, LONDON, SE1 2AF. See also Ernst & Young Europe LLP

DEUCHAR, Mr. Robert Lindsay, FCA *1975;* Old Dean Farm, Singleborough, MILTON KEYNES, MK17 0RF.

DEUCHARS-MURPHY, Mrs. Bryony, BSc ACA *2004;* 51 Manchuria Road, LONDON, SW11 6AF.

DEUTSCH, Mr. Alastair Michael, ACA *2009;* BSkyB Group Finance New Horizons Court 1 Ground Floor, British Sky Broadcasting Ltd, 7 Centaurs Business Centre Grant Way, ISLEWORTH, MIDDLESEX, TW7 5QD.

•**DEUTSCH, Mr. Stephen Soloman, FCA** *1977;* (Tax Fac), Stephen Deutsch, 102 Green Lane, EDGWARE, HA8 8EJ.

DEUTSCHLE, Mr. Karl Peter, BA ACA *1997;* with PricewaterhouseCoopers, Level 21, PWC Tower, 188 Quay Street, Private Bag 92162, AUCKLAND 1142 NEW ZEALAND.

•**DEV, Mr. Manish, BA(Hons) ACA** *2006;* MueDelta Accounting & Finance Consulting, 37 Quickswood Drive, LIVERPOOL, L25 4TP.

DEV, Mrs. Rajni, BA(Hons) ACA *2003;* 37 Quickswood Drive, LIVERPOOL, L25 4TP.

DEV, Mr. Vivek, FCA *1987;* Fox Fire, Old Long Grove, Seer Green, BEACONSFIELD, BUCKINGHAMSHIRE, HP9 2QH.

DEVA, Mr. Surendra, FCA *1962;* 4935 W. Louise Street, SKOKIE, IL 60077, UNITED STATES. (Life Member)

DEVADASON, Mr. Raj Mohan, MSc ACA *2002;* Flat B 29 Floor Block one, The Zenith, No 3 Wanchai road, WAN CHAI, HONG KONG ISLAND, HONG KONG SAR.
DEVAKI, Miss. Vaithianathan, ACA *1995;* 45 Richards Place, SINGAPORE 546363, SINGAPORE.
•①**DEVALIA, Miss. Dina Vasharam, BSc ACA** *1993;* Chantrey Vellacott D F K Russell Square House, 10-12 Russell Square, LONDON, WC1B 5LF. See also Chantrey Vellacott DFK LLP
DEVALIA, Mr. Pradipkumar Kanji, BA ACA *1984;* dph associates, Level 4, 61 Lavender Street, MILSONS POINT, NSW 2125, AUSTRALIA.
DEVANEY, Mr. Anthony John, FCA *1957;* Pastures, Chapel Street, Hinxworth, BALDOCK, SG7 5HW. (Life Member)
DEVANI, Ms. Aruna, ACA *1983;* 13 Newton Road, Canford Cliffs, POOLE, BH13 7EX.
DEVANI, Mr. Baiju, ACA *2008;* 42 Roxborough Park, HARROW, HA1 3AY.
DEVANI, Ms. Deepa, BA ACA *2007;* Flat 26 Clarendon Court, 20 Eastbury Avenue, NORTHWOOD, MIDDLESEX, HA6 3LN.
•**DEVANI, Mr. Kishor Mathuradas, FCA** *1962;* Flat 20 Farringdon House, 12 Strand Drive, RICHMOND, TW9 4EU.
DEVANI, Mr. Sandip Kishor, BA ACA *1991;* P.O. Box 476390, South Barsha, DUBAI, UNITED ARAB EMIRATES.
•**DEVANI, Mr. Shashikant Chandulal, FCA** *1964;* (Tax Fac), S.C. Devani & Co, 37 High Street, Acton, LONDON, W3 6ND.
DEVARAJAN, Mr. Samuel Mohaan, BSc(Hons) ACA *2002;* 21 Selbourne Avenue, SURBITON, SURREY, KT6 7NR.
DEVAUX, Mr. Frederick Nicholas Paul, CMG BSc FCA *1959;* P.O. Box 938, Coubaril, CASTRIES, SAINT LUCIA.
DEVCHAND, Mr. Dipesh, BSc(Econ) ACA *2001;* 133 Friern Barnet Road, LONDON, N11 3DY.
DEVENISH, Mrs. Maureen Denise, BSc ACA *1980;* Basketers, Colne Road, Great Tey, COLCHESTER, CO6 1AL.
•**DEVENNEY, Mrs. Helen Elizabeth, BA ACA** *1999;* Deloitte LLP, 2 New Street Square, LONDON, EC4A 3BZ. See also Deloitte & Touche LLP
DEVENNEY, Mrs. Samantha Kathryn Michele, BSc ACA *2005;* Flat 16, Axis Court, Woodland Crescent, Greenwich, LONDON, SE10 9UD.
•**DEVENNEY, Mr. Seamus, BSc ACA** *1999;* PricewaterhouseCoopers LLP, 1 Embankment Place, LONDON, WC2N 6RH. See also PricewaterhouseCoopers
DEVENNEY, Mr. William, MSc ACA *2005;* 360 First Avenue, 9G, NEW YORK, NY 10010, UNITED STATES.
DEVERELL, Miss. Gail Esther, BSc FCA *1980;* P.O. Box 1967, HAMILTON HM HX, BERMUDA.
•**DEVERELL, Mr. Giles Dalton, FCA** *1973;* G.D. Deverell, Asthill House, Aldbrough St. John, RICHMOND, NORTH YORKSHIRE, DL11 7ST.
DEVEREUX, Mr. Anthony, BSc ACA *2000;* 236 Old Clough Lane, Roe Green, Worsley, MANCHESTER, M28 2JD.
DEVEREUX, Mrs. Bettina Irene, BA ACA *1992;* 15 Leeson Road, BOURNEMOUTH, BH7 7AZ.
DEVEREUX, Ms. Carla, BSc ACA *2007;* Rose Cottage, 9 Kearsney Avenue, DOVER, CT16 3BU.
DEVEREUX, Mr. Guy William, BSc ACA *1993;* Apt 5D, 288 West 92nd Street, NEW YORK, NY 10025, UNITED STATES.
DEVEREUX, Mr. James William Robert, BSc ACA *1992;* Contract Fire Systems Ltd, C F S Business Park, Coleshill Road, SUTTON COLDFIELD, WEST MIDLANDS, B75 7FS.
•**DEVEREUX, Mr. John Howard Percy, FCA** *1963;* J.H.P Devereux, 7 Whitfield Road, Hughenden Valley, HIGH WYCOMBE, HP14 4NZ.
DEVEREUX, Mrs. Pallavi, BSc ACA *1990;* (Tax Fac), 21 Quineys Road, STRATFORD-UPON-AVON, WARWICKSHIRE, CV37 9BW.
DEVEREUX, Mrs. Rachel Elizabeth, BA ACA *1991;* Lancing College, LANCING, WEST SUSSEX, BN15 0RW.
•**DEVEREUX, Mr. Ronald, FCA** *1979;* (Tax Fac), Devereux Accountants Ltd, Empire House, Edgar Street, ACCRINGTON, LANCASHIRE, BB5 1PT.
DEVERICK, Mr. Jonathan Neil, FCA *1992;* 7, Partridge Close, BARNET, EN5 2DT.
DEVERILL, Mr. Graham, FCA *1972;* Enham Industries, Enham Alamein, ANDOVER, SP11 6JS.
•**DEVERILL, Mr. Ian Stuart, BSocSc FCA** *1990;* (Tax Fac), Ian Deverill, 18 Elgin Road, POOLE, DORSET, BH14 8ER. See also AIMS - Ian Deverill and Devcomp Limited
DEVERSON, Mr. David Leonard, FCA *1969;* Stream Cottage, Main Street, Kirkburn, DRIFFIELD, NORTH HUMBERSIDE, YO25 9DU.
•**DEVERSON, Mrs. Nicola, ACA** *1991;* (Tax Fac), Bespokes Ltd, Hilden Park House, 79 Tonbridge Road, Hildenborough, TONBRIDGE, KENT TN11 9BH. See also BSR Bespoke Limited
DEVES, Mr. Alan Douglas, BA ACA *1988;* May Cottage, Blandford Hill, Winterborne Whitechurch, BLANDFORD FORUM, DT11 0AE.
DEVESON, Mr. Geoffrey Reginald, FCA *1951;* 12 Carlton Place, Rickmansworth Road, NORTHWOOD, HA6 2JX. (Life Member)
DEVEY, Mr. Andrew John, BSc ACA *2005;* 6 Morris Avenue, Chilwell Beeston, NOTTINGHAM, NG9 6DE.
DEVEY, Miss. Colette Elizabeth, ACA *2000;* with Ernst & Young LLP, Apex Plaza, Forbury Road, READING, RG1 1YE.
DEVIDAYAL, Miss. Gauri, LLB ACA *2007;* 13 TYTAN, DUBASH LANE, NEPEAN SEA ROAD, MUMBAI 400036, INDIA.
DEVINE, Mrs. Ann, ACA ATII *1989;* G/F House F, The Royal Bank of Scotland Plc, PO Box 1000, EDINBURGH, EH12 1HQ.
DEVINE, Mr. Antony Kevin, BA ACA *1983;* 3rd Floor Princess Caroline House, 1 High Street, SOUTHEND-ON-SEA, SS1 1JE.
•**DEVINE, Mr. Bernard William Joseph, FCA** *1978;* Devine & Co, 242/242a Farnham Road, SLOUGH, SL1 4XE.
DEVINE, Mrs. Caroline Jane, BSc ACA *1993;* 4 Grange Drive, Burbage, HINCKLEY, LEICESTERSHIRE, LE10 2JR.
DEVINE, Mrs. Donna Jane, BSc ACA *2005;* The Sage Group plc, North Park, NEWCASTLE UPON TYNE, TYNE AND WEAR, NE13 9AA.
DEVINE, Mr. Francis Joseph, BCom FCA *1981;* 12 Turnstone Green, Langford Village, BICESTER, OX26 6TT.
DEVINE, Miss. Heather Jane, BA ACA ATII *1993;* Flat M, 49 Wellington Street, LONDON, WC2E 7BN.
DEVINE, Mrs. Jennifer Rose, ACA *2009;* 11 Arrow Close, SOUTHAMPTON, SO19 9TR.
DEVINE, Mrs. Joanne Elizabeth, BSc ACA *1992;* 5 Langley Road, Prestwich, MANCHESTER, M25 1NF.
DEVINE, Mr. Matthew James, BA(Hons) ACA *2000;* 26 Kimo Street, NORTH BALGOWLAH, NSW 2093, AUSTRALIA.
DEVINE, Miss. Rhiannon, BA ACA *2006;* 36 St. Johns Avenue, NORTHAMPTON, NN2 8RU.
DEVITT, Mrs. Joanne, BSc ACA *2000;* Danaher Central Boulevard, Blythe Valley Business Park, SOLIHULL, B90 8AG.
DEVITT, Mr. Michael Wyn, FCA *1968;* Pellery, Lotaet Garonne, 47370 THEZAC, FRANCE. (Life Member)
DEVITT, Mr. Paul Robert, BA ACA *2004;* 4th Floor, One The Esplanade, ST HELIER, JE2 3QA.
DEVITT, Mrs. Rachel Louise, BSc ACA *2004;* 73 Church Street, ST. ALBANS, HERTFORDSHIRE, AL3 5NG.
•**DEVITT, Mr. William Stuart, BSc FCA DChA** *1988;* Chantrey Vellacott DFK LLP, 35 Calthorpe Road, Edgbaston, BIRMINGHAM, WEST MIDLANDS, B15 1TS.
DEVJI, Mr. Mohamed Samji, FCA *1980;* SHOP ONE HUNDRED LTD, PO BOX 45746-00100, NAIROBI, KENYA.
DEVJI, Mrs. Nasim Mohamed, FCA *1977;* (Tax Fac), Diamond Trust Bank Kenya Ltd, 8th Floor Nation Centre, Kimathi Street, P.O. Box 61711 - 00200, City Square, NAIROBI 00200 KENYA.
DEVLIN, Mr. Addison, ACA *2011;* 43 Pexton Road, SHEFFIELD, S4 7DA.
DEVLIN, Miss. Charley-Jo, LLB ACA *2010;* 69 Windmill Way, GATESHEAD, TYNE AND WEAR, NE8 1NU.
•**DEVLIN, Mrs. Clare Louise, ACA** *1994;* 18 Westley Road, BURY ST. EDMUNDS, SUFFOLK, IP33 3RW.
DEVLIN, Miss. Diane Christine, FCA *1971;* 41 Argyle Road, WALSALL, WS4 2EU.
DEVLIN, Mr. Gary, ACA CPFA *2010;* 3a Lockharton Gardens, EDINBURGH, EH14 1AU.
DEVLIN, Mrs. Helen, BSc ACA *1993;* 38 Lenthall Close, NORWICH, NR7 0UU.
DEVLIN, Mr. Ian David, BSc FCA *1988;* with Deloitte LLP, Athene Place, 66 Shoe Lane, LONDON, EC4A 3BQ.
DEVLIN, Mr. John Edward, BSc(Econ) ACA *1997;* Colgate Palmolive Ireland, Unit 3054, Lake Drive, Citywest Business Campus, Naas Road, DUBLIN 24 COUNTY DUBLIN IRELAND.
DEVLIN, Ms. Karen, BSc ACA *2005;* 44 Tamar Way, WOKINGHAM, BERKSHIRE, RG41 3UB.
DEVLIN, Mrs. Marie-Aude Simonne, BA ACA *1983;* 14 Domaine de l'Oree du Bois, 78600 LE MESNIL LE ROI, FRANCE.
DEVLIN, Mr. Patrick David James, FCA *1973;* 9f 100 Lane 162, JingYe 3rd Road, TAIPEI, 10466, TAIWAN.
DEVLIN, Mr. Patrick Gerard James, BA ACA *1999;* 185 Trevelyan Road, LONDON, SW17 9LP.
DEVLIN, Mr. Roderick, BA FCA *1983;* KPMG S.A., Immeuble Le Palatin, 3 Cours Du Triangle, PARIS LA DEFENCE CEDEX, FRANCE.
DEVLIN, Mr. Roger Samuel Robert, BCom ACA *1998;* 61 Clarence Road, LONDON, SW19 8QF.
DEVLIN, Miss. Sara, ACA *2004;* Jolliffe Cork Consulting Ltd, 33 George Street, WAKEFIELD, WEST YORKSHIRE, WF1 1LX.
•**DEVLIN, Mrs. Sarah Jane, ACA** *2002;* Sum It Accounts Ltd, 29 Greenlands Road, NEWBURY, BERKSHIRE, RG14 7JS.
DEVLIN, Mr. Tom Stuart Whitmarsh, BA ACA *2006;* 51 Macquarie Quay, EASTBOURNE, EAST SUSSEX, BN23 5AT.
DEVNEY, Mr. Simon Mark, BA ACA *1990;* 31 Ranelagh Gardens, Stamford Brook Avenue, LONDON, W6 0YE.
•**DEVON, Mr. David John, FCA** *1972;* Crowe Clark Whitehill LLP, St Bride's House, 10 Salisbury Square, LONDON, EC4Y 8EH. See also Horwath Clark Whitehill LLP and Crowe Clark Whitehill
DEVON-LOWE, Mr. Karl Philip, BSc ACA AMCT *1991;* 43 High Road, Cookham, MAIDENHEAD, BERKSHIRE, SL6 9HR.
DEVONALD, Mr. Andrew John, BSc ACA *1993;* 9 Spring Close, Kilsby, RUGBY, CV23 8YZ.
DEVONALD, Mr. John Hamilton, FCA *1977;* Mill Farm House, Goodshawfold Road, ROSSENDALE, BB4 8QN.
DEVONALD, Mrs. Philippa Susan, ACA *1986;* Mill Farm House, Goodshaw Fold, ROSSENDALE, BB4 8QN.
DEVONPORT, Mr. James Robert, BSc ACA *1997;* Hillcrest, Roundham Crescent, PAIGNTON, TQ4 6DF.
DEVONPORT, Mrs. Karen, BA ACA *1990;* ASD Metal Services, Valley Farm Road, Stourton, LEEDS, WEST YORKSHIRE, LS10 1SD.
•**DEVOY, Ms. Anne Elizabeth, MA ACA** *1989;* PricewaterhouseCoopers LLP, 1 Embankment Place, LONDON, WC2N 6RH. See also PricewaterhouseCoopers
DEVOY, Miss. Catherine Victoria, BA ACA *2000;* with Deloitte LLP, Athene Place, 66 Shoe Lane, LONDON, EC4A 3BQ.
DEVOY, Mrs. Dionne, BA ACA *1993;* 15 The Cedars, Whickham, NEWCASTLE UPON TYNE, NE16 5TH.
DEVOY, Mr. Sean Michael, BA ACA *1993;* 25 Hazelmere Avenue, Melton Park, Gosforth, NEWCASTLE UPON TYNE, NE3 5QL.
DEVRAM, Mr. Jayesh Jehram, BA ACA *1994;* 136 Wolmer Gardens, EDGWARE, MIDDLESEX, HA8 8QE.
DEW, Mr. Beverley Edward John, MSc FCA *1998;* Bovis Construction Ltd, Bovis House, 142 Northolt Road, HARROW, MIDDLESEX, HA2 0EE.
DEW, Mr. Christopher Mark, BA(Hons) ACA *2001;* 1 Old Lodge Close, Eashing Lane, GODALMING, SURREY, GU7 2LA.
DEW, Mr. Ian, BSc ACA *1988;* Draka UK Ltd, PO Box 6500 Alfreton Road, DERBY, DE21 4ZH.
DEW, Mr. Nigel Francis James, BSc ACA *1979;* 33 St. Catherines Road, EASTLEIGH, SO50 4JT.
•**DEW, Mr. Peter Arthur, FCA** *1975;* Peter Dew, 22 Lattimore Road, Wheathampstead, ST. ALBANS, HERTFORDSHIRE, AL4 8QE.
DEW, Mr. Richard, ACA *2009;* 35a Niton Street, LONDON, SW6 6NH.
DEW, Mr. Ronald Beresford, MA LLB FCA *1947;* Wiveton Barn, HOLT, NR25 7TF. (Life Member)
DEW, Mr. Simon John, BSc ACA *2005;* with PKF (UK) LLP, Farringdon Place, 20 Farringdon Road, LONDON, EC1M 3AP.
DEWAN, Mr. Ranvir, FCA *1977;* TPG Capital, 80 Raffles Place, # 15-01 UOB Plaza, SINGAPORE 048624, SINGAPORE.
•**DEWANI, Mr. Ragesh Kantilal, FCA** *1994;* (Tax Fac), Dewanis Limited, Westbury House, 23-25 Bridge Street, PINNER, MIDDLESEX, HA5 3HR.
DEWAR, The Hon. Alexander John Edward, BA ACA MSI *1997;* Brewin Dolphin Limited, 7 Drumsheugh Gardens, EDINBURGH, EH3 7QH.
DEWAR, Miss. Alison Mary, BA ACA *1999;* Eastwater Cottage, Snowdenham Lane, Bramley, GUILDFORD, SURREY, GU5 0DB.
DEWAR, Miss. Amy Judith Louisa, ACA *2009;* Flat 6, 90 St. John's Hill, Battersea, LONDON, SW11 1SH.
•**DEWAR, Mr. Calum McNiel, MA ACA** *1992;* PricewaterhouseCoopers LLP, 1 Embankment Place, LONDON, WC2N 6RH. See also PricewaterhouseCoopers
DEWAR, Mr. Cameron John, ACA *2009;* La Maitrerie Farm Cottage, La Rue de la Maitrerie, St. Martin, JERSEY, JE3 6HZ.
DEWAR, Mr. David Stephen, BSc ACA *2006;* 8 Western Corner, EDINBURGH, EH12 5PY.
DEWAR, Mr. Gordon Duthie, BSc FCA *1974;* 19 Gilpin Avenue, East Sheen, LONDON, SW14 8QX.
DEWAR, Mr. Graham Jon, BSc FCA *1993;* 33 Ogden Road, Bramhall, STOCKPORT, SK7 1HL.
•**DEWAR, Mr. Ian Andrew, BA FCA** *1983;* KPMG LLP, 15 Canada Square, LONDON, E14 5GL. See also KPMG Europe LLP
DEWAR, Mr. Ian Campbell, FCA *1975;* Appletree Cottage, New Road, ESHER, KT10 9PG.
DEWAR, Mr. John David, BA ACA *1991;* Skeats Bungalow, Horn Lane, East Hendred, WANTAGE, OX12 8LD.
•**DEWAR, Mr. Robert David, FCA** *1964;* Robert Dewar, 31 Rivermill, 151 Grosvenor Road, LONDON, SW1V 3JN.
DEWAR, Mr. Robert Gordon, FCA *1955;* 6/20 The Avenue, CRAWLEY, WA 6009, AUSTRALIA. (Life Member)
DEWAR, Mrs. Sally Marie, BSc ACA *1995;* Rowans, Golf Club Road, WOKING, SURREY, GU22 0LU.
•①**DEWAR, Mr. Taylor Douglas Gibson, BCom ACA** *2000;* Ernst & Young LLP, 1 Bridgewater Place, Water Lane, LEEDS, LS11 5QR. See also Ernst & Young Europe LLP
DEWAR, Mrs. Vivien Mary, BA ACA *1985;* Pandas, 60, Tollhouse Road, Stoke Heath, BROMSGROVE, B60 3QL.
DEWBERRY, Mr. Paul Robert, BSc ACA *1999;* 17 Evelyn Road, Residences@Evelyn #08-06, SINGAPORE 309306, SINGAPORE.
DEWELL, Mr. Gordon Charles, FCA *1977;* P.O. Box 322, ABU DHABI, UNITED ARAB EMIRATES.
DEWEY, Mr. Adrian Francis, BSc ACA *1998;* 67b High Street, Greenfield, BEDFORD, MK45 5DD.
DEWEY, Mr. Anthony Frederick, FCA *1971;* 17 Artillery Road, Welgemoed North, BELLVILLE, WESTERN CAPE PROVINCE, 7530, SOUTH AFRICA.
DEWEY, Mrs. Julia Rachel, BA ACA *1983;* Dewey & Co, 17 St. Andrews Crescent, CARDIFF, CF10 3DB.
DEWEY, Mrs. Julie Catherine, BSc(Hons) ACA *2001;* 22 Brookhill Drive, NOTTINGHAM, NG8 2PS.
DEWEY, Miss. Katie Marie, ACA *2008;* Thermo Fisher Scientific, Wade Road, BASINGSTOKE, HAMPSHIRE, RG24 8PW.
•①**DEWEY, Mr. Peter Richard, BSc FCA** *1982;* Dewey & Co, 17 St Andrews Crescent, CARDIFF, CF10 3DB. See also Begbies Traynor(Central) LLP and Begbies Traynor Limited
DEWEY, Mr. Richard Michael, BSc FCA *1996;* Battles Ltd, Crofton Drive, LINCOLN, LN3 4NP.
DEWEY, Mr. Stephen Paul, BSc ACA *1981;* Ashdown House, Banbury Road, Lower Boddington, DAVENTRY, NN11 6XY.
DEWHIRST, Mr. Andrew David, BEng ACA *1985;* 59 Old Park View, ENFIELD, MIDDLESEX, EN2 7EQ.
DEWHIRST, Mr. Christopher Roswell, MEng ACA *2004;* 9 The Mount, FLEET, GU51 4PX.
DEWHIRST, Miss. Clare, BA ACA *1988;* 114 Wheathead Lane, KEIGHLEY, BD22 6NN.
DEWHIRST, Mr. Graham, BSc(Econ) FCA *1977;* Hopton Grove, 21 Hopton Hall Lane, Upper Hopton, MIRFIELD, WF14 8EA.
DEWHIRST, Mrs. Joanna Louise, BSc ACA *2004;* with Roffe Swayne, Ashcombe Court, Woolsack Way, GODALMING, GU7 1LQ.
DEWHIRST, Mr. John Philip, MA MBA ACIB FCA MSTP *1989;* 7 Beechwood Avenue, Moorhead, SHIPLEY, BD18 4JU.
DEWHIRST, Mrs. Sharon Ann, BSc ACA *1988;* 59 Old Park View, ENFIELD, MIDDLESEX, EN2 7EQ.
DEWHIRST, Mrs. Susan Elizabeth, BA ACA *1993;* (Tax Fac), Murray Smith LLP, Darland House, 44 Winnington Hill, NORTHWICH, CHESHIRE, CW8 1AU.
DEWHURST, Mr. Cyril William, FCA *1948;* Cottage 21, 4 Ridgeway North, P O Chisipite, HARARE, ZIMBABWE. (Life Member)
DEWHURST, Mr. David Mark, BCom ACA *1988;* Hyrons Manor, 2 Hyrons Lane, AMERSHAM, BUCKINGHAMSHIRE, HP6 5AS.
DEWHURST, Miss. Mary Christine, BA ACA *2005;* 13 Puma Court, LONDON, E1 6QG.
DEWHURST, Mrs. Mary Patricia, BCom ACA *1988;* Hyrons Manor, 2 Hyrons Lane, AMERSHAM, BUCKINGHAMSHIRE, HP6 5AS.
DEWHURST, Mr. Michael, BA ACA *2004;* 91 St Marks Road, Randwick, SYDNEY, NSW 2031, AUSTRALIA.

DEWHURST, Mr. Simon, BSc ACA *1995;* 3/F Bisney Road, POK FU LAM, HONG KONG ISLAND, HONG KONG SAR.

DEWHURST, Mrs. Susanne Louise, BSc ACA *1994;* 19 Heythrop Drive, Heswall, WIRRAL, CH60 1YQ.

DEWING, Mr. Andrew, ACA ACCA *2010;* 168 Westgate, GUISBOROUGH, CLEVELAND, TS14 6NL.

DEWING, Mr. Basil Richard, FCA *1963;* Wentworth House, 20 Priory Road, MALVERN, WR14 3DR. (Life Member)

DEWING, Mr. Ian Paul, MAEd BA FCA *1992;* 5 Penshurst Mews, Eaton, NORWICH, NR4 6JJ.

DEWING, Mr. Steven Charles, ACA MAAT *2009;* 29 Harry Blunt Way, Scarning, DEREHAM, NORFOLK, NR19 2TU.

DEWINTER, Mr. Justin Zakgerald, FCA *1993;* 18 Shirehall Gardens, LONDON, NW4 2QS.

DEWIS, Mr. Richard James, BA ACA *2004;* CALLE ALEMANIA 1 CASA 6, CUARTE DE HUERVA, 50410 ZARAGOZA, SPAIN.

DEWS, Mr. Geoffrey Philip, FCA *1954;* Waterloo Place, 107 Pall Mall, LONDON, SW1Y 5ER. (Life Member)

DEWS, Mr. Marcus John, BA ACA *2005;* First Rand Bank Ltd, 20 Gracechurch Street, LONDON, EC3V 0BG.

DEWS, Mr. Rodney, FCA *1963;* 10 Courtney Close, TEWKESBURY, GL20 5FB.

DEWS, Mr. Thomas Joseph, BA(Hons) ACA *2009;* with Ernst & Young LLP, 1 Bridgewater Place, Water Lane, LEEDS, LS11 5QR.

DEWSHI, Mr. Aziz Ali Mohamed, FCA *1966;* 53 Barnes End, NEW MALDEN, KT3 6PB. (Life Member)

DEWSON, Mr. Iain Edward, BSc(Hons) ACA *2003;* 6 Furze Place, Furze Hill, REDHILL, RH1 1ER.

DEWSON, Mr. Lawrence, FCA *1960;* 2 Willow Way, Dartnell Park Road, WEST BYFLEET, KT14 6PS. (Life Member)

DEXTER, Mr. Alan Michael, FCA *1964;* 42 Stone Hall Road, LONDON, N21 1LP.

•DEXTER, Mrs. Caroline Anne, BSc(Hons) ACA *2001;* Barkers Accountants Limited, Street Ashton Farm House, Stretton Under Fosse, RUGBY, WARWICKSHIRE, CV23 0PH.

DEXTER, Mr. David Alexander, FCA *1960;* 5 High Street, Carlton-le-Moorland, LINCOLN, LN5 9HT.

DEXTER, Mr. George Leonard, BSc ACA *1988;* 10 Kentish Gardens, TUNBRIDGE WELLS, TN2 5XU.

DEXTER, Mr. Graeme Peter Andrew, FCA *1973;* 72 Gorwel, LLANFAIRFECHAN, CONWY, LL33 0DT.

DEXTER, Mr. Paul Ivan, MSc BA FCA *1975;* 21 Park Lane, Allestree, DERBY, DE22 2DT.

DEXTER, Mrs. Samantha Jane, BA ACA *1993;* Marita Norchard Lane, Peopleton, PERSHORE, WORCESTERSHIRE, WR10 2ED.

DEXTER, Mr. Simon, BA ACA *2010;* 176a Kennington Park Road, LONDON, SE11 4BT.

DEXTER, Mr. Simon Peter, MA ACA *1983;* Aqualisa Products Ltd, Aqualisa Products Ltd Aqualisa, Westerham Trade Centre The Flyers Way, WESTERHAM, TN16 1DE.

DEXTER, Mr. Stephen Kenneth, FCA *1968;* Inanda, Main Street, Grove, WANTAGE, OX12 7HT.

DEXTER, Mr. William Mark, BSc ACA *1996;* Hendra Holiday Park, Lane, NEWQUAY, CORNWALL, TR8 4NY.

DEXTER-SMITH, Mr. Michael John, BSc FCA *1978;* 1050 Winter street, Xtremesoft suite 1000, WALTHAM, MA 02451, UNITED STATES.

DEY, Mr. Asish Kumar, MA ACA *1987;* Flat 3 Abingdon Mansions, Abingdon Road, LONDON, W8 6AD.

DEY, Mr. James Alexander Nash, ACA *2001;* The Royal Bank of Scotland Plc, 280 Bishopsgate, LONDON, EC2M 4RB.

DEY, Mr. James Scott Davidson, FCA *1938;* La Residence des Cedres, 10 Avenue du Parc, Thonon-les-Bains, 74200 PARIS, FRANCE. (Life Member)

•DEY, Mr. Joseph William, FCA *1973;* (Tax Fac), Dey & Co Ltd, Brookdale, 41 Clarence Road, CHESTERFIELD, S40 1LH. See also Dey & Co

DEY, Miss. Midula Rani, LLB ACA *2002;* The Jam factory, Flat 13 Block A, 27 Green Walk, LONDON, SE1 4TT.

DEY, Mr. Peter Anthony, FCA *1960;* 24 Priestlands Park Road, SIDCUP, DA15 7HR. (Life Member)

DEY, Miss. Sharmistha, BSc ACA *2011;* 62 Coombe Rise, Oadby, LEICESTER, LE2 5TW.

DEYCON, Mr. Tym N G, FCA *1971;* 11 The Green, Little Horwood, MILTON KEYNES, MK17 0PB.

DEYES, Mr. Peter Rathbone, BCom FCA *1963;* 6 Firs Crescent, LIVERPOOL, L37 1PT.

DEYONG, Miss. Jacqueline Susan, BA FCA *1978;* 192 Old Woking Road, WOKING, GU22 8HR.

•DEYONG, Mr. Lionel Saul, FCA *1973;* Scodie Deyong LLP, 85 Frampton Street, LONDON, NW8 8NQ.

DEZYK, Mr. Myron, BA ACA *1986;* Brocton, East End Way, PINNER, HA5 3BS.

DHADWAL, Mr. Amarjit Singh, BA(Hons) ACA *2003;* 101 Devonshire Road, SMETHWICK, B67 7QQ.

DHALA, Mr. Karim Tajdin Mohamedali, BSc ACA *1988;* Qualitas Healthcare Corporation Sdn Bhd, 301 Menara PJ Amcorp Trade Centre, Persiaran Barat, 46050 PETALING JAYA, SELANGOR, MALAYSIA.

DHALA, Mr. Mahmood Zulfikar, ACA *1980;* PO Box 43044 RPO Standard Life, 10405 Jasper Avenue, EDMONTON T5J 4M8, AB, CANADA.

DHALABHOY, Mr. Azim, FCA *1973;* A.Dhalabhoy, 371 Torbay Road, HARROW, HA2 9QD.

DHALIWAL, Mr. Amar Iqbal Singh, MSc ACA *1988;* 1258 Bracknell Place, NORTH VANCOUVER V7R 1V5, BC, CANADA.

DHALIWAL, Mrs. Davinder Kaur, BSc ACA *1997;* 31 Saturn Croft, Winkfield Row, BRACKNELL, RG42 6PA.

DHALIWAL, Miss. Hardish Kaur, MA FCA *1987;* 26 Eastmount Avenue, TORONTO M4K 1V1, ON, CANADA.

•DHALIWAL, Mr. Harvinder Singh, BA FCA FPC *1987;* (Tax Fac), Harvey & Co, 76a Uxbridge Road, Ealing, LONDON, W13 8RA.

DHALIWAL, Mr. Jaswinder Singh, BSc ACA *1997;* 31 Saturn Croft, Winkfield Row, BRACKNELL, RG42 6PA.

DHALIWAL, Mr. Randeep Singh, ACA *2008;* (Tax Fac), Flat 4, 353 Uxbridge Road, LONDON, W3 9RH.

DHALL, Mr. Sunil, MEng ACA *2001;* 41 Beresford Road, KINGSTON UPON THAMES, SURREY, KT2 6LP.

DHALLA, Mr. Gulamabbas Hassanali, FCA *1974;* 54 Moss Lane, PINNER, HA5 3AX.

DHALLU, Mr. Ravinder Singh, ACA *2010;* 53 Sunningdale Avenue, BARKING, ESSEX, IG11 7QF.

•DHALWANI, Mr. Pramod, FCA FPC *1999;* PDCA, 1 Scotch Firs, Wavendon Gate, MILTON KEYNES, MK7 7RR. See also Abiserve

DHAM, Miss. Shalini, BA ACA *2006;* 73 Hillfield Park, Winchmore Hill, LONDON, N21 3QJ.

DHAMECHA, Mr. Dipak, BA(Hons) ACA *2009;* 92 Carlyle Avenue, SOUTHALL, MIDDLESEX, UB1 2BJ.

DHAMI, Mrs. Gurdeep, BA ACA *2007;* 20 Church Street, Heath Town, WOLVERHAMPTON, WV10 0LU.

DHAMI, Mr. Gurdip Singh, MSc BSc ACA ACT *1994;* 41 Eton Road, STRATFORD-UPON-AVON, WARWICKSHIRE, CV37 7ER.

DHAMI, Mr. Kevin Singh, BSc ACA *2007;* 8 Horsted Way, ROCHESTER, KENT, ME1 2XY.

DHANANI, Mr. Ahmad Akbar, ACA *2011;* G/5 Hill Side Residency, Feroz Nana Road Bath Island, KARACHI 75530, PAKISTAN.

DHANANI, Mr. Aly Nizar, BEng ACA *1999;* PO Box 75653, DUBAI, UNITED ARAB EMIRATES.

•DHANANI, Mr. Bharat-Kumar Premchand, BSc FCA *1985;* (Tax Fac), DSJ Partners LLP, 2nd Floor, 1 Bell Street, LONDON, NW1 5BY.

DHANANI, Mr. Kunj, ACA *2010;* 47a Bridle Road, PINNER, MIDDLESEX, HA5 2SP.

DHANANI, Mr. Pravinchandra Meghji Sojpal, FCA *1971;* Spinners & Spinners Ltd, P.O.Box 46206, G.P.O, NAIROBI, 00100, KENYA.

DHANANI, Mr. Ravi, BEng ACA *2008;* PricewaterhouseCoopers, Dorchester House, 7 Church Street, HAMILTON HM 11, BERMUDA.

DHANANI, Mr. Rishi Vijaykumar, BSc ACA *2011;* 71 Merrion Avenue, STANMORE, MIDDLESEX, HA7 4RY.

•DHANANI, Mr. Sachin, BSc ACA *2003;* Innovata Business Solutions Limited, 26 Rofant Road, NORTHWOOD, MIDDLESEX, HA6 3BE.

•DHANANI, Mr. Sangeet Dinesh, BA ACA *1999;* Innovata Business Solutions Limited, 26 Rofant Road, NORTHWOOD, MIDDLESEX, HA6 3BE.

DHANANI, Mr. Shabir, ACA *1981;* 2803 - 1438 Richards Street, VANCOUVER V6Z 3B8, BC, CANADA.

DHANANI, Mr. Shafique Nazerali, FCA *1978;* 56 Chambertin, KIRKLAND H9H 5E3, QC, CANADA.

DHANANI, Miss. Tina, BSc ACA *2009;* 7 Castellane Close, STANMORE, MIDDLESEX, HA7 3TN.

DHANANI, Mrs. Urvashi, BSc ACA *1993;* 29 Pamela Gardens, PINNER, HA5 2QU.

DHAND, Mr. Hareesh, BSc FCA CF *1983;* The Station Mill, Station Road, ALRESFORD, HAMPSHIRE, SO24 9JQ.

•DHANDA, Mr. Ashish, BA FCA *1991;* Alexander Rosse Limited, 10 Linford Forum, Rockingham Drive, Linford Wood, MILTON KEYNES, MK14 6LY.

DHANDA, Mr. Gurminder Singh, BEng ACA *1995;* 53 Woodfield Road, SOLIHULL, B91 2DN.

DHANDA, Mr. Mohnish, BSc FCA *1992;* Solicitors Regulation Authority, Ipsley Court, Berrington Close, REDDITCH, WORCESTERSHIRE, B98 0TD.

DHANJEE, Mr. Amin Ahmedali, ACA *1990;* Broadway Nursing & Residential Care Home, 22-32 Flemington Avenue, LIVERPOOL, L4 8UD.

DHANJI, Mr. Iqbal, MBA BSc FCA *1992;* 8 Savery Drive, Long Ditton, SURBITON, KT6 5RH.

DHANOA, Mr. Sarbdayal Singh, MBA ACA ACMA *2009;* with Philips Lighting, Philips Centre, Guildford Business Park, GUILDFORD, SURREY, GU2 8XH.

DHANUKA, Mr. Sushil, ACA *2010;* 1605 Burlington, Hiranandani Estate, THANE 400607, INDIA.

DHAR, Mr. Panna Kanti, FCA *1964;* 13 Twin Oaks Road, PARSIPPANY, NJ 07054, UNITED STATES. (Life Member)

DHAR, Mr. Thomas Pradip, BSc ACA *2010;* 11 Westernmoor Road, NEATH, WEST GLAMORGAN, SA11 1BJ.

DHARAMSHI, Mrs. Barbara Joan, FCA *1965;* 13 Slave Hill, Haddenham, AYLESBURY, HP17 8AY. (Life Member)

DHARAMSHI, Mr. Nazeem John, MA ACA MBA *2000;* 56 Crystal Palace Road, East Dulwich, LONDON, SE22 9EY.

DHARAMSHI, Mr. Tajdeen Mohamedali Kanji, BA FCA *1967;* 13 Slave Hill, Haddenham, AYLESBURY, HP17 8AY.

DHARAMSI, Mr. Mohammed Iqbal, BA FCA *1984;* 10 Marina Court, Glacis Road, GIBRALTAR, GIBRALTAR.

DHARAMSI, Mr. Rahim Firozali, BA ACA *2002;* 4 Liberty Apartments, 19 Devon Road, WATFORD, WD24 4HS.

DHARANI, Mr. Babar, BA ACA *2005;* PAT Auto Ltd, PO Box 59509, 00200, NAIROBI, KENYA.

DHARMADHIKARI, Mr. Mukund Sadashiv, FCA *1976;* 12 Annie Besant Road, Worli, MUMBAI 400 018, INDIA.

DHARMAGUNAWARDENA, Miss. Varuni Samantha, ACA *2008;* Flat 28, 28 Bartholomew Close, LONDON, EC1A 7ES.

DHARSI, Mr. Ashid, CA FCA CTA *1979;* 6527 Balmoral Street, BURNABY V5E 1H9, BC, CANADA.

•DHARSI, Mr. Taha Mohammed, FCA *1974;* (Tax Fac), Dharsi & Co, Woodview, 92a Broadwood Avenue, RUISLIP, MIDDLESEX, HA4 7XT.

•DHARSI, Mr. Yasir, ACA *2008;* Thought Revolution Limited, 38a Station Road, North Harrow, HARROW, MIDDLESEX, HA2 7SE.

DHATT, Mrs. Amrit Roop, ACA *2011;* 48 Langley Road, SLOUGH, SL3 7AD.

•DHAUN, Mr. Ved Prakash, FCA *1977;* Ved Dhaun & Co, 20 Lansdowne Terrace, Gosforth, NEWCASTLE UPON TYNE, NE3 1HP.

DHAWAN, Mr. Anand Kumar, FCA *1965;* 55A Jorbagh, NEW DELHI 110 003, INDIA. (Life Member)

DHAWAN, Mrs. Melanie Helen, BCom ACA *2001;* 15 Vaughan Road, THAMES DITTON, KT7 0UF.

DHAWAN, Mr. Michael, ACA *2011;* 73 Grange Road, Fenham, NEWCASTLE UPON TYNE, NE4 9LB.

DHAYALAN, Mr. Hari, BEng ACA *2007;* 9 Jalan Hajijah, #04-06 Landbay, SINGAPORE 468704, SINGAPORE.

DHERI, Mr. Daljit Singh, BCom ACA *2005;* 21 Rowthorn Drive, Shirley, SOLIHULL, B90 4ST.

DHESI, Mrs. Balvir Kaur, BA(Hons) ACA *2004;* 13 Park Avenue, GRAVESEND, DA12 1NS.

•DHILLON, Mr. Abdul Azeem, ACA CTA IAC *1993;* Dhillons, 139 Blendon Road, BEXLEY, DA5 1BT.

DHILLON, Miss. Amanpreet Ruby, BCom ACA *2004;* 969 Garratt Lane, LONDON, SW17 0LW.

DHILLON, Mr. Balbir Singh, BSc ACA *1995;* 6B Boon Tiong Road. #09-53, SINGAPORE 165006, SINGAPORE.

DHILLON, Mrs. Baljit Kaur, ACA *2009;* 64a Shelley Crescent, HOUNSLOW, MIDDLESEX, TW5 9BJ.

DHILLON, Mr. Gurminder Singh, BA ACA *2004;* with Deloitte LLP, Athene Place, 66 Shoe Lane, LONDON, EC4A 3BQ.

DHILLON, Mrs. Harjit Kaur, ACA *2008;* 106 Yeading Lane, HAYES, MIDDLESEX, UB4 0EY.

DHILLON, Miss. Harmeet Kaur, BSc ACA *1998;* with PricewaterhouseCoopers, 145 King Street West, TORONTO M5H 1V8, ON, CANADA.

DHILLON, Miss. Inderpal, LLB ACA *2009;* 156 Wilmington Gardens, BARKING, IG11 9TZ.

DHILLON, Mrs. Kamal, BSc(Hons) ACA *2003;* with PricewaterhouseCoopers LLP, Pricewaterhousecoopers, 12 Plumtree Court, LONDON, EC4A 4HT.

DHILLON, Mrs. Kerandeep, ACA *2009;* with Littlejohn, 1 Westferry Circus, Canary Wharf, LONDON, E14 4HD.

DHILLON, Miss. Komal, ACA *2009;* Flat 6, 53 Regency Street, LONDON, SW1P 4AF.

DHILLON, Mr. Manmeet, ACA *2009;* Flat B, 57 Dartmouth Road, LONDON, NW2 4EP.

DHILLON, Mr. Navjyot Singh, BSc ACA *1994;* (Tax Fac), Barclays Capital, 5 The North Colonnade, Canary Wharf, LONDON, E14 4BB.

DHILLON, Mr. Parminder Singh, ACA *2009;* 177 Leigh Hunt Drive, LONDON, N14 6DQ.

•DHILLON, Mr. Philip Ranjit, BA FCA *1986;* Sterling House, Wavell Drive, Rosehill, CARLISLE, CA1 2SA. See also Saint & Co

DHILLON, Miss. Rajeet, BSc ACA *2011;* Meadow View, 1c Biddenham Turn, Biddenham, BEDFORD, MK40 4AT.

DHILLON, Mr. Ranvir, ACA *2011;* 27 Sutton Avenue, LANGLEY, BERKSHIRE, SL3 7AP.

•DHILLON, Ms. Sandeep, BA ACA *2001;* with PricewaterhouseCoopers LLP, 1 Embankment Place, LONDON, WC2N 6RH.

DHILLON, Mr. Sanvir, BSc ACA *2010;* Flat 21, Buckland Court, St. John's Estate, LONDON, N1 6TY.

•DHILLON, Mr. Satvir, MSc ACA *2007;* Chaucer, 64a Shelley Crescent, HOUNSLOW, TW5 9BJ.

DHILLON, Mr. Savraj Singh, MSc ACA *1999;* 284 Norwood Road, SOUTHALL, MIDDLESEX, UB2 4JH.

DHILLON, Ms. Sejal, BA ACA *1988;* GE Healthcare Ltd, Pollards Wood, Nightingales Lane, CHALFONT ST. GILES, BUCKINGHAMSHIRE, HP8 4SP.

DHILLON, Mr. Sukhbir Singh, BSc(Hons) ACA *2001;* Thales Telecom Services Ltd, 4 Thomas More Square, LONDON, E1W 1YW.

DHILLON, Mr. Sundeep, BEng ACA MBA *2000;* PO Box 1457, BELLEVUE, WA 98009, UNITED STATES.

DHILLON, Mr. Tarlochan Singh, FCA *1975;* 143 Olive Street, GRIMSBY L3M 5C9, ON, CANADA.

DHIMAN, Mr. Dev, BSc ACA *2009;* Flat 2 Griffith Court, 5 Madoc Close, LONDON, NW2 2BG.

DHIMAN, Mr. Jaswinder, ACA *2008;* 6 Verney Road, DAGENHAM, ESSEX, RM9 5LL.

DHIR, Mr. Pawan, BSc ACA *1995;* 11d Hornsey Lane Gardens, LONDON, N6 5NX.

•DHIR, Mr. Purshotam, FCA *1970;* Purshotam Dhir, A3 Chiragh Enclave, NEW DELHI 110048, INDIA. See also Mehra Dhir Bhatia & Co

DHIR, Mr. Ramesh Kumar, FCA *1965;* 121 Sunflower Apts, G.D. Somani Road, Cuffe Parade, MUMBAI 400005, MAHARASHTRA, INDIA.

DHIR, Mr. Sanjay Kumar, ACA *1993;* 23b Tregunter Tower 1, 14 Tregunter Path, MID LEVELS, HONG KONG ISLAND, HONG KONG SAR.

DHITAL, Mr. Ayush, MSc BSc ACA *2007;* Flat 12 Blemundsbury, Dombey Street, LONDON, WC1N 3PF.

DHODY, Mr. Jog, BCom ACA *2002;* 2 Rebecca Gardens, Penn, WOLVERHAMPTON, WV4 5PR.

•DHOKIA, Mrs. Joystna, BA ACA *1998;* 14 Ellerman Avenue, Whitton, TWICKENHAM, MIDDLESEX, TW2 6AS.

•DHOKIA, Mr. Suresh, MA ACA *1986;* Warr & Co, Mynshull House, 78 Churchgate, STOCKPORT, SK1 1YJ. See also Warr & Co Limited

DHOLAKIA, Mrs. Hardika, ACA CTA *1995;* with Hayles & Partners Limited, 39 Castle Street, LEICESTER, LE1 5WN.

DHONDY, Mr. Homi Behramji, MA FCA *1950;* H.B. Dhondy & Co, Taj Building, 2nd Floor, 210 Dr. Dadabhai Naoroji Road, MUMBAI 400 001, INDIA. (Life Member)

DHOOT, Mr. Jugjait Singh, BSc ACA *1992;* 22361 NE 6th Court, SAMMAMISH, WA 98074, UNITED STATES.

DHOOT, Mr. Kulwarn Singh, BSc FCA *1995;* 67 Langley Road, SLOUGH, SL3 7AJ.

DHOOT, Miss. Saranjit Kaur, LLB(Hons) ACA *2010;* 36 Rothbury Drive, ASHINGTON, NORTHUMBERLAND, NE63 8TQ.

DHOPATKAR, Mr. Dewesh Avinash, BSc ACA *1997;* Redstack, 58 Sanderstead Court Avenue, SANDERSTEAD, CR2 9AJ.

Members - Alphabetical DHUL - DICKINSON

DHUL, Mr. Sumeet, BSc ACA *1992;* 35 Otter Lane, Mountsorrel, LOUGHBOROUGH, LE12 7GF.
•**DHULL, Mrs. Kamlesh, ACA** *2010;* Homefield, Wood Lane, Iver Heath, IVER, SL0 0LE.
DHUNNOO, Mr. Twalha, MA MEng BA ACA *2002;* 47 College Gardens, LONDON, SW17 7UF.
DHUPELIA, Mr. Chandrakant Nitilal, FCA *1966;* Flat No 1, 64 Avenue Road, Highgate, LONDON, N6 5DR. (Life Member)
DHUPELIA, Miss. Suniti Ramila Chandrakant, BSc ACA *2005;* Flat 508, Cascades Tower, 4 Westferry Road, LONDON, E14 8JL.
DI CARA, Mr. Paul Stephen, FCA *1977;* 20 Barbuda Quay, EASTBOURNE, EAST SUSSEX, BN23 5TT.
DI CIACCA, Mr. Nicola Antonio, BA ACA *2001;* 60 New Broad Street, LONDON, EC2M 1JJ.
•**DI FRANCO, Mr. Marco, BSc ACA CTA** *1997;* (Tax Fac), Augmenture Ltd, 20 Links Side, ENFIELD, MIDDLESEX, EN2 7QZ.
•**DI GIUSEPPE, Mr. Peter Ettore, BSc FCA** *1971;* (Tax Fac), Peter Di Giuseppe, Witsend, 10 Poplar Close, Aller Park, NEWTON ABBOT, TQ12 4PG.
DI LELLIO, Mr. Riccardo, BA ACA *1995;* 42 Quilter Street, LONDON, E2 7BT.
•**DI LETO, Mr. Michael, ACA** *1994;* (Tax Fac), Saffery Champness, Lion House, Red Lion Street, LONDON, WC1R 4GB.
DI LORENZO, Mr. Alberto, ACA *2008;* 11 Brittens Lane, Salford, MILTON KEYNES, MK17 8BE.
DI LORENZO, Mr. Antonio, BA ACA *1993;* 25 Roseneath Road, LONDON, SW11 6AG.
DI MAMBRO, Miss. Hannah Mary Rose, BSc ACA CTA *1997;* Holly Cottage Kings Lane, Chipperfield, KINGS LANGLEY, HERTFORDSHIRE, WD4 9EP.
DI PAOLA, Mr. Paul Michael, ACA *2009;* 108 Clarence Road, LONDON, SW19 8QD.
DI PAOLA, Mrs. Sarah Elizabeth, BSc ACA *2006;* 108 Clarence Road, LONDON, SW19 8QD.
DI PAOLA, Mr. Sebastian Sergio Luigi, MA ACA ACT *1995;* PricewaterhouseCoopers AG, 50 Avenue Giuseppe-Motta, CH-1202 GENEVA, SWITZERLAND.
DI-STEFANO, Mr. Jonathan Graham, MA ACA *2000;* Telford Homes Plc, First Floor, Stuart House, Queensgate, Britannia Road, WALTHAM CROSS HERTFORDSHIRE EN8 7TF.
DI VITO, Mrs. Rachel Caroline Jane, BSc ACA ATII *1991;* Flat 2, 45 Queen's Gate Terrace, LONDON, SW7 5PN.
DIAB, Mr. Elias Tannous, FCA *1972;* Domallia, 11 Oswald Road, EDINBURGH, EH9 2HE. (Life Member)
•**DIACK, Mr. Stuart Mackenzie, LLB FCA** *1997;* with Deloitte LLP, 2 New Street Square, LONDON, EC4A 3BZ.
DIAL, Mr. Louis Harold, BA BSc ACA *1989;* Lane Heads House, Watery Gate Lane, Great Eccleston, PRESTON, PR3 0XH.
•**DIAMOND, Mr. Edward Anthony Gerard, BA FCA** *1993;* with Ernst & Young LLP, 1 Bridgewater Place, Water Lane, LEEDS, LS11 5QR.
DIAMOND, Miss. Emma Louise, LLB ACA *2006;* 21 Allendale Road, LOUGHBOROUGH, LEICESTERSHIRE, LE11 2HX.
DIAMOND, Mrs. Joanna, BA ACA *1999;* 28 Ivar Gardens, Lychpit, BASINGSTOKE, HAMPSHIRE, RG24 8YD.
DIAMOND, Mrs. Joanna Mary, BSc ACA *1989;* Citigroup, Canada Square, Canary Wharf, LONDON, E14 5LB.
DIAMOND, Mr. John Raymond, BSc ACA *1986;* Resolute Management Services Ltd Exchequer Court, 33 St. Mary Axe, LONDON, EC3A 8LL.
DIAMOND, Mrs. Julie Elizabeth, BSc ACA *1992;* 39 Nenthead Close, Great Lumley, CHESTER-LE-STREET, DH3 4SP.
DIAMOND, Mr. Laurence Stanley, FCA *1956;* 2a Stanhope Gardens, Highgate, LONDON, N6 5TS. (Life Member)
DIAMOND, Mr. Martin, MA FCA *1962;* Flat 22 87 Vincent Square, LONDON, SW1P 2PQ. (Life Member)
•**DIAMOND, Mr. Richard Edward, MA FCA** *1973;* Richard Diamond, 01 BP 7168, ABIDJAN, COTE d'IVOIRE.
DIAMOND, Mr. Shai, BA ACA *2008;* Ba'al HaSheiltot 8, Kiryat Moshe, JERUSALEM, ISRAEL.
DIAPER, Mr. Colin Malcolm, FCA *1962;* Sunny Cottage, The Street, Chilmark, SALISBURY, SP3 5AR. (Life Member)
•**DIAS, Mr. Denver Aloysius, FCA** *1980;* (Tax Fac), Williams, Jade House, 67 Park Royal Road, LONDON, NW10 7JJ.
DIAS, Mr. James Robert, BCom ACA *2004;* Basement Flat (entrance on Constitution Hill), 1 Bellevue, BRISTOL, BS8 1DA.
•**DIAS, Mr. Kenneth Peter, BA FCA** *1988;* Nyman Libson Paul, Regina House, 124 Finchley Road, LONDON, NW3 5JS.
DIAS, Mr. Raymond, FCA *1970;* 1 Castlereagh House, Lady Aylesford Avenue, STANMORE, MIDDLESEX, HA7 4FP. (Life Member)
DIAS, Mrs. Sarah, BSc ACA *2004;* 6 St. Marks Crescent, MAIDENHEAD, SL6 5DB.
DIAZ, Mr. Jay Mathew, BA ACA *2004;* 94 Cosmeston Street, CARDIFF, CF24 4LR.
DIBA - CAMPBELL, Mrs. Eva Elizabeth, BSc ACA *2002;* 9 Ormeley Road, Balham, LONDON, SW12 9QF.
DIBB, Mr. Ian Nigel, MBA BSc FCA *1979;* Devonshire Cottage, Bussage, STROUD, GL6 8BA.
DIBB, Mr. Peter, FCA *1973;* 86 Oakdale Drive, Heald Green, CHEADLE, CHESHIRE, SK8 3SW.
DIBB, Mr. Peter James, FCA *1960;* 31 Hillside Crescent, Newsome, HUDDERSFIELD, WEST YORKSHIRE, HD4 6LY. (Life Member)
DIBBEN, Mr. Francis Robert, ACA *2003;* Hays Specialist Recruitment Unit 5805-7 The Centre 99 Queen's Road, CENTRAL, HONG KONG SAR.
DIBBERN, Mr. Nick, ACA *2007;* Channel Four Television, 124-126 Horseferry Road, LONDON, SW1P 2TX.
DIBBLE, Mr. Edward, PhD MEng ACA *2009;* 78 Montreal House, Surrey Quays Road, LONDON, SE16 7AP.
DIBBO, Mr. James Malcolm, BSc(Econ) ACA *1997;* Fresh and Easy Neighborhood Market Inc, 2120 Park Place, EL SEGUNDO, CA 90245, UNITED STATES.
DIBDEN, Mr. Lindsay George, BSc ACA *1989;* H G Capital, 2 More London Riverside, LONDON, SE1 2AP.
DIBDEN, Mr. Rodney Gavin James, FCA *1966;* 6 Ovington Avenue, BOURNEMOUTH, BH7 6SB.
DIBLEY, Miss. Clare Hannah, BA ACA *1996;* Golf Tech Ltd Unit 5, Woodside Road South Marston Industrial Estate, SWINDON, SN3 4WA.
DIBLEY, Mr. Richard John, BSc FCA *1979;* Amberleaze, 2 Lower Green Road, Pembury, TUNBRIDGE WELLS, TN2 4DA.
DICEY, Mr. Clive Richard, FCA *1961;* 56 Feltham Hill Road, ASHFORD, MIDDLESEX, TW15 2DF.
DICHLER, Mr. Mark John, BSc ACA *1990;* 30 Almorah Road, Victoria Park, BRISTOL, BS3 4QQ.
DICK, Mr. Andrew Francis, FCA *1980;* Mulberry Cottage, Morris Street, HOOK, RG27 9NT.
DICK, Mr. Andrew Morris, BCom ACA *1995;* Deloitte, Private Bag 115033, Shortland Street, AUCKLAND, NEW ZEALAND.
•**DICK, Mr. Angus Handasyde, BA ACA** *1981;* Angus Handasyde Dick, Lower Shearlangstone, Modbury, IVYBRIDGE, PL21 0TQ.
DICK, Mr. Cameron James, BAcc ACA *2001;* 52 Hill Rise, RICKMANSWORTH, HERTFORDSHIRE, WD3 7NZ.
DICK, Mr. David John, FCA *1977;* 1 Bell House Place, 11 London Road South, Merstham, REDHILL, SURREY, RH1 3AZ. (Life Member)
DICK, Mrs. Denise Sarah, FCA *1980;* Honda Motor Europe Ltd, 470 London Road, SLOUGH, SL3 8QY.
•**DICK, Mr. George William, FCA** *1952;* G W Dick & Co LLP, Earl Grey House, 11 Beach Road, SOUTH SHIELDS, TYNE AND WEAR, NE33 2QA.
DICK, Mr. James Andrew, BA FCA *1971;* Kilnfield, Itchingwood Common, Limpsfield, OXTED, RH8 0RJ. (Life Member)
DICK, Miss. Justine, ACA *2008;* 41 Southborough Road, LONDON, E9 7EF.
DICK, Mr. Keith Joseph, FCA *1965;* 3 Deans Court, Milford on Sea, LYMINGTON, HAMPSHIRE, SO41 0SG. (Life Member)
DICK, Mr. Malcolm Gordon, FCA *1963;* Green Hollow, Lower Broad Oak Road, West Hill, OTTERY ST. MARY, DEVON, EX11 1XH. (Life Member)
•**DICK, Mr. Robert Learmonth, FCA** *1975;* R Learmonth Dick, 3a Headley Road, Woodley, READING, RG5 4JB. See also Cameron Browne
DICK, Mrs. Rosemary, BA ACA *1991;* Dolphin House, Charlton Park Gate, CHELTENHAM, GLOUCESTERSHIRE, GL53 7DJ.
DICK, Miss. Sharon Louise, LLB ACA *2006;* 214 Parklands, ROCHFORD, SS4 1SY.
DICK, Mr. Stuart John Macfarlane, MA ACA *2001;* Search Consultancy Ltd Campbell House, 215 West Campbell Street, GLASGOW, G2 4TT.
DICK, Mr. Trevor John, BSc FCA *1996;* Ernst & Young Advisory Services Ltd, 4/F Hutchison House, 10 Harcourt Road, CENTRAL, HONG KONG SAR.
•**DICK, Mr. William Robert Andrew, FCA** *1994;* (Tax Fac), G W Dick & Co LLP, Earl Grey House, 11 Beach Road, SOUTH SHIELDS, TYNE AND WEAR, NE33 2QA.
•**DICK-CLELAND, Mr. Alexander Henry George, BSc FCA** *1984;* Cleland & Co Limited, 1st Floor, Harbour Court, Les Amballes, St. Peter Port, GUERNSEY GY1 1WU.
DICKASON, Mr. Donovan, ACA CA(SA) *2010;* 2 Doull Road, Mayorswalk, PIETERMARITZBURG, KWAZULU NATAL, 3201, SOUTH AFRICA.
DICKEL, Mr. Antony John, BSc ACA *1986;* MRI Worldwide China Group, HONG KONG SAR Office, 2nd Floor, Wilson House, 19 - 27 Wyndham Street, CENTRAL HONG KONG ISLAND HONG KONG SAR.
DICKEN, Mr. Albert Bernard, FCA *1966;* 11 Boldmere Drive, SUTTON COLDFIELD, B73 5ES.
DICKEN, Mr. Paul Robert, BA ACA *1985;* 14 The Hollow, Hartford, HUNTINGDON, CAMBRIDGESHIRE, PE29 1YF.
DICKENS, Mr. Alfred Peter, FCA *1951;* 29 Meadsview Court, Clockhouse Road, FARNBOROUGH, Hampshire, GU14 7NW. (Life Member)
DICKENS, Mr. Christopher Paul, BA ACA *1998;* 9 Rocks Close, East Malling, WEST MALLING, KENT, ME19 6AE.
DICKENS, Mr. David John Hamilton, FCA TEP *1970;* Fulcrum Administration LLC, PO Box 49608, Atrium Centre - Suite 409, Khalid Bin Walid Street, DUBAI, UNITED ARAB EMIRATES.
•**DICKENS, Mr. Kevin, FCA** *1973;* (Tax Fac), 5 Long Acre, Weaverham, NORTHWICH, CW8 3PT.
DICKENS, Mr. Malcolm Welsh, FCA *1965;* 19 Naish Road, Barton on Sea, NEW MILTON, HAMPSHIRE, BH25 7PT. (Life Member)
DICKENS, Mr. Mark Christopher, BA FCA *1976;* (Tax Fac), Lee-Dickens Ltd, Rushton Road, Desborough, KETTERING, NN14 2QW.
•**DICKENS, Mrs. Melanie Gaenor, BSc(Hons) ACA** *1995;* Melanie Shepherd, 1 Vine Cottage, Village Green, Northchapel, PETWORTH, WEST SUSSEX GU28 9HU.
•**DICKENS, Mrs. Sophia Elizabeth, BSc ACA** *2005;* Sophia Dickens BSc ACA, 27 West Way, HARPENDEN, AL5 4RD.
DICKENS, Mr. Stephen Charles, BSc ACA *1979;* Flat 22, The Square, Chatham Way, BRENTWOOD, ESSEX, CM14 4AL.
•**DICKENS, Mr. Stephen Paul, BSc FCA** *1989;* 2a Lansdowne Road, SOUTHAMPTON, SO15 4HB.
DICKENSON, Mr. Alexis Ray, BSc ACA *2007;* 48 Dornoch Avenue, NOTTINGHAM, NG5 4DP.
DICKENSON, Mr. Maurice, FCA *1962;* (Tax Fac), 1 Corby Gate, Corby HallAshbrooke, SUNDERLAND, SR2 7JB. (Life Member)
DICKENSON, Mr. Stephen Edward, ACA *1982;* 81 Munster Road, TEDDINGTON, TW11 9LS.
DICKER, Mr. Adrian John Walter, MA FCA *1979;* 5 Tuscany Drive, PRINCETON JUNCTION, NJ 08550, UNITED STATES.
DICKER, Mr. Andrew John, BSc ACA *2005;* 2 Blencathra Cottages, St. Edmunds School, Portsmouth Road, HINDHEAD, GU26 6BH.
•**DICKER, Mr. Anthony Robin, FCA** *1974;* Tony Dicker Ltd, 29 Courtenay Road, Keynsham, BRISTOL, BS31 1JU.
•**DICKER, Mr. Christopher Hamilton, DL FCA DChA** *1973;* Trustee Training & Support Limited, Hill House, Ranworth, NORFOLK, NR13 6AB.
DICKER, Mr. John Charles, MSc FCA *1975;* 15 Sylvia Road, Claremont, CAPE TOWN, 7707, SOUTH AFRICA.
DICKER, Mrs. Julie Eleanor, BSc ACA *1999;* 48 Nursery Road, ALRESFORD, HAMPSHIRE, SO24 9JR.
DICKER, Mr. Norman Douglas, FCA *1955;* Minster Holdings Limited, 5 Longlands Close, Cheshunt, WALTHAM CROSS, HERTFORDSHIRE, EN8 8LW.
•**DICKER, Mr. Samuel Sidney, FCA** *1961;* (Tax Fac), Samuel S. Dicker, 32 Chatterton, LETCHWORTH GARDEN CITY, HERTFORDSHIRE, SG6 2JY.
•**DICKERSON, Mr. Peter James, BSc FCA** *1961;* P.J. Dickerson, 133 Marlborough Crescent, Riverhead, SEVENOAKS, TN13 2HN.
DICKETTS, Mr. Robert Anstey Ivor, FCA *1972;* Old Forge Cottage, Brenchley Road, Horsmonden, TONBRIDGE, KENT, TN12 8DN. (Life Member)
DICKEY, Mr. Steven James, MMath ACA *2010;* with Deloitte LLP, Athene Place, 66 Shoe Lane, LONDON, EC4A 3BQ.
DICKIE, Mr. Charles Stuart, BA ACA *1989;* Mandarin Oriental Hotel Group, 281 Gloucester Road, CAUSEWAY BAY, HONG KONG ISLAND, HONG KONG SAR.
DICKIE, Mr. Jamie Robert, MA ACA *1991;* Greenroyd House, Norwood Green, HALIFAX, HX3 8QE.
DICKIE, Mr. John Mckay, FCA *1956;* 63 Frogmore Park Drive, Blackwater, CAMBERLEY, GU17 0PJ. (Life Member)
DICKIE, Mr. William Douglas, FCA *1959;* 17 Grove Road, THORNTON HEATH, CR7 6HN. (Life Member)
•**DICKIN, Mr. Mark William, BSc(Hons) ACA** *2002;* Ellacotts LLP, Countrywide House, 23 West Bar Street, BANBURY, OXFORDSHIRE, OX16 9SA.
•**DICKINS, Mr. Paul Victor Robert, FCA** *1981;* Spencer Gardner Dickins Limited, 3 Coventry Innovation Village, Cheetah Road, COVENTRY, CV1 2TL. See also Spencer Gardner Dickins Audit LLP
DICKINSON, Mr. Alan Geoffrey, FCA *1959;* (Tax Fac), Little Manor, Lavant, CHICHESTER, PO18 0BQ.
DICKINSON, Mr. Allan, BA FCA *1985;* 24 Balmoral Drive, Formby, LIVERPOOL, MERSEYSIDE, L37 6EF.
DICKINSON, Mrs. Amanda Kate, BA ACA *1997;* 12 Harewood Road, SOUTH CROYDON, SURREY, CR2 7AT.
DICKINSON, Mr. Andrew, ACA *2011;* Maison Cosmos 202, Senoo 418, Minami-ku, OKAYAMA, 701-0205 JAPAN.
DICKINSON, Mr. Andrew Philip, BA ACA *1997;* Chiesi, Highfield, Cheadle Royal Business Park, CHEADLE, CHESHIRE, SK8 3GY.
DICKINSON, Mrs. Angela Denise, FCA *1970;* Fordhams, Church Lane, Ford End, CHELMSFORD, CM3 1LH. (Life Member)
DICKINSON, Mr. Angus Don, FCA *1977;* RSM Bird Cameron, Level 12 60 Castlereagh Street, SYDNEY, NSW 2000, AUSTRALIA.
DICKINSON, Mr. Antony John, BA FCA *1987;* 103 Eskdale Avenue, CHESHAM, HP5 3BD.
DICKINSON, Mr. Brian, FCA *1967;* 11 Siddington Road, Poynton, STOCKPORT, SK12 1SX.
DICKINSON, Miss. Caroline Louise, BA FCA *1991;* 275 Ashley Road, Hale, ALTRINCHAM, CHESHIRE, WA15 9NF.
DICKINSON, Miss. Charlotte Ann, BA ACA CIA *2004;* Haanat, Sandhills, Thorner, LEEDS, LS14 3DF.
DICKINSON, Mrs. Christine Linda, FCA *1977;* Waters Edge, Shore Road, Caldy, WIRRAL, CH48 2JL.
DICKINSON, Mr. Christopher, FCA *1973;* A5 Maison Victor Hugo, Greve D'azette, St. Clement, JERSEY, JE2 6PW. (Life Member)
DICKINSON, Mr. Christopher Keith, BSc ACA *2005;* 24 Temple Sheen, LONDON, SW14 7RP.
DICKINSON, Mrs. Claire Louise, BA ACA *2009;* 1 Manor Farm Cottages, Scaftworth, DONCASTER, SOUTH YORKSHIRE, DN10 6BL.
•**DICKINSON, Mr. David Anthony, ACA** *1992;* (Tax Fac), Broadside Business Services Limited, Hawkstone House, Portland Mews, Portland Street, LEAMINGTON SPA, WARWICKSHIRE CV32 5HD. See also Infocus Business Services Ltd
DICKINSON, Mr. Edward, ACA *2011;* 2 Darlington Road, DURHAM, DH1 4PE.
DICKINSON, Miss. Elspeth Joanne, MA FCA *1994;* Polarisavenue 39, 2132 JH HOOFDDORP, NETHERLANDS.
•**DICKINSON, Mr. Gary, FCA** *1989;* (Tax Fac), Gibson Booth, 12 Victoria Road, BARNSLEY, SOUTH YORKSHIRE, S70 2BB. See also Salary Solutions Limited
DICKINSON, Mr. Grahame Philip, FCA *1977;* Chaytor Cottage, Kirby Hill, RICHMOND, DL11 7JH.
DICKINSON, Miss. Hannah, ACA MAAT *2010;* 179 Stockport Road, Mossley, ASHTON-UNDER-LYNE, OL5 0RF.
DICKINSON, Mrs. Hazel Elizabeth, BA ACA *1987;* Djanogly City Academy Nottingham, Sherwood Rise, Nottingham Road, NOTTINGHAM, NG7 7AR.
•**DICKINSON, Miss. Helen Louise, BA FCA** *1992;* KPMG LLP, 15 Canada Square, LONDON, E14 5GL. See also KPMG Europe LLP
DICKINSON, Mr. Ian, BSc ACA *2004;* 11 Baildon Walk, LEEDS, LS14 2BW.
DICKINSON, Mr. Ian David, BA ACA *1990;* 13 Hoober Road, Ecclesall, SHEFFIELD, S11 9SF.
DICKINSON, Mr. Ian Joseph, ACA *1984;* Launceston Church Grammar School, PO Box 136, MOWBRAY, TAS 7248, AUSTRALIA.
DICKINSON, Miss. Joanna, BSc ACA *2006;* 47 Kingsley Flats, Old Kent Road, LONDON, SE1 5XB.
DICKINSON, Miss. Joanne Marie, BA ACA ACCA *1999;* 42 Melgund Road, LONDON, N5 1PT.
DICKINSON, Mr. John, FCA *1968;* 5 rue olivier de magny, marsinval, 78540 VERNOUILLET, FRANCE. (Life Member)

DICKINSON, Mr. John, FCA *1974;* 199A Dixon Road, ETOBICOKE M9P 2L9, ON, CANADA.
DICKINSON, Mr. John Finch Heneage, BA ACA *1992;* St. Johns Chambers, 101 Victoria Street, BRISTOL, BS1 6PU.
DICKINSON, Mr. John Graham, FCA *1975;* 52 Guisborough Road, Great Ayton, MIDDLESBROUGH, CLEVELAND, TS9 6AD.
DICKINSON, Mr. John Robert, BSc ACA *1993;* 22 Briers Close, Narborough, LEICESTER, LE19 2RB.
DICKINSON, Mr. John Robert, BSc FCA *1983;* Chollerton House, Chollerton, HEXHAM, NE46 4TH.
DICKINSON, Mrs. Karen, LLB ACA *2001;* 1 Leaside Way, WILMSLOW, CHESHIRE, SK9 1EW.
•DICKINSON, Ms. Lisa, ACA FCCA *2009;* Darnells, Quay House, Quay Road, NEWTON ABBOT, TQ12 2BU.
•DICKINSON, Mr. Mark John, FCA *1992;* Wise & Co, Wey Court West, Union Road, FARNHAM, SURREY, GU9 7PT. See also Firmvalue Payrolls Ltd
DICKINSON, Mr. Mark Robert, BA ACA *1999;* 12 Putney Close, OLDHAM, LANCASHIRE, OL1 2JS.
DICKINSON, Mr. Mark Vincent, MEng ACA *2004;* 55 Salisbury Place, LONDON, SW9 6UW.
DICKINSON, Mr. Michael Edward, BSc ACA FCCA *2009;* Flat 78 Melton Court, Onslow Crescent, LONDON, SW7 3JH.
DICKINSON, Mr. Michael John, FCA FSI *1975;* 3 Broad Lane, Upperthong, HOLMFIRTH, WEST YORKSHIRE, HD9 3JS.
DICKINSON, Mr. Michael Robert, BA FCA *1984;* 2 Wells Green Gardens, Netherthong, HOLMFIRTH, West Yorkshire, HD9 3HP.
DICKINSON, Mr. Neil Roger, BSc(Hons) ACA *2004;* Expro International Group Davidson House, The Forbury, READING, RG1 3EU.
DICKINSON, Mr. Oliver Peter Leigh, BA ACA CISA *2006;* Ty Gwyn, Waunfawr Road, CARDIFF, CF14 4SJ.
DICKINSON, Mr. Paul Christian, LLB ACA *2002;* 68 Ember Lane, ESHER, SURREY, KT10 8EN.
DICKINSON, Mr. Paul Michael, BA ACA ATII *1994;* Kesa Electricals plc, 22-24 Ely Place, LONDON, EC1N 6TE.
DICKINSON, Mr. Paul Michael, BSc ACA *1985;* The Alternative Board, 15 Hornbeam Square South, HARROGATE, NORTH YORKSHIRE, HG2 8NB.
•DICKINSON, Mr. Paul Winston John, BA FCA *1990;* WBD Accountants Ltd, Norton House, Fircroft Way, EDENBRIDGE, KENT, TN8 6EJ. See also Added Business Solutions LLP
DICKINSON, Mr. Peter, BSc ACA *1987;* Rue de la Prairie 28, CH-1196 GLAND, SWITZERLAND.
DICKINSON, Mr. Peter Denis, FCA *1970;* with PricewaterhouseCoopers, Building No 4, Arundel Office Park, Norfolk Road Mount Pleasant, HARARE, ZIMBABWE.
DICKINSON, Mr. Peter Hugh, FCA *1970;* Larksfield, Kent Hatch Road, Crockham Hill, EDENBRIDGE, TN8 6SX.
DICKINSON, Mr. Peter John Barron, MBA FCA *1969;* 255 Konihowski Road, SASKATOON S7S 1A9, SK, CANADA.
•DICKINSON, Mr. Philip Alexander, FCA *1973;* Philip A Dickinson Accountants Ltd, 103 High Street, HERNE BAY, KENT, CT6 5LA.
DICKINSON, Mr. Raymond Geoffrey, BCom FCA *1960;* 1 Viceroy Close, Edgbaston, BIRMINGHAM, B5 7UR. (Life Member)
DICKINSON, Mr. Richard Martin, BSc ACA *1994;* 7 Petty Whin Close, HARROGATE, NORTH YORKSHIRE, HG3 2YB.
DICKINSON, Mr. Simon John, BA ACA *1988;* I P C Media Blue Fin Building, 110 Southwark Street, LONDON, SE1 0SU.
DICKINSON, Mr. Stephen, BA FCA *1963;* Crow Hall, Bardon Mill, HEXHAM, NORTHUMBERLAND, NE47 7BJ. (Life Member)
DICKINSON, Mr. Stephen Geoffrey, BA FCA *1984;* Longacre Farm, Liverpool Road, Bickerstaffe, ORMSKIRK, L39 0EF.
DICKINSON, Mrs. Susan Jane, BA ACA *1993;* CHY CARA, 37 Penhale Road, FALMOUTH, CORNWALL, TR11 5UZ.
DICKINSON, Mr. Timothy Reginald, BSc FCA *1975;* Brackenhill, 144 Bouverie Avenue South, SALISBURY, SP2 8EB.
DICKINSON, Mr. Walton Peter, FCA *1954;* 23 Armstrong Cottages, BAMBURGH, NORTHUMBERLAND, NE69 7BA. (Life Member)
DICKINSON, Mr. William George Heneage, BSc FCA *1992;* Asset Protection Agency Eastcheap Court, 11 Philpot Lane, LONDON, EC3M 8UD.
DICKINSON GREEN, Mrs. Jane, BA ACA *1995;* with Brewers, Bourne House, Queen Street, Gomshall, GUILDFORD, SURREY GU5 9LY.
DICKMAN, Dr. Angela Marie, BSc ACA *2004;* 90 Hallamshire Road, SHEFFIELD, S10 4FP.
DICKMAN, Mr. Jeffery Lawrence, FCA *1972;* Flat 8, Frensham Court, 1 Alwyn Gardens, LONDON, NW4 4XW.
DICKS, Mr. Christopher, BA ACA *2003;* with KPMG LLP, 15 Canada Square, LONDON, E14 5GL.
DICKS, Mr. Christopher Joseph, FCA *1975;* The Cobb, 107 Manor Way, Aldwick, BOGNOR REGIS, PO21 4HU.
DICKS, Mr. Lawson Richard James, FCA *1960;* Riverside, Thorneyholme, Dunsop Bridge, CLITHEROE, BB7 3BB. (Life Member)
DICKSON, Mr. Andrew Christopher, BSc ACA *1999;* Flat 40, Priory Grove School, 10 Priory Grove, LONDON, SW8 2PH.
DICKSON, Mr. Andrew Richard, ACA *2009;* with Deloitte LLP, 2 New Street Square, LONDON, EC4A 3BZ.
DICKSON, Miss. Ashley Nicola Louise, MA ACA *2006;* with KPMG LLP, 15 Canada Square, LONDON, E14 5GL.
DICKSON, Miss. Catherine Mary, BSc ACA *2009;* with Morgan Cameron Limited, Wittas House, Two Rivers, Station Lane, WITNEY, OXFORDSHIRE OX28 4BH.
DICKSON, Mr. Charles James, BSc ACA *2004;* Unit 12, 7-9 Gilbert Street, MANLY, NSW 2095, AUSTRALIA.
•DICKSON, Miss. Christine Rose, BA FCA FRSA PGCE *1981;* Centre For Education & Finance Management Limited, Red Lion House, 9-10 High Street, HIGH WYCOMBE, BUCKINGHAMSHIRE, HP11 2AZ. See also Christine Dickson
DICKSON, Mr. Daniel Grant, ACA *2009;* 28 Witney Close, IPSWICH, IP3 9QF.
•DICKSON, Mr. David James, BA FCA *1980;* Garbutt & Elliott LLP, Arabesque House, Monks Cross Drive, Huntington, YORK, YO32 9GW.
DICKSON, Mr. David Russell, BSc(Hons) ACA *2004;* 87 Old Fort Road, SHOREHAM-BY-SEA, WEST SUSSEX, BN43 5HA.
DICKSON, Mr. Gordon Daniel, ACA *1979;* Pear Tree House, Thornton Steward, RIPON, NORTH YORKSHIRE, HG4 4BB.
DICKSON, Mr. James Robert, ACA *1993;* 7 Treble Close, Olivers Battery, WINCHESTER, SO22 4JN.
DICKSON, Mr. Jeremy David Fane, MA FCA *1967;* Upper Reach House, 36 Vantorts Road, SAWBRIDGEWORTH, HERTFORDSHIRE, CM21 9NB.
DICKSON, Mr. John, BCom FCA *1967;* Satron, Bridgford Close, Gorleston, GREAT YARMOUTH, NORFOLK, NR31 6SF.
•DICKSON, Mrs. Julia, BA ACA *1999;* PricewaterhouseCoopers LLP, Pricewaterhousecoopers, 12 Plumtree Court, LONDON, EC4A 4HT. See also PricewaterhouseCoopers
DICKSON, Mrs. Lynne, ACA *1995;* 3 Ramsey Gardens, Ingleby Barwick, STOCKTON-ON-TEES, CLEVELAND, TS17 5HN.
•DICKSON, Mr. Malcolm John, BA FCA *1981;* Bakers, Arbor House, Broadway North, WALSALL, WS1 2AN. See also Baker (Midlands) Limited
DICKSON, Mr. Michael John Rae, FCA *1974;* 12 Longnor Rd., Heald Green, CHEADLE, SK8 3BW.
DICKSON, Mr. Peter Maxwell, FCA FFA *1974;* Rum Runners Cay, The Moorings, Boss's Cove, PEMBROKE HM 01, BERMUDA.
DICKSON, Mrs. Philippa Ann, ACA *1981;* 57 Wallaceneuk, KELSO, ROXBURGHSHIRE, TD5 8BF.
DICKSON, Mr. Robert Alan, FCA *1977;* Rayner & Keeler Limited, Lowndes House, The Bury, Church Street, CHESHAM, HP5 1DJ.
DICKSON, Mr. Robert Henry, FCA *1946;* 11 Delamore Road, HILLCREST, KWAZULU NATAL, 3600, SOUTH AFRICA. (Life Member)
DICKSON, Miss. Sally, BSc ACA *2006;* Flat 4 Draymans Court, 41 Stockwell Green, LONDON, SW9 9QE.
DICKSON, Mr. Stephen Ross, FCA *1982;* Honeysuckle Cottage, High Street, Ticehurst, WADHURST, TN5 7AS.
DICKSON-GREEN, Mr. Benjamin Paul, ACA *2003;* 122 Newton Lane, DARLINGTON, COUNTY DURHAM, DL3 9HD.
DICKSON LEACH, Mr. James Seymour, FCA *1969;* 4655 Vantreight Drive, VICTORIA V8N 3W8, BC, CANADA.
•DIDAM, Ms. Susan, BSc FCA *1991;* Ernst & Young Gmbh, Wirtschaftspruefungsgesellschaft, Graf-Adolf-Platz 15, 40213 DUSSELDORF, GERMANY.
•DIDHAM, Mr. Andrew, BA FCA *1980;* NM Rothschild & Sons Ltd, New Court, St Swithins Lane, LONDON, EC4P 4DU.
DIDHAM, Mr. Oliver Rawdon, BSc ACA *2010;* Sproughton Manor, Sproughton, IPSWICH, IP8 3AE.
DIDHAM, Mr. William George Frank, FCA *1950;* 9 Stoneleigh, 17 Martello Road South, Canford Cliffs, POOLE, BH13 7HQ. (Life Member)
DIDIER, Miss. Christine, BA(Hons) ACA *2000;* 9 Rue Greneta, 75003 PARIS, FRANCE.
DIDLICK, Mr. Philip James, BSc(Hons) ACA *2002;* 79 Druidsville Road, LIVERPOOL, L18 3EN.
DIEBEL, Mr. Michael John Flower, FCA *1969;* Dalsland, Sandy Lane, EAST GRINSTEAD, WEST SUSSEX, RH19 3LP.
DIEC, Mr. Jonathan, ACA *2010;* 25 Chatsworth Drive, WELLINGBOROUGH, NORTHAMPTONSHIRE, NN8 5FD.
DIEDERICHS, Mr. Henning, ACA *2008;* with HM Treasury, 1 Horse Guards Road, LONDON, SW1A 2HQ.
DIEFFENTHALLER, Mr. George Anthony, BCom FCA *1964;* 123 Flamingo Avenue, Philippine, SAN FERNANDO, TRINIDAD AND TOBAGO. (Life Member)
DIEMKO, Mr. Janusz Ryszard, BSc ACA *1994;* 68 Boston Gardens, BRENTFORD, MIDDLESEX, TW8 9LP.
DIEPPE, Mrs. Claire Louise, BA(Hons) ACA *2001;* 7 Ombersley Road, DROITWICH, WORCESTERSHIRE, WR9 8JF.
DIEPPE, Mr. William, FCA *1972;* Oakwood, 71 Ducks Hill Road, NORTHWOOD, HA6 2SQ.
DIER, Mr. Timothy Spencer, ACA *2008;* 66 Harbour Way, SHOREHAM-BY-SEA, WEST SUSSEX, BN43 5HG.
DIETER, Mr. John Andrew, BSc ACA *1989;* PepsiCo QTG Division, 555 W. Monroe, CHICAGO, IL 60661, UNITED STATES.
DIETER, Mrs. Margaret Elizabeth, BSc ACA *1990;* 3204 Twilight Avenue, NAPERVILLE, IL 60564, UNITED STATES.
DIETMAN, Mr. David Kevin, ACA *1997;* 49 Hawkshead Lane, North Mymms, HATFIELD, HERTFORDSHIRE, AL9 7TD.
•DIETZ, Mr. Alan Arthur, FCA *1975;* with ICAEW, Metropolitan House, 321 Avebury Boulevard, MILTON KEYNES, MK9 2FZ.
DIEU, Miss. Maureen, ACA *2007;* 20 Walkers Mount, LEEDS, LS6 2SD.
DIEUDONNE, Mr. Kabongo, ACA CA(SA) *2008;* 14 Hillcroft, Douglas, ISLE OF MAN, IM2 7DW.
DIFFEY, Mr. Mark Leonard, BA ACA *2007;* with Deloitte LLP, Athene Place, 66 Shoe Lane, LONDON, EC4A 3BQ.
DIFFEY, Mr. Stuart, BA(Hons) ACA *2000;* 17 Monterey Drive, Locks Heath, SOUTHAMPTON, SO31 6NW.
DIGBY, Miss. Emma Louise, BSc ACA *2004;* 61 Heathfield South, TWICKENHAM, TW2 7SR.
DIGBY, Mrs. Helen Louise, BSc(Hons) ACA *2001;* 128 Nutbeem Road, EASTLEIGH, SO50 5JT.
DIGBY, The Hon. Henry Noel Kenelm, ACA *1979;* Minterne House, Minterne Magna, DORCHESTER, DT2 7AU.
DIGBY, Mr. Ian Stephen, BA ACA *1992;* Flat 6 Park House 72 West Hill Road, RYDE, ISLE OF WIGHT, PO33 1LW.
DIGBY, Mrs. Tracey Marie, BA ACA *1993;* Center Parcs Ltd, Head Office, One Edison Rise, New Ollerton, NEWARK, NOTTINGHAMSHIRE NG22 9DP.
•DIGBY-ROGERS, Mr. Jonathan, BSc FCA *1976;* J Digby-Rogers, 13 Gipsy Hill, LONDON, SE19 1QG.
DIGGES, Mr. Jonathan Charles Nigel, BA ACA *1997;* Mecom Group Plc, 5th FLoor, 70 Jermyn Street, LONDON, SW1Y 6NY.
DIGGINS, Mrs. Barbara Ann, LLB ACA *1986;* Warren Garth, The Drive, South Cheam, SUTTON, SM2 7DH.
DIGGINS, Mr. John Edward, MA FCA *1987;* Warren Garth, The Drive, SUTTON, SM2 7DH.
DIGGLE, Miss. Clare Suzanne, BA FCA *1994;* 30 Deans Farm, The Causeway, Caversham, READING, RG4 5JZ.
DIGGLE, Mr. Graham, BA ACA *1985;* Oxford Brookes University Wheatley Campus, Wheatley, OXFORD, OX33 1HX.
DIGGLE, Mr. Oliver John, MA FCA *1961;* with Diggle & Co, Waterfall House, Worthing Road, Swanton Morley, DEREHAM, NORFOLK NR20 4QD.
DIGGLE, Mr. Peter Hood, FCA *1973;* Church Farm House, Pipers Hill, Great Gaddesden, HEMEL HEMPSTEAD, HP1 3BY.
•DIGGLE, Mr. Simon, BA(Hons) ACA *2000;* with Pierce C A Ltd, Mentor House, Ainsworth Street, BLACKBURN, BB1 6AY.
DIGGLES, Mr. Stuart Richard, BEng ACA *1994;* B3 Cable Solutions, Delaunays House, Delaunays Road, Blackley, MANCHESTER, M9 8FP.
DIGHE, Mr. Rakesh, ACA CISA AMCT *1992;* Apartment 38, Hepworth Court, 30 Gatliff Road, LONDON, SW1W 8QN.
DIGHTON, Mr. Robert, BSc ACA *2010;* Flat C, 103 Goldhurst Terrace, LONDON, NW6 3HA.
DIGHTON, Mr. Simon Gerald, BSc FCA *1989;* 1st Credit Ltd Omnibus Building, Lesbourne Road, REIGATE, RH2 7JP.
DIGNAM, Mr. David, BA ACA *2009;* 641 Westhorne Avenue, LONDON, SE9 6JU.
DIGNAN, Mrs. Sarah Jane, BA(Hons) ACA CTA *2001;* with Jackson Stephen LLP, James House, Stonecross Business Park, 5 Yew Tree Way, Golborne, WARRINGTON CHESHIRE WA3 3JD.
DIGNE-MALCOLM, Mrs. Amanda, BA FCA *1989;* with ICAEW, Metropolitan House, 321 Avebury Boulevard, MILTON KEYNES, MK9 2FZ.
•DIGNUM, Mr. John Peter, MA FCA AMCT *1991;* Wheeler Rennen Limited, Dorset House, Regent Park, 297 Kingston Road, LEATHERHEAD, SURREY KT22 7PL.
DIGNUM, Mrs. Susan Michelle, BSc ACA *1992;* Gable End, Woodvill Road, LEATHERHEAD, KT22 7BP.
DIJK, Mrs. Amanda Louise, LLB ACA *2004;* 12 Francisco Close, Chafford Hundred, GRAYS, RM16 6YD.
•DILENA, Mr. Salvatore, BA(Hons) ACA *2008;* (Tax Fac), Dilena Limited, Nicholson House, 41 Thames Street, WEYBRIDGE, SURREY, KT13 8JG.
•DILKS, Mr. Ian Edwin, MA FCA *1977;* PricewaterhouseCoopers LLP, 1 Embankment Place, LONDON, WC2N 6RH. See also PricewaterhouseCoopers
DILKS, Mrs. Patricia Anne, BA FCA *1974;* Elm House, 10-16 Elm Street, LONDON, WC1X 0BJ.
•DILLAMORE, Mr. Robin Mark, MA FCA CTA *1991;* (Tax Fac), Dillamore & Co Limited, The Stables Offices, Stansty Park, Summerhill Road, WREXHAM, LL11 4YW. See also Finansure Limited and Dillamore & Co
DILLEY, Mr. Anthony John, BSc FCA *1979;* 13 Armiger Way, The Grove, WITHAM, CM8 2UY.
•DILLEY, Mr. Brian John, BSc FCA *1994;* KPMG LLP, 15 Canada Square, LONDON, E14 5GL. See also KPMG Europe LLP
DILLEY, Mr. Frank Kenneth, FCA *1945;* Springwood House, 8 Church Walk, Avonwick, SOUTH BRENT, DEVON, TQ10 9EJ. (Life Member)
DILLEY, Mr. James, ACA *2011;* 105 Dunstans Road, East Dulwich, LONDON, SE22 0HD.
DILLEY, Mr. Jonathan Christopher, ACA *2009;* 25A Walsworth Road, HITCHIN, HERTFORDSHIRE, SG4 9SP.
•DILLEY, Mr. Richard Charles, ACA FCCA *2007;* George Hay, Unit 1b, Focus 4, Fourth Avenue, LETCHWORTH GARDEN CITY, HERTFORDSHIRE SG6 2TU. See also GH Online Accounting Ltd
•DILLEY, Mr. Stephen William, FCA CF *1973;* Stephen Dilley & Associates Limited, 12 Barton Close, St. Annes Park, BRISTOL, BS4 4BA.
DILLISTONE, Miss. Nell Sarah Popert, BSc ACA *1989;* Gypsy Cottage, Mill Road, Shiplake, HENLEY-ON-THAMES, OXFORDSHIRE, RG9 3LW.
DILLON, Mrs. Anne Hazel, BSc ACA *1991;* Hinton Manor Farm, Hinton Manor Court, Woodford Halse, DAVENTRY, NN11 3NU.
DILLON, Miss. Claire Marie, BSc ACA *1999;* 17a Wilbury Grove, HOVE, EAST SUSSEX, BN3 3JQ.
DILLON, Mr. Geoffrey Michael William, BSc ACA *1998;* 22 Lawrence Road, WEST WICKHAM, KENT, BR4 9DB.
DILLON, Mr. John Eamon, ACA *1987;* with RJD Partners, 8-9 Well Court, Bow Lane, LONDON, EC4M 9DN.
DILLON, Mrs. Kim Geraldine, ACA *1985;* Colt Group Ltd, New Lane, HAVANT, HAMPSHIRE, PO9 2LY.
DILLON, Mr. Mark, ACA *2007;* 3 Mill Race, Stanstead Abbotts, WARE, HERTFORDSHIRE, SG12 8BZ.
DILLON, Mr. Martin Joseph, BSc ACA FCCA CPFA *2007;* A Floor, Belfast City Hospital, 51 Lisburn Road, BELFAST, BT9 7AB.
DILLON, Mr. Paul Nicholas, BSc FCA *1991;* Hinton Manor Farm Hinton Manor Court, Woodford Halse, DAVENTRY, NORTHAMPTONSHIRE, NN11 3NU.
•DILLON, Mr. Peter Marshall, FCA *1968;* Broomfield House, Bank Lane, Upper Denby, HUDDERSFIELD, HD8 8UT.
•DILLON, Mrs. Sarah Gail, BA(Hons) ACA *2001;* S G D Accountancy, 27 Linden Lea, Down Ampney, CIRENCESTER, GLOUCESTERSHIRE, GL7 5PF.
DILLON, Mr. Terence John, FCA *1961;* Cedar House, Church Lane, OXTED, SURREY, RH8 9LB.
DILLON, Mr. Thomas Michael John, LLB ACA *2007;* 53 St. Francis Avenue, SOLIHULL, B91 1EB.

DILLON-ROBINSON, Mr. Paul Mark, MBA FCA *1988;* Office of the Chief Executive, House of Commons, Houses of Parliament, LONDON, SW1A 0AA.
•**DILLOW, Mr. Nicholas John, BSc FCA** *1980;* (Tax Fac), N.J. Dillow, Vine Cottage, Hampton Hill, Swanmore, SOUTHAMPTON, SO32 2QN.
•**DILLOWAY, Mr. Larry David, FCA** *1985;* Dilloways Ltd, Weavers, 6 Hamlet Road, HAVERHILL, SUFFOLK, CB9 8EE.
DILNOT, Mrs. Catherine Elizabeth, MA ACA *1987;* Oxford Brookes University, Wheatley Campus, Wheatley, OXFORD, OX33 1HX.
DILREW, Miss. Lauren, ACA MAAT *2009;* 55 Solario Road, Costessey, NORWICH, NORFOLK, NR8 5EJ.
DILTON-HILL, Mr. Kevin George, ACA CA(SA) *2008;* 4 Arundel Terrace, BRIGHTON, BN2 1GA.
•**DILWORTH, Mr. Anthony John, FCA** *1969;* A.J. Dilworth, Annapurna House, Stag Lane, Great Kingshill, HIGH WYCOMBE, HP15 6EW.
DILWORTH, Mr. John Charles, MA ACA *1978;* P O Box N-1942, NASSAU, BAHAMAS.
DILWORTH, Mr. Nicholas, ACA *2008;* 27 Pirton Close, ST. ALBANS, HERTFORDSHIRE, AL4 9YJ.
DILWORTH, Mr. Nicholas Anthony, BSc ACA *2000;* Practice Plan Ltd, Kempthorne House, Park Avenue, OSWESTRY, SHROPSHIRE, SY11 1AY.
DILWORTH, Mr. Simon Richard, BA(Hons) ACA *2002;* 27 Queens Road, CLEVEDON, AVON, BS21 7TF.
DIMALINE, Mr. Kevin Peter, BA ACA *1982;* 20 Ladbrooke Crescent, Old Basford, NOTTINGHAM, NG6 0GQ.
DIMAMBRO, Miss. Julie, BCom ACA *2001;* 14 Holmwood Gardens, Westbury-on-Trym, BRISTOL, BS9 3EB.
DIMBLEBY, Mr. Andrew Peter, ACA *2008;* 50 Stainburn Road, LEEDS, LS17 6NN.
DIMBLEBY, Mr. Richard Henry, FCA *1973;* 20 Brook Road, Trentham, STOKE-ON-TRENT, ST4 8BH.
DIMELOW, Mrs. Ann Mary, FCA *1971;* New Hall Farm, Horsemans Green, WHITCHURCH, Shropshire, SY13 3BZ.
DIMELOW, Mr. James Allen, MA ACA *1979;* Mereton House Horsemans Green, WHITCHURCH, SHROPSHIRE, SY13 3DY.
DIMEO, Mrs. Sally Ann, BSc ACA *1993;* 32 Hayford Mills, Cambusbarron, STIRLING, FK7 9PN.
DIMES, Miss. Carly, ACA *2008;* Deloitte & Touche, 2 New Street Square, LONDON, EC4A 3BZ.
•**DIMES, Mr. Neil Edwin Stuart, BSc FCA** *1989;* PKF (UK) LLP, 2nd Floor, 1 Redcliff Street, BRISTOL, BS1 6NP.
DIMES, Mrs. Ruth Annabel Joan, BA ACA *2001;* M D A Ltd, Gillingham House, 38-44 Gillingham Street, LONDON, SW1V 1HU.
DIMITRIOU, Mr. Christos, MBA ACA *2006;* Porto Rafti & Dodekanisou, P.O. Box 1889, Porto Rafti, 19003 ATHENS, GREECE.
DIMITROV, Mrs. Nathalie Lydia Julia, BA(Hons) ACA *2000;* 86 Woodside Avenue, LONDON, N10 3HY.
DIMITROVA, Ms. Nadejda Panayotova, MA ACA *2005;* Sokratous 42, Moshato, 18345 ATHENS, GREECE.
DIMMELOW, Mr. Kevin Louis, LLB ACA *1983;* Age Concern, 8-10 Clemens Street, LEAMINGTON SPA, CV31 2DL.
•**DIMMICK, Mr. Christopher, FCA** *1989;* (Tax Fac), Rees Pollock, 35 New Bridge Street, LONDON, EC4V 6BW.
DIMMING, Mrs. Sangeeta, ACA *2009;* 198a Hermon Hill, LONDON, E18 1QH.
DIMMOCK, Mr. Andrew, BA FCA *1989;* Communaute Doulos, BP 4949, NOUAK-CHOTT, MAURITANIA.
DIMMOCK, Mr. Ian Richard, FCA *1974;* 22 Wivenhoe Road, Alresford, COLCHESTER, CO7 8AD.
DIMMOCK, Mr. James Leslie, FCA *1975;* Haddon Corner, Neston Road, Burton, NESTON, CH64 5SY.
DIMMOCK, Mrs. Judy, BA ACA *2004;* Institute of Chartered Accountants in England & Wales, Metropolitan House, 4 Rillaton Walk, MILTON KEYNES, MK9 2FZ.
DIMMOCK, Mr. Peter Charles, FCA *1969;* 25a Fallowfield, LUTON, LU3 1UL.
DIMMOCK, Mr. Peter David, BA ACA *1992;* 13 Lyttelton Road, Droitwich Spa, DROITWICH, WORCESTERSHIRE, WR9 7AA.
DIMMOCK, Mrs. Rosemary, MA ACA *2009;* 94 Leathermarket Court, LONDON, SE1 3HT.
DIMMOCK, Mr. Trevor Thomas, FCA *1971;* Ivy Lodge, Lodge Road, Cranfield, BEDFORD, MK43 0BQ.
DIMOCK, Mr. James Robert Chevalley, MA ACA *2009;* 26 Etna Road, ST. ALBANS, HERTFORDSHIRE, AL3 5NJ.
DIMOND, Miss. Anne Louise, LLB ACA *1989;* 30a Church Street, FARINGDON, OXFORDSHIRE, SN7 8AD.
DIMOND, Ms. Diane Marjorie, BSc FCA *1989;* New College Swindon, Queens Drive, SWINDON, WILTSHIRE, SN3 1AW.
DIMOND, Mrs. Ruth Patricia, BSc ACA *1986;* 101 Crow Green Road, Pilgrims Hatch, BRENTWOOD, CM15 9RP.
DIMOPOULOU, Miss. Zina, ACA MBA *2002;* Flat 5 Branksome Gower Road, WEYBRIDGE, SURREY, KT13 0HD.
DIMSDALE, Miss. Rebecca Katherine, ACA *2008;* Flat 4, 18 Louvaine Road, LONDON, SW11 2AG.
DIMSEY, Mrs. Kathryn Jane, BA ACA *1994;* Summercourt Cottage Kemsing Road, Wrotham, SEVENOAKS, TN15 7BP.
DIMSEY, Mr. Robert William Edward, BSc ACA *1994;* Ascot Underwriting Ltd Plantation Place, 30 Fenchurch Street, LONDON, EC3M 3BD.
DIN, Mr. Adrian Martin, BA FCA *1982;* 25 Stambourne Way, WEST WICKHAM, BR4 9NE.
DIN, Mr. Baber Nasim, BSc(Econ) ACA *2000;* with Deloitte LLP, Hill House, 1 Little New Street, LONDON, EC4A 3TR.
DIN, Mr. Munawar-Ud, FCA *1966;* 91-A New Muslim Town, LAHORE, PAKISTAN.
•**DIN, Mr. Nizamud, FCA** *1974;* N Din, 60 Sydney Road, West Ealing, LONDON, W13 9EY.
DIN, Miss. Shahina, FCA *1977;* 82 Wandsworth Bridge Road, Fulham, LONDON, SW6 2TF.
DINA, Miss. Parwin, BA ACA ATII *1998;* Parwin Dina, Bur Dubai, PO Box 122798, DUBAI, UNITED ARAB EMIRATES.
DINA, Mr. Rafiq Ahmed, FCA *1971;* 35 Pasir Ris Drive 3, Eastvale #11-05, SINGAPORE 519493, SINGAPORE.
DINA, Miss. Rubeena, BSc ACA *1999;* 71 Redfern Street, NORTH PERTH, WA 6006, AUSTRALIA.
DINAN, Mr. John Michael, FCA *1971;* PO Box 838, GEORGETOWN, GRAND CAYMAN, KY1-1103, CAYMAN ISLANDS.
DINAN, Mr. Marie Desire Pierre, BSc FCA *1964;* 11 E. Francois St, ROSE HILL, MAURITIUS.
DINAN, Mr. Paul Andrew, BSc FCA *1982;* 5 Carew Cottages, Village Green Lane, East Dean, EASTBOURNE, EAST SUSSEX, BN20 0DR.
DINAN DE SALDIVAR, Mrs. Valentine Marie-Aimee, BSc ACA *2002;* 25 Trotter Street, BEAU BASSIN, MAURITIUS.
DINARDO, Mr. Alessandro Carlo, BA ACA *2006;* Flat 12, 88 Stockwell Road, LONDON, SW9 9JQ.
DINDJER, Mr. Etem, BSc ACA *1984;* Yates Estates Ltd, 205 Walworth Road, LONDON, SE17 1RL.
•**DINE, Mrs. Marian, FCA** *1975;* M. Dine, Stoke Lodge, Aldersey Road, GUILDFORD, GU1 2ES.
•**DINEEN, Mr. Peter Bristow, FCA** *1972;* with Humphrey & Co, 7-9 The Avenue, EASTBOURNE, EAST SUSSEX, BN21 3YA.
DINEEN, Mrs. Susan Myra, MSc FCA FRSA *1976;* The Walmers, 50 Collington Lane West, BEXHILL-ON-SEA, EAST SUSSEX, TN39 3TA.
DINEEN, Mr. Terence John, FCA *1962;* 6 Mayals Green, Mayals, SWANSEA, SA3 5JR. (Life Member)
DINENI, Mrs. Stella, MSc ACA *1987;* 10 Somerset Road, Ealing, LONDON, W13 9PB.
•**DINER, Mr. Jeffrey Martin, FCA** *1976;* (Tax Fac), Benjamin Taylor & Co, 201 Great Portland Street, LONDON, W1W 5AB. See also Compubook Services Ltd and Wigmore Registrars Ltd
DINES, Miss. Catherine Mary, BA ACA *1989;* Chemin des Vergers 4, 1213 PETIT LANCY, SWITZERLAND.
DINES, Mr. Christopher John, BA ACA *1988;* 54 Balcaskie Road, Eltham, LONDON, SE9 1HQ.
DINES, Miss. Clare Louise, BA(Hons) ACA *2002;* Hilton International Maple Court Central Park, Reeds Crescent, WATFORD, WD24 4QQ.
DINES, Miss. Helen Elizabeth, LLB ACA *2004;* (Tax Fac), 73 Church Lane, Mill End, RICKMANSWORTH, HERTFORDSHIRE, WD3 8PT.
DINES, Mr. Stephen, BSc ACA *2003;* 18 Morley Gardens, Chandler's Ford, EASTLEIGH, SO53 1JF.
DING, Mr. Peter Yibing, BA ACA *1995;* Flat 2 2/F Block A, Villa Lotto, 18 Broadwood Road, HAPPY VALLEY, HONG KONG ISLAND, HONG KONG SAR.
•**DING, Mr. Raphael Wai Chuen, BCom ACA** *1985;* Guoco Group Limited, 50/F, The Center, 99 Queens Court Road, CENTRAL, HONG KONG SAR.
DINGLE, Mr. David Stephen, BSc ACA *1992;* with Francis Clark, Francis Clark LLP, Sigma House, Oak View Close, Edginswell Park, TORQUAY TQ2 7FF.
DINGLE, Mr. Jack, BA(Hons) ACA *2011;* Le Petit Verger, Duvaux Lane, St. Sampson, GUERNSEY, GY2 4XY.
DINGLE, Miss. Philippa, BA ACA *1995;* 2 Lower Barford Cottages, Bramshaw, LYNDHURST, SO43 7JN.
DINGLE, Mr. Richard James, BSc ACA *2004;* with Ernst & Young, Level 28, AL Attar Bus Tower, Sheikh Zayed Road, P.O. Box 9267, DUBAI UNITED ARAB EMIRATES.
DINGLE, Mrs. Sally Anne, MEng BA ACA *1999;* 13 Admirals Gate, LONDON, SE10 8JX.
DINGLE, Mr. Steven Paul, BSc ACA *1988;* 19 The Chase, Thundersley, BENFLEET, SS7 3BS.
DINGLEY, Mrs. Jane Mary, ACA *1984;* Buckland Place, Southampton Road, LYMINGTON, SO41 9GZ.
•**DINGLEY, Mr. Leslie George, FCA** *1975;* (Tax Fac), LD Financial + Management Services Ltd 2nd Floor, 145-157 St John Street, LONDON, EC1V 4PY.
•**DINGLEY, Mr. Peter Charles, BSc(Hons) FCA CTA** *1980;* Peter Dingley, Buckland Place, Southampton Road, LYMINGTON, HAMPSHIRE, SO41 9GZ.
•**DINGWALL, Mrs. Julie Patricia, ACA** *1980;* Julie Dingwall, 93 Willian Way, LETCHWORTH GARDEN CITY, HERTFORDSHIRE, SG6 2HY.
•**DINGWALL, Mr. Roger David, FCA** *1973;* (Tax Fac), Birkett Tomlinson & Co., Regency House, 67 Albert Road, COLNE, BB8 0BP.
DINGWELL, Miss. Laura, ACA *2010;* Flat 19 Maytree Gardens, 35-39 South Ealing Road, LONDON, W5 4QT.
DINHAM, Mr. Thomas, ACA *2011;* Flat 4, Brondesbury Court, 235 Willesden Lane, LONDON, NW2 5RR.
•**DINNAGE, Mrs. Jennifer Clare, FCA** *1993;* (Tax Fac), LD Financial + Management Services Limited, Unit 2, Birchden Farm, Broadwater Forest Lane, Groombridge, TUNBRIDGE WELLS KENT TN3 9NR.
DINNEN, Mr. Arnold David, FCA *1951;* 123 Brookside, BARNET, EN4 8TS. (Life Member)
•**DINNES, Mrs. Marie Colette, BSc FCA** *1988;* Phillips Dinnes Limited, Lyddons, Nailsbourne, TAUNTON, SOMERSET, TA2 8AF.
DINNIE, Mr. Andrew James, BSc ACA *1992;* Flat 8 Preston Court, 38 Station Road, BARNET, EN5 1QH.
DINNING, Mr. Andy, ACA *2009;* National Audit Office, 157-197 Buckingham Palace Road, LONDON, SW1W 9SP.
DINNING, Mrs. Clare, ACA *2007;* with PricewaterhouseCoopers LLP, Pricewaterhousecoopers, 12 Plumtree Court, LONDON, EC4A 4HT.
DINNING, Mr. Simon Neil, BA ACA *2006;* 43 Adys Road, LONDON, SE15 4DX.
DINOPOULOS, Mr. Demetri, ACA ACCA *2011;* 4 Hazlewood Mews, 373-377 Clapham Road, LONDON, SW9 9BL.
DINSDALE, Mr. Alain, BSc ACA *2001;* 2 Southern Rise, East Hyde, LUTON, LU2 9QB.
•**DINSDALE, Mr. Arthur James, BA FCA** *1990;* James Dinsdale FCA, 206A Lawn Lane, HEMEL HEMPSTEAD, HP3 9JF.
•**DINSDALE, Miss. Hilary Jane, MA ACA** *1984;* AIMS - Hilary Dinsdale, Pathways, Highland Street, IVYBRIDGE, DEVON, PL21 9AG.
DINSDALE, Mrs. Jayne Louise, BA ACA *1991;* West End Farm, Carperby, LEYBURN, DL8 4DJ.
DINSDALE, Mr. Phil James, MA FCA *1996;* 38 Clevedon Drive, Earley, READING, RG6 5XE.
DINSHAW, Mr. Ruiynton Faredun, FCA *1977;* Citibank, Citibank Centre, 33 Canada Square, Canary Wharf, LONDON, E14 5LB.
DINSMORE, Mr. Brian Geoffrey, BSc ACA *1988;* 5 Highcroft Drive, Wollaton, NOTTINGHAM, NG8 4DX.
DINSMORE, Mrs. Karen Elizabeth, BSc ACA *1987;* 5 Highcroft Drive, Wollaton, NOTTINGHAM, NG8 4DX.
DINWIDDIE, Mr. Andrew Maitland, ACA *2010;* 104 Kyrle Road, LONDON, SW11 6BA.
•**DINWIDDIE, Mr. Ian Maitland, BA FCA** *1976;* 35 Dover Street, LONDON, W1S 4NQ.
DINWIDDY, Mrs. Kate, MA ACA *2005;* 27 Holmesdale Avenue, LONDON, SW14 7BQ.
DINWIDDY, Mr. Tom, BSc ACA *2005;* Betfair Limited, Waterfront, Hammersmith Embankment, Chancellors Road, LONDON, W6 9HP.
DIOLA, Ms. Christiana, MA ACA *2000;* (Tax Fac), 39 Morfou Street, Enkomi, 2417 NICOSIA, CYPRUS.
DIOLA, Mr. John Joseph, BSc ACA *2004;* Ptolemaitos 4, Engoni, 2401 NICOSIA, CYPRUS.
DIOLA KIRMIZIS, Mrs. Emily Elia, BSc ACA *2004;* Ithakis 46, Tseri, 2480 NICOSIA, CYPRUS.
•**DIOMEDOU, Mr. Panayiotis, BA(Hons) ACA** *2003;* Advanta Business Services Limited, 29 Gildredge Road, EASTBOURNE, EAST SUSSEX, BN21 4RU.
•**DIOMEDOU, Mr. Steven, BA(Hons) ACA** *2001;* LMDB Limited, Railview Lofts, 19c Commercial Road, EASTBOURNE, EAST SUSSEX, BN21 3XE.
DIOMIDOUS, Miss. Phedra, BSc ACA *2011;* 24 Stylianou Lena, Aradhippou, 7102 LARNACA, CYPRUS.
DIONG, Mr. Chea Ming, MBA ACA *1991;* 176 LOYANG RISE, SINGAPORE 507425, SINGAPORE.
DIONG, Mr. Iek Ting, ACA *1979;* Armstrong Properties Plc, 49 Welbeck Street, LONDON, W1G 9XN.
DIONYSSIADES, Mrs. Maria Theodoros, LLB ACA *1993;* Emporiki Bank - Cyprus Limited, 4 Ionos street, 2406 Engomi, NICOSIA, CYPRUS.
DIOUMAN, Mr. Shamim, ACA *2005;* 130 Kempton Road, East Ham, LONDON, E6 2NE.
DIPLOCK, Mr. Graham George, BSc ACA *1993;* B G Group, 100 Thames Valley Park Drive, READING, RG6 1PT.
DIPLOCK, Miss. Karen Susan, BA(Hons) ACA *2001;* 12 Anisa Close, Kings Hill, WEST MALLING, ME19 4EW.
DIPLOCK, Mr. Roger Nicholas, FCA *1978;* 9 Broughton Avenue, RICHMOND, TW10 7TT.
DIPNARINE, Miss. Faye, ACA *2008;* 24 Woodleigh Avenue, LONDON, N12 0LL.
DIPPIE, Mr. John Alexander, BSc FCA *1978;* 24 Claremont Gardens, TUNBRIDGE WELLS, TN2 5DD.
•**DIPPLE, Mr. Simon Timothy, BSc FCA** *1991;* Sutton Dipple Limited, 8 Wheelwright's Corner, Old Market, Nailsworth, STROUD, GL6 0DB.
DIPROSE, Mr. Christopher Michael, MA ACA *1992;* 42 Orford Gardens, TWICKENHAM, TW1 4PL.
DIPROSE, Mr. Matthew Newton, BA(Econ) FCA *2000;* KPMG Centre, 18 Viaduct Harbour Avenue, AUCKLAND 1010, NEW ZEALAND.
DIQUE, Mr. Trevor Emmanuel Joseph, FCA *1971;* Peveril, 8 Woodwards Close, BURGESS HILL, WEST SUSSEX, RH15 0DS. (Life Member)
DIRAT, Mrs. Lisa Jane, BSc ACA *1996;* Sancreed, Hawksdown, Walmer, DEAL, KENT, CT14 7PJ.
DIRIENZO, Mr. Simeon Mark, BSc ACA *2009;* 17 Bryn Rhedyn, Coed-y-Cwm, PONTYPRIDD, MID GLAMORGAN, CF37 3DP.
DISBOROUGH, Miss. Jane Louise, MA ACA *1991;* Flat 4, Abingdon Mansions, Abingdon Road, LONDON, W8 6AD.
DISBOROUGH, Mr. Paul David, BSc ACA *1990;* Rossie Gamekeepers Cottage, Ladybank, CUPAR, FIFE, KY15 7UZ.
DISCHE, Mr. Jolyon Michael, BSc(Hons) ACA *2000;* Unit 3, 57 Shellcove Road, NEUTRAL BAY, NSW 2089, AUSTRALIA.
DISHMAN, Mr. James David, FCA *1985;* (Tax Fac), High Trees, 1 Corona Road, Langdon Hills, BASILDON, ESSEX, SS16 6HH.
DISHMAN, Mr. Stephen, BA ACA *1995;* Tarrant House, Springs Lane, Ellesborough, AYLESBURY, BUCKINGHAMSHIRE, HP17 0XD.
DISLEY, Mr. Andrew Guy, MA MBA FCA CTA AMCT *1985;* (Tax Fac), Allen & Overy Llp One, Bishops Square, LONDON, E1 6AD.
DISLEY, Mrs. Katherine Anita, BA(Hons) ACA *2002;* 14 Clover Crescent, BURNLEY, BB12 0EX.
•**DISNEY, Mr. Peter, ACA** *1981;* (Tax Fac), Wood & Disney Ltd, 1 Lodge Court, Lodge Lane, Langham, COLCHESTER, CO4 5NE.
DISS, Mr. Colin James, ACA *2009;* 2 Old Court, Arbour Lane, CHELMSFORD, CM1 7UF.
•**DISS, Mr. Nicholas John, BSc FCA** *1983;* Reardon & Co Limited, Ash House, Breckenwood Road, Fulbourn, CAMBRIDGE, CB21 5DQ. See also Reardon Holdings Limited
DISSANAYAKA, Mrs. Claire Sadie, ACA FCCA ACCA *2011;* 80 Beacon Drive, Bean, DARTFORD, DA2 8BG.
DISSANAYAKE, Mr. Balasuriya Kankanamalage Don, BSc FCA *1963;* 171 Locket Road, HARROW, MIDDLESEX, HA3 7NY. (Life Member)
DISTIN, Mr. Haydn Peter, BSc ACA *1983;* Willow Cottage, 11 Court Road, Cranfield, BEDFORD, MK43 0DR.
DISTON, Mr. Andrew John, BSc(Hons) ACA *2003;* Rexel UK Ltd, 11-13 Frederick Road Edgbaston, BIRMINGHAM, B15 1JD.

DISTON, Mrs. Claire, BSc ACA *2002;* 8 Pinley Way, SOLIHULL, B91 3YG.
DISTON, Mr. David George, FCA *1954;* 1320 Islington Avenue, Unit 1108, ETOBICOKE M9A5C6, ON, CANADA. (Life Member)
DISTON, Mr. Joseph, BA(Hons) ACA *2010;* Ernst & Young Ltd, Suite 6401, 62 Forum Lane, CAMANA BAY, GRAND CAYMAN, KY1-1106 CAYMAN ISLANDS.
DISTON, Mr. Robert, BSc FCA *1973;* (Tax Fac), 7 Moore Close, SUTTON COLDFIELD, B74 4XY.
DITCHFIELD, Mr. Graham, ACA *1981;* 3 Hillpark Crescent, Blackhall, EDINBURGH, EH4 7BG.
DITCHFIELD, Mrs. Helen Margaret, BA ACA *1986;* (Tax Fac), The Old Dairy, Anslow Lane, Rolleston-on-Dove, BURTON-ON-TRENT, DE13 9DS.
DITTON, Mr. Andrew John, BSc ACA *2007;* 69 Portland Close, SLOUGH, SL2 2LT.
DITTRICH, Mr. Leslie-John, BSc ACA *2006;* 21 St. Davids Square, LONDON, E14 3WA.
DIVALL, Mr. Gerald, FCA *1974;* 76 Lyford Road, LONDON, SW18 3JW.
DIVALL, Miss. Katherine Susan, BA ACA *2000;* 23 Boyd Cresent, WEST LAKES SHORE, SA 5020, AUSTRALIA.
DIVAN, Mr. Rahul Gautam, FCA *1995;* Rahul Gautam Divan & Associates, 134 Mittal Tower, C Wing, Nariman Point, MUMBAI 400021, INDIA.
•DIVECHA, Mr. Adil Rustom, FCA *1977;* Ward Divecha Limited, 29 Welbeck Street, LONDON, W1G 8DA.
DIVER, Mr. Stephen Edward, ACA *2011;* Flat 23, 'This Space', 212 Wandsworth Road, LONDON, SW8 2BP.
DIVER, Mr. Stephen Paul, MA FCA *1981;* 8 Riseholme Lane, Riseholme, LINCOLN, LN2 2LD.
DIVES, Mr. William Martin, FCA *1975;* 56 Milverton Road, LONDON, NW6 7AP.
DIX, Mr. Alan Nigel, BA ACA *1985;* Tilbrook Distribution Ltd Bradbourne Drive, Tilbrook, MILTON KEYNES, MK7 8BE.
DIX, Mr. Anthony Stanley, FCA *1969;* 19 Weare Gifford, Shoeburyness, SOUTHEND-ON-SEA, SS3 8AB.
DIX, Mr. Bryan John, BA FCA *1987;* 31 Cornflower Road, Haydon Wick, SWINDON, SN2 3SA.
•DIX, Mr. Christopher John, FCA *1970;* Christopher Dix, Eskdale, The Street, Claxton, NORWICH, NR14 7AS.
•DIX, Mr. Christopher William, BA FCA *1982;* Dix Vogan Limited, 2 Chancery Lane, WAKEFIELD, WEST YORKSHIRE, WF1 2SS.
DIX, Mr. James Scott, BSc(Hons) ACA *2006;* 11 Myrtle Drive, Burwell, CAMBRIDGE, CB25 0AJ.
•DIX, Mr. Jonathan James, BA(Hons) ACA *1990;* Impact Accounting Services Ltd, The Gatehouse, Llanvithyn, Llancarfan, BARRY, SOUTH GLAMORGAN CF62 3AT.
DIX, Mr. Michael John, ACA *2009;* Group Internal Audit First Floor Millstream West, Centrica Plc Millstream, Maidenhead Road, WINDSOR, SL4 5GD.
DIX, Mr. Michael John, BA ACA *1983;* Old Gatecombe House, Littlehempston, TOTNES, DEVON, TQ9 6LW.
DIX, Mr. Roger Patrick, FCA *1968;* Greenah Cragg, Berrier, Troutbeck, PENRITH, CA11 0SQ.
DIX, Miss. Sarah Elizabeth, FCA *1990;* 4 Hawfield Bank, Chelsfield, ORPINGTON, KENT, BR6 7TA.
DIX, Miss. Susan Margaret, FCA *1986;* 13 Cross Lane Gardens, Ticehurst, WADHURST, EAST SUSSEX, TN5 7HY.
•DIXIE, Mr. David Robin, FCA *1972;* Dixie Associates Ltd, AIMS Accountants for Business, 34 Swarthmore Road, Selly Oak, BIRMINGHAM, B29 4JS. See also AIMS - David Dixie
DIXIE, Miss. Monica Ruth, ACA *2009;* 26 Fuchsia Close, Reayrt Ny Keylley Peel, ISLE OF MAN, IM5 1GL.
DIXIT, Mr. Jitin Ratilal, BA ACA *2005;* Cantos Communications Ltd, 16 Lincoln's Inn Fields, LONDON, WC2A 3ED.
•DIXON, Mr. Adrian, BSc ACA *2003;* Dixon & Stone Limited, Fielding House, 43 Thornbury Close, Rhiwbina, CARDIFF, CF14 1UT. See also Dixon & Stone
DIXON, Mr. Adrian Charles, BSc ACA *1993;* 7 Granby Avenue, HARPENDEN, HERTFORDSHIRE, AL5 5QP.
DIXON, Mr. Alan Colin, FCA *1973;* 52 Woodlands Drive, Thelwall, WARRINGTON, WA4 2JL.
DIXON, Mr. Alastair, ACA *2010;* 16 St. Philips Avenue, EASTBOURNE, EAST SUSSEX, BN22 8LU.
DIXON, Miss. Alison Jayne, BSc ACA *2008;* 27 Davys Place, GRAVESEND, DA12 4DL.
DIXON, Miss. Amanda, ACA *1989;* Rosien, Bay View Road, Port Erin, ISLE OF MAN, IM9 6NA.
DIXON, Mrs. Amanda Jane, BSc ACA *1989;* Holly House, Hollins Lane, Greenfield, OLDHAM, OL3 7NR.
DIXON, Mrs. Amanda Louise, ACA *1996;* 1 Sutleye Court, Shenley Church End, MILTON KEYNES, MK5 6EA.
DIXON, Mr. Andrew, BSc ACA *1988;* 2 HEAD CROFT, FLAX BOURTON, BRISTOL, BS48 1US.
•DIXON, Mr. Andrew, BA ACA *1992;* with Grant Thornton UK LLP, Grant Thornton House, Kettering Parkway, Kettering Venture Park, KETTERING, NORTHAMPTONSHIRE NN15 6XR.
DIXON, Mr. Andrew Charles, BEng FCA *1989;* The Independent Chapel, Main Street, North Newington, BANBURY, OXFORDSHIRE, OX15 6AJ.
•DIXON, Mr. Andrew John, BSc FCA *1988;* Spain Brothers & Co, 29 Manor Road, FOLKESTONE, KENT, CT20 2SE.
DIXON, Mr. Andrew John, FCA *1976;* 23 Greenacres Avenue, Kirkham, PRESTON, PR4 2TX.
•DIXON, Mr. Andrew Paul, BA FCA *1987;* (Tax Fac), Wrigley Partington, Sterling House, 501 Middleton Road, Chadderton, OLDHAM, OL9 9LY.
DIXON, Mr. Andrew Philip Graham, BA FCA MIFT AMCT *1993;* 67 Wynches Farm Drive, ST. ALBANS, HERTFORDSHIRE, AL4 0XH.
DIXON, Mr. Andrew Stephen, BSc ACA *1992;* 18B Woodside Avenue, WALTON-ON-THAMES, KT12 5LG.
DIXON, Mr. Andrew Mark Luke, BA ACA *2011;* Ridgmont, The Crofts, Castletown, ISLE OF MAN, IM9 1LY.
DIXON, Mrs. Angela, BSc ACA *1985;* 26A Farringford CLose, ST. ALBANS, AL2 3HS.
DIXON, Mrs. Angela Marie, BA ACA *2005;* 4 Park View, Hodsoll Street, SEVENOAKS, KENT, TN15 7LN.
DIXON, Mr. Anthony John, MA FCA *1985;* 5 Walpole Rd, Strawberry Hill, TWICKENHAM, TW2 5SN.
DIXON, Mr. Brian, FCA *1957;* with Wrigley Partington, Sterling House, 501 Middleton Road, Chadderton, OLDHAM, OL9 9LY. (Life Member)
DIXON, Mr. Bruce James, BA ACA *1999;* 35 Carrick Court, Kennington Park Road, LONDON, SE114EE.
DIXON, Mrs. Carla Cassandra, MA ACA *2001;* Ashurst, Broadwalk House 5 Appold Street, LONDON, EC2A 2HA.
DIXON, Ms. Caroline Rebecca Louise, BSc ACA *1993;* Mylan, Albany Gate, Darkes Lane, POTTERS BAR, HERTFORDSHIRE, EN6 1AG.
DIXON, Mrs. Catherine Barbara, BSc ACA *1990;* Altro Limited, Works Road, LETCHWORTH GARDEN CITY, SG6 1NW.
DIXON, Mr. Charles Ernest, MA FCA *1966;* Pear Tree Cottages, The Street, Walberton, ARUNDEL, BN18 0PY.
DIXON, Mr. Charles Kendal, ACA *2008;* K P M G Llp, 15 Canada Square, LONDON, E14 5GL.
DIXON, Mr. Charles William, FCA *1971;* 5 Kiln Lane, LOUTH, LINCOLNSHIRE, LN11 0LG.
DIXON, Mr. Christopher Ian, BA ACA *2004;* B S N Block C Willerby Hill Business Park, Beverley Road Willerby, HULL, HU10 6FE.
DIXON, Mr. Christopher Raymond, BSc FCA *1983;* 7 Faulkner Road, Northcote Point, NORTH SHORE CITY, NEW ZEALAND.
DIXON, Mr. Clive, MA ACA *1990;* Theatres Trust, 22 Charing Cross Road, LONDON, WC2H 0QL.
DIXON, Mr. Clive Owen, FCA *1970;* 9 Glenrock Park, BROUGH, NORTH HUMBERSIDE, HU15 1HF.
•DIXON, Mr. Clive Owen Luke, BA FCA *1981;* Moore Stephens, P O Box 25, 26-28 Athol Street, Douglas, ISLE OF MAN, IM99 1BD. See also Moore Stephens Limited
DIXON, Mr. Conrad, BA FCA *1987;* 8 Heybridge Road, INGATESTONE, ESSEX, CM4 9AG.
DIXON, Mr. Craig Stephen, BSc ACA *1989;* Florian House, Leatherhead Road, Oxshott, LEATHERHEAD, KT22 0ET.
DIXON, Mr. Daniel Thomas, BA(Econ) ACA AMCT *1998;* Carnanton, Camden Park, TUNBRIDGE WELLS, TN2 5AE.
DIXON, Mrs. Danielle Samantha, ACA *2005;* 15 Laurel Gardens, ALDERSHOT, HAMPSHIRE, GU11 3TQ.
DIXON, Mr. David Alfred, FCA *1951;* 6 Cedar Drive, Everton, LYMINGTON, SO41 0ZB. (Life Member)
DIXON, Mr. David George, MBA BA FCA *1981;* 3 Lea Road, Ampthill, BEDFORD, MK45 2PR.
DIXON, Mr. David George, BMus ACA *1995;* 31 Poplar Road, Shalford, GUILDFORD, SURREY, GU4 8DH.
DIXON, Mr. David Philip, BA ACA *1988;* Holly Tree House, Butchers Lane, Preston, HITCHIN, SG4 7TR.
DIXON, Mrs. Deborah Anne, BA ACA *1983;* Bridgewater, Canal Side, Grappenhall, WARRINGTON, WA4 3EX.
DIXON, Mr. Eric Gordon, FCA *1974;* Koyunbaba, Little Valley Villas No.7, Gumusluk, BODRUM, MUGLA PROVINCE, TURKEY.
DIXON, Mr. Gary, BSc FCA *1991;* Lanchester House, Main Street, Great Glen, LEICESTER, LE8 9GH.
DIXON, Mr. Gary Frank, BA(Hons) ACA *2002;* (Tax Fac), 4 Park View, Hodsoll Street, SEVENOAKS, KENT, TN15 7LN.
DIXON, Mr. Gavin William, MA ACA *1991;* Woori Aviva Life Insurance, 8F V Tower, 283 Dangsan, Dong Yeongdungpo, SEOUL, 150 046 KOREA REPUBLIC OF.
DIXON, Mr. Graeme George, BSc ACA AMCT *2003;* Port of Tyne Authority, Maritime House, Tyne Dock, SOUTH SHIELDS, TYNE AND WEAR, NE34 9PT.
DIXON, Mrs. Heather Tracey, BA FCA *1989;* Brathay Hall Trust Brathay Hall, Clappersgate, AMBLESIDE, CUMBRIA, LA22 0HP.
DIXON, Mr. Hugh Frederick, FCA *1957;* The Old House, 89 Town Green Street, Rothley, LEICESTER, LE7 7NW. (Life Member)
DIXON, Mr. Ian, BA ACA QICA *1994;* 2 Huntly Road, WHITLEY BAY, TYNE AND WEAR, NE25 9UR.
DIXON, Mr. Ian Clive, BSc ACA *1978;* 11 Ridgelands, Fetcham, LEATHERHEAD, SURREY, KT22 9DB. (Life Member)
DIXON, Mr. Ian James, FCA *1963;* 10 Greenacres, Darras Hall, NEWCASTLE UPON TYNE, NE20 9RT. (Life Member)
DIXON, Mr. Ian James, BA ACA *2007;* Ground Floor Flat, 121 Bedford Hill, LONDON, SW129HE.
DIXON, Mr. Ian Richard, ACIB ACA *1993;* The Forge, Harland Rise Farm, Harland Way, COTTINGHAM, HU16 5TB.
DIXON, Mr. Ian Stephen, BA ACA *1991;* with Business Link Northwest, City Office, Brian Johnson Way, PRESTON, PR2 5PE.
DIXON, Mr. Ian Stuart, MA ACA *1989;* 25 Milton Road, Broughton, MILTON KEYNES, MK10 9RA.
•DIXON, Mr. Ian Stuart, PhD FCA *1989;* with PricewaterhouseCoopers, 7 More London Riverside, LONDON, SE1 2RT.
DIXON, Mr. James, FCA *1950;* Riverside House, Acomb, HEXHAM, NE46 4QJ. (Life Member)
DIXON, Mr. James Lee, MA(Cantab) BA ACA *2000;* 43 Queens Crescent, ABERDEEN, AB15 4AZ.
DIXON, Mr. James Robert Patrick, BA ACA *1992;* Hewlett Packard Ltd, Cain Road, BRACKNELL, RG12 1HN.
DIXON, Mr. James Rylott, FCA *1954;* Rylotts, 19A Crawley Lane, Poundhill, CRAWLEY, WEST SUSSEX, RH10 7TQ. (Life Member)
DIXON, Mr. James Wolryche, MA FCA *1973;* (Tax Fac), 5 Burleigh Place, Cambalt Road, Putney, LONDON, SW15 6ES. (Life Member)
•DIXON, Mrs. Jane Louise, BSc ACA ATII *1993;* (Tax Fac), ACL Tax and Accountancy Limited, Quorum 16, Quorum Business Park, Benton Lane, NEWCASTLE UPON TYNE, NE12 8BX.
DIXON, Mrs. Janice Dawn, FCA *1992;* The Willows, 40a Brook Street, Colne Engaine, COLCHESTER, CO6 2JD.
DIXON, Mr. Jeffrey Paul, BSc(Hons) ACA *2001;* 67 Princes Road, RICHMOND, SURREY, TW10 6DQ.
DIXON, Mrs. Joanne, ACA *1989;* 22 Church Walk, Station Road, WINCANTON, SOMERSET, BA9 9FG.
DIXON, Mrs. Joanne, BSc ACA *1996;* Apartado de Correos 20, 07814 SANTA GERTRUDIS DE FRUITERA, SPAIN.
DIXON, Mr. John, FCA *1972;* Unit 1 La Orquidea, Calle Don Jose Orbaneja s/n, Sitio de CalahondaMijas Costa, 29647 MALAGA, SPAIN. (Life Member)
DIXON, Mr. John Bradford, FCA *1968;* Fairlawn, Court Drive, LICHFIELD, WS14 0JQ.
DIXON, Mr. John Edwin, MA FCA *1974;* 14 Jalan Tunku Selekoh, Bukit Tunku, 50480 KUALA LUMPUR, FEDERAL TERRITORY, MALAYSIA.
DIXON, Mr. John Ernest, FCA *1953;* 18 Howard Place, Reigate Hill, REIGATE, SURREY, RH2 9NP. (Life Member)
DIXON, Mr. John Featherstone, BCom FCA *1954;* Flat 17 Lansdown Court, Malvern Road, CHELTENHAM, GL50 2JS. (Life Member)
DIXON, Mr. John Graham, FCA *1968;* 63 Redesmere Drive, ALDERLEY EDGE, SK9 7UR. (Life Member)
DIXON, Mr. John Nicholas Russell, FCA *1971;* Little Holme, Ockham Road North, WOKING, SURREY, GU23 6PD.
DIXON, Mr. John Norman, FCA *1968;* 45 Westercroft Lane, Northowram, HALIFAX, WEST YORKSHIRE, HX3 7EN.
DIXON, Mr. John Paul, ACA *1983;* Pricewaterhousecoopers, 89 Sandyford Road, NEWCASTLE UPON TYNE, NE1 8HW.
DIXON, Miss. Josephine, BSc ACA *1987;* Hotspur House, Allendale, HEXHAM, NE47 9BW.
DIXON, Mr. Julian David Edward, FCA *1967;* Chateau De Betous, BETOUS, 32110 GERS, FRANCE.
DIXON, Mr. Keith William, BSc FCA *1969;* 171 Wood Street, KIDDERMINSTER, WORCESTERSHIRE, DY11 6UF. (Life Member)
•DIXON, Mr. Kevin John, FCA *1989;* Brooks & Co, Hampton House, High Street, EAST GRINSTEAD, WEST SUSSEX, RH19 3AW.
DIXON, Mr. Lawrence, BSc ACA *1979;* 105 Chemin Des Cretes, 24140 VILLAMBLARD, DORDOGNE, FRANCE.
•DIXON, Mr. Lee Howard, BSc FCA CTA *1994;* (Tax Fac), Gibbons, Carleton House, 136 Gray Street, WORKINGTON, CUMBRIA, CA14 2LU. See also Gibbons & Company
DIXON, Mr. Leon James, BA ACA *2007;* 8 Elizabeth Street, Whitefield, MANCHESTER, M45 6BP.
DIXON, Mrs. Linda, BA ACA *1991;* Lanchester House, Main Street, Great Glen, LEICESTER, LE8 9GH.
DIXON, Mrs. Lucy Victoria, BA ACA *2003;* 4 Clarendon Avenue, ANDOVER, HAMPSHIRE, SP10 2LX.
•DIXON, Mr. Malcolm, FCA *1969;* Hightrees, 10 The Orchards, Off Lady Lane, BINGLEY, BD16 4AZ.
DIXON, Mr. Mark James, BSc BCom CertICM ACA MCT *1992;* 53G/26/1, Land Rover Gaydon Test Centre, Banbury Road Gaydon, WARWICK, CV35 0RG.
DIXON, Mr. Mark John, BSc(Hons) FCA *2000;* Cognis Capital Partners Llp, 25-26 Albemarle Street, LONDON, W1S 4HX.
DIXON, Mr. Mark Laurence, BA ACA *1990;* 8 Gillercomb Close, West Bridgford, NOTTINGHAM, NG2 6SE.
DIXON, Mr. Mark Robert Graham, BSc ACA *1990;* Harperley, Penn Lane, Tanworth-In-Arden, SOLIHULL, WARWICKSHIRE, B94 5HH.
DIXON, Mr. Matthew, MSc ACA *2011;* Grant Thornton UK LLP, 101 Cambridge Science Park Milton Road, CAMBRIDGE, CB4 0FY.
DIXON, Mr. Matthew John, BSc ACA *2010;* 214a Archway Road, LONDON, N6 5AX.
DIXON, Mr. Michael, BA ACA *1997;* 15 Marlborough Gate, ST. ALBANS, HERTFORDSHIRE, AL1 3TX.
DIXON, Mr. Michael, BSc ACA *1987;* 3 Deakin Avenue, HABERFIELD, NSW 2045, AUSTRALIA.
DIXON, Mr. Michael Andrew Morley, BSocSc ACA *1986;* Charities Aid Foundation, 25 Kings Hill Avenue Kings Hill, WEST MALLING, KENT, ME19 4TA.
DIXON, Mr. Michael Christopher, BSc ACA *1993;* Huntsman Tioxide, Haverton Hill Road, BILLINGHAM, CLEVELAND, TS23 1PS.
DIXON, Mr. Michael John, BSc ACA *2010;* 6126 W Colgate Ave, Park La Brea, LOS ANGELES, CA 90036, UNITED STATES.
DIXON, Ms. Natalie Claire, BA ACA *1994;* with PricewaterhouseCoopers, Royal Trust Tower, Suite 3000 TD Centre, Box 82, 77 King Street West, TORONTO M5K 1G8 ON CANADA.
DIXON, Mrs. Nicola Joanne, MA ACA *1997;* 54 Langdon Avenue, AYLESBURY, BUCKINGHAMSHIRE, HP21 9UT.
•DIXON, Mr. Nigel Anthony, FCA *1973;* Caulkhead Investments Ltd, Manor Farm House, Winterslow Road, Porton, SALISBURY, SP4 0JZ.
DIXON, Mr. Nigel Richard, BA FCA *1983;* Birchdale Dalefords Lane, Whitegate, NORTHWICH, CHESHIRE, CW8 2BN.
DIXON, Mr. Norman William, FCA *1953;* 6 Chestnut Walk, SHEPPERTON, TW17 8QP. (Life Member)
DIXON, Miss. Pamela Ann, BSc ACA *1985;* Dryden Associates, P O Box 61, Alderney, GUERNSEY, GY9 3JT.
DIXON, Mrs. Patricia Ann, BA FCA *1981;* Ridgmont The Crofts, Castletown, ISLE OF MAN, IM9 1LY.
DIXON, Mr. Paul, MA(Oxon) MChem ACA *2007;* with KPMG LLP, Bow Valley Square II, 205-5th Avenue SW Suite 1200, CALGARY T2P 4B9, AB, CANADA.
•DIXON, Mr. Paul Frank, FCA *1973;* Paul Dixon & Associates, Byeways, Mill Road, Lower Shiplake, HENLEY-ON-THAMES, RG9 3LW.
DIXON, Mr. Paul James, FCA *1973;* Bonningtons Stanstead Road, Hunsdon, WARE, HERTFORDSHIRE, SG12 8PS.
DIXON, Mr. Paul John, BSc FCA *1994;* Cathedral Capital Ltd, Fitzwilliam House, 10 St. Mary Axe, LONDON, EC3A 8BF.

DIXON, Mr. Paul Robert, ACA *1989;* Industrial Supplies & Services Ltd, Redfield Road, Lenton Lane Industrial Estate, NOTTINGHAM, NG7 2UJ.
DIXON, Mrs. Penny Anna, BA ACA *1997;* 47 Anlaby Road, TEDDINGTON, MIDDLESEX, TW11 0PB.
•DIXON, Mr. Peter Brian, FCA *1986;* Maynard Heady LLP, 40-42 High Street, MALDON, ESSEX, CM9 5PN. See also Maynard Heady
DIXON, Mr. Peter John, BA FCA *2000;* 243 Crystal Palace Road, East Dulwich, LONDON, SE22 9JQ.
DIXON, Mr. Peter Matthew, BSc FCA *1979;* 26 Rydal Drive, Hale Barns, ALTRINCHAM, WA15 8TE.
DIXON, Mr. Peter Rae, FCA *1969;* Canons Farm, Worminster, North Wootton, SHEPTON MALLET, SOMERSET, BA4 4AJ. (Life Member)
DIXON, Mr. Philip John, BA ACA *1986;* (Tax Fac), Nomura Code Securities, 1 Carey Lane, LONDON, EC2V 8AE.
DIXON, Mr. Philip Martin, BA FCA *1974;* 23 Broadoak Road, Worsley, MANCHESTER, M28 2TL.
•DIXON, Mr. Richard Mark, BA ACA *1992;* Wrigley Partington, Sterling House, 501 Middleton Road, Chadderton, OLDHAM, OL9 9LY.
DIXON, Mr. Richard Thomas, BA ACA *1989;* Bleak Hall Cottage, Chambers Lane, Ickleford, HITCHIN, HERTFORDSHIRE, SG5 3YA.
•DIXON, Mr. Roger, FCA *1955;* Dixon & Co, Bird in Eye Farm, Bird in Eye Hill, Framfield, UCKFIELD, EAST SUSSEX TN22 5HA.
DIXON, Mr. Roger Edwin, ACA *1979;* 23 Glenton Close, Rise Park, ROMFORD, RM1 4AN.
DIXON, Mrs. Sallyanne, BA ACA *1997;* Whitley Grange, South Otterington, NORTHALLERTON, DL7 9HU.
DIXON, Miss. Sarah, BSc ACA *2010;* 92 Newport Road, NEWBURY, RG14 2AS.
DIXON, Miss. Sarah Kate, ACA *2008;* Forensic Services, Pricewaterhousecoopers, 101 Barbirolli Square, MANCHESTER, M2 3PW.
DIXON, Mrs. Sarah Melland, BSc ACA *1983;* Flint House, Hardwick Road, Whitchurch-on-Thames, READING, RG8 7HH.
DIXON, Mr. Simon Roger, MPhil BA ACA *2000;* Spire, Cambridge Lea Hospital, 30 New Road, Impington, CAMBRIDGE, CB24 9EL.
DIXON, Mrs. Stephanie Susan, LLM LLB ACA CTA *1988;* (Tax Fac), Leeds Business School The Rose Bowl (417), Leeds Metropolitan University Portland Gate, LEEDS, WEST YORKSHIRE, LS1 3HM.
DIXON, Mr. Stephen Kay, FCA *1970;* Keepers Cottage, Tidmarsh, READING, RG8 8EB.
DIXON, Mr. Stephen Sheldon, BEng ACA *1997;* Pear Tree House, Bunbury Lane, Bunbury, TARPORLEY, CHESHIRE, CW6 9QS.
DIXON, Mr. Stuart Roy, BSc ACA *1987;* (Tax Fac), Rivermede, Weare Street, Ockley, DORKING, RH5 5NH.
DIXON, Mrs. Susan Mary, BA ACA *1992;* 3 Comfrey Close, Walnut Tree, MILTON KEYNES, MK7 7BY.
DIXON, Mr. Thomas Christopher, ACA *2007;* Flat 7, 135 Haverstock Hill, LONDON, NW3 4RU.
•①DIXON, Mr. Thomas Ernest, BSc ACA MABRP *1989;* with Baker Tilly Tax and Accounting Limited, 3 Hardman Street, MANCHESTER, M3 3HF.
DIXON, Mr. Thomas Mark, BA ACA *2005;* (Tax Fac), with PKF (UK) LLP, Farringdon Place, 20 Farringdon Road, LONDON, EC1M 3AP.
•DIXON, Mr. Thomas Pieter Hendrik, FCA *1974;* Rua Jose Viana 78, 2765-238 ESTORIL, PORTUGAL.
DIXON, Mr. William Dewar, FCA *1966;* Upton Lodge, Upton, BUDE, CORNWALL, EX23 0LY. (Life Member)
DIXON, Mr. William John, BSc FCA *1980;* Wyndham House, Llandogo, MONMOUTH, NP25 4TW.
DIXON, Mr. William Thomas Dalziel, BA FCA *1951;* Cobwood, The Street, Plaxtol, SEVENOAKS, KENT, TN15 0QQ. (Life Member)
DIXON-BROWN, Miss. Cecily Anne, BA ACA *2007;* Prudential PLC, Minster House, 12 Arthur Street, LONDON, EC4R 9AQ.
DIXON-CLARKE, Mr. Peter John, BA ACA *1994;* Beech House, East Winterslow, SALISBURY, SP5 1BG.
•DIZADJI, Mr. Farhad, BSc FCA *1979;* (Tax Fac), Roberts & Partners, 47 Queen Anne Street, LONDON, W1G 9JG.
DIZADJI, Miss. Tanaz, BSc ACA *2010;* Auguste Cottage, Hammers Lane, LONDON, NW7 4DD.
DIZER, Mr. Christopher James, BSc ACA MCT *1984;* 37 Compton Road, LONDON, SW19 7QA.
•DJANOGLY, Mr. Daniel, BA FCA FCIArb *1985;* Daniel Djanogly, 25 Southampton Buildings, LONDON, WC2A 1AL.
DO, Miss. Nguyen Thuy Dao, ACA *2011;* 5 Tran Quy Cap, Ward 12, Binh Thanh District, HO CHI MINH CITY, VIETNAM.
DOA, Miss. Claire Michelle, BSc ACA *2004;* Flat 313 Riverside Mansions, Milk Yard, LONDON, E1W 3TA.
DOAL, Miss. Manjeet, BSc ACA *2011;* Woodlands, Nursery Road, LOUGHTON, ESSEX, IG10 4EA.
DOAN, Miss. Kim Linh, BSc ACA *2006;* 4 andleon court, CLAYTON, VIC 3169, AUSTRALIA.
DOAR, Mr. Richard Jonathan, BSc ACA *2006;* with Deloitte LLP, 1 Woodborough Road, NOTTINGHAM, NG1 3FG.
DOBBIE, Miss. Catriona Margaret, MA ACA *1988;* 67 Church Road, RICHMOND, TW10 6LX.
DOBBIE, Ms. Lisa Margaret, ACA CA(NZ) *2010;* Flat 93, Hurlingham Court, Ranelagh Gardens, LONDON, SW6 3UR.
DOBBIN, Mr. Anthony Michael Chetwynd, MA FCA *1970;* (Tax Fac), Greystoke, 3 Seale Hill, REIGATE, RH2 8HZ.
•DOBBIN, Mr. Julian, BSc ACA *2002;* Mercer & Hole, Silbury Court, 420 Silbury Boulevard, MILTON KEYNES, BUCKINGHAMSHIRE, MK9 2AF.
DOBBIN, Mr. Thomas Joseph Christopher, FCA *1963;* 207 Childwall Road, LIVERPOOL, L15 6UT. (Life Member)
•DOBBINS, Mr. Matthew Stuart, BA ACA *2002;* with Dunkley & Co Limited, Woodlands Grange, Woodlands Lane, Bradley Stoke, BRISTOL, BS32 4JY.
DOBBINS, Mr. Rob, ACA *2009;* O M V UK Ltd, Ryder Court, 14 Ryder Street, LONDON, SW1Y 6QB.
DOBBINS, Mr. Simon Philip, BA FCA *1998;* Yoyogi Nishihara Park Mansion 301, 3-40-19 Nishihara, Shibuya-ku, TOKYO, 151-0066 JAPAN.
DOBBS, Mr. Andrew Christopher, LLB ACA *1993;* 28 Hall Meadow Croft, Halfway, SHEFFIELD, S20 4XB.
DOBBS, Mr. David, BA(Hons) ACA ACMA *2007;* Bramblings Church Lane, Marshchapel, GRIMSBY, SOUTH HUMBERSIDE, DN36 5TW.
DOBBS, Miss. Julia Carol, BSc ACA *1997;* 61 Old Station Road, Hampton In Arden, SOLIHULL, B92 0HA.
DOBBS, Mr. Nicholas Martin, ACA BEng(Hons) *1995;* The Blenheims, Main Street, Chilton, DIDCOT, OXFORDSHIRE, OX11 0RZ.
DOBBS, Mr. Philip James, ACA *2008;* 66 St. Martins Road, Thorngumbald, HULL, HU12 9PL.
DOBBS, Mr. Richard, BSc ACA *2001;* 12 Sherburn Street, CLEETHORPES, SOUTH HUMBERSIDE, DN35 8TQ.
DOBBS, Mr. Richard Noel, FCA *1963;* Salterns Cottage, Salterns Road, SEAVIEW, PO34 5AH.
•DOBBY, Mr. Francis Walter, FCA *1970;* 1 Ailsa Dell, Howley Mill Lane, BATLEY, WEST YORKSHIRE, WF17 0BL.
DOBBY, Mr. Matthew Christopher, BSc ACA *2002;* with HMRC, H M Revenue & Customs:, Alexander House, 21 Victoria Avenue, SOUTHEND-ON-SEA, SS99 1AA.
DOBBYN, Mr. Francis, BSc ACA *1980;* Highfield House, High Street, Semington, TROWBRIDGE, WILTSHIRE, BA14 6JN.
DOBBYN, Mrs. Laura Frances, MA ACA *2002;* 137 Disraeli Road, LONDON, SW15 2DZ.
DOBBYN, Mr. Michael Ian, BA ACA *1989;* Marie Heinekenplein 502, 1072 ML AMSTERDAM, NETHERLANDS.
DOBBYN, Mr. Sam, ACA *2008;* 137 Disraeli Road, LONDON, SW15 2DZ.
DOBELL, Mr. Anthony Russell, FCA *1971;* Pear Tree Farm, Peover Heath, KNUTSFORD, WA16 8UN. (Life Member)
DOBELL, Mr. Mark Timothy, BA FCA *1976;* The Moss, Peat Inn, CUPAR, KY15 5LH.
•DOBELL, Mr. Patrick John, MA ACA *1978;* Portsmouth Diocesan Trust, St. Edmund House, Edinburgh Road, PORTSMOUTH, PO1 3QA.
DOBERMAN, Mr. Jonathan Peter, BSc ACA *2004;* Flat 3, Laxmi Court, 52 Dollis Avenue, LONDON, N3 1BH.
DOBIE, Mr. Alisdair John, MA FCA *1994;* Ardfern, Bowriefauld, FORFAR, ANGUS, DD8 2LX.
DOBINSON, Mr. David William, BA FCA *1975;* 40 Vernon Road, LEIGH-ON-SEA, SS9 2NG.
DOBINSON, Mr. John Leslie, BA ACA *1989;* Dirry Mor Cottage, Fulmer Chase Stoke Common Rd, Fulmer, SLOUGH, SL3 6HB.
DOBINSON, Mr. Martyn, ACA *2008;* 55 Middlewich Road, Holmes Chapel, CREWE, CW4 7ER.
DOBINSON, Mr. Paul Robert, ACA *2010;* 113-119 The Terrace, PO Box 243, WELLINGTON 6140, NEW ZEALAND.
DOBLE, Mr. Alan Leslie, FCA *1969;* 24 Vicarage Gardens, Marshfield, CARDIFF, CF3 2PS.
DOBLE, Mrs. Julie Russell, BSc ACA *1984;* 9 Homewood Road, ST. ALBANS, AL1 4BE.
DOBLE, Miss. Sarah Elizabeth, BCom ACA *2005;* 6 Collins Road, WALSALL, WS8 7AW.
DOBNEY, Mr. Laurence Michael, ACA *1978;* 36 Redbridge, Werrington, PETERBOROUGH, PE4 5DP.
DOBRASZCZYC, Miss. Naomi, BA(Hons) ACA *2003;* 56 Russell Crescent, NOTTINGHAM, NG8 2BQ.
DOBREE, Mr. Peter Noel, FCA *1969;* 26 Lower Road, Fetcham, LEATHERHEAD, SURREY, KT22 9EW. (Life Member)
DOBREE, Mr. Ronald Bonamy, MA FCA *1969;* 102 Shinfield Road, READING, RG2 7DA.
•DOBRIN, Mr. Anthony Philip, FCA *1968;* Anthony P Dobrin FCA, 31 Church Mount, LONDON, N2 0RW.
•DOBRIN, Mr. Michael Morris, ACA *1984;* The Glendower Group Ltd, Island Farm House, Island Farm Road, WEST MOLESEY, SURREY, KT8 2TR.
DOBRUCKI, Mr. Jan Alexander, BSc ACA *1990;* 41 Southlands Drive, Fixby, HUDDERSFIELD, HD2 2LT.
DOBSON, Mr. Alan, ACA *1981;* Moore and Smalley, Priory Close St Mary's Gate, LANCASTER, LA1 1XB.
DOBSON, Mrs. Alyson Carole, MA ACA *2002;* Culmdale, Rewe, EXETER, EX5 4ES.
•DOBSON, Mrs. Andrea, BSc ACA *1999;* Andrea Dobson Limited, 10 Freshfields, KNUTSFORD, CHESHIRE, WA16 0NR.
•DOBSON, Mrs. Anne Eilidh, MA(Hons) ACA *2003;* Anne Dobson Limited, 133 Comiston Road, EDINBURGH, EH10 6AQ. See also Anne Dobson
DOBSON, Mr. Arthur Gilmour, BSc ACA *1989;* 35 South Road, West Bridgford, NOTTINGHAM, NG2 7AG.
DOBSON, Mr. Arthur Stephen, BSc FCA *1985;* 16 John Muir Crescent, DUNBAR, EH42 1GE.
DOBSON, Mrs. Christine, BSc ACA *1996;* 34 Almond Drive, Dunston Park, THATCHAM, RG18 4DZ.
DOBSON, Captain Christopher George, MA BA(Hons) ACA *2002;* Grove House, East Ferry Road, Susworth, SCUNTHORPE, LINCOLNSHIRE, DN17 3AS.
DOBSON, Mr. Christopher Neil Young, FCA *1973;* Sopers Ride, Selsfield Road, Turners Hill, CRAWLEY, RH10 4PP.
DOBSON, Mr. Clive, FCA *1969;* Maple Leaf, Scales, ULVERSTON, LA12 0PB. (Life Member)
DOBSON, Mr. David Michael, BSc ACA *2006;* 34 Montgomery Avenue, LEEDS, LS16 5RW.
DOBSON, Miss. Elizabeth Jane, MA MPhil ACA *2004;* Zone 4/26, Department of Transport Great Minster House, 76 Marsham Street, LONDON, SW1P 4DR.
DOBSON, Mr. Geoffrey John, FCA *1970;* 6 Epsom Lane South, TADWORTH, SURREY, KT20 5SX.
•DOBSON, Mrs. Geraldene Lea, ACA CA(SA) *2009;* (Tax Fac), Hemisphere Accounting Limited, Mornington, Maybourne Rise, WOKING, SURREY, GU22 0SH.
DOBSON, Miss. Gillian Louise, MA ACA DChA *1992;* Tees Valley Leisure Eston Sports Centre, Normanby Road, MIDDLESBROUGH, CLEVELAND, TS6 9AE.
•DOBSON, Mr. Graham Maurice, FCA *1975;* Chaytor Steele & Co, 9a Derby Street, ORMSKIRK, L39 2BJ.
DOBSON, Mrs. Helen Margaret, BA ACA *1991;* 129A The Mount, YORK, YO24 1DU.
DOBSON, Mr. Hugh Andrew Philip, BA FCA *1971;* Forest Cottage, Godshill Green, FORDINGBRIDGE, SP6 2LH.
DOBSON, Mrs. Isabel Claire, BA ACA *1987;* Daniel J Edelman Ltd, 105 Victoria Street, LONDON, SW1E 6QT.
DOBSON, Mr. James Edward, BSc(Hons) ACA *2003;* Bewdley, Dyffryn, NEATH, WEST GLAMORGAN, SA10 7AZ.
DOBSON, Mrs. Joanna Claire, BSc ACA *2003;* 40 Highfields Road, DRONFIELD, DERBYSHIRE, S18 1UW.
DOBSON, Miss. Joanna Louise, BA ACA *2002;* 29 Gladstone Grove, STOCKPORT, CHESHIRE, SK4 4BX.
•DOBSON, Mr. Jonathan, BA(Hons) ACA *2003;* Greenbank Accountancy Services Ltd, 23 Littlejohn Avenue, EDINBURGH, EH10 5TG.
DOBSON, Miss. Katherine Louise, MChem ACA *2010;* 30 Weavers Mead, HAYWARDS HEATH, WEST SUSSEX, RH16 4FR.
DOBSON, Mr. Kenneth, BSc ACA *2010;* 15 Spinners Yard, Fisher Street, CARLISLE, CA3 8RE.
DOBSON, Mr. Kevin Michael, MA FCA *1990;* 3 Grantham Road, Radcliffe-on-Trent, NOTTINGHAM, NG12 2HB.
DOBSON, Mrs. Kirstie Emma, LLB ACA *2000;* Humber Refinery, Eastfield Road, South Killingholme, IMMINGHAM, SOUTH HUMBERSIDE, DN40 3DW.
DOBSON, Mr. Mark, ACA *2010;* K P M G, 1 The Embankment, LEEDS, LS1 4DW.
DOBSON, Mr. Nigel Hewitt, FCA *1972;* Red Lodge, The Parade, Minis Bay, BIRCHINGTON, KENT, CT7 9LX.
DOBSON, Mr. Paul Robert, BA ACA *1996;* 9 Whinmoor Drive, Silkstone, BARNSLEY, SOUTH YORKSHIRE, S75 4NR.
DOBSON, Mr. Philip, FCA *1973;* Victoria House, Andrews Road, Llandaff North, CARDIFF, CF14 2JP.
DOBSON, Mr. Philip David, BEng ACA *1996;* Upper House Farm, Little Hereford, LUDLOW, SHROPSHIRE, SY8 4LQ.
DOBSON, Miss. Rachel Louise, MChem ACA CTA *2007;* 14 Maybury Close, Frimley, CAMBERLEY, SURREY, GU16 7HH.
DOBSON, Mr. Richard Iain, BA ACA *1999;* 143 Vernon Road, Poynton, STOCKPORT, SK12 1YS.
•DOBSON, Mr. Richard Mark, BA ACA *1988;* Ernst & Young Slovakia spol. s r.o., Hodzovo namestie 1A, 811 06 BRATISLAVA, SLOVAK REPUBLIC. See also Ernst & Young Europe LLP
•DOBSON, Mr. Robert Kirton, FCA *1966;* (Tax Fac), R.K. Dobson, 37 Walton Gardens, FOLKESTONE, CT19 5PR.
•DOBSON, Mr. Roger Charles, BCom ACA *1981;* R.C. Dobson & Co, Bredon View, Hollybush, LEDBURY, HR8 1ET.
DOBSON, Miss. Ruth Margaret, BA ACA *2000;* with PricewaterhouseCoopers, 11//F, PricewaterhouseCoopers Center, 2 Corporate Avenue, 202 Hu Bin Road, SHANGHAI 200021 CHINA.
DOBSON, Mrs. Sarah Jane, BA ACA *1990;* Spaldings Farmhouse, Laundry Lane, Thornham Magna, EYE, IP23 8HG.
DOBSON, Miss. Sasha, BA ACA *1997;* 20 Murray Street, YORK, YO24 4JA.
DOBSON, Mr. Stephen Mark, FCA *1981;* The Spinney, 6 Hawthorne Close, Lepton, HUDDERSFIELD, HD8 0BR.
•DOBSON, Mr. Steven Mark, MA ACA *1994;* Ernst & Young LLP, 1 More London Place, LONDON, SE1 2AF. See also Ernst & Young Europe LLP
DOBSON, Mr. Terence Bryan, BA ACA *1988;* Tudor House, 34 New Rd, HAVERFORDWEST, SA61 1TY.
DOBSON, Mr. Timothy Turney, FCA *1963;* Ampleforth Abbey, Ampleforth Lodge, YORK, YO62 4EN.
DOCHERTY, Dr. Gordon, BSc ACA *2007;* 38 Hyde Lane, Kinver, STOURBRIDGE, DY7 6AF.
DOCHERTY, Mrs. Helen Ruth, BSc ACA *2000;* 15 Ben Rhydding Drive, ILKLEY, LS29 8AY.
DOCHERTY, Mr. Ian Joseph, BA ACA *1988;* 274 Harborne Park Road, BIRMINGHAM, B17 0BL.
DOCHERTY, Miss. Jane Alison, MA LLB ACA CTA *1999;* 39 Chaucer Way, Wimbledon, LONDON, SW19 1UJ.
•DOCHERTY, Miss. Kathleen, BA FCA FCMA FCIPD *1993;* (Tax Fac), C&M Services (Bristol) Ltd, 19 The Park, Bradley Stoke, BRISTOL, BS32 0AP.
DOCHERTY, Mr. Mark James, BEng FCA *1992;* XKE Capital LLP, November House Hudnall Lane, Little Gaddesden, BERKHAMSTED, HERTFORDSHIRE, HP4 1QQ.
DOCHERTY, Mr. Stuart Andrew John, MA ACA *1998;* 18 Strathmore Gardens, LONDON, N3 2HL.
DOCHERTY, Miss. Susan, BA ACA *2011;* 144b Putney Bridge Road, LONDON, SW15 2NQ.
DOCKAR, Mr. Neil Kelvin, BA FCA *1981;* Frampton Cottage Pankridge Street Crondall, FARNHAM, SURREY, GU10 5QU.
•DOCKER, Mr. Alan William, FCA *1961;* Alan W. Docker, 8 Milton Close, Headless Cross, REDDITCH, WORCESTERSHIRE, B97 5BQ.
•DOCKER, Mr. Darren Martin, BA ACA *1996;* PricewaterhouseCoopers LLP, 7 More London Riverside, LONDON, SE1 2RT. See also PricewaterhouseCoopers
DOCKER, Mr. Donald Bruce, FCA *1958;* 11 The Glade, Shevington, WIGAN, WN6 8DJ. (Life Member)
DOCKER, Mrs. Jennifer Louise, BSc ACA *2001;* 178a Hale Road, Hale, ALTRINCHAM, CHESHIRE, WA15 8SQ.
DOCKER, Mr. Nicholas William Thomas, BSc ACA *2008;* 93 Sterndale Road, LONDON, W14 0HX.
DOCKER, Mrs. Patricia Anne, BA ACA *1984;* 4 Kinsbourne Close, HARPENDEN, AL5 3PB.
•DOCKERILL, Mrs. Caroline Mary, BSc ACA *1988;* (Tax Fac), Caroline Dockerill, 487 Chemin de la Contettaz, 74110 MORZINE, FRANCE.

DONALD - DOO **Members - Alphabetical**

DONALD, Mr. Robert, FCA *1957;* 3 Oakhurst, Grayshott, HINDHEAD, GU26 6JW. (Life Member)

DONALD, Mr. Scott William, ACA *2009;* 40 Colonel Grantham Avenue, AYLESBURY, BUCKINGHAMSHIRE, HP19 9AP.

•DONALD, Mr. Stephen George, MA ACA MBA *1993;* Stephen G Donald MA (Hons) MBA ACA, 12 Kincarrathie Crescent, PERTH, PH2 7HH.

DONALD, Mr. Steve Leslie, BSc ACA *1996;* 37 Darras Road, Darras Hall Estate, NEWCASTLE UPON TYNE, NORTHUMBERLAND, NE20 9PD.

DONALD, Miss. Suzanne, MA ACA *2010;* Deloitte & Touche Hill House, 1 Little New Street, LONDON, EC4A 3TR.

DONALD, Miss. Tanya Emma, ACA *2009;* 16 St. Maur Road, LONDON, SW6 4DP.

DONALD, Mr. William Pennington, FCA *1961;* Lyndon, Flitwick Road, Westoning, BEDFORD, MK45 5AA.

DONALDSON, Mr. Alan Charles John, MA FCA *1971;* Les Sourcils, Belmont Road, St Peter Port, GUERNSEY, GY1 1PY. (Life Member)

•DONALDSON, Mr. Andrew Francis Winton, ACA *1996;* Andrew Donaldson, Oak Tree House, 17 Lake Walk, Adderbury, BANBURY, OXFORDSHIRE OX17 3PF.

DONALDSON, Mr. Andrew James, BSc ACA *1997;* 11a Seaway Avenue, CHRISTCHURCH, DORSET, BH23 4EU.

DONALDSON, Mr. Andrew James, BSc ACA *2010;* BAA Bar Ltd, 7 Myrtle Street, LIVERPOOL, L7 7DN.

DONALDSON, Mr. Andrew Peter, BA ACA FRSA *1989;* RSM Tenon, Charter House Legge Street, BIRMINGHAM, B4 7EU.

DONALDSON, Mr. Andrew William, BA ACA *1986;* 37 The Avenue, Loansdean, MORPETH, NORTHUMBERLAND, NE61 2DF.

DONALDSON, Mr. Anthony Andrew, BSc FCA *1989;* 18 Oak View Rise, Harlow Wood, MANSFIELD, NOTTINGHAMSHIRE, NG18 4UT.

DONALDSON, Mrs. Caroline Ann, MA ACA *1986;* Flat 174 Berglen Court, 7 Branch Road, LONDON, E14 7JY.

DONALDSON, Miss. Catherine Julia, BSc ACA *1990;* 15 Rectory Road, FARNBOROUGH, HAMPSHIRE, GU14 7BU.

DONALDSON, Miss. Clare, LLB(Hons) ACA *2010;* 14 Orchard Mews, LONDON, N1 5BS.

DONALDSON, Mr. David Andrew Thomas, BA ACA *1986;* Eddystone, Shirenewton, CHEPSTOW, GWENT, NP16 6RL.

•DONALDSON, Mr. Edward Frederic Colin, BSc FCA *1979;* 32 New Concordia Wharf, Mill Street, LONDON, SE1 2BB.

DONALDSON, Miss. Elizabeth Jane, ACA *1986;* P.O. Box 527, (Private Boxes), HILLARYS, WA 6923, AUSTRALIA.

DONALDSON, Mr. Gregg David, ACA *2011;* Kalimna, Le Chemin Du Portelet, St Brelades, JERSEY, JE3 8AU.

DONALDSON, Mr. James, MA ACA *1997;* 9 St. Leonards Square, LONDON, NW5 3HL.

DONALDSON, Mr. John Alistair, BSc ACA *1993;* Station House, Station Road, Cliddesden, BASINGSTOKE, RG25 2NL.

DONALDSON, Mrs. Juliet Brianna, MA ACA *1993;* 2 Farm Pond Lane, FRANKLIN, MA 02038, UNITED STATES.

DONALDSON, Mr. Marcus Ian, BA ACA MIoD *1994;* 273 Petersham Road, RICHMOND, TW10 7DA.

•DONALDSON, Mr. Matthew Eric, ACA *2007;* Deloitte LLP, 2 New Street Square, LONDON, EC4A 3BZ. See also Deloitte & Touche LLP

DONALDSON, Mr. Michael, MA ACA *2010;* Flat 7, 53 Britton Street, LONDON, EC1M 5UQ.

DONALDSON, Mr. Neil David, ACA *2006;* with Deloitte Touche Tohmatsu, Grosvenor Place, 225 George Street, P.O. Box N 250, SYDNEY, NSW 2000 AUSTRALIA.

•DONALDSON, Mr. Robert Henry, ACA CF *1996;* Baker Tilly Tax and Advisory Services LLP, 25 Farringdon Street, LONDON, EC4A 4AB. See also Baker Tilly Corporate Finance LLP

DONALDSON, Mrs. Sonya Lois, ACA *2001;* 100 The Drive, BECKENHAM, BR3 1EG.

DONALDSON, Mrs. Stella Margaret, FCA *1967;* Chimney Corner, Castle Street, BEAUMARIS, LL58 8BB. (Life Member)

DONALDSON, Mr. Stephen, BSc ACA *1980;* 1 Collier Way, Stapleford, CAMBRIDGE, CB22 5DZ.

DONALDSON, Mr. Steven David Barry, BA FCA *1987;* Park House, 1a Park Drive, Hale, ALTRINCHAM, CHESHIRE, WA15 9DW.

DONALDSON, Mr. Stuart Greenwood, FCA *1952;* Troutbeck House, Leeds Road, Lightcliffe, HALIFAX, HX3 8SD. (Life Member)

DONALDSON, Mr. William Alexander, FCA *1970;* S H G, San Bernardo 139, Garda, 37016 VERONA, ITALY.

DONATI, Mr. Marcus Adrian Brownlow, BA FCA *1968;* 21 Oxberry Avenue, LONDON, SW6 5SP. (Life Member)

DONAU, Mr. Michael Henry, FCA *1952;* 9 Goffers House, Duke Humphrey Rd Blackheath, LONDON, SE3 0TT. (Life Member)

DONBAVAND, Mr. Timothy John, ACA *1991;* 111 Goodhart Way, WEST WICKHAM, BR4 0EU.

DONE, Ms. Frances Winifred, CBE BA FCA *1975;* 4 Greenwood Road, LYMM, WA13 0LA.

DONE, Mr. Martin John, FCA *1969;* 4300 De Maisonneuve Boulevard, West Apartment 735, WESTMOUNT H3Z 1K8, QUE, CANADA.

DONE, Mr. Michael William, ACA *1985;* Oxford Instruments Ltd: Research Instrum, Tubney Wood, ABINGDON, OXFORDSHIRE, OX13 5QX.

DONE, Mr. William Joseph, FCA *1973;* 172 Maney Hill Road, SUTTON COLDFIELD, B72 1JW.

DONEGAN, Mrs. Rebecca Jane, BSc ACA *1993;* 70 Janes Lane, BURGESS HILL, WEST SUSSEX, RH15 0QR.

DONEGAN, Mr. Roy, BSc ACA CTA *2007;* 175 Blythe Road, LONDON, W14 0HL.

DONELLY, Miss. Laura, BA ACA *2003;* John N Dunn Group Ltd Phoenix House, Kingfisher Way Silverlink Business Park, WALLSEND, TYNE AND WEAR, NE28 9NX.

DONERT, Mr. Philip Henry, BA ACA *2006;* Floor 04, Morgan Stanley, 20 Bank Street, LONDON, E14 4AD.

•DONEY, Mr. Robert George William, FCA *1968;* (Tax Fac), Robert G W Doney Limited, Sunnyfield, Church Road, West Lavington, MIDHURST, WEST SUSSEX GU29 0EH.

DONG, Miss. Wei, ACA *2011;* Flat 9, Studley Court, 4 Jamestown Way, LONDON, E14 2DA.

•DONGWORTH, Mr. Frank Peter, FCA *1971;* Dongworth Limited, First Floor, 30 London Road, SAWBRIDGEWORTH, HERTFORDSHIRE, CM21 9JS. See also Dongworth Frank P & Co

DONHUE, Mr. Peter Graham, BA ACA *1989;* 35 Bow Lane, LONDON, N12 0JR.

DONINGTON-SMITH, Mr. Roderick Hugo, FCA *1973;* Greta Cottage, Penrith Road, KESWICK, CUMBRIA, CA12 4JS.

DONKER, Mr. John William, BSc ACA *1989;* PricewaterhouseCoopers, Prince's Building, 22/F, 10 Chater Road, CENTRAL, HONG KONG ISLAND HONG KONG SAR.

DONKER, Mr. Mark Richard, BMet ACA *1993;* Standard Motor Products Europe Ltd, European Headquarters Little Oak Drive, SHERWOOD PARK, NOTTINGHAMSHIRE, NG15 0DR.

DONKERSLEY, Miss. Kathryn, ACA *2008;* Flat 6, 127-133 High Road, LONDON, N2 8BW.

DONLEA, Mr. Patrick Kevin Fitzgerald, FCA *1968;* The Old Vicarage, Great Offley, HITCHIN, SG5 3DX.

DONLEVY, Miss. Lesley Anne, ACA *2010;* 4 Maple Court, Bastins Close Park Gate, SOUTHAMPTON, SO31 1DX.

DONN, Mr. Arnold Joseph, FCA *1957;* 65 Goodyers Avenue, RADLETT, HERTFORDSHIRE, WD7 8AZ. (Life Member)

DONNACHIE, Mr. Martin Thomas, BA ACA *1993;* 101 Oldfield Road, ALTRINCHAM, WA14 4BL.

•DONNAN, Mr. Michael, BSc FCA *1989;* (Tax Fac), Howard Worth, Drake House, Gadbrook Park, NORTHWICH, CHESHIRE, CW9 7RA.

DONNAN, Miss. Michelle, ACA *2009;* Ringtons Ltd PO Box 3, Heaton, NEWCASTLE UPON TYNE, NE6 2YN.

DONNAN, Mrs. Rebecca Stephanie, BSc(Hons) ACA *2002;* E D & F ManSugar Limited, Seventh Floor, Cottons Centre, Hays Lane, LONDON, SE1 2QE.

DONNE, Mrs. Annabel, BA ACA *1992;* blowUP media UK Ltd, The Media Centre, 3-8 Carburton Street, LONDON, W1W 5AJ.

DONNE, Mr. John Adrian, BSc ACA *1992;* Stapleton Mill, Stapleton, MARTOCK, SOMERSET, TA12 6AN.

DONNELLY, Mr. Alan Ernest, FCA *1952;* 16a Palmerston Way, Alverstoke, GOSPORT, PO12 2LZ. (Life Member)

DONNELLY, Miss. Andrea, ACA FCCA ATT *2010;* with Spenser Wilson & Co, Equitable House, 55 Pellon Lane, HALIFAX, WEST YORKSHIRE, HX1 5SP.

DONNELLY, Mr. Ben, BA ACA *2011;* Wincelow Hall, Wincelow Hall Road, Hempstead, SAFFRON WALDEN, ESSEX, CB10 2PJ.

DONNELLY, Mrs. Bridget Clare, MA ACA *1988;* Creasys Education The Cottage, 53 Northcourt Road, ABINGDON, OXFORDSHIRE, OX14 1PJ.

DONNELLY, Mrs. Clare Louise, BA(Hons) ACA *2006;* Holly House Church Road, Greenstead Green, HALSTEAD, CO9 1QR.

DONNELLY, Mr. Desmond Cyril, FCA *1957;* Lamond, 7 Adlington Drive, SANDBACH, CW11 1DX. (Life Member)

DONNELLY, Miss. Emma Elizabeth Cecilia, MA ACA *2001;* with PricewaterhouseCoopers LLP, The Atrium, 1 Harefield Road, UXBRIDGE, UB8 1EX.

DONNELLY, Mr. Gerard Martin, BA ACA *1994;* Vantis BRS, 104-106 Colmore Row, BIRMINGHAM, B3 3AG.

DONNELLY, Mrs. Jennifer Margaret, BEng ACA *2002;* 18 Fullerton Road, LONDON, SW18 1BX.

DONNELLY, Mr. John, FCA *1976; (ACA Ireland 1954);* Glenbevan, Cross Avenue, BLACKROCK, COUNTY DUBLIN, IRELAND. (Life Member)

DONNELLY, Mr. John, MA ACA *1996;* Silk Road Lodge, 229 Abdumomunova Street, BISHKEK 72033, KAZAKHSTAN.

DONNELLY, Mr. John, FCA *1958;* 9 Greenacres, Turton, BOLTON, BL7 0QG. (Life Member)

DONNELLY, Mr. John, FCA *1958;* 85 Duxford Road, Great Barr, BIRMINGHAM, B42 2JD. (Life Member)

DONNELLY, Mr. John Michael, BSc ACA *1981;* Jehu Project Services Ltd Waterton Park, Waterton, BRIDGEND, MID GLAMORGAN, CF31 3PH.

DONNELLY, Mr. Liam Edwin, BA FCA *1980;* Wincelow Hall, Hempstead, SAFFRON WALDEN, CB10 2PJ.

DONNELLY, Mr. Mark Stephen, BSc ACA *1997;* 27a Bowes Road, WALTON-ON-THAMES, SURREY, KT12 3HT.

DONNELLY, Mrs. Martina Hilda Marjorie, BSc ACA *1991;* 3 Croft Park Grove, BARROW-IN-FURNESS, CUMBRIA, LA13 9NJ.

DONNELLY, Mr. Michael James, FCA *1971;* 5 Hale Avenue, NEW MILTON, BH25 6EZ.

DONNELLY, Mr. Michael Patrick, BSc(Hons) ACA *2002;* Anglo American Plc Anglo American House, 20 Carlton House Terrace, LONDON, SW1Y 5AN.

DONNELLY, Mrs. Naomi, ACA *2002;* 36 Hazell Road, Prestwood, GREAT MISSENDEN, BUCKINGHAMSHIRE, HP16 0LS.

DONNELLY, Mr. Paul John, BSc ACA *1991;* Macquarie Capital Markets Canada Ltd., Brookfield Place, 181 Bay Street, Suite 3100, TORONTO M5J 2T3, ON CANADA.

DONNELLY, Mr. Peter, ACA *2010;* 19 Foreshore, LONDON, SE8 3AQ.

•DONNELLY, Mr. Peter Joseph, BA FCA *1987;* with RSM Tenon Audit Limited, Clive House, Clive Street, BOLTON, BL1 1ET.

DONNELLY, Mr. Peter Norman, BSc ACA *1991;* 16412 Peacock Lane, LOS GATOS, CA 95032, UNITED STATES.

DONNELLY, Mrs. Rosalind, BSc FCA *1991;* 73 Elliott Street, Hawthorne, BRISBANE, QLD 4171, AUSTRALIA.

DONNELLY, Mr. Sean Patrick, BA ACA *2004;* 30 Dapdune Road, GUILDFORD, GU1 4NY.

DONNELLY, Mrs. Susan Charlotte, BSc ACA *1989;* 198 Summerwood Lane, Halsall, ORMSKIRK, L39 8RH.

•DONNELLY, Mrs. Tracey Anne, BA FCA *1993;* (Tax Fac), Fold House Farm, Westgate, BISHOP AUCKLAND, COUNTY DURHAM, DL13 1NS.

•DONNELY, Mr. Michael, BSc FCA *1984;* Michael Donnely & Co, Clevelands, Fordwater Road, CHICHESTER, PO19 6PS.

DONNET, Mrs. Christine Julia, BSc ACA *1997;* 13 Wick Avenue, Wheathampstead, ST. ALBANS, HERTFORDSHIRE, AL4 8QD.

DONNISON, Mrs. Pamela Margaret, FCA *1973;* 1 Blue Cedars, Warren Road, BANSTEAD, SM7 1NT.

DONOGHUE, Mr. Kieran James, ACA *1999;* 88 Keith Avenue, EDITHVALE, VIC 3196, AUSTRALIA.

DONOGHUE, Mr. Mark Richard, ACA *1991;* (Tax Fac), 115 London Road, NEWBURY, RG14 2AH.

DONOGHUE, Ms. Stella Mary, MBA BA ACA CDir *1992;* 2 Denmead Close, GERRARDS CROSS, BUCKINGHAMSHIRE, SL9 7LX.

•DONOHOE, Mrs. Angela Jane, ACA *1987;* Donnellys C.A. Limited, Peel House, 2 Chorley Old Road, BOLTON, BL1 3AA.

DONOHOE, Miss. Geraldine Mary, BSc ACA *1992;* 13 Gilpin Avenue, East Sheen, LONDON, SW14 8QX.

DONOHOE, Mr. James Fergus, BSc ACA *1991;* 6 Amberley Close, Storrington, PULBOROUGH, RH20 4JA.

•DONOHOE, Mr. John, ACA *2003;* Arram Berlyn Gardner, 30 City Road, LONDON, EC1Y 2AB.

DONOHOE, Mr. Patrick, BA(Hons) ACA *2003;* 24 Sandringham Close, ENFIELD, MIDDLESEX, EN1 3JH.

DONOHOE, Mr. Stephen John, MA ACA *2000;* 2 Harvest Road, MACCLESFIELD, CHESHIRE, SK10 2LH.

DONOHUE, Miss. Gayle, BSc ACA *2000;* with PricewaterhouseCoopers, Prince's Building, 22/F, 10 Chater Road, CENTRAL, HONG KONG ISLAND HONG KONG SAR.

DONOHUE, Mr. Nicholas Henry, FCA *1959;* 7 The Rosegarden, Fields Park Avenue, NEWPORT, NP20 5BS.

DONOHUE, Mr. Philip Edward, BA ACA *2009;* with Ballard Dale Syree Watson LLP, Oakmoore Court, Kingswood Road, Hampton Lovett, DROITWICH, WORCESTERSHIRE WR9 0QH.

DONOUGHER, Mr. Mark John, BSc ACA *1992;* Glaed Hame, Pasture Road, LETCHWORTH GARDEN CITY, HERTFORDSHIRE, SG6 3LW.

DONOVAN, Miss. Anna Louise, ACA CA(AUS) *2009;* 101 Wigmore Street, LONDON, W1U 1QU.

DONOVAN, Mr. Arthur James, FCA *1958;* 8 Amesbury Crescent, HOVE, BN3 5RD. (Life Member)

DONOVAN, Miss. Catherine Ann, BA ACA *2010;* 11 Whitehall Road, MANCHESTER, M20 6RY.

DONOVAN, Mr. Cecil William, FCA *1980; (ACA Ireland 1960);* 6 The Yew, Carysfort Hall, BLACKROCK, COUNTY DUBLIN, IRELAND.

DONOVAN, Mr. Chris Paul, BSc ACA *2005;* Flat 11 Rudyard Court, 127 Long Lane, LONDON, SE1 4PW.

DONOVAN, Mr. Christopher Alexander, BA ACA *2009;* 349 Quayside Drive, COLCHESTER, CO2 8GT.

DONOVAN, Miss. Helen Lorraine, BA ACA *2005;* Little Challows Wellfield Road, Marshfield, CARDIFF, CF3 2UB.

DONOVAN, Mr. James Daniel, FCA *1952;* The Fairway, Golf Club Road, Hook Heath, WOKING, GU22 0LT.

DONOVAN, Mrs. Janet Rachel, BSc ACA *1998;* 87 Southmoor Road, OXFORD, OX2 6RE.

DONOVAN, Mr. John Denis, FCA *1977;* 1228 18A St NW, CALGARY T2N 2H4, AB, CANADA.

DONOVAN, Mr. John Edward, FCA *1955;* 56 Molesey Park Road, WEST MOLESEY, KT8 2JZ. (Life Member)

DONOVAN, Mr. Michael James, FCA *1956;* 59 Berrylands Road, SURBITON, KT5 8PB. (Life Member)

DONOVAN, Mr. Michael Kevin, FCA *1960;* Hilltop House, Holly Bank, Trentham Park, STOKE-ON-TRENT, STAFFORDSHIRE, ST4 8FT. (Life Member)

DONOVAN, Mr. Nelson, BSc(Hons) ACA *2000;* Wilhelmstrasse 8b, 61381 FRIEDRICHSDORF, GERMANY.

DONOVAN, Mr. Nicholas Paul, BSc ACA *2008;* Singer Capital Markets Ltd, 1 Hanover Street, LONDON, W1S 1YZ.

DONOVAN, Mr. Patrick Paul, BA ACA *1998;* Carillion Carillion Building, 981 Great West Road, BRENTFORD, MIDDLESEX, TW8 9DN.

DONOVAN, Mr. Peter William, FCA *1973;* First Title, 33-39 Elmfield Road, BROMLEY, BR1 1LT.

•DONOVAN, Mr. Sean Dermot, FCA *1987;* AGL, Prudence House, Ashleigh Way, Langage Business Park, PLYMOUTH, PL7 5JX. See also AGL Accountants Limited

DONOVAN, Mr. Simon Grant Stevenson, BA ACA *1998;* Urb. Real del Campanario, Bloque 1 Esc 2-D, 29688 ESTEPONA, MALAGA, SPAIN.

DONOVAN, Mr. Stephen Patrick, BA ACA *1989;* 70 Ferry Parade, Herald Island, AUCKLAND 1008, NEW ZEALAND.

DONOVAN, Mr. Terence John, MBA BSc FCA *1975;* Glebe House, The Terrace, Boston Spa, WETHERBY, LS23 6AH.

DONOVAN-POTE, Mr. Michael, BSc ACA *2005;* 38 Fawcett Close, LONDON, SW11 2LU.

DONOWHO, Mr. Simon Christopher, BA ACA *1992;* KPMG, 8/F Prince's Building, 10 Chater Road, CENTRAL, HONG KONG ISLAND, HONG KONG SAR.

DONSON, Mr. Peter, BA(Hons) ACA *2011;* High Green House, Troutbeck, WINDERMERE, CUMBRIA, LA23 1PN.

DOO, Mr. Alan James William, BA ACA *1985;* 2242 Ridge Avenue, EVANSTON, IL 60201, UNITED STATES.

DOO, Miss. Caroline Yen Ny, BSc ACA *1993;* 3A Oxford Garden, 18 Cornwall Street, KOWLOON TONG, KOWLOON, HONG KONG SAR.

DOO, Miss. Daphne Wai-Fun, BSc ACA *1985;* Flat 10D Hilltop, 60 Cloud View Road, NORTH POINT, Hong Kong Island, HONG KONG SAR.

Members - Alphabetical DOO - DOUGALL

DOO, Mr. Darwin Wai-Keung, MA ACA *1981;* 1A Cavendish Heights, Block 8 33 Perkins Road, JARDINE'S LOOKOUT, Hong Kong Island, HONG KONG SAR.
DOO, Mr. Sonny Wilber Yuen Sun, ACA *1983;* PricewaterhouseCoopers, Prince's Building, 22/F, 10 Chater Road, CENTRAL, HONG KONG ISLAND HONG KONG SAR.
DOOBOREE, Mr. Aswaneesingh, BA ACA *2003;* Celtic Pharma Management L.P, Cumberland House, 1 Victoria Street, 4th Floor, HAMILTON HM 11, BERMUDA.
DOODY, Miss. Helenne Kerry, BSc(Hons) ACA *2003;* Lower Ground, 35a Kelvin Road, LONDON, N5 2PR.
DOODY, Miss. Kirsten Rachel, MS BSc ACA *1996;* 8 Parsifal Road, LONDON, NW6 1UH.
DOODY, Mr. Neil Beresford, FCA *1964;* The Forge, The Village, Finchampstead, WOKINGHAM, BERKSHIRE, RG40 4JN.
DOOGAN, Mrs. Susan Patricia, BSc(Hons) ACA *2002;* 3 Park Lane, Park Hall, OSWESTRY, SHROPSHIRE, SY11 4AE.
DOOKHEE, Mr. Rinesh, ACA *2009;* with RSM Tenon Limited, Davidson House, Forbury Square, READING, RG1 3EU.
DOOKUN, Mr. Arno Ari Jawaheer Robin Ranjiv, BSc ACA *2003;* Mon Desir, VACOAS, MAURITIUS.
DOOLAN, Mrs. Siobhan Michelle, BSc ACA *2010;* 83 Scott Road, BISHOP'S STORTFORD, HERTFORDSHIRE, CM23 3QN.
DOOLEY, Mr. Benjamin Martin, ACA *2008;* 6 Barn Crescent, STANMORE, MIDDLESEX, HA7 2RY.
DOOLEY, Mr. Carl Jonathan, ACA *2009;* 11 Lawford Place, Lawford, MANNINGTREE, CO11 2PT.
DOOLEY, Ms. Cateriona Mary, BA ACA *1995;* 21 Cahair Mhor, Cluain Minse, TULLAMORE, COUNTY OFFALY, IRELAND.
DOOLEY, Miss. Christine, BA ACA *1994;* 21 St. Dunstans Road, LONDON, W6 8RE.
DOOLEY, Mr. Donald, FCA *1954;* 95 Station Road, HARPENDEN, HERTFORDSHIRE, AL5 4RL.
DOOLEY, Mr. Jonathan Mark, MA FCA *1972;* Kingswillow House, St. Ives Road, Hilton, HUNTINGDON, PE28 9NL.
DOOLEY, Mrs. Kerry, BSc ACA *2005;* 7 Ennismore Green, LUTON, LU2 8UP.
DOOLEY, Miss. Lynne, BAcc ACA *1997;* 38 Bolton Drive, Eccleshill, BRADFORD, BD2 2AB.
DOOLEY, Mrs. Margaret, BSc FCA ATII *1972;* Land & Zeechicht, 2 Patrys Avenue, SOMERSET WEST, WESTERN CAPE PROVINCE, 7130, SOUTH AFRICA.
DOOLEY, Miss. Nicola Gillian, ACA CTA *2007;* (Tax Fac), Flat 23 China House, 14 Harter Street, MANCHESTER, M1 6HP.
•DOOLEY, Mrs. Ruth, MA FCA *1993;* Hazlewoods LLP, Windsor House, Barnett Way, Barnwood, GLOUCESTER, GL4 3RT.
DOOLITTLE, Mr. Robert Edward, BSc ACA *1991;* 39 Williams Grove, Long Ditton, SURBITON, KT6 5RW.
DOOMUNKHAN, Mr. Naweed Ahmad, BA ACA *2004;* with Grant Thornton UK LLP, 30 Finsbury Square, LONDON, EC2P 2YU.
DOONA, Mr. Paul Ernest, BA FCA *1977;* Victoria House, 10 Hartopp Road, Four Oaks, SUTTON COLDFIELD, B74 2RQ.
DOONER, Mr. Nigel Thomas, ACA *1981;* 35 Almond Grove, BRENTFORD, MIDDLESEX, TW8 8NL.
DOORGA, Miss. Poonam, ACA *2009;* Flat 32 Hennessy Court, 127 Leyton Green Road, LONDON, E10 6DQ.
DOORGAKANT, Mr. Maheshwar, BA ACA *2002;* 29 Avenue Ibis, Sodnac, QUATRE-BORNES, MAURITIUS.
•DOOTSON, Mr. Gordon Peter, BSc FCA *1991;* Deloitte LLP, Hill House, 1 Little New Street, LONDON, EC4A 3TR. See also Deloitte & Touche LLP
•DOOTSON, Mr. John Kevin, BSc FCA *1989;* (Tax Fac), Cyprotex Plc, 15 Beech Lane, MACCLESFIELD, CHESHIRE, SK10 2DR.
DOOTSON, Mr. Stuart John, ACA *1991;* 20 Oakhill Road, SEVENOAKS, TN13 1NP.
DORAI RAJ, Mr. Diren Peter, BA FCA *1994;* 1 Adam Drive, SINGAPORE 289961, SINGAPORE.
•DORAM, Mr. Joseph Edward, FCA *1961;* Alder View, 37 The Friary, LICHFIELD, WS13 6QH.
•DORAN, Mr. Charles Joseph, FCA *1972;* 121 North Street, GREENWICH, CT 06830-4722, UNITED STATES.
•DORAN, Mr. Colm Paul, BSc FCA *1977;* Paloma Consulting Limited, Thorney House, 26 The Barton, COBHAM, SURREY, KT11 2NJ.
DORAN, Mr. Edward Anthony, MA FCA *1979;* 39 Garden Road, Sundridge Park, BROMLEY, BR1 3LU.
DORAN, Miss. Francesca, LLB ACA *2011;* 102 The Drive, BECKENHAM, KENT, BR3 1EG.
DORAN, Miss. Joanne, BA ACA *1997;* Apartment 55, 39 Wellington Road Timperley, ALTRINCHAM, CHESHIRE, WA15 7RD.
•DORAN, Mr. John, FCA *1967;* The Doran Consultancy, 1-2 Hill End House, Norwood Green, HALIFAX, HX3 8QE.
DORAN, Mr. Kevin, BA ACA *1996;* Mc Donald's Restaurants Limited, 11-59 High Road, East Finchley, LONDON, N2 8AW.
DORAN, Mrs. Maria Lynn, BSc(Hons) ACA *2001;* Crestview, Enborne Row, Wash Water, NEWBURY, BERKSHIRE, RG20 0LX.
DORAN, Mr. Matthew Timothy, BA(Hons) ACA *2001;* Crestview, Enborne Row, Wash Water, NEWBURY, BERKSHIRE, RG20 0LX.
•DORAN, Mr. Michael John, BA FCA *1988;* Toad Hall, Ashorne, WARWICK, CV35 9DR.
DORAN, Mr. Nicholas Alexander, ACA *2008;* 20 Harleyford, Upper Park Road, BROMLEY, BR1 3HW.
DORAN, Mrs. Nicola Janis, BA ACA *1993;* Bayer Plc, Bayer House, Strawberry Hill, NEWBURY, RG14 1JA.
DORAN, Mr. Paul, MSocSc BA ACA *1999;* The Old Vicarage Shoreham Road, Otford, SEVENOAKS, TN14 5RL.
DORAN, Mr. Paul William, BSc ACA *2002;* V M Ware Theta Building, Lyon Way Frimley, CAMBERLEY, GU16 7ER.
DORAN, Mr. Peter John Leslie, FCA *1969;* 19 Nightingale Road, EAST MOLESEY, KT8 2PQ.
DORANS, Mr. Brian Raymond, FCA *1966;* Presterud Alle 20, 1357 BEKKESTUA, NORWAY. (Life Member)
DORANS, Mr. David, BA FCA *1991;* Channel Four Television, 124-126 Horseferry Road, LONDON, SW1P 2TX.
DORATI, Ms. Myria, BSc ACA *2011;* 9 Favierou Str., 2nd Monovolikos, Lemesos, 4151 LIMASSOL, CYPRUS.
DORBIN, Mr. Ned, BSc ACA *2002;* 73 Victoria Road, LONDON, N22 7XG.
•DORE, Mr. Andrew Michael, BA ACA *1987;* (Tax Fac), Wellers, Millweye Court, 73 Southern Road, THAME, OX9 2ED. See also Wellers Contractors Limited
DORE, Mr. Brian James, FCA *1958;* 38 Sunningwell, Sunningwell, ABINGDON, OXFORDSHIRE, OX13 6RB. (Life Member)
DORE, Mr. Carl Nicholas, FCA *1963;* Willowfield, Ladycroft, ALRESFORD, SO24 0QS.
DORE, Mr. Geoffrey William, BA ACA *1993;* 16A Druid Stoke Avenue, BRISTOL, BS9 1DD.
DORE, Mr. Martin John Alban, BSc FCA *1976;* 37 Sussex Gardens, Highgate, LONDON, N6 4LY.
DORE, Mr. Richard Kem, FCA *1977;* Forge House, Udimore, RYE, EAST SUSSEX, TN31 6AY.
DOREE, Mr. Herbert John, BA FCA *1970;* Wastlands, Mayes Green, Ockley, DORKING, RH5 5PN.
DOREE, Mr. Mark Richard, ACA *2009;* 54 Salcombe Close, Chandler's Ford, EASTLEIGH, HAMPSHIRE, SO53 4PJ.
DOREY, Mr. Andrew John Christopher, BA ACA *2005;* with PricewaterhouseCoopers, Darling Park Tower 2, 201 Sussex Street, GPO Box 2650, SYDNEY, NSW 1171 AUSTRALIA.
DOREY, Mrs. Anne Helen, ACA *1987;* La Bernauderie, Les Landelles, Castel, GUERNSEY, GY5 7DH.
DOREY, Mr. Arthur, ACA *2010;* Flat 2, 87 Larkhall Rise, Clapham, LONDON, SW4 6HR.
DOREY, Mr. Geoffrey Stuart, FCA *1952;* 11 Riverside Way, DROITWICH, WR9 8UP. (Life Member)
DOREY, Mr. Simon Peter John, BA ACA *1983;* 4434 Strathcona Road, NORTH VANCOUVER V7G1G3, BC, CANADA.
DOREY, Mr. William Francis, FCA *1966;* 2 Faesten Way, BEXLEY, DA5 2JB.
DORIS, Mr. Michael, BA ACA *2006;* Av. Brigadeiro Faria Lima 3064 - 2° andar Itaim Bibi, SAO PAULO, 01451000, BRAZIL.
DORJE, Mr. Orgyan, BSc(Hons) ACA *2004;* Flat 21 Scotia Building, 5 Jardine Road, LONDON, E1W 3WA.
DORJE, Mrs. Sarah Teresa, BSc ACA *2007;* Flat 21, Scotia Building, 5 Jardine Road, LONDON, E1W 3WA.
DORLAY, Mr. Stephen John, FCA *1969;* 60 Westering, ROMSEY, HAMPSHIRE, SO51 7LY.
DORLING, Mr. Jeremy James, BA ACA *1991;* Heuvel 13, 5674 RR NUENEN, NETHERLANDS.
•DORLING, Mr. Malcolm Peter, BA ACA ATII *1987;* M.P. Dorling, The Firs, Levens Green, Old Hall Green, WARE, SG11 1HD.
DORMAN, Mr. Antony James, FCA *1965;* 38 Kew Green, Kew, RICHMOND, TW9 3BH.
•DORMAN, Mr. David Edward, BA FCA DChA *1977;* JWPCreers, Genesis 5, Innovation Way, Heslington, YORK, YO10 5DQ.
DORMAN, Mr. David Rory Bruno, BA ACA *2004;* Halftimbers, Bepton, MIDHURST, WEST SUSSEX, GU29 0JB.
DORMAN, Mr. Paul Charles, BA ACA *1990;* 53 Evelyn Road, LONDON, SW19 8NT.
DORMAN, Mr. Sean Anthony, BA(Hons) ACA *2010;* 7 Kings Court, Beddington Gardens, WALLINGTON, SM6 0HR.
DORMAN, Mr. Trevor Edward, ACA *1985;* Stonewall, La Fosse A L'Ecrivain, St. Saviour, JERSEY, JE2 7HU.
•DORMAN, Mrs. Wendy Jane, BA ACA *1988;* PricewaterhouseCoopers CI LLP, Twenty Two Colomberie, St Helier, JERSEY, JE1 4XA.
DORMAN, Mr. William Henry Wolsey, MSc LLB FCA *1973;* Drake Kryterion Inc, 7776 South Pointe Parkway West, Suite 250, PHOENIX, AZ 85004, UNITED STATES.
DORMER, Mrs. Jennifer Susan, BSc ACA *1993;* 4 Woodend Lane, Cam, DURSLEY, GL11 5LR.
DORMER, Mr. Mark Stephen, BA ACA MCT *1991;* 33 Oley Meadows, CONSETT, DH8 0JF.
DORN, Mr. Charles Frederick Herbert, FCA *1977;* 95a High Street South, Stewkley, LEIGHTON BUZZARD, BEDFORDSHIRE, LU7 0HU.
DORNAN, Mr. Patrick John, FCA *1971;* PO Box 26976, MANAMA, BAHRAIN.
DORNER, Mr. Ian Clinton, BSc FCA *1977;* 3149 Gloria Terrace, LAFAYETTE, CA 94549, UNITED STATES.
DORNING, Mr. Paul Robert, BA ACA *1989;* 11 Mill View Road, BEVERLEY, HU17 0UP.
DORON, Mr. Oren, BSc ACA *2011;* 22 Wessex Gardens, LONDON, NW11 9RT.
DORR, Mr. James Adam, BSc ACA *2005;* 2 The Sidings, Hagley, STOURBRIDGE, WORCESTERSHIRE, DY8 2XT.
DORRI-ESFAHANI, Mr. Abdol Rasoul, FCA *1974;* ABIC Group, 45 Neshat St, TEHRAN, IRAN.
DORRINGTON, Mrs. Rebecca Anne, BSc(Hons) ACA CTA *2002;* 1 Moorcroft, Ashill, Nr Cullompton Devon, CULLOMPTON, EX15 3NN.
•DORRINGTON-WARD, Mr. Simon, FCA *1975;* M.W. Burrough & Co, 10 South St, BRIDPORT, DT6 3NJ.
DORRITY, Mr. Lachlan, BSc ACA *2009;* Flat 1, 19 Longbeach Road, LONDON, SW11 5SS.
DORSETT, Mrs. Claire Louise, BSc(Hons) ACA *2001;* 131 Birmingham Road, SUTTON COLDFIELD, WEST MIDLANDS, B72 1LX.
DORSETT, Dr. Jason Warren Rutherford, MA DPhil ACA *2004;* 44 Blenheim Road, Caversham, READING, RG4 7RS.
DORUDOTTIR, Ms. Stefania Maria, BA ACA *1992;* Managed Networks Ltd, 6-8 Bonhill Street, LONDON, EC2A 4BX.
DOS SANTOS, Mr. Manuel Carvalho De Sousa, ACA CA(SA) *2010;* 6 Woodberry Drive, Walmley, SUTTON COLDFIELD, WEST MIDLANDS, B76 2RH.
DOSANI, Mr. Mohammed Amin, FCA *1979;* 17 Grafton Close, WORCESTER PARK, SURREY, KT4 7JY.
DOSANI, Mr. Mohammed Arif, BCom FCA *1967;* Elmbray, Dene Close, The Avenue, WORCESTER PARK, KT4 7HQ.
DOSANI, Mr. Mohammed Rafiq, FCA *1972;* 90 Risebrough Avenue, NORTH YORK M2M 2E3, ON, CANADA.
DOSANI, Mr. Mohammed Yusuf, FCA *1971;* 2 Alford Close, Burpham, GUILDFORD, SURREY, GU4 7YL.
•DOSANI, Mr. Sachin, BA ACA *2007;* About Corporate Finance Limited, 10th Floor, Met Building, 22 Percy Street, LONDON, W1T 2BU.
DOSANJH, Mr. Gurchetan Singh, BSc FCA *1987;* 7 Ganton Way, GRANTHAM, LINCOLNSHIRE, NG31 9FD.
DOSANJH, Mr. John Singh, BEng FCA *1993;* P O Box 668, DOUBLE BAY, NSW 1360, AUSTRALIA.
DOSANJH, Mrs. Kamaljit Kaur, MA BA ACA *2003;* 53 Julius Hill, Warfield, BRACKNELL, BERKSHIRE, RG42 3UN.
DOSANJH, Miss. Mandip, BA(Hons) ACA *2003;* Bridge Cottage, 25 Old Ferry Drive, Wraysbury, STAINES, MIDDLESEX, TW19 5EH.
DOSANJH, Mrs. Sandeep, BSc ACA *2004;* 61 Dowland Close, SWINDON, SW25 2GD.
DOSANJH, Mrs. Sukhdev Kaur, ACA *1989;* 4 Windycroft Close, Woodcote Grange, PURLEY, CR8 3HW.
DOSHI, Mr. Anil Jayantilal, FCA *1967;* Apartment 1201, K G Tower, P O Box 262484, Dubai Marina, DUBAI, UNITED ARAB EMIRATES.
DOSHI, Mr. Anup Jyotindra, BSc ACA CTA *2002;* 47 Myrtleside Close, NORTHWOOD, MIDDLESEX, HA6 2XQ.
DOSHI, Mr. Avinash Jayant, BA(Hons) ACA *2010;* 3 Nursery Gardens, Goffs Oak, WALTHAM CROSS, HERTFORDSHIRE, EN7 6RZ.
DOSHI, Mr. Benjamin, ACA *2008;* 2/16 Denby Lane, Northcote Point, NORTH SHORE CITY 0627, AUCKLAND, NEW ZEALAND.
DOSHI, Mrs. Deepa Hemal, BSc FCA *1997;* BDO East Africa, 12th Floor, Loita House, Loita Street, PO Box 10032 -, NAIROBI 00100 GPO KENYA.
•DOSHI, Mr. Dilipkumar Keshavlal, FCA *1971;* Sterling, 505 Pinner Road, HARROW, MIDDLESEX, HA2 6EH.
•DOSHI, Mr. Kirtikumar Vikamshi, FCA *1975;* Brebners, The Quadrangle, 180 Wardour Street, LONDON, W1F 8LB.
DOSHI, Mrs. Nayna Neelesh, BSc ACA *1995;* 37 Connaught Gardens, Palmers Green, LONDON, N13 5BP.
DOSHI, Mr. Rahul, ACA *2009;* 101 Langham Road, LONDON, N15 3LR.
DOSHI, Mr. Samir Navinchandra, MEng ACA *1997;* Abu Dhabi Investment Investment Council, PO Box 61999, ABU DHABI, UNITED ARAB EMIRATES.
DOSHI, Ms. Serena Wei Lee, BA FCA *1997;* 8 Newark Road, WINDLESHAM, SURREY, GU20 6NE.
DOSHI, Mr. Vijay Chandrakant Ratilal, BA ACA CISA *1995;* Shell India Markets Pvt Ltd, Campus 4A; RMZ Millenia Business Park 143 Dr M G R Road, CHENNAI 600-096, INDIA.
DOSSA, Miss. Alaisha, ACA *2008;* Glen Acre, 20 Totteridge Common, LONDON, N20 8NG.
DOSSA, Mr. Imtiaz Sultan, FCA *1975;* 11 Warrington Road, RICHMOND, SURREY, TW10 6SJ. (Life Member)
DOSSA, Mr. Mohamed Hussein Meghji, FCA *1973;* Glenacre, 20 Totteridge Common, LONDON, N20 8NG.
DOSSA, Mr. Shirazali, FCA *1975;* 3511 WASS CRES., OAKVILLE L6L6G3, ON, CANADA.
DOSSAL, Mr. Amir Akbar, FCA *1975;* 26 Old Lyme Road, SCARSDALE, NY 10583, UNITED STATES. (Life Member)
DOSSANI, Mr. Afzal Hussein, ACA *1982;* Rafaqat Mansha Mohsin Dossani Masoom & Co, Suite 113 3rd Floor, Hafeez Centre, KCHS Block 7&8, Shahra-e-Faisal, KARACHI 75350 PAKISTAN.
DOSSER, Mr. Brian, FCA *1961;* 12 East Hills, Cranfield, BEDFORD, MK43 0EA.
DOSSETT, Dr. David Michael, BSc ACA *2007;* 19 Southville Road, THAMES DITTON, KT7 0UL.
•DOSSETT, Mr. Rodney Michael, FCA *1981;* Rodney M. Dossett, 55 Grand Parade, LEIGH-ON-SEA, SS9 1DT.
DOSSETT, Mrs. Tracy Anne, MA ACA CTA *2001;* with BDO LLP, 55 Baker Street, LONDON, W1U 7EU.
DOSWELL, Mr. Sean Edward, BA ACA *2003;* Northern Rock, Northern Rock House, Gosforth, NEWCASTLE UPON TYNE, NE3 4PL.
DOTCHIN, Mr. Graham John, BSc ACA *2007;* 3 Eastfield Terrace, NEWCASTLE UPON TYNE, NE12 8BA.
DOTIWALLA, Mr. Phiroze Jal, FCA *1971;* 158 Chipwood Crescent, WILLOWDALE M2J 3X7, ON, CANADA.
DOUBLE, Mr. Brian Keith, FCA *1952;* 12 Rean Drive Suite 811, TORONTO M2K 3C6, ON, CANADA. (Life Member)
DOUBLE, Mr. Michael Stockwell, MA FCA *1963;* 37 Grovewood Close, Chorleywood, RICKMANSWORTH, WD3 5PX. (Life Member)
DOUBLE, Miss. Sarah, BSc ACA *2008;* 78 Lavenham Road, IPSWICH, IP2 0JZ.
DOUBLEDAY, Miss. Lucy Ann, BA(Hons) ACA AMCT *2001;* Exchequer Funds and Accounts Team Room 3/04, H M Treasury, 1 Horse Guards Road, LONDON, SW1A 2HQ.
DOUBLEDAY, Mr. Peter Ernest, BA ACA *1987;* 2121 277th Ave SE, SAMMAMISH, WA 98075, UNITED STATES.
•DOUBLEDAY, Mr. Timothy John, BSc ACA *1988;* Doubleday & Co, The Swallows, Marsh Green Farm, Vicarage Lane Elworth, SANDBACH, CW11 3BU.
DOUCE, Mr. Andrew James, BSc ACA *2006;* (Tax Fac), 4 William Smith Close, CAMBRIDGE, CB1 3QF.
DOUCE, Mr. Jeffrey Thomas, FCA *1968;* 2 Lychgate Park, Locking, WESTON-SUPER-MARE, AVON, BS24 8DE. (Life Member)
DOUCH, Mr. Peter John, FCA *1971;* 38 Albion Way, VERWOOD, BH31 7LR.
DOUGAL, Mr. John James, MBA BSc ACA *1992;* Accuread, 14 Silver Fox Way, NEWCASTLE UPON TYNE, NE27 0QJ.
DOUGALL, Mr. Ninian, FCA *1941;* 84 Bulstrode Road, HOUNSLOW, TW3 3AL. (Life Member)

DOUGALL, Mr. Robert James, ACA *1987;* Centennial Coal Company Ltd, Level 18, 1 Market Street, SYDNEY, NSW 2000, AUSTRALIA.
DOUGHERTY, Mr. Charles Alma Keith, FCA *1982;* Gorse Lawn, 1 Turnberry Avenue, Howstrake Heights, Onchan, ISLE OF MAN, IM3 2JS. (Life Member)
•DOUGHERTY, Mr. Christopher Patrick John, BA FCA *1995;* Lakin Rose Limited, Pioneer House, Vision Park, Histon, CAMBRIDGE, CB24 9NL.
DOUGHERTY, Mr. Edward Wynn, FCA *1960;* P.O.Box 41017, NAIROBI, KENYA. (Life Member)
•DOUGHERTY, Mr. George Julian, BSc ACA *1991;* George Dougherty, Chestnuts, Lower Farm Road, Effingham, LEATHERHEAD, SURREY KT24 5JJ.
•DOUGHERTY, Mrs. Tracy Jane, FCA *1990;* TJM Dougherty Ltd, 7 The Coppice, Great Barton, BURY ST. EDMUNDS, SUFFOLK, IP31 2TT.
DOUGHTY, Mr. Dermot Peter, BA ACA *1984;* Independent Trust Corporation Unit 5 Wychwood Court, Cotswold Business Village London Road, MORETON-IN-MARSH, GL56 0JQ.
DOUGHTY, Mr. Gavin Mark, BSc ACA *1995;* 8 Roman Way, LECHLADE, GL7 3BP.
DOUGHTY, Mr. Paul, BSc ACA *1993;* Moneysupermarket House, St. Davids Park, Ewloe, DEESIDE, CLWYD, CH5 3UZ.
DOUGHTY, Mr. Robert William, BA FCA *1983;* Gillingham House 5th Floor, 38-44 Gillingham Street, LONDON, SW1V 1HU.
DOUGLAS, Mr. Adrian James, BSc ACA *1999;* 78 Woodland Road, LEEDS, LS15 7DJ.
DOUGLAS, Mr. Alexander James, ACA *2008;* 72 Lloyds Avenue, SCUNTHORPE, SOUTH HUMBERSIDE, DN17 1BX.
DOUGLAS, Ms. Amanda Jane Sholto, BSc ACA *2009;* Flat 2, 131 Blythe Road, LONDON, W14 0HL.
DOUGLAS, Mr. Andrew Vladimir, BA FCA *1983;* Flat 10, Priory Mansions, 90 Drayton Gardens, LONDON, SW10 9RG.
DOUGLAS, Mr. Aoin Kay Hugo, BSc(Hons) ACA *2002;* Finance Dept. FML002A, Liverpool Hope University College Hope Park, Taggart Avenue, LIVERPOOL, L16 9JD.
DOUGLAS, Mr. David Keith, BSc FCA *1986;* The Eurotech Group Plc, Dinan Way, EXMOUTH, EX8 4RZ.
DOUGLAS, Mrs. Felicity Elizabeth MacPherson, BA ACA *1984;* Grangeneuve, Bouteilles-St Sebastien, 24320 VERTEILLAC, FRANCE.
DOUGLAS, Miss. Fiona Pauline, BA ACA *1994;* Corhope, Princes Street, CORBRIDGE, NORTHUMBERLAND, NE45 5DG.
DOUGLAS, Mr. Giles Leonard, ACA *1997;* PO Box 652099, BENMORE, 2010, SOUTH AFRICA.
•DOUGLAS, Mr. Graham Thomas, BSc ACA *1980;* Douglas Shaw Limited, 7 Brenkley Way, Blezard Business Park, Seaton Burn, NEWCASTLE UPON TYNE, NE13 6DS.
DOUGLAS, Miss. Helen, BCom FCA *1986;* 56 Oakbank Drive, CUMNOCK, AYRSHIRE, KA18 1BD.
•DOUGLAS, Mr. Ian Alan, BSc FCA *1977;* Duncan Sheard Glass, 45 Hoghton Street, SOUTHPORT, MERSEYSIDE, PR9 0PG. See also DSG Accountancy and Taxation Services Limited
•DOUGLAS, Mr. James Alastair, BA FCA CTA *1980;* James Douglas Accounting Limited, 21 Trent View Gardens, Radcliffe-on-Trent, NOTTINGHAM, NG12 1AY. See also Douglas & Co
DOUGLAS, Mr. James Charles Robert, MA MSc ACA *1992;* Lower Green Farm, Horton-cum-studley, OXFORD, OX33 1AP.
DOUGLAS, Mr. James David, BSc ACA *2000;* 1 White Horse Road, HORSHAM, WEST SUSSEX, RH12 4UL.
DOUGLAS, Mr. John Alexander George, BSc ACA *1991;* 24b Douglas Crescent, EDINBURGH, EH12 5BA.
DOUGLAS, Mr. John Andrew, BSc FCA *1976;* A J 3 D PO Box 1937, SHEFFIELD, S11 9WP.
DOUGLAS, Mr. Justin Maxwell, BSc ACA CMC LRPS MIBC *1998;* 9 Lower Dagnall Street, ST. ALBANS, AL3 4PE.
DOUGLAS, Miss. Kate Emily, ACA *2009;* 226 Leigh Road, Chandler's Ford, EASTLEIGH, HAMPSHIRE, SO53 3AY.
DOUGLAS, Miss. Katharine Bridget, MA ACA ACT *1986;* 5 Dale Drive, CHATHAM, NJ 07928, UNITED STATES.
DOUGLAS, Mrs. Katherine Rose, BSc ACA *2001;* Oversley, 101 New Road, BROMSGROVE, WORCESTERSHIRE, B60 2LL.
•DOUGLAS, Ms. Katrina, MSc FCA *1990;* (Tax Fac), Katrina Douglas, The Chapel House, The Cross, Nympsfield, STONEHOUSE, GLOUCESTERSHIRE GL10 3TU. See also AIMS - Katrina Douglas
DOUGLAS, Mr. Keith, BSc ACA *1993;* 260 Sunny Ridge Rd, HARRISON, NY 10528, UNITED STATES.
DOUGLAS, Miss. Kelly, BA ACA *2007;* with PricewaterhouseCoopers LLP, 89 Sandyford Road, NEWCASTLE UPON TYNE, NE1 8HW.
DOUGLAS, Miss. Lucy, BSc ACA *2007;* Flat 74, Barrington Court, Colney Hatch Lane, LONDON, N10 1QH.
DOUGLAS, Mr. Mark Kennedy, BSc FCA *1993;* Fairlight, 3 Clos de Ruette Braye, St Martins, GUERNSEY, GY1 1PJ.
DOUGLAS, Miss. Mary Bridget, BA ACA *1993;* 47a The Avenue, SURBITON, SURREY, KT5 8JW.
DOUGLAS, Mr. Neil, BA ACA *2010;* 19 Saleby Close, Lower Earley, READING, RG6 3BE.
DOUGLAS, Mr. Neil Robert John, BSc FCA *1988;* Brush Electrical Machines Ltd, Falcon Works, PO Box 18, Nottingham Road, LOUGHBOROUGH, LEICESTERSHIRE LE11 1HJ.
DOUGLAS, Mr. Neil Stewart, BA FCA *1980;* 22 Ainslie Place, EDINBURGH, EH3 6AJ.
DOUGLAS, Mr. Nicholas Paul, BA ACA *1991;* WPP, 27 Farm Street, LONDON, W1J 5RJ.
•DOUGLAS, Mr. Nigel Darrell, FCA *1974;* Laburnum, Gainsborough Road, Middle Rasen, MARKET RASEN, LINCOLNSHIRE, LN8 3JS.
DOUGLAS, Mr. Paul Michael, FCA *1951;* 10 Pine Tree Lodge, 7 Durham Avenue, BROMLEY, BR2 0QA. (Life Member)
DOUGLAS, Mr. Paul Richard, BA ACA *1992;* Flat 4, 4 Stannary St, LONDON, SE11 4AA.
DOUGLAS, Mr. Peter Alaric, FCA *1970;* (Member of Council 1994 - 2004), Laurel Cottage Chapmans Town Road, Rushlake Green, HEATHFIELD, EAST SUSSEX, TN21 9PS.
DOUGLAS, Mr. Peter Henry, BA FCA *1994;* Westpac, Group Financial Control, Group Finance, Level 19 275 Kent Street, SYDNEY, NSW 2000 AUSTRALIA.
DOUGLAS, Mr. Peter Michael George, BSc ACA *1982;* c/o York House, PO Box 4, Hillhouse International, THORNTON-CLEVELEYS, LANCASHIRE FY5 4QD.
DOUGLAS, Mr. Raymond Leslie Scott, BA FCA *1978;* 16 The Fairway, Flackwell Heath, HIGH WYCOMBE, HP10 9NF.
•DOUGLAS, Mr. Richard Edward, FCA *1975;* Rawlinson & Hunter, Windward 1, Regatta Office Park, PO Box 897, GEORGE TOWN, GRAND CAYMAN KY1 - 1103 CAYMAN ISLANDS. See also Deloitte & Touche
DOUGLAS, Mr. Robert Granville, BSc FCA *1982;* The Shottery, 39 Four Oaks Road, SUTTON COLDFIELD, B74 2XU.
DOUGLAS, Mr. Robert Julian, BSc ACA *1979;* 2 Hollycroft, Brereton Heath Lane, Somerford, CONGLETON, CHESHIRE, CW12 4SH.
DOUGLAS, Mr. Robin Michael, BA ACA *1985;* 10 Exchange Square, LONDON, ec2a 2by.
DOUGLAS, Mrs. Rosamund Jane, BSc ACA *1980;* The Shottery, 39 Four Oaks Road, SUTTON COLDFIELD, WEST MIDLANDS, B74 2XU.
DOUGLAS, Mrs. Ruth Ingela Astrid, BA ACA *1993;* (Tax Fac), The Children's Society, Unit 17, Castle Road, Kings Norton Business Centre, Kings Norton, BIRMINGHAM B30 3HZ.
DOUGLAS, Mrs. Samantha Jane, MChem ACA *2010;* 34 Rosefield Avenue, WIRRAL, MERSEYSIDE, CH63 5JT.
DOUGLAS, Mrs. Sandra Belinda, BA ACA *1992;* Ty Cerrig, Golwg-y-Mor, Square & Compass, HAVERFORDWEST, SA62 5HP.
DOUGLAS, Miss. Sarah Louise, ACA *2009;* B M I Business Services, 10 Eden Place, CHEADLE, CHESHIRE, SK8 1AT.
DOUGLAS, Mrs. Sarah Rachael Elizabeth, BA ACA *1996;* Fairlight, 3 Clos de Ruette Braye, St Martins, GUERNSEY, GY1 1PJ.
DOUGLAS, Mr. Stanley, FCA *1949;* 80 College Road North, Blundellsands, LIVERPOOL, L23 8UU. (Life Member)
•DOUGLAS, Mr. Stephen, MPhil LLB ACA *1999;* Bannerdale Accountancy Services Limited, Cornwell House, Amotherby, MALTON, NORTH YORKSHIRE, YO17 6UN.
DOUGLAS, Mr. Steven, BSc(Econ) FCA *1999;* Oversley 101 New Road, BROMSGROVE, WORCESTERSHIRE, B60 2LL.
DOUGLAS, Mr. Timothy William, FCA *1969;* 8 Park Drive, East Sheen, LONDON, SW14 8RD.
DOUGLAS-HOME, Mr. Andrew, FCA *1975;* The Lees, Kelso Road, COLDSTREAM, BERWICKSHIRE, TD12 4LF.
•DOUGLAS-PENNANT, Mr. Philip Morton, FCA *1971;* Tisbury House, Tisbury, SALISBURY, SP3 6PZ.
DOUGLASS, Mr. Christopher William, LLB ACA *1999;* 6 Cable Cove, MOSMAN PARK, WA 6012, AUSTRALIA.
•DOUGLASS, Mr. Ian, BA FCA *1980;* (Tax Fac), The Coach House, Tarn House Farm, Barton Lane, PRESTON, PR3 5AX.
DOUGLASS, Mr. Ian Leslie, BA FCA ATII *1975;* Burnt Tree Vehicle Hire Burnt Tree House, Knights Way Battlefield Enterprise Park, SHREWSBURY, SY1 3AB.
DOUGLASS, Miss. Joanne, BA(Hons) ACA *2007;* 8 Jubilee Road, Gosforth, NEWCASTLE UPON TYNE, NE3 3UQ.
DOUGLASS, Mr. John Charles, FCA *1971;* Chantry House, 45 King Street, CHESHAM, HP5 1LZ.
DOUGLASS, Mr. John Edward, FCA *1977;* 12 Girdwood Road, Southfields, LONDON, SW18 5QS.
DOUGLASS, Mr. Lee Paul, ACA *2006;* 6 Rosebury Drive, NEWCASTLE UPON TYNE, NE12 8RG.
DOUGLASS, Mrs. Roselle Margaret, BA FCA *1976;* 12 Girdwood Road, Southfields, LONDON, SW18 5QS.
DOUIE, Mr. Francis Arthur James Wigan, CA FCA *1955;* 7 Churchill Avenue, Alexandra Park, HARARE, ZIMBABWE. (Life Member)
DOULL, Mr. Alun Edward Manley, BA ACA *1990;* 10 East Rise, Llanishen, CARDIFF, CF14 0RJ.
DOUMAS, Mr. Christos, ACA *2011;* Flat 8, 10 Leinster Gardens, LONDON, W2 6DR.
DOURAS, Ms. Laura Catherine, BSc ACA *2007;* 21 Redston Road, LONDON, N8 7HL.
DOUSE, Miss. Gemma, LLB ACA *2010;* Flat 3, 1 The Beeches, MANCHESTER, M20 2BG.
DOUSE, Mr. James Alexander, BA ACA *2004;* 138 Tubbenden Lane, ORPINGTON, KENT, BR6 9PR.
•DOUST, Mr. Clive Howard, BSocSc FCA ATII *1985;* (Tax Fac), Clive Howard Doust, 63 Pampisford Road, PURLEY, CR8 2NJ.
DOUTHWAITE, Mr. Alan Homer, BSc ACA *1990;* 99 Mt Albert Road, Mt Albert, AUCKLAND 1025, NEW ZEALAND.
DOUTHWAITE, Mr. John Antony, FCA *1953;* 16 Mapperley Gardens, Moseley, BIRMINGHAM, B13 8RN. (Life Member)
DOUTHWAITE, Mr. William John, FCA MBA *1980;* 2 Bagots Court, Bagot Street, Abbots Bromley, RUGELEY, WS15 3DA.
•DOVE, Mrs. Diana Mary, BA FCA *1979;* (Tax Fac), Diana Dove, 115 High Street, Prestwood, GREAT MISSENDEN, HP16 9EU.
DOVE, Miss. Ellen Astrid, BA ACA *2005;* with PricewaterhouseCoopers LLP, Cornwall Court, 19 Cornwall Street, BIRMINGHAM, B3 2DT.
DOVE, Mr. Graham Alfred, BA ACA *1980;* 15 Rue St Martin, Les Champs St Martin, 17770 ST HILAIRE DE VILLEFRANCHE, FRANCE.
DOVE, Mr. Graham Roger, ACA *2004;* 21/F. Sunshine Plaza, 353 Lockhart Road, WAN CHAI, HONG KONG ISLAND, HONG KONG SAR.
DOVE, Mr. Jack Richard, FCA *1956;* 29 Abington Park Crescent, NORTHAMPTON, NN3 3AD. (Life Member)
DOVE, Mr. Jonathan Mark, LLB ACA *1989;* Merck Chemicals Ltd, Boulevard Industrial Park, Padge Road, Beeston, NOTTINGHAM, NG9 2JR.
DOVE, Mr. Martin David John, BA FCA AKC *1983;* Rosemary, 3 Coombe Road, WOTTON-UNDER-EDGE, GLOUCESTERSHIRE, GL12 7LU.
DOVE, Mr. Nicholas Simon, FCA *1972;* P.O. Box Hm 1521, HAMILTON HM FX, BERMUDA.
DOVE, Mr. Philip, BSc ACA *1993;* Conifers Fundenhall Road, Hapton, NORWICH, NR15 1SG.
DOVE, Mr. Robert Alexander John, MA FCA *1980;* 16 Mayow Road, LONDON, SE23 2XG.
DOVE, Mr. Samuel Stuart, FCA *1957;* 27/15 King David Street, JERUSALEM, 94101, ISRAEL. (Life Member)
DOVE-EDWIN, Mr. Bassey Tokumboh, BA ACA *1993;* 311a Clive Court, Maida Vale, LONDON, W9 1SF.
•DOVER, Mr. Anthony, FCA *1991;* Tony Dover FCA, 11 Defender Court, Hylton Riverside Enterprise Park, SUNDERLAND, SR5 3PE.
•DOVER, Mr. Daniel Isaac, BA FCA *1979;* (Tax Fac), BDO LLP, 55 Baker Street, LONDON, W1U 7EU. See also BDO Stoy Hayward LLP
DOVER, Mr. Gerard Vernon, BSc ACA *1993;* 48 Bradleys Head Road, MOSMAN, NSW 2088, AUSTRALIA.
DOVER, Mr. James William, BSc ACA *1999;* Longfield House Austenwood Lane, Chalfont St. Peter, GERRARDS CROSS, BUCKINGHAMSHIRE, SL9 8SF.
DOVER, Mrs. Victoria Jane, BSc ACA *1999;* Longfield House, Austenwood Lane, Chalfont St. Peter, GERRARDS CROSS, BUCKINGHAMSHIRE, SL9 8SF.
DOVER ARYEH, Ms. Wendy Miriam Irene, LLB FCA CPA *1990;* 13/2 Hanamer Street, Malha, 96954 JERUSALEM, ISRAEL.
DOVEY, Mr. Charles Frederick, FCA *1981;* (Tax Fac), 110 Westley Road, Acocks Green, BIRMINGHAM, B27 7UL.
DOVEY, Miss. Clare, ACA *1994;* 113 Chartridge Lane, CHESHAM, BUCKINGHAMSHIRE, HP5 2RG.
DOVEY, Mr. George Trevor Ieuan, FCA *1959;* Leeways, Whitenap Lane, ROMSEY, SO51 5RS. (Life Member)
•DOVEY, Mr. Richard Peter, FCA *1971;* Richard Dovey & Co, 61 Malmains Way, BECKENHAM, BR3 6SB.
DOVEY, Mrs. Samantha, BA ACA CFA *1997;* La Conchee, La Corbiere Rue Des Hougues, Castel, GUERNSEY, GY5 7QH.
DOW, Mr. David Malcolm Edward, ACA *1983;* 55 Sutherland Avenue, ORPINGTON, BR5 1QY.
DOW, Mr. David McDiarmid, MA FCA *1979;* Scottish Government Victoria Quay, Leith Docks, EDINBURGH, EH6 6QQ.
•DOW, Mr. James Alexander Thomas, BCom ACA CF *1987;* Dow Schofield Watts Corporate Finance Limited, 7700 Daresbury Park, Daresbury, WARRINGTON, CHESHIRE, WA4 5BS.
DOW, Mr. Nicoll Lany, FCA *1972;* Conifers The Green, Frant, TUNBRIDGE WELLS, TN3 9DS.
DOW, Ms. Rhianydd Elisabeth, BA FCA *2000;* 5 Pelham Crescent, Churchdown, GLOUCESTER, GL3 2BN.
DOWALL, Mr. David Philip, ACA *2008;* Apartment 102, Two Porto Arabia, The Pearl Qatar, DOHA, QATAR.
•DOWD, Mr. Anthony Edward, BA ACA *1981;* A.E. Dowd, Roentgen Court, Roentgen Road, Daneshill, BASINGSTOKE, HAMPSHIRE RG24 8NT.
DOWD, Mr. Anthony Thomas, BSc FCA *1954;* 23 North Frith Park, Hadlow, TONBRIDGE, KENT, TN11 9QW. (Life Member)
DOWD, Mr. John Alan, LLM LLB ACA *2010;* 11 Bredon Close, LYTHAM ST. ANNES, FY8 4LP.
DOWD, Mr. Joseph Thomas, BSc ACA *1993;* Goldman Sachs JBWere, Governor Phillip Tower, 1 Farrar Place, SYDNEY, NSW 2000, AUSTRALIA.
DOWD, Mr. Michael, BA ACA *1993;* Ryohin Keikakau Europe, 8-12 Leeke Street, LONDON, WC1X 9HT.
DOWD, Mr. Nicholas Martin, BA ACA *1989;* 1507 Calumet Place, MISSISSAUGA L5J 3B1, ON, CANADA.
DOWDALL, Miss. Kay Louise, BA ACA *1996;* 67 Ffordd Dryden, Killay, SWANSEA, SA2 7PD.
DOWDALL, Mr. Robert Edward, MA FCA *1972;* Midwicket, Brantridge Park, Balcombe, HAYWARDS HEATH, RH17 6JT.
DOWDE, Miss. Lorna Joanne, BA ACA *1996;* with Deloitte LLP, 4 Brindley Place, BIRMINGHAM, B1 2HZ.
DOWDEN, Mr. Michael Christopher, FCA *1956;* 67 High Street, Roade, NORTHAMPTON, NN7 2NW. (Life Member)
DOWDESWELL, Mr. Alexander Stuart, BSc(Hons) ACA *2001;* 17 Goldsmith Way, ST. ALBANS, HERTFORDSHIRE, AL3 5LH.
DOWDESWELL, Mr. Frederick Charles, LLB ACA *1992;* Broseley Wood House Simpsons Lane, Broseley Wood, BROSELEY, SHROPSHIRE, TF12 5RF.
DOWDESWELL, Mr. Peter Robert, FCA *1971;* Sycamore Cottage, Preston Candover, BASINGSTOKE, RG25 2DU.
DOWDING, Mrs. Georgina Frances, BA ACA *2006;* with Deloitte LLP, Abbots House, Abbey Street, READING, RG1 3BD.
DOWDING, Mr. Ian John, BA(Hons) ACA *2000;* 12 Forge Close, UCKFIELD, EAST SUSSEX, TN22 5BQ.
DOWDING, Mr. Keith Stuart, BCom FCA *1975;* 12150 Big Cottonwood Canyon, 1101 The Crossings, BRIGHTON, UT 84121, UNITED STATES.
•DOWDING, Mr. Mark Timothy, ACA FCCA *2010;* MacIntyre Hudson LLP, Boundary House, 4 County Place, CHELMSFORD, CM2 0RE.
DOWDING, Mr. Raymond John, FCA *1974;* Woodclose, Borrowdale Road, KESWICK, CUMBRIA, CA12 5DD.
DOWDING, Mr. Roger Peter, FCA *1976;* 9 Fairlawns, Laustan Close, GUILDFORD, GU1 2QU.
DOWDS, Mr. Andrew McLean, LLB ACA *1985;* 27 St. Pauls Avenue, LYTHAM ST. ANNES, LANCASHIRE, FY8 1ED.
DOWDS, Mr. Brian Darren, BA ACA *1991;* 6 St Andrew Street, LONDON, EC4A 3AE.

DOWDS, Mrs. Justine, BSc ACA *1999;* 27 St. Pauls Avenue, Fairhaven, LYTHAM ST. ANNES, LANCASHIRE, FY8 1ED.
DOWDY, Mr. Richard Stephen, FCA *1966;* The Barn, Pix's Lane, Rolvenden, CRANBROOK, KENT, TN17 4HN.
DOWE, Mr. Stephen William, FCA *1978;* 10 Breary Lane East, Bramhope, LEEDS, LS16 9BJ.
DOWELL, Mr. David John, BA ACA CTA *1990;* Ritson Smith, 16 Carden Place, ABERDEEN, AB10 1FX.
DOWELL, Mr. Peter Derrick, FCA *1950;* 77 De Bohun Avenue, Southgate, LONDON, N14 4PZ. (Life Member)
DOWEN, Miss. Sharon Lesley, BSc ACA *1995;* 12 Glenfern Road, BILSTON, WV14 9HW.
DOWER, Mr. Nigel, BEd FCA *1989;* Wynfield, Chapel Hill, Gweek, HELSTON, TR12 7AE.
DOWERS, Mr. Steven, BA FCA ATII *2000;* 35 High Worple, Rayners Lane, HARROW, HA2 9SX.
DOWGILL, Mr. Peter Ronald, BSc ACA *1991;* 18 Parklands, Bramhope, LEEDS, LS16 9AJ.
DOWIE, Mr. Charles Michael, FCA *1966;* 3 The Chestnuts, HEMEL HEMPSTEAD, HP3 0DZ.
•DOWIE, Mr. Jon Mark, BSc ACA *1998;* KPMG LLP, 15 Canada Square, LONDON, E14 5GL.
DOWIE, Mrs. Julie, BA ACA *1988;* 4 Batts Hill, REDHILL, RH1 2DH.
DOWIE, Mr. Simon Joshua, BA ACA *1996;* 14 Cornhill, LONDON, EC3.
DOWIE, Mr. Tom Lightbody, MA ACA PGCE *1980;* Kilspindie House, Kilspindie, Errol, PERTH, PH2 7RX.
DOWLE, Mr. John Michael, FCA *1958;* 1 Mill Meadow, Milford on Sea, LYMINGTON, HAMPSHIRE, SO41 0UG. (Life Member)
DOWLE, Mr. Stuart Andrew, FCA *1968;* 6 Dewi Court, Cardiff Road, Llandaff, CARDIFF, CF5 2ET.
DOWLER, Mr. Andrew Stewart Haxton, FCA *1975;* 27 Albany Road, STRATFORD-UPON-AVON, CV37 6PG.
DOWLER, Mr. Jeremy, BA FCA *1974;* (Tax Fac), 23 Starling Close, BUCKHURST HILL, IG9 5TN.
DOWLER, Mr. Robert Michael, FCA *1949;* Marrington, 17 Park Road, BUXTON, SK17 6SG. (Life Member)
DOWLEY, Mr. Laurence Justin, MA FCA *1980;* 8 Norland Square, LONDON, W11 4PX.
DOWLEY, Mr. Robert Charles, BSc ACA *1998;* 8 McDougall Road, BERKHAMSTED, HERTFORDSHIRE, HP4 2WQ.
•DOWLING, Mr. Anthony John, BA ACA *1992;* (Tax Fac), SMP Accounting and Tax Limited, PO Box 227, Clinch's House, Lord Street, Douglas, ISLE OF MAN IM99 1RZ.
DOWLING, Mr. Christopher Bruce, BA ACA *1978;* Challenger Group, 21 Palmer Street, LONDON, SW1H 0AD.
DOWLING, Mrs. Esme Ann, BAcc ACA *2002;* 3 Cowper Road, BERKHAMSTED, HERTFORDSHIRE, HP4 3DA.
DOWLING, Mrs. Joanna Elaine, BSc ACA *1994;* with PricewaterhouseCoopers LLP, 1 Embankment Place, LONDON, WC2N 6RH.
DOWLING, Mrs. Joanne, BA(Hons) ACA *2002;* 6 Pulford Road, SALE, CHESHIRE, M33 3LP.
DOWLING, Mr. Joseph Anthony, BSc ACA *1984;* 4 South Frith, London Road Southborough, TUNBRIDGE WELLS, KENT, TN4 0UQ.
DOWLING, Mr. Kevin Mary, BCom ACA ATII *1991;* 162 Ballyroan Road, RATHFARNHAM Dublin 16, COUNTY DUBLIN, IRELAND.
DOWLING, Mr. Lee Antony, BSc ACA *2001;* 38 Kelso Close, RAYLEIGH, ESSEX, SS6 9RT.
DOWLING, Mr. Mark Stephen, BSc ACA AMCT *1992;* 16 Travertine Road, CHATHAM, ME5 9LQ.
DOWLING, The Revd. Paul Martin, BA ACA *1979;* 24 rue Jacques Coeur, 36000 CHATEAUROUX, FRANCE.
DOWLING, Mr. Peter James, BSc ACA *2004;* 16 Lyndhurst Road, Elvetham Heath, FLEET, HAMPSHIRE, GU51 1EH.
DOWLING, Mr. Peter John Osmond, FCA *1965;* Abbotswell Abbotswell Road, Frogham, FORDINGBRIDGE, HAMPSHIRE, SP6 2JD.
DOWLING, Mr. Philip Peter, FCA *1968;* Milton Rise, Milton Street, POLEGATE, BN26 5RP. (Life Member)
•DOWLING, Mr. Robert Wheatley, FCA *1986;* (Tax Fac), Carpenter Box LLP, Amelia House, WORTHING, WEST SUSSEX, BN11 1QR.
DOWLING, Mrs. Sally Anne, BSc ACA *1999;* Dawn Foods Ltd, Worcester Road, EVESHAM, WORCESTERSHIRE, WR11 4QU.
DOWLING, Mr. Simon, BSc ACA *2005;* The Mileage Co Ltd Astral Towers, Betts Way, CRAWLEY, WEST SUSSEX, RH10 9XY.
•DOWLING, Mr. Timothy Herbert, FCA *1970;* Tim Dowling, 16 Gordon Road, Claygate, ESHER, SURREY, KT10 0PQ.
DOWMAN, Miss. Sarah Margaret, BA ACA *2000;* Flat 5 Collette Court, Eleanor Close, LONDON, SE16 6PW.
DOWN, Mr. Christopher Jonathan Alderson, BA ACA *2000;* C/o Hearthstone Investments, New Broad Street House, 35 New Broad Street, LONDON, EC2M 1NH.
DOWN, Mr. Derek Herbert Ashford, FCA *1952;* High Trees, Thakeham Copse, Storrington, PULBOROUGH, WEST SUSSEX, RH20 3JW. (Life Member)
DOWN, Mr. Duncan William, LLB ACA *2003;* with Deloitte LLP, 3 Rivergate, Temple Quay, BRISTOL, BS1 6GD.
DOWN, Mrs. Gillian Margaret, BSc ACA *1992;* EJBC Business Consultants, 2b Park Street, NEWBURY, BERKSHIRE, RG14 1EA.
DOWN, Mr. Keith William, BA ACA *1992;* 8 The Drive, Wheathampstead, ST. ALBANS, HERTFORDSHIRE, AL4 8LF.
DOWN, Mr. Michael Kennedy, FCA *1955;* 8 Eylesden Court, Bearsted, MAIDSTONE, KENT, ME14 4BF. (Life Member)
DOWN, Mr. Richard Charles Alastair, FCA *1973;* The Orchard House, Efford Park, LYMINGTON, SO41 0JD.
DOWN, Mr. Robert Leigh, BSc ACA *2007;* 29 Lower Ebor Street, YORK, YO23 1AY.
DOWN, Mr. Russell Peter, BA FCA *1990;* Hyder Cosulting Plc, 29 Bressenden Place, LONDON, SW1E 5DZ.
DOWN, Mr. Stephen Howard, ACA *1980;* La Rocque Taille, Route De Carteret, Cobo Castel, GUERNSEY, GY5 7YS.
•DOWN, Mr. Terence John, FCA *1967;* (Tax Fac), Terence J. Down & Co., Brook House, Park Avenue, VENTNOR, ISLE OF WIGHT, PO38 1LE.
•DOWNER, Mr. Jonathan Mark, BA FCA *1997;* with KPMG LLP, 15 Canada Square, LONDON, E14 5GL.
•DOWNER, Mr. Michael John, BA ACA *1998;* Downer & Co Associates Limited, 125 Broadclyst Gardens, Thorpe Bay, SOUTHEND-ON-SEA, ESSEX, SS1 3QY.
DOWNER, Mr. Michael Thomas, FCA *1974;* Tower View, Copplestone, CREDITON, EX17 5NR.
DOWNER, Mr. Stephen James, FCA *1969;* 15 Avenue Road, TEDDINGTON, TW11 0BT.
DOWNES, Mr. Adam Nicholas, BSc(Hons) ACA *2002;* Premier Oil Plc, 23 Lower Belgrave Street, LONDON, SW1W 0NR.
•DOWNES, Mr. Andrew John, BA ACA *1996;* Deloitte LLP, Hill House, 1 Little New Street, LONDON, EC4A 3TR. See also Deloitte & Touche LLP
DOWNES, Mr. Andrew John, ACA MBA *2002;* 1 Dunkirk Bank, Amberley, STROUD, GLOUCESTERSHIRE, GL5 5AX.
•DOWNES, Mr. Andrew Nicholas, BA ACA *1995;* Mayfield & Company, 2nd Floor, 27 The Crescent, King Street, LEICESTER, LE1 6RX. See also Mayfield & Co (Accountants) Ltd
DOWNES, Mr. Barry Trouncer, FCA *1934;* P.O. Box 213, RAMSGATE, KWAZULU NATAL, 4285, SOUTH AFRICA. (Life Member)
DOWNES, Mrs. Belinda, BA ACA *2007;* Flat 20 Sylva Court, 81 Putney Hill, LONDON, SW15 3NX.
DOWNES, Mr. Charles, MSc BSc(Hons) ACA *2011;* 10 Hanover Square, Apartment 10R, NEW YORK, NY 10005, UNITED STATES.
DOWNES, Mr. Charles Anthony John, BSc ACA *1991;* 38 Elizabeth Crescent, CHESTER, CH4 7AZ.
DOWNES, Mrs. Emma Jane, BSc ACA *2003;* 24 Sparkes Close, BROMLEY, BR2 9GE.
DOWNES, Mr. Gareth, BSc ACA *2003;* (Tax Fac), Kelso Place Asset Management, 110 St. Martin's Lane, LONDON, WC2N 4BA.
DOWNES, Mr. Gerard John, BCom FCA *1967;* 59 Thomastown Road, Dun Laoghaire, DUBLIN, COUNTY DUBLIN, IRELAND. (Life Member)
DOWNES, Mr. Gerard Scot, BSc ACA *1992;* Ivy House Ccoking Lane Addingham Moorside, ILKLEY, LS29 0QQ.
DOWNES, Mr. James Findlay Reid, BSc ACA *1981;* Flat 15, Denne Park House, Denne Park, HORSHAM, WEST SUSSEX, RH13 0AZ.
•DOWNES, Mr. James Henry, FCA *1962;* DEKM Limited, 5 Trinity Terrace, London Road, DERBY, DE1 2QS.
DOWNES, Mr. John Charles, FCA *1959;* 1 Aber Drive, LLANDUDNO, GWYNEDD, LL30 3AN. (Life Member)
DOWNES, Mr. Jonathan Simon, MA ACA *1993;* Commerzbank, 30 Gresham Street, LONDON, EC2V 7PG.
DOWNES, Mrs. Julie, BA(Hons) ACA *2004;* Kerry Foods Ltd, Thorpe Lea Manor, Thorpe Lea, EGHAM, SURREY, TW20 8HY.
DOWNES, Mr. Martin Bruce James, BA FCA *1985;* N M Rothschild & Sons Ltd, PO Box 185, LONDON, EC4P 4DU.
DOWNES, Mrs. Melanie, BSc FCA *1989;* Box 1265, Bragg Creek, CALGARY T0L 0K0, AB, CANADA.
DOWNES, Mr. Michael, MMath ACA *2006;* 7 Hollinside Terrace, Lanchester, DURHAM, DH7 0RQ.
DOWNES, Mr. Oliver Thomas Andrew, BSc ACA *2006;* Flat 20, Sylva Court, 79 Putney Hill, LONDON, SW15 3NX.
DOWNES, Mr. Paul William Edwin, BSc FCA *1979;* Seven Acres, Horsell Common, WOKING, SURREY, GU21 4XY.
DOWNES, Mr. Richard Anthony Stewart, BA(Hons) ACA *2002;* 10 Priory Grange, Ambleside Road, WINDERMERE, CUMBRIA, LA23 1BF.
DOWNES, Mr. Richard George, BSc ACA *2005;* The Gable, Helmdon Road, Greatworth, BANBURY, OXFORDSHIRE, OX17 2DL.
•DOWNES, Mr. Roger Frank, FCA *1977;* Andorran Limited, 6 Manor Park Business Centre, Mackenzie Way, CHELTENHAM, GL51 9TX.
DOWNES, Mr. Steven Richard, ACA *1980;* 20 Derwent Road, Palmers Green, LONDON, N13 4PU.
DOWNEY, Miss. Deborah Caroline, BSc ACA *1999;* 2 Fourth Cross Road, TWICKENHAM, TW2 5EL.
DOWNEY, Mr. Gary Gerard, BA ACA *1981;* with Mazars LLP, Donaldson House, 97 Haymarket Terrace, EDINBURGH, EH12 5HD.
DOWNEY, Mrs. Gillian, BA FCA *1977;* 58a Queens Park Avenue, BOURNEMOUTH, BH8 9EY.
DOWNEY, Mr. James Andrew, BA ACA *1991;* 3 Ross Avenue, Moreton, WIRRAL, CH46 2SA.
DOWNEY, Mr. James Peter Edward, MA ACA *2004;* 1 Grantham Drive, YORK, YO26 4UE.
•DOWNEY, Mrs. Jane Elizabeth, BSc ACA *1992;* The Countryside Restoration Trust, Haslingfield Road, BARTON, CAMBRIDGESHIRE, CB23 7AG.
DOWNEY, Mr. Nigel Alexander, BA FCA *1982;* 4 Cornwall Close, CAMBERLEY, GU15 3UA.
DOWNEY, Mr. Patrick Joseph, BCom FCA *1970;* 2 Belmont Tce, Galloping Green, BLACKROCK, COUNTY DUBLIN, IRELAND.
DOWNEY, Mr. Peter John, BA ACA *1990;* 13 Pewley Way, GUILDFORD, GU1 3PX.
DOWNEY, Miss. Rachel, BA(Hons) ACA *2010;* Wilson Henry Partnership, 145 Edge Lane Edge Hill, LIVERPOOL, L7 2PF.
DOWNEY, Ms. Rachel Sara, BA ACA *1993;* 4 Christchurch Road, Prenton, WIRRAL, MERSEYSIDE, CH43 5SE.
DOWNEY, Mr. Richard Leslie, BCom FCA *1975;* 10 Ryfold Road, LONDON, SW19 8BZ.
DOWNEY, Mr. Ricky James, BA ACA *2005;* 18 Boundary Road, UPMINSTER, ESSEX, RM14 2QS.
DOWNEY, Mr. Sean Lincoln, BA ACA *1992;* STG, Hamriyah Free Zone, PO Box 41961, SHARJAH, UNITED ARAB EMIRATES.
DOWNEY, Miss. Sinead Ellen, BEng ACA *2001;* 49A Portland Street, LEAMINGTON SPA, WARWICKSHIRE, CV32 5EY.
DOWNEY, Mrs. Victoria Jane, BSc ACA *2004;* 3 Tannery Close Leonard Stanley, STONEHOUSE, GLOUCESTERSHIRE, GL10 3PH.
DOWNEY, Mr. William James, MA FCA *1962;* 6 Lancaster Gardens, LONDON, SW19 5DG. (Life Member)
DOWNHAM, Mr. Christopher, BA(Hons) ACA *2002;* Atlantic Books Limited, Ormond House 26-27 Boswell Street, LONDON, WC1N 3JZ.
DOWNHAM, Mr. David, MA ACA *1999;* Adderley Featherstone Bowcliffe Court, Great North Road Bramham, WETHERBY, WEST YORKSHIRE, LS23 6LW.
•DOWNHAM, Mr. Lee Michael, BEng ACA *2000;* Ernst & Young LLP, 1 More London Place, LONDON, SE1 2AF. See also Ernst & Young Europe LLP
DOWNHILL, Miss. Susan Katrina, ACA *1993;* rue Albert de Latour 47, 1030 BRUSSELS, BELGIUM.
DOWNIE, Mr. Douglas Marshall, BA ACA *1980;* 127 Heythorp Street, LONDON, SW18 5BT.
DOWNIE, Mr. Finnian Robert, BA ACA *2006;* 60 High Street, Bollington, MACCLESFIELD, CHESHIRE, SK10 5PF.
DOWNIE, Mr. George Edward Alexander, FCA *1972;* Bruce House Barn, Top Wath Road, Pateley Bridge, HARROGATE, NORTH YORKSHIRE, HG3 5PG.
DOWNIE, Mrs. Helen Marie, MA ACA *1999;* Flat 3, 11 Queens Avenue, Muswell Hill, LONDON, N10 3PE.
DOWNIE, Mr. Ian Michael Stuart, MA FCA *1976;* Beech Hill, Easton, WINCHESTER, SO21 1ED.
DOWNIE, Mr. James Cleyton, MA ACA *1992;* 71 Cambridge Street, LONDON, SW1V 4PS.
DOWNIE, Mr. James Rougvie, BA FCA *1958;* 178 Shed Road, DOUGLASVILLE, PA 19518, UNITED STATES. (Life Member)
DOWNIE, Mr. Michael James, BSc FCA *1977;* Legh Court, 21 Leycester Road, KNUTSFORD, WA16 8QR.
•DOWNING, Mr. Christopher Paul, ACA *2006;* Transparent Accountancy Limited, 48 Dean Park Road, BOURNEMOUTH, BH1 1QA.
DOWNING, Miss. Claire Elizabeth, BSc ACA *1998;* JPMorgan Audit 370B, Chaseside, BOURNEMOUTH, DORSET, BH7 7DA.
DOWNING, Mr. Derek Michael Raymond, FCA *1969;* 18 Millers Turn, CHINNOR, OX39 4JZ.
DOWNING, Mr. Eric Edward, FCA *1954;* Kingsmead, 6 Ringley Park Road, REIGATE, RH2 7BJ. (Life Member)
DOWNING, Miss. Helen Mary, BA ACA *2010;* 118 Church Lane, Meanwood, LEEDS, LS6 4NR.
•DOWNING, Mrs. Hilary Carole Emily, FCA *1972;* Taylor & Co, 20 Edenhurst Court, Parkhill Road, TORQUAY, TQ1 2DD.
DOWNING, Mr. Ian, BA ACA *1982;* Bibby Financial Services Ltd, 105 Duke Street, LIVERPOOL, L1 5JQ.
DOWNING, Ms. Jean Frances, BSc FCA *1979;* 3 Lake Hill Drive, COWBRIDGE, CF71 7HR.
DOWNING, Mr. Jonathan Clifford, BA ACA *1979;* Crew Farm, Crew Lane, KENILWORTH, WARWICKSHIRE, CV8 2LA.
DOWNING, Mr. Michael Eric, ACA *1980;* 6 Ringley Park Road, REIGATE, RH2 7BJ.
DOWNING, Mr. Michael Thomas, FCA *1971;* (Tax Fac), 14 Chaomans, LETCHWORTH GARDEN CITY, SG6 3UB.
DOWNING, Mr. Phill, ACA *2011;* 6 St. Annes Close, HENLEY-ON-THAMES, OXFORDSHIRE, RG9 1XA.
DOWNING, Mrs. Sara Jane, BA ACA *1992;* Lilac Croft, Pool Close, Little Comberton, PERSHORE, WR10 3EL.
DOWNING, Mr. Simon Jonathan, MEng ACA *2004;* with PricewaterhouseCoopers LLP, 101 Barbirolli Square, Lower Mosley Street, MANCHESTER, M2 3PW.
DOWNING, Mr. Stephen Nicholas, BA ACA *1982;* 57 Maison, L - 6837 BROUCH, LUXEMBOURG.
•DOWNING, Mr. Thomas George Mackay, LLB ACA *1991;* Deloitte LLP, 4 Brindley Place, BIRMINGHAM, B1 2HZ. See also Deloitte & Touche LLP
DOWNING, Mr. Victor Stanford, FCA *1963;* Villa Lily, 15 Triq il-Minfah, NAXXAR NXR 2652, MALTA. (Life Member)
DOWNING, Mr. Wadham St John, BSc ACA *1992;* Legal & General Group plc, One Coleman Street, LONDON, EC2R 5AA.
DOWNS, Miss. Amanda Wendy, BA ACA *1998;* 1088 Shoal Point Road, AJAX L1S 6Y9, ON, CANADA.
DOWNS, Mr. Andrew Peverly, FCA *1962;* 7 Alfreton Close, Wimbledon Parkside, LONDON, SW19 5NS.
DOWNS, Mr. Andrew Terence, BA ACA *1989;* Newton Investment Management, 160 Queen Victoria Street, LONDON, EC4V 4LA.
DOWNS, Mr. Anthony John, BA(Hons) ACA *2001;* 100 Horsehead Lane, Bolsover, CHESTERFIELD, DERBYSHIRE, S44 6XH.
DOWNS, Mr. Brian, FCA *1961;* 14 Ash Grove, CLEVEDON, AVON, BS21 7JS.
DOWNS, Mr. Gavin Dalziel, BSc FCA FCIS *1980;* Equiniti Limited, Aspect House, Spencer Road, Lancing, WORTHING, WEST SUSSEX BN99 6DA.
DOWNS, Mr. James Andrew Abbotson, BEng ACA *1992;* Flexiform Ltd, 1392 Leeds Road, BRADFORD, BD3 7AE.
DOWNS, Mr. Jason, BSc ACA *1995;* Coors Brewers Ltd, 137 High Street, BURTON-ON-TRENT, STAFFORDSHIRE, DE14 1JZ.
DOWNS, Mrs. Joanne Marie, ACA MAAT *2003;* 162a Compstall Road, Marple Bridge, STOCKPORT, CHESHIRE, SK6 5HA.
DOWNS, Mr. John Roger, BSc ACA *1990;* 25 Crawshaw Avenue, Beauchief, SHEFFIELD, S8 7DZ.
DOWNS, Miss. Julie, BSc ACA *1978;* 23 Cole Park Road, TWICKENHAM, TW1 1HP.
•DOWNS, Mr. Phillip Langford, ACA *1985;* P.L Downs, Michaelmas Cottage, Roundle Square Road, Felpham, BOGNOR REGIS, PO22 8JX.
DOWNS, Mr. Richard Sidney John, BSc ACA *1992;* Iglu Com, 165 The Broadway, LONDON, SW19 1NE.
DOWNS, Mr. Stephen Graham, PhD BSc ACA *2003;* 162a Compstall Road, Marple Bridge, STOCKPORT, CHESHIRE, SK6 5HA.
DOWNS, Mr. William, BSc ACA *1983;* 59 Maltings Place, LONDON, SW6 2BX.

DOWNTON, Mr. Matthew, ACA ACMA *2009;* with ICAEW, Metropolitan House, 321 Avebury Boulevard, MILTON KEYNES, MK9 2FZ.
DOWNTON, Mrs. Nicola Jane, BA(Hons) ACA *2002;* 2 Woodway, BEACONSFIELD, BUCKINGHAMSHIRE, HP9 1DH.
DOWSE, Mr. Anthony Roy, FCA *1969;* 6 Strawberry Fields, Meriden, COVENTRY, CV7 7SA.
DOWSE, Mr. Paul Barry, FCA *1962;* 27 Mayfair House, Piccadilly, YORK, YO1 9QJ.
DOWSE, Mr. Robert, BSc(Hons) ACA *2011;* Apartment 8, Q, 20 Newhall Hill, BIRMINGHAM, B1 3JA.
•DOWSETT, Mr. Alan John, BSc FCA *1981;* Dowsett Moore, 17 Station Road, HINCKLEY, LE10 1AW. See also Dowett A J & Co
DOWSETT, Mr. Andrew Ames, BSc ACA *1996;* 32 Albert Street, DURHAM, DH1 4RJ.
DOWSETT, Mrs. Carol Jean, BA ACA *1992;* 26a Aldershot Road, FLEET, HAMPSHIRE, GU51 3NN.
DOWSETT, Mr. Colin Graham, BA ACA *1990;* 26a Aldershot Road, FLEET, HAMPSHIRE, GU51 3NN.
DOWSETT, Mr. Peter Ames, FCA *1957;* 36 Monkhams Drive, WOODFORD GREEN, IG8 0LE. (Life Member)
DOWSON, Mr. Colin John, FCA *1967;* Colin Dowson, 1748 West 2nd Avenue, VANCOUVER V6J 1H6, BC, CANADA.
•DOWSON, Mr. David William, FCA *1974;* (Tax Fac), Lloyd Dowson Limited, Medina House, 2 Station Avenue, BRIDLINGTON, YO16 4LZ.
•DOWSON, Mrs. Hilary, BA FCA *1984;* Coates and Partners Limited, 51 St. John Street, ASHBOURNE, DERBYSHIRE, DE6 1GP.
DOWSON, Mr. Ian Gerald, FCA *1978;* Real Estate Associates Ltd, 1 Heddon Street, LONDON, W1B 4BD.
DOWSON, Mr. Jonathan Mark, MA ACA *2003;* 37 Wood Lane, CASTLEFORD, WEST YORKSHIRE, WF10 5PQ.
DOWSON, Mr. Paul Bourne, MA FCA *1965;* 4 Northgate Mews, North Street, MIDHURST, GU29 9DR.
DOWSON, Mr. Peter Lewis, FCA *1958;* The Old Farrowing House, Church Hill, Starston, HARLESTON, NORFOLK, IP20 9PF. (Life Member)
DOWSON, Mr. Philip, MA ACA *1991;* Kitelands House, Micheldever, WINCHESTER, SO21 3AZ.
•DOWSON, Mr. Trevor Charles Arnot, FCA *1972;* Trevor Dowson, Sackville Place, 44-48 Magdalen Street, NORWICH, NR3 1JU.
DOWTHWAITE, Mrs. Tanya Kate, BA FCA *1986;* The Old Bakehouse, Pudding Lane, Headbourne Worthy, WINCHESTER, SO23 7JL.
•DOWTY, Mr. John Michael Stewart, TD MA ACA *1984;* PricewaterhouseCoopers LLP, 7 More London Riverside, LONDON, SE1 2RT. See also PricewaterhouseCoopers
DOWZALL, Mr. James Frederick, FCA *1958;* Rosebank, 10 Briarfield Avenue, BRADFORD, BD10 8QR. (Life Member)
•DOXEY, Mr. Paul Laurent Evers, MA FCA CFE *1992;* Midtown, 322 High Holborn, LONDON, WC1V 7PB.
DOXEY, Mr. Peter, FCA *1958;* 2 Abbey Fields, Whalley, CLITHEROE, LANCASHIRE, BB7 9RS. (Life Member)
DOXSEY, Miss. Natalie, BSc ACA *2011;* 102 Park Lane, WALLINGTON, SURREY, SM6 0TL.
DOYLE, Mr. Alan John, FCA *1977;* Kerascouet, 56930 PLUMELIAU, FRANCE.
•DOYLE, Mr. Andrew Stephen, BSc FCA *1982;* Hart Moss Doyle Ltd, 69 High Street, Dodworth, BARNSLEY, SOUTH YORKSHIRE, S75 3RQ.
DOYLE, Ms. Anne Louise, BA ACA *1985;* The Old Co-op, Hart Moss Doyle Ltd, 69 High Street Dodworth, BARNSLEY, SOUTH YORKSHIRE, S75 3RQ.
DOYLE, Mr. Anthony, BA(Hons) ACA *2003;* 76 Glenmore Drive, Stenson Fields, DERBY, DERBYSHIRE, DE24 3HT.
DOYLE, Mr. Anthony Basil Christopher, BCom FCA *1957;* Pine Cottage, North Road, Middleham, LEYBURN, NORTH YORKSHIRE, DL8 4PJ. (Life Member)
DOYLE, Mr. Anthony John, BSc ACA *1990;* 82 Ealing Park Gardens, LONDON, W5 4EU.
DOYLE, Mr. Ben, BSc ACA *2004;* Hurst House, Straford Road, HENLEY-IN-ARDEN, B95 6AB.
DOYLE, Mr. Bryan Sean Kendall, BSc(Hons) ACA *1994;* 24a Portsmouth Road, CAMBERLEY, SURREY, GU15 1JX.
DOYLE, Mrs. Camilla Helene Sears, BSc ACA *2002;* 61 Richmond Way, LONDON, W14 0AS.
•DOYLE, Mr. Christopher Alan, BSc FCA *1973;* Lakesel Ltd, PO Box 47168, LONDON, W6 6AY.
DOYLE, Mr. Craig, ACA *2008;* Flat 61 Boss House, 2 Boss Street, LONDON, SE1 2PT.
DOYLE, Mr. Daniel Michael, BA ACA *1979;* 3 Seafield Road, KILLINEY, COUNTY DUBLIN, IRELAND.
DOYLE, Mr. David, BSc ACA *2009;* 116 Nutley, BRACKNELL, RG12 7HF.
DOYLE, Mr. David Corin, FCA *1970;* The End House, Park Copse, DORKING, RH5 4BL.
DOYLE, Mr. Declan, MAcc BCom ACA *1997;* 14 Billers Chase, Springfield, CHELMSFORD, CM1 6BD.
DOYLE, Mr. Desmond Mark, BA ACA *1991;* 250 Fowler Avenue, FARNBOROUGH, GU14 7JP.
DOYLE, Mrs. Elizabeth Katherine, BSc ACA *1994;* with PricewaterhouseCoopers LLP, Marlborough Court, 10 Bricket Road, ST. ALBANS, HERTFORDSHIRE, AL1 3JX.
•DOYLE, Ms. Eva, LLB FCA ATII *1992;* KPMG, Pobrezni 1a, 186 00 PRAGUE, CZECH REPUBLIC.
DOYLE, Mrs. Flavia Josephine Clare McNeill, MA ACA *2004;* Dancing Tide, 12 Devondale Drive, DEVONSHIRE DV07, BERMUDA.
DOYLE, Mrs. Florence Danielle, FCA *1974;* Lorien, Gorse Ride North, Finchampstead, WOKINGHAM, RG40 4ES.
DOYLE, Mr. Gregory Kevin, MSc BSc ACA *2010;* with PricewaterhouseCoopers LLP, Hays Galleria, 1 Hays Lane, LONDON, SE1 2RD.
DOYLE, Mr. Heikki Michael, BA ACA *2007;* 21 Knight Close, CHIPPENHAM, SN15 3FL.
DOYLE, Mr. John Edward David, BSc ACA *1991;* 8 Chesterholm, Bancroft, MILTON KEYNES, MK13 0PG.
DOYLE, Mr. John Oliver, ACA *2009;* Flat 7, 4 Carminia Road, LONDON, SW17 8AW.
DOYLE, Mr. Joseph Anthony, BSc ACA *1983;* 192 Walton Road, SALE, M33 4FG.
DOYLE, Mr. Kevan-Peter, BSc FCA CF *1995;* 34 Park Road, TWICKENHAM, TW1 2PX.
DOYLE, Mr. Kevin John Martin, FCA *1973;* 23 Coalecroft Road, Putney, LONDON, SW15 6LW.
DOYLE, Miss. Laura Ruth, BSc(Hons) ACA *2002;* Inchcape Plc, 22a St James Square, LONDON, SW1Y 5LP.
DOYLE, Mrs. Lisa Jayne, ACA *1993;* High Wyck, Sleepers Hill, WINCHESTER, HAMPSHIRE, SO22 4NB.
DOYLE, Mrs. Lorraine Carol, BSc ACA *1992;* Elsley Lodge, 17 Elsley Road, Tilehurst, READING, RG31 6RP.
DOYLE, Mrs. Maria Bernadette, BSc ACA *1998;* Killanena, CAHER, COUNTY CLARE, IRELAND.
DOYLE, Mr. Mark Christopher, BA ACA *1979;* 66 Thames Side, STAINES, MIDDLESEX, TW18 2HF.
DOYLE, Mr. Martin Patrick, BA FCA *1973;* 10 Onslow Way, Pyrford, WOKING, SURREY, GU22 8QX.
DOYLE, Mr. Michael William George, FCA *1972;* Belsey Gate Farmhouse, Soulby, KIRKBY STEPHEN, CUMBRIA, CA17 4PL.
•DOYLE, Mr. Patrick James, ACA *1979;* Doyle & Co, 7 The Courtyard, Gaulby Lane, Stoughton, LEICESTER, LE2 2FL.
•DOYLE, Mr. Patrick Joseph, FCA *1971;* P.J. Doyle & Co., 45 Heather Drive, Rednal, BIRMINGHAM, B45 9RA.
DOYLE, Mr. Paul, BSc ACA *1990;* The Ashford & St. Peters Hospitals N H S Trust, Guildford Road, CHERTSEY, KT16 0PZ.
DOYLE, Mr. Paul, BA(Hons) ACA *2010;* Flat 4, 27 Demesne Road, Douglas, ISLE OF MAN, IM1 3DZ.
•DOYLE, Mr. Peter, BSc ACA *1993;* Nortons Group, Highlands House, Basingstoke Road, Spencers Wood, READING, RG7 1NT. See also Nortons Recovery Limited, Nortons Group LLP
DOYLE, Mr. Peter Anthony, FCA CTA *1963;* Heathcrest, 28 Oldfield Way, Heswall, WIRRAL, CH60 6RH.
•DOYLE, Mr. Peter Edward, FCA *1965;* (Tax Fac), Peter E. Doyle, 18 Borrowbydale Avenue, KNARESBOROUGH, NORTH YORKSHIRE, HG5 0NF.
DOYLE, Mr. Peter Lawrence, MA FCA *1979;* Grosvenor, 70 Grosvenor Street, LONDON, W1K 3JP.
DOYLE, Mr. Philip John, MA FCA *1975;* 64 Woodcote Hurst, EPSOM, KT18 7DT. (Life Member)
DOYLE, Mrs. Rachel Elizabeth, BSc(Hons) ACA *2002;* 22 Post Hill, TIVERTON, DEVON, EX16 4ND.
•DOYLE, Mr. Richard Howard, FCA CTA *1992;* (Tax Fac), Auker Rhodes Professional Services LLP, Sapphire House, Albion Road, Greengates, BRADFORD, WEST YORKSHIRE BD10 9TQ. See also Auker Rhodes Tax & Financial Planning Ltd
DOYLE, Mr. Robert Alexander, BA ACA *1998;* 2 Antoinette Close, WARRAWEE, NSW 2074, AUSTRALIA.
DOYLE, Mrs. Samantha Jane, BA ACA *1995;* 24a Portsmouth Road, CAMBERLEY, SURREY, GU15 1JX.
DOYLE, Miss. Sarah, ACA *2010;* 20 Carrs Lane, Cudworth, BARNSLEY, SOUTH YORKSHIRE, S72 8EJ.
DOYLE, Mr. Stephen Conor, BA ACA *1997;* Unit 4, 806 3rd Street, CANMORE T1W 2J7, AB, CANADA.
DOYLE, Mr. Stephen Patrick, ACA *1982;* 30 Tydraw Road, Penylan, CARDIFF, CF23 5HB.
•DOYLE, Mr. Terence Anthony, BA FCA *1978;* Clive Owen & Co LLP, Oak Tree House, Harwood Road, Northminster Business Park, Upper Poppleton, YORK YO26 6QU.
DOYLE, Mr. Thomas Edward, FCA *1959;* 24 Grange Park Drive, Cottingley, BINGLEY, WEST YORKSHIRE, BD16 1NR. (Life Member)
•DOYLE, Mrs. Valerie Patricia, FCA *1999;* Riley, 51 North Hill, PLYMOUTH, PL4 8HZ.
DOYLE-LINDEN, Miss. Sally Margaret, BA ACA *1985;* Guildables Place, Guildables Lane, EDENBRIDGE, KENT, TN8 6QU.
DRABBLE, Mr. David Anthony, BA ACA *2003;* Aimia Foods Ltd, Penny Lane, Haydock, ST. HELENS, MERSEYSIDE, WA11 0QZ.
DRABBLE, Mr. David Robert, BA FCA *1973;* 10-11 Sampford Brett, TAUNTON, SOMERSET, TA4 4JU.
DRABBLE, Mr. Michael John, FCA *1975;* Halldale Hallmoor Road, Darley Dale, MATLOCK, DE4 2HF.
•DRABBLE, Mr. Peter, ACA *1979;* Drabble & Co, 1 Wellington Road, Bollington, MACCLESFIELD, SK10 5JR.
DRABBLE, Mr. Thomas Peter Kentigern, BA ACA *1981;* Hedgeways, Aldenham Grove, RADLETT, WD7 7BN.
DRACE-FRANCIS, Mrs. Emma Jane Loughlin, BSc FCA *1999;* 22 Werter Road, Putney, LONDON, SW15 2LJ.
DRACE-FRANCIS, Mr. James, BA FCA *1997;* 22 Werter Road, Putney, LONDON, SW15 2LJ.
DRACOPOLI, Mr. Andrew John, BA FCA *1972;* Worrell Investment Co., P.O. Box 5386, CHARLOTTESVILLE, VA 22905, UNITED STATES.
DRACUP, Mr. Andrew John, BA ACA *1992;* 10 Woodview Close, Horsforth, LEEDS, LS18 5TA.
DRAFFAN, Mr. Michael, BSc ACA *1993;* (Tax Fac), 12 Redcliffe Road, TORQUAY, TQ1 4QG.
DRAFFIN, Mr. Michael Alexander Francis, BSc FCA *1976;* 1 Spinney Court, Burleigh, STROUD, GL5 2PY.
DRAGATSIS, Mr. Nicholas, MEng ACA *2008;* 3 Alamanas, Flat 201, Engomi, 2415 NICOSIA, CYPRUS.
•DRAGE, Mr. Colin John Fleming, FCA *1971;* (Tax Fac), Drage & Co., 62 The Rise, SEVENOAKS, TN13 1RN.
DRAGE, Mr. Geoffrey Nicholas, BSc FCA *1971;* Ashleigh House, Snowdenham Links Road, Bramley, GUILDFORD, GU5 0BX.
DRAGICEVIC, Mr. Michael Miodrag, BSc FCA *1982;* 31 Royd Croft, Quarmby, HUDDERSFIELD, HD3 4EQ.
DRAGONETTI, Mr. Peter Hugh, ACA *1979;* Covert Cottage, Hill Bottom, Whitchurch Hill, READING, RG8 7PT.
DRAIN, Mr. Antony Peter, BSc ACA *1986;* 10 Forest View, LONDON, E4 7AY.
•DRAIN, Mr. David Charles, FCA *1979;* Edmund Carr LLP, 146 New London Road, CHELMSFORD, CM2 0AW. See also EC (Management Services) Ltd
DRAIN, Mr. Peter John, ACA *1981;* 83 Galleywood Road, Great Baddow, CHELMSFORD, CM2 8DN.
•DRAINEY, Mr. Francis Gerard, FCA *1983;* DHF Accounting Limited, 20 Market Street, ALTRINCHAM, CHESHIRE, WA14 1PF.
•DRAINEY, Mrs. Helen Caroline, BA ACA *1986;* DHF Accounting Limited, 20 Market Street, ALTRINCHAM, CHESHIRE, WA14 1PF.
DRAISEY, Mrs. Catherine Jane, BA ACA *1999;* 39 Links Drive, SOLIHULL, B91 2DJ.
DRAISEY, Mr. Mark Stewart, BCom ACA MBA CPA *1993;* 22 Oakfield Road, Selly Park, BIRMINGHAM, B29 7EJ.
DRAKE, Miss. Angela Denise, BSc ACA *2005;* Apartment 119 City South 39 City Road East, MANCHESTER, M15 4QE.
•DRAKE, Mr. Brian, FCA *1979;* Brian Drake & Co, The Counting House, Forest Road, New Ollerton, NEWARK, NG22 9QS.
DRAKE, Mr. Christopher, FCA *1973;* 4 Chapel Fold, Lower Wyke, BRADFORD, BD12 9AE.
DRAKE, Mr. Daniel, BSc ACA *2011;* 20 Doudney Court, Bedminster, BRISTOL, BS3 4AP.
DRAKE, Mr. David Anthony, BSc FCA *1988;* P O Box 2162, GRACEVILLE, QLD 4075, AUSTRALIA.
DRAKE, Mr. David Keith, FCA *1955;* 15 Eaton Court, Boxgrove Avenue, GUILDFORD, GU1 1XD. (Life Member)
DRAKE, Mr. Edward Ewan Hall, FCA *1965;* Blue Moon Promotions Ltd, Unit 8A, Pool Street Ind Est, Pool Street, MACCLESFIELD, CHESHIRE SK11 7NX.
DRAKE, Miss. Emma, ACA *2008;* Grant Thornton UK Llp, 300 Pavilion Drive, NORTHAMPTON, NN4 7YE.
DRAKE, Mr. Francis Desmond, MA FCA *1979;* Higher Luson Farm Luson, Yealmpton, PLYMOUTH, PL8 2JD. (Life Member)
DRAKE, Mr. Francis Ian, FCA *1973;* Heathfield, Lindon Avenue Off Town Lane, Denton, MANCHESTER, M34 2BU.
DRAKE, Mr. Gordon Alexander Miles, BSc ACA *1996;* Kingdom Hotel Investments, Dubai International Financial Centre, PO Box 121223, DUBAI, UNITED ARAB EMIRATES.
DRAKE, Mr. Graham Andrew, BSc ACA *1992;* Rygor Group Ltd., The Broadway West Wilts Trading Estate, WESTBURY, BA13 4JX.
DRAKE, Mr. Hugh Charles, MA FCA *1972;* Scremby Manor, Scremby, SPILSBY, PE23 5RP.
DRAKE, Ms. Janice, BCom FCA *1985;* 3 Old Eagley Mews, BOLTON, BL1 7HR.
•DRAKE, Mr. John Albert, FCA *1965;* J.A. Drake, 51 High Street, Cheveley, NEWMARKET, Suffolk, CB8 9DQ.
DRAKE, Mr. John Alwyn, BA FCA *1986;* 28 Bewdley Close, HARPENDEN, AL5 1QX.
DRAKE, Mr. Jonathan Martin, BA ACA *1999;* Taylor Wimpey Plc, 80 New Bond Street, LONDON, W1S 1SB.
DRAKE, Mr. Jonathan Paul, ACA *2008;* 5 Badger Close, KNEBWORTH, HERTFORDSHIRE, SG3 6NA.
DRAKE, Mr. Jonathan Paul, BA ACA *1997;* C/- Genesis Trust & Corporate Services Ltd, 2nd Floor Compass Centre, PO Box 448, GEORGETOWN, GRAND CAYMAN, KY1-1106 CAYMAN ISLANDS.
DRAKE, Mrs. Julie Anne, BSc ACA *1982;* Garden Cottage, Ockham Lane, Hatchford, COBHAM, KT11 1LP. (Life Member)
DRAKE, Miss. Julie Elizabeth, BA FCA *1992;* Treetops, 126 Leeds Road, Oulton, LEEDS, LS26 8JY.
DRAKE, Miss. Juliet Susannah, BSc(Hons) ACA *2010;* 138 Glengall Road, WOODFORD GREEN, ESSEX, IG8 0DS.
DRAKE, Miss. Katherine Mary, BA(Hons) ACA *2001;* 66 Gillmans Road, ORPINGTON, BR5 4LB.
•DRAKE, Mr. Keith Robert, FCA *1976;* (Tax Fac), Drake Fletcher & Co, Sheaf House, 1-3 Sheaf Street, DAVENTRY, NN11 4AA.
DRAKE, Ms. Lucy Janet, BA ACA *1993;* 27 Home Way, Mill End, RICKMANSWORTH, HERTFORDSHIRE, WD3 8QL.
DRAKE, Mr. Martin Francis, FCA *1974;* Connolly Europe Limited, 7 Arlington Court, Whittle Way, Arlington Business Park, STEVENAGE, HERTFORDSHIRE SG1 2FS.
DRAKE, Mr. Michael Brian, BSc ACA *1985;* 7 Tattersall Close, WOKINGHAM, RG40 2LP.
DRAKE, Mr. Oliver, BA ACA *2007;* IRIS WORLDWIDE LTD, 185 Park Street, LONDON, SE1 9DY.
DRAKE, Mr. Paul Anthony, FCA *1975;* Rowlands, 51 Oak Road, Rivenhall End, WITHAM, ESSEX, CM8 3HF.
DRAKE, Mr. Paul Jonathan, BA ACA *1984;* 48 Darlow Drive, STRATFORD-UPON-AVON, CV37 9DG.
DRAKE, Mr. Paul Stephen, BA ACA *2001;* Unit 4, 14 Mount Wyndham Dive, HAMILTON CR 04, BERMUDA.
DRAKE, Mr. Peter James, MA ACA *2000;* Athene House, 66 Shoe Lane, LONDON, EC4A 3BQ.
•DRAKE, Mr. Raymond John, FCA *1976;* (Tax Fac), Drake & Co, Drake House, 80 Guildford Street, CHERTSEY, KT16 9AD. See also Drake.com Limited
DRAKE, Mrs. Rebecca Elizabeth, BA ACA *2002;* Mount Wyndham Unit 4, 14 Mount Wyndham Drive, HAMILTON CR 04, BERMUDA.
DRAKE, Mrs. Rhian Eirlys, BSc ACA *1985;* Berthen Gron, Llanfwrog, RUTHIN, CLWYD, LL15 2AH.
DRAKE, Mr. Richard Charles, ACA *2009;* 19, Byron Road, WEST BRIDGFORD, NOTTINGHAMSHIRE, NG2 6DY.
DRAKE, Miss. Sara, BA(Hons) ACA *2004;* Flat 12 Dene House, 79 Frances Road, WINDSOR, SL4 3FE.
•DRAKE, Mrs. Shirley, BSc ACA *1992;* 80 Guildford Street, CHERTSEY, SURREY, KT16 9AD.
DRAKE, Mr. Stephen, BA ACA *1998;* PricewaterhouseCoopers, Emirates Towers Offices, PO Box 11987, Level 40, Sheikh Zayed Road, PO Box 11987 DUBAI UNITED ARAB EMIRATES.
DRAKE, Mr. Stephen John, FCA *1970;* Valance Manor Lodge, Valance Road, Clavering, SAFFRON WALDEN, CB11 4RS.

DRAKE, Mr. Stuart Jeffrey, ACA *1991;* Bays Farm, Shalford Green, BRAINTREE, ESSEX, CM7 5AZ.
DRAKE, Mrs. Susan, BSc ACA *1999;* 10 Chaucer Close, STRATFORD-UPON-AVON, WARWICKSHIRE, CV37 7PQ.
•**DRAKE, Mr. Timothy William, BSc FCA** *1981;* Tim Drake, Garden Cottage Ockham Lane, Hatchford, COBHAM, KT11 1LP.
DRAKE, Mrs. Tracy Ann, BSocSc ACA *1996;* 11 Homewood Cottages, Tanyard Hill, Shorne, GRAVESEND, KENT, DA12 3LE.
DRAKE-BROCKMAN, Mrs. Linda Margaret, FCA *1972;* 59 Sunnyside, Culloden Moor, INVERNESS, IV2 5ES.
DRAKEFORD, Mr. Andrew Jefferson, FCA *1971;* 2 Weston House, Ballfield Road, GODALMING, GU7 2HB.
DRAKEFORD, Mr. Simon John, BA ACA *1989;* House 29, Lane 1400 Beijing Xi Lu, Jingan District, SHANGHAI 200040, CHINA.
DRAKEFORD-LEWIS, Mr. Nigel Vincent, BA FCA *1986;* 5 Sonning Gate, Pound Lane, Sonning, READING, RG4 6GQ.
DRAKEFORD-LEWIS, Mrs. Suzanne Marie, BSc ACA *1991;* 5 Sonning Gate, Pound Lane, Sonning, READING, RG4 6GQ.
DRAKESMITH, Mrs. Deborah Rheims, BA ACA *1990;* 1 Baskerville Road, LONDON, SW18 3RJ.
DRAKESMITH, Mr. Nicholas Timon, BSc FCA *1990;* 1 Baskerville Road, LONDON, SW18 3RJ.
DRAKOS, Miss. Elena Eva, ACA *2011;* Flat 25 Eyre Court, 3-21 Finchley Road, LONDON, NW8 9TT.
DRAKOS, Mr. Frixos Loizou, FCA *1968;* Andrea Zakoy No 7, Strovolos, 2059 NICOSIA, CYPRUS. (Life Member)
DRAKOS, Mr. Markos, BSc FCA *1985;* 66 Acropolis Avenue, PO Box 27233, CY 2012 STROVOLOS, CYPRUS.
DRAKOU-GEORGHIOU, Ms. Marina, BSc ACA *1991;* 32 Alekou Constantinou Str.(Flat 301), DasoupolisStrovolos, 2024 NICOSIA, CYPRUS.
•**DRANSFIELD, Mr. Anthony James, BSc FCA** *1983;* (Tax Fac), Cripps Dransfield, 206 Upper Richmond Road West, LONDON, SW14 8AH.
DRANSFIELD, Mrs. Philippa Louise, BA FCA *1989;* 31 Church Lane, Wicklewood, WYMONDHAM, NORFOLK, NR18 9QH.
DRAPE, Miss. Fiona, BA FCA ACA *1991;* 1 Fishermans Cottages, Route de la Lague, St. Pierre Du Bois, GUERNSEY, GY7 9BU.
DRAPE, Mr. John Spencer, FCA *1958;* 8 Ash Grove, off York Road, ALTRINCHAM, WA14 3EG. (Life Member)
DRAPE, Mr. Nicholas Mark, ACA *2008;* Apartment 94 The Albany, 8 Old Hall Street, LIVERPOOL, L3 9EL.
DRAPER, Mrs. Abigail Sarah, BSc ACA *1996;* 265 Chester Road, Helsby, FRODSHAM, WA6 0PN.
•**DRAPER, Mr. Alan Richard, FCA** *1980;* 19 Velator Close, BRAUNTON, EX33 2DT.
DRAPER, Miss. Alison, BA ACA *2010;* 59 Elmswood Road, LIVERPOOL, L17 0DH.
DRAPER, Miss. Angela Julia, BCom ACA *2004;* 4/98 Dodds Street, SOUTHBANK, VIC 3006, AUSTRALIA.
•**DRAPER, Mrs. Anna Heather, MBA BA(Hons) ACA** *2002;* BDO LLP, Emerald House, East Street, EPSOM, SURREY, KT17 1HS. See also BDO Stoy Hayward LLP
•**DRAPER, Mr. Barry William, BSc FCA** *1983;* Forensic Accounting Services, 1st Floor Aztec Centre, Aztec West, Almondsbury, BRISTOL, BS32 4TD.
DRAPER, Mr. Bryan Patrick, BA ACA *1981;* PO BOX 341077, DUBAI, UNITED ARAB EMIRATES.
DRAPER, Mr. Christopher Neil, BSc ACA *1990;* c/- CMC, PO Box 1570, EAGLE FARM, QLD 4009, AUSTRALIA.
•**DRAPER, Mr. Derek George, FCA** *1958;* (Tax Fac), Derek Draper, The Glen, Adsett, WESTBURY-ON-SEVERN, GL14 1PH.
DRAPER, Miss. Eunice Julia, ACA *2008;* Harpswell, Elm Road, Horsell, WOKING, SURREY, GU21 4DY.
DRAPER, Mrs. Helen, MMath(Hons) ACA *2010;* with Pearson May, 37 Great Pulteney Street, BATH, BA2 4DA.
DRAPER, Mr. James, BA ACA *1999;* 2416 Blackstone Drive, WALNUT CREEK, CA 94598, UNITED STATES.
DRAPER, Mr. Jeffrey Thomas, BSc ACA *1989;* 2 Howick Park Avenue, Penwortham, PRESTON, PR1 0LS.
•**DRAPER, Mr. Jeremy Paul, FCA** *1983;* (Tax Fac), J D 2000 Ltd, Glan-yr-Afon, Clocaenog, RUTHIN, LL15 2BB.
DRAPER, Mr. John Anthony, FCA *1972;* 7 Bankside, Hale Barns, ALTRINCHAM, WA15 0SP.
•**DRAPER, Mr. John Edward, MA BSc(Hons) ACA** *1998;* J E Draper, 15 Main Street, Addingham, ILKLEY, WEST YORKSHIRE, LS29 0PD.
DRAPER, Mrs. Karen, BA ACA *1999;* 2416 Blackstone Drive, WALNUT CREEK, CA 94598, UNITED STATES.
DRAPER, Miss. Maxine Moss, BA ACA *2005;* 3 Westergate Road, LONDON, SE2 0DR.
DRAPER, Mr. Michael William, FCA *1953;* Flat 25, Clift House, Langley Road, CHIPPENHAM, WILTSHIRE, SN15 1DS. (Life Member)
DRAPER, Mr. Neil, BSc ACA *1982;* Clearview, Northend Lane, LIVERPOOL, L26 5QB.
•**DRAPER, Mr. Paul, BSc ACA** *1991;* Clarke Nicklin LLP, Clarke Nicklin House, Brooks Drive, Cheadle Royal Business Park, CHEADLE, CHESHIRE SK8 3TD.
•**DRAPER, Mr. Richard Alfred, FCA** *1977;* Noble Accountancy Services, Unit 4, Denby Dale Industrial Park, Wakefield Road, Denby Dale, HUDDERSFIELD HD8 8QH.
DRAPER, Mr. Roderick John, FCA *1957;* P.O. Box 267, WESTVILLE, KWAZULU NATAL, 3630, SOUTH AFRICA. (Life Member)
•**DRAPER, Mrs. Wendy Julia, BSc FCA** *1987;* JAD Audit Ltd, 4 Bloors Lane, Rainham, GILLINGHAM, KENT, ME8 7EG. See also JAD Associates Ltd
DRASAR, Mr. Francis, MA FCA *1979;* Lime Tree Cottage, Orleton, Stanford Bridge, WORCESTER, WR6 6SX.
DRASTIK, Mr. Thomas Veit, BA ACA *2002;* Koeniginstrasse 37, 80539 MUENCHEN, GERMANY.
DRASUTIS, Miss. Sarah Marion, BA ACA *2005;* 6 Spinners Drive, Sutton, ST. HELENS, MERSEYSIDE, WA9 3GF.
DRAVERS, Mr. Peter Barry, FCA *1968;* Seymour Pierce Limited, 20 Old Bailey, LONDON, EC4M 7EN.
DRAWBRIDGE, Mrs. Susan Mary, BSc ACA *1996;* 25 Maes y Llan, CONWY, GWYNEDD, LL32 8NB.
DRAXLBAUER, Miss. Katharine, BSc ACA *2010;* Flat 29, Lloyd Square, 16 Niall Close, BIRMINGHAM, B15 3LX.
•**DRAY, Mr. Adrian Clive, BSc FCA** *1991;* KPMG LLP, Arlington Business Park, Theale, READING, RG7 4SD. See also KPMG Europe LLP
DRAY, Mr. Andrew James, BA ACA *2010;* 20 St. Stephens Hill, CANTERBURY, KENT, CT2 7AX.
DRAY, Mr. Simon John, BSc FCA *1995;* 24 Benford Road, HODDESDON, HERTFORDSHIRE, EN11 8LL.
DRAYCOTT, Mr. Jack Iain, BSc ACA *2007;* with BDO LLP, Kings Wharf, 20-30 Kings Road, READING, RG1 3EX.
•**DRAYCOTT, Mr. Roger Mansfield, FCA** *1966;* Draycott & Kirk, Cleveland House, 92 Westgate, GUISBOROUGH, CLEVELAND, TS14 6AP.
DRAYSEY, Mrs. Zelda Alison, BEng ACA *2004;* Fleets Cottage, Pound Lane, Burley, BOURNEMOUTH, HAMPSHIRE BH24 4ED.
DRAYTON, Miss. Amy Clare, BSc ACA *2007;* with Grant Thornton UK LLP, 30 Finsbury Square, LONDON, EC2P 2YU.
DRAYTON, Mr. Daniel Edward, ACA *1987;* Anritsu Ltd, 200 Capability Green, LUTON, LU1 3LU.
DRAYTON, Mr. Robin Michael, FCA *1971;* Church Farm, Hawstead, BURY ST. EDMUNDS, SUFFOLK, IP29 5NT.
DRAZIN, Ms. Susannah Clare, BSc ACA *2005;* National Audit Office, 157-197 Buckingham Palace Road, LONDON, SW1W 9SP.
DREAN, Mr. Richard Trevor, BA ACA *1982;* 36 Grange Road, Elstree, BOREHAMWOOD, WD6 3LY.
DREESE, Miss. Sarah, BA ACA *2011;* (Tax Fac), 56 Tuscany Gardens, CRAWLEY, WEST SUSSEX, RH10 8EX.
DREEZER, Mr. Stephen, FCA *1966;* 51 Dell Park Avenue, TORONTO M6B 2T7, ON, CANADA.
DRENDA, Mr. Krzysztof Jacek, ACA *2009;* 98 Blenheim Gardens, LONDON, NW2 4NT.
•**DRENNAN, Mr. Andrew Cawthorne, BCom FCA** *1972;* A C Drennan, 73 Ashgate Avenue, CHESTERFIELD, DERBYSHIRE, S40 1JD. See also Scarsdale Trust Limited
DRENNAN, Miss. Catriona Hall, BSc ACA *1986;* North House, Wheldrake Lane, Crockey Hill, YORK, YO19 4SQ.
DRENNAN, Mr. Gary Paul, BA FCA *1997;* with BDO Seidman LLP, 233 North Michigan Avenue, CHICAGO, IL 60601, UNITED STATES.
•**DRENNAN, Mr. Richard Gordon, BSc FCA** *1972;* (Tax Fac), Drennan & Co, 64 Belsize Park, LONDON, NW3 4EH. See also Drennan Management Services Limited
DRENNAN, Mr. Richard Gregory, ACA *1988;* PO box HM 1475, HAMILTON HMFX, BERMUDA.
•**DRENNAN, Mr. Robert, FCA CF** *1976;* with Rawlinson & Hunter, Eighth Floor, 6 New Street Square, New Fetter Lane, LONDON, EC4A 3AQ.
DRENNEN, Mr. Peter Reginald Mayhew, FCA *1967;* 13 Edinburgh Gardens, WINDSOR, SL4 2AN. (Life Member)
DREON, Mr. Gary Robert, MSc ACA *1999;* 37 Edgecote Drive, Newhall, SWADLINCOTE, DE11 0LD.
DRESNER, Mr. William Johnathan, BSc ACA *2000;* 174 Ember Lane, EAST MOLESEY, KT8 0BS.
DRESSLER, Mr. Michel David Jacques, FCA *1967;* Casa Fortuna, Apartado 1219, 8401-910 CARVOEIRO, PORTUGAL.
DREVER, Mr. Norman Thomas, BA ACA *1984;* 13 Northumberland Street, EDINBURGH, EH3 6LL.
DREVER, Mrs. Peng Geik, ACA *1984;* 13 Northumberland Street, EDINBURGH, EH3 6LL.
DREW, Mr. Alastair, ACA *2010;* 10 The Shrublands, West Pottergate, NORWICH, NR2 4BS.
DREW, Miss. Alice, BSc ACA *2006;* with BDO LLP, 55 Baker Street, LONDON, W1U 7EU.
DREW, Miss. Anna Lee, ACA *2009;* The Larches, Chalkpit Lane, MARLOW, BUCKINGHAMSHIRE, SL7 2PN.
DREW, Miss. Anna Marian, BA ACA *1979;* (Tax Fac), 2 Branstone Road, Kew Gardens, RICHMOND, TW9 3LB.
DREW, Mr. Anthony Powell, FCA *1975;* Barton Products Ltd, Barton Road, Long Eaton, NOTTINGHAM, NG10 2FN.
DREW, Mr. Barry Gordon, FCA *1955;* Greenmantle, 18 Highland Way, KNUTSFORD, WA16 9AN. (Life Member)
•**DREW, Mr. Barry John, FCA** *1972;* (Tax Fac), Kitchen & Brown, Alpha House, 40 Coinagehall Street, HELSTON, TR13 8EQ.
DREW, Mr. Christopher Alexander, BSc ACA *2007;* with PricewaterhouseCoopers LLP, 1 Embankment Place, LONDON, WC2N 6RH.
DREW, Mr. Christopher John, BA FCA *1985;* 34 Waverley Lane, FARNHAM, SURREY, GU9 8BJ.
•**DREW, Mr. Clayton Peter, FCA** *1975;* 11 Bassett Crescent East, Bassett, SOUTHAMPTON, SO16 7PF.
DREW, Miss. Clementine, BSc(Hons) ACA *2010;* 11 Bassett Crescent East, SOUTHAMPTON, SO16 7PF.
DREW, Mr. Dan Hamilton, FCA *1962;* Lower Poswick, Whitbourne, WORCESTER, WR6 5SS.
DREW, Mr. David Ronald, BA ACA *1987;* Allianz Insurance plc, 57 Ladymead, GUILDFORD, GU1 1DB.
DREW, Mr. Edmond Robert, BA ACA *1990;* 46 Highfields, South Cave, BROUGH, HU15 2AJ.
DREW, Mr. Edward Nicholas, BA FCA *1975;* The Lodge, Barton Turf, NORWICH, NR12 8AS.
DREW, Mr. Gerald Charles, FCA *1961;* Duxhurst Place, Duxhurst Lane, REIGATE, RH2 8QQ.
•**DREW, Mrs. Helen Catherine, BA FCA** *1987;* Crowe Clark Whitehill LLP, Black Country House, Rounds Green Road, OLDBURY, WEST MIDLANDS, B69 2DG. See also Horwath Clark Whitehill LLP and Crowe Clark Whitehill
DREW, Mr. Ian Robert, MA ACA *1992;* 135 Fawe Park Road, LONDON, SW15 2EG.
DREW, Mr. John, FCA *1969;* Vue Desvert, Gorey Village Main Road, Grouville, JERSEY, JE3 9EP. (Life Member)
DREW, Mr. John Anthony, FCA *1965;* 4 Willis Court, Shipton-under-Wychwood, CHIPPING NORTON, OX7 6NS.
DREW, Mr. John Dickin, FCA *1965;* 4 Platte Saline, Alderney, GUERNSEY, GY9 3YA. (Life Member)
DREW, Mr. John Farley, BA FCA *1960;* Mutters Moor, 15 Hare Hill Close, Pyrford, WOKING, GU22 8UH. (Life Member)
DREW, Mr. Jonathan Gordon, BA FCA *1980;* Hillocks Farm, Whalley Old Road, Billington, CLITHEROE, LANCASHIRE, BB7 9JE.
DREW, Mr. Jonathan Robert, MA ACA *1990;* HSBC, Level 15, 1 Queens Road, CENTRAL, HONG KONG SAR.
•**DREW, Miss. Julie Amanda, BA FCA CTA** *1989;* (Tax Fac), Leslie Ward & Drew, Kingston House, Pierrepont Street, BATH, BA1 1LA.
DREW, Mrs. Katherine Anne, LLB ACA *1994;* The Vicarage, Church Lane, Marshfield, CHIPPENHAM, SN14 8NT.
DREW, Mr. Martin Stuart, BSc ACA *2005;* 69 Woodstock Road, WITNEY, OXFORDSHIRE, OX28 1EB.
DREW, Mr. Michael Philip, ACA *1994;* Gravelly House, 54 King Street, TRING, HP23 6BJ.
DREW, Mr. Patrick Keith, FCA *1959;* (Tax Fac), Cosawes Barton, Ponsanooth, TRURO, CORNWALL, TR3 7EJ.
DREW, Mr. Philip Charles, MBA BA FCA *1987;* 7 Earls Road, TUNBRIDGE WELLS, TN4 8EE.
DREW, Miss. Rachel Bryony, BSc ACA *2010;* West Trees, Mildenhall, MARLBOROUGH, SN8 2LP.
DREW, Mr. Raymond William Jeffery, FCA *1967;* 11 West Avenue, PINNER, HA5 5BZ.
DREW, Miss. Rebecca Kate, ACA *2008;* Deloitte & Touche, 4 Brindley Place, BIRMINGHAM, B1 2HZ.
DREW, Mr. Richard John, MA FCA FIMC *1978;* Bank House, 12 Calverley Park, TUNBRIDGE WELLS, TN1 2SH.
DREW, Mr. Richard Kenneth, ACA *2009;* Trafigura Beheer BV, Gustav MahlerPlein 102, Ito Tower, 1082 MA AMSTERDAM, NETHERLANDS.
DREW, Mr. Robin Patrick Barry, FCA *1979;* 17 Petrel Croft, BASINGSTOKE, RG22 5JY.
DREW, Mr. Spencer Tony, BSc ACA *2001;* 73 The Maltings, Pentwyn, CARDIFF, CF23 8EQ.
•**DREW, Mr. Stephen David, FCA** *1992;* Smith & Williamson Ltd, 25 Moorgate, LONDON, EC2R 6AY. See also Nexia Audit Limited
DREW, Mr. Stephen Peter, MA ACA *1980;* 2 The Finches, Highfield, SOUTHAMPTON, SO17 1UB.
DREW, Mr. Timothy, BSc ACA *1994;* 38 Redhill Drive, BRIGHTON, BN1 5FH.
•**DREW, Mr. Timothy Allen, BA ACA** *1984;* PKF (UK) LLP, Farringdon Place, 20 Farringdon Road, LONDON, EC1M 3AP.
DREW-BURRAGE, Mrs. Yvonne, BSc ACA *1992;* Garden Cottage, Tilford Road, HINDHEAD, SURREY, GU26 6QY.
DREWE, Mr. Christopher Robert, ACA *2008;* 3 The Meadows, WALSALL, WS9 0LB.
DREWE, Mrs. Linda Frances, FCA *1968;* 26 Aldeburgh Way, CHELMSFORD, CM1 7PD.
DREWELL, Mr. Alan, FCA *1962;* 5 Croft Bridge, Oulton, LEEDS, LS26 8LB.
•**DREWERY, Mr. Gary, BA ACA** *1987;* (Tax Fac), Gary Drewery, 27 Canewdon Road, WESTCLIFF-ON-SEA, ESSEX, SS0 7NE.
•**DREWETT, Mr. David Alexander Robertson, BSc ACA** *1978;* PKF (Isle of Man) LLC, PO Box 16, Analyst House, Douglas, ISLE OF MAN, IM99 1AP. See also Northwest Trust Company Limited
DREWETT, Mr. Heath Stewart, MA ACA *1993;* Our House, 30 Windsor Road, GERRARDS CROSS, BUCKINGHAMSHIRE, SL9 7NE.
DREWETT, Miss. Muriel Jean, FCA *1949;* 53 Ancastle Green, HENLEY-ON-THAMES, RG9 1TS. (Life Member)
DREWIENKA, Mr. David, ACA CA(SA) *2008;* 3 Trinity Avenue, LONDON, N2 0LX.
DREWITT, Miss. Catherine Mary Blair, ACA *1981;* Woodyard Cottage, Vicarage Lane, Podington, WELLINGBOROUGH, BEDFORDSHIRE, NN29 7HR.
DREWITT, Mr. Lionel Frank, BSc FCA *1962;* 9 Courtenay Place, LYMINGTON, SO41 3NQ.
DREWITT, Ms. Susan, BSc ACA *1987;* 99 Lansdowne Road, LONDON, W11 2LE.
DREWS, Mr. John Sears, FCA *1966;* 75 Ladbrooke Drive, POTTERS BAR, HERTFORDSHIRE, EN6 1QW. (Life Member)
•**DREXLER, Mr. Victor Robert, BCom FCA** *1969;* Littlestone Martin Glenton, 73 Wimpole Street, LONDON, W1G 8AZ.
DREYFUS, Mrs. Joanne Helen Louise, BSc ACA *2000;* 40 Boulevard du Général Gallieni, 94360 BRY SUR MARNE, FRANCE.
DRIBBELL, Mr. Geoffrey Leigh Daniel, BSc FCA *1978;* 53 Tycehurst Hill, LOUGHTON, ESSEX, IG10 1BZ.
•**DRIFFIELD, Mr. Alan Edward, FCA** *1978;* (Tax Fac), Driffield & Co, 11 Grenfell Close, Parkgate, NESTON, CH64 6TU.
DRIFFIELD, Mr. Christian Leslie, ACA *2007;* 57 Hill End Crescent, LEEDS, LS12 3PW.
DRILLINGCOURT, Mr. David William, BA ACA *1995;* 29 Regency Park, WIDNES, CHESHIRE, WA8 9PH.
•**DRING, Mr. Colin Richard, FCA** *1970;* 24 Vicarage Drive, East Sheen, LONDON, SW14 8RX.
DRING, Mr. David James, BSc(Hons) ACA *2000;* 4 Echo Barn Lane, Wrecclesham, FARNHAM, SURREY, GU10 4NP.
DRING, Mr. Edmund Roger, FCA *1963;* Garden End, Motts Hill Lane, TADWORTH, SURREY, KT20 5BE. (Life Member)
DRING, Mrs. Lea Jane, MA ACA *1994;* 6124 150 A Street, SURREY V3S 7W9, BC, CANADA.
DRING, Mrs. Susan Mary, LLB ACA *1987;* 1 Ferens Close, DURHAM, DH1 1JX.
DRINKWATER, Mr. Andrew David, ACA FCCA *2008;* with Charcroft Baker, 5 West Court, Enterprise Road, MAIDSTONE, KENT, ME15 6JD.
DRINKWATER, Mr. Andrew Robert, BA ACA *1990;* 1 rue Nicolas Welter, L - 2740 LUXEMBOURG, LUXEMBOURG.
DRINKWATER, Mr. David Neil, BSc ACA *1991;* 60 E 1st Street, Apt 4a, NEW YORK, NY 10003, UNITED STATES.
DRINKWATER, Mrs. Jennifer Susan, BA ACA *1990;* 6c rue de Syren, Alzingen, L5870 LUXEMBOURG, LUXEMBOURG.

DRINKWATER, Miss. Joanna Louise, BSc(Hons) ACA *2011;* 101 Hillaries Road, Erdington, BIRMINGHAM, B23 7QS.
•**DRINKWATER, Mr. Michael John, FCA** *1978;* Spider Associates Limited, 1 Hamlet Way, STRATFORD-UPON-AVON, WARWICKSHIRE, CV37 0AL. See also AIMS - Michael Drinkwater
DRINKWATER, Mr. Neil Anthony, FCA *1986;* flat 4, 14 Old Compton Street, LONDON, W1D 4TH.
DRINKWATER, Ms. Rosemary Ann, BA FCA *1984;* finance office, University of Warwick University House, Kirby Corner Road, COVENTRY, CV4 8UW.
DRINKWATER, Mrs. Sian Carol, BA ACA *1997;* 4 Dan-y-Coed Road, CARDIFF, CF23 6NA.
•**DRISCOLL, Mr. Christopher John, FCA** *1968;* (Tax Fac), C.J. Driscoll, The Old Surgery, 19 Mengham Lane, HAYLING ISLAND, PO11 9JT.
DRISCOLL, Mr. James Daniel, BA ACA *1999;* 130 Brynland Avenue, Bishopston, BRISTOL, BS7 9DY.
DRISCOLL, Mr. James Ronald, FCA *1964;* 232 Buckingham Road, BICESTER, OX26 4EL. (Life Member)
DRISCOLL, Miss. Karen Louise, BA ACA *1992;* 16 Eastdale Close, Kempston, BEDFORD, MK42 8LZ.
DRISCOLL, Mr. Kevin Timothy Eugene, FCA *1967;* 21 St. James Drive, PRESTATYN, CLWYD, LL19 8EJ. (Life Member)
DRISCOLL, Ms. Maureen Elizabeth, FCA *1973;* GPO Box 1923, HOBART, TAS 7000, AUSTRALIA.
DRISCOLL, Dr. Patrick Michael, PhD MA ACA *2010;* 26 York Street, CAMBRIDGE, CB1 2PY.
DRISCOLL, Mr. Philip Stuart, FCA *1980;* Airedale N H S Trust, Airedale General Hospital, Skipton Road, Steeton, KEIGHLEY, WEST YORKSHIRE BD20 6TD.
DRISCOLL, Mr. Stephen Gerard, BSc ACA *1991;* 3 Oakfield Close, Bramhall, STOCKPORT, SK7 1JE.
DRITSAS, Mr. Alexis, BSc(Hons) ACA *2011;* Flat 202, Sergides & Nicodemos Court, 57 Michail Karaoli, Ypsonas, 4184 LIMASSOL, CYPRUS.
DRIVER, Ms. Anne, BEng ACA *1991;* Level 7, 82 Pitt Street, SYDNEY, NSW 2000, AUSTRALIA.
DRIVER, Mrs. Carol Ann, BA ACA *1995;* 3 Gill Beck Close, Baildon, SHIPLEY, WEST YORKSHIRE, BD17 6TJ.
•**DRIVER, Mr. Christopher David Graham, BSc FCA** *1981;* with BDO LLP, Arcadia House, Maritime Walk, Ocean Village, SOUTHAMPTON, SO14 3TL.
DRIVER, Mr. David, FCA *1969;* The Old Vicarage, Little Salkeld, PENRITH, CA10 1NN.
•**DRIVER, Mr. David John Antony, BSc FCA** *1984;* GGDD llp, 2nd Floor, Compton House, 29-33 Church Road, STANMORE, MIDDLESEX HA7 4AR.
DRIVER, Miss. Fiona Louise, BSc ACA *1988;* WDR - Mail Code 2428, Disney Corporation, 3 Queen Caroline Street, LONDON, W6 9PE.
DRIVER, Mr. Iain, BSc(Hons) ACA *2011;* 13 Briardale Road, LIVERPOOL, L18 1DA.
•**DRIVER, Miss. Jacqueline Diane, BSc FCA** *1987;* KPMG LLP, 15 Canada Square, LONDON, E14 5GL. See also KPMG Europe LLP
DRIVER, Mr. John, BCom FCA *1974;* 5 Park Gates Avenue, Cheadle Hulme, CHEADLE, SK8 7DG.
DRIVER, Miss. Lisa Jane, BA(Hons) ACA *2001;* 5 Victoria Road, ILKLEY, WEST YORKSHIRE, LS29 9BA.
•**DRIVER, Mr. Neil Marcel, FCA FCCA** *1988;* Davis Grant LLP, Treviot House, 186-192 High Road, ILFORD, ESSEX, IG1 1LR.
DRIVER, Mr. Paul Robert, BA ACA *2000;* Hogg Robinson Plc Global House, Victoria Street, BASINGSTOKE, HAMPSHIRE, RG21 3BT.
DRIVER, Mr. Philip, BSc ACA *1981;* One Franklin Plaza, P.O. Box 7929, FP 2435, PHILADELPHIA, PA 19101, UNITED STATES.
DRIVER, Mr. Richard Stephen, FCA *1968;* Dibdin, 359 Chambersbury Lane, Leverstock Green, HEMEL HEMPSTEAD, HP3 8LW.
DRIVER, Ms. Tracey Ann, BA ACA CPA *1999;* with KPMG, 10 Shelley Street, SYDNEY, NSW 2000, AUSTRALIA.
DRIZEN, Mr. Lawrence, FCA FCCA *1960;* Suite 3, Third Floor, 1 Duchess Street, LONDON, W1W 6AN. (Life Member)
DRIZEN, Mr. Nicholas Simeon, BA(Econ) ACA CTA *1999;* Willow Cottage, 1a Willow Way, RADLETT, WD7 8DU.
DROBIS, Miss. Lucie, MSc BComm ACA *2010;* Box 510, GEORGE TOWN, GRAND CAYMAN, KY1-1106, CAYMAN ISLANDS.
DROESE, Miss. Nicola, ACA *2011;* 142 Pembroke Street, LONDON, N1 0DP.
DROLE, Mr. Klemen, ACA *2010;* Flat 54 Dorset House, Gloucester Place, LONDON, NW1 5AE.
DROUSHIOTIS, Mr. George, BSc ACA *2006;* Levantas 37, Panthea, 4007 LIMASSOL, CYPRUS.
DROUTSAS, Mr. Constantinos, ACA MBA *2010;* 5B Dimitsanas Str., Maroussi, 15125 ATHENS, GREECE.
DROUVÉ, Mrs. Kathryn Antonia, BCom ACA *2008;* Clarenbachstrasse 6, 50931 COLOGNE, GERMANY.
DROVER, Mr. Richard John, BSc ACA *1992;* Bramley House Hatch Lane, HASLEMERE, WEST SUSSEX, GU27 3LJ.
•**DROWN, Mr. Peter Loring, FCA** *1974;* Beavis Morgan LLP, 82 St. John Street, LONDON, EC1M 4JN.
DROZD, Mr. John Joseph, BSc FCA *1989;* 29 Beacon Road, SUTTON COLDFIELD, WEST MIDLANDS, B73 5ST.
DRRAH, Mr. Abdelmonem, ACA *2008;* 43 Alexandra Road South, MANCHESTER, M16 8GH.
DRUBRA, Mr. Harjeet Singh, BSc ACA *1993;* 39 Ledborough Lane, BEACONSFIELD, BUCKINGHAMSHIRE, HP9 2DB.
DRUCE, Mr. Christopher Edward, MA FCA *1963;* Rose Cottage, Lower End, Salford, CHIPPING NORTON, OX7 5YW. (Life Member)
DRUCE, Mr. Gareth Miles, BSc ACA *1997;* with KPMG, KPMG Crescent, 85 Empire Road, Parktown, JOHANNESBURG, 2193 SOUTH AFRICA.
DRUCE, Miss. Kathryn Louise, MSc ACA *2006;* Apartment 15 Seagrove Court, La Rue de la Corbiere St. Brelade, JERSEY, JE3 8HN.
DRUCE, Mr. Paul, ACA ACMA *2009;* 11 Mead Way, KIDLINGTON, OXFORDSHIRE, OX5 2BJ.
DRUCKMAN, Mr. Darryl Martin, FCA *1977;* 5 Coombe Gardens, LONDON, SW20 0QU.
DRUCKMAN, Mr. Leonard Reginald, ACA CA(SA) *2008;* 23 The Hawthorns, 4 Carew Road, EASTBOURNE, EAST SUSSEX, BN21 2BF. (Life Member)
DRUCKMAN, Mr. Paul Bryan, FCA FBCS CITP *1979;* (President 2004 - 2005) (Member of Council 1997 - 2007), Brackendene, Ditton Grange Drive, SURBITON, KT6 5HG.
DRUDY, Mr. Iain Alexander, BSc(Hons) ACA *2003;* 12 Haverdale Rise, BARNSLEY, SOUTH YORKSHIRE, S75 2AJ.
DRUMMOND, Mr. Andrew Robert, BSc ACA *1992;* 16 West Farm Close, ASHTEAD, KT21 2LJ.
DRUMMOND, Mr. Benjamin Wayne, ACA *2008;* 20 Ings View, Tollerton, YORK, YO61 1PR.
DRUMMOND, Mr. David Nicholas, MA FCA *1978;* 54 Princes Road, Wimbledon, LONDON, SW19 8RB.
•**DRUMMOND, Mr. Hugh Redvers, FCA** *1982;* (Tax Fac), Drummonds, Heritage House, 235 Main Street, GIBRALTAR, GIBRALTAR.
DRUMMOND, Mr. Jamie Andrew Duff, BA ACA *1999;* Flat B, 11 King's Gate, ABERDEEN, AB15 4EL.
DRUMMOND, Mr. John, ACA CA(SA) *2009;* Transportation Claims Limited, Abbey Gardens, Abbey Street, READING, RG1 3BA.
DRUMMOND, Mr. John Humphrey Hugo, BA ACA *1993;* 418 Fulham Palace Road, LONDON, SW6 6HX.
DRUMMOND, Ms. Karen, BSc ACA *2006;* Flat A, 639A Garratt Lane, LONDON, SW18 4SX.
DRUMMOND, Mr. Michael, ACA *1994;* 18 The Elms, Shotley Bridge, CONSETT, COUNTY DURHAM, DH8 0UA.
DRUMMOND, Mr. Peter John Vaughan, MA FCA *1989;* with HMRC, H M Revenue & Customs:, Alexander House, 21 Victoria Avenue, SOUTHEND-ON-SEA, SS99 1AA.
DRUMMOND, Mr. Robert James, BSc ACA *1987;* Flat 8, 20 Russell Gardens, Roseburn, EDINBURGH, EH12 5PP.
DRUMMOND, Mr. Robert Malcolm, MBA LLB FCA *1969;* Inwood Manor Hogs Back, Seale, FARNHAM, GU10 1HE.
DRUMMOND, Mr. Scott, BA BCom ACA *2011;* Flat 2, 65 Windsor Road, Ealing, LONDON, W5 3UJ.
•**DRUMMOND, Mr. Stewart James Albert, FCA** *1976;* KBDR, The Old Tannery, Hensington Road, WOODSTOCK, OXFORDSHIRE, OX20 1JL.
•**DRUMMOND, Mrs. Susan Elaine, ACA** *1983;* S.E.S. Consultancy Limited, 6 Fallowfield, Beyton, BURY ST. EDMUNDS, SUFFOLK, IP30 9BN.
DRUMMOND-MURRAY, Mrs. Beverley Jayne, LLB ACA *1992;* 2131 Wilderness Court, FRISCO, TX 75034, UNITED STATES.
DRURY, Mr. Alan, FCA *1970;* 15 Broomhouse Close, Denby Dale, HUDDERSFIELD, HD8 8UX.
DRURY, Mr. Alan Peter, FCA *1974;* Oak's Reach, 9 Larkspur Close, BISHOP'S STORTFORD, CM23 4LL.
DRURY, Mr. Alan Peter, MA FCA CTA *1977;* with Ernst & Young LLP, Blenheim House, Fountainhall Road, ABERDEEN, AB15 4DT.
DRURY, Miss. Alison Katherine, BSc ACA *2003;* 60 Francis Street, MIRFIELD, WEST YORKSHIRE, WF14 9BB.
DRURY, Ms. Amy, BA ACA *2004;* Apartment 3E, 24 Peck Slip, NEW YORK, NY 10038, UNITED STATES.
DRURY, Mr. Carl Stephen, BA ACA *1991;* 28 Ladbroke Drive, Wamley, SUTTON COLDFIELD, B76 2SD.
DRURY, Mr. David Peter, BA ACA *1983;* 3 Nook Green, Tingley, WAKEFIELD, WF3 1ER.
DRURY, Mr. Edward Martin, BSc FCA *1973;* (Tax Fac), 5 Victoria Close, Calderstones Park, Whalley, CLITHEROE, BB7 9JR.
DRURY, Mrs. Emma, BSc ACA *2006;* (Tax Fac), 4 Rowden Lane, CHIPPENHAM, WILTSHIRE, SN15 2AS.
DRURY, Mr. Graham Roger, FCA *1967;* 3 Gandalf Gardens, Fleet Road Twyning, TEWKESBURY, GLOUCESTERSHIRE, GL20 6DG.
DRURY, Mr. James Aubrey, BA ACA *1995;* Stamford House, 8 Chequers Lane, Grendon, NORTHAMPTON, NN7 1JP.
DRURY, Mr. John Charles, BA FCA *1980;* 27 Hardings Drive, DURSLEY, GL11 4LP.
•**DRURY, Mr. John Joseph, BA ACA CTA** *1986;* (Tax Fac), J J Drury, 65 Wattleton Road, BEACONSFIELD, HP9 1RY.
DRURY, Mr. John Michael, BSc FCA *1972;* Hague House, Old Stone Trough Lane, Kelbrook, COLNE, BB8 6LW.
DRURY, Mr. John Victor, FCA *1959;* 3 Millyford Close, Barton-on-Sea, NEW MILTON, BH25 7SZ. (Life Member)
DRURY, Miss. Kay Elizabeth, BSc ACA *1999;* with KPMG LLP, 100 Temple Street, BRISTOL, BS1 6AG.
DRURY, Mr. Lawrence Robert, MA FCA *1966;* Arden Cottage, Godshill Wood, FORDINGBRIDGE, HAMPSHIRE, SP6 2LR.
DRURY, Mrs. Lynne Marie, BSc ACA *1999;* 11 Roestock Gardens, Colney Heath, ST. ALBANS, HERTFORDSHIRE, AL4 0QJ.
DRURY, Mrs. Margaret Elizabeth, BSc ACA *1988;* Llandaff Diocese BSR, The Court, Coychurch, BRIDGEND, MID GLAMORGAN, CF35 5EH.
DRURY, Mr. Martin Edward, LLB ACA *1994;* Rose Briars, 26 Stonegate, SPALDING, LINCOLNSHIRE, PE11 2PH.
DRURY, Miss. Nicola Lea, LLM ACIB ACA *2002;* 25 Wicksteed House, Green Dragon Lane, BRENTFORD, MIDDLESEX, TW8 0DW.
DRURY, Mr. Philip James, BA FCA *1983;* 6 Springbook Court, Cashmere, BRISBANE, QLD 4500, AUSTRALIA.
•**DRURY, Mr. Sean Michael, BA ACA** *1998;* (Tax Fac), PricewaterhouseCoopers LLP, Pricewaterhousecoopers, 12 Plumtree Court, LONDON, EC4A 4HT. See also PricewaterhouseCoopers
DRURY, Mr. Stuart, BEng ACA CTA *2002;* Boparan Investments, 9 Colmore Row, BIRMINGHAM, B3 2BJ.
DRURY, Mr. Thomas Neville Dru, ACA *2009;* 21 Addison Grove, LONDON, W4 1EP.
DRY, Mr. Gordon, FCA *1961;* The Helm, 18 Littledale, KENDAL, LA9 7SG. (Life Member)
DRYBURGH, Mr. Terence Arnold, FCA *1975; (CA Scotland* Shorts, 6 Fairfield Road, CHESTERFIELD, DERBYSHIRE, S40 4TP.
DRYDEN, Mr. Douglas Cecil, MA FCA *1954;* P.O. Box 191, HARARE, ZIMBABWE. (Life Member)
DRYDEN, Mr. Martyn George, ACA *2008;* 65 Hawkhurst Way, WEST WICKHAM, BR4 9PE.
DRYDEN, Mr. Stephen William, BEng ACA *1993;* Home Farm, Arlescote, BANBURY, OXFORDSHIRE, OX17 1DQ.
DRYE, Mrs. Sarah, DPhil MEng ACA CTA *2003;* 131 chemin du Poizat, 01710 THOIRY, FRANCE.
DRYER, Mr. Christopher, ACA MAAT *2010;* 5 Willow Close, STAFFORD, ST17 0NQ.
DRYLIE, Mr. Ewan Andrew, ACA *2010;* Sterling Insurance Co Ltd, 50 Kings Hill Avenue, WEST MALLING, ME19 4JX.
DRYNAN, Mr. John Peter, FCA *1967;* 42 Elm Grove, Barnham, BOGNOR REGIS, WEST SUSSEX, PO22 0HL.
DRYSCH, Mr. Andrew, BSc ACA *1990;* with Ernst & Young LLP, 1 More London Place, LONDON, SE1 2AF.
DRYSDALE, Mr. Clive Douglas, ACA *1987;* The Hollies, Bath Road, MAIDENHEAD, BERKSHIRE, SL6 4LH.
DRYSDALE, Mr. Ian John, BA FCA *1990;* 15 Valley Gardens, Low Fell, GATESHEAD, NE9 5EB.
DRYSDALE, Mrs. Karen Joan, MA ACA *1995;* 9 Lyndhurst Drive, SEVENOAKS, KENT, TN13 2HD.
•**DRYSDALE, Mr. Malcolm John, MA ACA** *1991;* Deloitte LLP, Athene Place, 66 Shoe Lane, LONDON, EC4A 3BQ. See also Deloitte & Touche LLP
DRYSDALE, Mr. Patrick, BSc ACA *2011;* 4 Lamberts Place, Horsmonden, TONBRIDGE, KENT, TN12 8AG.
DRYSDALE, Mr. Simon Christopher, BSc ACA *1992;* Unit 128 Great Guildford Business Square, 30 Great Guildford Street, LONDON, SE1 0HS.
DSOUZA, Mr. Christopher Anthony, LLB ACA *1987;* Blankstone Sington Limited, Walker House, Exchange Flags, LIVERPOOL, L2 3YL.
DU, Miss. Lun, BA ACA *2009;* Credit Suisse, 1 Cabot Square, Canary Wharf, LONDON, E14 4QJ.
DU, Miss. Pauline, MSc ACA *1991;* Flat H 34th Floor, Block 15 South Horizons, 15 South Horizons Drive, AP LEI CHAU, HONG KONG ISLAND, HONG KONG SAR.
DU BOULAY, Mr. Alan Houssemayne, FCA *1975;* 1 Guston Farm Cottages, Guston Ash, CANTERBURY, CT3 2NH.
DU BRUYN, Mrs. Lucy, MA ACA *2005;* 4 St. Stephens Close, Up Nately, HOOK, HAMPSHIRE, RG27 9PP.
DU CROS, Mr. Ewart Alan, FCA *1954;* 4A Hillside Road, West Kirby, WIRRAL, CH48 8BB. (Life Member)
DU CROS, Mr. Ian Peter, BSc ACA *1986;* 5 The Heights, Brooklands, WEYBRIDGE, SURREY, KT13 0NY.
DU FEU, Miss. Marie Wellman, ACA *1983;* Ifg Fund Administration (Jersey) Ltd, Ifg House, Union Street, St Heliet, JERSEY, JE1 1FG.
DU-GAY, Mr. Christopher, BSc ACA *1986;* 78 York Mansions, Prince of Wales Drive, LONDON, SW11 4BW.
DU MEE, Mr. Pierre Roger De Chasteigner, FCA *1955;* 12 Ridgewood, PO Box 1943, MECC, 4301, SOUTH AFRICA. (Life Member)
DU PLESSIS, Mrs. Annelie, ACA CA(SA) *2008;* 53 Quicks Road, LONDON, SW19 1EY.
DU PLESSIS, Mrs. Celeste Melodie, ACA CA(SA) *2009;* 18 The Sidings, Dunton Green, SEVENOAKS, KENT, TN13 2YD.
DU PLESSIS, Mr. Jacques Willem, ACA CA(SA) *2009;* 10 Scawen Road, LONDON, SE8 5AG.
DU PLESSIS, Mr. Johannes Petrus Cornelius, ACA CA(SA) *2008;* 3900 Bow Valley Square II, 205 - 5th Ave SW, CALGARY T2P 2V7, AB, CANADA.
DU PLESSIS, Mr. Lodewicus Johannes, ACA CA(SA) *2008;* 53 Quicks Road, LONDON, SW19 1EY.
DU PLESSIS, Mr. Pieter Christiaan, ACA CA(SA) *2009;* 74A Lake Side dr, MILLBURN, NJ 07041, UNITED STATES.
DU PRE, Mr. Ian Alastair, FCA *1969;* 84 Palace Gardens Terrace, LONDON, W8 4RS.
DU PREEZ, Mr. Jacques, ACA *2003;* 45 Mill Road, BURGESS HILL, WEST SUSSEX, RH15 8DY.
DU PREEZ, Mrs. Susanna Magdalena, ACA CA(SA) *2009;* 41 Churchfield Road, WALTON-ON-THAMES, SURREY, KT12 2TX.
•**DU PREEZ, Mr. Vivian Rabey, ACA** *2011;* (Tax Fac), Very Useful Solutions Limited, BM 6885, LONDON, WC1N 3XX.
DU-ROSE, Mr. Keith, BSc ACA *1990;* Ecovision, Barley Court, Doughton, TETBURY, GLOUCESTERSHIRE, GL8 8TQ.
DU TOIT, Mr. Charles Sidney, FCA *1956;* 3-2590 Carberry Way, OAKVILLE L6M 5G2, ON, CANADA. (Life Member)
DUA, Mr. Harish, ACA *1982;* C-58 Soami Nagar, NEW DELHI 110 017, INDIA.
DUA, Mr. Ishwer Chander, FCA *1978;* 43746 Mink Meadows Street, SOUTH RIDING, VA 20152-3698, UNITED STATES.
DUA, Mr. Kamal, ACA MBA CPA *1985;* One Battery Park Plaza, Att: Mitchell & Titus LLP, NEW YORK, NY 10004, UNITED STATES.
•**DUA, Mr. Rakesh Kumar, BSc FCA** *1988;* (Tax Fac), Dua & Co Limited, 3 Century Court, Tolpits Lane, WATFORD, WD18 9PU. See also Virtual Back Office Limited and Dua LLP
DUA, Mr. Ravi, FCA *1985;* Integris Estates Ltd, Unit 15D, Oakcroft Road, CHESSINGTON, SURREY, KT9 1RH.
DUA, Mr. Robin, MEng ACA *2006;* 73 Ventnor Drive, LONDON, N20 8BU.
DUANCE, Mr. Thomas, BSc(Hons) ACA *2011;* 17 Crossgate Mews, STOCKPORT, CHESHIRE, SK4 3AP.
DUBASH, Mr. Farokh Adi, FCA *1972;* 24 Holland Gardens, BRENTFORD, MIDDLESEX, TW8 0BE.
DUBASH, Mr. Hormusji Noshir, ACA *1990;* 56 Coronation Road West, 02-04 Astrid Meadows, SINGAPORE 269269, SINGAPORE.

DUBASH, Mr. Merwan, FCA *1971;* 1300 Islington Avenue, # 801, TORONTO M9A 5C4, ON, CANADA.
DUBASH, Mr. Rustom Boman, ACA *1981;* R.B. Dubash & Co, Firuz-Ara, 160 Maharishi Karve Road, Cooperage, MUMBAI 400021, MAHARASHTRA INDIA.
DUBASH, Mr. Sarosh Rustomji, FCA *1975;* 24A Dinshaw Avari Colony, Parsi Gate Mehmoodabad, KARACHI 75500, PAKISTAN.
•DUBB, Mr. Sharn Pal, BA FCA *1994;* Nielsens, 453 Cranbrook Road, ILFORD, ESSEX, IG2 6EW.
DUBBURY, Mr. John Richard, BSc ACA *1981;* 65 Penrhyn Crescent, Beeston, NOTTINGHAM, NG9 5PA.
•DUBELL, Mr. Melvyn, FCA *1976;* Dubell & Co, 16 Hartfield Avenue, Elstree, BOREHAMWOOD, WD6 3JE.
DUBENS, Mr. Timothy Samuel Daiches, FCA *1979;* (Tax Fac), Timothy Dubens, 10 Mermaid Quay, NOOSAVILLE, QLD 4566, AUSTRALIA.
DUBERLEY, Mr. Keith, MBA BA ACA *1992;* Swallow Cottage Church Road, Stoke Fleming, DARTMOUTH, DEVON, TQ6 0PX.
•ⒹDUBEY, Mr. Shagun Sunil, FCA *1989;* 20 North Audley Street, LONDON, W1K 6WE. See also AlixPartners Ltd
DUBINA, Mr. Sergey Nikolayevich, MA ACA *1998;* Man Investments Limited, Sugar Quay Lower Thames Street, LONDON, EC3R 6DU.
•DUBOFF, Mr. Peter Edward, BA FCA *1979;* Duboff & Co, Trafalgar House, Grenville Place, LONDON, NW7 3SA.
•DUBOIS, Mr. James, FCA *1968;* Body Dubois Limited, The Bellbourne, 103 High Street, ESHER, SURREY, KT10 9QE.
DUBOIS, Mrs. Johanna Elizabeth, MA ACA *2001;* (Tax Fac), 40 Parklands, Darras HAll, Ponteland, NEWCASTLE UPON TYNE, NE20 9LL.
DUBOIS, Mr. Martin Henry, FCA *1954;* Flat 1, Sanderstead Heights, 3 Addington Road, SOUTH CROYDON, SURREY, CR2 8RE. (Life Member)
DUBOIS, Mr. Richard, FCA *1966;* 24 bis bd de Chanternerle, 73100 AIX LES BAINS, FRANCE.
DUBOIS, Mr. Stephane, ACA *2010;* 59d Battersea Bridge Road, LONDON, SW11 3AU.
DUCAT, Mr. Stephen Paul, BSc ACA *1990;* 1 Victoria Mews, Earlsfield, LONDON, SW18 3PY.
DUCE, Mrs. Claire Alexandra, BSc FCA *1992;* with PricewaterhouseCoopers, Emirates Towers Offices, PO Box 11987, Level 40, Sheikh Zayed Road, PO Box 11987 DUBAI UNITED ARAB EMIRATES.
DUCE, Mr. Gregory Ian, BA ACA *1983;* Lindisfarne Smethwick Lane, Brereton, SANDBACH, CHESHIRE, CW11 2ST.
DUCE, Mr. Peter Nigel, FCA *1975;* Grange Ventures Ltd, 103 The Chine, Grange Park, Winchmore Hill, LONDON, N21 2EG.
DUCE, Mr. Robert Angus, BA ACA *1994;* PO Box 11987, c/o Claire Duce, PricewaterhouseCoopers, Al Sufouh Tower, Dubai Media City, DUBAI UNITED ARAB EMIRATES.
DUCE, Mrs. Victoria Emily, BSc ACA *1992;* 12 Riverside Road, BURNHAM-ON-CROUCH, CM0 8JY. (Life Member)
DUCHEZEAU, Mr. Fernand Andre, FCA *1952;* Redwood Cottage, Bull Lane, GERRARDS CROSS, SL9 8RF. (Life Member)
•DUCIE, Mr. David Norbert, BSc FCA *1986;* Wrigley Partington, Sterling House, 501 Middleton Road, Chadderton, OLDHAM, OL9 9LY.
DUCK, Mrs. Barbara, FCA *1969;* 4 Somerton Avenue, Wilford, NOTTINGHAM, NG11 7FD.
DUCK, Mr. Christopher John, BSc ACA *2010;* 3 Comfrey Court, CAMBRIDGE, CB1 9YJ.
DUCK, Mr. Derek Edward, FCA *1959;* 20 Nelmes Crescent, HORNCHURCH, RM11 2QB. (Life Member)
DUCK, Miss. Jennifer, ACA *2008;* 48 Broadway, BLYTH, NORTHUMBERLAND, NE24 2PR.
DUCK, Mr. Thomas Joseph, BA ACA *2004;* 13 St Gowan Avenue, CARDIFF, CF14 4JX.
DUCKELS, Miss. Emma Louise, BSc ACA *2003;* 4 Burtons Gardens, Old Basing, BASINGSTOKE, HAMPSHIRE, RG24 7AF.
DUCKENFIELD, Mr. James Frederick, FCA *1949;* 3 Ringinglow Mews, 304 Ringinglow Road, SHEFFIELD, S11 7PX. (Life Member)
DUCKER, Mr. Andrew James, BCom ACA *1988;* 63a Lillington Road, LEAMINGTON SPA, CV32 6LF.
DUCKER, Mr. Benjamin Anthony, ACA *2008;* 2 Vanburgh Gardens, BASINGSTOKE, HAMPSHIRE, RG22 4UQ.
DUCKER, Mr. Bernard John, FCA *1949;* Merrileas, Leatherhead Road, Oxshott, LEATHERHEAD, KT22 0EZ. (Life Member)
DUCKER, Mr. Brian Charles, MA FCA *1972;* PO Box 457, WOOLLAHRA, NSW 1350, AUSTRALIA.
DUCKER, Mr. Justin Francis, BSc ACA *1991;* 28 Beauchamp Road, TWICKENHAM, TW1 3JD.
DUCKER, Miss. Lindsey Anne, ACA *2009;* 4 Stanmore Mount, LEEDS, LS4 2RH.
DUCKER, Mr. Stephen James, MA ACA *1990;* PricewaterhouseCoopers, 26F Office Tower A, Beijing Fortune Plaza, 23 Dongsanhuan Beilu, Chaoyang District, BEIJING 100020 CHINA.
DUCKER, Mr. Tremayne Anthony, BSc ACA *1996;* 1 Alnwick View, West Park, LEEDS, LS16 5RP.
•DUCKETT, Mr. Christopher David Nicholas, BA ACA *1991;* Chris Duckett, Thorn Office Centre, Straight Mile Road, Rotherwas, HEREFORD, HR2 6JT. See also Chris Duckett Limited
DUCKETT, Mr. Edward John, MA ACA *2007;* N M Rothschild & Sons Ltd, New Court, St Swithins Lane, LONDON, EC4P 4DU.
•DUCKETT, Mr. Jeremy Ernest, FCA *1962;* Silverley, Red Lane, Burton Green, KENILWORTH, CV8 1PB.
DUCKETT, Mr. John Nigel, BSc FCA *1991;* 229 Kings Causeway, Brierfield, NELSON, LANCASHIRE, BB9 0HD.
DUCKETT, Mr. Roger Anthony, FCA *1966;* Petroc, Somerford Keynes, CIRENCESTER, GL7 6EN. (Life Member)
DUCKETT, Mr. Simon John, BSc ACA *1991;* 10 Manor Heath, Copmanthorpe, YORK, YO23 3SJ.
DUCKHOUSE, Mr. David, BA ACA *1984;* Reed Smith The Broadgate Tower, 20 Primrose Street, LONDON, EC2A 2RS.
•DUCKMANTON, Mr. Terrence Paul, FCA *1979;* 15 Lowfield Road, COVENTRY, CV3 1LA.
DUCKWORTH, Mr. Anthony Harold, MA ACA *1988;* 4-703 Wanda Plaza, 93 Jiangguo Road, Chaoyang District, BEIJING, CHINA.
DUCKWORTH, Mr. Charles, MA ACA *1986;* 51 St. Josephs Vale, Blackheath, LONDON, SE3 0XG.
•DUCKWORTH, Mr. David John, FCA *1975;* (Tax Fac), D.J Duckworth Limited, 20 Bank Street, ACCRINGTON, BB5 1HH.
DUCKWORTH, Miss. Emma Jane, MSc ACA *1995;* 41 The Twitchell, BALDOCK, HERTFORDSHIRE, SG7 6DW.
DUCKWORTH, Mr. Geoffrey Keith, FCA *1968;* 261 Longhurst Lane, Mellor, STOCKPORT, SK6 5PW.
DUCKWORTH, Miss. Helen Catherine, BA ACA *2001;* 4 Canberra Mews, PORT MELBOURNE, VIC 3207, AUSTRALIA.
•DUCKWORTH, Mr. James Richard, FCA *1977;* Freeman Rich Ltd, 284 Clifton Drive South, LYTHAM ST. ANNES, LANCASHIRE, FY8 1LH. See also Freeman Rich
DUCKWORTH, Mr. Jeremy Dyce, BA ACA *1989;* Swinbrook Cottage, Swinbrook, BURFORD, OXFORDSHIRE, OX18 4DZ.
DUCKWORTH, Mr. Justin Patrick, BA ACA *2000;* 15 Ringmer Avenue, LONDON, SW6 5LP.
DUCKWORTH, Miss. Katie Louise, ACA *2011;* 9 Dearden Court, DARWEN, LANCASHIRE, BB3 3BB.
DUCKWORTH, Mr. Mark Riley, BA ACA ATII *1985;* Meadow End, Hudnall Lane, Little Gaddesden, BERKHAMSTED, HERTFORDSHIRE, HP4 1QQ.
•DUCKWORTH, Mr. Myles Ronald Holden, MA ACA *2000;* Deloitte LLP, Horton House, Exchange Flags, LIVERPOOL, L2 3PG. See also Deloitte & Touche LLP
DUCKWORTH, Mr. Neil Antony, BSc ACA *1999;* 48 Eastbourne Road, BRENTFORD, MIDDLESEX, TW8 9PF.
DUCKWORTH, Mr. Norman John, BSc FCA *1974;* Piers Meadow, Lowe Lane, Wolverley, KIDDERMINSTER, DY11 5QR.
•DUCKWORTH, Mrs. Patricia, FCA *1969;* MP Associates (Warwick) Ltd, Holly Cottage, Moreton Paddox, Moreton Morrell, WARWICK, CV35 9BU.
DUCKWORTH, Mr. Philip Roy, FCA *1974;* (Tax Fac), Forza Doors Ltd Unit 24a, Star Road Partridge Green, HORSHAM, WEST SUSSEX, RH13 8RA.
DUCKWORTH, Mr. Richard Harold, BA ACA *1997;* 5555 Glenridge Connector, Suite 800, ATLANTA, GA 30342, UNITED STATES.
DUCKWORTH, Mr. Roger Julian, BA FCA *1995;* 87 Kingfisher Circuit, FLAGSTAFF HILL, SA 5159, AUSTRALIA.
DUCKWORTH, Mr. Russell Stephen Peter, BSc ACA *1986;* Flat 6, 40 Chester Square, LONDON, SW1W 9HT.
DUCKWORTH, Mrs. Sally Louise, BA ACA *1994;* Eaton House, 7 Eaton Park, COBHAM, SURREY, KT11 2JF.
DUCKWORTH, Mrs. Sarah Ann, BA ACA MBA *1998;* Kellogg Company, Talbot Road, Stretford, MANCHESTER, M16 0PU.
DUCKWORTH, Mr. Simon Charles, BA ACA *1985;* 13 Beverley Road, Monkseaton, WHITLEY BAY, TYNE AND WEAR, NE25 8JH.
DUCKWORTH, Mr. Stephen Roger, MA FCA *1964;* 43 Pangbourne Avenue, LONDON, W10 6DJ.
•DUDA, Mr. George Joseph, BA ACA *1985;* GJ Duda, Tree Tops, Outwood Common, Outwood, REDHILL, RH1 5PW.
DUDACK, Mr. Lee Joseph, BA ACA *1989;* The Laurels, 29 Aldenham Avenue, RADLETT, WD7 8HZ.
DUDAREVA, Ms. Marianne, BSc ACA *2009;* Derevnya Kopische, Ulitsa Podgornaya 67-63, MINSK 220125, BELARUS.
DUDDELL, Mr. Howard John, BCom ACA *1985;* Burgess Group PLC, PO Box 46, Victory Mill, Priestmans Lane, Thornton Dale, PICKERING NORTH YORKSHIRE YO18 7RU.
DUDDELL, Mrs. Susan Edith, BA ACA *1983;* Crab Butts, 33 Beacon Park, First Avenue, PICKERING, YO18 8AQ.
DUDDLE, Mr. Michael Paul, BSc(Hons) ACA *2010;* 2 Ellesmere Green, Eccles, MANCHESTER, M30 9EZ.
DUDDRIDGE, Mrs. Helene Marie, BSc ACA *1992;* 48 Beattie Rise, Hedge End, SOUTHAMPTON, SO30 2RF.
DUDDRIDGE, Miss. Katrina Tzana, FCA *1984;* Linden, Rowhills, FARNHAM, GU7 9AU.
DUDDY, Mr. Martin Roger, FCA *1976;* 27 Lister Drive, NORTHAMPTON, NN4 9XE.
DUDDY, Mrs. Rosemary Louise, FCA *1977;* 27 Lister Drive, NORTHAMPTON, NN4 9XE.
DUDDY, Mr. Stuart, BSc(Hons) ACA *2011;* Top Floor Carling House, Coors Brewers Ltd, 137 High Street, BURTON-ON-TRENT, STAFFORDSHIRE, DE14 1JZ.
DUDEK, Mr. Adam, ACA *2010;* 5 Farthing Lane, REDDITCH, WORCESTERSHIRE, B97 6TE.
DUDENEY, Mrs. Susan Patricia, MSc ACA *1993;* 8 Haydn Avenue, PURLEY, CR8 4AE.
•DUDFIELD, Mr. Simon Thomas, BA FCA *1986;* (Tax Fac), Little & Company, 45 Park Road, GLOUCESTER, GL1 1LP.
DUDGEON, Mr. Anthony Oliver Batchen, ACA *2008;* 11th Floor, K P M G Llp, 15 Canada Square, LONDON, E14 5GL.
DUDGEON, Mr. David John, BA ACA *1998;* 39 Marshall Square, SOUTHAMPTON, SO15 2PB.
DUDGEON, Mr. James Edward, FCA *1964;* Broad Oaks, Lewes Road, HAYWARDS HEATH, RH17 7SP.
•DUDGEON, Mr. Jonathan Robert, BA ACA *2002;* (Tax Fac), Blu Sky Tax Ltd, 17 Northumberland Square, NORTH SHIELDS, TYNE AND WEAR, NE30 1PX. See also Blu Sky
•DUDGEON, Mr. Mark Nicholas, BSc FCA *1983;* Etyek Consulting, Dorottya utca 11, 1051 BUDAPEST, HUNGARY.
DUDGEON, Mr. Martin Andrew, BSc FCA *1990;* Riddarevagen 7, 191 33 SOLLENTUNA, SWEDEN.
DUDHIA, Mr. Mohamed Zunaid, BA ACA *1992;* 5 Stanhope Gate, LONDON, W1K 1AH.
DUDHIA, Mrs. Radha, BSc ACA *1992;* (Tax Fac), 10 Hillside Grove, Mill Hill, LONDON, NW7 2LR.
•DUDHIA, Mr. Zaheer, BSc ACA CTA *2001;* Z Dudhia & Company Limited, 4 Hornton Place, LONDON, W8 4LZ. See also Dudhia Lewin Myers Associates Limited
DUDLEY, Mr. Alexander Michael Paul, BA ACA *2010;* 28 Hubbard Close, Twyford, READING, RG10 0XU.
DUDLEY, Mr. Barry Peter, BSc FCA *1993;* Naked Communications Ltd, 159-173 St. John Street, LONDON, EC1V 4QJ.
DUDLEY, Miss. Emma Marie, BSc ACA *2010;* 16 Telok Blangah Crescent #11-316, SINGAPORE 090016, SINGAPORE.
DUDLEY, Mr. Frank Thomas, FCA *1975;* Beco Mgt Services, 61 6th Avenue, Inanda, JOHANNESBURG, 2196, SOUTH AFRICA.
DUDLEY, Mr. Graham Herbert, FCA *1957;* 20 Sir Josephs Walk, HARPENDEN, HERTFORDSHIRE, AL5 2DT. (Life Member)
DUDLEY, Mr. Guilford Paul Julian, FCA *1971;* 53 Marlow Hill, HIGH WYCOMBE, HP11 1SX.
DUDLEY, Miss. Helen, BSc ACA *2009;* Brambley Hedge, Forest Road, Hale, FORDINGBRIDGE, HAMPSHIRE, SP6 2NT.
DUDLEY, Mr. Ian, MChem ACA *2010;* 109a South Park Road, LONDON, SW19 8RU.
DUDLEY, Miss. Jacqueline Anne, BSc ACA *1999;* Ennismore, High Street, Yatton Keynell, CHIPPENHAM, SN14 7BG.
DUDLEY, Mr. John Leslie, FCA *1968;* 5 Friarstown Park, Ballyclough, LIMERICK, COUNTY LIMERICK, IRELAND.
DUDLEY, Mr. John Mark, BSc ACA *1996;* 124 Eagle Way, Hampton Vale, PETERBOROUGH, PE7 8EA.
•DUDLEY, Mr. Johnathan Geoffrey, FCA *1986;* (Tax Fac), Crowe Clark Whitehill LLP, Hatherton House, Hatherton Street, WALSALL, WS1 1YB. See also Horwath Clark Whitehill LLP and Crowe Clark Whitehill
•DUDLEY, Mr. Jonathan, BA ACA *1992;* with RSM Tenon Audit Limited, 5 Ridge House, Ridge House Drive, Festival Park, STOKE-ON-TRENT, ST1 5SJ.
DUDLEY, Mr. Joseph Gilbert, FCA *1935;* 10 Golden Stains Road, Avondale, HARARE, ZIMBABWE. (Life Member)
•DUDLEY, Mr. Martin Paul, FCA *1982;* (Tax Fac), Horsebrook House, 51 Old Farm Drive, Codsall, WOLVERHAMPTON, STAFFORDSHIRE, WV8 1GF.
DUDLEY, Mr. Michael, MA BSc FCA *1978;* Green Templeton College, 43 Woodstock Road, OXFORD, OX2 6HG.
DUDLEY, Mrs. Patricia Josephine, BSc FCA *1977;* The Beeches, Waterhouse Lane, Kingswood, TADWORTH, SURREY, KT20 6HT.
DUDLEY, Mr. Paul Hugh, BSc FCA *1974;* 2 Redwoods Duncombe Road, Bengeo, HERTFORD, SG14 3BT.
DUDLEY, Mr. Paul James, BSc ACA *1998;* 2 Gasden Drive, Witley, GODALMING, SURREY, GU8 5QQ.
DUDLEY, Mr. Paul Martin, BSc FCA *1984;* 17 Field View, Chandlers Ford, EASTLEIGH, SO53 4LJ.
•DUDLEY, Mr. Robert Howard, BSc FCA *1984;* (Tax Fac), 30 Ashlone Road, Putney, LONDON, SW15 1LR.
DUDLEY, Mr. Simon John, LLB ACA *1992;* 15 Kingswood Gardens, LEEDS, LS8 2BT.
DUDLEY, Mr. Timothy Paul, BA ACA *1993;* 9 Riversdale Road, THAMES DITTON, KT7 0QL.
DUDLEY-HAMMATT, Mr. Nicholas Andrew, ACA *2010;* 6 Kestrel Close, Ewshot, FARNHAM, GU10 5TW.
DUDMAN, Mr. Jonathan Andrew, BA FCA *1991;* Catella Monaco SAM, Est - Ouest, 24 Boulevard Princesse Charlotte, 98000 MONACO, MONACO.
DUERDEN, Mr. Anthony, FCA *1971;* 6 Whinnysty Lane, Heysham, MORECAMBE, LANCASHIRE, LA3 1PB.
DUERDEN, Mr. Christopher James, ACA *2008;* Seven Seas Ltd, 1301 Hedon Road, HULL, HU9 5NJ.
DUESBERY, Mr. Paul Gerard, BA(Hons) ACA *1990;* PGD Business Solutions Limited, 6 West End Drive, Horsforth, LEEDS, LS18 5JZ.
DUFF, Mr. Andrew Kenneth, ACA *1984;* 97 Cecily Street, Lilyfield, SYDNEY, NSW 2040, AUSTRALIA.
DUFF, Mrs. Catherine Christine, BA ACA *2004;* Flat 5, 12 Royal Crescent, BATH, BA1 2LR.
DUFF, Mr. Christian Henry, MSc BSc FCA *1974;* 147-101 Parkside Drive, PORT MOODY V3H 4W6, BC, CANADA.
DUFF, Mr. Colin Holman, FCA *1948;* 15 Holmesdale Park, Coopers Hill Road, Nutfield, REDHILL, RH1 4NW. (Life Member)
DUFF, Mr. Oliver Miles Christian, BA ACA *1995;* Level 3, H S B C, 8-16 Canada Square, LONDON, E14 5HQ.
DUFF, Mr. Peter Edward, MA ACA *1997;* Network Rail Infrastructure Ltd Kings Place, 90 York Way, LONDON, N1 9AG.
DUFF, Mr. Peter John, BSc FCA *1973;* 6601 Highland Park Drive, FORT SMITH, AR 72916, UNITED STATES.
DUFF, Mr. Peter Murray, FCA *1964;* 19 Lawn Crescent, RICHMOND, SURREY, TW9 3NR.
DUFF, Mr. Rory John Andrew, MEng ACA *2004;* Flat 105, Thanet House, Thanet Street, LONDON, WC1H 9QG.
DUFF, Miss. Rosemary Helen, ACA *2008;* 22 Riverside Court, LEEDS, LS1 7BU.
DUFF, Mr. Rupert Peter, BSc(Hons) ACA *2009;* 27 Nigel Road, LONDON, SE15 4NP.
DUFFELL, Mrs. Brenda Margaret, FCA *1965;* 32 The Ridgeway, ENFIELD, EN2 8QH.
•DUFFELL, Mr. Brent Simon, ACA *1985;* Cranfields, Suite 2, 3rd Floor, Leon House, 233 High Street, CROYDON CR0 9XT.
•DUFFELL, Mr. Peter Morris, FCA *1963;* Peter Duffell, 32 The Ridgeway, ENFIELD, EN2 8QH.
DUFFEN, Mr. Andrew Mark, BA ACA *1991;* 10 Southdale Road, Summertown, OXFORD, OX2 7SD.
DUFFETT, Mr. Anthony Martin, BSc FCA *1975;* 27 Church Rise, Forest Hill, LONDON, SE23 2UD.
DUFFIELD, Mr. Andrew Nicholas, BSc ACA *1993;* 5 Kingsmead, Upton, CHESTER, CH2 1EF.
DUFFIELD, Mr. Frank John, BA(Hons) FCA *1963;* 10 Aspen Road, Chartham, CANTERBURY, KENT, CT4 7TB.

DUFFIELD, Mr. Peter, BSc(Hons) ACA *2000;* GE Financial Markets, Le Pole House, Ship Street Great, DUBLIN 8, COUNTY DUBLIN, IRELAND.

•DUFFIELD, Mr. Peter David, LLB FCA *1980;* Smailes Goldie, Regents Court, Princess Street, HULL, HU2 8BA.

•DUFFILL, Miss. Elaine Louise, ACA *1983;* Fullard Duffill, 106 Birmingham Road, BROMSGROVE, B61 0DF.

•DUFFILL, Mr. Julian Mark, BA(Hons) ACA *2001;* Carter Dutton Limited, 65-66 St. Mary Street, CHIPPENHAM, WILTSHIRE, SN15 3JF.

DUFFILL, Mr. Robert Frank, FCA *1968;* (Tax Fac), 3 Mount Street, BATTLE, EAST SUSSEX, TN33 0EG.

DUFFILL, Mrs. Shelagh Mary, FCA *1977;* 3 Mount Street, BATTLE, EAST SUSSEX, TN33 0EG.

DUFFIN, Mr. Adrian James, ACA *1992;* 27 Fellows Way, Hillmorton, RUGBY, WARWICKSHIRE, CV21 4JP.

DUFFIN, Mrs. Ann Christine, BSc ACA *1986;* 93 Grove Avenue, Beeston, NOTTINGHAM, NG9 4DX.

DUFFIN, Mr. Anthony Louis, BSc ACA *1982;* 82 Little Herberts Road, Charlton Kings, CHELTENHAM, GL53 8LN.

DUFFIN, Mr. Christopher John, BA ACA *1986;* (Tax Fac), 9 Aidan Close, AYLESBURY, HP21 9XQ.

DUFFIN, Mr. Ian Andrew, BCom FCA *1982;* Princess Yachts International Plc, Newport Street, PLYMOUTH, PL1 3QG.

•DUFFIN, Mr. Paul William, BA FCA *1981;* Smith Cooper, Mansfield House, 57 Mansfield Road, ALFRETON, DE55 7JJ. See also F B 40 Limited

DUFFIN-JONES, Mrs. Fiona Martine, BSc FCA *1990;* 24 Pattison Lane, Woolstone, MILTON KEYNES, MK15 0AX.

DUFFITT, Mr. Neil James, ACA *2009;* Apartment 77, Springfield Court, 2 Dean Road, SALFORD, M3 7EH.

DUFFUS, Mr. Geoffrey Roger, BA ACA *2002;* 25 The Meer, Fleckney, LEICESTER, LE8 8UN.

•DUFFY, Mrs. Amanda Jane, BSc FCA *1991;* (Tax Fac), Robert Hayden & Co, 195 Bramhall Lane, Davenport, STOCKPORT, SK2 6JA.

DUFFY, Mr. Charles Bernard, FCA *1972;* 6 Dunscombe Road, WARWICK PARISH WK08, BERMUDA.

DUFFY, Miss. Clare Margaret, LLB ACA *2002;* Tesco Bank, Interpoint Building, 22 Haymarket Yards, EDINBURGH, EH12 5BH.

DUFFY, Mr. Daniel James, MEng ACA *2007;* 17 St James Drive, BRIDGNORTH, WV15 6BN.

DUFFY, Miss. Erin, BA(Hons) ACA *2003;* Flat B 25 Tregothnan Road, LONDON, SW9 9LD.

DUFFY, Mrs. Gillian Avril, LLB ACA *1989;* unit 42, 260 Vulture Street, SOUTH BRISBANE, QLD 4101, AUSTRALIA.

DUFFY, Miss. Helen Sarah, BA ACA *2004;* 80 Earlswood Street, LONDON, SE10 9ES.

DUFFY, Mr. John S F, ACA *2007;* Blue Oil Services Ltd 3rd Floor, 14/16 Bruton Place, LONDON, w1j6lx.

DUFFY, Dr. Karen Theresa Irene, FCA *1992;* H M Revenue & Customs 1 Munroe Court, White Rose Office Park Millshaw Park Lane, LEEDS, LS11 0EA.

•DUFFY, Mr. Kevin Victor, BA(Hons) ACA *2001;* with RSM Tenon Audit Limited, Sumner House, St. Thomas's Road, CHORLEY, LANCASHIRE, PR7 1HP.

DUFFY, Miss. Marie Kathleen, FCA *1974;* 39 Chestnut Avenue, BEVERLEY, HU17 9QX.

DUFFY, Mr. Martin Robert Anthony, FCA *1973;* Biwater Holdings LimitedBiwater House, Station Approach, DORKING, RH4 1TZ.

DUFFY, Ms. Patricia Mary, BSc FCA *1984;* Woodside Farm, Green Lane, Appleton, WARRINGTON, WA4 5NG.

DUFFY, Mr. Paul, BSc ACA *1995;* Baker & McKenzie Global Services LLC, One Prudential Plaza Suite 2500, 130 East Randolph Street, CHICAGO, IL 60601, UNITED STATES.

DUFFY, Mr. Paul Francis, FCA *1991; (FCA Ireland 1979);* Ernst & Young LLC, Rose House, 51-59 Circular Road, Douglas, ISLE OF MAN, IM1 1AZ.

DUFFY, Mr. Peter Thomas, BSc ACA *2004;* Flat 54 Russell Quay, West Street, GRAVESEND, DA11 0BP.

•DUFFY, Mr. Philip Francis, BSc ACA *1991;* MCR, The Chancery, 58 Spring Gardens, MANCHESTER, M2 1EW.

DUFFY, Mrs. Ruth, BA FCA *1996;* 7 South Park Drive, BLACKPOOL, FY3 9PZ.

DUFFY, Mrs. Ruth Patricia, BCom ACA *1980;* 53 Cottenham Park Road, LONDON, SW20 0SB.

DUFFY, Mrs. Samantha, BSc ACA MBA *1997;* 28 Kingsway Place, LONDON, EC1R 0LU.

DUFFY, Mrs. Sarah, MA ACA *2003;* 7 Anson Road, Benson, WALLINGFORD, OXFORDSHIRE, OX10 6DU.

DUFFY, Ms. Siobhan Elizabeth-Anne, BA FCA *1993;* Ulster Television Media Plc, Ormeau Road, BELFAST, BT7 1EB.

DUFFY, Mr. Stephen Michael, BA ACA *1987;* 2 Wainwright Road, ALTRINCHAM, WA14 4BS.

DUFFY, Mr. Steven, MEng ACA *2004;* 21 Fountain Court, Hastings Lane St. Helier, JERSEY, JE2 4HD.

DUFFY, Mr. Thomas William, ACA MAAT *2010;* (Tax Fac), 40 Pendower Way, NEWCASTLE UPON TYNE, NE15 6SP.

DUFFY, Mrs. Zoe Jane, ACA *2002;* 122 Chadderton Park Road, Chadderton, OLDHAM, OL9 0QD.

DUFTON, Mr. Colin, FCA *1972;* with Dufton Kellner Limited, Barnston House, Beacon Lane, Heswall, WIRRAL, CH60 0EE.

•DUFTON, Mr. Gareth Norman, BA(Hons) ACA *2001;* Gareth Dufton ACA, 61 Page Hill, WARE, HERTFORDSHIRE, SG12 0RZ.

DUFTON, Mr. Peter Anthony Howes, FCA *1971;* 123 The Chine, Grange Park, LONDON, N21 2EG.

DUFTY, Mr. Michael, FCA *1959;* The Mill House, Stratford Road, Wootton Wawen, HENLEY-IN-ARDEN, WEST MIDLANDS, B95 6BY.

DUGARD, Mr. John Roe, FCA *1958;* 66 Stanhome Drive, West Bridgford, NOTTINGHAM, NG2 7FU. (Life Member)

DUGDALE, Mrs. Anna Maria, ACA *1990;* 30 Newmarket Road, NORWICH, NR2 2LA.

DUGDALE, Ms. Carolyn Helen, BA ACA *1985;* Flat 1, 120 Nightingale Lane, LONDON, SW12 8NN.

•DUGDALE, Mr. Christopher John, BA ACA *1992;* with MA Partners LLP, 7 The Close, NORWICH, NORFOLK, NR1 4DJ.

DUGDALE, Mr. David John, FCA *1965;* Icomb Bank, Icomb, CHELTENHAM, GL54 1JD. (Life Member)

•DUGDALE, Mr. John Christian, BCom FCA *1977;* Whitehead & Howarth, 327 Clifton Drive South, LYTHAM ST. ANNES, FY8 1HN.

DUGDALE, Mrs. Judith Ann, BSc ACA *2004;* Woodlands Beechthorpe Avenue, Waddington, CLITHEROE, LANCASHIRE, BB7 3HT.

DUGDALE, Mr. Keith Stuart, MA FCA *1955;* The Old Carpenters Shop, The Street, Kelling, HOLT, NORFOLK, NR25 7EL. (Life Member)

DUGDALE, Mr. Mark, BSc ACA *1995;* 62 Guernsey Avenue, Buckshaw Village, CHORLEY, PR7 7AH.

DUGDALE, Mr. Michael Ian, BA ACA *1986;* 5 Hawthorn Place, Penn, HIGH WYCOMBE, BUCKINGHAMSHIRE, HP10 8EH.

DUGGAL, Mr. Anil Kumar, BA ACA *1985;* 5 The Burrows Narborough, LEICESTER, LE19 3WS.

DUGGAL, Mr. Mukesh Kumar, BA(Econ) ACA *2000;* 26 Medway Crescent, ALTRINCHAM, CHESHIRE, WA14 4UB.

DUGGAL, Mr. Rajesh Kumar, MSc FCA *1996;* 520 The Village #411, REDONDO BEACH, CA 90277, UNITED STATES.

•DUGGAL, Mr. Sudarshan Kumar, FCA *1971;* S.K. Duggal, 13 Pelham Court, NEWCASTLE UPON TYNE, NE3 2YL.

DUGGAL, Mr. Sunil, BSc ACA *2000;* 99 Church Road, LONDON, SW19 5AL.

DUGGAN, Mr. Alan Laurence, BA ACA CF *2005;* Flat 3, 16 Lancaster Park, RICHMOND, SURREY, TW10 6AB.

DUGGAN, Mr. Anthony James, BSc ACA *1997;* Flat 54 Gun Place, 86 Wapping Lane, LONDON, E1W 2RX.

•DUGGAN, Mr. Christopher Peter, LLB ACA *1991;* (Tax Fac), Griffins, Griffins Court, 24-32 London Road, NEWBURY, RG14 1JX. See also Griffins Business Advisers LLP

DUGGAN, Mr. David James, BA ACA *1991;* 68 rue du petit train, 31170 TOURNEFEUILLE, FRANCE.

•DUGGAN, Ms. Diana Margaret, BSc FCA *1974;* (Tax Fac), Diana Duggan & Co, 27 East Street, HEREFORD, HR1 2LU.

DUGGAN, Mr. Ian James, BSc(Hons) ACA *2004;* 43 Shelley Street, SWINDON, SN1 3PW.

•DUGGAN, Mr. James Joseph, BA FCA *1979;* 28 Lodge Road, Little Houghton, NORTHAMPTON, NN7 1AE.

DUGGAN, Mr. Jeffrey, FCA *1964;* 9 School Lane, SHEFFORD, SG17 5XA.

•DUGGAN, Mr. John, BSc FCA *1992;* (Tax Fac), Edwards, 409-411 Croydon Road, BECKENHAM, KENT, BR3 3PP.

DUGGAN, Mrs. Judith Ellen, MSc ACA *1992;* 68 rue du Petit Train, 31170 TOURNEFEUILLE, FRANCE.

DUGGAN, Miss. Katherine Josephine, ACA *2009;* 17 St. Margarets Avenue, ASHFORD, MIDDLESEX, TW15 1DR.

DUGGAN, Mrs. Lynn Catherine, BSc ACA *1993;* 50 Nightingale Road, LIVERPOOL, L12 0QN.

DUGGAN, Mr. Mark Thomas, FCA *1974;* 17A North Road, LILYDALE, VIC 3140, AUSTRALIA.

•DUGGAN, Mr. Neil Alan, PhD BSc FCA *1989;* KPMG LLC, Heritage Court, 41 Athol Street, Douglas, ISLE OF MAN, IM99 1HN. See also KPMG Audit LLC

DUGGAN, Mr. Richard Whitman, BSc FCA *1971;* BP 15, 73550 MERIBEL LES ALLUES, FRANCE.

DUGGAN, Mr. Robert Edward, ACA *1993;* 44 Hillfield Road, Selsey, CHICHESTER, PO20 0LF.

DUGGAN, Mrs. Valerie Janet, ACA *1992;* 4a Longmoor Road, LIPHOOK, GU30 7NY.

•①DUGGINS, Mr. David Kenneth, FCA *1982;* 43 Butlers & Colonial Wharf, LONDON, SE1 2PX.

DUGGLEBY, Mr. Adrian, BSc ACA *1991;* 2 Scrubbitts Park Road, RADLETT, HERTFORDSHIRE, WD7 8JW.

DUGMORE, Mrs. Catherine Thea, BA ACA *1993;* 20 West Common Grove, HARPENDEN, HERTFORDSHIRE, AL5 2AT.

•DUGMORE, Mr. Ian Martin Walter, LLB ACA *1992;* Ainsworths Limited, The Globe Centre, St. James Square, ACCRINGTON, LANCASHIRE, BB5 0RE.

DUGMORE, Mrs. Madeline, ACA *2007;* Ground Floor, 199 Kingston Road, LONDON, SW19 3NG.

DUHALDE, Miss. Tarka Isabella Carradine, BSc ACA *2006;* 4 Heathway, Tilehurst, READING, RG31 5AP.

DUHRA, Mr. Gurvinder Singh, BA ACA *1993;* Hohlstrasse 602, P.O. Box, CH-8010 ZURICH, SWITZERLAND.

DUHRE, Mr. Gurdial Singh, MBA BSc FCA *1984;* Seomar Sealladh, 2 Princes Crescent East, DOLLAR, FK14 7BU.

DUJCZYNSKI, Mr. Bartlomiej Adam, LLB ACA *2004;* 33 Lefroy Road, LONDON, W12 9LF.

DUKE, Mr. Alastair Stephen, BA(Hons) ACA *2003;* Littlejohn, 1 Westferry Circus, LONDON, E14 4HD.

DUKE, Mr. Daniel James Maxwell, MA ACA *1995;* 76 Sheldons Court, Winchcombe Street, CHELTENHAM, GL52 2NR.

DUKE, Mrs. Jennifer Mary, BCom ACA *1989;* 55 Bellevue Parade, NORTH CURL CURL, NSW 2099, AUSTRALIA.

DUKE, Mr. John William, BSc ACA *1990;* Nationwide Building Soc, Nationwide House, Pipers Way, SWINDON, SN38 3LN.

•DUKE, Mr. Mason David, BA FCA *1978;* Nunn Hayward, Sterling House, 20 Station Road, GERRARDS CROSS, SL9 8EL.

DUKE, Mrs. Melanie Kathryn, BSc ACA MCT *1990;* Church Barn, Draughton, NORTHAMPTON, NN6 9JQ.

DUKE, Mr. Stanley Timothy, FCA *1961;* 12 Langdale Close, Horsell, WOKING, SURREY, GU21 4RS.

DUKE, Mrs. Yasmin Jafferali Fazal, FCA *1979;* 11 Fairmead Close, BROMLEY, BR1 2JS.

DUKEK, Mr. Georg, BA FCA *1995;* Up'n Hoff 12, D-22927 GROSSHANSDORF, GERMANY.

•DUKER, Mr. Steven Gregory, FCA *1978;* (Tax Fac), Fredericks Limited, 5th Floor, Newbury House, 890-900 Eastern Avenue, Newbury Park, ILFORD ESSEX IG2 7HH.

DUKES, Mr. David Lawrence, FCA *1957;* 4a Caistor Road, BARTON-UPON-HUMBER, DN18 6AH. (Life Member)

•①DUKES, Mrs. Karen Lesley, BSc ACA *1991;* PricewaterhouseCoopers LLP, 7 More London Riverside, LONDON, SE1 2RT. See also PricewaterhouseCoopers

DUKES, Mr. Paul, BA FCA *1972;* 24 Monmouth Street, Topsham, EXETER, EX3 0AJ.

DULAI, Mrs. Gurpreet Kaur, MSc BSc ACA *2009;* K P M G, 1 The Embankment, LEEDS, LS1 4DW.

DULAI-GILL, Mrs. Kulvinder Kaur, ACA *1987;* 7123 Selkirk Street, VANCOUVER V6P 6J4, BC, CANADA.

•DULEY, Mr. Alan, BA ACA *1993;* Baker Tilly Tax & Advisory Services LLP, 12 Gleneagles Court, Brighton Road, CRAWLEY, WEST SUSSEX, RH10 6AD.

DULEY, Mrs. Donna Marie, BA(Hons) ACA *2001;* 68 Wildcroft Drive, North Holmwood, DORKING, SURREY, RH5 4TX.

DULEY, Mr. James Arthur, FCA *1972;* 257 Warwick Road, SOLIHULL, B92 7AB.

DULIEU, Mr. Rodney Owen, FCA *1972;* Bruntsfield, 37 Courtauld Rd., BRAINTREE, CM7 9BE. (Life Member)

DULLEY, Mr. Tim, BA FCA *2002;* Gamma Telecom, Victoria House, 64 Paul Street, LONDON, EC2A 4TT.

DULSON, Mr. Drew Richard, ACA *2008;* 18 Oakfield Road, Wordsley, STOURBRIDGE, DY8 5XS.

DULSON, Mr. Matthew Robert, BA ACA *2007;* 28 Oakwood Drive, LEEDS, LS8 2JB.

DULY, Mrs. Rosemary Ann, MA(Oxon) ACA CTA *1988;* 17 Glasshouse Studios, Fryern Court Road Burgate, FORDINGBRIDGE, SP6 1QX.

DUMA, Mr. Phillip Andreij, BSc ACA *2007;* with PricewaterhouseCoopers LLP, 31 Great George Street, BRISTOL, BS1 5QD.

•DUMASIA, Mr. Sharukh Tehmurasp, BSc ACA *1992;* KPMG LLP, 15 Canada Square, LONDON, E14 5GL. See also KPMG Europe LLP

•DUMBELL, Mr. Marc Rene George, BA(Hons) ACA *2002;* 7 Sarre Road, LONDON, NW2 3SN.

•①DUMBELL, Mr. Paul Nicholas, BA ACA *1993;* with KPMG LLP, St. James's Square, MANCHESTER, M2 6DS.

DUMBILL, Miss. Elizabeth, MA ACA *2010;* 7 Hearthstone Close, CHEADLE, CHESHIRE, SK8 2NW.

•DUMBLETON, Mr. Andrew Muir, BSc ACA *1986;* BDO LLP, 6th Floor, 3 Hardman Street, Spinningfields, MANCHESTER, M3 3AT. See also BDO Stoy Hayward LLP

DUMBLETON, Mr. David, BA ACA *2009;* Pricewaterhousecoopers, 33 Wellington Street, LEEDS, LS1 4JP.

DUMBLETON, Miss. Louise Emma, BA ACA *2004;* Brawn GB Team Operations Centre, 5a, BRACKLEY, NORTHAMPTONSHIRE, NN13 7BD.

•DUMBRELL, Mr. Carl Francis, ACA CA(AUS) *2008;* CDTL, GPO Box 5360, SYDNEY, NSW 2001, AUSTRALIA. See also CDTL Ireland

DUMBRILL, Mrs. Kathryn Elizabeth, BSc FCA *1987;* Paramount Software UK Ltd Empress Business Centre, 380 Chester Road, MANCHESTER, M16 9EA.

DUMBRILL, Mr. Nigel John, BSc ACA *1994;* 6 Mace Walk, CHELMSFORD, CM1 2GE.

DUMERESQUE, Mrs. Jane Grace, MBA ACA *1984;* Harvest Hill House Burgess Hill Road, Ansty, HAYWARDS HEATH, WEST SUSSEX, RH17 5AH.

DUMMER, Mr. Norman John, FCA FCCA *1967;* 97 Bluecoat Pond, Christs Hospital, HORSHAM, WEST SUSSEX, RH13 0TN. (Life Member)

DUMMETT, Mrs. Elaine Maria May-Ling, BA ACA *1997;* Tay House, 19 St. Albans Gardens, TEDDINGTON, MIDDLESEX, TW11 8AE.

DUMMETT, Mr. Robin Piers, BEng ACA *1997;* Tay House, 19 St. Albans Gardens, TEDDINGTON, MIDDLESEX, TW11 8AE.

DUMMETT, Mr. Toby, BA ACA *2009;* 18a Battersea Rise, LONDON, SW11 1EE.

DUMOND, Mr. Paul George, BSc ACA *1981;* CIM Investment Management Ltd, 1 Regent Street, LONDON, SW1Y 4NS.

DUMPLETON, Mr. Anthony William, MA(Hons) MSc ACA *2000;* 84 Berrylands, SURBITON, SURREY, KT5 8JY.

•DUNBAR, Mr. David Randolph Michell, FCA *1962;* (Tax Fac), with WSM Partners LLP, Pinnacle House, 17/25 Hartfield Road, Wimbledon, LONDON, SW19 3SE.

DUNBAR, Miss. Deborah Vanessa Rebecca, BA ACA *2002;* 33a Thorparch Road, LONDON, SW8 4SX.

DUNBAR, Mrs. Helene Margrethe Bekker-Nielsen, FCA *1999;* Henningsens Allé 14, DK2900 HELLERUP, DENMARK.

DUNBAR, Mr. Ian Malcolm Duncan, BSc ACA *1988;* 10 Grove Park, Redland, BRISTOL, BS6 6PP.

DUNBAR, Ms. Lucie Katherine, BA ACA *2007;* 19 Moberly Way, KENLEY, SURREY, CR8 5GP.

DUNBAR, Mr. Michael John, FCA *1958;* Swallows, Royce Way, West Wittering, CHICHESTER, PO20 8LN. (Life Member)

DUNBAR, Mr. Raymond John, BA ACA *1980;* 5 Hereford Copse, WOKING, GU22 0LX.

•DUNBAR, Mr. Stephen John, BA(Hons) FCA *1994;* Summit Accounting Solutions LLP, 74 Gartside Street, Spinningfields, MANCHESTER, M3 3EL.

•DUNBAVAND, Mrs. Barbara, BA FCA *1989;* Hall Livesey Brown, 10 Nicholas Street, CHESTER, CH1 2NX.

DUNCALF, Miss. Emma Jane, MA ACA *2002;* 28 Thornton Drive, COLCHESTER, CO4 5WB.

DUNCAN, Mr. Adam James, BSc ACA *1989;* Christies International Plc, 8 King Street, St. James, LONDON, SW1Y 6QT.

•①DUNCAN, Mr. Adrian Stewart, ACA CA(AUS) *2008;* Jackal Advisory Ltd, Level 19, Portland House, Bressenden Place, LONDON, SW1E 5RS.

DUNCAN, Mr. Alexander James, BA FCA *2000;* 67 Mexfield Road, LONDON, SW15 2RG.

DUNCAN, Mr. Alexander Robert, ACA *2008;* with Deloitte LLP, Athene Place, 66 Shoe Lane, LONDON, EC4A 3BQ.

•DUNCAN, Ms. Alison M M, BA ACA *1996;* Ernst & Young LLP, 1 More London Place, LONDON, SE1 2AF. See also Ernst & Young Europe LLP

•**DUNCAN, Mrs. Alison Miller, BSc ACA** *1995;* Imperial London Hotels Ltd, C/o Directors Office, Imperial Hotel, Russell Square, LONDON, WC1B 5BB.

DUNCAN, Mr. Andrew James McIntosh, BSc ACA *1994;* 16 Mortar Rock Road, WESTPORT, CT 06880, UNITED STATES.

•①**DUNCAN, Mr. Andrew John, ACA CA(AUS)** *2011;* with Leonard Curtis Limited, 1 Great Cumberland Place, LONDON, W1H 7LW.

DUNCAN, Mr. Andrew Malcolm, BA ACA *1992;* 8 Woodlea, Boston Spa, WETHERBY, LS23 6SB.

DUNCAN, Mr. Andrew Sinclair, BA FCA *1978;* Environmental Business Products Ltd, 214 Acton Lane, LONDON, NW10 7NH.

•**DUNCAN, Mr. Bret Stuart, ACA CTA** *1992;* Duncan Noice Limited, 5 Cherrytree, Union Road, Nether Edge, SHEFFIELD, S11 9EF.

DUNCAN, Mr. Bruce, BA ACA *2003;* 3 Schoolgate, Barwick in Elmet, LEEDS, LS15 4PF.

DUNCAN, Mr. Calum, ACA *2011;* Flat 4, 10 Church Walk, Newington Green, LONDON, N16 8QE.

DUNCAN, Mrs. Caroline Louise, BSc(Econ) ACA *2000;* 8 Beverley Close, MARLOW, BUCKINGHAMSHIRE, SL7 2RD.

DUNCAN, Mr. Colin Gordon, BA ACA *1986;* 39 Wiggett Grove, Binfield, BRACKNELL, RG42 4DY.

DUNCAN, Mr. Craig, MA(Hons) ACA DChA *2003;* 143 Raversby Road, CARNOUSTIE, DD7 7NJ.

DUNCAN, Mr. Cuan, ACA CA(SA) *2008;* Group Finance, Al-Futtaim Private LLC, PO Box 152, DUBAI, UNITED ARAB EMIRATES.

DUNCAN, Mr. David Graham, MA ACA *1983;* Heinrich-Pette-Str. 7, 65191 WIESBADEN, GERMANY.

DUNCAN, Mr. David Gregor, MA ACA *1992;* Flat 43, The Piper Building, Peterborough Road, LONDON, SW6 3EF.

DUNCAN, Mr. David Richard Louis, FCA *1962;* Mill Hill Cottage, Mill Hill, LONDON, SW13 0HS. (Life Member)

DUNCAN, Miss. Else Herforth, BA ACA *1996;* 24 Ursula Street, LONDON, SW11 3DW.

DUNCAN, Mr. George, BSc FCA *1962;* 16 Belgrave Mews West, Belgravia, LONDON, SW1X 8HT. (Life Member)

DUNCAN, Mr. Gordon Barclay, BSc ACA *1982;* 12 Burton Court, Franklins Row, Chelsea, LONDON, SW3 4TA.

DUNCAN, Mr. Graham John William, ACA CF *1989;* 170 Murray Road, Ealing, LONDON, W5 4DA.

DUNCAN, Mr. Guy Sebastian, BA ACA *1998;* Trafalgar House, Great Yarmouth Borough Council, Town Hall, GREAT YARMOUTH, NORFOLK, NR30 2QF.

DUNCAN, Mrs. Hilary Anne, BSc ACA *1988;* 79 North End, Meldreth, ROYSTON, HERTFORDSHIRE, SG8 6NU.

DUNCAN, Mr. Iain David Schilder, BA(Hons) ACA *2002;* 10 Greenwich Court, Park View Close, ST. ALBANS, AL1 5TR.

DUNCAN, Mr. Iain Stuart, BSc ACA *1995;* 1 Elm Close, LEATHERHEAD, SURREY, KT22 8HA.

DUNCAN, Mr. Ian, BA FCA *1970;* Residence Les Fonceaux, 52 Route Du Pave Des Gardes, 92310 SEVRES, FRANCE.

DUNCAN, Mr. Ian Barnet, MA ACA *1986;* 79 North End, Meldreth, ROYSTON, HERTFORDSHIRE, SG8 6NU.

•**DUNCAN, Mr. Ian Stuart, FCA** *1971;* Ian S Duncan Limited, 68 Brecon Way, BEDFORD, MK41 8DE.

DUNCAN, Mrs. Jane Catherine, BA(Hons) ACA *2000;* Room 516, Associated Newspapers Ltd Northcliffe House, 2 Derry Street, LONDON, W8 5TT.

DUNCAN, Mrs. Jill, BA ACA AMCT *2005;* Grainger Plc Citygate, St. James Boulevard, NEWCASTLE UPON TYNE, NE1 4JE.

DUNCAN, Mrs. Joanne Lesley, BA ACA *1997;* 8 Woodlea, Boston Spa, WETHERBY, LS23 6SB.

•**DUNCAN, Mr. John, FCA** *1975;* Gilbert Allen & Co, Churchdown Chambers, Bordyke, TONBRIDGE, TN9 1NR. See also Gilbert Allen Ltd

DUNCAN, Mr. John Paul, BSc ACA *1986;* (Tax Fac), with PricewaterhouseCoopers LLP, 101 Barbirolli Square, Lower Mosley Street, MANCHESTER, M2 3PW.

DUNCAN, Mr. Jonathan Richard, BSc ACA *1988;* Facility Management UK Ltd, c/o Corby Power Station, Mitchell Road, Phoenix Parkway, CORBY, NORTHAMPTONSHIRE NN17 5QT.

DUNCAN, Mr. Keith David, MBA BSc ACA *1986;* 216 Baltic Quay, 1 Sweden Gate, LONDON, SE16 7TG.

DUNCAN, Mr. Kenneth, FCA *1949;* 55 Beach Priory Gardens, SOUTHPORT, PR8 2SA. (Life Member)

•**DUNCAN, Miss. Lucy Jane, BSc ACA TEP** *2002;* (Tax Fac), Arnold Hill & Co LLP, Craven House, 16 Northumberland Avenue, LONDON, WC2N 5AP. See also Arnold Hill & Co

DUNCAN, Mr. Malcolm Ian, BCom FCA FCCA *1959;* 85 Whitmore Road, NEWCASTLE, STAFFORDSHIRE, ST5 3LZ.

DUNCAN, Mr. Mark, BA ACA *1998;* Halifax Share Dealing Ltd, Water Lane, LEEDS, LS98 3HX.

•**DUNCAN, Mr. Neil John, BSc FCA** *1992;* Nero Accounting Limited, Crows Nest Business Park, Ashton Road, Billinge, WIGAN, LANCASHIRE WN5 7XX.

DUNCAN, Mr. Neil Jonathan, BSc ACA *2009;* 56 Dore Road, SHEFFIELD, S17 3NB.

DUNCAN, Mr. Peter Lyne, BA FCA *1955;* Gatesgarth, Main Road, Glen Vine, ISLE OF MAN, IM4 4BQ. (Life Member)

DUNCAN, Mr. Robert Andrew, BSc ACA *2007;* 5 Eton Grove, LONDON, SE13 5BY.

DUNCAN, Mr. Robert Struan, FCA *1982;* Crofts End, 1 Cloister Way, LEAMINGTON SPA, WARWICKSHIRE, CV32 6QE.

DUNCAN, Mr. Robin John Grant, FCA *1977;* Ashott Cottage, Ashotts Lane, Chartridge, CHESHAM, BUCKINGHAMSHIRE, HP5 2TY.

DUNCAN, Mr. Roger, FCA *1971;* Orana, Bells Folly, Potters Bank, DURHAM, DH1 3RR.

•**DUNCAN, Mr. Ronald Paul, BA FCA** *1987;* HW, Sterling House, 22 St. Cuthberts Way, DARLINGTON, COUNTY DURHAM, DL1 1GB. See also Haines Watts

DUNCAN, Mr. Ross, BSc ACA *2002;* 44 Beaumont Avenue, ST. ALBANS, HERTFORDSHIRE, AL1 4TJ.

DUNCAN, Mr. Tom Patrick, MSc BSc ACA *2009;* with H W, Sterling House, 5 Buckingham Place, Bellfield Rd West, HIGH WYCOMBE, HP13 5HQ.

DUNCAN, Mrs. Tracey Marie, BA ACA *2000;* Ideal Shopping Direct Plc Ideal Home House, Newark Road, PETERBOROUGH, PE1 5WG.

DUNCANSON, Mr. Martin William, ACA *2008;* 33 Vaughan Williams Close, LONDON, SE8 4AW.

•**DUNCKLEY, Mr. David John, BSc ACA** *1998;* Grant Thornton UK LLP, 30 Finsbury Square, LONDON, EC2P 2YU. See also Grant Thornton LLP

DUNCKLEY, Mrs. Lisa Jean, BSc ACA *1998;* 170 Springbank Road, LONDON, SE13 6SU.

DUNCKLEY, Mr. Peter John, FCA *1971;* Capital Group, 22-24 Worple Road, LONDON, SW19 4DD.

DUNCOMBE, Mrs. Fiona Margaret, BA ACA *1993;* 16 Georgian Close, Maidenbower, CRAWLEY, RH10 7RE.

•**DUNCOMBE, Mr. Jeremy Robert, BSc FCA** *1985;* (Tax Fac), Duncombe & Co, Beech Hill, Glassenbury Road, CRANBROOK, TN17 2QJ.

DUNCOMBE, Mr. Norman Roger, FCA *1960;* Green Spinney, Oldhill Wood, Studham, DUNSTABLE, BEDFORDSHIRE, LU6 2NF. (Life Member)

•**DUNCUMB, Mrs. Nicola Jenny, MA FCA ATII** *1987;* (Tax Fac), N 4 Tax Limited, The Old Vicarage, Scamblesby, LOUTH, LN11 9XL.

DUNCUMB, Mr. William Richard, BSc FCA *1994;* Deloitte & Touche Hill House, 1 Little New Street, LONDON, EC4A 3TR.

DUNDAS, Mr. Peter, BSc ACA *1980;* 34 Burnmill Road, MARKET HARBOROUGH, LE16 7JF.

DUNDERDALE, Mr. Andrew Paul, ACA *2008;* 25 Gales Gardens, Bethnal Green, LONDON, E2 0EJ.

DUNDERDALE, Miss. Keri, ACA MAAT *2010;* 57 The Limes, Kempsey, WORCESTER, WR5 3LG.

DUNDJEROVIC, Miss. Alison, BSc ACA *2003;* 59 Firwood Avenue, ST. ALBANS, HERTFORDSHIRE, AL4 0TD.

DUNFIELD-PRAYERO, Mr. Gordon James, BA ACA *2001;* with Ernst & Young, 680 George Street, SYDNEY, NSW 2000, AUSTRALIA.

DUNFORD, Mr. Andrew Michael, MMath ACA *2004;* Helical Bar Plc, 11-15 Farm Street, LONDON, W1J 5RS.

DUNFORD, Miss. Emma, BSc ACA *2011;* 116 Hut Farm Place, Chandler's Ford, EASTLEIGH, HAMPSHIRE, SO53 3LR.

DUNFORD, Mrs. Hilary Jane, BSc ACA *1982;* 26 High Trees Avenue, BOURNEMOUTH, BH8 9JX.

•**DUNFORD, Mr. John Mark, BSc ACA** *1985;* Curtain Bluff, Rue Des Pointues Rocques, St. Sampson, GUERNSEY, GY2 4HW.

DUNFORD, Mr. John Philip, BSc ACA *1985;* Bourne Leisure Group Ltd, 1 Park Lane, HEMEL HEMPSTEAD, HERTFORDSHIRE, HP2 4YL.

DUNFORD, Mr. Malcolm, FCA *1963;* 57 Rowland Road, SCUNTHORPE, DN16 1SP.

•**DUNFORD, Mr. Richard John, ACA** *1984;* Richard Dunford & Co, 26 High Trees Avenue, BOURNEMOUTH, BH8 9JX. See also Richard Dunford Limited

DUNFORD, Mr. Stephen Charles, FCA *1981;* with Hillier Hopkins LLP, Charter Court, Midland Road, HEMEL HEMPSTEAD, HERTFORDSHIRE, HP2 5GE.

DUNFORD, Mrs. Theresa Margaret, BSc ACA *1992;* Cringleford, Bay Road, Freshwater Bay, FRESHWATER, PO40 9QS.

DUNFORD, Mr. Tim Peter, PhD MChem ACA *2010;* Smith & Williamson Ltd Imperial House, 18-21 Kings Park Road, SOUTHAMPTON, SO15 2AT.

DUNFOY, Mr. Mark Patrick, BA ACA *1993;* 11 Heathview Gardens, LONDON, SW15 3SZ.

DUNGARWALLA, Miss. Fatema Saifudin, ACA *2008;* 63 Kersey Drive, SOUTH CROYDON, SURREY, CR2 8SX.

DUNGARWALLA, Mr. Hatimalli, BA ACA *1992;* (Tax Fac), Whitefriars Ltd, 352 Brighton Road, SOUTH CROYDON, CR2 6AJ.

DUNGATE, Mr. Ian John, BA ACA *1989;* Britannia House, St Georges Street, Douglas, ISLE OF MAN, IM1 1JE.

DUNGEY, Mr. Paul Frederick, ACA CF *1996;* 118 Treffry Road, TRURO, CORNWALL, TR1 1WE.

DUNGEY, Mr. Phillip Edward, BSc ACA *1995;* Atos Origin, 4 Triton Square, Regents Place, LONDON, NW1 3HG.

DUNGWORTH, Miss. Alison Sara, BSc FCA *1986;* 11 Mayfly Close, Eastcote, PINNER, MIDDLESEX, HA5 1PD.

•**DUNGWORTH, Ms. Eliza Jane, LLB ACA ATII** *1993;* Deloitte LLP, Hill House, 1 Little New Street, LONDON, EC4A 3TR. See also Deloitte & Touche LLP

DUNHAM, Mr. Geoffrey John, FCA *1962;* Carr House, Tinkers Lane, Strumpshaw, NORWICH, NR13 4HT.

DUNHAM, Miss. Kate, BA ACA *1995;* 1 Thames Street, WEYBRIDGE, SURREY, KT13 8JG.

•**DUNHAM, Mr. Matthew, BSc ACA** *1991;* Grant Thornton UK LLP, 4 Hardman Square, Spinningfields, MANCHESTER, M3 3EB. See also Grant Thornton LLP

•**DUNHAM, Mr. Michael Fawcett, FCA** *1957;* TFD Dunhams, 11 Warwick Road, Old Trafford, MANCHESTER, M16 0QQ.

•**DUNHAM, Mrs. Vanessa Phyllis Robina, BSc FCA** *1976;* 49 Park Avenue South, Hornsey, LONDON, N8 8LX.

DUNHILL, Miss. Amy, MPhys ACA *2011;* Flat 8, 248 Finchley Road, LONDON, NW3 6DJ.

DUNHILL, Ms. Andrea Jean, MBA BA FCA *1978;* (Member of Council 2007 - 2011), The Riding, High Road, Chipstead, COULSDON, SURREY, CR5 3SD.

•**DUNHILL, Mr. Nicholas Vernon Aidan, MA ACA** *1994;* with N Dunhill & Co, 23A Moreton Terrace, Pimlico, LONDON, SW1V 2NS.

•**DUNHILL, Mrs. Rachel Ann, ACA** *1993;* Rachel Dunhill, 31 Crown Street, Scissett, HUDDERSFIELD, HD8 9JN.

DUNK, Mr. Andrew Peter, FCA *1968;* with Hedley Dunk Limited, Trinity House, 3 Bullace Lane, DARTFORD, DA1 1BB.

•**DUNK, Mrs. Bridget Mary, BA ACA** *1998;* B M Dunk, 70 Windermere Road, WEST WICKHAM, BR4 9AW.

DUNK, Mr. Geoffrey Michael Beswick, FCA *1972;* 80 Abingdon Road, Standlake, WITNEY, OXFORDSHIRE, OX29 7RN.

DUNK, Mr. John Emmerson, FCA *1952;* 37 Dale Avenue, HASSOCKS, BN6 8LP. (Life Member)

DUNK, Mr. John Julian, FCA *1968;* The Sawmill, Outlane, Hathersage, HOPE VALLEY, S32 1BQ.

DUNK, Mr. Paul Nicholas Hillam, FCA *1970;* Little Maldron Mill, Torphins, BANCHORY, AB31 4NE.

DUNKERLEY, Mr. Andrew John, BSc ACA *1980;* 30 Fairthorne Way, Shrivenham, SWINDON, SN6 8EA.

DUNKERLEY, Mr. Eric, FCA *1964;* 21 The Paddock, Ainsdale, SOUTHPORT, PR8 3PT. (Life Member)

DUNKERLEY, Mr. Guy, BA ACA *1992;* The Gatehouse, 2 Blacksmiths Close, Thrussington, LEICESTER, LE7 4UJ.

DUNKERLEY, Mr. John Harold, FCA *1974;* 179 Middle Street, DEAL, KENT, CT14 6LW.

DUNKERLEY, Mr. John Howard, ACA *1980;* 42 Belmont Avenue, Springhead, OLDHAM, OL4 4RS.

•**DUNKERLEY, Mr. Peter, FCA** *1979;* Street Farmhouse, The Street, Troston, BURY ST. EDMUNDS, SUFFOLK, IP31 1EW.

DUNKERLEY, Mr. Peter James, BEng ACA *2003;* PricewaterhouseCoopers, Dorchester House, 7 Church Street, PO Box HM1171, HAMILTON HMEX, BERMUDA.

DUNKERLEY, Mrs. Veronica Anne, BEng ACA *2002;* with PricewaterhouseCoopers, Dorchester House, 7 Church Street West, PO Box HM1171, HAMILTON HM EX, BERMUDA.

DUNKERS, Mr. Andrew Robert, BSocSc ACA *1991;* Cherry Tree Farm, Rowney Green Lane, Rowney Green, Alvechurch, BIRMINGHAM, B48 7QS.

DUNKERTON, Mrs. Gillian Christine, BA ACA *1989;* 18 Manor Drive Hilton, YARM, CLEVELAND, TS15 9LE.

DUNKLEY, Mr. Adrian Paul, ACA *1991;* (Tax Fac), 16 The Avenue, DRONFIELD, DERBYSHIRE, S18 2LS.

DUNKLEY, Mr. Alistair David, BCom FCA *1975;* Head Performance Analysis, Strategic Planning and Policy Directorate, HQ West Bay 1, PO Box 3212, DOHA, QATAR.

DUNKLEY, Mr. Andrew Albert, BSc FCA *1993;* 20 High Street, Nash, MILTON KEYNES, MK17 0EP.

DUNKLEY, Mr. Andrew Paul, FCA *1973;* Caistead, 40a Benwick Road, Doddington, MARCH, CAMBRIDGESHIRE, PE15 0TG.

DUNKLEY, Mr. James Francis, MBA FCA JDipMA *1949;* 4/52 Shephard Street, HOVE, SA 5048, AUSTRALIA. (Life Member)

DUNKLEY, Mr. Leighton, BSc ACA *2003;* 15 Hastings Parade, Devonport, NORTH SHORE CITY 0624, NEW ZEALAND.

DUNKLEY, Mr. Mark Graham, BA ACA *1986;* Dept for Work & Pensions, Level N2, Moorfoot Government Buildings, SHEFFIELD, S1 4PQ.

•**DUNKLEY, Mr. Michael Robert Paul, FCA** *1983;* Dunkley & Co Limited, Woodlands Grange, Woodlands Lane, Bradley Stoke, BRISTOL, BS32 4JY. See also Matrix Accountancy and Taxation Services Ltd

DUNKLEY, Mr. Norman Frederick, FCA *1958;* 78 Furnace Lane, Nether Heyford, NORTHAMPTON, NN7 3JT. (Life Member)

DUNKLEY, Mr. Paul Kevin, BSc ACA *1992;* Incentive FM, 22D Leathermarket Street, LONDON, SE1 3HP.

DUNKLEY, Mr. Richard Charles, BSc ACA *1989;* 64 Mayflower Way, Farnham Common, SLOUGH, SL2 3UB.

DUNKLEY, Mr. Richard John, BA ACA *1995;* H J Banks & Co Ltd Inkerman House, St. Johns Road Meadowfield Industrial Estate, DURHAM, DH7 8XL.

DUNKLEY, Mr. Rodney Patrick, FCA *1967;* 20 Aviemore Gardens, West Hunsbury, NORTHAMPTON, NN4 9XJ.

DUNKLEY, Mr. Roger, BSc ACA *1984;* Oakside, 9 Arbor Meadows, Winnersh, WOKINGHAM, RG41 5ED.

DUNKLEY, Mrs. Sara Jane, BA(Hons) ACA *2001;* 16 The Avenue, DRONFIELD, DERBYSHIRE, S18 2LS.

DUNKLING, Miss. Samantha Anne, BA ACA *2006;* 36 Farnesdown Drive, WOKINGHAM, RG41 1LD.

DUNKLING, Mr. Stephen, BA FCA CTA *1991;* Hermes Fund Managers Ltd, 1 Portsoken Street, LONDON, E1 8HZ.

DUNLAP, Mrs. Tracey Susan, BSc ACA *1989;* 1251 Pennsylvanie Street. No 1, DENVER, CO 80203, UNITED STATES.

DUNLEAVEY, Mr. Rory, BA ACA *2002;* 52 Fromond Road, Weeke, WINCHESTER, SO22 6EG.

DUNLEY, Mr. Christopher John Stewart, BA FCA *1994;* 7 Church Road, HAYWARDS HEATH, WEST SUSSEX, RH16 3NY.

DUNLEY, Mr. Jonathan James Stewart, MA ACA AMCT *1995;* Alfred House, 23-24 Cromwell Place, LONDON, SW7 2LD.

DUNLOP, Mr. Barney, BA ACA *2007;* Flat B, 224 Walm Lane, LONDON, NW2 3BS.

DUNLOP, Mr. Brian William, MA ACA *1988;* with Allen & Overy, One Bishops Square, LONDON, E1 6AD.

DUNLOP, Mr. Bruce William, FCA *1977;* 29th Floor, Caroline Centre, Lee Gardens Two, CAUSEWAY BAY, HONG KONG ISLAND, HONG KONG SAR.

•**DUNLOP, Mrs. Carol Elizabeth, BSc ACA** *1987;* Carol Dunlop, Pinnolds, Upton Lane, Brookthorpe, GLOUCESTER, GL4 0UT.

DUNLOP, Mrs. Caroline Susan, BA ACA *1991;* Haulfre, 64 Oldfield Road, Heswall, WIRRAL, MERSEYSIDE, CH60 6SG.

DUNLOP, Ms. Fiona Deirdre, MA ACA *1987;* 30 Corbiehill Avenue, EDINBURGH, EH4 5DX.

DUNLOP, Mr. Hamish Alexander, FCA *1974;* Kirkstone, Crabtree Green, Collingham, WETHERBY, LS22 5AB.

DUNLOP, Mr. Henry John, MA ACA *2003;* Merrill Lynch Financial Centre, 2 King Edward Street, LONDON, EC1A 1HQ.

DUNLOP, Miss. Janet Mary, BA ACA *1987;* 1 Harmsworth Street, Walworth, LONDON, SE17 3TJ.

DUNLOP, Mr. John Alexander, BSc FCA *1986;* Little Paddock Romsey Road, Whiteparish, SALISBURY, SP5 2SD.

DUNLOP, Mr. Julian Christopher Hamilton, FCA *1973;* Highfield Farm, 45 Stumpfield Road, KENSINGTON, NH 03833, UNITED STATES.
DUNLOP, Mr. Logan Graham Napier, MBA BA FCA *1975;* 18 Royal Crescent, ARMADALE, VIC 3143, AUSTRALIA.
DUNLOP, Mrs. Lynn, BSc ACA *2004;* The Downs School, Charlton Drive, Wraxall, BRISTOL, BS48 1PF.
DUNLOP, Mr. Neil Robert Harrison, MA ACA *1986;* 16 Russells Crescent, HORLEY, SURREY, RH6 7DN.
•DUNLOP, Mr. Robert Andrew, FCA *1971;* Spofforths LLP, 9 Donnington Park, 85 Birdham Road, CHICHESTER, WEST SUSSEX, PO20 7AJ.
DUNLOP, Mr. Robert John Harrison, BA ACA *1987;* 30 Corbiehill Avenue, EDINBURGH, EH4 5DX.
DUNLOP, Mr. Robert Layard, FCA *1946;* Ashwell Grange, BALDOCK, SG7 5NB. (Life Member)
DUNLOP, Mr. Timothy, ACA *2003;* Watchtower Bible & Tract Society, The Ridgeway, LONDON, NW7 1RN.
•DUNMORE, Mr. Eric Maurice, BA ACA *1989;* with The Third Space Group Limited, 13 Golden Square, LONDON, W1F 9JN.
DUNMORE, Miss. Jaine, BA ACA *1985;* Smiths Gloucester Ltd Allkerton Court, Alkerton Eastington, STONEHOUSE, GLOUCESTERSHIRE, GL10 3AQ.
DUNMORE, Mr. Robert John, BA ACA *1987;* 5 Carr Hill Way, RETFORD, NOTTINGHAMSHIRE, DN22 6TB.
DUNMORE, Miss. Sarah Elizabeth, BSc ACA MBA *2003;* 524 Saint Johns Place, Apt 3C, BROOKLYN, NY 11238, UNITED STATES.
DUNMOW, Mr. David Alan, BSc FCA *1989;* 51 Oak Lodge Tye, Springfield, CHELMSFORD, CM1 6GY.
DUNN, Ms. Alexandra Frances, ACA *2009;* Many Trees, Southfields Road, Woldingham, CATERHAM, SURREY, CR3 7BG.
DUNN, Mrs. Alice Margaret, LLB ACA *1986;* 2 Mill Close, Piccotts End, HEMEL HEMPSTEAD, HERTFORDSHIRE, HP1 3AX.
DUNN, Mrs. Amanda, BA ACA *1993;* Marling House, Station Road, WADHURST, TN5 6RT.
•DUNN, Mr. Andrew David, BSc FCA *1995;* 46 Ard Reayrt, Ramsey Road, Laxey, ISLE OF MAN, IM4 7QP.
DUNN, Mr. Andrew George Stewart, MA BSc(Hons) ACA *2010;* 16 Orchard Street, CANTERBURY, KENT, CT2 8AP.
DUNN, Mr. Andrew James, BA ACA *1991;* 5 Campion Way, WOKINGHAM, RG40 5YG.
•DUNN, Mrs. Anne-Maree, FCA *1992;* (Tax Fac), Williamson Morton Thornton LLP, 47 Holywell Hill, ST. ALBANS, HERTFORDSHIRE, AL1 1HD.
DUNN, Mr. Anthony Kendall, BA ACA *1989;* 14 Highbridge, Gosforth, NEWCASTLE UPON TYNE, NE3 2HA.
DUNN, Mr. Benjamin Paul, BA ACA *1998;* Clark McKay & Walpole, 90 Tottenham Court Road, LONDON, W1T 4TJ.
•DUNN, Mr. Brian Russell, FCA *1959;* B.R. Dunn, Manton Cottage, Westhorpe, SOUTHWELL, NOTTINGHAMSHIRE, NG25 0NE.
DUNN, Mr. Christopher James, FCA *1973;* Staple Fitzpaine Manor, Staple Fitzpaine, TAUNTON, TA3 5SW.
DUNN, Mr. Colin, BA ACA *1992;* PO Box 1103, MALENY, QLD 4552, AUSTRALIA.
DUNN, Mr. Edward John Charles, MA FCA *1983;* Orchard House Foods Ltd, 79 Manton Road, Earlstrees Industrial Estate, CORBY, NORTHAMPTONSHIRE, NN17 4JL.
•ⒾDUNN, Mr. Gareth Neil Stuart, BA ACA *1996;* 204 Loughborough Road, Ruddington, NOTTINGHAM, NG11 6NX.
•DUNN, Mr. Harold James, MSc FCA *1974;* Many Trees, Southfields Road, Woldingham, CATERHAM, CR3 7BG.
DUNN, Mrs. Hayley Marie, BA ACA *2003;* (Tax Fac), 4 Catchfrench Crescent, LISKEARD, CORNWALL, PL14 3WP.
DUNN, Mr. Ian Martin, BSc ACA *1989;* 3 Harestock Close, WINCHESTER, HAMPSHIRE, SO22 6NP.
DUNN, Mr. Jeremy Charles, ACA *1980;* Manor Cottage, Main Street, Wysall, NOTTINGHAM, NG12 5QS.
DUNN, Miss. Joanna, BSc ACA *2007;* (Tax Fac), 23 Withdean Court, London Road, Preston, BRIGHTON, BN1 6RN.
DUNN, Mr. John Anthony, FCA *1948;* Stable Cottage, Woodmancote, EMSWORTH, HAMPSHIRE, PO10 8RD. (Life Member)
DUNN, Mr. John Anthony Roberts, BA ACA *1994;* 8 Valley View, TUNBRIDGE WELLS, KENT, TN4 0SY.
•DUNN, Mr. John Eric Shiers, FCA *1961;* J.E.S. Dunn, Yew Tree Cottage, Unthank Lane, Holmesfield, DRONFIELD, S18 7WF.
DUNN, Mr. John Hirst, FCA *1972;* Cherry Garth, 2 Manor Park, Seaton, HULL, HU11 5RF.
DUNN, Mr. John Whitelaw, FCA *1972;* 3 Charlotte Square, Rhiwbina, CARDIFF, CF14 6ND.
DUNN, Mr. Jonathan Ashford Frank, BSc FCA *1988;* Bramblewick Cottage, The Green, Tostock, BURY ST. EDMUNDS, IP30 9NY.
DUNN, Mr. Jonathan David, ACA CF *1991;* B C M S Corporate Ltd Unit 14 Plantaganet House, Kingsclere Park Kingsclere, NEWBURY, RG20 4SW.
DUNN, Miss. Julia Mary Roberts, BA ACA *1993;* 27 Norfolk House Road, LONDON, SW16 1JJ.
DUNN, Miss. Kelly Anne, BSc(Hons) ACA *2003;* 62 Riversmead, HODDESDON, HERTFORDSHIRE, EN11 8DP.
•DUNN, Mr. Kevan Peter, ACA *1982;* Kevan Dunn, 18 Clavering Walk, BEXHILL-ON-SEA, TN39 4TN.
DUNN, Mr. Kevin Stephen, BSc(Hons) ACA *2000;* Fairbairn Private Bank (Iom) Ltd St Marys Court, 20 Hill Street Douglas, ISLE OF MAN, IM1 1EU.
DUNN, Mr. Lee Paul, LLB ACA CTA *2002;* National Grid Plc, N G T House, Warwick Technology Park, Gallows Hill, WARWICK, CV34 6DA.
DUNN, Mrs. Lesley Ann, PhD BSc ACA *1993;* Catterall Hall Farm, Catterall Lane, Catterall, PRESTON, PR3 0PA.
DUNN, Mrs. Lisa Jayne, BA ACA *1995;* 204 Loughborough Road, Ruddington, NOTTINGHAM, NG11 6NX.
DUNN, Mrs. Lucy Helen Mary, BA ACA *1989;* 35 Park Lane, Roundhay, LEEDS, LS8 2EH.
DUNN, Mr. Malcolm David, FCA *1968;* PO Box 69988, BRYANSTON, 2021, SOUTH AFRICA.
DUNN, Mr. Martin John, BSc ACA *1997;* with BDO LLP, 55 Baker Street, LONDON, W1U 7EU.
DUNN, Mr. Matthew James, MRes BSc ACA *2002;* Eerste Helmersstraat 198-3, 1054EM AMSTERDAM, NOORD HOLLAND, NETHERLANDS.
DUNN, Mr. Michael Edward, BSc FCA *1992;* St. Mowden Properties Plc, 7 Ridgeway, Quinton Business Park, Quinton, BIRMINGHAM, B32 1AF.
DUNN, Mr. Michael James, BA FCA *1989;* 35 Park Lane, Roundhay, LEEDS, LS8 2EH.
DUNN, Mr. Oliver, ACA *2011;* 47 Stanmore Crescent, LEEDS, LS4 2RY.
•DUNN, Mr. Perry Stephen, BA(Hons) ACA *2002;* Thornton Springer LLP, 67 Westow Street, Upper Norwood, LONDON, SE19 3RW. See also Chelepis Watson Limited
DUNN, Mr. Peter Antony, FCA *1968;* 67 Russell Hill Road, PURLEY, SURREY, CR8 2LL.
DUNN, Mr. Peter Damian, BSc ACA *1996;* 9 Tudorville Road, WIRRAL, MERSEYSIDE, CH63 2HT.
DUNN, Mr. Peter Harold, LLB FCA *1949;* 10 High Street, HAMPTON, TW12 2SJ. (Life Member)
DUNN, Mr. Peter Scholey, FCA *1978;* 74 Boulevard D'Italie, MC98000 MONACO, MONACO.
DUNN, Mr. Philip Alan, FCA *1966;* Orchid House, Trefgarn-Owen, HAVERFORDWEST, DYFED, SA62 6NE. (Life Member)
DUNN, Mr. Philip Graham, FCA *1974;* 18 Holita Road, TORONTO M2M 4C2, ON, CANADA.
DUNN, Mrs. Rachel Emma, BA ACA *2001;* 45 Kirkwood Drive, Kenton, NEWCASTLE UPON TYNE, NE3 3AR.
DUNN, Mr. Robert Dominic, BSc ACA *1992;* Van Breestraat 175 HS, 1071 ZN AMSTERDAM, NETHERLANDS.
DUNN, Mr. Robert John, BSc ACA *2007;* 322 Armidale Place, BRISTOL, BS6 5BQ.
DUNN, Mr. Robert John, BEng FCA *1977;* (Tax Fac), South Ridge, Narberth Road, TENBY, DYFED, SA70 8HT.
DUNN, Mr. Robin, FCA *1965;* 128 Hawcoat Lane, BARROW-IN-FURNESS, CUMBRIA, LA14 4HS.
•DUNN, Miss. Sabrina, ACA *2004;* Landau Morley LLP, Lanmor House, 370-386 High Road, WEMBLEY, MIDDLESEX, HA9 6AX.
DUNN, Mr. Simon Charles, PhD BSc ACA *2000;* 7 Riverdale Road, Beeston, NOTTINGHAM, NG9 5HU.
•DUNN, Mr. Stephen Gerard, BSc FCA CTA FSI *1979;* with KPMG LLP, Edward VII Quay, Navigation Way, Ashton-on-Ribble, PRESTON, PR2 2YF.
DUNN, Mrs. Suzanne Frances, BSc(Hons) ACA *2002;* 92 Jessett Drive, Church Crookham, FLEET, HAMPSHIRE, GU52 0XU.
DUNN, Mr. Timothy, FCA *1960;* The Brambles, Station Lane, Burton Leonard, HARROGATE, HG3 3RU. (Life Member)
•DUNN, Mr. Timothy Paul, BA FCA *1999;* Menzies LLP, Heathrow Business Centre, 65 High Street, EGHAM, SURREY, TW20 9EY.
DUNN-MASSEY, Ms. Patricia Louise, BA ACA *1988;* SRH Systems Ltd, Evesham House, Whittington Hall, Whittington Road, WORCESTER, WR5 2ZX.
DUNN-MASSEY, Mr. Steven Justin, BSc ACA *1987;* 25 Tower Road, WORCESTER, WR3 7AF.
DUNNE, Miss. Bronwen Mary Eleanor, BA ACA *1997;* 31 Temple Road, CROYDON, CR0 1HU.
DUNNE, Miss. Christine Theresa, BA(Hons) ACA *2001;* 65 Baker Street, ENFIELD, EN1 3EU.
DUNNE, Mr. Ciaran John, BA(Econ) ACA *1997;* 14 York Avenue, ROCHDALE, OL11 5HL.
DUNNE, Mr. Conall Murray, BCom ACA *1983;* 3207 W Parkland Blvd, TAMPA, FL 33609, UNITED STATES.
DUNNE, Mr. Cormac Vincent, BA ACA *1999;* QAS Ltd, George West House, 2-3 Clapham Common North Side, LONDON, SW4 0QL.
DUNNE, Mr. Ian James, BSc ACA *2004;* 19 Hawarden Way, Mancot, DEESIDE, CH5 2EL.
DUNNE, Miss. Jemma, BA(Hons) ACA *2010;* 66 Frederick Road, SUTTON, SURREY, SM1 2HU.
DUNNE, Mr. Jeremy, BSc ACA *1992;* 4 Woodlea Garth, Meanwood, LEEDS, LS6 4SG.
DUNNE, Mrs. Joanna, BA ACA *1997;* 19 Whitefield Road, Stockton Heath, WARRINGTON, WA4 6LZ.
DUNNE, Mr. John Anthony, BSc FCA *1980;* 19 Armley Grange Mount, LEEDS, LS12 3QB.
•DUNNE, Mr. Joseph Charles, FCA *1973;* (Tax Fac), Woolford & Co LLP, Hillbrow House, Hillbrow Road, ESHER, SURREY, KT10 9NW. See also Dixcart International Limited
•DUNNE, Mr. Martin Conrad, BSc FCA *1998;* (Tax Fac), Sayers Butterworth LLP, 3rd Floor, 12 Gough Square, LONDON, EC4A 3DW.
DUNNE, Mr. Michael David, FCA *1975;* 10 Lammas Road, Watton-at-Stone, HERTFORD, SG14 3RH.
DUNNE, Mr. Michael Edward, MEng BA ACA *2010;* with Deloitte Touche Tohmatsu, 550 Bourke Street, MELBOURNE, VIC 3000, AUSTRALIA.
DUNNE, Mr. Ronan James, FCA *2002; (FCA Ireland 1986);* O2, 260 Bath Road, SLOUGH, SL1 4DX.
DUNNE, Mr. Steven Michael, BA ACA *1993;* Credit Solutions Holdings Ltd, Capella Court, 725 Brighton Road, PURLEY, SURREY, CR8 2PG.
DUNNE, Mr. Timothy Vaughan, FCA *1975;* 103 Timberstone Court, CALGARY T3Z 3M6, AB, CANADA.
DUNNE, Mrs. Yvette Mandy, MA ACA *1993;* City of London Freemens School, Ashtead Park, ASHTEAD, SURREY, KT21 1ET.
DUNNETT, Mrs. Annette Elizabeth, MSci ACA *2007;* 88 Sandhill Oval, LEEDS, LS17 8EE.
DUNNETT, Mr. James Hanbury, FCA *1971;* Suite 1502, 1790 Bayshore Drive, VANCOUVER V6G 3G5, BC, CANADA.
DUNNETT, Mrs. Janice, ACA *1994;* House A, Little Palm Villa, Hang Hau Wing Lung Road, CLEARWATER BAY, NEW TERRITORIES, HONG KONG SAR.
DUNNETT, Mr. John-Paul Wanless, BA(Hons) ACA *2009;* 5 Admiral Square, Chelsea Harbour, LONDON, SW10 0UU.
DUNNETT, Mr. Paul Alexander, FCA *1973;* 5 Admiral Square, Chelsea Harbour, LONDON, SW10 0UU.
DUNNETT, Mr. Robert, BSc ACA *2007;* 88 Sandhill Oval, LEEDS, LS17 8EE.
•DUNNETT, Mr. Roger Phillip, FCA *1973;* WalkerDunnett & Co, 29 Commercial Street, DUNDEE, DD1 3DG.
•DUNNING, Mr. Alun, FCA *1968;* Alun Dunning, 25 Front Street, Hetton-le-Hole, HOUGHTON LE SPRING, DH5 9PF.
•DUNNING, Mr. Barrie John, FCA *1976;* (Tax Fac), Beavis Morgan Audit Limited, 82 St. John Street, LONDON, EC1M 4JN. See also Beavis Morgan LLP
DUNNING, Mr. Gordon Moore, BSc ACA *1979;* 250 Yonge Street, Suite 3110, P.O. Box 23, TORONTO M5B 2L7, ON, CANADA.
•DUNNING, Mr. Henry Edward, FCA *1954;* H.E. Dunning, HighleighNant-Y-Gamar Road, Craig-Y-Don LLANDUDNO, Clwyd, LL30 3BD.
DUNNING, Mr. Jack, ACA *2003;* 120 Chudleigh Road, LONDON, SE4 1HH.
DUNNING, Mr. James Alexander, BSc ACA *1988;* PricewaterhouseCoopers, Darling Park Tower 2, 201 Sussex Street, SYDNEY, NSW 2000, AUSTRALIA.
•DUNNING, Mrs. Janet Linda, BA FCA *1983;* Linda Dunning, The Dormers, 92 Bell Lane, AMERSHAM, HP6 6PG.
DUNNING, Mrs. Kathryn Eleanor, ACA *2003;* Endways, Mill Road, Banham, NORWICH, NR16 2HU.
DUNNING, Mrs. Lis Jenny, BA ACA *2003;* 120 Chudleigh Road, LONDON, SE4 1HH.
DUNNING, Miss. Lisa Maria, BSc(Hons) ACA *2001;* 28 Hesley Lane, Thorpe Hesley, ROTHERHAM, SOUTH YORKSHIRE, S61 2PS.
DUNNING, Mr. Mark Steven, BSc ACA *1993;* Ansa Elevators Unit 21 Broadgate, Oldham Broadway Business Park Chadderton, OLDHAM, OL9 9XA.
•DUNNING, Mr. Matthew William, BCom FCA *1986;* Hollows & Hesketh, 9 Sandy Lane, SKELMERSDALE, WN8 8LA.
DUNNING, Mr. Nicholas Anthony Robert, MA ACA *1988;* (Tax Fac), Hare Hatch House, Tag Lane, Hare Hatch, READING, BERKSHIRE, RG10 9SA.
DUNNING, Mr. Norman Edward, FCA *1948;* Walnut Lodge, 4 Annefield Close, MARKET DRAYTON, SHROPSHIRE, TF9 1HT. (Life Member)
DUNNING, Mrs. Rachel Margaret, BA ACA *1995;* 417 Mockingbird Way, HOCKESSIN, DE 19707, UNITED STATES.
DUNNING, Mr. Richard Glyn, FCA *1971;* 26 Mastmaker Road, LONDON, E14 9UB.
•DUNNING, Mr. Robert William, FCA *1972;* Kenneth Easby LLP, Oak House, Market Place, 35 North End, BEDALE, NORTH YORKSHIRE DL8 1AQ.
•DUNNING, Mr. Seton, FCA *1961;* S. Dunning FCA, 8 Dunlin Rise, Merrow, GUILDFORD, GU4 7DX. See also S. Dunning
DUNNINGHAM, Mr. Gordon Watson, FCA *1949;* P.O. Box 2583, KNYSNA, C.P., 6570, SOUTH AFRICA. (Life Member)
DUNNINGHAM, Mr. Timothy, FCA *1978;* Avranche Farm, La Ruette D'Avranches, St. Lawrence, JERSEY, JE3 1GJ.
DUNNINGTON, Mrs. Lisa Marie, BSc ACA *1993;* Jepps Barn, Jepps Lane, Barton, PRESTON, PR3 5AR.
DUNPHY, Ms. Elaine, ACA *2008;* 81 Avenue des Ternes, 75017 PARIS, FRANCE.
DUNPHY, Mr. Niall, BA ACA *1999;* 63 St. Ronans Crescent, WOODFORD GREEN, ESSEX, IG8 9DQ.
DUNS, Mr. Roy Alexander, FCA *1977;* 53 Middle Drive. Darras Hall, Ponteland, NEWCASTLE UPON TYNE, NE20 9DN.
DUNSBIER, Mr. James Frederick, BSc ACA *1995;* 31 Fielding Road, LONDON, W4 1HP.
DUNSBY, Mr. Adrian Bruce, BA(Hons) ACA CISA *1995;* with PricewaterhouseCoopers Inc, PO Box 2799, CAPE TOWN, C.P., 8000, SOUTH AFRICA.
DUNSBY, Mr. Peter, BSc ACA *1996;* 16 Balcombe Road, HAYWARDS HEATH, RH16 1PB.
•DUNSCOMBE, Mr. Raymond John, FCA *1964;* R.J. Dunscombe, 68 Hillmead, HORSHAM, RH12 2PX.
DUNSFORD, Mr. John Alexander, MSc BSc ACA *2003;* Apartment 11, Langham Place, 21-27 Valley Drive, HARROGATE, NORTH YORKSHIRE, HG2 0JL.
DUNSIRE, Mr. Andrew Robert Grant, BSc FCA *1980;* Chelwood, 10 Church Street, HAMPTON, TW12 2EG.
DUNSTAN, Mrs. Hayley Frances, BSc ACA *1995;* Lynthorpe, Tylers Lane, Bucklebury, READING, RG7 6TN.
DUNSTAN, Mr. John Curzon, BSc ACA *1992;* Interflora F T D A (B U) Ltd Interflora House, Watergate, SLEAFORD, LINCOLNSHIRE, NG34 7TB.
•DUNSTAN, Mrs. Lisa, ACA *2001;* (Tax Fac), The LK Partnership LLP, Rowan House, Hill End Lane, ST. ALBANS, HERTFORDSHIRE, AL4 0RA.
DUNSTAN, Mr. Stephen, BA ACA *1996;* 15 Boleyn Court, Dalkeith Avenue, BLACKPOOL, FY3 9SA.
•DUNSTAN, Mr. Stuart Andrew, FCA *1981;* Stuart Dunstan & Co, 105 Oak Hill, WOODFORD GREEN, IG8 9PF.
DUNSTER, Mr. Alexander David, BSc ACA *1999;* Diageo Plc Lakeside Drive, Park Royal, LONDON, NW10 7HQ.
DUNT, Mr. Keith Silvester, MBA BA FCA *1973;* Flat 2, 41 Queen's Gate Terrace, LONDON, SW7 5PN. (Life Member)
DUNTHORNE, Mr. Peter Richard, BSc ACA *1992;* I M O Car Wash Group Ltd, 35-37 Amersham Hill, HIGH WYCOMBE, BUCKINGHAMSHIRE, HP13 6NU.
•DUNTON, Mr. Barry, FCA *1968;* B. Dunton & Co, Millstone, Off Barleyfields, Wooburn Moor, HIGH WYCOMBE, HP10 0NH.
DUNTON, Mrs. Yanina Melody Gemma, BSc ACA *1998;* 3 Streamside Close, Hildenborough, TONBRIDGE, TN11 9AL.
•DUNWELL, Mr. Alan Jeffrey, BA FCA *1992;* RSM Tenon Audit Limited, 2 Wellington Place, LEEDS, LS1 4AP.
DUNWELL, Miss. Laura Amy, ACA *2009;* Flat 7, Kent Well Court, High Road, BENFLEET, ESSEX, SS7 5HX.

DUNWOODIE, Mr. Martin Christopher, MA ACA CFA *1998;* 15 Crabtree Lane, HARPENDEN, AL5 5TA.
DUNWOODIE, Mr. Paul Andrew, BSc FCA *1978;* Conoco Phillips, Portman House, 2 Portman Street, LONDON, W1H 6DU.
DUO, Ms. Shujie, ACA *2011;* Flat 97 New Atlas Wharf, 3 Arnhem Place, LONDON, E14 3ST.
DUONG, Mr. Dai, ACA CA(AUS) *2008;* with KPMG LLP, 15 Canada Square, LONDON, E14 5GL.
DUPARC, Mr. Robert Anthony, FCA *1959;* The Bynn, Village Way, Little Chalfont, AMERSHAM, HP7 9PU. (Life Member)
DUPEROUZEL, Miss. Adele, BA(Hons) ACA *2004;* Flat 6, The Cloisters, Gordon Square, LONDON, WC1H 0AG.
DUPEYRON, Mrs. Tracey, BSc ACA *1989;* Valley Farm, Golden Valley, Horsley Woodhouse, ILKESTON, DE7 6BA.
DUPLOCK, Mr. Ian Richard, BSc ACA *1997;* 36 Elm Place, NEW CANAAN, CT 06840, UNITED STATES.
DUPONT, Mr. Christophe, MBA ACA *1998;* Shin Caterpillar Mitsubishi, 3700 Tana, SAGAMIHARA, KANAGAWA, 229 1192 JAPAN.
DUPPA-MILLER, Mr. Charles Christopher, FCA *1965;* 6 The Old Walled Garden, Compton Verney, WARWICK, CV35 9HJ. (Life Member)
DUPUY, Mr. Mark Stuart, BSc ACA *1992;* Crestwood, #3 Crestwood Drive, PEMBROKE HM01, BERMUDA.
DUPUY, Mr. Richard, FCA *1969;* 4 Bron y Gamlas, Pontcysyllte, LLANGOLLEN, CLWYD, LL20 7YQ.
DUQUEMIN, Mr. Andrew Mark, BA ACA FCSI CF *1985;* Elysium Fund Management Ltd, PO Box 650, GUERNSEY, GY1 3JX.
DUQUEMIN, Mrs. Michelle Ann, BA ACA *1992;* Glengariff Route de Cobo, Castel, GUERNSEY, GY5 7UL.
DUQUEMIN, Mr. Philip John, FCA *1980;* Pre Du Rivage Rue de la Maladerie, St. Saviour, GUERNSEY, GY7 9QZ.
DUQUEMIN, Mr. Sean Richard, BSc ACA *1994;* PO Box 90239, SAN JOSE, CA 95109, UNITED STATES.
DUQUENOY, Mr. Philip James, BSc ACA *1997;* 71 Bray Road, GUILDFORD, GU2 7LJ.
DURACK, Mr. Sean Patrick, BSc ACA *1991;* C D L London Unit 1, Fitzroy Business Park Sandy Lane, SIDCUP, DA14 5NL.
DURAISINGHAM, Miss. Sai Lalitha, ACA *2010;* 14 Crescent Rise, LONDON, N22 7AW.
DURANCE, Mr. Peter Anthony, FCA *1981;* (Tax Fac), Beck House, 16 Main Street, Scothern, LINCOLN, LN2 2UJ.
DURAND, Mr. John Sebastian, BA ACA *1992;* 9 Woodlawn Road, LONDON, SW6 6NQ.
DURAND-HAYES, Mrs. Sabine Marie, ACA *1992;* 18 Rue Du Chemin Vert, 92 500 RUEIL MALMAISON, FRANCE.
DURANT, Mr. Christopher John, FCA *1975;* 5A Cuckoo Lane, Stubbington, FAREHAM, PO14 3PJ.
DURANT, Mr. Ian Charles, BA FCA FCT *1984;* Capital & Counties Properties PLC, 15 Grosvenor Street, LONDON, W1K 4QZ.
DURANT, Mr. Paul Anthony, BEng ACA *2004;* Flat A, 46 Solent Road, LONDON, NW6 1TX.
•DURANT, Mr. Richard Andrew, BA FCA *1990;* Midtown, 322 High Holborn, LONDON, WC1V 7PB.
DURANT, Mr. Tony Frank, BSc ACA *1983;* 10 Squirrel Green, Freshfield Formby, LIVERPOOL, L37 1NZ.
DURBACZ, Mrs. Angela Mary, BA ACA *1986;* Applecross, Water Lane, Butleigh, GLASTONBURY, BA6 8SP.
DURBACZ, Mr. Antony, BSc ACA *1992;* Rexam Plc, 4 Millbank, LONDON, SW1P 3XR.
•DURBER, Mr. Russell Paul, ACA *1981;* Pargetters, 19 Church Avenue, STOKE-ON-TRENT, ST2 7DA.
•DURBIN, Mr. Andrew Michael, BA FCA CF *1986;* Smith Cooper, Wilmot House, St James Court, Friar Gate, DERBY, DE1 1BT. See also Smith Cooper LLP
•DURBIN, Mr. Clark Robert, ACA *1983;* Clark R. Durbin & Co, 92 Western Avenue, NEWPORT, NP20 3QZ.
DURBIN, Mrs. Geraldine, BSc ACA *1993;* Castle Acre, 6 Church Lane, Bardsey, LEEDS, LS17 9DH.
DURBIN, Miss. Lucy Georgina, ACA *2009;* 114 Surrey Road, POOLE, DORSET, BH12 1HJ.
DURBIN, Mr. Peter Bernard, BA ACA *1988;* Castleacre, 6 Church Lane, Bardsey, LEEDS, LS17 9DH.
DURBIN, Mr. Peter Charles Robertson, MA FCA *1971;* (Tax Fac), 8 Anselm Close, Parkhill, CROYDON, CR0 5LY.
DURDIN, Mrs. Margaret Anne, FCA *1983;* (Tax Fac), with John A Roberts & Co Ltd, 42 Sheffield Road, CHESTERFIELD, DERBYSHIRE, S41 7LL.
DURE-SMITH, Mrs. Elizabeth Christine, BA ACA *1994;* 33 Broadshard Lane, RINGWOOD, HAMPSHIRE, BH24 1RP.
DURELL, Mr. James Tristan, BA ACA *2008;* 54 Scott Close, Ditton, AYLESFORD, KENT, ME20 6QP.
DURELL, Mr. Richard Geoffrey Adrian, BA ACA *2002;* with MacIntyre Hudson LLP, New Bridge Street House, 30-34 New Bridge Street, LONDON, EC4V 6BJ.
DUREY, Mr. Howard Ernest, BA ACA *1983;* 42 Chenies Avenue, AMERSHAM, HP6 6PP.
DURGAN, Mr. Graham Richard, BSc(Econ) ACA *1982;* MEMBER OF COUNCIL (Member of Council 1995 - 2010), Fielding House, Jubilee Road, Littlewick Green, MAIDENHEAD, SL6 3QU.
DURGAN, Mr. Paul William, BA FCA *1991;* 8 College Gardens, LONDON, SE21 7BE.
DURHAM, Miss. Charlotte, BA(Hons) ACA *2011;* 16 Swanfield Street, LONDON, E2 7DS.
DURHAM, Mr. Christopher John Walter, FCA *1967;* White Lion House, 64a Highgate High Street, LONDON, N6 5HX.
DURHAM, Mrs. Deborah, ACA *1991;* Asset Risk Consultants, 7 New Street, St. Peter Port, GUERNSEY, GY1 2PF.
DURHAM, Mr. James Alexander Edward, BEng ACA *1995;* 18 Sunderland Avenue, ST. ALBANS, AL1 4HJ.
DURHAM, Mrs. Joanne Lesley, BSc ACA ATII *1997;* with KPMG LLP, 1 The Embankment, Neville Street, LEEDS, LS1 4DW.
•DURHAM, Mr. Malcolm Gordon, LLB FCA *1986;* DFM Limited, 100 Fenchurch Street, LONDON, EC3M 5JD. See also F D Solutions
DURHAM, Mr. Michael Francis, BSc(Econ) FCA *1991;* Mobile Projects Ltd, 17 Abell Gardens, Pinkneys Green, MAIDENHEAD, BERKSHIRE, SL6 6PS.
DURHAM, Mr. Paul, BA FCA *1977;* Niriidon 7, Voula, 16673 ATHENS, GREECE.
DURHAM, Miss. Rosemary Judith, ACA *2008;* MITIE Group Plc, Unit 1, Harlequin Office Park, Fieldfare, Emersons Green, BRISTOL BS16 7FN.
DURHAM, Mr. Stephen Patrick, BSc ACA *1982;* Invensys, Manor Royal, CRAWLEY, WEST SUSSEX, RH10 9SJ.
DURICA, Miss. Bojana, ACA *2009;* 12 Churchfield Road, LONDON, W13 9NG.
DURIE, Mr. Alistair John Lindsay, MA FCA *1969;* Colnebrook, Blois Road, Steeple Bumpstead, HAVERHILL, CB9 7BN. (Life Member)
DURIE, Mr. Thomas Michael, BA ACA *1982;* Kings Head House, The Street, Sissinghurst, CRANBROOK, TN17 2JE.
DURKAN, Mr. John Raymond, BSc BEng ACA *2001;* 2 Victoria Mews, Horsforth, LEEDS, LS18 4SS.
DURKIN, Mr. Ian, MChem ACA *2010;* 23 Heckenhurst Avenue, BURNLEY, LANCASHIRE, BB10 3JN.
DURKIN, Mr. John Joseph, FCA *1977;* 23 Heckenhurst Avenue, Worsthorne, BURNLEY, LANCASHIRE, BB10 3JN.
DURKIN, Mr. Mark, BA FCA *1989;* Antenna Media Centre, Beck Street, NOTTINGHAM, NG1 1EQ.
DURLING, Mr. Richard John, FCA *1966;* 2 Park Road, GODALMING, GU7 1SH.
DURNEY, Miss. Jane Harriet, BA ACA *1997;* 3 Charles Street, BERKHAMSTED, HERTFORDSHIRE, HP4 3DG.
DURNFORD, Mr. Arthur Richard Patrick, FCA *1975;* Granville Chambers, J E Beale Plc, 21 Richmond Hill, BOURNEMOUTH, BH2 6BJ. (Life Member)
DURNO, Mr. Paul Casimir, BA ACA *1996;* 67 Barnfield Road, ST. ALBANS, HERTFORDSHIRE, AL4 9UD.
•DUROE, Mr. Robert Ian Kelvin, FCA *1973;* Robert I.K. Duroe, 4 Lansdowne Road, Frimley, CAMBERLEY, GU16 9UW.
•DUROJAIYE, Mr. Solomon Ajibade, FCA *1963;* Ajibade Durojaiye & Co, 27 Ajay Aina Street, Ifako Gbagada, PO Box 70305 Victoria Island, LAGOS, NIGERIA.
DUROSE, Mr. Stephen, BSc ACA *1992;* Fitch Ratings, Level 15, 77 King Street, SYDNEY, NSW 2000, AUSTRALIA.
DUROSE, Mrs. Storme Tamara, ACA *2009;* Unit 309 Fort Dunlop, Fort Parkway, BIRMINGHAM, B24 9FD.
DUROSINMI-ETTI, Mr. Oladapo, ACA *2008;* Flat 53, Regency Lodge, Adelaide Road, LONDON, NW3 5ED.
DUROW, Mrs. Joanna Kate, BA ACA *1990;* Old House Farm, Mangerton Lane, Bradpole, BRIDPORT, DT6 3SF.
DURRAN, Mr. John Raymond Charles, FCA *1976;* 118 St. Dunstans Avenue, LONDON, W3 6QL.
DURRANCE, Mrs. Emma Jane, BSc ACA *1997;* 38 Wick Road, TEDDINGTON, TW11 9DW.
DURRANCE, Mr. Simon Richard, BA ACA *1999;* Chemin de Beau-Rivage 7, 1006 LAUSANNE, SWITZERLAND.
DURRANDS, Dr. Paul Kenneth, ACA *1990;* Three Peaks Associates Ltd, Linkside Cottage, Abingdon Road, Tubney, ABINGDON, OXFORDSHIRE OX13 5QL.
•DURRANI, Mr. Farouk Salim Khan, FCA *1974;* (Tax Fac), Haines Watts Gatwick LLP, 3rd Floor, Consort House, Consort Way, HORLEY, SURREY RH6 7AF.
•DURRANS, Mr. Ian Willcox, BA ACA *1985;* PricewaterhouseCoopers LLP, 7 More London Riverside, LONDON, SE1 2RT. See also PricewaterhouseCoopers
DURRANS, Mr. Peter Gunston, FCA *1955;* 2 Springfield Place, The Street, Old Basing, BASINGSTOKE, HAMPSHIRE, RG24 7DR. (Life Member)
DURRANS, Mrs. Susan Jane, BSc ACA *1987;* Overdales, 5 Longdown Road, GUILDFORD, GU4 8PP.
•DURRANT, Mrs. Alexandra Beryl, FCA *1976;* (Tax Fac), Alexandra Durrant, 10A/12A High Street, EAST GRINSTEAD, RH19 3AW.
DURRANT, Mr. Andrew Mark, BSc ACA *1999;* 148 Palewell Park, LONDON, SW14 8JH.
DURRANT, Mr. Anthony Richard Charles, BA ACA *1984;* 1 Woodborough Road, Putney, LONDON, SW15 6PX.
DURRANT, Mr. Anthony Thomas, FCA *1969;* Cedar Lodge, School Road, Drayton, NORWICH, NR8 6HJ. (Life Member)
DURRANT, Mr. Benjamin William, FCA *1960;* 844 Dogwood Dell Lane, MIDLOTHIAN, VA 23113-6389, UNITED STATES. (Life Member)
DURRANT, Mr. Christopher Simon Peter, MA ACA *1999;* 3 Gleave Close, ST. ALBANS, HERTFORDSHIRE, AL1 4QG.
•DURRANT, Miss. Elaine Margaret, BSc ACA *1992;* (Tax Fac), Milsted Langdon LLP, Motivo House, Alvington, YEOVIL, SOMERSET, BA20 2FG.
DURRANT, Mr. John, FCA *1975;* Chislehurst Business Centre, 1 Bromley Lane, CHISLEHURST, BR7 6LH.
DURRANT, Mr. Mark Robert, FCA *1986;* Mussett Engineering Ltd, Little Money Road, Loddon, NORWICH, NR14 6JD.
DURRANT, Mr. Michael John, ACA *1986;* 12 Stokewood Road, BOURNEMOUTH, BH3 7NA.
DURRANT, Mr. Michael Reginald, FCA *1971;* Yew Tree Cottage, Rusper, HORSHAM, RH12 4PY. (Life Member)
DURRANT, Mr. Nevil Alexander, BA(Econ) ACA *1999;* Old Post Office High Street, Blackford, WEDMORE, SOMERSET, BS28 4NN.
DURRANT, Mr. Nigel Peter, BSc(Econ) FCA ASIP *1971;* 1 Raleigh Court, Kent AvenueEaling, LONDON, W13 8BG.
DURRANT, Mr. Owen Victor, FCA *1952;* 10 Claremont Road, NORWICH, NR4 6SH. (Life Member)
•DURRANT, Mrs. Patricia Chorlton Prichard, BA FCA *1978;* (Tax Fac), Holeys, Stuart House, 15/17 North Park Road, HARROGATE, HG1 5PD. See also Holeys Limited
•DURRANT, Mr. Paul Anthony, ACA *1980;* Wilson Durrant, 2 The Quadrant, COVENTRY, CV1 2DX.
•DURRANT, Mr. Richard Norman, FCA FCCA *1971;* Durrant & Company, Tankard Hall, Morton, OSWESTRY, SHROPSHIRE, SY10 8BQ.
DURRANT, Mrs. Suzannah Elizabeth Simons, BA ACA *1999;* 148 Palewell Park, LONDON, SW14 8JH.
DURRANT, Miss. Teresa Marie, BSc ACA *2003;* Flat 10, Woodstock House, Highbury Grange, LONDON, N5 2QF.
DURRINGTON, Mr. Ben, BA ACA CFA *2000;* 78 Belgrade Road, LONDON, N16 8DJ.
•DURST, Mr. Michael Bernard, FCA *1979;* (Tax Fac), Landau Baker Limited, Mountcliff House, 154 Brent Street, LONDON, NW4 2DR.
DURSTON, Miss. Vicki Clare, BSc ACA *2007;* Amplivox Ultratone, Ultravox House, Styal Road, MANCHESTER, M22 5WY.
•DURTNALL, Mr. Alan Robert, FCA *1965;* (Tax Fac), 48 Thorne Park Road, TORQUAY, TQ2 6RU.
•DURWARD, Mr. Keith James, BSc FCA *1990;* KPMG LLP, 15 Canada Square, LONDON, E14 5GL. See also KPMG Europe LLP
•DURY, Mr. Michael Raymond, ACA *1986;* (Tax Fac), M R Dury & Co Ltd, 51 Peaslands Road, SIDMOUTH, DEVON, EX10 9BE.
DUSAUTOY, Mr. Pierre Francis Collingwood, FCA *1973;* 7 Kings Road, BURNHAM-ON-CROUCH, ESSEX, CM0 8PP. (Life Member)
•DUSGATE, Mr. Christopher Ian, BSc FCA *1989;* (Tax Fac), C. Dusgate & Co, Fir Tree Cottage, Llanmadoc, Gower, SWANSEA, SA3 1DB.
DUSHYNSKY, Mr. Liam, ACA *2009;* 18 Willow Walk, HONITON, DEVON, EX14 2FX.
DUTCH, Miss. Hannah Rachel Mary, MA ACA *1993;* Mitie Group plc, Unit 1, Harlequin Office Park, Fieldfare, Emersons Green, BRISTOL BS16 7FN.
DUTCHMAN-SMITH, Mr. John Stewart, FCA *1967;* (Member of Council 1997 - 2001), 22 Lower Hill Drive, Heath Charnock, CHORLEY, LANCASHIRE, PR6 9JP.
DUTFIELD, Mr. Raymond John, FCA *1948;* 3 Woodward Place, Loughton Lodge, MILTON KEYNES, BUCKINGHAMSHIRE, MK8 9LG. (Life Member)
DUTHIE, Miss. Gemma, ACA *2011;* 84 Kirklees Drive, Farsley, PUDSEY, WEST YORKSHIRE, LS28 5TE.
DUTHIE, Mr. Robert Alan, FCA *1939;* 11 Kirkbeck Close, CARLISLE, CA3 0PS. (Life Member)
•DUTHIE, Mr. Robert Gerald Benton, MA FCA *1963;* Online Financial & Accountancy Ltd, 71 Bexley High Street, BEXLEY, DA5 1AA.
DUTHIE, Mr. William O'Kane, FCA *1973;* Fraxinus, Cleaghmore, BALLINASLOE, COUNTY GALWAY, IRELAND.
•DUTHOIT, Miss. Julie Margaret, BA ACA *1983;* Al Wilanowska 259, 02-730 WARSAW, POLAND.
DUTSON, Mr. Simon, BSc ACA *1988;* 188 Gleniffer Road, BELLINGEN, NSW 2454, AUSTRALIA.
DUTT, Mr. Dhanraj, BA ACA *1994;* 90 Salcombe Gardens, Mill Hill, LONDON, NW7 2NT.
DUTT, Mr. Dipankar, MSc FCA *1977;* Flat 3D Sanskaar, 8 Lake Range, CALCUTTA 700 026, INDIA.
DUTT, Mr. Monish Kant, FCA *1988;* World Bank Group, 4201 Blagden Avenue NW, WASHINGTON, DC 20011, UNITED STATES.
DUTT, Mr. Nilanjan, ACA *2008;* Flat 286 Russell Court, Woburn Place, LONDON, WC1H 0NF.
DUTT, Mr. Raibat Moon, MSc FCA *1975;* c/o National Foundation for India, Core 4A UGF, India Habitat Centre, Lodhi Road, NEW DELHI 110 003, INDIA.
DUTT, Mr. Subir, ACA *1980;* 18 Russell Road, NORTHOLT, UB5 4QR.
DUTTA, Mr. Ajit Singh, FCA *1970;* 2790 Marshall Lake Drive, OAKTON, VA 22124, UNITED STATES. (Life Member)
DUTTA, Ms. Ronita, BSc ACA *2002;* Protiviti, 5th Floor, Grand Buildings, 1-3 Strand, LONDON, WC2N 5AB.
DUTTA, Mr. Shaibal, BSc ACA *2000;* 2 Castle Yard, LONDON, N6 5DZ.
DUTTA, Dr. Shelah, MBA MBChB ACA *1994;* 35/5 Mid Steil, EDINBURGH, EH10 5XB.
DUTTON, Mr. Alan George Frederick, FCA *1958;* 130 Wades Hill, Winchmore Hill, LONDON, N21 1EH. (Life Member)
DUTTON, Mr. Andrew Robert Piers, ACA *1979;* Bunbury House, Bunbury, TARPORLEY, CW6 9PP.
DUTTON, Mr. Brian, FCA *1974;* 2 Makepeace Close, Vicars Cross, CHESTER, CH3 5LU.
•DUTTON, Mrs. Carolyn, ACA FCCA *2009;* with DTE Business Advisory Services Limited, DTE House, Hollins Mount, Hollins Lane, BURY, BL9 8AT.
DUTTON, Mr. Christopher, LLB ACA *1998;* Flat 4 Viscount Court, 1 Pembridge Villas, LONDON, W2 4XA.
DUTTON, Mr. David Allan, BA ACA *1997;* 17 Evendine Corner, Colwall Green, MALVERN, WORCESTERSHIRE, WR13 6DX.
DUTTON, Mr. David Brian, BA ACA *1985;* 20 Station Road, Marsden, HUDDERSFIELD, HD7 6DG.
DUTTON, Mr. David John, BSc(Hons) ACA *2006;* 47 Marshwood Croft, HALESOWEN, B62 0EY.
DUTTON, Mr. Derek Thomas, FCA *1952;* 7 Conyngham Road, NORTHAMPTON, NN3 9TA. (Life Member)
DUTTON, Mrs. Elizabeth Osborne, BSc ACA *1982;* 2 Freestone Road, SOUTHSEA, HAMPSHIRE, PO5 2NT.
DUTTON, Mr. George Alfred, BA ACA MBA *1982;* Unit 39E2, Tower B, Millennium Residences, Sukhumvit Soi 20, Klongtoey, BANGKOK 10110 THAILAND.
DUTTON, Miss. Helen Rebecca, BSc(Hons) ACA *2002;* Prudential Plc Group Finance, 12 Arthur Street, LONDON, EC4R 9AQ.
•DUTTON, Mr. Ian, MA ACA *1991;* (Tax Fac), Smith Cookson Accountants Limited, 4 Yorke Street, Hucknall, NOTTINGHAM, NG15 7BT. See also The Payroll Agency Limited
•DUTTON, Mr. John Roy, FCA *1969;* 40a Elms Road, HARROW, MIDDLESEX, HA3 6BH. See also Mountsides Limited

DUTTON, Mr. Jonathan Derek, BSc FCA *1984;* 7 Methley Street, LONDON, SE11 4AL.
DUTTON, Mr. Joseph Lawrence, FCA *1975;* 8-10 Buckley Terrace, Buckley Farm Lane, ROCHDALE, OL12 9DW.
DUTTON, Mr. Mark Richard, BA ACA *1995;* 51 Hobbs Avenue, PERTH, WA 6850, AUSTRALIA.
DUTTON, Miss. Paula Frances, BSc ACA *1992;* Westfields, 239 London Road, WEST MALLING, KENT, ME19 5AD.
DUTTON, Mr. Peter Trevor, ACA *1978;* Jacques Scott Group Ltd, PO Box 488 G.T., Crewe Rd., GEORGE TOWN, GRAND CAYMAN, KY1-1106 CAYMAN ISLANDS.
DUTTON, Mr. Philip, BA ACA *1985;* 23 Quarry Dene, LEEDS, LS16 8PA.
•**DUTTON, Mr. Richard William, FCA** *1983;* Carter Dutton Limited, 65-66 St. Mary Street, CHIPPENHAM, WILTSHIRE, SN15 3JF.
DUTTON, Mr. Stuart John, ACA *2009;* 25 Broomfield Close, WINSFORD, CHESHIRE, CW7 2US.
DUTTON, Mrs. Virginia Mary, BSc ACA *1993;* Dutton Phillips ltd, 6 Staincross Common, Staincross, BARNSLEY, SOUTH YORKSHIRE, S75 6JL.
•**DUVAL, Mr. Alexander Edward, BSc ACA MBCS** *1999;* with PricewaterhouseCoopers LLP, 1 Embankment Place, LONDON, WC2N 6RH.
DUVAL, Mr. Charles Gaetan Xavier-Luc, BA FCA *1986;* Nexia Baker & Arenson, 5th Floor, C&R Court, Labordonnas Street, PORT LOUIS, MAURITIUS.
DUVALL, Mr. David John Stewart, MA FCA *1973;* 39 Hudson Road, Woodley, READING, RG5 4EN.
DUVALL, Mr. Edward Hugh, FCA *1949;* Bayton, Crown Road, Llanfrechfa, CWMBRAN, NP44 8UE. (Life Member)
DUVEEN, Mr. Terence, FCA *1979;* Suite 9B, 818 Pittwater Road, DEE WHY, NSW 2099, AUSTRALIA.
DUXBERRY, Mr. Colin James, BSc ACA *1990;* 6 Shires Close, ASHTEAD, SURREY, KT21 2LT.
•**DUXBURY, Mr. Andrew James, BA(Hons) ACA** *2000;* with PricewaterhouseCoopers LLP, The Atrium, 1 Harefield Road, UXBRIDGE, UB8 1EX.
DUXBURY, Mr. Andrew John, BSc ACA *1989;* 72 Loweswater Drive, LOUGHBOROUGH, LE11 3RS.
DUXBURY, Mr. Glen Mark, BSc ACA *1992;* Northern College Wentworth Castle, Lowe Lane Stainborough, BARNSLEY, SOUTH YORKSHIRE, S75 3ET.
•**DUXBURY, Mrs. Helen Mary, BSc ACA** *1992;* The Duxbury Partnership Limited, 58 Sandringham Drive, Brinscall, CHORLEY, PR6 8SU.
DUXBURY, Mrs. Jacqueline, BCom ACA *1985;* Tamarind, Arthington Lane, Pool-in-Wharfedale, OTLEY, LS21 1JZ.
DUXBURY, Mrs. Jennifer Claire, BSc ACA *1992;* Barkston Ltd, 221 Pontefract Lane, LEEDS, LS9 0DX.
DUXBURY, Mrs. Karen Marie, BSc ACA *1991;* 12 Circus Street, Greenwich, LONDON, SE10 8SN.
DUXBURY, Mr. Kenneth, FCA *1958;* 2 Acorn Way, Pool In Wharfedale, OTLEY, LS21 1TY. (Life Member)
DUXBURY, Miss. Marian, ACA *2009;* 42 Quantock Road, BRISTOL, BS3 4PE.
•**DUXBURY, Mr. Nicholas James, BA FCA** *1993;* Integra Corporate Finance Limited, 1 Whitehall Quay, Whitehall Road, LEEDS, LS1 4HR.
DUXBURY, Mr. Nigel John, BSc ACA *1985;* The Royal Circus Tea, Warehouse, 12 Circus Street, Greenwich, LONDON, SE10 8SN.
DUXBURY, Mrs. Pamela Jane, BA ACA *2001;* 18 Shawbrook Close, Euxton, CHORLEY, PR7 6JY.
DUXBURY, Mr. Richard Graham, BSc ACA *1988;* Tamarind, Arthington Lane, Pool-in-Wharfedale, OTLEY, LS21 1JZ.
DUZNIAK, Ms. Jadwiga, LLB ACA *1993;* 8 Chapman Square, LONDON, SW19 5QQ.
DVORAK, Mr. Marcus, MBA ACA *2003;* Skansvagen 18, 191 45 SOLLENTUNA, SWEDEN.
DWAN, Mr. Gerald, FCA *1960;* 1 Mendip Close, Heald Green, CHEADLE, CHESHIRE, SK8 3LG. (Life Member)
DWANE, Mr. Neil Peter, BA ACA *1988;* Hartley Court, Hartley Lane, Hartley Wespall, HOOK, HAMPSHIRE, RG27 0BJ.
DWESAR, Mr. Sandeep, BA FCA *1989;* 70 Purley Downs Road, Sanderstead, SOUTH CROYDON, SURREY, CR2 0RB.
DWIGHT, Mr. Richard, BSc ACA *2011;* 3 Blount Close, Penkridge, STAFFORD, ST19 5JJ.
•**DWYER, Mr. Barry, FCA** *1968;* Barry Dwyer & Co, 25 Pishiobury Drive, SAWBRIDGEWORTH, HERTFORDSHIRE, CM21 0WT.
•**DWYER, Mr. Brendan Thomas Patrick, BA FCA** *1995; (FCA Ireland* Harbinson Mulholland, IBM House, 4 Bruce Street, BELFAST, BT2 7JD.
DWYER, Mr. David, BA ACA *2004;* 105 Leigh Hunt Drive, LONDON, N14 6DF.
DWYER, Mr. Francis Finnigan, BA ACA *1995;* 22 Rockleigh Road, SOUTHAMPTON, SO16 7AR.
DWYER, Mr. John Henry, BCom FCA *1975;* Fernfield Lodge, 2 Chase Farm Barns, Whaddon Road, Little Horwood, MILTON KEYNES, MK17 0QB.
DWYER, Mr. John Maurice, FCA *1966;* with Raymarsh Ford Limited, Ground Floor, 41 High Street, Kingswood, BRISTOL, BS15 4AA. (Life Member)
DWYER, Mr. John Peter Richard, BA ACA *2000;* Macquarie Bank, Citypoint, 1 Ropemaker Street, LONDON, EC2Y 9HD.
DWYER, Mr. Mark Roger, BSc ACA *2004;* Flat141, Penn Place, Solomons Hill, RICKMANSWORTH, HERTFORDSHIRE, WD3 1GY.
DWYER, Mrs. Sarah, BSc ACA *2008;* KPMG, c/o Sarah Lowe, PO Box 493, Century Yard, Cricket Square, GEORGE TOWN GRAND CAYMAN KY1-1106 CAYMAN ISLANDS.
DWYER, Mr. Stephen John, MA ACA *1987;* 3 Juggs Close, LEWES, BN7 1QP.
DWYER, Mr. Timothy John, LLB ACA *1998;* 5 Redwood Drive, ASCOT, SL5 0LW.
DY MO, Mr. Hua Cheung Philip, ACA *2008;* Flat C 24th Floor Block 35, City One Shatin, SHA TIN, HONG KONG SAR.
DYADINA, Miss. Ekaterina, ACA *2009;* Ikarou Street 6, Apt 1, Agios Omologites, 1085 NICOSIA, CYPRUS.
•**DYAS, Miss. Lisa, ACA** *1999;* Mill House Accountancy Limited, Medical Life, Priestly Court, Gillette Close, Staffordshire, STAFFORD HEIGHTS ST18 0LQ.
DYASON, Ms. Chantel, BA(Hons) ACA *2010;* Bank of America Merrill Lynch, 2 King Edward Street, LONDON, EC1A 1HQ.
DYBALL, Miss. Davena Frances, BSc FCA *1977;* 109 Leighswood Avenue, Aldridge, WALSALL, WS9 8BB.
DYCE, Mr. Craig, BA ACA *1993;* Mariposa, Wenden Road, Arkesden, SAFFRON WALDEN, ESSEX, CB11 4HB.
DYCE, Mrs. Wendy Anna, BA ACA *1992;* Mariposa, Wenden Road, Arkesden, SAFFRON WALDEN, ESSEX, CB11 4HB.
DYCKHOFF, Mr. Andrew Michael, MA ACA *1986;* 10 Swan Lane, Stock, INGATESTONE, ESSEX, CM4 9BQ.
DYCKHOFF, Mr. Michael, LLB FCA *1973;* 27 Blackthorn Way, Kingsnorth, ASHFORD, KENT, TN23 3QB. (Life Member)
DYE, Mrs. Maureen Penelope, FCA *1971;* 10 Salisbury Road, BARNET, EN5 4JP.
DYE, Mr. Michael Dalziel, FCA *1960;* 13 Mossley Court, Lyndhurst Avenue, Mossley Hill, LIVERPOOL, L18 8AR. (Life Member)
DYE, Miss. Rachel Hannah, BA ACA *2005;* 192 Earlsfield Road, LONDON, SW18 3DU.
DYE, Mr. Richard Geoffrey, BSc ACA *1987;* Fazenda Raio Luminoso, Altoparaiso, BRASILIA, 73770000, BRAZIL.
DYE, Mrs. Sarah Louise, BSc ACA *1992;* 77 Philip Avenue, Nuthall, NOTTINGHAM, NG16 1EB.
DYER, Mr. Alan Watson, FCA *1953;* The Old Vicarage, Oakridge Lynch, STROUD, GL6 7NS. (Life Member)
DYER, Mr. Arthur Frederick, FCA *1943;* 11 Norwood Close, KNARESBOROUGH, HG5 0NN. (Life Member)
DYER, Mr. Brian William, FCA *1974;* 30 Barshaw Gardens, Appleton, WARRINGTON, WA4 5FA.
DYER, Mrs. Faye Laura, BA ACA *2005;* 1 Tippet Close, BLACKBURN, BB2 3WX.
DYER, Mr. Graham John, FCA *1976;* Serco Plc, Palm Court, 4 Heron Square, RICHMOND, SURREY, TW9 1EW.
DYER, Mr. Howard James Ely, BSc ACA *1995;* St Mary's Cottage, 32 Vantorts Road, SAWBRIDGEWORTH, HERTFORDSHIRE, CM21 9NB.
DYER, Mr. James Norris, BEng ACA *1998;* The Firs, 1d Strawberry Lane, WILMSLOW, CHESHIRE, SK9 6AQ.
DYER, Mr. John Patrick, FCA *1966;* 1 Rue du Couderc, St Baudille, 81660 PONT DE LARN, FRANCE.
DYER, Mr. Jonathan Stephen, MA ACA *2002;* Flat 53 Printing House Square, Martyr Road, GUILDFORD, GU1 4AJ.
DYER, Mr. Keith, FCA *1971;* Little Garth, Cranebrook Lane, Hilton, LICHFIELD, WS14 0EX.
DYER, Mrs. Marion Jane, BA ACA *1984;* 10 Gatesden Road, Fetcham, LEATHERHEAD, KT22 9QR.
•**DYER, Mr. Mark Edward, BA FCA** *1984;* (Tax Fac), The Dyer Partnership Limited, 17 Westminster Court, Hipley Street, WOKING, SURREY, GU22 9LG.
DYER, Mr. Matthew Stephen, BSocSc ACA *1996;* 43 Wentworth Road, Harborne, BIRMINGHAM, B17 9SN.
•**DYER, Mr. Michael Karl Remane, ACA MAAT** *1996;* (Tax Fac), Reeves & Co LLP, 37 St. Margarets Street, CANTERBURY, KENT, CT1 2TU.
DYER, Mr. Michael Kenneth, FCA *1966;* Pen-y-Feidr, Llandissilio, CLYNDERWEN, DYFED, SA66 7JJ. (Life Member)
•**DYER, Mr. Neill Alan, FCA** *1984;* Dyer & Co Services Limited, Onega House, 112 Main Road, SIDCUP, KENT, DA14 6NE. See also Dyer & Co Accountants Limited
DYER, Mr. Nicholas John, FCA *1990;* 12 Waybrook Crescent, READING, RG1 5RG.
•**DYER, Mr. Paul Graham, FCA** *1969;* P G Dyer, 133 Bramcote Avenue, Chilwell, NOTTINGHAM, NG9 4EY.
•**DYER, Mr. Ramon Clifford, ACA** *1980;* Ray Dyer Accountants Ltd, Inglenook, Main Road, Nutbourne, CHICHESTER, PO18 8RR.
DYER, Mr. Richard Alan, FCA *1970;* 20 Herbert Road, BURNHAM-ON-SEA, SOMERSET, TA8 2HE.
DYER, Mr. Thomas Arthur Frederick, BA FCA *1973;* 32 Darrington Road, East Hardwick, PONTEFRACT, WF8 3DS.
DYER, Mr. Timothy Mark, BSc ACA *1996;* Addex Pharmaceuticals Ltd, Chemin des Aulx 12, Plan-les-Ouates, CH 1228 GENEVA, SWITZERLAND.
DYER, Mr. William Edward, FCA *1962;* (Tax Fac), Te-Dappa, Windmill Park, Wrotham Heath, SEVENOAKS, TN15 7SY. (Life Member)
DYER BARTLETT, Mrs. Diane, BA ACA *1988;* Ketton House Rectory Road, Kedington, HAVERHILL, SUFFOLK, CB9 7QL.
DYER BARTLETT, Mr. Dudley Richard Max, MA FCA *1981;* Ketton House, Rectory Road, Kedington, HAVERHILL, CB9 7QL.
•**DYER-SMITH, Mr. Christopher Simon Paul, FCA** *1975;* (Tax Fac), Dyer-Smith & Co, 7A High Street, EMSWORTH, PO10 7AQ.
DYET, Miss. Rachel Lucy Caroline, LLB ACA *1998;* 99 Grove Road, SUTTON, SURREY, SM1 2DB.
•**DYKE, Mr. Christopher John, BSc ACA** *1990;* (Tax Fac), C J Dyke & Company, The Old Police Station, Priory Road, ST. IVES, CAMBRIDGESHIRE, PE27 5BB.
DYKE, Mr. John Gordon, FCA *1957;* 31 Church Crescent, Whetstone, LONDON, N20 0JR. (Life Member)
DYKE, Mr. Martin James, ACA *2008;* Pavilion End Hall Road, Thorndon, EYE, SUFFOLK, IP23 7LU.
DYKE, Mr. Percy John, FCA *1937;* Pentlands, Little Badminton Lane, Lea., MALMESBURY, SN16 9NG. (Life Member)
DYKE, Mr. Philip Charles, FCA *1979;* 74 Cinnamon Lane, Fearnhead, WARRINGTON, WA2 0AP.
DYKE, Mr. Rhys, BSc(Hons) ACA *2011;* 26 Sandmere Road, LONDON, SW4 7QJ.
DYKES, Mr. Edward James, BA ACA *1997;* 12 Ursula Street, LONDON, SW11 3DW.
DYKES, Mr. Geoffrey Lynton, BSc ACA *1990;* 25 Carriage Drive, FRODSHAM, WA6 6DY.
DYKES, Mr. Graeme Alan, BSc FCA *1992;* 15 Ellis Close, HODDESDON, HERTFORDSHIRE, EN11 9FE.
•**DYKES, Mr. Ian Francis, BA ACA ATII** *1996;* PricewaterhouseCoopers LLP, Cornwall Court, 19 Cornwall Street, BIRMINGHAM, B3 2DT. See also PricewaterhouseCoopers
•**DYKES, Mr. Philip, BSc ACA** *1984;* Philip Dykes & Co, 1 Roebuck Lane, SALE, M33 7SY. See also Formaco Ltd
•**DYKES, Mrs. Rosemary, BA ACA** *1985;* Baker Tilly Tax & Advisory Services LLP, 1210 Centre Park Square, WARRINGTON, WA1 1RU. See also Formaco Ltd
DYKES, Mrs. Sadie Nicola, BSc ACA *1997;* Rosewood, 16 Redditch Road, Alvechurch, BIRMINGHAM, B48 7RZ.
•**DYMEK, Mr. Christopher John, FCA** *1978;* (Tax Fac), Lawford & Co, Union House, Walton Lodge, Bridge Street, WALTON-ON-THAMES, SURREY KT12 1BT. See also Lawfords Consulting Limited
DYMENT, Mr. Adrian Mark Oliver, BA ACA *2006;* 13 Bexley Street, WINDSOR, BERKSHIRE, SL4 5BP.
DYMIOTIS, Mr. Stelios, BSc FCA *1993;* 26 Lonsdale Drive, Oakwood, ENFIELD, MIDDLESEX, EN2 7LH.
DYMOCK, Mrs. Kay Lesley, BSc ACA *1984;* PO Box 5569, SHARJAH, UNITED ARAB EMIRATES.
DYMOKE, Mr. Simon Peter John, BA ACA *1985;* Brynards Hill House, Brynards Hill, Wootton Bassett, SWINDON, SN4 7ER.
DYMOND, Mrs. Elizabeth Lucy, MA FCA *1992;* H M Treasury, 1 Horse Guards Road, LONDON, SW1A 2HQ.
DYMOTT, Mr. James Graham, BA ACA *1993;* 185, Finchampstead Road, WOKINGHAM, RG40 3HD.
DYNE, Ms. Julie Elizabeth, BA ACA *2005;* Abaris Holdings Limited, Chalfton House, Oxford Road, Denham, UXBRIDGE, MIDDLESEX UB9 4DX.
DYRBUS, Mr. Robert, BSc FCA *1978;* 44 Wakehurst Road, LONDON, SW11 6BX.
•**DYSCH, Mr. Andrew, BSc ACA** *1987;* Sigma 2002 LLP, 45-47 Cornhill, LONDON, EC3V 3PF.
DYSON, Mr. Alan Campbell, BA ACA CTA *1980;* (Tax Fac), Mayflower, South View Road, Danbury, CHELMSFORD, CM3 4DX.
DYSON, Mr. Alexander James, FCA *1978;* 4 Hillkirk Drive, Shawclough, ROCHDALE, OL12 7HD.
DYSON, Mr. Alwyn Mark, BSc FCA *1960;* 18 Conway Road, Wimbledon, LONDON, SW20 8PA. (Life Member)
DYSON, Mr. Andrew John, MA ACA *1989;* 55 Wessenden Head Road, Meltham, HOLMFIRTH, WEST YORKSHIRE, HD9 4ET.
①**DYSON, Miss. Anne Elizabeth Exley Brooksbank, FCA** *1970;* with Ernst & Young LLP, 1 More London Place, LONDON, SE1 2AF.
DYSON, Mr. Bernard, BSc ACA *1991;* 1008 Carrington Drive, RALEIGH, NC 27615, UNITED STATES.
DYSON, Miss. Camilla Mary, BSc ACA *1994;* Hawkswick, 10 Denton Road, ILKLEY, LS29 0AA.
DYSON, Miss. Catherine Elizabeth, BA ACA *2004;* Santander UK Plc, 2-3 Triton Square, LONDON, NW1 3AN.
DYSON, Miss. Catherine Lucy, BEng ACA *2001;* 18 Knaresborough Drive, HUDDERSFIELD, HD2 2PR.
DYSON, Mr. Christopher Charles, BSc ACA *1986;* 3 Oak Cottages, Hungerford Lane Shurlock Row, READING, RG10 0PH.
•**DYSON, Mr. David Malcolm, ACA ATT** *1982;* AIMS - David Dyson, 115 Crosland Road, Oakes, HUDDERSFIELD, HD3 3PW.
DYSON, Mr. David Richard, BSc(Econ) ACA *1995;* 3 UK Ltd, 20 Grenfell Road, MAIDENHEAD, BERKSHIRE, SL6 1EH.
DYSON, Mr. David Victor, BSc FCA *1983;* The Barn Moorside Farm, Mottram, HYDE, CHESHIRE, SK14 6SG.
DYSON, Miss. Emily Cara, ACA *2011;* Flat 12, Gainsborough Mansions, Queen's Club Gardens, LONDON, W14 9RJ.
DYSON, Mr. Fernley Keith, MA FCA *1989;* The Grange, 100 High Street, Odell, BEDFORD, MK43 7AS.
DYSON, Mr. Francis Donald Guy, MA ACA *1989;* 214 The Pavilion, St Stephens Road, NORWICH, NR1 3SN.
DYSON, Mr. Geoffrey, BSc ACA *1985;* Diocese House, Lady Wootons Green, CANTERBURY.
DYSON, Mr. Howard Bernard, BSc FCA *1975;* 3 Grange Close, Bardsey, LEEDS, LS17 9AX. (Life Member)
DYSON, Mr. Ian, BA ACA *1987;* Field House, Manor Way Knott Park, Oxshott, LEATHERHEAD, KT22 0HS.
DYSON, Mr. John Christopher, MA FCA *1973;* 1 Dauntsey Court Duck Street, West Lavington, DEVIZES, SN10 4LR.
DYSON, Mr. John Hilton, FCA *1960;* Gronsundveien 65, 1394 NESBRU, NORWAY. (Life Member)
DYSON, Mr. John Howard, MA FCA *1973;* Bodalair House, Sandford Lane, Hurst, READING, RG10 0SU.
DYSON, Mr. John Nigel, FCA *1978;* Ashley Glebe Farm House Ashley, Kings Somborne, STOCKBRIDGE, SO20 6RJ.
DYSON, Dr. John Richard, FCA *1965;* 14 Coniston Avenue, POULTON-LE-FYLDE, LANCASHIRE, FY6 7NG. (Life Member)
DYSON, Mr. Jonathan, BA ACA *1983;* 5 Tennyson Road, Hutton, BRENTWOOD, ESSEX, CM13 2SJ.
DYSON, Mrs. Judith Mary, BSc FCA *1975;* Alveston, Main Street, Follifoot, HARROGATE, NORTH YORKSHIRE, HG3 1DU.
DYSON, Mr. Julian David Hadfield, BSc ARCS ACA *1997;* 3 Inglis Court, 15 Creffield Road, LONDON, W5 3HP.
DYSON, Mr. Keith Ashley David, ACA *2011;* Deloitte & Touche, PO Box 500, 2 Hardman Street, MANCHESTER, M60 2AT.
DYSON, Mr. Mark Edward, BA ACA *1987;* Fairview House, Rocky Lane, WIRRAL, MERSEYSIDE, CH60 0BZ.
DYSON, Mr. Matthew Damian, MA ACA CTA *1996;* 3 Dilly Lane, Barton on Sea, NEW MILTON, HAMPSHIRE, BH25 7DQ.
DYSON, Mr. Michael, MSc BSc ACA *2003;* 110 East 40th Street, Suite 903, NEW YORK, NY 10016-1801, UNITED STATES.
DYSON, Mr. Michael Frederick, FCA *1954;* 364 Wakefield Road, Dalton, HUDDERSFIELD, HD5 8DY. (Life Member)

DYSON, Mr. Patrick John, MA ACA *1986;* (Tax Fac), Spear & Jackson plc, Atlas Way, Atlas North, SHEFFIELD, S4 7QQ.
DYSON, Mr. Paul Derek, BSc ACA *1992;* Oak House, Coombe Park, KINGSTON UPON THAMES, KT2 7JD.
DYSON, Mr. Peter, FCA *1950;* 30 Park Avenue, Roundhay, LEEDS, LS8 2JH. (Life Member)
•DYSON, Mr. Peter, FCA *1986;* Bairstow & Atkinson, Carlton House, Bull Close Lane, HALIFAX, HX1 2EG.
DYSON, Mr. Richard George, MA FCA *1974;* (President 2006 - 2007) (Member of Council 2001 - 2010), Portinscale, 45 Arthog Road, Hale, ALTRINCHAM, WA15 0LU. (Life Member)
DYSON, Mrs. Samantha Jane, BA ACA *1995;* Cranmer House, Grubwood Lane, Cookham, MAIDENHEAD, BERKSHIRE, SL6 9UD.
•DYSON, Mrs. Toni Adele, BSc ACA *1987;* L E C G Ltd Davidson Building, 5 Southampton Street, LONDON, WC2E 7HA.
DYSON, Mrs. Valerie Anne, FCA *1983;* Park House Farm, Chelford Road, Henbury, MACCLESFIELD, CHESHIRE, SK11 9PG.
DYTE, Mr. Keith David, BCom ACA *1982;* The Beeches, Goathurst Common, SEVENOAKS, TN14 6BU.
•DZIALOWSKI, Mr. Benjamin, ACA *1979;* Alexander & Company, 220 The Vale, LONDON, NW11 8SR. See also Varbeck Limited
DZIEDZIC, Mr. Adam, ACA *2009;* Unit 2, 22 Blackly Row, Cockburn Central, PERTH, WA 6164, AUSTRALIA.
DZURUS BRADLEY, Mrs. Susan Leigh, BA ACA *2000;* 27 Kitsbury Road, BERKHAMSTED, HERTFORDSHIRE, HP4 3EA.
•EADE, Mr. Donald Keith, FCA *1967;* 11 Wildgoose Drive, HORSHAM, WEST SUSSEX, RH12 1TU.
EADE, Mrs. Dympna Marie, BA ACA *1983;* 186 Vines Avenue, THE VINES, WA 6069, AUSTRALIA.
EADE, Mr. Mark, BSc ACA *2005;* 46 Brouncker Road, LONDON, W3 8AQ.
EADE, Mr. Mark Edward, MSc ACA CTA *2004;* with Smith & Williamson Ltd, 25 Moorgate, LONDON, EC2R 6AY.
EADE, Mr. Matthew James, BA(Hons) ACA *2003;* 13 Nelson Road, TUNBRIDGE WELLS, KENT, TN2 5AW.
EADE, Miss. Rachel Jane, BA(Hons) ACA *2001;* Wolters Kluwer Health, Chowley Oak Business Park, Chowley Oak Lane, Tattenhall, CHESTER, CH3 9GA.
EADE, Mr. Roger Alexander, FCA *1973;* Nutek Ltd 20 Triumph Way, Woburn Road Industrial Estate Kempston, BEDFORD, MK42 7QB.
EADE, Mr. Thomas, MEng ACA *2002;* KPMG, 10 Shelley Street, SYDNEY, NSW 2000, AUSTRALIA.
EADES, Mr. Brian, FCA *1965;* 7 Wentworth Close, Farnborough, ORPINGTON, BR6 7EJ. (Life Member)
EADES, Mr. Colin William, FCA *1956;* 56 Clarendon Avenue, LEAMINGTON SPA, WARWICKSHIRE, CV32 4SA. (Life Member)
EADES, Mrs. Lisa Anne, BSc FCA *1992;* 4 Moorland Road, Maidenbower, CRAWLEY, RH10 7JB.
EADES, Miss. Victoria Alice, BSc ACA *2007;* with PricewaterhouseCoopers LLP, 1 Embankment Place, LONDON, WC2N 6RH.
EADIE, Mr. Alastair Kenneth, BSc FCA AMCT *1992;* 2 Burnaby Street, Chelsea, LONDON, SW10 0PH.
EADIE, Miss. Carolyn Claire, MA FCA *1980;* 86 Vincent Square, LONDON, SW1P 2PG.
EADIE, Mr. Christopher John, BA ACA *1998;* 50 Lillieshall Road, LONDON, SW4 0LP.
•EADIE, Mr. Douglas Young, BA FCA *1993;* Eadie Young Ltd, Chart House, Milton Road, Bloxham, BANBURY, OXFORDSHIRE OX15 4HD.
EADIE, Mr. Edward Charles, BSc ACA *2000;* 16 Hamilton Road, RD1, WAIMAUKU 0881, NEW ZEALAND.
EADIE, Mr. Paul Anthony, BA FCA *1991;* Hormann UK Limited, Gee Road, COALVILLE, LE67 4JW.
•EADIE, Mrs. Tracy Samantha, BCom FCA *1995;* Eadie Young Ltd, Chart House, Milton Road, Bloxham, BANBURY, OXFORDSHIRE OX15 4HD.
•EADON, Mr. David William, BSc FCA *1982;* BFE Brays Ltd, Building Society Chambers, Wesley Street, OTLEY, WEST YORKSHIRE, LS21 1AZ. See also Edward Ramsden Ltd
•EADON, Mr. Martin James Albert, MA FCA *1984;* 13 College Road, LONDON, SE21 7BG.
EADY, Mrs. Fiona, ACA *2002;* 8a Frog Lane, Upper Boddington, DAVENTRY, NORTHAMPTONSHIRE, NN11 6DJ.
EADY, Mrs. Jane Louise, BSc ACA *2003;* 246 Barry Road, LONDON, SE22 0JS.
EADY, Mr. Neil, BSc ACA *2003;* 246 Barry Road, East Dulwich, LONDON, SE22 0JS.
EADY, Mr. Richard Charles, ACA *1979;* North Staffordshire Combined Healthcare N H S Trust, Bucknall Hospital Eaves Lane, STOKE-ON-TRENT, ST2 8LD.
EAGAN, Mr. James Alexander, BSc ACA *2007;* Experian Ltd 6th Floor Cardinal Place, 80 Victoria Street, LONDON, SW1E 5JL.
EAGER, Miss. Anne, BSc ACA CTA *1994;* (Tax Fac), 77 Finnart Close, WEYBRIDGE, KT13 8QF.
EAGLAND, Mrs. Annalisa Mary, ACA *1990;* 2 The Green, WOODFORD GREEN, ESSEX, IG8 0NF.
•EAGLAND, Mr. Paul Mark, ACA ATII *1988;* BDO LLP, 55 Baker Street, LONDON, W1U 7EU. See also BDO Stoy Hayward LLP and Chiltern Tax Support for Professionals Limited
EAGLE, Mr. Alan Hugh, BA FCA *1975;* 48 Smithbarn, HORSHAM, RH13 6DX. (Life Member)
EAGLE, Miss. Caroline, BA ACA *1997;* Massey House, Flat 8 Massey House, 181 Brooklands Road, SALE, CHESHIRE, M33 3PJ.
•EAGLE, Mr. David Malcolm, BSc FCA *1982;* BDO LLP, Emerald House, East Street, EPSOM, SURREY, KT17 1HS. See also BDO Stoy Hayward LLP
EAGLE, Mr. James Charles, FCA *1954;* 25 Hospital Road., Swinton, MANCHESTER, M27 4EY.
EAGLE, Miss. Joanna Michele, MEng ACA *1997;* P O Box 771, NEW FARM, QLD 4005, AUSTRALIA.
EAGLE, Mr. Mark Frank, FCA *1993;* MacIntyre Hudson Llp, 30-34 New Bridge Street, LONDON, EC4V 6BJ.
EAGLE, Mr. Melvyn Nathan, FCA *1963;* 21 Newlands Avenue, RADLETT, WD7 8EH.
EAGLE, Mr. Nicholas David, BA ACA *1999;* 7 - 1238 Eastern Drive, PORT COQUITLAM V3C 6C5, BC, CANADA.
•EAGLE, Mr. Philip James, BSc FCA *1991;* (Tax Fac), Hallidays LLP, Riverside House, Kings Reach Business Park, Yew Street, STOCKPORT, CHESHIRE SK4 2HD. See also Hallidays Accountants LLP
EAGLE, Mrs. Rachel, BSc ACA *1996;* 3 Brentwood Road, Brincliffe, SHEFFIELD, S11 9BU.
EAGLE, Mr. Robert John, BA ACA *1998;* 13 Garsdale Crescent, Baildon, SHIPLEY, BD17 6TQ.
EAGLE, Dr. Simon Paul, MSc ACA *2001;* Osmington, Gloucester Road, ROSS-ON-WYE, HR9 5LR.
EAGLES, Mr. Darren Richard, BSc ACA *2003;* 4 Heys Close, ROSSENDALE, BB4 7LW.
•EAGLES, Mr. David Paul, MA ACA *1992;* PKF (UK) LLP, 16 The Havens, Ransomes Europark, IPSWICH, IP3 9SJ.
EAGLES, Mr. Jeremy John, BA ACA *1998;* Catlin Holdings Ltd, 3 Minster Court, LONDON, EC3R 7DD.
EAGLES, Mr. Simon Robert, BA ACA *1991;* Monument Securities, 25 St. James's Street, LONDON, SW1A 1HA.
EAGLESTONE, Mr. Adrian Alexis, BA ACA *1994;* Longmeadow, Downington, LECHLADE, GL7 3DL.
EAGLETON, Mr. Antony Sean, BSc ACA *1991;* 12 Union Drive, SHEFFIELD, S11 9EQ.
EAGLETON, Mr. Stephen William, FCA *1966;* 56 The Avenue, Kew, RICHMOND, SURREY, TW9 2AH.
EAGLING, Mr. Lee Elliot, BA(Hons) ACA *2011;* 19 Spring Gardens, NOTTINGHAM, NG8 4JN.
EAGLING, Mr. Stephen John, BSc ACA *2000;* 39 Lodge Farm Drive, NORWICH, NR6 7LP.
EAKHURST, Mr. Geoffrey Samuel, FCA *1954;* Post Cottage, The Square, Allithwaite, GRANGE-OVER-SANDS, LA11 7QF. (Life Member)
EAKINS, Mrs. Louise, BSc ACA *1996;* 17 Swansea Road, Penllegaer, SWANSEA, SA4 9AQ.
EAKINS, Mr. Simon Mark, BSc(Econ) ACA *1998;* 4 Seymour Avenue, BRISTOL, BS7 9HJ.
EALES, Mr. Christopher Owen Staniford, FCA *1955;* 4 Witley, 387 Sandbanks Road, POOLE, BH14 8HR. (Life Member)
EALES, Mr. Darryl Charles, BA ACA *1986;* 1 Vine Street, LONDON, W1J 0AH.
•EALES, Mrs. Helen, FCA *1979;* (Tax Fac), Pinder & Ratki, 7 Lansdowne Terrace, Gosforth, NEWCASTLE UPON TYNE, NE3 1HN.
EALES, Mrs. Joanne, BSc ACA *1989;* Pinfield House, 27 Cherry Hill Road, Barnt Green, BIRMINGHAM, B45 8LN.
EALES, Mr. Lyndon John, MEng ACA *1992;* Garth, Danzey Green, Tanworth-in-Arden, SOLIHULL, WEST MIDLANDS, B94 5BG.
EALES, Mr. Martin Wentworth, BA ACA *1997;* 34 Barham Road, West Wimbledon, LONDON, SW20 0ET.
EAMES, Mr. Alan Charles, ACA *1983;* Chewton Glen Hotel, Christchurch Road, NEW MILTON, HAMPSHIRE, BH25 6QS.
EAMES, Mr. Andrew, ACA *2009;* Ground Floor Flat, 7 Saville Place, BRISTOL, BS8 4EJ.
EAMES, Mr. Anthony Howard, FCA *1972;* Flat 11, The Yoo Building, 17 Hall Road, LONDON, NW8 9RF.
EAMES, Miss. Catharine Ursula, BA ACA *1994;* 49 Aubreys, LETCHWORTH GARDEN CITY, SG6 3TU.
EAMES, Mr. Christopher David, BSc ACA *1998;* 6 Symeon Place, Caversham, READING, RG4 7AS.
EAMES, Mrs. Clare Elizabeth, BSc ACA *1999;* 60 Monk Road, Bishopston, BRISTOL, BS7 8NE.
EAMES, Mr. Jason Anthony, BSc ACA *1998;* 60 Monk Road, Bishopston, BRISTOL, BS7 8NE.
EAMES, Mr. Richard Malcolm, BA ACA *1986;* 36 Orchard Avenue, BERKHAMSTED, HP4 3LG.
•EAMES, Mr. Robert Nigel, BSc ACA *1979;* 11 Oak Avenue, UPMINSTER, ESSEX, RM14 2LB.
•EAMES, Mr. Russell Mark, MSc ACA *1996;* Knox & Eames Limited, The Business Centre, Greys Green Farm, Rotherfield Greys, HENLEY-ON-THAMES, RG9 4QG.
•EAMES, Mr. Stephen, BA ACA *1986;* Mazars LLP, The Pinnacle, 160 Midsummer Boulevard, MILTON KEYNES, MK9 1FF.
EAMES, Mr. Stephen Richard, LLB FCA DChA *1996;* Flat 32 Belgrave House, 1-7 Clapham Road, LONDON, SW9 0JP.
EAMES, Mr. Thomas Richard Deane, BSc ACA *2002;* Albert Goodman, 57 Fore Street, CHARD, SOMERSET, TA20 1QA.
EAPEN, Mrs. Carol Patricia, BSc ACA *1982;* 206 Winston Road, PALMWOODS, QLD 4555, AUSTRALIA.
EAPEN, Mr. Mammen, ACA *1986;* (Tax Fac), Cambridge Consultants Ltd, 29 Science Park, Milton Road, CAMBRIDGE, CB4 0DW.
EARDLEY, Mr. Anthony Leighton, MA ACA *2011;* 26 Northpoint Square, LONDON, NW1 9AW.
EARDLEY, Mr. David Neil, BSc ACA *1996;* AstraZeneca AB, Sweden Operations, B337:9, 18160 LIDINGO, SWEDEN.
•EARDLEY, Mr. John Graham, BSc ACA *1984;* AIMS - Graham Eardley, 17 Wilsthorpe Road, Breaston, DERBY, DERBYSHIRE, DE72 3EA.
EARDLEY, Mr. Matthew William, ACA *2009;* 34 Oster Street, ST. ALBANS, HERTFORDSHIRE, AL3 5JL.
EARDLEY, Mr. Paul, BSc(Hons) ACA *2004;* 16 Grant Street, WEST CALDER, WEST LOTHIAN, EH55 8AG.
•EARDLEY, Mr. Philip James, PhD FCA *1988;* Haines Watts, Sterling House, 11 Omega Court, 350 Cemetery Road, SHEFFIELD, SOUTH YORKSHIRE S11 8FT.
•EARDLEY, Mr. Stephen, ACA FCCA *2009;* Howsons Accountants Limited, 18-20 Moorland Road, STOKE-ON-TRENT, ST6 1DW. See also Howsons
EARL, Mrs. Amy Jane, BA ACA *2002;* 34 Flint Lane, Barrow upon Soar, LOUGHBOROUGH, LEICESTERSHIRE, LE12 8GS.
EARL, Mr. Andrew Christopher, BA ACA *1998;* 24 Ford Road, SHEFFIELD, S11 7GZ.
EARL, Mr. Brian George, FCA *1964;* 6 Lordship Close, Hutton, BRENTWOOD, ESSEX, CM13 2QY.
EARL, Mr. David, FCA *1957;* P.O. Box 7121, ST ANNS, TRINIDAD AND TOBAGO. (Life Member)
EARL, Mrs. Emma, BSc ACA *2007;* 32a Portland Rise, LONDON, N4 2PP.
•EARL, Mrs. Fiona Diane, ACA *1983;* (Tax Fac), F.D. Earl, 3 Harvey Drive, SITTINGBOURNE, ME10 4UR.
EARL, Mr. Jonathan Christopher, ACA *2009;* Field Farm, Nether Westcote, CHIPPING NORTON, OXFORDSHIRE, OX7 6SD.
EARL, Mr. Jonathan Gareth, BSc ACA *2001;* 34 Flint Lane, Barrow upon Soar, LOUGHBOROUGH, LEICESTERSHIRE, LE12 8GS.
EARL, Mr. Mark, BA ACA *2010;* Flat 64 The Cedars, Park Road, NEWCASTLE UPON TYNE, TYNE AND WEAR, NE4 7DX.
EARL, Mr. Matthew James, MSc ACA *2006;* with Kingston Smith & Partners LLP, Devonshire House, 60 Goswell Road, LONDON, EC1M 7AD.
EARL, Mr. Patrick Martin, MA ACA *2003;* Linklaters CIS, Paveletskaya Square 2 bld. 2, 115054 MOSCOW, RUSSIAN FEDERATION.
•EARL, Mr. Peter Harvey, FCA *1969;* Pine Tree Cottage, Lodge Hill Lane, Ditchling, HASSOCKS, BN6 8SP.
EARL, Mr. Peter Robert, BA FCA *1984;* BAE Systems Programmes & Support Division, PO BOX 87 York House Farnborough Aerospace Centre, FARNBOROUGH, GU14 6YU.
EARL, Mr. Philip James, ACA *1997;* Doctors Net UK Ltd, 90 Milton Park Milton, ABINGDON, OXFORDSHIRE, OX14 4RY.
EARL, Miss. Rebecca, ACA *2011;* Flat 16, 89a Avenue Road Extension, LEICESTER, LE2 3EQ.
EARL, Mr. Robert Michael, ACA *2008;* 35 St. Marks Avenue, HARROGATE, NORTH YORKSHIRE, HG2 8AF.
EARL, Mr. Robin Michael, BSc ACA *1994;* 1 N G Baltic Place, South Shore Road, GATESHEAD, TYNE AND WEAR, NE8 3AE.
EARL, Mrs. Rosemary Jane, BSc ACA *1988;* Dept For Work & Pensions, GW33, Quarry House, Quarry Hill, LEEDS, LS2 7UA.
EARL, Mr. Simon William, ACA *2002;* 44, Crownfields, Weavering, MAIDSTONE, ME14 5TH.
•EARL, Mr. Stephen John, FCA *1977;* S.J. Earl, 22 The Fairway, LEIGH-ON-SEA, SS9 4QL.
EARL, Miss. Susan Elizabeth, BA ACA *1999;* Alliance & Leicester Plc, Bridle Road, BOOTLE, MERSEYSIDE, L30 4GB.
EARL, Mr. Tim, MEng ACA *2007;* Sainsburys Supermarkets Ltd, 33 Holborn, LONDON, EC1N 2HT.
EARL, Ms. Vicky Elizabeth, MA ACA *1998;* 30 Capel Road, WATFORD, HERTFORDSHIRE, WD19 4AE.
EARLAND, Mr. Paul, BSc ACA MCT *1987;* Trafigura Ltd, Portman House, 2 Portman Street, LONDON, W1H 6DU.
EARLAND, Mrs. Suzanne, BA ACA *1991;* Maple Haven, Eyhurst Close, Kingswood, TADWORTH, SURREY, KT20 6NR.
EARLE, Miss. Alison Claire, BSc ACA *2000;* Merck Sharp & Dohme Ltd, Shotton Lane, CRAMLINGTON, NORTHUMBERLAND, NE23 3JU.
EARLE, Mr. David Anthony, BSc FCA CTA *1976;* Beacon Firs Cottage, Seven Crosses, TIVERTON, ex16 6js.
EARLE, Mrs. Fiona Caroline, BA(Hons) ACA CIA *1991;* 1221 SW 4th Avenue Room 310, PORTLAND, OR 97204, UNITED STATES.
EARLE, Mr. George Newton, BA ACA *1993;* Roche House, Main Street, Oldcotes, WORKSOP, S81 8JF.
EARLE, Mr. George William Eric David, BTech ACA *1979;* 15 Castello Avenue, Putney, LONDON, SW15 6EA.
EARLE, Mr. Martin Stewart, FCA *1970;* Carramore House, 50 Vineyards Road, Northaw, POTTERS BAR, HERTFORDSHIRE, EN6 4PD.
•EARLE, Mr. Peter Philip, FCA *1980;* Menzies LLP, Ashcombe House, 5 The Crescent, LEATHERHEAD, KT22 8DY.
EARLE, Mr. Philip Reginald, BSc ACA *2007;* 58 St. Julians Farm Road, LONDON, SE27 0RS.
EARLE, Mr. Quentin Maurice, BSc FCA *1989;* Alliotts Imperial House, 15 Kingsway, LONDON, WC2B 6UN.
EARLE, Mrs. Sarah Florence, BA ACA *1993;* 62 Kingfisher Drive, GREENHITHE, DA9 9RT.
•EARLEY, Mr. David Walter, BSc FCA *1973;* David Earley (2005) Limited, Ketts House, Winchester Road, Chandler's Ford, EASTLEIGH, HAMPSHIRE SO53 2FZ. See also David Earley Limited
EARLY, Mrs. Caroline Ann, MA ACA *1996;* 84 Connaught Road, Brookwood, WOKING, GU24 0HF.
EARLY, Mr. Casey, MSc ACA *2004;* Peer House, Verulam Street, LONDON, WC1X 8LZ.
EARLY, Miss. Catriona, MEng ACA *2010;* Flat 311, Fellows Court, Weymouth Terrace, Hackney, LONDON, E2 8LA.
EARLY, Mr. Gavin Daniel, BSc ACA *2009;* Flat 7, 726a Wilmslow Road, MANCHESTER, M20 2DW.
EARLY, Mrs. Helen, BA FCA *1983;* 23 Deancroft Road, Chalfont St. Peter, GERRARDS CROSS, SL9 0HF.
EARLY, Mr. John Dalton, FCA *1970;* 3 Mayfair Park, Mersey Road, MANCHESTER, M20 2JW.
EARLY, Mr. Simon Jonathan, BSc ACA *1996;* 84 Connaught Road, Brookwood, WOKING, GU24 0HF.
EARNDEN, Mrs. Anna, BA(Hons) ACA *2011;* Valley View Holmside Lane, Burnhope, DURHAM, DH7 0DP.
•EARNSHAW, Mr. Andrew James, FCA *1981;* Josolyne & Co, Silk House, Park Green, MACCLESFIELD, CHESHIRE, SK11 7QW. See also Josolyne Medical Services Ltd
EARNSHAW, Mr. Charles Fenton, FCA *1946;* 6 Mulberry Close, CONWY, LL32 8GS. (Life Member)
EARNSHAW, Mr. Jeremy Waring, BEng FCA *1991;* Living Care Group, 63 Harrogate Road, LEEDS, LS7 3PQ.

EARNSHAW, Mrs. Julie Anne, BA ACA *1995;* 191 Colliers Break, Emersons Green, BRISTOL, BS16 7ED.
•**EARNSHAW, Mrs. Karen Esme, BA ACA** *1983;* Top Farm, Stocksmoor Road, Midgley, WAKEFIELD, WEST YORKSHIRE, WF4 4JQ.
EARNSHAW, Miss. Kathryn Jane, BA(Hons) ACA *2002;* 7 Industrial Street, Hightown, LIVERSEDGE, WEST YORKSHIRE, WF15 6NW.
EARNSHAW, Mr. Michael David, BSc ACA *1998;* First Data International F D R House, Christopher Martin Road, BASILDON, SS14 9AA.
EARNSHAW, Mr. Roger, FCA *1969;* 12 The Close, Rayners Lane, PINNER, HA5 5DU.
EARNSHAW, Miss. Ruth Elizabeth Grace, BSc ACA *1991;* 8 Alfred Road, BRENTWOOD, Essex, CM14 4BT.
EARP, Mr. Daniel James, BSc ACA *1999;* 89 Broom Park, TEDDINGTON, TW11 9RR.
•**EARP, Mr. James, BSc ACA** *1981;* Grant Thornton UK LLP, 30 Finsbury Square, LONDON, EC2P 2YU. See also Grant Thornton LLP
EARP, Mr. John, FCA *1972;* 199 Wingletye Lane, HORNCHURCH, ESSEX, RM11 3AL.
EARP, Mr. Matthew, BSc ACA *2007;* 4 Medway Drive, Bingham, NOTTINGHAM, NG13 8YD.
EARPS, Mr. Hugh Boyd, BA FCA *1975;* 3 St Davids Drive, Great Sutton, ELLESMERE PORT, CH66 2XE.
EARSMAN, Mr. Alan Mack, BA ACA *1993;* RBS Citizens, 100 Sockanosset Cross Road, CRANSTON, RI 02920, UNITED STATES.
EARTHROWL, Miss. Joanne, BSc ACA *2007;* 18 Colson Way, LONDON, SW16 1SD.
EARWICKER, Mr. David James, ACA *2005;* 5 Nash Drive, REDHILL, RH1 1LH.
EASBY, Mr. David Michael Wastell, FCA *1970;* 10 Holmcroft, Walton-on-the-Hill, TADWORTH, KT20 7XG.
EASBY, Mr. Peter John, FCA *1971;* Spratts Green Barn Spratts Green, Aylsham, NORWICH, NR11 6TX. (Life Member)
•**EASBY, Mr. Robert Philip, ACA** *2001;* Denmark Forrester Limited, First Floor, 1A High Street, SOUTHMINSTER, ESSEX, CM0 7AA.
EASDALE, Mr. Hamish Tait, MA FCA *1953;* 16 Vicarage Way, GERRARDS CROSS, BUCKINGHAMSHIRE, SL9 8AS. (Life Member)
EASDALE, Mr. Peter Ian Tait, FCA *1975;* 3 Badgers Glade, Burghfield Common, READING, RG7 3RQ. (Life Member)
EASDON, Mrs. Diane Catherine, BSc(Hons) ACA *1991;* Bates Tavner Resources International, 1st Floor, International House, 1 St. Katharines Way, LONDON, E1W 1UN.
EASEMAN, Mr. Antony James, BA ACA *1993;* 8 Dales Way, Guiseley, LEEDS, LS20 8JN.
EASEMAN, Mrs. Ruth Ann, BA ACA *1994;* 8 Dalesway, Guiseley, LEEDS, LS20 8JN.
EASLEA, Miss. Carolyn Margaret, BA ACA *1992;* 3 Highland Road, EMSWORTH, HAMPSHIRE, PO10 7JL.
EASLEA, Mr. Paul James Roger, ACA *2006;* Willmott Dixon Ltd Spirella Building, Bridge Road, LETCHWORTH GARDEN CITY, HERTFORDSHIRE, SG6 4ET.
EASON, Mr. Desmond Hugh Bernard, FCA *1954;* 3 Beechwood Avenue, Aylmerton, NORWICH, NR11 8QQ. (Life Member)
EAST, Mr. Bryan Martin Ford, BSc ACA *1983;* 8 Kestrel Close, Ewshot, FARNHAM, GU10 5TW.
EAST, Mr. Christopher Richard, BSc ACA *1991;* Fieldgate, Redbourn Lane, HARPENDEN, AL5 2AZ.
EAST, Mr. David Henry, FCA *1962;* 25 Havana Court, EASTBOURNE, EAST SUSSEX, BN23 5UH.
•**EAST, Mr. David John, FCA** *1973;* David J. East, Ashcroft House, 1 St Pauls Road, NEWTON ABBOT, DEVON, TQ12 2HP.
EAST, Miss. Emily, BSc ACA *2005;* 4 Pottery Street, Bermondsey, LONDON, SE16 4PH.
EAST, Mr. Graeme Philip, BSc ACA *1985;* 6 New Road, Forest Green, DORKING, RH5 5SA.
EAST, Mr. Mark John, BA ACA *1993;* Vondelstraat 118, 1054 GS AMSTERDAM, NETHERLANDS.
EAST, Mr. Michael Peter, FCA *1969;* Eastcastle, Management Group Ltd, 40-44 Newman Street, LONDON, W1T 1QD.
EAST, Mr. Peter Barnard, FCA *1962;* 56 Broome Grove, Wivenhoe, COLCHESTER, CO7 9QU. (Life Member)
EAST, Mr. Stephen John, BSc FCA FCT *1982;* White Ladies, Birch Hill, CROYDON, CR0 5HT.
EAST, Mr. Steven Peter, BSc ACA *1998;* 10 Westcombe Park Road, LONDON, SE3 7RB.
EAST, Mrs. Virginia Claire, ACA *1985;* 8 Kestrel Close, Ewshot, FARNHAM, GU10 5TW.
EASTAUGH, Mr. Colin Roy, BSc ACA *1982;* 58 Foyle Road, LONDON, SE3 7RH.
EASTAUGH, Mr. Guy Edward, MA ACA AMCT *1988;* 107 Cheapside, LONDON, EC2V 6DN.
•**EASTAWAY, Mr. Nigel Antony, FCA** *1966;* (Tax Fac), BDO LLP, 55 Baker Street, LONDON, W1U 7EU. See also BDO Stoy Hayward LLP
EASTBURN, Miss. Ruth Abigail, BSc(Hons) ACA *2002;* 20 Smith Avenue, ALLAMBIE HEIGHTS, NSW 2100, AUSTRALIA.
EASTCOTT, Mr. Mark, BSc ACA *1985;* 25 Merton Hall Road, LONDON, SW19 3PR.
EASTEAL, Mr. Christopher James, BA ACA *1995;* Kelvin Hughes Ltd, New North Road, ILFORD, IG6 2UR.
EASTELL, Mr. James Willoughby, BSc ACA *2002;* 141 Russell Road, LONDON, SW19 1LN.
•**EASTELL, Mr. Rupert John, BSc ACA** *1986;* Baker Tilly Tax and Advisory Services LLP, 25 Farringdon Street, LONDON, EC4A 4AB.
EASTER, Mrs. Annabelle, BA(Hons) ACA *2011;* 96 Victoria Road, Harborne, BIRMINGHAM, B17 0AE.
EASTER, Mr. David Henry, FCA *1964;* 227 Sycamore Road, FARNBOROUGH, HAMPSHIRE, GU14 6RQ.
EASTER, Mr. Granville Edward Dixon, ACA *1995;* Penfield, Doggetts Wood Close, CHALFONT ST. GILES, BUCKINGHAMSHIRE, HP8 4TL.
EASTER, Mr. Gregory Owen, BSc ACA *2010;* 96 Victoria Road, Harborne, BIRMINGHAM, B17 0AE.
EASTER, Mr. Jonathan Paul, BA ACA *1984;* 16 Damson Way, ST. ALBANS, AL4 9XU.
EASTERBROOK, Mr. Adrian Charles, FCA *1964;* 17 Westhill Road, PAIGNTON, TQ3 2ND. (Life Member)
EASTERBROOK, Mrs. Beatrix Mary, BSc FCA *1992;* High Brecks Lincoln Road, East Markham, NEWARK, NOTTINGHAMSHIRE, NG22 0SN.
EASTERBROOK, Mr. Deven Edward Cyril, FCA *1960;* Pine Cottage, Lennox Avenue, SIDMOUTH, DEVON, EX10 8TX. (Life Member)
EASTERBROOK, Mr. Horace Frederick, FCA *1951;* 7925 E.Meseto Avenue, MESA, AZ 85209-5086, UNITED STATES. (Life Member)
EASTERBROOK, Mr. Paul, BA ACA *2004;* 50 Boddens Hill Road, Heaton Mersey, STOCKPORT, SK4 2DG.
EASTERBROOK, Mr. Peter John, ACA *2009;* 50 Boddens Hill Road, STOCKPORT, CHESHIRE, SK4 2DG.
EASTERBROOK, Mr. Stephen James, BSc ACA *1994;* 56 Marsham Way, GERRARDS CROSS, BUCKINGHAMSHIRE, SL9 8AP.
EASTERBROOK, Mr. Stephen Keith, ACA *2009;* 50 Boddens Hill Road, STOCKPORT, CHESHIRE, SK4 2DG.
EASTERBROOK, Mrs. Susan Patricia, BSc ACA *1994;* Greenbanks, 56 Marsham Way, GERRARDS CROSS, BUCKINGHAMSHIRE, SL9 8AP.
EASTHAM, Mrs. Carol, BSc ACA *1981;* 16 Hamptons Lane, SOUTHAMPTON SN 02, BERMUDA.
EASTHAM, Miss. Charlotte Antonia, BA(Hons) ACA *2010;* 15 New Barton Street, SALFORD, M6 7WN.
EASTHAM, Mr. Keith William, BSc ACA *1988;* Intake Farm, Stangtop Road, Roughlee, NELSON, BB9 6NZ.
EASTHAM, Mr. Robert Murrough, FCA *1971;* Goytre, Llanfihangel Brynpabuan, BUILTH WELLS, POWYS, LD2 3PS.
EASTHAM, Mr. Robert William, BSc ACA *1981;* 16 Hamptons Lane, SOUTHAMPTON SN 02, BERMUDA.
EASTHILL, Mr. Henry John Dowson, MA FCA *1962;* 5 Jockey Road, WEDNESBURY, WS10 9BB. (Life Member)
EASTHOPE, Mr. Tony Stuart, ACA *1989;* Veyance Technologies UK Limited, Unit 25 Robins Road Burntwood Business Park, BURNTWOOD, STAFFORDSHIRE, WS7 3XB.
EASTICK, Mr. Jonathan Louis Peter, BSc ACA *1993;* Ul Dluga 22B, 05-822 Milanowek, WARSAW, POLAND.
EASTLAKE, Mr. David Gordon, BA ACA HKICPA *1989;* Apartment 2227, Four Seasons Place, 8 Finance Street, CENTRAL, HONG KONG ISLAND, HONG KONG SAR.
EASTLAKE, Mr. Edward Charles Philip, BSc FCA *1977;* 13 Morland Drive, Lamberhurst, TUNBRIDGE WELLS, KENT, TN3 8HZ.
EASTMAN, Mr. Bruce David, FCA *1977;* A C C A, 29 Lincoln's Inn Fields, LONDON, WC2A 3EE.
EASTMAN, Mr. Christopher James Robert, MEng ACA *2005;* with Deloitte LLP, 3 Rivergate, Temple Quay, BRISTOL, BS1 6GD.
EASTMAN, Mr. Henry Guy, BA ACA *1982;* 55 Britannia Road, LONDON, SW6 2JR.
EASTMAN, Mr. Mike, MSc BA ACA *2010;* 7100 Shannon Drive, EDINA, MN 55439, UNITED STATES.
EASTMAN, Mrs. Rachel Kate Geraldine, BSc ACA *1992;* Barkston House, Back Lane, Barkston House, TADCASTER, LS24 9PL.
EASTMENT, Mrs. Stephanie Mary, BSc ACA *1989;* Strathallan, 9 Mile House Lane, ST. ALBANS, HERTFORDSHIRE, AL1 1TH.
EASTMOND, Mr. Deyman Gregory, MA FCA *1961;* 8 Hartington Road, Chiswick, LONDON, W4 3UA. (Life Member)
•**EASTMOND, Mr. Stephen Reginald, FCA** *1973;* (Tax Fac), Eastmond & Co Limited, 4 Cordwallis Street, MAIDENHEAD, BERKSHIRE, SL6 7BE.
EASTOE, Mr. Anthony Paul, ACA *2008;* 65 Roseleigh Road, SITTINGBOURNE, KENT, ME10 1RR.
EASTOE, Mr. Basil Eric, FCA *1953;* P.O. Box 67704, BRYANSTON, GAUTENG, 2021, SOUTH AFRICA. (Life Member)
EASTOE, Mr. Sidney Howard, FCA *1966;* 3 Dene Road, NORTHWOOD, HA6 2AE. (Life Member)
EASTON, Dr. Caroline Susan, MBBS ACA *2000;* Flat 6 199, Southwark Bridge Road, LONDON, SE1 0ED.
EASTON, Miss. Genevieve, BA(Hons) ACA *2010;* 11a Blackstock Road, LONDON, N4 2JF.
EASTON, Mr. Gregory Alan, BSc ACA *2000;* Meadow Vale, Langfords Lane, High Littleton, BRISTOL, BS39 6HN.
•**EASTON, Mr. Jack Edward, BA FCA** *1982;* UHY Hacker Young LLP, Quadrant House, 4 Thomas More Square, LONDON, E1W 1YW.
EASTON, Mr. Malcolm Stewart, FCA *1972;* Court Cottage, South Street, Dolton, WINKLEIGH, EX19 8QS. (Life Member)
EASTON, Mr. Mark Andrew, ACA *2001;* Bauerlegasse 18 30+31, 1200 VIENNA, AUSTRIA.
EASTON, Mr. Paul Stephen, FCA *1976;* 18 Torcross Close, Glenfield, LEICESTER, LE3 8AP.
EASTON, Mr. Peter Francis, BA FCA *1955;* 28 Broad Street, WOKINGHAM, RG40 1AB. (Life Member)
EASTON, Mr. Richard John, FCA *1963;* Pheasants Oak, Burford Lane, Shelfield, ALCESTER, B49 6JH.
EASTON, Ms. Sally Elizabeth, BSc ACA *2001;* 33 Sistova Road, LONDON, SW12 9QR.
EASTON, Miss. Samantha, BSc ACA *2000;* Richardson groves, Cleveland House, Sydney Road, BATH, BA2 6NR.
EASTON, Mrs. Sarah Elizabeth, BSc ACA *1991;* Wype Doles Farm, Angle Bridge, Whittlesey, PETERBOROUGH, PE7 2HL.
EASTON, Mr. Stephen John, BSc FCA *1995;* 10 Devonshire Road, Belmont, DURHAM, DH1 2BQ.
EASTWOOD, Mr. Alan Roy, BCom ACA *1982;* Flint Management Ltd, 31 Moor Lane, RICKMANSWORTH, HERTFORDSHIRE, WD3 1LE.
EASTWOOD, Mr. Andrew Michael, ACA *1993;* 72 Cornfield, STALYBRIDGE, CHESHIRE, SK15 2UB.
EASTWOOD, Mrs. Anne Mairi, BSc FCA *1976;* Flexneys House, Main Road, Stanton Harcourt, WITNEY, OX29 5RP.
•**EASTWOOD, Mr. Anthony George, FCA** *1972;* (Tax Fac), A.G. Eastwood & Co, 2 Brook Place Cottages, Ide Hill, SEVENOAKS, TN14 6BL.
•**EASTWOOD, Mr. David Geoffrey Radcliffe, MA FCA** *1986;* KPMG LLP, 15 Canada Square, LONDON, E14 5GL. See also KPMG Europe LLP
EASTWOOD, Mr. Derek Arthur, FCA *1953;* 113 Laidon Avenue, Wistaston, CREWE, CHESHIRE, CW2 6QH. (Life Member)
EASTWOOD, Miss. Elizabeth Jane, BSS ACA *1986;* (Tax Fac), A E S Electric Ltd, 37 Kew Foot Road, RICHMOND, SURREY, TW9 2SS.
•**EASTWOOD, Mr. Jeremy Colin, BA ACA** *1978;* AIMS - Jeremy Eastwood ACA, 10 Broad Close, Barford St. Michael, BANBURY, OXFORDSHIRE, OX15 0RW.
EASTWOOD, Mr. John, FCA *1974;* 87 Chesterfield Drive, SEVENOAKS, KENT, TN13 2EQ.
EASTWOOD, Mr. John David, FCA *1956;* Flat 9, Ivy Park Court, 35 Ivy Park Road, SHEFFIELD, S10 3LA. (Life Member)
EASTWOOD, John Helperos Ritzema, Esq OBE FCA *1931;* Flat 3 5 Second Avenue, HOVE, BN3 2LH. (Life Member)
EASTWOOD, Mr. John Stuart, BCom FCA *1984;* 36 Miller Gardens, Riverside, PRESTON, PR1 8EW.
EASTWOOD, Ms. Karel, BSc ACA *1996;* 3 North Road, LONDON, N6 4BD.
EASTWOOD, Mr. Martin Leonard, BSc FCA CPA *1969;* M L Eastwood, P.O. Box 2033, REEDS SPRING, MO 65737, UNITED STATES.
EASTWOOD, Mr. Michael Alan, FCA *1966;* 14 Fir Tree Close, DUKINFIELD, SK16 5HW.
EASTWOOD, Mr. Neville, FCA *1952;* 55 Alms Hill Road, SHEFFIELD, S11 9RR. (Life Member)
EASTWOOD, Mr. Nicholas John, BA ACA *1985;* Rugby Football Union, 200 Whitton Road, TWICKENHAM, TW2 7BA.
EASTWOOD, Mr. Paul, LLB ACA *2002;* (Tax Fac), with Deloitte LLP, PO Box 403, Lord Coutanche House, 66-68 Esplanade, St Helier, JERSEY JE4 8WA.
EASTWOOD, Mr. Paul, MA ACA *2004;* 550 North Kingsbury Street, Unit 509, CHICAGO, IL 60654, UNITED STATES.
EASTWOOD, Miss. Paula Marie, BSc ACA *1989;* PricewaterhouseCoopers LLP, 17-00 PWC Building, 8 Cross Street, SINGAPORE 048424, SINGAPORE.
EASTWOOD, Mr. Robert, BA ACA *1986;* University of Liverpool Foundation Building, Brownlow Hill, LIVERPOOL, L69 7ZX.
EASTWOOD, Mr. Roger Clive, FCA *1981;* Meadow Cottage, Butcherfield Lane, HARTFIELD, EAST SUSSEX, TN7 4LD.
EASTWOOD, Mr. Rupert John Anthony, MA ACA *1993;* 4th Floor, 35 Davies Street, LONDON, W1K 4LS.
EASTWOOD, Mrs. Tracey, BA(Hons) ACA CTA *2003;* Winkleigh Cottage, La Grande Route de Rozel, St. Martin, JERSEY, JE3 6AP.
EASUN, Mrs. Claire Jane, BA ACA *2006;* 2 Boundary Road, Beeston, NOTTINGHAM, NG9 2RF.
EASUN, Miss. Lorraine Jennifer, MSci ACA CTA *2003;* (Tax Fac), 8 Furzedown Close, EGHAM, SURREY, TW20 9PY.
EATHERINGTON, Mr. John Arthur, FCA *1949;* 123 Breckhill Road, Mapperley, NOTTINGHAM, NG3 5JP. (Life Member)
EATOCK, Mrs. Elizabeth Louise, BSc ACA *2005;* Leeds City Council, Public Private Partnerships Unit, Civic Hall, Calverley Street, LEEDS, LS1 1UR.
EATOCK, Mr. Matthew Joseph, BSc ACA *2004;* 53 Jackson Avenue, LEEDS, LS8 1NS.
EATON, Mr. Andrew, BA ACA *1992;* Systagenix World Management, 2 City Place, Beehive Ring Road, London Gatwick Airport, GATWICK, WEST SUSSEX RH6 0PA.
EATON, Mr. Andrew John, BSc ACA *1991;* 66 Queen Victoria Road, SHEFFIELD, S17 4HU.
EATON, Mr. Anthony Francis, FCA *1962;* 40 Mill Road, Henham, BISHOP'S STORTFORD, HERTFORDSHIRE, CM22 6AB.
EATON, Mr. Benjamin, BA ACA *1999;* Flat 29 Esme House, Ludovick Walk, LONDON, SW15 5LJ.
EATON, Mr. Benjamin William, BSc ACA *2007;* 21 Ash Grove, ILKLEY, WEST YORKSHIRE, LS29 8EP.
EATON, Mrs. Carley Ann, ACA *2009;* 29 Levendale Road, LONDON, SE23 2TP.
EATON, Mrs. Clare, BSc ACA *2004;* E D F Energy, 40 Grosvenor Place, LONDON, SW1X 7EN.
EATON, Mr. David Andrew, MBE BA BSc FCA *1983;* (Tax Fac), The Cedars School Lane, Great Barton, BURY ST. EDMUNDS, SUFFOLK, IP31 2RQ.
EATON, Mr. David Michael, BSc ACA *2010;* 30 Havelock Road, WOKINGHAM, RG41 2XU.
EATON, Mr. Derek James, BSc ACA *1994;* 53 Cedars Road, BECKENHAM, BR3 4JG.
EATON, Mr. Desmond Trevor, FCA *1951;* Jan Van Beierenlaan 970, 2722 VB ZOETERMEER, NETHERLANDS. (Life Member)
EATON, Mr. Geoffrey Dennis, BA ACA *1983;* Uniq Plc, No1 Chalfont Park, GERRARDS CROSS, BUCKINGHAMSHIRE, SL9 0UN.
EATON, Mr. Gregory Paul, BSc FCA *1990;* 33 Carlton Road, Caversham, READING, RG4 7NT.
EATON, Ms. Gretchen Zoe, BA ACA *1999;* 49 Mysore Road, LONDON, SW11 5RY.
•**EATON, Mr. Guy Ashley, FCA** *1974;* 17 Honeyman Close, LONDON, NW6 7AZ.
•**EATON, Mr. John, FCA** *1971;* The Stables, Coupass Cottages, Feckenham, REDDITCH, WORCESTERSHIRE, B96 6HW.
EATON, Mr. John Edward Peter, FCA *1973;* Westgrove, Kestell Road, SIDMOUTH, EX10 8JJ.
EATON, Mr. Kenneth Ronald, BA ACA *1980;* 19 Falcon Wood, LEATHERHEAD, SURREY, KT22 7TF.
EATON, Miss. Lucy, BSc ACA *2004;* with Grant Thornton UK LLP, Hartwell House, 55-61 Victoria Street, BRISTOL, BS1 6FT.
EATON, Mr. Marc David, BSc ACA *1998;* 21 Seven Acres, THAME, OX9 3JQ.
EATON, Mrs. Maria, BSc ACA *2000;* Lark Rise, Hollybush Close, Potten End, BERKHAMSTED, HERTFORDSHIRE, HP4 2SN.

EATON, Mr. Mark Charles, BSc ACA CTA *1996;* (Tax Fac), 22 Witley Avenue, SOLIHULL, B91 3JD.
EATON, Mr. Mark Rayner, BA ACA *1980;* Adecco management & consulting SA, Sagereistrasse 10, P. O. Box, CH 8152 GLATTBRUGG, SWITZERLAND.
EATON, Mr. Michael Charles, FCA *1975;* 6 Woodland Crescent, BRACKNELL, BERKSHIRE, RG42 2LH.
•EATON, Mr. Paul Douglas, ACA *1992;* P D Eaton & Co, 32 Main Street, Lambley, NOTTINGHAM, NG4 4PN. See also K J Eaton & Company and K.J.Eaton & Co (Accountants) Ltd
EATON, Mr. Paul William, FCA *1975;* Bentley Systems UK Limited, North Heath Lane, HORSHAM, WEST SUSSEX, RH12 5QE.
EATON, Miss. Rebecca Louise, MEng ACA *2009;* 65 Twyn Road, Abercarn, NEWPORT, GWENT, NP11 5JY.
EATON, Mr. Roy Stanley, FCA *1973;* Flat 4, 79 Jasmin Croft, Kings Heath, BIRMINGHAM, B14 5AX.
EATON, Mr. Simon, BSc ACA *2007;* Flat 5, 41 Priory Road, LONDON, NW6 4NS.
EATON, Mrs. Suzanne Jane, BA ACA *1989;* 33 Carlton Road, Caversham Heights, READING, RG4 7NT.
•EATOUGH, Mrs. Diane Louise, BA FCA *1977;* (Tax Fac), PM+M Solutions for Business LLP, Greenbank Technology Park, Challenge Way, BLACKBURN, BB1 5QB. See also PM & M Corporate Finance Limited
EATWELL, Mr. Robert, BA ACA *2000;* 10 Serviden Drive, BROMLEY, BR1 2UB.
EAVES, Mr. Christopher Barry, MSc BA(Econ) FCA *1978;* 6 Cargate Lane, Upton, NORWICH, NR13 6AU.
EAVES, Mr. Damian Walmsley, BA ACA *1992;* 9 Spout Spinney, Stannington, SHEFFIELD, S6 6EQ.
EAVES, Mr. Mark, BA ACA CTA *2004;* (Tax Fac), 8 Waterford Gate, Pine Street, AYLESBURY, BUCKINGHAMSHIRE, HP19 7HX.
•EAVES, Mr. Paul Nigel Thomas, BSc FCA *1989;* (Tax Fac), Eaves and Co, 11 Part Street, SOUTHPORT, MERSEYSIDE, PR8 1HX.
EAVES, Miss. Shirley Jean, FCA *1971;* Flat 5, Hurstbourne Priors, 19 Harewood Road, SOUTH CROYDON, SURREY, CR2 7AT.
EAYRES, Mr. John Alfred, FCA *1970;* Rowan, 17 Station Road, Leziate, KING'S LYNN, PE32 1EJ.
EBANKS, Miss. Lorraine Dawn, BA ACA *1993;* 55 Norman Crescent, PINNER, MIDDLESEX, HA5 3QH.
EBBAGE, Mr. Kenneth Alan, FCA *1975;* Pentana, Gate House, Fretherne Road, WELWYN GARDEN CITY, HERTFORDSHIRE, AL8 6RD.
EBBATSON, Mr. Derek William, BA FCA *1980;* 20A Castle Hill Drive, Brockworth, GLOUCESTER, GL3 4PQ.
EBBATSON, Mrs. Emma Jane, BA ACA *2004;* 53 Swallow Lane, Golcar, HUDDERSFIELD, HD7 4NB.
EBBELS, Miss. Louise Elizabeth, BA(Hons) ACA *2010;* 12 Pennington Place, TUNBRIDGE WELLS, KENT, TN4 0AQ.
EBBETT, Ms. Neela, BSc ACA *1993;* Flat 5, 83 Canfield Gardens, LONDON, NW6 3EA.
EBBS, Mr. John Arthur, FCA *1970;* 2nd Floor Flat, The PLAS, High Street, HARLECH, LL46 2YA. (Life Member)
EBDON, Mr. James George, FCA *1969;* Cool Bawn, 15 Tamesis Gardens, WORCESTER PARK, KT4 7JX.
•EBDON, Miss. Lydia Margaret, BSc FCA *1996;* L M Ebdon Ltd, Lund Farm, The Lund, Easingwold, YORK, YO61 3PA.
EBDON, Mr. Neil, BSc ACA *2010;* 58 Carisbrooke Road, LEEDS, LS16 5RU.
EBEL, Mr. Antony Gerard, LLB FCA *1968;* The Annexe, 56a The Close, SALISBURY, SP1 2EL.
EBELING, Mr. Michael George, BA FCA *1963;* (Tax Fac), 9 The Ridings, COTTINGHAM, NORTH HUMBERSIDE, HU16 5NW.
EBENEZER, Mr. John Edward, MBE FCA JDipMA *1961;* Perefrith Barn, Fairdene, Hogscross Lane, Chipstead, COULSDON, SURREY CR5 3SJ.
EBERHARDT, Mr. Martin, BSc ACA *1986;* Marlyn, 39 Broad Ha'penny, Boundstone Road, FARNHAM, GU10 4TF.
EBERHART, Ms. Katharine Sue, ACA *1989;* White Cottage, The Enterdent, GODSTONE, RH9 8EG.
EBERST, Mr. Mark Simon, BA ACA *2000;* with KPMG Slovensko, Dvorakovo nabrezie 10, P. O. Box 7, 811 02 BRATISLAVA, SLOVAK REPUBLIC.
•EBERT, Mr. Ahron, BSc FCA *1983;* (Tax Fac), Ebert & Co, 9 Windsor Court, Golders Green Road, LONDON, NW11 9PP.
EBIED, Mr. Paul Zaid, ACA *2009;* 27b St. Anns Villas, LONDON, W11 4RT.
EBLETT, Mr. Kieran James, BA ACA *2006;* 2 Valley Court, LEEDS, LS17 6LU.
EBLING, Mr. Paul, BA ACA *1983;* 7 Kilcorral Close, EPSOM, KT17 4HX.
EBLING, Mr. Richard John, FCA *1968;* Apartado 24, Casa do Mar E81, 8401-951 LAGOA, ALGARVE, PORTUGAL. (Life Member)
EBNER, Mr. Mark Benjamin, BA FCA *1993;* 24 St Georges Road, LONDON, NW11 0LR.
EBRAHIM, Mr. Aasif Osman, ACA *2011;* 20 Pinewood Grove, LONDON, W5 2AG.
EBRAHIM, Mr. Abdool Rashid Aboobaker, FCA *1974;* Rashid Ebrahim, 71 Dr. Lesur Street, Unit 7, BEAU BASSIN, MAURITIUS.
•EBRAHIM, Mr. Afsar Azize Abdulla, FCA CF *1991;* BDO De Chazal du Mee, P.O. Box 799, 10 Frere Felix, De Valois Street, PORT LOUIS, MAURITIUS.
•EBRAHIM, Mr. Arifhusein, FCA *1975;* Ebrahim, 252 Uxbridge Road, RICKMANSWORTH, WD3 8EA.
EBRAHIM, Mr. Moiz, ACA *2009;* 63 Franklins, Maple Cross, RICKMANSWORTH, HERTFORDSHIRE, WD3 9SY.
EBRAHIM, Mr. Muhammad Masood, ACA FCCA *2009;* with KPMG LLP, 15 Canada Square, LONDON, E14 5GL.
•EBRAHIM, Mr. Sherali, FCA *1959;* (Tax Fac), S. Ebrahim, 5 Porlock Avenue, HARROW, MIDDLESEX, HA2 0AP.
EBRAHIMJI, Mr. Murtaza, BSc ACA *1997;* PO BOX 506526, DUBAI, UNITED ARAB EMIRATES.
EBRAHIMJI SAEED, Mr. Murtaza Saifudin, FCA *1975;* PO Box 1208, MOMBASA, 80100, KENYA.
EBREY, Mr. Robert Mark, BA ACA *2000;* 2 Wharf Cottage, Station Road, Padworth, READING, RG7 4JN.
EBSWORTH, Mr. Steven David, BA FCA *1991;* 119 Passage Road, BRISTOL, AVON, BS9 3LF.
EBURAH, Mr. Peter James, BSc ACA *1979;* 1 Kingsland Cottage, Benover Road, Yalding, MAIDSTONE, ME18 6EL.
ECCLES, Mr. Antony David Edward, BA ACA *1999;* Dresdner Kleinwort Benson, 20 Fenchurch Street, LONDON, EC3P 3DB.
ECCLES, Mr. David John, ACA *1984;* 13 Empress Avenue, FARNBOROUGH, Hampshire, GU14 8LU.
ECCLES, Mrs. Emma Mary Anna, BA ACA *2006;* Champion Consulting Ltd 1 Worsley Court, High Street Worsley, MANCHESTER, M28 3NJ.
ECCLES, Mrs. Eve, BA ACA *1986;* 9 les Bastides, Chemin de la Carraire, 83600 LES ADRETS DE L'ESTREREL, FRANCE.
ECCLES, Mr. George William O'Neale, LLB FCA *1977;* 9 Les Bastides, Quartier La Beilesse, 83600 LES ADRETS DE L'ESTREREL, FRANCE.
ECCLES, Mr. John William, BSc FCA *1976;* 89 Angotts Mead, STEVENAGE, SG1 2NJ.
ECCLES, Mr. Jonathan Allen, BA(Hons) ACA ACCA *2007;* 22b Colwell Road, LONDON, SE22 8QP.
•ECCLES, Mr. Jonathan Philip, ACA *2001;* (Tax Fac), with Prism Group Limited, The Old Sawmill, Copyhold Lane, Lindfield, HAYWARDS HEATH, WEST SUSSEX RH16 1XT.
ECCLES, Mr. Nigel Peter, BSc ACA *1991;* 36 Kimpton Road, Wheathampstead, ST. ALBANS, HERTFORDSHIRE, AL4 8LD.
•ECCLES, Mr. Richard Mark, BA FCA *1995;* with RSM Tenon Audit Limited, Charterhouse, Legge Street, BIRMINGHAM, B4 7EU.
ECCLES, Miss. Stephanie Anne, BA(Hons) ACA *2010;* 173 Vale Road, Woolton, LIVERPOOL, L25 7RY.
ECCLES-WILLIAMS, Mr. Simon Gavin Piers, MA ACA *1980;* Oak Hall, Pleshey, CHELMSFORD, CM3 1JD.
ECCLESHALL, Mr. George Linney, MA FCA *1947;* 17 Kingsdowne Road, SURBITON, KT6 6JZ. (Life Member)
ECCLESHALL, Miss. Joanne Elizabeth, MA ACA *1988;* 15 Harebell Hill, COBHAM, SURREY, KT11 2RS.
ECCLESTON, Mr. David John, FCA *1964;* White Top, Pistyll Hill, Marford, WREXHAM, LL12 8LE.
ECCLESTON, Mrs. Elen, BA ACA *2004;* 7 Bramblewood Close, Chirk Bank, WREXHAM, CLWYD, LL14 5LP.
ECCLESTON, Mr. John David, BA ACA *1991;* C/Zigordia 51 2A, 20800 ZARAUTZ, SPAIN.
ECCLESTON, Mr. Nathan, BA ACA *1999;* 23 Elton Road, HERTFORD, HERTFORDSHIRE, SG14 3DW.
ECCLESTON, Mr. Robert John, FCA *1966;* 18 Wordsworth Avenue, Headlers Cross, REDDITCH, B97 5BG.
ECHALIER, Miss. Fiona Helen, ACA *2008;* 14 Chatham Road, LONDON, E17 6EU.
ECHEVERRIA-VALDA, Mr. Fernando Timothy, BSc(Econ) ACA *1999;* 261 river valley road 0628 Aspen Heights, SINGAPORE, SINGAPORE.
ECKARDT, Mr. Philip Irving, BSc ACA *2010;* 19 Wykeham Way, Haddenham, AYLESBURY, BUCKINGHAMSHIRE, HP17 8BL.
ECKERSALL, Miss. Patricia Joan, BCom FCA *1983;* 176 The Circle, Queen Elizabeth Street, LONDON, SE1 2JL.
ECKERSLEY, Mr. Dennis William, BCom FCA *1953;* Birtles Cottage, 28 Goughs Lane, KNUTSFORD, WA16 8QL. (Life Member)
ECKERSLEY, Mr. Jonathan Lewis, ACA *1985;* 6 Haile Drive, Worsley, MANCHESTER, M28 1SL.
ECKERSLEY, Mr. Mark Robert, BSc ACA *1984;* 7 The Spinney, St Catherines, Newfield Lane, Dore Sheffield, SHEFFIELD, S17 3AL.
ECKERSLEY, Mr. Martin William, ACA *1980;* Cedar House, Hervines Road, AMERSHAM, BUCKINGHAMSHIRE, HP6 5HS.
•ECKERSLEY, Mr. Paul Norman, BSc FCA *1987;* SMP Accounting and Tax Limited, PO Box 227, Clinch's House, Lord Street, Douglas, ISLE OF MAN IM99 1RZ.
ECKERSLEY, Mr. Thomas Geoffrey, BA FCA *1969;* 1 Swancourt, Twyford, READING, RG10 0AZ. (Life Member)
ECKFORD, Mr. Andrew, BSc FCA *1999;* 12 Kirkhill Bank, Cubley, Penistone, SHEFFIELD, S36 9UX.
ECKFORD, Mr. James Conway, MA FCIB FCA *1969;* 1 The Oval, WALLASEY, MERSEYSIDE, CH45 6UX.
ECKHARDT, Mr. David, FCA *1968;* 29 Montpelier Sqaure, LONDON, SW7 1JY.
•ECKHARDT, Mr. James Daniel, FCA *1996;* James Eckhardt, 2 Queensborough Court, North Circular Road, LONDON, N3 3JP.
•ECKLAND, Mrs. Mary, BSc ACA *1979;* Decameas Ltd, 17 Berceau Walk, WATFORD, WD17 3BL.
ECKLES, Ms. Elizabeth Anne, MA ACA *1996;* 1 Hazel View, Marple, STOCKPORT, CHESHIRE, SK6 7JF.
ECKLEY, Mr. Neville Richard, FCA FCCA MIPA MICM FCMI FABRP *1965;* Coppers Roost, Holcombe Rogus, WELLINGTON, SOMERSET, TA21 0NB. (Life Member)
ECKSTEIN, Mr. Ian, FCA *1977;* Har Nof, 66-22 Harov Shaulson Street, PO Box 43005 JERUSALEM, 95400, ISRAEL.
•ECOB, Mr. Gary David, BSc ACA *1999;* Orbis Partners LLP, Third Floor, 35 Newhall Street, BIRMINGHAM, B3 3PU.
•ECOB, Mrs. Josephine Simone, BA ACA *1980;* (Tax Fac), Abrams Ecob Limited, 41 St. Thomas's Road, CHORLEY, LANCASHIRE, PR7 1JE.
ECOB, Mrs. Nikki, BSc ACA *2007;* with Deloitte LLP, 4 Brindley Place, BIRMINGHAM, B1 2HZ.
•ECONOMIDES, Mr. Constantinos, BSc ACA *2003;* Fidelico Limited, G Pavlides Court, 5th Floor, 2 Arch Kyprianou & Ayiou Andreou Street, 3036 LIMASSOL, CYPRUS.
ECONOMIDES, Miss. Elena, BSc ACA *2003;* Kyprianides Nicolaou & Economides, 4 Evagora Papachristoforou, Themis Court, Office 301, 3030 LIMASSOL, CYPRUS.
•ECONOMIDES, Mr. George Ioakim, FCA FCCA *1980;* Kyprianides Nicolaou & Economides, 4 Evagora Papachristoforou, Themis Court, Office 301, 3030 LIMASSOL, CYPRUS.
ECONOMIDES, Mr. Heraclis Andreas, BA ACA *1988;* 50 Cholmeley Crescent, LONDON, N6 5HA.
ECONOMIDES, Mr. Ioannis Frixou, BSc ACA *2000;* 125 grigori afxentiou street kokkinotrimithia, 2660 NICOSIA, CYPRUS.
ECONOMIDES, Mr. James George, BSc FCA *1982;* Wolsey House, Wolsey Close, LONDON, SW20 0DD.
ECONOMIDES, Miss. Thalia Amelia, BSc(Econ) ACA *2001;* 35 Aesop Street, Aglanjia, 2113 NICOSIA, CYPRUS.
ECONOMIDOU, Mrs. Marita Liassi, BA FCA *1996;* Electricity Authority of Cyprus, Head Office, Amfipoleos 11, Strovolos, 2025 NICOSIA, CYPRUS.
ECONOMOU, Mr. Kirk, BSc(Hons) ACA *2003;* 40 Wilmot Road, LONDON, N17 6LH.
ECONOMOU, Mr. Michael, BA FCA CTA *1991;* PricewaterhouseCoopers, 1719 N Vine Street, CHICAGO, IL 60614, UNITED STATES.
•ED, Mrs. Lynne Janice, BA ACA *1979;* Ernst & Young LLP, 1 More London Place, LONDON, SE1 2AF. See also Ernst & Young Europe LLP
EDBROOKE, Mrs. Suzanne Lesley, BSc ACA *1997;* 26-34 Liverpool Road, LUTON, LU1 1RS.
EDDEN, Mr. Paul Graham, BA FCA *1967;* Hemenhale House, The Street, Hempnall, NORWICH, NR15 2AD. (Life Member)
EDDEN, Mr. Robert James, ACA *1995;* 118 Oakleigh Road, Clayton, BRADFORD, BD14 6QD.
•EDDINS, Mr. Paul Francis Rowe, FCA *1970;* (Tax Fac), Paul Eddins, 214 Whitchurch Road, CARDIFF, CF14 3ND.
EDDISON, Miss. Catherine Sophie, ACA *2005;* (Tax Fac), Gostling Ltd, Unit 6, Acorn Business Park, Keighley Road, SKIPTON, NORTH YORKSHIRE BD23 2UE.
EDDISON, Mr. David William, MA FCA *1962;* Langley Farm, Bethersden, ASHFORD, TN26 3HF. (Life Member)
•EDDISON, Mr. Timothy Richard William, FCA *1975;* Eddisons, 16-18 Devonshire Street, KEIGHLEY, WEST YORKSHIRE, BD21 2DG. See also Eddison & Co Ltd
EDDLESTON, Mr. David Francis, BSc ACA *1992;* 18 Gable Close, ABBOTS LANGLEY, WD5 OLD.
EDDLESTON, Mr. Ian Marshall, BSc FCA *1991;* Ernst & Young, 725 Figueroa Street, Fifth Floor, LOS ANGELES, CA 90017-5418, UNITED STATES.
EDDLESTON-MCGRATH, Mr. Stephen Francis, BCom ACA *1996;* 103 Durning Road, LONDON, SE19 1JS.
•EDDOWES, Mr. Roger Niall, ACA FCCA *2008;* Chancery Hartwell LLP, 30 Ashby Road, TOWCESTER, NORTHAMPTONSHIRE, NN12 6PG. See also Chancery (UK) LLP
EDDOWES, Mrs. Susan Rosemary, BA ACA *1994;* Lawn Cottage Mustard Lane, Sonning, READING, RG4 6GH.
EDDY, Mr. Andrew Iwan Michael, BSc(Hons) ACA *2000;* U B S Investment Bank, 100 Liverpool Street, LONDON, EC2M 2RH.
•EDDY, Mr. Jonathan Fraser, BA FCA *1988;* 3 Clos Y Gwyddfid, Radyr Gardens, Morganstown, CARDIFF, CF15 8EX.
EDDY, Mrs. Sarah Judith, BSc ACA *1993;* Gordon Bros Nations House, 103 Wigmore Street, LONDON, W1U 1QS.
EDDY, Mrs. Sophie Tamara, ACA MAAT *1997;* The Elms, 61 Green Lane, REDRUTH, CORNWALL, TR15 1LS.
EDDY, Mr. Stephen John, BSc ACA *1997;* 119 Huddleston Road, LONDON, N7 0EH.
EDE, Mr. Anthony William, FCA *1982;* Sunnydale, North Bersted Street, BOGNOR REGIS, WEST SUSSEX, PO22 9AH.
EDE, Mr. Gareth Thomas Brett, BSc ACA *2004;* 12 Nursery Court, Nether Poppleton, YORK, YO26 6LR.
EDE, Mr. Graham Hewett, FCA *1979;* Moorings Woodland Drive, East Horsley, LEATHERHEAD, KT24 5AN.
EDE, Mr. Jeremy, BA ACA *1990;* Form 1, 17 Bartley Wood Business Park, Bartley Way, HOOK, RG27 9XA.
•EDE, Mr. Maurice Gordon, FCA *1969;* (Member of Council 1988 - 2010), Network 4M Limited, Suite 1, Park Farm Barn, Brabourne, ASHFORD, KENT TN25 6RG.
•EDE, Mr. Nigel Ramon, BSc FCA *1990;* 31 Grantchester Road, CAMBRIDGE, CB3 9ED.
EDE, Miss. Tracey Michelle, BSc ACA *1996;* White Horse Inn White Horse Lane, Meopham, GRAVESEND, KENT, DA13 0UE.
EDELMAN, Mr. David Laurence, BCom FCA MCT *1972;* 34 Links Way, NORTHWOOD, HA6 2XB.
•EDELMAN, Mr. Jeffery, FCA *1961;* Jeffery Edelman & Co., 22 Draycot Road, LONDON, E11 2NX.
EDELMAN, Mr. Nicholas Mark, BA ACA *2006;* 18 Lonsdale Road, LONDON, W11 2DE.
EDELMANN, Mrs. Christiane, BA ACA *1999;* Garnbachstr 15, 86926 GREIFENBERG, GERMANY.
EDELSHAIN, Mr. Adam, MA ACA *2011;* 8 Tudor Close, LONDON, NW7 2BG.
EDELSTEN, Mr. Mark, BA ACA *1985;* 34 Clifton Road, WINCHESTER, SO22 5BU.
EDELSTEN, Mr. Peter Melvin, BA ACA AMCT *1983;* Nieuwe Haven 63D, 3116 AA SCHIEDAM, NETHERLANDS.
EDEN, Mr. Anthony Richard, FCA *1968;* West End House, West End Road, Tiptree, COLCHESTER, CO5 0QN.
EDEN, Mr. Christopher Guy, BA ACA *2006;* Flat 111, Holcroft Court, Clipstone Street, LONDON, W1W 5DF.
EDEN, Mr. Gary John, ACA *2011;* 98 Sherwood Drive, WIGAN, LANCASHIRE, WN5 9RZ.
•EDEN, Mr. James Edward, FCA *1977;* Suite G4, Aspen Waite-Edens Chartered Accountants Suite G/4, Waterside Centre North Street, LEWES, EAST SUSSEX, BN7 2PE.
EDEN, Mrs. Judith Elizabeth, BSc ACA *1992;* 53 Lyndhurst Drive, SEVENOAKS, TN13 2HG.
•EDEN, Mr. Martin Howard, MBA BSc FCA *1972;* 300 625 11th AVENUE SW, CALGARY T2R 0E1, AB, CANADA.
•EDEN, Mr. Matthew Richard, BCom ACA *2003;* Cognitor Audit Services Limited, Cognitor Ltd, 3 Birch House, Harris Business Park, Hanbury Road, Stoke Prior BROMSGROVE WORCESTERSHIRE B60 4DJ.
EDEN, Mr. Richard Peter, BSc ACA *1993;* 12766 E Sahuaro Drive, SCOTTSDALE, AZ 85259, UNITED STATES.

EDEN, Miss. Sarah Ann, ACA *2009;* NHS Southside, 105 Victoria Street, LONDON, SW1E 6QT.
•EDEN, Mr. Stacy Adam, BA FCA *1998;* Crowe Clark Whitehill LLP, St Bride's House, 10 Salisbury Square, LONDON, EC4Y 8EH. See also Horwath Clark Whitehill LLP
EDEN, Miss. Tamsin Jane, BSc ACA *2005;* Flat 15, Parker Court, Denmark Avenue, LONDON, SW19 4HJ.
•EDENBOROUGH, Mr. Kevin, BA ACA *1999;* (Tax Fac), Eden Wood Accountants Limited, 2 Beaconsfield Road, Knowle, BRISTOL, BS4 2JF.
EDERER, Mr. John Michael, FCA *1984;* Ruetiholz Str.8, CH-8136 GATTIKON, SWITZERLAND.
EDERY, Mr. Daniel, BA(Hons) ACA *2002;* Barclays Capital, 5 North Colonnade, LONDON, E14 4BB.
EDEY, Mr. Russell Philip, FCA *1967;* Starling Leeze, East Street, Coggeshall, COLCHESTER, CO6 1SL.
EDGAR, Mr. Barnaby James Guy, BA ACA *1999;* Diageo Plc Lakeside Drive, Park Royal, LONDON, NW10 7HQ.
EDGAR, Mr. David John, PhD BA ACA *1988;* 98 Copenhagen Place, LONDON, E14 7DE.
EDGAR, Miss. Gemma, MA(Cantab) ACA *2011;* Apartment 66, 874 Wilmslow Road, MANCHESTER, M20 5AB.
EDGAR, Mr. James Bernard Shelley, FCA *1964;* 11 St. Johns Road, Bathwick, BATH, BA2 6PX. (Life Member)
EDGAR, Ms. Janice, MA FCA *1993;* with KPMG LLP, 15 Canada Square, LONDON, E14 5GL.
EDGAR, Miss. Jill, BA ACA *2011;* 56A Station Road, West Horndon, BRENTWOOD, Essex, CM13 3TW.
EDGAR, Mr. John Alister, BSc ACA *1998;* 61 Nunnery Lane, DARLINGTON, DL3 9PW.
EDGAR, Mr. John William McCredie, MSc BSc ACA *1988;* 310 West 28th. Street, NORTH VANCOUVER V7N 2J1, BC, CANADA.
EDGAR, Miss. Nicola Susan, BA ACA *2000;* 20a Frithwood Avenue, NORTHWOOD, MIDDLESEX, HA6 3LX.
EDGAR, Mrs. Penny Jane, ACA *2003;* 29 The Crescent, UPMINSTER, ESSEX, RM14 1JZ.
EDGAR, Mr. Peter David, FCA *1971;* 1 Cruxton Cottages, Cruxton, DORCHESTER, DT2 0DZ.
EDGAR, Mrs. Trina, AICD ACA CTA AMCT *1993;* Commonwealth Bank, St Australia, Level 2, 120 Putt Street, SYDNEY, NSW 2000 AUSTRALIA.
•EDGE, Mr. Adrian David, BSc ACA *1980;* David Edge, 2 Sandlebridge Lane, KNUTSFORD, WA16 7SD.
•EDGE, Mr. Bernard Michael, MSc FCA *1982;* Bernard Edge & Co, The Old Courts, 147 All Saints Road, NEWMARKET, SUFFOLK, CB8 8HH.
EDGE, Mrs. Catherine Ann, BA ACA *1995;* 31 Silhill Hall Road, SOLIHULL, B91 1JX.
EDGE, Mr. Chris William, BSc FCA *1996;* 7 Castle Drive, MAIDENHEAD, BERKSHIRE, SL6 6DB.
•EDGE, Mrs. Corinna Moira, BSc FCA *1983;* Mrs C.M. Edge BSc FCA, 2 Kingswood Road, LONDON, SW19 3NE.
EDGE, Mr. Edward William, FCA *1975;* Ashwood, Back Lane, Newton Poppleford, SIDMOUTH, EX10 0EY. (Life Member)
•EDGE, Mr. Francis Andrew, BSc ACA *1992;* (Tax Fac), Accountsource Ltd, 4 Beaufort, Parklands, Railton Road, GUILDFORD, SURREY GU2 9JX.
EDGE, Mr. Hubert Cary, FCA *1948;* 34 Cumberland Avenue, Beeston, NOTTINGHAM, NG9 4DH. (Life Member)
•EDGE, Mr. John Malcolm, FCA *1966;* Nairne Son & Green, 477 Chester Road, MANCHESTER, M16 9HF.
•EDGE, Mr. Karl Peter, BA FCA *1995;* KPMG LLP, One Snowhill, Snow Hill Queensway, BIRMINGHAM, B4 6GN. See also KPMG Europe LLP
EDGE, Miss. Katie, BSc ACA *2011;* 19 Thornbrook Way, Ettiley Heath, SANDBACH, CHESHIRE, CW11 3ZB.
•EDGE, Mr. Malcolm Clive Greenhalgh, BSc FCA *1978;* (Tax Fac), KPMG LLP, St. James's Square, MANCHESTER, M2 6DS. See also KPMG Europe LLP
EDGE, Mr. Martin Andrew, BSc(Hons) ACA *2003;* 56 Watkin Road, Clayton-le-Woods, CHORLEY, LANCASHIRE, PR6 7PX.
EDGE, Mr. Martin Ewart, MA ACA *1983;* Standard Chartered Bank, 5th Floor, 4 Sandown Valley Crescent, SANDTON, 2196, SOUTH AFRICA.
EDGE, Mr. Nicholas, BA ACA *2010;* 1101 Strata, 8 Walworth Road, LONDON, SE1 6EG.
EDGE, Mr. Peter David, BSc ACA *1982;* Murco Petroleum Ltd, 4 Beaconsfield Road, ST. ALBANS, AL1 3RH.
EDGE, Mrs. Rachael, BA(Hons) ACA *2001;* with BDO LLP, Fourth Floor, One Victoria Street, BRISTOL, BS1 6AA.
EDGE, Mrs. Rebecca Louise, BA ACA *2002;* Packsaddle Barn, Wigan Road, Euxton, CHORLEY, LANCASHIRE, PR7 6JZ.
EDGE, Mr. Roderick Boris Clifford, BSc ACA *1990;* Water Tower, Knoll Road, GODALMING, SURREY, GU7 2EJ.
EDGE, Mr. Stewart David, BA FCA *1977;* 28 Beavers Road, FARNHAM, GU9 7BD.
•EDGE, Mr. Timothy, BSc ACA *1995;* Deloitte LLP, PO Box 500, 2 Hardman Street, MANCHESTER, M60 2AT. See also Deloitte & Touche LLP
EDGE, Mrs. Tracey Ann, BSc ACA *2001;* 56 Watkin Road, Clayton-le-Woods, CHORLEY, LANCASHIRE, PR6 7PX.
EDGE, Mr. Warren Mark, BA ACA *1992;* Kirkstone Villa, Lanchester Road Hospital, Lanchester Road, DURHAM, DH1 5RD.
EDGE-PARTINGTON, Mr. Julian James, BA ACA *1979;* 2 Mapperley Drive, WOODFORD GREEN, IG8 9NZ.
EDGECLIFFE-JOHNSON, Mr. Paul, LLB FCA AMCT *1998;* Blythewood, The Highlands, East Horsley, LEATHERHEAD, SURREY, KT24 5BQ.
EDGECOMBE, Miss. Lynne, BA(Hons) ACA *2003;* 6 Orme Road, WORTHING, WEST SUSSEX, BN11 4EX.
EDGELL, Mr. Adrian Bruce, FCA *1967;* 4 Glenmore Court, 67 Nore Road, Portishead, BRISTOL, BS20 6JZ.
EDGELL, Mr. Jonathan William Farley, FCA *1969;* 3 Dunnock Way, Wargrave, READING, RG10 8LR. (Life Member)
EDGELL, Mr. Malcolm John, BSc FCA *1974;* 146A Golf Links Road, FERNDOWN, BH22 8DA.
EDGELL, Mr. Richard John, MA ACA *1982;* The Cottage, East End Green, HERTFORD, SG14 2PD.
EDGER, Mr. Andrew Ian, MBA FCA *1993;* c/o 3 Turner Place, College Town, SANDHURST, BERKSHIRE, GU47 0FW.
EDGER, Miss. Gillian, ACA *1987;* Keyhaven Capital Partners Limited, 1 Maple Place, LONDON, W1T 4BB.
EDGERTON, Mr. Brian Gerald, FCA *1960;* Flat 1, 7 Chesham Place, BRIGHTON, BN2 1FB. (Life Member)
•EDGERTON, Mr. Gary, FCA CertPFS *1986;* Fairhurst, Douglas Bank House, Wigan Lane, WIGAN, WN1 2TB.
EDGERTON, Mr. Graham John, BSc ACA *1988;* Redwoods, Mill Lane, WESTERHAM, KENT, TN16 1SG.
EDGERTON, Mr. Nigel Guy, ACA CA(SA) *2010;* 16 St. Stephen's Gardens, Manfred Road, Putney, LONDON, SW15 2RR.
EDGHILL, Mr. Mark Dugdale, BSc FCA *1988;* Z Energy Ltd, Level 2 Willeston Centre, 22-28 Willeston St, WELLINGTON 6140, NEW ZEALAND.
•EDGINGTON, Mr. Michael Arthur, FCA *1976;* Michael A. Edgington, 16 Park Hall Close, WALSALL, WS5 3HQ.
EDGINGTON, Mr. Neil James, BA ACA *2009;* 9 Carlos Street, GODALMING, GU7 1BP.
EDGINGTON, Mr. Simon James, FCA *1972;* Gentian Cottage, Rowplatt Lane, Felbridge, EAST GRINSTEAD, RH19 2NY.
EDGINTON, Miss. Claire Helen Rose, BSc ACA *2010;* Flat 23, 23 Hulse Road, SOUTHAMPTON, SO15 2QZ.
EDGINTON, Mr. Stewart, BA ACA ASIP *1998;* Hornweg 11, 8700 KUSNACHT, SWITZERLAND.
EDGLEY, Mrs. Carla Rhianon Pel, MA FCA *1990;* MEMBER OF COUNCIL, Gwern-y-Figyn Uchaf, Trallong, BRECON, LD3 8HW.
EDGLEY, Mr. Roy Edward, FCA *1966;* 2 Taylor Drive, The Green, Throop, BOURNEMOUTH, BH8 0PZ. (Life Member)
EDGSON, Mr. Daniel Paul, BA ACA *2007;* (Tax Fac), Flat 4 275 Kilburn High Road, LONDON, NW6 7JR.
EDGSON, Mr. Paul Frederick, ACA *1980;* PO Box 320188, Woodlands, LUSAKA, ZAMBIA.
EDHOLM, Mr. Peter Rolf, BSc ACA *1983;* 8 Dennis Drive, Westminster Park, CHESTER, CH4 7RG.
EDHOUSE, Mrs. Beverley Jane, BSc ACA *1988;* 102 High Street, Newington, SITTINGBOURNE, ME9 7JH.
•EDIE, Mrs. Greta Maud, ACA *1983;* (Tax Fac), Wright & Co, 57 High Street, South Norwood, LONDON, SE25 6EF.
EDIS, Mr. Alan Michael, FCA *1963;* Broadfield, Quarry Park Road, Pedmore, STOURBRIDGE, DY8 2RE.
EDIS, Mr. Michael, BSc FCA *1978;* Jardine Lloyd Thompson Ltd Jardine House, 6 Crutched Friars, LONDON, EC3N 2PH.
EDIS, Mr. Michael Allan, BA ACA *1987;* Beechwood, 1 Manor Close, Pyrford, WOKING, GU22 8SA.
EDIS, Mr. Richard Michael, BSc ACA *2010;* Raffles Rigg, Shenstone Hill, Gravel Path, BERKHAMSTED, HERTFORDSHIRE, HP4 2PA.
EDISBURY, Mr. Bryan Anthony, FCA *1960;* 148 Bradshaw Meadows, Bradshaw, BOLTON, BL2 4ND. (Life Member)
•EDISS, Mrs. Sarah Gail, BSc ACA *2002;* Spofforths LLP, 2nd Floor, Comewell House, North Street, HORSHAM, WEST SUSSEX RH12 1RD.
EDKINS, Mrs. Nicola Louise, ACA *2010;* 14 Powlett Road, ROCHESTER, ME2 4RD.
EDKINS, Mr. Simon David, ACA *2010;* Flat 19 Cuff Point, Columbia Road, LONDON, E2 7PP.
EDLER, Mr. Henry James, FCA *1955;* 48 Dale View Crescent, Chingford, LONDON, E4 6PQ. (Life Member)
EDLEY, Mr. Peter John, ACA *1991;* 6 Lakeside Cottages, Foggathorpe, SELBY, NORTH YORKSHIRE, YO8 6PS.
EDMANDS, Mr. David James Rosewall, ACA *1995;* 16 Kings Chase, Willesborough, ASHFORD, Kent, TN24 0LQ.
EDMANDS, Mr. James Benjamin Bell, MSc BA ACA *2007;* with National Audit Office, 157-197 Buckingham Palace Road, Victoria, LONDON, SW1W 9SP.
EDMANDS, Mrs. Michelle Elizabeth, BA ACA *2006;* Bunzl Vending Services Ltd, 19 Aintree Road Perivale, GREENFORD, MIDDLESEX, UB6 7LG.
EDMANS, Mr. Philip James, ACA *2009;* 27 Devonshire Park, READING, RG2 7DX.
EDMEAD, Mrs. Charlotte, LLB ACA *2002;* Burgate Broad Road, Hambrook, CHICHESTER, WEST SUSSEX, PO18 8RG.
EDMEADES, Mr. Robin John, BA FCA *1972;* 68a Fitzgeorge Avenue, LONDON, W14 0SW.
EDMEADS, Mr. John Colin, ACA *2005;* Large Cases Division, Revenue Commissioners, Setanta Centre, Nassau Street, DUBLIN, COUNTY DUBLIN IRELAND.
•EDMOND, Mr. James Michael, FCA *1977;* (Tax Fac), Charterhouse (Accountants) LLP, 88-98 College Road, HARROW, MIDDLESEX, HA1 1RA.
•EDMOND, Mr. Mark David, BSc ACA *1986;* RSM Tenon Limited, The Poynt Building, 45 Wollaton Street, NOTTINGHAM, NG1 5FW. See also Premier Strategies Limited
EDMOND, Mr. Michael Joseph, BSc ACA *1993;* 26 Blackmore Way, Wheathampstead, ST. ALBANS, HERTFORDSHIRE, AL4 8LJ.
EDMOND, Mr. Robert Maurice, FCA *1970;* The Spinney, Spinney Lane, Itchenor, CHICHESTER, PO20 7DJ. (Life Member)
EDMONDS, Mr. Alan Eric, BA FCA *1975;* Westways, 19 Washington Lane, Euxton, CHORLEY, PR7 6DE.
•EDMONDS, Mr. Andrew Graham, BSc ACA *1984;* Edmonds & Co, 9 Clun Terrace, Cathays, CARDIFF, CF24 4RB.
•EDMONDS, Mr. Andrew John, BSc ACA *2000;* Nexia Smith & Williamson Audit Limited, Imperial House, 18-21 Kings Park Road, SOUTHAMPTON, SO15 2AT. See also Smith & Williamson Ltd and Nexia Audit Limited
EDMONDS, Mr. Ben Luther James, BSc ACA *2008;* Graygill, Staunton, COLEFORD, GLOUCESTERSHIRE, GL16 8PB.
EDMONDS, Mr. David, BA ACA *1992;* 11 Harts Close, EXETER, DEVON, EX1 3RY.
EDMONDS, Mr. David Clifford, FCA *1970;* 20 Glanafon Street, Bethesda, BANGOR, GWYNEDD, LL57 3AL. (Life Member)
•EDMONDS, Mr. David Kenrick, FCA CTA *1976;* David Edmonds Ltd, Land Court Lane House, Tytherley Road, Winterslow, SALISBURY, SP5 1PZ.
EDMONDS, Mr. Glenn Kevin, BSc ACA *1997;* Ash Cottage, 14 Tollgate Road, Hamsterley Mill, ROWLANDS GILL, TYNE AND WEAR, NE39 1HF.
EDMONDS, Mrs. Helen Victoria, BSc(Hons) ACA *2000;* 5 Pepys Road, Westpoint Condominium, 03-04, SINGAPORE 118443, SINGAPORE.
•EDMONDS, Mr. Hugh Francis, BA FCA *1973;* Scotty Group Plc, Building A, Trinity Court, Wokingham Road, BRACKNELL, BERKSHIRE RG42 1PL.
EDMONDS, Miss. Jemima Ann, ACA *2009;* 29 Cornflower Way, Ludgershall, ANDOVER, HAMPSHIRE, SP11 9TF.
EDMONDS, Mr. Jonathan Steven, BSc ACA *1996;* 36 Redland Park, BATH, BA2 1SL.
EDMONDS, Miss. Juliet Louise, BSc ACA *1994;* 15 Druid Road, Stoke Bishop, BRISTOL, BS9 1LJ.
EDMONDS, Miss. Karen Hazel, ACA *1993;* 9 Longfield, Leverstock Green, HEMEL HEMPSTEAD, HERTFORDSHIRE, HP3 8HN.
EDMONDS, Mr. Maurice, FCA *1975;* Maynard Edmonds Ltd, 23 Tylers Hill Road, Botley, CHESHAM, BUCKINGHAMSHIRE, HP5 1XW.
•EDMONDS, Mr. Nicholas John, BA ACA *1995;* KPMG LLP, 15 Canada Square, LONDON, E14 5GL. See also KPMG Europe LLP
EDMONDS, Mrs. Nina Anne, BSc ACA *2000;* Top Floor Flat, 18 Bellevue, Clifton, BRISTOL, BS8 1DB.
EDMONDS, Miss. Phillippa Susan, BSc ACA *1995;* The Bungalow, Ballamanaugh Road, Sulby, ISLE OF MAN, IM7 2HB.
•EDMONDS, Mr. Roger John, FCA *1975;* Roger Edmonds, 18 Bradley Croft, Balsall Common, COVENTRY, CV7 7PZ.
EDMONDS, Mrs. Sarah Elizabeth, BSc(Hons) ACA *2004;* 204 Gorse Cover Road, Severn Beach, BRISTOL, BS35 4NT.
EDMONDS, Mr. Stephen Robert, FCA *1977;* Treetops, Church Street, Brixworth, NORTHAMPTON, NN6 9BZ.
EDMONDSON, Mr. Colin Michael, MBA BA ACA *1984;* 31 Heron Park, Basing, BASINGSTOKE, RG24 8UJ.
EDMONDSON, Mr. Craig, BSc ACA *1999;* 11 Moore Close, SUTTON COLDFIELD, B74 4XY.
EDMONDSON, Mr. Howard Barry, BSc FCA *1977;* Infodata Systems Limited, Mill Reef House, 9-14 Cheap Street, NEWBURY, RG14 5DD.
EDMONDSON, Mr. James Martin, BSc FCA *1975;* Arab Banking Corporation, PO Box 5698, MANAMA, BAHRAIN.
EDMONDSON, Mr. Mark Moses, BA(Hons) ACA *2009;* Pricewaterhousecoopers, 89 Sandyford Road, NEWCASTLE UPON TYNE, NE1 8HW.
EDMONDSON, Mr. Martin Richard, ACA *1983;* 3 Beeston Road, SALE, M33 5AQ.
EDMONDSON, Mr. Michael, BA(Hons) ACA *2003;* 10 Orchard Road, Shere, GUILDFORD, GU5 9HU.
EDMONDSON, Mr. Nigel Kenneth, BSc FCA *1973;* 4 Broadway, SALE, CHESHIRE, M33 6NR.
•EDMONDSON, Mr. Paul Robert, BSc ACA *1980;* (Tax Fac), Edmondson & Co, 170A London Road, Hazel Grove, STOCKPORT, SK7 4DJ.
•EDMONDSON, Mr. Paul Thomas, FCA *1983;* Edmondson's Associates Ltd, 1 Tye Green Paddock, Glemsford, SUDBURY, SUFFOLK, CO10 7TS.
EDMONDSON, Mr. Peter Robert, ACA *1981;* 56 Trinity Park, CALNE, WILTSHIRE, SN11 0QD.
EDMONDSON, Miss. Rebecca, BA ACA *2011;* 7 West Pasture Close, Horsforth, LEEDS, LS18 5PB.
EDMONDSON, Mr. Richard Worsley, FCA *1972;* 27 Hollycombe Close, LIPHOOK, HAMPSHIRE, GU30 7HR. (Life Member)
EDMONDSON, Mr. Ronald Hunter, FCA *1973;* The Tower Oldbury Place, Spring Lane Ightham, SEVENOAKS, KENT, TN15 9DR.
EDMONDSON, Mrs. Sheila, FCA *1956;* 81 Overstone Road, HARPENDEN, AL5 5PL. (Life Member)
EDMONDSON, Miss. Shelley, BA(Hons) ACA *2003;* 102 Asia House, 82 Princess Street, MANCHESTER, M1 6BD.
EDMONDSON, Mr. Stephen James, FCA *1970;* Bucyrus Aurols Limited, PO BOX 25 Westlands, HALIFAX, HX3 9TW.
EDMONDSON, Mr. William Somerville, BSc ACA *1995;* 21 Cromwell Road, HENLEY-ON-THAMES, OXFORDSHIRE, RG9 1JH.
EDMONSTONE, Mr. William Henry Neil, FCA *1969;* Broadgate House, Nether Wallop, STOCKBRIDGE, HAMPSHIRE, SO20 8HA.
•EDMUND, Mr. Huw John, FCA *1979;* Huw J Edmund Limited, Garth House, Unit 7, Ty-Nant Court, Morganstown, CARDIFF CF15 8LW.
EDMUNDS, Brian James Marchand, Esq MBE FCA ACMA *1951;* 3 Nunns Close, Coggeshall, COLCHESTER, ESSEX, CO6 1AN. (Life Member)
EDMUNDS, Mrs. Carole Elizabeth, BA FCA *1991;* with A.C. Mole & Sons, Riverside House, Riverside Business Park, Wylds Road, BRIDGWATER, TA6 4BH.
EDMUNDS, Mr. David Rhys, BA ACA *1994;* 12 Upton Court, 3 The Downs, LONDON, SW20 8JB.
EDMUNDS, Mr. Guy William, FCA *1963;* PO Box HG 41, Highlands, HARARE, ZIMBABWE. (Life Member)
•EDMUNDS, Mr. Henry Roger, MSc BSc FCA *1975;* Edmunds Richmond Limited, Suite 404, Albany House, 324-326 Regent Street, LONDON, W1B 3HH.
EDMUNDS, Mr. Keith Alexander Marchand, MA ACA *1984;* 124 Cranley Gardens, Muswell Hill, LONDON, N10 3AH.
EDMUNDS, Miss. Rebecca Anne, BSc ACA *2003;* The Wellcome Trust, 183-193 Euston Road, LONDON, NW1 2BE.
EDMUNDS, Mr. Robert William George, MA ACA *2006;* 6 Devon Chase, Warfield, BRACKNELL, RG42 3JN.

EDMUNDS, Mrs. Rosemary Margaret, BSc ACA *1989;* 2 Dyke Road Place, BRIGHTON, BN1 5LD.
EDMUNDS, Miss. Sarah Jayne, BSc ACA *2003;* Woodpecker Cottage Southampton Road, Cadnam, SOUTHAMPTON, SO40 2NH.
EDMUNDSON, Mr. Stuart, BA ACA *1996;* 44a Oakley Road, LONDON, N1 3LS.
EDMUNTON, Mr. Julian Victor, FCA *1972;* 84 Ninian Road, CARDIFF, CF23 5EP.
EDNEY, Mr. Alexander Charles, BSc ACA *2010;* Flat 7 Shiredene, 1 Shire Oak Road, LEEDS, LS6 2WF.
EDNEY, Mrs. Caroline Avril Monica, LLB ACA CTA *2004;* with Deloitte LLP, PO Box 500, 2 Hardman Street, MANCHESTER, M60 2AT.
•EDNEY, Mr. Colin Peter, BA FCA *1991;* Warrener Stewart Limited, Harwood House, 43 Harwood Road, LONDON, SW6 4QP.
•EDNEY, Mr. Peter William, FCA *1974;* Peter Edney & Co, 95 Station Road, HAMPTON, MIDDLESEX, TW12 2BD.
EDRICH, Mr. Jasper Timothy William, FCA FCMA CA(SA) *1972;* PO Box 2417, EDENVALE, GAUTENG, 1610, SOUTH AFRICA.
•EDRICH, Mr. Simon, BA ACA *1995;* PG&E Professional Services Limited, 3 Novara Row, Calabria Road, LONDON, N5 1JL.
EDSELL, Miss. Samantha, BA ACA *2004;* Field House, Blandford Road, Coombe Bissett, SALISBURY, SP5 4LH.
EDSER, Mr. Mark, ACA *2011;* 57 Portsmouth Road, SURBITON, SURREY, KT6 4HR.
EDSER, Mr. Mark Ansell, BSc FCA *1977;* 40 Eastmont Road, ESHER, SURREY, KT10 9AZ.
EDWARD, Miss. Elleanor Bernadette, BSc ACA *2007;* 8 Delamere Gardens, LONDON, NW7 3EB.
EDWARD, Mr. John Richard Mackay, FCA *1966;* 594 Derby Road, Adams Hill, NOTTINGHAM, NG7 2GZ. (Life Member)
EDWARD, Mr. Mark Philip Salter, BA FCA CPA *1991;* 11709 Roberts Glen Court, POTOMAC, MD 20854, UNITED STATES.
EDWARDES JONES, Mr. James Humphrey, BSc ACA *1990;* Oakwood, 5 Oak Way, West Common, HARPENDEN, HERTFORDSHIRE, AL5 2NT.
•EDWARDES-KER, Mr. Anthony Gordon, FCA *1974;* 128 Craneford Way, TWICKENHAM, TW2 7SQ.
•EDWARDES-KER, Mrs. Gillian Carole, BA ACA *1981;* Gillian Edwardes-Ker, 29 Shalstone Road, Mortlake, LONDON, SW14 7HP.
EDWARDS, Mr. Adrian Wynn, BA ACA ATII *1996;* 4 Alder Close, LICHFIELD, WS14 9UT.
EDWARDS, Mr. Alan Clifford, JP BA FCA *1961;* 29 Woodside Road, SEVENOAKS, KENT, TN13 3HF.
EDWARDS, Mr. Alan Thomas Henry, FCA *1973;* 26 Station Road, Nailsea, BRISTOL, BS48 4PD.
EDWARDS, Mr. Alasdair Ross, BSc FCA *1974;* Barn Court, Lapworth Street, Lowsonford, HENLEY-IN-ARDEN, WARWICKSHIRE, B95 5ET.
EDWARDS, Mrs. Alison Jane, ACA *2008;* 39 St. Clair Wynd, Newburgh, ELLON, AB41 6DZ.
EDWARDS, Mrs. Alison Jane, BSc ACA *1996;* 4 Alder Close, LICHFIELD, WS14 9UT.
EDWARDS, Mrs. Alison Patricia, BSc ACA *1993;* Murree, 2 Lonsdale Road, DORKING, SURREY, RH4 1JP.
EDWARDS, Mr. Alun Francis, FCA MAAT DChA *1997;* with Reeves & Co LLP, 37 St. Margarets Street, CANTERBURY, KENT, CT1 2TU.
EDWARDS, Mrs. Amy Louise, BA ACA *2006;* 4 Percy Road, EXETER, EX2 8JY.
EDWARDS, Mr. Andrew Boucher, FCA *1968;* 24 The Priory, Priory Road, Abbotskerswell, NEWTON ABBOT, DEVON, TQ12 5PP.
EDWARDS, Mr. Andrew Charles, BA ACA *1993;* 65 Summerdown Road, EASTBOURNE, BN20 8DQ.
EDWARDS, Mr. Andrew Colin, MA ACA *1981;* Room AB479, University of Nottingham Ningbo China, 199 Taikang East Road, NINGBO 315100, CHINA.
EDWARDS, Mr. Andrew Norman, BSc ACA *1983;* Linksview, Beechcroft, CHISLEHURST, BR7 5DB.
EDWARDS, Mrs. Anne Patricia, BA FCA *1985;* Moor End, Hyde, FORDINGBRIDGE, SP6 2QH.
EDWARDS, Mr. Anthony, FCA *1957;* Arbor, Rannoch Road, CROWBOROUGH, EAST SUSSEX, TN6 1RB. (Life Member)
•EDWARDS, Mr. Anthony, FCA *1962;* Hillcote, 4 Old Kittle Road, Kittle, SWANSEA, SA3 3JU.
EDWARDS, Mr. Anthony, FCA *1971;* 62 New Penkridge Road, CANNOCK, STAFFORDSHIRE, WS11 1HW.
EDWARDS, Mr. Anthony, BSc ACA *2011;* 20 Fairburn Road, Randlay, TELFORD, SHROPSHIRE, TF3 2NJ.
EDWARDS, Mr. Anthony Alan, BA FCA CF *1998;* with RSM Tenon Limited, Ferryboat Lane, SUNDERLAND, SR5 3JN.
EDWARDS, Mr. Anthony Avon, FCA *1965;* 43 Linkside Avenue, OXFORD, OX2 8JE.
•EDWARDS, Mr. Anthony Brian, BSc FCA TEP *1975;* (Tax Fac), landtax LLP, Mitre House, Lodge Road, Long Hanborough, Business Park, WITNEY OXFORDSHIRE OX29 8SS.
EDWARDS, Mr. Anthony James, BSc ACA *1987;* 14 Hayes Avenue, Kingspark, BOURNEMOUTH, BH7 7AD.
EDWARDS, Mr. Anthony John, FCA *1970;* 19 Hazelwood Road, Cudham, SEVENOAKS, KENT, TN14 7QU.
EDWARDS, Mr. Anthony Robert, FCA *1991;* impetus Finance, 8 Edgewood Road, Meols, WIRRAL, MERSEYSIDE, CH47 6AL.
EDWARDS, Mr. Antony Kenneth, BA ACA *1989;* Payne, Giltway, Giltbrook, NOTTINGHAM, NG16 2GT.
•EDWARDS, Mr. Arthur, BA FCA CTA *1987;* (Tax Fac), Berkeley Hamilton LLP, 5 Pullman Court, Great Western Road, GLOUCESTER, GL1 3ND.
EDWARDS, Mr. Ashley John, BSc ACA *1984;* 40 Henley Grove, Henleaze, BRISTOL, BS9 4EG.
EDWARDS, Mr. Barry, FCA *1958;* La Vieille Grange, Domaine de la Serre, 34630 ST THIBERY, FRANCE. (Life Member)
EDWARDS, Mr. Benjamin, ACA *2008;* 31 Roseden Way, NEWCASTLE UPON TYNE, NE13 9BD.
EDWARDS, Mr. Bernard Hammerton, FCA *1961;* Water Cottage, Duck Street, Elham, CANTERBURY, CT4 6TW. (Life Member)
EDWARDS, Mr. Brian Charles, FCA *1973;* Sequoia, Grassy Lane, SEVENOAKS, TN13 1PL.
EDWARDS, Mr. Brynmor Richards, FCA JDipMA *1963;* 79 Lightwater Meadow, LIGHTWATER, GU18 5XJ.
EDWARDS, Mrs. Caroline Laura, BA ACA *1999;* AHB Accountants, Westway Farm, Wick Road, Bishop Sutton, BRISTOL, BS39 5XP.
EDWARDS, Miss. Caroline Michelle, ACA *2009;* 13 Longmeadow Road, Knowsley, PRESCOT, MERSEYSIDE, L34 0HN.
EDWARDS, Mrs. Catherine, BSc ACA *2004;* 18 Highland Road, Twerton, BATH, BA2 1DY.
EDWARDS, Mrs. Catherine, ACA *2011;* 7 Apley Road, STOURBRIDGE, DY8 4PA.
•EDWARDS, Mrs. Catherine Anne, BA ACA *1988;* 5 Littlecote Gardens, Appleton, WARRINGTON, WA4 5DL.
EDWARDS, Mr. Cecil Arthur Wignarajah, FCA *1971;* 335 Banbury Road, WILLOWDALE M2L 2V2, ON, CANADA.
EDWARDS, Mr. Charles Philip Houghton, BA ACA *1996;* 35 Woodland Road, SHORT HILLS, NJ 07078, UNITED STATES.
EDWARDS, Mrs. Charlotte Anne, BSc ACA *2007;* 26 Lightfoot Street, Hoole, CHESTER, CH2 3AJ.
•EDWARDS, Mr. Christopher, ACA *1984;* Chris Edwards, Clamarpen, 17 Napier Court, Gander Lane, Barlborough, CHESTERFIELD DERBYSHIRE S43 4PZ.
EDWARDS, Mr. Christopher Alan, BSc FCA *1981;* Level 32 HSBC Main Building, 1 Queens Road, CENTRAL, HONG KONG ISLAND, HONG KONG SAR.
EDWARDS, Dr. Christopher Howard, BSc ACA *1999;* Hurst Barn, London Road, HOOK, RG27 9EF.
EDWARDS, Mr. Christopher James, FCA *1982;* Tekram Properties Ltd, Burnham House, Archer Mews 6 Windmill Road, Hampton Hill, HAMPTON, MIDDLESEX TW12 1RH.
EDWARDS, Mr. Christopher John, MA FCA *1964;* Lande A Geon, St. Peter, JERSEY, JE3 7EA.
EDWARDS, Mr. Christopher John, BA ACA *1999;* with Deloitte LLP, 3 Rivergate, Temple Quay, BRISTOL, BS1 6GD.
EDWARDS, Mrs. Claire Jane Victoria, BA ACA *1992;* 65 Summerdown Road, EASTBOURNE, EAST SUSSEX, BN20 8DQ.
EDWARDS, Mrs. Claire Louise, BEng ACA *1998;* 20 Grange Road, Ampthill, BEDFORD, MK45 2PA.
EDWARDS, Miss. Claire Louise, BSc ACA CF *2004;* with Ernst & Young LLP, The Paragon, Counterslip, BRISTOL, BS1 6BX.
EDWARDS, Mrs. Clare Lisa, FCA *1995;* 67 Peterborough Avenue, UPMINSTER, RM14 3LL.
EDWARDS, Mrs. Clare Louise, BA ACA *1996;* 2 Onslow Place, JOONDALUP, WA 6027, AUSTRALIA.
EDWARDS, Mr. Clive, FCA *1976;* 46 Firvale Road, Walton, CHESTERFIELD, S42 7NN.
•EDWARDS, Mr. Clive Stuart, ACA *1997;* Haines Watts Wales LLP, 7 Neptune Court, Vanguard Way, CARDIFF, CF24 5PJ.
EDWARDS, Mr. Colin, FCA *1970;* 11 Gleneagles Drive, WATERLOOVILLE, HAMPSHIRE, PO7 8RX. (Life Member)
EDWARDS, Mr. Colin Brian, BSc ACA *1991;* PO Box 379, FORTITUDE VALLEY, QLD 4006, AUSTRALIA.
EDWARDS, Mr. Conor Robert Lyth, BA FCA *1993;* 3 Dicconsons Lane, Halsall, ORMSKIRK, L39 7HR.
EDWARDS, Mr. Daniel Martin, MA ACA *1978;* Soberman LLP, 2 St Clair Avenue East, Suite 1100, TORONTO M4T 2T5, ON, CANADA.
EDWARDS, Miss. Danielle Zoe, BEng ACA *1999;* 45 Clarence Road, Harborne, BIRMINGHAM, B17 9LA.
EDWARDS, Mr. David, FCA *1964;* 29415 Fairway Bluff, FAIR OAKS, TX 78006, UNITED STATES. (Life Member)
EDWARDS, Mr. David, ACA *1982;* 45 The Moors, REDHILL, SURREY, RH1 2PD.
•EDWARDS, Mr. David Cottelle, MA ACA *1992;* (Tax Fac), Lewis Golden & Co, 40 Queen Anne Street, LONDON, W1G 9EL.
•EDWARDS, Mr. David Frederick, MA FCA *1973;* David F. Edwards, Victoria House, Victoria Street, CWMBRAN, NP44 3JS.
EDWARDS, Mr. David Hadley, BA ACA *1995;* 194 White Lion Road, AMERSHAM, BUCKINGHAMSHIRE, HP7 9NU.
•EDWARDS, Mr. David John, MA FCA *1984;* Sunny Clough, 243 Bass Lane, Summerseat, BURY, BL9 5NS.
EDWARDS, Mr. David John, BA ACA *1985;* Canterbury Cottage, Freefolk Priors, Freefolk, WHITCHURCH, RG28 7NJ.
EDWARDS, Mr. David John, BA ACA *1986;* 58 Cairn Wynd, INVERURIE, ABERDEENSHIRE, AB51 5HQ.
EDWARDS, Mr. David Joseph, BCom ACA *1985;* North Staffordshire Combined Healthcare N H S Trust, Bucknall Hospital Eaves Lane, STOKE-ON-TRENT, ST2 8LD.
EDWARDS, Mr. David Lindsey, MBA MCMI ACA *1991;* 27 Hampton Drive, MARKET DRAYTON, SHROPSHIRE, TF9 3RP.
EDWARDS, Mr. David Lloyd, FCA *1968;* Twin Oaks, The Drive Ifold, Loxwood, BILLINGSHURST, RH14 0TE. (Life Member)
EDWARDS, Mr. David Timothy Winston, BA(Econ) ACA *1998;* 12 Coogee Street, Mount Hawthorn, PERTH, WA 6016, AUSTRALIA.
EDWARDS, Mrs. Dawn Louise, BCom ACA *1996;* 21 Evergreen Way, STOURPORT-ON-SEVERN, WORCESTERSHIRE, DY13 9GH.
•EDWARDS, Mrs. Deborah Jayne, BA ACA *2007;* Headland Accounting Solutions Ltd, 42 East Street, NEWQUAY, CORNWALL, TR7 1BE. See also Harland Accountants (Newquay) Limited
EDWARDS, Mrs. Denise, FCA *1953;* 97 Lingmoor Rise, Heron Hill, KENDAL, LA9 7PL. (Life Member)
EDWARDS, Mr. Dennis David, FCA *1957;* 47 Llwyn-Y-Grant Road, Penylan, CARDIFF, CF23 9HL. (Life Member)
•EDWARDS, Mr. Dennis John, FCA *1960;* Edwards & Hartley, PO Box 237, Peregrine House, Peel Road, Douglas, ISLE OF MAN IM99 1SU. See also Edwards & Hartley Limited
EDWARDS, Mr. Donald Lloyd, FCA *1951;* Flat 12 Aspley Court, 1 Warwick Avenue, BEDFORD, MK40 2UH. (Life Member)
EDWARDS, Mr. Duncan Roderick Alan, BA ACA *1987;* CL/5/GP, Halifax Plc, Trinity Road, HALIFAX, WEST YORKSHIRE, HX1 2RG.
EDWARDS, Mr. Duncan William, FCA *1981;* 36 Dover Rise, Dover Parkview, Tower B #03-12, SINGAPORE 138685, SINGAPORE.
EDWARDS, Mr. Elton Percy, FCA *1951;* Casita, 7 Yew Tree Gardens, Kings Acre, HEREFORD, HR4 0TH. (Life Member)
EDWARDS, Mr. Eric Warren Goddard, FCA *1962;* Urbanizacion Balcon al Mar, Buzon 562, Calle Carl Nielson 25, Javea, 03738 ALICANTE, SPAIN. (Life Member)
•EDWARDS, Mr. Esmond Barry, FCA *1973;* (Tax Fac), Edwards Veeder (Oldham) LLP, Block E, Brunswick Square, Union Street, OLDHAM, OL1 1DE.
•EDWARDS, Mr. Esmond James, ACA *1980;* with Whiting & Partners, Garland House, Garland Street, BURY ST. EDMUNDS, SUFFOLK, IP33 1EZ.
EDWARDS, Ms. Fiona Jane, BSc ACA *1991;* 23 Brampton Drive, CARTERTON, OXFORDSHIRE, OX18 3SA.
EDWARDS, Mr. Francois Wyndham, MA LLB FCA *1958;* The Old Mill House, Micheldever, WINCHESTER, SO21 3AG. (Life Member)
EDWARDS, Mr. Frank, FCA *1970;* MEMBER OF COUNCIL, Ford Farm, Llancarfan, BARRY, SOUTH GLAMORGAN, CF62 3AG.
•EDWARDS, Mr. Frederick George, BSc ACA *1990;* The CM Edwards Partnership, Chiltern House, 45 Station Road, HENLEY-ON-THAMES, OXFORDSHIRE, RG9 1AT.
•EDWARDS, Mr. Frederick Noel, FCA *1971;* Edwards + Co, Harefield House Alderley Road, WILMSLOW, CHESHIRE, SK9 1RA.
EDWARDS, Mr. Gareth, BSc ACA *2006;* 04-09 D'Casita, 38 Lorong Marzuki, SINGAPORE 417104, SINGAPORE.
EDWARDS, Mrs. Gayle Janet, BSc ACA *1986;* Tremelling, 7 Oakhurst Avenue, HARPENDEN, AL5 2NB.
EDWARDS, Miss. Gaynor Ann, BA ACA *1988;* 16 Black Butt Cottages, Sutton Road, Cookham, MAIDENHEAD, BERKSHIRE, SL6 9RE.
EDWARDS, Mrs. Gemma Alice, BA ACA *2006;* 31 Western Road, HENLEY-ON-THAMES, OXFORDSHIRE, RG9 1JN.
EDWARDS, Mr. Geoffrey, BSc ACA *1995;* SA Brain & Co. Ltd, The Cardiff Brewery Crawshay Street, CARDIFF, CF10 1SP.
EDWARDS, Mr. Geoffrey Ivor, BSc FCA *1981;* (Tax Fac), B&W Group Ltd, Dale Road, WORTHING, WEST SUSSEX, BN11 2BH.
EDWARDS, Mr. Geoffrey James, BA ACA *1994;* 27 Nook Rise, LIVERPOOL, L15 7JB.
EDWARDS, Mr. Geoffrey Keith, ACA *1988;* 5 Nepondi Court, FAIRVIEW PARK, SA 5126, AUSTRALIA.
•EDWARDS, Mr. George, FCA *1972;* George Edwards, 10 Starts Close, Locksbottom, ORPINGTON, BR6 8NU.
EDWARDS, Mr. Gordon Frank, FCA *1950;* 8 Third Avenue, EXETER, EX1 2PJ. (Life Member)
EDWARDS, Mr. Gordon James Charles, ACA *2008;* 39 St. Clair Wynd, Newburgh, ELLON, AB41 6DZ.
EDWARDS, Mr. Gordon Keith, FCA *1974;* 35 Shiplake Bottom, Peppard Common, HENLEY-ON-THAMES, OXFORDSHIRE, RG9 5HH.
EDWARDS, Mr. Gordon William Francis, FCA ATII *1959;* 4A Argyle Terrace, Milford, North Shore City, AUCKLAND 0620, NEW ZEALAND. (Life Member)
EDWARDS, Mr. Graeme Anthony, ACA *2010;* 1 Shipton Close, WIDNES, CHESHIRE, WA8 4LZ.
EDWARDS, Mr. Graham, MA ACA ACT *1990;* 35 Church Mount, LONDON, N2 0RW.
EDWARDS, Mr. Graham Mark, MEng&Man ACA *1997;* Gull Meadow Gull Lane, Framingham Earl, NORWICH, NR14 7PN.
EDWARDS, Mr. Gregory Desmond, BSc ACA *1992;* 108 A Priory Road, LONDON, NW6 3NS.
EDWARDS, Mr. Gregory Mark, BSc ACA *1995;* with Credit Suisse, One Cabot Square, LONDON, E14 4QJ.
EDWARDS, Ms. Hannah Tamsin, BA ACA *1988;* Laneside House, Westfield Hoe Lane, Abinger Hammer, DORKING, RH5 6RS.
EDWARDS, Miss. Heidi Faye, BA ACA *2003;* 129 Tawe Park, Ystradgynlais, SWANSEA, SA9 1GW.
EDWARDS, Miss. Helen, ACA *2011;* 1 Chaseport Close, Ravenstone, OLNEY, BUCKINGHAMSHIRE, MK46 5AG.
EDWARDS, Miss. Helen Gayle, LLB ACA *2002;* 14 Vetchwood Gardens, West Timperley, ALTRINCHAM, CHESHIRE, WA14 5ZG.
EDWARDS, Mrs. Helga Jane, BSc ACA *1991;* 43 Harrowby Road, GRANTHAM, LINCOLNSHIRE, NG31 9ED.
EDWARDS, Mr. Huw Goronwy Owen, FCA *1973;* 34 Capstan Square, LONDON, E14 3EU.
EDWARDS, Mr. Huw Llewelyn, BSc ACA *1987;* 25 Ael Y Bryn Tanerdy, Caerfyrddin, CARMARTHEN, SA31 2HB.
EDWARDS, Mr. Huw Stanley, BA ACA *1999;* Legar Meidrim Road, Bancyfelin, CARMARTHEN, DYFED, SA33 5NJ.
EDWARDS, Mr. Ian, BA ACA *2007;* 12 Banksia Place, Yangebup, PERTH, WA 6164, AUSTRALIA.
•EDWARDS, Mr. Ian Nigel, ACA *1982;* (Tax Fac), Ian N. Edwards, 141 Grasmere Way, LEIGHTON BUZZARD, LU7 2QH.
EDWARDS, Mr. Ian Robert Michael, BSc ACA *1978;* Fenns Farm, Fenns Lane, West End, WOKING, GU24 9QF.
•EDWARDS, Mrs. Iona Elisabeth, ACA *2002;* Iona Edwards, Hen Dy, Plas Madoc, Llansannan, DENBIGH, CLWYD LL16 5LF.
EDWARDS, Mrs. Jacqueline Anne, BSc(Hons) ACA *2002;* 42 Fielding Road, STREET, SOMERSET, BA16 9PG.
EDWARDS, Mr. James Andrew McArthur, ACA MAAT *2003;* Maestaf, Upper High Street, Cefn Coed, MERTHYR TYDFIL, CF48 2HW.
EDWARDS, Mr. James Francis Hurle, BA ACA *1997;* 30 Vandon Court, 64 Petty France, Westminster, LONDON, SW1H 9HE.
EDWARDS, Mr. James Stelfox, BSc(Econ) ACA *1997;* 35 Rudloe Road, LONDON, SW12 0DR.
EDWARDS, Miss. Jane Patricia, BSc FCA *1985;* 74 Bidston Road, PRENTON, MERSEYSIDE, CH43 6TN.

EDWARDS, Mrs. Janet Elizabeth Heathcote, ACA *2008;* Finance & Leasing Association Imperial House, 15-19 Kingsway, LONDON, WC2B 6UN.
EDWARDS, Miss. Jennifer Jane, BSc ACA *1993;* Liberata UK Ltd, Caerleon House, Cleppa Park, NEWPORT, GWENT, NP10 8BA.
EDWARDS, Mr. Jeremy Charles, BA FCA *1962;* 26 Rooksmead Road, SUNBURY-ON-THAMES, TW16 6PD. (Life Member)
EDWARDS, Miss. Jessica Mary, ACA *2010;* Flat 148, The Mill, Enderley Street, NEWCASTLE, STAFFORDSHIRE, ST5 2AN.
EDWARDS, Mr. John Alexander, FCA *1952;* 245 Holyhead Road, Wellington, TELFORD, TF1 2EA. (Life Member)
•EDWARDS, Mr. John Brynmor, BSc FCA *1983;* Sully & Co, Sully House, 7 Clovelly Road Industrial Estate, BIDEFORD, DEVON, EX39 3HN. See also Haines Watts North Devon LLP
EDWARDS, Mr. John David, BSc ACA *1979;* 174 Rectory Road, SUTTON COLDFIELD, B75 7RT.
EDWARDS, Mr. John Malcolm, BSc ACA *1989;* Augusta & Co, 20 Gresham Street, LONDON, EC2V 7JE.
EDWARDS, Mr. John Michael, BSc FCA *1971;* 23 Marshals Drive, ST. ALBANS, HERTFORDSHIRE, AL1 4RB. (Life Member)
•EDWARDS, Mr. John Owen, MEng FCA *1991;* KPMG LLP, 15 Canada Square, LONDON, E14 5GL. See also KPMG Europe LLP
EDWARDS, The Revd. John Ralph, BSc FCA *1974;* (Member of Council 1998 - 2002), Green Hedges, 25 St John's Street, CROWTHORNE, RG45 7NJ.
EDWARDS, Prof. John Richard, MSc BSc FCA CTA *1971;* Cardiff Business School, University Of Wales, Colum Drive, CARDIFF, CF10 3EU.
EDWARDS, Mr. John Robert, FCA *1970;* 5 Howden Dyke, Leven Park, YARM, TS15 9UP.
•EDWARDS, Mr. John William, BA ACA *1987;* Baldwins, 33-35 Coton Road, NUNEATON, WARWICKSHIRE, CV11 5TP.
EDWARDS, Mr. John William, FCA *1973;* Saltings, Orwell Rise, Pin Mill, IPSWICH, IP9 1JL.
EDWARDS, Mr. Jonathan, MEng ACA FSI *2001;* Flat F, 179-181 West End Lane, LONDON, NW6 2LH.
EDWARDS, Mr. Jonathan Allan, BA(Hons) ACA *2002;* 68 Deacon Road, KINGSTON UPON THAMES, KT2 6LU.
EDWARDS, Mr. Jonathan Guy, BSc ACA DChA *1998;* 8 Parkway, HORLEY, SURREY, RH6 7HX.
EDWARDS, Mr. Joseph Thomas, MSc BSc(Hons) ACA *2009;* 12 Bishops Avenue, BROMLEY, BR1 3ES.
EDWARDS, Mrs. Julie Ann, BSc ACA *1999;* T W Thomas & Co Ltd, Unit 6b, Lion Way, Swansea Enterprise Park, SWANSEA, SA7 9FB.
EDWARDS, Miss. Julie Rosaline, FCA *1973;* 4 Beverley Close, SUTTON COLDFIELD, WEST MIDLANDS, B72 1YF.
EDWARDS, Mrs. Karen Julie, FCA *1988;* 16 Rooksbury Road, ANDOVER, HAMPSHIRE, SP10 2LW.
EDWARDS, Mr. Karl Frank Richard, BSc ACA *1999;* EMCH Ltd, 17th Floor Metro Tower, 30 Tian Yao Qiao Road, SHANGHAI 200030, CHINA.
EDWARDS, Miss. Kate, BA ACA *1998;* 2327 West 34th Avenue, VANCOUVER V6M 1G8, BC, CANADA.
EDWARDS, Miss. Katherine, BA(Hons) ACA *2002;* 64 Queen Elizabeth Way, WOKING, SURREY, GU22 9AJ.
•EDWARDS, Mr. Keith Geoffrey, BA FCA *1992;* (Tax Fac), Alan James & Co, Quantum House, 59-61 Guildford Street, CHERTSEY, SURREY, KT16 9AX.
•EDWARDS, Mr. Keith William, BSc ACA *1986;* James Holyoak & Parker Limited, 1 Knights Court, Archers Way, Battlefield Enterprise Park, SHREWSBURY, SHROPSHIRE SY1 3GA.
•EDWARDS, Miss. Kellie Ann, BA(Hons) ACA *2001;* 126 Marlborough Road, LONDON, N19 4NN.
EDWARDS, Mr. Kenneth Royston, FCA *1977;* Cartref, 6, Beach Avenue, Barton On Sea, NEW MILTON, BH25 7EJ.
•EDWARDS, Mr. Kevin Alan, BSc(Hons) ACA CTA *2003;* MacIntyre Hudson LLP, 8-12 Priestgate, PETERBOROUGH, PE1 1JA.
EDWARDS, Mr. Kevin Gareth, BSc ACA *2003;* Clio Oyamadai Ichibankan #204, Oyamadai 3-22-11, Setagaya-ku, TOKYO, 158-0086 JAPAN.
EDWARDS, Mr. Kevin Neil, BA ACA *1981;* 15 Rothesay Avenue, CHELMSFORD, CM2 9BU.
EDWARDS, Mr. Kevin Paul, BSc ACA *1983;* Manor House, 16a Manor Way, Hail Weston, ST. NEOTS, PE19 5LG.
•EDWARDS, Mr. Kevin William, BSc FCA *1987;* Kevin and Anne Edwards, Moor End, Hyde, FORDINGBRIDGE, HAMPSHIRE, SP6 2QH.
EDWARDS, Miss. Kirsten, MSc BA(Hons) ACA *2004;* 73 Garnet Street, LONDON, E1W 3QS.
EDWARDS, Mr. Lance William, FCA *1980;* F & C Assett Management Plc, Exchange House, 12 Primrose Street, LONDON, EC2A 2NY.
EDWARDS, Mr. Lawrence, BA ACA *2007;* Eton Court, Flat 2, 1 Queenston Road, MANCHESTER, M20 2WZ.
EDWARDS, Mr. Lawrence Sebastian, MA FCA *1994;* 17/8 East Silvermills Lane, Stockbridge, EDINBURGH, EH3 5BG.
•EDWARDS, Mr. Lee Sheridan, BSc ACA *1998;* KPMG LLP, 15 Canada Square, LONDON, E14 5GL. See also KPMG Europe LLP
EDWARDS, Mr. Leigh Gareth, BSc ACA *2007;* 46 Beverley Court, Wellesley Road, LONDON, W4 4LQ.
EDWARDS, Mr. Leo John, FCA *1970;* Kew Lodge, Belmont, WANTAGE, OXFORDSHIRE, OX12 9AS.
EDWARDS, Mr. Leslie Frank, FCA *1975;* 4 Baines Avenue, BLACKPOOL, FY3 7LA.
EDWARDS, Miss. Lindsey Elisabeth, ACA *2008;* Flat 2, 124 Sheen Road, RICHMOND, TW9 1UR.
EDWARDS, Mrs. Lindy, BA ACA *1988;* 1 The Old Vicarage, Top Wath Road, Pateley Bridge, HARROGATE, NORTH YORKSHIRE, HG3 5PG.
EDWARDS, Mrs. Lisa Jane, BSc ACA *1997;* Malmesbury Accountancy Ltd, 46 High Street, MALMESBURY, SN169AT.
EDWARDS, Miss. Lisa Michelle, ACA *2008;* 10, Brook Close, EAST GRINSTEAD, WEST SUSSEX, RH19 3XZ.
EDWARDS, Mr. Malcolm Andrew, MA ACA *1979;* 14 Wendover Road, BROMLEY, BR2 9JX.
EDWARDS, Mrs. Margaret Jennifer, BSc FCA *1970;* 2 Gowan Park, CUPAR, FIFE, KY15 4AZ.
EDWARDS, Mr. Mark, BSc ACA *1993;* Beazley, 60 Great Tower Street, LONDON, EC3R 5AD.
EDWARDS, Mr. Mark Harvey, ACA *1994;* 4 Archers Close, Swaffham Bulbeck, CAMBRIDGE, CB25 0NG.
EDWARDS, Mr. Mark James Timothy, MA ACA *1984;* T Rowe Price International Inc, 60 Queen Victoria Street, LONDON, EC4N 4TZ.
EDWARDS, Mr. Mark John, BSc FCA *1979;* A I M Aviation (Jecco) Ltd Jecco House, Boscombe Grove Road, BOURNEMOUTH, BH1 4PD.
EDWARDS, Mr. Mark John, ACA *2009;* 7/36 Southport Street, WEST LEEDERVILLE, WA 6007, AUSTRALIA.
EDWARDS, Mr. Mark R A, MA(Oxon) ACA *2007;* Flat 4, Malling House, Abbey Park, BECKENHAM, KENT, BR3 1PZ.
EDWARDS, Mr. Mark Trevarthian, BA ACA *1986;* EBRD, 1 Exchange Square, LONDON, EC2A 2JN.
EDWARDS, Mr. Mark William, BA ACA *1983;* 25 Harvey Road, GUILDFORD, GU1 3LU.
EDWARDS, Mr. Mark William, BA ACA *1985;* Wall House, Bowley Lane, Bodenham, HEREFORD, HR1 3LF.
EDWARDS, Mr. Martin, BA ACA *1991;* UK Platforms Ltd Unit 3, Dialog Fleming Way, CRAWLEY, WEST SUSSEX, RH10 9NQ.
EDWARDS, Mr. Martin Ellis, ACA *1980;* Wenallt, Llanrhaeadr, DENBIGH, LL16 4PL.
EDWARDS, Mr. Martin Francis, BSc ACA *2007;* with PricewaterhouseCoopers CI LLP, Twenty Two Colomberie, St Helier, JERSEY, JE1 4XA.
•EDWARDS, Mr. Martin Wyn, FCA *1972;* Martin Edwards & Co, La Fantaisie, St Martin, JERSEY, JE3 6HE.
EDWARDS, Mr. Martyn, BA ACA *1998;* 20 Coed Camlas, New Inn, PONTYPOOL, NP4 8RR.
EDWARDS, Mr. Martyn Lomax, FCA *1963;* 9 Lyon Close, CHELMSFORD, CM2 8NY.
EDWARDS, Mr. Mathew David, MMath ACA *2006;* with PricewaterhouseCoopers, 101 Barbirolli Square, Lower Mosley Street, MANCHESTER, M2 3PW.
EDWARDS, Mr. Matthew James, BA ACA *2009;* 701 Commercial Road, LONDON, E14 7LA.
•EDWARDS, Miss. Meg Katharine, BSc ACA *1990;* Rutherford Accountancy Limited, 34 Pettitts Lane, Dry Drayton, CAMBRIDGE, CB23 8BT.
EDWARDS, Miss. Melanie, ACA *2010;* Flat 4 Rutland Lodge, 81-85 Perry Hill, LONDON, SE6 4LJ.
EDWARDS, Miss. Melissa, ACA *2011;* 33 Felsham Road, Putney, LONDON, SW15 1AY.
EDWARDS, Mr. Melvyn Morris, FCA *1964;* 15 Eton Road, FRINTON-ON-SEA, CO13 9JA.
•EDWARDS, Mr. Mervyn William Barclay, FCA *1971;* M.W.B. Edwards, Gracegarth, Wetherby Road, KNARESBOROUGH, HG5 8LQ.
EDWARDS, Mr. Michael, MBA BSc ACA *1993;* 27 Borrowdale Drive, LEAMINGTON SPA, WARWICKSHIRE, CV32 6NY.
•EDWARDS, Mr. Michael Alan, FCA *1968;* M A Edwards Accountants Limited, 30a The Green, Kings Norton, BIRMINGHAM, B38 8SD.
EDWARDS, Mr. Michael Andrew, FCA *1975;* 2 St Johns Road, LEATHERHEAD, KT22 8SE.
EDWARDS, Mr. Michael Ian, FCA *1989;* Home Mead Barn, Kelston, BATH, BA1 9AF.
EDWARDS, Mr. Michael Robert, BA ACA ATII *1995;* Ch Du Verger 3, 1278 LA RIPPE, SWITZERLAND.
EDWARDS, Mr. Michael Victor, FCA *1966;* 6 Homefield, Wootton Bassett, SWINDON, SN4 8DE.
•EDWARDS, Mrs. Michaela June, FCA *1992;* Bourne & Co, 6 Lichfield Street, BURTON-ON-TRENT, DE14 3RD.
EDWARDS, Ms. Natalie Ellen, MA(Hons) ACA *2002;* c/o RBS, RBS Tower, 88 Phillip St, SYDNEY, NSW 2000, AUSTRALIA.
EDWARDS, Mr. Neil Pryce, ACA *1980;* 1586 Folkestone Terrace, WESTLAKE VILLAGE, CA 91361, UNITED STATES.
•EDWARDS, Mr. Neil Richard, BSc ACA AMCT *2002;* PricewaterhouseCoopers LLP, 1 Embankment Place, LONDON, WC2N 6RH. See also PricewaterhouseCoopers
•ⒾEDWARDS, Mr. Nicholas Guy, BA FCA *1989;* Deloitte LLP, Athene Place, 66 Shoe Lane, LONDON, EC4A 3BQ. See also Deloitte & Touche LLP
EDWARDS, Mr. Nicholas James, MSc ACA *2004;* 10 Canberra Court, West Avenue, Ramsey, HUNTINGDON, CAMBRIDGESHIRE, PE26 1EY.
•ⒾEDWARDS, Mr. Nicholas John, BA ACA *1989;* Cooper Parry LLP, 14 Park Row, NOTTINGHAM, NG1 6GR.
EDWARDS, Mr. Nicholas Vernon, BSc ACA *2009;* with Zolfo Cooper LLP, 10 Fleet Place, LONDON, EC4M 7RB.
EDWARDS, Mr. Nicholas William John, BA ACA *2000;* Nightingale House, Moorfield Group Ltd, 65 Curzon Street, LONDON, W1J 8PE.
EDWARDS, Mr. Nick, ACA *2008;* Trowers & Hamlins Sceptre Court, 40 Tower Hill, LONDON, EC3N 4DX.
EDWARDS, Miss. Nicola, ACA *2008;* Flat 4/M Grove End House, Grove End Road, LONDON, NW8 9HP.
EDWARDS, Mrs. Nicola Jane, BSc ACA *1996;* C & J Clarks Ltd, 40 High Street, STREET, SOMERSET, BA16 0EQ.
EDWARDS, Mrs. Nicola Janet, BSc ACA *1983;* 2505 26th Street, SANTA MONICA, CA 90405, UNITED STATES.
•EDWARDS, Mr. Nigel Denison, FCA *1970;* Nigel Edwards, Cross Gate, Shute Hill, Bishopsteignton, TEIGNMOUTH, DEVON TQ14 9QL.
EDWARDS, Mr. Norman John, MA FCA *1955;* 20 Warren Avenue, Cheam, SUTTON, SM2 7QN. (Life Member)
EDWARDS, Mr. Norman Taylor, BA FCA *1973;* Flat 4 Regents Apartments, Redland Court Road, BRISTOL, BS6 7BH.
EDWARDS, Mr. Norman William, FCA *1966;* 20 Succombs Place, Southview Road, WARLINGHAM, CR6 9JQ.
EDWARDS, Mr. Oliver Graham McCordall, BA ACA *2005;* 140 Underhill Road, East Dulwich, LONDON, SE22 0QJ.
EDWARDS, Mr. Owen Hugh, FCA *1963;* 47B Twatling Road, Barnt Green, BIRMINGHAM, B45 8HS.
EDWARDS, Mr. Paul, MA(Oxon) ACA *1992;* 13 St Saviours Court, Alexandra Park Road, LONDON, N22 7AZ.
EDWARDS, Dr. Paul, PhD MSc BSc ACA FSI *1998;* Arete Consulting Ltd, Nestor House, 4 Playhouse Yard, LONDON, EC4V 5EX.
EDWARDS, Mr. Paul Alexander, FCA *1991;* Go-Ahead Group Plc, 41-51 Grey Street, NEWCASTLE UPON TYNE, NE1 6EE.
EDWARDS, Mr. Paul David, BA LLB ACA *2002;* 25 Eastbourne Road, BRENTFORD, MIDDLESEX, TW8 9PE.
EDWARDS, Mr. Paul Martin, BSc ACA *1987;* 12 Brewery Square, LONDON, EC1V 4LE.
EDWARDS, Mrs. Penelope Dawn, BSc ACA *1990;* Silverdale, 15 Chadfield Road, Duffield, BELPER, DERBYSHIRE, DE56 4DU.
•EDWARDS, Mr. Peter, MA FCA *1954;* Fiscalis Management Ltd, Dunraven House, 6 Meadow Court, 41-43 High Street, WITNEY, OX28 6ER.
EDWARDS, Mr. Peter, BSc ACA *2007;* Ivy Cottage Lower Kingsdown Road, Kingsdown, CORSHAM, SN13 8AZ.
•EDWARDS, Mr. Peter Alan, BA FCA *1995;* with Grant Thornton UK LLP, Unit 2, Broadfield Court, SHEFFIELD, S8 0XF.
•EDWARDS, Mr. Peter Geoffrey, FCA *1977;* Hope Jones, Lymington House, 73 High St, LYMINGTON, SO41 9ZA.
EDWARDS, Mr. Peter James, BA ACA *2006;* (Tax Fac), 58 Whitecross Avenue, Whitchurch, BRISTOL, BS14 9JD.
•EDWARDS, Mr. Peter John, ACA ACCA *2010;* Warr & Co, Mynshull House, 78 Churchgate, STOCKPORT, SK1 1YJ. See also Warr & Co Limited
•EDWARDS, Mr. Peter John, FCA *1974;* (Tax Fac), Alliotts, Friary Court, 13-21 High Street, GUILDFORD, SURREY, GU1 3DL.
•EDWARDS, Mr. Peter John, ACA *1979;* (Tax Fac), Sandison Rouse & Co, Richmond House, 48 Bromyard Road, St Johns, WORCESTER, WR2 5BT.
EDWARDS, Mr. Peter Thomas, BA ACA *1992;* 39 Mayfield Avenue, CARDIFF, CF5 1AL.
EDWARDS, Mr. Philip George, FCA *1966;* with Everett & Son, 35 Paul Street, LONDON, EC2A 4UQ.
EDWARDS, Mr. Philip George, FCA *1974;* G Force Tyres Exhausts & Batteries, 183 Ash Road, ALDERSHOT, HAMPSHIRE, GU12 4DD.
•EDWARDS, Mr. Philip James, BCom FCA *1994;* (Tax Fac), with Vanilla Accounting Limited, 3 Oakmere Close, Edwalton, NOTTINGHAM, NG12 4FJ.
•EDWARDS, Mr. Philip Rennie, BSc FCA *1983;* Rockwells Ltd, 17 Church Road, TUNBRIDGE WELLS, KENT, TN1 1LG.
EDWARDS, Mr. Phillip Sion, BA ACA *1999;* 9 Rosemount Road, Flax Bourton, BRISTOL, BS48 1UP.
EDWARDS, Mrs. Rachel Louise, BSc ACA *1990;* Proudreed Limited, 16 Carlton Crescent, SOUTHAMPTON, SO15 2ES.
•EDWARDS, Mr. Ramon Edgar Monnier, FCA *1960;* Edwards & Co, 2 Stud Farm, Burrough Green, NEWMARKET, Suffolk, CB8 9NH.
EDWARDS, Mr. Randall James, BSc ACA *1988;* Springfield, Broughton, COWBRIDGE, SOUTH GLAMORGAN, CF71 7QR.
EDWARDS, Mr. Raymond Brunton, BCom FCA *1962;* Beech House, Long Wood Drive, Jordans, BEACONSFIELD, HP9 2SS.
EDWARDS, Mr. Raymond George, FCA *1959;* 18 Russells Crescent, HORLEY, RH6 7DN. (Life Member)
EDWARDS, Miss. Rhiannon Sasha Hately, BSc ACA *2007;* Vann Cottage, Vann Drive, Ockley, DORKING, SURREY, RH5 5TE.
EDWARDS, Mr. Richard, BA(Hons) ACA *2011;* Belmont, Rushton Spencer, MACCLESFIELD, CHESHIRE, SK11 0SE.
•EDWARDS, Mr. Richard Andrew, ACA *2009;* (Tax Fac), Randall Greene, Parallel House, 32/34 London Road, GUILDFORD, SURREY, GU1 2AB.
EDWARDS, Mr. Richard Aneurin, FCA *1958;* Burford House, The Common, Chipperfield, KINGS LANGLEY, WD4 9BY. (Life Member)
EDWARDS, Mr. Richard Charles, ACA *2008;* Sequoia, Grassy Lane, SEVENOAKS, KENT, TN13 1PL.
EDWARDS, Mr. Richard David Lewis, BSc ACA *1985;* Grove Cottage, 22 Epping Road, Toothill, ONGAR, CM5 9SQ.
EDWARDS, Mr. Richard Douglas, BSc FCA *1980;* 9 Rosehill Drive, BRIDGNORTH, SHROPSHIRE, WV16 5BP.
•EDWARDS, Mr. Richard James, FCA *1975;* Richard Edwards & Co The Maltings, Rosemary Lane, HALSTEAD, CO9 1HZ.
EDWARDS, Mr. Richard John, BEd ACA *1992;* 8 Brewin Close, BRACKLEY, NORTHAMPTONSHIRE, NN13 6NX.
EDWARDS, Mr. Robert Alan, ACA *1981;* Encon Insulation Brunswick House, Deighton Close, WETHERBY, WEST YORKSHIRE, LS22 7GZ.
•EDWARDS, Mr. Robert Blake, MA FCA *1982;* HedgeStart Partners LLP, St Albans House, 57/59 Haymarket, LONDON, SW1Y 4QX.
EDWARDS, Mr. Robert Clive, BSc ACA *2000;* 118 Avondale Avenue, STAINES, MIDDLESEX, TW18 2NF.
EDWARDS, Mr. Robert Jack Henderson, FCA *1960;* Magnolia Cottage, Harrowbeer Lane, YELVERTON, DEVON, PL20 6EA. (Life Member)
EDWARDS, Mr. Robert James, FCA *1973;* 32 Heywood Avenue, DISS, IP22 4DN. (Life Member)
EDWARDS, Mr. Robert John, FCA *1973;* Sycamore Lodge, La Rue de L'Eglise, St Peter, JERSEY, JE3 7YH.
EDWARDS, Mr. Robert John, BSc ACA *1998;* Balfour Beatty Capital, 350 Euston Road, Regent's Place, LONDON, NW1 3AX.
EDWARDS, Mr. Robert Kenneth, FCA *1979;* 61 Hemwood Road, WINDSOR, SL4 4YX.
EDWARDS, Mr. Robert Leslie, FCA *1956;* Culter Place, Coulter, BIGGAR, ML12 6PZ. (Life Member)
EDWARDS, Mr. Robert Mark, LLM LLB ACA *2002;* (Tax Fac), 11 Gleneagles Drive, WATERLOOVILLE, HAMPSHIRE, PO7 8RX.

EDWARDS, Mr. Robert Peter, MA FCA *1971;* I S Solutions Windmill House, 91-93 Windmill Road, SUNBURY-ON-THAMES, TW16 7EF.
EDWARDS, Mr. Robin Michael, BSc ACA *1985;* Willow, 40 Tehidy Gardens, CAMBORNE, TR14 0ET.
EDWARDS, Mr. Robin Miles, BSc FCA *1992;* Squirrels, Cowes Lane, Warsash, SOUTHAMPTON, SO31 9HD.
EDWARDS, Mr. Robin Warwick, FCA *1972;* 10 Kensington Gate, LONDON, W8 5NA.
EDWARDS, Miss. Rosemary Anne, BA(Hons) ACA *2002;* 3 Deergrass Walk, Knowle, FAREHAM, PO17 5GD.
EDWARDS, Miss. Rosie Alice, ACA *2010;* Flat 1, 84 Alderney Street, LONDON, SW1V 4EY.
EDWARDS, Mr. Roy Anthony, BA ACA *1988;* 23 Imperial Square, CHELTENHAM, GLOUCESTERSHIRE, GL50 1QZ.
•**EDWARDS, Mr. Rupert John Aldington, FCA** *1972;* Edwards & Keeping, Unity Chambers, 34 High East Street, DORCHESTER, DT1 1HA.
EDWARDS, Mr. Ryan David, ACA *2003;* 20 Grange Road, Ampthill, BEDFORD, MK45 2PA.
EDWARDS, Mrs. Sandra Jane, BA ACA *1999;* 6a Chatsworth Road, Silverstream, UPPER HUTT 5019, NEW ZEALAND.
EDWARDS, Mrs. Sarah Jayne, BSc(Hons) ACA *2001;* with National Audit Office, 157-197 Buckingham Palace Road, Victoria, LONDON, SW1W 9SP.
EDWARDS, Ms. Sarah Jean, BA ACA CPA *2002;* 4 Hopwood Close, LONDON, SW17 0AG.
•**EDWARDS, Mrs. Sharon Janet, FCA** *2000;* Mapus-Smith & Lemmon LLP, 48 King Street, KING'S LYNN, NORFOLK, PE30 1HE.
EDWARDS, Mr. Simon Jeremy, BSc ACA ATII *1987;* (Tax Fac), Coney Berry Coneyhurst Lane, Ewhurst, CRANLEIGH, GU6 7PL.
EDWARDS, Mr. Simon John, ACA *1997;* 6 Beningfield Drive, Napsbury Park, ST. ALBANS, HERTFORDSHIRE, AL2 1UJ.
EDWARDS, Mr. Simon Patrick, BSc FCA *1991;* Sector Hall, Sector Lane, AXMINSTER, DEVON, EX13 5RZ.
EDWARDS, Mr. Simon Richard, JP FCA *1972;* 26 Green Villa Park, WILMSLOW, CHESHIRE, SK9 6EJ.
EDWARDS, Mr. Stephen, BA ACA *2003;* Flat 1, 31 Rutland Drive, HARROGATE, NORTH YORKSHIRE, HG1 2NS.
EDWARDS, Mr. Stephen Colin, BSc ACA *1999;* 134 Havelock Road, LONDON, SW19 8HB.
•**EDWARDS, Mr. Stephen George, FCA** *1974;* (Tax Fac), 1 The Old Vicarage, Top Wath Road, Pateley Bridge, HARROGATE, NORTH YORKSHIRE, HG3 5PG.
EDWARDS, Mr. Stephen James, FCA *1982;* 108 Blagreaves Lane, Littleover, DERBY, DE23 7FP.
EDWARDS, Mr. Stephen Peter, BA ACA *1991;* Core Capital LLP, 9 South Street, LONDON, W1K 2XA.
•**EDWARDS, Mr. Stephen Richard, FCA** *1989;* (Tax Fac), HW, 30 Camp Road, FARNBOROUGH, HAMPSHIRE, GU14 6EW. See also Haines Watts and Haines Watts Consulting
EDWARDS, Mr. Stephen William, BA ACA *1999;* Grianan Road, Speenogue, BURT, COUNTY DONEGAL, IRELAND.
EDWARDS, Mr. Stewart, ACA *1993;* 50 Montrose Avenue, LUTON, LU3 1HR.
EDWARDS, Mr. Stewart, BA ACA *1991;* 110 Wessex Road, DIDCOT, OX11 8BN.
•**EDWARDS, Mr. Stuart, BA ACA** *1983;* (Tax Fac), Stuart Edwards & Company, Garden Studios, 11-15 Betterton Street, LONDON, WC2H 9BP.
•**EDWARDS, Mr. Stuart Ian, FCA** *1968;* (Member of Council 1999 - 2001), (Tax Fac), Malcolm Wood & Co., Shrubbery House, 47 Prospect Hill, REDDITCH, WORCESTERSHIRE, B97 4BS.
EDWARDS, Mr. Stuart Thomas, BSc ACA *1984;* 1 Grosvenor Place, LONDON, SW1X 7HJ.
EDWARDS, Mrs. Susan, BA ACA *1986;* 2 Fairlawn Park, WOKING, GU21 4HT.
EDWARDS, Mrs. Susan Jane, BA FCA *1985;* 17 Denby Dale, Hardwicke Park, WELLINGBOROUGH, NN8 5QR.
EDWARDS, Miss. Susannah Judith, ACA *2008;* 05-08 The Cornwall, 2 The Cornwall, SINGAPORE 269632, SINGAPORE.
EDWARDS, Mrs. Suzanne Elizabeth, BSc ACA *2004;* 37 Holtwood Drive, Woodlands, IVYBRIDGE, DEVON, PL21 9TH.
•**EDWARDS, Mr. Terence, FCA CFA** *1966;* (Tax Fac), Bullimores LLP, Old Printers Yard, 156 South Street, DORKING, SURREY, RH4 2HF.
EDWARDS, Mr. Thomas Michael, BSc ACA *2009;* 37 Hartham Road, LONDON, N7 9JQ.
EDWARDS, Mr. Thomas Stephen, BSc FCA *1990;* 1 Chestnut Close, Acton Turville, BADMINTON, GL9 1JN.
EDWARDS, Mr. Timothy David Warneford, MA ACA *1986;* Bayworth Cleave, Bayworth, ABINGDON, OX13 6QS.
•**EDWARDS, Mr. Timothy Francis, MBA BA ACA CF** *1990;* 17 Peel Moat Road, STOCKPORT, SK4 4PL.
EDWARDS, Mr. Timothy Peter Warren, ACA *1980;* Paynes Hill House, Steeple Aston, BICESTER, OX25 4SQ.
EDWARDS, Mr. Trevor William, FCA *1969;* Christmas House, Shenstone, KIDDERMINSTER, DY10 4ES.
EDWARDS, Mrs. Vanessa Caroline, BSc ACA *1999;* 8 Hatherall Close, Stratton St. Margaret, SWINDON, SN3 4LQ.
EDWARDS, Miss. Victoria Jane, BSc(Hons) ACA *2004;* Group Financial Business Solutions, Level 16 St Helen's, 1 Undershaft, LONDON, EC3P 3DQ.
EDWARDS, Miss. Victoria Kate, BSc(Hons) ACA *2010;* 78 Barkers Lane, SALE, CHESHIRE, M33 6SD.
EDWARDS, Mr. William John, FCA *1961;* Dibbins Hey, Tarporley Road, Clotton, TARPORLEY, CW6 0EH.
EDWARDS, Mr. William John, FCA *1958;* 47 Saxby Road, BURGESS HILL, RH15 8UL. (Life Member)
EDWARDS, Mr. William John, BSc ACA *1981;* 83 Baytree Road, Fairfield Park, BATH, BA1 6NF.
EDWARDS-BROWN, Mr. Allan David, BSc ACA *2011;* 4 Church Street, Carlton, BARNSLEY, SOUTH YORKSHIRE, S71 3EY.
•**EDWARDS-BROWN, Mr. David, BA FCA** *1977;* DEB, DEB House, 19 Middleswood Way, Wharncliffe Business Park, Carlton, BARNSLEY SOUTH YORKSHIRE S71 3HR.
•**EDWARDS-BROWN, Mrs. Janice, ACA FCCA** *2008;* DEB, DEB House, 19 Middleswood Way, Wharncliffe Business Park, Carlton, BARNSLEY SOUTH YORKSHIRE S71 3HR.
EDWARDS-MOSS, Mr. Thomas Michael, BA ACA *2006;* Credit Suisse, 17 Columbus Courtyard, LONDON, E14 4DA.
EDWARDSON, Mr. Andrew Richard, MA FCA *1989;* 5 Brooklyn Drive, Emmer Green, READING, RG4 8SR.
EDWICK, Mr. Paul Andrew, FCA *1978;* Trade Glaze Housae, Dowding Road, LINCOLN, LN3 4PH.
EDWIN, Mr. Ashton Antony, BSc ACA *2004;* 308 Balfour Road, ILFORD, IG1 4HZ.
EDWIN, Miss. Oluwabunmi Onadjefe, MSc BEng ACA *2009;* 4040 South Jackson Drive, No.206, INDEPENDENCE, MO 64057, UNITED STATES.
•**EDWORTHY, Mr. Christopher John, FCA** *1982;* Chris Edworthy, St John House, Trusham, NEWTON ABBOT, TQ13 0NR.
•**EDWORTHY, Mr. David William, BSc FCA** *1980;* (Tax Fac), D.W. Edworthy BSc FCA, The Old Rectory, Rectory Way, Lympsham, WESTON-SUPER-MARE, AVON BS24 0EW.
EDYVEAN, Miss. Lowena Jane Yasmin, ACA *2008;* Deloitte & Touche Llp, 3 Rivergate, BRISTOL, BS1 6GD.
EE, Miss. Angela Meng Yen, BA ACA *1995;* 65 Dunbar Walk, SINGAPORE 459442, SINGAPORE.
EE, Mr. Beng Wat, FCA *1975;* 23 Jalan Mandarin 2, Taman Mandarin, 31650 IPOH, PERAK, MALAYSIA.
EE, Mr. Beng Yew, ACA *1980;* 12 First Avenue, SINGAPORE 268748, SINGAPORE.
EE, Mrs. Chong Kong, ACA *1983;* 20 Formby Way, BULL CREEK, WA 6149, AUSTRALIA.
EE, Mr. Mark Yang Wei, BA ACA CFA *2007;* 23 Chiltern Drive, SINGAPORE 359742, SINGAPORE.
EE, Mr. Tiang Peng, FCA *1972;* 37 Headland Road, Castle Cove, SYDNEY, NSW 2069, AUSTRALIA.
EELES, Mrs. Clare Pearl, BA ACA *1988;* 26 De Lisle Road, BOURNEMOUTH, DORSET, BH3 7NF.
EELES, Mr. Jonathan David, ACA *1992;* 38 Beggars Lane, LEEK, STAFFORDSHIRE, ST13 8XE.
EELES, Miss. Marian Sara Hughes, ACA *2008;* 7b Thirsk Road, LONDON, SW11 5SU.
EFEYINI, Miss. Ethima Olanrewaju, BA(Hons) ACA *2001;* Flat 1-4, 96 Kensington Avenue, THORNTON HEATH, CR7 8BZ.
EFFAH, Mr. Edward Oppong, ACA *1990;* Fidelity Bank Limited PMB 43 Cantonments, ACCRA, GHANA.
•**EFFENDI, Mr. Ahmed Raza, BA(Hons) ACA** *2002;* KJA Huque Chaudhry Limited, 199 Roundhay Road, LEEDS, LS8 5AN. See also ACT Yorkshire Limited
•**EFFENDI, Mrs. Naheed, BA(Hons) FCA CTA** *2001;* KJA Kilner Johnson Limited, Network House, Stubs Beck Lane, Bradford, CLECKHEATON, WEST YORKSHIRE BD19 4TT.
EFRAIMIDOU, Miss. Ipatia, ACA *2009;* 45 Beamish View, Birtley, CHESTER LE STREET, DH3 1RS.
EFSTATHIADIS, Mrs. Clea, ACA *1993;* 81 Springvale Drive, WEETANGERA, ACT 2614, AUSTRALIA.
EFSTATHIOU, Ms. Argyroulla, BA ACA *2005;* Argous 12, Flat 301, 2311 LAKATAMIA, CYPRUS.
•**EFSTRATIOU, Mr. Charalambos, BA FCA** *1999;* Moore Stephens (Limassol) limited, Areil Corner, 1st Floor Office 101, 196 Arch Makarios Avenue, CY 3030 LIMASSOL, CYPRUS.
•**EFTEKHAR, Mr. Mehran, ACA** *1978;* Nest Investments (Holdings) Limited, Ariadne House, 2nd Floor, 333 28th October Street, 3106 LIMASSOL, CYPRUS.
•**EFTHYMIADES, Mr. Paris, BSc ACA** *1989;* Deloitte Hadjipavlou Sofianos & Cambanis S.A, 3a Fragoklissias & Granikou Str, Maroussi, 15125 ATHENS, GREECE.
EFTHYMIOU, Miss. Charoula, BSc ACA *2003;* 15 M.Kousoulide Street, Tseri, 2480 NICOSIA, CYPRUS.
EFTHYMIOU, Miss. Christiana, ACA *2010;* Barclays Bank PLC - Spanish Branch, PLAZA DE COLON 1, CIF:W0061418J, 28046 MADRID, SPAIN.
EFTHYMIOU, Mr. Chrysovalantis, BA ACA *2009;* 7 Thymariou Street, Panthea, Mesa Gitonia, 4007 LIMASSOL, CYPRUS.
EFTHYMIOU, Mr. Demetris, ACA CFA *2009;* Flat 8, 7 Cleveland Square, LONDON, W2 6DH.
EFTYCHIOU, Mr. Eftychios, MA ACA *1998;* PricewaterhouseCoopers Limited, Julia House, 3 Themistocles Dervis Street, CY-1066 NICOSIA, CYPRUS.
EGADDU, Mr. George William, BA FCA *1971;* George Egaddu, 6 Clement Hill Road, PO Box 3736, KAMPALA, UGANDA.
EGAN, Mr. Anthony Trevor, BA ACA *1989;* 11 Oakfield Close, Bramhall, STOCKPORT, SK7 1JE.
EGAN, Miss. Caroline Jane, MA ACA *2000;* Beechwood, 10 Woodhall Lane, Stanningley, PUDSEY, LEEDS, WEST YORKSHIRE LS28 7TT.
EGAN, Mr. David Anthony, BBS FCA *1975;* Flat 1, 11 Egliston Road, LONDON, SW15 1AL.
EGAN, Mrs. Emma Jane, BA ACA *2002;* 5 Station Road, TRING, HERTFORDSHIRE, HP23 5NG.
EGAN, Mr. Gary, ACA *1983;* Wincanton Plc, Methuen Park, CHIPPENHAM, SN14 0WT.
EGAN, Mr. Henry Anthony, FCA *1966;* 9 Bridge End, Billington, CLITHEROE, BB7 9NU.
EGAN, Mr. John, BA(Hons) ACA *2011;* 82 Cross Oak Road, BERKHAMSTED, HERTFORDSHIRE, HP4 3HZ.
EGAN, Mr. Michael, BA ACA *1995;* (Tax Fac), 36 Brighouse Road, Queensbury, BRADFORD, WEST YORKSHIRE, BD13 1QE.
•**EGAN, Mr. Michael, FCA** *1973;* (Tax Fac), Mike Egan & Co, 166-170 Lee Lane, Horwich, BOLTON, BL6 7AF.
•**EGAN, Mr. Michael Patrick William, MA FCA** *1982;* UHY Hacker Young LLP, Quadrant House, 4 Thomas More Square, LONDON, E1W 1YW. See also UHY Corporate Finance Limited
•**EGAN, Mr. Patrick David, FCA** *1974;* 2 Culverland Close, EXETER, EX4 6HR.
•**EGAN, Mr. Sean Michael, BA FCA** *1992;* Hale & Company LLP, Ground Floor, Belmont Place, Belmont Road, MAIDENHEAD, BERKSHIRE SL6 6TB. See also Hale & Company
EGAN, Mr. Terence Michael, FCA *1959;* Sabin, Firs Road, KENLEY, CR8 5LG.
EGAN, Dr. Thomas Andrew, PhD BSc FCA *1983;* Flat 1, 128 Sheen Road, RICHMOND, TW9 1UR.
EGAN, Mr. Timothy John, FCA *1969;* 7 Route du Puits Roulle Crotte, Sansais, Commune de Pers, 79190 PERS, FRANCE.
EGDELL, Mrs. Kathrin Kristina Faulkner, MA ACA *1992;* Lake House, Leek Old Road, Sutton, MACCLESFIELD, CHESHIRE, SK11 0HZ.
EGEDESO, Mr. Karsten, ACA *2007;* PricewaterhouseCoopers, Strandvejen 44, DK-2900, HELLERUP, DENMARK.
EGERT, Mr. James, BSc ACA *2003;* 42 Dalgarno Gardens, LONDON, W10 6AB.
EGERTON, Mrs. Caroline Louise, BSc ACA *2002;* The Body Shop International Plc, Watersmead, LITTLEHAMPTON, WEST SUSSEX, BN17 6LS.
EGERTON, Mr. Charles Edward, BSc FCA ATII *1974;* Far Hornsby Gate, Armathwaite, CARLISLE, CA4 9QZ.
EGERTON, Mr. Peter John, FCA FCCA JDipMA *1970;* Monkerton House, Stoke Prior, LEOMINSTER, HR6 0NB.
EGERTON BROWNE, Mr. Nicholas, BSc FCA *1977;* Prospect House, Tonagh, Mountnugent, KELLS, COUNTY MEATH, IRELAND.
EGERTON-KING, Mrs. Nicola Sian, BSc ACA *1987;* Winton House, Gravel Path, BERKHAMSTED, HP4 2PH.
EGERTON-KING, Mr. Nigel David, BA ACA *1986;* Winton House, Gravel Path, BERKHAMSTED, HERTFORDSHIRE, HP4 2PH.
EGGAR, Mr. Jonathan Neil, BSc ACA *2002;* 51 Littleton Street, LONDON, SW18 3SZ.
EGGAR, Mrs. Zoe Michelle, BSc ACA *2002;* 51 Littleton Street, LONDON, SW18 3SZ.
EGGERS, Miss. Sara, ACA *2008;* (Tax Fac), Flat 7, 27 Lingfield Road, LONDON, SW19 4PU.
EGGINGTON, Mr. Andrew John, MEng ACA *1991;* 23 St. Leonards Road, Claygate, ESHER, KT10 0EL.
EGGINTON, Mr. Peter George, BA FCA *1990;* PO Box 44151, DUBAI, UNITED ARAB EMIRATES.
EGGLENTON, Mr. Melvyn John, FCA *1981;* 8 Valley Road, West Bridgford, NOTTINGHAM, NG2 6HG.
EGGLESHAW, Mr. John Ross, FCA *1967;* 57 Elizabeth Street, PADDINGTON, NSW 2021, AUSTRALIA. (Life Member)
EGGLESHAW, Mr. Richard Andrew, BA ACA *2002;* 56 Emet Grove, Emersons Green, BRISTOL, BS16 7EG.
EGGLESTON, Mr. Andrew James, BA(Hons) ACA *2003;* Flat 3 30 Lytton Grove, LONDON, SW15 2HB.
•**EGGLESTON, Mr. Andrew Keith, BSc ACA** *2005;* Eggleston Wiley LLP, 20 Anchor Terrace, 3-13 Southwark Bridge Road, LONDON, SE1 9HQ.
EGGLESTON, Mr. Steven Andrew, LLB ACA *1999;* 1 Whitenbrook Dell, HYTHE, KENT, CT21 5WD.
•**EGGLESTONE, Mr. Edward, FCA** *1969;* (Tax Fac), Edward Egglestone & Company, 3-5 Scarborough Street, HARTLEPOOL, TS24 7DA.
EGGLETON, Mr. Gary John, BA ACA *2004;* 1/251, Ford Motor Co Ltd Eagle Way, Great Warley, BRENTWOOD, CM13 3BW.
•**EGGLETON, Mr. Guy David Christopher, FCA CF** *1991;* Old Mill Audit LLP, Leeward House, Fitzroy Road, Exeter Business Park, EXETER, EX1 3LJ. See also Old Mill Accountancy LLP
EGGLETON, Miss. Kathryn Mary, BSc FCA *1981;* Glendyke, 38 Caldy Road, WIRRAL, MERSEYSIDE, CH48 2HQ.
EGGLETON, Mr. Richard Arthur, ACA *2008;* Flat 11 Charlemont House, 35 Cheam Road, EPSOM, KT17 1QX.
•**EGGLISHAW, Mr. David John Jepson, ACA** *1992;* PO Box 31356 SMB, SEVEN MILE BEACH, GRAND CAYMAN, KY1-1206, CAYMAN ISLANDS.
•**EGGLISHAW, Mr. Philip Jepson, BA FCA** *1978;* T.A. Jehan & Co, Ingouville House, Ingouville Lane, St. Helier, JERSEY, JE4 8SP.
•**EGGLISHAW, Mr. Richard Jepson, BSc FCA** *1972;* T.A. Jehain & Co, Ingouville House, Ingouville Lane, St. Helier, JERSEY, JE4 8SP.
EGGS, Mr. Clive Harold, ACA *1987;* 23 Elmstead Gard, WORCESTER PARK, KT4 7BD.
EGINGTON, Miss. Angela, BSc ACA *2009;* 9 Robert Moffat, High Legh, KNUTSFORD, CHESHIRE, WA16 6PS.
•**EGINTON, Mr. Anthony Charles Thomas, BA FCA TEP** *1975;* (Tax Fac), Tony Eginton & Co, 1 Upper Gladstone Road, CHESHAM, BUCKINGHAMSHIRE, HP5 3AF.
EGLEN, Mr. David, BSc ACA *1992;* 7 Matham Road, EAST MOLESEY, KT8 0SX.
EGLEN, Ms. Sarah-Jane, BSc ACA *1997;* 101 Cranley Gardens, LONDON, N10 3AD.
EGLETON, Mr. Christopher William, FCA *1969;* 23 Karneadou Street, ATHENS, GREECE.
EGLETON, Mrs. Julie Louise, BSc ACA *1996;* 2 Abbotts Close, AYLESBURY, BUCKINGHAMSHIRE, HP20 1HZ.
EGLINGTON, Miss. Sarah Rebecca, ACA *2009;* Athene Place, 66 Shoe Lane, LONDON, EC4A 3BQ.
EGLINTINE, Mr. Neil, FCA *1981;* 6 Gladstone Mews, BLYTH, NE24 1HS.
•**EGLINTON, Mr. Kenneth Philip, BA FCA** *1982;* with Ernst & Young LLP, 1 More London Place, LONDON, SE1 2AF.
EGLINTON, Mr. Timothy Read, FCA *1975;* (Tax Fac), 153 Highlands Boulevard, LEIGH-ON-SEA, SS9 3TJ.
EGMORE, Mr. Stuart Arthur, BSc FCA *1992;* 45 West Road, Apt 4A, ORLEANS, MA 02653, UNITED STATES.
EHIEMUA, Mr. Emmanuel Oigiangbe, BSc FCA *1974;* Ehiemua & Co, 24 Commercial Road, Capl House, 1st Floor Apapa, P O Box 8096, Marina LAGOS NIGERIA.
•**EHLERS, Mr. George Thomas, FCA** *1967;* George T. Ehlers, Trendlewood, Ditchling Common, BURGESS HILL, RH15 0SE.
•**EHREICH, Mr. Bernhard, FCA** *1974;* B. Ehreich & Co, 113 Manor Road, LONDON, N16 5PB.

EHRENZWEIG, Mr. Neil Dominic, MEng ACA *2001;* Flat 7, 2 Gainsford Street, LONDON, SE1 2NE.

EICHMEYER, Mr. Axel, MA ACA *1997;* Axel Eichmeyer, Annastrasse 25, 60322 FRANKFURT AM MAIN, GERMANY.

EICHMULLER DE SOUZA, Mr. Alexander, BSc ACA *2000;* 6 Nightingale Square, LONDON, SW12 8LN.

•EICHMULLER DE SOUZA, Mr. Michael Walter, BSocSc ACA *2002;* with KPMG Audit, 9 Allee Scheffer, 2520 LUXEMBOURG, LUXEMBOURG.

EIFION-JONES, Mr. Jonathan Richard, FCA *1980;* Sumitomo Mitsui Banking Corporation Ltd, 99 Queen Victoria Street, LONDON, EC4V 4EH.

EIGENHEER, Mrs. Ruth Margaret, FCA *1959;* 31 Chemin de Planta, 1223 COLOGNY, SWITZERLAND. (Life Member)

EIGHTEEN, Mr. Brian Patrick, ACA *1982;* The Chestnuts, Tydehams, NEWBURY, RG14 6JT.

EIGHTEEN, Mrs. Rebecca Jane, ACA *2006;* 29b Britannia Road, WESTCLIFF-ON-SEA, ESSEX, SS0 8BP.

EILBECK, Mr. David Maurice, BA FCA *1981;* Metrix UK 4th Floor, Ministry of Defence St. Georges Court, 2-12 Bloomsbury Way, LONDON, WC1A 2SH.

•EILBECK, Mrs. Janet, BA FCA *1980;* The Garden House, Windmill Road, SEVENOAKS, TN13 1TN.

EILE-PARKER, Ms. Ilga, BSc ACA *1999;* with National Audit Office, 157-197 Buckingham Palace Road, Victoria, LONDON, SW1W 9SP.

EILERTSEN, Mrs. Lynne, BA ACA *1991;* The Bungalow, Kidbrooke Park Road, Blackheath, LONDON, SE3 0LW.

EILLEDGE, Elwyn Owen Morris, Esq CBE MA FCA *1963;* (Member of Council 1990 - 1992), Whitehorn House, Long Grove, Seer Green, BEACONSFIELD, HP9 2QH. (Life Member)

EILLES, Mr. Christopher Alan, FCA *1969;* 185 RIVERWOOD, BOERNE, TX 78006, UNITED STATES.

EILOART, Mr. Ian Robert, FCA *1954;* Little Haye, Holtye Road, EAST GRINSTEAD, WEST SUSSEX, RH19 3PP. (Life Member)

•EINOLLAHI, Mr. Maghsoud, MSc BSc FCA CF *1982;* Meecham House, Parkway, Bramhall, STOCKPORT, CHESHIRE, SK7 3DH.

EINOLLAHI, Miss. Sara, ACA *2009;* 201 Vauxhall Bridge Road, LONDON, SW1V 1ER.

EIREF, Mr. Zvi, MA FCA *1965;* 221 Dodds Lane, PRINCETON, NJ 08540, UNITED STATES.

•EISEN, Mr. Russell David, BA ACA *1989;* (Tax Fac), Elman Wall Limited, 5-7 John Princes Street, LONDON, W1G 0JN.

EISENBERG, Ms. Eva Ruth, BSc FCA *1977;* 18 Margaret Avenue, Shenfield, BRENTWOOD, CM15 8RF.

EJAZ, Mr. Faheem, BSc ACA ACCA *2010;* Deloitte & Touche Bakr Abulkhair & Co., Saudi Business Center Madina Road P.O. Box 442 Jeddah 21411 Saudi Arabia, JEDDAH, SAUDI ARABIA.

EKAIREB, Mr. Jason Haskel, BSc ACA *1993;* 5 Eden Close, LONDON, NW3 7UL.

EKAIREB, Mr. Rex Solomon, FCA *1972;* R&R Wholesal Jewellers, 45 Hatton Garden, LONDON, EC1N 8EX.

EKE, Miss. Caroline Elizabeth, BSc ACA *2006;* 9 Red Lion Court, Great North Road, HATFIELD, HERTFORDSHIRE, AL9 5BW.

EKE, Mr. Michael Ronald, FCA *1970;* Tigh na Birse, Birse, ABOYNE, ABERDEENSHIRE, AB34 5BY. (Life Member)

EKE, Mr. Richard John Sylvester, FCA *1981;* Tree Tops, Darkes Lane, POTTERS BAR, HERTFORDSHIRE, EN6 1BZ.

EKE, Mr. Roy Clive Ndubuisi, MSc BA(Hons) ACA *2004;* G A M Ltd, 12 St. James's Place, LONDON, SW1A 1NX.

EKERHOLM, Mrs. Marie Carina, BSc ACA *1996;* Freya Design, 32 Aberaman, Emmer Green, READING, RG4 8LD.

EKERMANS, Mrs. Issebel, ACA CA(SA) *2009;* (Tax Fac), Flat C, 45 Vineyard Hill Road, LONDON, SW19 7JL.

EKHAESE, Mr. Aitua Osa, BA ACA *1986;* 3 The Covert, NORTHWOOD, MIDDLESEX, HA6 2UD.

EKINS, Mr. Eric Walker, FCA *1960;* 3 Manor Close, Blunsdon, SWINDON, SN26 7BD. (Life Member)

EKINS, Mr. Martin, BCom ACA *1985;* Les Reinettes Les Rue Frairies, St. Andrew, GUERNSEY, GY6 8XT.

•EKKESHIS, Mr. Constantinos, MSc BSc ACA TEP *2007;* Ekkeshis Ierodiakonou Ltd, 39 Themistocles Dervis Street, Office 102, CY-1066 NICOSIA, CYPRUS.

EKSTEIN, Mr. Daniel, BA(Hons) ACA *2009;* 17a Woodland Gardens, LONDON, N10 3UE.

EL-ALI, Miss. Rita, BA(Hons) ACA *2000;* 1520 O Street NW, Apt 307, WASHINGTON, DC 20005, UNITED STATES.

•EL-BAHRANI, Mr. Izel-Din Salim, BA FCA *1961;* I.S.Bahrani, Faris Building, South Gate, BAGHDAD, IRAQ.

EL-BAZ, Mrs. Kim Ruth, BSc FCA *1994;* 16 Lion Gate Gardens, RICHMOND, SURREY, TW9 2DW.

EL-DADA, Mr. Youssef, BSc(Hons) ACA *2002;* 3 The Common, ASHTEAD, SURREY, KT21 2ED.

EL-ENBABY, Mr. Mohamed Salemm, FCA *1959;* El Makrizi Street, Flat 151, Zamalek, CAIRO, EGYPT. (Life Member)

EL HASSAN, Mr. Khalid, ACA *2009;* First Floor, 11 Hugon Road, LONDON, SW6 3HB.

EL-HAWI, Mrs. Christina Zaher, BA(Hons) ACA *2004;* Chubb Insurance Company of Europe, Cottons Centre, Hays Lane, LONDON, SE1 2QP.

EL-KALLAWI, Mr. Tamer Sami, ACA CA(SA) *2010;* P.O. Box 9313 - Eros, WINDHOEK, NAMIBIA.

EL-KOUR, Mr. Ala, BEng ACA *2004;* Flat C, 9 Winthorpe Road, LONDON, SW15 2LW.

EL-MARIESH, Mr. Anis, BSc ACA *1998;* 13 Percheron Drive, Knaphill, WOKING, SURREY, GU21 2QY.

•EL-RAMI, Mr. Andre Nadim, BSc FCA *1986;* R & G Chartered Accountants, 8th Floor, Jal al Dib Highway, Jal al Dib, BEIRUT, LEBANON.

EL SHERBINI, Mr. Mohamed Magdi Kamel, FCA *1963;* 10 Irak Street, Mohandseen, GIZA, EGYPT. (Life Member)

ELAHI, Mrs. Arifa, BA ACA *2004;* Building #18 Dubai Internet City, P.O. Box 11549 Dubai, United Arab Emirates, DUBAI, UNITED ARAB EMIRATES.

ELAMIN, Mr. Mansour Ismail, MSc BSc FCA *1973;* PO Box 8148, DUBAI, UNITED ARAB EMIRATES.

ELBORN, Mr. Keri John, BA ACA *1998;* 48 Ruskin Walk, Herne Hill, LONDON, SE24 9LZ.

ELBORN, Mr. Mark Horst, BA ACA *1990;* Gartenstrasse 12, 60594 FRANKFURT AM MAIN, GERMANY.

•ELBOURNE, Mr. Christopher Warren, FCA CTA *1969;* Elbourne & Company, 5 St. Marys Place, Meppershall, SHEFFORD, BEDFORDSHIRE, SG17 5NL.

ELBOURNE, Mrs. Julie Victoria Lindop, BA FCA *1985;* White Thorn, 27 Stoke Road, COBHAM, KT11 3BB.

ELCOCK, Mr. Bruce Davidson, BSc ACA *1990;* 28 Brae Burn Drive, PURCHASE, NY 10577, UNITED STATES.

ELCOCK, Mrs. Claire, ACA *2008;* with Grant Thornton UK LLP, 1 Whitehall Riverside, Whitehall Road, LEEDS, WEST YORKSHIRE, LS1 4BN.

ELCOCK, Mr. Derek Frank, FCA *1971;* (Tax Fac), 9 Upper Cheyne Row, LONDON, SW3 5JW.

ELCOCKS, Miss. Trudy Louise, BSc ACA *2002;* 196 Ocean Road, OHOPE 3121, BAY OF PLENTY, NEW ZEALAND.

ELCOMBE, Mr. Graham Ralph Stuart, MA FCA *1957;* Sandal Cottage, Church Lane, PINNER, HA5 3AA. (Life Member)

•ELDER, Mr. David John, ACA *1986;* (Tax Fac), East Partnership Limited, Mill House, 103 Holmes Avenue, HOVE, BN3 7LE.

ELDER, Mrs. Henrietta Elizabeth, BSc ACA *1993;* 24 Wilton Grove, LONDON, SW19 3QX.

ELDER, Mr. James Stuart, MA ACA *1993;* 24 Wilton Grove, LONDON, SW19 3QX.

ELDER, Mr. John, BA ACA *1999;* 15 Trelorrin Gardens, PLYMOUTH, PL3 4QD.

ELDER, Mrs. Lucy Sarah, MA ACA *1995;* Flat 15, Brendon House, 3 Nottingham Place, LONDON, W1U 5LB.

ELDER, Mr. Mark Christopher, BA ACA *2005;* Ashtree Farm Spondon Road, Dale Abbey, ILKESTON, DERBYSHIRE, DE7 4PS.

ELDER, Mr. Pearse Declan, MBA BA ACA *1982;* 17 Priory Road, Kew, RICHMOND, SURREY, TW9 3DQ.

ELDER, Mr. Robert Bruce, FCA *1959;* (Tax Fac), Cathcart, Hampden Gate, Speen, PRINCES RISBOROUGH, HP27 0RU. (Life Member)

ELDER, Mr. Vincent Leonard, BSc FCA MBA *1980;* Sir William Siemens Square, FRIMLEY, GU16 8QD.

ELDER, Mrs. Virginia Elizabeth, MA ACA *1989;* Potts Durtrees, Otterburn, NEWCASTLE UPON TYNE, NE19 1HW.

ELDERFIELD, Mr. Christopher John, BSc ACA *1981;* 5 St. Edmunds Grove Milngavie, GLASGOW, G62 8LS.

ELDERFIELD, Mrs. Katie Jane, BSc ACA *1998;* Stone Cross Cottage The Village, North Bovey, NEWTON ABBOT, DEVON, TQ13 8RA.

ELDERFIELD, Mr. Maurice, FCA *1949;* Hadleigh, 15 Keeil Pharick, Glen Vine, ISLE OF MAN, IM4 4EW. (Life Member)

ELDERFIELD, Mrs. Toni Martina, ACA *2008;* Flat 3 Hamilton House, 8 Victory Place, LONDON, E14 8BQ.

ELDERKIN, Mr. John David, BA ACA *1991;* 6 North Road, Stokesley, MIDDLESBROUGH, CLEVELAND, TS9 5DU.

ELDON-EDINGTON, Mr. Mark Alexander, BA ACA *1989;* 204 Hillary Lane, PENFIELD, NY 14526, UNITED STATES.

ELDRED, Mr. Nicholas John, BSc ACA MCIM DipM *1992;* 5 Osborne Close, WILMSLOW, SK9 2EE.

ELDRID, Mrs. Amanda Jane, BA ACA *1990;* Furze House, Heath Road, Soberton, SOUTHAMPTON, SO32 3QH.

ELDRID, Mr. Dean Michael, BSc ACA *1990;* Furze House, Heath Road, Soberton, SOUTHAMPTON, SO32 3QH.

•ELDRIDGE, Mr. Antony Michael, BSc ACA *1992;* PricewaterhouseCoopers LLP, Hays Galleria, 1 Hays Lane, LONDON, SE1 2RD. See also PricewaterhouseCoopers

ELDRIDGE, Mr. Colin Maurice Julian, FCA *1962;* Winding Wood Farm House, HUNGERFORD, RG17 9RN.

ELDRIDGE, Mr. Cyril Henry, FCA JDipMA *1951;* The Dower Barn, Gold Hill East, GERRARDS CROSS, SL9 9DN. (Life Member)

ELDRIDGE, Mr. Dennis William, FCA *1957;* 6 Woodberry Way, North Chingford, LONDON, E4 7DX. (Life Member)

ELDRIDGE, Mr. Derek Neil, FCA *1957;* 6 Darnley Close, FOLKESTONE, KENT, CT20 3NR. (Life Member)

ELDRIDGE, Mr. Gregg David, BCom ACA *2005;* 7 Rometta Way, Sinagra, PERTH, WA 6065, AUSTRALIA.

•ELDRIDGE, Mr. John Edward, FCA *1974;* McBrides Accountants LLP, Nexus House, 2 Cray Road, SIDCUP, KENT, DA14 5DA. See also McBrides Corporate Finance Limited

ELDRIDGE, Mr. Jonathan Howard, BSc ACA *2005;* Pricewaterhousecoopers, 1 Embankment Place, LONDON, WC2N 6RH.

ELDRIDGE, Mr. Karl, BA ACA MCT *1990;* 35 Wentworth Grange, Airlie Road, WINCHESTER, SO22 4HZ.

ELDRIDGE, Mr. Keith Richard, BA FCA *1993;* 2 Meadow Close, Goring, READING, RG8 0AP.

ELDRIDGE, Miss. Lucy Jayne, ACA *2008;* 170a Reading Road, WOKINGHAM, RG41 1LH.

ELDRIDGE, Dr. Michael David, PhD MA BD FCA *1964;* 112 Coombe Lane, CROYDON, CR0 5RF. (Life Member)

ELDRIDGE, Mr. Paul, ACA FCCA *2009;* 7 Byron Road, Hutton, BRENTWOOD, ESSEX, CM13 2RU.

ELDRIDGE, Mr. Peter, MA BA ACA *2005;* 65 Pymers Mead, LONDON, SE21 8NJ.

ELDRIDGE, Mrs. Rebecca Louise, BSc ACA *2004;* 17 Stratfield Park Close, Winchmore Hill, LONDON, N21 1BU.

ELDRIDGE, Mr. Richard Anthony, BSc FCA *1966;* Trevose Barton, Trevose Head, PADSTOW, PL28 8SL.

ELDRIDGE, Mr. Richard Paul Burgess, FCA *1973;* 8 Chalkhill Barrow, Melbourn, ROYSTON, SG8 6EQ.

ELDRIDGE, Mr. Simon John, FCA *1968;* P.O. Box 14546, FARRARMERE, GAUTENG, 1518, SOUTH AFRICA.

•ELDRIDGE, Mr. Simon Robert, BA FCA *1992;* SRE Associates Limited, 15 Ryeish Green Cottages, Hyde End Lane, Spencers Wood, READING, RG7 1ET. See also SRE Consultancy Limited

ELDRIDGE, Mr. Simon William, BA FCA *2000;* 28 Berkeley Gardens, LEIGH-ON-SEA, SS9 2TE.

ELDRIDGE, Mr. Steven, BA ACA *2010;* 97 Quickley Lane, Chorleywood, RICKMANSWORTH, HERTFORDSHIRE, WD3 5PG.

ELDRIDGE, Mr. William Henry, FCA *1953;* Chilterns, 11 The Heythrop, INGATESTONE, CM4 9HG. (Life Member)

ELEFTHERIADOU, Miss. Marie, ACA *2011;* 25d Priory Terrace, LONDON, NW6 4DG.

ELEFTHERIOU, Mr. Leftery, BA ACA *1996;* Unit 3, Delta Way, LONDON, TW20 8RX.

ELEFTHERIOU, Mr. Terry, BSc FCA *1984;* 2 Chuckanut Lane, HOUSTON, TX 77024-7301, UNITED STATES.

ELEMENT, Mr. David Viner, FCA *1958;* Walnut Cottage, The Street, Claxton, NORWICH, NR14 7AS. (Life Member)

•ELEMENT, Mr. Gregory Charles, BSc FCA *1984;* Element Leadership Consulting Ltd, Woodlands, Home Farm, Cefn Mably, CARDIFF, CF3 6LP.

ELEY, Mr. Benjamin Douglas, BA ACA *2008;* 42 Tiber Road, North Hykeham, LINCOLN, LN6 9TY.

ELEY, Mr. David Richard, BSc ACA *1989;* March Cottage, Moyleen Rise, MARLOW, BUCKINGHAMSHIRE, SL7 2DP.

ELEY, Mr. Mark Philip John, BSc ACA *2006;* Flat 7 Zenith, 594 Commercial Road, LONDON, E14 7JR.

ELEY, Mr. Norman Edward, MSc BA FCA *1980;* 11 Shepherds Way, CROWTHORNE, RG45 6AJ.

ELEY, Mr. Richard Stanley, MA FCA *1985;* 15 Fernbrook Road, Caversham Heights, READING, RG4 7HG.

ELEY, Ms. Sarah Jane, BA ACA *1998;* Flat 17, Crescent Mansions, Ronalds Road, LONDON, N5 1XD.

ELFICK, Mr. Richard Stanley, FCA *1957;* 29 Aberdeen Avenue, CAMBRIDGE, CB2 8DL. (Life Member)

ELFORD, Mr. Jonathan, ACA *2008;* Bethbarah, Stowey Road, Clutton, BRISTOL, BS39 5TG.

ELFORD, Mr. Julian Francis, BA ACA *1980;* (Tax Fac), 19 Templar Place, HAMPTON, MIDDLESEX, TW12 2NE.

•ELFORD, Mr. Keith Ernest, FCA *1974;* 5 Rymers Green, LIVERPOOL, L37 3HT.

ELFORD, Mr. Simon, BSc ACA *1987;* Flat 10, 9 Downleaze, Stoke Bishop, BRISTOL, BS9 1NA.

ELGAR, Ms. Christine Elizabeth, BA ACA *1987;* 35 Ferntower Road, LONDON, N5 2JE.

ELGAR, Mr. Richard Michael, ACA *1986;* 4 Ashton Place, Kintbury, HUNGERFORD, BERKSHIRE, RG17 9XS.

ELGAR, Mr. Simon John, BA ACA *1986;* (Tax Fac), International House, International House Business Centre, 1-6 Yarmouth Place, LONDON, W1J 7BU.

ELGEY, Miss. Catherine Jean, BSc ACA *1990;* Sherwoods (Darlington) Ltd, Chesnut Street, DARLINGTON, DL1 1RJ.

ELGIE, Mrs. Nicola Jane, MSci ACA *2005;* 101 Atkins Road, Balham, LONDON, SW12 0AL.

ELGIE, Mr. Ross, MSc BA ACA *2007;* 280 Mulberry St Apt #5B, NEW YORK, NY 10012, UNITED STATES.

ELIA, Mr. Falah Dawod, FCA *1968;* 6195 Oak Park Avenue, LAS VEGAS, NV 89118, UNITED STATES.

ELIA, Ms. Maria, BSc ACA *2006;* 28 London Street, Ayios Dometios, 2363 NICOSIA, CYPRUS.

ELIA, Mr. Michael John, BSc FCA *1983;* TraQs Consulting, 59 High Street, ASCOT, SL5 7HP.

ELIA, Mr. Paraskevas Sparsi, BA(Hons) ACA *2003;* 6 Agiou Demetriou Street, Anaphotia, 7573 LARNACA, CYPRUS.

•ELIADES, Mr. Constantinos, BSc ACA *2002;* CE&GE Professional Services Ltd, 7 Dositheou Street, Parabuilding Block C, 1st Floor, Office C102, 1071 NICOSIA CYPRUS.

ELIADES, Mr. George, BSc ACA *2011;* 135 West 50th Street, NEW YORK, NY 10020, UNITED STATES.

ELIADES, Mr. Haris, BSc ACA *2008;* 37 Christaki Kranou, Yermasoyia, 4041 LIMASSOL, CYPRUS.

ELIADES, Miss. Irene, BA(Hons) ACA *2000;* 30 Kavafi Street, Aglanjia, 2121 NICOSIA, CYPRUS.

ELIADES, Mrs. Sharon, BA ACA *1986;* 28 Kings Road, WILMSLOW, SK9 5PZ.

ELIADOU, Miss. Elle, ACA *2010;* 5 Nicolaou Yiangou Street, CY-3020 LIMASSOL, CYPRUS.

•ELIAS, Mr. Antoun, FCA *1975;* (Tax Fac), A. Elias, Coldharbour House, Coldharbour Lane, Bletchingley, SURREY, RH1 4NA.

•ELIAS, Mr. Edgar, FCA *1971;* Edgar Elias & Co, Trinominis House, First Floor, 125-129 High Street, EDGWARE, HA8 7DB.

ELIAS, Mr. Edward Anthony, FCA *1962;* Oakleigh, Grove Lane, Tettenhall Wood, WOLVERHAMPTON, WV6 8NH.

ELIAS-JONES, Miss. Rachel, MA(Hons) ACA *2011;* 4 Stephen Neville Court, SAFFRON WALDEN, CB11 4DX.

ELIASSON, Mr. Ian Michael Boyton, FCA *1974;* 93 Rickmansworth Road, WATFORD, WD18 7JB. (Life Member)

ELIATAMBY, Ms. Paulina Renuka, BSc(Econ) ACA *1988;* 55 Englands Lane, LOUGHTON, ESSEX, IG10 2QX.

•ELIJAH, Mr. Samson, ACA *1983;* Elijah & Co, 49 Watford Way, LONDON, NW4 3JH.

ELILIO, Mr. David, BA ACA *1997;* 15a Drummond Place, EDINBURGH, EH3 6PJ.

ELIS-WILLIAMS, Mrs. Katherine Elizabeth, BA ACA *1982;* 22 Ffriddoedd Road, BANGOR, GWYNEDD, LL57 2TW.

ELKERTON, Mr. Michael Rhodes, FCA *1973;* Lochiel, Horsham Road, CRANLEIGH, GU6 8DY.

ELKERTON, Mr. William James Stuart, MSc BA ACA *2010;* 1 Acol Road, LONDON, NW6 3AA.

ELKES, Mr. John Owen, FCA *1963;* 46 Cotswold Way, ENFIELD, EN2 7HJ. (Life Member)

ELKIES, Mr. Alexander George, ACA *1979;* 20 Nallur Rd, SINGAPORE 456637, SINGAPORE.

ELKIN, Mr. Colin Frederick, FCA *1956;* 168 Ridgewood Road, WEST HILL M1C 2X2, ON, CANADA. (Life Member)

ELKIN, Mr. David Edmund, FCA *1973;* 23 Soper Grove, BASINGSTOKE, HAMPSHIRE, RG21 5PU.

ELKIN, Mr. Edward Christian, BSc(Econ) ACA *2000;* Flat 28 Cannon Court 5 Brewhouse Yard, LONDON, EC1V 4JQ.

ELKIN, Mrs. Maria, BA ACA AMCT *1999;* Logica Plc, 250 Brook Drive, READING, RG2 6UA.

ELKINGTON, Mr. Charles Edward Nicholas, BSc ACA *1997;* Electra Partners LLP, Paternoster House, 65 St. Paul's Churchyard, LONDON, EC4M 8AB.

ELKINGTON, Mrs. Emma Jane, BSc FCA *1997;* 25 Palmer Road, HERTFORD, SG14 3LH.

ELKINS, Mr. Alan Richard, FCA *1972;* 3 Meadow Heights, St. Owens Cross, HEREFORD, HR2 8NP.

•ELKINS, Mr. Bruce Alan, FCA *1982;* CW Fellowes Limited, Templars House, Lulworth Close, Chandlers Ford, EASTLEIGH, SO53 3TL.

ELKINS, Mr. Chris, BSc(Hons) ACA *2009;* 15 Glebe Meadow, Overton, BASINGSTOKE, HAMPSHIRE, RG25 3ER.

ELKINS, Mr. Matthew, BA ACA *1995;* 12 James Road, PORTSMOUTH, PO3 6FP.

ELKINS, Mr. Thomas, ACA *2011;* 3/46A Moruben Road, MOSMAN, NSW NSW 2088, AUSTRALIA.

ELKS, Mr. Justin Philip, BA FCA *1996;* South Lodge Gennings Lughorse Lane, Hunton, MAIDSTONE, ME15 0QU.

ELL, Mrs. Joanne, BA ACA *2003;* 89 Mountbatten Avenue, WAKEFIELD, WEST YORKSHIRE, WF2 6HH.

ELLABY, Mr. Hugh Jonathan, BA ACA *1991;* 25 Primrose Close, BISHOP'S STORTFORD, CM23 4QG.

ELLABY, Mr. Martin John, BA ACA *2003;* Legal & General Assurance Society Ltd Legal & General House, St. Monicas Road Kingswood, TADWORTH, KT20 6EU.

ELLABY, Miss. Miranda Jane, BA ACA *1993;* Grosvenor Estate Eaton Estate Office, Eaton Park Eccleston, CHESTER, CH4 9ET.

•①ELLABY, Mr. Victor Henry, BA FCA *1985;* 39 Bromley Heath Road, Downend, BRISTOL, BS16 6HY. See also Rogers Evans (Bristol) Limited

ELLACOTT, Mr. Geoffrey John Stuart, FCA *1953;* 2 Barley Croft, Barley Close, Bloxham, BANBURY, OX15 4LW. (Life Member)

•ELLACOTT, Mr. John Lambert, MA FCA *1988;* KPMG LLP, 1 The Embankment, Neville Street, LEEDS, LS1 4DW. See also KPMG Europe LLP

ELLACOTT, Mrs. Susan Lesley, BA FCA *1994;* 12 Albert Road, WILMSLOW, CHESHIRE, SK9 5HT.

ELLAM, Mr. Clifford John, BA ACA *1985;* 64 Parkdale Drive, West Heath, BIRMINGHAM, B31 4RW.

ELLAM, Mr. David John, BA ACA *1990;* Biomarin Europe Ltd, 164 Shaftesbury Avenue, LONDON, WC2H 8HL.

ELLAM, Mr. James Anthony, FCA *1966;* Moorside Farm, Brockholes Lane, Brockholes, HOLMFIRTH, HD9 7EB. (Life Member)

ELLAM, Miss. Lorraine J, ACA *2009;* Flat 2, 24 Adelaide Road, SURBITON, KT6 4SS.

ELLAM, Mr. Mohammed Imran, BCom ACA *1997;* 23 Gwynne Avenue, BRADFORD, BD3 7DT.

ELLAM, Mr. Robert James, FCA *1976;* Sycamore House, Rectory Road, Hampton Bishop, HEREFORD, HR1 4JU.

ELLARBY, Mrs. Amanda, BA FCA *2000;* Vinnolit Hillhouse Ltd, Hillhouse International Business Park, Fleetwood Road North, THORNTON-CLEVELEYS, LANCASHIRE, FY5 4QD.

ELLARD, Mr. Paul Frederick, ACA CTA *1983;* Lambden CottageLambden Road, Pluckley ASHFORD, Kent, TN27 0RB. (Life Member)

ELLAWAY, Mr. John Edward, BSc FCA *1971;* 19 Knocksinna Crescent, Foxrock, DUBLIN, COUNTY DUBLIN, IRELAND. (Life Member)

ELLAWAY, Mr. Richard George, BA ACA ATII *1995;* Frights Bridge Farm, Woodchurch, ASHFORD, KENT, TN26 3PR.

ELLEN, Mr. Michael George, BA FCA *1976;* Alderney Gambling Control Commission, St. Annes House, Queen Elizabeth II Street, Alderney, GUERNSEY, GY9 3TB.

ELLEN, Mr. Thomas George, BA ACA *2005;* Flat 3, 21 Rastell Avenue, Streatham Hall, LONDON, SW2 4XP.

ELLENDER, Mr. Steven James, BSc(Hons) ACA *2004;* B G L Group Pegasus House Southgate Park, Bakewell Road Orton Southgate, PETERBOROUGH, PE2 6YS.

ELLERAY, Mr. James Stanley, FCA *1978;* 5 Gordon Avenue, Woolston, WARRINGTON, WA1 3UJ.

ELLERBY, Mr. Kevin Graham, ACA *2004;* with Richardson Jones, Mercury House, 19/21 Chapel Street, MARLOW, BUCKINGHAMSHIRE, SL7 3HN.

ELLERBY, Mr. Mark, BA FCA *1987;* Burton Grange, Burton Leonard, HARROGATE, HG3 3SU.

ELLERBY, Mr. Philip Andrew, BA ACA *2011;* Flat 1 Tollington House, 598-602 Holloway Road, LONDON, N19 3PG.

ELLERBY, Mr. Robert Brian, MA FCA *1980;* 27 Manor Road, HENLEY-ON-THAMES, RG9 1LT.

ELLERKER, Mr. Christopher James, LLB ACA *2002;* Flat 5, 146 Lavender Hill, LONDON, SW11 5RA.

ELLERTON, Mr. Hugh Brooke, FCA *1972;* EFG Trust Company (Singapore) Ltd, 25 North Bridge Road #07-00, EFG Bank Building, SINGAPORE 179104, SINGAPORE.

•ELLERTON, Mr. Ralph John, FCA *1969;* Appletons, Suite 1, Armcon Business Park, London Road South, Poynton, STOCKPORT CHESHIRE SK12 1LQ. See also Compliant Accounting Limited

ELLERTON, Mr. Stephen, BSc FCA *1990;* 9 Albany Road, LEIGHTON BUZZARD, BEDFORDSHIRE, LU7 1NS.

ELLES-HILL, Mr. Michael Patrickk, FCA *1961;* 16 Post Office Square, TUNBRIDGE WELLS, KENT, TN1 1BQ. (Life Member)

ELLICE, Mr. Mark James, BSc(Hons) ACA *2002;* 9 Jordon Close, STANSTED, CM24 8SH.

ELLICOTT, Mr. Dominic Lawrence, BA ACA *1999;* Interflora British Unit, Interflora House, Watergate, SLEAFORD, LINCOLNSHIRE, NG34 7TB.

ELLIFF, Mr. Stephen Robert, BSc ACA *1994;* 14 Hill View, BERKHAMSTED, HP4 1SA.

ELLIMAN, Mrs. Judith, BA FCA *1993;* Hillside Farm, Off Beverley Road, Blacko, NELSON, BB9 6LX.

•ELLINAS, Mr. Charalambos Georgiou, ACA *1982;* Charles Ellinas & Co, 15 York Gate, Southgate, LONDON, N14 6HS.

ELLINAS, Mr. Christodoulos, BSc ACA *1988;* SFS Group Public Co Ltd, Ellinas House, 6 Theotokis Str, PO Box 22379, 1521 NICOSIA, CYPRUS.

ELLINGHAM, Miss. Kathryn Clare, LLB ACA *2004;* 11 Park Road, Blaby, LEICESTER, LE8 4ED.

ELLINGHAM, Mr. Oliver Bernard, BA ACA *1984;* Tanhurst, Tanhurst Lane, Holmbury St. Mary, DORKING, SURREY, RH5 6LU.

ELLINGHAM, Mr. Paul, BSc ACA *1983;* Flat 10 Duncroft Manor, Vicarage Road, STAINES, MIDDLESEX, TW18 4XX.

ELLINGHAM, Ms. Sharon Amanda, BA ACA *1992;* 1 Stafford Crescent, BRAINTREE, CM7 9PS.

•ELLINGHAM, Mr. Simon Jeremy Lister, BA FCA DChA *1989;* Fawcetts, Windover House, St Ann Street, SALISBURY, SP1 2DR.

ELLINGHAM, Mrs. Sonia Margaret, BA ACA *1986;* Synergy Housing Group Ltd Link House, 25 West Street, POOLE, DORSET, BH15 1LD.

ELLINGHAM, Mr. Tony, ACA *1984;* Gamlyn Gay, Gayton Close, AMERSHAM, BUCKINGHAMSHIRE, HP6 6DW.

ELLINGTON, Ms. Geraldine Mary, MA ACA *1982;* 3 The Coach House, 55 Putney Hill, LONDON, SW15 6RZ.

ELLINGTON, Mr. Richard Thomas Padfield, FCA *1964;* 98 Pymers Mead, Dulwich, LONDON, SE21 8NJ. (Life Member)

ELLINGTON, Mrs. Susan Jane, BSc ACA *1991;* 16 Cambridgeshire Close, WOKINGHAM, RG41 3BD.

ELLINGWORTH, Mr. Martin Andrew, BA FCA *1983;* 4 Elm Drive, MARKET HARBOROUGH, LEICESTERSHIRE, LE16 9DS.

ELLINGWORTH, Mrs. Sarah Louise, BA ACA *1992;* 11 High Oaks Road, WELWYN GARDEN CITY, HERTFORDSHIRE, AL8 7BJ.

ELLINOR, Mr. David, LLB ACA *1992;* Mileta Sports Ltd, Spen Vale Street, HECKMONDWIKE, WF16 0NQ.

ELLINOR-DREYER, Mrs. Jodie Amber, BA(Hons) ACA CA(SA) *2003;* 48 Muirfield Road, GREENSIDE, GAUTENG, 2193, SOUTH AFRICA.

ELLINS, Mr. David Michael, FCA *1972;* 4 Huntersfield Close, REIGATE, RH2 0DX.

ELLINSON, Mr. Jacob, BSc FCA *1964;* 58 Princes Park Avenue, LONDON, NW11 0JT.

ELLIOT, Mr. David Anthony, BSc ACA *2000;* 52 The Oval, OTLEY, WEST YORKSHIRE, LS21 2EE.

ELLIOT, Mr. David Antony, FCA *1977;* Box 5, Oude Beurs 21, B-2000 ANTWERP, BELGIUM.

ELLIOT, Mrs. Gail, ACA *1981;* 35 Cote Lane, Thurgoland, SHEFFIELD, S35 7AE.

ELLIOT, Mr. Glenn William, FCA *1974;* 48 Churchill Avenue, Kooringal, WAGGA WAGGA, NSW 2650, AUSTRALIA.

ELLIOT, Mrs. Helen, BA ACA *1992;* Orchard House, Richardson Close, Mildrove, BOURNE, PE10 9YN.

ELLIOT, Mr. Ian Douglas Murray, FCA *1971;* Fern Lea, 209 Cromwell Road, WHITSTABLE, KENT, CT5 1NE.

•ELLIOT, Mr. James Arthur, FCA *1987;* Elliot & Co LLP, 84 Portland Road, Wyke Regis, WEYMOUTH, DORSET, DT4 9AB.

ELLIOT, Mr. John Andrew, FCA *1976;* Barton Lodge, Oxford Road, Steeple Aston, BICESTER, OX25 5QH.

•ELLIOT, Mr. Leonard Ralph, FCA *1981;* PCLG Limited, Equinox House, Clifton Park Avenue, Clifton Park, Shipton Road, YORK YO30 5PA.

ELLIOT, Mr. Michael David, BA ACA *2010;* 4 St. Aidans Avenue, DURHAM, DH1 5BB.

•ELLIOT, Mr. Paul Thomas, BSc ACA *1991;* Baker Tilly Corporate Finance LLP, 25 Farringdon Street, LONDON, EC4A 4AB. See also Baker Tilly Tax and Advisory Services LLP

ELLIOT, Mr. Peter Martin, BA ACA *1982;* Yew Tree Cottage, Clevedon Lane, Clapton-in-gordano, BRISTOL, BS20 7RH.

ELLIOT, Mr. Raymond Faber, MSocSc FCA *1960;* Greystones, 17 Newland Street, Eynsham, WITNEY, OX29 4LB. (Life Member)

ELLIOT, Mr. Richard Emmerson, BSc ACA *1991;* Kent Messenger Group Newspapers, Messenger House, New Hythe Lane, Larkfield, AYLESFORD, KENT ME20 6SG.

ELLIOT, Miss. Ruth Elizabeth, BA ACA *2001;* 9 Dart Drive, DIDCOT, OXFORDSHIRE, OX11 7XX.

ELLIOT, Miss. Victoria Louise, BA(Hons) ACA *2006;* 5 Warblington Close, Chandler's Ford, EASTLEIGH, HAMPSHIRE, SO53 3PP.

ELLIOT-SMITH, Dr. Andrea, PhD MBiochem ACA *2009;* 81A, High Street Chesterton, CAMBRIDGE, CAMBRIDGESHIRE, CB4 1NJ.

ELLIOTT, Mr. Alan James, BEng ACA *1997;* with PricewaterhouseCoopers, GPO Box 1331L, MELBOURNE, VIC 3001, AUSTRALIA.

ELLIOTT, Mr. Alastair Russell, BSc(Econ) ACA *1995;* 180 Surplus St, DUXBURY, MA 02332, UNITED STATES.

ELLIOTT, Mr. Andrew Martin Peter, BA ACA *1992;* L & F Indemnity Ltd, Belvedere Building, 69 Pitts Bay Road, PEMBROKE HM08, BERMUDA.

ELLIOTT, Mr. Andrew Vernon, BSc ACA *1980;* 39 The Homestead, KIDLINGTON, OX5 1SS.

ELLIOTT, Miss. Annabel Gillian Louise, ACA DChA *2009;* Danbury Court, 26 Danbury Street, LONDON, N1 8JU.

ELLIOTT, Mr. Anthony Edmund, BSc ACA *1998;* 29 Holyoake Street, Enderby, LEICESTER, LEICESTERSHIRE, LE19 4NS.

ELLIOTT, Mr. Anthony Gordon, FCA *1955;* 4 Latimer Way, Woodchester Park, Knotty Green, BEACONSFIELD, HP9 2UD. (Life Member)

•ELLIOTT, Mr. Anthony Reginald, FCA *1975;* Elliott & Company, 1a Station Buildings, Station Road, Gobowen, OSWESTRY, SY11 3LX.

ELLIOTT, Mr. Antony Gareth, BSc ACA *2003;* Leematt, 8926 KAPPEL AM ALBIS, SWITZERLAND.

ELLIOTT, Mr. Benjamin David, ACA *2009;* 43 Harker Drive, COALVILLE, LEICESTERSHIRE, LE67 4GG.

ELLIOTT, Mr. Bernard, FCA *1954;* 2 Edgemoor, Park Road, Bowdon, ALTRINCHAM, CHESHIRE, WA14 3JN. (Life Member)

•ELLIOTT, Mrs. Beverley Anne, BSc FCA CTA *1981;* (Tax Fac), Griffins, Griffins Court, 24-32 London Road, NEWBURY, RG14 1JX. See also Griffins Business Advisers LLP

ELLIOTT, Mrs. Breanne Elizabeth, ACA *2009;* 30 Osprey Heights, Bramlands Close, LONDON, SW11 2NP.

ELLIOTT, Mr. Brian Peter, ACA *1984;* Sutton Estates, 14 Bolton Street, LONDON, W1J 8BF.

•ELLIOTT, Mr. Bruce Graham, FCA *1973;* Maurice Andrews, Grove House, 25 Upper Mulgrave Road, Cheam, SUTTON, SM2 7BE.

ELLIOTT, Mr. Christopher Douglas, BSc FCA *1987;* 24 St Margarets Grove, Great Kingshill, HIGH WYCOMBE, HP15 6HP.

ELLIOTT, Mr. Christopher Richard Fetherston, BSc ACA *1985;* White Cottage, Battle Lane, Wanshurst Green, Marden, TONBRIDGE, TN12 9DF.

ELLIOTT, Miss. Claira Jane, ACA *2009;* Geay Varrey Ballacollister Road, Laxey, ISLE OF MAN, IM4 7JR.

ELLIOTT, Mrs. Clare Elizabeth, ACA *1992;* The Chestnuts, 13 Birches Close, EPSOM, KT18 5JG.

•ELLIOTT, Mr. Colin Geoffrey Grahame, BSc FCA *1971;* AIMS - Colin Elliott, The Paddock, Bishopsbourne, CANTERBURY, CT4 5HT.

•ELLIOTT, Mr. Colin Robert, FCA *1982;* (Tax Fac), Elliott Clark Limited, 1 Lamorna Court, 43 Wollaton Road, Beeston, NOTTINGHAM, NG9 2NG.

•ELLIOTT, Mr. David Charles, BSc FCA *1990;* Elliott Business Advisory Services Ltd, Manchester Business Park, 3000 Aviator Way, MANCHESTER, M22 5TG.

ELLIOTT, Mr. David John, FCA *1973;* Temple View, Banners Lane, Barston, SOLIHULL, B92 0JY.

•ELLIOTT, Mr. David John, FCA *1990;* KPMG LLP, Quayside House, 110 Quayside, NEWCASTLE UPON TYNE, NE1 3DX.

•①ELLIOTT, Mr. David Ronald, ACA *1991;* Moore Stephens LLP, Victory House, Quayside, Chatham Maritime, CHATHAM, KENT ME4 4QU.

•ELLIOTT, Mr. David Stirland Maclaren, FCA *1972;* David S M Elliott & Company Limited, Southdown, 59 Grove Road, Coombe Dingle, BRISTOL, BS9 2RT.

•ELLIOTT, Miss. Dawn, BA ACA *1989;* (Tax Fac), KPMG LLP, 15 Canada Square, LONDON, E14 5GL. See also KPMG Europe LLP

ELLIOTT, Mr. Derek James, BSc ACA *1995;* 27 Charlwood Road, LONDON, SW15 1QA.

ELLIOTT, Miss. Diane Clare, BA FCA *1994;* (Tax Fac), 71 Long Lane, LONDON, N3 2HY.

ELLIOTT, Mr. Douglas Geoffrey, LLB FCA *1963;* Llancaut Corner, Woodcroft, CHEPSTOW, NP16 7JB. (Life Member)

ELLIOTT, Mrs. Elizabeth Margaret, BA ACA *1983;* 10 The Hawthorns, CHALFONT ST. GILES, BUCKINGHAMSHIRE, HP8 4UJ.

ELLIOTT, Miss. Fiona, BA ACA *2007;* 1/3 Walker Street, EDINBURGH, EH3 7JY.

•ELLIOTT, Mr. Garry, FCA *1985;* Baker Tilly Tax & Advisory Services LLP, 1 St. James Gate, NEWCASTLE UPON TYNE, NE1 4AD. See also Baker Tilly UK Audit LLP

ELLIOTT, Mr. Gavin Charles, BA(Hons) ACA *2002;* Taylor Wimpey UK Ltd Gate House, Turnpike Road, HIGH WYCOMBE, BUCKINGHAMSHIRE, HP12 3NR.

ELLIOTT, Mr. Giles, BSc ACA *1995;* Pit Folly, The Avenue, Wilton, SALISBURY, SP2 0BU.

ELLIOTT, Mr. Graham Nicholas, MA ACA AMCT *1988;* Flat 57 Cinnabar Wharf Central, 24 Wapping High Street, LONDON, E1W 1NQ.

ELLIOTT, Mr. Grahame Nicholas, CBE FCA *1963;* 26 Harrop Road, Hale, ALTRINCHAM, CHESHIRE, WA15 9DQ.

ELLIOTT, Mrs. Hannah Lucy, MA BA ACA *2011;* Apartment 36, 55-57 Whitworth Street, MANCHESTER, M1 3NT.

ELLIOTT, Mr. Hayward Mackenzie, FCA *1966;* 23 Over Links Drive, POOLE, DORSET, BH14 9QU. (Life Member)

•ELLIOTT, Mrs. Helen Charlotte Elisabeth, BA FCA DChA *1983;* Sayer Vincent, 8 Angel Gate, City Road, LONDON, EC1V 2SJ.

ELLIOTT, Mrs. Helena Lorraine, BSc ACA *1995;* Pit Folly The Avenue, Wilton, SALISBURY, SP2 0BU.

ELLIOTT, Mr. Hugh, FCA *1975;* 11 Blythe Way, SOLIHULL, B91 3EY.

•ELLIOTT, Mr. Ian Henry, BA ACA *1992;* PricewaterhouseCoopers LLP, Benson House, 33 Wellington Street, LEEDS, LS1 4JP. See also PricewaterhouseCoopers

ELLIOTT, Mr. Ian Nichol, BSc FCA *1993;* 12 Oasthouse Close, Stoke Heath, BROMSGROVE, B60 4NW.

ELLIOTT, Mr. Ian Sheppard, MA FCA *1978;* Polymark France SAS, 2 Rue Augustin Fresnel, Za Du Clos Reine, 78410 AUBERGENVILLE, FRANCE.

ELLIOTT, Mr. Ian Walter, FCA *1979;* Kidmorie, 3 Warren Drive, Dorridge, SOLIHULL, B93 8JY.

•ELLIOTT, Mr. Ian William, FCA *1970;* 10 Windsor Road, RICHMOND, SURREY, TW9 2EL.

ELLIOTT, Miss. Isabel Rose, BSc ACA *2006;* (Tax Fac), Cobwebs Stunts Green, Herstmonceux, HAILSHAM, EAST SUSSEX, BN27 4PR.

ELLIOTT, Mrs. Jennifer Christine, ACA *2010;* UCL-Qatar, PO Box 23689, Georgetown building - second floor, Education City, DOHA, QATAR.

ELLIOTT, Miss. Joanne, ACA *2009;* 89 The Woodlands, Melbourne, DERBY, DE73 8DQ.

ELLIOTT, Ms. Joanne Catherine, MSc BSc ACA *2001;* Shakerley Main Street, Great Longstone, BAKEWELL, DERBYSHIRE, DE45 1TZ.

ELLIOTT, Miss. Joanne Lesley, BSc ACA *1989;* Thames River Capital (UK) Ltd, 51 Berkeley Square, LONDON, W1J 5BB.

ELLIOTT, Mrs. Joanne Mary, ACA MAAT *2011;* 45 Moorwood Drive, OLDHAM, OL8 2XD.

ELLIOTT, Mr. John, MA FCA *1963;* 29 Arden Road, CHELTENHAM, GLOUCESTERSHIRE, GL53 0HG. (Life Member)

ELLIOTT, Mr. John Patrick, BSc ACA *1994;* 14 Greystones Drive, REIGATE, SURREY, RH2 0HA.

•**ELLIOTT, Mrs. Joyce Elspeth Bain, BCom FCA** *1969;* (Tax Fac), J.E. Elliott, 63 Greenhill Road, Moseley, BIRMINGHAM, B13 9SU.

ELLIOTT, Mrs. Julia, ACA *2009;* 216 Mottingham Road, LONDON, SE9 4SU.

ELLIOTT, Mr. Julian Christopher, BA ACA *1996;* PC100A Design Services, D M L Devonport Royal Dockyard Ltd, H M Dockyard, PLYMOUTH, PL1 4SG.

ELLIOTT, Mrs. Karen Ann, BA ACA *1994;* Richmond, Swindon Lane, CHELTENHAM, GLOUCESTERSHIRE, GL50 4PF.

ELLIOTT, Miss. Kate, ACA *2010;* Flat 17 Warnford Court, 5 Archers Road, SOUTHAMPTON, SO15 2LQ.

ELLIOTT, Miss. Kate Jane, BA ACA *1995;* 27 Tolverne Road, West Wimbledon, LONDON, SW20 8RA.

•**ELLIOTT, Mr. Keith Malcolm, FCA** *1964;* (Tax Fac), K.M.Elliott, 8 The Spinney, BEACONSFIELD, BUCKINGHAMSHIRE, HP9 1SB.

•**ELLIOTT, Mr. Kenneth Duncan, FCA** *1974;* Kenneth D. Elliott, 22 Oaklands Avenue, ISLEWORTH, TW7 5PX.

ELLIOTT, Mr. Kevin Malcolm, MSc FCA *1982;* 42 Rylett Road, LONDON, W12 9ST.

ELLIOTT, Mr. Laurence James, BA ACA *2004;* 15 Shelton Road, LONDON, SW19 3AT.

•**ELLIOTT, Mr. Lawrence John, FCA** *1971;* Elliott & Partners, 1 Sudley Terrace, High Street, BOGNOR REGIS, WEST SUSSEX, PO21 1EY.

ELLIOTT, Mr. Leslie, FCA *1954;* Heath Ridge, Sandy Down, Boldre, LYMINGTON, SO41 8PL. (Life Member)

ELLIOTT, Mrs. Lindsay, ACA *2002;* Southern Co-operative Ltd, 44 High Street, FAREHAM, HAMPSHIRE, PO16 7BN.

ELLIOTT, Miss. Lorna Helen, BA(Hons) ACA *2002;* Pearson Language Tests Mezzanine Level, 80 Strand, LONDON, WC2R 0RL.

ELLIOTT, Mrs. Lucy, ACA *2008;* 6 The Orchard, Whickham, NEWCASTLE UPON TYNE, NE16 4HD.

ELLIOTT, Miss. Lucy Eleanor Catherine, MA ACA *1990;* World Food Programme, Via Cesare Giulio Viola 68/70, 00148 ROME, ITALY.

ELLIOTT, Miss. Margaret Elaine, MA ACA *1983;* 3 Orlando Road, LONDON, SW4 0LE.

ELLIOTT, Ms. Margaret Frances, BSc ACA *2000;* 16 Colchester Avenue, Glendowie, AUCKLAND 1071, NEW ZEALAND.

ELLIOTT, Mr. Mark Andrew, BSc ACA *1989;* Rütschistrasse 25, 8037 ZURICH, SWITZERLAND.

ELLIOTT, Mr. Mark Daniel, BA ACA *2004;* Oakhurst House Oakhurst, London Road, HENFIELD, WEST SUSSEX, BN5 9QL.

ELLIOTT, Mr. Mark Henry, FCA *1976;* 2 The Firs, BEXLEY, DA5 2AX.

ELLIOTT, Mr. Mark John Bertram, BA ACA *2000;* Barclays, PO Box 1891, DUBAI, UNITED ARAB EMIRATES.

ELLIOTT, Mr. Mark Westcombe, FCA *1983;* ICE Partners Ltd, 40 Oxford Drive, LONDON, SE1 2FB.

ELLIOTT, Mr. Martin Daniel, BSc FCA *2001;* Greystones, Quarterbridge Road, Douglas, ISLE OF MAN, IM2 3RL.

ELLIOTT, Mr. Martin John, FCA *1968;* The Lynches, Clungunford, CRAVEN ARMS, SHROPSHIRE, SY7 0PL. (Life Member)

ELLIOTT, Mr. Matthew John, BA ACA *2000;* 91 Mackenzie Way, GRAVESEND, DA12 5UH.

•**ELLIOTT, Mr. Michael John, FCA** *1969;* Beeches, Lodge Lane, HASSOCKS, WEST SUSSEX, BN6 8LU.

ELLIOTT, Mr. Michael John, FCA *1974;* 18 Dickens Way, YATELEY, GU46 6XX.

ELLIOTT, Mr. Michael Philip, MA ACA *1982;* 2 Whitehorns Farm Road, Charlton, WANTAGE, OX12 7HH.

ELLIOTT, Mr. Neil, BA ACA *1988;* 22 Station Road, THAMES DITTON, SURREY, KT7 0NR.

•ⒹELLIOTT, **Mr. Nicholas James, ACA MABRP** *1998;* Amberley House, 1 Weare Close, Billesdon, LEICESTER, LE7 9DY.

•**ELLIOTT, Mr. Nicholas James, BSc FCA** *1992;* 10 Park Avenue, SALE, M33 6HE.

ELLIOTT, Miss. Nicola Jane, MA FCA *1989;* 39 Burghley Hall Close, Wimbledon, LONDON, SW19 6TN.

ELLIOTT, Mr. Nicolas, MA ACA *2007;* Flat (6-I) Green Lake Apartments, House 9 Road #127, Gulshan 1, DHAKA 1212, BANGLADESH.

•**ELLIOTT, Mr. Norman, FCA** *1976;* N. Elliott & Co., 2 Gilsland Grove, Northburn Vale, CRAMLINGTON, NORTHUMBERLAND, NE23 3SY.

ELLIOTT, Mr. Paul Christopher, BSc ACA *1993;* 20 Puddingstone Dr, Boonton, NEW JERSEY, NJ 07005, UNITED STATES.

ELLIOTT, Mrs. Peggy Ilene, FCA *1945;* 11 Shelley Drive, Stratford-Sub-Castle, SALISBURY, SP1 3JZ. (Life Member)

•**ELLIOTT, Mr. Peter Albert, BA FCA** *1955;* (Tax Fac), Collett Smith Elliott & Co, The Old Coach House, 179 Moss Lane, PINNER, HA5 3AL.

ELLIOTT, Mr. Peter Arthur, FCA *1964;* 39 Daleview Road, SHEFFIELD, S8 0EJ. (Life Member)

•**ELLIOTT, Mr. Peter George Leonard, FCA** *1975;* Elliott & Co, 15 Dragon Close, BURNHAM-ON-CROUCH, CM0 8PW.

ELLIOTT, Mr. Philip John, MA(Oxon) ACA *2006;* (Tax Fac), 54 Hulme Hall Road, Cheadle Hulme, CHEADLE, CHESHIRE, SK8 6JZ.

•**ELLIOTT, Mr. Ralph Edgar, FCA** *1977;* RE Elliott, 25 Westrow Gardens, Seven Kings, ILFORD, ESSEX, IG3 9NE.

ELLIOTT, Mr. Rex Hayton Drummond, ACA CA(SA) *2009;* 16 Victoria Road, HOLYWOOD, COUNTY DOWN, BT18 9BD.

ELLIOTT, Mr. Richard Giles, BA ACA *1983;* 7 Fairoak Close, KENLEY, CR8 5LJ.

ELLIOTT, Mr. Richard James, FCA *1974;* 11 Quarryfields, Quarry CloseLeek Wootton, WARWICK, CV35 7RS.

ELLIOTT, Mr. Richard John Leslie, BSc FCA *2000;* 6 Balcombe Close, BEXLEYHEATH, DA6 8GA.

ELLIOTT, Mr. Robert, ACA CA(AUS) *2011;* Macquarie Bank, Level 25 Citypoint, 1 Ropemaker Street, LONDON, EC2Y 9HD.

ELLIOTT, Mr. Robert Alan, FCA *1963;* RAE The Croft Trustees Ltd, The Croft, Grange Garth, YORK, YO10 4BS.

ELLIOTT, Mr. Robert Alastair Duncan, BA ACA *1981;* 10 The Hawthorns, CHALFONT ST. GILES, BUCKINGHAMSHIRE, HP8 4UJ.

ELLIOTT, Mr. Robert Cassleton, MA ACA *1993;* 41 Berrylands, SURBITON, SURREY, KT5 8JT.

ELLIOTT, Mr. Robert Clive, FCA *1969;* Greentiles, Elm Close, Farnham Common, SLOUGH, SL2 3NA.

•**ELLIOTT, Mr. Robert Tregellas, ACA** *1980;* (Tax Fac), Saffery Champness, Lion House, Red Lion Street, LONDON, WC1R 4GB. See also Collett Smith Elliott & Co

ELLIOTT, Mr. Robert William, ACA *2009;* Flat 30 Osprey Heights, 7 Bramlands Close, LONDON, SW11 2NP.

ELLIOTT, Mr. Roger Martin, FCA *1975;* 64 Burdon Lane, Cheam, SUTTON, SM2 7BY.

•**ELLIOTT, Mr. Ronald, FCA** *1958;* Ronald Elliott & Co, 26 Catsey Woods, Bushey Heath, BUSHEY, WD23 4HS.

ELLIOTT, Mr. Rory Guy, BA ACA *2001;* 45 Sopwell Lane, ST. ALBANS, HERTFORDSHIRE, AL1 1RN.

ELLIOTT, Mrs. Ruth Elizabeth, LLB ACA *2002;* 23 Grange Road Cuddington, NORTHWICH, CHESHIRE, CW8 2QT.

ELLIOTT, Mrs. Sarah Frances, BA ACA *1992;* 14 Greystones Drive, REIGATE, SURREY, RH2 0HA.

ELLIOTT, Mr. Shane Lindsay, BSc ACA *1984;* 28 Oxford Road, FARNBOROUGH, HAMPSHIRE, GU14 6QT.

ELLIOTT, Mrs. Sharon Patricia, BA(Hons) ACA *2001;* 7 Morningside Drive, MANCHESTER, M20 5PQ.

ELLIOTT, Mr. Simon John, BSc ACA *1994;* 3 Worths Way, STRATFORD-UPON-AVON, WARWICKSHIRE, CV37 0RR.

ELLIOTT, Mr. Simon Martyn, BA ACA *1998;* 29 Belitha Villas, LONDON, N1 1PE.

•**ELLIOTT, Mr. Simon Timothy, FCA** *1980;* (Tax Fac), Rothman Pantall LLP, 10 Oxford Street, Southampton, SOUTHAMPTON, SO14 3DJ.

ELLIOTT, Mr. Stephen, BSc ACA *1983;* Failand, Middle Lane, Kingstone Seymour, CLEVEDON, BS21 6XP. (Life Member)

ELLIOTT, Mr. Steven, MA ACA *1980;* 35 Ringley Chase, Whitefield, MANCHESTER, M45 7UA.

ELLIOTT, Ms. Susan Patricia, BSc ACA *1984;* 37 Scawfell Road, CHORLEY, LANCASHIRE, PR7 2JP.

ELLIOTT, Mr. Thomas James George, ACA *2009;* 32 Amies Street, LONDON, SW11 2JN.

ELLIOTT, Mr. Timothy, FCA *1977;* Corfeira, 14 Pine Ridge Drive, Lower Bourne, FARNHAM, GU10 3JR.

ELLIOTT, Mr. Timothy Lance, BA ACA *1986;* 11 Latham Road, TWICKENHAM, TW1 1BN.

ELLIOTT, Mr. Timothy Stephen, ACA *2008;* 9 Tollemache Terrace, CHESTER, CH2 3ED.

ELLIOTT, Mr. William Thomas, BSc FCA *1980;* with Ernst & Young LLP, 1 Bridgewater Place, Water Lane, LEEDS, LS11 5QR.

ELLIOTT FREY, Mr. Andrew Stephen Timothy, BSc ACA *1979;* Village Office, 60 High Street Wimbledon, LONDON, SW19 5EE.

ELLIS, Mr. Aidan Mark, MA ACA CTA *1997;* BPP Professional Education ; 1st Floor, Merchants Court ; 2-12 Lord Street, LIVERPOOL, L2 1TS.

ELLIS, Mr. Alan David, BSc FCA *1974;* 2 Mercia Road, BALDOCK, HERTFORDSHIRE, SG7 6RZ.

ELLIS, Mrs. Alexandra Beth, BMedSc ACA *2005;* 11 Stockholm Close, YORK, YO10 4NU.

ELLIS, Mrs. Alison Jane, BA ACA *2000;* Cornerwood House, Swan Lane, The Lee, GREAT MISSENDEN, BUCKINGHAMSHIRE, HP16 9NU.

ELLIS, Mr. Alun Wyn, BA ACA *1982;* 28 Woodville Gardens, Ealing, LONDON, W5 2LQ.

ELLIS, Miss. Amanda Jane, BA ACA *1997;* 8 Redwood Glade, LEIGHTON BUZZARD, BEDFORDSHIRE, LU7 3JT.

ELLIS, Miss. Amie Marie, ACA *2009;* 12 Tree House Avenue, ASHTON-UNDER-LYNE, OL7 9PA.

•**ELLIS, Mrs. Andrea, BSc ACA** *1994;* Andrea Ellis, 6 Shaftesbury Avenue, Radcliffe-on-Trent, NOTTINGHAM, NG12 2NH.

ELLIS, Mr. Andrew Jackson, FCA *1961;* 60 London Road, CHELTENHAM, GL52 6EQ. (Life Member)

ELLIS, Mr. Andrew Neil, BSc FCA *1989;* Oakside House, 19 Iris Road, Bisley, WOKING, GU24 9HG.

ELLIS, Mr. Andrew Norman, BA ACA *1987;* 16 Thompson Close, East Leake, LOUGHBOROUGH, LE12 6HP.

ELLIS, Mr. Andrew Robert Iain, LLB ACA *1993;* 16 Kingfisher Close, Wheathampstead, ST. ALBANS, HERTFORDSHIRE, AL4 8JJ.

•**ELLIS, Mr. Andrew St John, FCA** *1972;* Andrew St J Ellis, 1 High Street, Bramham, WETHERBY, WEST YORKSHIRE, LS23 6QQ. See also Andrew St J Ellis FCA

•**ELLIS, Mr. Andrew Timothy, FCA** *1979;* (Tax Fac), Axel, 3 Minshull Street, KNUTSFORD, WA16 6HG.

ELLIS, Mr. Andrew Webster, BA ACA *1997;* PO Box 500666, DUBAI, UNITED ARAB EMIRATES.

ELLIS, Mrs. Angela Claire Armstrong, ACA *1995;* 121 Guildford Road, West End, WOKING, GU24 9LS.

ELLIS, Mrs. Anna Jayne, BA(Hons) ACA *2003;* 115 Smithills Dean Road, BOLTON, BL1 6JZ.

ELLIS, Mrs. Anne Dorothy, BA ACA *1993;* 16 Kingfisher Close, Wheathampstead, ST. ALBANS, AL4 8JJ.

ELLIS, Mr. Anthony, FCA *1964;* 17 Kewferry Road, NORTHWOOD, HA6 2NS. (Life Member)

ELLIS, Mr. Anthony John, BSc ACA *1997;* Flat 57, 20 Abbey Road, LONDON, NW8 9BJ.

ELLIS, Miss. Atina Lucia, ACA *2010;* Kaine Farm Bungalow, Breach Lane, Upchurch, SITTINGBOURNE, KENT, ME9 7PH.

ELLIS, Mrs. Belinda, BA(Econ) ACA *1996;* 24 Eatonville Road, LONDON, SW17 7SL.

ELLIS, Mr. Bruce John, BA ACA *1991;* 16 Soudan Road, LONDON, SW11 4HH.

ELLIS, Miss. Caroline, BSc(Hons) ACA *2003;* 5 Bakers Walk, Weston Turville, AYLESBURY, BUCKINGHAMSHIRE, HP22 5YW.

ELLIS, Miss. Catherine, BA ACA *2005;* 6 Maslen Road, ST. ALBANS, HERTFORDSHIRE, AL4 0GT.

ELLIS, Mrs. Catherine Emma, MBA BCom ACA *1992;* Carriers Croft Sheepy Road Sibson, NUNEATON, WARWICKSHIRE, CV13 6LE.

ELLIS, Mr. Charles, BSc ACA *2007;* Flat 9 Cyril Mansions, Prince of Wales Drive, LONDON, SW11 4HR.

•**ELLIS, Mr. Charles Robert, FCA** *1975;* (Tax Fac), Ellis & Co., 114/120 Northgate Street, CHESTER, CH1 2HT.

ELLIS, Mr. Charles Steven, BA ACA *2006;* 14 Houghton Close, Asfordby Hill, MELTON MOWBRAY, LE14 3QL.

ELLIS, Mrs. Charlotte Jane, BA ACA ACII *1996;* 45 Lindfield Road, LONDON, W5 1QS.

ELLIS, Miss. Chloe Jade, BA ACA *2005;* (Tax Fac), Hilltop Cottage, Houghley Lane, Bramley, LEEDS, LS13 2DT.

ELLIS, Mr. Christopher, ACA *2011;* Flat 6, 4 East Avenue, BOURNEMOUTH, BH3 7BY.

ELLIS, Mr. Christopher John, ACA *1984;* Hill House, 3 Eaton Park Road, COBHAM, KT11 2JG.

ELLIS, Mr. Clive Edward, BSc FCA *1985;* (Tax Fac), 1 Elm Grove, ORPINGTON, BR6 0AA.

ELLIS, Mr. Colin, FCA *1963;* 42 Danesfield Avenue, Waltham, GRIMSBY, DN37 0QE. (Life Member)

ELLIS, Mr. Colin Peter, BA ACA *2006;* Flat 7, Selhurst Court, 119 Gordon Road, CAMBERLEY, SURREY, GU15 2JQ.

ELLIS, Mr. Dan, FCA *1948;* Bryn Awel, Hill Street, PORTHMADOG, GWYNEDD, LL49 9BD. (Life Member)

ELLIS, Mr. Darren Paul, LLB ACA *2005;* 135 Tylney Road, BROMLEY, BR1 2SD.

ELLIS, Mr. David Anthony, BA(Hons) ACA *2001;* Apartment 3W, 500 Broadway, NEW YORK, NY 10012, UNITED STATES.

ELLIS, Mr. David George, FCA *1975;* Millicent House Wood Lane, Huyton, LIVERPOOL, L36 6EJ.

ELLIS, Mr. David James, BA ACA *1983;* St Martins House, 1 Gesham Street, LONDON, EC2V 7BX.

ELLIS, Mr. David John, BSc FCA *1976;* 44 Kingsmead Avenue, Lower Sunbury, SUNBURY-ON-THAMES, MIDDLESEX, TW16 5HJ.

ELLIS, Mr. David John, BA FCA *1970;* Oldfield Barn, Appleby Road, Docker, KENDAL, CUMBRIA, LA8 9BJ.

ELLIS, Mr. David Michael, FCA *1972;* Magna Trust, Sheffield Road, Templeborough, ROTHERHAM, S60 1DX.

ELLIS, Mr. David William, BSc ACA *2010;* 6 Harescroft, TUNBRIDGE WELLS, KENT, TN2 5XE.

ELLIS, Mr. Desmond, FCA *1971;* 11 Bell House Gardens, WOKINGHAM, RG41 2BD.

ELLIS, Mr. Donald John, FCA *1962;* 182 Handside Lane, WELWYN GARDEN CITY, AL8 6TD. (Life Member)

ELLIS, Mr. Dudley Stormont, FCA *1958;* 2219 Gladwin Drive, WALNUT CREEK, CA, 94596-6332, UNITED STATES. (Life Member)

ELLIS, Mr. Edward James, ACA *2008;* with Moore Stephens LLP, 150 Aldersgate Street, LONDON, EC1A 4AB.

ELLIS, Miss. Elizabeth, MA MMath ACA *2011;* 45 Grove Lane, COULSDON, SURREY, CR5 2QD.

ELLIS, Miss. Elizabeth Anne, BSc ACA *2004;* 12/5 Church Hill, EDINBURGH, EH10 4BQ.

ELLIS, Mrs. Elspeth, FCA *1981;* 26 Hammondstreet Road, Cheshunt, WALTHAM CROSS, HERTFORDSHIRE, EN7 6NT.

ELLIS, Miss. Fiona Elizabeth, BA ACA *1992;* 78 Ave Des Champs Elysees, Porte 673, 75008 PARIS, FRANCE.

ELLIS, Mr. Gary Frederick, FCA *1974;* 3 Brettargh Close, Haverbreaks, LANCASTER, LA1 5BU.

•**ELLIS, Mr. Gary John, BA FCA** *1987;* Clive Owen & Co LLP, Aire House, Mandale Business Park, Belmont Ind Estate, DURHAM, DH1 1TH.

ELLIS, Mr. Gary Winston, BSc FCA *1989;* Monahans Second & Third Floors, Clarks Mill Stallard Street, TROWBRIDGE, BA14 8HH.

•**ELLIS, Mr. Geoffrey, FCA** *1963;* (Tax Fac), Geoffrey Ellis & Co., Kirby Grange, Cold Kirby, THIRSK, NORTH YORKSHIRE, YO7 2HL.

ELLIS, Mr. Geoffrey John, BSc ACA *1987;* Travel Channel International Ltd, 64 Newman Street, LONDON, W1T 3EF.

ELLIS, Mr. Glenn Charles, BA FCA *1980;* 5 Tower Cottages, Sandpit Lane, BRENTWOOD, Essex, CM14 5QD.

ELLIS, Mr. Gordon, FCA *1974;* 7 Anson Close, Saltford, BRISTOL, BS31 3DY. (Life Member)

ELLIS, Mr. Graham Robert, ACA *2008;* 25 Hollybank Road, LIVERPOOL, L18 1HP.

ELLIS, Mr. Gregory, ACA *2011;* 191 London Road, RAYLEIGH, ESSEX, SS6 9DN.

ELLIS, Mr. Guy Butterworth, BSc FCA *1985;* (Tax Fac), Hutchison Whampoa (UK,) Ltd, Hutchison House, 5 Hester Road, LONDON, SW11 4AN.

ELLIS, Mr. Guy Graham, ACA *1987;* Flat 21, Lynton Grange, Fortis Green, LONDON, N2 9EU.

ELLIS, Mr. Howard William Hancock, FCA *1960;* White Garth, 37 The Uplands, LOUGHTON, ESSEX, IG10 1NQ. (Life Member)

ELLIS, Mr. Hugh David Stacey, FCA *1969;* Woodsden, Water Lane, Hawkhurst, CRANBROOK, TN18 5AP.

ELLIS, Mr. Hugh Lloyd, BSc ACA *2007;* with PricewaterhouseCoopers LLP, 1 Embankment Place, LONDON, WC2N 6RH.

ELLIS, Mr. Huw Maldwyn, BA ACA ATII *1985;* 19 Moreall Meadows, COVENTRY, CV4 7HL.

ELLIS, Mr. Ian, ACA *2002;* A P N House, Temple Crescent, LEEDS, LS11 8BP.

•**ELLIS, Mr. Ian, BSc FCA** *1977;* McCabe Ford Williams, Bank Chambers, 1 Central Ave., SITTINGBOURNE, ME10 4AE.

ELLIS, Mr. Ian Anthony, BA ACA *1989;* 25 Peacock Close, Killamarsh, SHEFFIELD, S21 1BF.

ELLIS, Mr. James Alexander, BSc ACA *2001;* Close Asset Management Holdings Ltd, 10 Exchange Square Primrose Street, LONDON, EC2A 2BY.

ELLIS, Mr. James Colin, ACA *2009;* 351a Fair Oak Road, EASTLEIGH, HAMPSHIRE, SO50 8AA.

ELLIS, Mr. James Frederick Paul, FCA *1973;* Stourfield, Back Lane, Sturminster Marshall, WIMBORNE, BH21 4BP.

ELLIS, Miss. Jane Charlotte, MA ACA *1996;* The National Gallery, Trafalgar Square, LONDON, WC2N 5DN.

•ELLIS, Ms. Janette Roselyn, LLB ACA *1991;* Ellisfoster LLP, 1 High Street, Lindfield, HAYWARDS HEATH, WEST SUSSEX, RH16 2HG. See also EF21 Limited

ELLIS, Mrs. Janine Elizabeth, BA ACA *1993;* 113 Ack Lane East, Bramhall, STOCKPORT, SK7 2AB.

•①ELLIS, Mrs. Jean McKay, BA FCA CTA *1994;* Duncan Sheard Glass, Castle Chambers, 43 Castle St, LIVERPOOL, L2 9TL. See also DSG Accountancy and Taxation Services Limited

ELLIS, Mr. Jeremy Adam Hirst, FCA *1961;* 9a Wrights Lane, Prestwood, GREAT MISSENDEN, BUCKINGHAMSHIRE, HP16 0LH.

ELLIS, Mr. John, BA ACA *1988;* with Streets LLP, Tower House, Lucy Tower Street, LINCOLN, LINCOLNSHIRE, LN1 1XW.

ELLIS, Mr. John Andrew, BSc ACA *1994;* The Old Vicarage, Vicarage Road, Rhydymwyn, MOLD, CLWYD, CH7 5HL.

•ELLIS, Mr. John Andrew Jackson, FCA *1981;* (Tax Fac), 59 Poland Street, LONDON, W1F 7NS.

•ELLIS, Mr. John Gelling, FCA *1974;* John Ellis & Co, The Barn, 173 Church Road, Northfield, BIRMINGHAM, B31 2LX.

ELLIS, Mr. John Henry, FCA *1961;* 101 Mortlake High Street, LONDON, SW14 8HQ. (Life Member)

•ELLIS, Mr. John Michael, BSc ACA *1996;* PricewaterhouseCoopers LLP, 1 Embankment Place, LONDON, WC2N 6RH. See also PricewaterhouseCoopers

•ELLIS, Mr. John Richard, FCA *1971;* Ellis & Co, 1 Peach Street, WOKINGHAM, BERKSHIRE, RG40 1XJ.

•ELLIS, Mr. Jonathan Felix Hugh, FCA *1975;* The Old Rectory, Thurning, DEREHAM, NR20 5QX.

ELLIS, Mr. Jonathan Matthew, ACA *2008;* Flat 7, Girton House, Manor Fields, LONDON, SW15 3LN.

•ELLIS, Mr. Julian, FCA *1970;* Julian Ellis, 15A Bull Plain, HERTFORD, SG14 1DX.

ELLIS, Mrs. June, FCA *1976;* (Tax Fac), 10 Borrowdale Grove, MORECAMBE, LA4 5XJ.

ELLIS, Mrs. Karen Lesley, BA(Hons) ACA *2001;* 11 Brisbane Avenue, Wimbledon, LONDON, SW19 3AF.

ELLIS, Mrs. Katharine Ann, BSocSc ACA *1998;* National Grid Wireless House, Warwick Technology Park Gallows Hill, WARWICK, CV34 6DD.

ELLIS, Miss. Katharine Frances Margaret, BSc FCA DChA *1980;* The Royal Society of, Edinburgh, 22-24 George Street, EDINBURGH, EH2 2PQ.

ELLIS, Mrs. Katherine Diana, BSc ACA *2005;* 127b Abbeville Road, LONDON, SW4 9JL.

ELLIS, Mrs. Katherine Frances Louise, BA ACA *2007;* 27 Holmes Road, Breaston, DERBY, DE72 3BT.

ELLIS, Mrs. Kathryn Elizabeth, BSc ACA *1994;* 35 Denbigh Gardens, RICHMOND, TW10 6EL.

ELLIS, Mr. Keith John, BA FCA *1977;* 4 Broadmeadows Close, New Invention, WILLENHALL, WV12 5JW.

•①ELLIS, Mr. Kevin James David, BA ACA *1988;* PricewaterhouseCoopers LLP, 1 Embankment Place, LONDON, WC2N 6RH. See also PricewaterhouseCoopers

ELLIS, Mr. Kevin Nicholas, BSc ACA *2006;* 47 Whitton Road, TWICKENHAM, TW1 1BH.

ELLIS, Mr. Kevin Stewart, BSc ACA *1989;* 10 Marshalls Way, Wheathampstead, ST. ALBANS, HERTFORDSHIRE, AL4 8HY.

ELLIS, Mr. Kieron Gordon, BA ACA *2009;* 35 Savannah Place, Great Sankey, WARRINGTON, WA5 8GN.

ELLIS, Miss. Laura, BA ACA *2006;* Google Australia, Level 5, 48 Pirrama Road, PYRMONT, NSW 2009, AUSTRALIA.

ELLIS, Miss. Laura Elizabeth, BSc ACA *2010;* 157 Edgware Road, LONDON, W2 2HR.

ELLIS, Mrs. Louise Michelle Baxter, BSc(Hons) ACA *2001;* 21 Lea Road, Sonning Common, READING, RG4 9LH.

ELLIS, Mr. Luke Thomas, MA FCA *2001;* Oracle Corporation (UK) Ltd, Oracle Parkway, READING, RG6 1RA.

ELLIS, Mr. Marc Peter, BSc ACA *1998;* Nice-Pak International Ltd Aber Park, Aber Road, FLINT, CLWYD, CH6 5EX.

ELLIS, Miss. Margaret Hannah, BSc FCA *1977;* Accent Group Ltd, Charlestown House, Acorn Park, Otley Road, SHIPLEY, WEST YORKSHIRE BD17 7SW.

•ELLIS, Dr. Mark Charles, BSc ACA *1997;* PricewaterhouseCoopers LLP, One Kingsway, CARDIFF, CF10 3PW. See also PricewaterhouseCoopers

ELLIS, Mr. Mark David, BA(Hons) ACA *2009;* 15/1 Ruabon Road, TOORAK, VIC 3142, AUSTRALIA.

ELLIS, Mr. Mark Richard, BA ACA *2002;* PricewaterhouseCoopers, 201 Sussex Street, GPO Box 2650, SYDNEY, NSW 1171, AUSTRALIA.

•ELLIS, Mr. Mark Richard, BA FCA *1980;* (Tax Fac), Duttellis Productions Ltd, 1 Ramsay Court, Kingfisher Way, Hinchingbrooke Business Park, HUNTINGDON, CAMBRIDGESHIRE PE29 6FY. See also AIMS - Mark Ellis

ELLIS, Mr. Mark St John, BA FCA CPA *1987;* 374 Roaring Brook Road, CHAPPAQUA, NY 10514, UNITED STATES.

ELLIS, Mr. Martin, BSc FCA *1987;* 144 Westbury Lane, NEWPORT PAGNELL, BUCKINGHAMSHIRE, MK16 8PT.

ELLIS, Mr. Martin Alexander, BA ACA *2005;* 40 Ferncroft, LIVERSEDGE, WEST YORKSHIRE, WF15 8DT.

•ELLIS, Mr. Martin Gilbert, BA FCA *1983;* Grant Thornton UK LLP, 30 Finsbury Square, LONDON, EC2P 2YU. See also Grant Thornton LLP

ELLIS, Mr. Matthew David, BCom ACA *1996;* 5102 S 47th St, ROGERS, AR 72758, UNITED STATES.

ELLIS, Mr. Matthew James, BA ACA *1997;* Greenways, Grove Road, Mollington, CHESTER, CH1 6LG.

ELLIS, Miss. Melanie, BCom ACA *1997;* Flat 27 Oakhill Court, Upper Richmond Road, LONDON, SW15 2QH.

ELLIS, Mrs. Melanie, BA ACA *1998;* West Berkshire District Council Council Offices, Faraday Road, NEWBURY, RG14 2AF.

•ELLIS, Mr. Mervyn Brian, FCA *1975;* (Tax Fac), with Stonehage Trust Holdings (Jersey) Ltd, Sir Walter Raleigh House, 48-50 Esplanade, St Helier, JERSEY, JE1 4HH.

ELLIS, Mr. Michael Charles Anthony, FCA *1970;* Dukes Cottage, Cox Green, Rudgwick, HORSHAM, WEST SUSSEX, RH12 3DF.

ELLIS, Mr. Michael D'arcy, FCA *1970;* Cliffmore Bungalow, Cheadle Road, Alton, STOKE-ON-TRENT, ST10 4DH.

ELLIS, Mr. Michael David Colvin, FCA *1973;* 32 Homebank House, 1 Bidston Road, PRENTON, MERSEYSIDE, CH43 2GB.

ELLIS, Mr. Michael John, BSc ACA *1992;* Little Trodgers, Honor End Lane, Prestwood, GREAT MISSENDEN, BUCKINGHAMSHIRE, HP16 9HG.

ELLIS, Mr. Michael John Irving, FCA *1958;* Zelaa, 2 The Barn, Front Street, Chedzoy, BRIDGWATER, SOMERSET TA7 8RE.

ELLIS, Mr. Nathan John, BSc ACA *1999;* Newtown House Newtown Road, Awbridge, ROMSEY, HAMPSHIRE, SO51 0GG.

•ELLIS, Mr. Neil, FCA *1979;* Forrester Boyd, 26 South Saint Mary's Gate, GRIMSBY, NORTH LINCOLNSHIRE, DN31 1LW. See also Dataplan Payroll Limited

•ELLIS, Mr. Neil Grant, BSc ACA MBA *1996;* Neil Ellis Consulting Limited, 1 Friary, Temple Quay, BRISTOL, BS1 6EU.

•ELLIS, Mr. Neville Trevor, BA FCA *1975;* Ellis Lloyd Jones LLP, Alan House, 2 Risca Road, NEWPORT, GWENT, NP20 4JW.

ELLIS, Mr. Nigel George, FCA *1963;* Willmead Farm, Bovey Tracey, NEWTON ABBOT, TQ13 9NP.

ELLIS, Mr. Norman Lewis, FCA *1958;* 8 Warley Mount, BRENTWOOD, Essex, CM14 5EN. (Life Member)

ELLIS, Ms. Patricia Dorothy, BA(Hons) ACA CTA CIOT *2001;* Marshalls Plc, Birkby Grange, 85 Birkby Hall Road, HUDDERSFIELD, HD2 2XB.

ELLIS, Mr. Paul, BA FCA *1969;* Sarnia, Chestnut Walk, Little Baddow, CHELMSFORD, CM3 4SP. (Life Member)

•ELLIS, Mr. Paul James, FCA *1973;* (Tax Fac), PKF (UK) LLP, Regent House, Clinton Avenue, NOTTINGHAM, NG5 1AZ.

ELLIS, Mr. Paul Murray, MA MBA FCA CPA *1984;* 10 Roland Drive, DARIEN, CT 06820, UNITED STATES.

ELLIS, Mr. Paul Stuart, BSc ACA *1987;* (Tax Fac), 3 Newby Walk, Connah's Quay, DEESIDE, CH5 4RN.

ELLIS, Mr. Peter, BA ACA *1993;* 6 Angus Close, Bedfordview, JOHANNESBURG, 2007, SOUTH AFRICA.

ELLIS, Mr. Peter John, BSc ACA *2006;* with Shipleys LLP, 10 Orange Street, Haymarket, LONDON, WC2H 7DQ.

ELLIS, Mr. Peter Macloim, FCA *1977;* Malvern House, The Common, Potten End, BERKHAMSTED, HERTFORDSHIRE, HP4 2QF.

ELLIS, Mr. Peter Vivian, BA LLB ACA *1983;* 16 Christchurch Avenue, LONDON, N12 0DE.

ELLIS, Mr. Peter William, FCA *1972;* Beacon Rise, High Street, Gringley-on-the-Hill, DONCASTER, DN10 4RG. (Life Member)

ELLIS, Mr. Peter-John Anthony, BA ACA *2007;* 41 Victoria Road, LONDON, N4 3SJ.

•ELLIS, Mr. Philip David, ACA CF *1990;* Optima Corporate Finance LLP, 32 Bedford Row, LONDON, WC1R 4HE.

ELLIS, Mr. Philip Geoffrey, ACA *1979;* 1 Basegreen Crescent, SHEFFIELD, SOUTH YORKSHIRE, S12 3FD.

•ELLIS, Mr. Philip Harold, BSc ACA *1989;* (Tax Fac), Kingsmead Accounting Ltd, 3 North Street, Oadby, LEICESTER, LE2 5AH.

ELLIS, Mrs. Rachel Caroline, MA FCA *1981;* (Tax Fac), 2 Firgrove, St. Johns, WOKING, SURREY, GU21 7RD.

ELLIS, Miss. Rebecca, BSc ACA CTA *2011;* 15 Rowan Close, Nelson, TREHARRIS, MID GLAMORGAN, CF46 6EN.

ELLIS, Mr. Richard David, ACA *1992;* Fenner plc, Hesslewood Country Office, Park, Ferriby Road, HESSLE, HU13 0PW.

•ELLIS, Mr. Richard David, BA(Hons) ACA *2003;* (Tax Fac), Ellis Lloyd Jones LLP, Alan House, 2 Risca Road, NEWPORT, GWENT, NP20 4JW.

•ELLIS, Mr. Richard Francis, FCA *1979;* 33 Grimsdyke Crescent, BARNET, HERTFORDSHIRE, EN5 4AQ.

ELLIS, Mr. Richard James, BSc ACA *1992;* 113 Ack Lane East, Bramhall, STOCKPORT, SK7 2AB.

ELLIS, Mr. Richard Paul, BA FCA *1994;* Yew Croft, Lumb Lane, Almondbury, HUDDERSFIELD, HD4 6SZ.

ELLIS, Mr. Robert Goldie, FCA *1969;* Beech Hill House, Abergavenny Road, USK, NP15 1HX. (Life Member)

•ELLIS, Mr. Robert Paul, FCA *1970;* John Cheatle Ltd, 32 Charles Street, LEICESTER, LE1 3FG. See also Ellis R.P.

•①ELLIS, Mr. Robin Arthur, BSc FCA *1957;* 9 The Elms, Church Road, Claygate, ESHER, KT10 0JT. See also R.A. Ellis & Co

ELLIS, Mr. Roderick George Howard, BA ACA *1992;* 790 Stovall Blvd, ATLANTA, GA 30342, UNITED STATES.

•ELLIS, Mr. Roderick Peter, FCA *1977;* R.P. Ellis, The Priory, 414 Newark Road, LINCOLN, LN6 8RX.

ELLIS, Mr. Roger Antony, FCA *1967;* Fairway, 4 Wigton Chase, Alwoodley, LEEDS, LS17 8SG.

ELLIS, Mr. Roland Richard, FCA *1952;* Russets, Tarrant Hinton, BLANDFORD FORUM, DT11 8JA. (Life Member)

ELLIS, Mr. Roy, FCA *1963;* 43 Alpes Road, Vainona, HARARE, ZIMBABWE.

ELLIS, Mr. Roy George, BA FCA *1995;* 57 St. Lawrence Park, CHEPSTOW, NP16 6DP.

ELLIS, Mr. Russell James, ACA *2009;* Flat B, 13 Finsbury Park Avenue, LONDON, N4 1DQ.

ELLIS, Mr. Samuel Michael Howard, ACA CA(AUS) *2010;* Macquarie Bank Limited, Level 30 Citypoint, 1 Ropemaker St, LONDON, EC2Y 9HD.

ELLIS, Mrs. Sara Felicity Booth, BA ACA *1984;* Sandisons Ltd, Badger House, Salisbury Road, BLANDFORD FORUM, DORSET DT11 7QD.

ELLIS, Mrs. Sarah Jane, BSc ACA *1990;* Homelea, Moor Road, Langham, COLCHESTER, CO4 5NR.

ELLIS, Mrs. Sarah Louise, BA(Hons) ACA *2001;* 44 Tolverne Road, LONDON, SW20 8RA.

ELLIS, Miss. Sarah Victoria, BA ACA *1998;* Flat 1, 7 West Cliffe Grove, HARROGATE, NORTH YORKSHIRE, HG2 0PS.

ELLIS, Mr. Simon Hugh, FCA *1968;* Balima, New Road, Wormley, GODALMING, GU8 5SU.

ELLIS, Mr. Simon James, MEng ACA *2007;* 70 Lavender Sweep, LONDON, SW11 1HD.

ELLIS, Mr. Simon Kevin, FCA *1981;* (Tax Fac), Avete, South Hanningfield Road, South Hanningfield, CHELMSFORD, CM3 8HJ.

ELLIS, Mr. Simon Matthew, BSc(Hons) ACA *2000;* with Grant Thornton UK LLP, 1 Whitehall Riverside, Whitehall Road, LEEDS, WEST YORKSHIRE, LS1 4BN.

•①ELLIS, Mr. Stephen Andrew, BSc ACA *1990;* PricewaterhouseCoopers LLP, Benson House, 33 Wellington Street, LEEDS, LS1 4JP. See also PricewaterhouseCoopers

ELLIS, Mr. Stephen Mark, BSc ACA *1990;* 4 Hilton Mews, Bramhope, LEEDS, LS16 9LF.

•ELLIS, Mr. Steven David, MA ACA *2001;* Staffords Cambridge LLP, CPC1, Capital Park, Fulbourn, CAMBRIDGE, CB21 5XE.

ELLIS, Mr. Steven John, BSc FCA MCT *1991;* Fieldridge, Broombarn Lane, GREAT MISSENDEN, BUCKINGHAMSHIRE, HP16 9JD.

ELLIS, Mr. Steven John, BA ACA *2006;* 27 Holmes Road, Breaston, DERBY, DE72 3BT.

ELLIS, Mr. Stuart Richard, ACA *2011;* 8 Kingsbury Court, NEWCASTLE UPON TYNE, NE12 8RP.

ELLIS, Miss. Susan, BSc ACA *1997;* 29 Montcliffe Crescent, MANCHESTER, M16 8GR.

ELLIS, Ms. Tamsin, BA ACA *1998;* Information Management West First, Boots the Chemists Ltd D90 Head Office, Thane Road, NOTTINGHAM, NG90 1BS.

ELLIS, Mr. Thomas David, BA ACA *2006;* 59 Parish Gardens, LEYLAND, PR25 3UF.

ELLIS, Mr. Timothy Frazer, BA ACA *1989;* 9 Tawini Road, Titirangi, AUCKLAND 0604, NEW ZEALAND.

ELLIS, Mr. Timothy Paul, BA ACA *1987;* 4 Keats Close, Ewloe, DEESIDE, CH5 3TG.

ELLIS, Mrs. Wendy, BA ACA *1997;* Greenways, Grove Road, Mollington, CHESTER, CH1 6LG.

ELLIS, Mr. Wilfred, BA FCA *1972;* Barn How, Kendal Road, Bowness-On-Windermere, WINDERMERE, LA23 3HP. (Life Member)

ELLIS, Mr. William Derek, BSc ACA *1991;* Ellis of Richmond Ltd, Richmond House, 1 The Links, Popham Close, HANWORTH, FELTHAM MIDDLESEX TW13 6JE.

ELLIS, Mr. William Edwin Gordon, FCA *1953;* Gordon Ellis & Co Trent Lane, Trent Lane Industrial Estate Castle Donington, DERBY, DE74 2PY. (Life Member)

ELLIS, Mr. William Ewart, BA FCA *1954;* Flat 3, Poplar Court, Kings Road, LYTHAM ST.ANNES, FY8 1NZ. (Life Member)

ELLIS, Mr. William George Edward, FCA *1954;* P O Box 1348, HOWICK, 3290, SOUTH AFRICA. (Life Member)

•ELLIS-BANKS, Ms. Claire Elizabeth, BA(Hons) FCA *2001;* Ellis Banks, 49 Sandbeck Court, Kingswood, Bawtry, DONCASTER, SOUTH YORKSHIRE DN10 6XP. See also Banks Ellis

ELLIS-JONES, Mr. David Christopher, FCA *1964;* Hope House, St. Peters Street, Bishops Waltham, SOUTHAMPTON, SO32 1AD.

ELLISDON, Mr. Mark Christopher, BSc ACA *1994;* Merribelle, Bickley Park Road, BROMLEY, BR1 2AY.

ELLISON, Mrs. Carol Ann, MA FCA *1984;* Beech House, Clease Way, Compton, WINCHESTER, HAMPSHIRE, SO21 2AL.

ELLISON, Mr. David Alfred, BA ACA *1983;* Orchard End, Harberton, TOTNES, DEVON, TQ9 7SN.

ELLISON, Mr. David Charles, BA ACA *1996;* Flat 1 The Chapters, 107 Badshot Lea Road Badshot Lea, FARNHAM, GU9 9LP.

ELLISON, Mr. David Graham, FCA *1966;* 4 Grosvenor Court, Pinfold Hill, Shenstone, LICHFIELD, STAFFORDSHIRE, WS14 0JW.

ELLISON, Mr. David Robert, FCA *1965;* The Lodge, Northwick Park, MORETON-IN-MARSH, GL56 9RL.

ELLISON, Mr. Douglas Bernard, BA ACA *1987;* 491 Essex Avenue, BLOOMFIELD, NJ 07003, UNITED STATES.

ELLISON, Mr. Gary, BA FCA *1987;* 16 Summer St, Stanley Point, NORTH SHORE CITY 0624, NEW ZEALAND.

ELLISON, Mr. James Nicholas, BA FCA *1975;* 5 Petit Port Close, La Route Du Petit Port St. Brelade, JERSEY, JE3 8HJ.

•ELLISON, Mr. Jeremy Simon, BSc FCA *1987;* Jeremy Ellison BSc FCA, Delamore, Long Lane, Shaldon, TEIGNMOUTH, DEVON TQ14 0HB.

ELLISON, Mrs. Joanne Tina, BA ACA *1998;* 18 The Croft, Euxton, CHORLEY, LANCASHIRE, PR7 6LH.

ELLISON, Mr. John, FCA *1964;* High Candovers, Hartley Mauditt, ALTON, GU34 3BP.

•ELLISON, Mr. John Maynard Hardy, FCA *1976;* with KPMG LLP, 15 Canada Square, LONDON, E14 5GL.

ELLISON, Mr. John Stuart, FCA *1975;* 51 Whirlow Park Road, Whirlowdale, SHEFFIELD, S11 9NN.

ELLISON, Miss. Lisa-Jane, BA ACA *2004;* 49 Chorley Old Road, Whittle-le-Woods, CHORLEY, LANCASHIRE, PR6 7LD.

•ELLISON, Mr. Malcolm, FCA *1980;* Jacob House, 139 Farndon Road, NEWARK, NG24 4SP.

ELLISON, Mr. Mark Benedict, MA FCA *1976;* 1 Rue Antoine Arnauld, 75016 PARIS, FRANCE.

•ELLISON, Mr. Nicolas Duncan, FCA *1976;* Humphrey & Co, 7-9 The Avenue, EASTBOURNE, EAST SUSSEX, BN21 3YA.

ELLISON, Mr. Paul, BSc ACA *2010;* 19 Barnfield Road, BROMSGROVE, WORCESTERSHIRE, B61 7BJ.

•①ELLISON, Mr. Paul William, BA ACA *1985;* with RSM Tenon Limited, Davidson House, Forbury Square, READING, RG1 3EU.

ELLISON, Mr. Richard John, FCA *1958;* Craigfield, Lake Road, Bowness On Windermere, WINDERMERE, LA23 2JF. (Life Member)

ELLISON, Mr. Robert Mark, ACA *1980;* 10 Willesden Green, Nuthall, NOTTINGHAM, NG16 1QF.

ELLISON, Miss. Sandra Jane, BA ACA *1988;* 65 Pinnington Road, Whiston, PRESCOT, L35 3TY.

ELLISON, Mrs. Stephanie Joy, BSc ACA *1982;* 11 Cedarwood, Cuddington, NORTHWICH, CW8 2XR.

•ELLISON, Mrs. Susan Theresa, BA FCA *1994;* (Tax Fac), Susan Ellison, 30 Whitchurch Close, Padgate, WARRINGTON, WA1 4JZ.

ELLISS, Mr. William Derrick, FCA *1972;* 50 Broadway, Duffield, BELPER, DERBYSHIRE, DE56 4BU.

ELLISTON, Mr. Bryan Richard, BSc FCA *1985;* Parkers Green Cottage, Hadlow Road East, TONBRIDGE, TN11 0AE.

ELLISTON, Mrs. Hannah Elizabeth, ACA *2009;* 26 Sebright Avenue, WORCESTER, WR5 2HH.

ELLISTON, Mr. Roger James, LLB FCA *1978;* Longridge House, 264 Chartridge Lane, CHESHAM, HP5 2SG.

ELLITHORNE, Mrs. Joy Audrey, BSc ACA *1994;* 6 Old Rectory Close, Broughton Astley, LEICESTER, LE9 6PP.

ELLMAN, Mr. Daniel David, BA ACA *2009;* 109a Theobald Street, BOREHAMWOOD, HERTFORDSHIRE, WD6 4PT.

ELLMER, Mr. Roland Charles, BSc FCA *1974;* The Holocaust Centre, Beth-Shalom, Laxton, NEWARK, NOTTINGHAMSHIRE, NG22 0PA.

•ELLMERS, Mr. Stephen, FCA *1981;* Day Smith & Hunter, Globe House, Eclipse Park, Sittingbourne Road, MAIDSTONE, KENT ME14 3EN.

ELLOWAY, Dr. Clare Rachel, BSc ACA ATII *2001;* 1a Waterpath, Westford, WELLINGTON, SOMERSET, TA21 0DS.

ELLS, Mr. Christopher John, FCA *1973;* Suite 12, 30 Churchill Business Centre, Kings Hill, WEST MALLING, KENT, ME19 4YU.

ELLS, Mr. Stuart John, FCA *1983;* Huntsmoor Templewood Lane, Farnham Common, SLOUGH, SL2 3HW.

ELLSE, Mr. Simon Richard, BA ACA *1984;* Spring House, 6a Hogshill Lane, COBHAM, SURREY, KT11 2AQ.

ELLSMORE, Mrs. Kerry, BSc ACA *2000;* 12 Yates Croft, SUTTON COLDFIELD, B74 4YB.

ELLSON, Mr. John William, FCA *1972;* Stoneleigh, 1 Brooklyn Road, Wilpshire, BLACKBURN, BB1 9PP. (Life Member)

ELLSON, Mr. Peter William, FCA *1958;* 14 Oakhurst Rise, CARSHALTON, SM5 4AG. (Life Member)

ELLSON, Mrs. Philippa Jane, BA ACA *1991;* Holly Tree Cottage, 54 Church Road, Catworth, HUNTINGDON, CAMBRIDGESHIRE, PE28 0PA.

•ELLSON, Mr. Stephen, FCA *1979;* Filer Knapper LLP, 10 Bridge Street, CHRISTCHURCH, DORSET, BH23 1EF.

ELLSWORTH, Mr. Robert Lewis, BSc FCA *1977;* 109 Brookfield Road, Churchdown, GLOUCESTER, GL3 2PN.

•ELLUM, Mr. Stephen Francis, ACA *1986;* Steve Ellum & Associates Limited, 18 Bryn Terrace, LLANELLI, SA15 2PD.

•①ELLWARD, Mr. Patrick Brian, BA ACA *1989;* with RSM Tenon Limited, The Poynt Building, 45 Wollaton Street, NOTTINGHAM, NG1 5FW.

ELLWOOD, Mrs. Alison Sara Penelope, BSc ACA *1989;* 11 Grant Walk, ASCOT, BERKSHIRE, SL5 9TT.

ELLWOOD, Mr. Clive Graham, ACA *1981;* Old Barn Quarry Farm, Claverton Down, BATH, BA2 6EE.

•ELLWOOD, Miss. Fiona Elizabeth, BSc FCA *1993;* Fiona E Davies, 3 Barton Common Lane, NEW MILTON, HAMPSHIRE, BH25 5PS.

ELLWOOD, Miss. Kirsten Paula, BSc ACA *1994;* The Anchorage, Houghton, STOCKBRIDGE, SO20 6LW.

•ELLWOOD, Mr. Peter Eric, BA FCA *1996;* robinson+co, Oxford Chambers, New Oxford Street, WORKINGTON, CA14 2LR. See also Robinson J.F.W. & Co

•ELLWOOD, Mr. Steven John, FCA *1968;* Steven Ellwood, 94 Biddulph Road, CONGLETON, CW12 3LY.

ELLYARD, Mr. Luke, BA ACA *2003;* KPMG, Level 32 Emirates Towers, Sheikh Zayed Road, P.O. Box 3800, DUBAI, 3800 UNITED ARAB EMIRATES.

ELMAN, Mr. Charles, FCA *1951;* 1 Chadwick Road, WESTCLIFF-ON-SEA, SS0 8LS. (Life Member)

ELMAN, Mr. Jeremy Mark, BSc ACA *2004;* 18/30A Lavender Street, LAVENDER BAY, NSW 2060, AUSTRALIA.

•ELMAN, Mr. Paul Jeremy, FCA *1981;* Francis James & Partners LLP, 1386 London Road, LEIGH-ON-SEA, ESSEX, SS9 2UJ.

ELMAN, Mr. Ralph Julian, BSc FCA *1978;* 8 Graces Mews, Abbey Road, LONDON, NW8 9AZ.

ELMER, Miss. Hannah Victoria, BSc ACA *2004;* 27 Harwich Road, Little Oakley, HARWICH, CO12 5JG.

ELMER, Mr. Jonathan Richard, BA ACA *1987;* Landis & Gyr Ltd, 1 Lysander Drive, Northfields Industrial Estate, Market Deeping, PETERBOROUGH, PE6 8FB.

•ELMES, Mr. Christian Alexander, BSc ACA *2000;* Elmes & English, 121 London Road, KNEBWORTH, HERTFORDSHIRE, SG3 6EX.

•ELMORE, Mr. David John, FCA *1980;* Briant Elmore & Co., 155 Station Road, Histon, Impington, CAMBRIDGE, CB24 9NP.

ELMORE, Mr. Paul Martin, FCA *1984;* 89 Durrell Drive, Cawston, RUGBY, CV22 7GW.

•ELMS, Mr. David John, MA FCA FSI *1989;* KPMG LLP, 15 Canada Square, LONDON, E14 5GL. See also KPMG Europe LLP

ELMS, Mr. Gerald John, BSc FCA *1978;* 220 EDELWEISS DRIVE NW, CALGARY T3A 4A3, AB, CANADA.

ELMS, Mrs. Nicola Louise, MA ACA *1998;* with Deloitte LLP, Stonecutter Court, 1 Stonecutter Street, LONDON, EC4A 4TR.

ELMS, Miss. Phillippa Mary, ACA *2008;* Ellacotts LLP, 23 West Bar, BANBURY, OXFORDSHIRE, OX16 9SA.

ELMS, Mrs. Sarah Victoria, ACA CTA *2004;* with PKF (UK) LLP, 16 The Havens, Ransomes Europark, IPSWICH, IP3 9SJ.

ELMS, Mr. Simon Paul, BSc ACA *1995;* 122 Ack Lane East, Bramhall, STOCKPORT, CHESHIRE, SK7 2AB.

ELPHICK, Ms. Anna Jo Karen, LLB ACA CTA *2002;* 38 Quarry Bank, TONBRIDGE, KENT, TN9 2QZ.

ELPHICK, Mr. David John, FCA *1959;* Saint Alphege, Exton, EXETER, EX3 0PP. (Life Member)

ELPHICK, Mr. John Oscar, FCA *1950;* 1 Aston Court, Blandford Road, Iwerne Minster, BLANDFORD FORUM, DORSET, DT11 8QN. (Life Member)

ELPHICK, Mr. Oliver Richard, BA ACA *1979;* 1 Botlan, 22340 PAULE, FRANCE.

ELPHICK, Mr. Paul Dennis, FCA *1972;* Roebuck Interim Executives Ltd, 59 Dartmouth House, Royal Quarter, Seven Kings Way, KINGSTON UPON THAMES, SURREY KT2 5BJ.

ELRINGTON, Mrs. Catherine Anne, LLB ACA *1992;* One North East, Stella House, Goldcrest Way, Newburn Riverside, NEWCASTLE UPON TYNE, NE15 8NY.

•ELS, Mr. Jan Ernst Albertus, ACA CA(SA) *2010;* ElsAcc Limited, 18 The Hemsleys, Pease Pottage, CRAWLEY, WEST SUSSEX, RH11 9BX.

ELSAM, Mr. Richard Leon, BA FCA *1974;* 22 Copse Road, CLEVEDON, AVON, BS21 7QL.

•ELSBY, Mr. Carl Anthony, ACA *1992;* Elsby & Co (Sywell) Ltd, Thistledown Barn, Holcot Lane, Sywell, NORTHAMPTON, NN6 0BG. See also Elsby & Co(Northampton) LLP

•ELSDEN, Mr. Neil Richard, BA FCA *2000;* (Tax Fac), Banks Limited, 14 Devizes Road, Old Town, SWINDON, SN1 4BH.

ELSDON, Miss. Katie, BA ACA *2007;* 9 Dalmuir Close, Eaglescliffe, STOCKTON-ON-TEES, TS16 9HY.

ELSE, Mr. Charles Derek, FCA *1965;* Mercantile Credit Bank Ltd, 8 Port Bell Road, P.O. Box 620, KAMPALA, UGANDA.

ELSE, Mrs. Joanne Lesley, BSc ACA *2004;* Barn 2 Lea End Lane, Hopwood Alvechurch, BIRMINGHAM, B48 7AY.

ELSE, Mr. Jon Paul, LLB ACA *2003;* Ashdene Vicarage Lane, Bowdon, ALTRINCHAM, CHESHIRE, WA14 3AS.

ELSE, Mr. Mark Peter, BSc ACA *2002;* Barn 2 Lea End Lane, Hopwood Alvechurch, BIRMINGHAM, B48 7AY.

ELSE, Mrs. Rachel Helen, BSc ACA *1995;* 59 Broadhurst, ASHTEAD, KT21 1QD.

ELSEGOOD, Mr. Philip Graham, BSc ACA *1985;* Gosland House, Bowes Gate Road, Bunbury, TARPORLEY, CW6 9QA.

ELSEY, Mr. Aron, BSc(Hons) ACA *2010;* Flat 29 Fairmont House, Needleman Street, LONDON, SE16 7AW.

•ELSEY, Mr. Christopher, FCA *1971;* (Tax Fac), Barter Durgan & Muir Limited, 35 Lavant Street, PETERSFIELD, HAMPSHIRE, GU32 3EL.

ELSEY, Mr. David Bryan, ACA *1983;* 26 Buxton Avenue, Gorleston, GREAT YARMOUTH, NR31 6HG.

ELSEY, Mr. Keith Anthony Lambert, FCA *1965;* Cleeves, Timberidge, Loudwater, RICKMANSWORTH, WD3 4JD. (Life Member)

ELSEY, Mr. Walter Philip Joseph, FCA *1971;* PO Box 3387, Richmond, NELSON, NEW ZEALAND. (Life Member)

ELSIGOOD, Mr. Steven Deryck, BSc ACA *1989;* with KPMG LLP, 15 Canada Square, LONDON, E14 5GL.

ELSMORE, Mr. Robert John, FCA *1962;* 40 Hill Village Road, SUTTON COLDFIELD, B75 5BA. (Life Member)

ELSOM, Mrs. Alison Jane, BSc ACA *1991;* 4 Marker Road, OCEAN REEF, WA 6027, AUSTRALIA.

ELSOM, Mr. David John, BA ACA *1988;* 2 Rutland Park, SHEFFIELD, S10 2PD.

ELSOM, Miss. Nicola Louise, BA ACA *1994;* 41 Thirlmere Road, Muswell Hill, LONDON, N10 2DL.

ELSON, Mrs. Joyce Emily Maria, BSc ACA *1986;* Lyshott House, Lyshott Heath Golf Club, Millbrook, BEDFORD, MK45 2JB.

ELSON, Mr. Peter Frederic Alan, BSc FCA *1975;* 18 St Laurent, NEWPORT COAST, CA 92657, UNITED STATES.

ELSTON, Mr. Andrew Henry, BA ACA *1993;* Stamford House, Stoke Row Road, Peppard Common, HENLEY-ON-THAMES, OXFORDSHIRE, RG9 5JD.

•ELSTON, Mr. Anthony Christopher Rupert, BA FCA *1993;* Lane End, 95 Bolling Road, Ben Rhydding, ILKLEY, WEST YORKSHIRE, LS29 8QH.

ELSTON, Mr. Christopher Thomas, FCA *1968;* 6 Towles Pastures Castle Donington, DERBY, DE74 2RX. (Life Member)

•ELSTON, Mr. David Vincent, BSc FCA *1983;* David V Elston & Co Ltd, 51 Molesworth Street, WADEBRIDGE, CORNWALL, PL27 7DR.

ELSTON, Miss. Jane Elizabeth, BSc ACA *1996;* Orchard House The Fosse, Eathorpe, LEAMINGTON SPA, CV33 9DF.

ELSTON, Mr. John, FCA *1964;* 71 Longcroft Road, Dronfield Woodhouse, DRONFIELD, DERBYSHIRE, S18 8XU.

ELSTON, Mr. John David, BA FCA *1973;* Tara, Woodland Rise, SEVENOAKS, TN15 0HZ.

ELSTON, Mr. Robin Nigel, BSc ACA *1991;* 2 Pakington Road, WORCESTER, WR2 6EF.

•ELSTON, Mr. Timothy Arthur Robert, BA FCA *1995;* Percy Westhead & Company, Greg's Buildings, 1 Booth Street, MANCHESTER, M2 4AD.

ELSTON, Mr. Trevor John, FCA *1974;* 70 Church Lane, Fradley, LICHFIELD, WS13 8NN.

ELSTONE, Mr. Henry Claude, FCA *1968;* Valley House, Valley Road, Darrington, PONTEFRACT, WF8 3BT.

ELSTONE, Mrs. Nicola Rachel, BA ACA *1991;* 3 Chancellery Mews, BURY ST. EDMUNDS, SUFFOLK, IP33 3AB.

ELSTONE, Mr. Robert Colin, BSc ACA *1989;* 12 Thorn Road, Bramhall, STOCKPORT, CHESHIRE, SK7 1HQ.

ELSTONE, Mrs. Tina Denise, BSc ACA *1987;* Riversdale Cottage, Coopers Lane, CROWBOROUGH, TN6 1SG.

•ELSTUB, Mr. Maurice Clifford, FCA *1967;* BP6, 06740 CHATEAUNEUF DE GRASSE, FRANCE.

ELSTUB, Mr. Nathan Mark, MA ACA *1995;* 8 Ralliwood Road, ASHTEAD, KT21 1DE.

ELSWORTH, Mrs. Elizabeth Joanna, ACA *1992;* (Tax Fac), 7 Margaret Avenue, Shenfield, BRENTWOOD, ESSEX, CM15 8RF.

•ELSWORTH, Mr. Graham Stewart, BCom FCA *1985;* BDO LLP, 125 Colmore Row, BIRMINGHAM, B3 3SD. See also BDO Stoy Hayward LLP

•ELSWORTH, Mr. Stephen Anthony, BA ACA *1992;* with BDO LLP, 55 Baker Street, LONDON, W1U 7EU.

ELSWORTH, Mr. Stephen Mark, BSc FCA *1984;* Yorkshire Bldg Soc Yorkshire House, Yorkshire Drive, BRADFORD, WEST YORKSHIRE, BD5 8LJ.

ELTON, Mr. Christopher Peter, BSc ACA *1988;* 70B High Street, Hook, GOOLE, DN14 5NY.

ELTON, Mr. Neil Anthony, MA ACA *1998;* Sagentia Ltd Harston Mill, Royston Road Harston, CAMBRIDGE, CB22 7GG.

ELTON, Mr. Richard James, BA ACA *1999;* 103 Woodford Road, Bramhall, STOCKPORT, CHESHIRE, SK7 1QB.

ELTRINGHAM, Mr. Jeffrey, FCA *1972;* 1322 Brock Road RR4, DUNDAS L9H 5E4, ON, CANADA.

ELVER, Mr. Keith Edward, BA FCA *1982;* Curlew House, Water Street, Morland, PENRITH, CA10 3AY.

ELVEY, Mr. Gordon Chester, BSc ACA *1993;* 44 Grange Gardens, PINNER, MIDDLESEX, HA5 5QE.

•ELVIDGE, Mr. Brian Patrick, FCA *1973;* with Smailes Goldie, Regents Court, Princess Street, HULL, HU2 8BA.

ELVIDGE, Mrs. Carol Ann, BSc ACA *1989;* 35 Claremont Avenue, Bramcote, NOTTINGHAM, NG9 3DG.

ELVIDGE, Mr. Christopher Edric David, BA ACA *1987;* 35 Claremont Avenue, Bramcote, NOTTINGHAM, NG9 3DG.

ELVIDGE, Mr. Hamish Murray Andrew, FCA *1978;* Arrow Lane House, Arrow Lane, Hartley Wintney, HOOK, RG27 8LR.

ELVIDGE, Mrs. Helen Katherine, BA ACA CTA *2005;* with PricewaterhouseCoopers LLP, Abacus House, Castle Park, CAMBRIDGE, CB3 0AN.

ELVIDGE, Mrs. Richarda Anne, BBS ACA *1995;* Park Farm House, Heythrop, CHIPPING NORTON, OXFORDSHIRE, OX7 5TW.

ELVIN, Mr. John Lloyd, FCA *1972;* 22 Beamish Way, Winslow, BUCKINGHAM, MK18 3EU.

ELVIN, Mr. Jonathan Robert, BSc FCA *1983;* 12 Beaumaris Grove, Shenley Church End, MILTON KEYNES, MK5 6EN.

ELVIN, Mr. Richard Alfred, FCA *1973;* Axa UK Plc, Civic Drive, IPSWICH, SUFFOLK, IP1 2AN.

ELVISS, Mr. Michael Anthony, FCA *1972;* Overdale, St Johns Park, Menston, ILKLEY, LS29 6ES.

ELVY, Mr. Brian Warwick, FCA *1968;* Walnut Tree House, 34 Chapel Lane, Blean, CANTERBURY, CT2 9HE.

ELWARD, Miss. Nicola Rachel, ACA *2008;* 74 Lincoln Road, ENFIELD, MIDDLESEX, EN1 1JU.

ELWELL, Mr. David Geoffrey, BSc ACA *2005;* 1 Fentham Close, Hampton-in-Arden, SOLIHULL, B92 0BE.

ELWELL, Mr. Geoffrey Michael, FCA *1993;* 7 Ryan Close, Ruislip Manor, RUISLIP, MIDDLESEX, HA4 9LB.

ELWELL, Miss. Karen Marie, BSc FCA *1987;* 23 Gladstone Road, Dorridge, SOLIHULL, B93 8BX.

ELWELL, Mr. Mark, BSc ACA *1998;* 23 Craven Hill Mews, LONDON, W2 3DY.

ELWES, Mr. George Romano Cary, LLB FCA *1975;* Blunham House, Blunham, BEDFORD, MK44 3NJ.

•ELWICK, Mr. Brian, FCA *1977;* (Tax Fac), Brian Elwick and Co Limited, 35 Mill Road, Swanland, NORTH FERRIBY, NORTH HUMBERSIDE, HU14 3PJ.

ELWIG, Mr. Simon Philip, BSc ACA *1992;* Level 2 Tower 1, 201 Sussex Street, SYDNEY, NSW 2000, AUSTRALIA.

ELWIN, Mr. George Andrew, BSc FCA *1990;* 77 Laustrasse, Sonnenberg, 70597 STUTTGART, GERMANY.

ELWIN, Mr. John Alured, FCA *1960;* 10 Lindsay Avenue, Cheadle Hulme, CHEADLE, CHESHIRE, SK8 7BQ. (Life Member)

ELWOOD, Mr. Michael Edward, FCA *1961;* 68 Watt Lane, SHEFFIELD, S10 5RE.

ELY, Mr. Adam David, ACA *2010;* Flat 14, Vibeca Apartments, 7 Chicksand Street, LONDON, E1 5LD.

ELY, Mr. Thomas Anthony, FCA *1963;* Coneygree, High Street, Harlaxton, GRANTHAM, NG32 1JD. (Life Member)

EMADI ALLAHYARI, Miss. Aida, BSc ACA *2009;* Pricewaterhousecoopers Llp, 1 Hays Lane, LONDON, SE1 2RD.

•EMAMY, Mr. Ali, BSc(Hons) ACA *2002;* Accounts Function Limited, 77 Bassett Green Close, Bassett, SOUTHAMPTON, SO16 3QX.

EMANUEL, Mr. John Clive Lloyd, FCA *1965;* J C L Emanuel, 40 Freemans Close, Stoke Poges, SLOUGH, SL2 4ER.

•EMANUEL, Mr. Justin Olabode, FCA *1960;* PO Box 1443, LAGOS, NIGERIA.

•EMANUEL, Mr. Maurice Seymour, FCA *1978;* M. Emanuel, 5 Lexham Gardens Mews, Kensington, LONDON, W8 5JQ.

EMARA, Mrs. Helen, ACA *1998;* 270 Higham Hill Road, LONDON, E17 5RQ.

EMARY, Mr. Simon Paul, MA BA FCA *1988;* 1 Poplar Rise, Wappenham, TOWCESTER, NORTHAMPTONSHIRE, NN12 8RR.

EMBERSON, Mrs. Catherine Mary, ACA *1990;* Red Linch, 19 Rothamsted Avenue, HARPENDEN, AL5 2DN.

EMBERSON, Mrs. Ellen, ACA *2003;* 10 Church Lane, WALLINGFORD, OXFORDSHIRE, OX10 0DX.

EMBERSON, Mr. John, ACA *1984;* Red Linch, 19 Rothamsted Avenue, HARPENDEN, AL5 2DN.

EMBERTON, Mr. Barry Antony, BSc ACA *1989;* 22 Brentwood Road, Swinton, MANCHESTER, M27 0EE.

•EMBIRICOS, Mr. Alexander Peter, FCA *1964;* with Watts Gregory LLP, Elfed House, Oak Tree Court, Mulberry Drive, Cardiff Gate Business Park Pontprennau, CARDIFF CF23 8RS.

EMBLEM, Mr. Marc Gareth Patrick, BSc ACA *2006;* U B S AG, 100 Liverpool Street, LONDON, EC2M 2RH.

EMBLETON, Mrs. Bernice Ann, BSc ACA *2003;* Talk Talk Group, 11 Evesham Street, LONDON, W11 4AR.

EMBLEY, Miss. Deborah Jayne, BA ACA *1990;* Flat 1, 64 Cromwell Avenue, LONDON, N6 5HQ.

EMBLEY, Mr. Mark, LLB ACA *1992;* 29 Pilkington Avenue, SUTTON COLDFIELD, WEST MIDLANDS, B72 1LA.

EMBREY, Mrs. Jacqueline Gaylor, BA ACA *1982;* 131 Northfield Road, Kings Norton, BIRMINGHAM, B30 1EA.

EMBREY, Mr. John Derek, FCA *1968;* Nimrod House, Muckhart, DOLLAR, CLACKMANNANSHIRE, FK14 7JH.

EMBUREY, Mrs. Pauline Teresa, BA ACA *1985;* Winterstoke, Logs Hill Close, CHISLEHURST, BR7 5LP.

EMBUREY, Mr. Philip George, BA FCA *1980;* Winterstoke, Logs Hill Close, CHISLEHURST, BR7 5LP.

EMBY, Mr. Alan Trevor, FCA *1958;* 54 Eastern Esplanade, BROADSTAIRS, CT10 1DU. (Life Member)

EMEMBOLU, Mr. Oranye, BA ACA *2005;* Floor 5 Tower Place East, Marsh Ltd, 1 Tower Place West, LONDON, EC3R 5BU.

EMENS, Mr. Timothy Michael, BA ACA *1992;* Lexmark Canada Inc, 50 Leek Crescent, Richmond Hill, RICHMOND HILL L4B 4J3, ON, CANADA.

EMERSON, Mr. Brian, BA FCA *1973;* Exmert Building Products Group Ltd, Greatham Street, HARTLEPOOL, TS25 1PR.

•EMERSON, Mrs. Claire, BA ACA CTA *1998;* GN Emerson Ltd, Common House, Gelt Road, BRAMPTON, CUMBRIA, CA8 1QQ. See also Emerson & Co

EMERSON, Mr. Clive Lewis, BA ACA *1996;* 9 West Wick, Downton, SALISBURY, SP5 3FH.

EMERSON, Mr. Duncan, BSc ACA *1982;* Huntsman Europe BVBA, Everslaan 45, 3078 EVERBERG, BELGIUM.

EMERSON, Mrs. Heather Margaret, MA ACA *1981;* 6 Church Close, Benson, WALLINGFORD, OX10 6TA.

EMERSON, Mr. John, MSc BA ACA *1982;* Matrix Group Ltd, 1 Vine Street, LONDON, W1J 0AH.

EMERSON, Mrs. Katherine Mary, MA ACA *1978;* Tudor Glade, 12 Ashley Rise, WALTON-ON-THAMES, KT12 1ND.

EMERSON, Mr. Matthew Charles, BA ACA *1993;* 30 Nightingale Road, GUILDFORD, GU1 1ER.

EMERSON, Mr. Michael John, BA ACA *1982;* Scholekster 1, 3755 EA EEMNES, NETHERLANDS.

EMERSON, Mr. Richard John, FCA *1972;* Creeve, The Mount, Barley, ROYSTON, SG8 8JH.

EMERSON, Mr. Robert Daniel, MA FCA *1956;* The Old Rectory, 5-6 Prima Road, LONDON, SW9 0NA. (Life Member)

EMERSON, Mr. Roger, MA FCA *1975;* 12 Ashley Rise, WALTON-ON-THAMES, SURREY, KT12 1ND. (Life Member)

EMERTON, Ms. Caroline Mary, MA FCA DChA *1982;* 20 Beaufort Road, TWICKENHAM, TW1 2PQ.

EMERTON, Mrs. Elizabeth Jane, BSc ACA *1986;* 59 Wolsey Road, EAST MOLESEY, SURREY, KT8 9EW.

•EMERTON, Mr. Leslie David, FCA *1981;* 26 Hinton Wood Avenue, Highcliffe, CHRISTCHURCH, DORSET, BH23 5AH.

EMERTON, Mr. Richard Paul, BA ACA *1986;* Korn Ferry Whitehead Mann, Ryder Court, 14 Ryder Street, LONDON, SW1Y 6QB.

EMERY, Mr. Alan Michael, FCA *1968;* 202 Castle Hill Road, WALSALL, WS9 9DB.

EMERY, Miss. Anna Marie, BSc ACA *2003;* Flat 2, 128 Old Woolwich Road, LONDON, SE10 9PR.

EMERY, Mr. Antony Steven, BA ACA *1986;* Financial Limited, 78 Woolbrook Road, SIDMOUTH, DEVON, EX10 9XB.

EMERY, Mr. Christopher Charles, BA ACA *1997;* 17 Daneacre Road, RADSTOCK, BA3 3JS.

EMERY, Mr. David, FCA *1971;* 1 Whitebirk Close, Greenmount, BURY, LANCASHIRE, BL8 4HE. (Life Member)

EMERY, Mr. David, BEng ACA *2011;* Orianda, 4 Allez Court, La Ramee, St Peter Port, GUERNSEY, GY1 2EW.

EMERY, Mr. Dominic, ACA *2008;* 29 Highbury Park, LONDON, N5 1TH.

EMERY, Mrs. Gillian Ann, BA ACA *1990;* 90 Ridgeway Road, Long Ashton, BRISTOL, BS41 9HA.

EMERY, Mr. James Richard William, FCA *1968;* Tretawn, St Christophers Cl, Little Kingshill, GREAT MISSENDEN, HP16 0DU. (Life Member)

EMERY, Miss. Joanna Catherine, BSc ACA *2006;* with Moore Stephens LLP, 150 Aldersgate Street, LONDON, EC1A 4AB.

•EMERY, Mr. John Cochrane, FCA CTA *1972;* John C. Emery & Co, 20 Bodiam Road, Greenmount, BURY, BL8 4DW.

EMERY, Mr. John Keith, FCA *1971;* Tudor CottageWye Road, Boughton Aluph ASHFORD, Kent, TN25 4HZ.

EMERY, Mr. John Richard, FCA *1961;* 23 Highview Way, Patcham, BRIGHTON, BN1 8WS.

EMERY, Miss. Kate Anne, ACA *2004;* John Wiley & Sons Ltd, The Atrium, Southern Gate, Terminus Road, CHICHESTER, WEST SUSSEX PO19 8SQ.

•EMERY, Mr. Kenneth John, FCA *1955;* (Tax Fac), Kenneth Emery, 7 Stencills Drive, WALSALL, WS4 2HP.

•EMERY, Mrs. Margaret Ruth, FCA *1971;* Margaret Emery, Tretawn, St Christopher Close, Little Kingshill, GREAT MISSENDEN, HP16 0DU.

EMERY, Mrs. Marie Lovise, ACA *2008;* with PricewaterhouseCoopers DA, Bjørvika, Postboks 748, Sentrum, NO-0106 OSLO, NORWAY.

EMERY, Mr. Martin Edwin, FCA *1966;* High Hurst, Reigate Hill, REIGATE, SURREY, RH2 9PL.

•EMERY, Mr. Michael Joseph, ACA *1981;* Michael J Emery & Co Limited, 22 St. John Street, NEWPORT PAGNELL, BUCKINGHAMSHIRE, MK16 8HJ.

EMERY, Mr. Michael Peter, FCA *1957;* 18 The Brambles, Clayton, NEWCASTLE, ST5 4JJ. (Life Member)

EMERY, Mr. Paul Stephen, BSc(Hons) ACA *2001;* (Tax Fac), 11 Henderson Place, Epping Green, HERTFORD, SG13 8GA.

EMERY, Mr. Peter Francis, FCA *1981;* 1988 West 4th Avenue, VANCOUVER V6J 1M5, BC, CANADA.

EMERY, Mr. Philip John, BA ACA *1989;* 4 Blyth's Wharf, Narrow Street, LONDON, E14 8BF.

EMERY, Mr. Richard St John, BA ACA *1995;* 15 Dighton Road, LONDON, SW18 1AN.

EMERY, Mr. Richard William, BSc FCA *1976;* 3 Clendon Court, VERMONT SOUTH, VIC 3133, AUSTRALIA.

EMERY, Mr. Robert George, MA FCA *1963;* 7 Tassel Road, BURY ST. EDMUNDS, SUFFOLK, IP32 7LN.

EMERY, Mrs. Samantha Wing Yeung, BSc ACA *2006;* Carillion Contruction, Construction House, 24 Birch Street, WOLVERHAMPTON, WV1 4HY.

EMERY, Miss. Sarah Jane, BSc(Hons) ACA *2002;* 8 Riverbanks Close, HARPENDEN, HERTFORDSHIRE, AL5 5EJ.

•①EMERY, Mr. Simon David, MA ACA *1997;* with Moorfields Corporate Recovery LLP, 88 Wood Street, LONDON, EC2V 7QR.

EMERY, Mr. Simon David John, BSc ACA *1988;* 90 Ridgeway Road, Long Ashton, BRISTOL, BS41 9HA.

EMERY, Mr. Simon Richard, BSc ACA *1995;* Barclays Capital, 1 Snowhill, BIRMINGHAM, B2 5AL.

EMERY, Mrs. Stephanie, ACA *1985;* 14 Chestnut Grove, FLEET, GU51 3LW.

•EMERY, Mr. Stephen William, ACA *1979;* Condy Mathias, 6 Houndiscombe Road, PLYMOUTH, PL4 6HH.

EMERY, Mrs. Vikki-Louise, BA ACA *2002;* 3 Brighton Avenue, WIGSTON, LEICESTERSHIRE, LE18 1JA.

EMES, Mr. David, MEng ACA *2000;* 80 Tolworth Park Road, SURBITON, SURREY, KT6 7RH.

EMES, Mr. Michael William, BSc ACA *2004;* with PricewaterhouseCoopers LLP, 1 Embankment Place, LONDON, WC2N 6RH.

EMKES, Mr. Daniel Georg, BA ACA *1986;* Harrow School The Bursary, 5 High Street, HARROW, HA1 3HP.

EMKES, Mrs. Jacqueline Mary, MEd BSc ACA *1987;* 10 Rothsay Gardens, BEDFORD, MK40 3QB.

EMLY, Mrs. Hollie, BSc ACA *2005;* with BDO LLP, 2 City Place, Beehive Ring Road, GATWICK, WEST SUSSEX, RH6 0PA.

EMLY, Mr. Timothy James, BA ACA *2005;* 63 Camden Road, SEVENOAKS, TN13 3LU.

EMM, Mr. Andrew Timothy, ACA *1979;* 79 Kelvin Road, LEAMINGTON SPA, CV32 7TG.

EMM, Mr. Philip Anthony, FCA *1949;* 28 The Fairways, LEAMINGTON SPA, CV32 6PR. (Life Member)

EMMANOUILIDIS, Mr. Alexander, MSc FCA *1989;* Calea Dorobantilor 36-40, Ap. 42, Sc.B Et. 5, 010573 BUCHAREST, ROMANIA.

EMMANUEL, Miss. Eileen Elizabeth, LLB FCA *1996;* 47 Brynland Avenue, Bishopston, BRISTOL, BS7 9DX.

EMMANUEL, Mr. Maurice Balendran, ACA ACMA MBA *2007;* 11 Crescent Gardens, RUISLIP, MIDDLESEX, HA4 8SZ.

EMMENS, Miss. Katherine Louise, MA ACA MCT *1993;* Casinostr 10, 4052 BASEL, SWITZERLAND.

EMMERSON, Mr. David Michael Irvin, FCA *1964;* Wellfield, Alnmouth, ALNWICK, NE66 2RA. (Life Member)

EMMERSON, Mr. Duncan James, BA ACA *2000;* 62 Chaworth Road, West Bridgford, NOTTINGHAM, NG2 7AD.

EMMERSON, Mr. George Alexander, BA FCA *1971;* Sperrbergstrasse 49, 2384 BREITENFURT, AUSTRIA. (Life Member)

EMMERSON, Mr. Martyn Lewis, MA ACA *1996;* Flat 3, 9a Dallington Street, LONDON, EC1V 0BQ.

EMMERSON, Mr. Michael, ACA *1980;* Mechelsestraat 1, 2587 XW THE HAGUE, ZUID HOLLAND, NETHERLANDS.

EMMERSON, Mr. Nicholas John, ACA *2009;* Icap Middle East 43rd Floor Bahrain Financial Harbour, MANAMA, PO BOX5488, BAHRAIN.

EMMERSON, Mr. Patrick John Maclean, FCA *1972;* 23 Richmond Drive, Mapperley, NOTTINGHAM, NG3 5EL.

•EMMERSON, Mr. Paul, BSc ACA *1991;* Smith Emmerson Accountants LLP, H5 Ash Tree Court, Nottingham Business Park, NOTTINGHAM, NG8 6PY. See also Smith Emmerson Audit Limited

EMMERSON, Mr. Philip Raymond, BA ACA *2000;* 24 Stamford Road, Exton, OAKHAM, LE15 8AZ.

EMMERSON, Mr. Richard John, ACA *1994;* 10 Beverley Road, WHITLEY BAY, TYNE AND WEAR, NE25 8JH.

EMMERSON, Mr. Robert Ian, BSc FCA *1971;* 2 Tynedale Terrace, HEXHAM, NE46 3JE.

EMMERSON, Mr. Robin Wade, MA(Oxon) ACA *2009;* La Motte, La Motte Road, St. Martin, GUERNSEY, GY4 6ER.

EMMERSON, Mrs. Victoria Jane, MA ACA *1995;* Kenmore, Harwoods Lane, EAST GRINSTEAD, WEST SUSSEX, RH19 4NQ.

EMMET, Mr. Robert Anthony Bernard, BSc FCA *1986;* Seabeach House, Halnaker, CHICHESTER, PO18 0LX.

EMMETT, Mr. Andrew James Skene, FCA *1982;* 10 Highfields, Fetcham, LEATHERHEAD, KT22 9XA.

•EMMETT, Mr. Clive, FCA *1959;* Emmett & Co (Nelson) Ltd, 11 Market Square, NELSON, BB9 7LP.

EMMETT, Mr. Danny, MSc BA(Hons) ACA *2009;* 42 Fairywell Road, Timperley, ALTRINCHAM, CHESHIRE, WA15 6UZ.

EMMETT, Miss. Elizabeth Claire, BSc ACA *2009;* Chy Nyverow, Newham Road, TRURO, tr12dp.

EMMETT, Mr. John Sydney Douglas, FCA *1969;* PO Box 1727, CPO Seeb, Postal Code 111, 111 MUSCAT, OMAN.

EMMETT, Mr. Matthew Dominic, BA ACA *2000;* 23, Eton Grove, NOTTINGHAM, NG8 1FT.

•EMMETT, Mr. Richard Alan, MA ACA *1984;* 33 Alderside Walk, Englefield Green, EGHAM, SURREY, TW20 0LX.

EMMINS, Mr. Mark Anthony, BSc ACA *1994;* Goldman Sachs International Internal Audit, Peterborough Court 133 Fleet Street, LONDON, EC4A 2BB.

EMMOTT, Mr. Adam James, BA ACA *2004;* 1 Airedale Drive, Horsforth, LEEDS, LS18 5ED.

EMMOTT, Mr. Andrew Richard, BSc ACA *1999;* The Old Vicarage, Bilton-in-Ainsty, YORK, YO26 7NN.

•EMMOTT, Mr. Niel Jonathan, BA FCA CF FSI *1993;* 41a Hill Top Road, Newmillerdam, WAKEFIELD, WEST YORKSHIRE, WF2 6PZ.

EMMOTT, Mrs. Rachel Elizabeth, BSc ACA *2006;* 1 Airedale Drive, Horsforth, LEEDS, LS18 5ED.

EMMOTT, Mr. Richard David, BA ACA *1984;* 3 The Boulevard Ascot Road, WATFORD, WD18 8AG.

EMMS, Mr. Anthony Leonard, FCA *1982;* 33 Hume Avenue #09-05, Symphony Heights, Upper Bukit Timah, SINGAPORE 598734, SINGAPORE.

EMMS, Ms. Hannah Elizabeth, BSc ACA *2005;* Capital & Regional PLC, 52 Grosvenor Gardens, LONDON, SW1W 0AU.

EMMS, Mr. Paul David, BA ACA *1992;* 28 Dragon View, HARROGATE, NORTH YORKSHIRE, HG1 4DG.

EMMS, Mr. Theodore Robert, MA FCA *1972;* Frogmore House, Drakelow Lane, Wolverley, KIDDERMINSTER, DY11 5XE.

EMNEY, Mr. Mark, BSc ACA *1994;* 29 Coronation Street, EAST BRIGHTON, VIC 3187, AUSTRALIA.

EMNEY, Mr. Paul, BA ACA *1991;* Barclays Bank Plc, 1 Churchill Place, LONDON, E14 5HP.

EMONSON, Mrs. Ruth Anne, BSc ACA *2002;* 8 College Gardens, Radbrook, SHREWSBURY, SHROPSHIRE, SY3 9BF.

EMPEY, Mrs. Rachel Clare, MA ACA *2001;* Danzigerstrasse 3, 80805 MUNICH, GERMANY.

EMPRINGHAM, Mrs. Catherine Mary, BSc ACA *1997;* 18 Lyndhurst Close, Downley, HIGH WYCOMBE, BUCKINGHAMSHIRE, HP13 5JD.

EMPSON, Mr. Christopher Anthony, BA(Hons) ACA *2000;* 39 Brockhurst Lane, Dickens heath, SOLIHULL, B90 1RG.

EMPSON, Ms. Gina, BSc FCA *1983;* ICS Corporate Services S.A., Quai du Mont-Blanc 29, 1201 GENEVA, SWITZERLAND.

EMPSON, Miss. Kirsten Louise, BA ACA *2006;* 16 Bracon, Belton, DONCASTER, SOUTH YORKSHIRE, DN9 1QP.

EMPSON, Mrs. Lisa, BSc(Hons) ACA *2000;* 103b Doncaster Road, Tickhill, DONCASTER, SOUTH YORKSHIRE, DN11 9JB.

EMPSON, Mrs. Lucy Rachel, BA(Hons) ACA *2000;* 39 Brockhurst Lane, Shirley, SOLIHULL, B90 1RG.

EMRITH, Miss. Firdaus Bibi, ACA *2008;* Flat b, 53 Woodland Way, LONDON, NW7 2JP.

EMSDEN, Mr. Kenneth Victor, FCA *1958;* 14 Priory Drive, Abbey Wood, LONDON, SE2 0PP. (Life Member)

EMSDEN, Miss. Lucy Elizabeth Naomi, BA ACA *1988;* 38 Bridge End, WARWICK, CV34 6PB.

EMSDEN, Mr. Reginald Christopher, FCA *1960;* (Tax Fac), Derwent, Keswick Road, ORPINGTON, KENT, BR6 0EU. (Life Member)

EMSLEY, Mrs. Anna, ACA *2010;* 23 Oakwood Close, REDHILL, RH1 4BE.

EMSLEY, Mrs. Christine, BSc ACA *1979;* 4 Old School Orchard, Watton-at-Stone, HERTFORD, SG14 3SS.

•EMSLEY, Mr. Paul Stewart, BSc FCA *1981;* Clement Rabjohns, 111-113 High Street, EVESHAM, WR11 4XP. See also Clemrab LLP and Clement Rabjohns Limited

EMSLEY, Mr. Stephen, ACA *2011;* 56 Leathermarket Court, LONDON, SE1 3HS.

EMSLIE, Mrs. Caroline Patricia, BSc ACA *1994;* (Tax Fac), 4 Trimmers Wood, HINDHEAD, GU26 6PN.

EMSON, Mr. Alan Leslie, FCA *1965;* 93 Fitz Roy Avenue, Harborne, BIRMINGHAM, B17 8RG. (Life Member)

EMSON, Mr. Stephen Paul, MA FCA *1984;* 10 Magnolia Close, Park Street, ST. ALBANS, AL2 2PP.

•ENDACOTT, Mr. Jonathan Leonard, BSc(Econ) FCA CTA *1992;* (Tax Fac), Winter Rule LLP, Lowin House, Tregolls Road, TRURO, CORNWALL, TR1 2NA. See also Francis Clark LLP

ENDACOTT, Mr. Richard John, FCA *1965;* Appletree Cottage, 11 Hocketts Close, Whitchurch Hill, READING, RG8 7PZ.

•ENDEACOTT, Mr. Jonathan Craig, BA ACA *1994;* (Tax Fac), Jon Endeacott Ltd, 66 Meols Drive, Hoylake, WIRRAL, MERSEYSIDE, CH47 4AW. See also Endeacott Jon C

ENDEAN, Mr. Stephen Charles, BSocSc ACA *1987;* Tradex Insurance Company Limited, Victory House, 7 Selsdon Way, LONDON, E14 9GL.

ENDEMANO, Mrs. Alison, BSc ACA *1998;* 32 Kingston Road, TEDDINGTON, MIDDLESEX, TW11 9HX.

ENDEMANO, Mr. Mark, BSc FCA *1996;* Buena Vista International Television, 3 Queen Caroline Street, Hammersmith, LONDON, W6 9PE.

ENDERBY, Miss. Leonie Jane, BA ACA *2002;* G/A 38 Siena One, DISCOVERY BAY, HONG KONG SAR.

ENDERBY, Miss. Tracey Margaret, BSc FCA *1997;* International Dept 4th Floor, British Red Cross Society, 44 Moorfields, LONDON, EC2Y 9AL.

ENDERSBEE, Mr. Bryan Joseph, FCA *1960;* 8 Ambrose Close, ORPINGTON, KENT, BR6 9UD. (Life Member)

ENDERSBY, Mr. Mark Richard, BA ACA *1992;* Funding Solutions UK Ltd The Lansdowne Building, 2 Lansdowne Road, CROYDON, SURREY, CR9 2ER.

ENDERSBY, Mr. Paul, LLB ACA *2004;* LivingstonePartners, Correos 12 1° 1ª, 46002 VALENCIA, SPAIN.

•ENDICOTT, Mr. David John, FCA *1970;* (Tax Fac), David Endicott, 47 Ashwood Drive, BROADSTONE, DORSET, BH18 8LN. See also David Endicott & Co

ENDICOTT, Mrs. Linda Doreen, BA FCA *1983;* Scords Farmhouse, Scords Lane, Toys Hill, WESTERHAM, TN16 1QE.

ENDICOTT, Mr. Peter, BSc FCA *1967;* 54 Conyngham Road, Weston Favell, NORTHAMPTON, NN3 9TA.

ENEFER, Mr. Steven Charles, BA ACA *2004;* 17 Upland Drive, COLCHESTER, CO4 0QA.

ENEVOLDSON, Mrs. Leigh, BSc ACA *1985;* 50 Grandison Road, LONDON, SW11 6LW.

•ENEVOLDSON, Mr. William Anderson, BA FCA *1984;* KPMG LLP, St. James's Square, MANCHESTER, M2 6DS. See also KPMG Europe LLP

•ENG, Mr. Ernest, FCA *1959;* Ernest Eng, Lynwood, Mayfield Road, WEYBRIDGE, KT13 8XD.

ENGEL, Mr. Ian, MA FCA *1956;* Well Cottage, 22d East Heath Road, LONDON, NW3 1AJ. (Life Member)

•ENGEL, Mrs. Karen Louise, BA ACA *2000;* Business Nurture Limited, 54 Farmleigh Gardens, Great Sankey, WARRINGTON, WA5 3FA.

•ENGEL, Mr. Kevin Michael, ACA *1995;* Grant Thornton UK LLP, 4 Hardman Square, Spinningfields, MANCHESTER, M3 3EB. See also Grant Thornton LLP

ENGELBERTS, Mrs. Jacqueline Tracey, BSc ACA *1996;* Prins Hendriklaan 31, 3721 AN BILTHOVEN, NETHERLANDS.

ENGELBRECHT, Mrs. Sally Elizabeth Anne, BA ACA *2004;* 49 Holtspur Top Lane, BEACONSFIELD, BUCKINGHAMSHIRE, HP9 1DR.

ENGELMANN, Miss. Veronique, BA(Hons) ACA *2010;* 3 Beulah Street, KING'S LYNN, NORFOLK, PE30 4DN.

•ENGELSMAN, Mr. Henry Louis, FCA *1979;* Engelsman & Co, The Estate House, 201 High Road, CHIGWELL, ESSEX, IG7 5BJ. See also DTA Services Ltd

ENGIDA, Mr. Getachew, MBA BA FCA *1984;* Deputy Director-General, UNESCO, 7 Place de Fontenoy, 75352 PARIS, FRANCE.
ENGINEER, Mr. Ferjan Jamshed, FCA *1972;* Engineer & Mehta, 45/47 Bombay Samachar Marg, Bank of Maharashtra Building, 5th Floor, MUMBAI 400 023, MAHARASHTRA INDIA.
•**ENGINEER, Mr. Ratan Jal, FCA** *1977;* Ernst & Young LLP, 1 More London Place, LONDON, SE1 2AF. See also Ernst & Young Europe LLP
ENGLAND, Mr. Andrew Mark, BA ACA CTA *2001;* (Tax Fac), with Menzies LLP, 3rd Floor Kings House, 12-42 Wood Street, KINGSTON UPON THAMES, SURREY, KT1 1TG.
ENGLAND, Mr. Anthony David, MSocSc FCA *1967;* Luce's Farm, Rockhampton, BERKELEY, GL13 9DU.
ENGLAND, Mr. David Michael, MA ACA *1988;* 119 Teddington Park Road, TEDDINGTON, MIDDLESEX, TW11 8NG.
ENGLAND, Mr. Gordon Edward Richard, FCA *1964;* 2 Hepburn Court, Kings Avenue, CHRISTCHURCH, DORSET, BH23 1NS. (Life Member)
ENGLAND, Mr. Graham Martyn, BA FCA *1981;* (Tax Fac), 3a Hillside Way, WELWYN, AL6 0TY.
ENGLAND, Mr. James, BSc ACA *2011;* 94 Upper Meadow Road, Quinton, BIRMINGHAM, B32 1NS.
ENGLAND, Mr. James Joseph, BSc ACA *1979;* 6 Minster Drive, Bowdon, ALTRINCHAM, WA14 3FA.
ENGLAND, Mr. John, FCA *1972;* 9 Beverley Avenue, LONDON, SW20 0RL.
ENGLAND, Mr. John, BSc FCA *1984;* 37 Midhaven Rise, WESTON-SUPER-MARE, AVON, BS22 9LT.
ENGLAND, Mr. John Christopher, FCA *1961;* Town Head House, 28 Town Head, Honley, HOLMFIRTH, HD9 6BW.
ENGLAND, Mrs. Julie, MA BSc FCA ILTM *1991;* 42 Maes Gweryl, CONWY, GWYNEDD, LL32 8RU.
ENGLAND, Mrs. Karen Jean, BA ACA *1987;* Woodlands, Bradley Lane, PUDSEY, LS28 8LH.
ENGLAND, Miss. Karen Margaret, BA ACA *1995;* The Morocco Store, Flat 3, 1 Leathermarket Street, LONDON, SE1 3HN.
ENGLAND, Mr. Lawrence Geoffrey, FCA *1954;* 11 Laburnum Crescent, Wadham Park, CREWKERNE, TA18 7BS. (Life Member)
ENGLAND, Mr. Nigel, FCA *1985;* Suite #231, Private Bag X1, Melrose Arch, JOHANNESBURG, 2076, SOUTH AFRICA.
ENGLAND, Mr. Norman Clifford, FCA *1952;* Saxbre, Birchen Lane, HAYWARDS HEATH, RH16 1SA. (Life Member)
ENGLAND, Mrs. Patricia Anne, MSc BSc ACA *1983;* 12 Claystones, West Hunsbury, NORTHAMPTON, NN4 9UY.
ENGLAND, Miss. Sally Yolanda, FCA *1974;* 40A Campden Hill Court, Campden Hill Road, LONDON, W8 7HU.
•**ENGLAND, Mrs. Theresa Man Tuen, ACA** *2004;* England & Co, 18 Trevecca Terrace, LISKEARD, CORNWALL, PL14 6RH.
ENGLAND, Mr. William James Guy, MA ACA *1995;* The Sundial, Horn Lane, East Hendred, WANTAGE, OXFORDSHIRE, OX12 8LD.
ENGLARD, Mr. Jonathan Aron, FCA *1992;* 49 Russell Gardens, LONDON, NW11 9NJ.
ENGLEBERT, Mr. Mark, BCom ACA *1994;* 1 Hickory Road, Quinns Rocks, PERTH, WA 6030, AUSTRALIA.
ENGLEBRIGHT, Mr. Drew, BSc ACA *1996;* Mediaedge CIA, 1 Paris Garden, LONDON, SE1 8NU.
ENGLEFIELD, Mr. Edward Ashton, FCA *1968;* Westering, Grays Close, HASLEMERE, SURREY, GU27 2LJ.
ENGLER, Mr. Daniel David Merlin, BA ACA *1997;* 83 Corncrake Way, BICESTER, OXFORDSHIRE, OX26 6UF.
ENGLISH, Mr. Adam James, BA ACA *1995;* 27 Pandora Road, LONDON, NW6 1TS.
ENGLISH, Mr. Alfred James, FCA *1964;* 6 The Laurels, Potten End, BERKHAMSTED, HP4 2SP. (Life Member)
ENGLISH, Miss. Claire Joanne, BSc ACA *2007;* 5 Sir Gil Simpson Drive Burnside PO Box 13244, CHRISTCHURCH 8141, NEW ZEALAND.
ENGLISH, Miss. Claire Louise, BSc ACA *2002;* 80 Greenacres, Preston Park Avenue, BRIGHTON, BN1 6HR.
ENGLISH, Mr. Darren John, BA FCA *1993;* Hyder Consulting Pty Ltd, Level 5 141 Walker Street, NORTH SYDNEY, NSW 2060, AUSTRALIA.
ENGLISH, Mr. David Edward, FCA *1965;* Greatwood Cottage, Marley Lane, BATTLE, EAST SUSSEX, TN33 0DQ. (Life Member)
ENGLISH, Mr. David Mark, BA ACA *1995;* with Harold Sharp, Holland House, 1-5 Oakfield, SALE, M33 6TT.
ENGLISH, Miss. Dawn Marie, BSc(Hons) BA(Hons) ACA *2001;* Imperial Tobacco Ltd, PO Box 244, BRISTOL, BS99 7UJ.
ENGLISH, Ms. Elizabeth Anne, BA(Hons) ACA *2000;* 22 Fernleigh Avenue, Levenshulme, MANCHESTER, M19 3LU.
•**ENGLISH, Mrs. Ellen Margaret Mary, MA ACA** *1980;* (Tax Fac), Ellen English, 99 St. James's Drive, LONDON, SW17 7RP.
ENGLISH, Mr. Gerald Anthony, BSc FCA *1974;* 11 Allee du Gaillet, 38240 MEYLAN, FRANCE. (Life Member)
ENGLISH, Miss. Jo, BSc ACA *2004;* 10 Robert Lennox Drive, NORTHPORT, NY 11768, UNITED STATES.
ENGLISH, Mr. John Howard, BSc ACA *1987;* 69 Gloucester Avenue, Shinfield, READING, RG2 9GA.
ENGLISH, Mr. John Owen, FCA *1977;* 111Fairway Drive, HAINES CITY, FL 33844, UNITED STATES.
ENGLISH, Mr. Nicholas Spencer Charles, BSc ACA *1997;* 10 Cromwell Road, HENLEY-ON-THAMES, OXFORDSHIRE, RG9 1JH.
•**ENGLISH, Mr. Nigel Keith, FCA** *1975;* Keith English & Co, Kings Cote, 151B Kings Road, WESTCLIFF-ON-SEA, ESSEX, SS0 8PP.
ENGLISH, Mr. Paul Robert, BA(Hons) ACA *2000;* Tottenham Hotspur Football Club, 748 High Road, LONDON, N17 0AP.
ENGLISH, Mrs. Paula Michelle, BSc ACA *1993;* 22 Baliol Road, HITCHIN, SG5 1TT.
ENGLISH, Mr. Philip Mark, BSc ACA *1994;* APM Terminals Suite 1809, Executive Heights Tecom Site C, Al Barsha, DUBAI, PO 361007, UNITED ARAB EMIRATES.
ENGLISH, Mrs. Philippa Jane, BA ACA *2004;* 4 Cornwell Court, NEWCASTLE UPON TYNE, NE3 1TT.
ENGLISH, Ms. Rachel June, MA FCA *1989;* 139 Maze Hill, LONDON, SE3 7UB.
ENGLISH, Mrs. Rosemary Anne, BSc FCA *1977;* 5 Friston Downs, Off The Brow, Friston, EASTBOURNE, EAST SUSSEX, BN20 0ET.
ENGLISH, Mr. Roy Frederic Charles, FCA *1949;* Flat 16, Hallgate, Blackheath Park, LONDON, SE3 9SG. (Life Member)
ENGLISH, Miss. Sarah, ACA *2009;* Unit 12A/ 21 Manning Road, DOUBLE BAY, NSW 2028, AUSTRALIA.
ENGLISH, Mrs. Sarah Jane, MA ACA *1996;* 17 Madely Close, HORNCASTLE, LN9 6RQ.
ENGLISH, Mrs. Sarah Louise, BSc ACA *2007;* 35 Charles Avenue, GRIMSBY, SOUTH HUMBERSIDE, DN33 2DA.
•**ENGLISH, Mr. Stephen Paul, BA(Hons) ACA CTA** *1999;* with RSM Tenon Audit Limited, 1 Bede Island Road, Bede Island Business Park, LEICESTER, LE2 7EA.
•**ENGLISH, Mr. William, FCA** *1964;* W. English & Co, 121 London Road, KNEBWORTH, HERTFORDSHIRE, SG3 6EX.
ENGLISH, Mr. William Henry, BSc FCA *1979;* with Deloitte & Touche LLP, 3000 Scotia Centre, 700-2nd Street S.W., CALGARY T2P 0S7, AB, CANADA.
ENGWELL, Mrs. Rachel, LLB ACA CTA *2002;* with Ernst & Young LLP, 1 Bridgewater Place, Water Lane, LEEDS, LS11 5QR.
ENNALS, Mrs. Elizaveta, MSc BSc ACA *2009;* Flat 43 Anchorage Point, 42 Cuba Street, LONDON, E14 8NE.
ENNETT, Mr. John Joseph, BCom FCA *1972;* Selbourne House, 32 Mount Hermon Road, WOKING, SURREY, GU22 7UN.
ENNIS, Mrs. Claire Elizabeth, BSc ACA *1990;* Hapag Lloyds (UK) Ltd, Hapag Lloyd House, 48a Cambridge Road, BARKING, ESSEX, IG11 8HH.
ENNIS, Miss. Sarah Louise, BSc(Hons) ACA *2000;* 11 Colbert Avenue, SOUTHEND-ON-SEA, SS1 3BH.
ENOCH, Mr. Melvyn Stuart, FCA *1964;* Traybon Ltd, 8 Rees Drive, STANMORE, MIDDLESEX, HA7 4YN.
ENOCH, Mr. Samuel James, BA ACA *2005;* 346 Hauser Blvd Apt. 414, LOS ANGELES, CA 90036, UNITED STATES.
•**ENOTIADES, Mr. Andrew Michael, MA FCA CF** *1985;* Voutira 22, 16673 ATHENS, GREECE.
ENOTIADOU, Miss. Melina, ACA *2011;* 6 Omirou Street, Engomi, 2407 NICOSIA, CYPRUS.
ENRIGHT, Miss. Ellie Maeve, ACA *2009;* K P M G, 100 Temple Street, BRISTOL, BS1 6AG.
•**ENRIGHT, Mr. Guy Thomas, MA ACA** *1998;* with Deloitte LLP, Athene Place, 66 Shoe Lane, LONDON, EC4A 3BQ.
ENRIGHT, Mrs. Helen Johnstone, MA ACA *1984;* 2nd Floor Alexander House, Church Path, WOKING, GU21 6EJ.
ENRIGHT, Miss. Katherine, ACA *2010;* Flat B, 14 Barnsbury Park, LONDON, N1 1HQ.
ENRIGHT, Mr. Matthew Jonathon, BA ACA *2005;* Trendsetter Home Furnishings Ltd Unit 10, Blackmore Road Stretford, MANCHESTER, M32 0QY.
ENRIGHT, Mr. Michael John, FCA *1977;* 30 Chepstow Place, LONDON, W2 4TA.
•**ENRIGHT, Mr. Peter Maurice, FCA** *1964;* (Tax Fac), M.C. Associates Ltd, 80c Asquith Road, Wigmore, GILLINGHAM, KENT, ME8 0JB.
ENSELL, Mr. David Philip, BSc FCA *1975;* EH Smith Companies, Westhaven House, Arleston Way, Shirley, SOLIHULL, WEST MIDLANDS B90 4LH.
•**ENSER, Mr. David Francis Penhorwood, FCA CF** *1980;* with Bird Luckin limited, Aquila House, Waterloo Lane, CHELMSFORD, CM1 1BN.
ENSKAT, Mr. Matthew Kevin, BSc ACA *1993;* Ridgeway, 15 Claremont Road, Claygate, ESHER, SURREY, KT10 0PL.
•**ENSOR, Miss. Alison Lindsay, BSc FCA** *1992;* (Tax Fac), Foremans LLP, Clayton House, Sandpiper Court, Chester Business Park, CHESTER, CH4 9QU. See also Foremans Company Services Ltd
ENSOR, Miss. Debbie Jayne, BA ACA CTA *1997;* (Tax Fac), 10 Westridge, DUDLEY, DY3 3TQ.
•**ENSOR, Mr. Jonathan Arthur, FCA** *1977;* (Tax Fac), H.G.Field & Co, 2 Guildford Street, CHERTSEY, KT16 9BQ.
ENSOR, Mr. Nicholas Lee, ACA *1983;* 20 Sorrel Close, Wootton, NORTHAMPTON, NORTHAMPTONSHIRE, NN4 6EY.
ENSUM, Mrs. Sally Anne, BA ACA *1990;* Finance Department, University of Hertfordshire, College Lane, HATFIELD, HERTFORDSHIRE, AL10 9AB.
ENTEKHABI, Mr. Massoud, FCA *1979;* Zenith Equity Partners, PO Box 3150, AGOURA HILLS, CA 91376-3150, UNITED STATES.
ENTICKNAP, Mr. Andrew, ACA *1992;* 15 Shakespeare Road, ST.IVES, CAMBRIDGESHIRE, PE27 6TR.
ENTICKNAP, Mr. Matthew, FCA *1973;* 1602 Mathews Terrace, PORTSMOUTH, VA 23704, UNITED STATES.
ENTICOTT, Miss. Kathryn Ann, BSocSc ACA *2002;* I H S Energy Enterprise House, Ilsom, TETBURY, GLOUCESTERSHIRE, GL8 8RX.
ENTICOTT, Mr. Ray, FCA *1957;* Ravens Croft, Plough Lane, Christleton, CHESTER, CH3 7BA. (Life Member)
ENTICOTT, Mr. Robert Frederick, BA ACA *1998;* 400 Campus Drive, FLORHAM PARK, NJ 07932, UNITED STATES.
•**ENTICOTT, Mr. Ronald David, FCA** *1968;* Airde Accountancy, Brant House, 83 Church Road, ADDLESTONE, KT15 1SF.
ENTRACT, Mr. Jonathan Mark, BA ACA *1999;* Karelia, 21 Weybridge Park, WEYBRIDGE, SURREY, KT13 8SQ.
ENTRACT, Mr. Michael, BA FCA *1964;* (Member of Council 1989 - 1993), 20 Walmer Gardens, LONDON, W13 9TS.
ENTWISLE, Mr. James Peter Hallamore, BA ACA *1995;* 5 Abbotswood, Speen, PRINCES RISBOROUGH, BUCKINGHAMSHIRE, HP27 0SR.
ENTWISTLE, Mr. David Graham, BA ACA *1987;* 1 Chaucer Mews, London Road, Upper Harbledown, CANTERBURY, KENT, CT2 9BF.
•**ENTWISTLE, Mr. Leonard, BSc ACA** *1986;* (Tax Fac), Wistle Limited, 290 Blackburn Road, Lynwood, DARWEN, LANCASHIRE, BB3 0AA. See also Len Entwistle
ENTWISTLE, Mr. Mark Ian, BSc ACA *1985;* Fairhurst Douglas Bank House, Wigan Lane, WIGAN, WN1 2TB.
ENTWISTLE, Mr. Paul Joseph, BSc ACA *1982;* 3 Masefield View, ORPINGTON, BR6 8PH.
ENTWISTLE, Mr. Robert William, FCA *1971;* Abercrombie Kent Kenya Ltd, PO Box 59749, NAIROBI, 00200, KENYA.
ENTWISTLE, Mr. Simon Graham, ACA *2009;* 174 The Edge, Clowes Street, SALFORD, M3 5NF.
ENTWISTLE, Mrs. Susan Ruth, BSc ACA *1981;* 711 Checker Drive, BUFFALO GROVE, IL 60089, UNITED STATES.
•**ENTWISTLE, Mr. Timothy John, FCA** *1985;* PKF (UK) LLP, 4th Floor, 3 Hardman Street, MANCHESTER, M3 3HF.
ENZER, Dr. Ian, PhD MSc FCA *1978;* 22 Exeter Walk, Bramhall, STOCKPORT, SK7 2QL.
EPAMINONDAS, Mr. Tassos, BA ACA *2005;* 6 Alkistidos Street, Acropolis, 2007 NICOSIA, CYPRUS.
EPHGRAVE, Mr. Richard Paul, FCA *1976;* 14 Seymour Road, EAST MOLESEY, KT8 0PB.
EPIE, Mr. Loxly Massango, ACA MBA *1993;* GAVI Alliance, 2 Chemin des Mines, 1202 GENEVA, SWITZERLAND.
EPIPHANIOU, Mr. Stelios, BA ACA *2006;* ONISILOU 7, 3075 LIMASSOL, CYPRUS.
EPLETT, Mr. Clive Roger, BCom FCA *1984;* Lower Pitford, 7 Critchmere Lane, HASLEMERE, GU27 1PR.
EPPEL, Mrs. Valerie Helen, BA ACA *1993;* Claridge House, 24 Valencia Road, STANMORE, HA7 4JH.
EPPS, Mr. John Edward, FCA *1962;* P.O.Box 2257, HAMILTON HMJX, BERMUDA.
EPPS, Mr. Stuart Lewis, BA ACA *1997;* 17 Idencroft Close, Pontprennau, CARDIFF, CF23 8PH.
•**EPSTEIN, Mr. Anthony, BSc FCA** *1990;* Gateway Partners Auditing UK Limited, 2nd Floor, 43 Whitfield Street, LONDON, W1T 4HD.
EPSTEIN, Mr. Anthony John, FCA *1962;* 3 Kingsdale Court, 367 Cockfosters Road, BARNET, HERTFORDSHIRE, EN4 0JF.
EPSTEIN, Mr. David, FCA *1966;* with Kingston Smith LLP, Devonshire House, 60 Goswell Road, LONDON, EC1M 7AD.
EPSTEIN, Mr. David Leslie, FCA *1966;* 5 Crooked Usage, Finchley, LONDON, N3 3HD.
•**EPSTEIN, Mr. Edward Ralph, BA FCA** *1974;* Epstein Consultancy, 1 Oakwell Drive, SALFORD, M7 4PY.
•**EPSTEIN, Mr. Gary John, FCA** *1978;* (Tax Fac), with UHY Hacker Young (S.E) Ltd, 168 Church Road, HOVE, EAST SUSSEX, BN3 2DL.
EPSTEIN, Mr. Gerald, FCA *1971;* Tree Tops, Devisdale Road, ALTRINCHAM, WA14 2AT.
•**EPSTEIN, Mr. Jeremy David, ACA** *1980;* Dodd Harris, 35/37 Brent Street, Hendon, LONDON, NW4 2EF.
EPSTEIN, Mr. Maurice, FCA *1955;* 12 Holly Lodge Gardens, Highgate, LONDON, N6 6AA. (Life Member)
•**EPSTEIN, Mr. Michael, BA FCA ATII** *1972;* Abbot & Co, 35 Cavendish Road, SALFORD, M7 4WP.
EPSTEIN, Mr. Raymond, FCA *1955;* 16 Winscombe Way, STANMORE, HA7 3AU. (Life Member)
EPSTEIN, Mr. Stuart David, BA FCA *2000;* 4 Deansway, East Finchley, LONDON, N2 0JF.
EPSTEIN, Mr. Warren Marc, BA ACA *1990;* 10 Adelaide Close, STANMORE, MIDDLESEX, HA7 3EL.
•**EPTON, Mr. Anthony John Walter, BA FCA** *1990;* (Tax Fac), Goldwins Limited, 75 Maygrove Road, West Hampstead, LONDON, NW6 2EG.
EPTON, Mr. Michael Robert, ACA MAAT *2009;* Mitton Aftercare Ltd, Ronnie Hellewell House, 451 Cleckheaton Road, Low Moor, BRADFORD, WEST YORKSHIRE BD12 0HS.
ER, Mr. Boon Chiew, FCA *1974;* Er & Co, 336 Smith Street, 04-302 New Bridge Centre, SINGAPORE 050336, SINGAPORE.
ERACLEOUS, Mr. Andreas, BSc ACA *1996;* IMH Media Ltd, PO Box 52549, 4065 LIMASSOL, CYPRUS.
ERACLEOUS, Miss. Elena, ACA *2011;* 8 Chryseleousis Str, Vorios Polos, 1026 NICOSIA, CYPRUS.
•**ERASMUS, Mr. Andrew David, BSc FCA** *1992;* Aston Hughes & Co, Selby Towers, 29 Princes Drive, COLWYN BAY, LL29 8PE.
ERASMUS, Ms. Magdalena Maria, ACA CA(SA) *2011;* (Tax Fac), Fifth Street 79, Northmead, BENONI, 1501, SOUTH AFRICA.
ERASMUS, Mr. Rupert Edward George, BSc(Hons) ACA *2002;* 147 Westmead Road, SUTTON, SURREY, SM1 4JR.
ERASMUS, Mr. Stefan Oliver, LLB FCA *1997;* 431 Mountain Park Drive SE, CALGARY T2Z 2N9, AB, CANADA.
ERATNE, Mr. Chaminda Lahiru, BSc ACA *2000;* 9 Holly Close, Walmley, SUTTON COLDFIELD, B76 2PD.
ERATNE, Mrs. Sonali Kisara, BSc ACA *2006;* 9 Holly Close, Walmley, SUTTON COLDFIELD, B76 2PD.
ERB, Mr. Jonathan, BSc ACA *1995;* 2 Kingswood Road, West Bridgford, NOTTINGHAM, NG2 7HS.
ERBAN, Mr. Christopher Ferry, BA FCA *1974;* 4 Highwaymans Ridge, WINDLESHAM, GU20 6JY.
ERDAL, Mr. Eral, BSc ACA *2003;* Erdal & Co, 100 Bedrettin Demirel CAD, PO Box 410, LEFKOSA MERSIN 10, TURKEY.
•**ERDAL, Mr. Hussein, FCA** *1968;* Erdal & Co, 100 Bedrettin Demirel CAD, PO Box 410, LEFKOSA MERSIN 10, TURKEY.
ERFANI, Mr. Majid, BSc FCA *1974;* 235 Water Street, Apt. # 406, PRESCOTT K0E 1T0, ON, CANADA.
ERHARDT, Mr. David Anthony, MA ACA *1997;* 4 Marina Views, GIBRALTAR, GIBRALTAR.
ERHARDT, Miss. Louise Catherine, BA ACA *2007;* 14a Selwyn Avenue, RICHMOND, SURREY, TW9 2HA.
•**ERICSON, Mr. Jonathan Mark, BA FCA** *1995;* Baker Tilly Tax & Advisory Services LLP, 12 Gleneagles Court, Brighton Road, CRAWLEY, WEST SUSSEX, RH10 6AD. See also Baker Tilly UK Audit LLP
•**ERICSSON, Mr. Nicholas William Henry, FCA** *1978;* Clark Brownscombe Limited, 8 The Drive, HOVE, EAST SUSSEX, BN3 3JT.

ERIKSEN, Mr. Duncan, ACA *2002;* Flat B, 2nd Floor, Best View Court, 68 MacDonnell Road, MID LEVELS, HONG KONG SAR.

ERIYAGOLLA, Miss. Udani, ACA *2011;* 17 Hoveland Lane, TAUNTON, SOMERSET, TA1 5DD.

ERKUL, Mr. Kenan Thomas, BA(Hons) ACA *2010;* 14 Ludlow Way, Croxley Green, RICKMANSWORTH, HERTFORDSHIRE, WD3 3SH.

ERMAK, Mr. Yusuf, ACA *2009;* 35 Albert Road, LONDON, E10 6NU.

ERMAN, Mr. Alper Ozer, BSc(Econ) ACA *1995;* 26 Finland Street, Surrey Quays, LONDON, SE16 7TP.

ERMAN, Mr. Ozer Kemal, MSc BSc FCA *1968;* 41 Greenfield Avenue, SURBITON, KT5 9HP.

•**ERMEAV, Mr. Stanley John Paul, FCA** *1971;* Horwath Belize, 35a Regent Street, P O Box 756, BELIZE CITY, BELIZE.

ERNEST, Mr. Martin John, BA ACA *1989;* Sameer Investments, 49 Riverside Drive, P.O Box 55358 - 00200, NAIROBI, KENYA.

ERO, Mrs. Charlotte Virginia, BA ACA *1996;* 140 Cambridge Way, PIEDMONT, CA 94611, UNITED STATES.

ERRINGTON, Mrs. Andrea Lynne, BSc ACA CF *1998;* Carabid Consultants LLP, The Station Mill, Station Road, ALRESFORD, HAMPSHIRE, SO24 9JQ.

ERRINGTON, Mr. Christopher Mark, BSc FCA *1996;* Birkdale, Green Lane, Chilworth, SOUTHAMPTON, SO16 7JW.

ERRINGTON, Mr. David, BSc ACA *1982;* Sleepy Hollow, 6 Sandy Way, BOURNEMOUTH, DORSET, BH10 7DL.

•**ERRINGTON, Mr. David Grant, BA ACA** *1983;* The Old Vicarage, 9 Endsleigh Gardens, SURBITON, SURREY, KT6 5JL.

ERRINGTON, Mr. David John, BSc ACA *1993;* Foxstone House, Filedways Forest Green, Nailsworth, STROUD, GL6 0DY.

ERRINGTON, Mr. Graham Paul, FCA *1968;* 31 Firs Walk, Tewin Wood, WELWYN, AL6 0NY.

ERRINGTON, Mr. Mark, ACA *1987;* P J H Group Ltd, Alder House, Slackey Brow, Kearsley, BOLTON, BL4 8SL.

ERRINGTON, Miss. Nadine, ACA *2009;* 2 Queensbury Gate, NEWCASTLE UPON TYNE, NE12 8JW.

ERRINGTON, Mr. Paul, ACA *2008;* 37 Caernarvon Road, NORWICH, NR2 3HZ.

ERRINGTON, Mr. Peter, FCA *1954;* 46 Heol-y-Pentre, Pentyrch, CARDIFF, CF15 9QE. (Life Member)

ERRINGTON, Mr. Richard Roger, BA ACA *1982;* T Crossling & Co Ltd., P.O. Box 5, Coast Road, NEWCASTLE UPON TYNE, NE6 5TP.

•**ERRINGTON, Mr. Robert Norman, FCA** *1972;* Errington Langer Pinner, Pyramid House, 956 High Road, Finchley, LONDON, N12 9RX.

ERRINGTON, Mr. Steven, BA ACA *1998;* 40 Willow Way, Ponteland, NEWCASTLE UPON TYNE, NE20 9RF.

ERRINGTON, Mr. Terence Lee, BSc ACA *2005;* Bank of Scotland, 40 Spring Gardens, MANCHESTER, M2 1EN.

ERSKINE, Miss. Helen Mary, MA FCA *1980;* P O Box 1745, TOPANGA, CA 90290, UNITED STATES.

ERSKINE, Miss. Linda Pauline, BA(Hons) ACA *2002;* Flat 1, 194 Tressillian Road, LONDON, SE4 1XY.

ERSKINE, Mr. Mark David, BA ACA *1996;* 61 Pepys Road, West Wimbledon, LONDON, SW20 8NL.

ERSKINE, Mr. Robert Iain Thomas, BSocSc ACA *1993;* La Rondelle, La Rue De Neuilly, St. Martin, JERSEY, JE3 6JG.

•**ERSKINE, Mr. Simon David, MA FCA FCIE DChA** *1980;* Gotham Erskine LLP, Friendly House, 52-58 Tabernacle Street, LONDON, EC2A 4NJ. See also MacIntyre Hudson LLP

ERTAC, Miss. Meryem, ACA *2010;* with Price Bailey LLP, 7th Floor Dashwood House, 69 Old Broad Street, LONDON, EC2M 1QS.

ERVINE, Mrs. Angela Jane, ACA *2009;* 33 Pirbright Road, LONDON, SW18 5NB.

ERWIN, Mr. Steven, BCom ACA *2000;* 47 Courtland Road, OXFORD, OX4 4HZ.

ESAM, Mr. John Charles, MA FCA *1975;* Mayfield Lodge, 1 Main Road, Biddenham, BEDFORD, MK40 4BB.

ESAU, Mr. Gareth Paul, BA ACA *1981;* Church Mission Society, Watlington Road, Cowley, OXFORD, OX4 6BZ.

ESCHE, Mr. Ben, MSc BA ACA *2011;* 258 Casson Street, ATLANTA, GA 30307, UNITED STATES.

ESCOLME, Miss. Nicola, LLB(Hons) ACA *2010;* 52 Norwich Road, Claydon, IPSWICH, IP6 0DF.

ESCOLME, Mr. Vernon, FCA *1952;* Flat 17, Rosewood Court, 18 Park Avenue, Roundhay, LEEDS, LS8 2BL. (Life Member)

•①**ESCOTT, Mr. Charles William Anthony, BA FCA** *1994;* PKF (UK) LLP, Pannell House, 6 Queen Street, LEEDS, LS1 2TW.

ESCOTT, Mrs. Dawn, BSc FCA *1993;* Oakroyd, 14 Staveley Road, SHIPLEY, BD18 4HD.

ESCOTT, Mr. Sean Patrick, MA ACA *1992;* 1166 Evesham Road, Astwood Bank, REDDITCH, WORCESTERSHIRE, B96 6DT.

ESCOTT, Mrs. Siobhan Clare, BSc ACA *1993;* 132 Donaghadee Road, BANGOR, COUNTY DOWN, BT20 4NH.

•**ESCOW, Mr. Maurice, FCA** *1955;* with Elliotts Shah, 2nd Floor, York House, 23 Kingsway, LONDON, WC2B 6UJ.

ESCREET, Mr. David, BA ACA *1990;* 7 Hall Orchards Avenue, WETHERBY, LS22 6SN.

ESCRITT, Mr. Ian, BSocSc ACA *2003;* 2 St. Stephens Avenue, ST. ALBANS, HERTFORDSHIRE, AL3 4AD.

ESCUDIER, Mr. Brian John, FCA *1961;* 9 Badgers Copse, NEW MILTON, HAMPSHIRE, BH25 5PE. (Life Member)

ESHAI, Mr. Mujahid, FCA *1974;* 37-M, GULBERG-3, LAHORE 5400, PAKISTAN.

ESHELBY, Mr. Stephen, BSc(Hons) ACA *2006;* 53 Caxton Road, LONDON, SW19 8SJ.

ESHER, Mrs. Alison Jane, BSc FCA *1976;* 35 Doveridge Road, Hall Green, BIRMINGHAM, B28 0LT.

ESHER, Mr. David John Swinton, FCA *1973;* 35 Doveridge Road, Hall Green, BIRMINGHAM, B28 0LT.

ESKANDARI, Mr. Mohammad, FCA *1974;* PO Box 94179, ABU DHABI, UNITED ARAB EMIRATES.

ESKDALE, Mr. Christopher Robert, MA ACA *1994;* C/O Old Mill Hey, Mill Lane, Willaston, NESTON, CH64 1RQ.

ESKELL, Mr. Lawrence Paul, ACA CA(SA) *2010;* 99 Bartholomews Square, Horfield, BRISTOL, BS7 0QB.

ESKELL, Miss. Penelope Jane, BA ACA *2005;* Pricewaterhousecoopers Llp, 1 Hays Lane, LONDON, SE1 2RD.

ESLAMI, Mr. Davood, BSc FCA ATII *1995;* 28 The Close, HARPENDEN, AL5 3NB.

•**ESLER, Mr. Roger William Henry, BA ACA CF** *1993;* Deloitte LLP, 1 City Square, LEEDS, WEST YORKSHIRE, LS1 2AL. See also Deloitte & Touche LLP

•**ESMAIL, Mr. Salim, BSc FCA** *1987;* (Tax Fac), Auditex Limited, 20 Broadwick Street, LONDON, W1F 8HT.

ESMAIL, Miss. Shenil, ACA *1983;* 62 Winners Circle, TORONTO M4L 3Z7, ON, CANADA.

ESMAIL, Mr. Zoheir Ali, ACA *2008;* 3 Bridle Road, PINNER, MIDDLESEX, HA5 2SL.

ESMAILJI, Mr. Murtaza, BSc ACA *2011;* 18 Oldborough Road, WEMBLEY, HA0 3PR.

ESME-LEONARD, Mr. Simon Peter, BSc ACA *2003;* 8806 Peach Oak Crossing, KATY, TX 77494, UNITED STATES.

ESMOND, Mr. Michael Burnett, FCA *1968;* 19 Shadwell Park Court, Shadwell Park, LEEDS, LS17 8TS.

ESPIE, Mr. Daniel, BSc ACA *1993;* Bank House, Tweed Green, PEEBLES, PEEBLESSHIRE, EH45 8AP.

ESPITALIER-NOEL, Mr. Joseph Bernard, FCA *1970;* 54 Chester Street, EPPING, NSW 2121, AUSTRALIA. (Life Member)

ESPITALIER-NOEL, Mr. Marie Maxime Hector, ACA *1983;* ENL Limited, 7th Floor, Swan Group Centre, 10 Intendance Street, PORT LOUIS, MAURITIUS.

ESPLEN, Mr. William, FCA *1974;* 4 De Grouchy Street, West Kirby, WIRRAL, MERSEYSIDE, CH48 5DX.

ESPLEY, Mr. Thomas Paul, BA ACA *2004;* c/o Jennifer Sanders, 4 Ludgate Drive, East Bridgford, NOTTINGHAM, NG13 8NW.

ESPLEY-AULT, Mrs. Olivia Jean, BA(Hons) ACA *2003;* with Ernst & Young, 700 West Georgia Street, (P.O. Box 10101), VANCOUVER V7Y 1C7, BC, CANADA.

ESS, Mr. Eric William, ACA *1987;* Mellor Bellamy, 2 The Crescent, WISBECH, PE13 1EH.

ESSA, Mr. Luqmaan, BA ACA *2006;* with Cassons, St Crispin House, St. Crispin Way, Haslingden, ROSSENDALE, LANCASHIRE BB4 4PW.

ESSA, Mr. Sohail Haji, BCom ACA *1996;* 51 Bassingham Road, WEMBLEY, HA0 4RJ.

ESSACK, Mr. Ismail, ACA CA(SA) *2010;* 3 Ryfold Road, LONDON, SW19 8DF.

•**ESSAM, Mr. Jonathan Charles Seymour, ACA** *1989;* (Tax Fac), Jon Essam & Co Ltd, Cottingham Way, Thrapston, KETTERING, NORTHAMPTONSHIRE, NN14 4PL.

ESSAYAN, Mr. Steven Lucas, BA ACA *1985;* 7 Goodrich Road, East Dulwich, LONDON, SE22 9EQ.

ESSE, Mr. William Nicholas, BSc ACA *1992;* with Stow Estate Trust, Home Farm, Lynn Road, Stow Bardolph, KING'S LYNN, NORFOLK PE34 3HT.

ESSERY, Mr. Gary Paul, BA ACA *2009;* Flat 18, 1A Archers Rd, SOUTHAMPTON, HAMPSHIRE, so15 2ta.

ESSERY, Miss. Margaret Constance, BSc ACA *1984;* 91 Parkinson Drive, CHELMSFORD, ESSEX, CM1 3GU.

ESSEX, Mrs. Alison Jane, BA(Hons) ACA *2001;* with Moore Stephens LLP, 150 Aldersgate Street, LONDON, EC1A 4AB.

ESSEX, Mr. Arthur Christian, FCA *1949;* (Member of Council 1973 - 1982), Flat 3E Cedar Lodge, Lythe Hill Park, HASLEMERE, GU27 3TD. (Life Member)

•**ESSEX, Mr. Charles Randall, FCA** *1968;* Rayner Essex LLP, Faulkner House, Victoria Street, ST. ALBANS, HERTFORDSHIRE, AL1 3SE.

ESSEX, Mr. David Anthony Dampier, MSc FCA *1969;* 7 Crescent Road, Wimbledon, LONDON, SW20 8EY. (Life Member)

ESSEX, Mr. Lawrence Randall, FCA *1963;* 12 Farmhouse Mews, THATCHAM, BERKSHIRE, RG18 4NW. (Life Member)

ESSEX, Mrs. Rekha, BA ACA *1995;* Rosebank Cottage, 44 Tennyson Road, Mill Hill, LONDON, NW7 4AS.

•**ESSEX, Mr. Simon James, FCA** *1994;* Rayner Essex LLP, Tavistock House South, Tavistock Square, LONDON, WC1H 9LG.

ESSEX, Mr. Simon Richard, MA FCA *1979;* Dutco Group, P O Box 233, DUBAI, UNITED ARAB EMIRATES.

ESSEX, Miss. Victoria Claire, BSc ACA *2011;* 51a Brighton Road, PURLEY, SURREY, CR8 2LR.

ESSON, Mr. James George, BSc(Hons) ACA *2001;* 3 Beech Close, Wilpshire, BLACKBURN, BB1 9JF.

ESSON, Mr. Robert Max Ross, MA FCA *1979;* 5731 N. Polk Drive, KANSAS CITY, MO, 64151-2697, UNITED STATES.

ESSOP, Miss. Iman, ACA *2008;* 26 Somerford Way, LONDON, SE16 6QW.

•**ESTCOURT, Mr. Paul, FCA** *1978;* (Tax Fac), P & C E Services Limited, 1 Cheyney Avenue, Salhouse, NORWICH, NR13 6RJ.

•**ESTELLA, Mr. Michael Joseph, ACA** *2008;* Harding Lewis Limited, 34 Athol Street, Douglas, ISLE OF MAN, IM1 1JB.

ESTERHUYSE, Ms. Elsa, ACA CA(SA) *2010;* Flat 28, 49 Hallam Street, LONDON, W1W 6JW.

ESTERHUYSEN, Ms. Katherine, ACA CA(SA) *2009;* Hertford College, Catte Street, OXFORD, OX1 3BW.

ESTERMAN, Mr. Melvyn, FCA *1971;* 11 Ascot Close, Elstree, BOREHAMWOOD, HERTFORDSHIRE, WD6 3JH.

ESTLIN, Mr. Peter Kenneth, BSc FCA *1985;* Barclays Bank Plc, 1 Churchill Place, LONDON, E14 5HP.

ESUFALLY, Mr. Abbasally Nuruddin, FCA *1976;* Hemas Holdings Ltd, 6th Floor, 75 Braybrooke Place, COLOMBO 2 COLOMBO, SRI LANKA.

ESURUOSO, Mr. Obafemi Adeniyi, BSc ACA *1992;* 7 Winston Close, HITCHIN, SG5 2HB.

ESWARAN, Mr. Meenakshi Sundaram Bagavathy, ACA FCCA FCMA *2008;* Towell Mattress & Furniture Industry, PO Box 28958, SHARJAH, UNITED ARAB EMIRATES.

ETCHELL, Mrs. Irene Swee Wah, ACA *1979;* 16 Brentwood Ave, WARRAWEE, NSW 2074, AUSTRALIA.

ETCHELL, Mr. Stephen Charles, ACA *1980;* Colonial Centre, Level 6, 52 Martin Place, SYDNEY, NSW 2074, AUSTRALIA.

ETCHELL, Mr. William John, BA ACA *1999;* 25 Baring Crescent, BEACONSFIELD, BUCKINGHAMSHIRE, HP9 2NG.

ETCHELLS, Mr. Adrian Paul, ACA MAAT *1996;* J E Hartley Ltd, Roth Hill Lane, Thorganby, YORK, YO19 6DJ.

ETCHELLS, Mr. David John, FCA *1970;* Old Malthouse, Fullerton Road, Wherwell, ANDOVER, SP11 7JS.

ETCHELLS, Mr. John Graham, FCA *1972;* 2958 Moggill Road, PINJARRA HILLS, QLD 4069, AUSTRALIA. (Life Member)

ETCHELLS, Mrs. Kate, MMath ACA *2011;* 264 Talbot Road, HYDE, CHESHIRE, SK14 4EQ.

ETCHELLS, Mr. Mark, BSc FCA *1990;* 50 Lisvane Street, CARDIFF, CF24 4LL.

ETCHELLS, Mr. Paul Kenneth, BA FCA *1974;* 3A Sakura Court, 58-60 Kennedy Road, WAN CHAI, HONG KONG ISLAND, HONG KONG SAR.

ETCHES, Mr. Nicholas Peter, FCA *1971;* Flat A Ground Floor Block 6, Stanford Villa, 7 Stanley Village Road, STANLEY, HONG KONG ISLAND, HONG KONG SAR.

ETESON, Mr. David Alan, FCA *1960;* Victoria House, 9 School Lane, Long Preston, SKIPTON, BD23 4PN. (Life Member)

ETHELL, Mr. Bernard Dale, MA FCA *1954;* 8 Felden Street, LONDON, SW6 5AF. (Life Member)

ETHELSTON, Mr. Edward Philip, MA ACA *2002;* 86 Beaconsfield Road, SURBITON, KT5 9AP.

ETHELSTON, Mr. William Frederick, MA BA(Hons) ACA *2003;* 1 Ivy Cottages, Lower Link, St. Mary Bourne, ANDOVER, HAMPSHIRE, SP11 6BY.

ETHERIDGE, Mr. Brian Robert, FCA *1973;* 3 Mountney Road, EASTBOURNE, EAST SUSSEX, BN21 1RJ.

ETHERIDGE, Mr. Hugh Charles, FCA *1974;* 5 Springfield Place, BATH, BA1 5RA.

ETHERIDGE, Mrs. Julia Martin, BSc ACA *1984;* 6 Paddock Fields, Old Basing, BASINGSTOKE, RG24 7DB.

ETHERIDGE, Mr. Mark Charles, BSc ACA *1992;* (Tax Fac), 3 Chartridge, Eskdale Road, UXBRIDGE, UB8 2RT.

ETHERIDGE, Mr. Neville, FCA *1962;* Greater Manchester Transport, Social & Athletic Society, Hyde Road Busdepot, Ardwick, MANCHESTER, M12 6JS.

ETHERIDGE, Mr. Stephen Michael David, BEng ACA *1990;* 44 King Edward Road, Oldfield Park, BATH, BA2 3PB.

ETHERIDGE, Mrs. Tracey Anne, BA ACA *1990;* 6 Pilgrims Way, Shere, GUILDFORD, GU5 9HR.

ETHERINGTON, Mr. Bernard John, BSc FCA *1987;* 117 Benson Road, Remuera, AUCKLAND, NEW ZEALAND.

ETHERINGTON, Mr. David Neil, MA ACA *1995;* 31 The Ridge, Berrylands, SURBITON, KT5 8HU.

ETHERINGTON, Mr. Jody Leonard, ACA *2009;* Flat 18 Timber Yard, Station Approach, BRAINTREE, CM7 3TB.

ETHERINGTON, Miss. Julie Elizabeth, ACA *1994;* Church Folde, 2 New Street, Mawdesley, ORMSKIRK, L40 2QP.

ETHERINGTON, Mrs. Leanne Michelle, BA(Hons) ACA *2002;* Newcastle Building Society, Portland House, New Bridge Street West, NEWCASTLE UPON TYNE, NE1 8AL.

ETHERINGTON, Mr. Lee, BA ACA *1997;* 34 Chipchase Mews, NEWCASTLE UPON TYNE, NE3 5RH.

ETHERINGTON, Mr. Nicholas Eric Jean, MA BA(Hons) ACA *2011;* Flat 3, Lexington, 42 Chorlton Street, MANCHESTER, M1 3HW.

•**ETHERINGTON, Mr. Paul Michael David, BSc FCA CF** *1993;* Grant Thornton UK LLP, Churchill House, Chalvey Road East, SLOUGH, SL1 2LS. See also Grant Thornton LLP

ETHERTON, Mr. James Howard, MA ACA *1987;* Construction Industry Solutions Ltd, 10 The Grove, SLOUGH, SL1 1QP.

ETHERTON, Mr. John Robert, BSc ACA *1982;* Weston Aerospace, 124 Victoria Road, FARNBOROUGH, GU14 7PW.

ETON, Mr. David Alexander, BSc FCA *1982;* 4 Thurlow Road, LONDON, NW3 5PJ.

ETTLING, Mr. Michael Ernest, ACA CA(SA) *2011;* 10 Chacombe Place, BEACONSFIELD, BUCKINGHAMSHIRE, HP9 2WS.

ETTY, Mrs. Amanda, ACA *2009;* 4 Rowan Close, Desborough, KETTERING, NORTHAMPTONSHIRE, NN14 2GP.

•**ETTY, Mrs. Helen Mary, BA ACA** *1990;* Startup Consultancy, 67 Endowood Road, Millhouses, SHEFFIELD, S7 2LY.

ETTY GOUNDER, Mr. Subramaniam, ACA *1985;* No 77, Jalan KE 3/1, Peridot Precint, Kota Emerald, 48000 RAWANG, SELANGOR MALAYSIA.

EU, Mr. Stuart Sze Gunn, MBA BSc(Hons) ACA *2000;* Flat 110 Clarence Gate Gardens, Glentworth Street, LONDON, NW1 6AL.

EUGENIOU, Mr. Eugenios, ACA *2002;* Mesaorias 7, Nea Ledra, Dali, 2549 NICOSIA, CYPRUS.

EUGSTER, Mr. Maximillian Brian Michael, BA ACA *1995;* Flat 2, 211 St. Margarets Road, TWICKENHAM, TW1 1LU.

EUINTON, Mr. Anthony Charles, FCA *1964;* 23 New Market, BECCLES, SUFFOLK, NR34 9HD.

EUMAN, Ms. Caroline Sally, BEng ACA *1997;* 10 Bunch Way, HASLEMERE, SURREY, GU27 1ER.

EUSTACE, Miss. Alexandra Rosemary, BA(Hons) ACA *2004;* Foreland Shipping Limited, Dexter House, 2 Royal Mint Court, LONDON, EC3N 4XX.

•**EUSTACE, Mr. Andrew Charles, BA ACA** *1988;* Silbury Business Advisers Ltd, Venture House, Calne Road, Lyneham, CHIPPENHAM, WILTSHIRE SN15 4PP. See also Silbury Woking Ltd

EUSTACE, Miss. Claire Frederica, BSc ACA *2011;* Apartment 9, 7 Blackthorn Avenue, Islington, LONDON, N7 8AJ.

EUSTACE, Mr. Dudley Graham, BA(Econ) FCA *1962;* Avalon, Old Barn Lane, Churt, FARNHAM, SURREY, GU10 2NA.

EUSTACE, Mr. Francis John, BA FCA *1978;* 4 Arch Grove, Long Ashton, BRISTOL, BS41 9BW.

EUSTACE, Mr. Jamie, BSc ACA *1998;* 416 Fulwood Road, SHEFFIELD, S10 3GH.

EUSTACE, Mr. Mark Edward, BEng ACA *1992;* 6 Europa Court, SHEFFIELD, S9 1XE.

EUSTACE, Mr. Stuart John, BA ACA *1989;* 55 Harbour Square, #PH11, TORONTO M5J 2L1, ON, CANADA.

EVA, Mr. Robin John Pedlar, BA FCA *1980;* The Old Barn, Rossmill Lane, Hale Barns, ALTRINCHAM, CHESHIRE, WA15 0BU.

•**EVAGORA, Mr. Evagoras, BA FCA** *1987;* (Tax Fac), EA (UK) LLP, 869 High Road, LONDON, N12 8QA. See also EA Associates

EVAGOROU, Miss. Clea, ACA *2009;* First Floor Flat, 26 Gordon Place, LONDON, W8 4JE.

EVAGOROU, Mr. Evagoras, ACA *2011;* Flat 31, 12 Doiranis, Akropoli, Strovolos, 2012 NICOSIA, CYPRUS.

EVAN-COOK, Mr. Paul, FCA *1969;* 4 Impasse Des Costettes, Hautes Roches, 34320 NIZAS, FRANCE.

EVANGELOU, Mr. Andreas Stavrinou, BSc ACA *1995;* 36 Brabourne Rise, BECKENHAM, KENT, BR3 6SG.

•**EVANGELOU, Mr. Evangelos, FCA** *1988;* Timenides & Evangeli, PO Box 21560, 1510 NICOSIA, CYPRUS.

•**EVANGELOU, Mr. George, ACA FCCA CPA** *2009;* CE&GE Professional Services Ltd, 7 Dositheou Street, Parabuilding Block C, 1st Floor, Office C102, 1071 NICOSIA CYPRUS.

EVANGELOU, Mr. Ioannis, FCA *1970;* 146 El Venizelou, Nea Erythrea, 146 71 ATHENS, GREECE.

EVANGELOU, Mr. Kostas, ACA *2008;* Analipseos 20, K Polemidia, 4154 LIMASSOL, CYPRUS.

EVANS, Mrs. Aarti, MA ACA *1993;* 149 Old Church Road, GREENWICH, CT 06830, UNITED STATES.

EVANS, Mrs. Abigail Mary, BSc(Hons) ACA *2003;* 6 Byron Close, YATELEY, GU46 6YW.

EVANS, Mrs. Agatha Zandile, BSc ACA *1992;* Flat 8, Winsmoor Court, 1a Glebe Avenue, ENFIELD, MIDDLESEX, EN2 8NU.

EVANS, Mr. Alan, FCA *1972;* Astwood House, 123 Derby Road, Draycott, DERBY, DE72 3NX.

EVANS, Mr. Alan Baxter, MA FCA *1955;* Hall & Watts Ltd, 266 Hatfield Road, ST. ALBANS, AL1 4UN. (Life Member)

•**EVANS, Mr. Alan George, FCA** *1973;* (Tax Fac), HATS Gloucester Ltd, 162 Hucclecote Road, GLOUCESTER, GL3 3SH.

EVANS, Mr. Alan John, FCA *1957;* MARTLETS, Llanfihangel-torymynydd, USK, GWENT, NP15 1DT. (Life Member)

•**EVANS, Mr. Alan Martin, FCA CTA** *1980;* (Tax Fac), Rimmer & May, 19 Murray Street, LLANELLI, DYFED, SA15 1AQ.

•**EVANS, Mr. Alan Morgan, FCA** *1964;* (Tax Fac), Meco Accountancy Services, Holmwood, Pentwyn, TREHARRIS, MID GLAMORGAN, CF46 5BS.

EVANS, Prof. Alan William, PhD BA FCA *1961;* Lianda, Hill Close, HARROW, MIDDLESEX, HA1 3PQ. (Life Member)

EVANS, Mr. Alasdair David, MA FCA *1987;* 8 Copsem Lane, ESHER, SURREY, KT10 9EU.

EVANS, Mrs. Alexandra Elizabeth, BSc ACA *1999;* 2 Firtree Close, Acomb, YORK, YO24 4EU.

EVANS, Mrs. Alexandra Jean, BSc(Hons) ACA *2004;* West Coast Energy Mynydd Awel, Mold Business Park Maes Gwern, MOLD, CLWYD, CH7 1XN.

EVANS, Miss. Alison Jacqueline, ACA *2000;* 405 NEPTUNE HOUSE, MARINA BAY, GIBRALTAR, GIBRALTAR.

•**EVANS, Mrs. Alison Jane, BA ACA CTA** *1991;* AJE, Little Garth, St. Johns Road, Bishop Monkton, HARROGATE, NORTH YORKSHIRE HG3 3QU.

EVANS, Mrs. Alison Jayne, BA FCA *1989;* 59 Ffordd Naddyn, Glan Conwyn, COLWYN BAY, Clwyd, LL28 5NH.

EVANS, Mrs. Alison Wendy, BA ACA *1989;* Threshing Barn West, Gonalston Lane, Hoveringham, NOTTINGHAM, NG14 7JH.

EVANS, Mr. Alun, BA ACA *1980;* 23 Tanllwyfan, Old Colwyn, COLWYN BAY, LL29 9LQ.

•①**EVANS, Mr. Alun, BCom FCA** *1989;* (Tax Fac), Alun Evans, Langdon House, Langdon Road, SA1 Swansea Waterfront, SWANSEA, SA1 8QY.

EVANS, Mr. Alun Lloyd, BA FCA MBA *1982;* 327 Banbury Road, OXFORD, OX2 7PL.

EVANS, Mr. Alyn Ifor, FCA *1966;* 11 Whitegate Fields, Green Street, Holt, WREXHAM, LL13 9JE.

•**EVANS, Mr. Andrew Curtis, BSc FCA** *1978;* Khalij Fiduciaire SA, Le Forum 1er Étage Grand'Rue 3, CP 317, CH-1820 MONTREUX, VAUD, SWITZERLAND.

EVANS, Mr. Andrew David, BSc ACA *1997;* Flat A 14/f, Caroline Height, 1 Link Road, HAPPY VALLEY, HONG KONG SAR.

EVANS, Mr. Andrew David, BSc(Econ) ACA *2004;* Flat 19, Oakhill Court, Upper Richmond Road, LONDON, SW15 2QH.

EVANS, Mr. Andrew David, BA FCA *1995;* 115 Louisa Street, Openshaw, MANCHESTER, M11 1GJ.

EVANS, Mr. Andrew James, BSc ACA *1991;* 28 Hollyfield Close, TRING, HERTFORDSHIRE, HP23 5PL.

EVANS, Mr. Andrew James, FCA *1979;* 6 Claremont Road, TWICKENHAM, TW1 2QY.

EVANS, The Revd. Andrew John, FCA *1975;* 16a Hillcrest, ELLESMERE, SHROPSHIRE, SY12 0LJ.

EVANS, Mr. Andrew John, FCA *1971;* 36 Highfield Avenue, Newbold, CHESTERFIELD, S41 7AX.

EVANS, Mr. Andrew Jonathan, BSc ACA *2006;* 63 Parkside Way, BIRMINGHAM, B31 5ES.

EVANS, Mr. Andrew Keith, BSc FCA *1990;* 177 Burtons Road, Hampton Hill, HAMPTON, MIDDLESEX, TW12 1DX.

EVANS, Mr. Andrew Mark, BSc ACA *1994;* with Ernst & Young LLP, 20 Chapel Street, LIVERPOOL, L3 9AG.

EVANS, Mr. Andrew Martin, BA ACA *1993;* Seronera Glebe Lane, Rushmoor, FARNHAM, GU10 2EW.

EVANS, Mr. Andrew Thomas Stephen, BA FCA *1978;* Style Matters, The Grange, Pickmere Lane, Pickmere, KNUTSFORD, CHESHIRE WA16 0JJ.

EVANS, Mrs. Angela, FCA *1989;* Unit 1 Andoversford Industrial Estate, Gloucester Road Andoversford, CHELTENHAM, GLOUCESTERSHIRE, GL54 4LB.

EVANS, Miss. Anita Gillian, BSc ACA *1995;* Silex Administration SA, Rue Kleberg 6, 1201 GENEVA, SWITZERLAND.

•**EVANS, Mrs. Ann Ellen, BA FCA** *1990;* Owain Bebb a'i Gwmni, 32 Y Maes, CAERNARFON, GWYNEDD, LL55 2NN.

EVANS, Mrs. Anna, BSc ACA *1993;* 1/F Shan Kwong Court, 30 Shan Kwong Road, HAPPY VALLEY, HONG KONG ISLAND, HONG KONG SAR.

EVANS, Mrs. Anne Therese, BSc FCA *1979;* 114 Merthyrmawr Road, BRIDGEND, Mid Glamorgan, CF31 3NY.

EVANS, Mr. Anthony Christopher, BA ACA *1982;* 4 Grovelands Road, Palmers Green, LONDON, N13 4RH.

•**EVANS, Mr. Anthony John, FCA** *1977;* A.J. Evans, 186 Longfield, FALMOUTH, CORNWALL, TR11 4ST.

EVANS, Mr. Anthony John, MA ACA *1990;* 7 Westmayne Industrial Park, Bramston Way, BASILDON, SS15 6TP.

EVANS, Mrs. Anwen, BA ACA *1996;* Tan-y-coed, Ffordd Morfa Bychan, PORTHMADOG, LL49 9UR.

EVANS, Mr. Arwel Owen, MA ACA *1988;* 75 Coombe Road, WIRRAL, MERSEYSIDE, CH61 4UW.

EVANS, Mr. Barry John, FCA *1962;* Lake Veiw Cottage, 15 Castle Hill, Little Virginia, KENILWORTH, WARWICKSHIRE, CV8 1NB. (Life Member)

EVANS, Mr. Barry Lawrence, BCom FCA *1974;* 29 Riversdale Road, THAMES DITTON, KT7 0QN.

EVANS, Mr. Barton Edward, FCA *1951;* PO Box 65-077, Mairangi Bay, AUCKLAND, NEW ZEALAND. (Life Member)

EVANS, Mr. Benjamin, BSc ACA *2004;* 54 Englewood Road, LONDON, SW12 9NY.

EVANS, Miss. Beth Louisa, ACA CTA *2002;* 7 Shrubbery Street, KIDDERMINSTER, WORCESTERSHIRE, DY10 2QZ.

EVANS, Mrs. Brenda, BA ACA *1985;* 8414 Blackgum Street, PARKER, CO 80134, UNITED STATES.

EVANS, Mr. Brent Ross, BA ACA *2002;* Via Cairoli 5 Int 9, 16124 GENOA, LIGURIA, ITALY.

EVANS, Mr. Brian, BSc FCA *1988;* The Lodge, Dobford Grange, North Rode, CONGLETON, CHESHIRE, CW12 2NY.

EVANS, Mr. Brian Charles, BSc ACA *1992;* Mill House, Windmill Hill, Upchurch, GILLINGHAM, KENT, ME8 7XA.

EVANS, Mr. Brian Nigel, MA FCA *1975;* Abbott Diabetes Care, Range Road, WITNEY, OXFORDSHIRE, OX29 0YL.

EVANS, Miss. Carly Jayne Lucia, LLB(Hons) ACA *2010;* 6 Saylittle Mews, Longlevens, GLOUCESTER, GL2 0XG.

•**EVANS, Mrs. Carol Ann, BSc ACA ATII** *1992;* (Tax Fac), C.A. Evans & Company, Spring Royd, Clapham Road, Austwick, LANCASTER, LA2 8BE.

EVANS, Miss. Caroline Sian, BA FCA *1990;* 15 Franklin Place, Lewisham, LONDON, SE13 7ES.

EVANS, Mrs. Carolyn Jane, BA ACA *1994;* 1 Sandown Close, STRATFORD-UPON-AVON, WARWICKSHIRE, CV37 9BZ.

EVANS, Miss. Caryl Eleri, BA(Hons) ACA *2010;* 56 St. Lawrence Quay, SALFORD, M50 3XT.

EVANS, Mrs. Catherine, LLB ACA *1986;* 3 The Willows, Edlesborough, DUNSTABLE, LU6 2JH.

EVANS, Ms. Catherine Elizabeth, MA ACA *1990;* 2/F 49B Robinson Road, MID LEVELS, HONG KONG ISLAND, HONG KONG SAR.

EVANS, Mrs. Catherine Sarah Jane, MA ACA *1998;* Oak Tree House, Wintringham, MALTON, NORTH YORKSHIRE, YO17 8HX.

EVANS, Miss. Catherine Rachel, ACA *2011;* Lan, Meidrim, CARMARTHEN, DYFED, SA33 5NY.

EVANS, Miss. Catrin Mair, BSc ACA *2001;* 58 Edgehill Street, READING, RG1 2PX.

•**EVANS, Mr. Charles David, BA FCA DChA** *1982;* Francis Clark, North Quay House, Sutton Harbour, PLYMOUTH, PL4 0RA. See also Francis Clark LLP

EVANS, Mrs. Charlotte Louise, BA(Hons) ACA *2001;* 8 Coppice Drive, HARROGATE, NORTH YORKSHIRE, HG1 2JE.

EVANS, Mrs. Charlotte Marjorie, BSc ACA *1999;* 39 Delaporte Point, NASSAU, CB 13016, BAHAMAS.

EVANS, Mr. Christopher, BA FCA *1988;* 1 The Grange, Shepherds Lane, Caversham Heights, READING, RG4 7HZ.

•**EVANS, Mr. Christopher, BA ACA** *2004;* Ballard Evans Corporate Finance Limited, Lowry House, 17 Marble Street, MANCHESTER, M2 3AW.

EVANS, Mr. Christopher Bryn, BSc ACA *2002;* 7521 Piper Place, LOS ANGELES, CA 90245, UNITED STATES.

EVANS, Mr. Christopher John, BSc ACA *1979;* Little Grange, Water Lane, Titsey, OXTED, RH8 0SA.

•**EVANS, Mr. Christopher John, BSc ACA** *1995;* with Target Accountants Limited, Lawrence House, Lower Bristol Road, BATH, BA2 9ET.

EVANS, Mr. Christopher John Lucas, FCA *1963;* 8 Wade Court Road, HAVANT, PO9 2SU.

EVANS, Mr. Christopher Michael, BSc ACA *1999;* GPO Box 5284, BRISBANE, QLD 4001, AUSTRALIA.

EVANS, Mr. Christopher Michael, BSc FCA *1973;* 69 Douglas Road, SURBITON, SURREY, KT6 7RZ.

EVANS, Mr. Christopher Neil, LLB ACA *1987;* 2 Wellfield, Bishopston, SWANSEA, SA3 3EP.

EVANS, Ms. Claire, BSc ACA *1992;* 182 Cyncoed Road, CARDIFF, CF23 6BQ.

EVANS, Mrs. Claire Elizabeth Carmichael, BSc ACA *1996;* 30 Wentworth Street, RANDWICK, NSW 2031, AUSTRALIA.

EVANS, Mrs. Claire Jane, BA ACA *1995;* (Tax Fac), with PricewaterhouseCoopers, Cornwall Court, 19 Cornwall Street, BIRMINGHAM, B3 2DT.

EVANS, Mrs. Claire Louise, BSc ACA *1986;* 40 Belwell Lane, Four Oaks, SUTTON COLDFIELD, B74 4TR.

EVANS, Mr. Clint, BSc FCA *1991;* 5 Church Road, KINGSTON UPON THAMES, SURREY, KT1 3DJ.

•**EVANS, Mr. Colin Clive, BA FCA** *1967;* C.C.Evans, 25 Clarefield Drive, Pinkneys Green, MAIDENHEAD, SL6 5DW.

EVANS, Mr. Colin John, MA ACA *1985;* Colas Rail Ltd, 19 Dacre Street, LONDON, SW1H 0DJ.

EVANS, Mr. Colin William, FCA *1970;* Denehurst, 4 Oakdene Road, Great Bookham, LEATHERHEAD, KT23 3HE.

EVANS, Mr. Colin Wilson, BCom ACA *1985;* with PricewaterhouseCoopers LLP, 31 Great George Street, BRISTOL, BS1 5QD.

EVANS, Miss. Crystal Eleanor, ACA *2007;* 2 The Orchard, Slip End, LUTON, LU1 4HL.

EVANS, Mr. Dafydd Iestyn, BA ACA *2006;* 1 Winstanley Road, LONDON, SW11 2EZ.

EVANS, Mr. Dafydd Rhys, MA(Hons) ACA *2001;* 161 MacMillan Way, Church Lane, LONDON, SW17 6AU.

EVANS, Mr. Damian Michael, BSc ACA *1996;* Dove Cottage, Park Street, FAIRFORD, GLOUCESTERSHIRE, GL7 4JL.

EVANS, Mr. Daniel, ACA *2011;* 48 Chasefield Road, LONDON, SW17 8LN.

EVANS, Mr. Daniel Thomas, BSc ACA *2009;* 5 Richmond Road, SOUTHAMPTON, SO15 3FT.

EVANS, Mr. David, BSc ACA *2007;* 22 Ufford Street, LONDON, SE1 8QD.

EVANS, Mr. David, BA(Hons) ACA *2011;* 41 Green Avenue, Davenham, NORTHWICH, CHESHIRE, CW9 8HZ.

EVANS, Mr. David, ACA *2010;* 51 Kenilworth Avenue, LOUGHBOROUGH, LEICESTERSHIRE, LE11 4SJ.

•**EVANS, Mr. David, FCA** *1979;* Moss & Williamson, Booth Street Chambers, Booth Street, ASHTON-UNDER-LYNE, OL6 7LQ. See also Moss & Williamson Ltd

EVANS, Mr. David Alan, MSc ACA MBA *1999;* Efyrnwy, Park Street, DENBIGH, CLWYD, LL16 3DE.

EVANS, Mr. David Albert, FCA *1979;* 1 Ashby Court, READING, RG2 8PG.

EVANS, Mr. David Alexander Richard, BSc ACA *1987;* Salem Communications, 4880 Santa Rosa Road, CAMARILLO, CA 93012, UNITED STATES.

EVANS, Mr. David Alun Valentine, BSc FCA *1991;* 126 Westbourne Road, PENARTH, SOUTH GLAMORGAN, CF64 3HH.

EVANS, Mr. David Anthony, FCA *1957;* 35 Gwel-an-Nans, Probus, TRURO, TR2 4ND. (Life Member)

EVANS, Mr. David Barrington, BCom FCA *1976;* Towy Finance Ltd, The Old Creamery, Pensarn Road, CARMARTHEN, DYFED, SA31 2BS.

•**EVANS, Mr. David Byron, BA(Hons) FCA** *1995;* Delta Accountancy Services, 57 Stotfold Road, Maypole, BIRMINGHAM, B14 5JD.

EVANS, Mr. David Charles, MBA BA FCA *1980;* 2 The Oaks, EPSOM, KT18 5HH.

EVANS, Mr. David Charles, BSc ACA *2010;* Flat 15, Beresford House, Rubens Place, LONDON, SW4 7RB.

EVANS, Mr. David Charles, ACA *1979;* 4 Humberdale Drive, Ferriby High Road, NORTH FERRIBY, HU14 3LB.

•**EVANS, Mr. David Christopher, BA FCA** *1990;* D.C. Evans, Cae Nant, Llandyrnog, DENBIGH, CLWYD, LL16 4HB.

EVANS, Mr. David Drew, BA FCA *1986;* 5 Lintin Close, Heighington, LINCOLN, LN4 1RW.

•**EVANS, Mr. David Edward, BA ACA** *1981;* (Tax Fac), David Evans & Co, PO Box 113, FRODSHAM, WA6 7WS.

EVANS, Mr. David Gareth, BSc ACA *2006;* 13 Lime Tree Place, ST. ALBANS, HERTFORDSHIRE, AL1 3BD.

EVANS, Mr. David Graham, FCA *1976;* 45 Marshwood Croft, HALESOWEN, B62 0EY.

EVANS, Mr. David Graham, BA ACA *1987;* 1 Edward Street, Bamber Bridge, PRESTON, PR5 6FB.

EVANS, Mr. David Graham Charles, BSc ACA *2006;* with KPMG LLP, 303 East Wacker Drive, CHICAGO, IL 60601-5255, UNITED STATES.

EVANS, Mr. David Hugh Birkett, FCA *1962;* Trevalyn Estates Ltd, The Mill House, Rossett, WREXHAM, LL12 0HL.

•**EVANS, Mr. David Humphrey, FCA** *1980;* (Tax Fac), David H Evans Limited, Unit 2, The Old Sawmill, Shaw Bridge Street, CLITHEROE, LANCASHIRE BB7 1LY.

EVANS, Mr. David James, LLB ACA *2000;* 89 Cherry Grove, Sketty, SWANSEA, SA2 8AX.

EVANS, Mr. David John, FCA *1963;* 35 Mountbatten Avenue, KENILWORTH, WARWICKSHIRE, CV8 2PY. (Life Member)

•**EVANS, Mr. David John, ACA FCCA MAAT** *2009;* Lancaster & Co, Granville House, 2 Tettenhall Rd, WOLVERHAMPTON, WV1 4SB. See also Lancaster Haskins LLP

•**EVANS, Mr. David John, LLB ACA** *1997;* Deloitte LLP, Athene Place, 66 Shoe Lane, LONDON, EC4A 3BQ. See also Deloitte & Touche LLP

•**EVANS, Mr. David John, FCA** *1973;* MEMBER OF COUNCIL, Mazars LLP, Tower Bridge House, St. Katharines Way, LONDON, E1W 1DD.

•**EVANS, Mr. David John, BA ACA** *1991;* KPMG Fiduciaire de France, 480 Avenue du Prado, Cedex 08, 13272 MARSEILLE, FRANCE. See also KPMG

EVANS, Mr. David Julian, FCA *1956;* 3 Cathedral Court, The Cathedral Green, CARDIFF, CF5 2EB. (Life Member)

EVANS, Mr. David Kelvin, BSc FCA *1972;* 5 Templeton Close, Dorridge, SOLIHULL, B93 8LS.

EVANS, Mr. David Llewelyn, BSc ACA *2005;* with Ernst & Young, 700 West Georgia Street, (P.O. Box 10101), VANCOUVER V7Y 1C7, BC, CANADA.

•**EVANS, Mr. David Lloyd, BA ACA** *1992;* (Tax Fac), Guilfoyle Sage & Co, 21 Gold Tops, NEWPORT, NP20 4PG. See also Guilfoyle Sage LLP

EVANS, Mr. David Mark, BSc FCA CPA *1989;* with PricewaterhouseCoopers LLP, 301 Commerce Street, Tower II Suite 2350, FORT WORTH, TX 76102-4140, UNITED STATES.

•**EVANS, Mr. David Rhys, BA FCA** *1984;* Marks Bloom Limited, 60 Old London Road, KINGSTON UPON THAMES, SURREY, KT2 6QZ.

EVANS, Mr. David Robert, BSc ACA *1989;* Ernst & Young Llp, 1 More London Place, LONDON, SE1 2AF.

EVANS, Mr. David Robert, BSc FCA *1980;* (Tax Fac), 25 Parkwood Avenue, ESHER, KT10 8DE.

EVANS, Mr. David Samuel, BEng ACA *1990;* 26 Grange Farm Drive, Stockton, SOUTHAM, CV47 8FT.

EVANS, Mr. David Stephen, BSc FCA *1977;* St Mungo's, 2nd Floor, Griffin House, 161 Hammersmith Road, LONDON, W6 8BS.

EVANS, Mr. David Timothy Chisnall, BEng ACA *1991;* 24 Scholars Green, LYMM, WA13 0QA.

EVANS, Mrs. Deborah Erin, BA(Hons) ACA *2004;* 17 Mescott Meadows, Hedge End, SOUTHAMPTON, HAMPSHIRE, SO30 2JT.

EVANS, Mr. Deryck John, BA FCA *1993;* Wales Audit Office, 24 Cathedral Road, CARDIFF, CF11 9LJ.
EVANS, Mr. Dominic William Edward, BA ACA *1994;* 14B The Government Quarters, 122 Pok Fu Lam Road, POK FU LAM, HONG KONG ISLAND, HONG KONG SAR.
EVANS, Mr. Donald Eric, FCA *1953;* 19 Carlton Road, Ainsdale, SOUTHPORT, PR8 2PG. (Life Member)
EVANS, Mr. Douglas William, FCA *1959;* 2 Gardeners Way, St Issey, WADEBRIDGE, PL27 7RN. (Life Member)
EVANS, Miss. Dulcie Rose, ACA *2009;* Flat 60, Constable House, Cassilis Road, LONDON, E14 9LH.
EVANS, Mr. Dylan James David, BSc ACA *1988;* Star Computers Building 3, Hatters Lane, WATFORD, WD18 8YG.
•**EVANS, Mr. Dylan Vaughan, BA ACA** *1988;* (Tax Fac), Hill & Roberts, 87 High Street, BALA, LL23 7AE.
EVANS, Mr. Ean Teare, BSc ACA *2003;* 22 Railway Parade, ANNANDALE, 2038, AUSTRALIA.
EVANS, Mr. Edwin Charles Lorance, BSc ACA *2003;* 10 Gresham Street, LONDON, EC2V 7AE.
EVANS, Miss. Elin Catrin, BSc ACA *2004;* Ystradbran, Cynghordy, LLANDOVERY, DYFED, SA20 0LF.
EVANS, Ms. Elizabeth Sarah, BSc ACA *1990;* Glebe Barn, Church Street, Ashley, NEWMARKET, SUFFOLK, CB8 9DU.
EVANS, Miss. Emily Mary, ACA *2009;* Flat 18, Stonebury, 5 Norfolk Road, Edgbaston, BIRMINGHAM, B15 3PS.
EVANS, Mrs. Emma, BEng ACA *2005;* 132 Trowbridge Road, BRADFORD-ON-AVON, WILTSHIRE, BA15 1EW.
EVANS, Mrs. Emma Clare, ACA *2004;* Church Farm Church Road, Bradley Green, REDDITCH, WORCESTERSHIRE, B96 6SN.
EVANS, Mrs. Emma Jane, LLB ACA *2004;* with KPMG LLP, St. James's Square, MANCHESTER, M2 6DS.
EVANS, Mr. Eric, FCA *1975;* The Rookery Coach House, 149 Clevedon Road Tickenham, CLEVEDON, AVON, BS21 6RF.
EVANS, Mr. Ernest Michael Selwyn, FCA *1956;* 6 Heol Brofiscin, Groesfaen, PONTYCLUN, CF72 8RR. (Life Member)
EVANS, Mr. Ernest Selwyn, FCA *1949;* 3 Cherry Orchard Close, CHIPPING CAMPDEN, GL55 6DH. (Life Member)
•**EVANS, Mrs. Fiona Lucy, BA(Hons) ACA** *2005;* Fiona Evans, 11 Perches Close, Membland, Newton Ferrers, PLYMOUTH, PL8 1HZ.
EVANS, Mrs. Frances Nadeen, BA ACA *1992;* 27 Ridge Avenue, HARPENDEN, AL5 3LT.
EVANS, Mr. Frederick Leonard, FCA *1952;* 8 Friary Gardens, WINCHESTER, HAMPSHIRE, SO23 9AF. (Life Member)
EVANS, Miss. Gabriella Lucia, BSc(Econ) ACA *1999;* 21 Whitehall Road, LONDON, W7 2JE.
EVANS, Mrs. Gail Elizabeth, BSc ACA ACCA *1996;* 23 The Drive, ESHER, SURREY, KT10 8DH.
EVANS, Mr. Gareth, BSc ACA CFA AMCT *2005;* Flat 13, Turner House, Cassilis Road, LONDON, E14 9LJ.
EVANS, Mr. Gareth Alun, BA ACA *2007;* with Menzies LLP, 3rd Floor Kings House, 12-42 Wood Street, KINGSTON UPON THAMES, SURREY, KT1 1TG.
EVANS, Mr. Gareth Huw, BA ACA *1992;* Bizspace Ltd, Sovereign House, 1 Albert Place, 11-19 Ballards Lane, LONDON, N3 1QA.
EVANS, Mr. Gareth Leigh, BSc(Hons) ACA *2000;* with PricewaterhouseCoopers LLP, 1 Embankment Place, LONDON, WC2N 6RH.
EVANS, Mr. Gareth Rawlett, BSc ACA *1993;* 3 Dudley Avenue, ROSEVILLE, NSW 2069, AUSTRALIA.
EVANS, Mr. Gareth Richard, BA ACA *1999;* Witts End, The Cricket Green, Hambledon, GODALMING, SURREY, GU8 4HF.
EVANS, Mr. Gareth Robin, BA FCA CTA *1997;* Carpenter Box, Grafton Lodge, Grafton Road, WORTHING, WEST SUSSEX, BN11 1QR.
EVANS, Mr. Gareth William, BSc ACA *2006;* 8 Hopwood Close, LONDON, SW17 0AG.
EVANS, Mr. Gareth Wynne, BA ACA *2003;* 32 Bentham Road, LANCASTER, LA1 4JX.
EVANS, Mr. Garry, BCom FCA *1986;* 6 Fosseway Close, MORETON-IN-MARSH, GLOUCESTERSHIRE, GL56 0DX.
EVANS, Mr. Garry Paul, BSc(Hons) ACA *2001;* 3 Tagg Wood View, Ramsbottom, BURY, LANCASHIRE, BL0 9XP.
EVANS, Miss. Gaynor, BA ACA *1993;* 189 Cyncoed Road, Cyncoed, CARDIFF, CF23 6AJ.
EVANS, Mrs. Gaynor Elisabeth, BSc FCA *1992;* 9 Squirrel Walk, Fforest, Pontarddulais, SWANSEA, SA4 0UH.
EVANS, Mr. George Henry, FCA *1956;* Sequoia, 18 Perton Grove, Wightwick, WOLVERHAMPTON, WV6 8DH. (Life Member)
EVANS, Mrs. Georgina Ellen, FCA *1975;* (Tax Fac), 20 Whitmore Road, BECKENHAM, BR3 3NT.
EVANS, Mr. Geraint Adrian, BA ACA *1989;* 3 The Glen, Torphichen Road, BATHGATE, EH48 4LJ.
•**EVANS, Mr. Geraint Llewelyn, BA ACA** *1999;* F E Metcalfe & Co, 40A Market Place, RIPON, NORTH YORKSHIRE, HG4 1BZ.
EVANS, Miss. Geraldine Jane, LLB ACA *1999;* 3 Middlegates, ST. AGNES, CORNWALL, TR5 0UH.
EVANS, Mr. Gethin, ACA *2011;* 15 Queen Street, Stony Stratford, MILTON KEYNES, MK11 1EG.
•**EVANS, Mrs. Gillian, BA ACA** *1991;* Gillian Evans, 71 allee du Largado, 13190 ALLAUCH, FRANCE.
•**EVANS, Mr. Glyn, FCA** *1980;* Bates Weston Audit Limited, The Mill, Canal Street, DERBY, DE1 2RJ. See also BW Business Services Limited
EVANS, Mr. Graham Richard, FCA *1974;* 34 Rue Beethoven, 78640 VILLIERS ST FREDERIC, FRANCE.
EVANS, Mr. Grenville Alun, BSc ACA *1979;* 72 Camberley Drive, Bamford, ROCHDALE, OL11 4BA.
EVANS, Mr. Guy Christopher, MA ACA CISA *1996;* 2 Millcroft Road, SUTTON COLDFIELD, WEST MIDLANDS, B74 2EE.
EVANS, Mr. Gwyn, BSc ACA *1992;* Griffin Windows Unit 37, Abergorki Industrial Estate, TREORCHY, MID GLAMORGAN, CF42 6DL.
EVANS, Mrs. Heather Louise, BSc ACA *1992;* 55 Aylesbury Road, Hockley Heath, SOLIHULL, WEST MIDLANDS, B94 6PD.
EVANS, Mrs. Helen Elizabeth, MA ACA DChA *1995;* 30 Burnham Road, ST. ALBANS, AL1 4QW.
EVANS, Dr. Helen Mary Elizabeth, PhD MA BSc ACA *2011;* 62 Catharine Street, CAMBRIDGE, CB1 3AW.
EVANS, Mrs. Hilary Clare, BSc ACA *1998;* Grey Gables Oakley Road, Battledown, CHELTENHAM, GLOUCESTERSHIRE, GL52 6NZ.
EVANS, Mr. Howard, BSc FCA *1976;* Charlton Park House, Charlton Park Gate, CHELTENHAM, GL53 7DJ.
EVANS, Mr. Howard John, FCA *1961;* with Williams Ross Ltd, 4 Ynys Bridge Court, Gwaelod Y Garth, CARDIFF, CF15 9SS.
EVANS, Mr. Howard Owen, BSc FCA *1972;* 242 Onslow Place, WEST VANCOUVER V7S 1K5, BC, CANADA.
EVANS, Mr. Hugh William, BA ACA *1992;* 149 Old Church Road, GREENWICH, CT 06830, UNITED STATES.
EVANS, Mr. Hugo, ACA *2011;* 37 Melody Road, LONDON, SW18 2QW.
EVANS, Mr. Huw, BSc ACA MBA *1998;* 9 Camden Road, BRECON, POWYS, LD3 7BU.
EVANS, Mr. Huw, BSc ACA *1992;* 124 Heol Cwmgarw, Brynaman, AMMANFORD, SA18 1DA.
EVANS, Mr. Huw Griffith, MA ACA *1983;* La Bigotterie, Berthelot Street, St. Peter Port, GUERNSEY, GY1 1JS.
EVANS, Mr. Iain Richard, BSc FCA *1975;* L E K Consulting Llp, 40 Grosvenor Place, LONDON, SW1X 7JL.
EVANS, Mr. Ian Geoffrey, BSc FCA *1986;* 38 Crooksbury Road, FARNHAM, SURREY, GU10 1QE.
•**EVANS, Mr. Ian Malcolm, BSc FCA** *1979;* (Tax Fac), Grant Thornton UK LLP, Grant Thornton House, 22 Melton Street, Euston Square, LONDON, NW1 2EP. See also Grant Thornton LLP
EVANS, Mr. Ian Michael, BSc ACA *1993;* 20 Avoca Street, BONDI, NSW 2026, AUSTRALIA.
EVANS, Mr. Ian Philip, FCA *1982;* 347 Geddes Street, ELORA N0B 1S0, ON, CANADA.
EVANS, Mr. Iestyn, BA(Hons) ACA *2001;* 10 Heol Wen, CARDIFF, CF14 6EF.
EVANS, Mr. Iwan, BSc ACA *2011;* 15 Lomond Way, STEVENAGE, HERTFORDSHIRE, SG1 6AJ.
EVANS, Mrs. Jacqueline Rhiannon, BSc FCA *1989;* SSC 1st Floor, Department for Transport, Shared Service Centre, Sandringham Park, Swansea Vale, SWANSEA SA7 0EA.
EVANS, Miss. Jaime Louise, BSc ACA *2002;* with PricewaterhouseCoopers LLP, 1 Embankment Place, LONDON, WC2N 6RH.
EVANS, Mr. James Anthony, BA ACA MRICS *2005;* King Sturge Llp, 30 Warwick Street, LONDON, W1B 5NH.
EVANS, Mr. James Elliot Morgan, FCA *1965;* 327 Locust St, SAN FRANCISCO, CA 94118, UNITED STATES.
•**EVANS, Mr. James Owen, FCA** *1985;* J.O. Evans, Green Banks, The Hill, Merrywalks, STROUD, GLOUCESTERSHIRE GL5 4EP.
EVANS, Mr. James Peter, FCA *1965;* 2 Denning Mead, ANDOVER, HAMPSHIRE, SP10 3LG. (Life Member)
EVANS, Mrs. Jane, BSc ACA *1992;* 87 High Street, TARPORLEY, CHESHIRE, CW6 0AB.
EVANS, Mrs. Jane Michelle, BSc ACA *1995;* 9 Pickenfield, THAME, OXFORDSHIRE, OX9 3HG.
•**EVANS, Miss. Jane Thompson, MA FCA CTA TEP** *1992;* (Tax Fac), Jane Evans Taxation Limited, 20 St. Leonards Road, EXETER, EX2 4LA.
•①**EVANS, Mr. Jason Mark, BSc ACA MABRP** *2005;* H R Harris & Partners (2010) Limited, 44 St. Helens Road, SWANSEA, SA1 4BB. See also H R Harris & Partners Ltd
EVANS, Mr. Jeffrey, BA FCA *1972;* Apartment G/2 Eaton House, 38 Westferry Circus, LONDON, E14 8RN.
EVANS, Mrs. Jennifer Catherine, BSc ACA *1992;* 48 Selwyn Avenue, RICHMOND, TW9 2HA.
EVANS, Mr. Jeremy Paul, MA FCA ATII *1989;* 5 Dunmow Hill, FLEET, HAMPSHIRE, GU51 3AN.
EVANS, Mrs. Joanne Louise, BSc ACA *1996;* 74 Chaul End Road, Caddington, LUTON, LU1 4AS.
EVANS, Mrs. Joanne Susan, BSc ACA *1997;* 24 Parrys Grove, Stoke Bishop, BRISTOL, BS9 1TT.
EVANS, Mr. John, FCA *1972;* 8 Gill Street, SUTTON-IN-ASHFIELD, NOTTINGHAMSHIRE, NG17 1FP.
EVANS, Mr. John, ACA *2008;* 5 Weavers Way, Twyford, READING, RG10 9GX.
EVANS, Mr. John Andrew, BSc ACA *1978;* John Evans Mgmt Services Ltd, 66 Floral Farm, Canford Magna, WIMBORNE, DORSET, BH21 3AU.
EVANS, Mr. John Arnold, MSc BA FCA *1973;* (Tax Fac), Gower Consultants Ltd, 20 Davigdor Road, HOVE, BN3 1TT.
EVANS, Mr. John David, FCA *1971;* 1 Martyns Way, Weedon, NORTHAMPTON, NN7 4RS. (Life Member)
•**EVANS, Mr. John David, ACA** *1980;* David Evans & Co, Stowegate House, 37 Lombard Street, LICHFIELD, STAFFORDSHIRE, WS13 6DP.
•**EVANS, Mr. John Gernos Morda, MA FCA** *1983;* KPMG AG Wirtschaftsprufungsgesellschaft, Tersteegenstrasse19-31, 40474 DUSSELDORF, GERMANY.
•**EVANS, Mr. John Ian, FCA** *1969;* with Alexander & Co, 17 St Ann's Square, MANCHESTER, M2 7PW.
EVANS, Mr. John Martin, BEng FCA *1988;* 12th Floor, Barclays Bank Plc, 1 Churchill Place, LONDON, E14 5HP.
EVANS, Mr. John Meric Charles, MA FCA *1985;* Le Vert Cottage, 19 rue d'Agnou, 78580 MAULE, FRANCE.
•**EVANS, Mr. John Michael, BSc FCA** *1978;* (Tax Fac), Gerald Thomas & Co, Furze Bank, 34 Hanover Street, SWANSEA, SA1 6BA.
EVANS, Mr. John Raymond, FCA *1965;* Bryn Estates Ltd, 13 Trinity Square, LLANDUDNO, GWYNEDD, LL30 2RB.
EVANS, Mr. John Reginald, TD FCA *1963;* 4 Lea Terrace, Moortown, LEEDS, LS17 5BB.
EVANS, Mr. John Richard Foster, BA ACA *1999;* Curdworth House 51 Coleshill Road Curdworth, SUTTON COLDFIELD, WEST MIDLANDS, B76 9HA.
EVANS, Mr. John Sidney, FCA *1951;* 252 Hillbury Road, WARLINGHAM, CR6 9TP. (Life Member)
EVANS, Mr. John Spencer Garrick, FCA *1966;* Nantmawr Farm Bungalow, Ferwig, CARDIGAN, DYFED, SA43 1QQ.
•**EVANS, Mr. John William, FCA** *1978;* S & J Accountants, 27 Wildmoor Lane, Catshill, BROMSGROVE, B61 0NT.
EVANS, Mr. Jonathan, BA(Hons) ACA *2002;* Antiquities Village Road, Denham, UXBRIDGE, MIDDLESEX, UB9 5BE.
•**EVANS, Mr. Jonathan, BEng ACA CISA** *1992;* J Evans, 10 Walmer Crescent, WORCESTER, WR4 0ES.
EVANS, Mr. Jonathan, ACA *2007;* 12 West Park Apartments, La Route de St. Aubin, St. Helier, JERSEY, JE2 3PZ.
EVANS, Mr. Jonathan, ACA *2009;* 36c Wimbledon Hill Road, LONDON, SW19 7PA.
EVANS, Mr. Jonathan Ceri, BEng ACA *1992;* Orchard House, Outwood Lane, Bletchingley, REDHILL, RH1 4LR.
EVANS, Mr. Jonathan David, BSc ACA *2006;* 103a Messina Avenue, LONDON, NW6 4LG.
EVANS, Mr. Jonathan Denvir, BCom ACA *1987;* 91 Back Lane, Whittington, LICHFIELD, WS14 9SA.
EVANS, Mr. Jonathan Gary, FCA *1990;* 2 Portreeve Close, Llantrisant, PONTYCLUN, MID GLAMORGAN, CF72 8DU.
EVANS, Mr. Jonathan Gerard, BSc ACA *2011;* 8 Rhyd yr Helyg, Sketty, SWANSEA, SA2 8DH.
EVANS, Mr. Jonathan James, MSc ACA CTA *2004;* 58 Broadway Avenue, Giffard Park, MILTON KEYNES, MK14 5QJ.
EVANS, Mr. Jonathan Mark, BSc ACA *2006;* 20 Kingsholm Road, Southmead, BRISTOL, BS10 5LH.
EVANS, Mr. Jonathan Samuel, ACA *2007;* 69 Hill Avenue, BRISTOL, BS3 4SU.
EVANS, Mr. Jonathan Robert, BSc ACA *2011;* 32 Carmarthen Street, CARDIFF, CF5 1QG.
EVANS, Mr. Joseph Alan, FCA *1970;* 65 Whitestone Crescent, Yeadon, LEEDS, LS19 7JS.
EVANS, Miss. Judith, BA FCA *1985;* 6 Kenwood Park Road, SHEFFIELD, S7 1NF.
EVANS, Mrs. Judith, BSc ACA *1992;* 41 The Shires, Marshfield, CARDIFF, CF3 2AZ.
EVANS, Miss. Judith Mary, MMath ACA *2009;* Flat E, 28 Harold Road, LONDON, SE19 3PL.
EVANS, Mrs. Julia Ann, BA ACA *1996;* 3 Hillside, Wombourne, WOLVERHAMPTON, WV5 8AL.
EVANS, Mrs. Julie Elizabeth, BSS ACA *1991;* 24 Scholars Green Lane, LYMM, WA13 0QA.
EVANS, Mrs. Julie Margaret, BA ACA *1981;* 32 Ravenscroft Park, BARNET, EN5 4NH.
EVANS, Mrs. Karen, BSc ACA *1988;* 91 Back Lane, Whittington, LICHFIELD, WS14 9SA.
EVANS, Mrs. Karen Beverley, BSc ACA *2005;* 33 Brooklands Lane, Menston, ILKLEY, WEST YORKSHIRE, LS29 6PL.
EVANS, Miss. Kate, BA ACA *2003;* 35a Glenton Road, LONDON, SE13 5RS.
EVANS, Miss. Katharine Julia, MA ACA ATII *1997;* (Tax Fac), 10 Rochford Avenue, Shenfield, BRENTWOOD, CM15 8QN.
EVANS, Mrs. Kathleen, LLB ACA *1984;* Royal College of Ophthalmologists, 17 Cornwall Terrace, LONDON, NW1 4QW.
EVANS, Miss. Kathleen Margaret, BSc FCA *1973;* 9 Boyd Close, KINGSTON-UPON-THAMES, KT2 7RL. (Life Member)
EVANS, Miss. Kathryn, ACA *2008;* 84 Moorland Road, CARDIFF, CF24 2LP.
EVANS, Mrs. Kathryn, ACA *2005;* 16 Kite Grove, Meir Park, STOKE-ON-TRENT, STAFFORDSHIRE, ST3 7GD.
•**EVANS, Mr. Keith, MA FCA** *1978;* PricewaterhouseCoopers LLP, Savannah House, 3 Ocean Way, Ocean Village, SOUTHAMPTON, SO14 3TJ. See also PricewaterhouseCoopers
•**EVANS, Mr. Keith, FCA** *1973;* Gravestock & Owen Ltd, 75 New Road, WILLENHALL, WV13 2DA.
•**EVANS, Mr. Keith, FCA ATII** *1979;* (Tax Fac), Thompson Wright Limited, Ebeneezer House, Ryecroft, NEWCASTLE, STAFFORDSHIRE, ST5 2BE.
EVANS, Mr. Keith John, FCA *1964;* 32 The Green, Rush Green Road, CLACTON-ON-SEA, CO16 7BH.
EVANS, Miss. Kelly Leigh, ACA MAAT *2011;* 12 Rhodfa Flint, Bodelwyddan, RHYL, CLWYD, LL18 5WP.
EVANS, Mr. Kenneth, FCA *1955;* 7 Warland Gate End, Walsden, TODMORDEN, OL14 6UP. (Life Member)
EVANS, Mr. Kenneth Morda, FCA *1950;* 3 Morford Way, Eastcote, RUISLIP, HA4 8SL. (Life Member)
EVANS, Mr. Kenneth Royston, FCA *1961;* 10 Jean Lawrie Court, St. Boswells, MELROSE, ROXBURGHSHIRE, TD6 0BF. (Life Member)
EVANS, Mrs. Kerrie Amanda, BA(Hons) ACA *2003;* 28 Ryder Close, Biddenham, BEDFORD, MK40 4GN.
EVANS, Mr. Kevin Charles, BSc ACA *1990;* Holly Tree Farm, Ham Lane Oldbury-on-Severn, Thornbury, BRISTOL, BS35 1PZ.
EVANS, Mr. Kevin Robert, ACA *2007;* Hospital Innovations Ltd, 19 Willowbrook Technology Park, Llandogo Road, CARDIFF, CF3 0EF.
EVANS, Mr. Kieran David, BSc ACA *1999;* Doosan Power Systems Doosan House, Crawley Business Quarter Manor Royal, CRAWLEY, WEST SUSSEX, RH10 9AD.
EVANS, Mrs. Laura, ACA *2008;* with Garbutt & Elliott LLP, Stable Court, Beechwoods, Elmete Lane, LEEDS, LS8 2LQ.
EVANS, Mrs. Laura Louise, LLB ACA *1988;* Lawnswood, 8 Burntwood Road, SEVENOAKS, KENT, TN13 1PT.
EVANS, Miss. Lauren Margaret, BSc ACA *2010;* 27 Winterstoke Road, LONDON, SE6 4UG.
EVANS, Mr. Lawrence Joseph, FCA *1951;* 1 Pickhill Hall, Bangor-Is-Y-Coed, WREXHAM, LL13 0UG. (Life Member)
EVANS, Mr. Lee Craig, ACA *2009;* 46 Blakeley Road, WIRRAL, MERSEYSIDE, CH63 0NA.

EVANS, Mrs. Linda Anne, BA FCA *1999;* 3 Bryan Grove, Mynydd Isa, MOLD, CLWYD, CH7 6UW.
EVANS, Mrs. Linda Dawn, BSc ACA *1994;* S J Roberts Constructions Ltd, Lowfield, Marton, WELSHPOOL, POWYS, SY21 8JX.
EVANS, Miss. Lisa, BSc ACA *2011;* Penbryn Uchaf, Gwalchmai, HOLYHEAD, GWYNEDD, LL65 4SL.
EVANS, Mr. Lloyd Douglas, BSc ACA ATII *1990;* 3 Ashcroft, BRIDGNORTH, SHROPSHIRE, WV16 5PG.
EVANS, Mrs. Lorraine, BA ACA *2005;* 11 Greenacres, BENFLEET, ESSEX, SS7 2JB.
EVANS, Miss. Louise Margaret, BSc ACA *1997;* Williams Grand Prix Engineering Ltd, Grove, WANTAGE, OXFORDSHIRE, OX12 0DQ.
EVANS, Ms. Lowri, BCom ACA *1981;* Rue Du Noyer 338, 1030 BRUSSELS, BELGIUM.
EVANS, Mrs. Lucy Helen Margaret, LLB ACA *1991;* 17 Pownall Road, Larkhill, SALISBURY, SP4 8LX.
EVANS, Mrs. Mairead, ACA *2008;* Willow House, Harborough Road, Maidwell, NORTHAMPTON, NN6 9JA.
EVANS, Mr. Malcolm Cavell, FCA *1970;* Wainscote Cottage, 36 Kivernell Road, Milford on Sea, LYMINGTON, HAMPSHIRE, SO41 0PQ.
•EVANS, Mr. Malcolm David, BA FCA *1981;* (Tax Fac), Breeze & Co (Llandudno) Ltd, 9 Lloyd Street, LLANDUDNO, CONWY, LL30 2UU.
•EVANS, Mr. Malcolm John, FCA *1975;* 2 South Road, NOTTINGHAM, NG7 1EB.
EVANS, Mr. Malcolm Thomas, BSc FCA *1956;* Flat 4 Wolsey Place, Mill Road, WORTHING, WEST SUSSEX, BN11 4LR. (Life Member)
EVANS, Mr. Marcus David, BSc ACA MBA *2007;* 10 Finsen Road, LONDON, SE5 9AX.
EVANS, Miss. Marion Elizabeth, FCA *1966;* 161 Cathedral Road, CARDIFF, CF11 9PL. (Life Member)
•EVANS, Mr. Mark, ACA *1993;* Ernst & Young LLP, 1 More London Place, LONDON, SE1 2AF. See also Ernst & Young Europe LLP
EVANS, Mr. Mark, BA FCA *1981;* 9 Dovecote Close, Haddenham, AYLESBURY, HP17 8BS.
EVANS, Mr. Mark, BA ACA *2007;* Flat 5, 42-44 Leverton Street, LONDON, NW5 2PG.
EVANS, Mr. Mark, BSc ACA *1998;* Willow House, 34 Halton Lane, Wendover, AYLESBURY, BUCKINGHAMSHIRE, HP22 6AR.
EVANS, Mr. Mark Andrew, BA FCA MCT MBA *1997;* Grey Gables, Chapel Lane, North Leigh, WITNEY, OXFORDSHIRE, OX29 6SD.
EVANS, Mr. Mark Christopher, MA FCA ATII CTA *1984;* (Tax Fac), with RSM Tenon Limited, 66 Chiltern St, LONDON, W1U 4JT.
EVANS, Mr. Mark Gareth, BA ACA *2000;* Pricewaterhousecoopers, 101 Barbirolli Square, MANCHESTER, M2 3PW.
EVANS, Mr. Mark Hywel, BSc FCA *1990;* Lawnswood, 8 Burntwood Road, SEVENOAKS, KENT, TN13 1PT.
•EVANS, Mr. Mark John, FCA *1985;* Tildesley & Tonks Limited, Unit 8, Pendeford Place, Pendeford Business Park, Wobaston Road, WOLVERHAMPTON WV9 5HD.
•EVANS, Mr. Mark Ward, ACA *1995;* RSM Tenon Audit Limited, 3 Hollinswood Court, Stafford Park, TELFORD, TF3 3BD.
EVANS, Mr. Martin John, BSc ACA *1991;* 6 Bellcast Close, Appleton, WARRINGTON, WA4 5SA.
EVANS, Mr. Martin Robert, FCA *1969;* with Evans & Partners, 9 Bank Road, Kingswood, BRISTOL, BS15 8LS.
EVANS, Mr. Martin William, BSc ACA *1988;* 26 Moss Lane, Bramhall, STOCKPORT, CHESHIRE, SK7 1EH.
EVANS, Mr. Martyn Drew, BA ACA *1981;* 19 Ashley Park Crescent, WALTON-ON-THAMES, SURREY, KT12 1EX.
EVANS, Mr. Matthew Brian Elliott, BSc ACA *1999;* 66 Aldwickbury Crescent, HARPENDEN, HERTFORDSHIRE, AL5 5SD.
EVANS, Mr. Matthew Dillwyn, BSc ACA *1999;* 317 Camp Road, ST. ALBANS, HERTFORDSHIRE, AL1 5NZ.
EVANS, Mr. Matthew Glyn, BA ACA *1999;* 2 TREVOR TERRACE, PAREMATA, WELLINGTON, NEW ZEALAND.
EVANS, Mr. Matthew Jesse, BSc ACA *2001;* 7 Devereux Road, WINDSOR, BERKSHIRE, SL4 1JJ.
EVANS, Mr. Matthew Stephen, BA ACA *2001;* Gainsborough House Winkfield Lane, Winkfield, WINDSOR, SL4 4RU.
•EVANS, Mr. Maurice Roy, FCA *1954;* M.R. Evans & Co, Birchwood, 5 Castle Way, Ewell, EPSOM, KT17 2PG.
EVANS, Miss. May Edwina, MMath ACA *2010;* Flat 53, Buckingham Court, 78 Buckingham Gate, LONDON, SW1E 6PE.
EVANS, Mr. Meurig Fon, BSc ACA *2006;* Swn y Nant, Rhosmeirch, LLANGEFNI, GWYNEDD, LL77 7NQ.
•EVANS, Mr. Michael, FCA *1969;* Evans Mockler Limited, Highstone House, 165 High Street, BARNET, HERTFORDSHIRE, EN5 5SU. See also Evans Mockler
EVANS, Mr. Michael, MBA BA FCA *1992;* Standard Life Investments Inc., Suite 1000, 1001 de Maisonneuve Blvd. West, MONTREAL H3A 3C8, QC, CANADA.
EVANS, Mr. Michael, BSc ACA *1986;* Jones Lang LaSalle, 22 Hanover Square, LONDON, W1S 1JA.
EVANS, Mr. Michael Albert, FCA *1969;* 62 Madeira Park, TUNBRIDGE WELLS, TN2 5SX.
•EVANS, Mr. Michael Anthony Cazel, ACA CA(SA) *2010;* Fifty Business Services Ltd, 5th Floor, 63 St Mary Axe, LONDON, EC3A 8AA.
EVANS, Mr. Michael David, BSc FCA *1992;* 1st Floor Shan Kwong Court, 30 Shan Kwong Road, HAPPY VALLEY, HONG KONG SAR.
EVANS, Mr. Michael Derrick, BA BSc(Hons) CEng DipComp ACA CITP MBCS *1982;* 46 Tytherton Road, LONDON, N19 4QA.
EVANS, Mr. Michael George, BA ACA *1979;* 3 Longfield Road, Ealing, LONDON, W5 2DH.
EVANS, Mr. Michael John, FCA *1970;* Souniou 5, Konia Village, 8300 PAPHOS, CYPRUS.
•EVANS, Mr. Michael John, BSc ACA *1991;* (Tax Fac), Hargreaves Brown & Benson, 1 Bond Street, COLNE, LANCASHIRE, BB8 9DG.
•EVANS, Mr. Michael Kevin Llewelyn, FCA *1971;* Kevin LLewelyn-Evans Limited, 21 Northampton Square, LONDON, EC1V 0AJ.
EVANS, Mr. Michael Norman Gwynne, BSc FCA *1966;* 144 Grove Lane, Cheadle Hulme, CHEADLE, SK8 7NH.
EVANS, Mr. Michael Richard Dugdale, BSc ACA *1980;* 46 Station Road, THAMES DITTON, KT7 0NS.
EVANS, Mr. Michael Robert Nesbit, FCA *1958;* 3 Deer Park Way, SOLIHULL, B91 3HU. (Life Member)
EVANS, Mrs. Michelle Joanne, BSc ACA *2003;* 29 Hurdlers Green, WATLINGTON, OXFORDSHIRE, OX49 5JD.
EVANS, Mr. Mitchell, BA FCA *1998;* 9 Oldfield Road, LONDON, SW19 4SD.
•EVANS, Mr. Nathan Charles, LLB ACA *2005;* Nathan Evans Limited, 16 Cambrian Way, Marshfield, CARDIFF, CF3 2WB.
EVANS, Mr. Nathan Jon, BSc ACA *2004;* Flat 20 Castle Court, 1 Brewhouse Lane, LONDON, SW15 2JJ.
EVANS, Mr. Neil David, BSc ACA *1993;* T U I UK, Wigmore House, Wigmore Place, Wigmore Lane, LUTON, LU2 9TN.
EVANS, Mr. Neil James, FCA *1980;* Zurich Financial Services, UK Life Ltd, Life Centre, Station Road, SWINDON, SN1 1EL.
EVANS, Mr. Nicholas Donald, BSc FCA *1974;* 2 The Parade, Castletown, ISLE OF MAN, IM9 1LG.
EVANS, Mr. Nicholas Gareth, ACA *1984;* 3 Kingsmead, Edlesborough, DUNSTABLE, LU6 2JN.
EVANS, Mr. Nicholas John, BA ACA *1983;* Redcroft, 4 Culcheth Road, ALTRINCHAM, WA14 2LU.
EVANS, Mr. Nicholas John Charles, MA ACA *1995;* 65 Broomleaf Road, FARNHAM, SURREY, GU9 8DQ.
EVANS, Mr. Nicholas Robert, BSc ACA *2008;* Vanguard Investments UK Ltd, 50 Cannon Street, LONDON, EC4N 6JJ.
•EVANS, Mr. Nicholas Stewart, FCA FRSA *1980;* (Tax Fac), Cansdales, Bourbon Court, Nightingales Corner, Little Chalfont, AMERSHAM, HP7 9QS. See also Cansdales Ltd
EVANS, Mr. Nicholas Terrey, FCA *1972;* 6 Mayford Cl, WOKING, GU22 9QS.
EVANS, Mrs. Nicola Jane, BA FCA CF *1989;* 40 Tydraw Road, Penylan, CARDIFF, CF23 5HB.
EVANS, Mrs. Nicola Odette, BSc ACA *1997;* Group Finance, Wincanton Plc, Methuen Park, CHIPPENHAM, SN14 0WT.
EVANS, Mr. Nigel Derek, BSc ACA *1993;* 9 Wallcroft Close, Binfield, BRACKNELL, RG42 4UD.
EVANS, Mr. Nigel Edward, BSc ACA *1994;* West Mercia Supplies, Holsworth Park, Oxon Business Park, Bicton Heath, SHREWSBURY, SY3 5HJ.
•EVANS, Mr. Norman Robert, BA FCA *1984;* Norman R Evans & Co Limited, 25-27 Station Street, Cheslyn Hay, WALSALL, WS6 7ED.
•EVANS, Mr. Oliver James, ACA *1995;* Evans & Partners, 9 Bank Road, Kingswood, BRISTOL, BS15 8LS.
EVANS, Mr. Owain Mortlock, FCA *1966;* 14 Oldway, Bishopstone, SWANSEA, SA3 3DE. (Life Member)
EVANS, Mrs. Pamela Diane, BSc ACA *2001;* with PKF (UK) LLP, 2nd Floor, 1 Redcliff Street, BRISTOL, BS1 6NP.
EVANS, Mrs. Patricia Joan, ACA *1980;* Dyke Yaxley Ltd, 1 Brassey Road, Old Pottsway, SHREWSBURY, SHROPSHIRE, SY3 7FA.
EVANS, Mr. Paul, BSc ACA *2010;* 26 Salisbury Place, LONDON, SW9 6UW.
EVANS, Mr. Paul Andrew Dale, MA BSc FCA *1968;* c/o Paladin Capital Management LLC, 235 Montgomery Street Suite 1146, SAN FRANCISCO, CA 94104, UNITED STATES.
•EVANS, Mr. Paul Anthony Brereton, BA FCA *1976;* 1 Love Lane, ABBOTS LANGLEY, HERTFORDSHIRE, WD5 0QA.
EVANS, Mr. Paul Anthony James, FCA *1972;* Association of the British Pharmaceutical Industry, 12 Whitehall, LONDON, SW1A 2DY.
EVANS, Mr. Paul Anthony Richard, FCA *1965;* 7 Hawksley Close, TWICKENHAM, TW1 4TR.
EVANS, Mr. Paul Daniel, BSc(Hons) ACA *2001;* Credit Suisse Trust Ltd, PO Box 122, St Peter Port, GUERNSEY, GY1 4EE.
EVANS, Mr. Paul Douglas, BSc ACA *2004;* 18 Manorway, WOODFORD GREEN, IG8 7QZ.
•EVANS, Mr. Paul Herbert, FCA *1979;* (Tax Fac), Stephenson Smart & Co, Stephenson House, 15 Church Walk, PETERBOROUGH, PE1 2TP.
EVANS, Mr. Paul James, BSc ACA *1990;* 73 Hatherley Road, CHELTENHAM, GLOUCESTERSHIRE, GL51 6EG.
EVANS, Mr. Paul Llewelyn, BSc ACA *1980;* High Elms, Mill Lane, Codsall, WOLVERHAMPTON, WV8 1EG.
EVANS, Mr. Paul Martin, FCA *1971;* 122 New Road, BROMSGROVE, B60 2LD.
EVANS, Mr. Paul Raymond James, BA(Hons) FCA *2001;* Flat 1, Isabella House, Othello Close, LONDON, SE11 4RT.
EVANS, Mr. Paul Timothy, BA ACA *1985;* 32 Ravenscroft Park, BARNET, EN5 4NH.
EVANS, Mr. Paul William John, ACA FCCA *1998;* 6 Spinney Close, Whittle-le-Woods, CHORLEY, LANCASHIRE, PR6 7PW.
EVANS, Miss. Penelope Ann, BSc ACA *1996;* 10 Prospect Road, Childs Hill, LONDON, NW2 2JT.
EVANS, Dr. Peter, ACA *1990;* City Learning Ltd, 4 Chiswell Street, LONDON, EC1Y 4UP.
•EVANS, Mr. Peter Andrew, MA FCA *1979;* PricewaterhouseCoopers, 7 More London Riverside, LONDON, SE1 2RT. See also PricewaterhouseCoopers LLP
EVANS, Mr. Peter Anthony, BSc FCA *1986;* Fitch Ratings Ltd, 30 North Colonnade, LONDON, E14 5GN.
EVANS, Mr. Peter Burnett, FCA *1961;* The Private Trust Corp Ltd, Charlotte House, Charlotte Street, PO Box N-65, NASSAU, BAHAMAS.
EVANS, Mr. Peter David, BA ACA *1992;* 4 Corfe Close, ASHTEAD, KT21 2HA.
EVANS, Mr. Peter David, BSc ACA *1992;* Ryvangs Alle 20, 2100 COPENHAGEN, DENMARK.
EVANS, Mr. Peter David Graham, FCA *1972;* 20 Westgate, COWBRIDGE, SOUTH GLAMORGAN, CF71 7AR.
EVANS, Mr. Peter Gordon, FCA *1961;* Twyneham House, Watery Lane, Upper Clatford, ANDOVER, HAMPSHIRE, SP11 7PS.
EVANS, Mr. Peter James Roderick, FCA *1971;* Woodstock, 45 St. Michaels Road, Crosby, LIVERPOOL, L23 7UN.
EVANS, Mr. Peter John, FCA *1963;* Chessgrove Cottage, Chessgrove Lane, LONGHOPE, GL17 0LE. (Life Member)
EVANS, Mr. Peter Jonathan Michael, BA FCA *1990;* Luk (UK) Ltd, Waleswood Road, Kiveton Park, SHEFFIELD, S26 5PN.
EVANS, Mr. Peter Leonard, ACA *1980;* 9 Windmill Close, WOKINGHAM, RG41 3XQ.
EVANS, Mr. Peter Michael, ACA *1979;* 4 Church Close, Middleton St. George, DARLINGTON, COUNTY DURHAM, DL2 1DT.
EVANS, Mr. Peter Mounshire, BA ACA *1988;* with Ernst & Young LLP, 1 More London Place, LONDON, SE1 2AF.
EVANS, Mr. Peter Richard, BSocSc ACA *1992;* 1 Sandown Close, STRATFORD-UPON-AVON, WARWICKSHIRE, CV37 9BZ.
EVANS, Mr. Phil Martin, BSc(Hons) ACA *2001;* 18 Baliol Square, DURHAM, DH1 3QH.
EVANS, Mr. Philip Christopher, BSc ACA *2003;* 132 Trowbridge Road, BRADFORD-ON-AVON, BA15 1EW.
•EVANS, Mr. Philip Grant, BSc FCA *1988;* Philip G Evans, Chartered Accountant and Business Adviser, PO Box 219, CHESTER LE STREET, COUNTY DURHAM, DH3 9BF.
EVANS, Mr. Philip Griffiths, FCA *1972;* Gwynfryn, College Street, AMMANFORD, SA18 2BU.
EVANS, Mr. Philip James, BSc ACA *1985;* 68 Joiners Road, Three Crosses, SWANSEA, SA4 3NY.
•EVANS, Mr. Philip John, BSc FCA *1987;* (Tax Fac), PJE, 3 Oakfield Court, Oakfield Road, Clifton, BRISTOL, BS8 2BD.
EVANS, Mr. Philip Kenneth, BA ACA *2004;* 22 Carbis Avenue, Grimsargh, PRESTON, PR2 5LU.
EVANS, Mr. Philip Trevor, BA ACA *1986;* 3978 Holden Drive, ANN ARBOR, MI 48103, UNITED STATES.
EVANS, Mrs. Philippa Jane, ACA *1995;* with Baker Tilly Tax & Advisory Services LLP, Hartwell House, 55-61 Victoria Street, BRISTOL, BS1 6AD.
•EVANS, Mr. Phillip Peter, ACA *1979;* Phillip P. Evans, Crown House, London Road, Loudwater, HIGH WYCOMBE, HP10 9TJ. See also P P Evans Limited
EVANS, Miss. Rachel Alison, MA(Hons) ACA *1996;* 5 Charlesbye Avenue, ORMSKIRK, LANCASHIRE, L39 2XY.
EVANS, Miss. Rachel Sian, BSc ACA *1991;* The Croft, 38 Kingswood Road, TADWORTH, KT20 5EG.
EVANS, Mr. Raymond, BSc FCA *1975;* 46 St. Catherines Road, HAYLING ISLAND, HAMPSHIRE, PO11 0HF.
•EVANS, Mr. Rennie Graham, BCom FCA *1981;* R O C G Prospero, 1 Portland Street, MANCHESTER, M1 3BE. See also Prospero Accounting Ltd
EVANS, Mr. Rhodri Huw, BSc ACA *2005;* 26a Duntshill Road, LONDON, SW18 4QL.
EVANS, Mr. Rhodri Rogers, BSc ACA *2001;* KPMG, 235 St Georges Terrace, PERTH, WA 6000, AUSTRALIA.
EVANS, Mr. Rhys Lloyd, BSc ACA *2010;* 7 Nant Glas, Tircoed Forest Village Penllergaer, SWANSEA, SA4 9SW.
EVANS, Mr. Richard Ceri, BA ACA *1992;* 58 Dan y Coed Road, Cyncoed, CARDIFF, CF23 6NE.
EVANS, Mr. Richard Charles, BSc ACA *1993;* 1 Lapwing Way, ABBOTS LANGLEY, WD5 0GG.
EVANS, Mr. Richard David, BA(Hons) ACA MSI *1988;* 6 Alstead Avenue, Hale, ALTRINCHAM, WA15 8BS.
EVANS, Mr. Richard David, BSc ACA *2004;* Flat 2, 13 St. Martin's Road, LONDON, SW9 0SP.
EVANS, Mr. Richard George, MSc ACA *1998;* 31 Denmark Road, LONDON, W13 8RQ.
EVANS, Mr. Richard Henry, FCA *1969;* Anchor Security Services Ltd The Steam Mill Business Centre, Steam Mill Street, CHESTER, CH3 5AN.
EVANS, Mr. Richard Henry, BSc FCA *1979;* Media Communication Group Plc, 66 Hammersmith Road, LONDON, W14 8UD.
EVANS, Mr. Richard Henry, MBA BA FCA *1979;* 2 Glasshouse Lane, KENILWORTH, WARWICKSHIRE, CV8 2AJ.
EVANS, Mr. Richard Henry, BA FCA *1977;* Hendrewenyn, Llanarthne, CARMARTHEN, SA32 8LJ.
EVANS, Mr. Richard James, BSc(Hons) ACA *2002;* W F Electrical, 313 Rainham Road South, DAGENHAM, ESSEX, RM10 8SX.
•EVANS, Mr. Richard James, BSc ACA *1984;* Reay & King, 87 High Street, Wimbledon, LONDON, SW19 5EG.
EVANS, Mr. Richard Jean Llewellyn, BSc FCA *1984;* 4 Courtland Avenue, LONDON, SW16 3BB.
EVANS, Mr. Richard John, BA ACA *1993;* 41 King Edwards Grove, TEDDINGTON, TW11 9LZ.
EVANS, Mr. Richard Julian, BSc ACA *2001;* 278d Earls Court Road, LONDON, SW5 9AS.
EVANS, Mr. Richard Llewelyn, FCA *1970;* Allhaven Ltd, 19 Berkeley Street, LONDON, W1J 8ED.
EVANS, Mr. Richard Llewelyn, BA FCA *1985;* 23 Holyrood Close, Caversham, READING, RG4 6PZ.
•EVANS, Mr. Richard Matthew, BA ACA *1998;* Harold Sharp, Holland House, 1-5 Oakfield, SALE, M33 6TT.
EVANS, Mr. Richard Murton, FCA *1965;* Jalan Eretan II/102, Kel. Balekambang, Kramat Jati, JAKARTA, 13530, INDONESIA.
EVANS, Mr. Richard Randall, BA(Hons) ACA *2003;* 101 Arthur Street, DERBY, DE1 3EJ.
EVANS, Mr. Richard Stephen, BSc ACA *2005;* 10 Llyswen Road, CARDIFF, CF23 6NG.
•EVANS, Mr. Richard Vaughan, BSc ACA *1989;* KPMG LLP, St. James's Square, MANCHESTER, M2 6DS. See also KPMG Europe LLP
EVANS, Mr. Richard William, BSc ACA *2002;* Tribal Education Ltd, 1-4 Portland Square, BRISTOL, BS2 8RR.
EVANS, Mr. Robert, BA ACA *1995;* 28 Beeches Road, Bloxwich, WALSALL, WS3 1EZ.
EVANS, Mr. Robert Angus, BSc ACA *1983;* Great House Barn, Llanhennock, NEWPORT, NP18 1LU.

EVANS, Mr. Robert Ieuan, BSc ACA *2003;* Westfield Contributory Health Scheme Westfield House, 87 Division Street, SHEFFIELD, S1 1HT.

•EVANS, Mr. Robert James, BSc ACA *1983;* Robert Evans, 23 Clifton Hill, St Johns Wood, LONDON, NW8 0QE.

EVANS, Mr. Robert James, BA ACA *1979;* 4 Home Farm, Corkhill Lane, Normanton, SOUTHWELL, NG25 0PR.

EVANS, Mr. Robert John, BA(Hons) ACA *2000;* Wilson Bowden Developments Ltd Cartwright Way, Forest Business Park Bardon Hill, COALVILLE, LEICESTERSHIRE, LE67 1UB.

EVANS, Mr. Robert John, MSc FCA *1978;* Homestead 46 Princes Avenue, CHATHAM, ME5 8AQ.

•EVANS, Mr. Robert Leslie, BSc FCA *1982;* Hall Livesey Brown, 68 High Street, TARPORLEY, CW6 0AT.

EVANS, Mr. Robert Owen, BSc FCA *1985;* Meadow Court, Whitton, LUDLOW, SHROPSHIRE, SY8 3DB.

EVANS, Mr. Robert Price, BSc ACA *1992;* Bryn Derw, Ffordd Gyffylog, Eglwysbach, COLWYN BAY, CLWYD, LL28 5SF.

•EVANS, Mr. Roger, FCA *1969;* Chartwell Accountants LLP, 79 High Street, SAFFRON WALDEN, ESSEX, CB10 1DZ. See also Chartwell

EVANS, Mr. Roger Clifford, FCA *1981;* 5 Connaught Gardens, BERKHAMSTED, HP4 1SF.

EVANS, Mr. Roger David Loveden, FCA *1971;* The Mill House, Scarah Mill, Ripley, HARROGATE, HG3 3EB.

EVANS, Mr. Roger Lewis, FCA *1964;* Kingston, Dale Brow, Prestbury, MACCLESFIELD, SK10 4BN.

EVANS, Mrs. Rosemary Cheryl, BSc ACA *2008;* 104 Alan Road, IPSWICH, IP3 8EZ.

EVANS, Ms. Rosemary Claire, LLB ACA *1991;* 32 Victoria Road, Mortlake, LONDON, SW14 8EX.

EVANS, Mrs. Rosemary Elizabeth, BSocSc FCA *1978;* 21 Woodman Close, HALESOWEN, B63 3EH.

EVANS, Mr. Russell John, BSc(Econ) ACA *2001;* 26 Lochranza Road, THIRSK, NORTH YORKSHIRE, YO7 1GB.

EVANS, Miss. Ruth, BA ACA *1998;* The Co-operative Travel, Hamil Road, STOKE-ON-TRENT, ST6 1AJ.

EVANS, Mrs. Ruth Annette, BSc ACA *1991;* 2 Wellfield, Bishopston, SWANSEA, SA3 3EP.

EVANS, Mrs. Ruth Mary, ACA *1986;* Dickons Nook, Wharf Lane, Sutton Cheney, NUNEATON, CV13 0AL.

EVANS, Mr. Ryan Andrew, BA(Hons) ACA *2010;* 39 Grange Road, SOUTH CROYDON, CR2 0NE.

EVANS, Mr. Sam Cavell, BA(Hons) ACA *2001;* with KPMG, 10 Shelley Street, SYDNEY, NSW 2000, AUSTRALIA.

EVANS, Mr. Samuel Mark, BSc(Hons) ACA *2009;* Malthouse & Co, America House, 8b Rumford Court, Rumford Place, LIVERPOOL, L3 9DD.

EVANS, Miss. Sara, BSc ACA *2011;* 49 Hambleton Road, HALESOWEN, B63 1HH.

•EVANS, Mrs. Sara Catrin, BSc FCA *1990;* (Tax Fac), Cyfri Cyfrifwyr Cyfyngedig, 1st Floor, Storws Fawr, Drury Lane, ABERAERON, DYFED SA46 0BP.

EVANS, Mrs. Sarah, BA ACA *1986;* La Bigoterie, Berthelot Street, St. Peter Port, GUERNSEY, GY1 1JS.

EVANS, Mrs. Sarah Anne, BA ACA *2001;* 53 Micklefield Way, SEAFORD, EAST SUSSEX, BN25 4EU.

EVANS, Mrs. Sarah Elizabeth, BSocSc ACA *1997;* Always Winchester Road Waltham Chase, SOUTHAMPTON, SO32 2LG.

EVANS, Miss. Sarah Elizabeth, LLB ACA *1999;* 25 Salisbury Road, WATFORD, WD24 4DT.

•EVANS, Mrs. Sarah Jane, BA FCA *1990;* (Tax Fac), 29 Tan y Bryn Road, Rhos on Sea, COLWYN BAY, CLWYD, LL28 4AD.

EVANS, Mrs. Sarah Louise, BSc FCA *1998;* Willow End, 61 Bedford Road, SHEFFORD, BEDFORDSHIRE, SG17 5DR.

EVANS, Mr. Sean Thomas, BA ACA *1993;* 30 Burnham Road, ST. ALBANS, HERTFORDSHIRE, AL1 4QW.

EVANS, Dr. Sian, MA ACA *2001;* 1 Fort Road, GUILDFORD, GU1 3TB.

EVANS, Miss. Sian, BA ACA *1999;* 30 Cobbett Close, SWINDON, SN25 4GZ.

EVANS, Mr. Simon David, BCom ACA *1989;* Dechra Pharmaceuticals Plc, Dechra House, Jamage Industrial Estate, Talke Pits, STOKE-ON-TRENT, ST7 1XW.

EVANS, Mr. Simon Gavin, BA FCA *1996;* 15 Borrowdale Drive, LEAMINGTON SPA, WARWICKSHIRE, CV32 6NY.

•EVANS, Mr. Simon James, BA ACA *1999;* Flat 38, 12a Islington Green, LONDON, N1 2XN.

•EVANS, Mr. Simon John, BSc FCA *1991;* with PricewaterhouseCoopers LLP, Cornwall Court, 19 Cornwall Street, BIRMINGHAM, B3 2DT.

EVANS, Mr. Simon Peter Carbery, BA(Hons) ACA *2001;* with BDO LLP, 55 Baker Street, LONDON, W1U 7EU.

EVANS, Mr. Simon Timothy, BA FCA DChA *1983;* STE Enterprise Limited, 56 Poles Hill, CHESHAM, BUCKINGHAMSHIRE, HP5 2QR.

EVANS, Mrs. Siobhan Annette, MA ACA *1986;* Welbeck, 147 Victoria Grove, BRIDPORT, DORSET, DT6 3AG.

EVANS, Miss. Sioned Eleri, MEng ACA *2010;* KPMG, PO Box HM897, HAMILTON HMDX, BERMUDA.

EVANS, Mr. Stephen Christopher, MA ACA *1981;* Wards Solicitors, 52 Broad Street, BRISTOL, BS1 2EP.

EVANS, Mr. Stephen Dudley, BA FCA *1967;* Fig Tree Cottage, Cocklake, WEDMORE, SOMERSET, BS28 4HB.

EVANS, Mr. Stephen Edmund Lyn, BSc ACA *1989;* Threshing Barn West, Gonalston Lane, Hoveringham, NOTTINGHAM, NG14 7JH.

EVANS, Mr. Stephen Geoffrey, BSc ACA *1982;* The Orchard, 58 Huddersfield Road, Skelmanthorpe, HUDDERSFIELD, HD8 9AS.

EVANS, Mr. Stephen Romilly, FCA *1975;* 71 Seven Star Road, SOLIHULL, B91 2BZ.

•EVANS, Mr. Stephen William, FCA *1973;* William Evans & Partners, 20 Harcourt Street, LONDON, W1H 4HG.

EVANS, Mr. Steven Robert, BA ACA *1995;* 26 Coed Y Cadno, Pen-Y-Fai, BRIDGEND, MID GLAMORGAN, CF31 4GA.

EVANS, Mr. Stuart Edward, BA(Hons) ACA *2000;* 76 Railway Road, TEDDINGTON, MIDDLESEX, TW11 8RZ.

EVANS, Miss. Susan, BA ACA *1990;* 19 Luctons Avenue, BUCKHURST HILL, IG9 5SG.

EVANS, Mrs. Susan Elizabeth, BSc ACA *1984;* (Tax Fac), Grey Roofs, The Scop, Almondsbury, BRISTOL, BS32 4DU.

EVANS, Mrs. Susan Mary, BA ACA *1990;* 3 Ashcroft, BRIDGNORTH, WV16 5PG.

•EVANS, Mrs. Suzanne Joan, BA(Hons) ACA *2002;* (Tax Fac), Nathan Evans Limited, 16 Cambrian Way, Marshfield, CARDIFF, CF3 2WB.

•EVANS, Mrs. Tahira, BSc FCA *1984;* (Tax Fac), TMB & Co, Tynycae, Briw, Llangedwyn, OSWESTRY, SY10 9LB.

EVANS, Miss. Tanya Elisabeth, BA ACA *1991;* 53 Thames Close, HAMPTON, TW12 2ET.

EVANS, Mr. Teifion Morgan, BSc FCA *1968;* 9 Hillside Close, Heddington, CALNE, SN11 0PZ. (Life Member)

•①EVANS, Mr. Terry Christopher, FCA *1971;* Rogers Evans, 20 Brunswick Place, SOUTHAMPTON, SO15 2AQ. See also Chantrey Vellacott DFK LLP

EVANS, Mrs. Tessa Louise, BA FCA *1996;* 74 Swansea Road, Pontlliw, SWANSEA, SA4 9EF.

EVANS, Mr. Thomas Charles, BSc ACA *2007;* 21 Holme Drive, Burton-upon-Stather, SCUNTHORPE, SOUTH HUMBERSIDE, DN15 9DA.

EVANS, Mr. Thomas Edward, ACA *2008;* 82 Sherwood Road, HARROW, MIDDLESEX, HA2 8AR.

EVANS, Mr. Thomas James, BSc ACA *2009;* 25 Inglefield Avenue, CARDIFF, CF14 3PY.

EVANS, Mr. Thomas James William, FCA *1951;* 46 Les Blancs Bois, Rue Cohu, Castel, GUERNSEY, GY5 7SY. (Life Member)

EVANS, Mr. Timothy David John, BA ACA *1979;* Hortus Ockham Drive, West Horsley, LEATHERHEAD, SURREY, KT24 6PG.

EVANS, Mr. Timothy Dominic, BA ACA *2000;* 83 John Archer Way, LONDON, SW18 2TT.

•EVANS, Mr. Timothy James, BSc(Hons) FCA CTA *2001;* Harold D. Pritchard & Co, Old Oak House, 49-51 Lammas Street, CARMARTHEN, DYFED, SA31 3AL.

EVANS, Mr. Timothy Martin, BSc ACA *1990;* Thomas Miller & Co Ltd, 90 Fenchurch Street, LONDON, EC3M 4ST.

EVANS, Mr. Timothy Philip Andrew, BA ACA *1995;* Whip Cottage 447 Luton Road, HARPENDEN, HERTFORDSHIRE, AL5 3QE.

•EVANS, Mr. Timothy William, BA ACA CF *2001;* 15 Parkgate Mews, LONDON, N6 5NB.

EVANS, Mr. Toby Harrie, BA ACA *1997;* 47 Lessar Avenue, LONDON, SW4 9HW.

EVANS, Mr. Trefor Williams, BA FCA *1957;* Ardwyn, 86 Kings Road, LLandybie Carms, AMMANFORD, SA18 2TN. (Life Member)

EVANS, Mr. Treve Nicholas, ACA *1991;* 1 Belmont Road, HELSTON, TR13 8UA.

EVANS, Mr. Trevor Gerald, FCA FRSA *1978;* 2 Herring Gull Close, BLYTH, NORTHUMBERLAND, NE24 3RH.

•①EVANS, Mrs. Victoria Suzanne, BSc(Hons) ACA MABRP *2002;* with Chantrey Vellacott DFK LLP, 35 Calthorpe Road, Edgbaston, BIRMINGHAM, WEST MIDLANDS, B15 1TS.

EVANS, Miss. Vivienne, ACA *2010;* Metropolitan House, 321 Avebury Boulevard, MILTON KEYNES, BUCKINGHAMSHIRE, MK9 2FZ.

EVANS, Mr. Wayne David, BSc FCA MCT MBA *1983;* WD Evans Ltd, 4 Arncliffe Way, COTTINGHAM, NORTH HUMBERSIDE, HU16 5DH.

•EVANS, Mr. William Albert Glyn, FCA *1972;* W.Glyn Evans & Co, Wyecroft, Holme Lacy, HEREFORD, HR2 6LJ.

EVANS, Mr. William Arnold, FCA *1961;* Drayton Hill Cottage, Royston Road, Wendens Ambo, SAFFRON WALDEN, CB11 4JX. (Life Member)

EVANS, Mr. William David, FCA *1977;* 30 The Downsway, SUTTON, SM2 5RN.

EVANS, Mr. William Edward Frank, BA ACA *2000;* Tribal Group plc, 1-4 Portland Square, BRISTOL, BS2 8RR.

•EVANS, Mr. William Emyr, BSc ACA *1987;* Agincourt Limited, 9 Deryn Court, Pentwyn Business Centre, Wharfedale Road, Pentwyn, CARDIFF CF23 7HB.

•EVANS, Mrs. Yvonne Ann, BSc FCA *1992;* (Tax Fac), Aviaccs Limited, 29 Moor Close Lane, Queensbury, BRADFORD, WEST YORKSHIRE, BD13 2NS.

EVANS, Mrs. Zoe, BA ACA *2005;* 91 Ringley Meadows, Stoneclough, MANCHESTER, M26 1ER.

•EVANS-DUDLEY, Mrs. Deborah Jane, BA ACA *1997;* CHD Associates LLP, Ground Floor, Eden Point, Three Acres Lane, Cheadle Hulme, CHEADLE CHESHIRE SK8 6RL.

•EVANS-JONES, Mr. Brian, BSc ACA *1985;* Mwldan Business Park, Bath House Road, CARDIGAN, CEREDIGION, SA43 1JY.

•EVANS-JONES, Mr. Owen, MSc FCA *1989;* O. Evans-Jones, Bod Marian, Glan Conwy, COLWYN BAY, LL28 5SY.

EVANS-MAILLARD, Mr. Huw David, MA FCA *1980;* 55 Raleigh Park Road, North Hinksey, OXFORD, OX2 9AZ.

EVANSON, Mr. Peter Nixon, FCA *1956;* 3 Padwick Road, HORSHAM, RH13 6BN. (Life Member)

EVE, Mr. Andrew James, BA ACA *2004;* 46 Rose Terrace, Horsforth, LEEDS, LS18 4QA.

•EVE, Mr. Charles Harry, BA ACA *2000;* Carpenter Box LLP, Amelia House, WORTHING, WEST SUSSEX, BN11 1QR.

EVE, Mr. Dennis Paul, BSc FCA *1970;* (Tax Fac), North Lodge, 77 High Road, HOCKLEY, ESSEX, SS5 4SZ.

EVE, Miss. Henrietta Frances, BSc ACA *2009;* MSPC CPA, 340 North Avenue, CRANFORD, NJ 07016, UNITED STATES.

•EVE, Mr. Maurice Anthony, FCA *1982;* (Tax Fac), M A EVE, 5 Julien Road, COULSDON, CR5 2DN.

EVE, Mrs. Sarah Carleton, BA FCA *1973;* Pedington Elm, Stone, BERKELEY, GLOUCESTERSHIRE, GL13 9LQ.

•EVE, Mr. Timothy Clive, BA ACA *1998;* Aston Ventrues Consultants Ltd Blackfriars House, Parsonage, MANCHESTER, M3 2JA.

EVE, Mr. Timothy George Frederick, BA ACA *1981;* 68 Hamble Road, BEDFORD, MK41 7XW.

EVE, Dr. Tom, PhD MChem ACA *2010;* 6 Pitt Crescent, LONDON, SW19 8HS.

EVELEGH, Mr. Nigel Markham Aldridge, BSc FCA *1967;* Organford Manor, Organford, POOLE, DORSET, BH16 6ES.

EVELEIGH, Mr. Brendan Anthony, FCA *1975;* Bahia de Casares 47, 29690 CASARES, MALAGA, SPAIN.

EVELEIGH, Mr. Justin Francis, BSc(Hons) ACA *2000;* Dubai Internet City, DUBAI, UNITED ARAB EMIRATES.

EVELEIGH, Mrs. Lesley Anne, BSc ACA *1992;* 11, Acer Drive, YEOVIL, BA21 3DH.

EVELING, Mr. Andrew James, ACA *2008;* 43 Beech Road, Biggin Hill, WESTERHAM, KENT, TN16 3UY.

EVEMY, Mr. John Kenneth, FCA *1952;* 51 Trull Road, TAUNTON, TA1 4QN. (Life Member)

•EVENDEN, Miss. Jill Marie, BA ACA *1990;* (Tax Fac), EBS Accountants Ltd, Gothic House, Barker Gate, NOTTINGHAM, NG1 1JU.

EVENDEN, Mr. Stephen Geoffrey, BSc ACA AMCT *2001;* 34 Hayes Garden, BROMLEY, BR2 7DG.

EVENETT, Mr. Rupert William, MA FCA *1992;* 49 Hyde Vale, LONDON, SE10 8QQ.

EVENHUIS, Mr. Patrick Henry, FCA *1951;* 45 St Stephens Close, Avenue Road St Johns Wood, LONDON, NW8 6DD. (Life Member)

EVENNETT, Mr. David Ernest, FCA *1955;* Box 625, Vale do Lobo, 8135 ALMANCIL, PORTUGAL. (Life Member)

•EVENS, Mrs. Alison Ruth, BA ACA *1982;* (Tax Fac), Evens & Co. Ltd, Hamilton House, Hamilton Terrace, MILFORD HAVEN, PEMBROKESHIRE, SA73 3JP.

•EVENS, Mr. Bruce Kingcome, BA ACA *1982;* Evens & Co. Ltd, Hamilton House, Hamilton Terrace, MILFORD HAVEN, PEMBROKESHIRE, SA73 3JP.

EVENS, Mr. Jonathan David Newton, BSc ACA *1988;* 46 Alder Close, BALDOCK, HERTFORDSHIRE, SG7 6HN.

EVENS, Mr. Mark David, MA FCA *1978;* High Mosser Gate, Mosser, COCKERMOUTH, CUMBRIA, CA13 0SR.

EVENSEN, Mr. James Peter, BA ACA *1979;* Alkon Ltd, 21 St. Annes Road St. Annes Park, BRISTOL, BS4 4AB.

EVERALL, Mr. Adam Mark, MBA BA ACA *1988;* 221 Red Bank Road, Bispham, BLACKPOOL, FY2 9EA.

EVERALL, Mr. Andrew John, BA ACA *1994;* Shereford House, Shereford, FAKENHAM, NORFOLK, NR21 7PP.

•EVERALL, Mr. Richard James, BA FCA *1980;* (Tax Fac), Razzle Limited, 8 Blandfield Road, LONDON, SW12 8BG.

•EVERALL, Mr. Stephen Richard, FCA *1986;* Stephen Everall FCA, 12 Hillside, Sawston, CAMBRIDGE, CB22 5BL.

EVERARD, Mr. Alan John, FCA *1970;* Walden Cottage, 59 The Street, Little Waltham, CHELMSFORD, CM3 3NT. (Life Member)

EVERARD, Mr. Gordon Geoffrey Ellis, FCA *1953;* The Annexe, 48 Mayfield Road, RYDE, ISLE OF WIGHT, PO33 3PR. (Life Member)

•EVERARD, Mr. Nigel Conrad, BA FCA *1986;* Hunter Gee Holroyd, Club Chambers, Museum Street, YORK, YO1 7DN. See also Hunter Gee Holroyd Limited

•EVERATT, Mr. David James, BA ACA *1994;* (Tax Fac), Forrester Boyd, 26 South Saint Mary's Gate, GRIMSBY, NORTH LINCOLNSHIRE, DN31 1LW.

EVERED, Miss. Ruth Mary, BSc ACA *2009;* Manton House, Eastgate, BOURNE, LINCOLNSHIRE, PE10 9LB.

•EVEREST, Mr. Clive Mark Llewellyn, MA ACA *1988;* PricewaterhouseCoopers LLP, Marlborough Court, 10 Bricket Road, ST. ALBANS, HERTFORDSHIRE, AL1 3JX. See also PricewaterhouseCoopers

EVEREST, Mrs. Jane Mary, BSc ACA *1986;* (Tax Fac), 18 Henley Road, IPSWICH, IP1 3SL.

•EVEREST, Mr. Philip James, FCA *1978;* (Tax Fac), Lucraft Hodgson & Dawes, 2/4 Ash Lane, Rustington, LITTLEHAMPTON, BN16 3BZ.

EVEREST, Mr. Richard Anthony, MA FCA *1966;* 2 Palfrey Close, ST. ALBANS, AL3 5RE.

EVEREST, Mrs. Susan Mary, ACA *1984;* 7 Portman Close, ST. ALBANS, AL4 9TW.

EVEREST-GREENE, Mrs. Maura Angela, BA ACA *1992;* Orchard House, 120 High Street, South Milford, LEEDS, LS25 5AQ.

•EVERETT, Mrs. Chai Hung, ACA *1991;* (Tax Fac), Everett Wong Limited, 51 The Mall, Southgate, LONDON, N14 6LR.

EVERETT, Mr. Christopher John Hugo, FCA *1960;* Brook House, High Street, Selborne, ALTON, GU34 3LG. (Life Member)

EVERETT, Mr. David, ACA *2009;* Babcock International Group, Devonport Royal Dockyard, PC 305B, PLYMOUTH, PL1 4SG.

EVERETT, Mr. Jamie Douglas, MA ACA *2006;* Ground floor flat, 39 Bronsart Road, LONDON, SW6 6AJ.

EVERETT, Mr. Jeffrey Graeme, FCA *1980;* Linkbase Ltd, Woodlands, 415 Limpsfield Road, WARLINGHAM, SURREY, CR6 9HA.

EVERETT, Mrs. Karen, BSc FCA *1988;* 18 Wyre Close, Chandler's Ford, EASTLEIGH, SO53 4QR.

EVERETT, Mr. Kenneth Allan John, FCA *1953;* 17 Essex Road, Leyton, LONDON, E10 6HP. (Life Member)

EVERETT, Mrs. Kirsty Jane, BA ACA *2003;* 10 Burrard Road, LONDON, NW6 1DB.

EVERETT, Mr. Mark, ACA *2009;* 33 Rushmore Grange, WASHINGTON, TYNE AND WEAR, NE38 7LF.

EVERETT, Mr. Martyn John, BSc FCA *1983;* Wealden Lodge, Oakleigh Road, PINNER, MIDDLESEX, HA5 4HB.

EVERETT, Mrs. Michelle Julie, ACA *1999;* 16 Greenfield Way, Wrenthorpe, WAKEFIELD, WEST YORKSHIRE, WF2 0TN.

EVERETT, Mr. Phillip John, MA FCA *1990;* 99 Warwick Road, LONDON, N11 2SR.

EVERETT, Mr. Richard Anthony Sharman, FCA *1963;* Sandfield House, 58 Lynn Road, DOWNHAM MARKET, PE38 9NN.

EVERETT, Mr. Richard Charles, BSc ACA *1990;* The Wood House Upper Green Road, Shipbourne, TONBRIDGE, TN11 9PQ.

EVERETT, Miss. Sara Jane, BA ACA *1996;* Ascot Racecourse, High Street, ASCOT, BERKSHIRE, SL5 7JX.

EVERETT, Mr. Scott Peter, BA ACA *2002;* 16 Greenfield Way, Wrenthorpe, WAKEFIELD, WF2 0TN.

EVERETT, Mr. Tobias John Deaton, ACA *1986;* 34 Teddington Park Road, TEDDINGTON, TW11 8ND.

EVERETT, Mr. Toby Douglas, FCA *1973;* Woodhill Farm, Frensham, FARNHAM, GU10 3EN.

EVERETT, Miss. Verity, BA ACA *2003;* 96 Gloucester Road, HAMPTON, TW12 2UJ.

•EVERIN, Mrs. Ann, FCA *1988;* Ann Everin, 24 Victoria Ave, Saltaire, SHIPLEY, BD18 4SQ.

EVERINGHAM, Mr. Paul John, BEng FCA CF *1997;* 31 St. Matthews Road, BRISTOL, BS6 5TU.

EVERINGHAM, Miss. Susan Jane, BSc ACA *1991;* 1 The Mews, Queniborough Hall Drive Queniborough, LEICESTER, LE7 3DZ.

EVERIST, Mr. Charles Roland Giles, BSc ACA *1993;* 18 Genesta Crescent, DALKEITH, WA 6009, AUSTRALIA.

EVERIST, Mr. John Colin, FCA *1971;* The Chesters, Rannoch Road, CROWBOROUGH, TN6 1RB.

EVERITT, Mrs. Amanda Jane, ACA *1989;* (Tax Fac), Vocis Driveline Controls, The American Barns, Banbury Road, Lighthorne, WARWICK, CV35 0AE.

EVERITT, Mr. Anthony David, BA ACA *1988;* 23 Dunford Road, Bedminster, BRISTOL, BS3 4PN.

EVERITT, Mr. Barrie, FCA *1972;* The Conkers, 28 Knedlington Road, Howden, GOOLE, NORTH HUMBERSIDE, DN14 7ER. (Life Member)

•EVERITT, Mr. David Terence, FCA *1961;* Everitt James & Co., 7 Ison Close, Biddenham, BEDFORD, MK40 4BH.

EVERITT, Mrs. Denise Kim, BA ACA *1982;* Room 131, University of Kent at Canterbury, The Registry, CANTERBURY, CT2 7NZ.

EVERITT, Mrs. Gillian Bahar, BA ACA *2006;* 16 Sandcroft Road, Caversham, READING, RG4 7NP.

EVERITT, Mr. James Victor Golden, MA FCA *1966;* 1 Greatford Gardens, Greatford, STAMFORD, PE9 4PX.

EVERITT, Mrs. Jennifer Claire, BSc ACA *2001;* 30 Mickleover Manor, Mickleover, DERBY, DE3 0SH.

EVERITT, Ms. Mary Elizabeth, MSc FCA *1972;* 16 Dorian Road, HORNCHURCH, RM12 4AW.

•EVERITT, Mrs. Michelle Dawn, BSc ACA *1995;* Michelle Everitt, 37 North Hill, LONDON, N6 4BS.

EVERITT, Mrs. Nicola, BSc(Hons) ACA *2010;* 3 Hayes Close, CHELMSFORD, CM2 0RN.

EVERITT, Mr. Peter Charles, FCA ATII *1972;* 36 Donington Avenue, Barkingside, ILFORD, ESSEX, IG6 1DP. (Life Member)

•EVERITT, Mr. Tony Kim, BSc FCA *1991;* Tony Everitt, 11B Soham Road, Fordham, ELY, CAMBRIDGESHIRE, CB7 5LB.

EVERITT, The Revd. William Frank James, BA FCA *1963;* 27 Lark Hill Crescent, RIPON, HG4 2HN.

EVERITT, Mr. William James Haydn, BA FCA *1964;* Neroche, 10 The Beacon, ILMINSTER, TA19 9AH.

EVERS, Mr. Martyn David, ACA CA(SA) *1980;* P.O. Box 69306, BRYANSTON, GAUTENG, 2021, SOUTH AFRICA.

EVERS, Mr. Robert George, FCA *1952;* Little Oaks, 33 Beacon Road, BROADSTONE, BH18 9JP. (Life Member)

EVERSDEN, Mr. Will Robert, BA ACA *2002;* with Deloitte LLP, Hill House, 1 Little New Street, LONDON, EC4A 3TR.

•EVERSFIELD, Mr. Geoffrey William Claude, BSc ACA *1989;* PricewaterhouseCoopers LLP, 1 Embankment Place, LONDON, WC2N 6RH. See also PricewaterhouseCoopers

EVERSHAM, Mr. Andrew John, BSc ACA *1996;* 23 Middle Croft Abbeymead, GLOUCESTER, GL4 4RL.

EVERSHED, Mr. Jonathan, BSc ACA *1992;* 98 London Road, WOKINGHAM, BERKSHIRE, RG40 1YG.

EVERSON, Mrs. Lynn Elizabeth, BSc ACA *1995;* Coppers View Uphill, Urchfont, DEVIZES, SN10 4SB.

EVERSON, Mr. Matthew Neil, BSc ACA *2005;* with Deloitte LLP, 3 Rivergate, Temple Quay, BRISTOL, BS1 6GD.

EVERSON, Mr. Peter Leslie, BSc ACA *1979;* Sea Cloud, Mizzentop, Longford Road, WARWICK PARISH WK 06, BERMUDA.

EVERSON, Mr. Roger Frank, FCA *1971;* Response Organisation A G Palmer House, Morrell Crescent Littlemore, OXFORD, OX4 4SU.

EVERSON, Ms. Rowena Helen Scholastica, BSc ACA *1998;* Robinson Road Post Office, PO Box 278, SINGAPORE, SINGAPORE.

EVERSON, Mr. Terence Fred, FCA *1963;* 7 Wolfreton Garth, Kirk Ella, HULL, HU10 7AB.

EVERSON-DAVIS, Mr. Godfrey Miles, FCA *1971;* Castle Acre, 3 The Close, Avon Castle, RINGWOOD, BH24 2BJ.

EVERTON, Mr. Cecil Frederick, FCA *1950;* 1 Wilfred Close, Merrimans Hill, WORCESTER, WR3 8XQ. (Life Member)

EVERTON, Mr. Jason Lee, BA ACA *1998;* 9 Drakes Hill Close, Wollaston, STOURBRIDGE, DY8 3LE.

EVERTON, Mr. John, BA ACA *2007;* Skanska UK Ltd Condor House, 5-10 St. Paul's Churchyard, LONDON, EC4M 8AL.

EVERTON, Mrs. Julie Ann, BSc ACA *1999;* 9 Drakes Hill Close, STOURBRIDGE, DY8 3LE.

EVERTON, Mr. Stephen Christopher Jim, BSc ACA *1985;* 3 Pond Close Welton, LINCOLN, LN2 3UE.

EVERY, Mr. Donald Cochrane, FCA *1974;* New Barn Garage, 65-67 Aldwick Road, BOGNOR REGIS, WEST SUSSEX, PO21 2NW.

EVERY, Mr. Edward, BSc ACA *2007;* Mallard House Medbourne Road, Ashley, MARKET HARBOROUGH, LE16 8DA.

EVERY, Sir Henry John Michael, Bt DL FCA *1971;* Cothay, 26 Fishpond Lane, Egginton, DERBY, DE65 6HJ.

EVERY, Mr. Simon Flower, MA FCA *1956;* The White House, Crawley, WINCHESTER, SO21 2PR. (Life Member)

EVES, Mr. Christopher, BA(Hons) ACA *2010;* 30 Victoria Avenue, Douglas, ISLE OF MAN, IM2 4AN.

EVESON, Dr. Robert Eric, BSc(Hons) ACA *2002;* 52 Kelmscott Road, BIRMINGHAM, B17 8QN.

•EVGENIOU, Mr. Evgenios, BEng FCA *1993;* PricewaterhouseCoopers Limited, Julia House, 3 Themistocles Dervis Street, CY-1066 NICOSIA, CYPRUS.

EVINGTON, Mr. Mark Ian, BA ACA *1987;* Cogent Breeding Ltd/Grosvenor Farms Ltd, Lea Lane, Aldford, CHESTER, CH3 6JQ.

EVINGTON, Mr. Terence, FCA *1965;* Southview, 9 The Pickerings, NORTH FERRIBY, NORTH HUMBERSIDE, HU14 3EJ. (Life Member)

EVISON, Miss. Anita Glenys, BA FCA *1975;* The Stables, Radcliffe Road, Holme Pierrepont, NOTTINGHAM, NG12 2LT.

EVISON, Mrs. Claire, BA ACA *2003;* 12 Pradoe View, West Felton, OSWESTRY, SHROPSHIRE, SY11 4GA.

EVISON, Mrs. Coralie Louise, BA ACA *1997;* 4 Beechwood Avenue, RICHMOND, SURREY, TW9 4DE.

•EVISON, Mr. David Paul, FCA *1971;* Garner Pugh & Sinclair, 3 Belgrave Place, 19 Salop Road, OSWESTRY, SHROPSHIRE, SY11 2NR.

EVISON, Mrs. Emma Louise, BSc ACA *1995;* Mars UK, Master Foods Freeby Lane, Waltham on the Wolds, MELTON MOWBRAY, LEICESTERSHIRE, LE14 4RS.

•EVISON, Mr. John Edward, FCA *1960;* Falconhurst, 6 Bryn y Bia Road, LLANDUDNO, GWYNEDD, LL30 3AS.

EVISON, Miss. Laura, BA ACA *1999;* 14 Woodland Way, WEYBRIDGE, SURREY, KT13 9SW.

•EVISON, Mr. Michael Philip, BA ACA *2003;* Garner Pugh & Sinclair, 3 Belgrave Place, 19 Salop Road, OSWESTRY, SHROPSHIRE, SY11 2NR.

EVISON, Mr. William John, BSc ACA *2009;* Flat 21, Overy House, Webber Row, LONDON, SE1 8QX.

EVITT, Ms. Joanna, ACA *2010;* 11 Redcliffe Parade East, BRISTOL, BS1 6SW.

•EVRY, Mr. Martin George, FCA *1986;* Ernst & Young Beograd d.o.o, 115d Bulevar, Miharjla Pupina, 11070 BELGRADE, SERBIA. See also Ernst & Young Europe LLP

EWAN, Mrs. Jill Mary, BA FCA *1983;* 8 Wycherley Avenue, Linthorpe, MIDDLESBROUGH, CLEVELAND, TS5 5HH.

EWART, Mr. Andrew, ACA ACCA *2009;* 55 Salisbury Street, HULL, HU5 3DU.

EWART, Mrs. Elizabeth Anne, BSc ACA *2001;* Ashview, Kite Hill, Wanborough, SWINDON, WILTSHIRE, SN4 0AW.

EWART, Mr. Philippe Pelham, BSc ACA *1993;* 1 Avenue General de Gaulle, 06230 VILLEFRANCHE-SUR-MER, FRANCE.

EWART-WHITE, Mr. David Vincent Ewart, FCA *1966;* 3 Pinecroft, St Georges Road, WEYBRIDGE, SURREY, KT13 0EN.

EWBANK, Mr. Alfred Norman, FCA *1952;* 26 Fidlers Walk, Wargrave, READING, RG10 8BA. (Life Member)

EWBANK, Mr. Richard John, BSc ACA *1990;* 17 Broadhurst Gardens, REIGATE, RH2 8AW.

EWE, Miss. Lee How, BSc ACA *1984;* 19 Brynmawr Road, CAMBERWELL, VIC 3124, AUSTRALIA.

EWE, Mr. Pang Kooi, BA FCA *1981;* 7 SHENTON WAY #01-02, SINGAPORE CONFERENCE HALL, SINGAPORE 068810, SINGAPORE. See also EWE, LOKE & PARTNERS

•EWEN, Mr. Norman Edward, FCA *1984;* (Tax Fac), Norman Ewen & Co, The Barn, Monument Offices, Maldon Road, Woodham Mortimer, MALDON ESSEX CM9 6SN.

EWEN, Mr. Peter, FCA *1971;* 19 Wessex Road, DIDCOT, OX11 8BU.

•EWEN, Mr. Philip Kenneth Shelley, FCA *1982;* Calder & Co, 1 Regent Street, LONDON, SW1Y 4NW.

EWEN, Miss. Rebecca Rachel, BSc ACA *2010;* 1 Church Road, Hilgay, DOWNHAM MARKET, NORFOLK, PE38 0JF.

EWEN, Miss. Sarah, MA ACA *2006;* 5/121, Ocean Street, Edgecliffe, SYDNEY, NSW 2027, AUSTRALIA.

EWENS, Mr. Colin Neil, FCA *1975;* 10 The Coppice, Kelvedon Common, BRENTWOOD, Essex, CM15 0DB.

EWENS, Mr. Samuel Edward, BSc ACA *2009;* 8 Flock Mill Place, LONDON, SW18 4QJ.

EWER, Mr. Adrian James Henry, FCA *1977;* John Laing Plc, Allington House, 150 Victoria Street, LONDON, SW1E 5LB.

EWER, Mrs. Sharon Veronica, BA ACA *1994;* 13 Foxenden Road, GUILDFORD, GU1 4DL.

EWER-SMITH, Mr. Geoffrey Charles, FCA *1975;* 8 Clarence Road, WALTON-ON-THAMES, KT12 5JU. (Life Member)

EWERS, Mr. Andrew William, MA FCA *1985;* Prime Care Holdings Ltd, Talland Parade, High Street, SEAFORD, EAST SUSSEX, BN25 1PJ.

EWERS, Ms. Hilary Jane, BSc ACA *1992;* 32 Red Lion Road, Chobham, WOKING, GU24 8RG.

EWERS, Mr. Robert Andrew, BA ACA *1989;* Swallow Cottages, Fryern Road, Storrington, PULBOROUGH, RH20 4NT.

EWERS, Mrs. Suzanne Elizabeth, MA ACA *1990;* Swallows Cottage Fryern Road, Storrington, PULBOROUGH, WEST SUSSEX, RH20 4NT.

•EWIN, Mr. Alexander David, BA ACA *2007;* Alex Ewin, Flat 7 Strathaird Court, 39 Grove Road, SUTTON, SURREY, SM1 2AH.

•EWIN, Mrs. Barbara Ann, BSc FCA *1979;* Barbara Ewin Ltd, Pear Tree Cottage, Old Durham, DURHAM, DH1 2RY.

EWIN, Mr. Stephen Joseph, MBA FCA *1973;* 4 Lickey End Buildings, Barnsley Hall Drive, BROMSGROVE, B61 0EX.

EWING, Mrs. Alison Arnot, BSc FCA *1991;* with Grant Thornton UK LLP, 4 Hardman Square, Spinningfields, MANCHESTER, M3 3EB.

EWING, Mr. Andrew James, BA ACA *1986;* Rookwood, 2 St John's Avenue, CLEVEDON, BS21 7TQ.

•EWING, Mr. David, BSc ACA *1989;* Evolve FD Ltd, 11 North Road, LIVERPOOL, L19 0LP. See also DE Consultancy Ltd

EWING, Mr. Justin Anthony Charles, BEng ACA *1994;* 2066 E Trolley Ct, BOISE, ID 83712, UNITED STATES.

•EWING, Mrs. Margaret, BA FCA *1981;* Deloitte LLP, 2 New Street Square, LONDON, EC4A 3BZ. See also Deloitte & Touche LLP

EWING, Mr. Mark Patrick James, MA ACA *2003;* 28 Northway Road, LONDON, SE5 9AN.

EWING, Miss. Melanie Clare, BA ACA *1999;* Apfelmatte 2, 8804 AU ZH, SWITZERLAND.

EWING, Mr. Paul Neil, BA ACA *2000;* 29/F The Center, 99 Queens Road, CENTRAL, HONG KONG ISLAND, HONG KONG SAR.

•EWING, Mr. Philip Gordon, BSc FCA *1984;* Harrison Beale & Owen Limited, Harrison Beale, 15 Queens Road, COVENTRY, CV1 3DE. See also Harrison Beale & Owen Management Services

EWING, Mr. Robert, BSc ACA *1991;* Kingston University, River House, 53-57 High Street, Kingston, KINGSTON UPON THAMES, KT1 1LQ.

EWING, Mr. Robert Stuart David, ACA *2011;* Flat 4, 18 The Mount, LONDON, NW3 6ST.

EWING, Mr. Tim Muir, BA ACA *1998;* 43 Hornsey Street, ROZELLE, NSW 2039, AUSTRALIA.

EWINGS, Ms. Lucy Amelia, BA ACA *2006;* 29 Higher Town, Sampford Peverell, TIVERTON, DEVON, EX16 7BR.

EWINS, Mr. Peter Colin, MSc ACA *1979;* Church Urban Fund, Corporation of the Church House, 27 Great Smith Street, LONDON, SW1P 3AZ.

EWINS, Mr. Thomas Richard, BSc ACA *2007;* 240 Bath Road, Keynsham, BRISTOL, BS31 1TG.

EWLES, Mr. Michael John, BA ACA *1989;* P.O. Box HM 3076, HAMILTON HM NX, BERMUDA.

•①EXELL, Mr. David John, FCA *1965;* David Exell Associates, PO Box 1601, Broad Street, Wrington, BRISTOL, BS40 5WA.

EXELL, Miss. Emily Claire, MA ACA *2006;* Flat 3, Dunbar Court, 6 Durham Road, BROMLEY, BR2 0SQ.

EXETER, Mr. Daniel Charles, BA(Hons) ACA *2001;* Level 4, 222 Bourke Street, MELBOURNE, VIC 3000, AUSTRALIA.

EXETER, Mr. Gordon Charles, FCA *1966;* 17 Deepdene, Hindhead Road, HASLEMERE, GU27 1RE.

•EXLEY, Mr. Andrew Nicholas, ACA *1993;* Sterling Corporate Finance LLP, 12 York Place, LEEDS, LS1 2DS.

•EXLEY, Mrs. Caroline Anne, BA FCA *2000;* Accountancy & Business Advice Lymm Limited, 22 Pepper Street, LYMM, CHESHIRE, WA13 0JB.

EXLEY, Mr. Colin Peter, ACA *1982;* 70 Monkton Farleigh, BRADFORD-ON-AVON, BA15 2QJ.

EXLEY, Mr. Ian James, BSc ACA *1979;* 22 Bedford Road, HORSHAM, RH13 5BJ.

EXLEY, Mr. Steven James, BA DipHE ACA *2006;* 10 King Cup Close, GLOSSOP, DERBYSHIRE, SK13 8UE.

EXTANCE, Mr. Paul Anthony, MA FCA *1988;* 7 Mardley Heights, WELWYN, HERTFORDSHIRE, AL6 0TX.

EXTON, Mr. Alan, FCA *1977;* Tigh Darach, 18 Lucerne Rd, Oakwood, DERBY, DE21 2XF.

EXTON, Mr. Brian Everard, FCA *1960;* Brian E Exon Management Services, 90 Glenburnie Road, VERMONT, VIC 3133, AUSTRALIA.

EXWOOD, Mr. Roger John William, BSc ACA *1991;* (Tax Fac), 10 Lamberts Place, HORSMONDEN, KENT, TN12 8AG.

EYKYN, Mr. William James, FCA *1964;* Abbotts Hill, Duntisbourne Abbotts, CIRENCESTER, GL7 7JN.

EYLES, Mr. Christopher, BA FCA *1974;* Laminar Medica Ltd, Unit 4A, Icknield Way Industrial Estate, Icknield Way, TRING, HERTFORDSHIRE HP23 4JX.

EYLES, Mr. Christopher David, BA ACA *1978;* 73 Calder Avenue, Brookmans Park, HATFIELD, AL9 7AJ.

EYLES, Mr. Colin John, BSc ACA *1992;* The Half Way, Whittonditch Road, Ramsbury, MARLBOROUGH, SN8 2PX.

EYLES, Mr. Peter Francis, ACA *1990;* 15 Croft Lane, Roade, NORTHAMPTON, NN7 2QZ.

EYLES, Mrs. Rosalind Marjorie, BA ACA *1993;* The Halfway, Whittonditch Road, Ramsbury, MARLBOROUGH, SN8 2PX.

EYLEY, Mr. Eric, FCA *1955;* 136 Ashby Road, BURTON-ON-TRENT, DE15 0LQ. (Life Member)

EYNON, Mr. Douglas, FCA *1959;* 17 Fox Wood, Hemblington, NORWICH, NR13 4RZ. (Life Member)

EYNON, Mr. James Sinclair, BSc ACA *2010;* Flat 1, 20 Acfold Road, LONDON, SW6 2AL.

EYNON, Mr. Lewis Charles, MA ACA *1985;* 62 Tavistock Road, CALLINGTON, CORNWALL, PL17 7DU.

EYNON, Mr. Philip James, FCA *1976;* The Anchorage, Dockyard Drive, ENGLISH HARBOUR, ANTIGUA AND BARBUDA.

EYRE, Miss. Alison Jane, BSc ACA *1993;* 54 Sumatra Road, LONDON, NW6 1PR.

EYRE, Mr. Andrew John Duncan, BSc ACA *1989;* 10 Stratford Way, Huntington, YORK, YO32 9YW.

EYRE, Mrs. Christine Joyce, FCA *1970;* 77 Lathe Road, Whiston, ROTHERHAM, S60 4LL. (Life Member)

•EYRE, Mr. Daniel Adrian, LLB ACA *1998;* Ernst & Young LLP, 1 More London Place, LONDON, SE1 2AF. See also Ernst & Young Europe LLP

EYRE, Mr. Douglas, FCA *1968;* 1 Kirby Way, West Southbourne, BOURNEMOUTH, BH6 3HZ.

•EYRE, Mrs. Elizabeth Leah, BSc FCA *1994;* Elizabeth Eyre Limited, 112-114 West Malvern Road, MALVERN, WORCESTERSHIRE, WR14 4NB.

EYRE, Mr. Geoffrey Peter, BEng ACA *1998;* Garden Flat, 51 Buckland Crescent, LONDON, NW3 5DJ.

EYRE, Mr. James Alexander, BSc ACA *2010;* 38 Hillbrook Road, LONDON, SW17 8SG.

EYRE, Mr. James David, BA(Hons) ACA *2001;* 6 The Meade, WILMSLOW, CHESHIRE, SK9 2JF.

EYRE, Mrs. Jill Alexandra, ACA *1986;* 16 Lodwick, Shoeburyness, SOUTHEND-ON-SEA, SS3 9HW.

EYRE, Mr. John Rees, FCA *1972;* Eyre & Elliston Ltd, 185-191 Chatsworth Road, CHESTERFIELD, DERBYSHIRE, S40 2BD.

EYRE, Mrs. Nicola Jayne, BSc ACA *2005;* 72 Morfa Street, BRIDGEND, Mid Glamorgan, CF31 1HD.

EYRE, Mr. Roger Michael, BSc ACA *2005;* 5 West End, Ashwell, BALDOCK, HERTFORDSHIRE, SG7 5PH.

EYRE, Mr. Thomas Frank Alexander, BA ACA FSI *1991;* Rensburg Limited, Quayside House, Canal Wharf, Holbeck, LEEDS, LS11 5PU.
•**EYRE-WALKER, Mr. James Philip, MBA BSc FCA** *1986;* Howsons Accountants Limited, 18-20 Moorland Road, STOKE-ON-TRENT, ST6 1DW.
EYRE-WALKER, Mrs. Louise, ACA *2008;* 44 Ashlea Road, WIRRAL, MERSEYSIDE, CH61 5UN.
•**EYTON, Mr. Nicholas, FCA** *1983;* Ernst & Young LLP, 1 More London Place, LONDON, SE1 2AF. See also Ernst & Young Europe LLP
EZEANAKA, Miss. Flora, BSc ACA *2010;* Flat 304 Utah Building, Deals Gateway, LONDON, SE13 7RP.
EZEKIEL, Mr. David, MSc FCA *1971;* International Advisory Ser Ltd, PO Box 1760, 44 Church Street, HAMILTON, BERMUDA.
EZEKIEL, Mr. David Richard Simon, FCA *1953;* 47 Leigh Hill Road, COBHAM, KT11 2HU. (Life Member)
EZEKIEL, Mr. Ivan Howard, BSc FCA ATII CF *1991;* 71 Kingsley Way, LONDON, N2 0EL.
EZRA, Mr. Raymond Leonard, FCA *1977;* 51 Braemar Crescent, LEIGH-ON-SEA, SS9 3RJ.
EZRA, Mr. Robert, LLB ACA *1980;* 79 Torrington Park, LONDON, N12 9PN.
EZRA, Mrs. Sally Torr, MA ACA *1979;* 110 Birchwood Drive, ITHACA, NY 14850, UNITED STATES.
EZRA, Mrs. Tanya, BSc ACA *2007;* 6 Heton Gardens, LONDON, NW4 4XS.
EZZAT, Mr. Taymour Ismail, BSc ACA *1992;* Herald Investment Management Ltd, 10/11 Charterhouse Square, LONDON, EC1M 6EE.
FABB, Mr. Alan Charles, BSc FCA *1959;* 41a Beaufort Avenue, Langland, SWANSEA, SA3 4PB. (Life Member)
FABB, Ms. Denise Ann, BSc ACA *1994;* 86 Birches Lane, KENILWORTH, CV8 2AG.
FABEN, Mr. Nigel Bertram John, FCA *1974;* 97 Rooks Street, Cottenham, CAMBRIDGE, CB24 8QZ.
FABER, Mr. Bernard, BSc FCA *1963;* 18 Highfield Gardens, LONDON, NW11 9HB.
FABER, Mr. Hamilton Stuart, MA ACA *1995;* 104 Narbonne Avenue, LONDON, SW4 9LG.
•**FABER, Mr. Paul, ACA** *2002;* Landau Morley LLP, Lanmor House, 370-386 High Road, WEMBLEY, MIDDLESEX, HA9 6AX.
FABER, Mr. Robin Henry Grey, MA FCA *1980;* St Catherine's Court, Berkeley Place, CLIFTON, SOMERSET, BS8 1BQ.
•**FABES, Mrs. Caroline Jane, BSc ACA** *1981;* Jane Fabes, Frilford Lodge, Sheepstead Road, Marcham, ABINGDON, OXFORDSHIRE OX13 6QG.
FABES, Mr. Warren Austin, MA FCA *1995;* 11 Gorse Avenue, WORTHING, BN14 9PG.
FABIAN, Mr. Andrew Mark, MA FCA FCT *1989;* Statpro Group plc, Statpro House, 81-87 Hartfield Road, Wimbledon, LONDON, SW19 3TJ.
FABIAN, Mr. Daniel, BSc ACA *2007;* 2 Reddings Close, LONDON, NW7 4JL.
•**FABIAN, Mr. Ross Marc, BSc(Hons) ACA** *2003;* Blick Rothenberg, 12 York Gate, Regent's Park, LONDON, NW1 4QS.
FABIAN-HUNT, Mr. Carl Nicholas, BSc ACA *1995;* Midhurst, Old Boars Hill, OXFORD, OX1 5JQ.
FABRIS, Mrs. Julie Carol, FCA *1992;* Birds Eye Iglo Group, 5 New Square, FELTHAM, MIDDLESEX, TW14 8HA.
FACCENDA, Miss. Helen Ann, BA(Hons) ACA *2000;* 34 Eccles Road, LONDON, SW11 1LZ.
FACER, Mr. Jonathan James, BSc ACA *1993;* 11 Friars Road, CHRISTCHURCH, DORSET, BH23 4EB.
FACER, Mr. Jonathan Mark, BA ACA *1983;* 37 Raikes Wood Drive, SKIPTON, BD23 1NA.
FACER, Mr. Paul Steven, BA(Hons) ACA *2002;* with PricewaterhouseCoopers Audit S.R.L, Lakeview Office, 301-311 Barbu Vacarescu Street, RO-020276 BUCHAREST, ROMANIA.
FACEY, Mrs. Catherine Sophie, MA ACA *2005;* 60 Nelson Road, LONDON, SW19 1HX.
FACEY, Mr. Christopher Peter John, BA(Hons) ACA *2001;* 3 Groes Lon, CARDIFF, CF14 6JT.
FACEY, Mr. David Alan, BSc ACA *1990;* Hunters, Frensham, FARNHAM, SURREY, GU10 3EB.
FACEY, Mr. Derrick Edward, FCA *1957;* 16 Badcock Road, Haslingfield, CAMBRIDGE, CB23 1LF. (Life Member)
FACEY, Mrs. Elizabeth, BSc ACA *1995;* University College Falmouth, Wood Lane, FALMOUTH, CORNWALL, TR11 4RH.
•**FACEY, Mr. Lee Cameron, BSc ACA** *2001;* Lubbock Fine, Russell Bedford House, City Forum, 250 City Road, LONDON, EC1V 2QQ.
FACHIRI, Mr. James Andrew Harrison, BA ACA *1990;* 84 Watermint Quay, Craven Walk, LONDON, N16 6DD.
FACKEY, Mr. Brian Arthur, BSc(Econ) FCA *1965;* 10 Tarn Brow, Aughton, ORMSKIRK, L39 4SS.
•**FACKLER, Mr. Joseph, FCA** *1974;* Swindells LLP, 20-21 Clinton Place, SEAFORD, EAST SUSSEX, BN25 1NP.
FACKNEY, Mr. Carl Jason, ACA CA(NZ) *2009;* 11 Alfred Close, Chiswick, LONDON, W4 5UW.
FACKRELL, Mr. Gideon Paul Jeffrey, BA ACA *1998;* The Garden House, 18a Bolton Road, LONDON, W4 3TB.
FACKRELL, Mrs. Joanne Louise, BA ACA *2000;* 71 Simmonds View, Stoke Gifford, BRISTOL, BS34 8HQ.
FACTOR, Mr. Bernard, BSc FCA *1992;* Mutschellenstrasse 6, 8002 ZURICH, SWITZERLAND.
FACTOR, Mr. David, FCA *1962;* 3 Warwick Road, Derwen Fawr, SWANSEA, SA2 8DZ. (Life Member)
FACTOR, Mr. Laurence Gerald, CA *1977; (CA Scotland 1965);* with RDP Newmans LLP, Lynwood House, 373-375 Station Road, HARROW, MIDDLESEX, HA1 2AW.
•**FADAVI-ARDEKANI, Mr. Majid, BSc FCA** *1983;* Fadavi & Co Limited, 8b Accommodation Road, LONDON, NW11 8ED.
FADDEN, Mr. Christopher Guy, BSc ACA *1991;* 39 Fulmare Road, Brickhill, BEDFORD, MK41 7JZ.
FAFALIOS, Mr. Mark George, FCA *1977;* 46 Sawfish Court, KISSIMMEE, FL 34759, UNITED STATES.
FAFALIOS, Mrs. Victoria Marjorie Jean, BSc ACA *1993;* Victoria House, Samaritans Purse International Victoria House, Victoria Road, BUCKHURST HILL, IG9 5EX.
FAGAN, Miss. Anna Marie, BSc ACA *2004;* John Fairhurst & Co Douglas Bank House, Wigan Lane, WIGAN, LANCASHIRE, WN1 2TB.
FAGAN, Mr. Eamon Francis, MSc BSc ACA *1984;* O'Rahilly Building, AFIS, University College Cork, CORK, COUNTY CORK, IRELAND.
•**FAGAN, Mr. Kevin Patrick, ACA CA(SA)** *2009;* KPF Accountancy Limited, 13 Cambridge Street, EXETER, EX4 1BY.
•**FAGAN, Mr. Lindsay Neil, FCA** *1977;* Civvals, 50 Seymour Street, LONDON, W1H 7JG. See also Civvals Ellam Ltd
FAGAN, Mr. Marc, BA ACA *2006;* Ivy House, Little Stainton, STOCKTON-ON-TEES, CLEVELAND, TS21 1HN.
FAGAN, Mr. Peter Gervais, BA FCA *1982;* 30 Trent Avenue, Garforth, LEEDS, LS25 2AY.
•**FAGANDINI, Mr. Ugo, FCA** *1973;* Joseph Miller & Co, Floor A, Milburn House, Dean Street, NEWCASTLE UPON TYNE, NE1 1LE.
•①**FAGELMAN, Mr. Michael Joseph, FCA** *1975;* (Tax Fac), MFA Accountants Limited, 6a The Gardens, FAREHAM, HAMPSHIRE, PO16 8SS.
FAGENCE, Miss. Caroline Lucy, BA ACA *2000;* with Peters Elworthy & Moore, Salisbury House, Station Road, CAMBRIDGE, CB1 2LA.
FAGG, Mr. Andrew Robert, BSc ACA *1997;* 63 Chilbolton Avenue, WINCHESTER, HAMPSHIRE, SO22 5HJ.
FAGG, Mrs. Catherine Ann, BA ACA *1999;* Serco Plc, Bartley Wood Business Park, Bartley Way, HOOK, HAMPSHIRE, RG27 9UY.
FAGGETTER, Ms. Ann Elizabeth, BSc FCA CTA *1992;* Lower Sent, Okewood Hill, DORKING, RH5 5NB.
FAGHIHI, Mr. Mahmoud, MSc ACA *1984;* Centrica Queensberry House, 3 Old Burlington Street, LONDON, W1S 3AE.
FAHEY, Mr. David Anthony, ACA *1984;* Aggar Hill Cottage, Finney Green, LeycettStaffs, NEWCASTLE, ST5 6AB.
FAHEY, Miss. Frances Mary, BEng ACA *1992;* 17 Mimosa Street, LONDON, SW6 4DS.
FAHID, Mr. Farhad, BSc ACA *1985;* Flat 32, Abingdon Court Abingdon Villas, LONDON, W8 6BT.
FAHRENHEIM, Mr. Donald Gavan, FCA *1986;* Aecom, 18 Upper Marlborough Road, ST. ALBANS, HERTFORDSHIRE, AL1 3UT.
FAHY, Mr. Brendan Patrick, BA ACA *1990;* (Tax Fac), South Lyn, 2 Mount Close, WOKING, SURREY, GU22 0PZ.
FAHY, Mr. Michael Francis, FCA *1965;* Unit 18, 21 Mt Wyndham Drive, HAMILTON CR04, BERMUDA.
FAHY, Mrs. Sarah Jayne, BCom ACA CTA *1990;* 5th Floor, 51-53 Great Marlborough Street, LONDON, W1F 7JT.
FAID, Miss. Emma Louise, MA ACA *1996;* 40 Scotland Road, CAMBRIDGE, CB4 1QG.
•**FAID, Mr. Stephen, BSc FCA** *1992;* Hendersons, Sterling House, Brunswick Industrial Estate, NEWCASTLE UPON TYNE, NE13 7BA.
•**FAIERS, Mr. Colin Charles, FCA** *1982;* Colin Faiers, 4 Elm Way, Willingham, CAMBRIDGE, CB24 5JS.
FAIERS, Ms. Tamsin Alethea, BA ACA *1998;* Farmhouse, Ancroft South Moor, BERWICK-UPON-TWEED, TD15 2TD.
FAIL, Mrs. Angela, ACA *1987;* Barbara M Thompson Chartered Certified Accountants, Summerdale Head Dyke Lane Pilling, PRESTON, PR3 6SJ.
•**FAIL, Mr. Nicholas James, BA FCA** *1987;* DTE Business Advisory Services Limited, DTE House, Hollins Mount, Hollins Lane, BURY, BL9 8AT. See also DTE Risk and Financial Management Ltd
FAIL, Mrs. Pauline Lesley, BSc ACA CTA *1982;* (Tax Fac), PGS Exploration (UK) Ltd, 4 The Heights, Brooklands, WEYBRIDGE, KT13 0NY.
FAIL, Mr. Robert James, FCA *1970;* 16 Barford Road, Seabridge, NEWCASTLE, ST5 3LF.
•**FAINT, Miss. Carol Elizabeth, BA ACA** *1983;* (Tax Fac), Tax & Accounts Solutions Ltd, The Old School House, Lyndhurst Road, BROCKENHURST, HAMPSHIRE, SO42 7RH.
FAINT, Mrs. Hazel Ann, MA ACA *1991;* 30 Russet Glade, Emmer Green, READING, RG4 8UJ.
FAINT, Mr. Simon Richard, MA ACA *1991;* Verizon UK Limited, Reading International Business Park, Basingtoke Road, READING, RG2 6DA.
FAIR, Mr. Bruce Nicholas, BEng ACA *2002;* 102 Kensington Church Street, LONDON, W8 4BU.
FAIR, Mr. Howard Russell, FCA *1967;* Highview, 8 Egypt Copse, COWES, PO31 8BA.
FAIR, Mr. Robert James, BA ACA *1986;* Keyham Farm, Buttons Lane, Priors Dean, ALTON, GU34 3SD.
•**FAIRBAIRN, Mrs. Anja, BSc(Hons) ACA** *2004;* Anja Fairbairn, 26 Kimberley Road, SOUTHSEA, HAMPSHIRE, PO4 9NS.
FAIRBAIRN, Mr. David William, FCA *1971;* 15 Chestnut Avenue, RICKMANSWORTH, WD3 4HA.
FAIRBAIRN, Miss. Fiona Julie, MA(Oxon) ACA *2009;* Flat 7 Salisbury House, 3 Drummond Gate, LONDON, SW1V 2HJ.
FAIRBAIRN, Mr. Ian James, FCA *1967;* 23 Ardern Lea, Alvanley, FRODSHAM, WA6 9EQ.
FAIRBAIRN, Mr. James Paul Clifford, FCA *1976;* 32 Grosvenor Gardens, LONDON, SW1W 0DH.
FAIRBAIRN, Mr. Lindsay, FCA *1978;* 38 Kelthorpe Close, Geeston, Ketton, STAMFORD, PE9 3RS.
FAIRBAIRN, Mr. Mark David, ACA *2009;* 15 Chestnut Avenue, RICKMANSWORTH, HERTFORDSHIRE, WD3 4HA.
FAIRBAIRN, Mr. Michael Charles, BA ACA *1987;* E7 The Engineering Offices, The Old Gasworks 2 Michael Road, LONDON, SW6 2AD.
FAIRBAIRN, Mr. Nigel Scott David, BA ACA *1992;* 45 Riefield Road, LONDON, SE9 2QE.
FAIRBAIRN, Mr. Noel Kenneth, FCA *1977;* (Tax Fac), 26 Weysprings, HASLEMERE, SURREY, GU27 1DE.
FAIRBAIRN, Mrs. Willa Alexia, BSc ACA CTA *2003;* Unit 3, Brook Business Centre, Cowley Mill Road, Cowley, UXBRIDGE, MIDDLESEX UB8 2FX.
FAIRBAIRN, Mr. William Andrew, FCA *1964;* Oulton House, Oulton, STONE, ST15 8UR. (Life Member)
FAIRBANK, Mr. Alex, MA ACA *2003;* 11 Elmdale Drive, Aldridge, WALSALL, WS9 8LQ.
•**FAIRBANK, Mr. David Michael, BCom FCA CA(SA)** *1973;* PricewaterhouseCoopers Inc, PO Box 2799, CAPE TOWN, C.P., 8000, SOUTH AFRICA.
FAIRBANK, Mrs. Valerie Ruth, BSc ACA *1981;* The Willows, Stert, DEVIZES, WILTSHIRE, SN10 3JD. (Life Member)
FAIRBANKS, Mr. Richard Stephen, BA ACA *1992;* 41 Crown Close, Martlesham, WOODBRIDGE, IP12 4UH.
FAIRBANKS, Mr. Victor John, FCA *1973;* 6 Boundary Road, West Bridgford, NOTTINGHAM, NG2 7BY.
FAIRBOTHAM, Mr. Jeffrey Alan, FCA *1980;* Williams Group, 2 Vincent Way, Raikes Lane, BOLTON, BL3 2NB.
•**FAIRBOTHAM, Mr. Michael Grant, BSc FCA** *1977;* MGF Associates Limited, 11 Simpkins Close, Weston Under Wetherley, LEAMINGTON SPA, CV33 9GE. See also Aims - Michael Fairbotham
FAIRBROTHER, Mr. Michael, BSc ACA *1979;* 99 Meeting House Lane, Balsall Common, COVENTRY, CV7 7GD.
FAIRBROTHER, Mrs. Nicola Jane, BA ACA *2000;* Oakwood House, 3 Grove Road, BEACONSFIELD, BUCKINGHAMSHIRE, HP9 1UR.
FAIRBURN, Mr. Donald, FCA *1959;* Stepalong, Conordon, Braes, Portree, ISLE OF SKYE, IV51 9QH. (Life Member)
FAIRBURN, Mr. Joseph William, FCA *1949;* Birds Corner, Trench Lane Old Town, St. Mary's, ISLES OF SCILLY, TR21 0PA. (Life Member)
FAIRCHILD, Mr. David John, ACA *1991;* Acabill, Franklin Road, North Fambridge, CHELMSFORD, CM3 6NF.
FAIRCHILD, Mr. Jonathan George, BA ACA AMCT *2002;* 13 Matford Hill, CHIPPENHAM, WILTSHIRE, SN15 3NX.
FAIRCHILD, Mr. Patrick Charles, FCA *1963;* 48 Court Hill, Sanderstead, SOUTH CROYDON, Surrey, CR2 9NA.
FAIRCHILD, Mr. Paul Jonathan, MA FCA *1994;* Athelstan Hall, Main Street, Ingoldsby, GRANTHAM, LINCOLNSHIRE, NG33 4EJ.
•**FAIRCHILD, Mr. Simon Charles, BSc FCA** *1991;* PricewaterhouseCoopers LLP, 1 Embankment Place, LONDON, WC2N 6RH. See also PricewaterhouseCoopers
FAIRCLOTH, Mr. Benedict Ralph George, BA ACA MBA *1997;* 12 Hillfield Road, LONDON, NW6 1PZ.
FAIRCLOTH, Mrs. Jill Helen, MA ACA *1997;* 12 Hillfield Road, LONDON, NW6 1PZ.
FAIRCLOTH, Miss. Rebecca Kate, BSc FCA *1996;* Hall Cottage South Green, Mattishall, DEREHAM, NORFOLK, NR20 3JZ.
FAIRCLOTH, Mr. Richard Charles, BSc ACA *2004;* Black Horse House, Castle Park, CAMBRIDGE, CB3 0AR.
•**FAIRCLOUGH, Miss. Amanda Ann Catherine, BSc FCA** *1992;* 7 Time Park, Whiston, PRESCOT, MERSEYSIDE, L35 7NU.
FAIRCLOUGH, Mr. David John, BA FCA *1990;* 6 Doeford Close, Culcheth, WARRINGTON, WA3 4DL.
•**FAIRCLOUGH, Mr. Geoffrey Charles, BSc(Econ) FCA** *1980;* Haines Watts Limited, 11A Park House, Milton Park, ABINGDON, OXFORDSHIRE, OX14 4RS. See also Haines Watts Corporate Finance (NW), HW Corporate Finance LLP, HW Technology Limited, Haines Watts, Haines Watts Corporate Services, H W and Haines Watts
FAIRCLOUGH, Mr. Graham Kenneth, BSc ACA ACCA *1995;* Flat 25, 79 Piccadilly, MANCHESTER, M1 2BU.
FAIRCLOUGH, Mr. Hugh, BA ACA *2007;* with Baker Tilly UK Audit LLP, 2 Whitehall Quay, LEEDS, LS1 4HG.
FAIRCLOUGH, Mr. Jeffrey William, BA ACA *1983;* 7 Strickland Close, WARRINGTON, WA4 3LJ.
FAIRCLOUGH, Mr. John William Percy, FCA MCT *1974;* 13 Park Hill Road, WALLINGTON, SURREY, SM6 0SD.
FAIRCLOUGH, Mr. Michael James, FCA *1972;* M F Associates Inc, 8409 N Military Trail Suite 119, PALM BEACH GARDENS, FL 33410, UNITED STATES.
FAIRCLOUGH, Miss. Sarah Jane, BA(Hons) ACA *2011;* 4 Berwick Close, Worsley, MANCHESTER, M28 1DT.
FAIRCLOUGH, Mr. Timothy Mark, BA FCA *1993;* Unit 3, 3 Clare Street, Blackburn, MELBOURNE, VIC 3130, AUSTRALIA.
•**FAIRE, Mr. Simon Edward, BA FCA** *1983;* E T Peirson & Sons, 21 The Point, Rockingham Road, MARKET HARBOROUGH, LEICESTERSHIRE, LE16 7NU.
FAIRES, Mr. Roland Clive, FCA *1972;* Charthire Ltd, No 2, The Coach House, Tollerton Hall, Tollerton, NOTTINGHAM NG12 4GQ.
FAIREY, Mr. Michael Craig, BSc ACA *1996;* BRAMBLES, 4 Manor Croft, Bishop Wilton, YORK, YO42 1TG.
FAIRFAX, Mr. Robert Alexander, BSc ACA *1998;* with Deloitte LLP, Athene Place, 66 Shoe Lane, LONDON, EC4A 3BQ.
FAIRFAX-LUCY, Mr. Duncan Cameron Ramsay, FCA *1956;* Grange Orchard, Grange Gardens, Wellesbourne, WARWICK, WARWICKSHIRE, CV35 9RL. (Life Member)
FAIRFIELD, Mr. Neil Barry, BA ACA *1999;* 1726 N Winchester Avenue, CHICAGO, IL 60622, UNITED STATES.
FAIRGRIEVE, Mr. Peter Lloyd, FCA *1973;* 13 Groeswen, LLANTWIT MAJOR, SOUTH GLAMORGAN, CF61 2UA.
FAIRHALL, Mr. Alex, ACA *2011;* 12 Livingstone Road, SOUTHSEA, HAMPSHIRE, PO5 1RT.
FAIRHALL, Mr. Benjamin Simon, BSc ACA *2004;* 36 Merritt Road, LONDON, SE4 1DY.
FAIRHEAD, Mr. Daniel James, ACA *2009;* Basement Flat, 1 Prima Road, LONDON, SW9 0NA.
FAIRHEAD, Mr. Nigel Derek, FCA *1977;* 53 Bonaly Cres, EDINBURGH, EH13 0EP.
FAIRHEAD, Mr. Roger James, BSc(Hons) ACA *1994;* 12 Winkworth Place, BANSTEAD, SM7 2AA.
FAIRHURST, Mr. Andrew David, MA FCA *1988;* Birkenkamp 4, 59302 OELDE, GERMANY.

FAIRHURST, Mrs. Ann, BSc ACA *1984;* PO Box 1949, Wilton, REDCAR, CLEVELAND, TS10 4YG.
FAIRHURST, Mrs. Bridgit Ann, BSc ACA *1989;* 150 Appleylane North, Appley Bridge, WIGAN, WN6 9DX.
•FAIRHURST, Mrs. Catherine, BSc ACA ATII *1989;* Ernst & Young LLP, 20 Chapel Street, LIVERPOOL, L3 9AG. See also Ernst & Young Europe LLP
FAIRHURST, Mr. Darryl, ACA *2008;* 7a Simpson Street, BONDI, NSW 2026, AUSTRALIA.
•FAIRHURST, Mr. David Geoffrey, BSc ACA *1994;* Ernst & Young LLP, 1 More London Place, LONDON, SE1 2AF. See also Ernst & Young Europe LLP
•FAIRHURST, Mr. David John, FCA *1961;* FCF Limited, 150 Appley Lane North, Appley Bridge, WIGAN, WN6 9DX.
FAIRHURST, Mr. John Andrew, BA ACA *1994;* 18 Bryanstone Road, LONDON, N8 8TN.
•FAIRHURST, Mr. John Bennett Stuart, BA(Hons) FCA *1990;* Fairhurst, Douglas Bank House, Wigan Lane, WIGAN, WN1 2TB. See also FCF Limited
FAIRHURST, Mr. Jonathan Mark, BA ACA *1994;* 25 Evelyn Road, LONDON, SW19 8NU.
•FAIRHURST, Mr. Mark, BSc FCA MAE *1984;* PKF (UK) LLP, 5 Temple Square, Temple Street, LIVERPOOL, L2 5RH.
FAIRHURST, Mr. Martin Paul, BSc(Hons) ACA *2001;* 47 Boscombe Road, SOUTHEND-ON-SEA, SS2 5JE.
FAIRHURST, Mr. Michael, BA ACA *1979;* London Scottish Bank Plc, 201 Deansgate, MANCHESTER, M3 3NW.
•FAIRHURST, Mr. Michael Christopher, BA FCA *1990;* Baker Tilly Tax & Advisory Services LLP, 1210 Centre Park Square, WARRINGTON, WA1 1RU. See also Baker Tilly UK Audit LLP
FAIRHURST, Mr. Nigel Robert, BSc ACA *1989;* 62 Lebanon Gardens, Wandsworth, LONDON, SW18 1RH.
FAIRHURST, Miss. Victoria Jane, BSc ACA *2006;* 7 Gainsborough, Cookham, MAIDENHEAD, SL6 9DR.
FAIRLESS, Mr. Mark Alexander, ACA *2009;* 3a Westgrove Lane, LONDON, SE10 8QP.
FAIRLEY, Mr. Andrew John Buchanan, BEng ACA *1995;* 44 Fullerton Road, Wandsworth, LONDON, SW18 1BX.
FAIRLEY, Mr. James, BSc ACA *1981;* Field Cottage Treacle Lane, Rushden, BUNTINGFORD, HERTFORDSHIRE, SG9 0SL.
FAIRLEY, Mr. John, FCA *1970;* 1 Kewferry Drive, NORTHWOOD, HA6 2NT. (Life Member)
FAIRLEY, Mr. John, BSc ACA *1991;* Pricewaterhousecoopers, 33 Wellington Street, LEEDS, LS1 4JP.
FAIRLEY, Mr. Neil Duff, BSc ACA *1988;* 72 Carr Road, Calverley, PUDSEY, LS28 5RH.
FAIRLEY, Mr. Peter James, FCA CPA *1974;* J H Cohn LLP, 14th Floor, 1212 Avenue of the Americas, NEW YORK, NY 10036, UNITED STATES.
FAIRLEY, Mr. Peter Robert, BA ACA *1995;* Hyperama Cash & Carry Ltd, Bull Close Road, NOTTINGHAM, NG7 2UT.
FAIRMAN, Mrs. Alison, BA ACA *2001;* with Crowe Clark Whitehill LLP, 10 Palace Avenue, MAIDSTONE, KENT, ME15 6NF.
FAIRMAN, Mrs. Emma Jane, BSc ACA *1992;* 5 Culcheth Road, ALTRINCHAM, WA14 2LU.
FAIRMAN, Mr. Richard William Mark, BA FCA *1995;* The Homestead, High Common, Swardeston, NORWICH, NR14 8DL.
FAIRMAN, Mr. Robert Timothy, MA ACA *1992;* Atos Origin, 4 Triton Square, LONDON, NW1 3HG.
•FAIRPO, Mr. Henry Charles, MA(Oxon) FCA CF *1993;* Castaing & Co Limited, The Chapel, Silver Street, Witcham, ELY, CAMBRIDGESHIRE CB6 2LF. See also Vigar & Associates Limited
FAIRRIS, Mr. Sami, Bsc ACA *2009;* Flat 10, Richmond Heights, 1-2 Richmond Hill, BRISTOL, BS8 1BL.
FAIRS, Miss. Catherine Anne, ACA *2008;* 29 Oakmead Road, LONDON, SW12 9SN.
FAIRS, Mr. Jonathan Patrick, BSc ACA *2003;* The Beat House Whitmore Vale Road, Grayshott, HINDHEAD, GU26 6LU.
FAIRS, Mr. Michael, BSc ACA *2011;* 174 Goring Road, Goring-by-Sea, WORTHING, WEST SUSSEX, BN12 4PH.
FAIRTHORNE, Mrs. Ann Elizabeth, FCA *1981;* 102 Sherwood Park Avenue, SIDCUP, DA15 9JJ.
FAIRTLOUGH, Miss. Amapola, LLB ACA *2001;* Via Ciamber 15, 32012 FORNO DI ZOLDO, ITALY.
FAIRWEATHER, Mr. Albert, FCA *1967;* 8 The Orchard, Westfield, WOKING, SURREY, GU22 9PA.
FAIRWEATHER, Miss. Carol Ann, BA ACA *1987;* 8 Fanthorpe Street, LONDON, SW15 1DZ.
FAIRWEATHER, Mr. Charles Philip, FCA *1972;* 8 Queen Street, LONDON, W1J 5PD.
FAIRWEATHER, Mr. Cyril Paul, MA FCA *1977;* Bolts Cross House, Rotherfield Greys, HENLEY-ON-THAMES, OXFORDSHIRE, RG9 5LG.
FAIRWEATHER, Mr. Ian Mcintyre, ACA *1979;* 74 St. Michael's Road, Llandaff, CARDIFF, CF5 2AQ.
FAIRWEATHER, Miss. Kathryn Elizabeth, BA(Hons) ACA *2002;* 7 Parkfield Drive, Boston Spa, WETHERBY, LS23 6EF.
FAIRWEATHER, Mr. Kenneth Michael, FCA *1967;* 29 Cloisters Road, LETCHWORTH GARDEN CITY, SG6 3JR.
FAIRWEATHER, Mr. Paul, ACA *2008;* 73 Derbyshire Lane, Stretford, MANCHESTER, M32 8BN.
FAIRWEATHER, Ms. Sharon Alison Mailston, BSc ACA *1989;* 67 Duddingston Road, EDINBURGH, EH15 1SE.
FAISAL, Mrs. Rabecca, BA ACA *1993;* 383 Birmingham Road, REDDITCH, WORCESTERSHIRE, B97 6RH.
FAISAL, Miss. Zara, BSc(Hons) ACA *2009;* No 36 Jalan 5/15, 46000 PETALING JAYA, MALAYSIA.
FAITHFULL, Mr. Jonathan Alwyn, MEng ACA *2001;* 3, Telford Close, Rogerstone, NEWPORT, NP10 0DL.
FAITHFULL, Mr. Peter David, FCA *1962;* Plaza Fuente Luminosa, Edificio Granca 11B, LAS PALMAS, Canary Islands, SPAIN. (Life Member)
•FAIZ, Mr. Javier, LLB ACA *2001;* Ernst & Young LLP, 1 More London Place, LONDON, SE1 2AF. See also Ernst & Young Europe LLP
•FAIZ-MAHDAVI, Mr. Behzad, BSc FCA *1984;* (Tax Fac), Audit Network Limited, 23 Mountside, STANMORE, MIDDLESEX, HA7 2DS. See also Faiz & Co Limited
FAIZI, Mr. Khalid, ACA *1982;* Khalid Faizi & Co, 50C Margalla Road, ISLAMABAD 44000, ISLAMABAD CAPITAL TERRITORY, PAKISTAN.
FAIZI, Mr. Tariq, BSc ACA *2002;* Flat 1 Sandhurst Court, Acre Lane, LONDON, SW2 5TX.
FAKE, Mr. Adrian Mark, BSc(Econ) ACA *2002;* 5 Hollins Park, Kippax, LEEDS, LS25 7RR.
FAKEY, Mr. Nickhill, BSc ACA *2007;* Flat 3, 30 Hillside Gardens, LONDON, N6 5ST.
FAKIM, Mr. Ehsan Issop, BSc FCA *1982;* Courts (Mauritius) Ltd, PO Box 791, Bell Village, PORT LOUIS, MAURITIUS.
FALCON, Miss. Sophie Anne, ACA *2009;* Pricewaterhousecoopers Llp Central Business Exchange, Midsummer Boulevard, MILTON KEYNES, MK9 2DF.
FALCONER, Mr. Alexander Peter, FCA *1957;* Fairview, 11 Fernside, BUCKHURST HILL, ESSEX, IG9 5TY. (Life Member)
FALCONER, Mr. Angus William, ACA *2008;* Flat 4 The Oriels, 146 Kingston Road, LONDON, SW19 3NB.
FALCONER, Mr. Douglas James, BA(Hons) ACA *2003;* 105 Raddlebarn Farm Drive, Selly Oak, BIRMINGHAM, B29 6UN.
FALCONER, Mrs. Elizabeth Medora, BA ACA *1984;* 43 Hargrave Road, MAIDENHEAD, SL6 6JR.
FALCONER, Mr. James Roderick, BSc ACA *2005;* 12 Burlington Gate, 42 Rothesay Avenue, Wimbledon Chase, LONDON, SW20 8JU.
FALCONER, Mr. Jamie Edward, LLB ACA *2007;* 99 Oxford Street, Totterdown, BRISTOL, BS3 4RL.
FALCONER, Mr. Mark Thomas, MMath ACA *2011;* 102 Becketts Park Drive, LEEDS, LS6 3PL.
•FALCONER, Mr. Matthew George, BA(Hons) ACA *2002;* PricewaterhouseCoopers, Sumitomo Mita Building, 12F, 5-37-8 Shiba, Minato-ku, TOKYO 108-0023 JAPAN. See also PricewaterhouseCoopers LLP
FALCONER, Mr. Peter George, MA FCA *1975;* Royal Bank Of Canada Europe Limited 11th Floor, Exchange Tower 19 Canning Street, EDINBURGH, EH3 8EG.
FALCONER, Miss. Susan Jean, BA ACA *1988;* 4 Marsh Road, PINNER, HA5 5NH.
FALCONER HALL, Mr. Simon James, ACA *1985;* Paradigm House, Macrae Road Ham Green, BRISTOL, BS20 0DD.
FALDU, Mr. Minesh, ACA *2009;* 30 Silkfield Road, LONDON, NW9 6QU.
FALEIRO, Ms. Rachel, BSc ACA *2001;* 8 Higher Green, EPSOM, KT17 3BA.
FALEK, Mr. Leo, BSc FCA *1961;* 1 Bradby House, Carlton Hill, LONDON, NW8 9XE.
FALERO, Mr. Javier, BSc ACA *2003;* 11 Tiepigs Lane, BROMLEY, BR2 7HJ.
FALEY, Mr. Robert Bernard, FCA *1972;* 48 Hackness Road, SCARBOROUGH, YO12 5RY.
FALEYE, Chief Olusola, FCA *1966;* 38 Balarabe Musa Crescent, PO Box 75361, Victoria Island, LAGOS, NIGERIA. (Life Member)
FALINSKI, Mr. Paul Edward, BCom FCA *1973;* Pinecroft, Checkendon, READING, RG8 0TD.
FALK, Mr. Fergus Antony, TD BSc(Econ) FCA *1969;* Brackendale House, Debden Road, SAFFRON WALDEN, CB11 4AB. (Life Member)
FALK, Mr. Harold Raymond, FCA *1961;* with Edwards Veeder LLP, Alex House, 260-268 Chapel Street, SALFORD, M3 5JZ.
FALK, Mr. Howard Warren, BA ACA *1989;* 26 The Rise, Elstree, BOREHAMWOOD, HERTFORDSHIRE, WD6 3JU.
FALK, Mr. Leslie, BA FCA *1976;* (Tax Fac), with Grant Thornton UK LLP, Grant Thornton House, 22 Melton Street, Euston Square, LONDON, NW1 2EP.
FALK, Mr. Vincent James, ACA *1996;* UniCredit Bank AG Moor House, 120 London Wall, LONDON, EC2Y 5ET.
FALK, Mr. William Edward, FCA *1966;* 32 Kingsley Way, Hampstead Garden Suburb, LONDON, N2 0EW.
FALKENBERG, Mr. Glenn, ACA CA(SA) *2008;* 27 Brockwell Park Row, LONDON, SW2 2YL.
FALKENBERG, Ms. Regina, BA ACA *1998;* 27 Brockwell Park Row, LONDON, SW2 2YL.
FALKINER, Mrs. Alison Clare, LLB ACA *2001;* Lyons Sleeman & Hoare, Nero Brewery, Brew House Lane, Hartley Wintney, HOOK, HAMPSHIRE RG27 8QA.
FALKINER, Mr. Gary Ian, MBS BA ACA *1998;* Willowbrook, 6 Forest Road, LYDNEY, GL15 5LB.
FALKINGHAM, Mrs. Lindsey Ann, BSc ACA *1994;* 11389 Terwilligerscreek Drive, CINCINNATI, OH 45249, UNITED STATES.
FALKINGHAM, Mr. Trevor, FCA *1963;* 9 South View Close, Yeadon, LEEDS, LS19 7JB. (Life Member)
•FALKNER, Mrs. Anne Elaine, FCA *1977;* 1 Temple Cottage, Ravenstone Lane Horton, NORTHAMPTON, NN7 2BH.
•FALKNER, Mrs. Karen Margaret, BSc ACA *1989;* H & M Ltd, 1-5 Alma Terrace, SKIPTON, NORTH YORKSHIRE, BD23 1EJ.
•FALKNER, Mr. Richard Iain, ACA *1984;* Richard Falkner & Co, Lowfield House, 222 Wellington Road South, STOCKPORT, CHESHIRE, SK2 6RS.
FALKNER, Mr. Robert Edward, FCA *1971;* 43 Montholme Road, LONDON, SW11 6HX.
•FALL, Mrs. Joanne Elizabeth, BA ACA *1995;* Ability Accounting Services Limited, 11 Westbourne Grove, CHELMSFORD, ESSEX, CM2 9RT.
FALLA, Mr. Charles Simon, BSc(Hons) ACA *2003;* 42 Charmouth Court, Kings Road, RICHMOND, SURREY, TW10 6EW.
•FALLA, Mr. Clive Stuart, FCA *1976;* Collenette Jones Limited, Crossways Centre, Braye Road, Vale, GUERNSEY, GY3 5PH.
FALLA, Mrs. Donna, BA ACA *2007;* Iguassu, 27 La Jaoniere Clos, Landes Du Marche, Vale, GUERNSEY, GY6 8DQ.
FALLA, Mr. John Martyn, BSc ACA *1988;* La Fontaine Farm St. Clair Hill, St. Sampson, GUERNSEY, GY2 4DS.
FALLA, Mr. Nicholas John, MBA BSc FCA AMCT *1983;* Xocoatl Limited, The Chimes, La Grande Lande, St. Saviour, GUERNSEY, GY7 9YY.
FALLE, Miss. Lisa, BA ACA *2008;* Nissaki 37 Parcq Du Pont Marquet, La Petite Route Des Mielles St. Brelade, JERSEY, JE3 8FB.
FALLEN, Mr. Malcolm James, BA ACA *1987;* Madleigh House, Village Road, Coleshill, AMERSHAM, BUCKINGHAMSHIRE, HP7 0LQ.
FALLER, Mr. Guy Nicholas Anthony, BSc FCA *1982;* 180 Hermitage Road, WOKING, GU21 8XQ.
FALLICK, Mr. John William, FCA *1962;* The Bell Tower, Treluggan Court, Ruan High Lanes, TRURO, TR2 5LP.
FALLMAN, Mr. Miles Adam, BA FCA *1987;* 31/32 Eastcastle Street, WEST END, W1W 8DL.
FALLON, Mr. Damien Jude, BA ACA *1983;* 46 Monastery Gardens, ENFIELD, MIDDLESEX, EN2 0AE.
FALLON, Mr. David Ian, BA(Hons) ACA *2001;* with Deloitte LLP, Abbots House, Abbey Street, READING, RG1 3BD.
FALLON, Mr. John Edward, FCA *1972;* The Gardeners Cottage, Old Hall Drive, Widmerpool, NOTTINGHAM, NG12 5PZ.
•FALLON, Mrs. Marianne Gina, BA ACA *1994;* KPMG LLP, 1 Forest Gate, Brighton Road, CRAWLEY, WEST SUSSEX, RH11 9PT.
FALLON, Mr. Paul, BSc ACA *1993;* 45 Pacific Drive, Banksia Beach, BRIBIE ISLAND, QLD 4507, AUSTRALIA.
FALLON, Mr. Paul, BSc(Hons) ACA *2011;* 233 Prescot Road, Aughton, ORMSKIRK, LANCASHIRE, L39 5AE.
FALLON, Mr. Peter James, FCA *1973;* 96 Woodville Road, Hartshorne, SWADLINCOTE, DERBYSHIRE, DE11 7EX.
FALLON, Mr. Philip Godfrey, BA FCA *1989;* 9 Fellowes Way, Hildenborough, TONBRIDGE, KENT, TN11 9DG.
FALLON-KHAN, Mrs. Martina Jane, BA ACA *1993;* 8 Lloyd Road, HOVE, EAST SUSSEX, BN3 6NL.
FALLOWFIELD, Mr. Robert James, FCA *1975;* Harrods Holdings Ltd, 87-135 Brompton Road, LONDON, SW1X 7XL.
FALLOWFIELD-SMITH, Mr. James Louis, BA(Hons) ACA *2011;* The Firs, Hare Lane, Little Kingshill, GREAT MISSENDEN, BUCKINGHAMSHIRE, HP16 0EF.
FALLOWFIELD-SMITH, Mr. Mark Edward, MSc ACA *2010;* Wireless Information Network 1 Cliveden Office Village, Lancaster Road Cressex Business Park, HIGH WYCOMBE, BUCKINGHAMSHIRE, HP12 3YZ.
•FALLOWS, Miss. Caroline Louise, BA ACA *1988;* The Cottage, Old Rectory Lane, Denham, UXBRIDGE, UB9 5AH.
•FALLOWS, Mr. Guy Richard, BSc FCA *1992;* Guy Fallows Enterprises Limited, Archway House, 81-82 Portsmouth Road, SURBITON, SURREY, KT6 5PT.
FALLOWS, Mr. Michael Joseph, FCA *1975;* 11 Greville Drive, Edgbaston, BIRMINGHAM, B15 2UU.
FALLOWS, Mrs. Natasha Jane, BA ACA *2000;* 15 Ferguson Avenue, ROMFORD, RM2 6RB.
FALLOWS, Mr. Roger William, FCA *1966;* 7 Spen Lane, Treales, PRESTON, PR4 3TE. (Life Member)
FALOON, Ms. Rebecca Irene, BSc ACA *1994;* PO Box 183, FRANKLIN, TAS 7113, AUSTRALIA.
FALVEY, Miss. Julia Elisabeth, MA(Cantab) BA ACA *2009;* 119 Winton Drive, Croxley Green, RICKMANSWORTH, HERTFORDSHIRE, WD3 3QS.
•FALVEY, Mr. Paul Timothy, BA FCA *1987;* (Tax Fac), Baker Tilly Tax & Advisory Services LLP, Hartwell House, 55-61 Victoria Street, BRISTOL, BS1 6AD. See also Spiers and Company
FALZARANO, Mrs. Sarah Ann, BSc(Econ) ACA *1998;* Musica Viva Australia, PO Box 1687, STRAWBERRY HILLS, NSW 2012, AUSTRALIA.
FALZON, Mr. Michael, BSc ACA *2007;* Deloitte & Touche, 4 Brindley Place, BIRMINGHAM, B1 2HZ.
FAMILY, Ms. Yasmin, MSc ACA *1996;* Flat 20, The Glass House, 3 Royal Oak Yard, LONDON, SE1 3GE.
FAN, Mr. Kwai Hung, ACA *2008;* Flat F 29/F, Block 10, City One Shatin, 1 Tak Kei Street, SHA TIN, NEW TERRITORIES HONG KONG SAR.
FAN, Mr. Lin Chi, ACA *2005;* Flat E 42/F Tower 1, The Metropolis, 8 Mau Yip Road, Tseung Kwan O, SAI KUNG, NEW TERRITORIES HONG KONG SAR.
FAN, Mrs. Lucetta Chui Fong, BSc ACA *1994;* 8 Maple Way, Cranfield, BEDFORD, BEDFORDSHIRE, MK43 0DY.
FAN, Mr. Mark Wai Man, ACA *2008;* Orix Asia Limited, 30/F United Centre, 95 Queensway, CENTRAL, HONG KONG ISLAND, HONG KONG SAR.
FAN, Mr. Paul Chi Fai, BA ACA *1991;* 16B Block 4, Cavendish Heights, 33 Perkins Road, JARDINE'S LOOKOUT, HONG KONG ISLAND, HONG KONG SAR.
FAN, Mr. Pengyuan, MA BA ACA *2009;* U B S AG, 100 Liverpool Street, LONDON, EC2M 2RH.
FAN, Miss. Siu Kwan, BA FCA *1992;* Suites 4201-03, One Island East, 18 Westlands Road, QUARRY BAY, HONG KONG ISLAND, HONG KONG SAR.
FAN, Mr. Wai Yuen, ACA *2007;* Rooms 1404-5 14th Floor, Two Grand Tower, 625 Nathan Road, MONG KOK, KOWLOON, HONG KONG SAR.
FAN, Mr. Wai-Ming Ray, ACA *2011;* 11a St. Fremund Way, LEAMINGTON SPA, WARWICKSHIRE, CV31 1AB.
FAN, Mr. Yick Man Christopher, MSc ACA *1998;* 19 Lorian Close, LONDON, N12 7DW.
•FANCOURT, Mr. Michael Peter, FCA *1975;* Butler Fancourt, Boon Court, Papyrus Road, Werrington, PETERBOROUGH, PE4 5HQ.
FANCY, Miss. Clare Helen, BA ACA *2005;* 6 Tydings Close, Long Ashton, BRISTOL, BS41 9FJ.
FANE, Mr. Andrew William Mildmay, MA FCA *1974;* 64 Ladbroke Road, LONDON, W11 3NR.
FANE-HERVEY, Mr. Kevin Charles, FCA *1973;* Bardens, Church Street, Ticehurst, WADHURST, TN5 7DL.
FANG, Miss. Lai Ming, ACA *2008;* Flat 305, Block L, Amoy Garden, 77 Ngau Tau Kok Road, NGAU TAU KOK, KOWLOON HONG KONG SAR.

FANKO, Mr. Graham Ernest, FCA *1970;* 38 Campbells Ride, Holmer Green, HIGH WYCOMBE, BUCKINGHAMSHIRE, HP15 6TQ. (Life Member)

FANNING, Mr. Alastair Scott, BEng ACA AMCT *1993;* Sony United Kingdom Ltd, The Heights, Brooklands, WEYBRIDGE, KT13 0XW.

FANNING, Mr. John Paul, MBA LLB ACA *1991;* 19/4 Montpelier Park, EDINBURGH, EH10 4LX.

FANNING, Mr. Sean Thomas, BSc(Hons) *2009;* 64 The Riding, Woodham, WOKING, SURREY, GU21 5TD.

•①**FANSHAWE, Mr. Antony Robert, BSc FCA** *1980;* Begbies Traynor (Central) LLP, 41 Castle Way, SOUTHAMPTON, SO14 2BW.

FANSHAWE, Mr. James Henry Dalrymple, BA FCA *1974;* Oak Farm, Naseby, NORTHAMPTON, NN6 6BX.

•**FANSON, Mrs. Angela Mary, ACA** *1990;* A.M. Fanson, Trelawney Court, 25a Lynstone Road, BUDE, EX23 8LR.

FANTHOME, Ms. Fiona, MA ACA *2004;* British Broadcasting Corporation, Media Centre, 201 Wood Lane, LONDON, W12 7TQ.

•**FANTHOME, Mrs. Heather Christine, FCA** *1984;* (Tax Fac), King Loose & Co, 5 South Parade, Summertown, OXFORD, OX2 7JL.

FANTHOME-HODGSON, Mr. Neil, MBA LLB ACA *1992;* Hedgefield House, Marden Road, Staplehurst, TONBRIDGE, TN12 0PD.

FANTIN, Mr. Mario Luca, BA ACA *2007;* 15 Orchard Rise, NEWCASTLE UPON TYNE, NE15 8XR.

FANTOM, Miss. Lisa Jane, BSc ACA *1993;* 3 Martree Court, Elworth, SANDBACH, CHESHIRE, CW11 3BN.

•**FAQUIR, Mr. Nazir Naveed, BSc ACA ATII** *1992;* (Tax Fac), PricewaterhouseCoopers LLP, 1 Embankment Place, LONDON, WC2N 6RH. See also PricewaterhouseCoopers

FARADAY, Mrs. Helen Claire, ACA *2008;* 80 The Drive, Roundhay, LEEDS, LS8 1LN.

FARADAY, Mr. Mathew, BSc ACA *1999;* 4 Ember Lane, ESHER, SURREY, KT10 8ER.

FARADAY, Mr. Neil James, MPhys ACA *2010;* Flat A, 18 Leconfield Road, LONDON, N5 2SN.

FARADOON, Mr. Mohammed Saqib, BSc ACA *2010;* 40 Clive Road, OXFORD, OX4 3EL.

FARAFONOV, Mr. Vitalij, BSc ACA *2005;* 10 Lyttelton Road, WARWICK, CV34 5EW.

FARAGHER, Mrs. Emma Ruth, BSc ACA *2009;* Keynote Tower 1, 303-220 12 Avenue SE, CALGARY T2G 0R5, AB, CANADA.

FARAGHER, Mr. Gordon John, BCom ACA CTA *1986;* 1 Oldcott Close, Worsley, MANCHESTER, M28 1UN.

FARAGHER, Mrs. Karen Ann, BSocSc FCA *1994;* with KPMG LLP, One Snowhill, Snow Hill Queensway, BIRMINGHAM, B4 6GN.

FARAGO, Mrs. Alison Jill, BSc ACA *1988;* A T C Ltd Unit 17, Perrywood Business Park Honeycrock Lane, REDHILL, RH1 5JQ.

FARAH, Mr. Habib, BA ACA *2010;* 102 Nearchou Court, 7a Mesimvrias Street, Ayios Athansios, 4100 LIMASSOL, CYPRUS.

FARAHAT, Mr. Raoul Vita, BA FCA *1932;* 13 Rue du Dragon, 75006 PARIS, FRANCE. (Life Member)

•**FARAM, Mr. David Paul, BSc ACA** *1979;* (Tax Fac), Control Accountancy Services, 1 Hawkwood Close, St Margaret's Banks, ROCHESTER, KENT, ME1 1HW.

FARANDA BELLOFIGLIO, Dr. Nunzio, BA FCA *1993;* (Tax Fac), 12 Webster Road, AYLESBURY, HP21 7FJ.

•**FARAROOY, Mr. Jamshyd, BSc FCA** *1978;* TadvinCo - Ernst & Young Iran, 1303 Vali-e-Asr Avenue, TEHRAN, 15178, IRAN.

FARAZI, Mr. Dilawer Jehan Sharyar, BA(Hons) ACA *2004;* with Grant Thornton UK LLP, 30 Finsbury Square, LONDON, EC2P 2YU.

FARAZMAND, Mr. Habib Sayed, BSc ACA *2009;* (Tax Fac), Ernst & Young, 1 Colmore Square, BIRMINGHAM, B4 6HQ.

FARAZMAND, Mrs. Madeline Rachel, ACA *2009;* 25 Pine Tree Close, BURNTWOOD, STAFFORDSHIRE, WS7 4TE.

FARBER, Mr. Harvey Martin, FCA *1975;* Ravutzki 7d, RA'ANANA, 43220, ISRAEL.

FARBER, Mr. Lester, FCA *1960;* 99 Higher Ainsworth Road, Radcliffe, MANCHESTER, M26 4JJ. (Life Member)

FARBRACE, Miss. Kim Lorraine, ACA *1986;* C17 Regalia Bay, 88 Wong Ma Kok Road, STANLEY, HONG KONG SAR.

FARBRIDGE, Miss. Alaina, BA ACA *1988;* 151 Worksop Road, Aston, SHEFFIELD, S26 2EB.

FARBRIDGE, The Revd. Nicholas Brisco, FCA *1956;* 55 Curling Vale, Onslow Village, GUILDFORD, GU2 7PH. (Life Member)

•**FARDELL, Mrs. Penelope Joyce, BSc FCA ATII** *1982;* (Tax Fac), Hollings Crowe Storr & Co, 14 Beech Hill, OTLEY, LS21 3AX.

FAREBROTHER, Miss. Rachel, BEng ACA *1998;* 7A West End Grove, FARNHAM, GU9 7EG.

FAREED, Mrs. Shirin Bano, BA(Hons) ACA *2000;* 23 Dunnock Avenue, BRADFORD, BD6 3XH.

FAREY, Mr. Christopher John, FCA *1972;* Moorside Cottage, Hutton-le-Hole, NORTH YORK, YO62 6UA.

FAREY, Mr. Jonathan Francis, BCom ACA *1984;* Wincanton Group Limited c/o H.J.Heinz NDC, Fourmarts Road Martland Park, WIGAN, LANCASHIRE, WN5 0LR.

FARGHER, Mr. Anthony Eric, BSc ACA *1995;* (Tax Fac), 11 Chaucer Close, WINDSOR, BERKSHIRE, SL4 3ER.

FARGHER, Mr. James Basil, FCA *1966;* Camelia Cottage, Old Lyndhurst Road, Cadnam, SOUTHAMPTON, SO40 2NL. (Life Member)

•**FARGHER, Mr. John Charles, BA FCA** *1974;* Charles Fargher, Ballafreer House, Union Mills, Douglas, ISLE OF MAN, IM4 4AT.

FARGHER, Mr. William Geoffrey, FCA *1957;* The Byre, Astley, SHREWSBURY, SY4 4BP. (Life Member)

FARID, Mr. Farhan, FCA CISA *1990;* Gulf Drilling International, Main Airport Road Building No. 4718, P O Box 9072, DOHA, QATAR.

FARIDI, Mr. Kamran, ACA *1979;* 4665 Black Rock Turnpike, FAIRFIELD, CT 06824, UNITED STATES.

FARIS, Mr. John Brian, FCA *1961;* 18 Tolmers Avenue, Cuffley, POTTERS BAR, EN6 4QA. (Life Member)

FARISH, Mr. Edwin James, BSc ACA *1987;* 1/11 Broderick Street, BALMAIN, NSW 2041, AUSTRALIA.

FARLEY, Miss. Alexandra Jane, LLB ACA *2004;* 32 Heath Road, ST. ALBANS, HERTFORDSHIRE, AL1 4DP.

FARLEY, Mr. Conor Francis, BSc(Hons) ACA *2001;* with Grant Thornton, Level 17, 383 Kent Street, SYDNEY, NSW 2000, AUSTRALIA.

FARLEY, Mr. David, ACA *1992;* Highland Bagley, WEDMORE, SOMERSET, BS28 4TD.

FARLEY, Mr. Duncan Karl, BA ACA *1990;* 43 Brodrick Road, LONDON, SW17 7DX.

FARLEY, Mr. Edward McMurdo, BA(Hons) ACA *2001;* 9 Balmuir Gardens, LONDON, SW15 6NG.

FARLEY, Mr. Elliot Neil, BSc ACA *2000;* 21 Mill Hill Leys, Wymeswold, LOUGHBOROUGH, LEICESTERSHIRE, LE12 6UU.

FARLEY, Mrs. Georgina Rosemary, MA ACA *2002;* B P P Professional Education, 137 Stamford Street, LONDON, SE1 9NN.

FARLEY, Mr. Ian Thomas, BSc ACA *1999;* (Tax Fac), B D O Stoy Hayward Lindsay House, 10 Callender Street, BELFAST, BT1 5BN.

FARLEY, Mr. John Martin, FCA *1959;* Shay Grove, 50 Green Lane, Glusburn, KEIGHLEY, WEST YORKSHIRE, BD20 8RU. (Life Member)

FARLEY, Mrs. Katie, BSc ACA *2005;* Barris House, Lapford, CREDITON, DEVON, EX17 6PU.

FARLEY, Mr. Michael George, BSc ACA *1978;* 43 Great Meadow Road, Bradley Stoke, BRISTOL, BS32 8DE.

•**FARLEY, Mr. Michael William, ACA** *1983;* Michael Farley & Associates Limited, 426-428 Holdenhurst Road, BOURNEMOUTH, DORSET, BH8 9AA.

FARLEY, Mr. Peter, FCA *1960;* 38 Potterdale Drive, Little Weighton, COTTINGHAM, HU20 3UX. (Life Member)

FARLEY, Mr. Shaun Robert, ACA *2009;* 9 Wesley Street Flat, 10-12 Wesley Street St. Helier, JERSEY, JE2 4SN.

FARLOW, Mr. David, BSc ACA *1998;* 4 Violet Grove, THATCHAM, BERKSHIRE, RG18 4DQ.

•**FARLOW, Mr. Mark Timothy, BSc ACA** *1986;* KPMG LLP, 15 Canada Square, LONDON, E14 5GL. See also KPMG Europe LLP

FARMAHAN, Mr. Sanjay Daniel, BSc ACA *2006;* Ty Cwm, Whitlow, SAUNDERSFOOT, DYFED, SA69 9AE.

FARMAN, Mr. Christopher, BSc ACA *1983;* 23 South Side, Hutton Rudby, YARM, CLEVELAND, TS15 0DD.

FARMAN, Mrs. Coral Ann, BA ACA *1992;* 78a Elm Road, LEIGH-ON-SEA, SS9 1SJ.

•**FARMAN, Mr. Denis John, BSc FCA** *1975;* Denis Farman, 28 Park Gate, Mount Avenue, Ealing, LONDON, W5 1PX.

FARMAN, Mr. John Harry, BSc ACA *1981;* Technicon International Management Services Ltd, Technicon House 905 Capability Green, LUTON, LU1 3LU.

•**FARMAR, Mr. Mark Philip, BA FCA** *1977;* Buzzacott LLP, 130 Wood Street, LONDON, EC2V 6DL. See also Buzzacott Livingstone Ltd and Fiscal Solutions Ltd

•**FARMBROUGH, Mr. James Yalden, MA FCA** *1985;* Baker Tilly Tax & Advisory Services LLP, The Pinnacle, 170 Midsummer Boulevard, MILTON KEYNES, MK9 1BP. See also Baker Tilly Corporate Finance LLP

•**FARMER, Mrs. Alexandra Victoria Hollis, LLB FCA** *1984;* Hollis & Co, The Rookery, Freasley, TAMWORTH, B78 2EZ.

FARMER, Mr. Andrew Peter, FCA *1971;* 65a Bidston Road, Oxton, PRENTON, MERSEYSIDE, CH43 6TR.

FARMER, Mr. Andrew Robert, BSc ACA *1996;* Waldingfield Lodge, The Street, Great Waldingfield, SUDBURY, SUFFOLK, CO10 0TJ.

FARMER, Mr. Christopher James, LLB ACA *2007;* Flat C, 8 Aristotle Road, LONDON, SW4 7UZ.

FARMER, Miss. Clare Simone, BA(Hons) ACA CTA *2001;* 9 Nether Street, Belton in Rutland, OAKHAM, LE15 9LD.

•**FARMER, Mr. Colin Charles, FCA** *1981;* Alliotts, Imperial House, 15 Kingsway, LONDON, WC2B 6UN.

FARMER, Mr. David, BA ACA *1995;* 39 Newbury Road, BROMLEY, BR2 0QN.

FARMER, Mr. David, BSc ACA *1985;* (Tax Fac), 13 Cow Lane Fulbourn, CAMBRIDGE, CB21 5HB.

FARMER, Mr. David Gordon, BA ACA *2007;* with PricewaterhouseCoopers LLP, 9 Greyfriars Road, READING, RG1 1JG.

FARMER, Mr. Ian Michael, ACA *1985;* 19 Beauty Point Road, MOSMAN, NSW 2088, AUSTRALIA.

FARMER, Mr. James Michael, BA ACA *1987;* 5 Kingsmill Close, Alverstoke, GOSPORT, PO12 2PG.

•**FARMER, Miss. Janet Margaret, ACA DChA** *1987;* 1 Castle Drive, ILFORD, IG4 5AE.

•**FARMER, Mr. John Anthony, BA FCA CF** *1979;* JWPCreers, 20-24 Park Street, SELBY, NORTH YORKSHIRE, YO8 4PW.

FARMER, Mr. John Anthony Cotton, FCA *1957;* The Peppers, The Street, Crookham Village, FLEET, HAMPSHIRE, GU51 5SG. (Life Member)

FARMER, Mr. John Davenport, FCA *1962;* Agar Nook, 14a Bower Road, Hale, ALTRINCHAM, CHESHIRE, WA15 9DT. (Life Member)

FARMER, Mr. Julian Derek, FCA *1973;* Flat 1, 20 Winton Road, Bowdon, ALTRINCHAM, WA14 2PB.

FARMER, Mr. Keith Edward John, BA FCA *1977;* T4i, Kampung Warisan, Jalan Jelatek, 54200 KUALA LUMPUR, FEDERAL TERRITORY, MALAYSIA.

FARMER, Mrs. Lesley Elizabeth, MBA BSc ACA *1992;* Legal & General Assurance Society Ltd Legal & General House, St. Monicas Road Kingswood, TADWORTH, KT20 6EU.

FARMER, Mr. Marc John, ACA *1998;* 14 Rookery Close, Kennington, ASHFORD, KENT, TN24 9RP.

FARMER, Mr. Martin Ian, FCA *1976;* Bearwood, Glendale Park, FLEET, GU51 5JL.

FARMER, Mr. Neville, FCA *1949;* 9 Broadsands Court, Broadsands Road, PAIGNTON, DEVON, TQ4 6LD. (Life Member)

•**FARMER, Mr. Nicholas, BSc FCA** *1977;* Burman & Co, Brunswick Hse, Birmingham Rd, REDDITCH, B97 6DY.

FARMER, Mr. Nicholas John, BSc ACA *1996;* 32 Allee de la Petite Savanna, Domain de la Belle Vue, Belle Vue Harel, PAMPLEMOUSSES, MAURITIUS.

•**FARMER, Mr. Nicholas Michael, BSc ACA** *1997;* (Tax Fac), Menzies LLP, Heathrow Business Centre, 65 High Street, EGHAM, SURREY, TW20 9EY.

FARMER, Mr. Paul Ronald, MPhil LLB ACA *1981;* Dorsey & Whitney, 21 Wilson Street, LONDON, EC2M 2TD.

FARMER, Mr. Peter Neil, BCom ACA CTA *1996;* 8 Oaklands, CIRENCESTER, GLOUCESTERSHIRE, GL7 1FA.

FARMER, Mr. Peter Richard Campbell, FCA *1972;* Peter Farmer Consultancy, Cavendish House, 9 Market End, Coggeshall, COLCHESTER, CO6 1NH.

FARMER, Mrs. Rachael Anne, BA(Hons) ACA *2004;* 21 Bryanston Road, Wirral, PRENTON, CH42 8PT.

FARMER, Ms. Rebecca, BSc ACA *2001;* with National Audit Office, 157-197 Buckingham Palace Road, Victoria, LONDON, SW1W 9SP.

FARMER, Mrs. Rebecca Jane, BSc ACA *1992;* 3 Chapel Lane, Barrowden, OAKHAM, LE15 8EB.

FARMER, Dr. Rebecca Jeanne, DPhil BA ACA *2001;* with Ernst & Young LLP, Apex Plaza, Forbury Road, READING, RG1 1YE.

FARMER, Mrs. Renata, BSc ACA *2001;* 50 Hilldrop Road, LONDON, N7 0JE.

•**FARMER, Mr. Richard James, ACA** *2008;* 394 Swindon Road, CHELTENHAM, GLOUCESTERSHIRE, GL51 9JZ.

FARMER, Mrs. Rosemarie Elvina, FCA *1971;* 6 Seys Close, COWBRIDGE, SOUTH GLAMORGAN, CF71 7BW.

•**FARMER, Mr. Roy Edward, BSc ACA CF** *1997;* Dains LLP, Charlotte House, Stanier Way, The Wyvern Business Park, DERBY, DE21 6BF.

FARMER, Miss. Sarah Elizabeth, BSc ACA *1993;* c/o Langdale, 40 West Street, Long Buckby, NORTHAMPTON, NN6 7QE.

FARMER, Ms. Sharon Lynne, BA ACA *1985;* 7 Milton Road, EASTBOURNE, EAST SUSSEX, BN21 1SG.

FARMERY, Miss. Anna Louise, ACA *1991;* 57 Roedhelm Road, East Morton, KEIGHLEY, WEST YORKSHIRE, BD20 5RF.

FARMERY, Mr. David Charles Edwin, FCA *1961;* 50 Lees Hall Avenue, Norton Lees, SHEFFIELD, S8 9JF.

FARMERY, Mr. David Keith, BSc ACA AMCT *1985;* Message Automation, c/o City Networks, Warnford Court, 29 Throgmorton Street, LONDON, EC2N 2AT.

FARMERY, Mr. Richard John, BA ACA *1989;* 35 Chartridge Lane, CHESHAM, BUCKINGHAMSHIRE, HP5 2JL.

FARMILOE, Mr. Gordon Trevarthen, ACA *1987;* Perrymill Farm, Perrymill Lane, Bradley Green, REDDITCH, B96 6RR.

FARMILOE, Mrs. Hilary Alison, BA ACA *1988;* 10 Denehurst Close, Barnt Green, BIRMINGHAM, B45 8HR.

•**FARNAN, Mr. David John, FCA** *1975;* 110 Martens Avenue, BEXLEYHEATH, KENT, DA7 6AN.

FARNAN, Miss. Patricia, MA(Oxon) ACA *2009;* Ernst & Young Llp The Paragon, Counterslip, BRISTOL, BS1 6BX.

•**FARNDALE, Mr. John Martin, FCA** *1975;* BFE Brays Ltd, 6 Cambridge Crescent, HARROGATE, NORTH YORKSHIRE, HG1 1PE. See also Edward Ramsden Ltd

FARNDON, Miss. Catherine Louise, BSc ACA *1997;* with Dixon Wilson, 22 Chancery Lane, LONDON, WC2A 1LS.

•**FARNDON, Mr. Michael Alan, ACA** *1983;* (Tax Fac), Warren Place, Birch Vale, COBHAM, SURREY, KT11 2PX.

FARNELL, Mr. Adrian Colin, BA FCA *1987;* The Royal Bank of Scotland Plc, Global Banking & Markets, 135 Bishopgate, LONDON, EC2M 3UR.

FARNELL, Mr. David Roy, FCA *1963;* 8 Deyncourt Darras Hall, Ponteland, NEWCASTLE UPON TYNE, NE20 9RP.

FARNELL, Mr. David Timothy, BSc ACA *2005;* 13 Page Heath Lane, BROMLEY, BR1 2DR.

•**FARNELL, Mr. Jonathan Graham, BSc ACA** *1996;* KPMG Europe LLP, 15 Canada Square, LONDON, E14 5GL.

•**FARNELL, Mr. Jonathan Sean William, BSc FCA** *1990;* Burgis & Bullock Corporate Finance Ltd, 2 Chapel Court, Holly Walk, LEAMINGTON SPA, CV32 4YS. See also Burgis & Bullock

FARNELL, Mr. Peter Samuel, FCA *1965;* 12 Berwick Road, BLACKPOOL, FY4 2PS.

FARNELL, Mr. Russell Austin, BA ACA *1997;* 166 Oak Drive, SAN RAFAEL, CA 94901, UNITED STATES.

FARNELL, Mr. Sean Paul, BA ACA *1997;* 1 Harewood Cottage, Steeton, KEIGHLEY, WEST YORKSHIRE, BD20 6TA.

•**FARNELL-SMITH, Mr. Robert Charles, BSc FCA** *1984;* RFS, The Coach House, 1A Watt Place, Cheadle, STOKE-ON-TRENT, STAFFORDSHIRE ST10 1NY.

•**FARNES, Mr. Gary Charles, ACA FCCA** *2010;* Mercer & Hole, Silbury Court, 420 Silbury Boulevard, MILTON KEYNES, BUCKINGHAMSHIRE, MK9 2AF.

FARNFIELD, Mr. Ian Murray, BSc ACA *1980;* The Chapter House, Outwood Common, Outwood, REDHILL, RH1 5PW.

FARNHAM, Mr. Adrian John Winston, BSc ACA *1990;* Turquoise, 23 Austin Friars, LONDON, EC2N 2QP.

FARNHAM, Mr. Mark Robert, BSc ACA *1990;* Stonecroft, High Road, Ashton Keynes, SWINDON, SN6 6NX.

FARNHAM, Mrs. Susan, BCom ACA *1991;* Stonecroft, High Road, Ashton Keynes, SWINDON, SN6 6NX.

FARNHILL, Mr. Howard Benjamin, FCA *1965;* 33 Archibald Street, Gosforth, NEWCASTLE UPON TYNE, NE3 1EB. (Life Member)

FARNILL, Mr. Frank, FCA *1962;* 44 Mount Pleasant, Bentham, LANCASTER, LA2 7LA.

FARNILL, Mr. Harry, FCA *1957;* 3 Prince Henry's Road, OTLEY, WEST YORKSHIRE, LS21 2BE. (Life Member)

FARNON, Mrs. Sally-Ann, FCA *1983;* Les Villets Farm, Les Villets, Forest, GUERNSEY, GY8 0HP.

•**FARNSWORTH, Mr. David William, FCA** *1977;* Feltons (Bham) Limited, 8 Sovereign Court, 8 Graham Street, BIRMINGHAM, B1 3JR.

FARNSWORTH, Mr. Iain Stewart, BSc FCA *1991;* Rose End, 103A The Drive, RICKMANSWORTH, WD3 4DY.

FARNSWORTH, Mrs. Jane, ACA *1984;* 93 Hall Cottages Church Road, Quarndon, DERBY, DE22 5JA.

FARNSWORTH, Mr. John Graham, FCA *1975;* 15 Noirmont Way, Northfield GreenEast Moorside, SUNDERLAND, SR3 2SS.
•**FARNSWORTH, Mr. John Peter, FCA CF** *1982;* Smith Cooper, Wilmot House, St James Court, Friar Gate, DERBY, DE1 1BT. See also Smith Cooper LLP
FARNSWORTH, Mr. Richard James, MA FCA *1991;* with PricewaterhouseCoopers LLP, 1 Embankment Place, LONDON, WC2N 6RH.
•**FARNWORTH, Mr. Anthony John, BA ACA** *1987;* Deloitte LLP, PO Box 500, 2 Hardman Street, MANCHESTER, M60 2AT. See also Deloitte & Touche LLP
FARNWORTH, Mr. Myles Mark Hurst, FCA *1958;* Blair Cottage, 52 Moss Road, ALDERLEY EDGE, SK9 7JB. (Life Member)
FARNWORTH, Mr. Oliver George, LLB ACA *1999;* (Tax Fac), with Deloitte Touche Tohmatsu, 35/F One Pacific Place, 88 Queensway, CENTRAL, HONG KONG ISLAND, HONG KONG SAR.
FAROOQ, Mr. Adnan, ACA FCCA *2007;* 4th Floor D.I. House, Dubai Investment Park 1, DUBAI, 3045, UNITED ARAB EMIRATES.
FAROOQ, Mr. Faisal, BA ACA *1996;* 186-D, Model Town, LAHORE 54700, PAKISTAN.
FAROOQ, Mr. Hassan Arshad, MSc BSc ACA *2002;* Ernst & Young, PO BOX 140, MANAMA, BAHRAIN.
FAROOQ, Mr. Mohammad Junaid, BSc FCA *1980;* 5 S.N. Srivastava Road, Panditnagar, LUCKNOW 226018, INDIA.
FAROOQ, Ms. Samar, BA ACA CTA *2004;* 15 Redbridge Court, Redbridge Lane East, ILFORD, IG4 5DG.
•**FAROOQ, Mr. Umar, FCA** *1974;* (Tax Fac), Farooq & Co (London) Limited, Wembley Point, 1 Harrow Road, WEMBLEY, MIDDLESEX, HA9 6DE.
FAROOQI, Mr. Aamir Zaheer, ACA *1983;* 300 Beach Road The Concourse #23-01, SINGAPORE 199555, SINGAPORE.
•**FAROOQI, Mr. Hammad, FCA** *1994;* with Azure Global Limited, Argyll House, 23 Brook Street, KINGSTON, KT1 2BN.
FAROOQI, Mr. Mohammad Javed, FCA *1974;* 336 Loma Avenue, LONG BEACH, CA 90814, UNITED STATES.
•**FAROOQI, Mr. Shajar Ahmad, FCA** *1974;* (Tax Fac), Sammar & Co Limited, Baet-Ul-Zafar, 14 Albury Avenue, Cheam, SUTTON, SM2 7JT.
FAROOQI, Mr. Zakria, BSc ACA *2010;* 4 Smeaton Road, LONDON, SW18 5JH.
•**FAROUK, Mr. Farhan, BA FCA** *1987;* Deloitte & Touche Bakr Abulkhair & Co, PO Box 442, 12 Floor, Saudi Business Center, Madinah Road, JEDDAH 21411 SAUDI ARABIA. See also Athar Khan & Co.
FARQUHAR, Mr. Andrew James, BSc ACA *1994;* 34 Mount Park, CARSHALTON, SM5 4PS.
FARQUHAR, Mr. Andrew Mark, BSc FCA *1989;* Area Directors Office HMCS - Cleveland Durham & Northumbria, Green Lane Old Elvet, DURHAM, COUNTY DURHAM, DH1 3RG.
•**FARQUHAR, Mrs. Ann, MA FCA ATII** *1987;* (Tax Fac), Farquhar Partnership LLP, Saville Court, Saville Place, Clifton, BRISTOL, BS8 4EJ.
FARQUHAR, Mr. Colin Alexander, ACA CA(SA) *2009;* Deloitte LLP, 4th Floor, Ahere Place, 66 Shoe Lane, LONDON, EC4A 3BQ.
FARQUHAR, Mr. Iain Edward Mark, FCA *1961;* 2 Pembroke Drive, Ponteland, NEWCASTLE UPON TYNE, NE20 9HS.
FARQUHAR, Mr. Michael Frank Banner, BSc FCA *1988;* Apple Tree Cottage, Bigfrith Lane, Cookham, MAIDENHEAD, SL6 9PH.
FARQUHAR, Mr. Paul Neil, BA ACA *1989;* 3 Duxbury Park, WASHINGTON, TYNE AND WEAR, NE38 8BJ.
•**FARQUHAR, Mr. Robert Mackenzie, FCA** *1964;* (Tax Fac), Robert Farquhar, 55 High Street, Topsham, EXETER, EX3 0DY.
FARQUHAR, Miss. Sarah, MA BA(Hons) ACA *2010;* 4 Sea View, ST. BEES, CUMBRIA, CA27 0BB.
FARQUHARSON, Mrs. Catherine Elizabeth, BSc ACA *1984;* Parkside, Bealings Road, Martlesham, WOODBRIDGE, IP12 4RW.
FARQUHARSON, Mr. Derek Mcbain, FCA *1959;* Parsons Field, The Hamlet, Potten End, BERKHAMSTED, HP4 2RD. (Life Member)
FARQUHARSON, Mrs. Fiona Ann, ACA *1985;* 139/395 Antill Street, WATSON, ACT 2602, AUSTRALIA.
FARQUHARSON, Mr. Ian James, BA ACA *1986;* 4 Heathlands Close, WOKING, GU21 4JH.
FARQUHARSON, Miss. Karen Anne, BSc ACA *1992;* 19 St Georges Close, Toddington, DUNSTABLE, LU5 6AT.
FARQUHARSON, Miss. Katherine, ACA *2011;* 43 The Avenue, SUTTON, SM2 7QA.
FARQUHARSON, Mr. Richard Graham Spencer, BA ACA *1991;* Chemin Du Petit-Record 62, Echallens, CH-1040 VAUD, SWITZERLAND.
FARQUHARSON, Mrs. Virginia Anne, BA ACA *1984;* Avalon, 4 Heathlands Cl, Kettlewell Hill Horsell, WOKING, GU21 4JH.
FARQUHARSON-PRATT, Mr. Christopher Howard, FCA *1966;* 36 Hopton Road, Upper Cam, DURSLEY, GL11 5PB.
FARR, Mr. Angus John, MA FCA MCIPD *1998;* 156 Mayall Road, LONDON, SE24 0PH.
FARR, Mr. Daniel John, ACA *2008;* 38 Minley Road, FARNBOROUGH, HAMPSHIRE, GU14 9RS.
FARR, Mr. Gordon Ingram, FCA *1953;* The Hermitage, 150 Above Town, DARTMOUTH, TQ6 9RH. (Life Member)
FARR, Miss. Jacqueline, BSc ACA *1994;* 8 Maple Road, SURBITON, KT6 4AB.
FARR, Mrs. Julie, BA ACA *1991;* 10 Summerfield Road, Ealing, LONDON, W5 1ND.
FARR, Mrs. Katherine Spencer, BA ACA *1989;* 45 Ennerdale Road, RICHMOND, TW9 2DN.
•**FARR, Miss. Kathryn Olwen, BA FCA ATII** *1992;* (Tax Fac), K.A.Farr & Co, 6-8 Botanic Road, Churchtown, SOUTHPORT, PR9 7NG.
FARR, Mr. Kenneth Anthony, FCA *1957;* Manderley, Hares Lane, Scarisbrick, SOUTHPORT, PR8 5LG. (Life Member)
FARR, Mr. Lance Denis, BSc(Hons) ACA *1995;* Overseas Courier Service Ltd, Global House, Poyle Road, Colnbrook, SLOUGH, BERKSHIRE SL3 0AY.
FARR, Mrs. Linda Rosemary, BSc FCA *1976;* 10 Birchitt Close, Bradway, SHEFFIELD, S17 4QJ.
FARR, Mrs. Margaret Alice, BSc FCA *1976;* High Pastures, Harpenden Road, Wheathampstead, ST. ALBANS, AL4 8DX.
FARR, Mr. Matthew, ACA *2009;* 89 School Road, ASHFORD, MIDDLESEX, TW15 2AL.
•**FARR, Mr. Nicholas, BSc FCA** *1990;* Moore Green, 22 Friars Street, SUDBURY, SUFFOLK, CO10 2AA. See also Moore Green Ltd
•**FARR, Mr. Nicholas Edward, MA ACA** *1998;* (Tax Fac), Grant Thornton UK LLP, Grant Thornton House, 22 Melton Street, Euston Square, LONDON, NW1 2EP. See also Grant Thornton LLP
FARR, Dr. Paul Gerard, ACA *2009;* Deloitte & Touche Llp Horton House, Exchange Flags, LIVERPOOL, L2 3PG.
•**FARR, Mr. Richard Eric, BCom FCA** *1982;* BDO LLP, 55 Baker Street, LONDON, W1U 7EU. See also BDO Stoy Hayward LLP
FARR, Mrs. Sarah Louise, BSc ACA *2005;* 11 North Road, Kirkburton, HUDDERSFIELD, HD8 0NX.
FARR, Mr. Simon Michael, BA(Econ) ACA *2010;* 20 Clearwater Drive, MANCHESTER, M20 2ED.
FARR, Mrs. Susan Jane, BA ACA *1988;* 15 Fir Road, Ashurst, SOUTHAMPTON, SO40 7AZ.
FARR, Mr. William John Maclean, FCA *1970;* 10 Birchitt Close, Bradway, SHEFFIELD, S17 4QJ.
FARRADAY, Mr. David Russell, BSc ACA *2004;* 2/19 Reynolds Street, CREMORNE, NSW 2090, AUSTRALIA.
FARRAGHER, Mr. Peter James, BCom FCA MBA *1976;* 130 Castleknock Park, DUBLIN 15, COUNTY DUBLIN, IRELAND.
FARRAGHER, Mr. Raymond, BA ACA *2007;* 44 Langdon House, Leather Lane, LONDON, EC1N 7TN.
FARRALL, Mrs. Katrina Wendy, BA ACA *1996;* 195 Vicarage Hill, BENFLEET, ESSEX, SS7 1PF.
FARRALL, Mr. Steven Michael, MA ACA *1996;* 195 Vicarage Hill, BENFLEET, SS7 1PF.
FARRAN, Mr. Charles Michael Darley, FCA *1981;* with Chantrey Vellacott DFK LLP, 35 Calthorpe Road, Edgbaston, BIRMINGHAM, WEST MIDLANDS, B15 1TS.
•**FARRAND, Mr. Colin Eric, FCA** *1971;* (Tax Fac), Farrand & Co, Canada Del Tejar 3, Alhaurin el Grande, 29120 MALAGA, SPAIN.
•**FARRAND-LAINE, Mrs. Colette Marilynne, BSc FCA** *1999;* (Tax Fac), Farrand-Laine Limited, 81 High Street, Little Paxton, ST. NEOTS, CAMBRIDGESHIRE, PE19 6QH.
FARRANT, Miss. Hayley, ACA *2010;* Flat 3, Newton House Mansions, 36 Bristol Road Lower, WESTON-SUPER-MARE, AVON, BS23 2PS.
FARRANT, Mr. Jonathan, ACA *2009;* Sightsavers, Grosvenor Hall, Bolnore Road, HAYWARDS HEATH, WEST SUSSEX, RH16 4BX.
FARRANT, Mr. Leslie John, BA FCA *1960;* 1 Sonning Meadows, Sonning, READING, RG4 6XB. (Life Member)
•**FARRANT, Mr. Matthew Granby, ACA CTA** *1984;* (Tax Fac), Barnett Spooner, The Old Steppe House, Brighton Road, GODALMING, SURREY, GU7 1NS.
FARRANT, Mr. Nicholas Charles, MSc BA ACA *2007;* White Cottage, Chapel Lane, High Street, Bishops Lydeard, TAUNTON, SOMERSET TA4 3AX.
FARRANT, Mr. Norman Frank, FCA *1956;* 75 Richmond Hill Court, Richmond Hill, RICHMOND, TW10 6BG. (Life Member)
FARRANT, Mrs. Patricia Margaret, ACA *1979;* 1 Broadlands Close, YEOVIL, SOMERSET, BA21 5XR.
•**FARRANT, Mr. Roy David, BSc FCA AKC** *1980;* Roy Farrant & Co Ltd, 14 Le Corte Close, KINGS LANGLEY, HERTFORDSHIRE, WD4 9PS.
FARRANT, Ms. Ruth Sylvena, BA(Hons) FCA *1994;* Via Paolo di Dono 44, 00142 ROME, ITALY.
•**FARRANT, Mr. Stephen James, BA FCA** *1990;* Day Smith & Hunter, Globe House, Eclipse Park, Sittingbourne Road, MAIDSTONE, KENT ME14 3EN.
FARRANT, Mr. Stuart Anthony, BSc(Hons) ACA *2000;* Marsh Ltd, 1 Tower Place West, LONDON, EC3R 5BU.
FARRANT, Miss. Suzanne Louise, ACA *2001;* 267 Mallorca Way, SAN FRANCISCO, CA 94123, UNITED STATES.
FARRAR, Mrs. Ailegh, BA ACA *2002;* 50 Fairfield Avenue, Kirk Ella, HULL, HU10 7UH.
FARRAR, Mr. Ben, BA(Hons) ACA *2001;* 8 Spring Gardens, Burley in Wharfedale, ILKLEY, WEST YORKSHIRE, LS29 7DA.
•**FARRAR, Mr. Christopher, FCA** *1968;* (Tax Fac), Farrars, Acorn House, 4 Mill Fields, Bassingham, LINCOLN, LN5 9NP.
FARRAR, Mr. Ian Peter, BA FCA *1997;* Flat F-13 Scenic Villas, 12 Scenic Villa Drive, POK FU LAM, HONG KONG ISLAND, HONG KONG SAR.
FARRAR, Mr. Jonathan Edward David, BSc ACA *1998;* The Homerton Hospital NHS Foundation Trust, Homerton Row, LONDON, E9 6SR.
FARRAR, Mrs. Kathryn Elena, ACA *2002;* 8 Hill Crest Drive, LOUGHBOROUGH, LEICESTERSHIRE, LE11 2GX.
FARRAR, Mr. Mark Jonathan, BSc FCA AMCT *1988;* Construction Skills, Bircham Newton, KING'S LYNN, NORFOLK, PE31 6RH.
FARRAR, Mr. Mark Richard, MA ACA *1997;* 40 Dry Hill Park Road, TONBRIDGE, TN10 3BU.
FARRAR, Mr. Paul Morgan, BA ACA *2002;* 50 Fairfield Avenue, Kirk Ella, HULL, HU10 7UH.
FARRAR, Mr. Peter John, BA FCA *1972;* North Downs House, The Ridge, Woldingham, CATERHAM, CR3 7AH.
FARRAR, Mr. Richard Alexis, BA FCA *1973;* 23 Hall Cliffe, Baildon, SHIPLEY, WEST YORKSHIRE, BD17 6ND. (Life Member)
FARRAR, Mr. Richard John Piercy, FCA *1967;* 25 Stoneglen Drive, ETOBICOKE M9C 2V6, ON, CANADA. (Life Member)
FARRAR, Mr. Roland Martin, FCA *1976;* 40 Chiltern Road, Bray, MAIDENHEAD, SL6 1XA.
FARRAR, Ms. Rosemary Joy, BA FCA *1984;* Southern Housing Group, Fleet House, 59-61 Clerkenwell Road, LONDON, EC1M 5LA.
FARRAR, Miss. Sarah Catherine, BSc(Hons) ACA *2003;* Validus Holdings, 29 Richmond Road, HAMILTON HM 08, BERMUDA.
FARRAR, Mr. Steven, BA FCA *1982;* 3 Lark Hill, Moulton, NEWMARKET, Suffolk, CB8 8RT.
•**FARRAR, Mr. Timothy Edgar, BA(Hons) ACA** *2002;* Farrars, 8 Hillcrest Drive, LOUGHBOROUGH, LEICESTERSHIRE, LE11 2GX. See also Farrars Limited
FARRELL, Mrs. Alexandra Mary, MBChB ACA *1992;* 17 Gledhow Park Drive, LEEDS, LS7 4JT.
FARRELL, Mrs. Alison Marie, BA ACA *1994;* 6 Poyntz Gardens, Dallington, NORTHAMPTON, NN5 7RY.
FARRELL, Mr. Brendan, BCom FCA CF *1983;* Stelfox House, 7 Chapel Lane Letty Green, HERTFORD, SG14 2PA.
FARRELL, Mr. Brian Patrick, FCA *1971;* Camelot, Stone House, Stillorgan Road, Donnybrook, DUBLIN 4, COUNTY DUBLIN IRELAND.
FARRELL, Mr. Brian Thomas, BAI BA ACA *2005;* Westferry Point, Flat 6, 156 Westferry Road, LONDON, E14 3QA.
FARRELL, Mr. Colin Andrew, MA FCA *1984;* (Tax Fac), PricewaterhouseCoopers, 21/F Edinburgh Tower, 15 Queen's Road Central, CENTRAL, HONG KONG ISLAND, HONG KONG SAR.
FARRELL, Mr. David Charles, BSc ACA CF *1992;* 1621 35th Street NW, WASHINGTON, DC 20007, UNITED STATES.
FARRELL, Mr. Duncan, FCA *1967;* 41 Reedsdale Gardens, Gildersome, Morley, LEEDS, LS27 7JD.
FARRELL, Mr. Grant James, BSc ACA *1991;* 29 Clarence Road, WINDSOR, BERKSHIRE, SL4 5AX.
FARRELL, Mr. Gregory James, BSc ACA *2006;* 175 Mead Way, BROMLEY, BR2 9ES.
FARRELL, Mrs. Jane Erica, BSc FCA *1985;* 17 Midhurst Avenue, Muswell Hill, LONDON, N10 3EP.
FARRELL, Mr. John Patrick, FCA *1955;* Broadcroft, Little Hallingbury, BISHOP'S STORTFORD, CM22 7QU. (Life Member)
FARRELL, Mrs. Julia Danielle, BSc(Hons) ACA *2002;* 730 Columbus Avenue, Apt 9F, NEW YORK, NY 10025, UNITED STATES.
FARRELL, Miss. Julia Diane, BA ACA *1997;* Croft House, 3 Chestnut Grove, Calverley, PUDSEY, WEST YORKSHIRE, LS28 5TN.
FARRELL, Mrs. Karen Juliette, BSc ACA *1993;* 21 Vowles Close, Wraxall, BRISTOL, BS48 1PP.
FARRELL, Mrs. Karen Michele, BSc ACA *1994;* 31 Ruscombe Gardens, Datchet, SLOUGH, SL3 9BG.
FARRELL, Mr. Kevin Anthony, FCA *1977;* Beau Vallon, High Street, Leintwardine, CRAVEN ARMS, SY7 0LQ.
FARRELL, Mr. Kevin Richard, BA ACA *1983;* Ernst & Young Tower, 222 Bay Street, PO Box 251, TORONTO M5K 1J7, ON, CANADA.
FARRELL, Miss. Maria Anne, BSc ACA *1993;* 114 Creighton Avenue, LONDON, N2 9BJ.
FARRELL, Mr. Michael, FCA *1959;* Preston Hill House, Pettiford Lane, Wootton Wawen, HENLEY-IN-ARDEN, B95 6ES. (Life Member)
•**FARRELL, Mrs. Michelle Dominique, BCom ACA** *2005;* Farrell Accountants, 175 Mead Way, BROMLEY, BR2 9ES.
FARRELL, Mr. Paul Anthony, BSc ACA *1994;* 81 Clarendon Drive, LONDON, SW15 1AN.
FARRELL, Mr. Peter John, BA FCA *1972;* Flat 2, 15 Tudor Hill, SUTTON COLDFIELD, B73 6BD.
FARRELL, Mr. Peter Rowland, BSc ACA *2001;* 182 Tythe Barn Lane Shirley, SOLIHULL, B90 1PF.
FARRELL, Miss. Sharnett, ACA *2011;* 12 Felspar Road, Southdene, Kirkby, LIVERPOOL, L32 3XX.
FARRELL, Mr. Stephen Francis, ACA *2009;* 73 Ashen Grove, LONDON, SW19 8BL.
FARRELL, Mr. Stephen Lee, BSc ACA *2000;* Stella Travel Services, Level 4, 77 Berry Street, NORTH SYDNEY, NSW 2060, AUSTRALIA.
FARRELLY, Mr. Barry Brendan, FCA *1970;* 38 The Grove, UPMINSTER, RM14 2ET.
FARRELLY, Ms. Finula Kathleen, BSc ACA *2001;* Flat 2, 6 Portland Rise, Finsbury Park, LONDON, N4 2PP.
FARRELLY, Mr. Jon Paul, BA ACA *2006;* 9 Brotherhood Drive, Sutton, ST. HELENS, MERSEYSIDE, WA9 3ZB.
FARRELLY, Mrs. Karen Jane, ACA *2001;* 1 Fairway, Shelfield, WALSALL, WS4 1RP.
FARRELLY, Mrs. Kirsty, BA ACA *2007;* 9 Brotherhood Drive, ST. HELENS, MERSEYSIDE, WA9 3ZB.
FARRELLY, Mr. Peter, ACA *2007;* Flat 1, 14 Ivanhoe Road Aigburth, LIVERPOOL, L17 8XQ.
FARRELLY, Mr. Thomas Paul, BSc ACA *1983;* PO Box 3585, DOUALA, CAMEROON.
FARREN, Mr. Raymond Edward, BA FCA *1985;* with ICAEW, Metropolitan House, 321 Avebury Boulevard, MILTON KEYNES, MK9 2FZ.
FARREN, Mr. Robert Stefan, ACA *2008;* K P M G Llp, 15 Canada Square, LONDON, E14 5GL.
•**FARREN, Mrs. Samantha, BSc ACA DChA** *2001;* Sam Farren BSc ACA DChA, 107 Noahs Ark, Kemsing, SEVENOAKS, KENT, TN15 6PD.
FARREN, Mr. Stuart Neil Peter, BA(Hons) FCA *1998;* Bnp Paribas, 10 Harewood Avenue, LONDON, NW1 6AA.
FARREN, Mr. William John, BSc ARCS ACA *2002;* with Baker Tilly UK Audit LLP, 25 Farringdon Street, LONDON, EC4A 4AB.
•①**FARRER, Mrs. Lindsay Marie, BA(Hons) ACA MABRP** *2002;* Saint & Co., Sterling House, Wavell Drive, Rosehill, CARLISLE, CA1 2SA.
FARRER, Mrs. Louise Mary, BA ACA *2004;* with Deloitte LLP, Athene Place, 66 Shoe Lane, LONDON, EC4A 3BQ.
FARRER, Mr. Mark Alan, MA ACA AMCT *2004;* 34 Clarendon Drive, LONDON, SW15 1AE.
•**FARRER, Mr. Stuart, BA FCA DChA** *1995;* Saint & Co., Sterling House, Wavell Drive, Rosehill, CARLISLE, CA1 2SA.
FARRES, Mr. Alan Ernest, FCA *1968;* 1058 Spar Drive, COQUITLAM V3H 3G8, BC, CANADA. (Life Member)

•**FARRES, Mr. Peter Robert, FCA** *1971;* College Farm, College Avenue, MAIDSTONE, ME15 6YJ.
FARREY, Mrs. Sara Ann, ACA *1991;* 13 Elm Court, Whickham, NEWCASTLE UPON TYNE, NE16 4PS.
FARRIER, Mr. Roger Neilson Mark, FCA *1977;* Campbell Saunders & Co, Suite 500-1055, West Broadway, VANCOUVER V6H 1E2, BC, CANADA.
FARRIMOND, Mr. Damian Dey, BA ACA *2004;* 141 Thunder Lane, NORWICH, NR7 0JG.
•**FARRIMOND, Mr. Darren James, BSc ACA** *1993;* Maskat Limited, 7 Cedargrove, Hagley, STOURBRIDGE, WEST MIDLANDS, DY9 0DR.
FARRIMOND, Mr. David, FCA *1976;* La Ramee Farmhouse, La Ramee, St Peter Port, GUERNSEY, GY1 2TP.
FARRIMOND, Miss. Jacqueline Caryll, MA ACA *1987;* 33 Clarendon Road, SHEFFIELD, S10 3TQ.
FARRIMOND, Mrs. Joanne, BSc ACA *1992;* 7 Cedargrove, Hagley, STOURBRIDGE, WEST MIDLANDS, DY9 0DR.
FARRINGTON, Mrs. Carol Jayne, BSc ACA *1982;* Oak Lodge, Wellington Heath, LEDBURY, HEREFORDSHIRE, HR8 1NB.
FARRINGTON, Mrs. Catherine Mary, BSc ACA *1993;* with Dains LLP, Unit 306, Third Floor, Fort Dunlop, Fort Parkway, BIRMINGHAM B24 9FD.
•①**FARRINGTON, Mr. Christopher James, BSc ACA** *1993;* with Deloitte LLP, 1 Woodborough Road, NOTTINGHAM, NG1 3FG.
FARRINGTON, Miss. Elizabeth Sarah Jane, MMath ACA CTA *2003;* 7 Foxhill, Kelsall, TARPORLEY, CHESHIRE, CW6 0NR.
FARRINGTON, Mr. Ian, FCA *1982;* 44 McArthur Drive, Kings Hill, WEST MALLING, KENT, ME19 4GW.
FARRINGTON, Mr. Jonathan, BA FCA MBA *1998;* Maxwell Stamp Plc, Abbots Court, 34 Farringdon Lane, LONDON, EC1R 3AX.
FARRINGTON, Mr. Nicholas Peter John, BA ACA *2001;* Eastwood, Willington Corner, TARPORLEY, CHESHIRE, CW6 0NE.
FARRINGTON, Mr. Paul, BA FCA *1976;* 159 Mendip Road, Lutley, HALESOWEN, B63 1JH.
FARRINGTON, Mr. Paul Graham, BSc ACA *2010;* 25 Rushwood Park, Standish, WIGAN, LANCASHIRE, WN6 0GH.
FARRINGTON, Mr. Robert William, FCA *1971;* 12 Oak Tree Drive, Cutnall Green, DROITWICH, WORCESTERSHIRE, WR9 0QY.
FARRINGTON-BROWN, Mrs. Sarah Jane, BSc ACA *1997;* 39 Glebe Road, Barnes, LONDON, SW13 0DZ.
FARRIS, Miss. Clare Louise, ACA *1994;* 11512 - 50 Ave, EDMONTON T6H 0J6, AB, CANADA.
FARRIS, Mrs. Rachel Pamela, BSc ACA CTA *2005;* 9 Maxfield Place, Epsom, AUCKLAND 1051, NEW ZEALAND.
FARROW, Mrs. Beth, BA ACA *2002;* Old Laundry Catslip Nettlebed, HENLEY-ON-THAMES, OXFORDSHIRE, RG9 5BL.
FARROW, Mrs. Beverley, BA ACA *1988;* Corso Sempione 11, MILAN, 20145, ITALY.
FARROW, Miss. Brenda, ACA *2007;* 109 Portswood Road, SOUTHAMPTON, SO17 2FU.
•**FARROW, Mr. Brian Keith, FCA** *1969;* Harrison Farrow, Newnham House, 3 Kings Road, NEWARK, NG24 1EW.
FARROW, Mrs. Deborah Lyn, BSc ACA *1992;* 4 Burnet Close, West End, WOKING, GU24 9PB.
FARROW, Mr. Frederick Charles, FCA *1961;* Auchengillian, 4 Osprey Gardens, Hazel Grove, Elburton, PLYMOUTH, PL9 8PP. (Life Member)
FARROW, Miss. Gayle Elizabeth, BA ACA *2002;* Flat 3, 24 Rothschild Road, LONDON, W4 5HS.
FARROW, Mr. Gerald, FCA *1962;* Bramble Lodge, 99 Rangell Gate, Low Fulney, SPALDING, PE12 6EW.
FARROW, Mr. Gordon Michael, FCA *1968;* 40 Aldenham Avenue, RADLETT, HERTFORDSHIRE, WD7 8HX.
FARROW, Mr. John Reginald, FCA *1968;* 2 Cefn Court, Stow Park Circle, NEWPORT, GWENT, NP20 4HQ.
•**FARROW, Mr. Jonathan Mark, BA FCA** *1992;* Midgley Snelling, Ibex House, Baker Street, WEYBRIDGE, SURREY, KT13 8AH.
FARROW, Miss. Julia Louise, BSc ACA *1997;* 46 Seaford Road, WOKINGHAM, BERKSHIRE, RG40 2EL.
FARROW, Mr. Kelvin Mark, BSc ACA *1996;* 3825 Canfield Road, PASADENA, CA 91107, UNITED STATES.
FARROW, Mr. Matthew James, BA(Hons) ACA *2001;* 34 Lychgate Close, Burbage, HINCKLEY, LEICESTERSHIRE, LE10 2ES.
FARROW, Ms. Maxine Jeannette, BA ACA *1995;* Flat 4, 27 Shortheath Road, FARNHAM, SURREY, GU9 8SN.
FARROW, Mr. Michael, BSc FCA *1958;* 27 The Avenue, Norton, MALTON, YO17 9EF. (Life Member)
FARROW, Mr. Michael Alfred, FCA *1966;* 4 Fendon Road, CAMBRIDGE, CB1 7RT.
•**FARROW, Mr. Nicholas Charles, BA FCA** *1989;* (Tax Fac), Farrow Accounting & Tax Ltd, Worple Court, 94-95 South Worple Way, LONDON, SW14 8ND.
FARROW, Mr. Paul Charles, BSc FCA *1976;* 2600 Ne Minnehaha St, C34, VANCOUVER, WA 98665, UNITED STATES.
•**FARROW, Mr. Paul Edward, ACA FCCA MAAT** *2008;* (Tax Fac), Mapus-Smith & Lemmon LLP, 23 London Road, DOWNHAM MARKET, NORFOLK, PE38 9BJ.
FARROW, Mr. Richard Albert, FCA *1968;* La Pre Broomrigg, La Rue de la Genestiere, Faldouet, St. Martin, JERSEY, JE3 6DA.
FARROW, Mr. Richard Kneen, BA ACA *1991;* Vicarage Consultancy Ltd, 31 Vicarage Fields, Overton Road, Ruabon, WREXHAM, CLWYD LL14 6LG.
FARROW, Miss. Sharon Joanne, BSc ACA *2005;* Flat 45, The Cloisters, 83 London Road, GUILDFORD, SURREY, GU1 1FY.
FARROW, Mr. Simon Frederick, BA ACA *1980;* Dial Court, 198 Burley Rd Thorney Hill, Bransgore, CHRISTCHURCH, BH23 8DF.
FARROW, Mr. William Stephen, FCA *1980;* Templemount, Blakes Road, Wargrave, READING, RG10 8LA.
FARRUGIA, Mr. Louis Anthony, FCA *1973;* Simonds Farsons Cisk Plc, The Brewery, MRIEHEL, BKR 01, MALTA.
FARRUGIA, Mr. Palmiero, BSc ACA *1979;* PT Sun Life Finanical Indonesia, World Trade Center, 8th Floor, Jl. Jend Sudirman Kav 29-31, JAKARTA, 12920 INDONESIA.
•**FARRUKH, Mr. Shehzad, ACA** *1990;* 2 Taunton Drive, LONDON, N2 8JD.
FARSHCHI-HEIDARI, Mr. Daryush, MChem ACA *2007;* FLAT F, 144 Bedford Hill, LONDON, SW12 9HW.
FARSIANI, Mrs. Angela May, BA ACA *1990;* 10 Northaw Road East, Cuffley, POTTERS BAR, HERTFORDSHIRE, EN6 4LT.
FARTHING, Miss. Carolyn Jill, BSc ACA *1991;* Nine Looms, Leighton Road, NESTON, CH64 3SW.
FARTHING, Mr. David Alan, BSc FCA *1990;* 16 Hollins Lane, Marple Bridge, STOCKPORT, SK6 5BB.
FARTHING, Mr. John, BSc FCA *1988;* with Kingston Smith & Partners LLP, Devonshire House, 60 Goswell Road, LONDON, EC1M 7AD.
FARTHING, Miss. Natalie, MSci ACA *2011;* 37 The Swallows, WELWYN GARDEN CITY, HERTFORDSHIRE, AL7 1BX.
FARTHING, Mrs. Nicola Louise, BA ACA *2002;* 9a Angel Road, THAMES DITTON, SURREY, KT7 0AU.
FARTHING, Miss. Sheila Miller, BSc ACA CTA *1985;* 53 Kingsley Street, Battersea, LONDON, SW11 5LF.
FARUQI, Mr. Hassan Ahmad, FCA *1971;* 30 Binden Road, LONDON, W12 9RJ. (Life Member)
FARUQI, Mr. Mohammad Ali, BA ACA *1994;* 4 The Squirrels, PINNER, MIDDLESEX, HA5 3BD.
FARWELL, Miss. Elizabeth Anne, BSc ACA *1981;* 13058 River Road, LOS ANGELES, CA 90049, UNITED STATES.
•**FARWELL, Mr. Michael Neil, MA FCA DChA** *1986;* James Cowper LLP, Mill House, Overbridge Square, Hambridge Lane, NEWBURY, BERKSHIRE RG14 5UX. See also JC Payroll Services Ltd
FARZAD, Mr. Salar, BSc ACA *1992;* Flat 10, Unwin Mansions, Queen's Club Gardens, LONDON, W14 9TH.
FARZADI, Mr. Hamed, BA ACA *2006;* Deloitte Corporate Finance Limited, Currency House Building 1, Dubai International Finance Centre, DUBAI, 282056, UNITED ARAB EMIRATES.
FARZADI, Mr. Mohammed, BSc ACA *2007;* with PricewaterhouseCoopers LLP, Pricewaterhousecoopers, 12 Plumtree Court, LONDON, EC4A 4HT.
FASEY, Mr. Nigel Gregg, BA ACA *1994;* The Barns St. Annes Manor, Hungary Lane Sutton Bonington, LOUGHBOROUGH, LE12 5NB.
FASIH, Mr. Anjum, ACA *1979;* D 34 Navy Housing Scheme, Clifton Block 9, KARACHI 75600, PAKISTAN.
FASOULIOTIS, Mr. Agathoklis, BA ACA *2001;* 4 Tamassou, 2411 Engomi, NICOSIA, CYPRUS.
FASS, Mr. Richard Andrew, FCA *1968;* 3 The Lane, LONDON, NW8 0PN.
FASS, Mr. Stephen Ivor, FCA *1969;* The Orchard, Westfield Park, Hatch End, PINNER, MIDDLESEX, HA5 4JJ.
•**FASSAM, Mr. Christopher John, ACA** *1983;* (Tax Fac), Atom Consulting Limited, Premier House, 50-52 Cross Lances Road, HOUNSLOW, TW3 2AA.
FASSIHI, Miss. Hilda, BSc ACA *2008;* Flat 3, 106 Tachbrook Street, LONDON, SW1V 2ND.
FASSIOMS, Mr. Richard Alan, BSc ACA *2010;* Cowgill Holloway, 45-51 Chorley New Road, BOLTON, BL1 4QR.
FATAH, Mr. Riswan, BA ACA *1991;* 35c Cambridge Gardens, LONDON, W10 5UA.
FATAKIA, Mr. Aspy Nariman, FCA *1959;* Ora-Tech Systems (Pvt.) Ltd., 190-A Block A S.M.C.H.S, Shahrah-e-Faisal, KARACHI 74400, PAKISTAN. (Life Member)
FATANI, Mr. Ishaq, BSc ACA *1997;* PO Box 94096, Khalidiya Post Office, ABU DHABI, UNITED ARAB EMIRATES.
•**FATANIA, Mrs. Reepa, BSc ACA** *1999;* Abaci Accountancy Ltd, 38 Drummond Drive, STANMORE, HA7 3PD.
FATEH MOHAMED, Mr. Mohamed Omar, MSc BSc ACA *2008;* 8 Lorong Bruas Kiri, Damansara Heights, 50490 KUALA LUMPUR, FEDERAL TERRITORY, MALAYSIA.
FATEMI, Mr. Ahmad, BSc FCA *1966;* No.39, 2nd Floor, 7th Alley, Sarafraz Ave., Dr. Beheshti Ave., TEHRAN 83816 IRAN.
FATHALI, Mr. Bahram, FCA *1969;* Sharak-E-Ghods, Khovardin Blvd., Bakashi Street, Iran Zamin Residental Complex, TEHRAN, 1465953541 IRAN.
FATHERS, Mr. Ronald, FCA *1950;* 2 Edmund Court, Pucklechurch, BRISTOL, BS16 9PW. (Life Member)
FATKIN, Mr. David Anthony, BA ACA *1984;* 8 Castle Park, LANCASTER, LA1 1YQ.
•**FATONA, Mr. Emmanuel Aibinu, BSc FCA** *1971;* (Tax Fac), Eafton & Co, 143 Varley Road, LONDON, E16 3NR. See also Joseph Anderson Beadle & Co
FATTAL, Mr. Daniel, MSc ACA *2003;* Flat 4 Monkton House, 130a Haverstock Hill, LONDON, NW3 2AY.
•**FATTORINI, Mr. Andrew Hugh Thomas, MBA BSc FCA** *1992;* Linpac Packaging Verona SRL, Via Monte Pastello 40, 37057 VERONA, ITALY.
•**FATTORINI, Mr. Michael James, FCA** *1973;* (Tax Fac), Lince Salisbury, Avenue House, St Julian's Ave, St Peter Port, GUERNSEY, GY1 1WA. See also BKR Lince Salisbury Limited
FATTUHI, Mr. Imad Simon, MEng ACA *2007;* 22 Primezone Mews, LONDON, N8 9JP.
FATZIKMANOLI, Miss. Maria, ACA *2004;* Kleovoulou 9-11, 15344 GERAKAS, ATTICA, GREECE.
FAU, Mrs. Laure, BSc ACA *1999;* 4 Alexander Place, LONDON, SW7 2SF.
FAUCHEUX, Mr. Anthony Armand, FCA *1954;* No 50, Deanfield Road, HENLEY-ON-THAMES, RG9 1UU. (Life Member)
•**FAULCONBRIDGE, Mr. Paul David, ACA** *1989;* Paul D. Faulconbridge, 16 Trinity Gardens, THORNTON-CLEVELEYS, FY5 2UA.
FAULDING, Mr. William Allen, FCA *1982;* 8 Westway, Eldwick, BINGLEY, BD16 3LZ.
FAULKES, Mr. Michael George Wyndham, FCA *1964;* Faulkes Properties Ltd, 35 Augustus Road, Edgbaston, BIRMINGHAM, B15 3PQ.
•**FAULKNALL, Mr. Mark Harold, BSc FCA** *1983;* Sherwoods, 1 Ferndale Grove, HINCKLEY, LEICESTERSHIRE, LE10 0EH.
FAULKNER, Mr. Anthony Robert, MEng ACA *2001;* 16 West End Lane, BARNET, EN5 2SA.
•**FAULKNER, Mrs. Bibi Sakineh, BSc ACA** *1991;* Faulkner Associates, The Maltings, 10 Beanacre, Hook Norton, BANBURY, OX15 5UA.
•**FAULKNER, Mrs. Claire, BA ACA** *1999;* Deloitte LLP, 2 New Street Square, LONDON, EC4A 3BZ. See also Deloitte & Touche LLP
FAULKNER, Mr. David Charles, ACA *1985;* I T B Pension Funds, 23 King Street, WATFORD, WD18 0BJ.
FAULKNER, Miss. Denyse Virginia, BA ACA *1985;* Box 86019 Eros, WINDHOEK, NAMIBIA.
FAULKNER, Mr. Hugh Edmund Brooke, BA ACA ATII *1979;* (Tax Fac), 77 Laurel Way, Totteridge, LONDON, N20 8HT.
FAULKNER, Mr. Ian Richard, FCA *1966;* 12 West Hill Court, Sherbrook Hill, BUDLEIGH SALTERTON, DEVON, EX9 6BN. (Life Member)
FAULKNER, Mr. James Alexander, FCA *1961;* Paddocks, Birch Grove, Chilbolton, STOCKBRIDGE, HAMPSHIRE, SO20 6BH. (Life Member)
FAULKNER, Mrs. Jennifer Helen, ACA *2009;* 20 St. Katherines Court, DERBY, DE22 3AY.
•**FAULKNER, Mr. John, FCA** *1970;* Keelings Limited, Broad House, 1 The Broadway, Old Hatfield, HATFIELD, HERTFORDSHIRE AL9 5BG.
FAULKNER, Mr. John Shaun Gabriel, BCom ACA *1994;* 58 Mansfield Road, LONDON, NW3 2HT.
FAULKNER, Mr. Mark Nicholas John, BSc ACA *1986;* c/o Mr K Yamakawa, 5-83-222 Nakakiyoto, Kiyose-shi, TOKYO, T204-0012 JAPAN.
FAULKNER, Mr. Martin James, MPhil BSc(Hons) ACA *2001;* 17 Gander Green, HAYWARDS HEATH, WEST SUSSEX, RH16 1RB.
FAULKNER, Mrs. Maryke, ACA CA(SA) *2011;* 3 Cutmore Place, CHELMSFORD, ESSEX, CM2 9XJ.
FAULKNER, Miss. Nadine Alex, LLM BA ACA *2007;* 32 Maple Avenue, FARNBOROUGH, HAMPSHIRE, GU14 9UR.
FAULKNER, Mrs. Natalie Allegra, ACA *2002;* with PricewaterhouseCoopers, Darling Park Tower 2, 201 Sussex Street, GPO Box 2650, SYDNEY, NSW 1171 AUSTRALIA.
FAULKNER, Mr. Noel Samuel Constantine, FCA *1962;* Chemin des Oisillons 9, 1009 PULLY, SWITZERLAND. (Life Member)
FAULKNER, Mr. Paul Robert, BSc ACA *1986;* 100 University Road, SINGAPORE 297904, SINGAPORE.
FAULKNER, Mr. Peter, BA ACA *1982;* 5 Brackenwood, CAMBERLEY, SURREY, GU15 1SX.
•**FAULKNER, Mr. Richard, BSc ACA** *1999;* with KPMG LLP, 15 Canada Square, LONDON, E14 5GL.
•**FAULKNER, Mr. Richard Ian, LLB FCA** *1964;* (Tax Fac), Ian Faulkner & Co, Esker Cottage, Quab Lane, WEDMORE, SOMERSET, BS28 4AR.
•**FAULKNER, Mr. Richard John, BEng ACA** *1989;* PKF (UK) LLP, Pannell House, Park Street, GUILDFORD, SURREY, GU1 4HN.
FAULKNER, Mr. Russell John, BEng ACA *2003;* (Tax Fac), 25 St George St, LONDON, W1S1FS.
FAULKNER, Mr. Samuel Gareth, ACA *2009;* 31 Silverthorne Loft Apartments, 400 Albany Road, LONDON, SE5 0DJ.
•**FAULKNER, Mrs. Sharon, BCom ACA** *1996;* (Tax Fac), Sharon Faulkner, 6795 Lake Rd, PONCA CITY, OK 74604-5179, UNITED STATES.
FAULKNER, Mr. Stephen John David, BSc ACA *2007;* Community Integrated Care, 2 Old Market Court Miners Way, WIDNES, CHESHIRE, WA8 7SP.
FAULKNER, Mr. Steven, BA ACA *1983;* 28 Rue Feron-Boussely, Franconville, 95130 PARIS, FRANCE.
•**FAULKNER, Mrs. Susan Jane, BSc ACA** *1987;* S J Faulkner, Willow Farm, Wood Lane, Quadring Eaudyke, SPALDING, LINCOLNSHIRE PE11 4SS.
FAULKNER, Mrs. Tessa Lindsey, BSc ACA *1987;* 35 Ellar Gardens, Menston, ILKLEY, LS29 6QA.
FAULKNER, Mr. Trevor David, BSc ACA *1987;* 35 Ellar Gardens, Menston, ILKLEY, LS29 6QA.
FAULKNER-TUCK, Mr. David John, BA ACA *2006;* 15 Harbury Road, BRISTOL, BS9 4PN.
FAULKS, Mr. Cecil Arthur, FCA *1949;* Palings, Cliff Lane, Calver, HOPE VALLEY, S32 3XD. (Life Member)
•**FAULL, Mr. Maurice Leon, MA FCA MAE** *1987;* with Hilton Sharp & Clarke, 30 New Road, BRIGHTON, BN1 1BN.
FAULL, Mr. Robert David, FCA *1954;* 3 Park Road, RAMSGATE, KENT, CT11 7QN. (Life Member)
FAUNCE, Mr. Charles Edmund, BSc FCA *1974;* (Tax Fac), 3 Foalhurst Close, TONBRIDGE, KENT, TN10 4HA.
FAUNDEZ, Miss. Antonia, MSc BSc ACA *2011;* Deloitte & Touche Llp, 3 Rivergate, BRISTOL, BS1 6GD.
FAURE, Miss. Anna Olivia, BSc ACA *2000;* 64 Pembridge Villas, LONDON, W11 3ET.
FAURE, Mr. Peter Stafford, FCA *1969;* Talk Business, 32C Rue Van Der Meulen, L 2152 LUXEMBOURG, LUXEMBOURG.
FAURE-WALKER, Mr. Rupert Roderick, BSc FCA CF *1972;* Woodhill, Danbury, CHELMSFORD, CM3 4AN.
FAURE WALKER, Mr. William Mark, BA ACA *1998;* 22 Court Road, TUNBRIDGE WELLS, KENT, TN4 8ED.
•**FAUTLEY, Miss. Janet Patricia, BA FCA** *1989;* Spofforths LLP, 2nd Floor, Comewell House, North Street, HORSHAM, WEST SUSSEX RH12 1RD.
FAUTLEY, Mr. John Bernard, FCA *1956;* 133 Marine Parade, LEIGH-ON-SEA, SS9 2RF. (Life Member)
FAUTLEY, Mr. Mark Stephen, BA ACA *2006;* 68 Locarno Avenue, GILLINGHAM, KENT, ME8 6ES.

•**FAUTLEY, Mr. Robin Graham, FCA** *1970;* (Tax Fac), Robin G. Fautley, 9 Lynton Road, Thorpe Bay, SOUTHEND-ON-SEA, SS1 3BE.
FAUX, Mr. Graham Alan, ACA *1983;* The Limes, East Hanningfield Road, Sandon, CHELMSFORD, CM2 7TQ.
•**FAVA, Mr. Anthony Joseph Leopold, FCA** *1968;* 11, Finkle Street, RICHMOND, NORTH YORKSHIRE, DL10 4QA.
•**FAVA, Mr. Paul Joseph, BA ACA** *1996;* Hindsight Tax Partners LLP, 12 The Riverside Studios, Amethyst Road, NEWCASTLE UPON TYNE, NE4 7YL.
FAVAGER, Mr. Neil John, BA ACA *1997;* 21 Kitchener St, Balgowlah, SYDNEY, NSW 2093, AUSTRALIA.
FAVARD, Mr. Hugues Ronan, ACA *2001;* 3 Impasse de la Ramme, 74560 ESSERTS SALEVE, FRANCE.
FAVELL, Mr. Martin Rowland, BA(Econ) FCA *1967;* Mayfields, Holton St. Mary, COLCHESTER, CO7 6NL. (Life Member)
•**FAWBERT, Mr. Antony Keith, FCA** *1986;* John A Roberts & Co Ltd, 42 Sheffield Road, CHESTERFIELD, DERBYSHIRE, S41 7LL.
FAWBERT, Mr. William Edward, BSc ACA *1997;* 11 Upper Pines, BANSTEAD, SURREY, SM7 3PU.
FAWCETT, Ms. Amanda Jean, BSc ACA *2001;* Unit 100, 2-18 Buchanan Street, BALMAIN, NSW 2041, AUSTRALIA.
FAWCETT, Mr. Anthony Christopher Foyle, BSc FCA *1973;* Old School House, Itchenor, CHICHESTER, PO20 7AB.
FAWCETT, Mr. Benjamin Hall, FCA *1961;* 29 Horncastle Road, WOODHALL SPA, LINCOLNSHIRE, LN10 6UY.
FAWCETT, Mr. Bernard Henry Irwin, FCA *1969;* Fernhill, Hitchen Hatch Lane, SEVENOAKS, TN13 3AY. (Life Member)
FAWCETT, Mr. James Burnett, LLB ACA *2001;* Craven Cottage, 16 Craven Terrace, SALE, M33 3GA.
FAWCETT, Mrs. Jane Clea Nadine, BA ACA *1990;* 58 Palewell Park, East Sheen, LONDON, SW14 8JH.
FAWCETT, Mr. Jeremy Lee, BA ACA *1980;* 13 Cragg Terrace, Rawdon, LEEDS, LS19 6LF.
FAWCETT, Mr. Michael Ronald, FCA *1968;* Stone Cottage, 36 Main Road, Watnall, NOTTINGHAM, NG16 1HT.
FAWCETT, Mr. Ralph Michael, BSc FCA *1972;* 1 Tynedale View, HEXHAM, NE46 3JG.
FAWCETT, Dr. Raymond John, PhD MA ACA *1996;* 2 Holmes Park, Headington, OXFORD, OX3 0FG.
FAWCETT, Mr. Robin James, FCA *1976;* 39 Lilyville Road, LONDON, SW6 5DP.
FAWCETT, Mr. Sam, BA(Hons) ACA *2011;* The Cottage Carberry Tower, Carberry, MUSSELBURGH, MIDLOTHIAN, EH21 8PY.
FAWCETT, Miss. Sarah Jane, BA(Hons) ACA *2010;* with Ernst & Young, 3 Bermudiana Road, HAMILTON HM11, BERMUDA.
FAWCETT, Mr. Scott, BSc ACA *2003;* Hayloft Main Street, Hillam, LEEDS, LS25 5HH.
FAWCETT, Mr. William Robin, ACA *2008;* Flat 89, Price's Court, Cotton Row, LONDON, SW11 3YS.
FAWCITT, Mr. Richard Quentin, FCA *1979;* Tour Société Générale, 17 cours Valmy, 92972 PARIS, FRANCE.
FAWCUS, Mrs. Carole, FCA *1974;* 2 Chapel Cottages, Station Road, East Garston, HUNGERFORD, BERKSHIRE, RG17 7HF.
•**FAWCUS, Mr. David John, BA** *1982;* Millbrook, Station Road, Great Shefford, HUNGERFORD, BERKSHIRE, RG17 7DR.
FAWCUS, Mr. David Stafford, MA FCA *1960;* Stables Cottage The Fields, Keevil, TROWBRIDGE, BA14 6NH.
FAWDINGTON, Mr. Eric Alexander, BTech ACA *1981;* 2 The Arbour, Middleton, ILKLEY, LS29 0EY.
FAWDRY, Mr. Michael Andrew, BA FCA *1982;* Griggs Farm, Knighton, Newchurch, SANDOWN, PO36 0NT.
FAWKE, Mr. Leonard, LLB FCA *1976;* Begbies Traynor, 9 Bond Court, LEEDS, LS1 2JZ.
FAWKES, Miss. Caroline Dawn, BA(Hons) ACA *2001;* 54 Corinth Street, HOWRAH, TAS 7018, AUSTRALIA.
FAWSSETT, Mr. Brian Uvedale, FCA MBCS *1958;* Glenwood, Shire Lane, Chorleywood, RICKMANSWORTH, WD3 5NH. (Life Member)
•**FAWTHROP, Mr. Russell Howard, BSc FCA** *1982;* (Tax Fac), Fawthrop Williams, Old Buttermere Works, 15 Buttermere Road, SHEFFIELD, S7 2AX.
•**FAY, Mr. Andrew Patrick Armand, BA FCA** *1981;* AIMS - Andrew Fay, 30 West Street, Dunster, MINEHEAD, SOMERSET, TA24 6SN.
FAY, Mr. Anthony William, BCom FCA *1963;* Gatesdene House, Little Gaddesden, BERKHAMSTED, HP4 1PB.
FAY, Mr. Bernard Anthony, FCA *1954;* with UHY International Limited, Quadrant House, 17 Thomas More Street, LONDON, E1W 1YW. (Life Member)
FAY, Mr. Duncan Edward, BA ACA *1990;* I M G Unit 1 Axis Centre, Hogarth Business Park Burlington Lane, LONDON, W4 2TH.
FAY, Miss. Geraldine, BA ACA *2002;* with National Audit Office, 157-197 Buckingham Palace Road, Victoria, LONDON, SW1W 9SP.
FAY, Mr. Ian Michael, BEng FCA CTA *1995;* with Deloitte Touche Tohmatsu, 10 Brandon Street, PO Box 1990, WELLINGTON, NEW ZEALAND.
FAY, Mrs. Janet Anne, BSc ACA *1986;* The Orchard, Woodhurst Lane, OXTED, SURREY, RH8 9HD.
FAY, Mr. Michael Alan, FCA *1957;* Bradshaws Barn, Bepton, MIDHURST, GU29 0NA. (Life Member)
FAY, Mr. Michael John, BA(Hons) ACA *2003;* 11B Parsons Way, Innaloo, PERTH, WA 6018, AUSTRALIA.
FAY, Mr. Michael Roberts, FCA *1962;* 102 Hall Road, HULL, HU6 8SB. (Life Member)
•**FAY, Mr. Paul, BA FCA** *1986;* (Tax Fac), Crowe Clark Whitehill LLP, St Bride's House, 10 Salisbury Square, LONDON, EC4Y 8EH. See also Horwath Clark Whitehill LLP and Crowe Clark Whitehill
FAY, Mr. Paul Anthony, ACA *1995;* KPMG, 20 Kingsmead Boulevard, DURBAN, KWAZULU NATAL, 4000, SOUTH AFRICA.
•**FAY, Mr. Stephen Mark, BSc ACA** *2000;* Fylde Tax Accountants Limited, Offices 11 & 12, Bispham Village Chambers, 335 Red Bank Road, BLACKPOOL, FY2 0HJ.
FAYADH, Mr. Khalid Jawad, BSc ACA *2005;* 26 Ridgewood Crescent, South Gosforth, NEWCASTLE UPON TYNE, NE3 1SQ.
FAYERS, Miss. Emma, BSc ACA *2003;* with Haslers, Old Station Road, LOUGHTON, ESSEX, IG10 4PL.
FAYERS, Mr. Kenneth Bryan, BSc ACA *1991;* Goldenberg Hehmeyer & Co, 50 Bank Street, LONDON, E14 5NS.
•**FAYERS, Mrs. Susan Lesley, FCA** *1984;* (Tax Fac), Ballams, Crane Court, 302 London Road, IPSWICH, IP2 0AJ.
•**FAYLE, Mr. Michael John, FCA** *1977;* KPMG Audit LLC, Heritage Court, 39-41 Athol Street, Douglas, ISLE OF MAN, IM1 1LA. See also KPMG LLC
•**FAYYAZ, Mr. Sarfraz, ACA** *2007;* Fintax, 2 Hebe Court, Montpelier Road, SUTTON, SURREY, SM1 4PE.
FAZACKERLEY, Mr. George William, FCA *1948;* 27 Waterside Court, Church Street, St. Neots, ST. NEOTS, PE19 2BL. (Life Member)
FAZACKERLEY, Mrs. Jennifer, BA(Hons) ACA *2010;* 37 Summit Drive, Freckleton, PRESTON, PR4 1PP.
FAZACKERLEY, Mr. John Charles, BA FCA *1979;* 48 Ridgeway, Weston Favell, NORTHAMPTON, NN3 3AN.
FAZAKERLEY, Mr. Edmund, BA ACA *1994;* 12 Heaton Close, STOCKPORT, CHESHIRE, SK4 4DQ.
FAZAKERLEY, Mr. John, FCA *1975;* Bredon, Walton Pool, Walton Rise, STOURBRIDGE, DY9 9RT.
•**FAZAKERLEY, Mr. Nicholas, FCA** *1974;* Adam Cottage, Cheverells Green, Markyate, ST ALBANS, AL3 8AD.
FAZAKERLEY, Mrs. Samantha Jane, BSc ACA *1993;* 12 Heaton Close, Heaton Moor, STOCKPORT, CHESHIRE, SK4 4DQ.
FAZAL, Mr. Mehdi Gulamabbas, BA FCA *1977;* 9 Ardross Avenue, NORTHWOOD, MIDDLESEX, HA6 3DS.
•**FAZAL, Mr. Michael David, BEng ACA MBA** *1998;* ASE Audit LLP, Rowan Court, Concord Business Park, MANCHESTER, M22 0RR.
•**FAZAL, Mr. Zahir, FCA** *1972;* 23 Westland Drive, GLASGOW, G14 9NY.
FAZEL, Mr. Mushtaqali Abdul Hussein, ACA *1979;* 19 Winter Creek Crescent, MARKHAM L6C-3E4, ON, CANADA.
FAZLI, Mr. Syed Adnan, BSc(Hons) ACA *2004;* Deloitte & Touche FAS, 44th Floor Tower A, Business Central Towers, Dubai Media City, PO Box 282056, DUBAI UNITED ARAB EMIRATES.
FEAKES, Mr. Alexander David, MSc ACA *2001;* 80 Perry Rise, LONDON, SE23 2QL.
FEAKIN, Mr. Danny, FCA *1972;* 17 The Gardens, KETTERING, NORTHAMPTONSHIRE, NN16 9DU.
FEAR, Mr. Alistair Graham, BSc ACA *1998;* Ferry Point Lodge, Meikleferry, TAIN, ROSS-SHIRE, IV19 1NL.
FEAR, Mr. Andrew John, BEng ACA *2001;* 22 Pollard Road, WESTON-SUPER-MARE, AVON, BS24 7DT.
FEAR, Mr. Mark Alan, BSc ACA *1995;* 1 Bluetail Close, STOWMARKET, SUFFOLK, IP14 5GA.
FEAR, Mr. Raymond Bernard, FCA *1969;* 3 Clare Close, WEST BYFLEET, KT14 6RD.
FEARE, Mr. William Robert, BSc ACA *1979;* Robert Teal Ltd, Trent View, Carlton-on-Trent, NEWARK, NOTTINGHAMSHIRE, NG23 6NR.
FEARN, Mrs. Amy Elizabeth, BSc ACA *2003;* Swann Cottage, 3 High Street, Packington, ASHBY-DE-LA-ZOUCH, LEICESTERSHIRE, LE65 1WJ.
FEARN, Mr. Andrew Keith, BA ACA *2000;* 25 Cumberland Drive Redbourn, ST. ALBANS, HERTFORDSHIRE, AL3 7PG.
FEARN, Mr. Antony David, MA MEng ACA *1995;* 31 Fulmer Drive, GERRARDS CROSS, BUCKINGHAMSHIRE, SL9 7HG.
FEARN, Mr. John David, FCA *1961;* The Orangery, 1 Rock House, Derby Road, Cromford, MATLOCK, DERBYSHIRE DE4 3RP.
FEARN, Mr. Matthew Robin, BA ACA *1991;* Wildernesse Chase Wildernesse Avenue, Seal, SEVENOAKS, TN15 0ED.
FEARN, Mr. Paul Roland, BTech ACA *1992;* Henley Hill Barn, Ashwicke, CHIPPENHAM, SN14 8AE.
FEARN, Mr. Peter Hugh Colin, FCA *1976;* Hunter's Lodge, Pot Kiln Lane, Goring Heath, READING, RG8 7SR.
•**FEARN, Mr. Peter Stuart, BSc ACA CTA** *1993;* (Tax Fac), Forrester Boyd, 26 South Saint Mary's Gate, GRIMSBY, NORTH LINCOLNSHIRE, DN31 1LW. See also Dataplan Payroll Limited
FEARNHEAD, Mrs. Jennifer, BA(Hons) ACA *2004;* Premier Farnell Plc, 150 Armley Road, LEEDS, LS12 2QQ.
FEARNLEY, Mr. Albert Eric, FCA *1959;* 33 Chiltern Road, Culcheth, WARRINGTON, WA3 4LQ. (Life Member)
FEARNLEY, Mr. James Robert, FCA *1973;* The Moorings, Waterside Walk, Wood Lane, MIRFIELD, WF14 0EB.
FEARNLEY, Mr. Peter Allen, ACA *2008;* 40 Inglemire Lane, HULL, HU6 7TA.
FEARNLEY, Mr. Peter William, ACA *2008;* 14 White Hart Wood, SEVENOAKS, TN13 1RR.
FEARNLEY, Mr. Roger, FCA *1968;* Walton Head House Walton Head Lane, Kirkby Overblow, HARROGATE, NORTH YORKSHIRE, HG3 1HG.
FEARNLEY, Prof. Stella Marie, BA FCA *1973;* (Member of Council 1991 - 2004), 102 Canford Cliffs Road, POOLE, DORSET, BH13 7AE.
FEARNLEY, Mr. Steven Ray, BA ACA *2006;* Deloitte & Touche, 2 New Street Square, LONDON, EC4A 3BZ.
FEARNS, Mr. David, FCA *1978;* 10 Prince Wood Lane, Birkby, HUDDERSFIELD, HD2 2DG.
FEARNS, Mr. David Warren, BSc FCA *1972;* 29 Longton Road, Barlaston, STOKE-ON-TRENT, ST12 9AA. (Life Member)
•**FEARNSIDE, Mr. David John Richard, FCA** *1974;* (Tax Fac), Fearnside & Co, 6 Foundry Yard, Boroughbridge, YORK, YO51 9AX.
•**FEARON, Mr. James Patrick, BSc ACA** *2002;* BDO LLP, Emerald House, East Street, EPSOM, SURREY, KT17 1HS. See also BDO Stoy Hayward LLP
FEARS, Mr. Nicholas Alan, BSc ACA *1987;* 36 Bryant Place, WESTWOOD, NJ 07675, UNITED STATES.
•**FEASEY, Mrs. Michelle Anne Elizabeth, FCA** *1992;* (Tax Fac), Michelle Feasey & Co Limited, Unit 1, West Street Business Park, West Street, STAMFORD, LINCOLNSHIRE PE9 2PR.
FEAST, Mr. James Anthony, FCA *1969;* 11 Manor Gardens, SOUTH CROYDON, SURREY, CR2 7BU.
FEATHER, Mr. Adrian Michael, FCA *1970;* Les Plumes, La Brousse, 50240 ARGOUGES, FRANCE. (Life Member)
FEATHER, Mrs. Clare Frances, BSc ACA *1997;* Ernst & Young, 400 Capability Green, LUTON, LU1 3LU.
•**FEATHER, Mr. Daniel Edmund, MA ACA** *1997;* Ernst & Young LLP, 1 More London Place, LONDON, SE1 2AF. See also Ernst & Young Europe LLP
FEATHER, Mr. Martin Raymond, BA ACA *1998;* 49 Earlham Road, NORWICH, NR2 3AD.
•**FEATHER, Mr. Roy, FCA** *1973;* (Tax Fac), Burton & Co, Sovereign House, Bradford Road, Riddlesden, KEIGHLEY, BD20 5EW.
FEATHERMAN, Mr. Peter Maxwell, MA FCA *1974;* 15a Queens Gardens, LONDON, W2 3BA.
FEATHERMAN, Mr. Simeon Louis Joel, BSocSc ACA *2001;* 27b Eccleston Square, LONDON, SW1V 1NZ.
FEATHERS, Mrs. Carol, ACA *1983;* Appleby Management (Bermuda) Ltd, Argyle House 41a Cedar Avenue, PO Box HM1179, HAMILTON HMEX, BERMUDA.
FEATHERSTONE, Mrs. Bina Autamchand, BSc ACA *1994;* 7 Langdale Gardens, CHELMSFORD, CM2 9QH.
FEATHERSTONE, Mr. Gordon Alan, FCA *1972;* 61 Circle Gardens, Merton Park, LONDON, SW19 3JT.
FEATHERSTONE, Mrs. Jacqueline, BSc ACA *1988;* 3 Headswell Avenue, BOURNEMOUTH, BH10 6JU.
FEATHERSTONE, Mr. John Robson, FCA *1958;* The Old Vicarage, Bishop Monkton, HARROGATE, HG3 3QQ. (Life Member)
FEATHERSTONE, Mrs. Karen Louise, ACA *2009;* 7 Strathspey Gate Broughton, MILTON KEYNES, MK10 7DU.
•**FEATHERSTONE, Mrs. Marjorie Dean, BSc ACA** *1991;* Mrs M Featherstone ACA, 13 Wentworth Road, Harborne, BIRMINGHAM, B17 9SH.
FEATHERSTONE, Mr. Michael Rodney, FCA *1970;* 14 Pinewood Court, South Downs Road, Hale, ALTRINCHAM, CHESHIRE, WA14 3HY.
FEATHERSTONE, Mrs. Nicola Kay, BA FCA *1991;* Hitachi Capital Vehicle Solutions Ltd, 54a Kiln Road, NEWBURY, RG14 2NU.
•**FEATHERSTONE, Mr. Roger David, BA BSc FCA** *1968;* Century Accounting Ltd, PO Box 56 Century House, Victoria Street, Alderney, GUERNSEY, GY9 3UF.
FEATHERSTONE, Mr. Roland Arthur, FCA *1972;* The Old Rectory, Halsham, HULL, HU12 0DD.
FEATHERSTONE, Mr. Simon Mark, BA FCA *1977;* 116, Eastern Way, Ponteland, NEWCASTLE UPON TYNE, NE20 9RQ.
FEATHERSTONE, Miss. Yvonne Margaret, BSc FCA *1978;* Woolford & Co Hillbrow House, Hillbrow Road, ESHER, KT10 9NW.
FEAVEARYEAR, Mr. Thomas Hedley, FCA *1956;* 31 Sunningdale Close, Bessacarr Grange, DONCASTER, DN4 6UR. (Life Member)
FEAVER, Mr. Michael Edward, FCA *1966;* Karenza, Farnham Lane, HASLEMERE, GU27 1HE. (Life Member)
FEAVERS, Mr. Charles Michael, FCA *1955;* Willowbank, 14 New Close, Acle, NORWICH, NR13 3BG. (Life Member)
FEBRY, Mr. Christopher Miles, BSc FCA *1990;* 12 Manorcrofts Road, EGHAM, SURREY, TW20 9LU.
FEBRY, Mrs. Jennifer Anne, BA FCA *1989;* 12 Manorcrofts Road, EGHAM, SURREY, TW20 9LU.
FECCI, Ms. Maria Luisa, BA FCA *1987;* 38 Briar Avenue, Euxton, CHORLEY, LANCASHIRE, PR7 6BQ.
•**FECHER, Mr. Marc Darren, ACA CF** *2008;* Kingston Smith LLP, Devonshire House, 60 Goswell Road, LONDON, EC1M 7AD. See also Kingston Smith Limited Liability Partnership, Devonshire Corporate Services LLP, Kingston Smith Consulting LLP and Devonshire Corporate Finance Limited
FEDARB, Mrs. Christina Helen, FCA *1976;* 22 President Road, Lexden, COLCHESTER, CO3 9ED.
FEDARB, Mr. Peter James, FCA *1976;* 22 President Road, Lexden, COLCHESTER, CO3 9ED.
FEDARB, Mr. Stephen, ACA *2008;* 22 President Road, COLCHESTER, CO3 9ED.
FEDER, Mr. Ilan Maxwell, BA(Hons) ACA *2001;* 85 Warwick Way, LONDON, SW1V 1QP.
•**FEDERER, Mr. Antony Henry Charles, ACA FCCA CF** *2008;* Rayner Essex LLP, Faulkner House, Victoria Street, ST. ALBANS, HERTFORDSHIRE, AL1 3SE.
FEDERMAN, Mr. Raoul Grant, MBA BA ACA *1996;* 103 Greenway, LONDON, N20 8EL.
FEDERMAN, Mr. Stewart Dean, BA ACA *2006;* Flat 38, Albany Court, 18 Plumbers Row, LONDON, E1 1EP.
FEDIAEVA, Miss. Elena, ACA *1999;* Apartment 53, Galleria Court, Sumner Road, LONDON, SE15 6PW.
FEE, Mr. Arthur John, BD FCA *1961;* 11 Thoresby Avenue, NEWARK, NOTTINGHAMSHIRE, NG24 4DJ.
FEECHAN, Mr. Glen John, BA ACA *1996;* Pinetree Centre, Durham Road, BIRTLEY, COUNTY DURHAM, DH3 2TD.
•**FEECHAN, Mr. Paul Elliott, BA ACA** *1989;* Deloitte LLP, One Trinity Gardens, Broad Chare, NEWCASTLE UPON TYNE, NE1 2HF. See also Deloitte & Touche LLP
•**FEEKE, Mr. Andrew James, BSocSc ACA** *2003;* with CLB Coopers, Ship Canal House, 98 King Street, MANCHESTER, M2 4WU.
FEELEY, Mr. Cyril Vincent, FCA *1962;* 294 Chapel Lane, New Longton, PRESTON, PR4 4AB. (Life Member)
FEELEY, Mrs. Katherine Suzanne, MA ACA CTA *1995;* 128 Brook Farm Road East, BEDFORD, NY 10506, UNITED STATES.
FEELEY, Mr. Mark Andrew, MA ACA *1994;* 128 Brook Farm Road East, BEDFORD, NY 10506, UNITED STATES.
FEELY, Mrs. Helen, LLB ACA *2003;* Clearbrook, 21 Low Wood Grove, Barnston, WIRRAL, MERSEYSIDE, CH61 1AN.
FEELY, Mr. Michael Andrew, BA ACA *1995;* 12 Cromlix Close, CHISLEHURST, BR7 5SJ.
FEENEY, Mr. Eamonn, BA FCA *1982;* 155 Heath End Road, Flackwell Heath, HIGH WYCOMBE, BUCKINGHAMSHIRE, HP10 9ES.

Members - Alphabetical **FEENEY - FENN**

FEENEY, Mr. James Michael, FCA *1975;* 18 Westlands Road, Moseley, BIRMINGHAM, B13 9RH.

FEENEY, Mr. James Patrick, BSc CA ACA MCT *1989;* 155 Highfields Park Drive, DERBY, DE22 1BW.

FEENEY, Mr. John Francis, FCA *1958;* 4 Balmoral Place, HILTON HEAD ISLAND, SC 29926, UNITED STATES. (Life Member)

•FEENEY, Mr. Mark John, BSc ACA *1990;* Consergo Limited, Regency House, 3 Albion Place, NORTHAMPTON, NN1 1UD.

FEENEY, Mr. Michael John, BSc ACA *1985;* 52 Orchard Drive, WOKING, SURREY, GU21 4BW.

FEENEY, Mrs. Penelope Mary Doel, BSc ACA *1983;* Duquesa Business Centre (A096), Apartado 157, 29692 SABINILLAS, MALAGA, SPAIN.

FEENEY, Mr. Timothy, FCA *1977;* 7 Antonio Way, PERTH K7H 3M9, ON, CANADA.

FEENY, Mr. Nicholas Derek, BA ACA *1985;* 7 Molyneux Street, LONDON, W1H 5HP.

FEENY, Mr. William Peter, BA FCA *1977;* 20 Sion Hill, BATH, BA1 2UJ.

FEETHAM, Miss. Ann Gaynor, BA ACA *1987;* Cronite Castings Limited, Blacknell Lane, CREWKERNE, SOMERSET, TA18 7HE.

FEETHAM, Mr. Paul James, BSc ACA *1999;* PricewaterhouseCoopers, Royal Trust Tower, Suite 3000 TD Centre, Box 82, 77 King Street West, TORONTO M5K 1G8 ON CANADA.

FEGAN, Mr. Adam Mark, BA ACA *2007;* 4 Mulberry Gardens, Shenley, RADLETT, HERTFORDSHIRE, WD7 9LB.

FEGAN, Mr. Michael Melvyn, BA FCA *1984;* 39 Palace Road, Llandaff, CARDIFF, CF5 2AG.

FEGAN READ, Mrs. Alexandra Claire, BSc(Hons) ACA *2003;* (Tax Fac), Hardy House Southwood Road, Beighton, NORWICH, NR13 3AB.

•FEHMI, Mr. Firuz Hasan, BA FCA *1981;* Erdal & Co, 100 Bedrettin Demirel CAD, PO Box 410, LEFKOSA MERSIN 10, TURKEY.

FEHNERS, Mrs. Sarah, BSc ACA *2005;* 84 Updown Hill, HAYWARDS HEATH, WEST SUSSEX, RH16 4GD.

FEI, Mr. Peter Benedetto, BA ACA *1980;* 29 Airedale Avenue, LONDON, W4 2NW.

FEIBUSCH, Mrs. Melanie Claire Frances, BA ACA *1992;* Arisaig, 2 Gong Hill Drive, Lower Bourne, FARNHAM, GU10 3HG.

•FEIGENBAUM, Mr. Alan, FCA FCMI *1969;* Fenton & Co, 7 Bancroft Avenue, LONDON, N2 0AR.

•FEIGER, Mr. Malcolm Myer, FCA *1958;* 25 Draycott Avenue, HARROW, HA3 0BL.

•FEIGHERY, Mr. Andrew, ACA *2010;* 272 Harold's Cross Road, DUBLIN 6, COUNTY DUBLIN, IRELAND. See also CGC Associates

FEILDING, Mrs. Harriet, BA ACA *1985;* The Old Manor House, Whiteheads Lane, BRADFORD-ON-AVON, WILTSHIRE, BA15 1JU.

•FEILDING, Mr. Peter Rudolph, FCA *1965;* Feilding & Co, Highfields, 11 Marlow Road, HIGH WYCOMBE, HP11 1TA.

FEINBERG, Mrs. Diana, ACA *1995;* PO Box 52752, SAXONWOLD, GAUTENG, 2132, SOUTH AFRICA.

•FEINGOLD, Mr. Eliot Hugh, BSc FCA *1974;* (Tax Fac), Purcells, 4 Quex Road, LONDON, NW6 4PJ.

FEINGOLD, Mr. Joshua Gerald, FCA ATII *1964;* Rechar Efrata 29/6, Arnona, 93384 JERUSALEM, ISRAEL.

FEINGOLD, Mr. Limor, BA ACA *1997;* 49 Austin Avenue, POOLE, DORSET, BH14 8HD.

FEINMESSER, Mr. James Simon, ACA *2009;* 12/5 Rivka Imeinu, MODI'IN, ISRAEL.

FEINMESSER, Mr. Jonathan Andrew, BA(Econ) ACA *1998;* 36 Broadfields Avenue, EDGWARE, HA8 8PG.

FEIRN, Mr. Nigel Stuart, BSc ACA *1992;* 15 Tickhill Way, Rossington, DONCASTER, DN11 0FJ.

•FEIST, Mr. Paul Richard, FCA *1987;* (Tax Fac), Feist Hedgethorne Limited, Preston Park House, South Road, BRIGHTON, BN1 6SB.

FEIZI, Mr. Behzad, FCA *1975;* no. 28 Shadab Street, S.Gharani Avenue, TEHRAN, 1598975533, IRAN.

•FELD, Mr. Robert Leslie, BCom FCA MAE *1976;* Bright Grahame Murray, 131 Edgware Road, LONDON, W2 2AP.

FELDMAN, Mrs. Barbara, FCA *1969;* P O Box 68055, 91680 JERUSALEM, ISRAEL.

FELDMAN, Mr. Christopher Alexander Cowper, FCA *1960;* 66 Hadley Road, BARNET, HERTFORDSHIRE, EN5 5QS. (Life Member)

FELDMAN, Mr. David Jonathan, BSc ACA *1994;* 17 Burnham Green Road, Datchworth, KNEBWORTH, HERTFORDSHIRE, SG3 6SE.

•FELDMAN, Mr. Gerald Isaac, FCA *1967;* G Feldman & Co Limited, 5 Stone Hall Road, LONDON, N21 1LR.

FELDMAN, Mr. Graham Lee, FCA *1968;* PO Box 68055, 91680 JERUSALEM, ISRAEL.

FELDMAN, Mr. Maurice Ronnie, BA FCA *1973;* Old School Cottage, Combrook, WARWICK, CV35 9HP. (Life Member)

FELDMAN, Mrs. Sheryl Joanne, BA ACA *2006;* 50 Brady Road, BENTLEY EAST, VIC 3165, AUSTRALIA.

FELDMAN, Mr. Stanley Leslie, FCA *1966;* 7 Pinfold Court, Whitefield, MANCHESTER, M45 7NZ. (Life Member)

FELDMAN, Mr. Terence Irvin, FCA *1966;* 23 Camlet Way, BARNET, HERTFORDSHIRE, EN4 0LH. (Life Member)

FELDMANN, Mr. Robert Gregory, MA ACA *1994;* 26 Winchester Road, LONDON, NW3 3NT.

FELGATE, Ms. Frances Caroline, BA ACA *1990;* 180 Erlanger Road, LONDON, SE14 5TJ.

FELIX, Mrs. Katharine Margaret, MA FCA *1986;* Eastlake & Beachell Ltd, The Crescent, King Street, LEICESTER, LE1 6RX.

•FELIX, Mr. Robert David, BA FCA *1980;* Robert Felix, 33 Broomhill Road, WOODFORD GREEN, ESSEX, IG8 9HD.

FELL, Mr. Alexander John, BA ACA *2002;* 7 One North Gateway, #10-24, One North Residences, SINGAPORE 138642, SINGAPORE.

FELL, Mrs. Andrea Margaret, BA ACA *1993;* 1 Monarch Close, RUGBY, WARWICKSHIRE, CV21 1NX.

FELL, Mr. Brian Jonathan, BSc ACA *1978;* The Bury, Brent Pelham, BUNTINGFORD, HERTFORDSHIRE, SG9 0AN. (Life Member)

FELL, Mr. Bruce Paul Gregson, BSc(Econ) ACA *1983;* 6 Redwood Lodge, Grange Road, CAMBRIDGE, CB3 9AR.

•FELL, Mr. David Hall, FCA *1976;* 9 Haverwood, Woodhouse, MILNTHORPE, LA7 7LN.

•FELL, Mrs. Hannah Amelia, BA ACA *2007;* Windsor Audit Limited, 111 Eddington Crescent, WELWYN GARDEN CITY, HERTFORDSHIRE, AL7 4SX.

FELL, Mr. James Thomas, BA ACA *1998;* 24 Waterside Gardens, READING, RG1 6QE.

•FELL, Mr. John Andrew, FCA *1972;* JA Fell & Company, White Cross, South Road, LANCASTER, LA1 4XQ.

FELL, Miss. Judith Anne, MA FCA *1977;* 15 Kitts Moss Lane, Bramhall, STOCKPORT, SK7 2BG.

FELL, Mrs. Linda Mary, ACA *1993;* 32 Lincoln Drive, Pyrford, WOKING, GU22 8RN.

FELL, Mr. Malcolm Alexander, BSc ACA MCT *1997;* 1 Monarch Close, RUGBY, WARWICKSHIRE, CV21 1NX.

FELL, Mr. Michael Howard, BA(Hons) ACA *2001;* Lucite International, Cassel Works, New Road, PO Box 8, BILLINGHAM, CLEVELAND TS23 1LE.

FELL, Mr. Michael William, BA ACA *1984;* M W B, 344-354 Gray's Inn Road, LONDON, WC1X 8BP.

FELL, Mr. Neil Anthony, BA FCA *1990;* Wapiti Lodge, Rue Des Longcamps, St. Saviour, GUERNSEY, GY7 9YN.

•FELL, Mr. Patrick William, BA FCA *1983;* with PricewaterhouseCoopers LLP, 1 Embankment Place, LONDON, WC2N 6RH.

FELL, Miss. Rebecca, MA MPhil BA ACA *2002;* with Deloitte LLP, 2 New Street Square, LONDON, EC4A 3BZ.

•FELL, Mr. Richard Archer, FCA *1962;* Richard A. Fell, Albion Lodge, Fordham Road, NEWMARKET, SUFFOLK, CB8 7AQ.

FELL, Mr. Stephen John, BSc ACA *1993;* 15 The Oval, WAKEFIELD, WF1 3QB.

•FELL, Mr. William Rees, FCA *1955;* W R Fell & Co, 11 Lingdales, Formby, LIVERPOOL, L37 7HA.

FELLER, Mr. Jamie, ACA *2009;* 27 Clonard Way, PINNER, MIDDLESEX, HA5 4BT.

•FELLER, Mr. Terence Bruce Lance, BSc FCA *1973;* Wilkins Kennedy, Cecil House, 52 St Andrew Street, HERTFORD, SG14 1JA.

FELLINGHAM, Mrs. Emma Clare, BSc ACA *1998;* Laurel Farm, Singleborough, MILTON KEYNES, MK17 0RF.

FELLINGHAM, Miss. Louise Lindsey, BSc(Hons) ACA *2010;* Flat 3, 39 Kirkstall Road, LONDON, SW2 4HD.

FELLOWES, Mr. Michael Dennis Drake, FCA *1966;* 3 St. Michaels Close, Stewkley, LEIGHTON BUZZARD, LU7 0HN.

FELLOWS, Mrs. Amy, MSc ACA *2006;* 12 Lodge Avenue, EASTBOURNE, EAST SUSSEX, BN22 0JD.

FELLOWS, Mr. Andy, ACA *2008;* 7 Atlas Road, BRISTOL, BS3 4QS.

FELLOWS, Mr. Anthony Edward Max, FCA *1964;* Clevedon Lodge, Sid Road, SIDMOUTH, DEVON, EX10 9AJ. (Life Member)

•FELLOWS, Mrs. Carol, ACA *1980;* Fellows Financial Managment Limited, 10 Hall Lane, KETTERING, NORTHAMPTONSHIRE, NN15 7LJ.

FELLOWS, Mrs. Cheryl Louise, BSc ACA *2002;* 4 The Croft, Drighlington, BRADFORD, WEST YORKSHIRE, BD11 1JG.

FELLOWS, Mr. Colin John, BSc ACA *1993;* 68 Lion Meadow, Steeple Bumpstead, HAVERHILL, CB9 7BY.

FELLOWS, Mr. Jeremy Robert Llewellyn, MA FCA *1989;* MWR Infosecurith Ltd, 1/3 St. Clement House, Alencon Link, BASINGSTOKE, HAMPSHIRE, RG21 7SB.

•FELLOWS, Miss. Joanne, BA ACA *1993;* F & A Consulting Limited, 2 Dublin Crescent, Henleaze, BRISTOL, BS9 4NA.

FELLOWS, Mr. Jon, BSc ACA *2005;* Flight Refuelling Ltd, Brook Road, WIMBORNE, BH21 2BJ.

•FELLOWS, Miss. Marilyn Gwyneth, FCA *1972;* M.G. Fellows, 1 Rhodfa Heilyn, Gwelfor Park, Dyserth, RHYL, CLWYD LL18 6LW.

FELLOWS, Mr. Matthew John, BA(Hons) ACA *2001;* 16 Old Fold View, BARNET, HERTFORDSHIRE, EN5 4EB.

•FELLOWS, Mr. Nigel John, FCA *1985;* (Tax Fac), Wells Professional Partnership LLP, 10 Lonsdale Gardens, TUNBRIDGE WELLS, KENT, TN1 1NU. See also QED Partnership LLP

•FELLOWS, Mr. Richard Keith, FCA *1975;* Howard Lee Fellows & Co, 11-13 First Floor, The Meads Business Centre, 19 Kingsmead, FARNBOROUGH, HAMPSHIRE GU14 7SR.

FELLOWS, Mr. Roger David, FCA *1962;* 21 Ash Hill, WOLVERHAMPTON, WV3 9DR.

•FELLOWS, Mr. Roy Timothy, FCA *1981;* Fellows Financial Managment Limited, 10 Hall Lane, KETTERING, NORTHAMPTONSHIRE, NN15 7LJ.

FELLS, Mr. Benjamin Vincent James, BSc(Hons) ACA *1999;* 71 Brampton Road, ST. ALBANS, HERTFORDSHIRE, AL1 4QA.

FELLS, Mrs. Parminder Kaur, BSc ACA *1999;* 71 Brampton Road, ST. ALBANS, HERTFORDSHIRE, AL1 4QA.

•FELMAN, Mr. Matthew David, ACA *2004;* Hayvenhursts, Fairway House, Links Business Park, St. Mellons, CARDIFF, CF3 0LT. See also Hayvenhursts Limited

•FELMAN, Mr. Philip Terry, FCA *1971;* Hayvenhursts Limited, Fairway House, Links Business Park, St. Mellons, CARDIFF, CF3 0LT. See also Hayvenhursts

FELSTEAD, Mrs. Angela, BSc ACA *1990;* Honeywell House, Arlington Business Park, Downshire Way, BRACKNELL, BERKSHIRE, RG12 1EB.

FELSTEAD, Mr. Dennis William, FCA *1955;* 63a Ramley Road, LYMINGTON, HAMPSHIRE, SO41 8GZ. (Life Member)

FELSTEAD, Mr. Derek Maurice, FCA *1968;* Flat 24, Tignel Court, Boddington Gardens, LONDON, W3 9AR.

FELSTEAD, Mrs. Sarah Jane, BSc FCA *1992;* Appletree Court, Vicarage Lane, HESSLE, NORTH HUMBERSIDE, HU13 9LQ.

FELSTEIN, Mr. Simon Michael, ACA *1994;* 40 Brooklands Road, Prestwich, MANCHESTER, M25 0ED.

FELSTEIN, Mr. Stefan Gary, ACA *1993;* 9B Moshe Levin Street, 42753 NETANYA, ISRAEL.

FELTHAM, Mr. Graham Mark Thomas, BSc(Hons) ACA *2002;* 2 Little Orchard Place, ESHER, KT10 9PP.

FELTHAM, Mr. Ian David, BA ACA *1992;* 2 Fox Wood, Hemblington, NORWICH, NR13 4RZ.

FELTHAM, Mr. John Gordon, ACA *2008;* Bank of America, 5 Canada Square, LONDON, E14 5AQ.

FELTHAM, Mr. John Herbert, FCA *1950;* Houndown, Tilford Road, HINDHEAD, GU26 6RN. (Life Member)

FELTHAM, Mrs. Julie Carol, BA ACA *1992;* 2 Fox Wood, Hemblington, NORWICH, NORFOLK, NR13 4RZ.

•FELTHAM, Mr. Richard Guy, LLB ACA CF *1986;* River House, Ure Bank Terrace, RIPON, NORTH YORKSHIRE, HG4 1JG.

FELTHAM, Mr. Terence Michael, BSc ACA *1994;* 134/41 Rocklands Road, WOLLSTONECRAFT, NSW 2065, AUSTRALIA.

•FELTHOUSE, Mr. Anthony Richard, BA ACA *1994;* with KPMG LLP, One Snowhill, Snow Hill Queensway, BIRMINGHAM, B4 6GN.

FELTON, Mr. Andrew Peter, ACA *1990;* Mead House, 7 Drayton Mill Milton Road, Drayton, ABINGDON, OX14 4FD.

FELTON, Mr. Anton Peter, FCA *1961;* 6 Fallowfield, STANMORE, MIDDLESEX, HA7 3DF. (Life Member)

FELTON, Mr. Benjamin Thomas, BEng ACA *2007;* 19 Giggs Hill Gardens, THAMES DITTON, KT7 0AS.

FELTON, Mr. David John, FCA *1971;* (Tax Fac), Dendy Neville, 3-4 Bower Terrace, MAIDSTONE, ME16 8RY.

FELTON, Mr. Gary, BSc ACA *1985;* 33 Marshals Drive, ST. ALBANS, HERTFORDSHIRE, AL1 4RB.

FELTON, Mr. John Christopher, BSc ACA *1987;* Woof Wear Ltd. Athenaeum House, Carminnow Road, BODMIN, CORNWALL, PL31 1EP.

FELTON, Mr. Keith David, BSc FCA *1984;* Highclere, Oak Way, REIGATE, RH2 7ES.

•FELTON, Mr. Keith William, FCA *1977;* Berkeley Hamilton LLP, 5 Pullman Court, Great Western Road, GLOUCESTER, GL1 3ND.

FELTON, Mr. Michael John, FCA *1973;* 70 Harpur Crescent, Alsager, STOKE-ON-TRENT, ST7 2SY.

FELTON, Mr. Monty, DFC FCA *1949;* 14 Sudbury Hill Close, WEMBLEY, HA0 2QR. (Life Member)

FELTON, Mr. Philip Edward, FCA *1948;* 5 Church Farm Court, Church Farm Lane, East Wittering, CHICHESTER, PO20 8SD. (Life Member)

FELTON, Mr. Richard John, BSc FCA *1970;* 4 Station Road Woburn Sands, MILTON KEYNES, MK17 8RW. (Life Member)

FELTON, Mr. Roy, FCA *1953;* 158 Prince George Avenue, LONDON, N14 4TB. (Life Member)

FELTON, Mr. Timothy Edward, BA ACA *2003;* Brevan Howard Asset Management, 55 Baker Street, LONDON, W1U 8EW.

FELTON, Mr. Wayne Harold, BCom FCA *1986;* MITIE Property Solutions Ltd Cotton Centre Ground Floor East, Cottons Lane, LONDON, SE1 2QG.

FELTON-SMITH, Mr. Paul Jonathan, BA ACA *1986;* Keyzaston House, Sutton End, Sutton, PULBOROUGH, WEST SUSSEX, RH20 1PY.

FENBY, Mr. Andrew Mark, ACA *2011;* 24 College Avenue, Rhos on Sea, COLWYN BAY, CLWYD, LL28 4NT.

FENBY, Mrs. Jane Frances, BA ACA *1991;* Great Hockham Hall Wretham Road, Great Hockham, THETFORD, NORFOLK, IP24 1NZ.

FENBY, Mr. Paul Jeremy Martin, BA ACA *1990;* West Mount Barn, 23 West Street, Swinton, MALTON, NORTH YORKSHIRE, YO17 6SP.

FENBY, Mr. Stephen Barry, BSc ACA *1988;* Great Hockham Hall Wretham Road, Great Hockham, THETFORD, NORFOLK, IP24 1NZ.

FENCHELLE, Mr. Mark Stephen, BSc ACA *1989;* 59 Arbuthnot Road, LONDON, SE14 5NP.

•FENCZUK, Mr. Antoni John, BSc ACA *1982;* Fenczuk & Co, 6 Sefton Drive, WILMSLOW, SK9 4EL.

•FENDALL, Mr. Alan David, BCom FCA *1979;* Deloitte LLP, PO Box 500, 2 Hardman Street, MANCHESTER, M60 2AT. See also Deloitte & Touche LLP

•①FENDER, Mr. Andrew, FCA *1977;* Sanderlings LLP, Sanderling House, 1071 Warwick Road, Acocks Green, BIRMINGHAM, B27 6QT.

FENDLEY, Mr. John Mark, FCA *1950;* 75 Longlands Road, CARLISLE, CA3 9AE. (Life Member)

FENELON, Mr. Mark John, BBLS ACA *2000;* 9 Bushy Park House, Templeogue Road, Terenure, DUBLIN 6, COUNTY DUBLIN, IRELAND.

FENEMORE-JONES, Mr. Claude Andrew Robert, BSc FCA *1980;* 173 Park Road, TEDDINGTON, TW11 0BP.

•FENEZ, Mr. Marcel Robert, BSc FCA *1984;* PricewaterhouseCoopers, Prince's Building, 22/F, 10 Chater Road, CENTRAL, HONG KONG ISLAND HONG KONG SAR.

FENG, Miss. Hengyi, MSc ACA *2005;* 308 Cobalt Point Lanterns Court, 38 Millharbour, LONDON, E14 9JT.

FENG, Miss. Wai Ping, BSc ACA *2007;* 8 Clockhouse Place, LONDON, SW15 2EL.

FENLEY, Mr. William Laurence John, VRD MA FCA *1958;* 30 Sussex House, Triq Ta'L Ibragg, ST ANDREWS, STJ03, MALTA. (Life Member)

FENLON, Mr. Andrew Paul, FCA *1981;* 6 Spring Street, SANDRINGHAM, VIC 3191, AUSTRALIA.

FENN, Mr. Alexander David, BSc ACA *2007;* 22 Thorpe Road, ST. ALBANS, HERTFORDSHIRE, AL1 1RG.

FENN, Mrs. Charlotte Josephine, ACA *1980;* 6 THE COACH HOUSE, 88 CHRISTCHURCH ROAD, WINCHESTER, HAMPSHIRE, SO23 9TE.

•FENN, Mr. David Michael, FCA *1977;* Wilkins Kennedy, 1-5 Nelson St, SOUTHEND-ON-SEA, SS1 1EG.

•FENN, Mr. David Robert, FCA *1974;* (Tax Fac), 11 Stuart Road, Wash Common, NEWBURY, RG14 6QX.

FFOULKES-JONES, Mr. John Dillwyn, FCA *1955;* Shenstones, Maesmawr Road, LLANGOLLEN, LL20 7PG. (Life Member)
FFOULKES-JONES, Mr. Robert Garson, MBA FCA *1966;* 33 Lakeside Road, POOLE, DORSET, BH13 6LS.
FFOULKES ROBERTS, Mr. Gavin Alexander, ACA *1982;* Jln Tirtayasa IX No 10, Kebayoran Baru, JAKARTA, 12160, INDONESIA.
FFRENCH, Mr. Ian James, FCA *1972;* Le Sol, L'Etacq, Jersey, ST OUEN, JE3 2FF.
FIALKO, Mr. Craig Steven, BSc ACA *1983;* Nokia siemens Networks, St. Martin strosse 76, 81541 MUNICH, GERMANY.
•**FIALKO, Mr. Michael John, MSc BSc FCA** *1972;* 10 Beech Avenue, Whetstone, LONDON, N20 9JT.
FIANDER, Mr. Alan Edward, FCA *1968;* PO Box 1110, MARGARET RIVER, WA 6285, AUSTRALIA.
FIANDER, Mr. Ian James, BA ACA *1993;* 12 Mount Nod Way, Mount Nod, COVENTRY, CV5 7GX.
FIANDER, Mr. Raymond Herbert, FCA *1969;* 343 Route de la Vie Chenaille, 01170 ECHENEVEX, FRANCE.
FIANU, Mr. Martin Mensah, ACA *1983;* 58 First Street, PELHAM, NY NY 10803, UNITED STATES.
FIAZ, Mr. Shazad, BA(Hons) ACA *2002;* 154 Agbrigg Road, WAKEFIELD, WEST YORKSHIRE, WF1 5BL.
FIBBINS, Mr. Michael, BSc ACA *1984;* University of London Stewart House, 32 Russell Square, LONDON, WC1B 5DN.
FICE, Mr. Michael John, BSc FCA *1977;* 4 Forge End, Portbury, BRISTOL, BS20 7TY.
FICENEC, Mr. John Paul Grant, BA ACA *2008;* 5 Creskeld Crescent, Bramhope, LEEDS, LS16 9EH.
FICKLING, Mr. Paul Marshall, MA MBA FCA *1971;* 34 Gatehill Road, NORTHWOOD, HA6 3QQ.
FICKLING, Mr. Simon, BA(Oxon) ACA *2010;* Exane BNP Paribas, 20 St James St, LONDON, SW1A 1ES.
FIDDAMAN, Mr. Paul, BA ACA *1991;* 26 Consett Road, Castleside, CONSETT, DH8 9QL.
FIDDLEMAN, Mr. Anthony, BSc ACA *1986;* Fairwinds, Kingswood Rise, Englefield Green, EGHAM, TW20 0NG.
FIDDLER, Mr. Damian Paul, BSc ACA *1988;* 4 Duddon Close, Standish, WIGAN, WN6 0UJ.
FIDGE, Miss. Danielle, BA(Hons) ACA *2011;* 51 South Primrose Hill, CHELMSFORD, CM1 2RF.
•**FIDGEON, Mrs. Kathleen Elizabeth, ACA** *1981;* Corner Cottage, Foscot, CHIPPING NORTON, OXFORDSHIRE, OX7 6RL.
FIDLER, Miss. Claire, BA ACA *2007;* 27 Cummings Street, STOKE-ON-TRENT, ST4 7NT.
FIDLER, Mr. Elliot Richard, BA ACA *1997;* 3b Rechov Otniel, Baka, 93503 JERUSALEM, ISRAEL.
FIDLER, Mr. Iain Martin, MA ACA *1992;* 1 Appold Street, Deutsche Bank, PO Box 135, LONDON, EC2A 2HE.
FIDLER, Mr. Mark William, MA FCA AMCT *1986;* 95 Marlborough Crescent, SEVENOAKS, KENT, TN13 2HL.
FIDLER, Mr. Martin Edward, FCA *1964;* 50 Ridge Langley, Sanderstead, SOUTH CROYDON, Surrey, CR2 0AR.
FIDLER, Mr. Nicholas George, BA ACA *2008;* Graysonside Farm, Lorton Road, COCKERMOUTH, CUMBRIA, CA13 9TQ.
•**FIDLER, Mr. Robert William, BA FCA** *1980;* Burgess Farm, Kintbury Holt, NEWBURY, BERKSHIRE, RG20 0HY.
FIDLER, Miss. Sarah, ACA *2011;* 2 Irwin Avenue, WALLSEND, TYNE AND WEAR, NE28 7QX.
FIDLER, Mrs. Stella Maria, BA ACA *1990;* 39 Chew Brook Drive, Greenfield, OLDHAM, OL3 7PD.
FIDLER, Mr. Stuart James, BA ACA *1996;* 8 Elm Bank Drive, BROMLEY, BR1 2ST.
FIDOCK, Mr. Ian, BSc ACA *1999;* The Firs, Trottiscliffe Road, Addington, WEST MALLING, KENT, ME19 5AZ.
FIDOE, Mr. David Thomas, ACA *2004;* Glenmore Lodge, Glenmore, AVIEMORE, INVERNESS-SHIRE, PH22 1QU.
FIELD, Mr. Andrew Gordon, BA ACA *1989;* 3 Holywell Close, ABINGDON, OXFORDSHIRE, OX14 2PU.
FIELD, Mr. Andrew Robert, ACA *1981;* Deltenne House, Netley Hill Estate, SOUTHAMPTON, SO19 6AN.
FIELD, Mrs. Angela Cheryl, BA ACA *1988;* 6 Pine Meadows School Lane, Kirk Ella, HULL, HU10 7NS.
FIELD, Dr. Anthony, CBE FCA *1955;* 152 Cromwell Tower, Barbican, LONDON, EC2Y 8DD. (Life Member)
FIELD, Mr. Anthony David, BA ACA *1985;* (Tax Fac), 368 Chemin du Serriers No 13, 06320 LA TURBIE, FRANCE.
FIELD, Mr. Ben Casper, ACA *2009;* 9 Soleoak Drive, SEVENOAKS, TN13 1QD.
FIELD, Mr. Brian James, FCA *1963;* 181 Goldstone Cres, HOVE, BN3 6BD.
FIELD, Mrs. Caroline Patricia, MBBS ACA *1988;* (Tax Fac), 168 Osborne Road, Jesmond, NEWCASTLE UPON TYNE, NE2 3LE.
FIELD, The Revd. Catherine Philippa, BSc(Hons) FCA *1995;* 22 Rutland Terrace, Barlow, DRONFIELD, DERBYSHIRE, S18 7SS.
FIELD, Mr. Christopher Paul, BA ACA *1995;* 16a Rooms Lane, Morley, LEEDS, LS27 9PB.
FIELD, Mr. Christopher Simon, MA FCA *1978;* 1610 Stonebridge Tr, WHEATON, IL 60187, UNITED STATES.
FIELD, Mr. Colin Howard, BA FCA *1999;* Harptree House, 9 Hall Close, Naseby, NORTHAMPTON, NN6 6AJ.
FIELD, Mr. David, MA BA ACA *2011;* Ground Floor Flat, 211 Botley Road, OXFORD, OX2 0HG.
FIELD, Mr. David Ernest, FCA *1966;* 9 The Longacre, The Woodlands, Codsall, WOLVERHAMPTON, WV8 2EG.
FIELD, Miss. Dawn, ACA *2007;* 81 Vistula Crescent, SWINDON, WILTSHIRE, SN25 1QG.
•**FIELD, Mr. Derek Bernard Melvin, FCA** *1962;* (Tax Fac), Derek Field & Co, 2nd Floor, Crown House, 37 High Street, EAST GRINSTEAD, RH19 3AF.
FIELD, Mr. Douglas John, BA FCA *1998;* Powergen, Wherstead Park, Wherstead, IPSWICH, IP9 2BJ.
FIELD, Miss. Emma Jane, BA ACA *1998;* Eboracum, 8 Threlfall Drive, Habberley Coppice, BEWDLEY, DY12 1HU.
FIELD, Mr. Geoffrey Keith, BA ACA *1982;* Thomson Directories Ltd, Thomson House, 296 Farnborough Road, FARNBOROUGH, HAMPSHIRE, GU14 7NU.
FIELD, Mr. Howard Michael, FCA *1966;* 58 Williams Way, RADLETT, HERTFORDSHIRE, WD7 7HB.
FIELD, Mr. Hugh John Gordon, BCom FCA *1982;* 33 Westleigh Avenue, Putney, LONDON, SW15 6RQ.
FIELD, Miss. Jessica Helen, BSc ACA *2007;* Deloitte & Touche, PO Box 500, MANCHESTER, M60 2AT.
FIELD, Mr. Joel, BSc ACA *2006;* with Ernst & Young LLP, 1 More London Place, LONDON, SE1 2AF.
FIELD, Mrs. Julia Elaine, BA ACA *1992;* Grange Services SA, Rue Du Rhone 63, CH1204 GENEVA, SWITZERLAND.
FIELD, Mr. Julian Mark, BA FCA ATII AMCT *1987;* 20 Box Ridge Avenue, PURLEY, CR8 3AP.
FIELD, Miss. Karen Ann, BSc ACA *2004;* 138 Woodhead Drive, CAMBRIDGE, CB4 1YX.
FIELD, Mr. Kenneth Noel, BSc LLB FCA *1954;* 2 Homefield Court, Little Marston Road, Marston Magna, YEOVIL, SOMERSET, BA22 8DJ. (Life Member)
FIELD, Mr. Laurence Alan, MA ACA *1993;* 99 Cavell Drive, BISHOP'S STORTFORD, HERTFORDSHIRE, CM23 5PX.
FIELD, Miss. Lesley Ann, BSc ACA *1985;* Royal Mail, 3rd Floor, 35-50 Rathbone Place, LONDON, W1T 1HQ.
FIELD, Mr. Mark, BSc ACA *1996;* Lloyds TSB Bank Plc, Canons House, BRISTOL, BS99 7LB.
FIELD, Mr. Martin Patrick, BSc ACA *1989;* 230 John O'Gaunts Way, BELPER, DE56 0DF.
•**FIELD, Mr. Martin Victor, BA FCA** *1984;* (Tax Fac), Clifford Roberts, Pacioli House, 9 Brookfield, Duncan Close, Moulton Park, NORTHAMPTON NORTHAMPTONSHIRE NN3 6WL.
FIELD, Mr. Matthew Anthony, BA(Hons) ACA *2002;* 6 West Way, RICKMANSWORTH, HERTFORDSHIRE, WD3 7EP.
FIELD, Mrs. Maxine Darcy, ACA *1990;* International Press Production Ltd Unit 8-9, Herringston Barn Herringston, DORCHESTER, DORSET, DT2 9PU.
•**FIELD, Dr. Meyrick Edward, FCA** *1991;* M R Salvage Limited, 7-8 Eghams Court, Boston Drive, BOURNE END, BUCKINGHAMSHIRE, SL8 5YS.
FIELD, Mr. Michael John, FCA *1965;* Radford House, 2 Newfield Road, Hagley, STOURBRIDGE, DY9 0JP.
FIELD, Mr. Michael Robert, BSc FCA *1977;* 56 Westcroft Square, LONDON, W6 0TA.
FIELD, Mr. Nicholas Peter, BSc ACA *2004;* 2 Woodcutter Place, Penn Road, Park Street, ST. ALBANS, HERTFORDSHIRE, AL2 2SP.
FIELD, Mr. Norman, FCA *1948;* 100 Booth Road, LONDON, NW9 5JY. (Life Member)
•**FIELD, Mr. Paul Michael Antony, FCA** *1968;* (Tax Fac), P.A. Field & Co, Hare Knap, Lewes Road, Ditchling, HASSOCKS, WEST SUSSEX BN6 8TY.
FIELD, Mr. Peter, LLB ACA *2001;* Flat 11, 112 Belgrave Road, LONDON, SW1V 2BL.
•**FIELD, Mr. Peter John, FCA** *1961;* P.J. Field, Monkey Lodge, Skirmett Road, Hambleden, HENLEY-ON-THAMES, RG9 6SX.
•**FIELD, Mr. Phillip Richard, FCA** *1961;* Flat 3, Queens Lodge, 28 Uxbridge Road, STANMORE, MIDDLESEX, HA7 3SZ.
FIELD, Dr. Rachel Ann, ACA *1989;* Loxley Print Ltd, Kiln Street, SHEFFIELD, S8 0YS.
FIELD, Miss. Rachel Marie, ACA *2009;* 34 Aspen Road, Caister-on-Sea, GREAT YARMOUTH, NORFOLK, NR30 5BG.
FIELD, Mr. Robert James, ACA *2005;* with Burgess Hodgson, Camburgh House, 27 New Dover Road, CANTERBURY, CT1 3DN.
•**FIELD, Mr. Robert William, BSc FCA** *1989;* AIMS - Robert W Field BSc ACA, 9 Hinton Wood Avenue, CHRISTCHURCH, DORSET, BH23 5AB.
FIELD, Mr. Ronald Gordon, FCA *1966;* 57 Admirals Walk, West Cliff Road, BOURNEMOUTH, BH2 5HG. (Life Member)
FIELD, Mr. Simon Andrew, BSc ACA *2004;* Apartment 310, 417 Wick Lane, LONDON, E3 2JJ.
FIELD, Mr. Simon John, BA ACA *1992;* Alpine Lifestyle Partners, Place de L'Eglise 2, 1870 MONTHEY, VALAIS, SWITZERLAND.
FIELD, Mr. Stephen James, BSocSc FCA *1989;* 64 Waresley Park, Hartlebury, KIDDERMINSTER, WORCESTERSHIRE, DY11 7XE.
FIELD, Mr. Stephen Mark, BA ACA *1983;* Actavis Group, 6th Floor, Lex House, 17 Connaught Place, LONDON, W2 2ES.
FIELD, Mr. Stephen Michael, FCA *1982;* 17 Les Bois, High Road, Layer De La Haye, COLCHESTER, CO2 0EX.
•**FIELD, Ms. Susan, FCA** *1972;* MEMBER OF COUNCIL, (Tax Fac), Susan Field Limited, Neptune House, 70 Royal Hill, LONDON, SE10 8RF.
FIELD, Mr. Timothy Duncan Richard, BA FCA *1995;* Swan House, South Chailey, LEWES, EAST SUSSEX, BN8 4AS.
FIELD, Mr. William Graham, ACA *1980;* with Ernst & Young LLP, 1 More London Place, LONDON, SE1 2AF.
FIELD, Mr. William Michael Craik, BA ACA *1990;* 125 Chevening Road, Queen's Park, LONDON, NW6 6DU.
FIELDEN, Mr. David, FCA *1968;* Beechcroft, Lewes Road, Lindfield, HAYWARDS HEATH, RH16 2LQ. (Life Member)
•**FIELDEN, Mr. Julian Scott, BSc FCA** *1981;* O C F Plc Unit 5 Rotunda Business Centre, Thorncliffe Road Chapeltown, SHEFFIELD, S35 2PG.
FIELDEN, Mr. Nicholas Mark, BA ACA *1992;* 38 Cartbridge Lane, WALSALL, WS4 1SB.
FIELDEN, Mrs. Rosamund Gillian, BSc ACA *1987;* c/o PT HM Sampoerna TBK, 17th floor One Pacific Place, Sudirman Central Business District, Jl. Jend. Sudirman Kav. 52-53, JAKARTA, 12190 INDONESIA.
FIELDEN, Mr. Thomas Edward, BA ACA *1997;* The White House, Kirkby Wharfe, TADCASTER, NORTH YORKSHIRE, LS24 9DD.
FIELDER, Miss. Alison, BA ACA *2005;* 3 Lulworth Avenue, Goffs Oak, WALTHAM CROSS, HERTFORDSHIRE, EN7 5LA.
FIELDER, Mr. John Anthony, FCA *1949;* 7 Gressland Court, Mead Drive, Kesgrave, IPSWICH, IP5 2HJ. (Life Member)
FIELDER, Mr. John Robert, BA ACA *1989;* Kent Barn, East Harting, PETERSFIELD, GU31 5LS.
•**FIELDER, Mr. Michael Hilton, FCA** *1956;* Michael H Fielder, Sutie One The Gomez Building, PO Box N1608, NASSAU, BAHAMAS.
FIELDER, Mr. Michael Paul, FCA *1969;* 10 Boarley Court, Sandling Lane, MAIDSTONE, ME14 2NL. (Life Member)
FIELDER, Mr. Robert, MA ACA *2009;* 6 Ambra Vale South, BRISTOL, BS8 4RN.
FIELDHOUSE, Mr. David Anthony, BSc ACA *2006;* Burberry Ltd Horseferry House, Horseferry Road, LONDON, SW1P 2AW.
•**FIELDHOUSE, Mr. Derek, FCA** *1970;* Derek Fieldhouse, 39 Newton Court, Oakwoood Grange Lane, LEEDS, LS8 2PH.
FIELDHOUSE, Mr. Ian William, MA FCA *1983;* 5 Mayfield Drive, WINDSOR, SL4 4RB.
FIELDHOUSE, Mr. James Brian, BA ACA *2007;* with BDO LLP, 6th Floor, 3 Hardman Street, Spinningfields, MANCHESTER, M3 3AT.
FIELDHOUSE, Mr. Paul, BA(Hons) ACA *2002;* Lansdowne Partners Ltd, 15 Davies Street, LONDON, W1K 3AG.
FIELDHOUSE, Mr. Roger, FCA FCMA *1961;* Flat 9 Silverdale, Lancaster Road, SOUTHPORT, MERSEYSIDE, PR8 2LF.
FIELDING, Mr. Alan, FCA *1956;* 26 Saltdean Way, Cooden, BEXHILL-ON-SEA, TN39 3SS. (Life Member)
•**FIELDING, Mr. Alan, BCom FCA** *1974;* Alan Fielding, 18 The Walk, ROCHDALE, LANCASHIRE, OL16 1EP.
FIELDING, Mr. Andrew John, BSc ACA *1988;* Zelezna Cesta 10 Apartment 17, 1000 LJUBLJANA, SLOVENIA.
FIELDING, Mrs. Christine Carol, BSc ACA *1983;* (Tax Fac), 1 Lapin Lane, Hatch Warren, BASINGSTOKE, RG22 4XH.
FIELDING, Mr. Christopher Michael, BA FCA *1983;* 34 The Avenue, LONDON, W4 1HT.
FIELDING, Mr. David, MA FCA *1976;* 4 Osprey Close, BLACKBURN, BB1 8LP.
FIELDING, Mr. David Hope, FCA *1964;* 15 Georgian Close, BEXHILL-ON-SEA, EAST SUSSEX, TN40 2NN.
FIELDING, Mr. David Michael, BA ACA *1995;* 21 Ibbetson Oval, Morley, LEEDS, LS27 7RY.
FIELDING, Mr. Dean Andrew, BSc ACA *1989;* Woodhouse Farm, Daffy Lane, Crayke, YORK, YO61 4TH.
FIELDING, Mrs. Elizabeth, BA FCA *1986;* 4 Osprey Close, BLACKBURN, BB1 8LP.
FIELDING, Mr. Geoffrey Peter, FCA *1987;* 2 Hoghton Close, LANCASTER, LA1 5UF.
FIELDING, Mr. George, FCA *1965;* 20 Pinos (Urb. Puerto Rey), Garrucha, 4630 ALMERIA, SPAIN.
•**FIELDING, Mrs. Gillian, BA ACA** *1986;* Hopefield, The Summer House, Soldiers Field Lane, Findon, WORTHING, WEST SUSSEX BN14 0SH.
•**FIELDING, Mr. Graham, ACA** *1978;* MHA Fieldings, The Post House, Astley Abbotts, BRIDGNORTH, SHROPSHIRE, WV16 4SW.
FIELDING, Mr. Herbert James Colin, FCA *1960;* 52 Upper George Street, CHESHAM, BUCKINGHAMSHIRE, HP5 3EH. (Life Member)
FIELDING, Dr. John Anthony, MSc FCA *1966;* 11 Wood Street, Woburn Sands, MILTON KEYNES, MK17 8PH. (Life Member)
FIELDING, Mr. John Keith, FCA *1952;* 25 South Western Road, TWICKENHAM, TW1 1LG. (Life Member)
FIELDING, Mr. John William, BSc ACA *2002;* 2 Southway Road, BRADFORD-ON-AVON, BA15 1UW.
FIELDING, Mr. Keith Baxter, BSc FCA *1965;* The Cottage, Clough House, Stones Lane, Linthwaite, HUDDERSFIELD, HD7 5PP.
FIELDING, Mrs. Kirsten Andree, BA ACA *2005;* 11 Mill Street, REDHILL, SURREY, RH1 6PA.
FIELDING, Mr. Mark, MA(Hons) ACA *2002;* Harcourt Capital LLP, 271 Regent Street, LONDON, W1B 2ES.
•**FIELDING, Mr. Mark, BSc FCA** *1996;* Simpson Wood, Bank Chambers, Market Street, HUDDERSFIELD, HD1 2EW.
FIELDING, Mr. Martin Leslie, ACA *1979;* The Summer House, Nepcote Lane, Findon, WORTHING, WEST SUSSEX, BN14 0SG.
FIELDING, The Revd. Michael Robert, FCA *1960;* Collingholme Barn Cottage, Cowan Bridge, CARNFORTH, LA6 2JL. (Life Member)
FIELDING, Mr. Paul Howard, MA(Hons) ACA *2000;* Asda Stores Limited, Asda House, South Bank, Great Wilson Street, LEEDS, LS11 5AD.
FIELDING, Mr. Peter James, FCA *1967;* 2 Mansion House Apartments, 60 Queens Road, SOUTHPORT, MERSEYSIDE, PR9 9JF. (Life Member)
FIELDING, Miss. Rebecca Louise, ACA CTA *2006;* Flat 2, 120 Gowers Walk, LONDON, E1 8GG.
FIELDING, Mr. Richard, BA ACA *1994;* The Old Rectory, Church Hill, Plumtree, NOTTINGHAM, NG12 5ND.
•**FIELDING, Mr. Robin Daniel, MA FCA** *2001;* RDF Financial Solutions, Dove Cottage, Liphook Road, Headley, BORDON, HAMPSHIRE GU35 8LL.
FIELDING, Mrs. Susie Mary, BSc ACA *1989;* Highfield, New Road, Highley, BRIDGNORTH, WV16 6NN.
FIELDING, Dr. Trevor Joseph, ACA *1991;* Highfield, New Road, Highley, BRIDGNORTH, WV16 6NN.
FIELDING, Mr. William Adolphus Crosbie, MA ACA *1986;* Thornfield Claughbane Road, Ramsey, ISLE OF MAN, IM8 2HL.
•**FIELDMAN, Mr. Derek Howard, FCA** *1971;* The Leaman Partnership LLP, 51 Queen Anne Street, LONDON, W1G 9HS.
FIELDMAN, Mr. Jeremy John, BSc ACA *2006;* Linpac Plastics Wakefield Road, Featherstone, PONTEFRACT, WEST YORKSHIRE, WF7 5DE.
FIELDS, Mr. Christopher George, FCA *1970;* Yare Shipping Stores G.W. Field & Sons (Great Yarmouth), Hewett Road Gapton Hall Ind. Est., GREAT YARMOUTH, NR31 0NN.
FIELDS, Mrs. Michele Cecile Edith, BA ACA *1982;* P.O. Box N682, NASSAU, BAHAMAS.
FIELDS, Mr. Paul Anthony, BA ACA *1994;* with KPMG LLP, Arlington Business Park, Theale, READING, RG7 4SD.

FIELDS, Miss. Samantha Michelle, BA(Hons) ACA *2003;* 19 Lord Avenue, Clayhall, ILFORD, ESSEX, IG5 0HP.
•**FIELDS, Mr. Stephen Andrew, BA FCA** *1987;* (Tax Fac), Forrester Boyd, 66-68 Oswald Road, SCUNTHORPE, SOUTH HUMBERSIDE, DN15 7PG.
FIELDSEND, Mr. Ian, BA(Hons) ACA *2000;* Flat 114 Lait House, 1 Albemarle Road, BECKENHAM, BR3 5LP.
FIELDSEND, Mr. Mark, ACA *2008;* with Grant Thornton UK LLP, Pinnacle Building, 20 Tudor Road, READING, RG1 1NH.
•**FIELDWICK, Miss. Diana Mary, FCA** *1979;* Fieldwick Kemsley & Partners Limited, 12 Heathfield South, TWICKENHAM, TW2 7SS.
FIELON, Mr. Alan Douglas, BSc FCA *1981;* 11 Paradise Lane, FAREHAM, HAMPSHIRE, PO16 8RA.
FIENNES, Mrs. Claire Elizabeth, BSc ACA *2000;* 341 Carolina Lane, PALO ALTO, CA 94306, UNITED STATES.
FIENNES, Mrs. Hilary Linda, BSc ACA *1988;* 122 Kelburn Parade, Kelburn, WELLINGTON, NEW ZEALAND.
FIETH, Mr. Robin Paul, BA FCA *1990;* with ICAEW, Chartered Accountants' Hall, Moorgate Place, LONDON, EC2P 2BJ.
FIETTA, Mr. Glendon Anthony, BSc ACA *1999;* Glamis, Waterend Lane, Redbourn, ST. ALBANS, HERTFORDSHIRE, AL3 7JZ.
FIFIELD, Mr. Clifford John, FCA *1977;* Joint Replacement Instrumentation Limited, 10A Chandos Street, LONDON, W1G 9DQ.
FIFIELD, Miss. Joanna Kate, BA ACA *2000;* 29 Lannesbury Crescent, ST. NEOTS, CAMBRIDGESHIRE, PE19 6AG.
FIFIELD, Mr. Richard Charles, BSc ACA *1989;* 90 London Road, WOKINGHAM, RG40 1YF.
•**FIFIELD, Mr. Richard Mark, BSc FCA** *1988;* Dapplewood, Ashtead Lane, GODALMING, GU7 1SY.
FIGG, Mr. David William, BSc ACA *1990;* 15 Inkerman Way, Denby Dale, HUDDERSFIELD, HD8 8UU.
FIGGETT, Mr. Christopher Maurice, FCA *1971;* 94b Feckenham Road Headless Cross, REDDITCH, WORCESTERSHIRE, B97 5AJ.
•**FIGGINS, Mr. Graham Peter, FCA** *1974;* with The Taylor Cocks Partnership Limited, 3 Acorn Business Centre, Northarbour Road, Cosham, PORTSMOUTH, PO6 3TH.
FIGGINS, Mr. Paul, BA ACA *2002;* 42 Frederick Road, Edgbaston, BIRMINGHAM, B15 1HN.
•**FIGGIS, Mr. Patrick Adam Fernesley, FCA** *1983;* PricewaterhouseCoopers LLP, 1 Embankment Place, LONDON, WC2N 6RH. See also PricewaterhouseCoopers
•**FIGGIS, Mr. Simon Richard Frank, LLB FCA** *1981;* KPMG LLP, 15 Canada Square, LONDON, E14 5GL. See also KPMG Europe LLP
FIGUS, Miss. Elena, ACA *2002;* World Food Programme, OSA Office - Internal Audit, Via Cesare Giulio Viola 68, 00148 ROME, ITALY.
•**FIKRI, Mr. Ali Taner, FCA** *1973;* Fikri & Co, Ali Tanner Fikri Building, Kyrenia Avenue No.78, LEFKOSA MERSIN 10, TURKEY.
FILATOVA, Miss. Victoria, ACA *2008;* 2 Claremont Flats, 117 Don Road St. Helier, JERSEY, JE2 4QD.
•**FILBEE, Mr. Andrew Philip, BA FCA** *1993;* (Tax Fac), Gardners Accountants Ltd, Brynford House, Brynford Street, HOLYWELL, CLWYD, CH8 7RD. See also Gardner Salisbury Limited
FILBEE, Miss. Beth Salena, BSc ACA *1990;* W W Giles(Smithfield) Ltd, 22a Horseshoe Business Park, Horseshoe Road, Pangbourne, READING, BERKSHIRE RG8 7JW.
FILBEE, Mrs. Sarah May, BSc ARCS ACA CTA *1998;* 107 Maze Hill, Greenwich, LONDON, SE10 8XQ.
FILBEY, Mr. Jonathan, BA ACA *2010;* 17 Florence Street, LONDON, N1 2DX.
FILBIN, Miss. Joanne, ACA *2008;* Flat 18, Dean Court, 10 Queens Road, KINGSTON UPON THAMES, SURREY, KT2 7SD.
FILBY, Mr. Christopher Brian Terrence, BSc ACA *1985;* (Tax Fac), The Reapers, 25 St Mary's Road, LEATHERHEAD, KT22 8HB.
FILBY, Mr. Mark John, BA ACA *1995;* PO BOX 95061, ABU DHABI, UNITED ARAB EMIRATES.
FILBY, Mr. Robert Lucien Albert, FCA *1983;* 102 Broadwood Avenue, RUISLIP, MIDDLESEX, HA4 7XT.
FILBY, Mr. Stuart, BA ACA *2005;* Level 25, 363 George Street, SYDNEY, NSW 2000, AUSTRALIA.
FILDER, Mr. Cyril Herbert, FCA *1953;* Sandrock, 25A Banks Road, West Kirby, WIRRAL, CH48 0QX. (Life Member)
FILECCIA, Mrs. Annette, BSc ACA *1986;* 87 Derby Road, Risley, DERBY, DE72 3SY.
FILECCIA, Mr. Piero, BA FCA *1985;* 87 Derby Road, Risley, DERBY, DE72 3SY.
FILEK, Mr. Michael, BMus LLB ACA CTA *2001;* Robert Jones & Agnes Hunt District Orthopaedic Hospital, Gobowen, OSWESTRY, SHROPSHIRE, SY10 7AG.
•**FILER, Ms. Lucy Jane, FCA** *1999;* Filer Knapper LLP, 10 Bridge Street, CHRISTCHURCH, DORSET, BH23 1EF.
FILER, Mr. Mark Howard, BSc FCA *1992;* 6 Beeches Wood, TADWORTH, SURREY, KT20 6PR.
FILER, Mr. Michael Harold, FCA *1963;* 8 Boscombe Cliff Road, BOURNEMOUTH, BH5 1JL. (Life Member)
FILER, Mr. Paul Andrew, MA FCA *1982;* 28 Meadowbank, Primrose Hill, LONDON, NW3 3AY.
FILER, Mr. Roy Montague, FCA *1950;* 4 Park Grove, EDGWARE, HA8 7SJ. (Life Member)
FILER, Mr. Samuel Max, MA(Oxon) ACA *2007;* 2808 Hilgard Avenue, BERKELEY, CA 94709, UNITED STATES.
FILI, Mr. Kyriakos, ACA *2009;* Kendea Kasianou 283A, Soin. Agiou Georgiou, Vrysoulles, 5522 FAMAGUSTA, CYPRUS.
FILLARY, Mr. David Raymond, ACA *1981;* 115 Lodge Avenue, ROMFORD, RM2 5AD.
FILLENHAM, Mr. Jeremy Laurence, FCA *1973;* Libbyvagen 32, 187 62 TABY, SWEDEN. (Life Member)
FILLERY, Mr. Graham Winston, BSc ACA *1989;* 4 Elm Tree Close, Palterton, CHESTERFIELD, DERBYSHIRE, S44 6RW.
FILLERY, Mr. Robert James, BSc ACA *1999;* Old Fishbourne Cottage, 5 Salthill Road, Fishbourne, CHICHESTER, WEST SUSSEX, PO19 3QX.
FILLEUL, Mr. Leonard Thomas Le Sueur, FCA *1947;* 9 Southwoods, YEOVIL, BA20 2QQ. (Life Member)
•**FILLEY, Mr. Jeremy, BSc FCA** *1999;* with RSM Tenon Audit Limited, Vantage, Victoria Street, BASINGSTOKE, HAMPSHIRE, RG21 3BT.
•**FILLINGHAM, Mr. James Spencer John, BA ACA** *1995;* PricewaterhouseCoopers LLP, 7 More London Riverside, LONDON, SE1 2RT. See also PricewaterhouseCoopers
FILLINGHAM, Mr. Neil Douglas, BA ACA *1985;* 9 Wilsford Close, Lower Earley, READING, RG6 4BP.
FILLINGHAM, Mr. Stuart Barry David, BA FCA *1989;* 31 Anthian Close, Woodley, READING, RG5 4XA.
FILLMORE, Mrs. Elizabeth Anne, BSc FCA *1976;* Church Barn, Pillerton Hersey, WARWICK, CV35 0QJ.
•**FILLMORE, Mr. Malcolm Peter, FCA** *1970;* Atherton Bailey LLP, Arundel House, 1 Amberley Court, Whitworth Road, CRAWLEY, WEST SUSSEX RH11 7XL. See also East Park Services Ltd
FILMER, Mrs. Angela Shirley, MA FCA *1959;* 19 Belvedere Court, Lyttelton Road, LONDON, N2 0AG. (Life Member)
FILMER-WILSON, Mr. James Arthur, FCA *1965;* Chelsea Securities Ltd, Room 704, Yu Yuet Lai Building, 43/55 Wyndham Street, CENTRAL, HONG KONG ISLAND HONG KONG SAR.
•**FILMORE, Mr. David Charles, FCA** *1972;* 13 Briarwood Crescent, Wibsey, BRADFORD, BD6 1SD.
•**FILOSE, Mr. Nicholas John, FCA** *1978;* (Tax Fac), Nicholas Filose, Greenmead, Waters Grn, BROCKENHURST, SO42 7RG.
FILSELL, Mr. Mark Andrew, ACA *1992;* with Knill James, One Bell Lane, LEWES, EAST SUSSEX, BN7 1JU.
FILSHIE, Mr. Alexander, BSc FCA AMCT *1992;* 60 Buckingham Palace Road, LONDON, SW1W 0RR.
FILSHIE, Mrs. Joanna Ruth, BA ACA *1994;* 38 Conduit Mews, LONDON, W2 3RE.
FINAN, Mr. Kevin, ACA *2010;* 72 Askwith Road, RAINHAM, ESSEX, RM13 8ER.
FINAN, Mr. Patrick Robert, ACA *2009;* 149 Haberdasher Street, LONDON, N1 6EH.
FINBERY, Mr. Simon Mark, BSc ACA *1992;* 9 Robin Bailey Way, Hucknall, NOTTINGHAM, NG15 7UP.
FINCH, Mr. Alexander John, BSc(Hons) ACA *2000;* 28 Nursery Place, SEVENOAKS, TN13 2RH.
FINCH, Mr. Andrew Daniel, LLB ACA *2003;* 80 Hyde Road, SOUTH CROYDON, SURREY, CR2 9NQ.
FINCH, Mr. Andrew Stewart, BSc ACA *2010;* 30 Highgate Edge, Great North Road, LONDON, N2 0NT.
FINCH, Mr. Christopher Graham, BSc FCA *1972;* 4 Noel Road, LONDON, N1 8HA.
FINCH, Mr. Christopher John, FCA *1973;* 17 Woodbridge Street, LONDON, EC1R 0LL.
FINCH, Mr. David James, BA FCA *1981;* 59 Ridgway Place, Wimbledon, LONDON, SW19 4SP.
FINCH, Mr. David John, BSc ACA *1989;* 4 Winchendon Road, LONDON, SW6 5DR.
FINCH, Mr. David Matthew, ACA *2008;* 31 Fraser Road, HIGH WYCOMBE, BUCKINGHAMSHIRE, HP12 4RR.
FINCH, Mr. David Roger Barnes, BA ACA *1985;* The Threshing Barn, North Weston, THAME, OXFORDSHIRE, OX9 2HA.
FINCH, Mr. Dean Kendal, BSc ACA *1991;* National Express Group Plc, 60 Charlotte Street, LONDON, W1T 2NU.
FINCH, Mr. Duncan Alistair, BEng ACA *1991;* Heather Bank, Bracken Lane, Storrington, PULBOROUGH, WEST SUSSEX, RH20 3HR.
•**FINCH, Mr. Edward Alexander, BA ACA** *1994;* Buzzacott LLP, 130 Wood Street, LONDON, EC2V 6DL.
FINCH, Miss. Fiona Kirsten, MSc BA ACA *2010;* G 4 S Plc The Manor, Manor Royal, CRAWLEY, WEST SUSSEX, RH10 9UN.
FINCH, Mrs. Hayley Jane, BA ACA *1993;* 3 Twyford Fields, Twyford, BANBURY, OXFORDSHIRE, OX17 3LE.
•**FINCH, Mrs. Jacqueline Ann, BSc FCA** *1987;* J.A. Finch, 30 Sweetings Road, Godmanchester, HUNTINGDON, PE29 2JS.
FINCH, Mrs. Joanne Sarah, BSc ACA *1996;* Baird House, Vodafone Group Plc Vodafone House, The Connection, NEWBURY, RG14 2FN.
FINCH, Mr. John, FCA *1966;* 2909 Cartier St. S.W., CALGARY T2T 3J5, AB, CANADA. (Life Member)
FINCH, Mr. John Peter, BA ACA *1994;* Pemberton Leisure Homes Ltd, Woodhouse Lane, WIGAN, WN6 7NF.
FINCH, Miss. Leanne, ACA *2008;* Mazars Tower Bridge House, St. Katharines Way, LONDON, E1W 1DD.
•**FINCH, Mr. Mark, ACA FCCA** *2008;* McPhersons CFG Limited, 23 St. Leonards Road, BEXHILL-ON-SEA, EAST SUSSEX, TN40 1HH.
FINCH, Mr. Mark Andrew, ACA *1985;* Mills & Reeve, 1 St. James Court, NORWICH, NR3 1RU.
•①**FINCH, Mr. Michael, LLB(Hons) ACA MIPA MABRP** *2002;* Moore Stephens LLP, 3-5 Rickmansworth Road, WATFORD, HERTFORDSHIRE, WD18 0GX.
•**FINCH, Mr. Michael Clifford, FCA** *1980;* (Tax Fac), S.W.Frankson & Co, Bridge House, 119-123 Station Road, HAYES, MIDDLESEX, UB3 4BX.
FINCH, Mr. Michael Henry Ainsworth, MA FCA *1958;* Darwin House, Darwin Lane, SHEFFIELD, S10 5RG. (Life Member)
FINCH, Mr. Oliver James, BA ACA *2008;* Flat 1, The Mount House, 16 Busbridge Lane, GODALMING, GU7 1PU.
FINCH, Mr. Peter John, BSc ACA ATII *1991;* 57 Greenwood Terrace, SINGAPORE 286861, SINGAPORE.
•**FINCH, Mr. Peter John Charles, BA FCA** *1979;* 6 Little Acres, WARE, SG12 9JW.
FINCH, Mr. Richard Lewis Crichton, BA FCA *1985;* 58 Torrington Drive, POTTERS BAR, EN6 5HS.
FINCH, Mr. Russell Guy, BA ACA *1991;* 51 Ellis Road, CROWTHORNE, BERKSHIRE, RG45 6PR.
FINCH, Mr. Simon Bancroft, BA ACA *1993;* Dytecna Limited, Unit 2, Horizon Business Village, 1 Brooklands Road, WEYBRIDGE, SURREY KT13 0TJ.
FINCH, Mr. Simon Charles, BA ACA *2004;* 7 La Ville Au Roi, La Rue de Trachy St. Helier, JERSEY, JE2 3JR.
FINCH, Mr. Simon Leigh, BSc FCA *1977;* 16 Broom Water West, TEDDINGTON, TW11 9QH. (Life Member)
FINCHAM, Mr. Arthur Douglas, FCA *1932;* 2 Wickham Way, BECKENHAM, BR3 3AA. (Life Member)
FINCHAM, Mr. Stewart Nicholas, BA FCA *1980;* 11 Anne Hathaway Drive, Churchdown, GLOUCESTER, GL3 2PX. (Life Member)
FINDING, Mr. Michael John, FCA *1967;* West Lodge, 97 Lower Bristol Road, WESTON-SUPER-MARE, BS23 2TX. (Life Member)
FINDLATER, Mr. Alexander John Maxwell, BA ACA *1979;* The Grammar House, The Hill, LANGPORT, TA10 9PU.
FINDLATER, Mr. John Quentin Alexander, FCA *1968;* Comp House, Binfield Heath, HENLEY-ON-THAMES, RG9 4NB.
FINDLATER, Mrs. Kerry Rachel, BEng ACA *1996;* Finance Department, Kraft Foods UK Ltd St. Georges House, Bayshill Road, CHELTENHAM, GL50 3AE.
FINDLAY, Mr. Alastair Ian, BA FCA *1978;* High Billinge House Quarry Bank Utkinton, TARPORLEY, CHESHIRE, CW6 0LA.
•①**FINDLAY, Mr. Alisdair James Fraser, ACA MBA** *1993;* Findlay James, Saxon House, Saxon Way, CHELTENHAM, GLOUCESTERSHIRE, GL52 6QX.
FINDLAY, Mr. Andrew Robert, BSc ACA *1996;* Marks & Spencer Plc, Waterside House, 35 North Wharf Road, LONDON, W2 1NW.
FINDLAY, Mr. Andrew William Thomas, BA ACA *1995;* 72 Louisville Road, LONDON, SW17 8RU.
FINDLAY, Mrs. Caroline Jane, MA ACA *1995;* 2 Beechwood Close, Battledown, CHELTENHAM, GLOUCESTERSHIRE, GL52 6QQ.
FINDLAY, Mr. Craig, LLB ACA *1991;* 21 Thomson Drive, Bearsden, GLASGOW, G61 3PA.
FINDLAY, Ms. Deborah Joan, BA FCA CTA *1986;* 33 Gubyon Avenue, Herne Hill, LONDON, SE24 0DU.
FINDLAY, Mrs. Georgina Louise, BA FCA *1986;* 79 Wrottesley Road, Tettenhall, WOLVERHAMPTON, WV6 8SQ.
FINDLAY, Mr. Ian, LLB ACA *1983;* Flat 4 Spencer Court, 14 Spencer Place, LONDON, N1 2AX.
FINDLAY, Mr. Ian, BA ACA *1982;* Bradford Grammar School, Keighley Road, BRADFORD, WEST YORKSHIRE, BD9 4JP.
FINDLAY, Mr. Ian Scott, FCA *1974;* Bombela Concesion Co (Pty) Ltd, P.O Box 1115, KELVIN, 2054, SOUTH AFRICA.
FINDLAY, Dr. John Duncan, PhD BSc ACA *2003;* 18a Lansdowne Grove, LONDON, NW10 1PR.
FINDLAY, Mr. Ralph Graham, BSc FCA *1988;* 79 Wrottesley Road, Tettenhall, WOLVERHAMPTON, WV6 8SQ.
FINDLAY, Mr. Stephen William, BSc ACA *2005;* M W B Business Exchange, 53 Chandos Place, LONDON, WC2N 4HS.
FINDLAY-COULSON, Mr. Timothy Paul Patrick, LLB ACA *1999;* 200 E 94th Street, Apt 411, NEW YORK, NY 10128, UNITED STATES.
FINDLER, Mr. Jonathan Paul, MBA FCA *1974;* Westwood House, Heathfield Avenue, Sunninghill, ASCOT, SL5 0AL.
FINDLEY, Mr. Derek Kenneth, BA ACA *1983;* 18 Westwood Avenue, KENDAL, LA9 5BB.
FINDLOW, Mrs. Lynne, BA ACA *2001;* 11 Millbeck Green, Collingham, WETHERBY, WEST YORKSHIRE, LS22 5AJ.
FINE, Mr. Alan Geoffrey, FCA *1952;* Dennis F Rose & Associates, 19350 Business Center Drive, Suite 100, NORTHRIDGE, CA 91324 6432, UNITED STATES. (Life Member)
•**FINE, Mr. Anthony Gordon, FCA** *1961;* Anthony G. Fine, 9 The Regents, Norfolk Road, BIRMINGHAM, B15 3PP.
FINE, Mr. Anthony Karl, BSc ACA *1999;* 310 w85th Street, Apt 2A, NEW YORK, NY 10024, UNITED STATES.
•**FINE, Mr. Barry, BA FCA** *1983;* Alexander Bursk, Parkgates, Bury New Road, Prestwich, MANCHESTER, M25 0JW.
•**FINE, Mr. Daniel Boruch, ACA** *2004;* Melinek Fine LLP, Ground Floor, Forframe House, 35-37 Brent Street, LONDON, NW4 2EF.
FINE, Mr. Jeffrey Joseph, FCA *1958;* 38 York Terrace East, Regents Park, LONDON, NW1 4PT. (Life Member)
FINE, Mr. Simon Daniel, BA ACA *1994;* 11 Elmsway, Hale Barns, ALTRINCHAM, CHESHIRE, WA15 0DZ.
•**FINE, Mr. Simon David, FCA** *1970;* David Fine & Co, Dolphin House, 12 Beaumont Gate, RADLETT, HERTFORDSHIRE, WD7 7AR.
FINEBERG, Mr. David Anthony, BA(Hons) FCA *2001;* 5 Octavia Mews, LONDON, W9 3LQ.
FINEGAN, Mrs. Alison Clare, ACA *1991;* Oxton Old Hall, Talbot Road, Oxton, PRENTON, CH43 2HJ.
FINEGAN, Mr. Paul Frank, BEng ACA *1993;* 56 Manor Park Drive, Finchampstead, WOKINGHAM, RG40 4XE.
FINELY, Miss. Helen Rachel, BA ACA *1999;* 4 Beech Copse, BROMLEY, BR1 2NX.
FINEMAN, Mr. Alan, FCA *1965;* Gwent House, Caroland Close, Smeeth, ASHFORD, KENT, TN25 6RY. (Life Member)
•**FINER, Mr. Ian Michael, FCA** *1974;* Finer Heymann LLP, Premier House, 112 Station Road, EDGWARE, HA8 7BJ.
FINERAN, Mrs. Joanne Caroline, BA ACA *2002;* with PricewaterhouseCoopers LLP, Benson House, 33 Wellington Street, LEEDS, LS1 4JP.
FINERAN, Mr. Paul Michael, BA(Hons) ACA *2002;* 4 Priest Hill Gardens, WETHERBY, WEST YORKSHIRE, LS22 7UD.
•**FINERTY, Mr. Bernard Francis, FCA** *1984;* (Tax Fac), Finerty Brice, Endeavour House, 78 Stafford Road, WALLINGTON, SM6 9AY.
•**FINESILVER, Mr. Jack Malcolm, BSc FCA** *1979;* (Tax Fac), Goodman Jones LLP, 29-30 Fitzroy Square, LONDON, W1T 6LQ.
FINESILVER, Mr. Morris Barrie, FCA *1975;* 30 Ebrington Road, HARROW, HA3 0LT.
•**FINESTEIN, Mr. Daniel John, BA FCA** *1990;* Infinity Asset Management LLP, 26th Floor, City Tower, Piccadilly Plaza, MANCHESTER, M1 4BD.
FINESTON, Miss. Gillian, BSc(Hons) ACA *2002;* 37 Frensham Drive, Putney Vale, LONDON, SW15 3EB.
•**FINGER, Mr. Laurence Warren, ACA** *1979;* SRLV, 89 New Bond Street, LONDON, W1S 1DA.

FINGERHUT, Mrs. Beatrice, FCA *1949;* 76 Green Lane, EDGWARE, HA8 7QA. (Life Member)
•FINGLETON, Mr. Paul John, BA FCA *1988;* (Tax Fac), Montpelier Professional (Lancashire) Limited, Charter House, Pittman Way, Fulwood, PRESTON, PR2 9ZD. See also Montpelier Audit Limited
FINILL, Mr. Christopher Tom, BSc ACA *1986;* 5 Cameron Close, CRANLEIGH, SURREY, GU6 8EB.
•FINK, Mr. Mark Richard, BA ACA CTA *1989;* (Tax Fac), Mark Fink Chartered Tax Adviser, Grove House, Back Rowarth, GLOSSOP, DERBYSHIRE, SK13 6ED.
FINK, Mr. Stanley, ACA *1982;* ISAM, 52 Queen Anne Street, LONDON, W1G 8HL.
FINKELSTEIN, Mr. Errol, ACA CA(SA) *2009;* 25 Crosby Way, FARNHAM, SURREY, GU9 7XG.
FINLAY, Mr. Alan Neilson, FCA *1959;* 136 Murray Avenue, BROMLEY, BR1 3DT. (Life Member)
FINLAY, Miss. Clara, ACA *2011;* Flat 16 Bellmaker Court, 136 St. Pauls Way, LONDON, E3 4AD.
FINLAY, Mr. David Malcolm, BA FCA *1979;* The National Audit Office, 151 Buckingham Palace Road, LONDON, SW1W 9SP.
•FINLAY, Mr. David Michael Gordon, FCA *1969;* 2 Rogerstone Grange Cottages, St. Arvans, CHEPSTOW, GWENT, NP16 6EX.
FINLAY, Mr. Fabian John Adam, LLB FCA *1981;* 36 Lancaster Mews, LONDON, W2 3QF.
FINLAY, Mrs. Jennifer Louise, BA ACA *1996;* 2 Rothamsted Avenue, HARPENDEN, HERTFORDSHIRE, AL5 2DB.
FINLAY, Mr. Jonathan Stewart, BSc FCA *1986;* 2 Luker Drive, PETERSFIELD, GU31 4SN.
FINLAY, Mr. Mark, ACA *2008;* 6 Havercroft Park, BOLTON, BL1 5AB.
FINLAY, Mr. Mark Stephen, BA FCA *1981;* 94 Station Road, Oakley, BEDFORD, MK43 7RE.
FINLAY, Ms. Pauline, MSc(Econ) ACA *1991;* 60 Swanshurst Lane, BIRMINGHAM, B13 0AL.
FINLAY, Mr. Philip, FCA *1951;* 20 Hawsted, BUCKHURST HILL, ESSEX, IG9 5SS. (Life Member)
FINLAY, Mr. Ross Frazer, BSc ACA *1996;* Renewable Energy Systems Ltd Beaufort Court, Egg Farm Lane, KINGS LANGLEY, HERTFORDSHIRE, WD4 8LR.
FINLAY, Mrs. Susan Wendy, FCA *1959;* Susan Finlay, 7 Helena Close, BARNET, HERTFORDSHIRE, EN4 0JA. (Life Member)
FINLAYSON, Mr. Graeme Thomson, ACA *2008;* Flat 3 Teviotdale House, 15 Parsonage Square, GLASGOW, G4 0TA.
FINLAYSON, Miss. Helen Louise, ACA *2010;* Ground Floor, 78 Priory Road, LONDON, NW6 3NT.
•FINLAYSON, Mrs. Monica Elaine StJohn, BSc FCA *1983;* FBR McGarry Harvey, 38-39 New Forest Enterprise Ctr, Rushington Business Park, Totton, SOUTHAMPTON, SO40 9LA.
•FINLAYSON, Mr. Neil Michael, BSc FCA DChA *1984;* Kingston Smith LLP, Devonshire House, 60 Goswell Road, LONDON, EC1M 7AD. See also Kingston Smith Limited Liability Partnership, Devonshire Corporate Services LLP and Kingston Smith Consulting LLP
FINLEY, Mr. Frank William, FCA *1950;* 35 Villa Rosa, Shrubbery Road, WESTON-SUPER-MARE, BS23 2JB. (Life Member)
FINLEY, Mr. Simon, BSc ACA *2004;* 11 Barnsley Way, Bourton-on-the-Water, CHELTENHAM, GLOUCESTERSHIRE, GL54 2GA.
FINLEY, Mr. Simon Gerard, ACA *1992;* 15 Chichele Road, OXTED, RH8 0AE.
FINLOW, Mr. Alexis John, MSc FCA *1992;* Castle House, Castle Hill Avenue, FOLKESTONE, CT20 2TN.
•FINN, Mr. Alexander William Galletly, BSc FCA *1987;* PricewaterhouseCoopers LLP, Hays Galleria, 1 Hays Lane, LONDON, SE1 2RD. See also PricewaterhouseCoopers
FINN, Mr. Andrew Mark, BA ACA *1992;* Totty Construction Group Limited, Woodland House, Woodland park Bradford Road, Chain Bar, CLECKHEATON, BD19 6BW.
FINN, Mrs. Annabella Jane, BA ACA *1988;* Deluxe Sticher International, Old Parish, Dungarvan, WATERFORD, COUNTY WATERFORD, IRELAND.
FINN, Miss. Anne Maria, BSc ACA *1997;* Salford Student Homes 24 Crescent, SALFORD, M5 4PF.
FINN, Mr. Anthony David, BA FCA *1975;* Apartment 4, 1 The Springs, Park Road, Bowdon, ALTRINCHAM, CHESHIRE WA14 3JH.
FINN, Mr. Anthony Harold, FCA *1963;* 2 Send Lodge, Send Road, Send, WOKING, SURREY, GU23 7EN. (Life Member)
•FINN, Mr. Anthony Harvey, BSc FCA *1971;* Purcells, 4 Quex Road, LONDON, NW6 4PJ.
•FINN, Mr. David Michael, FCA *1990;* RDP Newmans LLP, Lynwood House, 373/375 Station Road, HARROW, MIDDLESEX, HA1 2AW. See also Leonard Finn & Co Services Ltd
FINN, Mrs. Denise, FCA *1988;* Cherry Tree House, 32 Oast Road, OXTED, RH8 9DU.
FINN, Mrs. Diane Rachel, ACA *1997;* 124 Moreton Road, BUCKINGHAM, MK18 1PW.
FINN, Mr. Graham Robert, BSc ACA *1996;* Flat 7, 36 Buckingham Gate, LONDON, SW1E 6PB.
FINN, Mrs. Helen Lisa, BA(Hons) ACA *2001;* 17 Barrasford Close, ASHINGTON, NORTHUMBERLAND, NE63 8XT.
FINN, Mr. Joseph, BCom ACA *1992;* 7 Padua Road, BROMSGROVE, WORCESTERSHIRE, B60 2SF.
FINN, Miss. Kate Emily, ACA *2007;* 15 Wood Street, Horwich, BOLTON, BL6 6BN.
•FINN, Mrs. Katharine Elizabeth, BA ACA *1994;* PricewaterhouseCoopers LLP, 31 Great George Street, BRISTOL, BS1 5QD. See also PricewaterhouseCoopers
•FINN, Mr. Leonard Ian, FCA *1958;* Leonard Finn & Co Services Ltd, Brentmead House, Britannia Road, LONDON, N12 9RU. See also Shelley & Partners
FINN, Dr. Malcolm, BA ACA *2004;* Flat A, 10 Heathfield Park, LONDON, NW2 5JD.
•FINN, Mr. Mark Jeremy, BA ACA *1992;* MJ Finn & Co, Salters Brook Cottage, Stanton Wick, Pensford, BRISTOL, BS39 4DA.
FINN, Mr. Martin, BA ACA *2006;* 40 Wooburn Manor Park, Wooburn Green, HIGH WYCOMBE, BUCKINGHAMSHIRE, HP10 0ET.
FINN, Mr. Michael Anthony, MA FCA *1965;* Flat 24, 32 Grosvenor Street, LONDON, W1K 4QS.
FINN, Miss. Nicola Alison, MA(Oxon) BA ACA *2010;* KPMG, 10 Shelley Street, SYDNEY, NSW 2000, AUSTRALIA.
FINN, Mr. Owen Francis, FCA *1981;* MEMBER OF COUNCIL, 48 Spindlewood, Elloughton, BROUGH, HU15 1LL.
•①FINN, Mr. Paul Howard, FCA *1964;* Finn Associates (Businesscare) Limited, Central Administration, Tong Hall, Tong Lane, BRADFORD, WEST YORKSHIRE BD4 0RR.
•FINN, Mr. Russell A, BSc ACA *2009;* 28 Willow Green, KNUTSFORD, CHESHIRE, WA16 6AX.
FINN, Ms. Sarah Helen, BA ACA *1995;* Maliestraat 26, 3581 SN UTRECHT, NETHERLANDS.
FINN, Mr. Shaun Raymond, BSc FCA *1988;* The Covert, 11 Nottingham Road, Lowdham, NOTTINGHAM, NOTTINGHAMSHIRE, NG14 7AL.
FINN, Mrs. Simone Jari, BA ACA *1995;* 14 Dartmouth Park Avenue, LONDON, NW5 1JN.
FINN, Mr. Stuart Michael, BSc FCA *1975;* Handen FarmBank Road, Aldington ASHFORD, Kent, TN25 7DE.
FINN-KELCEY, Mr. John Richard Ernest, OBE FCA *1959;* 3 Tatchell Drive, Charing, ASHFORD, KENT, TN27 0GY. (Life Member)
FINNAMORE, Miss. Amanda Ellen, BA FCA *1992;* Sellen Tree, 15 Ferring Close, Ferring, WORTHING, BN12 5QT.
FINNAMORE, Mrs. Rebecca Jane, ACA *2008;* 7 Temperley Road, LONDON, SW12 8QQ.
•FINNEGAN, Mrs. Anne Caroline, BA ACA *1989;* Ashville Henderson, 33-35 Old Chester Road, Bebington, WIRRAL, MERSEYSIDE, CH63 7LE. See also Ashville Accountancy Limited
•FINNEGAN, Mr. James Joseph, MA(Oxon) FCA *2001;* Bishop Fleming, Stratus House, Emperor Way, Exeter Business Park, EXETER, EX1 3QS.
FINNEGAN, Mrs. Margaret Cecilia, ACA *1985;* 44 Copthorne Road, Croxley Green, RICKMANSWORTH, HERTFORDSHIRE, WD3 4AQ.
FINNEGAN, Mr. Patrick Anthony, FCA *1964;* Gull Cottage, SeaFront, WICKLOW, COUNTY WICKLOW, IRELAND.
•FINNEGAN, Mr. Patrick John, ACA *1982;* P J Finnegan, 10 Rutland Drive, Mickleover, DERBY, DE3 9FW.
FINNEGAN, Mr. Terence John, BA ACIB ACA *2001;* Roman Catholic Archdiocese of Liverpool, Lace, Croxteth Drive, Sefton Park, LIVERPOOL, L17 1AA.
•FINNEGAN, Mr. Vincent Michael, FCA *1963;* 4 Fulmer Chase, Stoke Common Road, Fulmer, SLOUGH, SL3 6HB.
FINNEGAN-BLAIR, Mrs. Claire Paula, BSc ACA *1998;* 68 Overtoun Terrace, Hataitai, WELLINGTON 6021, NEW ZEALAND.
•FINNEMORE, Mr. Jeffrey Michael, FCA *1971;* (Tax Fac), Finnemores Ltd, 10 St. Edwards Walk, Charlton Kings, CHELTENHAM, GLOUCESTERSHIRE, GL53 7RS. See also Finnemores
FINNERAN, Mr. Andrew Bernard, BSc ACA *1986;* Richmond Foods Plc, Leeming Bar Industrial Estate, NORTHALLERTON, NORTH YORKSHIRE, DL7 9UL.
FINNERTY, Mr. Jonathan Charles, BSc ACA *1991;* 6 The Crescent, Rutherway, Jericho, OXFORD, OX2 6QY.
FINNEY, Mrs. Diana, BA ACA *1999;* 9 Buckingham Drive, Kingsmead, NORTHWICH, CHESHIRE, CW9.
FINNEY, Mr. Guy Edward, BA ACA *1991;* Resolute Management Services Ltd Exchequer Court, 33 St. Mary Axe, LONDON, EC3A 8LL.
FINNEY, Mrs. Helen Elizabeth, BSc(Hons) ACA *2002;* 253 Whittingham Drive, Ramsbottom, BURY, LANCASHIRE, BL0 9NY.
FINNEY, Mr. Ian Robert, BA ACA *1996;* 67 Beech Avenue, Rode Heath, STOKE-ON-TRENT, ST7 3SH.
•FINNEY, Mr. James Joseph, FCA *1968;* J J Finney, 4 Chiltern Drive, Winstanley, WIGAN, WN3 6DY.
•FINNEY, Mr. Jeffrey Harry, FCA *1977;* with Barringtons Limited, 570-572 Etruria Road, NEWCASTLE, ST5 0SU.
FINNEY, Mr. Mark Ian, BA ACA *1989;* Top Floor Flat, 7 Belsize Avenue, Belsize Park, LONDON, NW3 4BL.
FINNEY, Mrs. Natalie Ellen, BSocSc ACA *2000;* 8 Lindrosa Road, SUTTON COLDFIELD, B74 3JY.
FINNEY, Miss. Rachel, BSc ACA *2010;* 51 Wrockwardine Road, Wellington, TELFORD, SHROPSHIRE, TF1 3DA.
FINNEY, Mr. Steven Terry, BA ACA *1985;* 631 International Parkway Suite 100, RICHARDSON, TX 75081, UNITED STATES.
FINNICK, Mr. John Reginald, LLB ACA ATII *1984;* Burness Solicitors, 50 Lothian Road, EDINBURGH, EH3 9WJ.
FINNIE, Miss. Katherine Louise, BA ACA *1993;* City of York Council, Mill House, North Street, YORK, YO1 6JQ.
FINNIE, Mr. Roger James, BSc FCA *1988;* Unit 6 1/Floor Cloud Nine, 9 Plunkett's Raod, THE PEAK, HONG KONG ISLAND, HONG KONG SAR.
•FINNIESTON, Miss. Catherine Mary, ACA *1987;* Finnieston Berry Partnership Limited, Europa House, 72-74 Northwood Street, BIRMINGHAM, B3 1TT.
FINNIGAN, Mr. Anthony James, ACA *2009;* 2 The Acorns, Wynchlands Crescent, ST. ALBANS, HERTFORDSHIRE, AL4 0XZ.
FINNIGAN, Mrs. Carol Ann, BA ACA *1983;* 15 Hawkswood Drive, Balsall Common, COVENTRY, CV7 7RD.
FINNIGAN, Mr. Liam Martin, BA(Hons) ACA *2004;* 7 Greenbank Road, Penwortham, PRESTON, PR1 9QN.
FINNIGAN, Mr. Robert David, BSc ACA *1983;* 15 Hawkswood Drive, Balsall Common, COVENTRY, CV7 7RD.
FINNIMORE, Mrs. Susan Marie, BSc ACA *1988;* 20 Dene Way, Ashurst, SOUTHAMPTON, SO40 7BX.
FINNING, Mr. Denis Sydney Robert, MA FCA *1971;* 44 Platts Lane, Hampstead, LONDON, NW3 7NT. (Life Member)
FINNIS, Mr. Martyn Stuart, ACA *1995;* 7 Mallards Way, Downswood, MAIDSTONE, KENT, ME15 8XH.
FINNITY, Mrs. Janet Elizabeth, BSc ACA *1987;* Chestnut House, Hollington, ASHBOURNE, DE6 3GB.
FINTA, Mr. Carl, BA ACA *1990;* The Old Barn House, Main Street, Thornganby, YORK, YO19 6DA.
FINUCANE, Mr. James Gerard, BA ACA *2008;* P.O. Box 6127, ABU DHABI, UNITED ARAB EMIRATES.
FIONDA, Mr. Ian, BSc ACA *2004;* C/O 66 Foxgloves, Coulby Newham, MIDDLESBROUGH, CLEVELAND, TS8 0XA.
FIORE, Miss. Fiorella, BSc ACA *1993;* Flat 9, 53 Drayton Gardens, South Kensington, LONDON, SW10 9RX.
FIRBAN, Mr. Nigel Howard, ACA *1981;* Personal Assurance Plc, John Ormond House, 899 Silbury Boulevard, MILTON KEYNES, BUCKINGHAMSHIRE, MK9 3XL.
FIRBAN, Mr. Thomas Norman, FCA *1951;* 460 Uppingham Road, LEICESTER, LE5 2GG. (Life Member)
•FIRBANK, Mr. Martin Andrew, BA(Hons) ACA *2003;* with Cooper Parry LLP, 14 Park Row, NOTTINGHAM, NG1 6GR.
FIRBANK, Mrs. Pamela Ruth, BSc ACA *1997;* 63 Church Drive, East Keswick, LEEDS, LS17 9EP.
FIRBANK, Mr. Steven, BSc ACA *1998;* 63 Church Drive, East Keswick, LEEDS, LS17 9EP.
FIREBRACE, Mr. James Peter Aylmer, BSc ACA *2000;* Catts Grove, Hadlow Down Road, CROWBOROUGH, EAST SUSSEX, TN6 3RG.
FIREBRACE, Mr. Patrick David Richard, LLB ACA *2001;* Beachcroft Llp Portwall Place, Portwall Lane, BRISTOL, BS1 6NA.
FIRKINS, Mr. Jonathan, BEng ACA *2002;* Flat 2, 4b Tyers Gate, LONDON, SE1 3HX.
FIRMAN, Mr. David Kenneth, ACA *2008;* Flat 14 Alaska Apartments, 22 Western Gateway, LONDON, E16 1BW.
FIRMAN, Miss. Ella, BSc ACA *2006;* Flat 2 Brooklands Court, Cavendish Road, LONDON, NW6 7XW.
•FIRMAN, Mr. Michael, FCA *1973;* Price Firman, Prince Consort House, Albert Embankment, LONDON, SE1 7TJ.
FIRMAN, Mr. Michael Peter Robert, FCA *1984;* Larkspur, 325 Eagle Park, Marton, MIDDLESBROUGH, TS8 9QR.
FIRMAN, Dr. Roger Andrew, FCA *1976;* 58 Birkdale, BEXHILL-ON-SEA, EAST SUSSEX, TN39 3TG.
FIRMIN, Mr. Barry Howard, FCA *1974;* Kingston Manor The Street, Kingston, LEWES, EAST SUSSEX, BN7 3PD.
•①FIRMIN, Mr. Mark Granville, BSc ACA MABRP *1996;* KPMG LLP, 1 The Embankment, Neville Street, LEEDS, LS1 4DW. See also KPMG Europe LLP
FIRMINGER, Mr. Marco Franco Emilio, BSc ACA *1990;* 8 Regency Gardens, WEYBRIDGE, SURREY, KT13 0DY.
FIRMSTON-WILLIAMS, Mr. Andrew Simon, BSc ACA *1985;* 30 Linkside, NEW MALDEN, SURREY, KT3 4LB.
FIRRELL, Mr. Philip David Rogerson, BA ACA *1990;* 9511 Greystone Parkway, BRECKSVILLE, OH 44141, UNITED STATES.
FIRTH, Mr. Alexander Jackson, BA FCA *1987;* 14 Kingfisher Close, Wheathampstead, ST.ALBANS, AL4 8JJ.
FIRTH, Mr. Alexander James, BA ACA *2004;* 50 Talfourd Avenue, READING, RG6 7BP.
FIRTH, Mrs. Alexandra Mary, BSc(Hons) ACA *1999;* 26 Gledhow Avenue, Roundhay, LEEDS, LS8 1LD.
FIRTH, Mr. Andrew, BSc ACA *2010;* 15 Dale Close, West Bridgford, NOTTINGHAM, NG2 6LH.
FIRTH, Mr. Andrew Gregory, BA FCA *1991;* 2, Heath Road, WEYBRIDGE, KT13 8AP.
•FIRTH, Mr. Andrew Timothy Robert, FCA *1974;* Garden Flat 92 Denbigh Street, LONDON, SW1V 2EX.
FIRTH, Miss. Ann, BA ACA *1987;* 22 Kingsway, WOKING, SURREY, GU21 6NU.
FIRTH, Mr. Arthur Gregory, FCA *1957;* Westridge House, Belvoir Close, Colsterworth, GRANTHAM, NG33 5JU. (Life Member)
FIRTH, The Revd. Barry, FCA *1960;* 51 Bolehill Park, Hove Edge, BRIGHOUSE, HD6 2RS. (Life Member)
FIRTH, Mr. Brian, FCA *1968;* 29 Hillston Close, Naisberry Park, HARTLEPOOL, TS26 0PE.
FIRTH, Mr. Brian Gilbert, BCom ACA *1992;* 28 North Road, Gedney Hill, SPALDING, LINCOLNSHIRE, PE12 0NL.
FIRTH, Mr. Christopher Neil, BA ACA *1988;* J Speak & Co Ltd, North Dean Mills, Stainland Road, HALIFAX, WEST YORKSHIRE HX4 8LS.
FIRTH, Mr. David, BSc FCA *1971;* with Sheards, Vernon House, 40 New North Road, HUDDERSFIELD, HD1 5LS.
FIRTH, Mr. David Andrew, BA FCA *1980;* 5 Meadow Croft, Barkisland, HALIFAX, WEST YORKSHIRE, HX4 0FB.
FIRTH, Prof. David Richard, ACA *1992;* School of Business, University of Montana, MISSOULA, MT 59812, UNITED STATES.
FIRTH, Mr. David Samuel Peter, BSc FCA *1986;* Woods Mill House, Shoreham Road, HENFIELD, BN5 9SD.
FIRTH, Mr. Dean, ACA *2008;* 40 Willington Road, SWINDON, SN25 2HB.
FIRTH, Mrs. Denise Jane, BA ACA *1993;* Cherry Trees, Childsbridge Lane, Seal, SEVENOAKS, TN15 0BU.
FIRTH, Mr. Edward Hugo Anson, BSc ACA *1992;* Financial Dynamics Ltd, 26 Southampton Buildings, LONDON, WC2A 1PB.
FIRTH, Mr. Graham Michael, FCA *1966;* Hunters Lodge, Abbots Road, Cinderford, GLOUCESTER, GL14 3BN.
FIRTH, Mr. James William, BA ACA *2009;* 26 Horkstow Road, BARTON-UPON-HUMBER, SOUTH HUMBERSIDE, DN18 5DZ.
FIRTH, Mrs. Janice, BA ACA *1989;* Ambridge, Braye Road, St. Sampson, GUERNSEY, GY2 4RD.
FIRTH, Mr. John Anthony, BA FCA *1985;* Ridgemount, 32 Talbot Avenue, Edgerton, HUDDERSFIELD, HD3 3BG.
FIRTH, Mr. John Barry, ACA ATII *1996;* (Tax Fac), 23 Pavilion Way, Meltham, HOLMFIRTH, WEST YORKSHIRE, HD9 5QN.

FIRTH, Mr. John Michael, FCA *1960;* Green Ridge, Tockwith Lane, Cowthorpe, WETHERBY, LS22 5EZ. (Life Member)

FIRTH, Mr. Jonathan Hodgson, MBA BTech FCA *1977;* Apartment 14 Hush House, Weaver Street, CHESTER, CH1 2BQ.

FIRTH, Mr. Jonathan James, BA ACA *2003;* Inisfail, La Route Des Cotils, Grouville, JERSEY, JE3 9AP.

FIRTH, Mrs. Kate, BSc(Hons) ACA DChA *2004;* with Crowe Clark Whitehill LLP, Aquis House, 49-51 Blagrave Street, READING, RG1 1PL.

•FIRTH, Mr. Martin, BA(Hons) ACA *2001;* Chipchase Manners, 384 Linthorpe Road, MIDDLESBROUGH, TS5 6HA. See also Chipchase, Manners & Co

•FIRTH, Mr. Michael, BA ACA *1993;* 28 Colwyn Loop, Tapping, PERTH, WA 6065, AUSTRALIA.

FIRTH, Mr. Michael Arthur, FCA *1969;* Dept of Finance & Insurance, Lingnan University, TUEN MUN, NEW TERRITORIES, HONG KONG SAR.

•FIRTH, Miss. Nicola, BSc(Hons) ACA MAAT *2006;* (Tax Fac), Business Focus & Systems Limited, 4 Chevin Mill, Leeds Road, OTLEY, WEST YORKSHIRE, LS21 1BT.

FIRTH, Mr. Patrick Anthony Seymour, BSc ACA *1991;* Ambridge, Braye Du Valle, St Sampson, GUERNSEY, GY2 4RD.

FIRTH, Mr. Paul Graham, FCA *1977;* Aedas, Norwich Union House, High Street, HUDDERSFIELD, HD1 2LF.

FIRTH, Mr. Paul Jonathan Mark, BA FCA *1992;* K & K Electronics EAD, 361 Tsarigradsko Chaussee Blvd, 1138 SOFIA, BULGARIA.

FIRTH, Mr. Paul Malcolm, BSc ACA MBA *1983;* 23 Rue Capouillet, B-1060 BRUSSELS, BELGIUM.

FIRTH, Mr. Peter, FCA *1975;* P O Box 529, Ashgrove, BRISBANE, QLD 4060, AUSTRALIA.

FIRTH, Mr. Peter Charles, BSc ACA *1991;* 470 W 24 Street, Apt 2B, NEW YORK, NY 10011, UNITED STATES.

FIRTH, Mr. Peter James, BEng ACA *1999;* 49 Culcheth Hall Drive, Culcheth, WARRINGTON, WA3 4PT.

FIRTH, Mr. Richard Paul, MBA ACA *1994;* 6302 Sharps Drive, CENTREVILLE, VA 20121, UNITED STATES.

FIRTH, Mr. Robert Edward, FCA *1981;* 18 Coudray Road, SOUTHPORT, PR9 9NL.

FIRTH, Mrs. Sally Ann, FCA CTA *1975;* (Tax Fac), Urquhart Dykes & Lord LLP, Chartered Patent Attorneys, Tower North Central, Merrion Way, LEEDS, LS2 8PA.

FIRTH, Mrs. Sarah Louise, BA ACA *2004;* SR Technics Limited, Diamond Hangar, Long Border Road, London Stansted Airport, STANSTED, ESSEX CM24 1RE.

FIRTH, Mrs. Susan Louise, BSc ACA *1989;* Burcot House, Headley Road, Grayshott, HINDHEAD, GU26 6JG.

FIRTH, Mr. Tony, BSc ACA *1999;* 26 Gledhow Avenue, LEEDS, LS8 1LD.

FIRTH, Miss. Victoria Mary, MA ACA *1995;* 54 Sutton Court, Sutton Court Road, Chiswick, LONDON, W4 3JE.

FISCHEL, Mr. David Andrew, BA ACA *1983;* Capital Shopping Centres Group Plc, 40 Broadway, LONDON, SW1H 0BT.

•FISH, Mr. Alistair John, ACA *1989;* MA Partners LLP, 7 The Close, NORWICH, NORFOLK, NR1 4DJ.

FISH, Mr. Andrew Christopher, FCA *1993;* Colbourne Cottage, Prince Albert Road, St. Peter Port, GUERNSEY, GY1 1EY.

FISH, Mr. Andrew John, BSc ACA *1993;* Cherry Tree Cottage, Manor Close, East Horsley, LEATHERHEAD, KT24 6SA.

FISH, Mr. Andrew Stuart, BA ACA *1999;* Stadium City Ltd, Welton Grange, Welton, BROUGH, NORTH HUMBERSIDE, HU15 1NB.

FISH, Mr. Angus Malcolm Alexander, MA ACA *1991;* 55 Highfield Avenue, HARPENDEN, HERTFORDSHIRE, AL5 5TZ.

FISH, Mr. Brian, FCA *1959;* Merrydown Grange Drive, Wooburn Green, HIGH WYCOMBE, HP10 0QD.

FISH, Mr. Brian Howard, FCA *1953;* 14 Stoke Hill, Stoke Bishop, BRISTOL, BS9 1JH. (Life Member)

FISH, Mrs. Caroline Kathryn Mary, FCA *1973;* 3 Summer Avenue, EAST MOLESEY, KT8 9LU.

FISH, Mr. Christopher Timothy Galloway, BSc FCA *1969;* Le Jardin, Rue Du Torval, Castel, GUERNSEY, GY5 7DD.

•FISH, Mr. Colin Andrew Everitt, BSc FCA *1989;* (Tax Fac), Lovewell Blake LLP, 102 Prince of Wales Road, NORWICH, NORFOLK, NR1 1NY.

FISH, Mr. David, ACA *2007;* 7 Glendale Road, North Seaton, ASHINGTON, NORTHUMBERLAND, NE63 9SN.

FISH, Mrs. Diane, BSc ACA *1987;* 137 Marine Drive Rhos on Sea, COLWYN BAY, CLWYD, LL28 4HY.

FISH, Mr. Ian Peter, BSc ACA *1995;* 73 Bishops Close, Thorpe St Andrew, NORWICH, NR7 0DY.

FISH, Mrs. Jane Belinda, BSc ACA *1993;* 55 Highfield Avenue, HARPENDEN, HERTFORDSHIRE, AL5 5TZ.

FISH, Mr. Martin Warwick, FCA *1966;* Brooklands, Station Road, NORTH FERRIBY, NORTH HUMBERSIDE, HU14 3DJ. (Life Member)

FISH, Mr. Michael Alan, ACA *1982;* Crown Dry Dock, Tower Street, HULL, HU9 1TY.

FISH, Mr. Nigel Timothy, BA ACA *1993;* Capita Registrars Ltd, The Registry, 34 Beckenham Road, BECKENHAM, KENT, BR3 4TU.

•FISH, Mr. Peter John, FCA *1961;* Peter J Fish, Culvers Hill, Rowington, WARWICK, CV35 7AB.

FISH, Mr. Robert Nigel Buckland, FCA *1976;* Stromness, Sandy Lane, Kingswood, TADWORTH, KT20 6NQ.

FISH, Mr. Rory Stuart, LLB ACA *1987;* 137 Marine Drive Rhos on Sea, COLWYN BAY, CLWYD, LL28 4HY.

FISH, Mr. Stephen, FCA *1970;* 7 Church Road, Sevington, ASHFORD, KENT, TN24 0LE.

•FISH, Mr. Stephen James, BSc ACA *1995;* Ernst & Young d.o.o, Milana Sachsa 1, 10000 ZAGREB, CROATIA. See also Ernst & Young Europe LLP

•FISH, Mr. Stephen John, BSc ACA *1982;* PricewaterhouseCoopers LLP, 31 Great George Street, BRISTOL, BS1 5QD. See also PricewaterhouseCoopers

FISH, Mr. Stephen Robert, BA ACA *1994;* 5 Percy Drive, Airmyn, GOOLE, DN14 8NZ.

FISH, Mr. Tom Hilton, FCA *1954;* 59 Ilsham Road, Wellswood, TORQUAY, TQ1 2JF. (Life Member)

FISHBURN, Mr. Ben Graham Frederick, BSc ACA *2002;* 23 Glebe Court, Rothwell, LEEDS, LS26 0WR.

FISHBURN, Mrs. Margaret Sally Ann, FCA *1971;* 10 Old Convent, Moat Road, EAST GRINSTEAD, WEST SUSSEX, RH19 3RS.

•FISHBURN, Mr. Michael James Engledew, BSc ACA *1990;* (Tax Fac), 108 Taxes Limited, Northend, Malbrook Road, Putney, LONDON, SW15 6UH.

FISHBURN, Mr. Paul Engledew, FCA *1957;* Oak Farm, Hog Lane, Ashley Green, CHESHAM, BUCKINGHAMSHIRE, HP5 3PS. (Life Member)

•FISHBURN, Mr. Simon Ephraim, BA FCA *1972;* AIMS - Simon Fishburn FCA, 10 The Old Convent, EAST GRINSTEAD, WEST SUSSEX, RH19 3RS.

FISHBURNE, Mrs. Fiona, MA FCA *1991;* 24 Star Avenue Stoke Gifford, BRISTOL, BS34 8RG.

FISHBURNE, Mr. Neil Robert, BEng FCA *1991;* 24 Star Avenue, Stoke Gifford, BRISTOL, BS34 8RG.

•FISHEL, Mr. David Harvey, FCA CTA *1978;* David Fishel Accountancy Services Limited, 59A Brent Street, LONDON, NW4 2EA.

FISHER, Mr. Alexander Richard, BSc ACA *2001;* State Street, No. 78 Sir John Rogersons Quay, DUBLIN 2, COUNTY DUBLIN, IRELAND.

FISHER, Mrs. Alison Jane, BA ACA *1991;* The Wynns, Chapel Street, Welford-on-avon, STRATFORD-UPON-AVON, CV37 8PX.

FISHER, Mr. Andrew Charles, BA FCA *1983;* Provident Financial Plc, Colonnade, Sunbridge Road, BRADFORD, WEST YORKSHIRE, BD1 2LQ.

FISHER, Mr. Andrew James, BA ACA *1993;* 70 Marina Avenue, Great Sankey, WARRINGTON, WA5 1JQ.

FISHER, Mr. Andrew Jonathan, MA FCA *1994;* 801 Glenferrie Road, HAWTHORN, VIC 3122, AUSTRALIA.

FISHER, Mr. Andrew Leslie, FCA *1973;* 5 Allandale Avenue, LONDON, N3 3PJ.

FISHER, Mr. Andrew Mark, BEng ACA *2000;* 4418 Village Forest Drive, SUGARLAND, TX 77479, UNITED STATES.

•FISHER, Mr. Andrew Simon, ACA FCCA *2008;* John Graham & Co, 30 Birkenhead Road, Hoylake, WIRRAL, CH47 3BW.

FISHER, Mr. Andrew Simon David, BEng ACA *1996;* 45 The Stables, Wynyard, BILLINGHAM, TS22 5SG.

•FISHER, Mr. Andrew Stephen, BA FCA *1987;* Alanbrookes Ltd, PO Box 258, STROUD, GLOUCESTERSHIRE, GL6 8WZ.

FISHER, Mr. Angus William Murray, ACA *1980;* Coledown House, Vicarage Lane, Curdridge, SOUTHAMPTON, SO32 2DP.

FISHER, Mrs. Anna Katherine, BA FCA *2000;* 181 Broad Lane, HAMPTON, MIDDLESEX, TW12 3BT.

FISHER, Mrs. Anne, FCA *1967;* Bela House, Beetham Road, MILNTHORPE, CUMBRIA, LA7 7QR.

FISHER, Mr. Anthony John, FCA *1952;* 14 Bluecoat Pond, Christs Hospital, HORSHAM, WEST SUSSEX, RH13 0NW. (Life Member)

FISHER, Mr. Anthony Robert, FCA *1972;* 35 South Avenue, EASTBOURNE, BN20 8PD.

•FISHER, Mr. Brian Jonathan, FCA *1971;* Fisher Berger & Associates, Devonshire House, 582 Honeypot Lane, STANMORE, MIDDLESEX, HA7 1JS. See also Fisher Brian

FISHER, Mr. Brian Shillson, BA FCA *1950;* 20 The Glebe, Queen Camel, YEOVIL, BA22 7PR. (Life Member)

FISHER, Mr. Carl John, ACA *1991;* Boss House Barn The Common Dunston, NORWICH, NR14 8PF.

FISHER, Mrs. Catherine Emma Jane, BA ACA *1992;* 1160 Pittsford Victor Road, PITTSFORD, NY 14534, UNITED STATES.

•FISHER, Mrs. Catherine Jane, BA ACA *1994;* C.J. Fisher & Co., 11 Oakwood Road, Henleaze, BRISTOL, BS9 4NP.

FISHER, Mrs. Catherine Mary, BSc ACA *1990;* 815 University Avenue, PALO ALTO, CA 94301, UNITED STATES.

FISHER, Mr. Charles John Hamilton, FCA *1968;* 15 Foskett Road, LONDON, SW6 3LY.

FISHER, Mr. Christian Alexander, ACA *2009;* 46 Northway Road, LONDON, SE5 9AN.

FISHER, Mr. Christopher Nigel, BA ACA *1998;* Deloitte, Rosenheimerplatz 4, 81669 MUNICH, GERMANY.

FISHER, Mr. Christopher Paul, FCA *1980;* Stewart Group, Alex Stewart (Assayers) Ltd Caddick Road, Knowsley Business Park, PRESCOT, MERSEYSIDE, L34 9HP.

FISHER, Mr. Darren John, BA ACA *1994;* 97 Lucien Road, LONDON, SW17 8HS.

FISHER, Mr. David, FCA *1954;* 62 Mount Stewart Avenue, HARROW, MIDDLESEX, HA3 0JU. (Life Member)

FISHER, Mr. David Craig, FCA *1963;* 3 Somerset Court, BELMONT, CA 94002, UNITED STATES. (Life Member)

FISHER, Mr. David Frank, BA ACA *1984;* 12a Bridge Road, CHERTSEY, KT16 8JL.

•FISHER, Mr. David Henry, MSc FCA CF *1972;* Grant Thornton, Al Fattan Currency House, Dubai International Centre, PO Box 482017, DUBAI, UNITED ARAB EMIRATES.

•FISHER, Mr. David John, FCA *1973;* Fisher Wilkinson, 44 Cheltenham Mount, HARROGATE, HG1 1DL.

FISHER, Mr. David John, BSc(Econ) ACA *1999;* 3 Dereham Road, Hingham, NORWICH, NR9 4HU.

•FISHER, Mr. Don, MA FCA *1981;* (Tax Fac), Don Fisher & Co, 309 Winston House, 2 Dollis Park, Finchley, LONDON, N3 1HF. See also DF Taxation Services Ltd

FISHER, Miss. Dorothy Jane, BA ACA *1981;* Lanntair, Cowden, DOLLAR, CLACKMANNANSHIRE, FK14 7PJ.

•FISHER, Mrs. Elaine Denise, BSc ACA *1990;* EDF Accountancy, 78 Brocket Road, WELWYN GARDEN CITY, HERTFORDSHIRE, AL8 7TU.

FISHER, Miss. Eleanor Grace, BSc FCA *2001;* PO Box 1102, GEORGETOWN, GRAND CAYMAN, KY1-1102, CAYMAN ISLANDS.

FISHER, Mr. Geoffrey Hugh, FCA *1972;* Little Timewell, Morebath, TIVERTON, DEVON, EX16 9AN. (Life Member)

•FISHER, Mr. Geoffrey Vincent, FCA *1979;* G.V. Fisher FCA, Flint House, 58 Worple Road, EPSOM, SURREY, KT18 5EL.

FISHER, Mr. Geoffrey William, FCA *1966;* Cruachan, Le Mont Isaac, St. Lawrence, JERSEY, JE3 1GB. (Life Member)

•FISHER, Mr. Guy Norman, MA FCA *1973;* Shipleys LLP, 10 Orange Street, Haymarket, LONDON, WC2H 7DQ.

FISHER, Mr. Hugo Hamilton, BA ACA *1996;* 87 Finlay Street, LONDON, SW6 6HF.

FISHER, Mrs. Jacqueline, BA ACA *1996;* 126 Quebec Quay, LIVERPOOL, L3 4ER.

FISHER, Mr. James, MA ACA *2003;* 246 High Street, Wickham Market, WOODBRIDGE, SUFFOLK, IP13 0RF.

FISHER, Mr. James Michael, BCom ACA *2003;* 2 Charlotte Close, ST. ALBANS, HERTFORDSHIRE, AL4 0TS.

FISHER, Mr. James Stephen, ACA *2010;* 11 Glencoe Road, WEYBRIDGE, KT13 8JY.

FISHER, Mr. John Albert Louis, FCA *1977;* Driftwood, Hook Park Road, Warsash, SOUTHAMPTON, SO31 9HA.

FISHER, Mr. John David, BCom ACA *1980;* 151 Cowan Way, WIDNES, WA8 5BW.

FISHER, Mr. John David, BSc ACA *1986;* KPMG Somekh Chaikin, 17 Ha'arba'a Street, TEL AVIV, 64739, ISRAEL.

•FISHER, Mr. John James Norman Waldron, BA FCA *1991;* PricewaterhouseCoopers LLP, 7 More London Riverside, LONDON, SE1 2RT. See also PricewaterhouseCoopers

FISHER, Mr. John Keith, MA ACA *1999;* 4 Eaton Park Road, COBHAM, KT11 2JH.

•FISHER, Mr. John Liam, FCA *1973;* J. L. Fisher, 15 Portsmouth Court, Harbour Views, GIBRALTAR, 111111, GIBRALTAR.

•FISHER, Mr. John Michael, FCA *1975;* (Tax Fac), Deeks Evans, 3 Boyne Park, TUNBRIDGE WELLS, TN4 8EN.

•①FISHER, Mr. John Peter, ACA *2001;* with Debt Free Direct Limited, Fairclough House, Church Street, Adlington, CHORLEY, LANCASHIRE PR7 4EX.

•FISHER, Mr. John Richard, BSc FCA DChA *1984;* Roffe Swayne, Ashcombe Court, Woolsack Way, GODALMING, GU7 1LQ.

FISHER, Mr. John Ronald, FCA *1966;* 35 St. Thomas Road, Mount Merrion, DUBLIN, COUNTY DUBLIN, IRELAND. (Life Member)

FISHER, Mr. John Stuart, FCA *1965;* 2 St Lucia Avenue, 4th Floor, St Andrew, KINGSTON 5, JAMAICA.

FISHER, Mr. Jonathan, ACA *2010;* Flat 2, 3 Cleve Road, LONDON, NW6 3RG.

FISHER, Mr. Jonathan David, BSc ACA *1983;* 36 Shelley Drive, Broadbridge Heath, HORSHAM, RH12 3NT.

FISHER, Mr. Jonathan David, BSc ACA *1999;* (Tax Fac), Warren Barn Church Lane, Gawsworth, MACCLESFIELD, CHESHIRE, SK11 9QY.

FISHER, Mr. Joseph Timothy, FCA *1962;* Brook Cottage, School Road, Bursledon, SOUTHAMPTON, SO31 8BW.

FISHER, Mr. Julian, BSc ACA MBA *1997;* 145 West 67 Street, Apt 41B, NEW YORK, NY 10023, UNITED STATES.

FISHER, Miss. Karen, BSc ACA *2007;* (Tax Fac), Chavereys, Mall House, The Mall, FAVERSHAM, ME13 8JL.

FISHER, Mrs. Karen Laura, BSc ACA CTA *2000;* 79b Riddlesdown Road, PURLEY, CR8 1DH.

FISHER, Mrs. Katherine, BA ACA *2002;* 95 Totterdown Road, WESTON-SUPER-MARE, AVON, BS23 4LN.

FISHER, Mrs. Kathryn Grace, ACA *2007;* with Baker Tilly, The Steam Mill, Steam Mill Street, CHESTER, CH3 5AN.

FISHER, Miss. Katie Louise, ACA *2008;* Pricewaterhousecoopers The Atrium, St. Georges Street, NORWICH, NR3 1AG.

FISHER, Mr. Kevin, ACA MAAT *2003;* MGL Group Limited, Davison House, Rennys Lane, DURHAM, DH1 2RS.

•FISHER, Mr. Kevin Christopher, BA FCA CTA *1986;* Myrus Smith, Norman House, 8 Burnell Road, SUTTON, SURREY, SM1 4BW.

FISHER, Mr. Kieron, MSc BA ACA *2003;* 20 Blenheim Park Road, SOUTH CROYDON, CR2 6BB.

FISHER, Mrs. Kirsty Charlotte, BSc ACA *2006;* 11 Geneva Crescent, Crowle, WORCESTER, WR7 4AW.

•FISHER, Miss. Laura Jayne, ACA *2006;* LJ Accountancy Services Ltd, 45 Riversleigh Drive, STOURBRIDGE, WEST MIDLANDS, DY8 4YQ.

FISHER, Mr. Mark Richard, BSc ARCS ACA *1987;* The Lane, Butts Lane, EASTBOURNE, EAST SUSSEX, BN20 9EP.

FISHER, Mr. Martin Henry McIntosh, FCA *1953;* Thorington Cottage, Thorington Street, Stoke By Nayland, COLCHESTER, CO6 4SP. (Life Member)

FISHER, Mr. Michael John, FCA *1978;* 88 Harnham Road, SALISBURY, SP2 8JW.

FISHER, Mr. Michael Lawrence, BA ACA *1992;* 12 Dalcross Way, DUNFERMLINE, KY12 7RT.

•FISHER, Mrs. Michelle, BSc FCA *1984;* Sobell Rhodes LLP, Monument House, 215 Marsh Road, PINNER, MIDDLESEX, HA5 5NE. See also Expecto Patronum Limited

FISHER, Miss. Michelle Sian, BSc ACA *2003;* Technical Department, Deloitte Touche Tohmatsu, 35/F One Pacific Place, 88 Queensway, Admiralty, Hong Kong ADMIRALTY HONG KONG ISLAND HONG KONG SAR.

FISHER, Mr. Nicholas Stephen, BA FCA *1996;* 5 The Foxes, WIRRAL, MERSEYSIDE, CH61 7YH.

FISHER, Mrs. Nicola Jane, BSc ACA CTA *1983;* Woodvale Cottage, Box, STROUD, GLOUCESTERSHIRE, GL6 9HW.

•FISHER, Mrs. Nicola Jane, BA ACA *1980;* (Tax Fac), Nicola Fisher Financial Planning Limited, 2 Inchford Close, NUNEATON, WARWICKSHIRE, CV11 6UF.

FISHER, Mrs. Olwen, BSc ACA *1996;* 87 Finlay Street, LONDON, SW6 6HF.

•FISHER, Mr. Paul James, PhD MA FCA *1983;* Coulston House, 24 Coulston, WESTBURY, BA13 4NY.

FISHER, Mrs. Paula, BA ACA *1988;* 13 Brook Street, Whiston, ROTHERHAM, SOUTH YORKSHIRE, S60 4HU.

•FISHER, Mr. Philip, FCA *1976;* (Tax Fac), Fisher & Company Limited, Kingfisher House, 65 Market Place, Market Weighton, YORK, YO43 3AN.

FISHER, Mrs. Rachael Anne, BSocSc ACA AMCT *1993;* Keypoint, Unit 5 West Point Row, Great Park Road Bradley Stoke, BRISTOL, BS32 4QG.

FISHER, Miss. Rebecca, BSc ACA MAAT *2010;* 3 Meadowgate Lane, SPALDING, LINCOLNSHIRE, PE11 1NF.

FISHER, Mr. Richard Ian Brook, FCA *1969;* 4 Victoria Mews, 7 Balfour Road, WEYBRIDGE, SURREY, KT13 8JB.

FISHER, Mr. Richard John, ACA *2008;* Riversdale, Bristol Road, MALMESBURY, SN16 0QQ.

FISHER, Mr. Richard John, BSc ACA *1999;* 132 Trentham Street, Southfields, LONDON, SW18 5DJ.

•FISHER, Mr. Richard Welby, ACA *1982;* (Tax Fac), Baker Tilly Tax & Advisory Services LLP, Spring Park House, Basing View, BASINGSTOKE, HAMPSHIRE, RG21 4HG. See also Baker Tilly UK Audit LLP

FISHER, Mr. Robert Arthur, FCA *1951;* 2 Arnesby Avenue, SALE, M33 2WJ. (Life Member)

FISHER, Mr. Robert Christopher Aldridge, FCA *1971;* 4 Treesdale Close, Birkdale, SOUTHPORT, MERSEYSIDE, PR8 2EL.

FISHER, Mr. Robert Eric John, FCA *1961;* 105 Dorridge Road, Dorridge, SOLIHULL, B93 8BP. (Life Member)

FISHER, Mr. Robert John, BA(Hons) ACA *2000;* 103 Thorndike Avenue, Alvaston, DERBY, DE24 8NY.

FISHER, Mr. Robert Stewart, FCA *1964;* Greenways Sunset Lane, West Chiltington, PULBOROUGH, WEST SUSSEX, RH20 2NY. (Life Member)

FISHER, Mr. Rodney Brian Neville, FCA *1964;* 3 St. Marys Road, LISS, GU33 7AH. (Life Member)

FISHER, Mr. Roland Barnabas Spencer, MA ACA *1998;* Gastin Development, Hazeley Enterprise Park, Hazeley Road, Twyford, WINCHESTER, HAMPSHIRE SO21 1QA.

FISHER, Mr. Roy, FCA *1970;* Phoenix Gaming Ltd, 92 Lupus Street, LONDON, SW1V 3HH.

FISHER, Mrs. Sacha Jayne, BSc(Hons) ACA PGCE *2003;* 39 Reynes Drive, Oakley, BEDFORD, MK43 7SL.

FISHER, Mrs. Sally-Anne, BSc ACA *1990;* 77 Langfield Road, Knowle, SOLIHULL, B93 9PS.

FISHER, Mrs. Sara Louise, BSc ACA *2002;* Windyridge Mill Lane, Fenny Compton, SOUTHAM, CV47 2YF.

•FISHER, Mr. Scott Alexander, BSc ACA *1994;* C.J. Fisher & Co., 11 Oakwood Road, Henleaze, BRISTOL, BS9 4NP.

•FISHER, Mr. Simon Charles, MA FCA *1975;* Beech House, Moorend Lane, Slimbridge, GLOUCESTER, GL2 7DG.

FISHER, Mr. Simon James, MA FCA *1975;* RSM Ashvir, PO Box 349, NAIROBI, 00606, KENYA.

FISHER, Mrs. Sonia Carol, BSc ACA *2005;* 3 Blackbrook Walk, PAIGNTON, DEVON, TQ4 7NE.

FISHER, Mr. Stephen Mark, MA ACA PGCE DChA *2002;* 9 Sunnycroft Road, LONDON, SE25 4TB.

FISHER, Mr. Stephen Martin, BA ACA *1986;* 30 Collingwood Avenue, SURBITON, SURREY, KT5 9PU.

FISHER, Mr. Stephen Paul, BSc ACA *1998;* Willow Grange Broompark, Torphichen, BATHGATE, WEST LOTHIAN, EH48 4NL.

FISHER, Mr. Thomas Lomond Elliott Lewis, BA ACA *1996;* Flat 28 Lavender Court, Lavender Close, LEATHERHEAD, KT22 8LE.

FISHER, Mr. Toby Christopher, BSc ACA *2001;* 39 Reynes Drive, Oakley, BEDFORD, MK43 7SL.

FISHER, Mr. Wayne Gary, BA ACA *1994;* 20a Quarry Street, LIVERPOOL, L25 6HE.

FISHER, Mr. William Shelly, FCA *1970;* 40 The Close, NORWICH, NR1 4EG.

FISHER, Mr. William Thomas, FCA *1972;* 33 Essex Court, Station Road, LONDON, SW13 0ER. (Life Member)

FISHER, Mr. William Thomas, BSc FCA *1981;* The Square House, Churt Road, HINDHEAD, GU26 6HY.

•FISHLEIGH, Mr. Martin John, FCA *1968;* (Tax Fac), Martin J. Fishleigh, Mount Cottage, Mount Pleasant, Westleigh, BIDEFORD, EX39 4LJ.

FISHLEY, Mr. Simon Mark, BA ACA *2006;* Travessa Percy Withers 50, Apt 302, CURITIBA, 80240-190 PARANA STATE, BRAZIL.

FISHLOCK, Mrs. Maria, BSc ACA *1989;* 53 Upton Close, Barnwood, GLOUCESTER, GL4 3EX.

FISHLOCK, Mr. Martin Gerard John, MSc FCA *1988;* 35 Woodcote Road, WOLVERHAMPTON, WV6 8LP.

FISHLOCK, Mr. William John, FCA *1968;* 41 Windsor Road, SWINDON, SN3 1JP.

•FISHMAN, Mr. Irvin, FCA *1975;* Montpelier Audit Limited, Montpelier House, 62-66 Deansgate, MANCHESTER, M3 2EN. See also Montpelier Professional (West End) Ltd

FISHMAN, Mr. Laurence, BA ACA *2006;* Auerbach Hope, Epatra House, 58-60 Berners Street, LONDON, W1T 3JS.

•①FISHMAN, Mr. Martin, BA FCA *1979;* Ernst & Young LLP, 1 More London Place, LONDON, SE1 2AF. See also Ernst & Young Europe LLP

FISHMAN, Mr. Robert Scott, ACA *2008;* 7 Acorn Terrace, Archway Road, LONDON, N6 4BF.

FISHPOOL, Mr. Paul, FCA *1966;* 121 Hadham Road, BISHOP'S STORTFORD, CM23 2QG. (Life Member)

FISHWICK, Mr. Anthony Noel John, FCA *1957;* 74 Moss Lane, Maghull, LIVERPOOL, L31 9AQ. (Life Member)

FISHWICK, Mr. Colin Andrew, BA ACA MBA *1989;* Rue du Stade 42, 68220 LEYMEN, FRANCE.

FISHWICK, Mr. Ian Guy, BA ACA *1986;* 7 Bishops Close, Bowdon, ALTRINCHAM, CHESHIRE, WA14 3NB.

FISK, Mr. Adrian Richard, BA FCA *1992;* 32 Ballingdon Road, LONDON, SW11 6AJ.

FISK, Mr. Christopher Jeffery, MEng ACA CTA *2005;* Armajaro Trading Limited, 6th Floor Nightingale House, 65 Curzon Street, LONDON, W1J 8PE.

FISK, Mrs. Claire, BA(Hons) ACA *2000;* 7 Baldock Road, LETCHWORTH GARDEN CITY, HERTFORDSHIRE, SG6 3LB.

FISK, Mr. David Robert, BA ACA *1995;* 59 Margravine Gardens, LONDON, W6 8RN.

FISK, Mr. Frank, ACA *2010;* 13 Lower Millfield, DUNMOW, CM6 1EN.

FISK, Mr. Graham Martin, BA FCA MCT *1984;* 29 School Lane, Chalfont St. Peter, GERRARDS CROSS, SL9 9AZ.

FISK, Miss. Jennifer Clare, BSc ACA *1990;* with PricewaterhouseCoopers LLP, 1 Embankment Place, LONDON, WC2N 6RH.

FISK, Mr. Michael George, FCA *1974;* 3 Parr Avenue, East Ewell, EPSOM, KT17 2RW.

FISK, Mr. Richard Keay, FCA *1960;* New Timbers, 61 Plainwood Close, CHICHESTER, PO19 5YB. (Life Member)

FISK, Miss. Teresa Mary, MA ACA *1994;* 5 Randall Road, Cliftonwood, BRISTOL, BS8 4TP.

FISON, Mr. David Robert, FCA *1965;* Vine Cottage, 38 Ham Common, RICHMOND, TW10 7JG. (Life Member)

FISON, Mr. Jonathan Rupert, BSc ACA *1991;* Freshfields, Falkenham, IPSWICH, IP10 0QY.

FISZZON, Mr. Michael John, FCA *1960;* 20 Golf Close, STANMORE, HA7 2PP.

FITCH, Mr. Alexander Stuart, BSc ACA *2009;* 97 Test Road, Sompting, LANCING, WEST SUSSEX, BN15 0EP.

•FITCH, Mrs. Anna Louise, BA ACA *2004;* DNA Logistics Limited, 2 Toft Villas, Kites Hardwick, RUGBY, WARWICKSHIRE, CV23 8AD.

•FITCH, Mr. Ian Robert, FCA *1990;* (Tax Fac), Larking Gowen, King Street House, 15 Upper King Street, NORWICH, NR3 1RB. See also Larking Gowen Corporate Finance Limited

FITCH, Mr. Joshua Edward Peregrine, BA ACA *1998;* 27 East Street, Rippingale, BOURNE, LINCOLNSHIRE, PE10 0SS.

FITCH, Mr. Michael, BA FCA *1969;* 15 Old School Close, Melrose Road, Merton Park, LONDON, SW19 3HY.

FITCH, Mr. Raymond Kenneth, FCA CTA *1976;* 42 The Drive, LOUGHTON, ESSEX, IG10 1HG.

FITCH, Mr. Richard Evelyn Murray, FCA CTA *1963;* The Old Vicarage, 25 Beauchamp Hill, LEAMINGTON SPA, CV32 5NS.

FITCH, Mr. Ronald, FCA *1958;* 16 Beech Mews, Devonshire Park RoadDavenport, STOCKPORT, SK2 6LB. (Life Member)

FITCHETT, Mr. David John, BSc FCA *1977;* 22 Lynwood Heights, RICKMANSWORTH, HERTFORDSHIRE, WD3 4ED.

FITCHETT, Mrs. Zoe Maria, BSc ACA *2005;* 6 Ingham Road, West Timperley, ALTRINCHAM, CHESHIRE, WA14 5PX.

FITCHFORD, Mr. Andrew Michael John, BA ACA *1991;* The Old House, The Green, Tanworth-in-Arden, SOLIHULL, B94 5AJ.

•FITT, Mr. Peter Wilfrid Edgar, FCA *1971;* Peter Fitt, 7 Coast Road, West Mersea, COLCHESTER, CO5 8QE.

•FITTALL, Mr. Colin John, BA FCA *1991;* Sturt Cottage, 24 Sturt Road, HASLEMERE, SURREY, GU27 3SD.

FITTER, Mr. Ian Paul, BA ACA *1983;* Harvington Properties Ltd, 417 Finchley Road, LONDON, NW3 6HJ.

FITTER, Mr. Richard John, MA(oxon) ACA *2008;* 20 Barkham Terrace, LONDON, SE1 7PS.

FITTON, Mr. Anthony George, BSc ACA *1996;* 15 Cob Lane Close, Digswell, WELWYN, HERTFORDSHIRE, AL6 0DD.

FITTON, Mr. David, FCA *1955;* 7 Goring Road, STEYNING, BN44 3GF. (Life Member)

FITTON, Mr. Garry John, BSc ACA *1997;* 15 Halstow Road, Greenwich, LONDON, SE10 0LD.

FITTON, Mr. Geoffrey, FCA *1955;* 32 White Rose Lane, WOKING, SURREY, GU22 7JY. (Life Member)

FITTON, Mr. Graham, BSc ACA *1985;* Sagar Hill Farm, Higham, BURNLEY, BB12 9BP.

FITTON, Mr. Ian Peter, BA ACA *1990;* 4 Grosvenor Court, Brook Road, CHEADLE, SK8 1PE.

•FITTON, Mr. Kelvin, BA FCA *1994;* Smith Craven, Kelham House, Kelham Street, DONCASTER, DN1 3RE.

•FITTON, Miss. Louise Marion, ACA *2009;* D.R.E. & Co (Audit) Limited, 7 Lower Brook Street, OSWESTRY, SHROPSHIRE, SY11 2HG. See also DRE & Co (Knighton) Limited and DRE & Co

FITTON, Mr. Maxwell Graham Livesey, FCA *1958;* 14 Solomon Cres, LATHAM, ACT 2615, AUSTRALIA. (Life Member)

FITTON, Mr. Michael, FCA *1965;* 5 Verica Gardens, Pamber Heath, TADLEY, HAMPSHIRE, RG26 3EU.

FITTON, Mrs. Pamela Kay, BA ACA *1987;* Sagar Hill Farm, Higham, BURNLEY, BB12 9BP.

FITTON, Mr. Paul Worrall, BA ACA *1980;* King George Chambers, 1 St. James Square, BACUP, OL13 9AA.

FITTON, Mr. Peter Lindsay, FCA *1974;* 180 Perry Rd, Sherwood, NOTTINGHAM, NG5 1GL.

FITTON, Mr. Richard, Ba ACA *2011;* Fox Lodge, 4 Manor Farm Close, Hardwick, WELLINGBOROUGH, NORTHAMPTONSHIRE, NN9 5GL.

FITZ-GERALD, Mrs. Natalie Emma, BSc ACA *1999;* 88 St. Johns Road, SEVENOAKS, KENT, TN13 3NE.

FITZ-GERALD, Mr. Nicholas John Purcell, ACA *1984;* 35 Elms Avenue, POOLE, BH14 8EE.

FITZ-GERALD, Mr. Philip, BA ACA *2000;* with Audit Inspection Unit, Financial Reporting Council, 5th Floor, Aldwych House, 71-91 Aldwych, LONDON WC2B 4HN.

FITZ-JOHN, Mr. Paul, FCA MBA *1969;* 9 Gover Close, WAREHAM, DORSET, BH20 5BU. (Life Member)

FITZAKERLEY, Mr. Nigel, BSc ACA *2007;* N G U, 469-471 Durham Road, Lowell, GATESHEAD, TYNE AND WEAR, NE9 5EX.

•FITZGERALD, Mr. Alan John, BTech FCA *1978;* Fitzgerald Mithia, Newgate House, 431 London Road, CROYDON, CR0 3PF.

FITZGERALD, Mr. Alden Gregory, MSc FCA *1970;* Charltons CJC P/L, Level 9, 130 Elizabeth Street, SYDNEY, NSW 2000, AUSTRALIA.

FITZGERALD, Mr. Alexander James Broun, BSc ACA *1999;* Flagship Housing Group Suite, 11-12 Keswick Hall, NORWICH, NR4 6TJ.

FITZGERALD, Mr. Andrew, ACA *2008;* 15 Victory Way, LONDON, SE16 6QH.

FITZGERALD, Mr. Andrew, FCA *1970;* Trotts Farm House, Methersgate Hall Estate, Sutton, WOODBRIDGE, IP12 3JL.

FITZGERALD, Mrs. Anna Danuta, BA ACA *1992;* Unit 6, 249 East 4th, NORTH VANCOUVER V7L1J1, BC, CANADA.

FITZGERALD, Mr. Brian, ACA *1982;* 188 Cooden Drive, BEXHILL-ON-SEA, EAST SUSSEX, TN39 3AH.

FITZGERALD, Mr. Christopher John, BSc ACA *1982;* Field View Cottage, Main Street, Farthingstone, TOWCESTER, NN12 8EZ.

FITZGERALD, Mr. Colin Michael, ACA CTA *1979;* 1 Earlsdon Road, Hanbury Park, WORCESTER, WR2 4PF.

FITZGERALD, Mr. David Anthony, FCA *1953;* 3930 Marine Drive, VANCOUVER V7V 1N4, BC, CANADA. (Life Member)

FITZGERALD, Mr. Derek Frank, FCA *1965;* 218 Eastwood Road, RAYLEIGH, SS6 7LY. (Life Member)

FITZGERALD, Mr. Desmond, BCom FCA *1994;* The Westend1320 21st St NW, Apt 207 WASHINGTON, DC 20036, UNITED STATES.

FITZGERALD, Mr. Donald Dennis, BA ACA *1983;* The Mill House Hawkcombe, Porlock, MINEHEAD, SOMERSET, TA24 8QN.

FITZGERALD, Mr. Duncan George, BSc FCA *1992;* with PricewaterhouseCoopers, 33/F Cheung Kong Center, 2 Queen's Road, CENTRAL, HONG KONG ISLAND, HONG KONG SAR.

•FITZGERALD, Mr. Graham, BA FCA *1998;* Evolution Audit LLP, 10 Evolution, Wynyard Park, BILLINGHAM, CLEVELAND, TS22 5TB.

FITZGERALD, Mr. Ian Keith, BA ACA *1980;* 10 Apley Close, HARROGATE, NORTH YORKSHIRE, HG2 8PS.

FITZGERALD, Mrs. Jillian Mary, MA ACA *1992;* Specialist Publications (UK) Ltd Clifton Heights, Triangle West, BRISTOL, BS8 1EJ.

FITZGERALD, Mr. John, ACA *2011;* Upper Stanbridge Farm Sopworth Road, Sherston, MALMESBURY, SN16 0QB.

FITZGERALD, Miss. Julie, BEng ACA *1993;* Susenbergstrasse 173, 8044 ZURICH, SWITZERLAND.

FITZGERALD, Miss. Mary, MA ACA *1989;* 255 Arcadia Road, #10-26 Hillcrest Arcadia, SINGAPORE 289850, SINGAPORE.

FITZGERALD, Mr. Michael George, FCA *1977;* Restormel Estates, Liddicoat Road, LOSTWITHIEL, PL22 0HD.

FITZGERALD, Mr. Michael George, MA ACA *1999;* Societe Generale, GLFI/CMF/SEC, Tours Societe Generale, 17 cours Valmy, La Defence CEDEX, 92987 PARIS FRANCE.

FITZGERALD, Mr. Michael Thomas, BA FCA *1982;* 14 Leonard Avenue, Otford, SEVENOAKS, KENT, TN14 5RB.

FITZGERALD, Mr. Nicholas John, MA FCA *1972;* c/o Grange Barn, Cranford Road, KETTERING, NN15 5JL. (Life Member)

FITZGERALD, Miss. Nicola, BA ACA *2007;* 42 Derbyshire Road South, SALE, CHESHIRE, M33 3JQ.

•FITZGERALD, Mr. Patrick, ACA *1979;* PricewaterhouseCoopers, Paseo de la Alameda, 35-7a Floor, 46023 VALENCIA, SPAIN.

FITZGERALD, Mr. Patrick Richard, LLB FCA *1971;* Woodlands, Glen Vine Road, Glen Vine, ISLE OF MAN, IM4 4HF.

FITZGERALD, Peter Gilbert, Esq OBE DL FCA *1972;* Fitzgeralds Lighting Cornwall Ltd, 30 Normandy Way, BODMIN, CORNWALL, PL31 1EX.

FITZGERALD, Mr. Richard, BA ACA *1981;* 34 Kings Avenue, LONDON, N10 1PB.

FITZGERALD, Mr. Richard John Norman, BA ACA *1988;* 21 Becketts Place, Hampton Wick, KINGSTON UPON THAMES, KT1 4EQ.

FITZGERALD, Mr. Rodney Arnold, BSc FCA *1980;* Walker Crips Stockbrokers Ltd Finsbury Tower, 103-105 Bunhill Row, LONDON, EC1Y 8LZ.

FITZGERALD, Mrs. Sarah Jane, BA ACA *1994;* 90 Westfield Road, Carlton, WAKEFIELD, WEST YORKSHIRE, WF3 3RJ.

•FITZGERALD, Ms. Sarah Jayne, ACA *1993;* Sarah J Fitzgerald, Briar Cottage, Hurston Lane, Storrington, PULBOROUGH, WEST SUSSEX RH20 4HH.

FITZGERALD, Mr. Sean Andrew, BA ACA *1992;* Standard Life Investments Investment House, 1 George Street, EDINBURGH, EH2 2LL.

•FITZGERALD, Mr. Thomas Joseph, BSc FCA *1973;* Fitzgeralds, 40 Ringford Road, LONDON, SW18 1RR.

FITZGIBBON, Mr. Christopher Paul Julian, BA FCA *1982;* Drimina House, SNEEM, COUNTY KERRY, IRELAND.

FITZGIBBON, Mr. Denis, BCom FCA *1975;* St. Leonard's Dale, WINDSOR, SL4 4AQ.

FITZGIBBON, Miss. Kate, ACA *2009;* 18 Baryntyne Crescent, Hoo, ROCHESTER, KENT, ME3 9GE.

FITZHUGH, Mr. David George, FCA *1963;* 20 Foxford Close, NORTHAMPTON, NN4 9UH. (Life Member)

FITZHUGH, Mr. Derek Alfred, FCA *1965;* 21 Reddings, WELWYN GARDEN CITY, AL8 7LA. (Life Member)

FITZJOHN, Miss. Julie, BSc ACA *1997;* Metropolis Group Ltd, 70 Chiswick High Road, LONDON, W4 1SY.

FITZMAURICE, Mr. Barry Timothy, BSc ACA *1994;* 28 Greenford Gardens, GREENFORD, MIDDLESEX, UB6 9LY.

FITZMAURICE, Mrs. Sinead, ACA *2010; (ACA Ireland 2001);* 10 Dowsleys Barn, NEW ROSS, COUNTY WEXFORD, IRELAND.

FITZPATRICK, Mr. Antony Simon, BSc ACA *1992;* 15 The Orchard, Bearsted, MAIDSTONE, KENT, ME14 4QL.

•FITZPATRICK, Mr. Barry John, FCA *1971;* Holmwood, Oaken Drive, Claygate, ESHER, KT10 0DL.

FITZPATRICK, Mr. Benjamin Joseph, BA(Hons) ACA *2003;* 205 Walthery Avenue, RIDGEWOOD, NJ 07450, UNITED STATES.

FITZPATRICK, Miss. Claire Helen, BSc ACA *1994;* BP Exploration Alaska, 900 E.Benson Boulevard, ANCHORAGE, AK 99506, UNITED STATES.

FITZPATRICK, Mr. Clifford, BSc ACA *2005;* 10 Hutley Drive, COLCHESTER, CO4 5FU.

FITZPATRICK, Mr. David William, BSc FCA *1992;* 11 Playfield Crsecent, East Dulwich, LONDON, SE22 8QR.

FITZPATRICK, Mr. Edward Hamilton Barnaby, MBA FCA *1969;* Flat 20 Ridgway, 87 - 89 Ararat Road, RICHMOND, SURREY, TW10 6PR.

FITZPATRICK, Miss. Elaine Patricia, BSc ACA *2005;* River Island Clothing Co Chelsea House, West Gate, LONDON, W5 1DR.

FITZPATRICK, Mr. John, BSc FCA *1978;* 1 Corn Mill Bottom, Shelley, HUDDERSFIELD, HD8 8JJ.

•FITZPATRICK, Mr. John Colin, BA FCA ACIArb *1983;* Fitzpatrickroyle, 105 Moorside North, Fenham, NEWCASTLE UPON TYNE, NE4 9DY.

FITZPATRICK, Mr. John-Mark, ACA CA(SA) *2010;* 20 Newlyn, 69 Oatlands Avenue, WEYBRIDGE, SURREY, KT13 9TL.
FITZPATRICK, Mr. Kevin Paul, BSc FCA *1996;* (Tax Fac), 7 Burnside, ASHTEAD, SURREY, KT21 1SB.
FITZPATRICK, Mr. Liam, BSc ACA *2007;* 48 Criffel Avenue, LONDON, SW2 4BN.
•FITZPATRICK, Mr. Maurice Charles, FCA *1976;* (Tax Fac), 12 Dehar Crescent, LONDON, NW9 7BD.
FITZPATRICK, Miss. Nicola Louise, BAcc ACA *2002;* 257 Imperial Court, 225 Kennington Lane, Kennington, LONDON, SE11 5QN.
FITZPATRICK, Mr. Paul Francis Joseph, ACA *1987;* Woodlea Brook Road, BUCKHURST HILL, IG9 5TR.
FITZPATRICK, Mr. Peter, BA FCA *1979;* Silvermist, 2 Convent Lane, Portmarnock, DUBLIN, COUNTY DUBLIN, IRELAND.
FITZPATRICK, Mr. Richard Joseph, FCA *1965;* 2 Yacht Street, SOUTHPORT, QLD 4215, AUSTRALIA. (Life Member)
FITZPATRICK, Mr. Robert Michael, BSc(Hons) ACA *2001;* 41 The Bramleys, Portishead, BRISTOL, BS20 7LL.
FITZPATRICK, Miss. Tamsin, BSc ACA *2010;* Unit 2, 1201 9th Street SW, CALGARY T2R 1 C5, AB, CANADA.
FITZPATRICK, Mr. Timothy Hugh, BSc ACA *1986;* H S B C, 8-14 Canada Square, LONDON, E14 5HQ.
•FITZPATRICK, Mr. William Joseph, MA BSc FCA *1993;* Fitzpatrick, 88 Church Road, HOLYWOOD, COUNTY DOWN, BT18 9BX.
FITZPATRICK, Mr. William Russell Stewart, BSc ACA *1987;* Dewynters Ltd, Communications House, 48 Leicester Square, LONDON, WC2H 7QD.
FITZSIMMONS, Mr. Andrew David, MSc ACA *2005;* 29 Greystone Road, Broadgreen, LIVERPOOL, L14 6UD.
FITZSIMMONS, Mr. Harry, FCA *1960;* 42 South Park Drive, BLACKPOOL, FY3 9QA. (Life Member)
FITZSIMMONS, Mr. James Andrew, MA MSc ACA *2001;* The Brand Union, 11-33 St. John Street, LONDON, EC1M 4AA.
FITZSIMMONS, Mrs. Karen Elizabeth, BA ACA *1994;* Murry General Steels Group Ltd, Brightgate House, Cobra Court, Trafford Park, MANCHESTER, M32 0TB.
FITZSIMMONS, Mr. Matthew Vincent, ACA *2011;* 57 Passingham Avenue, BILLERICAY, CM11 2TB.
FITZSIMMONS, Mr. Neil, BA ACA *1984;* 31 Rean Meadow, Tattenhall, CHESTER, CH3 9PU.
FITZSIMMONS, Mr. Simon John, LLB ACA *2007;* with Mazars LLP, Tower Bridge House, St. Katharines Way, LONDON, E1W 1DD.
FITZSIMMONS, Mr. Stefan, BA ACA *1999;* 74 Montagu Mansions, LONDON, W1U 6LE.
FITZSIMMONS, Mr. Stuart Charles, BA ACA *1998;* Hertz Europe Limited, Hertz House, 11 Vine Street, UXBRIDGE, MIDDLESEX, UB8 1QE.
FITZSIMMONS, Mr. Trevor Morrison, BA ACA *1987;* c/o Jardine Matheson & Co Ltd, 25/F Devon House, Taikoo Place, 979 King's Road, QUARRY BAY, HONG KONG SAR.
FITZSIMON, Mr. Eric William, FCA *1976;* 4 Mereside, Farnborough, ORPINGTON, BR6 8ET.
FITZSIMON, Mrs. Natalie Jane, BA ACA *1989;* 3853 Vandorf Road, STOUFFVILLE L4A 7X5, ON, CANADA.
FITZSIMON, Mr. Paul, BSc ACA *1991;* 3853 Vandorf Road, STOUFFVILLE L4A 7X5, ON, CANADA.
FITZSIMONS, Mrs. Claire Louise, BSc FCA CFE *1992;* Hill Top, 7 Bagnall Close, Uppermill, OLDHAM, OL3 6DW.
FITZSIMONS, Mr. George William, MA FCA *1989;* Charles Taylor Consulting Standard House, 12-13 Essex Street, LONDON, WC2R 3AA.
FITZSIMONS, Mr. Paul, ACA *1985;* Kennel Moor, Lower Moushill Lane, Milford, GODALMING, SURREY, GU8 5JX.
FITZWILLIAM, Mr. Peter David Campbell, BSc ACA *1985;* 20 Dunmore Road, West Wimbledon, LONDON, SW20 8TN.
FIVASH, Mr. Nicholas John, BSc ACA *1998;* 1 Severn View, Tabernacle Walk, Rodborough, STROUD, GL5 3UJ.
FLACK, Mr. Andrew Charles, BA ACA *1989;* 8416 Brook Road, MCLEAN, VA 22102, UNITED STATES.
FLACK, Mr. Charles Michael, BA ACA *1982;* 5 Old Mill Court, Station Road, Plympton, PLYMOUTH, PL7 2AJ.
FLACK, Ms. Debby Marie, BA ACA CTA *1988;* (Tax Fac), 12 Heathfield Close, GODALMING, SURREY, GU7 1SL.
FLACK, Mr. Graham Norman, FCA *1979;* 16 Cawdell Drive, Long Whatton, LOUGHBOROUGH, LE12 5BW.
FLACK, Mr. John Drage, FCA *1954;* 2c Earlswood Road, REDHILL, RH1 6HE. (Life Member)
FLACK, Mr. Kevin, BSc ACA *2006;* 16A Carlingford Road, LONDON, NW3 1RX.
FLACK, Mr. Mark, BA ACA *1991;* with Grant Thornton UK LLP, Grant Thornton House, 22 Melton Street, Euston Square, LONDON, NW1 2EP.
FLACK, Mr. Robin Anthony, MSc FCA *1973;* 18/2 Rogal Place, MACQUARIE PARK, NSW 2113, AUSTRALIA.
FLACKETT, Mr. Daniel, BA ACA *1999;* 178 Camden Road, LONDON, NW1 9HG.
•FLAHERTY, Mr. John Cameron, BSc FCA *1986;* Ernst & Young LLP, 1 Colmore Square, BIRMINGHAM, B4 6HQ. See also Ernst & Young Europe LLP
FLAHERTY, Mr. John Patrick, BA ACA *1999;* IPF PLC, 3 Leeds City Office Park, Meadow Lane, LEEDS, LS11 5BD.
•FLAIN, Mr. Kevin, ACA *2003;* Kevin Flain Accountancy Services, 52 Woodlands Road, Baughurst, TADLEY, HAMPSHIRE, RG26 5NS.
FLAM, Mrs. Chloe Horner, BA ACA *1994;* PO Box 776381, STEAMBOAT SPRINGS, CO 80477, UNITED STATES.
FLAMANK, Mr. Simon Alexander, FCA FCCA *1982;* 32 South Road, Chorleywood, RICKMANSWORTH, HERTFORDSHIRE, WD3 5AR.
FLANAGAN, Mr. Andrew Paul, BSc ACA *1990;* with Digita International Ltd, Liverton Business Park, EXMOUTH, DEVON, EX8 2NR.
FLANAGAN, Miss. Anne Teresa, BSc FCA *1989;* 11 Alister Street, North Fitzroy, MELBOURNE, VIC 3068, AUSTRALIA.
•FLANAGAN, Mr. Anthony John, FCA *1975;* Champion Accountants LLP, 1 Worsley Court, High Street, Worsley, MANCHESTER, M28 3NJ.
•FLANAGAN, Mr. Colin William, BA FCA *1987;* Sherwood Hall Associates Limited, 1st Floor, Langton House, Bird Street, LICHFIELD, STAFFORDSHIRE WS13 6PY.
FLANAGAN, Miss. Harriet Elizabeth, BA(Hons) ACA *2002;* 47 Park Drive, HARROGATE, NORTH YORKSHIRE, HG2 9AX.
FLANAGAN, Mr. Jeffrey Paul, BSc ACA *1988;* 19 Broadoaks Way, BROMLEY, BR2 0UA.
•FLANAGAN, Mrs. Joanne, BA FCA *1988;* Fusion@Magna, Magna Way, ROTHERHAM, SOUTH YORKSHIRE, s60 1fe.
•FLANAGAN, Mrs. Kay, FCA *1985;* MacMahon Leggate Ltd, Charter House, 18-20 Finsley Gate, BURNLEY, LANCASHIRE, BB11 2HA.
FLANAGAN, Miss. Lisa, BA(Hons) ACA *2010;* 334 Liverpool Road, SOUTHPORT, MERSEYSIDE, PR8 3BZ.
•FLANAGAN, Miss. Marie Patricia, BA ACA *1992;* Ernst & Young LLP, 1 More London Place, LONDON, SE1 2AF. See also Ernst & Young Europe LLP
FLANAGAN, Mr. Mark Thomas Charles, BA ACA *2007;* 19 Seaford Avenue, Wollaton, NOTTINGHAM, NG8 1LA.
FLANAGAN, Mrs. Mary Anne Glenda, BSc ACA *1994;* Shepherd Neame, 17 Court Street, FAVERSHAM, ME13 7AX.
FLANAGAN, Mr. Nicholas Guy, BSc ACA *1988;* The Old Bakery, 10 Cobden Hill, RADLETT, HERTFORDSHIRE, WD7 7JR.
FLANAGAN, Mr. Peter Francis, BCom FCA *1976;* 39 Holland Gardens, WATFORD, WD25 9JN.
FLANAGAN, Mr. Ross, ACA *2008;* 21 Hindley Street, ASHTON-UNDER-LYNE, LANCASHIRE, OL7 0BX.
FLANAGAN, Mrs. Sally Deborah, BSc ACA *1988;* The Old Bakery, 10 Cobden Hill, RADLETT, HERTFORDSHIRE, WD7 7JR.
FLANAGAN, Miss. Sarah Jane, BA ACA *2001;* 39 Hazelwell Crescent, BIRMINGHAM, B30 2QD.
FLANAGAN, Mrs. Stacy Jane, BSc ACA *1999;* with Deloitte Touche Tohmatsu, 35 Smith Street, (P.O.Box 38 2124), PARRAMATTA, NSW 2150, AUSTRALIA.
FLANAGAN, Mr. Timothy John Michael, BSc FCA *1979;* Marcelo T de Alvear 1239 1C, Capital Federal, BUENOS AIRES, C1058AAS, ARGENTINA.
FLANAGAN, Ms. Zoey Kim, ACA *1998;* 29 Junction Road, NORWICH, NR3 2JQ.
•FLANAGHAN, Mr. John Peter, FCA *1976;* JFA Accountancy Limited, 24 Foregate Street, WORCESTER, WR1 1DN.
FLANDERS, Mrs. Glynis Bethelda, MBA BA FCA *1980;* 8 Field Close, WHITBY, NORTH YORKSHIRE, YO21 3LR.
•FLANDERS, Mr. John Barry, FCA *1956;* Flanders & Company, Bunkers, 8 Ladycroft Paddock, Allestree, DERBY, DE22 2GA.
FLANDERS, Mr. Mark William, BA(Hons) ACA *2003;* ScanSafe/Cisco, Qube, 90 Whitfield Street, LONDON, W1T 4EZ.
FLANDERS, Mr. Martin Charles, ACA *1983;* 11 South Avenue, Darley Abbey, DERBY, DE22 1FB.
FLANIGAN, Mr. Martin Barrie, BSc ACA *1993;* (Tax Fac), 14 Rhodfa Felin, BARRY, SOUTH GLAMORGAN, CF62 6LX.
•FLANNAGAN, Mr. Terence Michael, ACA *1992;* (Tax Fac), MD Accountants Ltd, Frederick House, Dean Group Business Park, Brenda Road, HARTLEPOOL, CLEVELAND TS25 2BW.
FLANNERY, Miss. Caroline, BA ACA *2004;* Apple Tree House Ardargie, Forgandenny, PERTH, PH2 9DF.
FLANNERY, Miss. Catherine, BA ACA *2009;* Flat 4, 5 Kingsland Passage, LONDON, E8 2BA.
FLANNERY, Mrs. Karen Patricia, BA ACA *2000;* 38 Waggon Road, BARNET, HERTFORDSHIRE, EN4 0HL.
FLANNERY, Mrs. Kate Victoria, BSc ACA *1998;* 91 Beamish Close, Appleton, WARRINGTON, WA4 5RJ.
FLANNERY, Mr. Malcolm John, BSc ACA *2000;* 91 Beamish Close, Appleton, WARRINGTON, WA4 5RJ.
FLANNERY, Mr. Thomas Daniel, FCA *1972;* 199 Greenways, CONSETT, DH8 7DW.
FLANNIGAN, Mr. Paul, BSc ACA *1990;* 3 Waller Road, Walkley, SHEFFIELD, S6 5DP.
•FLASHER, Mr. Laurence Anthony, FCA *1980;* Josephs, Suite 2, Chapel Allerton House, 114 Harrogate Road, LEEDS, LS7 4NY.
FLASHMAN, Mr. Clive Samuel, BA ACA *1992;* 77 Cavendish Crescent, Elstree, BOREHAMWOOD, HERTFORDSHIRE, WD6 3JW.
FLATAU, Mr. Richard Percival, FCA *1971;* Matham Manor, Matham Road, EAST MOLESEY, SURREY, KT8 0SU.
•FLATHER, Mr. David Michael, FCA *1956;* D M Flather, 15 Goodwood, Owler Park Road, ILKLEY, LS29 0BY.
FLATHER, Mr. Simon Michael, FCA *1981;* Croft House, Apple Tree Gardens, Skipton Road, ILKLEY, WEST YORKSHIRE, LS29 9TG.
FLATLEY, Mr. Michael Derek, FCA *1951;* 9 Furlong Place, AXBRIDGE, SOMERSET, BS26 2JH. (Life Member)
•FLATLEY, Mr. Paul, BSc FCA *1994;* Grant Thornton UK LLP, 30 Finsbury Square, LONDON, EC2P 2YU. See also Grant Thornton LLP
FLATMAN, Mr. Mark, ACA *1984;* 3 Highfield Mews, Compayne Gardens, LONDON, NW6 3GB.
FLATMAN, Mr. Richard Anthony, BA FCA *1985;* 35 Gippingstone Road, Bramford, IPSWICH, IP8 4DR.
FLATT, Mr. Alan Raymond, ACA *1991;* Gas Transportation Co Unit 23 Woolpit Business Park, Windmill Avenue Woolpit, BURY ST. EDMUNDS, SUFFOLK, IP30 9UP.
FLATT, Mr. Andrew James, FCA *1974;* 43 Bellevue Road, Ealing, LONDON, W13 8DF.
FLATT, Mr. Andrew Robert Foster, BSc ACA *1993;* Marsh House, Kingston St. Mary, TAUNTON, SOMERSET, TA2 8HH.
FLATT, Mr. David Maurice, FCA *1965;* 324 Station Road, WESTCLIFF-ON-SEA, ESSEX, SS0 8DZ.
FLATTERS, Ms. Bernadette, BSc ACA *1997;* 11 Cleveland Road, Markyate, ST. ALBANS, HERTFORDSHIRE, AL3 8LB.
FLATTERS, Mr. David Richard Antony, MSc ACA *1999;* St. Ives Direct Ring Road, Seacroft, LEEDS, LS14 1NH.
•FLATTERS, Mrs. Jacqueline Anne, FCA *1968;* (Tax Fac), Hall Hayes & Co, Prospect House, 24 Prospect Road, OSSETT, WEST YORKSHIRE, WF5 8AE.
FLATTERS, Mr. Richard, ACA *2006;* Mayfair Business Park Broad Lane, BRADFORD, WEST YORKSHIRE, BD4 8PW.
FLATTERY, Mr. Brendan Peter, BA FCA *1989;* 84 Edge Hill, Darras Hall, Ponteland, NEWCASTLE UPON TYNE, NE20 9JQ.
FLATTERY, Mrs. Helen, BA ACA *1997;* Infineum UK Ltd, Milton Hill, Business & Technology Park, PO Box 1, ABINGDON, OXFORDSHIRE OX13 6BB.
FLAUM, Mr. Paul Charles, BA ACA *1995;* Premier Inn, Whitbread Court, Porz Avenue, Houghton Hall Park, Houghton Regis, DUNSTABLE BEDFORDSHIRE LU5 5XE.
FLAVELL, Mr. Jeremy Charles, FCA *1982;* Thomas Edge House Tunnell Street, St. Helier, JERSEY, JE2 4LU.
•FLAVELL, Mr. John Stanley, FCA *1964;* (Tax Fac), SRC Taxation Consultancy Ltd, Blenheim House, 56 Old Steine, BRIGHTON, BN1 1NH.
FLAVELL, Mr. Mark John, MEng ACA *2001;* with PricewaterhouseCoopers, Emirates Towers Offices, PO Box 11987, Level 40, Sheikh Zayed Road, PO Box 11987 DUBAI UNITED ARAB EMIRATES.
FLAVELL, Miss. Natalie, BSc ACA *2007;* 161 Burntwood Lane, LONDON, SW17 0AL.
FLAVELL, Miss. Sarah, ACA *2010;* 1 Elvington Lane, Hawkinge, FOLKESTONE, CT18 7AF.
•FLAVELLE, Mrs. Carole, BSc ACA *1979;* Flavelle & Co, Penventinnie Barn, TRURO, CORNWALL, TR4 9EG.
FLAVELLE, Mr. Michael Gerard, FCA *1983;* GUL International Ltd, Callywith Gate, Launceston Road, BODMIN, CORNWALL, PL31 2RQ.
FLAWN, Mr. Matthew James, BSc(Hons) ACA *2003;* Redbridge Worldfresh Ltd Tolworth Tower, Ewell Road, SURBITON, SURREY, KT6 7EL.
FLAXBEARD, Mr. Damon Alexander, LLB ACA *2001;* 63 Park Rise, HARPENDEN, HERTFORDSHIRE, AL5 3AN.
FLAXBEARD, Mr. Jason Richard, BSc ACA CPCU *1996;* 8390 E Crescent Parkway, Suite 200, GREENWOOD VILLAGE, CO 80111, UNITED STATES.
FLAXMAN, Mr. Gavin Charles, BA ACA *1986;* 74 Kings Road, WALTON-ON-THAMES, SURREY, KT12 2RB.
•FLAXMAN, Mr. Peter Edward, BSc FCA *1984;* Your Finance Team Limited, The Meads Business Centre, 19 Kingsmead, FARNBOROUGH, HAMPSHIRE, GU14 7SR. See also Flaxman Accounting Services Limited
FLAY, Mr. Terence Hubert, FCA *1966;* The Old Cottage, West Green, Hartley Wintney, HOOK, RG27 8JD.
FLEAR, Mrs. Claire Alison, BSc ACA *1990;* with Cooper Parry LLP, 14 Park Row, NOTTINGHAM, NG1 6GR.
FLEAR, Miss. Helen Elizabeth, BA ACA *1993;* with PricewaterhouseCoopers LLP, Donington Court, Pegasus Business Park, Castle Donington, DERBY, DE74 2UZ.
•FLEAR, Mrs. Sarah Louise, BA ACA *1998;* with Smith Cooper, Wilmot House, St James Court, Friar Gate, DERBY, DE1 1BT.
FLEAR, Mr. Simon Richard, BSc ACA *1989;* Intygra PPL, Unit 1, Wilford Business Park, Ruddington Lane, NOTTINGHAM, NG11 7EP.
FLECK, Mr. Peter Geoffrey, MA FCA *1977;* Hawthorn House, Albion Terrace, SALTBURN-BY-THE-SEA, TS12 1LT.
FLEET, Mrs. Caroline Ruth, BSc ACA *1999;* (Tax Fac), 12 Walden House Road, Great Totham, MALDON, ESSEX, CM9 8PN.
FLEET, Mrs. Emma, ACA *2009;* (Tax Fac), 2 Sedgegarth, Thorner, LEEDS, LS14 3LB.
FLEET, Mr. George, BA ACA *1995;* Broomy Croft, Cotmans Ash Lane, Kemsing, SEVENOAKS, KENT, TN15 6XD.
FLEET, Mrs. Helen Marie, LLB ACA *1999;* 1 Scott Place, Hardman Street, MANCHESTER, M3 3NN.
FLEET, Mr. Kenneth Jarvis, FCA *1954;* Leathley, 156 Radcliffe Road, West Bridgford, NOTTINGHAM, NG2 5HF.
FLEETWOOD, Dr. Allison Jane, BA ACA *2000;* 4 Bowes Road, WALTON-ON-THAMES, SURREY, KT12 3HS.
FLEETWOOD, Mr. Andrew Edwin Colin, ACA *2008;* 73 New Road, WORTHING, WEST SUSSEX, BN13 3JP.
•FLEETWOOD, Mr. Bernard, FCA *1958;* B. Fleetwood, 62 Chapel Street, BILLERICAY, CM12 9LS.
FLEETWOOD, Mr. Christopher John, BA FCA *1977;* 4 The Meadows, RICHMOND, DL10 7DU.
FLEETWOOD, Miss. Emma Caroline, LLB ACA *2006;* 5 Mountview Close, Vange, BASILDON, ESSEX, SS16 4RN.
FLEETWOOD, Mr. Jonathan Richard Alan, BSc ACA *1995;* Depuy International Ltd, Number 1, White Rose Office Park, Millshaw Park Lane, LEEDS, LS11 0EA.
FLEETWOOD, Mr. Mark Christopher, BA ACA *2005;* Brewin Dolphin Time Central, 32 Gallowgate, NEWCASTLE UPON TYNE, NE1 4SR.
•FLEETWOOD, Mr. Martin Christopher, BSc ACA *1992;* (Tax Fac), PricewaterhouseCoopers LLP, Waterfront Plaza, 8 Laganbank Road, BELFAST, COUNTY ANTRIM, BT1 3LR. See also PricewaterhouseCoopers
FLEIG, Mr. Mario Constantin Naoki, ACA *2010;* 14 Avenue de la Liberté, L-1930 Luxembourg, L-1930 LUXEMBOURG, LUXEMBOURG.
FLEMING, Mr. Andrew Selby, BA FCA *1976;* Fleming & Partners Pty Ltd, 8 Hunter Street, YARRALUMLA, ACT 2600, AUSTRALIA.
FLEMING, Mrs. Anne Catherine, BCom ACA *1995;* 62 Abbott Avenue, LONDON, SW20 8SQ.
FLEMING, Mrs. Caroline Janet, BA ACA *1999;* with PricewaterhouseCoopers LLP, 1 Embankment Place, LONDON, WC2N 6RH.
FLEMING, Miss. Christian Elisabeth, ACA *1991;* 53 Ashbourne Grove, East Dulwich, LONDON, SE22 8RN.
FLEMING, Mr. Christopher John, BSc ACA *1997;* 3 Marlin End, BERKHAMSTED, HERTFORDSHIRE, HP4 3GB.

FLEMING, Ms. Claire Alison, BCom ACA *2010;* 19f Upper Richmond Road, LONDON, SW15 2RF.
FLEMING, Mr. David Ivor James, FCA *1974;* Carey Group, Millennium House, Ollivier Street, Alderney, GUERNSEY, GY9 3TD.
FLEMING, Mr. David John, FCA *1964;* Well House Barn, Brown Bank Lane, Silsden, KEIGHLEY, WEST YORKSHIRE, BD20 0LL.
FLEMING, Mr. David Oliver, JP BSc ACA *1990;* 8 Heights Crescent, Middle Cove, SYDNEY, NSW 2068, AUSTRALIA.
FLEMING, Mrs. Elizabeth Anne, BSc ACA *1997;* 3 Marlin End, BERKHAMSTED, HERTFORDSHIRE, HP4 3GB.
FLEMING, Mrs. Elizabeth Anne, LLB ACA *1998;* Hockhams House, Martley, WORCESTER, WR6 6QR.
•FLEMING, Mr. Francesco Paolo, BSc ACA *1991;* KPMG SpA, Via Vittor Pisani 25, 20124 MILAN, ITALY.
FLEMING, Mr. Iain Moray, BSc ACA *1996;* Sotheby's, 34-35 New Bond Street, LONDON, W1A 2AA.
FLEMING, Mr. Ian James, MA FCA *1979;* Holtye Croft, Cansiron Lane, Cowden, EDENBRIDGE, TN8 7EE.
•FLEMING, Mr. Ian Robert, BA ACA *1992;* with Alvarez & Marsal - London Office, First Floor, One Finsbury Circus, LONDON, EC2M 7EB.
FLEMING, Mr. James Roland, BA FCA *1972;* P.O. Box 1, Northleach, CHELTENHAM, GL54 3JB.
FLEMING, Mrs. Jane Michelle, BEng FCA ACA *1992;* 23 Minnehaha Avenue, TAKAPUNA 0622, AUCKLAND, NEW ZEALAND.
FLEMING, Mr. Jeremy Ian, BA ACA *1992;* Old Cottage, High Barn Corner, Hascombe Road, GODALMING, SURREY, GU8 4AE.
•FLEMING, Mr. John Christopher, FCA *1974;* (Tax Fac), GlewDunn & Co, 83 Spring Bank, HULL, HU3 1AG.
FLEMING, Mr. Jonathan Peter, FCA *1967;* Hendra, 61 Woburn Road, Heath And Reach, LEIGHTON BUZZARD, LU7 0AP. (Life Member)
FLEMING, Mr. Kenneth Harry, FCA *1971;* 21 Millers Green Close, ENFIELD, MIDDLESEX, EN2 7BD.
FLEMING, Mrs. Lesley, BSc ACA DChA *1987;* 24b Abbey Road, KNARESBOROUGH, NORTH YORKSHIRE, HG5 8HY.
FLEMING, Ms. Linda Jane, BA FCA *1985;* 5 Devonshire Terrace, GLASGOW, G12 0XE.
FLEMING, Miss. Lorna, ACA *2010;* with PricewaterhouseCoopers LLP, 1 Embankment Place, LONDON, WC2N 6RH.
FLEMING, Mrs. Louise Juliet, BA ACA *1998;* The Coach House, Church Lane, Freshford, BATH, BA2 7WD.
FLEMING, Mr. Mark, BSc ACA *1992;* Poppyfields, 10 Winders Corner, Barlborough, CHESTERFIELD, S43 4WH.
FLEMING, Mr. Mark Jonathan, BA ACA *2004;* Royal Bank of Canada (C I) Ltd, P C F S, JERSEY, JE1 1PB.
FLEMING, Mr. Martin Alan, ACA *2006;* Burnside, Holme Street, APPLEBY-IN-WESTMORLAND, CUMBRIA, CA16 6QU.
FLEMING, Mrs. Mary Joanna, BSc ACA *1985;* Haydon Bridge High School, Haydon Bridge, HEXHAM, NORTHUMBERLAND, NE47 6LR.
FLEMING, Mr. Matthew Thomas, ACA *2008;* Flat 16a, Nightingale Mansions, 48 Nightingale Lane, LONDON, SW12 8TN.
FLEMING, Mrs. Melinda Katharine, LLB ACA *1994;* Hillside, 51 Silver Street, Ashwell, BALDOCK, HERTFORDSHIRE, SG7 5QL.
FLEMING, Miss. Nicola Jayne, ACA *2009;* Karringal, Romsey Road, Cadnam, SOUTHAMPTON, SO40 2NY.
FLEMING, Mrs. Nicola Michelle, BSc ACA *1995;* 31 Cliveden Road, LONDON, SW19 3RD.
•FLEMING, Mr. Patrick Joseph, FCA *1974;* 16 Burnley Road, Dollis Hill, LONDON, NW10 1EJ.
FLEMING, Mr. Paul Adam, BSc ACA *2006;* 7 Le Clos Du Bourg, La Grande Route de la Cote, St. Clement, JERSEY, JE2 6SL.
•FLEMING, Mr. Paul James, FCA *1981;* Parkin S. Booth & Co, Yorkshire House, 18 Chapel Street, LIVERPOOL, L3 9AG.
FLEMING, Mr. Peter, FCA CTA *1989;* 3 New Bridge Road, HULL, HU9 2LR.
FLEMING, Miss. Rachel Louise, BA ACA *2007;* 30 Greenfield Road, NEWCASTLE UPON TYNE, NE3 5TP.
FLEMING, Mr. Richard Alexander, MA ACA *1997;* 20 Huntleys Park, TUNBRIDGE WELLS, TN4 9TD.
•FLEMING, Mr. Richard Dixon, ACA CA(AUS) *2008;* KPMG Europe LLP, 15 Canada Square, LONDON, E14 5GL. See also KPMG LLP
FLEMING, Mr. Robert, BA ACA *1996;* 3 Buttercup Place, THATCHAM, RG18 4BT.
FLEMING, Mr. Ronald Malcolm, BA ACA *1985;* 67 Bearcroft, Weobley, HEREFORD, HR4 8TA.
FLEMING, Mr. Russell Robert, FCA *1960;* 29 Conifers, WEYBRIDGE, SURREY, KT13 9TJ.
FLEMING, Mrs. Sarah Lee, BSc ACA *1996;* 675 Hertford Road, ENFIELD, EN3 6NH.
FLEMING, Mr. Stephen Robert, BA ACA *1995;* Branches, Clandon Road, Send, WOKING, SURREY, GU23 7LA.
FLEMING, Mr. Thomas Anthony, BA(Hons) ACA *1993;* 10 Fletcher Drive, Bowdon, ALTRINCHAM, CHESHIRE, WA14 3FZ.
FLEMING, Mr. Timothy Russell, BSc ACA *1998;* 37 Tennyson Road, HARPENDEN, HERTFORDSHIRE, AL5 4BD.
FLEMING, Mrs. Tracy Ann, BSc ACA *1995;* 53 Berrylands Road, SURBITON, SURREY, KT5 8PB.
•FLEMING, Mr. Wayne Paul, BSc FCA CTA *1992;* Wayne Fleming Associates Limited, Greenfields, Swanton Road, DEREHAM, NORFOLK, NR20 4PS.
FLEMING-SMITH, Mr. William, BSc ACA *2003;* 55A Moore Park Road, LONDON, SW6 2HH.
•FLEMONS, Mrs. Anne Margaret, BA FCA *1979;* 2AG Solutions Limited, 76 Birches Lane, KENILWORTH, WARWICKSHIRE, CV8 2AG.
•FLEMONS, Mr. Graham Barry, BA FCA *1979;* (Tax Fac), 2AG Solutions Limited, 76 Birches Lane, KENILWORTH, WARWICKSHIRE, CV8 2AG.
•FLENK, Mr. Richard John, FCA *1972;* 91 Sub Road, Butleigh, GLASTONBURY, SOMERSET, BA6 8SR.
FLENK, Mr. Thomas Samuel, BA ACA *2004;* Top Floor Flat, 1 Caledonia Place, Clifton, BRISTOL, BS8 4DH.
FLESHER, Mr. Peter Stewart, FCA *1966;* Woodridge, 11 Bridle Dene, HALIFAX, HX3 7NR. (Life Member)
FLETCHER, Mr. Adam Michael, BA(Hons) ACA *2002;* Watzmannstrasse 42, 85598 BALDHAM, GERMANY.
FLETCHER, Miss. Alison, BSc ACA *1995;* 78 Kingscourt Road, LONDON, SW16 1JB.
FLETCHER, Mrs. Amanda Jill, FCA *1993;* (Tax Fac), 22 Gunners Park, Bishops Waltham, SOUTHAMPTON, SO32 1PD.
FLETCHER, Mr. Andrew Michael, BA FCA *1998;* Trafalgar House The Promenade, Clifton Down, BRISTOL, BS8 3NG.
FLETCHER, Mr. Andrew Peter, BA ACA *1990;* 57 Tunnel Wood Road, WATFORD, WD17 4GD.
•FLETCHER, Mr. Andrew Richard, MA ACA *1981;* Lowfield House 25 Dearneside Road Denby Dale, HUDDERSFIELD, HD8 8TL.
FLETCHER, Mr. Andrew William, BSc ACA *1988;* Hexagon Place, 6 Falcon Place, WELWYN GARDEN CITY, HERTFORDSHIRE, AL7 1TW.
FLETCHER, Mrs. Anna Elizabeth, ACA *1993;* 25 Mellow Lane West, Hillingdon, UXBRIDGE, UB10 0QU.
FLETCHER, Mrs. Anne, MA(Cantab) ACA *1992;* Newton Bungalow, Gatelawbridge, THORNHILL, DUMFRIESSHIRE, DG3 5EA.
•FLETCHER, Ms. Anne Carolyn, FCA *1974;* Fletcher Naessens, 4 Copperfield Way, CHISLEHURST, BR7 6RY. See also Fletcher A.C.
FLETCHER, Mr. Anthony, BA ACA *2003;* 42 Farmer Street, RICHMOND, VIC 3121, AUSTRALIA.
FLETCHER, Mr. Anthony Gerard, MA ACA *1991;* FAO, Room D280, Finance Division, Via Delle Terme Di Caracalla, 00100 ROME, ITALY.
FLETCHER, Mr. Anthony John, FCA *1963;* 3 The Glade, WELWYN GARDEN CITY, AL8 7LG. (Life Member)
FLETCHER, Mr. Anthony John, FCA *1970;* 9 Rectory Close, Ockley, DORKING, SURREY, RH5 5TN.
•FLETCHER, Mr. Anthony John, BSc FCA *1978;* Cobbs Orchard, High Street, North Moreton, DIDCOT, OXFORDSHIRE, OX11 9AT.
FLETCHER, Mr. Barrie William, FCA *1960;* 19 Kruger Gardens, Admiralty Way, Summerstrand, PORT ELIZABETH, C.P., 6001 SOUTH AFRICA. (Life Member)
FLETCHER, Mrs. Caroline Anne Jury, BA ACA *1993;* 350-B Plaza Office Building, ConocoPhillips, 315 Johnstone Avenue, BARTLESVILLE, OK 74004, UNITED STATES.
•FLETCHER, Mr. Charles Malcolm, FCA *1979;* (Tax Fac), Fletchers, Albion House, 163-167 King Street, DUKINFIELD, CHESHIRE, SK16 4LF.
•FLETCHER, Mrs. Chloe Elizabeth, MA ACA *2004;* Chloe Fletcher, 4 West View Orchard, Freshford, BATH, BA2 7TT.
FLETCHER, Mr. Chris, ACA *2011;* Flat 41 Portland Square, Portland Road, NOTTINGHAM, NG7 4HS.
FLETCHER, Mr. Christopher Charles, ACA *2011;* 48 Stirling Avenue, LEAMINGTON SPA, WARWICKSHIRE, CV32 7HR.
FLETCHER, Mr. Christopher Martin, BSc ACA *2006;* 15 Bartholomew Green, Markyate, ST. ALBANS, HERTFORDSHIRE, AL3 8RX.
FLETCHER, Mrs. Claire Joanne, BA ACA *1999;* 2232 Carmichael Dr, VIENNA, VA 22181, UNITED STATES.
FLETCHER, Mr. Colin James, BSc FCA *1965;* 13 Butt Furlong, Fladbury, PERSHORE, WORCESTERSHIRE, WR10 2QZ. (Life Member)
•FLETCHER, Mr. Colin Malcolm, FCA *1973;* H W, Sterling House, 5 Buckingham Place, Bellfield Rd West, HIGH WYCOMBE, HP13 5HQ. See also HW Corporate Finance LLP, Westernshare Limited and Haines Watts
•FLETCHER, Mr. Colin Peter, BA FCA *1990;* Sawford Bullard, 6 Hazelwood Road, NORTHAMPTON, NN1 1LW.
FLETCHER, Mr. Craig Stewart, ACA *2005;* Arriva Plc, 1 Admiral Way, Doxford International Business Park, SUNDERLAND, SR3 3XP.
FLETCHER, Mr. David Charles, FCA *1975;* Rose Theatre, 24-26 High Street, KINGSTON UPON THAMES, KT1 1HL.
FLETCHER, Mr. David Christopher, MSc FCA *1968;* 106 Westerfield Road, IPSWICH, IP4 2XN. (Life Member)
•FLETCHER, Mr. David Clifford, BSc ACA *1996;* (Tax Fac), Double Espresso & Friends Ltd, 3 The Paddock, Timperley, ALTRINCHAM, CHESHIRE, WA15 7NR.
FLETCHER, Mr. David Faviell, BA ACA *1980;* 2 St. Simon's Avenue, Putney, LONDON, SW15 6DU.
FLETCHER, Mr. David Geoffrey, BSc ACA *2005;* 20 Hesketh Avenue, MANCHESTER, M20 2QW.
FLETCHER, Mr. David Harry, BSc ACA *1984;* 2 Brompton Close, Lower Earley, READING, RG6 3XF.
•FLETCHER, Mr. David Ian, BCom ACA *1989;* KPMG LLP, 15 Canada Square, LONDON, E14 5GL. See also KPMG Europe LLP
FLETCHER, Mr. David John, BA FCA MCT *1987;* 1 Clare Croft, Middleton, MILTON KEYNES, MK10 9HD.
FLETCHER, Mr. David Robert, FCA *1961;* 19 Greycourt Close, Idle, BRADFORD, WEST YORKSHIRE, BD10 8QJ.
FLETCHER, Mr. David Robert, ACA *2009;* Holly Cottage, 43 Chantry Lane, HATFIELD, HERTFORDSHIRE, AL10 9HW.
FLETCHER, Mr. David Stuart Vincent, FCA *1969;* The Old School House, Gate Helmsley, YORK, YO41 1NL. (Life Member)
FLETCHER, Mr. Derek Frederick, FCA *1958;* 1 Halls Close, Hobbs Hill, WELWYN, HERTFORDSHIRE, AL6 9DF. (Life Member)
FLETCHER, Mr. Derek John, FCA *1950;* 13 Rue des Saints Peres, 75006 PARIS, FRANCE. (Life Member)
FLETCHER, Mr. Desmond Percy Cedric, FCA *1955;* 4 Cragside, WHITLEY BAY, NE26 3DU. (Life Member)
FLETCHER, Mr. Edward Stuart, FCA *1960;* 49 St. Johns Road, HELSTON, TR13 8HP. (Life Member)
FLETCHER, Mrs. Emma Louise, BA ACA *1995;* 38 Stradella Road, LONDON, SE24 9HA.
FLETCHER, Mr. Frank David, FCA *1969;* 9 St. Johns View, Bellerby, LEYBURN, NORTH YORKSHIRE, DL8 5QQ.
•FLETCHER, Mr. Geoffrey Michael, MBA FCA *1972;* J Camilo & Associados SROC, Rua Odette de Saint-Maurice 3 L, Piso -1 Escritorio A, 1700-921 LISBON, PORTUGAL.
FLETCHER, Mr. Giles, FCA *1961;* Apple Tree House, Middle Woodford, SALISBURY, SP4 6NG.
FLETCHER, Mr. Glenn Anthony, BSc ACA *1991;* H20 - Lake View Drive, Sherwood Park, NOTTINGHAM, NOTTINGHAMSHIRE, NG15 0HT.
FLETCHER, Mr. Harrison, FCA *1958;* The Croft, 3 Welburn Drive, West Park, LEEDS, LS16 5QD. (Life Member)
FLETCHER, Miss. Heather Clare, BSc ACA *1997;* 33a Church Town, Backwell, BRISTOL, BS48 3JQ.
FLETCHER, Mr. Ian Charles, BA FCA *1990;* Hurcott Farm, Broadheath, TENBURY WELLS, WORCESTERSHIRE, WR15 8QU.
FLETCHER, Mr. Ian Frederick, FCA *1972;* 11 Pontfaen, Llanbedr, CRICKHOWELL, POWYS, NP8 1SJ.
•FLETCHER, Mr. Ian Jack, FCA *1975;* (Tax Fac), Fletcher Greenwood & Co, 11-13 Broad Street, BRADFORD, WEST YORKSHIRE, BD1 4QT.
FLETCHER, Mr. James, ACA CTA *1997;* 36 Clarendon Road, Edgbaston, BIRMINGHAM, B16 9SE.
•FLETCHER, Dr. James, MA DPhil FCA DChA *1993;* (Tax Fac), Fletcher & Partners, Crown Chambers, Bridge Street, SALISBURY, SP1 2LZ.
FLETCHER, Mr. James Christian, ACA *2011;* 5 The Courtyard, Haydon Way, Battersea, LONDON, SW11 1YF.
FLETCHER, Mr. James David, BA ACA *2006;* Rugby Estates Plc, Rosebery House, 4 Farm Street, LONDON, W1J 5RD.
FLETCHER, Mr. James Jeremy Edward, BA ACA *2003;* Strutt & Parker, Walwers Lane, LEWES, EAST SUSSEX, BN7 2JX.
FLETCHER, Mr. James William, LLB ACA *2003;* 1 Holly Mount, Wickersley, ROTHERHAM, SOUTH YORKSHIRE, S66 1JR.
FLETCHER, Mrs. Joanne, BSc ACA *1995;* 39 Freestone Way, Katherine Park, CORSHAM, WILTSHIRE, SN13 9UA.
FLETCHER, Mrs. Joanne, BA ACA *1998;* 162 High Lane East, West Hallam, ILKESTON, DERBYSHIRE, DE7 6HZ.
FLETCHER, Mrs. Jodie, ACA *2009;* 14 Hawley Court, Newton Road Great Barr, BIRMINGHAM, B43 6AF.
FLETCHER, Mr. John, MA FCA *1977;* Rose Cottage Pluckley Road, Charing, ASHFORD, TN27 0AH.
FLETCHER, Mr. John David, FCA *1968;* 6 Chanctonbury View, HENFIELD, BN5 9TW.
FLETCHER, Mr. John David, BSc ACA *1979;* 45 Pebworth Road, HARROW, HA1 3UD.
FLETCHER, Mr. John Giovanni, BA(Hons) ACA *2004;* Apartment 18, Miller, 61 St. Pauls Square, BIRMINGHAM, B3 1QS.
FLETCHER, Mr. John Leo, FCA *1966;* 4 Westmoreland Close, Bowdon, ALTRINCHAM, CHESHIRE, WA14 3QR.
FLETCHER, Mr. John Michael, FCA *1961;* Ivy Cottage, Cholesbury, TRING, HP23 6ND. (Life Member)
FLETCHER, Mr. John Richard, FCA *1972;* 7 Caravaggio Court, T5F, Tigne Point, SLIEMA TP 01, MALTA.
FLETCHER, Mrs. Julie Karen, BA ACA *1997;* 18 Manor Close, Shrivenham, SWINDON, SN6 8AE.
•FLETCHER, Mrs. Kamini, BSc FCA *1990;* Kamini Fletcher Limited, Russett House, Northampton Road, Chapel Brampton, NORTHAMPTON, NN6 8AE.
FLETCHER, Miss. Kate Charlotte, BSc ACA *2001;* Flat 21, 10 The Grange, LONDON, SE1 3AG.
•FLETCHER, Miss. Kathryn Jane, FCA *1993;* Fletcher Thompson, Mill House, 21 High Street, Wicken, ELY, CAMBRIDGESHIRE CB7 5XR.
FLETCHER, Miss. Katrina Jane, ACA *2009;* 6 Kings Court, Market Weighton, YORK, YO43 3FN.
FLETCHER, Mr. Kevin John, BSc ACA *1991;* 129 Sydney Street, WILLOUGHBY, NSW 2068, AUSTRALIA.
FLETCHER, Mr. Lawrence Desmond, BSc ACA *1990;* 76 Cauldwell Lane, Monkseaton, WHITLEY BAY, TYNE AND WEAR, NE25 8LW.
FLETCHER, Mr. Lloyd Irving, FCA *1969;* 73 rue Gabriel Peri, Grigny, F91350 PARIS, FRANCE.
FLETCHER, Miss. Lynne Barbara, BSc ACA *1983;* 8 Woodcote Park Road, EPSOM, KT18 7EX.
FLETCHER, Mr. Malcolm Lewis, FCA *1953;* Greenhills, Steppey Lane, Mancetter, ATHERSTONE, CV9 2RG. (Life Member)
FLETCHER, Mr. Marcus, ACA *2007;* 71 Linton Avenue, BOREHAMWOOD, HERTFORDSHIRE, WD6 4QY.
FLETCHER, Mr. Marek Christopher, BA(Hons) ACA *2001;* (Tax Fac), 2 Ealing Park Gardens, LONDON, W5 4EU.
•FLETCHER, Mr. Mark, BSc ACA *1999;* Crombies Corfield Accountants Limited, 34 Waterloo Road, WOLVERHAMPTON, WV1 4DG. See also Crombies Accountants Limited
FLETCHER, Mr. Mark Shears, BSc ACA *1983;* 41 Ash Hayes Drive, Nailsea, BRISTOL, BS48 2LQ.
FLETCHER, Mr. Mark Timothy, BSc ACA *1994;* (Tax Fac), 7 Pageant Walk, CROYDON, CR0 5UG.
FLETCHER, Mr. Martin Lee, MA BA(Hons) ACA FPC *2010;* 16 John Archer Way, Wandsworth Common, LONDON, SW18 2TQ.
FLETCHER, Mr. Martyn, BSc FCA *1985;* Ansvar Insurance Co Ltd, Ansvar House, 31 St. Leonards Road, EASTBOURNE, BN21 3UR.
FLETCHER, Mr. Michael Brent, FCA *1977;* 7 Chetwyn Court, Gresford, WREXHAM, LL12 8EG.
FLETCHER, Mr. Michael James, BA ACA *2000;* 40 Browning Drive, Winwick, WARRINGTON, WA2 8XL.
FLETCHER, Mrs. Michelle Anne, BA ACA *2002;* 59 Braeburn Way, Kings Hill, WEST MALLING, KENT, ME19 4EA.
FLETCHER, Mr. Neil Arthur, FCA *1981;* Oak Trees, 30 Capesthorne Road, Christleton, CHESTER, CH3 7GA.

FLETCHER, Mr. Neil James, BSc(Hons) ACA *2001;* 25 Walkley Road, SHEFFIELD, S6 2XL.
•**FLETCHER, Mr. Neil Jason, BA ACA** *1994;* PricewaterhouseCoopers LLP, 7 More London Riverside, LONDON, SE1 2RT. See also PricewaterhouseCoopers
FLETCHER, Mr. Nicholas, BSc ACA *1997;* 14 Fiddicroft Avenue, BANSTEAD, SURREY, SM7 3AD.
FLETCHER, Mr. Nicholas Charles, BSc ACA *1998;* Longwood Lunghurst Road, Woldingham, CATERHAM, SURREY, CR3 7EJ.
FLETCHER, Mr. Nicholas John, BA ACA *1985;* Jasmine Cottage, 16 Raglan Road, REIGATE, SURREY, RH2 0DP.
FLETCHER, Mrs. Nicola, BSc ACA ATII *1996;* 21 Roundstone Close, NEWCASTLE UPON TYNE, NE7 7GH.
FLETCHER, Mr. Paddy John Paul, MSc BA ACA *2010;* 67a Richborne Terrace, LONDON, SW8 1AT.
FLETCHER, Mr. Patrick, LLB ACA *2004;* with RSM Tenon Limited, The Poynt Building, 45 Wollaton Street, NOTTINGHAM, NG1 5FW.
FLETCHER, Mr. Paul Edward, BSc ACA MCT *1991;* Bunge SA, 13 Route De Florissant, PO Box 518, 1211 GENEVA, SWITZERLAND.
•**FLETCHER, Mrs. Penelope Jane, FCA** *1994;* DEKM Limited, 5 Trinity Terrace, London Road, DERBY, DE1 2QS.
FLETCHER, Miss. Penny Ruth, ACA *2009;* 25 Flask Walk, LONDON, NW3 1HH.
FLETCHER, Mr. Peter, MMath BSc FCA MInstP *1993;* 1 Argyle Street, IPSWICH, IP4 2NA.
FLETCHER, Mr. Philip Anthony, FCA *1973;* MP Evans Group Plc, 3 Clanricarde Gardens, TUNBRIDGE WELLS, TN1 1HQ.
FLETCHER, Mrs. Rachel Louise, ACA *2005;* 73 Fairfield Road, Hugglescote, COALVILLE, LEICESTERSHIRE, LE67 2HT.
FLETCHER, Mr. Richard Anthony, ACA *2008;* 68 Stocks Lane, BARNSLEY, SOUTH YORKSHIRE, S75 2DD.
FLETCHER, Mr. Richard David, BA ACA *1990;* 9-11 Hall Carr Mill Cottages, ROSSENDALE, BB4 7QD.
FLETCHER, Mr. Richard Edward, BCom FCA *1983;* Mendip Cottage, Renfrew Road, KINGSTON-UPON-THAMES, KT2 7NT.
•**FLETCHER, Mr. Richard Geoffrey, BA ACA** *1990;* Baker & McKenzie LLP, 100 New Bridge Street, LONDON, EC4V 6JA.
FLETCHER, Mr. Richard James, FCA *1973;* 19A Belsize Crescent, LONDON, NW3 5QY. (Life Member)
FLETCHER, Dr. Richard Jason, BSc(Hons) ACA *2000;* Tree Tops, 21 Dearneside Road, Denby Dale, HUDDERSFIELD, HD8 8TL.
FLETCHER, Mr. Robert Martin, BA ACA *2002;* Deutsche Bank Winchester House, 1 Great Winchester Street, LONDON, EC2N 2DB.
FLETCHER, Miss. Sarah Jane, ACA *2008;* Quest Management Services Ltd, F.B. Perry Building, 40 Church Street, P.O.Box HM 2062, HAMILTON HM HX, BERMUDA.
FLETCHER, Mrs. Sarah Jennifer, BSc ACA *2002;* 30 Tom Blower Close, Wollaton, NOTTINGHAM, NG8 1JQ.
FLETCHER, Mrs. Sarah Louise, BA(Hons) ACA *2004;* 2 Wantage View, LIVERPOOL, L36 4QP.
FLETCHER, Mr. Sean Andrew, BA(Hons) ACA *2001;* (Tax Fac), 30 Tom Blower Close, NOTTINGHAM, NG8 1JQ.
FLETCHER, Ms. Sharron, BA ACA *1998;* (Tax Fac), 8 Weavers Park, Copmanthorpe, YORK, YO23 3XA.
FLETCHER, Mr. Simon, BA ACA *2001;* Vonderstraat 1, 6241 BUNDE, NETHERLANDS.
FLETCHER, Mr. Simon Malcolm, BA(Hons) ACA *2004;* 16 Avocet Circuit, CRANEBROOK, NSW 2749, AUSTRALIA.
FLETCHER, Mrs. Stacey Caroline, BA(Hons) ACA *2003;* 34 Renton Avenue, Guiseley, LEEDS, LS20 8EE.
•**FLETCHER, Mr. Stanley, FCA** *1975;* Fletcher & Co, 25 York Close, Freshfield, LIVERPOOL, L37 7HZ.
FLETCHER, Mr. Stephen George, MA FCA *1982;* 11 Methuen Drive, Hoghton, PRESTON, PR5 0JL.
FLETCHER, Mr. Stephen Maxwell, BSc FCA *1977;* 20 Garners Road, GERRARDS CROSS, SL9 0EZ.
•**FLETCHER, Mr. Steven Paul, FCA** *1980;* Robert Miller & Company (Cleadon) Limited, 43a Front Street, Cleadon Village, SUNDERLAND, SR6 7PG.
FLETCHER, Mr. Thomas John, BEng ACA *2005;* Flat 7, 3 Foundation Street, IPSWICH, IP4 1BS.
•**FLETCHER, Mrs. Vanessa Anne, FCA** *1984;* Vanessa Fletcher FCA, Wrentham House, Southwold Road, Wrentham, BECCLES, SUFFOLK NR34 7JF.
FLETCHER, Mrs. Vicky Catherine, BSc ACA *1998;* 5 Vicarage Hill, Kingsteignton, NEWTON ABBOT, DEVON, TQ12 3BA.
FLETCHER, Mr. Walter Karl, MA FCA *1971;* 3 Cobbittee Street, MOSMAN, NSW 2088, AUSTRALIA.
FLETCHER, Mr. William Edward, FCA *1963;* C/o Hurcot Farm, Broadheath, TENBURY WELLS, WORCESTERSHIRE, WR15 8QU.
FLETCHER, Mr. William Neil, FCA *1982;* Manor Farmhouse, Maidwell, NORTHAMPTON, NN6 9JB.
FLETCHER-BLACKWOOD, Mr. Neil Sinclair, FCA *1949;* 580 Diane Circle, Casselberry, CASSELBERRY, FL 32707, UNITED STATES. (Life Member)
•**FLETCHER-COOKE, Mr. Charles Louis Brander, MA FCA** *1972;* Westlands Bride Road, Ramsey, ISLE OF MAN, IM8 3UL.
FLETT, Mr. John Leslie, FCA *1968;* 29 St. Simon Street, SOUTH SHIELDS, TYNE AND WEAR, NE34 9SD.
FLEVILL, Mrs. Kay Michelle, BA(Hons) ACA *2001;* U H Y Hacker Young Turnaround & Recovery, St. James Buildings, 79 Oxford Street, MANCHESTER, M1 6HT.
•**FLEWITT, Mr. John Allan, BSc FCA** *1986;* Menzies LLP, Heathrow Business Centre, 65 High Street, EGHAM, SURREY, TW20 9EY.
•**FLIGHT, Mr. Graham Leslie, FCA** *1978;* Place Flight, Montrose House, 22 Christopher Road, EAST GRINSTEAD, RH19 3BT.
FLIGHT, Miss. Kitty, BEd ACA *2004;* with Freeman and Partners Limited, St. Brides House, 10 Salisbury Square, LONDON, EC4Y 8EH.
FLINDALL, Mr. Craig Richard, BSc ACA *2002;* 39 Sandhills Crescent, SOLIHULL, WEST MIDLANDS, B91 3UE.
FLINDERS, Mr. David Charles, ACA *1984;* Merlewood, Lochwinnoch Road, KILMACOLM, PA13 4DZ.
FLINDERS, Mrs. Rachael, BSc ACA *1997;* The Consumers Association, 2 Marylebone Road, LONDON, NW1 4DF.
FLINDERS, Mr. Stephen Matthew, BSc ACA *2009;* Flat 4 East View Place, East Street, READING, RG1 4AW.
FLINN, Mrs. Caroline Jane, BSc ACA *2002;* 19 Campion Drive, ROMSEY, HAMPSHIRE, SO51 7RD.
FLINT, Mr. Brian William, FCA *1961;* 3 Mill Row, West Hill Road, BRIGHTON, BN1 3SU.
FLINT, Mr. Christopher Graham John, LLM ACA *2002;* Flat 4a, 152 Rosendale Road, West Dulwich, LONDON, SE21 8LG.
FLINT, Mr. Cyril Arthur, FCA *1948;* 156 Merrow Down Country Club, Private Bag XII, BRYANSTON, GAUTENG, 2021, SOUTH AFRICA. (Life Member)
•**FLINT, Mr. David Bruce, FCA** *1970;* 39 Peverell Drive, BIRMINGHAM, B28 9DG.
FLINT, Mr. Eric Victor, FCA *1959;* Birchfield House, Aston Lane, Hope, HOPE VALLEY, DERBYSHIRE, S33 6SA. (Life Member)
FLINT, Mr. Henry Lawrence, BSc FCA *1990;* Mead House High Road, Broad Chalke, SALISBURY, SP5 5EH.
FLINT, Mr. Jeffrey, BSc ACA *1978;* Dove Dale Farm, Norwood Lane, Teversal, SUTTON-IN-ASHFIELD, NG17 3JR.
FLINT, Mr. John Dudley, FCA *1959;* Southway, Thorpe Green, Thorpe Morieux, BURY ST.EDMUNDS, IP30 0NZ. (Life Member)
FLINT, Mr. Martin, BA ACA *1999;* K P M G Salisbury Square House, 8 Salisbury Square, LONDON, EC4Y 8BB.
FLINT, Mr. Matthew James, BSc FCA *1999;* 20 Lovelace Walk, Hucknall, NOTTINGHAM, NG15 7ST.
•①**FLINT, Mr. Paul Andrew, BA FCA** *1991;* with KPMG LLP, St. James's Square, MANCHESTER, M2 6DS.
FLINT, Mr. Peter James, FCA *1970;* 23 Mayfield Heights, Brookhouse Hill, Fulwood, SHEFFIELD, S10 3TT.
FLINT, Mr. Robert James, FCA *1957;* Pinewood Farm, Chelford Road, Marthall, KNUTSFORD, WA16 8SY. (Life Member)
FLINT, Mrs. Samantha Jeanette, BA ACA *2001;* 2 Kingswood Avenue, LEEDS, LS8 2DB.
FLINT, Mrs. Sarah Louise, BSc ACA *2000;* 48 Durrell Drive, Cawston, RUGBY, CV22 7GW.
FLINT, Mr. Stuart, BA(Hons) ACA *2009;* 14 Goldcrest Close, HARTLEPOOL, CLEVELAND, TS26 0RY.
FLINT, Mr. Victor Iain, ACA *1978;* Valkenburgerplein 18, 2103 AT HEEMSTEDE, NETHERLANDS.
FLINT, Mr. William Malcolm, FCA *1967;* 40 Stamford Road, West Bridgford, NOTTINGHAM, NG2 6GE.
FLINT, Mr. William Richard, LLB ACA *1995;* Daily Mail & Gen Trust plc, 2 Derry Street, LONDON, W8 5TT.
FLINTOFF, Mrs. Anita Elizabeth, BSc ACA *2003;* Basement Flat, 33 Cadogan Road, SURBITON, KT6 4DJ.
FLINTOFF, Mr. Collin Edward, FCA *1973;* Ledgers Accountancy Ltd, 76 High Street, NEWPORT PAGNELL, BUCKINGHAMSHIRE, MK16 8AQ.
•**FLINTOFF, Mrs. Julie Amanda, BA ACA** *1993;* with RSM Tenon Audit Limited, Sumner House, St. Thomas's Road, CHORLEY, LANCASHIRE, PR7 1HP.
FLINTOFF, Mr. Robert Thomas, BSc ACA *1979;* 29 Homefield Road, Chiswick, LONDON, W4 2LW.
FLINTOFF, Mr. Thomas David, BSc ACA *1995;* 7 Beechwood Avenue, Kew, RICHMOND, SURREY, TW9 4DD.
FLINTOFF, Mr. Timothy Jonathan, BSc ACA *1989;* 92 Mallard Drive, GREENWICH, CT 06830, UNITED STATES.
FLIPPANCE, Mr. Brian John, BA ACA *1996;* 34 Benham Road, Greens Norton, TOWCESTER, NORTHAMPTONSHIRE, NN12 8DB.
FLISHER, Mr. John Rankine, MA FCA *1949;* 130 The Water Gardens, LONDON, W2 2DE. (Life Member)
FLITCROFT, Mr. Andrew John Alec, BA(Hons) FCA *1992;* 23 Mentmore Gardens, Appleton, WARRINGTON, WA4 3HF.
FLITMAN, Mr. Samuel, BA ACA *2011;* Flat 13, Lanesborough Court, 1 Chillingworth Road, LONDON, N7 8QQ.
FLITT, Mr. Kevin Paul, ACA *2008;* 19 North Larches, DUNFERMLINE, FIFE, KY11 4NX.
•**FLITTER, Mr. Julian Robert, BA FCA** *1991;* Goodman Jones LLP, 29-30 Fitzroy Square, LONDON, W1T 6LQ.
FLITTERMAN, Mr. Laurence Jon, BA FCA *1967;* Hollybrook Old Melton Rd, Normanton-on-the-Wolds, Keyworth, NOTTINGHAM, NG12 5NN.
FLITTON, Mr. James Stuart, FCA *1952;* 6 Richmond Drive, WATFORD, WD17 3BG. (Life Member)
FLIXON, Miss. Wendy Gillian, BSc ACA ATII *1986;* South Ridge, Narberth Road, TENBY, DYFED, SA70 8HT.
FLOCA, Mr. Marius Radu, ACA *2005;* 43 Avante Court, The Bittoms, KINGSTON UPON THAMES, KT1 2AN.
FLOOD, Mr. Alexander Stephen, FCA *1991;* 12 Chester Avenue, Westmere, AUCKLAND, NEW ZEALAND.
FLOOD, Mrs. Andrea Clair, BA(Hons) ACA *2000;* 15 Sandpiper Close, Bingham, NOTTINGHAM, NOTTINGHAMSHIRE, NG13 8QJ.
FLOOD, Mr. Christopher, BSc(Hons) ACA *2003;* 5 Heron Walk, Waterbeach, CAMBRIDGE, CAMBRIDGESHIRE, CB25 9BZ.
FLOOD, Mr. Christopher James, ACA *2008;* Lake Street Manor, Lake Street, MAYFIELD, EAST SUSSEX, TN20 6PP.
FLOOD, Mr. Edward Francis, ACA *1995;* 6 Weardale Avenue, South Bents, SUNDERLAND, SR6 8AS.
FLOOD, Mr. John Antony, FCA *1960;* 84 Malleson Road, Gotherington, CHELTENHAM, GL52 9EX. (Life Member)
•**FLOOD, Miss. Judith, BA FCA** *1987;* (Tax Fac), Thomas Westcott, 26-28 Southernhay East, EXETER, DEVON, EX1 1NS.
FLOOD, Mr. Martyn Trevor, BA(Hons) ACA *1987;* Linden Homes, Linden House, 14 Bartram Road, Totton, SOUTHAMPTON, SO40 9PP.
FLOOD, The Revd. Nicholas Roger, FCA *1970;* The Sanctuary, Salisbury Road, Plaitford, ROMSEY, HAMPSHIRE, SO51 6EE.
•**FLOOD, Mr. Paul Andrew, FCA** *1982;* (Tax Fac), Spain Brothers & Co, Westgate House, 87 St. Dunstans Street, CANTERBURY, KENT, CT2 8AE.
FLOOD, Mr. Paul John, BSc ACA *1993;* Flat 33 Roberts Court, 45 Barkston Gardens, LONDON, SW5 0ES.
FLOOD, Mr. Peter Sinclair, FCA *1969;* The Old Rectory, Ripley Lane, West Horsley, LEATHERHEAD, KT24 6JL.
FLOOD, Dr. Sophie Louisa, PhD BSc ACA *2008;* 38 Hencliffe Way, Hanham, BRISTOL, BS15 3TH.
FLOOD, Mrs. Susannah Louise, BSc ACA *1999;* 12 Rusland Close, Chandler's Ford, EASTLEIGH, HAMPSHIRE, SO53 1SD.
FLOOD, Mr. Timothy James, FCA *1969;* 31A Hook Hill, Sanderstead, SOUTH CROYDON, Surrey, CR2 0LB.
FLOOD, Mrs. Vanessa Janine, BA(Hons) ACA *2001;* 14 Chalkhill Barrow, Melbourn, ROYSTON, HERTFORDSHIRE, SG8 6EQ.
FLOODGATE, Mrs. Gemma Louise Joanne, BSc ACA *2004;* 71 Mithras Gardens, Wavendon Gate, MILTON KEYNES, MK7 7SY.
•**FLOOK, Mr. Gavin, BA FCA** *1993;* with Deloitte Audit S.P Z.O.O, Al Jan Pawla II 19, 00 854 WARSAW, POLAND.
FLOOK, Mrs. Lisa Diane, BSc ACA *1997;* (Tax Fac), 30 Belfry Close, Burbage, HINCKLEY, LE10 2GY.
FLOOK, Mr. Nigel Graham, BA ACA *1998;* 30 Belfry Close, Burbage, HINCKLEY, LE10 2GY.
FLOOK, Mr. Richard, BSc ACA *1989;* Elemis Ltd, The Lodge, 92 Uxbridge Road, HARROW, MIDDLESEX, HA3 6DQ.
•**FLOOK, Mr. Robert James, BSc(Hons) ACA** *2003;* CH4 Accounts Limited, 13 Seymore Mews, New Cross Road, LONDON, SE14 6AG.
FLORA, Mr. Ajitpal Singh, BSc ACA *1996;* 5 Bramley Hill, SOUTH CROYDON, Surrey, CR2 6LU.
FLORA, Miss. Anjalie, ACA *2009;* 16 Mortimer Road, Kempston, BEDFORD, MK42 8RE.
FLORA, Miss. Jaspal Kaur, BSc ACA *2007;* 2 Boston Gardens, Hanwell, LONDON, W7 2AN.
FLORENCE, Mrs. Nicola Jane, BSc ACA *1999;* Partridge Court, Old Vicarage Lane, Kemble, CIRENCESTER, GL7 6BB.
FLORES, Ms. Vickie, BSc ACA *1996;* Flat 23, Dundee Court, 73 Wapping High Street, LONDON, E1W 2YG.
FLOREY, Mr. Michael Andrew, BA ACA *1991;* 18 Hazelhurst Road, Castle Bromwich, BIRMINGHAM, B36 0BH.
FLOREY, Mr. Tim, BEng ACA *2003;* 35 Miller Way, Great Cambourne, CAMBRIDGE, CB23 5FJ.
FLORIDES, Mr. Andrew, BA ACA *1993;* 33A Trent Gardens, SOUTHGATE, LONDON, N14 4QA.
FLORIDES, Mr. Nicos, ACA *2002;* with Ten Group Services Limited, 1 Nikis Avenue, PO Box 21135, CY-1502 NICOSIA, CYPRUS.
•**FLORINGER, Mr. Brian James, FCA** *1993;* (Tax Fac), Lovewell Blake LLP, The Gables, Old Market Street, THETFORD, NORFOLK, IP24 2EN.
FLORSHEIM, Mr. Daniel Robert, BA ACA *1991;* (Tax Fac), FRM AMERICAS LLC, 888 Seventh Avenue, NEW YORK, NY 10019, UNITED STATES.
FLORY, Mr. Peter Clifford, MA FCA *1956;* The Old Rectory, Haselbech, NORTHAMPTON, NN6 9LJ. (Life Member)
•**FLORY, Mr. Simon John, FCA FCCA FICPA** *1984;* (Tax Fac), S J Flory LLP, 66 Haven Way, NEWHAVEN, EAST SUSSEX, BN9 9TD. See also Intelligent Blue Limited
FLOUQUET, Ms. Melanie Anne, ACA MBA *2000;* 20 Rue de l'Odeon, 75006 PARIS, FRANCE.
FLOURI, Miss. Ioulia, BA ACA *2004;* CORNER M. KARAOLI AND GR. AFXENTIOU, 1441 NICOSIA, CYPRUS.
FLOUROS, Mr. Marios, BSc FCA *1995;* 3 Miaoulis Street, 2368 AYIOS DOMETIOS, CYPRUS.
FLOWER, Mr. Andrew John, BA FCA *1989;* FTI Consulting Inc, 3 Times Square, 11th floor, NEW YORK, NY 10036, UNITED STATES.
FLOWER, Miss. Elaine Edna, ACA *1981;* Flat 3 Hillside, Kitnocks Hill, Curdridge, SOUTHAMPTON, SO32 2HJ.
FLOWER, Mr. Ian Campbell, FCA *1978;* Boldavon, Holbrook Road, Stutton, IPSWICH, IP9 2RY.
FLOWER, Mr. James Herbert, FCA *1974;* Flat 5, Waveney House, 30 Ormonde Gate, LONDON, SW3 4HA.
FLOWER, Mr. John Francis, BSc FCA *1961;* Schulweg 6c, 63688 GEDERN, GERMANY. (Life Member)
•**FLOWER, Mr. Matthew John, BSc FCA** *1996;* Zolfo Cooper LLP, 10 Fleet Place, LONDON, EC4M 7RB.
FLOWER, Mrs. Suzanne, BSc ACA *1995;* Oakleawood, 29 Kennel Lane, Fetcham, LEATHERHEAD, SURREY, KT22 9PQ.
FLOWER, Mr. Timothy William, BA(Hons) ACA *2001;* 30 Tasso Road, LONDON, W6 8LZ.
FLOWER, Mrs. Tracey Jayne, ACA *1998;* 144 Bedowan Meadows Tretherras, NEWQUAY, CORNWALL, TR7 2TB.
FLOWERDAY, Mrs. Rachel Sara, BA ACA *2005;* 105 Lady Bay Road, West Bridgford, NOTTINGHAM, NG2 5DT.
FLOWERDEW, Miss. Laura Ann, BA(Hons) ACA *2002;* Anglo American Plc, Anglo American House, 20 Carlton House Terrace, LONDON, SW1Y 5AN.
FLOWERDEW, Mrs. Lesley Ann, BSc ACA MCT *1995;* (Tax Fac), 40 Sole Farm Road, Bookham, LEATHERHEAD, SURREY, KT23 3DJ.
FLOWERDEW, Mr. Lewis Glyn, BCom ACA *1990;* 1 Samsara Road, BROMSGROVE, WORCESTERSHIRE, B60 2TQ.
FLOWERS, Mr. Brett William, BSc ACA *1999;* 3 Admington Drive, Hatton Park, WARWICK, CV35 7TZ.
FLOWERS, Miss. Helen Kate, ACA *2008;* 40 Eastfield Road, Westbury-on-Trym, BRISTOL, BS9 4AD.
FLOWERS, Mr. John Peter, BSc ACA *1992;* Qatargas Operating Company Ltd, P.O. Box 22666, DOHA, QATAR.

FLOWERS, Miss. Karen, ACA *1989;* 2 Lovage Road, Whiteley, FAREHAM, PO15 7LD.
•**FLOWERS, Mr. Martin David, BSc FCA** *1984;* Martin D. Flowers, 1 Paradise Square, SHEFFIELD, S1 2DE.
FLOWERS, Mr. Richard Dominic, MA ACA *1999;* (Tax Fac), Clarins (UK) Ltd, 10 Cavendish Place, LONDON, W1G 9DN.
FLOWITT-HILL, Mr. Stephen Richard, BA FCA *1984;* Saffron Housing Trust, Swan Lane, Long Stratton, NORWICH, NR15 2UY.
FLOYD, Mr. Allen Edward, FCA *1967;* 1 Aldon House, Dorchester Road, YEOVIL, SOMERSET, BA20 2RH.
FLOYD, Mr. Andrew James, BSc ACA *2005;* Bruntwood Management Services Ltd, 24th Floor, City Tower, MANCHESTER, M1 4BD.
FLOYD, Mr. Andrew Paul, BA ACA *1992;* 26 Conifers, WEYBRIDGE, SURREY, KT13 9TJ.
FLOYD, Mr. David Henry Cecil, FCA CF *1983;* Manor Farm, Bowerchalke, SALISBURY, SP5 5BU.
FLOYD, Mr. Hamish Ramsey, BA ACA *2002;* Elm Villa, Crazies Hill, Wargrave, READING, RG10 8LU.
•**FLOYD, Mr. Peter John Laurence, MA FCA** *1982;* Timberfield Ltd, 87a Hadlow Road, TONBRIDGE, KENT, TN9 1QD.
FLOYD, Mrs. Rebecca Jane, BSc ACA *1999;* Malvern Hills District Council The Council House, Avenue Road, MALVERN, WORCESTERSHIRE, WR14 3AF.
•**FLOYD, Mr. Richard Eaglesfield, FCA** *1962;* Jeremy Knight & Co LLP, 29 Roseacre Gardens, Chilworth, GUILDFORD, SURREY, GU4 8RQ. See also Richard Floyd & Co
FLOYDD, Mrs. Louise Kathleen, BSocSc ACA *1996;* St. Catherines, Chinthurst Lane, Bramley, GUILDFORD, SURREY, GU5 0DR.
•**FLOYDD, Mr. Maxwell John, FCA** *1985;* (Tax Fac), Saffery Champness, Edinburgh Quay, 133 Fountainbridge, EDINBURGH, EH3 9BA.
FLOYDD, Mr. William James Spencer, BSocSc ACA *1996;* Logica Chaucer House, The Office Park Springfield Drive, LEATHERHEAD, KT22 7LP.
FLOYDE, Mrs. Jessica Emily, BSc ACA *2005;* 31 Charles Avenue, Stoke Gifford, BRISTOL, BS34 8LW.
FLOYER-LEA, Ms. Anna Marie, ACA *2008;* 26 Heron Island, Caversham, READING, RG4 8DQ.
FLUDE, Dr. James Paul Maurice, BSc ACA *2004;* 2 Bittern Croft, Horbury, WAKEFIELD, WEST YORKSHIRE, WF4 5PD.
FLUKER, Mr. Patrick James, BA FCA *1980;* 39 Fingal Avenue, GLENHAVEN, NSW 2156, AUSTRALIA.
FLUSKEY, Mr. Allan, BA FCA *1976;* 88 Elmswood Gardens, NOTTINGHAM, NG5 4AW.
FLUSS, Mr. James Gordon, BSc(Econ) FCA *1991;* 13 Ravenshurst Avenue, LONDON, NW4 3EE.
FLUX, Mr. David, FCA *1976;* 23 Marina East, 30 Colley Terrace, GLENELG, SA 5045, AUSTRALIA.
FLUX, Mr. Nicholas Keith, BSc(Hons) FCA *2001;* 2 Thorpe View, ASHBOURNE, DERBYSHIRE, DE6 1SY.
FLYNN, Mr. Anthony John, FCA *1965;* Herbert Reeves & Co, 44 Great Eastern Street, LONDON, EC2A 3EP.
•**FLYNN, Mr. Anthony Joseph, BA FCA** *1987;* (Tax Fac), Benson Flynn Ltd, 4 Abbey Square, CHESTER, CH1 2HU. See also Abbey Tax Services Limited
•①**FLYNN, Mr. Anthony Norman, FCA** *1985;* with Re10 (UK) Plc, Albemarle House, 1 Albemarle Street, LONDON, W1S 4HA.
•**FLYNN, Mr. Bartholomew, BSc FCA** *1982;* Ernst & Young LLP, 20 Chapel Street, LIVERPOOL, L3 9AG. See also Ernst & Young Europe LLP
FLYNN, Miss. Bernadette Marie, BSc ACA *1986;* Llewelyn-Davies, Brook House, Torrington Place, LONDON, WC1E 7HN.
FLYNN, Mrs. Caitriona Anne, BA ACA *1995;* Grays Cottage, 16 Warwick Road, Upper Boddington, DAVENTRY, NORTHAMPTONSHIRE, NN11 6DH.
•**FLYNN, Ms. Caroline Louise, BCom ACA** *1994;* KPMG, 1 Stokes Place, St. Stephen's Green, DUBLIN 2, COUNTY DUBLIN, IRELAND.
FLYNN, Mr. Christopher, BSc ACA *1994;* 32 Keppoch Court, Dannemora, AUCKLAND 2016, NEW ZEALAND.
FLYNN, Mrs. Claire Suzanne, BA ACA *1998;* 755 Crossbrook Drive, MORAGA, CA 94556, UNITED STATES.
FLYNN, Mr. Craig Andrew, BSc ACA *1999;* 33 Rixtonleys Drive, Irlam, MANCHESTER, M44 6RN.
FLYNN, Mrs. Elaine Wendy, BA ACA *1982;* 10 Willow Lane, AMERSHAM, HP7 9DW.
FLYNN, Mr. Francis George Arthur, FCA *1949;* Tarn House, 7 Aston Park, Aston Rowant, WATLINGTON, OXFORDSHIRE, OX49 5SW. (Life Member)
FLYNN, Mrs. Gillian Patricia, BSc ACA *1992;* 9 Glen Road, Burton Joyce, NOTTINGHAM, NG14 5BQ.
FLYNN, Mr. James, BCom ACA *1994;* E8 Network Enterprise Park, Kilkloole, WICKLOW, COUNTY WICKLOW, IRELAND.
FLYNN, Mr. James Anthony, MA BSc ACA *2009;* 15 Coles Green Road, Dollis Hill, LONDON, NW2 6ED.
FLYNN, Miss. Joanne Elizabeth, ACA *2006;* 29 Cormorant Way, LEIGHTON BUZZARD, BEDFORDSHIRE, LU7 4UY.
•**FLYNN, Mr. John, BA FCA** *2000;* Sirius Business Solutions Limited, 2 Wimpole Close, YORK, YO30 5GG.
FLYNN, Miss. Julia, LLB ACA *1996;* 77 Oak Road, Horfield, BRISTOL, BS7 8RZ.
FLYNN, Miss. Kathryn, BSc(Hons) ACA *2011;* 242a Warrington Road, Ince, WIGAN, WN3 4NH.
FLYNN, Miss. Lauren, ACA *2009;* 124D Grove Park, LONDON, SE5 8LD.
FLYNN, Dr. Mark Barry Johnston, FCA FRSA *1990;* 185 College Street, Long Eaton, NOTTINGHAM, NG10 4GE.
•**FLYNN, Mr. Michael George, BA FCA** *1991;* with McCranors Limited, Clifford House, 38-44 Binley Road, COVENTRY, CV3 1JA.
FLYNN, Mr. Niall, BEng ACA *2005;* Experian Group Services Limited, Newenham House, Northern Cross, Malahide Road, DUBLIN 17, COUNTY DUBLIN IRELAND.
FLYNN, Mr. Patrick James, FCA *1963;* 29 Heybridge Avenue, Streatham, LONDON, SW16 3DY.
FLYNN, Mr. Paul Anthony, BSc ACA *1995;* Blossden Cottage, Salmons Road, Effingham, LEATHERHEAD, SURREY, KT24 5QJ.
FLYNN, Mr. Paul James, BA ACA *1993;* Balfour Beatty Ltd Kings Business Park, Kings Drive, PRESCOT, MERSEYSIDE, L34 1PJ.
FLYNN, Mr. Philip Stanley, BSc FCA *1986;* La Porte La Rue de Cambrai Trinity, JERSEY, JE3 5AL.
FLYNN, Miss. Rebecca Louise, BA ACA *2006;* 6 Glenville Road, KINGSTON UPON THAMES, SURREY, KT2 6DD.
FLYNN, Miss. Sarah, ACA *2008;* with Alliott Wingham Limited, Kintyre House, 70 High Street, FAREHAM, HAMPSHIRE, PO16 7BB.
FLYNN, Mr. Stuart Adrian, BA ACA *1993;* 7 Overslade Road, SOLIHULL, B91 3NA.
FLYNN, Mrs. Susan Deborah Leigh, BSc ACA *1982;* Hermes Pensions Management Ltd Lloyds Chambers, 1 Portsoken Street, LONDON, E1 8HZ.
FLYNN, Mr. Victor, BSc ACA *1988;* Chevin Housing Group, Harrison Street, WAKEFIELD, WF1 1PS.
•**FLYNN, Mr. William Brendan, FCA** *1976;* (Tax Fac), Southgate Accounting and Computer Consultants Ltd, 81 Ulleswater Road, Southgate, LONDON, N14 7BN. See also Flynn & Co
FOAKES, Mr. Robert David, FCA *1973;* QED Centre, Welsh Assembly Government South Division, Q E D Centre Treforest Industrial Estate, PONTYPRIDD, MID GLAMORGAN, CF37 5YR.
FOALE, Mr. Adrian John, FCA *1971;* 32 Hawe Farm Way, HERNE BAY, CT6 7UB.
FOALE, Mr. Graham Douglas Kenneth, JP FCA *1964;* 8 Blue Haze Close, Glenholt, PLYMOUTH, PL6 7HR.
FODEN, Mr. Cyril, FCA *1953;* 77 Walton Road, SALE, M33 4BB. (Life Member)
FODEN, Mr. George Harrington, FCA *1958;* The Red House, Bearswood End, BEACONSFIELD, BUCKINGHAMSHIRE, HP9 2NR. (Life Member)
FODEN, Mr. Karl James, ACA *1987;* Standard Bank Isle of Man Ltd Standard Bank House One, Circular Road Douglas, ISLE OF MAN, IM1 1SB.
FODEN, Mr. Kenneth Ernest, FCA *1969;* 61 Adelaide Road, Bramhall, STOCKPORT, SK7 1NR.
FODEN, Miss. Margaret Mary, BSc FCA *1996;* 43 Riding Dene, Mickley, STOCKSFIELD, NE43 7DQ.
•**FOFARIA, Mr. Kirtikumar Navalchand, BSc FCA** *1975;* K Fofaria, 30 Ilmington Road, HARROW, MIDDLESEX, HA3 0NH.
•**FOGARTY, Mrs. Gemma Louise, ACA** *2009;* Sadler Davies & Co LLP, 25A Essex Road, DARTFORD, DA1 2AU.
FOGARTY, Mr. Gerard Patrick, ACA *1992;* Currabaha, Templederry, Nenagh, TIPPERARY, COUNTY TIPPERARY, IRELAND.
FOGARTY, Miss. Katharine Mary Elizabeth, BA(Hons) ACA *2000;* Ground Floor Flat, 8, Hazelbourne Road, LONDON, SW12 9NS.
FOGARTY, Mrs. Sara Jane, BSocSc ACA *1992;* Regulatory & Operational Risk 3rd Floor, Ulster Bank Ltd, 11-16 Donegall Square East, BELFAST, BT1 5UB.
FOGDEN, Mrs. Ellen, BA ACA *1990;* 52 West End Lane, Horsforth, LEEDS, LS18 5JP.
FOGDEN, Mr. Jason, BA ACA *1998;* Erlenmattstrasse 22 (T4), CH-4058 BASEL, SWITZERLAND.
FOGERTY, Ms. Helen Elizabeth, BSc ACA *2005;* 14 St. James Drive, HARROGATE, NORTH YORKSHIRE, HG2 8HT.
FOGG, Mr. Christopher Michael, MBA BSc FCA *1968;* Connect London Ltd, 8 The Coles Shop, Abbeys Mills, Merton, LONDON, SW19 2RD.
FOGG, Mr. Jonathan, MSc BCom ACA *2011;* Flat 5, Wesley Court, Scotland Road, CAMBRIDGE, CB4 1GE.
•**FOGG, Mr. Martyn Guy, FCA** *1970;* 10 Dilliway Court, Western Road, BURNHAM-ON-CROUCH, ESSEX, CM0 8HY.
FOGG, Mr. Michael John, FCA *1972;* 7003 Greentree Drive, NAPLES, FL 34108, UNITED STATES. (Life Member)
FOGG, Miss. Natalie Louise, BSc ACA *2004;* 14/1 Simper Street, Wembley, PERTH, WA 6014, AUSTRALIA.
FOGG, Mr. Nicholas James, BSc ACA *1991;* Swiss RE, 30 St. Mary Axe, LONDON, EC3A 8EP.
•**FOGG, Mr. Richard Alan, MA ACA** *1980;* Richard A Fogg MA ACA, 98 Erddig Road, WREXHAM, LL13 7DR.
FOGGIN, Mr. Graham, BSc ACA *1991;* 8 Figgswood, COULSDON, SURREY, CR5 1RY.
FOGGO, Mrs. Melba Margaret, BA ACA *1999;* OakTree Cottage, 139 Tortoiseshell Way, BRAINTREE, CM7 1ZL.
FOISTER, Mr. David Richard, BA ACA *1985;* 34 Bayes Street, KETTERING, NORTHAMPTONSHIRE, NN16 8EH.
FOK, Mr. Chi Tak, ACA *2006;* Flat A 1/F, Tower 1, Beacon Heights, KOWLOON TONG, KOWLOON, HONG KONG SAR.
FOK, Mr. Hei Yuen Paul, ACA *2005;* Tang and Fok, Rooms 1801-3 18/Floor, Tung Ning Building, 249-253 Des Voeux Road Central, CENTRAL, HONG KONG ISLAND HONG KONG SAR.
FOK, Dr. Kai Kwong, ACA *2008;* Flat 1 16th floor, Block A, Peninsula Heights, 63 Broadcast Drive, KOWLOON TONG, KOWLOON HONG KONG SAR.
FOK, Ms. Kin Wah, ACA *2007;* 2A, Century Tower 1, 1 Tregunter Path, CENTRAL, HONG KONG ISLAND, HONG KONG SAR.
FOK, Mr. Michael Hin Keung, MSc ACA *1994;* 22 Repulse Bay Garden, 17th Floor, 18-40 Belleview Drive, REPULSE BAYHong Kong Island, HONG KONG SAR.
FOK, Mr. Ming Fuk, ACA *2005;* Suite A 47th Floor Tower 6, Bel-Air No.8, 8 Bel-Air Peak Avenue, Island South, CENTRAL, HONG KONG SAR.
FOK, Ms. See Wai, ACA *2007;* 30C Tower 5, The Belcher's, 89 Pok Fu Lam Road, POK FU LAM, HONG KONG ISLAND, HONG KONG SAR.
FOK, Mr. Sek Chi, ACA *2008;* FC Partners CPA Limited, Room 1902-4, 19/F Richful Centre, 11-12 Tak Hing High Street, TSIM SHA TSUI, KOWLOON HONG KONG SAR.
FOK, Ms. Siu Yung Feather, ACA *2007;* House 49, Fifth Street, Hong Lok Yuen, TAI PO, NEW TERRITORIES, HONG KONG SAR.
FOK KAM, Mr. Andre Eugene, BSc FCA *1979;* 4251 Kimber Street, PIERREFONDS H9H 5C5, QC, CANADA.
FOKES, Mr. Brian Ronald, FCA *1971;* 34 Rowan Way, Rottingdean, BRIGHTON, BN2 7FP. (Life Member)
FOKIAS, Mr. George, FCA *1977;* ul.gornoslaska 48/4, 62-800 KALISZ, POLAND.
•**FOKIAS, Mrs. Ruth Betiwyn, FCA** *1975;* Bright Brown Limited, Exchange House, St. Cross Lane, NEWPORT, ISLE OF WIGHT, PO30 5BZ.
FOKIDES, Mr. Marios, BA ACA *2007;* Flat 301, Ellados 10 Street, Acropolis, 2003 NICOSIA, CYPRUS.
FOLDES, Mr. John Henry Roger, MA ACA *1989;* 1 St. Winifreds Court, Kingston-on-Soar, NOTTINGHAM, NG11 0DQ.
•**FOLEY, Mr. Anthony John, BSc ACA** *1984;* (Tax Fac), A.J. Foley, Gwylfa, 16 Cefn Mably Park, CARDIFF, CF3 6AA.
FOLEY, Mrs. Clare, BA ACA *1992;* 16 Glenathol Road, Calderstones, LIVERPOOL, L18 3JS.
FOLEY, Mr. Edward Michael, FCA *1948;* 25 Northern Shadows Lane, SEDONA, AZ 86336, UNITED STATES. (Life Member)
FOLEY, Mrs. Emma, BA ACA *2002;* 8 Oak Avenue, Burley in Wharfedale, ILKLEY, WEST YORKSHIRE, LS29 7PH.
FOLEY, Ms. Gillian Mary, BA ACA *1990;* 5 Wrights Yard, Back Lane, GREAT MISSENDEN, BUCKINGHAMSHIRE, HP16 0BZ.
FOLEY, Mr. Grant Jeffrey, BA FCA *1998;* 10 Meadowside Road, UPMINSTER, ESSEX, RM14 3YT.
FOLEY, Mrs. Jane Marie, BA ACA *1990;* 27 St. Marys Park, ROYSTON, SG8 7XB.
•**FOLEY, Mr. John, FCA** *1964;* John Foley, 5 Sedge Mead, Netley Abbey, SOUTHAMPTON, SO31 5EY.
FOLEY, Mr. John Robert, BA ACA *1982;* Sandon House, Main Street, Bishampton, PERSHORE, WORCESTERSHIRE, WR10 2LX.
FOLEY, Mr. John Stephen, FCA *1973;* Mayerling, Blundell Road, Hightown, LIVERPOOL, L38 9EE.
FOLEY, Mrs. Julie Denise, BSc ACA *1993;* 12 Brookside Walk, LEIGHTON BUZZARD, BEDFORDSHIRE, LU7 3LA.
FOLEY, Mr. Kenneth, FCA *1949;* 1057 Den Mills Road, Apt 311, TORONTO M3C 1W9, ON, CANADA. (Life Member)
FOLEY, Mr. Kevan Paul, ACA *1981;* 18 Alderwood Avenue, EASTLEIGH, SO53 4TH.
•**FOLEY, Mr. Martin John, BA FCA** *1976;* (Tax Fac), Zandan Limited, 4 Grotes Place, Blackheath, LONDON, SE3 0QH.
•**FOLEY, Mr. Michael John Mitchell, FCA** *1970;* Foley & Co, 44A Oriental Road, WOKING, GU22 7AR.
FOLEY, Mr. Nicholas Roger, MA ACA *1980;* Manor House, 29 Broadway, Chilton Polden, BRIDGWATER, SOMERSET, TA7 9DP.
FOLEY, Mr. Richard John, FCA *1975;* PO Box 5167, SYDNEY, NSW 2001, AUSTRALIA. (Life Member)
FOLEY, Mr. Seamus, BSc FCA *1974;* 203 Courthouse Road, MAIDENHEAD, SL6 6HP.
FOLEY, Mr. Sean Liam, MA ACA *2003;* Westfield Shopping Towns Ltd, 71 High Holborn, LONDON, WC1V 6EA.
FOLEY, Mr. Simon David, BSc ACA *2001;* Cable & Wireless Panama SA, Piso 7 Torre B, Apartado Postal 659, PANAMA CITY 9A, PANAMA.
FOLEY, Mr. Stephen Anthony, BSc ACA *1989;* G. H. Warner Footwear PLC, Mercury House, Lea Road, WALTHAM ABBEY, ESSEX, EN9 1AT.
FOLEY, Miss. Suzanne Mary, MSc ACA *2001;* 14 Burnaby Gardens, LONDON, W4 3DT.
FOLEY, Mr. Terence Patrick, ACA *1981;* Oakwood Shopfitting, Southway, ANDOVER, HAMPSHIRE, SP10 5AG.
FOLKARD, Mr. Gordon David, BSc ACA *1989;* Beckington Cottage, 75 Milton Lane, WELLS, BA5 2QT.
FOLKES, Mrs. Claire Louise, BSc ACA *1999;* Willow Barn, Duddenhoe End, SAFFRON WALDEN, ESSEX, CB11 4UU.
FOLKES, Mr. Ian Arthur, BSc ACA *1992;* Young & Rubicam, 50 Scotts Road #03-01, SINGAPORE, SINGAPORE.
FOLKES, Mr. Keith Anderson, BA FCA *1968;* Lidsey Lodge, Sack Lane, BOGNOR REGIS, PO22 9PE.
FOLKS, Miss. Rachel Clare, BSc ACA *2003;* 10 Rum Close, LONDON, E1W 3QX.
FOLLAND, Mrs. Jolly, BA ACA *1987;* 91 Abingdon Road, LONDON, W8 6QU.
FOLLAND, Mr. Russell Graeme, MA ACA *1986;* 91 Abingdon Road, LONDON, W8 6QU.
FOLLETT, Mr. Barry, FCA *1965;* 334 Reigate Road, Epsom Downs, EPSOM, KT17 3LX. (Life Member)
FOLLETT-SMITH, Mr. Christopher Robert, FCA *1970;* PO Box 1355, WANDSBECK, 3631, SOUTH AFRICA.
FOLLEY, Mr. Keith, FCA *1967;* Coniston, 9 Noyna View, COLNE, BB8 7AU.
FOLLEY, Mr. Matthew Alan, BA(Hons) ACA *2007;* 109 Cranworth Gardens, LONDON, SW9 0NT.
FOLLEY, Mr. Stuart, BSc ACA *1992;* The Gables, Dewlands Common, VERWOOD, DORSET, BH31 6JL.
FOLLIS, Ms. Marion Jean, BA(Hons) ACA *2000;* 13 Carberry Road, LONDON, SE19 3RU.
FOLLISS, Mr. John Roy, BSc ACA *1983;* Dog Kennel Lodge, Burton Road, Whittington, LICHFIELD, WS13 8QE.
•**FOLLOWS, Mr. Andrew Gordon Dewdney, BEng FCA DChA** *2000;* Kingston Smith LLP, 105 St Peters Street, ST. ALBANS, HERTFORDSHIRE, AL1 3EJ. See also Kingston Smith Limited Liability Partnership, Devonshire Corporate Services LLP and Kingston Smith Consulting LLP
FOLLWELL, Mrs. Valerie, BSc FCA *1978;* Church House Farm, Chapel Chorlton, NEWCASTLE, STAFFORDSHIRE, ST5 5JN.
FOLMAN, Ms. Lisa-Marie, BSc ACA *2005;* Flat 1, 3 Private Road Sherwood, NOTTINGHAM, NG5 4DD.
FOLWELL, Mr. Andrew, BSc ACA *2004;* 118 Darley Green Road, Knowle, SOLIHULL, B93 8PN.
FOLWELL, Mrs. Catherine Sarah, MSc BSc ACA *2003;* 118 Darley Green Road, Knowle, SOLIHULL, WEST MIDLANDS, B93 8PN.

•**FOLWELL-DAVIES, Mrs. Kathryn, BA ACA CF** *1999;* Deloitte LLP, Athene Place, 66 Shoe Lane, LONDON, EC4A 3BQ. See also Deloitte & Touche LLP

FON-SING, Mr. Max Danny Kim Shiam, BSc ACA *1993;* Bois Cheri Road, MOKA, MAURITIUS.

FON-SING, Mr. William Voo Chongn, FCA *1969;* 22 Fr Folix de Valois, PORT LOUIS, MAURITIUS.

FONE, Mr. Christopher Mark, BA ACA *1992;* Summerfield, Little London, HEATHFIELD, EAST SUSSEX, TN21 0NU.

FONE, Mr. Douglas John, LLB ACA *1991;* Level 4, 95 Pitt Street, SYDNEY, NSW 2000, AUSTRALIA.

FONE, Mrs. Lakshmi Tara, ACA *2009;* 11 Shandy Street, LONDON, E1 4LX.

FONE, Mrs. Madeleine Louise Hearsum, BSc ACA DChA *1984;* 6 Days Lane, Biddenham, BEDFORD, MK40 4AD.

FONE, Miss. Valerie, MBE FCA *1962;* 11 Broad Oak, WOODFORD GREEN, IG8 0LH.

•**FONE, Mr. William John, FCA** *1968;* Bill Fone, Bear Place Farm, Blakes Lane, Hare Hatch, READING, RG10 9TA.

FONG, Mr. Andrew Fu-Chiu, BSc ACA *1992;* Flat E 58/F Tower 5, The Belchers, 89 Pok Fu Lam Road, POK FU LAM, HONG KONG ISLAND, HONG KONG SAR.

FONG, Mr. Andrew Yik Cheong, MSc BSc ACA *1992;* 12251 Trites Road, RICHMOND V7E 3R6, BC, CANADA.

FONG, Mr. Augustine Ts'oi Tuck, ACA *1983;* 12 PEEL ROAD, SINGAPORE 248616, SINGAPORE.

FONG, Mr. Chi Ho, ACA *2007;* C-5-1, Fairview Park, YUEN LONG, NEW TERRITORIES, HONG KONG SAR.

FONG, Mr. Chi Wing, ACA *2008;* Flat G 32/F, Tower 5 Aqua Marine, No.8 Sham Shing Road, SHAM SHUI PO, KOWLOON, HONG KONG SAR.

FONG, Ms. Ching Yin, ACA *2008;* Flat A, 7/F, Block 29, Laguna City, KWUN TONG, HONG KONG SAR.

FONG, Mr. Chun Fai, ACA *2007;* Flat 4 14/F Tower C, Fortress Metro Tower, No.238 Kings Road, NORTH POINT, HONG KONG ISLAND, HONG KONG SAR.

FONG, Mr. Danny Siu Lung, ACA *2005;* 26/F Flat H, Block 22, South Horizons, AP LEI CHAU, HONG KONG SAR.

FONG, Mr. Eddy Ching, BA FCA *1972;* Securities & Futures Commission, 8th Floor, Chater House, 8 Connaught Road, CENTRAL, HONG KONG ISLAND HONG KONG SAR.

FONG, Mr. Fuk Wai, ACA *2008;* Chinese Overseas Town (Asia) Holdings Ltd, 3203 Tower 6 The Gateway, Harbour City, TSIM SHA TSUI, KOWLOON, HONG KONG SAR.

FONG, Miss. Grace Kit-Yee, BSc ACA *1987;* Flat 1269 Tower 12, HONG KONG SAR Parkview, 88 Tai Tam Reservoir Road, STANLEY, HONG KONG ISLAND, HONG KONG SAR.

FONG, Mr. Hok Yin, ACA *2010;* Flat B 13th Floor, Kelford Mansion, 168 Hollywood Road, SHEUNG WAN, HONG KONG ISLAND, HONG KONG SAR.

FONG, Ms. Hon Fan, ACA *2005;* Flat B 15/F Block 10, 8 On Pong Road, Tai Po Centre, TAI PO, NEW TERRITORIES, HONG KONG SAR.

•**FONG, Mr. Hup, FCA** *1971;* Deloitte Touche Tohmatsu, 35/F One Pacific Place, 88 Queensway, CENTRAL, HONG KONG ISLAND, HONG KONG SAR. See also Kwan Wong Tan & Hong

FONG, Mr. Joe King, BSc ACA *1982;* Viale delle Terme di Caracalla, 00153 ROME, ITALY.

FONG, Mr. Joe Kwong Yat, ACA *2005;* Suite 1104, HONG KONG SAR Club Building, 3A Chater Road, CENTRAL, HONG KONG ISLAND, HONG KONG SAR.

FONG, Mr. Kin Kong Raymond, ACA *2007;* Room 903, Fu Yat House, Fu Keung Court, WANG TAU HOM, KOWLOON, HONG KONG SAR.

•**FONG, Mr. Laval Robert, ACA** *1982;* L.R. Fong, 1050 Schubert Street, BROSSARD J4X 1X1, QUE, CANADA.

FONG, Mr. Mark Chung, MSc FCA *1977;* with Grant Thornton, 6th Floor, Sunning Plaza, 10 Hysan Avenue, CAUSEWAY BAY, HONG KONG SAR.

FONG, Mrs. Nellie Kut Man, FCA *1973;* Room 1602 16/Fl, 9 Queen's Road Central, CENTRAL, HONG KONG SAR.

FONG, Miss. Phoebe, FCA *1978;* 11A Mount Rosie Road, SINGAPORE 3080 48, SINGAPORE.

FONG, Mr. Raymond King-Man, MBA BSc FCA *1985;* A5 Repulse Bay Towers, 119a Repulse Bay Road, REPULSE BAY, HONG KONG ISLAND, HONG KONG SAR.

FONG, Mr. Seow Kee, BA FCA *1983;* 5 Lengkok Setiabistari, Bukit Damansara, 50490 KUALA LUMPUR, FEDERAL TERRITORY, MALAYSIA.

FONG, Mr. Tat Wah David, ACA *2008;* David TW Fong & Co, Unit B 23/F, North Cape Commercial Building, 388 Kings Road, NORTH POINT, HONG KONG SAR. See also Nexia Charles Mar Fan & Co

FONG, Mr. Wai Kwong, ACA *2007;* 6983 Main Street, VANCOUVER V5X 3H6, BC, CANADA.

FONG, Mr. Yew Meng, BSc ACA *1978;* 28 Leonie Hill #23-30, Leonie Towers-A, SINGAPORE 239227, SINGAPORE.

FONG, Mr. Yew Meng, BSc ACA *1990;* with PricewaterhouseCoopers LLP, 1 Embankment Place, LONDON, WC2N 6RH.

FONG, Mr. Yuk Kee Maurice, ACA *2004;* Maurice Fong & Company, Unit 2201-2 22/F, Chinachem Johnston Plaza, 178-186 Johnston Road, WAN CHAI, HONG KONG ISLAND HONG KONG SAR.

FONSECA-VOYIATZIS, Mrs. Marta Maria, MSc BA(Hons) ACA *2002;* University of Arts, 5 Richbell Place, LONDON, WC1N 3LA.

FONSEKA, Mr. Marcus Andrew, FCA *1988;* 12511 Boheme Dr., HOUSTON, TX 77024, UNITED STATES.

FONTAINE, Mr. Mark Philip, BSc FCA *1987;* Oakdean Hampstead Norreys Road, Hermitage, THATCHAM, RG18 9RT.

FONTBIN, Mr. Philip Lawrence, ACA ATT MBA *1999;* Avanti, 66 Grove Gardens, TRING, HP23 5PY.

FONTENEAU, Mr. Jerome, BSc ACA *1994;* Flat 6, 22 Gledhow Gardens, South Kensington, LONDON, SW5 0AZ.

FONTES, Mr. Adrian Victor, BA FCA *1968;* Flat 7 Netley Castle, Abbey Hill Netley Abbey, SOUTHAMPTON, SO31 5FA.

FOO, Mr. Charles Loke Fay, BSc ACA *1988;* 37 Holly Gardens, West End, SOUTHAMPTON, SO30 3RU.

FOO, Miss. Chekwan, BSc ACA *1994;* Blk 318, Clementi Avenue 4, Apt 12-87, SINGAPORE 120318, SINGAPORE.

FOO, Miss. Him Tiem, BSc ACA *1992;* Apartment 2003, Block 2, Oasis Riviera, 883 Shui Cheng Rd, SHANGHAI 200051, CHINA.

FOO, Miss. Li Wah, ACA *1988;* 12 Jalan USJ 4/6B, UEP Subang Jaya, 47600 SUBANG, SELANGOR, MALAYSIA.

FOO, Mr. Nyap-Peen, BA FCA *1985;* PO Box 10692, The Terrace, WELLINGTON 6011, NEW ZEALAND.

FOO, Mr. San Kan, FCA *1973;* G-6-1 Hijauan Kiara, No. 6 Jalan Kiara 5, Mont Kiara, 50480 KUALA LUMPUR, FEDERAL TERRITORY, MALAYSIA.

FOO, Dr. See Liang, FCA *1983;* SOA SMU Level 5, 60 Stamford Road, SINGAPORE 178900, SINGAPORE.

FOO, Mr. Siak Chung, BSc ACA *2001;* F-8-2 Hijauan Kiara, No 6 Jalan Kiara 5, Mont Kiara, 50480 KUALA LUMPUR, FEDERAL TERRITORY, MALAYSIA.

FOO, Mr. Siang Mong Robert, FCA *1971;* 15 Balmoral Road, #02-04 Belmond Green, SINGAPORE 259801, SINGAPORE. (Life Member)

FOO, Mr. Tiang-Sooi, MSc FCA *1976;* 1C Victoria Park Road, SINGAPORE 266481, SINGAPORE.

FOO, Miss. Tina Ai Lynn, BA ACA *1999;* 152 Claremont Avenue, Motspur Park, NEW MALDEN, KT3 6QR.

FOO, Mr. Zhi Yong, ACA *2011;* Flat 154, 41 Millharbour, LONDON, E14 9ND.

FOO KUNE, Mr. Jean Nicolas, ACA *2011;* Flat 23, Centre Heights, 137 Finchley Road, LONDON, NW3 6JG.

FOODY, Mr. Cormac James Anthony D, BA ACA *2009;* 10 Linnet Close, NEWTON-LE-WILLOWS, MERSEYSIDE, WA12 9XJ.

FOOGOOA, Mr. Ashwin, MA ACA *2001;* 46 Waterside Close, Barnham Drive, off Central Way, Thamesmead, LONDON, SE28 0GS.

FOOKES, Mr. Melvyn, ACA *1981;* Mayerton Refractories Europe Ltd, Unit 7, Hockley Court, 2401 Stratford Road, Hockley Heath, SOLIHULL WEST MIDLANDS B94 6NW.

FOOKES, Mr. Richard Charles, BEng ACA *1993;* 1 Willingale Road, BRAINTREE, ESSEX, CM7 9FA.

FOOKS, Mr. John Anthony, MA FCA *1959;* Woodgate House, Beckley, RYE, TN31 6UH. (Life Member)

FOOKS, Mrs. Sara Louise, BSc ACA *1992;* 41 King Edwards Grove, TEDDINGTON, TW11 9LZ.

FOON, Miss. Siew Yin, BA(Hons) ACA *2004;* Flat 6830 Jalan Rajion, Off Jalan Johan Setia, Kampung Jalan Kebun, 42450 KLANG, SELANGOR, MALAYSIA.

FOONG, Mr. Daw Ching, FCA *1978;* Baker Tilly TFWLCL, 15 Beach Road, Apt. 03-10Beach Centre, SINGAPORE 189677, SINGAPORE.

FOONG, Dr. Soon Yau, PhD MBA BSc FCA *1977;* 34 Jalan BU 7/6, Bandar Utama, 47800 PETALING JAYA, Selangor, MALAYSIA.

FOONG PEN AHLIN, Miss. Meelain, ACA *1996;* 288 Old Church Road, Chingford, LONDON, E4 8BN.

FOORD, Mr. Alan Kenneth, FCA *1974;* 1 West Terrace, Milford, BELPER, DERBYSHIRE, DE56 0RF.

FOORD, Mr. David James, BA FCA MIoD *1989;* Januarys Consultant Surveyors, 7 Dukes Court, 54-62 Newmarket Road, CAMBRIDGE, CB5 8DZ.

FOORD, Mr. Derek Fergus Richard, FCA *1953;* 3 Alcroft Close, Abbey Grange, NEWCASTLE UPON TYNE, NE5 1QX. (Life Member)

FOORD, Mr. Jonathan Dryden, BA ACA *1994;* Fleet View The Pound Cookham, MAIDENHEAD, BERKSHIRE, SL6 9QD.

•**FOOT, Mr. Darren, ACA** *2002;* D B Foot Limited, 10 Prestwick Road, KINGSWINFORD, WEST MIDLANDS, DY6 9DZ.

FOOT, Mrs. Denise Elisabeth, BSc ACA *1992;* Fernside, 37 Dorchester Road, WEYBRIDGE, KT13 8PE.

•**FOOT, Mr. Ivan Ernest, FCA** *1973;* Foot & Ellis-Smith, Abacus House, 68A North Street, ROMFORD, RM1 1DA. See also Foot & Ellis-Smith Ltd

FOOT, Miss. Joanne Louise, MSc ACA *2006;* 22 Chepstow Close, KETTERING, NORTHAMPTONSHIRE, NN15 5EP.

FOOT, Mr. Julian, FCA *1970;* Menorca 42, 6 Dcha, 28009 MADRID, SPAIN. (Life Member)

•**FOOT, Mr. Nicholas Charles, BA FCA** *1979;* 6 Sherwood Place, Purley on Thames, READING, RG8 8RZ.

FOOT, Mr. Peter John Lewis, BA ACA *1989;* 65 Swithland Lane, Rothley, LEICESTER, LE7 7SG.

FOOT, Mr. Peter Nicholas, BSc ACA *1992;* AB World Foods, 42 Kings Hill Avenue, WEST MALLING, ME19 4AJ.

FOOT, Mr. Richard John, FCA *1957;* Fermain House, Casthorpe Road, Barrowby, GRANTHAM, LINCOLNSHIRE, NG32 1DP. (Life Member)

•**FOOT, Mr. Richard William David, FCA** *1975;* (Tax Fac), Foot Davson, 17 Church Road, TUNBRIDGE WELLS, TN1 1LG.

FOOT, Mr. Thomas, BA(Hons) ACA *2011;* 42 Milland Way, Oxley Park, MILTON KEYNES, MK4 4GU.

FOOTE, Mrs. Claire Louise, BSc ACA *2005;* 208 Bitterne Road West, Bitterne, SOUTHAMPTON, SO18 1BE.

FOOTE, Mr. David James, BSc(Hons) ACA *2001;* 85 Elm Road, Earley, READING, RG6 5TB.

FOOTE, Dr. Diane Mary, FCA *1988;* 5 Wellington Road, Turton, BOLTON, BL7 0EG.

FOOTE, Mrs. Elizabeth Sarah, BA(Hons) ACA *2004;* 85 Elm Road Earley, READING, RG6 5TB.

FOOTE, Miss. Laura Jane, ACA *2010;* Redevco UK, 1 James Street, LONDON, W1U 1DR.

•**FOOTE, Mr. Malcolm George, ACA** *1982;* (Tax Fac), Moss & Williamson, Booth Street Chambers, Booth Street, ASHTON-UNDER-LYNE, OL6 7LQ. See also Moss & Williamson Ltd

FOOTE, Mr. Matthew Michael, MSc BSc ACA *2011;* 3 Oaklands Avenue, Adel, LEEDS, LS16 8NR.

•**FOOTE, Mr. Michael Leonard, FCA** *1965;* Michael L Foote FCA, 8 Bates Lane, Weston Turville, AYLESBURY, BUCKINGHAMSHIRE, HP22 5SL.

FOOTE, Mrs. Natalie Gonella, MSc BSc ACA *2005;* Bickerton, Reading Road, Burghfield Common, READING, RG7 3EG.

FOOTE, Mr. Robin Timothy, ACA *2003;* 10 Ashwood Place, Ashwood Road, WOKING, SURREY, GU22 7JR.

FOOTE, Mr. Stephen, BA(Hons) ACA *2003;* 13a Golf Road Park, BRECHIN, ANGUS, DD9 6YJ.

FOOTE, Mr. Timothy David, BSc ACA *2005;* 208 Bitterne Road West, SOUTHAMPTON, SO18 1BE.

FOOTERMAN, Mr. Jonathan Bernard, ACA *1980;* 34 Valetta Road, LONDON, W3 7TN.

FOOTS, Mr. John Richard, BSc ACA *1995;* Camerons Brewery Ltd, Main Gate House, Lion Brewery, Waldon Street, HARTLEPOOL, CLEVELAND TS24 7QS.

FOOTTIT, Mrs. Helen Jane, ACA *2008;* 12 Victoria Crescent, POOLE, DORSET, BH12 2JH.

FOOTTIT, Mr. Nigel Mark, BA FCA CF *1996;* Mazars Unit 7-8, 2 New Fields Business Park Stinsford Road, POOLE, DORSET, BH17 0NF.

FOOTTIT, Miss. Sarah Margaret, BA ACA *1991;* Ivy House Farm, 7 Rugby Road, Barby, RUGBY, CV23 8UA.

FORADARI, Miss. Christina, BSc ACA *2009;* 11 Mykonos Str, Appartment 12, 1066 NICOSIA, CYPRUS.

•**FORADARIS, Mr. George Koumettou, BSc FCA CF** *1978;* PricewaterhouseCoopers Limited, Julia House, 3 Themistocles Dervis Street, CY-1066 NICOSIA, CYPRUS.

FORADARIS, Mr. Ioannis, ACA *2011;* Flat 11 Brockway House, 257 Holloway Road, LONDON, N7 8HF.

FORAN, Mrs. Emily, BA ACA *2002;* 5 Prowse Close, LEE-ON-THE-SOLENT, PO13 9JF.

FORBES, Mr. Adrian Nicholas, BA ACA *1989;* 72 Manor Road, HARROW, MIDDLESEX, HA1 2PE.

FORBES, Mrs. Alexandra Emily Louise, BA(Hons) ACA *2002;* 6 Ellis Fields, ST. ALBANS, HERTFORDSHIRE, AL3 6BQ.

FORBES, Mr. Andrew Duncan, FCA *1976;* 2869 Bottlebrush Drive, LOS ANGELES, CA 90077, UNITED STATES.

FORBES, Mr. Andrew Graham, BA ACA *1981;* 15 Loxwood Rd, Lovedean, WATERLOOVILLE, PO8 9TU.

FORBES, Mr. Andrew Nicholas, MEng ACA *2000;* 10 Erridge Road, LONDON, SW19 3JB.

FORBES, Mrs. Carey Nichola Roxanne, BA ACA *1987;* 25 Frensham Vale, Lower Bourne, FARNHAM, SURREY, GU10 3HS.

FORBES, Mr. Christopher David, LLB FCA *1982;* Sherbourne House, Newlands Corner, Shere Road, GUILDFORD, GU4 8SE.

FORBES, Mr. Christopher Stephen, BSc FCA *1974;* Flat 4 Combe Down, Shawford, WINCHESTER, HAMPSHIRE, SO21 2AA.

FORBES, Mrs. Clare, BA(Hons) ACA *2002;* with KPMG LLP, One Snowhill, Snow Hill Queensway, BIRMINGHAM, B4 6GN.

FORBES, Mr. David, ACA *2009;* Flat 1 Epstein Court, 27a Essex Road, LONDON, N1 2TP.

FORBES, Mr. Derek James, BA(Hons) ACA *2002;* 6 Ellis Fields, ST ALBANS, HERTFORDSHIRE, AL3 6BQ.

FORBES, Mr. Edward, BA ACA *2004;* Flat 2 The Warwick, 68-70 Richmond Hill, RICHMOND, TW10 6RH.

FORBES, Miss. Elizabeth, MA ACA *2001;* 7 Sandringham Mews, HAMPTON, MIDDLESEX, TW12 2LF.

FORBES, Miss. Gabrielle, BA ACA *1997;* Flat 40 Tower 2, Middleton Towers, 140 Pokfulam Road, POK FU LAM, HONG KONG ISLAND, HONG KONG SAR.

•**FORBES, Mr. Graeme Robert, BA FCA** *1981;* G R Forbes, 20 Harrowby Lane, GRANTHAM, LINCOLNSHIRE, NG31 9HX.

FORBES, Mr. Ian Duncan, FCA *1969;* 21 Brittany Woods, 3049 Brittany Drive, VICTORIA V9B 5P8, BC, CANADA.

•**FORBES, Mr. Ian Robert, BSc ACA CTA** *1996;* (Tax Fac), Tolverne Tax Services Limited, Tolverne, White Cross, Cury, HELSTON, CORNWALL TR12 7BH.

FORBES, Mrs. Jane Catherine, MA BA ACA *2005;* Pricewaterhousecoopers, 101 Barbirolli Square, MANCHESTER, M2 3PW.

FORBES, Mr. John Charles, FCA *1954;* 18 South Edge, SHIPLEY, BD18 4RA. (Life Member)

•**FORBES, Mr. John David, FCA** *1976;* (Tax Fac), Forbes Ltd, Suite 5, Melville House, High Street, DUNMOW, ESSEX CM6 1AF.

•**FORBES, Mr. John Davies, MA ACA** *1991;* PricewaterhouseCoopers LLP, Hays Galleria, 1 Hays Lane, LONDON, SE1 2RD. See also PricewaterhouseCoopers

FORBES, Mr. John James, MA ACA *1991;* 62 Carminia Road, LONDON, SW17 8AH.

FORBES, Mr. Jonathan Paul, ACA *2006;* (Tax Fac), 73 Quinta Drive, BARNET, HERTFORDSHIRE, EN5 3BW.

FORBES, Mrs. Louise Marie, BA ACA *1999;* 21 Caird's Wynd, BANCHORY, AB31 5XU.

FORBES, Mr. Mark St John Graham, FCA *1982;* Experience Hotels Ltd, The Mill House Trebarwith, TINTAGEL, CORNWALL, PL34 0HD.

FORBES, Mr. Matthew Edward Michael, BA(Hons) ACA *2009;* 7 Bayley Road, Willaston, NANTWICH, CHESHIRE, CW5 6RL.

FORBES, Mr. Nicholas David, LLB ACA *2002;* 6 Neptune Place, WAIKIKI, WA 6169, AUSTRALIA.

FORBES, Mr. Peter Christopher, FCA *1953;* Brandon House, Millwood Lane, Burnham Market, KING'S LYNN, PE31 8DP. (Life Member)

FORBES, Mr. Richard Nicol, BSc ACA *1992;* (Tax Fac), 66 Shanklin Road, SOUTHAMPTON, SO15 7RF.

FORBES, Mr. Robert Mackenzie, FCA *1971;* Innisfree, 30b Salterns Way, POOLE, DORSET, BH14 8JR.

FORBES, Mr. Ronald Harold, MA FCA *1975;* Vale House, Ham, MARLBOROUGH, SN8 3QR.

FORBES, Ms. Ruth Helen Sutherland, BA ACA *2002;* Floor 6, Victoria House, Southampton Row, LONDON, WC1B 4AD.

FORBES, Mrs. Sharon Annette, BSc ACA *1996;* Tolverne, White Cross, Cury, HELSTON, CORNWALL, TR12 7BH.
FORBES, Mrs. Sophy Louise, BSc(Hons) ACA *2000;* 3 Monks Horton Way, ST. ALBANS, HERTFORDSHIRE, AL1 4HA.
FORBES, Mr. Stuart Sanford, BSc FCA *1965;* 4 Gable Court Lawrie Park Avenue, LONDON, SE26 6HR. (Life Member)
•FORBES, Mr. Thayne Andrew, MA FCA *1987;* Intangible Business Ltd, 9 Maltings Place, 169 Tower Bridge Road, LONDON, SE1 3JB.
FORBES, Mr. Wyndham Kinloch, FCA *1935;* Croit-E-Ferish, Tynwald Road, Peel, ISLE OF MAN, IM5 1JL. (Life Member)
•FORBES-CABLE, Mr. John Michael, FCA *1962;* (Tax Fac), Forbes-Cable Ltd, 8 Albert Place, ABERDEEN, AB25 1RG. See also Forbes-Cable
FORD, Mr. Adrian Craig, BSc ACA *1985;* 1A Karloo Street, TURRAMURRA, NSW 2074, AUSTRALIA.
•FORD, Mr. Alan Steven, FCA *1976;* Alsford Limited, 306 The Greenway, EPSOM, SURREY, KT18 7JF.
FORD, Mr. Alex, BSc(Hons) ACA *2010;* 1 The Banks, Hinton Parva, SWINDON, SN4 0DH.
FORD, Mr. Alex Leon, BSc ACA *2009;* 71 Rye Road, HODDESDON, HERTFORDSHIRE, EN11 0JH.
FORD, Miss. Amelia, BCom ACA *2004;* 102 North Road, GLOSSOP, DERBYSHIRE, SK13 7AX.
FORD, Mr. Andrew Philip, BSc ACA *1989;* KALEVANKATU 18 A 5, 00100 HELSINKI, FINLAND.
FORD, Mrs. Anna, BA ACA *1999;* 11 Leverton Street, LONDON, NW5 2PH.
•FORD, Mr. Anthony John, BA FCA *1984;* Ford Campbell Corporate Finance LLP, Bass Warehouse, 4 Castle Street, Castlefield, MANCHESTER, M3 4LZ. See also Ford Campbell Freedman LLP
FORD, Mr. Anthony William, ACA *1980;* 1 Jarrah Lane, MOUNT CLAREMONT, WA 6010, AUSTRALIA.
FORD, Mr. Brian Geoffrey, FCA *1972;* 9 St Ives Park, Ashley Heath, RINGWOOD, BH24 2JX.
FORD, Mrs. Catherine Mary, BA(Hons) ACA *2002;* 19 Pennywell Drive, Holymoorside, CHESTERFIELD, DERBYSHIRE, S42 7EZ.
•FORD, Mr. Christopher Barry, BSc FCA *1991;* (Tax Fac), Raymarsh Ford Limited, Ground Floor, 41 High Street, Kingswood, BRISTOL, BS15 4AA.
FORD, Mr. Christopher James, BSc ACA *1995;* CycleActive Limited, Brougham Hall, PENRITH, CUMBRIA, CA10 2DE.
•FORD, Mr. Christopher John, FCA *1986;* (Tax Fac), Lucraft Hodgson & Dawes, Ground Floor, 19 New Road, BRIGHTON, BN1 1UF.
FORD, Mr. Christopher Mark, BSc ACA *1990;* 69 Sillswood, OLNEY, BUCKINGHAMSHIRE, MK46 5PN.
FORD, Mr. Colin Donald, BCom ACA *2004;* with Macilvin Moore Reveres LLP, 7 St John's Road, HARROW, HA1 2EY.
FORD, Mr. Craig John, BA ACA *2010;* 96 Junction Gardens, PLYMOUTH, DEVON, PL4 9AS.
FORD, Mr. David John, FCA *1971;* 2 Old Hall Gardens, Brooke, NORWICH, NR15 1JZ.
FORD, Mr. David Vincent, FCA *1971;* 4 Campden Close, Uppingham, OAKHAM, LE15 9TE.
•FORD, Mr. David William, FCA *1982;* Merchant & Co., 84 Uxbridge Road, West Ealing, LONDON, W13 8RA.
FORD, Mr. Derek, FCA FCT *1964;* Whistlers Wood, 75 Bois Lane, Chesham Bois, AMERSHAM, HP6 6DF.
FORD, Mr. Dominic Charles Patrick, BA ACA *1994;* 25a Bassein Park Road, LONDON, W12 9RN.
FORD, Miss. Elizabeth Jane, BSc ACA *1998;* Molewood House, Molewood Road, HERTFORD, SG14 3LT.
FORD, Mrs. Fiona Mary, BSc ACA *2004;* 8 King James Avenue, Cuffley, POTTERS BAR, HERTFORDSHIRE, EN6 4LR.
FORD, Mrs. Frances Ann, BA ACA *1983;* 34 Vicarage Rd, East Sheen, LONDON, SW14 8RU.
FORD, Mr. Graham, BSocSc FCA *1996;* 263 River Valley Road, 01-24 Aspen Heights, SINGAPORE 238309, SINGAPORE.
FORD, Mr. Ian, BA ACA *1992;* 29 Alwyne Road, LONDON, SW19 7AB.
FORD, Mr. Ian Howard, FCA *1956;* 14 Fairfield Road, EASTBOURNE, EAST SUSSEX, BN20 7LR. (Life Member)
FORD, Mrs. Jane Ann, BA ACA *1989;* 1 Otaki Place, St. Ives Chase, SYDNEY, NSW 2075, AUSTRALIA.
•FORD, Mr. John Warren Stransham, FCA *1980;* Box 861, PLETTENBERG BAY, WESTERN CAPE PROVINCE, 6600, SOUTH AFRICA.
FORD, Mr. John William, FCA *1970;* 141 Andover Avenue, Middleton, MANCHESTER, M24 1JQ. (Life Member)
FORD, Mr. Johnathan Richard, BSc ACA *1995;* Orchard House, Elmbridge, DROITWICH, WR9 0NH.
FORD, Mr. Jonathan Howard, BSc ACA *1989;* Riverbank House, Tibberton, NEWPORT, SHROPSHIRE, TF10 8NN.
•FORD, Mr. Jonathan Mark, BA FCA *1999;* with PricewaterhouseCoopers, 1 Embankment Place, LONDON, WC2N 6RH.
•FORD, Mr. Jonathan Robert, BSc FCA *1994;* Jonathan Ford & Co Limited, The Coach House, 31 View Road, Rainhill, PRESCOT, MERSEYSIDE L35 0LF.
FORD, Mr. Julian Michael John, BSc ACA *1983;* 6 Wheatlands Grove, HARROGATE, NORTH YORKSHIRE, HG2 8JH.
FORD, Miss. Karen Louise, BSc(Econ) ACA *2001;* 16 / 80 Middle Street, RANDWICK, NSW 2031, AUSTRALIA.
FORD, Miss. Karen Louise, BSc ACA *2007;* 13 Weyland Drive, Stanway, COLCHESTER, CO3 0RG.
FORD, Ms. Katherine Anne, BA ACA *1996;* Department for International Development, 1 Palace Street, LONDON, SW1E 5HE.
•FORD, Mr. Keith Robert, FCA *1965;* K.R. Ford FCA, Brook House, Main Street, Beckley, RYE, EAST SUSSEX TN31 6RL.
•FORD, Mr. Keith Vernon, BA FCA *1988;* The Ford Partnership, Pointers Gallows Green, Alton, STOKE-ON-TRENT, ST10 4BN.
FORD, Mr. Kelvin Derrick, BSc ACA *1989;* 5 Holm Oak Drive, Madeley, CREWE, CW3 9HR.
FORD, Mr. Kevin John Sidney, FCA *1969;* 301-30 Speers Road, OAKVILLE L6K 2E4, ON, CANADA.
FORD, Mr. Laurence Tony, BSc FCA *1985;* 7 Lichfield Close, Toton, NOTTINGHAM, NG9 6JZ.
FORD, Mrs. Louise Jane, BA ACA *1997;* 31 View Road, Rainhill, PRESCOT, L35 0LF.
•FORD, Mrs. Margaret Cicely Alice, BSc ACA ATII *1984;* Prescott Skellorn Green, Adlington, MACCLESFIELD, CHESHIRE, SK10 4NU.
FORD, Mr. Martyn, BSc ACA *2010;* 96a Torriano Avenue, LONDON, NW5 2SE.
FORD, Mr. Michael, FCA *1975;* Hyde Industrial Holdings Ltd, Stamford House, 185 Stamford Street, STALYBRIDGE, CHESHIRE, SK15 1QZ.
FORD, Mr. Michael, FCA *1974;* 67 Seatonville Road, West Monkseaton, WHITLEY BAY, NE25 9DR.
FORD, Mr. Michael James, BSc(Hons) ACA *2004;* 22 St. Andrews Meadow, Kirkby Malzeard, RIPON, NORTH YORKSHIRE, HG4 3SW.
•FORD, Mr. Neil Robert, BSc FCA CTA *1989;* with Torr Waterfield Ltd, Park House, 37 Clarence Street, LEICESTER, LE1 3RW.
FORD, Mrs. Nicola, ACA *2003;* Tower Cottage, 1 Tower Road, BELVEDERE, KENT, DA17 6HX.
FORD, Mr. Nigel Derek George, BSc ACA *1991;* Wheatfields, 3 Gill Croft Court, Easingwold, YORK, YO61 3GX.
•FORD, Mr. Patrick, FCA *1970;* Patrick Ford, Leybourne Lodge, Combe Lane, Wormley, GODALMING, GU8 5TP.
FORD, Mr. Paul Leslie, MBA BSc FCA CPA AMCT *1995;* Flat 3, 25 Arlington Gardens, Chiswick, LONDON, W4 4EZ.
•FORD, Mr. Paul Walter, FCA *1976;* Paul Ford & Co, 26 Cherwell Road, Keynsham, BRISTOL, BS31 1QT.
FORD, Mr. Peter James, BSc FCA *1982;* Old Homend, Stretton Grandison, LEDBURY, HEREFORDSHIRE, HR8 2TW.
FORD, Mr. Peter John, FCA *1971;* High Glen, 15 Scotlands Close, HASLEMERE, GU27 3AE.
FORD, Mr. Peter Michael, BA FCA *1970;* Whitestrake, Hawksdown Road, Walmer, DEAL, KENT, CT14 7PW.
FORD, Mr. Richard Joseph, FCA *1964;* Borrowdale, 15 Deepdene Drive, DORKING, SURREY, RH5 4AH.
FORD, Mr. Richard Michael, FCA *1953;* 17 Hornby Hall Close, Hornby, LANCASTER, LA2 8LB. (Life Member)
FORD, Mr. Richard William, MPhil BA ACA PGCE *1999;* with PricewaterhouseCoopers LLP, 1 Embankment Place, LONDON, WC2N 6RH.
FORD, Mr. Robert, BCom FCA *1980;* Mayfield, Tarporley Rd, Tarvin, CHESTER, CH3 8NF.
FORD, Mr. Robert Edward, MBA FCA *1969;* 23 Abbot Street, ANDOVER, MA 01810, UNITED STATES.
FORD, Mr. Robert Geoffrey, FCA *1970;* Ford Component Mfg Ltd, East Side, Tyne Dock, SOUTH SHIELDS, TYNE AND WEAR, NE33 5ST.
FORD, Mr. Robert Henry, BSc ACA *1981;* Zenimax Europe Limited Grafton House, 2-3 Golden Square, LONDON, W1F 9HR.
•FORD, Mr. Robert John, FCA *1976;* 14 Stoatley Rise, HASLEMERE, SURREY, GU27 1AF.
FORD, Mr. Robert William, ACA MAAT *2010;* 88 Franchise Street, KIDDERMINSTER, WORCESTERSHIRE, DY11 6SP.
FORD, Mr. Roger Anthony, FCA *1974;* 5 Bourdillon Close, Fenstanton, HUNTINGDON, PE28 9HW. (Life Member)
FORD, Mr. Russell Arnold, FCA *1966;* Hook Hill, Cousley Wood, WADHURST, TN5 6HJ. (Life Member)
FORD, Mr. Russell Brian, BA ACA *1997;* Applegarth, Blundel Lane, Stoke D'Abernon, COBHAM, SURREY, KT11 2SY.
FORD, Miss. Sarah, BSc ACA *2007;* with Grant Thornton UK LLP, 30 Finsbury Square, LONDON, EC2P 2YU.
FORD, Ms. Sarah Elizabeth, BA ACA *1991;* 6 Bulmershe Road, READING, RG1 5RJ.
FORD, Mr. Simon Daniel, BA(Hons) ACA *2002;* 22 Waldron Road, LONDON, SW18 3TE.
FORD, Mr. Simon William Frederick, ACA *1979;* 63 Glebe Street, DUMFRIES, DG1 2LZ.
FORD, Mr. Stephen John, FCA *1972;* Avenida Profesor Lora Tamayo num 38, Orgiva, 18400 GRANADA, SPAIN.
FORD, Mr. Stephen John, MA ACA *1996;* 51 Princess Court, Queensway, LONDON, W2 4RD.
FORD, Mr. Stuart Duncan, MA ACA *2001;* 13 Station Road, BILLERICAY, ESSEX, CM12 9DP.
FORD, Mr. Stuart James, BSc ACA *2002;* 36 Orchehill Avenue, GERRARDS CROSS, BUCKINGHAMSHIRE, SL9 8QJ.
FORD, Mrs. Susan Elizabeth, BSc ACA *1987;* Metric Property Investments, 1-3 Mount Street, LONDON, W1K 3NB.
FORD, Mr. Trevor Ashley, BA FCA *1990;* Mayfield Cottage, 44 Fox Lane, Hoghton, PRESTON, PR5 0JQ.
FORD, Ms. Wanda Janina, BA FCA *1985;* Mid Cheshire College of Further Education Hartford Campus, Chester Road Hartford, NORTHWICH, CHESHIRE, CW8 1LJ.
FORD-HORNE, Mr. Martin Gregory, FCA *1975;* 3 Brunstead Place, Branksome, POOLE, BH12 1EW.
FORD-MCNICOL, Mrs. Oana Delia, BSc ACA *2004;* Broadway Park, South Gyle Broadway, South Gyle, EDINBURGH, EH12 9JZ.
FORDE, Mrs. Caroline Sarah, MMath ACA *2006;* 48 Cleaveland Road, SURBITON, KT6 4AJ.
FORDE, Mrs. Gillian Elizabeth, BSc ACA *1980;* Tir Na Nog, 16 Downs Road, COULSDON, CR5 1AA.
FORDE, Mr. James, BA ACA *1997;* 83 Lichfield Grove, LONDON, N3 2JL.
FORDE, Mr. Matthew Peter, MSci ACA *2006;* 1 Lower Hill Road, EPSOM, SURREY, KT19 8LS.
FORDE, Mr. Michael Anthony, BCom ACA *1992;* Sleepy Hollow, Ladytown, NAAS, COUNTY KILDARE, IRELAND.
FORDE, Mr. Nicholas Stafford Paul, BSc FCA *1972;* 12 Midhurst Road, LONDON, W13 9XT.
FORDER, Mr. David Robert, BA ACA *1991;* 8 Bridge Street, Packington, ASHBY-DE-LA-ZOUCH, LEICESTERSHIRE, LE65 1WB.
FORDER, Mrs. Lisa Jayne, ACA *1996;* 8 Bridge Street, Packington, ASHBY-DE-LA-ZOUCH, LEICESTERSHIRE, LE65 1WB.
FORDHAM, Mr. Scott, BA(Hons) ACA *2001;* Wagoners Cottage, Dodford, NORTHAMPTON, NN7 4SZ.
FORDYCE, Mr. Michael William, FCA *1965;* Greystone House, Winforton, HEREFORD, HR3 6EA.
FOREHAND, Miss. Joan Innes Moffat, BSc ACA *1991;* Standard Life Plc, Standard Life House, 30 Lothian Road, EDINBURGH, EH1 2DH.
FOREMAN, Mr. Andrew Mark, BA FCA *1999;* with Lovewell Blake LLP, 102 Prince of Wales Road, NORWICH, NORFOLK, NR1 1NY.
FOREMAN, Mr. David, BA ACA *2000;* May Gurney Integrated Services Plc, Trowse, NORWICH, NR14 8SZ.
FOREMAN, Mr. David, LLB ACA *2007;* 99 The Edge, Clowes Street, SALFORD, M3 5ND.
FOREMAN, Mr. David Antony, MA ACA *1991;* 15 Davis Road, WEYBRIDGE, SURREY, KT13 0XH.
FOREMAN, Mr. David Tristan, BSc ACA *2004;* Seymour Pierce Limited, 20 Old Bailey, LONDON, EC4M 7EN.
FOREMAN, Mr. James Douglas, FCA *1972;* 3 An Mainistir, Fenagh, BALLINAMORE, COUNTY LEITRIM, IRELAND.
FOREMAN, Miss. Jane Louise, BA ACA DChA *1993;* 96 Bertram Road, Hendon, LONDON, NW4 3PP.
FOREMAN, Mr. John Anthony, BA FCA *1977;* Dunelm Pinfarthings, Amberley, STROUD, GLOUCESTERSHIRE, GL5 5JJ.
FOREMAN, Mr. Jonathan Richard William, BEng ACA *1992;* Normec (Manchester) Ltd, Westwood Industrial Estate, Arkwright Street, OLDHAM, OL9 9LZ.
FOREMAN, Mr. Keith Douglas, BSc ACA *1986;* 4 Jennys Way, COULSDON, SURREY, CR5 1RP.
FOREMAN, Miss. Lesley Anne Martin, FCA *1976;* 74 The Avenue, Kew, RICHMOND, TW9 2AH.
FOREMAN, Miss. Lianne Joyce, ACA *2009;* 14 Amberwood, FERNDOWN, DORSET, BH22 9JT.
FOREMAN, Mr. Neil Anthony, BSc ACA *1992;* Seacon (Europe) Ltd, Seacon House, Hewett Road, GREAT YARMOUTH, NORFOLK, NR31 0RB.
FOREMAN, Mr. Paul Andrew, BSc FCA *1990;* 8 Quarry Lane, Swaffham Bulbeck, CAMBRIDGE, CB25 0LU.
FOREMAN, Mr. Peter, FCA *1959;* L'Hermitage, Wirksworth Road, Kirk Ireton, ASHBOURNE, DERBYSHIRE, DE6 3JX. (Life Member)
FOREMAN, Mr. Peter Barry, FCA *1963;* 4 Barn Piece, BRADFORD-ON-AVON, WILTSHIRE, BA15 1XB.
FOREMAN, Mrs. Rachel Mary, BA(Hons) ACA *2004;* Meadow Barn, Purwell Mill, Purwell Lane, HITCHIN, HERTFORDSHIRE, SG4 0NF.
FOREMAN, Mr. Raymond Jeffrey, MA FCA *1976;* 7 Brockenhurst Close, Horsell, WOKING, GU21 4DS.
FOREMAN, Mr. Robin James, LLB ACA *1997;* 7 Brodrick Road, LONDON, SW17 7DZ.
FOREMAN, Mr. Roger Anthony, FCA *1971;* 13 Pottery Lane, CHELMSFORD, CM1 4HH.
FOREMAN, Mr. Russell Ian, BA ACA *1986;* 64 Gloucester Road, BARNET, HERTFORDSHIRE, EN5 1NB.
•FOREMAN, Mrs. Ruth Ann, BA ACA *1980;* Baker Tilly UK Audit LLP, Hartwell House, 55-61 Victoria Street, BRISTOL, BS1 6AD. See also Baker Tilly Tax and Advisory Services LLP
FOREMAN, Miss. Sandra, LLB ACA *2006;* Forsyth House, Cromac Place, BELFAST, BT2 8LA.
FOREMAN, Miss. Sarah, BA(Hons) ACA *2002;* Flat 4, 181-183 Stanstead Road, LONDON, SE23 1HP.
FOREMAN, Miss. Sarah Catherine, BSc(Hons) ACA *2003;* 18 Bradmore Avenue, Ruddington, NOTTINGHAM, NG11 6BL.
•FOREMAN, Mr. Simon Charles, FCA *1984;* Peter Howard Foreman & Co, 1 Wharfe Mews Cliffe Terrace, WETHERBY, LS22 6LX. See also Peter Howard Foreman Limited and Peter Howard & Co
FOREMAN, Mr. Terence David, ACA *1990;* 4 Old Fold, Chestfield, WHITSTABLE, KENT, CT5 3NL.
FOREMAN, Mr. Thomas Lee, BSc ACA *2003;* Meadow Barn, Purwell Lane, HITCHIN, HERTFORDSHIRE, SG4 0NF.
FOREMAN, Mrs. Tracy Kim, BSc ACA *2000;* 12 Robusta Court, BANKSIA BEACH, QLD 4507, AUSTRALIA.
FOREMAN, Mr. William Howard, FCA *1969;* Chester House, 10, Orchard GroveMinster, SHEERNESS, ME12 3PD.
FORES, Mr. Nicholas, MA ACA *1992;* 5 Acres Hall Crescent, PUDSEY, LS28 9DY.
FORFAR, Mr. David Fergus, BSc(Hons) ACA *2003;* 48 Fairway, LONDON, SW20 9DN.
FORGAN, Mrs. Janet Elizabeth, BSc ACA *2002;* Flat 1, 19 Strathblaine Road, LONDON, SW11 1RG.
FORGAN, Mr. John Marius Robin, BA FCA *1983;* Flat 2 Ravens Court, Upper Brighton Road, SURBITON, SURREY, KT6 6JU.
FORGE, Mr. David Lindus, FCA *1981;* Kingfisher House, Willow Wents, Mereworth, MAIDSTONE, KENT, ME18 5NF.
FORGUSON, Mr. Geoffrey Lynd, BPhil ACA *1992;* 14 Amelia Street, TORONTO M4X 1E1, ON, CANADA.
FORINTON, Mr. David Andrew, LLB ACA *2005;* 48 Alexandra Road, Englefield Green, EGHAM, SURREY, TW20 0RR.
FORLENZA, Miss. Maria Clothilde, BSocSc ACA *2004;* with Deloitte LLP, Athene Place, 66 Shoe Lane, LONDON, EC4A 3BQ.
FORMAN, Mr. Alasdair George Grant, BEng ACA *1991;* Furzegrove Farm, Cinder Hill, North Chailey, LEWES, EAST SUSSEX, BN8 4HP.
FORMAN, Mr. Anthony John, FCA *1970;* 82 Hackington Road, Tyler Hill, CANTERBURY, CT2 9NQ.
FORMAN, Mr. Bennet Robert, BSc(Hons) ACA *2000;* 37 Priest Avenue, WOKINGHAM, RG40 2LT.
FORMAN, Miss. Elizabeth, ACA *2007;* 395 South End Avenue, Apartment 25M, NEW YORK, NY 10280-1033, UNITED STATES.

FORMAN, Mrs. Fiona Mary Aird, BSc ACA *1991;* Furzegrove Farm Cinder Hill, North Chailey, LEWES, EAST SUSSEX, BN8 4HP.
FORMAN, Mrs. Jill Alexandra, BSc(Hons) ACA *2000;* 6 Henri Mussard, 1208 GENEVA, SWITZERLAND.
FORMAN, Mr. Nicholas Timothy, BSc FCA *1985;* Willoughby House, 73 High Street, Dorchester-on-Thames, WALLINGFORD, OXFORDSHIRE, OX10 7HN.
FORMAN, Mr. Patrick William, FCA *1970;* The Orchard, 19 Eastend Kirmington, ULCEBY, DN39 6YS. (Life Member)
FORMAN, Mr. Paul Alan, BSc ACA *2001;* 15 Rydal Gardens, ASHBY-DE-LA-ZOUCH, LEICESTERSHIRE, LE65 1FJ.
FORMAN, Mr. Saul Johnathan, BA(Hons) ACA *2001;* Credo Group, 83 Pall Mall, LONDON, SW1Y 5ES.
FORMAN, Mr. Stephen John, FCA *1967;* 51 Barham Avenue, Elstree, BOREHAMWOOD, HERTFORDSHIRE, WD6 3PW.
FORMBY, Mr. Paul, BCom ACA *1986;* Lex Vehicle Leasing, Heathside Park, Heathside Park Road, Cheadle, STOCKPORT, CHESHIRE SK3 0RB.
•FORMBY, Mr. Richard Francis, FCA *1985;* (Tax Fac), Monahans, Lennox House, 3 Pierrepont Street, BATH, BA1 1LB.
FORMOSA-GAUCI, Mr. Josef, BA ACA *1995;* 236/7 Tower Road, SLIEMA, MALTA.
•FORMOY, Mr. Steven Robert, BA(Hons) ACA *2003;* 4 Anston Close, Lower Earley, READING, RG6 4AQ.
FORRAI, Mr. Forbes Malcolm, BA ACA *1992;* 125 Elmsleigh Drive, LEIGH-ON-SEA, SS9 3DS.
FORREST, Mr. Andrew Derek, BEng FCA *1993;* (Tax Fac), Carr Head Farm, Noggarth Road, Roughlee, BURNLEY, LANCASHIRE, BB12 9PR.
FORREST, Mr. Arthur Thomas, FCA *1967;* Lawley, Highlands Road, Heath End, FARNHAM, GU9 0LX.
•FORREST, Mrs. Barbara Anne, MSc FCA *1982;* Barbara Forrest, 17 Orchard Way, Hurst Green, OXTED, RH8 9DJ.
•FORREST, Miss. Brenda, FCA *1981;* Brenda Forrest, 33 St. Georges Terrace, EAST BOLDON, TYNE AND WEAR, NE36 0LU.
FORREST, Mr. Christopher James, BSc ACA *2005;* H S B C Private Bank Ltd, 78 St. James's Street, LONDON, SW1A 1JB.
FORREST, Mr. David, FCA *1959;* Kendall House, Derwent Lane, Dunnington, YORK, YO19 5RR.
•FORREST, Mr. David, BA FCA CF *1985;* Ingram Forrest Corporate Finance LLP, 2 Rutland Park, SHEFFIELD, S10 2PD. See also Barber Harrison & Platt
FORREST, Mr. Donald Dunlop, MA FCA *1975;* Nexxtdrive Ltd, 3rd Floor, 11 Strand, LONDON, WC2N 5HR.
FORREST, Ms. Edwina Lesley, ACA FCCA *2010;* The Barn, La Fontaine, La Route Des Cotils, Grouville, JERSEY, JE3 9AP.
FORREST, Miss. Gemma Elizabeth, BSc ACA *2011;* 2 Francis Avenue, Rhos on Sea, COLWYN BAY, CLWYD, LL28 4DL.
FORREST, Mr. Gregory Robert Ewing, BA ACA *1992;* Little Choppins Stud, Coddenham, IPSWICH, IP6 9TN.
FORREST, Mrs. Jane Louise, BA(Hons) ACA *2000;* 65 Button Lane, Bearsted, MAIDSTONE, KENT, ME15 8DW.
FORREST, Mrs. Karen Mary, ACA *1997;* 7 Glen Hazel, Hook End, BRENTWOOD, ESSEX, CM15 0PE.
FORREST, Ms. Lisa, BA ACA *1992;* 95 Village Court, WHITLEY BAY, NE26 3QB.
FORREST, Mr. Martin Lee, FCA *1984;* 76 Schools Hill, CHEADLE, SK8 1JD.
FORREST, Mr. Michael Roger, MA FCA *1978;* 70 Upper Cranbrook Road, Westbury Park, BRISTOL, BS6 7UP.
FORREST, Mr. Peter, FCA *1969;* 44 Winn Road, Lee, LONDON, SE12 9EX. (Life Member)
•FORREST, Mr. Peter Anthony, ACA *1987;* Forrest & Co, 30 Heron Close, BLACKBURN, BB1 8NU. See also Forrest Consultancy Ltd
FORREST, Mr. Peter William, MSci ACA *2004;* 39 Clive Road, LONDON, SE21 8DA.
FORREST, Mr. Robert John, BA FCA *1977;* 20 Larchmont Avenue, LARCHMONT, NY 10538, UNITED STATES.
FORREST, Miss. Sarah Helen, BSc ACA *2001;* 85 Moss Lane, ALDERLEY EDGE, CHESHIRE, SK9 7HP.
FORREST, Mr. Simon, BSc ACA *2000;* 25 Polton Road, LASSWADE, MIDLOTHIAN, EH18 1AF.
FORREST, Mr. Simon James, BSc ACA *2001;* 141 Cherry Tree Road, BEACONSFIELD, BUCKINGHAMSHIRE, HP9 1BD.
FORREST, Mr. Stephen Phillip, FCA *1990;* Pike Stone Bank House, Slater Ing Lane Heptonstall, HEBDEN BRIDGE, HX7 7PD.
FORREST, Mr. Steven Colin, BSc ACA *1992;* Start Creative Ltd, 2 Sheraton Street, LONDON, W1F 8BH.
FORREST, Mr. Steven Terence, BA ACA *1996;* 54 Plantation Gardens, LEEDS, LS17 8SX.
FORRESTER, Mr. Andrew Craig, BEng ACA *1994;* 33 Osprey Avenue, BRACKNELL, BERKSHIRE, RG12 8AT.
FORRESTER, Mr. Andrew John, ACA *1986;* The Shieling, 70 Tiddington Road, STRATFORD-UPON-AVON, WARWICKSHIRE, CV37 7BA.
FORRESTER, Mr. Andrew Neil, BSc FCA *1992;* 1 Tower Mews, Elloughton, BROUGH, NORTH HUMBERSIDE, HU15 1GZ.
FORRESTER, Mrs. Claire Margaret, BSc ACA *2007;* with Ernst & Young LLP, The Paragon, Counterslip, BRISTOL, BS1 6BX.
FORRESTER, Miss. Diane Leonie, BSc ACA *1988;* Jasmine Cottage, Ascot Road Nuptown, Warfield, BRACKNELL, RG42 6HS.
FORRESTER, Miss. Fiona Maureen, BA FCA *1986;* 22 Elm Bank Gardens, LONDON, SW13 0NT. (Life Member)
FORRESTER, Mr. Iain, MChem ACA *2010;* National Audit Office, 157-197 Buckingham Palace Road, LONDON, SW1W 9SP.
FORRESTER, Mr. Jason Pierpoint, BSc FCA *1993;* Appartment 2202, 12 Cuscaden Walk, Four Seasons Park, SINGAPORE 249694, SINGAPORE.
FORRESTER, Mrs. Joanne, BA ACA *2004;* Experian Ltd, Riverleen House, Electric Avenue, NOTTINGHAM, NG80 1RH.
FORRESTER, Mr. Mark Andrew, BA ACA *1992;* with Ernst & Young, 18/F, Two International Finance Centre, 8 Finance Street, CENTRAL, HONG KONG ISLAND HONG KONG SAR.
FORRESTER, Mr. Mark Roy, BSc ACA *2000;* 69 Staunton Road, KINGSTON UPON THAMES, SURREY, KT2 5TN.
FORRESTER, Mrs. Melissa Jane, BSc ACA *1999;* 69 Staunton Road, KINGSTON UPON THAMES, SURREY, KT2 5TN.
FORRESTER, Mr. Neil Richard, MA FCA *1975;* PO Box 49, Ermioni, 21051 ARGOLIDAS, GREECE.
•FORRESTER, Mr. Nicholas, FCA *1980;* Forrester & Company (Malvern) Limited, 33 Graham Road, MALVERN, WORCESTERSHIRE, WR14 2HU. See also Forrester & Co.
FORRESTER, Mr. Nigel Raymond, FCA *1973;* 25 Melville Beach Road, APPLECROSS, WA 6153, AUSTRALIA.
FORRESTER, Mr. Peter Robert, MA FCA *1975;* Pipers Corner School, Pipers Lane, Great Kingshill, HIGH WYCOMBE, BUCKINGHAMSHIRE, HP15 6LP.
FORRESTER, Mr. Robert Thomas, MA ACA *1994;* 38 Moor Crescent, Gosforth, NEWCASTLE UPON TYNE, NE3 4AQ.
FORRESTER, Mr. Stuart Robert, BA ACA *1996;* High Clere, 3 Oaklands Close, HOLMFIRTH, WEST YORKSHIRE, HD9 3RN.
FORRESTER, Mrs. Susan, BSc ACA *1992;* 15 The Chase, Cottam, PRESTON, PR4 0NT.
FORROW, Mrs. Victoria Kathryn, MChem ACA *2006;* 63 Morden Hill, LONDON, SE13 7NP.
FORSBERG, Mr. Peter John, AICD FCA ASIA *1989;* 25 Cook Road, KILLARA, NSW 2071, AUSTRALIA.
•FORSDICK, Mr. Michael James, MA FCA *1981;* 14 Cove Street, BIRCHGROVE, NSW 2041, AUSTRALIA.
FORSEY, Mrs. Natalie Joanne, BSc ACA *2005;* 47 Strathallan Wynd, East Kilbride, GLASGOW, G75 8GU.
•FORSEY, Mr. Peter John, BA FCA *1990;* Money Debt & Credit M D & C House, 45 Clarendon Road, WATFORD, WD17 1SZ.
FORSHAW, Mr. Andrew Christopher, BA ACA *1983;* 9 Cleveley Park, Allerton, LIVERPOOL, L18 9UT.
FORSHAW, Mr. Andrew Robert, BSc ACA *1980;* 21 Manor Garth, Wigginton, YORK, YO32 2WZ.
FORSHAW, Mr. Christopher Michael John, FCA *1972;* 44 Kerris Way, Earley, READING, RG6 5UW.
FORSHAW, Mr. Christopher Thomas, MA ACA *1995;* Crane Electronics, PO Box 97005, 10301 Willows Rd NE, REDMOND, WA 98073-9705, UNITED STATES.
•FORSHAW, Mr. Darren William, BSc ACA *1997;* Endless LLP, 3 Whitehall Quay, LEEDS, LS1 4BF.
FORSHAW, Mr. Desmond John, FCA *1960;* 6 Hill Top Walk, ORMSKIRK, LANCASHIRE, L39 4TH. (Life Member)
FORSHAW, Miss. Hannah Louise, ACA *2008;* 22 St. Marys Street, WALLASEY, MERSEYSIDE, CH44 5TX.
FORSHAW, Mr. James David, FCA *1973;* Compass Group Holdings Plc, Immeuble Le Carat, 200 Avenue de Paris, 92326 CHATILLON, FRANCE.
FORSHAW, Mr. John Robert, BSc ACA *1993;* 25 Pullman Lane, GODALMING, SURREY, GU7 1XY.
•FORSHAW, Mr. Mathew Thomas, BA ACA *1995;* Finton Doyle, Preston Technology Centre, Marsh Lane, PRESTON, PR1 8UQ.
•FORSHAW, Mr. Michael John, BA FCA *1990;* M.J. Forshaw, 7 Oak Drive, Burscough, ORMSKIRK, LANCASHIRE, L40 5BQ. See also Haines Watts
FORSHAW, Mrs. Nicola, BSc ACA *2005;* Rockpools, Rue Des Crabbes, St. Saviour, GUERNSEY, GY7 9QH.
FORSHAW, Mr. Rodney William, FCA *1972;* Croit Veg, Ballacaley Road, Sulby, ISLE OF MAN, IM7 2HS. (Life Member)
FORSHAW, Mr. Roger, FCA *1964;* Winburn House, Zannies Lane, Witchampton, WIMBORNE, BH21 5BY.
FORSHAW, Mrs. Veronica Jayne, BA ACA *1985;* Sysco Management Consultants Ltd, Sysco Business Skills Academy Ltd, Threlfall Building, Trueman Street, LIVERPOOL, L3 2BA.
FORSKITT, Miss. Mary Anne, BSc ACA *1988;* Stoney Bank, Single Hill, Shoscombe, BATH, BA2 8LZ.
FORSS, Mr. Derek Nigel, MA ACA APMI *1982;* 4 Manor Gardens, RICHMOND, TW9 1XX.
FORSTER, Mr. Antony John, BA(Hons) ACA *2001;* 90 Fedden Village, Nore Road, Portishead, BRISTOL, BS20 8EJ.
FORSTER, Mrs. Catherine, BA(Hons) ACA *2004;* with PricewaterhouseCoopers LLP, 10-18 Union Street, LONDON, SE1 1SZ.
FORSTER, Mr. Christopher Paul, ACA *1987;* Icom House, 1/5 Irish Town, Suite No 6/ 312, PO Box 561, GIBRALTAR, GIBRALTAR.
FORSTER, Mr. Craig, ACA *2008;* 14 Oakfield Avenue, CHEADLE, CHESHIRE, SK8 1EF.
FORSTER, Mr. David Anthony, FCA *1955;* 4028 Bush Crescent, BEAMSVILLE L0R 1B9, ON, CANADA. (Life Member)
FORSTER, Mrs. Fiona Caroline, MEng BA ACA *2004;* with Deloitte LLP, Hill House, 1 Little New Street, LONDON, EC4A 3TR.
FORSTER, Mrs. Hannah Jane, MChem ACA *2003;* 96 Huntingdon Road, LONDON, N2 9DU.
FORSTER, Mrs. Helen Theresa, BSc ACA *1990;* 106 Wotton Drive, Ashton-in-Makerfield, WIGAN, WN4 8XR.
FORSTER, Mr. John Henry Knight, FCA *1965;* 12 Winchfield Court, Winchfield, HOOK, RG27 8SP.
FORSTER, Mr. John Michael, BCom FCA *1962;* Apartano 71, Casa Nas Salinas, 8501 903 MEXILHOEIRA, ALGARVE, PORTUGAL.
FORSTER, Miss. Louise Claire, BSc(Hons) FCA *2000;* 20 Rothbury Avenue, NEWCASTLE UPON TYNE, NE3 3HH.
FORSTER, Mr. Michael Kay, FCA *1948;* The Clearing, Deepdene Wood, DORKING, RH5 4BQ. (Life Member)
FORSTER, Mr. Michael William, BSc ACA *1983;* Flat 1, 61 Selsdon Road, West Norwood, LONDON, SE27 0PQ.
FORSTER, Mr. Neil Andrew, BSc ACA *1997;* Trealaw, Portsmouth Road, Milford, GODALMING, SURREY, GU8 5HW.
FORSTER, Dr. Nicola Louise, ACA *1992;* PwC, Private Bag x36, Sunninghill, JOHANNESBURG, 2157, SOUTH AFRICA.
FORSTER, Mr. Paul, ACA *1983;* Braeside, Leicester Road, Uppingham, OAKHAM, LE15 9SD.
FORSTER, Mr. Paul Crawford, BSc FCA *2000;* 94 Clare Road, BRAINTREE, ESSEX, CM7 2PF.
FORSTER, Mr. Peter John, ACA *1980;* 24-2828 Richmond Rd, OTTAWA K2B 8S1, ON, CANADA.
FORSTER, Mr. Peter Nicholas, BSc ACA *1979;* 28 The Quadrant, RICHMOND, SURREY, TW9 1DN.
FORSTER, Mr. Robert, LLB ACA MBA *1999;* 33 Field Lane, Appleton, WARRINGTON, WA4 5JR.
FORSTER, Mrs. Sally, BA ACA *1997;* 23 Bellevue Crescent, BRISTOL, BS8 4TE.
FORSTER, Mr. Sean Nicholas, BA ACA *2004;* with PricewaterhouseCoopers LLP, 1 Embankment Place, LONDON, WC2N 6RH.
FORSTER, Mr. Simon Robert, MA ACA *1980;* 11 Church Road, Ketton, STAMFORD, LINCOLNSHIRE, PE9 3RD.
•FORSTER, Mr. Stewart John, FCA *1979;* (Tax Fac), Friend-James Ltd, 169 Preston Road, BRIGHTON, EAST SUSSEX, BN1 6AG.
FORSTER, Miss. Suzanne Marie, BA ACA *1995;* 26 Oakwood Drive, BILLERICAY, ESSEX, CM12 0SA.
FORSYTH, Mr. Alan Neil, BA FCA *1954;* 17 Wren Way, Mickleover, DERBY, DE3 0UF. (Life Member)
FORSYTH, Mrs. Amanda Jean, MA ACA FRSA ASIP *1994;* 5 Dalrymple Crescent, EDINBURGH, EH9 2NU.
FORSYTH, Mr. Andrew, BEng ACA *1999;* Provident Financial, 1 Godwin Street, BRADFORD, BD1 2SU.
FORSYTH, Miss. Claire, BSc ACA *2011;* 29 Darkie Meadow, Bunbury, TARPORLEY, CHESHIRE, CW6 9RB.
FORSYTH, Miss. Clare, BSc ACA *2011;* 5 Coates Close, BASINGSTOKE, RG22 4EE.
•FORSYTH, Mr. David Thomas, FCA *1975;* (Tax Fac), David T Forsyth, 13 Barn Crescent, MARGATE, KENT, CT9 5HF.
•FORSYTH, Mr. Douglas Clayton Spencer, BSc ACA *2004;* Douglas Forsyth, Roydon Cottage, Sandy Down, Boldre, LYMINGTON, HAMPSHIRE SO41 8PL.
FORSYTH, Mr. Duncan Gavin, BSc ACA *1992;* West Coast, Arrowhead Road, Theale, READING, BERKSHIRE, RG7 4AH.
FORSYTH, Mr. Duncan Ryder Douglas, MSc ACA *2003;* 4th Floor, 41 Moorgate, LONDON, EC2R 6PP.
FORSYTH, Mr. Gordon Scott, BSc ACA *1993;* The Old Chequers, 68 High Street, Wilburton, ELY, CAMBRIDGESHIRE, CB6 3RA.
FORSYTH, Mr. Gordon Stuart, BA FCA *1978;* Thornfield Acre, Pudding Lane, Tiverton, TARPORLEY, CHESHIRE, CW6 9SN.
FORSYTH, Mr. Ian James, TD MA FCA *1960;* 70 West Common, HARPENDEN, AL5 2LD. (Life Member)
FORSYTH, Mr. Ian Stuart, BSc ACA *1979;* 18 Hillcrest Road, PURLEY, CR8 2JE.
•FORSYTH, Mr. Jeremy Clifford, BSc ACA *1988;* J Forsyth, 19 Cutenhoe Road, LUTON, LU1 3NB.
FORSYTH, Mr. Jonathan Charles, BSc ACA *1990;* Circle Anglia, 6 Central Avenue St. Andrews Business Park, NORWICH, NR7 0HR.
FORSYTH, Mr. Kevin James, BA ACA *1981;* 28 Uplands Road, KENLEY, CR8 5EF.
FORSYTH, Miss. Marion Jane, BA ACA *1998;* Glasgow 2014 Ltd Monteith House, 11 George Square, GLASGOW, G2 1DY.
FORSYTH, Miss. Melanie Christine, BA ACA *2008;* 4 Compton Terrace, LONDON, N1 2UN.
FORSYTH, Mr. Neil Cathcart, FCA *1962;* Sarsden House, Maugersbury, Stow-on-the-Wold, CHELTENHAM, GL54 1HR. (Life Member)
•FORSYTH, Mr. Nicholas, FCA *1989;* (Tax Fac), Lambert Chapman LLP, 3 Warners Mill, Silks Way, BRAINTREE, ESSEX, CM7 3GB.
FORSYTH, Mrs. Patricia, BSc ACA *1982;* Folkton House, Folkton, SCARBOROUGH, NORTH YORKSHIRE, YO11 3UG.
FORSYTH, Mr. Paul, BSc ACA *2006;* 9 Rossiter Road, LONDON, SW12 9RY.
FORSYTH, Mr. Paul Graham, MSc BA ACA *1979;* Level 5 The Fairmont, Sheikh Zayed Road, PO Box 27363, DUBAI, UNITED ARAB EMIRATES.
•FORSYTH, Mrs. Rosemary Jane, BA ACA *1994;* Wilkins & Co, 36 Chalklands, BOURNE END, BUCKINGHAMSHIRE, SL8 5TJ.
FORSYTH, Mrs. Sophie Jane, BMus ACA *2000;* with KPMG LLP, Quayside House, 110 Quayside, NEWCASTLE UPON TYNE, NE1 3DX.
FORSYTHE, Mr. Alex, ACA *2008;* 3/120 Brighton Boulevard, NORTH BONDI, NSW 2026, AUSTRALIA.
FORSYTHE, Mr. Bruce Hector William, BSc ACA *1990;* 35 Barlings Road, HARPENDEN, HERTFORDSHIRE, AL5 2AW.
FORSYTHE, Mrs. Jennifer Haydn, BSc ACA *1990;* 35 Barlings Road, HARPENDEN, HERTFORDSHIRE, AL5 2AW.
FORSYTHE, Mrs. Katharine Mary, BSc ACA ACII *1987;* 15 Pequot Road, MARBLEHEAD, MA 01945, UNITED STATES.
FORSYTHE, Mr. Macdonald Alexander, FCA *1967;* Hillside, 7 Robson Close, Chalfont St Peter, GERRARDS CROSS, SL9 0PS. (Life Member)
FORT, Mr. Alan James, BA ACA *1981;* Woodside, Barnet Wood Road, Bromley Common, BROMLEY, BR2 8HJ.
•FORT, Mr. David Mark, FCA *1994;* Haines Watts (Lancashire) LLP, Northern Assurance Buildings, 9-21 Princess Street, MANCHESTER, M2 4DN. See also Haines Watts Corporate Finance (NW)
FORT, Mr. Michael William, BA ACA *1990;* 24 Henbury View Road, Corfe Mullen, WIMBORNE, DORSET, BH21 3TT.
FORT, Mrs. Rosemary, BSc ACA *1980;* Enalder, Red Lane, COLNE, LANCASHIRE, BB8 7JR.
FORTE, Sir Rocco John Vincent, Kt MA FCA *1973;* Rocco Forte Collection, 70 Jermyn Street, LONDON, SW1Y 6NY.
FORTESCUE, Miss. Harriet Susan, ACA *2008;* Deloitte, 225 George Street, SYDNEY, NSW 2000, AUSTRALIA.

FORTESCUE, Mr. John Edward, FCA *1926;* 604 Woodside, Kloof Street, Tamboers Kloof, CAPE TOWN, C.P., 8001 SOUTH AFRICA. (Life Member)
FORTESCUE, Miss. Natalie Jayne, BA ACA *1997;* 84 Douglas Road, SURBITON, SURREY, KT6 7SB.
FORTESCUE, Mrs. Sandra, FCA *1970;* Tudor Timbers, Lewes Road, HAYWARDS HEATH, RH17 7SP.
FORTH, Mr. Andrew, BCom ACA *1992;* 175 Blossom Street, BOSTON, MA 02114, UNITED STATES.
FORTH, Mr. David Alexander, LLB FCA *1981;* Forth de Avellar Limited, 54 Dalmore Road, LONDON, SE21 8HB.
FORTH, Mrs. Fiona Mary, ACA CA(NZ) *2010;* 123 The Thatchers, BISHOP'S STORTFORD, HERTFORDSHIRE, CM23 4GU.
FORTH, Mr. Joe, BA ACA *2011;* 205 Farm View Road, Kimberworth, ROTHERHAM, SOUTH YORKSHIRE, S61 2BL.
•FORTH, Mr. Richard Ian Elinah, BSc ACA *1996;* Forth Associates Ltd, The Station, 77 Canal Road, LEEDS, LS12 2LX.
FORTH, Mr. William Henry, FCA *1959;* 4 Scots Hill Close, Croxley Green, RICKMANSWORTH, WD3 3AF. (Life Member)
FORTUNE, Mr. Gary, LLB ACA *1991;* 89 Abbots View, HADDINGTON, EH41 3QJ.
FORTUNE, Mr. Kenneth Frank, FCA *1971;* 32 Millbeck Drive, Harden, BINGLEY, WEST YORKSHIRE, BD16 1TF.
•FORTUNE, Mrs. Lisa Joanne, BA ACA *2009;* (Tax Fac), Fortune Hart, Green Hay Barn, Pershall, Eccleshall, STAFFORD, ST21 6NE.
FORTUNE, Mr. Nicholas John, BSc ACA *1989;* GBI, Qatar Science & Technology Park, PO Box 5825, DOHA, QATAR.
FORWARD, Mr. Charles Heaton, ACA MAAT *2001;* Birchlands Crawley Hill, West Wellow, ROMSEY, SO51 6AP.
FORWARD, Ms. Margaret Emily, BSc ACA *1991;* Langhorne Cottage, Reeth, RICHMOND, DL11 6SY.
FORWARD, Mr. Peter John, FCA *1969;* 3 Lubbock Road, CHISLEHURST, BR7 5JG.
•FORWOOD, Mr. Antony Alexander, FCA *1964;* (Tax Fac), with Wilkins Kennedy, Bridge House, London Bridge, LONDON, SE1 9QR.
FORWOOD, Mr. Edward Langton Homfray, MA ACA *1982;* Moat House Farm, Keepers Lane, Little Glemham, WOODBRIDGE, SUFFOLK, IP13 0BB.
FOSH, Mr. Nicholas, MPhys ACA *2011;* Apartment 6, Lime Tree Place, 2a Hunston Road, SALE, CHESHIRE, M33 4RP.
FOSH, Mr. Norman Sidney, FCA *1950;* The End House, Lingmere Close, CHIGWELL, IG7 6LH. (Life Member)
•FOSH, Mr. Simon Arthur, FCA *1982;* Gardiner Fosh Limited, 31 St. Johns, WORCESTER, WR2 5AG. See also Gardiner Fosh
•FOSKETT, Mr. Colin John Crafer, FCA *1956;* Foskett & Co., Beechcroft, Northleigh Lane, Colehill, WIMBORNE, BH21 2PN.
•FOSKETT, Mr. James Ronald, BSc FCA DChA *1987;* (Tax Fac), Cansdales, Bourbon Court, Nightingales Corner, Little Chalfont, AMERSHAM, HP7 9QS. See also Cansdales Ltd
FOSKETT, Mr. John Anthony, BSc(Hons) ACA *2000;* 6 Pinta Drive, STOURPORT-ON-SEVERN, WORCESTERSHIRE, DY13 9RY.
FOSKETT, Mr. Nicholas, ACA *2002;* 127 Hempstalls Lane, NEWCASTLE, ST5 9NZ.
FOSKETT, Mr. Robert William, FCA *1951;* Flat 3, Challoner Court, 224-226 Bromley Road, Shortland, BROMLEY, BR2 0AB. (Life Member)
FOSS, Mr. Christopher John, BSc(Econ) ACA *1997;* Northern Petroleum Plc, Martin House, 5 Martin Lane, LONDON, EC4R 0DP.
FOSSA, Mr. Riccardo Clifford, ACA CA(SA) *2011;* (Tax Fac), 860 Slington House, Rankine Road, BASINGSTOKE, HAMPSHIRE, RG24 8PH.
FOSSE, Mr. Peter William, ACA *1999;* 54 Meridian Place, LONDON, E14 9FE.
FOSSETT, Mr. Roy James, FCA *1958;* Roy James Fossett, 18 Flamingo Drive, WANTIRNA SOUTH, VIC 3152, AUSTRALIA. (Life Member)
FOSSEY, Miss. Leona June, BA ACA *2005;* 35 Beeches Mews, BRIGADOON, WA 6069, AUSTRALIA.
FOSSEY, Mr. Liam, MEng ACA *2007;* 22 Collings Close, LONDON, N22 8RL.
FOSTER, Mr. Adam, ACA *2011;* 1A Haydn Road, NOTTINGHAM, NG5 2JX.
•FOSTER, Mr. Albert Trevor, FCA *1974;* Foster & Company, 5 South Terrace, Moorgate, ROTHERHAM, S60 2EU.
FOSTER, Mr. Andrew, ACA CA(AUS) *2011;* 21 Aldersmead Road, LONDON, BR3 1NA.
FOSTER, Mr. Andrew Paul, BA ACA *1986;* Banbury House, Westend Road, Bradninch, EXETER, EX5 4HZ.
FOSTER, Mr. Andrew Richard James, BSc ACA *1992;* Whitfield Green Farm, Hague Street, GLOSSOP, SK13 7PJ.
•FOSTER, Mrs. Angela, BA(Hons) ACA CTA *2004;* Tindles LLP, Scotswood House, Teesdale South, STOCKTON-ON-TEES, CLEVELAND, TS17 6SB.
FOSTER, Mrs. Annette Claire, BSc ACA *1995;* Mitel Networks Ltd, Castlegate Business Park, CALDICOT, GWENT, NP26 5YR.
FOSTER, Mr. Anthony, BSc FCA *1960;* Cedar Cottage, Bridle Way, Goring-On-Thames, READING, RG8 0HS. (Life Member)
FOSTER, Mr. Anthony Roy, BSc ACA *1991;* Walnut House, Upper Basildon, READING, RG8 8LS.
FOSTER, Mrs. Bethan, BSc ACA *1984;* The Hollies, Windmill Lane, Balsall Common Solihull, COVENTRY, CV7 7GY.
•FOSTER, Mr. Brian Antony, FCA *1964;* Foster & Co, Foxbourne Business Centre, Heath Mill Close, Wombourne, WOLVERHAMPTON, WV5 8EX.
FOSTER, Mr. Brian Edgar, FCA *1951;* 17 Station Road, Shrivenham, SWINDON, SN6 8ED. (Life Member)
FOSTER, Ms. Carli-Louan, MA(Hons) MSc ACA *2011;* 25a Mycenae Road, LONDON, SE3 7SF.
FOSTER, Mrs. Carol Anne, BA ACA *1995;* 11 Thirlfield Wynd, LIVINGSTON, WEST LOTHIAN, EH54 7ER.
FOSTER, Mr. Charles Anthony, MA FCA *1969;* 34 Harvest Hill, EAST GRINSTEAD, RH19 4BT. (Life Member)
FOSTER, Mr. Christopher, BSc ACA *1995;* 26 Beach Road, Hartford, NORTHWICH, CHESHIRE, CW8 4BB.
FOSTER, Mr. Christopher Adrian Kenneth, FCA *1969;* 16 Atkinson Walk, Kennington, ASHFORD, KENT, TN24 9SB. (Life Member)
FOSTER, Mr. Christopher Norman, FCA *1969;* The Old Vicarage, Great Durnford, SALISBURY, SP4 6AZ.
FOSTER, Ms. Clare Louise, BA ACA *2002;* 20 Chanctonbury Road, HOVE, EAST SUSSEX, BN3 6EL.
FOSTER, Mr. Clifford John Hamilton, FCA *1976;* PO Box 63524, NAIROBI, 00619, KENYA.
FOSTER, Mr. Colin, BCom FCA *1955;* 18 Royal Avenue, Fulwood, PRESTON, PR2 9XP. (Life Member)
•FOSTER, Mr. Colin Gerald, BA FCA *1992;* Expert Accountancy Limited, 341 Lytham Road, BLACKPOOL, FY4 1DS.
FOSTER, Mr. Craig Garry, BA ACA *1994;* 38 Triangle West, Oldfield Park, BATH, BA2 3JA.
FOSTER, Mr. Daniel Joseph, ACA *2006;* 6 Maxted Road, LONDON, SE15 4LL.
FOSTER, Mr. David, FCA *1962;* Cart's House, Church End, Kensworth, DUNSTABLE, LU6 3RA.
FOSTER, Mr. David, BA(Hons) ACA *2001;* Flat 309 Dakota Building, Deals Gateway, LONDON, SE13 7QE.
FOSTER, Mr. David, BSc ACA *2011;* Flat 2, 20 Regent Street, Clifton, BRISTOL, BS8 4HG.
FOSTER, Mr. David Byrom, FCA *1958;* Bath Cottage, Aymestrey, LEOMINSTER, HR6 9TJ. (Life Member)
FOSTER, Mr. David Eric, BSc ACA *1992;* 8 Sicklinghall Road, WETHERBY, WEST YORKSHIRE, LS22 6AA.
FOSTER, Mr. David Ian, BA ACA *1991;* 42 Speldhurst Road, Chiswick, LONDON, W4 1BZ.
FOSTER, Mr. David John, FCA *1960;* Pradal, 46230 LALBENQUE, FRANCE. (Life Member)
FOSTER, Mr. David John, BSc ACA *1992;* Austrasse 39, 8045, ZURICH, SWITZERLAND.
FOSTER, Mr. David Richard, BSc ACA *1995;* 9 The Rigg, YARM, TS15 9XA.
FOSTER, Mr. David William, FCA *1972;* 3 Pines Close, GREAT MISSENDEN, BUCKINGHAMSHIRE, HP16 0HR.
FOSTER, Mr. Edward Charles, FCA *1967;* 159 Oakmount Road S.W., CALGARY T2V 4X3, AB, CANADA.
FOSTER, Mr. Edward James, LLB ACA *2000;* 1 Heydons Close, ST. ALBANS, HERTFORDSHIRE, AL3 5SF.
FOSTER, Mr. Eric Lancelot, FCA *1959;* 49 Mauldeth Rd, Heaton Mersey, STOCKPORT, SK4 3NB. (Life Member)
FOSTER, Ms. Gabrielle Catherine, ACA CA(AUS) *2010;* PO Box 2740, Dunearn LPO, DANDENONG, VIC 3175, AUSTRALIA.
FOSTER, Miss. Gail, BA ACA *1996;* 81 Mandrake Road, LONDON, SW17 7PX.
FOSTER, Mr. Gary Alistair, BAcc ACA *1999;* 4 Deyncourt, Ponteland, NEWCASTLE UPON TYNE, NE20 9RP.
FOSTER, Mr. Geoffrey Hilton, FCA *1970;* 8 Bell Acre, LETCHWORTH GARDEN CITY, HERTFORDSHIRE, SG6 2BS. (Life Member)
FOSTER, Mr. Geoffrey Iain, BSc ACA *1984;* The Hollies, Windmill Lane, Balsall Common, COVENTRY, CV7 7GY.
FOSTER, Mr. Geoffrey William, FCA *1959;* 8 School Drive, SHERBORNE, DORSET, DT9 3SB. (Life Member)
FOSTER, Mr. George Jonathan, BA ACA *1984;* Tarragona, Claypit Lane, Ledsham, South Milford, LEEDS, LS25 5LP.
FOSTER, Mr. Graham Peter, BSc ACA *1984;* G 4 S Plc The Manor, Manor Royal, CRAWLEY, WEST SUSSEX, RH10 9UN.
FOSTER, Mrs. Hilary Mary, FCA *1983;* 16 Richmond Road, Romiley, STOCKPORT, SK6 4PP.
•FOSTER, Mr. Hugh David, BA FCA *1990;* Fosters, Unit 3, Friends School, Low Green Rawdon, LEEDS, LS19 6HB.
FOSTER, Mr. Ian, BSc FCA *1992;* 3 Imperial Way, HEMEL HEMPSTEAD, HERTFORDSHIRE, HP3 9FJ.
•FOSTER, Miss. Isobel Muriel, BA FCA *1980;* Lambhill, Bride, Nr Ramsey, ISLE OF MAN, IM7 4BL.
FOSTER, Mr. James, MA BA ACA *2004;* 2 Hollow Rise, HIGH WYCOMBE, BUCKINGHAMSHIRE, HP13 5NU.
FOSTER, Mr. James, BA ACA *2005;* 157 Phoenix Way, Portishead, BRISTOL, BS20 7GP.
FOSTER, Mr. James Brian, FCA *1957;* Junipers, 38 St Mary Well Street, BEAMINSTER, DT8 3BB. (Life Member)
FOSTER, Mr. James Stephen, BSc FCA *1977;* 4a Spareleaze Hill, LOUGHTON, IG10 1BT.
FOSTER, Mrs. Janette Victoria, BSc FCA *1993;* 18 Rue Belair, L-5318 CONTERN, LUXEMBOURG.
FOSTER, Mr. Jason, ACA *2009;* 9 Mount Pleasant Road, LONDON, NW10 3EG.
•FOSTER, Mr. Jeremy Mark Russell, BA ACA *1986;* PricewaterhouseCoopers LLP, 7 More London Riverside, LONDON, SE1 2RT. See also PricewaterhouseCoopers
•FOSTER, Miss. Jill Kathryn, BA ACA *1991;* Foster & Co Ltd, 80 Lytham Road, Fulwood, PRESTON, PR2 3AQ.
FOSTER, Mr. John Alma, FCA *1957;* 7 Ravenswood Drive, SOLIHULL, B91 3NL. (Life Member)
•FOSTER, Mr. John David, BA FCA *1989;* Blue Cube Business Ltd, 10 Cheyne Walk, NORTHAMPTON, NN1 5PT.
FOSTER, Mr. John Ernest, FCA *1967;* 26a Ring Road, West Park, LEEDS, LS16 6EJ. (Life Member)
•FOSTER, Mr. John Gerard, BSc FCA *1981;* 43 Albany Road, SALISBURY, SP1 3YQ.
FOSTER, Mr. John Henry, FCA *1972;* 48 Meadow Road, PINNER, MIDDLESEX, HA5 1ED.
FOSTER, Mr. John Laurence, BA ACA *1983;* Annerly, Dartnell Avenue, WEST BYFLEET, KT14 6PJ.
FOSTER, Mr. John Leslie, BA ACA *1997;* RBC Dexia Investor Services (ESCH G17), 14 Porte de France, ESCH-SUR-ALZETTE, LUXEMBOURG.
FOSTER, Mr. John Leslie, MA FCA *1980;* Aegis Media UK & Ireland Ltd, Parker Tower 43-49 Parker Street, LONDON, WC2B 5PS.
•FOSTER, Mr. John Martin Graham, FCA *1974;* West and Foster Limited, 2 Broomgrove Road, SHEFFIELD, SOUTH YORKSHIRE, S10 2LR.
FOSTER, Mr. John Michael, FCA *1968;* 525 Fulwood Road, SHEFFIELD, S10 3QB.
•FOSTER, Mr. John Michael, FCA *1972;* John Foster & Co, Office Four, 3 Edgar Buildings, BATH, BA1 2FJ.
FOSTER, Mr. John Paul, BSc ACA *2003;* St Philips Point, Temple Row, BIRMINGHAM, WEST MIDLANDS, B2 5AF.
FOSTER, Mr. John William, FCA *1964;* 24 East Witton, LEYBURN, DL8 4SH.
FOSTER, Mr. John William, FCA *1975;* 34 Temple Road, EPSOM, KT19 8HA.
FOSTER, Mr. Jonathan Scott, BSc FCA *1986;* 3 Wyndcroft Close, ENFIELD, MIDDLESEX, EN2 7BJ.
FOSTER, Mr. Jordan John, BA(Hons) ACA *2003;* with KPMG LLP, St. James's Square, MANCHESTER, M2 6DS.
FOSTER, Mr. Joseph Christopher, FCA *1962;* Flat 1, 15 Otley Road, HARROGATE, HG2 0DJ.
FOSTER, Mrs. Judith Claire, FCA *1979;* 294 Molesey Road, Hersham, WALTON-ON-THAMES, SURREY, KT12 4SQ.
FOSTER, Mr. Julian Anthony, MA ACA MCT *1981;* Cross Keys Homes, Shrewsbury Avenue, PETERBOROUGH, PE2 7BZ.
FOSTER, Mr. Julian Roberts, BSc ACA *1994;* 6/20 Cleland Road, ARTARMON, NSW 2064, AUSTRALIA.
FOSTER, Mrs. Julie Denise, BSc ACA *1999;* with KPMG LLP, Arlington Business Park, Theale, READING, RG7 4SD.
FOSTER, Mrs. Julie Mari, BA ACA *1995;* 9 Tulum Approach, ILUKA, WA 6028, AUSTRALIA.
FOSTER, Mrs. Karen Lyn, BSc ACA *1988;* 21 Speedwell Drive, Balsall Common, COVENTRY, CV7 7AU.
FOSTER, Mrs. Kathryn, BSc ACA *1990;* 42 Speldhurst Road, Chiswick, LONDON, W4 1BZ.
FOSTER, Mrs. Kathryn Louise, BA ACA *1995;* (Tax Fac), Chaplin Associates, 35 Milldown Road, Goring on Thames, READING, RG8 0BA.
FOSTER, Mr. Kenneth, MA FCA *1957;* 18 Lawrence Avenue, Simonstone, BURNLEY, BB12 7HX. (Life Member)
FOSTER, Mr. Kenneth Martin Robert, FCA *1969;* 70 Glengall Road, WOODFORD GREEN, IG8 0DL. (Life Member)
•FOSTER, Mr. Kevin Lee, BSc ACA *1997;* Crouch Chapman, 62 Wilson Street, LONDON, EC2A 2BU.
FOSTER, Mrs. Kirsten Louise, BA ACA *2005;* Rank Group, New Statesman House, Stafferton Way, MAIDENHEAD, BERKSHIRE, SL6 1AY.
FOSTER, Mr. Leslie John, FCA *1955;* 19 Three Tuns Lane, Formby, LIVERPOOL, L37 4AG.
•FOSTER, Mr. Leslie Raymond, ACA *1979;* (Tax Fac), Foster & Co, 144 Malvern Avenue, NUNEATON, CV10 8NB.
FOSTER, Mrs. Linda, BSc ACA *1992;* Vale of Aylesbury Housing, Fairfax House, 69 Buckinghamshire Street, AYLESBURY, BUCKINGHAMSHIRE, HP20 2NJ.
•FOSTER, Miss. Linda Carol, BA ACA *1993;* Apley Accounting, 4 Apley Road, Wollaston, STOURBRIDGE, WEST MIDLANDS, DY8 4PA.
FOSTER, Mrs. Linda Margaret, BSc ACA *1983;* Brockhurst Davies Limited, Unit 11 The Office Village, North Road, LOUGHBOROUGH, LEICESTERSHIRE, LE11 1QJ.
FOSTER, Miss. Linda Mary, BA FCA *1993;* 30a Hayes Lane, BROMLEY, BR2 9EB.
FOSTER, Mrs. Louise Claire, ACA *1993;* Microsoft, Microsoft Campus, Thames Valley Park, READING, RG6 1WG.
FOSTER, Miss. Lucy Clare, ACA *2009;* 314 Saville Court, Potato Wharf, Castlefield, MANCHESTER, M3 4NB.
FOSTER, Mr. Luke, BSc ACA *2007;* 22 Salisbury Road, SEAFORD, BN25 2DD.
FOSTER, Mr. Mark, ACA *2002;* 2 Greenfield Avenue, Balsall Common, COVENTRY, CV7 7UG.
FOSTER, Mr. Mark Hardwick, BA FCA *1989;* Inglenook Cottage, 17 Cooper Lane, Potto, NORTHALLERTON, NORTH YORKSHIRE, DL6 3HG.
FOSTER, Mr. Mark Ian, ACA *2009;* 134 Derby Street, SHEFFIELD, S2 3NG.
FOSTER, Mr. Martin, BSc ACA *2003;* Ocon Construction Ltd, Ducie Street, MANCHESTER, M1 2TP.
•FOSTER, Mr. Martin, BSc ACA *1982;* Martin Foster & Co Limited, Offices 2 & 3, Shannon Court, High Street, SANDY, BEDFORDSHIRE SG19 1AG.
FOSTER, Mr. Martin Andrew, BA ACA *1992;* 7 The Square, Snaithwood Drive, Rawdon, LEEDS, LS19 6SZ.
FOSTER, Mr. Michael Albert, FCA *1962;* 8 Princes Mews, Hereford Road, LONDON, W2 4NX. (Life Member)
FOSTER, Mr. Michael John, ACA *2011;* 26 Edwin Avenue, Guiseley, LEEDS, LS20 8QJ.
FOSTER, Mr. Michael Raymond, FCA *1982;* Rowley House South Herts Office Campus, Elstree Way, BOREHAMWOOD, HERTFORDSHIRE, WD6 1JH.
FOSTER, Mrs. Mondane Louise, BSc(Hons) ACA MAAT *2009;* 40 Derby Road, Swanwick, ALFRETON, DERBYSHIRE, DE55 1AB.
FOSTER, Mr. Neil, BA ACA *1992;* Inspectorate International Limited, PO Box 49400, DUBAI, UNITED ARAB EMIRATES.
FOSTER, Mr. Neil Gavin, BA ACA *1997;* Trinity Estates Property Management, Vantage Point, 23 Mark Road, Hemel Hempstead Industrial Estate, HEMEL HEMPSTEAD, HERTFORDSHIRE HP2 7DN.
FOSTER, Mr. Nicholas, BA ACA *2011;* The Old Vicarage, Great Durnford, SALISBURY, SP4 6AZ.
FOSTER, Mr. Nicholas James, BA FCA *1976;* The Conduit Mead Co Ltd Unit 3b, Nettlefold Place, LONDON, SE27 0JW.
FOSTER, Mr. Nigel Alan, MA ACA *1986;* 21 Speedwell Drive, Balsall Common, COVENTRY, CV7 7AU.
FOSTER, Mr. Paul Brian, MSc ACA *1983;* with Endless LLP, 3 Whitehall Quay, LEEDS, LS1 4BF.
FOSTER, Mr. Paul Simon, BSc ACA *2001;* 61 Congreve Road, LONDON, SE9 1LW.
FOSTER, Mrs. Penelope Jane, ACA *1989;* Woodward Hale, 38 Dollar Street, CIRENCESTER, GLOUCESTERSHIRE, GL7 2AN.
FOSTER, Mr. Peter Anthony, FCA *1971;* 7 The Causeway, Selsey, CHICHESTER, WEST SUSSEX, PO20 9BY.

FOSTER, Mr. Philip Anthony, BEng ACA *1998;* Level 2 Finance, News International Finance, 1 Virginia Street, LONDON, E98 1FN.
FOSTER, Mr. Philip Joseph, BA ACA *1992;* The Coach House, 7 Douces Manor, St. Leonards Street, WEST MALLING, KENT, ME19 6UB.
FOSTER, Mrs. Rachel Jane, BSc ACA *1995;* 9 High Drive, NEW MALDEN, KT3 3UJ.
FOSTER, Miss. Rachel Victoria, MA ACA *2009;* Flat 24 West Kensington Mansions, Beaumont Crescent, LONDON, W14 9PE.
•**FOSTER, Mr. Richard Antony Nainby, BSc ACA ATII** *1989;* IMP Business Consulting Limited, The Homestead, 60 Church Street, Willingham, CAMBRIDGE, CB24 5HT.
FOSTER, Mr. Richard Croydon, BA(Hons) ACA FSI *1995;* Wells Fargo, Mac D1113-026, 1525 W WT Harris Blvd, CHARLOTTE, NC 28262-8522, UNITED STATES.
FOSTER, Mr. Richard Neil, ACA CPFA *2009;* 13 Summershades Lane, Grasscroft, OLDHAM, OL4 4ED.
•**FOSTER, Mr. Robert William, FCA** *1974;* Peake House, Main Street, Seaton, OAKHAM, LE15 9HU.
FOSTER, Mr. Roger John, BSc ACA *1991;* Rectory Farm, Madingley Road, Coton, CAMBRIDGE, CB23 7PG.
•**FOSTER, Mr. Ronald William, ACA** *1980;* R Foster & Co (Accountants) Ltd, Orchid House, 243 Elliott Street, Tyldesley, MANCHESTER, M29 8DG.
FOSTER, Mr. Ross Gregory, MA ACA *1996;* 40 Ferndene Road, Herne Hill, LONDON, SE24 0AB.
FOSTER, Mr. Roy William John, FCA *1955;* 16 Pauls Place, Farm Lane, ASHTEAD, SURREY, KT21 1HN. (Life Member)
FOSTER, Mr. Russell Glen, FCA *1971;* R G Foster Textile Machinery Ltd, Bull Close Road, NOTTINGHAM, NG7 2UL.
FOSTER, Mrs. Sara Catrin, ACA *2010;* 23 Phoenix Way, CARDIFF, CF14 4PR.
FOSTER, Mrs. Sarah, BA ACA *1991;* with The TACS Partnership, Graylaw House, Mersey Square, STOCKPORT, CHESHIRE, SK1 1AL.
FOSTER, Mr. Simon, ACA *2007;* Flat 5, 235 Upper Richmond Road, LONDON, SW15 6SN.
FOSTER, Mr. Simon Charles, BA(Hons) ACA *2001;* 12 Oak Road, Ballawattleworth, Peel, ISLE OF MAN, IM5 1WN.
•**FOSTER, Mr. Simon David Thomas, MA ACA** *1997;* KPMG, Naberezhnaya Tower Complex, Block C, 10 Presnenskaya Naberezhnaya, 123317 MOSCOW, RUSSIAN FEDERATION. See also KPMG Europe LLP
•**FOSTER, Mr. Simon William Knight, BA FCA** *1983;* 8650 Hopewell Road, CINCINNATI, OH 45242, UNITED STATES.
•**FOSTER, Dr. Stephen, ACA** *1991;* Blomfields, The Courtyard, 33 Duke Street, TROWBRIDGE, WILTSHIRE, BA14 8EA. See also S Foster (BOA) Ltd
•**FOSTER, Mr. Stephen, BSc ACA** *1996;* Abrahamson Foster Ltd, Atkins Building, Lower Bond Street, HINCKLEY, LEICESTERSHIRE, LE10 1QU.
FOSTER, Mr. Stephen Edmund, MA ACA *1988;* 38 Bridge End, WARWICK, CV346PB.
FOSTER, Mr. Stephen John, BA(Hons) ACA *2000;* 23 Brick Kiln Lane, Rufford, ORMSKIRK, L40 1SY.
•**FOSTER, Mr. Stephen Mark, BA FCA** *1991;* (Tax Fac), Maurice J. Bushell & Co, Curzon House, 64 Clifton Street, LONDON, EC2A 4HB. See also C.M.G. Associates
FOSTER, Mr. Steven Anthony, BSc ACA *1987;* ul. Hrubieszowska 2, 01-209 WARSAW, POLAND.
•**FOSTER, Mr. Stuart Geoffrey, BA FCA** *1980;* Hobsons, Alexandra House, 43 Alexandra Street, NOTTINGHAM, NG5 1AY.
•**FOSTER, Mrs. Susan Martha, FCA** *1984;* (Tax Fac), Knill James, One Bell Lane, LEWES, EAST SUSSEX, BN7 1JU.
FOSTER, Mr. Timothy Harrison, BA FCA *1987;* Unit 602, 30 Cliff Street, MILSONS POINT, NSW 2061, AUSTRALIA.
FOSTER, Mr. Trevor James, FCA *1957;* 30C Hayes Lane, BROMLEY, BR2 9EB. (Life Member)
FOSTER, Miss. Victoria Leanne, BSc ACA *2003;* Flat 5 Marncrest Court, 39 Westcar Lane Hersham, WALTON-ON-THAMES, SURREY, KT12 5ER.
FOSTER, Mr. Warren Michael, BCom ACA *1987;* 23 Whiston Grange, ROTHERHAM, S60 3BG.
FOSTER, Mrs. York Kee, ACA *1993;* Micklefield Croft, Micklefield Road, Rawdon, LEEDS, LS19 6AY.
FOSTER-BROWN, Mr. Robin Stephen, FCA *1964;* Osborne House, 16 Lady Street, DULVERTON, TA22 9BZ. (Life Member)
FOSTER-KEMP, Mr. Charles William, LLB ACA *2000;* Bullfinches Farm, Eridge Green, TUNBRIDGE WELLS, TN3 9LJ.
FOSTER THOMAS, Mr. John, BSc FCA *1974;* The Cross Church Road, Llanblethian, COWBRIDGE, CF71 7JF.
FOSTON, Mr. Nicholas Peter, FCA *1976;* 24 Moor Lane, Bramcote Hills, NOTTINGHAM, NG9 3FH.
FOSTON, Mr. Peter Wilfred, FCA *1948;* 6 St.Nicholas Close, Allestree, DERBY, DE22 2JW. (Life Member)
FOTHERBY, Mr. Nigel Terence Chell, BCom FCA *1981;* Morland House, 2 Chapel Street, WATLINGTON, OX49 5QT.
FOTHERGILL, Mr. James, MA ACA *1993;* 10 Calluna Court, WOKING, GU22 7HU.
FOTHERGILL, Mrs. Lynsey Hunter, LLB ACA *2001;* with PricewaterhouseCoopers, 89 Sandyford Road, NEWCASTLE UPON TYNE, NE1 8HW.
FOTHERGILL, Mr. Paul, MA ACA *1983;* 76 Rue Du Tir, 78600 MAISONS LAFFITTE, FRANCE.
FOTHERGILL, Mr. Paul John, BA ACA *1994;* 1 Gibson Mews, TWICKENHAM, TW1 2NS.
FOTHERINGHAM, Mr. David, ACA *2009;* 65 Cavendish Way, GRANTHAM, LINCOLNSHIRE, NG31 9FN.
•**FOTHERINGHAM, Mr. George Andrew, BA FCA CF** *1982;* Evolution Business and Tax Advisors LLP, 10 Evolution, Wynyard Park, Wynyard, BILLINGHAM, CLEVELAND TS22 5TB.
FOTHERINGHAM, Mr. Ian West, TD MA FCA FCMA *1959;* Far End, 42 France Hill Drive, CAMBERLEY, GU15 3QE. (Life Member)
•**FOTI, Mr. Michael, FCA** *1982;* The Springfield Accountancy Network Ltd, 17 The Ridgeway, Fetcham, LEATHERHEAD, SURREY, KT22 9BA.
FOULDS, Mr. Christopher John Michael, BSc ACA *2006;* Beau Geste, La Rue de la Hauteur, St. Helier, JERSEY, JE2 3FB.
FOULDS, Mr. David Michael, BSc ACA *1985;* Translinc Ltd Jarvis House, 157 Sadler Road, LINCOLN, LN6 3RS.
FOULDS, Mrs. Emma Louise, ACA *2008;* 96 Winding Way, LEEDS, LS17 7RQ.
•**FOULDS, Mrs. Julia Anne, FCA** *1984;* Zebra Accounting (Thames Valley) Ltd, 7 Kingsland House, 135 Andover Road, NEWBURY, BERKSHIRE, RG14 6JL.
FOULDS, Mr. Julian Marcus, BSc ACA *1996;* 30 Beaufort Road, EXETER, EX2 9AB.
FOULDS, Mr. Lawrence Patrick, MA FCA *1976;* 14 Ladbroke Walk, LONDON, W11 3PW.
FOULDS, Miss. Lindsay, BSc ACA *2005;* Flat 2 Southlands Court, Church Avenue, HAYWARDS HEATH, WEST SUSSEX, RH16 1EQ.
FOULDS, Mr. Martin John, BSc FCA *1985;* 2 Angel Court, LONDON, SW1Y 6QF.
FOULDS, Mr. Michael Arthur, JP FCA *1956;* 100 Cropwell Road, Radcliffe-on-Trent, NOTTINGHAM, NG12 2JG. (Life Member)
FOULDS, Ms. Penelope Jane, BA ACA *1997;* 14 Gwynne Close, TRING, HERTFORDSHIRE, HP23 5EN.
FOULDS, Mr. Peter Edmund, BSc ACA *1999;* 15 Rue Notre Dame, L-2240 LUXEMBOURG, LUXEMBOURG.
FOULERTON, Mr. Geoffrey Richard Douglas, FCA *1978;* Bushfurlong Dairy House, Isle Brewers, TAUNTON, SOMERSET, TA3 6QT.
FOULGER, Mr. Adrian Anthony, BSc ACA *1993;* 10 Kay Siang Road, SINGAPORE 248926, SINGAPORE.
•**FOULGER, Mrs. Caroline Jean, BA FCA** *1986;* with PricewaterhouseCoopers, Dorchester House, 7 Church Street West, PO Box HM1171, HAMILTON HM EX, BERMUDA.
FOULGER, Mr. Geoffrey David, FCA *1972;* 13 Sunbury Avenue, East Sheen, LONDON, SW14 8RA.
FOULGER, Mr. Julian St John, FCA *1980;* Spissenstrasse 82, 6045 MEGGEN, SWITZERLAND.
FOULIS, Mr. David, BSc ACA *2011;* Installation & Service, 2 Callis Court Road, BROADSTAIRS, KENT, CT10 3AE.
FOULKE, Mr. Andrew Mark, ACA *1988;* 26 Albert Road, RIPLEY, DE5 3FZ.
FOULKES, Mrs. Christine Amy, BA FCA *1984;* 17 Farrar Drive, Barton Park, MARLBOROUGH, SN8 1TP.
FOULKES, Mr. Gareth John, ACA *2009;* 26 Beverley Gardens, MAIDENHEAD, SL6 6SN.
•**FOULKES, Mr. Geoffrey Stephen, FCA** *1975;* with Built Off Site Ltd, London House, Shawbury Business Park, SHREWSBURY, SY4 4EA.
FOULKES, Mrs. Lesley, LLB ACA *1984;* Willow Cottage, 12 Pulens Lane, PETERSFIELD, GU31 4DB.
FOULKES, Mr. Liam Andrew, BSc ACA *2006;* PricewaterhouseCoopers, Level 19, Freshwater Place, 2 Southbank Boulevard, Southbank, MELBOURNE VIC 3006 AUSTRALIA.
FOULKES, Mr. Michael, BSc ACA *2010;* 76 Murhill, Limpley Stoke, BATH, BA2 7FB.
•**FOULKES, Mr. Michael John, BSc FCA** *1982;* Manchula Ltd, 7 Fulwith Close, HARROGATE, NORTH YORKSHIRE, HG2 8HP.
FOULKES, Mr. Paul David, BA ACA *1984;* Barley Cottage, North Lane, South Harting, PETERSFIELD, HAMPSHIRE, GU31 5NN.
FOULKES, Mr. Stephen John, ACA *2008;* (Tax Fac), 38 School Lane, RIPLEY, DERBYSHIRE, DE5 3GT.
FOULKES, Mr. Stephen William, BSc ACA *2006;* 18b The Green, Deanshanger, MILTON KEYNES, MK19 6HL.
FOULSER, Mr. Benjamin James, BA(Hons) ACA *2010;* Broadmead Rickman Hill Road, Chipstead, COULSDON, CR5 3LB.
FOULSTONE, Mr. Jamie, MSci ACA *2005;* 3 Plumbley Hall Mews, Mosborough, SHEFFIELD, S20 5BF.
FOUND, Mr. Dale Andrew, BA ACA *1994;* 11 - 875 Sahali Terrace, KAMLOOPS V2C 6W9, BC, CANADA.
FOUND, Mr. James Leon, BSc ACA *1997;* 270 Badminton Road, Downend, BRISTOL, BS16 6NT.
FOUND, Mr. Nicholas Stephen James, ACA *2008;* 15, Canada Square, LONDON, E145GL.
FOUNTAIN, Mr. Christopher James, MBA BSc ACA *1992;* Technology Strategy Board North Star House, North Star Avenue Hawksworth Trading Estate, SWINDON, SN2 1JF.
FOUNTAIN, Miss. Emma Jayne, BSc(Hons) FCA *2000;* with Bates Weston Audit Limited, The Mill, Canal Street, DERBY, DE1 2RJ.
FOUNTAIN, Mr. Ian Richard, BSc ACA *1992;* 19 Heights Close, WEST WIMBLEDON, LONDON, SW20 0TH.
FOUNTAIN, Mr. Mark Jonathan, BA ACA *1993;* 67 Brookside Crescent, Cuffley, POTTERS BAR, EN6 4QP.
FOUNTAIN, Mr. Michael John, FCA *1960;* Flat 9, Wray Mill House, Batts Hill, REIGATE, SURREY, RH2 0LJ. (Life Member)
FOURACRE, Mr. Alan David, BA ACA *1996;* 55 Glasnevin Drive, Casebrook, CHRISTCHURCH 8051, NEW ZEALAND.
FOURACRE, Mr. Tim, ACA *2008;* Clear Books, 107 Hammersmith Road, LONDON, W14 0QH.
FOURNIER, Mr. Jean Stephane Alain, BSc ACA *2000;* Route de Perreret 9, 1134 VUFFLENS-LE-CHATEAU, SWITZERLAND.
FOURNIER, Mr. Mark Anthony Taylor, BA ACA *2005;* Flat 61 Medland House, 11 Branch Road, LONDON, E14 7JT.
FOUX, Ms. Melissa Lou-Anne, BSc ACA *1996;* 56 Flanders Road, LONDON, W4 1NG.
FOVARGUE, Miss. Alison Elizabeth, BA ACA *2007;* The Farmhouse, West Farm, Farm Town, Coleorton, LEICESTER, LE67 8FH.
FOWELL, Mr. Henry Ernest John, FCA *1950;* 29 Cardinal Avenue, BEECROFT, NSW 2119, AUSTRALIA. (Life Member)
FOWER, Mrs. Susan Frances, MA ACA *1992;* 4 Lilac Grove, Luston, LEOMINSTER, HR6 0EF.
FOWER, Mr. Todd, BA ACA *1991;* 29 Lingen Avenue, HEREFORD, HR1 1BY.
FOWKE, Mr. Jeremy, BA(Hons) ACA *2001;* 44 Nunnery Lane, YORK, YO23 1AJ.
FOWKES, Mr. Mark, BA ACA *2007;* 62 Milliners Court, Lattimore Road, ST. ALBANS, HERTFORDSHIRE, AL1 3XT.
FOWKES, Mr. Timothy, FCA *1968;* (Tax Fac), 19 Stag Lane, Chorleywood, RICKMANSWORTH, WD3 5HP.
FOWLE, Mr. Christopher James, FCA *1959;* Willow Cottage, The Green, Pulham Market, DISS, NORFOLK, IP21 4SU. (Life Member)
FOWLE, Mr. David John, BSc ACA *1992;* 10 The Heythrop, INGATESTONE, CM4 9HG.
FOWLE, Mr. Mark Andrew, BA ACA *2001;* 1 Shorefields, Rainham, GILLINGHAM, KENT, ME8 8SA.
FOWLE, Mr. William Michael Thomas, CBE MA FCA *1965;* 31 Myddelton Square, LONDON, EC1R 1YB.
FOWLER, Mr. Adrian James Kennedy, BEng ACA *1986;* 794 Portugal Dept 3, QUITO, ECUADOR.
FOWLER, Mr. Alan, FCA *1957;* Chy Coggan, Trencrom, Lelant Downs, HAYLE, CORNWALL, TR27 6NU. (Life Member)
FOWLER, Miss. Alison Claire, BSc ACA *1996;* GB 15; 15/4B F04A, Dunton Research & Development Centre, LAINDON, SS16 6EE.
FOWLER, Mr. Andrew John, BSc ACA *2007;* Flat 3, 1 Marshall Street, LEEDS, LS11 9AB.
FOWLER, Mrs. Caroline Margaret, ACA *1995;* Laurel Cottage, Ferndale Barns, Lower Swell, CHELTENHAM, GLOUCESTERSHIRE, GL54 1LP.
•**FOWLER, Mr. Charles Roderick Spencer, TD DL FCA** *1973;* Competex Ltd, Orchard House, Park Lane, REIGATE, SURREY, RH2 8JX.
FOWLER, Miss. Cherry Denise, ACA *1993;* May Cottage, Hollybush Lane, Burghfield Common, READING, RG7 3JS.
FOWLER, Mr. Clyde Yoshimune, LLB ACA *2002;* 36 All Saints Avenue, MAIDENHEAD, SL6 6NA.
•**FOWLER, Mr. Colin Peter, BSc FCA** *1989;* Colin Fowler, The Woodlands, Mold Road, Cefn-y-Bedd, WREXHAM, CLWYD LL12 9YG.
FOWLER, Mr. David, BA ACA *1980;* 53 Blendon Drive, BEXLEY, DA5 3AA.
FOWLER, Mr. David John, BA ACA *1984;* 13319 Barryknoll Ln, HOUSTON, TX 77079, UNITED STATES.
FOWLER, Mr. Edward Joseph, BSc(Hons) ACA *2002;* 12 King Henry Road, FLEET, HAMPSHIRE, GU51 1JH.
FOWLER, Miss. Emma Louise, ACA *2007;* Build A Bear Workshop, St. Stephens House, Arthur Road, WINDSOR, BERKSHIRE, SL4 1RU.
FOWLER, Mrs. Fiona Claire, BA ACA *1995;* 16 Lindfield Road, Ealing, LONDON, W5 1QR.
FOWLER, Mr. Gareth Graham, BA ACA *1991;* 9 Park House Green, Spofforth, HARROGATE, HG3 1BP.
FOWLER, Mr. Gary Steven, BSc ACA *1992;* 8A Primrose Way, Horbury, WAKEFIELD, WEST YORKSHIRE, WF4 6AW.
FOWLER, Mr. Graeme Henry, BSc(Hons) ACA *1981;* Opella Ltd, Twyford Road, Rotherwas Industrial Estate, HEREFORD, HR2 6JR.
FOWLER, Miss. Heidi, ACA *2007;* 1 Fallowfield Court, West Lane, PENRITH, CUMBRIA, CA11 7DJ.
FOWLER, Mrs. Helen Lorraine, BSc ACA *1993;* Whiteridge, Chalkpit Lane, MARLOW, BUCKINGHAMSHIRE, SL7 2JE.
FOWLER, Mr. Ian, BA FCA *1959;* Old Court Bungalow Henley Road, Misterton, CREWKERNE, SOMERSET, TA18 8LS. (Life Member)
FOWLER, Mr. Ian Russell, FCA *1961;* 40 Davis Court, Marlborough Road, ST. ALBANS, AL1 3XU.
FOWLER, Mr. James, ACA *2010;* 35, 35 Cecil Road, LONDON, SW19 1JR.
FOWLER, Mr. James Dominic, BA ACA *1994;* 30 Curzon Road, LONDON, W5 1NF.
•**FOWLER, Mrs. Jane Marie, LLB FCA** *1995;* 26 Church Road, RICHMOND, SURREY, TW9 1UA.
FOWLER, Miss. Joanna, BA(Hons) ACA *2001;* Crows Cottage Low Road, Friskney, BOSTON, LINCOLNSHIRE, PE22 8NW.
FOWLER, Mrs. Joanne Claire, ACA *2010;* Langdale Main Street, Frolesworth, LUTTERWORTH, LEICESTERSHIRE, LE17 5EG.
FOWLER, Mr. John Charles, FCA *1950;* Brookwood, Station Road, Blockley, MORETON-IN-MARSH, GL56 9DT. (Life Member)
FOWLER, Mr. John Geoffrey, FCA *1969;* 235 Metcalfe No 506, Westmount, MONTREAL H3Z 2H8, QC, CANADA.
FOWLER, Mr. John Kenneth, BA ACA *1990;* 16 Varsity Drive, TWICKENHAM, TW1 1AG.
FOWLER, Mr. John Richard Francis, FCA *1966;* 56 Heath Road, PETERSFIELD, HAMPSHIRE, GU31 4EJ. (Life Member)
FOWLER, Mr. John Stuart Preston, BA ACA *1995;* Laurel Cottage, Ferndale Barns, Lower Swell, CHELTENHAM, GLOUCESTERSHIRE, GL54 1LP.
•**FOWLER, Mr. Malcolm, FCA** *1977;* (Tax Fac), Malcolm Fowler, 21 St. Johns Square, Wilton, SALISBURY, SP2 0DW.
FOWLER, Mr. Mark, BSc ACA CF *2000;* Astrazeneca T458/8 Alderley House, Alderley Park, MACCLESFIELD, CHESHIRE, SK11 4TF.
FOWLER, Mr. Mark Allan, BA(Hons) ACA *2004;* Credit Suisse, 5 Cabot Square, LONDON, E14 4QR.
FOWLER, Mr. Martin Edward, FCA *1970;* St Clair, Petrockstow, OKEHAMPTON, EX20 3QJ.
FOWLER, Mr. Matthew John, BA(Hons) ACA *2001;* 35 Broad Walk, WILMSLOW, CHESHIRE, SK9 5PL.
FOWLER, Mr. Maurice Anthony, FCA *1961;* 3 Albany Reach, Queens Road, THAMES DITTON, KT7 0QH. (Life Member)
FOWLER, Mr. Norman Alfred, FCA *1951;* 5 Astra Court, Hythe Marina VillageHythe, SOUTHAMPTON, SO45 6DZ. (Life Member)
FOWLER, Mr. Paul Anthony, BSc ACA *1992;* 9 St Peters Close, Upper Welland, MALVERN, WR14 4JS.
FOWLER, Mr. Paul David, BCom ACA *1992;* 10 Bailiffs Close, AXBRIDGE, BS26 2AZ.
FOWLER, Mr. Paul Reginald Nepean, MA FCA *1980;* 26 Church Road, RICHMOND, SURREY, TW9 1UA.
•**FOWLER, Mr. Peter Edward Hamilton, FCA** *1971;* Fowler & Hare, Pennant House, Glyndwr, LLANGEFNI, LL77 7EF.
FOWLER, Mr. Philip Michael, BSc ACA *1999;* J D W Griffin House, 40 Lever Street, MANCHESTER, M60 6ES.

•**FOWLER, Mr. Raymond Charles, FCA** *1974;* (Tax Fac), Fowler & Trembling, 2 Forge Close, Chipperfield, KINGS LANGLEY, WD4 9DL.

FOWLER, Mr. Reginald Frederick, FCA *1962;* 27 Ward Avenue, GRAYS, RM17 5RE.

•**FOWLER, Mrs. Sara Anne, BA FCA** *1984;* Ernst & Young LLP, 1 Colmore Square, BIRMINGHAM, B4 6HQ. See also Ernst & Young Europe LLP

FOWLER, Miss. Sarah Louise, BSc ACA DChA *2006;* with Sheen Stickland LLP, 7 East Pallant, CHICHESTER, WEST SUSSEX, PO19 1TR.

FOWLER, Mr. Stevan Lloyd, ACA *1984;* 22b Lightridge Road, HUDDERSFIELD, HD2 2HE.

•**FOWLER, Mrs. Theresa Demo, BA FCA** *1988;* Conley Ward, 1168/1170 Melton Road, Syston, LEICESTER, LE7 2HB.

FOWLER, Mr. Tim Stephen, BSc ACA *1998;* with Synergy Health PLC, Ground Floor Stella, Windmill Hill Business Park, Whitehill Way, SWINDON, SN5 6NX.

•**FOWLER-COLWELL, Mrs. Anne, BSc ACA** *1991;* (Tax Fac), Lightlink Ltd, 15 Kingston Street, DERBY, DE1 3EZ.

•**FOWLER-TUTT, Mr. Geoffrey, FCA** *1970;* Geoffrey Fowler-Tutt, 22 St. Heliers Avenue, HOVE, EAST SUSSEX, BN3 5RE.

FOWLES, Mr. Alexander Paul, BSc ACA *1992;* Flat 10, 51 Tanner Street, LONDON, SE1 3PL.

FOWLES, Miss. Caroline Ann, BSc ACA *1999;* Akle Haywoods Lane, Chalford Hill, STROUD, GLOUCESTERSHIRE, GL6 8LH.

FOWLES, Miss. Christine Margaret, FCA *1980;* (Tax Fac), 33 West Drive, Cheam, SUTTON, SM2 7NB.

FOWLES, Mr. Simon Peter, BEng ACA *2004;* with Moore Stephens LLP, 150 Aldersgate Street, LONDON, EC1A 4AB.

FOWLIE, Mr. John, CA *2010; (CA Scotland* Robertson Craig, 3 Clairmont Gardens, GLASGOW, G3 7LW. See also Robertson Craig & co

FOWLIS, Mrs. Wendy Carol, BSc ACA *1991;* Volkswagen Group UK Ltd, Yeomans Drive, Blakelands, MILTON KEYNES, MK14 5AN.

FOX, Ms. Adele, BSc ACA *1990;* 16 James Dawson Drive, Meriden, COVENTRY, CV5 9QJ.

FOX, Mrs. Alison Elizabeth, BSc FCA *1987;* Old Barnsgate Cottage, Herons Ghyll, UCKFIELD, TN22 4DB.

FOX, Miss. Amy Hester Martha, BA(Hons) ACA *2003;* Financial Dynamics Ltd, 26 Southampton Buildings, LONDON, WC2A 1PB.

FOX, Mr. Andrew Howard Paton, FCA *1964;* 10 Beaumanor Gardens, Woodhouse, LOUGHBOROUGH, LEICESTERSHIRE, LE12 8UR.

FOX, Mr. Andrew Joseph, ACA *1986;* Hallmark Industries Ltd, 17 Deer Park Road, Wimbledon, LONDON, SW19 3XJ.

•**FOX, Mr. Andrew Michael, FCA** *1986;* (Tax Fac), Fox & Co (Anglia) Limited, The Priory, Church Street, DEREHAM, NORFOLK, NR19 1DW.

•**FOX, Mr. Andrew Peter Charles, BA ACA** *1988;* George Hay & Company, 83 Cambridge Street, Pimlico, LONDON, SW1V 4PS.

FOX, Mr. Andrew Robert Milner, BA FCA MBA *1984;* Malthouse Cottage, Malthouse Lane, Froggatt, Calver, HOPE VALLEY, S32 3ZA.

FOX, Mr. Andrew Staley, FCA *1970;* Andrew Fox & Co, 4 Dukes Road, Lindfield, HAYWARDS HEATH, WEST SUSSEX, RH16 2JH.

FOX, Mr. Anthony Kenneth, ACA *1979;* 1079 West Hathersage, DAINFERN, GAUTENG, 2055, SOUTH AFRICA.

FOX, Mr. Anthony Maxwell, BA ACA *1984;* Maraiken, Heversham, MILNTHORPE, CUMBRIA, LA7 7ER.

•**FOX, Mr. Ashley Noel, FCA** *1972;* Aspens Ltd, Suite G4, Waterside Centre, North Street, LEWES, BN7 2PE.

FOX, Mr. Barry James, ACA *1980;* 51 High Street Brampton, HUNTINGDON, CAMBRIDGESHIRE, PE28 4TQ.

FOX, Mr. Brian, CA *2010; (CA Scotland* Robertson Craig, 3 Clairmont Gardens, GLASGOW, G3 7LW. See also Robertson Craig & co

•**FOX, Mr. Brian Geoffrey, FCA** *1975;* Sundt & Co Ltd, Court Lodge, Luddesdown Road, Luddesdown, GRAVESEND, KENT DA13 0XE. See also Fox & Company

FOX, Mr. Brian Harry, BSc ACA *1986;* Hillboro, Grange Lane, Alvechurch, BIRMINGHAM, B48 7DJ.

•**FOX, Mrs. Caroline Susan, BA FCA** *1989;* Caroline Fox, Limeburners, Old Horsham Road, Beare Green, DORKING, RH5 4PW.

FOX, Mrs. Catherine Lisa, BSc ACA *1991;* 176 Newton Drive, BLACKPOOL, FY3 8JD.

FOX, Ms. Christine Elizabeth, BA FCA *1985;* 1 The Poplars, Guiseley, LEEDS, LS20 9PF.

FOX, Mr. Christopher Jonathan, BSc FCA *1973;* 173, Worplesdon Road, GUILDFORD, GU2 9XD. (Life Member)

FOX, Mr. Colin David, FCA *1971;* 21 Coledale Dr, STANMORE, HA7 2QE.

FOX, Mr. David Andrew, BA ACA *1993;* 2 Dartmouth Road, Chorlton, MANCHESTER, M21 8XJ.

FOX, Mr. David Anthony, BEng ACA *1995;* 7 Oakhill Road, SEVENOAKS, TN13 1NQ.

FOX, Mr. David Christopher, BSc ACA *1990;* 38 Barley Close, Mistley, MANNINGTREE, CO11 1GA.

•**FOX, Mr. David Hamilton, MA FCA** *1971;* Allnuts, The Street, Brightwell-cum-Sotwell, WALLINGFORD, OXFORDSHIRE, OX10 0RR.

FOX, Mr. David John, BSc ACA *1998;* 1 Pibrac Avenue, WARRAWEE, NSW 2074, AUSTRALIA.

FOX, Miss. Dawn Victoria, ACA *2011;* 11 Pendennis Avenue, Lostock, BOLTON, BL6 4RS.

FOX, Mr. Duncan Peter, BSc FCA *1995;* Style Group, La Rue Fondon, St. Peter, JERSEY, JE3 7BF.

•**FOX, Mr. Edward Michael, FCA** *1973;* (Tax Fac), Hardings, 6 Marsh Parade, NEWCASTLE, ST5 1DU.

FOX, Mrs. Elaine Anne, LLB ACA *1999;* 16 Hamson Drive Bollington, MACCLESFIELD, CHESHIRE, SK10 5SS.

FOX, Miss. Elizabeth, BSc ACA *2006;* 8 Thurlow Close, LONDON, E4 9XE.

FOX, Miss. Eloise Jayne Mortimore, BSc ACA *2002;* Flat 69 Vanilla & Sesame Court, Curlew Street, LONDON, SE1 2NN.

FOX, Mr. Gavin, BSc ACA *1993;* Ansbacher & Co Ltd Two, London Bridge, LONDON, SE1 9RA.

FOX, Mr. Geoffrey Raymond, BA FCA *1956;* Strode House, Lacock, CHIPPENHAM, WILTSHIRE, SN15 2PQ. (Life Member)

FOX, Mr. George Frederick, BSc ACA *1981;* 8 Brookdale Avenue, ILFRACOMBE, DEVON, EX34 8DB.

FOX, Miss. Hannah Lucy Mary, BA(Hons) ACA *2001;* with PKF (UK) LLP, Pannell House, 6 Queen Street, LEEDS, LS1 2TW.

FOX, Mrs. Helen Elizabeth, BSc ACA *2003;* 6 Alderson Road, HARROGATE, NORTH YORKSHIRE, HG2 8AS.

FOX, Mrs. Helen Elizabeth, BSc ACA *2004;* John Fairhurst & Co Douglas Bank House, Wigan Lane, WIGAN, LANCASHIRE, WN1 2TB.

FOX, Mr. Howard, MA FCA *1963;* 3 Shakespeare Gardens, LONDON, N2 9LJ.

•**FOX, Mr. Howard, FCA** *1974;* Fox Associate LLP, Britannic House, 17 Highfield Road, LONDON, NW11 9LS. See also Fox Associates

FOX, Mr. James Richard, MA BA ACA *2002;* 50 Osborne Road, BRIGHTON, BN1 6LQ.

FOX, Miss. Janine Anne, FCA DChA *1985;* with Mazars LLP, The Lexicon, Mount Street, MANCHESTER, M2 5NT.

FOX, Miss. Jennifer Hilda, ACA *1986;* 110 Springvale Road, Kings Worthy, WINCHESTER, HAMPSHIRE, SO23 7NB.

FOX, Mr. Jeremy John, BSc(Econ) FCA *1982;* PO Box 8000, Old Queen Street, LONDON, SE11 5EN.

FOX, Mrs. Joanna Susan, BSc(Hons) ACA *2003;* 20 St. Brannocks Road, Cheadle Hulme, CHEADLE, CHESHIRE, SK8 7LA.

FOX, Miss. Joanne, BA ACA *2004;* 10 Elmgrove Road, Gorleston, GREAT YARMOUTH, NORFOLK, NR31 7PP.

FOX, Miss. Joanne Patricia, BA FCA *1990;* 29 Croft Road, GODALMING, GU7 1DB.

•**FOX, Mr. John Harry, BSc FCA CTA** *1980;* John H Fox & Co, 14 North Park Grove, Roundhay, LEEDS, LS8 1JJ.

FOX, Mr. John Keith Trevor, BA FCA *1963;* 17 Ireland Close, Browns Wood, MILTON KEYNES, MK7 8EQ. (Life Member)

FOX, Mr. John Staley, FCA *1959;* 35d Arterberry Road, LONDON, SW20 8AG. (Life Member)

•**FOX, Mr. John William Alfred, BA FCA** *1984;* (Tax Fac), John W A Fox, 270 Singlewell Road, GRAVESEND, KENT, DA11 7RE.

FOX, Mr. Jonathan Michael, BA(Hons) ACA *1993;* Finance, British Gypsum Ltd Central Accounts Department, East Leake, LOUGHBOROUGH, LE12 6JU.

FOX, Mr. Jonathan Walter, FCA *1975;* 300 Old Army Road, SCARSDALE, NY 10583, UNITED STATES.

FOX, Mrs. Julia, BSc ACA *1999;* 9 Conway Close, RYTON, NE40 3NZ.

FOX, Miss. Karen Theresa, BA ACA *1993;* Flat 16, Gemini Court, 852 Brighton Road, PURLEY, SURREY, CR8 2FD.

FOX, Mr. Keith Dennis, FCA *1977;* 6 Mill Street, Longtown, CARLISLE, CA6 5TF.

FOX, Ms. Krista Margaret, ACIB ACA *1999;* (Tax Fac), The Old Cottage, Silver Street, North Clifton, NEWARK, NG23 7AU.

FOX, Miss. Leah Elizabeth Rose, ACA *2008;* 16 Constance Street, SHIPLEY, WEST YORKSHIRE, BD18 4LX.

•**FOX, Mrs. Lesley Jane, BSc ACA** *1994;* Mazars LLP, 8 New Fields, 2 Stinsford Road, Nuffield, POOLE, DORSET BH17 0NF.

FOX, Mr. Mark Jeremy, BSc ACA *1991;* Campbell Arnotts, 24 George Street, NORTH STRATHFIELD, NSW 2137, AUSTRALIA.

FOX, Mr. Martin Anthony Joseph, MA FCA *1965;* Les Hauts De Bizkarbidea, 8 Rue Biscarbidea, 64500 ST JEAN DE LUZ, FRANCE.

FOX, Mr. Matthew, BSocSc ACA *2002;* Ace Group The Ace Building, 100 Leadenhall Street, LONDON, EC3A 3BP.

FOX, Mr. Michael Adrian, BA FCA *1963;* 131 Ducks Hill Road, NORTHWOOD, HA6 2SQ.

•**FOX, Mr. Michael Bingham, FCA** *1978;* Torevell Dent Audit LLP, 4th Floor, 153/155 Sunbridge Road, BRADFORD, BD1 2NU. See also Torevell Dent Ltd

FOX, Mr. Michael Niall, BA ACA *1983;* Goodwill, 3 Grange Fell Road, GRANGE-OVER-SANDS, CUMBRIA, LA11 6BJ.

•**FOX, Mr. Michael Patrick Joseph, MBA MSc BCom FCA** *1987;* Flat 16 Hartland, Royal College Street, LONDON, NW1 0RY.

FOX, Mr. Michael Peter Hugh, FCA *1965;* 12a Wedderburn Road, LONDON, NW3 5QG.

FOX, Mr. Michael Stuart Elgar, MSc ACA *1999;* 59 Keats Road, Greenmount, BURY, LANCASHIRE, BL8 4EP.

•**FOX, Mr. Neil, ACA** *1992;* Greywalls Accountants Limited, Greywalls, Silver Street, Minety, MALMESBURY, WILTSHIRE SN16 9QU.

FOX, Miss. Nereide Elizabeth, MA ACA *2006;* 48 Bridewell Place, LONDON, E1W 2PB.

FOX, Mr. Nicholas Howard, BA(Hons) ACA *2001;* 57 Eldon Road, CHELTENHAM, GL52 6TX.

FOX, Mr. Nigel Adrian Dawson, BA ACA *1988;* The School House, Winchester Road, Ampfield, ROMSEY, HAMPSHIRE, SO51 9BQ.

•①**FOX, Mr. Nigel Ian, BSc FCA** *1990;* with RSM Tenon Limited, Highfield Court, Tollgate, Chandler's Ford, EASTLEIGH, HAMPSHIRE SO53 3TY.

FOX, Mr. Nigel Trevor Antony, BCom ACA *1982;* Broadfield, Broadfield Road, Peaslake, GUILDFORD, SURREY, GU5 9RD.

FOX, Miss. Oriana, MA(Oxon) ACA *2007;* 75 Dibdin Road, SUTTON, SM1 2PQ.

FOX, Mr. Paul Joseph, MA FCA *1966;* The Battery, The Bayle, FOLKESTONE, CT20 1SQ. (Life Member)

FOX, Mr. Paul Julian, BCom FCA *1979;* Yeoman Oast, Manor Farm, Laddingford, MAIDSTONE, ME18 6BX.

FOX, Mr. Paul Simon, BSocSc ACA CTA *2003;* (Tax Fac), 42 Tretawn Gardens, Mill House, LONDON, NW7 4NR.

FOX, Mr. Peter Frederick George, BSc ACA *1983;* 14 Yew Tree Drive, BROMSGROVE, B60 1AL.

FOX, Mr. Peter James Ernest, BA FCA *1966;* The Garden House, Tarrington, HEREFORD, HR1 4HZ.

FOX, Mr. Peter John, BA ACA *1984;* Morris Vermaport Ltd, 14 Vickery Way, Chilwell, NOTTINGHAM, NG9 6RY.

FOX, Mr. Peter Jonathan Geoffrey, BA ACA *2005;* Canterbury of New Zealand limited, First Floor, Houldsworth Mill, Houldsworth Street, Reddish, STOCKPORT CHESHIRE SK5 6DS.

FOX, Mr. Philip Anthony, BA ACA *1986;* F Cross & Sons Ltd, Normanby Road, SCUNTHORPE, SOUTH HUMBERSIDE, DN15 8QZ.

FOX, Mr. Richard Murray, MA FCA *1959;* The Old Rectory, Itchenor, CHICHESTER, PO20 7AB. (Life Member)

FOX, Mr. Robert Parkin, BA FCA *1972;* 6 Lee Lane East, Horsforth, LEEDS, LS18 5RE. (Life Member)

FOX, Mr. Robin Bretten, MSc FCA *1968;* 6 Church Street, Little Shelford, CAMBRIDGE, CB22 5HG.

FOX, Mr. Roger Granville, FCA *1967;* 42 King George V Avenue, Berry Hill, MANSFIELD, NOTTINGHAMSHIRE, NG18 4FR. (Life Member)

•**FOX, Mrs. Sarah Fiona Scott, FCA** *1979;* Sarah Fox, Edgeworth House, Edgeworth, STROUD, GL6 7JQ.

FOX, Ms. Sarah Vivian, FCA *1979;* 10 Kelly Court, MAROOCHYDORE, QLD 4558, AUSTRALIA.

FOX, Mr. Sean David, MA MBA FCA MInstP *1990;* 54 Norbury Court Road, LONDON, SW16 4HT.

•**FOX, Mr. Sean Joseph, ACA** *2007;* (Tax Fac), Fox Reynard Ltd, PO Box 963, AYLESBURY, HP22 9JL.

FOX, Mrs. Sharon Elizabeth, ACA *1987;* 41 Church Lane, Fulbourn, CAMBRIDGE, CB21 5EP.

FOX, Mr. Shaun Joseph, BSc ACA *2001;* 10 Beckman Road, STOURBRIDGE, DY9 0TZ.

FOX, Mr. Simon Stephen, BA ACA *2005;* 42 Cowper Road, BOURNEMOUTH, BH9 2UJ.

FOX, Mr. Stephen, BSc ACA *1992;* 9 Blenheim Road, LONDON, W4 1UB.

FOX, Mr. Steve, BA(Hons) ACA *2002;* 84 Woodstock Way, MITCHAM, SURREY, CR4 1BB.

FOX, Mr. Thomas Peter Kenyon, FCA *1956;* Hill House, School Lane, Blockley, MORETON-IN-MARSH, GL56 9HX. (Life Member)

•**FOX, Mr. Timothy George, FCA** *1968;* Tim Fox, Pawlies Farm, Loxwood, BILLINGSHURST, WEST SUSSEX, RH14 0QN.

FOX, Mr. Tom, ACA *2008;* K P M G Arlington Business Park, Theale, READING, RG7 4SD.

FOX, Mr. Trevor Laurence, BA FCA *1977;* 37 Dalkeith Grove, STANMORE, MIDDLESEX, HA7 4SQ.

FOX, Mrs. Victoria Ann, BA FCA CTA *1980;* (Tax Fac), 69 St. Thomas Avenue, HAYLING ISLAND, HAMPSHIRE, PO11 0EU.

FOX, Miss. Victoria Elizabeth, MA ACA *1996;* 137 Kennington Park Road, Kennington, LONDON, SE11 4JJ.

FOX, Mr. Wayne Richard, BA FCA *1986;* The Willows, Whitson, NEWPORT, NP18 2PN.

FOX, Mr. William Ernest, FCA *1955;* 19 Woodbourne Drive, Claygate, ESHER, KT10 0DR. (Life Member)

FOX, Mr. William James Staley, BSc ACA *1993;* (Tax Fac), Sparrow Hill Cottage, Weare, AXBRIDGE, BS26 2LE.

FOX-ANDREWS, Mr. Peter Gauntlett, FCA *1970;* 46 Rodney Road, West Bridgford, NOTTINGHAM, NG2 6JH.

FOX-MILLER, Mrs. Alison Kay, BA ACA *1983;* 65 N Taylor Street, BERGENFIELD, NJ 07621, UNITED STATES.

FOXALL, Mrs. Carolyn Jane, ACA *1985;* 2 Kensington Gardens, KINGSTON UPON THAMES, KT1 2JU.

FOXCROFT, Mr. Craig, ACA *2009;* 35 Belah Road, CARLISLE, CA3 9RE.

FOXCROFT, Mr. Jonathan Charles Laurence, BA ACA *1989;* 11 Crawshaw Drive, Reedsholme, ROSSENDALE, BB4 8PR.

FOXCROFT, Miss. Sarah, BA ACA *1991;* 5 The Green Horton-cum-Studley, OXFORD, OX33 1AE.

FOXLEY, Ms. Linda Jayne, BSc ACA *1991;* Choice Quote Insurance G D H House, Green Lane Old Swan, LIVERPOOL, L13 7EB.

FOXLEY, Mr. Russell Barry James, FCA FCCA *1973;* Rossley, Snow Hill, CRAWLEY, RH10 3HA.

FOXLOW, Miss. Leisa Marie, BA ACA *1996;* Flat 6, 16 Fernbank Road, BRISTOL, BS6 6PZ.

FOXON, Mr. John Charles, FCA *1968;* Smith Cooper, 2 Lace Market Square, NOTTINGHAM, NG1 1PB.

•**FOXON, Mr. Paul Nicholas, BA ACA** *1986;* Kemp Taylor LLP, The Oval, 14 West Walk, LEICESTER, LE1 7NA.

FOXTON, Mr. Daniel, BSc ACA *2006;* Lovell Park, H B O S Plc, PO Box 93, LEEDS, LS1 1NS.

FOXTON, Mr. James Andrew, ACA *2004;* Surgery 1 Alderson House, Hull Royal Infirmary, Anlaby Road, HULL, HU3 2JZ.

FOXTON, Miss. Joanne Mary, BA ACA *1990;* 12 Warren House Walk, Walmley, SUTTON COLDFIELD, WEST MIDLANDS, B76 1TS.

•**FOXWELL, Mr. Alan Geoffrey, FCA** *1972;* F.W. Berringer & Co, Lygon House, 50 London Road, BROMLEY, BR1 3RA.

FOXWELL, Mr. Alan Vaughan, BSc ACA *1985;* 1 Ragley Close, Knowle, SOLIHULL, B93 9NU.

FOXWELL, Mr. John Francis, BSc ACA *2003;* 2 Ainslee Place, SEAFORTH, NSW 2092, AUSTRALIA.

FOXWELL, Mr. Michael John, FCA *1959;* 12 The Mount House, Sudbury Hill, HARROW, HA1 3NH. (Life Member)

FOXWELL, Mr. Nigel Anthony, BSc FCA MBA *1975;* Sleepy Hollow 101 Rogers Lane Stoke Poges, SLOUGH, SL2 4LP.

•**FOXWELL, Miss. Rebecca Anne, ACA** *2009;* G Foxwell & Co, Foxwell House, Libanus Road, EBBW VALE, GWENT, NP23 6YY.

FOXWELL, Miss. Victoria Helen, ACA *2010;* Flat 5, 2 All Saints Road, BRISTOL, BS8 2JH.

•**FOY, Miss. Jane Barbara, BSc FCA** *1991;* (Tax Fac), Jane Foy & Co, 24 Mosswood Road, WILMSLOW, CHESHIRE, SK9 2DR.

FOY, Miss. Tara, ACA *2008;* 100 Blendworth Crescent, HAVANT, HAMPSHIRE, PO9 2BQ.

FOYE, Mr. Anthony Martin, BA ACA *1987;* Lynwood, White Lane, Oakley, TADLEY, HAMPSHIRE, RG26 5TN.

FOYE, Ms. Sharon, BSc ACA *1996;* 8B Hamilton Park, Highbury, LONDON, N5 1SJ.

•FOYLE, Miss. Angela Louise, MA ACA 1988; BDO LLP, 55 Baker Street, LONDON, W1U 7EU. See also BDO Stoy Hayward LLP
FOYLE, Mrs. Bindi Jayantilal Jivraj, BSc ACA 1998; 5 Ingle Close, PINNER, MIDDLESEX, HA5 3BJ.
FOYLE, Mr. James John Lewis, BSc(Hons) ACA 2000; 5 Ingle Close, PINNER, HA5 3BJ.
FOYLE, Mr. John Lewis, MA FCA 1973; Brookmead, Moat Farm Chase, Chipping Hill, WITHAM, CM8 2JU.
FOZARD, Mr. Ian, FCA 1976; Market Town Taverns Plc, 6 Green Dragon Yard, KNARESBOROUGH, HG5 8AU.
FOZZARD, Mrs. Caroline Rose, BSc ACA 1998; Hazelhurst, Central Avenue, Hullbridge, HOCKLEY, SS5 6AU.
FRADIN, Mrs. Gemma Harriet, MA ACA 1999; 102 Ribblesdale Road, LONDON, SW16 6SR.
FRADIN, Mr. Timothy James, BA(Hons) ACA 2000; 102 Ribblesdale Road, LONDON, SW16 6SR.
FRADLEY, Mrs. Alison, BSc ACA 1988; 24 Woodcrest Place, CHERRYBROOK, NSW 2126, AUSTRALIA.
FRADLEY, Mrs. Catherine Susan, ACA 1991; 37 St. Catherine Drive, Hartford, NORTHWICH, CHESHIRE, CW8 2FE.
FRAIN, Mrs. Pamela Anne, BA FCA 1982; (Tax Fac), 10 Moor Lane, Ponteland, NEWCASTLE UPON TYNE, NE20 9AD.
•FRAIS, Mr. Adam Richard, BSocSc ACA ATII 1995; (Tax Fac), BDO LLP, 55 Baker Street, LONDON, W1U 7EU. See also BDO Stoy Hayward LLP
FRAKES, Mr. Mark, ACA 2005; Apt 201 Maison Dor Blanc, 15-4 Shirokane 4-Chome, TOKYO, 108-0072 JAPAN.
FRALL, Mr. Anthony James, FCA 1967; 19 Long Grove, Seer Green, BEACONSFIELD, BUCKINGHAMSHIRE, HP9 2YN. (Life Member)
•FRAME, Mr. David Richard McLean, MA FCA 1976; Littlejohn LLP, 1 Westferry Circus, Canary Wharf, LONDON, E14 4HD.
FRAME, Mr. Malcolm Henry, FCA 1962; 38 Lowndes Park, DRIFFIELD, YO25 5BG. (Life Member)
FRAME, Mr. Michael, MEng ACA 2004; 99a Milton Grove, LONDON, N16 8QX.
FRAME, Mr. Michael Andrew, BCom FCA 1991; 2 Carrington Lane, SALE, CHESHIRE, M33 5ND.
FRAME, Mr. Philip, BA(Hons) ACA 2010; 58 St. Andrews Close, Fearnhead, WARRINGTON, WA2 0EJ.
•FRAMJEE, Mr. Peshotan Rustom, FCA DChA 1984; Crowe Clark Whitehill LLP, St Bride's House, 10 Salisbury Square, LONDON, EC4Y 8EH. See also Horwath Clark Whitehill LLP and Crowe Clark Whitehill
FRAMJI, Mr. Kaikhosrou Kavasji, MA FCA 1974; 1350 Beverley Road, Suite No 115-147, MCLEAN, VA 22101, UNITED STATES.
•FRAMPTON, Mr. David John, FCA 1967; Higgisons, Higgison House, 381/383 City Road, LONDON, EC1V 1NW.
•ⒹFRAMPTON, Mr. Giles Richard, MA FCA 1982; Richard J. Smith & Co, 53 Fore Street, IVYBRIDGE, PL21 9AE.
FRAMPTON, Mrs. Jacqueline Anne, ACA 1990; 15 Cheriton Way, Rushmere, NORTHAMPTON, NN1 5SB.
FRAMPTON, Mr. Michael Gordon Samuel, FCA 1955; H.L. Brown & Son Ltd., 2 Barkers Pool, SHEFFIELD, S1 1LZ.
FRAMPTON, Mr. Nicholas John, FCA 1968; U59 Calle Altavista, Hacienda Guadalupe, Sabinillas, 29692 MALAGA, SPAIN. (Life Member)
FRAMPTON, Mrs. Sally Louise, BSc ACA 1982; 2688 Timberglen Drive, WEXFORD, PA 15090, UNITED STATES.
FRANCE, Mrs. Alison, BSc ACA 1997; 12 Warbleton Road, Chineham, BASINGSTOKE, RG24 8RF.
FRANCE, Mr. Brian William, MBE FCA 1963; 5 Grantley Gardens, GUILDFORD, GU2 8BS. (Life Member)
FRANCE, Mr. Charles Malcolm, FCA 1971; 20 Drake Road, SKEGNESS, LINCOLNSHIRE, PE25 3BH.
FRANCE, Miss. Donna Louise, ACA 2010; 10 Glendower Court, Greenfields, SHREWSBURY, SHROPSHIRE, SY1 2RG.
FRANCE, Mr. Edward William Glossop, FCA 1960; The Willows, 40 Aylesbury Road, THAME, OXFORDSHIRE, OX9 3AW. (Life Member)
FRANCE, Miss. Gemma Louise, MA ACA 2004; Deloitte Athene Place, 66 Shoe Lane, LONDON, EC4A 3BQ.
FRANCE, Mr. Gregor, MSci ACA 2005; Level 19, 20 Martin Place, SYDNEY, NSW 2000, AUSTRALIA.
FRANCE, Mr. John Richard, ACA 1980; Parkside Care Homes, Fieldside, 9 Canadian Avenue, LONDON, SE6 3AU.
FRANCE, Mrs. Kathreen Sarah, BA FCA 1990; 30 Brookside, East Leake, LOUGHBOROUGH, LEICESTERSHIRE, LE12 6PB.
FRANCE, Mr. Peter David, BSc ACA 1993; Flash Green Cottage, Bett Lane, Wheelton, CHORLEY, PR6 8JH.
FRANCE, Mr. Richard Henry Stewart, FCA 1975; Sandycroft Newcastle Road, Woore, CREWE, CW3 9SN.
FRANCE, Mr. Robin Geoffrey, BA(Econ) FCA 1966; North Farm House, Barker Hades Road, Letwell, WORKSOP, S81 8DF. (Life Member)
•FRANCE, Mr. Stephen John Richard, FCA 1976; Lodge Farm, Little Henny, SUDBURY, SUFFOLK, CO10 7EA.
FRANCES, Miss. Anne J, BSocSc FCA 1992; Cliff Cottage, 9 Golden Avenue Close, East Preston, LITTLEHAMPTON, WEST SUSSEX, BN16 1QS.
FRANCES, Mr. Paul Riccardo, FCA 1959; 119 Chilton Way, HUNGERFORD, RG17 0JF. (Life Member)
•FRANCHINI, Mr. Roberto Nicola Achille, BSc FCA 1980; Reconta Ernst & Young, Via Della Chiusa 2, 20123 MILAN, ITALY. See also Ernst & Young Europe LLP
•FRANCIES, Mr. Glyn John, FCA 1981; Baker Tilly Tax & Advisory Services LLP, 1st Floor, 46 Clarendon Road, WATFORD, WD17 1JJ. See also Baker Tilly UK Audit LLP
FRANCIES, Mr. Jonathan, FCA 1972; 58 Portobello Road, LONDON, W11 3DL.
FRANCIS, Mr. Alasdair Bruce Vaughan, BSc(Hons) ACA CF 2002; Ivy Bank, Beckford, TEWKESBURY, GLOUCESTERSHIRE, GL20 7AD.
FRANCIS, Mr. Alexander Iorwerth, BSc FCA 1980; Hastings College of Arts & Technology, Tower Block Room 310, Archery Road, ST. LEONARDS-ON-SEA, EAST SUSSEX, TN38 0HX.
FRANCIS, Mrs. Alison Louise, BSc ACA 1992; 41 Bobbin Lane, Westwood, BRADFORD-ON-AVON, BA15 2DL.
•FRANCIS, Miss. Amanda Susannah, BSc ACA 1988; Buzzacott LLP, 130 Wood Street, LONDON, EC2V 6DL.
FRANCIS, Mr. Andrew Mark, BSc ACA 2000; O M V Trading Services Ltd Ryder Court, 14 Ryder Street, LONDON, SW1Y 6QB.
FRANCIS, Mr. Anthony, BA(Hons) ACA 2002; 14 Moralee Close, NEWCASTLE UPON TYNE, NE7 7GE.
FRANCIS, Mr. Anthony Rowland, FCA 1971; Star Cottage, Alfriston, POLEGATE, EAST SUSSEX, BN26 5TJ.
•FRANCIS, Mrs. Anzo Gloreen, BA FCA 1988; (Tax Fac), James Francis & Company, 32 Wontner Road, Upper Tooting, LONDON, SW17 7QT.
FRANCIS, Ms. Caitlin, MPH BA(Hons) ACA 2000; with PricewaterhouseCoopers, Darling Park Tower 2, 201 Sussex Street, GPO Box 2650, SYDNEY, NSW 1171 AUSTRALIA.
FRANCIS, Miss. Christina Ruth, BSc ACA 1997; OTV SA, 1 Place Moutgolfier, 94417 ST MAURICE, FRANCE.
FRANCIS, Mr. Christopher Joseph Sutherland-Campbell, FCA 1981; (Tax Fac), Meech International, Network Point, WITNEY, OXFORDSHIRE, OX29 0YN.
FRANCIS, Mr. Daniel Fernley, FCA 1972; 11 Marlborough Road, Chandler's Ford, EASTLEIGH, HAMPSHIRE, SO53 5DJ.
FRANCIS, Mr. David Alfred, FCA 1964; 125 Widney Lane, SOLIHULL, WEST MIDLANDS, B91 3LH. (Life Member)
FRANCIS, Mr. David Christopher, MA ACA 1991; 21 Campbell Road, EDINBURGH, EH12 6DT.
FRANCIS, Mr. David John, ACA 1994; 16 The Greenway, Pattingham, WOLVERHAMPTON, WV6 7DD.
FRANCIS, Mr. David Mark, MA ACA 2000; Diageo Plc, Lakeside Drive, Park Royal, LONDON, NW10 7HQ.
FRANCIS, Mr. David Paul, FCA 1966; 26 The Spinney, Marlow Hill, HIGH WYCOMBE, HP11 1QE.
FRANCIS, Mr. Douglas Edward, FCA 1967; Tattletrees, 17 Holtwood Avenue, AYLESFORD, ME20 7QH.
FRANCIS, Mr. Douglas John, FCA 1966; 23 Cliveden Gages, Taplow, MAIDENHEAD, SL6 0GA. (Life Member)
FRANCIS, Miss. Eleanor Jeannette, ACA 2008; 92 Maysoule Road, LONDON, SW11 2BW.
FRANCIS, Miss. Elizabeth, BSc ACA 2010; National Audit Office, 157-197 Buckingham Palace Road, LONDON, SW1W 9SP.
FRANCIS, Miss. Emma Amanda, BA ACA 2003; 110 Tilt Road, COBHAM, KT11 3HQ.
FRANCIS, Mr. Emyr-Wyn, BSc(Econ) ACA 2003; 8 Clos Onnen, Coed Hirwaun, Margam, PORT TALBOT, WEST GLAMORGAN, SA13 2TZ.
FRANCIS, Mr. Frank, BA ACA 1988; 37 Lady Penrhyn Dr, Beacon Hill, SYDNEY, NSW 2100, AUSTRALIA.
•FRANCIS, Mr. Gary Eisenhower, BSc ACA 1979; Francis & Co., 100 Clarence Road, LONDON, E5 8HB.
FRANCIS, Mr. Gary Pearson, BEng ACA 1991; Hayes Control Systems Ltd, The Boathouse, Station Road, HENLEY-ON-THAMES, OXFORDSHIRE, RG9 1AZ.
FRANCIS, Mr. Gavin Andrew, BSc ACA 1991; Harvest Barn, Heydon Lane, Elmdon, SAFFRON WALDEN, CB11 4NH.
FRANCIS, Mr. Glenn Ian, BSc ACA 1996; 72 Flatford Place, KIDLINGTON, OX5 1TJ.
•FRANCIS, Mr. Graham John, BA FCA 1986; Moore Stephens (South) LLP, City Gates, 2-4 Southgate, CHICHESTER, WEST SUSSEX, PO19 8DJ. See also Moore Secretaries Limited
FRANCIS, Mr. Hugh Anthony, BSc ACA 1993; Avonlea, Hope Gardens, Whiteparish, SALISBURY, SP5 2SS.
FRANCIS, Mr. Hugh Roy, FCA 1982; 40 Topstreet Way, HARPENDEN, HERTFORDSHIRE, AL5 5TT.
•FRANCIS, Mr. Ian David, BSc ACA 1988; Thomas Edward Dixon & Company, 376 London Road, Hadleigh, BENFLEET, SS7 2DA.
FRANCIS, Mr. Ian Raymond, ACA 1992; Silveriey, 3 Harebell Hill, COBHAM, SURREY, KT11 2RS.
FRANCIS, Mr. James Alexander, BA ACA 2004; 6 Dunblane Drive, Orton Southgate, PETERBOROUGH, PE2 6SH.
FRANCIS, Mr. James Simon, ACA 2004; Circle Anglia, 6 Central Avenue, St. Andrews Business Park, NORWICH, NR7 0HR.
FRANCIS, Mr. Jeffrey Kenneth, ACA 2008; Flat 32 Mandeville House, Worsopp Drive, LONDON, SW4 9QT.
•FRANCIS, Mr. Jeremy Inglesby, MA FCA 1975; (Tax Fac), Jeremy Francis, 8 De Freville Avenue, CAMBRIDGE, CB4 1HR.
FRANCIS, Mr. John David, ACA 1979; 5 Brookview Close, Willow FarmThornhill, CARDIFF, CF14 9AZ.
•FRANCIS, Mr. John Stuart, BSc FCA DChA 1977; Lindeyer Francis Ferguson, North House, 198 High Street, TONBRIDGE, TN9 1BE. See also Lindeyer Francis Ferguson Limited
FRANCIS, Mr. John William, BSc FCA 1980; Kings Elms, 10 Kingswood Court, MAIDENHEAD, SL6 1DD.
FRANCIS, Mr. Jonathan Raymond, BA ACA 1992; 4 Leith Road, EPSOM, SURREY, KT17 1DA.
FRANCIS, Mr. Joseph Thomas, BSc ACA 2000; Apartment 404, Coptain House, Eastfields Avenue, LONDON, SW18 1JX.
•FRANCIS, Mr. Julian Paul, BA FCA 1982; (Tax Fac), Francis James & Partners LLP, 1386 London Road, LEIGH-ON-SEA, ESSEX, SS9 2UJ.
FRANCIS, Mrs. Karen, BSc FCA 1991; 8 Sapphire Drive, Denby, RIPLEY, DE5 8NL.
FRANCIS, Miss. Keren Mary, MA ACA 1981; 56 Pursewardens Close, LONDON, W13 9PW.
FRANCIS, Mrs. Kiran Monica, BSc(Hons) ACA 2002; 13 Burgh Heath Road, EPSOM, SURREY, KT17 4LP.
FRANCIS, Mrs. Lucy, LLB ACA 2004; 23 Sherwood Drive, HAYWARDS HEATH, WEST SUSSEX, RH16 1EW.
FRANCIS, Mr. Mark Cameron, BSc FCA FCSI 1981; 373 Park Avenue South, Floor 6, NEW YORK, NY 10016, UNITED STATES.
FRANCIS, Mr. Mark Edward, BSc ACA 1998; 2 Spring Close, Great Horwood, MILTON KEYNES, MK17 0QU.
FRANCIS, Mr. Mark Jonathan, BA ACA 1995; Westwood House Radcliffe Road, Golcar, HUDDERSFIELD, HD7 4EX.
FRANCIS, Mr. Mark Kevin, BSc ACA 2005; Higgins Group Plc, One Langston Road, LOUGHTON, ESSEX, IG10 3SD.
FRANCIS, Mr. Matthew, ACA 2011; Flat 31 John Bowles Court, 69 Schoolhouse Lane, LONDON, E1W 3AH.
FRANCIS, Mr. Matthew Richard, ACA 2007; 150 Aldersgate Street, LONDON, EC1A 4AB.
FRANCIS, Mr. Michael James, ACA CA(SA) 2008; The Stables, Garnons, HEREFORD, HR4 7JU.
FRANCIS, Mr. Michael Richard, BSc FCA 1992; 5 Bois Avenue, AMERSHAM, BUCKINGHAMSHIRE, HP6 5NS.
FRANCIS, Mrs. Michelle Lisa, ACA 2009; 69 Elmhurst Drive, HORNCHURCH, ESSEX, RM11 1NZ.
FRANCIS, Mr. Neil, BEng ACA PgDip 2009; 10 Woodham Close, Rubery, Rednal, BIRMINGHAM, B45 9YP.
FRANCIS, Mr. Nicholas Hugh, MA ACA 1986; (Tax Fac), with PricewaterhouseCoopers LLP, The Atrium, St. Georges Street, NORWICH, NR3 1AG.
FRANCIS, Mr. Nicholas William, ACA 2008; 7b-7c Meath Street, LONDON, SW11 4JA.
FRANCIS, Mr. Paul Andrew, BA ACA 1988; Flat 18 Royal Standard House, Standard Hill, NOTTINGHAM, NG1 6FX.
FRANCIS, Mr. Paul Antony, FCA 1975; Serendipity, Knocknacally, YOUGHAL, COUNTY CORK, IRELAND.
FRANCIS, Mr. Paul David, FCA 1971; 2 Mark Way, GODALMING, GU7 2BE.
FRANCIS, Mr. Paul Edward, BSc ACA 2008; Flat 2, Tom Browns, 47 High East Street, DORCHESTER, DORSET, DT1 1HU.
FRANCIS, Mr. Peter Charles, BA ACA 1995; 51 West Hill, DUNSTABLE, BEDFORDSHIRE, LU6 3PN.
FRANCIS, Mr. Peter John, BSc ACA 2005; 29 Barnmead, HAYWARDS HEATH, RH16 1UY.
FRANCIS, Mr. Peter John Chandler, BSc ACA 1994; Crossways Cottage, Woodspeen, NEWBURY, BERKSHIRE, RG20 8BT.
•FRANCIS, Mr. Peter Lawrence, MA ACA 1986; with KPMG LLP, 100 Temple Street, BRISTOL, BS1 6AG.
FRANCIS, Mr. Peter Michael, ACA 2009; 7 Meadow Drive, Tyla Garw, PONTYCLUN, MID GLAMORGAN, CF72 9FR.
FRANCIS, Mr. Peter Raymond, FCA 1966; Cranford, Camden Road, LINGFIELD, RH7 6AF. (Life Member)
FRANCIS, Mr. Philip George, BSc FCA 1963; 1 Montolieu Gardens, Putney, LONDON, SW15 6PB. (Life Member)
FRANCIS, Mrs. Rhian Sian, BA(Hons) ACA 2001; Gosling Cottage, Chapel Rd, Broughton, COWBRIDGE, CF71 7QR.
FRANCIS, Mr. Richard, BA ACA 1998; 76 Fairview Way, STAFFORD, ST17 0AX.
FRANCIS, Mr. Richard, ACA 2011; 8th Floor, Deloitte & Touche, 2 New Street Square, LONDON, EC4A 3BZ.
FRANCIS, Mr. Richard, LLB FCA 1987; Ravenswood House, Coventry Road, SOUTHAM, WARWICKSHIRE, CV47 1BG.
•FRANCIS, Mr. Richard Charles Alexander, BA FCA 1987; LB Group Ltd, 82 East Hill, COLCHESTER, CO1 2QW.
FRANCIS, Mr. Richard David, ACA 1979; Hillsborough, Maidstone Road, Horsmonden, TONBRIDGE, TN12 8NE.
FRANCIS, Mr. Richard David, BSc ACA 1994; 19 Ridgeway Crescent, TONBRIDGE, TN10 4NP.
FRANCIS, Mr. Richard John, MBA MSc FCA 1975; 107 Bouverie Ave South, SALISBURY, SP2 8EA.
FRANCIS, Mr. Richard Stewart Clement, BA FCA 1996; 18 The Robins, BRACKNELL, BERKSHIRE, RG12 8BU.
FRANCIS, Mr. Robert Frederick, FCA 1966; East Downend Farm, Egloskerry, LAUNCESTON, PL15 8SH. (Life Member)
FRANCIS, Mr. Robert Guy, FCA 1969; 19 Frobisher Court, Cleveland RoadWest Ealing, LONDON, W13 8BD. (Life Member)
•FRANCIS, Mr. Robin James, FCA 1974; R J Francis & Co Limited, Franklin House, 3 Commercial Road, HEREFORD, HR1 2AZ.
FRANCIS, Mr. Roger, BSc FCA 1978; 70 Norton Lees Lane, SHEFFIELD, S8 9BE.
FRANCIS, Mrs. Rosalind Elaine, BA FCA 1993; Thistledown, Rectory Lane, Fowlmere, ROYSTON, HERTFORDSHIRE, SG8 7TJ.
FRANCIS, Mrs. Sarah Jane, BSc(Hons) ACA 2002; Ivy Bank, Beckford, TEWKESBURY, GLOUCESTERSHIRE, GL20 7AD.
FRANCIS, Ms. Sharon Lesley, BA ACA 1996; 16 Primrose Close, SPENNYMOOR, COUNTY DURHAM, DL16 7YE.
FRANCIS, Mr. Simon Russell, BSc ACA 1992; Flay 0361 Tower 10, HONG KONG SAR Park View, 88 Tai Tam Reservoir Road, STANLEY, HONG KONG SAR.
•FRANCIS, Mr. Stephen Walter, FCA 1982; Garners Limited, Bermuda House, 45 High Street, Hampton Wick, KINGSTON UPON THAMES, SURREY KT1 4EH.
FRANCIS, Mr. Stuart Paul Chandler, BA ACA 1993; Brooklands, Coed Morgan, ABERGAVENNY, GWENT, NP7 9UU.
FRANCIS, Mrs. Susan Kathryn, BA ACA 1983; Hedgerows, Lower Way, Harpford, SIDMOUTH, EX10 0NQ.
•FRANCIS, Mr. Warren Brynley, ACA 1993; Francis & Co Limited, Festival House, Jessop Avenue, CHELTENHAM, GLOUCESTERSHIRE, GL50 3SH. See also W Francis & Co Ltd
FRANCIS, Mrs. Yvonne Lesley, BSc FCA 1982; 1 Berrycroft, BRACKNELL, RG12 2HR.
•FRANCO, Mr. Faustino, BSc FCA 1990; Perlin Franco Ltd, Trojan House, 34 Arcadia Avenue, LONDON, N3 2JU.
•FRANCO CARR, Ms. Maria del Mar, BSc ACA 1984; Afimar Accountants SLU, c/- Alfonso XIII s/n, Edf Terminal 13-8, 29640 FUENGIROLA, Malaga, SPAIN.
FRANCOIS, Mr. Andre Paul Maurice, BA ACA 2008; Flat 4, 63 Allfarthing Lane, LONDON, SW18 2AR.
FRANCOIS, Mr. Kevin Kuuku, BA ACA 1985; 11 Cavendish Road, OXFORD, OX2 7TN.

FRANCOM, Mr. Steven, BA ACA MCT *1998;* Innospec Ltd Innospec Manufacturing Park, Oil Sites Road, ELLESMERE PORT, CH65 4EY.

FRANCOMBE, Mr. Andrew Kevin, BSc FCA *1989;* 21 Foster Road, Chiswick, LONDON, W4 4NY.

•**FRANEK, Mr. Paul, BSc FCA** *1992;* Deloitte LLP, 2 New Street Square, LONDON, EC4A 3BZ. See also Deloitte & Touche LLP

FRANGESKIDOU, Miss. Marina, BA ACA *2007;* Amyklon 16 Halandri, 15231 ATHENS, GREECE.

FRANGI, Mrs. Dawn Rebecca, BSc ACA *2003;* C C L A Investment Management Ltd, 80 Cheapside, LONDON, EC2V 6DZ.

•**FRANGLETON, Mr. David John, FCA** *1980;* Mitchell Charlesworth, Centurion House, 129 Deansgate, MANCHESTER, M3 3WR.

FRANGLETON, Mrs. Jennifer Ann, BA ACA *2000;* Harwood, Ramsley, South Zeal, OKEHAMPTON, EX20 2LB.

FRANGOS, Mr. Alexander, BSc ACA *2005;* Flat 22 Finch Lodge, Admiral Walk, LONDON, W9 3TB.

•**FRANGOS, Mrs. Anastasia, BA ACA** *2004;* haysmacintyre, Fairfax House, 15 Fulwood Place, LONDON, WC1V 6AY.

FRANGOS, Mr. Antonis, BSc ACA *2011;* 25 Parthenonos Strovolos, 2021 NICOSIA, CYPRUS.

FRANGOS, Mr. Antonis Photiou, MSc BEng ACA *2001;* 20 Torbay Road, Chorlton, MANCHESTER, M21 8XD.

FRANGOU, Mrs. Claire Ellen, BSc(Econ) ACA CF *1998;* 20, Torbay Road, MANCHESTER, M21 8XD.

•**FRANGOU, Mr. Iacovos Kyriacos, BA FCA** *1999;* (Tax Fac), IKF Business Services Ltd, 84 Crescent Road, BARNET, HERTFORDSHIRE, EN4 9RJ.

FRANGOUDES, Miss. Yiouli, BA ACA *2009;* 4 Mesolongiou Street, Ayia Triada, 3032 LIMASSOL, CYPRUS.

•**FRANGOUS, Mr. Zacharias, BA ACA** *2002;* 11 Elassonos Street, Ayia Fila, CY 3115 LIMASSOL, CYPRUS.

FRANK, Mr. Anthony Frederick, BA FCA *1975;* 10 St. Georges Road, LONDON, NW11 0LR.

FRANK, Mr. Christopher John, ACA *2008;* 90A, 90 Bermondsey Street, LONDON, SE1 3UB.

FRANK, Mr. Clement Mcbean, FCA *1961;* 10 Luxford Road, Lindfield, HAYWARDS HEATH, WEST SUSSEX, RH16 2LZ.

FRANK, Mr. Gordon, ACA *1994;* 31 Reedfield, Reedley, BURNLEY, BB10 2NJ.

FRANK, Mr. Howard, FCA *1973;* 2 Kingsmead Close, Cromwell Road, TEDDINGTON, TW11 9EP.

FRANK, Mr. John Michael Bruce, FCA *1967;* Kings Hill Cottage, Kings Hill, Netheravon, SALISBURY, SP4 9PL.

FRANK, Miss. Mona Maria, BA ACA *2003;* 23 Wellington Road, ST. ALBANS, HERTFORDSHIRE, AL1 5NJ.

FRANK, Mr. Nicholas Robert, BA ACA *1986;* Flat 2, 110 Vineyard Hill Road, Wimbledon, LONDON, SW19 7JJ.

FRANK, Mr. Paul, FCA *1969;* Flat 68 Keverstone Court, 97 Manor Road, BOURNEMOUTH, BH1 3BY.

FRANK, Mr. Selwyn Boris, FCA *1951;* 9/635 Blue Mist, Pacific Highway, KILLARA, NSW 2071, AUSTRALIA. (Life Member)

FRANKE, Mr. John Adrian, BSc FCA *1986;* Compass Group Plc Compass House, Guildford Street, CHERTSEY, KT16 9BQ.

•**FRANKE, Mr. Malcolm David, BSc FCA** *1981;* Malcolm Franke & Co Ltd, Campania, Links Road, South Milton, KINGSBRIDGE, DEVON TQ7 3JR. See also Malcolm Franke

FRANKEL, Mr. John Frederic Horatio, MA FCA *1985;* 4 Chelsea Drive, LIVINGSTON, NJ 07039, UNITED STATES.

FRANKEN, Mr. Stefan, ACA *2000;* Route de Meribel 1123, Residence du Mont Chanay, 01170 ECHENEVEX, FRANCE.

FRANKHAM, Miss. Alice Michelle, ACA *2010;* 40 St. Welcumes Way, Harrietsham, MAIDSTONE, ME17 1BD.

FRANKHAM, Miss. Vivienne, BSc ACA *1999;* 16, Ealing Village, LONDON, W5 2LY.

FRANKIEWICZ, Miss. Marta, MSc BSc ACA *2009;* Room 4, 207 Clapham Road, LONDON, SW9 0QH.

FRANKISH, Mrs. Katy Josephine, BA(Hons) ACA *2003;* 1 Springs Terrance, Dark Lane, Wheelton, CHORLEY, LANCASHIRE, PR6 8AF.

•**FRANKISH, Mr. Michael Neil, BCom ACA** *2000;* with KPMG LLP, St. James's Square, MANCHESTER, M2 6DS.

FRANKL, Mr. Michael, MA ACA *1982;* 55 Illingworth, WINDSOR, SL4 4UP.

•**FRANKL, Mr. Robert Ian, FCA** *1977;* Freedman Frankl & Taylor, Reedham House, 31 King Street West, MANCHESTER, M3 2PJ.

FRANKLAND, Mr. Christopher John, FCA *1965;* 29 Montalt Road, WOODFORD GREEN, IG8 9RS. (Life Member)

FRANKLAND, Mr. John Richard, BSc FCA *1992;* 6 Cairndale Drive, LEYLAND, PR25 3BX.

FRANKLAND, Mrs. Linda Patricia, BSc ACA *1992;* 6 Cairndale Drive, LEYLAND, PR25 3BX.

FRANKLAND, Miss. Michele, LLB ACA *2003;* 101 Eland Road, LONDON, SW11 5LB.

FRANKLAND, Mrs. Patricia Mary, MA ACA *1981;* Fernbrook, The Street, BETCHWORTH, RH3 7DJ.

FRANKLAND, Mr. Stuart Anthony, BSc ACA *2005;* Flat 12 Hollywood Lofts, 154 Commercial Street, LONDON, E1 6NU.

FRANKLIN, Mr. Alan, FCA *1975;* 7 Towri Close, ST.IVES 2075, NSW 2075, AUSTRALIA.

FRANKLIN, Mr. Andrew James, FCA *1974;* Anglican Consultative Council, St. Andrews House, 16 Tavistock Crescent, LONDON, W11 1AP.

•**FRANKLIN, Mr. Andrew James, MA FCA** *1985;* Franklin Chartered Accountants, 320 Garratt Lane, Earlsfield, LONDON, SW18 4EJ. See also Franklin

FRANKLIN, Mr. Andrew Timothy, BEng ACA *1992;* 4 Clevedon Road, Tilehurst, READING, RG31 6RL.

FRANKLIN, Mr. Angus John, MA ACA *1992;* 17 St. Catherines Place, EDINBURGH, EH9 1NU.

FRANKLIN, Miss. Clare Amanda, LLB ACA CTA *2002;* with Deloitte LLP, 2 New Street Square, LONDON, EC4A 3BZ.

FRANKLIN, Mr. Clive Robert, ACA *1980;* 12 Walnut Tree Close, Radyr, CARDIFF, CF15 8SX.

•**FRANKLIN, Mr. David James, BA FCA** *1983;* Franklins, Bury Road, Hitcham, IPSWICH, IP7 7PP.

FRANKLIN, Mr. David James, BA ACA *2005;* Prometic Biosciences Ltd, 211 Cambridge Science Park, Milton Road, CAMBRIDGE, CB4 0WA.

FRANKLIN, Mr. David John, BA ACA *2007;* 104 Overstone Road, HARPENDEN, HERTFORDSHIRE, AL5 5PL.

FRANKLIN, Mrs. Davina Mary Elizabeth Ruth, FCA CTA *1973;* 5 Princes Plain, BROMLEY, BR2 8LH. (Life Member)

•**FRANKLIN, Mr. Dean Anthony, BSc FCA** *1990;* Franklin and Co Limited, Manor Cottage, Delmonden Lane, Hawkhurst, CRANBROOK, KENT TN18 4XJ.

FRANKLIN, Mr. Dennis Austin, FCA *1956;* Crosss Lanes Fruit Farm, Mapledurham, READING, RG4 7UW. (Life Member)

FRANKLIN, Mrs. Eliza, ACA *2004;* 25a Dallas Road, LONDON, NW4 3JB.

FRANKLIN, Miss. Elizabeth, ACA *2011;* C L S Holdings Plc, 86 Bondway, LONDON, SW8 1SF.

FRANKLIN, Mr. Geoffrey, FCA *1950;* Flat 2, Merlswood 33 Meads Road, EASTBOURNE, BN20 7ES. (Life Member)

•**FRANKLIN, Mr. Grant David, ACA** *1990;* Hillier Hopkins LLP, Charter Court, Midland Road, HEMEL HEMPSTEAD, HERTFORDSHIRE, HP2 5GE. See also Grant Franklin Limited

FRANKLIN, Mr. Howard William, FCA *1954;* Stonehey, 74 Warren Rd, Blundellsands, LIVERPOOL, L23 6UG. (Life Member)

FRANKLIN, Mr. Irvin Howerd, FCA *1958;* 32 Albany Manor Road, BOURNEMOUTH, BH1 3EN. (Life Member)

FRANKLIN, Mrs. Janine, BA(Hons) ACA *2003;* Little Innage Barns, Mathern, CHEPSTOW, GWENT, NP16 6JA.

FRANKLIN, Mr. Jason Mark, BCom ACA *1992;* 9a Briarwood, Finchampstead, WOKINGHAM, RG40 4XA.

FRANKLIN, Ms. Jean-Mare, ACA CA(SA) *2009;* 104 Overstone Road, HARPENDEN, HERTFORDSHIRE, AL5 5PL.

FRANKLIN, Mr. John Anthony, FCA *1972;* The Latch, Holly Bush Lane, Priors Marston, SOUTHAM, CV47 7RW.

FRANKLIN, Mr. John Herbert, FCA *1957;* Hall Cottage, South Green, SOUTHWOLD, IP18 6EU. (Life Member)

•**FRANKLIN, Mr. Kevin Nigel, BA FCA** *1988;* Am Brunnen, Tunworth Road, Mapledurwell, BASINGSTOKE, HAMPSHIRE, RG25 2LG.

FRANKLIN, Miss. Kimberley Jemma, ACA *2011;* 3/46A Moruben Road, MOSMAN, NSW 2088, AUSTRALIA.

FRANKLIN, Mrs. Lesley Susan, MA(Oxon) MSc FCA *1978;* The Old Manse, High Street, Weston, TOWCESTER, NN12 8PU.

FRANKLIN, Miss. Louise, ACA *2011;* 33 Ballingdon Road, Battersea, LONDON, SW11 6AJ.

FRANKLIN, Mr. Mark, BA ACA *1980;* The Haylings, 11 Lower Westfields, BROMYARD, HR7 4EN.

•**FRANKLIN, Mr. Mark Stephen, ACA** *1982;* M. Franklins, 84 Albion Court, Attleborough Road, NUNEATON, WARWICKSHIRE, CV11 4JJ.

FRANKLIN, Mrs. Maureen Anne, BSc ACA *1982;* Orchard House, 9 Camden Close, CHISLEHURST, BR7 5PH.

FRANKLIN, Mr. Michael, FCA *1966;* 17 Paddock Close, St.Ives, RINGWOOD, BH24 2LD.

FRANKLIN, Mr. Michael Graham, BSc FCA *1985;* 52 The Drive, SEVENOAKS, TN13 3AF.

FRANKLIN, Mr. Neil Graham, FCA *1976;* 92 Shefford Road, Meppershall, SHEFFORD, SG17 5LL.

FRANKLIN, Mr. Neville Malcolm, FCA *1973;* 1740 Summerlands Crescent, ORLEANS K1E 2Y2, ON, CANADA.

FRANKLIN, Mrs. Nikola, ACA *1987;* Oak Cottage, Little Heath Lane, Potten End, BERKHAMSTED, HERTFORDSHIRE, HP4 2RY.

FRANKLIN, Mr. Noah Felix Kalman, MA ACA *1986;* 19 Brookfield Park, LONDON, NW5 1ES.

FRANKLIN, Mrs. Penelope Jane, BSc ACA *1992;* (Tax Fac), 4 Clevedon Road, Tilehurst, READING, RG31 6RL.

FRANKLIN, Mr. Peter, FCA *1973;* 68 Rotary Way, THATCHAM, RG19 4SA.

FRANKLIN, Mr. Peter, LLB FCA *1978;* 3 Mill Close, Shipdham, THETFORD, NORFOLK, IP25 7HX.

FRANKLIN, Mr. Peter Mark, LLB ACA *2002;* Rose Cottage The Street, Rotherwick, HOOK, HAMPSHIRE, RG27 9BL.

FRANKLIN, Mr. Richard Alan, FCA *1968;* 3001 Corte Portofino, NEWPORT BEACH, CA 92660, UNITED STATES.

•**FRANKLIN, Mr. Richard Colin, FCA** *1978;* Franklins Accountants Limited, Astor House, 2 Alexandra Road, Mutley Plain, PLYMOUTH, PL4 7JR. See also Franklins Accountants LLP and Franklin & Marsland Ltd

FRANKLIN, Ms. Stephanie Anne, BA ACA ACIS *1994;* 128 St. Margarets Drive, NORWICH, NR7 8DB.

•**FRANKLIN, Mr. Stephen, FCA** *1975;* (Tax Fac), Stephen Franklin FCA CTA, 45 Membris Way, Woodford Halse, DAVENTRY, NN11 3QZ.

FRANKLIN, Mr. Stephen James, PhD BSc FCA *1976;* 58 Park View, Sharnford, HINCKLEY, LE10 3PT.

•**FRANKLIN, Mr. Stephen Roy, FCA** *1978;* Franklin Chartered Accountants, 320 Garratt Lane, Earlsfield, LONDON, SW18 4EJ. See also Franklin

•**FRANKLIN, Mr. William, BSc FCA** *1985;* Pett Franklin & Co LLP, Victoria House, 116 Colmore Row, BIRMINGHAM, B3 3BD.

FRANKLING, Mr. Barry Wingard, FCA *1972;* Toll Cottage, 25 Chesterton, BRIDGNORTH, SHROPSHIRE, WV15 5NX.

FRANKOW, Miss. Monika Anna, MSc BSc ACA *2005;* 213 Forest Road, LOUGHBOROUGH, LEICESTERSHIRE, LE11 3HS.

FRANKPITT, Mr. Alex, BSc ACA *2002;* with Baker Tilly Tax & Advisory Services LLP, Hartwell House, 55-61 Victoria Street, BRISTOL, BS1 6AD.

FRANKS, Mr. Adam Stephen, FCA *1996;* Blue Lizzard, 34 Jamestown Road, LONDON, NW1 7BY.

FRANKS, Mrs. Agnes Caroline, BSc ACA *1981;* The Old Top Shop, 74 High Street, Standon, WARE, SG11 1LB.

FRANKS, Mr. Alexander, FCA *1962;* 5 Oakwood Court, 12 Gordon Road, North Chingford, LONDON, E4 6BX.

FRANKS, Mr. Barry Anthony, FCA *1970;* Apt de Correos, No 29, Xativa, 46800 VALENCIA, SPAIN. (Life Member)

FRANKS, Mr. Daniel John, BSc ACA *2001;* 38 Windmill View, Patcham, BRIGHTON, BN1 8TU.

FRANKS, Mr. David John, FCA *1953;* 13 St Bridget Avenue, Crownhill, PLYMOUTH, PL6 5BB. (Life Member)

FRANKS, Mr. David Louis, FCA *1969;* 5 The Coppice, Rhinefield Road, BROCKENHURST, SO42 7QZ.

FRANKS, Mr. David Simmonds, BCom FCA *1970;* Blevins Franks, Gasan Centre, Mriehel By Pass, Mriehel, ATTARD, MALTA.

FRANKS, Mrs. Deborah Lynn, BCom ACA *1984;* 7 Royal Road, SINGAPORE 118308, SINGAPORE.

FRANKS, Mrs. Gina Valerie, BA ACA *1994;* Barden Furnace Farm, Barden Road, Speldhurst, TUNBRIDGE WELLS, TN3 0LH.

FRANKS, Mr. Harold Leon, BA FCA *1955;* Cedars, 25 The Spinney, CHEADLE, SK8 1JA. (Life Member)

FRANKS, Mr. Ian Charles, BSc ACA *1990;* 89 Swanland Road, HESSLE, HU13 0NS.

FRANKS, Mr. Jeremy Michael, MA ACA ATII *1985;* 21 Teignmouth Road, LONDON, NW2 4HR.

FRANKS, Miss. Jessica, LLB ACA *2007;* (Tax Fac), 29a Glenfield Road, LONDON, SW12 0HQ.

•**FRANKS, Mr. Jonathan Leslie, FCA** *1986;* Hillier Hopkins LLP, Dukes Court, 32 Duke Street, St James's, LONDON, SW1Y 6DF.

FRANKS, Mr. Jonathan Malcolm, BA ACA *1986;* The Water Gardens, Patrick Brompton, BEDALE, DL8 1JN.

FRANKS, Mr. Laurence Lee, BA ACA *1995;* 7 Price Drive, EDISON, NJ 08817, UNITED STATES.

•**FRANKS, Mr. Marc Ian, BSc ACA** *1999;* (Tax Fac), Silver Levene LLP, 37 Warren Street, LONDON, W1T 6AD.

FRANKS, Mr. Martin David, MA ACA *1999;* 36 Dorchester Road, WEYBRIDGE, SURREY, KT13 8PE.

FRANKS, Mr. Paul Jonathan, BSc ACA *1997;* Holly House, Daisy Lane, Alrewas, BURTON-ON-TRENT, STAFFORDSHIRE, DE13 7EW.

FRANKS, Mrs. Sally Amanda, ACA *1992;* E12 SEA VIEW VILLA, 102 CHUK YEUNG ROAD, SAI KUNG, NT, HONG KONG SAR.

FRANKS, Mrs. Sara Jacqueline, BSc ACA *1997;* 15 Neville Drive, LONDON, N2 0QS.

•**FRANKS, Mr. Thomas Kenric, BSc FCA** *1991;* KPMG LLP, 15 Canada Square, LONDON, E14 5GL. See also KPMG Europe LLP

•**FRANKTON, Mr. Terence John, BSc FCA** *1984;* (Tax Fac), Luckmans Duckett Parker Limited, 44-45 Queens Road, COVENTRY, CV1 3EH.

•①**FRANSES, Mr. Ian Soloman Robert, FCA** *1972;* Ian Franses Associates, 24 Conduit Place, LONDON, W2 1EP.

FRANTZI, Miss. Elpiniki, ACA *2008;* 6 Elia Venezi, Platy, Aglantzia, 2112 NICOSIA, CYPRUS.

FRANTZIS, Mr. Christos, BSc ACA *2004;* 6 Elia Venezi Street, Aglanjia, 2112 NICOSIA, CYPRUS.

FRANZMANN, Ms. Julia Joanna Szwajkowska, BSc ACA *2004;* 297 Laleham Road, STAINES, MIDDLESEX, TW18 2NY.

FRAPWELL, Miss. Sara Louise, BSc ACA *1992;* 52 Kyrle Road, LONDON, SW11 6BA.

FRASER, Miss. Aimee, LLB(Hons) ACA *2009;* Flat 9 Fettes House, Wellington Road, LONDON, NW8 9SU.

FRASER, Mr. Alastair Douglas, BSc ACA *1991;* Durrants Farm, Hadleigh, IPSWICH, IP7 6LA.

FRASER, Mr. Alastair Thomas, FCA *1959;* 2 Hawthorn Way Darras Hall, Ponteland, NEWCASTLE UPON TYNE, NE20 9RU. (Life Member)

FRASER, Mr. Alistair Ian, FCA *1974;* 16 Hallam Grange Croft, Fulwood, SHEFFIELD, S10 4BP.

•**FRASER, Mr. Alistair John, BA FCA** *1991;* Mazars LLP, Tower Bridge House, St. Katharines Way, LONDON, E1W 1DD.

FRASER, Mr. Andrew Hector, BSc ACA *1998;* 26 Rochester Road, SOUTHSEA, HAMPSHIRE, PO4 9BA.

FRASER, Mr. Andrew John, BCom ACA *1992;* Flat 1403, 20 Palace Street, LONDON, SW1E 5BB.

FRASER, Mr. Andrew John, ACA *2008;* 60 Borough Hill, CROYDON, CR0 4LN.

FRASER, Mr. Angus James, BEng ACA *1992;* Weatherford Oil Tools, Floor 28 Reef Tower, DUBAI, PO 4627, UNITED ARAB EMIRATES.

FRASER, Mr. Benjamin Paul, BA ACA *1999;* KazMunaiGas Exploration Production, 17 Kabanbay Batyr, Left bank Ishim River, ASTANA 010000, KAZAKHSTAN.

FRASER, Mr. Bruce Simon St John, FCA *1973;* Les Châtaigniers, Caplong, 33220 GIRONDE, FRANCE.

FRASER, Mrs. Carole, BSc ACA *2006;* Cowgill Holloway LLP, Regency House, 45-51 Chorley New Road, BOLTON, BL1 4QR.

FRASER, Mr. Christopher Stuart, BA ACA *1989;* 100 Dockham Shore Road, GILFORD, NH 03249, UNITED STATES.

FRASER, Mr. David, BSc ACA *1985;* 17 Sanderling Drive, LEIGH, WN7 1HU.

FRASER, Mr. David Baird, FCA *1963;* 50 South Eaton Place, LONDON, SW1W 9JJ.

FRASER, Mrs. Deborah Louise, BCom ACA *1998;* 12 Howards Meadow, Kings Cliffe, PETERBOROUGH, PE8 6YJ.

FRASER, Mr. Donald Charlton, BSc ACA *1979;* 1 The Cloisters, NEWCASTLE UPON TYNE, NE7 7LS.

FRASER, Mr. Donald John, BSc FCA *1975;* Kirrin House, 8 Blyton Close, BEACONSFIELD, BUCKINGHAMSHIRE, HP9 2LX.

FRASER, Mrs. Emma, BSc ACA *2007;* with Gallaher Ltd, Members Hill, Brooklands Road, WEYBRIDGE, SURREY, KT13 0QU.

FRASER, Mr. Eric Malcolm, FCA *1952;* 11 The Gabriels, Andover Road, NEWBURY, BERKSHIRE, RG14 6PZ. (Life Member)

•**FRASER, Mrs. Fiona Frances, ACA** *1982;* Fiona, 33 Talisker Place, PERTH, PH1 3GW.
FRASER, Mr. Geoffrey, BSc FCA CTA *1989;* (Tax Fac), with Thompson Jenner LLP, 1 Colleton Crescent, EXETER, EX2 4DG.
FRASER, Mrs. Gillian Deborah, BSc ACA *1992;* 24 Millway, LONDON, NW7 3RB.
FRASER, Mr. Gordon Charles, MEng ACA AMIChemE AMCT *1999;* Stansted House Malthouse Road, Stansted, SEVENOAKS, TN15 7PH.
FRASER, Mr. Greig Craig, BAcc ACA *2001;* Flat 504 Hallmark Court, 6 Ursula Gould Way, LONDON, E14 7FX.
FRASER, Mr. Iain, FCA *1970;* 44 East Park Road, Kintore, INVERURIE, AB51 0FE.
FRASER, Mr. Ian Anthony, FCA *1971;* Monte Carlo House Appt 35, 31 Boulevard des Moulins, MC 98000 MONTE CARLO, MONACO. (Life Member)
FRASER, Mr. Ian Dawson, FCA *1975;* 44 Millfield Drive, COWBRIDGE, CF71 7BR.
•**FRASER, Mr. Ian James, BA FCA ATII** *1978;* (Tax Fac), RSM Tenon Audit Limited, 2 Wellington Place, LEEDS, LS1 4AP.
•**FRASER, Mr. Ian John, FCA** *1980;* Bishop Fleming, Chy Nyverow, Newham Road, TRURO, TR1 2DP.
•**FRASER, Mr. Ian Stuart, BSc FCA** *1977;* (Tax Fac), Rupp & Fraser, 7 St. Paul's Road, NEWTON ABBOT, TQ12 2HP.
•**FRASER, Mr. James Alexander Gordon, BA ACA** *2003;* 13 Sion Road, TWICKENHAM, TW1 3DR.
FRASER, Mr. James Andrew, BEng ACA *2007;* 51 Tomlinson Road, Elsecar, BARNSLEY, S74 8DH.
FRASER, Mr. James Colin Hugh, ACA *2008;* 86 Liberty Street, LONDON, SW9 0EF.
FRASER, Mr. James Richard Alastair, BSc ACA *2002;* Independent Slate Supplies Ltd, 6 Gilston Road, SALTASH, CORNWALL, PL12 6TW.
FRASER, Miss. Jane Helen Anne, BA ACA *1998;* 49 Gowrie Road, LONDON, SW11 5NN.
FRASER, Miss. Jean Marguerite, BSc(Hons) ACA *2000;* 75 Coopers Gate, BANBURY, OX16 2WD.
FRASER, Mrs. Jill Margaret, ACA *2008;* 8 Highbarns, HEMEL HEMPSTEAD, HERTFORDSHIRE, HP3 8AG.
FRASER, Mr. Joe Alexander, BA ACA *2005;* 191 Rue Saint Charles, 75015 PARIS, FRANCE.
FRASER, Mr. John, BSc ACA *1995;* Floor 6A, Woolworths House, 93 Longmarket Street, CAPE TOWN, 8000, SOUTH AFRICA.
•**FRASER, Mr. Jonathan Ian, BSc FCA** *1992;* Nyman Libson Paul, Regina House, 124 Finchley Road, LONDON, NW3 5JS.
FRASER, Ms. Karen Jill, BSc ACA *1988;* Gamestec Leisure Ltd Low Lane, Horsforth, LEEDS, LS18 4ER.
FRASER, Miss. Kate, BSc ACA *2010;* 37 Mount View Road, SHEFFIELD, S8 8PH.
FRASER, Miss. Kathryn Elizabeth, LLB ACA *2000;* with KPMG LLP, 15 Canada Square, LONDON, E14 5GL.
FRASER, Miss. Kirsten Helen, BSc ACA *1989;* 17 Littlejohn Road, EDINBURGH, EH10 5GN.
FRASER, Mr. Lee, BCom ACA *2004;* Flat 2, 40 Altenburg Gardens, LONDON, SW11 1JL.
FRASER, Mr. Malcolm, BSc FCA *1979;* 12 Beamish View, East, STANLEY, DH9 0XB.
FRASER, Mr. Marten Charles Griffin, FCA *1970;* 22 Park Wharf, Haslam Street, NOTTINGHAM, NG7 1FA.
FRASER, Mr. Martyn Stuart, BSc FCA CF *2000;* with Smith & Williamson Ltd, Portwall Place, Portwall Lane, BRISTOL, BS1 6NA.
•**FRASER, Mrs. Mary Elizabeth, FCA** *1980;* Fraser & Associates, 1 Imperial Square, CHELTENHAM, GLOUCESTERSHIRE, GL50 1QB.
•**FRASER, Mr. Neil Geoffrey, BSc ACA** *1985;* Fraser Price Consulting Limited, Suite 1, Enness Building, East Street, Bingham, NOTTINGHAM NG13 8DS.
FRASER, Mr. Nicholas Graham, BSc FCA *1976;* 39 Bark Place, LONDON, W2 4AT.
FRASER, Mr. Nicholas Grant, BSc ACA *1998;* 24 SCENIC CRESCENT, COOMERA, QLD 4209, AUSTRALIA.
FRASER, Mrs. Olga, BSc(Econ) ACA *2004;* 26 Star Street, LONDON, W2 1QB.
FRASER, Mr. Paul Nicholas, BA FCA *1972;* 504 Route des Lentisques, 83400 HYERES, FRANCE.
FRASER, Mr. Peter Kenneth, FCA *1973;* Ferme de la Platane, rue de Lourmarin, Ansouis, 84240 VAUCLUSE, FRANCE.
FRASER, Mr. Richard Mark, BA ACA *1989;* 43 Rivington Close, Birkdale, SOUTHPORT, PR8 4DP.
FRASER, Mr. Roderick Charles, FCA ATII *1981;* Hampton Lodge, Hampton Court Road, EAST MOLESEY, KT8 9BP.
FRASER, Mr. Rupert James, MA ACA *1984;* 98 Clarendon Drive, LONDON, SW15 1AH.
•**FRASER, Mrs. Sharon Julia, BA ACA** *1990;* Deloitte LLP, PO Box 500, 2 Hardman Street, MANCHESTER, M60 2AT. See also Deloitte & Touche LLP
FRASER, Mr. Simon James, BA FCA *1990;* with Lloyds TSB Corporate Markets, 4th Floor, 25 Gresham Street, LONDON, EC2V 7HN.
FRASER, Mr. Stephen Brian, BA ACA *1992;* Sinclair Goldberg Price Ltd, 243 Brook Street, BIRKENHEAD, MERSEYSIDE, CH41 3SE.
FRASER, Mr. Stephen John, BA ACA *1989;* St Swithuns House, Bournemouth Churches Housing Association, 21 Christchurch Road, BOURNEMOUTH, BH1 3NS.
•**FRASER, Mr. Stephen Michael, BSc ACA** *1990;* PricewaterhouseCoopers LLP, Hays Galleria, 1 Hays Lane, LONDON, SE1 2RD. See also PricewaterhouseCoopers
•**FRASER, Mr. Steven George, FCA DChA** *1983;* Monahans, 38-42 Newport Street, SWINDON, SN1 3DR.
FRASER, Miss. Susan Elisabeth, BSc ACA *1990;* 194 Oxford Road, MARLOW, SL7 2PR.
FRASER, Mr. Timothy Martin, BA ACA *1987;* Monotype Imaging Unit 2, Perrywood Business Park Honeycrock Lane, REDHILL, RH1 5DZ.
FRASER, Mrs. Victoria Louise, BSc ACA *1998;* 3 Mayston Mews, LONDON, SE10 0LY.
FRASER-ALLEN, Mr. William Thomas, BA ACA *1997;* 45 Ouseley Road, LONDON, SW12 8ED.
FRASER-DALE, Mr. Andrew David, BSc FCA *1998;* Long Port Properties, PO Box 158, GUERNSEY, GY1 4EX.
FRASER-HARRIS, Mr. Adam Howard, BSc ACA *1995;* with Baker Tilly Corporate Finance LLP, The Clock House, 140 London Road, GUILDFORD, SURREY, GU1 1UW.
FRASER-HARRIS, Ms. Anna Carin, BSc ACA *1993;* 8 Andover Road, SOUTHSEA, HAMPSHIRE, PO4 9QG.
FRASER-HARRIS, Mr. Brian David, FCA *1964;* 55 Granada Road, SOUTHSEA, PO4 0RQ. (Life Member)
FRASER-SMITH, Mr. Richard Geoffrey, BSc ACA *1992;* Halcrow Group Limited Elms House, 43 Brook Green, LONDON, W6 7EF.
•**FRASI, Mr. Sonam Tsering, FCA** *1985;* Sonam Frasi & Co, The Bridge House, 256a Ladysmith Road, ENFIELD, MIDDLESEX, EN1 3AF.
FRATER, Ms. Fiona Elaine, BSc ACA *2002;* 10 Severn Road, Maidenbower, CRAWLEY, WEST SUSSEX, RH10 7ZF.
•**FRAY, Mr. Charles Robert, BA ACA** *1984;* Baker Tillly Tax & Advisory Services LLP, St Philips Point, Temple Row, BIRMINGHAM, B2 5AF. See also Baker Tilly Corporate Finance LLP
FRAY, Mrs. Frances Marie, ACA *1982;* 54 Princes Gardens, Codsall, WOLVERHAMPTON, WV8 2DH.
FRAY, Mr. Martyn George, FCA *1970;* The Witterings, Woolston, KINGSBRIDGE, DEVON, TQ7 3BH.
•**FRAY, Mr. Peter James, FCA** *1975;* P.J Fray, Keepers Cottage, Upton Bishop, ROSS-ON-WYE, HR9 7UE.
FRAYNE-JOHNSON, Mr. Paul, BA ACA *2003;* (Tax Fac), 12 Monmouth Grove, Kingsmead, MILTON KEYNES, MK4 4AY.
FRAZER, Mr. Ian William, FCA *1955;* 1 Westferry Circus, Canary Wharf, LONDON, E14 4HD.
FRAZER, Mrs. Katherine Rachel, BA ACA *2000;* Priory Woods School, Tothill Avenue, Netherfields, MIDDLESBROUGH, CLEVELAND, TS3 0RH.
FRAZER, Mrs. Pauline Harrison, FCA *1948;* Carpenter's Cottage, Riverside, West Kirby, WIRRAL, CH48 3JB. (Life Member)
FRAZER, Mrs. Trudi Hildegard, BSc(Hons) ACA *2000;* 16 Furzen Close, DUNSTABLE, BEDFORDSHIRE, LU6 3EN.
FREAKE, Mr. Benjamin Alistair, BSc ACA *2001;* Credit Suisse Financial Products, CS First, 1 Cabot Square, LONDON, E14 4QJ.
•**FREAKLEY, Mr. Simon Vincent, BCom FCA** *1988;* Zolfo Cooper LLP, 10 Fleet Place, LONDON, EC4M 7RB.
•**FREAN, Mr. John Raymond, FCA** *1969;* Spofforths LLP, A2 Yeoman Gate, Yeoman Way, WORTHING, WEST SUSSEX, BN13 3QZ.
FREAR, Mr. Alan Geoffrey, FCA *1976;* Pangor, Penwartha Coombe, PERRANPORTH, TR6 0AY.
•**FREARSON, Mr. John Stuart Simon, BSc FCA** *1976;* Frearson & Co, 187 Ringwood Road, EASTBOURNE, EAST SUSSEX, BN22 8UW.
FREARSON, Mr. Peter, MBA FCA *1970;* 93a Hartfield Road, FOREST ROW, EAST SUSSEX, RH18 5LY.
FREATHY, Mr. Angus Ralph, FCA *1970;* 11621 Twin Oaks Drive, BERLIN, MD 21811-2728, UNITED STATES.
FRECKLETON, Ms. Lucy Victoria, BSc ACA *1995;* 29 Edward Avenue, EASTLEIGH, SO50 6EH.
FRECKNALL HUGHES, Dr. Jane, PhD MA LLM ACA CTA *1990;* (Tax Fac), 12 Rose Hill Drive, Dodworth, BARNSLEY, S75 3LY.
FREDERICKS, Miss. May Sharon, BA ACA *1997;* flat 8, 32 Evelyn Gardens, LONDON, SW7 3BJ.
FREDERICKS, Mr. Peter George, BSc ACA *1990;* 6 Broadlands Close Calcot Park, READING, RG31 7RP.
FREDERIKSEN, Mr. Benjamin Paul, BA(Hons) ACA *2003;* Lion Nathan, Level 7, 68 York Street, SYDNEY, NSW 2000, AUSTRALIA.
•**FREDRICKS, Mr. Michael Edward, FCA** *1967;* 34 Aldwick Felds, BOGNOR REGIS, WEST SUSSEX, PO21 3ST.
FREDRIKSSON, Mr. Nicholas Martin Ware, BA ACA *1998;* Flat 19 Horse Shoe Court, 11 Brewhouse Yard, LONDON, EC1V 4JU.
FREE, Mr. Ian Edward Theodore, FCA *1957;* 19 Vale Leaze, Little Somerford, CHIPPENHAM, SN15 5JS. (Life Member)
FREE, Mr. Richard Victor, BA FCA *1973;* 1693 Howat Crescent, MISSISSAUGA L5J 4G6, ON, CANADA.
FREE, Mrs. Sarah Louise, BSc ACA *1988;* Halifax Fan Ltd Unit 11, Brookfoot Business Park Brookfoot, BRIGHOUSE, WEST YORKSHIRE, HD6 2SD.
FREEAR, Prof. John, MA FCA *1967;* 3 Ffrost Drive, DURHAM, NH 03824-3107, UNITED STATES. (Life Member)
FREEAR, Mr. Mark Andrew, BA ACA *2000;* 25a Truro Road, Sandringham, AUCKLAND 1025, NEW ZEALAND.
•**FREEAR, Mr. Stephen John, FCA** *1973;* 46/22 Normanby Road, Mount Eden, AUCKLAND 1024, NEW ZEALAND.
FREEBODY, Mr. John Benjamin, BSc ACA *2004;* Flat 27B, Marmion Road, LONDON, SW11 5PD.
FREEBODY, Mr. Richard John, FCA *1965;* Cherry Tree House, 29 Matlock Road, CATERHAM, CR3 5HP. (Life Member)
FREEBORN, Mr. Edward, BCom FCA *1973;* Little Hickmotts, The Lodge, Marden, TONBRIDGE, KENT, TN12 9DB.
FREEBORN, Mr. Philip John, BSc ACA *1990;* 3 Horseshoe Lane, LONDON, N20 8NJ.
FREEBORN, Mr. Timothy Charles Adrian, BA ACA *1985;* Evolution Securities, 100 Wood Street, LONDON, EC2V 7AN.
FREEBOROUGH, Ms. Janet Margaret, BSc ACA *1995;* Springfield Holtwood, Holt, WIMBORNE, BH21 7DT.
FREED, Mr. Gavin Mark, BA ACA *1997;* Paragon Skills, 79 Lynch Lane, WEYMOUTH, DORSET, DT4 9DW.
FREED, Mr. Mark Robin, ACA *1980;* (Tax Fac), 33 Trumpledor Street, 49403 PETACH TIKVA, ISRAEL.
•**FREED, Mr. Wallace Michael, FCA** *1965;* Jayes Freed, C P House, Otterspool Way, WATFORD, WD25 8HP.
FREEDA, Mrs. Gloria, FCA *1959;* 6 Burlington Park House, Dennis Lane, STANMORE, MIDDLESEX, HA7 4LA. (Life Member)
FREEDA, Mr. Raymond, FCA *1961;* 6 Burlington Park House, Dennis Lane, STANMORE, MIDDLESEX, HA7 4LA. (Life Member)
•**FREEDA, Miss. Suzanne Natalie, BA FCA** *1985;* FMCB, Hathaway House, Popes Drive, Finchley, LONDON, N3 1QF.
FREEDBERG, Mr. Ross Melvin, BA ACA *2006;* 12 Francis House, 552 Kings Road, LONDON, SW1X 7HH.
FREEDER, Mr. David Benjamin, BSc ACA *2007;* 37 Finch Lane, BUSHEY, WD23 3AJ.
•**FREEDMAN, Mr. Barry Stephen, FCA** *1966;* (Tax Fac), Stephen Daniel & Co., 138 Pinner Road, HARROW, HA1 4JE.
FREEDMAN, Mr. David, ACA *2008;* Flat 8 Mapesbury Court, 59-61 Shoot up Hill, LONDON, NW2 3PU.
•**FREEDMAN, Mr. David Charles Nathaniel, FCA** *1976;* (Tax Fac), Gates Freedman & Company, 9th Floor, Hyde House, The Hyde, LONDON, NW9 6LQ.
FREEDMAN, Mr. David Norman, BA(Econ) ACA *1999;* WSP Cantor Seinuk, 228 East 45th St, 3rd Floor, NEW YORK, NY 10017, UNITED STATES.
•**FREEDMAN, Mr. Henry Samuel, FCA** *1979;* Freedmans, Northway House, 5th Floor Suite 504-505, 1379 High Road, Whetstone, LONDON N20 9LP.
•**FREEDMAN, Mr. Howard, FCA** *1981;* Baker Tilly Tax and Advisory Services LLP, 25 Farringdon Street, LONDON, EC4A 4AB. See also Baker Tilly UK Audit LLP
FREEDMAN, Mr. Jerome David, FCA *1959;* 5 Thanescroft Gardens, CROYDON, CR0 5JR. (Life Member)
FREEDMAN, Mr. Jonathan Sydney, BA FCA *1976;* 8 Marsh Point, Marsh Road, PINNER, MIDDLESEX, HA5 5ND.
FREEDMAN, Mr. Kevin David, ACA *1986;* Freedman International Plc Unit 401 India House, 45 Curlew Street, LONDON, SE1 2ND.
FREEDMAN, Miss. Laura, BSc ACA *2007;* Flat 32 Cunard Court, Brightwen Grove, STANMORE, MIDDLESEX, HA7 4WY.
FREEDMAN, Mr. Lloyd Hugh, FCA *1987;* Oakthrift Corporation Ltd, Unit 9c Chester Road, BOREHAMWOOD, HERTFORDSHIRE, WD6 1LT.
FREEDMAN, Mr. Mark Edward, BSc ACA *1992;* 1 Spareleaze Hill, LOUGHTON, ESSEX, IG10 1BS.
FREEDMAN, Mr. Maurice, FCA *1957;* 16 Stanmore Hall, Wood Lane, STANMORE, HA7 4JY. (Life Member)
•**FREEDMAN, Mr. Michael, BCom FCA** *1962;* with Ford Campbell Freedman LLP, 34 Park Cross Street, LEEDS, LS1 2QH.
FREEDMAN, Mr. Michael, FCA *1959;* 126 17th Street, Linksfield West, JOHANNESBURG, GAUTENG, 2192, SOUTH AFRICA. (Life Member)
FREEDMAN, Mr. Michael Augustus, FCA *1960;* BPH Wealth Management LLP, Oddstones House, Thompsons Close, HARPENDEN, HERTFORDSHIRE, AL5 4ES.
•**FREEDMAN, Mr. Michael Gerald, MSc FCA** *1965;* Landau Morley LLP, Lanmor House, 370-386 High Road, WEMBLEY, MIDDLESEX, HA9 6AX.
•**FREEDMAN, Mr. Michael Jacob, FCA** *1969;* (Tax Fac), MJF, 23 Oaks Way, Long Ditton, SURBITON, SURREY, KT6 5DX.
FREEDMAN, Mr. Norman Ralph, FCA *1967;* 21/2 Rechov Hamiyasdim, 3900 ZICHRON YAAKOV, ISRAEL.
FREEDMAN, Mr. Paul Maurice, BA ACA *1995;* 11 Upton Lodge Close, BUSHEY, WD23 1AG.
FREEDMAN, Mr. Peter Malcolm, MA ACA MBA *1980;* 13a Downshire Hill, LONDON, NW3 1NR.
FREEDMAN, Mrs. Rebecca Jane, BSc ACA *1996;* 1 Spareleaze Hill, LOUGHTON, ESSEX, IG10 1BS.
•**FREEDMAN, Mr. Richard Allen, FCA** *1970;* (Tax Fac), Richard Freedman, Suite 2, Fountain House, 1a Elm Park, STANMORE, MIDDLESEX HA7 4AU.
FREEDMAN, Mr. Robert James, ACA *2010;* 8 Ladyfields, LOUGHTON, IG10 3RR.
FREEDMAN, Mr. Samuel Kenneth, FCA *1968;* 7 Ascot Close, Elstree, BOREHAMWOOD, HERTFORDSHIRE, WD6 3JH.
FREEDMAN, Mr. Scott James, BCom ACA *2006;* 22 Addison Way, LONDON, NW11 6AJ.
FREEDMAN, Mr. Simon Michael, BSc ACA *1991;* 44 Beechcroft Avenue, NEW MALDEN, KT3 3EE.
FREEDMAN, Mr. Steven Paul, BA FCA *1981;* 3 Wyatt Close, BUSHEY, WD23 4GT.
FREEGARD, Mr. Francis Edward Charles, FCA *1962;* 49 Cronk Drean, Douglas, ISLE OF MAN, IM2 6AT. (Life Member)
•**FREELAND, Mr. Julien Ivor Nicholas, FCA** *1979;* PricewaterhouseCoopers, Strathvale House, PO Box 258, GEORGE TOWN, GRAND CAYMAN, KY1-1104 CAYMAN ISLANDS.
FREELAND, Mr. Mark Alan, ACA *2003;* 11 Abergavenny Gardens, Copthorne, CRAWLEY, WEST SUSSEX, RH10 3RU.
FREELAND, Mr. Mark Philip, BA ACA *1995;* 2/59 Fancourt Street, Meadowbank, AUCKLAND 1072, NEW ZEALAND.
FREELAND, Mr. Michael, BSc ACA *1992;* 29 Dryburgh Road, Putney, LONDON, SW15 1BN.
FREELY, Mr. Dominic Peter, BSc ACA *1987;* 40 Eaton Rise, Ealing, LONDON, W5 2ER.
FREEMAN, Mr. Alan Douglas, MA FCA *1951;* Sallow Copse, Silchester, READING, RG7 2PH. (Life Member)
•**FREEMAN, Mr. Alan Gregory, FCA** *1977;* HWS, 1st Floor St Giles Hse, 15-21 Victoria Road, Bletchley, MILTON KEYNES, BUCKINGHAMSHIRE MK2 2NG.
FREEMAN, Mr. Alan Henry, MA FCA *1964;* Oberblattstrasse 11, 8832 WOLLERAU, SWITZERLAND. (Life Member)
FREEMAN, Mr. Alan Philip, BA FCA *1971;* Deerwood House, Woodlands Road, BROMLEY, BR1 2AD.
FREEMAN, Mr. Andrew Graham Winston, BA ACA *2003;* with Deloitte LLP, Hill House, 1 Little New Street, LONDON, EC4A 3TR.
FREEMAN, Ms. Angela, ACA CA(SA) *2009;* 26 Alacross Road, LONDON, W5 4HT.
•**FREEMAN, Mrs. Angela Judith, FCA CTA** *1985;* with ICAEW, Metropolitan House, 321 Avebury Boulevard, MILTON KEYNES, MK9 2FZ.
FREEMAN, Mrs. Anne Felicity, MA FCA *1983;* Les Fontaines, La Rue de L'Etocquet, St John, JERSEY, JE3 4AE.
FREEMAN, Mr. Benjamin Elliot, BA FCA *1997;* Bridgepoint, 30 Warwick Street, LONDON, W1B 5AL.
FREEMAN, Mr. Benjamin James, BSc ACA *2005;* 15 Farleigh Crescent, SWINDON, SN3 1JY.

FREEMAN, Mr. Benjamin Patrick, ACA *1984;* Flat D Royston, 55 Putney Hill, LONDON, SW15 6RZ.
FREEMAN, Mr. Charles Truscott, FCA *1981;* (Tax Fac), 9 The Uplands, HARPENDEN, HERTFORDSHIRE, AL5 2PG.
FREEMAN, Mr. Christopher George, ACA CA(NZ) *2010;* Suite 256, 235 Earls Court Road, LONDON, SW5 9FE.
FREEMAN, Mr. Christopher John Ogle, FCA *1969;* Casa Granado S.A., Rua Primeiro De Marco 16, RIO DE JANEIRO, 20010-000, BRAZIL.
FREEMAN, Mrs. Claire, ACA *2007;* 2 Sandstar Close, Longlevens, GLOUCESTER, GL2 0NR.
•**FREEMAN, Mr. Crispin Patrick, FCA** *1975;* (Tax Fac), Perkins Copeland, 15 Gildredge Rd, EASTBOURNE, BN21 4RA.
•**FREEMAN, Mr. Daniel Marc, BSc ACA** *1997;* Financialmodelling.com Ltd, 19 South View, East Preston, LITTLEHAMPTON, WEST SUSSEX, BN16 1PX.
FREEMAN, Mr. David, FCA *1966;* 16 Hoffmann Road, CANTON, CT 06019, UNITED STATES.
•**FREEMAN, Mr. David Derek, FCA** *1960;* (Tax Fac), D. Freeman & Co, Gateways Lodge, 76A Oakleigh Park North, LONDON, N20 9AS.
FREEMAN, Mr. David Hawten, FCA *1955;* 2028 Marlowe Avenue, MONTREAL H4A 3L5, QUE, CANADA. (Life Member)
•**FREEMAN, Mr. David Neal, FCA** *1982;* 11616 Milbern Drive, POTOMAC, MD 20854, UNITED STATES.
FREEMAN, Mr. Derek John, BA FCA *1966;* 71 Beaconsfield Road, Blackheath, LONDON, SE3 7LG. (Life Member)
FREEMAN, Mr. Donald Anthony, BSc ACA *1994;* 57 Mayford Road, LONDON, SW12 8SE.
FREEMAN, Mr. Edward Charles, BA ACA *2005;* 26 Stephen Hill, SHEFFIELD, S10 5NU.
FREEMAN, Mrs. Elaine Joy, BSc FCA *1991;* (Tax Fac), 25 Rectory Road, SOLIHULL, B91 3RJ.
FREEMAN, Miss. Elizabeth Jane, BSc ACA *1993;* Office Gold Ltd Unit 3 Quadrum Park, Old Portsmouth Road Peasmarsh, GUILDFORD, GU3 1LU.
FREEMAN, Mr. Geoffrey Marks, ACA *1983;* 12a Rehov HaRav Toledano, 42755 NETANYA, ISRAEL.
•**FREEMAN, Miss. Gillian Joan, BSc ACA** *1989;* Milsted Langdon LLP, Motivo House, Alvington, YEOVIL, SOMERSET, BA20 2FG.
FREEMAN, Miss. Hannah Charlotte, BA ACA *2003;* 19 Martingale Close, CAMBRIDGE, CB4 3TA.
FREEMAN, Mr. Harvey Barnett, BA FCA *1991;* 15 Fairview Way, EDGWARE, HA8 8JE.
FREEMAN, Mrs. Helena Rosemary, BA ACA *1993;* Wooda Farm, Wooda Road, Northam, BIDEFORD, DEVON, EX39 1NB.
•**FREEMAN, Mr. Howard Kimberley, BSc FCA** *1995;* Shorts, 6 Fairfield Road, CHESTERFIELD, DERBYSHIRE, S40 4TP.
FREEMAN, Mr. Ian, BSc ACA *2010;* 76 Villiers Road, WATFORD, WD19 4AJ.
FREEMAN, Miss. Jackie Doreen, BSc ACA *1990;* Pizza Express, 2 Balcombe Street, LONDON, NW1 6NW.
FREEMAN, Mr. James David, ACA MAAT *2010;* Flat 12 Richmond Court, St. Marys Road, LEAMINGTON SPA, CV31 1DA.
FREEMAN, Mrs. Janet Susan, BSc ACA CF *1988;* The Lodge, School Lane, Hamble, SOUTHAMPTON, SO31 4JD.
FREEMAN, Ms. Janine, MA(Oxon) ACA *1999;* 24 Greatheed Road, LEAMINGTON SPA, WARWICKSHIRE, CV32 6ES.
FREEMAN, Mrs. Jennifer Jane, BA ACA *1997;* The Water Barn, Hill Farm, Ford End, CHELMSFORD, CM3 1LH.
FREEMAN, Mr. John Anthony, BCom FCA *1961;* Stuart House, Down End, Hook Norton, BANBURY, OXFORDSHIRE, OX15 5LW.
FREEMAN, Mr. Jonathan Mark, BSc ACA ATII *1996;* with Deloitte LLP, 4 Brindley Place, BIRMINGHAM, B1 2HZ.
FREEMAN, Miss. Julie Ann, BA ACA *1999;* Woodview, Mill Road, Bethersden, ASHFORD, KENT, TN26 3DA.
•**FREEMAN, Mrs. Karen Jayne, BA ACA** *1998;* Impact Accounting (South West) LLP, 2 Coombe Lane, Cargreen, SALTASH, CORNWALL, PL12 6PB.
FREEMAN, Mr. Keith Michael, FCA FCCA *1967;* Ford Bank, 30 Albany Road, ST. LEONARDS-ON-SEA, EAST SUSSEX, TN38 0LN.
FREEMAN, Miss. Kelly Marie, BA(Hons) ACA *2002;* 110 Cravells Road, HARPENDEN, HERTFORDSHIRE, AL5 1BQ.
FREEMAN, Mr. Kevin, BSc ACA *2006;* Kilmarth, Love Lane, IVER, SL0 9QT.
FREEMAN, Mr. Laurence, FCA *1962;* 158 Old Bedford Road, LUTON, LU2 7HN.
FREEMAN, Mr. Lee Steven, BA ACA *1992;* 27 Elmwood, SAWBRIDGEWORTH, CM21 9NN.
FREEMAN, Mr. Leonard David, FCA *1973;* 30 Crow Hill Lane, Great Cambourne, CAMBRIDGE, CB23 5AW. (Life Member)
FREEMAN, Mrs. Lisa Jayne, BA ACA *1990;* Torrent Trackside Ltd Unit 23, Europa Way Britannia Enterprise Park, LICHFIELD, STAFFORDSHIRE, WS14 9TZ.
FREEMAN, Mrs. Louise Emma, BA ACA *2004;* Larking Gowen Kingstreet House, 15 Upper King Street, NORWICH, NR3 1RB.
FREEMAN, Ms. Marcia Louise, ACA CA(AUS) *2009;* Investec Bank (UK) Ltd, 2 Gresham Street, LONDON, EC2V 7QP.
FREEMAN, Mr. Marcus Roderick, BA ACA *1994;* PO Box 261075, Jebel Ali Free Zone, DUBAI, UNITED ARAB EMIRATES.
•**FREEMAN, Mr. Martin George, BA ACA** *2000;* Impact Accounting (South West) LLP, 2 Coombe Lane, Cargreen, SALTASH, CORNWALL, PL12 6PB.
FREEMAN, Mr. Martin Gill, FCA *1958;* 5 Gullet Lane, Kirby Muxloe, LEICESTER, LE9 2BL. (Life Member)
FREEMAN, Mr. Martin Howard, BSc FCA *1972;* 96 Park Road, Prestwich, MANCHESTER, M25 0DY.
FREEMAN, Mr. Martin William, FCA *1976;* 41 Merynton Avenue, Cannon Hill, COVENTRY, CV4 7BL.
FREEMAN, Mr. Matthew Albert, ACA *2010;* 91 Copenhagen Way, NORWICH, NR3 2RB.
FREEMAN, Mr. Matthew John, BA ACA *2003;* 2104, 1420 West Georgia Street, VANCOUVER V6G 3K4, BC, CANADA.
•①**FREEMAN, Mr. Michael Anthony, FCA MIPA FABRP** *1980;* Tony Freeman FCA MIPA, New Maxdov House, 130 Bury New Road, Prestwich, MANCHESTER, M25 0AA.
FREEMAN, Mr. Michael Asher, FCA *1959;* 1 Stockleigh Hall, Prince Albert Road, LONDON, NW8 7LA. (Life Member)
FREEMAN, Mr. Michael Millice, FCA *1960;* 20 Seymour Road, Wimbledon Common, LONDON, SW19 5JS.
FREEMAN, Mr. Neil, BSc ACA *2002;* Lend Lease Corporation, Level 5, 30 The Bond, 30 Hickson Road, MILLERS POINT, NSW 2000 AUSTRALIA.
FREEMAN, Mr. Neil John, BSc ACA *1994;* GRAAF JANLAAN 14, 1181 EC AMSTELVEEN, NETHERLANDS.
•**FREEMAN, Mr. Nicholas John, BSc ACA** *1979;* Turner Peachey Incorporating Ridgway Wall & Co, 12 West Castle St, BRIDGNORTH, WV16 4AB. See also Ridgeway Wall & Co
•**FREEMAN, Mrs. Nicola, ACA ATII** *1993;* PricewaterhouseCoopers LLP, First Point, Buckingham Gate, London Gatwick Airport, GATWICK, WEST SUSSEX RH6 0NT. See also PricewaterhouseCoopers
FREEMAN, Mrs. Nicole Lisa, MA MBA ACA *1997;* 38 Oakleigh Avenue, Whetstone, LONDON, N20 9JJ.
FREEMAN, Mr. Paul Alan, BA ACA *2008;* 14 Withey Close West, BRISTOL, BS9 3SX.
FREEMAN, Mr. Paul Andrew John, MA ACA *2007;* 16 St Johns Lane, Hartley, DARTFORD, DA3 8ET.
FREEMAN, Mr. Paul James, BA ACA *1986;* 16 Ludgate Street, Tutbury, BURTON-ON-TRENT, DE13 9NG.
FREEMAN, Mr. Paul Michael, MMath ACA CTA *2006;* (Tax Fac), 57a Temple Road, LONDON, NW2 6PN.
FREEMAN, Mr. Paul Ronald, FCA *1979;* 108 Shenfield Pl, Shenfield, BRENTWOOD, CM15 9AJ.
FREEMAN, Mr. Paul Stephen, BA FCA *1986;* (Tax Fac), 28 Station Road, PRINCES RISBOROUGH, HP27 9DL.
•**FREEMAN, Mr. Peter Edward, FCA** *1971;* (Tax Fac), Shorts, 6 Fairfield Road, CHESTERFIELD, DERBYSHIRE, S40 4TP.
FREEMAN, Mr. Philip Robert, BA ACA *1993;* 10 Sheridan Place, Roxborough Park, HARROW, HA1 3BQ.
FREEMAN, Mr. Philip Thomas, FCA *1974;* 32 Chessington Way, WEST WICKHAM, BR4 9NZ.
FREEMAN, Mr. Philip William, BCom FCA *1975;* Unit 4 The Moorings Business Park, Channel Way, Exhall, COVENTRY, CV6 6RH.
FREEMAN, Mr. Richard, ACA *2009;* 64 Coleridge Way, BOREHAMWOOD, HERTFORDSHIRE, WD6 2AR.
•**FREEMAN, Mr. Richard Charles Peter, MA FCA** *1982;* FCA Solutions Ltd, 44 Kelling Way, Broughton, MILTON KEYNES, MK10 9NW.
FREEMAN, Mr. Richard John, BSc ACA *1991;* Flat 33 The Westbourne, 1 Artesian Road, LONDON, W2 5DL.
FREEMAN, Mr. Robert Kenneth, FCA *1984;* 63 Sefton Gardens, Aughton, ORMSKIRK, LANCASHIRE, L39 6RY.
FREEMAN, Mr. Robert William, LLB ACA *2001;* 16 Kelvedon Road, Coggeshall, COLCHESTER, CO6 1RG.
FREEMAN, Mr. Roger Oswald Oldaker, FCA *1962;* High Meadow, Martens Lane, Polstead, COLCHESTER, CO6 5AG.
FREEMAN, Mrs. Rosemary Jane, ACA *1981;* Rowan House, Speen Lane, Speen, NEWBURY, RG14 1RJ.
FREEMAN, Mrs. Sarah Louise, BSc ACA *1992;* Metapraxis Ltd, Kingstons House, Coombe Road, KINGSTON UPON THAMES, SURREY, KT2 7AB.
FREEMAN, Mr. Seymour, FCA *1960;* 16370 mirasol way, DELRAY BEACH, FL 33446, UNITED STATES. (Life Member)
FREEMAN, Mr. Simon Mark, BSocSc ACA *1998;* 37 Frys Hill, OXFORD, OX4 7GW.
FREEMAN, Miss. Stephanie Elizabeth, BSc FCA *1989;* (Tax Fac), 102 Kenilworth Road, EDGWARE, MIDDLESEX, HA8 8XD.
FREEMAN, Mrs. Stephanie Louise, LLB(Hons) ACA *2009;* Apartment 418 Islington Gates, 14 Fleet Street, BIRMINGHAM, B3 1JL.
•**FREEMAN, Mr. Stephen Andrew, FCA** *1980;* (Tax Fac), Freeman Lawrence & Partners Ltd, Spectrum Studios, 2 Manor Gardens, LONDON, N7 6ER.
•**FREEMAN, Mr. Stephen Kenneth, BA ACA** *1993;* Ophelia House, 4 Blytheswood, Sheethanger Lane Felden, HEMEL HEMPSTEAD, HERTFORDSHIRE, HP3 0BQ.
FREEMAN, Mr. Thomas Charles, ACA *2008;* 21 Hopkins Mead, CHELMSFORD, CM2 6SS.
•**FREEMAN, Mr. Timothy James, BSc FCA** *1975;* King Freeman, 1st Floor, Kimberley House, Vaughan Way, LEICESTER, LE1 4SG.
FREEMAN, Mr. Timothy Peter, ACA *1995;* 26 London Road, REIGATE, RH2 9QT.
FREEMAN, Mr. Trevor Anthony, FCA *1972;* 2 Acorn Grove, Codsall, WOLVERHAMPTON, WV8 2AU.
FREEMAN, Mr. William Ian Bede, MBA FCA *1975;* Herons Cottage, Ferry Lane, Medmenham, MARLOW, BUCKINGHAMSHIRE, SL7 2EZ.
FREEMAN, The Revd. William Rodney, MA FCA *1962;* Lavender Cottage, Harkstead, IPSWICH, IP9 1BN.
FREEMANTLE, Mr. Adam Thomas, MMath ACA *2004;* BBDO Europe, 151 Marylebone Road, LONDON, NW1 5QE.
•**FREEMANTLE, Mr. Gavin Harry, FCA** *1973;* (Tax Fac), Merchant & Co., 84 Uxbridge Road, West Ealing, LONDON, W13 8RA.
FREEMANTLE, Mr. James Paul, BSc ACA *1997;* Hyde Cottage East Meon, PETERSFIELD, HAMPSHIRE, GU32 1NJ.
FREEMANTLE, Mrs. Julie Elizabeth, BA ACA *2000;* Hyde Cottage, East Meon, PETERSFIELD, HAMPSHIRE, GU32 1NJ.
FREER, Mr. Andrew Malcolm Bruce, ACA CA(SA) *2008;* (Tax Fac), 45a Walham Grove, LONDON, SW6 1QR.
FREER, Mrs. Christine, BSc FCA *1974;* 9 Hornbeam Way, WIMBORNE, DORSET, BH21 2QE.
FREER, Mrs. Claire Louise, BA ACA *1989;* Bridge Farmhouse, Suspension Bridge, Welney, WISBECH, CAMBRIDGESHIRE, PE14 9TF.
FREER, Mr. Edward Frederick, FCA *1962;* G.P.O. Box 9877, CENTRAL, HONG KONG ISLAND, HONG KONG SAR. (Life Member)
FREER, Mr. Mark Conway, BSc FCA *1974;* 9 Hornbeam Way, WIMBORNE, DORSET, BH21 2QE.
FREER, Mr. Mark Stephen, BSc ACA *1992;* 35 Barker Road, SUTTON COLDFIELD, WEST MIDLANDS, B74 2NZ.
FREER, Mr. Richard Charles, BSc ACA *1996;* A C S Cobham International School Heywood, Portsmouth Road, COBHAM, KT11 1BL.
FREER, Mr. Robert Ian, BSc ACA *1991;* Lloyds TSB Bank Plc Princess House, 1 Suffolk Lane, LONDON, EC4R 0AX.
FREERIKS, Mr. Mark, MSc BA ACA *2010;* 46 St. Olaf's Road, LONDON, SW6 7DL.
FREESTON, Mr. Julian Garner, BSocSc ACA *1997;* Zodiak Media Ltd, The Gloucester Building, Avonmore Road, LONDON, W14 8RF.
FREESTONE, Mr. Kaveh, BSc ACA *2006;* PO Box 5126, MANAMA, BAHRAIN.
FREESTONE, Mr. Richard John, BSc ACA *2008;* 12 St Martins Approach, RUISLIP, HA4 7QD.
•**FREESTONE, Mr. Robert Charles, BA FCA** *1980;* Freestone & Co, 1 The Centre, The High Street, GILLINGHAM, Dorset, SP8 4AB.
FREESTONE, Mr. Robert Edward, LLB FCA CTA *1980;* Enesco Ltd Brunthill Road, Kingstown Industrial Estate, CARLISLE, CA3 0EN.
FREESTONE, Mr. Robin Anthony David, BA ACA *1984;* Pearson Plc Shell Mex House, 80 Strand, LONDON, WC2R 0RL.
FREI, Mr. Alfred, FCA ATII *1964;* 49/8 Hizkiyahu Hamelech, Katamon, 93224 JERUSALEM, ISRAEL. (Life Member)
FREIER, Mr. Matthew, BSc ACA *2004;* 177 Grove Lane, Cheadle Hulme, CHEADLE, CHESHIRE, SK8 7NG.
FREIMANIS, Miss. Claire, ACA *2009;* Misys Plc, 1 Kingdom Street, LONDON, W2 6BL.
FREIRE, Mr. Diogo Bandeira, BSc FCA *2000;* 8 Culmstock Road, LONDON, SW11 6LX.
FREMANTLE, Mr. Edward Vigant Eardley, MA FCA *1968;* White Cottage, Horseshoe Lane, Great Hormead, BUNTINGFORD, HERTFORDSHIRE, SG9 0NQ. (Life Member)
•**FRENCH, Mr. Adam Daniel, BEng FCA** *1992;* Hailwood Accountants Ltd, 392-394 Hoylake Road, WIRRAL, MERSEYSIDE, CH46 6DF.
FRENCH, Mr. Adrian Francis Sansom, ACA *1984;* Perryways, Chessels Lane, Charlton Adam, SOMERTON, SOMERSET, TA11 7BJ.
FRENCH, Miss. Alisa Margaret, BSc ACA *2000;* 22 Rythe Road, Claygate, ESHER, SURREY, KT10 9DF.
FRENCH, Mr. Allan Neal Gavin, BSc ACA *1989;* 103 Bradgate Road, LONDON, SE6 4TR.
FRENCH, Mrs. Amanda Brenda Christina, BA ACA *1989;* 1 Shires Close, ASHTEAD, KT21 2LT.
FRENCH, Mr. Andrew John, BSc ACA *1980;* Hodgkyns, Brook Road, COLCHESTER, CO6 3RW.
•**FRENCH, Mr. Bernard, FCA** *1973;* Adams, 22 Whitworth Terrace, SPENNYMOOR, DL16 7LD.
FRENCH, Mrs. Bethany Joan, BSc ACA *1996;* Gallets Fulvens, Peaslake, GUILDFORD, GU5 9PG.
•**FRENCH, Mr. Bruce Harvey John, BSc FCA** *1974;* B H.J. French, Ancholme house, Hall Lane, Elsham, BRIGG, DN20 0SX.
FRENCH, Mrs. Catherine Anne, BSc ACA *2003;* 2133-1177 West Hastings Street, VANCOUVER V6E 2K3, BC, CANADA.
FRENCH, Dr. Catherine Louise, ACA *2010;* Deloitte & Touche, 2 New Street Square, LONDON, EC4A 3BZ.
•**FRENCH, Mrs. Catherine Marie, MA FCA DChA** *1992;* Malthouse & Company Ltd, America House, Rumford Court, Rumford Place, LIVERPOOL, L3 9DD.
FRENCH, Mr. Charles Matthew, BSc ACA *2005;* A B N Amro Bank NV, 250 Bishopsgate, LONDON, EC2M 4AA.
FRENCH, Mr. Charles Peter, BA(Hons) ACA *2000;* Newton Investment Mgmt, Mellon Financial Centre, 160 Queen Victoria Street, LONDON, EC4V 4LA.
FRENCH, Mrs. Chloe Katrina, BSc ACA *1986;* Freshford Hall, Staples Hill, Freshford, BATH, BA2 7WJ.
FRENCH, Mr. Christopher Dennis, FCA *1975;* 18 Celtic Avenue, BROMLEY, BR2 0RU.
FRENCH, Mr. Christopher Graham, ACA *1984;* Goldman Sachs, 10-15 Newgate Street, LONDON, EC1A 7HD.
FRENCH, Miss. Claire Elizabeth, MA ACA *2004;* 6 Crossgate Moor Gardens, DURHAM, DH1 4HS.
FRENCH, Mr. Colin, BA ACA *1985;* 34 School Lane, Brereton, SANDBACH, CHESHIRE, CW11 1RN.
FRENCH, Mr. Colin David, ACA *2004;* 130 Blakedown Road, HALESOWEN, WEST MIDLANDS, B63 4QL.
•**FRENCH, Mr. Colin Edward Marfleet, FCA** *1958;* (Tax Fac), 11 Carlton Road, LONDON, W5 2AW.
FRENCH, Mr. Colin Graham, FCA *1966;* The Garden House, Beacon Road, Ditchling, HASSOCKS, BN6 8XB.
FRENCH, Mr. Colin James, BSc FCA *1972;* Tile Cottage, Luxford Lane, CROWBOROUGH, EAST SUSSEX, TN6 2PE.
FRENCH, Mr. Craig, BSc ACA *2011;* 103 Cooper Lane, HALIFAX, WEST YORKSHIRE, HX3 7RG.
•**FRENCH, Mr. Daniel, BA ACA** *2007;* Leading Performance Limited, 21 Driftwood Avenue, ST. ALBANS, HERTFORDSHIRE, AL2 3DE.
FRENCH, Mr. David John, FCA *1971;* 14 Crossbush Road, Felpham, BOGNOR REGIS, PO22 7LS.
FRENCH, Mr. David Martin, BSc(Econ) FCA *1998;* 40 Golden Aspen Crest, CALGARY T3Z 3E6, AB, CANADA.
FRENCH, Mr. David Weston, BSc ACA *1994;* 38 Six Acres, Slinfold, HORSHAM, WEST SUSSEX, RH13 0TH.
FRENCH, Mr. Derrick Thomas, FCA *1957;* Highfield Cottage, Portinscale, KESWICK, CUMBRIA, CA12 5RF. (Life Member)
FRENCH, Mrs. Elizabeth Mary, BSc FCA *1977;* Buckinghamshire County Council, Culture & Learning, Gallery Suite, County Hall, AYLESBURY, BUCKINGHAMSHIRE HP20 1UU.

•**FRENCH, Miss. Ellen Rose, ACA** *2002;* Per Annum Accounting Limited, Flat A, The Chestnuts, 5 Kenilworth Road, NOTTINGHAM, NG7 1DD.

•**FRENCH, Mrs. Gillian Elizabeth Ann, BSc ACA** *1989;* DNA Accountants Limited, Regency House, 61a Walton Street, Walton on the Hill, TADWORTH, SURREY KT20 7RZ.

•**FRENCH, Mr. Graham Stuart, BSc(Hons) ACA** *2003;* DSC, Tattersall House, East Parade, HARROGATE, NORTH YORKSHIRE, HG1 5LT. See also DSC Accountants Limited

FRENCH, Miss. Helen Jane, BCom ACA *1989;* Swan Farm, Mill Lane, LOWER STONNAL, STAFFORDSHIRE, WS9 9HN.

•**FRENCH, Mr. Ian, BA ACA** *1989;* DNA Accountants Limited, Regency House, 61a Walton Street, Walton on the Hill, TADWORTH, SURREY KT20 7RZ.

•**FRENCH, Mr. James, BA(Hons) ACA** *2002;* with PricewaterhouseCoopers LLP, Marlborough Court, 10 Bricket Road, ST. ALBANS, HERTFORDSHIRE, AL1 3JX.

•**FRENCH, Mrs. Jane Louise, BSc ACA** *1991;* Neville Weston & Company, 3 High Street, St. Lawrence, RAMSGATE, KENT, CT11 0QL.

FRENCH, Miss. Jennifer Claire, BSc(Hons) ACA *2004;* 15 Stuyvesant Oval, Apt 7A, NEW YORK, NY 10009, UNITED STATES.

•**FRENCH, Mr. Jeremy John, BSc FCA** *1975;* French Ludlam & Co Ltd, 661 High Street, KINGSWINFORD, DY6 8AL.

•ⓘ**FRENCH, Mr. Jeremy Stuart, ACA** *1982;* FRP Advisory LLp, 43-45 Butts Green Road, HORNCHURCH, ESSEX, RM11 2JX.

FRENCH, Ms. Joanne Louise, BSc ACA *2004;* 3 Chapel Cottages, Townwell, Cromhall, WOTTON-UNDER-EDGE, GLOUCESTERSHIRE, GL12 8AG.

•**FRENCH, Mr. John, FCA** *1976;* (Tax Fac), Sellens French, 93/97 Bohemia Road, ST. LEONARDS-ON-SEA, EAST SUSSEX, TN37 6RJ.

FRENCH, Mr. John Alison Read Russell, MA FCA *1969;* 72 Palace Gardens Terrace, LONDON, W8 4RR.

FRENCH, Mr. John Beaumont, BCom FCA *1974;* 3 Acacia Walk, HARPENDEN, AL5 1SH.

FRENCH, Mr. John Edward, BSc ACA *1981;* Queen Elizabeth II The Conference Centre, Broad Sanctuary, LONDON, SW1P 3EE.

FRENCH, Mr. John Richard, BSc ACA *1985;* Tumblewood, Rodmell Road, TUNBRIDGE WELLS, TN2 5ST.

FRENCH, Mr. Julian Alexander Howard, BA(Hons) ACA *2002;* 32 Baxendale Street, LONDON, E2 7BY.

FRENCH, Mrs. Karen Vanessa, BSc ACA *1991;* Saxonmead, Borde Hill Lane, HAYWARDS HEATH, WEST SUSSEX, RH16 1XP.

FRENCH, Mr. Keith William, BSc ACA *1985;* 1 The Meadows, Haslingfield, CAMBRIDGE, CB23 1JD.

FRENCH, Mr. Leslie Eric, FCA *1964;* Rose Cottage, Winterhay, ILMINSTER, SOMERSET, TA19 9PN.

FRENCH, Miss. Madeleine, ACA *1995;* 18 Candlemas Lane, BEACONSFIELD, BUCKINGHAMSHIRE, HP9 1AH.

FRENCH, Mrs. Mary Anne, BA ACA *2006;* 10 South View, WETHERBY, WEST YORKSHIRE, LS22 7QE.

FRENCH, Mr. Michael, ACA *2011;* 183 Richmond Road, LONDON, E8 3NJ.

•**FRENCH, Mr. Michael David, FCA** *1977;* Harrison Hill Castle & Co., Melbury House, 34 Southborough Road, Bickley, BROMLEY, BR1 2EB.

•**FRENCH, Mr. Michael Frank, FCA** *1955;* (Tax Fac), M.F. French, Coleridge, 92 Leamington Road, KENILWORTH, CV8 2AA.

FRENCH, Mr. Michael Levick, BSc FCA *1978;* 40 Hertford Avenue, East Sheen, LONDON, SW14 8EQ.

FRENCH, Mr. Neil Barry, ACA *2005;* with Musker & Garrett Limited, Edward House, North Mersey Business Centre, Woodward Road, Knowsley Industrial Park, LIVERPOOL L33 7UY.

FRENCH, Mr. Neil Edward John, FCA *2000;* c/o KPMG, PO Box 357, PROVIDENCIALES, TURKS AND CAICOS ISLANDS.

FRENCH, Mr. Nigel, BCom ACA *1984;* 5 Adelaide Road, LEAMINGTON SPA, CV31 3PN.

FRENCH, Mr. Nigel Geoffrey, MA FCA *1977;* 20 Valentine Way, CHALFONT ST.GILES, HP8 4JB.

FRENCH, Mrs. Penelope Ann, BA ACA *2005;* with KPMG LLP, Aquis Court, 31 Fishpool Street, ST. ALBANS, HERTFORDSHIRE, AL3 4RF.

FRENCH, Mr. Peter Edmund, BA ACA *1990;* 13 Old Sneed Avenue, BRISTOL, BS9 1SD.

FRENCH, Mr. Peter Jason, BSc ACA *1992;* 2705 32nd Ave S, SEATTLE, WA 98144, UNITED STATES.

FRENCH, Mr. Peter John, FCA *1962;* 15 Pennyman Way, Stainton, MIDDLESBROUGH, CLEVELAND, TS8 9BL.

FRENCH, Mr. Peter John, BA ACA *2007;* Briar Cottage, Churn Lane, Horsmonden, TONBRIDGE, KENT, TN12 8HN.

•**FRENCH, Mr. Richard Alexander James, BA ACA** *2000;* PricewaterhouseCoopers, 1 Embankment Place, LONDON, WC2N 6RH. See also PricewaterhouseCoopers LLP

•**FRENCH, Mr. Robert Anthony, FCA** *1973;* R A French Ltd, 12 Lychgate, Higher Walton, WARRINGTON, WA4 6TF.

FRENCH, Mr. Robert Arnold, FCA *1978;* (Tax Fac), Brook House, 16 The Street, Honingham, NORWICH, NR9 5BL.

•**FRENCH, Mr. Robert Henry, FCA** *1968;* French Associates, The Swan Centre, Fishers Lane, Chiswick, LONDON, W4 1RX.

FRENCH, Mr. Robert John, FCA *1973;* 18 Fulmer Way, GERRARDS CROSS, BUCKINGHAMSHIRE, SL9 8AH.

•**FRENCH, Mrs. Sally Kathryn, BA FCA** *1983;* Greenman French Limited, Byways, The Batch, Bishop Sutton, BRISTOL, BS39 5US.

FRENCH, Mrs. Sarah Catherine Mary, BSc ACA *2002;* 14 Elm Lawns Close, Avenue Road, ST. ALBANS, HERTFORDSHIRE, AL1 3RE.

FRENCH, Mr. Sebastian, MA ACA *2007;* 18 Stable Lane, Seer Green, BEACONSFIELD, BUCKINGHAMSHIRE, HP9 2YT.

FRENCH, Ms. Stephanie Franziska Karen, BSc ACA *1992;* 5 Garth Mews, Greystoke Gardens Ealing, LONDON, W5 1HF.

FRENCH, Mr. Steven, ACA *2006;* Tom Ford, 7 Howick Place, LONDON, SW1P 1BB.

FRENCH, Mr. Thomas Jeremy, FCA *1964;* Ashley Green, 3a South Downs Road, Hale, ALTRINCHAM, CHESHIRE, WA14 3HU. (Life Member)

FRENCH, Mrs. Victoria Rosamond, MSc ACA *1999;* 29 Trewsbury Road, Sydenham, LONDON, SE26 5DP.

FRENCH-WOLLEN, Mrs. Jocelyn, ACA *2009;* 24 Wells Place, Kingham Close, Earlsfield, LONDON, SW18 3AW.

FRENDO, Mr. Nicholas Paul, BA ACA *2004;* 11 Imber Grove, ESHER, KT10 8JD.

FRENDO, Mr. Paul Anthony, FCA *1970;* 4 High Pewley, GUILDFORD, GU1 3SH.

•**FRENKEL, Mr. John Richard, BA FCA** *1978;* Frenkels Limited, Churchill House, 137 Brent Street, LONDON, NW4 4DJ.

FRENKEL, Mr. Roman, MEng ACA *2004;* 26 Hastings Street, LONDON, SE18 6SY.

FRENKEL, Mr. Vitek, BSc ACA *2005;* Frenkels Chartered Accountants, Churchill House, 137 Brent Street, LONDON, NW4 4DJ.

FRERE, Mr. Lionel Peter Dyve, FCA *1955;* 4 Harting Combe, ST. LEONARDS-ON-SEA, EAST SUSSEX, TN38 0XQ. (Life Member)

FRESHFIELD, Mr. Godfrey Raymond, FCA *1963;* 2 Kings Brook Close, Rempstone, LOUGHBOROUGH, LEICESTERSHIRE, LE12 6RR.

FRESHNEY, Mr. Mark Andrew, BSc ACA *2005;* 4th Floor, 1 Cabot Square, LONDON, E14 4QJ.

FRESSON, Mrs. Alice Shu Tshin, BA ACA *1990;* 6 Waldeck Road, Ealing, LONDON, W13 8LY.

FRESSON, Mr. Mark Gerald, BA ACA *1990;* (Tax Fac), 6 Waldeck Road, LONDON, W13 8LY.

•**FRETT, Mr. Richard William, FCA** *1979;* with Target Accountants Limited, Lawrence House, Lower Bristol Road, BATH, BA2 9ET.

FRETWELL, Mr. Alan Victor, FCA *1967;* 5 Dale Garth, Baildon, SHIPLEY, WEST YORKSHIRE, BD17 5TF. (Life Member)

FRETWELL, Mr. James, FCA *1949;* Lea Croft, Lee Green, MIRFIELD, WF14 0AB. (Life Member)

•**FRETWELL, Mrs. Karen, BA ACA** *1995;* R L & Associates Limited, Unit 9 Acorn Business Park, Woodseats Close, SHEFFIELD, S8 0TB. See also CFC Accountancy Services Ltd

FRETWELL, Mrs. Mary Louise, BA ACA *1992;* The Red House, 8 Stanley Avenue, BECKENHAM, BR3 6PX.

FREUDENTHAL, Mr. John Julius, FCA *1981;* 10A Valley Close, PINNER, HA5 3UR.

FREW, Miss. Emma-Jane, BA(Hons) ACA *2000;* 37 Painswick Road, CHELTENHAM, GLOUCESTERSHIRE, GL50 2EZ.

FREW, Mr. Gordon, FCA *1949;* 41a Eighth Avenue, Parktown North, JOHANNESBURG, GAUTENG, 2193, SOUTH AFRICA. (Life Member)

FREW, Mr. Iain, BA ACA *2006;* Flat 6 Nathan House, Reedworth Street, LONDON, SE11 4PG.

FREW, Mr. Patrick Joseph, BSc FCA *1976;* 20 Byron Avenue, South Woodford, LONDON, E18 2HQ.

FREW, Mrs. Sally Gail, LLB ACA *2003;* 2 Speedwell Close, RUGBY, CV23 0SG.

FREWER, Mr. John Edwin, BA FCA *1961;* 67 Westwood Park Drive, LEEK, ST13 8NW.

FREWER, Mrs. Rebecca Catharine Russell, BA(Hons) ACA *2001;* 4 Ridgway Hill Road, FARNHAM, GU9 8LS.

FREWIN, Mr. Dale Anthony, ACA *2009;* BMA House, British Medical Association B M A House, Tavistock Square, LONDON, WC1H 9JP.

FREY, Mr. Keith Gordon, MA FCA *1965;* 5 White Woods Lane, WESTPORT, CT 06880-1837, UNITED STATES.

FREY, Mr. Martin Rudolf, BSc ACA *1988;* Huenenbergweg 36, 6415 ARTH AM SEE, SWITZERLAND.

FRICKER, Mrs. Cherry Juliette, BMus ACA *2002;* 52 Westminster Road, YORK, YO30 6LY.

FRICKER, Miss. Elaine Joyce, BA ACA *1988;* Ground Floor Flat, 15 Drakefield Road, LONDON, SW17 8RT.

•**FRICKER, Mr. Harry William, FCA** *1976;* (Tax Fac), HWFCA Ltd, Flat 1, 32 Clifftown Parade, SOUTHEND-ON-SEA, SS1 1DL.

FRICKER, Miss. Janet Lynn, BSc ACA *1997;* 30 Highfield Park, MARLOW, BUCKINGHAMSHIRE, SL7 2DE.

FRICKER, Mr. Robert Edwin Colin, BA ACA *2008;* 45 Vicarage Road, OXFORD, OX1 4RE.

FRIDAY, Ms. Abbie Louise, ACA *2009;* 13 Lumiere Court, 209 Balham High Road, LONDON, SW17 7BQ.

FRIDAY, Mr. Terrence Michael, BA ACA *2009;* 18 Forest Road, CROWTHORNE, RG45 7EH.

FRIDD, Mr. Ralph David, MA FCA *1978;* Wiltshire P C T, Southgate House, Pans Lane, DEVIZES, WILTSHIRE, SN10 5EQ.

•**FRIDLINGTON, Mr. Stephen Andrew, BSc FCA** *1990;* (Tax Fac), Dexter & Sharpe, The Old Vicarage, Church Close, BOSTON, LINCOLNSHIRE, PE21 6NE.

•**FRIEDE, Mr. Philip Mark, BA FCA** *1981;* (Tax Fac), Philip Friede & Co Ltd, Third Floor, Premier House, 12-13 Hatton Garden, LONDON, EC1N 8AN.

FRIEDLER, Mr. Michael Bernard, BA ACA *1981;* Heatherby, Beech Drive, Kingswood, TADWORTH, KT20 6PP.

FRIEDLOS, Mr. Nicholas Robert, LLB FCA *1983;* 10 Lawn Road, LONDON, NW3 2XS.

FRIEDMAN, Miss. Irene Eleanor, BA ACA *1996;* Flat 1 Downhurst Court, 49 Parson Street, LONDON, NW4 1QT.

•**FRIEDMAN, Mr. Jonathan Richard, BA FCA** *1978;* Friedmans, Summit House, 13 High Street, Wanstead, LONDON, E11 2AA.

FRIEDMAN, Mr. Julian Arthur, FCA CA(SA) *1953;* 33 Woodlands Close, Golders Green, LONDON, NW11 9QR. (Life Member)

FRIEDMAN, Mr. Mortimer James, BCom FCA *1968;* 33 The Crescent, Alwoodley, LEEDS, LS17 7LY.

FRIEDMAN, Mr. Timothy William, BSc ACA *1994;* 44 Tyzack Road, HIGH WYCOMBE, HP13 7PU.

•**FRIEDMANN, Mr. Leonard Edward, FCA** *1977;* L.E. Friedmann, 110 Achuza Street, RA'ANANA, 43450, ISRAEL.

•**FRIEDNER, Mr. Marshall Anthony Barry, BSc FCA** *1974;* Marshall Friedner & Co, 9 Tycehurst Hill, LOUGHTON, ESSEX, IG10 1BX.

•**FRIEL, Mr. Edward James, BSc FCA** *1978;* (Tax Fac), Edward Friel & Co Limited, James House, 40 Lagland Street, POOLE, DORSET, BH15 1QG.

FRIEL, Mr. John, BSc(Hons) ACA CTA AMCT *1992;* (Tax Fac), Croft End Cottage Stag Lane, Great Kingshill, HIGH WYCOMBE, BUCKINGHAMSHIRE, HP15 6EF.

FRIELL, Mrs. Julie Patricia, BA ACA *1988;* Trees, 6 Bridle Road, Hannington, NORTHAMPTON, NN6 9SY.

FRIEND, Mr. Benjamin David, BSc ACA *2007;* 69 Ludlow Road, GUILDFORD, GU2 7NW.

•**FRIEND, Mrs. Denise, BSc(Econ) FCA** *1977;* Friend LLP, Eleven Brindley Place, 2 Brunswick Square, BIRMINGHAM, B1 2LP.

FRIEND, Mr. Graham Paul, MA MPhil ACA *1996;* Chalet Les Gentianes, 65 Chemin du Sommet, 1934 VERBIER, SWITZERLAND.

FRIEND, Mr. Henry John, FCA *1962;* Flat 1, Windacres 27 Warren Road, GUILDFORD, GU1 2HG. (Life Member)

•**FRIEND, Mr. Ian, ACA** *1986;* Oury Clark, PO Box 150, Herschel House, 58 Herschel Street, SLOUGH, SL1 1HD.

FRIEND, Mr. James Ernest, BCom FCA *1953;* Thraxbee Lodge, 28 Station Road, South Cave, BROUGH, HU15 2AA. (Life Member)

FRIEND, Mr. Jonathan Edward, BA FCA *1975;* 11 Lysander Way, ABBOTS LANGLEY, HERTFORDSHIRE, WD5 0TN.

•**FRIEND, Mr. Malcolm David, MSc FCA** *1971;* Friend LLP, Eleven Brindley Place, 2 Brunswick Square, BIRMINGHAM, B1 2LP.

FRIEND, Mr. Mark, BA ACA *1991;* 81 Teignmouth Road, LONDON, NW2 4EA.

•**FRIEND, Mr. Mark Anthony, BSc ACA** *1989;* Friend & Grant Ltd, Bryant House, Bryant Road, Strood, ROCHESTER, KENT ME2 3EW.

FRIEND, Mr. Nigel Andrew, BA ACA *1990;* 192 Sheen Lane, Sheen, LONDON, SW14 8LF.

FRIEND, Mr. Peter Henry, FCA *1975;* Oak Lodge, 197 Worlds End Lane, Chelsfield Park, Chelsfield, ORPINGTON, KENT BR6 6AT.

•**FRIEND, Mr. Philip Henry, ACA** *1987;* Friends Accounting Services, 51 Elm Park, STANMORE, MIDDLESEX, HA7 4AU.

FRIEND, Mr. Shaun, BA ACA *1986;* 24 Horsley Drive, KINGSTON UPON THAMES, KT2 5GG.

•**FRIEND, Mr. Simon David Anthony, MA FCA** *1985;* PricewaterhouseCoopers LLP, 1 Embankment Place, LONDON, WC2N 6RH. See also PricewaterhouseCoopers

•**FRIEND, Mr. Steven, MSc DIC ACA** *1997;* Amicustax Limited, 16 Dover Street, Mayfair, LONDON, W1S 4LR. See also Steven Friend & Co Ltd

FRIEND, Mr. Tony Peter, FCA *1978;* 19 Prince of Wales Drive, LONDON, SW11 4SB.

FRIEND-JAMES, Mr. William, BSc ACA *1998;* 4 Peninsular Close, Wellington Park, CAMBERLEY, SURREY, GU15 1QW.

FRIENDSHIP, Mr. Martin John Lloyd, BEng FCA AMCT *1991;* 20 Bridleways, VERWOOD, DORSET, BH31 6LA.

FRIENDSHIP, Mr. Martin William Elson, FCA *1965;* 38 Victoria Street, BOX HILL, VIC 3128, AUSTRALIA. (Life Member)

FRIER, Mr. Bernard Reginald, FCA *1953;* Tamesa, Trewsbury Coates, CIRENCESTER, GL7 6NY. (Life Member)

FRIER, Mr. Ian James, FCA *1953;* 142 Whytecliffe Road North, PURLEY, CR8 2AS. (Life Member)

FRIES, Mr. Brian Douglas, BA FCA *1971;* 20 Anthony Wall, Warfield, BRACKNELL, RG42 3UL. (Life Member)

FRIES, Ms. Jessica, MSc ACA *2003;* with PricewaterhouseCoopers LLP, 1 Embankment Place, LONDON, WC2N 6RH.

•**FRIEZE, Mr. Charles Adrian, MA(Oxon) FCA** *1963;* Charles Frieze MA(Oxon) FCA, 5 The Miltons, 13 Milton Crescent, CHEADLE, CHESHIRE, SK8 1NT.

FRIHMAT, Mr. Rachid, ACA *2008;* 2 Saumarez Street, St. Peter Port, GUERNSEY, GY1 2PT.

FRIPP, Mr. Derek Richard, FCA *1967;* The Cottage, North Road, Bunwell, NORWICH, NR16 1RB.

FRIPP, Mr. Matthew James, BA ACA *2002;* Samguri, Bendarroch Road, West Hill, OTTERY ST. MARY, DEVON, EX11 1TS.

FRIPP, Mr. Nigel Valentine, FCA *1975;* 130 Eagle Pass, PORT MOODY V3H 5E8, BC, CANADA.

•**FRISBY, Mrs. Chee-Hwan, ACA** *1979;* Frisby Wishart Ltd, 2 Lavender Lane, Rowledge, FARNHAM, SURREY, GU10 4AY. See also Frisby Wishart

FRISBY, Mr. Edward John Hope, BEng ACA *2002;* Finncap, 60 New Broad Street, LONDON, EC2M 1JJ.

FRISBY, Mr. Gordon James, BSc ACA *1990;* Copper Coin Stubbles Lane, Cookham, MAIDENHEAD, BERKSHIRE, SL6 9PX.

FRISBY, Mrs. Jill, BA ACA *1985;* 5 Bereweeke Avenue, WINCHESTER, HAMPSHIRE, SO22 6BH.

FRISBY, Mr. Kevin John, BSc ACA *1989;* Lane Clark & Peacock LLP, St. Pauls House, St. Pauls Hill, WINCHESTER, HAMPSHIRE, SO22 5AB.

•**FRISBY, Mr. Kevin Michael, BA FCA CF** *1990;* Ford Campbell Freedman LLP, 34 Park Cross Street, LEEDS, LS1 2QH.

•**FRISBY, Mr. William John, FCA** *1970;* WJ & JA Frisby, 27a Park Road, BUXTON, DERBYSHIRE, SK17 6SG.

FRISWELL, Mr. David John, FCA *1963;* Le Chalet Rouge, La Rue Des Bouillons, Trinity, JERSEY, JE3 5BB. (Life Member)

FRITH, Mr. Alexander William, BA ACA *2005;* 1st Floor, 6 St Andrew Street, LONDON, EC4A 3AE.

FRITH, Miss. Bethany, ACA *2011;* Ground Floor Flat, 33 Lancaster Road, Wimbledon, LONDON, SW19 5DF.

FRITH, Mr. David William, BA ACA CF *1982;* with Deloitte LLP, 1 City Square, LEEDS, WEST YORKSHIRE, LS1 2AL.

FRITH, Mrs. Fiona Elizabeth, BSc ACA *1998;* with PKF (UK) LLP, Farringdon Place, 20 Farringdon Road, LONDON, EC1M 3AP.

FRITH, Miss. Gloria Leona, ACA *2007;* 20 Finchfield Road, WOLVERHAMPTON, WV3 9LS.

FRITH, Mr. Godfrey William, BSocSc FCA *1979;* Merton Croft, 498 Streetsbrook Road, SOLIHULL, WEST MIDLANDS, B91 1RH.

FRITH, Miss. Janet, BA(Hons) ACA *2009;* 76 Lingfield Road, Clayton, MANCHESTER, M11 4ND.

FRITH, Mr. Michael, FCA *1965;* Viewpoint, 8 Netherswell Manor, Netherswell Stow on the Wold, CHELTENHAM, GLOUCESTERSHIRE, GL54 1JZ.

•FRITH, Mr. Robert Michael, FCA *1980;* (Tax Fac), Frith & Co, Moorgate House, 7b Station Road West, OXTED, SURREY, RH8 9EE. See also Frith Accountants Limited
FRITH, Mr. Russell Anthony John, BA ACA *1984;* 59 Long Cram, HADDINGTON, EH41 4NS.
FRITH, Mr. Steven, ACA *2010;* Hill Carr Farm, South Darley, MATLOCK, DERBYSHIRE, DE4 2LQ.
FRITZSCHE, Mr. Matthew Tobias, ACA *2009;* 6 Lincoln Road, Caythorpe, GRANTHAM, LINCOLNSHIRE, NG32 3DD.
•FRIXOU, Mr. John, BA FCA *1986;* (Tax Fac), Frixou & Co, 71 Goldhawk Road, Shepherds Bush, LONDON, W12 8EG.
•FRIZE, Mrs. Samantha Margaret Victoria, BA ACA *1996;* Samantha Frize Ltd, Lhag Dhoo, Pinfold Hill, Laxey, ISLE OF MAN, IM4 7HJ.
FROBISHER, Mrs. Stephanie Jutta, BA ACA *1997;* Linkside, 119 Middlewich Road, SANDBACH, CW11 1FH.
FROGGATT, Mr. Andrew James, MA MSci ACA *2007;* 406 Station Road, Dorridge, SOLIHULL, B93 8EU.
•FROGGATT, Mr. Christopher James, BA ACA *1992;* Ford Campbell Corporate Finance LLP, Bass Warehouse, 4 Castle Street, Castlefield, MANCHESTER, M3 4LZ. See also Ford Campbell Corporate Finance Ltd
FROGGATT, Mr. Christopher Mark Davidson, BA ACA *2001;* 125 Hartington Street, CHESTER, CH4 7BP.
•FROGGATT, Mr. James Mostyn, BA ACA *1992;* 1 Paddock Way, HEMEL HEMPSTEAD, HERTFORDSHIRE, HP1 2PE.
FROGLEY, Mr. John Clement, MA FCA *1973;* Frogleys Inc, 250 South End Avenue, Suite 7D, NEW YORK, NY 10280, UNITED STATES.
FROGLEY, Mrs. Nicolette Ann, BA(Hons) ACA *2002;* 38 Lavant Down Road, Lavant, CHICHESTER, WEST SUSSEX, PO18 0DJ.
FROLOVA, Ms. Yulia, ACA *2011;* Kashirskoe highway 90 build.1 app.83, 115551 MOSCOW, RUSSIAN FEDERATION.
•FROMBERG, Mr. Laurence, FCA *1983;* 20 Green Park, Prestwood, GREAT MISSENDEN, HP16 0PZ.
FROME, Mr. Andrew Paul, BSc ACA *1988;* Fawkners, Preston Candover, BASINGSTOKE, HAMPSHIRE, RG25 2DU.
FROOD, Mr. David Graham, BA ACA *1987;* (Tax Fac), with PricewaterhouseCoopers LLP, Hays Galleria, 1 Hays Lane, LONDON, SE1 2RD.
•FROOM, Mr. Michael Christopher, BSc ACA *1993;* KPMG LLP, One Snowhill, Snow Hill Queensway, BIRMINGHAM, B4 6GN. See also KPMG Europe LLP
•FROOM, Mr. Robert Howard, BBS FCA *1974;* (Tax Fac), R H Froom BBS FCA, 93 Mill Green, CONGLETON, CHESHIRE, CW12 1GD.
FROSDICK, Miss. Carolyn, BCom ACA *2006;* 26a Duntshill Road, LONDON, SW18 4QL.
FROSDICK, Miss. Kathryn, BSc ACA *2007;* 78 Old Farm Drive, LEEDS, LS16 5DX.
FROST, Mr. Adam Charles, BSc ACA *2006;* 14 Burman Road, Shirley, SOLIHULL, B90 2BD.
FROST, Mr. Adrian David, BA ACA *1992;* 2 Edwards Road, SUTTON COLDFIELD, B75 5NG.
FROST, Mr. Alan Kenneth, BA ACA *1999;* Fisher and Paykel Appliances Ltd, Maidstone Road, Kingston, MILTON KEYNES, MK10 0BD.
FROST, Mrs. Alison Jane, BA ACA *1985;* 32 Edward Gardens, Woolston, WARRINGTON, WA1 4QT.
FROST, Miss. Anna Hazel, BSc ACA *2009;* Deloitte LLP, 3 Rivergate, Temple Quay, BRISTOL, BS1 6GD.
FROST, Miss. Barbara St John, FCA *1958;* Flat 18 Latchmoor Court, Brookley Road, BROCKENHURST, HAMPSHIRE, SO42 7PY. (Life Member)
FROST, Mr. Brian Frank, FCA *1966;* Windrush, Woodhill Road, Sandon, CHELMSFORD, CM2 7SE.
FROST, Mr. Brian Jeffrey, BSc ACA *1989;* Moon Consulting, 14 Market Place, Winford, BRISTOL, BS40 8AT.
FROST, Mr. Bryan Michael William, FCA *1970;* Windyridge, Second Avenue, Trimley St. Mary, FELIXSTOWE, IP11 0UA.
FROST, Ms. Caroline Mary Frances, BA ACA *1995;* (Tax Fac), with J P Morgan Chase Bank, 125 London Wall, LONDON, EC2Y 5AJ.
FROST, Mr. Darren Michael, BSc ACA *2010;* 15 Eastwood Close, HAYLING ISLAND, PO11 9DY.
FROST, Mr. David Ewen, FCA *1967;* Wallberry, Brackley Avenue, Hartley Wintney, HOOK, RG27 8QU.
FROST, Mr. David Michael, FCA *1969;* Lower Barn, 13 The Bight, South Woodham Ferrers, CHELMSFORD, CM3 5GJ. (Life Member)
FROST, Mr. David William, BA FCA *1986;* Cestria Consultancy, 43 Anthony Street, ORMOND, VIC 3204, AUSTRALIA.
FROST, Ms. Debra Anne, MA ACA *1996;* 52 Hardy Road, LONDON, SW19 1HY.
FROST, Mr. Duncan James, BSc(Hons) ACA *2002;* 66 Mayfield Avenue, LONDON, N12 9JD.
FROST, Mr. Duncan Paul, BSc FCA *1976;* 133 Weeden Drive, Vermont South, MELBOURNE, VIC 3133, AUSTRALIA.
FROST, Mr. Edward, BSc ACA *2009;* with AGL, Prudence House, Ashleigh Way, Langage Business Park, PLYMOUTH, PL7 5JX.
FROST, Miss. Elizabeth, MSc BSc ACA *2010;* 9 Ainsley View, LEEDS, LS14 5QN.
FROST, Mr. Gavin Christopher, BSc FCA *1999;* Coutts, 440 Strand, LONDON, WC2R 0QS.
•FROST, Mr. Geoffrey Alan, BSc(Hons) FCA *2000;* Blue Spire South LLP, Cawley Priory, South Pallant, CHICHESTER, WEST SUSSEX, PO19 1SY.
FROST, Mr. Gerard Bernard John, FCA CTA *1966;* 27 Ditchley Road, Charlbury, CHIPPING NORTON, OX7 3QS. (Life Member)
FROST, Miss. Hannah Alice, BA ACA *2009;* 52 Benson Court, Ingram Crescent East, HOVE, EAST SUSSEX, BN3 5LY.
FROST, Mrs. Helen Ann, BA FCA *1986;* 19 Lyndhurst Drive, HARPENDEN, AL5 5QW.
•FROST, Mrs. Jacqueline Lesley, BSc ACA *1992;* Baker Chapman & Bussey, Magnet House, 3 North Hill, COLCHESTER, CO1 1DZ.
FROST, Mr. James Edward Ernest, BSc ACA *1991;* Universal Leasing Ltd, Cassiobury House, 11-19 Station Road, WATFORD, WD17 1AP.
FROST, Mr. James Metford, BSc ACA *1996;* Rose Cottage High Street, Longworth, ABINGDON, OX13 5DU.
•FROST, Mrs. Jennifer Doris, BSc ACA *1992;* J D Frost Accountants, 7 Links View, CIRENCESTER, GLOUCESTERSHIRE, GL7 2NF.
FROST, Miss. Joanna, BSc ACA *1984;* Regent Exhibitions Ltd, The Agora, First Floor, Ellen Street, HOVE, EAST SUSSEX BN3 3LN.
FROST, Mr. Jonathan Mark, BA ACA *1994;* Burg. van Tuyllkade 113 bis, 3553 AE UTRECHT, NETHERLANDS.
•FROST, Mr. Jonathan Park, BA ACA *1986;* FirstFD, Greengables, Peterston-super-Ely, CARDIFF, CF5 6LH.
•FROST, Mr. Julian Charles Hazelwood, BA FCA *1996;* BDO LLP, Kings Wharf, 20-30 Kings Road, READING, RG1 3EX. See also BDO Stoy Hayward LLP
FROST, Miss. Katrina, BSc ACA *2001;* 94 Villiers Avenue, SURBITON, SURREY, KT5 8BH.
FROST, Mr. Kenneth Arthur, MA FCA *1989;* 60 Albion Hill, BRIGHTON, BN2 9NW.
FROST, Miss. Lianne, BA FCA *1992;* Friends Provident, 100 Wood Street, LONDON, EC2V 7AN.
FROST, Mrs. Manon, BA(Hons) ACA *2002;* Society of Chemical Industry, 14-15 Belgrave Square, LONDON, SW1X 8PS.
FROST, Miss. Marguerite Jane, BA ACA *1988;* VCCP Ltd, Greencoat House, Francis Street, LONDON, SW1P 1DH.
FROST, Mr. Martin, BA ACA *1990;* Featherbed Lane, ST JOHN, BARBADOS.
•FROST, Mr. Maurice Nigel, FCA *1981;* Richard Place Dobson Services Limited, Ground Floor, 1-7 Station Road, CRAWLEY, WEST SUSSEX, RH10 1HT. See also Richard Place Dobson LLP
FROST, Mr. Michael Fenton, FCA *1984;* 32 Edward Gardens, Woolston, WARRINGTON, WA1 4QT.
FROST, Mr. Michael Robert, BSc(Hons) ACA *2001;* 19 Longstomps Avenue, CHELMSFORD, CM2 9BY.
FROST, Mr. Niall Graham Hyde, BSc(Hons) ACA *2010;* 54 Bachelor Gardens, HARROGATE, NORTH YORKSHIRE, HG1 3EE.
FROST, Mr. Nicholas Aaron, MA(Cantab) ACA *2010;* 50 Lower Dagnall Street, ST. ALBANS, HERTFORDSHIRE, AL3 4QF.
•FROST, Mr. Nicholas Iain, BSc ACA *1991;* Lambert Roper & Horsfield Limited, The Old Woolcombers Mill, 12-14 Union Street South, HALIFAX, WEST YORKSHIRE, HX1 2LE.
FROST, Mr. Nicholas Mark, BA ACA *1986;* Quest Management Services Ltd, Church Street, PO Box HM 2062, HAMILTON HMHX, BERMUDA.
•FROST, Mr. Nicholas Miles, BA ACA *1996;* KPMG LLP, 15 Canada Square, LONDON, E14 5GL. See also KPMG Europe LLP
•FROST, Mr. Nicholas William, BSc ACA *1981;* AIMS - Nick Frost, 1 The Maples, Great Alne, ALCESTER, WARWICKSHIRE, B49 6HL.
FROST, Miss. Nicola Rose, BA ACA *2009;* 33 Ribbledale Road, Mossley Hill, LIVERPOOL, L18 5HD.
FROST, Mr. Nigel David, FCA CTA *1970;* Bernham House, Bramshaw, LYNDHURST, HAMPSHIRE, SO43 7JN.
FROST, Mr. Paul James, BA ACA *2004;* 6 Mandeville Close, GUILDFORD, SURREY, GU2 9YA.
•FROST, Mr. Peter Harley, BEng ACA *1989;* 38 Eskdale Gardens, PURLEY, CR8 1EZ.
FROST, Mr. Peter Harry, FCA *1969;* 1575 WYNDHAM DRIVE, YORK, PA 17403, UNITED STATES.
FROST, Mr. Peter James, BSc ACA *2010;* 20 Chiltern Drive, Hale, ALTRINCHAM, CHESHIRE, WA15 9PN.
FROST, Mr. Peter John, BA FCA *1966;* 129 Rosendale Road, LONDON, SE21 8HE.
•FROST, Mr. Peter Richard James, BA ACA *1991;* Hazlewoods LLP, Windsor House, Barnett Way, Barnwood, GLOUCESTER, GL4 3RT.
FROST, Mr. Philip Donald, BA ACA *1984;* 21 Tealby Cl, Gilmorton, LUTTERWORTH, LE17 5PT.
FROST, Mrs. Rebecca Eve, ACA *2008;* Lovewell Blake, 102 Prince of Wales Road, NORWICH, NR1 1NY.
•FROST, Mr. Richard Anthony, MA FCA *1984;* MEMBER OF COUNCIL, Hawsons, Pegasus House, 463a Glossop Road, SHEFFIELD, S10 2QD.
FROST, Mr. Richard James, MMath ACA *2005;* with Grant Thornton UK LLP, Hartwell House, 55-61 Victoria Street, BRISTOL, BS1 6FT.
FROST, Mr. Robert James, ACA *2007;* 42 Norfolk Road, ROMFORD, RM7 9DL.
•FROST, Mr. Robert Martyn, FCA MIFT ASTP *1975;* arca group Ltd, The Old Chapel, Union Way, WITNEY, OXFORDSHIRE, OX28 6HD. See also Arca Group
FROST, Mr. Robin Charles, BSc ACA *1993;* 29047 Snapper Point, TEGA CAY, SC 29708, UNITED STATES.
FROST, Ms. Sandra Mary, BSc(Econ) ACA *2001;* 98 Sugden Road, LONDON, SW11 5EE.
FROST, Mrs. Sharon Lesley Anne, BSc ACA *1996;* 6 Cherry Tree Walk, Amotherby, MALTON, NORTH YORKSHIRE, YO17 6TR.
FROST, Mr. Simon David Lloyd, BEng FCA *1992;* 94 Wise Lane, LONDON, NW7 2RD.
FROST, Mr. Simon Henry, BA(Hons) ACA *2003;* 1 Twitchell Road, GREAT MISSENDEN, BUCKINGHAMSHIRE, HP16 0BQ.
•FROST, Mr. Stephen, BA FCA *1990;* Frosts C. A. Limited, 51 Bernard Street, EDINBURGH, EH6 6SL.
FROST, Mr. Stephen Anthony, BA ACA *1993;* Bacardi Limited, PO Box HM720, HAMILTON HMCX, BERMUDA.
FROST, Mr. Stephen John, ACA *1993;* 12 The Beeches, West Park, Silsoe, BEDFORD, BEDFORDSHIRE, MK45 4FD.
•FROST, Mr. Stephen John, ACA *1984;* Frost & Company (CA) Limited, Redcotts House, 1 Redcotts Lane, WIMBORNE, DORSET, BH21 1JX.
•FROST, Mr. Steven Paul, ACA *2008;* Fisher Phillips, Summit House, 170 Finchley Road, LONDON, NW3 6BP. See also Fisher Phillips 2010 Ltd
FROST, Mrs. Susan Elizabeth, MA ACA *1992;* 3 Cottage Gardens, Rednal, BIRMINGHAM, B45 9QZ.
•FROST, Mr. Thomas Anthony, FCA *1979;* 27 Oaklands Park, Grasscroft, OLDHAM, OL4 4JY.
FROST, Mr. William, FCA *1967;* 13 Petercroft Lane, Dunnington, YORK, YO19 5NQ.
FROST, Mr. William John, BSc FCA *1982;* Quill House, Main Street, Aberlady, LONGNIDDRY, EH32 0RB.
•FROSTICK, Mr. Richard John, BSc FCA *1988;* with Ernst & Young LLP, PO Box 3, Lowgate House, Lowgate, HULL, HU1 1JJ.
•FROSTWICK, Mr. Christopher James Newton, MA ACA *1986;* Grant Thornton UK LLP, Regent House, 80 Regent Road, LEICESTER, LE1 7NH. See also Grant Thornton LLP
•FROUD, Mr. Brian Keith, BSc FCA *1986;* Bew & Co Limited, 130 High Street, MARLBOROUGH, WILTSHIRE, SN8 1LZ.
•FROUD, Mr. Nicholas Edward, BA FCA *1987;* (Tax Fac), Nick Froud, 16 Shorewood Close, Warsash, SOUTHAMPTON, SO31 9LB.
FROW, Mrs. Alexandra Chloe Jane, BA(Hons) ACA *2003;* with PKF (UK) LLP, Pannell House, 159 Charles Street, LEICESTER, LE1 1LD.
FROW, Mr. Nigel, FCA *1977;* 4 Home Paddock, Waltham, GRIMSBY, SOUTH HUMBERSIDE, DN37 0JH.
FROW, Mr. Paul, BSc ACA *2006;* 47 Barons Close, Kirby Muxloe, LEICESTER, LE9 2BW.
•ⒹFROWDE, Mr. Peter Roderick, FCA *1971;* McCabe Ford Williams, Bank Chambers, 1 Central Ave., SITTINGBOURNE, ME10 4AE.
FROY, Mr. Christopher Neil, BSc ACA *1983;* N Froy & Sons Ltd Unit 200, Focal Point Fleming Way, CRAWLEY, WEST SUSSEX, RH10 9DF.
FRUDD, Miss. Eloise, ACA *2009;* 38 Lea Side Gardens, HUDDERSFIELD, HD3 4XP.
•FRUMIN, Mr. David Hilbre, FCA *1965;* (Tax Fac), DFA (Accountancy) Ltd, 48 Queen Street, EXETER, EX4 3SR.
FRUMKIN, Mr. Simon Leslie Elliott, BA ACA *1995;* T-Mobile (UK) Ltd Unit 1, Mosquito Way, HATFIELD, HERTFORDSHIRE, AL10 9BW.
FRY, Mr. Alec Walter, FCA *1960;* 69 Eastgate Street, WINCHESTER, HAMPSHIRE, SO23 8DZ. (Life Member)
•FRY, Mr. Anthony Edward, BA FCA *1978;* KPMG LLP, 15 Canada Square, LONDON, E14 5GL.
FRY, Mr. Anthony Edward, FCA *1977;* Rasa Ria 2a Redwood Grove Chilworth, GUILDFORD, SURREY, GU4 8NU.
•FRY, Mr. Anthony John, FCA *1973;* Geoffrey Cole & Co Ltd, 4 Reading Road, Pangbourne, READING, RG8 7LY. See also Pryor, Begent, Fry & Co.
FRY, Mr. Benjamin, BSc ARCS ACA *2011;* 144b Putney Bridge Road, LONDON, SW15 2NQ.
FRY, Mr. Carl Duncan, BSc FCA *1976;* Journey Group Plc, Unit 1-3, The Encompass Centre, International Avenue, Heston, HOUNSLOW TW5 9NJ.
FRY, Miss. Carol Ann, FCA *1996;* The Cottage Church Lane Adderbury, BANBURY, OXFORDSHIRE, OX17 3LR.
FRY, Mrs. Caroline Jane, BSc ACA *2010;* 10 Pengilly Road, FARNHAM, GU9 7XQ.
FRY, Mr. Charles Anthony, BA ACA *1999;* 119 Fairfax Road, TEDDINGTON, MIDDLESEX, TW11 9BU.
•FRY, Mr. Christopher Basil, FCA *1974;* Christopher B. Fry & Co, Claire House, Bridge Street, LEATHERHEAD, SURREY, KT22 8BZ.
FRY, Mr. Christopher James, BA ACA *1982;* 5 Woodlands Road, SURBITON, KT6 6PR.
•FRY, Mr. Christopher Ramon, BA FCA *1989;* (Tax Fac), KPMG LLP, St. James's Square, MANCHESTER, M2 6DS. See also KPMG Europe LLP
FRY, Mr. Clifford Ronald Charles, FCA *1973;* St John's House, 23 St John's Square, Wilton, SALISBURY, SP2 0DW.
FRY, Mr. David Michael, BSc ACA *1985;* P A Consulting Group, 123 Buckingham Palace Road, LONDON, SW1W 9SR.
•FRY, Miss. Elizabeth Catherine, BA ACA *1991;* White Corfield & Fry Limited, 420 Brighton Road, SOUTH CROYDON, SURREY, CR2 6AN.
•FRY, Mrs. Fiona Christina, BSc ACA *1985;* KPMG LLP, 15 Canada Square, LONDON, E14 5GL. See also KPMG Europe LLP
FRY, Mr. Gregory John, ACA *1983;* St George plc, St George House, 76 Crown Road, TWICKENHAM, TW1 3EU.
FRY, Mrs. Helen Jane, BSc ACA *1990;* Debenhams Plc Bedford House, Park Street, TAUNTON, SOMERSET, TA1 4DB.
FRY, Mr. Jeremy Colin, BA ACA *1985;* 49 Park Grove, Henleaze, BRISTOL, BS9 4LG.
FRY, Mr. John, FCA *1961;* 13 Foxbury Close, LUTON, LU2 7BQ. (Life Member)
•FRY, Mr. John Carmichael, FCA *1967;* Condy Mathias, Suite 26, 3 Atlas House, West Devon Business Park, TAVISTOCK, PL19 9DP.
FRY, Mrs. Julia Susan, BA ACA *1993;* Bellsfield, Oakley Close, EAST GRINSTEAD, WEST SUSSEX, RH19 3UG.
FRY, Mr. Kevin, BA ACA *1998;* 5 Great Severals, Kintbury, HUNGERFORD, BERKSHIRE, RG17 9SN.
FRY, Mr. Kevin William, ACA *1991;* 88 Northfield Road, RINGWOOD, HAMPSHIRE, BH24 1ST.
FRY, Mrs. Lisa Jayne, BSc ACA *2005;* 2 Landywood Lane, Cheslyn Hay, WALSALL, WS6 7AH.
•FRY, Mr. Malcolm George, FCA *1970;* Malcolm G. Fry, 12 Oak Grove, HERTFORD, SG13 8AT.
FRY, Miss. Margaret Ann, FCA *1963;* 9 Layton Park Croft, Rawdon, LEEDS, LS19 6PN.
FRY, Miss. Melanie Jacqueline, BCom ACA *2004;* Pricewaterhousecoopers, 1 Embankment Place, LONDON, WC2N 6RH.
FRY, Mrs. Melody Jane, ACA *1990;* West Lodge, Bordean Manor, Langrish, PETERSFIELD, GU32 1EP.
FRY, Mr. Nicholas Rodney Lowther, MA FCA *1971;* Flat 7, Hurlingham Court, Ranelagh Gardens, LONDON, SW6 3SH.
•FRY, Mr. Nigel Paul, BSc FCA *1989;* Milsted Langdon LLP, Winchester House, Deane Gate Avenue, TAUNTON, SOMERSET, TA1 2UH.

•**FRY, Mr. Peter Graham, FCA** *1974;* (Tax Fac), P.G. Fry & Co, Hatherley House, Bisley Green, Bisley, WOKING, SURREY GU24 9EW.
FRY, Mr. Richard Alan, MA FCA *1977;* Pondsmead House, Corscombe Road, Halstock, YEOVIL, BA22 9RY.
FRY, Mr. Roger William, FCA *1969;* Dell House, Epping New Road, BUCKHURST HILL, ESSEX, IG9 5UA. (Life Member)
FRY, Mr. Simon David, FCA *1982;* Flexbury End, Poughill Road, BUDE, CORNWALL, EX23 8NZ.
•**FRY, Mr. Stephen Alan, FCA** *1983;* Monahans, 3 Landmark House, Wirrall Park Road, GLASTONBURY, SOMERSET, BA6 9FR.
FRY, Mr. Stephen John, FCA *1972;* 23 Beechwood Park, South Woodford, LONDON, E18 2EH. (Life Member)
FRY, Mrs. Wendy Elizabeth, BSc ACA *1984;* 24 Evesham Close, REIGATE, RH2 9DN.
FRY, Mrs. Wendy Kristina, BA ACA *1992;* I N G Direct, 410 Thames Valley Park Drive, READING, RG6 1RH.
FRY, Mr. William Andrew, LLB FCA *1973;* 3726 Ella Lee Lane, HOUSTON, TX 77027, UNITED STATES.
FRY, Mr. Wilton George, BA ACA *2000;* Rustlings, 1 Burntwood Road, SEVENOAKS, TN13 1PS.
FRYATT, Mrs. Aoife Catherine, BSc(Hons) ACA *2003;* Kaplan Financial Thames Tower, Station Hill, READING, RG1 1LX.
FRYATT, Mr. David Richard, MA FCA FCIBS *1977;* 24 Spital Road, WIRRAL, CH63 9JE.
FRYATT, Mr. Ewan Michael, BSc(Hons) ACA CTA *2006;* 48 Meadvale Road, LONDON, W5 1NR.
FRYE, Mr. Roger Eric, FCA *1975;* Oakwood House, Tilford Road, HINDHEAD, SURREY, GU26 6RB.
FRYER, Mr. Alastair Ian, BA FCA *1977;* 3 Hayes Barton, Pyrford, WOKING, GU22 8NH.
FRYER, Miss. Andrea, BSc ACA *1994;* 85 Queens Road, RICHMOND, SURREY, TW10 6HJ.
FRYER, Mr. Anthony Robert, BSc ACA *1999;* 13 Beresford Road, ST. ALBANS, HERTFORDSHIRE, AL1 5NW.
FRYER, Mrs. Carolyn Jane, BSc ACA *1987;* Oakwood, 8 Bracken Close, Farnham Common, SLOUGH, SL2 3JP.
FRYER, Miss. Catherine Anne, BA ACA *2005;* 2738 N Southport #3W, CHICAGO, IL 60614, UNITED STATES.
FRYER, Mr. Donald William, FCA *1953;* 3 Malton Drive, Hazel Grove, STOCKPORT, CHESHIRE, SK7 6HQ. (Life Member)
FRYER, Mr. John Edward, FCA *1971;* 7 Norwich Close, LICHFIELD, STAFFORDSHIRE, WS13 7SJ.
FRYER, Mr. Jonathan Roger Anson, MMath ACA *2007;* Mazars (Thailand) Ltd., 12th Floor Empire Tower, 195 South Sathorn Road, BANGKOK 10120, THAILAND.
•**FRYER, Mr. Kenneth Wade, BA FCA** *1983;* (Tax Fac), Ken Fryer, 8 Coronation Road, BATH, BA1 3BH.
FRYER, Mrs. Lisa Marie, BSc ACA *1991;* Southwest Audit Partnership, CO/Somerset County Council, County Hall, TAUNTON, SOMERSET, TA1 4DY.
FRYER, Mr. Mark Rupert Maxwell, BA ACA *1991;* Burleigh, Old Church Road, Colwall, MALVERN, WORCESTERSHIRE, WR13 6EZ.
FRYER, Mr. Nicholas John, BA ACA *2005;* 104 Manor Park Road, YATELEY, GU46 6JH.
•**FRYER, Mr. Noel, FCA** *1966;* Guy Walmsley & Co, 3 Grove Road, WREXHAM, LL11 1DY.
FRYER, Mr. Paul Ian, BSc ACA *1983;* 7 Greenway Gardens, Shirley, CROYDON, CR0 8QJ.
FRYER, Mr. Philip Anthony Raymond, BA ACA *1979;* Flat 5, 39 Deptford High Street, LONDON, SE8 4AD.
FRYER, Mr. Robert Arthur, BA ACA *1980;* Financial Reporting Review Panel, 5th Floor, Aldwych House, 71-91 Aldwych, LONDON, WC2B 4HN.
•**FRYER, Mr. Stephen Mark, ACA** *1993;* (Tax Fac), Hedley Dunk Limited, Trinity House, 3 Bullace Lane, DARTFORD, DA1 1BB.
FRYER, Mrs. Tessa Helen, BA ACA *1994;* The Chambers, 53 Guildhall Street, PRESTON, PR1 3NU.
•**FRYER, Miss. Victoria, FCA FMAAT** *2000;* (Member of Council 2003 - 2005), Naylor Wintersgill Ltd, Carlton House, Grammar School Street, BRADFORD, WEST YORKSHIRE, BD1 4NS.
FRYERS, Mrs. Catherine Sarah, BA ACA *1997;* West Ridge, Shoulton, Hallow, WORCESTER, WR2 6PX.
•**FRYERS, Mr. Kevin William, FCA** *1971;* Fryers Bell & Co, 27 Athol Street, Douglas, ISLE OF MAN, IM1 1LB.
FRYMANN, Mr. Jonathan Paul, MA ACA *1999;* 115 Hillview Avenue, REDWOOD CITY, CA 94062, UNITED STATES.
FRYMANN, Mr. Peter David, BA FCA *1970;* The Old Chapel, 116 Church Road, Quarndon, DERBY, DE22 5JA.
FRYS, Mr. Michal, ACA *2008;* Hoza 58/60/39, 00-682 WARSAW, POLAND.
FTOUH, Miss. Thouraya, BSc ACA *2007;* 121 Pomeroy Street, LONDON, SE14 5BT.
FU, Mr. Chi Kwong Joseph, ACA *2008;* JFU CPA, Suite 2808, 28F Exchange Tower, 33 Wang Chiu Road, KOWLOON BAY, KOWLOON HONG KONG SAR.
FU, Mr. Hebin, ACA *2011;* Room 1502, Building 20, JiHua 7 Road, YiCui MeiGui Yuan, FOSHAN 528200, CHINA.
FU, Mr. Ho Kee, MSc BA ACA *2002;* PricewaterhouseCoopers, 33/F Cheung Kong Center, 2 Queen's Road Central, CENTRAL, HONG KONG SAR.
FU, Mr. Kwong Chi, ACA *2008;* 30B Ko Fung Court, 5 Fook Yum Road, NORTH POINT, HONG KONG SAR.
FU, Mrs. Shau-Ying, BSc ACA *1981;* 1422 E Charleston Avenue, PHOENIX, AZ 85022, UNITED STATES.
FU, Ms. Tao, ACA *2009;* 50 Apollo Building, 1 Newton Place, LONDON, E14 3TS.
FUCHS, Dr. Markus, ACA *2008;* K P M G Salisbury Square House, 8 Salisbury Square, LONDON, EC4Y 8BB.
FUCHS-WATSON, Mrs. Marie-Josee Elisabeth, ACA MBA *1992;* 145 rue de Macherin, 77630 ARBONNE-LA-FORET, FRANCE.
FUDGE, Mr. Anthony Michael, BA ACIB ACA *1984;* Villa 216U, Eid Villas, PO Box 92851, Near Exit – 9, Ghornata, Riyadh 11663 Kingdom of Saudi Arabia. RIYADH SAUDI ARABIA.
FUDGE, Mrs. Diana Marion, FCA *1974;* (Tax Fac), 34 Marks Tey Road, Stubbington, FAREHAM, PO14 3LE.
FUDGE, Mr. Nicholas John, BSc FCA *1976;* with Roger Hopkins, 18 Princes Street, NORWICH, NR3 1AE.
•**FUGE, Mr. Jeffrey Peter, BSc ACA** *2003;* (Tax Fac), Foxmain Associates Limited, 60 Stoke Lane, Westbury-on-Trym, BRISTOL, BS9 3SW.
FUGGLE, Miss. Charlotte Amelia, ACA *2007;* 5 Cromwell Place, LONDON, SW14 7HA.
FUGGLE, Mr. James, BA(Hons) ACA *2009;* Top Floor Flat, 57 Moreton Street, LONDON, SW1V 2NY.
FUGGLE, Mr. Nicholas Andrew, BA(Hons) ACA *2000;* Unit 1, 147 Gilles Street, ADELAIDE, SA 5000, AUSTRALIA.
FUKUMURA, Mr. Toshio, ACA *2000;* 1-3-2-805 Meguro, Meguro-ku, TOKYO, 153-0063 JAPAN.
FUKUMURO, Mr. Eiji, BA ACA *1994;* No. 3-9-2, Kitamachi, Kichijoji, Musashino, TOKYO, 1800001 JAPAN.
FULBROOK, Mr. Andrew, BA FCA *1987;* 79 Southgate Road, Island Bay, WELLINGTON 6002, NEW ZEALAND.
FULCHER, Mr. Alex William Robert, BSc(Hons) ACA *2009;* 12 Sandy Mead, MAIDENHEAD, SL6 2YS.
FULCHER, Mr. Daniel, ACA *2011;* 10 Herbs End, FARNBOROUGH, GU14 9YD.
FULCHER, Mr. Derick John, FCA *1970;* Ker Low, Surrey Gardens, Effingham Junction, LEATHERHEAD, KT24 5HF.
FULCHER, Mr. Ian Jack, ACA *1985;* Cambridge Computer Systems Rosemary House, Lanwades Business Park Kennett, NEWMARKET, SUFFOLK, CB8 7PN.
•**FULENA, Mr. Rewtiraman, ACA** *1980;* (Tax Fac), R Fulena And Co, 41 Britten Close, LONDON, NW11 7HQ.
FULFORD, Mr. Garrath David, BSc ACA *1993;* Royal Bank of Scotland, 135 Bishopsgate, LONDON, EC2M 3UR.
•**FULFORD, Mr. Graham Ronald, FCA** *1970;* (Tax Fac), 3 Mill Street, WARWICK, CV34 4HB.
FULFORD, Mrs. Jane Caroline Anne, BEng ACA *1989;* Novartis Pharma AG, Forum 2-3.01.30, CH4002 BASEL, SWITZERLAND.
FULFORD, Miss. Kelly, BA ACA *2009;* 33 Mary Street, Bovey Tracey, NEWTON ABBOT, DEVON, TQ13 9HQ.
FULFORD, Mrs. Linda Mary, BSc FCA *1974;* Carpenters Cottage, Church Street, Plumstead, NORWICH, NR11 7LG.
FULFORD, Mr. Michael John, FCA *1959;* Ruth Cottage, Main Street, East Langton, MARKET HARBOROUGH, LE16 7TW. (Life Member)
FULFORD, Mr. Robert Ian, BSc ACA *2004;* 4 Sulleys Hill, Lower Raydon, IPSWICH, IP7 5QQ.
FULFORD-BROWN, Mr. Michael David, LLB FCA *1974;* Chaff Barn, Eartham, CHICHESTER, WEST SUSSEX, PO18 0LP.
FULGONI, Mr. John Dominic Marc, BA FCA *1981;* 2472 West C Ave., KALAMAZOO, MI 49009, UNITED STATES.
FULHAM, Mr. James Christopher, BA ACA *1983;* 68 Newton Street, DARWEN, LANCASHIRE, BB3 0HG.
FULKER, Mrs. Katherine Louise, BA ACA *1997;* Fidelity Investments Ltd Beech Gate, Millfield Lane Lower Kingswood, TADWORTH, KT20 6RP.
FULKER, Mr. Timothy David, BSc FCA *1993;* St Hampden Limited, 57 London Road, HIGH WYCOMBE, HP11 1BS.
FULLARD, Mr. Andrew George, BA ACA CTA *1985;* 4 Oughtrington View, LYMM, WA13 9HD.
•**FULLARD, Mr. Colin Dennis, FCA** *1973;* Fullard Duffill, 106 Birmingham Road, BROMSGROVE, B61 0DF.
•**FULLARD, Mr. Stephen William, ACA** *1983;* (Tax Fac), Kingscott Dix (Cheltenham) Limited, Malvern View Business Park, Stella Way, Bishops Cleeve, CHELTENHAM, GLOUCESTERSHIRE GL52 7DQ.
FULLARTON, Mr. James Boyd, FCA *1970;* 25 West Downs Close, FAREHAM, PO16 7HW.
FULLARTON, Mr. Jonathan, BSc(Hons) ACA *2011;* Spain Brothers & Co, 87 St. Dunstans Street, CANTERBURY, KENT, CT2 8AE.
FULLELOVE, Mr. Glyn William, MA ACA *1990;* Informa Group Plc Informa House, 30-32 Mortimer Street, LONDON, W1W 7RE.
FULLER, Mr. Aidan Charles, BA ACA *1986;* 9 Barkworth Way, West Chiltington, PULBOROUGH, RH20 2PQ.
FULLER, Mr. Albert Joseph, BSc FCA *1977;* Orchard House, 9 Lanes End, Heath and Reach, LEIGHTON BUZZARD, LU7 0AE.
FULLER, Mr. Alexander Paul, BA(Hons) ACA *2002;* 2 Lydiard Close, AYLESBURY, BUCKINGHAMSHIRE, HP21 9XU.
FULLER, Mrs. Alison Claire, BSc ACA *1994;* 15 Pembroke Lane, Milton, ABINGDON, OX14 4EA.
FULLER, Mr. Andrew Jonathan, BA ACA *1989;* 28 Woodlands Park, Whalley, CLITHEROE, LANCASHIRE, BB7 9UG.
•**FULLER, Mr. Andrew Timothy, BA ACA** *1989;* Hillside, Bayford Hill, WINCANTON, BA9 9LR.
FULLER, Mr. Brian Harold, FCA *1954;* White House, Church Street, Teston, MAIDSTONE, ME18 5AG. (Life Member)
FULLER, Mr. Christopher Charles, FCA *1975;* The Barn, Grange Drive, WOKING, GU21 4BU.
FULLER, Mr. David Graham Maitland, FCA *1966;* Alanhurst, 61 Marsham Way, GERRARDS CROSS, BUCKINGHAMSHIRE, SL9 8AW. (Life Member)
FULLER, Mr. David Ronald, FCA *1971;* Gral. Ion Dragalina 23, Apt. 9, 050565 BUCHAREST, ROMANIA.
•**FULLER, Mr. Denis John Sanderson, FCA** *1972;* Inglenook, 11b Kings Ride, CAMBERLEY, SURREY, GU15 4HU.
FULLER, Mr. Gordon Andrew, BSc ACA *1993;* 1 Charlton Close, Windsor Meadows, Cippenham, SLOUGH, SL1 9HD.
FULLER, Miss. Jacqueline Amanda, BSc ACA *1993;* First Floor Flat, 3 Clyde Park, BRISTOL, BS6 6RR.
•**FULLER, Mrs. Janice, FCA** *1980;* Fullers, The Glebe, Shipley Hills Road, Meopham, GRAVESEND, DA13 0AD.
FULLER, Miss. Jennifer Caroline, LLB(Hons) ACA *2010;* 2 Warriner Gardens, LONDON, SW11 4EB.
FULLER, Miss. Joanna, ACA *2010;* 10 Edwin Close, BEXLEYHEATH, DA7 5QH.
FULLER, Mr. John Graham, FCA *1973;* 2 Swanley Lane, Ravensmoor, NANTWICH, CHESHIRE, CW5 8PX.
•**FULLER, Mr. John Stewart, FCA** *1980;* Fuller Accountants Limited, The Counting House, Church Farm Business Park, Corston, BATH, BA2 9AP.
FULLER, Mr. Jonathan Tom Telford, BSc ACA *1987;* Elm Cottage, Bowers Lane, Aston, STONE, ST15 0BN.
•**FULLER, Mr. Keith, BSc FCA** *1980;* Fullers, The Glebe, Shipley Hills Road, Meopham, GRAVESEND, DA13 0AD.
FULLER, Mrs. Kirsty Marie, ACA *2008;* 25 Stevensons Road, Longstanton, CAMBRIDGE, CB24 3GY.
FULLER, Mr. Leslie Ronald, FCA *1982;* Scruttons Farm, 37 Coldharbour Road, Northfleet, GRAVESEND, DA11 8AF.
FULLER, Miss. Lucille, BSc ACA *1984;* with Smith & Nephew plc, 15 Adam Street, LONDON, WC2N 6LA.
FULLER, Mr. Mark Anthony, BA ACA *1994;* 2 The Limes, South Milford, LEEDS, LS25 5NH.
FULLER, Mr. Mark Stephen Charles, BSc ACA *1991;* 14 Brookfield House, Wilmslow Road, CHEADLE, CHESHIRE, SK8 1HJ.
FULLER, Mr. Matthew Peter, LLB(Hons) ACA *2010;* Flat 5 Beaufort Place, 2 Evans Close, MANCHESTER, M20 2SQ.
FULLER, Mr. Michael Stewart, BA ACA *1995;* 4 Nutham Lane, Southwater, HORSHAM, WEST SUSSEX, RH13 9GG.
•**FULLER, Mr. Neil Stuart, FCA** *1984;* 178 Hastings Parade, NORTH BONDI, NSW 2026, AUSTRALIA.
FULLER, Mr. Patrick, ACA DChA *2008;* 40 Flemming Avenue, Ruislip, HILLINGDON, MIDDLESEX, HA4 9LF.
FULLER, Mr. Peter Denis, FCA *1952;* 2 Coopers Mews, Leyton Road, HARPENDEN, AL5 2JL. (Life Member)
FULLER, Mr. Richard Mark, BEng ACA FPC *2002;* The Hawthorns, 4 Manor Farm Close, Litchborough, TOWCESTER, NORTHAMPTONSHIRE, NN12 8JW.
FULLER, Mr. Robert, BA(Hons) ACA *2001;* 25 Hatherley Road, SIDCUP, KENT, DA14 4AR.
FULLER, Mrs. Sally Santos, BA(Hons) ACA CTA *2003;* 17 Wood Lane, Appleton, WARRINGTON, WA4 3DB.
FULLER, Mr. Simon James, BSc ACA *2005;* Flat 3, Old Silver Works, 54A Spencer Street, BIRMINGHAM, B18 6JT.
FULLER, Mr. Simon Jeremy Ian, BA(Hons) ACA *2001;* Bay Tree House, 10 Daltons Shaw, Orsett, GRAYS, ESSEX, RM16 3GY.
FULLER, Mr. Stewart Alfred, FCA *1952;* Dunain, Grasmere, AMBLESIDE, LA22 9RL. (Life Member)
FULLER, Mr. William George Henry, FCA *1968;* E & R Fuller Ltd, Tewes Farm, Little Sampford, SAFFRON WALDEN, ESSEX, CB10 2QQ.
FULLERTON, Mrs. Adrienne Hilary, BSc ACA *1986;* Barmer Strasse 3, 40545 DUSSELDORF, GERMANY.
FULLERTON, Mr. Andrew, MA ACA *1987;* 7 Mortlake Road, RICHMOND, TW9 3JE.
FULLERTON, Mr. Andrew, BA ACA *1986;* Alt Heerdt 59, 40549 DUSSELDORF, GERMANY.
FULLERTON, Miss. Ann Elizabeth, BA FCA *1983;* 20 Ledsham Park Drive, Little Sutton, WIRRAL, MERSEYSIDE, CH66 4XZ.
FULLERTON, Mr. Ian George, ACA *1986;* 26 Macdonald Street, PADDINGTON, NSW 2021, AUSTRALIA.
•**FULLERTON, Mr. John Richard, MSc FCA** *1972;* Fullertons, Westbourne House, 60 Bagley Lane, Farsley, PUDSEY, WEST YORKSHIRE LS28 5LY.
•**FULLERTON, Mr. Kevin, FCA** *1969;* Pinner Darlington, HSBC Bank Chambers, Listley St., BRIDGNORTH, WV16 4AW.
FULLERTON-ROME, Mrs. Elizabeth, MA ACA *1999;* 143 Mallinson Road, LONDON, SW11 1BH.
FULLMAN, Mr. Keith Charles, BA ACA *1988;* 105 Portway, WELLS, BA5 2BR.
FULLWOOD, Miss. Louise Pamela, MA BA(Hons) ACA *2006;* with BDO LLP, 125 Colmore Row, BIRMINGHAM, B3 3SD.
•**FULLWOOD, Mr. Malcolm, FCA** *1972;* Alphaline Consultants Ltd, 8 Histons Drive, Codsall, WOLVERHAMPTON, WV8 2ET.
FULLWOOD, Mr. Timothy Michael James, ACA *1982;* The Law Debenture Corporation Plc, 100 Wood Street, LONDON, EC2V 7EX.
FULTON, Mr. Anthony John, FCA *1954;* Flat 13 Cotswold Mill, Lewis Lane, CIRENCESTER, GL7 1EL. (Life Member)
FULTON, Mr. Barry Alan, BSc ACA *2003;* 27 Upper Cairns Terrace, RED HILL, QLD 4059, AUSTRALIA.
FULTON, Miss. Chantelle Marie, ACA *2011;* La Quatrieme, La Rue Des Pres, St. Ouen, JERSEY, JE3 2FG.
FULTON, Mr. Ian Robert Graham, ACA *1988;* 65 Fordbridge Road, ASHFORD, MIDDLESEX, TW15 2SS.
FULTON, Mrs. Joanna Kate, BA ACA *1997;* 309 Lonsdale Road, Barnes, LONDON, SW13 9PY.
FULTON, Mr. John Ballantyne, BA FCA *1978;* 25 The Orchards, Eaton Bray, DUNS, LU6 2DD.
FULTON, Mr. John Robert, BA ACA *2010;* The Rigs, Mount Auldyn, RAMSEY, IM8 3PJ.
•**FULTON, Mr. Keith Stewart, BA ACA** *1997;* (Tax Fac), with Chapman Davis LLP, 2 Chapel Court, LONDON, SE1 1HH.
FULTON, Miss. Laura, BA ACA *2001;* 61 Haldon Road, LONDON, SW18 1QF.
FULTON, Mr. Martin, BSc(Hons) ACA *2010;* 23 Queensway, MANCHESTER, M19 1QP.
FULTON, Mr. Nigel James, BSc FCA *1993;* 20 Platts Lane, LONDON, NW3 7NS.
FULTON, Mr. Peter John, BA ACA *2005;* St. Teresa, Cherry Orchard Close, ORPINGTON, BR5 4BN.
FULTON, Mr. Robert James, FCA *1966;* The Cottage, Bridge Hill, Bridge, CANTERBURY, KENT, CT4 5AX.
FULTON, Mrs. Veronica, FCA *1972;* The Law Debenture Pension Trust Corporation plc, Fifth Floor, 100 Wood Street, LONDON, EC2V 7EX.
FULTON, Mr. William David, JP DL FCA *1968;* The White House, Puddington, NESTON, CH64 5SR. (Life Member)
FULWELL, Mr. John, FCA *1959;* Terms End Lower Street, Withycombe, MINEHEAD, SOMERSET, TA24 6PZ. (Life Member)

FUNDREY, Mr. Jonathan Kenneth, BSc ACA MBCS *1985;* HMRC, 100 Parliament Street, LONDON, SW1A 2BQ.
FUNG, Ms. Carlin Helen Ka Ming, BSc ACA *1992;* 256 Doris Avenue Suite 1607, TORONTO M2N 6X8, ON, CANADA.
FUNG, Miss. Cheryl Yuen-Man, BSc ACA *1992;* KPMG, 8/F Prince's Building, 10 Chater Road, CENTRAL, HONG KONG ISLAND, HONG KONG SAR.
FUNG, Mr. Chi Hoi, ACA *2006;* c/o Nortel Networks (Asia) Limited, 5/F Cityplaza 4, TAIKOO SHING, HONG KONG ISLAND, HONG KONG SAR.
FUNG, Mr. Chi Keung, ACA *2007;* Fung Chi Keung & Company, Room 1102, 11/F Henan Building, 90 Jaffle Road, WAN CHAI, HONG KONG SAR.
FUNG, Mr. Chi Kwan Nicholas, ACA *2005;* 22B Tower 1 Maritime Bay, 18 Pui Shing Road, TSEUNG KWAN O, NEW TERRITORIES, HONG KONG SAR.
FUNG, Ms. Chi Ling Irene, ACA *2006;* Flat E, 19th Floor Block 5, Central Park, 18 Hoi Ting Road, TAI KOK TSUI, KOWLOON HONG KONG SAR.
FUNG, Ms. Ching Mei, ACA *2007;* Flat D, 11th Floor, Block B, Grammy Centre, 238 Yee Kuk Street, SHAM SHUI PO KOWLOON HONG KONG SAR.
FUNG, Mr. Chiu Kit, BSc ACA *1990;* (Tax Fac), 2 Charter Place, STAINES, MIDDLESEX, TW18 2HN.
FUNG, Mr. Chun Chung, LLB FCA *1964;* Unit 1313, HONG KONG SAR Plaza, 188 Connaught Road West, SAI YING PUN, HONG KONG ISLAND, HONG KONG SAR. (Life Member)
FUNG, Mr. David, BA ACA *1994;* C-11 Craigmount, 34 Stubbs Road, WAN CHAI, HONG KONG ISLAND, HONG KONG SAR.
FUNG, Mr. Henry, ACA *2007;* FTW & Partners CPA Limited, Suite 1001-3, 10th Floor, Manulife Provident Funds Place, 345 Nathan Road, KOWLOON CITY HONG KONG SAR.
FUNG, Mr. Hoi Fung, ACA *2007;* Fung Hoi Fung & Co, Flat B, 8/F, THY (Yuen Long) Commercial Building, 2 - 8 Tai Cheung Street, YUEN LONG NEW TERRITORIES HONG KONG SAR.
FUNG, Miss. Joan Hang Yu, BA ACA *2007;* 7 Talman Grove, STANMORE, MIDDLESEX, HA7 4UQ.
FUNG, Mr. Ka Kit, ACA *2010;* Flat 2107, Fu Wo House, Fu Keung Court, WANG TAU HOM, KOWLOON, HONG KONG SAR.
FUNG, Mr. Kin, ACA *2008;* Room 1306 Block 24, Heng Fa Chuen, CHAI WAN, HONG KONG SAR.
FUNG, Mr. King Cheung Vasco, ACA *2005;* c/o Shriro Pacific Ltd., Suites 4201-3 One Island East, 18 Westlands Road, QUARRY BAY, HONG KONG ISLAND, HONG KONG SAR.
FUNG, Mr. Kun Cheong, ACA *2007;* Lui & Mak C.P.A., Rooms 604-7 Dominion Centre 43-59, Queen's Road, East, WAN CHAI, HONG KONG SAR.
FUNG, Mr. Lak, ACA *2005;* Lak & Associates C.P.A. Ltd, 1603-1606 Alliance Building, 130-136 Connaught Road, CENTRAL, HONG KONG SAR.
•FUNG, Miss. Lily Yuk Chun, BA ACA *1991;* Tax Key Limited, 2nd Floor, Astoria House, 62 Shaftesbury Avenue, LONDON, W1D 6LT.
FUNG, Mr. Man Yin Sammy, BA FCA *1985;* Flat B 19/F, Woodgreen Crt, Parkvale Village, LANTAU ISLAND, NEW TERRITORIES, HONG KONG SAR.
FUNG, Ms. Mei Fung, ACA *2006;* ATSA CPA & Co, Room B 19/F, 88 Commercial Building, 28-34 Wing Lok Street, SHEUNG WAN, HONG KONG ISLAND HONG KONG SAR.
FUNG, Miss. Mei Yim, BSc FCA *1995;* 7E Block 2, Villa Premiere, 99 Fung Cheung Road, YUEN LONG, NEW TERRITORIES, HONG KONG SAR.
FUNG, Miss. Melanie, BSc ACA *2001;* 3 McNaught Street, BEAUMARIS, VIC 3193, AUSTRALIA.
FUNG, Miss. On Na, ACA *2010;* Flat D 81F Block 1, Dragon Inn, Tsing Ha Lane, TUEN MUN, HONG KONG SAR.
FUNG, Mr. Pak Wai Alex, ACA *2006;* Flat F 29/F, Tower 32, South Horizons, AP LEI CHAU, HONG KONG ISLAND, HONG KONG SAR.
FUNG, Mr. Pak Yue, ACA *2007;* Ground Floor, 40 B Tseng Lan Shue Village, SAI KUNG, NT, HONG KONG SAR.
FUNG, Ms. Pammy Yee, ACA *2005;* CCIF CPA Limited, 1/F Sunning Place, 10 Hysan Avenue, CAUSEWAY BAY, HONG KONG ISLAND, HONG KONG SAR. See also Charles Chan, Ip & Fung CPA Ltd
FUNG, Mr. Peter Shing Kwong, ACA *1982;* Flat 21b, Cumine Court, 52 King's Road, NORTH POINT, HONG KONG ISLAND, HONG KONG SAR.
FUNG, Mr. Po Fai, ACA *2005;* 8/F Flat F Grevillea Court, New Town Plaza (Phase 3), SHA TIN, NEW TERRITORIES, HONG KONG SAR.
FUNG, Mr. Pui Cheung, ACA *2005;* Pan-China (Hong Kong) CPA Limited, 20/F, HONG KONG SAR Trade Centre, 161-167 Des Voeux Road, CENTRAL, HONG KONG SAR. See also NCN CPA Limited
FUNG, Mrs. Sau Man Christina, BCom FCA *1990;* Flat 8A, 70 Sing Woo Road, HAPPY VALLEY, HONG KONG ISLAND, HONG KONG SAR.
FUNG, Mr. Shawn Fatt, BSc ACA *1983;* 33E Chancery Lane 01-19 The Chancery Residence, SINGAPORE 309555, SINGAPORE.
FUNG, Mr. Shiu Lam, JP FCA *1961;* Fung Yu & Co, Hong Kong Trade Centre 7/F, 161-7 Des Voeux Road Central, CENTRAL, HONG KONG ISLAND, HONG KONG SAR.
FUNG, Mr. Sik Kwong, ACA *2007;* Flat A 16/F, Block 3 Monte Vista, Sha on Street, Ma on Shan, SHA TIN, NEW TERRITORIES HONG KONG SAR.
FUNG, Mr. Tommy Hon Kwong, BSc FCA *1989;* with Ernst & Young, 62/F, One Island East, 18 Westlands Road, QUARRY BAY, HONG KONG ISLAND HONG KONG SAR.
FUNG, Mr. Tsan Sing Libon, BSc ACA *1992;* University of London, Birkbeck College, Malet Street, LONDON, WC1E 7HX.
FUNG, Mr. Tze Wa, ACA *2007;* 5\F Far East Consortium Building, 121 Des Voeux Road Central, CENTRAL, HONG KONG SAR.
FUNG, Mr. Wai Ming Stephen, ACA *2007;* Flat B, 19/F Wai King Mansion, 22 Aberdeen Main Road, ABERDEEN, HONG KONG SAR.
FUNG, Miss. Wai-Yan, BA ACA *2002;* 9 Millbank Place Bestwood Village, NOTTINGHAM, NOTTINGHAMSHIRE, NG6 8EF.
FUNG, Ms. Wing Ting Clarissa, ACA *2006;* Flat B, 42nd Floor, Goldwin Heights, 2 Seymour Road, MID LEVELS, HONG KONG ISLAND HONG KONG SAR.
FUNG, Mr. Wing Yuen, ACA *2004;* Fung & Pang CPA Limited, 1/F & 2/F Xiu Ping Commercial Building, 104 Jervois Street, SHEUNG WAN, HONG KONG ISLAND, HONG KONG SAR.
FUNG, Mr. Ying Wai Wilson, ACA *2007;* 48th Floor Jardine House, Connaught Road Central, CENTRAL, HONG KONG SAR.
FUNG, Mr. Yuk Kan Peter, BSc FCA *1992;* KPMG, 8th Floor, Tower E2, Oriental Plaza, 1 East Chang An Avenue, BEIJING 100738 CHINA.
FUNG-ON, Mr. Eton Gregory, FCA *1972;* 35 Ravensbourne Avenue, SHOREHAM-BY-SEA, WEST SUSSEX, BN43 6AA.
•FUNG-ON, Mr. Neil Anthony Robert, BSc(Hons) ACA *2000;* BDO LLP, 55 Baker Street, LONDON, W1U 7EU. See also BDO Stoy Hayward LLP
FUNNELL, Mr. James David, BSc ACA *2006;* 91 Livingstone Road, GRAVESEND, KENT, DA12 5DN.
FUNNELL, Mr. Nicholas John, MA ACA *1999;* 33 St Andrews Road, Gorleston, GREAT YARMOUTH, NR31 6LT.
FUNNELL, Mr. Robert William, BA FCA *1974;* 52 Craithie Road, Vicars Cross, CHESTER, CHESHIRE, CH3 5JL.
FUNNING, Mr. Michael, BSc FCA *1976;* St. John's Villa, Dawney Hill, Pirbright, WOKING, GU24 0JB.
FURBER, Mr. Jonathan Peter, BCom ACA *2000;* Vistorm Ltd, Vistorm House, 3200 Daresbury Park, Daresbury, WARRINGTON, WA4 4BU.
FURBER, Mr. Michael Richard, BSc ACA *1995;* 17 Lancaster Gardens, LONDON, SW19 5DG.
FURBER, Mr. Nicholas John, BSc ACA *1998;* 2327 West 34th Avenue, VANCOUVER V6M 1G8, BC, CANADA.
FURBER, Mr. Paul John, BSc ACA *1979;* The Forge, Wichenford, WORCESTER, WR6 6YY.
FURBER, Mr. Simon Mark, BA ACA *1994;* 67 Ryecroft Road, Frampton Cotterell, BRISTOL, BS36 2HJ.
FURBER, Mr. Timothy John, BSc ACA *1995;* 4 Waglands Garden, BUCKINGHAM, MK18 1EA.
FURBERT, Mrs. Elaine Marie, ACA *1981;* P.O. Box CR 137, CRAWL CR BX, BERMUDA.
FURBY, Mr. Derek John, FCA *1962;* Daisy Cottage, Market Street, Laxfield, WOODBRIDGE, SUFFOLK, IP13 8DR. (Life Member)
FUREY, Mr. Colin Paul, FCA *1967;* 10 Larch Road, Oswaldtwistle, ACCRINGTON, BB5 3AN.
FUREY, Mrs. Susan Elizabeth, BSc FCA *1992;* Aston University, The Aston Triangle, BIRMINGHAM, B4 7ET.
FURLAN, Miss. Lauren, ACA *2011;* 1235 South Prairie Avenue, Apt 3601, CHICAGO, IL 60605, UNITED STATES.
FURLEY, Mrs. Barbara Ann, FCA *1968;* 3 Woodfields, Chipstead, SEVENOAKS, KENT, TN13 2RA.
FURLEY, Mr. John Roger, ACA *1998;* United Kingdom Passport Agency Globe House, 89 Eccleston Square, LONDON, SW1V 1PN.
FURLONG, Mr. David Charles, BA FCA *1988;* 22 Wellington Court, Glenbuck Road, SURBITON, KT6 6BL.
FURLONG, Mrs. Elizabeth, BA ACA *2005;* 131 Papillon Drive, LIVERPOOL, L9 9HL.
FURLONG, Miss. Sharon Imeldest, BA ACA *1992;* Laurel House, 49 Richmond Avenue, LONDON, SW20 8LA.
FURLONG, Dr. Shaun Antony, DPhil BSc ACA *2004;* 1 The Potteries, Ridgewood, UCKFIELD, EAST SUSSEX, TN22 5TQ.
FURLONGE-KELLY, Mr. Wilhelm Hartmut Siegfried, MEng ACA *1993;* Amsterdamseweg 457, 1181BP AMSTELVEEN, NETHERLANDS.
FURLONGER, Mr. Marc, MEng BSc ACA *2001;* The British Land Co Ltd York House, 45 Seymour Street, LONDON, W1H 7LX.
FURMSTON, Miss. Jennifer Joanne, BSc ACA *2001;* 9 Dorset Square, Flat 4, LONDON, NW1 6QB.
FURMSTON, Mr. Nicholas James, BSc ACA *2004;* Balfour Beatty Capital - 6th Floor, Broadgate Estates, 350 Euston Road, LONDON, NW1 3AX.
FURMSTON, Mr. Roger Lloyd, BA FCA *1965;* Cladagh, Coulsdon Lane, Chipstead, COULSDON, SURREY, CR5 3QH. (Life Member)
FURNEAUX, Mr. Nigel Richard, FCA *1970;* Paludes, Sandisplatt Road, MAIDENHEAD, SL6 4NB.
•FURNEAUX, Mr. Paul Edward, BA ACA *1991;* KPMG LLP, 15 Canada Square, LONDON, E14 5GL. See also KPMG Europe LLP
FURNEAUX, Mr. Roland Geoffrey Ambrose, ACA *2007;* 72 Front Road, Woodchurch, ASHFORD, TN26 3SA.
FURNELL, Mr. David Joseph, FCA *1955;* 243 Bournemouth Road, Parkstone, POOLE, DORSET, BH14 9HX. (Life Member)
FURNELL, Mrs. Frances Lesley, BSc ACA *1987;* Mill House, The Green, Hollowell, NORTHAMPTON, NN6 8RW.
FURNELL, Mr. Timothy Paul, ACA *2008;* 35 The Oval, Wood Street Village, GUILDFORD, SURREY, GU3 3DL.
•FURNESS, Mr. Alan John, FCA *1961;* Furness Consultancy, 30 Sonning Meadows, Sonning - on -Thames, READING, RG4 6XB.
•FURNESS, Mr. Benjamin, BSc(Hons) ACA CTA *2004;* Allens Accountants Limited, 123 Wellington Road South, STOCKPORT, SK1 3TH.
•FURNESS, Mr. Brian Jeffrey, BA ACA *1992;* PricewaterhouseCoopers LLP, Hays Galleria, 1 Hays Lane, LONDON, SE1 2RD. See also PricewaterhouseCoopers
FURNESS, Mr. George, FCA *1954;* Cleft Cottage, 11 Garner Lane, Kirkburton, HUDDERSFIELD, HD8 0QX. (Life Member)
FURNESS, Mrs. Jennifer Margaret Banks, MA ACA *1997;* Prestbury, 74 Park Road, WOKING, SURREY, GU22 7DH.
FURNESS, Mr. John Christopher, FCA *1972;* Barn Ridge, Coopers Hill Road, South Nutfield, REDHILL, RH1 5PD.
FURNESS, Dr. Karen, PhD ACA *2005;* 42 New Zealand Lane, Duffield, BELPER, DERBYSHIRE, DE56 4BZ.
FURNESS, Mr. Michael Joseph, BA ACA *2001;* Warakirri Asset Management, Level 3, 53 Queen Street, MELBOURNE, VIC 3000, AUSTRALIA.
FURNESS, Mr. Neville Atkinson, FCA *1959;* Broomhaugh Farm, RIDING MILL, NE44 6EG.
FURNESS, Mr. Timothy Stefan, BSc ACA *2004;* Financial Services Compensation Scheme, 7th Floor, Lloyds Chambers, 1 Portsoken Street, LONDON, E1 8BN.
FURNESS, Miss. Vicki Louise, ACA *2009;* Deloitte & Touche, Corner House, Church and Parliament Streets, PO Box HM 1556, HAMILTON, BERMUDA.
FURNESS-SMITH, Mr. Charles Edwin, BSc ACA *1980;* The Cartwheel, London Road East, AMERSHAM, HP7 9DT.
FURNISS, Mr. Andrew John, LLB(Hons) ACA *2010;* 9 Lime Close, LUDLOW, SHROPSHIRE, SY8 2PP.
FURNISS, Mr. David, BA FCA *1975;* 42 Redhead Street, Doolandella, BRISBANE, QLD 4077, AUSTRALIA.
FURNISS, Mr. Edward John, FCA *1949;* with F.W. Smith Riches & Co, 15 Whitehall, LONDON, SW1A 2DD.
FURNISS, Miss. Helen Victoria, LLB ACA *2004;* 50 Astwood Drive, Flitwick, BEDFORD, MK45 1HW.
FURNISS, Mr. Ian William, BSc ACA *1989;* Middle Field, 2 Woodlands Close, HOLT, NORFOLK, NR25 6DU.
FURNISS, Mr. Jonathan Paul, BA ACA *1996;* 4 Trinity Fold, South Cave, BROUGH, NORTH HUMBERSIDE, HU15 2BJ.
FURNISS, Mrs. Julie Ann, BSc ACA *1990;* 101 Dorchester Way, Belmont, HEREFORD, HR2 7ZW.
FURNISS, Mrs. Sarah Elizabeth, BSc ACA *2009;* Caynton Lodge, Caynton, NEWPORT, SHROPSHIRE, TF10 8NE.
FURNISS-PLANT, Mrs. Leanne, BA ACA *2006;* XCel Superturn GB Ltd, Millstone Works, 32 Atlas Way, Atlas North, SHEFFIELD, S4 7QQ.
FURPHY, Mr. Stanley Paul, FCA *1972;* 136 Nestles Avenue, HAYES, UB3 4QF. (Life Member)
•FURRER, Mr. Paul Steven, BA FCA *1979;* (Tax Fac), Paul Furrer & Co, 2nd Floor Tuition House, 27-37 St. Georges Road, Wimbledon, LONDON, SW19 4EU.
•FURSDON, Mr. Jonathan Malcolm, BSc FCA ATII *1983;* (Tax Fac), Fursdon Consulting Ltd, The Old Stables, Grange Manor, Shipley Bridge Lane, Shipley Bridge, HORLEY SURREY RH6 9TL.
FURSE, Mr. Simon William, BSc ACA *1983;* 19 Chislehurst Road, BROMLEY, BR1 2NN.
FURSE-ROBERTS, Mr. David Maxwell, BSc FCA *1973;* The Hey Wey, High Street, Dadford, BUCKINGHAM, MK18 5JX.
•FURST, Mr. David Anthony, FCA *1973;* (President 2008 - 2009) (Member of Council 2002 - 2011), Crowe Clark Whitehill LLP, St Bride's House, 10 Salisbury Square, LONDON, EC4Y 8EH. See also Horwath Clark Whitehill LLP and Crowe Clark Whitehill
FURST, Mrs. Susan, FCA *1974;* (Tax Fac), 46 Broadhurst, ASHTEAD, KT21 1QF.
FURTH, Mr. Adam Charles Montgomery, BSc FCA *1975;* The Post Office, 151 Cwmamman Road, Garnant, AMMANFORD, SA18 1NB.
FURZE, Mr. Anthony Derek, FCA *1969;* 191 Bodmin Road, TRURO, TR1 1RA.
FURZE, Mr. Richard David, BA ACA *1981;* 57 Cannon Grove, Fetcham, LEATHERHEAD, KT22 9LP.
FUSCHILLO, Mr. Sam Paul, ACA *2009;* Deloitte & Touche Hill House, 1 Little New Street, LONDON, EC4A 3TR.
•FUSS, Mr. Ronald Leslie, FCA *1966;* Ronald Fuss & Co, Flat 7, Aspen Court, 86 Holders Hill Road, LONDON, NW4 1LW.
•FUSSELL, Mr. Andrew, FCA *1968;* Edwin Fussell & Co., 109 Footshill Road, Hanham, BRISTOL, BS15 8HB.
FUSSELL, Mr. Douglas Charles, FCA *1966;* Oakdene, 16 The Avenue, POTTERS BAR, EN6 1EB.
•FUSSELL, Mr. Paul, BA FCA CF *1999;* Hazlewoods LLP, Windsor House, Barnett Way, Barnwood, GLOUCESTER, GL4 3RT.
FUSSELL, Mr. Sidney William, FCA *1945;* Summerdown House, Bratton, WESTBURY, BA13 4SN. (Life Member)
FUSSELL, Mr. Simon Charles, BA ACA *1988;* 15 Kings Close, BUXTON, DERBYSHIRE, SK17 7NT.
•FUSSELL, Mr. Stewart Raymond, FCA *1974;* (Tax Fac), Berke Fine Fussell Limited, Beren Court, Newney Green, CHELMSFORD, CM1 3SQ. See also Nativearrow Limited
FUSSELL, Mr. Thomas Cyrus, BSc FCA *1997;* 38 Sandy Lane, RICHMOND, TW10 7EL.
•FUSSELL, Mr. Timothy George, BSc FCA ATII *1987;* Baker Tilly Tax and Advisory Services LLP, 25 Farringdon Street, LONDON, EC4A 4AB.
•FUTCHER, Mr. Ian Richard, ACA *1998;* Blackwood Futcher & Co, 9 St. Georges Yard, Castle Streeet, FARNHAM, SURREY, GU9 7LW.
FUTCHER, Miss. Kelly Anne, ACA *2007;* 27 The Close, Hedge End, SOUTHAMPTON, SO30 4DZ.
FUTCHER, Mr. Stephen Roy Lewis, FCA *1973;* 17 Christopher Way, EMSWORTH, PO10 7QZ.
•FUTERS, Mr. Austin, BA ACA *1982;* Futers Accountancy & Finance, 1 Westwood Avenue, NEWCASTLE UPON TYNE, NE6 5QT.
FUTTER, Mrs. Rosalind, BA ACA *2003;* 56 Elmstead Avenue, CHISLEHURST, KENT, BR7 6EG.
FYFE, Miss. Alexandra Adamantia, MA ACA *1990;* 36 Donovan Court, Drayton Gardens, LONDON, SW10 9QT.
FYFE, Mr. David, BA ACA *1984;* Court Dreve, 73 Weeping Cross, STAFFORD, ST17 0DQ.
FYFE, Mrs. Eleanor Anne, BSc ACA *1986;* 22 Bonnytoun Avenue, LINLITHGOW, WEST LOTHIAN, EH49 7JS.

FYFE, Mr. Ian Robert, FCA ACMA *1958;* 16 Hunter Close, EAST BOLDON, NE36 0TB. (Life Member)
FYFE, Ms. Karen Elizabeth, MA ACA *1991;* 116 Queen Victoria Drive, GLASGOW, G14 9BL.
FYFE, Miss. Lisa, BSc ACA *2010;* 1 Greenleaves, Clays Hill Bramber, STEYNING, WEST SUSSEX, BN44 3XA.
FYFE, Miss. Michelle Katie, BA(Hons) ACA *2009;* 37 Farm Drive, Tilehurst, READING, RG31 4EU.
•FYFFE, Miss. Amanda Eve, BA(Hons) ACA *2001;* with RGL LLP, 8th Floor, Dashwood, 69 Old Broad Street, LONDON, EC2M 1QS.
FYFFE, Mr. Graham George, BA FCA *1955;* 19 Gingells Farm Road, Charvil, READING, RG10 9DJ. (Life Member)
•FYLES, Mr. Stephen, FCA *1981;* (Tax Fac), Fenleys, 1st Floor, 168 High Street, WATFORD, WD17 2EG.
FYVIE, Mrs. Susan, LLB ACA *2002;* 5 Kilmailing Road, GLASGOW, G44 5UH.
GAASTRA, Mr. Stephen, BSc ACA *1983;* Lambert Smith Hampton United Kingdom House, 180 Oxford Street, LONDON, W1D 1NN.
GABARDI, Mr. Roberto Attilio, FCA *1970;* Via F Cavallotti 16, 43100 PARMA, ITALY.
GABAY, Mr. Adam Jonathan, BSc ACA *2001;* 8 Brookway, LONDON, SE3 9BJ.
GABB, Mrs. Emma, BA ACA *2004;* 32 Jasmine Close, WOKING, GU21 3RQ.
GABB, Mr. Jonathan Haydn, MEng ACA *2006;* Ove Arup & Partners, 8 Fitzroy Street, LONDON, W1T 4BJ.
GABB, Mr. Leslie Ian, BA ACA ATII *1988;* Advent Venture Partners, 25-28 Buckingham Gate, LONDON, SW1E 6LD.
GABBE, Mr. Martin Eric, BSc ACA *2002;* 59 Highbank, HAYWARDS HEATH, WEST SUSSEX, RH16 4TT.
•GABBERTAS, Mr. Richard Kenneth, MA FCA *1984;* KPMG LLP, 1 The Embankment, Neville Street, LEEDS, LS1 4DW. See also KPMG Europe LLP
GABBEY, Miss. Katherine, BEng ACA *2007;* PO BOX 9588, NEWMARKET 1149, NEW ZEALAND.
GABBI, Mr. Prem Kumar, BA(Hons) ACA AICM(Cert) *1995;* National Grid Plc N G T House, Warwick Technology Park Gallows Hill, WARWICK, CV34 6DA.
GABBIE, Mr. Neil Harold, BA ACA *1996;* Kellogg Europe Trading Limited, The Kellogg Building, Lakeshore Drive, Airside Business Park, SWORDS, COUNTY DUBLIN IRELAND.
GABBIE, Mr. Philip Henry, FCA *1963;* 28 Park Lodge Close, CHEADLE, CHESHIRE, SK8 1HU.
GABBIE, Mrs. Sarah Ruth, BSc ACA *1999;* 2 Warren Manor, MALAHIDE, COUNTY DUBLIN, IRELAND.
GABLE, Mr. James, ACA *2011;* 53 Church Way, Sanderstead, SOUTH CROYDON, SURREY, CR2 0JU.
GABRIEL, Mr. Alan, BSc ACA *1980;* 28 Avenue Road, FROME, SOMERSET, BA11 1RP.
•GABRIEL, Mrs. Barbara, FCA *1982;* Barbara Gabriel, 156 Clarence Avenue, NEW MALDEN, KT3 3DY.
GABRIEL, Mr. David Llewelyn, BA FCA *1989;* with Grant Thornton UK LLP, 30 Finsbury Square, LONDON, EC2P 2YU.
GABRIEL, Mr. David Ronald, BA FCA *1966;* 30 Grange Court Road, Henleaze, BRISTOL, BS9 4DR.
GABRIEL, Mr. Graham Ewen, MA ACA *2000;* Milners Lodge, Whitwell, YORK, YO60 7JJ.
GABRIEL, Mr. Michael Clifford, FCA *1967;* 56 Walham Grove, LONDON, SW6 1QR.
GABRIEL, Mr. Neil Hay, MEng ACA *2002;* Aldgate House, 33 Aldgate High Street, LONDON, EC3N 1DL.
GABRIEL, Mr. Nicholas Alexander, BSc ACA *1993;* 28176 Rey de Copas, MALIBU, CA 90265, UNITED STATES.
GABRIEL, Mr. Trevor Maurice, FCA *1969;* Villa Pompeo, 27 rue du Portier, MC 98000 MONTE CARLO, MONACO.
GABRIELCZYK, Mr. Jerzy Jozef, BSc FCA *1976;* Ul Dorohuska 17, 01-472 WARSAW, POLAND.
GABRIELE, Mr. Robert, BA FCA *1984;* 35 Charlwood Street, LONDON, SW1V 2DU.
GABRILATSOU, Miss. Eleni, BA(Hons) ACA *2011;* 14 Beckett Drive, Winwick, WARRINGTON, WA2 8XJ.
GAC, Miss. Alice Caroline, BA ACA *1993;* Lloyd's, Lloyds Building, 1 Lime Street, LONDON, EC3M 7HA.
GADD, Mr. Bernard, FCA *1955;* 40 Kirkmuir Drive, Stewarton, KILMARNOCK, AYRSHIRE, KA3 3HP. (Life Member)
GADD, Mr. Darren, BA(Hons) ACA *2000;* Infor Global Solutions Infor House, 1 Lakeside Road, FARNBOROUGH, GU14 6XP.
GADD, Miss. Fiona Kathryn, BA ACA *1991;* 22 Langcliffe Close, Culcheth, WARRINGTON, WA3 4LR.
GADD, Mrs. Kathlyn Joy, MSc ACA *1991;* Cockswood, Cocks Lane, Stockton Brook, STOKE-ON-TRENT, ST9 9PJ.
GADDES, Mr. Graham Stuart Mark, BA ACA *1989;* 17 Claybank Drive, Tottington, BURY, BL8 4BU.
GADHAVI, Mr. Dharmesh, ACA *2008;* 17 Strafford Gate, POTTERS BAR, HERTFORDSHIRE, EN6 1PW.
GADHAVI, Miss. Shejal, BSc ACA *2008;* 150 Kilmorie Road, LONDON, SE23 2SR.
GADHER, Mr. Nimish Kumar Pradip, BA(Hons) ACA *2010;* 5 St. Heliers Avenue, HOUNSLOW, TW3 3SL.
•GADHIA, Mr. Anil H, BA FCA *1981;* Guardians, 24 Spencer Walk, RICKMANSWORTH, HERTFORDSHIRE, WD3 4EE.
•GADHIA, Mr. Hitesh Valji, BSc ACA *1990;* Shaw Wallace Limited, 43 Manchester Street, LONDON, W1U 7LP.
GADHIA, Mrs. Jayne-Anne, BA ACA *1989;* Virgin Money, 17-23 Calton Road, EDINBURGH, EH8 8DL.
GADHIA, Mr. Ketan, BSc ACA *1999;* 46 Copse Wood Way, NORTHWOOD, MIDDLESEX, HA6 2UA.
GADHIA, Mrs. Ram Priya, BSc ACA *1988;* Honeysuckle, Loudhams Wood Lane, CHALFONT ST. GILES, BUCKINGHAMSHIRE, HP8 4AP.
GADHOK, Mr. Amrit Pal, BCom FCA *1966;* 201 Brabazon Road, Heston, HOUNSLOW, TW5 9LW.
GADHOKE, Mr. Harveen, FCA *1982;* with Deloitte & Touche, Deloitte Place, Waiyaki Way, Muthangari, P O Box 40092, GPO 00100 NAIROBI KENYA.
GADHOKE, Mr. Hitesh, BSc ACA *1996;* 10 Perry Way, LIGHTWATER, GU18 5LB.
•GADHVI, Miss. Raksha, BA ACA *1989;* Garlands CA Ltd, 6 Oakroyd Avenue, POTTERS BAR, HERTFORDSHIRE, EN6 2EH. See also Garlands Ltd
•GADOROS, Mr. Andrew Bela, BA FCA *1989;* 187 Miles Limited, The Quadrant Centre, Limes Road, WEYBRIDGE, SURREY, KT13 8DH.
GADSBY, Mr. Andrew Paul, BSc ACA *1993;* Barn Owl Cottage, 32 Agates Lane, ASHTEAD, KT21 2ND.
GADSBY, Mrs. Angela Ann, BSc ACA *2006;* with Allen & Overy, One Bishops Square, LONDON, E1 6AD.
•①GADSBY, Mr. Graeme Roy, BA FCA *1984;* G R Gadsby, The Orchard, Manor Park, CHISLEHURST, KENT, BR7 5QE.
•GADSBY, Mrs. Lisa Margaret, BSc ACA *1992;* Lisa Gadsby Book Keeping Services, Barn Owl Cottage, 32 Agates Lane, ASHTEAD, SURREY, KT21 2ND.
•GADSDEN, Mr. Bernard Leigh, FCA *1970;* Gadsden Grillo & Co, P.O.Box 35931, LUSAKA, ZAMBIA. See also Gadsden B.L.
GADSDEN, Mr. Michael John, FCA *1967;* 33 Beaumont Avenue, ST. ALBANS, AL1 4TL.
GADSDON, Miss. Natasha Claire, BA ACA *1995;* 7 Higher Compton Road, PLYMOUTH, PL3 5HY.
GAFF, Mr. Robert, FCA *1960;* 256 Montee de L'Eglise, 69250 CURIS AU MONT D'OR, FRANCE.
GAFFAR, Mr. Kassim, MSc ACA *1997;* Level 2, H S B C, 8-14 Canada Square, LONDON, E14 5HQ.
GAFFEY, Mr. Michael Gerard, MEng ACA *2004;* with PKF, AMP Place, Level 6, 10 Eagle Street, BRISBANE, QLD 4000 AUSTRALIA.
•GAFFNEY, Mr. Christopher Noel, FCA *1984;* Gaffneys, 2 Longsight Road, Holcombe Brook, BURY, LANCASHIRE, BL0 9TD.
•GAFFNEY, Mr. Geoffrey Howard, FCA *1967;* Rouse Audit LLP, 55 Station Road, BEACONSFIELD, BUCKINGHAMSHIRE, HP9 1QL. See also Rouse Partners LLP
GAFFNEY, Mr. Gordon James, MSc BA ACA *2001;* Failte Ireland, Amiens Street, DUBLIN 1, COUNTY DUBLIN, IRELAND.
GAFFNEY, Mr. Michael, BSc ACA *1994;* 2003 Nolte Drive, WEST DEPTFORD, NJ 08066, UNITED STATES.
GAFFNEY, Mr. Richard James, ACA *1998;* Siemens Sir William Siemens Square, Frimley, CAMBERLEY, GU16 8QD.
GAFFNEY, Mrs. Sarah Louise, MEng ACA *1997;* 631 Buyers Road, COLLEGEVILLE, PA 19426, UNITED STATES.
GAFFNEY, Miss. Sarah-Jane, ACA *2009;* 27 Oak Farm Close, Blackwater, CAMBERLEY, SURREY, GU17 0JU.
GAFFNEY, Mr. Timothy Linus, BSc ACA *1983;* 21 Watts Way, Long Buckby, NORTHAMPTON, NN6 7QX.
GAGE, Mr. Jonathan Moreton, ACA *1983;* Fox House, Little Coxwell, FARINGDON, SN7 7LW.
GAGE, Ms. Margaret Ann, MSc ACA *1982;* PGI Group Ltd, 81 Carter Lane, LONDON, EC4V 5EP.
•GAGE, Mr. Timothy James, FCA *1985;* Tim Gage, 45 Flitwick Road, Ampthill, BEDFORD, BEDFORDSHIRE, MK45 2NS.
GAGEN, Mrs. Valerie Ann, BSc ACA *1988;* 71 Manor Road, BARNET, EN5 2LG.
GAGER, Mr. Duncan James, BA ACA *1988;* 9 Allandale Place, Chelsfield, ORPINGTON, BR6 7TH.
GAGER, Mr. Eric Robert, FCA *1956;* Hylmalen, 2a Malyons Road, SWANLEY, KENT, BR8 7RE. (Life Member)
GAGGS, Mr. Bryan Geoffrey, FCA *1957;* 222 East Carrillo Street, Suite 209, SANTA BARBARA, CA 93101-7196, UNITED STATES. (Life Member)
GAGLANI, Mr. Vimal Mahendra, BSc(Hons) ACA *2006;* 93 Chelveston Crescent, Aldermoor, SOUTHAMPTON, SO16 5SB.
GAGLANI-PATEL, Mrs. Hina, BSc(Hons) ACA *2003;* 3 Baron Close, PENARTH, SOUTH GLAMORGAN, CF64 3UF.
GAGOO, Mr. Chetan, BSc ACA *2011;* 23 Priory Gardens, WEMBLEY, MIDDLESEX, HA0 2QG.
•GAHAGAN, Mr. Christopher John, LLB FCA *1991;* Premier Financial Direction Ltd, Kestrel Court, Harbour Road, Portishead, BRISTOL, BS20 7AN. See also DRC Forensics Limited
GAHAN, Mrs. Claire Amanda, BA ACA *1996;* 28 Furnival Street, SANDBACH, CHESHIRE, CW11 1DJ.
GAHAN, Mr. John Richard, BSc FCA *1995;* 22 Warren Drive, Dorridge, SOLIHULL, WEST MIDLANDS, B93 8JY.
GAHERTY, Mrs. Morag Ailsa, MA ACA *1992;* Arcady, 16 Hill Brow, Bearsted, MAIDSTONE, ME14 4AW.
GAIBANI, Mrs. Katherine Anne, BSc(Hons) ACA *2002;* Rosebank, 119 Cranbrook Drive, MAIDENHEAD, SL6 6SR.
GAILEY, Miss. Sarah Louise, BCom ACA *2008;* 69 Lyric Road, LONDON, SW13 9QA.
GAIN, Miss. Sarah Louise, LLB ACA CTA *2003;* 162 Moor Lane, UPMINSTER, ESSEX, RM14 1HE.
GAIND, Mr. Deepak, FCA *1976;* Dragonfly Apartments, Unit 26, St. James's Road, LONDON, SE16 4QJ.
•GAINEY, Mr. Stephen Leslie, BA FCA *1987;* (Tax Fac), Robinson Reed Layton, Peat House, Newham Road, TRURO, CORNWALL, TR1 2DP. See also DCN & Co. Limited
GAINSFORD, Mr. Alan Noel, FCA *1959;* Flat 25, 2 Mansfield Street, LONDON, W1G 9NF. (Life Member)
•GAIR, Mr. David Ronald, ACA *1988;* Mitchells, Suite 4, Parsons House, Parsons Road, WASHINGTON, TYNE AND WEAR NE37 1EZ.
GAIR, Miss. Paula, BSc ACA CTA *1996;* 52 Partridge Road, BIRMINGHAM, B26 2DA.
•GAIRDNER, Mr. James Andrew Campbell, FCA *1963;* Gairdners, 17 Larpent Avenue, Putney, LONDON, SW15 6UP.
GAIRDNER, Mr. Martin Hugh Temple, BA FCA *1966;* Keepers Cottage, Berwick Road, Berwick St. James, SALISBURY, WILTSHIRE, SP3 4TQ. (Life Member)
GAIRNS, Ms. Lesley Anne, BA ACA *1998;* 180 St. Ann's Hill, LONDON, SW18 2RS.
GAISFORD, Mr. James Dominic, BSc ACA *1986;* Priors Court, Sunnyfield, Broadclyst, EXETER, EX5 3EU.
GAIT, Mr. Christopher Doman, FCA *1962;* Barnbrook Lodge, New Street, Napton, SOUTHAM, CV47 8LR. (Life Member)
GAITSKELL, Mr. Andrew Christopher, BSc ACA *1992;* 55 Alleyn Road, Dulwich, LONDON, SE21 8AD.
GAITZSCH, Mr. Andreas Richard, BA(Hons) ACA *2001;* Lloyds Banking Group, 25 Gresham Street, LONDON, EC2V 7HN.
GAJENDRAN, Mr. Vijayasegaram, ACA ACMA *2011;* 29 Brookdene Drive, NORTHWOOD, MIDDLESEX, HA6 3NS.
GAJLEWICZ, Mr. David, BSc ACA *2006;* 33 New Road, STAINES, MIDDLESEX, TW18 3DA.
GAJPARIA, Mrs. Jaimi, MSc BSc ACA *2009;* Flat 1 Tunstall House, 3 Park Place, CHELTENHAM, GLOUCESTERSHIRE, GL50 2QS.
GAJRAJ, Mrs. Mithra Nelun, BSc FCA *1978;* 4 St Martins Drive, WALTON-ON-THAMES, KT12 3BW.
GAJRI, Mr. Ramesh Kumar, FCA *1975;* H.S Dev. & Co. Ltd., Unit 27, The Business Village, Wexham Road, SLOUGH, SL2 5HF.
GALAIYA, Mr. Dipesh Hashwin, BSc ACA *2005;* Flemmings Chartered Accountants, 76 Canterbury Road, CROYDON, CR0 3HA.
GALAIYA, Mr. Hiten Ratilal, BSc ACA *2006;* (Tax Fac), 84 Peel Road, HARROW, MIDDLESEX, HA3 7QU.
GALAIYA, Mr. Niraj, BSc(Hons) ACA *2000;* 38 Church Avenue, PINNER, MIDDLESEX, HA5 5JQ.
GALAN, Mr. David, BA ACA *2000;* 20 Lawrence Avenue, LONDON, NW7 4NN.
GALANTINI, Mr. Fabio Mirko, MA ACA CTA *1996;* 52 Gunhild Way, CAMBRIDGE, CB1 8RB.
GALAUN, Mr. Jack, BSc(Econ) FCA *1971;* 91 Michleham Down, LONDON, N12 7JL.
GALBRAITH, Mr. Andrew Gareth, BSc ACA *1996;* 10 Sprucewood View, Douglas, ISLE OF MAN, IM4 3HA.
GALBRAITH, Mr. Andrew James, BA ACA *1998;* A Plan Insurance Blue Boar Court, 9 Alfred Street, OXFORD, OX1 4EH.
GALBRAITH, Miss. Angela, ACA *2008;* Flat 6, Flat 2-7, 14a Highbury Place, LONDON, N5 1QP.
GALBRAITH, Mr. Benjamin David, BA ACA *1999;* 65 Hollins Lane, Marple, STOCKPORT, CHESHIRE, SK6 6AW.
GALBRAITH, Miss. Fiona, BSc ACA *2002;* Flat 34 Emerald House, 8 Merrivale Mews, MILTON KEYNES, MK9 2FL.
GALBRAITH, Mr. Geoffrey David, BSc(Hons) ACA *2001;* 6 Ingress Park Avenue, GREENHITHE, KENT, DA9 9XJ.
GALBRAITH, Mr. John Peter, FCA *1970;* 22 Hacketts Lane, WOKING, GU22 8PP.
GALBRAITH, Mrs. Lindsay Jean, BA(Hons) ACA *2002;* 6 Ingress Park Avenue, GREENHITHE, KENT, DA9 9XJ.
GALE, Mrs. Adele Marguerite, ACA *2009;* La Houssaye, Rosaire Avenue, St. Peter Port, GUERNSEY, GY1 1XU.
GALE, Mrs. Alison Margaret, BA FCA *1988;* 7 Norfolk Cottages, Bury, PULBOROUGH, RH20 1PA.
GALE, Mr. Andrew Peter, MSc ACA CPA *1996;* Woodside, 8 The Green, Woolley, WAKEFIELD, WEST YORKSHIRE, WF4 2JG.
GALE, Miss. Anna Louise, BSc ACA *2001;* with PricewaterhouseCoopers LLP, Cornwall Court, 19 Cornwall Street, BIRMINGHAM, B3 2DT.
GALE, Mr. Barry, MSc(Econ) ACA *2000;* 40 Southway, LONDON, SW20 9JQ.
•GALE, Mr. Brian Wilkin, FCA *1965;* BW Gale, Yew Tree House, Penn Lane, Kings Stanley, STONEHOUSE, GLOUCESTERSHIRE GL10 3PT.
GALE, Mrs. Caroline Madge, BSc ACA *1992;* Longmoor, 10 Durbin Park Road, CLEVEDON, AVON, BS21 7EU.
GALE, Mr. David John, LLB FCA *1973;* Public & Commercial Services Union, 160 Falcon Road, LONDON, SW11 2LN.
GALE, Mr. David Robert, BA FCA *1974;* 3 Loombah Avenue, LINDFIELD, NSW 2070, AUSTRALIA.
GALE, Mr. Graham Peter Michael, BA ACA *1997;* 30 City Road, CAMBRIDGE, CB1 1DP.
GALE, Mr. Harold Watson, FCA *1952;* Little Abbots, Argos Hill, Rotherfield, CROWBOROUGH, EAST SUSSEX, TN6 3QL. (Life Member)
•GALE, Mrs. Helen Jane, ACA *2002;* 4 La Place Du Puits, La Rue de la Capelle, St. Ouen, JERSEY, JE3 2DQ.
GALE, Mr. James William, MSc BSc(Hons) ACA *2010;* 33 Swan Hill, Mickleover, DERBY, DE3 0UW.
GALE, Mr. John Henry, FCA *1949;* 28 Swans Ghyll, Priory Road, FOREST ROW, RH18 5PA. (Life Member)
GALE, Mr. John Richard, FCA *1963;* 3601 Equestrian Way, TOMS RIVER, NJ 08755, UNITED STATES. (Life Member)
•GALE, Mr. John Robert, FCA *1979;* (Tax Fac), John Gale Associates, 415 Hillcross Avenue, MORDEN, SM4 4BZ.
GALE, Mr. Jonathan Edward Swinfen, BA ACA *2011;* 32 Carisbrooke House, Courtlands, Sheen Road, RICHMOND, SURREY, TW10 5AZ.
GALE, Mrs. Julie Joanna, BA ACA *1997;* 30 City Road, CAMBRIDGE, CB1 1DP.
GALE, Mr. Keith Henry, BA ACA *1984;* AHLI United Bank, PO Box 2424, MANAMA, BAHRAIN.
•GALE, Mr. Kevin Alexander, FCA *1989;* (Tax Fac), Grant Thornton UK LLP, Grant Thornton House, Kettering Parkway, Kettering Venture Park, KETTERING, NORTHAMPTONSHIRE NN15 6XR. See also Grant Thornton LLP
GALE, Mr. Kevin Jonathan, BSc ACA *1990;* Blue Sky Access Ltd, P.O. Box 3833, MARLOW, BUCKINGHAMSHIRE, SL7 2DP.
•GALE, Miss. Lisa Marie, BA ACA *2005;* with Barnett Spooner, The Old Steppe House, Brighton Road, GODALMING, SURREY, GU7 1NS.
•GALE, Mr. Michael John, FCA *1987;* Michael Gale & Co Limited, 1 Chaloner Street, GUISBOROUGH, CLEVELAND, TS14 6QD.
•GALE, Mr. Nicholas David, FCA *1980;* (Tax Fac), Bourne & Co, 3 Charnwood Street, DERBY, DE1 2GY.
GALE, Mr. Nicholas Paul, BSc ACA *1984;* Bowen State Building, Bowen Street, P.O.Box 12136, WELLINGTON, NEW ZEALAND.

GALE, Mr. Nicholas Tibor, FCA *1954;* 14 Ebrington Road, HARROW, HA3 0LR. (Life Member)
GALE, Mr. Peter Bradley, BA FCA *1976;* (Tax Fac), 2 Briar Hill, PURLEY, SURREY, CR8 3LE.
•GALE, Mr. Peter John, FCA *1972;* Swindells LLP, New Olives, High Street, UCKFIELD, EAST SUSSEX, TN22 1QE.
GALE, Mr. Philip Andrew, BSc FCA *1984;* Springfields 8 Walford Road Sibford Ferris, BANBURY, OXFORDSHIRE, OX15 5BL.
•GALE, Mr. Philip Antony, BSc FCA *1989;* (Tax Fac), Adler Shine LLP, Aston House, Cornwall Avenue, LONDON, N3 1LF.
•GALE, Mr. Philip John, BSc(Hons) ACA *2002;* RSM Tenon Audit Limited, Cedar House, Breckland, Linford Wood, MILTON KEYNES, MK14 6EX.
•GALE, Mr. Raymond David, FCA *1975;* R.D. Gale FCA, 94a Strines Road, Marple, STOCKPORT, CHESHIRE, SK6 7DU.
GALE, Mr. Richard John, BA ACA *1984;* The Tile House, Marston St. Lawrence, BANBURY, OXFORDSHIRE, OX17 2DA.
GALE, Mr. Richard Martin, ACA *1983;* Rosscot, Thomas Edge House Tunnell Street, St. Helier, JERSEY, JE2 4LU.
•GALE, Mr. Richard Sheehan, ACA *1984;* Coolbell Limited, Wigley Manor, Romsey Road, Ower, ROMSEY, HAMPSHIRE SO51 6AF.
•GALE, Mr. Robert, FCA *1969;* (Tax Fac), Robert Gale & Co, 8 Adelaide Row, SEAHAM, SR7 7EF.
GALE, Mr. Robert Charles, BSc ACA *1985;* 42 Station Road, THAMES DITTON, KT7 0NS.
•GALE, Mr. Robert John, BA FCA *1972;* Run Cottage, Carrs Road, Hassingham, NORWICH, NR13 4HJ.
•GALE, Mr. Russell John, BA FCA *1983;* 15 Cundy Close, Plympton, PLYMOUTH, PL7 4QH.
GALE, Mr. Stephen Dudley, MEng ACA CTA *2003;* 18 Fossil Road, LONDON, SE13 7DE.
•GALE, Mr. Stephen James, BSc FCA *1992;* Crowe Clark Whitehill LLP, St Bride's House, 10 Salisbury Square, LONDON, EC4Y 8EH. See also Horwath Clark Whitehill LLP and Crowe Clark Whitehill
•GALE, Mrs. Susan Ann, BA ACA *1985;* (Tax Fac), S.A. Gale, The Tile House, Marston St Lawrence, BANBURY, OX17 2DA.
•GALE, Mr. Terence Malcolm, FCA *1979;* Kings House, 12-42 Wood Street, KINGSTON UPON THAMES, SURREY, KT1 1TG. See also Menzies LLP
GALE, Ms. Yvonne, FCA *1993;* 5 Etal Avenue, WHITLEY BAY, TYNE AND WEAR, NE25 8QF.
GALEA, Mr. Daniel, ACA *2004;* Bella Vista, Raba Nemel, RABAT RBT 4344, MALTA.
GALER, Mr. Ian Richard, BA ACA *1982;* Wesleyan Assurance Society, Colmore Circus Queensway, BIRMINGHAM, B4 6AR.
GALES, Mrs. Lucy Jane, BSc ACA *1999;* 2398 Sandstone Dr, OAKVILLE L6M 4Y8, ON, CANADA.
GALETZKA, Mr. Peter Rene, BA ACA *1978;* 42 Palmerston Place, (First Floor Flat), EDINBURGH, EH12 5BJ.
•GALIA, Mr. Faruk Buda Bachu, BSc ACA *1990;* Mainstream Accountancy Services, 9 Crondal Place, Edgbaston, BIRMINGHAM, B15 2LB.
GALJAARD, Mr. Stephen Mark, BA ACA *1999;* 47 Hackthorn Road, Welton, LINCOLN, LN2 3LY.
GALKA, Mr. Zbyszek Bernard, FCA *1974;* 5 Howe Road, Douglas, Onchan, ISLE OF MAN, IM3 2AP.
GALKOWSKI, Mr. Tadeusz Julian, BA ACA *1989;* Enterprise Investors, Warsaw Financial Centre, Emilii Plater 53, WARSAW, 00-113, POLAND.
GALL, Mr. Daniel, ACA *1997;* 8/11 Bridge Road, Pelikan Complex, EAST MACKAY, QLD 4740, AUSTRALIA.
GALLACHER, Miss. Allison Rosalind Geraldine, BA ACA *1991;* Meisenrain 22c, 8044 GOCKHAUSEN, SWITZERLAND.
GALLACHER, Mrs. Helen Ruth, BSc(Hons) ACA *2000;* County Hall, Fishergate Hill, PRESTON, PR1 0LD.
GALLACHER, Mr. James Ian Sutherland, BSc FCA *1974;* 5 Carbery Avenue, Acton, LONDON, W3 9AD.
GALLACHER, Dr. John, BA FCA *1981;* York St. John University, Lord Mayors Walk, YORK, YO31 7EX.
GALLACHER, Mr. Martin John, BSc ACA *2007;* 57 Smyth Road, BRISTOL, BS3 2DS.
GALLACHER, Mr. Paul Nigel, BSc FCA *1996;* RBS Insurance, Churchill Court, Westmoreland Road, BROMLEY, BR1 1DP.
GALLAFANT, Mrs. Claire, ACA *2005;* 155 Foredyke Avenue, HULL, HU7 0DW.
•GALLAGHER, Mr. Andrew James, ACA *1994;* Moore Stephens & Company, L' Estoril Bloc C, 31 Avenue Princesse Grace, MONTE CARLO, MC 98000, MONACO. See also Moore Stephens LLP
GALLAGHER, Mr. Arthur Robin, FCA *1963;* Longley Old Hall, Longley, HUDDERSFIELD, HD5 8LB.
GALLAGHER, Mr. Carl Stephen, MSci ACA *2009;* 1 Grangedale Close, NORTHWOOD, MIDDLESEX, HA6 2YX.
GALLAGHER, Mrs. Carolyn, BSc ACA *1992;* Rowan House, 11a Orchard Garth, Copmanthorpe, YORK, YO23 3YP.
GALLAGHER, Mr. Daniel Joseph, ACA *2008;* 1 Lower Burgh Way, CHORLEY, PR7 3TJ.
GALLAGHER, Mr. David, BA ACA *1996;* 32 Danvers Road, Mountsorrel, LOUGHBOROUGH, LE12 7JQ.
GALLAGHER, Mr. David Francis, BA FCA *1980;* 21 Harvest Drive, Sindlesham, WOKINGHAM, RG41 5RF.
•GALLAGHER, Mr. David John, FCA *1985;* Calder & Co, 1 Regent Street, LONDON, SW1Y 4NW.
GALLAGHER, Miss. Deirdre Mary, BCom ACA *1997;* 77 Wainsfort Road, Terenure, DUBLIN 6, COUNTY DUBLIN, IRELAND.
GALLAGHER, Mrs. Denise, BAcc ACA *2003;* 14 Melford Avenue, Giffnock, GLASGOW, G46 6NA.
GALLAGHER, Mrs. Donna Louise, ACA *1989;* (Tax Fac), 23 Claremont Road, Bishopston, BRISTOL, BS7 8DL.
GALLAGHER, Miss. Elizabeth Maureen, BA ACA *1984;* 1 Althorp Close, MARKET HARBOROUGH, LE16 8EL.
GALLAGHER, Mr. Geoffrey David, BSc ACA *1992;* 21 Bewdley Close, HARPENDEN, AL5 1QX.
GALLAGHER, Mr. Ian William, MA FCA *1988;* 22 BRIDIE DRIVE, UPPER COOMERA, QLD 4209, AUSTRALIA.
GALLAGHER, Mrs. Irene Denise, MSc BA FCA *1969;* Apartment 2 Langham Mount, East Downs Road Bowdon, ALTRINCHAM, CHESHIRE, WA14 3NL.
GALLAGHER, Miss. Jacqueline Anne, BSc ACA *1996;* 5 Cleland Crescent, BALDIVIS, WA 6171, AUSTRALIA.
•GALLAGHER, Mr. James Joseph, FCA *1980;* (Tax Fac), Gallaghers, 33a High Street, Stony Stratford, MILTON KEYNES, MK11 1AA.
GALLAGHER, Mr. Jason Scott, BSc ACA *1994;* 71 Etherington Road, HULL, HU6 7JR.
GALLAGHER, Mr. Jeremiah Gerard, BA ACA *1992;* 14 Lime Avenue, Wheathampstead, ST. ALBANS, HERTFORDSHIRE, AL4 8LG.
GALLAGHER, Mr. Joel Richard, BSc(Hons) ACA CTA *2004;* Acal Plc, 2 Chancellor Court, Occam Road, Surrey Research Park, GUILDFORD, SURREY GU2 7AH.
•GALLAGHER, Mr. John Edward Masterson, FCA *1975;* Gallagher & Brocklehurst, 4 Plantagenet Road, BARNET, EN5 5JQ.
GALLAGHER, Mr. Joseph Gerald, FCA *1967;* 3 Ardilea Wood, Ardilea, DUBLIN 14, COUNTY DUBLIN, IRELAND.
GALLAGHER, Mrs. Julie Louise, ACA *1986;* The Gatehouse, Stansted Road, Birchanger, BISHOP'S STORTFORD, CM23 5PT.
GALLAGHER, Ms. Karen Jane, FCA *1972;* P.O. Box 4090, GUMDALE, QLD 4154, AUSTRALIA.
GALLAGHER, Miss. Kerry, BSc ACA DChA *2006;* 138 Britten Road, BASINGSTOKE, HAMPSHIRE, RG22 4HP.
GALLAGHER, Mrs. Lisa, BSc ACA *2005;* with Deloitte LLP, Athene Place, 66 Shoe Lane, LONDON, EC4A 3BQ.
GALLAGHER, Mr. Matthew Gerard, BA FCA *1994;* 1065 Nash Drive, CELEBRATION, FL 34743-4310, UNITED STATES.
GALLAGHER, Mr. Michael, ACA *1980;* 95 Eton Wick Road, Eton Wick, WINDSOR, SL4 6NQ.
GALLAGHER, Mr. Michael Francis, MEng ACA *1995;* 204 Alexandra Park Road, Wood Green, LONDON, N22 7UQ.
GALLAGHER, Mr. Michael James, MA(Hons) ACA *2000;* Flat 3 Eagle House, 30 Eagle Wharf Road, LONDON, N1 7EH.
GALLAGHER, Mr. Neil Christopher, BSc ACA *1995;* Nexus Telecommunications Plc Zicon House, Belgrave Street, LEEDS, LS2 8DD.
GALLAGHER, Mr. Patrick James, BA ACA *1989;* Rank Group Gaming Division New Statesman House, Stafferton Way, MAIDENHEAD, SL6 1AY.
GALLAGHER, Mr. Paul, BA(Hons) ACA *2010;* 3 Maidenwell Close, Navenby, LINCOLN, LN5 0EQ.
•GALLAGHER, Mr. Peter Richard, FCA *1968;* Gallagher & Co, Ivydene House, Uckinghall, TEWKESBURY, GL20 6ES.
GALLAGHER, Miss. Rachel Claire, BSc ACA *1999;* 43 Manor Road, TEDDINGTON, TW11 8AA.
GALLAGHER, Mr. Ronan Kannan, BSc(Hons) ACA *2002;* 9 Cavendish Meads, Sunninghill, ASCOT, SL5 9TB.
•GALLAGHER, Mr. Simon Patrick, BA ACA *1993;* Moore Stephens LLP, 150 Aldersgate Street, LONDON, EC1A 4AB. See also Moore Stephens & Co
GALLAGHER, Mr. Stephen Taylor, BSc ACA *1987;* 55 Mead Road, Leckhampton, CHELTENHAM, GLOUCESTERSHIRE, GL53 7DY.
GALLAGHER, Mrs. Suzanne Julia, ACA *2009;* Deloitte & Touche, Abbots House, Abbey Street, READING, RG1 3BD.
•①GALLANAGH, Mr. Eugene Patrick, BA ACA *1988;* 10 Glen Finlet Crescent, Neilston, GLASGOW, G78 3QT.
GALLANT, Mrs. Claire Alexandra, BSc ACA *1992;* Old Wheel Wrights, Cross Street, Hoxne, EYE, SUFFOLK, IP21 5AJ.
•GALLANT, Mr. John Claude James, BSc FCA *1978;* (Tax Fac), Bird Luckin Limited, Gateway House, 42 High Street, DUNMOW, ESSEX, CM6 1AH.
•GALLANT, Mr. Lee Andrew John, BEng ACA *1999;* Gallant Accountancy Services, 4 Johnsons Drive, HAMPTON, MIDDLESEX, TW12 2EQ. See also Lee Gallant
•GALLANT, Mr. Michael David, FCA *1969;* Michael Gallant & Co, 95 Sutton Heights, Albion Road, SUTTON, SURREY, SM2 5TD.
•GALLANT, Mr. Paul Terence, FCA *1976;* Smethurst & Buckton Ltd, 12 Abbey Road, GRIMSBY, SOUTH HUMBERSIDE, DN32 0HL. See also Smethurst & Buckton
GALLEMORE, Mr. John, BA ACA *1993;* 25 Deneford Road, MANCHESTER, M20 2TE.
•GALLER, Mr. Alfred Michael, FCA *1983;* (Tax Fac), Leskin Galler, The Linney, Oak Farm, Waddicombe, DULVERTON, SOMERSET TA22 9RX.
GALLEWAY, Mr. William Henry, BCom FCA *1955;* (Member of Council 1983 - 1995), Streonshalh, 1 North Promenade, WHITBY, YO21 3JX. (Life Member)
GALLEY, Mr. Bruce Buchanan, FCA *1969;* 16 Parolles Road, LONDON, N19 3RD.
GALLEY, Miss. Fiona Patricia, BSc ACA *1990;* 7 Dovewood Court, Littleover, DERBY, DE23 3ZF.
•GALLI, Mr. Andy, BSc ACA *1996;* Moore Stephens LLP, 150 Aldersgate Street, LONDON, EC1A 4AB. See also Moore Stephens & Co
GALLI, Mrs. Sara Lesley, BSc ACA *1996;* 62 Orchard Lane, AMERSHAM, BUCKINGHAMSHIRE, HP6 5AA.
GALLIANO, James Patrick, Esq MBE FCA *1962;* Church Lane Trustees Limited, P.O. Box 299, 10/3 ICC Building, Casemates Square, GIBRALTAR, GIBRALTAR.
GALLICK, Mr. Anthony David, FCA *1973;* 16 Reddings Close, LONDON, NW7 4JL.
GALLICO, Mr. Christopher Huish, MA MBA BSc FCA *1971;* 294 Warren Road, Bluebell Hill, CHATHAM, ME5 9RF.
GALLIENNE, Mr. Anthony Charles, BSc ACA *1982;* Norman Piette Ltd, PO Box 88, GUERNSEY, GY1 3EE.
GALLIENNE, Mr. Jeremy, BSc ACA *1980;* 15 South West High Street, GRANTOWN-ON-SPEY, MORAYSHIRE, PH26 3QH.
GALLIER, Mr. Philip Simon, ACA *2011;* 12 Lyme Street, LONDON, NW1 0EH.
GALLIERS, Mr. Andrew, BA(Hons) ACA *2011;* 42 Amethyst Grove, WATERLOOVILLE, PO7 8SG.
•GALLIERS, Mr. Colin Steven, FCA *1986;* (Tax Fac), Galliers & Co., Wizzard's Knoll, 33 Cockshot Road, MALVERN, WR14 2TT.
GALLIGAN, Mr. Dean Matthew, BSc FCA *2001;* 1 Spencer Hill, LONDON, SW19 4NZ.
GALLIMORE, Miss. Claire Joy, BA ACA *2006;* 46 Charnley Drive, LEEDS, LS7 4ST.
•GALLIMORE, Mr. Peter Charles, BA FCA AMCT *1999;* Deloitte LLP, 4 Brindley Place, BIRMINGHAM, B1 2HZ. See also Deloitte & Touche LLP
GALLIVAN, Mr. Nicholas David, BSc ACA *1995;* 28 Kelston Road, Whitchurch, CARDIFF, CF14 2AJ.
GALLIVER, Mr. Mark Scott, BA ACA *1999;* 28 Eaton Drive, KINGSTON UPON THAMES, KT2 7QT.
GALLO, Mrs. Charlotte, BA ACA *2001;* 11 Ashley Drive, Bramhall, STOCKPORT, CHESHIRE, SK7 1EW.
GALLON, Dr. Daniel, DPhil MChem ACA *2011;* Flat 44, Raleigh Court, Clarence Mews, LONDON, SE16 5GB.
GALLOP, Mr. Adam, BA ACA *1999;* 9 Ferry End, Ferry Road, Bray, MAIDENHEAD, BERKSHIRE, SL6 2AS.
GALLOP, Mr. Jonathan Howard, FCA *1973;* 7 Widdicombe Avenue, Parkstone, POOLE, BH14 9QW.
GALLOP, Mr. Thomas David, MA ACA *1999;* 65 High Street, Chippenham, ELY, CAMBRIDGESHIRE, CB7 5PP.
GALLOW, Mr. Jeffrey, BSc ACA *2005;* Flat 3 Sommerville Court, Alconbury Close, BOREHAMWOOD, HERTFORDSHIRE, WD6 4QH.
GALLOWAY, Mr. Andrew John, BA(Hons) ACA *2000;* 2 Ashcroft, BRIDGNORTH, SHROPSHIRE, WV16 5PG.
①GALLOWAY, Mr. Anthony John, FCA *1967;* 106 Park Hall Road, WALSALL, WS5 3LZ.
GALLOWAY, Miss. Caroline, ACA *2011;* 9 Clare Park, AMERSHAM, BUCKINGHAMSHIRE, HP7 9HW.
GALLOWAY, Mr. David Allistair, FCA *1968;* Moat House, Chapel Lane, West Wittering, CHICHESTER, PO20 8QG.
GALLOWAY, Mr. Duncan John, MA FCA *1976;* Hillcrest, Bradda West Road, Port Erin, ISLE OF MAN, IM9 6PL. (Life Member)
GALLOWAY, Mr. Graham Mackenzie, FCA *1978;* Cloister House, Brough Park, RICHMOND, NORTH YORKSHIRE, DL10 7PJ.
GALLOWAY, Mr. Ian Edward, BSc ACA *1999;* B G Group Plc, 100 Thames Valley Park Drive, READING, RG6 1PT.
GALLOWAY, Mr. Norman Locke, FCA *1950;* 31 Tiffany Close, WOKINGHAM, BERKSHIRE, RG41 3BN. (Life Member)
•GALLOWAY, Mr. Peter Ian Vivian, FCA *1977;* Mackenzie Field, Hyde House, The Hyde, Edgware Road, LONDON, NW9 6LA.
GALLOWAY, Mrs. Philippa Mary, FCA *1993;* 5 Middlewood, Sandringham Park Lowton, WARRINGTON, WA3 2QG.
GALLOWAY, Mrs. Rachel Elizabeth, ACA *1982;* Woodlands Surgery, 32-34 Station Road, CAMBRIDGE, CB1 2JH.
•GALPERT, Mr. John Bernard, FCA *1977;* S.L. Galpert & Co Ltd, 6 Montpelier Rise, LONDON, NW11 9SS.
GALPIN, Mrs. Imogen Charlton, BSc ACA *2007;* Newton House New Street, Marnhull, STURMINSTER NEWTON, DORSET, DT10 1PY.
GALPIN, Mr. Paul, BA ACA *2006;* 938 Garratt Lane, LONDON, SW17 0ND.
•GALPIN, Mr. Peter Richard, BA FCA *1984;* PricewaterhouseCoopers LLP, 1 Embankment Place, LONDON, WC2N 6RH. See also PricewaterhouseCoopers
GALT, Mr. Peter John McFarlane, FCA *1965;* 33 Cleveland Avenue, DARLINGTON, DL3 7HF.
GALVIN, Mr. Andrew Michael, ACA *1992;* North Longlands, Leeds Road, HALIFAX, WEST YORKSHIRE, HX3 8SX.
GALVIN, Mrs. Annette, BA ACA *2007;* 50 Castle Garden, SLANE, COUNTY MEATH, IRELAND.
GALVIN, Ms. Catherine, BSc FCA *1989;* 28 Friern Watch Avenue, North Finchley, LONDON, N12 9NT.
GALVIN, Mr. Christian John, MBA BSc FCA AMCT *1976;* 73 Gowan Avenue, LONDON, SW6 6RH.
GALVIN, Mrs. Glenda Joan, BA ACA *1991;* 59 Holmes Avenue, HOVE, BN3 7LB.
GALVIN, Mr. Graham, BA(Hons) ACA *2002;* Breast Cancer Care, 5-13 Great Suffolk Street, LONDON, SE1 0NS.
GALVIN, Mr. Ian, BA ACA CFA *1992;* PO Box 22688, DUBAI, UNITED ARAB EMIRATES.
GALVIN, Mr. John Noel, MA ACA *1992;* 21 Bloomfield Road, HARPENDEN, AL5 4DD.
GALVIN, Miss. Laura Jane, BSc ACA *2005;* Kingston Communications Melbourne House, Brandy Carr Road Wrenthorpe, WAKEFIELD, WEST YORKSHIRE, WF2 0UG.
•GALVIN, Mr. Martin Christopher, FCA *1971;* Martin C. Galvin, 1 Duke Street, GLOSSOP, SK13 8JD.
GALVIN, Mr. Peter James, FCA *1956;* April Cottage, Bates Hill, Ightham, SEVENOAKS, TN15 9HB. (Life Member)
GALVIN, Mr. Peter John, FCA *1957;* 8 Marlborough Way, ASHBY-DE-LA-ZOUCH, LE65 2NN. (Life Member)
GALVIN, Mrs. Ruth Elizabeth, BMus ACA *1992;* 105 Lyndon Road, SOLIHULL, B92 7RG.
GALVIN, Mr. Simon John, BA FCA *1977;* Great Oaks, 21 Grove Road, BEACONSFIELD, HP9 1UR.
GAMAGE, Mr. Alastair Richard, BSc ACA *1985;* Woodgable, 114 Nottingham Road, Ravenshead, NOTTINGHAM, NG15 9HL.
•GAMAGE, Mr. Nigel John, ACA *1980;* (Tax Fac), 14 Calstone, CALNE, WILTSHIRE, SN11 8PZ.
GAMBEL, Mr. Richard Dudley, BSc ACA *1992;* 17 Downs Wood, EPSOM, SURREY, KT18 5UH.
GAMBERONI, Mr. Denis Charles Pasquale, FCA *1963;* 7 Ainslies Belvedere, BATH, BA1 5HT. (Life Member)
GAMBIER, Mr. Andrew James, MA FCA *1998;* with ICAEW, Chartered Accountants' Hall, Moorgate Place, LONDON, EC2P 2BJ.
GAMBIN, Mr. Patrick, ACA *2002;* AL NABOODA GENERAL ENTERPRISES HOLDING (LLC), P.O.BOX 626, DUBAI, UNITED ARAB EMIRATES.

GAMBLE, Mr. Andrew Bernard, FCA *1973;* Brook Farm, Gaddesby Lane, Rearsby, LEICESTER, LE7 4YL.
GAMBLE, Mr. Anthony Charles, BSc FCA *1963;* 55 Hurlingham Court, Ranelagh Gardens, LONDON, SW6 3UP.
GAMBLE, Mr. Barry Thomas, BSc FCA *1974;* Manorfields Farm, Southam Road, Great Bourton, BANBURY, OX17 1AS.
GAMBLE, Mr. David, FCA *1969;* The Poplars, 37 Granville Road, Wigston Fields, WIGSTON, LE18 1JQ. (Life Member)
GAMBLE, Mr. Gareth David, BA(Hons) ACA *2002;* Flat 5, 77 Putney Bridge Road, Putney, LONDON, SW15 2NA.
GAMBLE, Mr. Jacob Alan, MA ACA *1987;* 40 Trafalgar Drive, Flitwick, BEDFORD, MK45 1EF.
GAMBLE, Mr. Karl, BSc ACA *2006;* 20 Upper Wood Close, Shenley Brook End, MILTON KEYNES, MK5 7GH.
GAMBLE, Mr. Nigel Charles, LLB ACA *1986;* 38 Illingworth Way, ENFIELD, EN1 2PA.
GAMBLE, Mr. Philip John, FCA *1969;* 5 The Glen, 166 Canford Cliffs Road, POOLE, BH13 7ES. (Life Member)
GAMBLE, Mr. Richard Arthur, FCA *1962;* Chart Hall Farm, Green Lane, Chart Sutton, MAIDSTONE, ME17 3ES.
GAMBLE, Mr. Roger Michael, BA ACA *2002;* 60 Coleman Crescent, RAMSGATE, KENT, CT12 6AE.
GAMBLE, Mr. Simon Richard, BSc ACA *1996;* (Tax Fac), 10 Bowerdean Street, LONDON, SW6 3TW.
GAMBLE, Mrs. Ursula Miriam, BCom ACA *1991;* Waltham Forest Town Hall, Forest Road, LONDON, E17 4JA.
•GAMBLEN, Mr. Nigel John, FCA CTA *1981;* (Tax Fac), Lentells Limited, Ash House, Cook Way, Bindon Road, TAUNTON, SOMERSET TA2 6BJ.
GAMBLES, Mrs. Claire Elizabeth, BSc ACA *2001;* with Deloitte LLP, 4 Brindley Place, BIRMINGHAM, B1 2HZ.
GAMBLES, Mr. Daniel Philip, BA(Hons) ACA CF *2001;* with Deloitte LLP, 4 Brindley Place, BIRMINGHAM, B1 2HZ.
•GAMBLIN, Mr. David Michael, BSc ACA ATII *1978;* David Gamblin, 71 The Hundred, ROMSEY, HAMPSHIRE, SO51 8BZ.
GAMBLING, Ms. Clare Mary, BA ACA *1990;* 13 Cranbrook Road, LONDON, W4 2LH.
GAMBLING, Mr. Stuart, BSc ACA *1992;* 2 Cassidy Gardens, Middleton, MANCHESTER, M24 5ND.
GAMBOLD, Mr. Bleddyn John, BA ACA *1982;* 161 Kanangra Road, Terrey Hills, SYDNEY, NSW 2084, AUSTRALIA.
•GAMBOLD, Mr. Matthew William, BSc MCIPS ACA *2004;* (Tax Fac), Chaddesley Sanford LLP, Longcroft House, 2-8 Victoria Avenue, LONDON, EC2M 4NS.
GAMBRELL, Mr. Andrew Paul, BSc ACA *1991;* English National Opera, London Coliseum, 38 St. Martin's Lane, LONDON, WC2N 4ES.
GAMBRELL, Mr. Christopher Charles, BA ACA *1991;* Courtil Charente, Rue Du Gele, Castel, GUERNSEY, GY5 7LP.
GAMBRELL, Miss. Jacqueline Mary, BA ACA *1979;* 115 Wickham Way, Park Langley, BECKENHAM, BR3 3AP.
GAME, Mr. Jonathan, BSc ACA *1989;* 5 Willow Mead, EAST GRINSTEAD, RH19 4TA.
GAME, Mr. Leigh, BSc(Hons) ACA *2009;* Unit 22, 16 Fritholme Gardens, PAGET PG04, BERMUDA.
GAME, Mr. Paul Martin, FCA *1968;* 46 Plough Hill, Cuffley, POTTERS BAR, EN6 4DS.
GAME, Mr. Ralph, FCA *1961;* 10 Cowslip Lane, SHERINGHAM, NORFOLK, NR26 8XL. (Life Member)
GAMESON, Miss. Amanda Valerie, BSc ACA *1992;* Arcadia Housing, 2 Station Road, Worle, WESTON-SUPER-MARE, AVON, BS22 6AP.
GAMESTER, Mr. Peter Anthony, BA FCA ATII *1977;* Lamorna, Chapel Road, Great Totham, MALDON, CM9 8DA.
GAMMAGE, Miss. Alexandra Clare, ACA *2009;* 11 Bat & Ball Lane, Wrecclesham, FARNHAM, GU10 4RA.
GAMMAGE, Mr. Antony Marshall, FCA *1957;* 9 Hartland Road, EPPING, CM16 4PH. (Life Member)
GAMMELL, Miss. Fiona Marlis, BSc(Hons) ACA *2001;* 137 High Street, NORTH SYDNEY, NSW 2060, AUSTRALIA.
GAMMIE, Mr. Peter Geoffrey, FCA *1974;* Alstone House, 243 Farleigh Road, WARLINGHAM, SURREY, CR6 9EL.
GAMMON, Mr. Alyn Huw, BSc ACA *1998;* 12 Lon y Cadno, Church Village, PONTYPRIDD, MID GLAMORGAN, CF38 2BQ.
GAMMON, Mr. John Edward Robert, FCA *1955;* T. Geddes Grant Ltd Pension Fund Plan, 61/63 Edward Street, PORT OF SPAIN, TRINIDAD AND TOBAGO. (Life Member)
•GAMMON, Mr. Jonathan Michael, BSc FCA *1984;* Magee Gammon Corporate Limited, Henwood House, Henwood, ASHFORD, KENT, TN24 8DH. See also Magee Gammon Partnership LLP
GAMMON, Mr. Roger Beauchamp, FCA *1974;* Flat 1, Beech Spinney, Lorne Road, Warley, BRENTWOOD, ESSEX CM14 5HH.
GAMMON, Miss. Sara Jane, MMath ACA *2009;* (Tax Fac), 80 Perivale, Monkston Park, MILTON KEYNES, MK10 9PE.
GAMMON, Mr. Stephen Thomas, BSc ACA *2006;* 9 Merlyn Avenue, Didsbury, MANCHESTER, M20 6FQ.
GAMMON-HARDAWAY, Mr. Mark Andrew, BA ACA *1987;* 2a Noreuil Road, PETERSFIELD, GU32 3BA.
•GAMON, Mrs. Jill Irene, FCA *1973;* with Johns Jones & Lo Limited, 14 Lambourne Crescent, Cardiff Business Park, Llanishen, CARDIFF, CF14 5GF.
•GAMSON, Mr. Peter John, BSc ACA *1999;* Grant Thornton UK LLP, Grant Thornton House, 22 Melton Street, Euston Square, LONDON, NW1 2EP. See also Grant Thornton LLP
GAMWELL, Mr. Andrew James, BSc ACA *2006;* 242 Westmount Road, LONDON, SE9 1YA.
GAN, Dato' Ah Tee, JP FCA CF *1983;* No.1 Lorong Setiabistari 2, Bukit Damansara, 50490 KUALA LUMPUR, FEDERAL TERRITORY, MALAYSIA.
GAN, Miss. Bee Eng, FCA *1976;* Blk 11, Dairy Farm Road, Apt 02-06, SINGAPORE 679040, SINGAPORE.
GAN, Mr. Chee Leong, ACA *1983;* 3 Persiaran Begonia, Desa Impian Menghijau, Planters Haven, 71800 NILAI, NEGERI SEMBILAN, MALAYSIA.
GAN, Mr. Henry, ACA *1979;* B12 Desa Ukay Condominium, 12 Jalan Terbrau Ukay Heights, 68000 AMPANG, SELANGOR, MALAYSIA.
GAN, Mr. Hock Soon, BSc CA ACA CPA *2010;* 153-15-3 Menara Duta, Jalan Dutamas Raya, 51200 KUALA LUMPUR, FEDERAL TERRITORY, MALAYSIA.
GAN, Mr. Hui Beng, BSc FCA *1979;* 137 Sunset Way #02-16, SINGAPORE 597159, SINGAPORE.
GAN, Ms. Hwee Leng, FCA *1991;* 501 Sembawang Road, 02-14 Seletaris, SINGAPORE 757706, SINGAPORE.
GAN, Mr. Ker Wei, BSc(Econ) ACA *2001;* Unit F 22/F Tower 1, The Belchers, 89 Pok Fu Lam Road, SAI WAN HO, HONG KONG ISLAND, HONG KONG SAR.
GAN, Mr. Kong Chin, BA FCA *1983;* 88 Old South Head Road, VAUCLUSE, NSW 2030, AUSTRALIA.
GAN, Ms. Li-Kim, ACA *2009;* 35 Jalan SS22/3 Damansara Jaya, 47400 PETALING JAYA, SELANGOR, MALAYSIA.
GAN, Mr. Nga Kok Jacob, BSc ACA *1984;* 5 Marine Vista #11-51, SINGAPORE 449029, SINGAPORE.
GAN, Mr. Soo Jin, FCA *1974;* No 3 Jln Athinahapan 3, Taman Tun Dr Ismail, 60000 KUALA LUMPUR, FEDERAL TERRITORY, MALAYSIA.
GAN, Miss. Stephanie Siew Lin, BA ACA *1994;* 18 Lorong Kemaris 4, Bukit Bandaraya, 59100 KUALA LUMPUR, FEDERAL TERRITORY, MALAYSIA.
GAN, Mr. Tin Hua, FCA *1967;* 73 Nim Road 07-02, Nim Gardens, SINGAPORE 807584, SINGAPORE.
GAN, Mr. Wee Shien, ACA *2010;* 129B Hornsey Park Road, LONDON, N8 0JX.
GANASALINGAM, Miss. Saraswathy, BSc ACA *1992;* 353 Burwood Highway, FOREST HILL, VIC 3131, AUSTRALIA.
GANATRA, Mr. Chandravadan Vithaldas, FCA *1972;* 9A Sandy Lodge Road, RICKMANSWORTH, WD3 1LP.
GANATRA, Mr. Dipesh, BA(Hons) ACA *2000;* 19 Lancaster Road, HARROW, MIDDLESEX, HA2 7NN.
GANATRA, Mr. Kantilal Ranchhoddas, FCA *1960;* 16 Hayesford Park Drive, BROMLEY, BR2 9DB. (Life Member)
GANATRA, Mr. Praful, BA ACA CTA *1989;* 69 Little Bushey Lane, BUSHEY, HERTFORDSHIRE, WD23 4RA.
GANATRA, Mr. Shamil Dinesh, ACA *2008;* Flat 25, 26 Spital Square, LONDON, E1 6DX.
GANDEE, Mr. David James, BSc ACA *1998;* 26 Tithby Road, Bingham, NOTTINGHAM, NG13 8GN.
GANDELL, Mr. Andrew William Pearse, ACA *2008;* Swallow Barn, Well Road, Crondall, FARNHAM, SURREY, GU10 5PW.
GANDERTON, Mr. Allan Rikki, ACA *1980;* 23 Curtis Crescent, KING CITY L7B 1C3, ON, CANADA.
GANDESHA, Mr. Daniel Mark, ACA *2008;* Flat 2, 56 Larkhall Rise, LONDON, SW4 6JY.
GANDESHA, Mr. Kartik, BA(Hons) ACA *2003;* 22 Northumberland Avenue, Wanstead, LONDON, E12 5HD.
GANDESHA, Miss. Nisha, BSc ACA *2007;* Flat 63 Naxos Building, 4 Hutchings Street, LONDON, E14 8JR.
GANDHI, Mr. Achal, BSc ACA *2008;* 10 Becmead Avenue, Kenton, HARROW, MIDDLESEX, HA3 8EY.
GANDHI, Mr. Arunkumar Ramanlal, FCA *1968;* Tata Sons Ltd, Bombay House, 24 Homi Mody Street, MUMBAI 400 006, MAHARASHTRA, INDIA.
GANDHI, Mr. Homi Dosabhai, BSc FCA *1967;* 704 Harristown Road, GLEN ROCK, NJ 07452, UNITED STATES.
GANDHI, Mr. Jainil, MA(Cantab) BA(Hons) ACA *2006;* 19 Elston Road, ALDERSHOT, HAMPSHIRE, GU12 4HX.
•GANDHI, Mr. Jayant Bhikhabhai, FCA *1966;* (Tax Fac), Gandhi & Co, 113 Kingsley Road, HOUNSLOW, TW3 4AJ.
GANDHI, Mr. Kaushal, BSc(Econ) ACA *2001;* 5 Manor Court, Bonnersfield Lane, HARROW, MIDDLESEX, HA1 2LD.
GANDHI, Mr. Mehul Mansukhlal, ACA *2008;* Edith Cowan University, 270 Joondalup Drive, JOONDALUP, WA 6027, AUSTRALIA.
GANDHI, Mr. Minoo Dadabhoy, FCA *1951;* Flat 4 Ness Baug, Annexe 2, Nana Chowk, MUMBAI 400 007, MAHARASHTRA, INDIA. (Life Member)
•GANDHI, Mr. Mital, BA(Hons) ACA *2003;* with S H Landes LLP, 3rd Floor, Fairgate House, 78 New Oxford Street, LONDON, WC1A 1HB.
GANDHI, Mr. Mukul, BA FCA *1985;* Tconsult Business Solutions, 21 The Embankment, BEDFORD, MK40 3PD.
GANDHI, Mr. Naresh Manherlal, BA FCA *1999;* 18 Pasture Close, North Wembley, WEMBLEY, HA0 3JE.
GANDHI, Mr. Nikesh, BSc(Hons) ACA *2002;* 15 Trevelyan Crescent, HARROW, MIDDLESEX, HA3 0RN.
GANDHI, Miss. Nita, BSc ACA *1995;* 12 Constitution Way, JERSEY CITY, NJ 07305-5414, UNITED STATES.
GANDHI, Mr. Pragnesh, BSc(Hons) ACA *2004;* 105 Argyll Avenue, LUTON, LU3 1EJ.
GANDHI, Miss. Puja, BSc ACA *2006;* 65 Du Cros Drive, STANMORE, MIDDLESEX, HA7 4TL.
•GANDHI, Mr. Pulin Mahendrakumar, BA ACA *1984;* PSJ & Associates, P.O. Box 90393, MOMBASA, KENYA.
GANDHI, Mr. Samir, BSc ACA *1993;* 25 Hazlitt Drive, Queens Avenue, MAIDSTONE, ME16 0EG.
GANDHI, Mr. Sanjay, BA ACA *1994;* 19 Longcrofte Road, EDGWARE, MIDDLESEX, HA8 6RR.
•GANDHI, Mr. Sanjeev Kumar, BSc ACA *1995;* with Grant Thornton UK LLP, Grant Thornton House, 22 Melton Street, Euston Square, LONDON, NW1 2EP.
GANDHI, Mr. Shirin, BA ACA *1992;* KPRG Business Services Limited, 26 Hillcrest Road, LOUGHTON, IG10 4QQ.
GANDHI, Mrs. Smita, BSc ACA *1998;* Little Stirrups, Church Road, Hartley, LONGFIELD, KENT, DA3 8DJ.
GANDHI, Mr. Viraf Hormasji, FCA *1969;* The Hoare Partnership Ltd, T/A Universal Showcards, 23 Stonefield Way, RUISLIP, HA4 0YF.
GANDY, Ms. Bridget Scott, BA ACA *1992;* Fimalac, 30 North Colonnade, LONDON, E14 5GN.
•GANDY, Mr. Howard Edward, BA(Hons) FCA *2000;* HG Professional Limited, Office F5, Building 67, Europa Business Park, Bird Hall Lane, Cheadle Heath STOCKPORT CHESHIRE SK3 0XA.
GANDY, Mr. Martin Frank, FCA *1977;* Cedar Rest, Cedar Avenue West, CHELMSFORD, CM1 2XA.
GANDZ, Mr. Benjamin Lee, BA ACA *2010;* Apartment A303, Gan Regency, 1 Ramat Yam, 46851 HERZLIA PETUACH, ISRAEL.
•GANDZ, Mr. Melvyn, FCA *1979;* (Tax Fac), BSG Valentine, Lynton House, 7/12 Tavistock Square, LONDON, WC1H 9BQ.
GANE, Miss. Jennifer Sara, ACA *2008;* 73 Myddelton Square, LONDON, EC1R 1XP.
GANESATHASAN, Miss. Menaka, MA ACA *1983;* Office of Research Services, University of Hawaii at Manoa, Sakamaki Hall C 200, Dole Street, HONOLULU, HI 96822 UNITED STATES.
GANESHWARAN, Mr. Ben Beeshmen, BA(Hons) ACA *2007;* Flat 45 Radley House, Gloucester Place, LONDON, NW1 6DP.
GANGE, Mr. Stephen Michael, BA ACA *1989;* Saudi Aramco, PO Box 2626, DHAHRAN, 31311, SAUDI ARABIA.
•GANGOLA, Mr. Amitabh Riki, BSc(Econ) FCA *1995;* RDP Newmans LLP, Lynwood House, 373/375 Station Road, HARROW, MIDDLESEX, HA1 2AW.
GANGULI, Mr. Amal, FCA *1962;* J-6/7, DLF Qutab Enclave Phase II, Guragaon, HARYANA 122002, INDIA.
GANGULI, Mr. Anupam, FCA *1992;* 128 Emmanuel Road, LONDON, SW12 0HS.
GANGULI, Mrs. Helen Sabina, MSc ACA *1991;* 5 Martins Shaw, Chipstead, SEVENOAKS, TN13 2SE.
GANGULI, Mr. Parbati Charan, FCA *1951;* 49C, Block CNew Alipore, CALCUTTA 700 053, INDIA. (Life Member)
GANGULI, Mr. Ranjan Kumar, BSc ACA *1991;* 5 Martins Shaw, Chipstead, SEVENOAKS, TN13 2SE.
GANGULY, Mr. Arnab, BSc ACA *2006;* 35 The Ridgeway, North Harrow, HARROW, HA2 7QL.
GANGULY, Mr. Pramit, BA(Hons) ACA *2009;* 35 The Ridgeway, North Harrow, HARROW, MIDDLESEX, HA2 7QL.
GANGULY, Mr. Sukanta, FCA *1981;* PO Box 73205, DUBAI, UNITED ARAB EMIRATES.
GANGULY, Mr. Swagata, BA(Hons) ACA *2001;* 51 Eton Avenue, LONDON, NW3 3EP.
GANI, Miss. Sabeena Hasan, BSc(Hons) ACA *2003;* Deutsche Bank Winchester House, 1 Great Winchester Street, LONDON, EC2N 2DB.
GANLEY, Mrs. Denise Claire, BA FCA *1997;* 10 Stewart Road, HARPENDEN, HERTFORDSHIRE, AL5 4QB.
GANNAWAY, Mrs. Elaine Blakely, BSc ACA *1993;* 35 Lauderdale Road, BIRKDALE 1310, NEW ZEALAND.
GANNON, Mr. Luke James, ACA *2010;* 5 Hadleigh Green, Lostock, BOLTON, BL6 4EB.
GANNON, Mr. Mark Simon, BA ACA MBA *1994;* Flat 19 Northpoint, Sherman Road, BROMLEY, BR1 3JN.
GANNON, Mr. Paul Ronald, BA ACA *1998;* 113 Endlesham Road, Balham, LONDON, SW12 8JP.
•GANPATSINGH, Mr. Roger Ian, BEng ACA *2000;* Throgmorton UK Limited, 4th Floor, Reading Bridge House, Reading Bridge, George Street, READING RG1 8LS. See also Throgmorton
GANSBUEHLER, Mrs. Caroline Emma, BSc ACA *2003;* The Old Mill Office, Boyton Hall Boyton Hall Lane, Roxwell, CHELMSFORD, CM1 4LN.
GANT, Mrs. Debbie, BSc ACA *1997;* 72 High Lane West, West Hallam, ILKESTON, DERBYSHIRE, DE7 6HQ.
GANT, Mr. Ian Tetley, FCA *1969;* (Tax Fac), 18 Fieldway, BERKHAMSTED, HP4 2NX.
•GANT, Mrs. Jane Farley, ACA *1980;* (Tax Fac), Gant Massingale, Fairlight, Meadway, BERKHAMSTED, HP4 2PN.
GANT, Mrs. Sian Elizabeth, BSc ACA *2005;* 5 Longcliff Close, Old Dalby, MELTON MOWBRAY, LE14 3LU.
GANT, Mr. Stephen John, BA FCA *1973;* 21 Kysbie Close, ABINGDON, OXFORDSHIRE, OX14 1XZ.
GANT, Mr. Stephen William, BA ACA *1990;* 23 Heath Drive, Theydon Bois, EPPING, CM16 7HL.
GANT, Mr. Timothy James, MA ACA *1992;* 36 Water Lane, COBHAM, KT11 2PB.
GANTEAUME, Mr. Henry Peter Geoffrey, FCA *1969;* Guardian Holdings Ltd, 1 Guardian Drive, West Moorings SE, WESTMOORINGS, TRINIDAD AND TOBAGO.
GANZ, Mr. Eli, BSc ACA *2011;* Flat 12, Pembroke Hall, Mulberry Close, LONDON, NW4 1QW.
GANZ, Ms. Rebecca Jane, MA ACA *1995;* 33 Spinnaker Drive, Te Atatu North, AUCKLAND 8, NEW ZEALAND.
GAO, Miss. Rong, ACA *2008;* 32 Toyne Way, LONDON, N6 4EG.
GAO, Mrs. Yan, BSc ACA *2009;* Level 5 Ernst&Young Tower, Oriental Plaza, No.1 East Chang An Avenue, DongCheng District, Beijing, BEIJING 100738 CHINA.
GAON, Mr. Isaac Joseph John, BA FCA *1975;* 38 Avenue Road, Suite 1101, TORONTO M5R 2G2, ON, CANADA.
•GARA, Mr. Michael, FCA *1971;* Trevelyan & Company Ltd, Charles House, 20/22 Elland Road, Churwell Hill, LEEDS, LS27 7SS.
•GARABEDIAN, Mr. Garo, BA FCA *1968;* (Tax Fac), Garo & Co., 27 Daventry Street, LONDON, NW1 6TD.
GARAVELLO, Mr. Marco John, BA ACA *2003;* with KPMG LLP, 8 Princes Parade, LIVERPOOL, L3 1QH.
GARAY, Mrs. Lydia, FCA *1976;* Villa Garay, Vista de la Brisa, Villa 1, Lote 4, Manzana 8, Joyas de Brisamar CP 39865 ACAPULCO MEXICO.
•GARBETT, Mr. Graham Stuart, BA FCA *1992;* with G & E Professional Services Limited, Arabesque House, Monks Cross Drive, Huntington, YORK, YO32 9GW.
GARBETT, Miss. Hayley Elizabeth, BA(Hons) ACA *2011;* 35 St. Andrews Avenue, Pelsall, WALSALL, WS3 4EN.

GARBETT, Mrs. Helen Elizabeth, BA BSc ACA *1989;* with KPMG LLP, 15 Canada Square, LONDON, E14 5GL.

GARBETT, Mr. Julian, BEng ACA *1983;* Horse Shoe House, West Winterslow, SALISBURY, SP5 1RY.

GARBUTT, Mr. Anthony James, BSc FCA *1983;* 51 Foxcote, Finchampstead, WOKINGHAM, BERKSHIRE, RG40 3PG.

GARBUTT, Mr. John Paul William, MA ACA *1994;* with Ernst & Young LLP, 1 More London Place, LONDON, SE1 2AF.

•GARBUTT, Mr. John Peter, BA(Hons) ACA *2007;* DSC, Tattersall House, East Parade, HARROGATE, NORTH YORKSHIRE, HG1 5LT. See also DSC Accountants Limited

GARBUTT, Mr. Neil, ACA *1978;* Fairway, Shibden Head Lane, Queensbury, BRADFORD, BD13 2NH.

•GARBUTT, Mr. Stephen, ACA *1985;* Axholme Associates Limited, Melbourne House, 27 Thorne Road, DONCASTER, SOUTH YORKSHIRE, DN1 2EZ.

•GARBUTTA, Mr. Stephen Michael, FCA *1971;* Harris & Trotter LLP, 65 New Cavendish Street, LONDON, W1G 7LS.

GARCHA, Miss. Sabreet, BSc(Econ) ACA *2011;* 77 Beaulieu Close, Datchet, SLOUGH, SL3 9DD.

GARCHA, Mr. Sarvjeet Singh, MA MPhil ACA MBA *1998;* Faradean, Temple Gardens, STAINES, MIDDLESEX, TW18 3NQ.

GARCIA, Mrs. Antonia Claire, BSc ACA *2000;* 162 Harefield Road, UXBRIDGE, MIDDLESEX, UB8 1PP.

GARCIA, Miss. Christina, ACA *2010;* 13 Clowders Road, LONDON, SE6 4DA.

•GARCIA, Mr. Daniel Alexis, BA FCA *1996;* (Tax Fac), Adler Shine LLP, Aston House, Cornwall Avenue, LONDON, N3 1LF.

GARCIA, Mr. Philip, MEng ACA *2010;* 29 Gloucester House, Courtlands, Sheen Road, RICHMOND, SURREY, TW10 5BB.

GARCIA-RIVAS, Mr. Eduardo, ACA *1998;* Barclays Bank Plc, Business Risk - 3030, Mateo Inurria 15, 28036 MADRID, SPAIN.

GARD, Mr. David Pascoe, BSc ACA *1995;* The Oast House, Bodiam Road, Sandhurst, CRANBROOK, KENT, TN18 5LE.

GARD, Mr. Graham Cecil Haidon, FCA *1955;* 193 Amber Valley, Private Bag X30, HOWICK, KWAZULU NATAL, 3290, SOUTH AFRICA. (Life Member)

GARD, Mr. William Henry, FCA *1957;* 38 Knowsley Way, Hildenborough, TONBRIDGE, TN11 9LQ. (Life Member)

GARDEN, Mr. Iain Graham, BA ACA *1984;* 10 Prairie Street, LONDON, SW8 3PU.

GARDEN, Mr. John Anthony, FCA *1957;* 23 Bracknell Gardens, Hampstead, LONDON, NW3 7EE. (Life Member)

GARDENER, Mr. Christopher Michael, BSc ACA *1993;* 18a The Crescent, WITNEY, OX28 2EL.

GARDENER, Mr. David John, BSc ACA *2010;* Reckitt Benckiser Plc, 103-105 Bath Road, SLOUGH, SL1 3UH.

GARDENER, Mr. Niall Philip, BSc ACA *2005;* with PKF (UK) LLP, Farringdon Place, 20 Farringdon Road, LONDON, EC1M 3AP.

•GARDENER, Mrs. Rebecca Joy Mary, BA ACA *1989;* Cardiff Bay Accountancy, Braeside, 7 Heol Y Pentre, Pentyrch, CARDIFF, CF15 9QD.

GARDENER, Mrs. Vivien Helen, BA ACA *1994;* 1 Lottage Road, Aldbourne, MARLBOROUGH, WILTSHIRE, SN8 2DL.

GARDENER, Mr. William Kenneth, BA FCA *1952;* 15 Ennismore Mews, LONDON, SW7 1AP.

GARDEZI, Mr. Raza Louis, BA(Hons) ACA *2001;* Total Security Services Limited, 485 Hale End Road, Highams Park, LONDON, E4 9PT.

GARDEZI, Mr. Syed Ihsan Ali Shah, FCA *1975;* C/21 Casa. 641, Urb. Guadalmina Alta, San Pedro de Alcantara, 29670 MARBELLA, MALAGA, SPAIN. (Life Member)

GARDIN, Mr. Thomas Henry, FCA *1963;* Greencroft, Appleton Wiske, NORTHALLERTON, NORTH YORKSHIRE, DL6 2AJ. (Life Member)

GARDINER, Mr. Adam, ACA *2011;* 85 Carisbrooke Road, LEEDS, LS16 5RX.

GARDINER, Mr. Andrew, MA BSc ACA *2003;* 2 Oak Lane, WINDSOR, BERKSHIRE, SL4 5EU.

GARDINER, Mr. Arthur Edward George, LLB FCA *1970;* 25 Vernon Road, Greenmount, BURY, BL8 4DD. (Life Member)

GARDINER, Mr. Benjamin Stefan Don, ACA *2009;* 27 Jasmond Road, PORTSMOUTH, PO6 2SY.

GARDINER, Mr. Christopher James, ACA *2010;* 100 Camden Road, IPSWICH, IP3 8JN.

•GARDINER, Mr. David Kim, FCA *1970;* D.K. Gardiner & Co., 15F Postgate, GLENROTHES, KY7 5LH.

GARDINER, Mr. Francis Michael Hugh, FCA *1952;* Shenleigh, Main Street, Welburn, YORK, YO60 7DX. (Life Member)

•GARDINER, Mr. Gavin Peter, BA FCA *1985;* Gardiner Fosh Limited, 31 St. Johns, WORCESTER, WR2 5AG. See also Gardiner Fosh

•GARDINER, Mr. Glen Colin, ACA *1993;* Accountancy Matters (South East) Limited, 6 Alder Close, Ash Vale, ALDERSHOT, HAMPSHIRE, GU12 5QS.

GARDINER, Mr. James Richard Peter, LLB ACA *2001;* Gardiner Bros Unit F-g Quedgeley West Business Park, Bristol Road Hardwicke, GLOUCESTER, GL2 4PH.

•GARDINER, Mr. Jeremy David, BSc ACA *1979;* J.D. Gardiner & Co, Chisholm House, 9 Queens Square, CORBY, NORTHAMPTONSHIRE, NN17 1PD.

GARDINER, Miss. Karen Elizabeth, BA ACA *1986;* 9 Bronte Road, Ballinaskeagh, BANBRIDGE, COUNTY DOWN, BT32 5BR.

GARDINER, Ms. Katherine Anne, BSc ACA *1985;* 11 Coombs Street, Islington, LONDON, N1 8DJ.

GARDINER, Mrs. Katherine Emily, ACA *2008;* 9 Quarry Road, Headington, OXFORD, OX3 8NT.

GARDINER, Mr. Keith, FCA *1971;* 86 Ellesmere Road, BOLTON, BL3 3JP.

•GARDINER, Mr. Laurence Walter, FCA *1960;* Laurence W. Gardiner, Fermain, 124 Glaziers Lane, Normandy, GUILDFORD, GU3 2DQ.

GARDINER, Mr. Leslie Henry, FCA *1952;* 3 Andrew Court, 68 Wickham Road, BECKENHAM, KENT, BR3 6RG. (Life Member)

GARDINER, Mr. Luke Alec, FCA *1970;* 3 Honeyhanger, Hindhead Road, HINDHEAD, GU26 6BA.

GARDINER, Miss. Lynda, ACA *2009;* 24 Alder Grove, Hoole, CHESTER, CH2 3EU.

•GARDINER, Mr. Mark Charles James, BA ACA *1985;* PricewaterhouseCoopers LLP, 1 Embankment Place, LONDON, WC2N 6RH. See also PricewaterhouseCoopers

GARDINER, Mr. Mark William, BA ACA MCT *1991;* The Random House Group Ltd, 20 Vauxhall Bridge Road, LONDON, SW1V 2SA.

GARDINER, Mr. Michael Henry, FCA *1955;* (Tax Fac), Coly House, Colyford, COLYTON, DEVON, EX24 6HE. (Life Member)

GARDINER, Mr. Michael Ian Macleod, MA FCA *1972;* Rogues Roost, Heath Road, WEYBRIDGE, KT13 8TL.

GARDINER, Mr. Paul William, MA FCA *1987;* Flat 7C, 7th Floor Shan Kwong Mansions, No 7C Shan Kwong Road, HAPPY VALLEY, HONG KONG SAR.

•GARDINER, Mr. Peter Edward, FCA *1970;* Abbotts House, 11 Abbots Road, COLCHESTER, CO2 8BE.

GARDINER, Mr. Peter George, FCA CTA FSI *1963;* Shepherds Farm Shepherds Lane, Halsall, ORMSKIRK, L39 7LB.

GARDINER, Mr. Peter Giles, FCA *1965;* Gardiner Bros, Unit F & G, Quedgeley West Business Park, Bristol Road, Hardwicke, GLOUCESTER GL2 4PH.

GARDINER, Miss. Polly Rosemary, BA ACA AKC *2004;* 23a Aliwal Road, LONDON, SW11 1RB.

GARDINER, Mr. Richard Jolyon, FCA *1962;* Gardiner Bros Unit F-g Quedgeley West Business Park, Bristol Road Hardwicke, GLOUCESTER, GL2 4PH.

•GARDINER, Mr. Robert Geoffrey, MA FCA *1988;* St John's Innovation Centre, Cowley Road, CAMBRIDGE, CB4 0WS.

GARDINER, Mr. Roger David, BSc FCA *1973;* BFD Holdings Ltd, 1 Mill Court, Mill Lane, NEWBURY, BERKSHIRE, RG14 5RE.

GARDINER, Mr. Simon John, MSci ACA *2004;* with KPMG LLP, 15 Canada Square, LONDON, E14 5GL.

•GARDINER, Mr. Stephen James, ACA ATII *1983;* John Goulding & Co Ltd, 4 Southport Road, CHORLEY, LANCASHIRE, PR7 1LD.

GARDINER, Mr. Tim Campbell, BSc ACA *1989;* 35/5 Darnell Road, EDINBURGH, EH5 3PH.

GARDINER, Mr. Tony Peter, BSc ACA *1995;* 12 Hoodhill Road, Harley, ROTHERHAM, S62 7US.

GARDINER CURRIE, Mrs. Britt, BSc FCA *1990;* 54 Prebend Gardens, LONDON, W6 0XU.

GARDNER, Mrs. Abigail Mary, BSc ACA *1997;* 14 Brayburne Avenue, LONDON, SW4 6AA.

GARDNER, Mr. Adrian David Edmund, BA ACA *1989;* P A Consulting Group, 123 Buckingham Palace Road, LONDON, SW1W 9SR.

GARDNER, Mr. Adrian Trevor, BSc ACA *2008;* Trevine, Station Road, BAMPTON, OXFORDSHIRE, OX18 2LQ.

GARDNER, Mr. Alan Frank, FCA *1955;* 1 Woodfield Drive, WINCHESTER, SO22 5PY. (Life Member)

•GARDNER, Mr. Alan Keith, BSc FCA CMC *1973;* HW, Keepers Lane, The Wergs, WOLVERHAMPTON, WEST MIDLANDS, WV6 8UA. See also Haines Watts

GARDNER, Miss. Alison Caroline, BSc(Hons) ACA *2002;* The Gables, 19 Woodchester Road, BRISTOL, BS10 5EX.

GARDNER, Mr. Andrew, BA ACA *1991;* Leeds University, Brotherton Library Office, University of Leeds, LEEDS, LS2 9JT.

GARDNER, Mr. Andrew Jeremy, BSc ACA *1997;* Prospect House, Brookhouse Group Ltd, 168-170 Washway Road, SALE, CHESHIRE, M33 6RH.

GARDNER, Mrs. Angela Mary, BA ACA *1997;* with KPMG LLP, 15 Canada Square, LONDON, E14 5GL.

GARDNER, Miss. Ann Georgina, ACA *1982;* (Tax Fac), 51 Glycena Road, LONDON, SW11 5TP.

•GARDNER, Mr. Anthony Edward, BA FCA *1991;* with Lopian Gross Barnett & Co, 6th Floor, Cardinal House, 20 St. Marys Parsonage, MANCHESTER, M3 2LG.

GARDNER, Mrs. Barbara Ann, FCA *1976;* with CLB Coopers, Fleet House, New Road, LANCASTER, LA1 1EZ.

GARDNER, Mrs. Barbara Lesley, BA FCA *1990;* 56 Cole Lane, IVYBRIDGE, PL21 0PN.

GARDNER, Mr. Calum Richard, BA ACA *1991;* 250 W 89th Street, Apartment 12G, NEW YORK, NY 10024, UNITED STATES.

•GARDNER, Mrs. Carol Jane, BSc ACA *1998;* Carol Gardner, 13 High Green, Thorpe Hamlet, NORWICH, NR1 4AP.

GARDNER, Mrs. Caroline Jane, MA FCA *1996;* Rose Cottage, Hillborough Avenue, SEVENOAKS, KENT, TN13 3SG.

GARDNER, Mrs. Catherine Anne, BSc ACA *1993;* with Ernst & Young LLP, 1 More London Place, LONDON, SE1 2AF.

GARDNER, Mr. Charles Richard Exton, FCA *1967;* Windwhistle, 2 Onslow Road, Burwood Park, WALTON-ON-THAMES, KT12 5BB.

GARDNER, Dr. Christopher, PhD BSc ACA *1984;* 5a Tournament Court, Edgehill Drive, WARWICK, CV34 6LG.

GARDNER, Mr. Christopher Brian, MA ACA *1991;* Church Cottage High Street, Rattlesden, BURY ST. EDMUNDS, SUFFOLK, IP30 0RA.

GARDNER, Mr. Christopher Frank, ACA *2009;* 17 Heysham Hall Drive, Heysham, MORECAMBE, LANCASHIRE, LA3 2QX.

GARDNER, Mr. Christopher John, BA ACA *1992;* 35 Cotysmore Road, SUTTON COLDFIELD, WEST MIDLANDS, B75 6BL.

GARDNER, Mrs. Claire Nadine, BA(Hons) ACA *2002;* 72 Avonmore Road, LONDON, W14 8RS.

•GARDNER, Miss. Clare Mary, BSc ACA *1986;* 11 The Chine, Muswell Hill, LONDON, N10 3PX.

GARDNER, Mr. Colin, FCA *1974;* 26 Julius Drive, Coleshill, BIRMINGHAM, B46 1HL.

GARDNER, Mr. David, ACA *2006;* 96 Quins Croft, LEYLAND, PR25 3UX.

GARDNER, Mr. David James, BSc ACA *1999;* 24 Peter Avenue, OXTED, SURREY, RH8 9LG.

GARDNER, Mr. David James, BA ACA *1999;* Arden Lodge, Arden Drive, Dorridge, SOLIHULL, B93 8LL.

GARDNER, Mr. David Nicholas, BSc ACA *2005;* 26 Salisbury avenue, ST. ALBANS, AL1 4TU.

GARDNER, Mr. David Robert, BSc ACA *1996;* 15 Barons Way, REIGATE, SURREY, RH2 8EU.

GARDNER, Mr. David William Leslie, FCA *1959;* Trees Whitepost Lane, Culverstone, Meopham, GRAVESEND, DA13 0TW.

GARDNER, Mr. Dominic Joseph, BA ACA *2006;* 40 Rockliffe Road, MIDDLESBROUGH, CLEVELAND, TS5 5DN.

GARDNER, Mr. Douglas Charles, BSc ACA *1991;* Oakside Cottage, Church Road, Scaynes Hill, HAYWARDS HEATH, WEST SUSSEX, RH17 7NH.

GARDNER, Mr. Duncan Michael, FCA TEP *1986;* Morris Crocker, Station House, 50 North Street, HAVANT, HAMPSHIRE, PO9 1QU.

GARDNER, Mr. Edward Ian, FCA *1983;* Summerfield, Park Road, WINCHESTER, SO22 6AA.

•GARDNER, Mr. Errol Wayne, ACA *1994;* Ernst & Young LLP, 1 More London Place, LONDON, SE1 2AF. See also Ernst & Young Europe LLP

GARDNER, Miss. Frances Ruth, BA ACA *2010;* Flat 5, West Lodge, 12a Beckenham Grove, Shortlands, BROMLEY, BR2 0JU.

GARDNER, Miss. Gemma Elizabeth, BA(Hons) ACA *2001;* Wych-Elms, Kenwyn Church Road, TRURO, CORNWALL, TR1 3DR.

GARDNER, Mr. Graham, ACA *2009;* with Jackson & Graham, Lynn Garth, Gillinggate, KENDAL, CUMBRIA, LA9 4JB.

•GARDNER, Mr. Graham Alan James, BSc FCA *1981;* (Tax Fac), JPCA Limited, 15a City Business Centre, Lower Road, LONDON, SE16 2XB.

GARDNER, Mrs. Helen, BCom ACA *2000;* 50a Furlong Lane, Alrewas, BURTON-ON-TRENT, STAFFORDSHIRE, DE13 7EE.

GARDNER, Mr. Ian Mark, BA ACA *1996;* 3 Martindale Road, Balham, LONDON, SW12 9PW.

GARDNER, Mr. Ian Richard, FCA *1976;* Taku-Fort-Str 13c, 81827 MUNICH, BAVARIA, GERMANY.

•GARDNER, Ms. Ingrid Lilian, BA FCA *1992;* PricewaterhouseCoopers LLP, Cornwall Court, 19 Cornwall Street, BIRMINGHAM, B3 2DT. See also PricewaterhouseCoopers

GARDNER, Mr. James Frederick, ACA *2008;* with KPMG LLP, 15 Canada Square, LONDON, E14 5GL.

GARDNER, Mr. James Paul, BA(Hons) ACA *2010;* 31 Park Hill, HARPENDEN, HERTFORDSHIRE, AL5 3AT.

GARDNER, Mr. James Robert, BA(Hons) ACA *2011;* 12 Edwardian Row, Bulkeley Road, CHEADLE, SK8 2AD.

•GARDNER, Mrs. Jane, BSc FCA *1989;* Jane Gardner, 13 Great Oaks Park, Rogerstone, NEWPORT, GWENT, NP10 9AT.

GARDNER, Mr. Jeffrey Michael, BSc ACA *2003;* with PricewaterhouseCoopers, Benson House, 33 Wellington Street, LEEDS, LS1 4JP.

•GARDNER, Mr. Jeremy Andrew Kightley, BSc ACA *1997;* Roffe Swayne, Ashcombe Court, Woolsack Way, GODALMING, GU7 1LQ.

•GARDNER, Mr. John Derrick, BA FCA *1980;* (Tax Fac), Gardner Brown, Calderwood House, 7 Montpellier Parade, CHELTENHAM, GL50 1UA.

•GARDNER, Mr. John Richard, FCA *1984;* (Tax Fac), Gardners Accountants Ltd, Brynford House, Brynford Street, HOLYWELL, CLWYD, CH8 7RD. See also Gardner Salisbury Limited

GARDNER, Mr. Jonathan Paul, BSc ACA *1993;* Barclays Capital, 5 North Colonnade, LONDON, E14 4BB.

GARDNER, Mr. Jonathan Richard, ACA *2009;* 28260 130th Street, SLEEPY EYE, MN 56085, UNITED STATES.

GARDNER, Mrs. Karen Elizabeth, BA(Hons) ACA *2003;* H M Revenue & Customs, 1 Munroe Court, White Rose Office Park, Millshaw Park Lane, LEEDS, LS11 0EA.

GARDNER, Mr. Kevin George, MSc BA ACA *2001;* Flat 12, Rye Apartments, 10 East Dulwich Road, LONDON, SE15 4EY.

GARDNER, Mr. Leonard Thomas, FCA *1949;* Flat 22, Victory Court, 23 Marine Parade West, LEE-ON-THE-SOLENT, HAMPSHIRE, PO13 9LN. (Life Member)

GARDNER, Ms. Lisa Michelle, BA ACA *1992;* 30 St Oswalds Road, Redland, BRISTOL, BS6 7HT.

GARDNER, Mr. Malcolm Arthur, FCA *1951;* 12 Brizlincote Lane, Bretby, BURTON-ON-TRENT, DE15 0PR. (Life Member)

•GARDNER, Mr. Malcolm William, BA FCA *1982;* 18 Elm Grove Road, Ealing, LONDON, W5 3JJ.

GARDNER, Mr. Mark Thomas, PhD BSc ACA *1993;* 30 The Borough, Brockham, BETCHWORTH, RH3 7NB.

GARDNER, Mr. Martin Geoffrey Hall, MA FCA CPA *1987;* 320 Brockton Lane, PLYMOUTH, MN 55447, UNITED STATES.

•GARDNER, Mr. Martin Neil, BSc ACA *2000;* Grant Thornton UK LLP, 30 Finsbury Square, LONDON, EC2P 2YU. See also Grant Thornton LLP

GARDNER, Mr. Merlin Mark Swire, BEng ACA *1992;* 12 Carnarvon Road, BRISTOL, BS6 7DR.

GARDNER, Mr. Michael, BA FCA *1984;* Barregarrow House, Barregarrow, Kirk Michael, ISLE OF MAN, IM6 1AX.

GARDNER, Mr. Michael, ACA *2009;* 48 Beech Road, Headington, OXFORD, OX3 7SJ.

GARDNER, Mr. Michael John, FCA *1966;* The White House, 26 Longdown Road, Lower Bourne, FARNHAM, SURREY, GU10 3JL.

GARDNER, Mr. Michael John, BA FCA *1979;* Edge Lee, 68 Moss Road, ALDERLEY EDGE, SK9 7JB.

GARDNER, Mr. Nicholas, BA ACA *1992;* 9 Tamarisk Close, SOUTHSEA, PO4 9TS.

GARDNER, Mrs. Nicole Anna, BSc ACA *1992;* 12 Carnarvon Road, Redland, BRISTOL, BS6 7DR.

GARDNER, Mr. Nigel Exton, BA FCA MBA *1974;* 122 Bedens Brook Road, SKILLMAN, NJ 08558, UNITED STATES.

GARDNER, Mr. Norman Edward, FCA *1973;* 8 Manor Park, MIRFIELD, WF14 0EW.

GARDNER, Miss. Odiakachukwu Erimerakpo, BSc ACA *2002;* 58 Selvage Lane, LONDON, NW7 3SN.

•**GARDNER, Mr. Paul, BA FCA** *1983;* The Willows, 159 Inchbonnie Road, South Woodham Ferrers, CHELMSFORD, CM3 5ZW.
GARDNER, Mr. Paul Jonathan, BSc FCA *1996;* 9 Leechwell Court, TOTNES, DEVON, TQ9 5GJ.
GARDNER, Mr. Paul William David, BSc ACA *1998;* with Deloitte LLP, Stonecutter Court, 1 Stonecutter Street, LONDON, EC4A 4TR.
GARDNER, Mr. Peter Andrew Stuart, BSc ACA *2001;* Cluff Gold plc, 15 Cateret Street, LONDON, SW1H 9DJ.
GARDNER, Mr. Peter Jeremy, BSc ACA *1980;* Querns Cottage Collins End, Goring Heath, READING, RG8 7RH.
GARDNER, Mr. Peter John, FCA *1972;* Hansa Capital Partners LLP, 50 Curzon Street, LONDON, W1J 7UW.
GARDNER, Mr. Philip Jonathan, BA FCA *1989;* 40 High Street, Little Wilbraham, CAMBRIDGE, CB21 5JY.
GARDNER, Mr. Philip Mark, BA ACA *1989;* Steve Hopewell Holdings, Lindop Bros (Queensferry) Ltd, Station Road, Queensferry, DEESIDE, CLWYD CH5 2TE.
GARDNER, Mrs. Rachael Anne, ACA *1999;* 18 Plovers Down, Oliver's Battery, WINCHESTER, SO22 4HH.
GARDNER, Mr. Rhys Ioan Thomas, BSc ACA *1992;* Shaw Trust Shaw House, Epsom Square White Horse Business Park, TROWBRIDGE, BA14 0XJ.
GARDNER, Mr. Robert Charles, ACA *1982;* 1 The Boltons, South Wootton, KING'S LYNN, PE30 3NQ.
GARDNER, Mr. Robert Lyle, BA ACA *1980;* Redhill House, Maplebeck, NEWARK, NG22 0BS.
•**GARDNER, Mrs. Sally Anne, BCom FCA** *1991;* Prism Group Limited, The Old Sawmill, Copyhold Lane, Lindfield, HAYWARDS HEATH, WEST SUSSEX RH16 1XT.
GARDNER, Miss. Samantha Jayne, ACA *2011;* 44c Byrne Road, LONDON, SW12 9JD.
GARDNER, Mrs. Sarah Heather, ACA *2008;* 13 Saxon Road, WALTON-ON-THAMES, KT12 3HD.
GARDNER, Mrs. Sharon Kim, BSc ACA *1993;* Blissland House, St. Marys Road, Hay-On-Wye, HEREFORD, HR3 5EB.
GARDNER, Miss. Shelley, BSc(Hons) ACA *2003;* 28 Barrack Road, EXETER, EX2 5ED.
GARDNER, Mr. Stephen James, BSc ACA *1989;* Credit Suisse, Paradeplatz 8, CH 8070 ZURICH, SWITZERLAND.
GARDNER, Mr. Stephen John Christie, BA ACA *1990;* 6 Adam Drive, SINGAPORE 289966, SINGAPORE.
•**GARDNER, Mr. Stephen Watson, FCA** *1983;* (Tax Fac), King Hope & Co, 31 Victoria Road, DARLINGTON, DL1 5SB.
GARDNER, Mr. Steven, ACA *2011;* 13a Northwold Road, Stoke Newington, LONDON, N16 7HL.
GARDNER, Mr. Steven Mark, BSc FCA *2000;* Unit 4 Cobbett Park, 22-28 Moorfield Road, GUILDFORD, SURREY, GU1 1RU.
GARDNER, Mr. Stuart Arthur, BA ACA *2009;* Flat 16 Mount Tay, St. Johns Road St. Helier, JERSEY, JE2 3WE.
•**GARDNER, Mr. Stuart John Lawson, BA FCA** *1991;* (Tax Fac), R.J.G. Palmer Gardner, Norgar House, 10 East Street, FAREHAM, PO16 0BN.
•**GARDNER, Mr. Timothy James Fernley, BA ACA** *1996;* Gale Gardner & Co Limited, Kencot House, Kencot, LECHLADE, OXFORDSHIRE, GL7 3QX.
GARDNER, Mr. Timothy Marc, BA FCA *2001;* Glaxo Smithkline Plc, G S K House, 980 Great West Road, BRENTFORD, MIDDLESEX, TW8 9GS.
GARDNER-BROWN, Ms. Diana Marjorie, MA ACA *1993;* with PricewaterhouseCoopers LLP, Pricewaterhousecoopers, 12 Plumtree Court, LONDON, EC4A 4HT.
GARE, Mr. Charles William, ACA *1996;* Flat 10, Admiral House, 20 Manor Road, TEDDINGTON, MIDDLESEX, TW11 8BF.
•**GARE, Mr. James, ACA DChA** *2009;* Gotham Erskine LLP, Friendly House, 52-58 Tabernacle Street, LONDON, EC2A 4NJ. See also MacIntyre Hudson LLP
GARE, Mr. Michael Adrian, BA ACA CF *1998;* Instem Life Sciences Limited, Diamond Way, Stone Business Park, STONE, STAFFORDSHIRE, ST15 0JD.
•**GARE, Mr. Thomas, FCA** *1965;* Thomas Gare, 44 Ramillies Avenue, Cheadle Hulme, CHEADLE, SK8 7AL.
GAREY, Mrs. Ruth, BSc ACA *2004;* 14 Despard Road, LONDON, N19 5NW.
GAREZE, Mrs. Jane, BA ACA *1994;* Gravelye Farmhouse, Hanlye Lane, Cuckfield, HAYWARDS HEATH, WEST SUSSEX, RH17 5HR.
•**GAREZE, Mr. Thomas Andrew George, BA FCA** *1986;* (Tax Fac), GriffinTax, Gravelye Farm House, Hanlye Lane, Cuckfield, HAYWARDS HEATH, WEST SUSSEX RH17 5HR.
GARFATH-COX, Miss. Alexandra Virginia Elizabeth, ACA *2008;* 11b Danby Street, LONDON, SE15 4BS.
•**GARFEN, Mr. David Leon, FCA** *1970;* (Tax Fac), Shine Garfen & Co, 210 Hendon Way, LONDON, NW4 3NE.
•**GARFEN, Mr. Gerald, FCA** *1971;* (Tax Fac), Shine Garfen & Co, 210 Hendon Way, LONDON, NW4 3NE.
GARFEN, Mr. Nicholas Paul, BA ACA *2007;* 21 Elm Walk, RADLETT, HERTFORDSHIRE, WD7 8DP.
•**GARFIELD, Mr. Alfred Marcel, FCA** *1970;* (Tax Fac), A.M. Garfield, 120 Salmon Street, Kingsbury, LONDON, NW9 8NL.
GARFIELD, Mr. Arnold Louis, FCA *1965;* 39 Malford Grove, South Woodford, LONDON, E18 2DY.
GARFIELD, Mr. Clive Nicholas Charles, BSc ACA *2002;* 54 Addison Road, LONDON, E11 2RG.
GARFIELD, Mr. Daniel Henry, ACA *2010;* 1 Grey Fell Close, STANMORE, MIDDLESEX, HA7 3DQ.
GARFIELD, Mr. Paul Andrew James, BA ACA *1998;* Lexisnexis Butterworth, Halsbury House, 35 Chancery Lane, LONDON, WC2A 1EL.
GARFITT, Mr. Alexander Jonathan, ACA *2008;* K P M G, 100 Temple Street, BRISTOL, BS1 6AG.
GARFITT, Mr. Ross, ACA *2005;* with Langdowns DFK, Fleming Court, Leigh Road, Eastleigh, SOUTHAMPTON, SO50 9PD.
GARFORD, Mr. Adrian Matthew, ACA *2008;* 7 Broom Avenue, Swanwick, ALFRETON, DERBYSHIRE, DE55 1DQ.
GARFORTH, Mr. Andrew Daniel, BA FCA CISA CISM *1988;* with Ernst & Young LLP, 20 Chapel Street, LIVERPOOL, L3 9AG.
GARFORTH, Mr. Stuart Andrew, BA ACA *2000;* Flat 15, Cornwall Court, Cleaver Street, LONDON, SE11 4DF.
GARFORTH-BLES, Mr. Hugh Charles, BA FCA *1975;* c/o Peter Dudgeon Ltd, Brompton Place, LONDON, SW3 1QE.
•**GARFORTH-BLES, Mr. Robert Michael, FCA** *1973;* Bles & Co, Lower Moor Farm, Charlton, MALMESBURY, SN16 9DY.
GARG, Mr. Rajiv Kumar, ACA *1988;* 860 United Nations Plaza, #14E, NEW YORK, NY 10017, UNITED STATES.
GARGAN, Mrs. Katherine Helena, MA FCA *1987;* Manor Cottage, 90 Cornwall Road, HARROGATE, HG1 2NG.
GARGAN, Mrs. Katherine Joan, BSc ACA *1990;* P O Box 1959, MAREEBA, QLD 4880, AUSTRALIA.
GARGENT, Mr. Francis Patrick Gerard, MA MSc FCA *1976;* King's Fund, 11-13 Cavendish Square, LONDON, W1G 0AN.
GARIBALDINOS, Mr. Savvas Nicou, BSc ACA *1992;* Flat 401, 2 Ermocleous Street, Acropolis, NICOSIA, CYPRUS.
•**GARLAND, Mr. Brian George, BA ACA** *1986;* Gerald Thomas & Co, Furze Bank, 34 Hanover Street, SWANSEA, SA1 6BA.
GARLAND, Mr. Clive Malachi James, BSc ACA *1994;* 18 Smith Street, DARWIN, NT 0800, AUSTRALIA.
GARLAND, Mr. David Anthony, BSc ACA *1981;* Royal Bank of Scotland, 5th Floor, Trinity Quay 2, Avon Street, BRISTOL, BS2 0PT.
•**GARLAND, Mr. Denis Ian, BA FCA** *1975;* D.I. Garland, 7 Highlands Road, Long Ashton, BRISTOL, BS41 9EN.
GARLAND, Mr. Douglas Walter, FCA *1957;* Pond House, Dalton, THIRSK, YO7 3HS. (Life Member)
GARLAND, Mr. Ian Richard, ACA *1988;* 2 Gorse Lane, Wrecclesham, FARNHAM, GU10 4SD.
GARLAND, Mr. Jamie, ACA MAAT *2011;* 5 County Gardens, FAREHAM, HAMPSHIRE, PO14 3JA.
GARLAND, Mr. Jeremy Neil, BA ACA *1985;* Witwood Food Products Ltd, 1 Lombard Way, BANBURY, OXFORDSHIRE, OX16 4TJ.
GARLAND, Mrs. Lynda Ruth, BA ACA *1990;* 36 Kendor Grove, MORPETH, NE61 2BU.
GARLAND, Mr. Michael Charles, BSc ACA *1983;* 21 Lichfield Road, Kew, RICHMOND, TW9 3JR.
GARLAND, Mr. Michael John, BA FCA *1975;* 53 Gordon Road, Ealing, LONDON, W5 2AL.
GARLAND, Mr. Michael John, FCA *1972;* 1 Newlyn Gardens, NOTTINGHAM, NG8 5GW.
GARLAND, Mr. Oliver Charles, MA ACA *1992;* 2 Bartlett Close, WALLINGFORD, OXFORDSHIRE, OX10 9EW.
GARLAND, Mr. Peter Keble, FCA *1965;* Rowes, Horndon, Mary Tavy, TAVISTOCK, PL19 9NQ. (Life Member)
GARLAND, Mr. Richard John Keble, FCA *1971;* Flat 1, Brakspear Mews, 47 New Street, HENLEY-ON-THAMES, OXFORDSHIRE, RG9 2BP.
GARLAND, Mr. Stephen Edward, FCA *1981;* Rosedale, 35 Crookham Road, FLEET, GU51 5DT.
GARLICK, Mrs. Anne Sylvia, FCA *1946;* 11 Springfield Park, TROWBRIDGE, BA14 7HT. (Life Member)
GARLICK, Mr. Christopher John, BSc ACA *1978;* Fugnerova 247, 252 28 CERNOSICE, CZECH REPUBLIC.
GARLICK, Mr. David Ross, ACA *1979;* Hazelfield, Legh Road, KNUTSFORD, WA16 8LS.
GARLICK, Mr. David William, FCA *1955;* 4 Chaddesley Glen, Canford Cliffs, POOLE, BH13 7PF. (Life Member)
•**GARLICK, Mrs. Diane, ACA FCCA** *2009;* Horne Brooke Shenton, 21 Caunce Street, BLACKPOOL, FY1 3LA.
GARLICK, Miss. Helen Mary, MA FCA *1980;* 6 Lambly Hill, VIRGINIA WATER, GU25 4BF.
•**GARLICK, Mrs. Kathryn Ann, FCA** *1994;* (Tax Fac), Kathryn Garlick, 15 Waterslea Drive, BOLTON, BL1 5FA.
GARLICK, Mr. Marc James, ACA *2011;* 6 Kennedy Close, NEWBURY, BERKSHIRE, RG14 6QL.
GARLICK, Mr. Richard Mark, BEng ACA *1987;* Lloyds Banking Group Corporate Markets, 10 Gresham Street, LONDON, EC2V 7AE.
GARLICK, Mr. Robert, BSc ACA *1978;* 2 The Close, Alwoodley, LEEDS, LS17 7RD.
GARLICK, Mr. Roger Harry, FCA *1970;* Cobblers Cottage, Station Approach, Oxshott, LEATHERHEAD, KT22 0TA. (Life Member)
GARMAN, Mr. Derek Owen, FCA *1957;* 20 Blackbridge Lane, HORSHAM, WEST SUSSEX, RH12 1RP. (Life Member)
GARMENT, Mr. Andrew, BSc(Hons) ACA *2001;* UBS, 26/F, Li Po Chun Chambers, 189 Des Voeux Road Central, CENTRAL, HONG KONG SAR.
GARMESON, Mr. Ian, MA ACA *1983;* Turret Group Limited, 173 High Street, RICKMANSWORTH, HERTFORDSHIRE, WD3 1AY.
GARMSTON, Mr. Matthew, LLB ACA *1995;* The Nook North Street, Islip, KIDLINGTON, OX5 2SL.
GARN, Mr. Christopher Kenneth, FCA *1969;* 17 Fairholme Avenue, Gidea Park, ROMFORD, ESSEX, RM2 5UP.
GARNER, Mr. Aiden Roy William, BA ACA *1992;* New Barn Lodge, 195 High Road, CHIGWELL, ESSEX, IG7 5AS.
GARNER, Mr. Alan Anthony, BSc ACA *1983;* 10601 Inverness Street, FORT SMITH, AR 72908, UNITED STATES.
•**GARNER, Mr. Andrew Scott, BA(Hons) ACA** *2002;* Harrison Black Limited, Pyle House, 137 Pyle Street, NEWPORT, ISLE OF WIGHT, PO30 1JW.
GARNER, Mr. Aubrey Edward, FCA *1956;* Ellehaven 34, 2950 VEDBAEK, DENMARK. (Life Member)
GARNER, Mr. Bernard Roger, FCA *1956;* 15 Broom Close, Taverham, NORWICH, NORFOLK, NR8 6FS.
GARNER, Mrs. Carolyn Anne, MA FCA CTA *1989;* Burghfield, Shootersway, BERKHAMSTED, HERTFORDSHIRE, HP4 3NJ.
GARNER, Mr. Christopher, MSc(Econ) ACA *2011;* 32 Audric Close, KINGSTON UPON THAMES, KT2 6BP.
GARNER, Mr. Christopher, BSc ACA *1997;* 10 rue J-Sébastien Clérambourg, 78112 FOURQUEUX, FRANCE.
GARNER, Mr. David, ACA *1995;* 14 Chancery Mews, LONDON, SW17 7TD.
GARNER, Mr. David, FCA *1973;* Wood Lea, Twemlow Green, Holmes Chapel, CREWE, CW4 8BN.
GARNER, Miss. Dawn, BA FCA *1992;* The Summit Group Ltd, Melita House, 124 Bridge Road, CHERTSEY, SURREY, KT16 8LH.
GARNER, Mr. Edward Piers, BSc(Hons) ACA *2002;* 33/128 Mounts Bay Road, Acacia Apartments, PERTH, WA 6000, AUSTRALIA.
GARNER, Mr. Gareth Erik, BA ACA *2000;* 33 Bridgewater Road, BERKHAMSTED, HERTFORDSHIRE, HP4 1HP.
GARNER, Mr. Gary Edward, MBA BSc FCA *1979;* PO Box 212416, DUBAI, UNITED ARAB EMIRATES.
GARNER, Mr. Graham Charles, FCA *1963;* PO Box N 1491, NASSAU, BAHAMAS.
GARNER, Miss. Hannah Lauren, BSc(Hons) ACA *2004;* with Hilton Sharp & Clarke, 30 New Road, BRIGHTON, BN1 1BN.
GARNER, Mr. James Adam, BA ACA *2004;* Virgin Active, 21 North Fourth Street, MILTON KEYNES, MK9 1HL.
GARNER, Mr. John, BA ACA *1999;* The Old Dairy, 67 North Road, West Bridgford, NOTTINGHAM, NG2 7NG.
GARNER, Mr. John Anthony, FCA *1964;* Ingleton, Church Lane, Barnham, BOGNOR REGIS, WEST SUSSEX, PO22 0DG. (Life Member)
GARNER, Mrs. Kelly Louise, BSc(Hons) ACA *2001;* 9 Greenland Gardens, Great Baddow, CHELMSFORD, CM2 8ZF.
GARNER, Mr. Laurence Edwin, FCA *1969;* The Stable, Merries Barns Cury, HELSTON, CORNWALL, TR12 7RA.
•**GARNER, Mr. Malcolm Robert, FCA** *1973;* Garner & Co, Rest Harrow, Welland, MALVERN, WORCESTERSHIRE, WR13 6NQ.
GARNER, Mr. Matthew James, ACA *2008;* 9 Bosville Road, SEVENOAKS, TN13 3JD.
GARNER, Mr. Michael Frederick, MA FCA *1964;* Old Drews, Knotty Green, BEACONSFIELD, HP9 2TT. (Life Member)
GARNER, Mr. Nicholas, BSc ACA *2011;* 9 Copse Close, SLOUGH, SL1 5DT.
GARNER, Mr. Nicholas David, ACA *2004;* Solar Contact, 1 Lakeside, CHEADLE, CHESHIRE, SK8 3GW.
GARNER, Mr. Nicholas Paul, BSc ACA *1989;* 120 High Street, Meldreth, ROYSTON, HERTFORDSHIRE, SG8 6LB.
GARNER, Mr. Nigel, BSc FCA *1987;* 16 Hall Park Hill, BERKHAMSTED, HP4 2NH.
GARNER, Mr. Oliver, ACA *2006;* 5 Heaton Road, SOLIHULL, WEST MIDLANDS, B91 2DY.
GARNER, Mr. Patrick Francis, FCA *1984;* Pinewood Shepperton Plc, Pinewood Road, IVER, BUCKINGHAMSHIRE, SL0 0NH.
GARNER, Mr. Peter Rex, FCA *1966;* 40 Elm Road, Sheen, LONDON, SW14 7JQ. (Life Member)
GARNER, Mr. Peter William, FCA *1974;* Morden Hall, Trap Road, Guilden Morden, ROYSTON, HERTFORDSHIRE, SG8 0JE.
GARNER, Mr. Philip John, FCA *1978;* 5 Mollington Grove, Hatton Park, WARWICK, CV35 7TU. (Life Member)
GARNER, Mr. Richard Edward, BSc(Econ) FCA *1994;* X L Insurance, 70 Gracechurch Street, LONDON, EC3V 0XL.
•**GARNER, Mr. Richard William, FCA** *1972;* Richard & Sue Garner, 7 Kingsland House, 135 Andover Road, NEWBURY, BERKSHIRE, RG14 6JL. See also Zebra Accounting (Thames Valley) Ltd
•**GARNER, Mr. Simon James, BSc ACA** *2002;* The Jamesons Partnership Limited, 92 Station Road, CLACTON-ON-SEA, CO15 1SG.
GARNER, Mr. Simon John, ACA *1993;* Rashleigh, Bagshot Road, Worplesdon Hill, WOKING, GU22 0QY.
•**GARNER, Mr. Stephen Charles John, FCA** *1967;* (Tax Fac), Stephen CJ Garner, Rookery Farm, Back Lane, Kingston Seymour, CLEVEDON, AVON BS21 6XB.
GARNER, Mr. Steven, BA FCA *1991;* 37 Scarsdale Villas, LONDON, W8 6PU.
•**GARNER, Mrs. Susan, ACA** *1981;* Richard & Sue Garner, 7 Kingsland House, 135 Andover Road, NEWBURY, BERKSHIRE, RG14 6JL.
•**GARNER, Mr. Thomas Ian, BA FCA** *1987;* (Tax Fac), Harrisaccounts LLP, Marland House, 13 Huddersfield Road, BARNSLEY, SOUTH YORKSHIRE, S70 2LW. See also T I Garner Limited
GARNER-WINSHIP, Mrs. Linda Louise, BA ACA *2004;* Floor 2, Hammerson Plc, 10 Grosvenor Street, LONDON, W1K 4BJ.
GARNER-WINSHIP, Mr. Peter Stephen, MA(Oxon) ACA *2009;* Anglo American Plc Anglo American House, 20 Carlton House Terrace, LONDON, SW1Y 5AN.
GARNETT, Mr. Anthony James, BA ACA *1998;* 12 Malvern Drive, ALTRINCHAM, CHESHIRE, WA14 4NQ.
GARNETT, Mr. Anthony Richard, BA FCA MBA CMIIA *2001;* 54 Dalton Crescent, DURHAM, DH1 4FB.
GARNETT, Mr. David John Edward, BA FCA *1981;* 13 Cunliffe Drive, SALE, M33 3WS.
GARNETT, Mrs. Hannah Louise, ACA *2009;* Croton Park Brick Bank Lane, Allostock, KNUTSFORD, CHESHIRE, WA16 9LX.
GARNETT, Mr. Ian Robert, BA ACA *1986;* Terrace 2c, Nichada Thani, BANGKOK BK 10210, THAILAND.
GARNETT, Mr. John Howard William, BSc FCA *1972;* 21 Argarmeols Road, Formby, LIVERPOOL, L37 7BX.
GARNETT, Mr. John Stewart, FCA *1969;* 33 Ashingdon Heights, ROCHFORD, SS4 3TH.
GARNETT, Mr. Michael, ACA *2008;* Diageo Plc Lakeside Drive, Park Royal, LONDON, NW10 7HQ.
GARNETT, Mr. Neal Charles, BA ACA *1992;* De Lage Landen Leasing Limited, 1111 Old Eagle School Road, WAYNE, PA 19087, UNITED STATES.

GARNETT, Mrs. Sally Patricia, BA ACA *1994;* 10 Greenfield Road, Bollington, MACCLESFIELD, SK10 5NE.
GARNETT, Mr. Samuel Raymond, FCA *1952;* Scalby Mount, 33 Church Lane, MIRFIELD, WF14 9HX. (Life Member)
GARNETT, Mr. Simon Paul, BEng ACA *1995;* 145 Oldfield Road, ALTRINCHAM, CHESHIRE, WA14 4HX.
GARNHAM, Mrs. Jennifer Alice, BA ACA *1995;* 147 Melton Road, West Bridgford, NOTTINGHAM, NG2 6FG.
GARNHAM, Mr. Kevin John, BSc ACA *1989;* The Willows, Livermere Road, Great Barton, BURY ST. EDMUNDS, IP31 2QE.
GARNHAM, Mr. Neil, MMath ACA *2007;* with Grant Thornton UK LLP, 4 Hardman Square, Spinningfields, MANCHESTER, M3 3EB.
GARNHAM-SMITH, Mr. Bruce Miles, BSc(Econ) FCA *1989;* 54 Compit Hills, CROMER, NR27 9LP.
GARNIER, Mr. Martin Frederick, FCA *1968;* M. F. Garnier, 2 Cumbria Close, Thornbury, BRISTOL, BS35 2YE.
GARNISH, Ms. Lesley Joyce, MA ACA CTA *1999;* 6 Hanson Close, Southend Road, BECKENHAM, BR3 1WJ.
GARNON, Mr. Michael, BSc ACA *1993;* 44 The Octagon, TAUNTON, SOMERSET, TA1 1RT.
GARNSWORTHY, Mr. Duncan Charles, ACA *2009;* Perricone MD Cosmeceuticals UK Ltd, 55 Conduit Street, LONDON, W1S 2YE.
GARNSWORTHY, Mr. Randall William, FCA *1951;* 4 Pine Walk, VERWOOD, BH31 6TJ. (Life Member)
GARPOZOS, Mr. Petros, BSc ACA *2007;* 39B Machaira, Anavargos, 8025 PAPHOS, CYPRUS.
GARRAD, Mr. Peter Justin, MEng ACA *1994;* 6 Old Rectory Green, Fladbury, PERSHORE, WORCESTERSHIRE, WR10 2QX.
GARRAGHAN, Mr. Philip, ACA *2009;* 24 Hall Street, CHEADLE, CHESHIRE, SK8 1PJ.
•**GARRAN, Mr. Andrew, FCA** *1967;* AIMS - Andrew Garran, 61 Beckwith Road, LONDON, SE24 9LQ.
GARRARD, Mr. Andrew Martin, BA(Hons) ACA *2001;* 38 Florence Road, West Bridgford, NOTTINGHAM, NG2 5HR.
GARRARD, Mrs. Catherine Patricia, BA ACA CTA *1999;* with PricewaterhouseCoopers LLP, Donington Court, Pegasus Business Park, Castle Donington, DERBY, DE74 2UZ.
GARRARD, Miss. Jane Elizabeth, BSc ACA *1995;* 50 Onslow Gardens, Muswell Hill, LONDON, N10 3JX.
GARRARD, Ms. Linda, BA ACA *1988;* Jardin A Frenes, Longue Rue, St. Saviour, GUERNSEY, GY7 9XU.
GARRARD, Mr. Mark Richard, BA ACA *2002;* 9 Hornbeam Drive, Poringland, NORWICH, NR14 7WE.
•**GARRARD, Mr. Paul Richard, FCA** *1981;* Walter Wright, 89 High Street, Hadleigh, IPSWICH, IP7 5EA. See also Walter Wright Consultancy Ltd
•**GARRARD, Mr. Richard Anthony, BA FCA** *1985;* Deloitte LLP, PO Box 137, Regency Court, Glategny Esplanade, St Peter Port, GUERNSEY GY1 3HW. See also Deloitte & Touche LLP
GARRARD, Mr. Ross, BSc ACA *2004;* Le Coin Farm Lodge Le Mont Du Coin, St. Brelade, JERSEY, JE3 8BE.
GARRARD, Mrs. Sarah Helen, BA(Hons) ACA *2002;* 35 Vinery Road, BURY ST. EDMUNDS, SUFFOLK, IP33 2LB.
GARRARD, Miss. Sheila, BA ACA *1980;* Copperhurst, Knoll Hill, Aldington, ASHFORD, KENT, TN25 7BZ.
•**GARRARD, Mr. Stewart John, BSc FCA** *1977;* Saffery Champness, Lion House, Red Lion Street, LONDON, WC1R 4GB.
GARRATT, Mr. Andrew David, BA FCA *1989;* 25 Ely Gardens, TONBRIDGE, TN10 4NZ.
GARRATT, Mr. Antony, BA ACA *2000;* Eastlands Homes Partnership Ltd Belle Vue House, 27 Garratt Way, MANCHESTER, M18 8HE.
GARRATT, Mr. David Harry, BA ACA *1991;* The Farndens, Compton, CHICHESTER, PO18 9HD.
GARRATT, Mr. Giles William, MA ACA *2006;* Flat 8 Morton Court, 10 St. Gregorys Road, STRATFORD-UPON-AVON, WARWICKSHIRE, CV37 6UH.
GARRATT, Mr. Ian Anderson, FCA *1969;* 5 Brasted Place, High Street, Brasted, WESTERHAM, TN16 1JE. (Life Member)
GARRATT, Mrs. Janice, ACA *1979;* 34 Littlebrook Road, SALE, M33 4WG.
GARRATT, Mrs. Marie Elaine, BSc(Econ) ACA *1997;* 60, Chatsworth Road, Hazel Grove, STOCKPORT, SK7 6BN.
GARRATT, Mr. Mark Jonathan, BA FCA MIoD *1990;* (Tax Fac), 21 Stradella Road, Herne Hill, LONDON, SE24 9HN.
GARRATT, Mr. Michael Steven, BSc FCA *1975;* The Manor, Fern Road, Cropwell Bishop, NOTTINGHAM, NG12 3BU.
GARRATT, Mr. Robin, BA FCIB ACA *1979;* 107 Wansunt Road, BEXLEY, DA5 2DN.
GARRATT, Mrs. Rosalind Alexandra, BSc ACA *1993;* 4 Rupert Crescent, NEWARK, NG24 4AP.
GARRED, Mr. John Martin, BA FCA *1984;* 1 Wilstrode Avenue, Binfield, BRACKNELL, RG42 4UW.
GARRETT, Mr. Alan Victor, FCA *1964;* 52 Blacketts Wood Drive, Chorleywood, RICKMANSWORTH, WD3 5QH. (Life Member)
GARRETT, Mr. Andrew, BSc ACA *1989;* PricewaterhouseCoopers, Emirates Towers Offices, PO Box 11987, Level 40, Sheikh Zayed Road, PO Box 11987 DUBAI UNITED ARAB EMIRATES.
•**GARRETT, Miss. Anneliese Edith, BA ACA** *2005;* Anneliese Garrett, 110 Speldhurst Road, TUNBRIDGE WELLS, KENT, TN4 0JD.
GARRETT, Mr. Barry Keith, FCA *1977;* Hereford House, 77 Tipton Road, Woodsetton, DUDLEY, WEST MIDLANDS, DY3 1BZ.
GARRETT, Mr. Charles John William, FCA CTA(Fellow) *1966;* 15 Darlow Drive, Biddenham, BEDFORD, MK40 4AX. (Life Member)
GARRETT, Mrs. Christine Deirdre, BA ACA *1984;* 6 Manor Road, Fringford, BICESTER, OX27 8DH.
GARRETT, Mr. Colin Alexander, ACA *1982;* Colin Garrett Associates Limited, 812 Warwick Road, SOLIHULL, B91 3EU.
GARRETT, Mr. David Richard, FCA *1960;* 3319 Terra Linda Drive, SANTA ROSA, CA 95404, UNITED STATES. (Life Member)
GARRETT, Miss. Deborah Susanne, ACA *1982;* 17 Water Meadow Way, Wendover, AYLESBURY, HP22 6RS.
GARRETT, Miss. Fiona Marie, BA ACA *1999;* (Tax Fac), 20 Amersham Road, Chalfont St. Peter, GERRARDS CROSS, BUCKINGHAMSHIRE, SL9 0NZ.
GARRETT, Mr. George Thomas Smith, FCA *1956;* Oaklands, Elm Road, Tokers Green, READING, RG4 9EG. (Life Member)
GARRETT, Mr. Glenn David, BSc ACA *1999;* N G T House, Warwick Technology Park, WARWICK, WARWICKSHIRE, CV34 6DA.
GARRETT, Mr. Graeme Ewart, ACA *1982;* Rose Cottage, 3 Nursery Gardens, Mere, WARMINSTER, BA12 6PP.
GARRETT, Mrs. Heather Ruth, BSc ACA *2007;* 14 Blakehill Drive, Great Sankey, WARRINGTON, WA5 1ZF.
•**GARRETT, Mrs. Helen, BA ACA CTA** *2003;* Wheelers, 16 North Street, WISBECH, CAMBRIDGESHIRE, PE13 1NE.
•**GARRETT, Mrs. Helen Joan, BSc FCA** *1991;* (Tax Fac), H G Accounting Solutions Limited, 17 St. James's Avenue, BECKENHAM, KENT, BR3 4HF.
GARRETT, Mr. Jack, ACA *2008;* White Knight, Burhill, WALTON-ON-THAMES, SURREY, KT12 4AZ.
GARRETT, Mrs. Joanne, ACA *1998;* Plumtree Cottage, Stoke Trister, WINCANTON, BA9 9PH.
•**GARRETT, Mr. John, FCA** *1990;* Musker & Garrett Limited, Edward House, North Mersey Business Centre, Woodward Road, Knowsley Industrial Park, LIVERPOOL L33 7UY.
GARRETT, Mr. John Edward, FCA *1962;* Yew Tree Cottage, 23 Broad Town Road, Broad Town, SWINDON, SN4 7RB. (Life Member)
GARRETT, Mr. Jonathan Charles, BA ACA *2001;* Deloitte & Touche Hill House, 1 Little New Street, LONDON, EC4A 3TR.
GARRETT, Mr. Kenneth John, MA FCA *1977;* Sycamore Lodge, 15 Harrowby Road, LEEDS, LS16 5HN.
GARRETT, Mr. Laurence Roy, BA ACA *1992;* 30 Middle Street, Thriplow, ROYSTON, HERTFORDSHIRE, SG8 7RD.
GARRETT, Mr. Lloyd, BSc(Hons) ACA *2000;* 8 Crest Way, Portslade, BRIGHTON, BN41 2EY.
GARRETT, Ms. Lorna Jane, ACA *2008;* 12 Coppice Way, LEEDS, LS8 4DB.
•**GARRETT, Mr. Mark, FCA** *1979;* Mark Garrett Tax & Accountancy Ltd, 1st Floor, 11 Laura Place, BATH, BA2 4BL.
GARRETT, Mr. Mark John Adam, BSc(Hons) ACA *2001;* (Tax Fac), 122 Hospital Street, NANTWICH, CHESHIRE, CW5 5RY.
GARRETT, Mrs. Melanie Elizabeth, BA FCA *1990;* 34 Lackford Close, Brundall, NORWICH, NR13 5NG.
GARRETT, Mr. Melvyn John, BA ACA *1984;* 5 Lenton Close, CHIPPENHAM, SN14 0UB.
•**GARRETT, Mr. Michael Geoffrey, BA FCA ATII** *1987;* CLB Coopers, Fleet House, New Road, LANCASTER, LA1 1EZ.
GARRETT, Mr. Michael John, MA ACA *1997;* Flat 3 22 Sheen Gate Gardens, LONDON, SW14 7NY.
GARRETT, Mr. Nicholas Julian, BA ACA *1988;* 2 Wilberforce Way, LONDON, SW19 4TH.
GARRETT, Mr. Paul Michael, BA ACA *1989;* 17 Coldharbour Lane, Hildenborough, TONBRIDGE, TN11 9JT.
GARRETT, Mr. Peter Anthony, ACA *1989;* Uvex House, Uvex UK Ltd, Farnham Trading Estate, FARNHAM, GU9 9NW.
GARRETT, Mrs. Sally Ruth, BA ACA *2006;* Bartfields (UK) Ltd Burley House, 12 Clarendon Road, LEEDS, LS2 9NF.
•**GARRETT, Mr. Simon Hamilton, BA FCA** *1981;* HW, Sterling House, 19-23 High Street, KIDLINGTON, OXFORDSHIRE, OX5 2DH. See also Haines Watts
•**GARRETT, Mr. Simon Nicholas, BSc ACA** *1985;* Pitcairn Cottage, 100 Lower Road, Fetcham, LEATHERHEAD, KT22 9NG.
GARRETT, Mr. Stephen George, FCA *1976;* Diana Farm, Stevenstone, TORRINGTON, DEVON, EX38 7HY.
•**GARRETT, Mr. Stephen George, BA ACA** *1999;* S Garrett ACA, 21 Cottonwood, Biddick Woods, HOUGHTON LE SPRING, TYNE AND WEAR, DH4 7TA.
GARRETT, Mrs. Victoria Jane, BA ACA *1991;* Beechcroft, Tilford Road, HINDHEAD, GU26 6RH.
•**GARRETT-BOWES, Mrs. Rosalind Josephine, BSc ACA CTA** *1984;* (Tax Fac), Ros Garrett Tax Services, Maple Lodge, Sycamore Close, AMERSHAM, BUCKINGHAMSHIRE, HP6 6BW.
GARRETY, Mr. Mark, BA(Hons) ACA *2003;* 16 Windmill Street, TUNBRIDGE WELLS, TN2 4UU.
GARRICK, Mr. Richard Michael, FCA *1969;* 2 The Lindens, LOUGHTON, ESSEX, IG10 3HS.
GARRIDO, Mr. Carlos Stephen, BA ACA *2001;* 6320 SW 104 Street, PINECREST, FL 33156, UNITED STATES.
GARRIGAN, Mr. Christopher, ACA *2010;* Birchtree Lodge, Long Lane, Wistow, SELBY, NORTH YORKSHIRE, YO8 3FY.
GARRIGAN, Mr. Dan, BA ACA *2008;* Flat 27 White House, Vicarage Crescent, LONDON, SW11 3LJ.
GARRIGAN, Mr. Peter Joseph, FCA *1967;* 11 Leyborne Park, Kew Gardens, RICHMOND, SURREY, TW9 3HB.
•**GARRINGTON, Miss. Sandra, ACA FCCA** *2008;* (Tax Fac), Finch House Properties Limited, Finch House, 28-30 Wolverhampton Street, DUDLEY, WEST MIDLANDS, DY1 1DB. See also Price Pearson Ltd
GARRIOCK, Mr. Trevor James, BA(Hons) ACA *2009;* 22 Megan Road, West End, SOUTHAMPTON, SO30 3FR.
•**GARRISON, Mr. Harvey, FCA** *1977;* H. Garrison, 10 Bickley Court, Aran Drive, STANMORE, MIDDLESEX, HA7 4NA.
•**GARRISON, Mrs. Kirsty Jane, BA FCA ATII** *1996;* Deloitte LLP, 2 New Street Square, LONDON, EC4A 3BZ. See also Deloitte & Touche LLP
•**GARRISON, Mr. Mark Andrew, BCom FCA DChA** *1988;* with Allotts, The Old Grammar School, 13 Moorgate Road, ROTHERHAM, SOUTH YORKSHIRE, S60 2EN.
GARRITY, Miss. Georgina Faye, BSc ACA *2003;* 2 Hulbert Close, Hilperton, TROWBRIDGE, WILTSHIRE, BA14 7FL.
GARROD, Mr. Daniel Ronald, MA ACA *1999;* 60A Manchuria Road, LONDON, SW11 6AE.
GARROD, Mr. John Albert, FCA *1962;* 6 Harbourside, HAVANT, PO9 1TJ. (Life Member)
GARROD, Mr. Kenneth John, BA FCA *1973;* 35 Heath Hurst Road, LONDON, NW3 2RU.
GARROD, Mr. Laurence Duncan, MA BA ACA *2005;* 47a Downshire Hill, LONDON, NW3 1NX.
GARROD, Mr. Miles Duncan, BA(Hons) ACA *2001;* 60 Harwood Close, WELWYN GARDEN CITY, HERTFORDSHIRE, AL8 7SN.
•**GARROD, Mr. Paul John, FCA** *1970;* (Tax Fac), Garrod Beckett & Co Ltd, 10 Town Quay Wharf, Abbey Road, BARKING, ESSEX, IG11 7BZ.
•**GARROD, Mr. Steven James, ACA** *2008;* with Clay Ratnage Strevens & Hills, Construction House, Runwell Road, WICKFORD, ESSEX, SS11 7HQ.
GARROOD, Dr. Anthony Peter, ACA *1986;* 23 George Road, GUILDFORD, GU1 4NP.
GARROOD, Mr. Charles William, BA ACA *2003;* 34 Bracken Avenue, LONDON, SW12 8BH.
GARROOD, Mrs. Shirley Jill, BSc ACA *1983;* Pilgrims View, Lower Warren Road, AYLESFORD, ME20 7EH.
GARROW, Mr. John Nicholas, FCA *1967;* 1 Pembroke Gardens, LONDON, W8 6HS.
GARROW, Mr. William James, FCA *1969;* V Degli Olivi 1, Castelnuovo di Porto, 00060 ROME, ITALY.
GARRY, Mr. Martin, BSc(Hons) ACA *2009;* 11 Holmfield Crescent, Lea, PRESTON, PR2 1PL.
GARRY, Mr. Paul Alan, BA ACA *1984;* Level 22, 100 Queen Street, MELBOURNE, VIC 3000, AUSTRALIA.
GARSIDE, Miss. Alex Keely, BSc ACA *2003;* 1230 Prince Street, HOUSTON, TX 77008, UNITED STATES.
GARSIDE, Mrs. Barbara Anne, BSc FCA *1976;* 26 Coppins Close, CHELMSFORD, ESSEX, CM2 6AY.
GARSIDE, Mr. Byron, BSc ACA *1997;* 3 Meadway, LONDON, N14 6NY.
GARSIDE, Mr. Edward Hilton, FCA *1955;* 8 Longbridge Close, Sherfield-on-Loddon, HOOK, HAMPSHIRE, RG27 0DQ. (Life Member)
GARSIDE, Mr. Edward Michael, BA FCA *1963;* 17 Delaunays Road, SALE, M33 6RX.
GARSIDE, Mr. Greg Andrew, BSc ACA *1999;* LA BIANCA, 63 SOUTH ROAD, SMITHS FL06, BERMUDA.
GARSIDE, Mr. John Frederick, FCA *1956;* 7-12-3 Twin Towers, PSN Tanjung Bungah, Ratu Mutiara, 11200 PENANG, MALAYSIA. (Life Member)
GARSIDE, Mr. Mark Andrew, FCA *1974;* La Borderie, Tarn et Garonne, 82150 VALEILLES, FRANCE.
•**GARSIDE, Mr. Paul Eli, ACA** *1981;* Deeks Evans, 3 Boyne Park, TUNBRIDGE WELLS, TN4 8EN. See also Deeks Evans Audit Services Limited, P E Garside Limited
GARSIDE, Mr. Philip Frederic, FCA *1961;* 674 Liverpool Road, Ainsdale, SOUTHPORT, PR8 3NA. (Life Member)
GARSIDE, Mr. Richard Dale, BSc FCA *1981;* CR Financial Solutions Limited, 12 Chinnock Close, FLEET, HAMPSHIRE, GU52 7SN.
GARSIDE, Mr. Roger George, FCA *1955;* 2 Roman Heights, Cogdean ElmsCorfe Mullen, WIMBORNE, BH21 3XQ. (Life Member)
•**GARSIDE, Mrs. Sarah Elizabeth, FCA** *1981;* Andorran Limited, 6 Manor Park Business Centre, Mackenzie Way, CHELTENHAM, GL51 9TX.
•**GARSIDE, Mr. Stephen Brian, BSc FCA** *1983;* (Tax Fac), Garside & Co LLP, 6 Vigo Street, LONDON, W1S 3HF.
GARSIDE, Mr. Stephen Howard, BA ACA *1984;* The Gables Yorkshire Side, Eastoft, SCUNTHORPE, SOUTH HUMBERSIDE, DN17 4PG.
GARSIDE, Mr. Thomas Edward Frederick, BA(Hons) ACA *2010;* 2 Warriner Gardens, LONDON, SW11 4EB.
GARSON, Mr. Stephen John Charles, BA FCA *1983;* MWH Constructors Inc, 370 Interlocken Blvd, BROOMFIELD, CO 80021, UNITED STATES.
GARSTANG, Mr. Matthew David, ACA *2007;* 10/2 Hopetoun Crescent, EDINBURGH, EH7 4AU.
GARSTIN, Mr. Anthony Simon, BSc FCA *1995;* 103 Canbury Avenue, KINGSTON-UPON-THAMES, KT2 6JR.
GARSTON, Mr. Andrew Jolyon, BSc ACA *1996;* Willis Group, 51 Lime Street, LONDON, EC3M 7DQ.
GARSTON, Mr. David Mark, BA ACA *1988;* West Haven, Station Road, HENLEY-IN-ARDEN, B95 5JQ.
GARTENBERG, Mr. Peter David, MA ACA *1985;* 18 Midcroft, RUISLIP, HA4 8ES.
GARTHWAITE, Mr. Charles Martin, BSc ACA *1994;* Aegon Plc Edinburgh Park, 1 Lochside Crescent, EDINBURGH, EH12 9SE.
GARTHWAITE, Mrs. Helen Elizabeth, BSc ACA *1992;* 1249 Green Lane Road, MALVERN, PA 19355, UNITED STATES.
GARTHWAITE, Mr. Joseph Edward, BA ACA *2001;* 42 Cawston Lane Dunchurch, RUGBY, WARWICKSHIRE, CV22 6QE.
GARTHWAITE, Mr. Keith, BSc ACA *1992;* 1249 Green Lane Road, MALVERN, PA 19355, UNITED STATES.
GARTHWAITE, Mr. Roy, MA FCA *1954;* Brown Butler, Leigh House, 28-32 St Paul's Street, LEEDS, LS1 2JT. (Life Member)
GARTHWAITE, Mr. Terence Brian, FCA *1970;* The Coach House, Grainge Chase, Great Horwood, MILTON KEYNES, MK17 0QE.
GARTNER, Miss. Caroline, MA BA ACA *2007;* Flat 72, Ormonde Court, Upper Richmond Road, LONDON, SW15 6TP.
GARTON, Mr. Andrew David, BA FCA *1989;* 6 Springlines, Wanbrough, SWINDON, SN4 0ES.
GARTON, Mr. Anthony William, BA(Hons) ACA *2002;* Cinven Services Ltd Warwick Court, 5 Paternoster Square, LONDON, EC4M 7AG.
GARTON, Miss. Elizabeth Catherine, MA BA(Hons) ACA *2010;* Brantingham Thorpe, BROUGH, NORTH HUMBERSIDE, HU15 1QE.
GARTON, Mr. Geoffrey Douglas, FCA *1971;* Northwest Development Agency, PO Box 37, WARRINGTON, WA1 1XB.
•**GARTON, Mr. Philip Miles, FCA** *1971;* (Tax Fac), Garton Graham & Co, 56 Grammar School Yard, HULL, HU1 2NB.

GARTSIDE, Mrs. Lucy Caroline, LLB ACA *2003;* 237 Leicester Road, Mountsorrel, LOUGHBOROUGH, LEICESTERSHIRE, LE12 7DD.
GARTSIDE, Mr. Philip Richard, MA FCA *1981;* 2 Vincent Hall, La Rue Du Becquet Vincent, Trinity, JERSEY, JE3 5FH.
GARVEN, Mr. Ian, BA(Hons) ACA *2003;* Arch Insurance Co, 60 Great Tower Street, LONDON, EC3R 5AZ.
GARVEY, Miss. Deborah, BSc ACA *2004;* 35 Randall Place, LONDON, SE10 9LA.
GARVEY, Mr. Dermot Martin, BA ACA *1988;* 36 Bamford Way, ROCHDALE, LANCASHIRE, OL11 5NB.
GARVEY, Mrs. Hazel Jean, FCA *1989;* with ICAEW, Metropolitan House, 321 Avebury Boulevard, MILTON KEYNES, MK9 2FZ.
GARVEY, Miss. Judith, BSc ACA *1992;* 8 St. Michaels Close, BROMLEY, BR1 2DX.
GARVEY, Mr. Martin James, FCA *1986;* 45 The Mount, Wrenthorpe, WAKEFIELD, WF2 0NZ.
GARVEY, Mr. Michael Peter Jack, FCA *1969;* The Lodge, The Drive, Hellingly, HAILSHAM, EAST SUSSEX, BN27 4EP.
GARVEY, Mr. Richard Thomas, FCA *1960;* 31 Clarence Crescent, SIDCUP, DA14 4DG. (Life Member)
GARVEY, Miss. Sally-Ann, MA ACA *2009;* 1/6 Auckland Road, Saint Heliers, AUCKLAND 1071, NEW ZEALAND.
GARVEY, Miss. Sandra Louise Mary, ACA *2008;* 5 Fan Avenue, COLCHESTER, CO4 5ZX.
GARVEY, Miss. Vivienne Elaine, LLB ACA *1999;* 1008 Franklin Ave, NEW ORLEANS, LA 70117, UNITED STATES.
GARVIN, Miss. Angela Jean, MA BA FCA *1981;* Irwell Valley Housing Association Ltd Paragon House, 48 Seymour Grove, MANCHESTER, M16 0LN.
GARVIN, Mr. John Alan, FCA TEP *1970;* with Ward Goodman Limited, 4 Cedar Park, Cobham Road, Ferndown Industrial Estate, WIMBORNE, DORSET BH21 7SF.
GARVIN, Mrs. Linda Mamie, MA ACA *1994;* 47 Radway Close, REDDITCH, B98 8RZ.
GARVIN, Mr. Michael John Moore, FCA *1967;* 46 Guildford Road, LONDON, SW8 2BU. (Life Member)
GARWOOD, Mr. Colin Philip, BA ACA *1988;* IHG Plc, Broadwater Park, North Orbital Road, Denham, UXBRIDGE, MIDDLESEX UB9 5HJ.
GARWOOD, Mr. Graham James, ACA *1979;* 76 Fairview Avenue, Hutton, BRENTWOOD, CM13 1NS.
GARWOOD, Mr. John Wonnacott, FCA *1954;* 90 Camlet Way, Hadley Wood, BARNET, EN4 0NX. (Life Member)
GARWOOD, Mr. Jonathan Mark, BA FCA *1993;* 15 Leconfield, DARLINGTON, COUNTY DURHAM, DL3 8HL.
•**GARWOOD, Mr. Paul Frederick, BSc FCA CTA TEP** *1983;* (Tax Fac), Smith & Williamson Ltd, 25 Moorgate, LONDON, EC2R 6AY.
•**GASCOIGNE, Mr. David Paul, BSc ACA** *1989;* KPMG LLP, 15 Canada Square, LONDON, E14 5GL. See also KPMG Europe LLP
GASCOIGNE, Mr. Garth Sinclair, BSc ACA *1988;* 30 Queen Annes Grove, Chiswick, LONDON, W4 1HN.
GASCOIGNE, Miss. Nicola, BSc ACA *2011;* 57 Coleridge Close, HITCHIN, HERTFORDSHIRE, SG4 0QX.
GASCOIGNE, Mr. Paul Andrew, BSc ACA *1993;* 35 Cavalier Drive, Apperley Bridge, BRADFORD, BD10 0UF.
•**GASCOIGNE, Mr. Roger James, BA FCA** *1992;* KPMG, Pobrezni 1a, 186 00 PRAGUE, CZECH REPUBLIC.
GASCOIGNE, Mr. Simon David, BA ACA *1993;* 3 Alwinton Drive, CHESTER-LE-STREET, DH2 3JH.
GASCOIGNE-PEES, Mr. Edward Max, BA ACA *2001;* Financial Dynamics Ltd, 26 Southampton Buildings, LONDON, WC2A 1PB.
•**GASCOYNE, Mr. Barry, FCA** *1971;* (Tax Fac), Gascoynes Limited, 15 Whiting Street, BURY ST. EDMUNDS, SUFFOLK, IP33 1NX.
GASCOYNE, Mr. Michael, MBA BEng ACA CFA *1992;* c/o The World Bank, 1818 H Street N.W., WASHINGTON, DC 20433, UNITED STATES.
•**GASCOYNE-RICHARDS, Mrs. Rebecca Jane, BSc FCA** *1986;* (Tax Fac), Lovewell Blake LLP, 102 Prince of Wales Road, NORWICH, NORFOLK, NR1 1NY.
GASELEE, Mrs. Sarah Persephone, MSc BA ACA *2001;* 16 Shouldham Street, LONDON, W1H 5FL.
GASH, Mrs. Christine Ann, BA FCA *1984;* 88 Plumtree Road, Thorngumbald, HULL, HU12 9QG.
•**GASH, Mr. Martin Arthur, BSc FCA** *1980;* with Atkinsons (Hull), 60 Commercial Road, HULL, HU1 2SG.
•**GASH, Mr. Neil, BSc FCA ACA** *1980;* Clough Taxation Solutions LLP, New Chartford House, Centurion Way, CLECKHEATON, WEST YORKSHIRE, BD19 3QB. See also Clough & Company LLP
•**GASH, Mr. Steven, FCA** *1974;* Clough & Company LLP, New Chartford House, Centurion Way, CLECKHEATON, WEST YORKSHIRE, BD19 3QB. See also Corporate Finance Services LLP, Clough Taxation Solutions LLP and Clough Management Services LLP
•**GASKELL, Mr. Andrew Nicholas, ACA** *1980;* Saffery Champness, Lion House, Red Lion Street, LONDON, WC1R 4GB.
•**GASKELL, Mrs. Bryony, BSc ACA** *2003;* Bryony Gaskell Accountancy Services, Monteverde, Stocks Road, Alfrick, WORCESTER, WR6 5HD.
GASKELL, Mrs. Clare Rosanna, BSc ACA *2004;* 6 Maunders Court, LIVERPOOL, L23 9YU.
GASKELL, Mr. David Perry, MA FCA *1979;* Grand Baie Trust, Ruisseau Creole, BLACK RIVER, MAURITIUS.
•**GASKELL, Mr. Duncan William, BSc FCA** *1977;* Duncan Gaskell, Pace Sports Management, 6 The Causeway, TEDDINGTON, MIDDLESEX, TW11 0HE.
GASKELL, Miss. Fiona Elizabeth, BSc ACA *1993;* (Tax Fac), Pricewaterhousecoopers Llp, 1 Hays Lane, LONDON, SE1 2RD.
GASKELL, Mr. Ian David, BA ACA *1996;* Geytescales, Lewth Lane, Woodplumpton, PRESTON, PR4 0TE.
•**GASKELL, Mr. Julian Robert, BA FCA** *1993;* with Hazlewoods LLP, Staverton Court, Staverton, CHELTENHAM, GLOUCESTERSHIRE, GL51 0UX.
•**GASKELL, Mr. Michael Arthur, FCA** *1969;* Michael Gaskell, 1 Woods Cottage, Farringdon, EXETER, EX5 2HY.
GASKELL, Mr. Michael John, BA ACA *1987;* Morris Group, Stratstone House, Altrincham Road, WILMSLOW, CHESHIRE, SK9 5NN.
GASKELL, Mr. Peter, BSc ACA *1979;* The Old Rectory, Station Road, Potterhanworth, LINCOLN, LN4 2DX.
GASKELL, Mr. Richard John, BSc ACA *2002;* with Zurich Financial Service UK Life, UK Life Centre, Station Road, SWINDON, SN1 1EL.
•**GASKELL, Mr. Richard John, FCA** *1983;* with Scott & Wilkinson LLP, Dalton House, 9 Dalton Square, LANCASTER, LA1 1WD.
GASKELL SYMS, Mr. Michael John, FCA *1970;* Pine Lodge, 4 Bay Tree Close, Orchard Road, BROMLEY, BR1 2TS.
GASKILL, Mr. Stephen, BSocSc ACA *1993;* PricewaterhouseCoopers (Vietnam) Ltd, 4th Floor Saigon Tower, 29 Le Duan Boulevard, District 1, HO CHI MINH CITY, VIETNAM.
GASKIN, Mr. Anthony, BSc ACA *1991;* 38 William Street, TAYPORT, FIFE, DD6 9HN.
GASKIN, Mr. David John, BSc ACA *1990;* 217 Woodlands Road, Upper Batley, BATLEY, WF17 0QS.
GASKIN, Mrs. Diane Catherine, BA FCA CTA *1989;* Beech Grove, East Chevin Road, OTLEY, LS21 3BN.
GASKIN, Mr. James Joseph, FCA *1970;* Altura, Brook Street, Kingston Blount, CHINNOR, OX39 4RZ.
GASKIN, Mr. Martin Joseph, BA ACA *1988;* Milton Gate, 60 Chiswell Street, LONDON, EC1Y 4AG.
GASKINS, Mr. Raymond Thomas, ACA *1986;* Lea House, Lawn Hill, Edgcott, AYLESBURY, HP18 0TT.
GASKINS, Mrs. Ruth Gael, BSc ACA *2000;* 61 Boddens Hill Road, Heaton Mersey, STOCKPORT, SK4 2DG.
GASPAR, Mr. Eamonn David, LLB ACA *1984;* 13 Jennings Lane, Harwell, DIDCOT, OX11 0EP.
GASPERINI, Mr. Laurence Robert, BEng ACA *1994;* 42 Church Road, LONDON, SW13 9HN.
GASS, Mr. Colin Malcolm, FCA *1952;* 46 King Edward Road, BARNET, EN5 5AS. (Life Member)
GASSER, Mr. Alan Neil, BA ACA CTA *2002;* 2 Wayfarer Close, Warsash, SOUTHAMPTON, SO31 9AU.
GASSON, Mr. Benjamin Daniel, MEng ACA *2005;* 74a Whitbread Road, LONDON, SE4 2BE.
GASSON, Mrs. Nicola Jane, BSc(Econ) ACA *2001;* 2 Herons Croft, WEYBRIDGE, KT13 0PL.
GASSON, Mr. Thomas William, BSc ACA *1991;* (Tax Fac), Goldman Sachs, Peterborough Court, 133 Fleet Street, LONDON, EC4A 2BB.
GASTER, Mr. Ben Charles, BEng ACA *2004;* 4 Cambridge Road, NOTTINGHAM, NG8 1FP.
GASTON, Mr. Christopher John, BSc ACA *2005;* Deutsche Bank, Floor 3 Tower 2, Logitech Park, MV Road, Sakinaka, MUMBAI 400072 INDIA.
GASTON, Mr. John Hallett, FCA *1957;* The Crofts, Fairwarp, UCKFIELD, TN22 3BG. (Life Member)
GASTON, Miss. Kirsty Anne, MSc BA ACA *1999;* 96 Brackenbury Road, LONDON, W6 0BD.
GASTON, Mr. Michael John, MBA BA ACA *1985;* 1 Dents Road, LONDON, SW11 6JA.
GATA, Mr. Henry, BA ACA *2011;* 15 Blacksmiths Close, ROMFORD, RM6 4XE.
GATAORA, Mr. Rajinder Singh, BA ACA *2003;* Flat 9 Princess Court, 105 Hornsey Lane, LONDON, N6 5XD.
GATE, Mr. Andrew Mark, BA ACA *1992;* 7 Ovington View, PRUDHOE, NE42 6RG.
GATEHOUSE, Mr. David, BSc FCA *1976;* 97 Broadley Drive, Livermead, TORQUAY, TQ2 6UT.
•**GATEHOUSE, Mr. Martin, BA ACA** *1995;* Eacotts Limited, Grenville Court, Britwell Road, Burnham, SLOUGH, SL1 8DF. See also Eacotts
GATELEY, Mr. Christopher, BSc ACA *1988;* Lambing Clough Farm, Lambing Clough Lane, Hurst Green, CLITHEROE, LANCASHIRE, BB7 9QN.
GATELEY, Miss. Jane Samantha, BSc ACA *1993;* 34 Fallow Fields, Great Woodcote Park, LOUGHTON, IG10 4QP.
GATELEY, Mr. John Kevin, MA ACA *1984;* 23 Brockenhurst Road, Martins Heron, BRACKNELL, RG12 9FJ.
GATELEY, Mr. Terence Michael, FCA *1977;* Elba Investments, 14 Petersham Place, Richmond Hill Road, BIRMINGHAM, B15 3RY.
GATELY, Mr. John, BA ACA *2010;* 2 Weylands Park, WEYBRIDGE, KT13 0JL.
GATENBY, Miss. Katie, MChem ACA *2007;* with PricewaterhouseCoopers LLP, 1 Embankment Place, LONDON, WC2N 6RH.
GATENBY, Mr. Michael Richard Brock, FCA *1970;* 11 Norland Square, LONDON, W11 4PX.
GATENBY, Mr. Patrick Dai, BA ACA *1992;* The Orcid Partnership, Herons Way, Chester Business Park, CHESTER, CH4 9QR.
GATENBY, Mrs. Rebecca Kay, BSc ACA *2004;* 10 Fryston Common Lane, Monk Fryston, LEEDS, LS25 5ER.
GATENS, Mr. Terence William, BSc ACA *1983;* I Q Chartered Accountants, 1-5 Seamer Road Corner, SCARBOROUGH, NORTH YORKSHIRE, YO12 5BB.
GATER, Mr. Colin, BSc ACA *2006;* 21 Ruffs Furze, Oakley, BEDFORD, MK43 7RR.
GATER, Mr. George, FCA *1970;* Tythe House, High Street North, Stewkley, LEIGHTON BUZZARD, BEDFORDSHIRE, LU7 0HJ.
GATER, Mr. Maxwell Cruickshank, FCA *1971;* Rowans, Marlborough Road, Ogbourne St. George, MARLBOROUGH, SN8 1TF.
•**GATES, Mrs. Anne-Marie, ACA FCCA** *2008;* Princecroft Willis LLP, The George Business Centre, Christchurch Road, NEW MILTON, HAMPSHIRE, BH25 6QJ. See also PW Business Solutions
GATES, Mrs. Clare, BA ACA *1999;* 11 Chartwell Drive, HAVANT, HAMPSHIRE, PO9 2QB.
GATES, Mr. David Peter, BSc ACA *1992;* Highview London Road, West Kingsdown, SEVENOAKS, TN15 6EW.
GATES, Mr. Edwin Peter, BSc ACA MCT *1982;* 5 Millhedge Close, COBHAM, KT11 3BE.
GATES, Mr. James David, BSc ACA *2002;* Hardvard International Plc, Hardvard House, The Waterfront, Elstree Road, ELSTREE, HERTFORDSHIRE WD6 3BS.
GATES, Ms. Jillian Sara, BA ACA *1992;* Manor Top Burwardsley Road, Burwardsley, CHESTER, CH3 9PH.
•**GATES, Mr. John Fairfax, FCA** *1969;* Myland Lodge, 301a Mile End Road, COLCHESTER, CO4 5EA. See also Humphreys & Gates
GATES, Mr. Kenneth Joseph, FCA *1963;* 40 Cotefield Drive, LEIGHTON BUZZARD, BEDFORDSHIRE, LU7 3DS. (Life Member)
GATES, Mrs. Lindsay Gayle, ACA *2009;* 3 Goldfinch Drive, Catterall, PRESTON, PR3 1TR.
GATES, Mr. Malcolm Derek, MA BA ACA *2002;* with PricewaterhouseCoopers LLP, 1 Embankment Place, LONDON, WC2N 6RH.
GATES, Mr. Martin Douglas Clift, FCA *1960;* 12 Marlborough Road, Chandlers Ford, EASTLEIGH, SO53 5DH. (Life Member)
GATES, Mr. Michael John, MBA FCA *1967;* Holmbushes Farm, Leigh, SHERBORNE, DT9 6HU.
GATES, Mr. Paul Jonathan, BSc ACA *1998;* WPP Group plc, 121-141 Westbourne Terrace, LONDON, W2 6JR.
GATES, Mr. Philip Anthony St Quentin, MA FCA *1967;* 4615 Russell Road, DUNCAN V9L 6N2, BC, CANADA.
GATES, Mr. Roger David, FCA *1962;* Broomy Green House, Checkley, Mordiford, HEREFORD, HR1 4NA. (Life Member)
GATES, Mrs. Sian Louise, BSc(Hons) ACA *2001;* 137 Tilehurst Road, LONDON, SW18 3EX.
GATES, Mr. Simon Barnaby, MA ACA *2000;* 137 Tilehurst Road, Earlsfield, LONDON, SW18 3EX.
•**GATES, Mr. Stephen John, MSc BA FCA ARPS** *1976;* (Tax Fac), Kiln Group Limited Furness House, 106 Frenchurch Street, LONDON, EC3M 5NR.
GATES, Mrs. Tracy, BSc(Hons) ACA *2002;* 2 Charlotte Close, Wing, LEIGHTON BUZZARD, BEDFORDSHIRE, LU7 0XJ.
GATES-SUMNER, Miss. Sophie Louise, BSc(Hons) ACA *2003;* 83 Thistledene, THAMES DITTON, KT7 0YW.
GATHA, Mr. Rajiv, BSc FCA *1996;* 12 Devonshire Park, READING, RG2 7DX.
GATHERCOLE, Mr. Clive David, BA ACA *1986;* St. Germain, The Warren, East Horsley, LEATHERHEAD, SURREY, KT24 5RH.
GATHERER, Mr. Benedict Matthew, BA(Hons) ACA *2009;* National Audit Office, 157-197 Buckingham Palace Road, LONDON, SW1W 9SP.
GATHIGI, Mr. Anthony Mureithi, ACA *1991;* PO BOX 11992, NAIROBI, 00400, KENYA.
GATHINJI, Mr. Ndungu, FCA *1971;* Hughes Building, Kenyatta Avenue, PO Box 42423, NAIROBI, KENYA. (Life Member)
GATHORNE-HARDY, The Hon. Hugh, MA FCA *1967;* Christies Care Ltd, The Old Post Office, High Street, SAXMUNDHAM, IP17 1AB.
•**GATLAND, Mr. Paul, FCA** *1982;* (Tax Fac), Burgess Hodgson, Camburgh House, 27 New Dover Road, CANTERBURY, CT1 3DN.
GATLAND, Mr. Simon Philip, BSc ACA *2005;* 56 Albert Road, LONDON, N22 7AH.
GATLIFF, Ms. Angela Ruth, BSc FCA *1982;* Flat 27, Queens Court, Queens Road, CHELTENHAM, GLOUCESTERSHIRE, GL50 2LU.
GATOFF, Mr. Alistair David, LLB ACA *1982;* 215 West 91 Street, Apt 122, NEW YORK, NY 10024, UNITED STATES.
GATOFF, Miss. Caroline Sarah, BSc(Hons) ACA *2002;* 18 Goodwyn Avenue, LONDON, NW7 3RG.
GATOFF, Mr. Leonard Henry, BA(Econ) FCA *1964;* (Member of Council 1987 - 1991), 78 Montagu Court, Gosforth, NEWCASTLE UPON TYNE, NE3 4JL. (Life Member)
GATRAD, Mr. Altaf Mahomed, BSc FCA *1980;* Park Lodge, 518 Wellinborough Road, NORTHAMPTON, NN3 3HX.
GATT, Mr. Jonathon, ACA CA(AUS) *2011;* GE Capital Finance Australasia Pty Limited, GE Corporate Finance Bank SAS London Branch, 30 Berkeley Square, LONDON, W1J 6EW.
GATTEI, Mr. Pierino Francesco, MA ACA *1999;* 15 Kingsnorth Road, Urmston, MANCHESTER, M41 8SL.
•**GATTER, Mr. Stephen Martin, BCom FCA** *1986;* (Tax Fac), ABACS Ltd, La Pineda, Upper Minety, MALMESBURY, WILTSHIRE, SN16 9PR.
GATUTHA, Mr. Paul Mwangi, ACA *1999;* P.O. Box HM 2274, HAMILTON HM JX, BERMUDA.
GATWARD, Mr. Bradly Neil, BA ACA ATII *1991;* 14 South Street, GODALMING, SURREY, GU7 1BF.
GATWARD, Mr. Edward John, MA FCA *1975;* Convent of Sisters of Nazareth Nazareth House, Hammersmith Road, LONDON, W6 8DB.
GATWARD, Ms. Sarah Jane, BSc ACA *1991;* 14 South Street, GODALMING, SURREY, GU7 1BF.
GAUDION, Miss. Diane Marie, BSc FCA *2000;* La Jaoniere, La Route De L'Islet, St. Sampson, GUERNSEY, GY2 4RS.
GAUGHAN, Ms. Lorraine Marie, BA ACA *1992;* 36 North Street, Caistor, MARKET RASEN, LINCOLNSHIRE, LN7 6QU.
GAUGHAN, Miss. Mary, BSc ACA *2011;* 41 Lancaster Road, LONDON, N18 1HP.
GAUGHAN, Mr. Thomas Luke, BSc ACA *2002;* 1 Hatchwood Close, WOODFORD GREEN, ESSEX, IG8 0SX.
GAUGHT, Mr. Ronald Edgar, FCA *1959;* The Acorns, Uplands Road, Denmead, WATERLOOVILLE, PO7 6HG. (Life Member)
GAUKROGER, Mr. Michael John, FCA *1984;* 14 Kestrel Drive, SUTTON COLDFIELD, B74 4XW.
•**GAUL, Mr. Nicholas, BA ACA** *1986;* Hannay & Co Limited, Norwood House, 73 Elvetham Road, FLEET, HAMPSHIRE, GU51 4HL.
GAULD, Mr. Robert John, MSc ACA *1998;* 65 Clement Road, Marple Bridge, STOCKPORT, CHESHIRE, SK6 5AG.
GAULD, Mr. Wyness Scott, FCA *1940;* 8 Harrowdene Court, Belvedere Drive Wimbledon, LONDON, SW19 7BY. (Life Member)

•**GHOSH, Mr. Dipankar Mohan, FCA** *1972;* 20 Russell Road, Moor Park, NORTHWOOD, MIDDLESEX, HA6 2LL.
GHOSH, Mrs. Emma, BA ACA *2001;* 39 Sevington Road, Hendon, LONDON, NW4 3RY.
GHOSH, Mr. Jyotirmoy, BSc FCA *1978;* 73 Hervey Close, Finchley Central, LONDON, N3 2HH.
GHOSH, Mrs. Leena, BA FCA *1987;* 8 Thurlow Court, 1a-1b Wellesley Road, LONDON, E11 2HG.
GHOSH, Mrs. Neelam Kumari, BA ACA ACCA *1996;* 151 New Hall Lane, BOLTON, BL1 5HP.
GHOSH, Miss. Nupur, BA(Hons) ACA *2001;* 28 North Park, Berry Hill, MANSFIELD, NG18 4PB.
•**GHOSH, Mr. Partha, FCA** *1991;* PricewaterhouseCoopers Ltd, 252 Veer Savarkar Marg, Shivaji Park Dadr, MUMBAI 400028, MAHARASHTRA, INDIA.
GHOSH, Mr. Pronab Kumar, FCA *1974;* (Tax Fac), 21 Chetwynd Avenue, BARNET, EN4 8NG.
GHOSH, Mr. Sanjay, BA FCA *1977;* Flat 35, Ormond House, Medway Street, LONDON, SW1P 2TB.
GHOSH, Mr. Satya Brata, FCA *1959;* No 84 S/ E, Block E, New Alipore, CALCUTTA 700 053, INDIA. (Life Member)
GHOSH, Miss. Shefali, MA ACA *1992;* Working Title Films, 26 Aybrook Street, LONDON, W1U 4AN.
GHOSH, Mr. Sidhartha, FCA *1975;* 5 Cambridge Ct, MEDFORD, NJ 08055, UNITED STATES.
GHOSH, Mr. Soumen, BSc ACA *1986;* Reliance Capital Ltd, 570 Rectifier House, Naigaum Cross Road, Wadala, MUMBAI 400031, INDIA.
GHOSH, Mr. Supryio, FCA *1965;* 10A Rawdon Street, KOLKATA 700017, WEST BENGAL, INDIA.
GHOSH, Mr. Sushovan, BSc FCA *1984;* SGI Group Limited, 14 St. Johns Road, WOKING, SURREY, GU21 7SE.
•**GHOSH, Mr. Ujjal Kanti, FCA ACA** *2011;* A S Kalsi & Co Limited, 124 Rookery Road, Handsworth, BIRMINGHAM, B21 9NN.
GHOTRA, Mr. Gurthian, BEng ACA CTA *1993;* McCormick Europe Ltd, Haddenham Business Park, Thame Road, Haddenham, AYLESBURY, BUCKINGHAMSHIRE HP17 8LB.
GHOWS, Mr. Abdul Hamid Bin Mohamed, FCA *1973;* 14 Jalan SS 19/4B, Subang Jaya, 47500 PETALING JAYA, SELANGOR, MALAYSIA.
GHUI, Mr. Hoi Wan, ACA *1993;* Hydro Sealing, Technology Sdn Bhd, 7 Jalan Kempas 2, Taman Tanah, Tampoi, 81200 JOHOR BAHRU MALAYSIA.
GHULAM, Mr. Shahnavaz, BSc ACA *2004;* 294a Amhurst Road, LONDON, N16 7UE.
GHUMAN, Mrs. Kiranjit, BA(Hons) ACA *2004;* Octavian Continental Limited, Oberoi Consulting, 19 St. Christophers Way Pride Park, DERBY, DE24 8JY.
GHUMRA, Mr. Imran, BA ACA CTA *2000;* KPMG, Tax, 111 Rue de Lyon, 1203 GENEVA, SWITZERLAND.
•**GHUMRA, Mr. Yusuf Omar, BSc FCA** *1986;* (Tax Fac), Ghumra & Co Limited, 24 Vulcan House, Vulcan Road, LEICESTER, LE5 3EF. See also Ghumra Accounting Limited
GHURA, Mr. Apinder Singh, BA ACA *1988;* Chan Casuals Ltd, The Chan Building, Comet Row, NEWCASTLE UPON TYNE, NE12 6DS.
GHURBURRUN, Mr. Soodarsansingh, ACA *2007;* 18 Worcester Road, LONDON, E17 5QR.
GIACOMETTO, Mrs. Claire Justine, BSc ACA *1994;* 14 Beech Road, Purley on Thames, READING, RG8 8DS.
GIAM, Miss. Mei Peng, BA ACA *2004;* 12B Tower 2, Centrestage, 108 Hollywood Road, CENTRAL, HONG KONG SAR.
GIANG, Mr. Tsz Lam, ACA *2009;* Rm 1C 3/F, 5 Hoi Ching Street, SAI WAN HO, HONG KONG SAR.
GIANNINI, Miss. Sarah Louise, ACA *2010;* 9 Pendennis Road, ORPINGTON, BR6 9BL.
GIAQUINTO, Mr. Umberto, BA ACA *2007;* with Baker Tilly (Gibraltar) Limited, Regal House, Queensway, PO Box 191, GIBRALTAR, GIBRALTAR.
GIBAUT, Mr. John Christopher, BSc ACA *1988;* 2684 Elm Drive, BRIER, WA 98036, UNITED STATES.
GIBB, Miss. Briony, ACA *2011;* Flat 3, Grove Hall, 10-12 West Grove, LONDON, SE10 8QT.
GIBB, Ms. Catherine Anne, BSc ACA *1987;* Rabys, South Park Lane, Bletchingley, REDHILL, RH1 4ND.
GIBB, Ms. Catherine Mary, BA ACA *1992;* SCC, James House, Warwick Road, Tyseley, Sparkhill, BIRMINGHAM B11 2LE.
GIBB, Mr. Christopher Howard, BA ACA *1991;* 16 Idsworth Close, Horndean, WATERLOOVILLE, PO8 0DW.
GIBB, Mrs. Claire Elizabeth, BSc(Hons) ACA *2001;* 4 Whinchat Tail, GUISBOROUGH, CLEVELAND, TS14 8PW.
GIBB, Mr. Dominic Iain, BSc ACA *1990;* 57 Hyde Vale, LONDON, SE10 8QQ.
GIBB, Mr. Ewan Kenneth, LLB ACA *1989;* China Industries Creative Industries Building, Mammoth Drive Wolverhampton Science Park, WOLVERHAMPTON, WV10 9TG.
GIBB, Mr. Michael, FCA *1975;* Denmark House, Norwich Road, Hardingham, NORWICH, NR9 4EG.
GIBB, Miss. Nemone Margaret Janet, BAcc ACA *2001;* Rose Cottage, Le Coin Farm, Le Mont Du Coin, St. Brelade, JERSEY, JE3 8BE.
•**GIBB, Mr. Nicholas Robert Pashley, MA FCA** *1982;* KPMG LLP, Arlington Business Park, Theale, READING, RG7 4SD. See also KPMG Europe LLP
GIBB, Mr. Nicolas John, BA FCA MP *1987;* Chapel Cottage Fisher Lane, South Mundham, CHICHESTER, WEST SUSSEX, PO20 1ND.
GIBB, Mr. Peter Harvey, BSc ACA *1992;* PO Box 25125, Gateway, DURBAN, 4321, SOUTH AFRICA.
•**GIBB, Mr. Richard David, BSc FCA** *1990;* Chisnall Comer Ismail & Co, Maria House, 35 Millers Road, BRIGHTON, BN1 5NP.
GIBB, Mr. Robert, FCA *1947;* 9 Oldway, Bishopston, SWANSEA, SA3 3DE. (Life Member)
GIBB, Mr. Robert Macnab Stormont, MA FCA *1973;* Felix Boix 710A, 28036 MADRID, SPAIN.
GIBB, Mr. Simon James Mark, BSc ACA *1987;* 106 Dunstable Road, Studham, DUNSTABLE, BEDFORDSHIRE, LU6 2QL.
GIBB-GRAY, Mr. Dominic James Michael, BA ACA *2006;* IBM, North Harbour, PORTSMOUTH, PO6 3AY.
GIBBARD, Mr. Dudley William, FCA *1969;* 144 Addington Rd., Irthlingborough, WELLINGBOROUGH, NN9 5UP. (Life Member)
GIBBARD, Dr. Jonathan Peter, ACA *2009;* with PricewaterhouseCoopers LLP, 9 Greyfriars Road, READING, RG1 1JG.
GIBBARD, Mr. Mark James, BSc FCA MCT *1987;* 53 Newstead Road, Barnwood, GLOUCESTER, GL4 3TQ.
GIBBENS, Barnaby John, Esq OBE FCA *1962;* 12 Kings Road, Wimbledon, LONDON, SW19 8QN.
•**GIBBENS, Mr. David Llewellyn, BSc FCA** *1992;* Gibbens Waterfield Ltd, Priory House, 2 Priory Road, DUDLEY, WEST MIDLANDS, DY1 1HH. See also Poole Waterfield Limited
•**GIBBENS, Mrs. Helen Clare, BSc(Econ) ACA FCCA** *2007;* Gibbens Waterfield Ltd, Priory House, 2 Priory Road, DUDLEY, WEST MIDLANDS, DY1 1HH. See also Poole Waterfield Limited
GIBBES, Mrs. Barbara, BA(Hons) ACA *2001;* Management Consulting Group Plc, 10 Fleet Place, LONDON, EC4M 7RB.
GIBBINGS, Mr. Thomas William McCormick, BSc(Econ) ACA *2004;* 22 Marcus Street, LONDON, SW18 2JT.
GIBBINS, Mr. Alan Bertram, BA FCA *1974;* Went House, 83 Swan Street, WEST MALLING, KENT, ME19 6LW.
GIBBINS, Mr. Allan Frederick, FCA *1986;* Salmons, Salmons Lane, WHYTELEAFE, CR3 0HB.
GIBBINS, Miss. Amanda, ACA *2007;* 11 Hall Close, Southery, DOWNHAM MARKET, NORFOLK, PE38 0NN.
GIBBINS, Mr. Christopher, FCA *1973;* 1 California, WOODBRIDGE, IP12 4DE.
GIBBINS, Mrs. Helen Katie, BA ACA *2006;* with KPMG LLP, St. James's Square, MANCHESTER, M2 6DS.
GIBBINS, Mrs. Jacqueline Ann, BSc ACA *1995;* 28 Corbet Avenue, Sprowston, NORWICH, NR7 8HS.
GIBBINS, Mr. Jonathan Martin, BSc ACA *1995;* 28 Corbet Avenue, Sprowston, NORWICH, NR7 8HS.
GIBBINS, Mr. Julian Ashley Nigel, BSc ACA *1991;* 15 Brim Hill, Hampstead Garden Suburb, LONDON, N2 0HD.
GIBBINS, Mr. Lance John, BA ACA *1991;* Hunters Lodge, Goodley Stock Road, Crockham Hill, EDENBRIDGE, KENT, TN8 6TA.
GIBBINS, Mr. Mark Robert, BA FCA *1984;* KPMG Romania, DN1 Sos bucuresti-ploesti nr 69-71, PO box 18-191 Sector 1, 013685 BUCHAREST, ROMANIA.
GIBBINS, Mr. Michael Edward Stanley, LVO FCA *1966;* 38 Clare Lawn Avenue, East Sheen, LONDON, SW14 8BG.
GIBBINS, Mr. Michael John, ACA *1986;* 22 Downham Crescent, WYMONDHAM, NR18 0SF.
GIBBINS, Mr. Robert Christopher, MA FCA *1966;* 101 - 1689 Duchess Avenue, WEST VANCOUVER V7V 1P7, BC, CANADA.
GIBBINS, Mrs. Sara Louise, ACA ATII MAAT *1996;* 15 Brim Hill, Hampstead Garden Suburb, LONDON, N2 0HD.
GIBBINS, Mr. Simon, ACA ATII ACT *1991;* 2 Sudbrooke Road, Wandsworth Common, LONDON, SW12 8TG.
GIBBON, Mrs. Amanda Elisabeth Owen, BA ACA *1990;* 43 Duncan Terrace, LONDON, N1 8AL.
GIBBON, Mr. Charles Henry Maitland, FCA *1971;* 30 Hill Crescent, BEXLEY, DA5 2DB.
GIBBON, Mr. David Keith Christopher, BA FCA *1985;* 14 Beaumont Road, WINDSOR, BERKSHIRE, SL4 1HY.
GIBBON, Mrs. Erica Jane, BA ACA *1994;* Flat 5 Tavistock, 15 Grosvenor Road, Birkdale, SOUTHPORT, PR8 2HT.
GIBBON, Mrs. Fiona, BA ACA *1997;* The Retreat, 2 Weston Road, PETERSFIELD, GU31 4JF.
•**GIBBON, Mr. Ian, FCA CF** *1977;* Alliotts, Congress House, 14 Lyon Road, HARROW, MIDDLESEX, HA1 2EN.
GIBBON, Miss. Katie Laura, BA ACA *2011;* 144 Limpsfield Road, SOUTH CROYDON, SURREY, CR2 9EF.
GIBBON, Mr. Mark, LLB FCA *1983;* Collegiate Management Services Ltd, 77 Mansell Street, LONDON, E1 8FE.
GIBBON, Mr. Mark, MA ACA *2004;* 5 Grove Road, HENLEY-ON-THAMES, OXFORDSHIRE, RG9 1DH.
GIBBON, Mr. Richard John, BA FCA *1992;* B P P Financial Education, 3 London Wall Buildings, LONDON, EC2M 5PD.
•**GIBBONS, Mr. Adrian Hugh Russell, BSc ACA** *1986;* Swat UK Limited, Block 2, Lower Ground, Angel Square, Islington, LONDON EC1V 1NY.
GIBBONS, Mr. Alastair Ronald, BSc ACA *1983;* 1 Hazlewell Road, LONDON, SW15 6LU.
GIBBONS, Mr. Arnold Edward Alexander, BA ACA *1986;* 102A Cole Park Road, TWICKENHAM, TW1 1JA.
GIBBONS, Mrs. Caroline Jane, BSc ACA CTA *1986;* 26 Eastwick Drive, Bookham, LEATHERHEAD, KT23 3PR.
GIBBONS, Mr. Clive Anthony, BA ACA *1984;* 5 Four Acre Coppice, HOOK, RG27 9NF.
GIBBONS, Mrs. Colette Mary, BSc FCA *1994;* P O Box 697, KAMPALA, UGANDA.
•**GIBBONS, Mr. David John, BSc ACA** *1986;* Menzies LLP, Woking Office, Midas House, 62 Goldsworth Road, WOKING, SURREY GU21 6LQ.
GIBBONS, Mr. David Paul, BSc ACA *1981;* 118 Jersey Rd Woollahra, SYDNEY, NSW 2025, AUSTRALIA.
GIBBONS, Mrs. Frances Jillian, BCom ACA *1989;* Shakespeare Putsman LLP, Somerset House, Temple Street, BIRMINGHAM, B2 5DJ.
•**GIBBONS, Mr. Godfrey George, FCA** *1969;* Complete Solutions 4U Limited, 43a High Street, Pelsall, WALSALL, WS3 4LT.
GIBBONS, Mr. Graham Ross, BAcc ACA *1988;* JT International (Jordan) Ltd, Moayyad Al-Shaar Str, Al-Muqablain, PO Box 630025, AMMAN, 11163 JORDAN.
GIBBONS, Miss. Isobel, BA(Hons) ACA *2011;* 30 Lower Farlington Road, PORTSMOUTH, PO6 1JH.
•**GIBBONS, Mrs. Jennifer Ann Cathleen, FCA** *1978;* (Tax Fac), CFW, 1 Sterling Court, Loddington, KETTERING, NN14 1RZ.
GIBBONS, Mr. John James, FCA *1960;* 215 Aylestone Lane, WIGSTON, LEICESTERSHIRE, LE18 1BE. (Life Member)
GIBBONS, Mr. Jonathan, FCA *1965;* 19 Dragons Hill Court, Keynsham, BRISTOL, BS31 1LW. (Life Member)
GIBBONS, Mr. Jonathan David Peter, MA ACA *2001;* Deloitte & Associes, 185 Avenue Charles de Gaulle, 92524 NEUILLY SUR SEINE CEDEX, FRANCE.
GIBBONS, Mr. Jonathan Marc, BSc ACA FCCA *2011;* 83 Longfield Avenue, Mill Hill, LONDON, NW7 2SA.
GIBBONS, Mr. Leslie Alan, FCA *1969;* 80 Mill Rise, Westdene, BRIGHTON, BN1 5GH.
GIBBONS, Mr. Leslie Robert, FCA *1957;* 16c South Cliff Tower, Bolsover Road, EASTBOURNE, BN20 7JW. (Life Member)
GIBBONS, Miss. Lindsey, BSc ACA *2006;* 10 The Vale, WOODFORD GREEN, IG8 9BT.
GIBBONS, Mr. Mark, BCom ACA *1991;* 24 Birch Street, WOLVERHAMPTON, WV1 4HY.
GIBBONS, Mr. Martin Anthony, BSc ACA *1993;* 23 Firs Road, SALE, CHESHIRE, M33 5EH.
GIBBONS, Mr. Matthew Francis, FCA *1973;* P.O N-7776, Lyford Cay, NASSAU, 00000, BAHAMAS.
•**GIBBONS, Mr. Michael Frederick, FCA** *1983;* (Tax Fac), Nabarro, 3/4 Great Marlborough Street, LONDON, W1F 7HH.
GIBBONS, Mr. Neil Barry, BA ACA *1989;* Fieldsview, 56a Rope Lane, CREWE, CHESHIRE, CW2 6RD.
GIBBONS, Mr. Nicholas Richard Charles, ACA *1982;* Van Heyningen Bros. Ltd, Runction Nursery, Lagness Road, Runcton, CHICHESTER, WEST SUSSEX PO20 1LJ.
GIBBONS, Miss. Nicola Jane, BSc(Hons) ACA *2001;* 59 Croftwood Road, STOURBRIDGE, WEST MIDLANDS, DY9 7EY.
GIBBONS, Mr. Nigel, FCA *1979;* Oakhurst Farm, Oakhurst Lane, Loxwood, BILLINGSHURST, WEST SUSSEX, RH14 0QR.
GIBBONS, Mr. Norman John, FCA *1978;* PO Box 466, HARPENDEN, HERTFORDSHIRE, AL5 9BB.
GIBBONS, Mr. Paul John Joseph, BSc ACA *1990;* Bayerische Landesbank, 13-14 Appold Street, LONDON, EC2A 2NB.
GIBBONS, Mr. Paul Joseph, BSc FCA *1992;* 138 Rockbourne Road, Sherfield-on-Loddon, HOOK, HAMPSHIRE, RG27 0SR.
•**GIBBONS, Mr. Philip Michael, FCA** *1971;* 13 Lowood Lodge, Lowther Terrace, LYTHAM ST. ANNES, FY8 5QG.
GIBBONS, Mr. Robert Michael, BSc ACA *1982;* MacFarlanes Solicitors, 20 Cursitor Street, LONDON, EC4A 1LT.
GIBBONS, Mr. Simon, BA FCA *1996;* PO Box 278, Madinat Qaboos, 112 MUSCAT, OMAN.
•**GIBBOR, Mr. Brian Jeffrey, BA FCA** *1982;* Gibbors Limited, 19 Ardross Avenue, NORTHWOOD, MIDDLESEX, HA6 3DS. See also Gibbors
GIBBS, Mr. Adam John, BSc ACA *2009;* Gotham Erskine, Friendly House, 52-58 Tabernacle Street, LONDON, EC2A 4NJ.
GIBBS, Mr. Andrew David, ACA *2008;* 79 London Road, WOKINGHAM, RG40 1YA.
GIBBS, Mr. Andrew Goldsworthy, MA FCA *1971;* 23 Shooters Hill Road, Blackheath, LONDON, SE3 7AS.
•**GIBBS, Mr. Andrew Mark, BA FCA ACII** *1986;* Driftwood, 1 Pokiok Crescent, SMITHS FL 05, BERMUDA.
GIBBS, Mrs. Angela Susan, ACA *2003;* Harland Accountants Parade House, The Parade, LISKEARD, CORNWALL, PL14 6AF.
GIBBS, Mr. Barry, BSc ACA *1999;* 42 Rowse Street, RANGIORA 7400, NEW ZEALAND.
GIBBS, Mr. Benjamin Morel Ohenaku, BA FCA *1998;* 119 Rue Pierre Ledent, 62170 MONTREUIL, FRANCE.
GIBBS, Mr. Colin Geoffrey, FCA *1964;* 1 Broadcote Close, Brooke, NORWICH, NR15 1HZ. (Life Member)
GIBBS, Mr. David Charles, FCA *1961;* Rotselaerlaan 28, 3080 TERVUREN, BELGIUM. (Life Member)
•**GIBBS, Mr. David Christopher, BSc FCA ATII** *1993;* (Tax Fac), PricewaterhouseCoopers LLP, Abacus House, Castle Park, CAMBRIDGE, CB3 0AN.
GIBBS, Mr. David Paul, BSc FCA *1987;* 42 Bonython Avenue, GLENELG NORTH, SA 5045, AUSTRALIA.
GIBBS, Mr. Dominic Vaughan, BA ACA *1993;* The Cayzer Trust Company Limited, 30 Buckingham Gate, LONDON, SW1E 6NN.
•**GIBBS, Mr. Geoffrey Charles, FCA FCCA** *1977;* Gibsons Financial Limited, Foresters Hall, 25-27 Westow Street, LONDON, SE19 3RY. See also Gibsons
GIBBS, Mr. Ian Shaun, BA ACA *1991;* Bromius Capital Pte Ltd, 50 Raffles Place, H33-02 Singapore Land Tower, SINGAPORE 048623, SINGAPORE.
•**GIBBS, Mr. John Alan, ACA** *1991;* AH Partnership, Stanley House, 49 Dartford Road, SEVENOAKS, KENT, TN13 3TE. See also AH Partnership Limited
GIBBS, Mr. John Andrew, BSc ACA *1992;* Polar Electro (UK) Ltd Polar House, Heathcote Way Heathcote Industrial Estate, WARWICK, CV34 6TE.
GIBBS, Mr. John Kenneth Andrew, FCA *1974;* Church Farmhouse, Batcombe, DORCHESTER, DORSET, DT2 7BG.
GIBBS, Mr. John William Barratt, FCA *1967;* 32 Pembroke Gardens Close, LONDON, W8 6HR. (Life Member)
GIBBS, Mr. Jonathan Philip, BA FCA *1974;* Mayfield Lodge, Grayswood Road, HASLEMERE, GU27 2BU.
GIBBS, Miss. Judith Elizabeth, BSc ACA CTA *2002;* Flat 4, 19 Eltham Road, LONDON, SE12 8ES.
GIBBS, Mrs. Julia Elizabeth, BA ACA *2001;* 21 Sheraton Drive, Wollaton, NOTTINGHAM, NG8 2PR.
GIBBS, Mr. Kenneth Philip, MSc ACA *1987;* Poolfield Farm, Charfield, WOTTON-UNDER-EDGE, GLOUCESTERSHIRE, GL12 8HY.
GIBBS, Miss. Marie Joanne, LLB ACA *2001;* 135 Craven Road, NEWBURY, BERKSHIRE, RG14 5NN.
GIBBS, Mrs. Marion, BA ACA *1995;* 37 Pantheon Road, Chandler's Ford, EASTLEIGH, SO53 2PD.

GIBBS, Mr. Mark Peter, BA ACA *1990;* (Tax Fac), The Old Sheepwash Barn, Stroxton Lane, Stroxton, GRANTHAM, LINCOLNSHIRE, NG33 5DA.

•**GIBBS, Mr. Martyn Russell, ACA** *1982;* 24 Cooper Close, Heathlands, BROMSGROVE, B60 3PJ.

•**GIBBS, Mr. Matthew Simon, BCom FCA** *1996;* Rice & Co, 14A Market Place, UTTOXETER, ST14 8HP.

GIBBS, Mr. Michael Peter, ACA *1990;* 27 Harcourt Street, DUNEDIN, NEW ZEALAND.

GIBBS, Mr. Michael William Bruce, FCA *1980;* P O Box 10027, GEORGE TOWN, GRAND CAYMAN, KY1-1001, CAYMAN ISLANDS.

GIBBS, Mr. Neville, FCA *1958;* 14 Goddards Close, CRANBROOK, TN17 3LJ. (Life Member)

GIBBS, Mr. Nigel Gerard, BCom FCA *1972;* 37 Windsor Road, Radyr, CARDIFF, CF15 8BQ.

GIBBS, Mr. Owen James, ACA *2011;* Flat 1, Lagare Apartments, 53 Surrey Row, LONDON, SE1 0DF.

GIBBS, Mrs. Penelope Marie, BA ACA *1995;* 22 Oakrits, Meldreth, ROYSTON, SG8 6JH.

GIBBS, Mr. Peter David Errington, FCA *1968;* Tremain, 4 Heights Close, Wimbledon, LONDON, SW20 0TH.

GIBBS, Mr. Peter John, BCom ACA *1986;* 61 Cottage Lane, Marlbrook, BROMSGROVE, WORCESTERSHIRE, B60 1DT.

GIBBS, Mr. Philip Martin Domville, MA FCA *1954;* 8 Peek Crescent, Wimbledon, LONDON, SW19 5ER. (Life Member)

GIBBS, Mr. Raymond John, BA FCA *1979;* 7 Danehurst Place, Locks Heath, SOUTHAMPTON, SO31 6PP.

GIBBS, Mr. Rory James, BBA ACA *2006;* Piper PE LLP, Eardley House, 182-184 Campden Hill Road, LONDON, W8 7AS.

GIBBS, Mr. Roy Clifford, FCA *1962;* 34 Marennes Crescent, Brightlingsea, COLCHESTER, CO7 0RU. (Life Member)

GIBBS, Miss. Sarah Louise, ACA MAAT *2009;* 19 Blandford Road, SHEPTON MALLET, SOMERSET, BA4 4FB.

GIBBS, Mrs. Sharon Jayne, BSc ACA *2005;* 53 Lochleven Road, CREWE, CW2 6RX.

GIBBS, Mr. Simon David, BSc ACA *1985;* Lost Cottage, Church Road, Penn, HIGH WYCOMBE, HP10 8EG.

GIBBS, Mr. Simon Francis Edmund, BA FCA FCCA *1980;* Percy House, Canoe Lake Road, RYDE, ISLE OF WIGHT, PO33 1LY.

GIBBS, Mr. Simon Vincent, BSc ACA *1999;* Financial Services Authority, 25 North Colonnade, Canary Wharf, LONDON, E14 5HS.

GIBBS, Mr. Stephen Frederick, BSc FCA *1976;* 13 Scott End, AYLESBURY, BUCKINGHAMSHIRE, hp19 8se.

GIBBS, Mr. Timothy David, BA(Hons) ACA *2001;* 21 Sheraton Drive, Wollaton, NOTTINGHAM, NG8 2PR.

GIBBY, Mr. Derek Robert, BSc FCA *1996;* Opus International Willow House, Brotherswood Ct Bradley Stoke, BRISTOL, BS32 4QW.

GIBLIN, Mr. Andrew John, BA ACA *1991;* 1 Kiln Close, STUDLEY, B80 7EF.

GIBLIN, Mr. Simon John, MA ACA *2001;* Flat 52 Finchley Court, Ballards Lane, LONDON, N3 1NH.

GIBLIN, Miss. Tracey Christine, BSc(Hons) FCA *2001;* Flat 2 Somersham, 26 Ray Park Avenue, MAIDENHEAD, SL6 8DY.

GIBLING, Miss. Lucy Anne-Marie, ACA *2008;* 27 Wellington Road, BROMLEY, BR2 9NG.

GIBNEY, Mr. Daniel James, BSc ACA *2005;* 7 Beaconsfield Road, ST. ALBANS, AL1 3RD.

GIBNEY, Mr. John Michael, ACA *1984;* Britvic House, Britvic Soft Drinks Ltd Britvic House, Broomfield Road, CHELMSFORD, CM1 1TU.

GIBNEY, Miss. Talitha, BSc(Hons) ACA *2001;* 41 Boleyn Drive, WEST MOLESEY, KT8 1RE.

GIBSON, Mr. Alan John, FCA *1965;* 119 Coulsdon Road, COULSDON, CR5 1EH.

GIBSON, Mr. Alex, MSc ACA *2004;* 15 Gerrard Crescent, BRENTWOOD, ESSEX, CM14 4JU.

GIBSON, Miss. Alexandra Mary, BA ACA CTA *2005;* 76 Panorama, 15 Conduit Road, MID LEVELS, HONG KONG ISLAND, HONG KONG SAR.

GIBSON, Mr. Andrew, BSc ACA *2007;* 3 Beech Paddocks, Hessett, BURY ST.EDMUNDS, IP30 9NR.

GIBSON, Mr. Andrew Christopher, BA ACA *1991;* 115 Franklin Road, HARROGATE, NORTH YORKSHIRE, HG1 5EN.

GIBSON, Mr. Andrew Colin, BA FCA *1975;* Bremvilla, East Village, CREDITON, EX17 4DP.

GIBSON, Mr. Andrew James, BSc FCA *1983;* Hill House Loamy Hill Road, Tolleshunt Major, MALDON, ESSEX, CM9 8LS.

GIBSON, Mr. Andrew Marc, BA(Hons) ACA *2004;* with KPMG LLP, 8 Princes Parade, LIVERPOOL, L3 1QH.

•**GIBSON, Mr. Andrew Robert, BA FCA** *1993;* Audit England Limited, Blackburn House, 32 Crouch Street, COLCHESTER, ESSEX, CO3 3HH.

GIBSON, Mr. Anthony John, FCA *1975;* Unit 20015, Bel'Aire Winelands Estate, SOMERSET WEST, WESTERN CAPE PROVINCE, 7130, SOUTH AFRICA.

GIBSON, Mr. Brian Thomas, MA ACA *1995;* 105 Little Walden Road, SAFFRON WALDEN, ESSEX, CB10 2DN.

•**GIBSON, Mr. Carl, ACA CTA** *2005;* TCG Accountancy Limited, 19 Chesterholm, CARLISLE, CA2 7XH.

GIBSON, Mr. Carl Brian, BA ACA *1995;* 3 Sussex Road, Maghull, LIVERPOOL, L31 5NS.

GIBSON, Mr. Chris, ACA *2009;* Flat 3, Falcon Heights, 89-91 Falcon Road, LONDON, SW11 2PF.

GIBSON, Mrs. Christine Elizabeth, BA FCA *1997;* 18 South Sands, Cliff Park Road, PAIGNTON, DEVON, TQ4 6NB.

GIBSON, Mr. Christopher Adam, BA ACA *2006;* 8 Crofters Close, NORTHAMPTON, NN4 0BJ.

GIBSON, Mr. Christopher Hugh Buckley, FCA *1974;* Black Down House, Petworth Road, HASLEMERE, SURREY, GU27 3AX.

GIBSON, Mr. Clive Anthony George, BSc(Econ) FCA *1977;* The Farm House, Sherrington, WARMINSTER, WILTSHIRE, BA12 0SN.

GIBSON, Mr. Colin, BA ACA *2006;* 40 Links Avenue, WHITLEY BAY, TYNE AND WEAR, NE26 1TG.

GIBSON, Mr. Colin John, FCA *1973;* 20 East Ninth Street, NEW YORK, NY, 10003, UNITED STATES.

GIBSON, Mrs. Corinne Patricia, BSc ACA *1991;* 65 Ennerdale Avenue, STANMORE, HA7 2LB.

GIBSON, Mr. Craig John, BSc ACA *1990;* Brindle Lodge, 10 Blackacres Close, SANDBACH, CW11 1YE.

GIBSON, Mr. David, BA ACA *1989;* Apartado De Correos 34, La Cala, Mijas Costa, 29649 MALAGA, SPAIN.

•**GIBSON, Mr. David Anthony, BA ACA** *1995;* (Tax Fac), Gibsons Accountants Ltd, 226 Oldham Road, ROCHDALE, LANCASHIRE, OL11 2ER.

•**GIBSON, Mr. David Arthur, MA FCA** *1980;* (Tax Fac), Saint & Co., 49 High Street, WIGTON, CA7 9NJ.

GIBSON, Mr. David Mcfarlane, ACA *1978;* C.da Busulmone, 96017 NOTO, ITALY. (Life Member)

GIBSON, Mrs. Dorothy Joyce, BA ACA *2006;* I T V Network Centre, 200 Gray's Inn Road, Holborn, LONDON, WC1X 8HF.

GIBSON, Mr. Douglas William, FCA *1949;* 7 Clevedon, WEYBRIDGE, SURREY, KT13 0PJ. (Life Member)

GIBSON, Mr. Edward James, BSc ACA *2006;* 201 Asia House, 82 Princess Street, MANCHESTER, M1 6BD.

GIBSON, Mrs. Emma Victoria, ACA *2008;* 8 Manor Close, Bramhope, LEEDS, LS16 9HQ.

GIBSON, Miss. Fiona Jane, BSc ACA *2001;* 28B Milton Road, High Gate, LONDON, N6 5QD.

GIBSON, Mr. Gareth, BSc ACA *2006;* 1 Llanerch Goed, Llantwit Fardre, PONTYPRIDD, MID GLAMORGAN, CF38 2TB.

GIBSON, Miss. Gemma, ACA *2010;* Hockway Ltd, Liu 22, Dubai Silicone Oasis, PO Box 440136, DUBAI, UNITED ARAB EMIRATES.

GIBSON, Mr. Geoffrey, BSc ACA *1980;* 39 Cardinal Gardens, DARLINGTON, COUNTY DURHAM, DL3 8SD.

GIBSON, Mr. Geoffrey, FCA *1974;* Adler & Allan Holdings Ltd, 80 Station Parade, HARROGATE, NORTH YORKSHIRE, HG1 1HQ.

GIBSON, Mr. Graeme David, BSc ACA *1995;* 12 Foxhills Close, Appleton, WARRINGTON, WA4 5DH.

GIBSON, Mrs. Helen Louise, BA ACA *1996;* with RSM Tenon Limited, Sumner House, St Thomas's Rd, CHORLEY, PR7 1HP.

GIBSON, Ms. Helen Victoria, BCom ACA *1993;* Flat B, 59 Eton Avenue, LONDON, NW3 3ET.

GIBSON, Mr. Iain Andrew, BA ACA *2005;* The Old Coach House, West Woodburn, HEXHAM, NORTHUMBERLAND, NE48 2RX.

GIBSON, Mr. Iain Garvie, BSc FCA *1983;* P.O. Box 47791, NAIROBI, 00100, KENYA.

GIBSON, Mr. Ian Jeffrey, BSc ACA *1987;* Stanmore House, 3 Silverdale Road, BURGESS HILL, WEST SUSSEX, RH15 0ED.

GIBSON, Mr. Ian Robert, BSc ACA *1993;* 30 Oxford Road, Gomersal, CLECKHEATON, BD19 4HN.

GIBSON, Mr. James Alan, MA FCA *1974;* The Bailiff's House, Hall Lane, Utkinton, TARPORLEY, CW6 0JQ.

GIBSON, Mr. James Ernest, MA ACA *1988;* Big Yellow Group PLC, 2 the Deans, Bridge Road, BAGSHOT, GU19 5AT.

GIBSON, Mr. James Henry, FCA *1960;* Quorn Court, High Street, Quorn, LOUGHBOROUGH, LE12 8DT. (Life Member)

GIBSON, Miss. Jane Charmian, BA ACA *1981;* 23 Hampton Drive, RINGWOOD, BH24 1SL.

GIBSON, Mr. Jay, ACA *2009;* 42 Abbotswood Close, REDDITCH, WORCESTERSHIRE, B98 0QD.

•**GIBSON, Mrs. Joanna Clare, BSc FCA** *1983;* (Tax Fac), J.C. Gibson & Company, Harbour Office, Gunsgreen Basin, EYEMOUTH, BERWICKSHIRE, TD14 5SD.

GIBSON, Mrs. Joanne, BSc(Hons) ACA *2001;* 17 Manorfields, Benton, NEWCASTLE UPON TYNE, NE12 8AG.

•**GIBSON, Mrs. Joelle, BSc ACA** *1995;* (Tax Fac), J Gibson & Co Limited, 12 Foxhills Close, Appleton, WARRINGTON, CHESHIRE, WA4 5DH.

GIBSON, Mr. John Alfred, FCA *1957;* 49 Windmill Av, WOKINGHAM, RG41 3XA. (Life Member)

GIBSON, Mr. John Christopher, BA ACA *1991;* (Tax Fac), GLOBAL HOUSE, Victoria Street, BASINGSTOKE, RG21 3BT.

GIBSON, Mr. John David, FCA *1971;* Elysium, London Road, CHALFONT ST.GILES, HP8 4ND.

GIBSON, Mr. John Michael, MA MSc ACA *1997;* 24 West Hill Avenue, LEEDS, LS7 3QH.

GIBSON, Mr. John Miller, BA FCA *1967;* 25 Fitzjohn Avenue, BARNET, HERTFORDSHIRE, EN5 2HH. (Life Member)

GIBSON, Mr. John Robert, MA FCA *1978;* 54B Tregunter Tower III, 14 Tregunter Path, MID LEVELS, HONG KONG ISLAND, HONG KONG SAR.

GIBSON, Mr. John Stewart Pym, FCA *1965;* Matford Vean, 14 Matford Avenue, EXETER, EX2 4PW. (Life Member)

GIBSON, Mr. Jonathan David Bruce, MA ACA *1983;* Viale Majno 24, 20129 MILAN, ITALY.

GIBSON, Mr. Joseph Henry, FCA *1926;* Section 0515, P.O. Box 02 5289, MIAMI, FL 33102, UNITED STATES. (Life Member)

GIBSON, Mr. Kevin Paul, BCom ACA *1985;* 9 Bolwarra Close, Redlynch, CAIRNS, QLD 4870, AUSTRALIA.

GIBSON, Mr. Kevin Richard, BSc ACA *1988;* 8 Turnberry, Knutshaw Bridge, BOLTON, BL3 4XJ.

GIBSON, Mrs. Laura, BA(Hons) ACA *2002;* Shipley & Keighley Pre School Learning Alliance, 2 Bradley Street Off Park Road, BINGLEY, WEST YORKSHIRE, BD16 4DU.

•**GIBSON, Ms. Linda Anne, BA FCA** *1992;* Linda Gibson, 44 Hillfield Road, Selsey, CHICHESTER, WEST SUSSEX, PO20 0LF.

•①**GIBSON, Ms. Lynn, BA FCA FABRP** *1979;* Gibson Hewitt & Co, 5 Park Court, Pyrford Road, WEST BYFLEET, SURREY, KT14 6SD. See also Gibson Hewitt Outsourcing Ltd

GIBSON, Mr. Malcolm James Brunton, FCA *1962;* Cruz Del Sur 1, 9c, 28007 MADRID, SPAIN.

•**GIBSON, Mrs. Marian Dorothy, BSc ACA** *1990;* Gibsons, Belmont, Church Road, St Mary's, ISLES OF SCILLY, TR21 0NA.

GIBSON, Mr. Mark Andrew, BA ACA *1989;* 37 Dunbottle Way, MIRFIELD, WEST YORKSHIRE, WF14 9JU.

GIBSON, Mr. Mark Jonathon, BA CA *1992; (CA Scotland 1983);* 15 Theed Street, WATERLOO, SE1 8ST.

•**GIBSON, Mr. Martin, ACA** *1983;* (Tax Fac), Bartfields (UK) Limited, 57a Commercial Street, Rothwell, LEEDS, LS26 0QD.

GIBSON, Mr. Matthew, BA ACA *1999;* 17 Grange Court, Alwoodley, LEEDS, LS17 7TX.

•①**GIBSON, Mr. Matthew David, MA FCA** *1994;* (Tax Fac), PKF (UK) LLP, 4th Floor, 3 Hardman Street, MANCHESTER, M3 3HF.

GIBSON, Mr. Michael, BA(Hons) FCA MIIA *1994;* 7 Bailey Way, Hetton-le-Hole, HOUGHTON LE SPRING, DH5 0HB.

•**GIBSON, Mr. Michael Ramsey, BA ACA** *1979;* Cooper Gibson, 32 Parkfield Gardens, HARROW, HA2 6JR.

GIBSON, Mr. Miles John, BA ACA *1989;* 18 Hampton Close, LONDON, N11 3PR.

GIBSON, Mr. Myles, LLB FCA *1974;* 17 Orchard Way, Stoke Goldington, NEWPORT PAGNELL, BUCKINGHAMSHIRE, MK16 8PE.

GIBSON, Mr. Nicholas, BSc ACA *1997;* 11 St. Helens Lane, LEEDS, LS16 8AB.

GIBSON, Mr. Oliver Martin, ACA *2008;* 19 Lytham Close, ST. LEONARDS-ON-SEA, EAST SUSSEX, TN38 0XE.

•**GIBSON, Mr. Paul Howey, MA FCA DChA** *1980;* Cobwebs, 22 Dalloway Road, ARUNDEL, BN18 9HW.

GIBSON, Mr. Paul Nigel, MA FCA *1984;* 6 Ivywell Road, BRISTOL, BS9 1NX.

GIBSON, Mrs. Paula Louise, BA ACA *1992;* Crown Lodge, Tintern, CHEPSTOW, GWENT, NP16 6TF.

GIBSON, Mr. Peter, BA FCA *1979;* Ian Farmer Associates, Unit 1, Bamburgh Court, Team Valley Trading Estate, GATESHEAD, TYNE AND WEAR NE11 0TY.

GIBSON, Mr. Peter David, BSc ACA *1979;* Internal Audit Manager, GASCO, PO Box. 665, ABU DHABI, UNITED ARAB EMIRATES.

GIBSON, Mr. Peter David Edward, MA ACA *1998;* 44 Knocklofty Park, BELFAST, BT4 3NB.

GIBSON, Mr. Peter George, FCA *1955;* North End Farm, Chiddingfold, GODALMING, GU8 4UX. (Life Member)

GIBSON, Miss. Rebecca, ACA *2008;* Unit 29 Mizzentop, Mizzentop Road, WARWICK WK 06, BERMUDA.

GIBSON, Mr. Richard Stanley, BA(Hons) ACA *2001;* 4 Ridgeway Gardens, WOKING, SURREY, GU21 4RB.

•**GIBSON, Mr. Robert Baird, BSc FCA** *1982;* (Tax Fac), G D Hakin & Co, 9 Stanley Street, BLYTH, NORTHUMBERLAND, NE24 2BS.

GIBSON, Mr. Robert Hounsfield, FCA *1979;* 35 Barrabooka Street, CLONTARF, NSW 2093, AUSTRALIA.

GIBSON, Mr. Robert John, FCA *1965;* 64 Avenue Road, RUSHDEN, NN10 0SJ.

GIBSON, Mr. Robert Neil, FCA *1959;* 107 The Meadows, Cherry Burton, BEVERLEY, HU17 7RL. (Life Member)

GIBSON, Mr. Robin Thomas, BA FCA *1959;* 13 Meadow Croft, Old Hall Park, Whitefield, MANCHESTER, M45 7ND. (Life Member)

GIBSON, Mr. Roger Kenneth, FCA *1969;* 42a High Street, Great Doddington, WELLINGBOROUGH, NN29 7TQ.

GIBSON, Mr. Ronald Thomas, FCA *1966;* 8 Cade Hill Road, STOCKSFIELD, NE43 7PB. (Life Member)

GIBSON, Miss. Rosalind Sarah, BA FCA *1998;* 21 Woodmoor, Finchampstead, WOKINGHAM, BERKSHIRE, RG40 3TT.

GIBSON, Mrs. Sara Helen, BSc ACA *1992;* Barlow Andrews, 78 Chorley New Road, BOLTON, BL1 4BY.

GIBSON, Miss. Shane, BSc ACA *2007;* 19 Otterbourne Walk, Sherfield-on-Loddon, HOOK, HAMPSHIRE, RG27 0SE.

GIBSON, Mr. Simon Charles Cecil, BSc ACA *1996;* Open Vantage Ltd, 1-4 King Street, LONDON, WC2E 8HH.

•**GIBSON, Mr. Simon John, FCA** *1991;* (Tax Fac), Simon J Gibson Limited, 7 Eskdale Close, Sleights, WHITBY, YO22 5EW.

•**GIBSON, Mr. Stephen, FCA** *1983;* NE Accountancy Services Limited, 9 Park Parade, Roker, SUNDERLAND, SR6 9LU.

GIBSON, Mr. Stuart James, BA ACA *1992;* White House Bartlow Road, Hadstock, CAMBRIDGE, CB21 4PF.

GIBSON, Mrs. Suzanne Jean, BA ACA *1988;* 53b Manchester Road, Denton, MANCHESTER, M34 2AF.

GIBSON, Mrs. Thea, ACA *2009;* 39 Welman Way, ALTRINCHAM, CHESHIRE, WA15 8WE.

GIBSON, Mr. Thomas Edward, ACA MAAT *2010;* Tithe Farm, Bolton Lane, Barmby Moor, YORK, YO42 4DE.

GIBSON, Mr. Timothy Charles, FCA *1968;* The Old Vicarage, Little Missenden, AMERSHAM, BUCKINGHAMSHIRE, HP7 0QX.

GIBSON, Mrs. Tracy Elizabeth, ACA *2007;* 19 Chesterholm, Sandsfield Park, CARLISLE, CA2 7XH.

GIBSON, Miss. Vivienne Lesley, BA ACA *1989;* c/o The Grange, Iveston Lane, CONSETT, DH8 7TB.

GIBSON, Mrs. Vivienne Margaret, BSc FCA MCT *1984;* Spirent Plc, Northwood Park, Gatwick Road, CRAWLEY, WEST SUSSEX, RH10 9XN.

GIBSON, Mr. William James, RD FCA *1966;* West Town House, Nempnett Thrubwell, Blagdon, BRISTOL, BS40 7XE. (Life Member)

GIDDENS, Mr. John Christian, BEng ACA *1999;* 37 Carolyn Place, FERNY GROVE, QLD 4055, AUSTRALIA.

•**GIDDENS, Mr. Mark, BSc FCA TEP** *1992;* (Tax Fac), UHY Hacker Young LLP, Quadrant House, 4 Thomas More Square, LONDON, E1W 1YW.

GIDDENS, Mr. Wayne Terry, BSc ACA *1998;* 27 Portmore Park Road, WEYBRIDGE, SURREY, KT13 8ET.

GIDDINGS, Mrs. Jennifer, BA(Hons) ACA *2000;* 3 Nailsworth Road, Dorridge, SOLIHULL, B93 8NS.

GIDDINGS, Mrs. Joanne, BA ACA *1991;* Avon Cosmetics Ltd, Nunn Mills Road, NORTHAMPTON, NN1 5PA.
GIDDINGS, Mr. Michael John, MEng ACA *2000;* Barclays Bank Plc, PO Box 3333, BIRMINGHAM, B3 2WN.
GIDDINGS, Mr. Michael Stephen, BSc(Hons) ACA *2010;* 48 Chandlers Way, HERTFORD, SG14 2ED.
GIDDINGS, Mrs. Michelle Clare, BA ACA *2005;* with ICAEW, Metropolitan House, 321 Avebury Boulevard, MILTON KEYNES, MK9 2FZ.
GIDDINGS, Mr. Philip Edward, BSc FCA *1974;* 2 The Paddock, La Rue Du Froid Vent St. Saviour, JERSEY, JE2 7LJ.
GIDDINGS, Mr. Simon Mark, MEng ACA *2002;* 8 Cote Park, BRISTOL, BS9 2AD.
GIDDINS, Mr. Alan Clifford Bence, BA ACA *1991;* 55 Chartfield Avenue, Putney, LONDON, SW15 6HW.
GIDDINS, Mrs. Joanna Catherine, BA ACA *1992;* 55 Chartfield Avenue, Putney, LONDON, SW15 6HW.
GIDDONS, Mr. Ian Robert, BA ACA *1979;* Harrison Parrott Ltd Unit 5-6, Albion Court Albion Place, LONDON, W6 0QT.
GIDLEY, Mrs. Helen Caroline, BSc(Hons) ACA *2003;* Thorne & Co, 1 St. Marys Street, ROSS-ON-WYE, HEREFORDSHIRE, HR9 5HT.
GIDLEY, Mr. Peter Robert, ACA *1980;* Copy Nook, Lothersdale, KEIGHLEY, BD20 8EQ.
•**GIDLEY, Mrs. Zoe Louise, MEng ACA** *1996;* Gidley Accounting, 1 Thornton Close, CRICK, NORTHAMPTONSHIRE, NN6 7GE.
GIDLEY-KITCHIN, Mr. Greville Courtenay Bartholomew, FCA *1950;* Wybournes, Kemsing, SEVENOAKS, TN15 6NE. (Life Member)
GIDLEY-KITCHIN, Mr. Thomas Edward, MA ACA *1981;* 10 Stamford Cottages, Billing Street, LONDON, SW10 9UP.
GIDLOW, Mr. Ian Trevor, BSc ACA *1992;* 52 Sidmouth Avenue, ISLEWORTH, MIDDLESEX, TW7 4DR.
•**GIDLOW, Mr. Richard John Cairns, FCA** *1979;* Leach & Co, Ashley House, 136 Tolworth Broadway, SURBITON, SURREY, KT6 7LA.
GIDMAN, Mr. Trevor Christopher, FCA *1959;* 29 The Millbank, Ifield, CRAWLEY, RH11 0JQ. (Life Member)
GIDNEY, Mr. Andrew, BA ACA *2000;* 49 Belle Avenue, SAN ANSELMO, CA 94960, UNITED STATES.
GIDNEY, Miss. Donna Marie, ACA *2008;* 104 North Brink, WISBECH, CAMBRIDGESHIRE, PE13 1LL.
GIDUMAL, Ms. Anita, BA ACA *1992;* 6B Ruby Court, Tower 1, 55 South Bay Road, REPULSE BAY, HONG KONG ISLAND, HONG KONG SAR.
•**GIEBEL, Mr. Francis Thomas, FCA** *1980;* F.T. Giebel & Co, 26 Menelik Road, LONDON, NW2 3RP.
•**GIESS, Mr. David John, FCA** *1973;* Briars Bank, 77a Sheering Road, HARLOW, CM17 0JN.
•**GIESSLER, Mr. Paul Christopher, BSc ACA** *1992;* (Tax Fac), Francis Clark, Hitchcock House, Hilltop Business Park, Devizes Road, SALISBURY, SP3 4UF. See also Francis Clark LLP
GIFFARD, Mr. Charles Berenger Gregory, BA FCA *1986;* Fidelity, 21/F Two Pacific Place, 88 Queensway, ADMIRALTY, HONG KONG SAR.
GIFFARD-TAYLOR, Mr. Barrie, FCA *1971;* Barnbridge Farm, East Tytherton, CHIPPENHAM, SN15 4LT.
GIFFIN, Mr. George Edward Patrick, FCA *1958;* 116 Marsham Court, Marsham Street, LONDON, SW1P 4LB. (Life Member)
GIFFIN, Mr. Giles Richard, BEng ACA *1996;* 2 Rosemount Road, Flax Bourton, BRISTOL, BS48 1UQ.
•**GIFFIN, Mrs. Lisa Ann, FCA** *1993;* Bray Giffin LLP, Langford Hall Barn, Witham Road, Langford, MALDON, ESSEX CM9 4ST.
GIFFIN, Mr. Michael, FCA *1957;* 19 Burntwood Road, SEVENOAKS, TN13 1PS. (Life Member)
GIFFIN, Mr. Michael William, BSc ACA *1992;* 14 Maze Road, RICHMOND, SURREY, TW9 3DA.
GIFFORD, Mr. Jonathan William James, ACA *2009;* 11 Devonshire Park, BIDEFORD, DEVON, EX39 5HZ.
GIFFORD, Mr. Mark Anthony, BA ACA *1994;* House of Fraser, 27 Baker Street, LONDON, W1U 8AH.
GIFFORD, Mr. Simon, FCA *1969;* Brissenden Farm, Swain Road, St. Michaels, TENTERDEN, KENT, TN30 6SN.
GIFFORD-GIFFORD, Mr. Mark Barry, MA MPhil FCA *1963;* Parkside, Salston Ride, Salston, OTTERY ST. MARY, DEVON, EX11 1RH.
GIGG, Miss. Karen Jane, FCA ATII *1994;* 11 Richard House Drive, LONDON, E16 3RE.
•**GIGG, Mrs. Kathryn Healy, FCA** *1984;* (Tax Fac), Kathryn Gigg, The Office, 20 Kings Lynn Road, HUNSTANTON, PE36 5HP.
GIGGINS, Mrs. Janet Anne, BA ACA *1985;* 143 Priory Road, HUNGERFORD, BERKSHIRE, RG17 0AP.
GIGLIA, Ms. Cheryl Lynn, ACA *1997;* 54 Balcombe Street, LONDON, NW1 6ND.
GIGOV, Mr. Emil Slavtchev, BA ACA *1997;* 10 Chapel Croft, INGATESTONE, CM4 0BU.
GIL, Mrs. Candida Jill, BSc ACA *1989;* 13 Cedar Park, Stoke Bishop, BRISTOL, BS9 1BW.
•**GILANI, Mrs. Avani, BA FCA** *1986;* Ernst & Young, Kenya Commercial Bank Bldg., Kenyatta Ave, (P.O. Box 45), NAKURU, 20100 GPO KENYA.
GILANI, Mr. Faiz, ACA *2010;* P.O Box 70 (20100), NAKURU, KENYA.
GILANI, Mr. Kamran Hussain, BSc ACA *2002;* Ty Blaidd, Leckwith Road, Llandough, PENARTH, SOUTH GLAMORGAN, CF64 2LY.
GILANI, Mrs. Munira Tajdin Kassam, FCA *1979;* Imperial Hotel, P.O. Box 1866, KISUMU, KENYA.
GILANI, Mr. Shamsher Gulamhussein, FCA CPA *1979;* P.O. Box 70, NAKURU, 20100, KENYA.
GILANI, Mr. Syed Tariq, BSc ACA *1982;* 90/2 Ninth Street, off KH Sehr, Defence Phase 6, KARACHI, PAKISTAN.
GILARDO, Mr. Stefano, ACA *2007;* Flat 2, Phillip House, Heneage Street, LONDON, E1 5LW.
GILBERT, Mr. Adrian Charles, BA ACA *1995;* DHL, Solstice House, 251 Midsummer Boulevard, MILTON KEYNES, MK9 1EQ.
GILBERT, Mrs. Ailish Patricia, BSc ACA *1990;* Ryefield, Packhorse Road, SEVENOAKS, KENT, TN13 2QP.
GILBERT, Mr. Alan Clifton, FCA *1956;* 68 Marlborough Avenue, Cheadle Hulme, CHEADLE, SK8 7AW. (Life Member)
GILBERT, Mr. Alexander, ACA *2011;* Flat 20 Pied Bull Court, Galen Place, LONDON, WC1A 2JR.
GILBERT, Miss. Alison, ACA *2008;* 70 Raffles House, 67 Brampton Grove, Hendon, LONDON, NW4 4BX.
GILBERT, Mr. Arieh Alexander, MA ACA *2003;* 11 Parsons Lodge, 65 Priory Road, LONDON, NW6 3NH.
GILBERT, Mr. Benjamin Charles, BA(Hons) ACA CTA *2003;* (Tax Fac), 22 Les Arches, La Route de la Cote St. Martin, JERSEY, JE3 6LA.
GILBERT, Mrs. Bernadette Mary, BA ACA *1991;* Treetops, 38 Hollybush Hill, Snaresbrook, LONDON, E11 1PS.
•**GILBERT, Mr. Brian John, FCA** *1975;* (Tax Fac), Gilbert & Co, Suite 2, Hilton Hall, Hilton Lane, Essington, WOLVERHAMPTON WV11 2BQ.
GILBERT, Mr. Brian Leonard, FCA *1958;* 12 St Nicholas Lodge, Church Street, BRIGHTON, BN1 3LJ. (Life Member)
GILBERT, Miss. Carina, ACA *2009;* 269 Rochester Road, Burham, ROCHESTER, KENT, ME1 3RT.
GILBERT, Mrs. Caroline, BA ACA *1988;* The Manse, 10 Shepley Street, Brookfield, GLOSSOP, DERBYSHIRE, SK13 6JG.
GILBERT, Mrs. Caroline Jane, BSc ACA *1985;* 75 Edinburgh Drive, Rushall, WALSALL, WS4 1HS.
GILBERT, Miss. Charlotte Hazel, BSc(Hons) ACA *2004;* Aviva Investors, 1 Poultry, LONDON, EC2R 8EJ.
GILBERT, Mr. Christopher, MEng ACA *2011;* 19 Old Dairy Close, FLEET, GU51 3SJ.
GILBERT, Mr. Christopher Lee, BAcc ACA *1999;* Hornbeam House Waltham Road White Waltham, MAIDENHEAD, SL6 3JD.
GILBERT, Mr. Dale Robert, BSc FCA *1987;* 1 Severn Close, WELLINGBOROUGH, NORTHAMPTONSHIRE, NN8 5WF.
GILBERT, Mr. David Alan, FCA *1982;* 61 Oakridge Avenue, RADLETT, WD7 8HB.
GILBERT, Mr. David Edward, FCA *1972;* 39 Merestones Drive, CHELTENHAM, GL50 2SU. (Life Member)
•**GILBERT, Mr. David Harry, FCA** *1979;* BDO LLP, 55 Baker Street, LONDON, W1U 7EU. See also BDO Stoy Hayward LLP
GILBERT, Mr. David John, BSc ACA *1995;* 16 Budbury Place, BRADFORD-ON-AVON, BA15 1QF.
GILBERT, Mr. Donald Peter, BA ACA *1993;* Flat B, 79 Grandison Road, LONDON, SW11 6LT.
GILBERT, Mr. Drummond, MA(Hons) ACA *2011;* 284 Lillie Road, Fulham, LONDON, SW6 7PX.
GILBERT, Mr. Edward Walter, FCA *1965;* 10 West Leys road, Swanland, NORTH FERRIBY, HU14 3LX.
GILBERT, Mrs. Elizabeth Anne, BA ACA *1981;* National Grid Plc N G T House, Warwick Technology Park Gallows Hill, WARWICK, CV34 6DA.
GILBERT, Miss. Emily Charlotte, BSc ACA *2006;* 8 St Heneras Court, 1 Brady Drive, BROMLEY, KENT, BR1 2FE.
GILBERT, Mrs. Emily Louise, BSc ACA *1999;* 99 Sandy Lane, SUTTON, SM2 7EP.
GILBERT, Mr. Frank William, FCA *1958;* 50 Ashbourne Road, DERBY, DE22 3AD. (Life Member)
GILBERT, Miss. Gemma Claire, BSc ACA *2007;* 16 Charterhouse Apartments, 21 Eltringham Street, LONDON, SW18 1AU.
GILBERT, Miss. Gemma Jade, BA(Hons) ACA *2010;* 4 41-42 East Esplanade, MANLY, NSW 2095, AUSTRALIA.
•**GILBERT, Mr. Geoffrey Roy Freeman, FCA** *1988;* (Tax Fac), Moffat Gilbert, 5 Clarendon Place, LEAMINGTON SPA, CV32 5QL.
GILBERT, Mr. Graham Allen, BSc ACA *1982;* Harcourt Cottage, Aune Cross, Bantham, KINGSBRIDGE, DEVON, TQ7 3AD.
GILBERT, Mr. Graham Geoffrey, BA(Hons) ACA *2002;* (Tax Fac), Whitlocks End Farmhouse, Bills Lane, Shirley, SOLIHULL, WEST MIDLANDS, B90 2PL.
•**GILBERT, Mr. Grahame Scott, FCA** *1980;* Cameron Hughes Ltd, 16 Jubilee Parkway, Jubilee Business Park, DERBY, DE21 4BJ.
GILBERT, Ms. Helen Kate, BA ACA *2007;* 4 Grange Avenue, Dronfield Woodhouse, DRONFIELD, DERBYSHIRE, S18 8PH.
•**GILBERT, Mr. Iain, BA FCA** *1985;* (Tax Fac), Fox & Co (Accountants) Ltd, Atticus House, 2 The Windmills, Turk Street, ALTON, HAMPSHIRE GU34 1EF.
GILBERT, Mr. Ian, ACA *2011;* Flat 9, Riverside Court, Lee Road, Blackheath, LONDON, SE3 9DG.
GILBERT, Mr. Ian Alfred, BSc FCA *1972;* Kennel Cottage, Itton, CHEPSTOW, NP16 6BS.
GILBERT, Mr. Ian Frank, BSc FCA *1951;* 902 Whitehall, 1120 Beach Drive, VICTORIA V8S 2N1, BC, CANADA. (Life Member)
GILBERT, Mr. James Edward, BSc ACA *2003;* 61 Stratford Way, Huntington, YORK, YO32 9YW.
GILBERT, Mr. Jeffrey Joseph Brams, BSc FCA *1972;* 1 Alleyn Place, WESTCLIFF-ON-SEA, ESSEX, SS0 8AT.
GILBERT, Mr. John, MBA FCA *1970;* Robert Brett & Sons Ltd, Milton Manor Farm, Ashford Road, Chartham, CANTERBURY, KENT CT4 7PP.
GILBERT, Mr. John Maurice, FCA *1969;* 6 Well Road, Hampstead, LONDON, NW3 1LH.
GILBERT, Mrs. Joy Margaret, BA FCA *1983;* 19 Stutton Road, TADCASTER, LS24 9HE.
GILBERT, Mrs. Kathryn Dorothy, BA ACA *1992;* 71 Scargill Road, West Hallam, ILKESTON, DE7 6LF.
•**GILBERT, Mr. Kevin Mark, FCA** *1977;* (Tax Fac), Morris Crocker Limited, Station House, 50 North Street, HAVANT, HAMPSHIRE, PO9 1QU. See also Morris Crocker
GILBERT, Mr. Kevin William Bruce, BA FCA *1972;* 20 Rumbold Road, Fulham, LONDON, SW6 2HX.
GILBERT, Mrs. Laura Anne, MA ACA *2001;* 6 Erridge Road, LONDON, SW19 3JB.
GILBERT, Mr. Laurence Martin, FCA *1969;* Lindow, 12 Apsley Grove, Bowdon, ALTRINCHAM, WA14 3AH.
GILBERT, Ms. Lesley Jane, BSc ACA *1992;* Nexus, 52a Cromwell Road, LONDON, SW7 5BE.
GILBERT, Mr. Malcolm Derek Edward, BSc ACA *1980;* Mythenquai 2, 8022 ZURICH, SWITZERLAND.
GILBERT, Mrs. Margaret Louise, ACA *1989;* 3, Northlea, Weston By Welland, MARKET HARBOROUGH, LE16 8HY.
GILBERT, Mr. Mark Stephen, BCom ACA *1987;* 17 Halcyon Close, Oxshott, LEATHERHEAD, KT22 0HA.
GILBERT, Mr. Martin, BSc ACA *1979;* 1 Ringley Close, Whitefield, MANCHESTER, M45 7HR.
GILBERT, Mr. Martin David, BA ACA *2006;* Flat 92C, 92 Mildmay Grove South, LONDON, N1 4PJ.
GILBERT, Mr. Martin John, BA FCA *1975;* 6 Little Russets, Hutton, BRENTWOOD, ESSEX, CM13 1RP.
GILBERT, Mrs. Meriel Ann, BA ACA *1982;* 20 Rumbold Road, LONDON, SW6 2HX.
GILBERT, Mr. Michael Andrew, BA ACA *1994;* 6 Balmoral Drive, Methley, LEEDS, LS26 9LE.
GILBERT, Mr. Michael George, BSc FCA *1975;* Brook House, Town Hill, Yoxall, BURTON-ON-TRENT, DE13 8NN.
•**GILBERT, Mr. Michael Harvey, FCA** *1974;* (Tax Fac), RMT, Gosforth Park Avenue, NEWCASTLE UPON TYNE, NE12 8EG. See also RMT Accountants and Business Advisors
GILBERT, Mrs. Natalie Barbara, BSc(Hons) ACA *2004;* 44 Fleece Road, Long Ditton, SURBITON, SURREY, KT6 5JN.
GILBERT, Mr. Neil Robin, BA ACA *1998;* 19 Briery Meadows, Hemingfield, BARNSLEY, SOUTH YORKSHIRE, S73 0QW.
•**GILBERT, Mr. Nicholas Jay, BA FCA** *1992;* Gilbert Finance & Accounting LLP, Amarna, Hillam Common Lane, Hillam, LEEDS, LS25 5HU.
GILBERT, Mr. Nicholas John, ACA *2009;* 37a Albert Road, LONDON, E17 7PR.
GILBERT, Mr. Nicholas Ronald James, BSc FCA *1973;* 229 Foley Road West, Streetly, SUTTON COLDFIELD, B74 3NU.
GILBERT, Mrs. Nicola Ann, BSc ACA *1992;* Alma Villa, 256 Henbury Road, BRISTOL, BS10 7QR.
GILBERT, Mr. Nigel, ACA *1985;* 71 Scargill Road, West Hallam, ILKESTON, DE7 6LF.
•**GILBERT, Mr. Norris, FCA** *1949;* Norris Gilbert, 143 Ivor Court, 209 Gloucester Place, LONDON, NW1 6BT.
GILBERT, Mr. Paul, BSc FCA *1978;* 45 First Avenue, WAKEFIELD, WF1 2HS.
GILBERT, Mr. Paul Andrew, BSc ACA *1999;* 25 Grove Road, Hazlemere, HIGH WYCOMBE, BUCKINGHAMSHIRE, HP15 7QY.
GILBERT, Mr. Paul David, BSc ACA *1991;* Alvarez & Marsal, 1 Finsbury Circus, LONDON, EC2M 7EB.
GILBERT, Mr. Paul John Thomas, BA FCA *1988;* The Old Field, St Marys Road, Bowdon, ALTRINCHAM, WA14 2PJ.
GILBERT, Mr. Peter Richard, BSc ACA *1992;* Hatton Court Hotel Upton Hill, Upton St. Leonards, GLOUCESTER, GL4 8DE.
GILBERT, Mrs. Philippa Anne, BSc ACA *1993;* 6 Toll Down Way, Burton, CHIPPENHAM, WILTSHIRE, SN14 7PD.
GILBERT, Miss. Rachael Sarah, BSc ACA *2004;* Flat 12 Walton Court, King Charles Street, PORTSMOUTH, PO1 2BP.
•**GILBERT, Mr. Richard, BA ACA** *1990;* Fitzroy House, 13-17 Epworth Street, LONDON, EC2A 4DL.
•**GILBERT, Mr. Richard Harvey, ACA** *2007;* with Mazars LLP, Tower Bridge House, St. Katharines Way, LONDON, E1W 1DD.
GILBERT, Mr. Richard Malcolm, ACA *1991;* 8 Church Bank, Cragg Vale, HEBDEN BRIDGE, HX7 5TF.
GILBERT, Mr. Richard Michael, FCA *1959;* 2 Collingwood Court, The Strand, Brighton Marina Village, BRIGHTON, BN2 5WH.
GILBERT, Mr. Robert Charles, BA FCA *1959;* Bradford Villa, 43 Church Lane, Nailsea, BRISTOL, BS48 4NG. (Life Member)
GILBERT, Mr. Simon, BA FCA *1981;* Rochesters, 3 Caroline Street, BIRMINGHAM, B3 1TR.
GILBERT, Mrs. Stephanie Ruth, BSc ACA *1989;* P.O. Box 922, Cramerview, Bryanston, JOHANNESBURG, 2060, SOUTH AFRICA.
GILBERT, Mr. Stephen Michael John, BA FCA *1990;* 9 Burlington Lodge, 32 Lubbock Road, CHISLEHURST, KENT, BR7 5QR.
GILBERT, Mrs. Tessa Joanna, BA FCA *1994;* Hillside Lodge, 37 Peppard Road, Sonning Common, READING, RG4 9SS.
GILBERT, Mr. Tom, ACA *2011;* PwC, 20 Rue Garibaldi, 69451 LYON, FRANCE.
•**GILBERT, Mr. William Richard, BA ACA** *2000;* YPO, The Granary, Haggs Farm Business Park, Haggs Road, HARROGATE, NORTH YORKSHIRE HG3 1EQ. See also YPOC
•**GILBERT, Mr. Winston Samuel, FCA** *1966;* Gilbert Allan & Co, 8 Rodborough Road, LONDON, NW11 8RY.
GILBERT, Mr. Zvi-Myer, ACA *2005;* 8 Rodborough Road, Golders Green, LONDON, NW11 8RY.
GILBERT-BARROW, Mr. Colin, BSc FCA *1977;* 5 Lower Hall Road, Lascelles Hall, HUDDERSFIELD, HD5 0AZ.
GILBERTSON, Mrs. Camilla Elizabeth, BSc ACA *1996;* 6 Balmoral Crescent #06-02, The Twins, SINGAPORE 259896, SINGAPORE.
GILBERTSON, Mrs. Caroline Joanna, BA ACA *2005;* K P M G Llp, 15 Canada Square, LONDON, E14 5GL.
•**GILBERTSON, Mr. John Gordon, BSc ACA** *1985;* (Tax Fac), Hanley & Co, 25 Main Street, Staveley, KENDAL, LA8 9LU.
GILBERTSON, Mr. Julian Giles, ACA *1991;* The Farmhouse, 6 The Square, Greta Bridge, BARNARD CASTLE, COUNTY DURHAM, DL12 9SD.
GILBERTSON, Mr. Philip James Francis, MA(Oxon) ACA *2004;* with KPMG LLP, 15 Canada Square, LONDON, E14 5GL.
GILBEY, The Hon. Anthony William, FCA *1963;* Rusko, Gatehouse of Fleet, CASTLE DOUGLAS, DG7 2BS.
GILBEY, Mr. Harry Newman, BSc ACA *2006;* 19 Queen's Gate, LONDON, SW7 5JE.
GILBEY, Mr. James William, BA ACA *2004;* 16 Braemar Avenue, LONDON, SW19 8AZ.

•**GILBEY, Ms. Joanne Lee, ACA ATII** *1993;* BDO LLP, 2 City Place, Beehive Ring Road, GATWICK, WEST SUSSEX, RH6 0PA. See also BDO Stoy Hayward LLP
GILBEY, Mr. Matthew Paul, ACA *2008;* with PricewaterhouseCoopers LLP, 1 Embankment Place, LONDON, WC2N 6RH.
GILBEY, Mr. Paul Hugh, FCA *1970;* Rievaulx, 29 Kingsmoor Road, HARLOW, CM19 4HP.
GILBEY, Mr. Richard Hubert Gordon, MA ACA *1991;* 46 Lavender Gardens, LONDON, SW11 1DN.
GILBEY, Mr. Walter Anthony, BSc ACA *1990;* Dean Place, Crazies Hill, Wargrave, READING, RG10 8QN.
GILBODY, Mrs. Caroline Ann, BA ACA *2010;* W K Finn-Kelcey Stourside Place, 35-41 Station Road, ASHFORD, TN23 1PP.
GILBRAITH, Mr. Henry Haslem, BSc FCA *1976;* Hall Moss Bungalow, Bull Hill, DARWEN, BB3 2TT.
GILBURN, Mr. David Alan, LLB FCA *1973;* (Tax Fac), Glenriding, 39 Blackwell Road, Barnt Green, BIRMINGHAM, WORCESTERSHIRE, B45 8BT. (Life Member)
GILCHREASTE, Miss. Claire, BA ACA *2006;* Manchester United, PO Box 270, Old Trafford, MANCHESTER, M16 0TY.
•**GILCHREASTE, Mr. Thomas Anthony, FCA** *1976;* (Tax Fac), with Hindle Jepson & Jennings Ltd, 10 Borough Road, DARWEN, LANCASHIRE, BB3 1PL.
GILCHRIST, Mr. Andrew John, BA ACA *1997;* Redcliffe, 24 South Road, Chorleywood, RICKMANSWORTH, HERTFORDSHIRE, WD3 5AR.
GILCHRIST, Miss. Anne-Marie, BA ACA *2001;* 55 Rydal Road, BOLTON, BL1 5LJ.
GILCHRIST, Mr. Edward David, BA(Hons) ACA *2004;* Electronic Arts Inc, 209 Redwood Shores Parkway, REDWOOD CITY, CA 94065, UNITED STATES.
•**GILCHRIST, Mr. Ian Robert, FCA** *1974;* Hartley Fowler LLP, 44 Springfield Road, HORSHAM, WEST SUSSEX, RH12 2PD.
GILCHRIST, Miss. Jodie Lavinia, BA BSc(Hons) ACA *2004;* 8 Albion Place, Bennetthorpe, DONCASTER, SOUTH YORKSHIRE, DN1 2EG.
GILCHRIST, Miss. Karen, ACA *2009;* 67 Eton Rise, Eton College Road, LONDON, NW3 2DA.
GILCHRIST, Miss. Karen May, MA ACA *2004;* 24 Merlin Way, Chandler's Ford, EASTLEIGH, HAMPSHIRE, SO53 4JB.
GILCHRIST, Mr. Oliver Campbell Radnor, BA ACA *1992;* Cerillion Technologies, 15 Adeline Place, LONDON, WC1B 3AJ.
GILCHRIST, Mr. Richard Andrew Marr, BSc ACA *1999;* 2 Saint Mary's Street, NEWTON LOWER FALLS, MA 02462, UNITED STATES.
GILDER, Mr. Adrian Raymond, BA ACA *1988;* 20 Blackwood Close, WEST BYFLEET, KT14 6PP.
GILDER, Mrs. Alexandra Louise, ACA *2009;* 12 Bridle Road, STOURBRIDGE, WEST MIDLANDS, DY8 4QE.
GILDER, Mrs. Helen Patricia, BSc ACA *1991;* 286 Ecclesall Road South, SHEFFIELD, S11 9PS.
•**GILDER, Mr. Stephen Robert, BSc FCA** *1986;* PricewaterhouseCoopers LLP, 1 Embankment Place, LONDON, WC2N 6RH. See also PricewaterhouseCoopers
GILDERSLEEVES, Mr. Paul Simon, MA ACA *1988;* (Tax Fac), The Old Stables, The Green, Charney Bassett, WANTAGE, OX12 0EU.
•**GILDERSON, Mrs. Jane Elizabeth, BSc FCA** *1991;* Gilderson & Co, Hawthorn House, High Levels, Sandtoft, DONCASTER, DN8 5SJ.
GILDING, Mr. Neil Michael, BA(Hons) ACA *2001;* 4 Collingwood Close, Poringland, NORWICH, NORFOLK, NR14 7WN.
GILDING, Mrs. Sally Jane, BSc ACA *2005;* 4 Collingwood Close, Poringland, NORWICH, NORFOLK, NR14 7WN.
GILDROY, Mrs. Lindsay Joanne, BA(Hons) ACA *2002;* 65 Upgang Lane, WHITBY, NORTH YORKSHIRE, YO21 3HZ.
GILES, Mr. Adrian Patrick Gordon, FCA FCIS *1967;* Keppel Lodge, 5 West Street, EMSWORTH, HAMPSHIRE, PO10 7DX.
•**GILES, Mr. Alan Keith, FCA** *1971;* (Tax Fac), Giles, 32 High Street, Winterbourne, BRISTOL, BS36 1JN.
GILES, Mr. Alexander Rennie, MA MPhil ACA *2000;* 8 Elmscott Gardens, LONDON, N21 2BP.
GILES, Mr. Alistair, ACA *2008;* Sandpipers, Hervines Road, AMERSHAM, BUCKINGHAMSHIRE, HP6 5HS.
GILES, Mr. Andrew David, BSc ACA *1997;* A Giles & r Williams, 36 Park Place, CARDIFF, CF10 3BB.
GILES, Mr. Andrew Martin, FCA *1970;* Humphrystown House, BLESSINGTON, COUNTY WICKLOW, IRELAND.
GILES, Mr. Calvin Sheldon, MA FCA *1987;* Wyre View, Button Oak, Kinlet, BEWDLEY, DY12 3AQ.
GILES, Mr. Carl, BA(Hons) ACA *2009;* 15 Heath Ridge Green, COBHAM, KT11 2QL.
GILES, Miss. Carol Elizabeth, BSc ACA *2004;* 26 Trellech Court, Abbey Manor Park, YEOVIL, BA21 3TE.
GILES, Mr. Christopher James, BSc ACA *1987;* The Old School House, Main Street, Rotherby, MELTON MOWBRAY, LE14 2LP.
•**GILES, Mr. David Benjamin, ACA** *2007;* Giles & Co, Humphrystown House, BLESSINGTON, COUNTY WICKLOW, IRELAND.
GILES, Mr. David Linton, FCA *1972;* Troup Curtis, 1 Catharine Place, BATH, BA1 2PR.
GILES, Mr. David Ralph, FCA *1958;* Tadworth Cottage, 9 Uitsig Road, CONSTANTIA, 7806, SOUTH AFRICA. (Life Member)
GILES, Mr. Edward John, BSc ACA *1984;* Hall Farm House, Charwelton Road, Preston Capes, DAVENTRY, NN11 3TA.
GILES, Mrs. Elizabeth Anne, BSc ACA *1987;* The Old School House, Main Street, Rotherby, MELTON MOWBRAY, LE14 2LP.
GILES, Mr. Grant Neil, BA ACA *2009;* 23 Sunny Hill, BRISTOL, BS9 2NG.
GILES, Ms. Hilary Joy, BA ACA *1987;* 94 Bent Street, LINDFIELD, NSW 2070, AUSTRALIA.
GILES, Mr. Ian Robert, BSc ACA *1984;* 12 Osprey Close, Lords Wood, SOUTHAMPTON, SO16 8EX.
GILES, Mr. John Christopher, BSc FCA *1970;* 58 Grove Park Terrace, LONDON, W4 3QE. (Life Member)
GILES, Mr. John William, FCA *1967;* 8 Dursley Drive, CANNOCK, WS11 1TN. (Life Member)
GILES, Mr. Jonathan, BSc ACA *1997;* Eurocopy (Gb) Ltd Northern House, Moor Knoll Lane East Ardsley, WAKEFIELD, WEST YORKSHIRE, WF3 2EE.
GILES, Mr. Lawrence Charles Anthony, BSc ACA *1983;* 63 Grenville Avenue, Wendover, AYLESBURY, BUCKINGHAMSHIRE, HP22 6AJ.
GILES, Mr. Leslie Alfred David, FCA *1939;* Southcroft, Rusper Road, Ifield, CRAWLEY, WEST SUSSEX, RH11 0LN. (Life Member)
•**GILES, Mrs. Linda, BSc ACA** *1988;* (Tax Fac), Linda Giles, 12 The Gap, Marcham, ABINGDON, OX13 6NJ.
•**GILES, Mrs. Lorraine Ann, FCA** *1978;* (Tax Fac), R & L Giles Limited, 21 St Ives Gardens, BOURNEMOUTH, BH2 6NS.
GILES, Mrs. Louise Elizabeth, BSc ACA DChA *2004;* 60 Someries Road, Warners End, HEMEL HEMPSTEAD, HP1 3PJ.
GILES, Mr. Matthew David, BSc ACA *1989;* 7 The Avenue, COULSDON, CR5 2BN.
GILES, Mr. Matthew Ernest Boothby, BSc(Hons) ACA *2001;* 28 Kensington Drive, Lodge Moor, SHEFFIELD, S10 4NF.
GILES, Mr. Michael John, BSc ACA *1984;* S J Berwin LLP, 10 Queen Street Place, LONDON, EC4R 1BE.
GILES, Mr. Neil Malcolm, BA ACA *2000;* 21 Stickleback Road, CALNE, WILTSHIRE, SN11 9RB.
GILES, Mr. Nicholas Peter, BSc ACA *2011;* 11a Ambleside Court, Ambleside Avenue, Telscombe Cliffs, PEACEHAVEN, EAST SUSSEX, BN10 7LT.
GILES, Mr. Oswald Adrian Robert, BA ACA *1986;* 74 Hamilton Road, LONDON, SW19 1JF.
GILES, Mr. Paul Anthony, FCA *1971;* 10 Boothbridge Lane, Thornton-in-Craven, SKIPTON, BD23 3TE.
•**GILES, Mr. Philip Howard, FCA** *1976;* GOODHEW CONSULTANCY LIMITED, 201 Borden Lane, Borden, SITTINGBOURNE, KENT, ME9 8HR.
•**GILES, Mr. Richard Edward, BSc FCA** *1977;* R & L Giles Limited, 21 St Ives Gardens, BOURNEMOUTH, BH2 6NS.
GILES, Mr. Richard Graham, MA ACA AMCT *2002;* 19 Meadway, HARPENDEN, HERTFORDSHIRE, AL5 1JN.
GILES, Mr. Richard K, FCA *1964;* 16026 Summers Pass, SAN ANTONIO, TX 78247, UNITED STATES.
GILES, Mr. Robert Lewis, ACA *1981;* 265 Flatrock Road, HURSTBRIDGE, VIC 3099, AUSTRALIA.
GILES, Mr. Simon James, BA ACA *2007;* 20 Horsham Road, Pease Pottage, CRAWLEY, WEST SUSSEX, RH11 9AL.
GILES, Mr. Simon Kenneth, LLB ACA *1999;* 401 New Hythe Lane, Larkfield, AYLESFORD, KENT, ME20 6US.
GILES, Mr. Stephen Paul, MA ACA *1986;* 115 Longmore Avenue, BARNET, EN5 1JU.
GILES, Mrs. Susan Jane, BA ACA *1998;* 21 Stickleback Road, CALNE, SN11 9RB.
GILES, Mr. Thomas Derek Bullivant, BA FCA *1963;* Castle Gotha, Porthpean, ST AUSTELL, CORNWALL, PL26 6AZ. (Life Member)
GILES, The Revd. Timothy David, FCA *1969;* Lea Cottage, Hillhead Road, Kergilliack, FALMOUTH, CORNWALL, TR11 5PA.
GILES KNOPP, Mr. Andrew David Anthony, BA ACA *1996;* 9 Moncur Street, WOOLLAHRA, NSW 2025, AUSTRALIA.
GILFELLON, Mr. Michael Gerard, BA ACA *1981;* 64 Duke Road, LONDON, W4 2DE.
GILFILLAN, Mr. Philip, BA FCA *1995;* 5 Kielder Close, BLYTH, NORTHUMBERLAND, NE24 4QH.
GILHAM, Mr. Clive Martin, BA FCA *1984;* 3 St. Johns Cottages, Hall Road Mount Bures, BURES, SUFFOLK, CO8 5AR.
GILHAM, Mr. Paul Martin, BA FCA *1999;* 6 Williamson Close, Winnersh, WOKINGHAM, RG41 5RY.
GILHAM, Mrs. Sara Margaret, BSc ACA *1996;* 10 Meadow Way, REIGATE, SURREY, RH2 8DR.
GILHESPIE, Mrs. Julie, LLB ACA *1990;* 11 Levington Wynd, Nunthorpe, MIDDLESBROUGH, CLEVELAND, TS7 0QD.
GILHOME, Mrs. Jill Elizabeth, MSc ACA *1992;* 27 Mainspring Road, Wilsden, BRADFORD, BD15 0EH.
GILJAM, Mr. Adriaan Alexander, ACA *1981;* 2 Talana Rd, Claremont, CAPE TOWN, 7708, SOUTH AFRICA.
GILKES, Mr. Brent Stephen, BSc ACA *1988;* 440 Millenium Ridge, ST THOMAS, BARBADOS.
GILKES, David Arthur, Esq MBE MA FCA *1964;* St Ambrose, The Drift, Levington, IPSWICH, IP10 0LF. (Life Member)
GILKES, Mr. John Garfield, BSc FCA *1992;* with Deloitte & Touche LLP, 555 12th Street NW, Suite 500, WASHINGTON, DC 20004, UNITED STATES.
GILKES, Mr. Robert Michael, BSc ACA *1991;* Bramber, Salty Lane, Shaldon, TEIGNMOUTH, DEVON, TQ14 0AP.
GILKISON, Miss. Fiona Margaret, BA(Hons) ACA *2002;* Specialist Investigations, H M Revenue & Customs Special Investigations, Trinity Bridge House 2 Dearmans Place, SALFORD, M3 5AQ.
GILKS, Mr. Alastair James Pearson, BSc ACA *1982;* The Farm House, Whatborough Farm, Nr. Tilton on the Hill, LEICESTER, LE7 9DJ.
GILKS, Mr. David John Ellis, FCA *1971;* Shamwari, Crampmoor Lane, Crampmoor, ROMSEY, HAMPSHIRE, SO51 9AJ. (Life Member)
GILKS, Mr. Lyndon Frederick, FCA *1975;* 40 Prospect Place, CIRENCESTER, GL7 1EZ.
GILL, Mr. Adrian Stuart, BSc ACA *1991;* Connells, Cumbria House, 16-20 Hockliffe Street, LEIGHTON BUZZARD, BEDFORDSHIRE, LU7 1HJ.
•**GILL, Mr. Ainsley, BA FCA** *1995;* McPhersons CFG Limited, 23 St. Leonards Road, BEXHILL-ON-SEA, EAST SUSSEX, TN40 1HH.
GILL, Mrs. Alison, BSc ACA *1991;* 14 Hitherside, Shirley, SOLIHULL, B90 1RT.
•**GILL, Mr. Alwyn, LLB ACA** *1984;* Elta Partnership Limited, Montrose House, Buildwas Road, Clayhill, NESTON, CH64 3RU.
GILL, Mr. Amardeep, BA(Econ) ACA *2011;* 69 Bulstrode Road, HOUNSLOW, TW3 3AN.
GILL, Mr. Amrik Singh, BCom ACA *1999;* 346 Sutton Road, WALSALL, WS5 3BB.
•**GILL, Mr. Andrew Derek, BSc(Hons) FCA** *1993;* A. G. Accounting Services Limited, 24 Mount Durand, St. Peter Port, GUERNSEY, GY1 1ED. See also Andy Gill Accounting Services
GILL, Mr. Andrew George, BSc ACA *1994;* Little Oaks Isington Road, Isington, ALTON, HAMPSHIRE, GU34 4PP.
GILL, Miss. Awara Kaur, BA ACA *1984;* with Chantrey Vellacott DFK LLP, Russell Square House, 10-12 Russell Square, LONDON, WC1B 5LF.
GILL, Mr. Balvinder, BCom ACA *1998;* c/o S Patel, P O Box 45086, NAIROBI, KENYA.
GILL, Mr. Billy, BA(Hons) ACA *2003;* 2 Palm Grove, SYDNEY, NSW 2076, AUSTRALIA.
GILL, Mr. Brett Richard Joseph, FCA *1965;* Reapers, Duke Street, Micheldever, WINCHESTER, SO21 3DF. (Life Member)
GILL, Mr. Brian Haydn, FCA *1959;* 16 Westwood Grove, SOLIHULL, B91 1QB. (Life Member)
•**GILL, Mr. Charles, ACA** *1978;* (Tax Fac), The Barker Partnership, 44 Kirkgate, RIPON, HG4 1PB. See also The Barker Partnership Limited
GILL, Mrs. Chhayabahen Mahendra, ACA *1991;* Amin & Co, 98-100 Fleetwood Road, LONDON, NW10 1NN.
GILL, Mr. Christopher, LLB FCA *1964;* 94 Claygate Lane, ESHER, KT10 0BJ.
GILL, Mr. Christopher Haydn, BSc ACA *1992;* 72 The Pastures, HEMEL HEMPSTEAD, HERTFORDSHIRE, HP1 2TW.
GILL, Mr. Christopher John, BSc ACA *1987;* Rowan House, 33 Meadow Court, Ponteland, NEWCASTLE UPON TYNE, NE20 9RB.
GILL, Mr. Christopher Marshall, BSc FCA *1983;* 63 Church Street, EPSOM, KT17 4QA.
GILL, Mr. Clifford William, MA ACA *1988;* Lexden Cottage, 2 Portley Wood Road, WHYTELEAFE, CR3 0BP.
•**GILL, Miss. Colette, BSc ACA MSFA TEP** *1998;* 2 Griffin Close, Eccleston, ST. HELENS, MERSEYSIDE, WA10 5BL.
GILL, Mrs. Corinne Jane, BA FCA *1988;* Oakleigh House, West Lane, Baildon, SHIPLEY, BD17 5DL.
GILL, Mr. Cranstoun Bygott Harold, MA FCA *1953;* The Croft, 3 Harrop Road, Hale, ALTRINCHAM, CHESHIRE, WA15 9BU. (Life Member)
GILL, Mr. Daniel, ACA *2003;* Pilot Partners, PO Box 7095, BRISBANE, QLD 4001, AUSTRALIA.
GILL, Mr. Daniel James, BA(Hons) ACA *2001;* 15 Southdean Gardens, LONDON, SW19 6NT.
GILL, Mr. David, ACA *2011;* 152 Dovers Green Road, REIGATE, SURREY, RH2 8BZ.
GILL, Mr. David Alan, BCom ACA *1981;* Spindles, St Marys Road, Bowdon, ALTRINCHAM, WA14 2PH.
GILL, Mr. David Barry, BSc ACA *1999;* 5 Mayflower Crescent, Buckshaw Village, CHORLEY, LANCASHIRE, PR7 7BF.
GILL, Mr. David Greatorex, FCA *1962;* Yew Tree House, Dunstall, BURTON-ON-TRENT, STAFFORDSHIRE, DE13 8BE.
GILL, Mr. David Harold, FCA *1969;* Halfpeny Croft, Heathway, Chaldon, CATERHAM, SURREY, CR3 5DL.
•**GILL, Mr. David Kevin, FCA DChA** *1973;* (Tax Fac), 7 Park Avenue, LYTHAM ST. ANNES, LANCASHIRE, FY8 5QU.
•**GILL, Mr. David Thomas, MA ACA** *2004;* with BDO LLP, 55 Baker Street, LONDON, W1U 7EU.
GILL, Mr. Derek, FCA *1959;* The Ochils, Ightenhill Park Lane, BURNLEY, BB12 0LL. (Life Member)
GILL, Mr. Edmund James, FCA *1961;* 41 Chantry Heath Crescent, Knowle, SOLIHULL, B93 9NJ. (Life Member)
•**GILL, Ms. Elanor Jane, MA ACA** *2001;* Deloitte LLP, Abbots House, Abbey Street, READING, RG1 3BD. See also Deloitte & Touche LLP
GILL, Miss. Eleanor, BMus ACA *2003;* Department of Transport Great Minster House, 76 Marsham Street, LONDON, SW1P 4DR.
GILL, Mr. Francis Douglas, FCA *1961;* 6 Ashway, Woolaston, LYDNEY, GL15 6QA. (Life Member)
GILL, Miss. Gemma Dorian, BSc ACA *2005;* 4 Church Drive East, Daybrook, NOTTINGHAM, NG5 6JG.
GILL, Mrs. Gillian Elizabeth, BA FCA *1990;* Rothschild Trust Guernsey Ltd, PO Box 472, GUERNSEY, GY1 6AX.
•**GILL, Mr. Gordon Melvyn, FCA** *1974;* (Tax Fac), with RSM Tenon Limited, The Poynt Building, 45 Wollaton Street, NOTTINGHAM, NG1 5FW.
GILL, Mr. Gurbrinder Singh, FCA *1971;* Roe Beech, Beaulieu Road, LYNDHURST, HAMPSHIRE, SO43 7DA.
•**GILL, Mr. Gurbrinder Singh, BA FCA** *1992;* 27 Clifton Road, AMERSHAM, BUCKINGHAMSHIRE, HP6 5PP.
GILL, Mr. Gurinderjeet, BSc ACA *2010;* 256 Chertsey Lane, STAINES, MIDDLESEX, TW18 3NF.
GILL, Mr. Gurvinder Singh, MSc BSc ACA *2003;* University Partnership Programme, Weston House, 246 High Holborn, LONDON, WC1V 7EX.
•**GILL, Miss. Hamdeep Tina, BSc ACA ATII** *1989;* Ernst & Young LLP, 1 More London Place, LONDON, SE1 2AF. See also Ernst & Young Europe LLP
•**GILL, Mr. Harminther Singh, BA ACA** *1989;* MacIntyre Hudson LLP, Euro House, 1394 High Road, Whetstone, LONDON, N20 9YZ.
GILL, Ms. Helen Nina, BA ACA *1992;* 89 Ashley Road, ALTRINCHAM, CHESHIRE, WA14 2LX.
GILL, Mr. Irving Peter, FCA *1948;* Ghyll Croft, 10 Banks Hill, BARNOLDSWICK, BB18 5XA. (Life Member)
GILL, Mr. Jaiprakash Singh, FCA *1985;* P.O Box 438, KILLARA, NSW 2071, AUSTRALIA.
GILL, Miss. Jaitinder, PhD BSc(Hons) ACA *2001;* Gainsborough House Winkfield Lane, Winkfield, WINDSOR, SL4 4RU.
GILL, Mr. James Chacliff, ACA *2010;* Flat 22 Queens Court, Hill Lane, SOUTHAMPTON, SO15 5RR.
GILL, Mr. Jasbir Singh, BSc ACA *1995;* Via Belgioioso 10, 22100 COMO, ITALY.

GILL, Mrs. Jean, FCA *1982;* 28 Penleigh Gardens, Wombourne, WOLVERHAMPTON, WV5 8EJ.
•**GILL, Mr. Jeffrey Edward, MA ACA** *1983;* (Tax Fac), Blanche & Co., The Lanterns, 16 Melbourn Street, ROYSTON, HERTFORDSHIRE, SG8 7BX.
GILL, Mrs. Jillian, BSc FCA *1988;* Castell Newydd, 30 Stryd y Brython, RUTHIN, CLWYD, LL15 1JA.
GILL, Mr. John, FCA *1961;* 25 Heyes Lane, Timperley, ALTRINCHAM, WA15 6EF. (Life Member)
GILL, Mr. John Anthony Samuel, FCA *1967;* Brae Rise, Berry Lane, Worplesdon, GUILDFORD, GU3 3QF.
GILL, Mr. Jonathan Aubrey, BCom ACA *1986;* 3 Friars Gorse, Off Hyperion Road, Stourton, STOURBRIDGE, WEST MIDLANDS, DY7 6SP.
GILL, Mr. Jonathan Brian, BEng ACA *1993;* Oakleigh House, West Lane, Baildon, SHIPLEY, BD17 5DL.
GILL, Mrs. Julie Carolyn, BSc ACA *1988;* 24 Parkwood Road, Wimbledon, LONDON, SW19 7AQ.
GILL, Mrs. Julie Rose, BA FCA *1993;* 1 Syddal Road, Bramhall, STOCKPORT, SK7 1AB.
GILL, Miss. Katherine, BA(Hons) ACA *2000;* 4 The Green, Welton, BROUGH, HU15 1NG.
•**GILL, Mr. Kevin Duncan, BA ACA ACII** *1992;* Ernst & Young LLP, 1 More London Place, LONDON, SE1 2AF. See also Ernst & Young Europe LLP
GILL, Mr. Kuldip Singh, BA ACA *1994;* 17 Ireton Road, Handsworth Wood, BIRMINGHAM, B20 2NB.
GILL, Mr. Lindsey Philip, BSc ACA *1993;* 61 The Parade, Greatstone, NEW ROMNEY, TN28 8RE.
GILL, Mrs. Louise, BA ACA *1999;* 10 The Paddock, HASLEMERE, GU27 1HB.
GILL, Mrs. Lucy Anne, BSc ACA *2007;* with PricewaterhouseCoopers, 9 Greyfriars Road, READING, RG1 1JG.
GILL, Miss. Lynette Kathryn, BA ACA *1994;* Stanwell Corporation Ltd, GPO Box 773, BRISBANE, QLD 4001, AUSTRALIA.
GILL, Mrs. Mandeep, BA ACA *2003;* 21 Rosemary Way, NUNEATON, WARWICKSHIRE, CV10 7ST.
GILL, Miss. Manjinder, BA(Hons) ACA *2003;* 118 Langbourne Place, LONDON, E14 3WW.
GILL, Mr. Manjit Singh, MSc ACA *1991;* 20 Roebig Street, ASPLEY, QLD 4034, AUSTRALIA.
GILL, Mrs. Marina, MSc ACA *2005;* 93 Sylvan Avenue, LONDON, N22 5JA.
•**GILL, Mr. Mark Andrew, BA FCA** *1995;* PricewaterhouseCoopers LLP, 1 Embankment Place, LONDON, WC2N 6RH. See also PricewaterhouseCoopers
•**GILL, Mr. Mark Ellis, BSc FCA** *1978;* Quarry Lodge, La Rue Du Paradis Vale, GUERNSEY, GY3 5BL.
GILL, Mr. Mark Richard, BA(Hons) ACA *2002;* 49a Oaklands, NEWCASTLE UPON TYNE, NE3 4YP.
GILL, Mr. Martin John, BSc ACA *1987;* 24 Parkwood Road, Wimbledon, LONDON, SW19 7AQ.
•**GILL, Mr. Martin John, BSc ACA** *1995;* PKF (UK) LLP, City Point, 65 Haymarket Terrace, EDINBURGH, EH12 5HD.
GILL, Miss. Marysia, ACA *2011;* 16 Kipling Road, EASTLEIGH, HAMPSHIRE, SO50 9EG.
GILL, Mr. Matthew, ACA *1999;* 55 Church Rise, CHESSINGTON, SURREY, KT9 2HA.
GILL, Mr. Matthew Clement Hugh, BSocSc ACA *1998;* 217 Rye Street, BISHOP'S STORTFORD, HERTFORDSHIRE, CM23 2HE.
GILL, Dr. Matthew James, PhD ACA *2002;* Financial Services Authority, 25 North Colonnade, LONDON, E14 5HS.
GILL, Mr. Matthew John David, BA ACA *1994;* Business Development, 8th Floor Emirates Group Headquarters, DUBAI, PO Box 686, UNITED ARAB EMIRATES.
GILL, Mr. Michael Charles, BSc FCA *1980;* with Carston & Co Limited, First Floor, Tudor House, 16 Cathedral Road, CARDIFF, CF11 9LJ.
GILL, Mr. Narinder, BEng ACA *1998;* HBOS Group Plc Tax Department Walton Street, AYLESBURY, BUCKINGHAMSHIRE, HP21 7QW.
GILL, Mr. Nicholas, BSc ACA *2010;* 58 Erroll Road, HOVE, EAST SUSSEX, BN3 4QG.
GILL, Mr. Oliver, MA ACA *2010;* 49c Chelverton Road, LONDON, SW15 1RN.
GILL, Ms. Parminder, BA ACA *1994;* Azzurri Communications Ltd St. Georges Business Park, Brooklands Road, WEYBRIDGE, KT13 0TS.
GILL, Mr. Paul Howard, BSc ACA *1983;* The Coach House, Foxley Road, MALMESBURY, SN16 0JQ.
GILL, Mr. Paul Michael, BA FCA *1979;* 10 Ringinglow Road, Ecclesall, SHEFFIELD, S11 7PP.
GILL, Mr. Peter Richard, BA FCA *1980;* 30 Sheen Common Drive, RICHMOND, TW10 5BN.
GILL, Mr. Peter Stephen, FCA *1973;* 11 Isinglass Close, NEWMARKET, SUFFOLK, CB8 8HX.
GILL, Mr. Philip, BSc ACA *2011;* Flat 4, Thyme Court, 205 Holders Hill Road, LONDON, NW7 1NJ.
•**GILL, Mr. Rajinder Singh, BCom ACA** *1998;* 37 West Drive, Handsworth, BIRMINGHAM, B20 3ST.
GILL, Mr. Rajul, BSc(Econ) ACA *2000;* 18 Dapdune Road, GUILDFORD, GU1 4NY.
GILL, Mrs. Rebekah Elizabeth, BSc ACA *2000;* 55 Church Rise, CHESSINGTON, SURREY, KT9 2HA.
GILL, Mr. Reginald Christopher, BA FCA *1980;* 8 Orchard Close, MARCH, PE15 9DF.
GILL, Mr. Richard John, BA ACA *1988;* 103 Tinker Lane, Walkley, SHEFFIELD, S6 5EA.
GILL, Mr. Robert Andrew Harrowby, BSc(Hons) ACA *2001;* Willow Cottage Barton Park Farm, Main Street Barton under Needwood, BURTON-ON-TRENT, STAFFORDSHIRE, DE13 8AB.
•**GILL, Mr. Robert James, FCA** *1981;* (Tax Fac), Robert J Gill FCA, 4 Rutland Drive, Mickleover, DERBY, DE3 9FW.
GILL, Mr. Rupert John, BSc ACA *1994;* Heather House, Burwash Road, Broad Oak, HEATHFIELD, EAST SUSSEX, TN21 8ST.
GILL, Miss. Sara Julie, BSc FCA *1986;* Les Meunieres, 38660 ST PANCRASSE, FRANCE.
GILL, Miss. Sarah, BSc ACA *1992;* 160 West 66th Street, Apartment 22 J, NEW YORK, NY 10023, UNITED STATES.
GILL, Mr. Simon, BSc ACA *2006;* 84 Chiltern Road, Caversham, READING, RG4 5JB.
GILL, Mr. Simon David, BSc ACA *2001;* Korn Ferry International Ltd, Ryder Court, 14 Ryder Street, LONDON, SW1Y 6QB.
GILL, Mr. Simon Guy, FCA *1976;* 152 Dovers Green Road, REIGATE, RH2 8BZ. (Life Member)
GILL, Mr. Simon Peter, ACA *2008;* Mazars Llp The Atrium, Park Street West, LUTON, LU1 3BE.
GILL, Mr. Stephen, BSc ACA *1981;* Ladye Place, London Road, ASCOT, SL5 7EG.
GILL, Mr. Sukhbinder, ACA *2009;* 18 Fellside, Ponteland, NEWCASTLE UPON TYNE, NE20 9JP.
GILL, Ms. Sukhjeet Kaur, BA ACA *1996;* 66 Solent Road, West Hampstead, LONDON, NW6 1TX.
GILL, Mrs. Sukhpal Kaur, ACA *2008;* 67 Mehdi Road, OLDBURY, WEST MIDLANDS, B69 2GE.
GILL, Mr. Sukraj Singh, BA(Hons) ACA *2010;* 119 Moorside Crescent, Sinfin, DERBY, DE24 9PT.
GILL, Mrs. Susan Carolyn, BA ACA *1987;* Rowan House, 33 Meadow Court, Ponteland, NEWCASTLE UPON TYNE, NE20 9RB.
GILL, Ms. Susan Doris, BSc ACA *1989;* 24 The Park, ST. ALBANS, AL1 4RY.
•**GILL, Miss. Suzie, BA ACA** *1999;* 57 Norrington Road, MAIDSTONE, KENT, ME15 9XD.
GILL, Miss. Tajinder Kaur, ACA *2006;* Ferrlian Bursnips Road, Essington, WOLVERHAMPTON, WV11 2RE.
GILL, Mr. Tejinder Singh, BSc ACA *2005;* 1 Rochester Drive, PINNER, HA5 1DA.
GILL, Mr. Timothy Stuart, ACA *1979;* (Tax Fac), 9 Vicarage Gardens, Grayshott, HINDHEAD, GU26 6NH.
•**GILL, Mrs. Tracy, BCom ACA** *1991;* Samuel George Limited, 14 Rogers Way, WARWICK, CV34 6PY.
GILL, Miss. Tracy Amanda, BSc ACA *2002;* 6 Clockhouse Avenue, BURNLEY, BB10 2SU.
GILL, Miss. Zoe Frances, ACA *2008;* 36 Britannia Close, LONDON, SW4 7NN.
GILL-CAREY, Mr. Peter Michael, FCA *1975;* 5 Minses Close, Elburton, PLYMOUTH, PL9 8DR.
GILL-WILLIAMS, Miss. Maria, BA(Hons) ACA *2010;* 193 Wellfield Road, LONDON, SW16 2BY.
GILLAH, Mr. Nigel Andrew, LLB FCA *1977;* 420 East 72nd Street, Apartment 9J, NEW YORK, NY 10021, UNITED STATES.
•**GILLAIN, Mr. Douglas Pascal Wilfred, FCA** *1963;* 135 Spencefield Lane, Evington, LEICESTER, LE5 6GG.
GILLAM, Mr. Andrew John, BA ACA *1997;* Walnut Lodge, 29 Melville Avenue, SOUTH CROYDON, CR2 7HZ.
GILLAM, Mr. Clive Adrian George, BCom FCA *1974;* 9 Minster Rd, OXFORD, OX4 1LX.
GILLAM, Mr. Malcolm John Christopher, BSc FCA MBA *1976;* 2215 de l'Academie, ST-LAZARE J7T 2B1, QUE, CANADA.
•**GILLAM, Mr. Neil Malcolm, ACA FCCA ATII** *1983;* (Tax Fac), haysmacintyre, Fairfax House, 15 Fulwood Place, LONDON, WC1V 6AY.
GILLAMS, Mr. Charles Alfred Richard, MA ACA *1981;* Meon House, Stratford Road, Mickleton, CHIPPING CAMPDEN, GL55 6SU.
GILLAN, Mrs. Charlotte Elizabeth, BA ACA *2000;* B H P Petroleum Ltd, 1 Neathouse Place, LONDON, SW1V 1LH.
GILLANDERS, Miss. Diane Elizabeth, BA ACA *1988;* 16 Normans Lane, ROYSTON, HERTFORDSHIRE, SG8 9BS.
GILLANDERS, Mr. William, FCA *1954;* 37 Glebe Rise, Littleover, DERBY, DE23 6GX. (Life Member)
GILLANI, Mr. Shamsher Esmail, FCA *1977;* (Tax Fac), with Gillani & Co, Conduit House, Conduit Lane, HODDESDON, EN11 8EP.
GILLARD, Mr. Andrew John, BA ACA *2000;* 35 Quick Road, LONDON, W4 2BU.
•**GILLARD, Mr. Colin Herbert, FCA** *1981;* Northams, 21/23 New Street, HONITON, EX14 1HA.
GILLARD, Mr. David James, BA ACA *1989;* Oxford University, Great Clarendon Street, OXFORD, OX2 6LY.
•**GILLARD, Mr. David John, BSc FCA** *1980;* (Tax Fac), Gillards Limited, 4 Heath Square, Boltro Road, HAYWARDS HEATH, RH16 1BL.
GILLARD, Mrs. Gillian Patricia, ACA *1982;* Southlands, 21 Ribblesdale Place, Higherford, NELSON, BB9 6AX.
•**GILLARD, Mr. Ian Douglas, FCA FCCA** *1983;* R D Owen, 18A Queen Square, BATH, BA1 2HR. See also R D Owen Services Limited and Pethericks & Gillard Ltd
GILLARD, Mr. James, BA ACA *2011;* 29 Grove Road, Headingley, LEEDS, LS6 2AQ.
GILLARD, Mr. Jeffrey George, BSc FCA *1978;* Room 410A, Rita Resort & Residence, 308/80 Moo 10, Trappaya Road, Nong Prue, Banglamung CHON BURI 20150 THAILAND.
GILLARD, Mr. Robert Michael, BCom FCA *1956;* 76 Staplegrove Road, TAUNTON, TA1 1DJ. (Life Member)
•**GILLARD, Mr. Roger, ACA** *1982;* (Tax Fac), Thomas Westcott, Timberly, South Street, AXMINSTER, DEVON, EX13 5AD.
GILLARD, Mrs. Stephanie Claire, BA ACA *1997;* 36 The Woodlands, ESHER, SURREY, KT10 8DB.
GILLATT, Mrs. Kathryn Isobel, BA FCA *1987;* Gables Farm, 73 Main Street, Long Whatton, LOUGHBOROUGH, LE12 5DF.
GILLBANKS, Mr. David Alexander, FCA *1963;* Monopol Holdings Ltd, 18 Hanover Street, LIVERPOOL, L1 4AA. (Life Member)
GILLBANKS, Mr. Neale William, BSc ACA *1989;* (Tax Fac), 25 Delph Way, Whittle-le-Woods, CHORLEY, LANCASHIRE, PR6 7TG.
GILLBANKS, Mr. Timothy Nicholas, BEng ACA *1992;* 7 Chester Road, LONDON, N19 5DE.
GILLBE, Ms. Clare, ACA *2009;* 17 Endsleigh Grove, BIRMINGHAM, B28 8NU.
•**GILLBE, Mrs. Jane Helen, BSc ACA** *1979;* (Tax Fac), Jane H. Gillbe, Annfield House, 5 Maori Road, GUILDFORD, GU1 2EG.
GILLBE, Mr. John Peter, MA ACA *1979;* 5 Maori Road, GUILDFORD, GU1 2EG.
•**GILLEARD, Mr. John, FCA** *1985;* Dutton Moore, 6 Silver Street, HULL, HU1 1JA.
GILLERAN, Mr. Keith Edward, FCA *1966;* 23 Danecourt Gardens, Park Hill Rise, CROYDON, CR0 5JN. (Life Member)
•**GILLESPIE, Mr. Alexander, MA ACA** *1990;* (Tax Fac), Gillespie Inverarity & Co, 33 Leslie Street, Blairgowie, PERTH, PH10 6AW. See also Gillespies
GILLESPIE, Mr. Alexander Matthew, ACA *2008;* with PKF (UK) LLP, Farringdon Place, 20 Farringdon Road, LONDON, EC1M 3AP.
GILLESPIE, Mr. Andrew James, FCA *1988;* Corrpro Companies Europe Ltd, Adam Street, Bowesfield Lane, STOCKTON-ON-TEES, CLEVELAND, TS18 3HQ.
GILLESPIE, Mr. Andrew Mark, BA ACA *1998;* Rentokil Ltd, 1 Grenfell Road, MAIDENHEAD, SL6 1ES.
•**GILLESPIE, Mr. Colin Stephen, BSc FCA CF** *1979;* PricewaterhouseCoopers LLP, 101 Barbirolli Square, Lower Mosley Street, MANCHESTER, M2 3PW. See also PricewaterhouseCoopers
GILLESPIE, Mr. David, FCA *1962;* 1a Hartfield Road, BEXHILL-ON-SEA, EAST SUSSEX, TN39 3EA. (Life Member)
GILLESPIE, Mr. David John, BA FCA *1975;* Pritchard Stockbrokers Ltd, Roddis House, Old Christchurch Road, BOURNEMOUTH, BH1 1LG.
GILLESPIE, Mr. Ewen James, BSc ACA *2001;* Group Finance, Lloyds Banking Group, Ettrick House, 37 South Gyle Crescent, EDINBURGH, EH12 9DS.
GILLESPIE, Mr. Francis, FCA *1960;* 72 Cambridge Road, MIDDLESBROUGH, CLEVELAND, TS5 5HG. (Life Member)
GILLESPIE, Mr. Graham Richard, MA ACA *1980;* The Old Rectory, Welford Road, Long Marston, STRATFORD-UPON-AVON, CV37 8RH.
GILLESPIE, Mr. Ian Andrew, FCA *1974;* Cornerways, 1 The Row, Pebble Hill, Toot Baldon, OXFORD, OX44 9ND.
GILLESPIE, Mrs. Janet Marion, ACA *1983;* 1 Aldgate, LONDON, EC3N 1LP.
GILLESPIE, Mrs. Janice, BSc ACA *1990;* Quadrant, North Tyneside Council, 16 The Silverlink North, NEWCASTLE UPON TYNE, NE27 0BY.
GILLESPIE, Mrs. Jennifer Mary, BSc ACA *1979;* The Greys, Pescot Avenue, New Barn, LONGFIELD, DA3 7NA.
GILLESPIE, Mr. John Francis, FCA *1968;* Bramley Lodge Borough Green Road, Wrotham, SEVENOAKS, TN15 7RA.
GILLESPIE, Mr. John Michael, FCA *1972;* The Old StablesWissenden, Bethersden ASHFORD, Kent, TN26 3EL.
GILLESPIE, Mr. John William Munro, BA(Hons) ACA *2002;* World Fuel Services Europe Ltd Portland House, Bressenden Place, LONDON, SW1E 5BH.
GILLESPIE, Mrs. Laura, ACA *1992;* 39 Oak Lane, Upchurch, SITTINGBOURNE, ME9 7AU.
GILLESPIE, Miss. Laura Elizabeth, BA ACA *2002;* 10 Rowan Court, DOUNE, FK16 6HS.
GILLESPIE, Miss. Lynda, BA ACA *2002;* 10 Rowan Court, DOUNE, FK16 6HS.
•**GILLESPIE, Mr. Mark, BA ACA** *2006;* Gillespie BS Limited, Henleaze House, Harbury Road, BRISTOL, BS9 4PN.
GILLESPIE, Mr. Mark Richard, BA ACA *2007;* Flat A-b, 236 Upper Street, LONDON, N1 1RU.
GILLESPIE, Mrs. Susan Louise, BA ACA *1991;* 11 Fulmer Drive, GERRARDS CROSS, BUCKINGHAMSHIRE, SL9 7HH.
GILLESPIE, Mr. Timothy John, ACA *2008;* Glenside, Glen Path, SUNDERLAND, SR2 7TU.
GILLETT, Mr. Alistair Nigel, BSc ACA *1985;* 1 Acacia Drive, Hale, ALTRINCHAM, WA15 8QZ.
GILLETT, Mr. Andrew John, FCA CTA *1970;* The Old Estate Office, Fifty One, Firle, LEWES, BN8 6LQ.
GILLETT, Mr. Dean Henry, BSc ACA *1990;* SEI Interconnect Products (Envelope) Ltd, Axis Court, Mallard Way, Riverside Business Park, Swansea Vale, SWANSEA SA7 0AJ.
GILLETT, Mr. Duncan Charles, BSc(Econ) ACA *1998;* Clearwell Mobility Ltd Unit 3, 21 Albert Drive, BURGESS HILL, WEST SUSSEX, RH15 9TN.
GILLETT, Mrs. Helen Denise, BSc ACA *1992;* 6 Devon Road, Merstham, REDHILL, RH1 3EU.
GILLETT, Mr. Jonathan Andrew Gurney, FCA *1969;* 125 Dovehouse Street, LONDON, SW3 6JZ.
GILLETT, Mr. Laurence David, FCA *1972;* 9 North Road, CHESTER-LE-STREET, DH3 4AQ.
GILLETT, Miss. Leanne, ACA *2007;* 186 Hamlin Lane, EXETER, EX1 2SH.
GILLETT, Mr. Mark, BSc FCA *1992;* 49 Winn Road, LONDON, SE12 9EY.
GILLETT, Mr. Martin Charles, BA(Hons) ACA *2000;* 41 St. Johns Way, Sandiway, NORTHWICH, CHESHIRE, CW8 2LX.
GILLETT, Mr. Michael Edmund, BCom FCA *1974;* 16 Wisbech Way, Hordle, LYMINGTON, HAMPSHIRE, SO41 0YQ.
GILLETT, Mrs. Nicola, BSc ACA *2000;* 41 St. Johns Way, Sandiway, NORTHWICH, CHESHIRE, CW8 2LX.
GILLETT, Mr. Paul Anthony, ACA *1984;* Minaun, Curraghtown, DRUMREE, COUNTY MEATH, IRELAND.
GILLETT, Mr. Peter Lewis, FCA *1966;* 83 Theydon Grove, EPPING, ESSEX, CM16 4PX.
GILLETT, Prof. Peter Richard, PhD MA FCA MBCS FCMI *1978;* 21 Hickory Lane, NORTH BRUNSWICK, NJ 08902-1311, UNITED STATES.
GILLETT, Mr. Philip John, BSc FCA FTII FCT *1976;* The Law Debenture Corporation Plc, 100 Wood Street, LONDON, EC2V 7EX.
GILLETT, Mr. Roger Alwyn, FCA *1968;* 3 Wick Farm, Wick Green, Southbourne, BOURNEMOUTH, BH6 4LY.
•**GILLETT, Miss. Rosalind Alice, ACA** *1983;* E&R Consulting Limited, 5 Highfield Park, MARLOW, BUCKINGHAMSHIRE, SL7 2DE.
GILLETT, Ms. Sharon Jacqueline, BSc ACA *2005;* 11 Chestnut Avenue, BUCKHURST HILL, ESSEX, IG9 6EN.
GILLETT, Mr. Timothy John, BMus FCA CTA *1989;* (Tax Fac), 233 Botley Road, CHESHAM, BUCKINGHAMSHIRE, HP5 1XY.

GILLETT, Mr. William Graham, FCA *1974;* Sopers Cottage, Markedge Lane, Chipstead, COULSDON, SURREY, CR5 3SL.

GILLHAM, Mr. Austin Nigel West, FCA *1973;* 16 Mindi Road, DOONAN, QLD 4562, AUSTRALIA.

GILLHAM, Mrs. Kirsty Marie, BSc ACA *2005;* 4 Healey Street, MOORABBIN, VIC 3189, AUSTRALIA.

GILLHESPY, Mr. Anthony James, BSc(Econ) ACA *1991;* 1 Timandra Close, Abbey Meads, SWINDON, SN25 4XN.

•GILLHESPY, Mr. Norman Richard, PhD MA FCA *1972;* N R Gillhespy, 172 Birmingham Road, SUTTON COLDFIELD, WEST MIDLANDS, B72 1BX. See also M R Gillhespy MA FCA Ltd

GILLIAM, Mr. Thomas, MA(Oxon) ACA AMCT *2003;* 6 Elmbridge Lane, WOKING, SURREY, GU22 9AW.

GILLIAN, Mr. Michael William, BA FCA *1964;* PO Box 134, ETTALONG BEACH, NSW 2257, AUSTRALIA. (Life Member)

GILLIANS, Mrs. Diane, BA ACA *1999;* 132 Hayes Road, RDI, West Melton, CHRISTCHURCH 7671, NEW ZEALAND.

GILLIAT, Mr. Christopher Douglas, MA FCA *1980;* Upton Mill, Mill Lane, Upton, NEWARK, NG23 5SZ.

•GILLIBRAND, Mr. John Hays, BA FCA CF *1985;* 40 Deakins Mill Way, Egerton, BOLTON, BL7 9YT.

•GILLIBRAND, Mr. Michael, FCA *1963;* Gould & Mansford, P O Box 151, Anvil Cottage, Anvil Lane, Letcombe Regis, WANTAGE OXFORDSHIRE OX12 9LA.

•GILLIBRAND, Mr. Michael James, LLB FCA *1986;* Stripes Solicitors Ship Canal House, 98 King Street, MANCHESTER, M2 4WU.

•GILLIBRAND, Mr. Michael Paul, ACA *1992;* Bright Partnership, Yarmouth House, Trident Business Park, Daten Avenue, Birchwood, WARRINGTON WA3 6BX.

GILLIES, Mr. Alaistair Carmichael, BSc ACA *1992;* 47 Mile Ash Lane, Darley Abbey, DERBY, DE22 1DE.

GILLIES, Mr. Alan Rickman, BA FCA *1958;* 1-2 St. Ann's Passage, LONDON, SW13 0AX. (Life Member)

GILLIES, Mr. Alasdair Christopher, BA ACA *1984;* UKLC G, Zurich Financial Services UK Life Centre, Station Road, SWINDON, SN1 1EL.

GILLIES, Mr. Andrew Sawyer, BSc ACA *1994;* 15 Cornwall Gardens, BRIGHTON, BN1 6RH.

GILLIES, Mr. Crawford Scott, MBA LLB ACA *1980;* CG Advisory Ltd, 101 George Street, EDINBURGH, EH2 3ES.

GILLIES, Mr. Iain, CA *2010; (CA Scotland* Robertson Craig, 3 Clairmont Gardens, GLASGOW, G3 7LW. See also Robertson Craig & co

GILLIES, Mr. Ian Leonard, BA FCA *1983;* Parmley Graham Ltd, Saltmeadows Road, GATESHEAD, TYNE AND WEAR, NE8 3BG.

GILLIES, Ms. Karen Islay, BCom ACA *2005;* 28 South Inch Park, PERTH, PH2 8BU.

GILLIES, Mr. Kenneth McLeod, BA ACA *1988;* J T C UK Ltd, 196 Bath Street, GLASGOW, G2 4HG.

GILLIGAN, Mr. Anthony Luke, FCA ATII CTA *1986;* Lex Vehicle Leasing, Heathside Park Road, STOCKPORT, CHESHIRE, SK3 0RB.

GILLIGAN, Mr. Derek John, FCA *1956;* 6 May Street, LARGS, AYRSHIRE, KA30 8EB. (Life Member)

GILLIGAN, Mr. Peter, BSc ACA *2011;* Nimes, 134 Wash Road, BASILDON, ESSEX, SS15 4BE.

GILLILAND, Mr. Michael Gerard, ACA *2003;* XL Re Ltd, XL House, One Bermudiana Road, PO Box HM 1066, HAMILTON HM EX, BERMUDA.

GILLILAND, Mrs. Morag D'Agnel, MA ACA *2004;* Pink Tiger, 29 White Sands Road, PAGET PG06, BERMUDA.

GILLILAND, Mr. Paul Rory, BA FCA *1978;* 15 Oak Lodge Tye, Springfield, CHELMSFORD, CM1 6GY.

GILLILAND, Mrs. Samantha, BSc ACA *1998;* 5 Lloyd Avenue, CREMORNE, NSW 2090, AUSTRALIA.

GILLIN, Mr. Richard Timothy, BA FCA *1998;* with Deloitte LLP, 2 New Street Square, LONDON, EC4A 3BZ.

GILLING, Mrs. Christine Mary, BA ACA *1996;* Landau Ltd, 5 Landau Court, Tan Bank, Wellington, TELFORD, SHROPSHIRE TF1 1HE.

GILLINGHAM, Mr. Alasdair, BA ACA *2007;* Flat 1, 243a Goldhurst Terrace, LONDON, NW6 3EP.

GILLINGHAM, Mr. Brian Paul, FCA *2001;* Citizen Watch UK Ltd, 19 The Business Centre Molly Millars Lane, WOKINGHAM, RG41 2QY.

GILLINGHAM, Mr. Thomas Richard, FCA *1973;* Shop Court, Milton Damerel, HOLSWORTHY, EX22 7NY.

GILLINGHAM, Mr. Timothy Mark, LLB ACA *1979;* Woodlands, Tannington Long Road, Brundish, WOODBRIDGE, SUFFOLK, IP13 8BE.

GILLINGS, Mr. Ian, BA FCA *1971;* Golden Eye, Bradda East, Port Erin, ISLE OF MAN, IM9 6QB.

GILLINGS, Mr. Michael Geoffrey Mills, FCA *1974;* 52 West Hill Way, LONDON, N20 8QS.

GILLINGS, Mr. Simon Robert, BSc ARCS ACA CF *1995;* 54 Cowslip Drive, Little Thetford, ELY, CB6 3JD.

GILLINGWATER, Mr. Alex Lee, ACA *1996;* 52 Sycamore Grove, Bracebridge Heath, LINCOLN, LN4 2RD.

•GILLINGWATER, Mr. John Robert, FCA *1959;* J R Gillingwater, 15 Pelham Avenue, GRIMSBY, DN33 3NA.

GILLION, Mr. Paul Martin, BSocSc ACA *1994;* Greenways Farm Road, Goring, READING, RG8 0AB.

•GILLIONS, Mr. Barry, FCA *1966;* Garden House, Chelwood Beacon, Chelwood Gate, HAYWARDS HEATH, WEST SUSSEX, RH17 7LH.

GILLIS, Ms. Alexandra Maya, BA ACA *1995;* 95a Sutherland Avenue, LONDON, W9 2HG.

GILLIS, Mrs. Caroline Louise, ACA *2004;* with Rawlinsons, Ruthlyn House, 90 Lincoln Road, PETERBOROUGH, PE1 2SP.

GILLIS, Mr. David Solomon, FCA *1971;* 11 Sedgley Park Road, Prestwich, MANCHESTER, M25 0BJ.

GILLIS, Miss. Jane Winifred, MA ACA *1992;* 28 Ardoch Road, Catford, LONDON, SE6 1SJ.

GILLIS, Mrs. Rosalyn, FCA *1977;* (Tax Fac), Russell House, 140 High Street, EDGWARE, HA8 7LW.

•GILLIS, Mrs. Ruth Jane Prescott, LLB FCA *1984;* (Tax Fac), Nether Kinfauns, Church Road, Kinfauns, PERTH, PH2 7LD.

GILLIVER, Mr. Neil Derek, BSc ACA *1991;* 10 Florence Park, Almondsbury, BRISTOL, BS32 4HE.

GILLMAN, Mr. Ian Richard, BSc FCA *1991;* 14 Hookstone Way, WOODFORD GREEN, ESSEX, IG8 7LF.

•GILLMAN, Mr. Peter Frederick, FCA *1974;* Price Bailey LLP, Causeway House, 1 Dane Street, BISHOP'S STORTFORD, HERTFORDSHIRE, CM23 3BT. See also Price Bailey Private Client LLP, PB Financial Planning Ltd and Colin Pickard & Company Limited

GILLMAN, Mr. Trevor Charles, BA ACA *1992;* 104 Nene Road, HUNTINGDON, PE29 1RF.

•GILLMORE, Mr. Frederick Charles, FCA *1963;* (Tax Fac), F C Gillmore & Co Limited, 198 Leesons Hill, CHISLEHURST, KENT, BR7 6QH.

GILLO, Mr. Geoffrey Michael, FCA CMILT *1976;* 103 Beach Street, DEAL, KENT, CT14 6JQ.

GILLOCH, Mr. Peter Gordon, FCA *1952;* 140 Normanshire Drive, Chingford, LONDON, E4 9HD. (Life Member)

GILLON, Mr. Anthony Sean, FCA *1977;* The Spinney, 19 Woodlands Road, Bickley, BROMLEY, BR1 2AD.

GILLON, Mr. Guy Michael L'Estrange, BSc(Hons) ACA *2003;* Bluebird Partners LLP, 64 Great Suffolk Street, LONDON, SE1 0BL.

GILLON, Mrs. Mary Clare, BSc FCA *1991;* 11 Windmill Lane, ALTON, HAMPSHIRE, GU34 2SN.

GILLOOLY, Mr. Adrian Michael, BSc ACA *1998;* Thorndean, Boyndon Road, MAIDENHEAD, SL6 4EU.

GILLOTT, Mr. David, FCA *1967;* 51 The Knoll, KINGSWINFORD, DY6 8JT.

GILLOTT, Prof. Elizabeth, BA FCA *1974;* (Tax Fac), 31 Gilbert Scott Court, Whielden Street, AMERSHAM, BUCKINGHAMSHIRE, HP7 0AP.

GILLOTT, Mrs. Elizabeth Sharon, BA ACA *1985;* (Tax Fac), Spa Street, OSSETT, WEST YORKSHIRE, WF5 0HP.

GILLOTT, Miss. Isobel Jane, BSc ACA *1999;* 8 Brecon Avenue, WORCESTER, WR4 0RJ.

GILLOTT, Mr. Justin James, BEng ACA *1998;* 68 Danecroft Road, LONDON, SE24 9NZ.

GILLOTT, Mr. Nicholas Frank, BCom ACA *2002;* 9 Birkdale Avenue, Blackwell, BROMSGROVE, WORCESTERSHIRE, B60 1BY.

GILLOTT, Mr. Simon Charles, ACA *2009;* with KPMG LLP, 15 Canada Square, LONDON, E14 5GL.

GILLOTT, Mr. Timothy Alan, BCom ACA *1999;* Ant-Sybex Ltd, Spirella Buildings, Bridge Road, LETCHWORTH GARDEN CITY, HERTFORDSHIRE, SG6 4ET.

GILLSON, Ms. Suzanne Jayne, ACA *1988;* Lilac Cottage, Tunnel Lane, Orleton, LUDLOW, SY8 4HY.

GILMAN, Mr. David William, BA FCA *1977;* Motability Operations, City Gate House, 22 Southwark Bridge Road, LONDON, SE1 9HB.

GILMAN, Mr. Melvyn Harvey, BA ACA *1985;* 10 Valley Road, CHEADLE, SK8 1HY.

GILMAN, Mr. Nicholas Charles, BSc ACA *1995;* 10 Kitson Road, Barnes, LONDON, SW13 9HJ.

GILMARTIN, Mrs. Emma, BSc ACA *2001;* 434 Bolton Road West, Ramsbottom, BURY, LANCASHIRE, BL0 9RY.

GILMARTIN, Dr. Mark, BSc ACA *1993;* (Tax Fac), 68 Ryecroft Road, LONDON, SW16 3EH.

•GILMARTIN, Mr. Matthew Francis, ACA *2001;* (Tax Fac), Sage & Company Business Advisors Limited, 102 Bowen Court, St Asaph Business Park, ST. ASAPH, CLWYD, LL17 0JE. See also MFG Holdings Limited

GILMORE, Mrs. Alix Louise, BBA ACA *2004;* 22 Cumberland Road, Atherton, MANCHESTER, M46 9LG.

GILMORE, Mr. Colin Michael, MA FCA *1965;* Oakfield, Albaston, GUNNISLAKE, CORNWALL, PL18 9EZ.

GILMORE, Mrs. Emma Elizabeth, BSc ACA *2001;* Braemar, Mount Auldyn, Ramsey, ISLE OF MAN, IM8 3PJ.

GILMORE, Mr. John, BA FCA *1989;* Sling Media Inc., 1051 East Hillsdale Blvd, Suite 500, FOSTER CITY, CA 94404, UNITED STATES.

GILMORE, Mr. John William Alexander, MA FCA *1985;* 45 Rugby Road, BELFAST, BT7 1PT.

GILMORE, Mr. Jonathan Caleb, BA(Hons) ACA *2003;* 44 Park Crescent, Elstree, BOREHAMWOOD, HERTFORDSHIRE, WD6 3PU.

GILMORE, Mr. Jonathan Paul, BA(Hons) ACA *2009;* 10 Perrygate Avenue, MANCHESTER, M20 1JR.

GILMORE, Mr. Liam, BA ACA *2000;* 15 Craiglea Drive, EDINBURGH, EH10 5PB.

GILMORE, Mr. Michael Joseph, BA ACA *2006;* (Tax Fac), with Grant Thornton UK LLP, Grant Thornton House, 22 Melton Street, Euston Square, LONDON, NW1 2EP.

GILMORE, Mr. Robin Myron, FCA *1963;* 7 Arncliffe Grange, LEEDS, LS17 6ST. (Life Member)

GILMORE, Miss. Sally-Ann, BA ACA *1996;* Moneygram International Ltd, 1 Bevington Path, LONDON, SE1 3PW.

GILMOUR, Mr. Archibald Lymburner, FCA *1969;* Dale Farm, Worcester Lane, SUTTON COLDFIELD, B75 5PR.

GILMOUR, Mr. Ewen Hamilton, MA FCA *1977;* St.Mary House, 20 Arthur Road, Wimbledon, LONDON, SW19 7DZ.

GILMOUR, Mr. Fergus William, BA ACA *1993;* Highclere International Investors Ltd, 2 Manchester Square, LONDON, W1U 3PA.

GILMOUR, Mr. Graham Stanley James, MA ACA *1989;* 27 Welwyn Hall Gardens, WELWYN, AL6 9LF.

GILMOUR, Mrs. Helena, BSc ACA *2007;* Flat 615 Block A, 27 Green Walk, LONDON, SE1 4TT.

GILMOUR, Mr. James, BSc ACA MCT *2002;* Tesco.Com, 1 Falcon Way Shire Park, WELWYN GARDEN CITY, HERTFORDSHIRE, AL7 1TW.

GILMOUR, Miss. Jennifer Jane, ACA *2009;* 21 Sunningdale Drive, Onchan, ISLE OF MAN, IM3 1EX.

GILMOUR, Mrs. Karen Marie, BSc ACA *1998;* 18 The Croft, KIDDERMINSTER, WORCESTERSHIRE, DY11 6LX.

GILMOUR, Ms. Lisa, ACA *1988;* ACCA, 29 Lincoln's Inn Fields, LONDON, WC2A 3EE.

GILMOUR, Miss. Lyndsey Emma, ACA *2008;* 227 Kenton Lane, NEWCASTLE UPON TYNE, TYNE AND WEAR, NE3 3EA.

GILMOUR, Mr. Matthew, BCom ACA *1998;* 3 Norwegian Wood, Rad Lane, Abinger Hammer, DORKING, SURREY, RH5 6RA.

GILMOUR, Mr. Mervyn Marshall, BA(Hons) ACA *1989;* ROYDON, St Kew, BODMIN, CORNWALL, PL30 3HH.

GILMOUR, Mr. Paul, BA ACA *2010;* 120 Latchmere Road, LONDON, SW11 2JT.

GILMOUR, Mr. Paul John, BSc ACA *1991;* 31 Belfield Road, Didsbury, MANCHESTER, M20 6BJ.

•GILMOUR, Mr. Paul Richard, LLB ACA *2001;* Mazars LLP, The Pinnacle, 160 Midsummer Boulevard, MILTON KEYNES, MK9 1FF.

•GILMOUR, Mr. Walter Allison, FCA *1954;* (Member of Council 1983 - 1993), (Tax Fac), W.A. Gilmour, 4 St Gilberts Close, Pointon, SLEAFORD, LINCOLNSHIRE, NG34 0NG.

GILPIN, Mr. Alan, ACA *2006;* 10a Lound Road, KENDAL, CUMBRIA, LA9 7DT.

GILPIN, Mr. David Philip, ACA *1978;* 13 Cornelius Vale, Chancellor Park, CHELMSFORD, CM2 6GY.

GILPIN, Mr. James Essery, BA ACA *1996;* Flat 329, Whitehouse Apartments, 9 Belvedere Road, LONDON, SE1 8YS.

•GILPIN, Mr. Jonathan Charles, BCom ACA *2001;* with PricewaterhouseCoopers LLP, Exchange House, Central Business Exchange, Midsummer Boulevard, MILTON KEYNES, MK9 2DF.

•GILPIN, Mr. Mark Julian, BA FCA *1984;* Gilpin and Harding, 15 St. Johns Place, Birtley, CHESTER LE STREET, COUNTY DURHAM, DH3 2PW.

GILPIN, Mr. Peter Frederick, FCA *1958;* 60 Northdown Road, SOLIHULL, B91 3ND. (Life Member)

GILPIN, Mr. William Edward, BA ACA *1994;* 7 Old Rectory Green, Aughton, ORMSKIRK, LANCASHIRE, L39 6TE.

GILROY, Mr. Angus Hugh, FCA *1963;* Grainingfold, Five Oaks, BILLINGSHURST, RH14 9AT.

GILROY, Mr. Brian Hugh, FCA *1963;* Hill Rise, Letch Hill Drive, Bourton-On-The-Water, CHELTENHAM, GL54 2DQ.

GILROY, Mr. George Cummings, FCA *1958;* 28 Richmomd Way, Barns Park, CRAMLINGTON, NE23 7XE. (Life Member)

GILROY, Mrs. Julie, BA ACA CTA *1993;* (Tax Fac), with PricewaterhouseCoopers LLP, 101 Barbirolli Square, Lower Mosley Street, MANCHESTER, M2 3PW.

•GILROY, Mr. Nigel Howard, FCA *1974;* (Tax Fac), Nigel H. Gilroy & Co, 6 Broomfield Road, SURBITON, KT5 9AZ.

GILROY, Mr. William Peter, FCA *1972;* 10 Northolt Avenue, Parkside Chase, CRAMLINGTON, NE23 1RJ.

GILSON, Mr. Mark Stephen, BSc ACA *1992;* Capital International Ltd Capital House, Circular Road Douglas, ISLE OF MAN, IM1 1AG.

•GILSON, Mr. Timothy Richard, FCA *1975;* Tim Gilson, 6 Homestead Close, Bredon, TEWKESBURY, GLOUCESTERSHIRE, GL20 7NN.

GILSON, Mrs. Victoria Kate, BSc ACA *2010;* Sunhillow, Norwood Lane, Meopham, GRAVESEND, KENT, DA13 0YF.

GILTHORPE, Mr. David Alexander, BA FCA *1984;* Lady Park Farm Cottage, Lady Park, GATESHEAD, NE11 0HD.

•GILTRAP, Mr. Peter John, BCom ACA *1989;* Eden Outsourcing Limited, Tuscam House, Trafalgar Way, CAMBERLEY, SURREY, GU15 3BN.

GILTROW, Miss. Clare Elizabeth, BSc ACA *1992;* Littlejohn, 1 Westferry Circus, LONDON, E14 4HD.

GIMBLETT, Mr. Lee Humphries, BSc ACA *1991;* 11 Anderton Retreat, MURDOCH, WA 6150, AUSTRALIA.

GIMMLER, Mr. Richard Robert, BSc ACA *1995;* Glebe House Church Walk, Ashton Keynes, SWINDON, SN6 6PB.

GIN, Mr. Russell, BSc ACA *2002;* Flat 25 Holly Lodge, 90 Wimbledon Hill Road, LONDON, SW19 7PB.

GINGELL, Mr. Carl, BSc ACA *2003;* Megachem (UK) Ltd, Castlegate Business Park, CALDICOT, GWENT, NP26 5AD.

•GINGELL, Mr. David John, MA FCA *1980;* David J. Gingell, 15 Raddenstile Lane, EXMOUTH, EX8 2JL.

GINGELL, Mrs. Mina Elizabeth, ACA *2008;* with Spofforths LLP, 2nd Floor, Comewell House, North Street, HORSHAM, WEST SUSSEX RH12 1RD.

GINGELL, Mr. Timothy, MA ACA *1991;* I2 Ltd The Visual Space, Capital Park Fulbourn, CAMBRIDGE, CB21 5XH.

•GINGLES, Mr. Darren Andrew, ACA MAAT *2004;* DG Accountancy Services Limited, 1 Canterbury Close, WORCESTER PARK, SURREY, KT4 8GR.

•GINMAN, Mr. Paul Richard, BA FCA *1981;* Baker Tilly Tax and Advisory Services LLP, 25 Farringdon Street, LONDON, EC4A 4AB.

GINMAN-JONES, Mrs. Maria Charlotta, ACA *1993;* 45 De Vere Gardens, LONDON, W8 5AW.

GINN, Mr. Alan, BSc ACA *2003;* Sunnyside Garden Centre Ltd, Leicester Road, IBSTOCK, LEICESTERSHIRE, LE67 6HL.

GINN, Mr. Christopher Michael, BA ACA *1986;* with PKF (UK) LLP, 16 The Havens, Ransomes Europark, IPSWICH, IP3 9SJ.

GINN, Mr. Daniel Richard, LLB ACA *2003;* WorleyParsons, Level 12, 141 Walker Street, NORTH SYDNEY, NSW 2060, AUSTRALIA.

GINN, Mr. Roland Bernard, FCA *1979;* 11 Hillside Gardens, BERKHAMSTED, HERTFORDSHIRE, HP4 2LE.

GINNINGS, Mr. Paul David, FCA *1970;* Gardeners Cottage, Pickwell, Georgeham, BRAUNTON, DEVON, EX33 1LA.

GINNIS, Mr. Neil Peter, ACA *2008;* La Barberie La Rue Du Pontlietaut, St. Clement, JERSEY, JE2 6LG.

GINSBERG, Mrs. Jacqueline Helen, ACA CA(SA) *2010;* The Ridings, 30 Hurstwood, ASCOT, BERKSHIRE, SL5 9SP.

GINSBERG, Mr. Lee, ACA CA(SA) *2010;* The Ridings, 30 Hurstwood, ASCOT, BERKSHIRE, SL5 9SP.

GINSBURG, Mr. Wolfie, FCA ACA *1995;* 18 Broadhurst Avenue, EDGWARE, MIDDLESEX, HA8 8TR.

GINTY, Mr. Michael Gerard, FCA *1983;* 12 Arlington Road, Stretford, MANCHESTER, M32 9HJ.

GIOIA, Mr. Filippo, MSc ACA *2005;* Flat 2, 26 Hartswood Road, LONDON, W12 9NF.

GIOKA, Ms. Ifigenia, MBA ACA *2004;* B H P Billiton Plc, Neathouse Place, LONDON, SW1V 1BH.

GIORGI, Miss. Maia Teresa, BA ACA *1993;* 17 Craddock Road, ENFIELD, EN1 3SR.

GIORGINO, Mr. Felice, ACA *2007;* Flat 1, Charnwood Court, 11 Ranelagh Road, LONDON, W5 5RJ.

GIPP, Miss. Helen Louise, BSc ACA *1996;* Old Sun Inn Skirwith, PENRITH, CUMBRIA, CA10 1RQ.

GIRACH, Miss. Tasneem, ACA *2011;* 24 Eden Road, Oadby, LEICESTER, LE2 4JP.

GIRAUD, Mrs. Nicola Margaret, BA ACA *2005;* 4 Clos de la Caroline, La Rue Des Sillons St. Peter, JERSEY, JE3 7DP.

GIRDLESTONE, Mr. Geoffrey Charles, FCA *1972;* 5 Urquhart Court, 109 Park Road, BECKENHAM, BR3 1QL.

•GIRDLESTONE, Mr. John, FCA *1965;* (Tax Fac), John Girdlestone, Waterside Court, Falmouth Road, PENRYN, TR10 8AW.

•GIRDLESTONE, Mr. Robert Paul, MA ACA *1993;* PricewaterhouseCoopers LLP, Marlborough Court, 10 Bricket Road, ST. ALBANS, HERTFORDSHIRE, AL1 3JX. See also PricewaterhouseCoopers

GIRLING, Mr. Adam Charles, MA ACA *2002;* 5 Times Square, NEW YORK, NY 10036, UNITED STATES.

GIRLING, Mr. Christopher Francis Gregory, FCA *1980;* Flat 6, Halliday House, Gunners Row, SOUTHSEA, HAMPSHIRE, PO4 9XE.

•GIRLING, Mr. Lee Phillip, BSc(Econ) ACA *1997;* Tax Partner Ltd, 21 Dennyview Road, Abbots Leigh, BRISTOL, BS8 3RD.

GIRLING, Mr. Michael John, BA FCA *1976;* ConocoPhilips Algeria Ltd, 5b Chemin Macklay, El Biar, ALGIERS, ALGERIA.

GIRLING, Mr. Norman, FCA *1956;* 7 The Views, George Street, HUNTINGDON, CAMBRIDGESHIRE, PE29 3BY. (Life Member)

•GIRLING, Mr. Roger Malcolm, ACA *1981;* (Tax Fac), Larking Gowen Ltd, Unit 1, Claydon Business Park, Great Blakenham, IPSWICH, IP6 0NL. See also Larking Gowen

•GIRLING, Mr. Simon Edward Jex, BA FCA MIPA *1991;* BDO LLP, Fourth Floor, One Victoria Street, BRISTOL, BS1 6AA. See also BDO Stoy Hayward LLP

GIRLING, Mr. Terry Edward, FCA *1979;* Deltec Bank & Trust Limited, P.O. Box N-3229, NASSAU, BAHAMAS.

•ⒾGIRN, Mr. Kanwaljit Singh, MSc FCA MBA FABRP *1989;* Gore & Company, QWest, International House, Great West Road, BRENTFORD, MIDDLESEX TW8 0GP.

GIRN, Mrs. Nina, BA ACA *2001;* 86 Gunnersbury Avenue, Ealing, LONDON, W5 4HA.

GIRNARY, Mr. Zaeem, BSc ACA *2003;* 70 High Street, Prestwood, GREAT MISSENDEN, BUCKINGHAMSHIRE, HP16 9EN.

GIROLAMI, Mr. Christopher Peter, MA ACA *1991;* 40B Waterford Road, LONDON, SW6 2DR.

GIROLAMI, Miss. Clare Nicola, BA ACA *1989;* Oxley Croft, Weetwood Lane, LEEDS, LS16 5NZ.

GIROLAMI, Sir Paul, Kt BCom FCA *1954;* 24 Chelsea Square, LONDON, SW3 6LF. (Life Member)

GIRTCHEN, Mr. Andrew John, BSc ACA *2007;* with PricewaterhouseCoopers, 26 Honeysuckle Drive, PO Box 798, NEWCASTLE, NSW 2300, AUSTRALIA.

GIRVAN, Mr. Matthew James, ACA *2009;* 1 Marlowe Close, STEVENAGE, HERTFORDSHIRE, SG2 0JJ.

•GIRVIN, Mrs. Louise Amanda, BA ACA *2002;* Louise Girvin, Fieldsway, 4A Pikemere Road, Alsager, STOKE-ON-TRENT, ST7 2SB.

GISBORNE, Mr. Michael Guy, FCA *1957;* The Spinney Shore Road, Castletown, ISLE OF MAN, IM9 1BF.

GISBY, Mr. Anthony Paul, BA ACA *1990;* Apt. 317 Chorlton Mill, 3 Cambridge Street, MANCHESTER, M1 5BZ.

GISLASON, Ms. Allison R, BA CA ACA *2009;* 264a Essex Road, LONDON, N1 3AR.

GISSEL, Mr. Peter, BSc ACA *1990;* Bridgepoint Capital Ltd, 30 Warwick Street, LONDON, W1B 5AL.

GISSING, Ms. Helen Rosemary, BSc ACA *1990;* Jan van Heelustraat 33, 5615 NC EINDHOVEN, NETHERLANDS.

GITLIN, Mr. Brian, ACA CA(SA) *2009;* 15th Floor Apt 1, C1 Columbia Palace, 11 Ave Princess Grace, 98000 MONACO, MONACO.

GITOGO, Mr. Tom Mbuthia, ACA *1998;* Pan Africa Life Assurance Limited, PO Box 44041, NAIROBI, 00100, KENYA.

GITOHO, Mrs. Valentine Wangui, FCA *1983;* P. O. Box 57077-00200, NAIROBI, KENYA.

GITSHAM, Mr. Alan Geoffrey, BA FCA *1975;* P.O.Box 41, KLOOF, KWAZULU NATAL, 3640, SOUTH AFRICA.

•GITTENS, Miss. Lynne, BSc ACA *1989;* Lynne Gittens ACA, 5 Crystal Wood Road, Heath, CARDIFF, CF14 4HU.

GITTENS, Miss. Natasha, ACA *2009;* 84 Rock Lane, Stoke Gifford, BRISTOL, BS34 8PG.

GITTER, Mr. Geoffrey, BSc FCA *1967;* 19 The Greenway, Rayners Lane, PINNER, HA5 5DR. (Life Member)

•GITTER, Mr. Jeffrey, BSc FCA *1975;* Lubbock Fine, Russell Bedford House, City Forum, 250 City Road, LONDON, EC1V 2QQ.

GITTINGS, Mr. Nicholas James, BA ACA *2002;* with Zolfo Cooper Ltd, The Zenith Building, 26 Spring Gardens, MANCHESTER, M2 1AB.

GITTINS, Mr. Andrew John, BA FCA *1987;* Low Field, Church Street, BROUGHTON-IN-FURNESS, CUMBRIA, LA20 6ER.

•GITTINS, Mr. Andrew John, BSc FCA *1979;* Westbury, 145/157 St John Street, LONDON, EC1V 4PY.

•GITTINS, Mr. Christopher David, MA FCA *1971;* Gittins & Co, 3 Tebbit Mews, Winchcombe Street, CHELTENHAM, GLOUCESTERSHIRE, GL52 2NF.

GITTINS, Mr. Edward Watkin, BA FCA *1975;* (Tax Fac), Ballavale Farm, Ballavale Road, Santon, ISLE OF MAN, IM4 1EH.

GITTINS, Mrs. Elizabeth Alexandra, BSc FCA ACA *1990;* Northfields, Forden, WELSHPOOL, SY21 8NN.

GITTINS, Mr. John Anthony, BSc ACA *1985;* East Wing, Leigton House, Leighton Road, Neston, NESTON, CH64 3SW.

GITTINS, Mr. Paul Trevor, BSc FCA *1984;* 5 South View, Farnhill, KEIGHLEY, WEST YORKSHIRE, BD20 9AZ.

•GITTINS, Mr. Peter Laurie, FCA *1953;* Coulthards Mackenzie, 9 Risborough Street, LONDON, SE1 0HF.

GITTINS, Mr. Philip Anthony, BA FCA *1986;* The Mallows, 63 Hoe Lane, Abridge, ROMFORD, RM4 1AU.

GITTINS, Miss. Rachel Louise, ACA *2010;* Lower Sylfaen, Golfa, WELSHPOOL, POWYS, SY21 9AG.

GITTINS, Mr. Richard Paul, BSc(Hons) ACA CTA *2001;* 27 Parkfields, ROCHESTER, ME2 2TW.

•GITTLESON, Mr. David Jacob, BA ACA *1992;* Ernst & Young LLP, 1 More London Place, LONDON, SE1 2AF. See also Ernst & Young Europe LLP

GITTUS, Mr. Graham William, MBA FCA FCMA *1972;* 22 Swanmore Road, Littleover, DERBY, DE23 3SD.

GIUFFREDI, Mr. Paul James, BA ACA *1990;* Baker Ross Ltd Unit 2-3, Forest Works Forest Road, LONDON, E17 6JF.

GIULIANI, Mrs. Priya, BSc FCA *2000;* with KPMG LLP, 15 Canada Square, LONDON, E14 5GL.

GIUSEPPI, Mr. Denis Paul, FCA *1938;* 4 Barleythorpe Road, OAKHAM, LE15 6NR. (Life Member)

•GIVANS, Mr. Roland John, BA FCA *1983;* UHY Wingfield Slater, 6 Broadfield Court, Broadfield Way, SHEFFIELD, S8 0XF.

•GIVEN, Mr. Andrew John, MA ACA *1992;* General Atlantic, 23 Savile Row, LONDON, W1S 2ET.

GIVEN, Ms. Catriona Ferguson, BA ACA *2006;* 7 Sir John Newsom Way, WELWYN GARDEN CITY, HERTFORDSHIRE, AL7 4FJ.

GIVEN, Miss. Claire Marie, BSc FCA *2000;* with Cassons, St Crispin House, St. Crispin Way, Haslingden, ROSSENDALE, LANCASHIRE BB4 4PW.

GIVEN, Mr. Conor, LLB ACA *2009;* 14 Kingisholt Court, 4 Wellington Road, LONDON, NW10 5LJ.

GIVEN, Mrs. Elizabeth Jane, MA ACA *1992;* Fairport Cottage, Lands End Road, Bursledon, SOUTHAMPTON, SO31 8DN.

•GIWA-OSAGIE, Mr. Alhaji Rilwan Oghogho Oritsejeminogho, FCA *1966;* Giwa-Osagie DFK & Co, 6 Ugbague Street, P.O. Box 16, BENIN CITY, NIGERIA.

GKAFA, Miss. Anna, ACA *2011;* Papagou 90, Kamatero, 13451 ATHENS, GREECE.

•GLADDERS, Mr. Kevin Michael, BA ACA *1982;* (Tax Fac), Kevin M Gladders, 40 Gildale, Werrington, PETERBOROUGH, PE4 6QY. See also A K & K Limited

GLADEN, Mr. Paul Jeremy, BA ACA *1992;* 1794 ELISON LANE APT 2, MISSOULA, MT 59802, UNITED STATES.

GLADING, Mrs. Hazel Helena, BSc ACA *1984;* ICG Electronics, 12 Second Drove Ind Estate, Fengate, PETERBOROUGH, PE1 5XA.

GLADISH, Mr. Angus John, BSc ACA MSI *2004;* 2 Forest Crescent, HARROGATE, NORTH YORKSHIRE, HG2 7EU.

GLADISH, Mrs. Sharon Louise, LLB ACA *1999;* 2 Forest Crescent, HARROGATE, NORTH YORKSHIRE, HG2 7EU.

GLADMAN, Mrs. Heather Fiona, BSc FCA *1992;* 45a Welcomes Road, KENLEY, SURREY, CR8 5HA.

GLADSTONE, Mrs. Alison Jane, BSc ACA *2005;* with Page Kirk LLP, Sherwood House, 7 Gregory Boulevard, NOTTINGHAM, NG7 6LB.

GLADSTONE, Mrs. Carolyn May, BA ACA *2002;* 6a Eliot Hill, LONDON, SE13 7EB.

GLADSTONE-MILLAR, Mrs. Charlotte Jean, BA FCA *1980;* 68 Penny Street, PORTSMOUTH, PO1 2NL.

GLADSTONE-MILLAR, Mr. Keith, BA FCA *1979;* 68 Penny Street, PORTSMOUTH, PO1 2NL.

GLADWELL, Mr. David Julian, BSc ACA *1995;* 5 Brookway, LONDON, SE3 9BJ.

GLADWELL, Mr. Eric Raymond, BSc FCA *1991;* FIL Investment Management Limited, 25 Cannon Street, LONDON, EC4 5TA.

GLADWELL, Mrs. Katharyn Jane, BA ACA *1999;* 5 Brookway, Blackheath, LONDON, SE3 9BJ.

GLADWIN, Mr. Andrew, BA ACA *1992;* Briarfield, 3 Sandy Lane, Dobcross, OLDHAM, OL3 5AG.

GLADWIN, Mr. John Leighton, FCA *1967;* Gladwin Associates Ltd, 4 Manor Close, Prestwood, GREAT MISSENDEN, BUCKINGHAMSHIRE, HP16 0PT.

GLADWIN, Mrs. Natalie Jayne, BSc ACA *2007;* 13 Marsh Way, BROMSGROVE, WORCESTERSHIRE, B61 0JD.

•GLADWIN, Miss. Pamela, ACA *1994;* (Tax Fac), PM&G Limited, Mainwood Farm, Kneesall, NEWARK, NOTTINGHAMSHIRE, NG22 0AH.

GLADWYN, Mr. David Andrew, FCA *1980;* 16 Frensham Grove, Horton Bank Top, BRADFORD, BD7 4AN.

GLAGOW, Ms. Susan Yvonne, ACA *1986;* 2900 Jazz Street, ROUND ROCK, TX 78664, UNITED STATES.

GLAISTER, Mr. Stephen Andrew, BA ACA *1996;* 15 Belah Crescent, CARLISLE, CA3 9TX.

GLANCEY, Mr. Michael Clement John, BA ACA *1987;* 2200 Laurens Road, GREENVILLE, SC 29607, UNITED STATES.

GLANCEY, Mr. Peter John, BSc ACA *1989;* Standard Bank Plc, 20 Gresham Street, LONDON, EC2V 7JE.

GLANCY, Mrs. Amanda Jane, BA ACA *1996;* R E A Services, First Floor, 32-36 Great Portland Street, LONDON, W1W 8QX.

GLANCY, Mr. Michael Paul, BA FCA *1987;* with Grant Thornton UK LLP, 4 Hardman Square, Spinningfields, MANCHESTER, M3 3EB.

GLANCY, Mr. William James, MMath ACA *2005;* 3 Les Cyclamens, Green Road, ST CLEMENT, JE2 6QA.

GLANFIELD, Mrs. Bryonie, MSc BSc ACA *1987;* Weston House, Milcote Road, Welford On Avon, STRATFORD-UPON-AVON, CV37 8EH.

GLANFIELD, Mrs. Helen Mary Anne, FCA *1977;* PO Box 1111, GEORGE TOWN, GRAND CAYMAN, KY1-1102, CAYMAN ISLANDS.

GLANFIELD, Mr. Martin James, BSc ACA FRSA *1985;* Weston House, Welford On Avon, STRATFORD-UPON-AVON, CV37 8EH.

GLANVILLE, Mr. Ian, MBA BSc ACA *1992;* The Logic Group Enterprises Ltd Logic House, Waterfront Business Park, FLEET, GU51 3SB.

•GLANVILLE, Mr. James Robert Daniel, BSc FCA *1990;* Mitchell Glanville Limited, 41 Rodney Road, CHELTENHAM, GL50 1HX.

GLANVILLE, Mr. Jonathan Craig, ACA *1996;* 19 Edgcumbe Green, ST AUSTELL, CORNWALL, PL25 5EE.

GLANVILLE, Miss. Laura, BA(Hons) ACA *2010;* Deloitte, Floor 5, Al Fattan Currency House, DIFC, DUBAI, UNITED ARAB EMIRATES.

GLANVILLE, Mrs. Marie Louise, MA BA ACA ACIS *1999;* 28 Bramhall Drive, High General's Wood, Rickleton, WASHINGTON, NE38 9DB.

GLANVILLE, Mr. Paul John, ACA *2000;* J A E Europe Ltd, 200 Fowler Avenue, FARNBOROUGH, GU14 7JP.

GLANVILLE, Mr. Spencer Trerise, BA ACA *1999;* 28 Bramhall Drive, High General's Wood, Rickleton, WASHINGTON, NE38 9DB.

GLANVILLE, Mrs. Victoria Jayne, BSc ACA *1992;* Park Farm, Bramley Road, Silchester, READING, RG7 2LJ.

GLASBY, Mr. John, FCA *1971;* Hawthorns, 9A Eaton Road, Cressington Park, LIVERPOOL, L19 0PN.

GLASBY, Mr. John Peter, ACA *2005;* 28 Cornel Close, WITHAM, CM8 2XH.

•GLASER, Mrs. Elizabeth Jane, BA ACA *1992;* Liz Glaser, Rookery, Pitney, LANGPORT, SOMERSET, TA10 9AS.

GLASER, Mr. Kenneth Morris, FCA *1968;* 4 Drayton Rise, BEXHILL-ON-SEA, EAST SUSSEX, TN39 3TH. (Life Member)

GLASGOW, Mr. Charles Lindsay, FCA *1967;* 22 Irvine Crescent, ST ANDREWS, FIFE, KY16 8LG.

GLASGOW, Miss. Kimberley Jaine, BSc(Econ) ACA *2010;* Grant Sellers Bank Court, 12a Manor Road, VERWOOD, DORSET, BH31 6DY.

•GLASMAN, Mr. Leslie, BSc FCA *1978;* (Tax Fac), Johnstone Howell & Co, Fairfield House, 104 Whitby Road, ELLESMERE PORT, CHESHIRE, CH65 0AB.

GLASMAN, Mr. Mark, BSc ACA *1983;* (Tax Fac), 87 Brookside, East Barnet, BARNET, EN4 8TS.

•GLASNER, Mr. Jonathan David, BSc FCA *1981;* (Tax Fac), Jon Glasner Limited, 21 Bedford Square, LONDON, WC1B 3HH.

GLASS, Mr. Andrew Michael, FCA *1975;* The Brainwave Centre Ltd, Huntworth Gate, Huntworth, BRIDGWATER, SOMERSET, TA6 6LQ.

GLASS, Mr. Bernard Beverley Wills, MA FCA *1978;* 31 Highbury Hill, Highbury, LONDON, N5 1SU.

GLASS, Mr. Blair Richard, BA ACA *1991;* 6/214 Sydney Street, WILLOUGHBY, NSW 2068, AUSTRALIA.

GLASS, Mrs. Clair, BA ACA *1997;* 6 Swallow Drive, Kelsall, TARPORLEY, CHESHIRE, CW6 0GD.

•GLASS, Mr. Colin, BSc(Econ) FCA *1971;* Winburn Glass Norfolk, Convention House, St. Mary's Street, LEEDS, LS9 7DP. See also TMC Accountancy Limited

GLASS, Mr. David, ACA *2011;* 5 Parksway, Prestwich, MANCHESTER, M25 0JE.

GLASS, Mrs. Hannah Joy, BSc ACA *2007;* Flat 8 Merillion Court, 2 Sunbury Gardens, LONDON, NW7 3GJ.

•GLASS, Miss. Jenny Louise, BSc ACA *1993;* (Tax Fac), J L Glass Ltd, Trafalgar House, Trafalgar Wharf, 223 Southampton Road, PORTSMOUTH, PO6 4PY.

GLASS, Mr. Jonathan Douglas, BSc ACA *1991;* 3 Palmerston Close, Royal Earlswood Park, REDHILL, SURREY, RH1 6TQ.

•GLASS, Mr. Julian Mark, LLB FCA *2001;* with FTI Forensic Accounting Limited, 322 High Holborn, LONDON, WC1V 7PB.

GLASS, Mrs. Katie Elizabeth, BSc ACA *2002;* 171 Queens Road, BUCKHURST HILL, ESSEX, IG9 5AZ.

GLASS, Mr. Malcolm Rae, FCA *1949;* 69 Merrowdown Country Club, Private Bag XII, BRYANSTON, GAUTENG, 2021, SOUTH AFRICA. (Life Member)

GLASS, Mr. Michael Stuart, BSc ACA *1987;* Natpoint Ltd, Edgware House, 389 Burnt Oak Broadway, EDGWARE, MIDDLESEX, HA8 5TX.

GLASS, Miss. Phillipa, BSc ACA *2003;* 26 Aragon Avenue, GLENDOWIE 1071, AUCKLAND, NEW ZEALAND.

GLASS, Miss. Rebecca Kathryn, BA ACA *2003;* 6 Kingsclere Drive, Bishops Cleeve, CHELTENHAM, GLOUCESTERSHIRE, GL52 8TG.

GLASS, Mr. Robert Jonathan, BSc(Hons) ACA *2010;* 86 Storks Road, LONDON, SE16 4DP.

GLASS, Mr. Russell Mark, BA ACA *1998;* Tui Travel Plc, Tui Travel House, Crawley Business Quarter, Fleming Way, CRAWLEY, WEST SUSSEX RH10 9QL.

GLASS, Mr. Simon Jeremy, BSc ACA *1987;* Mimosa House, 42 Ravenswood Avenue, CROWTHORNE, BERKSHIRE, RG45 6AY.

•GLASSCOCK, Mr. Ian William, FCA *1970;* 12 Harding Road, ABINGDON, OXFORDSHIRE, OX14 1SJ.

GLASSCOCK, Mr. Malcolm John, BSc FCA *1972;* 10 Little Robhurst, High Halden, ASHFORD, KENT, TN26 3NG.

GLASSE, Mr. John James Maxwell, DL FCA *1956;* The Old Rectory, Church End, Milton Bryan, MILTON KEYNES, MK17 9HR. (Life Member)

•GLASSMAN, Mr. David, FCA *1975;* (Tax Fac), Glassman & Company, 8 Holywell Hill, ST. ALBANS, HERTFORDSHIRE, AL1 1BZ. See also Glassman & Company Limited

GLASSMAN, Mr. David Michael, MBA FCA CMC *1968;* 1 Witney Close, PINNER, HA5 4UR.

GLASSOCK, Mr. Brian Sydney, FCA *1961;* 9 Regis Avenue, Aldwick Bay Estate, BOGNOR REGIS, WEST SUSSEX, PO21 4HQ. (Life Member)

GLASSOCK, Mr. Stephen Michael, BA FCA *1989;* 19 Osborne Road, LYTHAM ST. ANNES, FY8 1HS.

GLASSON, Mr. Christopher, BA ACA *2006;* 15 Elphinstone Street, LONDON, N5 1BS.
GLASSON, Mr. Christopher James, FCA *1976;* (Tax Fac), 91 Burbage Road, Dulwich, LONDON, SE24 9HD.
GLASSON, Mr. Peter, FCA *1963;* Danes Lye, Bratton, WESTBURY, BA13 4TB. (Life Member)
GLASSON, Mr. Richard Paul, BA ACA *1994;* Gyro International Ltd, 3rd Floor, The Chambers, Chelsea Harbour, LONDON, SW10 0XF.
GLASSPOOL, Mr. David Mark Payler, BSc ACA *1989;* SEB Enskilda, 2 Cannon Street, LONDON, EC4M 6XX.
GLASSPOOL, Mr. Richard Damien, BA FCA *1983;* 4 Broad Reach, The Embankment, BEDFORD, MK40 3PB.
GLASTONBURY, Mr. Howard Damian, BA ACA *1996;* 79 Lancer Place, WEBSTER, NY 14580, UNITED STATES.
GLATTER, Mrs. Helen, BSc FCA *1988;* (Tax Fac), 15a Stevenson Crescent, Lower Parkstone, POOLE, BH14 9NU.
•GLATTER, Mr. Robert, FCA FIIA *1960;* R G Consultancy, 12 York Gate, Regent's Park, LONDON, NW1 4QS.
GLAUM, Miss. Susan, BSc ACA *1991;* Worshipful Company of Goldsmiths Goldsmiths Hall, 13 Foster Lane, LONDON, EC2V 6BN.
•GLAVANIS, Mr. Christos Stergios, BSc FCA *1979;* Ernst & Young, 11Klm National Road, Athens-Lamia, Metamorphosi, 14451 ATHENS, GREECE.
GLAYSHER, Mr. Owen William, BA(Hons) ACA *2003;* 11 Longmead, LISS, HAMPSHIRE, GU33 7JX.
GLAZEBROOK, Mr. Michael, BSc ACA *1985;* 15 Lichfield Road, Kew, RICHMOND, TW9 3JR.
GLAZER, Mr. Donald, BA FCA *1961;* 8 Darnhills, Watford Road, RADLETT, WD7 8LQ. (Life Member)
GLAZER, Mr. Max, BSc ACA *2011;* 21 Silverbirch Walk, Maitland Park Road, LONDON, NW3 2HH.
•GLAZER, Mr. Robert David, BA FCA *1987;* Ripe LLP, 9a Burroughs Gardens, LONDON, NW4 4AU.
•GLAZIER, Mr. Alan, FCA *1974;* (Tax Fac), Alan Glazier & Co, 36 Upton Road, Claughton, BIRKENHEAD, MERSEYSIDE, CH41 0DF.
•GLAZIER, Mr. Christopher John, FCA *1983;* PricewaterhouseCoopers LLP, 1 Embankment Place, LONDON, WC2N 6RH. See also PricewaterhouseCoopers
GLAZZARD, Mr. Adam Matthew, BA ACA *2005;* 59a Gerald Road, STOURBRIDGE, WEST MIDLANDS, DY8 4SA.
GLAZZARD, Mrs. Sarah Jane, BA ACA *1997;* 2432 Caledonia Avenue, NORTH VANCOUVER V7G 1T9, BC, CANADA.
•GLEADEN, Mr. Alan Nigel, BEng FCA *1994;* 11 Northwick Crescent, SOLIHULL, B91 3TU.
GLEADEN, Mr. Alan William, BSc FCA *1979;* 11 Northwick Crescent, SOLIHULL, B91 3TU. (Life Member)
GLEADEN, Mr. Simon James, BSc FCA ATII *1990;* 26 Wollaton Rise, RETFORD, NOTTINGHAMSHIRE, DN22 7WT.
GLEADLE, Dr. Marie Pauline Rachel, BA ACA *1985;* Hill View House, Cokes Lane, CHALFONT ST.GILES, HP8 4TA.
GLEADLE, Mr. Stephen Derrick, BSc ACA *1983;* Hill View House, Cokes Lane, CHALFONT ST. GILES, BUCKINGHAMSHIRE, HP8 4TA.
GLEAVE, Mr. David Geraint, BSc ACA *2006;* (Tax Fac), 18 Wood Street, Wootton Bassett, SWINDON, SN4 7BD.
•GLEAVE, Mr. James John, BA FCA *1982;* Manor Garden, New Street, HENLEY-ON-THAMES, OXFORDSHIRE, RG9 2NH.
GLEAVE, Mr. Peter, FCA *1966;* Semper House, Bryning, Wrea Green, PRESTON, PR4 3PP. (Life Member)
GLEAVE, Mrs. Rebecca Clare, BA ACA *2009;* 54 The Sidings, DARWEN, LANCASHIRE, BB3 2BD.
GLEAVE, Mr. Simon John Edward, ACA *1992;* KPMG, 8/F Prince's Building, 10 Chater Road, CENTRAL, HONG KONG ISLAND, HONG KONG SAR.
GLEBOVA, Miss. Natalia, ACA *2010;* 4 Pegasus St. Apt 1, 1087 NICOSIA, CYPRUS.
GLEDHILL, Mr. Andrew Richard, BA ACA *1991;* Hill View, 14 South Royde Avenue, Skircoat Green, HALIFAX, HX3 0BL.
GLEDHILL, Mr. Ben Quentin, MA ACA *2000;* ABN AMRO, 38/F Cheung Kong Centre, 2 Queens Road, CENTRAL, HONG KONG ISLAND, HONG KONG SAR.
GLEDHILL, Mr. Christopher, BSc FCA *1973;* 6 Rainsborough Chase, Cox Green, MAIDENHEAD, SL6 3BL. (Life Member)
GLEDHILL, Miss. Claire Louise, ACA *2009;* The Glass House, 40 Malden Road, LONDON, NW5 3HH.
GLEDHILL, Miss. Gemma Louise, ACA *2008;* with BDO LLP, 55 Baker Street, LONDON, W1U 7EU.
GLEDHILL, Mrs. Jennifer, BSc ACA *1997;* 10 Messing Green, Messing, COLCHESTER, CO5 9GD.
GLEDHILL, Mr. Jeremy, FCA *1980;* 9 Black Fan Close, ENFIELD, EN2 0RL.
•GLEDHILL, Mr. Jeremy Lee, BA FCA *1996;* with KPMG LLP, 1 The Embankment, Neville Street, LEEDS, LS1 4DW.
GLEDHILL, Mr. John David, FCA *1975;* Woodford Consulting Ltd, 87-93 Westbourne Grove, LONDON, W2 4UL.
GLEDHILL, Mrs. Louise Marie Veronique, BA ACA *1998;* 66 Dunsford Close, SWINDON, SN1 4PW.
GLEDHILL, Mr. Mark, ACA *1992;* 39 New Hey Road, HUDDERSFIELD, HD3 4AL.
•GLEDHILL, Mr. Michael, FCA *1969;* Michael Gledhill, New Court Cottage, Whitsbury, FORDINGBRIDGE, SP6 3QB.
GLEDHILL, Mr. Peter James, BA(Hons) FCA *1978;* with Merchant & Co., 84 Uxbridge Road, West Ealing, LONDON, W13 8RA.
•GLEDHILL, Mr. Richard John, MA ACA *1982;* PricewaterhouseCoopers LLP, 7 More London Riverside, LONDON, SE1 2RT. See also PricewaterhouseCoopers
GLEDHILL, Miss. Sarah Louise, BSc ACA *2003;* 75 Whitton Road, TWICKENHAM, TW1 1BT.
GLEDHILL, Mr. Simon Roger, FCA MBA *1981;* Dunridge House, West Street, Misson, DONCASTER, DN10 6DX.
GLEDHILL, Mr. Stephen, BA FCA *1978;* 18 Knighton Drive, Four Oaks, SUTTON COLDFIELD, WEST MIDLANDS, B74 4QP.
GLEDHILL, Mr. Stuart David, BSc ACA *2005;* 420 Lynmouth Avenue, MORDEN, SURREY, SM4 4RU.
GLEDSON, Mr. James Neil, FCA *1962;* Village House, Tythby Road, Cropwell Butler, NOTTINGHAM, NG12 3AA.
GLEED, Mr. David Kenneth, MA ACA *1995;* 165 Bush Road, Cuxton, ROCHESTER, KENT, ME2 1HA.
GLEED, Mrs. Laura Emily, BA ACA *2006;* 3 Ives Road, HERTFORD, SG14 3AU.
GLEED, Mr. Mark Francis Nevill, BSc ACA *1992;* Cobham Plc, Brook Road, WIMBORNE, DORSET, BH21 2BJ.
•GLEED, Mr. Steven Whatley Nevill, BSc ACA *1997;* The Studio, Horton Road, Ashley Heath, RINGWOOD, BH24 2EE.
•GLEEK, Mr. David Jeffrey, FCA *1973;* Gleek Cadman Ross LLP, Credcoll House, 96 Marsh Lane, LEEDS, LS9 8SR. See also Gleek Cadman Ross Limited
GLEESON, Miss. Alayne Juliana, BA ACA *2005;* 24 rue Notre Dame, L-2240 LUXEMBOURG, LUXEMBOURG.
GLEESON, Mr. Anthony Darlow, FCA *1975;* 23 Creechberry Orchard, TAUNTON, SOMERSET, TA1 2EX.
GLEESON, Ms. Frances Mary, BA ACA *1996;* Aveva Solutions Ltd, Madingley Road, CAMBRIDGE, CB3 0HB.
GLEESON, Miss. Helene Elizabeth Claire, MMath(Hons) ACA *2010;* 23 Mill Lane, Hockwold, THETFORD, NORFOLK, IP26 4LR.
GLEESON, Mr. Jason John, BSc ACA *1997;* 500 East Pratt Street, Suite 1250, BALTIMORE, MD 21202, UNITED STATES.
GLEESON, Mr. Nicholas Robert, BSc ACA *1985;* 56 Sea Lane, Goring-by-Sea, WORTHING, BN12 4PY.
GLEESON, Mr. Ronan Joseph, BBLS ACA *2004;* 123 Hadley Road, BARNET, HERTFORDSHIRE, EN5 5QN.
GLEESON, Mrs. Sarah, BA ACA *1993;* Westgate Leisure Centre, Via Ravenna, CHICHESTER, WEST SUSSEX, PO19 1RJ.
•GLEGHORN, Mr. Grant Courtney, FCA *1985;* MacIntyre Hudson LLP, Euro House, 1394 High Road, Whetstone, LONDON, N20 9YZ.
GLEGHORN, Mr. Roger, ACA *1983;* 1 Brampton Close, Barton Seagrave, KETTERING, NORTHAMPTONSHIRE, NN15 6QQ.
GLEICH, Mr. Martin Francis, BSc ACA *1998;* 56 Chepstow Road, LONDON, W2 5BE.
GLEICHER, Mr. Lee Howard, BSc ACA *2010;* 54 Tryfan Close, ILFORD, ESSEX, IG4 5JY.
GLEIG, Miss. Joanne, BA ACA *1986;* 87 Cowlishaw Road, SHEFFIELD, S11 8XG.
•GLEN, Mr. Alan, BSc FCA *1992;* Deloitte Touche Tohmatsu, 35/F One Pacific Place, 88 Queensway, CENTRAL, HONG KONG ISLAND, HONG KONG SAR.
GLEN, Mr. Paul Edward, BSc FCA *1989;* Cardiff Pinnacle Insurance Management Services Plc, Pinnacle House Stangate Crescent, BOREHAMWOOD, HERTFORDSHIRE, WD6 2XX.
GLEN, Mr. Robert John, MA ACA MCT *1989;* 5 High Meadows, Wilsden, BRADFORD, WEST YORKSHIRE, BD15 0HN.
GLEN, Miss. Tara Louise Owen, BA ACA *1997;* E P Barrus Ltd, Granville Way, BICESTER, OXFORDSHIRE, OX26 4UR.
GLENCAIRN-CAMPBELL, Mr. Diarmid Cecil Brinton, FCA *1969;* (Tax Fac), Warridge Lodge Farm, Timberhonger Lane, BROMSGROVE, B61 9DW.
GLENCROSS, Mr. Arthur John, MA ACA *1980;* Calculus Capital Ltd, 104 Park Street, LONDON, W1K 6NF.
GLENCROSS, Mr. Colin James, ACA *1990;* 24 Merrow Woods, GUILDFORD, GU1 2LH.
•GLENCROSS, Mr. Roger Edmund, FCA *1966;* Alfred Neill & Co, 34 Hollington Crescent, NEW MALDEN, KT3 6RR.
GLENCROSS, Mrs. Sarah Elizabeth, BA ACA *1999;* 57 Amyand Park Road, TWICKENHAM, TW1 3HG.
GLENCROSS, Mr. Steven Martin, BA FCA *1979;* 24 St. Botolphs Road, SEVENOAKS, TN13 3AQ.
GLENDAY, Mr. Douglas Alexander, BSc(Hons) ACA *2000;* Johnson Matthey Plc, 5th Floor, 25 Farringdon Street, LONDON, EC4A 4AB.
GLENDENNING, Mr. Paul, BA(Hons) ACA *2001;* 24 Rosebery Crescent, Jesmond Vale, NEWCASTLE UPON TYNE, NE2 1EU.
GLENDINNING, Miss. Allison Claire, BA ACA *1996;* The Manor House Tumbling Hill, Carleton, PONTEFRACT, WEST YORKSHIRE, WF8 3SA.
GLENDINNING, Mr. Andrew, BSc FCA *1980;* TXO plc3rd Floor, 22 Newman Street, LONDON, W1T 1PH.
GLENDINNING, Mr. Andrew Edward, BA ACA *1998;* Jansen-Cilag Ltd, 50-100 Holmers Farm Way, HIGH WYCOMBE, BUCKINGHAMSHIRE, HP12 4EG.
•GLENDINNING, Mr. Simon Adrian, ACA *2005;* Unit 4 Brunel Buildings, Brunel Road, NEWTON ABBOT, DEVON, TQ12 4PB.
GLENISTER, Mr. John Frederick, FCA *1949;* 16 Hyde Lane, Danbury, CHELMSFORD, CM3 4QS. (Life Member)
•GLENISTER, Mr. Julian Reginald, FCA *1984;* Spain Brothers & Co, 29 Manor Road, FOLKESTONE, KENT, CT20 2SE.
•GLENISTER, Mrs. Lorna Alison, FCA *1981;* Lorna Glenister Limited, 5 The Square, BAGSHOT, SURREY, GU19 5AX.
GLENISTER, Mr. Nigel Edward, BSc(Econ) ACA *1995;* The Spinney, Church Lane, Lacey Green, PRINCES RISBOROUGH, HP27 0QX.
GLENN, Miss. Amanda Jane, ACA *1989;* c/o Nicholas Line, Flight Operations, FC 1048, PO Box 92, DUBAI, UNITED ARAB EMIRATES.
GLENN, Mr. Anthony Morgan, FCA *1968;* Soumoulou, California Lane, Bushey Heath, BUSHEY, WD23 1EP.
GLENN, Mr. Cecil, FCA *1951;* Little Marshall Green Farm, Witton-le-Wear, BISHOP AUCKLAND, DL14 0BQ. (Life Member)
GLENN, Mr. Jonathan Mark, MA ACA *2005;* Mark Royal House, D O E Water Service, 70-74 Donegall Street, BELFAST, BT1 2GU.
GLENN, Mr. Jonathan Martin, BA ACA *1997;* 13 Woodside Road, Bricket Wood, ST. ALBANS, HERTFORDSHIRE, AL2 3QL.
GLENN, Mr. Malcolm, FCA *1961;* Hale Barn, The Hale, Wendover, AYLESBURY, HP22 6QR. (Life Member)
GLENN, Miss. Rhoda Dorothy, ACA *2004;* 82c Ladywell, OAKHAM, LEICESTERSHIRE, LE15 6DB.
GLENN, Mrs. Susan Elizabeth, BA ACA *1984;* Kairidale, 348 Kairangi Road, RD 3, CAMBRIDGE 3495, NEW ZEALAND.
GLENN, Mr. Timothy John, ACA *2008;* 88A Argyle Street, CAMBRIDGE, CB1 3LS.
GLENNERSTER, Mrs. Samantha Clare, BSc(Hons) ACA PGCE *2000;* 10 Springlines, Wanborough, SWINDON, SN4 0ES.
GLENNISTER, Mr. David, BA ACA *2006;* 38 Churchfield Road, REIGATE, RH2 9RH.
GLENNON, Mr. Andrew Paul, BA ACA *1988;* 13 Broadway, Tranmere Park, LEEDS, LS20 8JU.
GLENNON, Miss. Eileen, BBS ACA *2011;* Flat A-b, 165 Latchmere Road, LONDON, SW11 2JZ.
GLENNON, Ms. Geraldine, BA ACA *1995;* 53 Leander Road, LONDON, SW2 2NB.
GLENNON, Mr. Liam Alexander, BSc ACIB ACA CF *1999;* 14 Beech Crescent, Poynton, STOCKPORT, SK12 1AW.
GLENNON, Ms. Nora Teresa, BCom ACA *1995;* Pier Road, Menlo, GALWAY, COUNTY GALWAY, IRELAND.
GLENNON, Mr. Stephen Matthew, BEng ACA *1992;* 168 Melton Road, Stanton-On-The-Wolds, Keyworth, NOTTINGHAM, NG12 5BQ.
GLENNY, Mr. Paul Martin, BA ACA *1980;* 541 Formosa Road, GUMDALE, QLD 4154, AUSTRALIA.
GLENNY, Mr. Trevor David, BSc ACA *1997;* 56 Main Road, Middleton Cheney, BANBURY, OX17 2LT.
•GLENTON, Mr. Anthony Arthur Edward, CBE TD DL FCA *1966;* Ryecroft Glenton, 32 Portland Terrace, Jesmond, NEWCASTLE UPON TYNE, NE2 1QP.
GLENTON, Mr. Peter James, ACA *2008;* with Ryecroft Glenton, 32 Portland Terrace, Jesmond, NEWCASTLE UPON TYNE, NE2 1QP.
GLEW, Mr. Christopher, BSc ACA *2011;* 5 Creaton Court, WIGSTON, LEICESTERSHIRE, LE18 3XX.
GLEW, Mr. Ian Robert, BSc ACA *1983;* Hall Farm House, Main Street, Ufford, STAMFORD, PE9 3BH.
GLEW, Mr. Mark Roy, BSc ACA CTA *2003;* 65 Ashurst Road, BARNET, HERTFORDSHIRE, EN4 9LH.
GLEW, Mr. Ramsay Macintyre, BSc ACA *1983;* Diagonal Solutions Ltd Waterside House, Kirkstall Road, LEEDS, LS4 2DD.
GLEW, Mr. Robert, BA ACA *1991;* 4 Wykehurst Cottages, Colwood Lane, Bolney, HAYWARDS HEATH, RH17 5QG.
GLEW, Mr. Steven Peter, BSc FCA *1981;* 22 Firs Walk, Trewin Wood, WELWYN, AL6 0NZ.
GLICHER, Mr. Julian Harvey, FCA *1971;* 75 Eastbury Road, NORTHWOOD, HA6 3AP.
•GLICHER, Mr. Steven Victor, FCA *1987;* Steven Glicher & Co., Eden Point, Three Acres Lane, Cheadle Hulme, CHEADLE, CHESHIRE SK8 6RL.
GLICK, Mrs. Kate Victoria, BA ACA *1995;* Edge Legal Limited, 1 Marylebone High Street, LONDON, W1V 4LZ.
GLICKMAN, Mr. Alan Leslie, FCA *1971;* Unit 101, 4723 Dawson Street, BURNABY V5C0A7, BC, CANADA.
GLICKMAN, Ms. Fiona Jane, BA ACA *1991;* 12 Midmar Drive, EDINBURGH, EH10 6BU.
GLICKMAN, Mr. Paul, MA FCA MBA *1990;* Unit 15F, Laguna Tower, The Residences, Opposite Greenbelt 2, Makati, MANILA PHILIPPINES.
GLICKMAN, Mrs. Sarah Jacqueline Saoirse, BA ACA *1996;* 1 Kermit Road, MAPLEWOOD, NJ 07040, UNITED STATES.
GLICKSMAN, Mr. Stanley Laurence, FCA *1967;* 28 Mulgrave Road, HARROW, HA1 3UG.
•GLIDDON, Mr. Richard William, FCA CTA *1977;* Michael J Dodden & Co, 34 & 38 North Street, BRIDGWATER, TA6 3YD.
•GLITHERO, Miss. Caroline Ellen, BA(Hons) FCA *1987;* Accountancy Consultants East Ltd, 58 North Street, BOURNE, LINCOLNSHIRE, PE10 9AB.
GLITHERO, Mr. Peter Bradley, BSc FCA *1986;* 24 Wellingborough Road, Mears Ashby, NORTHAMPTON, NN6 0DZ.
GLITHERO, Mr. Sean Robert, BA ACA *1998;* 262 Hyde End Road, Spencers Wood, READING, RG7 1DL.
•GLITHEROW, Mrs. Linda Mary, BA FCA ATII *1997;* LMG Taxation & Accountancy, 5 Foreman Way, Kemp Street, Crowland, PETERBOROUGH, PE6 0DJ.
GLITHRO, Mr. Owen, ACA *2011;* 3 Phillimore Road, Emmer Green, READING, RG4 8UR.
GLOBE, Mrs. Julie Ann, BSc ACA *1988;* Plaxton Limited, Plaxton Park, Cayton Low Road, Eastfield, SCARBOROUGH, NORTH YORKSHIRE YO11 3BY.
GLOOR, Mr. Gordon Adolf, FCA *1955;* 12 Athona Court, Godwin Road, Cliftonville, MARGATE, KENT, CT9 2HG. (Life Member)
GLOSSOP, Mr. Brian, FCA *1964;* 39 North Acre, BANSTEAD, SM7 2EG.
GLOSSOP, Miss. Bridgett Anne, FCA *1972;* Millar & Miller Ltd, P O Box 2648, WELLINGTON, NEW ZEALAND.
•GLOSSOP, Mr. David John, BA FCA *1982;* Baker Tilly Tax & Advisory Services LLP, 2 Whitehall Quay, LEEDS, LS1 4HG.
GLOSSOP, Mrs. Elizabeth Helen Margaret, ACA *1989;* 13 Dale CloseTranmere Pk, Guiseley, LEEDS, LS20 8JL.
GLOSTER, Miss. Katie Lynn, ACA *2008;* 57 Merrywood Road, BRISTOL, BS3 1EB.
GLOVER, Mr. Alan Myles, FCA *1965;* 2 Intake Way, HEXHAM, NORTHUMBERLAND, NE46 1RU.
•GLOVER, Mr. Andrew John, BSc FCA *1986;* Ernst & Young LLP, 1 More London Place, LONDON, SE1 2AF. See also Ernst & Young Europe LLP
GLOVER, Miss. Belinda Katherine, BSc ACA *1991;* 2 The Cross, Sibford Gower, BANBURY, OX15 5RP.
GLOVER, Miss. Beverley Jane, MA ACA DChA *1998;* Saffery Champness, Lion House, Red Lion Street, LONDON, WC1R 4GB.
GLOVER, Miss. Caroline Jane, BA FCA *1990;* with Morris & Co (2011) Limited, Chester House, Lloyd Drive, Chesire Oaks Business Park, ELLESMERE PORT, CHESHIRE CH65 9HQ.
GLOVER, Mrs. Caroline Louise, BSc ACA *1987;* 10 Beaumont Grove, SOLIHULL, WEST MIDLANDS, B91 1RP.

•**GLOVER, Mrs. Christine Patricia, MA FCA** *1980;* A.C. Mole & Sons, Stafford House, Blackbrook Park Avenue, TAUNTON, SOMERSET, TA1 2PX.

GLOVER, Mr. Christopher, ACA *2011;* Apt 3110, 10 Navy Wharf Court, TORONTO M5V 3V2, ON, CANADA.

•**GLOVER, Mr. Christopher Gerard, MSc FCA** *1966;* Christopher G Glover, 2 New Road, Cookham, MAIDENHEAD, BERKSHIRE, SL6 9HD.

GLOVER, Mr. Colin Edward, FCA *1964;* Sandy Lodge, Camilla Drive, Westhumble, DORKING, RH5 6BU. (Life Member)

•**GLOVER, Mr. Colin Stephen, FCA** *1969;* Colin Glover & Co, 23 Carlyle Court, Chelsea Harbour, LONDON, SW10 0UQ.

GLOVER, Mr. Craig, ACA *1990;* Waco Ltd Catfoss Airfield, Brandesburton, DRIFFIELD, NORTH HUMBERSIDE, YO25 8EJ.

GLOVER, Mr. David, ACA *1980;* 16 Burdock Close, Killinghall, HARROGATE, NORTH YORKSHIRE, HG3 2WF.

GLOVER, Mr. David Barrie, FCA *1962;* 10 Bourchier Close, SEVENOAKS, TN13 1PD.

GLOVER, Mr. David Fraser, BSc ACA *1985;* Van Line Nina Works, Gelderd Road, LEEDS, LS12 6NA.

GLOVER, Mr. David Hugh Kenneth, FCA *1969;* 1 Hillview Close, Tilehurst, READING, RG31 6YX.

GLOVER, Mr. David Lindsay, BA(Hons) ACA *2004;* Apartment 3A, Warwick Park Road, WARWICK WK 05, BERMUDA.

•**GLOVER, Mr. David Sidney, FCA** *1985;* John Kerr, 369-375 Eaton Road, West Derby, LIVERPOOL, L12 2AH.

GLOVER, Miss. Emily-Jane, ACA *2010;* 41 Pilling Lane, Preesall, POULTON-LE-FYLDE, LANCASHIRE, FY6 0EX.

•**GLOVER, Mrs. Emma Catharine, FCA CTA** *1991;* (Tax Fac), Rowlands, Rowlands House, Portobello Road, Birtley, CHESTER LE STREET, COUNTY DURHAM DH3 2RY.

GLOVER, Mr. Gordon, FCA *1956;* Roseacre, 879 Chester Road, Great Sutton, ELLESMERE PORT, CHESHIRE, CH66 2LP. (Life Member)

GLOVER, Mrs. Heather Marion, BA(Econ) ACA *2000;* Highlands Cholderton Road, Grateley, ANDOVER, SP11 8LH.

GLOVER, Mr. Herbert Michael John, FCA *1968;* South View House, Instow, BIDEFORD, DEVON, EX39 4HX. (Life Member)

GLOVER, Mr. Ian George, BSc ACA *1988;* 83 Hove Park Road, HOVE, EAST SUSSEX, BN3 6LN.

GLOVER, Mr. James Michael, BA(Hons) ACA *2004;* 75 Argento Tower, Mapleton Road, LONDON, SW18 4GB.

GLOVER, Mr. Joel Ralph, ACA *2008;* 5 Abbey Road, BEXLEYHEATH, KENT, DA7 4BD.

GLOVER, Mr. John, BSc ACA *1996;* April Cottage, Park Lane, Hamstead Marshall, NEWBURY, BERKSHIRE, RG20 0HL.

•**GLOVER, Mr. John Charles, FCA** *1957;* John C. Glover, 2 Deepdale, Wilnecote, TAMWORTH, B77 4PD.

GLOVER, Mr. John Derek, FCA *1954;* Western Farm, Harcombe, SIDMOUTH, DEVON, EX10 0PR. (Life Member)

GLOVER, Mr. John Edward, BSc ACA *2006;* Basement flat, 8a Arundel Place, LONDON, N1 1LS.

GLOVER, Mr. John Gerrard, BSc ACA *1984;* 66 The Avenue, WORCESTER PARK, KT4 7HJ.

•**GLOVER, Mr. John Martin, BA FCA** *1967;* (Tax Fac), JGCA Limited, Yew Tree Cottage, Northchapel, PETWORTH, WEST SUSSEX, GU28 9HL.

GLOVER, Mr. John Paul, BA ACA *2003;* B D O Stoy Hayward, 3 Hardman Street, MANCHESTER, M3 3AT.

GLOVER, Mr. John Selwyn, FCA *1960;* Woodlands House, Hareway Lane, Barford, WARWICK, CV35 8DD. (Life Member)

GLOVER, Mrs. Karen Patricia, FCA *1980;* 39 LIONEL GROVE, PENKHULL, STOKE-ON-TRENT, STAFFORDSHIRE, ST4 6RW.

GLOVER, Mr. Kenneth David, FCA *1955;* 31 Eskdale Cl, DEWSBURY, WF12 7PT. (Life Member)

GLOVER, Miss. Kerry, BSc(Hons) ACA *1999;* 146 West 57th Steet, Apt 66D, NEW YORK, NY 10019, UNITED STATES.

GLOVER, Mrs. Kerry Anita, BSc ACA *1997;* 26 Shortcroft, BISHOP'S STORTFORD, CM23 5QY.

•**GLOVER, Mr. Lindsey Richard, FCA** *1974;* (Tax Fac), Accountancy and Tax Solutions Ltd, Unit 2, Hockliffe Business Park, Hockliffe, LEIGHTON BUZZARD, BEDFORDSHIRE LU7 9NB.

GLOVER, Mr. Malcolm Norman, FCA *1954;* 23 Lilley Drive, Kingswood, TADWORTH, SURREY, KT20 6JA. (Life Member)

•①**GLOVER, Mr. Maurice Grisman John, FCA** *1970;* Maurice Glover, 31 Burnaby Gardens, LONDON, W4 3DR.

GLOVER, Mr. Michael, BSc ACA *1998;* Swansea College Tycoch Road, Sketty, SWANSEA, SA2 9EB.

GLOVER, Mr. Michael Paul, ACA *1988;* 12 Coniston Court, Windermere Crescent, Ainsdale, SOUTHPORT, MERSEYSIDE, PR8 3QT.

GLOVER, Mr. Neil Jonathan, BA FCA *1978;* (Tax Fac), 49 Crouch Hall Lane, Redbourn, ST ALBANS, AL3 7EU.

GLOVER, Mrs. Philippa Jane, BSc ACA *2000;* University of Warwick, Gibbet Hill Road, COVENTRY, CV4 7AL.

GLOVER, Mr. Richard Nathan, ACA *2008;* 120 Gatliff Close, Ebury Bridge Road, LONDON, SW1W 8QH.

GLOVER, Mr. Robin William Frank, FCA *1971;* 6 Westerley Close, Warsash, SOUTHAMPTON, SO31 9AX.

GLOVER, Mr. Ronald Anthony, FCA *1959;* Foxgloves, 16 Wyvern Road, SUTTON COLDFIELD, B74 2PT. (Life Member)

GLOVER, Mr. Russell Graham, FCA *1974;* 2502 Eagle Run Drive, WESTON, FL 33327, UNITED STATES.

GLOVER, Mr. Simon Edward, BA FCA *1977;* 21 Letchworth Avenue, CHATHAM, ME4 6NP.

GLOVER, Mr. Simon Shaw, BA ACA *1992;* 16 Warren Drive, Dorridge, SOLIHULL, WEST MIDLANDS, B93 8JY.

GLOVER, Mr. Stephen Charles, BSc FCA *1975;* Flat 4 Littlemere Court, 42 Ashley Road, ALTRINCHAM, CHESHIRE, WA14 2LZ. (Life Member)

GLOVER, Mr. Stephen John, ACA *1979;* 65 Church Walk, Euxton, CHORLEY, PR7 6HL.

GLOVER, Mr. Stuart Darryl, FCA *1974;* 24 Ibstock Road, Ravenstone, COALVILLE, LE67 2AL.

GLOVER, Mr. Thomas William, FCA *1961;* 148 St. Crispin Retirement Village, St. Crispin Drive, Duston, NORTHAMPTON, NN5 4RD. (Life Member)

GLOVER, Mr. Timothy Paul, BCom ACA *1997;* 26 Shortcroft, BISHOP'S STORTFORD, HERTFORDSHIRE, CM23 5QY.

GLOVER, Mrs. Victoria Helen, BSc ACA *2004;* 9 Bousley Rise, Ottershaw, CHERTSEY, SURREY, KT16 0JX.

GLOVER, Mr. William Derrick, FCA *1958;* 21 West End Way, LANCING, BN15 8RL. (Life Member)

GLOYNE, Mrs. Karen, BSc ACA *1994;* 39 Longfield Drive, AMERSHAM, BUCKINGHAMSHIRE, HP6 5HE.

GLOYNE, Mr. Martin Gordon, BA ACA *1990;* 39 Longfield Drive, AMERSHAM, BUCKINGHAMSHIRE, HP6 5HE.

GLUCINA, Miss. Stephanie, ACA CA(NZ) *2009;* 1d Claverton Street, LONDON, SW1V 3AY.

GLUCK, Mr. Maurice Bertram, FCA *1953;* 3 Snells Wood Court, AMERSHAM, HP7 9QT.

GLUSHKO, Mr. Valery Yurievich, ACA *1997;* 8 Fitzclarence House, 175-177, Holland Park Avenue, LONDON, W11 4UL.

GLYDE, Mr. Andrew, BSc(Hons) ACA *2000;* 1 Causeway Fold, Blackshaw Head, HEBDEN BRIDGE, WEST YORKSHIRE, HX7 7JF.

GLYDE, Mr. Brendan Francis William, FCA *1974;* 184 Shoebury Road, SOUTHEND-ON-SEA, SS1 3RQ.

GLYDE, Mr. Duncan Robert Thomas, BA ACA *1990;* 10 Rimside Gardens, Longframlington, MORPETH, NE65 8DE.

GLYDE, Mrs. Sarah Louise, BSc ACA ATII *1999;* Provident Financial Plc, Sunbridge Road, BRADFORD, WEST YORKSHIRE, BD1 2LQ.

GLYN, Mr. Malcolm Adam, BA ACA *1988;* 1 Pagoda Avenue, RICHMOND, TW9 2HQ.

GLYN, Mr. Michael, FCA *1965;* The Palms, 1c Shelley Close, EDGWARE, HA8 8DX.

•**GLYN DAVIES, Mr. Hewitt Murray, FCA** *1971;* U B S Warburg, 1-2 Finsbury Avenue, LONDON, EC2M 2PP.

GLYN JONES, Mrs. Vanessa Elizabeth, FCA *1970;* Torrley House, Stockland, HONITON, DEVON, EX14 9DQ.

•**GLYN-SMITH, Mr. Philip Anthony, BA FCA** *1994;* (Tax Fac), HSP Tax Ltd, Whiteacres, Cambridge Road, Whetstone, LEICESTER, LE8 6ZG. See also HSP Taxation Compliance Limited

GLYNN, Mr. Andrew David, BA ACA *1995;* 605-518 W 14th Ave, VANCOUVER V5Z 4N5, BC, CANADA.

GLYNN, Mr. Anthony David, BSc FCA *1989;* 24 Valley Road, Bramhall, STOCKPORT, SK7 2NN.

GLYNN, Mr. Damian Philip, BA(Hons) FCA FCILA *1990;* 189 Selly Oak Road, Kings Norton, BIRMINGHAM, B30 1HR.

•**GLYNN, Mrs. Jayne Alison, BSc ACA** *1989;* J Glynn & Associates Ltd, 24 Valley Road, Bramhall, STOCKPORT, SK7 2NN.

GLYNN, Mrs. Judith, BA(Hons) FCA FCILA *1973;* 6 Windsor Road, Prestwich, MANCHESTER, M25 0DZ.

GLYNN, Mr. Matthew, BA(Hons) ACA *2011;* with KPMG LLP, St. Nicholas House, 31 Park Row, NOTTINGHAM, NG1 6FQ.

•**GLYNN, Mr. Michael Boyde, FCA** *1973;* (Tax Fac), 5 Upper Glen Road, ST. LEONARDS-ON-SEA, EAST SUSSEX, TN37 7AX.

GLYNN, Mr. Paul James, BSc ACA *2001;* 69 Eastwood Road, Bramley, GUILDFORD, GU5 0DX.

GLYNN, Mr. Simon Graham, BSc ACA *1992;* 18 Wentworth House, Irving Mews, Alwyne Road, LONDON, N1 2FP.

GLYNNE, Mr. Anthony Stuart, FCA *1967;* 121 Alwoodley Lane, LEEDS, LS17 7PN.

GO, Mr. Chi Keung Jimmy, ACA *2007;* Flat E, 18/F, Fu Tien Mansion, Horizon Gardens, 13 Taikoo Wan Road, TAIKOO SHING HONG KONG SAR.

GO, Mr. Paul Kai Lung, BSc FCA *1989;* with Ernst & Young, 62/F, One Island East, 18 Westlands Road, QUARRY BAY, HONG KONG ISLAND HONG KONG SAR.

GOAD, Mr. Christopher Mark, ACA *2009;* Stephenson Smart & Co, 22-26 King Street, KING'S LYNN, NORFOLK, PE30 1HJ.

•**GOAD, Mr. Ian Richard, ACA FMAAT** *2008;* (Tax Fac), IMG, The Studio, 1 Wilkins Way, BEXHILL-ON-SEA, EAST SUSSEX, TN40 2RD.

GOAD, Mr. Thomas Peter, BSc ACA *2005;* with Ernst & Young, 41 Shortland Street, PO Box2146, AUCKLAND 1140, NEW ZEALAND.

GOADBY, Mr. Roger, FCA *1962;* Clevelands, Elm Tree Drive, HINCKLEY, LE10 2TX. (Life Member)

•**GOALEN, Mr. Ian Michael, BCom FCA** *1983;* KPMG LLP, St. James's Square, MANCHESTER, M2 6DS. See also KPMG Europe LLP, KPMG Audit plc

GOAMAN, Mr. Darren Paul, BSc ACA *2001;* 11 Edgar Road, SOUTH CROYDON, SURREY, CR2 0NJ.

•**GOAR, Mr. David Gustave, ACA** *1987;* Rawlinson & Hunter Limited, Trafalgar Court, 3rd Floor, West Wing, St Peter Port, GUERNSEY GY1 2JA.

•**GOATCHER, Mr. James, FCA** *1981;* (Tax Fac), Goatcher Chandler Limited, 10 Overcliffe, GRAVESEND, KENT, DA11 0EF.

•**GOATCHER, Mr. Richard John, FCA** *1969;* 8 Hornchurch Hill, WHYTELEAFE, SURREY, CR3 0DA.

GOATE, Mr. Christopher George Cubitt, FCA *1959;* 7 Bourne Banks, 20 Branksome Wood Road, BOURNEMOUTH, BH4 9JX.

GOATE, Mr. David Anthony, FCA *1960;* Furze Edge, Stodmarsh Road, CANTERBURY, CT3 4AG. (Life Member)

GOATE, Mr. Roland Edward, FCA *1934;* Villa 98 Peninsular Gardens, 56 Miller St., KIPPA RING, QLD 4021, AUSTRALIA. (Life Member)

•**GOATER, Mr. Edward Hugh, FCA** *1970;* E H Goater, 71 Burtons Road, Hampton Hill, HAMPTON, MIDDLESEX, TW12 1DE.

GOATER, Mr. Robert Alan, FCA *1973;* 6 Merrydown Lane, Chineham, BASINGSTOKE, RG24 8LU.

GOATLEY, Mr. Richard John, LLB ACA *1999;* Middlesex County Cricket Club, Marylebone Cricket Club, Lords Cricket Ground, St. Johns Wood Road, LONDON, NW8 8QN.

GOATMAN, Mr. Clive Edwin Charles, BA FCA *1974;* 4 Hawthorn Road West, NEWCASTLE UPON TYNE, NE3 4DN.

GOBAT, Mr. Anthony Theodore, FCA *1964;* 24 Milbourne Lane, ESHER, SURREY, KT10 9EA.

GOBEY, Mr. John Mayoss, FCA *1952;* Flat 21 Chorleywood Lodge, Rickmansworth Road, Chorleywood, RICKMANSWORTH, HERTFORDSHIRE, WD3 5BY. (Life Member)

GOBIRAJ, Mr. Manickavasagar, ACA *1991;* 11 Turnpike Link, Park Hill, CROYDON, CR0 5NT.

GOBRAN, Mrs. Helen Elizabeth, BSc(Hons) ACA *2002;* 9 Wales Lane, Barton under Needwood, BURTON-ON-TRENT, STAFFORDSHIRE, DE13 8JF.

GOCKELER, Mr. Martin, ACA *1993;* 2001 Topanga Court, FORT COLLINS, CO 80525, UNITED STATES.

GODALL, Mr. Ijaz, MSc ACA *1979;* 49 Gloucester Lea, Warfield, BRACKNELL, RG42 3XQ.

GODAUSKI, Ms. Solveig Josefine, BA ACA *2004;* 38 Bearslane Close, Totton, SOUTHAMPTON, SO40 2FF.

•**GODBEE, Mr. David Keith, BSc ACA** *1997;* PricewaterhouseCoopers LLP, 7 More London Riverside, LONDON, SE1 2RT. See also PricewaterhouseCoopers

GODBEE, Mr. Keith Andrew, BSc(Econ) FCA *1971;* Trees Cottage, Blackmore, INGATESTONE, CM4 0QX.

GODBEE, Mr. Michael Ian, BSc FCA *1969;* 99 The Avenue, LONDON, W13 8JT. (Life Member)

GODBEHERE, Mr. Anthony Keith, FCA *1962;* 7 Elmdene Close, The Elms Torksey, LINCOLN, LN1 2EU.

GODBER, Mr. Christopher Harold Frederick, BA FCA *1966;* Goldmine House, 26 Southbank, Great Budworth, NORTHWICH, CW9 6HG. (Life Member)

GODBER, Mr. Jonathan Mark, BEng ACA *1999;* Meadow View, 107 Dale Road, Swanland, NORTH FERRIBY, HU14 3QH.

•**GODBER, Mrs. Lorraine, BSc ACA** *2003;* Insite Corporate Management Limited, DeVirgo House, Valepits Road, Garretts Green, BIRMINGHAM, B33 0TD.

GODBER, Mr. Richard Anthony, BA FCA *1977;* Flat 67, Defoe House, Barbican, LONDON, EC2Y 8DN.

GODBOLD, Miss. Alison Jill, BA(Hons) ACA *2001;* The Expro Group, Morton Peto Road, GREAT YARMOUTH, NORFOLK, NR31 0LT.

GODBOLD, Mr. James Matthew, ACA *2008;* Alize, Shootersway Lane, BERKHAMSTED, HERTFORDSHIRE, HP4 3NP.

GODBOLD, Miss. Sarah Louise, BSc ACA *2007;* 32 Southampton Drive, Cressington Heath, LIVERPOOL, L19 2HE.

GODBOLD, Mr. Tony Keith, BSc FCA *1980;* National Bank of Greece SA, 75 King William Street, LONDON, EC4N 7BE.

GODDARD, Mrs. Anda, ACA *2009;* Flat 41/A West Kensington Mansions, Beaumont Crescent, LONDON, W14 9PF.

•**GODDARD, Mr. Andrew Keith, BA ACA** *1993;* Forshaws, Railex Business Centre, Crossens Way, Marine Drive, SOUTHPORT, MERSEYSIDE PR9 9LY.

GODDARD, Mr. Anthony Christopher, BA FCA *1974;* 2 Capernway Cottages, Gibbs Brook Lane, OXTED, RH8 9NX.

GODDARD, Mr. Anthony Gordon, BSc FCA *1977;* Clovelly, Lower Road, Charlton-All-Saints, SALISBURY, SP5 4HQ.

GODDARD, Mr. Anthony Michael, FCA *1962;* (Tax Fac), Calder, Grove Road, WANTAGE, OX12 7BY. (Life Member)

GODDARD, Mr. Christopher Michael, BA ACA *1999;* Ground Floor Flat, 6 Corney Road, Chiswick, LONDON, W4 2RA.

GODDARD, Mr. Colin Edward, BA FCA *1973;* 26 Petworth Avenue, Goring-by-Sea, WORTHING, BN12 4QL.

GODDARD, Mr. David Arthur, FCA *1973;* 7 Tudor Court, Florence Rd, SOUTHSEA, PO5 2NF.

•**GODDARD, Mr. David John, ACA** *1980;* Websters, Baker Street Chambers, 136 Baker Street, LONDON, W1U 6UD.

GODDARD, Mr. Derek Benjamin, FCA *1965;* 18 The Leas, Station Road, Rustington, LITTLEHAMPTON, WEST SUSSEX, BN16 3SE. (Life Member)

GODDARD, Mrs. Elizabeth Dawn, BA ACA *1991;* 26 Kiln Ride, Finchampstead, WOKINGHAM, RG40 3PL.

GODDARD, Mr. Geoffrey, FCA *1959;* 145 Bayview Avenue, BELVEDERE, CA 94920, UNITED STATES. (Life Member)

GODDARD, Mrs. Helen Elizabeth, BSc ACA *2005;* Wales Audit Office, 24 Cathedral Road, CARDIFF, CF11 9LJ.

•**GODDARD, Mr. Iain Jackson, FCA** *1979;* (Tax Fac), with Harrison Beale & Owen Limited, Highdown House, 11 Highdown Road, LEAMINGTON SPA, WARWICKSHIRE, CV31 1XT.

GODDARD, Mr. James Bowman, BSc ACA MCT *1985;* The Coach House, Winchcombe Road, Sedgeberrow, EVESHAM, WR11 7UA.

GODDARD, Dr. Jeffrey Paul, BSc ACA *1993;* Shetland Charitable Trust, 22-24 North Road, Lerwick, SHETLAND, ZE1 0NQ.

GODDARD, Mr. Joel Stephen, ACA *2011;* 3 Greenslade House, The Manor, Church Street, Beeston, NOTTINGHAM, NG9 1GB.

GODDARD, Mr. John, BA FCA *1982;* 2 Ashley Gardens, Petersham, RICHMOND, TW10 7BU.

GODDARD, Mr. John Albert, FCA *1957;* 32 Pagehurst Road, Addiscombe, CROYDON, CR0 6NR. (Life Member)

•**GODDARD, Mr. John Cedric, FCA** *1975;* J.C. Goddard, 30 Sansome Walk, WORCESTER, WR1 1LX.

GODDARD, Mr. John Geoffrey, BA FCA *1975;* 38 Delvino Road, LONDON, SW6 4AJ.

GODDARD, Mr. John Wolcott, FCA *1960;* 7 Radbrook Road, Radbrook, SHREWSBURY, SY3 9BB. (Life Member)

GODDARD, Mr. Joseph Nathaniel, MA FCA *1971;* Goddard Enterprises Ltd, P.O.Box 502, BRIDGETOWN, BARBADOS.

•**GODDARD, Mr. Kevin Joseph, BTech FCA CMC** *1973;* Goddards, 54 New Road, ESHER, SURREY, KT10 9NU.

GODDARD, Mr. Malcolm Ian, BCom ACA *1990;* Altima Partners LLP, 23 Savile Row, LONDON, W1S 2ET.

GODDARD, Mr. Mark John, BSc ACA *1995;* 8 Hall Lane, Hingham, NORWICH, NR9 4JX.

GODDARD, Mr. Mark Simeon, BSc ACA *1987;* 32 Appleton Road, Hale, ALTRINCHAM, CHESHIRE, WA15 9LP.

•**GODDARD, Mr. Martin Alan, FCA** *1977;* Grant Thornton UK LLP, 30 Finsbury Square, LONDON, EC2P 2YU. See also Grant Thornton LLP

GODDARD, Mr. Martin John, ACA ATII *1984;* 4 Reddings Close, SAFFRON WALDEN, CB11 4AZ.

•**GODDARD, Mr. Martin Philip, BA FCA** *1984;* M. Goddard & Co, 69 Tupwood Lane, CATERHAM, CR3 6DD.

•**GODDARD, Mr. Melvyn Francis, FCA** *1971;* Melvyn F. Goddard & Co, 1 Peerswood Court, Little Neston, NESTON, CH64 0US.

GODDARD, Mr. Michael, ACA *2007;* with Deloitte LLP, 4 Brindley Place, BIRMINGHAM, B1 2HZ.

GODDARD, Mr. Michael, BSc FCA *1969;* Chalet Simpatica, PO Box 27, 3780 GSTAAD, SWITZERLAND.

GODDARD, Mr. Michael Derek, MA ACA *1989;* 26 Kiln Ride, Finchampstead, WOKINGHAM, RG40 3PL.

GODDARD, Mr. Michael James, BSc ACA *1999;* APRA, Level 26, 400 George Street, SYDNEY, NSW 2000, AUSTRALIA.

GODDARD, Mr. Michael Richard, FCA *1959;* 75 Paines Lane, PINNER, HA5 3BX. (Life Member)

GODDARD, Mr. Nicholas Stuart, MA ACA *1991;* British Airways Plc, Waterside HAA3, PO Box 365, Harmondsworth, WEST DRAYTON, MIDDLESEX UB7 0GB.

•**GODDARD, Mr. Paul Frederick, ACA** *1979;* Bartfields (UK) Limited, Burley House, 12 Clarendon Road, LEEDS, LS2 9NF. See also Bartfields Business Services LLP

GODDARD, Mr. Paul Richard, BA ACA *1985;* 20 Holborn Close, Jersey Farm, ST. ALBANS, AL4 9YG.

•**GODDARD, Mrs. Penelope Janet, BSc FCA** *1984;* with James Holyoak & Parker Limited, 1 Knights Court, Archers Way, Battlefield Enterprise Park, SHREWSBURY, SHROPSHIRE SY1 3GA.

•**GODDARD, Mr. Peter Barry, FCA** *1979;* Peter Goddard & Co Ltd, 125 High Street, Odiham, HOOK, RG29 1LA.

GODDARD, Mr. Peter John, FCA *1969;* 34 Victoria Court, Hamilton Ave, HENLEY-ON-THAMES, OXFORDSHIRE, RG9 1XG.

GODDARD, Mrs. Rachel Jill-Elizabeth, BA ACA *2010;* 10 St. Augustine Gardens, SOUTHAMPTON, SO17 2XA.

GODDARD, Dr. Richard Neal Basire, MA FCA *1991;* 4 Chaussee Blanche, L-8014 STRASSEN, LUXEMBOURG.

GODDARD, Mr. Richard Thomas, MA FCA *1983;* 44 Woodlands Parkway, Timperley, ALTRINCHAM, WA15 7QU.

•**GODDARD, Mr. Robert Peter Colin, FCA** *1980;* Robert P.C. Goddard, 42 Theobalds Way, Frimley, CAMBERLEY, GU16 9RF.

GODDARD, Mr. Roger Alan, BA ACA CDir *1988;* Mockbridge Cottage Brighton Road, Shermanbury, HORSHAM, WEST SUSSEX, RH13 8HD.

GODDARD, Mr. Roger David, BA FCA *1977;* The Spinney, 35A Bollin Hill, WILMSLOW, SK9 4AN.

GODDARD, Mr. Ronald Arthur, FCA *1955;* 15 Lingfield Road, LONDON, SW19 4QD. (Life Member)

GODDARD, Miss. Ruth Elaine, BA FCA *1991;* Vine Cottage Main Street, Hethe, BICESTER, OXFORDSHIRE, OX27 8HD.

GODDARD, Mr. Simon John, BSc FCA *1977;* Raleigh UK Limited 136 Church Street Eastwood, NOTTINGHAM, NOTTINGHAMSHIRE, NG16 3HT.

GODDARD, Mr. Simon Richard Hector Brian, BEng ACA *1992;* 9 Rue Emile Dubois, 75014 PARIS, FRANCE.

GODDARD, Mr. Terence Ivor, FCA *1954;* Marymead, Fountains Park, Netley Abbey, SOUTHAMPTON, SO31 5FB. (Life Member)

GODDARD, Mr. Terry George, FCA *1981;* Quillets Mead, 51 Bell Road, EAST MOLESEY, SURREY, KT8 0SS.

GODDARD, Mr. Victor Albert Scott, FCA *1949;* Solveig, 35 The Ridgeway, Cuffley, POTTERS BAR, EN6 4BB. (Life Member)

GODDARD, Mrs. Yvonne, BSc ACA ATII *1992;* 28 Meredun Close, Hursley, WINCHESTER, HAMPSHIRE, SO21 2JB.

GODDARD-WAITE, Mrs. Sarah-Jayne, BSc ACA *2000;* 7a Springfield Crescent, Woodfalls, SALISBURY, SP5 2LS.

GODDEN, Mr. Andrew James Patrick, BA ACA *2001;* Module Co Ltd Malvern View Business Park, Stella Way Bishops Cleeve, CHELTENHAM, GL52 7DQ.

GODDEN, Mr. Anthony James, BA ACA *1992;* Appleton Cottage, North Elham, Elham, CANTERBURY, CT4 6UY.

GODDEN, Mr. Anthony Nicholas, FCA *1967;* Orchard Cottage, Coate, DEVIZES, WILTSHIRE, SN10 3LE.

GODDEN, Mr. Brian John, BSc FCA *1975;* Villa St Jude, Victoria Village Close, La Rue De La Boucterie, JERSEY, JE3 5HQ.

•**GODDEN, Mr. Christopher David, FCA** *1989;* Blenheim Consulting Limited, PO Box 464, BRISTOL, BS34 8SE.

•**GODDEN, Mrs. Diana Mary, BA FCA** *1979;* (Tax Fac), Diana Godden, 65 Alzey Gardens, HARPENDEN, AL5 5SY.

•**GODDEN, Mr. Duncan James, BSc ACA** *2004;* Duncan Godden ACA, 38 Sandringham Close, Haxby, YORK, YO32 3GL.

GODDEN, Mr. Graham Paul, FCA *1975;* 2 rue des Occitans, 11700 LAREDORTE, FRANCE.

•**GODDEN, Mr. James Thomas Charles, BSc ACA** *2005;* JTC Accountants, 7 Pelham Gardens, FOLKESTONE, KENT, CT20 2LF.

GODDEN, Miss. Jennifer Louise, ACA *2008;* 7 Woodside, BUXTON, DERBYSHIRE, SK17 6PW.

GODDEN, Mr. Mark Edwin, BA FCA *1987;* Baxter Healthcare Limited, Wallingford Road, Compton, NEWBURY, RG20 7QW.

•**GODDEN, Mr. Michael David, FCA** *1981;* Pitt Godden & Taylor, Brunel House, George Street, GLOUCESTER, GL1 1BZ.

GODDEN, Mr. Nicholas Peter Bernard, BA ACA *1985;* Black Cat House, 47 Courts Hill Road, HASLEMERE, GU27 2PN.

GODDEN, Mr. Nicholas Roger Bromfield, MA FCA *1962;* Church House, Staverton, DAVENTRY, NN11 6JJ. (Life Member)

GODDEN, Mr. Robert James, BSc ACA *2005;* 54 Orchard Avenue, Eltham North, MELBOURNE, VIC 3095, AUSTRALIA.

GODDEN, Mrs. Ruth Mary, FCA *1982;* (Tax Fac), Rickerbys LLP, Ellenborough House, Wellington Street, CHELTENHAM, GLOUCESTERSHIRE, GL50 1YD.

•**GODDIN, Mr. Timothy Peter James, FCA** *1969;* Grove Farm, Bennetts Road North, Corley, COVENTRY, CV7 8BG.

GODDING, Mr. David Edward, LLB FCA *1984;* Glebe Farm House, The Street, Daglingworth, CIRENCESTER, GL7 7AE.

GODDING, Mr. Martin Kenneth, FCA *1975;* Id Dar Taghna, 47 Mayfield Close, WALTON-ON-THAMES, SURREY, KT12 5PR.

GODEFROY, Mr. Nigel John, BA FCA *1993;* Sutton Harbour Holdings Plc, North Quay House, Sutton Harbour, PLYMOUTH, PL4 0RA.

•**GODEL, Mr. Mark John, BA FCA** *1992;* BBA Limited, Beachside Business Centre, La Rue du Hocq, St Clement, JERSEY, JE2 6LF.

GODFRAY, Mrs. Christine, BA ACA *1990;* PO Box 11302, GEORGE TOWN, GRAND CAYMAN, KY1-1008, CAYMAN ISLANDS.

•**GODFREE, Mrs. Kathryn Margaret, BA ACA** *1992;* Grant Thornton UK LLP, Enterprise House, 115 Edmund Street, BIRMINGHAM, B3 2HJ. See also Grant Thornton LLP

GODFREE, Mr. Richard Spencer, BSc ACA *1998;* 11 Highfield, Hatton Park, WARWICK, WARWICKSHIRE, CV35 7TQ.

•**GODFREY, Mr. Adrian, BSc FCA** *1993;* Ernst & Young Global Ltd, Becket House, 1 Lambeth Palace Road, LONDON, SE1 7EU. See also Ernst & Young Europe LLP and Ernst & Young LLP

•**GODFREY, Mr. Adrian Malcolm William, BA ACA** *1984;* Mazars LLP, Clifton Down House, Beaufort Buildings, Clifton Down, Clifton, BRISTOL, BS8 4AN.

GODFREY, Mr. Alexander, MA(Cantab) ACA *2003;* R J & A E Godfrey, Elsham Wolds, BRIGG, SOUTH HUMBERSIDE, DN20 0NU.

•**GODFREY, Ms. Alison, BA(Hons) ACA** *2002;* Godfrey Wilson Ltd, Unit 5.11 Paintworks, Bath Road, BRISTOL, BS4 3EH.

GODFREY, Mrs. Andrea Jane, BSc ACA *1986;* 116 Salisbury Road, LONDON, W13 9TT.

GODFREY, Mr. Andrew Graham, BA ACA *2003;* Rose Cottage, Broughton Poggs, Filkins, LECHLADE, GLOUCESTERSHIRE, GL7 3JH.

•**GODFREY, Mr. Brian Andrew, BA ACA** *2007;* BLG Accounts, 18 Hall Park, Barlby, SELBY, NORTH YORKSHIRE, YO8 5XR.

GODFREY, Mr. Bryan Stuart, FCA *1965;* 5 Coverham Close, NORTHALLERTON, NORTH YORKSHIRE, DL7 8SS.

GODFREY, Mrs. Caroline Mary, MA FCA *1983;* 38 Brecon Way, BEDFORD, MK41 8DD.

GODFREY, Mrs. Catriona Fyfe, BA ACA *1984;* PO Box HM 2294, HAMILTON HMJX, BERMUDA.

GODFREY, Mrs. Charlotte Mary, MA ACA *1990;* 42 Cromwell Grove, LONDON, W6 7RG.

GODFREY, Mr. Christopher James Race, BSc ACA *2006;* with Grant Thornton UK LLP, 30 Finsbury Square, LONDON, EC2P 2YU.

GODFREY, Miss. Claire Louise, BA ACA *2006;* 5 St. Nicholas Close, KETTERING, NORTHAMPTONSHIRE, NN15 5UH.

GODFREY, Mr. Colin, FCA *1977;* 255A Southend Road, STANFORD-LE-HOPE, SS17 7AB.

GODFREY, Mr. Daniel Shaun, BSc ACA *2008;* 1 Sorrel Close, Barham, IPSWICH, IP6 0SP.

GODFREY, Mr. David Haydn, BA ACA *1994;* Lindum House, 11 Beacon Hill Road, NEWARK, NOTTINGHAMSHIRE, NG24 1NT.

GODFREY, Mr. David John, BA ACA *1987;* 1 Wellington Road, Ealing, LONDON, W5 4UJ.

•**GODFREY, Mr. David John, BSc ACA** *1989;* Godfrey, 75 Queens Park Avenue, BOURNEMOUTH, BH8 9LJ.

GODFREY, Mr. Derek, BSc FCA *1988;* 8 Valley Drive, BRIGHTON, BN1 5FA.

GODFREY, Mr. Donald Robertson, FCA *1969;* 22 Heworth Hall Drive, YORK, YO31 1AQ. (Life Member)

GODFREY, Mr. Douglas, FCA *1970;* Turfgate Farm, Hartlington, Grassington, SKIPTON, BD23 5EE.

GODFREY, Mr. Edward Charles, FCA *1956;* 8 Shirley Road, LEICESTER, LE2 3LJ. (Life Member)

GODFREY, Mr. Edward John, BA FCA *1973;* 1 B Lote 1528, Av Dr Mario Moutinho, 1400-136 LISBON, PORTUGAL.

GODFREY, Mr. Eric George Henry, FCA *1957;* 4 Shirley Church Road, Shirley, CROYDON, CR0 5EE. (Life Member)

GODFREY, Mr. Ernest, FCA *1957;* 10 Sorrel Way, Narborough, LEICESTER, LE19 3PZ. (Life Member)

GODFREY, Mr. Hugh Edward, FCA *1966;* Thomas Ridley & Son Ltd, Unit 10, Rougham Industrial Estate, BURY ST.EDMUNDS, IP30 9ND.

•**GODFREY, Mr. Hugo John, BSc FCA** *1991;* (Tax Fac), Godfrey Accounting, 1 Farnham Road, GUILDFORD, SURREY, GU2 4RG.

GODFREY, Mr. Jeremy, ACA *2009;* 38b Steppingley Road, Flitwick, BEDFORD, MK45 1AN.

GODFREY, Mr. John, MA FCA *1970;* 69 Kew Green, RICHMOND, TW9 3AH.

GODFREY, Mr. John Arthur, BSc FCA *1974;* 6 Burnside Way, Penwortham, PRESTON, PR1 9JT. (Life Member)

GODFREY, Mr. John Arthur Cadas, CBE FCA *1971;* R J & A E Godfrey, Wootton Road Elsham Top, BRIGG, DN20 0NU.

GODFREY, Mrs. Judith Jane, BSc ACA *1991;* 109 Arthur Road, Wimbledon, LONDON, SW19 7DR.

GODFREY, Mr. Kevin, BSc ACA *2007;* with PricewaterhouseCoopers LLP, Savannah House, 3 Ocean Way, Ocean Village, SOUTHAMPTON, SO14 3TJ.

GODFREY, Mr. Mark Charles, BSc ACA *1989;* 2 Clouston Street, GLENDOWIE, AUCKLAND, NEW ZEALAND.

GODFREY, Mr. Mark Christopher, MA ACA *1991;* Basement Flat, 40 Ash Road, ALDERSHOT, GU12 4EZ.

GODFREY, Mr. Nigel Mark, BA ACA ACII *1982;* PO Box HM 2294, HAMILTON HM JX, BERMUDA.

GODFREY, Mr. Paul David, BA ACA *1985;* 3 Garden Court, Wheathampstead, ST.ALBANS, AL4 8RE.

GODFREY, Mr. Peter, FCA *1949;* (Member of Council 1984 - 1987), 2N Maple Lodge, Lythe Hill Park, HASLEMERE, GU27 3TE. (Life Member)

GODFREY, Mr. Peter Brian, FCA *1965;* 14 Victoria Court, Victoria Road, SHOREHAM-BY-SEA, BN43 5WS.

GODFREY, Mr. Peter Lea Race, FCA *1973;* Rectory Farm, Maidford, TOWCESTER, NN12 8HT.

GODFREY, Mr. Peter Walker, FCA *1952;* 7 Sunny Hill Court, Sunningfields Crescent, LONDON, NW4 4RB. (Life Member)

GODFREY, Mr. Ralph David, FCA *1977;* Flat 39 Dolphin Court, Kingsmead Road, HIGH WYCOMBE, HP11 1XE.

•**GODFREY, Mr. Robert Arthur, FCA** *1963;* Godfrey Edwards, Park Lodge, Rhosddu Road, WREXHAM, LL11 1NF.

GODFREY, Mr. Robert Peter, FCA *1977;* Schlagholzbusch 27, 40822 METTMANN, GERMANY.

GODFREY, Mr. Samuel, ACA *2005;* R J & A E Godfrey, Wooton Road, Elsham Top, BRIGG, SOUTH HUMBERSIDE, DN20 0NU.

•**GODFREY, Mr. Stephen, FCA** *1967;* (Tax Fac), Godfrey Anderson & Co., 6 Latchmoor Way, GERRARDS CROSS, SL9 8LP.

GODFREY, Mr. Stuart, MA ACA *2010;* Flat A-b, 63 Abbeville Road, LONDON, SW4 9JW.

GODFREY, Mr. Tom, BSc ACA *2006;* A O N Ltd, 8 Devonshire Square, LONDON, EC2M 4PL.

GODFREY, Mr. William Penton, FCA *1975;* Sarah Radclyffe Productions Ltd, 10-11 St. Georges Mews, LONDON, NW1 8XE.

GODFREY, Mr. William Seymour, FCA *1948;* 21 Sidney Road, WALTON-ON-THAMES, KT12 2NA. (Life Member)

•①**GODFREY-EVANS, Mr. Peter John, BA FCA** *1986;* Mercer & Hole, Silbury Court, 420 Silbury Boulevard, MILTON KEYNES, BUCKINGHAMSHIRE, MK9 2AF.

GODKIN, Mr. Richard Michael Aston, BSc ACA *1996;* The Grenville Homes Group UK Limited, The Bothy, Albury Park, Albury, GUILDFORD, SURREY GU5 9BH.

GODLEY, Miss. Bronwen Jane, BSc ACA *1992;* 9 Rosemary Close, Abbeydale, GLOUCESTER, GL4 5TL.

GODLEY, Mr. David Lawrence, FCA *1965;* April Cottage, Andrew Hill Lane, Hedgerley, SLOUGH, SL2 3UL.

GODLEY, Mr. Kevin Michael, BSc ACA *2008;* 3 Henderson Avenue, GUILDFORD, GU2 9LP.

GODLEY, Mr. Philip John, BA(Hons) FCA *2001;* Sanne Trust Company Ltd, 13 Castle Street, St Helier, JERSEY, JE4 5UT.

•**GODLEY, Mr. Ralph, FCA** *1972;* Streets Audit LLP, Tower House, Lucy Tower Street, LINCOLN, LN1 1XW. See also Streets Whitmarsh Sterland and SMS Corporate Partner Unlimited

GODLEY, Mrs. Siobhan Louise, BA ACA CTA *2000;* with Deloitte LLP, Hill House, 1 Little New Street, LONDON, EC4A 3TR.

•**GODLEY, Mr. William, ACA** *2006;* Stonegate Trinity LLP, 3rd Floor, 3 Brindley Place, BIRMINGHAM, B1 2JB.

GODLINGTON, Mr. Gerard David, BSc ACA *1985;* 146 Hartshead Lane, Hartshead, LIVERSEDGE, WEST YORKSHIRE, WF15 8AJ.

•**GODMON, Mr. Richard Alexander Robert, FCA CTA** *1990;* Menzies LLP, Wentworth House, 4400 Parkway, Whiteley, FAREHAM, HAMPSHIRE PO15 7FJ.

GODSAL, Mr. Hugh Colleton, MA ACA *1992;* Ink Publishing, 141-143 Shoreditch High Street, LONDON, E1 6JE.

GODSAL, Miss. Laura Christina, BA ACA *1995;* 19 Redcliffe Mews, LONDON, SW10 9JT.

GODSALL, Mr. Peter John, FCA *1973;* 1 The Haydens, TONBRIDGE, TN9 1NS.

•**GODSELL, Mr. James Martin, MSc FCA CTA** *1996;* (Tax Fac), JMG Accountancy Services Ltd, 7 The Brookmill, Coley Park Farm, READING, RG1 6DD.

GODSIFF, Mr. Philip John, MA ACA *1980;* 98 Humber Road, LONDON, SE3 7LX.

GODSMARK, Mr. Ian, BSc ACA *2011;* 21 Bulkington Avenue, WORTHING, WEST SUSSEX, BN14 7HH.

GODSMARK, Mr. James Robert, BSc ACA *1990;* 459 Green Lane, COVENTRY, CV3 6EL.

GODSMARK, Mr. Jonathan David Howard, BSc ACA *2007;* 515 W 52nd Street, Apt 17N, NEW YORK, NY 10019, UNITED STATES.

•**GODSMARK, Mr. Martin Richard, BSc FCA** *1979;* (Tax Fac), Carpenter Box LLP, Amelia House, WORTHING, WEST SUSSEX, BN11 1QR.

GODSMARK, Miss. Victoria, BA ACA *2006;* 24 Merrow Court, Levylsdene, GUILDFORD, GU1 2SA.

GODSON, Mr. Frederick, BA(Econ) FCA *1965;* 48 Fairfield Drive, West Monkseaton, WHITLEY BAY, TYNE AND WEAR, NE25 9SA.

GODSON, Ms. Lynn Vivienne, ACA *1988;* 7 Spital Street, LINCOLN, LN1 3EG.

GODSON, Mr. Michael, BA ACA *1986;* 17, Tinker Lane, SHEFFIELD, S10 1SE.

•**GODSON, Mr. Raymond George, BA FCA** *1968;* Godson & Co, 6/7 Pollen Street, LONDON, W1S 1NJ.

•**GODSON, Mr. Timothy George, FCA** *1992;* Duncan & Toplis, 5 Resolution Close, Endeavour Park, BOSTON, LINCOLNSHIRE, PE21 7TT.

GODULA, Mr. John, FCA *1976;* 55 Grosvenor Drive, WHITLEY BAY, NE26 2JR.

GODWIN, Mr. Charles Richard, FCA *1960;* Greencroft, Priest Lane, Cartmel, GRANGE-OVER-SANDS, LA11 6PT. (Life Member)

•**GODWIN, Mr. Dalton Piers, BSc ACA AITI** *1986;* Godwin & Company, 16 Railway Place, High Street, CORK, COUNTY CORK, IRELAND.

GODWIN, Mr. David Ross, BSc FCA *1990;* Marsh Ltd, 1 Tower Place West, LONDON, EC3R 5BU.

GODWIN, Mr. Edward Bruno Kelsall, BA(Hons) ACA *2002;* 12AF1-7, Astrazeneca Pharmaceutical Division, Mereside Alderley Park, MACCLESFIELD, CHESHIRE, SK10 4TG.

GODWIN, Mr. Hilary Edward, FCA *1963;* Moorswood, 330 Birchanger Lane, Birchanger, BISHOP'S STORTFORD, HERTFORDSHIRE, CM23 5QR.

GODWIN, Miss. Lisa Marie, BSc ACA *1997;* Sentinel House Floor 3, Aviva UK Life, PO Box 21, NORWICH, NR1 3NJ.

GODWIN, Mr. Malcolm George, FCA *1971;* 10 Hugon Close, Penylan, CARDIFF, CF23 9BY.

GODWIN, Mr. Michael John, BSc ACA *1983;* PricewaterhouseCoopers LLP, 111-5th Avenue SW Suite 3100, CALGARY AB T2P 5L3, AB, CANADA.
GODWIN, Mr. Richard Maxwell, BSc ACA *1994;* 221 Queensway, #04-11 Viz Holland, SINGAPORE 276750, SINGAPORE.
GODWIN, Mr. Richard Oliver, BSc ACA *2006;* N M Rothschild & Sons Ltd, 67 Temple Row, BIRMINGHAM, B2 5LS.
GODWIN, Mr. Simon Charles, BA ACA *1992;* 86 Teignmouth Road, LONDON, NW2 4DX.
GODWIN, Mr. Timothy Charles William, MA ACA *1986;* Orchard House, Fermoy Court, Little Brington, NORTHAMPTON, NN7 4JP.
GODZICZ, Mrs. Susan Mary, BSc ACA *1981;* Highfield, Church Road, Mabe, PENRYN, TR10 9HN.
GOECK, Mr. Henning Bruno Gerhard, ACA CA(SA) *2011;* Thalwiesenstrasse 1, 8302 KLOTEN, SWITZERLAND.
GOEDEKE, Mr. Eckhard, ACA CA(SA) *2009;* J6 Hollybank, 17 Rudd Road, Illovo, JOHANNESBURG, 2196, SOUTH AFRICA.
GOEL, Mrs. Anjali, ACA *2005;* 4463 Laird Circle, SANTA CLARA, CA 95054, UNITED STATES.
•GOEL, Mrs. Rachel Ann, ACA *1998;* Michael Thompson Accountants Ltd, 32 Surrey Street, NORWICH, NR1 3NY.
GOEL, Mr. Ritesh, ACA *2011;* Flat 28, Thackeray Court, Hanger Vale Lane, LONDON, W5 3AT.
GOEL, Mr. Rohit, MEng ACA *1999;* 31 Halsbury Road East, NORTHOLT, UB5 4PU.
GOENKA, Mr. Ashish, BSc ACA *2005;* Flat 104, Matilda House, St. Katharines Way, LONDON, E1W 1LF.
GOENKA, Miss. Neha, ACA *2007;* Padmaj 33, Jai Hind Society, 11th Road, JVPD Scheme, Juhu, MUMBAI 400 049 INDIA.
GOFF, Mr. Adam John Maynard, ACA *1999;* The Beeches, 11 Queens Drive Lane, ILKLEY, LS29 9QS.
•GOFF, Mr. Brian Leslie, FCA *1972;* (Tax Fac), Goff and Company, 89 Havant Road, EMSWORTH, HAMPSHIRE, PO10 7LF.
•GOFF, Mrs. Eileen Mary, ACA *2008;* Carpenter Box LLP, Amelia House, WORTHING, WEST SUSSEX, BN11 1QR.
GOFF, Ms. Joan Amanda, ACA *1982;* The Larches, Wood Ridge, NEWBURY, RG14 6NP.
GOFF, Miss. Joanna Louise, BA ACA *2004;* with PricewaterhouseCoopers LLP, Benson House, 33 Wellington Street, LEEDS, LS1 4JP.
GOFF, Miss. Katherine Fay, BA ACA *2002;* 15 Rivervale Grove, DUNLEER, COUNTY LOUTH, IRELAND.
GOFF, Mr. Mark Jonathan, BA ACA *2001;* Flat B 93 Louisville Road, LONDON, SW17 8RN.
GOFF, Mr. Michael Lee Johnson, ACA *1979;* G.J. GOFF Ltd, 297 Aylsham Road, NORWICH, NR3 2RY.
•GOFFE, Mr. James Robert, BA FCA *1986;* (Tax Fac), Melville & Co, Unit 17/18, Trinity Enterprise Centre, Furness Business Park, Ironworks Road, BARROW-IN-FURNESS CUMBRIA LA14 2PN.
GOFFE, Ms. Judith Ann, BSc FCA *1982;* Jamaica Buildings, St. Michael's Alley, LONDON, EC3V 9DS.
GOFFIN, Mr. Ralph Alan, FCA *1975;* 10 Cavendish Court, CHESTER, CH4 7LJ.
GOGA, Mr. Fakhruddin A, BCom FCA *1975;* Abu Dhabi Investment Authority, P.O. Box 3600, ABU DHABI, UNITED ARAB EMIRATES.
GOGARTY, Miss. Helen Mary, BCom ACA *1997;* 27 Mereworth Drive, NORTHWICH, CHESHIRE, CW9 8WY.
•GOGARTY, Mr. Robert John, FCA *1982;* Robgog Limited, Bank House, Southwick Square, Southwick, BRIGHTON, BN42 4FN. See also Clamp Gogarty Ltd
GOGAY, Mr. Kevan, BSc ACA *2002;* Alena Bridge Street, Great Kimble, AYLESBURY, BUCKINGHAMSHIRE, HP17 9TN.
GOGERTY, Mr. Richard Howard, BSc ACA *1990;* 2 Marriner Crescent, LINCOLN, LN2 1BB.
GOGGIN, Mr. Kevin Paul, BSc FCA *1988;* 9 Sycamore Drive, Frimley, CAMBERLEY, SURREY, GU16 8PN.
GOGGS, Mr. Andrew Quentin, BA FCA *1964;* 9 Rutts Lane, West Lavington, DEVIZES, SN10 4LN.
GOGUS, Mr. Selim, BSc ACA *2011;* East Lodge, Danson Park, BEXLEYHEATH, KENT, DA6 8HL.
GOH, Colonel Albert Thien Yew, FCA *1975;* Villa Lima, 241 Jalan PH3, Taman Putra Heights, Pengkalan Batu, 75150 MALACCA CITY, MALAYSIA.
GOH, Miss. Amanda Seng Doon, MSc BA(Hons) ACA *2002;* 2 Jalan Hujan Bukit, Overseas Union Garden, 58200 KUALA LUMPUR, FEDERAL TERRITORY, MALAYSIA.
GOH, Miss. Ann Nee, MBA BAcc ACA *1984;* 333A Onan Road, SINGAPORE 424725, SINGAPORE.
GOH, Mr. Chien Cheng, FCA *1972;* 53 Lily Avenue, SINGAPORE 277785, SINGAPORE.
GOH, Miss. Chu Kwong Esther, FCA *1980;* 58 Jalan Gumilang, SINGAPORE 668897, SINGAPORE.
GOH, Mr. Chung Seng, BA FCA *1982;* 27 Holland Hill, Apt 04-05 Holland Peak, SINGAPORE 278741, SINGAPORE.
GOH, Miss. Esther Hoon Chin, FCA *1973;* EHC Goh & Company, Apt 03-04 Balmoral Plaza, 271 Bukit Timah Road, SINGAPORE 259708, SINGAPORE.
GOH, Miss. Euleen Yiu Kiang, ACA *1979;* 50 Draycott Park, 10-01 The Draycott, SINGAPORE 259396, SINGAPORE.
GOH, Ms. Gina, FCA *1975;* 470 Faith Drive Unit 60, MISSISSAUGA L5R 4E9, ON, CANADA.
GOH, Mr. John Oon Par, BSc ACA *1991;* (Tax Fac), 35 Chambers Grove, WELWYN GARDEN CITY, HERTFORDSHIRE, AL7 4FG.
GOH, Miss. Kathryn Hoon Bee, ACA *1983;* 41 Newton Road, #03-03 Newton Lodge, SINGAPORE 307968, SINGAPORE.
GOH, Mr. Kee Meng, BSc ACA *2006;* 23 Stirling Road, LONDON, N22 5BL.
GOH, Miss. Li Wei, BA(Hons) ACA *2002;* 489 Taman Kota Jaya, Simpang, 3470 TAIPING, PERAK, MALAYSIA.
GOH, Miss. Lisa, BSc ACA *2000;* 3 Howitt Road, LONDON, NW3 4LT.
GOH, Miss. Mary Hui Hui, BSc ACA *2006;* 20 Great Woodcote Park, PURLEY, CR8 3QS.
GOH, Mr. Meng Kuan Ivan, FCA *1973;* Ivan Goh & Co, 604-1281 West Cordova St, VANCOUVER V6C 3R5, BC, CANADA. (Life Member)
GOH, Mr. Michael Keng Juay, BSc FCA *1973;* 25 Jalan Pantai 9/7, 46000 PETALING JAYA, Selangor, MALAYSIA.
GOH, Ms. Monnie, ACA *2008;* 866 Jalan Selesa, Happy Garden, Kucai Lama, 58200 KUALA LUMPUR, FEDERAL TERRITORY, MALAYSIA.
GOH, Ms. Sellina, ACA CA(AUS) *2011;* 24B Haverstock Street, LONDON, N1 8DL.
•GOH, Mr. Siak Chua, FCA *1979;* Joseph Goh & Co, Charlene House, 44 St Margarets Road, EDGWARE, HA8 9UU. See also Milton Avis
GOH, Mr. Tian Hock, BSc FCA *1992;* 11 Laluan Ipoh Permai 7, Taman Ipoh Permai, 31400 IPOH, PERAK, MALAYSIA.
GOH, Mr. Tieng Tak, FCA *1962;* 16-A Jalan Mariamah, 80100 JOHOR BAHRU, Johor, MALAYSIA. (Life Member)
GOH, Miss. Victoria, ACA *2009;* 468 Jurong West St 41 #10-453, SINGAPORE 640468, SINGAPORE.
GOH, Mr. Wei Sian, BA(Hons) ACA *2004;* with SQM, Suite 15.05 Level 15, City Square Office Tower, 106-108 Jalan Wong Ah Fook, 80000 JOHOR BAHRU, MALAYSIA.
GOH, Miss. Yee Hoon, BAcc ACA *2002;* 25 Taman Temenggong, Bukit Baru, 75150 MALACCA CITY, MALACCA STATE, MALAYSIA.
GOHARI, Mr. Shahriar, BA ACA *1980;* Gargash & Gargash, P.O. Box 71995, DUBAI, UNITED ARAB EMIRATES.
•GOHIL, Mr. Jayant Gopalji, BSc ACA CTA CPFA *1990;* 46 Meadway, ILFORD, ESSEX, IG3 9BH.
GOHIL, Miss. Sharmila, FCA *1988;* 85 Hillview Road, Hatch End, PINNER, HA5 4PB.
GOHILL, Mr. Naresh Amratlal, BA ACA *1986;* Dolphin Containers Limited, PO Box 34673, LUSAKA, 10101, ZAMBIA.
GOIDE, Mr. Dennis Ian, FCA *1953;* 18B Oakleigh Park South, LONDON, N20 9JU. (Life Member)
GOING, Mr. Patrick Michael Parker, FCA *1965;* Stevenston House, Oak Lane, SEVENOAKS, TN13 1UH.
GOKAL, Mr. Kamlesh Mahendra, BSc(Econ) ACA *1997;* c/o Gokal Intl Ltd, Units B-D 10th Flr, Winner Building, 27 D'Aguilar Street CENTRAL, Hong Kong Island, HONG KONG SAR.
GOKANI, Miss. Malini, BA(Hons) ACA *2004;* KPMG LLP Level 17, 10 Upper Bank Street, LONDON, E14 5GH.
•GOKANI, Mr. Pravin Ratanshi, FCA *1971;* PGK Associates Limited, Talbot House Business Centre, 204-226 Imperial Drive, Raynes Lane, HARROW, MIDDLESEX HA2 7HH. See also Ash Wilson Limited
GOKDOGAN, Mr. Ekrem, ACA *2009;* 29 Yeovilton Place, KINGSTON UPON THAMES, KT2 5GP.
GOKHOOL, Miss. Nivedita, BA(Hons) ACA *2004;* Omega Underwriting Holdings Ltd New London House, 6 London Street, LONDON, EC3R 7LP.
•GOKMEN, Mr. Ismail Hakki, BA FCA *1982;* Newbery Chapman LLP, Adam House, 14 New Burlington Street, LONDON, W1S 3BQ.
GOKOOL, Miss. Joanna Santos, ACA *2009;* (Tax Fac), Flat 28 Candlemakers Apartments, 112 York Road, LONDON, SW11 3RS.
GOLAN, Mr. Simon, BA(Econ) ACA *2002;* (Tax Fac), 7 Heronsgate, EDGWARE, MIDDLESEX, HA8 7LD.
•GOLBEY, Mr. Geoffrey Philip, FCA *1968;* (Tax Fac), Harold Everett Wreford LLP, 1st Floor, 44-46 Whitfield Street, LONDON, W1T 2RJ.
GOLBY, Mr. Ashley Lewis, FCA ATII *1979;* 3 Grenville Close, LONDON, N3 1UF.
•GOLBY, Mr. David Charles, MA ACA *1985;* David Golby, High Street Cottage, Compton, NEWBURY, RG20 6NL.
GOLBY, Mr. Marcus John Joseph Reynolds, BA ACA *1996;* 2 Thornhill Road, Middlestown, WAKEFIELD, WEST YORKSHIRE, WF4 4PD.
GOLBY, Mrs. Pamela Lennox, FCA *1951;* High Street Cottage, Compton, NEWBURY, RG20 6NL. (Life Member)
GOLBY, Mr. Peter David Holmes, MEng ACA *2002;* 21 Loudhams Road, Little Chalfont, AMERSHAM, BUCKINGHAMSHIRE, HP7 9NY.
•GOLBY, Mr. Stephen, BA FCA *1980;* A.C. Mole & Sons, Riverside House, Riverside Business Park, Wylds Road, BRIDGWATER, TA6 4BH.
GOLCHEHREH, Mr. Rahmin, BSc(Hons) ACA *2010;* Flat 5, 52 Cambridge Road, BROMLEY, BR1 4EA.
GOLCHER, Mr. Samuel Charles Benjamin, BSc(Hons) ACA CTA *2001;* Brambles, Unit 2, Weybridge Business Park, Addlestone Road, ADDLESTONE, SURREY KT15 2UP.
GOLD, Mr. Andrew John, MBA BSocSc ACA AMCT *1995;* Mutual One Limited, The Bailey, SKIPTON, NORTH YORKSHIRE, BD23 1DN.
GOLD, Mr. Andrew Paul, BA ACA *2003;* 51 Lower Park Road, LOUGHTON, ESSEX, IG10 4NB.
•GOLD, Mr. Anthony Brian, FCA *1967;* Tudor Lodge, 3 The Sycamores, RADLETT, HERTFORDSHIRE, WD7 7LJ.
GOLD, Mr. Colin Andrew, MA FCA *1975;* 1 Darnaway Street, EDINBURGH, EH3 6DW.
•GOLD, Mr. David Robert, BA FCA *1987;* Joseph Miller & Co, Floor A, Milburn House, Dean Street, NEWCASTLE UPON TYNE, NE1 1LE.
GOLD, Mr. Gideon Louis, BA ACA *2007;* 48 Clifton Gardens, Temple Fortune, LONDON, NW11 7EL.
GOLD, Mr. Henry Patrick, FCA *1962;* (Member of Council 1980 - 1981), Carlisle House, Chapel Street, Bildeston, IPSWICH, IP7 7EP. (Life Member)
•GOLD, Mr. Jack, FCA *1958;* Trent Raymond & Co, 4 Chartley Avenue, STANMORE, MIDDLESEX, HA7 3QZ.
GOLD, Mr. James John Norris, BSc FCA *1991;* 1 Portland Drive Clay Hill, ENFIELD, MIDDLESEX, EN2 9AT.
•GOLD, Mr. Jeffrey David, FCA *1966;* (Tax Fac), Jeffrey Gold & Co, Turnberry House, 1404-1410 High Road, Whetstone, LONDON, N20 9BH.
GOLD, Mrs. Kathryn Louise, BSc(Hons) ACA *2002;* 54 Holly Farm Close, Caddington, LUTON, LU1 4ET.
GOLD, Mr. Leonard Morris, FCA *1960;* 8 Andover House, 9A Eton Avenue, LONDON, NW3 3EL. (Life Member)
GOLD, Mrs. Moira Claudia, FCA *1976;* The Old Stables, Savages Close, Bishops Tachbrook, LEAMINGTON SPA, CV33 9RL.
GOLD, Mr. Nicholas Roger, BA FCA *1977;* 14 Northumberland Place, LONDON, W2 5BS.
GOLD, Mr. Paul David, BA ACA *1990;* 8 Rookley Close, TUNBRIDGE WELLS, TN2 4TS.
GOLD, Mr. Perry Laurence, BA FCA *1980;* with Ernst & Young LLP, 1 More London Place, LONDON, SE1 2AF.
GOLD, Mr. Ramon Rueben, FCA *1957;* 2 Norfolk House, Stratton Close, EDGWARE, HA8 6PS. (Life Member)
•GOLD, Mr. Richard Howard David, FCA *1976;* Barnett Ravenscroft LLP, 13 Portland Road, Edgbaston, BIRMINGHAM, B16 9HN.
GOLD, Mr. Simon David, BSc ACA *1986;* 4 Haslemere Avenue, LONDON, NW4 2PX.
GOLD, Mr. Stuart Morris, FCA *1959;* 6 Althorp Close, BARNET, EN5 2AY. (Life Member)
GOLD, Ms. Susan Natalia, BA(Hons) ACA *2001;* 93 Hydethorpe Road, LONDON, SW12 0JF.
GOLD, Miss. Tania Louise, BSc ACA *2005;* Flat B, 49 Howitt Road, LONDON, NW3 4LU.
GOLDACRE, Mrs. Judith, BA ACA *1996;* 515 Fulwood Road, SHEFFIELD, S10 3QB.
GOLDBART, Mr. Peter Michael, FCA *1965;* 656 Finchley Road, LONDON, NW11 7NT.
GOLDBERG, Mr. Arnold, FCA *1963;* 3 Beningfield Drive, Napsbury Park, London Colney, ST. ALBANS, HERTFORDSHIRE, AL2 1UJ.
GOLDBERG, Mr. Arthur, ACA CA(SA) *2010;* 40 Ambrose Avenue, LONDON, NW11 9AN.
GOLDBERG, Mr. Avram Lloyd, BA ACA *1990;* 32 Acacia Road, St Johns Wood, LONDON, NW8 6AS.
•GOLDBERG, Mr. David, BSc FCA DChA *1990;* (Tax Fac), Cohen Arnold, New Burlington House, 1075 Finchley Road, Temple Fortune, LONDON, NW11 0PU. See also Cohen Arnold & Co
GOLDBERG, Mr. Ivan Anthony, BSc ACA *1995;* 41 Highcroft, Cherry Burton, BEVERLEY, NORTH HUMBERSIDE, HU17 7SG.
GOLDBERG, Mr. Jeremy Michael, FCA *1962;* Stockwell Farmhouse, St. Dominick, SALTASH, PL12 6TF.
GOLDBERG, Mr. Martin Lee, FCA *1973;* 117 Fairmile Lane, COBHAM, KT11 2BS.
GOLDBERG, Mr. Michael, BCom ACA *1996;* Flat 34 Holly Lodge, 90 Wimbledon Hill Road, LONDON, SW19 7PB.
GOLDBERG, Mr. Richard Lionel, FCA *1971;* 2 Meadow View, HARROW, HA1 3DN.
GOLDBLATT, Mr. Harold, FCA *1954;* 9 Riverside Drive, Golders Green Road, LONDON, NW11 9PU. (Life Member)
GOLDBLATT, Mr. Stuart Mark, MA ACA *2006;* with KPMG LLP, St. James's Square, MANCHESTER, M2 6DS.
GOLDBY, Mr. Roger Barry, FCA *1970;* Alanod Ltd, Chippenham Drive, Kingston, MILTON KEYNES, MK10 0AN.
•GOLDEN, Mrs. Karen Veronica, BEng ACA *1999;* Karen Golden, 18 Crossley Drive, Heswall, WIRRAL, MERSEYSIDE, CH60 9JA.
GOLDEN, Lewis Lawrence, Esq OBE JP FCA *1947;* Little Leith Gate, Angel Street, PETWORTH, GU28 0BG. (Life Member)
GOLDEN, Miss. Melissa Frances, ACA *2010;* 39 Fanshawe Crescent, HORNCHURCH, ESSEX, RM11 2DD.
•GOLDEN, Mr. Michael, ACA FCCA *2009;* Martin & Company, 158 Richmond Park Road, BOURNEMOUTH, BH8 8TW.
GOLDEN, Mr. Thomas Patrick, FCA *1960;* 52 Windsor Park, Monkstown, DUBLIN, COUNTY DUBLIN, IRELAND. (Life Member)
•GOLDER, Mr. Robert William, FCA *1971;* R W Golder, 28 Beaufort Avenue, New Cubbington, LEAMINGTON SPA, CV32 7TA.
•GOLDER, Mr. Stephen Robert, FCA *1981;* Wilkins Kennedy, Bridge House, London Bridge, LONDON, SE1 9QR.
GOLDFARB, Mr. Elliot Simon, BA(Econ) ACA *1997;* William Pears Group, Haskell House 152 West End Lane, LONDON, NW6 1SD.
•ⒹGOLDFARB, Mr. Kevin Ashley, BSc FCA *1981;* Griffins, Tavistock House South, Tavistock Square, LONDON, WC1H 9LG. See also Rayner Essex LLP
GOLDFARB, Mr. Peter Howard, MA FCA *1973;* 50 Waterside Lane, WEST HARTFORD, CT 06107, UNITED STATES. (Life Member)
•GOLDHAWK, Mr. Michael Eric, FCA *1973;* 1 Parklands, Great Bookham, LEATHERHEAD, SURREY, KT23 3NB.
•GOLDICH, Mr. Lance Spencer, ACA *1986;* (Tax Fac), Brody Lee Kershaw & Co, 2nd Floor, Hanover House, 30-32 Charlotte Street, MANCHESTER, M1 4EX. See also Brody Lee Kershaw Ltd
GOLDIE, Mrs. Andrea, ACA *2008;* 208 / 2 NewQuay Promenade, DOCKLANDS, VIC 3008, AUSTRALIA.
•GOLDIE, Mr. Christopher Beal, ACA *1970;* Christopher Goldie & Co Limited, 11 Kings Road, BARNET, EN5 4EF.
•ⒹGOLDIE, Mr. Gordon Smythe, FCA *1981;* Tait Walker Advisory Services LLP, Bulman House, Regent Centre, Gosforth, NEWCASTLE UPON TYNE, NE3 3LS. See also Tait Walker Management Limited
•GOLDIN, Mr. Irving Arnold, BA FCA *1976;* Goldin & Co, 105 Hoe Street, Walthamstow, LONDON, E17 4SA.
GOLDING, Mr. Adam Jon, BSc FCA *1994;* 17 Woodland Way, WELWYN, HERTFORDSHIRE, AL6 0RZ.
GOLDING, Mr. Alan Jack, FCA *1954;* 67 Pine Grove, Brookmans Park, HATFIELD, AL9 7BL. (Life Member)
GOLDING, Mr. Andrew Colin, ACA *1990;* Waterlane Cottage, Water Lane, Selsley East, STROUD, GL5 5LW.
GOLDING, Mr. Andrew Peter, BSc FCA *1991;* Seaford College, Lavington Park, PETWORTH, WEST SUSSEX, GU28 0NE.
GOLDING, Mr. Andrew Shawn, ACA *1987;* 22 Grantham Crescent, IPSWICH, IP2 9PD.

•**GOLDING, Mr. Anthony Edward, FCA** *1975;* H W, Sterling House, 5 Buckingham Place, Bellfield Rd West, HIGH WYCOMBE, HP13 5HQ. See also Haines Watts
•**GOLDING, Mr. Anthony Peter, FCA** *1968;* (Tax Fac), Anthony Golding Limited, Blue Haze, Down Road, TAVISTOCK, DEVON, PL19 9AG.
GOLDING, Mr. Barry Lee, BSc ACA *1993;* Woubruggestraat 18-2, 1059VS AMSTERDAM, NETHERLANDS.
GOLDING, Mr. Bradley Spencer, BSc ACA *1986;* with PricewaterhouseCoopers LLP, Hays Galleria, 1 Hays Lane, LONDON, SE1 2RD.
•**GOLDING, Mr. Christopher John, MBA BA BSc FCA** *1982;* 9 Ruffetts Way, TADWORTH, KT20 6AF.
GOLDING, Mr. Eric Roger, FCA *1964;* Goldsmith Practise Services, Siena Court, Broadway, MAIDENHEAD, BERKSHIRE, SL6 1NJ.
GOLDING, Mr. Graham Philip, BA ACA *1985;* Flat 6 Pavilion House Copers Cope Road, BECKENHAM, KENT, BR3 1DS.
•**GOLDING, Mr. John Charles, MA ACA** *1983;* Grant Thornton UK LLP, Hartwell House, 55-61 Victoria Street, BRISTOL, BS1 6FT. See also Grant Thornton LLP
GOLDING, Mr. John William, BSc ACA *1991;* 11 Anise Close, SWINDON, SN2 2SQ.
•**GOLDING, Mr. Julian Edward, BSc ACA** *2001;* Wilkins Kennedy, 1-5 Nelson St, SOUTHEND-ON-SEA, SS1 1EG.
GOLDING, Mrs. Katherine Louise, BA ACA *2005;* 43 Albion Road, ST. ALBANS, HERTFORDSHIRE, AL1 5EB.
•**GOLDING, Mr. Lawrence John, BSc FCA** *1984;* CKLG Ltd, 9 Quy Court, Colliers Lane, Stow-cum-Quy, CAMBRIDGE, CB25 9AU.
GOLDING, Mr. Leonard John, FCA *1952;* Hernando De Aguirre 752, Depto 1108, Providencia, SANTIAGO, CHILE. (Life Member)
GOLDING, Miss. Lucy Anni Maija, MSc BSc(Hons) ACA *2011;* Meghills, Chelmsford Road, Leaden Roding, DUNMOW, ESSEX, CM6 1QJ.
•**GOLDING, Mrs. Lucy Emma, LLB ACA** *2002;* Foreshore Accountancy, Balmoral, Shotley Road, Chelmondiston, IPSWICH, IP9 1EE.
GOLDING, Mr. Mark David, BA ACA CF *1993;* 4 Brindley Close, OXFORD, OX2 6XN.
•**GOLDING, Mr. Michael Ezra, FCA** *1957;* Michael Golding, Pacazzo Surgente 5th Floor, via Serafino Balestra C, 6900 LUGANO, SWITZERLAND. See also Fidirevisa Italia S.P.A
GOLDING, Mr. Michael George David, FCA *1957;* 18 Elizabeth Road, KINGTON, HR5 3DB. (Life Member)
•**GOLDING, Mr. Michael John, BA FCA** *1991;* Golding West & Co Limited, 16 Station Road, CHESHAM, BUCKINGHAMSHIRE, HP5 1DH.
GOLDING, Mr. Nathan, ACA *2011;* 152 Elm Lane, SHEFFIELD, S5 7TY.
GOLDING, Mr. Nicholas Francis, ACA *1989;* (Tax Fac), BalfourBeatty PLC, Stockley House, 130 Wilton Road, LONDON, SW1V 1LQ.
GOLDING, Mr. Paul, BSc(Hons) ACA *2003;* K P M G Salisbury Square House, 8 Salisbury Square, LONDON, EC4Y 8BB.
GOLDING, Mr. Peter Edward, FCA *1970;* 6 Jeffries Close Rownhams, SOUTHAMPTON, SO16 8DS.
GOLDING, Miss. Sarah Louise, BA ACA *2004;* 6 Derby Road, CHATHAM, ME5 7JF.
GOLDING, Mr. Sean Thomas, BA ACA *1997;* (Tax Fac), 3 Ledsons Grove, Melling, LIVERPOOL, L31 1GB.
GOLDING, Mr. Siegfried Raglan Mortimer, BSc ACA *1982;* Coopervision, Delta Park, Concorde Way, Segensworth North, FAREHAM, HAMPSHIRE PO15 5RL.
GOLDING, Mr. Terence Edward, FCA *1956;* Pinn Cottage, Pinner Hill, PINNER, HA5 3XX. (Life Member)
GOLDING, Mrs. Victoria Elisabeth, BSc FCA *1997;* 18 Far Mead Croft, Burley-in-Wharfedale, ILKLEY, LS29 7RR.
GOLDINGAY, Mr. Anthony Percy, FCA *1977;* 31 Rosemary Road, Yardley, BIRMINGHAM, B33 8RB.
GOLDINGHAM, Mrs. Deanne Lauren, ACA *2008;* 11a Wix's Lane, LONDON, SW4 0AL.
GOLDINGHAM, Mr. Michael, ACA *2008;* 19a Linden Court, Upper Maze Hill, ST. LEONARDS-ON-SEA, EAST SUSSEX, TN38 0LG.
GOLDMAN, Mr. Alan Irving, FCA *1966;* 118 Stanmore Hill, STANMORE, MIDDLESEX, HA7 3BY.
GOLDMAN, Mr. Anthony Leopold, FCA *1968;* Flat 8, Malmesbury Park, 263 Harborne Road, Edgbaston, BIRMINGHAM, B15 3JA.
GOLDMAN, Mr. Clive, BA FCA *1977;* Beechwood House, 36 Tretawn Gardens, LONDON, NW7 4NR.
•**GOLDMAN, Mr. Clive Ian, BSc FCA** *1979;* Booth Ainsworth LLP, Alpha House, 4 Greek Street, STOCKPORT, CHESHIRE, SK3 8AB.
•**GOLDMAN, Mr. Jeffrey Philip, FCA** *1978;* Simmons Gainsford LLP, 5th Floor, 7-10 Chandos Street, Cavendish Square, LONDON, W1G 9DQ.
•**GOLDMAN, Mr. Mark Joseph, BA FCA** *2000;* MJG Accounts Ltd, Hollinwood Business Centre, Albert Street, OLDHAM, OL8 3QL.
•**GOLDMAN, Mr. Michael Ralph, ACA** *1979;* Brooks & Co, 27 Stanley Road, SALFORD, M7 4FR.
GOLDMAN, Mrs. Tracy Rosalind, BSc ACA *2005;* 6 Tretawn Gardens, LONDON, NW7 4NR.
GOLDRICK, Mr. Philip Joseph, BA ACA *1989;* 109 Bollington Road, Heaton Chapel, STOCKPORT, SK4 5ES.
GOLDRING, Mr. Dougal John William, BSc ACA *1992;* Royal Mail Royal Mail House, 100 Victoria Embankment, LONDON, EC4Y 0HQ.
GOLDRING, Mr. Howard David, BSc ACA *1980;* Delmore Asset Management Ltd, 111 Baker Street, LONDON, W1U 6SG.
GOLDS, Mr. Matthew James Alexander, BA(Econ) ACA *2009;* 23 Riddings Court, Timperley, ALTRINCHAM, CHESHIRE, WA15 6BG.
GOLDSACK, Mr. David Sydney, FCA *1973;* 30 Garratts Lane, BANSTEAD, SM7 2EA.
GOLDSBROUGH, Mr. Bryce, BSc ACA *1991;* 8 Duncan Street, BALLARAT, VIC 3350, AUSTRALIA.
GOLDSBROUGH, Mr. Mark Timothy, BA(Hons) ACA *2002;* 24 Lemur Drive, CAMBRIDGE, CB1 9XZ.
•**GOLDSBROUGH, Mr. Roy, FCA** *1980;* Roy Goldsborough, 10 Quantock Grove, Bingham, NOTTINGHAM, NG13 8SE.
•**GOLDSCHMIDT, Mr. Phillip David, BSc ACA** *1988;* with Berg Kaprow Lewis LLP, 35 Ballards Lane, LONDON, N3 1XW.
GOLDSHMID, Mrs. Galit, ACA *2007;* (Tax Fac), 116 Grove Road, Bladon, WOODSTOCK, OXFORDSHIRE, OX20 1RA.
GOLDSMITH, Mrs. Anna Katharine, MEng ACA *1994;* 34 Fitzroy Crescent, Staveley Road Chiswick, LONDON, W4 3EL.
GOLDSMITH, Mrs. Cherry Ann, BA FCA *1970;* 12 Barton Road, Haslingfield, CAMBRIDGE, CB23 1LL. (Life Member)
GOLDSMITH, Mr. Crispin Kinglake, BA(Hons) ACA *2002;* Royal Bank of Scotland 4th Floor, 135 Bishopsgate, LONDON, EC2M 3UR.
GOLDSMITH, Mr. Daniel Charles, MA ACA *1989;* 34 Fitzroy Crescent, Staveley Road Chiswick, LONDON, W4 3EL.
GOLDSMITH, Mr. David, BA ACA *2011;* Flat 15, Rehov HaGila 11, 42724 NETANYA, ISRAEL.
GOLDSMITH, Mr. David, BSc FCA *1969;* Flat 17, The Galleries, 9 Abbey Road, LONDON, NW8 9AQ.
GOLDSMITH, Mr. David Colin, FCA *1960;* Sunnymead, Tapsells Lane, Durgates, WADHURST, TN5 6RS. (Life Member)
GOLDSMITH, Miss. Erica Jane Ruth, BA ACA *2006;* with PricewaterhouseCoopers LLP, First Point, Buckingham Gate, London Gatwick Airport, GATWICK, WEST SUSSEX RH6 0NT.
GOLDSMITH, Mr. Fred, BA FCA *1948;* 38 Fairlawn, Hall Place Drive, WEYBRIDGE, KT13 0AY. (Life Member)
GOLDSMITH, Mrs. Jennifer Ann, ACA *2009;* Apartment 19, Central Court, Melville Street, SALFORD, M3 6DH.
GOLDSMITH, Mr. John Arthur, MA FCA *1951;* Langdale, Cobham Way, East Horsley, LEATHERHEAD, KT24 5BH. (Life Member)
GOLDSMITH, Mr. Jonathan Antony, BA ACA *1986;* 38 Gironde Road, Fulham, LONDON, SW6 7DZ.
GOLDSMITH, Miss. Laura Jane, BA(Hons) ACA *2001;* 6 Thornsett Place, Anerley, LONDON, SE20 7XD.
GOLDSMITH, Miss. Louise Jane, BA ACA *2010;* 17 Milton Road, LONDON, NW7 4AU.
GOLDSMITH, Mr. Nigel John, BA ACA *1987;* Rose Cottage, Manley Road, Alvanley, FRODSHAM, WA6 9DE.
GOLDSMITH, Mr. Paul William, BA FCA *1981;* 102 Fawnbrake Avenue, Herne Hill, LONDON, SE24 0BZ.
•**GOLDSMITH, Mr. Peter, FCA** *1976;* (Tax Fac), Goldsmith & Co, 61 Highgate High Street, LONDON, N6 5JX.
GOLDSMITH, Mr. Peter Ernest, FCA *1955;* 65 Hill Brow, HOVE, BN3 6DD. (Life Member)
GOLDSMITH, Mr. Richard, ACA *2011;* KPMG, St. James's Square, MANCHESTER, M2 6DS.
GOLDSMITH, Mr. Richard Daniel, ACA *2008;* 9 Heddon Court Avenue, Cockfosters, BARNET, HERTFORDSHIRE, EN4 9NE.
GOLDSMITH, Mr. Simon David, ACA *1983;* 5 Hive Road, Bushey Heath, BUSHEY, WD23 1JG.
GOLDSMITH, Mr. Simon Haydon, MA FCA *1989;* Swaynes Farm Guildford Road Rudgwick, HORSHAM, WEST SUSSEX, RH12 3JD.
•**GOLDSMITH, Mrs. Susan, ACA** *1978;* Susan Goldsmith Limited, 3 Kings Drive, EDGWARE, HA8 8EB.
GOLDSMITH, Mrs. Susan Janet, BA ACA *1989;* New Haven, Catteshall Lane, GODALMING, GU7 1LJ.
GOLDSMITH, Mrs. Suzanne Clare, ACA MAAT *2004;* 18 Gilbert Road, Clare, SUDBURY, SUFFOLK, CO10 8QW.
GOLDSMITH, Mr. Timothy, BA FCA *1987;* PricewaterhouseCoopers, 2 Southbank Boulevard, Southbank, MELBOURNE, VIC 3006, AUSTRALIA.
GOLDSMITH, Mr. Timothy Stephen, BA ACA *2008;* 71 Pinner Road, WATFORD, WD19 4EG.
GOLDSMITH, Mr. Walter Kenneth, FCA *1961;* 21 Ashurst Close, NORTHWOOD, HA6 1EL.
•**GOLDSMITH, Mr. William Richard Morgan, LLB FCA** *1972;* (Tax Fac), Goldsmiths Bayley Ltd, 7 Glentworth Road, Clifton, BRISTOL, BS8 4TB. See also Accede Financial Services Ltd
GOLDSPINK, Mr. Michael David, FCA *1959;* 11 Mulberry Walk, Woodmans Park, Heckington, SLEAFORD, LINCOLNSHIRE NG34 9GW. (Life Member)
GOLDSTEIN, Mr. Anthony James, ACA *2000;* 1A Church Mount, LONDON, N2 0RW.
GOLDSTEIN, Mr. Anthony Malcolm, FCA *1971;* Engimattstrasse 20, 8002, ZURICH, SWITZERLAND.
GOLDSTEIN, Mr. Anton Raymond, FCA *1967;* 5 West Heath Close, LONDON, NW3 7NJ.
GOLDSTEIN, Mr. Brian, FCA *1960;* Victorian Suite, 15 Dolphin Court, High Road, CHIGWELL, IG7 6PH. (Life Member)
•**GOLDSTEIN, Mr. Charles Henri, FCA** *1983;* Brindley Goldstein Ltd, 103 High Street, WALTHAM CROSS, EN8 7AN.
•**GOLDSTEIN, Mr. Henry Alexander, FCA** *1971;* Maurice J. Bushell & Co, Curzon House, 64 Clifton Street, LONDON, EC2A 4HB. See also C.M.G. Associates
GOLDSTEIN, Mr. Joel, BA(Hons) ACA *2002;* 10223 Meadow Lake Lane, HOUSTON, TX 77042, UNITED STATES.
GOLDSTEIN, Mr. Joshua Nathan, MA ACA *1986;* Flat 4/A Olivers Wharf, 64 Wapping High Street, LONDON, E1W 2PJ.
GOLDSTEIN, Mrs. Julie Ann, BSc ACA *1982;* Luxury Unveiled Ltd, 28 Grosvenor Street, LONDON, W1K 4QR.
GOLDSTEIN, Mr. Matthew David, BA ACA *1998;* 8 Roedhelm Road, East Morton, KEIGHLEY, WEST YORKSHIRE, BD20 5RF.
•**GOLDSTEIN, Mr. Michael, FCA FFTA** *1963;* (Tax Fac), Michael Goldstein & Co, 1 Harley Street, LONDON, W1G 9QD.
•**GOLDSTEIN, Mr. Michael David, MSc BA FCA** *1980;* (Tax Fac), Goodman Jones LLP, 29-30 Fitzroy Square, LONDON, W1T 6LQ.
•**GOLDSTEIN, Mr. Michael Howard, FCA** *1987;* BDO LLP, 55 Baker Street, LONDON, W1U 7EU. See also BDO Stoy Hayward LLP
•**GOLDSTEIN, Mr. Philip, FCA** *1978;* (Tax Fac), Benjamin Taylor & Co, 201 Great Portland Street, LONDON, W1W 5AB. See also Compubook Services Ltd and Wigmore Registrars Ltd
GOLDSTEIN, Mr. Philip Edward, BA(Hons) ACA *2004;* 1A Church Mount, Hampstead Gardens Suburb, LONDON, N2 0RW.
GOLDSTONE, Mr. Anthony Stewart, OBE DL BA FCA *1962;* 78 Stanhope Road, Bowdon, ALTRINCHAM, CHESHIRE, WA14 3JL.
GOLDSTONE, Mrs. Claire Louise, BA ACA *2011;* 35 Grove Avenue, FAREHAM, PO16 9EZ.
GOLDSTONE, Mr. Harvey Lennard, FCA *1969;* Villa Papageno, 1183 Route De Callian, 83440 MONTAUROUX, FRANCE.
GOLDSTONE, Miss. Jayne Amanda, MBA BA FCA AMCT *1993;* 3 Lincoln Court, Rickard Close, Hendon, LONDON, NW4 4XH.
•**GOLDSTONE, Mr. Nicholas Simon, BA ACA** *1998;* BDO LLP, 55 Baker Street, LONDON, W1U 7EU. See also BDO Stoy Hayward LLP
GOLDSTONE, Mrs. Sindy, LLB ACA *1995;* UK Facilities Barnett House, Viking Street, BOLTON, BL3 2RR.
•**GOLDSTRAW, Mr. Trevor Robert, FCA** *1977;* 73 Canterbury Road, Hawkinge, FOLKESTONE, KENT, CT18 7BP.
•**GOLDSTRONG, Mr. Simon Kenneth, MBA BSc ACA** *1986;* Goldstrong Accountants Ltd, 55 Heaton Road, Grange Park, BILLINGHAM, CLEVELAND, TS23 3GP.
•**GOLDSWORTHY, Mr. Andrew James, BA FCA** *1988;* Mazars LLP, Tower Bridge House, St. Katharines Way, LONDON, E1W 1DD.
GOLDSWORTHY, Mr. Edward Charles, BA ACA *2005;* 7 Junction Road, OXFORD, OX4 2NT.
GOLDSWORTHY, Mr. John Francis, FCA *1973;* 92 Aylesbeare, Shoeburyness, SOUTHEND-ON-SEA, SS3 8DB.
GOLDSWORTHY, Mr. John Norman, FCA *1974;* 43 Victoria Street, NEWARK, NG24 4UG.
GOLDSWORTHY, Mr. Laurence Cedric, BA FCA *1970;* 26 Barcheston Road, Knowle, SOLIHULL, WEST MIDLANDS, B93 9JS.
GOLDSWORTHY, Mr. Mark Stuart, BSc(Hons) ACA *2003;* Laing O'Rourke Plc, Bridge Place, Anchor Boulevard, Crossways, DARTFORD, DA2 6SN.
GOLDSWORTHY, Mrs. Mary Frances, FCA *1974;* 26 Barcheston Road, Knowle, SOLIHULL, WEST MIDLANDS, B93 9JS.
GOLDSWORTHY, Mr. Michael Sutherland Elston, BA ACA CFA *2001;* 20 Park Mansions, Prince Of Wales Drive, LONDON, SW11 4HG.
GOLDTHORPE, Mr. Arnold James, FCA *1973;* 1 Taylor Hill, Cawthorne, BARNSLEY, S75 4HB.
GOLDTHORPE, Mr. Clive Frederick, BA FCA *1982;* 6 April Close, ORPINGTON, BR6 6NA.
GOLDTHORPE, Mr. David Ian, BSc FCA *1971;* 16 Harley Road, SHEFFIELD, S11 9SD.
GOLDTHORPE, Mr. Jonathan Michael, BA ACA *1995;* 57 Corder Road, IPSWICH, IP4 2XD.
GOLDTHORPE, Mr. Keith Alan, FCA *1961;* 6 Darnhills, Watford Road, RADLETT, HERTFORDSHIRE, WD7 8LQ.
GOLDTHORPE, Mr. Rory Anthony, BA ACA *2005;* with PKF, Pannell House, 6 Queen Street, LEEDS, LS1 2TW.
GOLDWATER, Mr. Andrew Geoffrey, BA(Hons) ACA *2003;* Coach House Wylam Hall, Church Road, WYLAM, NORTHUMBERLAND, NE41 8AS.
GOLDWIN, Mr. James, ACA *2011;* Flat B, 12 Dornton Road, LONDON, SW12 9ND.
•**GOLDWIN, Mr. Paul Robert, BA FCA** *1990;* Linn Maggs Goldwin, 2-4 Great Eastern Street, LONDON, EC2A 3NT.
GOLDWYN, Mr. Stephen Howard, ACA *1980;* Better Properties Ltd, 129 Stamford Hill, LONDON, N16 5TW.
•**GOLEND, Mr. Laurence Max, BSc FCA** *1981;* Maurice Golend & Co, 271 Green Lanes, LONDON, N13 4XP.
GOLEND, Mr. Maurice, FCA *1952;* 31 Eversley Crescent, Winchmore Hill, LONDON, N21 1EL. (Life Member)
GOLESTAN-NEJAD, Mr. Hossein, FCA *1977;* 968 De Soto Lane, FOSTER CITY, CA 94404, UNITED STATES.
GOLLAN, Mr. Andrew Paul, BA ACA *1998;* Amberley, Long Mill Lane, Platt, SEVENOAKS, KENT, TN15 8LY.
GOLLAN, Mr. John Anthony, BA FCA *1981;* Cleves Lodge, Cleves Wood, WEYBRIDGE, KT13 9TH.
GOLLAND, Mrs. Jennifer Mary, ACA *1993;* 225 Nottingham Road, MELTON MOWBRAY, LE13 0NS.
GOLLCHER, Mr. Mark Frederick, FCA *1989;* 1 Annunciation Sq, SLIEMA, SLM 06, MALTA.
•**GOLLEDGE, Mr. David Kenneth, FCA** *1973;* Whyatt Pakeman Partners, Colkin House, 16 Oakfield Rd, Clifton, BRISTOL, BS8 2AP.
GOLLEDGE, Mr. Geoffrey, FCA *1951;* with Pawley & Malyon, 15 Bedford Square, LONDON, WC1B 3JA. (Life Member)
GOLLEDGE, Mr. Mark Hedworth, BA FCA *1985;* River House, 6 Riverside, Wraysbury, STAINES, TW19 5JN.
GOLLEDGE, Mr. Simon, MA FCA *1983;* 733 Braewood Drive, BRADBURY, CA 91010, UNITED STATES.
GOLLINGS, Mr. Denzil Richard, BSc ACA *1991;* Sunnybank, Woodhurst Lane, OXTED, RH8 9HD.
•**GOLLINGS, Mr. Nicolas Alexander, BA(Hons) ACA** *2001;* Haddon Cottage, Victoria Road, WEYBRIDGE, SURREY, KT13 9QH. See also Nicolas Gollings & Co
GOLLINS, Mr. Jonathan Matthew, MA ACA *1990;* 3 Heath Villas, Vale Of Health, LONDON, NW3 1AW.
•**GOLLOP, Geoffrey Richard, Esq OBE MA FCA** *1979;* (Tax Fac), Geoff Gollop & Co Limited, St Brandon's House, 29 Great George Street, BRISTOL, BS1 5QT.
GOLTON, Mr. Adam Charles Robert, BSc FCA *1990;* Inglenook, 4 Kingfisher Copse, St. John's Rd. Locks Heath, SOUTHAMPTON, SO31 6WT.
•**GOLTON, Mr. David Donald, LLB FCA** *1974;* F.F. Leach & Co, Kestrel House, 111 Heath Road, TWICKENHAM, TW1 4AH.

GOLTON, Mrs. Jayne, BA ACA *1990;* 4 Kingfisher Copse, Locks Heath, SOUTHAMPTON, SO31 6WT.

GOLUMBINA, Mr. Adrian Mihaita, BA ACA *2000;* Bay Tree House, Odell Road, Sharnbrook, BEDFORD, MK44 1JL.

•**GOLZ, Mr. Michael John, FCA** *1965;* M J Golz & Company, Odeon House, 146 College Road, HARROW, HA1 1BH.

GOMAN-SMITH, Mrs. Angela Lesley, FCA *1975;* Action for Carers (Surrey), Astolat, Coniers Way, Burpham, GUILDFORD, SURREY GU4 7HL.

GOMARSALL, Mr. Ralph Ian, BSc ACA *1992;* Thermal Ceramics Asia Pte, 150 Kampong Ampat, #05-06A KA Centre, SINGAPORE 368324, SINGAPORE.

GOMBITOVA, Miss. Tamara, BA(Hons) ACA *2010;* F, 49 Constantine Road, LONDON, NW3 2LN.

•**GOMER, Mr. Nicholas Kenwyn, BA ACA** *1982;* Ernst & Young LLP, 1 More London Place, LONDON, SE1 2AF. See also Ernst & Young Europe LLP

GOMER, Miss. Philippa, ACA *2011;* Flat 1, 196 Golders Green Road, LONDON, NW11 9AL.

•**GOMERSALL, Mr. Malcolm Antony, BSc FCA** *1991;* Grant Thornton UK LLP, Grant Thornton House, 202 Silbury Boulevard, MILTON KEYNES, BUCKINGHAMSHIRE, MK9 1LW. See also Grant Thornton LLP

GOMERSALL, Mr. Nicholas Jon, BSc ACA *1999;* Calderdale PCT, F Mill, Dean Clough Mills, HALIFAX, WEST YORKSHIRE, HX3 5AX.

GOMERSALL, The Revd. Richard, FCA *1968;* Dale View House, 14 Wignall Avenue, Wickersley, ROTHERHAM, SOUTH YORKSHIRE, S66 2AX.

GOMERSALL, Mrs. Sara-Jane, BSc ACA *1992;* 2 Cutenhoe Road, LUTON, LU1 3ND.

GOMES, Mr. Berchams, BA FCA *1960;* 503 Embassy Towers, Seven Bungalows Road, Versova, MUMBAI 400061, MAHARASHTRA, INDIA. (Life Member)

GOMES, Mr. Edwin Jose, ACA *1983;* #07-04 21 Oxford Road, SINGAPORE 218817, SINGAPORE.

GOMES, Mr. Frank George, FCA *1972;* 4423 Walsh Street, CHEVY CHASE, MD 20815, UNITED STATES.

GOMES, Mrs. Gwyneth Ann, BSc ACA *1987;* Rendah, 119 Fairmile Lane, COBHAM, KT11 2BS.

•**GOMES, Mr. Ian Pierre, MBA BCom FCA** *1982;* KPMG LLP, 15 Canada Square, LONDON, E14 5GL. See also KPMG Europe LLP

GOMES, Mr. Julian, ACA *2011;* 7 Chelsea Close, WORCESTER PARK, SURREY, KT4 7SF.

GOMES, Mr. Peter Denis, BSc FCA *1986;* Qualicum, Hermitage Lane, Cranage, CREWE, CW4 8HB.

GOMES, Mr. Ranjit Nihal, BA FCA *1977;* Koekoekdreef 41, Zoersel, B-2980 ANTWERP, BELGIUM. (Life Member)

GOMES, Miss. Simone Amelia, BSc(Hons) ACA *2011;* Flat 4 Gabrielle Court, 1-3 Lancaster Grove, LONDON, NW3 4EU.

GOMEZ, Mr. Jeffrey Gerard, FCA *1983;* Gomez & Co, 16-A 1st Fl, Jalan Tun Sambanthan 3, Brickfields, 50470 KUALA LUMPUR, FEDERAL TERRITORY MALAYSIA.

GOMEZ VILLAMOR, Miss. Lucia, ACA *2008;* with Endless LLP, 3 Whitehall Quay, LEEDS, LS1 4BF.

GOMM, Mr. Christopher Peter Maynard, MA BSc FCA *1965;* Frating Lodge, Frating, COLCHESTER, CO7 7DG.

GOMME, Mr. David Frank, FCA *1970;* Windrush House, Terrick, AYLESBURY, HP22 5XP.

GOMME, Mr. Edwin Michael, FCA *1978;* 54 Hotham Road, Putney, LONDON, SW15 1QJ.

•**GOMPELS, Mrs. Susan Irene, OBE FCA** *1969;* (Member of Council 1983 - 2003), (Tax Fac), S.I. Gompels & Co, 7 Heathfield, Stoke D'Abernon, COBHAM, KT11 2QY.

GONCALVES, Ms. Ariana Maria Guimaraes, ACA *2009;* Edificio BCI, Rua Rainha Ginga, 9th Floor, LUANDA, ANGOLA.

GONCALVES, Miss. Louise Pamela, BSc(Hons) ACA *2002;* 23 Buttercup House, Waterport Terraces, GIBRALTAR, GIBRALTAR.

GONDA, Mrs. Julie, BA ACA *1991;* 15 Castle Grove, Holcombe Brook, BURY, BL0 9TF.

GONEN, Mr. Ilan, BA ACA AMCT *2002;* 78 Linkside, LONDON, N12 7LG.

GONG, Mr. Felix Wooi Teik, FCA *1976;* GEP Associates, 25 Jalan 1/42A, Dataran Prima, 47301 PETALING JAYA, Selangor, MALAYSIA.

GONG, Miss. Ting, MSc ACA *2010;* 7 Hollies Lane, SALFORD, M5 3GX.

•**GONG, Mr. Wee Ning, FCA** *1972;* 23 Jalan Birah, Damansara Heights, 50490 KUALA LUMPUR, FEDERAL TERRITORY, MALAYSIA.

GONSALVES, Mr. Andrew Thomas, BSc(Hons) ACA *2002;* Volkswagen Financial Services (UK) Ltd, Brunswick Court, Yeomans Drive, Blakelands, MILTON KEYNES, MK14 5LR.

•**GONSALVES, Mr. Dev Anthony, FCA** *1980;* 7/125 Queen Street, NORTH STRATHFIELD, NSW 2137, AUSTRALIA.

GONSALVES, Mr. Wayne Joseph, MSc FCA *1986;* 79 Slough Lane, LONDON, NW9 8YB.

GONTI ZAMBOGLOU, Mrs. Maria, BA ACA *2009;* 6 Emmanouel Roides Street, Ayia Zoni, 3031 LIMASSOL, CYPRUS.

GONZAGA, Mr. Tim, MEng ACA *2007;* with Kingston Smith LLP, Devonshire House, 60 Goswell Road, LONDON, EC1M 7AD.

GONZALEZ, Mr. George Augustine, FCA *1974;* Hill House, Deepdene Park Road, DORKING, SURREY, RH5 4AW.

GONZALEZ, Mr. Louis, BSc ACA AMCT *1992;* 12 Berrymede Road, LONDON, W4 5JF.

GONZALEZ, Miss. Margaret, BSc ACA CTA *1989;* (Tax Fac), 18 Woodford Place, WEMBLEY, HA9 8TE.

•**GOOCH, Mr. Alan John, FCA** *1964;* (Tax Fac), The Carley Partnership, St. James's House, 8 Overcliffe, GRAVESEND, DA11 0HJ. See also Carleys Integrated Solutions Ltd

GOOCH, Mr. Brian James, MA FCA *1997;* Hawsons Pegasus House, 463a Glossop Road, SHEFFIELD, S10 2QD.

GOOCH, Mr. Jeffrey Andrew, MA ACA *1992;* 33 Marlborough Road, RICHMOND, SURREY, TW10 6JT.

GOOCH, Mr. Michael Douglas, FCA *1976;* Rushindo, 38A Shirley Road, ROSEVILLE, NSW 2069, AUSTRALIA.

•**GOOCH, Mr. Nicholas Henry Wyard, BA FCA CTA** *1992;* Francis Clark, Hitchcock House, Hilltop Business Park, Devizes Road, SALISBURY, SP3 4UF. See also Francis Clark LLP

•**GOOCH, Mr. Nigel Roland Noah, FCA** *1977;* Greystones, Green Lane, CROWBOROUGH, TN6 2BX.

GOOCH, Mrs. Sarah Jane, BSc ACA *2006;* 40 Bounty Road, BASINGSTOKE, RG21 3DD.

GOOD, Miss. Amy Rowen Mary, BA ACA *2005;* 3 Branksome Close, NORWICH, NR4 6SP.

•**GOOD, Ms. Anne, ACA** *1986;* Anne Good, 51 St. James Avenue, FARNHAM, SURREY, GU9 9QF.

GOOD, Mr. Charles Anthony, BSc FCA *1971;* 21 Victoria Grove, LONDON, W8 5RW.

GOOD, Mr. David John, FCA *1968;* 12A Wells Park Court, Taylors Lane, LONDON, SE26 6QP. (Life Member)

GOOD, Mr. David Saxty, FCA *1969;* Alnasr Tech. Trading, Agencies, PO Box 7355, ABU DHABI, UNITED ARAB EMIRATES.

GOOD, Mr. Derek Harry, FCA *1953;* Flat 7 Grand Mansions, Queens Gardens, BROADSTAIRS, CT10 1QF. (Life Member)

GOOD, Mrs. Fiona Anne, ACA *1992;* 1 Brennans Gate, Burbage, MARLBOROUGH, SN8 3GP.

•**GOOD, Mr. Gary Steven, FCA** *1990;* GGDD llp, 2nd Floor, Compton House, 29-33 Church Road, STANMORE, MIDDLESEX HA7 4AR.

•**GOOD, Mr. Geoffrey James, BSc FCA** *1973;* Good Financial Management, 18 Aylesbury Close, New Catton, NORWICH, NR3 3LB.

GOOD, Mr. James, BSc ACA *2011;* Flat 77, Stretton Mansions, Glaisher Street, LONDON, SE8 3JP.

•**GOOD, Mr. Jonathan William, BSc FCA** *1988;* (Tax Fac), Good & Co, The White House, 6 Nottingham Road, Cropwell Bishop, NOTTINGHAM, NG12 3BQ.

GOOD, Miss. Josie, BA(Hons) ACA *2004;* 12 Scratton Road, SOUTHEND-ON-SEA, SS1 1EN.

GOOD, Miss. Katharine Isobel Halina, MA ACA *2004;* with Deloitte LLP, Hill House, 1 Little New Street, LONDON, EC4A 3TR.

GOOD, Mrs. Kirsten Mary, BCom ACA *1989;* Itchel Cottage, Itchel Lane, Crondall, FARNHAM, GU10 5PT.

GOOD, Mr. Michael John, ACA *1991;* La Haute Lande, Les Abreuveurs, St. Sampson, GUERNSEY, GY2 4XB.

•**GOOD, Mr. Michael Stewart, BSc FCA** *1979;* Michael Good Ltd, Greyfriars Court, Paradise Square, OXFORD, OX1 1BE.

GOOD, Mr. Michael Victor, ACA *1986;* 34 Highfield Avenue, Dovercourt, HARWICH, CO12 4DP.

GOOD, Mr. Nicholas Charles Saxty, BSc ACA *2000;* 2 Eastern Terrace, BRIGHTON, BN2 1DJ.

GOOD, Mr. Nicholas Luke, MA FCA *1998;* with KPMG LLP, 15 Canada Square, LONDON, E14 5GL.

GOOD, Mr. Patrick Toby, BEng ACA *1994;* Rapsley Cottage, Coneyhurst Lane, Ewhurst, CRANLEIGH, SURREY, GU6 7PP.

GOOD, Mr. Sean Patrick, BA ACA *1986;* 22 Stanhope Road, ST. ALBANS, HERTFORDSHIRE, AL1 5BL.

GOOD, Mr. Stephen Paul, BA ACA *1987;* 32 Algarth Road, Pocklington, YORK, YO42 2HP.

GOOD, Mr. Timothy James, BA ACA *1979;* (Tax Fac), with The Professional Training Partnership, Cherwell Innovation Centre, 77 Heyford Park, Camp Road, Upper Heyford, BICESTER OXFORDSHIRE OX25 5HD.

GOOD, Mr. William Marsh, BSc FCA *1976;* Elite House, Eco Logic Elite House, 70 Warwick Street, BIRMINGHAM, B12 0NL.

GOODA, Mr. Robert Graham, FCA *1978;* Kamrath, Pastortiggesweg 7A, 48607 OCHTRUP, GERMANY.

GOODACRE, Prof. Alan, PhD BSc ACA *1979;* Accounting & Finance Division Stirling Management School, University of Stirling, STIRLING, FK9 4LA.

GOODACRE, Mr. David, ACA *2009;* 2 Brendon Drive, NOTTINGHAM, NG8 1JA.

GOODACRE, Mrs. Lorna Jane, ACA *2008;* 2 Brendon Drive, NOTTINGHAM, NG8 1JA.

GOODALE, Mrs. Hayley Amanda, BSc ACA *2002;* 2 Great Minster Street, WINCHESTER, SO23 9HA.

GOODALL, Mr. Alistair Nicolas Julian, BSc ACA *1994;* 36 Pierce Lane, Fulbourn, CAMBRIDGE, CB21 5DL.

GOODALL, Mr. Andrew Paul, ACA *2006;* 44 Ethelred Gardens, West Totton, SOUTHAMPTON, SO40 8UA.

GOODALL, Mr. Arthur Alan, FCA *1959;* Four Gables, 68 Pendre Avenue, PRESTATYN, LL19 9SL. (Life Member)

GOODALL, Mr. Barnaby William, BA ACA *2010;* Craigwell Lodge Remenham Hill, Remenham, HENLEY-ON-THAMES, OXFORDSHIRE, RG9 3HA.

GOODALL, Mrs. Beverley Paula, BA(Hons) ACA *2002;* 15 Sudbury Road, STOCKTON-ON-TEES, CLEVELAND, TS20 2SJ.

GOODALL, Miss. Carolyn Tracey, ACA DChA *1988;* 1 Northern Avenue, Shaw Cum Donnington, NEWBURY, BERKSHIRE, RG14 2JJ.

GOODALL, Mr. Colin Robert, FCA *1966;* Dana Petroleum Plc, 17 Carden Place, ABERDEEN, AB10 1UR. (Life Member)

GOODALL, Mr. Gareth, BSc ACA *2007;* Bertha Cottage, 8 Edward Street, Stapleford, NOTTINGHAM, NG9 8FJ.

GOODALL, Mr. Graeme, MBA BSc FCA *1986;* Milmega Limited, Park Road, RYDE, ISLE OF WIGHT, PO33 2BE.

GOODALL, Miss. Kimberley Louise, BA(Hons) ACA *2010;* 8 Salem Apartments, Burnt Lane, St Peter Port, GUERNSEY, GY1 1HL.

GOODALL, Ms. Lara Claire, BSc ACA *1996;* J P Morgan Fleming Asset Management, Finsbury Dials, 20 Finsbury Street, LONDON, EC2Y 9AQ.

GOODALL, Mr. Neil Martin, BA ACA *1982;* 31 Cheltenham Gardens, Hedge End, SOUTHAMPTON, SO30 2UB.

GOODALL, Mr. Peter, FCA *1976;* 2 Sherwood Avenue, Littleover, DERBY, DE23 1NF.

GOODALL, Mr. Richard James, BSc ACA *2009;* Apartment 305 Block 5 Spectrum, Blackfriars Road, SALFORD, M3 7BU.

GOODALL, Mr. Robert Andrew, BA ACA *1988;* Brunswick Developments Group plc, Administration Offices, Brighton Marina, BRIGHTON, BN2 5UF.

GOODALL, Mrs. Samantha Fiona, ACA *2002;* 47 Ashmole Avenue, BURNTWOOD, STAFFORDSHIRE, WS7 9QG.

GOODALL, Mr. Stanley, FCA *1964;* 53 Glebelands Rd, Prestwich, MANCHESTER, M25 1WF.

•**GOODALL, Mr. Timothy Michael Charles, FCA** *1973;* (Tax Fac), Goodall & Co, Abacus House, Manor Road, LONDON, W13 0AS.

GOODALL, Miss. Zoe Claire, LLM LLB CA ACA *2002;* PO Box 10194, The Terrace, WELLINGTON 6143, NEW ZEALAND.

GOODBAN, Mr. Christopher John, FCA *1964;* 36 Grosvenor Road, ST. ALBANS, AL1 3AE.

GOODBAN, Mr. Nicholas James, BSc ACA *2003;* Reliance Security Services Ltd, Boundary House, Cricket Field Road, UXBRIDGE, MIDDLESEX, UB8 1QG.

•**GOODBAND, Mr. Edward Mark Connell, FCA** *1980;* Goodband Viner Taylor, Ellin House, 42 Kingfield Road, SHEFFIELD, S11 9AS.

GOODBODY, Mr. George Edward, FCA *1965;* 7 Ashington Gardens, Ashington, WIMBORNE, DORSET, BH21 3DF. (Life Member)

GOODBODY, Mr. Graham George, FCA *1967;* 87 Histon Road, Cottenham, CAMBRIDGE, CB24 8UQ.

GOODBORN, Miss. Ann Caroline, BSc ACA *1991;* 8 Arden Leys, Tanworth-in-Arden, SOLIHULL, WEST MIDLANDS, B94 5JE.

GOODBOURN, Mr. Howard Charles, BSc FCA *1986;* Cotswold, Fox Hill Close, HAYWARDS HEATH, WEST SUSSEX, RH16 4RA.

GOODBURN, Mr. Andrew Robert, FCA *1969;* Deacons Hay, Beaconsfield Road, Chelwood gate, HAYWARDS HEATH, RH17 7LG.

GOODBURN, Mr. Christopher Joseph, BA ACA *1981;* 5190 Del Monte, VICTORIA V8Y 1X2, BC, CANADA.

GOODBURN, Mr. Steven Charles, BA ACA *2006;* 9 Bradford Street, CHELMSFORD, CM2 0BG.

GOODCHAP, Mr. John Austen, FCA *1951;* St James Residential Hotel, 66 Main Road, St James, CAPE TOWN, 7945, SOUTH AFRICA. (Life Member)

GOODCHILD, Mrs. Diana Marie, ACA *1985;* Spinneymead, Forest Road, East Horsley, LEATHERHEAD, KT24 5DJ.

GOODCHILD, Mr. Gordon Edwin, FCA *1952;* Little Grange, Higham, COLCHESTER, CO7 6LD. (Life Member)

•**GOODCHILD, Mr. Martin Roy, BA FCA ATII** *1979;* (Tax Fac), PKF (UK) LLP, Farringdon Place, 20 Farringdon Road, LONDON, EC1M 3AP.

GOODCHILD, Dr. Nicholas James, FCA *1990;* Chiltington House, High Croft, Shamley Green, GUILDFORD, SURREY, GU5 0UE.

GOODCHILD, Mrs. Penelope Jane, BSc ACA *1979;* Woodstock, 3 Broomfield Ride, Oxshott, LEATHERHEAD, KT22 0LR.

GOODCHILD, Mr. Peter Daniel, BSc ACA *2006;* 304/5 Cary Street, DRUMMOYNE, NSW 2047, AUSTRALIA.

GOODCHILD, Mr. Roger Duncan, BEng ACA *1991;* 16 Boxgrove Road, GUILDFORD, SURREY, GU1 2NF.

GOODCHILD-OKONKWO, Mr. Mark, BA ACA *2002;* Flat 36 Exchange House, 71 Crouch End Hill, LONDON, N8 8DF.

GOODE, Mr. Alan, FCA *1954;* 3 Greenfields Rise, WHITCHURCH, Shropshire, SY13 1EP. (Life Member)

GOODE, Mrs. Denise Elaine, BSc ACA *1986;* 20 Alton Road, WILMSLOW, SK9 5DX.

GOODE, Mr. James Richard, BA FCA *2000;* Flat 2, James House, 70 Webb's Road, LONDON, SW11 6SE.

GOODE, Miss. Lianne, BA(Hons) ACA *2010;* 53 High Ridge Road, HEMEL HEMPSTEAD, HERTFORDSHIRE, HP3 0AU.

GOODEN, Mr. James Kenneth, BA ACA *1995;* 20 Chisbury Close, BRACKNELL, BERKSHIRE, RG12 0TX.

GOODEN, Mr. Raymond John, FCA *1972;* 344 Williams Avenue, MILTON L9T 2G2, ON, CANADA.

GOODENOUGH, Mr. Angus Macleod, BSc ACA *1989;* Farnborough, The Sixth Form College, Prospect Avenue, FARNBOROUGH, GU14 8JX.

GOODENOUGH, Mr. John Matcham, FCA *1959;* 35 Tarragon Way, Burghfield Common, READING, RG7 3YU. (Life Member)

GOODENOUGH, Miss. Sharon Julie, BA FCA *1981;* 27 Monks Road, Hyde, WINCHESTER, SO23 7EQ.

GOODENOUGH, Mrs. Victoria Lucy, BA ACA *2002;* 28A Merlyn Park, Ballsbridge, DUBLIN 4, COUNTY DUBLIN, IRELAND.

GOODENOUGH-BAYLY, Mrs. Jane Clare, BSc ACA *1991;* 39 Old School Drive, Longton, PRESTON, LANCASHIRE, PR4 5YU.

GOODER, Mr. David William, FCA *1969;* Cathedral Leasing Ltd, 300 Relay Point, Relay Drive, TAMWORTH, STAFFORDSHIRE, B77 5PA.

GOODER, Mr. George, FCA *1969;* The Gate House, Shipton, MUCH WENLOCK, SHROPSHIRE, TF13 6JY.

GOODERHAM, Mr. Colin Peter, BSc ACA *1980;* Bakers Cottage, 1 Cole End Lane, Sewards End, SAFFRON WALDEN, CB10 2LQ.

•**GOODERHAM, Mr. Edwin Leigh, BSc ACA** *2002;* GPMG Limited, 7 New Street, Pontnewydd, CWMBRAN, GWENT, NP44 1EE.

GOODERHAM, Mr. Martin, BSc ACA *2011;* 9 Cricks Walk, Roydon, DISS, NORFOLK, IP22 5SN.

•**GOODERHAM, Mr. Nicolas John, FCA** *1970;* 14 Shalbourne Rise, CAMBERLEY, SURREY, GU15 2EJ.

GOODERICK, Mr. Robert Levison, BA FCA *1973;* 67 Southmoor Road, OXFORD, OX2 6RE.

GOODEVE, Mrs. Julie Anne, BA ACA *1995;* 8 Gilbey Avenue, BISHOP'S STORTFORD, CM23 5NX.

GOODEVE, Mr. Kevin John, BA FCA *1991;* 8 Gilbey Avenue, BISHOP'S STORTFORD, CM23 5NX.

•**GOODEY, Mr. Mark, BSc ARCS FCA** *1984;* Deloitte LLP, 2 New Street Square, LONDON, EC4A 3BZ. See also Deloitte & Touche LLP

•**GOODEY, Mr. Mark James Nicholas, MSc FCA** *1984;* (Tax Fac), M.J.N. Goodey, 109 Arundel Road, PEACEHAVEN, BN10 8HE.

•**GOODEY, Mr. Thomas Walter, FCA** *1973;* Flat 1, 162 Trinity Road, LONDON, SW17 7HT.
•**GOODFELLOW, Miss. Clare Dawn, ACA** *1995;* Traddles, Chapel Road, Tolleshunt D'Arcy, MALDON, ESSEX, CM9 8TL.
•**GOODFELLOW, Mr. David, FCA** *1988;* Flat 6, 143 Gloucester Terrace, LONDON, W2 6DX.
GOODFELLOW, Mrs. Jacqueline Mary, BSc ACA *1988;* 545 Te Moana Road, Pleasant Valley, RD21, GERALDINE 7991, NEW ZEALAND.
GOODFELLOW, Mr. James Robert, MA ACA *2003;* The Bank of England, Threadneedle Street, LONDON, EC2R 8AH.
GOODFELLOW, Miss. Lorna, BSc ACA *2001;* 34 Hyde Lane, Danbury, CHELMSFORD, CM3 4QT.
•**GOODFELLOW, Mr. Mark, ACA** *2008;* 77 St. Andrews Park, Tarragon Road, MAIDSTONE, ME16 0WD.
GOODFELLOW, Mr. Peter, ACA *2007;* 34 Parklawn Avenue, EPSOM, KT18 7SL.
GOODFELLOW, Mr. Ronald Henry, BSc ACA *1987;* 545 Te Moana Road, GERALDINE RD21 7991, NEW ZEALAND.
GOODGAME, Mr. Christopher John, BEng ACA PGCE *2001;* with Deloitte LLP, Athene Place, 66 Shoe Lane, LONDON, EC4A 3BQ.
GOODGAME, Mr. John David, BA ACA *1992;* Blaise End, 130 Westbury Lane, Coombe Dingle, BRISTOL, BS9 2PU.
GOODGER, Mr. Jeremy Paul, BSc ACA *1990;* Legal & General Group PLC, 1 Coleman Street, LONDON, EC2R 5AA.
GOODHAND, Mr. Stephen, FCA *1972;* La Boutonniere, Bouton, 71360 SULLY LE CHATEAU, FRANCE.
•**GOODHEAD, Mr. Christopher John, BSc FCA** *1990;* Knight Goodhead Limited, 7 Bournemouth Road, Chandler's Ford, EASTLEIGH, HAMPSHIRE, SO53 3DA.
•**GOODHEAD, Mr. Clive, BSc FCA** *1985;* Goodheads, Oceans End, Rose Hill, MARAZION, CORNWALL, TR17 0HB.
GOODHEW, Miss. Kathryn, ACA *2009;* Flat 23, The Maples, Granville Road, ST. ALBANS, HERTFORDSHIRE, AL1 5BU.
GOODHEW, Mr. Richard John, FCA *1976;* Earlywood Rise, Coronation Road, ASCOT, BERKSHIRE, SL5 9LH.
•**GOODHIND, Mr. Jason Richard, BA(Econ) FCA** *1996;* with BDO LLP, Prospect Place, 85 Great North Road, HATFIELD, HERTFORDSHIRE, AL9 5BS.
GOODIER, Mr. Geoffrey Charles, BEng ACA *1992;* 7 Fosse Road, KINGSBRIDGE, TQ7 1NG.
GOODIN, Mr. John George, FCA *1955;* 7 Woodside Road, NEW MALDEN, SURREY, KT3 3AH. (Life Member)
GOODING, Mr. David Gerald, BSc FCA *1972;* 12 Axeview Road, SEATON, DEVON, EX12 2JT.
GOODING, Miss. Hannah Frances, BA ACA *2005;* with Target Consulting Limited, Lawrence House, Lower Bristol Road, BATH, BA2 9ET.
GOODING, Mr. Jonathan Lloyd, MChem ACA *2005;* 21 Archers Fields, Sandridge Road, ST. ALBANS, HERTFORDSHIRE, AL1 4EL.
•**GOODING, Ms. Karen Elizabeth, BA FCA** *1990;* The Southill Partnership Limited, Southill Business Park, Cornbury Park, Charlbury, CHIPPING NORTON, OXFORDSHIRE OX7 3EW.
GOODING, Mrs. Katy, BSc ACA *2006;* with Pearson May, 5 Wicker Hill, TROWBRIDGE, BA14 8JS.
GOODING, Mr. Michael Henry, BSc ACA *1991;* 8 Mill Close, Deddington, BANBURY, OX15 0UN.
GOODING, Mr. Neil Richard, MEng ACA *1993;* Tile Barn, Hartest, BURY ST. EDMUNDS, SUFFOLK, IP29 4DW.
GOODING, Mr. Philip James, BSc FCA *1966;* Saxfield House, Blakeney Short Lane, Saxlingham, HOLT, NORFOLK, NR25 7JT.
GOODING, Mr. Robert Christopher, ACA *2009;* with PricewaterhouseCoopers LLP, Hays Galleria, 1 Hays Lane, LONDON, SE1 2RD.
GOODING, Mr. Roger Kenneth, FCA *1962;* 26 Parkfield Street, Rowhedge, COLCHESTER, CO5 7EL.
GOODINSON, Mr. Keith Ian, ACA *1980;* 119 Deer Park Drive, Arnold, NOTTINGHAM, NG5 8SA.
GOODKIN, Mr. Brian, FCA *1977;* 84 Wheelers Lane, Kings Heath, BIRMINGHAM, B13 0SF.
•**GOODKIND, Mr. Clive Warren, FCA** *1977;* (Tax Fac), Rayner Essex LLP, Tavistock House South, Tavistock Square, LONDON, WC1H 9LG.
GOODLAD, Miss. Jodie, ACA *2009;* 4 Newnham Terrace, HARROGATE, NORTH YORKSHIRE, HG2 7ST.
GOODLAND, Miss. Kirstie Lynn, MA BSc(Hons) ACA PGCE *2001;* Flat 1 Hadleigh Court, 245 Willesden Lane, LONDON, NW2 5RY.
GOODLET, Mr. Patrick, ACA *2008;* 33, King Street, LONDON, SW1Y6RJ.
GOODLEY, Miss. Sarah Louise, BA ACA *2005;* 51 Penton Avenue, STAINES, MIDDLESEX, TW18 2NA.
GOODLIFFE, Mr. Mark Robert, BA ACA *1991;* 40 Emperors Gate, LONDON, SW7 4HJ.
GOODLIFFE, Mr. Peter William, BSc FCA *1981;* 20 Park Lodge Close, CHEADLE, SK8 1HU.
GOODLIFFE, Mr. Richard George, FCA *1957;* Mallards Point, Bracken Close, Storrington, PULBOROUGH, RH20 3HT. (Life Member)
•①**GOODLUD, Mr. Stephen John, BSc ACA** *1992;* with KPMG LLP, 15 Canada Square, LONDON, E14 5GL.
•**GOODMAKER, Mr. Philip Harold, FCA ATII** *1970;* Philip Goodmaker, 18 Fallowfield, Middlesex, STANMORE, HA7 3DF.
GOODMAN, Mr. Adam Richard, BSc ACA *2002;* 1 Flaxland Close, MARKET HARBOROUGH, LEICESTERSHIRE, LE16 8EY.
GOODMAN, Mrs. Amanda Jean, BSc ACA *1997;* U B S AG, 100 Liverpool Street, LONDON, EC2M 2RH.
•**GOODMAN, Mr. Andrew Joseph, ACA** *1981;* Heath House Business Services, 14 Willow Close, Mylor Bridge, FALMOUTH, CORNWALL, TR11 5SG.
GOODMAN, Mr. Barry Robert, MA FCA *1981;* Trident Chambers, P.O.Box 146, ROAD TOWN, TORTOLA ISLAND, VG1110, VIRGIN ISLANDS (BRITISH).
GOODMAN, Mrs. Catherine Linda, MA BA ACA ATII *1994;* 45 Highfield Road, PURLEY, CR8 2JJ.
GOODMAN, Mr. Christopher John, BSc ACA *1993;* 26 King Street, COTTINGHAM, NORTH HUMBERSIDE, HU16 5QE.
•**GOODMAN, Mr. David, BA FCA** *1986;* (Tax Fac), Kitchen & Brown, Alpha House, 40 Coinagehall Street, HELSTON, TR13 8EQ.
GOODMAN, Mr. Duncan Clive, ACA *1981;* Cengage Learning (E M E A) Ltd Cheriton House, North Way Walworth Industrial Estate, ANDOVER, SP10 5BE.
GOODMAN, Ellis Martin, Esq CBE FCA *1959;* 69 Park Avenue, Glencoe, CHICAGO, IL 60022, UNITED STATES.
GOODMAN, Mr. Eric, FCA *1970;* 71 Kipton Field, Rothwell, KETTERING, NORTHAMPTONSHIRE, NN14 6ED. (Life Member)
GOODMAN, Mr. Geoffrey Ian, FCA *1971;* 11 Meadow Road, PINNER, HA5 1EB.
GOODMAN, Mr. Harold Gerald, BA FCA *1965;* 3 Montpellier Mews, Broughton Park, Salford, MANCHESTER, M7 4ZW.
•**GOODMAN, Mr. Huw Thomas William, BSc FCA** *1980;* Sinnett & Tansley Limited, 3 Richfield Place, Richfield Avenue, READING, RG1 8EQ.
GOODMAN, Mr. James, ACA *2011;* 85 George Road, GODALMING, GU7 3LU.
GOODMAN, Mr. James, BAcc FCA *2001;* R S M Tenon, 48 St. Vincent Street, GLASGOW, G2 5TS.
GOODMAN, Mrs. Jane Ellen, BSc ACA *1989;* 38 Winthorpe Drive, SOLIHULL, B91 3UW.
GOODMAN, Mr. Jeffrey Joel, JP FCA *1960;* The Studio, 125 Bow Lane, Finchley, LONDON, N12 0JL. (Life Member)
•**GOODMAN, Mr. Jonathan Harrison Moss, BSc FCA** *1995;* (Tax Fac), Moss Goodman, 24 Lyndhurst Gardens, Finchley, LONDON, N3 1TB. See also J Goodman Accounting Services Limited
GOODMAN, Mr. Keith, BA FCA *1961;* 59 Briar Gate, Long Eaton, NOTTINGHAM, NG10 4BQ.
GOODMAN, Mr. Keith Alexander, MA ACA *1992;* c/o Media Square (Asia) Limited, 1902 Chinachem Hollywood Ctr, 1 Hollywood Road, CENTRAL, HONG KONG ISLAND, HONG KONG SAR.
GOODMAN, Mr. Keith David, FCA *1971;* Leonard Curtis & Co, One Great Cumberland Place, LONDON, W1H 7LW. (Life Member)
GOODMAN, Mrs. Laura Anne, BSc(Hons) ACA *2002;* Trotts View, Trotts Lane, WESTERHAM, KENT, TN16 1SD.
•**GOODMAN, Mr. Laurence Howard, FCA** *1982;* Bridgebank Capital, Egerton House, Towers Business Park, Wilmslow Road, MANCHESTER, M20 2DX.
GOODMAN, Mrs. Lesley Nichola, BA ACA *1993;* 4 Rendells Meadow, Bovey Tracey, NEWTON ABBOT, TQ13 9QW.
GOODMAN, Mr. Mark David, BA ACA *1992;* 49 Main Street, Swannington, COALVILLE, LE67 8QL.
GOODMAN, Mr. Mark Simon, MA FCA *1990;* 26 Northey Avenue, Cheam, SUTTON, SM2 7HR.
GOODMAN, Mr. Neil Martin, FCA *1958;* Fernwood, Bracken Lane, Storrington, PULBOROUGH, RH20 3HR. (Life Member)
•**GOODMAN, Mr. Nigel Stephen, BA ACA** *2002;* with RSM Tenon Audit Limited, Davidson House, Forbury Square, READING, RG1 3EU.
GOODMAN, Mr. Nigel Timothy, FCA *1974;* Flat No.1 Ingrebourne Court, Chingford Avenue, LONDON, E4 6RL.
•**GOODMAN, Mr. Paul Joseph, BA FCA** *1970;* (Tax Fac), Paul Goodman, Mortons Cottage, The Green, Sarratt, RICKMANSWORTH, HERTFORDSHIRE WD3 6BH. See also Goodman Craig
GOODMAN, Mr. Paul Martin, ACA *2010;* 40 Fitzjohn Avenue, BARNET, HERTFORDSHIRE, EN5 2HW.
•**GOODMAN, Mr. Peter Albert, MA FCA CTA TEP** *1981;* (Tax Fac), Wilkins Kennedy, Bridge House, London Bridge, LONDON, SE1 9QR.
GOODMAN, Mr. Peter John, FCA *1972;* 106 Westfield Road, WOKING, GU22 9QP. (Life Member)
•**GOODMAN, Mr. Peter Martin, BA ACA** *2003;* Goodmans Accounting and Advisory Ltd, The Waterfront (ADI Office), Salts Mill Road, Saltaire, SHIPLEY, WEST YORKSHIRE BD17 7EZ.
•**GOODMAN, Mr. Philip Charles, BA FCA** *1992;* Goodman & Co, 14 Basing Hill, Golders Green, LONDON, NW11 8TH.
GOODMAN, Mr. Philip Stanley, BA ACA *1983;* 21 Dellcott Close, WELWYN GARDEN CITY, AL8 7BB.
•**GOODMAN, Mr. Richard Adrian, FCA** *1981;* Goodmans, 138 Bury Old Road, Whitefield, MANCHESTER, M45 6AT.
GOODMAN, Mr. Richard James, FCA *1976;* Wincanton, Methuen Park, CHIPPENHAM, WILTSHIRE, SN14 0WT.
GOODMAN, Mr. Richard John, BSc ACA *2007;* 26 Pondfield Lane, BRENTWOOD, CM13 2BX.
GOODMAN, Mrs. Sally Jane, BSc ACA *2002;* 1 Flaxland Close, MARKET HARBOROUGH, LEICESTERSHIRE, LE16 8EY.
GOODMAN, Mrs. Sara Elizabeth, BSc ACA *1991;* 26 Northey Avenue, SUTTON, SURREY, SM2 7HR.
GOODMAN, Mr. Simon James, FCA *1971;* 16 Lime Tree Road, NORWICH, NR2 2NQ.
GOODMAN, Mr. Thomas Andrew, ACA *2008;* Flat 4, 9 Hobury Street, LONDON, SW10 0JB.
•**GOODMAN, Mr. Timothy James, BEng ACA** *2003;* Ernst & Young LLP, 1 More London Place, LONDON, SE1 2AF. See also Ernst & Young Europe LLP
GOODRICH, Mr. Benjamin Harry, BSc ACA *2010;* 61 Kings Road, FLEET, HAMPSHIRE, GU51 3AS.
GOODRICH, Mrs. Nancy Elisabeth, BA ACA *1994;* 4 The Boulevard, LYTHAM ST. ANNES, FY8 1EH.
•**GOODRICH, Mr. Simon Reginald, FCA** *1971;* Goodrich Morrison & Co, 10 Durfold Road, HORSHAM, RH12 5HZ.
GOODRICH, Mrs. Vicky Elaine, ACA *2007;* 64 Sefton Road, CHESTER, CH2 3RS.
GOODRICK, Miss. Lisa, ACA *2006;* 11 Stane Drive, Bracebridge Heath, LINCOLN, LN4 2UL.
GOODRIDGE, Mrs. Clare Alexandra, BA ACA *1993;* Thornleigh, 18 Wood Road, Tettenhall Wood, WOLVERHAMPTON, WV6 8LS.
GOODRIDGE, Mr. Darius Jon, ACA *1989;* Abu Dhabi Future Energy Company, PO Box 54115, ABU DHABI, UNITED ARAB EMIRATES.
•**GOODRIDGE, Mr. David James, BA FCA DChA** *1985;* Kingston Smith & Partners LLP, 105 St. Peters Street, ST. ALBANS, HERTFORDSHIRE, AL1 3EJ. See also Kingston Smith Limited Liability Partnership, Kingston Smith LLP, Devonshire Corporate Services LLP and Kingston Smith Consulting LLP
•**GOODRIDGE, Mr. John Simon, BA ACA** *1995;* with Buzzacott LLP, 130 Wood Street, LONDON, EC2V 6DL.
GOODRIDGE, Mr. Nicholas John, ACA *1993;* Thornleigh, 18 Wood Road, Tettenhall Wood, WOLVERHAMPTON, WV6 8LS.
GOODRIDGE, Mr. Paul Garnet George, BA ACA *1990;* 16 Woollards Lane, Great Shelford, CAMBRIDGE, CB22 5LZ.
•**GOODRIDGE, Mr. Robin David, BA ACA** *1988;* Ashbys Business Consultants Limited, Morton House, 9 Beacon Court, Pitstone Green Business Park, Pitstone, LEIGHTON BUZZARD BEDFORDSHIRE LU7 9GY.
GOODRUM, Mr. Nicholas, BSc(Hons) ACA *2010;* 209/9-15 Central Avenue, MANLY, NSW 2095, AUSTRALIA.
GOODSELL, Mr. David Mark, BA ACA *2003;* 49 Burnham Road, ST. ALBANS, HERTFORDSHIRE, AL1 4QN.
GOODSELL, Mrs. Joanne Ruth, BA ACA *1998;* BoA Netherlands Coöperatieve U.A., Herengracht 469, 1017 BS AMSTERDAM, NETHERLANDS.
GOODSELL, Mr. Samuel Neil, ACA *2007;* 50 Fontmell Park, ASHFORD, Middlesex, TW15 2NJ.
•**GOODSELL, Mr. Terry James, FCA** *1975;* James Cowper LLP, 3 Wesley Gate, Queens Road, READING, RG1 4AP. See also JC Payroll Services Ltd
GOODSHIP, Mr. Mark David, BA(Hons) ACA *2002;* Scottish Widows, 5 Morrison Street, EDINBURGH, EH3 8BH.
GOODSIR, Mr. George Spiers, FCA *1961;* Stow Maries, Woodcote Park, EPSOM, KT18 7EN. (Life Member)
GOODSIR-CULLEN, Mr. Niall Jonathan Martin, FCA *1974;* Johnson Smith Associates Ltd., PO Box 2499, Elizabethan Square, Shedden Road, GEORGETOWN, GRAND CAYMAN KY1-1104 CAYMAN ISLANDS.
GOODSON, Mr. Alan Robin, BEng ACA *2001;* 1735 Market Street 32nd Floor, PHILADELPHIA, PA 19103, UNITED STATES.
GOODSON, Mrs. Andrea Elizabeth, BSc(Hons) ACA *2000;* 22 Old Library Mews, NORWICH, NR1 1ET.
GOODSON, Mrs. Hannah Patricia, BSc ACA *2002;* 9 Vicarage Mews, Conway Road, CARDIFF, CF11 9PD.
GOODSON, Mrs. Joanne, BA ACA *2000;* Barn 1, St Marys Court, Church End, Kensworth, DUNSTABLE, BEDFORDSHIRE LU6 3RA.
GOODSON, Mr. John Francis, BSc FCA *1968;* 19 Grasmere Avenue, HARPENDEN, HERTFORDSHIRE, AL5 5PT. (Life Member)
GOODSON, Mr. Jonathan James, BSc(Hons) ACA *2003;* 22 Old Library Mews, NORWICH, NR1 1ET.
GOODSON, Mr. Philip Steven, BA ACA *1996;* 10 Newlands Crescent, GUILDFORD, GU1 3JS.
•**GOODSON, Mrs. Suzanne Marie, BSc FCA** *1989;* (Tax Fac), 8 Summerfield Drive, Wootton, BEDFORD, MK43 9FE. See also Wright Connections Limited
GOODSON, Mr. Timothy, BSc(Hons) ACA *2002;* 42 St. Augustine Road, Heath, CARDIFF, CF14 4BE.
GOODSWEN, Ms. Anne, BA ACA *1989;* Olive Field, Church Lane, Awbridge, ROMSEY, HAMPSHIRE, SO51 0HN.
GOODSWEN, Miss. Julia Mary, BA ACA *1988;* Corrie, Shaftesbury Road, WOKING, GU22 7DU.
GOODWILL, Miss. Anne-Marie Christine, BSc ACA *2001;* 14 Jackson Close, EPSOM, SURREY, KT18 7RA.
GOODWIN, Mr. Alan David, FCA *1972;* 391 Crewe Road, Winterley, SANDBACH, CHESHIRE, CW11 4RS.
GOODWIN, Mr. Andrew John, BSc BCom ACA *1992;* Glenridding, 127 Meeting House Lane, Balsall Common, COVENTRY, CV7 7GD.
GOODWIN, Mr. Andrew Michael, ACA *2002;* 108 Letchworth Road, LEICESTER, LE3 6FH.
GOODWIN, Miss. Anne Elizabeth, BCom ACA *1999;* 31 Mariner Ave, Edgbaston, BIRMINGHAM, B16 9DF.
GOODWIN, Mr. Bernard, FCA *1955;* 6 Staffordshire House, Broughton Avenue, Finchely, LONDON, N3 3EG. (Life Member)
GOODWIN, Mr. Brent, ACA *1983;* 74 Desford Road, Kirby Muxloe, LEICESTER, LE9 2BD.
•**GOODWIN, Mr. Christopher, BA FCA** *1990;* (Tax Fac), Moore Stephens (Guildford) LLP, Priory House, Pilgrims Court, Sydenham Road, GUILDFORD, SURREY GU1 3RX.
GOODWIN, Mr. Christopher John, MA FCA *1980;* 14 Waters Meet, HUNTINGDON, CAMBRIDGESHIRE, PE29 3AY.
GOODWIN, Mr. Clive George Dalton, BSc ACA *1997;* 28 Wensleydale Road, HAMPTON, MIDDLESEX, TW12 2LW.
GOODWIN, Mr. Darryl Neil, MA FCA *1986;* 4 Merrileas Gardens, BASINGSTOKE, HAMPSHIRE, RG22 5JZ.
•**GOODWIN, Mr. David Gerard, BSc FCA** *1994;* Sturgess Hutchinson Limited, 10 Station Road, Earl Shilton, LEICESTER, LE9 7GA.
GOODWIN, Mr. David John, FCA *1964;* 41 Greenfields, MAIDSTONE, KENT, ME15 8ET. (Life Member)
GOODWIN, Mr. David Jonathan, FCA *1972;* Royals, Old Chapel Yard, Church Street, FALMOUTH, CORNWALL, TR11 3EF.
•**GOODWIN, Mrs. Deborah Louise Pearson, FCA** *1980;* PCA Limited, 12 Old Park Avenue, LONDON, SW12 8RH. See also Pearson
GOODWIN, Mr. Duncan Paul, BA FCA *1974;* The Cottage, Forest Road, Cotebrook, TARPORLEY, CHESHIRE, CW6 9EE.

GOODWIN, Miss. Emma Elizabeth Alice, MA ACA *2007;* 83 Boundary Lane, WELWYN GARDEN CITY, HERTFORDSHIRE, AL7 4EG.
•**GOODWIN, Mrs. Emma Jayne, ACA** *2002;* East Midlands Managed Account Service, 9 Trent View Gardens, Radcliffe-on-Trent, NOTTINGHAM, NG12 1AY.
GOODWIN, Mr. Frank, BA FCA *1960;* 24 Moulton Grove, STOCKTON-ON-TEES, TS19 7RH. (Life Member)
GOODWIN, Mr. Geoffrey Robert, FCA *1970;* 37 New Street, HENLEY-ON-THAMES, OXFORDSHIRE, RG9 2BP.
GOODWIN, Mr. George William Roy, FCA *1959;* 45 Brean Down Avenue, Henleaze, BRISTOL, BS9 4JE. (Life Member)
•**GOODWIN, Mr. Glynn Leslie, FCA** *1982;* (Tax Fac), Benten & Co., Abbey House, 51 High Street, SAFFRON WALDEN, ESSEX, CB10 1AF.
GOODWIN, Mr. Ian, BSc ACA *1987;* The Old Vicarage, Church Lane, Riseley, BEDFORD, MK44 1ER.
GOODWIN, Mr. Ian David, BSc ACA *1992;* 42 Ashley Street, CARLISLE, CA2 7BD.
GOODWIN, Mr. James Lawrence, BA FCA *1988;* Finkley Manor, Finkley, ANDOVER, HAMPSHIRE, SP11 6AE.
GOODWIN, Mr. Jason Richard, BSc(Hons) ACA *2001;* South Staffordshire Plc, Green Lane, WALSALL, WEST MIDLANDS, WS2 7PD.
GOODWIN, Mr. Jeremy Richard Frank, BA ACA *1982;* 98 Broom Road, TEDDINGTON, MIDDLESEX, TW11 9PF.
GOODWIN, Mr. John Paul, BSc FCA *1990;* 47 Route de St. Georges, Petit-Lancy, 1213 GENEVA, SWITZERLAND.
GOODWIN, Mrs. Karen Margaret, BA ACA *1986;* 133 Tanglewood Drive, EAST GREENWICH, RI 02818, UNITED STATES.
•**GOODWIN, Mrs. Laura Gaye, FCA** *1991;* Acadia Accounting Limited, 77 Woodville Drive, Marple, STOCKPORT, CHESHIRE, SK6 7QX.
GOODWIN, Mr. Lee David, BA FCA *1987;* Fox Corner, 76 Foston Gate, Wigston Harcourt, LEICESTER, LE18 3SD.
•**GOODWIN, Mr. Leigh John, BSc ACA** *1993;* L J Goodwin & Co Limited, 6 Parkside Court, Greenhough Road, LICHFIELD, STAFFORDSHIRE, WS13 7AU.
GOODWIN, Mrs. Lyndsie Sharon, BSc ACA CTA *2001;* 1 Stourside, Shotley Gate, IPSWICH, IP9 1QF.
GOODWIN, Mr. Lytton Balfour, FCA *1970;* Southmead, 156 Clifton Drive South, St Annes, LYTHAM ST. ANNES, FY8 1HG.
GOODWIN, Mr. Malcolm Duncan, BAcc ACA *2005;* Holyrood Park House, 106 Holyrood Road, EDINBURGH, EH8 8AE.
GOODWIN, Mr. Mark Gerald, BA ACA *1999;* 407 The Paddock, Birches, The Paddock, STOURBRIDGE, DY9 0RE.
GOODWIN, Mrs. Mary-Clare, BA ACA *1999;* 8 Queens Road, LONDON, SW14 8PJ.
GOODWIN, Mr. Michael John, FCA *1974;* 3 Follyfield, Hankerton, MALMESBURY, SN16 9LA.
GOODWIN, Mr. Mostyn Innes, MA BA ACA *2002;* The Paragon, 4a St Philips Way, LONDON, N1 7aj.
GOODWIN, Mr. Nicholas David, BCom ACA *1988;* Jeyes Ltd, Brunel Way, THETFORD, IP24 1HF.
GOODWIN, Mr. Paul Jeremy, FCA *1973;* Walnut Cottage, Church Walk, Headcorn, ASHFORD, KENT, TN27 9NR.
GOODWIN, Mr. Peter Reginald, FCA *1964;* 11 Ferndale Road, RAYLEIGH, SS6 9NN. (Life Member)
GOODWIN, Mr. Philip Walter, BA FCA *1991;* 16 Rowanvale, BANBRIDGE, COUNTY DOWN, BT32 4RU.
GOODWIN, Miss. Philippa Jane, BA ACA *1995;* 20 Park View, Hatch End, PINNER, MIDDLESEX, HA5 4LN.
GOODWIN, Mr. Randolph, FCA *1948;* Pitlock Farm, Old Tanhouse Lane, Cradley, MALVERN, WR13 5LZ. (Life Member)
•**GOODWIN, Mr. Robert Edward Osbon, FCA** *1966;* (Tax Fac), Goodwin Shaw, 39 Market Place, CHIPPENHAM, SN15 3HT. See also Robert Goodwin & Co
•**GOODWIN, Mr. Robert John, ACA** *1993;* C/o Ernst & Young, P O BOX 1750, RUWI 112, MUSCAT, OMAN.
GOODWIN, Mr. Roger, FCA *1980;* Griffin Mining Ltd, 6th Floor, 60 St. James's Street, LONDON, SW1A 1LE.
•**GOODWIN, Mr. Ronald Joseph, FCA** *1974;* Baker Tilly Tax & Advisory Services LLP, Festival Way, Festival Park, STOKE-ON-TRENT, ST1 5BB. See also Baker Tilly UK Audit LLP
GOODWIN, Miss. Sarah Jane, BSc(Hons) ACA *2011;* 120 Meadway, Bramhall, STOCKPORT, CHESHIRE, SK7 1NL.
•**GOODWIN, Mrs. Sarah Margaret, MA FCA** *1976;* Sarah M. Goodwin, Amber Hill, Amberley, STROUD, GL5 5AN.
GOODWIN, Mrs. Sharon, BSc ACA *1996;* 11 Barton Road, MAIDSTONE, KENT, ME15 7BU.
GOODWIN, Mr. Simon John, BA ACA *1992;* 20 Amberley Road, Palmers Green, LONDON, N13 4BJ.
GOODWIN, Mr. Stephen Mark, BA ACA *1988;* Bruf Contract Holdings Ltd, Gibbs Marsh Trading Estate, Stalbridge, STURMINSTER NEWTON, DORSET, DT10 2RX.
•**GOODWIN, Mr. Stephen Paul, MA FCA** *1985;* (Tax Fac), Goldwins Limited, 75 Maygrove Road, West Hampstead, LONDON, NW6 2EG.
GOODWIN, Mr. Steven John, BSc ACA *1992;* 1727 Sailmaker St, CHARLESTON, SC 29492, UNITED STATES.
GOODWIN, Mr. Timothy Robert Thomas, FCA *1962;* 33 Kent Avenue, Ealing, LONDON, W13 8BE.
GOODWIN, Mr. Trevor John, FCA *1973;* BayTree House, 59 Baldslow Road, HASTINGS, EAST SUSSEX, TN34 2EY.
GOODWIN, Mrs. Zoe Louise, BSc ACA *2000;* 1 Nant y Garn, Risca, NEWPORT, GWENT, NP11 7AS.
•**GOODWORTH, Mr. Thomas Edward, BA(Hons) ACA** *2004;* with BDO LLP, 55 Baker Street, LONDON, W1U 7EU.
GOODY, Mr. Andrew John, BA ACA *1992;* Bibby Line Ltd, 105 Duke Street, LIVERPOOL, L1 5JQ.
GOODY, Mr. David Hugh, BSc FCA MCT *1979;* 28 West Hill Road, LONDON, SW18 1LN.
GOODY, Miss. Rachel Mead, BA ACA DChA *1991;* 8 Adams Road, CAMBRIDGE, CB3 9AD.
GOODYEAR, Mrs. Alison Jane, BSc ACA *1990;* 10 Somerville Close, Bromborough, WIRRAL, CH63 0PH.
GOODYEAR, Mrs. Brooks Murray, MSc ACA *1987;* 89 Farrer Drive, #01-01 Sommerville Park, SINGAPORE 259288, SINGAPORE.
•**GOODYEAR, Mr. Geoffrey George, FCA** *1970;* (Tax Fac), Lubbock Fine, Russell Bedford House, City Forum, 250 City Road, LONDON, EC1V 2QQ.
GOODYER, Mr. Timothy Edward, BA(Hons) ACA *2003;* Crossways, 15 Jennings Road, SMITHS FL04, BERMUDA.
GOOI, Mr. Aaron Hsien-Liu, MBA BEng ACA *1995;* 2 Prose Street, North Balwyn, MELBOURNE, VIC 3104, AUSTRALIA.
GOOI, Mr. Lee Huat, BSc ACA *1984;* 10 Solok Jones, Pulau Tikus, 10250 PENANG, MALAYSIA.
GOOI, Mr. Richard Hock-Leok, FCA *1977;* 1/ 33 Francesca Street, Mont Albert North, MONT ALBERT, VIC 3129, AUSTRALIA.
•**GOOLD, Mr. Alan Clive Witchurch, FCA** *1970;* Alan Goold, 16 Bayliss Road, Wargrave, READING, RG10 8DR.
GOOLD, Mrs. Eleanor Joan, BSc ACA *2007;* 9 South Road, MAIDENHEAD, BERKSHIRE, SL6 1HF.
GOOLD, Mrs. Jane Louise, BSc ACA *1987;* (Tax Fac), Crosslanes Farm Reading Road, Arborfield, READING, RG2 9HP.
GOOLD, Mr. Nicholas David, ACA *1990;* 1 Robins Field, Wansford, PETERBOROUGH, PE8 6JW.
GOOLD, Mr. Peter Anthony, LLB FCA *1968;* Oxenber Cottage, Graystonber Lane, Austwick, LANCASTER, LA2 8BJ.
GOOLDEN, Mr. Michael Cyril Christopher, MA FCA *1972;* Foxes Bank Farm, Washwell Lane, WADHURST, TN5 6LN.
GOONERATNE, Mr. Amitha Lal, FCA *1979;* 27 Queen's Road, 3 COLOMBO, SRI LANKA.
GOONETILLAKE, Mr. Damayanth Sunimal, BA ACA *1986;* 33 Hillersdon Avenue, LONDON, SW13 0EG.
GOONTING, Mr. Anthony Gerard, ACA *1980;* Unit 23-07, Kiaramas Cendana Condominium, 10 Jalan Desa Kiara, 50480 KUALA LUMPUR, FEDERAL TERRITORY, MALAYSIA.
GOORWAPPA, Mr. Darren Marcus, BA ACA *1995;* 30 Long Acres, Greasby, WIRRAL, CH49 2SP.
GOOTT, Mr. Trevor Evan, BCom ACA *2002;* 7A Alexander Road, Bantry Bay, CAPE TOWN, 8005, SOUTH AFRICA.
GOPAL, Mr. Kishore Srinivas Ramaswami, BSc(Hons) ACA *2004;* 161 Pencisely Road, CARDIFF, CF5 1DN.
GOPAL, Miss. Rajshree Naresh, BA FCA *1999;* with ICAEW, Metropolitan House, 321 Avebury Boulevard, MILTON KEYNES, MK9 2FZ.
GOPAL, Mr. Ramchandran, BCom FCA ATT CPA *1993;* F/001 Vishal Apartments, Sir M V Road, Andheri East, MUMBAI 400069, MAHARASHTRA, INDIA.
GOPAL, Mr. Soomunsingh, ACA *2007;* 68 Exmouth Road, RUISLIP, MIDDLESEX, HA4 0UG.
GOPALAN, Mr. Bharat, ACA *2009;* Flat 38 Meridian Court, 9 Chambers Street, LONDON, SE16 4UE.
GOPAUL, Mr. Rajiv Kumar, BSc ACA *1992;* 33 Beechwood Gardens, ILFORD, ESSEX, IG5 0AE.
GOPINATHAN, Miss. Kavita, BSc ACA *2006;* Apartment 95, Becquerel Court, West Parkside, Greenwich Peninsula, LONDON, SE10 0QA.
GOPSILL, Mr. Michael Clement, FCA *1970;* (Tax Fac), Woodside, Church Lane, Longbank, BEWDLEY, DY12 2UH. (Life Member)
GOR, Mr. Vishal, BA(Hons) ACA *2002;* Royal & Sunalliance Plantation Place, 30 Fenchurch Street, LONDON, EC3M 3BD.
GORA, Mr. Ebrahim, ACA *2009;* 8 North Crescent, LONDON, N3 3LL.
•**GORACY, Mr. Alexander Jozef, FCA** *1981;* Albert Goodman CBH Limited, The Lupins Business Centre, 1-3 Greenhill, WEYMOUTH, DORSET, DT4 7SP. See also Coyne Butterworth Hardwicke Limited
GORARD, Mr. Anthony John, FCA *1952;* 6 Shetland Close, Leigh Park, WESTBURY, BA13 2GN. (Life Member)
GORASIA, Mr. Shashi, BSc(Hons) ACA *2003;* 36 Kensington Road, OLDHAM, OL8 4BZ.
GORASIA, Mr. Suresh, BEng ACA *1999;* 151 Frederick Street, OLDHAM, OL8 4DA.
GORAYA, Miss. Baljit Kaur, BSc ACA ACII *1994;* Pricewaterhousecoopers, Plumtree Court, LONDON, EC4A 4HT.
GORBACHEV, Mr. Nikolay, ACA *2007;* 37/3 Yubileynaya Street, Flat 131, MYTISCHY, MOSCOW REGION, RUSSIAN FEDERATION.
GORBATCHEVA, Miss. Maria, BA ACA *2005;* with PricewaterhouseCoopers LLP, Pricewaterhousecoopers, 12 Plumtree Court, LONDON, EC4A 4HT.
GORBATKO, Ms. Inga, MSc ACA *2003;* 68 Lauderdale Mansions, Lauderdale Road, LONDON, W9 1NF.
GORBUNOWA, Miss. Irina, ACA *2002;* 3 Ely Gardens, Ely Street, STRATFORD-UPON-AVON, CV37 6FB.
GORDON, Mr. Adrian, FCA *1963;* 71 Grove End Gardens, Grove End Road, LONDON, NW8 9LN.
GORDON, Mr. Alan Nicholas Chesterfield, BA FCA *1988;* 5 Woodcote Park Road, EPSOM, KT18 7EY.
GORDON, Mr. Alastair Neil, BA ACA *1986;* 64 Castelnau, LONDON, SW13 9EX.
GORDON, Mr. Alexander Duncan, MA FCA *1955;* A.D.Gordon, 4A Devonshire Mews North, LONDON, W1G 7BJ. (Life Member)
GORDON, Dr. Allan Laurence, PhD MBA FCA *1983;* 30 Elmgate Drive, Littledown, BOURNEMOUTH, BH7 7EG.
GORDON, Mr. Andrew Edward, BSc FCA *1978;* Ranmoor, 5 Fairmile Avenue, COBHAM, SURREY, KT11 2JA.
GORDON, Mr. Andrew Hugh, BA(Hons) ACA *2000;* Trewithen, Gravesend, TORPOINT, CORNWALL, PL11 2LX.
GORDON, Mr. Andrew Marc, BA(Econ) ACA CF *1997;* 9 Maurice Walk, LONDON, NW11 6JX.
GORDON, Mr. Andrew Stuart, BSc ACA *2006;* 29 Birch Road, Southville, BRISTOL, BS3 1PE.
GORDON, Mr. Andrew Todd, BA ACA *2005;* 114 Grosvenor Road, Jesmond, NEWCASTLE UPON TYNE, NE2 2RQ.
GORDON, Mrs. Anna Christine, BA ACA *1998;* with PricewaterhouseCoopers LLP, 1 Embankment Place, LONDON, WC2N 6RH.
GORDON, Mr. Anthony John Ramsay, BA FCA *1981;* The Bell House, Messing, COLCHESTER, CO5 9UA.
GORDON, Mr. Anton Joel, BA FCA *1985;* 223 Main Street, Shadwell, LEEDS, LS17 8LA.
GORDON, Mr. Atholl Stuart, BA ACA *1987;* F G H UK Ltd F G H House, Ingleby Road, BRADFORD, BD99 2XG.
•**GORDON, Mr. Barry Allan, FCA ATII** *1986;* (Tax Fac), Dua & Co Limited, 3 Century Court, Tolpits Lane, WATFORD, WD18 9PU. See also Dua LLP
GORDON, Mrs. Belinda-Jayne, BSc ACA *1991;* Amberley, The Birches, Cheadle, STOKE-ON-TRENT, STAFFORDSHIRE, ST10 1EJ.
GORDON, Mr. Brian Charles, FCA *1975;* Walsham Brothers & Co Ltd, 4 Fenchurch Avenue, LONDON, EC3M 5BS.
•**GORDON, Mr. Bruce Malcolm, BA ACA** *1987;* Thames Valley Capital Ltd, Davidson House Forbury Sq., READING, RG1 3EU.
GORDON, Mr. Carl Philip, BA ACA *2006;* 42 Truswell Avenue, SHEFFIELD, S10 1WJ.
GORDON, Mr. Carl Ronald, BSc ACA *1995;* C/O KPMG Limited, 10th floor Sun Wah Tower, 115 Nguyen Hue Street, District 1, HO CHI MINH CITY, VIETNAM.
GORDON, Miss. Catherine Anne Drummond, BSc FCA *1976;* 13 Belvedere Avenue, Wimbledon Village, LONDON, SW19 7PP.
GORDON, Ms. Catherine Lucy, BA ACA *1996;* with Deloitte LLP, 1 Woodborough Road, NOTTINGHAM, NG1 3FG.
GORDON, Mr. David John, FCA *1962;* 10 Aldeburgh Lodge Gardens, ALDEBURGH, IP15 5DP.
GORDON, Mr. David Jonathan, BA ACA *1985;* Flat 1Paul House, 41-43 Saffron Hill, LONDON, EC1N 8FH.
GORDON, Mr. David Sorrell, BA FCA *1968;* 255 West 94th Street, Apartment 16F, NEW YORK, NY 10025, UNITED STATES.
GORDON, Mr. Donald Grant, FCA *1969;* Brooklands, Mardy, ABERGAVENNY, NP7 6NU.
•**GORDON, Mrs. Elizabeth Anne, MSc BSc FCA** *1988;* Baker-Gordon, 23 Lindhurst Drive, Hockley Heath, SOLIHULL, WEST MIDLANDS, B94 6QD.
GORDON, Mr. Eugene, FCA *1955;* 13 Elm Tree Drive, Burbage, HINCKLEY, LE10 2TX. (Life Member)
GORDON, Mrs. Faye Danielle, LLB ACA *2001;* with PricewaterhouseCoopers LLP, 89 Sandyford Road, NEWCASTLE UPON TYNE, NE1 8HW.
GORDON, Mr. Graeme Robertson, BSc FCA *1992;* MEMBER OF COUNCIL, Praxity AISBL, Stephenson House, 2 Cherry Orchard Road, CROYDON, CR0 6BA.
GORDON, Mrs. Helen, BA ACA *2006;* 42 Truswell Avenue, SHEFFIELD, S10 1WJ.
GORDON, Mr. Henry Kenneth, FCA *1960;* Greenwoods, Oaklands Lane, BARNET, HERTFORDSHIRE, EN5 3JN. (Life Member)
GORDON, Ian, Esq OBE JP DL FCA *1962;* 6 Beach Way, Beach Road, NORTH SHIELDS, NE30 3ED.
GORDON, Mr. Ian Alfred, BSc FCA *1971;* 5 Elm Tree Close, St John's Wood, LONDON, NW8 9JS. (Life Member)
•**GORDON, Mr. Ian Peter, BA ACA** *1992;* 17 Lancaster Road, MANCHESTER, M20 2QU.
GORDON, Mr. James, MSc ACA *2010;* Flat B, 39 Uverdale Road, LONDON, SW10 0SN.
GORDON, Mr. James Beaton, BSc ACA *2000;* Rio Tinto, 2 Eastbourne Terrace, LONDON, W2 6LG.
•**GORDON, Mr. James Iain, BSc ACA** *1993;* with Ernst & Young LLP, 1 More London Place, LONDON, SE1 2AF.
GORDON, Mr. James Rupert, BSc(Econ) ACA *2003;* Moore Europe Research Services, 1 Curzon Street, LONDON, W1J 5HA.
GORDON, Miss. Jennifer Ruth, BA FCA *1989;* 57 Waterloo Road, Ramsey, ISLE OF MAN, IM8 1EG.
GORDON, Mr. John Brian, BA ACA *1991;* 19 Northwold Avenue, West Bridgford, NOTTINGHAM, NG2 7LQ.
GORDON, Mr. John David, FCA *1961;* La Petite Pompe, Les Mouilpieds, St. Martin, GUERNSEY, GY4 6TJ. (Life Member)
GORDON, Mr. John Edwin, MA FCA *1965;* Flat 15, 10 Berkeley Street, LONDON, W1J 8DP. (Life Member)
GORDON, Mr. John Roger, BSc(Econ) ACA *2002;* with Ferguson Maidment & Co, Sardinia House, Sardinia Street, Lincolns Inn Fields, LONDON, WC2A 3LZ.
GORDON, Mr. Jonathan Saul, BA ACA *2005;* 8 Brim Hill, LONDON, N2 0HF.
GORDON, Mr. Joseph Eric, ACA *2009;* 70A New Kings Road, Fulham, LONDON, SW6 4LT.
GORDON, Mrs. Katharine Grace, BA ACA *1992;* with PricewaterhouseCoopers, 1 Embankment Place, LONDON, WC2N 6RH.
GORDON, Dr. Kathleen Rosetta, DBA FCA *1979;* B22 Graeme Hall Park, CHRISTCHURCH, 15050, BARBADOS.
GORDON, Mr. Keith Michael, MA FCA CTA *1995;* with Atlas Chambers, 3 Field Court, Gray's Inn, LONDON, WC1R 5EP.
•**GORDON, Mr. Keith William, FCA** *1962;* (Tax Fac), K.W. Gordon & Co, 32 Hillcrest, WEYBRIDGE, KT13 8EB.
GORDON, Mr. Laurence Antony, FCA *1956;* 38 Rockingham Court, Acklam, MIDDLESBROUGH, TS5 7BN. (Life Member)
GORDON, Mr. Leslie Malcolm, MSc FCA *1968;* Claire House, 15 Highfields, ASHTEAD, KT21 2NL.
GORDON, Mr. Malcolm George, BSc ACA *1985;* 18 Balmoral Terrace, South Gosforth, NEWCASTLE UPON TYNE, NE3 1YH. (Life Member)
•**GORDON, Mr. Malcolm John, FCA** *1973;* AIMS - M J Gordon, 57 Taunton Road, BRIDGWATER, TA6 3LP.
GORDON, Mr. Mark Simon, BA(Hons) ACA *2003;* 74 Hawkstone Avenue, Whitefield, MANCHESTER, M45 7PR.
GORDON, Mr. Mark Webster, BSc ACA *1989;* The Old Vicarage, Church Road, East Harptree, BRISTOL, BS40 6AY.
GORDON, Mr. Martin, BSc FCA *2001;* 4 Swan Close, Crudwell, MALMESBURY, SN16 9DE.

GORDON, Mr. Martyn John, FCA *1965;* (Tax Fac), 9 Highview Avenue, EDGWARE, HA8 9TX.
GORDON, Mr. Matthew David, BA ACA *2000;* Sanofi - Aventis, 1 Onslow Street, GUILDFORD, SURREY, GU1 4YS.
GORDON, Mr. Matthew Millar, BA ACA *2002;* 41 Cedars Close, Belmont Hill, LONDON, SE13 5DP.
•**GORDON, Mr. Michael Donald, BA FCA** *1977;* Mitchell Gordon LLP, 43 Coniscliffe Road, DARLINGTON, COUNTY DURHAM, DL3 7EH.
GORDON, Mr. Michael John, BA ACA *1980;* 52 Grange Road, Aveley, SOUTH OCKENDON, RM15 4ER.
GORDON, Mrs. Pam, BA ACA *2007;* with Deloitte LLP, Hill House, 1 Little New Street, LONDON, EC4A 3TR.
GORDON, Mr. Paul David, MA BA FCA *1973;* 3 Swanston Grove, EDINBURGH, EH10 7BN.
•**GORDON, Mr. Paul Richard, BA ACA** *1997;* with Ernst & Young LLP, 1 More London Place, LONDON, SE1 2AF.
GORDON, Mr. Phillip James, BA ACA *1988;* 31 Larkfield Drive, Rawdon, LEEDS, LS19 6EL.
GORDON, Miss. Rachel, BA ACA *2007;* The Granary, Mitford, MORPETH, NORTHUMBERLAND, NE61 3QW.
GORDON, Mr. Rael, FCA *1952;* 701 Palatino, 187 Main Road, Green Point, CAPE TOWN, C.P., 8005 SOUTH AFRICA. (Life Member)
GORDON, Mr. Richard James, FCA *1978;* Direct Health Group Ltd, Suite C, First Floor, Darwin House, Birchwood Park, Birchwood WARRINGTON WA3 6FW.
GORDON, Mr. Robert Malcolm, FCA *1976;* Units 79 & 11 Paragon Way, Exhall, COVENTRY, CV7 9QS.
GORDON, Mr. Robert Michael, FCA *1961;* 12 Manor Farm Green, Twyford, WINCHESTER, HAMPSHIRE, SO21 1RA.
•**GORDON, Mr. Robert Nicholas Andrew, BA FCA** *1992;* PricewaterhouseCoopers LLP, Pricewaterhousecoopers, 12 Plumtree Court, LONDON, EC4A 4HT. See also PricewaterhouseCoopers
GORDON, Mr. Robert William, BSc ACA *1992;* 4 Thurmond Road, Stanmore, WINCHESTER, SO22 4DE.
•**GORDON, Mr. Robert William, FCA ATT FMAAT** *1999;* Gordon Consultancy Limited, Hamilton, 13 The Nurseries, Linstock, CARLISLE, CA6 4RR.
GORDON, Mr. Robin Lindsay, MA BBS ACA *1992;* Hewlett Packard, 450 Alexandra Rd #04-00, HPAS building, SINGAPORE 119960, SINGAPORE.
GORDON, Mr. Sidney, LLB FCA *1962;* Flat 2, 3 Rosecroft Avenue, LONDON, NW3 7QA. (Life Member)
GORDON, Mr. Simon, BSc ACA *1995;* 104 Salford Road, Aspley Guise, MILTON KEYNES, MK17 8HZ.
GORDON, Mr. Simon, BSc FCA *1977;* 33 Newberries Avenue, RADLETT, WD7 7EJ.
GORDON, Mr. Simon Peter Luis, ACA *1981;* Gerrards Farm, Farley Street, Nether Wallop, STOCKBRIDGE, HAMPSHIRE, SO20 8EL.
GORDON, Miss. Stella, BA ACA *2006;* Flat 2, 7 Wyneham Road, LONDON, SE24 9NT.
GORDON, Mr. Steven Morris, MA ACA *1992;* 5 York Road, Bowdon, ALTRINCHAM, CHESHIRE, WA14 3EQ.
GORDON, Mr. Stuart Linton, BSc ACA *1979;* 62 Parkhead Road, Ecclesall, SHEFFIELD, S11 9RB.
•**GORDON, Mr. Stuart Thomas, ACA** *1989;* (Tax Fac), Stuart Gordon, Suite 3 Capital House, Speke Hall Road, Hunts Cross, LIVERPOOL, L24 9GB.
GORDON, Mrs. Terry, BA ACA *1987;* Southways, 31 Larkfield Drive, Rawdon, LEEDS, LS19 6EL.
GORDON, Mr. Thomas Guy, BA ACA *1993;* 12 Grangeside, DARLINGTON, DL3 8QJ.
•**GORDON, Mr. Timothy Richard, BA ACA** *1987;* Ernst & Young, 5 Times Square, NEW YORK, NY 10036, UNITED STATES. See also Ernst & Young Europe LLP and Ernst & Young LLP
GORDON, Mrs. Tracy Jane, BSc ACA *1993;* 4 Pavilion Square, Beechcroft Road, LONDON, SW17 7DN.
GORDON, Mr. Vincent, FCA *1961;* 28 Alfred Road, CLAREMONT, WA 6010, AUSTRALIA.
•**GORDON, Mr. Warren Harvey, BA FCA** *1984;* 74 Hillcrest Gardens, ESHER, KT10 0BX.
GORDON, Mrs. Zena Marie, BSc ACA *2005;* Trewithen, Gravesend, TORPOINT, CORNWALL, PL11 2LX.
GORDON-BROWN, Mr. Robert Stanley, FCA *1948;* 31 Gretton Court, High Street Girton, CAMBRIDGE, CB3 0QN. (Life Member)
GORDON CLARK, Mr. Henry Toyne, BA ACA *2000;* Steward Farm, Moretonhampstead, NEWTON ABBOT, DEVON, TQ13 8SD.
GORDON-FINLAYSON, Mr. Robert Ian, BA FCA *1972;* Maizey Lodge, Ogbourne Maizey, MARLBOROUGH, SN8 1RY.
GORDON-HART, Mrs. Sheenagh Joy, MA FCA *1982;* Morgan Guaranty Ltd, 60 Victoria Embankment, LONDON, EC4Y 0JP.
GORDON-LENNOX, The Duke of Richmond Charles Henry, FCA *1956;* Molecomb, Goodwood, CHICHESTER, PO18 0PZ.
GORDON-PICKING, Mr. Bruce, MSc FCA *1969;* 18 Margaret Avenue, Shenfield, BRENTWOOD, CM15 8RF.
•**GORDON-SMITH, Mr. David Robyn, BA ACA CF CTA** *1999;* (Tax Fac), Donald Reid Limited, Prince Albert House, 20 King Street, MAIDENHEAD, BERKSHIRE, SL6 1DT. See also Coyne Butterworth (Dorchester) Limited
GORDON-STEWART, Mr. Alastair James, MA(Hons) ACA *2001;* Kier Group Plc, Tempsford Hall, SANDY, BEDFORDSHIRE, SG19 2BD.
•**GORDON STEWART, Mr. Julian Alistair, MA FCA** *1968;* (Tax Fac), J.A.Gordon Stewart & Co, 29 Greenside Road, LONDON, W12 9JQ.
GORE, Mr. Colin Spencer, FCA MBA *1977;* Institution of Occupational Safety and Health, The Grange, Highfield Drive, Wigston, WIGSTON, LE18 1NN.
GORE, Mr. Dudley Stuart, FCA *1968;* Dudley Gore & Co, 50 Queen Street, RAMSGATE, CT11 9EE.
GORE, Dr. James Pelham Overton, FCA *1982;* Department of Accounting, and Finance, The Management School, Lancaster University, LANCASTER, LA1 4YX.
GORE, Mr. Michael Arthur, MA FCA *1966;* 37 Epsom Lane South, TADWORTH, KT20 5TA. (Life Member)
GORE, Mr. Michael Balfour Gruberg, BA FCA *1963;* 19 Launceston Place, LONDON, W8 5RL. (Life Member)
GORE, Mr. Michael William, FCA *1965;* Westview Cottage, Sandy Lane, West Somerton, GREAT YARMOUTH, NR29 4DJ.
GORE, Mr. Nicholas David, ACA *1979;* Wisteria Cottage, Westcombe, SHEPTON MALLET, BA4 6ER.
GORE, Mr. Patrick Brian, BA ACA CF *1993;* 8 Duffryn Road, Cyncoed, CARDIFF, CF23 6NP.
GORE, Mr. Richard David St John, BSc ACA *1990;* CoasTel Communications Ltd, 57-59 Christian Mill Business Park, Tamerton Foliot Road, PLYMOUTH, DEVON, PL6 5DS.
GORE, Mr. Richard Thomas, FCA *1966;* 33 Parkfield Road, Ickenham, UXBRIDGE, MIDDLESEX, UB10 8LW. (Life Member)
GORE, Mr. Sanjiv Satish, FCA *1970;* 31 Castelnau Mansions, Castelnau, Barnes, LONDON, SW13 9QU.
GORE, Mrs. Sharon Amanda, ACA (SA) *1995;* (Tax Fac), Haycroft, High Street, Hermitage, THATCHAM, RG18 9RE.
GORE, Mr. Simon Christopher, BA ACA *2006;* 37 Belmont Crescent, MAIDENHEAD, SL6 6LS.
GORE, Mr. Stephen Roy, BSc ACA *1992;* V3, Imtech Telecom UK Ltd, Jays Close, BASINGSTOKE, RG22 4BS.
GORE-RANDALL, Mr. Philip Allan, MA FCA *1978;* 1 Newton Grove, LONDON, W4 1LB.
GORECKI, Miss. Karen Natalie, BA ACA *2003;* 10 Carter Road, Maidenbower, CRAWLEY, WEST SUSSEX, RH10 7NY.
GOREE, Mr. Mark Edward, BSc FCA *1996;* 123 Howard Road, Westbury Park, BRISTOL, BS6 7UZ.
•**GOREHAM, Mr. Alan Charles, FCA** *1969;* (Tax Fac), Alan Charles Associates, Abacus House, 19 Manor Close, TUNBRIDGE WELLS, TN4 8YB. See also MC Accounting Ltd
GOREHAM, Mr. Anthony Robert, MMath ACA *2006;* Flat 2 Sunnyside House, Sunnyside, LONDON, NW2 2QL.
•**GORHAM, Mr. Geoffrey Michael, FCA** *1972;* 43 Shepard Close, LEIGH-ON-SEA, ESSEX, SS9 5YR.
•**GORHAM, Mr. Ian David, BSc ACA** *1997;* 5 Cabot Rise, Portishead, BRISTOL, BS20 6NX.
GORHAM, Mr. Simon Edward, BA ACA *1985;* Teachers Building Society, Allenview House, Hanham Road, WIMBORNE, DORSET, BH21 1AG.
GORIN, Miss. Charlotte, ACA *2011;* Flat 14, Block A Cobblestones, La Retraite, Queens Road, St. Helier, JERSEY JE2 3WU.
•**GORING, Mr. Anthony Robert, FCA** *1979;* (Tax Fac), A R Goring, 91a Hassock Lane North, Shipley, HEANOR, DERBYSHIRE, DE75 7JB.
•**GORING, Mr. Keith Solomon, FCA FCCA** *1965;* (Tax Fac), K.S. Goring & Co, 35 Coombe Road, KINGSTON UPON THAMES, SURREY, KT2 7BA.
GORINGE, Mrs. Amanda Helen, MA ACA *1992;* 78 Queens Walk, STAMFORD, PE9 2QE.
GORINGE, Mr. Stephen John, MA FCA *1992;* H M Revenue & Customs Business Profits, 22 Kingsway, LONDON, WC2B 6NR.
GORKA, Mrs. Madeleine Alexandra Isabelle, ACA *2009;* Station House, Abbey Lane, SHEFFIELD, S8 0BY.
GORLE, Mr. Robert John Tayler, BSc ACA *2000;* Zattikka Ltd, Avanta Video House, 48 Charlotte Street, LONDON, W1T 2NS.
•**GORMAN, Mr. Christopher Stephen, ACA FCCA** *2007;* Chipchase Manners, 384 Linthorpe Road, MIDDLESBROUGH, TS5 6HA. See also Chipchase, Manners & Co
GORMAN, Mrs. Clare, BA ACA *1986;* Northumberland County Council, County Hall, MORPETH, NORTHUMBERLAND, NE61 2EF.
•**GORMAN, Mr. Ivor Dennis, FCA** *1973;* Ensors, 285 Milton Road, CAMBRIDGE, CB4 1XQ.
GORMAN, Miss. Jane Alexandra, MA ACA *2002;* 253 Bridge Road, FOREST LODGE, NSW 2037, AUSTRALIA.
•**GORMAN, Mr. Jeremy Philip, FCA** *1971;* The Garden Flat, 58d Clifton Gardens, LONDON, W9 1AU.
GORMAN, Mr. John Michael, FCA *1976;* 15 Shepherds Lea, BEVERLEY, NORTH HUMBERSIDE, HU17 8UU. (Life Member)
GORMAN, Mr. Joseph Michael, FCA *1962;* Pondside Cottage, Eyton, LEOMINSTER, HR6 0AH. (Life Member)
GORMAN, Ms. Maria Teresa, ACA *2009;* 15 Broxash Road, LONDON, SW11 6AD.
GORMAN, Mr. Mitchell John, ACA CA(AUS) *2011;* Shell International Trading & Shipping Co Ltd, Shell Mex House, 80 Strand, LONDON, WC2R 0ZA.
GORMAN, Mrs. Sally Elizabeth, MEng FCA CTA *1992;* 21 Twyford Crescent, Acton, LONDON, W3 9PP.
GORMAN, Miss. Sophie Louise, ACA *2008;* 5 Churchview Road, TWICKENHAM, TW2 5BT.
GORMAN, Mr. Steven, BSc(Hons) ACA *2004;* 25/3 Huntingdon Place, EDINBURGH, EH7 4AT.
GORMER, Mr. David Andrew, BSc ACA *2005;* 45 Carlisle Avenue, ST. ALBANS, HERTFORDSHIRE, AL3 5LX.
•**GORMLEY, Mr. John Bernard Arthur, FCA** *1977;* Gormley & Co, Plurenden Manor Farm, Plurenden Road, High Halden, ASHFORD, KENT TN26 3JW.
GORMLEY, Mr. Mark Paul, ACA *2010;* 254 Sadler Road, Keresley, COVENTRY, CV6 2LP.
GORMLEY, Mrs. Oonah, LLB ACA *1990;* 2 Gartclush Gardens, Bannockburn, STIRLING, FK7 8QA.
GORMLEY, Mr. Philip Andrew, MMath ACA *2004;* Punch Taverns Plc, Jubilee House, Second Avenue, BURTON-ON-TRENT, STAFFORDSHIRE, DE14 2WF.
GORMLEY, Mr. Philip Gerard, BSc FCA *1975;* 16 Thornhill Avenue, MAGHERAFELT, COUNTY LONDONDERRY, BT45 5JA.
GORNALL, Mr. Henry, BA ACA *2010;* 26 Vernon Avenue, LONDON, SW20 8BW.
•**GORNALL, Mr. Michael James, FCA** *1976;* (Tax Fac), Michael J Gornall Ltd, The Office at Woodcroft, 6 Byerworth Lane North, Garstang, PRESTON, PR3 1QA. See also Michael J. Gornall
GORNER, Mr. Christopher David, BSc FCA *1976;* 12 Austenway, GERRARDS CROSS, SL9 8NW.
GORRIDGE, Mrs. Heidi Michelle, ACA *2006;* 87 Bishopsteignton, Shoeburyness, SOUTHEND-ON-SEA, SS3 8AF.
•**GORRIDGE, Mr. Jonathan Richard, FCA** *1990;* MWS, Kingsridge House, 601 London Road, WESTCLIFF-ON-SEA, ESSEX, SS0 9PE.
GORRIE, Mr. Ian James, BSc ACA *1990;* Clovelly Court, Glencairn Road, KILMACOLM, PA13 4NR.
GORRIE, Mr. John Richard, BSc FCA *1977;* Robann House, 78 Hill Rise, GERRARDS CROSS, BUCKINGHAMSHIRE, SL9 9BQ.
GORRIE, Mr. John Robert, ACA *2008;* Flat 304, 35 Indescon Square, LONDON, E14 9DR.
•**GORRINGE, Mr. Christopher Mark, FCA** *1988;* Plummer Parsons Accountants Limited, 5 North Street, HAILSHAM, BN27 1DQ. See also Plummer Parsons
GORRINGE, Mr. John Pennington, BA FCA *1981;* 4 Palewell Park, East Sheen, LONDON, SW14 8JG.
GORRINGE, Miss. Vicky, BA(Hons) ACA *2004;* 11 Lysander Way, Cottingley, BINGLEY, WEST YORKSHIRE, BD16 1WF.
•**GORROD, Mr. David Charles, FCA** *1977;* (Tax Fac), Gorrod Nominees Ltd, 68 Ship Street, BRIGHTON, BN1 1AE.
GORROD, Mr. Derek Martin, ACA *1983;* Breck Farm House, Holt Road, Haveringland, NORWICH, NORFOLK, NR10 4QH.
GORROD, Mr. Nicholas John, LLB ACA *1985;* 2 Thornton Hall, Upper Kings Cliff, St. Helier, JERSEY, JE2 3GP.
•**GORROD, Mr. Philip Jeffrey, BSc FCA** *1978;* (Tax Fac), Philip Gorrod, High Hill House, 30 London Road, HALESWORTH, SUFFOLK, IP19 8LR.
GORROD, Mr. Roger Brian, BSc FCA *1990;* 178 Thunder Lane, Thorpe St Andrew, NORWICH, NR7 0AB.
GORRY, Mr. John, ACA *2011;* Flat 121, Tower House, 81 Fieldgate Street, LONDON, E1 1GW.
•**GORSE, Mr. John, BA FCA CTA** *1975;* (Tax Fac), Kingscott Dix Limited, 60 Kings Walk, GLOUCESTER, GL1 1LA.
•**GORSKI, Mr. Nigel Henry, BA ACA** *1992;* Nigel Gorski Consulting, 23 Hollinwood View, BINGLEY, WEST YORKSHIRE, BD16 2EF.
GORST, Mr. Allan Leslie, BCom FCA *1969;* Flat 3, Bryn y Bia Lodge, Bryn y Bia Road, LLANDUDNO, GWYNEDD, LL30 3AX. (Life Member)
•**GORST, Mr. Charles Arthur, FCA** *1970;* Lymewood, Melrose Crescent, Poynton, STOCKPORT, SK12 1UT.
GORST, Mr. William, FCA *1962;* 3 Beverley Close, CLITHEROE, BB7 1HX. (Life Member)
•**GORSUCH, Mr. Ian Malcolm, FCA CTA** *1982;* Haines Watts, Interwood House, Stafford Avenue, HORNCHURCH, RM11 2ER. See also Chakko Harris
•**GORSUCH, Mr. Richard Joseph Anthony, BSc ACA** *1995;* KPMG LLP, 15 Canada Square, LONDON, E14 5GL. See also KPMG Europe LLP
GORTON, Mr. Adam, ACA *2010;* Flat 9 Village Court, 1 Carrington Road Urmston, MANCHESTER, M41 6HT.
GORTON, Mr. Alastair Benjamin, BA ACA *2006;* 29a Basuto Road, LONDON, SW6 4BJ.
•**GORTON, Mr. David John, FCA CTA** *1993;* Gortons, Stanmore House, 64-68 Blackburn Street, Radcliffe, MANCHESTER, M26 2JS.
GORTON, Mr. Edward Stephen, BA ACA *1983;* 8 Beadnell Way, The Ings, REDCAR, TS10 2QU.
GORTON, Mrs. Fiona Elizabeth, BA ACA *1995;* Makants Farm, Blackburn Road, BOLTON, LANCASHIRE, BL1 7LH.
GORTON, Mr. Frank, BSc LLB FCA FCMA JDipMA *1960;* Ashlea House, 56 Loughborough Road, Bunny, NOTTINGHAM, NG11 6QT. (Life Member)
•**GORTON, Mr. Jim, BSc FCA** *1993;* (Tax Fac), Gortons, Stanmore House, 64-68 Blackburn Street, Radcliffe, MANCHESTER, M26 2JS.
GORTON, Mr. John Richard, ACA *1980;* Rexam, 100 Capability Green, LUTON, LU1 3LG.
GORTON, Mr. John Stanley, FCA *1960;* Beechcroft, Hollymount Lane, Greenmount, BURY, LANCASHIRE, BL8 4HP.
GORTON, Mr. Karl, BA ACA *1996;* 16 Athelstan Way, TAMWORTH, STAFFORDSHIRE, B79 8LB.
GORTON, Miss. Katherine, BA(Hons) ACA *2004;* 53 Brocklebank Road, LONDON, SW18 3AT.
GORTON, Mr. Robert Steven, ACA *1993;* 50 Lilyville Road, Fulham, LONDON, SW6 5DW.
GORTY, Mr. Andrew Mark, MSc BSc ACA *2002;* 2 Pacific Close, SOUTHAMPTON, SO14 3TX.
GORVETT, Mr. Stephen John, BA ACA *1981;* Badgers Cross, 2 Longwood Lane, Failand, BRISTOL, BS8 3TQ.
GORVY, Mr. Harold Aubrey, FCA *1950;* Stonehage Ltd, 56-58 Conduit Street, LONDON, W1S 2YZ. (Life Member)
GORVY, Mr. Manfred Stanley, FCA *1961;* Flat 69 Albert Hall Mansions, Kensington Gore, LONDON, SW7 2AQ.
GORWALA, Miss. Khushnaz Feroze, BA ACA *1994;* (Tax Fac), 8 Park Mead, South Harrow, HARROW, HA2 8NQ.
•**GOSCHALK, Mr. Stephen Lewis, BSc FCA** *1978;* 41 Meadway, LONDON, NW11 7AX.
GOSCOMB, Mr. Christopher Roderick John, FCA *1976;* Cyril Sweett Ltd, 60 Gray's Inn Road, LONDON, WC1X 8AQ.
GOSDEN, Mr. Andrew, MSc BA(Hons) ACA *2001;* Kenn Cottage, Christchurch Road, Downton, LYMINGTON, HAMPSHIRE, SO41 0LA.
GOSDEN, Mr. Anthony Frank, MA FCA *1974;* Portland House, 29 High Street, Botley, SOUTHAMPTON, SO30 2EA.
GOSDEN, Mr. Mark Richard, BA FCA *1991;* Signal Administration Inc, 64 Danbury Road, Suite 400, WILTON, CT 06897, UNITED STATES.
GOSHAWK, Mrs. Helen Janet, BA ACA *1991;* 8 Briar Close, BILLERICAY, CM11 2RJ.
GOSLAND, Miss. Kirstie Ann, BSc ACA *2003;* 7 Murrells Lane, CAMBERLEY, SURREY, GU15 2PY.

GOSLIN, Mrs. Cressida Blanche Katherine, BA ACA *1989;* Proteus, Back Street, West Camel, YEOVIL, BA22 7QF.

GOSLING, Mr. Andrew Thomas, MA FCA *1981;* CRANBORNE, 6 Fulwith Mill Lane, HARROGATE, NORTH YORKSHIRE, HG2 8HJ.

GOSLING, Mrs. Anne Elizabeth, BSc FCA *1976;* 1 Fawns Keep, Mottram Rise, STALYBRIDGE, SK15 2UL.

GOSLING, Mr. Charles David Vivian, MA FCA *1965;* 31 Yarmouth Road, NORTH WALSHAM, NR28 9AT. (Life Member)

GOSLING, Miss. Clare Louise, BA ACA *1998;* 5 Kings Road, SALE, CHESHIRE, M33 6QB.

•GOSLING, Mr. Geoffrey Hugh, ACA *1978;* Gosling Consulting, Unit 15, Hockley Court, 2401 Stratford Road, Hockley Heath, SOLIHULL WEST MIDLANDS B94 6NW.

•GOSLING, Mr. Graham Martin, FCA *1973;* (Tax Fac), Graham Gosling & Co, 1 Fawns Keep, Mottram Rise, STALYBRIDGE, SK15 2UL.

GOSLING, Mr. John Ceri Fabian, MSc ACA *1990;* 1 The Chantry, Bromham, CHIPPENHAM, WILTSHIRE, SN15 2ET.

GOSLING, Mr. Keith Derek, MA ACA *1985;* Edgecombe, Mill Lane, Corfe, TAUNTON, TA3 7AH.

GOSLING, Mr. Keith Graham, FCA *1971;* Jaggers End, Main Road, Hathersage, HOPE VALLEY, DERBYSHIRE, S32 1BB. (Life Member)

GOSLING, Mr. Kevin John, MA ACA *1988;* Royal Bank of Scotland, 90-100 Southwark Street, LONDON, SE1 0SW.

GOSLING, Mr. Mark David, BA ACA *1990;* York House, Ripley, HARROGATE, NORTH YORKSHIRE, HG3 3AY.

GOSLING, Mr. Mark Robert Fitch, BSc ACA *1987;* 2407 Shibley Avenue, SAN JOSE, CA 95125, UNITED STATES.

GOSLING, Mr. Michael, FCA *1958;* 20 Mill Road, Swanland, NORTH FERRIBY, HU14 3PL. (Life Member)

GOSLING, Mr. Richard, BSc ACA *2011;* 52 Kellerton Road, Lewisham, LONDON, SE13 5RD.

GOSLING, Mr. Stuart Peter, BSc BCom ACA *1986;* Schueco UK Ltd, Schueco International K G Whitehall Avenue, Kingston, MILTON KEYNES, MK10 0AL.

GOSLING, Mrs. Susan Jeanette, LLB FCA *1985;* Cranborne, 6 Fulwith Mill Lane, HARROGATE, NORTH YORKSHIRE, HG2 8HJ.

•GOSNEY, Miss. Eileen Florence, FCA *1993;* S V Bye, New Garth House, Upper Garth Gardens, GUISBOROUGH, TS14 6HA.

GOSNOLD, Mr. Peter, BSc ACA *2007;* 75 Woburn Drive, Hale, ALTRINCHAM, WA15 8NE.

•GOSRANI, Mr. Hasmukhlal, FCA *1975;* H. Gosrani, 12 Blakesley Road, Yardley, BIRMINGHAM, B25 8XU.

GOSRANI, Mr. Jignesh, BSc ACA ACCA *2006;* Flat 21 Elizabeth House, Elizabeth Drive, BANSTEAD, SURREY, SM7 2FE.

GOSS, Mr. Bryan John, MSc FCA *1956;* Bali H'ai, 51 Pastoral Way, Sketty, SWANSEA, SA2 9LY. (Life Member)

GOSS, Mr. Clive Michael, BA ACA *1992;* 26 Wilmington Avenue, LONDON, W4 3HA.

GOSS, Mr. Cyril, FCA *1953;* 9/1 Rehov David Alroi, German Colony, 92108 JERUSALEM, ISRAEL. (Life Member)

GOSS, Mr. Eric Seymour, MA MBA ACA *1989;* Vospers Motor House Ltd, Marsh Mills Retail Park, PLYMOUTH, PL6 8AY.

•GOSS, Mr. Graham John, FCA *1969;* HW Corporate Finance Anglia, 78 Tenter Road, Moulton Park Industrial Estate, NORTHAMPTON, NORTHAMPTONSHIRE, NN3 6AX. See also HW Kettering Limited, HW Laskey and Co Limited and HW Northamptonshire LLP

GOSS, Mr. Iain David, FCA *1974;* Maison des Fleurs, Lacotte, 24310 BRANTOME, FRANCE.

GOSS, Mr. Richard James, BA FCA *1993;* The Farmhouse, Ribbonwood Farm (off Marsh Lane), Anderson, BLANDFORD FORUM, DORSET, DT11 9HE.

GOSS, Mr. Roderick John, BA ACA *1980;* Top Yard, Castlegate, Castle Bytham, GRANTHAM, NG33 4RQ.

GOSSAGE, Mr. Andrew John, MA ACA *1996;* 50 Heathfield Road, Wavertree, LIVERPOOL, L15 9HA.

GOSSAGE, Mr. Neal Trevor, BA FCA *1979;* 20 Cawdell Drive, Long Whatton, LOUGHBOROUGH, LE12 5BW.

GOSSET, Mr. Robert Arthur, BA ACA *1980;* Los Arcos, Carretera Vieja de Finestrat 5, 03502 BENIDORM, ALICANTE, SPAIN.

GOSSLING, Mrs. Jane Frances Wharton, BA ACA *1992;* Cranog, Drove Road, Chilbolton, STOCKBRIDGE, SO20 6AB.

GOSSLING, Mr. Lionel Richard, FCA *1974;* Technik Ltd, 4 Riverpark Ind Est, Billet Lane, BERKHAMSTED, HERTFORDSHIRE, HP4 1HL.

•GOSTELOW, Mr. David Joseph, FCA *1983;* Hodgson & Oldfield, 20 Paradise Square, SHEFFIELD, S1 1UA.

•①GOSTELOW, Mr. Neil David, BSocSc ACA *2002;* with KPMG LLP, 15 Canada Square, LONDON, E14 5GL.

GOSTLING, Mr. Brian, FCA *1957;* 12 Lynndale Avenue, Cross Hills, KEIGHLEY, BD20 7DB. (Life Member)

GOSTLING, Mr. David John, BSc FCA *1988;* Diethelm Travel Management Ltd, 140/1 Wireless Road, Kian Gwan II Building, BANGKOK 10330, THAILAND.

•GOSTLING, Mr. Philip John, ACA *1994;* Gostling Ltd, Unit 6, Acorn Business Park, Keighley Road, SKIPTON, NORTH YORKSHIRE BD23 2UE.

GOSTLING, Mr. Richard Mark, BA ACA *1992;* Butlers, Tower Hill, HORSHAM, WEST SUSSEX, RH13 0AQ.

GOSWAMI, Mr. Asimdeb, FCA *1960;* 11 Anil Roy Road, KOLKATA 700 029, WEST BENGAL, INDIA. (Life Member)

GOSWAMI, Mr. Rakesh, ACA *1990;* TSTT, 1 Edward Street, PORT OF SPAIN, TRINIDAD AND TOBAGO.

•GOSWELL, Mr. Patrick, FCA *1961;* Dowsons, 195 Main Road, HARWICH, CO12 3PH.

GOTCH, Mr. Philip Andrew, BA(Hons) ACA *2002;* 3 Gladiator Close, Wootton, NORTHAMPTON, NN4 6LS.

GOTFRIED, Mr. Kenneth Richard, FCA *1968;* 15 Coral Tree Avenue, Subiaco, PERTH, WA 6008, AUSTRALIA. (Life Member)

GOTHAM, Mr. Dunstan Lewis Rhead, BSc ACA *1988;* RBS, 250 Bishopsgate, LONDON, EC2M 4AA.

•GOTHAM, Mr. Peter John, BA FCA DChA *1979;* (Tax Fac), MacIntyre Hudson LLP, New Bridge Street House, 30-34 New Bridge Street, LONDON, EC4V 6BJ. See also Gotham Erskines LLP

GOTHARD, Mrs. Bettina Hedwig Katharina Maria, BSc(Econ) ACA *1997;* Hoppers House, Cockpit Road, Great Kingshill, HIGH WYCOMBE, HP15 6ER.

GOTHARD, Mr. Guy Edwin, FCA *1959;* 90 Bawnmore Road, Bilton, RUGBY, CV22 6JP. (Life Member)

GOTHARD, Mr. Nigel, BSc ACA *1993;* 3 Chaucer Mews, London Road Upper Harbledown, CANTERBURY, KENT, CT2 9BF.

GOTHARD, Mr. Paul Averill, BA ACA *1993;* AP Group Charles House, Charles Street, ST HELIER, JE2 4SF.

GOTHARD, Mr. Ronald, FCA *1958;* 22 Hillside Drive, Swinton, MANCHESTER, M27 8XH. (Life Member)

GOTSELL, Mr. Lloyd Kevin, BSc ACA *1992;* 10 Rue de la Charite, 5 eme etage, 69002 LYON, FRANCE.

GOTT, Mr. Philip Arthur, BSc ACA *1983;* The Hollow Tree, Stoke Goldington, NEWPORT PAGNELL, MK16 8NP.

GOTTESMAN, Mr. John Michael, FCA *1959;* 1 Wells Road, COLCHESTER, CO1 2YN. (Life Member)

GOTTS, Mr. David James, BA ACA *2005;* 117 Downhall Park Way, RAYLEIGH, ESSEX, SS6 9QZ.

GOTTS, Mr. Michael John, FCA *1957;* 29 Woodland Drive, Thorpe End, NORWICH, NR13 5BH. (Life Member)

GOUDE, Mr. Matthew John, BA ACA *2006;* 27 Nettle Gap Close, Wootton, NORTHAMPTON, NN4 6AH.

•GOUDGE, Mrs. Catherine Anne, BSc FCA *1998;* Catherine Goudge, 33 Well Close, Long Ashton, BRISTOL, BS41 9NB.

GOUDGE, Mr. Charles William, FCA *1960;* Nova, Coppid Hill, Barkham Road, WOKINGHAM, BERKSHIRE, RG41 4TG. (Life Member)

GOUDIE, Miss. Lynne, BSc ACA *1996;* Flat 4, 32 Church Road, RICHMOND, SURREY, TW9 1UA.

GOUDOUFA, Ms. Dimitra, MSc BSc ACA *2005;* 17 Eyzonon Street, Kolonaki, 11521 ATHENS, GREECE.

GOUGH, Mrs. Abbey Elizabeth Meredith, BA ACA *2007;* 3 Vincent Road, CROYDON, CR0 6ED.

GOUGH, Ms. Alison Lorna, BSc ACA *2001;* 31 Wavell Road, MAIDENHEAD, BERKSHIRE, SL6 5AB.

GOUGH, Sir Charles Brandon, MA FCA *1964;* (Member of Council 1981 - 1984), The New Cottage, Long Barn Road, Weald, SEVENOAKS, KENT, TN14 6NH. (Life Member)

GOUGH, Mr. Christopher Michael, BA ACA *2008;* Lloyds TSB Bank Plc Tredegar Park, Pencarn Way Duffryn, NEWPORT, GWENT, NP10 8SB.

GOUGH, Mr. Colin Brian, BA FCA *1982;* 39 Siddeley Avenue, KENILWORTH, CV8 1EW.

GOUGH, Mr. David Allan, LLB ACA *1993;* 505 Court Street, Apartment 7A, BROOKLYN, NY 11231, UNITED STATES.

GOUGH, Miss. Heather Louise, BA(Hons) ACA *2000;* Financial Training Co Ltd, St. James Buildings, 79 Oxford Street, MANCHESTER, M1 6FQ.

GOUGH, Ms. Janet Frances, MA ACA *1989;* 21 Campden Hill Square, LONDON, W8 7JY.

GOUGH, Mrs. Janine Deborah Anne, BSc ACA *1983;* Wheatlands Cottage, Lines Road, Hurst, READING, RG10 0SP.

GOUGH, Miss. Joanna, BSc ACA *2007;* Flat 6, 106 Manor Park, LONDON, SE13 5RH.

GOUGH, Mr. John Michael, BA ACA *1988;* D04, 10 Veyses End, Stratford St. Mary, COLCHESTER, CO7 6NY.

GOUGH, Mr. John Richard Henry, FCA *1963;* 70 Manor House Lane, Yardley, BIRMINGHAM, B26 1PR.

GOUGH, Mr. Lawrence, BA ACA MIS *1997;* Flat 807, Cavalier House, 46-50 Uxbridge Road, LONDON, W5 2SU.

GOUGH, Mr. Lawrence John, FCA *1962;* 43 Woodbury Way, AXMINSTER, EX13 5RE. (Life Member)

GOUGH, Mr. Martin Craig, BSc ACA *1998;* Prysmian SpA, Edifico 307, 222 Viale Sarca, 20126 MILAN, ITALY.

GOUGH, Mr. Michael John, FCA *1962;* 3573 Knollwood Dr N.W., ATLANTA, GA 30305, UNITED STATES.

•GOUGH, Mr. Paul Bernard, BSc FCA FCCA FPC *1979;* L.V. Gough & Co, 7 West Drive, Cheam, SUTTON, SM2 7NB.

•GOUGH, Mr. Paul William, BA FCA *1988;* InTouch Accounting Limited, Bristol & West House, Post Office Road, BOURNEMOUTH, BH1 1BL.

GOUGH, Mr. Richard Edward Charles, MA ACA *1988;* 3 Avenue Gardens, TEDDINGTON, MIDDLESEX, TW11 0BH.

GOUGH, Mr. Richard Paul, BA(Hons) ACA *2003;* 194 Willow Avenue, BIRMINGHAM, B17 8HH.

GOUGH, Mrs. Sarah Parthina, BSc ACA *1996;* 3 Avenue Gardens, TEDDINGTON, TW11 0BH.

GOUGH, Miss. Selina, BA ACA *2010;* Flat B, 4 Killyon Road, LONDON, SW8 2XT.

GOUGH, Mr. Simon Andrew, BA ACA *2005;* Woodfold Park Stud, Woodfold Park, Further Lane, Mellor, BLACKBURN, BB2 7QA.

GOUGH, Mr. Simon Christopher, BSc ACA *1983;* 2 The Crescent, STONE, ST15 8JN.

GOUGH, Mr. Simon Paul, BA ACA *2006;* 36 Clonmel Close, Caversham, READING, RG4 5BF.

GOUGH, Mr. Simon Paul, BSc ACA *1990;* 67 Berkeley Street, HAWTHORN, VIC 3122, AUSTRALIA.

GOUGH, Mr. Stephen Christopher, BSc ACA *2006;* 3 Vincent Road, CROYDON, CR0 6ED.

GOUGH, Mr. Stephen John, FCA *1981;* 2 Clos De La Baule, Grouville, JERSEY, JE3 9HD. (Life Member)

GOUGH, Mrs. Tracey Joan, BSc ACA *1992;* 1 Mullein Close, Eaton Ford, ST. NEOTS, PE19 7GX.

GOUGH, Mr. Trevor Owen, ACA *1994;* 199 Bay Street, Commerce Court West, 4th Floor, TORONTO M5L 1A2, ON, CANADA.

GOUGH, Mrs. Vanessa Elizabeth, MA FCA *1992;* Johnson Matthey Plc 5th Floor, 25 Farringdon Street, LONDON, EC4A 4AB.

GOUGH-COOPER, Mr. James Henry, BA ACA *1997;* 29 Larkhall Rise, LONDON, SW4 6HU.

GOULBOURN, Mrs. Jacqueline Hazel, BSc FCA MBA *1995;* 8 Armonde Close, Boreham, CHELMSFORD, CM3 3GA.

GOULBOURNE, Mrs. Rebecca, MSc BA ACA *1999;* 10 Langdale Avenue, HARPENDEN, HERTFORDSHIRE, AL5 5QU.

GOULD, Mr. Alan, FCA *1959;* 98 Selby Road, West Bridgford, NOTTINGHAM, NG2 7BA. (Life Member)

GOULD, Mr. Alan Graham, FCA *1969;* Kingsley House, Lapley Lane, Stretton, STAFFORD, ST19 9LE. (Life Member)

•GOULD, Mr. Alastair Campbell, ACA *1978;* McEwan Wallace, 68 Argyle Street, Birkenhead, WIRRAL, CH41 6AF.

GOULD, Miss. Alice, BA(Hons) ACA *2011;* 35a Brunel Road, MAIDENHEAD, BERKSHIRE, SL6 2RP.

GOULD, Mr. Brian Philip, FCA *1959;* 31 Park View, Hatch End, PINNER, HA5 4LL. (Life Member)

GOULD, Mrs. Catherine Anne, BSc FCA *1997;* 26 Fairview Grove, Swaffham Prior, CAMBRIDGE, CB25 0LB.

•GOULD, Mr. David Charles, BSc ACA *1986;* Montpelier Accountancy Limited, 7 Montpelier, Quarndon, DERBY, DE22 5JW.

GOULD, Mr. David Jon, FCA *1964;* 25 Martiou 17, Kareas, 162 33 ATHENS, GREECE. (Life Member)

•GOULD, Mr. David Mark Thomas, BA ACA FCCA *1990;* (Tax Fac), Ashmole & Co, Williamston House, 7 Goat Street, HAVERFORDWEST, DYFED, SA61 1PX.

GOULD, Mr. David Neale, ACA *1982;* 7 Karen Close, IPSWICH, IP1 4LP.

GOULD, Mrs. Dawn, BCom ACA *2001;* Greenway, Salthill Road, CLITHEROE, LANCASHIRE, BB7 1PE.

GOULD, Mr. Gerald Anthony, FCA *1950;* 4 Whinmoor Close, Bidston, PRENTON, CH43 7XR. (Life Member)

GOULD, Mr. Gerard, BSc ACA *1992;* American Golf, Europa Boulevard, Westbrook, WARRINGTON, WA5 7YW.

GOULD, Harold, Esq OBE JP DL BA FCA *1950;* 12 Sutherland Street, LONDON, SW1V 4LB. (Life Member)

GOULD, Miss. Heather Louise, ACA *2009;* 12 Baxter Mews, SHEFFIELD, S6 1LW.

GOULD, Mrs. Heather Mary, FCA *1981;* 4 Delaware Cottage, Hever Road, EDENBRIDGE, TN8 7LD.

GOULD, Mrs. Joanna Margaret, BA FCA *1993;* 2 Whiteley Wood Road, SHEFFIELD, S11 7FE.

GOULD, Mrs. Joanne Mary, BA ACA *1993;* 18 Parkstone Avenue, Hill Top, BROMSGROVE, WORCESTERSHIRE, B61 7NS.

GOULD, Mr. John Robert, BA ACA *1993;* 11 Aston Hall Drive, NORTH FERRIBY, HU14 3EB.

GOULD, Mr. John Roger Beresford, MA FCA *1966;* (Member of Council 1995 - 2001), 4 The Park, Grasscroft, OLDHAM, OL4 4ES. (Life Member)

•GOULD, Mr. John Vincent, BSc FCA *1983;* Wenn Townsend, 30 St Giles', OXFORD, OX1 3LE. See also Wenn Townsend Accountants Limited

GOULD, Ms. Josephine Jayne Powell, BSc ACA *1986;* 2 The Priory, Cloverfield, LYMM, CHESHIRE, WA13 9WB.

GOULD, Mr. Kevin David, BA FCA *1993;* Little Trees Top Road, Sharpthorne, EAST GRINSTEAD, RH19 4NS.

GOULD, Mrs. Kirstie, BSc(Econ) ACA *1998;* The Cottage Church Hill, Horsell, WOKING, GU21 4QE.

GOULD, Mr. Lawrence Jonathon, BA ACA *1984;* 50 Wildwood Road, LONDON, NW11 6UP.

GOULD, Mr. Mark Philip, MA ACA *1987;* (Tax Fac), 45 The Woodlands, ESHER, KT10 8DD.

GOULD, Mr. Matthew Richard, BSc ACA *2006;* 1 Edgefield, West Allotment, NEWCASTLE UPON TYNE, NE27 0BT.

GOULD, Mr. Michael Philip, FCA CF *1969;* Laurels, Park Hill, LOUGHTON, IG10 4ES.

GOULD, Mr. Michael Stuart, BSc ACA *1994;* with PricewaterhouseCoopers, One North Wacker, CHICAGO, IL 60606, UNITED STATES.

GOULD, Mr. Nicholas John, BEng ACA *1999;* 2 Buckhurst Way, Earley, READING, RG6 7RL.

GOULD, Mr. Nigel John, ACA *1983;* Haddow Holdings Plc, Listers Mills, Heaton Road, BRADFORD, WEST YORKSHIRE, BD9 4SH.

GOULD, Mr. Peter Antony, BEng ACA *1997;* Chemin de mangette 13, 1260 NYON, VAUD, SWITZERLAND.

GOULD, Mr. Peter Christopher, BA ACA *1982;* 29 Lark Hill Rise, Rushmere St. Andrew, IPSWICH, IP4 5WA.

GOULD, Mr. Peter John, BSc ACA *2007;* 72a Dennis Avenue, Beeston, NOTTINGHAM, NG9 2PR.

GOULD, Mrs. Rachel Gregg, BA ACA *1994;* 6 Meadow Close, Farrington Gurney, BRISTOL, BS39 6UY.

GOULD, Mr. Roger Martin, FCA *1969;* 111 Lovibonds Avenue, ORPINGTON, BR6 8EP.

GOULD, Mrs. Sarah Bradbury, BA ACA *2001;* Trevelyan, Point Road Point Devoran, TRURO, CORNWALL, Tr3 6nz.

GOULD, Mr. Thomas Donald James, BSc ACA *1996;* La Yunta, Panamerica Sur KM7, Via Cuenca, Tarqui, CUENCA, ECUADOR.

•GOULD, Miss. Victoria Anne, MTh ACA *2000;* (Tax Fac), Apple Tree Accountancy & Taxation Services Ltd, The Barn, The Old Manor House, Poffley End, Hailey, WITNEY OXFORDSHIRE OX29 9UW.

•GOULD, Mr. William John, ACA *1980;* Rickard Keen LLP, 7 Nelson Street, SOUTHEND-ON-SEA, SS1 1EH. See also MGI Rickard Keen LLP

•GOULDEN, Mr. Andrew Paul, MA ACA *1983;* Deloitte LLP, Stonecutter Court, 1 Stonecutter Street, LONDON, EC4A 4TR. See also Deloitte & Touche LLP

GOULDEN, Mr. Charles David, FCA *1969;* 2a Sandycoombe Road, TWICKENHAM, TW1 2LX.

•GOULDEN, Mr. Christopher James, BA FCA *1980;* Chris Goulden FCA, 11 Rosebarn Avenue, EXETER, EX4 6DY.

•**GOULDEN, Mr. Peter Anthony, BSc FCA** *1975;* P.A. Goulden, Beechings, Water Street, Hampstead Norreys, THATCHAM, RG18 0SB.
GOULDER, Mr. Brian Roy, FCA *1953;* Danns Farm, Stunts Green, Herstmonceux, HAILSHAM, BN27 4PR. (Life Member)
GOULDER, Mr. Neil Renshaw, FCA DChA *1985;* Brawlings Barn Brawlings Lane, Chalfont St. Peter, GERRARDS CROSS, SL9 0RE.
GOULDER, Mr. Richard Martin, BA ACA ATII *1996;* 19 Rectory Close, SURBITON, KT6 5HR.
GOULDER, Mr. Stephen Charles, BA FCA *1993;* Stables, Main Road, Kingsley, BORDON, GU35 9NG.
GOULDING, Mr. Ian Don, BSc ACA *1989;* Q Hotels Ltd Wellington House Cliffe Park Way, Bruntcliffe Road Morley, LEEDS, LS27 0RY.
GOULDING, Mr. James Frederick, FCA *1950;* 38 Cumberland Avenue, Fixby, HUDDERSFIELD, HD2 2JJ. (Life Member)
GOULDING, Mr. John Geoffrey, FCA *1951;* 4 Napton Court, Frankton House, Cawston, RUGBY, WARWICKSHIRE, CV22 7SN. (Life Member)
GOULDING, Mr. John Michael, BCom FCA *1973;* 3 Craddock Road, SALE, M33 3QQ.
GOULDING, Mr. Kenneth Edward, BA ACA *1979;* 19 Aldenham Ave, RADLETT, WD7 8HZ.
GOULDING, Mr. Kenneth John, FCA *1962;* 2 Spring Royd, Luddendenfoot, HALIFAX, WEST YORKSHIRE, HX2 6HW.
GOULDING, Mr. Michael David, ACA *2009;* Chalgrave Otterbourne Road, Shawford, WINCHESTER, SO21 2DG.
GOULDING, Mr. Niall Alexander, BCom ACA *1996;* Broughton Brothers Ltd, Carter Lane, Shirebrook, MANSFIELD, NOTTINGHAMSHIRE, NG20 8AH.
GOULDING, Mr. Nicholas Clive, BSc FCA *1972;* Long Valley, Deane Down Drove, Littleton, WINCHESTER, HAMPSHIRE, SO22 6PP. (Life Member)
GOULDING, Mrs. Sarah Jane, ACA *2003;* 14 Staghorn Parade, NORTH LAKES, QLD 4509, AUSTRALIA.
GOULDING, Mr. Simon Mark, BCom ACA *1991;* Campbell Dallas, Sherwood House, 7 Glasgow Road, PAISLEY, RENFREWSHIRE, PA1 3QS.
GOULDING, Mr. Stanley, FCA *1972;* Old Timbers, 53 Church Street, MALDON, ESSEX, CM9 5HW.
GOULDING, Mr. Timothy Charles, BSc(Hons) ACA *2003;* 41 Russell Drive, CHRISTCHURCH, DORSET, BH23 3TW.
GOULDINGAY, Mr. David Charles, FCA *1975;* 430 Quinton Road West, BIRMINGHAM, B32 1QG.
GOULDMAN, Mrs. Lorraine, FCA *1990;* Freedman Frankl & Taylor Reedham House, 31 King Street West, MANCHESTER, M3 2PJ.
GOULSTON, Mr. Stephen, BSc ACA *1988;* The Wagon Wheel, Blashford, RINGWOOD, BH24 3PE.
GOULT, Mr. George, FCA *1960;* 135 Ongar Road, BRENTWOOD, ESSEX, CM15 9DL. (Life Member)
GOULTY, Mr. Simon Andrew, BA ACA *1999;* 69 Updown Hill, WINDLESHAM, GU20 6DS.
GOUNDAR, Miss. Santhie Lau, BSc ACA *2010;* Flat D, 349 Hither Green Lane, LONDON, SE13 6TJ.
GOUNDRY, Mr. Richard Gordon Fraser, BSc(Hons) ACA *2002;* Musikantenweg 20, 60316 FRANKFURT AM MAIN, GERMANY.
GOURD, Mr. Peter Alan, BSc FCA *1977;* Kilima, Lincoln Road, Chalfont St. Peter, GERRARDS CROSS, BUCKINGHAMSHIRE, SL9 9TG.
GOURGEY, Mr. Charles Richard, BA ACA *1983;* Amazon Properties PLC, 23 Spring Street, LONDON, W2 1JA.
•**GOURLAY, Mrs. Alison Rebecca, BSc ACA** *1999;* Cowden Consulting Ltd, Ruthin House, Southgate, Eckington, SHEFFIELD, S21 4FT.
GOURLAY, Mr. Anthony David, BSc FCA *1977;* Malleny, Eglington Rd, Tilford, FARNHAM, GU10 2DH.
GOURLAY, Mr. James, MA MSc ACA *2010;* Flat 2, 147 Alderney Street, LONDON, SW1V 4HD.
GOURLAY, Mr. John Cowden, FCA *1962;* Glenstocken, Colvend, DALBEATTIE, DG5 4QE. (Life Member)
GOURLAY, Mr. Nigel Timothy, BSc FCA *1980;* The Down House, Oxbottom Lane, Newick, LEWES, BN8 4HU.
GOURLEY, Mrs. Natalie Ann, BA(Hons) ACA *2001;* R N Store & Co, 50-54 Oswald Road, SCUNTHORPE, SOUTH HUMBERSIDE, DN15 7PQ.
GOUW, Mr. Peter Jan, BSc ACA ATII *1999;* (Tax Fac), with KPMG LLP, 191 West George Street, GLASGOW, G2 2LJ.
GOUWS, Mr. Craig Stuart, ACA CA(SA) *2011;* 3 The Coach House, Terrace Lane, RICHMOND, SURREY, TW10 6NF.
•**GOVAN, Mr. Philip Morrison, FCA** *1976;* (Tax Fac), Morrison Govan, Bull Farm Barn, Hartley, CRANBROOK, TN17 3QE.
GOVEAS, Ms. Patricia Ann, MA ACA *1998;* 104 Effra Road, LONDON, SW19 8PR.
GOVENDER, Mr. Bhashkaran, ACA CA(SA) *2011;* (Tax Fac), 34 Darrell Close, CHELMSFORD, CM1 4EL.
GOVER, Mr. Anthony David, MA FCA *1965;* 21 Somerset Square, Holland Park, LONDON, W14 8EE. (Life Member)
GOVER, Mr. Paul Lucien, BA ACA *1991;* Mayfair Chambers, 2 Charles Street, LONDON, W1J 5DB.
GOVER, Mr. Peter Julian, BA ACA *1991;* 11 Broadwater Road North, Hersham, WALTON-ON-THAMES, KT12 5DB.
GOVER, Mr. Roy Roland, FCA *1975;* GCG Consulting, Colchester Business Centre, George Williams Way, COLCHESTER, ESSEX, CO1 2JS.
GOVETT, Mr. Clement John, LVO MA FCA *1969;* 29 Marchmont Road, RICHMOND, TW10 6HQ.
GOVETT, Miss. Joanna Elizabeth, BA ACA *2007;* 7 Hunter Road, LONDON, SW20 8NZ.
GOVEWALLA, Miss. Ann, BA ACA *1997;* 51 Finchley Park, LONDON, N12 9JS.
•**GOVEY, Mr. Stephen James, MA FCA** *1982;* Mazars LLP, Tower Bridge House, St. Katharines Way, LONDON, E1W 1DD.
GOVIER, Mr. John Meldon, FCA *1962;* Shenstone, The Esplanade, SIDMOUTH, EX10 8BE. (Life Member)
GOVIER, Mr. Neil Leroy, BSc FCA CFA *1983;* 1 River Valley Close, 22-03, SINGAPORE 238427, SINGAPORE.
GOVIER, Mr. Peter John Hugh, FCA *1957;* 11 Rothesay Point, Wharncliffe Road, Highcliffe, CHRISTCHURCH, DORSET, BH23 5DB. (Life Member)
GOVIER, Miss. Sarah Jane, BSc ACA *1998;* Flat 3014, 1 Pan Peninsula Square, LONDON, E14 9HL.
GOVIL, Mr. Navin, FCA *1974;* 289 Reynolds Road, ELTHAM, VIC 3095, AUSTRALIA.
GOW, Mr. Iain, ACA *2010;* Zolfo Cooper, P.O. Box 1102, 4th Floor, Building 3, Cayman Financial Centre, GEORGETOWN KY1-1102 CAYMAN ISLANDS.
•**GOW, Mr. Malcolm John Arthur, FCA** *1978;* Arthur Gow Ltd, 21 Queens Road, Hale, ALTRINCHAM, CHESHIRE, WA15 9HE. See also Arthur Gow
GOW, Miss. Nicolette Lucy, BSc ACA *1991;* Finance department Trinity Suite, North Devon District Hospital, Raleigh Park, BARNSTAPLE, DEVON, EX31 4JB.
GOW, Mr. Noel Furse, BCom FCA *1965;* 177 Aylesbury Road, Wendover, AYLESBURY, BUCKINGHAMSHIRE, HP22 6AA.
GOW, Mr. Robin Eric, ACA *1983;* Hampshire Autistic Society, 1634 Parkway Whiteley, FAREHAM, PO15 7AH.
GOWAN, Miss. Nikki Lynn, BA(Hons) ACA *2002;* 114 East 91st Street, Apartment 5A, NEW YORK, NY 10128, UNITED STATES.
GOWANLOCK, Mr. John Robert, FCA *1961;* 4 Burges Close, Marnhull, STURMINSTER NEWTON, DT10 1QQ.
GOWANS, Mr. James David, BA ACA *2009;* Semperian PPP Investment Partners, 3rd Floor Redbridge House Lower Bristol Road, BATH, BA2 3RH.
•**GOWANS, Mr. Neil James, FCA CTA** *1979;* Baker Tilly Tax & Advisory Services LLP, 1210 Centre Park Square, WARRINGTON, WA1 1RU. See also Baker Tilly UK Audit LLP
GOWDIE, Mrs. Susan, BA ACA *1995;* 55 Ashbourne Drive, Coxhoe, DURHAM, DH6 4SP.
•**GOWDY, Mr. Barry Anthony, BA ACA** *1984;* (Tax Fac), 51 White Hart Road, PORTSMOUTH, PO1 2TY.
GOWEN, Mr. Robert, BA ACA *1995;* 22a Highridge Close, EPSOM, SURREY, KT18 5HF.
GOWER, Mrs. Angela Frances, ACA *1985;* Southerwold, Lustleigh, NEWTON ABBOT, DEVON, TQ13 9TL.
GOWER, Mr. Anthony Edward James, FCA *1972;* The Limes Bradford Road, Heronsgate, RICKMANSWORTH, HERTFORDSHIRE, WD3 5DA. (Life Member)
GOWER, Miss. Cleo Julia, BA ACA *1997;* 5 Hillcrest Court, HIGHTON, VIC 3216, AUSTRALIA.
GOWER, Mr. Francis Leslie, FCA *1947;* Norwood, 14 Park Road, IPSWICH, IP1 3ST. (Life Member)
GOWER, Mr. Ian James, FCA *1970;* 53 Alcester Drive, SUTTON COLDFIELD, B73 6PZ. (Life Member)
GOWER, Mrs. Joanna Louise, BSc ACA *1996;* 25 Pondmore Way, ASHFORD, Kent, TN25 4LU.
•**GOWER, Mr. Kevin Bryan, FCA** *1973;* Flat 64 Redruth House, Grange Road, SUTTON, SM2 6RU.
GOWER, Miss. Laura, ACA *2011;* Ground Floor Flat, 73 Harlescott Rd., LONDON, SE15 3DA.
•**GOWER, Mr. Nicholas John P, BSc FCA** *1984;* PricewaterhouseCoopers LLP, 101 Barbirolli Square, Lower Mosley Street, MANCHESTER, M2 3PW. See also PricewaterhouseCoopers
GOWER, Mr. Nigel' David, FCA *1991;* 3 Cherington Way, ASCOT, SL5 8TJ.
•**GOWER, Mr. Richard John, FCA** *1977;* Richard J Gower, Redferns, 35 The Lagger, CHALFONT ST. GILES, BUCKINGHAMSHIRE, HP8 4DH.
GOWER, Mr. Robin Patrick, FCA *1988;* 52 Bridge Down, Bridge, CANTERBURY, CT4 5BA.
GOWER, Mr. Roger Charles, BA ACA *2004;* Reqional Air Building, PO Box 1182, Flat No 1, Nairobi Road, ARUSHA, TANZANIA.
GOWER, Mr. Stuart Walton, MSc ACA *1994;* (Tax Fac), Ingouville House, Ingouville Lane, ST HELIER, JE2 4SG.
•**GOWER, Mr. Thomas Edwin Terence, FCA** *1966;* T.E.T.Gower, 12 Birdwood Road, MAIDENHEAD, SL6 5AP.
GOWER ISAAC, Mr. Edward Alexander, BA ACA *1996;* P R Donnelley Unit 3-5, Tower Close, HUNTINGDON, CAMBRIDGESHIRE, PE29 7YD.
GOWER-SMITH, Miss. Jennifer Mary, MSc ACA *2004;* 43 Cedar Terrace, RICHMOND, SURREY, TW9 2BZ.
•**GOWER-SMITH, Mr. Nicholas Mark, FCA FRSA** *1981;* (Tax Fac), Norman Cox and Ashby, Grosvenor Lodge, 72 Grosvenor Road, TUNBRIDGE WELLS, TN1 2AZ. See also Gower-Smith and Co
GOWERS, Mr. Adam Stanislaw, BA ACA *2007;* Flat 7 Hever House, The Avenue, SURBITON, KT5 8JN.
GOWERS, Mrs. Gemma Natalie, BSc ACA *2004;* 9 Main Street, Empingham, OAKHAM, LE15 8PR.
GOWERS, Mr. Paul James, BA ACA *2000;* 20 Denison Close, LONDON, N2 0JT.
GOWERS, Mr. Tobias Zachary, BSc ACA *2002;* 9 Main Street, Empingham, OAKHAM, LE15 8PR.
GOWING, Mr. David Frederick, MA FCA *1973;* 4 Kenilworth Avenue, BRACKNELL, BERKSHIRE, RG12 2JJ.
GOWING, Mr. Nigel Peter, MBA BSc FCA *1984;* 10 Loyd Close, ABINGDON, OX14 1XR.
GOWING, Mr. Richard James, BA ACA *1987;* HSBC Bank Plc, 8 Canada Square, Canary Wharf, LONDON, E14 5HQ.
GOWLER, Mrs. Josie Leah Collins, MA(Hons) ACA *1998;* 10 Burma Road, Duxford, CAMBRIDGE, CB22 4QP.
GOWLETT, Mr. Anthony Robert, FCA *1975;* 42 Buckingham Way, WALLINGTON, SM6 9LT.
GOWLETT, Mr. Robert William, FCA *1972;* Robert William Gowlett, 45 Green Moor Link, Winchmore Hill, LONDON, N21 2NN.
GOWLETT, Miss. Susan Florence, FCA *1973;* 2 Warwick Road, Little Canfield, DUNMOW, CM6 1GB.
GOWLING, Mrs. Kay, BA ACA *1987;* Barn Close Ham Lane, Prinsted, EMSWORTH, PO10 8XT.
GOWLLAND, Mr. Nicholas Tadeusz, BSc FCA *1994;* FLAT 9A, VILLAS SORRENTO, 64 MOUNT DAVIS ROAD, POK FU LAM, HONG KONG SAR.
GOWMAN, Ms. Nicola Sarah, CA ACA *2007;* 30 Tir yr Yspyty, Bynea, LLANELLI, DYFED, SA14 9AZ.
GOWMAN, Mr. Philip Robert, MA ACA *1989;* H S B C Bank Plc, Level 21, 8 Canada Square, LONDON, E14 5HQ.
GOWRIE, Miss. Gemma Ann, ACA *2009;* 6 Beech Road, ALDERLEY EDGE, CHESHIRE, SK9 7LX.
GOWTHORPE, Mrs. Catherine, BA FCA *1982;* 1 Church Lane, Mellor, BLACKBURN, BB2 7JL.
GOY, Miss. Anne Michelle, BSc ACA *1990;* 26 Park Farm Road, KINGSTON UPON THAMES, SURREY, KT2 5TQ.
•**GOY, Miss. Carol Anne, BA FCA** *1993;* Shaw Austin Limited, 45 City Road, CHESTER, CH1 3AE.
GOYAL, Mr. Avnish, BA ACA *1992;* 42 Mount Avenue, Hutton, BRENTWOOD, ESSEX, CM13 2NZ.
GOYAL, Miss. Deepti, BA ACA *2007;* 771a High Road, LONDON, N12 8JY.
GOYAL, Mr. Narvit Kumar, BA ACA *1996;* 10 Holmfield Avenue, LEICESTER, LE2 2BF.
GOZZARD, Mr. Hugh Douglas, BSc ACA *1991;* with Deloitte Touche Tohmatsu, 35/F One Pacific Place, 88 Queensway, CENTRAL, HONG KONG ISLAND, HONG KONG SAR.
GRABHAM, Mrs. Claire Anne, BTech ACA *1994;* 8 Panteg, Pentyrch, CARDIFF, CF15 9TL.
GRABHAM, Mr. Timothy Lynton, FCA *2000;* Freshfields Bruckhaus Deringer Llp, PO Box 561, LONDON, EC4Y 1HS.
GRABOWSKI, Mr. Andrew Bronislaw, MA FCA *1985;* Rickling House, Cambridge Road, Quendon, SAFFRON WALDEN, ESSEX, CB11 3XJ.
GRABOWSKI, Mr. Marek Tadeusz, MA FCA *1982;* Financial Reporting Council, 5th Floor, Aldwych House, 71-91 Aldwych, LONDON, WC2B 4HN.
GRACE, Miss. Alanna, ACA *2008;* P.O.Box 1363, GEORGE TOWN, GRAND CAYMAN, KY1-1108, CAYMAN ISLANDS.
GRACE, Mrs. Alison Mary, ACA *1988;* 38 Moores Lane, Eton Wick, WINDSOR, BERKSHIRE, SL4 6JX.
GRACE, Mr. Andrew Campbell, LLB ACA *1988;* 38 Brewery Road, WOKING, GU21 4NA.
GRACE, Mrs. Belinda Annette, BA ACA *1994;* 44 Maypole Road, OLDBURY, B68 0HL.
GRACE, Mrs. Christine Veronica, ACA *1988;* 32 Widney Manor Road, SOLIHULL, WEST MIDLANDS, B91 3JQ.
GRACE, Mr. Christopher Anthony, BA ACA *1983;* Pendower, 27 The Riding, Woodham, WOKING, GU21 5TA.
GRACE, Mr. Cyril John, FCA *1955;* 2 The Causeway, Victoria Road, DISS, IP22 4AW. (Life Member)
•**GRACE, Mr. David Alwyn, FCA** *1970;* Gorings, The Laurels, St. Mary Street, ILKESTON, DE7 8BQ.
•**GRACE, Mr. David William, LLB ACA** *1982;* PricewaterhouseCoopers LLP, Hays Galleria, 1 Hays Lane, LONDON, SE1 2RD. See also PricewaterhouseCoopers
GRACE, Mr. Donald, FCA *1958;* 6 St. Nicholas Croft, Askham Bryan, YORK, YO23 3RJ. (Life Member)
GRACE, Mrs. Georgina Bridget, ACA MAAT *2002;* 5 Braemar Drive, Oakley, BASINGSTOKE, RG23 7LX.
GRACE, Mr. Jason, ACA *2010;* 34 Piggotts Road, Caversham, READING, RG4 8EN.
GRACE, Mr. Jeremy Charles Hew, BSc ACA *1991;* 7 New Cottages, Oaken, WOLVERHAMPTON, WV8 2BD.
GRACE, Mrs. Joanne, BSc ACA *1997;* with Allied Textile Companies Limited, 1st Floor, 5 Morston Claycliffe Office Park, Whaley Road, BARNSLEY, SOUTH YORKSHIRE S75 1HQ.
GRACE, Mr. John Joseph, FCA *1973;* Gortrush, Piltown, KILKENNY, COUNTY KILKENNY, IRELAND. (Life Member)
•**GRACE, Mr. John Robert, FCA** *1969;* J.R. Grace & Co, Tanglin, 3A Highfield Road, SHANKLIN, ISLE OF WIGHT, PO37 6PP.
GRACE, Mrs. Julia Clare, BA ACA *1989;* Meadowview, 1 Ashwood, East Harptree, BRISTOL, BS40 6BW.
GRACE, Mr. Keith Frederick, BCom ACA MBA *1983;* The Old Vicarage, 53 York Road, Wollaston, WELLINGBOROUGH, NORTHAMPTONSHIRE, NN29 7SG.
GRACE, Mr. Michael, BSc(Hons) ACA *2003;* 60/22 Mosman Street, MOSMAN, NSW 2088, AUSTRALIA.
GRACE, Mr. Nigel George William, BSc ACA *1994;* 20 Moorgate, LONDON, EC2R 6DA.
GRACE, Mr. Noel Anthony, FCA *1985;* 32 Widney Manor Road, SOLIHULL, WEST MIDLANDS, B91 3JQ.
GRACE, Mr. Paul John, ACA *1992;* 37 Highfield Park Road, LAUNCESTON, CORNWALL, PL15 7DX.
GRACE, Mr. Peter Michael Vincent, MA(Cantab) FCA CFA *1989;* Grace & Associate Consulting Ltd, 3 - 4 Belgrad Rakpart ii 4, 1056 BUDAPEST, HUNGARY.
GRACE, Mr. Stephen David Michael, ACA *2010;* 21 Signal Court, Lightfoot Street Hoole, CHESTER, CH2 3BP.
GRACE, Mr. Steven Ian, BSc ACA DChA *1999;* 88a Ivy Cottages, Uxbridge Road Mill End, RICKMANSWORTH, HERTFORDSHIRE, WD3 8BW.
GRACE, Mr. Steven John, BCom ACA *1983;* 22 Browning Road, HARPENDEN, AL5 4TR.
GRACE, Ms. Virginia Helen, BSc ACA *1989;* The Poplars, 90 Aldreth Road, Haddenham, ELY, CAMBRIDGESHIRE, CB6 3PN.
GRACEY, Mr. John Charles, MA ACA *1982;* 16 Ambleside, EPPING, CM16 4PT.
GRACEY, Mr. Norman Robert, BSc ACA *1991;* 39 Fairholme, Putnoe, BEDFORD, MK41 9DA.
GRACEY, Mr. Patrick Richard Kirkwood, BSc ACA *1989;* 58 Norroy Road, LONDON, SW15 1PG.
GRACHVOGEL, Mr. Joseph George, FCA *1963;* 60 Park Avenue, Bush Hill Park, ENFIELD, EN1 2HW.
GRACIAS, Mr. Eugene Thomas, BSc ACA *1992;* The Northern & Sheel Building, Sojitz, 10 Lower Thames Street, LONDON, EC3R 6EQ.

GRANT - GRAVES Members - Alphabetical

GRANT, Mr. Graham Howard, FCA *1958;* The Old Barn, Cusworth, DONCASTER, DN5 7TR. (Life Member)
GRANT, Mr. Gregor, MA ACA *1993;* Brook House, Pettycrate Lane, Chideock, BRIDPORT, DORSET, DT6 6LB.
GRANT, Mr. Henry Robert Joseph, FCA *1964;* The Cottage New Road, Cutnall Green, DROITWICH, WORCESTERSHIRE, WR9 0PQ.
GRANT, Mr. Ian Caulfeild, FCA *1964;* 29 Parry Court, Hazel Grove, Mapperley, NOTTINGHAM, NG3 6DQ. (Life Member)
GRANT, Mr. Ian Douglas, FCA *1973;* August Equity LLP, 1st Floor, 10 Slingsby Place, St Martin's Courtyard, Covent Garden, LONDON WC2E 9AB.
•**GRANT, Mr. Ian Jonathan, BSc FCA CF** *1974;* (Tax Fac), Grants, 11 Park Place, LEEDS, LS1 2RX.
GRANT, Mr. Ian Mark, BSc FCA *1993;* 1 Ogden Close, Helmshore, ROSSENDALE, BB4 4NZ. (Life Member)
GRANT, Mr. Ian Richard, BA FCA *1982;* Mota Gur 2/5, KFAR SABA, 44405, ISRAEL.
GRANT, Mr. James, BA ACA *2010;* 62 Forum Lane, PO Box 510, GEORGE TOWN, GRAND CAYMAN, KY1 1106, CAYMAN ISLANDS.
GRANT, Mr. James Angus, BSc(Hons) ACA *2003;* KPMG, 10 Shelley Street, SYDNEY, NSW 2000, AUSTRALIA.
GRANT, Mr. James Burns, ACA *2009;* 52 Gladsmuir Road, LONDON, N19 3JU.
GRANT, Mr. James Edward, MSc BSc ACA *2006;* with PricewaterhouseCoopers LLP, 300 Madison Avenue, NEW YORK, NY 10017, UNITED STATES.
GRANT, Mr. James Patrick, BSc ACA *2004;* 11 Walnut Close, BROADSTAIRS, CT10 2EL.
•**GRANT, Mrs. Jane Barriff, FCA** *1975;* Winningtons, 1 Winnington Road, LONDON, N2 0TP.
GRANT, Mrs. Janet Irene, BEng ACA *1993;* 11 Greenside Drive, Hale, ALTRINCHAM, CHESHIRE, WA14 3HX.
GRANT, Mrs. Janine, ACA *1996;* (Tax Fac), 6 Dakenham Close, Salhouse, NORWICH, NR13 6PA.
GRANT, Mr. Jason Mark, BA ACA *2003;* Pinnick Lewis Handel House, 95 High Street, EDGWARE, MIDDLESEX, HA8 7DB.
GRANT, Mrs. Jennifer Mary Elizabeth, FCA *1964;* The Gables, Fen Road, Pakenham, BURY ST.EDMUNDS, IP31 2LS.
GRANT, Mrs. Joanna, BSc ACA *2011;* 12 Evenlode Drive, Berinsfield, WALLINGFORD, OXFORDSHIRE, OX10 7NY.
GRANT, Mr. John Duncan, BSc FCA *1978;* Jepson Clough Farm, Schoolfold Lane, Adlington, MACCLESFIELD, SK10 4PL.
GRANT, Mr. John Mackenzie, FCA *1969;* Old Orchard, Stoke Trister, WINCANTON, SOMERSET, BA9 9PG.
GRANT, Mr. John Reginald, LLB FCA *1958;* 10 St Johns Court, BRECON, POWYS, LD3 9EF. (Life Member)
GRANT, Mr. John Stanley, BSc FCA *1971;* PO Box 2617, FLORIDA, GAUTENG, 1710, SOUTH AFRICA.
•**GRANT, Mr. Jonathan Basil, FCA** *1986;* Grant Harrod Parkinson LLP, 49a High Street, RUISLIP, MIDDLESEX, HA4 7BD.
GRANT, Mr. Jonathan Edward Charles, BA FCA *1976;* Financial Reporting Council, Aldwych House, 71-91 Aldwych, LONDON, WC2B 4HN.
GRANT, Mr. Jonathan Paul, BA FCA *1995;* 15135 Memorial Drive, Apt 6303, HOUSTON, TX 77079, UNITED STATES.
•**GRANT, Mrs. Joyce Margaret, BSc ACA** *1990;* Grant Thornton UK LLP, Grant Thornton House, 22 Melton Street, Euston Square, LONDON, NW1 2EP. See also Grant Thornton LLP
GRANT, Mr. Keith William, FCA *1979;* 20 Kerrfield, Romsey Road, WINCHESTER, HAMPSHIRE, SO22 5EX.
GRANT, Mr. Kevin James, BSc ACA *2004;* 22 Brooklynn Close, Waltham Chase, SOUTHAMPTON, SO32 2RY.
GRANT, Miss. Laura, Bsc(Hons) ACA *2011;* 16 Horsmonden Road, LONDON, SE4 1RG.
•**GRANT, Mr. Leon John, FCA** *1969;* (Tax Fac), Winningtons, 1 Winnington Road, LONDON, N2 0TP.
GRANT, Miss. Lindsay Melanie, BA ACA *1993;* Wavegate Ltd, Churchill House, 137-139 Brent Street, LONDON, NW4 4DJ.
GRANT, Mrs. Lynne Margaret, BA ACA *1993;* 11 Dorchester Mews, TWICKENHAM, TW1 2LE.
GRANT, Mr. Martyn Ian, FCA *1984;* 76 Clyst Valley Road, Clyst St. Mary, EXETER, EX5 1DE.
GRANT, Mr. Matthew, MSc ACA *2007;* Gorse Farm Snitterfield Road, Bearley, STRATFORD-UPON-AVON, CV37 0EX.
GRANT, Mr. Matthew Paul, BA ACA *1990;* 13 Derwentwater Gardens, Whickham, NEWCASTLE UPON TYNE, NE16 4EY.
GRANT, Mr. Matthew William Alan, BA ACA *1998;* North Grange House, North Green Road, Pulham St. Mary, DISS, NORFOLK, IP21 4QZ.
GRANT, Mr. Maurice, FCA *1959;* 9 St Martin's Approach, RUISLIP, HA4 7QB. (Life Member)
GRANT, Mr. Michael Charles, MA ACA *1987;* Fernbank, Cardiff Road, Creigiau, CARDIFF, CF15 9NN.
GRANT, Mr. Michael John Granville, FCA *1968;* Church House, Church Road, East Brent, HIGHBRIDGE, SOMERSET, TA9 4HZ.
•**GRANT, Newton Keene, Esq OBE FCA FCCA FCIArb** *1960;* (Tax Fac), Treworlas House, Ruan High Lanes, TRURO, CORNWALL, TR2 5LN.
GRANT, Mr. Nicholas Airth, FCA *1954;* Flat 40 Belgravia Court, 33 Ebury Street, LONDON, SW1W 0NY. (Life Member)
GRANT, Mr. Nigel Cameron, BA ACA *1991;* 79b Frant Road, TUNBRIDGE WELLS, KENT, TN2 5LP.
GRANT, Mr. Nigel John, MA ACA MBA *1981;* 22 Upper Park Road, KINGSTON UPON THAMES, SURREY, KT2 5LD.
GRANT, Mrs. Pamela, ACA *1981;* 72 Clayhall Avenue, Clayhall, ILFORD, IG5 0LF.
GRANT, Mr. Paul Dorian, BA FCA *1993;* Calle Joan Cuadreas I Marcer 8D, ST Pere De Ribes, 08810 BARCELONA, SPAIN.
GRANT, Mr. Paul Lawrence, BA ACA *1993;* 67 Rocky Lane, Great Barr, BIRMINGHAM, B42 1PB.
GRANT, Mr. Paul Richard, MMath ACA *2006;* Flat 32 Dryden Court, Renfrew Road, LONDON, SE11 4NH.
GRANT, Mr. Peter Airth, FCA *1955;* Symonds House, Symonds Street, WINCHESTER, SO23 9JS. (Life Member)
GRANT, Mr. Peter David, FCA *1965;* 1739 Sunningdale Bend, MISSISSAUGA L5J 1G1, ON, CANADA. (Life Member)
GRANT, Mr. Peter Harvey, MA FCA *1995;* Ballyguinny, 8 Moor of Balvack, Monymusk, INVERURIE, AB51 7SQ.
GRANT, Mr. Peter Leatham Fraser, FCA *1952;* Farndon, 15 Riddings Road, Hale, ALTRINCHAM, CHESHIRE, WA15 9DS. (Life Member)
GRANT, Mr. Peter William, MA FCA *1980;* Cedar Cottage, 77 Lonesome Lane, REIGATE, RH2 7QT.
GRANT, Mrs. Rebecca, BSc ACA *2000;* 49 Endsleigh Park Road, PLYMOUTH, PL3 4NH.
GRANT, Mr. Richard Edward, FCA *1965;* 5/59 Wrights Road, Drummoyne, SYDNEY, NSW 2047, AUSTRALIA.
GRANT, Mr. Richard John, BA ACA *1979;* Cadogan Estates Limited, 18 Cadogan Gardens, LONDON, SW3 2RP.
GRANT, Mr. Robert Neil, BA ACA *1995;* 21 Woodshaw Mead, Wootton Bassett, SWINDON, SN4 8RB.
GRANT, Mr. Robert Raymond, BSc ACA *1993;* (Tax Fac), Freemantlemedia Ltd, 1 Stephen Street, LONDON, W1T 1AL.
GRANT, Mr. Robin Alexander, BA(Hons) ACA *2001;* Flat 45 Lait House, 1 Albemarle Road, BECKENHAM, KENT, BR3 5LN.
GRANT, Mr. Ronald Peter, FCA *1965;* Jabulani Guadalmina Alta 744, Calle 19e, San Pedro de Alcantara, 29670 MARBELLA, SPAIN.
GRANT, Mrs. Rosemary Glenys, BSc ACA *1985;* Fernbank, Llantwit Road, Creigiau, CARDIFF, CF15 9NN.
•**GRANT, Mr. Ryan Kevin, BSc(Hons) ACA** *2002;* with Zolfo Cooper Ltd, 35 Newhall Street, BIRMINGHAM, B3 3PU.
GRANT, Mrs. Sarah Elizabeth, BSc ACA *2003;* 12 Newmills Crescent, BALERNO, MIDLOTHIAN, EH14 5SX.
GRANT, Mrs. Sheila, BSc FCA *1979;* 29 Turnberry Drive, Acomb, YORK, YO26 5QP.
GRANT, Mr. Simon, BA ACA *2006;* 26 Sevington Road, LONDON, NW4 3RX.
GRANT, Mr. Simon Robert, BA FCA *1990;* 5 Lyn Close, Ingleby Barwick, STOCKTON-ON-TEES, CLEVELAND, TS17 0QU.
•**GRANT, Mr. Spencer Neil, BSc ACA** *1998;* 5 Pinks Farm, Rectory Lane, Shenley, RADLETT, HERTFORDSHIRE, WD7 9AW.
GRANT, Mr. Stephen, FCA *1974;* 258 Richardson Street, MIDDLE PARK, VIC 3206, AUSTRALIA.
•**GRANT, Mr. Stephen Paul, FCA MIPA CTA FABRP** *1985;* (Tax Fac), Wilkins Kennedy, Anglo House, Bell Lane Office Village, Bell Lane, AMERSHAM, BUCKINGHAMSHIRE HP6 6FA.
GRANT, Mr. Stephen Richard, BSc ACA *1999;* 12 Alma Road, Clifton, BRISTOL, BS8 2BY.
GRANT, Mr. Stuart Spencer, BSc ACA *1993;* 31 Royal Chase, TUNBRIDGE WELLS, KENT, TN4 8AX.
GRANT, Mrs. Susan Diana, ACA *1993;* 52 Cowles Road, MOSMAN, NSW 2088, AUSTRALIA.
GRANT, Mrs. Susan Wendy, BCom ACA *1984;* 11 Rothamsted Avenue, HARPENDEN, AL5 2DD.
•**GRANT, Mr. Terrence Bryan, FCA** *1980;* Sibbalds Ltd, Oakhurst House, 57 Ashbourne Road, DERBY, DE22 3FS.
GRANT, Mr. Timothy Andrew, ACA CTA *2000;* Rectory House, Ingham, BURY ST. EDMUNDS, SUFFOLK, IP31 1NS.
GRANT, Mr. Timothy James, BSc ACA *1989;* 2 Poyner Close, FAREHAM, PO16 7YQ.
GRANT, Mr. Trevor, BSc ACA *1986;* Vliegut 38, 3061 LEEFDAAL, BELGIUM.
GRANT, Ms. Wendy Jane, BSc ACA CTA *2003;* (Tax Fac), 1b Haneda Park, Drumahoe, LONDONDERRY, BT47 3RX.
GRANT WETHERILL, Mr. James William Richard, BA ACA *1994;* 35 Poole Road, SINGAPORE 437526, SINGAPORE.
•**GRANTHAM, Mr. Andrew Timothy De Lisle, BSc FCA** *1990;* AlixPartners UK LLP, 20 North Audley Street, LONDON, W1K 6WE.
GRANTHAM, Mr. Anthony Barrie, FCA *1956;* 2 Springfield Avenue, Elburton, PLYMOUTH, PL9 8PZ. (Life Member)
GRANTHAM, Mr. John William, ACA *2010;* 80 Tranby Lane, Anlaby, HULL, HU10 7DU.
GRANTHAM, Miss. Louise Christine, BA FCA *1989;* Repic, Repic House, Unit C3, Waterfold Park, BURY, LANCASHIRE BL9 7BR.
GRANTHAM, Mr. Mark Frederick, FCA *1979;* Mark Grantham, Dunas Douradas, Apartado 3164, 8135 ALMANCIL, PORTUGAL.
GRANTHAM, Mr. Rufus Alexis Henry, MA(Hons) ACA *2001;* 87 Westcombe Park Road, LONDON, SE3 7QS.
GRANTHAM, Miss. Sarah Elizabeth, BA ACA MBA *1992;* 85 Hazelhurst Road, Worsley, MANCHESTER, M28 2SW.
GRANTHAM, Mr. Stuart Anthony, BA ACA *1998;* 61 Ranelagh Grove, NOTTINGHAM, NG8 1HS.
GRANTLEY, Mr. Nicholas Terence, BA ACA *1989;* 29 Portland Rise, Finsbury Park, LONDON, N4 2PT.
GRANVILLE, Mr. Ian Langley, BA ACA *1992;* Foreshore, Greenbank Road, Devoran, TRURO, CORNWALL, TR3 6PQ.
GRANVILLE, Mr. Julian Philip, BA ACA *1993;* 9 Kildare Terrace, LONDON, W2 5JT.
GRANVILLE, Mrs. Rachael Anne, BA FCA *1996;* 33 Holtwood Drive, IVYBRIDGE, DEVON, PL21 9TH.
GRANVILLE, Mr. Simon Anthony Gordon, BSc ACA *1996;* 8/4 Paling Street, THORNLEIGH, NSW 2120, AUSTRALIA.
GRANVILLE-COLLIS, Mr. Frank, FCA FTII *1952;* Aux Vignaux II, Panassac, 32140 GERS, FRANCE. (Life Member)
GRANVILLE-SMITH, Mrs. Jocelin Pamela, BSc ACA *1992;* Plantation House, Sandbanks Lane, Graveney, FAVERSHAM, KENT, ME13 9DQ.
GRANVILLE-SMITH, Ms. Louise, ACA *2009;* 62 Oakfield Road, Clifton, BRISTOL, BS8 2BG.
GRAPES, Mr. John Christopher, FCA *1964;* Iona, Pooks Green, Marchwood, SOUTHAMPTON, SO40 4WP.
GRASBY, Dr. Timothy, PhD BEng ACA *2011;* 32 Silverbirch Road, SOLIHULL, WEST MIDLANDS, B91 2PJ.
•**GRASHOFF, Mr. Tudor, FCA** *1981;* Grashoff & Co Ltd, 35 Whellock Road, LONDON, W4 1DY. See also Grashoff & Co
GRASMANE, Mrs. Svetlana, BSc ACA *2004;* Ausmas 6a, RIGA LV-1006, LATVIA.
•**GRASS, Mr. Andrew Robert, ACA** *1990;* Andrew Grass, Vallehermoso 82, Baso, Izqda, Espana, 28015 MADRID SPAIN.
•**GRASSAN, Mr. John Frederick, BA FCA ATII** *1990;* (Tax Fac), Fredericks 2001 Limited, Highgate Business Centre, 33 Greenwood Place, LONDON, NW5 1LB.
•**GRASSBY, Mr. Stephen Duncan, FCA** *1990;* (Tax Fac), Grassbys, Lindsay House, 15 Springfield Way, Anlaby, HULL, HU10 6RJ.
GRASSI, Miss. Belinda Claire, BA ACA *1994;* 32 Melrose Road, Wandsworth, LONDON, SW18 1NE.
GRASSI, Mr. Jonathan, MA ACA CF *1989;* Lasham Hill House, Lasham, ALTON, GU34 5RU.
GRASSICK, Mr. Alun Clark, BSc FCA *1988;* KPMG, 8/F Prince's Building, 10 Chater Road, CENTRAL, HONG KONG ISLAND, HONG KONG SAR.
GRASSKE, Mr. Paul Martin, BSc ACA *1988;* 12 Queens Park Road, CHESTER, CH4 7AD.
GRASTY, Mrs. Ruth, BA ACA *2006;* 2 Gaunts Place, Farsley, PUDSEY, WEST YORKSHIRE, LS28 5GT.
GRATER, Mr. Bruce Walton, ACA CA(SA) *2009;* 33 Middleton Road, Newlands, CAPE TOWN, 7700, SOUTH AFRICA.
GRATER, Mr. Peter William, FCA *1972;* 9 41 Spruce Street, TORONTO M5A 2H8, ON, CANADA.
GRATTAGE, Mr. Carl, BA FCA *1995;* 19 The Woodlands, Cold Meece, STONE, STAFFORDSHIRE, ST15 0YA.
GRATTAN, Mr. David, BSc ACA *1980;* HOLME LEA STUBLEY NEW HALL, off FEATHERSTALL ROAD, LITTLEBOROUGH, OL15 8PH.
GRATTAROLA, Mr. Leonardo Giuseppe, BSc FCA *1984;* Principality Bldg Soc, PO Box 89, CARDIFF, CF10 1UA.
GRATTE, Mr. Jonathan Andre, BSc ACA *1997;* Financial Services Authority, 25 North Colonnade, LONDON, E14 5HS.
GRATTON, Mr. Andrew, ACA *2009;* Flat 41 Markham Quay, Camlough Walk, CHESTERFIELD, DERBYSHIRE, S41 0FT.
GRATTON, Miss. Annabel Victoria, ACA *2009;* 15 Regina Drive, LEEDS, LS7 4LR.
•**GRATTON, Mr. David Alan James, BSc FCA** *1984;* Duncan & Toplis, Enterprise Way, Pinchbeck, SPALDING, LINCOLNSHIRE, PE11 3YR.
GRATTON, Mr. David Martin, BSc ACA *1984;* 9 Warren Road, GUILDFORD, SURREY, GU1 2HB.
GRATTON, Mr. Gordon Cameron Paul, BA ACA *1981;* Hollybrook, 1 Beckside Gardens, Weetwood, LEEDS, LS16 5QZ.
•**GRATTON, Mrs. Liza Diane Lesley, ACA** *2007;* 7 Queen Elizabeth Drive, SWINDON, SN25 1WR.
GRATTON, Mr. Martin, BEng ACA *1996;* 5 Tudor Lawns, Roundhay, LEEDS, LS8 2JR.
GRATTON, Mr. Michael Henry Blackwell, FCA *1972;* 58 Watford Road, RADLETT, WD7 8LR.
•**GRATTON, Mr. Nicholas George, FCA** *1992;* Little & Company, 45 Park Road, GLOUCESTER, GL1 1LP.
•**GRATTON, Mr. Peter William Rutherford, BA FCA** *1988;* Deloitte LLP, Athene Place, 66 Shoe Lane, LONDON, EC4A 3BQ. See also Deloitte & Touche LLP
GRATTON, Mrs. Valerie, FCA *1971;* 58 Watford Road, RADLETT, WD7 8LR.
GRATWICK, Mrs. Diane May, BA ACA *1982;* Higher Lock Cottage, Bullgate Lane, North Rode, CONGLETON, CHESHIRE, CW12 2PB.
GRATWICK, Mr. Edward David, BA ACA *1979;* Croda Chemicals Europe Ltd, Foundry Lane, WIDNES, CHESHIRE, WA8 8UB.
GRATWICK, Mr. John Warwick, FCA *1973;* 11 Old School Court, Lewes Road, Lindfield, HAYWARDS HEATH, WEST SUSSEX, RH16 2LD. (Life Member)
GRATWICK, Mr. Richard Charles, BSc FCA *1977;* Top Lock Cottage, North Rode, CONGLETON, CHESHIRE, CW12 2PB.
GRATWICKE, Mr. Adrian Edward, BA ACA *1992;* Metcash Limited, 50 Waterloo Road, Macquarie Park, SYDNEY, NSW 2113, AUSTRALIA.
GRAVATT, Ms. Alison Helen, BA ACA *1989;* 5 Railway Cottages, Sulgrave Road, LONDON, W6 7RJ.
•**GRAVE, Mr. John Christopher, MSc ACA CTA** *2001;* Grave Solutions Limited, River Bend, Culgaith, PENRITH, CUMBRIA, CA10 1QE.
•**GRAVELIUS, Mr. Alan Jakob, FCA ATII** *1961;* A.J. Gravelius FCA ATII, 20 Halyards, Ferry Road, Topsham, EXETER, EX3 0JU.
•**GRAVELL, Mr. Nicholas John B, ACA FCCA** *2007;* Four Fifty Partnership Limited, 34 Boulevard, WESTON-SUPER-MARE, AVON, BS23 1NF. See also T P Lewis & Partners (WSM) Limited
GRAVEN, Mr. Richard Thomas, BA ACA *1994;* 12 Hatherden Avenue, POOLE, DORSET, BH14 0PJ.
•**GRAVENER, Mrs. Sharon S, ACA FCCA** *2009;* Scrutton Bland, Sanderson House, Museum Street, IPSWICH, IP1 1HE.
•**GRAVENEY, Mr. John Irving, FCA** *1973;* William Price & Co, Westbury Court, Church Road, Westbury-on-Trym, BRISTOL, BS9 3EF. See also Walbrook Bureau Services Limited
GRAVES, Mr. Alan Dennis, FCA *1964;* 2 Squires Wood Drive, CHISLEHURST, BR7 5RT. (Life Member)
GRAVES, Mr. Alex Matthew, ACA *2008;* 55 Greenhill Park, BISHOP'S STORTFORD, HERTFORDSHIRE, CM23 4EW.
GRAVES, Miss. Carla Elizabeth, BSc(Econ) CA ACA *2002;* with Fitzgerald and Law LLP, 8 Lincoln's Inn Fields, LONDON, WC2A 3BP.
•**GRAVES, Mr. Colin Alan, FCA** *1975;* Red Hill Farmhouse, Curry Rivel, LANGPORT, SOMERSET, TA10 0PH.
•**GRAVES, Mr. Daniel Robert, BA(Hons) ACA** *2002;* Wilkins Kennedy, Bridge House, London Bridge, LONDON, SE1 9QR.
GRAVES, Mr. Darren, BA ACA *2006;* with Deloitte LLP, Athene Place, 66 Shoe Lane, LONDON, EC4A 3BQ.
•**GRAVES, Mr. David William, FCA** *1964;* Profitright Ltd, 29 Wyatt Drive, LONDON, SW13 8AL.
GRAVES, Mr. James Leslie, FCA *1958;* 172 Hall Lane, UPMINSTER, RM14 1AT. (Life Member)

•**GRAVES, Mr. John Anthony, BSc FCA** *1973;* (Tax Fac), 23 Dows Road, BELFAST, BT8 8LB.

•**GRAVES, Mr. John Michael, FCA** *1980;* (Tax Fac), John Graves FCA, Heatherlea House, East End, LYMINGTON, SO41 5ST.

GRAVES, Mr. John Michael, FCA *1970;* Markham House, Rowrah Road, Rowrah, FRIZINGTON, CA26 3XJ. (Life Member)

GRAVES, Mr. John Osborne, BSc FCA *1979;* Little Paddocks, 3 White Beam Way, TADWORTH, KT20 5DL.

•**GRAVES, Mr. Mark, MEng FCA** *1998;* Blue Skies Accountancy Limited, 17 Millbrook Drive, Broughton Astley, LEICESTER, LE9 6UX. See also Blue Skies Financial Services Limited

GRAVES, Mr. Mark Simon, BA ACA *2002;* 159 London Road, REDHILL, RH1 2JH.

GRAVES, Mr. Martin John, ACA *1984;* 57 Ha'penny Bridge Way, Victoria Dock, HULL, HU9 1HD.

GRAVES, Mr. Raymond, FCA *1965;* St. Chads, 20 Uppleby, Easingwold, YORK, YO61 3BB.

•**GRAVES, Mr. Raymond James, BA ACA** *1986;* Ray Greaves & Co, 158 Cemetery Road, IPSWICH, IP4 2HL.

GRAVES, Mr. Richard Charles, BSc ACA *1995;* Roxar AS, Gamle Forusei 17, P O Box 112, N-4065 STAVANGER, NORWAY.

GRAVES, Mrs. Sarah, BSc ACA *1990;* Deeks Evans, 36 Cambridge Road, HASTINGS, EAST SUSSEX, TN34 1DU.

•**GRAVES, Mr. Simon Peter, FCA** *1989;* (Tax Fac), S P Graves, 27 All Saints Street, HASTINGS, EAST SUSSEX, TN34 3BJ.

GRAVES, Mrs. Susan Elizabeth, MA ACA *1996;* 1710 Havenwood Drive, RICHMOND, VA 23238, UNITED STATES.

GRAVES, Mrs. Susan Menzies, MA FCA *1986;* (Tax Fac), Towerwood Mugdock, Milngavie, GLASGOW, G62 8EJ.

•**GRAVES, Mr. Thomas Atkins, BA FCA** *1999;* Vitag Limited, 9 Laurel Avenue, GRAVESEND, KENT, DA12 5QP.

GRAVES, Ms. Tina Elveen, BSc ACA *1989;* The Cottages, Elmcote Lane, Cambridge, GLOUCESTER, GL2 7AS.

•**GRAVES, Mr. Tommas Henry, FCA** *1961;* T.H. Graves, 73 Fairfax Road, TEDDINGTON, TW11 9DA.

GRAVES, Miss. Tonia Alexandra Paola, BA ACA *1996;* with PricewaterhouseCoopers, 1 Embankment Place, LONDON, WC2N 6RH.

GRAVES, Mr. William Harvey, BSc FCA *1974;* Dorowa, Allan Court, WORKINGTON, CA14 3ET.

•**GRAVESTOCK, Mr. Iain Richard, MA ACA** *1999;* KPMG LLP, 15 Canada Square, LONDON, E14 5GL. See also KPMG Europe LLP

GRAVESTOCK, Mr. Peter Stanley, FCA *1967;* 2 Grasmere Avenue, Streetly, SUTTON COLDFIELD, WEST MIDLANDS, B74 3DG.

GRAVETT, Mr. Heath Jason, BA ACA *1992;* Level 33, Bankwest Tower, 108 St Georges Terrace, PERTH, WA, AUSTRALIA.

GRAVETT, Mrs. Julie, FCA *1986;* Peugeot Citroen Automobiles UK Ltd Pinley House, 2 Sunbeam Way, COVENTRY, CV3 1ND.

•**GRAVETT, Mr. Michael Louis, FCA** *1957;* (Tax Fac), 37 Matlock Way, NEW MALDEN, KT3 3AT.

•**GRAVETT, Mr. Philip James, BSc FCA** *1975;* Quantum Financial Solutions Limited, Ellerslie, Crawley End, Chrishall, ROYSTON, HERTFORDSHIRE SG8 8QJ.

GRAVETT, Mr. Simon Morford, FCA *1968;* Meadowside Main Street, Kings Norton, LEICESTER, LE7 9BF.

GRAVILL, Mr. Michael Duncan Disney, BSc ACA *1981;* Hilliards Barn, Amlets Lane, CRANLEIGH, GU6 7DH.

GRAVILLE, Mrs. Rachel Mary, MA ACA *2005;* 61 Greenfield Road, Harborne, BIRMINGHAM, B17 0EP.

GRAY, Mrs. Abbie Louise, ACA *2001;* Myrtle Cottage Doctors Hill, Sherfield English, ROMSEY, HAMPSHIRE, SO51 6JX.

GRAY, Mr. Adrian David, BA ACA *1990;* 1 Beechcroft Road, BUSHEY, HERTFORDSHIRE, WD23 2JU.

GRAY, Mr. Adrian Desmond Leslie, FCA *1974;* 1 Oakfield, Playden, RYE, EAST SUSSEX, TN31 7UA.

GRAY, Mr. Alan, FCA *1961;* 4 Parsonage Court, Portishead, BRISTOL, BS20 6PH.

GRAY, Mr. Alan David, FCA *1977;* The Leprosy Mission, 80 Windmill Road, BRENTFORD, MIDDLESEX, TW8 0QH.

GRAY, Mr. Alan James Thomas, FCA *1955;* 45 Birch Close, New Barn, LONGFIELD, DA3 7LH. (Life Member)

GRAY, Mr. Alan Leslie, FCA *1987;* Diesel Marine International, West Chirton Ind Estate, Gloucester Road, NORTH SHIELDS, TYNE AND WEAR, NE29 8RQ.

GRAY, Mr. Alan Saul, FCA *1976;* PO Box 1007, 8 Hayman Road, 40297 MIKHMORET, ISRAEL.

GRAY, Mr. Alec John, BA FCA *1975;* 7 Mill Bridge Mews, HERTFORD, SG14 1HE.

GRAY, Ms. Alexandra, BSc(Hons) ACA *2001;* Gilead Sciences Europe Ltd, 2 Roundwood Avenue, Stockley Park, UXBRIDGE, MIDDLESEX, UB11 1AF.

GRAY, Mrs. Alexandra Judith, BSc ACA *1994;* (Tax Fac), 6 Crossacres, Pyrford Woods, WOKING, GU22 8QS.

GRAY, Mrs. Alexandra Victoria, MA ACA *2004;* McCann Erickson, 42-48 St. John's Square, LONDON, EC1M 4EA.

GRAY, Mrs. Alison Margaret, BSc ACA *1989;* 92 London Road, KNEBWORTH, HERTFORDSHIRE, SG3 6HB.

GRAY, Mr. Allan Keith, MBA BSc FCA *1991;* D2 Wing Michael Young Building, The Open University, Walton Hall, MILTON KEYNES, MK7 6AA.

GRAY, Mrs. Andrea Jean, FCA *1970;* 23 Hope Avenue, Mickleover, DERBY, DE3 0FZ.

GRAY, Dr. Andrew Alexander, MChem ACA *2010;* 20 Route de Pré-Bois, ICC Building - Section H, GENEVA, SWITZERLAND.

GRAY, Mr. Andrew James, BEng ACA *2002;* Elm House, Abbey Lane, Aslockton, NOTTINGHAM, NG13 9AE.

•**GRAY, Mr. Andrew John, BA ACA** *1987;* PricewaterhouseCoopers LLP, Hays Galleria, 1 Hays Lane, LONDON, SE1 2RD. See also PricewaterhouseCoopers

GRAY, Mr. Andrew Jon, BSc ACA *2004;* 43 Shoalhaven Circuit, MAWSON LAKES, SA 5095, AUSTRALIA.

GRAY, Mr. Andrew Jonathan, BA(Hons) ACA *2000;* 15 Waterside Road, BEVERLEY, HU17 0PP.

GRAY, Mr. Andrew Philip, BSc ACA *1999;* Artemi Investment Management, 42 Melville Street, EDINBURGH, EH3 7HA.

GRAY, Mr. Andrew Robert, BSc ACA *1992;* 9 St Edmunds Road, IPSWICH, IP1 3QY.

GRAY, Mr. Andrew Robert, BSc FCA *1994;* Springfield, Lilbourne Road, Clifton upon Dunsmore, RUGBY, WARWICKSHIRE, CV23 0BB.

GRAY, Mr. Andrew Rutherford, FCA *1968;* Gossoms Cottage, Gossoms End, BERKHAMSTED, HP4 1DF.

GRAY, Mr. Andrew William Edward, MA ACA DChA *1999;* Toybox PO Box 5967, Bletchley, MILTON KEYNES, MK3 6WD.

GRAY, Mrs. Angela Helena, BSc ACA *1991;* 37 Mulberry Gardens, Shenley, RADLETT, WD7 9LB.

GRAY, Mrs. Ann Louise, BA ACA *1983;* 24 Matmore Gate, SPALDING, LINCOLNSHIRE, PE11 2PN.

GRAY, Mrs. Anne Elizabeth, BA FCA *1992;* 5 Pigeon Hill, Tiffield, TOWCESTER, NORTHAMPTONSHIRE, NN12 8AR.

•**GRAY, Mrs. Anne Lyn, FCA ATII** *1988;* Graybrowne Limited, The Counting House, Nelson Street, HULL, HU1 1XE.

GRAY, Mr. Anthony, FCA *1969;* Oak Villa Barn, Lower Mountain Road, Penyffordd, CHESTER, CH4 0EU.

•**GRAY, Mr. Anthony, BA ACA** *1987;* Anthony Gray & Co, 28 Church Lane, Culcheth, WARRINGTON, WA3 5DJ.

GRAY, Mr. Anthony John, FCA *1954;* 14 Ross Way Red House Farm, Gosforth, NEWCASTLE UPON TYNE, NE3 2BL. (Life Member)

GRAY, Mr. Anthony Lynne, ACA *1996;* 36 The Promenade, Mayland, CHELMSFORD, CM3 6AR.

GRAY, Mr. Anthony Richard, BA FCA *1980;* 54 Stirling Road, Talbot Woods, BOURNEMOUTH, BH3 7JH.

GRAY, Mr. Antony Charles, FCA *1978;* Heronslea, 104 Granary Lane, BUDLEIGH SALTERTON, DEVON, EX9 6EP.

GRAY, Mr. Basil Leslie, FCA *1960;* 12 Cliffe Lane, Hathersage, HOPE VALLEY, S32 1DE. (Life Member)

GRAY, Mrs. Beatrice Anne, BA ACA *1983;* King & Taylor, 10-12 Wrotham Road, GRAVESEND, KENT, DA11 0PE.

GRAY, Mr. Brian James, FCA *1973;* European Commission MADO 27/32, 1049 BRUSSELS, BELGIUM.

•**GRAY, Mr. Bruce Malcolm Lee, FCA** *1968;* (Member of Council 1999 - 2007), (Tax Fac), Bruce M.L. Gray, Suite 122, Airport House, Purley Way, CROYDON, CR0 0XZ.

GRAY, Mr. Bruce Nelson, BSc ACA *1995;* 96 Gillhurst Road, Harborne, BIRMINGHAM, B17 8PA.

GRAY, Miss. Caroline Elizabeth, BA ACA *2007;* with PricewaterhouseCoopers LLP, 1 Embankment Place, LONDON, WC2N 6RH.

GRAY, Mrs. Carolyn Patricia, ACA *1992;* C/O Wg Cdr RW Gray RAF, UKSU, NATO JWC, BFPO, 50.

GRAY, Mrs. Celia Mary, BSc ACA *1982;* 76 Gloucester Road, HAMPTON, TW12 2UJ.

GRAY, Mr. Charles Alexander, BSc(Hons) ACA *2003;* 112 Gloucester Road, KINGSTON UPON THAMES, SURREY, KT1 3QN.

GRAY, Mr. Charles Stuart MacLennan, BA FCA *1992;* 25 Waratah Street, FRESHWATER, NSW 2096, AUSTRALIA.

GRAY, Mr. Charles William, BEng ACA *1993;* 6 Gaddum Road, Didsbury, MANCHESTER, M20 6SZ.

GRAY, Mr. Christopher John, BA(Econ) FCA *1983;* Jan Teulingslaan 89, 1187 SH AMSTELVEEN, NETHERLANDS.

•①**GRAY, Mr. Christopher Michael, BSc ACA** *1987;* with Deloitte LLP, 3 Rivergate, Temple Quay, BRISTOL, BS1 6GD.

GRAY, Mr. Christopher Philip, BSc ACA *1992;* 10 Hall Park Gate, BERKHAMSTED, HERTFORDSHIRE, HP4 2NJ.

•**GRAY, Mrs. Claire Laura, BA FCA** *1986;* (Tax Fac), Integer Accountants Ltd, Unit 3, Uphall Farm, Salmons Lane, Coggeshall, COLCHESTER ESSEX CO6 1RY. See also Integer

•**GRAY, Mr. Colin, FCA** *1981;* Colin Gray & Co Limited, 26 Lower Kings Road, BERKHAMSTED, HERTFORDSHIRE, HP4 2AE. See also Priority Payroll Services Limited and Colin Gray & Co

•**GRAY, Mr. Colin Richard, BA ACA** *1990;* (Tax Fac), OMB Accountants Ltd, Holmwood Farm, Horsham Road, North Holmwood, DORKING, SURREY RH5 4JR.

GRAY, Mr. Darren, BA FCA ATII AMCT *1992;* 40 Roxborough Park, HARROW, HA1 3AY.

GRAY, Mr. David Alistair, MBA BA FCA *1981;* Darley Stud Management Co Ltd, The Main Office, Duchess Drive, NEWMARKET, SUFFOLK, CB8 9HE.

GRAY, Mr. David Anthony, FCA *1965;* 24 Buttershaw Lane, LIVERSEDGE, WEST YORKSHIRE, WF15 8HD.

GRAY, Mr. David Anthony, BA FCA *1981;* Coromandel, Hassop Road, BAKEWELL, DE45 1AP.

GRAY, Mr. David Ashley, BSc ACA *1991;* 137 Northwood Way, NORTHWOOD, MIDDLESEX, HA6 1RF.

GRAY, Mr. David Charles Norreys, FCA *1969;* Ivy Farm, 17 Smithfield End, Swanbourne, MILTON KEYNES, MK17 0SP.

GRAY, Mr. David Henry, FCA MCT *1975;* 34 Chestnut Avenue, RICKMANSWORTH, HERTFORDSHIRE, WD3 4HB.

GRAY, Mr. David John, FCA *1983;* Argent Holdings Ltd, 5th Floor, 9 Hatton Street, LONDON, NW8 8PL.

GRAY, Mr. David William, BSc ACA *1992;* 8 Lea Gardens, WEMBLEY, MIDDLESEX, HA9 7SE.

GRAY, Mr. David William, BA ACA *1990;* PricewaterhouseCoopers, White Square Office Center, 10 Butyrsky Val, 125047 MOSCOW, RUSSIAN FEDERATION.

GRAY, Mr. Derek Reginald, FCA *1954;* Driftwood, 43 Marine Drive West, West Wittering, CHICHESTER, WEST SUSSEX, PO20 8HH. (Life Member)

•**GRAY, Mr. Derek Richard, FCA** *1955;* (Tax Fac), SG Associates Limited, 82z Portland Place, LONDON, W1B 1NS.

•**GRAY, Mr. Donald Holm, BSc FCA CF** *1999;* Barber Harrison & Platt, 2 Rutland Park, SHEFFIELD, S10 2PD.

GRAY, Mr. Douglas John Paul, BA FCA *1982;* 90 Needlers End Lane, Balsall Common, COVENTRY, CV7 7AB.

GRAY, Mr. Duncan Stuart, BA FCA *1996;* 35 Chatsworth Terrace, YORK, NORTH YORKSHIRE, YO26 4RZ.

GRAY, Mr. Edward Baillie, BSc ACA *2002;* 56 Chaworth Road, West Bridgford, NOTTINGHAM, NG2 7AD.

GRAY, Mr. Edward Harrison, BSc ACA *2003;* Flat 34 Park Central Building, Fairfield Road, LONDON, E3 2US.

GRAY, Mr. Edward James, MEng ACA *2010;* Rowan Cottage, Church Road, Copthorne, CRAWLEY, WEST SUSSEX, RH10 3RA.

GRAY, Ms. Elizabeth Ann, BSc ACA *1992;* 14 Haytor Park, Stoke Bishop, BRISTOL, BS9 2LR.

GRAY, Mrs. Emily, BSc(Hons) ACA *2001;* 49 Sherbourne Place, Linden Fields, TUNBRIDGE WELLS, TN2 5QX.

GRAY, Miss. Fiona, BA(Hons) ACA *2010;* 82 Stamford Park Road, Hale, ALTRINCHAM, CHESHIRE, WA15 9ER.

GRAY, Mr. Frank Henry, FCA *1959;* 4 Lynwood Road, EPSOM, KT17 4LD. (Life Member)

•**GRAY, Mr. Gary Alan, ACA** *1990;* (Tax Fac), Charlton & Co, Saville Chambers, 4 Saville Street, SOUTH SHIELDS, NE33 2PR.

GRAY, Mr. Gavin Stewart, BEng ACA *1995;* Hellermanntyton Ltd Stoner House, London Road, CRAWLEY, WEST SUSSEX, RH10 8LJ.

GRAY, Mrs. Gillian Winifred Livingston, BA ACA *1985;* 1 Knighton Lodge, 39 Rydens Rd, WALTON-ON-THAMES, KT12 3AG.

GRAY, Mrs. Hannah, BA ACA *2000;* Holly Dene, Bower Heath, HARPENDEN, HERTFORDSHIRE, AL5 5EE.

GRAY, Mr. Harold Geoffrey, FCA *1949;* F L & J Properties Company, 2 Golf Course Road, Stanton on the Wolds, Keyworth, NOTTINGHAM, NG12 5BH.

•**GRAY, Miss. Hazel Margaret, BEng ACA** *1995;* (Tax Fac), 11 Ashley Park Drive, ABERDEEN, AB10 6RY.

GRAY, Mrs. Heather Joy, MA ACA *1985;* P.O.Box HM 789, HAMILTON HM CX, BERMUDA.

GRAY, Miss. Helen, ACA *2010;* 27 Redrock Road, ROTHERHAM, SOUTH YORKSHIRE, S60 3JP.

GRAY, Mrs. Helen Judith, BCom ACA *1991;* (Tax Fac), 23 Rectory Park, Sanderstead, SOUTH CROYDON, Surrey, CR2 9JQ.

•**GRAY, Mrs. Helen Lucinda, BA ACA** *1993;* Helen Gray Accounting Services, Hideaway House, Wilderness Rise, Dormans Park, EAST GRINSTEAD, WEST SUSSEX RH19 2LN.

GRAY, Mr. Iain Henderson, BCom FCA *1959;* 7 George Street, Cellardyke, ANSTRUTHER, KY10 3AS. (Life Member)

GRAY, Mr. Ian, BSc ACA *1995;* Seymours Ltd, PO Box 861, JERSEY, JE4 0ZX.

GRAY, Mr. Ian Archie, FCA *1976;* 6 Baronsmead Road, LONDON, SW13 9RR.

GRAY, Mr. Ian Peter William, FCA *1962;* 39 Old High Street, Headington, OXFORD, OX3 9HP. (Life Member)

•**GRAY, Mr. Ian Stephen, FCA** *1971;* (Tax Fac), Gray & Co, Springvale, Police Station Square, Mildenhall, BURY ST. EDMUNDS, IP28 7ER.

GRAY, Mr. Jack, FCA *1966;* The Priest Hall, Kentisbeare, CULLOMPTON, EX15 2BG. (Life Member)

GRAY, Mr. James Mckinnon, FCA *1964;* Lakehead District School Board, 2135 Sills Street, THUNDER BAY P7E 5T2, ON, CANADA.

GRAY, Miss. Jennifer Clare, BSc ACA *2010;* 130 Snowberry Crescent, WARRINGTON, CHESHIRE, WA5 1DA.

GRAY, Mr. Jeremy Bernard, BA(Hons) ACA *2004;* 28a Cheniston Gardens, LONDON, W8 6TH.

GRAY, Mrs. Joanna Jacqueline, BA ACA *2000;* 23 Dunstable Road, Toddington, DUNSTABLE, BEDFORDSHIRE, LU5 6DS.

GRAY, Mr. John Alan, FCA *1953;* Westgate Drive, BRIDGNORTH, WV16 4QF. (Life Member)

GRAY, Father John Bernard, FCA *1966;* 1 King Edwards Road, WARE, HERTFORDSHIRE, SG12 7EJ.

GRAY, Mr. John Marc Tully, BA ACA *2002;* 49 Brondesbury Villas, LONDON, NW6 6AJ.

GRAY, Mr. John Philip, FCA *1959;* 'Nonsuch', 33 Oaklands, Framingham Earl, NORWICH, NR14 7QS. (Life Member)

GRAY, Mr. John Stephen Christopher, MSc ACA *2000;* Rua Dr. Cincinato Braga 47, Sao Bernardo Do Campo, SAO PAULO, 09890-900, BRAZIL.

GRAY, Mr. John Timothy, FCA *1976;* William Raveis Real Estate, 47 Riverside Avenue, WESTPORT, CT 06880, UNITED STATES.

GRAY, Mr. John William, FCA *1974;* The Barn, Meadow View, Sedgley, DUDLEY, DY3 3EX. (Life Member)

GRAY, Mr. Jonathan, BSc ACA *1996;* The Rookery, 25 Raffin Lane, PEWSEY, WILTSHIRE, SN9 5HJ.

GRAY, Mr. Jonathan Brownlow, MA ACA *1981;* 8 Aston Close, ASHTEAD, SURREY, KT21 2LQ.

GRAY, Mr. Jonathan Paul, BSc ACA *1987;* AMP Ltd, Gaters Mill, West End, SOUTHAMPTON, SO18 3HW.

•**GRAY, Mr. Julian John, BA ACA** *1998;* Ernst & Young LLP, Wessex House, 19 Threefield Lane, SOUTHAMPTON, SO14 3QB. See also Ernst & Young Europe LLP

GRAY, Mrs. Julie, BA ACA *1992;* 15 Holly Avenue, Jesmond, NEWCASTLE UPON TYNE, NE2 2PU.

GRAY, Mrs. Justine Clare, BA ACA *1999;* 2a Cumberland Road, Headingley, LEEDS, LS6 2EF.

GRAY, Mrs. Karen Anne, BA ACA *1998;* South Wing, Aboyne Castle Business Centre, ABOYNE, AB54 5JP.

GRAY, Miss. Katharine Mary, BA ACA *1998;* 39 Ottways Lane, ASHTEAD, SURREY, KT21 2PL.

GRAY, Mrs. Kathryn Anne, BA ACA *1991;* 5 Merchiston Gardens, EDINBURGH, EH10 5DD.

GRAY, Mr. Kevin Alexander, BSc ACA *2000;* Laurel House, 3 Cedar Close, Worton, DEVIZES, SN10 5SD.

GRAY, Mrs. Lynnette, ACA *2002;* Luminus Group, Brook House, Ouse Walk, HUNTINGDON, CAMBRIDGESHIRE, PE29 3QW.

GRAY, Miss. Lysanne Mary, BSc ACA *1989;* Flat 2, 11 Cleve Road, West Hampstead, LONDON, NW6 3RH.

GRAY, Mr. Mark Andrew, MA ACA *1997;* 21 Kingsley Park Avenue, SHEFFIELD, S7 2HG.

GRAY, Mr. Martin John, BSc ACA *1983;* Dominion Insurance Co Ltd, 2 Knoll Rise, ORPINGTON, BR6 0NX.

•**GRAY, Mr. Matthew Grant, FCA** *1990;* (Tax Fac), Grant & Co (Accountants) Limited, 7 Manor Park Business Centre, Mackenzie Way, CHELTENHAM, GLOUCESTERSHIRE, GL51 9TX. See also M W Accountancy Limited

GRAY, Mr. Michael, BSc ACA *1990;* 401 Laws Brook Road, CONCORD, MA 01742, UNITED STATES.

GRAY, Mr. Michael Grenville, MA BSc FCA *1976;* 5 Thomson Lane, #27-01 Sky@Eleven, SINGAPORE 297724, SINGAPORE. (Life Member)

GRAY, Mr. Michael James, BSc ACA *1987;* 1 Knighton Lodge, 39 Rydens Rd, WALTON-ON-THAMES, KT12 3AG.

GRAY, Mr. Michael John, FCA *1965;* Paddock House, Ivy House Lane, BERKHAMSTED, HP4 2PP.

GRAY, Mr. Michael William Andrew, ACA *2009;* Flat B, 157 Ramsden Road, LONDON, SW12 8RF.

GRAY, Ms. Miriam Clare, MA ACA *1998;* 34 Rectory Road, Barnes, LONDON, SW13 0DT.

GRAY, Mr. Neil, BSc ACA *2006;* Deloitte Touche Tohmatsu, Level 2 Grosvenor Place, 225 George Street, SYDNEY, NSW 2000, AUSTRALIA.

•**GRAY, Mr. Neil Anthony, BA FCA CF** *1983;* with RSM Tenon Audit Limited, Davidson House, Forbury Square, READING, RG1 3EU.

•**GRAY, Mr. Neville Jason, ACA** *1996;* Ernst & Young LLP, 1 More London Place, LONDON, SE1 2AF. See also Ernst & Young Europe LLP

GRAY, Mr. Nicholas John Talbot, BSc FCA *1992;* Munich Re Underwriting Ltd, St Helens, 1 Undershaft, LONDON, EC3A 8EE.

GRAY, Mr. Nicholas Peter, BA ACA *1999;* Hollydene, Bower Heath, HARPENDEN, HERTFORDSHIRE, AL5 5EE.

GRAY, Miss. Nicola, BA ACA *2010;* 26 Finney Drive, Grange Park, NORTHAMPTON, NN4 5DT.

GRAY, Mrs. Nicola Jayne, BSc ACA *1996;* 51 Bracondale, NORWICH, NR1 2AT.

GRAY, Miss. Nicola Louise, ACA *1995;* 15 Park Avenue, Wynyard Village, BILLINGHAM, TS22 5RU.

GRAY, Mr. Paul Bradley, ACA *1986;* Flat 16 Paramount Building 206-212 St. John Street, LONDON, EC1V 4JY.

GRAY, Mr. Paul James, FCA *1974;* J L Farms Limited, Fulney Farm Centre, Rangell Gate, Low Fulney, SPALDING, LINCOLNSHIRE PE12 6EW.

GRAY, Mr. Paul Jonathan, BA ACA *2003;* Flat 3, 183 Goldhurst Terrace, LONDON, NW6 3ER.

GRAY, Mr. Paul Lawrence, BSc FCA *1987;* 25 Crosspaths, HARPENDEN, HERTFORDSHIRE, AL5 3HE.

GRAY, Mr. Peter, FCA *1969;* 21 Ulph Place, Burnham Market, KING'S LYNN, NORFOLK, PE31 8HQ.

GRAY, Mr. Peter Dougal, BSc FCA *1993;* New Ireland Assurance Company, 11/12 Dawson Street, DUBLIN 2, COUNTY DUBLIN, IRELAND.

GRAY, Mr. Peter Francis, MA FCA *1969;* 1 Bradbourne Street, LONDON, SW6 3TF.

GRAY, Mr. Peter John, BA ACA *2007;* 28 Cornel Road, NEWCASTLE UPON TYNE, NE7 7PT.

GRAY, Mr. Peter Leslie Montgomery, FCA *1962;* Barley House, Stedcombe Vale, Axmouth, SEATON, EX12 4BJ. (Life Member)

GRAY, Mr. Peter Mortimer, FCA *1968;* Witzigs, 5 George Edwards Road, FAKENHAM, NORFOLK, NR21 8NL.

GRAY, Mr. Philip, ACA *2011;* Flat 403, Icon 25, High Street, MANCHESTER, M4 1HG.

GRAY, Mr. Philip David, FCA *1968;* 3 Thurstans, HARLOW, CM19 4RS.

GRAY, Mr. Philip Denis, FCA *1956;* 61 Westridge Road, Kings Heath, BIRMINGHAM, B13 0DU. (Life Member)

GRAY, Mr. Philip Graham Walter, FCA *1961;* Apartment 302 Bridge House, Sion Place, BRISTOL, BS8 4BW.

GRAY, Mr. Philip John, BA FCA *1985;* 4 Brookland Place, Remuera, AUCKLAND 1050, NEW ZEALAND.

GRAY, Mr. Phillip Andrew, BSS ACA *1990;* 33 Barford Drive, WILMSLOW, CHESHIRE, SK9 2GA.

GRAY, Mrs. Rachel Clare, BA(Hons) ACA *2001;* Elm House Abbey Lane, Aslockton, NOTTINGHAM, NG13 9AE.

GRAY, Mr. Richard, BSc(Hons) ACA *2002;* 25 Home Pastures, Hose, MELTON MOWBRAY, LEICESTERSHIRE, LE14 4JB.

GRAY, Mr. Richard Anthony, FCA *1966;* 5, 5 Church Farm Barns, Aldworth Road Compton, NEWBURY, RG20 6RD.

•**GRAY, Mr. Richard James, BA ACA** *1996;* Ernst & Young LLP, 1 More London Place, LONDON, SE1 2AF. See also Ernst & Young Europe LLP

GRAY, Mr. Richard John, BA(Hons) ACA *2002;* S V B Syndicates Ltd, 71 Fenchurch Street, LONDON, EC3M 4HH.

GRAY, Mr. Richard John, ACA *1979;* 22 Vandyke Close, REDHILL, RH1 2DS.

GRAY, Mr. Richard Kempson, FCA *1977;* 76 Gloucester Road, HAMPTON, MIDDLESEX, TW12 2UJ.

GRAY, Mr. Richard Nicholas, FCA *1971;* FIFO Trust Ltd, Noble House, Les Baissieres, St. Peter Port, GUERNSEY, GY1 2UE.

GRAY, Mr. Richard Peter, BSc(Hons) ACA *2001;* PP B2B, British Telecom BT Centre, 81 Newgate Street, LONDON, EC1A 7AJ.

GRAY, Mr. Richard Talbot, BSc ACA *1987;* Man Investments AG, Huobstrasse 3, 8808 PFAFFIKON, SWITZERLAND.

GRAY, Mr. Richard Wharrick, FCA *1971;* Rookwood, Thornton-Le-Dale, PICKERING, YO18 7SD.

GRAY, Mr. Richard William, BA FCA *1968;* #20 Southdown Farm, 1 Buggy Whip Hill, SOUTHAMPTON SN 02, BERMUDA.

GRAY, Mr. Robert Andrew, FCA *1971;* 87 Davyhulme Road, Urmston, MANCHESTER, M41 7BU.

•**GRAY, Mr. Robert Edmund, FCA** *1974;* Robert Gray Accountancy Services Limited, 12 Exchange Street, RETFORD, NOTTINGHAMSHIRE, DN22 6BL.

GRAY, Prof. Robert Hugh, MBE PhD MA BSc(Econ) FCA FCCA *1976;* University of St. Andrews:, School of Mgmt, The Gateway, North Haugh, ST ANDREWS, FIFE KY16 9SS.

GRAY, Mr. Robert John, BA FCA *1975;* Wild Wood, Broad Lane, Newdigate, DORKING, RH5 5AS.

•**GRAY, Mr. Robert John, BSc FCA** *1985;* Francis Gray Limited, Ty Madog, 32 Queens Road, ABERYSTWYTH, DYFED, SY23 2HN. See also Francis, Jones & Davies Ltd

GRAY, Mr. Robin, FCA *1956;* Badgers, 1 Smithbrook Gate, CRANLEIGH, SURREY, GU6 8HS. (Life Member)

GRAY, Mr. Roderick James, MA ACA *1982;* 24 Matmore Gate, SPALDING, LINCOLNSHIRE, PE11 2PN.

GRAY, Mr. Roderick Stewart, BSc FCA *1972;* Pasadena, Cross Street, SUDBURY, SUFFOLK, CO10 2DL.

•**GRAY, Mr. Roger Stewart, FCA** *1973;* Grays Accountants Limited, Kings Works, Kings Road, TEDDINGTON, MIDDLESEX, TW11 0QB.

GRAY, Mr. Roy William, FCA *1954;* 19 Arundel Road, KINGSTON-UPON-THAMES, KT1 3RX. (Life Member)

GRAY, Miss. Sarah Georgina, ACA *2001;* 25 Dell Road, Oulton Broad, LOWESTOFT, NR33 9NS.

GRAY, Mrs. Sarah Lynn, BSc ACA *1987;* (Tax Fac), Target Bloxam Court, Corporation Street, RUGBY, WARWICKSHIRE, CV21 2DU.

GRAY, Miss. Sharon Lesley, BSc ACA *1995;* 8 Salford Road, SOUTHPORT, MERSEYSIDE, PR8 3JN.

GRAY, Mr. Simon, BA ACA *1992;* 42 Sixacres, Slinfold, HORSHAM, RH13 0TH.

•**GRAY, Mr. Simon, BSc FCA ATT CTA IIT(Dip)** *1998;* Henton & Co LLP, St. Andrews House, St. Andrews Street, LEEDS, LS3 1LF.

GRAY, Mr. Simon Anthony John, MA FCA *1984;* with PricewaterhouseCoopers, 2 Southbank Boulevard, Southbank, MELBOURNE, VIC 3006, AUSTRALIA.

GRAY, Mr. Simon Talbot, FCA *1961;* Brackens, Captains Row, LYMINGTON, SO41 9RP.

GRAY, Mr. Simon Timothy, BA(Hons) ACA *2000;* 1 Church Street, Bunny, NOTTINGHAM, NG11 6QW.

GRAY, Miss. Stephanie, BSc ACA *1992;* Chalet Makila Lotissement Lachaz, Montchavin, 73210 BELLENTRE, SAVOIE, FRANCE.

•**GRAY, Mr. Stephen, BSc FCA** *1985;* (Tax Fac), Crowther Jordan Ltd, 39 High Street, Wednesfield, WOLVERHAMPTON, WV11 1ST.

GRAY, Mr. Stephen Marius, BA FCA *1962;* with Dixon Wilson, 22 Chancery Lane, LONDON, WC2A 1LS.

GRAY, Mr. Stephen William, FCA *1978;* Allen House, Main Street, Acomb, HEXHAM, NE46 4PW.

GRAY, Mr. Stuart James, ACA *1997;* The Zenith Centre, Level 6 Tower A, 821 Pacific Highway, CHATSWOOD, NSW 2067, AUSTRALIA.

GRAY, Mr. Stuart Macdonald, BSc ACA *2003;* 82 Whitwell Road, SOUTHSEA, HAMPSHIRE, PO4 0QS.

GRAY, Mr. Terence, BSc FCA *1978;* 24 Moreton Road, Upton, WIRRAL, CH49 6LL.

GRAY, Mr. Timothy John, BA ACA *1988;* 3 The Fairway, Kirby Muxloe, LEICESTER, LE9 2EU.

GRAY, Mr. Timothy John, ACA *1980;* 62 Station Road, Pelsall, WALSALL, WS3 4BQ.

GRAY, Mr. Usher Benjamin, BSc ACA *2004;* Montifiore 6, 43335 RA'ANANA, ISRAEL.

GRAY, Mrs. Victoria, BSc ACA *2005;* 78a Marlow Bottom, MARLOW, BUCKINGHAMSHIRE, SL7 3NB.

GRAY, Mrs. Wendy Elizabeth, BSc ACA *1985;* 7 Dorothy Terrace, Sacriston, DURHAM, DH7 6LG.

GRAY MUIR, Mr. William John, BA ACA *1992;* Sundial Properties, 46 Charlotte Square, EDINBURGH, EH2 4HQ.

GRAYBURN, Miss. Sharon Elizabeth, BA ACA *1999;* Flat 15, 111 Warwick Way, LONDON, SW1V 4HT.

•**GRAYDON, Mr. John Anthony, BA ACA** *1997;* with RSM Tenon Audit Limited, 66 Chiltern Street, LONDON, W1U 4JT.

GRAYDON, Mrs. Verity, ACA *2002;* Rue Auguste Beernaert 41, Watermael Boitsfort, 1170 BRUSSELS, BELGIUM.

•**GRAYER, Mr. Michael David, FCA CF** *1987;* Menzies LLP, Heathrow Business Centre, 65 High Street, EGHAM, SURREY, TW20 9EY.

GRAYNOTH, Mr. Terence, MBA BSc FCA *1989;* 15 Forge End, ST. ALBANS, AL2 3EQ.

GRAYSON, Miss. Catherine Elizabeth, BSc ACA *1994;* Fsquared Ltd, Aeroworks, 5 Adair Street, MANCHESTER, M1 2NQ.

GRAYSON, Mr. Derrick William, FCA *1966;* Hambleton Hill, Tealby Road, MARKET RASEN, LN8 3UL. (Life Member)

GRAYSON, Mr. Edward Michael, FCA *1970;* Car & General (Kenya) Ltd, PO Box 20001, NAIROBI, 00200, KENYA.

GRAYSON, Mr. John Hugh, FCA *1968;* Bramley Farm, Ford Road, Marsh Lane, SHEFFIELD, S21 5RE.

GRAYSON, Mr. Jonathan Robert, BA ACA *1996;* Flat 2, 77 Ferndale Road, Clapham, LONDON, SW4 7RL.

GRAYSON, Mrs. Louise Marie, BA ACA *2005;* 42 Leyburn Close, Whelley, WIGAN, LANCASHIRE, WN1 3NF.

GRAYSON, Mr. Paul John, MA MSc ACA *2010;* Flat 157 Building 45, Hopton Road, LONDON, SE18 6TL.

•**GRAYSON, Mr. Richard William, FCA** *1984;* Nicholsons, Newland House, The Point, Weaver Road, LINCOLN, LN6 3QN.

GRAYSON, Mr. Toby Benjamin, LLB ACA *2000;* Eni China B.V., 15th Floor Unit HIJKL, Times Plaza, No.1 Taizi Road, Shekou, SHENZHEN 518067 GUANGDONG PROVINCE CHINA.

GRAYSON, Mrs. Wendy Monica, BSc ACA *1990;* The Willows, Springwood Park, TONBRIDGE, KENT, TN11 9LZ.

•**GRAYSTON, Mrs. Anne, BSc FCA** *1986;* 49 Gordon Road, South Woodford, LONDON, E18 1DW.

GRAYSTON, Mrs. Elizabeth Alice Jane, ACA *2004;* 36 Bentley Drive, OSWESTRY, SHROPSHIRE, SY11 1TQ.

GRAYSTON, Mr. Kevin, FCA *1977;* 3 Copse Close, BURY ST.EDMUNDS, IP33 2TD.

GRAYSTON, Mr. Lloyd Michael, BA(Hons) ACA CTA *1999;* 78 Richmond Park Road, KINGSTON UPON THAMES, KT2 6AJ.

GRAYSTON, Mr. Paul, BCom ACA *2004;* 17 Ospringe Road, LONDON, NW5 2JD.

GRAZEBROOK, Mr. Julian Spencer William, FCA *1978;* The Rectory, Gussage St. Michael, WIMBORNE, DORSET, BH21 5HX.

GRAZIER, Mrs. Judith Anne, BEd ACA *1989;* Sunnyside, 1A Langcliffe Avenue, HARROGATE, NORTH YORKSHIRE, HG2 8JQ.

GREALEY, Mrs. Eileen Frances, BA ACA *1990;* Rowington, Pound Close, Off Poolhead Lane, Earlswood, SOLIHULL, WEST MIDLANDS B94 5ET.

GREALISH, Miss. Dawn, BA ACA *2007;* 28 Recreation Avenue, ROMFORD, RM7 9ET.

GREALY, Ms. Christina, MA ACA *1998;* 15 Alison Way, Oramsmount, WINCHESTER, SO22 5BT.

GREANEY, Mr. Michael Christopher, BCom ACA *1996;* 13 Proby Park, Barnhill Road, Dalkey, DUBLIN, COUNTY DUBLIN, IRELAND.

GREASBY, Mr. Gary Peter, BSc ACA *1992;* 17 Turpins Ride, Oaklands, WELWYN, HERTFORDSHIRE, AL6 0QU.

GREASLEY, Miss. Alicia Sophie, ACA *2010;* second floor flat, 118 Brondesbury Villas, LONDON, NW6 6AE.

GREASLEY, Mr. Antony Frederick, BA FCA *1985;* Maple House, Clayton, DONCASTER, SOUTH YORKSHIRE, DN5 7DH.

GREASLEY, Mrs. Sheila, BSc FCA *1975;* Sheila Greasley, 41 Coopers Holt Close, Skellingthorpe, LINCOLN, LN6 5SY.

GREATBANKS, Mr. Eric James, FCA *1953;* 17 The Avenue, BILLERICAY, CM12 9HG. (Life Member)

GREATBATCH, Mr. Alan, MA ACA *1981;* 48 Heybridge Lane, Prestbury, MACCLESFIELD, CHESHIRE, SK10 4ER.

GREATBATCH, Mr. Kenneth John, FCA *1971;* The Chevin, Cokes Lane, CHALFONT ST.GILES, HP8 4UD.

GREATOREX, Mr. Anthony Nicholas, BA ACA *1992;* Lamorna, Scott Close, Farnham Common, SLOUGH, SL2 3HT.

GREATOREX, Mr. Colin Harold, FCA *1975;* 203 Woodfield Road, NOTTINGHAM, NG8 6HW.

GREATOREX, Mr. David Anthony, FCA *1968;* 13 Carlisle Close, DUNSTABLE, BEDFORDSHIRE, LU6 3PH.

GREATOREX, Mr. Ian Russell, BA ACA *1988;* Windrush, Castle Road, Horsell, WOKING, GU21 4ES.

GREATOREX, Mr. Mark Derrick, BSc ACA *1984;* Deckers Europe Limited, First Floor, 83/84 George Street, RICHMOND, SURREY, TW9 1HE.

GREATOREX, Mr. Raymond Edward, FCA *1965;* (Tax Fac), Beeches Brook, Wisborough Green, BILLINGSHURST, WEST SUSSEX, RH14 0HP.

GREATREX, Mrs. Heather Jane, BA ACA *1988;* 20 Letchmore Road, RADLETT, WD7 8HT.

•**GREATREX, Mr. Philip Robert, BSc FCA CTA** *1981;* CW Energy LLP, 4th Floor, 40 Queen Street, LONDON, EC4R 1DD. See also CW Energy Tax Consultants Ltd

GREATREX, Mrs. Sarah Jane, BA ACA *1994;* Manor Cottge, Nantwich Road, Wimboldsley, MIDDLEWICH, CW10 0LW.

GREAVES, Mrs. Alaine Louise, BSc ACA *1999;* 13 River Street, WILMSLOW, CHESHIRE, SK9 4AB.

GREAVES, Mr. Bryan Michael, FCA *1970;* 5 Mountbatten Avenue, Sandal, WAKEFIELD, WF2 6EY.

GREAVES, Mr. Cameron Geoffrey, FCA *1970;* (Tax Fac), VCG SIA, Baznicas iela 13/4, RIGA LV-1010, LATVIA.

GREAVES, Cllr Christopher Ian, FCA *1974;* 4 Croft Drive, Menston, ILKLEY, WEST YORKSHIRE, LS29 6LX.

•**GREAVES, Mr. Christopher Michael, FCA** *1971;* Greaves & Co, White Lodge, 33 Woodside Road, WOODFORD GREEN, IG8 0TW.

GREAVES, Mrs. Claire Elizabeth, FCA *1991;* University of Plymouth, Drake Circus, PLYMOUTH, PL4 8AA.

GREAVES, Mr. David Christopher, ACA *2009;* 43 Ditton Reach, THAMES DITTON, SURREY, KT7 0XB.

•**GREAVES, Mr. Ian Geoffrey, BA FCA ACMA** *1987;* KPMG LLP, One Snowhill, Snow Hill Queensway, BIRMINGHAM, B4 6GN. See also KPMG Europe LLP

GREAVES, Mr. Ian William, BSc ACA *1990;* Ruby Cottage, 123 Newtown Road, Warsash, SOUTHAMPTON, SO31 9GY.

①**GREAVES, Mr. John Peter Robert, FCA** *1974;* with KPMG LLP, 15 Canada Square, LONDON, E14 5GL.

GREAVES, Mr. John Rhodri Dyson, BA ACA *1986;* Broadlands Cottage, Camden Park, TUNBRIDGE WELLS, TN2 4TN.

GREAVES, Miss. Kathryn Linda, BSc ACA *1992;* Allen & Overy Llp One, Bishops Square, LONDON, E1 6AD.

GREAVES, Miss. Laura Jayne, ACA *2006;* 79 Rowan Tree Road, Killamarsh, SHEFFIELD, S21 1FA.

GREAVES, Mr. Leslie, FCA *1971;* Rowan Cottage, Doulting, SHEPTON MALLET, BA4 4QE.

•**GREAVES, Mr. Mark Andrew, FCA CF MBA** *1991;* Francis Clark, North Quay House, Sutton Harbour, PLYMOUTH, PL4 0RA. See also Francis Clark LLP

GREAVES, Mr. Mark John, BA ACA *1988;* The Old Rectory, Drayton Parslow, MILTON KEYNES, MK17 0JF.

GREAVES, Mr. Peter Alfred Fernan, FCA *1953;* Squirrel Cottage, 118 Fairmile Lane, Stoke D'Abernon, COBHAM, KT11 2BX. (Life Member)

GREAVES, Mrs. Susan Jean, FCA FCCA DipCG *1987;* 52 Chelsfield Way, Pendas Fields, LEEDS, LS15 8XE.

•**GREAVES, Mr. Terence John, FCA** *1971;* 4U Management Ltd, 8 Hodgson Fold, Addingham, ILKLEY, WEST YORKSHIRE, LS29 0HA. See also Greaves Terry J

GRECH, Mrs. Lucy Margaret, BA ACA *1998;* 47 Mandalay Drive, Brockhill Village, Norton, WORCESTER, WR5 2PL.

•**GREELEY, Mr. Paul William, FCA** *1961;* (Tax Fac), Four Stacks, 6 Peaks Hill, PURLEY, SURREY, CR8 3JE.

GREEN, Miss. Adele Louise, BSc ACA *2010;* 26 Silver Birches, Denton, MANCHESTER, M34 7RA.

GREEN, Mr. Adrian Phillip, MSc ACA *1998;* 8 Brookhill Close, Diggle, OLDHAM, OL3 5NH.

•GREEN, Mr. Alan Duncan, ACA *1985;* Alan Green Accountancy Limited, Verna House, 9 Bicester Road, AYLESBURY, BUCKINGHAMSHIRE, HP19 9AG.
GREEN, Mr. Alan Richard, ACA *2004;* 25 Jefferson Ave, MAPLEWOOD, NJ 07040, UNITED STATES.
GREEN, Mr. Alec Douglas, FCA *1969;* 4 Kent Terrace, Regents Park, LONDON, NW1 4RP.
GREEN, Mr. Alex Dominic John, BSc ARCS ACA *1996;* Pestalozzistrasse 13, Bern, 3007 CANTON, SWITZERLAND.
GREEN, Mr. Alexander David, BA ACA *2006;* 56 Springfield Park, Twyford, READING, RG10 9JH.
•GREEN, Mr. Alexander Sonny, FCA *1976;* (Tax Fac), Greenback Alan LLP, 11 Raven Wharf, Lafone Street, LONDON, SE1 2LR.
GREEN, Mrs. Alexandra, FCA *1977;* 16 Lynfield Lane, Chesterton, CAMBRIDGE, CB4 1DR.
GREEN, Mrs. Alison Elaine, BSc ACA *2003;* Jesus College, Jesus Lane, CAMBRIDGE, CB5 8BL.
GREEN, Mr. Allen Robert, BSc ACA *1979;* A K Industries Ltd, Foxwood Court, Rotherwas, HEREFORD, HR2 6JQ.
•GREEN, Mr. Andrew, LLB ACA *2004;* 10 The Vale, WOODFORD GREEN, IG8 9BT.
•GREEN, Mr. Andrew, FCA MIPA AFA *1971;* A. Green, Dal Ghorm House, Ardtoe, ACHARACLE, ARGYLL, PH36 4LD.
GREEN, Mr. Andrew, BA ACA *2001;* 4 Queens Gardens, LONDON, W5 1SF.
GREEN, Mr. Andrew Charles, BA FCA *1976;* 109 Eastern Esplanade, SOUTHEND-ON-SEA, ESSEX, SS1 2YP.
GREEN, Mr. Andrew James, ACA *2008;* PRS Investment Advisory, PO Box 10360, Strathvale House, 90 North Church Street, GEORGETOWN, GRAND CAYMAN KY1 1003 CAYMAN ISLANDS.
GREEN, Mr. Andrew James Duncan, BSocSc ACA *1997;* The White Cottage, Duddleswell, UCKFIELD, EAST SUSSEX, TN22 3BH.
•GREEN, Mr. Andrew Jonathan, FCA ATII *1983;* (Tax Fac), 49 Harwich Road, Mistley, MANNINGTREE, ESSEX, CO11 1NB.
GREEN, Mr. Andrew Peter, BSc ACA *1981;* Fairmile House, Sandy Lane, COBHAM, KT11 2EL.
GREEN, Mr. Andrew Simon, BSc ACA *1988;* Ernst & Young Llp, 1 More London Place, LONDON, SE1 2AF.
GREEN, Mr. Andrew Stephen Landon, MA ACA *2000;* Floor 7, Societe Generale S G House, 41 Tower Hill, LONDON, EC3N 4SG.
GREEN, Mr. Andrew William, ACA *2009;* 170 Crampton Street, LONDON, SE17 3AE.
GREEN, Mrs. Angela Mary, BA ACA *1998;* Woodside Watersplash Lane, ASCOT, BERKSHIRE, SL5 7QP.
GREEN, Mrs. Ann Marian, BCom ACA *1980;* 32 Holliers Close, THAME, OX9 2EN.
•GREEN, Mrs. Anna Katrine, BA ACA *1992;* AK Accountancy Ltd, 64 Coronation Road, Downend, BRISTOL, BS16 5SL.
GREEN, Mr. Anthony Charles, ACA *1979;* P O Box 97, MFUWE, ZAMBIA.
GREEN, Mr. Anthony David, BSc ACA *1995;* 52 Benomley Drive, HUDDERSFIELD, HD5 8LX.
GREEN, Mr. Anthony Gerhard, MA ACA *1980;* Merck Sharp & Dohme GmbH, Am Euro-Platz 2, Gebaude G - 5 Stock, 1120 VIENNA, AUSTRIA.
GREEN, Mr. Antony Brian, FCA *1954;* Timbers, Plymouth Road, BUCKFASTLEIGH, DEVON, TQ11 0DH. (Life Member)
GREEN, Mr. Antony Nicholas Lovell, BEng ACA *1994;* Bellevue, Swan Gardens, Tetsworth, THAME, OX9 7BN.
GREEN, Mr. Arthur, FCA *1950;* (President 1987 - 1988) (Member of Council 1972 - 1991), Up Yonder, Herbert Road, SALCOMBE, TQ8 8HP. (Life Member)
•GREEN, Mr. Barry Charles, FCA *1974;* B.C. Green, Neumattstrasse 13, 6313 MENZINGEN, SWITZERLAND.
GREEN, Mr. Barry Dennis, FCA *1976;* 42 Hahermon Street, 65153 TEL AVIV, ISRAEL.
GREEN, Mr. Barry Michael, BA ACA *1978;* 2195 Massachusetts Avenue, LEXINGTON, MA 02421, UNITED STATES.
GREEN, Mr. Brian, ACA *1988;* 7 Kirbys Drive, Bowburn, DURHAM, DH6 5GA.
GREEN, Mr. Brian, FCA *1971;* with UHY Torgersens Limited, 7 Grange Road West, JARROW, TYNE AND WEAR, NE32 3JA.
•ⒹGREEN, Mr. Brian, BA ACA *1986;* KPMG LLP, St. James's Square, MANCHESTER, M2 6DS. See also KPMG Europe LLP
GREEN, Mr. Brian John, FCA *1968;* The Coach House, Long Lane, Haughton, TARPORLEY, CW6 9RN.
GREEN, Mr. Brian Rex, MA FCA *1960;* Flat 5, 31 Queen's Gate Terrace, Kensington, LONDON, SW7 5PR. (Life Member)
GREEN, Mrs. Caroline Elizabeth, MA ACA *1993;* 79 Hightown Road, CLECKHEATON, BD19 5JP.
GREEN, Miss. Catherine Alexandra, ACA *2011;* 25 Shafton Road, ROTHERHAM, SOUTH YORKSHIRE, S60 3JG.
GREEN, Mrs. Catherine Anne, BSc(Hons) ACA *2000;* 63 Shimmer Pond Place, THE WOODLANDS, TX 77385, UNITED STATES.
GREEN, Mrs. Catherine Elizabeth, BSc ACA CTA *1998;* 8 Brookhill Close, Diggle, OLDHAM, OL3 5NH.
GREEN, Miss. Catherine Mary, BSc ACA *2000;* 58 Rocks Lane, LONDON, SW13 0DA.
GREEN, Mr. Charles Edward, ACA *1983;* Pyke House, Court Street, Sherston, MALMESBURY, WILTSHIRE, SN16 0LL.
GREEN, Mr. Charles Gordon Mitchell, FCA *1967;* Hill Top Farm, Colne Road, Oldfield, KEIGHLEY, BD22 0JJ.
•GREEN, Mr. Charles Richard, BCom ACA CTA *1988;* (Tax Fac), Clarkson Hyde LLP, 3rd Floor, Chancery House, St. Nicholas Way, SUTTON, SURREY SM1 1JB.
GREEN, Mr. Charles Richard, FCA *1983;* 27 Kelvedon Green, Kelvedon Hatch, BRENTWOOD, ESSEX, CM15 0XG.
GREEN, Mr. Charles Whitfield, MA FCA *1981;* The Wood, Maesbrook, OSWESTRY, SHROPSHIRE, SY10 8QU.
GREEN, Miss. Charlotte Emma, BSc ACA *1995;* Avenue Alfred Madoux 30, Woluwe St Pierre, 1150 BRUSSELS, BELGIUM.
GREEN, Miss. Charys Anne, BA(Hons) ACA *2003;* 9 St Albans Road, Claughton, PRENTON, CH43 8SB.
GREEN, Mrs. Cheryl Anne, ACA *1987;* PO Box HM 897, HAMILTON HM DX, BERMUDA.
GREEN, Mr. Christopher, ACA *2011;* 4 The Dell, Oakdale, BLACKBURN, BB2 4SG.
GREEN, Mr. Christopher Andrew, MSci ACA *2010;* Flat 13, Corinthian Court, Redcliff Mead Lane, BRISTOL, BS1 6FE.
GREEN, Mr. Christopher Anthony William, FCA *1968;* 40 Fenn Avenue, TORONTO M2L 1M8, ON, CANADA.
GREEN, Mr. Christopher Frederick, FCA *1963;* Barrowdale, 72 Sea Lane, Ferring, WORTHING, BN12 5EP. (Life Member)
GREEN, Mr. Christopher Howard, BA FCA *1979;* 24 Portman Gardens, UXBRIDGE, MIDDLESEX, UB10 9NT.
GREEN, Mr. Christopher James, MSc BA ACA *2006;* 1 Laburnum Close, CARTERTON, OXFORDSHIRE, OX18 1JT.
GREEN, Mr. Christopher John Hayden, BA FCA *1971;* Uplands, BUDLEIGH SALTERTON, DEVON, EX9 6NZ. (Life Member)
GREEN, Mr. Christopher Martin, BSc ACA *1987;* Neller, 164 Fullarton Road, DULWICH, SA 5065, AUSTRALIA.
GREEN, Mr. Christopher Michael, BSc ACA *1985;* South View House, North Bank, Haydon Bridge, HEXHAM, NE47 6LU.
GREEN, Miss. Clair, BA(Hons) ACA *2011;* 31 Severn Close, SANDHURST, BERKSHIRE, GU47 9RJ.
GREEN, Mrs. Claire Annabel, ACA *2011;* 18 Broome Close, HORSHAM, WEST SUSSEX, RH12 5XG.
•GREEN, Mr. Clifford Charles, LLB FCA *1985;* (Tax Fac), Eastbury Accounting Solutions Limited, Beechwood, Balnain, Drumnadrochit, INVERNESS, IV63 6TJ.
GREEN, Mr. Conrad David, BSc ACA *1990;* Pemajero, Cedar Avenue West, CHELMSFORD, CM1 2XA.
GREEN, Mr. Daniel Joseph, BA ACA *2007;* 26 Lennox Gate, BLACKPOOL, FY4 3JQ.
GREEN, Mr. Darren Paul, BA ACA *2001;* Fremantle Media Ltd, 1 Stephen Street, LONDON, W1T 1AL.
GREEN, Mr. David, BA ACA *1993;* 7 Forest Ridge, East Ardsley, WAKEFIELD, WF3 2EU.
GREEN, Mr. David, FCA *1979;* 5 Copperfields, SAFFRON WALDEN, CB11 4FG.
•GREEN, Mr. David, FCA *1974;* 111 Monks Road, Binley Woods, COVENTRY, CV3 2BY.
GREEN, Mr. David Alexander, BSc FCA *1988;* 62 Freshfield Road, Formby, LIVERPOOL, L37 7BQ.
GREEN, Mr. David Anthony, BSc FCA *1969;* 10 Coastal Road, East Preston, LITTLEHAMPTON, WEST SUSSEX, BN16 1SJ. (Life Member)
GREEN, Mr. David Anthony, BSc FCA *1985;* 78 Valley Fields Crescent, ENFIELD, MIDDLESEX, EN2 7QA.
GREEN, Mr. David Gordon, ACA *1985;* Merlot, Rockbeare, EXETER, EX5 2EG.
GREEN, Mr. David Harold, FCA *1962;* 55 Great Cranford Street, Poundbury, DORCHESTER, DORSET, DT1 3SQ. (Life Member)
GREEN, Mr. David John, FCA *1965;* Florestan, Graynfylde Drive, BIDEFORD, EX39 4AP.
GREEN, Mr. David Louis Brian, FCA *1959;* 2f Lindfield Gardens, LONDON, NW3 6PU. (Life Member)
GREEN, Mr. David Martin, BA ACA *1990;* Skanska UK PLC, Maple Cross House, Denham Way, Maple Cross, RICKMANSWORTH, WD3 9SW.
GREEN, Mr. David Martin, BA ACA *1980;* 3 Abberley Park, Sittingbourne Road, MAIDSTONE, KENT, ME14 5GD.
GREEN, Mr. David Martyn Jackson, FCA *1967;* 4 Longfield, Little Kingshill, GREAT MISSENDEN, BUCKINGHAMSHIRE, HP16 0EG.
GREEN, Mr. David Merrick, BSc ACA *1979;* David M. Green, 13 Bressey Grove, South Woodford, LONDON, E18 2HU.
•GREEN, Mr. David Michael, BSc FCA *1987;* (Tax Fac), Gowers Limited, The Old School House, Bridge Road, Hunton Bridge, KINGS LANGLEY, HERTFORDSHIRE WD4 8SZ.
•GREEN, Mr. David Michael Ewin, FCA *1968;* Jade Financial Management Ltd, 2 Tone Road, CLEVEDON, BS21 6LG.
GREEN, Mr. David Paul, BA ACA *2006;* Royal Mail, Rowland Hill House, Boythorpe Road, CHESTERFIELD, DERBYSHIRE, S49 1HQ.
GREEN, Mr. David Peter, BCom FCA *1981;* 425 Winter Road, DELAWARE, OH 43065, UNITED STATES.
GREEN, Mr. David Sebastian, BSc ACA *1994;* Via Cassarinetta 24, 6900 LUGANO, SWITZERLAND.
•GREEN, Mr. David Thomas, FCA DChA *1974;* Haines Watts Wales LLP, Pagefield House, 24 Gold Tops, NEWPORT, GWENT, NP20 4PG.
GREEN, Ms. Deborah Anne, MA ACA *1993;* Costal Housing Group, 11 Wind Street, SWANSEA, SA1 1DP.
GREEN, Miss. Deborah Louise, BA ACA *1994;* Westown, 1 Castle Road, KENILWORTH, WARWICKSHIRE, CV8 1NG.
GREEN, Miss. Denise Michelle, BSc ACA *2005;* Flat 7 Sycamore Court, 203 The Great North Way, Hendon, LONDON, NW4 1PN.
GREEN, Mr. Dennis Malcolm, FCA *1958;* 11 Woburn Court, Stanmore Road, RICHMOND, TW9 2DD. (Life Member)
GREEN, Mr. Dennis William, FCA *1953;* 54 Kingscote Hill, Gossops Green, CRAWLEY, RH11 8QA. (Life Member)
GREEN, Mr. Douglas Royston, BSc ACA *1986;* Manston, 33 Beaconsfield Road, Claygate, ESHER, SURREY, KT10 0PN.
GREEN, Mr. Edmund, FCA *1957;* Longlea, 46 Ferringham Lane, Ferring, WORTHING, BN12 5LU. (Life Member)
GREEN, Mr. Edward, BSc ACA *1990;* 8 Rutland Road, SOUTHPORT, PR8 6PB.
•ⒹGREEN, Mr. Elliot Harry, FCA MABRP *1999;* Oury Clark, PO Box 150, Herschel House, 58 Herschel Street, SLOUGH, SL1 1HD.
GREEN, Mr. Eric Alexander Luke, BSc(Hons) ACA *2010;* 64 Beaumont Leys Lane, LEICESTER, LE4 2BA.
GREEN, Mr. Eric Frank John, FCA *1940;* 20281 E. Country Club Drive, Apt 215, AVENTURA, FL 33180-3024, UNITED STATES. (Life Member)
GREEN, Mr. Eric Robinson, FCA *1954;* Bryn Arvon, 63 Harefield Road, RICKMANSWORTH, WD3 1ND. (Life Member)
GREEN, Miss. Esther Louise, BA ACA *1994;* 1 Palace Theatre Apartments, Market Street, RUGBY, CV21 3HJ.
GREEN, Mrs. Fiona Ann, ACA *1987;* Bellingham Marine, Churchill House, 12 Mosley Street, NEWCASTLE UPON TYNE, NE1 1DE.
•GREEN, Mrs. Fiona Elizabeth, BA(Hons) ACA CTA *2002;* DJH Accountants Ltd, Porthill Lodge, High Street, Wolstanton, NEWCASTLE, STAFFORDSHIRE ST5 0EZ.
GREEN, Mrs. Fiona Jane Jamieson, BSc ACA *1983;* 49 Monkhams Avenue, WOODFORD GREEN, ESSEX, IG8 0EX.
GREEN, Mr. Francis Anthony, FCA *1977;* 44 Nutbush Drive, BIRMINGHAM, B31 5SG.
GREEN, Mr. Fraser John, BSc ACA *1991;* 18 Caroline Terrace, EDINBURGH, EH12 8QY.
GREEN, Mr. Gary, MA BA ACA *2010;* 3 Chaucer Grove, BOREHAMWOOD, HERTFORDSHIRE, WD6 2FF.
GREEN, Mr. Gary Richard, FCA *1981;* 3608 Hampton Manor Drive, CHARLOTTE, NC 28226, UNITED STATES.
GREEN, Mr. Geoffrey Colin, FCA *1970;* Los Alcornoques B14, Monte Mayor Golf & Country Club, 29679 BENAHAVIS, MALAGA, SPAIN.
•GREEN, Mr. Geoffrey David, BSc FCA *1983;* 41 Warmans Close, WANTAGE, OX12 9XT.
GREEN, Mrs. Georgina Ruth, BA ACA *2006;* 37 Summerbridge Crescent, Gomersal, CLECKHEATON, WEST YORKSHIRE, BD19 4LW.
GREEN, Mr. Gordon, FCA *1964;* 1 Craven Road, CLEETHORPES, SOUTH HUMBERSIDE, DN35 7SQ.
GREEN, Mr. Harold Michael, FCA *1966;* Flat 5 Meltham Hall, Huddersfield RoadMeltham, HOLMFIRTHWest Yorkshire, HD9 4BQ.
GREEN, Mr. Harold Unsworth, FCA *1948;* 17 Flacca Court, Field Lane Tattenhall, CHESTER, CH3 9PW. (Life Member)
GREEN, Mrs. Helen, BSc ACA *1989;* The Greenhouse, 415 Luton Road, HARPENDEN, AL5 3QE.
•GREEN, Mrs. Helen Foster, FCA *1988;* Saffery Champness, P O Box 141, La Tonnelle House, Les Banques, St. Sampson, GUERNSEY GY1 3HS.
GREEN, Mrs. Helen Jane, BA ACA *2004;* British Telecom BT Centre, 81 Newgate Street, LONDON, EC1A 7AJ.
GREEN, Mrs. Helen Louise, BA ACA *1997;* Tinkerfield, Old Clitheroe Road, Dutton, PRESTON, PR3 2YU.
•GREEN, Mr. Hugh Grant Duffill, BSc FCA *1988;* KPMG LLP, 15 Canada Square, LONDON, E14 5GL. See also KPMG Europe LLP
•GREEN, Mr. Hugh Michael, FCA *1968;* Sunnybank, Far Hill, Llanishen, CHEPSTOW, NP16 6QZ.
GREEN, Mr. Ian Christopher, BSc FCA *1978;* 236 North Road, LONDON, SW19 1TR.
GREEN, Mr. Ian Colin, FCA *1968;* 7 Hill Road, PINNER, HA5 1JY. (Life Member)
•ⒹGREEN, Mr. Ian David, BA ACA *1991;* PricewaterhouseCoopers LLP, Benson House, 33 Wellington Street, LEEDS, LS1 4JP. See also PricewaterhouseCoopers
GREEN, Mr. Jack, FCA *1963;* Alston, 9 Farnham Lane, Ferrensby, KNARESBOROUGH, NORTH YORKSHIRE, HG5 9JG. (Life Member)
GREEN, Mr. Jake Edward Andrew, MA ACA *2003;* 6 Pollard Road, LONDON, N20 0UB.
GREEN, Mr. James, BA(Hons) ACA *2010;* Flat 19 Uno Apartments, 1 Sherman Road, BROMLEY, BR1 3GP.
•GREEN, Mr. James Edward, FCA *1980;* Duncan & Toplis, 26 Park Road, MELTON MOWBRAY, LE13 1TT.
GREEN, Mr. James Paul, BSc ACA *1998;* Spa Cottage, Sheepcote Green, Clavering, SAFFRON WALDEN, ESSEX, CB11 4SJ.
GREEN, Mrs. Jane, BSc ACA *1995;* Association for Financial Markets in Europe St Michael's House, 1 George Yard, LONDON, EC3V 9Dh.
•GREEN, Mrs. Jane Elizabeth, MSc FCA *1989;* Viridis Consulting Ltd, 9 Kenyons, West Horsley, LEATHERHEAD, SURREY, KT24 6HX.
GREEN, Mr. Jeffrey Johnstone, BA ACA *1987;* 27 Babylon Lane, Anderton, CHORLEY, PR6 9NR.
GREEN, Mrs. Jeniffer Mary, BSc FCA ATII *1973;* Willow Farm, Brickyard Lane, Navenby, LINCOLN, LN5 0LH.
GREEN, Ms. Jennifer, MSc BEng ACA *2001;* with Grant Thornton UK LLP, The Explorer Building, Fleming Way, Manor Royal, CRAWLEY, WEST SUSSEX RH10 9GT.
GREEN, Mrs. Jennifer Patricia, BSc ACA *1990;* 22 New Road, Twyford, READING, RG10 9PT.
GREEN, Mr. Jeremy John, BA ACA *1982;* Hunterswood, Northwich Road, Cranage, CREWE, CW4 8HL.
•GREEN, Mrs. Joanna Forbes, BSc ACA *2005;* Ward Mackenzie, Sussex House, Farningham Road, CROWBOROUGH, EAST SUSSEX, TN6 2JP.
GREEN, Miss. Joanna Kate, BA ACA *2009;* 28 Doria Road, LONDON, SW6 4UG.
GREEN, Mr. John Barrington Thomas, FCA *1965;* 3 The Haven, 27 Downs Park West, BRISTOL, BS6 7QH.
GREEN, Mr. John Charles, BSc ACA *1995;* Worldwide Clinical Trials Ltd Isaac Newton Centre, Nottingham Science Park, NOTTINGHAM, NG7 2RH.
•GREEN, Mr. John Derrick, BA FCA CF *1984;* Pierce C A Ltd, Mentor House, Ainsworth Street, BLACKBURN, BB1 6AY. See also Pierce Group Limited
GREEN, Mr. John Flannan, MSc FCA *1977;* 5 Dale Gardens, WIRRAL, MERSEYSIDE, CH60 6TQ.
GREEN, Mr. John Louis, BA FCA *1970;* Hursley House, The Warren, East Horsley, LEATHERHEAD, KT24 5RH.
GREEN, Mr. John Michael, FCA *1972;* 62 Binswood Avenue, LEAMINGTON SPA, CV32 5RY.
GREEN, Mr. John Owen, FCA *1968;* 604 Troon Circle, MARTINEZ, GA 30907, UNITED STATES.
GREEN, Mr. John Stephen, FCA *1975;* Chepstow Cottage, 6 Chepstow Close, BILLERICAY, CM11 1SH.
GREEN, Mr. John Vernon, FCA *1972;* 5 Orton Close, Rearsby, LEICESTER, LE7 4XZ.
GREEN, Mr. Jonathan, BSc ACA *2002;* 18 The Hall Close, Dunchurch, RUGBY, WARWICKSHIRE, CV22 6NP.
•GREEN, Mr. Jonathan Daniel, ACA FCCA *2010;* Lewis Brownlee, Avenue House, Southgate, CHICHESTER, WEST SUSSEX, PO19 1ES. See also Lewis Brownlee Sherlock

GREEN, Dr. Judith Margaret, FCA *1989;* (Tax Fac), Wooten Hall Cottage, Greendown, Litton, RADSTOCK, BA3 4RU.
GREEN, Ms. Judith Susan, BA FCA *1975;* Wellspring Cottage, 3 Castle Road, Lavendon, OLNEY, MK46 4JD.
GREEN, Mrs. Julie Kaye, FCA *1985;* PO Box 615, KYABRAM, VIC 3619, AUSTRALIA.
GREEN, Mrs. Julie Marion, ACA *2003;* 50 The Drove Way, Istead Rise, GRAVESEND, DA13 9JZ.
•GREEN, Mrs. Karen Jayne Lynn, BCom FCA TEP *1983;* BW Macfarlane LLP, 3 Temple Square, LIVERPOOL, L2 5BA.
GREEN, Miss. Katherine Helen, BSc ACA *2001;* 6 Wolf Run Drive, Riverwalk, SIMPSONVILLE, SC 29681, UNITED STATES.
GREEN, Mrs. Katherine Louise, BA ACA *1992;* Moulton Lodge, 15 Park Lane, Moulton, NORTHWICH, CW9 8QG.
GREEN, Mrs. Kathryn Ann, BCom ACA *2003;* 30 Phoenix Way, Portishead, BRISTOL, BS20 7JX.
•GREEN, Mr. Keith Anthony, FCA *1985;* (Tax Fac), Barter Durgan, 10 Victoria Road South, SOUTHSEA, PO5 2DA.
GREEN, Mr. Keith Charles, BSc FCA *1982;* (Tax Fac), 32 Holliers Close, THAME, OXFORDSHIRE, OX9 2EN.
GREEN, Mr. Kevin Jeffrey, BSc ACA *1991;* Q D Ltd, 93 Great Titchfield Street, LONDON, W1W 6RP.
•GREEN, Mr. Kim Daniel Patric, FCA *1978;* PricewaterhouseCoopers LLP, 1 Embankment Place, LONDON, WC2N 6RH.
GREEN, Mrs. Kym Margo, ACA *1989;* 19 Eyebrook Road, Bowdon, ALTRINCHAM, WA14 3LH.
GREEN, Miss. Laura Michelle, ACA *2009;* 3 Willow Close, BATH, BA2 2DZ.
GREEN, Miss. Laura Suzanne, ACA *2007;* 8 Harthill, Gildersome Morley, LEEDS, LS27 7EU.
GREEN, Mr. Leonard Walter, FCA *1958;* 82 Shalva Street, 46705 HERZLIA PETUACH, ISRAEL. (Life Member)
GREEN, Mr. Leslie, FCA *1953;* 3 Queen's Gardens, LONDON, NW4 2TR. (Life Member)
GREEN, Mr. Leslie Thomas, FCA *1966;* 1 Endway, SURBITON, KT5 9BU. (Life Member)
GREEN, Mrs. Linda, BSc ACA *1992;* Schiehallion, 18 Caroline Terrace, EDINBURGH, EH12 8QY.
GREEN, Miss. Lorna, ACA *2011;* PricewaterhouseCoopers, 201 Sussex Street, GPO Box 2650, SYDNEY, NSW 1171, AUSTRALIA.
•GREEN, Mrs. Lorna Gail, BSc ACA *1994;* Green Accounting Solutions Limited, 82 Vaughan Williams Way, Warley, BRENTWOOD, ESSEX, CM14 5WT.
GREEN, Miss. Lorna Katherine, ACA *2007;* 488 Stanks Drive, LEEDS, LS14 5BJ.
GREEN, Mrs. Louise Elizabeth, BA ACA *1994;* Foxcote Lodge, Jacksons Meadow, Bidford-on-Avon, ALCESTER, B50 4HQ.
•GREEN, Mr. Marc Jason, BA FCA *1988;* Tish Leibovitch, 249 Cranbrook Road, ILFORD, IG1 4TG.
GREEN, Mr. Marcus Conrad, BA(Hons) FCA *1998;* 27 New Park Street, Morley, LEEDS, LS27 0PT.
GREEN, Mr. Mark Alban, BA ACA *1983;* Greated Happiness Ltd, 157 Auckland Road, LONDON, SE19 2RH.
GREEN, Mr. Mark Ian, BA ACA *2008;* 50 Greenock Crescent, WOLVERHAMPTON, WV4 6BJ.
GREEN, Mr. Mark John, MSc BA ACA *2006;* 37 Castle Dyke Wynd, YARM, CLEVELAND, TS15 9DE.
GREEN, Mr. Mark Peter, BA ACA *1998;* 38 Chemin De La Cote, 1283 DARDAGNY, SWITZERLAND.
GREEN, The Revd. Martyn, FCA *1969;* 29 Park Row, KNARESBOROUGH, NORTH YORKSHIRE, HG5 0BJ.
GREEN, Mr. Matthew, ACA *2009;* 11 Brambler Court, BRENTFORD, MIDDLESEX, TW8 9QP.
GREEN, Mr. Matthew, BA ACA *2011;* 82 Palace Road, LONDON, SW2 3JY.
GREEN, Mr. Matthew Allan, ACA *2008;* 22 Manchester Square, LONDON, W1U 3PT.
GREEN, Mr. Matthew Barnaby, BA FCA *2000;* 5th Floor, 40 Portman Square, LONDON, W1H 6LT.
GREEN, Mr. Matthew Gilbert, MA BSc(Econ) ACA *1982;* 38 Broxash Road, LONDON, SW11 6AB.
GREEN, Mr. Matthew Newbery, BA(Hons) ACA *2002;* PO Box 24172, SAFAT, KUWAIT.
GREEN, Mr. Matthew Robert, ACA *2009;* 5 Arthur Milton Street, BRISTOL, BS7 9EB.
GREEN, Mr. Matthew William Schofield, ACA *2010;* La Cachette Val Plaisant, St. Helier, JERSEY, JE2 4TB.
GREEN, Mr. Michael, FCA *1957;* Flat 26 Hartsbourne Park, 180 High Road, Bushey Heath, BUSHEY, WD23 1SD. (Life Member)
•GREEN, Mr. Michael, FCA *1961;* (Tax Fac), The Old Coach House Services Limited, The Old Coach House, 40 Carey Street, READING, RG1 7JS. See also Jack & Co
GREEN, Mr. Michael Anthony, BSc FCA *1982;* 70 Spurgate, Hutton Mount, BRENTWOOD, ESSEX, CM13 2JT.
•GREEN, Mr. Michael Christopher, FCA *1974;* 229 Bills Lane, Shirley, SOLIHULL, WEST MIDLANDS, B90 2PJ.
GREEN, Mr. Michael Howard, BSc ACA *2005;* 7 Cedar Vale Lane, North Apartment, DEVONSHIRE DV06, BERMUDA.
GREEN, Mr. Michael James, FCA *1952;* 117 High Street, AMERSHAM, BUCKINGHAMSHIRE, HP7 0DY. (Life Member)
GREEN, Mr. Michael James, ACA *2008;* S O S Sahel UK The Old Music Hall, 106-108 Cowley Road, OXFORD, OX4 1JE.
GREEN, Mr. Michael James, BSc ACA *2010;* 6 Middlewich Close, DAVENTRY, NORTHAMPTONSHIRE, NN11 0GJ.
GREEN, Mr. Michael James Bay, FCA *1965;* 30 Gresham Street, Dresdner Kleinwort, PO Box 52715, LONDON, EC2P 2XY.
GREEN, Mr. Michael John, MA ACA *1993;* 1250 Merchant Lane, MCLEAN, VA 22101, UNITED STATES.
GREEN, Mr. Michael John, FCA *1970;* 116 Lambwath Road, HULL, HU8 0HE.
GREEN, Mr. Michael Jonathan, FCA *1965;* 12 Shackletons, Chipping, ONGAR, CM5 9AT.
GREEN, Mr. Michael Lawrence, BA FCA *1962;* 8 The Beeches, Heald Road, Bowdon, ALTRINCHAM, CHESHIRE, WA14 2HZ. (Life Member)
•GREEN, Mr. Michael Richard, BEng ACA *2005;* Oakwood, 99 Stockton Lane, YORK, YO31 1JA.
GREEN, Mr. Michael Robert, BA ACA *1992;* Ernst & Young, PO Box 136, ABU DHABI, UNITED ARAB EMIRATES.
•GREEN, Miss. Natalie Ursula, FCA *1991;* (Tax Fac), Natalie Green & Co, 7G Mobbs Miller House, Christchurch Road, NORTHAMPTON, NN1 5LL.
GREEN, Mr. Neil Anthony, BA ACA *1992;* 181 Brockwell Lane, CHESTERFIELD, DERBYSHIRE, S40 4EX.
GREEN, Mr. Nicholas Andrew, BSc ACA *2006;* 2 Bulls Lodge Farm Cottages, Generals Lane Boreham, CHELMSFORD, CM3 3HN.
GREEN, Mr. Nicholas Charles, BSc ACA *2008;* 2 Pinto Close, Whiteley, FAREHAM, HAMPSHIRE, PO15 7BZ.
GREEN, Mr. Nicholas Julian, BSc ACA *1990;* 9 Kenyons, West Horsley, LEATHERHEAD, KT24 6HX.
GREEN, Miss. Nicholette Elizabeth, BA(Hons) ACA *2001;* 22 Rockleigh Road, SOUTHAMPTON, SO16 7AR.
GREEN, Miss. Nicola, ACA *2008;* 30 Blenheim Gardens, READING, RG1 5QG.
GREEN, Mrs. Nicola Jayne, BSc ACA *2003;* 60 Morton Gardens, Halfway, SHEFFIELD, S20 8GJ.
GREEN, Miss. Nicola Marie, BA ACA *1999;* Helvetic Fund Administration, Suite 209, Neptune House, Marina Bay, GIBRALTAR, GIBRALTAR.
GREEN, Ms. Nicola Mary, BSc ACA *1998;* 16 Churchill Court, 3a Blenheim Grove, Peckham, LONDON, SE15 4QW.
GREEN, Mr. Nigel, FCA *1971;* 23 Honeycroft Hill, UXBRIDGE, MIDDLESEX, UB10 9NQ.
•GREEN, Mr. Nigel Ives, BSc FCA *1984;* GBJ LLP, Sterling House, 27 Hatchlands Road, REDHILL, RH1 6RW.
GREEN, Mr. Nigel Patrick, BA ACA *1985;* Elmwood Design Ltd Ghyll Royd, Guiseley, LEEDS, LS20 9LT.
GREEN, Mr. Norman Frank, MCom FCA *1969;* (Tax Fac), 28 Wolsey Road, ASHFORD, MIDDLESEX, TW15 2RB.
GREEN, Sir Owen Whitley, Kt FCA *1950;* Edgehill, Succombs Hill, WARLINGHAM, CR6 9JG. (Life Member)
GREEN, Mr. Patrick Arthur, ACA CA(SA) *2008;* 17 Flat C, Balham Grove, LONDON, SW12 8AZ.
•GREEN, Mr. Paul Andrew, BCom FCA *1986;* Carl Zeiss Vision UK Ltd, Unit 9 Holford Way, Holford, BIRMINGHAM, B6 7AX.
•GREEN, Mr. Paul Andrew, BSocSc FCA *1979;* 26 Heathcote Avenue, SOLIHULL, B91 1QL.
GREEN, Mr. Paul Charles, FCA *1966;* Hollybank House, Rue Des Huriaux, ST. MARTIN, JERSEY, JE3 6AF.
GREEN, Mr. Paul Granville, BA ACA *1990;* Creggameen, CASTLEREA, COUNTY ROSCOMMON, IRELAND.
GREEN, Mr. Paul Robert, BA FCA *1992;* PO Box 989, ABU DHABI, UNITED ARAB EMIRATES.
•GREEN, Mr. Paul Steven, BSc ACA *1989;* (Tax Fac), 3 Park Grove, EDGWARE, HA8 7SH.
GREEN, Mrs. Paula, BA ACA *2000;* 44 Westfield Road, SURBITON, KT6 4EJ.
GREEN, Miss. Penelope Katherine Marion, BA ACA *1996;* 46 Cholmeley Crescent, LONDON, N6 5HA.
•GREEN, Mr. Peter Bruno, BSc FCA *1995;* Flat 329, Willoughby House, Barbican, LONDON, EC2Y 8BL.
GREEN, Mr. Peter Charles Richard, BSc ACA *1993;* 57 St. Davids Drive, Scawsby, DONCASTER, SOUTH YORKSHIRE, DN5 8PW.
GREEN, Mr. Peter David Andrew, BA ACA *1987;* 30 Corringham Road, LONDON, NW11 7BU.
GREEN, Mr. Peter Francis, BSc FCA *1974;* 27 Blake Hall Crescent, Wanstead, LONDON, E11 3RH.
GREEN, Mr. Peter Hugh, FCA ACA *1987;* 21 Braemar Road, SUTTON COLDFIELD, B73 6LN.
GREEN, Mr. Peter James, FCA *1951;* 8 The Meadows, Portsmouth Road, GUILDFORD, GU2 4DT. (Life Member)
GREEN, Mr. Peter Michael, BSc ACA *1990;* 7 Ryecroft Avenue, Lowton, WARRINGTON, WA3 2TN.
GREEN, Mr. Peter Robert, BSc FCA *1979;* 4 Margaret Road, Crosby, LIVERPOOL, L23 6TR.
GREEN, Mr. Peter William, FCA *1967;* The Rectory, Wrights Green Lane, Little Hallingbury, BISHOP'S STORTFORD, HERTFORDSHIRE, CM22 7RE.
•GREEN, Mr. Philip Andrew, BSc FCA *1984;* Philip Green - Aims Accountants For Business, Copper Glade, Moss Lane, Yarnfield, STONE, STAFFORDSHIRE ST15 0PW.
GREEN, Mr. Philip Charles, BSc ACA *1989;* 52 Cherry Tree Walk, WEST WICKHAM, BR4 9EH.
GREEN, Mr. Philip Geoffrey, BSc ACA *1986;* Littlefield, Cavendish Road, St. Georges Hill, WEYBRIDGE, SURREY, KT13 0JP.
GREEN, Mr. Philip James, BSc ACA *1992;* 82 Vaughan Williams Way, Warley, BRENTWOOD, CM14 5WT.
GREEN, Mr. Philip James, BSc(Hons) ACA *2000;* 20 Devon Avenue, Upholland, WIGAN, LANCASHIRE, WN8 0DQ.
GREEN, Mr. Philip James, FCA *1966;* Greenacres, Dale Head Road, Prestbury, MACCLESFIELD, SK10 4BL.
GREEN, Mr. Philip Leslie, ACA *1981;* Miles & Miles Ltd, 18 Petersham Mews, LONDON, SW7 5NR.
•GREEN, Mrs. Philippa Jane, BA ACA *1981;* Ernst & Young LLP, 1 More London Place, LONDON, SE1 2AF. See also Ernst & Young Europe LLP
GREEN, Mr. Raymond John, FCA *1952;* Pemberley, 1 Great Lane, Frisby-On-The-Wreake, MELTON MOWBRAY, LE14 2PB. (Life Member)
•GREEN, Mr. Raymond Michael, FCA *1980;* (Tax Fac), Raymond M. Green, 25 Croft Close, Spondon, DERBY, DE21 7EF.
GREEN, Mr. Richard, MEng ACA *2002;* 74 Sparrow Farm Road, EPSOM, SURREY, KT17 2LR.
GREEN, Mr. Richard, BA ACA *1999;* 3 Brookfield Close, Hutton, BRENTWOOD, CM13 2RG.
GREEN, Mr. Richard Alan, BSc FCA *1975;* Dalton House, Huttons Ambo, YORK, YO60 7HJ.
GREEN, Mr. Richard Antony, BSc ACA *1988;* Clough Hey, Elland Road, Ripponden, SOWERBY BRIDGE, HX6 4HW.
GREEN, Mr. Richard David, BA ACA *1998;* 6 Meadway, Lawford, MANNINGTREE, ESSEX, CO11 2ER.
•GREEN, Mr. Richard Denis, FCA *1982;* Smith & Williamson Ltd, Imperial House, 18-21 Kings Park Road, SOUTHAMPTON, HAMPSHIRE, SO15 2AT. See also Nexia Audit Limited
GREEN, Mr. Richard Desmond, FCA *1971;* 8 St James Lane, WINCHESTER, SO22 4NX.
GREEN, Mr. Richard James, BA FCA CF *1987;* (Member of Council 2008 - 2011), with August Equity LLP, 1st Floor, 10 Slingsby Place, St Martin's Courtyard, Covent Garden, LONDON WC2E 9AB.
•GREEN, Mr. Richard James, BSc ACA *1998;* Franklin Underwood, 1 Pinnacle Way, Pride Park, DERBY, DE24 8ZS.
•GREEN, Mr. Richard John, FCA *1975;* Venthams Limited, Millhouse, 32-38 East Street, ROCHFORD, SS4 1DB.
•GREEN, Mr. Richard John, FCA *1994;* Garbutt & Elliott, 2 Stable Court, Elmete Lane, Beechwoods, LEEDS, LS8 2LQ. See also G & E (Holdings) Ltd and Garbutt & Elliott Limited
GREEN, Mr. Richard Jon, ACA CTA *1997;* 53 Queens Road, DUDLEY, WEST MIDLANDS, DY3 1HL.
GREEN, Mr. Richard Jonathan, BSc FCA *1982;* 19 Eyebrook Road, Bowdon, ALTRINCHAM, WA14 3LH.
•GREEN, Mr. Richard Jonathan, BSc FCA *1986;* PricewaterhouseCoopers LLP, 7 More London Riverside, LONDON, SE1 2RT. See also PricewaterhouseCoopers
GREEN, Mr. Richard Linton, BA(Hons) ACA *2000;* 27 Ballingdon Road, LONDON, SW11 6AJ.
GREEN, Mr. Richard Michael George, FCA *1965;* Tiffin Green, 11 Queens Road, BRENTWOOD, ESSEX, CM14 4HE.
GREEN, Mr. Richard Paul, FCA *1972;* Richard Green, Smithwood Farmhouse, Smithwood Common, CRANLEIGH, GU6 8QY.
GREEN, Mr. Richard Philip, BSc FCA *1976;* Grooms Lodge Foxcote, Andoversford, CHELTENHAM, GLOUCESTERSHIRE, GL54 4LW.
GREEN, Mr. Richard Stewart, BA ACA *2004;* 95 Hanley Road, LONDON, N4 3DQ.
GREEN, Mr. Richard Stuart, MA ACA *1991;* Kerkstraat 56, 2514KT THE HAGUE, NETHERLANDS.
GREEN, Mr. Robert Anthony, FCA *1975;* Yew Tree Cottage, South Lane, Nomansland, SALISBURY, SP5 2BZ.
GREEN, Mr. Robert Anthony George, BA ACA *1998;* 8 Oak Meadows Court, Rainhill, PRESCOT, L35 6QD.
GREEN, Mr. Robert David, MA ACA *1980;* 11 Whitworth Lane, Loughton, MILTON KEYNES, MK5 8EB.
GREEN, Mr. Robert Huelin, BA ACA *1992;* 16 Brooklands House, Lucas Court, LEAMINGTON SPA, CV32 5JL.
GREEN, Mr. Robert James, BSc ACA *2003;* 99 Hayward Road, THAMES DITTON, KT7 0BF.
GREEN, Mr. Robert John, BSc FCA *1991;* 55 Tom Blower Close, NOTTINGHAM, NG8 1JQ.
•GREEN, Mr. Robert Kirk, FCA *1976;* Green & Peter, The Limes, 1339 High Road, Whetstone, LONDON, N20 9HR. See also G.T. Associates
GREEN, Mr. Robert Matthew, BSc ACA *2002;* GE Equipment Services Europe, Rivierstaete, Amsteldijk 166, 1079 LH AMSTERDAM, NETHERLANDS.
•GREEN, Mr. Robert Tarrant Brunt, MA FCA *1968;* Tarrant Green & Co, 27 Old Gloucester Street, LONDON, WC1N 3AX.
GREEN, Mr. Roger Michael, FCA *1965;* 16 Green Lane, Poynton, STOCKPORT, SK12 1TJ.
GREEN, Mrs. Rosslyn Catriona, BA ACA *1992;* 55 Tom Blower Close, Wollaton, NOTTINGHAM, NG8 1JQ.
GREEN, Mr. Roy Samuel, FCA *1938;* 11 Garreg Drive, WELSHPOOL, POWYS, SY21 7HX. (Life Member)
GREEN, Mr. Royston, FCA *1969;* 9 Heol y Graig, Aberporth, CARDIGAN, DYFED, SA43 2HB.
GREEN, Mrs. Sally, BSc ACA *1989;* The Lindens Balmoral Road, Grappenhall, WARRINGTON, WA4 2EB.
GREEN, Ms. Sarah Elizabeth, ACA *2009;* Flat 5 Bridgewalk Heights, 80 Weston Street, LONDON, SE1 3QZ.
GREEN, Mrs. Sharon Jane, BSc ACA *1989;* 437a Huddersfield Road, OLDHAM, OL4 2HN.
GREEN, Mrs. Sharon Jane, BA ACA *1994;* 9 Obelisk Road, Finedon, WELLINGBOROUGH, NN9 5DW.
GREEN, Mr. Simon James, BA(Hons) ACA *2003;* Dexion Capital plc, 1 Tudor Street, LONDON, EC4Y 0AH.
GREEN, Mr. Simon Jonathan, BSc FCA *1984;* Pear Tree Cottage, The Green, West Peckham, MAIDSTONE, KENT, ME18 5JW.
GREEN, Mr. Simon Richard, BA ACA *1990;* 23 Waterston Gardens, HILLARYS, WA 6025, AUSTRALIA.
GREEN, Mr. Simon Stanley, MA ACA *1989;* International Office, Henan Polytechnic University, 2001 Century Avenue, JIAOZUO 454000, HENAN PROVINCE, CHINA.
GREEN, Mr. Stephen, ACA *2008;* 14 Orme Road, KINGSTON UPON THAMES, KT1 3SA.
GREEN, Mr. Stephen, BA FCA *1988;* PO Box HM897, HAMILTON HM DX, BERMUDA.
•GREEN, Mr. Stephen Michael, ACA *1982;* (Tax Fac), Greens Accountancy & Tax Services Limited, 106a Commercial Street, Risca, NEWPORT, NP11 6EE.
GREEN, Mr. Stephen Nathaniel, BSc ACA *1990;* Paddocks Farm, Golford Road, CRANBROOK, TN17 3NW.
GREEN, Mr. Stephen William, BA FCA *1977;* Proton Cars (UK) Ltd Unit 1-3, Crowley Way Avonmouth, BRISTOL, BS11 9YR.
GREEN, Mr. Steven, FCA *1982;* 48 Riverside Drive, Radcliffe, MANCHESTER, M26 1HU.
GREEN, Mr. Stuart, BA(Hons) ACA *2010;* 111 Park Hall Road, Mansfield Woodhouse, MANSFIELD, NOTTINGHAMSHIRE, NG19 8QS.
GREEN, Mr. Stuart, BSc ACA *2004;* 1 Winston Close, Spencers Wood, READING, RG7 1DW.

GREEN, Mr. Stuart Douglas, MBA BA FCA AMCT *1990;* 1 Martin Place, SYDNEY, NSW 2000, AUSTRALIA.
•**GREEN, Mr. Stuart Silverthorne Erskine, BSc FCA** *1973;* Stuart S.E. Green, The Glen, 19 Lingfield Common Road, LINGFIELD, RH7 6BU.
GREEN, Miss. Susan, BA ACA *1992;* with Watersheds Ltd, 8 Bath Road, Old Town, SWINDON, SN1 4BA.
GREEN, Miss. Susan Amanda, BSc ACA *1993;* 9 Bratch Lane, Wombourne, WOLVERHAMPTON, WV5 9AL.
•**GREEN, Miss. Susan Margaret, FCA** *1983;* (Tax Fac), Townends Accountants Limited, Fulford Lodge, 1 Heslington Lane, YORK, YO10 4HW.
•**GREEN, Mrs. Suzanne Elizabeth, FCA** *1991;* SL Accountants Ltd, 294 Warwick Road, SOLIHULL, WEST MIDLANDS, B92 7AF. See also SLA Tax Ltd
GREEN, Mrs. Suzanne Patricia, BA ACA *1991;* The Paddocks, Badgeworth Lane, Badgeworth, CHELTENHAM, GLOUCESTERSHIRE, GL51 4UH.
GREEN, Mr. Thomas Christopher, BA ACA AMCT *1994;* Plexus Cotton, 20 Chapel Street, LIVERPOOL, L3 9AG.
GREEN, Mr. Thomas Henry, BSc(Hons) ACA *2003;* with PricewaterhouseCoopers, Darling Park Tower 2, 201 Sussex Street, GPO Box 2650, SYDNEY, NSW 1171 AUSTRALIA.
GREEN, Mr. Timothy James, FCA *1980;* Burrow Cottage, Cottles Lane, Woodbury, EXETER, EX5 1EE.
GREEN, Mr. Timothy John Mackenzie, BSc ACA MCT *1993;* Cefas, Lowestoft Laboratory, Rakefield Road, LOWESTOFT, SUFFOLK NR33 0HT.
GREEN, Mr. Timothy Simon, ACA *1988;* GMT Communications Partners LLP, Sackville House, 40 Piccadilly, LONDON, W1J 0DR.
•**GREEN, Mr. Victor John Spiers, FCA** *1977;* Morris Green Accountants Limited, 1 Tregaron Court, Ash Bank, STOKE-ON-TRENT, ST2 9QL.
GREEN, Mr. Victor Maurice, FCA *1961;* The Old Rectory, Lower Road, Stoke Albany, MARKET HARBOROUGH, LEICESTERSHIRE, LE16 8PZ.
•**GREEN, Mr. Victor Stanley, FCA** *1974;* Victor S. Green & Co, 7 Inchlaggan Road, Fallings Park, WOLVERHAMPTON, WV10 9QX.
GREEN, Miss. Victoria Anne, BSc ACA *2009;* Top Floor Flat, 20 Solent Road, LONDON, NW6 1TU.
GREEN, Mrs. Victoria Jane, MA(Oxon) ACA *1999;* Euroway House, 1 White House Court, Hockliffe Street, LEIGHTON BUZZARD, BEDFORDSHIRE, LU7 1FD.
GREEN, Mr. William David, MA FCA *1976;* Lanma, TALYBONT, DYFED, SY24 5EQ.
GREEN, Mr. William Edward, BA FCA *1989;* 22 New Road, Twyford, READING, RG10 9PT.
GREEN, Mr. William Geoffrey Michael, BA ACA *2002;* 39 Norfolk Road, TONBRIDGE, TN9 1UL.
GREEN-ARMYTAGE, Mr. Jeremy John, MBA FCA *1991;* Brickyard Cottage, Marton Road, Long Itchington, SOUTHAM, CV47 9PZ.
GREEN-ARMYTAGE, Mr. Peter John, BSc ACA *1993;* 118b Mallinson Road, Battersea, LONDON, SW11 1BJ.
GREEN CHOW, Ms. Caroline Elaine, BSc ACA *1984;* 1034 Germano Way, PLEASANTON, CA 94566, UNITED STATES.
GREEN-WILKINSON, Mr. Edward John, ACA *2008;* Floor 4, B D O Stoy Hayward, 55 Baker Street, LONDON, W1U 7EU.
•**GREEN-WILKINSON, Mr. Richard Lumley, FCA** *1973;* CW Fellowes Limited, Templars House, Lulworth Close, Chandlers Ford, EASTLEIGH, SO53 3TL.
•**GREENACRE, Mr. Paul James, BA ACA** *1992;* P J Greenacre & Co Limited, The Old Bakery, Tiptoe Road, Wootton, NEW MILTON, BH25 5SJ.
GREENACRE, Mr. Stuart Clive, BSc ACA *1999;* Red House, Hadleigh Road, East Bergholt, COLCHESTER, CO7 6QT.
GREENALL, Miss. Clair, BSc ACA *2000;* 7 Herbert Street, Burtonwood, WARRINGTON, WA5 4HL.
GREENALL, Mrs. Emma Louise, ACA *2008;* with Plummer Parsons Accountants Limited, 5 North Street, HAILSHAM, BN27 1DQ.
•**GREENALL, Mr. Stephen David, ACA** *1982;* Mellieha, 16 Stryands, Hutton, PRESTON, PR4 5HD.
GREENALL, Mr. Timothy Paul, FCA *1973;* Boskalis Westminster Middle East Ltd, 224 Arch.Makarios III Avenue, Achilleos Building Block B 1st Floor, 3030 LIMASSOL, CYPRUS.
•**GREENALL, Mr. Walter James, ACA** *1979;* Codap Services Ltd, The Old Station, Station Road, Stow-cum-Quy, CAMBRIDGE, CB25 9AJ.
GREENAWAY, Mr. Brian Hedley, FCA *1962;* 5 Cade Lane, Brattle Wood, SEVENOAKS, KENT, TN13 1QX.
GREENAWAY, Mr. Brian James, FCA *1971;* Ilford Medical Centre, 61 Cleveland Road, ILFORD, ESSEX, IG1 1EE.
GREENAWAY, Mr. Carl Denham, MA ACA *1992;* Niscayah Ltd, Roding House, 970 Romford Road, LONDON, E12 5LP.
GREENAWAY, Miss. Laura Louise, BSc ACA *1990;* Nuffield Cottage, 17 Bradford Court, Bloxham, BANBURY, OX15 4RA.
GREENAWAY, Mr. Michael Philip, FCA *1974;* Criplands, Gravelye Lane, HAYWARDS HEATH, RH16 2SL. (Life Member)
GREENAWAY, Mr. Neil, ACA *2009;* Flat 5, 72 Grange Road, LONDON, W5 5BX.
GREENAWAY, Mr. Simon James, BSc ACA *2007;* 6 York Road, RICHMOND, SURREY, TW10 6DR.
GREENBAUM, Mr. Malcolm, ACA *1991;* 1 Princes Close, EDGWARE, HA8 7QB.
GREENBAUM, Mrs. Talia, LLB ACA *2002;* 8 Mayfield Gardens, Hendon, LONDON, NW4 2QA.
•**GREENBERG, Mr. Alan, FCA** *1966;* 2 Exeter Road, Southgate, LONDON, N14 5JY.
GREENBERG, Mr. Alan Manuel, BSc ACA *1988;* 13 Ringwood Avenue, Muswell Hill, LONDON, N2 9NT.
•**GREENBERG, Mr. Brian Stephen, BA FCA** *1976;* (Tax Fac), B.S. Greenberg & Co., 2 The Reddings, Mill Hill, LONDON, NW7 4JR.
GREENBLATT, Mr. Adam Bryce, ACA *2001;* Avenue House, Belsize Park Gardens, LONDON, NW3 4LA.
GREENBURY, Mr. David John, BSc ACA *1996;* 116 Sanctuary Way, Wybers Wood, GRIMSBY, DN37 9SA.
GREENE, Mr. Ben Richard Etienne, MA ACA *2004;* 3 Scholars Road, LONDON, SW12 0PF.
•**GREENE, Mr. Christopher Randall, FCA** *1972;* (Tax Fac), Randall Greene, Parallel House, 32/34 London Road, GUILDFORD, SURREY, GU1 2AB.
•**GREENE, Mr. David Antony, FCA** *1970;* (Tax Fac), Martin Greene Ravden LLP, 55 Loudoun Road, St John's Wood, LONDON, NW8 0DL. See also MGR Audit Limited
GREENE, Mr. David John, FCA *1977;* Vila Blanca, Calle Chaparros 9, Zona del Castillo, Fuengirola, 29640 MALAGA, SPAIN.
•**GREENE, Mr. Derek Lawrence, FCA** *1974;* Derek Greene & Co, 33 Minoan Drive, Apsley, HEMEL HEMPSTEAD, HERTFORDSHIRE, HP3 9WA.
•**GREENE, Mr. Gerald Michael, FCA** *1972;* The Greene Partnership, Durkan House, 5th Floor, 155 East Barnet Road, BARNET, HERTFORDSHIRE EN4 8QZ.
GREENE, Mr. Graham David, FCA *1976;* 820 Hedgegate Court, ROSWELL, GA 30075, UNITED STATES.
GREENE, Mr. Howard, BSc ACA *2006;* 2 Sedgefield Road, Radcliffe, MANCHESTER, M26 1YE.
•**GREENE, Mr. Lawrence, FCA** *1967;* Greene Miller & Co, 14 Woburn Close, BUSHEY, WD23 4XA.
•**GREENE, Mr. Michael Edwin, FCA** *1965;* (Tax Fac), Michael E Greene, 48 Western Road, BRENTWOOD, ESSEX, CM14 4SS.
GREENE, Mr. Michael John, FCA *1968;* 35 Ormskirk Ave Suite 611, TORONTO M6S 1A8, ON, CANADA.
•**GREENE, Mr. Paul, BA ACA PGCE** *2001;* Spain Accountants, Avenida Diagonal 4686, 08006 BARCELONA, SPAIN.
GREENE, Mr. Stephen Christopher, ACA *2010;* 5 Norfolk Road, Cliftonville, MARGATE, CT9 2HU.
GREENE, Mr. Stephen Paul, FCA *1969;* Rankvale Holdings Plc, Avenfield House, 118-127 Park Lane, LONDON, W1K 7AG.
GREENE, Mr. Thomas Richard Etienne, BSc ACA AMCT *2000;* Anmer, Lytton Road, WOKING, SURREY, GU22 7BH.
GREENER, Mr. Bryan, BA ACA *1991;* 3 Brooke Gardens, Dunmow Road, BISHOP'S STORTFORD, CM23 5JF.
GREENER, Mr. Hugh Thornton, FCA *1962;* 6 Tegfan, Maes-y-Felin, PONTYCLUN, CF72 9BP. (Life Member)
•**GREENER, Mr. Martin John, BSc ACA** *1983;* Lomond Accountancy Ltd, Acre Cottage, Clynder, HELENSBURGH, DUNBARTONSHIRE, G84 0QQ.
•**GREENER, Mrs. Pamela Anne, MA ACA** *1987;* (Tax Fac), The Deanery, 1 Cathedral Close, WAKEFIELD, WEST YORKSHIRE, WF1 2DP.
GREENFIELD, Mr. Alexander James, BA ACA *1999;* Calyon, Broadwalk House, 5 Appold Street, LONDON, EC2A 2DA.
GREENFIELD, Mr. David, BA FCA *1971;* 24 Lyttelton Road, DROITWICH, WR9 7AA.
•**GREENFIELD, Mr. Graeme Peter, BA ACA** *1988;* G.L. Barker & Co LLP, 45-49 Austhorpe Road, Crossgates, LEEDS, LS15 8BA.
GREENFIELD, Mr. Graham John, FCA *1962;* Norbridge, Bosbury, LEDBURY, HR8 1JX.
GREENFIELD, Mrs. Jane Elizabeth Louise, BA FCA *1985;* 4 Georgian Close, BROMLEY, BR2 7RA.
GREENFIELD, Mr. John Anthony Leslie, BSc FCA *1976;* 21 Ridley Road, WARLINGHAM, CR6 9LR.
GREENFIELD, Mr. Martin, FCA *1973;* 26 Coniston Road, Dronfield Woodhouse, DRONFIELD, DERBYSHIRE, S18 8PZ.
GREENFIELD, Dr. Paul Michael, PhD BSc ACA *2002;* 30 La Ville Vautier, St. Ouen, JERSEY, JE3 2WF.
GREENFIELD, Mr. Peter, FCA *1958;* 68 Moseley Wood Drive, LEEDS, LS16 7HJ. (Life Member)
GREENFIELD, Mr. Philip, BA FCA *1984;* 4 Georgian Close, BROMLEY, BR2 7RA.
GREENFIELD, Mr. Phillip Lee Richard, ACA *1981;* The Nook, Wharf Road, SHILLINGFORD, OXFORDSHIRE, OX10 7EW.
GREENFIELD, Mr. Richard Adrian, FCA *1981;* 20 Sandy Lane, SUTTON, SM2 7NR.
GREENFIELD, Mr. Richard Edward Keith, MA ACA *1981;* Byeways, Chester High Road, Neston, NESTON, CH64 7TA.
GREENFIELD, Mr. Robert Howard, FCA *1953;* Manor Top, Chestnut Hill, KESWICK, CA12 4LT. (Life Member)
GREENFIELD, Mr. Robert Tempest, BA FCA PGCE *1975;* Business School North East Worcs College, Osprey House, Albert Street, REDDITCH, WORCESTERSHIRE, B97 4DE.
GREENFIELD, Miss. Tania Francesca Anne, BA ACA *1995;* The Coach House, 5a Milton Road, HARPENDEN, HERTFORDSHIRE, AL5 5LA.
GREENFIELD, Mr. William Edward James, BA(Hons) ACA *2010;* Apartment 17 Dane House, 92 Northenden Road, SALE, CHESHIRE, M33 3UR.
•**GREENGARTEN, Mr. Abie, ACA CA(AUS)** *2008;* Gateway Partners Auditing UK Limited, 2nd Floor, 43 Whitfield Street, LONDON, W1T 4HD.
GREENGRASS, Mr. Adam, BSc ACA *1997;* 63 Quarrendon Road, AMERSHAM, BUCKINGHAMSHIRE, HP7 9EH.
•**GREENHALF, Mr. Niven Coats, BSc ACA** *1978;* (Tax Fac), Greenhalf & Associates, Elm Tree House, Britwell Salome, WATLINGTON, OXFORDSHIRE, OX49 5LG.
GREENHALGH, Mr. Alan, FCA *1959;* 4 Ryder Close, Aughton, ORMSKIRK, LANCASHIRE, L39 5HJ. (Life Member)
GREENHALGH, Mr. Andrew William, ACA *2009;* 723 Welford Road, LEICESTER, LE2 6HX.
GREENHALGH, Mr. Arthur Frederick, FCA *1957;* The Pebble, Somersal Herbert, ASHBOURNE, DERBYSHIRE, DE6 5PD. (Life Member)
GREENHALGH, Ms. Bridget Jane, MA ACA CTA *1987;* 58 Ferndene Road, LONDON, SE24 0AB.
GREENHALGH, Mr. Christopher, BA ACA *1996;* Manor House, The Green, Wolviston, BILLINGHAM, CLEVELAND, TS22 5LN.
GREENHALGH, Mr. Christopher John, ACA *2009;* 39 Abernethy Court, Abernethy Street Horwich, BOLTON, BL6 6FY.
GREENHALGH, Mr. David, FCA *1967;* Ellerburn, Doctors Hill, Burton Road Low Bentham, LANCASTER, LA2 7DZ.
GREENHALGH, Mr. David Alan, FCA *1970;* 60 South Road, Clifton upon Dunsmore, RUGBY, WARWICKSHIRE, CV23 0BZ.
GREENHALGH, Mr. David Michael, BEng ACA *1994;* ADIA, Internal Equities, PO Box 3600, ABU DHABI, UNITED ARAB EMIRATES.
•**GREENHALGH, Mr. Geoffrey Frank, FCA** *1964;* (Tax Fac), 22 Uplands Road, KENLEY, SURREY, CR8 5EF.
GREENHALGH, Mr. Harold, FCA *1960;* 1 Helena Road, Capel-le-Ferne, FOLKESTONE, KENT, CT18 7LG. (Life Member)
GREENHALGH, Mr. John Phillip, BCom FCA *1984;* Takapuna Services Ltd, 18 Dartmoor Drive, HUNTINGDON, CAMBRIDGESHIRE, PE29 6XT.
GREENHALGH, Mr. John Richard James, FCA *1968;* Brandlesome, Lillyfield, WIRRAL, CH60 8NT.
GREENHALGH, Miss. Kay Marie, BA ACA *1991;* Flat 5, 16 Mannering Road, Aigburth, LIVERPOOL, L17 8TR.
GREENHALGH, Mr. Keith Allen, BA FCA *1992;* Flat 1 Baltic Quay, 1 Sweden Gate, Surrey Quays, Southwark, LONDON, SE16 7TG.
GREENHALGH, Mrs. Kelly Vanessa, BSc ACA *2004;* 9 Shirebrook Drive, GLOSSOP, DERBYSHIRE, SK13 8RF.
GREENHALGH, Mr. Llewellyn Simon, BA ACA *1993;* Eccles Savings & Loans, Pearce House, Cawdor Street, Eccles, MANCHESTER, M30 0QF.
GREENHALGH, Mr. Malcolm, FCA *1967;* 7 Fircroft Close, WOKING, GU22 7LZ.
•**GREENHALGH, Mr. Melvyn, FCA** *1966;* (Tax Fac), Melvyn Greenhalgh, 34 Cedar Grove, North Runcton, KING'S LYNN, PE33 0QZ.
•**GREENHALGH, Mr. Melvyn Ellis, FCA** *1971;* (Tax Fac), MelG Limited, Boscarn, 2 Clijah Croft, South Downs, REDRUTH, CORNWALL TR15 2NR.
•**GREENHALGH, Mr. Michael, FCA** *1969;* Michael Greenhalgh & Co Ltd, Elland House, 22 High Street, Burgh le Marsh, SKEGNESS, LINCOLNSHIRE PE24 5JT.
GREENHALGH, Mr. Michael, MA FCA *1966;* 14 Castle Park, LANCASTER, LA1 1YQ. (Life Member)
GREENHALGH, Mr. Neil James, BSc ACA *1997;* 118 Scobell Street, Tottington, BURY, BL8 3DF.
•**GREENHALGH, Mr. Nigel Kent, FCA** *1983;* (Tax Fac), Wyatt Morris Golland & Co, Park House, 200 Drake Street, ROCHDALE, OL16 1PJ.
GREENHALGH, Mr. Paul, BA ACA *1984;* The Stables, Hoddlesden Hall, Hoddlesden, DARWEN, BB3 3NN.
GREENHALGH, Mr. Paul Michael, ACA *1982;* 24 Upper Shad Road, POUND RIDGE, NY 10576, UNITED STATES.
GREENHALGH, Mr. Richard Arthur James, BA(Hons) ACA MSI *2003;* Boothsdale Farm, Boothsdale, Willington, TARPORLEY, CHESHIRE, CW6 0NH.
GREENHALGH, Mr. Richard William, BA FCA *1977;* C/o Mainland Holdings Ltd, PO Box 196, LAE, 411, PAPUA NEW GUINEA.
GREENHALGH, Mrs. Wendy Hazel, BSc ACA *1979;* c/o Mott Macdonald, PO Box 47094, ABU DHABI, UNITED ARAB EMIRATES.
GREENHAM, Mr. Antony Crosby, MSc BA ACA *1996;* Old Tile Cottage, High Street, Ticehurst, WADHURST, EAST SUSSEX, TN5 7AL.
GREENHAM, Miss. Fiona Margaret, MSc ACA *2004;* 19 Grantley Heights, Kennet Side, READING, RG1 3EG.
GREENHAM, Mr. John, BA ACA *1980;* Farnham Lane House, Farnham Lane, HASLEMERE, GU27 1EU.
GREENHEAD, Mr. Martin Robert, BSc ACA *1993;* 65 Burnt Oak Lane, SIDCUP, DA15 9DE.
GREENHILL, Mr. Keith, FCA *1964;* 9 Gilstead Close, Thurnby, LEICESTER, LE7 9QD.
GREENHOUGH, Mr. James Arnold, FCA *1953;* Flat 12, Overdale, 60 Hollins Lane, Marple, STOCKPORT, CHESHIRE SK6 6AW. (Life Member)
GREENHOUGH, Mr. Rupert Harry David, BSc ACA *1991;* PO Box 8736, ARMADALE, VIC 3143, AUSTRALIA.
GREENHOUSE, Mr. Nicholas Paul, MEng ACA CTA *2003;* with Deloitte LLP, 2 New Street Square, LONDON, EC4A 3BZ.
GREENIDGE, Mr. Harold Ian, FCA CTA *1971;* 28 Marennes Crescent, Brightlingsea, COLCHESTER, CO7 0RU.
GREENING, Miss. Justine, BSc ACA MP *1995;* 41 Haldon Road, Wandsworth, LONDON, SW18 1QF.
GREENING, Mrs. Margaret, FCA *1969;* 32 Carlton Rd, SIDCUP, DA14 6AH. (Life Member)
GREENLAND, Mr. Andrew Rafael, ACA *2007;* 44 Godolphin Road, LONDON, W12 8JF.
GREENLAND, The Revd. Paul Howard, BSc ACA *1986;* The Vicarage, 88 Chignal Road, CHELMSFORD, CM1 2JB.
GREENLEAF, Mr. Andrew John, BCom ACA *1996;* PepsiCo UK, 1530 Arlington Business Park, Theale, READING, RG7 4SA.
GREENLEES, Mr. Alec Richard, BSc(Hons) ACA *2000;* 36 The Keep, Blackheath, LONDON, SE3 0AF.
GREENLEES, Mr. Graham Paul, ACA *1986;* with Wilkins Kennedy, Bridge House, London Bridge, LONDON, SE1 9QR.
GREENLEES, Mr. Loudon Ian, FCA *1976;* Thames River Capital (UK) Ltd, 51 Berkeley Square, LONDON, W1J 5BB.
GREENLEES, Mr. Peter Geoffrey, ACA *1981;* The Chartis Building, 58 Fenchurch Street, LONDON, EC3M 4AB.
GREENOUGH, Mr. John, FCA CPFA *1978;* Podnor Farm, Podnor Lane, Mellor, STOCKPORT, SK6 5PX.
GREENOUGH, Mr. Michael Anthony, FCA *1965;* 4 Larkhill Drive, Moorside, CLECKHEATON, BD19 6JS.
GREENSHIELDS, Mr. Martin William Tyzack, FCA *1975;* Hardy Transaction Management Ltd, Beehive Works Milton Street, SHEFFIELD, SOUTH YORKSHIRE, S3 7WL.
•**GREENSILL, Mr. David Thomas, ACA** *1981;* (Tax Fac), ABS - David Greensill, 63 Farrington Road, Ettingshall Park, WOLVERHAMPTON, WV4 6QJ. See also AIMS - David Greensill
•**GREENSILL, Mr. Steven Mark, BSc FCA** *1993;* (Tax Fac), Military House Limited, Military House, 24 Castle Street, CHESTER, CH1 2DS. See also Chester Accounting Services

GREENSLADE, Mr. Daniel Mark, BSc ACA *2002;* with PricewaterhouseCoopers LLP, First Point, Buckingham Gate, London Gatwick Airport, GATWICK, WEST SUSSEX RH6 0NT.

GREENSLADE, Mr. David John, FCA *1961;* Thaxted, Parkfield, SEVENOAKS, TN15 0HX. (Life Member)

GREENSLADE, Mrs. Joanna Avril Battersby, BA ACA *1997;* 21 Church End, Potterspury, TOWCESTER, NORTHAMPTONSHIRE, NN12 7PX.

GREENSLADE, Mr. Marc Richard, BA(Hons) ACA *2001;* 166 Southmead Road, Westbury-On-Trym, BRISTOL, BS10 5DR.

GREENSLADE, Mr. Martin Frederick, MA ACA *1991;* Thaxted, Parkfield, SEVENOAKS, KENT, TN15 0HX.

GREENSLADE, Mr. Peter Donald, BA FCA *1983;* Wood Edge Cottage, Bolney Road, Shiplake, HENLEY-ON-THAMES, RG9 3NT.

GREENSMITH, Mr. Anthony, BA ACA *1999;* 38 Carrwood Road, WILMSLOW, CHESHIRE, SK9 5DL.

GREENSMITH, Mrs. Carolyn Mary, BSc ACA *1993;* 8 Ennerdale Road, Kew, RICHMOND, SURREY, TW9 3PG.

GREENSMITH, Mrs. Emma Jane, BSc(Hons) ACA *2001;* North Cottage, 1a Saw Mill Lane, Addingham, ILKLEY, WEST YORKSHIRE, LS29 0ST.

GREENSMITH, Miss. Nicola Faye, BSc ACA *2005;* 111 Priory Wharf, BIRKENHEAD, MERSEYSIDE, CH41 5LD.

GREENSMITH, Mr. Paul John, BA FCA *1993;* 8 Ennerdale Road, Kew, RICHMOND, SURREY, TW9 3PG.

•**GREENSMITH, Mr. Peter, BSc ACA** *1981;* (Tax Fac), P. Greensmith & Co, 35 Pinecrest Drive, Thornhill, CARDIFF, CF14 9DS.

•**GREENSMITH, Mr. Peter James, FCA** *1972;* 6 Hocombe Wood Road, Chandler's Ford, EASTLEIGH, HAMPSHIRE, SO53 5PP.

GREENSPAN, Mr. Daniel James, BA(Hons) ACA *2001;* 40 Oakview Gardens, LONDON, N2 0NJ.

GREENSTED, Mrs. Jacqueline Karen, BSc ACA *1997;* Record Power Ltd, Unit B Adelphi Way, Ireland Industrial Estate, Staveley, CHESTERFIELD DERBYSHIRE S43 3LS.

GREENSTED, Mr. Robert, ACA *2011;* Flat 4, China Court, Asher Way, LONDON, E1W 2JF.

GREENSTREET, Mr. Ian, BSc FCA *1987;* Abbey Business Centres St. Martins House, 16 St. Martin's le Grand, LONDON, EC1A 4EN.

GREENUP, Dr. Alison Laura, PhD BSc ACA *2005;* 87 Burghley Road, LONDON, NW5 1UH.

GREENWAY, Mr. Anthony William, BA ACA *2004;* (Tax Fac), 4th Flr (4/02), G E Capital Finance, 30 Berkeley Square, LONDON, W1J 6EX.

GREENWAY, Miss. Caroline Margaret, BA ACA *2003;* with Deloitte & Touche LLP, 50 Fremont Street, SAN FRANCISCO, CA 94105, UNITED STATES.

GREENWAY, Mrs. Charlotte Susan, BSc ACA *1987;* Chiltern House, 34 Orchehill Avenue, GERRARDS CROSS, SL9 8QQ.

GREENWAY, Mr. Clive Stephen, BA ACA *1996;* 19 Clearwater Place, Long Ditton, SURBITON, SURREY, KT6 4ET.

GREENWAY, Mr. Darren John, ACA *1997;* with PricewaterhouseCoopers, Dorchester House, 7 Church Street West, PO Box HM1171, HAMILTON HM EX, BERMUDA.

GREENWAY, Mrs. Deborah Louise, BA ACA *1996;* 29 Uplands Road, KENLEY, CR8 5EE.

GREENWAY, Miss. Jennifer, BSc ACA *1986;* University of Warwick, University House, Kirby Corner Road, COVENTRY, CV4 8UW.

GREENWAY, Mr. Richard Ian, MEng ACA *1997;* 29 Uplands Road, KENLEY, CR8 5EE.

GREENWAY, Mr. Richard Ian, BA(Hons) ACA *2002;* 11 Beaufort Close, Burbage, HINCKLEY, LEICESTERSHIRE, LE10 2LF.

GREENWOOD, Mr. Alan, FCA *1956;* 17 Highgate, NELSON, BB9 0DU. (Life Member)

GREENWOOD, Miss. Alice Shirin, BA ACA *2007;* Flat A 5th Floor, Tak Mansions, 5 Leung Fai Terrace, MID LEVELS, HONG KONG ISLAND, HONG KONG SAR.

GREENWOOD, Mrs. Alison, BSc ACA *2007;* Heywood Shepherd, 1 Park Street, MACCLESFIELD, CHESHIRE, SK11 6SR.

GREENWOOD, Miss. Alison, BSc FCA *1984;* 29 Knoll Street, ROCHDALE, OL11 3JJ.

GREENWOOD, Mrs. Amanda Jane, ACA *1984;* Walnut House, Farnham Lane, HASLEMERE, GU27 1HE.

GREENWOOD, Mr. Andrew, MA FCA *1973;* (Tax Fac), Upper Rookes Hall, Rookes Lane, HALIFAX, HX3 8PU.

•**GREENWOOD, Mrs. Ann Margaret, BSc ACA** *1979;* Ann Greenwood, Wood Farm Cottage, Barton Lane, Thrumpton, NOTTINGHAM, NG11 0AU.

GREENWOOD, Mr. Anthony Colin, BSc ACA *1991;* 6 Hinchwick Court, Off Manor Road, Dorridge, SOLIHULL, WEST MIDLANDS, B93 8DF.

GREENWOOD, Miss. Caroline Suzanne, BSc ACA *2002;* 34 Carrington Place, TRING, HERTFORDSHIRE, HP23 5JZ.

GREENWOOD, Mr. Cedric, FCA *1955;* Fairlawn, Dryclough Lane, HALIFAX, HX3 0LD. (Life Member)

GREENWOOD, Mr. Christopher William, MA ACA *1983;* 3 Norfolk Gardens, SUTTON COLDFIELD, B75 6SS.

GREENWOOD, Miss. Ciaran, BSc ACA *2006;* 29 Telford Gardens, Hedge End, SOUTHAMPTON, SO30 2TQ.

GREENWOOD, Miss. Claire Jane, BSc ACA *2003;* 59 George Street, SHIPLEY, WEST YORKSHIRE, BD18 4PL.

GREENWOOD, Mr. Colin Blain, BSc FCA *1960;* 1a Station Road, Digswell, WELWYN, AL6 0DF. (Life Member)

GREENWOOD, Mr. Colin Brian, BA ACA *1983;* Club La Costa, Officinas Ejecutivos, URB Marina del Sol, Ctra de Cadiz, KM 206.5 Mijas Costa, MALAGA SPAIN.

GREENWOOD, Mr. David, BSc(Hons) ACA *2011;* 17 The Floats, Riverhead, SEVENOAKS, TN13 2QT.

GREENWOOD, Mr. David Alan, FCA *1976;* The Rowans, 12 Norwood Park, Birkby, HUDDERSFIELD, HD2 2DU.

•**GREENWOOD, Mr. David Michael, FCA** *1980;* (Tax Fac), Whitehead & Aldrich, 5 Ribblesdale Place, PRESTON, PR1 8BZ.

•**GREENWOOD, Mr. David Scott, FCA** *1977;* (Tax Fac), Connelly & Co Limited, Permanent House, 1 Dundas Street, HUDDERSFIELD, HD1 2EX.

GREENWOOD, Mrs. Dawn Margaret, BA(Hons) ACA *1996;* Mont Les Vaux Cottage, Le Mont Les Vaux, St. Brelade, JERSEY, JE3 8AF.

GREENWOOD, Mrs. Elizabeth Rowan, BA ACA *1998;* Windrush Barn Police Row, Therfield, ROYSTON, HERTFORDSHIRE, SG8 9QE.

GREENWOOD, Miss. Emma, BA(Hons) ACA *2011;* 8 Grosvenor Avenue, Whitefield, MANCHESTER, M45 6GN.

GREENWOOD, Mr. Ernest, FCA *1971;* 72 Shaw Lane, Oxenhope, KEIGHLEY, BD22 9QL.

GREENWOOD, Mr. Gary William, BA ACA *1999;* 38 Parr Lane, Eccleston, CHORLEY, LANCASHIRE, PR7 5SL.

GREENWOOD, Mrs. Genevieve, BSc ACA *2006;* Wilderhope, Blind Lane, BOURNE END, BUCKINGHAMSHIRE, SL8 5LF.

GREENWOOD, Mr. Gerald Ellis, FCA *1967;* Woodside, Long Lane, Colby, NORWICH, NR11 7EF.

GREENWOOD, Mr. Iain Stuart Charles, MA(Cantab) ACA CTA *1993;* 53 Hurst Park Road, Twyford, READING, RG10 0EZ.

GREENWOOD, Mr. Ian, BSc(Hons) ACA *2009;* with KPMG, 10 Shelley Street, SYDNEY, NSW 2000, AUSTRALIA.

GREENWOOD, Mr. Ian Robert, BA FCA *1999;* 72 Manchester Road, MACCLESFIELD, CHESHIRE, SK10 2JP.

GREENWOOD, Mr. Jack, FCA *1949;* 10443 All Bay Road, SIDNEY V8L 2N8, BC, CANADA. (Life Member)

•**GREENWOOD, Mr. James Hall, FCA** *1973;* (Tax Fac), James H. Greenwood & Co Ltd, Ava Lodge, Castle Terrace, BERWICK-UPON-TWEED, TD15 1NP. See also J.H. Greenwood & Company

GREENWOOD, Miss. Jenny, BSc ACA *2003;* Flat 37 Barry Court, Palatine Road, MANCHESTER, M20 3LQ.

GREENWOOD, Miss. Joanne Alison, BSc ACA *1992;* (Tax Fac), 37 Hillcrest, SUNDERLAND, SR3 3NL.

•**GREENWOOD, Mr. John, FCA** *1966;* (Tax Fac), Greenwood & Co, 5 Cherry Grove, ROCHDALE, LANCASHIRE, OL11 5YT.

GREENWOOD, Mr. John David, FCA *1965;* 1 Brookside, Euxton, CHORLEY, PR7 6HR.

•**GREENWOOD, Mr. John James, BSc ACA** *1981;* Baker Tilly (BVI) Limited, P.O. Box 650, Tropic Isle Building, Nibbs Street, Road Town, TORTOLA VIRGIN ISLANDS (BRITISH).

GREENWOOD, Mr. John Leonard, BA ACA *1998;* Glaxo Smith Kline, Temple Hill, DARTFORD, DA1 5AH.

GREENWOOD, Mr. John Michael, BSc ACA *2006;* Crick Software Ltd Crick House, Boarden Close Moulton Park Industrial Estate, NORTHAMPTON, NN3 6LF.

GREENWOOD, Mr. John Reid, FCA *1956;* Tall Trees, Owlwood Lane, Dunnington, YORK, YO19 5PH. (Life Member)

GREENWOOD, Mr. John Richard David, BSc ACA CF *1991;* 22 Main Street, Costock, LOUGHBOROUGH, LEICESTERSHIRE, LE12 6XD.

GREENWOOD, Mr. Jonathan, BA ACA *2001;* (Tax Fac), The Beacon, Leaze Road, MARLBOROUGH, WILTSHIRE, SN8 1JU.

GREENWOOD, Mrs. Karen Julia, BSc ACA *1993;* Universal Square Suite 3.1.4, Devonshire Street, MANCHESTER, M12 6JH.

GREENWOOD, Ms. Kathryn, BSc(Hons) ACA CTA *2001;* Whittingham Riddell LLP, Belmont House, Sitka Drive, Shrewsbury Business Park, SHREWSBURY, SY2 6LG.

GREENWOOD, Mr. Keith Alfred, FCA *1973;* Lime Tree Cottage, Branton Lane, Great Ouseburn, YORK, YO26 9RS.

GREENWOOD, Mr. Lynton John, MA ACA *2005;* 402 Street Lane, LEEDS, LS17 6RW.

•**GREENWOOD, Mrs. Margaret Joan, MA FCA** *1979;* Fairfield House, The Street, Didmarton, BADMINTON, AVON, GL9 1DS.

GREENWOOD, Mrs. Marie-Christine Genevieve, MSc ACA *1995;* Concateno Cozart, 92 Milton Park Milton, ABINGDON, OXFORDSHIRE, OX14 4RY.

GREENWOOD, Mr. Mark Christopher, BSc ACA *1989;* 258 Brooklands Road, MANCHESTER, M23 9HD.

GREENWOOD, Mr. Mark Christopher, BA ACA *2009;* 12 The Saltings, Littlestone, NEW ROMNEY, TN28 8AE.

GREENWOOD, Mr. Mark Francis, MBA BA FCA FCMI *1989;* Towergate Partnership Ltd, 77 Leadenhall Street, LONDON, EC3A 3DE.

GREENWOOD, Mr. Mark Stephen, BA ACA *1991;* 17 Merriwa Place, CHERRYBROOK, NSW 2126, AUSTRALIA.

GREENWOOD, Mr. Martin Andrew, BSc FCA *1982;* The Nest, Cricket Hill Lane, YATELEY, HAMPSHIRE, GU46 6BB.

GREENWOOD, Mr. Martin James, FCA *1977;* Stonecroft, Daisy Lea Lane, Edgerton, HUDDERSFIELD, HD3 3LL.

GREENWOOD, Mr. Martin Nicholas Winston, FCA *1965;* Half Mile, Taggs Island, HAMPTON, MIDDLESEX, TW12 2HA.

GREENWOOD, Mr. Michael, FCA *1964;* (Member of Council 1995 - 2007), The Trees, Lower Westhouse, CARNFORTH, LANCASHIRE, LA6 3NZ.

GREENWOOD, Mr. Michael Frank, BSc ACA *1990;* 51 Gloucester Road, RICHMOND, SURREY, TW9 3BT.

GREENWOOD, Mr. Nicholas, ACA *2008;* 15 Broomfield Ride, Oxshott, LEATHERHEAD, SURREY, KT22 0LR.

GREENWOOD, Mr. Nicholas Stephen Parker, BSc FCA *1977;* 10 Harden Beck, Harden, BINGLEY, BD16 1JQ.

•**GREENWOOD, Mr. Patrick John Aberneithy, FCA** *1974;* Wheatlands Farm, White Horse Lane, Finchampstead, WOKINGHAM, BERKSHIRE, RG40 4LZ.

GREENWOOD, Mr. Paul Huw, BA ACA *1989;* 54 Peckarmans Wood, LONDON, SE26 6RZ.

GREENWOOD, Mr. Paul Simon, ACA *1988;* 39A Barrett Street, WEMBLEY, WA 6014, AUSTRALIA.

GREENWOOD, Mr. Peter Astin, BA ACA *1995;* KPMG LLP, 777 Dunsmuir Street, PO Box 10426, VANCOUVER V7Y 1K3, BC, CANADA.

GREENWOOD, Mr. Philip John, MA FCA *1993;* Withermarsh Green Farm, Withermarsh Green, Stoke by Nayland, COLCHESTER, CO6 4TD.

GREENWOOD, Mr. Richard, BSc ACA *1997;* 7108 Carlisle Court, CLARKSVILLE, MD 21029, UNITED STATES.

GREENWOOD, Mr. Richard William, BA ACA *2007;* 7 Tithe Road, Kempston, BEDFORD, MK43 9BE.

•**GREENWOOD, Mr. Robert, ACA** *1979;* (Tax Fac), Sunderland Driver, Orchard House, Aire Valley Business Centre, KEIGHLEY, BD21 3DU.

GREENWOOD, Mr. Robert Andrew, FCA *1971;* 19 Chelsea Mansions, Northowram, HALIFAX, HX3 7HG.

GREENWOOD, Mr. Robin Erskine, MA FCA FSI TEP *1979;* Chilland Cottage, Lower Chilland Lane, Martyr Worthy, WINCHESTER, HAMPSHIRE, SO21 1EB.

GREENWOOD, Mr. Robin Michael, BSc(Hons) ACA *2004;* 608 The Hacienda, 15 Whitworth Street West, MANCHESTER, M1 5DE.

GREENWOOD, Mr. Roger Keith, BSc ACA *1992;* 142 Bedford Road, SUTTON COLDFIELD, B75 6AJ.

GREENWOOD, Miss. Sally, ACA *2010;* 7 Musgrave Close, Cheshunt, WALTHAM CROSS, HERTFORDSHIRE, EN7 6TZ.

GREENWOOD, Mr. Shane Alexander Mark, ACA *1991;* Old Tollgate Cottage, Cannock Road, Penkridge, STAFFORD, ST19 5DX.

GREENWOOD, Mr. Stephen Harold, FCA *1978;* The Fold, Cripton Lane Ashover, CHESTERFIELD, DERBYSHIRE, S45 0AW.

•**GREENWOOD, Mr. Steven, BCom FCA** *1985;* Cassons, St Crispin House, St. Crispin Way, Haslingden, ROSSENDALE, LANCASHIRE BB4 4PW. See also Cassons & Associates

GREENWOOD, Mr. Stuart Alan, FCA *1975;* centenary house, W Yeomans (Chesterfield) Ltd Centenary House, 11 Midland Way Barlborough, CHESTERFIELD, DERBYSHIRE, S43 4XA.

GREENWOOD, Mr. Thomas, MA FCA *1955;* Bundoran Cottage, Vicarage Lane, Laleham, STAINES, TW18 1UE. (Life Member)

•**GREENWOOD, Mr. Timothy Charles, BA ACA** *1993;* TC Greenwood, 22 Ullswater Road, Handforth, WILMSLOW, CHESHIRE, SK9 3NQ.

GREENWOOD, Mr. Tom Francis, BSc ACA *2007;* 15 St. Marks Crescent, LONDON, NW1 7TS.

GREENWOOD, Miss. Tracy Ann, BA ACA *2003;* Hartfield House, 41-47 Hartfield Road, LONDON, SW19 3RQ.

GREENWOOD, Mr. William, FCA *1953;* Woodbine House, 17 Tredrea Lane, St Erth, HAYLE, TR27 6JS. (Life Member)

GREENWOOD PAUS, Miss. Alyson Laraine, BSc ACA *1993;* Chemin des Courbes 13, CH-1247 ANIERES, SWITZERLAND.

GREEP, Mr. Nicolas William Gliddon, BSc ACA *1991;* 9 Cock Lane, Fetcham, LEATHERHEAD, SURREY, KT22 9TT.

•**GREER, Mr. Gary, FCA** *1983;* Afford Bond LLP, 31 Wellington Road, NANTWICH, CHESHIRE, CW5 7ED. See also Afford Astbury Bond LLP

GREER, Mr. Geoffrey David, BCom FCA *1973;* 2 Wayland Close, LEEDS, LS16 8LT.

GREER, Mr. Gordon Paul, ACA *1996;* Jomast Developments Ltd, Top Floor, Oriel House, Calverts Lane, Bishop Street, STOCKTON-ON-TEES CLEVELAND TS18 1SW.

GREER, Mrs. Shireen Elizabeth, BSc ACA *2003;* Haas group International, 1475 Phoenixville Pike, WEST CHESTER, PA 19380, UNITED STATES.

GREET, Mr. John Benjamin, FCA *1970;* 6010 Flagstaff Road, BOULDER, CO 80302, UNITED STATES.

•**GREEVE, Mr. Mark James, BA ACA** *1992;* Mark Greeve Accounting Limited, 10 Keswick Drive, FRODSHAM, WA6 7LU. See also Mark Greeve

GREEVES, Mr. Alastair Leopold, FCA *1972;* 2910 E. Orange Grove Blvd, PASADENA, CA 91107, UNITED STATES.

•**GREEVES, Mr. Christopher John, BSc FCA CTA** *1984;* (Tax Fac), Larking Gowen, 1 Tavern Lane, DEREHAM, NR19 1PX.

•**GREEVES, Mr. Edward William, BSc FCA** *1977;* (Tax Fac), Morris & Co (2011) Limited, Chester House, Lloyd Drive, Chesire Oaks Business Park, ELLESMERE PORT, CHESHIRE CH65 9HQ.

GREEVES, Mr. Peter John, LLB FCA *1973;* 82 Queens Court, Queens Road, RICHMOND, SURREY, TW10 6LB.

GREG, Mr. Anthony Nigel, BA FCA *1977;* 25 Bramble Gardens, BURGESS HILL, RH15 8UQ.

GREGG, Mr. Cornelius Joseph, BA ACA *1983;* 94 The Elms, Mount Merrion Avenue, BLACKROCK, COUNTY DUBLIN, IRELAND.

GREGG, Mr. David Stephen, ACA *1993;* 33 Heathside, ESHER, SURREY, KT10 9TD.

GREGG, Mrs. Jenna Suzanne, BSc(Hons) ACA *2010;* Floor 8, K P M G One Snowhill, Snow Hill Queensway, BIRMINGHAM, B4 6GH.

•**GREGG, Mr. Michael John, BA FCA** *1985;* Baker Tilly Tax & Advisory Services LLP, 3 Hardman Street, MANCHESTER, M3 3HF. See also Baker Tilly UK Audit LLP

GREGG, Mr. Richard Walter, BSc(Hons) ACA *2001;* 3 Bunyana Avenue, WAHROONGA, NSW 2076, AUSTRALIA.

GREGG, Mr. William Stewart, FCA *1972;* with Baker Tilly Tax & Advisory Services LLP, The Clock House, 140 London Road, GUILDFORD, SURREY, GU1 1UW.

GREGGAINS, Miss. Lucy Caroline, BSc FCA *1997;* 106 Prices Court, Cotton Row, Battersea, LONDON, SW11 3YW.

GREGGOR, Mr. Paul William, MA ACA *1982;* Esselte Ltd Waterside House, 4 Cowley Business Park High Street Cowley, UXBRIDGE, MIDDLESEX, UB8 2HP.

GREGGS, Mr. John Walter, FCA *1961;* 2 Shaws Garth, Shirdley Hill Halsall, ORMSKIRK, L39 8SZ. (Life Member)

GREGOR, Mr. Andrew James, BA(Hons) ACA *2002;* 8 Lyndale, GUISBOROUGH, CLEVELAND, TS14 8JN.

GREGOR, Mrs. Sarah Valerie, BSc ACA *1994;* 7 The Wardens, KENILWORTH, CV8 2UH.

GREGORIADES, Mr. Andreas, MEng ACA *2009;* 9 Leandrou Street, Kaimakli, 1036 NICOSIA, CYPRUS.

•**GREGORIADES, Mr. Angelos Michael, BSc FCA** *1984;* (Tax Fac), KPMG, 14 Esperidon Street, 1087 NICOSIA, CYPRUS. See also KPMG Metaxas Loizides Syrimis

GREGORIOU, Ms. Annita, BA ACA *1999;* 85 Limassol Avenue, CY-2121 Aglantzia Cyprus, P.O. Box 22032, NICOSIA, CYPRUS.

GREGORIOU, Miss. Loria, BSc ACA *2006;* with MGI Gregoriou & Co Ltd, Greg Tower, 7 Florina Street, P.O. Box 24854, 1304 NICOSIA, CYPRUS.
GREGORIOU, Mr. Stavros, ACA *2008;* with Deloitte LLP, Athene Place, 66 Shoe Lane, LONDON, EC4A 3BQ.
GREGORY, Mr. Adrian, BSc ACA *1993;* (Tax Fac), 4 South Row, LONDON, SE3 0RY.
GREGORY, Mr. Alfred Philip, FCA *1957;* Green Barn, Holt Road, Cley-next-the-Sea, HOLT, NR25 7TZ. (Life Member)
GREGORY, Mrs. Alison Clare, BA(Hons) ACA PGCE *2002;* (Tax Fac), 13 Brecon Close, Quedgeley, GLOUCESTER, GL2 4TS.
GREGORY, Mr. Andrew Douglas, FCA *1971;* The Business Advisory Group Limited, P O Box 1404, NAIROBI, 00502, KENYA.
GREGORY, Mr. Andrew Howard, ACA *2009;* R S M Bentley Jennison, 5 Ridge House Ridge House Drive, STOKE-ON-TRENT, ST1 5SJ.
•**GREGORY, Mr. Andrew John, BA FCA** *1985;* Gregory & Co, 80 Bowling Hall Road, BRADFORD, WEST YORKSHIRE, BD4 7TH.
GREGORY, Mr. Andrew Nicholas, BA ACA *1993;* 6 Holly Royde Close, MANCHESTER, M20 3HR.
GREGORY, Mrs. Barbara Elaine, BA ACA *1987;* Grange Vale Stokeinteignhead, NEWTON ABBOT, DEVON, TQ12 4QH.
•**GREGORY, Mr. Benjamin Paul, BA ACA** *2003;* with Ernst & Young LLP, 1 More London Place, LONDON, SE1 2AF.
GREGORY, Miss. Catharine Fiona, BSc ACA *2002;* 19 Rutland Place, MAIDENHEAD, BERKSHIRE, SL6 4JA.
GREGORY, Mrs. Catherine Ann, LLB ACA *2002;* (Tax Fac), H M Customs & Excise Lingate House, 102 Chapel Lane, WIGAN, WN3 4BJ.
GREGORY, Miss. Catherine Lynne, BA ACA *1995;* Flat 132 Globe Wharf, 205 Rotherhithe Street, LONDON, SE16 5XX.
GREGORY, Mrs. Cerys Louise, BSc(Econ) ACA *1999;* 9 Hazeltree Court, Bryncoch, NEATH, SA10 7SZ.
GREGORY, Mr. Charles Michaell, BSc FCA *1975;* Cresacre, 5 St. Marys Way, Chalfont St. Peter, GERRARDS CROSS, BUCKINGHAMSHIRE, SL9 9BL. (Life Member)
•**GREGORY, Mr. Christopher, BA FCA TEP** *1981;* Orbis Partners LLP, Third Floor, 35 Newhall Street, BIRMINGHAM, B3 3PU.
GREGORY, Mr. Christopher Harry, FCA *1974;* P O Box 72805, DUBAI, UNITED ARAB EMIRATES.
GREGORY, Mr. Christopher Michael, BSc FCA *1975;* 41 Ashdown Avenue, FARNBOROUGH, HAMPSHIRE, GU14 7DN. (Life Member)
•**GREGORY, Mr. Clive, BSc FCA** *1977;* (Tax Fac), AGM Partners LLP, Suite 9, Innovation Centre, 23 Cambridge Science Park, CAMBRIDGE, CB4 0EY.
GREGORY, Mr. Clive William, BA ACA *1996;* Ashley House Ashley Road, Bentworth, ALTON, GU34 5RH.
GREGORY, Mr. Dale Lawrence, LLB ACA *2000;* KPMG, Level 32, Emirates Towers, Sheikh Zayed Road, PO Box 3800, DUBAI UNITED ARAB EMIRATES.
GREGORY, Mr. David, BA ACA *1985;* 17 Leeson Road, BOURNEMOUTH, BH7 7AZ.
GREGORY, Mr. David Ernest, FCA *1972;* Flat 3, Kirklee, Green Walk, Bowdon, ALTRINCHAM, CHESHIRE WA14 2SL. (Life Member)
GREGORY, Mr. David Keith, BSc ACA *1997;* 62 Grove Way, ESHER, KT10 8HW.
GREGORY, Mr. David Michael, BSc ACA *1989;* (Tax Fac), Rose Cottage, 118 Vale Road, Ash Vale, ALDERSHOT, GU12 5HS.
•**GREGORY, Mr. David Noel, FCA JDipMA** *1969;* 15 Orchard Rise, RICHMOND, TW10 5BX.
•**GREGORY, Mr. Derek Edward, FCA** *1962;* Rosemary Cottage, Bowling Close, Stanton-by-Dale, ILKESTON, DE7 4QG.
GREGORY, Miss. Donna Louise, ACA *2010;* Apartment 181, 185 Water Street, MANCHESTER, M3 4JU.
•**GREGORY, Mr. Duncan, BSc(Hons) ACA CF MSI** *1999;* Moore Stephens LLP, 150 Aldersgate Street, LONDON, EC1A 4AB.
GREGORY, Mr. Edward Thomas, MPhil ACA *2009;* Flat 2-4, 49 South Hill Park, LONDON, NW3 2SS.
GREGORY, Miss. Ethel Mary, FCA *1961;* Carolina Cottage, 6 Hall Garth Lane, West Ayton, SCARBOROUGH, YO13 9JA. (Life Member)
GREGORY, Mr. Gareth Alan, BA(Econ) ACA *2005;* 129 Rue de Reckenthal, L-2410 STRASSEN, LUXEMBOURG.
GREGORY, Mr. Gareth Michael, MA ACA *2004;* Auckland Council, Private Bag 92300, AUCKLAND 1142, NEW ZEALAND.
GREGORY, Mr. Graeme Mark, BSc ARCS ACA *1998;* 16 Old Sawmill Close, VERWOOD, BH31 6PT.
GREGORY, Mrs. Helen Diana, BA ACA *1996;* (Tax Fac), with PricewaterhouseCoopers LLP, 1 Embankment Place, LONDON, WC2N 6RH.
GREGORY, Mrs. Helen Louisa, BA FCA *1995;* Our Cottage, Whitfield, WOTTON-UNDER-EDGE, GLOUCESTERSHIRE, GL12 8EA.
•**GREGORY, Mr. Hugh Richard Henry, BA FCA** *1977;* Hugh Gregory, 112 South Street, TAUNTON, TA1 3AG.
•**GREGORY, Mr. Ian Ellis, FCA** *1995;* Daw White Murrall, 1 George Street, WOLVERHAMPTON, WV2 4DG.
GREGORY, Mr. Ian William, LLB ACA *1991;* T.N. Robinson Ltd, Daw Bank, STOCKPORT, SK3 0EH.
•**GREGORY, Mrs. Jacqueline Ann, ACA** *1990;* Jacky Gregory, Church Lodge, Church Road, Warsash, SOUTHAMPTON, SO31 9GF.
GREGORY, Mr. James Andrew, FCA *1971;* 18 Harrowby Lane, GRANTHAM, NG31 9HX.
GREGORY, Mr. James Edward, BSc ACA *2000;* Bakers Corner Cottage, Oakhanger Road, Kingsley, BORDON, HAMPSHIRE, GU35 9NJ.
GREGORY, Mr. James Edward, ACA *2003;* 11 St. Johns Close, BEVERLEY, NORTH HUMBERSIDE, HU17 8FD.
GREGORY, Mr. James Robert, MA ACA *1992;* 63 Leverton Street, LONDON, NW5 2NX.
•**GREGORY, Mr. Jan Paul, FCA** *1977;* 36 Congleton Road, ALDERLEY EDGE, CHESHIRE, SK9 7AB.
GREGORY, Mrs. Jane Carey, BA ACA DChA *1981;* 22 Fox Hill, Upper Norwood, LONDON, SE19 2XE.
GREGORY, Mrs. Janis Anne, BSc FCA *1982;* 14 Chard Avenue, Whimple, EXETER, DEVON, EX5 2TU.
GREGORY, Ms. Jemma Jane, ACA *2000;* Bakers Corner Cottage, Kingsley, BORDON, HAMPSHIRE, GU35 9NJ.
GREGORY, Miss. Jill, BSc ACA *1988;* J Gregory, 12 Elmfield Grove, NEWCASTLE UPON TYNE, NE3 4XA.
GREGORY, Mr. Joe Lloyd, BSc ACA *2009;* 36 Congleton Road, ALDERLEY EDGE, CHESHIRE, SK9 7AB.
GREGORY, Mr. John, BSc *1990;* Kellogg Co of GB Ltd, The Kellogg Building, Talbot Road, Old Trafford, MANCHESTER, M16 0PU.
GREGORY, Mr. John Edward, BA ACA *1986;* St. Maxime La Rue de la Monnaie Trinity, JERSEY, JE3 5DG.
GREGORY, Mr. John Howard, FCA *1973;* Fern House, Whitchurch Road, Cublington, LEIGHTON BUZZARD, LU7 0LP.
GREGORY, Mr. Jonathan David Leigh, BSc FCA *1986;* The Beeches, Blackboard Lane, Urchfont, DEVIZES, WILTSHIRE, SN10 4RD.
GREGORY, Mrs. Katie Louise, ACA *2008;* 1 Arbour Tree Lane, Chadwick End, SOLIHULL, WEST MIDLANDS, B93 0AZ.
•**GREGORY, Mr. Keith Anthony, BSc ACA** *1983;* (Tax Fac), Keith Gregory, 26 Barley Close, Little Eaton, DERBY, DE21 5DJ.
GREGORY, Mr. Kenneth Alfred, FCA *1948;* 32 Bernard Hackett Court, ROSS-ON-WYE, HEREFORDSHIRE, HR9 5YU. (Life Member)
•**GREGORY, Mr. Kevin, ACA FCCA CF** *2009;* Hawsons, Pegasus House, 463a Glossop Road, SHEFFIELD, S10 2QD.
GREGORY, Mr. Kevin John, BSc FCA *1983;* 20, Edward Road, BROMLEY, BR1 3NQ.
•**GREGORY, Mrs. Linda Carol, FCA** *1983;* (Tax Fac), Gregory Wildman, The Granary, Crowhill Farm, Ravensden Road, Wilden, BEDFORD MK44 2QS.
GREGORY, Mr. Malcolm Ralph, BA ACA *1982;* Argeles-Bagneres, 65200 HAUTES-PYRENEES, FRANCE.
•**GREGORY, Mrs. Margaret Elizabeth, FCA** *1968;* (Tax Fac), Margaret E. Gregory, 5 Bryn Castell, Radyr, CARDIFF, CF15 8RA.
GREGORY, Mr. Mark, BA(Hons) ACA *2002;* Flat 12 Oxton Court, Rose Mount, Oxton, WIRRAL, MERSEYSIDE CH43 5SU.
GREGORY, Mr. Mark Charles, BSc ACA *1995;* Suite 211, Willmott Dixon Ltd Spirella Building, Bridge Road, LETCHWORTH GARDEN CITY, HERTFORDSHIRE, SG6 4ET.
GREGORY, Mr. Mark Julian, BSc ACA *1988;* Legal & General Assurance Society Ltd, Legal & General House, St. Monicas Road, Kingswood, TADWORTH, SURREY KT20 6EU.
GREGORY, Mr. Martin Paul, BA ACA *1987;* Dupont UK Ltd, Wedgewood Way, STEVENAGE, HERTFORDSHIRE, AL3 8HU.
•**GREGORY, Mr. Martyn, BSc ACA CF** *1995;* Deloitte LLP, 3 Rivergate, Temple Quay, BRISTOL, BS1 6GD. See also Deloitte & Touche LLP
GREGORY, Mr. Matthew, ACA *1994;* The Limes, 180 London Road, ST. ALBANS, HERTFORDSHIRE, AL1 1PL.
GREGORY, Mr. Matthew James, ACA *2007;* Flat 35 Jasper House, 9 Merrivale Mews, MILTON KEYNES, MK9 2FN.
GREGORY, Mr. Michael Christopher, FCA *1967;* 41 Old Sneed Road, Stoke Bishop, BRISTOL, BS9 1ES.
GREGORY, Mr. Michael David, FCA *1972;* RJ 116 KM 38, Condo Village Green II Lote 168, Cachoeiras De Macacu, RIO DE JANEIRO, 28.680-000, BRAZIL.
•**GREGORY, Mr. Michael George, ACA** *1988;* Gregory & Co, 12 Kikas & Frosos Sountia Street, 6016 LARNACA, CYPRUS.
GREGORY, Mr. Morris Gage, FCA *1952;* 13 Hepscott Drive, Beaumont Park, WHITLEY BAY, NE25 9XJ. (Life Member)
GREGORY, Mrs. Nicola Kerry, LLB ACA *2002;* 37 Wayneflete Tower Avenue, ESHER, KT10 8QQ.
GREGORY, Mr. Panos Barry George, MSc FCA *1993;* 110, Coleridge Road, CROYDON, CR0 7BR.
GREGORY, Mr. Peter Andrew, BA ACA *1991;* Apple Barn, South Barton, Brixton, PLYMOUTH, PL8 2DF.
GREGORY, Mr. Peter Michael, FCA *1966;* (Tax Fac), Flat 2, Chase Court, 28 Beaufort Gardens, LONDON, SW3 1QQ.
GREGORY, Mr. Philip Ashton, BA FCA *1977;* Stanton Ford House, Calver Road, Baslow, HOPE VALLEY, DERBYSHIRE, S32 3XF.
GREGORY, Mr. Philip Michael Robert, FCA *1979;* P O BOX 172, GUILDFORD, WA 6935, AUSTRALIA.
GREGORY, Mr. Philip Peter Clinton, BA ACA *1979;* 3 Ashlyns Park, Fairmile Avenue, COBHAM, KT11 2JY.
•**GREGORY, Mr. Raef Scott, BA FCA** *1997;* Brebners, The Quadrangle, 180 Wardour Street, LONDON, W1F 8LB.
GREGORY, Mr. Richard Peter, ACA MBA *1998;* Northern Rock Plc, Northern Rock House, Gosforth, NEWCASTLE UPON TYNE, NE3 4PL.
GREGORY, Mr. Richard Thomas, BSc FCA *1972;* Ashfield Lodge, Ashfield Crescent, ROSS-ON-WYE, HEREFORDSHIRE, HR9 5PH.
GREGORY, Mr. Robert, FCA *1986;* with Barnbrook Sinclair Limited, 1 High Street, Knaphill, WOKING, SURREY, GU21 2PG.
GREGORY, Mr. Robert George, BA ACA *1983;* 45 Kingsway, ROCHDALE, OL16 5HN.
GREGORY, Mr. Robert Paul, BA FCA *1967;* 10 Erica Close, West End, WOKING, GU24 9PE.
GREGORY, Mr. Robert William, FCA *1979;* Rose Homes Ltd, 11 Windmill Street, Whittlesey, PETERBOROUGH, PE7 1HJ.
GREGORY, Mr. Robin Guy, BSc ACA *1988;* (Tax Fac), 154 Boulevard de Magenta, 75010 PARIS, FRANCE.
GREGORY, Mrs. Sara Louise, BA ACA *1990;* Holly Tree House, Westdown Park, Burwash Common, ETCHINGHAM, TN19 7NW.
GREGORY, Mr. Scott Jonathan, ACA *1992;* The Limes, 73 Station Road, Great Massingham, KING'S LYNN, NORFOLK, PE32 2JQ.
GREGORY, Mr. Stephen, BAcc CA *2008;* 10 Outenique Avenue, Quellerina, NORTHCLIFF, 1709, SOUTH AFRICA.
GREGORY, Mr. Stephen, BA FCA *1973;* 10574 E. Fernwood Lane, SCOTTSDALE, AZ 85262, UNITED STATES.
•**GREGORY, Mr. Stephen Raymond, BA FCA** *1981;* Ernst & Young LLP, 1 More London Place, LONDON, SE1 2AF. See also Ernst & Young Europe LLP
GREGORY, Mr. Stephen Robert, BSc FCA *1975;* Corrosion Resistant Products Ltd, Todmorden Road, LITTLEBOROUGH, OL15 9EG.
GREGORY, Mr. Stuart Lloyd, FCA *1973;* Gore Cottage, Eastbourne Road, East Dean, EASTBOURNE, EAST SUSSEX, BN20 0BL.
GREGORY, Miss. Susan Hayley, MA FCA MBA *1991;* Charmant, 48 The Front, Middleton One Row, DARLINGTON, DL2 1AU.
GREGORY, Mr. Thomas Arthur William, FCA *1967;* 40 Church Road, Trull, TAUNTON, SOMERSET, TA3 7LQ.
•**GREGORY, Mr. Timothy Mark Thomas, BA FCA CTA** *1996;* (Tax Fac), Saffery Champness, Lion House, Red Lion Street, LONDON, WC1R 4GB.
GREGORY, Mr. Tom, ACA *2010;* 21 School Lane, Beeston, NOTTINGHAM, NG9 5EH.
GREGORY, Mr. Trevor John, BA ACA *1980;* The Hollies, Llanwarne, HEREFORD, HR2 8JE.
GREGORY, Mr. William Albert, BSc(Hons) ACA ACCA *2008;* Westlea, Woodroyd Close, Bramhall, STOCKPORT, CHESHIRE, SK7 3LT.
GREGORY, Mr. William Brian, BA ACA *1979;* 22 Fox Hill, LONDON, SE19 2XE.
•**GREGORY-JONES, Mrs. Anne Marie, BSc FCA** *1976;* (Tax Fac), haysmacintyre, Fairfax House, 15 Fulwood Place, LONDON, WC1V 6AY.
GREGORY-LILLEY, Mr. Calvin, BA ACA *1996;* Hadley House, Melfort Road, CROWBOROUGH, EAST SUSSEX, TN6 1QT.
GREGORY-SMITH, Mr. Samuel Robert, ACA *2008;* Ground Floor, 68 Grosvenor Park Road, LONDON, E17 9PG.
GREGSON, Mr. Andrew Paul, BSc ACA *1990;* Grove Lodge Grove Road, Seal, SEVENOAKS, TN15 0LE.
GREGSON, Mr. James, BSc ACA *2010;* 10 South Street, Newchurch, ROSSENDALE, LANCASHIRE, BB4 9HF.
GREGSON, Mr. John, MA FCA *1970;* Home Farm Cottage Grape Lane, Croston, LEYLAND, PR26 9HB.
GREGSON, Miss. Lorraine Mary, BA ACA *1992;* 97 St. Martins Road, BLACKPOOL, FY4 2DZ.
GREGSON, Mr. Martin, BSc ACA *1979;* 14 Bwllfa Road, Ynystawe, SWANSEA, SA6 5AL.
GREGSON, Mr. Michael Jonathan, BSc ACA *1983;* 33 Front Road, Woodchurch, ASHFORD, KENT, TN26 3QB.
GREGSON, Mr. Michael Stewart, MSc ACA *1991;* 67 Colchester Road, West Mersea, COLCHESTER, CO5 8JZ.
GREGSON, Mr. Nigel Christopher, BA ACA CPA *1990;* 460 Norristown Rd, Suite 350, BLUE BELL, PA 19422, UNITED STATES.
GREGSON, Mr. Piers Martin, FCA *1971;* Larkfields, Tadmarton Heath Road, Hook Norton, BANBURY, OX15 5DQ. (Life Member)
GREGSON, Mr. Robin Anthony, BSc FCA *1985;* 2 Lakeside, East Morton, KEIGHLEY, BD20 5UY.
GREGSON, Dr. Simon Anthony John, MA MSc FCA *1980;* Keepers Cottage, 17 High Street, Shipton-Under-Wychwood, CHIPPING NORTON, OX7 6DQ.
GREGSON, Mr. Stanley, FCA *1956;* Rua Ouro Preto 100, Vila Diva - Granja Viana, Carapicuiba, SAO PAULO, BRAZIL. (Life Member)
GREGSON, Mr. Stephen David, LLB ACA *2007;* 76 Culverden Road, LONDON, SW12 9LS.
GREGSON, Mr. Stephen John, BA ACA CF *1996;* Glenhurst, Cocker Bar Road, LEYLAND, LANCASHIRE, PR26 7TA.
GREHAN, Mr. Paul Anthony Matthew, BSc ACA *2011;* Flat 27, Welsby Court, Eaton Rise, LONDON, W5 2EY.
GREIG, Miss. Beryl Joyce Nance, FCA *1954;* 34 Heath Village, HACKETTSTOWN, NJ 07840, UNITED STATES. (Life Member)
GREIG, Mr. James Thomas, ACA *2010;* 16 Skinners Lane, ASHTEAD, KT21 2NR.
GREIG, Mr. Michael William, BSc ACA CTA *1980;* (Tax Fac), The Nestlings, School Lane, Denmead, WATERLOOVILLE, HAMPSHIRE, PO7 6NA.
GREIG, Mr. Peter Francis Mcneil, FCA *1968;* 14 West Street Lane, CARSHALTON, SM5 2PY.
GRENFELL, Mr. Joseph, FCA *1965;* 20 Ivanhoe Drive, Kenton, HARROW, HA3 8QP. (Life Member)
GRENFELL, Mr. Nicholas, FCA *1951;* Scott Simmonds & Co, 12 Pengarth Close, TRURO, CORNWALL, TR1 2BP. (Life Member)
GRENIER, Mr. Stephen Marcel, BSc ACA *1986;* The Spinneys, Swan Lane, EDENBRIDGE, KENT, TN8 6BD.
GRENNALL, Mr. David John, BSc ACA *1987;* 35 Victoria Mews, Barnt Green, BIRMINGHAM, B45 8NA.
GRENVILLE, Mr. Peter Anthony, BCom FCA *1978;* 6 Springvale Close, Leatherhead Road, Great Bookham, LEATHERHEAD, SURREY, KT23 4RD.
GRENVILLE, Miss. Philippa Leah, BSc(Hons) ACA *2011;* 4 The Hollies, Woolton, LIVERPOOL, L25 7AQ.
•**GRENVILLE-BARKER, Mrs. Carol Ann, BA FCA** *1984;* (Tax Fac), Grenville Barker & Co Limited, 15 Lingfield Avenue, KINGSTON UPON THAMES, SURREY, KT1 2TL.
GRESHAM, Mr. Daniel Joshua, BSc(Hons) ACA *2001;* Ard na Greina, Marley Lane, HASLEMERE, GU27 3RG.
GRESHAM, Mrs. Jutta Maria, BA ACA *1993;* Briar Lodge, 20 Ashleigh Road, HORSHAM, RH12 2LF.
•**GRESHAM, Mr. Paul Richard, BSc ACA** *1984;* KPMG LLP, 1 Forest Gate, Brighton Road, CRAWLEY, WEST SUSSEX, RH11 9PT. See also KPMG Europe LLP
•**GRESHAM, Mr. Roy, FCA** *1973;* Roy Gresham FCA, 40 Barcombe Road, Barnston, Heswall, WIRRAL, MERSEYSIDE CH60 1UZ.
GRESSWELL, Mr. Anthony Peter, FCA *1965;* The Old Rectory, Wytham, OXFORD, OX2 8QA.
GRESTY, Mr. Alan Sydney, FCA *1966;* 12 Jordan Close, KENILWORTH, CV8 2AE.

GRESTY, Mr. Graham Richard, LLB ACA *1987;* 11 Edinburgh Way, Queens Park, CHESTER, CH4 7AS.
GRESTY, Miss. Louise Mary, BSc ACA *2003;* 23 Hazelville Grove, BIRMINGHAM, B28 9PX.
•GRESTY, Mr. Peter John, FCA *1964;* 8 Fletcher Drive, Bowdon, ALTRINCHAM, WA14 3FZ.
GRETHE, Mr. Richard Paul, BA ACA *1998;* 19 Hill Rise, LONDON, NW11 6LY.
•GRETTON, Mrs. Carolynne Wendy, FCA *1987;* The Gretton Partnership Limited, 9 Brook Lane, Corfe Mullen, WIMBORNE, DORSET, BH21 3RD.
GRETTON, Mr. George Richard, BA ACA *1983;* 52 Mora Road, LONDON, NW2 6TG.
GRETTON, Ms. Mary Frances, MBA BA FCA CIA *1977;* 1717 California Road, PEKIN, IL 61554-9728, UNITED STATES.
GRETTON, Mr. Nicholas George, BA ACA *1990;* 274 Musters Road, West Bridgford, NOTTINGHAM, NG2 7DR.
GRETTON, Miss. Penni, BSc ACA *2006;* 16 Stanley Avenue, BIRMINGHAM, B32 2HB.
•GRETTON, Mr. Richard John, FCA *1976;* (Tax Fac), The Gretton Partnership Limited, 9 Brook Lane, Corfe Mullen, WIMBORNE, DORSET, BH21 3RD.
GRETTON, Miss. Stephanie, ACA *2008;* Apartment 12, 33 Highmarsh Crescent, MANCHESTER, M20 2AN.
GRETTON-WATSON, Dr. Simon Paul, PhD MEng ACA *2010;* 1 Ellery Road, LONDON, SE19 3QG.
GREVES, Mr. John Charles, FCA *1963;* 2 Ambleside Way, NUNEATON, WARWICKSHIRE, CV11 6AT. (Life Member)
GREVESON, Mrs. Rachel Louise, ACA *2010;* 27 Springfield Road, Morley, LEEDS, LS27 9PN.
GREW, Mr. Benjamin Jon, BSc ACA *2006;* Flat 506 Ginger Apartments, 1 Cayenne Court, LONDON, SE1 2PA.
GREW, Mrs. Kay, BSc ACA *1992;* 33 Richmond Drive, LICHFIELD, STAFFORDSHIRE, WS14 9SZ.
GREW, Mrs. Maria Lianne, MA ACA *2009;* 27 Rutland Close, BASILDON, SS15 6QX.
GREW, Mr. Stephen David, BSc ACA *2009;* 27 Rutland Close, BASILDON, SS15 6QX.
GREWAL, Ms. Abninder Kaur, BA ACA *1989;* Na Parcelach 228, Nebusice, 16400 PRAGUE, CZECH REPUBLIC.
GREWAL, Mr. Alekh Singh, FCA *1986;* Mannai Corporation, P.O. Box 76, DOHA, QATAR.
GREWAL, Mrs. Amandip, BSc ACA *2001;* 94 Mayfield Avenue, LONDON, W13 9UX.
GREWAL, Miss. Gagan, BA ACA *2002;* MGPA, 60 Sloane Avenue, LONDON, SW3 3XB.
GREWAL, Mr. Jaswinder Pal Singh, BSc ACA *1991;* 265 Waye Avenue, Cranford, HOUNSLOW, TW5 9SJ.
GREWAL, Mr. Kamaljit Singh, BSc ACA *1998;* 101 Howell Road, OAKVILLE L6H 5Z4, ON, CANADA.
GREWAL, Ms. Manjit Kaur, BSc ACA *1994;* 29 Chelmsford Road, LONDON, E18 2PW.
GREWAL, Mr. Ravinder Singh, BSc ACA *1993;* 17 Parkthorne Drive, North Harrow, HARROW, HA2 7BU.
GREWAL, Miss. Sandeep Kaur, ACA *2009;* Paul Grewal, 11 Amberley Road, SLOUGH, SL2 2LR.
•GREWER, Mr. Mark Russell, FCA *1997;* Hunter Gee Holroyd Limited, Club Chambers, Museum Street, YORK, YO1 7DN.
GREY, Mr. Andrew James Alexander, FCA *1966;* Littlethorpe, Furze Hill, Kingswood, TADWORTH, SURREY, KT20 6EP.
GREY, Miss. Annelie, BSc ACA *2005;* with Deloitte LLP, Hill House, 1 Little New Street, LONDON, EC4A 3TR.
GREY, Mr. Brian John Michael, FCA *1957;* Llwyuioli Farmhouse, Llantrisant Road, Groes Faen, PONTYCLUN, CF72 8NG. (Life Member)
•GREY, Mr. Bryan William, FCA *1975;* Bryan Grey & Co Limited, Broadfield House, 18 Broadfield Road, SHEFFIELD, S8 0XJ.
GREY, Mr. Colin James, FCA *1960;* Lissadel, Fairoak Lane, Oxshott, LEATHERHEAD, KT22 0TW. (Life Member)
•GREY, Mr. David Wolfe, FCA *1960;* David Grey & Co Ltd, 175/177 Temple Chambers, Temple Avenue, LONDON, EC4Y 0DB. See also Accounteasy Limited
GREY, Mr. Ernest Philip, MA FCA *1952;* 116 Park Avenue, ORPINGTON, BR6 9EE. (Life Member)
GREY, Miss. Gemma Marie, ACA *2009;* 29 Hardy Road, LONDON, SW19 1JA.
GREY, Mr. Ivar Andreas Robert John, FCA *1971;* 1 Clos Cefn Bychan, Pentyrch, CARDIFF, CF15 9PF.
GREY, Mr. John, FCA *1958;* 17 Well Ridge Park, WHITLEY BAY, TYNE AND WEAR, NE25 9PQ. (Life Member)
GREY, Mr. Jonathan Guthrie, FCA *1975;* Orchard Cottage Gaston Lane, South Warnborough, HOOK, HAMPSHIRE, RG29 1RH.
GREY, Miss. Lucy Caroline, MBA BA ACA *2007;* 44 Fordingley Road, LONDON, W9 3HF.
GREY, Mr. Malcolm Dominic Anthony, MA ACA *1993;* Schauenburgerstrasse 10, 4052 BASEL, SWITZERLAND.
GREY, Mr. Richard Michael, FCA *1974;* 78 Elmfield Road, Gosforth, NEWCASTLE UPON TYNE, NE3 4BD.
GREY, Mr. Richard William Arthur, BA ACA *1982;* 11 Tinto Grove, Bargeddie, Baillieston, GLASGOW, G69 7TJ.
GREY, Mr. Simon Ridley, ACA *1987;* Logic Consultancy Services Ltd, 184 Meadvale Road, Ealing, LONDON, W5 1LT.
GREY, Mr. Toby Guthrie, MA ACA *1980;* 3 Logan Mews, LONDON, W8 6QP.
GREYBROOK, Miss. Emily Rose, BA(Hons) ACA *2011;* Top Floor Flat, 94 Pembroke Road, Clifton, BRISTOL, BS8 3EG.
GRIBBEN, Mr. Leo Charles, BA ACA *1998;* 14 Sabin Drive, Weston under Wetherley, LEAMINGTON SPA, CV33 9GA.
GRIBBEN, Miss. Victoria Jane Elizabeth, MSc BA(Hons) ACA *2010;* 9 Cypress Grove, Wales, SHEFFIELD, S26 5QA.
GRIBBIN, Mr. Adrian Douglas, BSc ACA *1996;* Cornacausk, Streete, Rathowen, MULLINGAR, COUNTY WESTMEATH, IRELAND.
GRIBBIN, Mr. Gabriel Adam, BSc FCA *1991;* 96 Old Church Lane, STANMORE, MIDDLESEX, HA7 2RR.
GRIBBIN, Mr. Simon Daniel, BSc ACA *1986;* 38 The Ridgeway, Golders Green, LONDON, NW11 8QS.
GRIBBLE, Mrs. Cecilia Jane, BSc ACA *1986;* Pabulum Ltd 3rd Floor Flagship House, Reading Road North, FLEET, HAMPSHIRE, GU51 4WP.
GRIBBLE, Mr. Ian Robert, BEng ACA *2005;* Moose Lodge Clay Head Road, Baldrine, ISLE OF MAN, IM4 6DP.
GRICE, Mr. Andrew Stephen, BA FCA *1989;* 19 Kingfisher Close, BASINGSTOKE, HAMPSHIRE, RG22 5PJ.
•GRICE, Mr. Anthony Edward, BA FCA CertPFS *1975;* Allotts, The Old Grammar School, 13 Moorgate Road, ROTHERHAM, SOUTH YORKSHIRE, S60 2EN.
•GRICE, Miss. Karen, BA(Hons) ACA *2009;* Fouette Accountancy Solutions Limited, White Rose House, 5 Walnut Grove, Cotgrave, NOTTINGHAM, NG12 3AU.
•GRICE, Mr. Markham John, FCA *1977;* Mazars LLP, Tower Bridge House, St. Katharines Way, LONDON, E1W 1DD.
GRICE, Mrs. Pamela Joan, BSc ACA *1979;* 34 St. John's Avenue, KIDDERMINSTER, DY11 6AU.
GRICE, Mr. Trevor Charles, FCA *1965;* Hathenshaw Farm Hathenshaw Lane, Denton, ILKLEY, LS29 0HR. (Life Member)
•GRICKS, Ms. Catherine, BSc ACA *2009;* CGSM Accountants, 1 Engayne Gardens, UPMINSTER, ESSEX, RM14 1UY.
•GRICKS, Mr. Daniel David Thomas, BA FCA *1976;* (Tax Fac), Upminster Limited, 1 Engayne Gardens, UPMINSTER, ESSEX, RM14 1UY.
GRIECO, Mr. Piero, BA ACA *2002;* Flat 8 Stevens House, Jerome Place, KINGSTON UPON THAMES, KT1 1HX.
GRIER, Mrs. Emily Alice, BSc ACA *2005;* 24 Marlborough Crescent, SEVENOAKS, TN13 2HP.
GRIER, Mr. Peter William, BSc ACA *2002;* 24 Marlborough Crescent, SEVENOAKS, KENT, TN13 2HP.
GRIER, Mr. Robert, FCA *1971;* 93 Gardenfield, Skellingthorpe, LINCOLN, LN6 5TA. (Life Member)
GRIERSON, Mr. David William, FCA *1973;* 5 Belle Vue Drive, Ashbrooke, SUNDERLAND, SR2 7SF.
GRIERSON, Mr. Michael John, FCA *1970;* Edwards & Ward Ltd Unit 12, April Court Sybron Way, CROWBOROUGH, EAST SUSSEX, TN6 3DZ.
•GRIERSON, Mr. Robert McMorrine, FCA *1967;* Landin Wilcock & Co, Queen St Chmbrs, 68 Queen St, SHEFFIELD, S17 4BD.
GRIERSON, Mr. William Andrew, ACA CTA *1984;* Woodlands, 2A The Brae, Auchendinny, PENICUIK, EH26 0RB.
GRIESBACH, Mr. Philip Martin, LLB ACA *1990;* 29 Blythe Way, SOLIHULL, B91 3EY.
GRIESSNER, Miss. Barbara, ACA *2003;* 128 Henry Doulton Drive, LONDON, SW17 6DF.
GRIEVE, Miss. Alison Esther, MA FCA *1976;* 43 Larkhall Rise, LONDON, SW4 6HT.
•GRIEVE, Mr. Andrew David, BA FCA *1987;* Thompson Taraz LLP, 35 Grosvenor Street, Mayfair, LONDON, W1K 4QX.
GRIEVE, Mrs. Carolyn Elizabeth, BAcc ACA *2000;* 10 Downshire Park South, HILLSBOROUGH, COUNTY DOWN, BT26 6RT.
GRIEVE, Mr. Charles Ramsay, FCA *1982;* Securities & Futures Commission, 8th Floor Chater House, 8 Connaught Road, CENTRAL, HONG KONG ISLAND, HONG KONG SAR.
GRIEVE, Mrs. Kathleen Mary, BSc FCA *1977;* Springfield, Hillwood Rd, Four Oaks, SUTTON COLDFIELD, B75 5QW.
GRIEVE, Mr. Martin Richard, ACA *1990;* 30 St. Andrews Gardens, COBHAM, SURREY, KT11 1HG.
GRIEVE, Mr. Nigel David, FCA *1975;* 5 Marsham Court, Victoria DriveWimbledon, LONDON, SW19 6BB.
GRIEVE, Mr. Rorie George Speirs, FCA *1973;* Finance Owl Services Limited, Springfield, Hillwood Road, Four Oaks, SUTTON COLDFIELD, B75 5QW.
GRIEVE, Mr. Thomas Allan, ACA *2008;* Flat B, 20 Charteris Road, LONDON, N4 3AB.
GRIEVES, Mr. Colin, FCA *1966;* 1 Tennand Cl, Cheshunt, WALTHAM CROSS, EN7 6DJ. (Life Member)
GRIEVES, Mrs. Helen Mary, BSc ACA *1996;* 4 Luckmore Drive, READING, RG6 7RP.
GRIEVES, Mr. Karl Geoffrey, MSc FCA *1989;* 53 Cronk Drean, Douglas, ISLE OF MAN, IM2 6AT.
GRIEVESON, Mrs. Sarah Elizabeth, BSc ACA *1999;* with PricewaterhouseCoopers LLP, 1 Embankment Place, LONDON, WC2N 6RH.
•GRIEVSON, Mr. Allen, FCA *1970;* (Tax Fac), Mitchells Grievson Limited, Kensington House, 3 Kensington, BISHOP AUCKLAND, COUNTY DURHAM, DL14 6HX.
GRIEVSON, Miss. Hannah Elizabeth, ACA *2008;* 11/39 Stanton Road, Mosman, SYDNEY, NSW 2088, AUSTRALIA.
GRIEVSON, Mr. Richard James, FCA *1972;* Totterdown House, Inkpen, HUNGERFORD, RG17 9EA.
•GRIFFEE, Mr. Paul Robert, ACA *1992;* Garden Flat, 15c Apsley Road, Clifton, BRISTOL, BS8 2SH.
•GRIFFEN, Mr. Steven James, ACA FCCA *2007;* Plummer Parsons, 18 Hyde Gardens, EASTBOURNE, BN21 4PT. See also Plummer Parsons Accountants Ltd
GRIFFEY, Mr. Nigel John, PhD BSc ACA CPA *1983;* 19073 Quiver Ridge Drive, LEESBURG, VA 20176, UNITED STATES.
GRIFFIN, Mrs. Ailsa Louise, BA ACA *2002;* 12 Chalkwell Drive, WIRRAL, MERSEYSIDE, CH60 2UE.
•GRIFFIN, Mr. Alan Michael, BSc FCA *1976;* AM Griffin BSc FCA, Ladyacre, Stag Lane, Chorleywood, RICKMANSWORTH, HERTFORDSHIRE WD3 5HD.
GRIFFIN, Mrs. Andrea Louise, BA(Hons) ACA *2001;* 43 Muirfield Close, CONSETT, COUNTY DURHAM, DH8 5XE.
GRIFFIN, Mr. Andrew, ACA *2008;* 6 Pinewood Road, Drury, BUCKLEY, CLWYD, CH7 3JZ.
GRIFFIN, Mr. Andrew Wynn, BSc ACA *1993;* 1 Honeywell Road, LONDON, SW11 6EQ.
GRIFFIN, Mrs. Anita Kathryn, BA ACA CTA *1995;* 5 Widmerpool Lane, Willoughby On The Wolds, LOUGHBOROUGH, LE12 6TE.
GRIFFIN, Mr. Antony Denis Gage, FCA *1952;* Hollytree Cottage, 145 Worlebury Hill Road, WESTON-SUPER-MARE, BS22 9TH. (Life Member)
GRIFFIN, Mr. Ben Charles, MSc BSc ACA *2009;* (Tax Fac), The Elms Farm, Little Witley, WORCESTER, WR6 6LL.
•GRIFFIN, Mr. Byron Mark, BA ACA CF *1995;* 16 Sheridan Road, Wimbledon, LONDON, SW19 3HP. See also Deloitte & Touche LLP
GRIFFIN, Mr. Carl Stephen, LLB ACA *1982;* Old Vicarage Neen Savage, Cleobury Mortimer, KIDDERMINSTER, WORCESTERSHIRE, DY14 8JU.
GRIFFIN, Miss. Caroline, BA ACA *2000;* 9606 Orchard Hill, DALLAS, TX 75243, UNITED STATES.
•①GRIFFIN, Mr. Chad, BA ACA *1998;* with FTI Consulting Limited, 322 Midtown, High Holborn, LONDON, WC1V 7PB.
GRIFFIN, Miss. Claire, ACA *2010;* C/O KPMG, PO Box 493, Century Yard, Cricket Square, GEORGE TOWN, KY1-1106 CAYMAN ISLANDS.
GRIFFIN, Mrs. Clare Freda Proctor, FCA *1961;* 9 Woolbrook Meadows, SIDMOUTH, DEVON, EX10 9UH.
•GRIFFIN, Miss. Danielle Louise, MChem ACA *2007;* with Moore Stephens (Guildford) LLP, Priory House, Pilgrims Court, Sydenham Road, GUILDFORD, SURREY GU1 3RX.
GRIFFIN, Mr. Daryl Sumner, FCA *1969;* 23 Priory Road, West Kirby, WIRRAL, MERSEYSIDE, CH48 7ET.
GRIFFIN, Mr. David, LLB FCA *1961;* Cronk Beg Fort Island Road, Derbyhaven, ISLE OF MAN, IM9 1TZ. (Life Member)
GRIFFIN, Mr. David, ACA *2007;* with PricewaterhouseCoopers LLP, Savannah House, 3 Ocean Way, Ocean Village, SOUTHAMPTON, SO14 3TJ.
GRIFFIN, Mr. David Andrew, BA ACA *1987;* Barron & Barron Chartered Accountants, Bathurst House, 86 Micklegate, YORK, YO1 6LQ.
GRIFFIN, Mr. David Frank, ACA *1986;* 36 Meadow Road, Toddington, DUNSTABLE, LU5 6BB.
•GRIFFIN, Mr. David Henry, BA FCA *1978;* Albert Goodman LLP, Mary Street House, Mary Street, TAUNTON, SOMERSET, TA1 3NW. See also Coyne Butterworth Hardwicke Limited
GRIFFIN, Mr. David James, ACA *1990;* Beeswift Ltd, West Wing, Delta House, Delta Point, Greets Green Road, WEST BROMWICH WEST MIDLANDS B70 9PL.
GRIFFIN, Mr. David Jeremy, MSc ACA *2003;* with Deloitte LLP, 2 New Street Square, LONDON, EC4A 3BZ.
GRIFFIN, Mr. David Stewart, FCA *1965;* 9 Woolbrook Meadows, SIDMOUTH, DEVON, EX10 9UH. (Life Member)
GRIFFIN, Ms. Deborah, OBE BSc ACA *1983;* with Deloitte LLP, Athene Place, 66 Shoe Lane, LONDON, EC4A 3BQ.
GRIFFIN, Mr. Donald Caesar Patrick, FCA *1975;* Alcan Inc (Zurich branch), PO BOX 1954, Max Hogger-Strasse 6, CH-8048 ZURICH, SWITZERLAND.
GRIFFIN, Mr. Douglas Raymond, FCA *1936;* West Dene, West Hill, OTTERY ST.MARY, EX11 1TU. (Life Member)
GRIFFIN, Mr. Edward Arthur, BA ACA *1998;* Hodge Farm House, Bubhurst Lane, Frittenden, CRANBROOK, KENT, TN17 2BD.
GRIFFIN, Mrs. Emma Louise, BSc(Hons) ACA *2003;* Little Barnards, Henley Road, MARLOW, BUCKINGHAMSHIRE, SL7 2BZ.
GRIFFIN, Mrs. Fiona Jane, BA ACA *1990;* The Grant Considine Partnership, 46-48 High Street, BANCHORY, KINCARDINESHIRE, AB31 5SR.
GRIFFIN, Mr. Geoffrey John, BA FCA *1968;* 11 Highgate, SUTTON COLDFIELD, B74 3HW.
GRIFFIN, Mr. Geoffrey Nigel, BSc FCA *1985;* 6 Buckingham Road, Wanstead, LONDON, E11 2EB.
•GRIFFIN, Mrs. Grace Lai Fun, BSc FCA ATT *1983;* Griffin & Associates Limited, 312 Uxbridge Road, RICKMANSWORTH, HERTFORDSHIRE, WD3 8YL.
GRIFFIN, Mr. Harold, MA FCA *1958;* Penteli, Woods Hill Lane, Ashurstwood, EAST GRINSTEAD, RH19 3RF. (Life Member)
GRIFFIN, Mrs. Hillary Jane, BA ACA CTA *1985;* 1 Greenloons Drive, Formby, LIVERPOOL, L37 2LX.
•GRIFFIN, Mr. James, FCA *1980;* Everett & Son, 35 Paul Street, LONDON, EC2A 4UQ.
GRIFFIN, Mr. James Edward, ACA *2009;* The Elms Farm, Little Witley, WORCESTER, WR6 6LL.
GRIFFIN, Mr. James Finbarr, BEng ACA *1995;* Goodbody Stockbrokers, Ballsbridge Park, Ballsbridge, DUBLIN 4, COUNTY DUBLIN, IRELAND.
GRIFFIN, Mr. James Peter, BSc ACA *2005;* G417, Astrazeneca Alderley House, Alderley Park, MACCLESFIELD, CHESHIRE, SK10 4TF.
GRIFFIN, Mr. Jason Alexander, BA ACA *1995;* 1 Chantry Drive, INGATESTONE, ESSEX, CM4 9HR.
GRIFFIN, Mrs. Jessica Anne, BSc ACA *1995;* 22 The Esplanade, Huntingdon, HAMILTON, NEW ZEALAND.
GRIFFIN, Mrs. Johanna Rachel, BSc ACA *2005;* Three Lions Underwriting Limited, 35 Newhall Street, BIRMINGHAM, B3 3PU.
GRIFFIN, Mr. John Stanford, MA FCA *1959;* 12 Chenel Close Orchard Village, Lakeside, CAPE TOWN, 7945, SOUTH AFRICA. (Life Member)
GRIFFIN, Mr. Jonathan Lee, BA ACA *1995;* 43 Percheron Drive, Knaphill, WOKING, GU21 2QY.
GRIFFIN, Mrs. Kathryn, ACA *2010;* 22 Tolefrey Gardens, Chandler's Ford, EASTLEIGH, HAMPSHIRE, SO53 4HG.
•GRIFFIN, Mr. Kenneth Royston, MA FCA *1983;* 119 Reedley Road, Stoke Bishop, BRISTOL, BS9 1BE.
GRIFFIN, Mr. Lee Justin, BSc ARCS ACA *1997;* KPMG, One Snow Hill, BIRMINGHAM, B4 6GH.
GRIFFIN, Mr. Lionel Eric, FCA *1965;* 58 Childs Circuit, BELROSE, NSW 2085, AUSTRALIA.
GRIFFIN, Mr. Matthew John, BSc ACA *2005;* 13 Sedbergh Park, ILKLEY, WEST YORKSHIRE, LS29 8SZ.
GRIFFIN, Mr. Michael Richard, ACA *1981;* The Grocers Company, Grocers Hall, Princes Street, LONDON, EC2R 8AD.

GRIFFIN, Mrs. Michaela Paula, ACA *2005;* with BW Macfarlane LLP, 3 Temple Square, LIVERPOOL, L2 5BA.

GRIFFIN, Mr. Nicholas Charles, FCA *1956;* Spread Eagles Melbury Abbas, SHAFTESBURY, DORSET, SP7 0DU. (Life Member)

GRIFFIN, Mr. Paul Michael, BA ACA *1990;* 123 Wentworth Road, Harborne, BIRMINGHAM, B17 9SU.

GRIFFIN, Mr. Peter, FCA *1959;* 4 Fernhill Close, KENILWORTH, CV8 1AN. (Life Member)

GRIFFIN, Mr. Peter Francis, BA FCA *1984;* La Nouvelle Corderie, Rue St. Pierre, St. Pierre Du Bois, GUERNSEY, GY7 9SW.

GRIFFIN, Mrs. Rachel, BA ACA *2003;* 13 Sedbergh Park, ILKLEY, WEST YORKSHIRE, LS29 8SZ.

GRIFFIN, Mr. Raymond Michael, BSc(Hons) ACA *2003;* PO Box 1044, GEORGETOWN, GRAND CAYMAN, KY1-1102, CAYMAN ISLANDS.

GRIFFIN, Mrs. Rebecca, ACA *1995;* Ballawyllan Beg, East Baldwin, ISLE OF MAN, IM4 5ER.

GRIFFIN, Richard Arthur, Esq OBE FCA *1963;* Domaine de Peygonthier, 24240 POMPORT, FRANCE. (Life Member)

GRIFFIN, Mr. Richard Philip, MSc FCA *1974;* Oak House, Widmoor, Wooburn Green, HIGH WYCOMBE, BUCKINGHAMSHIRE, HP10 0JG.

GRIFFIN, Mr. Roger Francis Raby, BA FCA *1967;* Fraz Morra: Voc., No. 37 Molino di Scelta, 06012 CITTA DI CASTELLO, PROVINCE OF PERUGIA, ITALY.

GRIFFIN, Miss. Samantha Claire, BSc ACA *2005;* with Carter Backer Winter LLP, Enterprise House, 21 Buckle Street, LONDON, E1 8NN.

•**GRIFFIN, Mr. Terence James, FCA** *1975;* (Tax Fac), Kenneth Morris Ltd, 9-11 New Road, BROMSGROVE, WORCESTERSHIRE, B60 2JF.

GRIFFIN, Mr. Thomas Joseph, FCA *1964;* 38 Aldenham Avenue, RADLETT, WD7 8HX. (Life Member)

GRIFFIN, Miss. Vickie Margaret, BA(Hons) ACA *2003;* with Grant Thornton UK LLP, Unit 2, Broadfield Court, SHEFFIELD, S8 0XF.

GRIFFIN, Mr. William Bramwell, FCA *1956;* Villa Rossetti, 1117 Vale Do Lobo, 8135 ALMANCIL, ALGARVE, PORTUGAL. (Life Member)

GRIFFIN, Mr. William Thomas Jackson, MA FCA *1955;* 7 Lowndes Place, LONDON, SW1X 8DB. (Life Member)

GRIFFITH, Mrs. Allison Shiona, BSc ACA *1996;* 40 Links Side, ENFIELD, EN2 7QU.

GRIFFITH, Miss. Amy Hannah, ACA *2008;* 33 McDermott Close, LONDON, SW11 2LY.

GRIFFITH, Mr. Andrew John, BA ACA *1995;* British Sky Broadcasting Ltd, 7 Centaurs Business Centre Grant Way, ISLEWORTH, MIDDLESEX, TW7 5QD.

GRIFFITH, Mr. Andrew Patrick, BA ACA *1993;* 1 High Swinburne Place, NEWCASTLE UPON TYNE, NE4 6AT.

•**GRIFFITH, Mr. Bryn John, BA ACA** *1989;* Bryn Griffith, 24 Carleton Road, Poynton, STOCKPORT, CHESHIRE, SK12 1TL.

GRIFFITH, Mr. Campbell Lloyd, FCA *1975;* (Tax Fac), Woodway Lodge, 56 Aperfield Road, Biggin Hill, WESTERHAM, KENT, TN16 3LX. (Life Member)

GRIFFITH, Mr. Daniel Martin, BA ACA *2010;* CO JACK BENSON, 28 ROETELSTRASSE, 8006 ZURICH, SWITZERLAND.

GRIFFITH, Mr. David Richard, BA ACA *1988;* Medlar Cottage, 49 Gally Hill Road, Church Crookham, FLEET, GU52 6QE.

•**GRIFFITH, Mr. George Henry Wilson, ACA FCCA MABRP** *1980;* (Tax Fac), George H W Griffith Limited, Century House, 31 Gate Lane, SUTTON COLDFIELD, WEST MIDLANDS, B73 5TR.

GRIFFITH, Mrs. Hayley Elizabeth, BSc ACA *2005;* EFSC, Kellogg Co of GB Ltd The Kellogg Building, Talbot Road Old Trafford, MANCHESTER, M16 0PU.

GRIFFITH, Mr. Iwan Gwyn, BEng ACA *1991;* Symonds Hydroclean Ltd Wern Trading Estate, Rogerstone, NEWPORT, GWENT, NP10 9XX.

GRIFFITH, Mr. Jack Vaughan, FCA *1948;* 19 Cherry Holt Avenue, Heaton Mersey, STOCKPORT, CHESHIRE, SK4 3PT. (Life Member)

GRIFFITH, Mr. Jonathan Carey, BA FCA *1982;* 11 Lanelay Terrace, PONTYPRIDD, MID GLAMORGAN, CF37 1ER.

GRIFFITH, Mr. Jonathan Llewelyn, FCA *1970;* Little Kernborough, Kernborough, KINGSBRIDGE, DEVON, TQ7 2LL.

GRIFFITH, Mr. Lewis Charles, FCA *1963;* The Dell, Llidiarty-Y-Parc, CORWEN, LL21 9EL. (Life Member)

GRIFFITH, Mr. Mark, ACA *2008;* 87 Oaktree Road, SOUTHAMPTON, SO18 1PJ.

GRIFFITH, Mr. Maurice James, FCA *1972;* Taprobane, Sandisplatt Road, MAIDENHEAD, SL6 4NA.

GRIFFITH, Mr. Michael, FCA *1965;* 37 Fontenay Road, Ormonde, JOHANNESBURG, GAUTENG, 2091, SOUTH AFRICA.

GRIFFITH, Miss. Odile Lesley, BSc ACA *1979;* Upper House, Westburton, PULBOROUGH, WEST SUSSEX, RH20 1HD.

•**GRIFFITH, Mr. Paul Jeremy, FCA** *1971;* (Tax Fac), Griffith Clarke, 701 Stonehouse Business Park, Sperry Way, STONEHOUSE, GLOUCESTERSHIRE, GL10 3UT.

GRIFFITH, Mr. Rheinallt Wyn, BA ACA *1999;* Hen Gapel, Bodfari Road, Llandyrnog, DENBIGH, CLWYD, LL16 4HW.

•**GRIFFITH, Mr. Ross Grant Kendrick, FCA** *1982;* Vogue Management Services Limited, Units 6-10, Strawberry Lane Industrial Estate, Strawberry Lane, WILLENHALL, WV13 3RS.

GRIFFITH, Mrs. Samantha Georgina, BSc ACA *2003;* (Tax Fac), Signet Group Limited, 15 Golden Square, LONDON, W1F 9JG.

GRIFFITH, Mr. Simon Christopher, BSc(Econ) ACA *1998;* Stephenson Harwood, 1 Finsbury Circus, LONDON, EC2M 7SH.

GRIFFITH, Mrs. Susan, MA ACA *1981;* Lenvale Farmhouse Otham Street, Bearsted, MAIDSTONE, ME15 8SL.

GRIFFITH, Mrs. Traci Lynn, BSc FCA *1995;* Chinook Stables, Icart Road, St. Martin, GUERNSEY, GY4 6JG.

•**GRIFFITH-JONES, Mr. John Guthrie, TD MA ACA** *1978;* KPMG LLP, 15 Canada Square, LONDON, E14 5GL. See also KPMG Europe LLP, KPMG Audit plc, KPMG Holding plc

GRIFFITH-JONES, Mr. Peter Laugharne, MA ACA *1981;* Lockeridge House, Lockeridge, MARLBOROUGH, SN8 4EL.

GRIFFITHS, Miss. Aimee Laura, BA ACA *2004;* with Deloitte LLP, 2 New Street Square, LONDON, EC4A 3BZ.

GRIFFITHS, Mr. Alan John, BSc ACA *1993;* 4 Napier Avenue, LONDON, E14 3QB.

•**GRIFFITHS, Mr. Alan Joseph, BA ACA** *1993;* Ernst & Young Kft, H-1132 Budapest, Vaci ut 20, 62 PF.632, 1399 BUDAPEST, HUNGARY. See also Ernst & Young Europe LLP

•**GRIFFITHS, Mr. Alun Glyn, BEng FCA** *2000;* GS Ltd, Shiraz Loft Suite, Belvedere Hill, St. Saviour, JERSEY, JE2 7RP.

GRIFFITHS, Mr. Andrew Alexander, BA ACA *1999;* 19 Garden Court, Wheathampstead, ST. ALBANS, HERTFORDSHIRE, AL4 8RE.

•**GRIFFITHS, Mr. Andrew Bartholomew, FCA DChA** *1983;* (Tax Fac), Plummer Parsons, 18 Hyde Gardens, EASTBOURNE, BN21 4PT. See also A.B. Griffiths & Co Ltd

GRIFFITHS, Mr. Andrew Eric, BSc ACA *1992;* Deloitte & Touche GmbH, Franklinstrasse 50, 60486 FRANKFURT AM MAIN, GERMANY.

GRIFFITHS, Mr. Andrew Hugh Thomas, BA ACA *1990;* 14 Naval Parade, OCEAN REEF, WA 6027, AUSTRALIA.

GRIFFITHS, Mr. Andrew John, BSc(Hons) ACA *2002;* 49 Wilton Crescent, ALDERLEY EDGE, CHESHIRE, SK9 7RF.

GRIFFITHS, Mr. Andrew Michael, BA ACA *1991;* 657 Los Altos Avenue, LONG BEACH, CA 90814, UNITED STATES.

GRIFFITHS, Ms. Angela Susan, MA ACA *1983;* 24 Palestine Grove, LONDON, SW19 2QN.

•**GRIFFITHS, Mrs. Anne Thompson, MA ACA CTA** *1980;* (Tax Fac), Anne Griffiths, Lant Lodge Farm, Tansley, MATLOCK, DE4 5FW.

GRIFFITHS, Mr. Anthony Charles, FCA *1969;* (Tax Fac), Lansdowne Associates UK Ltd, Lansdowne House, 85 Fairfield Road, WINCHESTER, SO22 6SG.

GRIFFITHS, Mr. Anthony Nigel Clifton, FCA *1967;* Unit 360336/F, Lippo Centre, Tower II, 86 Queensway, ADMIRALTY, HONG KONG ISLAND HONG KONG SAR.

GRIFFITHS, Miss. Antonia, BSc ACA *2006;* British Gypsum Ltd, East Leake, LOUGHBOROUGH, LEICESTERSHIRE, LE12 6JQ.

GRIFFITHS, Mr. Brian Charles, MA(Cantab) ACA *1980;* 9 Bosserts Way, Highfields Caldecote, CAMBRIDGE, CB23 7PA.

GRIFFITHS, Mr. Brian John, FCA *1975;* Brambles, 11 The Daisycroft, HENFIELD, BN5 9LH.

GRIFFITHS, Mr. Carl John Marcus, MSc ACA *1993;* 6375 Breckenridge Place, KILBRIDE L7P 0K8, ON, CANADA.

GRIFFITHS, Mrs. Caroline Alexandra, BA ACA *2006;* Rydal, 3 Austenway, Chalfont St. Peter, GERRARDS CROSS, BUCKINGHAMSHIRE, SL9 8NN.

GRIFFITHS, Miss. Caroline Jane, ACA *2008;* KPMG, Dukes Keep, Marsh Lane, SOUTHAMPTON, SO14 3EX.

GRIFFITHS, Miss. Catherine Andrea, BSc ACA *1997;* 35 Western Road, Pontardawe, SWANSEA, SA8 4AJ.

GRIFFITHS, Ms. Catherine Jane, MA ACA *1996;* S G S United Kingdom Ltd, Rossmore Business Park, ELLESMERE PORT, CH65 3EN.

GRIFFITHS, Mrs. Catherine Victoria, ACA *2010;* with J Cleverdons Limited, 7 The Broadway, BROADSTAIRS, KENT, CT10 2AD.

GRIFFITHS, Mr. Charles Alexander, BA FCA *1973;* Monsoon Marketing Ltd, 63 Teignmouth Road, CLEVEDON, AVON, BS21 6DL.

GRIFFITHS, Mr. Charles De Beaufort, BA FCA *1975;* Red Lodge, Warren Road, KINGSTON UPON THAMES, SURREY, KT2 7HN.

GRIFFITHS, Mr. Charles Robert, BSc(Hons) ACA *2002;* 1a Swindell Road, STOURBRIDGE, DY9 0TN.

GRIFFITHS, Mr. Charles William, BSc ACA *1994;* 50 Conisboro Avenue, Caversham, READING, RG4 7JE.

GRIFFITHS, Mr. Christopher Huw, MEng BSc ACA *1999;* Ty Mefus Pentwyn Road, TREHARRIS, CF46 5BS.

GRIFFITHS, Mr. Christopher Thomas, FCA *1975;* 87 Woden Avenue, Stanway, COLCHESTER, CO3 0QY.

GRIFFITHS, Miss. Clare Ilona, BA(Hons) ACA *2009;* Riggindale, Roods Drive, Kirkoswald, PENRITH, CUMBRIA, CA10 1EH.

GRIFFITHS, Ms. Clare Imogen, BSc ACA *1986;* 17 Broxbourne Road, ORPINGTON, KENT, BR6 0AZ.

GRIFFITHS, Mr. Clive Thomas, BSc ACA *1991;* 5932 West Hedgehog Place, PHOENIX, AZ 85083, UNITED STATES.

GRIFFITHS, Mr. Colin, BSc ACA *1979;* Murata Electronics UK Ltd Oak House, Harvest Crescent, FLEET, GU51 2QW.

GRIFFITHS, Mr. Cromar William, MA ACA *2009;* Tower 2, 211 Sussex Street, SYDNEY, NSW 2000, AUSTRALIA.

GRIFFITHS, Mr. Damian, BA ACA *1989;* 57 Rosendale Road, West Dulwich, LONDON, SE21 8DY.

GRIFFITHS, Mr. Daniel Liam, ACA *2011;* 45 Kilby Road, STEVENAGE, HERTFORDSHIRE, SG1 2LT.

GRIFFITHS, Mr. Darryll Hurst, FCA *1972;* 45 Archers Court Road, Whitfield, DOVER, CT16 3HS.

•**GRIFFITHS, Mr. David, BA ACA** *1988;* DPC Accountants Limited, Vernon Road, STOKE-ON-TRENT, ST4 2QY. See also The DPC Group Limited

•**GRIFFITHS, Mr. David, BA FCA** *1977;* (Tax Fac), David Griffiths, Westville, Ober Road, BROCKENHURST, SO42 7ST. See also Profitplus Corporate Services Limited

GRIFFITHS, Mr. David Alexander, BA(Hons) ACA *2001;* 196 Riverside Road, ST. ALBANS, HERTFORDSHIRE, AL1 1SF.

GRIFFITHS, Mr. David Alexander, FCA *1965;* 54 Abbots Lane, KENLEY, CR8 5JH.

GRIFFITHS, Mr. David Charles, MA FCA *1978;* Hoye, Clenches Farm Lane, SEVENOAKS, TN13 2LX.

GRIFFITHS, Mr. David Colin, BA FCA *1961;* 9 Parklands, Corntown, BRIDGEND, Mid Glamorgan, CF35 5BE. (Life Member)

•**GRIFFITHS, Mr. David Gale, BA FCA** *1965;* RFW Rutherfords Ltd, Ardenham Court, Oxford Road, AYLESBURY, BUCKINGHAMSHIRE, HP19 8HT.

GRIFFITHS, Mr. David George, BSc FCA *1976;* 3 The Paddock, Baildon, SHIPLEY, BD17 7LL.

GRIFFITHS, Mr. David Graham, FCA *1966;* Bryn Croft, 40 Hastings Road, BATTLE, EAST SUSSEX, TN33 0TE. (Life Member)

GRIFFITHS, Mr. David Henry Clifton, FCA *1958;* 3 Phoebe Lane, Wavendon, MILTON KEYNES, MK17 8LR. (Life Member)

GRIFFITHS, Mr. David Howard, BA ACA *1979;* 10 Canon Street, Islington, LONDON, N1 7DB.

GRIFFITHS, Mr. David James, ACA *2009;* Flat 310, 9 Steedman Street, LONDON, SE17 3BA.

GRIFFITHS, Mr. David John, FCA *1969;* Mayfield, Windsor Lane, Wooburn Green, HIGH WYCOMBE, BUCKINGHAMSHIRE, HP10 0EG.

GRIFFITHS, Mr. David Kenneth Rannie, FCA *1969;* The Red House, 38 Victoria Street, Earls Barton, NORTHAMPTON, NN6 0LJ.

GRIFFITHS, Mr. David Lawrence, BA ACA *2007;* 7 Hunter Close, LONDON, SW12 8EQ.

GRIFFITHS, Mr. David Morgan, PhD FCA *1976;* 21 Adbolton Grove, West Bridgford, NOTTINGHAM, NG2 5AR.

•**GRIFFITHS, Mr. David Morley Arthur, BA FCA** *1993;* (Tax Fac), Griffiths Limited, Number One, 272 Kensington High Street, LONDON, W8 6ND.

GRIFFITHS, Mr. David Norris, FCA *1965;* 27 Somerville Road, SUTTON COLDFIELD, B73 6HH. (Life Member)

•**GRIFFITHS, Mr. David Philip, FCA CTA** *1975;* Griffiths & James Limited, Suite 5, Brecon House, Llantarnam Park, CWMBRAN, NP44 3AB.

GRIFFITHS, Mr. David Richard, BA ACA *1991;* 47 Templeoak Drive, Wollaton, NOTTINGHAM, NG8 2SF.

GRIFFITHS, Mr. David Thomas, FCA *1974;* with Copson Grandfield Ltd, 30-31 St James Place, Mangotsfield, BRISTOL, BS16 9JB.

GRIFFITHS, Mr. David William, BSc ACA *1990;* 4 Munster Road, TEDDINGTON, TW11 9LL.

GRIFFITHS, Mr. David William, FCA *1960;* 23 Green Acre, Great Waldingfield, SUDBURY, SUFFOLK, CO10 0SB. (Life Member)

GRIFFITHS, Mr. David Wyn, MA ACA *2001;* 4 Station Cottages, Trafford Road, GREAT MISSENDEN, BUCKINGHAMSHIRE, HP16 0BT.

•**GRIFFITHS, Mrs. Deborah, ACA** *1989;* (Tax Fac), Deloitte LLP, 2 New Street Square, LONDON, EC4A 3BZ. See also Deloitte & Touche LLP

GRIFFITHS, Mrs. Debra Jane, BA ACA *1993;* with BW Macfarlane LLP, 3 Temple Square, LIVERPOOL, L2 5BA.

GRIFFITHS, Miss. Denise Colette, BA ACA *1995;* Retail Manager Solutions Ltd, Castle Malwood, Minstead, LYNDHURST, HAMPSHIRE, SO43 7PE.

GRIFFITHS, Mr. Derrick Neil, BSc ACA *1989;* Stanley House, Douglass Grange Blakewater House, Phoenix Park, BLACKBURN, BB1 5RW.

GRIFFITHS, Mr. Dilwyn, ACA *2005;* 12 Gadsden Terrace, Success, PERTH, WA 6164, AUSTRALIA.

•**GRIFFITHS, Mr. Dorian Lyn, FCA** *1979;* (Tax Fac), O'Brien & Partners, 7A Nevill Street, ABERGAVENNY, GWENT, NP7 5AA. See also VAOB Group Limited

GRIFFITHS, Miss. Ella Kay Yvonne, BA ACA *1988;* 34 Lodge Gate, Great Linford, MILTON KEYNES, MK14 5EW.

GRIFFITHS, Mr. Elliot, JP FCA *1969;* 12 Stanley Place, Cadoxton, NEATH, SA10 8BE. (Life Member)

•**GRIFFITHS, Mr. Emlyn, FCA** *1967;* Griffith Williams & Co, 36 Stryd Fawr, PWLLHELI, LL53 5RT.

GRIFFITHS, Miss. Frances Elanor, BA(Hons) ACA ACCA *2002;* 42 Intake Road, PUDSEY, LS28 9BZ.

GRIFFITHS, Mrs. Frances Mary Henrietta, BSc ACA *1981;* Qinetiq, A8 Room GO26, Cody Technology Park, Old Ively Road, FARNBOROUGH, HAMPSHIRE GU14 0LX.

GRIFFITHS, Mr. Gareth David, ACA *2002;* 33 Tennant Street, NUNEATON, WARWICKSHIRE, CV11 4NT.

GRIFFITHS, Mr. Geoffrey, BSc FCA *1981;* Paddock House Paddock Lane, Dunham Massey, ALTRINCHAM, WA14 5RP.

•**GRIFFITHS, Mr. Gwyn James, BSc FCA** *1991;* Deloitte LLP, Hill House, 1 Little New Street, LONDON, EC4A 3TR. See also Deloitte & Touche LLP

GRIFFITHS, Mr. Haydn, ACA *2011;* Rye Salters, Horsley Road, Downside, COBHAM, SURREY, KT11 3NY.

GRIFFITHS, Miss. Hazel Jayne, ACA *2009;* 3 Granville Way, Brightlingsea, COLCHESTER, CO7 0SY.

GRIFFITHS, Mrs. Helen Elizabeth, BSc ACA *2005;* Mitchells & Butlers Retail Ltd, 27 Fleet Street, BIRMINGHAM, B3 1JP.

GRIFFITHS, Mr. Howard Rhidian, FCA *1967;* Hillfield Cottage, Danzey Green, Henley-In-Arden, SOLIHULL, B94 5BG.

GRIFFITHS, Mr. Howell James, FCA *1951;* 6 Robin Hill, DINAS POWYS, CF64 4TF. (Life Member)

GRIFFITHS, Mr. Ian Charles, BA ACA *1987;* 24 Glebe Court, Highfield, SOUTHAMPTON, SO17 1RH.

•**GRIFFITHS, Mr. Ian Robert, BSc ACA** *2000;* with KPMG LLP, 15 Canada Square, LONDON, E14 5GL.

GRIFFITHS, Mr. Ian Ward, MA ACA *1991;* 1 Rhymers Gate, Wyton, HUNTINGDON, PE28 2JR.

GRIFFITHS, Dr. Ieuan Wynn, PhD MA MSc FCA *1980;* 53 Cyncoed Road, CARDIFF, CF23 5SB.

•**GRIFFITHS, Mr. Iwan James Lawrence, BA ACA** *1998;* PricewaterhouseCoopers LLP, 7 More London Riverside, LONDON, SE1 2RT. See also PricewaterhouseCoopers

GRIFFITHS, Mr. James Reginald Eric, BSc(Hons) ACA *2001;* Hatsford, Aylton, LEDBURY, HR8 2QJ.

GRIFFITHS, Mr. Jeffrey, BA FCA *1974;* 50 Sir Geroge, STOUFFVILLE L4A 1P7, ON, CANADA.

GRIFFITHS, Mrs. Jennifer Ann, BSc ACA DChA *2000;* with PricewaterhouseCoopers LLP, First Point, Buckingham Gate, London Gatwick Airport, GATWICK, WEST SUSSEX RH6 0NT.

GRIFFITHS, Mrs. Jennifer Louise, BA ACA *2011;* 23 Plattbrook Close, MANCHESTER, M14 7AZ.
•GRIFFITHS, Mrs. Jill, BA(Hons) ACA *2001;* Insight NE, The Exchange, Manor Court, Jesmond, NEWCASTLE UPON TYNE, NE2 2JA. See also Insightne
GRIFFITHS, Miss. Joanna, BSc(Econ) ACA *2004;* 35 Morgan Street, LONDON, E3 5AA.
GRIFFITHS, Mr. John Adrian, FCA FCT *1964;* Highwell, Warborough Road, Letcombe Regis, WANTAGE, OX12 9LE.
GRIFFITHS, Mr. John Francis, BSc FCA *1978;* 75 Steli Avenue, CANVEY ISLAND, ESSEX, SS8 9QF.
GRIFFITHS, Mr. John Martin, BA FCA *1987;* 243 Burnt Ash Lane, BROMLEY, BR1 5DL.
GRIFFITHS, Mr. John Peter, BSc ACA *1980;* 93 Hazlemere Road, Penn, HIGH WYCOMBE, HP10 8AF.
•GRIFFITHS, Mr. John Price, BSc FCA *1993;* Peacheys CA Limited, Lanyon House, Mission Court, NEWPORT, GWENT, NP20 2DW.
GRIFFITHS, Mr. John Tibbott, FCA *1967;* Garth, School Lane, Hawthorn, PONTYPRIDD, CF37 5AL. (Life Member)
GRIFFITHS, Mr. Jolyon David Hewer, BSc FCA *1986;* (Tax Fac), Hazard Chase, 6 Lawrence Ave, Stanstead Abbotts, WARE, SG12 8JL.
GRIFFITHS, Mr. Jonathan Charles, BSc ACA *1979;* 42 Beulah Road, LONDON, E17 9LQ.
GRIFFITHS, Mr. Jonathan Mark, BA ACA *1999;* Darling Park Tower 2, 201 Sussex Street, SYDNEY, NSW 1171, AUSTRALIA.
GRIFFITHS, Mr. Jonathan Neil, MSc BA ACA *1997;* North Somerset Council, Town Hall, WESTON-SUPER-MARE, AVON, BS23 1UJ.
GRIFFITHS, Mr. Jonathan Wynn, BSc ACA *1986;* 7 Llantarnam Drive, Radyr, CARDIFF, CF15 8GA.
GRIFFITHS, Mr. Joseph Tristam, ACA *2008;* Flat 10 Eastry House, Hartington Road, LONDON, SW8 2HU.
GRIFFITHS, Mrs. Judith Mary, BA ACA *1992;* Somercotes, 18a Church Way, Grendon, NORTHAMPTON, NN7 1JE.
GRIFFITHS, Mrs. Julia Clare, BA ACA *1979;* (Tax Fac), Bowling Green Cottage, The Southend, LEDBURY, HR8 2HD.
GRIFFITHS, Dr. Julian Peter, BEng ACA *2003;* with PricewaterhouseCoopers, 2 Southbank Boulevard, Southbank, MELBOURNE, VIC 3006, AUSTRALIA.
GRIFFITHS, Mr. Julian Torquil, MA FCA *1977;* Life Sciences Research Ltd, Woolley Road, Alconbury, HUNTINGDON, PE28 4HS.
GRIFFITHS, Miss. Karen, BSc ACA *1993;* Willesden Cottage, Hollow Lane, Kingsley, FRODSHAM, WA6 6TX.
GRIFFITHS, Mr. Karl Mark, BSc ACA *2001;* 44 Clare Croft, Middleton, MILTON KEYNES, MK10 9HD.
GRIFFITHS, Mrs. Katharine Louise, BA(Hons) ACA *2002;* 1a Swindell Road, STOURBRIDGE, WEST MIDLANDS, DY9 0TN.
GRIFFITHS, Mrs. Katherine Laura, BA ACA *2004;* 44 Alma Road, ST. ALBANS, HERTFORDSHIRE, AL1 3BL.
GRIFFITHS, Mr. Keith, BSc FCA *1981;* 32 Tulip Way, LEEK, STAFFORDSHIRE, ST13 7AX.
GRIFFITHS, Miss. Kerry Emma, BSc ACA *2006;* Manor Cottage, Kingston Hill, KINGSTON UPON THAMES, KT2 7LN.
GRIFFITHS, Mr. Kevin Alun, BA ACA ATII *1996;* with Ernst & Young, PO Box 7878, Waterfront Place, 1 Eagle Street, BRISBANE, QLD 4001 AUSTRALIA.
GRIFFITHS, Mr. Kevin Roy, BSc ACA *1990;* 179 Vicarage Road, WATFORD, WD18 0HA.
GRIFFITHS, Miss. Laura, BCom ACA *2006;* 169 Boston Manor Road, BRENTFORD, MIDDLESEX, TW8 9LE.
GRIFFITHS, Mrs. Laura Elizabeth, BA ACA *2004;* 4 Holmes Close, East Dulwich, LONDON, SE22 9AR.
GRIFFITHS, Mr. Leslie Trevor, FCA *1975;* Frogson Waste Management Ltd, 20 Douglas Road, SHEFFIELD, S3 9SA.
GRIFFITHS, Mrs. Lisa-Marie, LLB ACA *2001;* Zurcherstrasse 73, 8142 UITIKON WALDEGG, SWITZERLAND.
GRIFFITHS, Miss. Louise Patricia, MChem ACA *2006;* Macquarie Bank, Citypoint, 1 Ropemaker Street, LONDON, EC2Y 9HD.
GRIFFITHS, Mrs. Margaret Denise, BA FCA *1972;* 38 Peterborough Close, ASHTON-UNDER-LYNE, OL6 8XW.
GRIFFITHS, Mr. Mark, BSc ACA CTA *2004;* 67 Harley Road, SALE, CHESHIRE, M33 7EP.
GRIFFITHS, Mr. Mark Andrew, BA ACA *1997;* 6 The Copse, Burley In Wharfedale, ILKLEY, LS29 7QY.
•GRIFFITHS, Mr. Mark Foster, BA FCA *1997;* Dyke Yaxley Limited, 1 Brassey Road, Old Potts Way, SHREWSBURY, SY3 7FA.
GRIFFITHS, Mr. Mark Frank, BA ACA *1991;* Croft Top Barn, Higham, BURNLEY, LANCASHIRE, BB12 9LX.
GRIFFITHS, Mr. Mark Howard, LLB ACA *1994;* Somercotes, 18A Church Way, Grendon, NORTHAMPTON, NORTHAMPTONSHIRE, NN7 1JE.
•GRIFFITHS, Mr. Martin William, BA ACA *1987;* Downspark Consulting Limited, 8 Norland Road, Clifton, BRISTOL, BS8 3LP.
GRIFFITHS, Mr. Michael John, BA FCA *1981;* 59 Sandridge Road, ST. ALBANS, AL1 4AG.
GRIFFITHS, Mr. Michael John, BMus ACA *1993;* 1271 Highland Road, SANTA YNEZ, CA 93460, UNITED STATES.
GRIFFITHS, Mr. Michael John, BSc ACA *1990;* 21 Adams Avenue, TURRAMURRA, NSW 2074, AUSTRALIA.
GRIFFITHS, Mr. Michael Thomas, BA FCA *1973;* The Dell, Fall Birch Road, Lostock, BOLTON, BL6 4LF.
GRIFFITHS, Mr. Nathan, LLB(Hons) ACA *2011;* 44 Beaufort Avenue, Langland, SWANSEA, SA3 4PB.
GRIFFITHS, Miss. Nicola Marie, BSc ACA *2010;* 7 Rheidol Drive, BARRY, SOUTH GLAMORGAN, CF62 7HA.
GRIFFITHS, Mr. Nigel George, LLB ACA *1991;* 17 Windsor Clive Drive, Rhyd Cafer, CARDIFF, CF5 6HQ.
GRIFFITHS, Mrs. Nina, BA ACA *2005;* Bryn Glas, Penybontfawr, OSWESTRY, SHROPSHIRE, SY10 0EW.
GRIFFITHS, Mr. Norman James, BSc FCA *1975;* High Pines, Pinewood Road, Ash, ALDERSHOT, GU12 6DG.
GRIFFITHS, Mr. Paul, BSc ACA *2002;* PricewaterhouseCoopers LLP, Fourth Floor One National Life Drive, MONTPELIER, VT 05604, UNITED STATES.
GRIFFITHS, Mr. Paul David, BA ACA *1995;* ZUERCHERSTRASSE 73, 8142 UITIKON WALDEGG, SWITZERLAND.
•GRIFFITHS, Mr. Paul David, FCA *1987;* Hepworth Griffiths, 47/49 Grove Street, RETFORD, NOTTINGHAMSHIRE, DN22 6LA.
GRIFFITHS, Mrs. Paula Jane, BSocSc ACA *1992;* 2 Radlett Park Road, RADLETT, WD7 7BQ.
GRIFFITHS, Mr. Peter Anthony, FCA *1971;* 62 The Albany, 8 Old Hall Street, LIVERPOOL, L3 9EL. (Life Member)
GRIFFITHS, Mr. Peter Brian, FCA *1973;* Osprey House, 4 Lakeside View, Ingbirchworth, SHEFFIELD, S36 7EX.
GRIFFITHS, Mr. Peter Charles, BA ACA ACII *1984;* Domestic & General Services Ltd Swan Court, 11 Worple Road, LONDON, SW19 4JS.
GRIFFITHS, Mr. Peter David, FCA *1971;* 7 Compton Close, REDDITCH, WORCESTERSHIRE, B98 7NL.
GRIFFITHS, Mr. Peter David, BA ACA *1986;* 107 Park Road, Chiswick, LONDON, W4 3ER.
GRIFFITHS, Mr. Peter Dudley, FCA *1951;* Lawnswood, Aberhafesp, NEWTOWN, SY16 3HL. (Life Member)
GRIFFITHS, Mr. Peter John, BSc(Econ) ACA *1999;* 2 April Glen, Mayow Road, LONDON, SE23 2XP.
•GRIFFITHS, Mr. Peter John, BSc FCA *1979;* Ernst & Young, P.O. Box 140, MANAMA, BAHRAIN.
GRIFFITHS, Mr. Peter John, MSc BA ACA *2005;* Microloan Foundation, 10 Barley Mow Passage, LONDON, W4 4PH.
GRIFFITHS, Mr. Peter Lowden, BCom FCA *1965;* 67 Gloucester Place, LONDON, W1U 8JL. (Life Member)
GRIFFITHS, Mr. Peter Neil, BSc FCA *1972;* 20 The Laurels, Potten End, BERKHAMSTED, HP4 2SP. (Life Member)
•GRIFFITHS, Mr. Peter Williams, BSc ACA *1984;* (Tax Fac), Alexander Partnership, Barclays Bank Chambers, 18 High Street, TENBY, PEMBROKESHIRE, SA70 7HD.
GRIFFITHS, Mr. Philip Cartwright, FCA *1975;* Business Risk Management Ltd, PO Box 116, ASHTON-UNDER-LYNE, LANCASHIRE, OL6 8YX.
GRIFFITHS, Mr. Philip David, BSc ACA *1992;* Glenbrook Cottage Glenbrook Wagon Lane, HOOK, HAMPSHIRE, RG27 9EJ.
GRIFFITHS, Mr. Philip John, BA FCA *1972;* 11 Bury Road, POOLE, DORSET, BH13 7DD.
•GRIFFITHS, Mr. Philip Leslie, BA FCA DChA *1988;* Mitchell Charlesworth, 5 Temple Square, Temple Street, LIVERPOOL, L2 5RH.
GRIFFITHS, Miss. Philippa, BSc ACA *2011;* 48 Maidendale Road, KINGSWINFORD, WEST MIDLANDS, DY6 9DD.
•GRIFFITHS, Mr. Rhys Gwyn Selyf, MEng ACA *2005;* Dolydd, Chwilog, PWLLHELI, LL53 6NX.
GRIFFITHS, Mr. Richard Denis, BSc(Hons) ACA *2003;* with Grant Thornton UK LLP, Enterprise House, 115 Edmund Street, BIRMINGHAM, B3 2HJ.
GRIFFITHS, Mr. Richard George, FCA *1971;* 112 Blackgate Lane, Tarleton, PRESTON, PR4 6UT.
GRIFFITHS, Mr. Richard Mark, BA ACA *1984;* 250 Howe Street Suite 700, VANCOUVER V6C 3S7, BC, CANADA.
GRIFFITHS, Mr. Richard Owen, Bsc(Hons) ACA *2009;* Top Floor Flat, 103 Ravenslea Road, LONDON, SW12 8RT.
GRIFFITHS, Mr. Richard Whitelaw, FCA *1970;* Route de Chanivaz 18, 1164 BUCHILLON, SWITZERLAND. (Life Member)
GRIFFITHS, Mr. Robert Ernest, BA ACA *1980;* Flat 7 Dovedale Gardens, 465 Battersea Park Road, LONDON, SW11 4LR.
GRIFFITHS, Mr. Robert Frederick, FCA *1954;* (Member of Council 1969 - 1975), 13 St. Marys Road, Harborne, BIRMINGHAM, B17 0EY. (Life Member)
GRIFFITHS, Mr. Robert James, FCA *1977;* 3 Westlook, Carlton Road, CARLTON, BB 24030, BARBADOS.
•GRIFFITHS, Mr. Robert John, BA FCA *1995;* Anavrin Limited, 51 Penyston Road, MAIDENHEAD, BERKSHIRE, SL6 6EJ.
GRIFFITHS, Mr. Robert John, BSc ACA *1996;* 45 Abingdon Road, Standlake, WITNEY, OXFORDSHIRE, OX29 7QH.
GRIFFITHS, Mr. Robert Mark, FCA *1977;* 4 Aveland Park Road, CALLANDER, FK17 8FD.
GRIFFITHS, Mr. Robin David, BEng FCA *1997;* PetroSantander Colombia Inc, Calle 70 No 7-60 Oficina 601, BOGOTA, COLOMBIA.
GRIFFITHS, Mr. Rodney James, FCA *1973;* 8 Little Dene Copse Pennington, LYMINGTON, HAMPSHIRE, SO41 8EW.
GRIFFITHS, Mr. Roger Murray, BCom FCA *1967;* 19 Pinegarth, Darras Hall, Ponteland, NEWCASTLE UPON TYNE, NE20 9LF. (Life Member)
GRIFFITHS, Mrs. Rose Hilary, BSc ACA ATII *1990;* Serco Ltd, Serco House, 16 Bartley Wood Business Park, Bartley Way, HOOK, HAMPSHIRE RG27 9UY.
GRIFFITHS, Mrs. Rosemarie Ann, ACA *1995;* 5 Derby Road, SURBITON, SURREY, KT5 9AY.
GRIFFITHS, Miss. Sarah, BCom ACA *2007;* Flat 40 Merchants House, Collington Street, LONDON, SE10 9LX.
•GRIFFITHS, Mrs. Sarah Jane, ACA MAAT *2001;* SJ Griffiths Consultancy, 16 Glenfield Close, SUTTON COLDFIELD, WEST MIDLANDS, B76 1LD.
GRIFFITHS, Mr. Scott, BA ACA *2001;* 2535 Pathway Ave, SIMI VALLEY, CA 93063, UNITED STATES.
GRIFFITHS, Mrs. Sian, BSc ACA *2006;* Control Techniques Plc, The Gro, Pool Road, NEWTOWN, POWYS, SY16 3BE.
GRIFFITHS, Mr. Simon, ACA CA(SA) *2010;* 7B Acton Street, LONDON, WC1X 9LX.
•GRIFFITHS, Mr. Simon, BSc FCA *1982;* Guy Walmsley & Co, 3 Grove Road, WREXHAM, LL11 1DY.
GRIFFITHS, Mr. Simon Graham, BSc ACA *1995;* 2 Archer Road, PENARTH, CF64 3LS.
GRIFFITHS, Mr. Simon Martin, BA ACA *1988;* Reciproca, 6 Grove Avenue, LONDON, N10 2AR.
GRIFFITHS, Mr. Sion Dyfri, BA ACA *2009;* Carnedd y Gors, Glandyfi, MACHYNLLETH, POWYS, SY20 8SS.
GRIFFITHS, Mr. Stephen, FCA *1978;* (Tax Fac), 78 Porlock Gardens, Nailsea, BRISTOL, BS48 2QZ.
•GRIFFITHS, Mr. Stephen Clive, FCA *1977;* (Tax Fac), Seahurst Limited, 156 Bath Road, SOUTHSEA, HAMPSHIRE, PO4 0HU.
GRIFFITHS, Mr. Stephen David, BSc ACA *1993;* 1351 NW 139th Ave, PEMBROKE PINES, FL 33028, UNITED STATES.
GRIFFITHS, Mr. Stephen Nigel John, BSc ACA *1997;* Rothschild, 1 Park Row, LEEDS, LS1 5AB.
GRIFFITHS, Mr. Stephen Peter, ACA *1984;* 6 Brambling Road, HORSHAM, RH13 6AY.
GRIFFITHS, Mr. Timothy John, BSc FCA MSI *1973;* 1904 Dusit Thani, Sheikh Zayed Road, P O Box 23335, DUBAI, UNITED ARAB EMIRATES.
GRIFFITHS, Mr. Tom, BSc ACA *2006;* McGrathNicol, Level 31, 60 Margaret Street, SYDNEY, NSW 2000, AUSTRALIA.
GRIFFITHS, Mr. Trevor Richard Arthur, MA ACA *1985;* Flanes Wood Cottage Stone Street, Seal, SEVENOAKS, TN15 0LQ.
•GRIFFITHS, Mr. Vaughan Wynne, BSc FCA *1981;* DNG Dove Naish, Eagle House, 28 Billing Road, NORTHAMPTON, NN1 5AJ.
GRIFFITHS, Mr. William Paul, FCA *1977;* 14 Loire Mews, HARPENDEN, HERTFORDSHIRE, AL5 1DR.
GRIFFITHS, Miss. Zoe Georgina, BA ACA *2006;* Flat 168 Leamore Court, 1 Meath Crescent, LONDON, E2 0QQ.
GRIGG, Mrs. Ann Jane, BA ACA *1999;* 35 Hermitage Way, KENILWORTH, WARWICKSHIRE, CV8 2DW.
GRIGG, Miss. Annelisa Edwina, MA MPhil ACA *1999;* 243 Barton Road, Comberton, CAMBRIDGE, CB23 7BU.
GRIGG, Mr. Brian Maurice, FCA *1963;* Greenhayn, Coggeshall Road, Feering, COLCHESTER, CO5 9QX.
GRIGG, Miss. Elizabeth Alexandra, BSc(Hons) ACA *2000;* 29 Charles Road, DEAL, CT14 9AT.
GRIGG, Mr. Jamie, ACA *2011;* 86 Colombo Square, Worsdell Drive, GATESHEAD, TYNE AND WEAR, NE8 2DF.
GRIGG, Miss. Jean Margaret, BSc ACA *1993;* (Tax Fac), 3 Thistledown, Walmer, DEAL, KENT, CT14 7XE.
GRIGG, Mrs. Julie Marie, BA FCA *1985;* 65 Rose Hill Park West, SUTTON, SURREY, SM1 3LA.
GRIGG, Ms. Lynne, BA ACA *1992;* The Holt, Chirk Bank, WREXHAM, CLWYD, LL14 5BU.
GRIGG, Mr. Robert Neil, BSc ACA *2008;* (Tax Fac), Burrow Farm, Broadclyst, EXETER, EX5 3JA.
GRIGG, Mr. Simon Kennedy, ACA *1980;* James Villa Holidays Ltd, 20/20 Business Park, St. Leonards Road, Allington, MAIDSTONE, KENT ME16 0LS.
GRIGGS, Mr. Adam Benjamin, LLB ACA *2003;* 5 Hillgarth Court, Elvington, YORK, YO41 4BD.
•GRIGGS, Mr. Andrew John Quentin, BA FCA CF *1990;* Reeves & Co LLP, Montague Place, Quayside, Chatham Maritime, CHATHAM, KENT ME4 4QU.
GRIGGS, Mrs. Angela Louise, BA ACA *2004;* 37 Roach Vale, COLCHESTER, CO4 3YN.
•GRIGGS, Mr. Geoffrey John, BSc FCA MSI *1978;* (Tax Fac), Geoffrey J. Griggs, 66 Lynwood Grove, ORPINGTON, KENT, BR6 0BH.
•GRIGGS, Mrs. Julie Anita, BSc FCA *1990;* (Tax Fac), Levicks, West Hill, 61 London Road, MAIDSTONE, ME16 8TX.
GRIGGS, Mrs. Karolina Catherine Alexandra, BA ACA *1994;* The Coach House, Abbots Hill, Ospringe, FAVERSHAM, KENT, ME13 0RR.
GRIGGS, Mr. Keith Graham, MA ACA *1983;* 89 Lammasmead, BROXBOURNE, HERTFORDSHIRE, EN10 6PG.
GRIGGS, Mr. Kenneth Donald, FCA *1976;* Les Floralies, 3 ave de Grande-Bretagne, 98000 MONTE CARLO, MONACO.
GRIGGS, Mr. Leonard Sidney, FCA *1956;* Whisperwood, Cullwood Lane, NEW MILTON, BH25 5QJ. (Life Member)
GRIGGS, Mr. Martyn Steven, BTech ACA *1980;* 19 Alexa Close NW, CALGARY T3R 1B9, AB, CANADA.
•GRIGGS, Mr. Neil Graham, BSc FCA *1995;* Kinetic Partners Audit LLP, One London Wall, Level 10, LONDON, EC2Y 5HB.
•GRIGGS, Mr. Nigel Paul, FCA *1981;* Carlton Haines Ltd, Carlton House, 28/29 Carlton Terrace, Portslade, BRIGHTON, BN41 1XF.
•GRIGGS, Mr. Richard Vincent, FCA *1988;* Lancasters (Accountants) Ltd, Manor Courtyard, Aston Sandford, Nr Haddenham, AYLESBURY, HP17 8JB.
GRIGGS, Mr. Simon John, BSc ACA *1989;* The London Stock Exchange, 10 Paternoster Square, LONDON, EC4M 7LS.
•GRIGGS, Mr. Stephen, BSc FCA *1990;* Deloitte LLP, 2 New Street Square, LONDON, EC4A 3BZ. See also Deloitte & Touche LLP
•GRIGGS, Mr. Stuart Arthur, FCA *1974;* (Tax Fac), Stuart A. Griggs, 99 High Street, Yatton, BRISTOL, BS49 4DR.
GRIGORIEV, Mr. Anton, ACA *2010;* 77 Building 1, Sadovnicheskaya, Moscow, 115035 MOSCOW, RUSSIAN FEDERATION.
GRIGSBY, Mrs. Susan Jayne, BSc ACA *2006;* Berry Lodge, Crawley Ridge, CAMBERLEY, SURREY, GU15 2AJ.
GRIGSON, Mr. David John, BA ACA *1979;* 16 Maple Road, HARPENDEN, HERTFORDSHIRE, AL5 2DU.
GRIGSON, Miss. Eleanor, BA(Hons) ACA *2001;* Al Attar Business Tower, Sheikh Zayed Road, DUBAI, 9267, UNITED ARAB EMIRATES.
GRILLO, Mr. Nicola Donatello, BA ACA *2003;* 183 Farnaby Road, BROMLEY, BR2 0BA.
GRILLS, Mr. Michael Louis, BA FCA *1999;* 17 Admirals Walk, GREENHITHE, DA9 9QP.
•GRILLS, Mr. Oliver James, BMus ACA *2003;* Lonsdale & Marsh, Orleans House, Edmund Street, LIVERPOOL, L3 9NG.
•GRIMBLY, Mr. Andrew Edgar, BA ACA *1997;* PricewaterhouseCoopers LLP, Savannah House, 3 Ocean Way, Ocean Village, SOUTHAMPTON, SO14 3TJ. See also PricewaterhouseCoopers
GRIMDITCH, Mr. Andrew Richard, BA ACA *1997;* Waste Recycling Group, 900 Pavilion Drive, NORTHAMPTON, NN4 7RG.
GRIMDITCH, Miss. Katherine, ACA *2011;* Flat 12, Medland House, 11 Branch Road, LONDON, E14 7JT.

GRIMDITCH, Mr. Kenneth Frederick, FCA *1962;* 23 Fieldhead Paddock, Boston Spa, WETHERBY, LS23 6SA. (Life Member)
GRIMDITCH, Mr. Mark, MSc ACA *1981;* Apartment 62, Eaton House, 38 Westferry Circus, LONDON, E14 8RN.
GRIMDITCH, Mrs. Sandra Joyce, BSc ACA MBA *1980;* Apartment 62, Eaton House, 38 Westferry Circus, LONDON, E14 8RN.
GRIME, Mr. Geoffrey John, FCA *1969;* Pine Farm, La Rue Des Landes, St. Mary, JERSEY, JE3 3EE.
GRIME, Mr. Jeremy Peter, ACA *1992;* Amber Court Chart Hill Road, Chart Sutton, MAIDSTONE, ME17 3RQ.
GRIME, Miss. Julia Margaret, LLB ACA *1990;* 40 Stockton Road, Chorlton, MANCHESTER, M21 9ED.
GRIMES, Mr. Darren Samuel, BA(Hons) ACA CTA AMCT *2003;* Deloitte LLP Horton House Exchange Flags, LIVERPOOL, L2 3PG.
GRIMES, Mr. David, BA FCA *1976;* DG Shipping Ltd, Lowland House, Gellibrands FCA, Shire Lane, Chalfont St. Peter, GERRARDS CROSS SL9 0QY.
GRIMES, Mr. David, BA ACA *1990;* 64 Lingmoor Drive, BURNLEY, BB12 8UY.
GRIMES, Mr. David Peter Justus, BA ACA ATII *1993;* Knauf Insulation Ltd, PO Box 10, Stafford Road, ST. HELENS, MERSEYSIDE, WA10 3NS.
GRIMES, Mr. Dominic, ACA *2010;* 11 Chadbury Close, Lostock, BOLTON, BL6 4JA.
•**GRIMES, Mr. Kenneth John, MSc FCA** *1982;* J M J Accountancy, 10 Watermark Way Foxholes Business Park, HERTFORD, SG13 7TZ.
GRIMES, Ms. Leonie Sophie, MA FCA CF *1991;* with Deloitte LLP, Athene Place, 66 Shoe Lane, LONDON, EC4A 3BQ.
•**GRIMES, Mr. Malcolm Patrick, FCA** *1977;* (Tax Fac), M.P. Grimes & Co, 154a Eltham High Street, Eltham, LONDON, SE9 1BJ. See also M P Grimes & Co Ltd
•**GRIMES, Mr. Neil Christopher, BA(Econ) ACA** *1998;* PricewaterhouseCoopers LLP, 1 Embankment Place, LONDON, WC2N 6RH. See also PricewaterhouseCoopers
•**GRIMES, Mr. Nicholas John, FCA** *1977;* Nicholas J. Grimes, Spindrift, 39 Dunthorne Road, COLCHESTER, CO4 0HZ.
GRIMES, Mr. Paul Anthony, MSc FCA *1975;* Manuli Packaging UK Ltd, 6 Leafield Industrial Estate, CORSHAM, SN13 9SW.
GRIMES, Mr. Thomas Edward, FCA *1955;* Field Cottage, The Laines, Chedworth, CHELTENHAM, GLOUCESTERSHIRE, GL54 4NS. (Life Member)
GRIMLEY, Mr. Anthony Robert, FCA *1955;* 57 Balmoral Drive, Beeston, NOTTINGHAM, NG9 3FT. (Life Member)
GRIMLEY, Mr. John Clive, FCA *1958;* 12 Woburn Close, LOUGHBOROUGH, LE11 4TB. (Life Member)
•**GRIMLEY, Mr. Peter Anton Ninian, FCA** *1980;* (Tax Fac), P A N Grimley Ltd, Hillcrest, Lawrenny Road, Cresselly, KILGETTY, DYFED SA68 0TB. See also P.A. N. Grimley
•**GRIMMER, Mrs. Julie Gail, FCA DChA** *1991;* (Tax Fac), Larking Gowen, King Street House, 15 Upper King Street, NORWICH, NR3 1RB. See also Larking Gowen Limited
GRIMMETT, Mrs. Alison Tina, BSc ACA *1999;* 5 The Rise, CROWTHORNE, RG45 6EJ.
GRIMMETT, Mr. Andrew, BSc ACA *1992;* 14 Kings Walk, SINGAPORE 268027, SINGAPORE.
GRIMSDELL, Mr. Colin Raymond, BSc ACA *1990;* Grayrigg, Mill Hill Lane, Winshill, BURTON-ON-TRENT, STAFFORDSHIRE, DE15 0BB.
•**GRIMSDELL, Mrs. Helen Margaret, BA FCA** *1990;* (Tax Fac), Brieley Grimsdell Ltd, 12 James Street, Kimberley, NOTTINGHAM, NG16 2LP.
•**GRIMSDELL, Mr. Michael Henry, BA FCA ATII** *1969;* Grimsdell & Co, P.O. Box 8080, Sitteen Street, RIYADH, 11482, SAUDI ARABIA.
GRIMSDICK, Mr. Nicholas Alexander, BSc ACA *2008;* Apartment 215 Romney House, 47 Marsham Street, LONDON, SW1P 3DR.
GRIMSHARE, Mr. Paul John, BSc ACA *1999;* Aviva plc, St. Helens, 1 Undershaft, LONDON, EC3P 3DQ.
GRIMSHAW, Mrs. Andrea Pamela, FCA *1977;* Sundays Hill House, Brinkworth, CHIPPENHAM, SN15 5AU.
GRIMSHAW, Mr. Andrew Michael, BA ACA *1982;* Wrengate Ltd, Wrengate House, 221 Palatine Road, MANCHESTER, M20 2EE.
GRIMSHAW, Mrs. Helen, MA(Hons) ACA *2001;* 22 Rothamsted Avenue, HARPENDEN, HERTFORDSHIRE, AL5 2DJ.
GRIMSHAW, Mrs. Jane Carol, ACA FCCA *2008;* with Ormerod Rutter Limited, The Oakley, Kidderminster Road, DROITWICH, WORCESTERSHIRE, WR9 9AY.
GRIMSHAW, Mrs. Karen Tracey, MA ACA *1996;* 5 Grantham Drive, Brandlesholme, BURY, BL8 1XW.
GRIMSHAW, Ms. Nicola, BA ACA *1988;* Apartment 602, 7 High Holborn, LONDON, WC1V 6DR.
GRIMSHAW, Mr. Norman Varcoe, FCA *1952;* 9 Huntsmans Way, Badsworth, PONTEFRACT, WF9 1BE. (Life Member)
GRIMSHAW, Ms. Paula Kirsten, MSc ACA *1994;* 56 Leopold Road, BRISTOL, BS6 5BS.
GRIMSHAW, Mr. Roger Clive, FCA *1963;* Home Farm, Tredington, TEWKESBURY, GL20 7BP. (Life Member)
GRIMSHAW, Mr. Roger Nicholas, MA ACA *1980;* 37 Belmont Court, Highbury New Park, LONDON, N5 2HA.
GRIMSHAW, Mr. Stephen Michael, BSc FCA *1977;* 3814 Great Springs Court, KATY, TX 77494, UNITED STATES.
GRIMSHAW, Mr. William George Peter, FCA *1951;* 961 Forest Road, LUGARNO, NSW 2210, AUSTRALIA. (Life Member)
GRIMSON, Mrs. Ina Denise, BA ACA *1991;* 36 Main Street, Cambusbarron, STIRLING, FK7 9NN.
•**GRIMSON, Mr. Neil Bernard Stuart, FCA** *1986;* (Tax Fac), Roy Pinnock & Co LLP, Wren House, 68 London Road, ST. ALBANS, HERTFORDSHIRE, AL1 1NG. See also Wren Accounting Ltd
•**GRIMSTER, Mr. Stuart John, ACA** *2003;* Old Mill, Number One, Goldcroft, YEOVIL, SOMERSET, BA21 4DX. See also Old Mill Accountancy LLP and Old Mill Audit LLP
GRIMSTON, Mr. Robert John Sylvester, BSc ACA *1985;* Elm Farm, Sibford Ferris, BANBURY, OX15 5AA.
•**GRIMSTONE, Mr. Andrew John, BA FCA** *1989;* Deloitte LLP, Athene Place, 66 Shoe Lane, LONDON, EC4A 3BQ. See also Deloitte & Touche LLP
GRIMSTONE, Mr. Ian Paterson, FCA *1966;* 7 Broadhurst, ASHTEAD, KT21 1QB.
GRIMSTONE, Mrs. Joanna Gabriela, BSc ACA *1992;* Rookfields, 24 Blanford Road, REIGATE, RH2 7DR.
GRIMWADE, Alfred Arthur, Esq OBE FCA *1949;* 12 Courtlands, 17 Court Downs Road, BECKENHAM, BR3 6LN. (Life Member)
GRIMWADE, Mr. Andrew Beverly, MA FCA *1978;* United Reformed Church, 86 Tavistock Place, LONDON, WC1H 9RT.
GRIMWADE, Mrs. Anne-Marie Frances, BSc ACA *2001;* New P H D Media Ltd, 5 North Crescent Chenies Street, LONDON, WC1E 7PH.
•**GRIMWADE, Mr. David Robert, FCA** *1962;* David Grimwade, Watermead, St Mary's Road, Mortimer, READING, RG7 3UE.
GRIMWADE, Mr. Michael Simon, MA ACA *1992;* 11 Ravensbourne Gardens, LONDON, W13 8EW.
GRIMWOOD, Mr. David Richard Neil, BA(Hons) ACA *2001;* Veolia Water UK Plc Kings Place 5th Floor, 90 York Way, LONDON, N1 9AG.
GRIMWOOD, Miss. Helen Victoria, BSc ACA *2006;* 50 Tottington Road, BOLTON, BL2 4BH.
GRIMWOOD, Mr. Mark Julian, FCA *1977;* 33 Presburg Road, NEW MALDEN, KT3 5AH.
GRIMWOOD, Mr. Melvyn John, BA ACA *1999;* Oak View, 3a Oxcroft, BISHOP'S STORTFORD, HERTFORDSHIRE, CM23 4AE.
GRIMWOOD, Mrs. Sally Joanne, BSc ACA *2001;* 5 Milk Hall Barns, Latimer Road, CHESHAM, BUCKINGHAMSHIRE, HP5 1QH.
GRIMWOOD, Mr. Simon Max, BEng ACA *1995;* 30 Langley Avenue, SURBITON, KT6 6QW.
GRIMWOOD, Mr. Victor Ernest, FCA *1954;* Maple Tree, Somerfield Road, London Road, MAIDSTONE, ME16 8JJ. (Life Member)
GRINAKER, Miss. Tarryn, ACA *2010;* 2 Rocklands Court, 59 Exner Avanue, Vredehoek, CAPE TOWN, WESTERN CAPE PROVINCE, 8001 SOUTH AFRICA.
GRINDAL, Mr. Christopher Richard Lancastre, BA ACA *1987;* Oxara Energy Group, 15-17 King Street, LONDON, SW1Y 6QU.
GRINDALL, Mr. Ian, BSc ACA *1991;* Goodrich Corporation, Four Coliseum Centre, 2730 West Tyvola Road, CHARLOTTE, NC 28217-4578, UNITED STATES.
GRINDELL, Mrs. Ann Caroline, FCA *1966;* 6a Victoria Place, RYDE, ISLE OF WIGHT, PO33 2PX.
•**GRINDELL, Mr. Christopher Philip, BSc ACA** *1984;* Monkton Accounting Services, Yetholmlaw House, Town Yetholm, KELSO, ROXBURGHSHIRE, TD5 8SH.
GRINDELL, Mrs. Elizabeth Margaret, BSc ACA *1991;* Yetholmlaw House, Town Yetholm, KELSO, ROXBURGHSHIRE, TD5 8SH.
•**GRINDELL, Mr. Julian Mark, BA ACA** *1989;* 1 Long Close, Lower Stanmore Lane, WINCHESTER, SO23 9QZ.
•**GRINDEY, Mr. Peter, BSc FCA** *1991;* Fearns Marriott Ltd, Ford House, Market Street, LEEK, STAFFORDSHIRE, ST13 6JA.
GRINDEY, Mr. Rodney James Hambleton, FCA *1974;* PO Box 33240, Petone, LOWER HUTT 5046, NEW ZEALAND.
GRINDLAY, Miss. Alexandra, FCA *1969;* Greystone, The Meadway, SHOREHAM-BY-SEA, WEST SUSSEX, BN43 5RP. (Life Member)
GRINDLE, Mr. Michael Mark, BSc ACA *1985;* Edge Search Ltd, 212 Piccadilly, LONDON, W1J 9HG.
GRINDLEY, Miss. Clair Louise, BSocSc CA ACA *1999;* 2 Queen Street East Suite 1200, TORONTO M5C 3G7, ON, CANADA.
GRINDLEY, Mrs. Maria Louisa, BSc FCA *1996;* Woodstock House, 5A Woodstock Road, WITNEY, OXFORDSHIRE, OX28 1EA.
GRINDLEY, Mr. Philip Robert Giles, ACA *1993;* with PricewaterhouseCoopers, Marie-Curie-Strasse 24-28, D-60439 FRANKFURT AM MAIN, GERMANY.
•**GRINDROD, Mr. Anthony Michael, BSc ACA** *1989;* Davies Grindrod & Co, 11 Queen Street, Wellington, TELFORD, TF1 1EH. See also Grindrod & Company Limited and Grindrod Davies & Co
GRINDROD, Mr. Ernest Clegg, FCA *1958;* P.O.Box SS-6882, Bay View, Eastern Rd, NASSAU, BAHAMAS. (Life Member)
GRINDROD, Mrs. Joanne, ACA *2006;* Flat B, 32 Oakhill Road, LONDON, SW15 2QR.
GRINDROD, Mr. Neil Stuart, BSc(Hons) ACA *2004;* 9 Meade Road, BILLERICAY, CM11 1DE.
GRINDROD, Mr. Peter John Edward, FCA *1955;* 84-30 123 Street, Kew Gardens, NEW YORK, NY 11415, UNITED STATES. (Life Member)
GRINDULIS, Mrs. Josephine Anne, BA ACA *1986;* 1 Highfield Road, Heath, CARDIFF, CF14 3RE.
GRINHAM, Mr. Arthur John, FCA *1952;* 26 Julian Road, BRISTOL, BS9 1LB. (Life Member)
GRINHAM, Mrs. Caroline Laura, LLB FCA *1986;* with Ernst & Young LLP, 1 More London Place, LONDON, SE1 2AF.
GRINHAM, Miss. Rachel Catherine, MA FCA *2001;* Unit 203, 605 Sydney Road, BRUNSWICK, VIC 3056, AUSTRALIA.
GRINSELL, Mr. John Richard, FCA *1973;* 10 Otterwood Bank, WETHERBY, LS22 7XT.
GRINSTED, Mr. Jeremy, BEng ACA *2003;* 30a Edward Road, FARNHAM, SURREY, GU9 8NP.
GRINSTED, Mr. Peter Meredith, FCA *1951;* Caloundra, Lyncroft Road, Pakefield, LOWESTOFT, SUFFOLK, NR33 7AT. (Life Member)
•**GRINSTED, Mr. Sean Andrew, ACA ATII CF TEP** *1991;* (Tax Fac), Francis Clark, Vantage Point, Woodwater Park, Pynes Hill, EXETER, EX2 5FD. See also Francis Clark LLP
GRINT, Mr. John Leslie Martin, MA ACA *1980;* 70 Old London Road, Badgers Mount, SEVENOAKS, TN14 7AE.
•**GRINTER, Mr. Simon John, ACA** *1981;* The Old Wool Barn Worston, Yealmpton, PLYMOUTH, PL8 2LN.
GRINYER, Mr. John Raymond, MSc FCA *1962;* 81b Dundee Road, Broughty Ferry, DUNDEE, DD5 1LZ. (Life Member)
GRISDALE, Mr. Ashley Paul Peter, BA ACA *1993;* 117 Wilberforce Road, LONDON, N4 2SP.
GRISDALE, Miss. Frances Jane, MA ACA *1984;* Little Paddock, Romsey Road, Whiteparish, SALISBURY, SP5 2SD.
GRISDALE, Mr. John Chester, FCA *1965;* PO Box 15510, Farrarmere, BENONI, GAUTENG, 1518, SOUTH AFRICA.
GRISMAN, Mr. Peter Edward Thomas, FCA *1977;* 9 Franklynn Road, HAYWARDS HEATH, WEST SUSSEX, RH16 4DG.
GRIST, Mr. Ashley Alexander, BSc ACA *1990;* 6A Boulevard Victor Hugo, 78100 SAINT-GERMAIN-EN-LAYE, FRANCE.
•**GRIST, Mr. Benjamin Carlyle, BA ACA CTA** *2007;* Dixon Wilson, 22 Chancery Lane, LONDON, WC2A 1LS.
GRIST, Mr. David Anthony, BSc ACA *1983;* 36 Castle Close, VENTNOR, ISLE OF WIGHT, PO38 1UD.
•**GRIST, Miss. Helen Elizabeth, BSc FCA** *1992;* (Tax Fac), Latrigg Limited, Latrigg, The Glen, Saltford, BRISTOL, BS31 3JP.
GRIST, Mr. Ivor George, FCA *1958;* Dumbledor, Beechwood Road, Combe Down, BATH, BA2 5JS. (Life Member)
GRIST, Mr. Michael Benjamin, MA(Hons) ACA *2001;* 65 Carthew Road, LONDON, W6 0DU.
GRIST, Mr. Nicholas Paul, BSc ACA *1999;* Royal Bank of Scotland, 90-100 Southwark Street, LONDON, SE1 0SW.
GRIST, Mr. Stephen John, BSc ACA *1992;* 39 Woodend Drive, ASCOT, SL5 9BD.
GRITTI, Miss. Joanne Marie, BA(Hons) ACA *2009;* with Experian plc, Landmark House, Experian Way, NOTTINGHAM, NG80 1ZZ.
GRITZMANN, Mr. Jan, BSc ACA *2006;* Flat 2, 56 Thurlow Park Road, LONDON, SE21 8HZ.
GRIX, Mr. Jonathan Philip, FCA *1989;* La Maison Des Vignes, 4 Place de la Republique, 11200 TOUROUZELLE, AUDE, FRANCE.
GROAT, Mr. Andrew Nicholas, BA ACA *2007;* 21 High Green, NORWICH, NR1 4AP.
GROAT, Mr. Maurice James Malcolm, MA MBA FCA FRSA *1988;* Apartment 631, Tas Sellum, MELLIEHA, MALTA.
GROBEL, Mr. Christian, BA ACA *2002;* FremantleMedia North America, 4000 W Alameda Ave 3rd Floor, BURBANK, CA 91505, UNITED STATES.
GROBLER, Mr. Nicholas, BSc(Hons) ACA *2010;* 24 Florence Drive, ENFIELD, MIDDLESEX, EN2 8DG.
GROCOCK, Mr. Alistair Finlay, BA FCA *1981;* Silver Birches, Woodside, Little Baddow, CHELMSFORD, CM3 4SR.
GROCOCK, Mr. Graham Finlay, BA FCA *1975;* 19 West Leake Lane, Kingston-on-Soar, NOTTINGHAM, NG11 0DN.
GROCOCK, Miss. Lisa Michelle, BSc ACA *1997;* 103/2 Pier Street, PORT MELBOURNE, VIC 3207, AUSTRALIA.
GROCOTT, Mr. Andrew Paul Reynard, BA ACA *1985;* 22 The Quadrant, West Wimbledon, LONDON, SW20 8SP.
GROCOTT, Mr. Paul Martin, MA ACA *1993;* (Tax Fac), with PricewaterhouseCoopers KFT, Wesselenyi u 16, BUDAPEST, H-1077, HUNGARY.
GROCOTT, Miss. Sarah Lindsay, MA ACA CTA *1995;* (Tax Fac), with PricewaterhouseCoopers LLP, Cornwall Court, 19 Cornwall Street, BIRMINGHAM, B3 2DT.
GROCOTT, Mr. Stephen, BA ACA *1992;* Bridewell UK Ltd, 25 Carbrook Hall Road, SHEFFIELD, S9 2EJ.
GROCOTT, Miss. Suzanne Ellen, BSc ACA SIA *1986;* 22 The Quadrant, LONDON, SW20 8SP.
GRODNER, Mr. Geoffrey Raymond, BA FCA *1988;* 6 Alders Road, EDGWARE, HA8 9QG.
GROENEN, Mr. Joseph Michael, BA ACA *2008;* Flat 4 Connaught Court, 13 Connaught Avenue, LONDON, E4 7AG.
GROENEN, Mr. Thomas Edward, BA ACA *2004;* with PricewaterhouseCoopers LLP, 300 Madison Avenue, NEW YORK, NY 10017, UNITED STATES.
GROENEWALD, Mr. Christo, ACA CA(SA) *2010;* (Tax Fac), 153 Shirland Road, LONDON, W9 2EP.
GROENEWALD, Mrs. Lydia Catherine, BA ACA *2007;* with PricewaterhouseCoopers LLP, 80 Strand, LONDON, WC2R 0AF.
GROGAN, Mr. Alan, BA ACA *2006;* 285 Upper Kilmacud Road, Goatstown, DUBLIN 14, COUNTY DUBLIN, IRELAND.
•**GROGAN, Mrs. Andrea, BA ACA** *1991;* JGA, St James's Court, Brown Street, MANCHESTER, M2 1DH.
GROGAN, Mr. Bernard, FCA *1969;* 1 Laund Hey View, Helmshore Road, Haslingden, ROSSENDALE, BB4 4BB.
GROGAN, Mr. Ian James, BEng ACA *1999;* Flat 3, 19 St. Johns Park, Blackheath, LONDON, SE3 7TD.
•**GROGAN, Mr. John Francis, MA FCA CTA MEWI** *1980;* JGA, St James's Court, Brown Street, MANCHESTER, M2 1DH.
GROGAN, Mr. Jonathan William, BA ACA *1983;* 95 Headstone Lane, HARROW, MIDDLESEX, HA2 6JL.
GROGAN, Mr. Tim Robert, BSc ACA *2006;* 47 High Elm Road, Hale Barns, ALTRINCHAM, CHESHIRE, WA15 0HZ.
•**GROMADZKI, Mr. Jan Grzegorz, BSc ACA** *1981;* Jan G Gromadzki, 13 Wolverhampton Road, Codsall, WOLVERHAMPTON, WEST MIDLANDS, WV8 1PT.
•**GROMAN, Mr. Anthony Israel, FCA** *1972;* (Tax Fac), Groman & Company, 5 Violet Hill, St. Johns Wood, LONDON, NW8 9EB.
GRONBECH, Mr. Ian Robert, MA ACA *1991;* Sluisweg 33, 3238 LE ZWARTEWAAL, NETHERLANDS.
GRONOW, Ms. Angela Louise, BSc ACA *1992;* Seestrasse 149, 8700 KUSNACHT, SWITZERLAND.
GRONOW, Mr. David Gareth, BSc ACA *1997;* 7 Brownhills, Gorseinon, SWANSEA, SA4 4AB.
GRONOW, Mrs. Deborah Elizabeth, BSc ACA *1993;* 7 Clyde Close, Pontlanfraith, BLACKWOOD, NP12 2FY.
•**GRONOW, Mr. Julian Rees, FCA** *1966;* Julian R Gronow Limited, Field House, Field Lane, Kemberton, SHIFNAL, SHROPSHIRE TF11 9LR.
GRONOW, Mr. Julian Windsor, BA ACA *1995;* 7 Clyde Close, Pontllanfraith, BLACKWOOD, NP12 2FY.
GRONTENRATH, Mr. John Edward, FCA *1970;* 12 St. Marys Park, OTTERY ST. MARY, DEVON, EX11 1JA.

GROOCOCK, Mr. Trevor Charles, FCA *1961;* 28 Pensford Avenue, Kew, RICHMOND, TW9 4HP.
GROOGAN, Miss. Michaela Edith, MA ACA *2004;* 54a Boileau Road, Ealing, LONDON, W5 3AJ.
GROOM, Mr. David Michael, BSc ACA *1993;* Bembridge Lodge, 114 High Street, BEMBRIDGE, PO35 5SQ.
GROOM, Mr. Denis James, BCom FCA *1959;* 778 Simcoe Street, BRIDGENORTH K0L 1H0, ON, CANADA. (Life Member)
GROOM, Mr. Geoffrey Christopher David, FCA *1970;* PO Box 10183, Bamburi, MOMBASA, KENYA.
•GROOM, Mrs. Gillian, FCA *1982;* 55 Fullarton Drive, TROON, AYRSHIRE, KA10 6LF.
•GROOM, Mr. John Alastair Huntley, BSc FCA *1992;* KPMG LLP, 15 Canada Square, LONDON, E14 5GL. See also KPMG Europe LLP
GROOM, Mr. Michael John, FCA *1964;* (President 2001 - 2002) (Member of Council 1975 - 2004), 14 High Meadows, Compton, WOLVERHAMPTON, WV6 8PH.
GROOM, Miss. Nicola Margaret, ACA *1991;* The Gap Inc, Castle Mound Way, RUGBY, WARWICKSHIRE, CV23 0WA.
GROOM, Mr. Nigel Wayne, BSc ACA *1994;* Pen-Y-Fan, Elm Road, East Bergholt, COLCHESTER, SUFFOLK, CO7 6SG.
GROOM, Mr. Richard Joseph, MA FCA *1971;* 1 Bath Lodge, Green Hill, London Road, WORCESTER, WR5 2AA. (Life Member)
GROOM, Mr. Robert Taylor, BSc ACA *1991;* 10 Dyer Road, Keephatch Park, WOKINGHAM, RG40 5PG.
GROOM, Mr. Simon James, BSc FCA ATT CTA *1987;* Butterworths Tolley Halsbury House, 35 Chancery Lane, LONDON, WC2A 1EL.
GROOM, Mr. Simon Patrick, BSc ACA *2003;* Synthomer Limited, Central Road, Temple Fields, HARLOW, ESSEX, CM20 2BH.
GROOM, Mr. Stuart John, BSc ACA *1989;* 1154 Oberon Drive, KING FERRY, NY 13081, UNITED STATES.
GROOM, Mrs. Wendy Jane, BSc ACA *2002;* 28 Bridle Stile Gardens, Mosborough, SHEFFIELD, S20 5EH.
GROOME, Mr. Deryck Michael, FCA *1952;* 14 Langton Road, Great Bowden, MARKET HARBOROUGH, LE16 7EZ. (Life Member)
GROOME, Mr. Gareth David, BA ACA *1994;* The Old Byre Plas Devon Court, Rossett Road, Holt, WREXHAM, LL13 9SY.
GROOME, Mrs. Nicola Jane, BSc ACA *2002;* with BDO LLP, 55 Baker Street, LONDON, W1U 7EU.
GROOT, Mr. James Pieter, MSc BSc ACA *2005;* 6 Foster Walk, Sherburn in Elmet, LEEDS, LS25 6EU.
GROSBERG, Mr. Ariel Raphael, BA ACA *2007;* 65 Leeside Crescent, LONDON, NW11 0JL.
GROSE, Mr. Douglas Andrews, FCA *1959;* Roselands, Chittlehamholt, UMBERLEIGH, EX37 9PD. (Life Member)
GROSE, Mr. Ian, BSc ACA *2006;* Unit 103, 27 Waruda Street, KIRRIBILLI, NSW 2061, AUSTRALIA.
GROSE, Mr. Peter William, BSc ACA *1983;* W Grose Ltd, Queens Park Parade, Kingsthorpe, NORTHAMPTON, NN2 6NJ.
GROSE, Mr. Rupert Molyneux, BA ACA *1994;* Street Farm House Main Street, Shudy Camps, CAMBRIDGE, CB21 4RA.
GROSE, Mrs. Shirley Verena, ACA *1996;* 14 Throop Close, BOURNEMOUTH, BH8 0DD.
•GROSELEY, Mr. Reginald Keith, FCA *1966;* (Tax Fac), R.K.Groseley, Lynwood House, Dudley Road, Lye, STOURBRIDGE, DY9 8DU. See also Poole Waterfield Limited
GROSS, Mr. Alexander, FCA *1952;* 22/6 KKL, 92465 JERUSALEM, ISRAEL. (Life Member)
•GROSS, Mr. Bernard, BCom BAcc FCA ACA *1995;* (Tax Fac), Winston Gross & Co, 34 Arlington Road, LONDON, NW1 7HU.
GROSS, Mr. Charles Edward Grant Kennedy, FCA *1971;* Cottage In The Wood, Turners Hill Road, Crawley Down, CRAWLEY, RH10 4EZ.
GROSS, Mr. Charles William Abbot, MA FCA CPA *1968;* PricewaterhouseCoopers, 600 Grant Street, PITTSBURGH, PA 15219, UNITED STATES.
GROSS, Mr. David Anthony, BSc ACA *1993;* Monkswell House, Monastery Road, ENNISKERRY, COUNTY WICKLOW, IRELAND.
GROSS, Miss. Emma Celia, BSc ACA *2009;* 10 Hinton Close, Rickerscote, STAFFORD, ST17 4HP.
GROSS, Mr. Ephraim, FCA *1951;* 1115 Princeton Apt. D., SANTA MONICA, CA 90403, UNITED STATES. (Life Member)
GROSS, Mr. Guy Edward Franklin, MA FCA *1963;* 70 Maidstone Road, ROCHESTER, ME1 3DE. (Life Member)
•GROSS, Mr. Howard Anthony, FCA FCCA CTA *1971;* MEMBER OF COUNCIL, (Tax Fac), Gross Klein, 6 Breams Buildings, LONDON, EC4A 1QL. See also Gross, Klein & Partners
GROSS, Mr. Ian Peter, BSc ACA *1989;* 64 Hopkins Close, Thornbury, BRISTOL, BS35 2PX.
GROSS, Mr. Lewis, BEng ACA *2002;* Haweswater House, Lingley Mere Business Park, Lingley Green Avenue, Great Sankey, WARRINGTON, WA5 3LP.
•GROSS, Mr. Philip Robert, BA ACA *1991;* Libra, 30 St Vincents Way, POTTERS BAR, EN6 2RF.
GROSS, Mr. Raymond Malcolm Victor, BA FCA *1968;* Apartment 7, High Lawn, East Downs Road, Bowdon, ALTRINCHAM, CHESHIRE WA14 2LG. (Life Member)
GROSSART, Miss. Sally Ann, MA ACA *1990;* 6 Carlton Street, EDINBURGH, EH4 1NJ.
GROSSE, Mr. David James, BA ACA *1992;* c/o CLSA 18th Floor, One Pacific Place, 88 Queensway Admiralty, ADMIRALTY, HONG KONG ISLAND, HONG KONG SAR.
•GROSSKOPF, Mr. Jonathan, MSc FCA *1975;* 85 Bishops Road, Prestwich, MANCHESTER, M25 0AS.
GROSSKOPF, Mrs. Therese, FCA *1968;* 22 Hurstdene Gardens, LONDON, N15 6NA.
GROSSMAN, Mr. Barrie Spencer, BA FCA *1974;* Boleyn House, 3 Wolsey Close, Drax avenue, LONDON, SW20 0DD.
GROSSMAN, Mr. Bernard Martin, FCA *1963;* 14 Hillersdon Avenue, EDGWARE, HA8 7SQ. (Life Member)
•GROSSMAN, Mr. Edward, FCA *1972;* (Tax Fac), 80 Erskine Hill, LONDON, NW11 6HG.
GROSSMAN, Mrs. Heather Jane, ACA *2007;* Staffordshire Fire & Rescue Service, Pirehill, STONE, STAFFORDSHIRE, ST15 0BS.
GROSSMAN, Mr. Jamie, CA *2009; (CA Scotland 2008);* Wilson Wright LLP, First Floor, Thavies Inn House, 3-4 Holborn Circus, LONDON, EC1N 2HA.
GROSSMAN, Mr. Josh, BSc(Hons) ACA *2011;* 35 Upper Park Road, SALFORD, M7 4JB.
GROSSMAN, Miss. Kim, LLB ACA *2011;* 79 Howberry Road, EDGWARE, MIDDLESEX, HA8 6TF.
GROSSMAN, Mr. Martin Kingsley, FCA *1975;* 15 Malmsmead House, Homerton, LONDON, E9 5RP.
•GROSSMAN, Mr. William Eric, FCA *1975;* Goodman Jones LLP, 29-30 Fitzroy Square, LONDON, W1T 6LQ.
•GROSSMARK, Mr. Peter Raphael Adrian, FCA *1985;* Silver Levene LLP, 37 Warren Street, LONDON, W1T 6AD.
GROSSMITH, Mr. Elliot Saul, BSc(Hons) ACA *2003;* 10a Ashbourne Avenue, LONDON, NW11 0DR.
GROSSNASS, Mr. Michael Percy, FCA *1968;* 29 Bridge Lane, LONDON, NW11 0ED.
GROSTERN, Mr. Stuart Jonathan, BSc ACA *1993;* 26 Beech Drive, East Finchley, LONDON, N2 9NY.
GROSVENOR, Mrs. Amanda Katherine, BA ACA *1999;* with PricewaterhouseCoopers LLP, The Atrium, 1 Harefield Road, UXBRIDGE, UB8 1EX.
GROSVENOR, Mrs. Claire, BA(Hons) ACA MCT *2001;* 74 High Street, Sunninghill, ASCOT, BERKSHIRE, SL5 9NN.
•GROSVENOR, Mr. Daniel, LLB ACA AMCT *2000;* Deloitte LLP, Athene Place, 66 Shoe Lane, LONDON, EC4A 3BQ. See also Deloitte & Touche LLP
GROSVENOR, Mr. James, ACA *2004;* 17a Rest Bay Close, PORTHCAWL, MID GLAMORGAN, CF36 3UN.
GROSVENOR, Mr. John Bernard, FCA *1972;* 58 Beechwood Road, SMETHWICK, B67 5EQ.
GROSVENOR, Mr. John Brian, FCA *1975;* Briarhedge, 33 Orchehill Avenue, GERRARDS CROSS, BUCKINGHAMSHIRE, SL9 8QE.
GROSVENOR, Mr. Jonathan Mark Nigel Sloley, MA ACA *1988;* 92b Banbury Road, OXFORD, OX2 6JT.
GROSVENOR, Mr. Stanley, FCA *1965;* 5 Egton Avenue, Nunthorpe, MIDDLESBROUGH, TS7 0QY. (Life Member)
GROSZ, Mr. George, BSc FCA *1960;* 93 Avenue de St. Mande, 75012 PARIS, FRANCE. (Life Member)
GROTT, Mr. Michal Stefan, FCA *1968;* 73 Richmond Park Road, KINGSTON UPON THAMES, KT2 6AF. (Life Member)
•GROU, Mr. John Alexander, FCA *1972;* John A Grou, Finches, Little Hill, West Chiltington, PULBOROUGH, RH20 2PU.
•GROUCOTT, Mr. Andrew Joseph, BA FCA *1988;* Groucott Moor Limited, Lombard House, Cross Keys, LICHFIELD, STAFFORDSHIRE, WS13 6DN.
GROUND, Mr. Mark George, BSc FCA *1997;* Mansell, Dedswell Drive, West Clandon, GUILDFORD, SURREY, GU4 7TQ.
•GROUNDS, Miss. Caroline, BA ACA *1988;* 198 Rivermead Court, Ranelagh Gardens, LONDON, SW6 3SG.
GROUNDS, Mr. Simon Peter, ACA *2007;* Hazeldean, Bath Road, STURMINSTER NEWTON, DORSET, DT10 1DS.
GROUNDWATER, Mr. Thomas Sanderson, FCA *1969;* 17 Baronsfield Road, St. Margarets, TWICKENHAM, TW1 2QT.
GROUNSELL, Mr. Jared Peter, BSc ACA *2004;* with Dean Statham LLP, 29 King Street, NEWCASTLE, STAFFORDSHIRE, ST5 1ER.
GROUPMAN, Mr. Clive De-Courcy, BSc FCA *1982;* 3 Clarence Road, WOTTON-UNDER-EDGE, GL12 7EX.
•GROUT, Mr. Andrew Philip, FCA *1972;* (Tax Fac), Midgley Snelling, Ibex House, Baker Street, WEYBRIDGE, SURREY, KT13 8AH.
GROUT, Mr. John William, BEng ACA *1990;* Larchmont, Vicarage Lane, East Farleigh, MAIDSTONE, KENT, ME15 0LX.
GROUT, Mr. Richard Douglas, FCA *1971;* 13-100 Laguna Parkway, BRECHIN L0K 1B0, ON, CANADA.
GROUT, Mr. William David, MA ACA *2010;* 14 Heene Road, ENFIELD, MIDDLESEX, EN2 0QG.
GROVE, Mr. Alistair Michael, BA FCA *1983;* Rooksmoor, Buckland Monachorum, YELVERTON, DEVON, PL20 7NN.
GROVE, Mrs. Amanda Margaret, LLB ACA *1991;* Piemans Way, 37 Lower Road, Fetcham, LEATHERHEAD, SURREY, KT22 9EL.
GROVE, Mr. Andrew John, BA ACA *1993;* 39 Maidstone Drive, Wordsley, STOURBRIDGE, DY8 5RQ.
GROVE, Ms. Annette Veronica, ACA CA(AUS) *2009;* (Tax Fac), 15 York House, Courtlands Sheen Road, RICHMOND, TW10 5BD.
GROVE, Mr. Christopher James, FCA *1976;* 5 Morley Close, LEWES, BN7 1NQ.
•GROVE, Mr. Christopher John, BSc FCA *1991;* BDO LLP, 55 Baker Street, LONDON, W1U 7EU. See also BDO Stoy Hayward LLP
GROVE, Mr. David Lawrence, BA FCA *1968;* 2 Greenfields Close, SHIPSTON-ON-STOUR, WARWICKSHIRE, CV36 4HA.
GROVE, Mr. David Leslie, OBE BA FCA *1973;* Badgers Holt, Rookery Lane, Lowsonford, SOLIHULL, B95 5EP.
•GROVE, Miss. Elizabeth Mary, FCA *1976;* E Mary Grove, Beechwood, Stoke Prior, LEOMINSTER, HEREFORDSHIRE, HR6 0LN.
•GROVE, Mr. Graham Slater, FCA *1968;* (Tax Fac), G S Grove, 7 Hillwood Common Road, Four Oaks, SUTTON COLDFIELD, B75 5QJ.
GROVE, Mr. Harvey Gordon Edwin, FCA *1975;* Top Farm, Bretforton, EVESHAM, WR11 5JJ.
GROVE, Miss. Jacqueline, BA ACA *1987;* 25 Edgcumbe Park Road, PLYMOUTH, PL3 4NL.
GROVE, Mr. Mark Allen, BSc ACA *2000;* 80 Kingfisher House, Juniper Drive, LONDON, SW18 1TY.
GROVE, Mr. Nicholas Matthew, ACA *2008;* Pricewaterhousecoopers Cornwall Court, 19 Cornwall Street, BIRMINGHAM, B3 2DT.
GROVE, Mr. Peter Hulbert, FCA *1958;* Stony Ridge, St. Catherines, WOKING, GU22 0HW. (Life Member)
GROVE, Mr. Robert Edward, BA ACA *1996;* 11 Nursery Way, Great Haywood, STAFFORD, ST18 0FY.
GROVE, Mr. Terence John, FCA *1958;* (Member of Council 1995 - 1999), 2 Savile Gardens, CROYDON, CR0 5QQ.
GROVE, Mr. William Hulbert, ACA *1991;* Spring Close, Millers Lane, Outwood, REDHILL, RH1 5PZ.
GROVE-WHITE, Mr. Patrick Alexander, FCA *1950;* 4 Walker Park, Nayland, COLCHESTER, CO6 4NE. (Life Member)
GROVER, Mr. Anthony Philip, BSc ACA *1992;* Indigo Capital Llp, 30 King Street, LONDON, EC2V 8EH.
GROVER, Mr. Jack Adam Charles, MA(Cantab) MSci ACA CTA *2007;* Yew Trees, Plough Lane, Harefield, UXBRIDGE, MIDDLESEX, UB9 6PF.
GROVER, Mr. Jason, BSc FCA ATII FCT *1990;* Mary Land Wood Lodge, Rough Road, WOKING, GU22 0RB.
GROVER, Miss. Joan Lucy, FCA *1960;* Moriah, 40 Furners Mead, HENFIELD, BN5 9JA. (Life Member)
GROVER, Mrs. Katherine Hazel, BSc FCA *1992;* Mary Land Wood Lodge, Rough Road, WOKING, SURREY, GU22 0RB.
•GROVER, Mr. Keith Alistair, BA FCA *1984;* HB Accountants, Amwell House, 19 Amwell Street, HODDESDON, HERTFORDSHIRE, EN11 8TS. See also Hardcastles Limited
GROVER, Mr. Pramod, FCA *1966;* Grant Thornton, L41 Connaught Circus, NEW DELHI 110001, INDIA.
•GROVER, Mr. Rajesh, BSc FCA *1990;* (Tax Fac), Grover & Co, Anmol House, 173 Uxbridge Road, Hanwell, LONDON, W7 3TH.
•GROVES, Mr. Andrew Paul William, BSc ACA *1986;* PricewaterhouseCoopers LLP, Exchange House, Central Business Exchange, Midsummer Boulevard, MILTON KEYNES, MK9 2DF. See also PricewaterhouseCoopers
GROVES, Mr. Andrew Peter, BA ACA *2007;* 89 Park Road, Chilwell Beeston, NOTTINGHAM, NG9 4DE.
GROVES, Mr. Anthony John Martin, BA ACA *1984;* Motion Recruitment Partners, 206 Newbury Street, BOSTON, MA 02116, UNITED STATES.
GROVES, Mrs. Cheryl Alice Lynda, BA(Hons) ACA *2000;* 1 Midway, ST. ALBANS, HERTFORDSHIRE, AL3 4BD.
GROVES, Mr. Clifford, FCA *1989;* 11 Hadley Court, Church Road, POLEGATE, EAST SUSSEX, BN26 5BY.
•GROVES, Mr. David Peter, ACA *1986;* Lemans, 29 Arboretum Street, NOTTINGHAM, NG1 4JA.
GROVES, Mr. David Robert, FCA *1973;* The Orchard, Temple Lane, East Meon, PETERSFIELD, GU32 1PZ.
•GROVES, Mr. Denys David, FCA *1959;* Groves & Co, 141 Cyncoed Road, CARDIFF, CF23 6AF.
GROVES, Miss. Diane Elizabeth, BA ACA *1998;* Level 3, 345 George Street, SYDNEY, NSW 2000, AUSTRALIA.
GROVES, Mrs. Helen Georgina, BA(Hons) ACA CTA *2001;* with Morris Owen, 43-45 Devizes Road, SWINDON, SN1 4BG.
GROVES, Mr. Ian Keith, ACA *1986;* Darlington Council for Voluntary Service, Church Row, DARLINGTON, COUNTY DURHAM, DL1 5QD.
GROVES, Mrs. Jacquetta Wheatley, BSc ACA *1991;* 6 West Avenue, Gosforth, NEWCASTLE UPON TYNE, NE3 4ES.
•GROVES, Mr. James Alan, FCA *1995;* Bromhead, Harscombe House, 1 Darklake View, Estover, PLYMOUTH, PL6 7TL. See also Bromhead Limited
GROVES, Mr. John Charles, FCA *1966;* 37 School Lane, Kirk Ella, HULL, HU10 7NP.
•GROVES, Mr. John Delwin, ACA *1987;* Delwin Groves, 7 Mill Close, Broom, ALCESTER, WARWICKSHIRE, B50 4HT. See also Flemons & Co Limited
GROVES, Mrs. Judy Ann, BSc ACA *1980;* 11 Harris Street, MARBLEHEAD, MA 01945, UNITED STATES.
GROVES, Mr. Julian Russell, BA ACA *1988;* 12 Denewood Close, WATFORD, WD17 4SZ.
GROVES, Miss. Laura Emily, ACA *2005;* The Flower House Lewes Road, Blackboys, UCKFIELD, EAST SUSSEX, TN22 5LF.
GROVES, Miss. Linda Mary, BSc ACA *1991;* 9 Mount Rise, REDHILL, RH1 6JY.
GROVES, Mr. Mark Richard, BSc ACA *1993;* 9 St. Francis Place, LONDON, SW12 8ER.
GROVES, Mr. Michael, BA FCA *1982;* 9 Magpie Close, Little Common, BEXHILL-ON-SEA, TN39 4EU.
GROVES, Mr. Michael Peter, BA ACA *1997;* Steria Ltd, Three Cherry Trees Lane, HEMEL HEMPSTEAD, HERTFORDSHIRE, HP2 7AH.
GROVES, Mr. Nathan Paul, BA ACA *2007;* 25 Ernesettle Crescent, Higher St Budeaux, PLYMOUTH, PL5 2ET.
•GROVES, Mr. Nicholas Timothy, MA ACA *2000;* PricewaterhouseCoopers LLP, 7 More London Riverside, LONDON, SE1 2RT. See also PricewaterhouseCoopers
GROVES, Mr. Nigel Jonathan Rothwell, ACA *1979;* 14 Dimple Park, Egerton, BOLTON, BL7 9QE.
•GROVES, Mr. Peter James, FCA *1981;* (Tax Fac), Baker Tilly Tax and Advisory Services LLP, Charter House, The Square, Lower Bristol Road, BATH, BA2 3BH.
GROVES, Mr. Peter Warland, BA FCA *1967;* 69 Willian Way, LETCHWORTH GARDEN CITY, HERTFORDSHIRE, SG6 2HJ. (Life Member)
GROVES, Mr. Richard Jeremy Ferris, FCA *1969;* 44 Merrivale Square, OXFORD, OX2 6QX.
GROVES, Mr. Richard William, BA ACA *1989;* 24 Ashley Piece, Ramsbury, MARLBOROUGH, SN8 2QE.
GROVES, Mr. Roger Edward Vane, PhD BCom FCA *1963;* 1 Forest Hill, Gilwern, ABERGAVENNY, GWENT, NP7 0DY. (Life Member)
GROVES, Mr. Russell John Thornton, ACA *1984;* 32 Pembroke Croft, Hall Green, BIRMINGHAM, B28 9EY.
GROVES, Mr. Sam James, BSc ACA *1996;* 38 Cuckoo Bushes Lane, Chandler's Ford, EASTLEIGH, HAMPSHIRE, SO53 1JY.
•GROVES, Mr. Simon Nicholas, BA FCA *1982;* Simon Groves & Co, 227 Cassiobury Drive, WATFORD, HERTFORDSHIRE, WD17 3AN.

GROVES, Mrs. Sophie Jane, MA ACA *1999;* 38 Cuckoo Bushes Lane, Chandler's Ford, EASTLEIGH, HAMPSHIRE, SO53 1JY.
GROVES, Mr. Timothy Michael, ACA *1992;* Cowper House, Cowper Road, BERKHAMSTED, HERTFORDSHIRE, HP4 3DE.
•**GROVES, Mrs. Tracey Jane, BA ACA** *1996;* PricewaterhouseCoopers LLP, Pricewaterhousecoopers, 12 Plumtree Court, LONDON, EC4A 4HT. See also PricewaterhouseCoopers
GROVES, Mr. William Raymond, FCA *1966;* 1 Pond Cottage, Studridge Lane, Speen, PRINCES RISBOROUGH, BUCKINGHAMSHIRE, HP27 0SA.
GROWER, Mr. Bennett Benjamin, FCA *1969;* 16 Boscombe Cliff Road, BOURNEMOUTH, BH5 1JL. (Life Member)
GROZIER, Mr. Graeme Hamilton, BSc FCA *1991;* H M Revenue & Customs, Crown House, 11 Regent Hill, BRIGHTON, BN1 3ER.
GRUBB, Mr. Albert Ernest, FCA *1948;* Stratford House, 192 Coleshill Road, ATHERSTONE, CV9 2AQ. (Life Member)
GRUBB, Mr. David John, BA(Hons) ACA *2002;* 101 Cannock Road, CANNOCK, WS11 5DA.
GRUBB, Mr. Ian Michael, BA ACA *1993;* 31 Curriers Lane, SHIFNAL, SHROPSHIRE, TF11 8EJ.
GRUBB, Mr. Richard De Cruce, BSc FCA *1975;* 29 Hofland Road, West Kensington, LONDON, W14 0LN.
GRUBB, Mr. Thomas Richard, BA ACA *2008;* with KPMG LLP, 15 Canada Square, LONDON, E14 5GL.
GRUBE, Miss. Sarah Jane, BSc ACA *2001;* (Tax Fac), Taxation Department, American Express Europe Ltd Sussex House, Civic Way, BURGESS HILL, RH15 9AQ.
GRUBER, Mrs. Frances Helen Louise, FCA *1983;* 12 Possum Street, TRINITY BEACH, QLD 4879, AUSTRALIA.
GRUDGINGS, Mr. Stafford, FCA *1976;* 6 Nevin Close, Menai, SYDNEY, NSW 2234, AUSTRALIA.
GRUGEON, Mr. David Hilton, FCA *1967;* 8 Montclair Street, ASPLEY, QLD 4034, AUSTRALIA.
GRUHN, Mr. Ernest Paul James, FCA CTA *1960;* Timbers, Williams Way, RADLETT, HERTFORDSHIRE, WD7 7EZ. (Life Member)
GRUMITT, Mr. John Paul George, BA ACA *1991;* 28 Mayfield Avenue, LONDON, W4 1PW.
GRUMMETT, Mr. Mark Elliott, BA ACA *1991;* 21 Lowther Drive, Garforth, LEEDS, LS25 1EW.
GRUMMITT, Mr. James, BSc ACA *2011;* 5 Hawthorn Road, LONDON, N8 7LY.
GRUMMITT, Mrs. Joanna Melanie, ACA MAAT *1997;* 26 London End, Woburn, MILTON KEYNES, MK17 9PU.
•**GRUMMITT, Mr. Nigel Charles, BSc FCA** *1990;* Mazars LLP, Tower Bridge House, St. Katharines Way, LONDON, E1W 1DD.
•**GRUNBERG, Mr. David, BA FCA** *1981;* Grunberg & Co., 10-14 Accommodation Road, Golders Green, LONDON, NW11 8ED. See also Grunberg & Co Limited
GRUNBERG, Mr. Michael, BSc FCA *1980;* New Century, 1 Pier Steps, St. Peter Port, GUERNSEY, GY1 2LF.
GRUNCELL, Mr. Frederick Ernest Joseph, FCA *1962;* 7 Beaulieu Gardens, Winchmore Hill, LONDON, N21 2HR.
GRUNDY, Mr. Adam, BSc ACA *2003;* Suite No.1104, Al Masaood Tower, Hamdan Street, P.O.Box 47322, ABU DHABI, UNITED ARAB EMIRATES.
GRUNDY, Mr. Alan, FCA *1965;* with Ashby Berry & Co, 48/49 Albemarle Crescent, SCARBOROUGH, YO11 1XU.
GRUNDY, Mr. Andrew James Fielding, MA ACA *1992;* 2 Larch Rise, The Lanes, Leckhampton, CHELTENHAM, GLOUCESTERSHIRE, GL53 0PY.
GRUNDY, Dr. Anthony Nigel, PhD MA MPhil MSc FCA MBA *1980;* 18 Summerhouse Lane, Harefield, UXBRIDGE, MIDDLESEX, UB9 6HX.
GRUNDY, Mr. Charles Richard, MA ACA *1983;* Avenue Walckiers 94, 1160 Auderghem, BRUSSELS, BELGIUM.
GRUNDY, Miss. Charlotte, BA(Hons) ACA *2010;* 51 Newington, Willingham, CAMBRIDGE, CB24 5JE.
GRUNDY, Mr. Christopher David, BSc(Hons) ACA *2001;* 1 Monks Drive, West Acton, LONDON, W3 0EG.
GRUNDY, The Revd. Christopher John, FCA *1972;* St. John's Vicarage, 383 Southcoates Lane, HULL, HU9 3UN. (Life Member)
•**GRUNDY, Mr. David Kenneth, BSc ACA** *1992;* Grant Thornton UK LLP, 4 Hardman Square, Spinningfields, MANCHESTER, M3 3EB. See also Grant Thornton LLP
GRUNDY, Mr. Guy Edward, BSc(Hons) FCA *2000;* 10 Wellington Close, SALE, CHESHIRE, M33 7BJ.
GRUNDY, Mr. Harry, FCA *1958;* The Farmhouse, Darwin Park, Abnalls Lane, LICHFIELD, WS13 8BJ. (Life Member)
GRUNDY, Mr. Humphrey Fielding, FCA *1961;* 25 Harrop Road, Hale, ALTRINCHAM, WA15 9DA. (Life Member)
GRUNDY, Mr. Ian, BA ACA *1992;* 2 Bradleys Yard, Plumtree, NOTTINGHAM, NG12 5NR.
GRUNDY, Mr. John Charles, BSc ACA *1998;* 15 Adam Drive, SINGAPORE 289974, SINGAPORE.
GRUNDY, Mr. John Edward, FCA *1971;* 8 Bunting Road, BURY ST. EDMUNDS, SUFFOLK, IP32 7BX.
•**GRUNDY, Mr. John Richard, BA FCA** *1976;* (Tax Fac), Ashgroves, 14 Albert Street, Douglas, ISLE OF MAN, IM1 2QA.
GRUNDY, Mr. Keith James, FCA *1974;* 40 Ganstead Lane Bilton, HULL, HU11 4BA.
GRUNDY, Mr. Michael, BCom FCA *1971;* 1 Harper Fold Road, Radcliffe, MANCHESTER, M26 3RU.
GRUNDY, Mr. Michael John, BSc FCA *1973;* 7 Nightingale Square, LONDON, SW12 8QJ.
GRUNDY, Mrs. Nicola Helen, BA ACA *1992;* The University of Nottingham Kings Meadow Campus, Lenton Lane, NOTTINGHAM, NG7 2NR.
•**GRUNDY, Mr. Oliver Wilson, MA FCA** *1984;* Deloitte LLP, Hill House, 1 Little New Street, LONDON, EC4A 3TR. See also Deloitte & Touche LLP
GRUNDY, Mr. Paul, BSc FCA *1981;* 74 Broad Walk, WILMSLOW, CHESHIRE, SK9 5PN.
GRUNDY, Mr. Paul John, BA ACA *1987;* 3 Peel Grove, Roe Green, Worsley, MANCHESTER, M28 2JN.
GRUNDY, Mr. Peter Thomas, FCA *1956;* Garden Cottage, Albury, GUILDFORD, GU5 9BE. (Life Member)
GRUNDY, Mrs. Rachel Melanie, BA ACA *2000;* 56 Midford Drive, BOLTON, BL1 7LY.
GRUNDY, Miss. Roseanna, ACA *2008;* Flat 3 Carlton Mansions, 380-382 Clapham Road, LONDON, SW9 9AR.
GRUNDY, Mrs. Sophie Katherine, BA(Hons) ACA *2003;* 10 Wellington Close, SALE, M33 7BJ.
GRUNDY, Mr. Thomas James, BSc ACA *1999;* 1 Felday Houses Holmbury St. Mary, DORKING, SURREY, RH5 6NJ.
GRUNEBERG, Mr. Andrew John, MA ACA *1998;* Little Croft, 6 Pilgrims Way East, Otford, SEVENOAKS, TN14 5QN.
GRUNSELL, Ms. Helen, BSc ACA *2001;* 3 Watlington Lane North, DEVONSHIRE DV 06, BERMUDA.
GRUNWALD, Mr. Leopold Ernest, ACA *1979;* 120 Caribou Road, TORONTO M5N 2B2, ON, CANADA.
GRUNWELL, Mr. Peter Higson, FCA *1959;* Woodfield, Croasdale Drive, Parbold, WIGAN, WN8 7HR. (Life Member)
GRUSELLE, Mr. Martin Harold, FCA *1961;* 25 Barley Road, Great Chishill, ROYSTON, HERTFORDSHIRE, SG8 8SB. (Life Member)
GRUSZCZYNSKI, Mr. Zdzislaw Michael, BSc ACA *1980;* Hazeldene, Hill Top Road, Hainworth, KEIGHLEY, BD21 5QN.
GRUT, Mr. Peter, BA FCA *1970;* SARL Gryon House, 5 Avenue Saint Laurent, MC 98000 MONTE CARLO, MONACO.
•**GRYGIER, Miss. Olga Barbara, BSc FCA** *1991;* PricewaterhouseCoopers Sp. z o.o., Al.Armii Ludowej 14, WARSAW, 00638, POLAND.
•**GRYLLS, Mr. Paul, BA ACA** *1988;* Newnorth Ltd, The Grange Business Centre, Belasis Avenue, BILLINGHAM, CLEVELAND, TS23 1LG.
GRYNYER, Miss. Kelly Jane, BSc(Hons) ACA *2000;* 5 Highfield, CHALFONT ST. GILES, BUCKINGHAMSHIRE, HP8 4HA.
•**GRZESKOWIAK, Mrs. Joan, PhD MA ACA** *1986;* 41 The Elms, HERTFORD, SG13 7UY.
GU, Ms. Shan Shan, ACA *2009;* 33/F, Cheung Kong Center, 2 Queens Road, CENTRAL, HONG KONG SAR.
GUAN, Mr. Michael, ACA *1979;* with Lee Corporatehouse Associates, No 11, 1st Floor, Regent Square, Simpang 150, BANDAR SERI BEGAWAN BRUNEI DARUSSALAM.
GUANO, Miss. Joanna Helen, BA ACA *1998;* 21 Wandle Road, LONDON, SW17 7DL.
•**GUBBAY, Mr. Jacob, FCA** *1967;* with Westbury, 145/157 St John Street, LONDON, EC1V 4PY.
GUBBAY, Mr. Jeremy Joseph, BA ACA *1989;* Fox Williams, 10 Dominion Street, LONDON, EC2M 2EE.
GUBBAY, Mr. Joshua, BA ACA *1995;* T U I UK Wigmore House, Wigmore Place Wigmore Lane, LUTON, LU2 9TN.
GUBBAY, Mr. Simon Joseph, BSc(Econ) ACA *2003;* Flat 3 Berkeley Court, 42 Neeld Crescent, LONDON, NW4 3RR.
GUDD, Mrs. Emma, BSc ACA *1991;* Stone Walls, Dodford, NORTHAMPTON, NORTHAMPTONSHIRE, NN7 4SX.
•**GUDERLEY, Mr. Henry, FCA** *1977;* H. Guderley & Co, 67 Lancaster Avenue, BARNET, EN4 0ER.
GUDGE, Miss. Louise, BSc ACA *2006;* 18 Devoncroft Gardens, TWICKENHAM, TW1 3PB.
GUDGEON, Miss. Deborah Jane, BSc ACA *1987;* Flat 6, 66 Shepherds Hill, Highgate, LONDON, N6 5RN.
GUDGEON, Mr. Martin Richard, BSc ACA *1992;* Cobble Cottage, Thorncombe Street, Bramley, GUILDFORD, GU5 0LZ.
GUDGEON, Mr. Richard Craven, FCA *1967;* 2 Woodsome Lane, Fenay Bridge, HUDDERSFIELD, HD8 0LQ.
GUDGIN, Mr. Edward Peter, FCA *1957;* Cornerways, 2 Collens Road, Beeson End, HARPENDEN, AL5 2AJ. (Life Member)
GUDKA, Mr. Ajay, BA ACA *2006;* 4 Pebworth Road, HARROW, HA1 3UB.
GUDKA, Mrs. Anandi, BSc ACA *2007;* 8 Sunny Nook Gardens, SOUTH CROYDON, CR2 6PX.
GUDKA, Mr. Anuj Amritlal, MA ACA *1989;* P.O. Box 80382, MOMBASA, 80100, KENYA.
GUDKA, Mr. Arun, ACA *1979;* 35 Kinross Close, Kenton, HARROW, HA3 0UE.
•**GUDKA, Mr. Chandrakant Raichand Virji, BSc FCA** *1974;* C.R.V. Gudka & Co, 306 Neasden Lane, LONDON, NW10 0AD.
•**GUDKA, Mr. Elesh Shantilal, BA ACA** *1987;* KSEG, Belfry House, Champions Way, Hendon, LONDON, NW4 1PX.
GUDKA, Mr. Ganesh Harshit Harakhchand, BA ACA *1992;* 5 Oldcastle Croft, Tattenhoe, MILTON KEYNES, MK4 3EN.
GUDKA, Mr. Manish Mansukhlal, BA ACA *1996;* Aprirose, Aprirose House, 48 High Street, EDGWARE, HA8 7EQ.
GUDKA, Mrs. Manisha, BA ACA *1991;* P.O. Box 80382, MOMBASA, 80100, KENYA.
GUDKA, Mr. Millan Mahendra, BEng ACA *2004;* Flat 32 Manor House, 250 Martlebone Road, LONDON, NW1 5NP.
GUDKA, Mr. Neil Ashok, BSc ACA *2010;* PO BOX 41522, NAIROBI, KENYA.
GUDKA, Mrs. Palvi, BSc ACA *1998;* (Tax Fac), 66 Parkside Drive, WATFORD, WD17 3AX.
GUDKA, Mr. Piyush Zaverchand, ACA *1981;* 90 Howberry Road, EDGWARE, MIDDLESEX, HA8 6SY.
GUDKA, Mr. Priyen, BSc ACA *1994;* 12 Winchfield Close, HARROW, HA3 0DT.
GUDKA, Miss. Rakhee, BSc ACA *2010;* 35 Kinross Close, HARROW, MIDDLESEX, HA3 0UE.
•**GUDKA, Mr. Ritesh, FCA CTA** *1992;* TG Associates Limited, Monument House, 215 Marsh Road, PINNER, HA5 5NE.
GUDKA, Mr. Sachen Laxmikant, BSc ACA *1992;* Po Box 65, Viwandani, NAIROBI, 00507, KENYA.
GUEFOR, Mr. Abdul, BEng ACA *1996;* Treasury [isw-12], Intel (UK) Ltd, Pipers Way, SWINDON, SN3 1RJ.
GUELOVANI, Mr. Herman Georgievitch, ACA *1995;* 27 Meriden Close, BROMLEY, BR1 2UF.
GUERIN, Mr. Andrew John Daintry, ACA *2001;* Web Recruit, 1 Northleigh House Thorverton Road, EXETER, EX2 8HF.
GUERIN, Mr. Stephen John, MSc BSc ACA *2007;* 68B FORTHBRIDGE ROAD, LONDON, SW11 5NY.
GUERRA FERNANDEZ, Mrs. Andrea, BA(Hons) ACA *2010;* 84 Orchard Place, SOUTHAMPTON, SO14 3BW.
GUERRIERO, Mr. Ricky, BSc ACA *2011;* 6 Summers Way, MARKET HARBOROUGH, LEICESTERSHIRE, LE16 9QE.
GUERTIN, Mrs. Jennifer, BSc ACA *2006;* 16 Hawthorn Road, Bamford, ROCHDALE, LANCASHIRE, OL11 5JQ.
GUESSOUM, Mr. Nadir, ACA *2011;* 123 Woodside Road, Beeston, NOTTINGHAM, NG9 2SA.
GUEST, Mr. Ben, ACA *2010;* 10 Foxford Close, SUTTON COLDFIELD, WEST MIDLANDS, B72 1YT.
GUEST, Mrs. Catherine, BSc ACA *1997;* Oak House Holt End Lane, Bentworth, ALTON, HAMPSHIRE, GU34 5LF.
GUEST, Mrs. Cheryl Jane, BSc ACA *1994;* 14 Nichols Way, WETHERBY, WEST YORKSHIRE, LS22 6AD.
•**GUEST, Mr. David Anthony, FCA** *1987;* (Tax Fac), UHY Hacker Young (S.E) Ltd, 168 Church Road, HOVE, EAST SUSSEX, BN3 2DL. See also UHY Hacker Young
GUEST, Mr. David James, BSc FCA *1977;* 3 Harvey Avenue, NANTWICH, CW5 6LE.
GUEST, Mr. David Paul, BA ACA *1999;* 3 Church Lane, Lympsham, WESTON-SUPER-MARE, AVON, BS24 0DS.
GUEST, Mr. David Thomas, FCA *1958;* 15 Dippons Drive, Tettenhall Wood, WOLVERHAMPTON, WV6 8HJ. (Life Member)
•**GUEST, Mr. David Thomas, FCA** *1970;* (Tax Fac), PPG Accountants Limited, Ferndale House, 3 Firs Street, DUDLEY, WEST MIDLANDS, DY2 7DN. See also David T. Guest
GUEST, The Hon. David William Graham, MA FCA *1969;* 14 Shandon Street, EDINBURGH, EH11 1QH.
GUEST, Mr. Edward Melville Horatio, BA FCA *1999;* 9 St. Ann's Hill, LONDON, SW18 2EZ.
GUEST, Mr. Jack Bernard, BSc FCA *1954;* 119 Albury Drive, PINNER, HA5 3RJ. (Life Member)
•**GUEST, Mr. James Arthur, FCA** *1966;* J A Guest Ltd, 91 Princess Street, MANCHESTER, M1 4HT. See also Guest & Company
GUEST, Mr. James Matthew, FCA *1975;* 34 Wellington Road, Ealing, LONDON, W5 4UH.
GUEST, Miss. Jennifer Mary, ACA *2009;* Pricewaterhousecoopers, 7 More London Riverside, LONDON, SE1 2RT.
GUEST, Mr. John Anthony, BSc(Hons) ACA *2008;* Baker Tilly, 3 Hardman Street, MANCHESTER, M3 3HF.
GUEST, Mr. John David, BA ACA *1989;* 36 Alder Drive, Timperley, ALTRINCHAM, WA15 7YG.
GUEST, Mr. Lawrence Kingsley, FCA *1960;* Shearwater House, 1 Sea Grove, Selsey, CHICHESTER, WEST SUSSEX, PO20 9HT. (Life Member)
GUEST, Mr. Michael John, BA ACA *1983;* Orchard Cottage, 7 Bowmere Road, TARPORLEY, CW6 0BS.
GUEST, Mr. Nicholas Leigh, BSc ACA *1992;* Wester Ballindean House, Inchture, PERTH, PH14 9QS.
GUEST, Miss. Nicole Elena, BA ACA CFA *1996;* Ambleside Bacombe Lane, Wendover, AYLESBURY, BUCKINGHAMSHIRE, HP22 6EQ.
•**GUEST, Mr. Paul, FCA** *1992;* Peplows, 2 Cranmere Court, Lustleigh Close, Matford Business Park, EXETER, DEVON EX2 8PW.
GUEST, Mr. Paul Nigel, FCA *1968;* 232 Boulevard St Germain, 75007 PARIS, FRANCE.
GUEST, Mr. Philip Justin, BA ACA *1993;* Oak House Holt End Lane, Bentworth, ALTON, HAMPSHIRE, GU34 5LF.
GUEST, Ms. Sarah Elizabeth, BSc ACA *2000;* 25 Baring Crescent, BEACONSFIELD, BUCKINGHAMSHIRE, HP9 2NG.
GUEST, Miss. Sophie, BA ACA *2008;* 106 Vineyard Hill Road, LONDON, SW19 7JJ.
GUEST, Miss. Sophie Clare, BA(Hons) ACA *2001;* 14 Chapel Lane, LEICESTER, LE2 3WE.
GUEST, Mr. Sydney Clifford, FCA *1960;* 3 Church Lane, Lympsham, WESTON-SUPER-MARE, AVON, BS24 0DS. (Life Member)
GUEST-GORNALL, Mr. Richard Foster Dawson, BA ACA *1997;* I M G, McCormack House, Burlington Lane, Chiswick, LONDON, W4 2TH.
GUFFOGG, Ms. Darryl, BA ACA *1994;* 14 Paynes Orchard, Cheddington, LEIGHTON BUZZARD, LU7 0SN.
GUGALKA, Mr. Raphael Leszek, ACA *2009;* 20 Beech Avenue, Denholme, BRADFORD, WEST YORKSHIRE, BD13 4LX.
GUGEN, Mr. Francis Robert, FCA *1974;* 38 Argyll Road, Kensington, LONDON, W8 7BS.
GUGEN, Mr. Roger Thomas, FCA *1976;* 60 Lonsdale Road, LONDON, SW13 9JS.
•**GUGGIARI, Mrs. Rosemarie Hilda, BSc ACA** *1983;* Acara Accountancy, Hadley Ridge, North End, Goxhill, BARROW-UPON-HUMBER, NORTH LINCOLNSHIRE DN19 7JX.
GUHA, Miss. Aindrila, BA ACA *2010;* Flat 507, Faraday Lodge, Renaissance Walk, LONDON, SE10 0QL.
GUHA, Mr. Jason, BSc ACA *1999;* Bldg H 2nd flr W175 S, British Petroleum Co Plc, Chertsey Road, SUNBURY-ON-THAMES, MIDDLESEX, TW16 7LN.
GUHA, Mr. Parthasarathi, BA ACA *1982;* 10 Biddle Street, MOOREBANK, NSW 2170, AUSTRALIA.
GUHAN, Mr. Tiruvadi Jagadisan, ACA *1982;* 2 Gannet Street, OTTAWA K1K 4T7, ON, CANADA.
GUHAROY, Mr. Somnath, FCA *1973;* Maximasia Consulting Assciates, 9th Floor Pasaraya Blok M Kebayoran Baru, JAKARTA, JAVA, 12160, INDONESIA.
•**GUIDUZZI, Mr. Pierluigi, ACA** *2002;* (Tax Fac), PLG Consulting Ltd, 2nd Floor Victory House, 99-101 Regent Street, LONDON, W1B 4EZ.
GUIGNARD, Mr. Richard Charles Peter, FCA *1967;* Moya Khatta, The Avenue, RADLETT, WD7 7DW. (Life Member)
GUILBERT, Mrs. Christina Margaret, BA ACA *1982;* 32 Fairfax Avenue, EPSOM, SURREY, KT17 2QW.

GUILBERT, Mrs. Morven Anna, MA ACA *1991;* Les Brises, Kings Road, St Peter Port, GUERNSEY, GY1 1QF.
GUILBERT, Mr. Richard Edward, BA ACA *1983;* 32 Fairfax Avenue, East Ewell, EPSOM, KT17 2QW.
GUILBERT, Mr. Simon, MA ACA *2011;* 8 Domaine de Beauport, Hauteville, St. Peter Port, GUERNSEY, GY1 1DL.
GUILFORD, Mr. Mark, BSc FCA *1987;* 1 Gillingham Road, KETTERING, NN15 7RA.
GUILFORD, Mr. Noel Denis, BA FCA MSI *1977;* Fourwinds House, Balderton, CHESTER, CH4 9LF.
•GUILFOYLE, Mr. Brendan Ambrose, FCA *1975;* The P&A Partnership, 1 Whitehall, LEEDS, LS1 4HR.
GUILFOYLE, Mr. Joseph John, BA(Hons) ACA *2004;* Jones Lang LaSalle, 22 Hanover Square, LONDON, W1S 1JA.
•GUILFOYLE, Mr. Paul St John, BA ACA *1987;* (Tax Fac), with Gibson Hewitt Outsourcing Ltd, 5 Park Court, Pyrford Road, WEST BYFLEET, KT14 6SD.
•GUILFOYLE, Mrs. Ruth Susan, BA(Hons) ACA *2003;* Target Consulting, Lawrence House, Lower Bristol Road, BATH, BA2 9ET.
GUILFOYLE, Mr. Thomas, FCA *1952;* 21 Afon Gardens, Ponthir, NEWPORT, GWENT, NP18 1PR. (Life Member)
GUILLE, Mrs. Kathleen, FCA *1982;* Beech Croft, Battersby, MIDDLESBROUGH, CLEVELAND, TS9 6LU.
•GUILLEBAUD, Mr. John Roger, BSc FCA *1969;* A4U Accountants for Us Ltd, Sweet Meadows, Clifford Bridge, Drewsteignton, EXETER, EX6 6QB. See also Roger Guillebaud & Co
•GUILLEM, Mr. Michael John Vincent, FCA *1978;* Helmores UK LLP, Grosvenor Gardens House, 35-37 Grosvenor Gardens, LONDON, SW1W 0BY.
GUILLERMIN, Miss. Marie-Aimee, ACA *2011;* 3/83 West Esplanade, MANLY, NSW 2095, AUSTRALIA.
•GUILLIATT, Mr. Glenn William, BSc ACA *1983;* (Tax Fac), PGU Accounting Ltd, St. Oswald House, St. Oswald Street, CASTLEFORD, WEST YORKSHIRE, WF10 1DH.
GUILLOU, Mr. Nic John Hatton, PhD ACA *1994;* The Mill House, Cliff Street, St. Peter Port, GUERNSEY, GY1 1LH.
GUINN, Mr. David John, FCA *1971;* 11 Wordsworth Drive, EASTBOURNE, BN23 7QP.
•GUINN, Mr. Peter Charles, FCA CF *1996;* (Tax Fac), Alliotts, Congress House, 14 Lyon Road, HARROW, MIDDLESEX, HA1 2EN.
GUINNESS, Mr. Geoffrey Neil, MA FCA *1963;* 64A Kings Road, RICHMOND, TW10 6EP. (Life Member)
•GUINNESS, Mr. Kevin Michael, ACA *1988;* Kevin Guinness & Co, Sibberton Lodge, Leicester Road, Thornhaugh, PETERBOROUGH, PE8 6NH.
GUIRY, Mr. Vincent Edward, FCA *1975;* (Tax Fac), 11 Taywood Close, STEVENAGE, SG2 9QP.
GUJADHUR, Mr. Chandra Kumar, FCA *1981;* 4th Floor Raffles Tower, 19 Cybercity, Ebene, QUATRE-BORNES, MAURITIUS.
GUJADHUR, Mr. Dimeshwar, BA ACA *1994;* 50 Av de Calabre, Woluwe St Lambert, 1200 BRUSSELS, BELGIUM.
GUJADHUR, Mr. Kunal, MSc BSc ACA *2011;* 2 Walmar Close, BARNET, HERTFORDSHIRE, EN4 0LA.
GUJADHUR, Mr. Sheo Shankar, BSc ACA *1993;* 2 Monseigneur Gonin St, P O Box 94, PORT LOUIS, MAURITIUS.
GUJADHUR, Mr. Tej Kumar, MA BSc ACA *1999;* 9th Floor Orange Tower, c/o GFin Corporate Services, Cybercity, EBENE, MAURITIUS.
GUJRAL, Mr. Bhupinder, BSc ACA *1999;* 2 Athenia Close, Goffs Oak, WALTHAM CROSS, HERTFORDSHIRE, EN7 5ES.
GUJRAL, Mr. Sukhdeep Singh, BSc FCA *1997;* Citigroup Centre, 33 Canada Square, LONDON, E14 5LB.
•GULABIVALA, Mr. Rajesh, ACA *1987;* (Tax Fac), Taylors, Battle House, 1 East Barnet Road, BARNET, EN4 8RR.
•GULAM HUSSEIN, Mr. Iqbal, FCA *1972;* I G. Hussein & Company, 3 Magdalen Place, DUNDEE, DD1 4NN.
•GULAMALI, Mrs. Shahin Begum, BA ACA *1994;* Icknield Limited, 3rd Floor, 63-66 Hatton Garden, LONDON, EC1N 8LE.
•GULAMHUSEIN, Mr. Murtaza Mohamedtaki, ACA *1992;* Saymur Accountants Limited, 1st Floor, 27 Peterborough Road, HARROW, MIDDLESEX, HA1 2AU.
•GULAMHUSEIN, Mr. Shaukatali Mohamedhusein, FCA *1972;* S.M.G. Daya & Co, P.O.Box 90071, MOMBASA, KENYA.
•GULAMHUSEINWALA, Mr. Vajiuddin Kalimuddin, FCA *1970;* Mainard Limited, 7 Kingfield Road, LONDON, W5 1LD.
•GULATI, Mr. Anurag, BA ACA *1995;* Hampton Wells, 2 Woolhampton Way, CHIGWELL, IG7 4QH.
GULATI, Mr. Arvind, BSc ACA *1986;* P O Box N 4774, NASSAU, BAHAMAS.
GULATI, Mr. Rakesh, MBA BA FCA *1984;* Haleakala, 25 Garners Road, Chalfont St. Peter, GERRARDS CROSS, SL9 0HA.
GULATI, Mr. Vineet, ACA *1993;* 3143 Middlefield Avenue, FREMONT, CA 94539, UNITED STATES.
•GULL, Mrs. Susan Valerie, BA FCA *1987;* Scrutton Bland, Sanderson House, Museum Street, IPSWICH, IP1 1HE.
GULLEY, Mr. Adam, BSc ACA *2009;* 20 Clos Du Ruisseau, La Grande Route de St Martin St. Martin, JERSEY, JE3 6UU.
GULLICK, Mr. Gareth Richard, BSc(Hons) ACA *2001;* 15 Dorking Road, Bookham, LEATHERHEAD, KT23 4PB.
GULLIVER, Mr. Christopher Robin, FCA *1967;* Leadershape Ltd, P O Box 480, ABINGDON, OXFORDSHIRE, OX14 1WW.
•GULLIVER, Mr. John, LLB ACA ATII CIOT *1992;* (Tax Fac), Mason Hayes & Curran, South Bank House, Barrow Street, DUBLIN 4, COUNTY DUBLIN, IRELAND.
GULLIVER, Mr. John Richard, BSc ACA *1988;* Eden Financial Ltd Moorgate Hall, 155 Moorgate, LONDON, EC2M 6XB.
GULLIVER, Mr. Keith Philip, BSc FCA *1972;* 10 Kielder Close, Chandler's Ford, EASTLEIGH, HAMPSHIRE, SO53 4RL.
GULLIVER, Mr. Ronald, LLB FCA *1963;* The Old Chapel, New Mill Lane, Eversley, HOOK, HAMPSHIRE, RG27 0RA. (Life Member)
GULLIVER, Mr. Steven James, BA ACA *1995;* 1 Springfield Villas, 27 Chapel Lane, Milford, GODALMING, SURREY, GU8 5HB.
GULLIVER, Mr. Thomas, BA ACA *2010;* 6 Boyne Rise, Kings Worthy, WINCHESTER, SO23 7RE.
GULMOHAMED, Mr. Faiz, BSc ACA *1998;* 8 Huson Close, LONDON, NW3 3JW.
GULMOHAMED, Mr. Farid Rashid, FCA *1970;* Flat 23, Hanover House, St. Johns Wood High Street, St Johns Wood, LONDON, NW8 7DX.
GULMOHAMED, Mr. Jason, BCom ACA *1999;* Northgate Information Solutions Peoplebuilding Estate, Maylands Avenue Hemel Hempstead Industrial Estate, HEMEL HEMPSTEAD, HERTFORDSHIRE, HP2 4NW.
•GULRAJANI, Mr. Ramesh, BSc FCA *1984;* BSG Valentine, Lynton House, 7/12 Tavistock Square, LONDON, WC1H 9BQ.
GULWELL, Mr. Derrick John, FCA *1969;* County Tyre Group, 16-17 Victoria Road St. Philips, BRISTOL, BS2 0UX.
GULWELL, Mr. Michael George, BSc ACA *1995;* Hollybank Cottage, Whitewall Lane, Felliscliffe, HARROGATE, HG3 2JZ.
•GULY, Mr. Damian Peter, BA FCA *1988;* PricewaterhouseCoopers LLP, 7 More London Riverside, LONDON, SE1 2RT. See also PricewaterhouseCoopers
GULZAR, Mr. Tariq, ACA CPA *2011;* Warid Telecom (PVT) Ltd, EFU House, 9th Floor, Jail Road, LAHORE 54000, PAKISTAN.
•GUMBLEY, Mr. Christopher David, FCA *1983;* (Tax Fac), Chris Gumbley and Co, 5 Mercury Quays, Ashley Lane, SHIPLEY, WEST YORKSHIRE, BD17 7DB.
GUMBLEY, Mr. James Howard, BA(Hons) ACA *2004;* with KPMG LLC, Heritage Court, 41 Athol Street, Douglas, ISLE OF MAN, IM99 1HN.
GUMBLEY, Mr. Terence Edmund, FCA *1974;* Oakhouse, St. Johns Lane, BEWDLEY, WORCESTERSHIRE, DY12 2QZ.
GUMEL, Mr. Farouk Mohammed, BSc ACA *2006;* with PricewaterhouseCoopers, Plot 252E Muri Okunola Street, Victoria Island, P O Box 2419, LAGOS, NIGERIA.
GUMERY, Mr. Raymond Sydney, FCA *1953;* 139 Springfield Road, Castle Bromwich, BIRMINGHAM, B36 0DU. (Life Member)
GUMIENNY, Mr. Marek Stefan, BSc ACA *1985;* 8 Westmead, LONDON, SW15 5BQ.
GUMM, Mr. Paul David, BEng ACA *1994;* Flat 24 Adams Quarter, Tallow Road, BRENTFORD, MIDDLESEX, TW8 8ER.
GUMMER, Mrs. Patricia Anne, BSc FCA *1977;* Harewood Grange, Harewood Road, Holymoorside, CHESTERFIELD, S42 7HR.
•GUMMERSON, Mr. James Robert Donald, FCA *1975;* Hadley & Co, Adelphi Chambers, 30 Hoghton Street, SOUTHPORT, PR9 0NZ.
GUMMERY, Mrs. Emma Frances Louise, BA FCA *1991;* 13 Redfern Avenue, WORCESTER, WR5 1PZ.
•GUMMERY, Mr. Keith John, MA FCA *1981;* The South House, Shortgrove, SAFFRON WALDEN, CB11 3TX.
GUMMOW, Mr. Antony, BSc FCA *1977;* Blue Elvan, Kellow, LOOE, CORNWALL, PL13 1LE.
•GUMMOW, Mr. Clive Freeman, BCom FCA *1963;* (Tax Fac), Clive Gummow, Cottage Farm, Pinley Green, Claverdon, WARWICK, CV35 8LX.
GUMUSH, Mr. Arseven Reshat, BSc FCA *1973;* 27 Barndicott House, Barndicott, WELWYN GARDEN CITY, HERTFORDSHIRE, AL7 2BS.
GUN, Mrs. Angela Jane, BA ACA *2005;* LGC Limited, Queens Road, TEDDINGTON, MIDDLESEX, TW11 0LY.
GUNAPALA, Mr. Sanjaya, MEng BEng ACA *2003;* 4 Elphinstone Close, Brookwood, WOKING, SURREY, GU24 0AF.
•GUNARATNASINGAM, Ms. Athena Meera, BA(Hons) ACA *2004;* (Tax Fac), AV Accountants Limited, 19 Harewood Road, ISLEWORTH, MIDDLESEX, TW7 5HB.
GUNARY, Mr. Brian Arthur, FCA *1951;* 18 The Meads, Ongar Road, BRENTWOOD, ESSEX, CM15 9GL. (Life Member)
GUNASEKARA, Miss. Sarah Frances, MA ACA *2010;* 34 Castle Hill, MAIDENHEAD, BERKSHIRE, SL6 4JJ.
GUNASENA, Mr. Steven Mark, MPhil FCA *1991;* GEMALTO SA, BATIMENT 5.1.239, 6 RUE DE LA VERRERIE, 92197 MEUDON, FRANCE.
GUNAWARDENA, Mr. Rohana Kithsiri, BSc FCA *1990;* 2733 Cowper Street, PALO ALTO, CA 94306-2448, UNITED STATES.
GUNAWARDHANA, Mr. Chamila Abewickrama, ACA *2008;* Flat 9 Waltham House, Boundary Road, LONDON, NW8 0JD.
GUNDRY, Prof. Stephen Walter, MSc FCA *1975;* University of Bristol, Water & Health Research Centre, Department of Civil Engineering, Merchant Venturers Building, Woodland Road, BRISTOL BS8 1UB.
GUNERATNE, Mr. Lewis Alexander, MEng BA(Hons) ACA *2006;* Flat 53 Stepney City Apartments, 49 Clark Street, LONDON, E1 3HS.
GUNES, Mr. Mehmet, MSc ACA *1999;* Tepecik Tolu, Sari Konaklar Sitesi B22 Dr 8, Etiler, ISTANBUL, TURKEY.
•GUNESH, Mr. Indar Raj, ACA *1993;* Wesley Pemberton LLP, 89 Vicars Moor Lane, LONDON, N21 1BL.
GUNEWARDENA, Mr. Desmond Anthony Lalith, BSc ACA *1982;* D & D (London) Ltd, 16 Kirby Street, LONDON, EC1N 8TS.
GUNEWARDENA, Mrs. Victoria, BSc ACA *1999;* South Warwickshire General Hospitals, NHS Trust, Finance Dept, Warwick Hospital, Lakin Road, WARWICK CV34 5BD.
•GUNGAH, Mr. Dharmanand Neil, MA ACA FCCA ATT *2008;* (Tax Fac), Neils Limited, 3 Dukes Court, Wellington Street, LUTON, BEDFORDSHIRE, LU1 5AF. See also Spiro Neil
•GUNGAH, Mr. Om Prakash, FCA FAIA *1980;* 4 The Drive, MORDEN, SURREY, SM4 6DQ.
GUNKEL, Mr. Peter Charles, FCA *1973;* Glenwood, 38 Kingswood Way, SOUTH CROYDON, Surrey, CR2 8QQ. (Life Member)
GUNLACK, Mr. Robert Henry, FCA *1969;* Treviades Barton, High Cross, Constantine, FALMOUTH, CORNWALL, TR11 5RG.
GUNN, Mr. Alastair James, BA ACA *2005;* 8 Quintin Avenue, LONDON, SW20 8LD.
GUNN, Miss. Alice, BA ACA *2005;* (Tax Fac), Flat 13 Park Mansions, 14 Stamford Brook Avenue, LONDON, W6 0YD.
GUNN, Mr. Andrew David Stewart, MBA FCA *1966;* 80 Northampton Road, Earls Barton, NORTHAMPTON, NN6 0HE. (Life Member)
•①GUNN, Mr. Cameron Frazer, ACA CA(AUS) *2009;* ReSolve Partners LLP, One America Square, Crosswall, LONDON, EC3N 2LB.
GUNN, Mr. Christopher Simon, BSc ACA *1982;* The Cottage, Bodsham, ASHFORD, KENT, TN25 5JQ.
GUNN, Miss. Claire Louise, ACA *2008;* 62b Mansfield Road, LONDON, NW3 2HU.
GUNN, Miss. Debra Jane, BA ACA *2001;* 13 Grayling Court, BERKHAMSTED, HERTFORDSHIRE, HP4 1TF.
GUNN, Miss. Helen Elizabeth, BA ACA *1996;* Bnp Paribas, 10 Harewood Avenue, LONDON, NW1 6AA.
GUNN, Mr. Ian Hugh Alexander, FCA *1967;* Baylaw, 2A Parry's Lane, Stoke Bishop, BRISTOL, BS9 1AA.
GUNN, Mr. James Rice, BA(Hons) ACA *2003;* 5 Butlers Grove, Great Linford, MILTON KEYNES, MK14 5DT.
GUNN, Mrs. Jennifer Barbara, BA ACA *1981;* Barker Brettell Llp, 100 Hagley Road Edgbaston, BIRMINGHAM, B16 8QQ.
GUNN, Mr. John Alexander, BA FCA *1956;* 16 Royal York Crescent, Clifton, BRISTOL, BS8 4JY. (Life Member)
GUNN, Mr. John Reginald, FCA *1965;* 85 Wild Duck Road, WILTON, CT 06897, UNITED STATES.
GUNN, Miss. Julia Katherine, BSc ACA *2004;* with KPMG, 10 Shelley Street, SYDNEY, NSW 2000, AUSTRALIA.
GUNN, Mrs. Kim, ACA *2009;* 94 Penkett Road, WALLASEY, MERSEYSIDE, CH45 7QA.
GUNN, Mrs. Lucia Marie, BA ACA *1999;* 83 The Street, Crowmarsh Gifford, WALLINGFORD, OXFORDSHIRE, OX10 8EF.
GUNN, Miss. Lynsey, BA ACA *2001;* Pricewaterhousecoopers Llp, 1 Hays Lane, LONDON, SE1 2RD. (Life Member)
GUNN, Mr. Matthew, MA ACA *2000;* 11G MOUNT SINAI LANE, 05-33 GLENTREES, SINGAPORE 277056, SINGAPORE.
•GUNN, Mr. Michael Peter, BA FCA *1982;* 2 Parsons Paddock, Exeter Road, Newton Poppleford, SIDMOUTH, DEVON, EX10 0FD.
GUNN, Mr. Peter Robert Francis, BSc(Econ) FCA *1978;* The Bluebells, 9 Redwood Place, Wattleton Road, BEACONSFIELD, HP9 1RP.
GUNN, Mr. Philip Graham, BA ACA *1979;* 24 Nicker Hill, Keyworth, NOTTINGHAM, NG12 5EN.
GUNN, Mr. Philip James, BSc ACA *1995;* GFI Group Pte Ltd, 16 Collyer Quay, #31-00 Hitachi Tower, SINGAPORE 049318, SINGAPORE.
GUNN, Mr. Philip Rice, FCA *1966;* 10 Whitefield Terrace, Greenbank Road, PLYMOUTH, PL4 8NH. (Life Member)
GUNN, Mr. Richard, MEng ACA *2002;* Alvarez & Marsal, 1 Finsbury Circus, LONDON, EC2M 7EB.
GUNN, Mr. Robert Charles, FCA *1972;* Corners, 3 Caledon Road, BEACONSFIELD, HP9 2BX.
GUNN, Mr. Robert Neil John, BA ACA *1993;* with RSM Tenon Audit Limited, Charterhouse, Legge Street, BIRMINGHAM, B4 7EU.
GUNN, Mrs. Sarah, MA ACA *1990;* 4 St. Bernards Crescent, EDINBURGH, EH4 1NP.
GUNN, Miss. Sharron Elizabeth, BA FCA *1990;* with ICAEW, Chartered Accountants' Hall, Moorgate Place, LONDON, EC2P 2BJ.
GUNN, Mr. Stefan Soutar, MA ACA *2007;* 27 Cheriton Place, Westbury-on-Trym, BRISTOL, BS9 4AW.
GUNN, Mr. Stephen Mark, BA ACA *1998;* 39 Ascough Wynd, Aiskew, BEDALE, NORTH YORKSHIRE, DL8 1AT.
GUNN, Mr. William Keith, BCom ACA *2010;* 171 Main Street, PO Box 4259, ROAD TOWN, VIRGIN ISLANDS (BRITISH).
GUNNELL, Mr. James Lidzey, FCA *1960;* 6 Ashcombe Drive, BEXHILL-ON-SEA, TN39 3UJ. (Life Member)
GUNNER, Mr. Alan Douglas, FCA *1974;* 3 Sherring Close, BRACKNELL, RG42 2LD.
GUNNER, Mr. Peter John, FCA *1973;* 21 Burge Crescent, Cotford St. Luke, TAUNTON, SOMERSET, TA4 1NU. (Life Member)
GUNNEY, Mr. Colin Hugh, FCA *1971;* (Tax Fac), Maer House Upper Widhill Lane, Blunsdon, SWINDON, SN26 8BX.
GUNNING, Mrs. Justine Amanda, BSc ACA *1998;* with PricewaterhouseCoopers LLP, Marlborough Court, 10 Bricket Road, ST. ALBANS, HERTFORDSHIRE, AL1 3JX.
GUNNING, Mr. Richard Vincent, BSc FCA *1978;* PO Box 360, DUBAI, UNITED ARAB EMIRATES.
GUNNING, Mr. Stephen William Lawrence, MEng&Man ACA *1993;* British Airways World Cargo Carrus (S122), PO Box 99, Sealand Road, HOUNSLOW, MIDDLESEX, TW6 2JS.
GUNNINGHAM, Mr. James Douglas, ACA *1985;* (Tax Fac), Novelis UK, 15 Bunbury Way, EPSOM, SURREY, KT17 4JP.
GUNSON, Mr. Andrew Digby, BSc ACA *2000;* Tanglewood, Parkside Road, KENDAL, CUMBRIA, LA9 7LG.
•GUNSON, Mr. Martin Edward, FCA FRSA *1980;* (Tax Fac), Martin Edward Gunson, Bank House, 9 Dicconson Terrace, Lytham, LYTHAM ST. ANNES, FY8 5JY.
GUNSON, Mr. Paul John, ACA *1984;* 45/75A Ross Street, Glebe, SYDNEY, NSW 2037, AUSTRALIA.
GUNSON, Mr. Peter John, FCA *1957;* Bridleway, Whins Lane, Simonstone, BURNLEY, LANCASHIRE, BB12 7QT. (Life Member)
GUNSON, Mr. Stephen John, MA MBA FCA *1989;* Glotterpfad 8, 79194 GUNDELFINGEN, GERMANY.
GUNSTON, Mrs. Christopher, FCA *1974;* Tudor House, Ghyll Road, HEATHFIELD, EAST SUSSEX, TN21 0XJ.
GUNSTON, Mr. Matthew Richard, BCom ACA *2001;* Calle Puero Rico 18 7d, 28016 MADRID, SPAIN.
GUNSTON, Mr. Richard John, ACA *2009;* 32 Westbourne Street, HOVE, EAST SUSSEX, BN3 5PG.

•**GUNTER, Mrs. Amanda Jane, ACA** *2002;* (Tax Fac), A.C. Mole & Sons, Stafford House, Blackbrook Park Avenue, TAUNTON, SOMERSET, TA1 2PX.

GUNTER, Mr. Michael Frederick, BSc ACA *1994;* Deluxe Entertainment Services Group Inc., 1377 N. Serrano Ave, LOS ANGELES, CA 91106, UNITED STATES.

GUNTERT, Mr. Andrew Nicholas, MSc FCA *1971;* (Member of Council 1996 - 2000), 7 Chalcot Place, Great Holm, MILTON KEYNES, MK8 9BZ.

GUNTHER, Mr. Steven Peter, ACA *2003;* 25 Chester Avenue, UPMINSTER, ESSEX, RM14 3JH.

GUNTON, Mr. John Neil, BSc ACA *1990;* 36 Links Road, Lower Parkstone, POOLE, BH14 9QS.

GUNTON, Mr. Michael Frederick, FCA *1972;* Michael Gunton Consulting, chemin de la Colline 4, Case Postale 39, 1197 PRANGINS, SWITZERLAND.

GUNTON, Mrs. Sarah Jane, ACA *2005;* Elm House, 7 Elm Road, STOWMARKET, SUFFOLK, IP14 1QW.

GUNTRIP, Mr. Anthony John, FCA *1971;* White Lodge, 30 Birchwood Road, Petts Wood, ORPINGTON, BR5 1NZ.

GUNYON, Mr. Steven Leslie, BSc ACA *1980;* 17 Snowshill Close, Barnwood, GLOUCESTER, GL4 3GE.

GUO, Miss. Linhong, BSc ACA *2011;* 98 Light Oaks Road, SALFORD, M6 8WP.

GUPPY, Mrs. Anjum, BSc ACA *1994;* 19 Dugdale Hill Lane, POTTERS BAR, EN6 2DP.

•**GUPPY, Mr. Jonathan Jeffrey, BSc ACA** *1987;* KPMG LLP, 15 Canada Square, LONDON, E14 5GL. See also KPMG Europe LLP

GUPPY, Mr. Paul Jeremy, BA ACA *1992;* 205 Sunnybank Road, POTTERS BAR, HERTFORDSHIRE, EN6 2NH.

GUPPY, Mr. Richard David, BEng ACA *1992;* The Old Chapel, West Woodburn, HEXHAM, NE48 2RA.

GUPTA, Mr. Abhinav, ACA *2011;* 122 Mandakini Enclave, NEW DELHI 110019, INDIA.

•**GUPTA, Mr. Ajay Kumar, MA FCA** *1982;* Ernst & Young, 220 South Sixth Street, 1400 Pillsbury Center, MINNEAPOLIS, MN 55402, UNITED STATES.

GUPTA, Mrs. Ameeka, BA ACA *2005;* M225, Greater Kailash Part 2, NEW DELHI 110048, CAPITAL TERRITORY OF DELHI, INDIA.

GUPTA, Mr. Ananda, FCA *1997;* 3400 Riverside Drive, Suite 13020, BURBANK, CA 91505, UNITED STATES.

GUPTA, Mr. Anil Kumar, ACA *1989;* DMC Healthcare, Nice Group Ltd Nice Business Park 19-35, Sylvan Grove, LONDON, SE15 1PD.

GUPTA, Mr. Arun, MSc ACA *2003;* 65 Stacey Avenue, Wolverton, MILTON KEYNES, MK12 5DN.

GUPTA, Mr. Arun Kumar, BSc FCA *1977;* 74 Warren Road, LONDON, NW2 7NJ.

GUPTA, Mr. Arvind Kumar, ACA ACMA *2000;* P O Box 129, Wendywood, JOHANNESBURG, GAUTENG, 2148, SOUTH AFRICA.

GUPTA, Mr. Ashok Kumar, FCA *1967;* 1 Coney Walk, Wimblington, MARCH, CAMBRIDGESHIRE, PE15 0RH.

•**GUPTA, Mr. Brijinder Kumar, BSc FCA CTA** *1992;* (Tax Fac), Murphy Salisbury, 15 Warwick Road, STRATFORD-UPON-AVON, CV37 6YW.

GUPTA, Mr. Dhruba, MPhil BSc FCA *1965;* 5510 MARGATE STREET, SPRINGFIELD, VA 22151, UNITED STATES.

•**GUPTA, Mr. Dibyendu, FCA** *1973;* 2 Highview Gardens, EDGWARE, HA8 9UE.

GUPTA, Mrs. Divya, ACA *2010;* Flat 15 Sheridan Place, 15 Roxborough Park, HARROW, MIDDLESEX, HA1 3BQ.

GUPTA, Miss. Elka, BCom ACA *2001;* 66 Greenfield Road, Harborne, BIRMINGHAM, B17 0EE.

GUPTA, Mrs. Jayshree, ACA *2010;* 9 Alandale Drive, PINNER, MIDDLESEX, HA5 3UP.

GUPTA, Mr. Madan, BSc FCA *1992;* PO Box 504603, DUBAI, UNITED ARAB EMIRATES.

GUPTA, Mrs. Monica, BSc ACA *2002;* 227 Leesons Hill, CHISLEHURST, KENT, BR7 6QJ.

GUPTA, Mr. Neel, BSocSc ACA *1996;* 5 South Drive, Sonning-on-Thames, READING, RG4 6GB.

GUPTA, Mr. Piyush, BA FCA *1995;* 3 Brook Close, MARCH, CAMBRIDGESHIRE, PE15 9UR.

GUPTA, Mr. Praveen, ACA CTA *1995;* with BDO LLP, 125 Colmore Row, BIRMINGHAM, B3 3SD.

GUPTA, Mrs. Preeti, MBA ACA CTA *2001;* 3 Beaumont Chase, BOLTON, BL3 4XH.

GUPTA, Mr. Rajesh, BSc ACA *1995;* 12 Shaftesbury Avenue, Kenton, HARROW, HA3 0QX.

GUPTA, Mr. Rajesh, BSc ACA *1998;* Morgan Stanley, 25 Cabot Square, Canary Wharf, LONDON, E14 4QA.

•**GUPTA, Mr. Rajiv, BSc FCA** *1987;* A.R.N. Gupta & Co, 501 Great West Road, HOUNSLOW, TW5 0BS.

GUPTA, Miss. Rakhee, BSc ACA *2003;* 28 Queens Gardens, HOUNSLOW, TW5 9DB.

•**GUPTA, Mr. Ranvir Kumar, FCA** *1975;* R.K. Gupta & Co, 89 Hook Rise South, SURBITON, SURREY, KT6 7NA.

GUPTA, Mr. Ravinder Kumar, BSc ACA *1997;* 31 Heath Drive, LONDON, NW3 7SB.

GUPTA, Miss. Rju, BA ACA *1993;* 10 Pavenham Drive, Edgbaston, BIRMINGHAM, B5 7TW.

GUPTA, Mr. Rohit, ACA *1993;* 6 Payne Close, BARKING, IG11 9PL.

GUPTA, Mr. Sachin, BA ACA *2001;* 11 Wellington Road, HAMPTON, MIDDLESEX, TW12 1JP.

GUPTA, Mr. Sandeep, BCom FCA *1990;* Glen Abbey, 320 Hayward Lane, ALPHARETTA, GA 30022-6440, UNITED STATES.

GUPTA, Mr. Sandeep, BSc ACA *2000;* 15 The Ridgeway, LONDON, W3 8LW.

GUPTA, Miss. Sehjal, BSc(Hons) ACA CTA *2007;* 89 Hook Rise South, SURBITON, KT6 7NA.

GUPTA, Mr. Shalet Kumar, BEng ACA *1997;* Anchor Trust, Valley Road, BRADFORD, WEST YORKSHIRE, BD1 4RP.

GUPTA, Miss. Shalini, BA ACA *1991;* 33 Longford Avenue, SOUTHALL, UB1 3QN.

GUPTA, Mrs. Shobhna, MSc FCA *1992;* Po Box 504603, DUBAI, UNITED ARAB EMIRATES.

GUPTA, Mr. Shyam, BSc ACA *2007;* Merrill Lynch Financial Centre, 2 King Edward Street, LONDON, EC1A 1HQ.

GUPTA, Mr. Simon, BA(Econ) ACA *1995;* (Tax Fac), 563 Reading Road, Winnersh, WOKINGHAM, RG41 5HJ.

•**GUPTA, Mrs. Sonia, ACA** *2011;* Abingdon Accountants Limited, The Manor, Sweetcroft Lane, UXBRIDGE, MIDDLESEX, UB10 9LE.

•**GUPTA, Mr. Sudheer, BA FCA** *1990;* (Tax Fac), Alliotts, Imperial House, 15 Kingsway, LONDON, WC2B 6UN.

•**GUPTA, Mr. Suneel, BCom ACA** *1995;* with Grant Thornton UK LLP, Enterprise House, 115 Edmund Street, BIRMINGHAM, B3 2HJ.

GUPTA, Mr. Sunil Kumar, FCA *1990;* 1 Woodhall Drive, LONDON, SE21 7HJ.

GUPTA, Mr. Tarsem Lal, FCA FCCA ACMA *1968;* 57 Silverdale Road, Gatley, CHEADLE, CHESHIRE, SK8 4QR.

GUPTA, Mr. Vikas, BA ACA *1999;* 9 Stoughton Road, LEICESTER, LE2 2EE.

GUPTA, Mr. Vinay Kumar, FCA *1973;* 13 Central Lane, Babar Road, NEW DELHI 110001, INDIA.

GUPTA, Mr. Yogesh, ACA *1989;* 1429 241st Place SE, SAMMAMISH, WA 98075, UNITED STATES.

•**GUPTA, Mr. Yogeshwar Kumar, FCA** *1969;* YG Eaton & Co Limited, Alpine House, Unit 2, 1st Floor, Honeypot Lane, LONDON NW9 9RX.

GUPWELL, Mr. Christopher John, FCA *1965;* Woodlands, Stock Green, REDDITCH, WORCESTERSHIRE, B96 6TB.

•**GURAM, Mrs. Narinder Kaur, ACA** *1982;* Guram & Co, 173 Homesdale Road, BROMLEY, KENT, BR1 2QL.

GURAV, Mr. Subhash Nivrutti, BA FCA CTA *1993;* (Tax Fac), 41 Greenhill Road, HARROW, MIDDLESEX, HA1 1LD.

GURBUTT, Mr. Michael James, ACA *2002;* 7314 Aynsley Lane, MCLEAN, VA 22102, UNITED STATES.

GUREJA, Mr. Nikhil, BEng ACA *2001;* Flat B, 12F Tregunter Tower 3, 14 Tregunter Path, MID LEVELS, HONG KONG ISLAND, HONG KONG SAR.

•**GURKIN, Mrs. Alison, ACA** *1990;* Alison Gurkin Consultants, 41 Culmington Road, Ealing, LONDON, W13 9NJ.

GURKIN, Mr. Nigel David, BSc ACA *1991;* Plus Shops Ltd, Langham House, 302-308 Regent Street, LONDON, W1B 3AT.

•**GURMIN, Mr. Steven, ACA** *1984;* Steven Gurmin, 122 Hamilton Avenue, HALESOWEN, B62 8SJ.

GURNER, Mr. Michael Stephen, FCA *1968;* Ryecotes, 35 Moor Park Road, NORTHWOOD, HA6 2DL.

GURNEY, Mr. Alistair, BA ACA *2011;* Flat 1, 44-48 Clerkenwell Road, LONDON, EC1M 5PS.

GURNEY, Mr. Brian Edwin, FCA *1952;* Highclere, 20 The Heath, LEIGHTON BUZZARD, LU7 3HL. (Life Member)

GURNEY, Mr. Charles Alfred, BSc ACA *1991;* Jigsaw Unit 2/B, 159 Mortlake Road, RICHMOND, TW9 4AW.

GURNEY, Mr. David John, BSc FCA *1983;* 24 Madeley Close, Rubery, BIRMINGHAM, B45 9XA.

GURNEY, Mr. Glenn Robert, ACA *2009;* 2 Melford Close, South Wootton, KING'S LYNN, NORFOLK, PE30 3XH.

GURNEY, Mr. John Michael Anthony, BA FCA *1954;* 4 Sycamore Avenue, ABERGAVENNY, GWENT, NP7 5JY. (Life Member)

GURNEY, Mr. Jonathan Paul, LLB ACA *1994;* 17 Turnstone Close, Winnersh, WOKINGHAM, RG41 5LQ.

GURNEY, Mr. Joseph, BA ACA *2011;* 53c Witherington Road, LONDON, N5 1PN.

GURNEY, Mr. Mark Simon Okey, BSc(Hons) ACA *2004;* Golfbreaks Ltd, 2 Windsor Dials, Arthur Road, WINDSOR, BERKSHIRE, SL4 1RS.

•**GURNEY, Mr. Martin Stuart, BA FCA** *1992;* (Tax Fac), HW, Old Station House, Station Approach, Newport Street, SWINDON, WILTSHIRE SN1 3DU. See also Haines Watts

GURNEY, Mr. Nigel John, BSc ACA *1993;* 9 Bedser Close, LONDON, SE11 5BE.

GURNEY, Mr. Robert Edward Quintin, BA ACA *1997;* Bawdeswell Hall, DEREHAM, NORFOLK, NR20 4SA.

GURNEY, Mr. Simon John, BA FCA *1993;* 1 Holiday Lane, Hanslope, MILTON KEYNES, MK19 7BU.

GURNEY, Mr. Simon John Okey, FCA *1969;* Sleepy Hollow, Bagshot Road, Worplesdon, GUILDFORD, GU3 3PX.

GURNEY, Mr. Steven David, BA(Hons) ACA *2001;* Flat 14 Beaulieu Court, 133-135 De La Warr Road, BEXHILL-ON-SEA, TN40 2JJ.

GURNEY, Mr. Trevor Robert, FCA *1974;* Brown Butler Apsley House, 78 Wellington Street, LEEDS, LS1 2JT.

GURNEY, Mr. William Stephen Claude, FCA *1969;* Lizard Farm, Foulsham, DEREHAM, NORFOLK, NR20 5RN.

GURNHILL, Mr. James Ian, LLB FCA *1972;* 45 Bowen Court, 31-35 The Drive, HOVE, EAST SUSSEX, BN3 3JF. (Life Member)

GURNHILL, Mr. Russell Charles, BSc ACA MCT *1995;* 14 Eynella Road, LONDON, SE22 8XF.

GURR, Mr. David James, BEng ACA *1997;* Enterprise House, 5 Roundwood Lane, HARPENDEN, HERTFORDSHIRE, AL5 3BW.

GURR, Mr. Jacob Matthew George, ACA *1999;* 66 Romney Drive, BROMLEY, BR1 2TE.

GURR, Mr. Peter Nicholas, ACA *1998;* with Deloitte LLP, 2 New Street Square, LONDON, EC4A 3BZ.

GURR, Mr. Stephen John, FCA *1971;* 12 Blagdens Close, Southgate, LONDON, N14 6DE.

GURREY, Mr. Niall, FCA *1950;* 180 City Road, Tilehurst, READING, RG31 5SD. (Life Member)

•**GURRIE, Mr. Leonard Alan, FCA** *1964;* L.A. Gurrie, 203 Collingwood House, Dolphin Square, LONDON, SW1V 3ND.

GURSAHANI, Mr. Mahendra S, ACA *1983;* Standard Chartered Bank, 9th Floor Executive Office, 6788 Ayala Avenue, MAKATI CITY, PHILIPPINES.

GURSAHANI, Mrs. Subh Manmohan, ACA *1982;* 3 Banaba Circle, South Forbes, Makati City, MANILA 1220, PHILIPPINES.

GURTNER, Mr. Vernon Frederick, BSc FCA *1975;* 3 Mason Close, WALTHAM ABBEY, ESSEX, EN9 3JW. (Life Member)

GURU, Miss. Akshawra, BSc(Hons) ACA *2011;* 162 Squires Lane, LONDON, N3 2QT.

•**GURYEL, Mrs. Seval, BSc(Hons) ACA** *2003;* Guryel & Co, 214 Lower Addiscombe Road, CROYDON, SURREY, CR0 7AB.

GUSEV, Mr. Victor, BSc ACA *2004;* FL 21, Deliana Court, 3106 LIMASSOL, CYPRUS.

GUSTAFSSON, Mrs. Hilary, BSc(Hons) ACA *2001;* Winter Rule Lowin House, Tregolls Road, TRURO, CORNWALL, TR1 2NA.

GUSTERSON, Mr. Ronald George, FCA *1953;* 10 Bilton Road, RUGBY, CV22 7AB. (Life Member)

GUTCH, Mr. Mathew John Watabe, ACA *2009;* 88 Hessel Road, LONDON, W13 9ET.

GUTCHER, Mrs. Amy Caroline, MA ACA DChA *2006;* 92 Clock House Road, BECKENHAM, BR3 4JT.

GUTCHER, Mr. Lee, BA ACA *2006;* 92 Clock House Road, BECKENHAM, BR3 4JT.

GUTHRIE, Mr. Alastair Donald, FCA *1975;* 9 Sturdee Close, EASTBOURNE, EAST SUSSEX, BN23 6AZ.

GUTHRIE, Mr. Andrew Micheal McDunphy, BA ACA *1985;* Integrate Preston & Chorley Ltd, 112-116 Tulketh Brow Ashton-on-Ribble, PRESTON, PR2 2SJ.

•**GUTHRIE, Mr. George Richard, BSc ACA** *1989;* (Tax Fac), Guthrie Accountancy Services Limited, Unit 1, 11 Eagle Parade, BUXTON, DERBYSHIRE, SK17 6EQ.

GUTHRIE, Mr. Hamish Kirk, BSc FCA *1976;* 2 Norman Macleod Crescent, Bearsden, GLASGOW, G61 3BF.

GUTHRIE, Mr. Jonathan, BSc ACA *1987;* MGT Limited, Cluny Court, The John Smith Business Park, KIRKCALDY, KY2 6QJ.

•**GUTHRIE, Mr. Mark Adrian, FCA** *1969;* Mark A. Guthrie & Co., 43-45 Acre Lane, LONDON, SW2 5TN.

GUTHRIE, Mrs. Mary, BSc FCA *1976;* 2 Norman Macleod Crescent, Bearsden, GLASGOW, G61 3BF.

GUTHRIE, Mr. Neal Robert, FCA *1975;* 20 Freathy Lane, Kennington, ASHFORD, Kent, TN25 4QR.

•**GUTHRIE, Mr. Roger David Charles, MA FCA CTA** *1979;* Peters Elworthy & Moore, Salisbury House, Station Road, CAMBRIDGE, CB1 2LA. See also PEM VAT Services LLP, PEM Corporate Finance LLP

GUTSELL, Mr. Ian Charles, BA BSc ACA *1990;* 6 Grosvenor Road, SEAFORD, BN25 2BL.

GUTTENSTEIN, Mr. Robin Francis Eric, FCA *1970;* Flat 2003 Yin Ren Mansion, Da Cheng Xiang 98, WUXI 214001, JIANGSU PROVINCE, CHINA.

GUTTERIDGE, Mrs. Elspeth Janet, BCom ACA *1989;* Ty Cottage, Southern Green, Rushden, BUNTINGFORD, HERTFORDSHIRE, SG9 0SW.

GUTTERIDGE, Mr. Jonathan Ralph, BSc ACA *1986;* 27 Lyndhurst Gardens, PINNER, HA5 3XD.

GUTTERIDGE, Mrs. Nicola Kay, BSc(Hons) ACA *2002;* Kendall Wadley Llp Granta Lodge, 71 Graham Road, MALVERN, WORCESTERSHIRE, WR14 2JS.

•**GUTTERIDGE, Miss. Sarah Elizabeth, MA FCA** *1996;* Deloitte LLP, Athene Place, 66 Shoe Lane, LONDON, EC4A 3BQ. See also Deloitte & Touche LLP

•**GUTTRIDGE, Mr. Robert Prime, MA ACA** *1987;* 4 Palmer Close, BRIDGWATER, SOMERSET, TA6 6UU.

GUTTRIDGE, Mr. Roy Clive, FCA *1965;* 4 Rockingham Hall Gardens, Hagley, STOURBRIDGE, DY9 9JQ. (Life Member)

GUY, Mrs. Alice, BA ACA *2003;* 57 Stratton Way, BIGGLESWADE, SG18 0NS.

GUY, Mr. Andrew Christopher, BA ACA *1991;* Hessenring 42, Eppstein-Bremthal, 65817 EPPSTEIN-VOCKENHAUSEN, GERMANY.

GUY, Mr. Andrew James, BA ACA *1995;* Sacred Heart Presbytery Bannockburn Road, Cowie, STIRLING, FK7 7BG.

•**GUY, Mrs. Caroline Rosemary, BSc(Hons) ACA** *2004;* CG Accounting Limited, 70 Eddington Crescent, WELWYN GARDEN CITY, HERTFORDSHIRE, AL7 4SQ.

GUY, Mr. Christian, ACA *2004;* 5 Vicq Farm Close, La Grande Route Des Sablons Grouville, JERSEY, JE3 9FL.

GUY, Mr. Christopher Patrick Edward, ACA *2008;* Flat 5, 114 Roman Way, LONDON, N7 8XJ.

GUY, Mrs. Claire Louise, BSc ACA *1993;* 4 Mill Lane, Horton-cum-Studley, OXFORD, OX33 1DH.

GUY, Mr. David Michael, BA ACA *1993;* Cascal Services Ltd, Biwater International Ltd Biwater House, Station Approach, DORKING, RH4 1TZ.

GUY, Mr. Derry Cameron Waterford, MBA BA ACA *1982;* 9 Cinnamon Row, LONDON, SW11 3TW.

GUY, Mr. James Julian, BSc ACA *1991;* Flat 1, 16 Grenville Place, LONDON, SW7 4RW.

•**GUY, Mrs. Jayne Elizabeth, ACA** *1984;* Guy & Co, Beechwood, 5 Hale End, Hook Heath, WOKING, GU22 0LH.

•**GUY, Mr. Jeremy Brooks, BA FCA** *1993;* West House Accountants Ltd, 14 High Street, Tettenhall, WOLVERHAMPTON, WV6 8QT. See also Bardsley Accountants Limited

GUY, Mr. John Andrew, BA ACA *1983;* 37 High Trees Road, REIGATE, RH2 7EN.

GUY, Mr. John Joseph, FCA *1973;* 9 Lockside Drive, Kinver, STOURBRIDGE, DY7 6NQ.

•**GUY, Mr. Joseph Henry George, FCA ATII** *1972;* (Tax Fac), Henry Guy, 20 Belmont Close, UXBRIDGE, UB8 1RF.

GUY, Mr. Julian, BSc ACA *1990;* Finnery House, Gartocharn, ALEXANDRIA, DUNBARTONSHIRE, G83 8SD.

•**GUY, Mr. Kevin Andrew, BA FCA** *1990;* (Tax Fac), BCG Accountants Limited, 111 South Road, Waterloo, LIVERPOOL, L22 0LT. See also BCG Accountancy Company Ltd

GUY, Mr. Michael, ACA *2010;* 122 Canal Wharf, 10 Waterfront Walk, BIRMINGHAM, B1 1SL.

GUY, Mr. Nigel David, BSc FCA *1974;* 16 Kingston Lane, TEDDINGTON, TW11 9HW. (Life Member)

GUY, Mr. Nigel Raymond Allen, FCA *1983;* 5 Hale End, WOKING, SURREY, GU22 0LH.

GUY, Mr. Paul Nelson, FCA *1962;* Goldfinch House, Swife Lane, Broad Oak, HEATHFIELD, EAST SUSSEX, TN21 8UR.

GUY, Mr. Richard Benjamin, BSc FCA *1976;* (Tax Fac), 3 New Street, HENLEY-ON-THAMES, OXFORDSHIRE, RG9 2BP.

GUY, Mr. Richard John, FCA *1971;* Keneam Lodge, 78 Shurdington Road, CHELTENHAM, GLOUCESTERSHIRE, GL53 0JH.

GUY, Dr. Robert, PhD MA ACA *2011;* 26 Holbrook Road, CAMBRIDGE, CB1 7ST.
GUY, Mr. Robert James, BSc ACA *2010;* 64 Radyr Avenue, Mayals, SWANSEA, SA3 5DT.
GUY, Ms. Sarah-Jayne, BSc ACA *2007;* Clearview House, 70 Ringsend Road, LIMAVADY, COUNTY LONDONDERRY, BT49 0QJ.
GUY, Mr. Stefan James, BA(Hons) ACA *2001;* 4 Edward Street, Stapleford, NOTTINGHAM, NG9 8FJ.
•**GUY, Mrs. Suzanne, ACA** *1987;* Caerus Financial Management Limited, 23 Larch Rise, Easingwold, YORK, NORTH YORKSHIRE, YO61 3RZ. See also Caerus
GUY, Mr. Timothy Stuart, MA ACA *2010;* Amnesty International Peter Benenson House, 1 Easton Street, LONDON, WC1X 0DW.
GUY - WILLIAMS, Mr. Richard David, BA FCA *1999;* 17 Green Lane, WALTON-ON-THAMES, SURREY, KT12 5HD.
GUY-BYRNE, Miss. Emily Louise, BSc ACA *2005;* Flat 68, 152 Grosvenor Road, LONDON, SW1V 3JL.
GUYAN, Miss. Victoria Ann, ACA *2010;* 20 Moorfield Drive, Wilberfoss, YORK, YO41 5PZ.
GUYATT, Mr. Adam, MA ACA *2010;* 2631 Alfred Crescent, REGINA S4V 1E6, SK, CANADA.
GUYATT, Mr. Angus Andrew Selby, BSc(Hons) ACA CTA *2004;* 31 McMullan Close, WALLINGFORD, OXFORDSHIRE, OX10 0LQ.
GUYATT, Mr. Benjamin John, BA ACA *2001;* 9 Normandy Road, Wroughton, SWINDON, SN4 0UJ.
GUYATT, Mr. Raymond Edwin, FCA *1966;* 4310 Montrose Avenue, WESTMOUNT H3Y 2A7, QUE, CANADA.
GUYER, Mrs. Nichola Jane, BSc ACA *2001;* Maison Du Haut Lowlands, La Rue de Samares St. Clement, JERSEY, JE2 6LX.
•**GUYERS, Mrs. Jacqueline Fenella, BA ACA** *1990;* J F Guyers Limited, 1 Hornby Chase, Old Hall Gardens, LIVERPOOL, L31 5PP.
GUYLER, Mr. Hugh Walter James, BA ACA *1988;* with Deloitte & Touche LLP, Two World Financial Center, NEW YORK, NY 10281-1414, UNITED STATES.
GUYTON, Mr. Neil Firth, BSc ACA *2006;* All About Food Ltd, Matrix Park, CHORLEY, LANCASHIRE, PR7 7NB.
•**GUYTON, Mr. Stuart Firth, FCA** *1973;* Virtual Business Source Limited, PO Box 501, The Nexus Building, Broadway, LETCHWORTH GARDEN CITY, HERTFORDSHIRE SG6 9BL.
•**GWATKIN, Mr. Philip, BSc FCA** *1984;* (Tax Fac), Gwatkin & Co, 98 Meols Parade, Meols, WIRRAL, CH47 5AY. See also Gwatkin & Co Limited
GWILLIAM, Prof. David Robert, MA FCA *1978;* The White House, Cae Melyn, ABERYSTWYTH, SY23 2HA.
GWILLIAM, Miss. Isobel Rosemary, BSc ACA *1990;* Dixton, Hadley Common, BARNET, HERTFORDSHIRE, EN5 5QG.
GWILLIAM, Miss. Katherine, ACA *2008;* with Deloitte LLP, 5 Callaghan Square, CARDIFF, CF10 5BT.
GWILLIAM, Miss. Lois Frances, BA ACA *2001;* Raised Ground Floor Front Studio, 25 Primrose Gardens, LONDON, NW3 4UJ.
GWILLIAM, Mr. Stephen Paul, ACA *1998;* 128 Barnett Lane, KINGSWINFORD, DY6 9PN.
GWILLIAM, Mr. Vincent Mitchell Lovell, BSc ACA *1984;* Lawnside, Meerut Road, BROCKENHURST, HAMPSHIRE, SO42 7TD.
GWILT, Mr. Arthur, FCA *1952;* Treetops, 6 Lowcross Road, POULTON-LE-FYLDE, FY6 8EA. (Life Member)
GWILT, Mr. Donald Thomas, FCA *1956;* 28 Rectory Way, Ickenham, UXBRIDGE, UB10 8BS. (Life Member)
GWILT, Mr. James Stanley, FCA *1966;* PO Box 382, RIVER CLUB, GAUTENG, 2149, SOUTH AFRICA.
GWILT, Mr. Jonathan Simon, BSc(Hons) ACA DChA *1992;* (Tax Fac), Kensington Temple, KT Summit House, 100 Hanger Lane, Ealing, LONDON, W5 1EZ.
GWYN, Mr. Hwfa Anthony Richard, ACA *2008;* Flat 16, Hildred House, Ebury Mews, LONDON, SW1W 9NU.
GWYN, Mr. Robin William Basil, BA ACA *1979;* W H Ireland Ltd, 11 St. James's Square, MANCHESTER, M2 6WH.
•**GWYNANT, Mrs. Catherine Mair, BSc FCA** *1992;* 2 Cae Bedw, CAERPHILLY, MID GLAMORGAN, CF83 2UU.
GWYNN, Mr. Andrew Philip, BSc ACA *2006;* 47 Garnet Street, LONDON, E1W 3QS.
GWYNN, Mr. Mark William, MSc BA ACA *1983;* 15 Curlew Crescent, ROYSTON, SG8 7XP.
GWYNNE, Miss. Catherine Jane, ACA *1998;* 34 Hillgate Place, LONDON, SW12 9ES.
GWYNNE, Mrs. Ceri Michelle, BA(Hons) ACA *2002;* 9 Williams Way, Higham Ferrers, RUSHDEN, NORTHAMPTONSHIRE, NN10 8AJ.
GWYNNE, Mr. Derek Edward John, BA ACA *1980;* 33 Marlow Drive, HAYWARDS HEATH, WEST SUSSEX, RH16 3SR.
GWYNNE, Mr. Desmond Francis, FCA *1963;* Mynthurst Close, Leigh, REIGATE, RH2 8RJ. (Life Member)
GWYNNE, Mr. John Graham, BSc FCA *1976;* Group Dynamics Ltd, 21 Wadsworth Road, GREENFORD, MIDDLESEX, UB6 7LQ.
•**GWYNNE-EVANS, Mr. David, BA ACA** *1995;* Gwynne-Evans & Co, 49 Sandy Lodge Way, NORTHWOOD, MIDDLESEX, HA6 2AR.
GWYNNE-JONES, Mr. Roger, FCA *1974;* Home Retail Group Plc, 489-499 Avebury Boulevard, MILTON KEYNES, MK9 2NW.
•**GWYTHER, Mr. Andrew Gordon, MA ACA** *1997;* Deloitte LLP, Hill House, 1 Little New Street, LONDON, EC4A 3TR. See also Deloitte & Touche LLP
GWYTHER, Mr. Bernard, FCA *1968;* 104 Rhyd-y-Defaid Drive, Sketty, SWANSEA, SA2 8AW.
•**GWYTHER, Mr. Hugh, FCA** *1958;* Gwyther B Perseus & Co, 4 Heath Halt Court, Heath Halt Road, CARDIFF, CF23 5QB.
GWYTHER, Mr. Hugh Michael, FCA *1952;* Grasmere, 7 Lamack Vale, TENBY, SA70 8DN. (Life Member)
GWYTHER, Miss. Julie Anne, BSc ACA *1993;* (Tax Fac), 48 Egmont Road, SUTTON, SURREY, SM2 5JN.
•**GYDE, Mr. Mark David Andrew, FCA DChA** *1986;* (Tax Fac), Carter A.J. & Co, 22B High Street, WITNEY, OX28 6RB.
GYI, Miss. Kim Chawsu, ACA CA(NZ) *2009;* 8a Vaughan Avenue, LONDON, W6 0XS.
GYLES, Mr. Richard Hywel, BA ACA *2007;* 16 Edison Court, Greenroof Way, LONDON, SE10 0DQ.
GYSELYNCK, Mr. Richard Kim, TD MA FCA *1979;* Sea Bank, Shore Road, Port Erin, ISLE OF MAN, IM9 6HW.
GYTE, Mr. Colin Thomas, ACA *2008;* 159 Hardhorn Road, POULTON-LE-FYLDE, LANCASHIRE, FY6 8ES.
GYTE, Mr. David, MPhys ACA *2011;* Oldfield, 159 Hardhorn Road, POULTON-LE-FYLDE, LANCASHIRE, FY6 8ES.
H'NG, Miss. Keng Yoong, BA(Hons) ACA *2004;* ACE Asia Pacific, 600 North Bridge Road, #17-01 Parkview Square, SINGAPORE 188778, SINGAPORE.
H'NG, Mr. Weng Sek, ACA *2008;* 85 Hamlet Gardens, LONDON, W6 0SX.
HA CHOW, Miss. Stephanie, BSc ACA *2004;* 62 Volcy Pougnet Street, PORT LOUIS, MAURITIUS.
HAAGNER, Miss. Lee-Ann, ACA *2008;* 53 Clarence Road, LONDON, SW19 8QF.
HAAN, Mr. John Edward, BA ACA *2006;* Equitix, 91 Charterhouse Street, LONDON, EC1M 6HL.
HAAN, Mr. Michael Robert Anthony, FCA *1969;* Holly House, Hasle Drive, Hedgehog Lane, HASLEMERE, SURREY, GU27 2PL.
HAAS, Mr. Raymond Colin, BCom FCA *1995;* 7 Welbeck Street, LONDON, W1G 9YE.
HAAS, Mr. Richard David Walter, BSc FCA *1986;* The Walled Garden, College Lane, Ellisfield, BASINGSTOKE, RG25 2QE.
HABBERSHON, Mr. Simon Nicholas, BSc FCA *1984;* Ingalls, Libra House, Murley Moss Business Village, Oxenholme Road, KENDAL, CUMBRIA LA9 7RL.
HABBERTON, Mr. Michael John, FCA *1966;* Cobham House, 51 High Street, Hillmorton, RUGBY, CV21 4EG. (Life Member)
HABBICK, Mr. Iain, BA ACA *1995;* 104 Beaumont Avenue, ST. ALBANS, HERTFORDSHIRE, AL1 4TP.
HABBITTS, Mr. David Arthur Victor, FCA *1962;* 132 Griffin Street, Benton Sands Estate, CALLALA BEACH, NSW 2540, AUSTRALIA. (Life Member)
HABER, Miss. Janet Susan, BA FCA *1981;* 31 Cromwell Tower, Barbican, LONDON, EC2Y 8DD.
•**HABERFELD, Mr. Mike, BSc FCA** *1991;* Landau Morley LLP, Lanmor House, 370-386 High Road, WEMBLEY, MIDDLESEX, HA9 6AX.
HABERFIELD, Mr. Mark Stuart Edwin, BSc ACA *1988;* 9 Bannoch Brae, DUNFERMLINE, KY12 7YF.
•**HABERMAN, Mr. Philip, MA FCA** *1980;* Ernst & Young LLP, 1 More London Place, LONDON, SE1 2AF. See also Ernst & Young Europe LLP
HABGOOD, Mrs. Sarah Louise, BSc FCA *1996;* Christmas Cottage, 22 Grove Road, BEACONSFIELD, BUCKINGHAMSHIRE, HP9 1UP.
HABIB, Mr. Faisal, ACA *1991;* 30 Holyrood Road, New Barnet, BARNET, HERTFORDSHIRE, EN5 1DG.
HACK, Mr. Jonathan Nicholas Bewick, BSc ACA *1992;* Resolution, 23 Savile Row, LONDON, W1S 2ET.
HACK, Mrs. Karen Lesley, BA ACA *1996;* 43 Bedford Gardens, LONDON, W8 7EF.
HACK, The Revd Canon Rex Hereward, MA FCA *1956;* Flat A, Marshmead, 8 Pownall Avenue, Bramhall, STOCKPORT, CHESHIRE SK7 2HE. (Life Member)
HACKEMANN, Mr. Sean, BSc ACA *2005;* Flat 32, Forest Croft, Taymount Rise, LONDON, SE23 3UN.
HACKENBROCH, Mr. Michael Akiva, BSc ACA *2002;* Telereal Bastion House, 140 London Wall, LONDON, EC2Y 5DN.
HACKER, Mr. John Raymond, FCA *1964;* 51 High Street, SEVENOAKS, KENT, TN13 1JF. (Life Member)
HACKER, Mrs. Liesl Ann, BSc ACA *2000;* Wirral University Teaching Hospital NHS Foundation Trust, Clatterbridge Hospital, Clatterbridge Road, Bebington, WIRRAL, MERSEYSIDE CH63 4JY.
HACKETT, Mr. Andrew Richard, BA ACA *1997;* Adidas (UK) Limited, P O Box 39 The Adidas Centre, Pepper Road, Hazel Grove, STOCKPORT, SK7 5SA.
HACKETT, Mrs. Claire Anne, ACA *2009;* 54 Oakhurst Drive, CREWE, CW2 6UF.
HACKETT, Mr. Craig Allan, BA(Hons) ACA *2003;* 1a Victoria Avenue, HALESOWEN, B62 9BL.
HACKETT, Mr. Darren, BSc ACA *1996;* 64 Priests Lane, Shenfield, BRENTWOOD, CM15 8BZ.
HACKETT, Mr. David, BSc(Hons) ACA CTA *2010;* 85 Ashton Drive, LANCASTER, LA1 2LQ.
•**HACKETT, Mr. David John, FCA** *1970;* David J Hackett, 100 Newland, LINCOLN, LN1 1YA.
HACKETT, Mr. David Monck Mason, FCA *1952;* PO Box 545, 43 Division Street N, BRIGHTON K0K 1H0, ON, CANADA. (Life Member)
HACKETT, Mrs. Hannah, ACA *2011;* 75 Limes Road, Hardwick, CAMBRIDGE, CB23 7XN.
HACKETT, Miss. Jennifer Karen, BA ACA *2003;* Blackpool Borough Council, Revenue Section, PO Box 50, Town Hall, BLACKPOOL, FY1 1NF.
HACKETT, Mr. Matthew, ACA *2007;* with Coates and Partners Limited, 51 St. John Street, ASHBOURNE, DERBYSHIRE, DE6 1GP.
HACKETT, Mr. Peter, BA FCA *1972;* 4 Hollyfield Ave, SOLIHULL, B91 1QJ.
•**HACKETT, Mr. Steven John, FCA** *1973;* Stema Services Ltd, 198 Station Road, LEIGH-ON-SEA, ESSEX, SS9 3BS.
HACKETT, Mr. Thomas Francis, BCom FCA *1976;* Fidelity Bank & Trust International Limited, PO Box N 4853, NASSAU, BAHAMAS.
HACKING, Mr. Andrew Timothy David, ACA *1989;* Vizards Tweedie Barnards Inn, 86 Fetter Lane, LONDON, EC4A 1AD.
HACKING, Mr. Christopher William, FCA *1975;* Aqua Cure Plc, Hall Street, SOUTHPORT, MERSEYSIDE, PR9 0SE.
HACKING, Mr. Greville Johnson, FCA *1950;* 20 Northdene Drive, ROCHDALE, OL11 5NH. (Life Member)
HACKING, Mr. Jeremy Stuart Thomas, FCA *1975;* 1324 Cambridge Drive, OAKVILLE L6J 1S3, ON, CANADA.
HACKING, Mrs. Joanna Marie, BA ACA *2005;* 17 Quidditch Lane, Lower Cambourne, CAMBRIDGE, CB3 6DD.
HACKING, Mr. Jonathan Edward Alexander, FCA *1969;* 7 Llys Y Wennol, Northop Hall, MOLD, CH7 6GE.
•**HACKING, Miss. Judith Mary, FCA** *1963;* Miss J.M. Hacking, 5 Mill Mead, Wendover, AYLESBURY, HP22 6BY.
HACKING, Mr. Matthew Ian, BSc ACA *2000;* 17 Quidditch Lane, Lower Cambourne, CAMBRIDGE, CB23 6DD.
HACKING, Mr. Michael Jeremy, FCA *1975;* 91 Chatburn Road, CLITHEROE, LANCASHIRE, BB7 2AS.
HACKLETON, Mr. Peter Bryan, BA(Hons) ACA *2003;* 59 Vestry Road, LONDON, SE5 8PG.
HACKNEY, Miss. Emily Christine, ACA *2008;* Flat 31B, Tower 1 Queens Terrace, 1 Queen Street, SHEUNG WAN, HONG KONG ISLAND, HONG KONG SAR.
•**HACKNEY, Mr. Howard Stanley, FCA** *1974;* (Tax Fac), Howard Hackney LLP, Firscroft, Firs Lane, Appleton, WARRINGTON, CHESHIRE WA4 5LD.
HACKNEY, Mr. James, BSc ACA *2007;* 67 Quail Meadows, TETBURY, GLOUCESTERSHIRE, GL8 8PQ.
•**HACKNEY, Mr. John Christopher, FCA** *1973;* (Tax Fac), Sowerby FRS LLP, Beckside Court, Annie Reed Road, BEVERLEY, NORTH HUMBERSIDE, HU17 0LF.
HACKNEY, Mr. John Procter, FCA *1962;* 14 West Green, Stokesley, MIDDLESBROUGH, CLEVELAND, TS9 5BB. (Life Member)
HACKNEY, Mr. Timothy Paul, BEng ACA *1993;* 1648 SW Buckskin Trl, STUART, FL 34997, UNITED STATES.
•**HACKSHALL, Mrs. Kirsty Alexandra, BA ACA** *1998;* Deloitte LLP, 2 New Street Square, LONDON, EC4A 3BZ. See also Deloitte & Touche LLP
HACKWOOD, Mr. David Malcolm, FCA *1972;* Yew Tree House, Harris Lane, Abbots Leigh, BRISTOL, BS8 3RZ.
HACON, Mr. Ian, FCA FRSA *1995;* Lyndhurst House, 2 Lyndhurst Close, Gorleston, GREAT YARMOUTH, NORFOLK, NR31 8BA.
HADADI, Mr. Muntazir, ACA *2009;* 34 Hurst Road, HINCKLEY, LE10 1AB.
HADANI, Mr. Harnish, BA ACA *1992;* 29 Columbine Road, West Hamilton, LEICESTER, LE5 1UG.
•**HADANI, Mr. Prashant Amratlal, FCA** *1986;* Hadleighs, Sai Krupa, 27 Beechcroft Road, BUSHEY, WD23 2JU.
HADAVINIA, Miss. Mahshid, BSc ACA *2010;* Flat 46, Balman House, Rotherhithe New Road, LONDON, SE16 2AF.
HADAWAY, Mr. Eric Aubrey, FCA *1947;* Four Winds, Hall Lane, Upper Farringdon, ALTON, HAMPSHIRE, GU34 3EA. (Life Member)
HADDEN, Mrs. Denise Ann, ACA *1989;* 2 Lakeview Stables, St. Clere Kemsing, SEVENOAKS, TN15 6NL.
•**HADDEN, Mr. Michael George Gordon, FCA** *1983;* M.G.G.Hadden & Co Ltd, 46A Grosvenor Road, Birkdale, SOUTHPORT, PR8 2ET.
HADDEN, Mr. Peter John, FCA *1969;* The Birches, Low Row, BRAMPTON, CUMBRIA, CA8 2LN.
HADDEN-PATON, Mr. Alasdair Kinloch, ACA *1980;* Lyckweed Farm, Lambourn Woodlands, HUNGERFORD, BERKSHIRE, RG17 7TJ.
HADDLETON, Mr. Christopher Richard, BSc ACA *2009;* Rathbone Kear Ltd Stephenson Way, Wakefield 41 Industrial Estate, WAKEFIELD, WEST YORKSHIRE, WF2 0XN.
HADDLETON, Mr. Michael, FCA *1960;* Squirrels, 118a Boundstone Road, Rowledge, FARNHAM, GU10 4AU. (Life Member)
HADDLETON, Mr. Sidney John, FCA *1953;* 8 Park Avenue, SOLIHULL, B91 3EJ. (Life Member)
HADDLETON, Mr. Timothy, FCA *1970;* 19 Silver Sands, PO Box 752 WB, GEORGE TOWN, KY1-1303, CAYMAN ISLANDS.
HADDOCK, Mr. Colin Rudyerd Gemmell, BA FCA *1977;* Virgin Gorda Financial Advisors Ltd, Box 1086, THE VALLEY, VIRGIN GORDA, VG1150, VIRGIN ISLANDS (BRITISH).
HADDOCK, Mrs. Helen Margaret, BSc FCA *1989;* Buzzacott, 12 New Fetter Lane, LONDON, EC4A 1AG.
•**HADDOCK, Mr. Mark William, ACA** *2001;* 25 Springtail Road, Pinewood, IPSWICH, SUFFOLK, IP8 3UA.
•**HADDOCK, Mr. Michael Spencer, MA FCA** *1991;* Mike Haddock FCA, 94 Oxford Road, CAMBRIDGE, CB4 3PL.
HADDOCK, Mr. William James, MA ACA *1990;* 12 Highland Road, LONDON, SE19 1DP.
HADDON, Miss. Clare, ACA *2010;* 47 Birch Meadow, BROSELEY, SHROPSHIRE, TF12 5LN.
HADDON, Mr. David, FCA *1960;* D Haddon (Financial Services) Ltd, Arden Cottage, Woodside, Little Baddow, CHELMSFORD, CM3 4SR. (Life Member)
HADDON, Mr. Ian William Maclean, FCA *1968;* 30 Drayton Road, Newton Longville, MILTON KEYNES, MK17 0BS. (Life Member)
HADDON, Mr. Jack Albert, FCA *1955;* Redbrook, Bosbury Road, Cradley, MALVERN, WORCESTERSHIRE, WR13 5JA.
HADDON, Mr. Jeremy John Walby, BA FCA MBA *1982;* 3B Oban Road, BOURNEMOUTH, BH3 7BG.
HADDON, Mr. Kenneth William, FCA *1960;* Greenacres, 11 Staines Green, HERTFORD, SG14 2LN. (Life Member)
HADDON, Mr. Michael John, ACA *1990;* 20 Yenakart Soi 2, Sathorn, BANGKOK 10120, THAILAND.
HADDON, Mr. Paul Gee Wai, BA ACA *2000;* 240 East 39th Street, Apt 46C, NEW YORK, NY 10016, UNITED STATES.
HADDON, Mr. Ronald Keith, BA FCA *1976;* Hillbrook, 15 Brook Lane, Renhold, BEDFORD, MK41 0LD.
HADDON-GRANT, Mr. Hugo, BA FCA *1982;* with Cavendish Corporate Finance, 40 Portland Place, LONDON, W1B 1NB.
HADDOW, Mr. Keith Alexander, BSc ACA *1992;* TTP Group Plc, Melbourn Science Park, Cambridge Road, Melbourn, ROYSTON, HERTFORDSHIRE SG8 6EE.
HADDOW, Miss. Rachel Helen Pirie, BSc FCA *1983;* (Tax Fac), 29 Harness Way, ST. ALBANS, AL4 9HA.

HADDOW, Miss. Sara Kiew, ACA *2008;* 2 Trellis Drive, Lychpit, BASINGSTOKE, HAMPSHIRE, RG24 8YU.
HADEN, Mr. David Neil, BA ACA *1984;* C M L Group Ltd Vittoria House, 296 Price Street, BIRKENHEAD, MERSEYSIDE, CH41 3PT.
•HADEN, Mrs. Dorota Malgorzata, ACA ACMA *2011;* Certax Northampton Ltd, 180 Bants Lane, NORTHAMPTON, NN5 6AH.
HADEN, Mr. John Brian, FCA *1958;* with Law & Co, Pool House, Arran Close, 106 Birmingham Road, Great Barr, BIRMINGHAM B43 7AD.
HADEN, Mrs. Lucy Samantha, ACA *2002;* with BDO LLP, 55 Baker Street, LONDON, W1U 7EU.
•HADEN, Mr. Timothy Mark, BA ACA *2002;* Deloitte LLP, 2 New Street Square, LONDON, EC4A 3BZ. See also Deloitte & Touche LLP
HADFIELD, Mrs. Barbara, BSc FCA *1979;* 4 London Mews, CIRENCESTER, GL7 1GE.
HADFIELD, Mr. Benjamin Graham, BA ACA *2010;* 403 Woodborough Road, NOTTINGHAM, NG3 5HE.
HADFIELD, Mr. Brian David, FCA *1973;* 143 Buryfield Road, SOLIHULL, WEST MIDLANDS, B91 2AY.
HADFIELD, Mr. Christopher, LLB ACA *2003;* 20 Grove Road, LONDON, SW13 0HQ.
HADFIELD, Miss. Fiona, MChem ACA *2009;* RN Media Company Ltd, 15 Kings Terrace, LONDON, NW1 0JP.
HADFIELD, Mrs. Helen Mary, ACA *2009;* 4 Halwick Close, HEMEL HEMPSTEAD, HERTFORDSHIRE, HP1 1XG.
HADFIELD, Mr. James William, BSc ACA *2003;* Hallfield House Coach Lane, Stanton-in-the-Peak, MATLOCK, DERBYSHIRE, DE4 2NA.
HADFIELD, Mr. John David, FCA *1954;* 349 Waterfall Hills Estate, Private Bag X5, SUNNINGHILL, 2152, SOUTH AFRICA. (Life Member)
HADFIELD, Mrs. Julie, BA ACA *2003;* with Ernst & Young LLP, 1 More London Place, LONDON, SE1 2AF.
HADFIELD, Mrs. Lynn Anne, BA ACA *2000;* 1 Huxley Close, MACCLESFIELD, CHESHIRE, SK10 3DG.
•HADFIELD, Michael Arthur, Esq OBE JP FCA *1966;* Hadfields, Commerce House, 658B Chatsworth Road, CHESTERFIELD, S40 3JZ.
•HADFIELD, Mr. Nicholas James, BSc FCA *1983;* (Tax Fac), N J Hadfield, Tobys Cottage, Blythburgh, HALESWORTH, SUFFOLK, IP19 9NG.
•HADFIELD, Mr. Patrick Rollo Heywood, PhD FCA *1991;* 5 Cumberland Road, LONDON, N22 7TD.
•HADFIELD, Mrs. Pauline Rose, BA FCA *1973;* Hadfield & Co, 17 King Street, KNUTSFORD, CHESHIRE, WA16 6DW. See also Cranford Computer Services Ltd
HADFIELD, Mr. Peter David Seton, FCA *1964;* 26 Redcliffe Square Management Company Ltd, Moorlea, Broomhall Lane, WOKING, GU21 4AN. (Life Member)
•HADFIELD, Mr. Philip James, FCA *1972;* (Tax Fac), Hadfield & Co, 17 King Street, KNUTSFORD, CHESHIRE, WA16 6DW. See also Cranford Computer Services Ltd
HADFIELD, Miss. Rachel Alexandra, BA ACA *2000;* 15 Baroona Road, NORTHBRIDGE, NSW 2063, AUSTRALIA.
HADFIELD, Mr. Scott James, BSc ACA *1997;* with PricewaterhouseCoopers, Darling Park Tower 2, 201 Sussex Street, GPO Box 2650, SYDNEY, NSW 1171 AUSTRALIA.
HADFIELD, Miss. Sharon, BA ACA *2002;* with Deloitte LLP, Hill House, 1 Little New Street, LONDON, EC4A 3TR.
HADFIELD, Mr. Stephen Anthony, BSc ACA *2004;* 5 Primley Gardens, LEEDS, LS17 7HT.
HADFIELD, Mr. Stephen William, BSc(Hons) ACA *2000;* 5 Campion Court, Reayrt Ny Keylley, Peel, ISLE OF MAN, IM5 1GF.
HADFIELD-STARR, Miss. Jessica, ACA *2009;* 38 Abbots Close, MACCLESFIELD, CHESHIRE, SK10 3PB.
HADI, Mr. Bilal Ahmad, ACA *2008;* 69a Jevington Way, LONDON, SE12 9NG.
HADI, Mr. Mustafa, MA ACA *2005;* L E C G Ltd, Davidson Building, 5 Southampton Street, LONDON, WC2E 7HA.
HADID, Mr. Foulath Mohammed, MA FCA *1966;* Flat 1, Eaton Square, LONDON, SW1W 9DA.
•HADJIANTONAS, Mr. Antonis, BSc FCA *1991;* House G11, Edison 9 Street, Lofos Edisson, Pallini, 153 51 ATHENS, GREECE.
HADJIARAPI, Miss. Eleni, ACA *2011;* P.O. Box 54211, 3722 LIMASSOL, CYPRUS.
HADJICHRISTODOULOU, Mr. Christos, MBA BA(Econ) ACA *1996;* 13 Kerynias St, 2008 NICOSIA, CYPRUS.
HADJICHRISTOU, Ms. Maria, ACA *2011;* 13 Gregory Afxentiou, Ayia Napa, 5330 FAMAGUSTA, CYPRUS.
HADJICHRISTOU, Mr. Stavros, ACA *2005;* Ilektras 30A, Kato Lakatamia, 2322 NICOSIA, CYPRUS.
HADJICHRYSANTHOU, Mr. Marios, MSc BSc ACA *2009;* 6 Elysion Street, Ayios Dhometios, 2364 NICOSIA, CYPRUS.
HADJICONSTANTINOU, Miss. Andrea, MPhil BSc ACA *2005;* P O Box 21894, 1514 NICOSIA, CYPRUS.
HADJICONSTANTINOU, Mr. Constantinos, FCA *1976;* Knossou 6, Aylantzia, CY2112 NICOSIA, CYPRUS.
•HADJICOSTI, Mr. Costas, BA ACA *1983;* Abacus Limited, Arianthi Court, 2nd Floor, 50 Agias Zonis Street, CY 3090 LIMASSOL, CYPRUS.
•HADJIDAMIANOU, Mr. Andreas, BA(Econ) FCA *2000;* Ernst & Young, 11 klm National Road, Athens-Lamia, PC 14451 METAMORFOSIS, GREECE. See also Ernst & Young Europe LLP
HADJIDAMIANOU, Mr. Marios, BA ACA *2002;* 35 Ayiou Neophytou Street, Archangelos, 2334 NICOSIA, CYPRUS.
HADJIEFTYCHIOU, Mr. Aristarchos, FCA *1998;* Farantaton 48 Apt. Z, 11527 ATHENS, GREECE.
HADJIEVANGELOU, Mr. Panayiotis, BA FCA *1991;* ATLANTIC INDUSTRIES, NASR CITY FREE ZONE, POBOX 7052, EIGTH DISTRICT, CAIRO, 11471 EGYPT.
HADJIGEORGIOU, Mr. Demetrios Christos, BA ACA *1994;* Holly Bank, 47 Turnpike, Newchurch, ROSSENDALE, BB4 9DU.
HADJIGREGORIOU, Mr. Spyros Aristodimou, BA(Econ) FCA ATII *1968;* S A Hadjigregoriou, PO Box 24780, 1303 NICOSIA, CYPRUS. (Life Member)
•HADJIHANNAS, Mr. Marios Felix, MBA BA ACA *1993;* (Tax Fac), HLB Afxentiou Limited, Palaceview House, Corner of Prodromos St & Zinonos Kitieos, POBox 16006, CY-2085 NICOSIA, CYPRUS.
•HADJIIOANNOU, Mr. Charilaos, BSc ACA *2006;* HTT Audit Limited, Elrini Tower, 27 Evagorou Street, 6th Floor, Office 61, 1066 NICOSIA CYPRUS.
HADJIJOSEPH, Mr. Stelios, BSc ACA *1980;* 11 Kleona Street, Strovolos, 2058 NICOSIA, CYPRUS.
HADJIKKOU, Miss. Andri, BA ACA *2004;* 5 Savva Zanou street, 2548 NICOSIA, CYPRUS.
HADJIKYRIACOU, Mr. Christos, BA ACA *2006;* 10 Dilou Str, Engomi, CY-2413 NICOSIA, CYPRUS.
HADJILIASIS, Mr. Evanthis, BA ACA *1999;* 3 Dionysou Street, Strovolos, 2060 NICOSIA, CYPRUS.
HADJILOIZOU, Mr. Loizos, BA ACA *2002;* No. 3 Garifalion Street, Oroklini, 7040 LARNACA, CYPRUS.
•HADJILOUCAS, Mr. Antonis, BSc(Hons) ACA *2000;* PricewaterhouseCoopers Limited, City House, 6 Karaiskakis Street, CY-3032 LIMASSOL, CYPRUS.
HADJILOUCAS, Mr. Loukianos, BA(Hons) ACA *2004;* 12 Evmeniou Panayiotou Str, 3077 LIMA, CYPRUS.
HADJIMAMAS, Miss. Sylvia, BSc ACA *2005;* 18 Makepeace Avenue, Highgate, LONDON, N6 6EJ.
HADJIMANOLIS, Mr. Manolis Stelios, BSc FCA *1999;* P.O Box 51358, 3504 LIMASSOL, CYPRUS.
•HADJIMARCOU, Mr. Yiannis, BA(Hons) FCA *2000;* Trevor Jones & Co., Old Bank Chambers, 582-586 Kingsbury Road, Erdington, BIRMINGHAM, B24 9ND.
HADJIMARKOS, Mr. Constantinos Paul, BSc ACA *1990;* PO Box 27376, 1644 NICOSIA, CYPRUS.
HADJIMICHAEL, Miss. Amalia, BA ACA *2004;* 8 Simou Menardou Street, Ria Court 8 1st floor, P.O.Box. 42633, 6015 LARNACA, CYPRUS.
HADJIMICHAEL, Mr. Lambros, ACA *2011;* Flat 56, Brampton Tower, Bassett Avenue, SOUTHAMPTON, SO16 7FB.
HADJIMICHAEL, Mr. Nicos, BA ACA *2005;* Vathilaka 14, Kiti, 7550 LARNACA, CYPRUS.
•HADJIMICHAEL, Mr. Panayiotis Mikis, BA FCA *1990;* P Hadjimichael, Office 5, 44 Hakket, 6045 LARNACA, CYPRUS.
HADJIMICHAEL, Mr. Stelios, BSc ACA *2009;* 6A Olympoy, K.Lakatamia, 2322 NICOSIA, CYPRUS.
HADJIMICHAEL, Ms. Tasoula Andrea, BA ACA *1988;* Laiki Bank, 167 Athalassas avenue, PO Box 22032, 1598 NICOSIA, CYPRUS.
HADJIMITSIS, Mr. Athos Nearchou, BSc ACA *1988;* P O Box 20862, 1664 NICOSIA, CYPRUS.
HADJIMITSIS, Mr. Christis Nearchos, BSc ACA *1985;* Bank of Cyprus Ltd, 57 Stassinos Street, Ayia Paraskevi, Strovolos, 1398 NICOSIA, CYPRUS.
HADJINEOPHYTOU, Mrs. Emma Michelle, BSc ACA *1999;* 15 Odyssea Eliti, Lakatamia, 2332 NICOSIA, CYPRUS.
HADJINEOPHYTOU, Mr. George, BEng ACA *1997;* 15 Odyssea Eliti, Lakatamia, 2332 NICOSIA, CYPRUS.
HADJINESTORA, Mrs. Lella, BSc FCA *1980;* 4 Patron Street, Strovolos, 2027 NICOSIA, CYPRUS.
•HADJINICOLAOU, Mr. Antonios, BSc ACA *1993;* 12 Jean Morea Street, Halandri, GR152-32 ATHENS, GREECE.
HADJINICOLAOU, Mr. Athanassios, BSc ACA *1988;* Poseidonos 78, 19005 NEA MAKRI, ATTIKI, GREECE.
•HADJINICOLAOU, Mr. Nicholas, BSc ACA *1989;* (Tax Fac), Nicholas Hadjinicolaou, 151 Longsight, Harwood, BOLTON, BL2 3JE.
HADJINICOLAOU, Mr. Yiangos, BSc FCA *1973;* (Tax Fac), 44a Compton Avenue, BRIGHTON, BN1 3PS.
HADJIOANNOU, Mr. Andreas, FCA *1968;* 23 Levidou Street, 145 62 KIFISIA, GREECE.
HADJIOANNOU, Mrs. Christina Anne, BSc(Econ) ACA *1996;* 6 Ragkava, Plaka, 10558 ATHENS, GREECE.
HADJIOANNOU, Mrs. Popi, BSc ACA *1995;* 3 Savva Rotsides Street, Dasoupolis, NICOSIA, CYPRUS.
HADJIPANAYIS, Mr. Alexis, BSc ACA *2007;* 10 Psycharis Street, 2123 NICOSIA, CYPRUS.
•HADJIPANTELA, Mr. Michalakis, MSc BA ACA CPA *2002;* P.O.Box 14193, 2154 AGLANTZIA, CYPRUS.
•HADJIPAVLOU, Mr. Alexis, ACA *2008;* Lefkotheas 7, Ekali, 14578 ATHENS, GREECE.
HADJIPAVLOU, Mr. George, LLB ACA *2007;* (Tax Fac), 7 Rega Fereou Street, Makedonitissa, 2413 NICOSIA, CYPRUS.
HADJIPAVLOU, Miss. Irene, MSc BSc ACA *2010;* 38 Nelsonos Street, STROVOLOS, 2021 NICOSIA, CYPRUS.
•HADJIPAVLOU, Mr. Michael, BSc FCA CF *1981;* Deloitte Hadjipavlou Sofianos & Cambanis S.A, 3a Fragoklissias & Granikou Str, Maroussi, 15125 ATHENS, GREECE.
•HADJIPIERIS, Mr. George, BA ACA *1999;* AGH Audit Ltd, 58 Agiou Athanasiou Avenue, El Greco Building, 2nd Floor, Office 201, 4102 LIMASSOL CYPRUS.
HADJIROUSOS, Mr. Avgoustinos, ACA *2009;* 27 Artemidos Street, 2058 NICOSIA, CYPRUS.
•HADJIROUSOU, Mr. Ninos Augustinou, FCA *1971;* 27 Artemidos Str, Strovolos, 2058 NICOSIA, CYPRUS.
HADJISAVVAS, Mr. Constantinos, BSc ACA *1998;* 83 Panicou Haraki, 4105 LIMASSOL, CYPRUS.
HADJISAVVAS, Mr. Savvas Constantinou, FCA *1975;* 10 SOULIOU STREET, AGLANTZIA, 2102 NICOSIA, CYPRUS.
HADJISOTIRIOU, Mrs. Paula, ACA *1980;* EFG Eurobank Ergasias SA, 20 Amalias Str, Souri 5, Syntagma Square, 10557 ATHENS, GREECE.
•HADJISPYRIDES, Mr. Georgios, FCA *1998;* Costouris Michaelides & Co(Overseas), PO Box 30980, DUBAI, UNITED ARAB EMIRATES.
HADJISTAVRIS, Mr. Christodoulos, BSc ACA *2008;* Flat 101, 11 Thessalonikis Street Aglantzia, 2122 NICOSIA, PLATEAU STATE, CYPRUS.
HADJITHOMAS, Mr. Panayiotis Charalambous, BA ACA *1995;* Atlantidon 8, 6058 LARNACA, CYPRUS.
HADJIVASSILIOU, Mr. Alexandros, ACA *2009;* Flat 01, 10 K Kolokasi St, Engomi, NICOSIA, CYPRUS.
HADJIVASSILIOU, Miss. Maria, BSc ACA *2003;* 17 Alkistidos Street, Acropolis, NICOSIA, 2007, CYPRUS.
•HADJIVASSILIOU, Mr. Vasilios Petrou, BA FCA *1986;* PricewaterhouseCoopers Limited, City House, 6 Karaiskakis Street, CY-3032 LIMASSOL, CYPRUS.
HADJIVASSILIOU, Mr. Vassilios Soteriou, FCA *1974;* 17 Alkistidos Str, Acropolis, 2007 NICOSIA, CYPRUS.
HADJIXENOPHONTOS, Dr. Andreas, MSc FCA *1989;* Corneliou street 17 Dasoupolis Strovolos, 2028 NICOSIA, CYPRUS.
HADJIYIANNAKOU, Miss. Androula, BSc ACA *2011;* Macariou 3, Athienou, Larnaca, 7606 LARNACA, CYPRUS.
•HADJIZACHARIAS, Mr. Eleftherios Z, FCA *1979;* KPMG Limited, P O Box 21121, 1502 NICOSIA, CYPRUS. See also KPMG Metaxas Loizides Syrimis
HADLEIGH, Mr. Simon Andrew, BSc ACA *1985;* 17 Shambrook Road, Cheshunt, WALTHAM CROSS, EN7 6WA.
HADLER, Mr. John Kenneth, FCA *1960;* 30 Chiswick Quay, LONDON, W4 3UR. (Life Member)
HADLEY, Mr. Christopher Frederick Bernard, BSc ACA CTA *1999;* 8 Partridge Close, CHESHAM, BUCKINGHAMSHIRE, HP5 3LH.
HADLEY, Mr. Clinton Geoff, ACA CA(SA) *2010;* 35 Hyde Close, WINCHESTER, HAMPSHIRE, SO23 7DT.
HADLEY, Mr. David Iain, BSc ACA *1986;* (Tax Fac), 1 Banks Drive, SANDY, BEDFORDSHIRE, SG19 1AE.
HADLEY, Mr. Derek John, FCA *1966;* 92 Gower Road, HALESOWEN, B62 9BT.
HADLEY, Miss. Emma Frances, BSc ACA *2007;* 31 Winterfold Close, LONDON, SW19 6LE.
HADLEY, Mr. Gary, BA FCA *1984;* 124 Upper Hoyland Road, Hoyland, BARNSLEY, SOUTH YORKSHIRE, S74 9NL.
HADLEY, Mr. James, ACA *2009;* 5 Mavins Road, FARNHAM, SURREY, GU9 8JT.
•HADLEY, Mr. John Henry, FCA *1973;* (Tax Fac), John H. Hadley, 28 Littlegreen Road, Woodthorpe, NOTTINGHAM, NG5 4LN. See also A. Hadley Ltd
HADLEY, Mr. John Stanley, MA FCA *1982;* with PricewaterhouseCoopers, 63 rue de Villiers, 92208 NEUILLY-SUR-SEINE, FRANCE.
HADLEY, Mrs. Kate Angharad, BA ACA *2004;* 47 Metchley Lane, BIRMINGHAM, B17 0HT.
HADLEY, Mr. Keith Edward, BSc ACA *1986;* Strix Ltd, Forrest house, Ronaldsway, Ballasalla, ISLE OF MAN, IM9 2AG.
HADLEY, Mr. Mark Derek, BSc ACA *1989;* 11 Andover Road, PORT WASHINGTON, NY 11050, UNITED STATES.
HADLEY, Mr. Michael John, FCA *1969;* PO Box 145, Calle Paseros 124, Urbanisation La Sierrezuela, Muas Costa, 29649 MALAGA, SPAIN.
HADLEY, Mr. Michael John, ACA *1979;* 175 Summerfields Avenue, HALESOWEN, WEST MIDLANDS, B62 9NU.
HADLEY, Mr. Philip Geoffrey, MA FCA *1978;* Apartment 8, 4 Maior Gheorghe Sontu, Sector 1, 011447 BUCHAREST, ROMANIA.
HADLEY, Mr. Philip John, BA FCA *1972;* 29 Ellesboro Road, Harborne, BIRMINGHAM, B17 8PU.
HADLEY, Mr. Raymond, FCA *1978;* 16 Farlow Croft, High Green, SHEFFIELD, S35 4DY.
HADLEY, Mr. Richard Luke, BSc ACA *1993;* 78 Purlewent Drive, BATH, BA1 4BA.
HADLEY, Mr. Richard Stephen, BSc ACA *2004;* 47 Metchley Lane, BIRMINGHAM, B17 0HT.
HADLEY, Mr. Robert Charles Wassell, FCA *1968;* 5 Littlefield, Wivenhoe, COLCHESTER, ESSEX, CO7 9LU.
HADNUM, Mr. Lee John, LLB ACA *2002;* BCB Bachstrasse 1, CH-9606 BUTSCHWIL, SWITZERLAND.
HADWIN, Mr. Richard Thomas, BSc ACA *1998;* The Dispensary, 8 Cleveland Place East, BATH, BA1 5DJ.
HADZOVIC, Ms. Melida, MSc ACA *2002;* 28-30 Mornington Avenue, 15A Mornington Avenue Mansions, LONDON, W14 8UW.
HAEDERLE, Mrs. Philippa Mary, BSc ACA *1990;* 9 Grassy Lane, MAIDENHEAD, SL6 6AU.
HAENEY, Mrs. Hollie Kate, BA ACA *1999;* 70 Church Street, North Cave, BROUGH, NORTH HUMBERSIDE, HU15 2LW.
HAENS, Mr. Stephen Henri, MA FCA *1982;* 48 POND VIEW DRIVE, KINGSTON, MA 02364, UNITED STATES.
•HAFEEZ, Mr. Abdul, ACA FCCA *2008;* RA & Co, Audit House, 260 Field End Road, RUISLIP, MIDDLESEX, HA4 9LT. See also RA Accountants LLP
HAFEEZ, Mrs. Fawzia, FCA *1976;* 21005 Scottsbury Drive, GERMANTOWN, MD 20876, UNITED STATES.
HAFEEZ, Mr. Mohammed Rohil, ACA *1981;* International Finance Corporation, 2121 Pennsylvania Avenue NW, WASHINGTON, DC 20433, UNITED STATES.
•HAFEEZ, Mr. Muhammad, FCA *1973;* Hafeez & Co, 2 Minto Street, EDINBURGH, EH9 1RG.
HAFEEZ, Mr. Omar, FCA *1994;* 10c Askari Apt, Ch Khaliq-uz-Zaman Road, KARACHI, PAKISTAN.
HAFFENDEN, Mr. Mark, BSc FCA *1980;* O2 Uk, 260 Bath Road, SLOUGH, SL1 4DX.
•HAFFENDEN, Mr. Richard Ian, MA FCA *1988;* (Tax Fac), Jacob Cavenagh & Skeet, 5 Robin Hood Lane, SUTTON, SURREY, SM1 2SW.
•HAFFNER, Mr. Aryeh Lawrence, ACA *1979;* Haffner Hoff LLP, 86 Princess Street, MANCHESTER, M1 6NP.
•HAFFNER, Mr. Stephen Efrem, BSc(Econ) FCA *1989;* Harris & Trotter LLP, 65 New Cavendish Street, LONDON, W1G 7LS.
HAFIZ, Mr. Shahid Hanif, FCA *1978;* Heidelberg Middle East Group, PO Box 52967, JEDDAH, 21573, SAUDI ARABIA.
HAFIZ, Mr. Sheikh Abdul, FCA *1973;* Rahman Rahman Huq, 9 Mohakhali Commercial Area, 11th & 12th Floors, DHAKA 1212, BANGLADESH.

HAFIZ, Miss. Zaineb, BSc ACA *2009;* KPMG, Level 32, Emirates Towers, Sheikh Zayed, PO Box 3800, DUBAI 3800 UNITED ARAB EMIRATES.
HAFNER, Mrs. Claire Andree, ACA *1989;* Vocalink Ltd Drake House, Homestead Road, RICKMANSWORTH, HERTFORDSHIRE, WD3 1FX.
HAGAN, Mr. Andrew David, ACA *2009;* Flat 6, 249 Lavender Hill, LONDON, SW11 1JW.
HAGAN, Mr. David Lloyd, FCA *1970;* Eastwoods, Pitmore Lane, Sway, LYMINGTON, HAMPSHIRE, SO41 6BW. (Life Member)
HAGAN, Dr. Desmond, BSc ACA *2001;* Flat C, 97 College Place, LONDON, NW1 0DR.
HAGAN, Miss. Irene, ACA *2009;* P.O.BOX CT82, CANTONMENTS, ACCRA, GHANA.
HAGAN, Mr. Michael John, BSc FCA *1973;* 11 Abbots Way, Westlands, NEWCASTLE, STAFFORDSHIRE, ST5 2ES.
HAGDRUP, Mrs. Fiona, MA ACA *1996;* 14 Rutland Street, LONDON, SW7 1EH.
HAGE, Mr. Iskandar, ACA *2011;* Flat 21, Palace Mansions, Earsby Street, LONDON, W14 8QW.
HAGELL, Mr. Stewart Michael, BSc ACA *2010;* 25 Graydon Avenue, CHICHESTER, WEST SUSSEX, PO19 8RF.
HAGEN, Mr. Martin John, FCA *1973;* MEMBER OF COUNCIL (President 2009 - 2010), Sunny Brae, 2 Belmont Road, WINSCOMBE, BS25 1LE.
HAGEN, Mr. Richard, ACA *2011;* Flat B, 416 Garratt Lane, LONDON, SW18 4HW.
HAGEN, Mr. Shaun, BA FCA *1989;* 12 Stainsborough Road, Hucknall, NOTTINGHAM, NG15 6TT.
•**HAGG, Mr. John Bevil, FCA** *1985;* (Tax Fac), J Hagg & Co, 75 Camborne Avenue, LONDON, W13 9QZ.
HAGGAN, Mr. Stephen, BA(Hons) ACA *2011;* Geoffrey Hannam Limited, 103 Castle Street, STOCKPORT, CHESHIRE, SK3 9AR.
HAGGAR, Mr. Anthony James, FCA *1955;* 3A Cowpers Way, Tewin Wood, WELWYN, AL6 0NU. (Life Member)
•**HAGGARD, Mr. Andrew David Debonnaire, BEng FCA** *1996;* Haggards Crowther, Heathmans House, 19 Heathmans Road, LONDON, SW6 4TJ.
•**HAGGARD, Mr. Tim Michael Debonnaire, BSc ACA** *1992;* Haggards Crowther, Heathmans House, 19 Heathmans Road, LONDON, SW6 4TJ.
•**HAGGART, Mr. Neil Robert, BSc FCA** *1973;* N. Haggart & Co, 114 Copse Avenue, WEST WICKHAM, BR4 9NP.
HAGGARTY, Mr. Ross, BA(Hons) ACA *2011;* Flat 6, 70 Wapping High Street, LONDON, E1W 2NN.
HAGGER, Mr. Andrew Latimer, BSc ACA *1993;* 10 School Lane, Chalfont St. Peter, GERRARDS CROSS, BUCKINGHAMSHIRE, SL9 9AU.
•**HAGGER, Mr. Barry Thomas, FCA** *1972;* (Tax Fac), B.T. Hagger, Shirebrook House, Fen Street, Buxhall, STOWMARKET, IP14 3DQ.
HAGGER, Mr. David John, FCA *1966;* 141 Cambridge Road, Linthorpe, MIDDLESBROUGH, CLEVELAND, TS5 5HL.
HAGGER, Mr. David Jonathan, BSc ACA *2004;* with Deloitte Touche Tohmatsu, Grosvenor Place, 225 George Street, P.O. Box N 250, SYDNEY, NSW 2000 AUSTRALIA.
HAGGER, Mrs. Glenda Florence Elizabeth, BA ACA *1997;* Toad House Brockley Way, Claverham, BRISTOL, BS49 4PA.
HAGGER, Mr. James David Cameron, BSc ACA *1992;* 174 West 76 Street, Appartment 13J, NEW YORK, NY 10023-8407, UNITED STATES.
HAGGER, Mr. Jonathan Osborne, FCA *1972;* Realty Insurances Ltd, 58 Davies Street, LONDON, W1K 5JF.
HAGGIE, Miss. Katharine Jane, ACA *2010;* 4 Whitefields Drive, RICHMOND, NORTH YORKSHIRE, DL10 7DB.
HAGGIPAVLOU, Mrs. Sarika, BSc ACA *1993;* 200 Upper Richmond Road, LONDON, SW15 2SH.
•**HAGLEY, Mr. Richard John, BSc FCA** *1995;* with Grant Thornton UK LLP, Grant Thornton House, 22 Melton Street, Euston Square, LONDON, NW1 2EP.
HAGON, Mr. Richard John, MA FCA *1972;* (Tax Fac), Erlestead 11, Woodmansterne Lane, BANSTEAD, SM7 3EX. (Life Member)
HAGON, Dr. Victoria Jane, PhD BA(Hons) ACA *2002;* 72 Shipton Road, YORK, YO30 5RQ.
HAGUE, Mr. Alan James, BSc ACA *2010;* 45 Main Street, Watton, DRIFFIELD, NORTH HUMBERSIDE, YO25 9AW.
•**HAGUE, Mr. Andrew John, BEng ACA** *2003;* Howard Worth, Bank Chambers, 3 Churchyardside, NANTWICH, CW5 5DE.
HAGUE, Mr. Andrew Nicholas, FCA *1966;* Lakeland Lodge, KESHCARRIGAN, COUNTY LEITRIM, IRELAND. (Life Member)
HAGUE, Mr. Brian John, BSc FCA *1978;* The Copse, 22 Sharp Lane, Almondbury, HUDDERSFIELD, HD4 6SW.
HAGUE, Mrs. Clare Louise, BA ACA *2003;* with Deloitte LLP, Stonecutter Court, 1 Stonecutter Street, LONDON, EC4A 4TR.
HAGUE, Mr. David Ian, MSc ACA *1999;* 1611 Egret Way, SUPERIOR, CO 80027, UNITED STATES.
•**HAGUE, Mr. David Richard, BSc FCA** *1977;* The Firs, Garston Lane, Marston Magna, YEOVIL, SOMERSET, BA22 8DN.
HAGUE, Dr. Elizabeth Helen, PhD BSc ACA *2006;* Brackendale Cottage, Brackendale Lane, Bradbourne, ASHBOURNE, DERBYSHIRE, DE6 1PB.
HAGUE, Mr. Gareth Richard, BA ACA *2006;* Apartment 16, Glenwood House, Glenwood Drive, SHEFFIELD, S6 1SR.
HAGUE, Miss. Gillian Anne, BA ACA *1991;* Oak Cottage, The Street, West Clandon, GUILDFORD, SURREY, GU4 7TG.
HAGUE, Miss. Janet, BA FCA *1980;* Orchard House, Whirlow Farm, Whirlow Lane, SHEFFIELD, S11 9QF.
HAGUE, Miss. Joanna, BA(Hons) ACA *2010;* 22 Gledhill Avenue, Penistone, SHEFFIELD, S36 6BD.
HAGUE, Mrs. Joanne, BA HND ACA *1996;* A F B Accountants, Unit 6, Coldharbour Business Park, SHERBORNE, DORSET, DT9 4JW.
HAGUE, Miss. Joanne Louise, BA ACA *2005;* Alderley House, Astrazeneca Pharmaceutical Division, Mereside Alderley Park, MACCLESFIELD, CHESHIRE, SK10 4TG.
HAGUE, Mr. John Leslie, FCA *1949;* 29 St.Martins Road, BLACKPOOL, FY4 2DT. (Life Member)
•**HAGUE, Mr. John Michael Richard, FCA** *1981;* (Tax Fac), Jackson & Graham, 4 Finkle Street, SEDBERGH, CUMBRIA, LA10 5BZ.
HAGUE, Miss. Katherine Jane, ACA *2008;* 24 Drew Close, POOLE, DORSET, BH12 5ET.
HAGUE, Mr. Mark Hamilton, FCA *1974;* 139 Judge Cushing Road, SCITUATE, MA 02066, UNITED STATES.
HAGUE, Mr. Peter James, BA ACA *2005;* with PricewaterhouseCoopers LLP, 1 Embankment Place, LONDON, WC2N 6RH.
HAGUE, Mr. Peter William, BA FCA *1968;* 13 Raleigh Drive, LONDON, N20 0UX.
HAGUE, Miss. Stephanie Jane, BSc(Hons) ACA *2010;* 152 Fleetwood Road North, THORNTON-CLEVELEYS, LANCASHIRE, FY5 4BL.
HAGUE, Mr. Terence Alan, FCA *1956;* 28 Wesley Road, Colehill, WIMBORNE, BH21 2PG. (Life Member)
HAGUE, Mrs. Victoria Louise, BA(Hons) ACA *2004;* 12 Beech Court Gardens, MAIDSTONE, ME15 6AJ.
HAGUE-HOLMES, Mr. Gerard Martin, BA FCA FSI *1986;* 27 Pollards Hill West, LONDON, SW16 4NU.
HAGUES, Mr. Ian James, BA FCA *1976;* Green Pastures, Lands Lane, KNARESBOROUGH, HG5 9DE.
HAGYARD, Mr. Martin Peter, BSc ACA *1988;* 24 Friary Road, LICHFIELD, WS13 6QL.
HAHM, Mr. Karl Andre, BSc ACA *1983;* West Winds, Oxmoor Lane, Biggin South Milford, LEEDS, LS25 6HJ.
HAHN, Mr. Stuart Ingram, BSc FCA *1986;* 5 Loseley Court, Great Holm, MILTON KEYNES, MK8 9HJ.
HAHN, Mr. Trevor Michael, BSc(Econ) ACA *1998;* 2 Delmar Avenue, HEMEL HEMPSTEAD, HERTFORDSHIRE, HP2 4LY.
HAI, Mr. Syed Ashfaque, MA MSc ACA *1985;* 3811 LAWRENCE AVENUE, KENSINGTON, MD 20895, UNITED STATES.
HAI, Mr. Zulfiqar Ali, BA FCA ATII AIIT *1995;* 55 Cameron Road, Seven Kings, ILFORD, IG3 8LG.
HAIDER, Mr. Imran, ACA *2005;* Delta House, 175-177 Borough High Street, LONDON, SE1 1HR.
HAIDER, Mr. Saeed, FCA *1972;* 21/1 Main Khayaban-e-Shahbaz, Phase VI, D.H.A., KARACHI, PAKISTAN.
•**HAIDER, Mr. Sajjad, FCA** *1959;* Sajjad Haider & Co, P.O. Box 3251, DUBAI, UNITED ARAB EMIRATES.
•**HAIDER, Mr. Shahab Bilal Sajjad, BSc FCA** *1993;* Sajjad Haider & Co, P.O. Box 3251, DUBAI, UNITED ARAB EMIRATES.
HAIDER, Miss. Shirley, LLB ACA *1999;* 10 Holly Lodge, 41 Lindsay Road, POOLE, DORSET, BH13 6BQ.
HAIG, Mr. Alan John, MSc FCA *1968;* 3 Queensfield, Dummer, BASINGSTOKE, RG25 2AY.
HAIG, Mr. Giles David Price, BSc ACA *1989;* 79 Springfield Road, WINDSOR, SL4 3PR.
HAIG-BROWN, Mr. Nigel Maurice, MSc FCA *1974;* 12 Hillcrest Gardens, ESHER, KT10 0BS.
•**HAIGH, Mr. Adrian Paul, MA(Cantab) ACA** *2004;* Stephenson Nuttall & Co, Ossington Chambers, 6-8 Castle Gate, NEWARK, NG24 1AX.
HAIGH, Mr. Alan, FCA *1963;* 18 Sycamore Avenue, Meltham, HOLMFIRTH, HD9 4EE.
HAIGH, Miss. Alison Sarah, FCA *1977;* (Tax Fac), 62 Browning Avenue, Hanwell, LONDON, W7 1AU.
HAIGH, Mr. Andrew John, BA FCA *1979;* Drewan, Fenay Lane, Almondbury, HUDDERSFIELD, HD5 8UJ.
HAIGH, Mr. Andrew Neil, ACA *2008;* Baker Tilly, 2 Whitehall Quay, LEEDS, LS1 4HG.
HAIGH, Mr. Andrew Peter, BSc ACA *1992;* Living Ventures, 6 Princess Street, KNUTSFORD, CHESHIRE, WA16 6DD.
HAIGH, Mr. Daniel Luke, BSc ACA *2005;* Youell House, 1 Hill Top, COVENTRY, CV1 5AB.
HAIGH, Mr. David Edward Bickerton, BA FCA *1981;* 31 Bolton Gardens, TEDDINGTON, TW11 9AX.
HAIGH, Mr. Drew Gareth, BA ACA *2006;* 145 West 10th Street, Flat 4D, NEW YORK, NY 10014, UNITED STATES.
HAIGH, Mr. George Sidney, MC FCA *1947;* Newlands House, Warley, HALIFAX, HX2 7SW. (Life Member)
HAIGH, Miss. Helen, BA ACA *1979;* 21 Park Lane, LEEDS, LS8 2EX.
HAIGH, Ms. Helen Hilda, BSc ACA *2002;* 105 Corporate Center Blvd, GREENSBORO, NC 27408, UNITED STATES.
HAIGH, Mr. John Douglas, FCA *1968;* Hartcliffe House, Denby Dale, HUDDERSFIELD, HD8 8QJ. (Life Member)
HAIGH, Mr. John Ernest, FCA *1972;* 101 La Haute Folie, 76790 LES LOGES, FRANCE.
•**HAIGH, Mr. Julian Robin David, BSc FCA** *1977;* Trenfield Williams, The Old Railway Station, Sea Mills Lane, Stoke Bishop, BRISTOL, BS9 1FF. See also Trenfield Williams Ltd
HAIGH, Mrs. Laura Jane, LLB ACA *2004;* 8 Moreton Road, Aston Upthorpe, DIDCOT, OXFORDSHIRE, OX11 9EP.
HAIGH, Mr. Malcolm, FCA *1974;* 2 The Rhyddings, Birtle Road, BURY, BL9 6UT.
HAIGH, Mr. Malcolm Crabtree, BA FCA *1985;* 52 Goldington Avenue, Oakes, HUDDERSFIELD, HD3 3PX.
HAIGH, Mrs. Margaret Wendy, BA(Hons) FCA *1984;* The Children's Hospital at Westmead, Corner Hawkesbury Road and Hainsw 2145 rth Street Westmead, SYDNEY, NSW 2145, AUSTRALIA.
HAIGH, Mrs. Maria Rose, BA ACA *1992;* 24 Brampton Avenue, MACCLESFIELD, SK10 3RH.
•**HAIGH, Mr. Peter Joseph, BA FCA** *1978;* (Tax Fac), Peter Haigh, The Old Estate Office, Westway Farm, Bishop Sutton, BRISTOL, BS39 5XP.
HAIGH, Mr. Rodney, FCA *1965;* Appartment G/1, The Court, St. Marys Place, SHREWSBURY, SY1 1DY. (Life Member)
HAIGH, Mr. Walter, FCA *1946;* 58 Castlecroft Road, Finchfield, WOLVERHAMPTON, WV3 8DA. (Life Member)
HAIGH-LUMBY, Mr. Peter Richard, FCA *1974;* 21 Theresa Road, Hammersmith, LONDON, W6 9AQ.
HAIGHT, Ms. Lynn Janice Gaye, MA FCA *1973;* 73 Heath Street West, TORONTO M4V 1T2, ON, CANADA.
HAIGNEY, Mr. Nicholas Steven, BSc FCA *1992;* Pricewaterhousecoopers Llp, 80 Strand, LONDON, WC2R 0AF.
HAIKNEY, Mr. David Robert, BSc ACA *1987;* Warfield Investments & Outsourcing, Clarendon Enterprise Centre Ltd, Bristol & West House, Post Office Road, BOURNEMOUTH, BH1 1BL.
HAILE, Mr. Bernard Edmund, FCA *1964;* 65 Kings Road, BERKHAMSTED, HP4 3BP.
HAILE, Miss. Elaine, ACA *2008;* Dafferns Llp, 1 Eastwood Business Village Harry Weston Road, COVENTRY, CV3 2UB.
HAILE, Mrs. Sarah Louise, BSc ACA *1999;* 48 Brodrick Road, LONDON, SW17 7DY.
HAILE-WOLDEMARIAM, Mr. Michael, BSc ACA *1999;* Flat 7 Concord Court, Winery Lane, KINGSTON UPON THAMES, KT1 3GF.
HAILES, Mr. Robert Ernest, FCA *1971;* Cartref, Ashley Gardens, WEMBLEY, HA9 8NP.
•**HAILEY, Mr. Colin, MA ACA** *1999;* Confluence Tax LLP, Fosters Wing, Anstey Hall, Maris Lane, Trumpington, CAMBRIDGE CB2 9LG.
HAILEY, Mr. David, ACA *2008;* 13 Pinnocks Close, BALDOCK, HERTFORDSHIRE, SG7 6DJ.
HAILEY, Mr. Edward John, BA ACA *1985;* The Cedars Mill Lane, Calcot, READING, RG31 7RS.
HAILEY, John Anthony, Esq OBE BA FCA *1967;* Bondyke House, St Margarets Avenue, COTTINGHAM, HU16 5NS. (Life Member)
HAILEY, Mr. Stephen Russell, FCA *1969;* 6 Dognell Green, WELWYN GARDEN CITY, HERTFORDSHIRE, AL8 7BL. (Life Member)
HAILEY, Mr. Terence Ronald, FCA *1966;* 23 Chichester Avenue, HAYLING ISLAND, PO11 9EZ.
HAILIS, Mr. Panayiotis, BSc ACA *2010;* 7 Kleovoulou Papakyriakou, 6018 LARNACA, CYPRUS.
HAILS, Miss. Clare Louise, BA ACA *1993;* 7 The Grove, Meltham, HOLMFIRTH, WEST YORKSHIRE, HD9 4EH.
HAILS, Mr. Trevor George, MA FCA *1978;* Bentley Heath Farm, Bentley Heath, BARNET, EN5 4RY.
HAILSTONE, Mr. Frank Nelder, FCA *1951;* 46 Hale Road, Wendover, AYLESBURY, HP22 6NF. (Life Member)
HAILSTONES, Mr. Frank, CA *1989; (CA Scotland 1982);* 10 Abercorn Close, SOUTH CROYDON, CR2 8TG.
•**HAILWOOD, Mr. Anthony Gordon, FCA** *1970;* Tony Hailwood Ltd, 14 Davenport Road, Heswall, WIRRAL, MERSEYSIDE, CH60 9LF.
HAILWOOD, Mr. John Leslie, BSc ACA *1982;* 1 Church Close, Peterstone Wentlooge, CARDIFF, CF3 2TP.
HAIM, Mr. Robert, BA ACA *1985;* Flat 6, 9 Evelyn Gardens, LONDON, SW7 3BE.
HAIMES, Mr. Kevin John, FCA *1999;* with Deloitte LLP, Hill House, 1 Little New Street, LONDON, EC4A 3TR.
HAIN, Mr. Graham Andrew Anderson, BA ACA *1999;* with RSM Tenon Limited, Salisbury House, 31 Finsbury Circus, LONDON, EC2M 5SQ.
•**HAIN, Miss. Karen, BA ACA** *1997;* Moore and Smalley LLP, Richard House, 9 Winckley Square, PRESTON, PR1 3HP.
HAINE, Mrs. Diana Elizabeth, FCA *1976;* 26 Cambridge Drive, WISBECH, PE13 1SE.
HAINE, Mr. Edward James Gray, ACA *2009;* 38 Oak Close, Exminster, EXETER, EX6 8ST.
HAINES, Mr. Alan John, BSc ACA *1984;* 1 Mandeville Road, HERTFORD, SG13 8JG.
•**HAINES, Mr. Anthony Edward, BSc ACA** *1992;* Wenn Townsend, 30 St Giles', OXFORD, OX1 3LE. See also Wenn Townsend Accountants Limited
HAINES, Mr. Charles Rupert, MA ACA *1994;* 65 Balglass Road, Howth, DUBLIN 13, COUNTY DUBLIN, IRELAND.
HAINES, Mr. Christopher Paul, BSc ACA *1994;* 27 Foxbrook Drive, CHESTERFIELD, DERBYSHIRE, S40 3JR.
HAINES, Mr. Christopher Robert, ACA *1980;* 7 Bowercourt Cl, SOLIHULL, B91 3YW.
HAINES, Mr. Daryl William, BSc FCA *1989;* 91 Woodlands Grove, COULSDON, CR5 3AP.
HAINES, Mr. Dennis George, FCA *1953;* 66 Spring Grove, LOUGHTON, IG10 4QE. (Life Member)
HAINES, Mrs. Diane Elizabeth, BA ACA *1999;* 65 Beaconsfield Road, EPSOM, SURREY, KT18 6HY.
HAINES, Mr. Gareth David, BSc ACA *1993;* The Cottage, Main Street, Newton Solney, BURTON-ON-TRENT, STAFFORDSHIRE, DE15 0SJ.
HAINES, Mr. Gareth Rhys, BCom ACA *2003;* 8 Tamarisk Close, Up Hatherley, CHELTENHAM, GLOUCESTERSHIRE, GL51 3WL.
HAINES, Mrs. Helen Ruth Irene, BA ACA *2006;* 5 Beechfield Road, BROMLEY, BR1 3BT.
HAINES, Mr. Howell David John, FCA *1950;* The Pines, 12 Judges Close, HEREFORD, HR1 2TW. (Life Member)
HAINES, Mr. Jason George, ACA CA(SA) *2010;* Farthing Acre, Standalone Warren, Haynes, BEDFORD, MK45 3QG.
HAINES, Mr. John, FCA *1964;* 8 Woodlands Rise, NORTH FERRIBY, NORTH HUMBERSIDE, HU14 3JT.
HAINES, Mr. John Cyril George, FCA *1959;* The Ridings, Little Welland Lane, Castlemorton, MALVERN, WORCESTERSHIRE, WR13 6BN. (Life Member)
HAINES, Mr. John Frank Henry, FCA *1949;* Longwood House, Churt, FARNHAM, GU10 2NX. (Life Member)
HAINES, Mrs. Kathryn Joy, MBA *1981;* 35 Newton Lane, Wigston Magna, WIGSTON, LEICESTERSHIRE, LE18 3SE.
HAINES, Mr. Kerry Benjamin, BSc ACA *2003;* 2 Longland Court, GLOUCESTER, GL2 9HQ.
HAINES, Mrs. Lorna, BSc ACA *2006;* 32 Brompton Road, MANCHESTER, M14 7GA.
HAINES, Mrs. Louise, BSc ACA *1991;* 48 Easthampstead Road, WOKINGHAM, RG40 2EF.
HAINES, Mr. Martyn Philip, BA FCA *1975;* Gaythorne, 29 Showell Lane, Lower Penn, WOLVERHAMPTON, WV4 4TZ.

HAINES, Mr. Matthew Charles, ACA *2010;* 1 Hessary Place, Poundbury, DORCHESTER, DORSET, DT1 3SP.

HAINES, Mr. Michael Clipson, BA FCA CPA *1981;* P O Box 320, Cold Spring, NEW YORK, NY 10516-0320, UNITED STATES.

HAINES, Mrs. Nathalie Caroline Denaux, BSc FCA *1998;* 106 Falcondale Road, Westbury on Trym, BRISTOL, BS9 3JD.

•**HAINES, Mr. Neil, BA CA FCA** *1983;* PricewaterhouseCoopers, Private Bag 92162, AUCKLAND 1142, NEW ZEALAND.

•**HAINES, Mr. Nicholas Matthew, BA FCA CTA** *1999;* Hazlewoods LLP, Windsor House, Bayshill Road, CHELTENHAM, GLOUCESTERSHIRE, GL50 3AT.

HAINES, Mr. Peter Iain, BSc ACA *2001;* Lynderville Rokeby Drive, Tokers Green, READING, RG4 9EN.

HAINES, Mr. Peter John, BA ACA *1987;* Hazel Dene, The Meadows, Cotton, STOWMARKET, IP14 4NZ.

HAINES, Mr. Richard Charles, BA ACA *1998;* Northgate Information Solutions, 15 Peoplebuilding Estate, Maylands Avenue, Hemel Hempstead Industrial Estate, HEMEL HEMPSTEAD, HERTFORDSHIRE HP2 4NW.

HAINES, Mr. Richard James, BA ACA *2006;* 8 Fairfield, Minety, MALMESBURY, SN16 9TR.

HAINES, Miss. Sarah, ACA *2011;* 7 Mount Hermon Close, WOKING, SURREY, GU22 7TU.

HAINES, Mr. Sean Christopher, BA ACA *2009;* 3 Sussex Road, Ickenham, UXBRIDGE, MIDDLESEX, UB10 8PL.

•**HAINES, Mr. Stuart Jonathan, BA ACA** *1991;* with Bloomer Heaven Limited, Rutland House, 148 Edmund Street, BIRMINGHAM, B3 2FD.

HAINES, Mrs. Susan Jane, ACA *1983;* 7 Bowercourt Close, SOLIHULL, B91 3YW.

HAINES, Ms. Susan Penelope, BSc ACA *1988;* 353 Widney Road, Bentley Heath, SOLIHULL, B93 9BQ.

HAINES, Mr. Thomas Stephen, BSc(Hons) FCA *1978;* Wigical Group, 3 Rue Renert, L-2422 LUXEMBOURG, LUXEMBOURG.

•**HAINING, Mr. Peter, FCA** *1980;* (Tax Fac), The Kings Mill Partnership, Ashdown House, High Street, Cross in Hand, HEATHFIELD, EAST SUSSEX TN21 0SR. See also Kingsmill Ltd

HAINSWORTH, Mr. Adam Lawrence John, BSc ACA *1999;* Be The Brand Experience, 42-44 Scrutton Street, LONDON, EC2A 4HH.

HAINSWORTH, Mr. Adam Wilson, ACA *1988;* The Coach House, The Grange, Calverley, PUDSEY, LS28 5QH.

HAINSWORTH, Mr. Alan, FCA *1964;* Ingleside, Thornton le Beans, NORTHALLERTON, NORTH YORKSHIRE, DL6 3SP.

HAINSWORTH, Mr. Brian, FCA *1960;* 5 Avondale Grove, SHIPLEY, WEST YORKSHIRE, BD18 4QT.

HAINSWORTH, Mr. Christopher Rowan William, BA ACA *2003;* AV Pictures, Caparo House, 103 Baker Street, 3rd Floor, LONDON, W1U 6LN.

HAINSWORTH, Mrs. Katherine Natalie, BA(Hons) ACA *2004;* 8 Greenacre Park Mews, Rawdon, LEEDS, WEST YORKSHIRE, LS19 6RT.

•**HAINSWORTH, Mrs. Krista Jane, BA FCA** *1991;* Hainsworth Kerry Practice, Old Links Rectory, Links Green, Hinstock, MARKET DRAYTON, TF9 2NH.

HAINSWORTH, Mr. Robert James, BA ACA *2004;* (Tax Fac), 8 Greenacre Park Mews, Rawdon, LEEDS, LS19 6RT.

HAINSWORTH, Mr. Robert Joseph, BSc ACA *1993;* Marsylka Manufacturing Co Ltd, 16 Roydsdale Way, Euroway Industrial Estate, BRADFORD, WEST YORKSHIRE, BD4 6SE.

HAINSWORTH, Mr. Roger Charles, BA FCA *1977;* A.W. Hainsworth & Sons, Spring Valley Mills, Stanningley, PUDSEY, WEST YORKSHIRE, LS28 6DW.

HAINSWORTH, Mr. Stewart, BA ACA *1993;* Plaw Hatch Hall, Plaw Hatch Lane, Sharpthorne, EAST GRINSTEAD, WEST SUSSEX, RH19 4JL.

HAIR, Mr. Bartholomew Ross, BA ACA *1993;* 132 Lower Ham Road, Ham, KINGSTON UPON THAMES, KT2 5BD.

HAIR, Mr. Ronald Eric, FCA *1965;* Hall Farmhouse, Canwick, LINCOLN, LN4 2RG. (Life Member)

HAIR, Mrs. Zoe Anne Alyson, BA ACA CTA *1994;* Group Tax House F The Royal Bank of Scotland Plc PO Box 1000, EDINBURGH, EH12 1HQ.

•**HAIRON, Mr. Karl John, BSc FCA** *1999;* PricewaterhouseCoopers CI LLP, Twenty Two Colomberie, St Helier, JERSEY, JE1 4XA.

HAIRSINE, Miss. Janet Elizabeth, BSc(Hons) ACA *2002;* Prime Life Ltd Caernarvon House, 121 Knighton Church Road, LEICESTER, LE2 3JN.

HAISMAN, Mr. George Bertram, FCA *1973;* Pump House Wycoller Road, Trawden, COLNE, BB8 8SY.

HAJDU-HOWE, Mrs. Andrea, LLB ACA *2006;* Tribeca by the Waterfront, 60 Kim Seng Road, #29-05, SINGAPORE 239497, SINGAPORE.

•**HAJEE ABDOULA, Mr. Abdul Sattar, FCA** *1985;* Grant Thornton, 2nd Floor, Fairfax House, 21 Mgr Gonin Street, PORT LOUIS, MAURITIUS.

HAJEE-ADAM, Mr. Muhammad Tahir Hassen Mohamed, ACA *1995;* 28 Brycedale Crescent, LONDON, N14 7EY.

HAJI, Mr. Irfan Ahmed, BA FCA *1991;* 29 Lime Grove, TWICKENHAM, TW1 1EL.

•**HAJI, Mr. Karim Khalid, BSc ACA** *1999;* KPMG LLP, 15 Canada Square, LONDON, E14 5GL. See also KPMG Europe LLP

•**HAJI, Mr. Salim Sadrudin Alibhai, FCA** *1978;* Ashburns Accountants Ltd, 79 Victoria Road, Ruislip Manor, RUISLIP, MIDDLESEX, HA4 9BH.

HAJI YAHYA, Mr. Mohamad Aanwar Bin, BSc ACA CF *1981;* PricewaterhouseCoopers, P.O.Box 10192, Level 10 1 Sentral, Jalan Travers, 50470 KUALA LUMPUR, FEDERAL TERRITORY MALAYSIA.

HAJIGEORGIOU, Ms. Nicola, MSc ACA *2009;* 2 Bramber Road, LONDON, N12 9NE.

HAJIGEORGIOU, Mr. Theodosis George, BSc FCA *2000;* 14 Gregoriou Louviq, Dasoupolis, 2015 NICOSIA, CYPRUS.

HAJIGEROU, Mr. Charilaos, FCA *1979;* c/o Electricity Authority, of Cyprus, P.O. Box 4506, 1399 NICOSIA, CYPRUS.

HAJIOFF, Mr. Isaac, BSc ACA *2007;* 7 Holders Hill Drive, LONDON, NW4 1NL.

HAJITTOFIS, Mr. Alkis Andreas, ACA *2009;* 5 Chanion Street, 2023 NICOSIA, CYPRUS.

HAJIYIANNI, Mrs. Antigoni, BA(Hons) ACA *2010;* P.O. Box 56775, 3310 LIMASSOL, CYPRUS.

HAJJAR, Mr. Karim Charles, BSc ACA *1988;* Ground and Lower Ground, 41 Cathcart Road, LONDON, SW10 9JG.

HAKE, Mr. Paul Joseph, BEng ACA *1999;* 50 Oakwood Drive, MADISON, CT 06443, UNITED STATES.

•**HAKEEM, Mr. Saleh, BA ACA** *2004;* SJH Accountancy, 295 Evesham Road, REDDITCH, WORCESTERSHIRE, B97 5HL.

HAKEMAN, Mr. Robert John, BSc ACA *1996;* 1 Hebron Close, Clive, SHREWSBURY, SY4 5QT.

HAKIM, Miss. Aniq Niaz, ACA *2008;* 6 Leywell Road, MANCHESTER, M9 4QR.

•**HAKIM, Mr. Azra Ramsay, FCA** *1974;* (Tax Fac), RHCO, 727-729 High Road, Finchley, LONDON, N12 0BP. See also Bellstar Associates Ltd

•**HAKIM, Mr. Jeremy Philip, FCA** *1973;* with Hakim Fry, 69-71 East Street, EPSOM, KT17 1BP.

HAKIM, Miss. Karen Joyce, BSc ACA *2004;* 22 Snaresbrook Drive, STANMORE, MIDDLESEX, HA7 4QW.

HAKIM, Mr. Maurice Robert, BA FCA *1993;* 31 Hogarth Hill, LONDON, NW11 6AY.

HAKIM, Mr. Peter Graham, FCA *1962;* Green View, The Green, Ewhurst, CRANLEIGH, GU6 7RT.

HAKONG, Mrs. Patricia Lee Pit Lan, ACA *1980;* Lloyd's Market Association Suite 358 Lloyd's, One Lime Street, LONDON, EC3M 7DQ.

HALAI, Mr. Jagdisha, ACA *1998;* 7 Mayfield Close, HARPENDEN, HERTFORDSHIRE, AL5 3LG.

HALAI, Mr. Sarang Karsan, ACA FCCA ACMA *2011;* 43 Whimbrel Parade, Beechbord, PERTH, WA 6063, AUSTRALIA.

HALBARD, Mr. Christopher Neal, BA ACA *1991;* Bowland Lewis Lane, Chalfont St. Peter, GERRARDS CROSS, BUCKINGHAMSHIRE, SL9 9TS.

HALBE, Mr. Benjamin Ovgaard, BA ACA *2007;* Onslow House, Onslow Street, GUILDFORD, SURREY, GU1 4TN.

•**HALBERSTADT, Mr. David, BSc FCA** *1978;* D. Hall & Co, 46 Broom Lane, SALFORD, M7 4FJ.

HALBERT, Mr. Keith, BA FCA *1980;* 10 Garlan Street, ELORA N0B 1S0, ON, CANADA.

HALBERT, Mr. Robert Stephen, BA FCA *1982;* GVA Grimley Limited, 10 Stratton Street, LONDON, W1J 8JR.

HALCROW, Dr. Debra Kathleen, BSc(Hons) ACA *2000;* with PricewaterhouseCoopers LLP, Benson House, 33 Wellington Street, LEEDS, LS1 4JP.

HALCROW, Mr. Michael David, BA ACA *1992;* 39 Durand Gardens, LONDON, SW9 0PS.

HALDENBY, Mr. Graham, BSc FCA *1976;* (Member of Council 1995 - 2001), 25 Ladysmith Road, Willerby, HULL, HU10 6HL.

HALDENBY, Mr. Ian Maurice, BA ACA *1997;* Department for Education, 2 St Pauls Place, SHEFFIELD, S1 2FJ.

HALDENBY, Mrs. Rachel Louise, BSc ACA *1999;* 11 Troon Close, Normanton, WAKEFIELD, WEST YORKSHIRE, WF6 1WA.

•**HALDER, Mr. Christopher William, BSc FCA** *1983;* (Tax Fac), Chris Halder Limited, 23 Ingham Road, LONDON, NW6 1DG.

HALDER, Mr. Graeme Robert, BA ACA *1988;* 74 High Street, Hardingstone, NORTHAMPTON, NN4 6DA.

HALE, Mr. Andrew Michael, BA FCA CTA *1987;* 24 Godwin Way, Bromham, BEDFORD, MK43 8JH.

HALE, Mr. Andrew Timothy, BA ACA *1991;* 97 Clarence Road, TEDDINGTON, TW11 0BN.

HALE, Mr. Anthony Peter, BSc FCA *1985;* 202 Greenock Road, LARGS, KA30 8SB.

HALE, Mr. Brian Richard, FCA *1963;* 5 Hamilton Green, MALTON, NORTH YORKSHIRE, YO17 7YH.

HALE, Mrs. Carla, BEng ACA *2001;* 10 Plaitford Close, RICKMANSWORTH, HERTFORDSHIRE, WD3 1NJ.

HALE, Mrs. Caroline Lindsay, BSc(Hons) ACA *2002;* 4 Cranbrook Drive, TWICKENHAM, MIDDLESEX, TW2 6HN.

HALE, Mrs. Carrie Elizabeth, BSc ACA *2004;* Monks Rest, Tidmarsh Road, Pangbourne, READING, RG8 7BA.

HALE, Mr. Clive Russell, FCA *1974;* 27 Elm Avenue, Pennington, LYMINGTON, SO41 8BD.

HALE, Mr. David Alan, BSc(Hons) ACA *2003;* 6 Corporal Way, LIVERPOOL, L12 4YW.

HALE, Mr. David John, MA ACA *1992;* Wenlock, 16 Kippington Road, SEVENOAKS, KENT, TN13 2LH.

HALE, Mr. Derrick Bernard, FCA *1966;* 35 Dorchester Court, Dexter Close, ST. ALBANS, HERTFORDSHIRE, AL1 5WD.

HALE, Mr. Donald Gordon Charles, ACA *1983;* Ware Garages, 356 Ware Road, HERTFORD, SG13 7ER.

HALE, Mr. Francis Aidan, BSc ACA *2001;* 36 Littlewood, Stokenchurch, HIGH WYCOMBE, HP14 3TF.

HALE, Mr. Ian Dennis, ACA MAAT *1998;* 5 Hopefield Place, Rothwell, LEEDS, LS26 0GQ.

HALE, Mrs. Jacqueline Alison, FCA *1988;* Journeys End, Old Church Path, Clophill, BEDFORD, MK45 4BP.

HALE, Mrs. Jane Margaret, BA FCA *1990;* 97 Clarence Road, TEDDINGTON, TW11 0BN.

HALE, Mr. Jason Michael, BSc(Hons) ACA *2000;* 10 Plaitford Close, RICKMANSWORTH, HERTFORDSHIRE, WD3 1NJ.

HALE, Mr. John Alexander, FCA *1954;* 75 Oakleigh Avenue, LONDON, N20 9JG.

HALE, Mr. John Corbyn, FCA *1967;* 29 Manor Road North, Edgbaston, BIRMINGHAM, B16 9JS. (Life Member)

HALE, Mr. John Selwyn, BSc FCA *1985;* 37 Chandlers Road, ST. ALBANS, AL4 9RT.

•**HALE, Mr. John Stuart, BSc ACA CTA** *1989;* (Tax Fac), Sully & Co, 18-22 Angel Crescent, BRIDGWATER, SOMERSET, TA6 3AL.

HALE, Mr. Jonathan Edward, BA ACA *1999;* 1008 Nautilus Penthouse, Royal Ocean Plaza, GIBRALTAR, GIBRALTAR.

HALE, Mr. Jonathan Richard, BA ACA *1990;* Appleby, 8 Marshalls Piece, Stebbing, DUNMOW, CM6 3RZ.

HALE, Mrs. Julie Kathryn, BA FCA *1983;* Garric, Pike Law Lane, Scapegoat Hill, Golcar, HUDDERSFIELD, HD7 4PL.

•**HALE, Mr. Kari Anthony, BA ACA** *1989;* Deloitte LLP, Hill House, 1 Little New Street, LONDON, EC4A 3TR. See also Deloitte & Touche LLP

•**HALE, Mr. Leslie, BSc FCA** *1976;* Hale Jackson Knight, Montague House, 4 St. Marys Street, ROSS-ON-WYE, HEREFORDSHIRE, HR9 5HT.

HALE, Mr. Mark Ian, BA ACA *1999;* 17 Sevenoaks Road, ORPINGTON, KENT, BR6 9JH.

HALE, Mr. Mark John William, BA ACA *1993;* Anam Cara, Birks Brow, Thornley, PRESTON, PR3 2TX.

HALE, Mr. Melvyn Leslie, FCA *1966;* Ashcroft, Parrotts Close, Croxley Green, RICKMANSWORTH, WD3 3JZ. (Life Member)

HALE, Mr. Michael Robert, FCA *1959;* Wynchmoor, Pursers Lane, Peaslake, GUILDFORD, GU5 9RE. (Life Member)

HALE, Mr. Nathaniel Jonathan, BSc(Hons) ACA *2010;* 35 Adams Court, KIDDERMINSTER, WORCESTERSHIRE, DY10 2SF.

•**HALE, Mr. Neil Andrew, ACA** *1993;* 3 Malton Way, TUNBRIDGE WELLS, KENT, TN2 4QE.

HALE, Miss. Nicola Kay, BSc ACA *1990;* 9 Chapel Close, Welford on Avon, STRATFORD-UPON-AVON, WARWICKSHIRE, CV37 8QJ.

HALE, Mr. Nigel Keith, BA FCA *1983;* 6 Highfield Close, SOUTHAMPTON, SO17 1QZ.

HALE, Mr. Paul David, BA ACA *2000;* with Ernst & Young, The Ernst & Young Building, 680 George Street, SYDNEY, NSW 2000, AUSTRALIA.

HALE, Mr. Paul Michael, BSc ACA *1994;* XL House, X L Insurance, 70 Gracechurch Street, LONDON, EC3V 0XL.

HALE, Mr. Peter Geoffrey Gwyn, FCA DChA *1978;* with Haines Watts (Lancashire) LLP, Northern Assurance Buildings, 9-21 Princess Street, MANCHESTER, M2 4DN.

HALE, Mrs. Petra Kim, BEng FCA *1993;* 12 Bailey Close, WINDSOR, BERKSHIRE, SL4 3RD.

•**HALE, Mr. Richard Kenneth, BSc FCA** *1977;* (Tax Fac), Woodward Hale, 38 Dollar Street, CIRENCESTER, GL7 2AN. See also Woodward Hale Limited

HALE, Mr. Robert, FCA *1967;* 71 Wheeleys Road, BIRMINGHAM, B15 2LN.

HALE, Mr. Roger Andrew, BA ACA *1992;* 12 Bailey Close, WINDSOR, SL4 3RD.

•①**HALE, Mr. Roger Gareth, BA FCA** *1987;* with PricewaterhouseCoopers LLP, One Kingsway, CARDIFF, CF10 3PW.

HALE, Mr. Ronald Alfred, FCA *1951;* 18 Chesworth Crescent, HORSHAM, RH13 5AN. (Life Member)

HALE, Mr. Russell Timothy, BA ACA *1995;* 57a Druidsville Road, LIVERPOOL, L18 3EN.

HALE, Mrs. Sarah Penelope, BA FCA *1973;* 59 Fordington Road, LONDON, N6 4TH.

HALE, Mr. Sean Colin, BSc ACA *1990;* 5 Gleneagles Drive, Bessacarr, DONCASTER, DN4 6UN.

HALE, Mr. Simon Robert, BSc FCA *1997;* 3 Kent Close, WOKINGHAM, BERKSHIRE, RG41 3AN.

•**HALE, Mr. Stephen, ACA FCCA** *2009;* Perrys, 32-34 St. Johns Road, TUNBRIDGE WELLS, KENT, TN4 9NT.

•**HALE, Mr. Stephen Charles, BSc ACA** *1994;* PricewaterhouseCopopers LLP, Exchange House, Central Business Exchange, Midsummer Boulevard, MILTON KEYNES, MK9 2DF.

HALE, Mr. Stephen Michael, BA ACA *1998;* 99 Park Hill Road, BIRMINGHAM, B17 9HH.

HALE-SUTTON, Miss. Holly, BA ACA *2007;* Pricewaterhousecoopers, 1 Embankment Place, LONDON, WC2N 6RH.

HALEEM, Mr. Shaik Yasin, BSc ACA *1999;* 29 The Grove, READING, RG1 4RB.

HALES, Mr. Colin James, FCA *1966;* 117 Evelyn Rd, Otford, SEVENOAKS, TN14 5PU. (Life Member)

HALES, Mr. Damian, BSocSc ACA *2000;* with Deloitte LLP, Athene Place, 66 Shoe Lane, LONDON, EC4A 3BQ.

HALES, Mr. Daniel Paul, MSc BSc ACA *2007;* 46 Cowslip Hill, LETCHWORTH GARDEN CITY, HERTFORDSHIRE, SG6 4EZ.

HALES, Mr. David, BA ACA *1993;* 54 Chestnut Road, LONDON, SW20 8EB.

•**HALES, Mr. David Martin, BSc ACA** *1990;* Ernst & Young LLP, Apex Plaza, Forbury Road, READING, RG1 1YE. See also Ernst & Young Europe LLP

HALES, Mrs. Janet Ann, BSc ACA *1991;* Tradewinds, Cheapside Road, ASCOT, BERKSHIRE, SL5 7DW.

HALES, Mr. Jonathan David Fritchley, BSc ACA *1991;* with Lithgow Nelson & Co, Unit F/1, Moor Hall, Sandhawes Hill, EAST GRINSTEAD, WEST SUSSEX RH19 3NR.

HALES, Mr. Joseph Edward, FCA *1965;* 25 Tredenham Road, St Mawes, TRURO, TR2 5AW. (Life Member)

HALES, Mr. Kevin, MA FCA *1988;* 123 Meyer Road, 28-05 The Makena, SINGAPORE 437934, SINGAPORE.

HALES, Mr. Kevin Peter, BSc ACA *1992;* Veolia Water Solutions Marlow International, Parkway, MARLOW, BUCKINGHAMSHIRE, SL7 1YL.

HALES, Mr. Nicholas, BSc ACA *2011;* 102a Highbury Park, LONDON, N5 2XE.

HALES, Mr. Nicholas James, BA(Hons) ACA *2002;* 52 Avante Court, The Bittoms, KINGSTON UPON THAMES, SURREY, KT1 2AN.

HALES, Miss. Rachel, BSc ACA *1996;* Seymour Place, 4 Sherwood Court, LONDON, W1H 5TH.

HALES, Mr. Robert Bryan, MA ACA *1990;* Booker Group plc, Equity House, Irthlingborough Road, WELLINGBOROUGH, NORTHAMPTONSHIRE, NN8 1LT.

HALES, Mr. Simon Alexander, ACA *1983;* 81 Willian Way, LETCHWORTH GARDEN CITY, SG6 2HJ. (Life Member)

HALES, Mr. Vernon Stanley, BSc ACA *1994;* Plymouth College Bursar's Office, Ford Park, PLYMOUTH, DEVON, PL4 6RN.

HALEWOOD, Mr. Edward George, BCom FCA *1974;* 3 Murat Grove, Waterloo, LIVERPOOL, L22 8QY.
HALEY, Mr. Christopher, MA ACA *1992;* 26 Glebe Way, OAKHAM, LE15 6LX.
•**HALEY, Mr. David Paul, LLB ACA** *2001;* with PricewaterhouseCoopers, Hay's Galleria, 1 Hays Lane, LONDON, SE1 2RD.
•**HALEY, Mr. John William, FCA** *1974;* John William Haley, Hame, Stodmarsh Road, CANTERBURY, CT3 4AP.
HALEY, Miss. Julie Karen, ACA *1992;* 20 Prince Wood Lane, Birkby, HUDDERSFIELD, HD2 2DG.
HALEY, Mr. Michael Timothy, BA FCA *1982;* La Maison Blanc, La Grande Route de la Cote, Pontac, St. Clement, JERSEY, JE2 6SE.
HALEY, Mr. Paul James, FCA *1979;* 9 The Elms, Stoke, PLYMOUTH, PL3 4BR.
•**HALEY, Mr. Peter, FCA** *1966;* P. Haley & Co, Poverty Hall, Lower Ellistones, Greetland, HALIFAX, HX4 8NG.
HALEY, Mrs. Rebecca Elizabeth, ACA *2008;* 101 Coneybury, Bletchingley, REDHILL, RH1 4PR.
HALEY, Mr. Richard Austin, BA FCA *1998;* The Old Dairy, Nightingales Lane, CHALFONT ST. GILES, BUCKINGHAMSHIRE, HP8 4SH.
HALEY, Mr. Stephen John, BA ACA *1986;* 11 Brook Mews North, LONDON, W2 3BW.
•**HALEY, Mr. Timothy John, BA FCA** *1985;* (Tax Fac), Electspace Limited, Thomas House, Meadowcroft Business Park, Pope Lane, Whitestake, PRESTON PR4 4AZ.
HALEY-BURROWS, Mr. Tristan, BA(Hons) ACA *2002;* Flat 12 Regents Gate House, 10 Horseferry Road, LONDON, E14 8DZ.
•**HALFHIDE, Mr. Geoffrey Bernard, BSc FCA** *1979;* High Skears, Aukside, Middleton-in-Teesdale, BARNARD CASTLE, COUNTY DURHAM, DL12 0QY.
HALFORD, Mr. Andrew Nigel, BA FCA *1984;* The Ox Drove House, Ox Drove, Burghclere, NEWBURY, BERKSHIRE, RG20 9HJ.
HALFORD, Mr. Anthony John, FCA *1971;* 63 Woodlands Drive, Thelwall, WARRINGTON, WA4 2JL.
HALFORD, Mr. Frank, FCA *1955;* 28 Coleridge Court, Milton Road, HARPENDEN, HERTFORDSHIRE, AL5 5LD. (Life Member)
HALFORD, Mr. Jonathan, BSc ACA *1993;* Tyrol House, Holywell Road, Malvern Wells, MALVERN, WORCESTERSHIRE, WR14 4LF.
•**HALFORD, Mr. Keith Andrew, ACA** *1982;* Halford & Co, Unit 14, Home Farm Business Centre, East Tytherley Road, Lockerley, ROMSEY HAMPSHIRE SO51 0JT. See also Halford Accountancy Services Ltd
•**HALFORD, Mr. Mark, FCA** *1983;* (Tax Fac), Harris Kafton, 11a Norwich Street, FAKENHAM, NORFOLK, NR21 9AF.
HALFORD, Mr. Miles Benjamin David, MA FCA *1962;* 5 Cannon Place, LONDON, NW3 1EH. (Life Member)
HALFORD, Mr. Thomas James, BSc FCA *1979;* 29 High Street, IPSWICH, IP1 3QH.
HALFORD, Mr. Timothy William, BSc ACA *1989;* Flat 3, 22 Castellain Road, LONDON, W9 1EZ.
HALFORD-MAW, Mr. Tristan, BA ACA *2001;* 86 Moorgreen, Newthorpe, NOTTINGHAM, NG16 2FB.
HALFORD-MAW, Mr. William Guy, MA BA ACA *2005;* Zurich Financial Services, Mythenquai 2, 8022 ZURICH, SWITZERLAND.
HALHEAD, Mr. Richard John, BA ACA MCT *1984;* Chevin Quarry Lodge, Firestone Hill, Hazelwood, BELPER, DE56 4AE.
HALIFAX, Mr. Keith Michael, ACA *2009;* 151 Pirie Street, ADELAIDE, SA 5000, AUSTRALIA.
HALIL, Mr. Ozgun Tahir, FCA *1983;* Flat 903 Whitehouse Apartments, 9 Belvedere Road, LONDON, SE1 8YW.
HALIM, Mr. Ismail Abdul, BCom ACA *1987;* 17 Jalan Balau, Damansara Heights, 50490 KUALA LUMPUR, FEDERAL TERRITORY, MALAYSIA.
•**HALIT, Mr. Aykout, BSc FCA** *1964;* Eren Bagimsiz Dentetim Ve YMM AS, Abidei Hurriyet Cad, No 285 Bolkan Center, C Blok, Sisli, ISTANBUL TURKEY. See also Ergin Uluslararasi Denetim ve YMM AS
HALIT ONGEN, Miss. Alev, ACA *2009;* 17 Bromley Grove, BROMLEY, BR2 0LP.
HALKES, Ms. Lyn Marie, BSc ACA *1982;* Westfield House, Milton Lilbourne, PEWSEY, SN9 5LQ.
•**HALKES, Mr. Nigel Leslie, BSc FCA** *1981;* Ernst & Young LLP, 1 More London Place, LONDON, SE1 2AF. See also Ernst & Young Europe LLP
HALL, Mr. Adam, BSc ACA *2011;* 2 Millfield, Sedgeberrow, EVESHAM, WORCESTERSHIRE, WR11 7US.
HALL, Mr. Adam Christian Roderick, MA ACA *1996;* Ferry Lodge Ferry Lane, GUILDFORD, SURREY, GU2 4EE.
HALL, Mr. Adrian Peter, MA FCA ACT *1991;* 33 Great Eastern Road, HOCKLEY, SS5 4BX.
HALL, Mr. Adrian Philip Vincent, FCA *1965;* Greenways, 19 Hillside Road, Radcliffe-On-Trent, NOTTINGHAM, NG12 2GZ. (Life Member)
HALL, Mr. Alan, FCA *1967;* Preston Tilery Farm, Brafferton, DARLINGTON, COUNTY DURHAM, DL1 3LF.
HALL, Mr. Alan Frederick, BA BD FCA *1953;* 8 Baillieknowe Cottages, Stichill, KELSO, TD5 7TB. (Life Member)
HALL, Mr. Alan Napier, FCA *1955;* 8 Winchester Crescent, Fulwood, SHEFFIELD, S10 4ED. (Life Member)
HALL, Mr. Alan Richard, FCA *1973;* Skye, High Street, Limpsfield, OXTED, RH8 0DR.
HALL, Mr. Alan Stanley, FCA *1969;* 84 The Rocks Road, East Malling, WEST MALLING, ME19 6AU. (Life Member)
HALL, Mr. Alan Stuart, BA FCA *1999;* Bank of New York, 1 Piccadilly Gardens, MANCHESTER, M1 1RN.
HALL, Mr. Alastair William, BA ACA *2003;* Flat B, 103 Putney Bridge Road, LONDON, SW15 2PA.
HALL, Mr. Alex James, BSc(Hons) ACA *2011;* Flat 3, Everett Court, Aldborough Close, Withington, MANCHESTER, M20 3DT.
HALL, Mrs. Alexis Emma, BA ACA *2007;* Rutland House, 22 Croft Road, Edwalton, NOTTINGHAM, NG12 4BW.
HALL, Miss. Alison Margaret, MA ACA *1990;* 79 Morningside Park, EDINBURGH, EH10 5EZ.
HALL, Mrs. Amanda Jane, BA ACA *1996;* with KPMG LLP, Arlington Business Park, Theale, READING, RG7 4SD.
HALL, Mr. Andrew, BEd FCA *1981;* 25 Middlefield La, Hagley, STOURBRIDGE, DY9 0PY.
•**HALL, Mr. Andrew, FCA** *1982;* Ronkowski & Hall Ltd, 12 Westgate, Baildon, SHIPLEY, WEST YORKSHIRE, BD17 5EJ.
HALL, Mr. Andrew Harrison, MBA BA ACA *1992;* Grand Rue 27, 1260 NYON, SWITZERLAND.
HALL, Mr. Andrew James, FCA *1979;* 3 Badingham Drive, HARPENDEN, HERTFORDSHIRE, AL5 2DA.
HALL, Mr. Andrew James, BA ACA *2009;* 27 The Crescent, King Street, LEICESTER, LE1 6RX.
HALL, Mr. Andrew John, BA ACA *1986;* 11 Brandwood, Chadderton, OLDHAM, OL1 2TP.
HALL, Mr. Andrew John Hume, BA ACA *1985;* 135 Old Brompton Road, LONDON, SW5 0LF.
HALL, Mr. Andrew Leonard, ACA *2008;* 9 Briergate, Haxby, YORK, YO32 3YP.
HALL, Mr. Andrew Leonard, BA ACA *1984;* 48 Thornbury Wood, Chandler's Ford, EASTLEIGH, HAMPSHIRE, SO53 5DQ.
HALL, Mr. Andrew Peter, MA ACA *2001;* 21 Fontaine Road, LONDON, SW16 3PB.
HALL, Mr. Andrew Reece, BA FCA *1993;* 7 Leamington Road, Urmston, MANCHESTER, M41 7AZ.
•**HALL, Mr. Andrew Robert, BA ACA** *1996;* Andrew Hall & Co, 71 Dominies Close, ROWLANDS GILL, TYNE AND WEAR, NE39 1PB.
•**HALL, Mr. Andrew Rowland, MA FCA** *1980;* Eurocontrol Asesores Contables, Oficina 48, Edificio Burgosol, Comunidad de Madrid 35 bis, Las Rozas de Madrid, 28230 MADRID SPAIN. See also Eurocontrol Auditores S.L.P
HALL, Mrs. Ann, LLB(Hons) CA ACA *1992;* Templar House, 85 The Green, Tudhoe Village, SPENNYMOOR, DL16 6LG.
HALL, Mrs. Anne, BA ACA *1990;* 71 Park Road North, CHESTER-LE-STREET, DH3 3SA.
HALL, Mrs. Anne Joan, BA ACA *1996;* Jaycroft, Furze View, Slinfold, HORSHAM, WEST SUSSEX, RH13 0RH.
HALL, Mr. Anthony, BSc FCA *1976;* 11 Horsley Close, Holmehall, CHESTERFIELD, S40 4XD.
HALL, Mr. Anthony Julian, FCA *1974;* 24 Surrenden Crescent, BRIGHTON, BN1 6WF. (Life Member)
HALL, Mr. Anthony Mark, BSc ACA *1998;* 88 Hamilton Avenue, HALESOWEN, B62 8SJ.
HALL, Mr. Antony Philip, BA ACA *2004;* Somers Hill Cottage, 21 Somers Hill Road, HAMILTON FL 04, BERMUDA.
HALL, Mrs. April Janette, BSc ACA DChA *1989;* Birmingham St. Marys Hospice, 176 Raddlebarn Road, Selly Park, BIRMINGHAM, B29 7DA.
HALL, Mr. Arthur Raymond, FCA *1947;* 33 Birch Close, Oxton, PRENTON, CH43 5XE. (Life Member)
HALL, Mr. Benjamin Robert, ACA *2007;* 87 Douglas Lane, Grimsargh, PRESTON, PR2 5JB.
HALL, Mr. Brendan James, ACA *2011;* 37 Renaissance Drive, Churwell, Morley, LEEDS, LS27 7GB.
HALL, Mr. Brian Arthur, FCA *1971;* 12 Alderbrook Road, LONDON, SW12 8AG.
HALL, Mr. Brian George, FCA *1958;* 4 Heather Lea Avenue, Dore, SHEFFIELD, S17 3DJ. (Life Member)
HALL, Mr. Brian John, MSc FCA *1977;* 10 North Drive, RUISLIP, HA4 8EZ.
HALL, Mr. Brian Neale, FCA *1955;* 57 Anglesey Avenue, MAIDSTONE, ME15 9TD. (Life Member)
HALL, Mrs. Bronia Corinne, FCA *1974;* 3 Crown Mill, Vernon Street, LINCOLN, LN5 7QD.
HALL, Mr. Carl, BSc ACA ATII *1996;* Flat 6, 81 Ravenhurst Road, BIRMINGHAM, B17 9SR.
HALL, Mrs. Carol, BA(Hons) ACA *2003;* 6 Hill Rise, ALTRINCHAM, CHESHIRE, WA14 4QB.
•**HALL, Mrs. Caroline Heather, BSc FCA** *1987;* (Tax Fac), D.R.E. & Co (Audit) Limited, 6 Claremont Buildings, Claremont Bank, SHREWSBURY, SHROPSHIRE, SY1 1RJ. See also DRE & Co (Knighton) Limited and DRE & Co
HALL, Mrs. Caroline Jane, MA ACA *1994;* 41 Manor Park Drive, Finchampstead, WOKINGHAM, RG40 4XE.
HALL, Miss. Catherine Ann, MA FCA *1994;* (Tax Fac), 103B Kelmscott Road, LONDON, SW11 6PU.
HALL, Mrs. Catherine Anne, BA ACA *2002;* Deloitte & Touche Ltd Global House, High Street, CRAWLEY, WEST SUSSEX, RH10 1DL.
HALL, Miss. Catherine Anne, BSc ACA *2005;* Flat 14, 9 Bell Yard Mews, LONDON, SE1 3UY.
HALL, Miss. Celia Jane, BSc(Hons) ACA *2003;* Flat F, 144 Bedford Hill, LONDON, SW12 9HW.
HALL, Mr. Charles Robert, FCA *1978;* Warborough Lodge, 11 Rusthall Road, TUNBRIDGE WELLS, TN4 8RA.
HALL, Miss. Chloe Patricia, LLB ACA *2005;* Appt 2704, 330 Burnhamthorpe Road West, MISSISSAUGA L5B 0E1, ON, CANADA.
HALL, Mr. Christian Richard, BA ACA *1997;* 1 Kevill Davis Drive, Little Plumstead, NORWICH, NR13 5FB.
•**HALL, Mr. Christopher Allan Lawrence, BSc ACA** *1981;* CS Lawrence & Co Limited, 10 Swan Bank, CONGLETON, CHESHIRE, CW12 1AH.
HALL, Mr. Christopher George, ACA *1984;* The Lawns, 21 Old Church Street, LEICESTER, LE2 8ND.
HALL, Mr. Christopher Harvey, MA FCA *1976;* Equity Trust, 31/F The Center, 99 Queen's Road, CENTRAL, HONG KONG ISLAND, HONG KONG SAR.
HALL, Mr. Christopher James, BSc FCA *1994;* The Undercroft Offices, Thorpe Underwood Estate, YORK, YO26 9SZ.
HALL, Mr. Christopher John, TD MA FCA *1972;* 26 Sand Lane, Northill, BIGGLESWADE, SG18 9AD.
HALL, Mr. Christopher John, BA FCA *1974;* 1E Old Tye Avenue, Biggin Hill, WESTERHAM, TN16 3LY.
HALL, Mr. Christopher John, MSc FCA *1985;* Risk Advisors Ltd, 49 Telfords Yard, 6 - 8 The Highway, Wapping, LONDON, E1W 2BQ.
HALL, Mr. Christopher Keith, MA FCA *1977;* Wessex Lodge, Green Lane, WOODSTOCK, OX20 1JY.
HALL, Mr. Christopher Robert, ACA *2008;* Flat 10, Jessel Mansions, Queen's Club Gardens, LONDON, W14 9SH.
•**HALL, Mr. Christopher Spencer, BA FCA** *1974;* Alpha BusinessServices Limited, Inverebrie, ELLON, ABERDEENSHIRE, AB41 8PX. See also Inverebrie Limited
HALL, Miss. Claire Katharine Victoria, BSc ACA *2010;* 50 Tilehouse Road, GUILDFORD, SURREY, GU4 8AJ.
HALL, Miss. Claire Louise, BA ACA *2005;* B Braun Avitum UK Ltd, Brookdale Road, Thorncliffe Park, SHEFFIELD, S35 2PW.
HALL, Mr. Clifford Arthur Charles, BSc ACA *1980;* Courtyard House, Church Street, Withersfield, HAVERHILL, CB9 7SG.
HALL, Mr. Clive Jonathan, MA FCA *1989;* Eventure Media Ltd, 32 Elsynge Road, Wandsworth, LONDON, SW18 2HN.
HALL, Mr. Danny, ACA *2011;* 57 High View Road, Douglas, ISLE OF MAN, IM2 5BJ.
HALL, Mr. Darren Anthony, BA ACA *1995;* 28 Kilvert Drive, SALE, M33 6PN.
HALL, Mr. David, ACA *2008;* 5 Alresford Road, Middleton, MANCHESTER, M24 1WU.
HALL, Mr. David, FCA *1968;* Ash Tree House, Leys Lane, Preston Bissett, BUCKINGHAM, MK18 4LJ.
HALL, Mr. David, FCA *1972;* 8 The Drive, Marple, STOCKPORT, CHESHIRE, SK6 6DR.
HALL, Mr. David, BCom ACA *1984;* Apartment 3 Brandesburton Hall, Redwood Drive Brandesburton, DRIFFIELD, NORTH HUMBERSIDE, YO25 8UJ.
•**HALL, Mr. David, FCA** *1987;* Hardwickes, Etruria Old Road, STOKE-ON-TRENT, ST1 5PE.
•**HALL, Mr. David, BSocSc FCA** *1988;* Deloitte LLP, 1 Woodborough Road, NOTTINGHAM, NG1 3FG. See also Deloitte & Touche LLP
•**HALL, Mr. David Cameron, FCA** *1983;* (Tax Fac), RHK Business Advisers LLP, Coburg House, 1 Coburg Street, GATESHEAD, TYNE AND WEAR, NE8 1NS. See also RHK Corporate Finance LLP
•**HALL, Mr. David Charles, ACA** *1984;* Marks & Co, 100 Church St, BRIGHTON, BN1 1UJ.
HALL, Mr. David George, MA ACA *2003;* Marsh Pty Ltd, Darling Park Tower 3, 201 Sussex Street, SYDNEY, NSW 2000, AUSTRALIA.
HALL, Mr. David Ian, BA ACA *1988;* 4 Ashfield Terrace, Appley Bridge, WIGAN, WN6 9AG.
HALL, Mr. David James, FCA *1968;* 33 Cheyne Avenue, LONDON, E18 2DP.
HALL, Mr. David James, BSc ACA *1993;* Greenfields House, Charter Way, BRAINTREE, CM77 8FG.
HALL, Mr. David John, FCA *1957;* 160 Browns Lane, Knowle, SOLIHULL, B93 9BD. (Life Member)
HALL, Mr. David John, ACA *2008;* Flat 167, Compass House, Smugglers Way, LONDON, SW18 1DJ.
HALL, Mr. David John, LLB ACA *2003;* 46 St. Aidans Road, LONDON, SE22 0RN.
HALL, Mr. David John, BSc ACA *1994;* Grand Lodge, 10 Gunners Vale, Wynyard Woods, Wynyard, BILLINGHAM, CLEVELAND TS22 5SL.
•**HALL, Mr. David John, BCom FCA** *1986;* The Hall Liddy Partnership, 12 St. John Street, MANCHESTER, M3 4DY. See also Hall Liddy
HALL, Mr. David Lee, BA FCA *1968;* 58 Causey Farm Road, Hayley Green, HALESOWEN, B63 1EL. (Life Member)
HALL, Mr. David Mackey, FCA *1970;* PO Box 1104, HUNTERS HILL, NSW 2110, AUSTRALIA.
HALL, Mr. David Oliver, BA ACA *2005;* 69 Wardle Road, SALE, CHESHIRE, M33 3DJ.
•**HALL, Mr. David William, BA FCA** *1989;* N H Accountants Limited, 6 Bedford Road, Barton-le-Clay, BEDFORD, MK45 4JU.
HALL, Mrs. Deborah Alison, BA FCA ACIS *1985;* 1 Redwood Close, HONITON, EX14 2XS.
HALL, Mr. Dennis Ernest, FCA *1963;* 38 College Drive, RUISLIP, HA4 8SB. (Life Member)
HALL, Mr. Derek, BA FCA *1977;* 122 Vancouver Quay, SALFORD, M50 3TX.
HALL, Mr. Dominic Marcus Tagholm, MA ACA *2000;* 14a Friday Street, HENLEY-ON-THAMES, OXFORDSHIRE, RG9 1AH.
HALL, Mr. Douglas Alan, BSc ACA *1992;* Yew Tree Garden Centre, Ball Hill, NEWBURY, RG20 0NG.
•**HALL, Mr. Douglas John, BA FCA** *1984;* Smith & Williamson Ltd, 25 Moorgate, LONDON, EC2R 6AY.
HALL, Mr. Duncan Roger, ACA *2010;* Third Floor Flat, 17 Baron's Court Road, LONDON, W14 9DP.
HALL, Mr. Edward, ACA *2009;* 37 Percival Drive, Harbury, LEAMINGTON SPA, WARWICKSHIRE, CV33 9GZ.
HALL, Mr. Edward Graham, BA ACA ATII *1992;* 33 Tunbridge Lane, Bottisham, CAMBRIDGE, CB25 9DU.
HALL, Mrs. Elaine, BSc ACA *1988;* 7 Ashford Grove, Abbey Grange, NEWCASTLE UPON TYNE, NE5 1QS.
HALL, Mrs. Fiona Catherine, BSc ACA *1994;* Wedgewood House, 3 Manor Gardens, Lower Bourne, FARNHAM, GU10 3QB.
HALL, Mrs. Fiona Marie, BA ACA *1993;* 14 Clappers Meadow, MAIDENHEAD, SL6 8TT.
HALL, Mrs. Frances Hilary, BA FCA *1990;* 28 Ox Lane, HARPENDEN, HERTFORDSHIRE, AL5 4HE.
HALL, Mr. Frank Ernest, FCA *1949;* 41 Monks Walk, REIGATE, RH2 0SS. (Life Member)
•**HALL, Mr. Frederic Martin, FCA** *1968;* Bakers Cottage, The Street, Sutton, PULBOROUGH, WEST SUSSEX, RH20 1PS.
•**HALL, Mrs. Gaynor Patricia, BSc FCA** *1996;* Sunnycroft, Glasshouses, HARROGATE, NORTH YORKSHIRE, HG3 5QY. See also Hall Accountancy Services Limited
HALL, Mr. Geoffrey Vernon, FCA *1977;* 110 Higher Lane, LYMM, CHESHIRE, WA13 0BY.
•**HALL, Mr. George Henry, FCA** *1974;* (Tax Fac), Hall & Co, 59 The Avenue, SOUTHAMPTON, SO17 1XS.
HALL, Dr. Gillian, BSc ACA *2005;* 28 Linley Road, SALE, CHESHIRE, M33 7EJ.

HALL, Mr. Glen, BSc ACA *2000;* 2 Spring Close, Upper Basildon, READING, RG8 8JQ.

HALL, Mr. Gordon Martyn, FCA *1965;* 2 The Stables, Rufford New Hall, Rufford Park Lane, Rufford, ORMSKIRK, LANCASHIRE L40 1XE. (Life Member)

HALL, Mr. Graham Matthew Ian, BSc ACA *2004;* 67 Farriers Lea, Bolnore Village, HAYWARDS HEATH, RH16 4FS.

HALL, Mr. Graham Neil, FCA *1960;* 29 Leyborne Park, Kew, RICHMOND, TW9 3HB. (Life Member)

•HALL, Mr. Gregory John, BA FCA *1997;* Mazars LLP, The Pinnacle, 160 Midsummer Boulevard, MILTON KEYNES, MK9 1FF.

HALL, Mr. Haddon Michael, FCA *1970;* Esteval Dos Mouros, CXP 224-Z, 8100-023, ALTE, ALGARVE, PORTUGAL.

HALL, Mrs. Hayley Maria, ACA *1989;* 8 Ragley Way, Whitestone, NUNEATON, CV11 6SU.

HALL, Mrs. Helen June, BEng ACA *1994;* Ernst & Young, 41 Shortland Street, PO Box 2146, AUCKLAND, NEW ZEALAND.

HALL, Mr. Holden, FCA *1962;* 29 Fox Covert Grove, EDINBURGH, EH12 6UJ. (Life Member)

HALL, Mr. Hugh Nigel, FCA *1972;* Highfield, The Rise, East Horsley, LEATHERHEAD, KT24 5BJ.

HALL, Mr. Iain Thomas, ACA *2011;* 91 Victoria Road, Stechford, BIRMINGHAM, B33 8AN.

HALL, Mr. Ian, FCA *1967;* The Beeches, 164 Chester Road, Hazel Grove, STOCKPORT, SK7 6HE. (Life Member)

HALL, Mr. Ian Michael, BA ACA *1993;* Astellas, Lovett House, Lovett Road, STAINES, MIDDLESEX, TW18 3AZ.

•HALL, Mr. Ian Thomas, BSc FCA *1988;* Ian Hall FCA, Brackendale House, Roundwell, Bearsted, MAIDSTONE, KENT ME14 4HJ.

•HALL, Mrs. Jacqueline Lesley, BA FCA *1985;* (Tax Fac), Baker Tilly Tax & Advisory Services LLP, 2 Humber Quays, Wellington Street West, HULL, HU1 2BN.

HALL, Mrs. Jacqueline Tracey, BCom ACA *1998;* Providence Cottage, 55 Trent Valley Road, LICHFIELD, STAFFORDSHIRE, WS13 6EZ.

HALL, Mr. James Alistair, BSc(Hons) ACA *2003;* 33 Wyvern Avenue, Roseville, SYDNEY, NSW 2069, AUSTRALIA.

HALL, Mr. James David, BA ACA *1994;* The Dovecote, 5 North Farm, Ramper Road, Letwell, WORKSOP, NOTTINGHAMSHIRE S81 8DR.

HALL, Mr. James Patrick, FCA *1961;* Harmony View, Glasson, ATHLONE, COUNTY WESTMEATH, IRELAND.

HALL, Mr. James Peter, BA ACA *2003;* Darley Japan KK, 3-2-1 Tomikawa Higashi, Hidaka-cho, SARU-GUN, 055-0004 JAPAN.

HALL, Mr. James Richard, ACA *2009;* 9 Lumiere Court, 209 Balham High Road, LONDON, SW17 7BQ.

•HALL, Mr. Jan Yanick Stephen, ACA *2004;* (Tax Fac), Business Builders (UK) Limited, Omnia One, 125 Queen Street, SHEFFIELD, S1 2DU.

HALL, Mrs. Jane Suzanne, BSc ACA *1993;* The Innovation Group Plc, 1300 Parkway, Whiteley, FAREHAM, HAMPSHIRE, PO15 7AE.

•HALL, Mr. Jason William, ACA FCCA MAAT *2008;* (Tax Fac), Mapus-Smith & Lemmon LLP, 48 King Street, KING'S LYNN, NORFOLK, PE30 1HE.

•HALL, Mrs. Jennifer, BA FCA *1990;* Brennan Neil & Leonard, 32 Brenkley Way, Blezard Business Park, Seaton Burn, NEWCASTLE UPON TYNE, NE13 6DS.

HALL, Mrs. Jennifer Anne, BSc(Hons) ACA PGCE *2000;* 17 Kelton Close, Lower Earley, READING, RG6 3BQ.

HALL, Miss. Jennifer Mary, BSc ACA *2006;* 40 Fusion Court, Broadmeads, WARE, HERTFORDSHIRE, SG12 9EJ.

HALL, Mr. Jeremy Charles, BSc ACA *1993;* 3 The Mall, LONDON, N14 6LR.

HALL, Mr. Jeremy John, BA ACA *1988;* Now Health International, Ground Floor, Al Shaiba Building, PO Box 502163, DUBAI, UNITED ARAB EMIRATES.

•HALL, Mr. Jeremy John, BSc ACA *2000;* with KPMG Fides Peat, Avenue de Rumine 37, CH-1002 LAUSANNE, SWITZERLAND.

HALL, Mr. Jeremy Mark Gregson, BA FCA *1986;* Old Vicarage, Littletown, Newlands Valley, KESWICK, CA12 5TU.

HALL, Miss. Joanne Clare, BCom ACA *2004;* 91 Windrush Close, Pelsall, WALSALL, WS3 4LJ.

HALL, Mr. John, FCA *1953;* Lake Brow, Gowbarrow Lane, Watermillock, PENRITH, CA11 0JP. (Life Member)

HALL, Mr. John, FCA *1965;* 11 South Fork, NEWCASTLE UPON TYNE, NE15 8TZ. (Life Member)

•HALL, Mr. John, FCA *1980;* J. Hall & Co Limited, 255 Breightmet Fold Lane, BOLTON, BL2 5NB.

•HALL, Mr. John Alan, FCA *1972;* Albert Goodman CBH Limited, The Lupins Business Centre, 1-3 Greenhill, WEYMOUTH, DORSET, DT4 7SP. See also Coyne Butterworth Hardwicke Limited

HALL, Mr. John Anthony, FCA *1968;* Apartido 6, 07710 SAN LUIS, MENORCA, SPAIN.

HALL, Mr. John David, BSc(Econ) FCA *1962;* 16 Ave de Montgolfier, 92430 MARNES LA COQUETTE, FRANCE. (Life Member)

HALL, Mr. John David, FCA *1960;* 95 Broome Street, COTTESLOE, WA 6011, AUSTRALIA. (Life Member)

HALL, Mr. John Edward, MA FCA ATII *1995;* Dennys Close, Temple End, Harbury, LEAMINGTON SPA, WARWICKSHIRE, CV33 9NE.

HALL, Mr. John Euston, FCA *1957;* 11 Brandwood, Chadderton, OLDHAM, OL1 2TP. (Life Member)

HALL, Mr. John George, FCA *1978;* Knightsbridge Vending Ltd, 18 Norbury Court, City Works, Openshaw, MANCHESTER, M11 2NB.

HALL, Mr. John Henry, FCA *1962;* Hallco Financial Services, PO Box 1081, BRAESIDE, VIC 3198, AUSTRALIA.

HALL, Mr. John Jeremy Brayshay, FCA *1975;* 29 Route de Niort, Lussais, 79110 CHEF BOUTONNE, FRANCE.

HALL, Mr. John Mark, BA(Hons) ACA *2001;* The Brambles Stowe Lane, Stowe-by-Chartley, STAFFORD, ST18 0NA.

HALL, Mr. John Michael, BA FCA *1975;* 33 Oaklands, Gosforth, NEWCASTLE UPON TYNE, NE3 4YQ.

•①HALL, Mr. John Michael, MA FCA *1989;* Invocas Group Plc, 2nd Floor, Capital House, Festival Square, EDINBURGH, EH3 9SU.

•HALL, Mr. John Richard, BA FCA *1993;* Walter Dawson & Son, Apex House, 38 Little Horton Lane, BRADFORD, WEST YORKSHIRE, BD5 0AL.

HALL, Mr. John Richard, FCA *1979;* 5 West End Grove, Horsforth, LEEDS, LS18 5JJ.

HALL, Mr. John Richard Malcolm, FCA *1968;* Norwood Grange, Norwood Lane, IVER, BUCKINGHAMSHIRE, SL0 0EW.

HALL, Mr. Jonathan, MBA BA FCA *1992;* Digby House, Fulshaw Park, WILMSLOW, CHESHIRE, SK9 1QQ.

HALL, Mr. Jonathan Adam Aikman, BA(Hons) ACA *2001;* Maven Capital Partners (UK) LLP, St. James House, 7 Charlotte Street, MANCHESTER, M1 4DZ.

HALL, Mr. Jonathan David, BA ACA *2002;* Saracens Rugby Club Unit 3, Sandridge Park Porters Wood, ST. ALBANS, HERTFORDSHIRE, AL3 6PH.

HALL, Mr. Jonathan David, MSc BSc ACA *2005;* with Yorkshire Bank PLC, Manchester Financial Solutions Centre, The Chancery, 58 Spring Gardens, MANCHESTER, M2 1YB.

HALL, Mr. Jonathan Edward, BA FCA *1993;* Saffron Bldg Soc, Saffron House, 1a Market Place, SAFFRON WALDEN, ESSEX, CB10 1HX.

HALL, Mr. Jonathan William Scambler, BA ACA *1998;* 2 Waverley Place, LEATHERHEAD, KT22 8AS.

HALL, Mr. Joseph, MEng ACA *2010;* 47 Keith Grove, LONDON, W12 9EY.

HALL, Mr. Joseph Stuart, BSc ACA FMAAT *2005;* R D Computers, 29-31 Eastways, WITHAM, CM8 3YQ.

HALL, Mr. Joseph William, FCA *1970;* Byways The Street, Shotley, IPSWICH, IP9 1LX.

HALL, Mrs. Judith Anne, BSc ACA *1992;* 35 Swiss Avenue, CHELMSFORD, CM1 2AD.

HALL, Mrs. Judith Clare, BA ACA *1993;* 4 Saddlewood Avenue, MANCHESTER, M19 1QN.

•HALL, Mr. Julian, FCA *1959;* (Tax Fac), Julian Hall, Larkfield, Ashlawn Road, RUGBY, CV22 5QE.

HALL, Mrs. Karen, BSc ACA *2000;* 26 Ruffle Close, WEST DRAYTON, UB7 9BP.

HALL, Miss. Kate Elizabeth, BA(Hons) ACA *2010;* 99 Disraeli Road, LONDON, SW15 2DY.

HALL, Miss. Katharine, BSc ACA *2007;* 18 Briardale Walk, ALTRINCHAM, CHESHIRE, WA14 5GU.

HALL, Miss. Katherine, BA(Hons) ACA *2009;* 26c Hammelton Road, BROMLEY, BR1 3PY.

HALL, Miss. Kathryn Mary Stratford, BCom FCA DChA MIIA *1985;* 65 Dover Road, Birkdale, SOUTHPORT, PR8 4TH.

•HALL, Mr. Keith, FCA *1975;* (Tax Fac), Hall & Company, 2 The Causeway, Longframlington, MORPETH, NORTHUMBERLAND, NE65 8BL.

•HALL, Mr. Keith David, BSc FCA *1993;* ACAX, Shilton House, 56 Park Avenue North, NORTHAMPTON, NN3 2JE.

•HALL, Mr. Keith Richard, FCA *1993;* Feist Hedgethorne Limited, Preston Park House, South Road, BRIGHTON, BN1 6SB.

HALL, Mr. Kevin Andrew, BSc ACA ATT *2007;* Old Tesco House, Tesco Stores Ltd Tesco House, Delamare Road Cheshunt, WALTHAM CROSS, HERTFORDSHIRE, EN8 9SL.

HALL, Mr. Kevin Neil, ACA *1980;* 61 Majestic Point, CALGARY T3Z 2Z9, AB, CANADA.

HALL, Mr. Kevin Robert, BA(Hons) ACA *2002;* (Tax Fac), 33 Wigmore Street, LONDON, W1U 1AU.

•HALL, Mr. Kevin Rodney Raymond, BSc ACA *1991;* with KPMG LLP, Arlington Business Park, Theale, READING, RG7 4SD.

HALL, Miss. Kirsty Louise, MEng BA ACA *2005;* 2001 Pierce St Apt33, SAN FRANCISCO, CA 94115, UNITED STATES.

HALL, Mrs. Ladan, BSc ACA *1991;* 13 Grange Park Place, LONDON, SW20 0EE.

HALL, Mrs. Leila Jane, ACA *2008;* Baringa Partners Llp, 53a High Street, ESHER, KT10 9RQ.

HALL, Mrs. Linette, BSc(Hons) ACA CTA *2001;* Meadow Lodge, Culgaith, PENRITH, CUMBRIA, CA10 1QL.

HALL, Mrs. Lynn Julie, ACA *1986;* 109 Oxford Road, Moseley, BIRMINGHAM, B13 9SG.

HALL, Mr. Malcolm Iain, MA FCA *1975;* Lashbrook Leys Mill Road, Shiplake, HENLEY-ON-THAMES, OXFORDSHIRE, RG9 3LT. (Life Member)

HALL, Mrs. Margaret Mary, BA ACA *1985;* 48 Retford Road, SHEFFIELD, S13 9LE.

HALL, Mrs. Marie Victoria, ACA *2002;* 3 Meadowcroft Close, Outwood, WAKEFIELD, WEST YORKSHIRE, WF1 3TG.

HALL, Miss. Marissa Anne Kedre, BA(Hons) ACA CTA *2002;* 41 Byton Road, Tooting, LONDON, SW17 9HH.

HALL, Mr. Mark, BSc ACA *1997;* Ashbury House, Hungate Lane, Bishop Monkton, HARROGATE, NORTH YORKSHIRE, HG3 3QL.

HALL, Mr. Mark, BA ACA *1999;* 4th Floor, One Esplanade, ST HELIER, JE2 3QA.

•HALL, Mr. Mark James, ACA CTA *2007;* (Tax Fac), Halls (UK) Limited, 49 Windsor Avenue, Ashton-on-Ribble, PRESTON, LANCASHIRE, PR2 1JD.

HALL, Mr. Martin, ACA *1995;* 41 Otterburn Road, NORTH SHIELDS, NE29 9BJ.

HALL, Mr. Martin Ernest, FCA *1982;* 15 Fennel Drive, Bradley Stoke, BRISTOL, BS32 0BX.

HALL, Mr. Martin Francis, FCA *1974;* Moor Mill Farmhouse, Common Road, Thorpe Salvin, WORKSOP, S80 3JH.

HALL, Mr. Martin Gerald, MA ACA *1982;* 37 Percival Drive, Harbury, LEAMINGTON SPA, CV33 9GZ.

HALL, Mr. Martin James, MA FCA MCT *1990;* Standard Chartered, 1 Basinghall Avenue, LONDON, EC2V 5DD.

HALL, Mr. Martin John, BSc ACA *2003;* with Dodd & Co., Clint Mill, Cornmarket, PENRITH, CA11 7HW.

HALL, Mr. Martin John Dennis, BSc ACA *1984;* The Firs Coaley, DURSLEY, GLOUCESTERSHIRE, GL11 5DX.

HALL, Mr. Matthew, BSc(Econ) ACA *2010;* 18 Southfield Gardens, NEWCASTLE UPON TYNE, NE16 4QR.

HALL, Mr. Matthew, BSc ACA *2005;* Crime Operations Economic Crime Unit, Northumbria Police, Ponteland, NEWCASTLE UPON TYNE, NE20 0BL.

HALL, Mr. Matthew Benjamin Luke, MA(Hons) ACA *2001;* with PricewaterhouseCoopers LLP, 9 Greyfriars Road, READING, RG1 1JG.

HALL, Mr. Matthew Geoffrey, BSc ACA *2010;* 23 Ashley Road, LONDON, N19 3AG.

HALL, Mr. Matthew James, BA ACA *2003;* 3a Woodhill Road, Portishead, BRISTOL, BS20 7EU.

•HALL, Mr. Matthew Robert, BA FCA *1999;* with Deloitte LLP, 3 Victoria Square, Victoria Street, ST. ALBANS, HERTFORDSHIRE, AL1 3TF.

HALL, Mr. Matthew William, MA ACA *1998;* 56 Long Park, AMERSHAM, BUCKINGHAMSHIRE, HP6 5LF.

HALL, Mr. Michael, MA FCA *1976;* Pool House, Hawkesbury Upton, BADMINTON, AVON, GL9 1AY.

HALL, Mr. Michael, BSc ACA *1990;* 89 Waddon New Road, CROYDON, CR0 4JB.

•HALL, Mr. Michael Anthony, FCA *1974;* Crowe Clark Whitehill LLP, Carrick House, Lypiatt Road, CHELTENHAM, GLOUCESTERSHIRE, GL50 2QJ. See also Horwath Clark Whitehill LLP and Crowe Clark Whitehill

HALL, Mr. Michael Arthur, BA ACA *1988;* 20, Burcote Drive, Outlane, HUDDERSFIELD, HD3 3FY.

HALL, Mr. Michael George Henry, BSc(Hons) ACA *2000;* Islwyn, Mold Road, RUTHIN, CLWYD, LL15 1SL.

HALL, Mr. Michael Robert, FCA *1964;* Selective Financial Services Ltd, Derventio House Buxton Road, Ashford-in-the-Water, BAKEWELL, DERBYSHIRE, DE45 1QP.

HALL, Mr. Michael Roy, FCA *1969;* 11 Jaypark Crescent, Spennells, KIDDERMINSTER, DY10 4JP. (Life Member)

•HALL, Mr. Nathan Jamie, MA ACA *2000;* (Tax Fac), KPMG LLP, 15 Canada Square, LONDON, E14 5GL.

•HALL, Miss. Nichola Lynne, BSc(Hons) ACA *2003;* Nichola Hall ACA, 65 Oakwood Close, MIDHURST, WEST SUSSEX, GU29 9QP.

HALL, Mr. Nicholas James, BSc FCA *1982;* 2 Faircross Way, ST. ALBANS, AL1 4SD.

HALL, Mr. Nicholas James Humphreys, MA FCA *1971;* Angus & Ross PLC, St Chad's House, 59 Piercy End, Kirkbymoorside, YORK, YO62 6DQ.

•HALL, Mr. Nicholas Malcolm, BSc FCA *1989;* (Tax Fac), Accurate Consulting LLP, Oakfield Lodge, Main Street, Grendon Underwood, AYLESBURY, BUCKINGHAMSHIRE HP18 0SL.

•HALL, Mr. Nicholas Peter, BA FCA *1990;* KPMG Europe LLP, 15 Canada Square, LONDON, E14 5GL. See also KPMG LLP

HALL, Miss. Nicola Elizabeth, ACA *2002;* Parkwood Leisure Little Bowbrook, Walton Road Hartlebury, KIDDERMINSTER, WORCESTERSHIRE, DY10 4JA.

HALL, Mrs. Nicola Tracy, BSc ACA *1993;* with Ensors, Cardinal House, 46 St Nicholas Street, IPSWICH, IP1 1TT.

HALL, Mr. Nigel Patrick, MA FCA *1980;* 9 Harmont House, 20 Harley Street, LONDON, W1G 9PH.

HALL, Mr. Oliver Matthew, MPhys ACA *2008;* 47b Chichele Road, LONDON, NW2 3AN.

HALL, Mrs. Paula, BA ACA *2003;* 31 Beauxfield, Whitfield, DOVER, CT16 3JW.

HALL, Mr. Peter, BA(Hons) ACA *2004;* 2 La Cahce de la Ronde Seapoint, La Grande Route de la Cote St. Clement, JERSEY, JE2 6BR.

HALL, Mr. Peter Alistair, BSc FCA *1981;* Hugill House, Swanfield Road, WALTHAM CROSS, HERTFORDSHIRE, EN8 7JR.

HALL, Mr. Peter Arthur, FCA *1962;* Beech House, 27 Quarry Road East, Heswall, WIRRAL, CH61 6XD. (Life Member)

HALL, Mr. Peter James, BA ACA *2006;* 13 St. Nicholas Road, HAVANT, HAMPSHIRE, PO9 3TN.

HALL, Mr. Peter John, BSc ACA *1990;* James Walker & Co Ltd, Gote Brow, COCKERMOUTH, CUMBRIA, CA13 0NH.

HALL, Mr. Philip, BSc FCA *1972;* Inglehurst, 49 Grove Road, ILKLEY, LS29 9PQ.

HALL, Mr. Philip, ACA *2008;* with PricewaterhouseCoopers, Dorchester House, 7 Church Street West, PO Box HM1171, HAMILTON HM EX, BERMUDA.

•HALL, Mr. Philip Jonathan, BA ACA *1995;* (Tax Fac), Grant Thornton UK LLP, Crown House, Crown Street, IPSWICH, IP1 3HS. See also Grant Thornton LLP

HALL, Mr. Philip Stephen, BSc ACA *1986;* 41 Eaton Hill, Cookridge, LEEDS, LS16 6SE.

HALL, Mrs. Rachel Anne, MSc ACA *2002;* 235 Kanohi Road, KAUKAPAKAPA 0873, AUCKLAND, NEW ZEALAND.

•HALL, Miss. Rachel Simone, ACA *1995;* R S Hall and Co, Dragon's Lair, 27 Belle Meade Close, Woodgate, CHICHESTER, WEST SUSSEX PO20 3YD.

HALL, Mrs. Rauna Kristiina, BA ACA *2006;* Peterboro, Little Aldershot, Baughurst, TADLEY, HAMPSHIRE, RG26 5JN.

HALL, Mr. Raymond George, FCA *1957;* 300 Mayplace Road East, BEXLEYHEATH, DA7 6JT. (Life Member)

•HALL, Mrs. Rebecca Jane, BA ACA *1997;* RJ Hall, Great Danegate, Danegate, Eridge Green, TUNBRIDGE WELLS, KENT TN3 9HU.

•HALL, Mrs. Rebecca Mary, BSc(Hons) ACA *2004;* RM Hall, Farm View, High Row, Kirby Misperton, MALTON, NORTH YORKSHIRE YO17 6XN.

HALL, Miss. Rebekah Marie, BA ACA *2006;* 17 The Driftway, 182 Grove Road, LONDON, E3 5TG.

HALL, Mr. Richard, BA ACA *2002;* 56 Cheswick Drive, Gosforth, NEWCASTLE UPON TYNE, NE3 5DU.

•HALL, Mr. Richard Alexander, BA ACA *1989;* Ernst & Young LLP, 1 More London Place, LONDON, SE1 2AF. See also Ernst & Young Europe LLP

HALL, Mr. Richard Charles, BSc FCA *1977;* Trelonk Vean Freshwater Lane, St. Mawes, TRURO, CORNWALL, TR2 5AR.

HALL, Mr. Richard Gordon, TD MA FCA *1966;* Farm Cottage, Heath House, WEDMORE, BS28 4UG.

•HALL, Mr. Richard John William, MA ACA CF *1996;* HW Corporate Finance LLP, 13-21 High Street, GUILDFORD, SURREY, GU1 3DG.

HALL, Mr. Richard Liam, MEng ACA *2000;* 4 Lee Court, Whitley, GOOLE, NORTH HUMBERSIDE, DN14 0GX.
HALL, Mr. Richard Martin, BA(Hons) ACA *2004;* (Tax Fac), with KPMG LLP, Dukes Keep, Marsh Lane, SOUTHAMPTON, HAMPSHIRE, SO14 3EX.
HALL, Mr. Robert, BA ACA *1996;* 2 Hud Hill, HALIFAX, HX3 7LH.
HALL, Mr. Robert, BCom FCA *1992;* c/o BAT, Globe House, 4 Temple Place, LONDON, WC2R 2PG, EGYPT.
HALL, Mr. Robert, BA ACA *1993;* 64 Longdean Park, CHESTER LE STREET, COUNTY DURHAM, DH3 4DG.
HALL, Mr. Robert Ernest, FCA *1969;* Route de Conde, 14410 VASSY, FRANCE.
•**HALL, Mr. Robert Jan, BSc FCA** *1996;* Mitchell Charlesworth, 24 Nicholas Street, CHESTER, CH1 2AU.
•**HALL, Mr. Robert Peter, BSc ACA** *1992;* with KPMG, P O Box 3800, Level 32, Emirates Towers, Sheikh Zayed Road, DUBAI UNITED ARAB EMIRATES.
HALL, Mr. Robert Stewart Aikman, FCA *1967;* Vicarage House, Kirkby Wharfe, TADCASTER, LS24 9DE.
HALL, Mr. Robin Alexander, FCA *1972;* Cinven Ltd, Warwick Court, Paternoster Square, LONDON, EC4M 7AG.
HALL, Mr. Robin Arnsby, BA ACA *1992;* 13 Grange Park Place, LONDON, SW20 0EE.
HALL, Mr. Rodney David Gibson, FCA *1975;* 1 Wellhouse Road, BECKENHAM, BR3 3JR.
HALL, Miss. Sally, BSc ACA ATII *1991;* 9 Bauhinia Road, South Forbes Park, MAKATI CITY 1219, PHILIPPINES.
HALL, Miss. Samantha Louise, BA ACA *2005;* 17 Jourdain Park, Heathcote, WARWICK, CV34 6FJ.
HALL, Ms. Sarah Elizabeth, BSc(Hons) FCA *1993;* 7 Agar's Hill, PEMBROKE HM05, BERMUDA.
HALL, Ms. Sarah Elizabeth, BSc ACA *1987;* 42 Oakdene Road, Brockham, BETCHWORTH, RH3 7JX.
HALL, Mrs. Sarah Jayne, BA ACA *2005;* The Lodge, 17 Great Oaks, Hutton, BRENTWOOD, ESSEX, CM13 1AZ.
HALL, Miss. Sarah Kirsten, BA ACA *1993;* 47 Carvers Croft, Woolmer Green, KNEBWORTH, SG3 6LX.
HALL, Mrs. Sarah Nicola, LLB ACA *2003;* 3 Meadow Bank, Wooldale, HOLMFIRTH, WEST YORKSHIRE, HD9 1QS.
HALL, Miss. Sheila Vivien Thurstans, FCA *1960;* 19 Timberdene, Holders Hill Road, LONDON, NW4 1LA. (Life Member)
HALL, Mr. Simon, BSc ACA *2011;* 517a Finchley Road, LONDON, NW3 7BB.
HALL, Mr. Simon, MA ACA PGCE *2006;* 40 Winifred Road, Heavily, STOCKPORT, SK2 6HG.
HALL, Mr. Simon Alexander, BSc ACA *1989;* 34 Mickleham Way, New Addington, CROYDON, CR0 0PN.
HALL, Mr. Simon Colin, BEng ACA *1994;* Wedgewood House, 3 Manor Gardens, Lower Bourne, FARNHAM, SURREY, GU10 3QB.
•**HALL, Mr. Simon David, BA ACA** *2002;* Simalls Limited, PO Box 773, Charles Bisson House, 30-32 New Street, St Helier, JERSEY JE4 0RZ.
HALL, Mr. Simon Edward, MEng ACA *2002;* 25 Chartridge Lane, CHESHAM, BUCKINGHAMSHIRE, HP5 2JL.
HALL, Mr. Simon John, BSc ACA *1995;* 6 Filey, Amington, TAMWORTH, STAFFORDSHIRE, B77 3QH.
HALL, Mr. Spencer, ACA *1979;* 75 Devonshire Road, Westbury Park, BRISTOL, BS6 7NH.
•**HALL, Mr. Spencer John, BA(Hons) ACA** *2001;* S Hall Associates Limited, 9 Wimpole Street, LONDON, W1G 9SG. See also Auia
HALL, The Revd. Stanley, BA FCA *1950;* 43 Glen Grove, Royton, OLDHAM, OL2 5SY. (Life Member)
HALL, Mr. Stephen, FCA *1963;* Longburgh Ridge, Burgh By Sands, CARLISLE, CA5 6AF.
•**HALL, Mr. Stephen, BSc(Hons) CA FCA** *1978;* CHA Business Advisors Limited, Great Clough House, Goodshaw Fold Close, Loveclough, ROSSENDALE, LANCASHIRE BB4 8PZ.
•①**HALL, Mr. Stephen George, BSc FCA** *1982;* with PricewaterhouseCoopers LLP, 31 Great George Street, BRISTOL, BS1 5QD.
HALL, Mr. Stephen Hargreaves, TD MA FCA *1960;* Hole Farm Lodge The Street, Great Waldingfield, SUDBURY, SUFFOLK, CO10 0TW. (Life Member)
HALL, Mr. Stephen James, BA(Hons) ACA *2009;* 16 Appleton Road, STOCKPORT, CHESHIRE, SK4 5NA.
HALL, Mr. Stephen John, BA(Hons) ACA *2002;* 3002B Kaipara Coast Highway, RD4, WARKWORTH 0984, NEW ZEALAND.
HALL, Mr. Stephen Lloyd, BSc ACA *1992;* 302 -122 East 3rd Street, NORTH VANCOUVER V7L 1E6, BC, CANADA.
HALL, Mr. Stephen Mallalieu, BSc FCA *1977;* 5 Merriefield Drive, BROADSTONE, DORSET, BH18 8BW.
HALL, Mr. Stephen Robert, BSc ACA *1980;* 1 Fernyhalgh Gardens, Fulwood, PRESTON, PR2 9NH.
HALL, Mr. Stephen William Frederick, BEng ACA *1999;* Gosforth Lodge, Rugby Lane, SUTTON, SURREY, SM2 7NF.
HALL, Mr. Steven, BSc ACA *2004;* Moorfield Group, 65 Curzon Street, LONDON, W1J 8PE.
HALL, Mr. Steven, ACA *2008;* 38 Langham Way, ELY, CAMBRIDGESHIRE, CB6 1DZ.
HALL, Mr. Steven John, BSc FCA *1983;* 59 Speer Road, THAMES DITTON, SURREY, KT7 0PJ.
HALL, Mr. Steven John, FCA *1983;* (Tax Fac), Stanway Cottage, Shipton, MUCH WENLOCK, SHROPSHIRE, TF13 6LD.
HALL, Mr. Steven John, MA MSci ACA CFA *2001;* 21 Pembroke Avenue, PINNER, MIDDLESEX, HA5 1JP.
HALL, Mr. Stuart Andrew, ACA *1993;* Warwick House, 18 Warwick Crescent, HARROGATE, NORTH YORKSHIRE, HG2 8JA.
HALL, Mr. Stuart Richard John, ACA *2002;* Silverfleet Capital Partners LLP, 1 New Fetter Lane, LONDON, EC4A 1HH.
•**HALL, Mrs. Susan Linda, BA ACA** *1985;* (Tax Fac), Peach & Co, 115 Byrkley Street, BURTON-ON-TRENT, DE14 2EG.
HALL, Mrs. Susannah Mary Louise, BSc ACA *1990;* North Lodge Tramhill, Brill, AYLESBURY, BUCKINGHAMSHIRE, HP18 9TX.
•**HALL, Mr. Tim John, ACA FCCA** *2011;* The Trevor Jones Partnership LLP, Springfield House, 99-101 Crossbrook Street, Cheshunt, WALTHAM CROSS, HERTFORDSHIRE EN8 8JR.
HALL, Mr. Timothy James Ashley, BSc ACA *2007;* K P M G Llp, 15 Canada Square, LONDON, E14 5GL.
HALL, Mr. Timothy John, MA FCA *1979;* Lynton House, 17 High Green, Great Ayton, MIDDLESBROUGH, TS9 6BJ.
HALL, Mr. Timothy Richard, BSc ACA *1989;* Lombard Medical Technologies Plc Lombard Medical House, Basil Hill Road, DIDCOT, OXFORDSHIRE, OX11 7HJ.
HALL, Mr. Timothy Stevenson, BA ACA *1995;* La Source, Harewood Road, Collingham, WETHERBY, LS22 5NE.
HALL, Mr. Timothy William, BSc(Eng) FCA *1989;* 53 Windsor Drive, BARNET, EN4 8UE.
HALL, Mrs. Tracy Ann, ACA *1992;* 54 Mowbray Road, NORTHALLERTON, NORTH YORKSHIRE, DL6 1QU.
HALL, Mr. Trevor, BA ACA *2006;* 32 Downs Park, HIGH WYCOMBE, BUCKINGHAMSHIRE, HP13 5LU.
HALL, Mr. Trevor, BA(Hons) ACA *2001;* Circle Anglia, 1-3 Highbury Station Road, LONDON, N1 1SE.
•**HALL, Mr. William Benedict David, FCA** *1988;* millhall consultants ltd, Carlson Suite, Vantage Point Business Village, MITCHELDEAN, GLOUCESTERSHIRE, GL17 0DD.
•**HALL, Mr. William Graham, FCA** *1975;* AIMS - William Hall, Sarratt House, Bridle Lane, Loudwater, RICKMANSWORTH, HERTFORDSHIRE WD3 4JA.
HALL, Mr. William John Raymond, BA ACA *2004;* 20 Cheyne Park Drive, WEST WICKHAM, KENT, BR4 9LQ.
HALL, Mr. William Lindop, FCA *1953;* Dearham House, Copsem Lane, ESHER, KT10 9HE. (Life Member)
HALL-BYRNE, Mrs. Anthea Patricia, MBA ACA *1985;* 1 Station Road, Rearsby, LEICESTER, LE7 4YX.
HALL-PALMER, Mr. Nicholas Charles, BA ACA *1992;* Orchard Cottage, Bradford-on-Tone, TAUNTON, SOMERSET, TA4 1HB.
HALL-ROBERTS, Mr. Joseph Richard, BA ACA *1983;* J D R Cable Systems Ltd, 177 Wisbech Road Littleport, ELY, CAMBRIDGESHIRE, CB6 1RA.
HALL-SMITH, Mr. Sean Patrickk, FCA *1969;* Apartado de Correos 228, 46780 OLIVA, VALENCIA PROVINCE, SPAIN. (Life Member)
•**HALL-STRUTT, Mr. Leslie Raymond, FCA** *1957;* L.R. Hall-Strutt, 25 Cloudesley Close, SIDCUP, KENT, DA14 6TF.
•**HALL-TOMKIN, Mr. Clive Neil, FCA** *1991;* (Tax Fac), Maxwells, 4 King Square, BRIDGWATER, SOMERSET, TA6 3YF.
HALLADAY, Mr. David Andrew, BCom ACA *1997;* 16a Oxford Road, LONDON, SW15 2LF.
HALLAH, Mr. David Francis Wynn, FCA *1969;* Hourne, 32410 LARROQUE ST SERNIN, FRANCE.
HALLAHANE, Ms. Bridget Catherine, BA ACA *2010;* 9 Hyde Vale, LONDON, SE10 8QQ.
HALLALA, Mr. Mark John, BCom ACA *1985;* 7 Beauchamp Road, EAST MOLESEY, KT8 0PA.
HALLAM, Mrs. Ann Lindsay, BA ACA *1986;* Linnet House, 9 Keepers Green, Braiswick, COLCHESTER, CO4 5UT.
HALLAM, Mr. Crispin John, BA ACA *1982;* Duck Pool, Ashleyhay, Wirksworth, MATLOCK, DERBYSHIRE, DE4 4AJ.
HALLAM, Mrs. Hazell, BSc ACA *2004;* 7d Underwood Street, LONDON, N1 7LY.
HALLAM, Mr. John Edward, FCA *1971;* Kings Mills Farm, Kings Mills Road, Castel, GUERNSEY, GY5 7JT.
HALLAM, Mr. Joseph, BSc ACA *2002;* Kenhill Barnett Lane, Wonersh, GUILDFORD, GU5 0RZ.
HALLAM, Miss. Laura Jayne, BA ACA *2009;* 2 Langdon Close, Long Eaton, NOTTINGHAM, NG10 4NX.
HALLAM, Mr. Mark William, BSc MNI FCA *1991;* R N L I, West Quay Road, POOLE, DORSET, BH15 1HZ.
HALLAM, Mr. Matthew, BA ACA *2000;* Windwood House The Edge, Eyam, HOPE VALLEY, DERBYSHIRE, S32 5QP.
HALLAM, Miss. Natalie Christina, ACA *2008;* St. Anora, 9 Brock Road, St. Peter Port, GUERNSEY, GY1 1RT.
HALLAM, Mr. Neil, BSc ACA *1985;* 1 Basevi Way, LONDON, SE8 3JU.
HALLAM, Mr. Paul Andrew, MA ACA *2002;* 604 Cascades Tower, 4 Westferry Road, LONDON, E14 8JN.
HALLAM, Mr. Richard John, FCA *1968;* Kato Entex Ltd, Glaisdale Drive, Bilbrough, NOTTINGHAM, NG8 4JY.
HALLAM, Mr. Simon, BA ACA *1991;* 39 Imogen Gardens, Heathcote, WARWICK, CV34 6FB.
HALLAM, Miss. Sophie Ann, BSc ACA *1994;* 14 Copperkins Lane, AMERSHAM, BUCKINGHAMSHIRE, HP6 5QF.
HALLAM, Dr. Timothy David, PhD BSc(Hons) ACA *2001;* 20 Elleray Road, Alkrington, Middleton, MANCHESTER, M24 1NY.
•**HALLAM, Mr. William John, FCA** *1973;* 2265 Sirocco Drive SW, CALGARY T3H 3M3, AB, CANADA.
HALLAN, Mr. James, BA(Hons) ACA *2010;* Flat 31 Stretton Mansions, Glaisher Street, LONDON, SE8 3JP.
HALLAS, Mr. Gordon, FCA *1964;* 81 The Village, Holme, HOLMFIRTH, HD9 2QG.
HALLAS, Mrs. Jacquelyn Margaret, FCA *1979;* 3 Garth Drive, LEEDS, LS17 5BE.
HALLAS, Mrs. Karen Elizabeth, BSc ACA *1995;* 30 Upper Bank End Road, HOLMFIRTH, HD9 1EW.
HALLAS, Mr. Rory, ACA *2008;* 188 Huntingfield Road, LONDON, SW15 5ES.
HALLATT, Mr. Peter, BSc ACA *2007;* 2 Rue Francois Faber, Limpertsberg, L-1509 LUXEMBOURG, LUXEMBOURG.
HALLERON, Mr. Martin Christopher, ACA *2008;* 33 Kirkside View, Hapton, BURNLEY, BB11 5RJ.
HALLETT, Mr. Brian James, FCA *1977;* 235 Hunts Pond Road, FAREHAM, PO14 4PJ.
•**HALLETT, Ms. Christina Susan Mary, BA ACA** *1986;* PricewaterhouseCoopers LLP, 80 Strand, LONDON, WC2R 0AF. See also PricewaterhouseCoopers
HALLETT, Miss. Clare Judith, BA ACA *2006;* New House Farm Thomas Chapel, Begelly, KILGETTY, DYFED, SA68 0XH.
•**HALLETT, Mr. David, ACA FCCA** *2010;* (Tax Fac), Derek J Read Limited, 107 North Street, MARTOCK, SOMERSET, TA12 6EJ.
•**HALLETT, Mr. John William, MBA FCA** *1971;* 11 Northumberland Place, RICHMOND, SURREY, TW10 6TS.
•**HALLETT, Mr. Justin Marc, ACA** *2002;* BDO Limited, PO Box 180, Place du Pre, Rue du Pre, St Peter Port, GUERNSEY GY1 3LL.
•**HALLETT, Mr. Nicholas Paul, FCA** *1982;* NPH Accountants Ltd, The Old Rectory, Church Road, Gisleham, LOWESTOFT, SUFFOLK NR33 8DS.
HALLETT, Mr. Oliver, BA ACA AKC *2011;* Flat 412, Seddon House, Barbican, LONDON, EC2Y 8BX.
HALLETT, Mr. Peter John, ACA *1981;* Goldfields, Glenhill Farm, Glendon Road, KETTERING, NN14 1QE.
•**HALLETT, Mr. Raymond, ACA** *1980;* with RSM Tenon Limited, Highfield Court, Tollgate, Chandler's Ford, EASTLEIGH, HAMPSHIRE SO53 3TY.
HALLETT, Mr. Richard James, BA FCA *1994;* Hargreave Hale Ltd, Accurist House, 44 Baker Street, LONDON, W1U 7AL.
HALLETT, Mr. Richard James, BA ACA *2010;* Orleton Grange, Orleton, Stanford Bridge, WORCESTER, WR6 6SU.
HALLETT, Mr. Ricky Courtney, BA ACA *1983;* Maskreys Ltd, 116-120 Whitchurch Road, CARDIFF, CF14 3YL.
•**HALLETT, Mr. Roderick Richard, ACA** *1979;* R.R. Hallett, Orleton Grange, Orleton, Stanford Bridge, WORCESTER, WR6 6SU.
HALLETT, Mr. Roy Graham, FCA *1954;* 160 Yarmouth Rd, LOWESTOFT, NR32 4AB. (Life Member)
•**HALLETT, Mr. Stephen Charles, BA FCA** *1979;* (Tax Fac), Gapfillers Limited, 5 Chargot Road, Llandaff, CARDIFF, SOUTH GLAMORGAN, CF5 1EW. See also AIMS - Steve Hallett FCA
•①**HALLEY, Mr. Myles Antony, BSc FCA** *1983;* The White House, 145 Main Street, Sutton Bonington, LOUGHBOROUGH, LEICESTERSHIRE, LE12 5PE.
HALLEZ, Mrs. Laura Anne, BSc ACA *2007;* with Mazars LLP, Regency House, 3 Grosvenor Square, SOUTHAMPTON, SO15 2BE.
HALLEZ, Mr. Regis Michel, ACA *2008;* 12 Poole Road, SOUTHAMPTON, SO19 2HD.
•**HALLGARTEN, Mr. Daniel Arthur, BSc ACA** *1989;* HGT Management LLP, 20 Manchester Square, LONDON, W1U 3PZ.
HALLIDAY, Mrs. Catherine Wendy, BA ACA *1990;* 176a Henwick Road, WORCESTER, WR2 5PE.
HALLIDAY, Mrs. Denise Carole, BSc ACA *1997;* 24 Warrington Avenue, EAST KILLARA, NSW 2071, AUSTRALIA.
HALLIDAY, Mr. Edward John, BSc ACA *2006;* 4 Foxhill Chase, STOCKPORT, SK2 5HJ.
HALLIDAY, Mr. James Charles, BSc FCA *1982;* Friends Provident, Pixham End, DORKING, SURREY, RH4 1QA.
•**HALLIDAY, Mr. James Frederick, BA ACA** *1988;* Halliday & Co, Victoria House, 45 Rutland Park, Botanical Gardens, SHEFFIELD, S10 2PB.
HALLIDAY, Mr. James Mcgowan, FCA *1973;* 8a Peggys Walk Littlebury, SAFFRON WALDEN, ESSEX, CB11 4TG.
HALLIDAY, Mr. Jeremy David, ACA *1981;* East Farm, Laverton, RIPON, NORTH YORKSHIRE, HG4 3SX.
HALLIDAY, Mr. John Craig, BSc ACA *1991;* 7909 East 25th Place, DENVER, CO 80238, UNITED STATES.
HALLIDAY, Miss. Katherine Elizabeth, BA(Hons) ACA *2010;* Albert Court, 18 Melville Place, LONDON, N1 8ND.
HALLIDAY, Miss. Laura, ACA *2010;* 406a Bearwood Road, SMETHWICK, B66 4EX.
HALLIDAY, Mr. Leslie Bruce, BA ACA *1995;* Gosling Syke, 84 Etterby Street, Stanwix, CARLISLE, CA3 9JD.
HALLIDAY, Mr. Martin John, BSc ACA *1985;* Group GTI Ltd, The Fountain Building, Nowsbery Park, WALLINGFORD, OXFORDSHIRE, OX10 6SL.
HALLIDAY, Mr. Neil, BSc ACA *1988;* 21, Beechwood, LINLITHGOW, EH49 6SD.
HALLIDAY, Mr. Nigel Kilayn, MA FCA *1970;* 62 The Street, Surlingham, NORWICH, NR14 7AJ. (Life Member)
•**HALLIDAY, Mr. Paul, BSc ACA** *1991;* (Tax Fac), with PricewaterhouseCoopers LLP, 141 Bothwell Street, GLASGOW, G2 7EQ.
HALLIDAY, Mr. Peter Edwin, BA FCA *1985;* c/o Majan Electricity company, PO Box 701, PC 116 MINA AL FAHAL, OMAN.
HALLIDAY, Mr. Philip Michael, FCA *1983;* (Tax Fac), 222 East 34th Street, Apartment 2022, NEW YORK, NY 10016-9843, UNITED STATES.
HALLIDAY, Mr. Robert William, BSc ACA *1986;* 12 Murieston Valley, Murieston, LIVINGSTON, EH54 9HB.
HALLIDAY, Mr. Robin Lance, BSc FCA *1985;* 13 Wraysbury Drive, Waterside Park, WEST DRAYTON, UB7 7FL.
•**HALLIDAY, Mr. Russell John, BSc ACA** *1986;* WBV Limited, 33 Heathfield, SWANSEA, SA1 6HD. See also Heathfield Tax Consultancy Ltd
HALLIDAY, Mr. Simon John Rhodes, MA ACA *1988;* 176a Henwick Road, WORCESTER, WR2 5PE.
HALLIDAY, Mr. Steven Don, BA ACA *1979;* Laneside, Wallbank Road, Bramhall, STOCKPORT, SK7 3AP.
HALLIDAY, Mrs. Susan Jane, BA ACA *1983;* (Tax Fac), CARDALE ASSET MANAGEMENT LTD, 2 Greengate, Cardale Park, HARROGATE, NORTH YORKSHIRE, HG3 1GY.
HALLIFAX, Mr. Guy Charles, MSc ACA *1985;* 53 Compton Road, Wimbledon, LONDON, SW19 7QA.
HALLINAN, Mr. Kieran John, BSc FCA *1991;* 22 Beeston Mount, Bollington, MACCLESFIELD, CHESHIRE, SK10 5QY.
HALLISSEY, Mr. Michael, MA FCA *1968;* Flat 66 Waterside Point, 2 Anhalt Road, LONDON, SW11 4PD.
HALLISSEY, Mr. Steven Peter, BAcc ACA *1999;* 92 Milestone Avenue, Charvil, READING, RG10 9TN.
HALLIWELL, Mr. Bruce, BSc(Hons) ACA *1994;* Jersey Steel Co (1935) Group, Goose Green Marsh, Beaumont, St Peter, JERSEY, JE3 7BU.
HALLIWELL, Mr. Edward, BA ACA *1998;* 9 Coppins Close, Helsby, FRODSHAM, CHESHIRE, WA6 9QL.

HALLIWELL, Mrs. Fiona Helen, ACA *1989;* 15 Hamilton Avenue, HENLEY-ON-THAMES, OXFORDSHIRE, RG9 1SH.
HALLIWELL, Mrs. Helen Claire, BA ACA *1992;* 6 Bolton Road, LONDON, W4 3TB.
HALLIWELL, Mr. James Dominic, BA ACA MCT *1987;* Syngenta International AG, Schwarzwaldallee 215, PO Box, CH-4002 BASEL, SWITZERLAND.
HALLIWELL, Miss. Jane, BSc ACA *1993;* 64 Granville Gardens, HODDESDON, EN11 9QD.
HALLIWELL, Mr. Keith Anthony, BSc FCA *1984;* Orbital Corporation Ltd, PO Box 901, BALCATTA, WA 6914, AUSTRALIA.
•**HALLIWELL, Mr. Kevin Michael, FCA** *1982;* Adams Lee Clark, Adam House, 71 Bell Street, HENLEY-ON-THAMES, RG9 2BD. See also Salary and Accounting Services Limited
HALLIWELL, Mr. Martin Paul, BA ACA *1989;* Appleton House, St. Marys Lane, Winkfield, WINDSOR, SL4 4SH.
HALLIWELL, Mr. Michael Robert, FCA *1965;* 20 Fairhaven Road, LYTHAM ST. ANNES, LANCASHIRE, FY8 1NN. (Life Member)
HALLIWELL, Mr. Neville, FCA *1965;* 3 Cherry Hill, ST. ALBANS, AL2 3AT.
HALLIWELL, Mr. Nigel Dennis, BSc ACA *1988;* 27 Hill House Close, Turners Hill, CRAWLEY, WEST SUSSEX, RH10 4YY.
HALLIWELL, Mr. Philip Neville, BSc ACA *1992;* 5 High Street, Colney Heath, ST. ALBANS, AL4 0NS.
HALLIWELL, Miss. Samantha, BSc ACA *2010;* 19 Standhills Road, KINGSWINFORD, WEST MIDLANDS, DY6 8DW.
HALLIWELL, Mr. Stephen Paul, BSc ACA *1995;* Woodlands Farm, Norwood Hill, HORLEY, RH6 0ET.
HALLIWELL, Mrs. Virginia Therese, LLB ACA *1981;* Monkswell, Vale Royal Drive, Whitegate, NORTHWICH, CHESHIRE, CW8 2BA.
•**HALLMARK, Mr. John Frederick, BSc(Hons) FCA MBIM** *1972;* (Tax Fac), John F Hallmark, Moonrakers, 29 Overton Shaw, EAST GRINSTEAD, RH19 2HN.
HALLMARK, Mr. Martin Robert, MA ACA *1995;* C V C, 111 Strand, LONDON, WC2R 0AG.
HALLORAN, Mr. Conrad Thomas, FCA *1955;* 446a Killinghall Road, BRADFORD, WEST YORKSHIRE, BD2 4SL. (Life Member)
HALLORAN, Miss. Marie Louise, BSc ACA *2004;* 91 Calvert Road, Greenwich, LONDON, SE10 0DG.
HALLOWELL, Mrs. Anne Victoria, BSc FCA DChA *1994;* North of England Civic Trust, Blackfriars, NEWCASTLE UPON TYNE, NE1 4XN.
HALLOWELL, Mr. Stephen John, BA ACA *1994;* 21 Carlisle Close, Holystone, NEWCASTLE UPON TYNE, NE27 0UT.
HALLOWES, Mr. Guy Rupert, FCA *1966;* 29A Johnston Crescent, Lane Cove, SYDNEY, NSW 2066, AUSTRALIA. (Life Member)
HALLOWS, Mr. John Douglas Whaley, FCA *1970;* Sokwe/Asilia Group Limited, PO Box 1111, ARUSHA, TANZANIA.
HALLOWS, Mrs. Katherine Emma, BSc ACA *1995;* Donard House, Birtle Road, BURY, BL9 6UT.
•**HALLOWS, Miss. Maria Margaret, BA FCA DChA** *1994;* Beever and Struthers, St George's House, 215-219 Chester Road, MANCHESTER, M15 4JE.
HALLOWS, Miss. Melissa Michelle, BSc ACA *2009;* 89 Lexicon Apartments, Mercury Gardens, ROMFORD, RM1 3HG.
HALLOWS, Mr. Richard Antony, MA MBA FCA MIOD *1971;* Gea Moutault & Associates, 46 Rue Du General Foy, 75008 PARIS, FRANCE.
HALLPIKE, Miss. Katrina Rachel, MA ACA *2009;* with PricewaterhouseCoopers LLP, 17-00 PWC Building, 8 Cross Street, SINGAPORE 048424, SINGAPORE.
•**HALLS, Mr. Adrian Trevor, BA(Hons) ACA FCCA CF** *1984;* Ashgates Corporate Services Ltd, 5 Prospect Place, Millennium Way, Pride Park, DERBY, DE24 8HG. See also Ashgates
HALLS, Mr. Andrew David, BSc(Hons) ACA *2003;* 21 Aspens Way, BROMSGROVE, WORCESTERSHIRE, B61 0UW.
HALLS, Mr. John Rosevear, FCA *1955;* 2 Metha Road, St.Newlyn East, NEWQUAY, TR8 5LP. (Life Member)
HALLS, Miss. Lisa, BA ACA *1995;* 35 Windfall Way, GLOUCESTER, GL2 0RP.
HALLS, Mrs. Lorna, BSc(Hons) ACA *2003;* 32 / 81 Point St, PYRMONT, NSW 2009, AUSTRALIA.
•**HALLS, Mrs. Nicola Ann, MA FCA** *1989;* (Tax Fac), Fletcher & Partners, Crown Chambers, Bridge Street, SALISBURY, SP1 2LZ.
HALLS, Mr. Nigel John, FCA *1961;* 3 Longford Court Barns, Tewkesbury Road, GLOUCESTER, GL2 9BN.
HALLS, Mr. Nigel Phillip, BSc FCA *1994;* Esso Petroleum Company Ltd, Mailpoint 12, Exxonmobil House, Ermyn Way, LEATHERHEAD, SURREY KT22 8UX.
HALLS, Mr. Robert James, BA ACA *2006;* HPB Management Ltd, HPB House, Old Station Road, NEWMARKET, SUFFOLK, CB8 8EH.
HALLS, Mr. Robert Lawrence, ACA *2008;* 12 Mulberry Lane, PORTSMOUTH, PO6 2QU.
HALLSWORTH, Mr. Christopher, BSc ACA *2006;* (Tax Fac), 7 Deerplay Court, BACUP, LANCASHIRE, OL13 8GE.
HALLSWORTH, Mr. Daniel, BSc ACA *2011;* Ballard Dale Syree Watson Llp Oakmoore Court, Kingswood Road Hampton Lovett, DROITWICH, WORCESTERSHIRE, WR9 0QH.
•**HALLSWORTH, Mr. John Anthony, BSc ACA** *1995;* KPMG LLP, 15 Canada Square, LONDON, E14 5GL. See also KPMG Europe LLP
•**HALLSWORTH, Mrs. Louise Mary, BA ACA** *1990;* Clifford Fry & Co LLP, St. Marys House, Netherhampton, SALISBURY, SP2 8PU.
HALLSWORTH, Mr. Norris Edward, FCA *1964;* 28 Shepshed Road, Hathern, LOUGHBOROUGH, LE12 5LL.
•**HALLSWORTH, Mr. Richard John, BCom ACA ACIM DipM** *2001;* Nicholsons, Newland House, The Point, Weaver Road, LINCOLN, LN6 3QN.
HALLWARD, Mr. Charles, BA(Hons) ACA *2000;* 71 Beryl Road, LONDON, W6 8JS.
HALLWOOD, Mr. Arthur, FCA *1951;* 58 Ballard Chase, ABINGDON, OX14 1XQ. (Life Member)
HALLWORTH, Mr. Bernard Theodore, FCA *1952;* 1 Garden Court, Hervines Road, AMERSHAM, BUCKINGHAMSHIRE, HP6 5HW. (Life Member)
HALLWORTH, Mr. Graham, ACA *1985;* Pennsylvania, 12 Summerhill Road, Prestbury, MACCLESFIELD, CHESHIRE, SK10 4AH.
HALLWORTH, Mr. Steven, ACA *1981;* Kenmare, Kelsey Lane, Balsall Common, COVENTRY, CV7 7GL.
•**HALLYBONE, Mr. Michael John, FCA** *1976;* (Tax Fac), Platt Rushton LLP, Sutherland House, 1759 London Road, LEIGH-ON-SEA, ESSEX, SS9 2RZ. See also Sutherland Corporate Services Ltd
HALM, Miss. Gloria, FCA *1973;* P.O. Box 4071, ACCRA, GHANA. (Life Member)
HALON, Mr. Richard Jonathan, BA ACA *1982;* 20A Bilu Street, 43581 RA'ANANA, ISRAEL.
HALPERN, Mr. Barry, FCA *1955;* Hillside, 7 Kingston Hill, CHEADLE, SK8 1JS. (Life Member)
•**HALPERN, Mr. David, FCA** *1966;* Halpern and Co, 20 Berkeley Street, LONDON, W1J 8EE.
•**HALPERN, Mr. David, BSc ACA** *2000;* Outsourced Accounts Department Ltd, 32 Winders Way, SALFORD, M6 6AR.
HALPIN, Miss. Abigail Hannah, BA ACA *2002;* 8 Chestnut Grove, LONDON, SW12 8JD.
HALPIN, Mr. Cecil Francis, FCA *1964;* Sutton House, Wonston, Sutton Scotney, WINCHESTER, SO21 3LS. (Life Member)
HALPIN, Mr. Clement Douglas, FCA *1963;* 75 Lynwood Road, LONDON, W5 1JG.
HALPIN, Mr. Conor, BCom ACA *1993;* National Instruments, Unit 302 Omni Business Park, Swords Road, Santry, DUBLIN 9, COUNTY DUBLIN IRELAND.
HALPIN, Mrs. Hilary Jane, BA FCA *1989;* Feniscliffe Long Moss Lane, Whitestake, PRESTON, PR4 4XN.
HALPIN, Mr. Nicholas John Blake, BA(Hons) ACA *2000;* 8 Chestnut Grove, LONDON, SW12 8JD.
HALPIN, Mr. Patrick Edward, MSc ACA *2001;* BP plc, 20 Canada Square, LONDON, E14 5NJ.
HALPIN, Mr. Peter Joseph, BA ACA *1988;* Feniscliffe Long Moss Lane, Whitestake, PRESTON, PR4 4XN.
HALSALL, Mrs. Alison Lindsay, BA ACA *2006;* 7 Connaught Close, WILMSLOW, CHESHIRE, SK9 2QS.
HALSALL, Mr. David, BSc ACA *2006;* 7 Connaught Close, WILMSLOW, CHESHIRE, SK9 2QS.
HALSALL, Mrs. Emma, BA ACA *2007;* 39 Granville Road, SOUTHPORT, MERSEYSIDE, PR8 2HU.
•**HALSALL, Mrs. Helen Mary Beatrice, BSc ACA** *1990;* 4 Heald Drive, Bowdon, ALTRINCHAM, CHESHIRE, WA14 2JA.
•**HALSALL, Dr. John Anthony Sydney, MA FCA** *1975;* Halsall & Co, Cherwell, Remenham Lane, Remenham, HENLEY-ON-THAMES, RG9 3DB.
HALSALL, Mr. Jonathan, ACA *2011;* Pricewaterhousecoopers, 1 Embankment Place, LONDON, WC2N 6RH.
HALSALL, Mr. Kieron Ashley, FCA *1982;* Mayville, Alexander Drive, Douglas, ISLE OF MAN, IM2 3QN.
•**HALSALL, Mr. Nicholas Mark, BA ACA** *1997;* PricewaterhouseCoopers, Sixty Circular Road, Douglas, ISLE OF MAN, IM1 1SA. See also PricewaterhouseCoopers LLC
HALSALL, Mr. Reginald Derek, FCA *1948;* Meadow View, Dray Road, Higher Odcombe, YEOVIL, BA22 8UG. (Life Member)
HALSALL, Miss. Stephanie Joanne, BA(Hons) ACA *2010;* 62 Westbourne Drive, Douglas, ISLE OF MAN, IM1 4BD.
HALSALL, Mrs. Susan, BSc ACA *1998;* 6 Milbury, Earls Barton, NORTHAMPTON, NN6 0PZ.
HALSALL, Mr. Thomas, BA FCA *1953;* 23 Clifford Road, Poynton, STOCKPORT, SK12 1HY. (Life Member)
HALSALL, Ms. Wendy Margaret, BA ACA ATII *1987;* Acomb Mill, Acomb, HEXHAM, NORTHUMBERLAND, NE46 4PQ.
HALSE, Mr. Michael Norman, FCA *1956;* 55 Rue Brancion, 75015 PARIS, FRANCE. (Life Member)
•**HALSEY, Mr. Adam Michael, BCom FCA DChA** *1998;* haysmacintyre, Fairfax House, 15 Fulwood Place, LONDON, WC1V 6AY.
•**HALSEY, Mrs. Alison Margaret, BA FCA** *1980;* KPMG LLP, 15 Canada Square, LONDON, E14 5GL. See also KPMG Europe LLP
HALSEY, Mrs. Amanda Jane, BA FCA *1987;* 18 Fairmile Lane, COBHAM, SURREY, KT11 2DJ.
HALSEY, Mr. Michael Frank, BSc ACA *1988;* MDFRC, University Drive, WODONGA, VIC 3690, AUSTRALIA.
HALSEY, Mr. Michael John, FCA *1973;* Sans Sourci, 1 Clos de la Perference, La Grande Route de St. Martin, St. Martin, JERSEY, JE3 6JB.
HALSEY, Mr. Michael John, BSc(Econ) FCA *1971;* Little Paddock, Guildford Road, Fetcham, LEATHERHEAD, SURREY, KT22 9DY. (Life Member)
HALSEY, Mrs. Natalie Cara, BA(Hons) ACA *2003;* 3 Darell Gardens, Frampton On Severn, GLOUCESTER, GLOUCESTERSHIRE, GL2 7HZ.
HALSEY, Mr. Niki James, BA ACA *2003;* Kingston Communications Melbourne House, Brandy Carr Road Wrenthorpe, WAKEFIELD, WEST YORKSHIRE, WF2 0UG.
HALSEY, Mr. Robert John, FCA *1982;* Cromwell East, 1777 S.E. 15th St, Suite 521, FORT LAUDERDALE, FL 33316, UNITED STATES.
HALSON, Mr. Gordon Henry, FCA *1956;* 36 Jessopp Avenue, BRIDPORT, DORSET, DT6 4ES. (Life Member)
HALSTEAD, Mr. Ben, ACA *2008;* with Howard Worth, Bank Chambers, 3 Churchyardside, NANTWICH, CW5 5DE.
•**HALSTEAD, Mr. Benjamin, BA(Hons) ACA** *2005;* Streets, Fairways, A1/A428 Interchange, Wyboston Lakes, Great North Road, BEDFORD BEDFORDSHIRE MK44 3BZ. See also Streets Whitmarsh Sterland
•**HALSTEAD, Mr. David Edward Michael, BSc FCA** *1994;* Deloitte LLP, City House, 126-130 Hills Road, CAMBRIDGE, CB2 1RY. See also Deloitte & Touche LLP
HALSTEAD, Mrs. Elizabeth Louise, BSc ACA *1986;* 4 Hartland Road, EPPING, CM16 4PE.
•**HALSTEAD, Mr. John Barrie, FCA** *1970;* Opus Services Limited, The Laurels, 2 St Leonards Road, HARROGATE, NORTH YORKSHIRE, HG2 8NX.
HALSTEAD, Mr. John Stephen, FCA *1971;* 1 Carr Hall Mews, Carr Hall Road, Barrowford, NELSON, LANCASHIRE, BB9 6QD.
•**HALSTEAD, Mr. John Stephen, FCA** *1972;* (Tax Fac), Halstead & Co, 434 Hale Road, Hale Barns, ALTRINCHAM, WA15 8TH.
•**HALSTEAD, Mr. Keith Erik, MA(Oxon) ACA** *1986;* Kingston Smith LLP, Surrey House, 36-44 High Street, REDHILL, RH1 1RH. See also Kingston Smith Limited Liability Partnership, Devonshire Corporate Services LLP and Kingston Smith Consulting LLP
•**HALSTEAD, Mrs. Margaret Elizabeth, FCA** *1980;* Halstead & Co, 434 Hale Road, Hale Barns, ALTRINCHAM, WA15 8TH.
HALSTEAD, Mr. Richard Graham, BA FCA *1981;* Ashton, 18 Brompton Terrace, Kinnoull, PERTH, PH2 7DQ.
HALSTEAD, Mr. Roger Malcolm, ACA *1980;* 33B Cremorne Road, CREMORNE POINT, NSW 2090, AUSTRALIA.
HALSTEAD, Mr. Stephen John, BSc ACA *1991;* 7 Vine Close, BAYVIEW HEIGHTS, QLD 4868, AUSTRALIA.
HALSTEAD, Mr. Stephen John, BA ACA *1994;* 2 Pitt Drive, ST. ALBANS, HERTFORDSHIRE, AL4 0GR.
HALSTEAD, Mr. William Richard, BSc ACA *1981;* William Halstead Ltd, PO Box 239, Stanley Mills, Edward Street, BRADFORD, WEST YORKSHIRE BD4 9RS.
HALSTED, Mr. Andrew Robert, ACA *1990;* Halsted Brothers (Pvt) Ltd, P.O. Box 3858, HARARE, ZIMBABWE.
HALTON, Miss. Amanda Kristina, ACA *2008;* Deloitte & Touche Hill House, 1 Little New Street, LONDON, EC4A 3TR.
HALTON, Mr. Angus John McAlpine, BA ACA *1993;* Barclays Bank Plc, 1 Churchill Place, LONDON, E14 5HP.
HALTON, Mr. Clive Alan, FCA *1963;* Orchard House, Frenchay Hill, BRISTOL, BS16 1LU.
HALTON, Mr. Eldred Charles William, MA ACA *1982;* 2 Woodside, Homer, MUCH WENLOCK, SHROPSHIRE, TF13 6NQ.
HALTON, Mr. Gary Robert, BA ACA *1993;* 8 Stainer Close, NEWTON-LE-WILLOWS, MERSEYSIDE, WA12 9WY.
HALTON, Mr. Ian Malcolm, BA ACA *1991;* 6 Chestnut Avenue, Walton, WAKEFIELD, WF2 6TE.
HALTON, Mr. John, BA FCA *1980;* Calypso Soft Drinks Ltd, Spectrum Business Park, Wrexham Industrial Estate, WREXHAM, LL13 9QA.
HALTON, Mr. Julian McDonald, BSc(Hons) ACA *2002;* Corrigan Associates, Venturers House, King Street, BRISTOL, BS1 4PB.
HALTON, Miss. Lesley Joan, FCA *1976;* 8 Roland Bailey Gardens, TAVISTOCK, PL19 0RB.
HALTON, Mrs. Nia, BA(Hons) ACA *2002;* 11 Mafeking Road, Penylan, CARDIFF, CF23 5DQ.
HALTON, Miss. Nicola Claire, BA ACA *2005;* Melbourne IT, Level 2, 120 King Street, MELBOURNE, VIC 3000, AUSTRALIA.
HALTON, Mrs. Sara Frances, MSc ACA *1992;* 24 Wellington Road, HAMPTON, MIDDLESEX, TW12 1JT.
HALTON, Dr. Sarah Elizabeth, BA ACA *2001;* Whitzend, 123 Woodside Road, AMERSHAM, BUCKINGHAMSHIRE, HP6 6AL.
•**HALTON, Mr. Terence, FCA** *1971;* Barra Accountancy Services, Kisimul, 9 Argyll Close, Horsforth, LEEDS, LS18 5SP.
HALY, Mrs. Mary Ruth, BSc FCA *1989;* 13 Orchard Rise, Coombe Lane West, KINGSTON-UPON-THAMES, KT2 7EY.
HAM, Mr. David Fenton, MA ACA *1992;* 25 Chestnut Avenue, TUNBRIDGE WELLS, TN4 0BT.
HAM, Miss. Frances Elizabeth, LLB ACA *1988;* 3 Highgrove Gardens, WORTHING, BN11 4SN.
•**HAM, Mr. John, BSc FCA** *1992;* (Tax Fac), J Ham & Co Ltd, 114 Heol Llanishen Fach, Rhiwbina, CARDIFF, CF14 6LG. See also John Ham
•**HAM, Mr. Kenneth Roy, FCA** *1968;* K.R.Ham, Brambles, Noman's Chapel, Thorverton, EXETER, EX5 5JP.
HAM, Mr. Michael Norman James, FCA *1973;* 23 Chemin Du Barrage, 42330 ST GALMIER, FRANCE.
•**HAM, Mr. Peter James, PhD BSc FCA** *1976;* Audit for Business Development and Solutions Ltd, 15 Oxford Street, SOUTHAMPTON, SO14 3DJ.
HAM, Mr. Richard David, BA ACA *1987;* 3 Sheraton Lane, RUMSON, NJ 07760, UNITED STATES.
HAM, Mr. Roy, FCA *1953;* 22 Burlington Rd., ALTRINCHAM, WA14 1HR. (Life Member)
HAM, Mr. Stephen John, BSc ACA *1987;* Tremarske, 1 St Mellons Road, Marshfield, CARDIFF, CF3 2TX.
HAM, Mr. Steven Johnston, BSc ACA *1990;* 103 College Road, NORWICH, NORFOLK, NR2 3JP.
HAM, Mr. Tom David, BSc ACA *2010;* Flat 32 Hunsaker, Alfred Street, READING, RG1 7AU.
HAMAD, Mr. Anthony Abu, ACA *1979;* Wehda Tower Suite 1501, P.O. Box 62130, ABU DHABI, UNITED ARAB EMIRATES.
HAMALAINEN, Dr. Paul Kalevi, PhD BSc ACA *1998;* The Gables, 48 Main Street, Woodnewton, PETERBOROUGH, NORTHAMPTONSHIRE, PE8 5EB.
HAMALAINEN-BENNETT, Mrs. Anna-Maria, BA(Hons) ACA *2000;* Harbourside, Halifax Bank of Scotland, 10 Canons Way, BRISTOL, BS1 5LF.
HAMANI, Ms. Lisa, BA ACA *2001;* 85 Leoforos Lemesou, CY-2121 NICOSIA, CYPRUS.
HAMBIDGE, Mr. Derek Cecil, MA FCA *1959;* High Beech, 45 Court Hill Road, HASLEMERE, GU27 2PN. (Life Member)
HAMBIDGE, Mr. Philip John, ACA *1988;* Hunters & Frankau Ltd, Hurlingham Business Park, Sulivan Road, LONDON, SW6 3DU.
•**HAMBLETON, Mr. Anthony Nicholas, BA FCA** *1994;* with KPMG Al Fozan & Al Sadhan, 13th Floor, Al Subeaei Towers, King Abdulaziz Street, PO Box 4803, AL KHOBAR 31952 SAUDI ARABIA.
HAMBLETON, Miss. Kathleen Mary, BSc ACA *1997;* 129 Sunnyhill Road, LONDON, SW16 2UW.

•①HAMBLIN, Mr. Brian James, BA FCA *1979;* PKF (UK) LLP, Farringdon Place, 20 Farringdon Road, LONDON, EC1M 3AP.
•HAMBLIN, Ms. Joanna Mary Margaret, BA(Hons) ACA FCCA *2007;* with Bird Luckin limited, Aquila House, Waterloo Lane, CHELMSFORD, CM1 1BN.
•HAMBLIN, Mr. John Alan, FCA *1973;* Pumphrey Dasalo Limited, 1 The Green, RICHMOND, SURREY, TW9 1PL.
HAMBLIN, Mr. Michael Anthony, FCA *1970;* 71 Heol Briwnant, Rhiwbina, CARDIFF, CF14 6QH.
HAMBLIN, Mr. Peter Robert, BSc ACA *1986;* The Barns, Main Street, Gumley, MARKET HARBOROUGH, LEICESTERSHIRE, LE16 7RU.
HAMBLIN, Mr. Richard John, BA ACA *1989;* 6 Troutbeck Crescent, Beeston, NOTTINGHAM, NG9 3BP.
HAMBLING, Mrs. Joanna Margaret, BA ACA *1992;* (Tax Fac), 3 Grange View Gardens, LEEDS, LS17 8NL.
HAMBLING, Mr. Peter Timothy William, MA ACA *1994;* 3 Grange View Gardens, LEEDS, LS17 8NL.
HAMBLION, Mr. David Malcolm, FCA *1990;* (Tax Fac), 9 Juniper Drive, CHRISTCHURCH, DORSET, BH23 4UT.
•HAMBLYN, Mr. Ian David, ACA *1993;* Watson Associates, 30-34 North Street, HAILSHAM, EAST SUSSEX, BN27 1DW.
HAMDORFF, Mr. David John, BSc ACA *1991;* Ragdale Hall Health Hydro, Ragdale, MELTON MOWBRAY, LE14 3PB.
HAMED, Ms. Malak, BSc ACA *2000;* Flat 5 Devonshire Court, 272 Cavendish Road, Balham, LONDON, SW12 0BS.
•HAMEDANI, Mr. Hossein, BSc ACA *1982;* Grant Thornton UK LLP, 30 Finsbury Square, LONDON, EC2P 2YU. See also Grant Thornton LLP
HAMEED, Mr. Asad, FCA *1978;* c/o Saudi Cable Company, P O Box 4403, JEDDAH, 21491, SAUDI ARABIA.
HAMEED, Mr. Faisal, MA FCA *1995;* 18 Warren Road, PURLEY, CR8 1AA.
HAMEER, Mr. Salim, ACA *2007;* 591 Uxbridge Road, PINNER, MIDDLESEX, HA5 4SN.
HAMEL, Mr. Brian Andrew, BA ACA *2006;* PricewaterhouseCoopers Ceska republika s.r.o., Katerinska 40, 120 00 PRAGUE, CZECH REPUBLIC.
HAMER, Mr. Alan David, BSc ACA *1995;* 7 Gileston Road, Pontcanna, CARDIFF, CF11 9JS.
HAMER, Mr. Andrew, ACA *2009;* Apartment 2, 11 Turnbull Road West Timperley, ALTRINCHAM, CHESHIRE, WA14 5UP.
HAMER, Mr. Andrew Mark, BA ACA *1990;* 42 Clifton Avenue, Stanley, WAKEFIELD, WF3 4HB.
HAMER, Mr. Andrew Woosnam, BSc ACA *1992;* with National Audit Office, 157-197 Buckingham Palace Road, Victoria, LONDON, SW1W 9SP.
HAMER, Mr. Anthony Marcel George, FCA *1964;* 9540 East Grand Avenue, GREENWOOD VILLAGE, CO 80111, UNITED STATES.
HAMER, Mr. Brian Albert, BSc ACA *1979;* 7 Glastonbury Drive, Poynton, STOCKPORT, CHESHIRE, SK12 1EN.
HAMER, Mr. David John, BSc ACA *1989;* Laurel Cottage, Botley Road, Shedfield, SOUTHAMPTON, SO32 2JG.
HAMER, Mr. Derrick, FCA *1954;* 645 Scott Hall Rd, LEEDS, LS17 5PD. (Life Member)
HAMER, Miss. Gwen, MA(Hons) ACA *2001;* 30/6 Forbes Road, EDINBURGH, EH10 4ED.
HAMER, Mr. Ian Michael, BSc FCA *1992;* Kontron UK Ltd, 9 Ben Turner Industrial Estate Oving Road, CHICHESTER, PO19 7ET.
HAMER, Mr. Jeremy John, FCA *1976;* with Financial Decisions, Great Down Farm, Great Down Lane, Marnhull, STURMINSTER NEWTON, DORSET DT10 1JY.
HAMER, Mrs. Jill Susan, BA ACA *1991;* I B M UK Ltd MP AGAC, PO Box 41, North Harbour, PORTSMOUTH, PO6 3AU.
HAMER, Mr. Jonathan, BSc ACA *1992;* 215 Nursery Road, Dinnington, SHEFFIELD, S25 2QU.
HAMER, Mr. Mark Geoffrey, BA ACA *1993;* 58 Oakley Lane, Oakley, BASINGSTOKE, HAMPSHIRE, RG23 7JX.
HAMER, Mr. Nicholas Charles, ACA *1989;* 8 Ash Way, NEWCASTLE, STAFFORDSHIRE, ST5 3UB.
HAMER, Mr. Robert James Childerstone, ACA *1995;* Rand Merchant Bank Limited, P O Box 786273, SANDTON, GAUTENG, 2146, SOUTH AFRICA.
HAMER, Mr. Stephen Wilson, BA ACA *1982;* Toad Hall, Church Lane, Gawsworth, MACCLESFIELD, SK11 9RJ.
HAMER, Mr. Timothy, BA ACA *2006;* 74 Merewood Avenue, Headington, OXFORD, OX3 8EF.
HAMER, Miss. Vanessa, BSc FCA *2000;* (Tax Fac), 314 Helmshore Road, Haslingden, ROSSENDALE, LANCASHIRE, BB4 4DJ.
HAMER, Mrs. Vanessa Jane, ACA *1993;* The Shooting Box, Old Hall Lane, Tabley, KNUTSFORD, WA16 0HX.
HAMES, Miss. Elspeth Elizabeth, BA ACA *2004;* with PricewaterhouseCoopers LLP, 1 Embankment Place, LONDON, WC2N 6RH.
HAMES, Miss. Gabrielle, BSc ACA CTA *2007;* 123 Sugden Road, LONDON, SW11 5ED.
HAMES, Mr. John David, FCA *1975;* 82 Carrick Point, Falmouth Road, LEICESTER, LE5 4WN.
HAMES, Miss. Katie Louise, BSc(Hons) ACA *2003;* 15 Furzebank, ASCOT, SL5 7BP.
HAMES, Miss. Laura, MA ACA *2010;* 49 Elers Road, LONDON, W13 9QB.
HAMI, Mrs. Aneesa, BA ACA *2006;* Flat 503 Washington Building, Deals Gateway, LONDON, SE13 7SE.
HAMID, Mr. Amjad, FCA *1972;* 2 Daffodil Place, HAMPTON, TW12 3RU.
HAMID, Mr. Mohamed Arif, MBA ACA *1981;* 11 Mackenzie Road, BIRMINGHAM, B11 4EP.
•HAMID, Mr. Mohamed Tariq, ACA *1988;* Hartmans, Trenleigh House, 3 Woodbridge Road, Moseley, BIRMINGHAM, B13 8EH.
HAMILL, Mr. John Barrie, MBA BA ACA *1995;* Bayview, Burray, ORKNEY, KW17 2SS.
HAMILL, Mr. Keith, BA FCA *1979;* Brambles, 7 Beechcroft, CHISLEHURST, BR7 5DB.
HAMILL, Mr. Mark John, BSc ACA *1993;* 31 Fernhill Road, Sandringham, MELBOURNE, VIC 3191, AUSTRALIA.
HAMILL, Mr. Patrick James, BA(Hons) ACA *2010;* 5 Shoreham Close, BEXLEY, DA5 3AG.
HAMILL, Mr. Paul William, BA ACA *2000;* HSBC Bank Middle East Ltd, 3rd Floor Building No.5 Emaar Square, PO BOX 502601, DUBAI, UNITED ARAB EMIRATES.
HAMILTON, Mr. Alan John, FCA *1970;* 1 Canterbury Road, Stubbington, FAREHAM, PO14 2LY.
HAMILTON, Mr. Alexander Gordon Kelso, MA FCA *1970;* 51 Chelsea Square, LONDON, SW3 6LH.
HAMILTON, Mrs. Alison Hilary Ewing, BSc ACA CTA *1989;* April Cottage, Laneside, Middleton In Teesdale, BARNARD CASTLE, COUNTY DURHAM, DL12 0RY.
HAMILTON, Ms. Alison Shirley, MA ACA *1996;* Seymour Distribution Ltd, 2 East Poultry Avenue, LONDON, EC1A 9PT.
HAMILTON, Mr. Alistair James, BSc ACA *2004;* Inflexion Private Equity Partners LLP, 43 Welbeck Street, LONDON, W1G 8DX.
HAMILTON, Mr. Andrew Charles, FCA *1967;* 65 Hazlewell Road, LONDON, SW15 6UT.
•HAMILTON, Mr. Andrew Nigel, FCA ATII *1974;* Andrew Hamilton & Co, 38 Dean Park Mews, EDINBURGH, EH4 1ED.
•HAMILTON, Miss. Anne Margaret, BA ACA *1985;* Deloitte LLP, Hill House, 1 Little New Street, LONDON, EC4A 3TR. See also Deloitte & Touche LLP
•HAMILTON, Mr. Anthony Richard, FCA *1963;* (Tax Fac), A.R. Hamilton, Roebuck House, 16 Somerset Way, IVER, SL0 9AF.
HAMILTON, Mr. Ashley Mark, BSc ACA *2003;* Flat 1 Villa Menorca, 15 Burton Road, POOLE, DORSET, BH13 6DT.
HAMILTON, Mr. Benedict Martin, ACA *2011;* 12 South Avenue, Burnage, MANCHESTER, M19 2WS.
HAMILTON, Mr. Bruce Allan, MA ACA *2001;* 37d Heathfield Road, LONDON, SW18 2PH.
HAMILTON, Mrs. Camilla, BA(Hons) ACA *2004;* 7 Sollershott West, LETCHWORTH GARDEN CITY, HERTFORDSHIRE, SG6 3PU.
HAMILTON, Mrs. Caroline Elizabeth, LLB ACA ATII *2000;* Pendragon Plc, 2 Oakwood Court, Little Oak Drive, Annesley, NOTTINGHAM, NG15 0DR.
HAMILTON, Ms. Claire, BA ACA *1992;* 194 The Boulevard, Ivanhoe East, MELBOURNE, VIC 3079, AUSTRALIA.
HAMILTON, Miss. Claire Louise, ACA *2009;* 61 Huntley Close, Abbeymead, GLOUCESTER, GL4 4GU.
HAMILTON, Miss. Claire Louise, BA ACA *1992;* 22 Lansdowne Gardens, Jesmond, NEWCASTLE UPON TYNE, NE2 1HE.
HAMILTON, Mr. Craig, BSc ACA *1992;* 64 Pine Avenue, GRAVESEND, DA12 1QZ.
HAMILTON, Mr. Damon James, ACA *2002;* PO Box 651588, Benmore, SANDTON, GAUTENG, 2010, SOUTH AFRICA.
HAMILTON, Mr. David Alistair, FCA *1966;* Brayford House, Fen Lane, East Keal, SPILSBY, LINCOLNSHIRE, PE23 4AY. (Life Member)
HAMILTON, Mr. David Francis, FCA *1972;* 16 Tichborne Close Frimley, CAMBERLEY, SURREY, GU16 8RP.
HAMILTON, Mr. David James, BSc ACA *1985;* The Barn, Drumcrosshall, By Bathgate, BATHGATE, EH48 4JT.
HAMILTON, Mr. David James Cochran, BSc ACA *1989;* 19a Grove Road, BEACONSFIELD, BUCKINGHAMSHIRE, HP9 1UR.
HAMILTON, Mr. David Macintyre, BSc FCA *1978;* 8 Tarham Close, HORLEY, RH6 8LD.
HAMILTON, Mr. David Nicholas, BSc ACA *1989;* Ticketmaster UK Ltd., 48 Leicester Square, LONDON, WC2H 7LR.
•HAMILTON, Mr. David Norman Peyton, MA FCA *1964;* (Tax Fac), Hamilton & Co, The White Cottage, Stock Lane, Landford Wood, SALISBURY, SP5 2ER. See also Hamilton Associates
•HAMILTON, Mr. David Patrick, FCA *1968;* Poinciana House, West Mall & Poiniciana, PO Box F44171, FREEPORT, BAHAMAS.
HAMILTON, Mr. Dominic, ACA *2009;* 23 Kings Avenue, LONDON, SW4 8DX.
HAMILTON, Mr. Donald, FCA *1949;* 4 Church Road, Ashton, CHESTER, CH3 8AB. (Life Member)
HAMILTON, Mr. Donald Mclaws, FCA *1954;* 58 Church Street, LEATHERHEAD, SURREY, KT22 8DW. (Life Member)
HAMILTON, Mr. Douglas Frank, BA FCA *1965;* Woodvale, WYLAM, NE41 8EP.
•HAMILTON, Mr. Douglas Howard, DipPFS FCA *1969;* (Tax Fac), Hamilton Brading, 1 Sopwith Crescent, WICKFORD, SS11 8YU.
HAMILTON, Mr. Edwin Stuart, BSc ACA *1987;* Box 53620, ABU DHABI, UNITED ARAB EMIRATES.
•HAMILTON, Mrs. Elizabeth, PhD FCA *1985;* S V Bye, New Garth House, Upper Garth Gardens, GUISBOROUGH, TS14 6HA.
HAMILTON, Mrs. Emma, BCom ACA *1988;* Northern Lights, La Rue Du Pont, St. Ouen, JERSEY, JE3 2DX.
HAMILTON, Mr. Ewen Maitland, ACA *1991;* Watts Tyres Ltd, Church Road, LYDNEY, GLOUCESTERSHIRE, Gl15 5EN.
HAMILTON, Miss. Fiona Anne, BSc ACA *2006;* 16 Hartledon Road, BIRMINGHAM, B17 0AD.
HAMILTON, Baron Gavin Goulburn, BSc ACA *1994;* Harrington Hall, Harrington, SHIFNAL, SHROPSHIRE, TF11 9DR.
HAMILTON, Mr. George, FCA *1953;* Little Knox Farmhouse, CASTLE DOUGLAS, KIRKCUDBRIGHTSHIRE, DG7 1NR. (Life Member)
HAMILTON, Dr. Gordon Fordyce, BSc ACA *1999;* Great Greenfields, Gransmore Green, Felsted, DUNMOW, ESSEX, CM6 3LA.
HAMILTON, Mr. Graham, FCA *1971;* Calle Osa Mayor 144, (J4 37/57) Urb La Florida, Orihuela Costa, 03189 ALICANTE, SPAIN.
HAMILTON, Mr. Grant Leslie, BA ACA *2005;* 303/97 Boyce Road, Maroubra, SYDNEY, NSW 2035, AUSTRALIA.
HAMILTON, Mrs. Heather Anne, BSc ACA *1987;* 4 Mallard View, Belfast Road, NEWTOWNARDS, COUNTY DOWN, BT23 4FB.
HAMILTON, Mrs. Helen Marie, BCom ACA *1999;* 11 Edgerton Garth, TADCASTER, NORTH YORKSHIRE, LS24 9QP.
HAMILTON, Mr. Iain Duncan, BSc ACA *1993;* 5 Tormore Close, Heapey, CHORLEY, PR6 9BP.
HAMILTON, Mr. Ian, BSc ACA *1990;* Flat 5 Invergarry House, 45 Carlton Vale, LONDON, NW6 5EP.
HAMILTON, Mr. Ian, BA ACA *1980;* Nettleden Grange, Nettleden, HEMEL HEMPSTEAD, HP1 3DQ.
HAMILTON, Mr. Ian Noel Craig, BA ACA *1985;* Speakerbus Ltd, Fourways House, 4-10 Ware Road, HODDESDON, EN11 9RS.
HAMILTON, Mr. James Edward Hume, FCA *1960;* 75/119 Sugarwood Street, MOGGILL, QLD 4070, AUSTRALIA. (Life Member)
•HAMILTON, Mr. James Phillip, LLB ACA *1999;* PKF (UK) LLP, Pannell House, 6 Queen Street, LEEDS, LS1 2TW.
HAMILTON, Mrs. Jane Alexandra, FCA *1978;* The Coach House, Sevenhills Road, IVER, SL0 0PA.
HAMILTON, Mrs. Janice Margaret Clark, BSc ACA *1986;* The Barn, Drumcrosshall, BATHGATE, WEST LOTHIAN, EH48 4JT.
HAMILTON, Miss. Jean Marion, ACA *1981;* 54 Wickhams Wharf, WARE, SG12 9PT.
•HAMILTON, Mr. John, FCA *1973;* Harbor Limited, 2 Mundy Street, HEANOR, DERBYSHIRE, DE75 7SB.
HAMILTON, Mr. John David Esmond, FCA *1960;* 1 Conway Road, Wimbledon, LONDON, SW20 8PB.
HAMILTON, Mr. John Philip, MA FCA *1968;* 6 Marlborough Crescent, Riverhead, SEVENOAKS, TN13 2HP. (Life Member)
HAMILTON, Mr. John Stephen, FCA *1971;* 29 lierstrase, 80639 MUNICH, BAVARIA, GERMANY.
HAMILTON, Mr. Julian Edward, MBA FCA *1962;* Jobtel Practice Merger Catalysts Ltd, Minster Chambers, Minister Centre, Church Street, SOUTHWELL, NOTTINGHAMSHIRE NG25 0HD. (Life Member)
HAMILTON, Miss. Kathryn Louise, MA ACA *2004;* with Deloitte LLP, 2 New Street Square, LONDON, EC4A 3BZ.
HAMILTON, Mr. Keith Osborne, BSc FCA *1980;* with Deloitte LLP, 4 Brindley Place, BIRMINGHAM, B1 2HZ.
HAMILTON, Mr. Keith Wallace, MA ACIB FCA FCMA *1970;* 149 Forest Road, TUNBRIDGE WELLS, TN2 5EX.
HAMILTON, Mr. Kenneth George Edward, FCA *1958;* 8212 Halyard Way, INDIANAPOLIS, IN 46236-9576, UNITED STATES. (Life Member)
HAMILTON, Mrs. Margaret Joyce, BSc FCA *1976;* 36 Windsor Gate, EASTLEIGH, SO50 4PU.
HAMILTON, Mr. Mark Richard, BSc(Hons) ACA *2001;* 35/4 Rattray Grove, EDINBURGH, EH10 5TL.
HAMILTON, Mr. Mark William, ACA *1993;* 135 Gaywood Road, KING'S LYNN, PE30 2QA.
HAMILTON, Mr. Neil Andrew, ACA *2004;* 15 Westgate House, ALNWICK, NORTHUMBERLAND, NE66 1XP.
HAMILTON, Mr. Neil David, BA ACA *1997;* Cornwall Council, County Hall, Treyew Road, TRURO, CORNWALL, TR1 3AY.
HAMILTON, Mr. Neil David, BA ACA *2004;* 21 Popes Grove, TWICKENHAM, TW1 4JZ.
HAMILTON, Mr. Nicholas David, MA ACA *1983;* Ridge Cottage, Rusper Road, Capel, DORKING, RH5 5HG.
HAMILTON, Mr. Nicholas Ian, BA FCA *1974;* Grey Oak, Tudor Close, PULBOROUGH, WEST SUSSEX, RH20 2EF.
HAMILTON, Mr. Nicholas Leonard James, FCA *1970;* 16 Churchfields, St. Martins, OSWESTRY, SHROPSHIRE, SY11 3HZ.
•HAMILTON, Mr. Nicholas Mark, FCA *1971;* DPMC Business Advisory Ltd, Flat Third Floor North, 6 Raymond Buildings, Gray's Inn, LONDON, WC1R 5BN.
HAMILTON, Mr. Nigel James, FCA *1965;* (Member of Council 1990 - 1995), Linden Wood, Cokes Lane, CHALFONT ST. GILES, BUCKINGHAMSHIRE, HP8 4UD. (Life Member)
HAMILTON, Mr. Peter, BSc ACA *2010;* 2 Caillard Road, Byfleet, WEST BYFLEET, SURREY, KT14 7JB.
HAMILTON, Mr. Peter Neil, MEng FCA *1999;* 3625 Caldwell Court, NASHVILLE, TN 37204, UNITED STATES.
•HAMILTON, Mr. Robert Christopher, FCA *1962;* Hamilton & Co., 7 Greave Close, The GrangeWenvoe, CARDIFF, CF5 6BU.
HAMILTON, Mr. Robert Patrick, BSc ACA CTA *1993;* (Tax Fac), 46 Ventnor Road, Haslingden, ROSSENDALE, LANCASHIRE, BB4 6QP.
HAMILTON, Mr. Ronald Esmond, BA FCA *1983;* 42 Windsor Crescent, BERWICK-UPON-TWEED, TD15 1NT.
HAMILTON, Mr. Roy, FCA *1978;* 21 Cayton Grove, Chapel House Estate, NEWCASTLE UPON TYNE, NE5 1HL.
•HAMILTON, Mrs. Sarah Margaret, FCA *1987;* Richard Sexton & Co, St. Margaret's, 3 Manor Road, COLCHESTER, CO3 3LU.
HAMILTON, Mr. Sean Iain, BA ACA MABRP *1992;* with PricewaterhouseCoopers LLP, 89 Sandyford Road, NEWCASTLE UPON TYNE, NE1 8HW.
HAMILTON, Mrs. Sharleen, BSc ACA *1997;* 8 Chestnut Way, LEEDS, LS16 7TN.
HAMILTON, Mrs. Sharon Amanda, BSc(Econ) ACA *1998;* with PricewaterhouseCoopers LLP, 1 Embankment Place, LONDON, WC2N 6RH.
HAMILTON, Mr. Stephen Arthur, BSc FCA *1976;* 105 Crescent Avenue, BURLINGAME, CA 94010, UNITED STATES.
HAMILTON, Mr. Stephen James, BSc ACA *1996;* Cargill Plc Knowle Hill Park, Fairmile Lane, COBHAM, KT11 2PD.
HAMILTON, Mrs. Stephne Margaret, ACA *2002;* 11 Buttercup Avenue, Weltevreden Park, ROODEPOORT, 1709, SOUTH AFRICA.
HAMILTON, Miss. Susan, ACA *2011;* Flat 3, 12 Smyrna Road, Kilburn, LONDON, NW6 4LY.
HAMILTON, Mrs. Tanya Michelle, BA FCA *1999;* Nexus House, Cray Road, SIDCUP, DA14 5DA.
HAMILTON, Miss. Victoria, BSc(Hons) ACA *2004;* 14/7a William Street, RANDWICK, NSW 2031, AUSTRALIA.
HAMILTON, Miss. Victoria Jain, BSc ACA *2010;* Flat 2, 40 Park Avenue, HARROGATE, NORTH YORKSHIRE, HG2 9BG.
HAMILTON, Miss. Victoria Louise, BSc ACA *2010;* Flat 18, Cuthbert Bell Tower, 4 Pancras Way, LONDON, E3 2SL.

HAMILTON, Mrs. Wendy Elizabeth, FCA 1972; Huggle Cottage, Hurlands Lane, Passfield, LIPHOOK, GU30 7XR.
HAMILTON-BURKE, Mr. Ian Douglas, FCA 1966; Bellisle, Quarry Street, Woolton, LIVERPOOL, L25 6DY.
HAMILTON-DEELEY, Mr. Gavin John, FCA 1977; 30 Settrington Road, LONDON, SW6 3BA.
HAMILTON-GRAY, Mr. Colin Armstrong, FCA 1958; White Lodge, Royston Place, Barton on Sea, NEW MILTON, HAMPSHIRE, BH25 7AJ. (Life Member)
HAMILTON-JAMES, Mrs. Helen, ACA 1997; with Deloitte Touche Tohmatsu, 35 Smith Street, (P.O.Box 38 2124), PARRAMATTA, NSW 2150, AUSTRALIA.
•HAMILTON-JONES, Mr. Charles Nugent, BSc FCA 1983; KPMG S.A., 1 Cours Valmy, Paris La Défense Cedex, 92923 PARIS LA DÉFENSE, FRANCE.
HAMILTON-MEIKLE, Mr. Andrew Tullis, MA FCA 1993; Ernst & Young Llp, 1 More London Place, LONDON, SE1 2AF.
HAMILTON-MEIKLE, Mr. Jonathan Patrick, BSc ACA 1992; 1b Arvácska Utca, H-1022 BUDAPEST, HUNGARY.
HAMILTON-PEARSON, Mrs. Lynne Susanna, BSc ACA 1994; Harbourview, 5A John Street, SHOREHAM-BY-SEA, WEST SUSSEX, BN43 5DL.
HAMILTON-SMITH, Mr. David Lewis, BA ACA 1981; 19956 Alexandria Drive, MONUMENT, CO 80132, UNITED STATES.
HAMILTON-SMITH, Mrs. Dorothea Neil, BA ACA 1988; Davison & Shingleton Boundary House, 91-93 Charterhouse Street, LONDON, EC1M 6HR.
HAMLET, Mr. Robert William, FCA 1970; 14 Montefiore Avenue, RAMSGATE, KENT, CT11 8BE.
HAMLET, Mr. Roger Ashington, FCA 1973; 33 Great Furlong, Bishopsteignton, TEIGNMOUTH, TQ14 9TU.
HAMLET, Mrs. Sarah Louise, BSc ACA 2001; 55 Lingfield Avenue, KINGSTON UPON THAMES, SURREY, KT1 2TL.
HAMLET, Mr. Stephen Robert, LLB ACA 2000; 55 Lingfield Avenue, KINGSTON UPON THAMES, SURREY, KT1 2TL.
HAMLEY, Mrs. Hester, ACA 1990; 19 Vapron Road, PLYMOUTH, PL3 5NJ.
HAMLIN, Mr. Andrew James, BA ACA 1995; 4 Ashling Crescent, BOURNEMOUTH, BH8 9JB.
•HAMLIN, Mr. Robert Myles, BSc ACA DChA 1991; Baker Tilly Tax & Advisory Services LLP, The Clock House, 140 London Road, GUILDFORD, SURREY, GU1 1UW. See also Baker Tilly UK Audit LLP
HAMLIN, Miss. Sarah, BSc ACA 1992; 12 The Mede, Whipton, EXETER, EX4 8ED.
HAMLIN, Mrs. Thea Louise, BA ACA 1999; 41 Anstey Lane, ALTON, HAMPSHIRE, GU34 2NF.
HAMLYN, Mr. John Michael, FCA 1969; Stoneridge Cottage, Green Lane, Disley, STOCKPORT, SK12 2AL. (Life Member)
HAMLYN, Mr. Malcolm Crawford, FCA 1965; 10 Green Close, Springfield, CHELMSFORD, CM1 7SL.
HAMLYN, Mr. Martin Paul, MA ACA 1981; 11 Lyncourt, 5 The Orchard, LONDON, SE3 0QT.
HAMLYN, Mr. Michael Cleveland, ACA 1981; 2 Medcroft Gardens, East Sheen, LONDON, SW14 7RN.
HAMLYN, Mr. Nicholas Jeremy, BSc(Hons) ACA 2002; Red Lion Inn High Street, Exbourne, OKEHAMPTON, DEVON, EX20 3RY.
HAMLYN WILLIAMS, Mr. Philip Leslie Anstee, FCA 1975; 23 Minster Yard, LINCOLN, LN2 1PY.
HAMMANS, Mrs. Julia Anne, BA ACA 1985; 34 Cole Park Road, TWICKENHAM, TW1 1HS.
•HAMMANS, Mr. Nicholas Charles, BSc ACA 1984; PricewaterhouseCoopers LLP, Hays Galleria, 1 Hays Lane, LONDON, SE1 2RD. See also PricewaterhouseCoopers
HAMMELL, Mr. Stephen John, BA ACA 1998; 2 Court Drive, SELBY, NORTH YORKSHIRE, YO8 4JJ.
HAMMENT, Mr. Denis Ernest, FCA 1955; 40 Rockleaze Road, Sneyd Park, BRISTOL, BS9 1NF. (Life Member)
•HAMMENT, Mr. Michael Graham, MA ACA 1990; MH (Oxford) Ltd, 16 Wentworth Road, OXFORD, OX2 7TQ.
•HAMMER, Mr. Aaron, BSc ACA 1988; (Tax Fac), Hammer & Co Accountants Ltd, 13 Alba Court, Alba Gardens, LONDON, NW11 9NP.
HAMMERSLEY, Mr. Benjamin David, BA ACA 1996; Keyline Brands, 2nd Floor, Central House, Balfour Road, HOUNSLOW, TW3 1HY.
HAMMERSLEY, Mr. David Peter, BA ACA 2003; Flat 3 Poppythorn Court, Poppythorn Lane Prestwich, MANCHESTER, M25 1ND.
•HAMMERSLEY, Mr. Derek, BA FCA 1975; Grineaux Hammersley, 20 Market Hill, SOUTHAM, CV47 0HF. See also Grineaux Accountants Limited
HAMMERSLEY, Mr. Scott, MA ACA 1996; 23 Poltimore Road, GUILDFORD, SURREY, GU2 7PT.
HAMMERSLEY, Mr. Sean, BA ACA 2005; 62a Ormiston Grove, LONDON, W12 0JS.
HAMMERSON, Mr. David Graham, FCA 1966; PO Box 121, RADLETT, HERTFORDSHIRE, WD7 8ZE. (Life Member)
HAMMERTON, Mr. Barry Victor, FCA 1965; 2-4631 Lochside Drive, VICTORIA V8Y 2S9, BC, CANADA.
HAMMERTON, Mr. John Lewis, BSc ACA 1983; 3 Riverview, Milford, BELPER, DERBYSHIRE, DE56 0QY.
HAMMERTON, Mr. Richard Wadsworth, BSc ACA 1988; Adams Hydraulics Ltd, PO Box 15, YORK, YO30 4TA.
HAMMERTON, Mr. Roger Lewis, FCA 1952; 16 Dorchester Close, Berry Hill, MANSFIELD, NG18 4QW. (Life Member)
HAMMERTON, Mrs. Sarah Louise, BSc ACA 1985; The Downings, Westwell, ASHFORD, TN25 4LQ.
•HAMMERTON, Mr. Simon, FCA 1982; (Tax Fac), with Beavis Morgan Audit Limited, 82 St. John Street, LONDON, EC1M 4JN.
HAMMETT, Mr. Christopher Eynon, BSc FCA 1986; 6 Egar Way, Bretton, PETERBOROUGH, PE3 9AE.
HAMMETT, Mr. Paul Edward, BSc(Hons) ACA 2002; 19 Park Rise, HARPENDEN, HERTFORDSHIRE, AL5 3AP.
HAMMETT, Mr. Peter Liam, BSc FCA 1974; PH-Associes Sarl, 50 Rue Marcel Dassault, 92100 BOULOGNE, FRANCE.
HAMMILL, Mrs. Sally, MA FCA 1978; (Tax Fac), Pyegreave Farm, Coalpit Lane, Langley, MACCLESFIELD, CHESHIRE, SK11 0DQ.
HAMMILL, Mr. Sean Wesley, ACA 2008; Flat 3 Tudor Mansions, Gondar Gardens, LONDON, NW6 1EY.
HAMMON, Mr. Russell John, BSc FCA 1975; 10 Fanthorpe Street, Putney, LONDON, SW15 1DZ.
HAMMOND, Mr. Andrew David, BA ACA 1992; 20 Bere Close, WINCHESTER, SO22 5HY.
HAMMOND, Mr. Andrew Fredrick, BSc(Hons) ACA 2004; Shell International Trading & Shipping Co Ltd, Shell Mex House 80 Strand, LONDON, WC2R 0ZA.
•HAMMOND, Mr. Andrew Raymond, BSc ACA 1999; PricewaterhouseCoopers LLP, Cornwall Court, 19 Cornwall Street, BIRMINGHAM, B3 2DT. See also PricewaterhouseCoopers
•HAMMOND, Miss. Barbara Jane, BSc ACA 1982; (Tax Fac), BJ Hammond & Co Ltd, 10c West Station Yard, MALDON, ESSEX, CM9 6TR.
HAMMOND, Mr. Barrie George, FCA 1956; 11 Whites Forge, Appleton, ABINGDON, OX13 5LG. (Life Member)
HAMMOND, Mr. Benjamin, BA(Hons) ACA 2000; 114 Cloudesley Road, Islington, LONDON, N1 0RU.
HAMMOND, Mr. Benjamin Edward John, ACA 2010; 22 The Grove, LEEDS, LS17 7BW.
HAMMOND, Mr. Christopher Mark, ACA FCCA 2010; Rosewood Cottage, Snow Hill, Great Easton, DUNMOW, ESSEX, CM6 2DR.
HAMMOND, Mrs. Clare Frances, BCom ACA 1992; Wynstone, Cunnery Road, CHURCH STRETTON, SHROPSHIRE, SY6 6AF.
•①HAMMOND, Mr. Clive Robert, FCA 1968; Marsh Hammond Limited, Peek House, 20 Eastcheap, LONDON, EC3M 1EB. See also Marsh Hammond & Partners LLP
•HAMMOND, Mrs. Colleen Elizabeth, ACA 1994; (Tax Fac), CEH Consulting and Accounting Limited, 41 Weeping Cross, STAFFORD, ST17 0DG.
•HAMMOND, Mrs. Cynthia Joy, FCA ATII ACIS 1976; (Tax Fac), Harrison Priddey & Co, 22 St John Street, BROMSGROVE, B61 8QY.
HAMMOND, Mr. David, BA ACA 1995; 33 Larches, Warfield Park, BRACKNELL, BERKSHIRE, RG42 3RR.
•HAMMOND, Dr. David Bruce, FCA CTA 1968; Little Court, Hall Place Lane, Burchetts Green, MAIDENHEAD, SL6 6QY.
•HAMMOND, Mr. David Glyndwr, FCA 1968; (Tax Fac), Hammond & Davies, 16-18 Pontardulais Road, Gorseinon, SWANSEA, SA4 4FE.
HAMMOND, Mr. David James, BSc ACA 1982; Temple Translations Ltd, 2 Bridewell Place, LONDON, EC4V 6AP.
HAMMOND, Mr. David John, BA FCA 1979; 52 Whitehorse Drive, EPSOM, KT18 7LY.
HAMMOND, Mr. David John, MBA BSc FCA 1991; 37 Conifer Drive, Warley, BRENTWOOD, ESSEX, CM14 5TZ.
•HAMMOND, Mr. David Paul, BA FCA 1983; (Tax Fac), 351A Darling Street, BALMAIN, NSW 2041, AUSTRALIA.
HAMMOND, Mr. David Thomas, BSc FCA 1992; Penyplock, Tillington, HEREFORD, HR4 8LF.
HAMMOND, Mr. David William, ACA 1987; 6 Tannery Lane, Odell, BEDFORD, MK43 7AJ.
HAMMOND, Mr. Derek John, BA(Hons) ACA 2001; with PricewaterhouseCoopers, Darling Park Tower 2, 201 Sussex Street, GPO Box 2650, SYDNEY, NSW 1171 AUSTRALIA.
HAMMOND, Mr. Frank, ACA 1980; 1 Croft Road, Great Longstone, BAKEWELL, DERBYSHIRE, DE45 1PA.
HAMMOND, Mr. Geoffrey Byard, BSc FCA 1992; Phoenix Computers Ltd Technology House, Hunsbury Hill Avenue, NORTHAMPTON, NN4 8QS.
HAMMOND, Mrs. Helen Jeannette, BSc ACA ATII 1994; Springdale, Clare Valley, NOTTINGHAM, NG7 1BU.
HAMMOND, Mrs. Janet, ACA 1990; Associated Newspapers Ltd Northcliffe House, 2 Derry Street, LONDON, W8 5TT.
HAMMOND, Mrs. Joanne, BA ACA 1993; Unit 42, Oriana Way Nursling Industrial Estate, SOUTHAMPTON, SO16 0YU.
HAMMOND, Mr. John, FCA 1964; 16 Purley Oaks Road, Sanderstead, SOUTH CROYDON, Surrey, CR2 0NP.
HAMMOND, Mr. John, BA ACA 2007; 7 Algernon Street, Eccles, MANCHESTER, M30 9QA.
HAMMOND, Mr. John Bateman, FCA 1956; 24 Cranford Road, Barton Seagrave, KETTERING, NN15 5JH. (Life Member)
HAMMOND, Mr. John Edgar Scaife, BCom FCA 1954; 32 Tame Porati St, Manakau, LEVIN 5573, NEW ZEALAND. (Life Member)
•HAMMOND, Mr. John Richard, BSc ACA 1990; Deloitte LLP, Athene Place, 66 Shoe Lane, LONDON, EC4A 3BQ. See also Deloitte & Touche LLP
HAMMOND, Mr. Julian Francis, ACA 1991; Ferndale House, Burndell Road, Yapton, ARUNDEL, WEST SUSSEX, BN18 0HT.
HAMMOND, Mrs. Karen, BA ACA 2006; 71 Coolgardie Avenue, CHIGWELL, ESSEX, IG7 5AX.
HAMMOND, Miss. Keely Jayne, BA(Hons) ACA 2001; 63 Glenside, Appley Bridge, WIGAN, LANCASHIRE, WN6 9EG.
HAMMOND, Mr. Keith Laurence, BSc ACA 1989; H F L Ltd Cranwell House, La Route Du Picquerel St. Sampson, GUERNSEY, GY2 4SD.
HAMMOND, Mr. Keith Robert, BA ACA 1987; Amaravati Buddhist Monastery, Great Gaddesden, HEMEL HEMPSTEAD, HERTFORDSHIRE, HP1 3BZ.
HAMMOND, Mr. Kenneth William, FCA 1954; New House, Duck Street, Wendens Ambo, SAFFRON WALDEN, CB11 4JU. (Life Member)
HAMMOND, Mrs. Lesley Harriman, BA ACA 1986; 62 Hallowell Road, NORTHWOOD, HA6 1DS.
HAMMOND, Miss. Lorraine, BSc(Hons) ACA 2004; 40 Sprowston Road, NORWICH, NR3 4QN.
HAMMOND, Miss. Louise Elizabeth, BCom ACA 2003; Cobwebs, Elcombes Close, LYNDHURST, SO43 7DS.
HAMMOND, Miss. Lucy Elizabeth, BSc ACA 2004; Spofforths Unit A/2, Yeoman Gate Yeoman Way, WORTHING, WEST SUSSEX, BN13 3QZ.
HAMMOND, Mr. Mark Raymond, MSc BA LLB ACA 1986; 1 Storrs Green Cottages, Storrs, SHEFFIELD, S6 6GY.
HAMMOND, Mr. Michael John, FCA 1965; Village End, Plompton Road, Follifoot, HARROGATE, NORTH YORKSHIRE, HG3 1DT.
HAMMOND, Mr. Michael Leslie, FCA 1971; St. Catherines School, Bramley, GUILDFORD, SURREY, GU5 0DF.
•HAMMOND, Mr. Michael Robert, FCA 1974; (Tax Fac), Cornerways, 15 The Drive, Angmering, LITTLEHAMPTON, BN16 1QL.
HAMMOND, Mrs. Nicola Kirsten, BSc ACA 1990; Dial House Longwater Road, Eversley, HOOK, HAMPSHIRE, RG27 0NW.
HAMMOND, Mr. Nigel Derek, BSc ACA 1990; Rust Hall, Langton Road, TUNBRIDGE WELLS, KENT, TN3 0BB.
HAMMOND, Mr. Paul John, BSc ACA 1993; Springdale, Clare Valley, NOTTINGHAM, NG7 1BU.
•HAMMOND, Mr. Paul Stephen, FCA 1970; Hammond Taxation Services Limited, Glenbrook, Torwoodhill Road, Rhu, HELENSBURGH, DUNBARTONSHIRE G84 8TG.
HAMMOND, Miss. Rebecca, ACA 2011; Tollgate Farm, Banbury Road, Bishops Tachbrook, LEAMINGTON SPA, WARWICKSHIRE, CV33 9QJ.
HAMMOND, Mr. Robert, ACA 2009; 2 Devey Close, KNEBWORTH, HERTFORDSHIRE, SG3 6EN.
HAMMOND, Mr. Robin Noel Craigmyle, FCA 1977; Stones Hill Farm, Sandford, CREDITON, DEVON, EX17 4EF.
•HAMMOND, Mr. Roger, FCA 1985; HW, 136-140 Bedford Road, Kempston, BEDFORD, BEDFORDSHIRE, MK42 8BH. See also Wilkinson & Company
HAMMOND, Mrs. Sarah Ann, BA ACA 1990; Mulberry, Icehouse Wood, OXTED, RH8 9DW.
HAMMOND, Mrs. Sharon, BA ACA 1992; Veolia Environnement UK plc, Kings Place 90 York Way, LONDON, N1 9AG.
•HAMMOND, Miss. Stephanie, ACA FCCA 2009; Beatons Limited, York House, 2-4 York Road, FELIXSTOWE, IP11 7QG. See also BG Outsourcing Ltd
HAMMOND, Mr. Stephen John, BSc ACA 1998; 39 The Glades, Aldridge, WALSALL, WS9 8RN.
HAMMOND, Mrs. Susan Louise, ACA 2005; 27 Clough Court, NOTTINGHAM, NG8 3FJ.
HAMMOND, Mrs. Susannah, BSc ACA 1990; 4 Heath Villas, HALIFAX, HX3 0BB.
HAMMOND, Mr. Tony Reginald, FCA 1972; 3 Harbour Hill Road, POOLE, DORSET, BH15 3PX. (Life Member)
•HAMMOND, Mr. William Gaunt, BSc ACA 1995; Highlands, Horsell Park, WOKING, GU21 4LW.
HAMMONDS, Mr. Harvey, BSc ACA 1992; 5 Wester Hill, Greenbank, EDINBURGH, EH10 5XG.
HAMMONDS, Mr. Timothy John, BA(Hons) ACA 2000; 2 Long Meadow, Thorley Park, BISHOPS STORTFORD, CM23 4HH.
HAMNETT, Mrs. Julia Ann, ACA 1995; Stone House Farm, The Woodside, Baldwins Gate, NEWCASTLE, STAFFORDSHIRE, ST5 5EB.
HAMNETT, Mr. Owen David, BA(Hons) ACA 2004; Courtlands, Glasllwch Lane, NEWPORT, GWENT, NP20 3PT.
•HAMON, Mr. Edward Charles, FCA 1978; Edward Hamon, Mirador, 1 Rue de L'Est, St. Helier, JERSEY, JE2 4UD.
HAMON, Mr. George Edward, BA ACA 2003; 15 Woodside Avenue, ESHER, SURREY, KT10 8JQ.
•HAMON, Mr. Peter John Buesnel, BA FCA 1990; (Tax Fac), Bromhead, Harscombe House, 1 Darklake View, Estover, PLYMOUTH, PL6 7TL. See also Bromhead Limited
•HAMON, Mr. Richard John Francis, BSc FCA 1974; RJF Hamon FCA, Le Mahier, La Rue Mahier, St Ouen, JERSEY, JE3 2DW. See also RJF Hamon
HAMON WATT, Mr. Kenneth Ian, BSc ACA 1980; 13 The Coppins, Ampthill, BEDFORD, MK45 2SW.
HAMOUDA, Mr. Ahmed Fouad Hassan, ACA 1980; Ernst & Young, Ring Road, Zone #10A, Rama Tower, P O Box 20, Kattameya CAIRO EGYPT.
HAMP, Mrs. Claire Andrea, BSc ACA 1998; 4 Handside Close, WELWYN GARDEN CITY, HERTFORDSHIRE, AL8 6SR.
•HAMPARTSOUMIAN, Mr. Hovnan, BA FCA 1979; Hovnan & Co Limited, 106 Ashurst Road, Cockfosters, BARNET, HERTFORDSHIRE, EN4 9LG.
HAMPARTSOUMIAN, Miss. Miranda, ACA 2008; 106 Ashurst Road, Cockfosters, BARNET, HERTFORDSHIRE, EN4 9LG.
HAMPDEN, Mr. Vinston Elisha, BSc FCA 1982; Aon Insurance Managers (Barbados) Ltd, P.O Box 1304, Sunrise House, Wildey Main Road, ST MICHAEL, BB11000 BARBADOS.
HAMPDEN SMITH, Mr. Paul Nigel, BSc FCA 1985; Travis Perkins plc, Lodge Way House, Lodge Way, NORTHAMPTON, NN5 7UG.
HAMPER, Mr. Gordon Rushforth, BA ACA 1994; 27 Pavillion Gardens, STAINES, TW18 1LS.
•HAMPER, Mr. Neil Douglas, FCA 1966; (Tax Fac), 68 Benfleet Road, BENFLEET, ESSEX, SS7 1QB.
HAMPER, Mr. Reginald Gordon, FCA 1969; 17 Badgers Field, PEACEHAVEN, BN10 8LQ. (Life Member)
HAMPSHIRE, Mr. David, ACA 1980; Little Oaks, Maydowns Road, Chestfield, WHITSTABLE, CT5 3LW.
HAMPSHIRE, Mr. James Justin, BSc ACA 1998; Ashbourne, Brook Street, Cuckfield, HAYWARDS HEATH, WEST SUSSEX, RH17 5JJ.
HAMPSHIRE, Mrs. Karen, BSc ACA 1991; 266 Hyde End Road, Spencers Wood, READING, RG7 1DL.
HAMPSHIRE, Mrs. Kathryn, ACA 1995; Peel Walker, 11 Victoria Road, ELLAND, HX5 0AE.
HAMPSHIRE, Mr. Mark, BSc ACA 2002; 27 Kellerton Road, LONDON, SE13 5RB.

•**HAMPSHIRE, Dr. Russell John, FCA** *1989;* (Tax Fac), KPMG LLP, Arlington Business Park, Theale, READING, RG7 4SD. See also KPMG Europe LLP

HAMPSHIRE, Mr. Thomas, BEng ACA *2010;* Barclays Bank Plc, 1 Churchill Place, LONDON, E14 5HP.

HAMPSHIRE-HORNSBY, Miss. Doris, MSc FCA *1977;* 21 Solar House, City Centre, SUNDERLAND, SR1 3EG. (Life Member)

HAMPSON, Mr. Alec David, ACA *1988;* Perceptive Infomatics, Lady bay House, Meadow Grove, NOTTINGHAM, NG2 3HF.

HAMPSON, Mr. Barnaby Michael John, BA(Hons) ACA *2002;* Hulgardsvej 4A, 2400 KOBENHAVN, NV, DENMARK.

•**HAMPSON, Mr. Barry Edward, FCA** *1977;* (Tax Fac), Barry Hampson, 63 Passmore, Tinkers Bridge, MILTON KEYNES, MK6 3DY.

HAMPSON, Mrs. Caroline Elizabeth, BA ACA *1996;* 1 Roehampton Gate, LONDON, SW15 5JR.

HAMPSON, Mrs. Ffion Eleri, BA FCA *1996;* 1 Rhodfa Cilcain, MOLD, CLWYD, CH7 1GR.

•**HAMPSON, Mr. Ian, FCA** *1983;* Hill Eckersley & Co, 62 Chorley New Road, BOLTON, BL1 4BY. See also Hill Eckersley & Co Limited

HAMPSON, Mr. James Brian, BA ACA *1997;* Visage House, Visage Imports Ltd, 56 Shaftesbury Avenue, SOUTH SHIELDS, TYNE AND WEAR, NE34 9PH.

HAMPSON, Mr. Jeffreys Kristen, BA(Hons) ACA *2001;* Maple House, Charndon, BICESTER, OXFORDSHIRE, OX27 0BL.

HAMPSON, Mr. Jeremy Stuart, BSc ACA *1996;* 15 Clark Walk, Ettington, STRATFORD-UPON-AVON, WARWICKSHIRE, CV37 7SE.

HAMPSON, Mrs. Karen Ann, BA ACA *2001;* P J Livesey Group Ltd, Beacon Road, Ashburton Road West, Trafford Park, MANCHESTER, M17 1AF.

HAMPSON, Mr. Keith, BA FCA *1979;* 69 Sheepmoor Close, Harborne, BIRMINGHAM, B17 8TD.

HAMPSON, Mr. Neil Edward John, MA ACA *1993;* Poplar Cottage, Avening Green, Totworth, WOTTON-UNDER-EDGE, GLOUCESTERSHIRE, GL12 8HD.

HAMPSON, Mr. Peter, BA FCA *1953;* Apartment 30, Sharoe Bay Court, Sharoe Green Lane, Fulwood, PRESTON, PR2 9HZ. (Life Member)

HAMPSON, Mrs. Rebecca, BCom ACA *1992;* 15 Clark Walk, Ettington, STRATFORD-UPON-AVON, WARWICKSHIRE, CV37 7SE.

HAMPSON, Mr. Richard John, MSc ACA *2008;* 7 The Cloisters, Millhams Street, CHRISTCHURCH, DORSET, BH23 1DN.

HAMPSON, Mr. Robert George, BA ACA *2001;* 7 Ruskin Drive, SALE, M33 5TQ.

HAMPSON, Mr. Stephen Anthony, BSc ACA *1998;* 3 Appleby Walk, KNARESBOROUGH, NORTH YORKSHIRE, HG5 9LT.

HAMPSON, Mrs. Trudy Ann, BA ACA *2001;* 23 Heaton Grove, CHATSWOOD 0626, NEW ZEALAND.

HAMPSTEAD, Mrs. Patricia Susan, BA ACA *1988;* 2 The Green, Tuttington, NORWICH, NORFOLK, NR11 6GT.

HAMPSTEAD, Mr. Robert Geoffrey, BA(Hons) ACA *2011;* 4 Princes Plantation, New Road, Firbeck, WORKSOP, NOTTINGHAMSHIRE, S81 8LB.

HAMPTON, Miss. Alix Yvonne, ACA *2005;* with Wilkins Kennedy, 1-5 Nelson St, SOUTHEND-ON-SEA, SS1 1EG.

HAMPTON, Miss. Catherine, MMath ACA *2011;* Flat 29, Hunsaker, Alfred Street, READING, RG1 7AU.

HAMPTON, Mr. Christopher James, ACA *2010;* 234 Vale Road, Ash Vale, ALDERSHOT, HAMPSHIRE, GU12 5JQ.

HAMPTON, Mr. Clifford Samuel Herbert, BA FCA *1972;* Highmoor Hall, Highmoor, HENLEY-ON-THAMES, RG9 5DH.

HAMPTON, Mr. David Kenneth, FCA *1966;* U T C Ghana Ltd, CT 1586, ACCRA, GHANA.

HAMPTON, Mrs. Eileen Mary, BSc ACA *1991;* 876 Southern Shore Drive, PEACHTREE CITY, GA 30269, UNITED STATES.

HAMPTON, Mr. Iain Stewart, FCA *1936;* P.O. Box 728, LONEHILL, 2062, SOUTH AFRICA. (Life Member)

HAMPTON, Mr. Jonathan James, BA FCA *1978;* The Engine House, 5 Park Road, Moira, SWADLINCOTE, DE12 6BJ.

HAMPTON, Miss. Justine, BSc ACA *2004;* 45 Babyon Court, HAMMONDS PLAINS B4B 0A2, NS, CANADA.

•**HAMPTON, Mr. Philip Peter, BA ACA** *2000;* Ashleigh Accountancy Ltd, 1 Ashleigh Rise, BOURNEMOUTH, BH10 4FB.

HAMPTON, Miss. Rebecca, BSc ACA *2011;* Flat 39, Northpoint House, 400 Essex Road, LONDON, N1 3GH.

HAMPTON, Mr. Robert Anthony, FCA *1970;* The Lodge, 17 Acol Road, LONDON, NW6 3AD.

HAMPTON, Mr. Robert Edward, FCA *1967;* 12 Rectory Gardens, Oldswinford, STOURBRIDGE, DY8 2HB.

•**HAMSHAW, Mr. David James, FCA** *1978;* Hamshaw & Co, 100 Wide Bargate, BOSTON, PE21 6SE.

HAMSHAW, Mr. John Peter, FCA *1973;* 117 Westbourne Terrace, LONDON, W2 6QT.

•**HAMSHAW, Mr. Paul Derek, FCA FRSA** *1981;* Xerox UK Ltd, Riverview, Oxford Road, UXBRIDGE, MIDDLESEX, UB8 1HS.

HAMSHERE, Mr. Paul William, BEng ACA *1994;* 67 Woodland Drive, ST. ALBANS, HERTFORDSHIRE, AL4 0EN.

HAMSHIRE, Mrs. Elenor, BSc ACA *2000;* 20 Littlegreen Road, Woodthorpe, NOTTINGHAM, NG5 4LN.

•**HAMSON, Mr. Peter Jon, BA FCA** *1977;* P J Hamson & Co Limited, 99 Wilsthorpe Road, Long Eaton, NOTTINGHAM, NG10 3LE.

HAMWIJK, Mr. Graham Alfred, BSc FCA *1980;* 3 Wildwood, NORTHWOOD, HA6 2DB.

HAMZAH, Miss. Rozanah, BSc ACA *2004;* 98 Persiaran Zaaba, Taman Tun Dr. Ismail, 60000 KUALA LUMPUR, FEDERAL TERRITORY, MALAYSIA.

HAN, Mr. Chan Juan, ACA *1980;* 58 Trevose Cresent, Apt 03-13, The Trevose, SINGAPORE 298089, SINGAPORE.

HAN, Mr. Liang, BSc ACA *2009;* 62 Kinburn Street, LONDON, SE16 6DW.

HAN, Miss. Nannan, MA BA ACA *2010;* 7 Rickfield Close, HATFIELD, HERTFORDSHIRE, AL10 8RP.

HAN, Mr. Wee Deng, FCA *1974;* 70G Fernhill Road, Fernhill Cottage, SINGAPORE 259151, SINGAPORE.

HANAFIAH, Dato' Bin Hussain, BA FCA *1957;* 49 Lorong 5/4 H, 46000 PETALING JAYA, Selangor, MALAYSIA. (Life Member)

•**HANAFIN, Mr. Michael Joseph, BA FCA** *1976;* (Tax Fac), Hanafin Klein, The House, High Street, Brenchley, TONBRIDGE, TN12 7NQ.

•**HANBURY, Mr. William John, BSc(Hons) ACA CTA** *2002;* Bishop Fleming, 50 The Terrace, TORQUAY, TQ1 1DD.

HANBY, Mr. Leonard, FCA *1957;* 343 Hagley Road, STOURBRIDGE, DY9 0RF. (Life Member)

HANBY, Mr. Peter Nicholas, FCA *1973;* 15 Dawpool Farm, Station Road, Thurstaston, WIRRAL, MERSEYSIDE, CH61 0HR.

HANCE, Mr. Julian Christopher, BA FCA *1981;* Furnace Pond Cottage, Slaugham, HAYWARDS HEATH, WEST SUSSEX, RH17 6AG.

HANCKE, Mr. Shaun, ACA CA(SA) *2008;* 70 Wissey Way, ELY, CAMBRIDGESHIRE, CB6 2WW.

HANCKE-TRUTER, Mrs. Maryke, BCom ACA *2007;* 7 Kings Close, THAMES DITTON, KT7 0TY.

HANCOCK, Mrs. Amanda Jane, BSc ACA *1993;* 1 Wadestown Road, Wadestown, WELLINGTON 6001, NEW ZEALAND.

HANCOCK, Mrs. Beverley Jayne, BSc ACA *1992;* 38 St Johns Road, Neville Cross, DURHAM, DH1 4NU.

HANCOCK, Mr. Christopher John, FCA *1971;* 3 Impasse De La Gavotte, 17770 MIGRON, FRANCE.

HANCOCK, Mr. Christopher Michael Jefferies, ACA *1994;* Cleaver House Headley Common Road, Headley, EPSOM, KT18 6NR.

HANCOCK, Ms. Clare Rachel Julien, BSc ACA *2000;* 139 The Ridgeway, ST. ALBANS, HERTFORDSHIRE, AL4 9XA.

HANCOCK, Mr. David Edmund, BSc ACA *1989;* Coast Business Solutions Ltd, I T T C Building, 2 Tamar Science Park, Davy Road, PLYMOUTH, PL6 8BX.

HANCOCK, Mr. David John, BSc ACA *1986;* 54 Otley Road, Eldwick, BINGLEY, BD16 3EE.

•**HANCOCK, Mr. David John Cyril, BSc FCA** *1980;* David Hancock & Co, Webb House, 20 Bridge Road, Park Gate, SOUTHAMPTON, SO31 7GE.

HANCOCK, Mr. David Stanley, BSc FCA *1978;* Hilston, 171 Lache Lane, CHESTER, CH4 7LU. (Life Member)

HANCOCK, Mr. Ernest Maurice, BA ACA *2000;* 87 Alderbrook Road, LONDON, SW12 8AD.

HANCOCK, Mr. Gareth Tristan, BSc ACA *1996;* Flat 3, 16 Amherst Avenue, Ealing, LONDON, W13 8NQ.

HANCOCK, Miss. Gemma Louisa, BSc(Hons) ACA *2004;* with KPMG LLP, 1 Forest Gate, Brighton Road, CRAWLEY, WEST SUSSEX, RH11 9PT.

HANCOCK, Mr. Graeme John, MA ACA MCT *1990;* 5 Nursery View, FARINGDON, SN7 8SJ.

HANCOCK, Mr. Graham Daniel, MA ACA *1996;* 17 The Avenue, TWICKENHAM, TW1 1QP.

HANCOCK, Mr. Ian Chater Wells, BCom FCA *1956;* 19 Hillbrow, Richmond Hill, RICHMOND, SURREY, TW10 6BH. (Life Member)

HANCOCK, Mr. Ivor Newton, FCA *1968;* 24 Heol Felyn Fach, Tondu, BRIDGEND, MID GLAMORGAN, CF32 9DE.

HANCOCK, Mr. James Frank, BA ACA *2002;* 21 Rews Meadow, EXETER, EX1 3QJ.

HANCOCK, Mr. John Stuart, BCom FCA *1965;* Somercombe House, 109 Higher Lane, Langland, SWANSEA, SA3 4PS.

HANCOCK, Mr. Malcolm Brian, FCA *1960;* Acer Lodge, Fornham All Saints, BURY ST. EDMUNDS, SUFFOLK, IP28 6JJ. (Life Member)

HANCOCK, Mr. Mark James, BSc FCA *1992;* 35 Smore Slade Hills, Oadby, LEICESTER, LE2 4UX.

HANCOCK, Mr. Mark Peter Skelcher, ACA *2005;* with Barnes Roffe LLP, 3 Brook Business Centre, Cowley Mill Road, Cowley, UXBRIDGE, MIDDLESEX UB8 2FX.

HANCOCK, Mr. Martin Ian, BCom FCA AMCT *1986;* 301 Bridgewater Place, Birchwood Park, Birchwood, WARRINGTON, WA3 6XF.

HANCOCK, Mrs. Mary Bernadette Conway, BSc ACA *1987;* 10 Amesbury Road, Moseley, BIRMINGHAM, B13 8LD.

•**HANCOCK, Mr. Michael Edward, BSc FCA** *1983;* (Tax Fac), Hancock M.E., 2 Burls Yard, Crown Street, Needham Market, IPSWICH, IP6 8AJ.

•**HANCOCK, Mr. Nicholas John, BA FCA** *1990;* Albert Goodman LLP, Mary Street House, Mary Street, TAUNTON, TA1 3NW.

HANCOCK, Mrs. Pandora Jane, BSc ACA *1983;* Birmingham City University, The Business School, Galton Building, Franchise Street, Perry Barr, BIRMINGHAM B42 2SU.

HANCOCK, Mr. Patrick Leslie, BA ACA *1994;* 63 Thornway, Bramhall, STOCKPORT, SK7 2AH.

HANCOCK, Mr. Paul Harold, BA ACA *1980;* 40 Manor Way, CHESHAM, BUCKINGHAMSHIRE, HP5 3BH.

HANCOCK, Mr. Philip David, ACA *2004;* with HSKS Limited, 18 St. Christophers Way, Pride Park, DERBY, DE24 8JY.

HANCOCK, Mrs. Priscila, ACA *2010;* 32 County Hall Apartments North Block, Chicheley Street, Waterloo, LONDON, SE1 7PJ.

HANCOCK, Miss. Rebecca Elizabeth, ACA *2010;* Flat A, Devonshire Court, 101-103 Gloucester Terrace, LONDON, W2 3HB.

•**HANCOCK, Mr. Richard John, MBA FCA CF ACIM** *1982;* Hancock & Company, 47 Winchester Road, ANDOVER, HAMPSHIRE, SP10 2EF.

HANCOCK, Mr. Roger Markham, FCA *1965;* (Tax Fac), Sugarswell Bungalow, Shenington, BANBURY, OXFORDSHIRE, OX15 6HW.

HANCOCK, Mr. Samuel Peter, BSc ACA *2006;* 24 Melton Road, BIRMINGHAM, B14 7DA.

•**HANCOCK, Mrs. Sarah Ann Gifford, BA FCA** *1992;* (Tax Fac), Brehon Limited, Mayfield House, Grand Rue, St Martin, GUERNSEY, GY4 6AA.

HANCOCK, Mr. Simon Gregory John, BEng FCA *1995;* 24 The Grove, RADLETT, HERTFORDSHIRE, WD7 7NF.

•**HANCOCK, Mr. Stephen, FCA** *1981;* Enconcert Ltd, 47 Upper High Street, WORTHING, WEST SUSSEX, BN11 1DR.

HANCOCK, Mr. Stephen Robert Edward, BSc FCA *1979;* 10 Amesbury Road, Moseley, BIRMINGHAM, B13 8LD.

HANCOCK, Mrs. Theresa, BSc ACA *1990;* The Cote, Healey House, Netherton, HUDDERSFIELD, HD4 7DG.

HANCOCK, Ms. Zoe Julie Clare, BA ACA *1998;* 139 The Ridgeway, ST. ALBANS, HERTFORDSHIRE, AL4 9XA.

HANCOCK, Miss. Zoe Louise, ACA *2004;* 10/174 Esplanade East, Port Melbourne, MELBOURNE, VIC 3207, AUSTRALIA.

HANCOCKS, Mr. Michael Ernest, FCA *1976;* (Tax Fac), 19 Woodlands Grove, Higher Heath, WHITCHURCH, Shropshire, SY13 2JB.

HANCOX, Mr. David Morgan, BEng ACA *1998;* Westfield, Faringdon Road, Southmoor, ABINGDON, OXFORDSHIRE, OX13 5BH.

HANCOX, Dr. Elizabeth Louise, PhD BSc ACA *2000;* Unichem Plc, Unichem House, Cox Lane, CHESSINGTON, SURREY, KT9 1SN.

HANCOX, Mrs. Jacqueline Louise, PhD BSc ACA *1987;* Summerhill, Newport Road, Edgmond, NEWPORT, TF10 8HD.

•**HANCOX, Mrs. Joanna Jane, BSc ACA CTA** *2001;* Hancox & Co Limited, 62 Market Street, Milnsbridge, HUDDERSFIELD, HD3 4HT. See also Milnsbridge Accountancy Limited

HANCOX, Mr. John Philip Dale, MA FCA *1966;* Offham Manor, Offham, WEST MALLING, ME19 5NJ.

•**HANCOX, Mr. Joseph Frederick, FCA** *1977;* Crowe Clark Whitehill LLP, Black Country House, Rounds Green Road, OLDBURY, WEST MIDLANDS, B69 2DG. See also Horwath Clark Whitehill LLP and Crowe Clark Whitehill

HANCOX, Mr. Matthew John, BSc ACA *1995;* I N G Corporate Finance, 60 London Wall, LONDON, EC2M 5TQ.

HANCOX, Mrs. Michaela Jane, BSc(Hons) ACA *1994;* 14 Highfield Avenue, HARPENDEN, HERTFORDSHIRE, AL5 5UA.

HANCOX, Miss. Wendy Rowena, BSc FCA *1980;* Ahead for Business Pty Ltd, Level 10, 420 St Kilda Road, MELBOURNE, VIC 3004, AUSTRALIA.

HAND, Mr. Anthony Peter Vaughan, FCA *1966;* Penn Moor, Vicarage Road, Penn, WOLVERHAMPTON, WV4 5HR. (Life Member)

HAND, Miss. Bridget, BSc ACA *2010;* 20 Cissbury Road, LONDON, N15 5QA.

HAND, Mrs. Fiona Elizabeth, MA ACA *1991;* The Oaks, Byfleet Road, COBHAM, SURREY, KT11 1EE.

HAND, Miss. Jennifer Alison, ACA *2009;* Mazars Llp, Cartwright House, Tottle Road, NOTTINGHAM, NG2 1RT.

HAND, Mr. Jeremy, BSc ACA *1988;* 10 Milbourne Lane, ESHER, KT10 9DX.

HAND, Mrs. Sharon Christina, BEng ACA *1998;* LH Woodhouse & Co Ltd, Wolds Farm, The Fosse, Cotgrave, NOTTINGHAM, NG12 3HG.

•**HAND, Mr. Simon Lawrence, BSc FCA** *1983;* (Tax Fac), Gulfstream Aerospace Hangar 63, Percival Way London Luton Airport, LUTON, LU2 9NT.

HANDA, Mr. Monish, MA ACA *2000;* 160 Squires Lane, LONDON, N3 2QT.

HANDA, Mr. Puneet Ramesh, BSc(Hons) ACA *2000;* P. O. Box 74330, NAIROBI, 00200, KENYA.

HANDA, Mr. Sandeep, BA ACA *1992;* Tanglewood, Royston Grove, PINNER, HA5 4HF.

HANDA, Mr. Subhash Chandra, FCA *1963;* Subhash C. Handa, PO Box 25223, NAIROBI, 00603, KENYA.

HANDCOCK, Mrs. Penelope Anne, FCA *1973;* 3 Lancaster Close, Middle Hill, Englefield Green, EGHAM, TW20 0LA.

HANDEL, Mrs. Cecilia Margery, MA ACA PGCE *2002;* 6 Pandan Valley, 13-604, SINGAPORE 597630, SINGAPORE.

HANDEL, Mr. John David, FCA *1963;* Pinehurst, Woodhill Road, Sandon, CHELMSFORD, CM2 7SE.

•**HANDFORD, Mr. Antony Philip Peard, ACA** *1984;* APH Accounting Limited, 1 The Hamlet, Hough Green, CHESTER, CH4 8JW.

HANDFORD, Mr. Jonathan, BSc ACA *2002;* 25 Lime Grove, Kirby Muxloe, LEICESTER, LE9 2DF.

HANDFORD, Mr. Stephen Michael, BSc FCA *1979;* 2 Priors Dean Road, Harestock, WINCHESTER, SO22 6HU.

HANDFORD, Mr. Timothy John, BSocSc ACA *2003;* ICI Paints, Wexham Road, SLOUGH, SL2 5DS.

•**HANDLER, Mr. Noam Dov, BA ACA** *2000;* Ernst & Young LLP, 100 Barbirolli Square, MANCHESTER, M2 3EY. See also Ernst & Young Europe LLP

•**HANDLEY, Mr. David, BSc FCA** *1998;* MCA Breslins Banbury Ltd, Greenway House, Sugarswell Business Park, Shenington, BANBURY, OXFORDSHIRE OX15 6HW. See also Breslin Banbury Limited

HANDLEY, Mr. David Michael, FCA *1979;* 13 Shillingstone Close, BOLTON, BL2 3PD.

HANDLEY, Mr. David Paul, BA ACA *1988;* 191a Moor Lane, UPMINSTER, RM14 1HN.

HANDLEY, Mr. David William Sampson, FCA *1973;* Pump International Ltd, Trevoole, Praze, CAMBORNE, CORNWALL, TR14 0PJ.

HANDLEY, Mr. George William, FCA *1968;* Spinney Farm House, Chapel Brampton, NORTHAMPTON, NN6 8AG. (Life Member)

•**HANDLEY, Mr. Jack, FCA** *1952;* Handley & Co, Fern Dene, Savile Rd, HALIFAX, HX1 2BA.

HANDLEY, Mr. John, FCA *1972;* 56 Yellowhammer Court, KIDDERMINSTER, DY10 4RR. (Life Member)

HANDLEY, Mr. John Martin, BSc ACA *1987;* Mintz Cottage, Cakebole, Chaddesley Corbett, KIDDERMINSTER, DY10 4RF.

HANDLEY, Mrs. Margaret Helen, BSc FCA *1976;* 9 Blunts Wood Crescent, HAYWARDS HEATH, RH16 1NE.

•**HANDLEY, Mr. Mark William Sampson, BA FCA** *1989;* with Grant Thornton UK LLP, Crown House, Crown Street, IPSWICH, IP1 3HS.

HANDLEY, Mr. Noel Andrew Ernest, FCA *1972;* 2 Cavalry Drive, MARCH, PE15 9EQ.

HANDLEY, Mr. Paul James Anthony, BA ACA *2006;* 17 Julius Close, BASINGSTOKE, HAMPSHIRE, RG24 9SJ.
•**HANDLEY, Mr. Paul John Weston, FCA** *1967;* Paul Handley, 6 Highbury Road, Streetly, SUTTON COLDFIELD, B74 4TF.
HANDLEY, Mr. Peter, FCA *1970;* 18 The Meadows, Westwoodside, DONCASTER, DN9 2HA.
•**HANDLEY, Mr. Philip Alan, FCA** *1990;* Greenhalgh Business Services Ltd, 2a Peveril Drive, NOTTINGHAM, NG7 1DE.
HANDLEY, Mr. Richard Simon, MA FCA *1979;* The Linhay, Ilsington, NEWTON ABBOT, DEVON, TQ13 9RS. (Life Member)
HANDLEY, Mr. Rupert Sacheverell, BSc FCA *1989;* 27b Druid Stoke Avenue, BRISTOL, BS9 1DB.
•**HANDLEY, Mr. Stephen Fryer, BA FCA** *1987;* No 2 Accommodation Road, LONDON, NW11 8ED.
HANDLEY, Mr. William Ernest Hartop, FCA *1951;* 29a Ferndale, TUNBRIDGE WELLS, KENT, TN2 3PJ. (Life Member)
•**HANDLEY, Mr. William John, BSc FCA CTA** *1979;* (Tax Fac), Handley Roberts, 1 The Courtyard, Chalvington, HAILSHAM, EAST SUSSEX, BN27 3TD.
HANDLEY-JONES, Mr. Nicholas, FCA *1973;* 23 Glenmore House, 64 Richmond Hill, RICHMOND, SURREY, TW10 6BQ.
•**HANDLEY POTTS, Mr. Julian Mark, FCA** *1979;* (Tax Fac), Winterstoke Financial Management Limited, Unit 1, Rivermead, Pipers Way, THATCHAM, BERKSHIRE RG19 4EP.
HANDMAN, Miss. Joanna Margaret Gillian, BA(Hons) ACA *2002;* 141 Darwin Road, Ealing, LONDON, W5 4BB.
HANDREN, Miss. Miriam Kate, BA ACA *1982;* Caer Wigau Uchaf Farm, Pendoylan, COWBRIDGE, CF71 7UJ.
HANDS, Mr. Antony Russell, FCA *1973;* 18 Grazing Lane, Webheath, REDDITCH, WORCESTERSHIRE, B97 5PE.
HANDS, Mr. David, FCA MCIH *1973;* 16 Trundalls Lane, Shirley, SOLIHULL, B90 1SS.
HANDS, Mr. David Bryan, FCA *1974;* March & Edwards, 8 Sansome Walk, WORCESTER, WR1 1LW.
HANDS, Mr. Gavin William Valentine, BA ACA FCCA *2000;* The Coach House, Finavon, FORFAR, DD8 3PX.
HANDS, Mr. Harry Frederick, FCA *1950;* P.O. Box 34, VLOTTENBURG, 7604, SOUTH AFRICA. (Life Member)
HANDS, Miss. Kaeti, BA ACA *2007;* 16 Little London Court, Mill Street, LONDON, SE1 2BF.
HANDS, Miss. Katie Jane, BSc(Hons) ACA *2000;* 12 Belvedere Mews, Blackheath, LONDON, SE3 7DF.
HANDS, Mr. Leonard Thomas, FCA *1958;* 5 Park Lane, Cheshunt, WALTHAM CROSS, EN7 6LY. (Life Member)
HANDS, Mr. Martin Jeffery, BA FCA *1977;* Lindley House, Naburn, YORK, YO19 4RU.
HANDS, Miss. Penelope Clare, BA ACA *2003;* Warren House, Warren Road, CROWBOROUGH, EAST SUSSEX, TN6 1TX.
HANDS, Mr. Peter George John, MA ACA *1979;* 62 High Street, Shirley, SOLIHULL, B90 1EY.
HANDS, Mr. Richard, FCA *1962;* Abbot's House, 48 Gander Hill, HAYWARDS HEATH, RH16 1RD. (Life Member)
HANDS, Mr. Richard James, BA FCA *1968;* 3 Hill Farm Court, Edwalton, NOTTINGHAM, NG12 4DP. (Life Member)
HANDS, Mr. Stuart Arthur, BA ACA *1996;* Fusion Corporate Finance, The Crescent, King Street, LEICESTER, LE1 6RX.
•**HANDSCOMB, Mr. Guy David, BSc ACA** *1987;* Helliwell Handscomb, 15 Littlethorpe Hill, Hartshead, LIVERSEDGE, WF15 8AZ.
•**HANDSCOMB, Mrs. Lynn, ACA** *1986;* Helliwell Handscomb, 15 Littlethorpe Hill, Hartshead, LIVERSEDGE, WF15 8AZ.
HANDSCOMB, Mr. Peter Ewart, BSc ACA *1993;* Temple Cottage, 10 Moor Park Lane, FARNHAM, GU10 1QS.
HANDSCOMBE, Mr. Kevin Paul, BA ACA *1983;* 3 Borrowdale Avenue, IPSWICH, IP4 2TN.
HANDY, Mr. Christopher Peter, BSc ACA *1991;* 5 Chantry Road, Moseley, BIRMINGHAM, B13 8DL.
HANDY, Mr. Guy Andrew, BA ACA *1984;* Robin Down, Fairview Lane, CROWBOROUGH, TN6 1BT.
HANDY, Mr. Kenneth Francis, FCA *1955;* 64 Hayes Chase, WEST WICKHAM, BR4 0JA. (Life Member)
HANDY, Mr. Nicholas John, BA ACA *1986;* Lansdowne House, 57 Berkeley Square, LONDON, W1J 6ER.
HANDYSIDE, Mr. Ethan, BA ACA *2004;* The Royal Bank of Scotland Plc, 280 Bishopsgate, LONDON, EC2M 4RB.
•**HANDYSIDE, Mr. Robert Graham, FCA** *1959;* Handyside & Company, Bank Chambers, 92 Newport Road, CARDIFF, CF24 1DG.
HANES, Mr. David John, FCA *1969;* The Lodge, 7 Lower Green Road, Pembury, TUNBRIDGE WELLS, TN2 4DZ.
HANFORD, Mr. David John, FCA *1979;* Six Limes, 6 Beeston Fields Drive, Beeston, NOTTINGHAM, NG9 3DB.
•**HANGER, Miss. Rachel Elizabeth, BA ACA** *1992;* KPMG LLP, 15 Canada Square, LONDON, E14 5GL. See also KPMG Europe LLP
HANIF, Mr. Asim, BSc ACA *2006;* 65 Stansfield Road, HOUNSLOW, TW4 7QR.
HANIMANN-ROBINSON, Mrs. Helen, BA ACA *1990;* Forchstrasse 157, 8127 FORCH, SWITZERLAND.
HANISON, Mr. Norman, FCA *1968;* 9 Church Mount, LONDON, N2 0RW. (Life Member)
HANKERS, Mr. Gary, ACA *2007;* 10 Bala Lake Crescent, Broughton, MILTON KEYNES, MK10 7BB.
HANKEY, Mr. John Barnard, FCA *1963;* 4 Park Lane, Appleton, ABINGDON, OX13 5JT. (Life Member)
HANKEY, Mr. Nicholas, ACA ACMA *1995;* 5 Beech Grove, TRING, HP23 5NU.
HANKIN, Mr. David John, FCA *1969;* Lambley Brook, Springhead Lane, Kilmington, AXMINSTER, DEVON, EX13 7SS.
HANKIN, Mr. James Andrew, ACA *2008;* 22 Kedleston Avenue, MANCHESTER, M14 5PT.
HANKIN, Mr. Sean, BSc FCA *1995;* The Law Society Ipsley Court, Berrington Close, REDDITCH, WORCESTERSHIRE, B98 0TD.
•**HANKINSON, Mr. Jonathan Marc Lindon, LLB ACA** *1990;* (Tax Fac), David Lindon & Co, Avaland House, 110 London Road, Apsley, HEMEL HEMPSTEAD, HP3 9SD.
HANKINSON, Mr. Simon John, BA ACA *1997;* 204 Hoffman Ave, Apt B, SAN FRANCISCO, CA 94114, UNITED STATES.
HANKS, Mr. Anthony Joseph Patrick, FCA *1957;* 11 Ralliwood Road, ASHTEAD, KT21 1DD. (Life Member)
HANKS, Mr. Brian Paul, ACA *1981;* 1 Lancaster Drive, Upper Rissington, CHELTENHAM, GL54 2QZ.
HANKS, Mr. Brian Richard, FCA *1959;* 9 Disraeli Park, Penn Road, BEACONSFIELD, BUCKINGHAMSHIRE, HP9 2QE. (Life Member)
HANKS, Mr. Gavin James, BA ACA *1996;* 2 The Hawthorns, Charvil, READING, RG10 9TS.
•**HANKS, Mr. John Martin, LLM FCA** *1987;* (Tax Fac), John M Hanks, 50 Thames Street, OXFORD, OX1 1SU.
HANKS, Mr. Kenneth, FCA *1960;* 28 Broadoaks Way, BROMLEY, BR2 0UB. (Life Member)
HANKS, Mr. Michael Richard, BSc FCA *1974;* 3 Victoria Road, SUTTON, SURREY, SM1 4RT.
HANKS, Miss. Rebecca, BSc ACA *2007;* with Knill James, One Bell Lane, LEWES, EAST SUSSEX, BN7 1JU.
HANKS, Mr. Richard, BA ACA *1989;* 106 Washington Road, PRINCETON, NJ 08540, UNITED STATES.
HANKS, Miss. Yvonne Catherine, BA FCA *1989;* Parade View, Burtle Road, Burtle, BRIDGWATER, SOMERSET, TA7 8NB.
•**HANLAN, Mrs. Karen Marie, BSc ACA** *1993;* Karen Hanlan Independent Examiner, Hollyoakes, School Lane, Lea Marston, SUTTON COLDFIELD, WEST MIDLANDS B76 0BW.
HANLEY, Mrs. Claire, BSc ACA *1995;* 27 Sir Thomas Mitchell Road, BONDI BEACH, NSW 2026, AUSTRALIA.
HANLEY, Mrs. Claire-Marie, BA ACA *2006;* 103 Ladywood Road, HERTFORD, SG14 2TB.
HANLEY, The Right Hon. Sir Jeremy James, KCMG FCA *1969;* 6 Butts Mead, Northgate, NORTHWOOD, HA6 2TL.
•**HANLEY, Mrs. Kirstie Louise, BA(Hons) ACA** *2004;* with PricewaterhouseCoopers LLP, 7 More London Riverside, LONDON, SE1 2RT.
HANLEY, Miss. Lisa Jane, BA ACA *2003;* Vere Cottage, Marsh, AYLESBURY, BUCKINGHAMSHIRE, HP17 8SP.
HANLEY, Mr. Michael James, BSc ACA *2004;* 39 Moffat Road, LONDON, SW17 7EZ.
•**HANLEY, Mr. Richard Martin, BA ACA** *1989;* KPMG LLP, 500 East Middlefield Road, MOUNTAIN VIEW, CA 94043, UNITED STATES.
HANLEY, Mr. Steven Ross, BA ACA *1982;* 3 Spring Close, Upper Basildon, READING, RG8 8JQ.
HANLEY, Mrs. Susan Helen, BSc ACA *1990;* PO Box 6053, NARRAWEENA, NSW 2099, AUSTRALIA.
HANLON, Mrs. Celia Ann, BSc FCA *1974;* Higher Nature Plc, The Nutrition Centre, Burwash Common, ETCHINGHAM, EAST SUSSEX, TN19 7LX.
•**HANLON, Mrs. Jennifer Elizabeth Imogen, ACA** *2002;* Jennifer Hanlon, Wisteria Cottage, Mendlesham Road, Cotton, STOWMARKET, SUFFOLK IP14 4RB.
HANLON, Mr. John Bryce, FCA *1970;* with Hawes Strickland, Federation House, 36/38 Rockingham Road, KETTERING, NORTHAMPTONSHIRE, NN16 8JS.
HANLON, Mr. Noble Murray, FCA *1972;* 7 Great Woodcote Park, West Purley, PURLEY, CR8 3QU.
HANLON, Mr. Norman Ian, FCA *1969;* with David Upstone, 9 Market Place, BRACKLEY, NORTHAMPTONSHIRE, NN13 7AB.
HANMAN, Mrs. Anne Mary, BA ACA *1988;* 16 Smethurst Road, Billinge, WIGAN, WN5 7DW.
HANMER, Mr. Paul Henry, FCA *1981;* 38 Beacon Park Drive, SKEGNESS, LINCOLNSHIRE, PE25 1HE.
•**HANMER, Mr. William Richard, FCA** *1973;* The New Ortani Garden Court 26F 4-1 Kioi-cho Chiyoda-ku, TOKYO, 102-0094 JAPAN. See also Richard Hanmer
HANN, Mr. Alan Simon Piers, BSc ACA *1988;* Ernst & Young LLP, 222 Bay Street Box 251, TORONTO M5K 1J7, ON, CANADA.
HANN, Mr. Harry Edwin, FCA *1952;* Greenacre, Hawks Hill Close, LEATHERHEAD, KT22 9DL. (Life Member)
HANN, Mr. Jonathan Hugh James, BSc(Hons) ACA *2003;* 9 Redfearn Mews, HARROGATE, NORTH YORKSHIRE, HG2 9QN.
HANN, Mr. Matthew, ACA *2010;* 4 Dalton Street, ST. ALBANS, HERTFORDSHIRE, AL3 5QQ.
HANN, Mr. Michael John, BSc ACA *1988;* 47 St. James's Road, SEVENOAKS, KENT, TN13 3NG.
•**HANN, Mrs. Nancy, FCA** *1977;* (Tax Fac), with Morris Crocker, Station House, 50 North Street, HAVANT, PO9 1QU.
HANN, Mr. Peter Anthony, BA ACA *1981;* (Tax Fac), 52 East India Way, CROYDON, CR0 6RZ.
HANNA, Miss. Deborah, BSc ACA AMCT *2003;* 17 Trevor Road, Flixton, MANCHESTER, M41 5GT.
HANNA, Miss. Georgina, BSc ACA *2008;* 51 AG Epiktitoy, Agios Athanasios, 4107 LIMASSOL, 4107 LIMASSOL, CYPRUS.
HANNA, Mrs. Gillian Violet, BSc ACA *2005;* 10 Penrhyn Gardens, NEWTOWNARDS, COUNTY DOWN, BT23 8JN.
HANNA, Mr. Hanna Youssif, MCom FCA *1953;* 27 Talaat Harb Street, CAIRO, EGYPT. (Life Member)
HANNA, Mr. Harold John Alexander, BSc FCA *1979;* (Tax Fac), Compton, 6 Cliffe Road, Barton-on-Sea, NEW MILTON, BH25 7PB.
HANNA, Mr. Jonathan Patrick Christopher, MA(Hons) ACA *2002;* 6 Henfold Cottages, Henfold Lane Newdigate, DORKING, SURREY, RH5 5AG.
HANNA, Mr. Kenneth George, FCA *1976;* Inchcape Plc, 22a St James Square, LONDON, SW1Y 5LP.
HANNA, Mrs. Lucy, BSc(Hons) ACA *2002;* 6 Henfold Cottages, Henfold Lane Newdigate, DORKING, SURREY, RH5 5AG.
HANNA, Ms. Patricia Niamh, LLB ACA *2001;* Flat 5, Kingsley House London Road, HARROW, HA1 3JQ.
HANNA, Mr. Peter Neil, FCA *1971;* La Valliere, Les Camps Du Moulin, St. Martin, GUERNSEY, GY4 6DZ.
HANNAFORD, Mr. John David, BA ACA *1991;* 12 Hobury Street, LONDON, SW10 0JB.
HANNAFORD, Mr. Richard Charles, BSc FCA *1972;* 14 Yew Tree Close, Langford, BRISTOL, BS40 5DP. (Life Member)
HANNAFORD, Mr. Robert, BA ACA *2006;* Coastal Energy, 3355 West Alabama Suite 500, HOUSTON, TX 77098, UNITED STATES.
•**HANNAFORD, Miss. Sarah, BA(Hons) FCA** *2000;* Wilkins Kennedy, Bridge House, London Bridge, LONDON, SE1 9QR.
HANNAH, Mr. Craig Robert, BA FCA *1983;* Morris & Hannah Ltd, Foxpad, St. Lythan's, CARDIFF, CF5 6BQ.
HANNAH, Mr. David, FCA *1967;* 5 The Lowes, Bowdon, ALTRINCHAM, WA14 3PE.
HANNAH, Mr. David Marshall, FCA *1959;* 6 Bron y Felin, MENAI BRIDGE, LL59 5UY.
HANNAH, Mr. David Warren, ACA *1984;* (Tax Fac), 18 Albert Street, Kibworth Harcourt, LEICESTER, LE8 0NA.
HANNAH, Mrs. Joanne Turner, BA FCA ACA *1993;* 40 Gonville Avenue, Sutton, MACCLESFIELD, SK11 0EG.
HANNAH, Mr. John, FCA *1956;* 31 Langstone Ley, WELWYN GARDEN CITY, HERTFORDSHIRE, AL7 1FR. (Life Member)
HANNAH, Mrs. Katherine Joan Loxton, BSc FCA CTA *1985;* Slaney House, Hunts Common, Hartley Wintney, HOOK, HAMPSHIRE, RG27 8AA.
HANNAH, Miss. Kathryn Louise, BSc ACA *1999;* 1 Upland Drive, Brookmans Park, HATFIELD, HERTFORDSHIRE, AL9 6PS.
HANNAH, Mr. Mark Stuart, BA ACA *1990;* 12 Charnock Crescent, SHEFFIELD, S12 3HB.
HANNAH, Mr. Paul George, ACA *1978;* 2 Falfield Close, Lisvane, CARDIFF, CF14 0GB.
HANNAH, Mr. Steven Peter, BA ACA *2010;* 12 Joseph Hall Avenue, Douglas, ISLE OF MAN, IM2 6PN.
HANNAM, Mr. Brian Neil, FCA *1964;* 42 Reynard Way, NORTHAMPTON, NN2 8QX.
HANNAM, Mr. David, ACA *2011;* 21 Wycliffe Road, LONDON, SW19 1ES.
•**HANNAM, Mr. Geoffrey, BA FCA** *1989;* (Tax Fac), Geoffrey Hannam Limited, 103 Castle Street, Edgeley, STOCKPORT, CHESHIRE, SK3 9AR.
•**HANNAM, Mr. Giles Philip, BA ACA** *1999;* PricewaterhouseCoopers LLP, 1 Embankment Place, LONDON, WC2N 6RH. See also PricewaterhouseCoopers
HANNAM, Mr. James Robert, MA ACA *1998;* Ernst & Young Llp, 1 More London Place, LONDON, SE1 2AF.
•**HANNAM, Mr. Mark Ashley, BSc FCA** *1989;* PricewaterhouseCoopers LLP, Benson House, 33 Wellington Street, LEEDS, LS1 4JP. See also PricewaterhouseCoopers
HANNAM, Ms. Melissa Jane, BA(Hons) ACA *2001;* 7 Brookside, Campton, SHEFFORD, SG17 5PA.
HANNAM, Mr. Philip, FCA *1953;* 59 Stanneylands Drive, WILMSLOW, SK9 4EU. (Life Member)
HANNAM, Mr. Richard Andrew, BSc(Hons) ACA *2003;* 14 Kingsdale Drive, Menston, ILKLEY, WEST YORKSHIRE, LS29 6QN.
HANNAM, Mr. Robert Michael, BSc ACA *1979;* Lee Farm, Lee Lane, Lambutts, TODMORDEN, OL14 6HS.
HANNAN, Mr. Aktar Uzzaman, BA ACA *2004;* JT International S.A., 1 rue de la Gabelle, 1211 GENEVA, SWITZERLAND.
HANNAN, Miss. Amanda Jane, MSc ACA *2000;* 81 rue Truffaut, 75017 PARIS, FRANCE.
HANNAN, Mr. Edward, BSc ACA *2005;* 35 Birkbeck Road, BECKENHAM, KENT, BR3 4SL.
•**HANNAN, Mrs. Leanne McDonald, ACA** *2002;* Pinstripe Busines Solutions, 28 Foxglove Close, NEWTON AYCLIFFE, COUNTY DURHAM, DL5 4PF.
HANNAN, Mr. Ommar, BSc(Hons) ACA *2001;* Shell Markets Middle East Ltd, 15th Floor, City Tower 2, Sheikh Zayed Road, PO Box 307, DUBAI UNITED ARAB EMIRATES.
HANNAN, Mr. Roger James, BSc FCA CPA CFP *1977;* Hannan & Associates, 732 Florsheim Drive #11, LIBERTYVILLE, IL 60048, UNITED STATES.
HANNANT, Mr. Charles Edward John, MEng ACA MCSI ACGI *2001;* Credit Suisse, 9th Floor, The Gate, Dubai International Financial Centre, P.O. Box 33660, DUBAI UNITED ARAB EMIRATES.
HANNANT, Mr. Christopher James, BA ACA *2000;* (Tax Fac), Zip Heaters UK Ltd, 14-16 Bertie Ward Way, DEREHAM, NORFOLK, NR19 1TE.
HANNANT, Mrs. Mary Elizabeth, BSc FCA *1980;* Brachers Solicitors, 57-59 London Road, MAIDSTONE, ME16 8JH.
HANNANT, Mr. Michael Francis, ACA *1982;* The Reading Room High Street, Newport, SAFFRON WALDEN, CB11 3QY.
•**HANNAWAY, Mr. Ivano, FCA** *1984;* (Tax Fac), 9 Berkeley Road, Loudwater, HIGH WYCOMBE, BUCKINGHAMSHIRE, HP10 9TT.
HANNAY, Mrs. Sarah Jane, BSc(Hons) ACA *2001;* Beeches House, 3 Foxley Grove, Burnham, SLOUGH, SL1 8ET.
•**HANNAY-WILSON, Mr. John Richard Hannay, FCA** *1968;* Flat 5, Building 7, Micro District 7, AKTAU 130002, KAZAKHSTAN.
HANNELL, Mr. Adrian Ralph, BA(Hons) ACA *2001;* 15 Onslow Way, WOKING, GU22 8QX.
HANNELL, Mrs. Stephanie Jane, BSc(Hons) ACA *2001;* 5 Watercress Place, HORSHAM, RH13 6TT.
HANNEN, Mr. James Troubridge John, FCA *1970;* 132 Hill Village Road, Four Oaks, SUTTON COLDFIELD, B75 5HN.
HANNER, Mrs. Jessica Alison, MA ACA *1998;* with PricewaterhouseCoopers LLP, 1 Embankment Place, LONDON, WC2N 6RH.
HANNEY, Mr. David Charles, BSc ACA *1994;* 1 Hazel Villas, Valley Road, Hayfield, HIGH PEAK, DERBYSHIRE, SK22 2LP.

HANNEY, Mr. Mark, BSc ACA *1994;* Downsgate 17 Epsom Lane South, TADWORTH, SURREY, KT20 5SX.
HANNEY, Mr. Peter Jonathan, MA FCA *1990;* 24 Oak Grove, HERTFORD, SG13 8AT.
HANNEY, Miss. Sally-Ann, BA ACA *2008;* with British American Tobacco plc, Globe House, 4 Temple Place, LONDON, WC2R 2PG.
HANNIBAL, Ms. Penelope, ACA *2007;* 7 Catherine Street, MACCLESFIELD, SK11 6ET.
HANNIDES, Mr. George Michael, BSc FCA *1982;* Suite G A 1, Oak House, Woodland Business Park, Linford Wood West, MILTON KEYNES, MK14 6EY.
HANNIGAN, Mr. Derek Henry, FCA *1958;* 136 Purley Downs Road, Sanderstead, SOUTH CROYDON, SURREY, CR2 0RE. (Life Member)
HANNIGAN, Mr. Thomas Kevin, FCA *1962;* 33 Perrinsfield, LECHLADE, GL7 3SD.
HANNON, Mr. Brian Francis, BA ACA *1985;* CQS Management Ltd, 5th Floor, 33 Grosvenor Place, LONDON, SW1X 7HY.
HANNON, Miss. Bridget Elizabeth Stewart-Moore, BA ACA *2007;* 26 Pinner Road, SHEFFIELD, S11 8UH.
HANNON, Ms. Cliona Carol, BCom ACA *1997;* with Nestle UK Ltd, St. Georges House, CROYDON, SURREY, CR9 1NR.
HANNON, Mr. James, BA ACA MBA *1999;* 13 Old Road, LONDON, SE13 5SU.
HANNON, Miss. Tracy Joanne, BSc FCA *1995;* 29 Dale Road, Marple, STOCKPORT, CHESHIRE, SK6 6EZ.
•**HANRAHAN, Mrs. Susan Anne, FCA** *1977;* (Tax Fac), Mattison & Co., 10A Royal Parade, CHISLEHURST, BR7 6NR.
HANS, Mr. Imran Lukman, BSc(Hons) ACA *2011;* 11 St. Anns Close, DEWSBURY, WEST YORKSHIRE, WF12 0BA.
HANSELL, Mr. Alan James, BSS FCA *1977;* Peacocks Medical Group Ltd, Peacock Medical Group Ltd, Benfield Business Park, Benfield Road, NEWCASTLE UPON TYNE, NE6 4NQ.
HANSELL, Mr. Timothy Lloyd, BA ACA *1998;* with Grant Thornton UK LLP, 101 Cambridge Science Park, Milton Road, CAMBRIDGE, CB4 0FY.
HANSEN, Mr. Adam John, BSc ACA *2007;* 54 Waterloo Road, SOUTHPORT, PR8 2NB.
•**HANSEN, Mr. Bo, ACA** *2009;* Pileurten 15, 5450 OTTERUP, DENMARK.
HANSEN, Mr. Carl Frederick, BA FCA *1984;* 28 Farthingale Lane, WALTHAM ABBEY, EN9 3NF.
HANSEN, Miss. Keta Jean, MA ACA *1997;* 153 Broomwood Road, LONDON, SW11 6JU.
HANSEN, Mr. Kim Gregory, BSc ACA *1978;* 37 Fairfield Avenue, UPMINSTER, ESSEX, RM14 3AZ.
•**HANSEN, Mr. Michael Groth, BA ACA** *2005;* with KPMG LLP, Borups Alle 177, Oest - Koebenhavn, 2000 FREDERIKSBERG, DENMARK.
HANSFORD, Mr. James Victor, MA FCA MCT *1983;* Lazard Alternative Investments LLC, 30 Rockefeller Plaza, NEW YORK, NY 10020, UNITED STATES.
HANSFORD, Mr. Jeremy, BA FCA *1992;* Winterflood Securities Ltd, The Atrium Building, 25 Dowgate Hill, LONDON, EC4R 2GA.
HANSFORD, Mr. Nigel Antony, BSc ACA *1989;* 10 Bramble Croft, Lostock, BOLTON, BL6 4GW.
HANSLIP, Mr. Peter Eric, ACA *2007;* 10 Greenheys Close, NORTHWOOD, MIDDLESEX, HA6 2FR.
HANSLIP, Miss. Zoe Yolanda Jane, BA ACA *2005;* Risk Management Division (HO-1 D-C), The Bank of England, Threadneedle Street, LONDON, EC2R 8AH.
HANSOM, Mrs. Sian, BSc ACA *1985;* 46 The Green, Ravensworth, RICHMOND, DL11 7ES.
HANSOM, Mr. Theodore Richard, FCA *1961;* Middle Lodge, Hillgrove, WELLS, BA5 3EL. (Life Member)
HANSON, Mr. Aaron James, ACA MAAT *2009;* 46 Hulme Road, Denton, MANCHESTER, M34 2WZ.
HANSON, Mrs. Alison Jane, BA ACA *1992;* The Cat Gallery The Raylor Centre, James Street, YORK, YO10 3DW.
HANSON, Mr. Andrew Frank, FCA *1974;* Woodcombe Lodge, Bratton Lane, MINEHEAD, SOMERSET, TA24 8SQ.
HANSON, Ms. Annette Maria, BSc ACA *1993;* 9 Pontoise Close, SEVENOAKS, KENT, TN13 3ES.
HANSON, Mr. Anthony Santino, ACA *2009;* 3E Mylne Street, LONDON, EC1r 1XY.
•**HANSON, Mr. Christopher Kenneth, FCA ATII** *1976;* The Hanson Partnership LLP, Suite A, Unit 16, Cirencester Office Park, Tetbury Road, CIRENCESTER GLOUCESTERSHIRE GL7 6JJ.
HANSON, Miss. Clare Bernice, BSc ACA *1987;* 6 Court Lane Gardens, Dulwich Village, LONDON, SE21 7DZ.
HANSON, Mr. David Christopher, BSc ACA *1982;* The Maltings, Highfield Court, Cross Lane Shepley, HUDDERSFIELD, HD8 8BG.
HANSON, Mr. David John, FCA *1957;* Scobitor, Widecombe-In-The-Moor, NEWTON ABBOT, TQ13 7TF. (Life Member)
•**HANSON, Mr. Derek Richard, FCA** *1971;* Newsham Hanson & Company, 1-5 Bellevue Road, CLEVEDON, AVON, BS21 7NP.
•**HANSON, Mr. Edward James, BSc ACA** *1997;* Deloitte LLP, 2 New Street Square, LONDON, EC4A 3BZ. See also Deloitte & Touche LLP
HANSON, Miss. Emma, ACA *1999;* 36 Lennon Close, Hillmorton, RUGBY, WARWICKSHIRE, CV21 4DT.
•**HANSON, Mr. Gary Edward, BSc FCA** *1979;* BDO LLP, First Floor, Clarendon House, Clarendon Road, CAMBRIDGE, CB2 8FH. See also BDO Stoy Hayward LLP
HANSON, Mr. George Maurice, FCA *1963;* The Warren, 6 Wayside Crescent, Scarcroft, LEEDS, LS14 3BD. (Life Member)
HANSON, Mr. Gregory Albert, BAcc ACA CTA *1986;* J & J Denholm Ltd, 18 Woodside Crescent, GLASGOW, G3 7UL.
HANSON, Mr. Harold, FCA *1950;* Flat 8, 2 Corscombe Close, WEYMOUTH, DORSET, DT4 0UG. (Life Member)
HANSON, Miss. Harriet, ACA *2010;* 7 Hengaston Street, BRISTOL, BS3 3HR.
HANSON, Mr. Ian Nigel, FCA *1968;* 14 Wentworth Avenue, Whirlowdale Park, SHEFFIELD, S11 9QX.
•**HANSON, Mr. Ian William, FCA** *1965;* 18 Grenville Avenue, Wendover, AYLESBURY, HP22 6AQ.
HANSON, Mr. Ivor William, BSc(Econ) FCA *1990;* with PKF (UK) LLP, St Hughs, 23 Newport, LINCOLN, LN1 3DN.
HANSON, Mrs. Jane Carolyn, JP BA(Hons) FCA *1996;* The Maltings, Highfield Court, Cross Lane, Shepley, HUDDERSFIELD, HD8 8BG.
HANSON, Mr. John, FCA *1960;* 4 Moorland Gardens, Moortown, LEEDS, LS17 6JT. (Life Member)
HANSON, Mr. John, BA FCA *1975;* 3A, Foss View, YORK, YO1 7NG.
HANSON, Mr. John, FCA *1972;* Howlands (Furniture) Ltd, 36 Dashwood Avenue, HIGH WYCOMBE, BUCKINGHAMSHIRE, HP12 3DX.
HANSON, Mr. John Douglas, LLB FCA *1955;* 84 Chichester Road, CROYDON, CR0 5NB. (Life Member)
•**HANSON, Mrs. Julie Elizabeth, BA ACA** *1988;* Julie Hanson, The Heights, High Molewood, HERTFORD, SG14 2PL.
HANSON, Mr. Leonard Gordon, BSc ACA *1998;* 18 Nelson Street, Syston, LEICESTER, LE7 2JQ.
HANSON, Mrs. Louise Katherine Joanna, BSc ACA *1992;* Clifton College: Office, 32 College Road, Clifton, BRISTOL, BS8 3JH.
•**HANSON, Mr. Luke Christopher, BSc ACA** *2003;* 16 Woodeson Lea, LEEDS, LS13 1RJ.
HANSON, Mr. Michael, ACA *2011;* 43 Link Way, HORNCHURCH, ESSEX, RM11 3RN.
•**HANSON, Mr. Michael John, BA ACIB FCA** *1982;* 3 Ack Lane West, Cheadle Hulme, CHEADLE, CHESHIRE, SK8 7EN.
HANSON, Mrs. Nicola, BA ACA *2004;* 22 Fitzpatrick Way, PADBURY, WA 6025, AUSTRALIA.
HANSON, Mr. Paul James, BA ACA *1985;* 6 Dalkeith Road, HARPENDEN, AL5 5PW.
HANSON, Mr. Paul Roy, BA FCA *1994;* 406 Easter Avenue, PO Box F-40031, FREEPORT, BAHAMAS.
HANSON, Mr. Peter Charles, BA ACA *1989;* 144 Worcester Road, Hagley, STOURBRIDGE, DY9 0NR.
HANSON, Mr. Philip Leighton, BA(Hons) ACA *2003;* Flat 3 Clement Court, Bakers Close, ST. ALBANS, HERTFORDSHIRE, AL1 5FH.
•**HANSON, Mr. Philip William, MA FCA** *1973;* HSKS Limited, 18 St. Christophers Way, Pride Park, DERBY, DE24 8JY.
HANSON, Mr. Richard James, BSc ACA *1995;* CA Europe Sarl, Lake Geneva Center, Route de la Longeraie 9, 1110 MORGES, SWITZERLAND.
HANSON, Mr. Roger Howard, ACA *1987;* P.O. Box 2586, GEORGE TOWN, GRAND CAYMAN, KY1-1103, CAYMAN ISLANDS.
HANSON, Mrs. Sally Cathleen, BA FCA DChA *1988;* Perennial Gardener Royal Benevolent Society, 115-117 Kingston Road, LEATHERHEAD, SURREY, KT22 7SU.
HANSON, Miss. Sara Elisa, BA ACA *2009;* 5 Aldermore Drive, SUTTON COLDFIELD, B75 7HW.
HANSON, Mr. Simon Gordon, BA ACA *1983;* 1 Broome Close, YATELEY, HAMPSHIRE, GU46 7SY.
HANSORD, Mr. James, ACA *2010;* 8 Braybrooke Place, CAMBRIDGE, CB1 3LN.
HANSPAL, Miss. Poonam Panna, BSc ACA *2011;* 69 Lascelles Road, SLOUGH, SL3 7PW.
HANSRANI, Mr. Vikash, BA(Hons) ACA *2009;* Flat 407, Platinum House, Lyon Road, HARROW, HA1 2EX.
HANSSON, Ms. Zelda, BA ACA *2003;* Disney Channel Unit 12 Chiswick Park, 566 Chiswick High Road, LONDON, W4 5AN.
HANSTOCK, Mrs. Fiona, BA ACA *1982;* 1 Longaston Close, Slimbridge, GLOUCESTER, GL2 7BA.
HANTON, Mr. Terence Michael, ACA *1980;* 15 Waterhall polo estate, ST JAMES, BARBADOS.
HANWELL, Mr. David Anthony, FCA *1973;* P.O. Box HM 3106, HAMILTON HMNX, BERMUDA.
HANWORTH, Mr. Paul Robert, MA ACA *1979;* Pan Jamaican Investment Trust, 60 Knutsford Boulevard, KINGSTON 5, JAMAICA.
HAO, Mr. Shu Yan, ACA *2006;* Flat A, 2/F Tower 2, One Beacon Hill, 1 Beacon Hill Road, KOWLOON TONG, KOWLOON HONG KONG SAR.
HAPPE, Miss. Judy Amanda, BSc ACA *2006;* Ground Floor Flat, 25 Cedars Road, LONDON, W4 3JP.
HAQ, Miss. Amber, MChem ACA *2002;* Via San Pantaleo 66, 00186, ROME, ITALY.
HAQ, Mrs. Anisha, BSc ACA *2004;* 41 Loweswater Road, CHELTENHAM, GLOUCESTERSHIRE, GL51 3AZ.
HAQ, Mr. Armaghan Ul, FCA *1987;* 22 Shortcroft, BISHOP'S STORTFORD, HERTFORDSHIRE, CM23 5QY.
HAQ, Miss. Hannah, ACA *2008;* 5 Greyfriars Court, Castle Road, COLCHESTER, CO1 1TL.
•**HAQ, Mr. Imran, ACA** *2002;* D-82 Block F, North Nazimabad, KARACHI, PAKISTAN.
HAQ, Mr. Manzurul, FCA *1974;* 295/2 Sarwar Road, LAHORE, PUNJAB, PAKISTAN.
HAQ, Mr. Nadeem, BAcc ACA *2002;* 15 Deaconsbank Gardens, Thornliebank, GLASGOW, G46 7UP.
HAQ, Mr. Salman-Ul, FCA *1982;* Level 13, 167 Macquarie Street, SYDNEY, NSW 2000, AUSTRALIA.
•**HAQ, Mr. Shaukat Hamid, FCA** *1973;* HAQ AND CO, Via Lombardia 30, 00187 ROME, ITALY.
HAQ, Mr. Sohail Atta, BA ACA *1991;* Bromford Housing Group Exchange Court, Bradbourne Avenue Wolverhampton Business Park, WOLVERHAMPTON, WV10 6AU.
•**HAQ, Mr. Vasim Ul, BA FCA ACMA** *1987;* with RSM Tenon Audit Limited, 66 Chiltern Street, LONDON, W1U 4JT.
•**HAQ, Mrs. Zabila, BSc ACA** *1998;* Javed & Co, 109 Hagley Road, Edgbaston, BIRMINGHAM, B16 8LA.
HAQUANI, Mr. Mohammed Kaleemuddin, FCA *1963;* 16 College Street, ST. ANDREWS, FIFE, KY16 9AA.
HAQUE, Mr. Anwarul, BSc ACA *2001;* Flat 1, Newminster Court, 47 The Ridgeway, ENFIELD, MIDDLESEX, EN2 8QW.
HAQUE, Mr. Majharul, BA ACA *1993;* 24A Clarence Road, LONDON, SW19 8QE.
•**HAQUE, Mr. Mohammed Atiqul, ACA** *2009;* MAH Professional Services Limited, 80-83 Long Lane, Barbican, LONDON, EC1A 9ET.
HAQUE, Mr. Mohammed Naved, BA(Hons) ACA *2002;* B D G Workfutures, 11-33 St. John Street, LONDON, EC1M 4AA.
HAQUE, Mr. Sajjad Akhtar, BA ACA *1994;* 44 Anne Boleyns Walk, SUTTON, SM3 8DF.
HAQUE, Mr. Sana-ul, BA(Hons) ACA *2003;* 201 Church Road, Harold Wood, ROMFORD, RM3 0SA.
HAQUE, Mrs. Shirin, BA ACA *1989;* Suite 14 5th Floor, Khyber Plaza Blue Area, ISLAMABAD, PAKISTAN.
HAQUE, Mr. Zahirul, BA ACA *2002;* Nationwide Bldg Soc, Kings Park Road, Moulton Park Industrial Estate, NORTHAMPTON, NN3 6NW.
HAQUE, Mr. Zaigham Abdul, ACA *1988;* P.O. Box 213786, DUBAI, UNITED ARAB EMIRATES.
HARALAMBOUS, Mr. Andrew, BA ACA *1999;* BOMMERSHEIMER WEG 9, 61348 BAD HOMBURG, GERMANY.
HARALAMBOUS, Ms. Chloe, BA ACA *2003;* Po Box 27127, 1642 NICOSIA, CYPRUS.
HARALAMBOUS, Mr. Haralambos, ACA *2008;* 3 Orfeos Street, Ayios Domedios, 2370 NICOSIA, CYPRUS.
HARALAMBOUS, Ms. Ivi, BSc ACA *2000;* Pobox 27127, CY1642 NICOSIA, CYPRUS.
HARALDSSON, Mr. Tom Johan Henrik, ACA *2008;* 6 r Guillaume Schneider, L-2522 LUXEMBOURG, LUXEMBOURG.
HARAN, Mrs. Abigail, BSc ACA *2001;* 37 Gatesden Road, Fetcham, LEATHERHEAD, KT22 9QW.
HARANGOZO, Miss. Ilona, BSc ACA *2011;* 2 Maple Court, Westover Gardens, Westbury-on-Trym, BRISTOL, BS9 3LD.
•**HARBACH, Mr. Paul John, FCA** *1976;* HTCA, Stepple Business Centrel, Catherton Road, Cleobury Mortimer, KIDDERMINSTER, WORCESTERSHIRE DY14 0LH.
HARBARD, Mr. Paul Joseph, FCA *1975;* 42 Ebury Bridge Road, LONDON, SW1W 8PZ.
•**HARBEN, Mr. David Antony, BSc FCA** *1993;* Rawcliffe & Co, West Park House, 7/9 Wilkinson Avenue, BLACKPOOL, LANCASHIRE, FY3 9XG.
•**HARBEN, Mr. James Richard, FCA** *1967;* with Harben Barker Limited, Drayton Court, Drayton Road, SOLIHULL, WEST MIDLANDS, B90 4NG.
HARBER, Mr. David Mark, FCA *1977;* 23 Reeveswood, Eccleston, CHORLEY, PR7 5RS.
HARBER, Mr. James Ian, FCA *1969;* 101 Oak Avenue, Bare, MORECAMBE, LANCASHIRE, LA4 6HY.
•**HARBER, Mr. Lionel Charles, BA FCA** *1967;* (Tax Fac), Lionel C Harber, 37 Charnhill Drive, Mangotsfield, BRISTOL, BS16 9JR.
HARBER, Mr. Neil Trevor, FCA *1969;* Priory Garth, 417 Streetsbrook Road, SOLIHULL, B91 1RE.
•**HARBER, Mr. Nicholas Edward, BSc FCA CF** *1998;* Baker Tilly Tax & Advisory Services LLP, Hartwell House, 55-61 Victoria Street, BRISTOL, BS1 6AD. See also Baker Tilly Corporate Finance LLP
HARBIDGE, Mr. Paul Michael, BA FCA *1976;* The Barn Woodside Farm, Barton Gate Barton under Needwood, BURTON-ON-TRENT, STAFFORDSHIRE, DE13 8AP.
HARBOR, Mr. John Liming, FCA *1970;* 24 Guildown Avenue, GUILDFORD, SURREY, GU2 4HB.
HARBORD, Mr. David Christopher, BA ACA *1987;* 6 Laurel Drive, BROADSTONE, DORSET, BH18 8LJ.
HARBORD, Miss. Kim Louise, BSC ACA *2009;* First Floor Flat, 76 Upper Tollington Park, LONDON, N4 4NB.
HARBORD, Mr. Michael Graham, BA ACA *1994;* Grufskeri, Butterrow Lane, STROUD, GLOUCESTERSHIRE, GL5 2NH.
HARBORD, Mr. Philip Richard, ACA *1987;* Walton House, The Cross, Walton, LUTTERWORTH, LEICESTERSHIRE, LE17 5RJ.
HARBORNE, Mrs. Eithne Faith Nixon, BSc FCA *1986;* with Sherwood Harborne Ltd, Sherwood House, 548 Birmingham Road, Lydiate Ash, BROMSGROVE, B61 0HT.
•**HARBORNE, Mr. Garry Paul, FCA** *1983;* Sherwood Harborne Ltd, Sherwood House, 548 Birmingham Road, Lydiate Ash, BROMSGROVE, B61 0HT.
HARBORNE, Mr. Richard, BSc ACA *1996;* 20 Raymond Road, NEUTRAL BAY, NSW 2089, AUSTRALIA.
HARBOTTLE, Mr. Derek John, FCA *1973;* 31 Green Street, Brockworth, GLOUCESTER, GL3 4LU.
•**HARBOTTLE, Mr. Ian Anthony, FCA** *1973;* (Tax Fac), 21 St. Thomas Street, BRISTOL, BS1 6JS. See also Jordans International Limited
HARBOUR, Mr. Adrian, ACA *2009;* Cameron House La Ruette de la Tour, Castel, GUERNSEY, GY5 7TR.
HARBOUR, Miss. Christina Louise, BA(Hons) ACA *2000;* Bay Tree Cottage, 7 Henley Street, Luddesdown, GRAVESEND, KENT, DA13 0XB.
•**HARBOUR, Mr. Grahame James, BA FCA** *1988;* Grahame J Harbour Limited, 1 Windrush Road, Keynsham, BRISTOL, BS31 1QL.
HARBOUR, Mr. Karel Frederick, BSc FCA *1975;* Rostherne Florance Lane, Groombridge, TUNBRIDGE WELLS, TN3 9SH.
HARBOUR, Mr. Ronald James, FCA *1961;* Cranford, 2 Connaught Close, SIDMOUTH, EX10 8TU. (Life Member)
HARBOUR, Mr. Timothy John, BSc ACA *2007;* 2 Easton Road, WITHAM, CM8 2DW.
HARBRIDGE, Mr. Simon Richard, BSc ACA *1992;* Charlbury House, Marlbrook Lane, Sale Green, DROITWICH, WORCESTERSHIRE, WR9 7LW.
HARBRON, Mr. Anthony Geoffrey, FCA *1969;* Brycefields, Hollington Lane, Stramshall, UTTOXETER, ST14 5EP.
HARBRON, Miss. Melanie Charlotte, BA(Hons) ACA *2004;* PO Box 30464, SEVEN MILE BEACH, GRAND CAYMAN, KY1-1202, CAYMAN ISLANDS.
HARBUT, Mr. David John, FCA FCMA FCT JDipMA *1959;* 1 Hoe Meadow, BEACONSFIELD, HP9 1TD. (Life Member)
HARBY, Miss. Lucy Elaine, BCom ACA *1990;* 3 Beaks Hill Road, BIRMINGHAM, B38 8BJ.
•**HARBY, Mr. Norman Eric, FCA** *1976;* Godwin Harby, Grays Court, 5 Nursery Road, BIRMINGHAM, B15 3JX.
HARCOMBE, Mrs. Sophie, BEng ACA *2002;* 10 Mill Field, Broadsword Park, Ilchester, YEOVIL, SOMERSET, BA22 8WG.

HARCOURT VERNON, Miss. Anne, BA FCA *1976;* (Tax Fac), 30 Felix Road, WALTON-ON-THAMES, KT12 2LB.

HARCOURT-WEBSTER, Mr. Julian Richard John, MA ACA *1987;* 8 Blenheim Gardens, KINGSTON-UPON-THAMES, KT2 7BW.

HARCOURT WILLIAMS, Mr. Martin Frederic, MA FCA *1961;* The Old Forge, East Hanningfield, CHELMSFORD, CM3 8AA. (Life Member)

HARD, Mr. James Alexander, BA ACA *2002;* 1 Yarm Court Road, LEATHERHEAD, KT22 8NY.

HARDACRE, Mrs. Sarah Judith, MA ACA *1993;* 172 North Road, BELFAST, BT4 3DJ.

HARDACRE, Mrs. Simone Elizabeth, BA(Hons) ACA *2003;* Abacus Trust Company Ltd, Sixty Circular Road, Circular Road, Douglas, ISLE OF MAN, IM1 1SA.

HARDAKER, Mr. Craig, MEng ACA *1997;* 15 Fir Rigg Drive, Marske-by-the-Sea, REDCAR, TS11 6BT.

•HARDAKER, Mr. Philip John, FCA *1970;* 1 Granville Road, SEVENOAKS, TN13 1ES.

•HARDBATTLE, Mr. John Francis, FCA *1972;* Hard Battles, The Cottage Limby Hall Lane, Swannington, COALVILLE, LE67 8QH.

HARDBATTLE, Mr. Michael Ian John, BSc ACA *2007;* with PricewaterhouseCoopers LLP, Cornwall Court, 19 Cornwall Street, BIRMINGHAM, B3 2DT.

HARDCASTLE, Mr. Graham Stuart, BA ACA *1989;* 22 Jerome Drive, ST. ALBANS, HERTFORDSHIRE, AL3 4LX.

•HARDCASTLE, Mr. John, FCA *1970;* (Tax Fac), John Hardcastle, 3 Church Green, Stanford in the Vale, FARINGDON, OXFORDSHIRE, SN7 8LQ.

HARDCASTLE, Mr. John Kenneth Willis, BSc ACA *1988;* Ridgecote 26 Dawstone Road, WIRRAL, MERSEYSIDE, CH60 0BU.

HARDCASTLE, Mr. John Neil, FCA *1965;* Elmwood House, Le Mont Cambrai, St. Lawrence, JERSEY, JE3 1JN.

HARDCASTLE, Mrs. Susan Deborah, BA ACA *1989;* 22 Jerome Drive, ST. ALBANS, AL3 4LX.

HARDCASTLE, Mr. Timothy William, BA ACA *1991;* 3 Walnut Tree Grove, Brampton, HUNTINGDON, PE28 4UG.

HARDCASTLE, Mr. Trevor, FCA *1954;* Fern Cottage, 9 Main Street, Ebberston, SCARBOROUGH, NORTH YORKSHIRE, YO13 9NR. (Life Member)

•HARDEN, Mr. Christopher Paul, FCA *1976;* (Tax Fac), Christopher Harden Ltd, 122a Nelson Road, TWICKENHAM, TW2 7AY.

HARDEN, Mr. John Albert Hilary, FCA *1957;* Kingsbrook, 12 Park Road, WOKING, GU22 7BW. (Life Member)

•HARDEN, Mr. Kim Peter, BA FCA *1988;* (Tax Fac), Accountancy Plus (Dorset) Limited, 4 New Street, Marnhull, STURMINSTER NEWTON, DT10 1PY.

HARDEN, Mr. Paul James, MA ACA CTA *1997;* (Tax Fac), with KPMG LLP, 15 Canada Square, LONDON, E14 5GL.

HARDEN, Mr. Robert John, MA ACA *1999;* Windy Farm, Capel Road, Bentley, IPSWICH, IP9 2DL.

•HARDEN, Mr. Trevor Thomas, FCA *1980;* Trevor T. Harden FCA, 35 Meadow Way, Farnborough Park, ORPINGTON, BR6 8LN.

HARDER, Ms. Susan Elizabeth, BA ACA *1993;* 8 Elgin Road, CROYDON, CR0 6XA.

HARDERN, Mrs. Carole Joy, MBA BA ACA *1986;* 64 The Fairway, Fixby, HUDDERSFIELD, HD2 2HU.

HARDIE, Mr. Alistair Peter, BSc FCA MCIM *1976;* Waveney Cottage, Hillgrove, Lurgashall, PETWORTH, GU28 9EW.

HARDIE, Mr. Charles Jeremy Mawdesley, CBE MA BPhil FCA *1969;* 23 Arlington Road, Mornington Crescent, LONDON, NW1 7ER.

HARDIE, Mr. Christopher Richard, BA ACA *1984;* 125 Old Broad Street, LONDON, EC2N 1AR.

HARDIE, Mrs. Claire Elizabeth, BSc(Hons) ACA *2001;* 4923 26th Street North, ARLINGTON, VA 22207, UNITED STATES.

HARDIE, Mr. Martin Alexander, BA FCA *1988;* 88 Cranley Gardens, LONDON, N10 3AH.

HARDIE, Mr. Nicholas Alan Scott, BA ACA *1980;* Hammerson Plc, 10 Grosvenor Street, LONDON, W1K 4BJ.

HARDIE, Mr. Peter Keir, BA FCA *1973;* 53A Chestnut Drive, LEIGH, WN7 3JW.

HARDIE, Mr. Reginald George, FCA FCT *1964;* 1 Ladybarn Crescent, Bramhall, STOCKPORT, SK7 2EZ.

HARDIE, Mr. Richard William John, MA FCA *1974;* U B S Investment Bank, 1Finsbury Avenue, LONDON, EC2M 2PP.

HARDIE, Mr. William Peter Fraser, ACA *1988;* 8 Dalesway, Eldwick, BINGLEY, BD16 3DU.

•HARDIE-BROWN, Mrs. Gael Mary, MBS BSc ACA *1987;* Hardie Brown & Co, Hilltown, BALLYMITTY, COUNTY WEXFORD, IRELAND.

•HARDIMAN, Mr. David Keith, BSc FCA *1984;* David K. Hardiman, 36-38 Meadow Street, WESTON-SUPER-MARE, AVON, BS23 1QQ.

HARDIMAN, Mr. Mark, BEng ACA *1999;* Flat 10, 14 Martello Street, LONDON, E8 3PE.

HARDIMAN, Mrs. Sian Elizabeth Wynn, LLB ACA *2001;* 5 Bewick Place, Hampton Vale, PETERBOROUGH, PE7 8EW.

HARDIMAN-EVANS, Mr. David John Gwyn, BA FCA *1994;* Cherwyn, Ockham Road South, East Horsley, LEATHERHEAD, SURREY, KT24 6SG.

HARDING, Mr. Alan, BSc ACA *1999;* 45 Stocks Lane, Boughton, CHESTER, CH3 5TE.

HARDING, Mr. Alvin Arthur, FCA *1967;* with Freeport Trust Company Limited, 4 Athol Street, Douglas, ISLE OF MAN, IM1 1LD.

HARDING, Mr. Andrew Howard, BSc ACA *1987;* 5 Ashley Close, WALTON-ON-THAMES, SURREY, KT12 1BJ.

HARDING, Mr. Andrew William, BSc ACA *1990;* North Barn, Brington Road, Old Weston, HUNTINGDON, CAMBRIDGESHIRE, PE28 5LP.

HARDING, Mr. Anthony Richard, FCA *1968;* 5 Broadfield House, 156 Noak Hill Road, BILLERICAY, CM12 9XA.

•①HARDING, Mr. Barrie Dunkin, FCA FIPA FABRP *1971;* MEMBER OF COUNCIL, Barrie Harding & Co, Hollyoak House, Mead Pastures, Woodham Walter, MALDON, CM9 6PY.

•HARDING, Mr. Barry Raymond, FCA *1970;* (Tax Fac), Harding Accountants Limited, 23 Frogmore Park Drive, Blackwater, CAMBERLEY, GU17 0PG.

HARDING, Mr. Brian Harry, ACA *1980;* 2 Nursery Road, Hook End, BRENTWOOD, Essex, CM15 0HE.

HARDING, Mr. Brian William, FCA *1951;* 17 Sovereign Way, RYDE, PO33 3DL. (Life Member)

HARDING, Mrs. Candace Melloney, BA ACA *1982;* 5 Ashley Close, WALTON-ON-THAMES, SURREY, KT12 1BJ.

HARDING, Mrs. Clare Helen, MA ACA *1996;* 225 George Street, SYDNEY, NSW 2000, AUSTRALIA.

HARDING, Mrs. Clare Louise, BA ACA *1993;* 28555 La Maravilla, LAGUNA NIGUEL, CA 92677, UNITED STATES.

HARDING, Mr. Craig, BA(Hons) ACA *2003;* with Deloitte LLP, 5 Callaghan Square, CARDIFF, CF10 5BT.

HARDING, Dr. David, DPhil MSci ACA *2011;* 51 South Primrose Hill, CHELMSFORD, CM1 2RF.

HARDING, Mr. David Henry, FCA *1955;* 25 The Fairway, UPMINSTER, ESSEX, RM14 1BS.

HARDING, Mr. David John, BA FCA *1977;* 1 Lon Aeron, RHYL, LL18 4JZ.

HARDING, Mr. David Robert, MA ACA *1998;* 16 The Ruddings, Wheldrake, YORK, YO19 6BP.

HARDING, Mr. David Robert, BA ACA *1992;* I T W Foils Kays & Kears Industrial Estate, Blaenavon, PONTYPOOL, GWENT, NP4 9AZ.

•①HARDING, Mr. David Samuel Alexander, BSc FCA *1989;* with Deloitte LLP, Hill House, 1 Little New Street, LONDON, EC4A 3TR.

HARDING, Mr. Derek John, BSc ACA *1998;* Drawback House, 50 Rotherfield Road, HENLEY-ON-THAMES, OXFORDSHIRE, RG9 1NN.

HARDING, Mr. Dominic David, BA(Econ) ACA *2000;* 4 The Green, Marcham, ABINGDON, OXFORDSHIRE, OX13 6NE.

HARDING, Mr. Edward Andrew, BA ACA *2000;* Flat 1, 15 Kings Gardens, HOVE, EAST SUSSEX, BN3 2PG.

HARDING, Mr. Edward James Douglas, MA ACA *1996;* Icon Corporate Finance, 5 Kings Court Little King Street, BRISTOL, BS1 4HW.

HARDING, Mr. Frederic Orriss, FCA *1958;* Edgehill, 108 Wodeland Avenue, GUILDFORD, GU2 4LD. (Life Member)

•HARDING, Mr. Gary, BSc ACA *1992;* Ernst & Young LLP, 100 Barbirolli Square, MANCHESTER, M2 3EY. See also Ernst & Young Europe LLP

•HARDING, Mr. Gary John, FCA *1981;* Gary J. Harding, 24 Brickfield Avenue, Leverstock Green, HEMEL HEMPSTEAD, HP3 8NP. See also GJH Accountants Ltd

HARDING, Mr. Gerald Dudley, BCom FCA *1955;* 1 Regency House, Newbold Terrace, LEAMINGTON SPA, CV32 4HD. (Life Member)

HARDING, Mr. Gilbert Ernest Frank, MA FCA *1954;* 4 Hill Top Lane, Ness, NESTON, CH64 4EL. (Life Member)

HARDING, Mr. Graham David, MBA BA ACA *1993;* Future Publishing Ltd, 30 Monmouth Street, BATH, BA1 2BW.

HARDING, Mr. Graham Leslie, BSc FCA *1972;* 12 Limehayes Road, OKEHAMPTON, DEVON, EX20 1NS.

HARDING, Mr. Harold Michael Denton, BSc FCA *1977;* Misty Meadows, Rednal, West Felton, OSWESTRY, SHROPSHIRE, SY11 4HR.

HARDING, Mr. Ian, BA ACA *1986;* 82 Beaconsfield Way, Earley, READING, RG6 5UX.

•HARDING, Mr. Ian, FCA *1980;* (Tax Fac), Gilpin and Harding, 15 St. Johns Place, Birtley, CHESTER LE STREET, COUNTY DURHAM, DH3 2PW.

HARDING, Mr. Ian, BCom ACA *1981;* Jasmine Cottage, Eglington Road, Tilford, FARNHAM, GU10 2DH.

HARDING, Mr. Ian Andrew, FCA *1988;* Oldenway, 80 Thorpe Hall Avenue, SOUTHEND-ON-SEA, SS1 3AS.

HARDING, Mr. Ian John, BSc ACA CTA *1999;* with Smith & Williamson Ltd, Old Library Chambers, 21 Chipper Lane, SALISBURY, SP1 1BG.

HARDING, Mrs. Jacqueline Ann, BSc ACA *1986;* 2 The Parklands, South Cave, BROUGH, HU15 2EL.

HARDING, Mr. James Arthur, BA ACA *1999;* Little Keysford, Treemans Road, Lewes Road, Horsted Keynes, HAYWARDS HEATH, WEST SUSSEX RH17 7EA.

HARDING, Mr. James Christopher, BSc ACA *1996;* 98A Avenue Road, MOSMAN, NSW 2088, AUSTRALIA.

HARDING, Mrs. Janet, BSc ACA *1989;* New Mill House, Research Machines Plc, 183 Milton Park Milton, ABINGDON, OXFORDSHIRE, OX14 4SE.

HARDING, Mr. Jason Keith, ACA *1995;* 15 Beaulieu Crescent, CARINDALE, QLD 4152, AUSTRALIA.

•HARDING, Mr. Joel Timothy, ACA ATII CTA *1999;* Field Cottage, Ashotts Lane, Chartridge, CHESHAM, BUCKINGHAMSHIRE, HP5 2TY.

HARDING, Mr. John, FCA *1973;* 4137 West 13 Avenue, VANCOUVER V6R 2T5, BC, CANADA.

HARDING, Mr. John Trevor, BSc ACA *1979;* Jelf Group Plc Unit 1500 Bristol Parkway North, Newbrick Road Stoke Gifford, BRISTOL, BS34 8YU.

HARDING, Mr. Julian St John, BSc FCA MSI ASIP *1994;* 20 Woodfields, SEVENOAKS, KENT, TN13 2RA.

HARDING, Mrs. Julie Anne, BSc ACA *1987;* Highfield View, Mill Lane, WEDMORE, BS28 4DW.

•HARDING, Mr. Kevin John, BSc FCA *1999;* RGL LLP, 8th Floor, Dashwood, 69 Old Broad Street, LONDON, EC2M 1QS.

HARDING, Mrs. Lorna Jane, BSc ACA *1995;* 43 Dirdene Gardens, EPSOM, KT17 4AZ.

•HARDING, Miss. Lorraine Marion, FCA *1988;* Harding & Co, Tiptree Cottage, 1 King Street, Markyate, ST. ALBANS, HERTFORDSHIRE AL3 8JY.

HARDING, Ms. Mairi Elizabeth, MA ACA *1999;* 16 Devonshire Park, READING, RG2 7DX.

•HARDING, Mr. Malcolm Christian, BSc FCA *1984;* with KPMG LLP, 1 The Embankment, Neville Street, LEEDS, LS1 4DW.

HARDING, Mr. Marc, BSc ACA *1997;* 35 Stroud Green Lane, Stubbington, FAREHAM, HAMPSHIRE, PO14 2HS.

HARDING, Mr. Mark David, BSc ACA *1995;* with KPMG LLP, 100 Temple Street, BRISTOL, BS1 6AG.

HARDING, Mr. Mark James, BA ACA *2003;* Holly View Darlington Road, Long Newton, STOCKTON-ON-TEES, CLEVELAND, TS21 1PE.

HARDING, Mr. Michael David, BA ACA *1994;* Summerlea, 12 Station Road, Hurst Green, ETCHINGHAM, EAST SUSSEX, TN19 7PL.

•HARDING, Mr. Michael Howard, BA FCA *1991;* Premiair Aviation Group Ltd, Business Aviation Centre, Blackbushe Airport, CAMBERLEY, SURREY, GU17 9LG. See also J E R Accounting Services Limited

•HARDING, Mr. Michael J, ACA FCCA *2008;* Brooks & Co, Mid-Day Court, 20-24 Brighton Road, SUTTON, SM2 5BN.

HARDING, Mr. Michael John, FCA *1956;* 1 Pickhill Oast, Smallhythe Road, TENTERDEN, TN30 7LZ. (Life Member)

•HARDING, Mr. Michael John, BSc FCA *1988;* 41 Hillcrest Avenue, MONA VALE, NSW 2103, AUSTRALIA.

•HARDING, Mr. Michael John, FCA *1971;* M J Harding, 7 Broad Elms Lane, Ecclesall, SHEFFIELD, S11 9RQ.

HARDING, Mr. Michael John, MA FCA *1962;* Well Waters Chatter Alley, Dogmersfield, HOOK, RG27 8SS. (Life Member)

HARDING, Mr. Michael Lawrence, FCA *1973;* Bramley House, Lovetts Plc Bramley House The Guildway, Old Portsmouth Road Artington, GUILDFORD, GU3 1LR.

HARDING, Mr. Michael Spencer, MSc BSc ACA *2007;* 17 Hillsale Piece, Littlemore, OXFORD, OX4 4GG.

•HARDING, Mr. Neil Charles, BA FCA *1987;* Bradshaw Johnson, 13 Bancroft, HITCHIN, HERTFORDSHIRE, SG5 1JQ. See also Bradshaw Johnson & Co

HARDING, Mr. Neil Charles Iliff, MA ACA *1985;* 3 I Group, 16 Palace Street, LONDON, SW1E 5JD.

HARDING, Mr. Neil Craig, BA(Hons) ACA *2003;* 32 St. Audreys Close, Histon, CAMBRIDGE, CB24 9JX.

HARDING, Mr. Nicholas David, MA ACA *2004;* Thomson Reuters Ltd Aldgate House, 33 Aldgate High Street, LONDON, EC3N 1DL.

HARDING, Mr. Nicholas James, BA FCA *1976;* Sciberscross Lodge, Strath Brora, ROGART, IV28 3YQ. (Life Member)

HARDING, Mr. Nicholas John, MA FCA *1974;* PS Co Ltd, Unit B, 1-3 Acre Road, READING, RG2 0SU.

HARDING, Mr. Paul Donkin, BA ACA *1988;* 1 Saddlers Mews, 34 St John's Road, Hampton Wick, KINGSTON UPON THAMES, KT1 4AW.

HARDING, Mr. Paul Ifold, FCA *1971;* P.O.Box 504, LONEHILL, 2062, SOUTH AFRICA.

HARDING, Mr. Peter Charles, BSc FCA *1983;* Birse Rail Ltd, Lyndon House, 58-62 Hagley Road, BIRMINGHAM, B16 8PE.

HARDING, Mr. Peter James, FCA *1978;* 7 High View, Darras Hall, NEWCASTLE UPON TYNE, NE20 9ET.

HARDING, Mr. Peter Martin, FCA *1952;* 11 Mere Close, Mountsorrel, LOUGHBOROUGH, LE12 7BP. (Life Member)

HARDING, Mr. Raymond, BSc ACA *1979;* University College London, Estates & Faculties Division, Gower Street, LONDON, WC1E 6BT.

•HARDING, Mr. Richard Andrew, BSc ACA *1998;* Ernst & Young LLP, 100 Barbirolli Square, MANCHESTER, M2 3EY. See also Ernst & Young Europe LLP

HARDING, Mr. Richard Anthony, BEng ACA *1997;* 30F AIA Central, 1 Connaught Road, CENTRAL, HONG KONG ISLAND, HONG KONG SAR.

HARDING, Mr. Richard Clive, FCA *1971;* Risley, 25 Lime Avenue, CAMBERLEY, GU15 2BS.

•HARDING, Mr. Richard Samuel, FCA *1974;* (Tax Fac), Thomas Moffatt & Co Ltd, 3rd Floor, The Sion, Crown Glass Place, BRISTOL, BS48 1RB.

•①HARDING, Mr. Robert James, BSc ACA *2003;* 38 St. Pauls Road, LONDON, N1 2QW.

•HARDING, Mr. Robert Sydney, FCA *1976;* R S Harding Ltd, 15 High Street, Redbourn, ST. ALBANS, HERTFORDSHIRE, AL3 7LE.

HARDING, Mr. Robert William, BA ACA *1995;* 80 Bridge Villas, 199 Tang An Rood, Pudong, SHANGHAI 201203, CHINA.

HARDING, Mr. Robin Charles Trevor, BEng ACA *2000;* 19 Lucien Road, Wimbledon Park, LONDON, SW19 8EL.

HARDING, Miss. Samantha Gay Louise, BSc ACA *1992;* 19 Edward Road, DORCHESTER, DORSET, DT1 2HL.

HARDING, Mrs. Sarah Elisabeth, BSc ACA *1993;* 6 Ashwood, East Harptree, BRISTOL, BS40 6BW.

HARDING, Mr. Simon Alvin, BSc ACA CTA *1999;* 11 Fernhurst Road, LONDON, SW6 7JN.

HARDING, Mr. Simon Matthew, BSc FCA *1994;* with KPMG LLP, 333 Bay Street, Suite 4600, TORONTO M5H 2S5, ON, CANADA.

HARDING, Mr. Simon Robert, BSc ACA *1995;* 389 Ivydale Road, LONDON, SE15 3ED.

HARDING, Mr. Stephen, BSc FCA *1997;* with Beever and Struthers, St George's House, 215-219 Chester Road, MANCHESTER, M15 4JE.

•HARDING, Mr. Stephen John, BA ACA *1993;* 35 Newbury Gardens, Stoneleigh, EPSOM, SURREY, KT19 0NS.

•HARDING, Mr. Stephen John, FCA *1969;* (Tax Fac), HardingRedmans Limited, Bridge House, Court Road, SWANAGE, DORSET, BH19 1DX.

HARDING, Mr. Steve, BA ACA *2003;* 46 Gathorne Road, BRISTOL, BS3 1LU.

HARDING, Mr. Stuart John, BSc ACA *1989;* Rose Cottage, Soake Road, Denmead, WATERLOOVILLE, PO7 6HY.

•HARDING, Mr. Terry, BA FCA *1989;* KPMG LLP, 15 Canada Square, LONDON, E14 5GL. See also KPMG Europe LLP

HARDING, Mrs. Victoria Alice, BSc ACA *2004;* 1 Brocks Close, GODALMING, SURREY, GU7 1NA.

HARDING, Mr. William, BA ACA *2011;* C/O KPMG Cayman Islands, PO Box 493, GEORGE TOWN, KY1 1106, CAYMAN ISLANDS.

•**HARDING-EDGAR, Mr. Jeremy Peter Charles, MA FCA** *1980;* Eclipse Consultancy Limited, 9 Limes Road, BECKENHAM, KENT, BR3 6NS.
HARDINGHAM, Mr. Alan Robert, ACA *2006;* Thorne House Ferry Road, Surlingham, NORWICH, NR14 7AR.
HARDINGHAM, Mr. Dean, ACA *2010;* with PricewaterhouseCoopers LLP, 1 Embankment Place, LONDON, WC2N 6RH.
HARDINGHAM, Mrs. Eleanor Marie, BSc FCA *1979;* 1 Royle Close, Orton Longueville, PETERBOROUGH, PE2 7LN.
HARDINGHAM, Miss. Jennifer Anne, ACA *2009;* 46 Princes Street, Douglas, ISLE OF MAN, IM1 1BD.
HARDINGS, Mr. Alan Clive, BA ACA *1996;* 1 Maltings Close, Stewkley, LEIGHTON BUZZARD, LU7 0UN.
HARDISTY, Mrs. Anne Christine, BSc FCA *1978;* Hope Cottage, 33 Harris Lane, Shenley, RADLETT, WD7 9EF.
HARDISTY, Mr. Peter Weatherhead, FCA *1970;* Ash Grove, Pound Street, LYME REGIS, DORSET, DT7 3JA.
HARDISTY, Miss. Sarah, BA ACA *1999;* I N G Bank, 60 London Wall, LONDON, EC2M 5TQ.
HARDISTY, Mr. Stephen Christopher, MA FCA *1966;* Winsec Financial Services Ltd, 1 The Centre, Church Road, Tiptree, COLCHESTER, CO5 0HF.
HARDLESS, Mr. Alan Cedric, FCA *1958;* 18 Coleman Court, Station Road, CLACTON-ON-SEA, CO15 6PY. (Life Member)
•**HARDLESS, Mr. David Roderick, BA ACA** *1989;* Park Place Corporate Finance LLP, 19 Park Place, LEEDS, LS1 2SJ.
HARDLESS, Mrs. Julie Susan, BA FCA *1989;* Stud Hall, Back Lane, Sicklinghall, WETHERBY, NORTH YORKSHIRE, LS22 4BQ.
HARDLESS, Miss. Sally Mei Lin, BA ACA *1993;* with PricewaterhouseCoopers LLP, 1 Embankment Place, LONDON, WC2N 6RH.
HARDMAN, Mr. Alastair John, BA ACA *2002;* Whhite Ladies Cottage, 7 Pickets Yard, St Thomas Street, PENRYN, CORNWALL, TR10 8JR.
HARDMAN, Mr. Andrew James, ACA *2011;* 8 Deerfold, CHORLEY, PR7 1UH.
HARDMAN, Mr. Dennis John, FCA *1968;* Thalassa, Porthilly, Rock, WADEBRIDGE, CORNWALL, PL27 6JX. (Life Member)
HARDMAN, Mr. Eric Robert, BA FCA *1967;* 32 Aintree Road, Little Lever, BOLTON, BL3 1EZ.
HARDMAN, Mr. Graham Arthur, FCA *1977;* Student Union Building, University of Central Lancashire, PRESTON, PR1 2HE.
HARDMAN, Mr. Graham Arthur Graham, MBA FCA *1965;* 151 Rideau Terrace, OTTAWA K1M 0Z4, ON, CANADA.
HARDMAN, Mr. James Malcolm Innes, BSc ACA *1993;* 14 Emanuel Avenue, LONDON, W3 6JH.
HARDMAN, Mr. John Andrew, ACA *1983;* Millbrook Cottage, Off Gateback Road, Endmoor, KENDAL, LA8 0HJ.
HARDMAN, Mr. John David, ACA *2008;* Level 28, Barclays Bank Plc, 1 Churchill Place, LONDON, E14 5HP.
HARDMAN, Mr. John Derrick, BSc ACA *1990;* 44 Girdwood Road, LONDON, SW18 5QS.
HARDMAN, Mr. John Nimrod, BCom FCA FRSA *1966;* Hillside, Spofforth Hill, WETHERBY, LS22 4SF.
HARDMAN, Mr. Mark David, BSc ACA *2004;* 5 Finbeck Way, Lower Earley, READING, RG6 4AH.
HARDMAN, Mrs. Mei Shuen, BA ACA *1996;* 7th Floor St Albans House, 57-59 Haymarket, LONDON, SW1Y 4QX.
•**HARDMAN, Mr. Michael Richard, FCA** *1963;* (Tax Fac), Michael Hardman, Oak House, Botley Road, CHESHAM, BUCKINGHAMSHIRE, HP5 1XG.
HARDMAN, Mr. Nicholas John, BSc ACA *1992;* Rosewood, Fearn Close, East Horsley, LEATHERHEAD, KT24 6AD.
HARDMAN, Mr. Nigel Stuart, FCA *1975;* Horwood Homewares Ltd, Avonmouth Way, BRISTOL, BS11 9HX.
HARDMAN, Mr. Paul Gareth, BSc(Hons) ACA *2004;* Netgear International Limited, Floor 1 Building 3, University Technology Centre, Curraheen Road, CORK, COUNTY CORK IRELAND.
HARDMAN, Mr. Roger Ratcliffe, FCA *1969;* The Barn, The Wildlife Trust The Barn, Berkeley Drive Bamber Bridge, PRESTON, PR5 6BY.
HARDMAN, Mrs. Sara Genine, BA ACA *1998;* 36 Falcon Road, BINGLEY, WEST YORKSHIRE, BD16 4DW.
•**HARDMAN, Mr. Thomas Martin, FCA** *1970;* Bay View Pen y Bryn Estate, Mynytho, PWLLHELI, GWYNEDD, LL53 7SE.
HARDON, Miss. Wendy Richardson, MA ACA *1990;* 6 Adam Drive, SINGAPORE 289966, SINGAPORE.
•**HARDOON, Mr. Henry, BSC ACA** *2008;* 18 Connaught Drive, LONDON, NW11 6BJ.
•**HARDS, Mr. Adrian James, FCA CTA** *1984;* (Tax Fac), Hards Tax Services Limited, Stanford House, Stanford Close, Frampton Cotterell, BRISTOL, BS36 2DG.
HARDS, Mr. Darryl Peter, ACA *2008;* with Deloitte LLP, Global House, High Street, CRAWLEY, RH10 1DL.
HARDS, Mr. David, ACA *1979;* (Tax Fac), Deutsche Bank A G, Prince George House, 20 Finsbury Circus, LONDON, EC2M 1NB.
HARDS, Mr. David Anthony, BA ACA *1991;* 164 Old Bath Road, CHELTENHAM, GL53 7DR.
HARDS, Mr. George Walter Patrick, BA ACA *1994;* Windyridge, 14 Moira Road, ASHBY-DE-LA-ZOUCH, LE65 2GA.
HARDWICK, Miss. Amy Victoria, BA ACA *2010;* Flat 3 Faroe, Gotts Road, LEEDS, LS12 1DF.
HARDWICK, Mr. David James, BSc ACA MAAT *2009;* 62 Weldon Road, Broadheath, ALTRINCHAM, CHESHIRE, WA14 4HG.
HARDWICK, Mr. John Frederick, BA FCA *1992;* Pailcare Ltd, Wolverton Depot, Stratford Road, Wolverton, MILTON KEYNES, MK12 5NT.
•**HARDWICK, Mr. Nicholas Andrew, BA FCA** *1989;* (Tax Fac), Hardwicks Accountants Ltd, Sarsfield House, Gillott Lane, Wickersley, ROTHERHAM, S66 1EH. See also Hardwicks
HARDWICK, Mr. Paul Edwin, FCA *1980;* Wyke Farms Ltd, White House Farm, Wyke Champflower, BRUTON, BA10 0PU.
HARDWICK, Mr. Paul Rene, FCA *1983;* (Tax Fac), Unit 6 Littlers Point, Second Avenue Trafford Park, MANCHESTER, M17 1LT.
•**HARDWICK, Mr. Philip Andrew, FCA CF** *1979;* Victoria Accountancy Limited, 3 St Augustines Mansions, Bloomburg Street, LONDON, SW1V 2RG.
HARDWICK, Miss. Stephanie Jane, BSc ACA *1989;* Shaw Group UK Ltd, Stores Road, DERBY, DERBYSHIRE, DE21 4BG.
•**HARDWICK, Ms. Stephanie Jane, BSc FCA** *1994;* (Tax Fac), The 41GP Partnership, 41 Great Portland Street, LONDON, W1W 7LA. See also The 41GP Partnership LLP
HARDWICK, Mr. Steven John, BSc ACA *1985;* Larsen & Ross Ltd, Hillside Villas, INVERNESS, IV2 3ES.
HARDWICK, Mr. William Derek, FCA *1950;* 22A Brookside Bar, CHESTERFIELD, S40 3PJ. (Life Member)
HARDWICK, Ms. Zoe Christina, MA(Oxon) ACA *2001;* Griechenplatz 22, D-81545 MUNICH, GERMANY.
HARDWICK SMITH, Mr. Martin Jonathan, FCA CTA *1973;* Little Foxes, Beredens Lane, Great Warley, BRENTWOOD, ESSEX, CM13 3JB.
HARDWIDGE, Miss. Kathryn Jane, BA FCA *1997;* O2, 260 Bath Road, SLOUGH, SL1 4DX.
HARDY, Mr. Alan John, MA ACA *1990;* 43 Brook Hill, WOODSTOCK, OXFORDSHIRE, OX20 1XH.
HARDY, Mrs. Alice, BA(Hons) ACA *2003;* 7/53 Helena Street, RANDWICK, NSW 2031, AUSTRALIA.
•**HARDY, Mrs. Amanda Jayne, ACA** *1997;* AJH Accountancy, 10 Westgate Park, Hough, CREWE, CW2 5GY. See also AJH
HARDY, Mr. Andrew James, BSc ACA *1992;* Finn Laurens Associates Ltd, 6 Fife Road, KINGSTON UPON THAMES, SURREY, KT1 1SZ.
HARDY, Mr. Andrew Michael, FCA *1968;* 11 Ivy Drive, Sandiway, NORTHWICH, CW8 2NL.
HARDY, Mrs. Ann Marina, BA ACA *1993;* 7 Tideswell Close, Ravenshead, NOTTINGHAM, NG15 9EX.
HARDY, Mrs. Audrey Frances, ACA *1980;* Weylands, 58 Chalfont Road, Seer Green, BEACONSFIELD, HP9 2QP.
HARDY, Mr. Brian, BSc FCA MBA *1966;* 8 Bardwell Road, OXFORD, OX2 6SW.
HARDY, Mr. Brian James, BSc FCA *1978;* Orchard House 16 High Street Low Pittington, DURHAM, DH6 1BE.
HARDY, Miss. Carol Margaret, BA ACA *1996;* 6 Bawson Court, Gomersal, CLECKHEATON, WEST YORKSHIRE, BD19 4SA.
HARDY, Mr. Charles Michael, BA ACA *1994;* 5 Granville Gardens, NEWCASTLE UPON TYNE, NE2 1HL.
HARDY, Mr. Clive Frank, BSc ACA *2003;* Lloyds TSB Bank Plc, Tredegar Park, Pencarn Way, Duffryn, NEWPORT, GWENT NP10 8SB.
HARDY, Mr. David Johnson, BA ACA *1996;* 109 Emlyn Road, LONDON, W12 9TG.
HARDY, Mr. David Michael, BSc FCA *1983;* Rylston Bannerdown Road, Batheaston, BATH, BA1 7PL.
HARDY, Sir David William, Kt FCA *1952;* (Member of Council 1975 - 1978), 17 Cranmer Court, LONDON, SW3 3HN. (Life Member)
HARDY, Mr. Duncan Ralph, FCA *1981;* Ilex Contracts Ltd, 2 Russley Park Stables, Russley Park, Baydon, MARLBOROUGH, SN8 2JY.
HARDY, Mrs. Frederique, ACA *2004;* 24 Rustat Avenue, CAMBRIDGE, CB1 3PF.
HARDY, Mrs. Gemma, BA ACA *2007;* Avenue Theodore-Weber 22, 1208 GENEVA, SWITZERLAND.
HARDY, Mr. George Barry Conyers, FCA *1972;* Apartment 6, The Bourne, Townsend Lane, HARPENDEN, HERTFORDSHIRE, AL5 2PW.
HARDY, Mr. George James Allan, MA FCA *1966;* 9 Regents Park Terrace, LONDON, NW1 7EE.
HARDY, Mr. Graham, FCA *1963;* 2 Gate Close, Hawkchurch, AXMINSTER, DEVON, EX13 5TY.
HARDY, Mr. Graham Leslie, BSc FCA *1975;* 23 The Spinney, Bar Hill, CAMBRIDGE, CB23 8ST.
HARDY, Mrs. Helen, BSc ACA *2001;* Grosvenor Estate, Eaton Estate Office, Eaton Park, Eccleston, CHESTER, CH4 9ET.
HARDY, Mr. James, MSc ACA *2005;* 21 Gregory Street, ERMINGTON, NSW 2115, AUSTRALIA.
HARDY, Mr. James Oliver, MSc BSc ACA *2003;* 3 West End Avenue, PINNER, HA5 1BH.
HARDY, Miss. Jennifer, ACA *2009;* 23 Dovedale Gardens, Pendas Fields, LEEDS, LS15 8UP.
HARDY, Mr. John, BA FCA *1977;* New Court, St Swithins Lane, LONDON, EC4P 4DU.
HARDY, Mr. John Anthony, LLB ACA *1991;* 19 St. James Road, WALLASEY, MERSEYSIDE, CH45 9LR.
•**HARDY, Mr. John Philip, BA FCA** *1986;* Jolliffe Cork Hardy LLP, Market Place, OSSETT, WEST YORKSHIRE, WF5 8BQ.
HARDY, Mr. Jonathan Edward, BA(Hons) ACA *2003;* 55 Baker Street, CHELMSFORD, CM2 0SA.
HARDY, Mr. Jonathan Martin, BSc ACA *1994;* CIT Bank Limited, Peninsular House, 36 Monument Street, LONDON, EC3R 8LJ.
HARDY, Mr. Karl Thomas, BA ACA *2003;* Unit 2a, Hylton Park, SUNDERLAND, SR5 3HD.
•**HARDY, Mrs. Katharine Sarah, BSc ACA** *1991;* Sarah Hardy Accountancy, 2 Quarry Bank, LIGHTWATER, SURREY, GU18 5PE.
•**HARDY, Mr. Keith John, FCA** *1972;* Smith Pearman Limited, Hurst House, High Street, Ripley, WOKING, SURREY GU23 6AY. See also Smith Pearman
HARDY, Mrs. Lynn, BA(Hons) ACA *2002;* 12 Blackthorne Drive, Chingford, LONDON, E4 6LR.
HARDY, Mrs. Lynne Marie, BSc ACA *1982;* 18 Lucy Hall Drive, Baildon, SHIPLEY, BD17 5BG.
HARDY, Mr. Malcolm Keith, FCA *1962;* 26 Murdoch Road, WOKINGHAM, RG40 2DF.
HARDY, Mr. Mark David, BA ACA *1992;* SRPHL, South Riding Point Holding Ltd, PO Box F-42530, FREEPORT, BAHAMAS.
HARDY, Mrs. Mary Munro, BA FCA *1979;* 2 Heathwood Close, LEIGHTON BUZZARD, BEDFORDSHIRE, LU7 3DU.
HARDY, Mr. Matthew, BSc ACA *1989;* 12 Oakdene Way, TARPORLEY, CW6 0BU.
HARDY, Mr. Matthew David, ACA *2009;* Upper Flat, 49 Spencer Rise, LONDON, NW5 1AR.
HARDY, Mr. Michael John, BSc FCA *1992;* Kazakhmys Plc, 28 Samal -1, ALMATY 050051, KAZAKHSTAN.
•**HARDY, Mr. Michael Ronald, BA FCA** *1997;* with PricewaterhouseCoopers Oy, Itamerentori 2, PO Box 1015, HELSINKI, FIN-00100, FINLAND.
HARDY, Miss. Michelle Suzanne, BA ACA *1996;* Over Newbold Farm, Newbold Road, CHESTERFIELD, S41 9RP.
•**HARDY, Mr. Nigel James, BSc FCA** *1988;* (Tax Fac), Baker Tilly Tax & Advisory Services LLP, Hartwell House, 55-61 Victoria Street, BRISTOL, BS1 6AD. See also Baker Tilly UK Audit LLP
HARDY, Mr. Paul Emerson, BSc ACA *2002;* 66 Abbey Road, WYMONDHAM, NORFOLK, NR18 9BY.
HARDY, Mr. Paul James, BSc FCA CF *1985;* Hardy Transaction Management Ltd, Beehive Works, Milton Street, SHEFFIELD, S3 7WL.
•**HARDY, Mr. Paul Kevin, FCA** *1970;* P K Hardy Ltd, 12 Shropshire Close, MIDDLEWICH, CW10 9ES.
HARDY, Mrs. Paula Geraldine, BSc ACA *1993;* Camrie High Street, Brasted, WESTERHAM, TN16 1HS.
HARDY, Mr. Peter, BA(Hons) ACA *2011;* Spain Bros & Co, 87 St. Dunstans Street, CANTERBURY, CT2 8AE.
HARDY, Mr. Philip Geoffrey, BA ACA *2006;* Holly Bush Farm Pickmere Lane, Tabley, KNUTSFORD, CHESHIRE, WA16 0HP.
HARDY, Mrs. Rachel Jayne, BSc ACA *2005;* with BDO LLP, Arcadia House, Maritime Walk, Ocean Village, SOUTHAMPTON, SO14 3TL.
•**HARDY, Mr. Richard David, ACA** *1985;* (Tax Fac), Adkin Hardy LLP, The White House, Holberrow Green, REDDITCH, B96 6SE.
HARDY, Mr. Richard Evelyn Whittelle, MSc FCA *1980;* The Mill House, Iden, RYE, EAST SUSSEX, TN31 7PT.
•**HARDY, Mr. Richard James, BSc FCA** *1982;* Duncan & Toplis, 14 All Saints Street, STAMFORD, LINCOLNSHIRE, PE9 2PA.
•**HARDY, Mr. Roger Stuart, FCA** *1975;* (Tax Fac), Mills & Black, Derwent House, 141-143 Dale Road, MATLOCK, DE4 3LU.
HARDY, Mr. Ronald Cragg, FCA *1952;* Apartment 3, The Holly, The Woodlands, Drake Lane, DURSLEY, GLOUCESTERSHIRE GL11 4HH. (Life Member)
HARDY, Mr. Ronald Owen, FCA *1962;* 2 Charleston, IRVINE, CA 92620, UNITED STATES. (Life Member)
HARDY, Miss. Sarah Jane, ACA *2008;* 196 Evans Bay Parade, Roseneath, WELLINGTON 6021, NEW ZEALAND.
HARDY, Mr. Simon Alexander, BEng ACA AMCT *2002;* 10 La Seiva Terrace, La Seiva Road, MARAVAL, TRINIDAD AND TOBAGO.
•**HARDY, Mr. Simon Charles, BSc FCA** *1981;* Deloitte LLP, Hill House, 1 Little New Street, LONDON, EC4A 3TR. See also Deloitte & Touche LLP
HARDY, Mr. Simon Martin, BSc ACA *1991;* 62 Hendham Road, LONDON, SW17 7DQ.
HARDY, Mr. Stephen Nicholas, BSc FCA *1987;* Swiftcover.com, Walnut Tree Place, Send, WOKING, SURREY, GU23 7HL.
•**HARDY, Mr. Stuart Frederick, FCA** *1970;* Sharman Fielding, 9 University Road, LEICESTER, LE1 7RA. See also Price G.D. & Co
•**HARDY, Mr. Timothy Edward, BA ACA** *2006;* Smith Pearman Limited, Hurst House, High Street, Ripley, WOKING, SURREY GU23 6AY. See also Smith Pearman
HARDY, Miss. Vanessa Kay, BSc ACA *2005;* Warwick Court, 5 Paternoster Square, LONDON, EC4M 7BP.
HARDY, Mr. William Robert, BA ACA *1984;* 116 Munster Road, TEDDINGTON, TW11 9LW.
HARDY, Ms. Yvonne, MSc BA ACA *1982;* with Ernst & Young LLP, 1 More London Place, LONDON, SE1 2AF.
HARDY-WATMOUGH, Ms. Anna Marie, BA ACA *2005;* 15 Orchard Grove, MANCHESTER, M20 2LB.
HARE, Mr. Adrian David, FCA *1972;* Newquay Zoo, Trenance Park, NEWQUAY, CORNWALL, TR7 2LZ.
HARE, Mr. Alexander Edward, BA ACA *2009;* 65 Eland Road, LONDON, SW11 5JZ.
HARE, Miss. Alison Lorraine, ACA *1994;* 18b Hill Road, FAREHAM, PO16 8LA.
HARE, Miss. Christine Sarah, BSc ACA *1994;* 5 St. Pauls on The Green, HAYWARDS HEATH, WEST SUSSEX, RH16 3BF.
HARE, Mr. Christopher George, FCA *1968;* 4 South View, Somerhill Avenue, HOVE, BN3 1RJ.
HARE, Mr. David Andrew, BSc BEng ACA *1987;* Umbro International Ltd Umbro House, 5000 Lakeside, CHEADLE, CHESHIRE, SK8 3GQ.
HARE, Mr. David Charles Radford, FCA *1973;* 13777 Ballantyne Corporate Parkway, Suite 305, CHARLOTTE, NC 28277, UNITED STATES.
HARE, Mr. Dominic Michael, BA ACA *1995;* Estate Office, Blenheim Palace Grounds, WOODSTOCK, OXFORDSHIRE, OX20 1PS.
HARE, Mrs. Emma, BSc ACA *2004;* Glover & Co Unit 2 Hockliffe Business Centre, Watling Street Hockliffe, LEIGHTON BUZZARD, BEDFORDSHIRE, LU7 9NB.
HARE, Mr. John Christopher Bruce, FCA *1970;* Old Well Cottage, Sevenoaks Road, Ightham, SEVENOAKS, KENT, TN15 9DS.
HARE, Mr. John Dudley, ACA *1981;* Pawpots, Hardings Lane, ILKLEY, LS29 0DZ.
HARE, Mr. John Lindsay Radford, FCA *1968;* Netherwood Byre, Netherwood Lane, Chadwick End, SOLIHULL, B93 0BB.
•**HARE, Mr. Jonathan Arthur, BA ACA** *1992;* PricewaterhouseCoopers LLP, Cornwall Court, 19 Cornwall Street, BIRMINGHAM, B3 2DT. See also PricewaterhouseCoopers
HARE, Mrs. Kimberley, LLB ACA *2002;* 21 Rock Road, Midsomer Norton, RADSTOCK, BA3 2AQ.
HARE, Mr. Martin Dudley, FCA *1971;* Higher Hollowshaw Farm, Chinley, High Peak, SK23 6AW. (Life Member)
HARE, Mr. Michael John, BA ACA *1979;* 5 Arnold Close, STEVENAGE, SG1 4TF.
HARE, Mr. Nigel David, BA ACA *1990;* 40 St. Clements Road, HARROGATE, HG2 8LX.

Members - Alphabetical HARE - HARLE

HARE, Mr. Peter Charles, FCA *1970;* 12D Bowes Road, WALTON-ON-THAMES, SURREY, KT12 3HS. (Life Member)
HARE, Mr. Philip Stephen, BSc ACA ATII *1992;* (Tax Fac), 2 Queen Anne's Close, Stotfold, HITCHIN, HERTFORDSHIRE, SG5 4LP.
HARE, Mr. Simon, ACA *2011;* Badgers Wood, St. Marys Hill, ASCOT, BERKSHIRE, SL5 9AP.
HARE, Mr. Stephen, BCom ACA *1986;* Flat 801 Peninsula Apartments, 4 Praed Street, LONDON, W2 1JJ.
HARE, Mr. Steven Graham, FCA *1981;* 2 Victoria Cottages, Victoria Road, HARROGATE, HG2 0HQ.
HARE, Mr. Trevor Austin, FCA *1969;* 56 Hall Lane, Hagley, STOURBRIDGE, DY9 9LH.
HARE, Mrs. Vera Sybille, ACA *1982;* 97 Coldershaw Road, LONDON, W13 9DU.
HARE-SCOTT, Mr. Nigel Trewren, BA FCA *1977;* 3 Staffords, HARLOW, ESSEX, CM17 0JR.
HAREL, Mr. Antoine Louis, BA FCA *1987;* Harel Mallac & Co Ltd, 18 Edith Cavell Street, PORT LOUIS, MAURITIUS.
HAREL, Mr. Joseph Maurice Antoine, FCA *1957;* 9 Reunion Lane, FLOREAL, MAURITIUS. (Life Member)
HAREL, Mr. Marie Francois Jacques, FCA *1959;* 5 Forest Lane, P O Box 71, FLOREAL, MAURITIUS. (Life Member)
HARESNAPE, Mr. Christopher Paul, BSc ACA *1989;* 3 Furness Close, Poynton, STOCKPORT, SK12 1QN.
•HARESNAPE, Mrs. Lesley Anne, BA FCA *1987;* with DTE Business Advisory Services Limited, DTE House, Hollins Mount, Hollins Lane, BURY, BL9 8AT.
HARFIELD, Mr. Jonathan Henry Martyn, MA MPhil PhB ACA *1992;* Flat 22, Capital Wharf, 50 Wapping High Street, LONDON, E1W 1LY.
HARFIELD, Miss. Victoria Louise, BSc ACA *2009;* Norwich Airport Ltd, Amsterdam Way, NORWICH, NR6 6JA.
HARFOOT, Miss. Martha, MSci ACA *2006;* with BDO LLP, Fourth Floor, One Victoria Street, BRISTOL, BS1 6AA.
HARFORD, Mr. Desmond, FCA *1974;* 145 Sussex Gardens, LONDON, W2 2RY.
HARFORD, Mr. William Patrick, BSc ACA *2003;* Barclays, 16th Floor 1 Churchill Place, LONDON, E14 5HP.
HARFORD-CROSS, Dr. Charles Frederick, MA DPhil ACA *2005;* Linpac Plastics Wakefield Road, Featherstone, PONTEFRACT, WEST YORKSHIRE, WF7 5DE.
HARFORD-CROSS, Mrs. Fiona Katharine, BA ACA *2002;* with KPMG LLP, 1 The Embankment, Neville Street, LEEDS, LS1 4DW.
HARFOUCHE, Miss. Roula, MSc ACA *2002;* Flat 6, 23 Frognal, LONDON, NW3 6AR.
HARGADEN, Mr. Jason Paul, BSc ACA *1994;* 11b Malcolm Road, LONDON, SW19 4AS.
•HARGATE, Mr. Mark Christopher, BA FCA *1993;* Dains LLP, Unit 306, Third Floor, Fort Dunlop, Fort Parkway, BIRMINGHAM B24 9FD.
•HARGOOD, Mrs. Pearl, BA ACA *1989;* Pearl Hargood BA ACA, Hafan, Heol y Mynydd, Penbre, Llanelli, BURRY PORT DYFED SA16 0AJ.
HARGRAVE, Mr. Ian George, BSc FCA MIAP CDir *1991;* 12 Harendon, TADWORTH, KT20 5TT.
HARGRAVE, Mr. John Charles, BA FCA *1984;* Sarik House, Pearson Road, Sonning, READING, RG4 6UH.
HARGRAVE, Ms. Lisa Jane, MA ACA *2000;* 4 Old Mill Close, Duffield, BELPER, DERBYSHIRE, DE56 4GQ.
HARGRAVE, Mrs. Nicola Peta, BEd ACA *1989;* 2 Aston Villa, Butts Lawn, BROCKENHURST, SO42 7TE.
HARGRAVE, Mr. Richard, BA ACA *1984;* c/o Starline USA LLC, 180 Teaticket Highway, FALMOUTH, MA 02536, UNITED STATES.
HARGRAVES, Mr. Andrew James, BA ACA *2000;* 6 Senna Lane, Comberbach, NORTHWICH, CHESHIRE, CW9 6BD.
HARGRAVES, Mr. Christopher Stanley, FCA *1964;* 10 Ivy Bank Close, Sharples, BOLTON, BL1 7EF. (Life Member)
•HARGRAVES, Mr. Jonathan Christopher, BA FCA *1991;* (Tax Fac), Bentleys, Hazlemere, 70 Chorley New Road, BOLTON, BL1 4BY.
HARGRAVES, Mr. Michael Graham, BSc FCA *1978;* The Old Forge House, Ferry Road, South Stoke, READING, OXFORDSHIRE, RG8 0JL.
HARGRAVES, Miss. Pauline Ann, BSc FCA *1982;* 5 Meadowside Cottages, Lower Platts Ticehurst, WADHURST, EAST SUSSEX, TN5 7DA.
HARGRAVES, Mrs. Tracey Ann, BSc ACA *2000;* 6 Senna Lane, Comberbach, NORTHWICH, CHESHIRE, CW9 6BD.
HARGREAVES, Mrs. Alison Ann, BSc ACA *1983;* 6556 Old Carversville Road, PO Box 268, CARVERSVILLE, PA 18913, UNITED STATES.
HARGREAVES, Mrs. Alison Jane, BA FCA *1985;* W T Johnson & Sons (Huddersfield) Ltd Bankfield Mills Wakefield Road Moldgreen, HUDDERSFIELD, HD5 9BB.
HARGREAVES, Mr. Alistair Simon, BSc ACA *2004;* Admiral Insurance Services Ltd Capital Tower, Greyfriars Road, CARDIFF, CF10 3AZ.
HARGREAVES, Mr. Andrew, BSc ACA *2005;* 98 Allison Road, LONDON, N8 0AS.
HARGREAVES, Mr. Anthony Butler, FCA *1953;* 902A Blinkwater, Disa Park, Clifford Avenue, Vredehoek, CAPE TOWN, 8001 SOUTH AFRICA. (Life Member)
HARGREAVES, Mr. Anthony Paul, FCA *1956;* Tannery House, Temple Sowerby, PENRITH, CUMBRIA, CA10 1SD. (Life Member)
HARGREAVES, Mrs. Carol, BSc FCA *1977;* 19 Grange Road, Rawtenstall, ROSSENDALE, BB4 7RU.
HARGREAVES, Miss. Catherine Elizabeth, MA(Oxon) ACA *2009;* Flat 2, 367 Wilmslow Road, MANCHESTER, M14 6AH.
HARGREAVES, Miss. Claire Elizabeth, BSc ACA *1993;* Apartado de Correos 559, 29680 ESTEPONA, MALAGA, SPAIN.
HARGREAVES, Mr. David, FCA *1953;* Willards Farm, Dunsfold, GODALMING, GU8 4LB. (Life Member)
HARGREAVES, Mr. David Anthony, FCA *1984;* Herne House, Mansfield Road, Hasland, CHESTERFIELD, DERBYSHIRE, S41 0JN.
HARGREAVES, Mr. David Harry, FCA *1972;* 153 The Park, Market Bosworth, NUNEATON, CV13 0LP.
HARGREAVES, Mr. David Neil, FCA *1967;* 10 Avenue Charles De Gaulle, 89000 AUXERRE, FRANCE. (Life Member)
•HARGREAVES, Miss. Deborah Anne, BA(Hons) ACA *2002;* (Tax Fac), Sellens French, 93/97 Bohemia Road, ST. LEONARDS-ON-SEA, EAST SUSSEX, TN37 6RJ.
•HARGREAVES, Mr. Eric Ronald, BSc FCA CTA *1993;* Windle & Bowker Limited, Croft House, Station Road, BARNOLDSWICK, LANCASHIRE, BB18 5NA.
HARGREAVES, Ms. Felicity Elinor, BA(Hons) ACA *2003;* 3 Seaton Drive, BEDFORD, MK40 3BQ.
HARGREAVES, Mr. Gary Leonard, BA ACA *1988;* The Quaerere Academy, Wilderness Lane, Great Barr, BIRMINGHAM, B43 7SD.
•HARGREAVES, Mr. Ian Robert, BA FCA *1999;* with CLB Coopers, Laurel House, 173 Chorley New Road, BOLTON, BL1 4QZ.
•HARGREAVES, Mr. James Andrew, BA FCA *1996;* Ratiocinator Limited, Cholmondeley House, Dee Hills Park, CHESTER, CH3 5AR.
HARGREAVES, Mr. Jarrod, ACA *1996;* 13 Hawthorn Road, Hale, ALTRINCHAM, CHESHIRE, WA15 9RQ.
HARGREAVES, Mr. John Cormac, BSc ACA *1978;* Snelling Cottages, 51 West Street, FARNHAM, SURREY, GU9 7DX.
HARGREAVES, Mr. John Malcolm, FCA *1963;* 456 Stonegate Road, LEEDS, LS17 5BG.
HARGREAVES, Mr. John Michael, BSc ACA *1990;* 14 Furness Avenue, Simonstone, BURNLEY, LANCASHIRE, BB12 7SU.
HARGREAVES, Mr. John Phillip, BCom ACA *1986;* Lakeside House, Squires Lane, LONDON, N3 2QL.
HARGREAVES, Mr. John Roger, FCA *1964;* 40 High Fawr Avenue, Hampton Park, OSWESTRY, SHROPSHIRE, SY11 1TB. (Life Member)
HARGREAVES, Mr. Julian Nicholas, BSc ACA *1995;* Coyne Airways Ltd, Roberts House, 103 Hammersmith Road, LONDON, W14 0QH.
HARGREAVES, Miss. Katharine, MSci ACA *2011;* Flat 12 Vibeca Apartments, 7 Chicksand Street, LONDON, E1 5LD.
HARGREAVES, Mrs. Katherine Jill, BA(Hons) ACA *2001;* 70 Elms Road, LONDON, SW4 9EW.
HARGREAVES, Mrs. Linda, BSc ACA *1997;* 16 The Chancery, Bramcote, NOTTINGHAM, NG9 3AJ.
HARGREAVES, Miss. Linda Carol, BA ACA *1989;* 47 Elm Drive, Holmes Chapel, CREWE, CW4 7QA.
HARGREAVES, Mrs. Lois Jane, BSc ACA *1996;* 3 Oak Ridge, WETHERBY, LS22 6GT.
HARGREAVES, Mr. Malcolm Stuart, BCom ACA *1983;* 2 Crossfield Road, Hale, ALTRINCHAM, WA15 8DU.
HARGREAVES, Mr. Mark Ian, BSc FCA *1984;* Briarfield Cottage, The Front, Middleton One Row, DARLINGTON, COUNTY DURHAM, DL2 1AU.
HARGREAVES, Mr. Martin Donald, BSc ACA *1992;* Trutex Ltd Jubilee Mill, Taylor Street, CLITHEROE, BB7 1NL.
HARGREAVES, Mr. Martin Robert, BSocSc ACA *2002;* 35 Wellington Hill West, Henleaze, BRISTOL, BS9 4SP.
HARGREAVES, Mrs. Maxine Jane, BSc ACA *1989;* 2 Watlington, HOOK, RG27 9TW.
HARGREAVES, Mrs. Melissa, BSc ACA *2002;* Bakersfield, Brockclough Road, ROSSENDALE, LANCASHIRE, BB4 9LG.
HARGREAVES, Mr. Michael Walter Wensley, FCA *1964;* Grange Cottage, Wilton, PICKERING, YO18 7LE.
HARGREAVES, Mr. Neil, BA ACA *1979;* Queens Court High Street, Newport, SAFFRON WALDEN, CB11 3PF.
HARGREAVES, Mr. Neil David, BSc ACA *1991;* West Point, St John's Park, Menston, ILKLEY, LS29 6ES.
HARGREAVES, Mr. Neil James, BSc ACA *2002;* 9 Farrier Way, Appley Bridge, WIGAN, LANCASHIRE, WN6 9AZ.
HARGREAVES, Mrs. Nicola Claire, BA(Hons) ACA *2002;* 36a Common Lane, East Ardsley, WAKEFIELD, WEST YORKSHIRE, WF3 2EF.
HARGREAVES, Mr. Peter Kendal, FCA *1970;* Hargreaves Lansdown, 1 College Square South Anchor Road, BRISTOL, BS1 5HL.
HARGREAVES, Mr. Peter William, ACA *1979;* La Cache Le Chemin Des Maltieres, Grouville, JERSEY, JE3 9EB.
HARGREAVES, Mrs. Rhiannon Elizabeth, BA ACA *2004;* 16 Westville Road, Penylan, CARDIFF, CF23 5AG.
HARGREAVES, Mr. Richard John, BSc FCA *1995;* 13 Newton Drive, ACCRINGTON, BB5 2JT.
HARGREAVES, Mrs. Ruth Mary, BCom ACA *1983;* 2 Crossfield Road, Hale, ALTRINCHAM, WA15 8DU.
HARGREAVES, Mr. Simon John, BSc ACA *1989;* Penridge Church Road, Penn, HIGH WYCOMBE, BUCKINGHAMSHIRE, HP10 8NU.
HARGREAVES, Miss. Stacey Joanne, ACA MAAT *2009;* 18 Chelmorton Place, Chaddesden, DERBY, DE21 4QL.
HARGREAVES, Mr. Theodore Henry, FCA *1955;* Grangemead, Fairfield Road, Shawford, WINCHESTER, SO21 2DB. (Life Member)
HARGREAVES, Mrs. Vesna, ACA *2009;* 76 Court Way, TWICKENHAM, TW2 7SW.
HARGREAVES, Mr. William, FCA *1951;* The Colony Hotel, 130 Daisy Street, Sandown, SANTON, 2196, SOUTH AFRICA. (Life Member)
HARIA, Mr. Bejjel, BSc ACA *1997;* 97 Wentworth Avenue, LONDON, N3 1YN.
HARIA, Mrs. Bela, BA ACA *1999;* 71 Green Lane, EDGWARE, MIDDLESEX, HA8 7PZ.
•HARIA, Mr. Chetan, BSc FCA *1990;* Cromwell Accountants, 29 Lansdowne Road, STANMORE, MIDDLESEX, HA7 2RX. See also David Summers & Co Limited and Cromwell Accountants Ltd
HARIA, Miss. Deepa, BSc ACA *2008;* 60 Portland Crescent, STANMORE, HA7 1NB.
•HARIA, Mr. Deepakkumar, BSc FCA CFE *1988;* Deloitte LLP, Hill House, 1 Little New Street, LONDON, EC4A 3TR. See also Deloitte & Touche LLP
HARIA, Mr. Harish, BA ACA MCT *1991;* 47 Briar Road, HARROW, MIDDLESEX, HA3 0DP.
HARIA, Mr. Jayendra Juthalal, FCA *1973;* 126 Malvern Gardens, HARROW, HA3 9PG.
HARIA, Mr. Kunjal, BSc ACA *2001;* 5 Wilmer Way, LONDON, N14 7JD.
HARIA, Mr. Mahesh Kumar Jayantilal, FCA *1977;* Karamshi Meghji Haria Investments Ltd, P.O. Box 41022, NAIROBI, KENYA.
•HARIA, Mr. Manoj, BSc ACA *1996;* Elliotts Shah, 2nd Floor, York House, 23 Kingsway, LONDON, WC2B 6UJ.
HARIA, Mr. Rajnikant Juthalal, FCA *1973;* 124 Malvern Gardens, HARROW, HA3 9PG.
HARIA, Miss. Reshma, BA ACA *1987;* 16 Totternhoe Close, HARROW, HA3 0HS.
HARIHARAN, Mr. Narayanan, BCom ACA *2005;* 15 Mersham Drive, Kingsbury, LONDON, NW9 9PP.
HARING, Mr. Ian Howard, FCA *1976;* 18 Holmdene Avenue, Mill Hill, LONDON, NW7 2NA.
HARING, Mr. Richard Anthony, ACA *2008;* 17 Evangelist Road, LONDON, NW5 1UA.
HARIRI, Mr. Maziyar, ACA *2008;* Flat 8/D, Portman Mansions, Porter Street, LONDON, W1U 6DE.
HARJEET SINGH, Ms. Anita Kaur, BSc ACA *2001;* No. 2, Jalan 6/1, 46000 PETALING JAYA, Selangor, MALAYSIA.
HARJEET SINGH, Ms. Sunita Kaur, BSc ACA *2001;* 23 Persiaran Wangsa Baiduri 4, Taman Wangsa Baiduri, 47500 SUBANG, SELANGOR, MALAYSIA.
HARKCOM, Mrs. Rebecca Joy Dean, BA ACA *1986;* Education for Health, 10 Church Street, WARWICK, CV34 4AB.
HARKER, Mr. Brian James, MBA FCA *1973;* 2427 Rensford Avenue, CHARLOTTE, NC 28207-2633, UNITED STATES.
HARKER, Mr. Godfrey Howard, FCA *1955;* Longlands, 69A Lewes Road, Ditchling, HASSOCKS, BN6 8TY. (Life Member)
•HARKER, Mr. Nigel John, BCom FCA *1998;* with KPMG LLP, 15 Canada Square, LONDON, E14 5GL.
HARKER, Mr. Peter, FCA *1958;* The Flour Barn, 7 Castle Ashby Road, Yardley Hastings, NORTHAMPTON, NN7 1EL. (Life Member)
HARKER, Mr. Peter Henry, ACA *2008;* Saffery Champness Lion House, 72-75 Red Lion Street, LONDON, WC1R 4GB.
HARKER, Mr. Richard, BA FCA *1979;* 303 Leake Road, Gotham, NOTTINGHAM, NG11 0LE.
•HARKER, Mr. Roderick Peter, MA FCA ATII *1976;* R.P. Harker, Maskani Yetu, 2 Garey Close, Foxdale, ISLE OF MAN, IM4 3EU.
HARKER, William Gibson, Esq MBE FCA *1939;* Coniston, Villa Road, BINGLEY, BD16 4EY. (Life Member)
HARKIN, Mr. Drummond James, BA ACA *2000;* 23 Paddocks Drive, NEWMARKET, SUFFOLK, CB8 9BE.
HARKIN, Dr. Francis Joseph Eammon, ACA *1991;* Corvalley House Howe Road, The Howe Port St. Mary, ISLE OF MAN, IM9 5PR.
HARKIN, Miss. Ruth, BA ACA *1991;* 121 Walton Road, SALE, CHESHIRE, M33 4DR.
HARKINS, Mr. James, BA ACA *1999;* 18 Cobbett Road, SOUTHAMPTON, SO18 1HH.
HARKNESS, Mr. Bruce Richard, BA(Hons) ACA *2002;* Floor 10 Building 2 82 Sadovnicheskya Street, 115035 MOSCOW, RUSSIAN FEDERATION.
HARKNESS, Mrs. Helen, BA ACA *1985;* Gretton Hill Farm, Winchcombe, CHELTENHAM, GL54 5EW.
HARKNESS, Mr. Ian George, BA ACA *1993;* 26A St Stephens Gardens, TWICKENHAM, TW1 2LS.
HARKNESS, Mrs. Katherine, ACA *2005;* 33 Penn Lane, RUNCORN, CHESHIRE, WA7 4TP.
HARKNESS, Mr. Keith Richard, FCA *1966;* Orchard House, 67 Ankle Hill, MELTON MOWBRAY, LEICESTERSHIRE, LE13 0QJ.
HARKNETT, Mr. Alistair John, MSc BA ACA *2009;* Unit 14, 366-368 Military Road, CREMORNE, NSW 2090, AUSTRALIA.
•HARKNETT, Mrs. Mary Denise, ACA *1986;* Michael Welfare & Company Ltd, 100 High Road, Byfleet, WEST BYFLEET, SURREY, KT14 7QT. See also MW & Co LLP
•HARLAND, Mr. Alan James, FCA *1973;* Alan J Harland, 380 Wokingham Road, Earley, READING, RG6 7HX.
HARLAND, Mr. Alwyn Laing, FCA *1939;* 41 Wilsham Road, ABINGDON, OXFORDSHIRE, OX14 5LE. (Life Member)
HARLAND, Mrs. Ann-Christine, BSc ACA *1987;* 19 Sondes Place Drive, DORKING, RH4 3ED.
HARLAND, Mr. Benjamin, BSc ACA *1990;* 333 East 14th Street Apt. 14E, NEW YORK, NY 10003, UNITED STATES.
•HARLAND, Mr. Christopher Robert, BA ACA *1993;* Mentor House, Ainsworth Street, BLACKBURN, BB1 6AY.
HARLAND, Mr. David William Romanis, BSc FCA *1978;* The Old Rectory, Church Lane, South Moreton, DIDCOT, OX11 9AF.
HARLAND, Mr. Edwin George, MA ACA CFE ALCM *1986;* with PricewaterhouseCoopers LLP, Pricewaterhousecoopers, 12 Plumtree Court, LONDON, EC4A 4HT.
HARLAND, Miss. Helen, ACA *2008;* 10 Berlin Road, STOCKPORT, CHESHIRE, SK3 9QD.
HARLAND, Miss. Jane Elizabeth, BSc ACA *2000;* with Baker Tilly Tax & Advisory Services LLP, 1 Old Hall Street, LIVERPOOL, L3 9SX.
HARLAND, Mr. John Michael, MA FCA *1977;* 25 Woodhill Drive, REDWOOD CITY, CA 94061-1826, UNITED STATES. (Life Member)
HARLAND, Mr. Keith Duncan, ACA *1980;* 93 Cashew Road, Apt 02-02 Cashew Heights, SINGAPORE 679664, SINGAPORE.
HARLAND, Mr. Neil Adrian, BA ACA *2004;* 27 Cross Lane, SHEFFIELD, S10 1WL.
•HARLAND, Mr. Robert Andrew, FCA *1989;* with Grant Thornton UK LLP, Grant Thornton House, 22 Melton Street, Euston Square, LONDON, NW1 2EP.
HARLAND, Mr. Simon Guy, BSc ACA *2000;* c/o Po Box 333888, Villa P-24, The Villa, DUBAI, UNITED ARAB EMIRATES.
HARLAND, Mr. Stephen John, BSc ACA *1985;* AXA PPP Healthcare, PPP House, Vale Road, TUNBRIDGE WELLS, KENT, TN1 1BJ.
HARLAND, Mrs. Susan, BA ACA *1986;* 98 Bankhead Road, NORTHALLERTON, NORTH YORKSHIRE, DL6 1HQ.
HARLE, Mr. Christian David, BSc ACA *1995;* 8 Park View Terrace, WORCESTER, WR3 7AG.

HARLE, Mrs. Jing Yee, BSc ACA *1996;* West Bromwich Bldg Soc: Principal Office, 374 High Street, WEST BROMWICH, WEST MIDLANDS, B70 8LR.
HARLE, Mr. Jonathan David, BSc FCA *1977;* Chemin Des Pontets IE, Commugny, 1291 GENEVA, SWITZERLAND.
HARLEY, Mr. Allan, MA ACA *1997;* The Royal Bank of Scotland Plc, 280 Bishopsgate, LONDON, EC2M 4RB.
•**HARLEY, Mr. Brian Woodall, FCA** *1974;* BWH and Company, Iveco House, Station Road, WATFORD, WD17 1DL. See also Northwood Payroll Services Ltd
HARLEY, Mrs. Emma Jo, BSc ACA *2004;* Tewkesbury Borough Council, Council Offices, Gloucester Road, TEWKESBURY, GLOUCESTERSHIRE, GL20 5TT.
HARLEY, Mrs. Gillian Margaret, BA ACA *1997;* 15 Cotland Acres, REDHILL, RH1 6JZ.
HARLEY, Mr. Glenn, BA ACA *1990;* 35 Spindlewood, Elloughton, BROUGH, HU15 1LL.
HARLEY, Mr. Ian, MA FCIB FCA *1976;* 28 Kingswood Way, SOUTH CROYDON, Surrey, CR2 8QP.
HARLEY, Mr. John Alfred, FCA *1958;* La Petite Grange, Pechbertie, 82150 BELVEZE, FRANCE. (Life Member)
•**HARLEY, Mr. John Henry, FCA CA(SA)** *1973;* Postern Heath, Postern Lane, TONBRIDGE, TN11 0QU.
HARLEY, Mr. Keith, FCA *1962;* 16 Melton Road, NORTH FERRIBY, NORTH HUMBERSIDE, HU14 3ET.
HARLEY, Mr. Leslie George, FCA CA(AUS) *1988;* PO Box 855, SAMFORD, QLD 4520, AUSTRALIA.
HARLEY, Mrs. Louise Emma, BA(Hons) ACA *2003;* 61 Foxes Close, HERTFORD, SG13 7UA.
HARLEY, Mrs. Nicola Jane, BA(Hons) ACA *2000;* with Ernst & Young LLP, 1 More London Place, LONDON, SE1 2AF.
HARLEY, Mr. Robert, BA FCA *1973;* Triumph Motorcycles Ltd, Dodwells Road, HINCKLEY, LEICESTERSHIRE, LE10 3BZ.
HARLEY, Mrs. Tracy Catherine, BSc ACA *1991;* 35 Spindlewood, Elloughton, BROUGH, HU15 1LL.
HARLING, Mr. Adrian Paul, BA FCA *1981;* 4 Wentworth Drive, Bramhall, STOCKPORT, SK7 2LQ.
HARLING, Ms. Annabelle Joy, BSc ACA *1999;* Churn Cottage Bohams Road, Blewbury, DIDCOT, OXFORDSHIRE, OX11 9HF.
HARLOW, Miss. Evlyn Mary, BSc ACA *2011;* Ty Halen, Salthouse Point, Crofty, SWANSEA, SA4 3RP.
HARLOW, Mr. Ian James, BSc ACA *1995;* Management Performance Ltd, 9 Reading Road Pangbourne, READING, RG8 7LR.
•**HARLOW, Mr. Michael Christopher George, FCA** *1977;* (Tax Fac), Acquis Limited, The Bell House, 57 West Street, DORKING, SURREY, RH4 1BS.
HARLOW, Mr. Stephen John, FCA *1976;* 3 Peacewood Mews, Les Vardes, St. Peter Port, GUERNSEY, GY1 1BY.
HARM, Miss. Marlane, BA(Hons) ACA *2011;* 30 Knightside Gardens, GATESHEAD, TYNE AND WEAR, NE11 9RL.
HARMAN, Mr. David Frankie, BA FCA FRSA *1981;* 61 Mycenae Road, LONDON, SE3 7SE.
HARMAN, Mr. Dominic Charles, BA(Hons) ACA *2003;* 16 McNaughton Close, FARNBOROUGH, GU14 0PX.
HARMAN, Mr. Gordon Cosworth, FCA *1970;* Withinlee Cottage, Withinlee Road, Mottram St. Andrew, MACCLESFIELD, CHESHIRE, SK10 4QE.
HARMAN, Mr. Greg Andrew, FCA *1994;* L E C G Ltd, Davidson Building, 5 Southampton Street, LONDON, WC2E 7HA.
HARMAN, Miss. Helen Judith, LLB ACA *2000;* 14 North Park, MANSFIELD, NG18 4PA.
•**HARMAN, Mr. Henry James William, FCA** *1969;* James Harman & Co, The Atrium, Curtis Road, DORKING, SURREY, RH4 1XA.
HARMAN, Mr. James Gwilym, FCA *1960;* 7 Rue Pasteur, 95220 HERBLAY, FRANCE.
HARMAN, Miss. Joanne Elizabeth, ACA *2000;* 3 Minshull Hall Court, Middlewich Road, CREWE, CHESHIRE, CW1 4RD.
HARMAN, Dr. John Sidney, PhD BA FCA *1975;* (Tax Fac), 1/10 The Paragon, Blackheath, LONDON, SE3 0NZ.
HARMAN, Mrs. Josephine Ann, BSc ACA *1992;* Springwell Chase, Goughs Lane, BRACKNELL, BERKSHIRE, RG12 2JR.
HARMAN, Miss. Katherine, BSc ACA *2004;* 50a Church Street, EVESHAM, WORCESTERSHIRE, WR11 1DS.
•**HARMAN, Mr. Nigel Edward, BSc FCA** *1985;* KPMG LLP, 15 Canada Square, LONDON, E14 5GL. See also KPMG Europe LLP
HARMAN, Mr. Paul, FCA CTA *1963;* Glenesk House, Newtown, St. Martin, HELSTON, CORNWALL, TR12 6DP.
•**HARMAN, Mr. Richard James, FCA** *1983;* (Tax Fac), Spencer Fellows & Co, 169 New London Road, CHELMSFORD, CM2 0AE.
•**HARMAN, Mr. Robert James, BA FCA CF** *1983;* Morris Owen, 43-45 Devizes Road, SWINDON, SN1 4BG.
HARMAN, Mr. Stephen Miles, ACA *1997;* 2647 Broadway #3S, NEW YORK, NY 10025, UNITED STATES.
HARMAN, Mr. Vaughn Eric, BSc ACA *1986;* 30 Cambridge Road, TEDDINGTON, TW11 8DR.
•**HARMAN, Mr. William Raymond, BA FCA CPA** *1977;* InC Blue Ltd, 100 Pall Mall, LONDON, SW1Y 5NQ.
HARMAN, Mrs. Yvonne, BSc FCA *2000;* 16 McNaughton Close, FARNBOROUGH, GU14 0PX.
HARMENS, Mr. Christiaan, FCA *1986;* Ryeford, 122 Park Road, Hale, ALTRINCHAM, CHESHIRE, WA15 9JW.
HARMER, Mr. Andrew Frederic, BSc ACA MBA *1994;* (Tax Fac), Little Orchard, Ickleton Road, Elmdon, SAFFRON WALDEN, CB11 4LT.
HARMER, Mr. Anthony James, BA ACA *1979;* 22 Swan Close, Martlesham Heath, IPSWICH, IP5 3SD.
•**HARMER, Mr. Colin Robert, FCA** *1969;* (Tax Fac), Harmer Slater Limited, Salatin House, 19 Cedar Road, SUTTON, SURREY, SM2 5DA. See also Service Charge Assurance Ltd
HARMER, Mr. David John, BSc ACA *1983;* Rte du Boiron 29, 1260 NYON, SWITZERLAND.
HARMER, Mr. Douglas Russell Eden, BA ACA *2000;* 159 Earlsfield Road, LONDON, SW18 3DD.
•**HARMER, Mr. Gregory Robert Peter, FCA** *1972;* 48 Shearwater Avenue, FAREHAM, HAMPSHIRE, PO16 8YQ.
HARMER, Mr. Ian, ACA *2009;* 3 Queen Anne Street, MILTON KEYNES, MK13 0BB.
HARMER, Mr. James Ian, BSc ACA *2009;* 13 High Street, Sherston, MALMESBURY, SN16 0LH.
HARMER, Mr. John Robert, BA FCA *1967;* 27 Shenfield Place, Shenfield, BRENTWOOD, ESSEX, CM15 9AH.
HARMER, Mrs. Kim, MA LLM ACA CTA *1996;* 66 Clarendon Way, TUNBRIDGE WELLS, TN2 5LD.
HARMER, Mr. Martin James, FCA *1977;* 631 Fairfield Circle, WESTFIELD, NJ 07090, UNITED STATES.
HARMER, Mr. Michael Thomas, FCA *1957;* Buckle Point, Marine Parade, SEAFORD, BN25 2QR. (Life Member)
HARMER, Mr. Robert Martin, BA FCA *1976;* Little Hays, Brickhouse Lane, GODSTONE, RH9 8JW.
HARMER, Miss. Rosemary Elizabeth, LLB ACA *2004;* 11 Ebley Street, BONDI JUNCTION, NSW 2022, AUSTRALIA.
HARMER, Mr. Simon James, ACA *2008;* Flat A, 4 Langland Gardens, LONDON, NW3 6PY.
HARMES, Mr. David Orlando Spencer, BSc FCA *1977;* 10 Lime Walk, MAIDENHEAD, BERKSHIRE, SL6 6QB.
HARMON, Miss. Catherine, BSc ACA *2002;* 3 Moorlay Crescent, Winford, BRISTOL, BS40 8DB.
HARMS, Mr. Patrick Keith, FCA *1970;* 8 Hartside Close, Gamston, NOTTINGHAM, NG2 6NW.
HARMSWORTH, Mr. John Francis, BA ACA *1983;* 21 Stanton Close, ST. ALBANS, AL4 9HT.
HARNDEN, Mr. John, FCA *1971;* John Harnden Consultancy Services, Rose Cottage, Snelson Lane, Marthall, KNUTSFORD, WA16 8SR.
HARNESS, Mr. Robert, MMath ACA *2011;* 97b Landor Road, Clapham, LONDON, SW9 9RT.
HARNETT, Mr. Anthony, ACA *2009;* Mewstone House, 19 Oldfield Road, Maybury Hill, WOKING SURREY GU22 8AN.
•**HARNETT, Mr. Harry Damien, BCom ACA** *1992;* Harnettaccountants, Weir Cottage, Teddington Studios, Broom Road, Teddington, TWICKENHAM TW11 9NT.
HARNETT, Mr. John Arthur, BA ACA *1982;* The Priory Beely Road, Oughtibridge, SHEFFIELD, S35 0FD.
HARNETT, Mr. Nicholas Paul, BSc ACA *2007;* E D F Energy, Networks Finance, 3rd Floor, Energy House, Harrier Business Park, CRAWLEY WEST SUSSEX RH10 1EX.
HARNETTY, Mr. Adam John, BSc ACA *1992;* The Well House, Lye Lane, Bricket Wood, ST. ALBANS, HERTFORDSHIRE, AL2 3TH.
HARNEY, Mr. Marc Timothy, MA ACA *1993;* Bamford, 60 Hollin Lane, Styal, WILMSLOW, SK9 4JJ.
HARNEY, Mr. Vincent John, BA ACA *1992;* Lordship V Jaime 1, 11000 PRAGUE, CZECH REPUBLIC.
HARNICK, Mr. Paul Richard, BSc(Hons) ACA *2006;* with KPMG LLP, 8 Princes Parade, LIVERPOOL, L3 1QH.
HAROLD, Mr. David Colin, BSc ACA *1978;* Aralonco Establishment, P.O. Box 1089, 1211 GENEVA, SWITZERLAND.
HAROLD, Ms. Theodora Caroline, MA ACA *2001;* 6 Albert Street, CAMBRIDGE, CB4 3BE.
HAROON, Mr. Naveen, BSc ACA *2009;* 22 Firs Park Avenue, LONDON, N21 2PT.
HARPER, Mr. Adam Brian, BSc FCA *1992;* 432 Old Long Ridge, STAMFORD, CT 06903, UNITED STATES.
HARPER, Mr. Alan, ACA *2010;* Flat 1, 29 Khama Road, LONDON, SW17 0EN.
HARPER, Mr. Alan Richard, ACA *2011;* 26 Kidmore Road, Caversham, READING, RG4 7LU.
HARPER, Mr. Andrew Robert, BSc FCA *1977;* Level 3, Pitney Bowes Software Europe Ltd, 6 Hercules Way Leavesden, WATFORD, WD25 7GS.
HARPER, Mr. Andrew William, BA(Hons) ACA *2002;* 218 Tinshill Road, LEEDS, LS16 7LE.
HARPER, Mr. Anthony, BSc ACA *1981;* 20 Barton Road, ELY, CAMBRIDGESHIRE, CB7 4DE.
HARPER, Mr. Anthony, ACA *2009;* Flat D/63 Du Cane Court, Balham High Road, LONDON, SW17 7JH.
HARPER, Mr. Anthony Geoffrey Carr, FCA *1970;* Flat 4, Lawnswood, Station Road, BEACONSFIELD, BUCKINGHAMSHIRE, HP9 1AB.
HARPER, Mr. Barrie Keith, BA FCA *1971;* Mill House, Grove Hill, Hellingly, HAILSHAM, BN27 4HF.
HARPER, Mr. Benjamin, MEng ACA *2011;* K P M G Salisbury Square House, 8 Salisbury Square, LONDON, EC4Y 8BB.
HARPER, Mrs. Beverley Claire, BSc ACA *1989;* 34 John Booth Street, Springhead, OLDHAM, OL4 5TG.
HARPER, Mr. Christopher John, ACA *2009;* 83 Bull Lane, RAYLEIGH, ESSEX, SS6 8LZ.
HARPER, Mr. Christopher John, BSc ACA *1987;* Baird Capital Partners Europe, Mint House 77 Mansell Street, LONDON, E1 8AF.
HARPER, Mr. Christopher Oliver, FCA *1967;* Bowling Green House Farm, High Moor, Wrightington, WIGAN, LANCASHIRE, WN6 9PT.
•**HARPER, Mr. Clive Anthony, BA FCA** *1983;* 1 Woodthorpe Glades, WAKEFIELD, WEST YORKSHIRE, WF2 6NF.
HARPER, Mr. David, ACA *2009;* 9 Towers Lane, COCKERMOUTH, CUMBRIA, CA13 9EA.
HARPER, Mr. David Andrew, BSc FCA *1991;* Level 2 477 Collins Street, MELBOURNE, VIC 3000, AUSTRALIA.
•**HARPER, Mr. David Leslie, FCA** *1975;* (Tax Fac), Fiander Tovell LLP, Stag Gates House, 63/64 The Avenue, SOUTHAMPTON, SO17 1XS.
•**HARPER, Mr. David Ronald, FCA** *1977;* Hardwickes, Etruria Old Road, STOKE-ON-TRENT, ST1 5PE.
HARPER, Mrs. Deborah, BA ACA *1993;* Valley Cottage, 8 Valley Lane, Lower Bourne, FARNHAM, SURREY, GU10 3NQ.
HARPER, Mr. Douglas John, FCA *1970;* 4 Lancaster Close, SOUTHPORT, MERSEYSIDE, PR8 2LD.
HARPER, Mr. Duncan Alfred, BA ACA *1997;* Aukett Fitzroy Robinson Cottam House, 36-40 York Way, LONDON, N1 9AB.
HARPER, Miss. Emma, BA ACA *2007;* ICI Paints, Building 154, Wexham Road, SLOUGH, SL2 5DS.
HARPER, Mr. Frank Welton, FCA *1934;* Reigate Beaumont, Colley Lane, REIGATE, SURREY, RH2 9JB. (Life Member)
HARPER, Mr. Geoffrey Ken, FCA *1966;* The Chestnuts, 14 Church Street, Guilden Morden, ROYSTON, HERTFORDSHIRE, SG8 0JD.
•**HARPER, Miss. Hilary Rachael, BCom ACA** *1992;* Hilary Harper Accoutancy Services Ltd, The Pines, Cranhill Farm, Harborough Road, Billesdon, LEICESTER LE7 9EL.
HARPER, Mr. Hugo Clive, BA FCA *1982;* 16 Hampden Road, HIGH WYCOMBE, HP13 6SX.
HARPER, Mr. Ian Frank Richard, FCA *1992;* Toshiba of Europe Ltd, 100 Ludgate Hill, LONDON, EC4M 7RE.
HARPER, Mr. Ian James, BA ACA *1998;* Morgan Stanley, 25 Cabot Square, Canary Wharf, LONDON, E14 4QA.
HARPER, Mrs. Isobel Janet, BSc ACA *1995;* Molecatcher's Cottage, 17 Cabbage Moor, Great Shelford, CAMBRIDGE, CB22 5NB.
HARPER, Mr. Jack, MMath ACA *2011;* Flat 6 Springfield, Highland Avenue, BRENTWOOD, CM15 9DD.
•**HARPER, Mr. James, FCA** *1991;* THS Accountants Limited, The Old School House, Leckhampton Road, CHELTENHAM, GLOUCESTERSHIRE, GL53 0AX.
HARPER, Mr. James, ACA *2011;* Flat 75, Admirals House, Gisors Road, SOUTHSEA, HAMPSHIRE, PO4 8GY.
HARPER, Miss. Jane Elizabeth, BA ACA *1980;* 2 Piccadilly, Back Way Great Haseley, OXFORD, OX44 7JP.
•**HARPER, Miss. Jane Ellen, BA(Hons) ACA** *2004;* Cobhams Limited, 73 Liverpool Road, Crosby, LIVERPOOL, MERSEYSIDE, L23 5SE.
HARPER, Ms. Janina Louise, BSc ACA *1995;* Kings Norton Engineering, Facet Road, BIRMINGHAM, B38 9PT.
HARPER, Mr. Jeremy, ACA *1984;* Leonard Cheshire Foundation Waterloo Court, 31 Waterloo Road, WOLVERHAMPTON, WV1 4XD.
HARPER, Mr. John Alfred, FCA *1959;* Dalegarth, 28 Alexandra Drive, Yoxall, BURTON-ON-TRENT, STAFFORDSHIRE, DE13 8PL. (Life Member)
HARPER, Mr. John Cecil, FCA *1976;* Suite 10, 55 Griva Digeni Street, Chlorakas, 8220 PAPHOS, CYPRUS. (Life Member)
HARPER, Mr. John Sidney, FCA *1969;* Plenty House, Shipton Lane, Burton Bradstock, BRIDPORT, DT6 4NQ.
HARPER, Mr. John Stanley, FCA *1960;* North Gables, 103 Altwood Road, MAIDENHEAD, SL6 4QD. (Life Member)
HARPER, Mr. Joseph Finlay, BSc ACA *2010;* Flat 5, Vision House, 50 Peerless Street, LONDON, EC1V 9AW.
HARPER, Mr. Julian, BA FCA TEP *1970;* 14 Derby Square, Douglas, ISLE OF MAN, IM1 3LS.
HARPER, Ms. Julie Michelle, BA ACA *1993;* Balmoral Capital, Cassini House, 57-59 St. James's Street, LONDON, SW1A 1LD.
HARPER, Mr. Laurent David Paul, ACA *2002;* 63 New Road, Ruscombe, READING, RG10 9LN.
HARPER, Mr. Leonard Herbert, FCA *1961;* 93 Nutley Crescent, Goring-by-Sea, WORTHING, WEST SUSSEX, BN12 4LB. (Life Member)
HARPER, Mrs. Lorraine, LLB ACA *2000;* 63 New Road, Ruscombe, READING, RG10 9LN.
HARPER, Mr. Mark Anthony, BSc ACA *1998;* 122 Acorn Avenue, Giltbrook, NOTTINGHAM, NG16 2WJ.
HARPER, Mr. Mark James, BA ACA *1995;* The Old Shop, Newham Bottom, RUARDEAN, GLOUCESTERSHIRE, GL17 9UB.
HARPER, Mr. Matthew Brian, BSc(Hons) ACA *2001;* Voyage Ltd Garrick House, 2 Queen Street, LICHFIELD, STAFFORDSHIRE, WS13 6QD.
HARPER, Mr. Michael, BSc ACA *2011;* 15 Mortlake Road, RICHMOND, SURREY, TW9 3JE.
•**HARPER, Mr. Michael Alan, BA FCA** *1974;* (Tax Fac), Mike Harper Tax & Accountancy Services Ltd, 58a High Street, Watton, THETFORD, NORFOLK, IP25 6AH.
•**HARPER, Mr. Michael John, BEng ACA** *1991;* KPMG LLP, 15 Canada Square, LONDON, E14 5GL. See also KPMG Europe LLP
HARPER, Mr. Nathanael James Gayford, BA ACA *2008;* Flat D, 57b Fulham High Street, LONDON, SW6 3JJ.
HARPER, Mrs. Nicola Jane, BSc ACA *2000;* 2 Cherry Grove, ILKLEY, WEST YORKSHIRE, LS29 9BS.
•**HARPER, Mr. Nigel Shirley Gayford, FCA** *1979;* Management Consultancy Services Limited, Carters Corner Farm, Cowbeech Hill, Cowbeech, HAILSHAM, EAST SUSSEX BN27 4JA. See also Holland Harper LLP
HARPER, Mr. Paul, FCA *1979;* 69 Sorrel Drive, Kingsbury, TAMWORTH, STAFFORDSHIRE, B78 2PJ.
HARPER, Mr. Peter Joseph, FCA *1958;* Mayhall Lodge, Oakway, AMERSHAM, HP6 5PQ. (Life Member)
HARPER, Mr. Peter Robert, FCA *1976;* Hawke Vale, Otterham, CAMELFORD, CORNWALL, PL32 9YP.
HARPER, Mr. Philip, FCA *1970;* 69 Winifred Avenue, UMINA BEACH, NSW 2257, AUSTRALIA.
HARPER, Mr. Philip Thomas, BA ACA *2010;* Flat 5 Woodley House, 34 Woodley Green, WITNEY, OXFORDSHIRE, OX28 1BF.
HARPER, Miss. Rachel Ann, BSc ACA *1991;* BP International Ltd, Chertsey Road, SUNBURY-ON-THAMES, MIDDLESEX, TW16 7LN.
HARPER, Mr. Richard Leslie Welton, FCA *1970;* 29 Roslyndale Avenue, Woollahra, SYDNEY, NSW 2025, AUSTRALIA.
HARPER, Mr. Robert Brett, ACA *1985;* Cardinham House, Cardinham, BODMIN, PL30 4BL.
HARPER, Mr. Robin Francis, FCA *1974;* Berry Palmer & Lyle, 150 Leadenhall Street, LONDON, EC3V 4QT.
•①**HARPER, Mr. Roger, BSc FCA** *1974;* Roger Harper, PO Box 4, Castletown, ISLE OF MAN, IM99 9YU. See also Roger & Co

HARPER, Mr. Ronald John, FCA *1938;* Whitegates, Philcote Street, Deddington, BANBURY, OX15 0TB. (Life Member)
HARPER, Mrs. Rosemary, BSc FCA *1988;* Bank Of New Zealand, PO Box 995, AUCKLAND, NEW ZEALAND.
HARPER, Mr. Simon Robert, BSc FCA *1992;* 30 Castle View, Ovingham, PRUDHOE, NE42 6AU.
HARPER, Mr. Stephen Ellis, BSc FCA *1965;* 10 Copperfields, 48 The Avenue, BECKENHAM, BR3 5ER.
HARPER, Mrs. Suzanne Lynne, BA ACA *1999;* with Baker Tilly Corporate Finance LLP, 1st Floor, 46 Clarendon Road, WATFORD, WD17 1JJ.
HARPER, Mrs. Suzanne Michelle, BSc ACA *2002;* 126 Aylward Road, LONDON, SW20 9AQ.
HARPER, Mr. Thomas, BSc ACA *2010;* Goldman Sachs, Petershill, 1 Carter Lane, LONDON, EC4A 5ER.
HARPER, Mr. Thomas Henry Wallis, BSc ACA *1993;* with Federal Home Loan Bank of Chicago, 200 E Randolph Drive, CHICAGO, IL 60601-6428, UNITED STATES.
HARPER, Mr. Thomas Richard Hellier, FCA *1971;* 5465 Elizabeth Street, VANCOUVER V5Y 3J7, BC, CANADA.
HARPER, Mrs. Tracey Ann, BA ACA *1993;* 12 Southway, LONDON, N20 8EA.
HARPER-TEE, Mr. Adrian, BEng ACA *1995;* Unit 308 6 Victoria Street, ST KILDA, VIC 3182, AUSTRALIA.
HARPHAM, Mr. Barry Edward, BSc FCA *1978;* Breakthrough Breast Cancer, 3rd Floor Weston House, 246 High Holborn, LONDON, WC1V 7EX.
HARPHAM, Mrs. Louise Karen, BA(Hons) ACA *2004;* 34 Tunstall Gardens, REDCAR, CLEVELAND, TS10 2TR.
HARPIN, Mr. Sidney Bryan, FCA *1954;* 14 Carisbrooke Avenue, LEICESTER, LE2 3PA. (Life Member)
HARPUR, Mr. Brian John, BA FCA CTA *1991;* 50 Bowes Hill, ROWLAND'S CASTLE, PO9 6BP.
HARPUR, Mr. John Henry Mark, BSc ACA ATII *1990;* Rosebank, 42 Big Brigs Way, Newtongrange, DALKEITH, MIDLOTHIAN, EH22 4DG.
HARPUR, Mr. Robert John, FCA *1970;* Stick Cottage, Birchwood, Storridge, MALVERN, WR13 5HA. (Life Member)
•**HARRAD, Mr. Mark David, ACA** *2002;* Synergy, 3-4 Moorside Court, Yelverton Business Park, YELVERTON, DEVON, PL20 7PE. See also Synergy Services(SW) Ltd
HARRADENCE, Mr. Michael Edward, FCA *1972;* 24 Camellia Way, WOKINGHAM, BERKSHIRE, RG41 3NB.
HARRADINE, Mr. David, ACA *2008;* Pricewaterhousecoopers, 33 Wellington Street, LEEDS, LS1 4JP.
HARRADINE, Mr. David John Louis, BSc ACA *1992;* 44 The Ridgeway, Down End, FAREHAM, HAMPSHIRE, PO16 8RE.
HARRAGHY, Mrs. Anne Elin, BA ACA *1988;* 25 Arlington Road, West Ealing, LONDON, W13 8PF.
•**HARRALL, Mr. Jeffrey Charles, FCA** *1968;* Colclough Harrall & Co, 50 King Street, NEWCASTLE, ST5 1HX.
HARRAND, Mr. Peter Mervyn, FCA *1966;* 8 Overdale Avenue, LEEDS, LS17 8TE.
HARRAP, Mrs. Betty Marjorie, FCA *1943;* 3 Weston La, Funtington, CHICHESTER, PO18 9LT. (Life Member)
HARRAP, Mr. Charles Anthony, FCA *1946;* The Grakens, Cromarty Mains, CROMARTY, ROSS-SHIRE, IV11 8XS. (Life Member)
HARRAP, Mr. Stephen Peter Douglas, MA FCA *1983;* HM Revenue & Customs, 132 Park Road, PETERBOROUGH, PE1 2TY.
HARRAWAY, Mr. James Keith, BA ACA *2005;* C V C, 111 Strand, LONDON, WC2R 0AG.
HARRAWAY, Mr. Peter, BA ACA *2007;* Flat 1, 67 Netherwood Road, LONDON, W14 0BP.
HARREX, Mr. Patrick, BA FCA *1974;* 21 Preston Drove, BRIGHTON, BN1 6LA.
HARRHY, Mr. Jonathan Andrew, ACA *2008;* 62 Foundry Road, Risca, NEWPORT, GWENT, NP11 6AL.
HARRIDENCE, Mrs. Caroline Matheson, BSc ACA *1996;* 7 Knoll Gardens, NEWBURY, BERKSHIRE, RG20 0NZ.
HARRIDENCE, Mr. Karl Stuart, MA MPhil ACA *1997;* 7 Knoll Gardens, Enbourne Row, NEWBURY, BERKSHIRE, RG20 0NZ.
HARRIES, Mr. Andrew David, BA FCA *1983;* 255 Streetsbrook Road, SOLIHULL, B91 1HE.
HARRIES, Mrs. Catherine, BSc ACA *1993;* 44 Durlston Road, KINGSTON UPON THAMES, SURREY, KT2 5RT.
HARRIES, Mrs. Charlotte Kate, BSc ACA *1995;* 45 South Eden Park Road, BECKENHAM, BR3 3BQ.
HARRIES, Mr. David Tom Lewis, BSc ACA *1991;* Flat 27 Blenheim Court, King and Queen Wharf, Rotherhithe Street, LONDON, SE16 5ST.
HARRIES, Mr. Gareth Adrian, MA BA ACA *2002;* 9 Hill Rise, ESHER, SURREY, KT10 0AL.
HARRIES, Mr. Gareth Wynn, BSc ACA *1996;* 13605 NW Hogan Street, PORTLAND, OR 97229, UNITED STATES.
HARRIES, Mr. Howard David, MA FCA *1975;* National Bank of Kuwait, NBK House, 13 George Street, LONDON, W1U 3QJ.
HARRIES, Mr. James Colin, FCA *1957;* PO Box 100, MIDLAND, WA 6936, AUSTRALIA. (Life Member)
HARRIES, Mr. John Michael, BSc FCA *1961;* Blithe Barn, Ampney St Peter, CIRENCESTER, GL7 5SH.
HARRIES, Mr. John Neil Hudson, BA ACA *1990;* 12 Comben Drive, Godmanchester, HUNTINGDON, CAMBRIDGESHIRE, PE29 2AU.
HARRIES, Mr. John Richard, BEng ACA *2005;* 22 Underhill, Moulsford, WALLINGFORD, OXFORDSHIRE, OX10 9JH.
HARRIES, Mr. John Richard, FCA *1973;* 93 Sea Bee Lane, DISCOVERY BAY, NEW TERRITORIES, HONG KONG SAR.
HARRIES, Miss. Katie Louise, ACA *2010;* 37 Mappleborough Road, Shirley, SOLIHULL, WEST MIDLANDS, B90 1AG.
HARRIES, Miss. Megan Elizabeth, ACA *2007;* 16 Nelson Street, NORWICH, NR2 4DN.
•**HARRIES, Mr. Neil, ACA ACCA** *2008;* Harries Watkins & Jones Ltd, First Floor, 85 Taff Street, PONTYPRIDD, MID GLAMORGAN, CF37 4SL.
HARRIES, Mr. Paul Ronayne, BSc ACA *1995;* 45 South Eden Park Road, BECKENHAM, BR3 3BQ.
•**HARRIES, Mr. Raymond Elwyn, BA FCA ATII** *1974;* (Tax Fac), 47 Barons Court Road, Penylan, CARDIFF, CF23 9DG.
HARRIES, Miss. Rhian Eiry, BSc(Hons) ACA *2010;* Eirianfa, Station Road, Nantgaredig, CARMARTHEN, DYFED, SA32 7LQ.
HARRIES, Mr. Roy Edward, FCA *1972;* with Harries Watkins & Jones Ltd, First Floor, 85 Taff Street, PONTYPRIDD, MID GLAMORGAN, CF37 4SL.
HARRIES, Mr. Stewart, BSc ACA *1988;* 13 Cumbrae Gardens, Long Ditton, SURBITON, SURREY, KT6 5EL.
•**HARRIES, Mr. Stuart, ACA ACCA** *2009;* WBV Limited, Woodfield House, Castle Walk, NEATH, SA11 3LN. See also SMJH Limited
HARRIES, Mr. Thomas David, BSc(Hons) ACA *2004;* with BDO LLP, 55 Baker Street, LONDON, W1U 7EU.
HARRIGAN, Mr. Glenn Sylvester, BSc ACA CF *1989;* Ellen L. Skelton Building, P.O. Box 681, ROAD TOWN, TORTOLA ISLAND, VG 1110, VIRGIN ISLANDS (BRITISH).
HARRIGAN, Mr. Michael John, ACA *1981;* A T C (International) Ltd The Old Office Block, 16 Elmtree Road, TEDDINGTON, MIDDLESEX, TW11 8ST.
HARRIHILL, Mr. David Ambrose, BA ACA *1995;* 10 Sandow Crescent, COROMANDEL VALLEY, SA 5051, AUSTRALIA.
HARRILD, Mr. Benjamin Henry, BA ACA *2003;* 38 Althorp Road, LONDON, SW17 7ED.
•**HARRILD, Mr. John, FCA** *1977;* (Tax Fac), John Harrild & Co., 501A Prescot Road, Old Swan, LIVERPOOL, L13 3BU.
HARRILL, Mr. Henry Reginald, FCA *1956;* 67 Lott Creek Hollow, CALGARY T3Z 3A9, AB, CANADA. (Life Member)
HARRIMAN, Mr. Karl James, LLB ACA ATII *2002;* 3 Wyndham Wood Close, Fradley, LICHFIELD, STAFFORDSHIRE, WS13 8UZ.
HARRIMAN, Mr. Paul, MA ACA *1993;* Apple Garth Denwood Street, Crundale, CANTERBURY, CT4 7EF.
HARRIMAN, Mr. Roger, FCA *1961;* 12 Woodstock Crescent, Dorridge, SOLIHULL, B93 8DA.
HARRIMAN, Mrs. Tatiyana Victorovna, ACA *1996;* Apple Garth Denwood Street, Crundale, CANTERBURY, KENT, CT4 7EF.
•**HARRINGTON, Mr. Alfred, ACA** *1979;* Rost Holme, Kirkbampton, CARLISLE, CA5 6HU.
HARRINGTON, Mr. Andrew Mark, ACA *1987;* 83 Oaklands, South, GODSTONE, RH9 8HX.
HARRINGTON, Mrs. Bara Jane, BSc ACA *2004;* 26 Murdoch Close, TRURO, CORNWALL, TR1 1RR.
HARRINGTON, Mr. Benjamin, MEng ACA *2011;* 22 Awsworth Lane, Cossall, NOTTINGHAM, NG16 2RZ.
HARRINGTON, Mrs. Carolyn, BSc ACA *1999;* 10 Thumbswood, WELWYN GARDEN CITY, HERTFORDSHIRE, AL7 4QE.
HARRINGTON, Mr. Christopher Daniel, BSc ACA *2000;* 10 Thumbswood, WELWYN GARDEN CITY, HERTFORDSHIRE, AL7 4QE.
HARRINGTON, Mr. Cornelius Michael, BCom ACA *2000;* 34 Ardfield Grove, Grange, Douglas, CORK, COUNTY CORK, IRELAND.
HARRINGTON, Mr. Daniel John, LLB ACA *2007;* 8a Steerforth Street, LONDON, SW18 4HH.
HARRINGTON, Mr. David, MA LLB FCA *1976;* 6 The Chase, Ballakillowey, Colby, ISLE OF MAN, IM9 4BL.
•**HARRINGTON, Mr. Denis Patrick Noel, FCA** *1988;* (Tax Fac), with PricewaterhouseCoopers, One Spencer Dock, North Wall Quay, DUBLIN 1, COUNTY DUBLIN, IRELAND.
HARRINGTON, Mr. Garrie Ernest, BSc ACA *1986;* Bay Tree House Fox Pond Lane, Pennington, LYMINGTON, SO41 8FW.
•**HARRINGTON, Mrs. Joanna Rae, BA(Hons) ACA** *1991;* Harrington & Co, 7 Hawthorn Wood, KENMARE, COUNTY KERRY, IRELAND.
HARRINGTON, Mrs. Julia Louise, BSc ACA *1991;* 13 St. Georges Square, WORCESTER, WR1 1HX.
HARRINGTON, Mr. Justin Peter, FCA *1977;* H C L Insurance B P O Services Ltd, 12-16 Addiscombe Road, CROYDON, CR0 0XT.
HARRINGTON, Miss. Karen, BA ACA *2000;* 42 Jack Close, Chandler's Ford, EASTLEIGH, SO53 4NU.
HARRINGTON, Miss. Kate, BSc ACA *2005;* 270B Sussex Way, LONDON, N19 4HY.
•**HARRINGTON, Mr. Keith Darryl, BSc ACA** *1991;* PricewaterhouseCoopers LLP, Cornwall Court, 19 Cornwall Street, BIRMINGHAM, B3 2DT. See also PricewaterhouseCoopers
•**HARRINGTON, Mrs. Laura Jane, BSc ACA** *2000;* with PricewaterhouseCoopers LLP, Cornwall Court, 19 Cornwall Street, BIRMINGHAM, B3 2DT.
HARRINGTON, Mr. Leslie Thomas, FCA *1964;* 2343 Chantrell Park Drive, SURREY V4A 9W8, BC, CANADA.
•**HARRINGTON, Mr. Mark Andrew, FCA** *1975;* 27 Bellair Avenue, LIVERPOOL, L23 9SN.
HARRINGTON, Mr. Mark James, BSc ACA *1994;* 24 Cumnor Road, Old Boars Hill, OXFORD, OX1 5JP.
HARRINGTON, Mr. Mark John, ACA *1996;* J A GLOVER LIMITED, UNIT 2 LORDSWOOD INDUSTRIAL ESTATE, CHATHAM, ME5 8UD.
HARRINGTON, Mr. Martin John, BSc ACA *1993;* 56 Oroua Street, Eastbourne, LOWER HUTT 5013, NEW ZEALAND.
HARRINGTON, Mr. Neil Simon, BSc ACA *1989;* Burcott Lodge, Burcott, LEIGHTON BUZZARD, BEDFORDSHIRE, LU7 0LZ.
HARRINGTON, Mr. Nicholas Joseph, FCA *1975;* 9 Kingsmead Avenue, WORCESTER PARK, KT4 8XB.
•**HARRINGTON, Mr. Patrick Bernard, BCom FCA** *1983;* (Tax Fac), BHG LLP, 77 Shrivenham Hundred Business Park, Majors Road, Watchfield, SWINDON, SN6 8TY.
HARRINGTON, Mr. Peter David, BA FCA *1978;* (Tax Fac), Buchanan House, 3 St. James's Square, LONDON, SW1Y 4JU.
HARRINGTON, Mr. Peter Joseph, ACA *2009;* 9c Stanhope Road, LONDON, N6 5NE.
HARRINGTON, Mr. Peter Taylor, ACA *1996;* with Dodd & Co., Clint Mill, Cornmarket, PENRITH, CA11 7HW.
HARRINGTON, Mr. Raymond Maxwell, FCA *1956;* 157 Wilmslow Road, Handforth, WILMSLOW, SK9 3JL. (Life Member)
HARRINGTON, Mr. Richard Hugh, BCom ACA *1985;* 46 Azalea Close, London Colney, ST. ALBANS, AL2 1UA.
HARRINGTON, Mr. Robert William, FCA *1956;* 11 Paddock Close, Blundellsands, LIVERPOOL, L23 8UX. (Life Member)
HARRINGTON, Mr. Roger Christopher, MA ACA *1991;* BP plc, Chertsey Road, SUNBURY-ON-THAMES, MIDDLESEX, TW16 7LN.
HARRINGTON, Miss. Sarah Elizabeth, BSc ACA *1992;* 129 Longfellow Road, WORCESTER PARK, KT4 8BA.
HARRINGTON, Mr. Stephen Thomas, FCA *1973;* Woodmans Yard, High Street, Damerham, FORDINGBRIDGE, HAMPSHIRE, SP6 3EU.
HARRINGTON, Mr. Terence Ralph, FCA *1973;* Strawberry Cottage, Frogwell, TIVERTON, DEVON, EX16 8BQ.
HARRIS, Mr. Adam, ACA *2011;* 122 Norman Lane, LEVITTOWN, NY 11756-1708, UNITED STATES.
HARRIS, Mr. Adam Howard, BSc FCA *1992;* Smithy House, Totteridge Green, LONDON, N20 8PE.
HARRIS, Mr. Adrian James, FCA *1971;* Bridge House, 31 Church Street, Brixworth, NORTHAMPTON, NN6 9BZ.
HARRIS, Mr. Alan John Fraser, FCA *1965;* The Old School Novington Lane East Chiltington, LEWES, EAST SUSSEX, BN7 3AX.
HARRIS, Mr. Alastair Charles, MBA BA ACA *1989;* 18 Palladium Drive, Littleover, DERBY, DE23 3XH.
HARRIS, Mrs. Alison, ACA *2009;* 12 Dyer Court, WEST LAKES, SA 5021, AUSTRALIA.
HARRIS, Mr. Alister David, BSc ACA CF *2004;* with Grant Thornton UK LLP, 4 Hardman Square, Spinningfields, MANCHESTER, M3 3EB.
HARRIS, Mr. Alvin, FCA *1974;* Oldfield, 9 The Grove, RADLETT, WD7 7NF.
HARRIS, Miss. Amy Caron, BSc ACA *2010;* 33 The Chase, SUTTON COLDFIELD, B76 1JS.
HARRIS, Mr. Andrew, BSc ACA *1993;* 91 Main Road, Jacksdale, NOTTINGHAM, NG16 5HR.
HARRIS, Mr. Andrew, BA ACA *1993;* 6 Sandale Close, Gamston, NOTTINGHAM, NG2 6QG.
HARRIS, Mr. Andrew Clive, BSc ACA *2002;* 29 Hollis Gardens, CHELTENHAM, GLOUCESTERSHIRE, GL51 6JH.
HARRIS, Mr. Andrew James, BA ACA *1984;* Silver Spring, Bray Road, MAIDENHEAD, SL6 1UQ.
HARRIS, Mr. Andrew Jonathon, BA ACA *1989;* 21 Haslemere Gardens, Finchley, LONDON, N3 3EA.
HARRIS, Mr. Andrew Paul, BSc ACA *2003;* 9 Merestones Drive, CHELTENHAM, GLOUCESTERSHIRE, GL50 2SU.
•**HARRIS, Mr. Andrew Simon, BSc FCA MBA** *1992;* Deloitte LLP, Hill House, 1 Little New Street, LONDON, EC4A 3TR. See also Deloitte & Touche LLP
HARRIS, Mr. Andrew Warren, MEng ACA *1999;* 17 Craigstown Road, Kells, BALLYMENA, COUNTY ANTRIM, BT42 3NA.
•**HARRIS, Mr. Andrew William, BSc ACA** *1997;* BDO LLP, 55 Baker Street, LONDON, W1U 7EU. See also BDO Stoy Hayward LLP
HARRIS, Mrs. Angela, BSc ACA *1999;* 10 Fircroft Drive, Chandler's Ford, EASTLEIGH, HAMPSHIRE, SO53 2HE.
HARRIS, Miss. Anne-Marie, BA ACA *1996;* Bridges Community Ventures Ltd, 1 Craven Hill, LONDON, W2 3EN.
HARRIS, Mr. Anthony Beauchamp, MSc FCA *1969;* 1 Norland Rd, Clifton, BRISTOL, BS8 3LP. (Life Member)
HARRIS, Mr. Anthony Liam Stuart, FCA *1967;* 55 Frenchgate, RICHMOND, NORTH YORKSHIRE, DL10 7AE.
HARRIS, Mr. Antony Charles, BA ACA *1993;* Rosemullion The Warren, East Horsley, LEATHERHEAD, SURREY, KT24 5RH.
HARRIS, Mr. Antony Guy David Bloxam, BSc FCA *1969;* The Oast House, Curtisden Green, Goudhurst, CRANBROOK, KENT, TN17 1LL.
HARRIS, Ms. Barbara Mary, BA ACA *1984;* PO Box 45, DAR ES SALAAM, TANZANIA.
HARRIS, Mr. Brian, FCA *1955;* 6 The Close, Broadsands, PAIGNTON, TQ4 6JQ. (Life Member)
HARRIS, Mr. Brian Andrew, MA FCA CTA *1988;* 17 St. Peters Road, CIRENCESTER, GLOUCESTERSHIRE, GL7 1RE.
•**HARRIS, Mr. Brian Edward, FCA** *1969;* Brian Harris & Co, Grosvenor Gardens House, 35-37 Grosvenor Gardens, LONDON, SW1W 0BS. See also Harris & Screaton Ltd
HARRIS, Mr. Brian Reginald, FCA *1964;* PO Box 34, WOY WOY, NSW 2256, AUSTRALIA.
HARRIS, Ms. Bridget Ann, MA ACA *1991;* British Academy, 10 Carlton House Terrace, LONDON, SW1Y 5AH.
HARRIS, Mrs. Carol Tracy, BA ACA *2001;* 16 Berceau Walk, WATFORD, WD17 3BL.
HARRIS, Miss. Carolyn June, BSc(Econ) ACA *2004;* 22a Granville Park, LONDON, SE13 7EA.
•**HARRIS, Mrs. Catharine Mary, FCA** *1981;* All About Business Limited, Audley House, Northbridge Rd, BERKHAMSTED, HERTFORDSHIRE, HP4 1EH.
HARRIS, Miss. Catherine, MA ACA *2003;* H M V UK Ltd, Film House, 142 Wardour Street, LONDON, W1F 8LN.
HARRIS, Mrs. Catherine, BA ACA *1999;* with Deloitte LLP, Athene Place, 66 Shoe Lane, LONDON, EC4A 3BQ.
HARRIS, Mrs. Catherine, BSc ACA *1996;* (Tax Fac), Walnut Cottage, Little Haseley, OXFORD, OX44 7LH.
•**HARRIS, Miss. Charlotte Emma, BA ACA** *2006;* Harris & Trotter LLP, 65 New Cavendish Street, LONDON, W1G 7LS.
HARRIS, Miss. Christalle Rebecca, BSc ACA *2011;* 10 Bullrush Lane, Great Cambourne, CAMBRIDGE, CB23 6BG.
HARRIS, Mr. Christiaan, BA ACA *2001;* 28 Louie Pollard Crescent, Great Harwood, BLACKBURN, LANCASHIRE, BB6 7TG.
HARRIS, Mr. Christopher David, BSc ACA *1982;* Rua Curitiba 195 Apto151, Paraiso, SAO PAULO, 04005-030 SP, BRAZIL.
HARRIS, Mr. Christopher Mark, FCA *1954;* Cobblestone, 6 Barnstaple Street, WINKLEIGH, EX19 8HT. (Life Member)

HARRIS, Mr. Christopher Matthew, BA ACA CPA *1999;* 31 Cooper Lane, BASKING RIDGE, NJ 07920, UNITED STATES.
HARRIS, Mr. Christopher Norman, FCA *1972;* 61 Elmer Road, BOGNOR REGIS, PO22 6EH.
HARRIS, Mr. Christopher Patrick Stedman, BCom ACA *1992;* 105 Ditton Road, SURBITON, KT6 6RJ.
HARRIS, Miss. Claire Rebecca, BA ACA *2007;* 6 Nodders Way, Biddenham, BEDFORD, MK40 4BJ.
HARRIS, Mrs. Claire Rosa, FCA *1973;* 8 Lodge Crescent, WARWICK, CV34 6BB.
HARRIS, Ms. Clare Elizabeth, BA ACA *1988;* 35 Milton Lane, WELLS, SOMERSET, BA5 2QS.
HARRIS, Mr. Clifford John, FCA *1961;* 27 Beverley Crescent, BEDFORD, MK40 4BX.
HARRIS, Mr. Clive, BSc ACA *1979;* Box 30142, GEORGETOWN, GRAND CAYMAN, KY1-1201, CAYMAN ISLANDS.
HARRIS, Mr. Clive Philip, FCA *1975;* 16A Grove Park, Wanstead, LONDON, E11 2DL.
HARRIS, Mr. Colin Anthony, BSc ACA *1979;* 38 Welford Place, Wimbledon, LONDON, SW19 5AJ.
HARRIS, Mr. Colin Michael, FCA *1959;* 3 Myrtleside Close, NORTHWOOD, HA6 2XQ. (Life Member)
HARRIS, Mr. Colin Peter, FCA *1974;* 26 Beechwood Close, Exning, NEWMARKET, Suffolk, CB8 7EL.
HARRIS, Mr. Craig, BA ACA *1990;* 12 Church Croft, BURY, BL9 8JD.
HARRIS, Mr. Crawford Charles Alexander, FCA *1974;* 61 Clifton Park Road, Clifton, BRISTOL, BS8 3HN.
HARRIS, Mr. Creighton, FCA *1951;* 85 Pantmawr Road, Rhiwbina, CARDIFF, CF14 7TD. (Life Member)
HARRIS, Mr. Cyril Peter, FCA *1952;* 54 Church Avenue, Clent, STOURBRIDGE, DY9 9QT. (Life Member)
HARRIS, Mr. Daniel Charles, BA ACA *2004;* 16 Church Road, Wickham Bishops, WITHAM, ESSEX, CM8 3LA.
HARRIS, Mr. Daren Robert, BA ACA *1990;* Willow House, 111 Reading Road, Finchampstead, WOKINGHAM, BERKSHIRE, RG40 4RD.
HARRIS, Mr. Darren Neil, BSc ACA *1993;* 1 Beacon Street, PENRITH, CA11 7UA.
HARRIS, Mrs. Daryl Maxine, BSc ACA *1990;* 17 Beech Avenue, Horsforth, LEEDS, LS18 4PA.
HARRIS, Mr. David, FCA *1963;* 877 Shaker Road, LONGMEADOW, MA 01106-2422, UNITED STATES.
HARRIS, Mr. David, FCA *1965;* Watermill House, Mill Road, Kettleburgh, WOODBRIDGE, SUFFOLK, IP13 7JS.
HARRIS, Mr. David, BA ACA *2010;* 15 Englefield Crescent, Cliffe Woods, ROCHESTER, KENT, ME3 8HB.
HARRIS, Mr. David, BCom ACA *2001;* Little Garth The Ridge, Little Baddow, CHELMSFORD, CM3 4RT.
•ⓁHARRIS, Mr. David Anthony, BA ACA *1979;* 2 Challoners Close, Rottingdean, BRIGHTON, BN2 7DG.
•HARRIS, Mr. David Forbes, FCA CTA *1985;* David Harris, Lyn House, 39 The Parade, Oadby, LEICESTER, LE2 5BB.
HARRIS, Mr. David Francis, BSc ACA *1998;* Autologic Holdings PLC, Boundary Way, Lufton Trading Estate, Lufton, YEOVIL, SOMERSET BA22 8HZ.
HARRIS, Mr. David George, FCA CTA *1970;* Paul Harris & Co Ltd, 59 West End, REDRUTH, CORNWALL, TR15 2SQ.
HARRIS, Mr. David Ian, MA ACA DChA *1978;* 3 Orchard Close, Boulton Moor, DERBY, DE24 5AE.
HARRIS, Mr. David John, FCA *1976;* 14 Cherry Orchard, Charlton, PERSHORE, WORCESTERSHIRE, WR10 3LD.
•HARRIS, Mr. David John, FCA *1966;* Brooks Green, Abbey House, 342 Regents Park Rd, LONDON, N3 2LJ.
HARRIS, Mr. David John, MSci ACA *2007;* with PricewaterhouseCoopers, Royal Trust Tower, Suite 3000 TD Centre, Box 82, 77 King Street West, TORONTO M5K 1G8 ON CANADA.
HARRIS, Mr. David John, MA ACA *1986;* 25 Redesmere Drive, ALDERLEY EDGE, SK9 7UR.
HARRIS, Mr. David Michael, BSc ACA *1979;* 175 Forest Road, TUNBRIDGE WELLS, TN2 5JA.
•HARRIS, Mr. David Robert, BSc FCA *1996;* 12 Thrush Lane, Cuffley, POTTERS BAR, HERTFORDSHIRE, EN6 4JU.
HARRIS, Miss. Dawn Kathleen, BSc ACA *2004;* Deloitte & Touche Abbots House, Abbey Street, READING, RG1 3BD.
HARRIS, Mr. Dean Sean, ACA *1991;* 45 Holmfield Road, LEICESTER, LE2 1SE.
HARRIS, Miss. Deborah Jacqueline, BEng ACA *1995;* 57 Carterhatch Road, ENFIELD, EN3 5LT.
•HARRIS, Mrs. Denise Hazel, ACA *1985;* (Tax Fac), Walker Harris, 27 St. David Street, BRECHIN, ANGUS, DD9 6EG.
HARRIS, Miss. Denise Mary, BA ACA *1989;* Thomas Westcott, 49 St. Peter Street, TIVERTON, DEVON, EX16 6NW.
HARRIS, Mr. Derek, FCA *1959;* 9 Jenner Court, Stavordale Road, WEYMOUTH, DT4 0AF. (Life Member)
HARRIS, Mr. Derek John, FCA *1970;* Greenbanks, 35 Furze Lane, PURLEY, CR8 3EJ.
HARRIS, Mr. Derek John Elliott, BSc FCA *1977;* 282 Newbury Street, Apartment 5, BOSTON, MA 02116, UNITED STATES.
HARRIS, Dr. Derek William, FCA *1965;* 19 Croft Close, Elford, TAMWORTH, STAFFORDSHIRE, B79 9BU.
HARRIS, Mr. Dominic Joseph, MSc ACA MBA *2001;* Flat 5 Chatten Court, 11 Swynford Gardens, LONDON, NW4 4XN.
•HARRIS, Mr. Dov Zvi, ACA *2005;* Cohen Arnold, New Burlington House, 1075 Finchley Road, Temple Fortune, LONDON, NW11 0PU. See also Cohen Arnold & Co
HARRIS, Mr. Edward Robin Dudley, FCA *1960;* 16 Priorsfield, MARLBOROUGH, SN8 4AQ. (Life Member)
HARRIS, Mrs. Elizabeth Jane, BA ACA *1988;* 26 Longstanton Road, Oakington, CAMBRIDGE, CB24 3BB.
•HARRIS, Mr. Elliot Stephen, FCA DChA *1977;* Chantrey Vellacott DFK LLP, Cheviot House, 53 Sheep Street, NORTHAMPTON, NN1 2NE.
HARRIS, Miss. Emily Katherine, ACA *2009;* Flat 217 Royle Building, 31 Wenlock Road, LONDON, N1 7SH.
HARRIS, Mrs. Emma, BA ACA *1997;* 50 Eyebrook Road, Bowdon, ALTRINCHAM, WA14 3LP.
HARRIS, Miss. Emma-Louise, ACA *2010;* 204/160 Fullarton Road, Rose Park, ADELAIDE, SA 5067, AUSTRALIA.
•HARRIS, Mrs. Felicity Ann Sarah, BA ACA *1985;* (Tax Fac), Tavistock Business Consultancy Limited, 28 Glanville Road, TAVISTOCK, DEVON, PL19 0EB.
HARRIS, Miss. Francesca Amy, ACA *2010;* Flat 15, Da Vinci House, 44 Saffron Hill, LONDON, EC1N 8FH.
HARRIS, Mr. Gareth, BA ACA *2001;* 67 Jackroyd Lane, MIRFIELD, WEST YORKSHIRE, WF14 8HS.
HARRIS, Mr. Gareth Addison, BSc FCA *1988;* 18 Painters Pightle, HOOK, RG27 9SS.
•HARRIS, Mr. Gary Andrew, BA ACA *1991;* (Tax Fac), G.A.Harris & Co Limited, Brulimar House, Jubilee Road, Middleton, MANCHESTER, M24 2LX. See also Levin Harris & Co Limited
HARRIS, Mr. Geoffrey David, FCA *1956;* 4 High Trees Road, Knowle, SOLIHULL, B93 9PR. (Life Member)
HARRIS, Mr. Geoffrey Michael, FCA *1966;* G Harris Consultants, The Beacon, 63 Alleyn Park, LONDON, SE21 8AT.
HARRIS, Mr. George Roy, FCA *1956;* 7 The Woodcotes, Bromborough, WIRRAL, CH62 6ER. (Life Member)
HARRIS, Mrs. Georgina Cecelia Strathearn, MA ACA *1999;* 69 Sedlescombe Road, LONDON, SW6 1RF.
HARRIS, Mr. Gerald, FCA *1958;* 37 Brooke Way, BUSHEY, WD23 4LE. (Life Member)
HARRIS, Mrs. Gillian Louise, BA ACA *1989;* Virgin Media Ltd, Bartley Wood Industrial Estate, HOOK, HAMPSHIRE, RG27 9UP.
HARRIS, Mr. Glyndwr, FCA *1970;* Larks Hill, Gravel Path, BERKHAMSTED, HP4 2PJ.
HARRIS, Mr. Gordon Roy, LLB FCA *1960;* 2 Rosings, The Springs, Bowdon, ALTRINCHAM, WA14 3JH. (Life Member)
HARRIS, Mr. Graeme Richard, BA ACA *1994;* 35 Allerton Road, LONDON, N16 5UF.
•HARRIS, Mr. Graham Barnett, BSc FCA TEP *1982;* (Tax Fac), 19 Copland Avenue, WEMBLEY, HA0 2EN.
HARRIS, Mr. Graham Bernard, BSc(Hons) ACA *2001;* 22 Hurst View Road, SOUTH CROYDON, SURREY, CR2 7AG.
HARRIS, Mr. Graham Warwick, MSc ACA *1989;* 31 West Square, LONDON, SE11 4SP.
HARRIS, Mr. Granville William, BA ACA *1979;* Total Systems Plc, 392-394 City Road, LONDON, EC1V 2QA.
HARRIS, Mr. Gregory Paul, BA ACA *2003;* (Tax Fac), 36 Athelstan Close, Bromborough, WIRRAL, MERSEYSIDE, CH62 2EX.
HARRIS, Mrs. Hayley, BSc ACA *1990;* 56 Langland Bay Road, Langland, SWANSEA, SA3 4QR.
•HARRIS, Mrs. Heidi Lorraine, MSc BSc ACA *2004;* Harris & Harris Accountancy Services CIC, Fort Dunlop, Fort Parkway, BIRMINGHAM, B24 9FE.
HARRIS, Mrs. Helen Elizabeth, ACA *2008;* 2 Brick House, Lampley Road, Kingston Seymour, CLEVEDON, AVON, BS21 6XS.
HARRIS, Mrs. Helene Caroline Marie, BSc(Hons) ACA *2001;* 16 Plane Avenue, Northfleet, GRAVESEND, KENT, DA11 9QB.
•HARRIS, Mr. Howard Andre, BA(Econ) ACA CTA TEP *1998;* (Tax Fac), Charterhouse (Accountants) LLP, 88-98 College Road, HARROW, MIDDLESEX, HA1 1RA.
HARRIS, Mr. Hugh Rhodri, BA FCA *1974;* 6 Vanbrugh Terrace, Blackheath, LONDON, SE3 7AP.
HARRIS, Mr. Iain Farlane Sim, BA ACA *1989;* 1 Red Lion Close, Aldenham, WATFORD, WD25 8BB.
•HARRIS, Mr. Ian, FCA *1984;* (Tax Fac), CBHC LLP, Carlton House, 101 New London Road, CHELMSFORD, CM2 0PP.
HARRIS, Mr. Ian, ACA *2011;* Pricewaterhousecoopers, 7 More London Riverside, LONDON, SE1 2RT.
HARRIS, Mr. Ian, BEng ACA *1998;* Shielfield Farm Cottage, LAUDER, BERWICKSHIRE, TD2 6PG.
HARRIS, Mr. Ian Louis, BA FCA *1989;* Flat 4, 12 Clanricarde Gardens, LONDON, W2 4NA.
HARRIS, Mr. Ian Michael Brian, BSc ACA *1988;* Club Support The Hangar, David Lloyd Leisure, PO Box 439, HATFIELD, HERTFORDSHIRE, AL10 1EF.
HARRIS, Mr. Ian Walter, MM FCA *1958;* 26 Walmer Road, Woodley, READING, RG5 4PN. (Life Member)
HARRIS, Mr. Jack, FCA *1962;* Jordans View, Deanwood Road, Jordans, BEACONSFIELD, HP9 2UU.
HARRIS, Mrs. Jacqueline Diane, BSc ACA *1995;* (Tax Fac), Sophos Plc The Pentagon, Abingdon Science Park, ABINGDON, OXFORDSHIRE, OX14 3YP.
HARRIS, Mr. James, FCA *1952;* 31 Bayhampton Court, TORONTO M3H 5L5, ON, CANADA. (Life Member)
HARRIS, Mr. James, BSc ACA *2007;* 37 Heron Road, LONDON, SE24 0HZ.
HARRIS, Mr. James Emerson, BSc ACA *2001;* 59 Beaconsfield Road, EPSOM, SURREY, KT18 6HY.
HARRIS, Mr. Jeff, ACA *2011;* Flat 4, 10 Fitzjohns Avenue, LONDON, NW3 5NA.
HARRIS, Mr. Jeffery Francis, BSc FCA *1973;* 20 Pensford Avenue, Kew, RICHMOND, SURREY, TW9 4HP.
•HARRIS, Mr. Jeffrey Alan, BSc ACA *1992;* PKF (UK) LLP, Farringdon Place, 20 Farringdon Road, LONDON, EC1M 3AP.
HARRIS, Mr. Jeremy, BSc ACA *2005;* with KPMG LLP, Arlington Business Park, Theale, READING, RG7 4SD.
HARRIS, Mr. Jeremy Donald, ACA *1978;* Trots Brook, Plum Lane, Shipton-under-Wychwood, CHIPPING NORTON, OXFORDSHIRE, OX7 6DZ.
HARRIS, Mr. Jeremy Mark Littleton, FCA *1955;* Myrtle Cottage, Stoke Bliss, TENBURY WELLS, WR15 8QJ. (Life Member)
HARRIS, Mr. Jeremy Paul, BSc FCA *1985;* Mylkehouse, Chapel Lane, Sissinghurst, CRANBROOK, KENT, TN17 2JN.
HARRIS, Mrs. Joan Marie, BSc ACA *1995;* 30 Balfern Grove, LONDON, W4 2JX.
HARRIS, Mrs. Joanne Maureen, BSc ACA *2007;* 6 Tollgate Road, Capel St. Mary, IPSWICH, IP9 2HB.
HARRIS, Mr. John Ambler, FCA *1956;* Overmead, Cheltenham Road, Painswick, STROUD, GLOUCESTERSHIRE, GL6 6XN. (Life Member)
HARRIS, Mr. John Dudley, FCA *1966;* 108 Main Street, Wolston, COVENTRY, CV8 3HP.
HARRIS, Mr. John Duncan, MA FCA *1972;* Chilland Barn, Martyr Worthy, WINCHESTER, SO21 1EB. (Life Member)
HARRIS, The Revd. John Francis Prest, FCA *1965;* Holy Spirit, 68 Sterrix Lane, Litherland, LIVERPOOL, L21 0DA. (Life Member)
•HARRIS, Mr. John Graham, BSc FCA *1982;* Hale Financial Limited, Spring Court, Spring Road, Hale, ALTRINCHAM, CHESHIRE WA14 2UQ.
HARRIS, Mr. John Graham, FCA *1970;* with Harris Watson Holdings Plc, Unit 3, First Floor, Dartmouth Middleway, Aston Science Park, BIRMINGHAM B7 4AZ.
HARRIS, Mr. John Hatfield, FCA MCT *1968;* Hatfield House, The Street, Luckington, CHIPPENHAM, SN14 6NP. (Life Member)
HARRIS, Mr. John Lawrence, FCA *1961;* La Mouchais, 22130 BOURSEUL, FRANCE. (Life Member)
HARRIS, Mr. John Lewis David, BSc ACA *1987;* Armour Group plc, Lonsdale House, 7-9 Lonsdale Gardens, TUNBRIDGE WELLS, KENT, TN1 1NU.
HARRIS, Mr. John Peter, BA ACA *1985;* Viale Emilio Po 380, 41126 MODENA, ITALY.
HARRIS, Mr. John Robert Charles, FCA *1972;* 18 Ashton Court, 4 Hayne Road, BECKENHAM, KENT, BR3 4XD.
•HARRIS, Mr. John Thomas George, ACA *1984;* Harris & Clarke LLP, 7 Billing Road, NORTHAMPTON, NN1 5AN.
HARRIS, Mr. Jolyon, BSc ACA *2006;* 10 Kineton Road, OXFORD, OX1 4PG.
HARRIS, Mr. Jonathan James, BSc ACA *2000;* Flat 2, 32a Broomfield Road, STOCKPORT, CHESHIRE, SK4 4ND.
•HARRIS, Mr. Jonathan Paul Boniface, FCA *1972;* (Tax Fac), Jonathan P B Harris FCA, The Paddock, Ulting Lane, Ulting, MALDON, CM9 6QY.
HARRIS, Mr. Jonathan Robert, MA ACA *1984;* Marc Ltd, 14-16 Bruton Place, LONDON, W1J 6LX.
HARRIS, Miss. Jordan Elizabeth, ACA *1989;* 19 New Barn Lane, WHYTELEAFE, CR3 0EX.
HARRIS, Mr. Joseph, MSci ACA *2005;* 25c Osborne Avenue, NEWCASTLE UPON TYNE, NE2 1JR.
HARRIS, Miss. Judith Esther, BCom FCA *1970;* 13 Montclair Drive, LIVERPOOL, L18 0HA.
HARRIS, Mrs. Julia Frances, BA ACA *1979;* 70 Condamine Street, Balgowlah Heights, SYDNEY, NSW 2093, AUSTRALIA.
HARRIS, Mrs. Juliet, BA ACA *1989;* 6 Avon Road, South Wootton, KING'S LYNN, NORFOLK, PE30 3LS.
HARRIS, Miss. Katherine, ACA *2007;* 5 Greswell Street, LONDON, SW6 6PR.
HARRIS, Miss. Katherine, ACA *2008;* 7 Blakeney Court, Oakwood, DERBY, DE21 2LF.
HARRIS, Mrs. Kay Rebecca, MA BA ACA *2000;* Lower Widgery Heath View, East Horsley, LEATHERHEAD, KT24 5EA.
HARRIS, Mr. Keith, BSc FCA *1972;* The Stone House, Little Wenlock, TELFORD, TF6 5BE.
HARRIS, Mr. Keith Michael, FCA *1975;* 17 Kingston Avenue, Saltford, BRISTOL, BS31 3LF.
HARRIS, Mr. Kelvin John, BSc ACA *1998;* 1130 Angelo Court NE, ATLANTA, GA 30319-1044, UNITED STATES.
•HARRIS, Mr. Kevin James, MBA BA FCA *1994;* Cooper Parry LLP, 1 Colton Square, LEICESTER, LE1 1QH.
HARRIS, Mr. Kevin Lee, ACA *2005;* 2b Baldur Close, BEDFORD, MK41 0UY.
HARRIS, Mr. Kevin Stuart, BA FCA *1989;* Nitritex Ltd Unit 4, Minton Enterprise Park Oaks Drive, NEWMARKET, SUFFOLK, CB8 7YY.
•HARRIS, Mr. Leon Elias, FCA *1980;* L. Harris, 38 Rehov Habrosh, BINYAMINA, 30500, ISRAEL.
•HARRIS, Mr. Leonard, CA *1987; (CA Scotland 1973);* Harris, 10th Floor, Alberton House, St. Marys Parsonage, MANCHESTER, M3 2WJ.
HARRIS, Mr. Leslie John, BCom FCA *1954;* 2 Trinity Square, Hospital Road, RETFORD, NOTTINGHAMSHIRE, DN22 7BD. (Life Member)
HARRIS, Mr. Lindsay Mark, BSc ACA CTA *1986;* (Tax Fac), Thompson Fryza Bannister Ltd, The Corner House 2 High Street, AYLESFORD, ME20 7BG.
HARRIS, Mr. Luke Edward, BA(Hons) ACA *2010;* 8/2 Oxford Terrace, EDINBURGH, EH4 1PX.
HARRIS, Miss. Mala Lucy, BA ACA *1993;* 977 Eldorado Drive, SUPERIOR, CO 80027, UNITED STATES.
•ⓁHARRIS, Mr. Malcolm Barry, FCA *1956;* Harris Kafton, 11a Norwich Street, FAKENHAM, NORFOLK, NR21 9AF.
HARRIS, Mr. Malcolm Walter, FCA *1955;* The Haven, 20 Hopton Road, Cam, DURSLEY, GL11 5PB. (Life Member)
HARRIS, Mrs. Margaret Evelyn, BSc ACA *1984;* Burrows Hill, Burrows Lane, Gomshall, GUILDFORD, GU5 9QE.
HARRIS, Mr. Mark, LLB ACA *2002;* 181 Franciscan Road, Tooting, LONDON, SW17 8HP.
•HARRIS, Mr. Mark, BSc FCA *1985;* (Tax Fac), Rawlinson & Hunter, Lower Mill, Kingston Road, Ewell, EPSOM, KT17 2AE.
•HARRIS, Mr. Mark Barry, FCA *1989;* Bakers, Arbor House, Broadway North, WALSALL, WS1 2AN. See also Baker (Midlands) Limited
HARRIS, Mr. Mark Edward, ACA *2009;* 60 Kim Seng Road #14-03, Tribeca by the Waterfront, SINGAPORE 239497, SINGAPORE.
HARRIS, Mr. Mark Jonathan, BA FCA *1989;* 41 Middleway, LONDON, NW11 6SH.
HARRIS, Mr. Mark Malcolm, BA ACA *1985;* 28th Floor, 5 Queens Road, CENTRAL, HONG KONG ISLAND, HONG KONG SAR.
HARRIS, Mr. Mark Nicholas, MEng ACA *2003;* 122D Shirland Road, LONDON, W9 2BT.
HARRIS, Mr. Mark Smeeth, BSc ACA *1989;* Esab Holdings Ltd, 322 High Holborn, LONDON, WC1V 7PB.

HARRIS, Mr. Mark Terence, BSc ACA *2004;* with KPMG, P O Box 493 Century Yard, Cricket Square, GEORGE TOWN, GRAND CAYMAN, KY1-1106 CAYMAN ISLANDS.
HARRIS, Mr. Martin, MEng ACA *2006;* 78 Clonmel Close, Caversham, READING, RG4 5BF.
HARRIS, Mr. Matthew, BA ACA *2007;* Amino Communications Ltd, Prospect House, Buckingway Business Park, Anderson Road, Swavesey, CAMBRIDGE CB24 4UQ.
HARRIS, Mr. Matthew Ian, BSc ACA *1997;* The Newtons, Newtons Road, Kewstoke, WESTON-SUPER-MARE, AVON, BS22 9LG.
HARRIS, Mr. Matthew James, BSc ACA *1997;* 1 Whywick Cottage, Davis Street Hurst, READING, RG10 0TJ.
HARRIS, Mr. Matthew Philip, BSc ACA *1984;* Severn Valley Railway (Holdings) Plc The Railway Station, Railway Station, BEWDLEY, WORCESTERSHIRE, DY12 1BG.
HARRIS, Mrs. Melanie Ann, BSc ACA *1988;* 1 Lochalsh Grove, Coppice Farm, New Invention, WILLENHALL, WV12 5FA.
HARRIS, Mr. Michael, FCA *1946;* 7 Regency Court, 4 South Cliff, EASTBOURNE, EAST SUSSEX, BN20 7AE. (Life Member)
•HARRIS, Mr. Michael, FCA *1967;* 12 Old Forge Close, STANMORE, HA7 3EB.
•HARRIS, Mr. Michael Andrew, ACA FCCA *2011;* Chegwidden & Co, Priestley House, Priestley Gardens, Chadwell Heath, ROMFORD, RM6 4SN.
•HARRIS, Mr. Michael Anthony, FCA *1968;* Landfall, Picket Piece, ANDOVER, HAMPSHIRE, SP11 6LY.
HARRIS, Mr. Michael James, ACA *1993;* Hazelridge, Cummings Cross, Liverton, NEWTON ABBOT, DEVON, TQ12 6HJ.
HARRIS, Mr. Michael James Robert, BSc ACA *1989;* Moorcroft, 11 Sandown Avenue, ESHER, SURREY, KT10 9NT.
•HARRIS, Mr. Michael John, FCA *1971;* M.J. Harris & Co, 35 Whitehill Road, GRAVESEND, KENT, DA12 5PE.
HARRIS, Mr. Michael Leonard, FCA *1955;* Flat 24, 9 Chelsea Embankment, LONDON, SW3 4LE. (Life Member)
HARRIS, Mr. Michael William, FCA *1971;* Ashleys, Mill Road, Friston, SAXMUNDHAM, SUFFOLK, IP17 1PH. (Life Member)
HARRIS, Miss. Michelle Louis, ACA *1994;* Yew Tree Cottage, Winsor Road, Winsor, SOUTHAMPTON, SO40 2HE.
•HARRIS, Mr. Naphtlia, FCA FCCA ATII *1958;* (Tax Fac), N H & Co LLP, Jaybee House, 155-157a Clapham High Street, LONDON, SW4 7SY.
HARRIS, Mr. Neil, FCA *1974;* Les Cedres, 55 Chemin De La mongie, 33420, GENISSAC, FRANCE.
HARRIS, Mr. Neil, BSc(Hons) ACA *2001;* 10 Grenville Drive, Stapleford, NOTTINGHAM, NG9 8PD.
•HARRIS, Mr. Neil Barry, BSc *1992;* Financial Reporting Council, 5th Floor, Aldwych House, 71-91 Aldwych, LONDON, WC2B 4HN.
•HARRIS, Mr. Neil Christopher, FCA *1974;* (Tax Fac), Marsh & Moss Limited, The Gables, Bishop Meadow Road, LOUGHBOROUGH, LEICESTERSHIRE, LE11 5RE.
HARRIS, Mr. Neil John, BSc ACA *1996;* 18 High Wood, ILKLEY, WEST YORKSHIRE, LS29 8SB.
HARRIS, Mr. Neil Richard, BA ACA ATII *1994;* (Tax Fac), Brackens Church Road, West Lavington, MIDHURST, WEST SUSSEX, GU29 0EH.
•HARRIS, Mr. Neil Russell, BA FCA *1982;* Deloitte LLP, Global House, High Street, CRAWLEY, RH10 1DL. See also Deloitte & Touche LLP
HARRIS, Mr. Nicholas James, ACA *2008;* 16 Charlemont Road, TEIGNMOUTH, DEVON, TQ14 8RP.
•HARRIS, Mr. Nigel Barnett, BA FCA *1988;* (Tax Fac), Harris & Company (C.A.) Limited, 4-6 Canfield Place, LONDON, NW6 3BT.
HARRIS, Mrs. Olivia Mary, BSc ACA *2000;* 22 Hurst View Road, SOUTH CROYDON, SURREY, CR2 7AG.
HARRIS, Mr. Patrick John, BA FCA *1974;* Pond Farm, Church Road, Yelverton, NORWICH, NR14 7PB.
HARRIS, Mr. Patrick John Neil, FCA *1952;* 3 Victorian Barns, Syerston Hall Park, Syerston, NEWARK, NG23 5NL. (Life Member)
HARRIS, Mr. Paul, FCA *1957;* 144 Reading Road South, Church Crookham, FLEET, GU52 6AH. (Life Member)
•HARRIS, Mr. Paul, FCA *1966;* Paul Harris & Company, PO Box 61 GT, GEORGE TOWN, GRAND CAYMAN, KY1 1102, CAYMAN ISLANDS.
HARRIS, Mr. Paul, BA ACA *1993;* La Haie Du Puits, La Grande Route de Rozel, St. Martin, JERSEY, JE3 6AP.
HARRIS, Mr. Paul, BSc FCA *1993;* 10205 Brimfield Drive, AUSTIN, TX 78726, UNITED STATES.
HARRIS, Mr. Paul, BA ACA *1996;* Finance, 2nd Floor, 20 Moorgate, LONDON, EC2R 6DA.
HARRIS, Mr. Paul Edward Woodstock, BEng ACA *1996;* 4 Eaton Terrace, LONDON, SW1W 8EZ.
•HARRIS, Mr. Paul Geoffrey, ACA FCCA *2009;* Chegwidden & Co, Priestley House, Priestley Gardens, Chadwell Heath, ROMFORD, RM6 4SN.
HARRIS, Mr. Paul James Warren, BSc ACA *2006;* The Pastures, 6A Station Road, Nassington, PETERBOROUGH, PE8 6QB.
HARRIS, Mr. Paul Jamie, MSc FCA *1997;* 400 9th St. Apt. W5D, HOBOKEN, NJ 07030, UNITED STATES.
HARRIS, Mr. Paul Michael, MA ACA *1984;* 17 Field Road, LICHFIELD, STAFFORDSHIRE, WS13 7RU.
HARRIS, Mr. Paul Richard, BSc ACA *1992;* 22 Murton Lane, Newton, SWANSEA, SA3 4TR.
•HARRIS, Mr. Paul Toyne, BSc ACA *1980;* (Tax Fac), UHY Hacker Young, First Floor, Pembroke House, Ellice Way, Wrexham Technology Park, WREXHAM CLWYD LL13 7YT.
HARRIS, Ms. Pauline Jane, FCA *1988;* Landcentral (Europe) ltd, Suite 413 Highlands House 165 The Broadway, LONDON, SW191NE.
HARRIS, Mr. Peter, FCA *1958;* Melody, 38 Heath Farm Road, STOURBRIDGE, WEST MIDLANDS, DY8 3BY. (Life Member)
HARRIS, Mr. Peter Christopher, MA MBA FCA *1966;* Suite 1602 The Center, 989 Changle Road, SHANGHAI 200031, CHINA. (Life Member)
•HARRIS, Mr. Peter James, FCA *1979;* All About Numbers Ltd, Audley House, North Bridge Road, BERKHAMSTED, HERTFORDSHIRE, HP4 1EH. See also Peter Harris & Company
HARRIS, Mr. Peter Jonathan, BA ACA *1988;* 381 Wimbledon Park Road, Wimbledon, LONDON, SW19 6PE.
HARRIS, Mr. Peter Laurence Meryon, FCA *1969;* 32A Newbury hill Extension, Glencoe, Point Cumana, PORT OF SPAIN, TRINIDAD AND TOBAGO.
•HARRIS, Mr. Peter Mark, FCA *1979;* Hotel Chocolat Ltd, Mint House, Newark Close, ROYSTON, HERTFORDSHIRE, SG8 5HL.
HARRIS, Mr. Peter Robert, BA FCA *1977;* Four Winds, Fireball Hill, Sunningdale, ASCOT, SL5 9PJ.
HARRIS, Mr. Peter Roland, FCA *1955;* Rocks Barn, Sydling St. Nicholas, DORCHESTER, DT2 9NX. (Life Member)
HARRIS, Mr. Peter Roy, BA ACA *2006;* with PricewaterhouseCoopers, 111 5th Avenue SW, Suite 3100, CALGARY T2P 5L3, AB, CANADA.
HARRIS, Mr. Peter William, BSc ACA *1987;* 21 Admiral House, 20 Manor Road, TEDDINGTON, MIDDLESEX, TW11 8BF.
HARRIS, Mr. Peter Woodstock, FCA *1957;* Sallow Copse, Ringshall, BERKHAMSTED, HP4 1LZ.
•HARRIS, Mr. Philip, ACA *1982;* Philip Harris & Co, 38 Woodruff Way, Thornhill, CARDIFF, CF14 9FP.
HARRIS, Mr. Philip John, BEng ACA *2006;* Flat 28 Hightrees House, Nightingale Lane, LONDON, SW12 8AQ.
•HARRIS, Mr. Philip Martyn, ACA *2007;* with Gordon Down & Partners, 144 Walter Road, SWANSEA, SA1 5RW.
•HARRIS, Mr. Phillip John, BA FCA *1981;* (Tax Fac), Harris & Co, 2 Pavilion Court, 600 Pavillion Drive, NORTHAMPTON, NN4 7SL.
HARRIS, Mrs. Rachel Alison, BA ACA *1993;* Rosemullion, The Warren, East Horsley, LEATHERHEAD, SURREY, KT24 5RH.
HARRIS, Mrs. Rachel Anne Hampton, BA ACA *1989;* Stratford Wine Shippers & Merchants Ltd High Street, Cookham, MAIDENHEAD, BERKSHIRE, SL6 9SQ.
HARRIS, Mr. Ralph William, BEng ACA *1992;* Casa Riccio, 2 Chandlers Drive, TAMWORTH, B77 4NY.
HARRIS, Mr. Raphael Alexander Simon, FCA *1980;* 2 Cranbourne Gardens, LONDON, NW11 0HP.
HARRIS, Mr. Raymond Anthony, BA ACA CF *1995;* Silver Birches Desford Road, Thurlaston, LEICESTER, LE9 7TE.
•HARRIS, Mr. Raymond Ian, FCA *1962;* (Tax Fac), Raymond Harris, 3 Golfside Close, LONDON, N20 0RD.
HARRIS, Mr. Richard Alan, FCA *1977;* 5 The Covert, BEXHILL-ON-SEA, EAST SUSSEX, TN39 4TP.
HARRIS, Mr. Richard Alexander, BSc ACA *1993;* 125 Gretton Road, Winchcombe, CHELTENHAM, GLOUCESTERSHIRE, GL54 5EL.
HARRIS, Mr. Richard Brendan, BEng ACA *1997;* 8 SIN MING ROAD, #04-03 SIN MING CENTRE, SINGAPORE 575628, SINGAPORE.
HARRIS, Mr. Richard Charles, BSc ACA *1990;* 3 Bellini Court, FIG TREE POCKET, QLD 4069, AUSTRALIA.
•HARRIS, Mr. Richard Christopher, BA ACA *1996;* Watson Associates, 30-34 North Street, HAILSHAM, EAST SUSSEX, BN27 1DW.
HARRIS, Mr. Richard John, MA FCA ATII MCT *1979;* 82 Broad Oaks Road, SOLIHULL, B91 1HZ.
HARRIS, Mr. Richard John, BSc ACA *1983;* Generic Software Consultants Ltd; St Andrews House, Caldecotte Lake Drive, MILTON KEYNES, MK7 8LE.
HARRIS, Mr. Richard John, ACA *1987;* Birthday Cottage, 25 Devon Point Lane, DEVONSHIRE FL05, BERMUDA.
HARRIS, Mr. Richard John Leslie, BSc ACA *1988;* 177 Barnett Wood Lane, ASHTEAD, KT21 2LP.
HARRIS, Mr. Richard Neal, ACA *2009;* Deloitte & Touche Llp, 3 Rivergate, BRISTOL, BS1 6GD.
•HARRIS, Mr. Richard Paul Howson, MA FCA CTA *1986;* (Tax Fac), Smith & Williamson Ltd, Old Library Chambers, 21 Chipper Lane, SALISBURY, SP1 1BG.
•HARRIS, Mr. Richard Rhys, BSc FCA *1985;* Owain Bebb a'i Gwmni, 32 Y Maes, CAERNARFON, GWYNEDD, LL55 2NN.
•HARRIS, Mr. Richard Samuel, FCA *1968;* (Tax Fac), Richard S Harris & Co Ltd, 45 Bell Common, EPPING, CM16 4DY. See also Richard S Harris & Co
HARRIS, Mr. Richard William, FCA *1970;* P.O. Box 557, SAVANNAH, GRAND CAYMAN, KY1-1502, CAYMAN ISLANDS.
HARRIS, Mr. Robert Caldicott, BA ACA *2002;* Bard Ltd, Forest House, Tilgate Forest Business Park, Brighton Road, CRAWLEY, WEST SUSSEX RH11 9BP.
HARRIS, Mr. Robert Leslie, FCA *1992;* 28632 Point Loma, LAGUNA NIGUEL, CA 92677, UNITED STATES.
HARRIS, Mr. Robert Llewellyn, BA ACA *1996;* Unit 4, 427 Alfred Street, NEUTRAL BAY, NSW 2089, AUSTRALIA.
HARRIS, Mr. Robert William, BSc FCA *1993;* 12 Bracken Avenue, LONDON, SW12 8BH.
HARRIS, Mr. Robin Andrew, ACA *1989;* Donnerville Cottage, Donnerville Gardens, Admaston, TELFORD, TF5 0DE.
HARRIS, Mr. Robin Arthur, FCA *1970;* 30 Martingale Road, BILLERICAY, CM11 1SG.
HARRIS, Mr. Roderick Charles, FCA *1970;* Troad y Llanw, High Street, BORTH, DYFED, SY24 5JP.
HARRIS, Mr. Rodney Hewer, BSc ACA *1991;* 16 Home Way, PETERSFIELD, HAMPSHIRE, GU31 4EE.
•HARRIS, Mr. Roger, FCA *1969;* ATS Associates - Roger Harris, Denebank, 117 Bolton Road, Hawkshaw, BURY, BL8 4JF. See also Harris Roger
HARRIS, Mr. Roger John, CBE FCA *1964;* Trevaunance, 41 Caradon Close, Derriford, PLYMOUTH, PL6 6BW.
HARRIS, Mr. Ronald, FCA *1951;* 10 Sands Lane, Elloughton, BROUGH, HU15 1JH. (Life Member)
•HARRIS, Mr. Ronald Michael, FCA *1975;* Harris & Trotter LLP, 65 New Cavendish Street, LONDON, W1G 7LS.
HARRIS, Mrs. Rosemary, BA ACA *1983;* 74 The Mount, GUILDFORD, GU2 4JB.
•HARRIS, Mr. Ross Aitken, BA(Hons) ACA *2004;* Glenburgh Limited, 136 Boden Street, GLASGOW, G40 3PX.
HARRIS, Mr. Rupert James, BEng ACA *1994;* Ludgate House, 245 Blackfriars Road, LONDON, SE1 9UY.
HARRIS, Mr. Russell Stuart, BSc FCA *1979;* Independent Regulator of NHS Foundation Trust, 4 Matthew Parker Street, LONDON, SW1H 9NP.
HARRIS, Mr. Sam, MSc ACA *2005;* 2 Northcliffe Drive, Totteridge, LONDON, N20 8JS.
HARRIS, Miss. Samantha Jane, ACA *1998;* Flat 12, Barness Court, 6-8 Westbourne Terrace, LONDON, W2 3UW.
HARRIS, Miss. Sarah, BA(Hons) ACA *2011;* 30 Port Rise, CHATHAM, ME4 6NQ.
•HARRIS, Mrs. Sarah Elizabeth, BA ACA CTA AIIT *2005;* Oury Clark, PO Box 150, Herschel House, 58 Herschel Street, SLOUGH, SL1 1HD.
HARRIS, Mrs. Sarah Jane, BSc ACA *1988;* 381 Wimbledon Park Road, LONDON, SW19 6PE.
HARRIS, Mr. Simon, BSc ACA *2002;* with Zurich Financial Service UK Life, UK Life Centre, Station Road, SWINDON, SN1 1EL.
HARRIS, Mr. Simon Charles, BSc ACA *1986;* 20 Belgrave Road, BILLERICAY, CM12 0TX.
HARRIS, Mr. Simon David, BEng ACA *1999;* 32 Upminster Road, HORNCHURCH, ESSEX, RM12 6PA.
HARRIS, Mr. Simon John, FCA *1965;* Hazleton Grange, Hazleton, CHELTENHAM, GL54 4EB.
HARRIS, Mrs. Siobhan Patricia, BSc ACA *1996;* 2 Hills Farm, Sudbury Road, Newton Green, SUDBURY, CO10 0QH.
HARRIS, Mr. Stanley Warrington, FCA *1952;* 26 Burses Way, Hutton, BRENTWOOD, CM13 2PL. (Life Member)
•①HARRIS, Stephen John, Esq ACA *1989;* with Ernst & Young LLP, 1 More London Place, LONDON, SE1 2AF.
HARRIS, Mr. Stephen John, BSc ACA *1999;* 4 Home Close, CRAWLEY, WEST SUSSEX, RH10 3AF.
•HARRIS, Mr. Stephen Mark, BSc FCA CF FRSA *1986;* Dove House, 5 Harewelle Way, Harrold, BEDFORD, MK43 7DW.
•HARRIS, Mr. Stephen Maxwell, BSc FCA *1976;* Stephen Harris & Co, Belgrave Place, 8 Manchester Road, BURY, LANCASHIRE, BL9 0ED.
HARRIS, Mr. Steven, BSc ACA *2003;* 28b, Trewint Street, LONDON, sw184hb.
HARRIS, Mr. Steven Charles Andrew, BSc ACA *1991;* Circassia Ltd, Magdalen Centre, The Oxford Science Park, OXFORD, OX4 4GA.
HARRIS, Mr. Steven James, ACA *2007;* with FTI Forensic Accounting Limited, 322 High Holborn, LONDON, WC1V 7PB.
•HARRIS, Mr. Steven John, BSc ACA *1997;* 226 Summers Lane, Finchley, LONDON, N12 0JY.
HARRIS, Mr. Stewart Anthony, FCA *1975;* Tadburn House, 20 Southampton Road, ROMSEY, SO51 8AF.
HARRIS, Mr. Stuart, BSc ACA ACIS *1992;* Flat 23 Falcon Lodge, Admiral Walk, LONDON, W9 3TA.
•HARRIS, Mr. Stuart, BA FCA ATII *1983;* (Tax Fac), NWN Blue Squared Ltd, 7 Bourne Court, Southend Road, WOODFORD GREEN, ESSEX, IG8 8HD.
HARRIS, Mr. Stuart Andrew, BSc(Econ) ACA *1997;* 370 Victoria Road, RUISLIP, HA4 0ET.
HARRIS, Mr. Stuart Irvine, FCA *1954;* 2426 Ecuadorian Way, Apt 60, CLEARWATER, FL 33763-3318, UNITED STATES. (Life Member)
HARRIS, Mr. Stuart William, FCA *1977;* 16 Redstock Road, SOUTHEND-ON-SEA, SS2 5DJ.
HARRIS, Mrs. Sue Marie, BSc ACA *2002;* 10 Midway Street, SAN FRANCISCO, CA 94133, UNITED STATES.
HARRIS, Miss. Susan, BA ACA *1992;* (Tax Fac), South View, Christmas Lane, Metfield, HARLESTON, IP20 0JZ.
HARRIS, Mrs. Susan Clare, BSc ACA *1998;* 18 High Wood, ILKLEY, WEST YORKSHIRE, LS29 8SB.
HARRIS, Miss. Susan Margaret, BSc ACA *1987;* 59 Westminster Drive, LONDON, N13 4NT. (Life Member)
•HARRIS, Miss. Susan Margaret, MA ACA *1992;* 4 Church Steadings, Waverton, CHESTER, CH3 7QX.
HARRIS, Mr. Thomas Peter Alexander, MSc BA ACA *2004;* with Moore Stephens LLP, 150 Aldersgate Street, LONDON, EC1A 4AB.
HARRIS, Mr. Thomas Ronald, BA ACA *1986;* Evendine Court, Evendine Lane, Colwall, MALVERN, WORCESTERSHIRE, WR13 6DT.
HARRIS, Mr. Timothy Charles, MA FCA *1972;* Catfield Hall, Catfield, GREAT YARMOUTH, NR29 5DB.
•HARRIS, Mr. Timothy Geoffrey, FCA *1972;* (Tax Fac), Tim Harris, Mill Cottage, Windmill Hill, Brenchley, TONBRIDGE, KENT TN12 7NR.
HARRIS, Mr. Timothy James, ACA *2009;* with Dixon Wilson, 22 Chancery Lane, LONDON, WC2A 1LS.
HARRIS, Mr. Timothy Mark, BA ACA *1997;* 11 Reed Street, CREMORNE, NSW 2090, AUSTRALIA.
HARRIS, Mr. Timothy Miles, BA ACA *1990;* 37 Cedar Road, STAMFORD, PE9 2JJ.
HARRIS, Mr. Timothy Richard, FCA *1969;* Penylan, Heathside Park Road, WOKING, GU22 7JE. (Life Member)
HARRIS, Mr. Timothy Walter, BSc *1994;* Aviva Plc, St. Helens, 1 Undershaft, LONDON, EC3P 3DQ.
HARRIS, Miss. Tina Joan, MA ACA *2009;* C W Fellowes Ltd Carnac Place, Carnac Court Cams Hall Estate, FAREHAM, PO16 8UY.
HARRIS, Mr. Toby Charles, BA(Hons) ACA *2002;* Flat 1, 21 Collingham Gardens, LONDON, SW5 0HL.
HARRIS, Mr. Trevor George Frederick, BSc FCA *1976;* 4 Leg Square, SHEPTON MALLET, SOMERSET, BA4 5LL.
HARRIS, Prof. Trevor Samuel, ACA CA(SA) *2011;* Columbia Business School, 3022 Broadway, 608 Uris Hall, NEW YORK, NY 10027, UNITED STATES.

HARRIS, Mrs. Vanessa Anne, ACA 1979; 5 The Covert, Clavering Walk, BEXHILL-ON-SEA, TN39 4TP.

HARRIS, Mr. Vernon George, BSc FCA 1963; Ladywood House, Pond Road, Hook Heath, WOKING, GU22 0JZ.

HARRIS, Mrs. Victoria Anne, BSc ACA 1984; Portman Settled Estates Ltd, 38 Seymour Street, LONDON, W1H 7BP.

HARRIS, Miss. Victoria Jane, BA ACA 1991; Basement Flat, 78 Randolph Avenue, LONDON, W9 1BG.

HARRIS, Mr. Wendell Murray, BA FCA 1970; Polar Advisors Ltd, Riverside Cottage, Micheldever, WINCHESTER, HAMPSHIRE, SO21 3DB.

HARRIS, Mr. William Andrew, BSc ACA 1992; 57 Drayton Road, Irthlingborough, WELLINGBOROUGH, NORTHAMPTONSHIRE, NN9 5TA.

•HARRIS, Mr. William Stuart, BSc FCA 1982; Avonglen Limited, 2 Venture Road, Southampton Science Park, Chilworth, SOUTHAMPTON, SO16 7NP.

HARRIS, Miss. Yvonne Mary, BSc ACA 1991; Hawkstone View, Longford, MARKET DRAYTON, SHROPSHIRE, TF9 3PW.

HARRISON, Mr. Adam Chapman, FCA 1962; 18 Corby Gate, Ashbrooke, SUNDERLAND, SR2 7JB. (Life Member)

HARRISON, Mr. Adrian Paul, MEng ACA 1991; 113 Leicester Road, Quorn, LOUGHBOROUGH, LE12 8BA.

•HARRISON, Mr. Alan Graham, BA FCA 1975; HSA Associates, 89 Chorley Road, Swinton, MANCHESTER, M27 4AA.

•HARRISON, Mr. Alan John, FCA 1974; Harrison Farrow, Newnham House, 3 Kings Road, NEWARK, NG24 1EW.

HARRISON, Mr. Alan Peter, LLB FCA TEP 1983; Cotswold, La Rue De L'etocquet, St. John, JERSEY, JE3 4AE.

•HARRISON, Mr. Albert, FCA 1961; (Tax Fac), Bay Cottage, 144 Howgate Road, BEMBRIDGE, ISLE OF WIGHT, PO35 5TW.

HARRISON, Mr. Alistair Stuart, LLB ACA 2003; 2 The Burltons, Cromhall, WOTTON-UNDER-EDGE, GLOUCESTERSHIRE, GL12 8BH.

HARRISON, Mrs. Amanda Jane, BA ACA 1991; 6210 Basilea, Carrasco, MONTEVIDEO, CP11501, URUGUAY.

HARRISON, Miss. Amie Louise, MMath(Hons) ACA CTA 2006; 221 Moorgate Road, ROTHERHAM, SOUTH YORKSHIRE, S60 3BD.

HARRISON, Mr. Amos Paul, FCA 1992; 8 Holt Park Drive, Adel, LEEDS, LS16 7RG.

HARRISON, Mrs. Andrea, LLB ACA 2000; 45 Tingley Crescent, Tingley, WAKEFIELD, WF3 1JF.

•HARRISON, Ms. Andrea Jane, ACA ACCA 2007; with Ernst & Young LLP, 100 Barbirolli Square, MANCHESTER, M2 3EY.

HARRISON, Mr. Andrew, BA ACA 1983; Argyll Business Centres Ltd, 78 Pall Mall, LONDON, SW1Y 5ES.

HARRISON, Mr. Andrew John, BA ACA 1987; Optix Software Limited, Postoptics Unit 1 Hudson Way, York Business Park Nether Poppleton, YORK, YO26 6RZ.

HARRISON, Mr. Andrew Mark, BSc(Hons) ACA 2000; 87 Fordwich Rise, HERTFORD, SG14 2DF.

HARRISON, Mr. Andrew Mark, ACA 1984; Capita Symonds, 25 Sackville Street, LONDON, W1S 3HQ.

HARRISON, Mr. Andrew Stephen, BSc ACA 1986; Winchester House - 5th floor, Deutsche Bank Winchester House, 1 Great Winchester Street, LONDON, EC2N 2DB.

HARRISON, Miss. Angela Louise, BA FCA 1993; with Mazars LLP, Tower Building, 22 Water Street, LIVERPOOL, L3 1PQ.

HARRISON, Miss. Anne, BA ACA 1993; 1 Rowton Bridge Road, Christleton, CHESTER, CH3 7BD.

•HARRISON, Mrs. Anne Frances, BSc FCA 1986; Rigby Lennon & Co, 20 Winmarleigh Street, WARRINGTON, WA1 1JY.

HARRISON, Mr. Anthony James, BSc 1986; with Cookson Group plc, 165 Fleet Street, LONDON, EC4A 2AE.

HARRISON, Mr. Anthony William, FCA 1973; Amberley, Blackboy Lane, Fishbourne, CHICHESTER, PO18 8BL.

HARRISON, Mr. Arthur Geoffrey, FCA 1958; 31 Birchvale Drive, Romiley, STOCKPORT, CHESHIRE, SK6 4LE. (Life Member)

HARRISON, Mr. Benjamin James Paul, ACA 2009; 154 Macpherson Street, Bronte, SYDNEY, NSW 2024, AUSTRALIA.

HARRISON, Mr. Brian George, MSc BA FCA 1955; 18 Bull Street, STRATFORD-UPON-AVON, WARWICKSHIRE, CV37 6DT. (Life Member)

HARRISON, Miss. Carol Anne, MA FCA DChA 1982; 20A Romberg Road, Tooting Bec, LONDON, SW17 8UA.

HARRISON, Miss. Caroline, ACA 2008; Alliance & Leicester Commercial Finance Plc, 298 Deansgate, MANCHESTER, M3 4HH.

HARRISON, Mrs. Caroline, BA FCA 1991; West Yorkshire Playhouse, Playhouse Square, Quarry Hill, LEEDS, LS2 7UP.

HARRISON, Mrs. Caroline Ruth, BSc ACA 1995; Pebble Cottage Milestone Avenue, Charvil, READING, RG10 9TN.

HARRISON, Miss. Catherine Laura, BSc(Hons) ACA 2010; 166 Acaster Lane, Bishopthorpe, YORK, YO23 2TD.

HARRISON, Mrs. Catherine Louise, BSc ACA 1991; 27 Grasmere Road, LONDON, N10 2DH.

HARRISON, Mrs. Catriona McKenzie, BSc FCA 1995; 15 Malthouse Passage, LONDON, SW13 0AQ.

HARRISON, Mr. Charles Nicholas, FCA 1973; 51 Hovedene, Cromwell Road, HOVE, EAST SUSSEX, BN3 3EH.

•HARRISON, Ms. Christine Anne, FCA 1980; Harrison & Co, St. Johns Kirk, Symington, BIGGAR, LANARKSHIRE, ML12 6JU.

HARRISON, Mr. Christopher Alan, BA FCA 1979; 29 Stoatley Rise, HASLEMERE, SURREY, GU27 1AG.

•HARRISON, Mr. Christopher Charles, FCA 1983; (Tax Fac), Ashworth Moulds, 1 Grange Crescent, Rawtenstall, ROSSENDALE, LANCASHIRE, BB4 7QT.

HARRISON, Mr. Christopher John, FCA 1975; 42 Avenue du Gueret, LIMAL, 1300, BELGIUM.

•HARRISON, Mr. Christopher John, FCA 1970; with Rawlcliffe & Co, West Park House, 7/9 Wilkinson Avenue, BLACKPOOL, LANCASHIRE, FY3 9XG.

HARRISON, Mr. Christopher John James, BSc ACA 1992; Drax Power Ltd Drax Power Station, Drax, SELBY, NORTH YORKSHIRE, YO8 8PH.

HARRISON, Mr. Christopher Mark, BA ACA 2006; Flat 121 Windsor Court, 18 Mostyn Grove, LONDON, E3 2LS.

HARRISON, Mr. Christopher Parker, BA ACA 1984; Horseman Capital Management, 9 Chester Close, LONDON, SW1X 7BE.

HARRISON, Miss. Claire Elizabeth, BSc(Econ) ACA 2004; Apt 3C, 646 Tenth Avenue, NEW YORK, NY 10036, UNITED STATES.

HARRISON, Miss. Claire Elizabeth, BA ACA 1994; 339 Bakers Ground, Stoke Gifford, BRISTOL, BS34 8GG.

HARRISON, Mr. Colin David, FCA 1971; 24 Gordon Road, Wanstead, LONDON, E11 2RB.

HARRISON, Mr. Colin Frederick, BCom ACA 1979; 77 Burkes Road, BEACONSFIELD, BUCKINGHAMSHIRE, HP9 1EE.

HARRISON, Mr. Colin Gilbert, FCA 1960; Cropthorne Green Lane, Oddingley, DROITWICH, WORCESTERSHIRE, WR9 7NF. (Life Member)

HARRISON, Mr. Colin Norman, BSc ACA 1999; 125 Meadway, BARNET, EN5 5JY.

HARRISON, Mr. Craig Darren, ACA 2004; Bausch & Lomb UK Ltd, 106-114 London Road, KINGSTON UPON THAMES, KT2 6TN.

HARRISON, Mr. Craig Simon, BSc ACA 1999; Pebble Cottage Milestone Avenue, Charvil, READING, RG10 9TN.

•HARRISON, Mr. Daniel James, ACA 2005; Harrisons Accountancy Limited, 14 Saffron Road, BIGGLESWADE, BEDFORDSHIRE, SG18 8DJ.

HARRISON, Mr. Daniel Robert, ACA 2010; 100 Leander Drive, ROCHDALE, OL11 2XE.

HARRISON, Mr. David, BSc ACA 1989; 42 Rockfields, PORTHCAWL, MID GLAMORGAN, CF36 3NS.

HARRISON, Mr. David, MA ACA 2010; 17 Oatlands Chase, Shinfield, READING, RG2 9FY.

HARRISON, Mr. David Anthony, FCA 1966; Foxhayes, 7 Ashleigh Park, Bampton, TIVERTON, EX16 9LF.

HARRISON, Mr. David Ashley, BSc FCA 1977; 6 Newton Drive, Greenmount, BURY, BL8 4DH.

HARRISON, Mr. David Bernard Kosta, MA FCA 1964; 14 Acfold Road, LONDON, SW6 2AL. (Life Member)

HARRISON, Mr. David Clifford, BA ACA 1993; T404/5, Astrazeneca Alderley House, Alderley Park, MACCLESFIELD, CHESHIRE, SK10 4TF.

HARRISON, Mr. David George, BA ACA 1989; Adelphi Group Limited, Adelphi Mill, Bollington, MACCLESFIELD, SK10 5JB.

HARRISON, Mr. David John, BSc ACA 1991; The Archway, Main Street, Winster, MATLOCK, DERBYSHIRE, DE4 2DH.

HARRISON, Mr. David John Anthony, BA ACA 1992; 39 Park Hall Road, West Dulwich, LONDON, SE21 8EX.

HARRISON, Mr. David Laughton, FCA 1972; The Peak, Ross Green, Wichensford, WORCESTER, WR6 6YU.

HARRISON, Mr. David Paul, BA ACA 2005; 34 Maple Drive, CHELMSFORD, CM2 9HR.

HARRISON, Mr. David William Spencer, FCA 1968; 42 Redcliffe Road, Mapperley Park, NOTTINGHAM, NG3 5BW.

HARRISON, Mrs. Deborah Ann, BSc ACA 1985; PKF (UK) LLP, 3 Hardman Street, MANCHESTER, M3 3HF.

HARRISON, Mr. Derek, FCA 1972; 10 Selkirk Grove, Northburn Lea, CRAMLINGTON, NE23 3LT.

HARRISON, Mr. Dominic Stephen, BA ACA 1990; 58 Penn Lane, Melbourne, DERBY, DE73 8EQ.

•HARRISON, Mrs. Dorothy Iris, BSc FCA 1974; 9 Ardilaun Road, LONDON, N5 2QR.

HARRISON, Mr. Edward, FCA 1958; 20 Barley Orchard, Gnosall, STAFFORD, ST20 0QT. (Life Member)

HARRISON, Mrs. Elizabeth, BA(Hons) ACA 2011; 33 Cowan Way, WIDNES, CHESHIRE, WA8 9BJ.

HARRISON, Miss. Elizabeth Claire, BA ACA 1993; Games Workshop Group Plc, Willow Road, Lenton, NOTTINGHAM, NG7 2WS.

HARRISON, Fred Brian, Esq CBE FCA 1950; (Member of Council 1981 - 1988), 11 Hillcrest, King Harry Lane, ST. ALBANS, AL3 4AT. (Life Member)

HARRISON, Mr. Gareth Alwin, MA ACA CTA 2003; (Tax Fac), Barclays Bank, 3rd Floor, Building 6, Emaar Square, DUBAI, POBox 1891 UNITED ARAB EMIRATES.

HARRISON, Mr. Gavin James, BA ACA 2001; (Tax Fac), 38 Springwell Road, TONBRIDGE, KENT, TN9 2LN.

HARRISON, Mr. Geoffrey, FCA 1962; Sunne House, 2 Westwood Close, Droitwich Spa, DROITWICH, WR9 0BD.

HARRISON, Mrs. Gillian Margaret, BSc ACA 1984; Manor Farm House, Great Somerford, CHIPPENHAM, SN15 5EH.

HARRISON, Mr. Guy Antony, FCA 1960; Flat 2 Lower Ground, 4 Surbiton Crescent, KINGSTON UPON THAMES, SURREY, KT1 2JP. (Life Member)

HARRISON, Mrs. Helen Janet, ACA 1991; Optima Health & Nutrition Ltd Concept House, Brackenbeck Road, BRADFORD, WEST YORKSHIRE, BD7 2LW.

HARRISON, Mrs. Helen Louise, BSc ACA 2007; 6 Tennyson Way, PONTEFRACT, WEST YORKSHIRE, WF8 1LD.

HARRISON, Miss. Helen Ruth, BA ACA 2005; Flat 1, 104 The Broadway, LONDON, SW19 1RH.

•HARRISON, Mr. Ian Christopher, BA(Hons) ACA 2006; Rawcliffe & Co, West Park House, 7/9 Wilkinson Avenue, BLACKPOOL, LANCASHIRE, FY3 9XG.

HARRISON, Mr. Ian David, FCA 1977; 785 Borough Road, Tranmere, BIRKENHEAD, CH42 6QN.

HARRISON, Mr. James, BA ACA 2004; 80b Upper Richmond Road West, LONDON, SW14 8BZ.

HARRISON, Mr. James Alexander, BSc ACA 1993; 19 Cardwells Keep, GUILDFORD, GU2 9PD.

•HARRISON, Mr. James Brian, FCA 1970; J Brian Harrison Limited, 4 Locks Common Road, PORTHCAWL, MID GLAMORGAN, CF36 3HU.

HARRISON, Mr. James Graham, FCA 1954; with Harrisons, 4 Brackley Close, South East Sector, Bournemouth International Airport, CHRISTCHURCH, DORSET BH23 6SE. (Life Member)

HARRISON, Miss. Jane, BSc ACA 2002; 3 Burgh Meadows, Eaves Green, CHORLEY, PR7 3LR.

HARRISON, Miss. Jane, BA ACA 2006; Experian, Background Checking Lambert House, Talbot Street, NOTTINGHAM, NG80 1LH.

•HARRISON, Miss. Jane Mary, BSc FCA 1990; Pilgers Ruh, Westmount Avenue, AMERSHAM, BUCKINGHAMSHIRE, HP7 0AY.

HARRISON, Ms. Jane Victoria, BSc(Hons) ACA 2000; 22 Martaban Road, LONDON, N16 5SJ.

HARRISON, Mr. Jeffrey Malcolm, BSc FCA 1977; 56 Smithbarn, HORSHAM, WEST SUSSEX, RH13 6DX.

HARRISON, Miss. Jennifer Anne, BA ACA 2005; The Bungalow, 35 Clifford Road, Boston Spa, WETHERBY, WEST YORKSHIRE, LS23 6DB.

HARRISON, Mrs. Jennifer Rachel, BA ACA 1998; with Deloitte LLP, Hill House, 1 Little New Street, LONDON, EC4A 3TR.

•HARRISON, Mr. Jeremy, BA ACA 2002; Catalyst Corporate Finance LLP, 9th Floor, Bank House, 8 Cherry Street, BIRMINGHAM, B2 5AL.

•HARRISON, Mr. Jeremy, BSc ACA 1986; 6 Chevin Avenue, Homestead Estate Menston, ILKLEY, WEST YORKSHIRE, LS29 6PE.

•HARRISON, Mr. Jeremy James, BEng FCA 1980; Whiting & Partners Limited, Garland House, Garland Street, BURY ST. EDMUNDS, SUFFOLK, IP33 1EZ. See also Whiting & Partners

HARRISON, Mr. John, BA FCA 1969; Goodwin Manor, Swaffham Prior, CAMBRIDGE, CB5 0LG.

HARRISON, Mr. John, BA FCA 1983; 33 Woodside, REDCAR, TS10 4NG.

•HARRISON, Mr. John, FCA 1973; John Harrison (Worksop) Limited, 78 Carlton Road, WORKSOP, S80 1PH.

HARRISON, Mr. John Barrie, BSc FCA 1980; c/o 8th Floor, Princes Building, Ice House Street, CENTRAL, HONG KONG SAR.

HARRISON, John Cannell, Esq MBE FCA 1947; 12 Downsway, SHOREHAM-BY-SEA, BN43 5GH. (Life Member)

HARRISON, Mr. John Dashwood St Clair, MA CA 1974; (CA Scotland 1954); 3 Pilmour Place, ST ANDREWS, FIFE, KY16 9HZ. (Life Member)

HARRISON, Mr. John David, FCA 1957; 7 Walker Grove, Stapleford, NOTTINGHAM, NG9 7GY. (Life Member)

HARRISON, Mr. John Douglas, FCA 1972; Hilltop House, 2 The Avenue, Nunthorpe, MIDDLESBROUGH, CLEVELAND, TS7 0AA.

HARRISON, Mr. John Douglas, BEng ACA 1998; 6 Cornwell Close, Isleham, ELY, CAMBRIDGESHIRE, CB7 5BF.

HARRISON, Mr. John Ernest, ACA 1990; 20 Cornford Close, BURGESS HILL, RH15 8TJ.

HARRISON, Mr. John Geoffrey, ACA CA(SA) 2010; Suite 730, P Bag X43, SUNNINGHILL, 2157, SOUTH AFRICA.

HARRISON, Mr. John Mark, BSc ACA 2009; 45 Tyler Street, BRISTOL, BS2 0LS.

HARRISON, Mr. John Maynard Colchester, FCA 1968; Skirmers, Aston Street, Aston Tirrold, DIDCOT, OXFORDSHIRE, OX11 9DQ. (Life Member)

•HARRISON, Mr. John Neil, FCA MIPA FABRP 1973; Harrisons Springfield House, Springfield Business Park Caunt Road, GRANTHAM, LINCOLNSHIRE, NG31 7FZ.

HARRISON, Mr. John Neville, MA FCA 1964; Fairfield, Chapel Lane, Long Marston, TRING, HP23 4QT.

HARRISON, Mr. John Nicholas, BCom FCA 1983; Westleigh Investments Ltd, Lakeside, St. Mellons, CARDIFF, CF3 0FB.

HARRISON, Mr. John Overend, BSc ACA 1981; UK Territorial Headquarters The Salvation Army, 99-101 Newington Causeway, LONDON, SE1 6BN.

HARRISON, Mr. John Paul, FCA 1973; 3 Old Vicarage Mews, Sileby, LOUGHBOROUGH, LEICESTERSHIRE, LE12 7FZ.

HARRISON, Mr. John Reeves, BSc FCA 1973; Northcourt, Shorwell, NEWPORT, ISLE OF WIGHT, PO30 3JG.

HARRISON, Mr. John Scott, MA FCA 1986; 47 Bedford Street, Ampthill, BEDFORD, MK45 2EX.

HARRISON, Mr. John Stewart, FCA 1972; Old Chapel, Main Street, Barkston Ash, TADCASTER, LS24 9PR.

HARRISON, Mr. John Trevor, BA FCA 1965; (Member of Council 1981 - 1988), Woodcote, 1B Harmer Dell, Digswell, WELWYN, AL6 0BE.

HARRISON, Mr. Jonathan Charles, FCA 1971; 18 Abinger Mews, Maida Vale, LONDON, W9 3SP.

HARRISON, Mr. Jonathan David, BA ACA 2006; 16/88 North Steyne, MANLY, NSW 2095, AUSTRALIA.

•HARRISON, Mr. Jonathan George, BA ACA 1992; PricewaterhouseCoopers LLP, First Point, Buckingham Gate, London Gatwick Airport, GATWICK, WEST SUSSEX RH6 0NT. See also PricewaterhouseCoopers

HARRISON, Mr. Jonathan James Hewetson, MA FCA 1959; Castle Farmhouse, Odell, BEDFORD, MK43 7BB. (Life Member)

HARRISON, Dr. Joseph Graham, BSc ACA 2001; 47 Sumerling Way, Bluntisham, HUNTINGDON, CAMBRIDGESHIRE, PE28 3XT.

HARRISON, Mr. Julian Peter, BSc ACA 1987; The Royal Bank of Scotland Plc, Premier Place, 2 Devonshire Square, LONDON, EC2M 4XB.

•HARRISON, Mrs. Julie Pamla, BSc(Hons) FCA CTA 1996; with Tait Walker LLP, Crutes House, Fudan Way, Teesdale Park, STOCKTON-ON-TEES, CLEVELAND TS17 6EN.

•HARRISON, Mrs. Kameliya Aleksandrova, ACA 2008; Tearle & Carver Limited, Chandos House, School Lane, BUCKINGHAM, MK18 1HD.

•HARRISON, Mrs. Karen Tracey Elliott, BA FCA CTA 1996; Censis, Exchange Building, 66 Church Street, HARTLEPOOL, TS24 7DN.

HARRISON, Miss. Katherine, BA ACA 2006; 209b Lordship Lane, LONDON, SE22 8HA.

HARRISON, Mr. Keith Anthony, BA ACA *1992;* English Heritage 1 Waterhouse Square, 138 Holborn, LONDON, EC1N 2ST.

HARRISON, Mr. Keith Anthony David, ACA *1982;* 10 Lim Tai See Walk, SINGAPORE 267773, SINGAPORE.

HARRISON, Miss. Laura, BA ACA *2006;* 24 Gordon Road, Wanstead, LONDON, E11 2RB.

HARRISON, Miss. Laura Elizabeth, BSc ACA *2007;* with G & E Professional Services Limited, Arabesque House, Monks Cross Drive, Huntington, YORK, YO32 9GW.

HARRISON, Mr. Laurence, ACA *2011;* 17 Erin Way, Port Erin, ISLE OF MAN, IM9 6EF.

HARRISON, Mr. Lee David, BSc ACA *2010;* 55 Oakworth Avenue, Broughton, MILTON KEYNES, MK10 9NU.

•**HARRISON, Mr. Leigh Gordon, BA FCA** *1984;* Peak House, The Ridge, Cold Ash, THATCHAM, BERKSHIRE, RG18 9HZ.

HARRISON, Mr. Leslie, FCA *1955;* Gartenstrasse 46, 73660 URBACH, GERMANY. (Life Member)

HARRISON, Mrs. Lorna, BSc ACA *1991;* Ivy House Brook Lane Beeston Castle, TARPORLEY, CW6 9TU.

HARRISON, Mrs. Louise Jane, BSc(Hons) ACA *2003;* 28 Surbiton Hill Park, SURBITON, SURREY, KT5 8ES.

HARRISON, Ms. Lucy, MA ACA *2002;* 84 Bedford Road, LONDON, N2 9DA.

HARRISON, Ms. Lynn, BA ACA *1990;* 8 Parkhouse Court, Parkhouse Lane, READING, RG30 2AZ.

HARRISON, Mrs. Lynne Janine, BCom ACA *1980;* 6 Lindisfarne Close, Winsley, BRADFORD-ON-AVON, WILTSHIRE, BA15 2HS.

HARRISON, Mr. Marcus Troy, ACA CA(SA) *2009;* 51 Graham Road, LONDON, SW19 3SW.

HARRISON, Mr. Mark, BSc ACA *2001;* with KPMG, 50th Floor Plaza 66, 1266 Nanjing West Road, SHANGHAI 200040, CHINA.

HARRISON, Mr. Mark Andrew John, BSc ACA ACT *1989;* 5 Orchard Avenue, HARPENDEN, HERTFORDSHIRE, AL5 2DW.

HARRISON, Mr. Mark David, BSc ACA *2007;* 183 Staines Road, TWICKENHAM, TW2 5BB.

•**HARRISON, Mr. Mark Richard, BA FCA** *1999;* Mark J Rees, Granville Hall, Granville Road, LEICESTER, LE1 7RU.

HARRISON, Mr. Mark Robert, ACA *1992;* 8 Oxford Road, TEDDINGTON, MIDDLESEX, TW11 0PZ.

HARRISON, Mr. Mark Seymour, FCA *1976;* 33 Silverdale, Keymer, HASSOCKS, BN6 8RD.

HARRISON, Mr. Martin, ACA *1986;* Ele Advanced Technologies Ltd, Cotton Tree Lane, COLNE, BB8 7BH.

HARRISON, Mr. Martin Christopher James, MA ACA ACT *1990;* Colt Telecom, Beaufort House, 15 St Boltophs Street, LONDON, EC3A 7QW.

HARRISON, Mr. Martin James, BCom ACA *1984;* 3 Breech Close, Streetly, SUTTON COLDFIELD, B74 2EB.

HARRISON, Mr. Martin John, MA ACA *1984;* Realstar Hotels (UK) Ltd, 161 Brompton Road, LONDON, SW3 1QP.

HARRISON, Mr. Martin John, BA ACA *1995;* Flat 1, 3 Park Drive, The Park, NOTTINGHAM, NG7 1DA.

HARRISON, Mr. Matthew Colin, MA ACA *1998;* 9a Woodland Avenue, WINDSOR, SL4 4AG.

HARRISON, Mr. Matthew John Maurice, MA FCA *1985;* Flat 32A Block 2, Ronsdale Garden, 25 Tai Hang Drive, TAI HANG, HONG KONG ISLAND, HONG KONG SAR.

HARRISON, Mr. Michael, FCA *1955;* 11 Lorraine Circle, WABAN, MA 02468, UNITED STATES. (Life Member)

HARRISON, Mr. Michael, BA ACA *1986;* Mainfirst Bank AG, Golden House, 30 Great Pulteney Street, LONDON, W1F 9LT.

HARRISON, Mr. Michael Alan Brian, MA FCA *1961;* Church End House, Church End, Horningsea, CAMBRIDGE, CB25 9JQ.

HARRISON, Mr. Michael Anthony, FCA *1975;* 22 Briarwood, LISKEARD, PL14 3QQ.

HARRISON, Mr. Michael Anthony, BA ACA *1995;* Crown House, Akzo Nobel Decorative Coatings Ltd, PO Box 37, DARWEN, LANCASHIRE, BB3 0BG.

•**HARRISON, Mr. Michael John, FCA** *1976;* (Tax Fac), Saffery Champness, City Tower, Piccadilly Plaza, MANCHESTER, M1 4BT.

HARRISON, Mr. Michael Martin, ACA *1978;* 31 Lymefield Drive, Worsley, MANCHESTER, M28 1NA.

HARRISON, Mr. Michael Patrick Joseph, FCA *1983;* (Tax Fac), Wrays Cottage Main Street, East Keswick, LEEDS, LS17 9EU.

•**HARRISON, Mr. Michael Stanley, FCA** *1979;* Sobell Rhodes LLP, Monument House, 215 Marsh Road, PINNER, MIDDLESEX, HA5 5NE. See also Windy Ridge Consulting Limited

•**HARRISON, Mr. Michael William, FCA** *1975;* Harrison Latham & Company, 97 Tulketh Street, SOUTHPORT, PR8 1AW.

HARRISON, Mrs. Michele Elisabeth, BSc ACA *1990;* 26 Darlow Drive, Biddenham, BEDFORD, MK40 4AY.

HARRISON, Miss. Miranda Clare, BSc ACA *2009;* 14 Peppermint Road, HITCHIN, HERTFORDSHIRE, SG5 1RY.

HARRISON, Dr. Neil Edward, PhD MA BSc FCA CPA *1974;* P.O. Box 423, LARAMIE, WY 82073, UNITED STATES.

•**HARRISON, Mr. Neil James, LLB ACA CTA** *2003;* Ernst & Young LLP, 1 Bridgewater Place, Water Lane, LEEDS, LS11 5QR. See also Ernst & Young Europe LLP

HARRISON, Mr. Neil Peter, BA ACA *2008;* 158 West Ella Road, Westella, HULL, HU10 7RP.

HARRISON, Mr. Nicholas Dudley, BA FCA *1973;* Rosebery House, 105 Tattenham Crescent, EPSOM, KT18 5NY.

HARRISON, Mr. Nicholas James, BSc(Hons) ACA *2011;* 2 Gloucester Court, HATFIELD, HERTFORDSHIRE, AL10 0UT.

HARRISON, Mr. Nicholas John Edward, BA FCA *1981;* 113 York Road, ALDERSHOT, HAMPSHIRE, GU11 3JQ.

HARRISON, Mr. Nicholas Michael, BA ACA *2000;* 2 Armstrong Street, SEAFORTH, NSW 2092, AUSTRALIA.

HARRISON, Mr. Nigel Radcliffe, FCA *1971;* 31 East Coast Road, Milford, NORTH SHORE CITY 0620, NEW ZEALAND.

HARRISON, Mr. Noel, BSc ACA *1986;* Condor Group Condor House, New Harbour Road South Hamworthy, POOLE, DORSET, BH15 4AJ.

HARRISON, Mr. Norman George Walter, FCA *1967;* 57 Heath Road, CHESTER, CH2 1HT.

HARRISON, Mrs. Pamela Elizabeth, ACA *1990;* Burford House, Park Lane, Bishop Wilton, YORK, YO42 1SS.

HARRISON, Mrs. Patricia Elizabeth, FCA *1976;* Old Chapel Main Street, Barkston Ash, TADCASTER, LS24 9PR.

•**HARRISON, Mr. Paul, MSc BSc FCA** *2000;* Waltons Clark Whitehill LLP, Oakland House, 40 Victoria Road, HARTLEPOOL, CLEVELAND, TS26 8DD. See also Horwath Clark Whitehill (North East) LLP

HARRISON, Mr. Paul Albert, BA ACA *2001;* Places for People, 4 The Pavilions Ashton-on-Ribble, PRESTON, PR2 2YB.

HARRISON, Mr. Paul Alec, BSc ACA *2001;* Ivy Cottage, The Green, Sarratt, RICKMANSWORTH, WD3 6AT.

HARRISON, Mr. Paul Anthony, BA ACA *1989;* Hermes Pensions Management Ltd, Lloyds Chambers, 1 Portsoken Street, LONDON, E1 8HZ.

HARRISON, Mr. Paul Anthony, FCA *1990;* 4720 Center Boulevard, Apartment 516, Long Island City, NEW YORK, NY 11109, UNITED STATES.

HARRISON, Mr. Paul David, BA ACA *2002;* Aztec Financial Services Ltd, PO Box 730, JERSEY, JE4 0QH.

HARRISON, Mr. Paul James, BSc ACA *1984;* Safinvest S.A, 14 Rue du Rhone, CH-1204 GENEVA, SWITZERLAND.

HARRISON, Mr. Paul Lee, MA FCA *1984;* 5 Kelvin Avenue, SALE, M33 3BL.

HARRISON, Mr. Paul Russell, ACA *1986;* Browne Jacobson LLP, 44 Castle Gate, NOTTINGHAM, NG1 7BJ.

HARRISON, Mr. Paul Scott, BA ACA *1991;* The Sage Group Plc, North Park Avenue, NEWCASTLE UPON TYNE, NE13 9AA.

•**HARRISON, Miss. Pauline, FCA ATII** *1977;* Harrison Jones & Co, Excelsior House, Mucklow Hill, HALESOWEN, B62 8EP.

HARRISON, Mrs. Penny Miller, BA ACA *1997;* 3 Tamarisk Close, Up Hatherley, CHELTENHAM, GLOUCESTERSHIRE, GL51 3WL.

•**HARRISON, Mr. Peter, FCA** *1979;* 158 West Ella Road, West Ella, HULL, HU10 7RP.

•**HARRISON, Mr. Peter, FCA** *1955;* (Tax Fac), Peter Harrison, Riggs House, Riggs Head, SCARBOROUGH, YO12 5TG. See also Harrison Peter and Harrison Ingham & Co

HARRISON, Mr. Peter Darrell, FCA *1955;* Whitburn, Surrey Gardens, Effingham Junction, LEATHERHEAD, KT24 5HH. (Life Member)

•**HARRISON, Mr. Peter David, BTech FCA** *1999;* Wright Vigar Limited, Britannia House, Marshalls Yard, GAINSBOROUGH, DN21 2NA. See also Camamile Limited

HARRISON, Mr. Peter John, MBM BA FCA *1989;* The Field House, 3 Mulberry Garth, Thorp Arch, WETHERBY, WEST YORKSHIRE, LS23 7AF.

HARRISON, Mr. Peter John, BSc FCA ATII CF *1990;* 36 Court Yard, LONDON, SE9 5QE.

•**HARRISON, Mr. Peter Owen, FCA** *1980;* 9 Marshals Drive, ST. ALBANS, AL1 4RB.

HARRISON, Dr. Peter Robert, PhD FCA *1959;* Peter Harrison Foundation, 2nd Floor, Fountain House, 42-48 London Road, REIGATE, RH2 9QQ. (Life Member)

HARRISON, Mr. Peter Stewart Malcolm, FCA *1971;* Granary Cottage, Ashurst, STEYNING, BN44 3AP.

•**HARRISON, Mr. Philip David, BSc ACA** *1988;* Cobham Murphy Limited, 116 Duke Street, LIVERPOOL, L1 5JW.

HARRISON, Mr. Philip Gordon, BSc(Econ) FCA *1960;* 28 Lynnbank Road, LIVERPOOL, L18 3HF. (Life Member)

•**HARRISON, Mr. Philip John, FCA** *1973;* (Tax Fac), Morris & Co (2011) Limited, Chester House, Lloyd Drive, Chesire Oaks Business Park, ELLESMERE PORT, CHESHIRE CH65 9HQ.

HARRISON, Mr. Piers Godfrey, ACA *2002;* 28 Alma Road, LONDON, SW18 1AB.

•**HARRISON, Mr. Piers Richard, BA FCA** *1996;* with BDO LLP, Prospect Place, 85 Great North Road, HATFIELD, HERTFORDSHIRE, AL9 5BS.

HARRISON, Mrs. Rachel Emma, BA ACA *1999;* 38 The Leavens, Apperley Bridge, BRADFORD, BD10 0UW.

HARRISON, Mr. Richard, BSc FCA *1974;* The Barn Main Street, Tibthorpe, DRIFFIELD, NORTH HUMBERSIDE, YO25 9LA.

HARRISON, Mr. Richard, BSc ACA *2009;* 5 King Henry Road, FLEET, GU51 1JH.

HARRISON, Mr. Richard Charles Vyvyan, BCom ACA *1995;* Glendon, Cricketfield Lane, BISHOP'S STORTFORD, CM23 2SR.

HARRISON, Mr. Richard James, FCA *1975;* 57 Spareleaze Hill, LOUGHTON, IG10 1BS.

HARRISON, Mr. Richard James, BEng ACA *2001;* First Floor Flat, 15 Mascotte Road, Putney, LONDON, SW15 1NN.

HARRISON, Mr. Richard John, BA ACA *2007;* 135 Block 3 Spectrum, Blackfriars Road, SALFORD, M3 7BP.

•**HARRISON, Mr. Richard John, FCA** *1975;* Harrison & Co Accountants Limited, 531 Denby Dale Road West, Calder Grove, WAKEFIELD, WEST YORKSHIRE, WF4 3ND.

HARRISON, Mr. Richard Keith, BSc ACA *1993;* 10 Bannister Gardens, ROYSTON, SG8 7XA.

HARRISON, Mr. Richard Lloyd, BA(Hons) ACA *2002;* dms Organization Ltd., dms House, PO Box 31910, Grand Cayman KY1-1208, Cayman Islands, GEORGETOWN CAYMAN ISLANDS.

HARRISON, Mr. Richard Samuel, ACA *2001;* Loft 304, The Box Works, Worsley Street, MANCHESTER, M15 4NU.

HARRISON, Mr. Richard W, ACA *2008;* 42 Ashfield Road, SALE, CHESHIRE, M33 7DT.

HARRISON, Mr. Robert Devereux, FCA *1964;* 10 Woodfield, Southwater, HORSHAM, WEST SUSSEX, RH13 9EN.

HARRISON, Mr. Robin Forster, FCA *1975;* Victoria Cottage, 55 Green Lane, Freshfield, LIVERPOOL, L37 7BH.

HARRISON, Mr. Ronald, FCA *1951;* 9 Robin Hill Drive, CAMBERLEY, GU15 1EG. (Life Member)

HARRISON, Mrs. Rosemarie Patricia, ACA *1982;* 428 Whirlowdale Road, Whirlow, SHEFFIELD, S11 9NL.

HARRISON, Miss. Rosemary Elizabeth, BA ACA *1993;* Hunters, Maresfield, UCKFIELD, TN22 2EE.

HARRISON, Mr. Russell, ACA *2010;* 42 Mount Pleasant Drive, BOURNEMOUTH, BH8 9JN.

HARRISON, Miss. Ruth Constance Mary, BA ACA *1993;* 31 Ashburnham Grove, LONDON, SE10 8UL.

HARRISON, Mrs. Samantha, BSc ACA *1995;* Junkanoo Cottage, 6 Bodiam Close, Shenley Church End, MILTON KEYNES, MK5 6HS.

HARRISON, Miss. Samantha Beatrice Susan, BA ACA CF *2003;* Old Change House, 128 Queen Victoria Street, LONDON, EC4V 4BJ.

•**HARRISON, Ms. Sandra Jean, BEd FCA CTA** *1991;* (Tax Fac), Wilkins Kennedy, Greytown House, 221-227 High Street, ORPINGTON, BR6 0NZ.

HARRISON, Mrs. Sarah, BA ACA *2004;* 48 Highfield Road, LYMM, CHESHIRE, WA13 0EF.

HARRISON, Mrs. Sarah, ACA *2003;* 42 Mount Pleasant Drive, BOURNEMOUTH, BH8 9JN.

HARRISON, Miss. Sarah Elizabeth, ACA *2010;* 12 Crystal Wood Road, CARDIFF, CF14 4HW.

HARRISON, Mrs. Sarah Jane, BA ACA CTA *1990;* 5 Orchard Avenue, HARPENDEN, AL5 2DW.

HARRISON, Mrs. Sarah Kate, BSc ACA *1993;* Ecolab Ltd, David Murray John Building, SWINDON, SN1 1NH.

HARRISON, Mr. Shaun, ACA *2006;* with HSBC Bank plc, 62-76 Park Street, LONDON, SE1 9DZ.

HARRISON, Mrs. Sheila Christine, BSc ACA *1990;* Girsby Green, Neasham, DARLINGTON, DL2 1PP.

HARRISON, Mr. Simon, ACA *2010;* 4 Tees Court, Bingham, NOTTINGHAM, NG13 8XE.

HARRISON, Mr. Simon David, BSc ACA *1997;* Coley Croft, Norwood Green, HALIFAX, HX3 8RD.

•**HARRISON, Mr. Simon Paul, FCA** *1990;* Townsend Harrison Limited, 13 Yorkersgate, MALTON, NORTH YORKSHIRE, YO17 7AA.

HARRISON, Mrs. Stephanie Clare, MA ACA *2002;* Stable Cottage Chiltern Rise, Reading Road Woodcote, READING, RG8 0QX.

HARRISON, Mrs. Stephanie Frances, BSc ACA *2009;* 1 The Spinney, Granville Road, LONDON, N12 0HR.

HARRISON, Mr. Stephen, MMath ACA *2010;* 250 Horn Lane, LONDON, W3 6TQ.

HARRISON, Mr. Stephen John, BA ACA *1987;* 2 Milburn Close, Riverside, CHESTER-LE-STREET, DH3 3QT.

HARRISON, Mr. Stephen Lee, BSocSc ACA *1993;* 89 Jalan Bunga Anggerik Dataran Ukay, 68000 AMPANG, MALAYSIA.

•**HARRISON, Mr. Stephen Patrick, BSc ACA** *1981;* (Tax Fac), PKF (UK) LLP, Farringdon Place, 20 Farringdon Road, LONDON, EC1M 3AP.

HARRISON, Mr. Stephen Paul, MA ACA *1979;* 341 Ivydale Road, LONDON, SE15 3ED.

HARRISON, Mr. Stephen Peter, BA(Hons) ACA *2002;* 3 Wensley Crescent, LEEDS, LS7 3QT.

•**HARRISON, Mr. Stephen William, BSc FCA** *1978;* 46 Westport Avenue, Mayals, SWANSEA, SA3 5EQ.

HARRISON, Mr. Steven, BA ACA *1991;* 16b St. Pauls Place, LONDON, N1 2QF.

HARRISON, Mr. Steven Joseph, MSc ACA *1996;* W L I Ltd Belvedere House, Basing View, BASINGSTOKE, RG21 4HG.

•**HARRISON, Mr. Stewart Clive, BSc FCA** *1989;* (Tax Fac), S Harrison, 6 Albany, 38-40 Alexandra Grove, North Finchley, LONDON, N12 8NN.

•**HARRISON, Mr. Stuart Paul, BA ACA** *2003;* Venthams Limited, Millhouse, 32-38 East Street, ROCHFORD, SS4 1DB.

HARRISON, Mrs. Susan, ACA MAAT *2002;* Autumn Cottage Randalls Green, Chalford Hill, STROUD, GLOUCESTERSHIRE, GL6 8EB.

HARRISON, Mrs. Susan Margaret, BSc ACA *1987;* 7 Sunnybank Road, Boldmere, SUTTON COLDFIELD, B73 5RE.

HARRISON, Mrs. Suzanne Louise, ACA *2000;* 6 Cornwell Close, Isleham, ELY, CAMBRIDGESHIRE, CB7 5BF.

HARRISON, Mrs. Suzy-Jayne Elizabeth, BSc ACA *2004;* 86 Whitefield Lane, Tarbock Green, PRESCOT, MERSEYSIDE, L35 1QX.

HARRISON, Mrs. Tamasine Clare, BSc ACA *1996;* 27 Montagu Road, Datchet, SLOUGH, BERKSHIRE, SL3 9DT.

HARRISON, Mr. Thomas Francis, FCA *1952;* 10 Fairfield Close, Penrhyn Bay, LLANDUDNO, CONWY, LL30 3HU. (Life Member)

HARRISON, Mr. Thomas Frederick George, FCA *1960;* Oakhaven, 5 Brockway West, Tattenhall, CHESTER, CH3 9EZ.

HARRISON, Mr. Thomas Paul, BA FCA *1982;* 9420 Bartons Creek Road, RALEIGH, NC 27615, UNITED STATES.

HARRISON, Mr. Timothy Parker, BA ACA *1982;* Spreakley House, Frensham, FARNHAM, SURREY, GU10 3EJ.

HARRISON, Mr. Trevor John, BA FCA *1983;* Svenska Handelsbanken, 3 Thomas More Square, LONDON, E1W 1WY.

HARRISON, Mr. Trevor Stewart, MA LLM FCA *1972;* Pashley Down, Montreal Road, SEVENOAKS, TN13 2EP. (Life Member)

HARRISON, Miss. Vanessa Elaine, BA ACA *2002;* 19g Westbourne Drive, LONDON, SE23 2UP.

HARRISON, Mrs. Victoria, BA(Hons) ACA *2002;* Flat 11 Triangle Court, 10 Redcross Way, LONDON, SE1 1TA.

HARRISON, Mr. William Charles, FCA *1957;* 5 Roseway Rosemary Ln Burton, Rossett, WREXHAM, LL12 0LF. (Life Member)

•**HARRISON, Mr. William Nigel, FCA** *1986;* Harrison Walker, Enterprise House, 2 Pass Street, OLDHAM, OL9 6HZ.

•**HARRISON-CRIPPS, Mr. William Lawrence, FCA MInstD CTA** *1973;* (Tax Fac), Tollgate, Lawbrook Lane, Peaslake, GUILDFORD, GU5 9QW.

HARRISON PLACE, Ms. Julia Mary, BA ACA *1987;* 21 Jubilee Close, SALISBURY, SP2 9HF.

HARRISON-TOPHAM, Mr. Thomas Roger Nevile, MA FCA *1968;* Ashes Farm, Caldbergh, LEYBURN, DL8 4RP.

•**HARRISSON, Mr. Mark William Damer, MA FCA** *1967;* Groupe Agora, 2 rue Joseph Sansboeuf, 75008 PARIS, FRANCE.
HARRISSON, Mr. Philip Timothy, FCA *1973;* Rheingold, 58 Brushfield Way, Knaphill, WOKING, GU21 2TQ.
HARRITY, Mr. Austin Paul, BA(Oxon) ACA *2006;* Flat 14 Amberley Court Mill Road, WORTHING, WEST SUSSEX, BN11 5HG.
HARROCKS, Mr. Denis, FCA *1949;* 51 Altys Lane, ORMSKIRK, L39 4RG. (Life Member)
•**HARROD, Mr. David, FCA** *1974;* Harrod Neilson & Company, 14 Woodstock Road, Bushey Heath, BUSHEY, HERTFORDSHIRE, WD23 1PH.
HARROD, Mr. Hugo, MSc ACA *2006;* 14 Ravenscourt Road, LONDON, W6 0UG.
HARROD, Miss. Sarah Barbara, BA ACA *2007;* 1 Newsham Close, NEWCASTLE UPON TYNE, NE5 1QD.
HARROLD, Mr. Alan Henry, BSc ACA *1981;* Cherry Tree House, The Drive, BOURNE END, BUCKINGHAMSHIRE, SL8 5RE.
HARROLD, Mr. Leslie Percy, FCA *1946;* 9 Coulston Court, East Common, GERRARDS CROSS, BUCKINGHAMSHIRE, SL9 7AA. (Life Member)
HARROLD, Dr. Nicola Elaine, BSc(Hons) ACA *2001;* Molson Coors Brewing Company (UK) Ltd, 137 High Street, BURTON-ON-TRENT, STAFFORDSHIRE, DE14 1JZ.
•**HARROLD, Mr. Philip Richard, BA FCA** *1986;* PricewaterhouseCoopers LLP, Donington Court, Pegasus Business Park, Castle Donington, DERBY, DE74 2UZ. See also PricewaterhouseCoopers
•**HARROLD, Mr. Rex, FCA** *1972;* (Tax Fac), Rex Harrold & Co, The Old Coach House, Theobalds Park Road, ENFIELD, EN2 9BD.
HARROLD, Mr. Tom, ACA *2010;* 6 Nesta Road, WOODFORD GREEN, ESSEX, IG8 9RG.
HARROLD, Mrs. Tracey, BSc ACA *1987;* Hawthorns, Stoney Lane, Ashmore Green, THATCHAM, RG18 9HF.
HARROP, Miss. Alison Claire, BSc ACA *1990;* P O Box N157, Grosvenor Place, SYDNEY, NSW 1220, AUSTRALIA.
HARROP, Mr. Andrew, ACA *2011;* 32 Station Road, HESSLE, NORTH HUMBERSIDE, HU13 0BG.
HARROP, Mr. Andrew David, FCA CTA *1990;* Mazars, Mazars House, Gelderd Road, Gildersome, Morley, LEEDS LS27 7JN.
HARROP, Mr. David Anthony, BA ACA *1996;* 2 Home Farm Mews, Bingley Road, Menston, ILKLEY, WEST YORKSHIRE, LS29 6BB.
HARROP, Mr. Matthew Jonathan, BSc ACA *2004;* 122 Strathville Road, LONDON, SW18 4RE.
HARROP, Mr. Michael John, FCA *1969;* Szerelmey Ltd, 369 Kennington Lane, Vauxhall, LONDON, SE11 5QY.
HARROP, Mr. Nicholas Charles, BA ACA *1992;* (Tax Fac), 99 Forge Fields, SANDBACH, CHESHIRE, CW11 3RD.
HARROP, Mr. Peter Edmund Morris, FCA *1960;* 3 Park Farm Cottages, Main Street, Carlton-On-Trent, NEWARK, NG23 6NW. (Life Member)
HARROP, Mrs. Sarah Louise, BA ACA *1997;* 2 Home Farm Mews, Bingley Road, Menston, ILKLEY, LS29 6BB.
HARROP, Mr. Simon Lawrence, BA FCA *1988;* 113 Dane Road, SALE, CHESHIRE, M33 7BL.
HARROW, Mrs. Christina Louise, MA ACA *2009;* 4 Murray Road, Wimbledon, LONDON, SW19 4PB.
HARROW, Mr. Peter James, FCA *1975;* 20 Redhill Drive, BRIGHTON, BN1 5FH.
HARROW, Mr. Stephen Giles, BA ACA *2000;* with Ernst & Young LLP, 1 More London Place, LONDON, SE1 2AF.
•**HARROWER, Mr. Ian, FCA** *1969;* Ian Harrower, 45 Ashlone Road, Putney, LONDON, SW15 1LS.
HARROWER, Mr. Scott John, BSc ACA *2006;* 3 Ash Vale Cottages, Ash Vale, Chiddingfold, GODALMING, GU8 4RD.
HARROWSMITH, Mr. John Anthony, BSc FCA *1968;* Plum Tree Cottage, Low Way, Bramham, WETHERBY, LS23 6QT.
•**HARRUP, Mr. Peter John, BSc ACA** *1989;* (Tax Fac), PKF (UK) LLP, 16 The Havens, Ransomes Europark, IPSWICH, IP3 9SJ.
•**HARRY, Mr. Christopher, ACA** *1979;* Butterfield Morgan Limited, Druslyn House, De La Beche Street, SWANSEA, SA1 3HJ.
HARRY, Mr. Daniel Peter, BA ACA *1996;* 64 Chestnut Manor Close, STAINES, MIDDLESEX, TW18 1AQ.
HARRY, Mr. Edward Charles Clement, BSc ACA *1992;* 17 Holly Grove, Lisvane, CARDIFF, CF14 0UJ.
HARRY, Mr. Mark Adrian, BSc ACA *1988;* Flat 5 Chesterfield Court, 76 Granville Park, LONDON, SE13 7DU.
HARRY, Mr. Oliver James, ACA *2008;* Grosvenor Villas, 4 Hamilton Road, Wimbledon, LONDON, SW19 1JF.
HARRY, Mr. Shane Edwin, MChem ACA *2009;* (Tax Fac), Flat 2 Fleet House, 6 Victory Place, LONDON, E14 8BG.
HARSANT, Mr. Raymond Peter, FCA *1959;* Beech Hill, 69 Kippington Road, SEVENOAKS, TN13 2LN. (Life Member)
HARSIANI, Mr. Kishor Ramesh, BA ACA *1998;* 16 Five Fields Close, WATFORD, WD19 5BZ.
HARSLEY, Mr. Michael John, BA ACA *1985;* Advanced Air, Burrell Way, THETFORD, NORFOLK, IP24 3QU.
HARSTON, Mr. Jonathan James, MA ACA *2002;* 23 Hazelbank, SURBITON, KT5 9RQ.
HART, Mr. Adam, ACA *2008;* with Deloitte & Touche, Regency Court, Glategny Esplanade, St Peter Port, GUERNSEY, GY1 3HW.
HART, Mr. Adam David, LLB ACA FRSA *1989;* London Bridge Capital Ltd, 33 Glasshouse Street, LONDON, W1B 5DG.
•**HART, Mr. Adrian Charles, BA FCA** *1973;* THP Limited, 34-40 High Street, Wanstead, LONDON, E11 2RJ. See also THP Company Secretarial LLP, THP Tax Solutions LLP and THP Wealth Structuring LLP
•**HART, Mr. Alan Gordon, BA FCA** *1972;* (Tax Fac), 3 Barkworth Close, Anlaby, HULL, HU10 7HL.
HART, Mr. Alan Graham, BSc ACA *1997;* Whits End, Cock Lane, Penn, HIGH WYCOMBE, BUCKINGHAMSHIRE, HP10 8DY.
HART, Mr. Alexander William, FCA *1964;* Heathfield, Raleigh Drive, Claygate, ESHER, SURREY, KT10 9DE. (Life Member)
HART, Mrs. Alice Catherine, ACA *2004;* Valley Farm Poultry LTD, Blacksmiths Meadow, Combs Lane, STOWMARKET, SUFFOLK, IP14 2NJ.
HART, Mrs. Amanda Judith, BA ACA *1999;* 5 Grange Close, WINCHESTER, SO23 9RS.
HART, Mr. Andrew John, LLB ACA *1992;* 17 Bramley Gardens, Whimple, EXETER, EX5 2SJ.
HART, Mr. Andrew Thomas James, ACA *2008;* with PricewaterhouseCoopers LLP, 1 Embankment Place, LONDON, WC2N 6RH.
HART, Mr. Anthony Gordon Kenneth, FCA *1965;* 16 Halyards, Topsham, EXETER, EX3 0JU. (Life Member)
HART, Mr. Anthony Gordon Seymour, FCA *1950;* Pitfield, Bayley's Hill, SEVENOAKS, TN14 6HS. (Life Member)
HART, Mr. Anthony Jason, BA(Hons) FCA *2000;* 7 Lytham Close, SKIPTON, BD23 2LF.
HART, Mr. Antony Ian, BSc ACA *2005;* 75 Trelawney Road, Peverell, PLYMOUTH, PL3 4JY.
HART, Mrs. Barbara Joan, BA FCA *1978;* 107 Lower Village Road, ASCOT, SL5 9BQ.
HART, Mr. Brian George, FCA *1971;* 81 Alumhurst Road, BOURNEMOUTH, BH4 8HR.
HART, Mr. Bryan, FCA *1964;* 5 Mercedes Avenue, HUNSTANTON, PE36 5EJ. (Life Member)
HART, Dr. Carol Jean, FCA *1984;* 55 Methuen Road, New Windsor, AUCKLAND 0600, NEW ZEALAND.
HART, Mr. Charles James, FCA *1969;* The Old Village Shop, 4 Heathview Cottages, Mill Lane, Great Warford, ALDERLEY EDGE, CHESHIRE SK9 7TY.
HART, Mrs. Charlotte Sophie, BSc ACA *2009;* 59 Eaststand Apartments, Highbury Stadium Square, LONDON, N5 1FF.
HART, Mr. Christopher, MA ACA *2011;* Flat 11, 19 St. Alphonsus Road, LONDON, SW4 7AW.
HART, Mr. Colin Kenneth, FCA *1972;* 2 Woods End, Dunholme, LINCOLN, LN2 3FT.
HART, Mr. Darren, BA ACA *1993;* 9 Siskin Close, Mickleover, DERBY, DE3 5UL.
HART, Mr. David, FCA *1957;* 19 Seafields, Seaburn, SUNDERLAND, SR6 8PQ. (Life Member)
HART, Mr. David, BA ACA *1990;* Lynton House, 17 Lorne Grove, Radcliffe-On-Trent, NOTTINGHAM, NG12 2FX.
•**HART, Mr. David Ernest, MA MBA FCA** *1973;* Mittelstrasse IC, 59872 MESCHEDE, GERMANY.
HART, Mr. David Glencairn Wilson, BSc ACA *1982;* (Tax Fac), 1 Glenask Court, London Road, Binfield, BRACKNELL, BERKSHIRE, RG42 4AB.
HART, Mr. David Mcknight, BA FCA *1978;* The Hunting Lodge, 127 London Road West, BATH, BA1 7JF.
HART, Mr. David Patrick, FCA *1955;* 15 Birdcroft Lane, ILKESTON, DE7 4BE. (Life Member)
HART, Mr. Derek Arthur, FCA *1972;* 24 Oaktree Drive, HOOK, RG27 9RN.
•**HART, Miss. Elizabeth Michelle, BSc ACA** *2004;* LBCA Limited, 8 Waterside, Station Road, HARPENDEN, HERTFORDSHIRE, AL5 4US.
HART, Mrs. Emma Louise, ACA *2004;* Schroders, 31 Gresham Street, LONDON, EC2V 7QA.
HART, Mr. Gerald Charles, FCA *1967;* 1 Beacon Walk, Gringley-on-the-Hill, DONCASTER, SOUTH YORKSHIRE, DN10 4TD.
HART, Mrs. Helen Mary, BA ACA *1991;* 11 The Vineyard, RICHMOND, SURREY, TW10 6AQ.
HART, Mr. Henry Corbett, MA FCA *1958;* 41 Sydenham Rise, LONDON, SE23 3XL. (Life Member)
HART, Dr. Ian James, PhD BA ACA *2004;* with National Audit Office, 157-197 Buckingham Palace Road, Victoria, LONDON, SW1W 9SP.
HART, Mr. Ian Keith, ACA *2007;* 37 Penterry Park, CHEPSTOW, GWENT, NP16 5AZ.
HART, Mr. Ian Keith, BA ACA *1990;* 11 The Vineyard, RICHMOND, SURREY, TW10 6AQ.
•**HART, Mr. Ian Peter, BA FCA** *1991;* Henton & Co LLP, St. Andrews House, St. Andrews Street, LEEDS, LS3 1LF.
HART, Mr. Ivor Malcolm, FCA *1957;* Flat 33 Theydon Bower, Bower Hill, EPPING, CM16 7AB. (Life Member)
HART, Mr. James Simon, BCom ACA *2001;* 25 The Avenue, NORTHWOOD, MIDDLESEX, HA6 2NJ.
HART, Mr. James Thomas, ACA *1997;* 14 Langthwaite Close, BROUGH, NORTH HUMBERSIDE, HU15 1TH.
HART, Mr. James Thomas Lewis, FCA *1969;* 15 Cremorne Road, SUTTON COLDFIELD, WEST MIDLANDS, B75 5AH.
HART, Miss. Jane, BSc(Hons) ACA *2011;* 3 Croft Gardens, Grappenhall Heys, WARRINGTON, WA4 3LH.
•**HART, Mrs. Janet Margaret, BSc FCA** *1979;* (Tax Fac), Harts, 3 Churchgates, Church Lane, BERKHAMSTED, HERTFORDSHIRE, HP4 2UB.
HART, Mr. Jeffrey Darrell, BSc FCA *1994;* 28a Dene Road, NORTHWOOD, MIDDLESEX, HA6 2BT.
HART, Mr. Jeffrey John, BCom ACA *1998;* 84 Cole Valley Road, BIRMINGHAM, B28 0DF.
HART, Miss. Jennifer Margaret, MSc BAcc ACA *2010;* Flat 14, Central, 5 Wharf Road, SALE, CHESHIRE, M33 2ZJ.
HART, Mr. Jeremy Colin, BSc FCA *1989;* (Tax Fac), Garthowen, 16 The Ridge, Yatton, BRISTOL, BS49 4DQ.
HART, Mr. John Anthony, FCA *1968;* 67 Lullington Garth, LONDON, N12 7BL.
HART, Mr. John Blair, FCA *1981;* Bretton House, Baldersby, THIRSK, NORTH YORKSHIRE, YO7 4PP.
HART, Mr. Jolyon Avery, BA FCA *1982;* Leicester Mercury, Northcliffe Accounting Centre, PO Box 6795, LEICESTER, LE1 1ZP.
HART, Mr. Jonathan David, BA ACA *1983;* 13 Dryden Road, ENFIELD, MIDDLESEX, EN1 2PR.
HART, Mr. Jonathan Paul, BSc ACA *1998;* Meadow Bank, The Avenue, GODALMING, GU7 1PE.
HART, Miss. Katherine Elizabeth, BSc ACA *2003;* Oak Farm Receptions, Oaks Farm, Oaks Lane, Shirley, CROYDON, CR0 5HP.
HART, Mrs. Katherine Rebecca, BSc ACA *2002;* Meadow Bank, The Avenue, GODALMING, GU7 1PE.
HART, Mr. Keith Alisdaire, BSc FCA *1972;* Maltings Farm, The Street, Great Wratting, HAVERHILL, SUFFOLK, CB9 7HQ.
HART, Mrs. Kirsty Lyn, BA ACA *1999;* Lavender Cottage, 4 Cryers Hill Lane, HIGH WYCOMBE, HP15 6AA.
HART, Miss. Lucy Emma, MA ACA *2011;* 21 Hillview, Queensferry Road, EDINBURGH, EH4 2AF.
HART, Miss. Lucy Katherine, BA ACA *2009;* 43 Campbell Road, SOUTHSEA, PO5 1RJ.
HART, Mrs. Maria, ACA CA(SA) *2008;* 28 Dorien Road, LONDON, SW20 8EJ.
•**HART, Mr. Mark Edward, BA ACA CTA** *1995;* Blick Rothenberg, 12 York Gate, Regent's Park, LONDON, NW1 4QS.
HART, Mr. Mark Jonathan, BA ACA *1986;* Carr End, Doods Way, REIGATE, SURREY, RH2 0JT.
HART, Mr. Mark Richard, BSc ACA *2006;* 59 Eaststand Apartments, Highbury Stadium Square, LONDON, N5 1FF.
HART, Mr. Marsden Colin Henry, FCA *1972;* 6 rue d Orgeval, 91400 ORSAY, FRANCE. (Life Member)
HART, Mr. Matthew, BSc ACA *2010;* 3 Ferrari House, Lowlands Road, Vale, GUERNSEY, GY3 5SZ.
HART, Mr. Matthew, ACA *2010;* 10 Troy Rise, Morley, LEEDS, LS27 8JH.
•**HART, Mr. Michael James, BA FCA** *1996;* (Tax Fac), Thompson Jenner LLP, 1 Colleton Crescent, EXETER, EX2 4DG.
HART, Mr. Michael John, FCA *1972;* 262 Watford Road, Croxley Green, RICKMANSWORTH, WD3 3DD.
HART, Mr. Michael Ross, BA(Hons) FCA *1972;* 36 Coleshill Street, SUTTON COLDFIELD, WEST MIDLANDS, B72 1SH.
HART, Mr. Nicholas, ACA *2008;* Flat 1 Tanners Court, 53 St. Andrew Street, HERTFORD, SG14 1HZ.
HART, Mr. Nicholas, BSc ACA *2007;* 200 W 26th Street, Apt 9I, NEW YORK, NY 10001, UNITED STATES.
HART, Miss. Nicola Stephanie, BSc ACA *2010;* 2 Redan Road, WARE, HERTFORDSHIRE, SG12 7NJ.
•**HART, Mr. Nigel Howard, FCA** *1978;* (Tax Fac), Nigel H Hart & Co, 99 Old Church Lane, STANMORE, MIDDLESEX, HA7 2RT.
HART, Mr. Oliver Nicolas Norwood, FCA *1956;* Mintwall House, Aldgate, Ketton, STAMFORD, PE9 3TD. (Life Member)
HART, Mr. Paul Andrew, BSc ACA *1992;* 22 Kinsbourne Close, HARPENDEN, HERTFORDSHIRE, AL5 3PB.
HART, Mr. Paul Ernest, FCA *1964;* 34 Parkhouse Road, MINEHEAD, SOMERSET, TA24 8AD. (Life Member)
HART, Mr. Paul James, BSc ACA *1993;* Manpower Limited Capital Court, 10 Windsor Street, UXBRIDGE, MIDDLESEX, UB8 1AB.
HART, Mr. Peter Robin, BA(Hons) ACA *2010;* 64 Tottenhall Road, LONDON, N13 6JB.
HART, Mr. Philip Martin, FCA *1974;* Urbanisation Puig Rosell, C d' Isabel Vila 18, 17251 CALONGE, SPAIN. (Life Member)
HART, Mr. Philip Michael, BSc ACA *2007;* 46 De Montfort Road, LONDON, SW16 1LZ.
HART, Mr. Philip Simon, MA MPhil FCA *2001;* Barclays Bank Plc, 1 Churchill Place, LONDON, E14 5HP.
•**HART, Mrs. Rachael, ACA** *2007;* Rachael Hart ACA, 3 Evelench Barns, Evelench Lane, Tibberton, DROITWICH, WORCESTERSHIRE WR9 7NY.
HART, Miss. Rachel Anna, BA ACA *1997;* 16/13 Stuart St, MANLY, NSW 2095, AUSTRALIA.
HART, Miss. Rebecca Louise, MEng ACA *2007;* B P P Holdings Plc Aldine House, 142-144 Uxbridge Road, LONDON, W12 8AA.
HART, Mr. Robert Edwin, BA ACA *2006;* 23 Wansbeck Close, STEVENAGE, HERTFORDSHIRE, SG1 6AA.
HART, Miss. Rosemary, ACA *1979;* (Tax Fac), with Smith & Williamson, Old Library Chambers, 21 Chipper Lane, SALISBURY, SP1 1BG.
HART, Mrs. Rosemary Ann, BA ACA *1979;* Bretton House, Baldersby, THIRSK, YO7 4PP.
HART, Ms. Rosemary Georgina, BSc ACA *1992;* 24 St. Mary's Road, LONDON, SW19 7BW.
HART, Dr. Samantha Elizabeth, PhD BA ACA ATII *1994;* with Deloitte LLP, 3 Rivergate, Temple Quay, BRISTOL, BS1 6GD.
HART, Miss. Samantha Leigh, ACA *2002;* 631 Chester Road, SUTTON COLDFIELD, WEST MIDLANDS, B73 5HY.
HART, Mrs. Sandra, BSc ACA *1992;* Bristol & London Plc, Harbour Place, Serbert Road, BRISTOL, BS20 7GF.
HART, Ms. Sara-Jane, BA(Hons) ACA *2001;* 4 Turnpike Close, DARLINGTON, DL1 3SH.
HART, Mrs. Sarah Louise, BA ACA *1995;* Pilgrims End Pilgrims Way Westhumble, DORKING, SURREY, RH5 6AP.
HART, Mr. Simon David, BA ACA *1990;* (Tax Fac), Arbil Limited, Providence Street, Lye, STOURBRIDGE, WEST MIDLANDS, DY9 8HS.
HART, Mr. Stephen, BSc ACA *1997;* Pricewaterhousecoopers Abacus House, Castle Park, CAMBRIDGE, CB3 0AN.
HART, Mr. Terence Alan, BSc ACA *1991;* Telstra Europe Ltd, Blue Fin Building, 2nd Floor, 110 Southwark Street, LONDON, SE1 0TA.
HART, Mr. Thomas John, ACA *1983;* 3 West Hartlepool Road, Wolviston, BILLINGHAM, CLEVELAND, TS22 5JZ.
HART, Mr. Thomas Richard Ogden, MA FCA *1967;* B I S (Integrated Solutions) UK Ltd Roman Way, Grange Park, NORTHAMPTON, NN4 5EA.
HART, Mr. Timothy Guy Collins, ACA *1980;* Kingswood House, The Lee, GREAT MISSENDEN, HP16 9NU.
•**HART, Mrs. Wendy Elizabeth, BA FCA CF** *1992;* Grant Thornton UK LLP, 3140 Rowan Place, John Smith Drive, Oxford Business Park South, OXFORD, OX4 2WB. See also Grant Thornton LLP
HART, Mrs. Zoe, ACA *2008;* Flat G, 105 Honor Oak Park, LONDON, SE23 3LB.
HART-DALE, Miss. Victoria Helena, BA(Hons) ACA *2002;* 36 Emerson Apartments, Chadwell Lane, LONDON, N8 7RF.

HART DYKE, Mr. James Paul, BSc ACA *1998;* British American Tobacco, Polska Trading Sp. z o.o., Wisniowy Business Park, Bud E, Ul. Llzecka 26, 02-135 WARSAW POLAND.
HART-SMITH, Mrs. Gabrielle Louise, BA BSc ACA *2002;* Willifield Hedgerow, Chalfont St. Peter, GERRARDS CROSS, BUCKINGHAMSHIRE, SL9 0HD.
HARTAS, Miss. Janet Marie, BA FCA *1990;* 14 Briar Hollow, Heaton Mersey, STOCKPORT, SK4 2EE.
HARTE, Miss. Audrey Patricia, BA ACA *1995;* 91 Binn Eadair View, Sutton, DUBLIN 13, COUNTY DUBLIN, IRELAND.
HARTE, Mr. Brian Arthur, BCom FCA *1978;* Royal Bank of Canada, 17/F Cheung Kong Centre, 2 Queens Road, CENTRAL, HONG KONG SAR.
•**HARTE, Miss. Claire Elaine, BEng FCA** *1996;* S.W.Frankson & Co, Bridge House, 119-123 Station Road, HAYES, MIDDLESEX, UB3 4BX.
HARTE, Mr. David Patrick, ACA *1983;* 15 Cotswold Meadow, WITNEY, OX28 5FA.
HARTE, Mr. Jason Maxwell, ACA *1989;* 64 Chestfield Road, Chestfield, WHITSTABLE, KENT, CT5 3JH.
HARTE, Mrs. Nicola Jane, BSc ACA *1994;* 12 Robins Close, Barford St Michael, BANBURY, OX15 0RP.
HARTE, Mr. Peter Richard, BSc FCA *1975;* 16 Osborne Road, LONDON, N13 5PS.
HARTE, Mrs. Sandra Anne Maude, BCom FCA *1979;* Flat 1B, Henredon Court, 8 Shouson Hill Road, SHOUSON HILL, HONG KONG SAR.
HARTE, Mrs. Tamara Joanne, MA FCA *1995;* 1 The Sycamores, Little London, SPALDING, LINCOLNSHIRE, PE11 2UD.
HARTE, Mr. William Nigel Bret, BA ACA *1992;* Unipart Leisure & Marine Parkwood House, Charter Avenue, COVENTRY, CV4 8DA.
HARTELL, Mr. Graham, BSc ACA *1981;* 17 Sunningdale Avenue, Rossall Park, FLEETWOOD, FY7 8HS.
•**HARTEY, Mr. Michael Denis, FCA** *1980;* Randomlight Ltd, 6-8 Old Hall Road, Gatley, CHEADLE, CHESHIRE, SK8 4BE.
HARTEY, Mr. Peter James, BA ACA *1989;* 3 Cedar Grove, STOCKPORT, SK4 4RN.
HARTFORD, Mr. Colin Anthony, FCA *1973;* 10 Broad Lane, LYMINGTON, HAMPSHIRE, SO41 3QP.
HARTGILL, Mr. Thomas Leonard, ACA *2002;* The Blade, Abbey Street, READING, RG1 3BA.
HARTHAN, Mr. David, FCA *1969;* (Tax Fac), Harbury Bungalow, 15a Rush Hill Road, Uppermill, OLDHAM, OL3 6JD.
HARTIGAN, Mr. A Spencer, BBS FCA *1972;* 973 Beaconsfield Road, NORTH VANCOUVER V7R 1T1, BC, CANADA.
HARTIGAN, Mr. John William, BA ACA *1995;* 1 Gannaway Court, Curlieu Lane, Norton Lindsey, WARWICK, CV35 8JR.
HARTIGAN, Mr. Timothy Mark, BA ACA *1985;* Bibby Financial Services, Packington House, 3-4 Horse Fair, BANBURY, OXFORDSHIRE, OX16 0AA.
HARTILL, Mr. Peter James Norman, FCA *1974;* 31a George Road, Edgbaston, BIRMINGHAM, B15 1PJ.
HARTILL, Mrs. Sarah Louise, BSc ACA *2006;* 9 Staten Gardens, TWICKENHAM, TW1 4HS.
HARTIS, Mr. Anthony Marc, MSci ACA *2004;* 23 Lurline Gardens, LONDON, SW11 4DB.
HARTLAND, Mr. Derek William, FCA *1969;* Elizabeth House, 8a Princess Street, KNUTSFORD, CHESHIRE, Wa16 6DD.
HARTLAND, Mr. Horace Howard, FCA *1948;* 95 Chestnut Drive, Erdington, BIRMINGHAM, B24 0DR. (Life Member)
HARTLAND, Mrs. Isabel Dalton, BSc ACA *1993;* 31 Endcliffe Glen Road, SHEFFIELD, S11 8RW.
HARTLAND, Mr. Jeremy Robert, MA ACA *2000;* 12 West Road, SAFFRON WALDEN, CB11 3DS.
HARTLAND, Mr. Malcolm Robert, BA ACA *1996;* Lockwood Rectory, 20 Solid, Woodhead Road, HUDDERSFIELD, HD4 6ES.
HARTLAND, Mr. Peter Conway, BSc ACA *1990;* 31 Endcliffe Glen Road, SHEFFIELD, S11 8RW.
HARTLE, Mr. Thomas Peter, FCA *1963;* west wold, 20 caistor road, MARKET RASEN, LINCOLNSHIRE, ln8 3fe. (Life Member)
HARTLEBURY, Mr. Thomas William, BSc ACA *2010;* 19 Pinewoods Avenue, Hagley, STOURBRIDGE, WEST MIDLANDS, DY9 0JF.
HARTLESS, Mr. Adrian Charles, BCom FCA *1976;* TI Automotive Ltd, 4650 Kingsgate, Cascade Way, OXFORD, OX4 2SU.
HARTLEY, Mr. Adam Oliver, ACA *2008;* 17 Hillary Avenue, NEWCASTLE UPON TYNE, NE12 9LS.
•**HARTLEY, Mr. Alan, FCA** *1965;* Alan Hartley, 5 West Lane, Pirton, HITCHIN, SG5 3RA.
HARTLEY, Mr. Alexander James, BA(Hons) ACA *2002;* with KPMG LLP, St. James's Square, MANCHESTER, M2 6DS.
HARTLEY, Miss. Alison Elizabeth, BA ACA *1989;* The Port House, 7 Royal Park, Mill Street, ULLAPOOL, ROSS-SHIRE, IV26 2XT.
HARTLEY, Mr. Andrew, BA ACA *1983;* The Brambles, 3 Manor Park, Arkendale, KNARESBOROUGH, NORTH YORKSHIRE, HG5 0QH.
HARTLEY, Mr. Andrew John, BSc FCA CF *1987;* UBS Ltd. Strategic Equity Solutions, 1 Finsbury Avenue, LONDON, EC2M2PP.
HARTLEY, Mr. Andrew John, BA ACA *1993;* 1 Singleton Road, Heaton Moor, STOCKPORT, SK4 4PW.
HARTLEY, Mr. Andrew Peter James, BSc ACA *2010;* 34 Caldervale Avenue, MANCHESTER, M21 7PD.
HARTLEY, Mr. Brian Newbitt, FCA *1957;* 33 The Limes, 34/36 Linden Gardens, LONDON, W2 4ET. (Life Member)
•**HARTLEY, Mrs. Caroline Elizabeth, BSc FCA** *1980;* Caroline Hartley FCA, 21 Anglesey Drive, Poynton, STOCKPORT, SK12 1BT.
HARTLEY, Mrs. Caroline Mary, BA ACA *1985;* Wellswood House, Birchley Road, Battledown, CHELTENHAM, GL52 6NY.
HARTLEY, Miss. Catherine Laurie, BA ACA *2003;* 198 Gisburn Road, Barrowford, NELSON, LANCASHIRE, BB9 6AU.
HARTLEY, Miss. Catherine Louise, BA ACA *2005;* BDO Seidman LLP, 4250 Executive Square, Suite 600, LA JOLLA, CA 92037, UNITED STATES.
HARTLEY, Mr. Charles Richard, BA FCA *1985;* Sunnyside Farm, Brearton, HARROGATE, HG3 3BX.
•**HARTLEY, Mr. Charles Thomas Michael, FCA** *1962;* (Tax Fac), Edwards & Hartley, PO Box 237, Peregrine House, Peel Road, Douglas, ISLE OF MAN IM99 1SU. See also Edwards & Hartley Limited
HARTLEY, Miss. Charlotte Louise, BSc ACA *2007;* 26 Vincent Road, NORWICH, NR1 4HH.
HARTLEY, Mrs. Christine, FCA *1972;* 67 Red Hall Lane, LEEDS, LS14 2EF. (Life Member)
HARTLEY, Mr. Christopher Iain, BA ACA *1999;* 90 Nelson Road, LONDON, N8 9RT.
HARTLEY, Mr. Clifford Roger, FCA *1964;* 2a Barnwood Road, Earby, BARNOLDSWICK, LANCASHIRE, BB18 6PB.
HARTLEY, Mr. Colin Stuart, FCA *1971;* 58-1295 Wharf St, PICKERING L1W 1A2, ON, CANADA.
•**HARTLEY, Mr. Daniel, BSc(Hons) ACA AMCT** *2006;* Dan Hartley Business Consulting, Manor Farm House East, Knaresborough Road, Follifoot, HARROGATE, NORTH YORKSHIRE HG3 1DT.
•①**HARTLEY, Mr. David, FCA** *1960;* with Summerhayes, Compass House, 6 Billetfield, TAUNTON, SOMERSET, TA1 3NN.
•**HARTLEY, Mr. David Alan, BA FCA** *1988;* (Tax Fac), Stewart & Co, Knoll House, Knoll Road, CAMBERLEY, GU15 3SY. See also Stewart & Co Accountancy Services Ltd
HARTLEY, Mr. David Alexander, BSc ACA *1986;* Four Embarcadero Center, Suite 550, SAN FRANCISCO, CA 94111, UNITED STATES.
HARTLEY, Mr. David Andrew, BSc ACA *1993;* 20 Chapel View, Loveclough, ROSSENDALE, LANCASHIRE, BB4 8FN.
HARTLEY, Mr. David Ellis, FCA *1955;* 54 Raikeswood Drive, SKIPTON, NORTH YORKSHIRE, BD23 1LY. (Life Member)
•**HARTLEY, Mr. David Nigel, BSc FCA** *1989;* (Tax Fac), Waite & Hartley, 66 North Street, WETHERBY, WEST YORKSHIRE, LS22 6NR.
HARTLEY, Ms. Elizabeth Kathleen, BSc ACA *1980;* PO box 600, Meadowbridge P.O., KINGSTON 19, JAMAICA.
HARTLEY, Mr. Ernest Christopher Fenton, FCA *1968;* 541 Le Grand Large, 42 Quai Jean Charles Rey, Fontvielle, MC 98000 MONACO, FRANCE. (Life Member)
HARTLEY, Mr. Frank, FCA *1960;* 221 Tinakori Road, Thorndon, WELLINGTON 6011, NEW ZEALAND. (Life Member)
HARTLEY, Mr. Gareth, ACA *2007;* 3 Ambler Road, LONDON, N4 2QT.
HARTLEY, Mr. Giles, MSc BSc ACA *2011;* Finchdean Farm House, Finchdean, WATERLOOVILLE, HAMPSHIRE, PO8 0AU.
HARTLEY, Mr. Ian, BSc ACA *1991;* 12 Badgerwood, Dechmont, BROXBURN, WEST LOTHIAN, EH52 6NZ.
HARTLEY, Mr. Ian Malcolm, BA FCA *1975;* Wool House, Roydsdale Way, Euroway Trading Estate, BRADFORD, BD4 6SE.
HARTLEY, Mr. Ian Michael, FCA *1976;* 29 Eynsford Rise, Eynsford, DARTFORD, DA4 0HS.
HARTLEY, Mr. James Matthew, BCom ACA *2000;* 16 Deepdale Green, Barrowford, NELSON, LANCASHIRE, BB9 8TB.
HARTLEY, Mr. James Peter, ACA *2007;* Grant Thornton UK Ltd, 1 Whitehall Riverside, LEEDS, LS1 4BN.
HARTLEY, Mr. James William, MA FCA *1970;* (Member of Council 1995 - 1999), 2 Spion Kop, Claypit Lane Thorner, LEEDS, LS14 3EB. (Life Member)
HARTLEY, Mrs. Jane, BA ACA *1989;* Sunnyside Farm, Brearton, HARROGATE, HG3 3BX.
HARTLEY, Mrs. Jennifer Michelle, BA(Hons) ACA *2004;* with Clough & Company LLP, 15/17 Devonshire Street, KEIGHLEY, BD21 2BH.
HARTLEY, Miss. Jenny Anne, BA(Hons) ACA *2001;* 37 Ashdales, ST. ALBANS, HERTFORDSHIRE, AL1 2RB.
HARTLEY, Mr. Jeremy Peter, BSc FCA *1992;* Audley House, Whalley Road, Barrow, CLITHEROE, LANCASHIRE, BB7 9BA.
HARTLEY, Mrs. Joanne Carol, BSc ACA *1998;* The Dean, Owslebury, WINCHESTER, SO21 1LN.
HARTLEY, Mr. John David Smith, BEng FCA *1982;* Impala Estates Ltd, The Steadings, Kildwick, KEIGHLEY, WEST YORKSHIRE, BD20 9AE.
HARTLEY, Mr. John Duncan, FCA *1950;* 29 Creskeld Lane, Bramhope, LEEDS, LS16 9EP. (Life Member)
HARTLEY, Mr. Jonathan Paul, BA ACA *1992;* Ernst & Young, P.O. Box 656, CAPE TOWN, C.P., 8000, SOUTH AFRICA.
HARTLEY, Mr. Jonathan Peter, BA FCA *1979;* 1 Homewood Crescent, Karori, WELLINGTON, NEW ZEALAND.
HARTLEY, Mrs. Judith, BA ACA *1988;* Northern Ballet Theatre Limited, 2 St Cecelia Street, LEEDS, LS2 7PA.
HARTLEY, Mrs. Kirsty Fiona, BA(Hons) ACA *2003;* Lloyds Banking Group, 155 Bishopsgate, LONDON, EC2M 3TQ.
•**HARTLEY, Mrs. Linda Ann, BCom FCA** *1984;* SL Accountants Ltd, 294 Warwick Road, SOLIHULL, WEST MIDLANDS, B92 7AF. See also SLA Tax Ltd
HARTLEY, Miss. Louise, BSc ACA *2011;* 41 Magellan House, Armouries Way, LEEDS, LS10 1JE.
HARTLEY, Miss. Louise, BSc ACA *1997;* Umbro House, Lakeside Cheadle Royal Business Park, CHEADLE, CHESHIRE, SK8.
HARTLEY, Mr. Michael Edward, BSc FCA *1975;* The Old Malthouse High Street, Everton, DONCASTER, SOUTH YORKSHIRE, DN10 5AU.
HARTLEY, Mr. Michael Jon, BSc(Econ) FCA *1985;* Kingfishers Green Lane, Prestwood, GREAT MISSENDEN, BUCKINGHAMSHIRE, HP16 0QA.
HARTLEY, Miss. Natasha, BA ACA *2011;* Clevedon House, 68 Ranmoor Road, SHEFFIELD, S10 3HJ.
HARTLEY, Mr. Nigel Denis Richard, BSc FCA *1979;* Le Mas, 630 Kareela Road, PENROSE, NSW 2579, AUSTRALIA.
HARTLEY, Mr. Nigel Jonathan, BA ACA *1988;* Darkstar Brewery Ltd, Unit 22, Star Road Trading Estate, Star Road, Partridge Green, HORSHAM WEST SUSSEX RH13 8RA.
HARTLEY, Mr. Paul, BSc ACA *2011;* 48 Mill Rise, BRIGHTON, BN1 5GH.
HARTLEY, Mr. Paul Edward, FCA *1980;* Gran Bahia 24-OA, Bahia De Marbella, ES-29603 MARBELLA, SPAIN.
•**HARTLEY, Mr. Paul Robert, FCA** *1971;* (Tax Fac), P.R.Hartley, PO Box 27075, LONDON, N2 0FZ.
HARTLEY, Mr. Peter Christopher, BSc FCA *1976;* Cranford, 17 Jacobean Lane, Knowle, SOLIHULL, B93 9LP.
HARTLEY, Mr. Raymond Vincent, FCA *1967;* 53 Belmont Road, BUSHEY, WD23 2JR. (Life Member)
HARTLEY, Mrs. Rebecca Claire, BA ACA *1993;* 23 Church Avenue, Haughton Green, Denton, MANCHESTER, M34 7PP.
HARTLEY, Mr. Richard Andrew, MA FCA *1976;* Mount Lodge, Malthouse Lane, Worplesdon, GUILDFORD, GU3 3PS. (Life Member)
•**HARTLEY, Mr. Richard Howard, FCA** *1972;* Richard H. Hartley, 142 Broadhurst Gardens, LONDON, NW6 3BH. See also Lance House Services Ltd
HARTLEY, Mr. Richard Matthew, BA FCA *1993;* (Tax Fac), with Baker Tilly Tax & Advisory Services LLP, 2 Whitehall Quay, LEEDS, LS1 4HG.
HARTLEY, Mr. Robert, BA FCA *1984;* Eddisons, Pennine House, Russell Street, LEEDS, LS1 5RN.
HARTLEY, Mr. Roger Everett, FCA *1970;* Macaple SAS, Rue Marc Sangnier, 45308 PITHIVIERS, FRANCE.
HARTLEY, Miss. Rosalind, BA ACA *1998;* 1 Littlebridge Cottage, Stoke Trister, WINCANTON, SOMERSET, BA9 9PP.
HARTLEY, Mrs. Ruth Theresa, BSc ACA *2002;* 4 Bolton Avenue, WORCESTER, WR4 0ST.
HARTLEY, Miss. Sarah Louise, BA ACA *2010;* 63 Thamesdale, London Colney, ST. ALBANS, HERTFORDSHIRE, AL2 1TA.
HARTLEY, Mr. Simon John, BSc ACA *1985;* Wellswood House, Birchley Road, Battledown, CHELTENHAM, GL52 6NY.
HARTLEY, Mrs. Steffanie Jennifer, MA MPhil ACA *2001;* 17 Deans Yard, LONDON, SW1P 3PB.
HARTLEY, Mr. Stephen Charles, BA FCA *1981;* 2 Mayfield, Hipperholme, HALIFAX, WEST YORKSHIRE, HX3 8JY.
•**HARTLEY, Mr. Stephen John, FCA** *1975;* Atkin Macredie & Co Ltd, Westbourne Place, 23 Westbourne Road, SHEFFIELD, S10 2QQ.
HARTLEY, Mr. Steven Michael, BSc ACA *1984;* 21 Anglesey Drive, Poynton, STOCKPORT, CHESHIRE, SK12 1BT.
HARTLEY, Mr. Steven Michael, BA ACA *2006;* 64 Lee Road, LONDON, SE3 9DA.
HARTLEY, Mr. Stuart Leslie, FCA *1960;* 1 Meadow Height Court, THORNHILL L4J IV5, ON, CANADA. (Life Member)
HARTLEY, Miss. Susan, BSc FCA AMCT *1988;* 4 Prestwick Fold, OSSETT, WEST YORKSHIRE, WF5 9LT.
HARTLEY, Mrs. Vanessa Sarah, BA ACA *1997;* 50 Durlston Road, KINGSTON UPON THAMES, SURREY, KT2 5RU.
HARTLEY, Miss. Victoria Kate, BA FCA *1995;* 23 Knowles Avenue, NORTH BONDI, NSW 2026, AUSTRALIA.
HARTLEY, Mr. Walter Colin Farrar, FCA JDipMA *1954;* Apartment 6, Willow Springs, Gilstead Way, ILKLEY, WEST YORKSHIRE, LS29 0DB. (Life Member)
HARTLEY-WILEY, Mr. Christopher John, ACA CA(SA) *2008;* 8 Redland Drive, Loughton, MILTON KEYNES, MK5 8EL.
HARTLEY-WILEY, Mr. Peter Gregory, ACA CA(SA) *2008;* Flat 24 Beacon House, 4 Burrells Wharf Square, LONDON, E14 3TJ.
HARTMAN, Mr. Raymond William, BA FCA *1963;* 22 Manor Road, South Hinksey, OXFORD, OX1 5AS.
HARTNACK, Mr. Michael David, BA ACA *1999;* Wilhelminastraat 43A, 2011VK, HAARLEM, NETHERLANDS.
HARTNALL, Mr. Michael James, FCA *1965;* Monkswood, Prior Hatch Lane, Hurtmore, GODALMING, GU7 2RJ.
HARTNELL, Mr. Alan John, BA ACA *2001;* Room 4520, British Broadcasting Corporation White City, 201 Wood Lane, LONDON, W12 7TS.
•**HARTNELL, Mrs. Clare Susannah, BA ACA** *1993;* (Tax Fac), Grant Thornton UK LLP, Grant Thornton House, 22 Melton Street, Euston Square, LONDON, NW1 2EP. See also Grant Thornton LLP
HARTNELL, Mr. Peter, BSc ACA *1992;* (Tax Fac), 6 Compton Way, FARNHAM, GU10 1QZ.
HARTNESS, Mrs. Joanne, BSocSc ACA *2000;* 22 Bankton Drive, LIVINGSTON, EH54 9EH.
HARTNETT, Mrs. Deborah Anne, BSc ACA *1995;* 5 Woodville Place, HERTFORD, SG14 3NX.
HARTNEY, Mr. Ronan Gerard, BA ACA *1994;* 145 High Street, TEDDINGTON, MIDDLESEX, TW11 8HH.
HARTNOLL, Mr. Christopher, BSc ACA *1981;* Jac's House, Ruddle Way, Langham, OAKHAM, LE15 7NZ.
HARTRIDGE, Mr. Donald Keith, FCA *1966;* 30 Bolton Crescent, WINDSOR, BERKSHIRE, SL4 3JQ. (Life Member)
HARTRY, Mr. Nicholas John, BSc(Hons) ACA *2000;* 9 Leader Street, PADSTOW, NSW 2211, AUSTRALIA.
HARTSHORN, Mr. Anthony Clive, FCA *1962;* 44 Les Chenevrieres, Le Bourg, 71290 RATENELLE, FRANCE. (Life Member)
HARTSHORN, Mr. Jonathan David, BSc FCA *1996;* 77 St Peters Terrace, Howth, DUBLIN 13, COUNTY DUBLIN, IRELAND.
HARTSHORN, Mr. Richard Godfrey, FCA *1966;* BRANDYGATE, 196 Thornhill Road, SUTTON COLDFIELD, WEST MIDLANDS, B74 2EP.
HARTSHORNE, Mr. David William, FCA *1975;* The University Of Birmingham, Finance Office - Treasury Management, Edgbaston, BIRMINGHAM, B15 2TT.
HARTSHORNE, Mr. Simon Andrew, BA ACA *1990;* 13 Lady Betty Road, NORWICH, NR1 2QU.
•**HARTSHORNE-FERGUSON, Mrs. Emma Jane, BA ACA** *2006;* Bell Tindle Williamson LLP, The Old Post Office, 63 Saville Street, NORTH SHIELDS, TYNE AND WEAR, NE30 1AY. See also BTW LLP and Bell Tindle Williamson Services Limited
•**HARTSTONE, Mr. Jeffrey Lionel, MA FCA** *1984;* Berg Kaprow Lewis LLP, 35 Ballards Lane, LONDON, N3 1XW. See also Jeff Hartstone Limited
HARTT, Mr. Richard John, BSc FCA *1981;* 37 Oak Tree Close, VIRGINIA WATER, GU25 4JG.

HASSAN, Mr. Mohammed Alawi, ACA FCCA *2010;* Albaraka Banking Group, PO Box 1882, MANAMA, BAHRAIN.
HASSAN, Mr. Muhammad, ACA *2010;* with PricewaterhouseCoopers, Emaar Square, Building 4 Level 8, PO Box 11987, DUBAI, UNITED ARAB EMIRATES.
HASSAN, Mr. Saeed-Ul, FCA *1965;* Saeed Methani Mushtaq & Co, 10/7 Al-Karam, Faiz Road, Old Muslim Town, LAHORE, PAKISTAN.
HASSAN, Mrs. Sarah Louise, BA(Hons) ACA *2002;* with KPMG LLP, Management Services Centre, 58 Clarendon Road, WATFORD, WD17 1DE.
HASSAN, Mr. Taher Amin, MCom FCA *1953;* 1127 Cornich El Nil, Maspiro, CAIRO, EGYPT. (Life Member)
HASSAN, Mr. Tolga, BA ACA *1996;* New HQ Block, Johnson Matthey Plc, Orchard Road, ROYSTON, HERTFORDSHIRE, SG8 5HE.
HASSAN, Mr. Yusuf, ACA CA(SA) *2010;* with KPMG, P O Box 28653, SHARJAH, UNITED ARAB EMIRATES.
HASSAN, Mr. Zia-ul, FCA *1965;* 13 Wayford Close, Longthorpe, PETERBOROUGH, PE3 9NL. (Life Member)
HASSAN KHAN, Mr. Sharjeel, BSc ACA *2008;* (Tax Fac), 2 Thyra Grove, LONDON, N12 8HD.
HASSANALLY, Mr. Murtaza, BSc FCA *1982;* 12 Woodberry Avenue, HARROW, MIDDLESEX, HA2 6AU.
•HASSAPIS, Mr. Panayiotis, BSc FCA *1986;* Hassapis & Co (Accountants Auditors) Ltd, Doma Building, 227 Arch Makarios III Avenue, PO Box 53104, 3300 LIMASSOL, CYPRUS.
•HASSARD-JONES, Mr. Hugh, FCA *1975;* Hassard-Jones Limited, 9 Northmead Road, Allerton, LIVERPOOL, L19 5NN.
•HASSECK, Mr. Richard Ian, FCA *1981;* (Tax Fac), Gateway Partners Auditing UK Limited, 2nd Floor, 43 Whitfield Street, LONDON, W1T 4HD.
HASSELDINE, Mr. Richard Howard John, FCA *1968;* 62/9 Struan Street, TOORAK, VIC 3142, AUSTRALIA. (Life Member)
HASSELL, Mr. Brett, MBA BSc FCA *1976;* 8 Montpelier Villas, BRIGHTON, BN1 3DH.
•HASSELL, Mr. Lewis Irving, BSc FCA *1978;* (Tax Fac), Lewis Hassell, 235 Bury New Road, Whitefield, MANCHESTER, M45 8QP.
•HASSELL, Miss. Sally-Ann Rose, MA FCA *1985;* Hassell Forensic Accounting Limited, Erry Lodge, 3 Wilkins Green Lane, HATFIELD, HERTFORDSHIRE, AL10 9RT.
HASSETT, Mr. John Gerard, BSc ACA *1991;* Military Road, Crinkle, BIRR, COUNTY OFFALY, IRELAND.
HASSIOTIS, Mr. Demetrius, BSc(Econ) CA FCA *1999;* with Credsure Pty Ltd, PO Box 3085, Broadwa 6009, NEDLANDS, WA 6009, AUSTRALIA.
HASSLACHER, Mr. Austin Robert Roche, FCA *1968;* Floudwood House, Froxfield, PETERSFIELD, GU32 1DR. (Life Member)
HASSON, Mr. Ian Robert, MA ACA *1992;* with PricewaterhouseCoopers SA, Birchstrasse 160, 8050 ZURICH, SWITZERLAND.
HASSON, Mr. Mark, ACA *2001;* 13 Peel Street, DOVER HEIGHTS, NSW 2030, AUSTRALIA.
HASSON, Mr. Peter Frank, MA MBA ACA *1990;* Cliffe, 14 Great Austins, FARNHAM, GU9 8JG.
•HASSON, Mr. Stephen David, BSc FCA *1981;* 27 Monellan Crescent, Caldecotte, MILTON KEYNES, MK7 8NA.
HASTEWELL, Mrs. Sian Mary, BA ACA *1986;* 60 Williston Road, AUBURNDALE, MA 02466, UNITED STATES.
HASTIE, Mr. Charles William, MA ACA *2004;* Financial Services Authority, 25 North Colonnade, LONDON, E14 5HS.
•HASTIE, Mr. Christopher Paul, FCA *1969;* (Tax Fac), Dawpool Accountancy Services Limited, 48 Brimstage Road, Heswall, WIRRAL, MERSEYSIDE, CH60 1XG.
HASTIE, Mr. David Gilbert, BSc FCA *1973;* UNON, PO Box 67578, NAIROBI, 00200, KENYA.
HASTIE, Mr. George Nelson Frederick, MBA FCA *1970;* 30 Goldsmith Close, WOKINGHAM, RG40 4YP.
HASTIE, Mr. James Edward Archibald, BA FCA *1996;* Brights Meadow, Ham, MARLBOROUGH, WILTSHIRE, SN8 3RB.
HASTIE, Mrs. Judith Claire, BA ACA *1992;* Chance House, Netherend, LYDNEY, GL15 6NS.
HASTIE, Mrs. Katharine Mary, BSc ACA *1995;* Brights Meadow, Ham, MARLBOROUGH, WILTSHIRE, SN8 3RB.
•HASTIE, Mr. Stuart Grant, BSc FCA *1981;* Disclosure Solutions Ltd, The Old Smithy, Radwinter Road, Ashdon, SAFFRON WALDEN, ESSEX CB10 2ET. See also Disclosure Solutions
HASTINGS, Mr. Charles Richard, BA ACA *1986;* Hollybush House, Pamington, TEWKESBURY, GL20 8LX.
HASTINGS, Mr. Christopher Alan, MA ACA *1993;* (Tax Fac), Flat 11, 85-87 Worple Road, Wimbledon, LONDON, SW19 4JH.
HASTINGS, Mr. Colin Raymond, BSc FCA *1974;* 46B Kensington Gardens, ILFORD, IG1 3EL.
HASTINGS, Mr. David, FCA *1970;* 11 Gorseway, FLEET, GU52 7NA.
•HASTINGS, Mr. David Michael, FCA *1977;* Newby Castleman, Eltham House, 6 Forest Road, LOUGHBOROUGH, LE11 3NP.
HASTINGS, Mr. Jamie, ACA *2008;* 3 Bewl Bridge Close, Flimwell, WADHURST, EAST SUSSEX, TN5 7NL.
•HASTINGS, Mr. John Laurence, FCA *1972;* (Tax Fac), J.L. Hastings, 3 Bewlbridge Close, Flimwell, WADHURST, TN5 7NL.
HASTINGS, Mr. Kevin Graham, BA ACA *1998;* 210 Perry Street, BILLERICAY, CM12 0NZ.
HASTINGS, Mrs. Louise Margaret, BSc ACA *2007;* 7 Warblers Way, BOGNOR REGIS, WEST SUSSEX, PO22 9LR.
HASTINGS, Mr. Roy, BA ACA *1996;* 20 Wallis Road, BASINGSTOKE, RG21 3DN.
HASTINGS-JONES, Mr. Phillip, MA(Oxon) ACA *2005;* Basement Flat, 98 Cloudesley Road, LONDON, N1 0EB.
HASWELL, Mr. Leslie, FCA *1973;* 11 Palmerston Road, TWICKENHAM, MIDDLESEX, TW2 7QX.
•HASWELL, Mrs. Rosalind Stella Elizabeth, BA ACA *1984;* Morley Haswell, 4 St James Court, Bridgnorth Road, Wollaston, STOURBRIDGE, DY8 3QG. See also Morley Haswell Consultants Limited
HASZCZYN, Mr. Donald Stephen, MSc BEng ACA *1991;* Habitat for Humanity International, Zochova 6-8, 811 03 BRATISLAVA, SLOVAK REPUBLIC.
•HATCH, Mr. Marcus Andrew, BSc FCA *1985;* PricewaterhouseCoopers, Financial Services Centre, Bishop's Court Hill, BRIDGETOWN, BARBADOS.
HATCH, Mr. Maurice Edward, DFC FCA *1947;* Hillbury Lodge, 248 Hillbury Road, WARLINGHAM, CR6 9TP. (Life Member)
HATCH, Mr. Michael Dennis, BSc FCA *1978;* 6 Elmwood Gardens, Colyford, COLYTON, DEVON, EX24 6PW.
HATCH, Mr. Michael Raymond, BSc ACA *1985;* 8 Lambridge Wood Road, HENLEY-ON-THAMES, RG9 3BS.
•HATCH, Mr. Richard George, FCA *1982;* (Tax Fac), Trudgeon Halling, The Platt, WADEBRIDGE, PL27 7AE. See also Trudgeon Halling Limited
HATCH, Mr. Richard James, BSc ACA *2007;* R B C Ceas International Ltd Exchange Tower, 19 Canning Street, EDINBURGH, EH3 8EG.
•HATCH, Mr. Robert William, FCA *1981;* Ensors, Saxon House, Moseleys Farm, Business Centre, Fornham All Saints, BURY ST. EDMUNDS SUFFOLK IP28 6JY.
HATCH, Mr. Stephen, BSc ACA *1991;* The Gate House, 23 South Park Drive, GERRARDS CROSS, SL9 8JJ.
HATCHARD, Mr. Adam, BA(Hons) ACA *2011;* 12 High Street, Hale Village, LIVERPOOL, L24 4AF.
•HATCHARD, Mr. Clive Alan, ACA *1991;* One Forbury Square, The Forbury, READING, RG13BB.
HATCHARD, Mr. David, BA ACA *2011;* 41 Maze Green Road, BISHOP'S STORTFORD, HERTFORDSHIRE, CM23 2PG.
•HATCHE, Mr. Terence John, FCA *1970;* Hatche & Co, 8 Streamside, TONBRIDGE, KENT, TN10 3PU.
HATCHER, Mr. Andrew James, FCA *1971;* 1 Britts Orchard, Buxted, UCKFIELD, TN22 4NA.
•HATCHER, Mr. Christopher David, BSc FCA *1981;* Watts Gregory LLP, Elfed House, Oak Tree Court, Mulberry Drive, Cardiff Gate Business Park Pontprennau, CARDIFF CF23 8RS.
•HATCHER, Mr. John George, FCA *1974;* (Tax Fac), Smith Hodge & Baxter, Thorpe House, 93 Headlands, KETTERING, NN15 6BL.
HATCHER, Mr. Peter Daniel, BSc FCA *1988;* Argos Ltd, 489-499 Avebury Boulevard, MILTON KEYNES, MK9 2NW.
HATCHER, Mr. Stephen Robert, BA ACA *1990;* North Cottage, Snowswick Lane, Buscot, FARINGDON, OXFORDSHIRE, SN7 8DP.
HATCHER, Mr. Thomas, ACA *2011;* 148 Quarry Street, Woolton, LIVERPOOL, L25 6HQ.
HATCHETT, Miss. Emma Rosamund, ACA *2007;* 20 Thorpewood Avenue, LONDON, SE26 4BX.
HATCHLEY, Mr. James Graham, BSc ACA *1993;* Flint House, Grange Park, Northington, ALRESFORD, SO24 9TG.
HATCHMAN, Mr. Paul Kenneth, FCA *1975;* 10 Elgin Avenue, Upton, MACCLESFIELD, SK10 3DX.
HATELEY, Mr. Joseph John, FCA *1965;* Wynwood House, Oaken Grove, Codsall, WOLVERHAMPTON, WV8 2AL.
HATELEY, Mr. Richard Ian, BSc FCA *1991;* 3 Birchmere Row, Blackheath, LONDON, SE3 0SS.
HATELY, Mr. Stuart, BSc ACA *1993;* 23 Moor End Lane, Silkstone Common, BARNSLEY, SOUTH YORKSHIRE, S75 4QT.
HATFIELD, Mr. Adam George Roland, BSc ACA *1990;* Old Berkeley Cottage Old Common Road, Chorleywood, RICKMANSWORTH, HERTFORDSHIRE, WD3 5LW.
•HATFIELD, Mr. Dale Andrew, BA ACA *1981;* Hatfield & John Ltd, 2 Market Street, ABERAERON, DYFED, SA46 0AS.
•HATFIELD, Mr. David Raymond, FCA *1968;* 49 Priors Close, New Waltham, GRIMSBY, DN36 4QZ.
HATFIELD, Mr. Edward Carl, ACA *2009;* 397 Woodham Lane, Woodham, ADDLESTONE, SURREY, KT15 3PP.
•HATFIELD, Mr. Ian, FCA *1997;* Hatfield & Co Accounting Services Ltd, South Normanton Business Centre, 40 High Street, NORMANTON, DERBYSHIRE, DE55 2BP.
HATFIELD, Mr. Nicholas, BEng ACA *2001;* 12 Aventine Court, 101 Holywell Hill, ST. ALBANS, HERTFORDSHIRE, AL1 1HR.
HATFIELD, Mr. Richard Thomas, BSc ACA CTA *1996;* (Tax Fac), 101 St. Johns Avenue, KIDDERMINSTER, WORCESTERSHIRE, DY11 6AX.
HATFIELD, Mr. Timothy Charles David, BA ACA *1982;* Hazlewood Hall, Aldeburgh Road, Friston, SAXMUNDHAM, SUFFOLK, IP17 1PD.
HATHAWAY, Mrs. Aileen Valerie, LLB ACA *1979;* 10 Mill Close, Broom, ALCESTER, B50 4HT.
HATHAWAY, Mr. James Andrew John, BSc ACA *2003;* 9 The Garden Mews, Farm Road, MAIDENHEAD, BERKSHIRE, SL6 5GZ.
HATHAWAY, Mr. Keith Victor, BA FCA *1972;* 49 Portsmouth Avenue, THAMES DITTON, KT7 0RU.
HATHAWAY, Mr. Martyn John, BSc ACA *1991;* 19 Gresham Road, Hall Green, BIRMINGHAM, B28 0JA.
•HATHAWAY, Mr. Maxwell, ACA *2004;* Coates and Partners Limited, 51 St. John Street, ASHBOURNE, DERBYSHIRE, DE6 1GP.
HATHAWAY, Mr. Richard Charles, BA FCA *1992;* 17 Chelwood Avenue, Goring-by-Sea, WORTHING, BN12 4QP.
•HATHAWAY, Mr. Richard Guy, MA FCA *1993;* KPMG LLP, 15 Canada Square, LONDON, E14 5GL. See also KPMG Europe LLP
HATHER, Mr. Christopher Ashley, BSc(Hons) ACA *2007;* 9 Holme Lane, Bottesford, SCUNTHORPE, DN16 3RP.
•HATHER, Mr. Jon, FCA *1975;* 55 Wray Common Road, REIGATE, SURREY, RH2 0NB.
HATHERLY, Mr. Andrew James, MSc BA ACA *2001;* 68b Hill Rise, RICHMOND, SURREY, TW10 6UB.
HATHERLY, Mr. David John, BSc FCA *1972;* 27 Willowbrae Avenue, EDINBURGH, EH8 7HE. (Life Member)
HATHERLY, Ms. Hannah Zoe, BA ACA *2006;* Flat D, 51 Highbury Hill, LONDON, N5 1SU.
HATHERLY, Mr. Peter John, ACA *1986;* 60 Four Ashes Road, Bentley Heath, SOLIHULL, B93 8LX.
HATHERLY, Mr. Robert Edward, BSc ACA *1999;* 8406/177 Mitchell Road, ERSKINEVILLE, NSW 2043, AUSTRALIA.
HATHI, Mr. Sudhir, FCA *1976;* Express Rent A Car Ltd, 90-91 Crawford Street, LONDON, W1H 2HD.
HATIMI, Miss. Anisa, BSc ACA *1991;* J P Morgan, 60 Victoria Embankment, LONDON, EC4Y 0DS.
HATJANTONAS, Mr. George John, MA MSc ACA CF *1999;* 1 RIMINI STREET, 1102 NICOSIA, CYPRUS.
HATRY, Mr. John Adrian, BCom FCA *1972;* 305 Second Avenue, OTTAWA K1S 2J1, ON, CANADA.
HATT, Mrs. Pamela Clare, BA ACA *1986;* 10 Hazeldown Road, Rownhams, SOUTHAMPTON, SO16 8DJ.
HATTAM, Mr. Christopher, BSc ACA *2010;* Flat 25 Somerston House, 24 St. Pancras Way, LONDON, NW1 0NY.
HATTAN, Miss. Elizabeth, MEng ACA *2005;* (Tax Fac), 24 Scylla Grove, Cove, ABERDEEN, AB12 3EH.
HATTER, Mr. David Geoffrey, BSc ACA *1982;* 68 Dorchester Road, SOLIHULL, B91 1LJ.
HATTER, Miss. Jennifer Mary Jane, BA ACA *2010;* 20b Severus Road, LONDON, SW11 1PL.
HATTER, Mr. Paul Antony, BSc ACA *1994;* The Gatehouse, Woodside Avenue, BEACONSFIELD, BUCKINGHAMSHIRE, HP9 1JL.
HATTERSLEY, Mr. Christopher John, BSc FCA *1980;* BNP Paribas, 10 Harewood Avenue, LONDON, NW1 6AA.
HATTERSLEY, Mr. Gordon, FCA *1958;* Berry Hill, Millthorpe Lane, Holmesfield, DRONFIELD, S18 7SA. (Life Member)
•HATTERSLEY, Mrs. Joan Dorothy, FCA *1968;* H.C.Samuel & Co., Glen View, Epsom Road, West Horsley, LEATHERHEAD, KT24 6AL.
HATTERSLEY, Mr. Jonathan Leslie, FCA FCSI *1974;* 32 Whirlow Park Road, SHEFFIELD, S11 9NP.
HATTERSLEY, Mr. Roger, BA ACA *1991;* 31 Wilkinsons Court, Easingwold, YORK, YO61 3GH.
HATTLE-SPENCE, Mr. Colin Alexander Edward, ACA *2005;* 21543 Oak Park Trails Drive, KATY, TX 77450, UNITED STATES.
HATTO, Mr. Andrew John, BSc ACA *2009;* 29 Ardern Lea, Alvanley, FRODSHAM, WA6 9EQ.
HATTON, Mr. Barry Peter, FCA *1970;* 7 Spring Gardens, GAINSBOROUGH, LINCOLNSHIRE, DN21 2AZ.
HATTON, Mr. Benedict John, BEng FCA ACT *1994;* 1 Gatesheath Cottages, Smithy Green, Tattenhall, CHESTER, CHESHIRE, CH3 9AJ.
•HATTON, Miss. Charlotte Jane, MSc ACA *1981;* Jane Hatton, Neville Lodge, 53 Newbridge Crescent, WOLVERHAMPTON, WV6 0LH.
HATTON, Mr. Christopher Gilbert, BSc FCA *1973;* The White House, Bockhanger LaneKennington, ASHFORDKent, TN24 9BP.
•HATTON, Mr. Colin John, ACA *1987;* 4 Seaton Park, Seaton, TORPOINT, CORNWALL, PL11 3JF.
HATTON, Mr. David James, BSc ACA *1997;* Haslenstrasse 12, CH8903 BIRMENSDORF, SWITZERLAND.
HATTON, Mrs. Helen Frances Sara, ACA *2008;* 19R Hillcrest Road, Hillcrest Villa, SINGAPORE 286797, SINGAPORE.
HATTON, Mr. Henry Robert, FCA *1965;* House 48/1, Greenmeadows Drive, PORT MACQUARIE, NSW 2444, AUSTRALIA.
•HATTON, Mr. Humphry Douglas Francis, BSc FCA *1988;* 61 Rusholme Road, LONDON, SW15 3LF.
HATTON, Mr. James Martin, ACA *2009;* 7 Hound Close, ABINGDON, OXFORDSHIRE, OX14 2LU.
•HATTON, Mr. Mark Arnold Bowes, BA FCA *1988;* Ernst & Young LLP, Citygate, St James' Boulevard, NEWCASTLE UPON TYNE, NE1 4JD. See also Ernst & Young Europe LLP
HATTON, Mr. Matthew, ACA *2010;* Flat D, 159 Goldhurst Terrace, LONDON, NW6 3EU.
HATTON, Mr. Neil James, BSc ARCS ACA *1995;* MF Global UK ltd, Sugar Quay, Lower Thames Street, LONDON, EC3R 6DU.
HATTON, Mr. Nicholas Julian, BSc FCA CTA *1999;* (Tax Fac), with PricewaterhouseCoopers LLP, 101 Barbirolli Square, Lower Mosley Street, MANCHESTER, M2 3PW.
HATTON, Mr. Paul Andrew, BA FCA *1992;* 47 Belluton Road, Knowle, BRISTOL, BS4 2DN.
HATTON, Mr. Stephen John, FCA FCMA MBA AMCT CertPRM *1981;* 35 Sylvan Tryst, BILLERICAY, CM12 0AX.
HATTON, Miss. Sylvia Pauline, BSc ACA *1986;* 116B Church Side, EPSOM, SURREY, KT18 7SY.
HATTON, Mr. Terence Paige, FCA ATII *1959;* 28 Maertop Way, Littabourne Park, BARNSTAPLE, EX31 1RZ. (Life Member)
HATTON, Mr. Thomas David Michael, BSc ACA *1984;* Geoffrey Osborne Ltd, 51 Fishbourne Road East, CHICHESTER, WEST SUSSEX, PO19 3HZ.
HATTON, Mr. Tony Roy, BA ACA *1996;* Flat 3, 37 Park Dale East, WOLVERHAMPTON, WV1 4TD.
HATTORI, Mr. Paul Kozo, BSc FCA *1989;* 19 Rona Road, LONDON, NW3 2HY.
HATTRELL, Mrs. Katherine Mary, BA ACA *1987;* 21 Crescent Grove, LONDON, SW4 7AF.
•HATTRELL, Mr. Richard William, BA FCA *1994;* Gilberts, Pendragon House, 65 London Road, ST. ALBANS, AL1 1LJ.
HATWELL, Mrs. Helen Victoria, BSc HND ACA *2001;* Mill House, The Common, Wacton, NORWICH, NR15 2UT.
HATZIGIANNIS, Mr. Efstratios Stratos, BSc ACA *1988;* 37 Chapel Street, LONDON, SW1X 7DD.
HAU, Miss. Diana, ACA *2008;* Flat 708 Wharfside Point South, 4 Prestons Road, LONDON, E14 9EL.

HAU, Mrs. Emma Louise, BSc ACA *1999;* 900 High School Way, No.2122, MOUNTAIN VIEW, CA 94041, UNITED STATES.
HAU, Mr. Kevin Yuen Yuk, ACA *2009;* Room 1704 17/F, Fu Fai Commertial Centre, 27 Hillier Street, SHEUNG WAN, HONG KONG ISLAND, HONG KONG SAR.
HAU, Mr. Kung Ming, BSc ACA *2004;* Prudential, 12 Arthur Street, LONDON, EC4R 9AB.
HAU, Mr. Kwan Ngan Charles, ACA *2008;* Room 403, Wing On House, 71 Des Voeux Road, CENTRAL, HONG KONG SAR.
HAU, Mr. Martin Siu-Chor, BSc ACA *1992;* P O Box 7146, General Post Office, CENTRAL, Hong Kong Island, HONG KONG SAR.
HAU, Miss. Michelle, ACA *2011;* 3 Hanover Mews, BRIGHTON, BN2 9HU.
HAU, Mr. Samuel Chung Fai, ACA *2008;* Room 7 12/F Block G, Tak BO Garden, KOWLOON BAY, HONG KONG SAR.
HAU, Miss. Yee Mann, BSc ACA *1994;* Flat 19B Tower 17, Pacific Palisades, 1 Braemar Hill Road, NORTH POINT, HONG KONG SAR.
HAU HANG SANG, Ms. Beatrice, BA ACA *1999;* 162 Blagdon Road, NEW MALDEN, SURREY, KT3 4AL.
•**HAUCK, Mr. Jonathan Ellis, BSc ACA** *2000;* 58 Summer Road, THAMES DITTON, SURREY, KT7 0QP.
HAUCK, Mrs. Lucy, BSc ACA *2000;* 58 Summer Road, THAMES DITTON, SURREY, KT7 0QP.
HAUGEN, Mr. Trond, ACA *2009;* with Deloitte & Touche LLP, Suite 1400, 181 Bay Street, TORONTO M5J 2V1, ON, CANADA.
•**HAUGH, Mr. Peter William, BSocSc FCA** *1980;* Old Mill Accountancy LLP, The Old Mill, Park Road, SHEPTON MALLET, SOMERSET, BA4 5BS.
HAUGHEY, Mr. James Robert, BA ACA *1992;* Burnell, Baslow Road, Holymoorside, CHESTERFIELD, DERBYSHIRE, S42 7HJ.
HAUGHEY, Mr. Niall, ACA *2008;* 240A, Sandycombe Road, KEW, TW9 2EQ.
HAUGHTON, Mr. Giles Henry Edward, MA(Hons) ACA *2001;* 11 Denbigh Close, LONDON, W11 2QH.
HAUGHTON, Mr. Mark James, BSc CEng ACA *1999;* 11 Jacques Lane, Clophill, BEDFORD, MK45 4BS.
HAUGHTON, Mr. Peter Kenneth, BSc ACA *2007;* Flat 11 Bayes House, Augustas Lane Barnsbury, LONDON, N1 1QT.
HAUGHTON, Mr. Roy Francis, FCA *1971;* Old Orchard, 1 Parsons Lane, Bierton, AYLESBURY, BUCKINGHAMSHIRE, HP22 5DF.
HAUKIM, Mr. Eshan, BSc(Hons) ACA *2011;* 38 Hunters Grove, HAYES, MIDDLESEX, UB3 3JE.
•**HAULKHAM, Miss. Jo-Anne, BSc(Hons) FCA** *2001;* Spofforths LLP, A2 Yeoman Gate, Yeoman Way, WORTHING, WEST SUSSEX, BN13 3QZ.
HAUNCH, Mr. Richard Antony, FCA *1971;* 40 Peregrine Place, Merefield, NORTHAMPTON, NN4 0SL.
HAUNTON, Dr. Kathleen Mary, BSc ACA CTA *1996;* with Deloitte LLP, Abbots House, Abbey Street, READING, RG1 3BD.
HAUSSMANN, Mr. Alexander Konstantin, FCA *1958;* Seefeldstrasse 45, PO Box 772, CH-8034 ZURICH, SWITZERLAND. (Life Member)
HAUXWELL, Mr. Philip John, BSc ACA *2006;* 38 Esher Park Avenue, ESHER, KT10 9NX.
HAVARD, Miss. Danielle Sandra Fergusson, BA ACA *2003;* Riddlesdown, 53 South Road, WARWICK WK08, BERMUDA.
HAVARD, Mr. John Stephen, BA FCA ATII *1975;* (Tax Fac), 4 Penfold Close, SHEFFORD, BEDFORDSHIRE, SG17 5DF.
HAVARD, Mrs. Lisa, ACA *2009;* 12 Stag Close, EASTLEIGH, SO50 8NX.
HAVARD, Miss. Rebecca Haddon, BA ACA *1999;* 138 Seely Road, LONDON, SW17 9QY.
•**HAVELL, Mr. Lance Steven, ACA** *1980;* Lance Havell, 77 Cumberland Avenue, GUILDFORD, GU2 9RH.
HAVEN, Mr. Andrew Paul, BSc ACA *2003;* 27 Cleveland Road, LONDON, E18 2AN.
HAVENS, Mr. David Edward, FCA *1961;* 31 Century Court, Montpellier Grove, CHELTENHAM, GL50 2XR. (Life Member)
HAVERCROFT, Mr. Colin Frank, FCA *1963;* Llygad Yr Haul, Ffordd Pentre Mynach, BARMOUTH, LL42 1EN. (Life Member)
•**HAVERS, Mr. Karl Jonathan, BA FCA** *1991;* Ernst & Young LLP, Apex Plaza, Forbury Road, READING, RG1 1YE. See also Ernst & Young Europe LLP
HAVERS, Mrs. Linda Ellen, FCA *1961;* 12 Mill Meadow, Milford-on-Sea, LYMINGTON, SO41 0UG.
HAVERTY-STACKE, Mr. Dylan, BA ACA MBA *1998;* PepsiCo Inc, 700 Anderson Hill Road, PURCHASE, NY 10577-1444, UNITED STATES.
•**HAVERY, Mr. Andrew James, MA FCA CTA MCT CISA** *1992;* Flat 68, Westminster Gardens, Marsham Street, LONDON, SW1P 4JG.
•**HAVILAND-NYE, Mr. Anthony, FCA** *1962;* (Tax Fac), Haviland & Co, 11 Biddulph Road, LONDON, W9 1JA.
HAVILL, Mr. Colin Grant, BSc FCA *1980;* 18 Sion Hill, BRISTOL, BS8 4AZ.
HAVILL, Mr. John Mark, ACA *1993;* 1 Deer Park Cottages, Brockhampton, CHELTENHAM, GLOUCESTERSHIRE, GL54 5SP.
•**HAW, Mr. Colin, FCA** *1983;* (Tax Fac), Barber Harrison & Platt, 57/59 Saltergate, CHESTERFIELD, S40 1UL.
•①**HAW, Mr. Matthew Robert, BSc ACA** *2000;* 1b St. Margarets Avenue, SIDCUP, KENT, DA15 7NP.
HAW, Mr. Peter John, FCA *1962;* Crummack Farm, Austwick, LANCASTER, LA2 8DJ.
•**HAWABHAY, Mr. Kaneyalall, FCA** *1975;* BDO De Chazal du Mee, P.O. Box 799, 10 Frere Felix, De Valois Street, PORT LOUIS, MAURITIUS.
HAWDON, Mr. Sidney, FCA *1951;* 70 Broadway, Tynemouth, NORTH SHIELDS, NE30 2LH. (Life Member)
•**HAWES, Mr. Alan John, FCA** *1972;* Ensors Trustee Company Ltd, Cardinal House, 46 St. Nicholas Street, IPSWICH, IP1 1TT.
•**HAWES, Mr. Bernard Harold, FCA** *1964;* Bernard Hawes, 52 Maids Causeway, CAMBRIDGE, CB5 8DD.
HAWES, Mr. David Michael, BSc FCA *1966;* 147 Shooters Hill Road, Blackheath, LONDON, SE3 8UQ.
HAWES, Mr. David Robert, BA ACA *2006;* Capita Financial Group, Beaufort House, 51 New North Road, EXETER, EX4 4EP.
HAWES, Mr. Derek George, FCA *1968;* (Tax Fac), 2 Oakfields, Hanbury, BURTON-ON-TRENT, DE13 8TP.
HAWES, Miss. Hazel Janet, BSc ACA *1996;* 11 Court Drive, Hillingdon, UXBRIDGE, UB10 0BL.
HAWES, Miss. Janine, BSc ACA *1988;* with KPMG LLP, 15 Canada Square, LONDON, E14 5GL.
HAWES, Mr. Nicholas James, BSc ACA *1989;* Keepers Cottage, Church Road, Scaynes Hill, HAYWARDS HEATH, RH17 7NH.
•**HAWES, Mr. Peter David, FCA** *1985;* PDH Accountants Limited, Timbers, Southview Road, CROWBOROUGH, TN6 1HW.
HAWES, Mr. Peter John, FCA *1958;* Flat 40, Edison Court, Exchange Mews, Culverden Park Road, TUNBRIDGE WELLS, KENT TN4 9TR. (Life Member)
HAWES, Mr. Richard Charles, FCA *1974;* 23 Humphries Way, Milton, CAMBRIDGE, CB24 6DL.
•①**HAWES, Mr. Richard Michael, BA FCA** *1991;* Deloitte LLP, 5 Callaghan Square, CARDIFF, CF10 5BT. See also Deloitte & Touche LLP
HAWES, Mr. Roger Geoffrey, FCA *1969;* c/o Jonathan C Evans, Orchard House, Outwood Lane, Bletchingley, REDHILL, RH1 4LR.
•**HAWES, Mrs. Sarah Mary, BSc FCA** *1977;* H & D Consultants Ltd, Braefield, Castle Walk, WADHURST, EAST SUSSEX, TN5 6DB.
•**HAWES, Mr. Simon John Sutcliffe, FCA MSI** *1983;* PricewaterhouseCoopers LLP, 7 More London Riverside, LONDON, SE1 2RT. See also PricewaterhouseCoopers
•**HAWES, Mr. Thomas James, FCA** *1978;* Hawes Strickland, Federation House, 36/38 Rockingham Road, KETTERING, NORTHAMPTONSHIRE, NN16 8JS. See also HMJT
HAWKARD, Mrs. Jane Anne, BA ACA *1992;* West Hill House, 23a Woodlands, BEVERLEY, HU17 8BT.
HAWKE, Mr. Christopher Edward, BSc ACA *2004;* 18b Gynn Lane, Honley, HOLMFIRTH, HD9 6LF.
HAWKE, Mr. Colin Rhys, MA ACA *1982;* 21 Jeffreys Road, LONDON, SW4 6QU. (Life Member)
HAWKE, Mr. David Christopher, BA ACA *1995;* 9 Kensington Gardens, Monkseaton, WHITLEY BAY, NE25 8AR.
HAWKE, Mr. Gerald Edward John, MSc FCA *1975;* 2 Mill Lane, Prestbury, CHELTENHAM, GLOUCESTERSHIRE, GL52 3NE.
HAWKE, Mrs. Marie, BSc ACA *2010;* West Cottage, Darkey Lane, LIFTON, DEVON, PL16 0DY.
HAWKEN, Mr. Jeremy, BA ACA *1998;* 35 Sunnybank, EPSOM, SURREY, KT18 7DY.
HAWKEN, Mr. Mark, MA ACA *1997;* Beechcroft, 31 Tangier Road, GUILDFORD, SURREY, GU1 2DF.
HAWKEN, Mr. Robert Humber, BSc ACA *1996;* 25 Abelia Close, West End, WOKING, SURREY, GU24 9PG.
HAWKER, Mr. Giles Richard Fort, BA(Hons) ACA *2002;* 35 Stoke Grove, BRISTOL, BS9 3SD.
HAWKER, Mr. John David, BSc ACA *1984;* 2 Fydlers Close, Woodside, WINDSOR, SL4 2DY.
•**HAWKER, Ms. Julie Mary, BSc ACA** *1992;* Arden Tax & Accountancy Limited, 2nd Floor, Cavendish House, 39-41 Waterloo Street, BIRMINGHAM, B2 5PP.
HAWKER, Mr. Michael Leslie, BSc FCA *1974;* Monkshorn, Main Road, East Boldre, BROCKENHURST, SO42 7WT.
HAWKER, Mr. Robert James, BA ACA *2005;* 2 Sevenoaks Drive, Spencers Wood, READING, RG7 1AZ.
HAWKES, Mr. Adam Richmond, BA ACA *1996;* 103 Delawyk Crescent, Herne Hill, LONDON, SE24 9JD.
HAWKES, Mr. Andrew John, BEng FCA *1995;* with Bishop Fleming, 16 Queen Square, BRISTOL, BS1 4NT.
HAWKES, Mrs. Ann, ACA *1981;* (Tax Fac), with Barber Harrison & Platt, 2 Rutland Park, SHEFFIELD, S10 2PD.
•**HAWKES, Mr. Bernard Alexander, LLB FCA** *1994;* Richardsons Financial Group Limited, 30 Upper High Street, THAME, OXFORDSHIRE, OX9 3EZ.
HAWKES, Mrs. Carolyn Jane, BSc ACA *1993;* 3 Waterstream Square, Chudleigh, NEWTON ABBOT, DEVON, TQ13 0PD.
HAWKES, Mrs. Christine Amanda, BA ACA *1985;* Windeggwegg 14, Wilen bei Wollerau, CH8832 WOLLERAU, SWITZERLAND.
HAWKES, Mr. Darren John, BSc ACA *1994;* 6 Birdbrook Close, Hutton, BRENTWOOD, CM13 1YG.
HAWKES, Mr. Derek Richard, BA ACA *1986;* Arcelor Mittal Sheffield Ltd Vulcan Works, Birley Vale Close, SHEFFIELD, S12 2DB.
HAWKES, Mr. Jeffrey Michael, FCA *1969;* (Tax Fac), 8 St.Faith's Close, Newton Longville, MILTON KEYNES, MK17 0BA.
HAWKES, Mr. Jonathan Mark, BSc ACA *1992;* Becton Dickinson UK Ltd The Danby Building, Edmund Halley Road, OXFORD, OX4 4DQ.
HAWKES, Mr. Malcolm Tudor, BSc ACA *1986;* 75 Blackmoor Wood, ASCOT, SL5 8EL.
HAWKES, Mr. Michael Gwyn, BSc ACA *1997;* 39 Effingham Road, SURBITON, SURREY, KT6 5JZ.
HAWKES, Mr. Paul Christopher, BSc(Hons) ACA *2001;* Skibound Holidays Ltd, Olivier House, 18 Marine Parade, BRIGHTON, BN2 1TL.
HAWKES, Mr. Paul Ernest, BA ACA *1986;* 64 Stockerstrasse, CH 8001 ZURICH, SWITZERLAND.
HAWKES, Mr. Robert Frank, FCA *1968;* 178 Cheswood Drive, SUTTON COLDFIELD, B76 1XY.
HAWKES, Mr. Stephen, BSc ACA *1985;* PO Box 435, TURRAMURRA, NSW 2074, AUSTRALIA.
HAWKEY, Mr. Richard Allan, BSc ACA *1999;* 10 Wychwood Place, WINCHESTER, HAMPSHIRE, SO22 6BE.
HAWKEY, Mr. Stephen, FCA *1973;* 29 Allee Jules Romains, Lotissement De La Garde, 87000 LIMOGES, FRANCE. (Life Member)
•**HAWKEY, Mr. Stephen Geoffrey, ACA** *1999;* (Tax Fac), Whitakers, Bryndon House, 5-7 Berry Road, NEWQUAY, TR7 1AD.
HAWKIN, Miss. Valerie Ann, BA ACA DChA *1985;* 126 Mile End Lane, Mile End, STOCKPORT, SK2 6BY.
HAWKINS, Mrs. Ailsa, BSc ACA *1997;* Lloyds TSB Asset Finance Div, St. William House, Tresillian Terrace, CARDIFF, CF10 5BH.
HAWKINS, Mr. Alan, FCA *1951;* Flat 49, Highland Lodge, 17 Carew Road, EASTBOURNE, EAST SUSSEX, BN21 2JQ. (Life Member)
•**HAWKINS, Mr. Alan Keith, BSc FCA** *1977;* A.K. Hawkins & Co, Lehing Farm, Headley Heath Lane, Headley Heath, BIRMINGHAM, B38 0DH.
HAWKINS, Mrs. Alison Linda, BSc(Econ) ACA *1999;* 5 Whitethorns Close, Swinford, LUTTERWORTH, LEICESTERSHIRE, LE17 6BF.
HAWKINS, Miss. Amy Elizabeth, BSc ACA *2009;* Flat 24, 57 Stamford Street, LONDON, SE1 9DJ.
•**HAWKINS, Mrs. Andrea Dawn, BSc FCA** *1993;* AD Hawkins & Co, 9 Barnes Close, West Wellow, ROMSEY, HAMPSHIRE, SO51 6ET.
•**HAWKINS, Mr. Andrew Douglas, BSc FCA** *1978;* with PricewaterhouseCoopers, 7 More London Riverside, LONDON, SE1 2RT.
HAWKINS, Mr. Andrew Peter, LLB ACA *1984;* Vision Capital Group LLP, 54 Jermyn Street, LONDON, SW1Y 6LX.
HAWKINS, Mr. Andrew Philip, ACA *1992;* Medina, Dimmocks Lane, Sarratt, RICKMANSWORTH, HERTFORDSHIRE, WD3 6AR.
HAWKINS, Mr. Anthony James, ACA *2009;* with Clarkson Hyde LLP, 3rd Floor, Chancery House, St. Nicholas Way, SUTTON, SURREY SM1 1JB.
HAWKINS, Mr. Anthony Rex, FCA *1969;* Green Acres Upham Street, Upham, SOUTHAMPTON, SO32 1JA.
HAWKINS, Mr. Anthony William, FCA *1962;* Taddiport, West Buckland, BARNSTAPLE, EX32 0SL.
HAWKINS, Miss. Brenda Janice, BSc ACA *1980;* 100 Beechwood Road, SOUTH CROYDON, Surrey, CR2 0AB.
HAWKINS, Mr. Brian, BSc FCA *1975;* 940 Hedge Drive, MISSISSAUGA L4Y 1G1, ON, CANADA.
HAWKINS, Mr. Brian Ernest, FCA *1960;* Firle Cottage Chapel Lane, Iden Green, CRANBROOK, KENT, TN17 4HQ. (Life Member)
HAWKINS, Mr. Brian Sydney, FCA *1968;* Copse End, 19 Knapps Drive, WINSCOMBE, BS25 1BD.
HAWKINS, Mr. Christopher Allan, FCA *1962;* 6 Court Rise, Llanddewi Rhydderch, ABERGAVENNY, NP7 9YH.
HAWKINS, Mrs. Claire Fiona, BSc ACA *1998;* 4 Appian Way, Baston, PETERBOROUGH, PE6 9PR.
HAWKINS, Miss. Claire Leanne, BSc ACA *2010;* 83 Deakin Road, BIRMINGHAM, B24 9AL.
•**HAWKINS, Mr. Colin Richard, BA FCA** *1976;* Fundi Professional Services Limited, Hambrook, Bethesda Street, Upper Basildon, Pangbourne, READING RG8 8NT.
HAWKINS, Mr. Cyril James, FCA *1951;* Beggars Roost, Thicket Grove, Newlands Drive, MAIDENHEAD, SL6 4LW. (Life Member)
HAWKINS, Mr. Daniel Russell, BSc ACA *2010;* 54 Sidney Street, GRANTHAM, LINCOLNSHIRE, NG31 8AZ.
HAWKINS, Mr. Darren, ACA CA(AUS) *2008;* MDT (UK) Limited, 5th Floor, 2 Savoy Court, Strand, LONDON, WC2R 0EZ.
HAWKINS, Mr. Darrin Anthony, BCom ACA *1991;* D H Consulting Ltd, 75 Larchwood Drive, Englefield Green, EGHAM, SURREY, TW20 0SL.
HAWKINS, Mr. David Edwin Charles, FCA *1952;* 26 Fringwood Close, NORTHWOOD, HA6 2TB. (Life Member)
HAWKINS, Mr. David Grant, BA FCA *1972;* 4 Wood Close, Lisvane, CARDIFF, CF14 0TT.
HAWKINS, Mr. David Ian, FCA *1975;* 2 Netherwood Road, BEACONSFIELD, BUCKINGHAMSHIRE, HP9 2BE.
•**HAWKINS, Mr. David Stuart Spencer, FCA** *1981;* Gibbons Mannington & Phipps, 20-22 Eversley Road, BEXHILL-ON-SEA, EAST SUSSEX, TN40 1HE.
HAWKINS, Mr. Douglas George, FCA *1971;* Wildhatch Greenview Avenue Leigh, TONBRIDGE, KENT, TN11 8QT. (Life Member)
HAWKINS, Mr. Edward John, MA ACA *1994;* 577/925 Srinakarin Road, Samrong Nua, SAMUT PRAKAN 10270, THAILAND.
•**HAWKINS, Miss. Elaine, BSc FCA** *1978;* Elaine Hawkins, Merok, 34 Camp Road, GERRARDS CROSS, BUCKINGHAMSHIRE, SL9 7PD.
HAWKINS, Mrs. Fiona Mary, MSc ACA *2002;* James Cowper Phoenix House, 50 Bartholomew Street, NEWBURY, RG14 5QA.
HAWKINS, Mr. Gary, BA ACA *1999;* 43 Woodlands Road, Baughurst, TADLEY, HAMPSHIRE, RG26 5PA.
•**HAWKINS, Mr. Gary Charles, ACA** *2005;* Hawkins Tilly Limited, 5 Canterbury Street, GILLINGHAM, KENT, ME7 5TP.
HAWKINS, Mr. Gary Neil, FCA MAAT *1997;* Store Property Holdings Ltd, Farr House, 4 New Park Road, CHICHESTER, WEST SUSSEX, PO19 7XA.
HAWKINS, Mr. Gavin, BSc ACA *1997;* 47 Chaucer Road, SIDCUP, DA15 9AP.
HAWKINS, Miss. Hazel Mary, BA FCA *1986;* Middle Farm, Lower Holditch, AXMINSTER, EX13 7AX.
HAWKINS, Mr. James Greville, BA FCA *1986;* with ICAEW, Metropolitan House, 321 Avebury Boulevard, MILTON KEYNES, MK9 2FZ.
•**HAWKINS, Miss. Jamie Louise, ACA** *2008;* 49 Newfoundland Way, Portishead, BRISTOL, BS20 7FP.
HAWKINS, Mrs. Joanna Margaret Ruth, LLB ACA *2002;* 135 Hale Drive, Mill Hill, LONDON, NW7 3EJ.
HAWKINS, Mr. John Anthony, FCA *1970;* Magnolia House, Candie Road, St. Peter Port, GUERNSEY, GY1 1UP.
HAWKINS, Mr. John Michael, BSc ACA *1991;* 40 Woodruff Way, Thornhill, CARDIFF, CF14 9FP.
•**HAWKINS, Mr. John Nicholas, FCA** *1974;* (Tax Fac), Pentins, Lullingstone House, 5 Castle Street, CANTERBURY, CT1 2FG. See also Pentins Business Advisers Limited

HAWKINS, Mr. Julian James Edward, MA ACA *1997;* Howie & Partners LLP, 3063 Walker Road, WINDSOR N8W 3R4, ON, CANADA.
•**HAWKINS, Mrs. Karen Ruth, BA FCA** *1992;* Hawkins, Dunelm, Longden Common Lane, Longden Common, SHREWSBURY, SY5 8AQ.
HAWKINS, Mrs. Kate Mary, BSc ACA *1997;* 1 Whitley Cottages, Whitley Hill, HENLEY-IN-ARDEN, WARWICKSHIRE, B95 5DJ.
HAWKINS, Mrs. Kay Louise, BA ACA *1986;* Farthings, 2 Monument View, Nynehead, WELLINGTON, TA21 0BH.
HAWKINS, Mr. Keith Raymond, FCA *1960;* 41 Bressey Grove, South Woodford, LONDON, E18 2HX. (Life Member)
HAWKINS, Mr. Kerry James, MA FCA *1970;* Coombe Farm, Dunsford, EXETER, EX6 7AD. (Life Member)
HAWKINS, Mr. Kevin Antony, BA ACA *1992;* 55 Hazelwood Grove, SOUTH CROYDON, SURREY, CR2 9DW.
HAWKINS, Mr. Mark, ACA *2002;* Woodbrook, Pottersheath Road, WELWYN, HERTFORDSHIRE, AL6 9SU.
•**HAWKINS, Mr. Mark Adrian, BA ACA** *1989;* MA Hawkins BA ACA, 212 Norcot Road, Tilehurst, READING, RG30 6AE.
HAWKINS, Mr. Mark John, BSc FCA *1984;* Langham House, 214 Ninfield Road, BEXHILL-ON-SEA, TN39 5DD.
•**HAWKINS, Mr. Mark Jonathan, MBA LLB ACA** *1991;* Ernst & Young, 59 Route de Chancy, 1213 GENEVA, SWITZERLAND. See also Ernst & Young Europe LLP
HAWKINS, Mr. Martyn Alan Steven, BSc ACA *2006;* 47 Harcourt Road, ALTRINCHAM, CHESHIRE, WA14 1NR.
HAWKINS, Mr. Matthew James, MSc BSc ACA *2000;* 7 Figsbury Close, SWINDON, SN25 1UA.
HAWKINS, Mr. Michael, FCA *1978;* Nilpeter Ltd, Unit 21, Priory Tec Park, Saxon Way, Priory Park, HESSLE NORTH HUMBERSIDE HU13 9PB.
HAWKINS, Mr. Michael Frank, FCA *1966;* The Old Rectory, Blisworth, NORTHAMPTON, NN7 3BJ.
HAWKINS, Mr. Michael Norman, ACA *2007;* 25 Wellesley Avenue, MANCHESTER, M18 8WJ.
HAWKINS, Mr. Neil John, BA ACA *1992;* Yorkshire House Floor 1, Aviva UK Insurance, 2 Rougier Street, YORK, YO90 1UU.
HAWKINS, Mr. Nicholas Bryan, BSc FCA *1988;* 3321 Caldeira Drive, LIVERMORE, CA 94550, UNITED STATES.
HAWKINS, Mr. Nigel Timothy John, BA ACA *1991;* 1 Hornbeam Road, Chandlers Ford, EASTLEIGH, SO53 4PA.
HAWKINS, Mr. Patrick Ferrer, OBE FCA *1955;* 4 Childs Hall Close, Bookham, LEATHERHEAD, KT23 3QE. (Life Member)
HAWKINS, Mr. Paul Ian, FCA *1977;* The Oasis, 39 Woodcote Road, WALLINGTON, SURREY, SM6 0LH.
HAWKINS, Mr. Peter John, MSc FCA *1970;* 12 Hill House Road, BRISTOL, BS16 5RT. (Life Member)
•**HAWKINS, Mr. Richard Fraser, FCA** *1971;* Richard F Hawkins Ltd, Linport, 59 Oaklands Avenue, Porthill, NEWCASTLE, STAFFORDSHIRE ST5 0DR. See also Richard F Hawkins
HAWKINS, Mr. Richard George, FCA *1974;* Wall House, Nash Lane, Scaynes Hill, HAYWARDS HEATH, WEST SUSSEX, RH17 7NJ.
HAWKINS, Mr. Robert Andrew, BSc ACA *2009;* Flat 3, 6 Blatchington Road, TUNBRIDGE WELLS, TN2 5EG.
•**HAWKINS, Mr. Robert Anthony, FCA** *1983;* PKF (UK) LLP, East Coast House, Galahad Road, Beacon Park, Gorleston, GREAT YARMOUTH NORFOLK NR31 7RU.
HAWKINS, Mr. Robert Frederick, BSc ACA *1993;* Barclays Bank Plc, Welland House, Westwood Business Park, COVENTRY, CV4 8JN.
HAWKINS, Mr. Roger Keith, FCA *1959;* 17 Fulford Walk, Etterby Park, CARLISLE, CA3 9RA. (Life Member)
HAWKINS, Mrs. Samantha, BSc ACA *2003;* 13 Daniell Close, Sully, PENARTH, SOUTH GLAMORGAN, CF64 5JY.
HAWKINS, Mrs. Samantha Joan, ACA *2007;* 31 Hectors Way, OAKHAM, LE15 6JZ.
HAWKINS, Mrs. Saskia Ruth, BA ACA CTA *2005;* with Ernst & Young LLP, 1 More London Place, LONDON, SE1 2AF.
HAWKINS, Miss. Sharon, BA(Hons) ACA *2002;* Burnt House, 85 Bush Road, East Peckham, TONBRIDGE, KENT, TN12 5LJ.
HAWKINS, Mr. Simon Edward, BA ACA *2000;* 3 Haydens, High Street, Wrington, BRISTOL, BS40 5QD.
HAWKINS, Mr. Simon James, BSc ACA *1998;* Christie & Co, 249 Upper Third Street, MILTON KEYNES, MK9 1DS.
HAWKINS, Mr. Simon Richard, BA(Hons) ACA *2001;* 3 Whitfield Avenue, Westlands, NEWCASTLE, ST5 2JH.
HAWKINS, Mr. Stephen Andrew, BA FCA *1974;* 33 Major Buttons Drive, MARKHAM L3P 3G6, ON, CANADA.
HAWKINS, Mr. Steven Patrick, LLB ACA *1998;* 4 Appian Way, Baston, PETERBOROUGH, PE6 9PR.
HAWKINS, Mr. Steven William, BSc ACA *2007;* 14 Kings Gate, 36 Hockley Road, RAYLEIGH, SS6 8GJ.
HAWKINS, Mrs. Susan Elizabeth, FCA *1953;* 4 Childs Hall Close, Bookham, LEATHERHEAD, KT23 3QE. (Life Member)
HAWKINS, Mr. Thomas Benjamin, MA ACA *1988;* 14 Darlan Road, LONDON, SW6 5BT.
HAWKINS, Mr. Timothy, BSc(Econ) ACA *2003;* with PricewaterhouseCoopers LLP, One Kingsway, CARDIFF, CF10 3PW.
HAWKINS, Mr. William Mark, MA(Hons) ACA *2002;* 32 Lennox Road, HOVE, EAST SUSSEX, BN3 5HY.
HAWKLEY, Mr. Christopher John, BSc FCA *1977;* 12 Ounty John Lane, STOURBRIDGE, DY8 2RG.
HAWKSFIELD, Mr. John Peter, FCA *1967;* (Tax Fac), Stone Lodge, Seaton, OAKHAM, LE15 9HU.
HAWKSLEY, Mr. Anthony Thomas, MA FCA *1977;* King's College School, Southside, Wimbledon Common, LONDON, SW19 4TT.
HAWKSLEY, Mr. Daniel, PhD MChem ACA *2010;* 28 Stour Green, ELY, CAMBRIDGESHIRE, CB6 2WX.
HAWKSLEY, Mr. John Richard, FCA *1966;* 25 Beach Road, Mundesley, NORWICH, NR11 8BQ.
HAWKSLEY, Mr. Paul Alan, ACA *2008;* 68 Bittams Lane, CHERTSEY, SURREY, KT16 9QX.
HAWKSWORTH, Mr. James William, BEng ACA *1996;* Hallmark Hotels, 12 Bruntcliffe Way, Morley, LEEDS, LS27 0JG.
HAWLEY, Mr. Brian, FCA *1953;* Higher Up, 30 Ashdale Close, Stapenhill, BURTON-ON-TRENT, DE15 9HN. (Life Member)
HAWLEY, Mr. Christopher John, ACA *2005;* 3 Newlands Close, HORLEY, SURREY, RH6 8JR.
HAWLEY, Mr. Christopher Matthew, BSc FCA *1997;* Linder Myers Llp, Phoenix House, 45 Cross Street, MANCHESTER, M2 4JF.
HAWLEY, Mr. Derek, FCA *1960;* Field House, 37 The Delves, Swanwick, ALFRETON, DE55 1AR. (Life Member)
•**HAWLEY, Mr. Geoffrey Stephen, FCA CTA** *1980;* (Tax Fac), Hawley and Company, First Floor Suite, 23 Trinity Square, LLANDUDNO, LL30 2RH.
HAWLEY, Mrs. Julia Elizabeth, BSc ACA *1994;* Hall Farm Main Road, Brentingby, MELTON MOWBRAY, LEICESTERSHIRE, LE14 4RX.
HAWLEY, Mr. Mark, BSc ACA *2011;* 44 Hardy Street, HULL, HU5 2PL.
HAWLEY, Mr. Michael Bingham, BSc FCA *1969;* MEMBER OF COUNCIL, with Beeley Hawley & Co Ltd, 44 Nottingham Road, MANSFIELD, NOTTINGHAMSHIRE, NG18 1BL.
HAWLEY, Mr. Peter Philip, FCA *1986;* with Dean Statham, Bank Passage, STAFFORD, ST16 2JS.
HAWORTH, Miss. Amy Elizabeth, BA ACA *2003;* with Deloitte LLP, Hill House, 1 Little New Street, LONDON, EC4A 3TR.
HAWORTH, Mr. Ashley Robert, BEng ACA *2006;* 73 Albert Road, Grappenhall, WARRINGTON, WA4 2PF.
HAWORTH, Mr. Benjamin, BSc ACA *2010;* 50 Abbott Avenue, Raynes Park, LONDON, SW20 8SQ.
HAWORTH, Mr. Christopher, BA FCA *1997;* 4 Carlton Road, SALE, CHESHIRE, M33 6PE.
HAWORTH, Mr. Christopher, BSc ACA *2011;* 56 Bardfield Way, RAYLEIGH, SS6 9SJ.
•①**HAWORTH, Mr. Christopher George Taylor, FCA** *1973;* Chris Haworth & Co, The Gables, Goostrey Lane, Twemlow Green, Holmes Chapel, CREWE CW4 8BH.
HAWORTH, Mr. David Edward, MA ACA *1994;* Mackerels, Ide Hill, SEVENOAKS, KENT, TN14 6BW.
HAWORTH, Mr. David Roger, FCA *1951;* 1769 Melton Road, Rearsby, LEICESTER, LE7 4YR. (Life Member)
HAWORTH, Mr. Ian Thomson, FCA *1986;* Plot 23195, PO Box 502450, GABORONE, BOTSWANA.
HAWORTH, Miss. Jane Kathryn, BSc ACA *2002;* 9 Rivermead Way, Whitefield, MANCHESTER, M45 8SF.
HAWORTH, Mr. John David, BEng ACA *1991;* Leathwood, Sunnymede Avenue, CHESHAM, HP5 3LE.
HAWORTH, Mr. John Roger, BA ACA *1986;* 41 Nassau Road, LONDON, SW13 9QF.
HAWORTH, Mr. John Ryder, FCA *1955;* 9 Woodlands Park, Whalley, CLITHEROE, BB7 9UG. (Life Member)
HAWORTH, Mr. Jonathan Paul Crichton, BSc ACA *2006;* Consort Medical Plc Breakspear Park, Breakspear Way, HEMEL HEMPSTEAD, HERTFORDSHIRE, HP2 4TZ.
HAWORTH, Mr. Leslie William, FCA *1965;* 1184 Dowland Crescent, BURLINGTON L7T 4C9, ON, CANADA. (Life Member)
HAWORTH, Mr. Mark John, MSc ACA *2004;* Top Flat, 1 Caledonia Place, Clifton, BRISTOL, BS8 4DH.
HAWORTH, Mr. Martin John, BA ACA *1987;* 29 Hayhurst Road Whalley, CLITHEROE, LANCASHIRE, BB7 9RL.
HAWORTH, Ms. Moira, BA ACA *1984;* (Tax Fac), 43 Haddon Road, Hazel Grove, STOCKPORT, SK7 6LD.
HAWORTH, Mr. Paul Melville, MA ACA *1998;* 17 The Greenway, Chalfont St. Peter, GERRARDS CROSS, BUCKINGHAMSHIRE, SL9 8LX.
•**HAWORTH, Mr. Philip John, BSc ACA** *1985;* Haworth & Co Limited, 21 Market Place, DEREHAM, NORFOLK, NR19 2AX.
HAWORTH, Mr. Ross Edward, BEng ACA *2000;* 56 Broadstraik Drive, Elrick, WESTHILL, ABERDEENSHIRE, AB32 6JG.
HAWORTH, Mrs. Sarah Jacqueline, BA ACA *1984;* 20 Clyde Street, SOWERBY BRIDGE, HX6 3PW.
HAWORTH, Mr. Steven Phillip, BSc ACA *1989;* 108 Templecombe Drive, BOLTON, BL1 7TD.
HAWORTH-BOOTH, Mr. James Nicolas, BA ACA *2005;* 74 Tonsley Hill, LONDON, SW18 1BD.
HAWORTH-MADEN, Mr. Michael, BA ACA *1990;* Audit Commission Millbank Tower, 21-24 Millbank, LONDON, SW1P 4HQ.
•**HAWSON, Mr. Keith Dennis, BA FCA** *1989;* Walters Hawson Limited, 26 Percy Street, ROTHERHAM, S65 1ED.
•**HAWTHORN, Mr. Alan Geoffrey, FCA** *1973;* (Tax Fac), Ashmole & Co, Williamston House, 7 Goat Street, HAVERFORDWEST, DYFED, SA61 1PX.
HAWTHORN, Mrs. Alison Mary, BSc ACA *1999;* with David Owen & Co, 126 High St, MARLBOROUGH, SN8 1LZ.
•**HAWTHORN, Mr. Brian Edward, FCA** *1977;* Brian E Hawthorn, 12 Cotham Road, BRISTOL, BS6 6DR.
HAWTHORN, Miss. Clare, ACA MAAT *2010;* 82 Wokingham Road, CROWTHORNE, BERKSHIRE, RG45 7QA.
HAWTHORN, Mr. John Edmund, BSc ACA *1985;* Mail Point 1.1, Commander in Chief Fleet Headquarters, The Admiral Sir Henry Leach Building Guardroom Road, PORTSMOUTH, PO2 8BY.
HAWTHORN, Miss. Louise, ACA *2011;* Ground Floor Flat, 19 Hubert Grove, LONDON, SW9 9PA.
HAWTHORN, Mr. Michael Raymond, FCA *1981;* 30 Lariggan Crescent, PENZANCE, CORNWALL, TR18 4NH.
HAWTHORN, Mr. Paul Richard, FCA *1973;* Brookside Farm, Laundry Lane, Vines Cross, HEATHFIELD, EAST SUSSEX, TN21 9ED.
HAWTHORN, Mrs. Susan Mary, BSc ACA *1992;* EZH Limited, Hop Kiln Cottage, Grit Lane, MALVERN, WORCESTERSHIRE, WR14 1UR.
HAWTHORNE, Mr. Charles Clayton, FCA *1959;* 108 Gage Road, WILTON, NH 03086, UNITED STATES. (Life Member)
HAWTHORNE, Mr. Giles Edward, BSc(Hons) ACA *2001;* 3 Edward Close, SANDY, BEDFORDSHIRE, SG19 1JT.
HAWTIN, Mr. Paul Andrew, FCA *1990;* 19 Ringshall Gardens, Bramley, TADLEY, RG26 5BW.
HAXBY, Mr. Adrian John, BA ACA *1985;* U B S, 1-2 Finsbury Avenue, LONDON, EC2M 2PP.
HAXBY, Mr. David Arthur, LLB FCA *1968;* Greyfriars, 61 Kent Road, HARROGATE, HG1 2NL.
HAXTON, Ms. Alexandra Jane, BA(Hons) ACA *2001;* 3 Squirrels Way, EPSOM, SURREY, KT18 7AQ.
HAXTON, Mr. Edward Paul, BA FCA *1988;* Middlewood, School Lane, Frisham, THATCHAM, RG18 9XB.
HAY, Mr. Alastair, BA ACA *2007;* Flat 20 Princess Court, Bryanston Place, LONDON, W1H 2DF.
HAY, Mrs. Christine, LLB ACA *1991;* Level Four Systems Ltd, 21 Cowal Crescent, GLENROTHES, FIFE, KY6 3PS.
HAY, Mr. David Stuart, BSc ACA *2010;* 58 Wheathampstead Road, HARPENDEN, HERTFORDSHIRE, AL5 1NE.
HAY, Mrs. Elizabeth Anne, BA ACA *1993;* The Grange, Cragg Lane, Newton, ALFRETON, DE55 5TN.
HAY, Mrs. Elizabeth Katherine Anne, BSc ACA *2009;* Ground Floor Building 3320, Century Way Thorpe Park, LEEDS, LS15 8ZB.
HAY, Mr. Eugene Andrew, FCA *1976;* Abney House, School Lane, Baslow, BAKEWELL, DE45 1RZ.
•**HAY, Mr. Graeme, BSc FCA** *1982;* Ashby Berry & Co, 48/49 Albemarle Crescent, SCARBOROUGH, YO11 1XU.
HAY, Mr. Hugh Cameron, MA FCA *1963;* The Coach House, Church Street, STURMINSTER NEWTON, DORSET, DT10 1DB. (Life Member)
•**HAY, Mr. Ian, ACA FCCA FMAAT** *2011;* Segrave & Partners, Turnpike House, 1208/1210 London Road, LEIGH-ON-SEA, SS9 2UA.
HAY, Mr. Ian Charles, ACA *1994;* 50 Amber Road, #04-01, Amber Residences, SINGAPORE 439888, SINGAPORE.
HAY, Mrs. Jacqueline Wendy Lauchlan, MA ACA *2001;* 38 The Moor, Melbourn, ROYSTON, CAMBRIDGESHIRE, SG8 6ED.
HAY, Mr. James Alexander, FCA *1962;* Mizpah Shorts Hill Treslothan, CAMBORNE, CORNWALL, TR14 9LW. (Life Member)
HAY, Mr. James Brian, FCA *1960;* 81a Allington Road, Newick, LEWES, BN8 4ND.
HAY, Mr. Malcolm Edward, MA ACA *1986;* The Oxford Trust, 1-5 London Place, OXFORD, OX4 1BD.
HAY, Mr. Mark Alistair, MA ACA *1983;* Alte Gladbacherstrasse 81, 47805 KREFELD, GERMANY.
HAY, Mr. Martin Charles, BSc FCA *1978;* 116 West Heath Road, LONDON, NW3 7TU.
HAY, Mr. Michael Douglas, BSc ACA *1992;* Level Four Systems Ltd, 21 Cowal Crescent, GLENROTHES, FIFE, KY6 3PS.
HAY, Mrs. Nicola Peta Roberts, BA ACA *1982;* The Mid Counties Co-operative Ltd, New Barclay House, 234 Botley Road, OXFORD, OX2 0HP.
HAY, Mr. Robert Andrew, BA ACA *1998;* Display Link (UK) Ltd Mount Pleasant House, Mount Pleasant, CAMBRIDGE, CB3 0RN.
HAY, Miss. Ruth, BSc ACA *2006;* 34 Barclay Road, LONDON, SW6 1EH.
HAY, Mr. Simon, ACA CA(AUS) *2011;* with KPMG LLP, 15 Canada Square, LONDON, E14 5GL.
HAY, Miss. Sonia Julie, MBA BA FCA *1993;* 4 Pine Ridge, London Road, ST. ALBANS, HERTFORDSHIRE, AL1 1JE.
HAY, Miss. Stephanie Louise, BSc ACA *1989;* 20 Cawdell Drive, Long Whatton, LOUGHBOROUGH, LE12 5BW.
•**HAY, Mr. Stephen, BSc ACA** *1992;* 2020 CA Ltd, 1 St. Andrew's Hill, LONDON, EC4V 5BY.
HAY, Mr. Stephen James, BSc FCA *1992;* Independent Regulator of NHS, Foundation Trust, 4 Matthew Parker Street, LONDON, SW1H 9NL.
•**HAY, Mr. Stuart Leslie, FCA** *1977;* (Tax Fac), Freeman Baker Associates, The Old Church, 48 Verulam Road, ST. ALBANS, AL3 4DH.
HAY, Mrs. Wendy Irene, LLB(Hons) ACA *2000;* Muirside Steading, Muirside Lane, Cairneyhill, DUNFERMLINE, KY12 8ND.
HAY-PLUMB, Mrs. Paula Maria, BSc ACA *1984;* Ventana, 8 Drews Park, Knotty Green, BEACONSFIELD, BUCKINGHAMSHIRE, HP9 2TT.
HAYAT, Mrs. Nadia, MA ACA *2007;* 14 Fairview Way, EDGWARE, MIDDLESEX, HA8 8JF.
HAYAT, Mr. Tariq Ahmed, ACA *2008;* 26 Traps Lane, NEW MALDEN, SURREY, KT3 4RT.
HAYCOCK, Mrs. Alicja Krystyna, BA ACA *1998;* 10 Meadow View Yockleton, SHREWSBURY, SY5 9PA.
HAYCOCK, Mrs. Jane, BSc ACA *1990;* 11 Brownsea View Avenue, Lilliput, POOLE, DORSET, BH14 8LG.
•①**HAYCOCK, Mr. Kevin Andrew, FCA** *1982;* Maytree Cottage, Button Oak, Kinlet, BEWDLEY, WORCESTERSHIRE, DY12 3AG.
HAYCOCK, Mr. Peter James, BSc(Econ) ACA *1996;* 10 Meadow View, Yockleton, SHREWSBURY, SY5 9PA.
HAYCOCK, Mr. Robert Owen, BSc FCA *1992;* 11 Brownsea View Avenue, Lilliput, POOLE, DORSET, BH14 8LG.
HAYCOCK, Mr. Roger David, BCom ACA *1980;* 47 Woodley Lane, ROMSEY, SO51 7JR.
HAYCOCK, Mr. Simon, BSc ACA *1989;* with Peters & Co, 1 Park Road, CATERHAM, CR3 5TB.
HAYCOCK, Mr. Stephen Lea, BSc ACA *1993;* Nevada Trees, 5 Loveridge Drive, Baschurch, SHREWSBURY, SY4 2DJ.
•**HAYCOCKS, Mr. Richard John, FCA CF** *1971;* 10 Courtenay Drive, BECKENHAM, KENT, BR3 6YE.
HAYCOX, Mr. Jonathon, ACA *2011;* 84 Colombo Square, Worsdell Drive, GATESHEAD, TYNE AND WEAR, NE8 2DF.
HAYCROFT, Mr. Paul Philip, BCom ACA *1989;* Pond Farm, Wymondham Road, Bunwell, NORWICH, NR16 1NB.
HAYDAY, Mr. Geoffrey Denis, FCA *1975;* 1 Cedar Drive, Barming, MAIDSTONE, KENT, ME16 9HD.

HAYDAY, Mr. Graham David, ACA *1979;* Overdale, 35 Blackacre Road, Theydon Bois, EPPING, CM16 7LT.

•**HAYDAY, Mr. Marcus Alexander, BSc FCA** *2000;* Grant Thornton (Gibraltar) Limited, 6A Queensway, PO Box 64, GIBRALTAR, GIBRALTAR.

HAYDEN, Mr. John Thomas Joseph, FCA *1968;* Ivy Cottage, 106 Wagon Lane, Olton, SOLIHULL, B92 7PD.

HAYDEN, Mr. Michael Henry, FCA *1966;* Little Wickham, 37 Wickham Hill, Hurstpierpoint, HASSOCKS, BN6 9NP. (Life Member)

HAYDEN, Mr. Michael Sean, BSc FCA *1992;* 8 Woodnook Road, Streatham Park, LONDON, SW16 6TZ.

•**HAYDEN, Mr. Philip Richard, FCA** *1974;* Richard Place Dobson Services Limited, Ground Floor, 1-7 Station Road, CRAWLEY, WEST SUSSEX, RH10 1HT. See also Richard Place Dobson LLP

HAYDEN, Mr. Richard Andrew, FCA *1976;* Flat 5, Grange Court, Grange Street, ST. ALBANS, HERTFORDSHIRE, AL3 5NE.

•**HAYDEN, Mr. Robert Leonard, FCA** *1972;* Robert Hayden & Co, 195 Bramhall Lane, Davenport, STOCKPORT, SK2 6JA.

HAYDEN, Mrs. Victoria Farne, MSci ACA *2004;* 12 Green Close, South Wonston, WINCHESTER, HAMPSHIRE, SO21 3EE.

HAYDEN-GARNER, Mrs. Michelle Kay, BSc ACA *1999;* with Uttridge Accounting Ltd, 36a Church Street, Willingham, CAMBRIDGE, CB24 5HT.

•**HAYDN-JONES, Mr. Simon, MSc ACA** *1998;* with KPMG LLP, One Snowhill, Snow Hill Queensway, BIRMINGHAM, B4 6GN.

HAYDOCK, Mr. David, LLB ACA *1990;* White House Port Lane, Brimscombe, STROUD, GL5 2QJ.

HAYDOCK, Mr. Paul Robert, BSc(Hons) ACA *2003;* 12 Kirkstead Road, Cheadle Hulme, CHEADLE, CHESHIRE, SK8 7PZ.

HAYDOCK, Mr. Peter Harvey, FCA *1972;* Faith Cottage, 58a Longden Coleham, SHREWSBURY, SY3 7EH.

HAYDOCK, Mr. Ross, ACA *2008;* 14 Triangle Place, LONDON, SW4 7HS.

HAYDON, Mr. Andrew Mansel, BA ACA *1981;* Chapman Entertainment Ltd, The Pavillion, 90 Point Pleasant, LONDON, SW18 1PP.

HAYDON, Mr. Daniel James, BA ACA *2005;* 13 Robin Hood Lane, Helsby, FRODSHAM, WA6 0DU.

HAYDON, Mr. David Noel, BSc FCA *1978;* Oaklands, Marl Lane, FORDINGBRIDGE, HAMPSHIRE, SP6 1JR.

HAYDON, Mr. Derek Henry, FCA *1961;* Heathfield, 4 The Avenue, Charlton Kings, CHELTENHAM, GL53 9BJ. (Life Member)

HAYDON, Mr. Mark Jeffery, BSc ACA *1983;* C/- Sigco, P O Box HM 3398, HAMILTON HM PX, BERMUDA.

HAYDON, Mr. Mark Norman, BA CA *1990; (CA Scotland 1979);* (Tax Fac), Whiting & Partners, The Old School House, Dartford Road, MARCH, PE15 8AE.

•**HAYDON, Mrs. Michelle Ann, BA(Hons) FCA** *2001;* (Tax Fac), Routeglow Limited, 83 Timberbank, Vigo, GRAVESEND, KENT, DA13 0SN.

HAYDON, Mr. Peter William, BA ACA *1988;* 4 Ivy Close, La Rue de la Croix, St. Ouen, JERSEY, JE3 2HA.

HAYDON, Mr. Richard James, ACA *2008;* 18 The Grove, BRIERLEY HILL, WEST MIDLANDS, DY5 3ES.

HAYDON, Mrs. Sarah Elizabeth, BSc ACA *1986;* PO Box 137-140, PARNELL 1151, AUCKLAND, NEW ZEALAND.

•**HAYDON, Mrs. Susan Jane, FCA** *1985;* S.J. Haydon, The Conifers, Stone Lane, Lydiard Millicent, SWINDON, SN5 3LD.

HAYEEMS, Mr. Benjamin Solomon, FCA *1950;* 25 Nomad Crescent, DON MILLS M3B 1S5, ON, CANADA. (Life Member)

•**HAYER, Miss. Aman, BA ACA** *1993;* (Tax Fac), Wheawill & Sudworth, P.O. Box B30, 35 Westgate, HUDDERSFIELD, HD1 1PA.

HAYER, Miss. Pavan, BA(Hons) ACA *1994;* IMS Health UK, 7 Harewood Avenue, LONDON, NW1 6JB.

HAYER, Mr. Ranjodh Singh, BSc ACA *1999;* 105 Drury Road, HARROW, MIDDLESEX, HA1 4BP.

HAYERS, Mr. David Charles, BSc FCA *1998;* Tanglewood Hooke Road, East Horsley, LEATHERHEAD, KT24 5DY.

HAYERS, Mrs. Fiona Clare, BSc ACA *1998;* Tanglewood, Hooke Road, East Horsley, LEATHERHEAD, SURREY, KT24 5DY.

HAYERS, Mr. Robert Michael, ACA *1981;* Panoramalaan 2, 3080 TERVUREN, BELGIUM.

HAYES, Mr. Adam Denis, BEng ACA *1989;* ADH Management Services Ltd, Paddock House, London Road, WINDLESHAM, SURREY, GU20 6PJ.

•**HAYES, Mr. Adam Martin, BA MEB ACA CTA** *2005;* (Tax Fac), SN Hayes Tax Partners Ltd, PO Box 318, 9 Hope Street, St Helier, JERSEY, JE4 9XQ.

HAYES, Mr. Adrian Nicholas, MA BA(Hons) CA FCA *1985;* 186 Idris Road, Bryndwr, CHRISTCHURCH 8052, NEW ZEALAND.

HAYES, Mr. Alan, FCA *1962;* Poppy Cottage, 3 Church Lane, Whalley, CLITHEROE, BB7 9SY. (Life Member)

HAYES, Mr. Alan Newton, FCA *1966;* 27 Cormorant Wharf, Queensway Quay, GIBRALTAR, GIBRALTAR. (Life Member)

HAYES, Mr. Albert Edward, BSc FCA *1975;* 21 Reson Way, HEMEL HEMPSTEAD, HP1 1NU.

HAYES, Mr. Alex, ACA *2011;* 87 Brooksfield, WELWYN GARDEN CITY, HERTFORDSHIRE, AL7 2AW.

HAYES, Mr. Andrew John, BSc ACA *1993;* 133 Rivermead Court, Ranelagh Gardens, LONDON, SW6 3SE.

HAYES, Mr. Andrew John, BA FCA *1977;* 99 Valley Road, LOUGHBOROUGH, LE11 3PY.

HAYES, Mr. Andrew Philip, BSc FCA *1992;* T W M Solicitors, 128 High Street, GUILDFORD, GU1 3HH.

HAYES, Ms. Ann, BA ACA *1984;* Whitepost Farm House, Cold Harbour Road, Chiddingstone Hoath, EDENBRIDGE, TN8 7DL.

•**HAYES, Mr. Anthony Gilbert, FCA** *1974;* Hayes & Company, 76 Old Woking Road, WEST BYFLEET, KT14 6HU.

HAYES, Mr. Benjamin Oliver, BSc(Econ) ACA *2006;* with Wenn Townsend, 30 St Giles', OXFORD, OX1 3LE.

HAYES, Miss. Brenda Rose, BA FCA *1975;* (Tax Fac), 4 Church Road, Earley, READING, RG6 1EY.

HAYES, Mr. Brian George, FCA *1958;* 43 Milton Street, NUNAWADING, VIC 3131, AUSTRALIA. (Life Member)

HAYES, Miss. Catherine Jane, BSc ACA *1999;* (Tax Fac), 12 Whitehart Close, Theale, READING, RG7 5QL.

HAYES, Mrs. Cecilia Josephine, FCA *1973;* 76 Old Woking Road, WEST BYFLEET, SURREY, KT14 6HU.

HAYES, Mr. Christopher Neal, LLB FCA *1964;* Dinwoodie, Middletown Lane, Sambourne, REDDITCH, WORCESTERSHIRE, B96 6NX. (Life Member)

HAYES, Mrs. Claire Emma, BSc ACA *1998;* 37 Parsonage Close, Upholland, SKELMERSDALE, LANCASHIRE, WN8 0JL.

HAYES, Mrs. Claire Tracy, BA FCA *1991;* Monahans Second & Third Floors, Clarks Mill Stallard Street, TROWBRIDGE, BA14 8HH.

•**HAYES, Mr. David Evan, FCA** *1974;* (Tax Fac), Arthur Gait & Company, 18 Gold Tops, NEWPORT, NP20 5WJ.

HAYES, Mr. David Malcolm, FCA *1953;* 64 Homefield Road, Pucklechurch, BRISTOL, BS16 9QA. (Life Member)

•**HAYES, Miss. Dawn, BSc ACA** *2005;* 1 Trinity Avenue, ENFIELD, EN1 1HP.

HAYES, Mr. Desmond Pierse, FCA *1967;* 3354 Clay Street, SAN FRANCISCO, CA 94118, UNITED STATES.

•**HAYES, Mr. Dominic Matthew, BA FCA** *1999;* Moore Stephens LLP, 150 Aldersgate Street, LONDON, EC1A 4AB.

HAYES, Mr. Edmund Joseph, FCA *1962;* Bewdley House, Canon Pyon Road, HEREFORD, HR4 7SQ.

HAYES, Mrs. Emma Jane, ACA *2008;* with Deloitte LLP, 1 Woodborough Road, NOTTINGHAM, NG1 3FG.

HAYES, Mr. Geoffrey Michael George, FCA *1955;* Glenburn, Cavendish Road, WEYBRIDGE, KT13 0JY. (Life Member)

HAYES, Mr. George Edward, FCA *1950;* Lismore, Park Lane, Mellor Brook, BLACKBURN, BB2 7PY. (Life Member)

HAYES, Mr. Harold Edward, DFC FCA *1953;* 974 Alenmede Crescent, OTTAWA K2B 8K5, ON, CANADA. (Life Member)

HAYES, Mrs. Helen Louise, BSc(Hons) ACA *2003;* Omega Underwriting Holdings Ltd New London House, 6 London Street, LONDON, EC3R 7LP.

HAYES, Mr. Iain Augustus Laurenson, ACA *1981;* 9 Darragh Street, TANNUM SANDS, QLD 4680, AUSTRALIA.

HAYES, Mr. Ian Dennis, ACA *1989;* Flat 2, 73 Park Hill, LONDON, SW4 9NS.

•**HAYES, Mr. Ian Edward, BA FCA** *1974;* MEMBER OF COUNCIL, (Tax Fac), The Ridgeway, 132 Waxwell Lane, PINNER, MIDDLESEX, HA5 3ES.

•**HAYES, Mr. Ian Mitchell, BA ACA** *1992;* Mills & Black, Derwent House, 141-143 Dale Road, MATLOCK, DE4 3LU.

HAYES, Mr. Ian Philip, BSc FCA *1977;* Amcor Flexibles, 1919 S. Butterfield Road, MUNDELEIN, IL 60060, UNITED STATES.

HAYES, Mr. Ian Walter, FCA *1964;* 63 Foljambe Avenue, Walton, CHESTERFIELD, S40 3EY.

HAYES, Mr. James Robert, BSc ACA *2003;* 31 Rae Street, RANDWICK, NSW 2031, AUSTRALIA.

HAYES, Miss. Jane Elizabeth, BSc ACA *1988;* 15 Derby Road, HASLEMERE, GU27 1BS.

•**HAYES, Mr. John Anthony, BSc FCA** *1981;* (Tax Fac), J.A. Hayes, Les Chalumaux, Val Au Bourg, St. Martins, GUERNSEY, GY4 6EP.

HAYES, Mr. John Brian, BSc FCA *1980;* 9 Alveston Drive, WILMSLOW, CHESHIRE, SK9 2GA.

HAYES, Mr. John Edward, BCom FCA *1960;* 30 Fowley Common Lane, Glazebury, WARRINGTON, WA3 5JN. (Life Member)

•**HAYES, Mr. John Forbes Raymond, MA FCA** *1975;* ST Hampden Limited, Hampden House, Great Hampden, GREAT MISSENDEN, BUCKINGHAMSHIRE, HP16 9RD.

HAYES, Mr. John Maurice, FCA *1970;* Chestnut Barn Tollerton Lane, Tollerton, NOTTINGHAM, NG12 4GA.

HAYES, Mr. John Robert, BA FCA *1981;* Whitepost Farm House, Cold Harbour Road, Chiddingstone Hoath, EDENBRIDGE, TN8 7DL.

HAYES, Mr. Julian Andrew, BA ACA *2000;* 6 Kilmington Close, Hutton, BRENTWOOD, CM13 2JZ.

HAYES, Mrs. Kate, BA ACA *2004;* 55 Woodside Avenue, Meanwood, LEEDS, LS7 2UL.

HAYES, Mrs. Katherine Janet, ACA *2004;* 9 Stonemill Rise, Appley Bridge, WIGAN, LANCASHIRE, WN6 9BH.

HAYES, Mrs. Katy Jane, BSc ACA *2003;* 31 Byron Hill Road, HARROW, MIDDLESEX, HA2 0JD.

HAYES, Mr. Kevin Andrew, FCA *1980;* 4 Elm Road, WINCHESTER, HAMPSHIRE, SO22 5AG.

HAYES, Mr. Laurence Christian, LLB ACA *2001;* Wood View, Baydon Road, Shefford Woodlands, HUNGERFORD, BERKSHIRE, RG17 7AD.

HAYES, Mr. Lee, BSc ACA *2011;* 24 Harden Close, Great Oakley, CORBY, NORTHAMPTONSHIRE, NN18 8JW.

HAYES, Mr. Leslie Stanhope, BSc FCA *1972;* Rua Pio Correia 110 ap 703, Jd Botanico, 22461-240 RIO DE JANEIRO, BRAZIL.

HAYES, Mrs. Lynn, BA ACA *1995;* 9 Castlefields, Bournmoor, HOUGHTON-LE-SPRING, DH4 6HH.

HAYES, Mr. Marcus Renny, BA ACA *1983;* 163 Hanham Road, RD1, Kumeu, AUCKLAND, NEW ZEALAND.

HAYES, Mr. Martin, FCA *1965;* The Knott, 18 Vicarage Lane, Dore, SHEFFIELD, S17 3GX.

HAYES, Mr. Matthew, BSc(Econ) ACA *2000;* One Houston Center, Suite 700, 1221 McKinney Street, HOUSTON, TX 77010, UNITED STATES.

HAYES, Miss. Melanie Anne, BA ACA *2006;* 6 Burmester Road, LONDON, SW17 0JN.

HAYES, Mrs. Melissa Margaret, ACA *2009;* 1 Wheelwright Mews, Warwick Road, Leek Wootton, WARWICK, CV35 7QY.

•**HAYES, Mr. Michael Christopher, FCA** *1974;* Michael C Hayes, 1 Fielding Mews, LONDON, SW13 9EY.

•**HAYES, Mr. Michael George, BA FCA** *1981;* (Tax Fac), Kingston Smith & Partners LLP, Devonshire House, 60 Goswell Road, LONDON, EC1M 7AD. See also Kingston Smith Limited Liability Partnership

HAYES, Mr. Nicholas, BA ACA *2011;* Hurst Farmhouse Church Road, Weald, SEVENOAKS, KENT, TN14 6LT.

HAYES, Mr. Nicholas John Gardner, MA ACA *1980;* Equity Trust, 6 St Andrew Street, LONDON, EC4A 3AE.

HAYES, Mr. Nigel Thornton, FCA *1973;* Meadow View, Banbury Road, Lower Boddington, DAVENTRY, NORTHAMPTONSHIRE, NN11 6XY.

HAYES, Mr. Paul Andrew, MEng&Man ACA *1992;* Oakwood, Oakhurst Avenue, HARPENDEN, HERTFORDSHIRE, AL5 2ND.

HAYES, Mr. Peter Jonathan, ACA *1978;* PO Box 31080, WHITEHORSE Y1A 5P7, YT, CANADA.

HAYES, Miss. Rebecca, BA ACA *2010;* 15 Skibereen Close, Pontprennau, CARDIFF, CF23 8PT.

HAYES, Mr. Richard George, FCA *1970;* Trudder Grange, NEWTOWN MOUNT KENNEDY, COUNTY WICKLOW, IRELAND.

HAYES, Mr. Richard James, FCA FRSA *1975;* 8 Cathedral Court, King Harry Lane, ST. ALBANS, HERTFORDSHIRE, AL3 4AF.

HAYES, Mr. Richard Walter, FCA *1973;* (Tax Fac), with KPMG LLP, 15 Canada Square, LONDON, E14 5GL.

•**HAYES, Mr. Robert William, FCA** *1970;* (Tax Fac), 51 Horndean Road, EMSWORTH, HAMPSHIRE, PO10 7PU.

HAYES, Mr. Roland Edward, MA ACA *1994;* 18 Princeton Street, LONDON, WC1R 4BB.

HAYES, Mr. Ross Phillip, ACA *2004;* PO Box 753, PADDINGTON, NSW 2021, AUSTRALIA.

HAYES, Mrs. Sarah Christina, BA(Hons) ACA *2000;* with PricewaterhouseCoopers LLP, 101 Barbirolli Square, Lower Mosley Street, MANCHESTER, M2 3PW.

HAYES, Mrs. Sarah Louise, ACA *2010;* R G L Forensics, Dashwood House, 69 Old Broad Street, LONDON, EC2M 1QS.

HAYES, Mrs. Sarah Marie, BA ACA *2005;* 7 Highmore Road, LONDON, SE3 7UA.

HAYES, Mr. Stephen Paul, BA ACA *1979;* 10 Cheyne Walk Green Park, Tickhill Road Bawtry, DONCASTER, DN10 6RS.

HAYES, Mr. Terence, FCA *1952;* The Coach House, 306 Dobbin Hill, SHEFFIELD, S11 7JG. (Life Member)

•**HAYES, Mr. Thomas Edward, BA(Hons) ACA** *2002;* MaxAim LLP, United Business Centre, 1 Mariner Court, Calder Park, WAKEFIELD, WEST YORKSHIRE WF4 3FL.

HAYES, Mr. Timothy Charles, ACA *1980;* 9 Carthew Villas, LONDON, W6 0BS.

HAYES, Mr. Tom James Michael, ACA *2010;* 45 Buckingham Way, WALLINGTON, SURREY, SM6 9LU.

HAYES, Mr. William Francis, FCA *1976;* P O Box 109, Armadale North, ARMADALE, VIC 3143, AUSTRALIA.

HAYES, Mr. William James, MA FCA *1977;* 181 Parkway, WELWYN GARDEN CITY, AL8 6JA.

•**HAYFIELD, Mr. Colin John, BSc FCA DChA** *1981;* Hardcastle Burton, 166 Northwood Way, NORTHWOOD, MIDDLESEX, HA6 1RB.

HAYFIELD, Mr. Robin Quentin, FCA *1969;* 15 Queen's Gate Gardens, LONDON, SW7 5LY.

HAYGARTH, Mr. Edward, BSc ACA *2000;* Grant Thornton UK Llp Grant Thornton House, 22 Melton Street, LONDON, NW1 2EP.

HAYGARTH, Mr. Edward James Anthony, BCom FCA *1956;* 14 Marlborough, 38-40 Maida Vale, LONDON, W9 1RW. (Life Member)

HAYGARTH, Mr. Nigel Charles, MA FCA *1969;* 5 Basire Street, LONDON, N1 8PN.

HAYGARTH, Mr. Richard Kenneth, BSc ACA *1990;* Flint Walls, Boxgrove, CHICHESTER, PO18 0EE.

HAYGARTH, Mrs. Sally Ann, BA ACA *1990;* Flint Walls, Boxgrove, CHICHESTER, PO18 OEE.

HAYHOW, Mr. Leonard William, FCA *1951;* 4 Heather Close, North Wootton, KING'S LYNN, PE30 3RH. (Life Member)

HAYHURST, Mrs. Carol Victoria, BSc ACA CTA AMCT *1998;* (Tax Fac), with PricewaterhouseCoopers LLP, 101 Barbirolli Square, Lower Mosley Street, MANCHESTER, M2 3PW.

HAYHURST, Miss. Cathryn Alice, BSc(Hons) ACA *2004;* 19 Well Row, Broadbottom, HYDE, SK14 6AR.

HAYHURST, Mr. John Andrew, BSc ACA *1995;* E C I Colchester House, 38-40 Peter Street, MANCHESTER, M2 5GP.

HAYHURST, Mr. Michael, ACA *1986;* Stadco Ltd, Harlescott Lane, SHREWSBURY, SY1 3AS.

HAYHURST, Mrs. Pamela Ann, FCA *1970;* 13 Crossford Drive, BOLTON, BL3 4UA.

HAYHURST, Mr. Paul, BSc ACA *1989;* Sphinx C S T Ltd, Woodside House, Sherwood Park, Annesley, NOTTINGHAM, NG15 0DS.

HAYHURST, Mr. William, FCA *1953;* Alston House, Robin Lane, Huby, YORK, YO61 1HH. (Life Member)

HAYHURST-FRANCE, Mr. James, BSc ACA *2011;* White Cottage Main Street, Chackmore, BUCKINGHAM, MK18 5JE.

HAYLE, Mr. Peter Richard, BA FCA *1990;* 4 The Grove, MORPETH, NORTHUMBERLAND, NE61 1HY.

HAYLE, Mr. Timothy, BA ACA *2008;* Flat 1, 35 Ivanhoe Road, Aigburth, LIVERPOOL, L17 8XF.

HAYLER, Mr. Richard, ACA *2008;* 30 Glenmere Row, LONDON, SE12 8RH.

HAYLES, Mr. Barry, FCA *1965;* Shackerstone Fields, Snarestone, SWADLINCOTE, DE12 7DE.

HAYLES, Mr. Gregory Peter, ACA *1991;* (Tax Fac), The Gate House, Duffield Lane, Stoke Poges, SLOUGH, SL2 4AA.

HAYLETT, Mrs. Lesley, BA ACA *1990;* 21 Spindlewood, Elloughton, BROUGH, HU15 1LL.

HAYLEY, Mr. Alec William, BSc FCA *1988;* EGL UK Limited, 38 Threadneedle Street, LONDON, EC2R 8AU.

HAYLEY, Mr. James Austin, MA ACA *2003;* Royal Bank of Scotland, 135 Bishopsgate, LONDON, EC2M 3UR.

HAYLEY, Mr. Keith, FCA *1977;* 19 Mountfield Gardens, TUNBRIDGE WELLS, TN1 1SJ.

HAYLING, Mr. Arthur John, FCA *1951;* BrinkhurstChurch Lane, Challock ASHFORD, Kent, TN25 4DD. (Life Member)
HAYLINGS, Miss. Nicola Zoe, ACA *2002;* 40 Abbey Gardens, LONDON, NW8 9AT.
HAYLLAR, Mr. Nicholas James, BA(Hons) ACA *2002;* 12 The Grove Mill, Grove Mill Lane, WATFORD, WD17 3TU.
HAYLLAR, Mr. Richard Frank, FCA *1949;* Rowfold, Piltdown, UCKFIELD, TN22 3XE. (Life Member)
HAYMAN, Mr. Alexander, ACA *2011;* 194 Weir Road, LONDON, SW12 0NP.
HAYMAN, Mr. Andrew James, BA ACA *2007;* 26 Boundary Park, SEATON, EX12 2UN.
•HAYMAN, Mr. Ashley, MA FCA CF CTA MEWI *1974;* (Tax Fac), Cassons, St Crispin House, St. Crispin Way, Haslingden, ROSSENDALE, LANCASHIRE BB4 4PW. See also Cassons & Associates
HAYMAN, Miss. Catherine Anne, BSc(Hons) ACA *2001;* 28 Burrator Drive, EXETER, EX4 2EN.
•HAYMAN, Mr. Christopher Bruce, FCA *1965;* C.B. Hayman, 9 Sutton Road, SEAFORD, BN25 1RU.
HAYMAN, Mr. David Jeremy, BA ACA *2001;* Flat 308, 83 Crampton Street, LONDON, SE17 3BT.
HAYMAN, Mr. Gavin James, BSc(Hons) ACA *2002;* 1 Courtil Mansell, Le Cornus, La Route Des Cornus, St. Martin, GUERNSEY, GY4 6UA.
•HAYMAN, Mr. Kevin, FCA *1972;* (Tax Fac), King & Taylor, 10-12 Wrotham Road, GRAVESEND, DA11 0PE.
HAYMAN, Mr. Mark Edwin, BSc ACA *1996;* 7 Hunsdon Manor Garden, Weston under Penyard, ROSS-ON-WYE, HEREFORDSHIRE, HR9 7FQ.
HAYMAN, Mr. Peter Ivor, BCom FCA *1950;* 12 Russell Close, LONDON, W4 2NU. (Life Member)
HAYMAN, Mr. Peter Laurence George, BSc ACA *1986;* Brambledene, 13 Pardown, Oakley, BASINGSTOKE, RG23 7DY.
HAYMAN, Miss. Rachael, BA ACA *2006;* 6 Louisa Street, SUMMER HILL, NSW 2130, AUSTRALIA.
HAYMER, Mr. Jonathan, MA FCA *1984;* Ravenscar, Alvanley Road, Helsby, FRODSHAM, WA6 9PS.
HAYMES, Mr. Donald Ewan, BSc ACA *1991;* 9 Browns Court, Bradley, KEIGHLEY, WEST YORKSHIRE, BD20 9BE.
HAYNES, Mr. Anthony David, BA ACA *1989;* 11 Glen Darragh Gardens, Glen Darragh Road Glen Vine, ISLE OF MAN, IM4 4DD.
HAYNES, Mr. Brian William Thomas, FCA *1965;* 26 Crabmill Close, Knowle, SOLIHULL, WEST MIDLANDS, B93 0NP.
HAYNES, Mr. Byron James MacBean, BA ACA *1992;* Georg-Coch-Platz 2, 1010 WIEN, AUSTRIA.
HAYNES, Ms. Caroline Elizabeth, BA ACA *2007;* 10 Manchuria Road, LONDON, SW11 6AE.
HAYNES, Mr. Chris John Latimer, BA ACA *1995;* Oakley House, Pinfold Lane, Ashampstead, READING, RG8 8SH.
HAYNES, Miss. Clare Elizabeth, BA ACA *1995;* 4 Delamere Road, Delapre, NORTHAMPTON, NN4 8QG.
HAYNES, Mr. Derek Leslie, FCA *1975;* with KPMG LLP, 15 Canada Square, LONDON, E14 5GL.
HAYNES, Miss. Eleanor, BSc ACA DChA *2005;* Burnett House, New Road, NEWBURY, RG14 7RY.
HAYNES, Miss. Eleanor Gwyneth, BSc ACA *2007;* Flat 26 Viscount Point, 199 The Broadway, LONDON, SW19 1NL.
HAYNES, Mrs. Elizabeth, MA ACA *2002;* 6 Henry Dane Way, Newbold Coleorton, COALVILLE, LEICESTERSHIRE, LE67 8PP.
•HAYNES, Mrs. Frances Ann, BA FCA *1991;* Frances A Haynes, 1 Church Hill Road, Hooe, PLYMOUTH, PL9 9SE.
HAYNES, Mrs. Gemma Louise, ACA *2010;* 29 The Glade, COULSDON, CR5 1SR.
HAYNES, Mr. John Christopher Charles, MA FCA *1965;* 4 Walpole Avenue, RICHMOND, TW9 2DJ.
HAYNES, Mr. John Frederick, FCA *1975;* Whistler, 6 Oxhayes Close, Balsall Common, COVENTRY, CV7 7PS.
HAYNES, Mr. John Stuart Richard, BCom FCA *1984;* 41 Main Street, Congerstone, NUNEATON, WARWICKSHIRE, CV13 6LZ.
HAYNES, Mrs. Julie Louise, BSc ACA *1997;* B G Group, Thames Valley Park Drive, READING, BERKSHIRE, RG6 1PT.
•HAYNES, Mrs. Katherine Ann, ACA *1994;* Kate Haynes Limited, 129 Woodlands Road, Little Bookham, LEATHERHEAD, KT23 4HN.
HAYNES, Dr. Kathryn, PhD FCA *1993;* Coach House, Firby, YORK, YO60 7LH.
HAYNES, Ms. Kelli Lynn, BA ACA *1999;* 10B Greenview Gardens, 125 Robinson Road, SAI YING PUN, HONG KONG SAR.
HAYNES, Mr. Lachlan, ACA CA(AUS) *2008;* 18 Winscombe Crescent, LONDON, W5 1AZ.
HAYNES, Miss. Laura Elizabeth, ACA *2008;* Unit 5, 4 Breezyway Lane, SMITHS FL06, BERMUDA.
•HAYNES, Mr. Leslie Clifton, BSc FCA DChA *1995;* Les Haynes, 30 Kemps Road, Twyford, BANBURY, OXFORDSHIRE, OX17 3JS.
HAYNES, Mr. Lionel John, MBA BSc FCA *1975;* Wickets, Picket Piece, ANDOVER, HAMPSHIRE, SP11 6LY.
HAYNES, Mr. Martin Gregory, FCA *1981;* 644 Main Street, PO Box 220, MONCTON E1C 8L3, NB, CANADA.
HAYNES, Mr. Martin Laurence, ACA *2008;* 35 Siskin Close, ROYSTON, HERTFORDSHIRE, SG8 7XX.
HAYNES, Mr. Maurice Frederick, FCA *1969;* 101 Rue des Becasses, Parc Des Ecureuils, 40170 LIT ET MIXE, FRANCE.
HAYNES, Mr. Neil, BSc ACA *2004;* 54 Trafalgar Street, ANNANDALE, NSW 2038, AUSTRALIA.
HAYNES, Mr. Neil Antony, BSc FCA *1988;* 23 Wadebridge Drive, Horeston Grange, NUNEATON, CV11 6SY.
•HAYNES, Mr. Paul Kevin, BSc(Econ) FCA *1984;* Paul K Haynes, 128 Malines Avenue, PEACEHAVEN, BN10 7RZ.
HAYNES, Mr. Peter Colin Frank, BSc FCA *1981;* Wolsey House, 4 Montpelier Row, TWICKENHAM, TW1 2NQ.
•HAYNES, Mr. Philip Edmund, FCA *1964;* (Tax Fac), Philip Haynes FCA, Briarsmead, Old Road, Buckland, BETCHWORTH, RH3 7DU.
HAYNES, Mr. Richard, ACA *2011;* 4 Moriatry Close, LONDON, N7 0EF.
HAYNES, Mr. Richard Arthur, FCA *1975;* The Old Bakery, Silk Path, Bincombe Lane, CREWKERNE, SOMERSET, TA18 7LY.
HAYNES, Mr. Richard John, MBA FCA *1975;* 62 St. Marys Road, KETTERING, NORTHAMPTONSHIRE, NN15 7BW.
HAYNES, Mr. Roger John, FCA *1962;* Beaufort Cottage, Budgenor Lane, MIDHURST, GU29 0AB. (Life Member)
HAYNES, Mr. Roland Nicholas Norman, FCA *1965;* Coddiford, Cheriton Fitzpaine, CREDITON, DEVON, EX17 4BD.
•HAYNES, Mrs. Sally Elizabeth, MSci ACA *2004;* Sally Haynes, 8 Burcott Road, WELLS, SOMERSET, BA5 2EQ.
HAYNES, Miss. Sara Kathryn, BSc ACA *2010;* PO Box 12272, Thorndon, WELLINGTON 6144, NEW ZEALAND.
•HAYNES, Mr. Simon Gover, FCA *1977;* Colin F Whitfield & Co Limited, Redbrook View, Redbrook, WHITCHURCH, SHROPSHIRE, SY13 3AD.
HAYNES, Mr. Simon Paul, BSc ACA *1999;* 15 Glenmore Road, SWINDON, SN25 1WH.
HAYNES, Mr. Stephen Robert, BA ACA *1993;* 27 West Road, SAFFRON WALDEN, ESSEX, CB11 3DS.
HAYNES, Miss. Susan, BSc ACA *1980;* 57 Church Street, CROWTHORNE, BERKSHIRE, RG45 7PD.
HAYNES, Mrs. Victoria Louise, BSc ACA AMCT *1996;* Holly Tree House, Southorpe, STAMFORD, LINCOLNSHIRE, PE9 3BX.
HAYNES, Miss. Victoria Rose, BSc ACA *2011;* 34 Amersham Road, HIGH WYCOMBE, BUCKINGHAMSHIRE, HP13 6QU.
HAYON, Mr. Laurence, BA ACA *1987;* Docusave Limited, Unit 4/C Henley Business Park, Pirbright Road Normandy, GUILDFORD, GU3 2DX.
HAYRE, Mr. Herbir, BEng ACA *1997;* 98 Parkway, Chellaston, DERBY, DE73 5QA.
HAYRE, Dr. Jaswant Singh, PhD BA(Hons) FCA *1993;* 3 Clemens Place, Kings Hill Park, Kings Hill, WEST MALLING, KENT, ME19 4QH.
HAYS, Miss. Angela Janette, BSc ACA *1991;* 41 Quick Road, LONDON, W4 2BU.
HAYS, Mr. Mark William, BSc(Econ) ACA *1998;* 69 Couchmore Avenue, ESHER, SURREY, KT10 9AX.
•HAYSOM, Mr. Robert Frank, MA FCA *1974;* Haysom Silverton & Partners Ltd, Norfolk House Centre, 82 Saxon Gate West, MILTON KEYNES, MK9 2DL.
HAYTER, Ms. Alison, BSc ACA *1986;* 54 Creighton Road, Ealing, LONDON, W5 4SJ.
HAYTER, Miss. Charlotte March, ACA *2009;* with Deloitte LLP, 2 New Street Square, LONDON, EC4A 3BZ.
HAYTER, Mr. Christopher William, BA ACA *1983;* 245 Stuart Road, PLYMOUTH, PL1 5LH.
•HAYTER, Mr. Gerald Frank, FCA *1967;* Gerald F Hayter, 324 London Road, WOKINGHAM, BERKSHIRE, RG40 1RD. See also Hayter, Gerald F
HAYTER, Mr. Kevin Nigel Scott, BEng ACA *2009;* 52 Richmond Place, BATH, BA1 5QA.
HAYTER, Mr. Martin John, BSc FCA *1993;* with Ernst & Young, 2323 Victoria Avenue, Suite 2000, DALLAS, TX 75219, UNITED STATES.
HAYTER, Mr. Nicolas John, BSc ACA *1990;* Floor 28, Metlife, 1 Canada Square, LONDON, E14 5AA.
•HAYTER, Mr. Richard James, FCA *1981;* (Tax Fac), Rawlinsons, Marian House, 3 Colton Mill, Bullerthorpe Lane, LEEDS, LS15 9JN.
HAYTER, Mr. Timothy Richard, BSc ACA FCT *1988;* Bunzl plc, York House, 45 Seymour Street, LONDON, W1H 7JT.
•HAYTHORNTHWAITE, Miss. Gillian Mary, FCA *1993;* J.L. Winder & Co., 125 Ramsden Square, BARROW-IN-FURNESS, LA14 1XA.
HAYTON, Mr. Clive John, BSc ACA *1983;* Retirement Villages Ltd, 57 Church Street, EPSOM, SURREY, KT17 4PX.
HAYTON, Mrs. Delyth Elizabeth, BA ACA *1993;* Braeside, Trenear, HELSTON, CORNWALL, TR13 0HH.
•HAYTON, Miss. Glynis Irene, FCA *1977;* Glynis I. Hayton FCA, 92 Valley Park, WHITEHAVEN, CUMBRIA, CA28 8BA.
•HAYTON, Mr. John Paul, MBA BSc FCA *1991;* Hayton Accountancy Limited, 22 The Boyle, Barwick in Elmet, LEEDS, LS15 4JN.
HAYTON, Mrs. Margaret Elisabeth, FCA *1968;* 75 High Ash Crescent, LEEDS, LS17 8RL. (Life Member)
•HAYTON, Mr. Michael, MA FCA *1978;* Cameron Hughes Ltd, 16 Jubilee Parkway, Jubilee Business Park, DERBY, DE21 4BJ.
HAYTON, Mr. Robert, FCA *1955;* 6 Newlands Avenue, Whitefield, MANCHESTER, M45 7WR. (Life Member)
HAYTON, Mr. Roger Peter, FCA *1973;* 2 Linton Drive, LEEDS, LS17 8QN.
•HAYTON, Mr. Scott, ACA MAAT *2001;* Haytons Limited, 20 Melbourne Avenue, FLEETWOOD, LANCASHIRE, FY7 8AY.
HAYWARD, Mr. Alastair Guy Craufurd, BSc ACA *1987;* Allianz House, 60 Gracechurch Street, LONDON, EC3V 0HR.
HAYWARD, Miss. Amy Alice, BSc ACA *2004;* Land Securities Properties Ltd, 5 Strand, LONDON, WC2N 5AF.
HAYWARD, Mr. Andrew Joseph, ACA *2008;* Hurricane Exploration Plc, Anstey Gate, 82 Anstey Road, ALTON, HAMPSHIRE, GU34 2RL.
HAYWARD, Mrs. Angela Diane, ACA *1987;* with Trafalgar Accountancy & Tax Limited, Trafalgar House, 261 Alcester Road South, BIRMINGHAM, B14 6DT.
•HAYWARD, Mrs. Angela Joy, ACA *1994;* Angela Hayward, 17 High Street, Needham Market, IPSWICH, IP6 8AL.
HAYWARD, Mrs. Carole Mary, BSc ACA *1988;* 38 Mayfield Road, WEYBRIDGE, KT13 8XB.
HAYWARD, Miss. Catherine Louise, BSc ACA *1992;* University College of Birmingham, Summer Row, BIRMINGHAM, B3 1JB.
HAYWARD, Miss. Chloe Amanda, BA ACA *1998;* 57 Springhead Cottage, Amberley Road, Parham, PULBOROUGH, RH20 4HN.
•HAYWARD, Mr. Christopher, BSc FCA *1984;* Rectory Cottage, Wicken Bonhunt, SAFFRON WALDEN, CB11 3UG.
HAYWARD, Mr. Christopher Timothy Esmond, MA FCA *1965;* (Member of Council 1995 - 1998), Springhead House, Amberley Road, Parham, PULBOROUGH, RH20 4HN. (Life Member)
HAYWARD, Mrs. Christy Ann, BSc ACA *1997;* 1 Harbour View Close, POOLE, DORSET, BH14 0PF.
HAYWARD, Mr. Darren John, LLB ACA *1996;* Wisdoms Lodge, Windmill End, EPSOM, KT17 3AQ.
HAYWARD, Mr. David, BSc ACA *1990;* The Paddocks, Buckholt Road, Cranham, GLOUCESTER, GL4 8HE.
HAYWARD, Mr. David Mowbray, BA(Hons) ACA *2002;* 77 Iancu Nicolae, Villa 6, 077190 BUCHAREST, ILFOV COUNTY, ROMANIA.
•HAYWARD, Mr. Derek William, ACA *1981;* (Tax Fac), Hayward & Co, 49 Dundalk Lane, Cheslyn Hay, WALSALL, WS6 7AZ.
HAYWARD, Mr. Donald John, FCA *1954;* 51 Summerley Lane, Felpham, BOGNOR REGIS, WEST SUSSEX, PO22 7HY. (Life Member)
HAYWARD, Miss. Donna Louise, ACA *2011;* 7 Brockenhurst Close, Wigmore, GILLINGHAM, KENT, ME8 0HG.
HAYWARD, Mr. Duncan Leigh, BA FCA *1991;* Pacific Life R E Ltd, Tower Bridge House, St. Katharines Way, LONDON, E1W 1BA.
HAYWARD, Miss. Elizabeth Marie, ACA *2008;* 76 Concorde Drive, BRISTOL, BS10 6PX.
HAYWARD, Mrs. Emma Suzanne, BSc(Hons) ACA *2001;* 52 Elmgrove Road, WEYBRIDGE, SURREY, KT13 8PD.
HAYWARD, Mr. Ernest Vincent, FCA *1961;* 169a Foley Road West, Streetly, SUTTON COLDFIELD, B74 3NY. (Life Member)
HAYWARD, Mr. Francis John, BCom FCA *1952;* 2 Broadway, NEWPORT, SHROPSHIRE, TF10 7TN. (Life Member)
HAYWARD, Mr. Geoffrey Stephen, ACA *1980;* 29a Blenheim Road, ST. ALBANS, HERTFORDSHIRE, AL1 4NS.
HAYWARD, Mr. Glenn Eric, BSc ACA *1998;* Nominet Minerva House, Edmund Halley Road, OXFORD, OX4 4DQ.
•HAYWARD, Mr. Gordon Harold George, FCA *1974;* James Kenney & Co, 202-204 Swan Lane, COVENTRY, CV2 4GD.
HAYWARD, Mr. Ian Charles, BSc FCA *1982;* 9 Wilderness Road, Earley, READING, RG6 7RU.
HAYWARD, Mr. James Alfred William, BA FCA *1984;* Equiniti Plc, Aspect House, Lancing Business Park, LANCING, WEST SUSSEX, BN99 6DA.
HAYWARD, Mr. James Duncan Henry, BSc ACA *1989;* 2 Winchendon Road, LONDON, SW6 5DR.
HAYWARD, Mrs. Jane Elizabeth, BA ACA *1986;* 9 The Borough, Yealmpton, PLYMOUTH, PL8 2LR.
HAYWARD, Mrs. Jane Margaret, FCA *1975;* 200 Chartwell Road, OAKVILLE L6J 3Z8, ON, CANADA.
•HAYWARD, Miss. Janice, BSc FCA *1985;* (Tax Fac), Villars Hayward LLP, Boston House, 2a Boston Road, HENLEY-ON-THAMES, OXFORDSHIRE, RG9 1DY.
•HAYWARD, Mr. John Anthony Irving, FCA *1961;* (Tax Fac), John Hayward Associates, 4 Marco Road, Hammersmith, LONDON, W6 0PN. See also Hayward J.A.I.
HAYWARD, Mr. John Richard, BA FCA *1983;* 5 Ethel Road, BIRMINGHAM, B17 0EL.
HAYWARD, Mr. Jonathan Ian, BA ACA *2007;* 7 Eccleston Close, Seddons Farm, BURY, BL8 2JF.
•HAYWARD, Mr. Jonathan James, MA FCA *1981;* Flat 26, Presidents Quay House, 72 St. Katharines Way, LONDON, E1W 1UF.
•HAYWARD, Mr. Kim Harry, BA FCA *1979;* BDO LLP, Arcadia House, Maritime Walk, Ocean Village, SOUTHAMPTON, SO14 3TL. See also BDO Stoy Hayward LLP
HAYWARD, Mr. Leslie, FCA *1953;* 26 De La Bere Crescent, Burbage, HINCKLEY, LE10 2EQ. (Life Member)
•HAYWARD, Mrs. Lindsay Helen, BSc(Hons) ACA *2000;* (Tax Fac), PricewaterhouseCoopers LLP, Erskine House, 68-73 Queen Street, EDINBURGH, EH2 4NH. See also PricewaterhouseCoopers
•HAYWARD, Mr. Martin Berkley, BSc ACA *1989;* (Tax Fac), Martin Hayward, 85 (a) High Street, BARRY, SOUTH GLAMORGAN, CF62 7DW. See also Focus 30 Limited
•HAYWARD, Mrs. Mary Elizabeth, FCA *1974;* Hayward Cooper & Co, 30 Bolton Road, Aspull, WIGAN, WN2 1YY.
HAYWARD, Mr. Neil Christopher, MEng ACA *2001;* PwC, PO Box 11987, DUBAI, UNITED ARAB EMIRATES.
•HAYWARD, Mr. Nicholas Charles Eyes, BA ACA *1988;* Nicholas C.E. Hayward, 5 Higher Actis, GLASTONBURY, SOMERSET, BA6 8DR.
•HAYWARD, Mr. Nicholas Richard, FCA *1975;* (Tax Fac), McCabe Ford Williams, Bank Chambers, High Street, CRANBROOK, TN17 3EG.
HAYWARD, Mrs. Nicola Jane Abigail, BA(Hons) ACA *2000;* 388 George Street, SYDNEY, NSW 2000, AUSTRALIA.
HAYWARD, Mr. Paul David, ACA ACMA *2007;* 47 The Dormers, Highworth, SWINDON, SN6 7NZ.
HAYWARD, Mr. Peter, ACA *2006;* Nomura International Plc, 1 Angel Lane, LONDON, EC4R 3AB.
HAYWARD, Mr. Peter Anthony, FCA *1966;* 5 Priestwell Court, East Haddon, NORTHAMPTON, NN6 8BT.
HAYWARD, Mr. Peter Martin, BA ACA *1991;* 18 Waine Close, BUCKINGHAM, MK18 1FG.
•HAYWARD, Mr. Peter Stuart, FCA *1973;* Nunn Hayward, 66-70 Coombe Road, NEW MALDEN, KT3 4QW.
HAYWARD, Mrs. Rachel Helen, BA ACA *2002;* Yoyogi Terrace Apartments, No. 214 32-27, Tomigaya 1, Chome Shibuya-ku, TOKYO, 151-0063 JAPAN.
•HAYWARD, Mr. Richard John, BA ACA *1988;* (Tax Fac), Ward Williams Group Limited, Park House, 25-27 Monument Hill, WEYBRIDGE, SURREY, KT13 8RT. See also Ward Williams Limited
HAYWARD, Mr. Richard Michael James, BSc FCA *1995;* 123 Parker Road, Oratia, Waitakere City, AUCKLAND, NEW ZEALAND.
HAYWARD, Mr. Richard Paul, ACA *2008;* 12 Watermead Close, STOCKPORT, CHESHIRE, SK3 8UX.

•**HAYWARD, Mr. Roderick James Hansell, FCA** *1969;* (Tax Fac), Argenta Associates Ltd, 15 Ernle Road, Wimbledon Common, LONDON, SW20 0HH.
HAYWARD, Mr. Sam Robert, BA ACA *1997;* Fernhill Cottage, New Lane, East Stour, GILLINGHAM, DORSET, SP8 5NA.
HAYWARD, Miss. Sophie Victoria, BA ACA *2003;* 8 Mount Lodge, 102 Clapham Park Road, LONDON, SW4 7BH.
HAYWARD, Mr. Stephen David, BSc ACA *2006;* 23 Wood End Hill, HARPENDEN, HERTFORDSHIRE, AL5 3EZ.
HAYWARD, Mr. Stephen John, BA ACA *1985;* Cedar Lodge, Bath Road, Oakhill, BATH, BA3 5AF.
HAYWARD, Mr. Stephen Peter, BA FCA *1982;* Meadow End Kingswood Road, Hillesley, WOTTON-UNDER-EDGE, GLOUCESTERSHIRE, GL12 7RB.
HAYWARD, Mr. Stuart, BA ACA *1985;* NC Book Keeping, Unit 6, Eckland Hodge, Desborough Road, MARKET HARBOROUGH, LEICESTERSHIRE LE16 8HB.
HAYWARD, Mr. Thomas William Roderick, BA ACA *1999;* The Coach House, Ferry Lane, Cookham, MAIDENHEAD, BERKSHIRE, SL6 9XH.
HAYWARD, Mr. Timothy Paul, FCA *1975;* 200 Chartwell Road, OAKVILLE L6J 3Z8, ON, CANADA.
HAYWARD, Mr. Toby Jonathan Langford, ACA *1984;* Coulsworthy House, Coulsworthy, Combe Martin, ILFRACOMBE, EX34 0PD.
HAYWARD, Mr. William Frank, FCA *1944;* Inveresk House, Bodenham, SALISBURY, SP5 4EY. (Life Member)
HAYWARD-SURRY, Mr. Jeremy Keith, OBE FCA *1965;* 191 Cove Road, Oyster Bay Cove, NEW YORK, NY 11771, UNITED STATES.
•**HAYWARD-WRIGHT, Mr. Alistair Graeme, ACA** *2005;* Hayward Wright Ltd, Prospect House, Church Green West, REDDITCH, WORCESTERSHIRE, B97 4BD.
HAYWOOD, Mr. Alfred, FCA *1957;* 65 Woolsery Avenue, Whipton, EXETER, EX4 8BR. (Life Member)
HAYWOOD, Mr. Allan, FCA *1950;* Meadow Croft, Cove Lane, Townhead, Grassington, SKIPTON, NORTH YORKSHIRE BD23 5BL. (Life Member)
HAYWOOD, Ms. Andrea Lynne, BSc ACA *1982;* West Downs Campus, The University of Winchester, Sparkford Road, WINCHESTER, SO22 4NR.
•**HAYWOOD, Mr. Christopher Warren, FCA** *1969;* Haywood & Co LLP, Kevan Pilling House, 1 Myrtle Street, BOLTON, BL1 3AH. See also Haywood & Co Ltd
HAYWOOD, Mr. Darren Paul, BA ACA *2000;* 13 Out Northgate, BURY ST. EDMUNDS, SUFFOLK, IP33 1JQ.
HAYWOOD, Mr. James Harry, TD FCA *1951;* 10 Smith Street, WARWICK, CV34 4HH. (Life Member)
HAYWOOD, Mrs. Jennifer Louise, ACA *1996;* Actuarial Education Co Ltd, 31 Bath Street, ABINGDON, OXFORDSHIRE, OX14 3FF.
HAYWOOD, Mr. Kevin Emanuel David, BSc ACA *1991;* with Ernst & Young LLP, 1 More London Place, LONDON, SE1 2AF.
•**HAYWOOD, Ms. Melanie Katherine, ACA** *1992;* Melanie Haywood, 5 Essendine Road, LONDON, W9 2LS.
•**HAYWOOD, Mr. Michael Henry, ACA MAAT** *2010;* Haywood & Co LLP, Kevan Pilling House, 1 Myrtle Street, BOLTON, BL1 3AH. See also Haywood & Co Ltd
HAYWOOD, Mrs. Nathalie Megan, BSc ACA *2004;* Conifers, Templewood Lane, Farnham Common, SLOUGH, BUCKINGHAMSHIRE, SL2 3HF.
•**HAYWOOD, Mr. Paul, FCA** *1976;* P Haywood, 61 Moxon Way, Manor Park, Ashton-in-Makerfield, WIGAN, WN4 8SW.
HAYWOOD, Mr. Paul, BA ACA *1986;* 28 Norman Road, Northfield, BIRMINGHAM, B31 2EW.
HAYWOOD, Mr. Robert Kenneth James, BSc ACA *1979;* 32 Weysprings, HASLEMERE, GU27 1DE.
HAYWOOD, Mr. Simon Philip, BA(Hons) ACA *2001;* 33 The Meadows, Grange Park, NORTHAMPTON, NN4 5BU.
HAYWOOD, Mr. Timothy Paul, BA FCA *1988;* The Yeoman House, Acton, STOURPORT-ON-SEVERN, DY13 9TF.
HAYWOOD CROUCH, Mr. Kevin, BA(Hons) ACA *2002;* with BDO LLP, 55 Baker Street, LONDON, W1U 7EU.
•**HAZAEL, Mr. Andrew Richard, BA FCA** *1973;* Jacob Cavenagh & Skeet, 5 Robin Hood Lane, SUTTON, SURREY, SM1 2SW.
HAZAN, Miss. Claire, ACA *2008;* Flat 30 Mapesbury Court, 59-61 Shoot up Hill, LONDON, NW2 3PU.
•**HAZARD, Miss. Carolyn Jane, BA ACA** *1996;* H W Fisher & Company, Acre House, 11-15 William Road, LONDON, NW1 3ER. See also Fisher Corporate Plc and H W Fisher & Company Limited
HAZEL, Mrs. Joanne, BSc ACA *2005;* Kaplan Financial, 1st Floor, City Exchange, 11 Albion Street, LEEDS, LS1 5ES.
•**HAZEL, Mr. Malcolm John, FCA** *1974;* M.J. Hazel & Co, 30 Brookfield, NEATH, SA10 7EH.
HAZEL, Mr. Paul Malcolm, FCA *1975;* RHH Business Consultancy, Roel Hill House, Hawling, CHELTENHAM, GLOUCESTERSHIRE, GL54 5AP.
HAZEL, Mr. Peter John Curwen, FCA *1968;* 45 Christchurch Hill, Hampstead, LONDON, NW3 1LA. (Life Member)
HAZELBY, Mr. Paul Vincent, BCom FCA *1976;* Silverglade, Heath Ride, Finchampstead, WOKINGHAM, RG40 3QJ.
HAZELDINE, Mr. Ian Geoffrey, BSc FCA *1985;* 566 London Road, Davenham, NORTHWICH, CHESHIRE, CW9 8LR.
HAZELL, Dr. Annalise Victoria, ACA *2008;* 25 Scotts Hill Lane, CHRISTCHURCH, DORSET, BH23 1HG.
•**HAZELL, Mr. Bernard Leonard, BA ACA** *1982;* (Tax Fac), Moore Stephens, Suite 5, Watergardens 4, Waterport, P O Box 743, GIBRALTAR GIBRALTAR. See also Moore Stephens Limited
HAZELL, Mr. David Ian, FCA *1971;* Clos Au Barbier, La Villette, St. Martin, GUERNSEY, GY4 6QD.
•**HAZELL, Mrs. Elizabeth Mildred, BA FCA DChA** *1987;* with PricewaterhouseCoopers LLP, 7 More London Riverside, LONDON, SE1 2RT.
HAZELL, Mr. Mark, MA FCA *1985;* 153 Burwell Drive, WITNEY, OXFORDSHIRE, OX28 5LP.
HAZELL, Mr. Mark Robert, BSc ACA *2009;* 30 Stanwell Gardens, Stanwell, STAINES, MIDDLESEX, TW19 7JY.
HAZELL, Mr. Matthew, MA ACA *2003;* 83 Waltham Way, LONDON, E4 8HD.
HAZELL, Mr. Matthew Stuart, ACA *2009;* Flat 4 58 Fordwych Road, LONDON, NW2 3TH.
HAZELL, Mrs. Victoria Jane, MA BA ACA *2003;* 144 Elm Road, NEW MALDEN, SURREY, KT3 3HT.
HAZELTON, Mr. John, MA FCA *1980;* Espley Hall, Espley, MORPETH, NORTHUMBERLAND, NE61 3DJ.
HAZELWOOD, Mr. Charles John Gore, LLB ACA *1990;* Bentley Lodge, Normans Lane, Higher Whitley, WARRINGTON, WA4 4PY.
HAZELWOOD, Miss. Sarah Jane, BSc FCA *1993;* 20 Goldsmid Road, TONBRIDGE, KENT, TN9 2BX.
HAZLEDINE, Mr. Scott Neil, BEng ACA *1992;* Orchard Cottage, Gwernesney, USK, GWENT, NP15 1DB.
HAZLEHURST, Mrs. Jennifer Louise, BSc ACA *2003;* 8 Stanway Drive, Hale, ALTRINCHAM, CHESHIRE, WA15 9HG.
•**HAZLEHURST, Mr. Paul Anthony, FCA** *1982;* Neal Frain, 53 York Street, HEYWOOD, LANCASHIRE, OL10 4NR.
HAZLEWOOD, Mr. Jonathan Charles, BSc ACA *1991;* 29 Cricketers Close, Ashington, PULBOROUGH, WEST SUSSEX, RH20 3JQ.
HAZLEWOOD, Dr. Mark, BSc ACA *1996;* Oakley, Quidenham, NORWICH, NR16 2PJ.
HAZON, Mrs. Gillian Ann, BSc ACA *1992;* Bield Housing Association, 79 Hopetoun Street, EDINBURGH, EH7 4QF.
•**HAZZARD, Mr. David Reginald, FCA** *1973;* David R Hazzard FCA, Dobsons Farm, Sandygate Lane, Broughton, PRESTON, PR3 5LA.
HAZZARD, Mrs. Laura, BA(Hons) ACA *2001;* 7 Le Clos Rondin, Le Rue Du Rondin, St. Mary, JERSEY, JE3 3EX.
HAZZARD, Mr. Timothy James, BSc ACA *1984;* 26 The Mall, SWINDON, SN1 4JG.
HAZZLEWOOD, Mr. David Gordon, BA ACA *1980;* 96 Davyhulme Road, Urmston, MANCHESTER, M41 7DL.
HE, Ms. Jing, ACA *2008;* Flat 10, 34 Madeley Road, LONDON, W5 2LH.
HE, Ms. Songmei, ACA *2005;* 70 Little West Street, Apt 19F, NEW YORK, NY 10004, UNITED STATES.
HE, Miss. Ying, ACA *2008;* 172 St. Davids Square, LONDON, E14 3WD.
HE, Mr. Yongliu, ACA *2011;* Deloitte & Touche Llp City House, 126-130 Hills Road, CAMBRIDGE, CB2 1RY.
HE, Miss. Yunyu, ACA *2008;* 81 Exeter Road, LONDON, NW2 4SE.
HEAD, Mr. Alan, FCA *1966;* Fiddlers Green, Church Farm Lane, Marsworth, TRING, HERTFORDSHIRE, HP23 4ND.
HEAD, Mr. Andrew Donald, BSc ACA *2005;* Level 4 Apartments, Casino Division, Tabcorp Holdings Limited, 80 Pyrmont Street, Ultimo, SYDNEY NSW 2007 AUSTRALIA.
HEAD, Mr. Arthur William, FCA *1972;* 38 Gundreda Road, LEWES, BN7 1PX.
HEAD, Mr. Barry Ronald, FCA *1954;* Conifers, Agates Lane, ASHTEAD, KT21 2NE. (Life Member)
HEAD, Mr. Brian Arthur Edward, FCA *1956;* Coxsole Farm, Stelling Minnis, CANTERBURY, CT4 6AQ. (Life Member)
HEAD, Mr. Bryan Cyril, FCA *1971;* Winton, 22 The Headway, Ewell, EPSOM, KT17 1UP.
HEAD, Mr. Christopher, MSc ACA *2007;* Brandbank Ltd, 28 Whiffler Road, NORWICH, NORFOLK, NR3 2AZ.
HEAD, Mrs. Danielle Michelle, BSc ACA *2010;* 53 Thanet Road, IPSWICH, IP4 5LB.
•**HEAD, Mr. David, BA ACA** *1990;* The Old Manse, 22 Boreham Road, WARMINSTER, BA12 9JR.
HEAD, Dr. Geoffrey Douglas, ACA *2008;* Flat 101 Roundwood Court, 3 Meath Crescent, LONDON, E2 0QL.
HEAD, Ms. Gillian Ruth, LLB ACA *1991;* 23 Vanbrugh Fields, LONDON, SE3 7TZ.
HEAD, Mr. Graham Charles, BSc ACA *1989;* (Tax Fac), with Grant Thornton UK LLP, Grant Thornton House, 202 Silbury Boulevard, MILTON KEYNES, BUCKINGHAMSHIRE, MK9 1LW.
HEAD, Mr. Mervyn Stuart Gordon, FCA *1965;* 13 Long Buftlers, HARPENDEN, HERTFORDSHIRE, AL5 1JF.
HEAD, Mr. Michael Edward, BSc ACA *1991;* 19 Felbridge Avenue, CRAWLEY, WEST SUSSEX, RH10 7BD.
HEAD, Mr. Michael John, BA ACA *1988;* 6 Angelica Gardens, Horton Heath, EASTLEIGH, HAMPSHIRE, SO50 7PB.
HEAD, Mr. Neil, BA ACA *1991;* Buffleigh, Reading Road, Mattingley, HOOK, RG27 8JZ.
HEAD, Mr. Paul David, MA FCA *1991;* CP 804 Batterie des Mazots, Rue du Chamossaire, 1972 ANZERE, VALAIS, SWITZERLAND.
HEAD, Mrs. Paula Louise, BA ACA *1995;* 66 Corrie Parade, CORLETTE, NSW 2315, AUSTRALIA.
HEAD, Mr. Peter Douglas, BSc FCA *1978;* Collingtree Cottage, Frieth Road, MARLOW, SL7 2JQ.
HEAD, Dr. Raymond, FCA *1954;* The Manse, Bridgehouse Gate, Pateley Bridge, HARROGATE, HG3 5HQ. (Life Member)
HEAD, Mr. Robert Harold, FCA *1955;* 27 Wittering Road, HAYLING ISLAND, PO11 9SP. (Life Member)
HEAD, Mr. Robert Michael, MA FCIB ACA ACII *1983;* Flat 1, 56 Vincent Square, LONDON, SW1P 2NE.
HEAD, Mr. Roger Burgess, BSc FCA *1972;* Fox Haven, Beechcroft, Yester Road, CHISLEHURST, BR7 5DB.
HEAD, Mr. Thomas Daniel, BSc(Hons) ACA *2002;* 20A Caroline Height, 1 Link Road, HAPPY VALLEY, HONG KONG SAR.
HEAD, Miss. Victoria Elizabeth Howard, FCA *1973;* 7 Preston Park Avenue, BRIGHTON, BN1 6HJ.
HEADDEY, Mr. Stephen, FCA *1969;* 2 Hollyhock Close, CROWTHORNE, BERKSHIRE, RG45 6TX.
HEADEY, Mr. Ivor Leslie, FCA *1949;* Newlands, Lower Broad Oak Road, West Hill, OTTERY ST.MARY, EX11 1XH. (Life Member)
HEADEY, Mr. Peter Gordon, TD FCA *1965;* Timbers, East Dean, CHICHESTER, PO18 0JG.
•**HEADICAR, Mr. Kenneth Lloyd, FCA** *1971;* Sussex Accountancy Services Ltd, 5 Bankside, HASSOCKS, BN6 8EL.
HEADING, Mrs. Catherine Louise, BA ACA *2000;* Braeside, Queensdown Road, Kingsdown, DEAL, KENT, CT14 8EE.
HEADING, Mr. Richard Anthony, BSc ACA *2000;* The Willis Building, 51 Lime Street, LONDON, EC3M 7DQ.
HEADINGS, Mrs. Catherine Mary, BA ACA *1994;* Sandycroft, St. Margarets Avenue, Dormans Park, EAST GRINSTEAD, RH19 2NG.
HEADINGS, Mr. John Mark, BEng ACA *1992;* Sandycroft, St. Margarets Avenue, Dormans Park, EAST GRINSTEAD, RH19 2NG.
HEADINGTON, Miss. Suzanne Marie, BSc ACA *2004;* Flat 6, Laxton House, 38 Lansdown Road, CHELTENHAM, GLOUCESTERSHIRE, GL51 6PU.
HEADLAM, Mrs. Penelope Anne, BA ACA *1997;* 8 The Mount, RINGWOOD, BH24 1XX.
HEADLAM, Mr. Robert Alexander, BA ACA *1998;* 8 The Mount, Poulner, RINGWOOD, BH24 1XX.
HEADLAM, Mr. Thomas Walter, MA *1992;* Flat B, 9 Richborne Terrace, LONDON, SW8 1AS.
HEADLAND, Mr. Anthony Thomas Paget, FCA *1962;* The Chestnuts, Little London Road, Silchester, READING, RG7 2PR.
HEADLAND, Mr. Michael William, FCA *1968;* Faro, Old Forge Lane, Granby, NOTTINGHAM, NG13 9PS.
HEADLEY, Mr. Andrew Nicholas, BSc ACA *1997;* Olleberrie Farm, Olleberrie Lane, Sarratt, RICKMANSWORTH, HERTFORDSHIRE, WD3 4NT.
•**HEADLEY, Mr. John Anthony, BSc ACA** *1991;* Ernst & Young LLP, 1 More London Place, LONDON, SE1 2AF. See also Ernst & Young Europe LLP
•**HEADLEY, Mr. Stephen Robert, BSc FCA** *1992;* JWP Creers, Foss Place, Foss Islands Road, YORK, YO31 7UJ. See also JWPCreers LLP
HEADON, Mr. Adrian Denis, BSc ACA *1992;* 500 5th Avenue, 52nd Floor, NEW YORK, NY 10110, UNITED STATES.
HEADON, Mrs. Fiona Helen, BSc ACA *1992;* Greenlea, Hedgehog Lane, HASLEMERE, GU27 2PJ.
•**HEADON, Mr. Steven Richard, ACA** *2008;* The Moore Scarrott Partnership LLP, Calyx House, South Road, TAUNTON, SOMERSET, TA1 3DY. See also Moore Scarrott Audit Limited
•**HEADY, Mr. John Nicholas, BSc ACA** *1985;* (Tax Fac), Heady & Co Limited, 27 City Business Centre, Hyde Street, WINCHESTER, SO23 7TA. See also Heady & Company(Business Services) Limited
HEAFFORD, Mrs. Stephanie Jayne, BA ACA CTA *1991;* (Tax Fac), 12 Douglas Road, Bingham, NOTTINGHAM, NG13 8EL.
HEAFIELD, Mr. Gustus John James, MA ACA *1991;* 1st Floor Admin Building, South London & Maudsley N H S Trust Maudsley Hospital, Denmark Hill, LONDON, SE5 8AZ.
HEAFORD, Mr. David John, BEng ACA *2007;* 1 Bishop Villas, Churchview Road, TWICKENHAM, MIDDLESEX, TW2 5GF.
HEAFORD, Mr. James Anthony, FCA *1960;* Bellevue, Publow Lane Publow, Nr Pensford, BRISTOL, BS39 4HP. (Life Member)
HEAFORD, Miss. Sally-Anne, BA FCA *1988;* High Bank, 54 Delamer Road, Bowdon, ALTRINCHAM, CHESHIRE, WA14 2LP.
HEAFORD, Mr. William Michael, BSc FCA *1973;* 14 Royal Gardens, Bowdon, ALTRINCHAM, WA14 3GX.
HEAGREN, Mr. Paul Neil, BSc ACA *1989;* Birch House, Samarkand Close, CAMBERLEY, SURREY, GU15 1DG.
HEAGREN, Mrs. Victoria Jane, ACA *1996;* Birch House, Samarkand Close, CAMBERLEY, SURREY, GU15 1DG.
HEAH, Mr. Gregory Sieu Eng, BA ACA *1989;* Westcott House, Lower Ground Floor 35 Portland Place, LONDON, W1B 1AE.
HEAH, Miss. Hoon Imm, BSc(Hons) ACA *2002;* Securities Commission New Zealand, Level 8 Unisys House, 56 The Terrace, PO Box 1179, WELLINGTON 6011, NEW ZEALAND.
HEAH, Mr. Sieu Lay, BA CA ACA CF *1981;* 1 Lorong 14/37 E, 46100 PETALING JAYA, Selangor, MALAYSIA.
HEAH, Miss. Wendy Tin-See, BSc FCA *1971;* 48 Leedon Road, SINGAPORE 267859, SINGAPORE.
•**HEAL, Mr. Colin Thomas, FCA** *1969;* Davisons Ltd, 41-42 High Street, BIDEFORD, DEVON, EX39 3AA.
HEAL, Miss. Emily, ACA *2008;* 12/122 Bower Street, MANLY, NSW 2095, AUSTRALIA.
HEAL, Mrs. Fui Sui, MA MSc ACA CTA *2000;* 8 Williams Grove, Long Ditton, SURBITON, SURREY, KT6 5RN.
HEAL, Mr. Mark William, FCA *1974;* 1 Springfield Close, Bolney, HAYWARDS HEATH, RH17 5PQ.
HEAL, Mr. Nicholas James, BA ACA *1989;* 35 Salmons Leap, CALNE, WILTSHIRE, SN11 9EU.
HEAL, Mr. Paul Bentley, BA FCA *1976;* Culberry Farm, East Pennard, SHEPTON MALLET, BA4 6TT.
HEAL, Mr. Rod, BSc ACA *2001;* with Ernst & Young LLP, 1 More London Place, LONDON, SE1 2AF.
HEAL, Mr. Ronald Stewart, FCA *1977;* 396 Kingston Road, EPSOM, KT19 0DW.
HEALD, Mr. Andrew Peter, BSc ACA *1999;* Schroders plc, Garrard House, 31Gresham Street, LONDON, EC2V 7QA.
HEALD, Mr. Ben, BSS ACA *1991;* Angel Meade, 22 Ridgeway Road, Long Ashton, BRISTOL, BS41 9ET.
HEALD, Mr. Charles, MChem ACA *2011;* Flat 87, Bedford Court Mansions, Bedford Avenue, LONDON, WC1B 3AE.
HEALD, Mr. Christopher John, BSc ACA *1986;* 21 Chiltern Road, Wendover, AYLESBURY, HP22 6DB.
HEALD, Mr. David Anthony, BSc ACA *1999;* 42 Park Mount Drive, MACCLESFIELD, CHESHIRE, SK11 8NT.
HEALD, Mr. Gareth Owen Davey, LLB ACA *2001;* 24 Salisbury Close, Stotfold, HITCHIN, HERTFORDSHIRE, SG5 4FL.

HEALD, Mrs. Helen Patricia, FCA *1976;* Four Winds, Chalfont Avenue, AMERSHAM, BUCKINGHAMSHIRE, HP6 6RF.
HEALD, Mr. John Arthur, FCA *1968;* 10 Warren Road Appleton, WARRINGTON, WA4 5AG.
HEALD, Miss. Judith Anne, BA FCA *1987;* Windybraes, Ferbies, Speldhurst, TUNBRIDGE WELLS, KENT, TN3 0NT.
HEALD, Mr. Malcolm Barclay, MA ACA *1981;* Horseshoe Hill House, Horseshoe Hill, Burnham, SLOUGH, SL1 8QE.
•HEALD, Miss. Rachel Sarah, BSc ACA *1997;* with PricewaterhouseCoopers LLP, Cornwall Court, 19 Cornwall Street, BIRMINGHAM, B3 2DT.
HEALD, Mr. Richard, BA ACA *2009;* 38 Staveley Close, LONDON, N7 9RS.
HEALD, Mr. Stephen John, FCA *1976;* Dunottar School, High Trees Road, REIGATE, RH2 7EL.
HEALE, Mrs. Shirley Susan Elspeth, FCA *1958;* 20 Cromwell Close, East Finchley, LONDON, N2 0LL. (Life Member)
HEALEY, Mr. David Edward, MA FCA *1959;* Lapwing House, Highcroft, Shamley Green, GUILDFORD, GU5 0UE. (Life Member)
HEALEY, Ms. Dawn, BEng ACA *1993;* PNAA Inc, 2192 Martin, Suite 140, IRVINE, CA 92612, UNITED STATES.
•HEALEY, Mr. Eric James George, FCA *1971;* 11 The Firs, Bowdon, ALTRINCHAM, WA14 2TG.
HEALEY, Mr. Gregory John, BA ACA *1994;* (Tax Fac), 12 Netherbury Road, LONDON, W5 4SP.
HEALEY, Mr. John, ACA *2008;* with PricewaterhouseCoopers, 1 Embankment Place, LONDON, WC2N 6RH.
HEALEY, Mr. John Joseph, FCA *1977;* 38 Elizabeth Jennings Way, OXFORD, OX2 7BN.
•HEALEY, Mr. Jonathan Paul, BA(Hons) ACA *2002;* Lindeyer Francis Ferguson, North House, 198 High Street, TONBRIDGE, TN9 1BE.
HEALEY, Miss. Joyce, BA FCA *1974;* 23 Hastings Way, HALIFAX, WEST YORKSHIRE, HX1 2QB.
HEALEY, Miss. Karen Jane, ACA *2009;* 1 Siskin Close, Bramcote, NOTTINGHAM, NOTTINGHAMSHIRE, NG9 3SX.
HEALEY, Mrs. Kathleen Anne, BSc FCA *1989;* 15 Whitworth Close, Wellesbourne, WARWICK, CV35 9NQ.
HEALEY, Mr. Mark Anthony, BA FCA *1987;* The Manor House, Calverley Road, Oulton, LEEDS, LS26 8JD.
HEALEY, Mr. Mark Vincent Andrew, BA ACA *1992;* Cyrano Cottage, La Grande Route de St. Pierre, St. Peter, JERSEY, JE3 7AY.
•HEALEY, Mr. Nigel Raymond, BA FCA *1989;* Hunter Healey Limited, Abacus House, 450 Warrington Road, Culcheth, WARRINGTON, WA3 5QX.
•HEALEY, Mr. Peter Edward, BA FCA *1978;* The Old Farmhouse, Rimington, CLITHEROE, LANCASHIRE, BB7 4DS.
•HEALEY, Mrs. Rebecca Jane, BSc FCA *2000;* Bennett Jones & Co, 94 Fore Street, BODMIN, PL31 2HR.
HEALEY, Mr. Richard Martin James, HND ACA *2005;* (Tax Fac), Maple Mews, Chelford Road, KNUTSFORD, CHESHIRE, WA16 8LU.
HEALEY, Mr. Robert Andrew, BSc ACA *1997;* 120 Route de Bouconne, 31700 CORNEBARRIEU, FRANCE.
HEALEY, Mr. Robert John, BSc ACA *1985;* Interval International, Coombe Hill House, Beverley Way, LONDON, SW20 0AR.
HEALEY, Mr. Simon Peter, BCom ACA *1999;* 110 Bennerley Road, LONDON, SW11 6DU.
HEALEY PEARCE, Mrs. Sarah Rachel, BA ACA *2002;* 10 Poppy Close, BURY ST. EDMUNDS, SUFFOLK, IP32 7JT.
HEALY, Mr. Calvin John, MBiochem ACA CTA *2003;* (Tax Fac), with Moore Stephens, 30 Gay Street, BATH, BA1 2PA.
•HEALY, Mr. Graham John, BSc FCA *1981;* Smith & Williamson Ltd, 1 Bishops Wharf, Walnut Tree Close, GUILDFORD, SURREY, GU1 4RA.
HEALY, Mrs. Jacqueline Anne Lilian, BA ACA *1992;* Diageo Plc Lakeside Drive, Park Royal, LONDON, NW10 7HQ.
HEALY, Miss. Jemma, BSc ACA *2009;* 71 Wanlip Road, LONDON, E13 8QR.
•HEALY, Mr. Jeremy Edward, BA(Hons) ACA *2000;* Alco Audit Limited, 12-14 Percy Street, ROTHERHAM, SOUTH YORKSHIRE, S65 1ED. See also Terence Houghton & Co Ltd
HEALY, Mr. Julian Rupert Francis, BA ACA *1990;* 20 Heatherbank, CHISLEHURST, KENT, BR7 5RE.
HEALY, Mrs. Louise Elizabeth Hamilton, BA ACA *1985;* Sparkes Place, Wonersh Common, Wonersh, GUILDFORD, GU5 0PH.
HEALY, Mrs. Lucy Elizabeth, BSc ACA *2006;* Ryobi Technologies Ltd, Medina House, Fieldhouse Lane, MARLOW, BUCKINGHAMSHIRE, SL7 1TB.
HEALY, Mr. Michael Brendan Anthony, FCA *1965;* PH5 1531 Camden Avenue, LOS ANGELES, CA 90025, UNITED STATES.
HEALY, Mr. Patrick Nicholas, BCL ACA *1995;* Basement Flat, 14 Ravensdon Street, LONDON, SE11 4AR.
HEALY, Mr. Stephen, ACA *2006;* 10 Gainsborough Close, Grange Farm, MILTON KEYNES, MK8 0NA.
HEALY, Mr. Timothy Joseph, FCA *1965;* 11 Saffron House, Kingsfield Road, BIGGLESWADE, BEDFORDSHIRE, SG18 8AT. (Life Member)
HEAMAN-DUNN, Mr. Stuart Anthony, BA FCA *1974;* Emhart Deutchland GMBH, Kaiserleistrasse 51, D-6050 OFFENBACH AM MAIN, GERMANY.
•HEANEY, Mr. Francis, FCA *1960;* F. Heaney, 22 Hillcrest Road, LOUGHTON, ESSEX, IG10 4QQ.
HEANEY, Mr. Quintin John, BA FCA *1983;* Beaufort House, 15 St Botolph St, LONDON, EC3A 7EE.
HEANEY, Mr. Richard Paul, BA ACA *2003;* 2 Idaho Walk, Washington Drive, Great Sankey, WARRINGTON, WA5 8GT.
•HEANEY, Mr. Stuart Alexander, BSc ACA *1997;* Meyer Williams, Queen Alexandra House, 2 Bluecoats Avenue, HERTFORD, HERTFORDSHIRE, SG14 1PB.
HEANEY, Mr. Timothy Colin Francis, BSc FCA *1986;* Honeysuckle Cottage, Woodside, Thornwood Common, EPPING, ESSEX, CM16 6LH.
HEANLY, Mr. Steven Warburton, BA ACA *1993;* 138 Westbourne Grove, LONDON, W11 2RR.
HEAP, Mrs. Alison, MA ACA CTA *1998;* Sleeches Farmhouse Fowley Lane, High Hurstwood, UCKFIELD, EAST SUSSEX, TN22 4BQ.
HEAP, Mrs. Emma, BA ACA *2005;* with PricewaterhouseCoopers LLP, 101 Barbirolli Square, Lower Mosley Street, MANCHESTER, M2 3PW.
HEAP, Mrs. Eva Susanne, BSc ACA *2002;* 26 Upper Grotto Road, TWICKENHAM, TW1 4NF.
HEAP, Mrs. Hilary, BSc ACA *1999;* with KPMG LLP, St. James's Square, MANCHESTER, M2 6DS.
HEAP, Mrs. Irene, FCA *1948;* 152 Reinwood Road, Lindley, HUDDERSFIELD, HD3 4DW. (Life Member)
HEAP, Mr. Jeremy Wilfrid, MA ACA *1988;* Lakeside House, 45 Home Park Road, LONDON, SW19 7HS.
HEAP, Mrs. Linda Catherine, MSc FCA *1978;* European Environmental Controls Limited, 28-30 Hall Street, SOUTHPORT, MERSEYSIDE, PR9 0SE.
HEAP, Mr. Michael, FCA *1970;* 9 de l' Heritage, KNOWLTON J0E 1V0, QC, CANADA.
HEAP, Mr. Michael Conrad, MA ACA *1995;* Sleeches Farmhouse Fowley Lane, High Hurstwood, UCKFIELD, EAST SUSSEX, TN22 4BQ.
HEAP, Mr. Richard James, BSc ACA *1999;* Leonard Curtis, 1 North Parade Parsonage Gardens, MANCHESTER, M3 2NH.
•HEAP, Mr. Richard Michael, BSc FCA *1994;* Kingston Smith LLP, Devonshire House, 60 Goswell Road, LONDON, EC1M 7AD. See also Kingston Smith Limited Liability Partnership, Devonshire Corporate Services LLP and Kingston Smith Consulting LLP
HEAP, Mr. Wallace Allan, JP BA LLB FCA *1938;* Brookfield Nursing Home, 8 Nab Wood Drive, SHIPLEY, WEST YORKSHIRE, BD18 4EJ. (Life Member)
HEAPHY, Mr. John Patrick, FCA *1978;* 51 Forest Grove Drive, TORONTO M2K 1Z4, ON, CANADA.
HEAPS, Mr. Adam, ACA *2009;* 95 High View Road, GUILDFORD, SURREY, GU2 7RY.
HEAPS, Mr. John Anthony, FCA *1982;* Le Picachon, La Rue de la Gabourellerie, St. Ouen, JERSEY, JE3 2BQ.
HEAPS, Mr. Michael John, FCA *1969;* 9 Rusper Road, HORSHAM, RH12 4BA.
HEAPS, Mr. Ryan, BSc ACA *2011;* Fir Tree Cottage, Catforth Road, Catforth, PRESTON, PR4 0HH.
•HEARD, Mr. Anthony John, FCA *1969;* J.R. Atkins & Co, 3 Beech Lane, MACCLESFIELD, SK10 2DR.
HEARD, Mrs. Clare, BA ACA *2000;* Diageo Plc Lakeside Drive, Park Royal, LONDON, NW10 7HQ.
HEARD, Mr. David John, BA ACA *1990;* Invista Textiles (UK) Ltd Ermin Street, Brockworth, GLOUCESTER, GL3 4HP.
HEARD, Mr. David John, BSc FCA *1977;* 5 Scammadine Close, Brinsworth, ROTHERHAM, S60 5JL.
HEARD, Mrs. Hannah Claire, BSc ACA *2000;* 1 Springshaw Close, SEVENOAKS, KENT, TN13 2QE.
•HEARD, Mr. John Alec, FCA *1977;* J.A. Heard & Co, 36 The Green, Long Whatton, LOUGHBOROUGH, LEICESTERSHIRE, LE12 5DB.
HEARD, Mr. John Michael, PhD MSc BSc FCA *1971;* 54 Wood Lodge Lane, WEST WICKHAM, BR4 9NA. (Life Member)
HEARFIELD, Mr. Karl Adam, ACA *2009;* Y M H A, 161 Briggate, LEEDS, LS1 6LY.
•HEARLD, Mr. Christopher Robert, BA FCA *1996;* KPMG LLP, 1 The Embankment, Neville Street, LEEDS, LS1 4DW. See also KPMG Europe LLP
HEARLEY, Mr. Matthew, ACA *2008;* with PricewaterhouseCoopers, Level 21, PWC Tower, 188 Quay Street, Private Bag 92162, AUCKLAND 1142 NEW ZEALAND.
HEARN, Mr. Barry Maurice William, FCA *1970;* Great Claydons, Chelmsford Road, East Hanningfield, CHELMSFORD, CM3 8AL.
HEARN, Mr. Benjamin James, BA ACA *2001;* 25 Beech Grove, EPSOM, KT18 5UG.
HEARN, Mr. Christopher, BSc ACA *2011;* 8 Brudenell Road, POOLE, DORSET, BH13 7NN.
HEARN, Mr. Christopher John, BA ACA *2004;* with KPMG LLP, 15 Canada Square, LONDON, E14 5GL.
HEARN, Mr. Christopher John, BSc FCA *1980;* 28 Green Bank Drive, Sunnyside, ROTHERHAM, SOUTH YORKSHIRE, S66 3ZP.
HEARN, Mrs. Collette, BSc ACA *2001;* 25 Beech Grove, EPSOM, KT18 5UG.
HEARN, Mr. David Gareth, BA ACA *1988;* Middle Prospect, New Road, BAMPTON, OXFORDSHIRE, OX18 2LF.
HEARN, Mr. David Victor, BSc FCA *1986;* with Stacey & Partners, 88 High Street, NEWMARKET, SUFFOLK, CB8 8JX.
HEARN, Mr. Dennis, FCA *1954;* 63 Ashley Park Avenue, WALTON-ON-THAMES, SURREY, KT12 1EU. (Life Member)
HEARN, Miss. Elizabeth Jane, BSc FCA *1981;* 11A Stourbridge Road, Fairfield, BROMSGROVE, B61 9LR.
HEARN, Mrs. Jenny, BMus ACA *2006;* Ground Floor Flat, 57 Agamemnon Road, LONDON, NW6 1EG.
HEARN, Mrs. Joanne, BSc ACA *2011;* 226 Dale Close, Stanway, COLCHESTER, CO3 0FT.
HEARN, Mr. John Richard Whitcombe, MA FCA *1975;* Grangebrook, Broomfield Park, ASCOT, SL5 0JT.
HEARN, Mr. John Robert, FCA *1952;* Apt 804 Delisle Avenue, TORONTO M4V 3C2, ON, CANADA. (Life Member)
HEARN, Mr. Mark, ACA CA(AUS) *2008;* Citibank Tower, Paseo de Roxas, MAKATI CITY 1200, PHILIPPINES.
HEARN, Mr. Mark David, BA ACA *1995;* Thales Transport & Securities Ltd Quadrant House, Thomas More Street 17 Thomas More Square, LONDON, E1W 1YW.
HEARN, Mr. Matthew Steven, BA ACA *2007;* 18 Ormonde Rise, BUCKHURST HILL, IG9 5QQ.
HEARN, Mr. Michael Ernest, FCA *1961;* Maple Lodge, Standen Close, Felbridge, EAST GRINSTEAD, RH19 2RL.
HEARN, Mr. Michael Thomas, FCA *1956;* 31 Home Farm Park, Lee Green Lane, Church Minshull, NANTWICH, CHESHIRE, CW5 6ED. (Life Member)
HEARN, Mr. Peter John, MA FCA *1977;* Flat 94, Cinnabar Wharf, 28 Wapping High Street, LONDON, E1W 1NG.
HEARN, Mr. Richard Andrew, BA(Hons) ACA *2003;* 353 Evergreen Circle SW, CALGARY T2Y 0B8, AB, CANADA.
HEARN, Mr. Richard Charles, BSc FCA *1980;* 28 Avenue Bugeaud, 75116 PARIS, FRANCE.
HEARN, Mr. Roger Andrew, BA ACA *1985;* 30 Glendale Avenue, EDGWARE, MIDDLESEX, HA8 8HQ.
HEARN, Mrs. Zanri, BCom BAcc ACA *2007;* 86 Meadway, HARPENDEN, HERTFORDSHIRE, AL5 1JQ.
HEARNDEN, Mrs. Denise, BA ACA *1991;* Hager & Elsasser UK Ltd, Field Place Estate, Field Place, Broadbridge Heath, HORSHAM, WEST SUSSEX RH12 3PB.
HEARNDEN, Mr. Robert Maurice, FCA *1960;* 21 The Butts, WESTBURY, BA13 3EU. (Life Member)
HEARNDEN, Mr. Trevor Michael, BA ACA *1992;* O C S Group Ltd, 79 Limpsfield Road, SANDERSTEAD, SURREY, CR2 9LB.
HEARNE, Mr. Andrew Nicholas, BSc FCA *1978;* 270 Tamarack Street, NORTH VANCOUVER V7N 1S4, BC, CANADA.
HEARNE, Miss. Jill, ACA *2011;* Flat E, The Lodge, 22 Leigham Court Road, LONDON, SW16 2PL.
•HEARNE, Mr. John Barry, FCA FCCA *1981;* THP Limited, 34-40 High Street, Wanstead, LONDON, E11 2RJ.
•HEARNE, Mr. Michael Bernard, FCA *1970;* Baker Tilly Tax & Advisory Services LLP, Lancaster House, 7 Elmfield Road, BROMLEY, BR1 1LT.
HEARNE, Mrs. Rachel, BA ACA *2006;* 66 Ryedale Avenue, MANSFIELD, NOTTINGHAMSHIRE, NG18 3GT.
•HEARNE, Mr. Richard Bruce, ACA *1980;* R H Accountancy Services Limited, 22 Beresford Road, HARROW, MIDDLESEX, HA1 4QZ.
HEARNE, Mr. Simon Michael, ACA *2008;* with Deloitte LLP, PO Box 500, 2 Hardman Street, MANCHESTER, M60 2AT.
•HEARNSHAW, Mr. Peter John, FCA *1959;* (Tax Fac), Peter J. Hearnshaw & Co, 2 Sankyns Green, Little Witley, WORCESTER, WR6 6LQ.
HEARNSHAW, Mr. Robert, FCA *1976;* Hobgrumble Ghyll, Town End, Out Rawcliffe, PRESTON, PR3 6TN.
HEARSEY, Mr. James Robert Anthony, BSc ACA *2010;* 47 Chillington Street, MAIDSTONE, ME14 2RT.
HEARSEY-MCKAY, Ms. Deborah June, BSc ACA *1989;* 22 Kiirfechstrooss, L-6834 BIWER, LUXEMBOURG.
HEARTH, Miss. Lucinda, BSc(Hons) ACA *2011;* Pricewaterhousecoopers LLP, 1 Embankment Place, LONDON, WC2N 6RH.
HEASLEY, Mrs. Joan Elizabeth, BA ACA *1982;* 3 Coniston Road, Beeston, NOTTINGHAM, NG9 3AD.
HEASLEY, Mrs. Shelagh Ellen, BCom ACA *1985;* 18 Peel Avenue, Frimley, CAMBERLEY, SURREY, GU16 8YT.
HEASMAN, Mr. John Philip Derek, MEng ACA *1996;* Rock UK Frontier Centre, Addington Road Irthlingborough, WELLINGBOROUGH, NORTHAMPTONSHIRE, NN9 5UH.
•HEASMAN, Mr. Richard William, BA ACA *1991;* Reeves & Co LLP, 37 St. Margarets Street, CANTERBURY, KENT, CT1 2TU.
•HEASON, Mr. Robert Andrew, FCA *1971;* 14 Plains Farm Close, Mapperley, NOTTINGHAM, NG3 5RE.
•HEATH, Mr. Alan, BSc FCA *1984;* (Tax Fac), AH Accounting Limited, 41 Kingfisher Road, BUCKINGHAM, MK18 7EX.
HEATH, Mrs. Allison Judith, MA BSc ACA *1988;* 42 The Ridgway, SUTTON, SURREY, SM2 5JU.
HEATH, Mr. Andrew James, BA FCA *1992;* Willow Tree Barn, Pickmere Lane, Pickmere, KNUTSFORD, CHESHIRE, WA16 0HS.
HEATH, Mr. Anthony Frederick, BA FCA *1969;* 36 Tadorne Road, TADWORTH, SURREY, KT20 5TF.
HEATH, Miss. Bryony Laura, ACA *2011;* Dog Kennels Farm, Grove, RETFORD, NOTTINGHAMSHIRE, DN22 0RN.
HEATH, Mrs. Caroline, BSc(Hons) ACA *2002;* Hyder Consulting Ltd, 29 Bressenden Place, LONDON, SW1E 5DZ.
HEATH, Mr. Charles Trevor, FCA *1963;* The New House, 1a The Mead, Ashton Keynes, SWINDON, SN6 6PL.
•HEATH, Mr. Clive John, FCA *1975;* Knipe Whiting Heath Ltd, Turpins, St. Weonards, HEREFORD, HR2 8QG.
•HEATH, Mr. Colin Arnold, FCA *1973;* (Tax Fac), 7 Wrights Close, TENTERDEN, KENT, TN30 6QN.
HEATH, Mr. Colin Jack, BSc(Econ) ACA *2003;* 409/10 Jaques Avenue, Bondi Beach, SYDNEY, NSW 2026, AUSTRALIA.
HEATH, Mr. David, ACA *2011;* 1 Norton Green, STEVENAGE, HERTFORDSHIRE, SG1 2DP.
HEATH, Mr. David Arthur, MBA FCA *1972;* E C 2 I Ltd, 18-19 Aviation Way Southend Airport, SOUTHEND-ON-SEA, SS2 6UN.
HEATH, Mr. David Edward, BEng ACA *2011;* 39 Keats Avenue, REDHILL, RH1 1AF.
HEATH, Mr. David William, ACA *1981;* Yew Tree Cottage, Broadmoor Common, Woolhope, HEREFORD, HR1 4QY.
HEATH, Mr. Duncan Michael, BA ACA *2001;* 62 Kemp's End, TRANENT, EAST LOTHIAN, EH33 2GZ.
HEATH, Mrs. Elizabeth, BA ACA *1988;* 30 Jenny Lane, Woodford, STOCKPORT, CHESHIRE, SK7 1PE.
HEATH, Miss. Elizabeth Sarah, BSc FCA *1982;* 1 rue Albert-Gos, 1206 GENEVA, SWITZERLAND.
HEATH, Mr. Frederick John, FCA *1960;* Gover Lodge, Mount Hawke, TRURO, TR4 8BQ. (Life Member)
HEATH, Mr. Glyn Anthony, BA ACA *1988;* PricewaterhouseCoopers, Box D198, G.P.O., PERTH, WA 6840, AUSTRALIA.
HEATH, Miss. Jacqueline, BA(Oxon) ACA *2011;* 31 Stafford Street, Brewood, STAFFORD, ST19 9DX.

HEATH, Mr. James, BA ACA *2004;* Nomura International Plc, 1 Angel Lane, LONDON, EC4R 3AB.
HEATH, Mr. Jamie Richard, BA ACA *2007;* 16 Ruskin Way, PRENTON, MERSEYSIDE, CH43 9HQ.
HEATH, Mr. Jamie Robert, BSc ACA *2006;* Kurt Salmon, 10 Fleet Place, LONDON, EC4M 7RB.
HEATH, Mrs. Joanna Clare, BSc ACA *1983;* Pinewood, 20 Millig Street, HELENSBURGH, DUNBARTONSHIRE, G84 9PJ.
HEATH, Mrs. Joyce Maureen, ACA *1982;* with Knipe Whiting Heath Ltd, Turpins, St. Weonards, HEREFORD, HR2 8QG.
HEATH, Mr. Kevin, BSc ACA *2002;* 11 Norfolk House Road, LONDON, SW16 1JJ.
HEATH, Mr. Laurence Mark, MSc BSc ACA *2009;* 66a Church Road, RICHMOND, TW10 6LN.
•HEATH, Mr. Martin Andrew, BSc ACA *1989;* PricewaterhouseCoopers LLP, 101 Barbirolli Square, Lower Mosley Street, MANCHESTER, M2 3PW. See also PricewaterhouseCoopers
•HEATH, Mr. Michael Francis Hemington, BSS ACA *1991;* KPMG, 15 Canada Square, LONDON, E14.
HEATH, Miss. Natalie Teresa, BSc ACA MSI *2003;* Flat 2 Leicester Court, 24 Clevedon Road, TWICKENHAM, TW1 2TB.
HEATH, Mr. Nicholas Benjamin, BA ACA *1989;* University of Oxford, 23-38 Hythe Bridge Street, OXFORD, OX1 2EP.
•HEATH, Mr. Nicholas Mark, MA ACA *1986;* Crouch Chapman, 62 Wilson Street, LONDON, EC2A 2BU.
HEATH, Mr. Peter Alexander Milnes, FCA *1969;* 16 Lanyard Place, WOODBRIDGE, SUFFOLK, IP12 1FE.
HEATH, Mr. Peter Francis, FCA *1972;* 193 Send Road, Send, WOKING, GU23 7ET.
HEATH, Mr. Peter John, FCA *1965;* Paxwood, 8 Condover Park, Condover, SHREWSBURY, SY5 7DU. (Life Member)
HEATH, Mr. Philip Glen, BA ACA ATII *1992;* 5 The Spinney, Harlow Wood, MANSFIELD, NG18 4TH.
•HEATH, Mr. Philip James, FCA *1979;* Brebners, The Quadrangle, 180 Wardour Street, LONDON, W1F 8LB.
HEATH, Mr. Philip Martin, BSc ACA *1993;* North Hill, Scot Lane, Chew Stoke, BRISTOL, BS40 8UN.
HEATH, Mr. Robert Christopher, FCA *1974;* 89 Drillfield Road, NORTHWICH, CHESHIRE, CW9 5HU.
HEATH, Mr. Robert Douglas, BEng ACA *1993;* 4 Ramsbury Drive, Earley, READING, RG6 7RT.
•HEATH, Mr. Robin David Jennings, FCA *1974;* Ernst & Young LLP, 1 More London Place, LONDON, SE1 2AF. See also Ernst & Young Limited, EYOP LLP, Ernst & Young Europe LLP
HEATH, Mr. Ronald Edwin, FCA *1963;* 1 Wellstones Close, IVYBRIDGE, PL21 0FE.
HEATH, Mrs. Sarah Louise, BA ACA *2007;* 16 Ruskin Way, PRENTON, MERSEYSIDE, CH43 9HQ.
•HEATH, Mr. Scott Daniel, ACA *2009;* Mitten Clarke Limited, Festival Way, Festival Park, STOKE-ON-TRENT, ST1 5TQ.
HEATH, Mr. Simon Barrie, BA ACA *1981;* Dog Kennels Farm, Grove, RETFORD, NOTTINGHAMSHIRE, DN22 0RN.
HEATH, Mr. Stephen Michael, BSc ACA *1983;* Fairfx Marc House, 13-14 Great St. Thomas Apostle, LONDON, EC4V 2BB.
HEATH, Mr. Steven James, BA ACA *1999;* 39 Tatton Road North, STOCKPORT, CHESHIRE, SK4 4QX.
•①HEATH, Mrs. Tracey McArdle, BSc FCA *1989;* with Ernst & Young LLP, 100 Barbirolli Square, MANCHESTER, M2 3EY.
HEATH, Miss. Victoria Clare, BSc ACA *2005;* 23 Foxglove Rise, MAIDSTONE, KENT, ME14 2AF.
HEATH-SMITH, Mr. David, FCA *1960;* 48 Derby Road, Bramcote, NOTTINGHAM, NG9 3FY. (Life Member)
HEATHCOAT-AMORY, The Right Hon. David Philip, FCA MP *1974;* 12 Lower Addison Gardens, LONDON, W14 8BQ.
HEATHCOCK, Mr. Martin John, FCA *1966;* 6 Hawthorn Coppice, Hagley, STOURBRIDGE, WEST MIDLANDS, DY9 0PE.
HEATHCOTE, Mr. Francis James, ACA *1980;* Crave Hall, Cow Lane, Great Chesterford, SAFFRON WALDEN, ESSEX, CB10 1RJ.
HEATHCOTE, Mr. Gilbert, FCA *1970;* Ravenscroft Heathcote Ltd, Stocks Green Old Road, Feering, COLCHESTER, CO5 9RN.
HEATHCOTE, Mr. James Arthur, FCA *1954;* Calle Castellet 7, Pedralbes, 08034 BARCELONA, SPAIN. (Life Member)
HEATHCOTE, Mr. Julian, BSc ACA *1997;* 5 Gordon Place, MANCHESTER, M20 3LD.
HEATHCOTE, Mrs. Kerry Louise, BSc(Hons) ACA *2001;* 89-91 High Street, Dilton Marsh, WESTBURY, WILTSHIRE, BA13 4DP.
HEATHCOTE, Mrs. Lindsay Claire, ACA *2009;* 7 Hartford Gardens, East Hartford, CRAMLINGTON, NORTHUMBERLAND, NE23 3BL.
HEATHCOTE, Miss. Marjorie Hannah Dora, BSc ACA *2010;* 281 Buxton Road, Furness Vale, HIGH PEAK, DERBYSHIRE, SK23 7PZ.
HEATHCOTE, Mr. Michael Barry John, FCA *1972;* 8 Wheelwrights Close, ARUNDEL, WEST SUSSEX, BN18 9TA.
HEATHCOTE, Mr. Robert Alexander Bridges, FCA *1964;* 46 St. Cross Road, WINCHESTER, SO23 9PS.
HEATHCOTE, Mrs. Sharon Elizabeth, BA ACA *1995;* 6 The Whitfields, MACCLESFIELD, SK10 3PX.
HEATHCOTE, Mr. Stephen, BA ACA *1995;* 13 Heriot Road, Lenzie Kirkintilloch, GLASGOW, G66 5AX.
HEATHCOTE, Mr. Steven Trevor, FCA *1974;* Conifers, 65 Croftdown Road, Harborne, BIRMINGHAM, B17 8RE.
HEATHER, Mr. Andrew John Charles, BA ACA *2005;* 733 West Waveland Avenue, CHICAGO, IL 60613, UNITED STATES.
HEATHER, Mr. Brian Hersee, FCA *1977;* 9 Gledhow Park Crescent, LEEDS, LS7 4JY.
HEATHER, Mr. Colin, FCA *1959;* 5 Calsay Gardens, Auchtermuchty, CUPAR, KY14 7LD. (Life Member)
HEATHER, Mr. David Murray, FCA *1963;* The Square, Ermin Street, Lambourn Woodlands, HUNGERFORD, RG17 7TR.
HEATHER, Mr. James, BA(Hons) ACA *2010;* A116 Le Capelain House, Castle Quay, La Rue de l'Etau, St Helier, JERSEY, JE2 3EA.
HEATHER, Miss. Lisa Samantha, ACA *2010;* 1 Cleveland Road, CHICHESTER, WEST SUSSEX, PO19 7AF.
HEATHER, Mrs. Lorraine Karen, BA ACA *1991;* Counsells Chartered Accountants, 48-50 Smithbrook Kilns, CRANLEIGH, GU6 8JJ.
HEATHER, Mr. Malcolm Thomas, BA ACA *1981;* Coombe Barn, London Road, Sayers Common, HASSOCKS, BN6 9HY.
HEATHER, Mr. Peter William, FCA *1973;* P.W. Heather, Brook Bungalow, Northchapel, PETWORTH, WEST SUSSEX, GU28 9EN.
HEATHER, Mr. Ronald Edward, FCA *1953;* Lingcroft, 4 Amey Drive, Bookham, LEATHERHEAD, KT23 4AL. (Life Member)
•HEATHER, Mr. Steven John, BA FCA *1986;* (Tax Fac), Heather & Co Ltd, Longlac, White House Lane, Jacobs Well, GUILDFORD, GU4 7PT.
•HEATHERINGTON, Mr. Peter, MA FCA *1975;* Peter Heatherington, Dene House, Hartburn, MORPETH, NORTHUMBERLAND, NE61 4JB.
HEATHERS, Miss. Stephanie, ACA *2011;* 12 Bracken Way, GUILDFORD, GU3 3AN.
HEATHERSHAW, Miss. Claire, ACA *2007;* 1 Limecroft View, Wingerworth, CHESTERFIELD, DERBYSHIRE, S42 6NR.
•HEATLEY, Mr. Michael John Russell, FCA CTA *1957;* (Tax Fac), Michael J.R. Heatley, 4 Gentian Glade, HARROGATE, HG3 2NT.
HEATLEY, Mr. Robert Frederick, BA ACA *1992;* 2016 Crist Drive, LOS ALTOS, CA 94024, UNITED STATES.
•HEATLIE, Mr. Christopher, BA ACA *1994;* BDO LLP, 6th Floor, 3 Hardman Street, Spinningfields, MANCHESTER, M3 3AT. See also BDO Stoy Hayward LLP
HEATON, Mr. Alan John, BSc ACA ACT *1988;* House B3, Chateau Royale, 1 Yung Yi Road, TAI PO, HONG KONG SAR.
HEATON, Miss. Anna-Louise, MA ACA *1998;* 41 Speldhurst Road, LONDON, W4 1BX.
HEATON, Mrs. Betty Patricia, FCA *1955;* Dolphins, Seagrove Farm Road, SEAVIEW, PO34 5HU. (Life Member)
HEATON, Mr. Charles Robert, BSc ACA *1989;* 26 Turnpike Close, MARKET HARBOROUGH, LE16 7TJ.
HEATON, Mrs. Christine Lynn, BA ACA *1988;* House B3, Chateau Royale, 1 Yung Yi Road, TAI PO, HONG KONG SAR.
HEATON, Mr. Christopher Charles Standring, BA ACA *1986;* (Member of Council 2009 - 2011), 6 Home Farm Court, Wortley, SHEFFIELD, S35 7DT.
HEATON, Mr. Christopher Luke, BA FCA *1989;* 6 Cornhill Close, Duffield, BELPER, DERBYSHIRE, DE56 4HQ.
HEATON, Mrs. Clare Lesley, BSc ACA *1988;* Vitaflo International Ltd, 11-16 Century Building, Brunswick Business Park, LIVERPOOL, L3 4BL.
•HEATON, Mr. David, LLB ACA *1999;* Deloitte LLP, PO Box 500, 2 Hardman Street, MANCHESTER, M60 2AT. See also Deloitte & Touche LLP
•HEATON, Mr. David Alan, BA FCA CTA *1985;* MEMBER OF COUNCIL, (Tax Fac), Baker Tilly Tax & Advisory Services LLP, 2 Whitehall Quay, LEEDS, LS1 4HG.
HEATON, Mr. David John, BSc FCA *1973;* The Old Manor, Manor Road, Landkey, BARNSTAPLE, DEVON, EX32 0JL. (Life Member)
HEATON, Mr. Douglas, FCA *1954;* 9 Ridgemont, Fulwood, PRESTON, PR2 3FQ. (Life Member)
HEATON, Mr. Iain Sholto, ACA *2009;* Nine Acres Watercress Lane, Mattishall, DEREHAM, NORFOLK, NR20 3RJ.
•HEATON, Mr. Jonathan, BSc FCA MAE *1978;* Resources, The Hermitage Tower, Elston Lane, Grimsargh, PRESTON, PR2 5LE. See also Financial Resources Limited
HEATON, Mr. Michael David George, BA ACA *2010;* 19 Brigantine Way, NEWPORT, GWENT, NP10 8EW.
HEATON, Mr. Nicholas Peter, BA ACA *1989;* Edificio Sao Fernando 1-E, Rua 5 De Outubro 33, 2790 CARNAXIDE, PORTUGAL.
HEATON, Mr. Norman James, FCA *1950;* (Tax Fac), Hadleigh, Moffats Lane, Brookmans Park, HATFIELD, HERTFORDSHIRE, AL9 7RU. (Life Member)
HEATON, Mr. Patrick John, BSc FCA *1999;* 9 Wheatroyd Lane, Almondbury, HUDDERSFIELD, HD5 8XS.
HEATON, Dr. Paul Anthony, PhD BSc ACA *2003;* 2 Calder Drive, Swinton, MANCHESTER, M27 9SY.
HEATON, Mr. Paul Anthony, MA FCA *1984;* 248 High Street, Boston Spa, WETHERBY, LS23 6AD.
HEATON, Mr. Paul Gordon, BSc ACA *1992;* 1 Gold View, SWINDON, SN5 8ZG.
HEATON, Mr. Phillip Geoffrey, BEng ACA *1999;* Topgrade Sportswear Unit B The Grandstand, Leacroft Road, WARRINGTON, CHESHIRE, WA3 6PJ.
HEATON, Mr. Robert Fergus, BA ACA *1992;* 21 St. Mary's Road, Wimbledon, LONDON, SW19 7BZ.
HEATON, Mr. Ronald Briggs, FCA *1949;* 7 Ings Lane, Waltham, GRIMSBY, DN37 0EX. (Life Member)
HEATON, Mr. Stephan James, BSc(Hons) ACA *2001;* 4 Garsdale Close, Great Sankey, WARRINGTON, WA5 3DL.
•HEATON, Mr. Timothy Clive, FCA *1979;* The Tax Partnership, Spring Cottage, 90 Monkton Deverill, WARMINSTER, WILTSHIRE, BA12 7EX.
HEATON, Mr. Timothy John Barclay, BA FCA *1976;* 3 Ridley Hill Farm, Ridley, TARPORLEY, CHESHIRE, CW6 9RX.
HEAUME, Miss. Carla Jane, ACA *2005;* Hillstead Candie Road, St. Peter Port, GUERNSEY, GY1 1UP.
HEAVEN, Mr. Dennis John, FCA *1957;* 172 Clarence Road, Four Oaks, SUTTON COLDFIELD, B74 4LB. (Life Member)
HEAVEN, Mr. Mark Jonathan, BA ACA *1995;* 26 Green Parade, SANDRINGHAM, VIC 3191, AUSTRALIA.
•HEAVEN, Mr. Michael Victor Rhodes, FCA *1969;* (Tax Fac), Michael Heaven & Associates Limited, Quadrant Court, 48 Calthorpe Road, Edgbaston, BIRMINGHAM, B15 1TH. See also Nettleton Management Services Limited
•HEAVEN, Mr. Paul Martin, ACA *1984;* Blue Sky Corporate Finance (Midlands) Ltd, 2nd Floor, 3 Brindley Place, BIRMINGHAM, B1 2JB.
HEAVEN, Miss. Susan Mary, BSc ACA *1994;* (Tax Fac), 2a Stevens Lane, Claygate, ESHER, KT10 0TE.
•HEAVENS, Mr. Neil James, BA FCA *1992;* 10 Oliver Close, The Prinnels, Lydiard Tregoz, SWINDON, WILTSHIRE, SN5 6NP.
HEAVENS, Mr. Reginald John, FCA *1953;* 64 Sandown Lodge, Avenue Road, EPSOM, KT18 7QU. (Life Member)
•HEAVER, Mr. Paul Malcolm, FCA *1973;* Pantiles, Rectory Road, Coleby, LINCOLN, LN5 0AJ.
HEAVERS, Mr. Paul Barry, FCA *1966;* The Thatched Cottage, Cherry Gardens, Wethersfield, BRAINTREE, CM7 4AQ.
HEAVEY, Mrs. Mary Rosanna, BSc ACA *1998;* 21 Brockwell, Oakley, BEDFORD, MK43 7TD.
HEAYBERD, Mr. Christopher Incledon, BA ACA *1981;* MacDonald & Co Property Ltd, 40a Dover Street, LONDON, W1S 4NW.
HEAZELL, Ms. Victoria, MA FCA *1995;* 74 Brook Drive, LONDON, SE11 4TS.
HEBB, Mr. Timothy, ACA *1983;* 7 Hall Walk, Walkington, BEVERLEY, NORTH HUMBERSIDE, HU17 8TF.
HEBBES, Mr. Marcus Llewellyn, BSc ACA *1999;* Parkholme, 9 Brookvale Road, Highfield, SOUTHAMPTON, SO17 1QN.
HEBBLETHWAITE, Mr. Marcus Dalby Andrew, BSc ACA *1987;* 45 Carlisle Road, LONDON, NW6 6TL.
•HEBBLETHWAITE, Mr. Paul, BA FCA *1982;* Haywood & Co., 18 Stalker Walk, SHEFFIELD, S11 8NF.
HEBBLETHWAITE, Mr. Richard Jeremy, TD BA FCA *1959;* 2 The Green, Evenley, BRACKLEY, NN13 5SQ. (Life Member)
HEBBLETHWAITE, Mr. Richard Neil, BA FCA *1971;* 1Les Bidons, La Grande Route de Faldouet, St. Martin, JERSEY, JE3 6UG.
HEBBORN, Mr. Stephen James, BA ACA *1993;* Fox Hollies, Tidenham Chase, Woodcroft, CHEPSTOW, GWENT, NP16 7JS.
HEBBRON, Mr. Albert George, FCA *1948;* 29 Fairacres, RUISLIP, HA4 8AN. (Life Member)
HEBBRON, Ms. Michelle, BA ACA *1993;* 24 Eastwood Road, Muswell Hill, LONDON, N10 1NL.
HEBDIGE, Miss. Claire Louise, ACA CTA *2002;* Longmeadow Cottage Hollee, Kirkpatrick Fleming, LOCKERBIE, DUMFRIESSHIRE, DG11 3NF.
HEBDITCH, Mrs. Laura Patricia, BSc ACA *2002;* 17 St. Ediths Road, Kemsing, SEVENOAKS, KENT, TN15 6PT.
HEBDITCH, Mr. Paul Donald, BA ACA *1991;* 10b Fortune Court, 18-20 Arbuthnot Road, CENTRAL, HONG KONG ISLAND, HONG KONG SAR.
•①HEBENTON, Mr. Robert James, BSc(Hons) ACA *2002;* with PricewaterhouseCoopers LLP, 101 Barbirolli Square, Lower Mosley Street, MANCHESTER, M2 3PW.
•HECEK, Mr. Raymond Vincent, ACA *1982;* (Tax Fac), Raymond Hecek, 615 London Road, WESTCLIFF-ON-SEA, ESSEX, SS0 9PE.
HECHT, Mr. Adam, ACA *2009;* Flat 7, Christie Court, 3 Aspern Grove, LONDON, NW3 2AB.
HECK, Mrs. Tracy Helen, BSc ACA *1996;* Nal Resources, 550 6th Ave SW, Suite 600, CALGARY T2P 0S2, AB, CANADA.
HECKELS, Mr. Paul John, BA ACA *1998;* 14 Sandleford Lane, Greenham, THATCHAM, RG19 8XW.
HECKER, Mr. Paul Stuart, BA FCA *1983;* 9 Thorndean Drive, Warninglid, HAYWARDS HEATH, RH17 5SX.
HECKFORD, Mr. Geoffrey Brittain, FCA *1952;* 14 The Hurdles, Thrapston Road, Brampton, HUNTINGDON, CAMBRIDGESHIRE, PE28 4WB. (Life Member)
HECKSCHER, Mr. Albert Richard, BSc FCA *1962;* (Tax Fac), 37 Highcroft Gardens, LONDON, NW11 0LY.
HECKSCHER, Mr. Robert, BA ACA *1998;* 92 Lancaster Avenue, LONDON, SE27 9EB.
•HECQUET, Mr. Robert Thomas, FCA *1970;* Davert Banks & Co, 11 St. Saviours Wharf, Mill Street, LONDON, SE1 2BE.
HECTOR, Mr. Gordon, FCA *1953;* 296 Blackburn Road, Edgworth Turton, BOLTON, BL7 0PL. (Life Member)
•HECTOR, Mr. John Philip, FCA *1973;* Philip Hector & Co Limited, Unit 6, Grange Road Workshops, Grange Road, Geddington, KETTERING NORTHAMPTONSHIRE NN14 1AL.
HECTORIDES, Mr. Christos Phidhia, BSc ACA *1990;* 10 Ionos Street, Engomi, NICOSIA, CYPRUS.
HEDAYATI, Miss. Yasaman, MSc BA ACA *2006;* Flat 7 Brunswick Court, 1 Darleston Road, LONDON, SW19 4LF.
HEDDEN, Miss. Rachel Louise, BA ACA *2005;* Flat 4, 137-139 Balham High Road, LONDON, SW12 9AU.
HEDDEN, Mr. Wayne Robert, BA ACA *1999;* with PricewaterhouseCoopers LLP, 488 Almaden Boulevard, SAN JOSE, CA 95110, UNITED STATES.
HEDDERMAN, Mr. Robert Patrick, FCA *1956;* 61 Wood Lodge Lane, WEST WICKHAM, BR4 9LY. (Life Member)
HEDDERSON, Mr. Thomas Joseph, FCA *1971;* Lane Head, Partridge Hill, Ashwell, BALDOCK, HERTFORDSHIRE, SG7 5QZ.
•HEDDITCH, Mr. David Laurence, MA FCA *1993;* Deloitte LLP, 5 Callaghan Square, CARDIFF, CF10 5BT. See also Deloitte & Touche LLP
HEDDLE, Mr. John Robert, FCA *1973;* The Colchester Consultancy Limited, 2 Sunbeam Close, Rowhedge, COLCHESTER, CO5 7DZ.
HEDEN, Mrs. Cara, BA(Hons) ACA *2003;* Alliance Healthcare, 43 Cox Lane, CHESSINGTON, KT9 1SN.
HEDGE, Mr. Colin John, FCA *1958;* 165 Buxton Road, Spixworth, NORWICH, NR10 3PL. (Life Member)
HEDGE, Mr. Leonard George, FCA *1938;* 5 Cavendish Place, Beeston, NOTTINGHAM, NG9 1BY. (Life Member)
HEDGE, Mr. Richard Huxley, MA FCA *1974;* 40 Stanley Street, INDOOROOPILLY, QLD 4068, AUSTRALIA. (Life Member)
HEDGE, Mr. Stephen David, BSc ACA *2003;* Alyn Cottage 12 Rowley Green Road, BARNET, HERTFORDSHIRE, EN5 3HJ.
HEDGE, Mrs. Victoria Jane, BA ACA *2002;* 6 Connaught Road, ST. ALBANS, HERTFORDSHIRE, AL3 5RX.
HEDGECOCK, Mr. Neil Bernard, BSc ACA *1994;* 7 Staffords Lane, West Haddon, NORTHAMPTON, NN6 7AT.

HEDGECOCK, Mrs. Sarah May, BSc ACA *1993;* 7 Staffords Lane, West Haddon, NORTHAMPTON, NN6 7AT.
HEDGER, Mr. Andrew, BA FCA *1993;* 73 Weald Road, SEVENOAKS, TN13 1QJ.
HEDGER, Mrs. Naomi Jane, ACA *2005;* 15 Church Lane, Isleham, ELY, CAMBRIDGESHIRE, CB7 5SQ.
HEDGER, Mrs. Sarah Ann, MEng ACA *1992;* 24 Huntsmans Causeway, LECHLADE, GL7 3DT.
HEDGES, Mrs. Anna, BSc ACA *1993;* 38 Welsh Road West, SOUTHAM, CV47 0JW.
HEDGES, Mr. Daniel John, ACA *2010;* 1 Boardwalk Way, Marchwood, SOUTHAMPTON, SO40 4AJ.
HEDGES, Mr. Darryn William, BSc ACA *1992;* Pavilion House, 60 Cold Bath Road, HARROGATE, NORTH YORKSHIRE, HG2 0PB.
•**HEDGES, Mr. David Anthony Roy, FCA** *1974;* (Tax Fac), Hedges & Co, The Leighs, Weston, SIDMOUTH, EX10 0PH.
HEDGES, Ms. Deborah Jane, BSc ACA *1986;* 1 The Droveway, HAYWARDS HEATH, RH16 1LL.
HEDGES, Mr. Gary, BSc ACA *1991;* (Tax Fac), 32 Tabard Gardens, NEWPORT PAGNELL, BUCKINGHAMSHIRE, MK16 0LX.
•**HEDGES, Mr. Ian Malcolm Grant, FCA** *1974;* Kyffin & Co., The Old Convent, Llanbadarn Road, ABERYSTWYTH, SY23 1EY.
•**HEDGES, Mr. James Alfred, FCA** *1980;* James A Hedges Limited, Westwood Cottage, Lower Gustard Wood, Wheathampstead, ST. ALBANS, HERTFORDSHIRE AL4 8RU.
HEDGES, Mr. James Killingworth, BSc ACA *1983;* Charlton House, SHAFTESBURY, SP7 0PL.
HEDGES, Mr. John Bernard, FCA *1956;* Flat 37, Homeregal House, Bellingham Lane, RAYLEIGH, ESSEX, SS6 7HN. (Life Member)
HEDGES, Mr. Michael, ACA *2011;* 21 Rochelle Close, LONDON, SW11 2RU.
HEDGES, Mr. Miles Stuart, MA FCA *1984;* The Open University, PO Box 77, Walton Hall, MILTON KEYNES, MK7 6BT.
•**HEDGES, Mr. Peter John, FCA** *1972;* Wood Ridings, Parkfield, SEVENOAKS, TN15 0HX.
•**HEDGES, Mr. Timothy Simon Guy, BSc FCA** *1983;* Hedges Chandler (Westcliff) Limited, Hamlet House, 366-368 London Road, WESTCLIFF-ON-SEA, ESSEX, SS0 7HZ. See also Hedges Chandler (Sudbury) Ltd, Hedges Bull Commercial Finance Ltd
•**HEDGETHORNE, Mr. Peter James, BSc FCA** *1981;* (Tax Fac), Feist Hedgethorne Limited, Preston Park House, South Road, BRIGHTON, BN1 6SB.
HEDGMAN, Mr. George Edward, FCA *1949;* 16 Lime Court, 2 Gipsy Lane, LONDON, SW15 5RJ. (Life Member)
HEDINGER, Mr. Witold George, BA FCA *1976;* LARRIVAL, 47400 VARES, LOT ET GARONNE, FRANCE.
HEDLEY, Mr. Adam David, MA ACA *1996;* Manor House, Exbourne, OKEHAMPTON, DEVON, EX20 3RT.
HEDLEY, Mr. Anthony Michael, FCA *1973;* Hedley & Co, Springwell House, 2 Shear Bank Road, BLACKBURN, BB1 8AD.
HEDLEY, Mr. Colin Robert, FCA *1974;* Ball Asia Pacific Limited, Units 1610-1618 Tower 1 Grand Century Place, Prince Edward Road West, MONG KOK, KOWLOON, HONG KONG SAR.
HEDLEY, Mr. Daniel Richard, ACA *2008;* Ground Floor Left, 5 Comiston Place, Morningside, EDINBURGH, EH10 6AF.
HEDLEY, Mr. David John, BA ACA *1987;* Sevogelstrasse 52, 4052 BASEL, SWITZERLAND.
HEDLEY, Mr. Hugh Bernard, FCA *1974;* with Rigby Taylor Ltd, Rigby Taylor House, Crown Lane, Horwich, BOLTON, BL6 5HP.
HEDLEY, Mrs. Julie, BSc FCA *1997;* British Pepper & Spice, Rhosili Road, Brackmills, NORTHAMPTON, NN4 7AN.
HEDLEY, Mr. Nicholas, ACA *2011;* 23 Walkley Street, SHEFFIELD, S6 3RF.
HEDLEY, Mr. Paul Ian, BA ACA *1995;* Direct Energy, 12 Greenway Plaza Suite 600, HOUSTON, TX 77046, UNITED STATES.
HEDLEY, Mr. Philip John Lane, FCA *1973;* 18 Eveline Avenue, PARKDALE, VIC 3195, AUSTRALIA.
HEDLEY, Miss. Ruth Alexandra, MA ACA *1992;* Flat 3 St Andrews Mansions, 157 Lower Clapton Road, LONDON, E5 8EX.
HEDLEY, Mr. Simon Nigel, MA FCA *1985;* 45 Woodlands, Gosforth, NEWCASTLE UPON TYNE, NE3 4YL.
HEDLEY, Mr. Simon Paul, BSc ACA *2003;* Flat 8 United House, Mayflower Street, LONDON, SE16 4JL.
HEDLEY, Mr. William Wilson, TD FCA *1960;* 2 Church Street, Bathford, BATH, BA1 7TU. (Life Member)
HEDLEY-DENT, Mr. Giles Edward, FCA *1974;* Thesis Asset Management Plc, Belmont House, Station Way, CRAWLEY, WEST SUSSEX, RH10 1JA.
HEDLEY LEWIS, Miss. Melissa, ACA *2009;* 11 Birkholme, Corby Glen, GRANTHAM, LINCOLNSHIRE, NG33 4LF.
HEDLEY LEWIS, Mr. Vincent Richard, FCA *1967;* Birkholme Farm, Birkholme Manor, Corby Glen, GRANTHAM, NG33 4LF. (Life Member)
HEDRICH-WIGGANS, Mrs. Annika, MA MSt ACA *2001;* Oakham School, Chapel Close, Market Place, OAKHAM, RUTLAND, LE15 6DT.
HEE KARSTADT, Ms. Lilian, ACA *1987;* 1 Wimbleton Crescent, ETOBICOKE M9A 3X5, ON, CANADA.
•**HEEGER, Mr. Christian, BSc FCA** *1991;* with Grant Thornton UK LLP, The Explorer Building, Fleming Way, Manor Royal, CRAWLEY, WEST SUSSEX RH10 9GT.
HEEKS, Mr. David Ian, BA ACA *1990;* 44 Heath Street, STOURBRIDGE, DY8 1SA.
HEELAS, Mr. John Henry Gale, FCA *1989;* Lower Fen, Scotland Street, Stoke By Nayland, COLCHESTER, CO6 4QD.
HEELEY, Mr. Adam John, BSc ACA *2002;* 10 Chesworth Crescent, HORSHAM, WEST SUSSEX, RH13 5AN.
HEELEY, Mr. Christopher Charles, BSc ACA *2010;* 1 Copperfield Court, 239 Dickens Heath Road, Shirley, SOLIHULL, WEST MIDLANDS, B90 1QD.
HEELEY, Mr. David, FCA *1975;* Oak Tree House, Candlemas Lane, BEACONSFIELD, BUCKINGHAMSHIRE, HP9 1AE.
HEELEY, Mr. Paul, MPhil BSc ACA *1999;* 70 Summerseat Lane, Ramsbottom, BURY, BL0 9RQ.
HEELEY, Mr. Robert Antony, BSc(Hons) ACA *2000;* 31 Rocklands Crescent, LICHFIELD, WS13 6DJ.
HEELEY, Mr. Rodger, MA ACA CTA *2007;* with PricewaterhouseCoopers LLP, 1 Embankment Place, LONDON, WC2N 6RH.
HEELEY, Mr. Stephen John, BSc ACA *1995;* Nationwide Bldg Soc, Kings Park Road, Moulton Park Industrial Estate, NORTHAMPTON, NN3 6NW.
HEELEY, Mrs. Victoria Frances, BSc ACA *2006;* Flat 11 Dennington House, Dennington Park Road, LONDON, NW6 1AU.
HEELS, Mr. David Edward, MA MBA ACA *1989;* 83 Thornhill Street, Calverley, PUDSEY, WEST YORKSHIRE, LS28 5PR.
HEELS, Mr. Richard Stephen, BCom FCA *1977;* 5 Laburnum Grove, Horbury, WAKEFIELD, WF4 6HG.
HEELS, Mr. Stephen, BSc ACA *2007;* 170 Wakefield Road, Horbury, WAKEFIELD, WF4 5HW.
HEENAN, Mr. Duncan, BSc FCA *1973;* Dolphins House, Boxers Lane, Niton, VENTNOR, PO38 2BH.
•**HEENAN, Mr. Michael Richard, BSc FCA** *1976;* (Tax Fac), Dean Statham, Bank Passage, STAFFORD, ST16 2JS.
HEENAN, Miss. Rosemary, BA FCA *1985;* (Tax Fac), The Plaza, 100 Old Hall Street, LIVERPOOL, MERSEYSIDE, L3 9QJ.
•**HEENAN, Mr. Stuart James, BSc ACA** *1981;* (Tax Fac), Heenans, KBC Kingston Exchange, 12-50 Kingsgate Road, KINGSTON UPON THAMES, SURREY, KT2 5AA.
HEENEMAN-WONG, Mrs. Alicia Caroline, LLB ACA *2004;* Flat 22 Ilchester Mansions, Abingdon Road, LONDON, W8 6AE.
HEENEY, Mr. George Francis, FCA *1952;* 19 Magdalene Court, Royston Road, BALDOCK, HERTFORDSHIRE, SG7 6PF. (Life Member)
•**HEENEY, Mr. John Paul, BA FCA** *1995;* RNS, 50-54 Oswald Road, SCUNTHORPE, NORTH LINCOLNSHIRE, DN15 7PQ.
HEEPS, Mrs. Katharine, MEng ACA DChA *1993;* 20 Cooper Close, Waterloo Road, LONDON, SE1 7QU.
HEER, Mr. Narinderpal Singh, BSc ACA *1992;* 80 Levett Gardens, ILFORD, IG3 9BU.
HEER, Mr. Rajkarnh Singh, BSc ACA *2010;* 113 Long Lane, Ickenham, UXBRIDGE, MIDDLESEX, UB10 8QS.
•**HEER, Mr. Sukhbinder Singh, BA ACA** *1989;* Gambit Corporate Finance LLP, 3 Assembly Square, Britannia Quay, Cardiff Bay, CARDIFF, CF10 4PL.
•**HEERAMANECK, Mr. Naval Jehangir, FCA** *1970;* (Tax Fac), NJHCo, 8th Floor, Tolworth Tower, Ewell Road, SURBITON, KT6 7EL. See also Heeramaneck N.J. & Co
HEERKENS, Mr. Tom Henricus Maria, BA ACA *2005;* Stokerkade 74, 1019 XB AMSTERDAM, NETHERLANDS.
HEERY, Mr. Allen, BSc ACA *1993;* 1308 Kobbe Avenue Apt B, SAN FRANCISCO, CA 94129, UNITED STATES.
HEFER, Mr. Hercules Viljoen, FCA *1956;* PO Box 784516, SANDTON, GAUTENG, 2146, SOUTH AFRICA. (Life Member)
HEFFER, Mr. Nicholas, MA FCA *1963;* 18 Rue du Maréchal Joffre, 09500 MIREPOIX, FRANCE. (Life Member)
HEFFERNAN, Mr. Andrew Peter, ACA *1993;* 22 Westbere Road, LONDON, NW2 2EP.
HEFFERNAN, Mr. Dermot Timothy Andrew, BSc ACA *1984;* 1 Struan Gardens, WOKING, GU21 4DJ.
HEFFERNAN, Mr. John Paul, BA ACA *2007;* 28 Dennis Road, EAST MOLESEY, KT8 9ED.
HEFFERNAN, Mr. Liam Anthony, BSc FCA *1999;* 5 Malthouse Meadows, LIPHOOK, GU30 7BD.
•**HEFFERNAN, Mr. Martin Michael, BSc FCA** *1992;* Thompson Taraz LLP, 35 Grosvenor Street, Mayfair, LONDON, W1K 4QX.
HEFFERNAN, Mr. Paul Alan, MSc BA ACA *1997;* with Grant Thornton UK LLP, Grant Thornton House, 22 Melton Street, Euston Square, LONDON, NW1 2EP.
•**HEFFRON, Mr. Andrew, BSc FCA** *1993;* Mazars LLP, Tower Bridge House, St. Katharines Way, LONDON, E1W 1DD.
HEFFRON, Mr. Christian Patrick, BSc ACA *1992;* 15423 Eagle Tavern lane, CENTREVILLE, VA 20120, UNITED STATES.
HEFFRON, Mr. John Joseph, BCom FCA *1960;* 81 Commerce Street, Melbourne, DERBY, DE73 8FT. (Life Member)
HEGARTY, Miss. Bernadette, BA ACA *1986;* 15 Augustus Court, Augustus Road, Southfields, LONDON, SW19 6NA.
HEGARTY, Mr. Brendan Patrick, MSc BA(Hons) ACA *2002;* 126 Mayfield Gardens, LONDON, W7 3RD.
•**HEGARTY, Mr. Bryan Patrick, FCA** *1949;* Wheeler Hegarty & Co, Forest Lodge, Kingston Hill, KINGSTON UPON THAMES, SURREY, KT2 7JZ.
HEGARTY, Mr. Colin, ACA *2008;* 44 Ballards Road, Dollis Hill, LONDON, NW2 7UG.
HEGARTY, Mr. Colin Michael, FCA *1973;* (Tax Fac), 15 Cornfields, YATELEY, GU46 6YT.
HEGARTY, Mr. Daniel, ACA *2011;* 6 Cobbetts Walk, Bisley, WOKING, SURREY, GU24 9DT.
HEGARTY, Mr. Matthew John, BSc ACA *2000;* Ellesmere, Tuesley Lane, GODALMING, SURREY, GU7 1SJ.
•**HEGARTY, Mrs. Pauline Anne, BSc ACA** *1985;* Pauline Hegarty, 18 Footherley Road, Shenstone, LICHFIELD, STAFFORDSHIRE, WS14 0NJ.
HEGARTY, Mr. Sean David, MA ACA *1998;* 19 West Way, HARPENDEN, HERTFORDSHIRE, AL5 4RD.
HEGARTY, Mr. Sean Michael, LLB ACA *2001;* 377 Ellerman Road, LIVERPOOL, L3 4FH.
HEGGIE, Mr. George Annan, FCA *1971;* Green Meads, 15 Green Lane, GUILDFORD, GU1 2LZ.
HEGINBOTHAM, Ms. Kay, MEng ACA *2005;* 30 King George Avenue, Exning, NEWMARKET, SUFFOLK, CB8 7ES.
HEGINBOTTOM, Mr. David, MA(Oxon) ACA *1996;* 5 Haywood Drive, HEMEL HEMPSTEAD, HERTFORDSHIRE, HP3 0SA.
HEIDARI, Mr. Many, MSc ACA *2010;* Flat A, 84 Pine Road, LONDON, NW2 6SA.
HEIDEN, Mr. Paul, BSc ACA *1982;* Bay Tree House, 20 Valley Road, West Bridgford, NOTTINGHAM, NG2 6HG.
•**HEIDENFELD, Mr. Thomas, BSc(Econ) ACA** *1995;* Mvenchner-Kindl-Weg, 81547 MUNICH, GERMANY.
HEIGL, Mrs. Anne Michelle, BA ACA *1995;* Guntherstrasse 21, 80639 MUNICH, GERMANY.
HEILBRON, Mr. Jonathan Charles Ian, BA FCA *1986;* Thomas Pink Ltd, 1 Palmerston Court, Palmerston Way, LONDON, SW8 4AJ.
HEILBRONN, Mr. Christopher John William, BA ACA *1979;* 18 Codrington Crescent, MISSION BAY 1071, NEW ZEALAND.
HEILMANN, Mrs. Lydia Kirsten, MA ACA CFE *2003;* 825 Fairfield Beach Road, FAIRFIELD, CT 06824, UNITED STATES.
HEIMBACH, Mrs. Susan Barbara, BSc ACA *1983;* Imperial College Healthcare NHS Trust Hammersmith Hospital, Du Cane Road, LONDON, W12 0HS.
HEIMS, Mr. Philip George, FCA *1976;* Pricewaterhousecoopers, 1 Embankment Place, LONDON, WC2N 6RH.
HEINEMANN, Miss. Emma, BA ACA *2011;* 47 Heath Street, NEWCASTLE, STAFFORDSHIRE, ST5 2BU.
•**HEINEMANN, Mr. Volker, ACA** *2002;* 7 Avebury Square, READING, RG1 5JH.
HEINICKE, Mr. Michael William, BA ACA *2006;* with PricewaterhouseCoopers LLP, 101 Barbirolli Square, Lower Mosley Street, MANCHESTER, M2 3PW.
HEIS, Mrs. Elizabeth Anne, BSc ACA *1989;* Chilling House, High Street, Leigh, TONBRIDGE, TN11 8RH.
•①**HEIS, Mr. Richard, LLB FCA** *1987;* KPMG LLP, 15 Canada Square, LONDON, E14 5GL. See also KPMG Europe LLP
HEISER, Mrs. Judith Rosalyn, BSc ACA *1989;* 10 Allenby Road, MAIDENHEAD, BERKSHIRE, SL6 5BB.
HEISTERS, Ms. Lia, BSc ACA *1990;* 30 St. Lawrence Terrace, LONDON, W10 5SX.
HEITON, Mr. John Miller, BEng ACA *2002;* (Tax Fac), Containental Offshore Ltd Cothal House Cothal View, Kirkton Avenue Pitmedden Industrial Estate Dyce, ABERDEEN, AB21 0BA.
HEKMATPANAH, Mr. Houshang, MSc ACA *1979;* 52 Bancroft Avenue, LONDON, N2 0AS.
HELDREICH, Mrs. Joanne Louise, BA ACA *2001;* East Midlands Housing Group Memorial House, Whitwick Business Park Stenson Road, COALVILLE, LE67 4JP.
HELDREICH, Mr. Robert John, BSc FCA *2000;* (Tax Fac), Porterbrook Leasing Ivatt House, The Point 7 Pinnacle Way Pride Park, DERBY, DE24 8ZS.
HELE, Mrs. Susan Amanda, BSc ACA *1981;* Lilley Green Farm, Lilley Green Road, Alvechurch, BIRMINGHAM, B48 7HA.
HELE KERGOZOU DE LA BOESSIERE, Mrs. Jacqueline Sara, FCA FRSA *1980;* (Tax Fac), Lilac Cottage The Street Draycott, CHEDDAR, SOMERSET, BS27 3TH.
HELEY, Mr. Stuart Craig, BA ACA *1990;* Dicom Ltd Lydford Road, Meadow Lane Industrial Estate, ALFRETON, DERBYSHIRE, DE55 7RQ.
HELFER, Mr. Martin Lister, BA ACA *1991;* 26 Tyne Road, Bishopston, BRISTOL, BS7 8EE.
HELFGOTT, Mrs. Thea, BA ACA *1995;* 28 Helenslea Avenue, Golders Green, LONDON, NW11 8ND.
HELKS, Mrs. Naomi Elizabeth, BA ACA CTA *1997;* 28 Shaw Avenue, NORMANTON, WEST YORKSHIRE, WF6 2TT.
•**HELLAWELL, Mr. Peter John, FCA CTA** *1979;* Petersons Accountants Limited, 28 High Street, WITNEY, OXFORDSHIRE, OX28 6RA.
HELLAWELL, Mr. Richard Andrew, BA FCA *1975;* 22 Kendal Walk, LEEDS, LS3 1NP.
HELLEM, Mr. Jonathan, BSc ACA *2011;* 72 Tamworth Drive, FLEET, GU51 2UP.
HELLEN, Mr. David Robert, FCA *1956;* 1 Mulberry Close, Gidea Park, ROMFORD, RM2 6DX. (Life Member)
HELLEN, Mr. Robert, BA ACA *1998;* 8 Swans Pasture, CHELMSFORD, CM1 6AF.
•**HELLER, Mr. Adrian, FCA** *1982;* Martin + Heller, 5 North End Road, LONDON, NW11 7RJ.
HELLER, Mr. Andrew Robert, MA ACA *1994;* Bisichi Mining Plc, 30-35 Pall Mall, LONDON, SW1Y 5LP.
HELLER, Mr. Michael Aron, MA FCA *1961;* London & Associated Properties Plc, Carlton House, St. James's Square, LONDON, SW1Y 4JH.
HELLER, Mr. Peter John, FCA *1975;* Manor Farm Cottage, Church Lane, PRINCES RISBOROUGH, BUCKINGHAMSHIRE, HP27 9AW.
HELLER, Mr. Ralph Nathan, BSc FCA *1969;* Burgmatt 15, PO Box 235, 6341 BAAR, SWITZERLAND.
HELLER, Mr. Samuel Chaim, FCA *1973;* 44 Princes Park Avenue, LONDON, NW11 0JT.
HELLEWELL, Mr. David Simpson, FCA *1961;* 4 Goodwood, Owler Park Road, ILKLEY, WEST YORKSHIRE, LS29 0BY.
HELLEWELL, Mr. Richard Geoffrey, BA FCA *1983;* Royal Blind, PO Box 500, Gillespie Crescent, EDINBURGH, EH10 4HZ.
HELLIAR, Prof. Christine Vivienne, PhD BSc FCA FRSA *1981;* Avenel, Ewanfield, CRIEFF, PH7 3DA.
HELLIER, Mr. Charles Peter Henry, MA ACA *1981;* Vale House, Wotton Vale Balchins Lane, Westcott, DORKING, RH4 3LP.
HELLIER, Mr. Kenneth Charles, FCA *1958;* 11 Cavendish Place, Avenue Road, LYMINGTON, HAMPSHIRE, SO41 9ET. (Life Member)
HELLINGS, Mr. Brian Aliol, FCA *1959;* 66a West River Road, RUMSON, NJ 07760, UNITED STATES. (Life Member)
HELLINGS, Mr. Edward, BA ACA *1993;* Queen Annes School Henley Road, Caversham, READING, RG4 6DX.
•**HELLINGS, Mrs. Geraldine Anne, BA ACA** *1992;* G A Hellings Ltd, 53 Queens Road, Wimbleon, LONDON, SW19 8NP.
HELLIWELL, Mr. David, FCA *1965;* 53 Bonython Road, NEWQUAY, CORNWALL, TR7 3AL.
HELLIWELL, Mr. Fergus James, ACA *2009;* 9a Ravenstone Street, LONDON, SW12 9ST.
HELLIWELL, Mr. James Malcolm, MEng ACA *2009;* Radickestrasse 45a, 21079 HAMBURG, GERMANY.
HELLIWELL, Mr. Patrick Arthur, FCA *1968;* 18 Savile Park, HALIFAX, HX1 3EA.
HELLIWELL, Mr. Robert Christopher Guy, FCA *1974;* Church Cottage, The Street, Stradishall, NEWMARKET, SUFFOLK, CB8 8YW.
HELLIWELL, Mr. Ronald, FCA *1955;* Newlyn, 2 Station Lane, Grotton, OLDHAM, OL4 5QY. (Life Member)
HELLMUTH, Mr. Daniel, BSc ACA *2011;* 14 Oatlands Road, Shinfield, READING, RG2 9DW.

HELLYAR, Mr. Barry John, FCA *1973;* 18607 Upper Bay Road, NASSAU BAY, TX 77058, UNITED STATES.
HELLYAR, Mr. Michael Francis, FCA *1964;* 16 Chapel Close, Petrockstow, OKEHAMPTON, DEVON, EX20 3HR.
HELLYAR, Mr. Stuart Thomas, BSc ACA *1996;* 33 Trimaran Road, Warsash, SOUTHAMPTON, SO31 9BE.
•HELLYER, Mr. James Robert, MA ACA *2006;* James Hellyer & Co, 7 Honey Street, Northam, BIDEFORD, DEVON, EX39 1DL.
HELLYER, Mr. Nicholos James, BSc ACA *1989;* Flat 15 Eagle Wharf East, 35 Narrow Street, LONDON, E14 8DP.
HELLYER, Mr. Robert Charles Orlando, BBS ACA *1980;* F F P Services Ltd, 15 Suffolk Street, LONDON, SW1Y 4HG.
HELM, Mr. Andrew, BSc ACA *1988;* Rose Cottage Pound Lane, Ampfield, ROMSEY, SO51 9BL.
HELM, Mr. Christopher, BSc ACA *2005;* 26 Millennium Wharf, Wharf Lane, RICKMANSWORTH, HERTFORDSHIRE, WD3 1AZ.
HELM, Mr. Christopher James Alfred, MSc BA ACA *1989;* African Development Bank (BAD), B.P.323 - 1002 Tunis Belvedere, TUNIS, TUNISIA.
HELM, Mrs. Clare Helen Everella, BA ACA *1990;* 165 Westchester Drive, Churton Park, WELLINGTON 6037, NEW ZEALAND.
HELM, Mr. David, MA ACA *1983;* 18 Whiteacre, Standish, WIGAN, WN6 0SH.
HELM, Mr. David Peter, BSc ACA *1986;* Orchard House, Rowan Close, SANDBACH, CHESHIRE, CW11 1XN.
HELM, Mrs. Jillian Anne, BA ACA *1992;* 53 Pilgrims Way, Standish, WIGAN, WN6 0AJ.
•HELM, Mr. John Mark Moxon, BA ACA *1992;* Simply Churches Limited, 17 Heathville Road, LONDON, N19 3AL.
HELM, Mr. Paul David, BA FCA *1989;* 165 Westchester Drive, Churton Park, WELLINGTON, NEW ZEALAND.
HELM, Mr. Stanley Vincent, FCA *1957;* 1 Railway Lane, CHATTERIS, CAMBRIDGESHIRE, PE16 6NE. (Life Member)
HELMAN, Mr. Henry, FCA *1940;* 523 Bonhill Road, LOS ANGELES, CA 90049, UNITED STATES. (Life Member)
HELME, Mr. Andrew Gareth, BSc ACA *2006;* 9th Floor, B D O Stoy Hayward, 1 Bridgewater Place Water Lane, LEEDS, LS11 5RU.
HELME, Mr. Christopher David, BSc ACA *2004;* 129 Tritonville Road, Sandymount, DUBLIN 4, COUNTY DUBLIN, IRELAND.
HELME, Mr. James, BA ACA *2004;* with Grant Thornton UK LLP, 30 Finsbury Square, LONDON, EC2P 2YU.
HELME, Mr. Jamie Robert, MA ACA *2004;* 15/14, Dean Park Street, EDINBURGH, MIDLOTHIAN, EH4 1JR.
HELME, Mrs. Sarah Elizabeth, BA(Hons) ACA *2001;* 129 Tritonville Road, SANDYMOUNT DUBLIN 4, COUNTY DUBLIN, IRELAND.
HELMER, Mr. Gavin Romald Helmerow, BSc ACA *1995;* Standard Bank Plc, 20 Gresham Street, LONDON, EC2V 7JE.
HELMER, Mr. Jamie, BEng ACA *2004;* Felton Pumphrey, 1 The Green, RICHMOND, TW9 1PL.
HELMORE, Mr. Max, BA ACA *2009;* 2 Trigon Road, LONDON, SW8 1NH.
HELMSLEY, Mrs. Deborah Karen, BSc ACA *2002;* The Compass Centre, Nelson Road, HOUNSLOW, MIDDLESEX, TW6 2GW.
HELMY, Mr. Abol Fazl, FCA *1974;* 1331 Brickell Bay Drive, Apt 4303, MIAMI, FL 33131, UNITED STATES.
HELPS, Mr. Andrew John, BSc ACA *1989;* 16 Birchall Road, Redland, BRISTOL, BS6 7TP.
HELPS, Mrs. Joanne Louise, BA ACA *1992;* Continu Forms Holdings Plc, Wells Road, RADSTOCK, BA3 3UP.
•HELPS, Mr. John Victor Robert, BSc ACA *1986;* (Tax Fac), Skingle Helps & Co, 28 Southway, Carshalton Beeches, CARSHALTON, SURREY, SM5 4HW.
•HELPS, Mr. Philip Stanley, FCA CTA *1993;* (Tax Fac), Stanley Joseph Limited, Suite 1, Liberty House, South Liberty Lane, BRISTOL, BS3 2ST.
HELPS, Mr. Simon Andrew, BA(Hons) ACA *2006;* Flat 2, 7 Wyneham Road, LONDON, SE24 9NT.
HELSBY, Miss. Carole Ann, BA ACA *1986;* 22 Breydon Gardens, ST HELENS, MERSEYSIDE, WA9 5WH.
HELSBY, Mrs. Elizabeth June, ACA *1982;* Mitchell & Co, 143-147 High Street, NEWTON-LE-WILLOWS, MERSEYSIDE, WA12 9SQ.
HELSBY, Mr. Ian, BA FCA *1980;* 170 Esperanza Way, PALM BEACH GARDENS, FL 33418, UNITED STATES.
HELSBY, Mr. Michael, BA(Hons) ACA *2001;* 45 Milton Road, HARPENDEN, HERTFORDSHIRE, AL5 5LZ.
HELSBY, Mr. Neil Tudor, BSc FCA *1975;* Oakbase Oakbase House, Trafford Street, CHESTER, CH1 3HP.
HELSON, Mr. Christopher Derek, BA ACA *2007;* 142c St. Albans Road, Sandridge, ST. ALBANS, HERTFORDSHIRE, AL4 9LL.
HELSON, Mr. Patrick Gerard, MA ACA *1992;* Actis Capital LLP, 1st Floor Cradock Heights, Corner of Cradock & Tyrwhitt Ave, ROSEBANK, 2196, SOUTH AFRICA.
HELT, Miss. Lyndsay, ACA *2010;* Creaseys Llp, 12-16 Lonsdale Gardens, TUNBRIDGE WELLS, TN1 1PA.
HELYER, Mr. George James, FCA *1964;* 247 Petersham Road, Petersham., RICHMOND, TW10 7DA.
HELYER, Mr. Jonathon Paul, BA ACA *2001;* 31 Eastheath Avenue, WOKINGHAM, BERKSHIRE, RG41 2PP.
HEMANI, Mr. Karim Ramzanali, FCA *1975;* Foxley Down, 23 Hadley Wood Rise, KENLEY, CR8 5LY.
HEMANI, Mr. Mohamed Magan Alibhai, FCA *1969;* 20 Badminton Close, NORTHOLT, UB5 4NA. (Life Member)
HEMANS, Mr. Alexander Patrick, BA ACA *1995;* 51 Rusthall Avenue, LONDON, W4 1BN.
HEMANS, Mr. Richard James, MA ACA *2000;* La Molliere, La Rue Des Fosses, Forest, GUERNSEY, GY8 0JA.
HEMATALLY, Mr. Feroz, ACA FCCA *2009;* with Invensys plc, Portland House, Bressenden Place, LONDON, SW1E 5BF.
HEMAYA, Mr. Fikry Mounir, BSc ACA *1982;* Les Bouleries, La Route de St. Jean, St. Mary, JERSEY, JE3 3EA.
HEMBERY, The Revd. Steven John, FCA *1974;* 19 Parkside, WESTCLIFF-ON-SEA, SS0 8PR.
HEMBLING, Mrs. Claire Helen, BSc ACA *1999;* 45 John Street, FORRESTERS BEACH, NSW 2260, AUSTRALIA.
•HEMBLYS, Mr. Richard, FCA *1981;* (Tax Fac), Spenser Wilson & Co, Equitable House, 55 Pellon Lane, HALIFAX, WEST YORKSHIRE, HX1 5SP.
HEMBROW, Miss. Kate, ACA *2011;* 61 Auckland Road, LONDON, KINGSTON UPON THAMES, KT1 3BQ.
•HEMERY, Mr. Leslie Stuart, FCA *1977;* PricewaterhouseCoopers, Avenida Andres Bello 2711, Torre Costanera Piso 5, SANTIAGO, CHILE.
•HEMING, Mr. Martin Clifton, BA FCA *1985;* Windle & Bowker Limited, Croft House, Station Road, BARNOLDSWICK, LANCASHIRE, BB18 5NA.
HEMINGTON, Mr. David, BSc FCA *1979;* 17 Bressingham Drive, Landmere Court, West Bridgford, NOTTINGHAM, NOTTINGHAMSHIRE, NG2 7PD.
HEMINGTON, Mr. Donald Robert, FCA *1952;* 27 Goddington Lane, ORPINGTON, BR6 9DR. (Life Member)
•HEMINGTON, Mr. Guy Richard, BSc FCA CF AMCT *1983;* Jasper CF Limited, 80 Caroline Street, BIRMINGHAM, B3 1UP.
•HEMINGTON, Mr. Peter James, MA ACA *1989;* BDO LLP, 55 Baker Street, LONDON, W1U 7EU. See also BDO Stoy Hayward LLP
HEMINGWAY, Mr. Adam, BSc(Hons) ACA *2010;* 20 Frances Street, YORK, YO10 4DW.
HEMINGWAY, Mr. Andrew Richard, BA ACA *2006;* 47 Byrne Road, LONDON, SW12 9HZ.
HEMINGWAY, Miss. Annabel, ACA *2004;* 21 Hanbury Square, PETERSFIELD, HAMPSHIRE, GU31 4QT.
HEMINGWAY, Mr. Ian Andrew, BSc ACA *2004;* 2 Blacksmith Mews, Robin Hood, WAKEFIELD, WF3 3TZ.
HEMINGWAY, Miss. Jayne, BSc FCA *1998;* HRMC Sherbourne House, Sherbourne House, 1 Manor House Drive, COVENTRY, CV1 2TA.
HEMINGWAY, Mr. John, FCA *1953;* 5 Denbigh Drive, Chatburn Park, CLITHEROE, BB7 2BH. (Life Member)
HEMINGWAY, Mr. Paul Andrew, BSc ACA ATII AMCT *1997;* 71 Southworth Road, NEWTON-LE-WILLOWS, MERSEYSIDE, WA12 0BL.
HEMINGWAY, Mr. Peter, FCA *1951;* Old Barn Cottage, Chapel Hill, Kearby, WETHERBY, LS22 4BU. (Life Member)
HEMINGWAY, Mr. Richard Peter, BSc ACA *1983;* 11 Ravens Holme, BOLTON, BL1 5TN.
HEMINSLEY, Mr. William, BSc ACA *2007;* British Broadcasting Corporation White City, 201 Wood Lane, LONDON, W12 7TS.
HEMMANT, Mr. Tom, BSc ACA *2007;* 82 Waldron Road, LONDON, SW18 3TD.
HEMMING, Mr. Andrew Gordon, FCA *1975;* 2343 Frances Drive, LOVELAND, CO 80537-6926, UNITED STATES.
•HEMMING, Mr. Carl Raymond, FCA ATT *1984;* 4 Exeter Drive, Wellington, TELFORD, SHROPSHIRE, TF1 3PR.
HEMMING, Mr. Charles Edwarde, LLB ACA *1981;* Park Grove Court, Lye Green, CROWBOROUGH, TN6 1UU.
•HEMMING, Mrs. Helen Claire, BSc ACA *1997;* with Ernst & Young LLP, 1 Colmore Square, BIRMINGHAM, B4 6HQ.
•HEMMING, Mr. John Anthony, FCA *1972;* (Tax Fac), J.A. Hemming, Unit 9a, High Grosvenor, Worfield, BRIDGNORTH, SHROPSHIRE WV15 5PN.
HEMMING, Mr. John David, ACA *1981;* (Tax Fac), The Wellcome Trust, 215 Euston Road, LONDON, NW1 2BE.
HEMMING, Mrs. Karen Jane, BA ACA *1992;* 2 Lavender Grove, BANCHORY, ABERDEENSHIRE, AB31 4FD.
HEMMING, Mr. Keith Blakemore, FCA *1951;* The Coach House, Walesby, MARKET RASEN, LN8 3UW. (Life Member)
HEMMING, Mr. Mark James, BSc FCA CF *1996;* Ernst & Young, 400 Capability Green, LUTON, LU1 3LU.
•HEMMING, Mr. Paul Gerard Edmund, BA FCA *1989;* Zolfo Cooper LLP, 10 Fleet Place, LONDON, EC4M 7RB.
HEMMING, Mr. Roger John William, ACA *1990;* N M Rothschild & Sons Ltd, 67 Temple Row, BIRMINGHAM, B2 5LS.
HEMMING, Mrs. Tamsin Louisa, BSc ACA *1993;* Desforges, Collards Lane, HASLEMERE, GU27 2HU.
•HEMMINGFIELD, Mr. Derek Norman, BCom FCA *1971;* UHY Wingfield Slater, 6 Broadfield Court, Broadfield Way, SHEFFIELD, S8 0XF.
•HEMMINGS, Mr. Adrian, BA FCA *2001;* Simpkins Edwards LLP, Michael House, Castle Street, EXETER, EX4 3LQ.
HEMMINGS, Miss. Amanda Louise, ACA *2009;* Flat 16 Leavesden Court, Mallard Road, ABBOTS LANGLEY, HERTFORDSHIRE, WD5 0GT.
•HEMMINGS, Mr. Christopher Francis, BSc ACA *1987;* PricewaterhouseCoopers, 7 More London Riverside, LONDON, SE1 2RT. See also PricewaterhouseCoopers LLP
HEMMINGS, Mr. Giles Edward, MA MBA FCA *1974;* Balnald Lodge, Kirkmichael, BLAIRGOWRIE, PH10 7NA. (Life Member)
HEMMINGS, Mr. Jonathan, BSc FCA *1994;* 31 Brashland Drive, NORTHAMPTON, NN4 0SS.
•HEMMINGS, Mr. Jonathan Mark, BSc(Hons) ACA *2003;* Nunn Hayward, Sterling House, 20 Station Road, GERRARDS CROSS, SL9 8EL.
HEMMINGS, Mr. Keith, BA FCA *1985;* Joe Manby Ltd, Hookstone Park, HARROGATE, NORTH YORKSHIRE, HG2 7DB.
HEMMINGS, Mr. Mark Andrew, ACA *2010;* 5 Siglap Road #11-49 Mandarin Gardens, SINGAPORE 448908, SINGAPORE.
HEMMINGS, Mr. Nicholas Scott, FCA *1993;* (Tax Fac), 50 Tinglesfield, Stratton, CIRENCESTER, GLOUCESTERSHIRE, GL7 2JL.
HEMMINGS, Mrs. Nicola Ann, BA ACA *1987;* Castle House, Dorking Road, Walton on the Hill, TADWORTH, SURREY, KT20 7TJ.
HEMMINGS, Mr. Paul, FCA *1966;* with Whyatt Pakeman Partners, Colkin House, 16 Oakfield Rd, Clifton, BRISTOL, BS8 2AP. (Life Member)
HEMMINGS, Mr. Richard, MA BA ACA *2005;* with PKF (UK) LLP, Farringdon Place, 20 Farringdon Road, LONDON, EC1M 3AP.
HEMMINGS, Mr. Richard Anthony, BSc FCA *1975;* 25 Whinfield Road, WORCESTER, WR3 7HF.
HEMMINGS, Mrs. Sarah Jane, ACA *2008;* 1 Church View Cottage, Westerleigh, BRISTOL, BS37 8QW.
HEMMINGS, Mrs. Shona, BSc ACA *2005;* 2 Milford Close, Wordsley, STOURBRIDGE, DY8 5RB.
HEMMINGS, Mr. Stephen James, BA ACA *2006;* (Tax Fac), Flat 8, 7 Blackdown Close, LONDON, N2 8JF.
HEMP, Mr. Clive Lloyd, FCA *1969;* 8 The Bryn, Derwen Fawr, SWANSEA, SA2 8DD. (Life Member)
HEMP, Mr. Stephen John, ACA *1982;* 39 The Street, Lound, LOWESTOFT, NR32 5LW.
HEMPSTEAD, Mrs. Jennifer Langford Allan, FCA *1965;* 4 Ascott Gardens, West Bridgford, NOTTINGHAM, NG2 7TH.
HEMRAJ, Mrs. Rita, ACA *2008;* 63 Addison Way, NORTHWOOD, MIDDLESEX, HA6 1SS.
HEMS, Mr. David Neil, ACA *1990;* 34 Foxland Avenue, Rednal, BIRMINGHAM, B45 9QE.
HEMS, Miss. Lauren, BA ACA *2010;* 25 Hall Park Avenue, WESTCLIFF-ON-SEA, ESSEX, SS0 8NP.
•HEMS, Mr. Peter Kenneth, FCA *1973;* 57 Main Street, Lyddington, OAKHAM, LEICESTERSHIRE, LE15 9LR.
HEMS, Mr. Raymond Anthony, BSc FCA *1976;* 25 Hall Park Avenue, WESTCLIFF-ON-SEA, SS0 8NP.
HEMS, Mr. Timothy Duncan, BA ACA *2009;* Apartment 31, 31 Watkin Road, LEICESTER, LE2 7HY.
HEMSHALL, Mrs. Rebecca Elizabeth, BSc(Hons) ACA *2001;* 63 Beech View Road Kingsley, FRODSHAM, WA6 8DG.
HEMSLEY, Mr. Alan David, FCA *1984;* Regus, 90 Long Acre, LONDON, WC2E 9RZ.
HEMSLEY, Mr. David Andrew, FCA *1972;* Springfield, Shaw Lane, Oxenhope, KEIGHLEY, BD22 9QL.
HEMSLEY, Miss. Faith Natalie, BSc(Hons) ACA *2001;* 12 Wasdale Close, West Bridgford, NOTTINGHAM, NG2 6RG.
HEMSLEY, Mr. Graeme, BA ACA *1992;* Aspin, Farm Lane, Ditchling, HASSOCKS, WEST SUSSEX, BN6 8UN.
HEMSLEY, Mrs. Jennifer Louise, BSc ACA *2000;* 44 Pentney Road, LONDON, SW12 0NX.
HEMSLEY, Mrs. Lorna Ann, BA ACA *1992;* Aspin, Farm Lane, Ditchling, HASSOCKS, WEST SUSSEX, BN6 8UN.
HEMSLEY, Mr. Maarten Duncan, FCA *1972;* 265 Washington Street, DUXBURY, MA 02332, UNITED STATES.
HEMSLEY, Mr. Matthew James, ACA *2009;* 1 Beresford Road, LONDON, N2 8AT.
HEMSLEY, Mr. Paul Jeremy, BA FCA *1985;* Ordnance Survey, Adanac Park, SOUTHAMPTON, SO16 0AS.
HEMSLEY, Miss. Rebecca Theresa, MA ACA *1997;* Xention Ltd Unit 1 Iconix Park, London Road Pampisford, CAMBRIDGE, CB22 3EG.
HEMSLEY, Mr. Richard Colwyn, MA FCA *1972;* 22 Moorway, Tranmere Park, Guiseley, LEEDS, LS20 8LB.
HEMSLEY, Mr. Robert James, ACA *2008;* Basement Flat, 84 Coronation Road, Southville, BRISTOL, BS3 1AT.
HEMSLEY, Mr. Simon James Dominic, BSc ACA *1999;* 44 Pentney Road, LONDON, SW12 0NX.
HEMSLEY, Mr. Stephen Glen, BA FCA *1982;* Madeira, Captains Row, LYMINGTON, HAMPSHIRE, SO41 9RP.
HEMSTALK, Mr. Steven Keith, BSc ACA *1999;* 750 Columbus Ave, #2X, NEW YORK, NY 10025, UNITED STATES.
•HEMSTED, Mrs. Marian Benham, FCA *1975;* Marian Hemsted, Reed House, The Street, Plaxtol, SEVENOAKS, TN15 0QL.
HEMSTED, Miss. Rebecca Anne, BA ACA *2007;* R M Education, 183 Milton Park Milton, ABINGDON, OXFORDSHIRE, OX14 4SE.
HEMSTRITCH, Mrs. Jane Sharman, BSc FCA *1977;* PO Box 2036, RICHMOND, VIC 3121, AUSTRALIA.
•HEMUS, Mr. Anthony John, ACA *1981;* PricewaterhouseCoopers LLP, 31 Great George Street, BRISTOL, BS1 5QD. See also PricewaterhouseCoopers
HEMUS, Mr. David John, FCA *1956;* 4 Upper Hall Estate, Worcester Road, LEDBURY, HR8 1JA. (Life Member)
HEMUSS, Mrs. Hazel Louise, BSc(Hons) ACA *2001;* 3 Ballagarey Close, Glen Vine, ISLE OF MAN, IM4 4EG.
HEMUSS, Mr. Joly Scott Adam, MEng ACA *2000;* 3 Ballagarey Close, Glen Vine, ISLE OF MAN, IM4 4EG.
HEN, Mr. Man Edmund, ACA *2005;* Flat G 20/F Block 5, Broadview garden, 1 Tsing Luk Street, TSING YI, NEW TERRITORIES, HONG KONG SAR.
HENBREY, Mr. Simon John, MA FCA *1987;* Halma Plc Misbourne Court, Rectory Way, AMERSHAM, BUCKINGHAMSHIRE, HP7 0DE.
HENBREY, Mr. William Alexander, FCA *1970;* 55 Windrush Court, Windrush Drive, HIGH WYCOMBE, BUCKINGHAMSHIRE, HP13 7UL.
•HENBURY, Mrs. Lynne Michelle, BSocSc ACA *2001;* with Moore Stephens, Oakley House, Headway Business Park, 3 Saxon Way West, CORBY, NORTHAMPTONSHIRE NN18 9EZ.
HENCHOZ, Miss. Laura Ann, BA ACA ATII *1995;* (Tax Fac), 27 Standish Road, LONDON, W6 9AL.
HENDEN, Mr. Lawrence Peter, BSc FCA *1972;* 35 Marigold Close, MELKSHAM, WILTSHIRE, SN12 6FT.
HENDER, Mr. David John, ACA *1990;* www Footyboots4Kids.com.ltd, Long Barn, Ockley Road, Beare Green, DORKING, SURREY RH5 4PU.
HENDER, Mrs. Linda, BSc ACA *1981;* 11 Page Furlong, Dorchester-on-Thames, WALLINGFORD, OX10 7PU.
•HENDERSON, Mr. Alexander James McKenzie, MA FCA CTA AMCT *1992;* PricewaterhouseCoopers LLP, 1 Embankment Place, LONDON, WC2N 6RH. See also PricewaterhouseCoopers
HENDERSON, Mr. Alistair, ACA *2011;* 16 Courtney Close, NOTTINGHAM, NG8 2BS.

HENDERSON, Mr. Alistair Robert Gordon, FCA *1966;* P.O. Box N.4820, NASSAU, BAHAMAS.
HENDERSON, Mr. Andrew Stuart, FCA *1972;* 5684 Little Grand Canyon Drive, PARADISE, CA 95969, UNITED STATES. (Life Member)
HENDERSON, Mr. Andrew William, BA ACA *2006;* with Deloitte LLP, PO Box 403, Lord Coutanche House, 66-68 Esplanade, St Helier, JERSEY JE4 8WA.
HENDERSON, Miss. Anne Patricia, FCA *1976;* 38 Jesmond Dene Road, NEWCASTLE UPON TYNE, NE2 3QL.
•**HENDERSON, Mr. Brian John, BA ACA** *2000;* with PricewaterhouseCoopers LLP, 1 Embankment Place, LONDON, WC2N 6RH.
HENDERSON, Mr. Callum James, BSc FCA *1991;* Assured Recruitment Solutions Ltd, I C 2 Building, Keele University, Science Park, Keele, NEWCASTLE STAFFORDSHIRE ST5 5NH.
HENDERSON, Mr. Charles Douglas, BA FCA *1984;* Invesco Perpetual, Perpetual Park, Perpetual Park Drive, HENLEY-ON-THAMES, OXFORDSHIRE, RG9 1HH.
HENDERSON, Mr. Christopher, BSc ACA *2010;* 6 Morlan Park, RHYL, CLWYD, LL18 3EG.
HENDERSON, Miss. Claire Elspeth, BA(Hons) ACA *2010;* 2 Midtown Cottages, Unthank Dalston, CARLISLE, CA5 7BA.
HENDERSON, Mrs. Clare, BA ACA *1994;* 34 Balcaskie Road, LONDON, SE9 1HQ.
HENDERSON, Mr. Clive, BSc FCA *1974;* The Bridge House, Church Lane, Lapworth, SOLIHULL, B94 5NU.
HENDERSON, Mr. Colin Coventry, BCom ACA *2001;* Daiwa Capital Markets Europe Limited, 5 King William Street, LONDON, EC4N 7DA.
HENDERSON, Mr. Colin Spencer, FCA *1970;* 17 Rawcliffe Lane, YORK, YO30 6NP. (Life Member)
•**HENDERSON, Mr. Crispin John, FCA** *1972;* Threadneedle Investments, St. Mary Axe House, 60 St. Mary Axe, LONDON, EC3A 8JQ.
HENDERSON, Mr. Damion John, BA ACA *1997;* KPMG, Crown House, 4 Par-la-Ville Road, HAMILTON HM 08, BERMUDA.
HENDERSON, Mr. David Alexander, MSc ACA *1999;* with KPMG, 8th Floor, Tower E2, Oriental Plaza, 1 East Chang An Avenue, BEIJING 100738 CHINA.
HENDERSON, Mr. David Lawrence, ACA *2009;* 40 Kenley Road, St Margarets, TWICKENHAM, TW1 1JU.
HENDERSON, Ms. Dawn, BSc ACA *1992;* Wetherby Business Centre, 14-18 York Road, WETHERBY, WEST YORKSHIRE, LS22 6SL.
HENDERSON, Mr. Derek, FCA *1963;* 8 Highcroft, Millbrook Green, Collingham, LEEDS, WEST YORKSHIRE, LS22 5AH.
HENDERSON, Mr. Derek Patrick, BSc ACA *2001;* 55 St. Davids Road South, LYTHAM ST. ANNES, FY8 1TY.
HENDERSON, Mr. Edward Douglas, FCA *1974;* 3 Lane Gardens, Claygate, ESHER, KT10 0NP.
HENDERSON, Mr. Edward Harvey, FCA *1952;* 2021 28th Street, WEST VANCOUVER V7V 4M2, BC, CANADA. (Life Member)
HENDERSON, Mrs. Elizabeth Denise, BA ACA *1991;* 3 McWilliam Close, Talbot Village, Wallisdown, POOLE, BH12 5HP.
HENDERSON, Mrs. Emma Jane, BSc(Hons) ACA *2000;* 11 Woodlands Close, GERRARDS CROSS, BUCKINGHAMSHIRE, SL9 8DQ.
HENDERSON, Miss. Fiona Louise, BSc FCA *1994;* 1 St. James Avenue, FARNHAM, SURREY, GU9 9QF.
•**HENDERSON, Mr. Gerald, ACA FCCA** *2008;* with Stokoe Rodger, St Matthews House, Haugh Lane, HEXHAM, NORTHUMBERLAND, NE46 3PU.
•**HENDERSON, Mr. Iain Anton Robert, MA FCA** *2000;* BDO LLP, 55 Baker Street, LONDON, W1U 7EU. See also BDO Stoy Hayward LLP
HENDERSON, Mr. Iain Donald, BCom FCA *1975;* 5 Compton Close, LOUGHBOROUGH, LE11 3SF.
HENDERSON, Mr. Ian Charles, FCA *1980;* H M Young Offender Institution, The Grove, Grove Road, Easton, PORTLAND, DORSET DT5 1DL.
HENDERSON, Mr. Ian Donald, MA ACA *1997;* M C F Corporate Finance, 53-54 Haymarket, LONDON, SW1Y 4RP.
HENDERSON, Mr. Ian Gordon, BSc ACA *1994;* Caledonian Brewing Company Ltd, 42 Slateford Road, EDINBURGH, EH11 1PH.
HENDERSON, Mr. Ian Ralph, BSc FCA *1958;* 2 Edge Hill, WHITEHAVEN, CA28 6DJ. (Life Member)
HENDERSON, Mr. Ian Ramsay, MA LLB FCA *1976;* 20 Westbourne Park Road, LONDON, W2 5PH.
HENDERSON, Mr. Ian Rutherford, FCA *1985;* One Aberdeen House, 22 - 24 Highbury Grove, LONDON, N5 2EA.
•**HENDERSON, Mr. Ian Stuart, LLB ACA** *1987;* (Tax Fac), A.H.Cross & Co, 16 Quay Street, NEWPORT, ISLE OF WIGHT, PO30 5BG.
HENDERSON, Mr. James, MA ACA *1994;* Thalia 21, Noord-Holland, 1188ET AMSTELVEEN, NETHERLANDS.
HENDERSON, Mr. James Alexander Whitecross, MA FCA *1976;* 32 Granard Avenue, LONDON, SW15 6HJ. (Life Member)
HENDERSON, Mr. James Antony, MEng ACA *2006;* 17 Borage Close, Pontprennau, CARDIFF, CF23 8SJ.
HENDERSON, Mr. James Iain, MA ACA *1989;* 1 Silverdale Way, Whickham, NEWCASTLE UPON TYNE, NE16 5SL.
HENDERSON, Ms. Jennifer Lesley, BSc ACA *2003;* 32 Meridian Close, Hardwick, CAMBRIDGE, CB23 7AN.
HENDERSON, Mr. Jeremy, BSc ACA *2007;* Asperity Employee Benefits Ltd, 90 Westbourne Grove, LONDON, W2 5RT.
HENDERSON, Mr. Jim, BSc(Hons) ACA *2001;* Hanögatan 10, PO Box 50559, SE-202 15 MALMO, SWEDEN.
HENDERSON, Mrs. Joanne Claire, BSc ACA *2002;* with Ernst & Young LLP, The Paragon, Counterslip, BRISTOL, BS1 6BX.
•**HENDERSON, Mr. John, FCA** *1977;* CBS (Nottingham) Ltd, 5 The Old Stables, Bestwood Country Park, NOTTINGHAM, NG5 8ND.
HENDERSON, Mr. John Edward, FCA *1961;* 31 Maple Avenue, Whitefield, MANCHESTER, M45 7EP.
•**HENDERSON, Mr. John Edwin, BSc FCA** *1971;* Ted Henderson Limited, Ben-y-Hone Cottage, 21 Dundas Street, Comrie, CRIEFF, PERTHSHIRE PH6 2LN.
HENDERSON, Mr. John Malcolm Edward, FCA *1970;* Larksfield, Cokes Lane, CHALFONT ST.GILES, HP8 4TN.
•**HENDERSON, Mr. John Roseby, FCA** *1973;* DNG Dove Naish, Eagle House, 28 Billing Road, NORTHAMPTON, NN1 5AJ.
HENDERSON, Miss. Julia Amanda, BSc ACA *2007;* The Montague, 310 Tadcaster Road, YORK, YO24 1HF.
HENDERSON, Miss. Karen Giselle, ACA *2010;* 23b Boundaries Road, LONDON, SW12 8ET.
HENDERSON, Miss. Kathryn, BSc ACA *2007;* Longview Solutions European Headquarters, 3rd Floor Viewpoint, 240 London Road, STAINES, MIDDLESEX, TW18 4JT.
HENDERSON, Mr. Lee Stuart, ACA *2009;* 26 Peartree Walk, Yaxley, PETERBOROUGH, PE7 3HQ.
HENDERSON, Mrs. Lesley Susan, BSc FCA *1983;* RED HORSE STABLES, HENLEY STREET, ALCESTER, B49 5QX.
HENDERSON, Mr. Leslie John, MA ACA *1980;* 2 Le Champ de la Vigne, Alliat, 09400 ARIEGE, FRANCE.
HENDERSON, Miss. Lucinda, BSc ACA *2004;* with Deloitte LLP, Athene Place, 66 Shoe Lane, LONDON, EC4A 3BQ.
HENDERSON, Mr. Malcolm George, FCA *1974;* 28 Torcross Way, CRAMLINGTON, NORTHUMBERLAND, NE23 1PX. (Life Member)
•**HENDERSON, Mrs. Margaret Robertson, MA FCA** *1973;* M.R. Henderson, 32 Granard Avenue, LONDON, SW15 6HJ.
HENDERSON, Mr. Mark, BSc ACA *1999;* 15 Princes Avenue, Grange Estate, Gosforth, NEWCASTLE UPON TYNE, NE3 2HR.
•**HENDERSON, Mr. Mark Armstrong, BSc FCA** *1990;* Moore Stephens LLP, 150 Aldersgate Street, LONDON, EC1A 4AB.
HENDERSON, Mr. Mark James, BA ACA AMCT *1994;* Holdfast End, Holdfast Lane, HASLEMERE, SURREY, GU27 2EU.
HENDERSON, Mr. Mark Norcott Graham, BBS ACA *1994;* Ospedaletti, Navigation Road, MALLOW, COUNTY CORK, IRELAND.
HENDERSON, Mr. Matthew Charles, BA ACA *2000;* 26 Park Road, Menston, ILKLEY, WEST YORKSHIRE, LS29 6EN.
HENDERSON, Mrs. Melanie Amanda, BA ACA *1991;* Kents Hall, Heath Road, Swaffham Prior, CAMBRIDGE, CB25 0LA.
•**HENDERSON, Mr. Michael, FCA** *1967;* 3 Cecil Avenue, BOURNEMOUTH, BH8 9EL.
HENDERSON, Mr. Michael John Glidden, FCA *1961;* Langdale, Woodland Drive, East Horsley, LEATHERHEAD, KT24 5AN.
HENDERSON, Mr. Neil Alistair, BA ACA *1995;* 34 Balcaskie Road, Eltham, LONDON, SE9 1HQ.
HENDERSON, Mrs. Nicola, ACA *2008;* Bell House, Therfield, ROYSTON, HERTFORDSHIRE, SG8 9PT.
HENDERSON, Mr. Paul Evan, BA FCA *1982;* Greenwoods, 13 The Grove, Parkfield Latimer, CHESHAM, HP5 1UE.
HENDERSON, Mr. Paul Robert, ACA *1984;* CENTRO 4, 20 - 23 MANDELA STREET, LONDON, NW1 0DU.
HENDERSON, Ms. Paula, BA ACA *1997;* (Tax Fac), 49 Starmead Drive, WOKINGHAM, BERKSHIRE, RG40 2JA.
HENDERSON, Mr. Peter, BEng ACA *2006;* 42 Bridgman Road, LONDON, W4 5BD.
HENDERSON, Mr. Peter, BTech ACA *1979;* 104 Stonnall Road, Aldridge, WALSALL, WS9 8JZ.
HENDERSON, Mr. Peter George, BA(Hons) ACA *2003;* 1502 Oleanas Residence, 42 Kim Yam Road, SINGAPORE 239347, SINGAPORE.
HENDERSON, Mr. Peter John William, BSc FCA *1978;* Westerlings, 5 Ellwood Road, BEACONSFIELD, BUCKINGHAMSHIRE, HP9 1EN.
HENDERSON, Mr. Philip Graeme, ACA *2009;* Deloitte Llp City House, 126-130 Hills Road, CAMBRIDGE, CB2 1RY.
HENDERSON, Mrs. Philippa Laura, BA(Hons) ACA *2002;* 104 Marlborough Crescent, SEVENOAKS, TN13 2HR.
HENDERSON, Mr. Richard, BA ACA *2004;* The Granary, Mitford, MORPETH, NORTHUMBERLAND, NE61 3QW.
HENDERSON, Mr. Richard John, BA(Hons) ACA *2001;* Tesco Personal Finance, 22 Haymarket Yards, EDINBURGH, EH12 5BH.
•**HENDERSON, Mr. Robert Buchan, BSc FCA** *1992;* Astute Services Ltd, 4 Daventry Road, Dunchurch, RUGBY, WARWICKSHIRE, CV22 6NS.
HENDERSON, Mr. Robert David Charles, FCA *1973;* 14 St. George Street, LONDON, W1S 1FE.
HENDERSON, Mr. Robert Stuart Craig, MA ACA *2001;* 22 Niagara Road, HENLEY-ON-THAMES, OXFORDSHIRE, RG9 1EB.
HENDERSON, Mr. Robert William, BA ACA *1998;* 12 Darnley Park, WEYBRIDGE, SURREY, KT13 8EY.
HENDERSON, Dr. Roger, ACA *2008;* with Deloitte LLP, 2 New Street Square, LONDON, EC4A 3BZ.
HENDERSON, Miss. Sarah Jane, BSc ACA *2005;* with Deloitte LLP, 1 City Square, LEEDS, WEST YORKSHIRE, LS1 2AL.
HENDERSON, Mrs. Shona Anne, BSc ACA *1990;* 17 Malwood Road, LONDON, SW12 8EN.
HENDERSON, Mr. Simon Anthony Glidden, BA(Econ) ACA *1996;* Broughton House, Rookery Lane, Broughton, STOCKBRIDGE, HAMPSHIRE, SO20 8AY.
HENDERSON, Mr. Simon Nicholas, BSc ACA *1993;* 17 Bury Close, Warbstow, LAUNCESTON, CORNWALL, PL15 8UZ.
HENDERSON, Mr. Stephen, FCA *1980;* 7 Megson Way, Walkington, BEVERLEY, HU17 8YA.
HENDERSON, Mr. Stephen Joseph, LLB DipLP ACA *2000;* Tesco, Heldrew House, Delamare Road, Cheshunt, WALTHAM CROSS, HERTFORDSHIRE EN8 9SL.
HENDERSON, Mr. Steven, LLB ACA *1995;* Claymore Group, PO Box 64, PROVIDENCIALES, TURKS AND CAICOS ISLANDS.
•**HENDERSON, Mr. Stuart Jonathan Brodie, BA ACA** *1987;* Deloitte LLP, City House, 126-130 Hills Road, CAMBRIDGE, CB2 1RY. See also Deloitte & Touche LLP
HENDERSON, Mrs. Susan, LLB ACA *2001;* 19 Alpin Drive, DUNBLANE, PERTHSHIRE, FK15 0FQ.
HENDERSON, Mrs. Suzannah, MA ACA *2002;* 118 Alderney Street, LONDON, SW1V 4HA.
HENDERSON, Mrs. Tessa Catherine, MA ACA *2003;* La Bastide St Jean, 2711 Rte de Draguignan, 83690 VILLECROZE, FRANCE.
HENDERSON, Mr. Thomas Cameron, MA ACA *2000;* 182 Northcote Road, LONDON, SW11 6RE.
HENDERSON, Mr. Toby John, BA ACA *2002;* 49 Kings Croft, Long Ashton, BRISTOL, BS41 9ED.
•**HENDERSON, Mr. William Buchan, FCA** *1952;* W.B. Henderson, Pachesham Gates, Oxshott Road, LEATHERHEAD, KT22 0ER.
HENDERSON-CASH, Mrs. Ruth Marie, ACA *1992;* 1 Lancaster Court, Well Place, CHELTENHAM, GLOUCESTERSHIRE, GL50 2PJ.
HENDERSON CLELAND, Mr. Hugh John, BSc ACA *1988;* Royal Bank of Scotland, 135 Bishopsgate, LONDON, EC2M 3UR.
HENDERSON-WILLIAMS, Mr. Frank, BA FCA *1963;* 21 Oakbury Road, LONDON, SW6 2NN. (Life Member)
HENDLE, Mr. Mark James, BSc ACA *2000;* Andersen Press, Random House, 20 Vauxhall Bridge Road, LONDON, SW1V 2SA.
•**HENDLEY, Mrs. Jacqueline Anne, FCA** *1990;* (Tax Fac), KPMG LLP, One Snowhill, Snow Hill Queensway, BIRMINGHAM, B4 6GN. See also KPMG Europe LLP
HENDON, Mr. Brian Thomas, FCA *1974;* Farthings, Earleydene, ASCOT, SL5 9JY.
•**HENDON, Mr. Ronald, FCA** *1964;* Ronald Hendon & Co, 16 The Callenders, Heathbourne Road, BUSHEY HEATH, WD23 1PU.
HENDRICK, Mr. Paul Anthony, MSc FCA CF MCT *1976;* 14 Park Crescent, LONDON, N3 2NJ.
HENDRICK, Mrs. Sally Louise, BA ACA *1993;* 16 Amberley Drive, Twyford, READING, RG10 9BZ.
HENDRIE, Miss. Cheryl Ann, ACA *2008;* Flat 17, 4 Balmes Road, LONDON, N1 5TQ.
HENDRIE, Miss. Elaine, BSc ACA *1990;* 2 Elm Barns, Cottenham, CAMBRIDGE, CB24 8DB.
•**HENDRIE, Mrs. Jill Maureen, BSc FCA** *1981;* Bessler Hendrie, Albury Mill, Mill Lane, Chilworth, GUILDFORD, SURREY GU4 8RU.
HENDRIE, Mr. Michael John, FCA *1975;* Sven Christiansen Plc, Unit 4 Riverway Estate, Portsmouth Road, GUILDFORD, GU3 1LZ.
HENDRIES, Mr. Michael Andrew Hugh, FCA *1962;* Heathlands, Samarkand Close, CAMBERLEY, SURREY, GU15 1DG. (Life Member)
HENDRIKS, Mr. Ian Alastair Nigel, BCom FCA *1966;* The Gatehouse, 53c Abingdon Road, LONDON, W8 6AN. (Life Member)
HENDRY, Mr. Anthony Paul, BA ACA *1996;* Financial Control Level 16 Barclays Wealth, Barclays Bank Plc, 1 Churchill Place, LONDON, E14 5HP.
HENDRY, Mr. Craig Archibald Macdonald, LLB ACA *1998;* Strathaden, 81 South Beach, TROON, AYRSHIRE, KA10 6EQ.
HENDRY, Mr. David Charles, ACA *1981;* 24 Maple Close, Pulloxhill, BEDFORD, MK45 5EF.
HENDRY, Mr. David Vaughn, ACA CA(SA) *2010;* Crawford & Company, Trinity Court, 42 Trinity Square, LONDON, EC3N 4TH.
HENDRY, Mrs. Diane Carole, BA ACA *1980;* 1 South Wing, Stoneleigh Abbey, KENILWORTH, WARWICKSHIRE, CV8 2LF.
HENDRY, Mrs. Karen, BSc ACA *1993;* 3 Mount Pleasant Drive, TADLEY, RG26 4XA.
HENDRY, Mrs. Louise Ruth, BA ACA *1997;* 71 Ourimbah Road, Mosman, SYDNEY, NSW 2088, AUSTRALIA.
HENDRY, Mr. Michael Hugh, BSc ACA *1994;* 10 Victoria Road, PENRITH, CA11 8HR.
HENDRY, Miss. Nicola, BSc(Hons) ACA *2010;* 19 Farrier Close, WASHINGTON, TYNE AND WEAR, NE38 8RW.
HENDRY, Mr. Philip Edward, BA(Hons) ACA *2003;* Flat 8 Masters Lodge, Johnson Street, LONDON, E1 0BE.
HENDRY, Mr. Roger James, MA FCA *1975;* 40 Seagry Road, Wanstead, LONDON, E11 2NH.
HENDRY, Mr. Scott Graeme, BCom ACA *2003;* 28 Thomas Street, NORTH MANLY, NSW 2100, AUSTRALIA.
HENDY, Mrs. Jane Elizabeth, BSc ACA *1992;* 97a Providence Square, LONDON, SE1 2EB.
HENEAGE, Miss. Elizabeth, BA ACA *2007;* 36 Iveley Road, LONDON, SW4 0EW.
HENEBERY, Miss. Ann Bernadette Marie, BSc ACA *1999;* 1 Ballinwillin, Mitchelstown, CORK, COUNTY CORK, IRELAND.
HENEBERY, Mr. Michael Patrick, BCom ACA CF *1990;* Palio Capital Partners Suite 1.09, 42 Brook Street, LONDON, W1K 5DB.
HENEBRY, Mr. Philip Edward, FCA *1976;* 84 Route du Lavoret, 74200 ANTHY SUR LEMAN, HAUTE SAVOIE, FRANCE.
HENEGHAN, Miss. Charlotte Elizabeth, BA ACA *2006;* 1 York Road, LONDON, N21 2JL.
HENEGHAN, Mrs. Elizabeth Mary, FCA *1973;* Hartwell & Co (Timber) Ltd, The Timber Yard, Weston Subedge, CHIPPING CAMPDEN, GLOUCESTERSHIRE, GL55 6QH.
HENEGHAN, Mrs. Margaret Ann, BA ACA *1984;* Criogan Ard, Tawnagh Srah, CLAREMORRIS, COUNTY MAYO, IRELAND.
HENEGHAN, Mrs. Paula Marie, BSc ACA *2000;* First Floor Campus Centre Building, De Montfort University, Mill Lane, LEICESTER, LE2 7DR.
HENEHAN, Miss. Nicola, BSc ACA *2010;* 89 Chelsham Road, SOUTH CROYDON, CR2 6HZ.
HENFREY, Mr. David John, FCA *1979;* (Tax Fac), Bird Luckin Ltd, Aquila House, Waterloo Lane, CHELMSFORD, CM1 1BN.
HENG, Mrs. Eileen Bik-York, FCA *1975;* 19 Lilian Road, FRAMINGHAM, MA 01701, UNITED STATES.
HENG, Mr. Franklin Ching Kuen, MA FCA *1992;* Flat B, 17th Floor, Kennedy Heights, 10-18 Kennedy Road, MID LEVELS, HONG KONG SAR.
HENG, Mr. Freddie Kim Chuan, BSc ACA *1980;* 26 Bedok Avenue, SINGAPORE 469937, SINGAPORE.

HENG, Mr. Gek Hwah, FCA *1972;* Sin Heng Chan Pte Ltd, 80 Tras Street, SINGAPORE 079019, SINGAPORE.
HENG, Miss. Khai Sing, ACA *2009;* Flat 36B Tower 1, The Palazzo, 28 Lok King Street, SHA TIN, HONG KONG SAR.
HENG, Mr. Kwoo Seng, FCA *1977;* c/o Morrison Heng, 7/F Allied Kajima Building, 138 Gloucester Road, WAN CHAI, HONG KONG SAR.
•HENISON, Mr. Marc Anthony, ACA *2006;* MGM Accountancy Ltd, 3rd Floor, 20 Bedford Street, LONDON, WC2E 9HP.
HENKE, Mrs. Deepa, BSc ACA CTA *2002;* (Tax Fac), 37 Watford Road, RADLETT, HERTFORDSHIRE, WD7 8LG.
HENKE, Mr. Klaus, BA ACA *1999;* 37 Watford Road, RADLETT, HERTFORDSHIRE, WD7 8LG.
HENKEL, Mr. Martin John Laurence, BSc FCA *1968;* Little Lords Ashford Road, Sheldwich, FAVERSHAM, ME13 0NJ. (Life Member)
•HENKHUZENS, Mr. Robert Henry, BA FCA *1977;* R.H. Henkhuzens Limited, PO Box 643, Ground Floor Office Suite, Colomberie Close, JERSEY, JE4 0YS.
HENLEY, Mr. Adrian John, FCA *1952;* 173 Marlborough Crescent, SEVENOAKS, TN13 2HW. (Life Member)
HENLEY, Mrs. Alison Therese, BA ACA *1987;* with Shaw Gibbs LLP, 264 Banbury Road, OXFORD, OX2 7DY.
HENLEY, Mr. Bernard, FCA *1961;* 114 Hummersknott Avenue, DARLINGTON, DL3 8RS.
HENLEY, Mr. David Antony, BA ACA *2004;* 46 Broadwater Road, Twyford, READING, RG10 0EU.
HENLEY, Mr. Keith John, FCA *1970;* Deer Run, Rudge End Farm, Woolhope, HEREFORD, HR1 4QH. (Life Member)
HENLEY, Mr. Mark David, FCA *1995;* Karenza Poole Road, Lytchett Matravers, POOLE, DORSET, BH16 6AF.
HENLEY, Mr. Raymond Alan, FCA *1968;* Ramridge Cottage, Weyhill, ANDOVER, SP11 0QG.
HENLEY, Miss. Sharon Barbara, ACA CA(AUS) *2008;* 40 Selhurst Close, LONDON, SW19 6AZ.
HENLEY-JONES, Mrs. Alison Christina, BSc ACA *2007;* 1a Palmer Avenue, SUTTON, SM3 8EF.
HENLEY-MARSHALL, Ms. Michelle Elise, BA ACA *2005;* (Tax Fac), 17 Conway Crescent, Carlton, NOTTINGHAM, NG4 2QA.
•HENMAN, Mrs. Jane Marion Ann, FCA DChA *1969;* Shipleys LLP, 3 Godalming Business Centre, Woolsack Way, GODALMING, SURREY, GU7 1XW.
HENMAN, Miss. Laura, BSc ACA *2011;* 168a Finchampstead Road, WOKINGHAM, BERKSHIRE, RG40 3EY.
HENNAH, Mr. Adrian Nevil, MA FCA *1983;* Speen House, Bath Road, Speen, NEWBURY, BERKSHIRE, RG14 1RH.
HENNAH, Mr. Kenneth Alan, BSc ACA *2003;* 4 Chase Hill, Geddington, KETTERING, NORTHAMPTONSHIRE, NN14 1AG.
HENNELL, Mrs. Alison, BSc ACA *1991;* New Haven, Penn Street, AMERSHAM, BUCKINGHAMSHIRE, HP7 0PY.
HENNELL, Mr. Bernard Macdonald, MA FCA *1952;* 37 Glenearn Court, Pittenzie Street, CRIEFF, PERTHSHIRE, PH7 3LE. (Life Member)
HENNELL, Mr. John Murray, FCA *1974;* with HBOS plc, 10 Canons Way, BRISTOL, BS1 5LF.
HENNELL, Mr. Peter, BSc FCA *1971;* Red Rose Villa, Church Street, Scothern, LINCOLN, LN2 2UA. (Life Member)
•HENNELL, Mr. Simon John Alexander, BA FCA *1986;* Simon Hennell Limited, Newhaven, Penn Street, AMERSHAM, BUCKINGHAMSHIRE, HP7 0PY.
HENNELL JAMES, Mr. Jeremy Rees, BEng ACA *1989;* 37 Days Green, Capel St.Mary, IPSWICH, IP9 2HZ.
HENNEM, Mr. Peter, FCA *1967;* 8 The Drive, ILFORD, IG1 3HT.
•HENNESSEY, Miss. Angela Mary, BSc FCA FCIArb *1982;* 35 Carbery Avenue, LONDON, W3 9AD.
HENNESSEY, Mr. Paul Simon, BSc(Hons) ACA *2004;* with BDO LLP, Prospect Place, 85 Great North Road, HATFIELD, HERTFORDSHIRE, AL9 5BS.
HENNESSY, Mr. Arthur, FCA *1969;* 32 Lauderdale Avenue, THORNTON-CLEVELEYS, FY5 3JP. (Life Member)
•ⒹHENNESSY, Mr. Daniel Paul, FCA *1984;* Aticus Recovery Limited, 5th Floor, Horton House, Exchange Flags, LIVERPOOL, L2 3PF.
HENNESSY, Mr. Richard Patrick, BA FCA *1979;* Oak Meadows, 65 Park Road, WOKING, SURREY, GU22 7BZ.
HENNESSY, Mr. Timothy David, ACA CPA *1995; (ACA Ireland 1973);* Haven Lodge, Killeady Road, Halfway Ballinhassig, CORK, COUNTY CORK, IRELAND.
HENNESSY-RENDERS, Mrs. Amy Claire, BSc ACA *2003;* 50 Mill Common, Undy, CALDICOT, GWENT, NP26 3JJ.
HENNIG, Mrs. Kate Helena, BSc ACA *2001;* 35 Burton Walk, East Leake, LOUGHBOROUGH, LE12 6LB.
HENNIGAN, Mr. John Anthony, BA ACA *1992;* 1 Woodlands Court, Oadby, LEICESTER, LE2 4QE.
HENNIGAN, Mr. Joseph Francis, ACA *2008;* Apartment 5E, 2250 Broadway, NEW YORK, NY 10024, UNITED STATES.
HENNING, Miss. Elaine Joanne, BA ACA *2006;* with Moore Stephens LLP, 150 Aldersgate Street, LONDON, EC1A 4AB.
HENNING, Mr. Michael William, BSc ACA *1987;* Kaplan Financial, Broadcasting House, 10 Havelock Road, SOUTHAMPTON, SO14 7FY.
HENNING, Mr. Paul Richard, BA(Hons) ACA *2002;* Calle de Alba 4, 11310 SOTOGRANDE, SPAIN.
HENNING, Mr. Simon Richard, FCA *1969;* Les Fauconnaires, St. Andrew, GUERNSEY, GY6 8UE. (Life Member)
HENREY, Mr. Michael Julian, FCA *1961;* 5 Greenside Road, Greenside, JOHANNESBURG, GAUTENG, 2193, SOUTH AFRICA. (Life Member)
HENREY, Mr. Robert John Edward, MA FCA *1964;* 349 North Maple Avenue, GREENWICH, CT 06830, UNITED STATES.
HENRICK, Mr. Jamie David, BEng ACA *2008;* 212 Crondall Street, LONDON, N1 6JQ.
HENRICKSEN, Mr. Roland Dennis, FCA *1966;* 4927 Windsong Crescent, KELOWNA V1W 4Y2, BC, CANADA.
HENRIKSEN, Mr. Peter, MSc(Econ) BSc(Econ) FCA CMC FIMC *1970;* Highshield, Heugh House Lane, Haydon Bridge, HEXHAM, NORTHUMBERLAND, NE47 6HJ.
HENRIKSEN, Mr. Rune, ACA *2004;* 21 Kissing Point Road, TURRAMURRA, NSW 2074, AUSTRALIA.
HENRIKSEN, Mr. Troels Bugge, BSc ACA *1990;* Bagley Cottage, Spring Copse, OXFORD, OX1 5BJ.
HENRY, Mr. Anthony Thomas, BSc(Econ) FCA *1962;* 87 Rue de la Culaz, Ornex, F01210 FERNEY VOLTAIRE, FRANCE. (Life Member)
HENRY, Mr. Calvin Paul, BSc ACA *1993;* 56a Carrington Lane, Milford on Sea, LYMINGTON, HAMPSHIRE, SO41 0RB.
HENRY, Miss. Catherine Anne, ACA *2008;* Flat 18 Palatine Place, 265 Palatine Road, MANCHESTER, M22 4ET.
HENRY, Mr. Christopher Michael, FCA *1975;* 14 Stanton Drive, LUDLOW, SY8 2PH.
HENRY, Mr. Damian, ACA *2008;* 279 Westrow Drive, BARKING, ESSEX, IG11 9BU.
HENRY, Mr. Dominic, BSc ACA *2006;* with Kaplan Financial, 1st Floor, City Exchange, 11 Albion Street, LEEDS, LS1 5ES.
HENRY, Mr. Dominick Hugh Mitcheson, BA FCA *1972;* Baytree House, Batcombe, SHEPTON MALLET, SOMERSET, BA4 6HD.
•HENRY, Ms. Hilene Susan, BSc(Hons) FCA FCCA *1984;* Wilson Henry LLP, 145 Edge Lane, Edge Hill, LIVERPOOL, L7 2PF.
HENRY, Mr. Hugh Richard, FCA *1954;* The Old House, Pirbright, WOKING, GU24 0JE. (Life Member)
HENRY, Mr. James Martin, MA ACA *1986;* 129 Rocky Lane, Eccles, MANCHESTER, M30 9LZ.
HENRY, Miss. Jessica, BSc ACA *2009;* 75 Austin Road, BROMSGROVE, WORCESTERSHIRE, B60 3ND.
•HENRY, Mr. John David, BSc ACA *1992;* JDH Business Services Ltd, Carreg Lwyd, Cefn Bychan Road, Pantymwyn, MOLD, CLWYD CH7 5EW.
HENRY, Mr. Jonathan William, BA ACA *1988;* Haycroft, Suckley, WORCESTER, WR6 5DJ.
HENRY, Miss. Judith, BA ACA *2006;* with PricewaterhouseCoopers LLP, 1 Embankment Place, LONDON, WC2N 6RH.
HENRY, Mr. Kevin Francis, FCA *1980;* 8 Hill Top Grove, Batley Road, West Ardsley, WAKEFIELD, WF3 1HP.
HENRY, Mr. Liam, ACA *2008;* (Tax Fac), 16 The Drive, Ickenham, UXBRIDGE, MIDDLESEX, UB10 8AF.
HENRY, Mr. Lyndon Sayers, MA ACA CTA *2001;* 8 Westward Way, Kenton, HARROW, MIDDLESEX, HA3 0SE.
HENRY, Mr. Marcus Peter, BSc FCA *1992;* 13 Norna Crescent, Kelburn, WELLINGTON, NEW ZEALAND.
HENRY, Miss. Marie-Noelle Lisebie, FCA *1977;* 74 Minnamurra Road, NORTHBRIDGE, NSW 2063, AUSTRALIA.
HENRY, Mr. Michael Julian, BA ACA *1993;* 228 St Margarets Road, TWICKENHAM, TW1 1NL.
HENRY, Miss. Monique, BA ACA *2005;* PO Box 10998, GEORGE TOWN, GRAND CAYMAN, KY1-1000, CAYMAN ISLANDS.
HENRY, Mr. Paul Charles, FCA *1974;* Emily House, 202-8 Kensal Road, LONDON, W10 5BN.
HENRY, Mr. Peter, FCA *1954;* 22 Vauxhall Gardens, DUDLEY, WEST MIDLANDS, DY2 8AH. (Life Member)
•HENRY, Mr. Raymond, BSc FCA *1991;* Flat 4/2, 14 Norval Street, GLASGOW, G11 7RX.
HENRY, Mr. Richard Charles, FCA *1966;* Bailiffs Farmhouse, Ibworth, TADLEY, HAMPSHIRE, RG26 5TJ. (Life Member)
HENRY, Ms. Roisin Mary, BA ACA *1998;* 22 Princes Court, Princes Road, WEYBRIDGE, SURREY, KT13 9BZ.
HENRY, Miss. Sarah Frances, BSc ACA *1990;* Flat 12, Parkchurch House, 108 Grosvenor Avenue, LONDON, N5 2NE.
•HENRY, Mrs. Sarah Margaret, BA FCA *1975;* Sarah Henry, 24 Frewin Road, LONDON, SW18 3LP.
•HENRY, Miss. Sonja, BA ACA *1995;* Cavendish, 4th Floor, Centre Heights, 137 Finchley Road, LONDON, NW3 6JG.
•HENRY, Mr. Stephen, FCA *1980;* Ridehalgh Limited, Guardian House, 42 Preston New Road, BLACKBURN, BB2 6AH.
HENRY, Mr. Thomas Rhys, BSc ACA *2010;* 125 Lavender Sweep, LONDON, SW11 1EA.
HENRY, Miss. Valerie Elizabeth, MBA BSc ACA *1989;* 10 Independence House, 6 Chapter Way, Merton Abbey Hills, Wimbledon, LONDON, SW19 2RX.
HENRY-BOCHAN, Ms. Josefa, BA(Hons) ACA *2010;* with Deloitte LLP, PO Box 500, 2 Hardman Street, MANCHESTER, M60 2AT.
HENRY LEPART, Mrs. Diane Patula, BA(Hons) FCA *1994;* Lazard Services & Co Ltd, 50 Stratton Street, LONDON, W1J 8LL.
HENSE, Ms. Stefanie, ACA *2008;* Philosophenweg 9, 61350 BAD HOMBURG, GERMANY.
HENSEY, Mr. John, BA FCA *1980;* 19 Kings Lea, Adlington, CHORLEY, PR7 4EN.
HENSHALL, Mr. Terence Howard, FCA *1977;* Holly Cottage Gravelly Hill, Ashley, MARKET DRAYTON, SHROPSHIRE, TF9 4PN.
HENSHAW, Mr. Adam Robert, BSocSc ACA *1998;* 21 Wortley Terrace, WOTTON-UNDER-EDGE, GLOUCESTERSHIRE, GL12 7JY.
HENSHAW, Mr. Alexander Graham Guy, FCA *1967;* Boathouse, Sandilands, Sutton-on-Sea, MABLETHORPE, LN12 2RH.
•HENSHAW, Mr. Andrew Derick, BSc FCA *1988;* Moore Stephens (South) LLP, City Gates, 2-4 Southgate, CHICHESTER, WEST SUSSEX, PO19 8DJ. See also Moore Secretaries Limited
HENSHAW, Mrs. Helen Claire, BSc ACA *2001;* 48 Parkside Avenue, Long Eaton, NOTTINGHAM, NG10 4AJ.
HENSHAW, Mr. John, BCom FCA *1962;* 6 Hollies Drive, Edwalton, NOTTINGHAM, NG12 4BZ. (Life Member)
HENSHAW, Mr. Kevin Richard, ACA *1992;* 16 Lakeside, South Cerney, CIRENCESTER, GL7 5XE.
HENSHAW, Mr. Lee Robert, ACA *2011;* 7 Torkard Court, Hucknall, NOTTINGHAM, NG15 6UJ.
•HENSHAW, Mr. Michael, BSc FCA *1991;* (Tax Fac), Greenhalgh Business Services Ltd, 2a Peveril Drive, NOTTINGHAM, NG7 1DE.
HENSHAW, Mr. Robert Henry, BA ACA *1995;* Pear Tree Cottage, 6 The Rake, Bromborough, WIRRAL, MERSEYSIDE, CH62 7AQ.
HENSHAW, Miss. Sally Ann, BA ACA *1994;* Greggs Adam House, Player Court Player Street, NOTTINGHAM, NG7 5LQ.
•HENSHAW, Mrs. Stephanie Jane, BA *1988;* Francis Clark, Vantage Point, Woodwater Park, Pynes Hill, EXETER, EX2 5FD. See also Francis Clark LLP
HENSHAW, Mr. Timothy Reginald, BSc(Hons) ACA *2004;* L A International Computer Consultants L, International House, Festival Way, STOKE-ON-TRENT, ST1 5UB.
•HENSMAN, Mr. Brian John, FCA *1973;* The Carley Partnership, St. James's House, 8 Overcliffe, GRAVESEND, DA11 0HJ. See also Carleys Integrated Solutions Ltd
HENSMAN, Mrs. Maureen Patricia, BSc ACA *1980;* 9 Lavant Road, CHICHESTER, PO19 5QY.
HENSMAN, Mr. Michael John, BSc FCA *1975;* 49 Sandstone Avenue, SHEFFIELD, S9 1AJ.
HENSMAN, Mr. Peter Richard Wavell, MA FCA *1973;* Maudlands, Maude Street, KENDAL, CUMBRIA, LA9 4QD.
HENSON, Mr. Brian Albert Voice, FCA *1956;* Dean House, Main Street, Offenham, EVESHAM, WORCESTERSHIRE, WR11 8QD. (Life Member)
•HENSON, Mr. Christopher, FCA *1975;* Phipps Henson McAllister, 4 South Bar Street, BANBURY, OXFORDSHIRE, OX16 9AA.
HENSON, Mr. Derek Edward, FCA *1955;* 11 Sandford Drive, Woodley, READING, RG5 4RR. (Life Member)
HENSON, Mrs. Eleanor Marian Athena, BSc ACA *1997;* Primrose Hill Farm, Primrose Hill, Tivetshall St. Mary, NORWICH, NR15 2BZ.
HENSON, Mr. Ian Richard, BSc ACA *1996;* Primrose Hill Farm, Primrose Hill, Tivetshall St. Mary, NORWICH, NR15 2BZ.
HENSON, Mr. Ian Robert, BSc ACA *1982;* 2 Shawbury Village, Shawbury Lane Shustoke, Coleshill, BIRMINGHAM, B46 2RU.
•HENSON, Mrs. Joanne Marie, ACA *2005;* 27 Hamilton Drive, NEWTON ABBOT, DEVON, TQ12 2TL.
HENSON, Mr. Martin Ashley David, BSc ACA *1989;* 215 Beamhill Road, BURTON-ON-TRENT, DE13 9QW.
HENSON, Mr. Neil Stuart, BA ACA *1988;* Chartwell, Woodcroft Lane, Woodcroft, CHEPSTOW, NP16 7PZ.
HENSON, Mr. Paul Robert, BA ACA *1987;* John Swire & Sons Ltd Swire House, 59 Buckingham Gate, LONDON, SW1E 6AJ.
HENSON, Mr. Peter Robert Voice, FCA *1962;* Eagle High, Sly Corner, Lee Common, GREAT MISSENDEN, HP16 9LD.
HENSON, Miss. Rebecca Jane, BA(Hons) ACA *2001;* 27 Kellerton Road, LONDON, SE13 5RB.
HENSTOCK, Mr. Barry Anthony, FCA *1961;* 1450 Lakeshore Road East, OAKVILLE L6J 1M1, ON, CANADA. (Life Member)
•HENTON, Mrs. Alison Lesley, BA ACA *1991;* Antrams, 44-46 Old Steine, BRIGHTON, BN1 1NH.
HENTON, Mr. Andrew Michael, MA ACA *1995;* Raglan House, Queens Road, St. Peter Port, GUERNSEY, GY1 1PU.
HENTON, Mr. Nigel Ian Plenderleith, BSc FCA *1977;* Natural Distribution(Holdings) Ltd, Unit E, Foster Road, Ashford Business Park, Sevington, ASHFORD KENT TN24 0SH.
HENTSCHEL, Mr. Richard John, BSc FCA *1986;* Odensegade 10 1 TH, 2100 COPENHAGEN, DENMARK.
HENTY, Mr. Anthony Arthur, FCA *1962;* 17 Chelwood Road, Earley, READING, RG6 5QG. (Life Member)
HENWOOD, Mr. Daniel Martin, ACA *2007;* 1 Trelawney Drive, Tilehurst, READING, RG31 5WQ.
•HENWOOD, Mrs. Elizabeth Jane, BSc ACA MBA *1996;* Lowe Henwood Limited, The Lodge, 149 Mannamead Road, PLYMOUTH, PL3 5NU.
HENWOOD, Mrs. Jennifer Elaine, BSc ACA *1998;* Penningtons Solicitors, De Vinci House, Basing View, BASINGSTOKE, HAMPSHIRE, RG21 4EQ.
HENWOOD, Mr. Jeremy David, BSc ACA *1993;* 6 Rosyth Gardens, NEWBURY, BERKSHIRE, RG14 7WD.
HENWOOD, Mrs. Sara Ann, ACA *1980;* Mole Cottage, 11 Carey Parade, NORTH TAMBORINE, QLD 4272, AUSTRALIA.
HENWORTH, Mr. David Julian, BA ACA *1994;* 1 Dairy Farm Barns, Little Saredon, Shares Hill, WOLVERHAMPTON, WV10 7LJ.
HENWORTH, Mrs. Rebecca Kate, BSc ACA *1999;* 1 Dairy Farm Barns, Little Saredon, WOLVERHAMPTON, WV10 7LJ.
HEPBURN, Mr. Allan Ritchie, CA *2003; (CA Scotland 1986);* c/o Ernst & Young Hua Ming, Level 16 Tower E3, Oriental Plaza, #1 East Chang An Avenue, Dong Chen District, BEIJING 100738 CHINA.
HEPBURN, Ms. Catherine Anne, ACA *2004;* 4 Betjeman Mews, GATESHEAD, TYNE AND WEAR, NE8 3BF.
HEPBURN, Miss. Emily, MEng ACA *2007;* Little Mew, Spring Road, PLYMOUTH, PL9 0AY.
HEPBURN, Ms. Harriet Rose, BA ACA *1992;* 37 Baalbec Road, LONDON, N5 1QN.
•HEPBURN, Mr. Philip Frankland, FCA *1972;* 28 Abbey Road, BRISTOL, BS9 3QW.
HEPBURN, Miss. Susan Elena, MA ACA *2005;* 4 Glenlockhart Valley, EDINBURGH, EH14 1DE.
HEPPELL, Mr. Alan Matthew, FCA *1969;* 22 Bere Close, WINCHESTER, SO22 5HY.
HEPPELL, Mr. Frank Neil, FCA *1958;* 3 Brooklands, NEWCASTLE UPON TYNE, NE20 9LZ. (Life Member)
HEPPELL, Dr. Michael, FCA *1971;* 15 Bayview Avenue, East Hawthorn, MELBOURNE, VIC 3123, AUSTRALIA. (Life Member)
HEPPELL, Mr. Richard Emlyn, BA ACA *1992;* 14 Kingsbury Avenue, ST. ALBANS, AL3 4TA.
•HEPPENSTALL, Miss. Clare Nicola, MA FCA *1992;* Mumby Heppenstall, Wellingore Hall, Wellingore, LINCOLN, LN5 0HX.
•HEPPENSTALL, Mrs. Jennifer Maria, BSc ACA *2004;* R L Ferris Limited, 64 Derby Lane, LIVERPOOL, L13 3DN.

HEPPENSTALL, Mr. Keith Desmond, BA FCA *1985;* 35 Knowle Lane, Ecclesall, SHEFFIELD, S11 9SL.
HEPPENSTALL, Mr. Richard Douglas Beaumont, BCom FCA *1971;* 1 Poplar Bank, Fenay Bridge, HUDDERSFIELD, HD8 0AE.
HEPPENSTALL, Mr. Richard Edward, BSc FCA *1988;* Ul.Sloneczna 34, 00-789 WARSAW, POLAND.
HEPPER, Mr. Richard John, MA FCA *1992;* Capital for enterprise Limited, 1 Broadfield Close, SHEFFIELD, SOUTH YORKSHIRE, S8 0XN.
HEPPER, Mr. Roger Anthony, BSc FCA *1987;* c/o JF Asset Management Ltd, 21st Floor, Chater House, 8 Connaught Road, CENTRAL, HONG KONG ISLAND HONG KONG SAR.
HEPPES, Mr. Keith Harry, FCA *1966;* 37 Leonards Road, P.O. Box 403, HILTON, KWAZULU NATAL, 3245, SOUTH AFRICA.
HEPPLE, Mr. Douglas Keith, FCA *1972;* 35 The Paddock, Walbottle, NEWCASTLE UPON TYNE, NE15 8JG.
HEPPLESTON, Dr. Erica Anne, ACA CA(NZ) *2009;* 27 Severn Drive, ESHER, KT10 0AJ.
HEPPLESTONE, Miss. Emma Louise, BA ACA *2007;* Ludgate House, 245 Blackfriars Road, LONDON, SE1 9UY.
•HEPPLEWHITE, Mr. Mark Francis, LLB FCA *1991;* Hepplewhite & Co, 20 Selborne Road, Southgate, LONDON, N14 7DH.
HEPTON, Miss. Kim Elizabeth, BCom FCA *1985;* The Dairy House Carlton Lane, East Carlton Yeadon, LEEDS, LS19 7BG.
HEPTON, Ms. Tansy Jane, BSc ACA *1985;* The Woodlands, 34 Dearnside Road, Denby Dale, HUDDERSFIELD, HD8 8TL.
HEPWORTH, Mr. Andrew Robert, FCA *1975;* 3 Lidget Croft, Bradley, KEIGHLEY, WEST YORKSHIRE, BD20 9DJ.
HEPWORTH, Miss. Anna Patricia, ACA *2011;* Apartment 27, Tempus Tower, 9 Mirabel Street, MANCHESTER, M3 1NN.
HEPWORTH, Mr. Christian David, BSc ACA *1999;* L12 333 Collins St, MELBOURNE, VIC 3000, AUSTRALIA.
•HEPWORTH, Mr. Colin John, ACA *1983;* (Tax Fac), Fourstones, Gallowlaw Burnhouse Road, WOOLER, NE71 6ST.
HEPWORTH, Mr. Derek Antony, ACA *1979;* 922 Schuyler Drive, WEST CHESTER, PA 19380, UNITED STATES.
HEPWORTH, Mr. Ian Richard, BA(Econ) FCA *1972;* 7 West Croft, Addingham, ILKLEY, WEST YORKSHIRE, LS29 0SP.
HEPWORTH, Mrs. Jennifer, BSc(Hons) ACA *2002;* 59 Woodville Road, BARNET, HERTFORDSHIRE, EN5 5NG.
•HEPWORTH, Mr. John Allan, ACA *1988;* Hepworth Griffiths, 47/49 Grove Street, RETFORD, NOTTINGHAMSHIRE, DN22 6LA.
HEPWORTH, Mr. John Charles, BA ACA *1995;* S I G Plc Hillsborough Works, Langsett Road, SHEFFIELD, S6 2LW.
HEPWORTH, Mr. Michael Ernley, BA FCA *1986;* 80 Victoria Street, Cardinal Place, LONDON, SW1E 5JL.
HEPWORTH, Mr. Paul, BA FCA *1974;* Palace House, 458 Padiham Road, BURNLEY, BB12 6TD.
HEPWORTH, Mr. Peter Hamby, MBA BA ACA *1989;* Wessex House, Callow Hill, VIRGINIA WATER, GU25 4LD.
HEPWORTH, Mr. Peter Newton, FCA *1953;* Langdale House, 108 Tadcaster Road, Dringhouses, YORK, YO24 1LT. (Life Member)
HEPWORTH, Mr. Roger Arthur Ambrose, FCA *1962;* Oaklands, Garden Reach, CHALFONT ST. GILES, HP8 4BE.
•HEPWORTH, Mr. Roland, FCA *1979;* (Tax Fac), Roland Hepworth, 2 Hall Croft, NORMANTON, WEST YORKSHIRE, WF6 2DN.
HEPWORTH, Mr. Simon, BA ACA *1988;* 44A Woodbury Road, St Ives, SYDNEY, NSW 2075, AUSTRALIA.
HERACLEOUS, Ms. Nicolina, ACA *2010;* Po Box 24528, 1307 NICOSIA, CYPRUS.
HERAGHTY, Mr. Denis, BAcc ACA *1996;* 292 Langside Road, GLASGOW, G42 8XW.
HERALD, Mr. Andrew Nicholas, FCA *1967;* Dowlands Farm House, Tangley, ANDOVER, HAMPSHIRE, SP11 0SH.
•HERATY, Mrs. Laura Jane, BSc ACA *1996;* Applewood LLP, 27 Little St Marys, Long Melford, SUDBURY, SUFFOLK, CO10 9HY.
•HERBERT, Mr. Alan Peter, FCA *1989;* with RSM Tenon Audit Limited, Stoughton House, Harborough Road, Oadby, LEICESTER, LE2 4LP.
HERBERT, Mr. Alastair Timothy Bruce, BSc ACA *1979;* Magnolia House, 3 Kingsfold Close, BILLINGSHURST, RH14 9HG.
HERBERT, Mr. Andrew Charles, BSc ACA *1989;* Hastoe Villa, 3 Western Road, TRING, HERTFORDSHIRE, HP23 4BE.
HERBERT, Mr. Barry Charles, FCA *1961;* Kaprifolgatan 20, 21362 MALMO, SWEDEN.
•HERBERT, Mr. Benjamin Paul, BCom ACA *2002;* Dennis & Turnbull Limited, Swatton Barn, Badbury, SWINDON, SN4 0EU. See also Dennis & Turnbull Holdings Limited
HERBERT, Mr. Benjamin William, BSc ACA *2009;* Ford Farm, Coleford, CREDITON, DEVON, EX17 5DG.
HERBERT, Mrs. Christine Gillian, BA FCA *1996;* Rosemead, High Street, Harwell, DIDCOT, OXFORDSHIRE, OX11 0EX.
HERBERT, Miss. Claire, ACA *2011;* 37 Richmond Way, Fetcham, LEATHERHEAD, SURREY, KT22 9NU.
HERBERT, Mr. Daniel Rhidian, ACA *1980;* Tirfelin, Mill Street, Tre-r-ddol, MACHYNLLETH, SY20 8PR.
HERBERT, Mr. David James, BSc ACA *1995;* 5925 Elm Lane, PEORIA, IL 61614, UNITED STATES.
•HERBERT, Mr. David John, FCA *1995;* David Herbert Limited, Regus Centre, Windmill Hill Business Park, Whitehill Way, SWINDON, SN5 6QR.
HERBERT, Mr. David Lee, ACA *2000;* 7 Diswell Brook Way, Deanshanger, MILTON KEYNES, MK19 6GA.
HERBERT, Mrs. Dawn Mary, BSc ACA *1993;* Greenacres, Burstall Lane, Sproughton, IPSWICH, IP8 3DJ.
HERBERT, Mrs. Diane Carol, BA FCA DChA *1988;* 35 Holly Walk, Silsoe, BEDFORD, MK45 4EB.
•HERBERT, Mr. Edward Peter, BSc FCA *1994;* Insight Practice Services, 1 Castleton Road, Hazel Grove, STOCKPORT, CHESHIRE, SK7 6LB.
•HERBERT, Mr. George Robert, FCA *1982;* Allen Sykes Limited, 5 Henson Close, South Church Enterprise Park, BISHOP AUCKLAND, COUNTY DURHAM, DL14 6WA.
•HERBERT, Mr. Graham Herbert, FCA *1959;* G.H.Herbert & Co, 227 Marlpool Lane, KIDDERMINSTER, DY11 5DL.
HERBERT, Mrs. Janet Margaret, BSc ACA *1988;* Beddgelert, Rushden Road, Bletsoe, BEDFORD, MK44 1QW.
HERBERT, Mr. John Shotton, FCA *1968;* Michelend, Lewes Road, Westmeston, HASSOCKS, BN6 8RH.
HERBERT, Miss. Julie, BA ACA *1994;* 1 Park Drive, Eccles, MANCHESTER, M30 9JR.
HERBERT, Mrs. Kathryn Jane, BA ACA *1993;* 16 Conway Road, West Wimbledon, LONDON, SW20 8PA.
HERBERT, Mr. Keith Barry, LLB FCA *1983;* McIntyre Hudson LLP New Bridge Street House, 30-34 New Bridge Street, LONDON, EC4V 4BJ.
HERBERT, Mrs. Linda Joy, BA ACA *1988;* Mulberry Lodge, Southwood, WOKINGHAM, RG40 2HF.
HERBERT, Miss. Lorna, ACA *2009;* 31 Roseden Way, NEWCASTLE UPON TYNE, NE13 9BD.
HERBERT, Mr. Mark Andrew, BEng FCA *1993;* 16 Conway Road, LONDON, SW20 8PA.
•HERBERT, Mr. Mark James, BA FCA *1990;* Malthouse & Company Ltd, America House, Rumford Court, Rumford Place, LIVERPOOL, L3 9DD.
HERBERT, Mr. Michael John, BSc(Hons) ACA *2006;* SRP 3, Detica Ltd Chancellor Court, Occam Road Surrey Research Park, GUILDFORD, GU2 7YP.
HERBERT, Mr. Nigel Paul Stewart, BSc FCA *1986;* Mulberry Lodge, Southwood, Southlands Road, WOKINGHAM, RG40 2HF.
HERBERT, Mrs. Olivia Zoe, LLB ACA *2005;* 21 Beningfield Drive, London Colney, ST. ALBANS, HERTFORDSHIRE, AL2 1UX.
HERBERT, Mrs. Paula Jeannie, BSc ACA *1998;* 20 Old Lands Hill, BRACKNELL, BERKSHIRE, RG12 2QX.
HERBERT, Prof. Peter John Alan, MSc FCA *1968;* Vivenda Tres moinhos, C P 116-Z, Barranco De Apra, 8100-226 LOULE, PORTUGAL. (Life Member)
HERBERT, Mr. Philip Robert, FCA *1967;* Kingfishers, 10 Rookwood Park, HORSHAM, RH12 1UB.
HERBERT, Mr. Richard, BA ACA *2010;* 49 Zealand Road, LONDON, E3 5RA.
HERBERT, Mr. Richard James, BSc FCA *1976;* Hovells, 10 Frogge Street, Ickleton, SAFFRON WALDEN, CB10 1SH.
HERBERT, Mr. Richard Kevin, ACA *2008;* 2 Fern Road, Aller Park, NEWTON ABBOT, DEVON, TQ12 4NR.
•HERBERT, Mr. Roger Leslie, FCA *1965;* R. Herbert & Co, 53 Cedar Lawn Avenue, BARNET, HERTFORDSHIRE, EN5 2LP.
•HERBERT, Miss. Sian Anne, BSc ACA *1992;* PricewaterhouseCoopers LLP, Pricewaterhousecoopers, 12 Plumtree Court, LONDON, EC4A 4HT. See also PricewaterhouseCoopers
HERBERT, Mr. Simon Ian, MPhil BSc ACA *1999;* 20 Old Lands Hill, BRACKNELL, BERKSHIRE, RG12 2QX.
HERBERT, Mr. Simon Paul, ACA *1990;* 9 Station Road, Lidlington, BEDFORD, MK43 0SA.
HERBERT, Mr. Stuart Sidney, ACA *1997;* c/o Marsh Management Services Singapore Pte Ltd, 18 Cross Street #04-00, Marsh & McLennan Centre, SINGAPORE 048423, SINGAPORE.
HERBERT, Mrs. Suzanne Jane, BA ACA *1994;* with PricewaterhouseCoopers LLP, 1 Embankment Place, LONDON, WC2N 6RH.
•HERBERT, Mr. Terry James, FCA ATII *1975;* G D Hakin & Co, 9 Stanley Street, BLYTH, NORTHUMBERLAND, NE24 2BS.
HERBERT, Mr. Timothy Charles, BCom ACA *2002;* (Tax Fac), 48 Oakhurst Road, EPSOM, SURREY, KT19 9SF.
•HERBINET, Mr. David, ACA *2001;* Mazars LLP, Tower Bridge House, St. Katharines Way, LONDON, E1W 1DD.
HERD, Mr. Andrew William, MA ACA *1983;* 4c Hill Road, St Johns Wood, LONDON, NW8 9QG.
HERD, Mr. George Alexander, BA ACA *2009;* 1507 Coventry Road, Yardley, BIRMINGHAM, B25 8LW.
•HERD, Mrs. Helen Margaret, BA ACA *2004;* Prospect Laithe, Saxelby Farm, Hebden, SKIPTON, NORTH YORKSHIRE, BD23 5DX.
HERD, Miss. Jennifer Lynne, BSc ACA *2006;* 111 Highbury New Park, LONDON, N5 2HG.
HERD, Mrs. Margaret Ann, BA ACA *1989;* 10 King's Cross Terrace, ABERDEEN, AB15 6BF.
HERD, Mr. Paul Geoffrey, BSc ACA *1992;* 3 Clenches Farm, Clenches Farm Road, SEVENOAKS, KENT, TN13 2NT.
HERDMAN, Mrs. Carol Sheila, BSc ACA *1994;* 15 Hawthorn Way, Gilberdyke, BROUGH, HU15 2YB.
HERDMAN, Mr. Geoffrey Howard Walker, FCA *1966;* Flat 24, 120 Wigmore Street, LONDON, W1U 3RU.
HERDMAN, Mrs. Julia, BCom ACA *1992;* 5 Bruces Way, Hathaway Grange, STRATFORD-UPON-AVON, WARWICKSHIRE, CV37 9JH.
HERDMAN, Mr. Mark Anthony, BA ACA *2005;* Flat 1 & 3, 66 Shakespeare Road, WORTHING, WEST SUSSEX, BN11 4AT.
HERDMAN, Miss. Michelle Pauline, BSc ACA *1991;* Standard Chartered Bank, 1 Basinghall Avenue, LONDON, EC2V 5DD.
•HERELLE, Mr. Patrick, FCA *1988;* Patrick Herelle, 88 Daneby Road, Catford, LONDON, SE6 2QG. See also Leigh Carr
HERFORD, Mr. George Oscar, ACA *1980;* 52A Chelsea Park Gardens, LONDON, SW3 6AD.
HERHOLDT, Mrs. Kerry, ACA CA(SA) *2011;* General-Wille Str 107, 8706 FELDMEILEN, SWITZERLAND.
HERIOT, Miss. Joanne Jean, ACA *2011;* 72 Park Grove Road, LONDON, E11 4PU.
HERIOT, Mrs. Katy Elizabeth, BA ACA *1999;* 27 Cross Road, Cholsey, WALLINGFORD, OX10 9PE.
HERITAGE, Mr. Dennis Francis, FCA *1951;* 1 Cann Lodge Gardens, SHAFTESBURY, DORSET, SP7 8HU. (Life Member)
HERITAGE, Ms. Joanna Leigh, BSc ACA *1991;* 6 Stuart Drive, Stockton Heath, WARRINGTON, WA4 2BT.
HERITAGE, Mr. Nicholas John, BEng ACA *1998;* 16 Old Forge Road, LONDON, N19 4AH.
HERITAGE, Ms. Sarah Kathryn, BSc ACA *2005;* 35 Kings Road, ST. ALBANS, HERTFORDSHIRE, AL3 4TQ.
HERITAGE, Mr. Vernon Henry, BSc FCA *1981;* 29-03 Riverine By The Park, 398 Kallang Road, SINGAPORE 339098, SINGAPORE.
HERKES, Mr. Andrew Richard, FCA *1973;* The Chalet, May Road, Turvey, BEDFORD, BEDFORDSHIRE, MK43 8DT.
HERKES, Mr. Richard Charles, MSc ACA *1981;* LLwyn Celyn, Ffawyddog, CRICKHOWELL, NP8 1PW.
•HERLIHY, Mr. Francis, ACA CF *1996;* Wilton Engineering Services Ltd, Port Clarence Road, Port Clarence, MIDDLESBROUGH, CLEVELAND, TS2 1RZ.
HERLIHY, Ms. Selina Anne, ACA CA(AUS) *2008;* 6a Highgate West Hill, LONDON, N6 6JR.
HERLINGER, Mr. Charles Edward Nield, BSc FCA *1981;* Winton Lodge, Milley Lane, Hare Hatch, READING, RG10 9TL.
HERLINGER, Mrs. Diane Elizabeth, BA ACA *1982;* 117 Oakwood Court, LONDON, W14 8LA.
HERMAN, Mr. Daniel, BA(Com) FCA *1960;* Bow House, 3 Bow Green Road, Bowdon, ALTRINCHAM, WA14 3LY. (Life Member)
HERMAN, Mr. David Peter, FCA *1972;* Sabaidee, Norwich Road, Mulbarton, NORWICH, NR14 8JT.
•HERMAN, Ms. Irene, FCA *1979;* (Tax Fac), Herman & Co, Clapper Cottage, Bondleigh, NORTH TAWTON, DEVON, EX20 2AU.
HERMAN, Mr. Jeffrey Michael, FCA *1975;* Royston, 64 Park View, Hatch End, PINNER, HA5 4LN.
HERMAN, Miss. Kellie Luanne, ACA *2008;* 25 Gore Road, LONDON, SW20 8JN.
HERMAN, Miss. Louise, ACA *2009;* 3 Red Lodge, Red Road, BOREHAMWOOD, HERTFORDSHIRE, WD6 4SN.
HERMAN, Mr. Paul Stephen, BSc ACA *1998;* with Cavendish Corporate Finance, 40 Portland Place, LONDON, W1B 1NB.
HERMAN, Mr. Stephen Paul, BSc ACA *1979;* 27 Hartopp Road, SUTTON COLDFIELD, WEST MIDLANDS, B74 2RE.
HERMANS, Mr. Dirk, ACA *2003;* Apartment 3009, The Prudential Tower Residences, 2-13-14 Nagatacho, Chiyoda-ku, TOKYO, JAPAN.
HERMER, Mr. David Benjamin, BSc ACA *2009;* 24 Myddleton Avenue, Finsbury Park, LONDON, N4 2DP.
•HERMISTON, Mr. Gordon James, BCom ACA FRSA *1995;* Kesworth Limited, 8 Highgate Drive, TELFORD, SHROPSHIRE, TF2 9FE.
HERMISTON, Mr. James Jeffrey Alexander, MA ACA *1987;* Flat D, 560 Great Western Road, Mannofield, ABERDEEN, AB10 6PU.
HERMISTON-HOOPER, Mr. Edward, ACA *2009;* BDO Corporate Finance, Floor 33 East, Al Fattan Currency Tower, DIFC, DUBAI, 506802 UNITED ARAB EMIRATES.
•HERMITAGE, Mr. Toby James, BSc ACA *2009;* 29 Nutbeem Road, EASTLEIGH, HAMPSHIRE, SO50 5JP.
HERMON-TAYLOR, Mr. Christopher Guy, FCA *1967;* Trumley Barns East, West Lavant, CHICHESTER, WEST SUSSEX, PO18 9AY. (Life Member)
HERNANDEZ, Mr. Robert Finbar, BSc ACA *1995;* Fir Croft, The Highlands, East Horsley, LEATHERHEAD, SURREY, KT24 5BQ.
HERNE, Mrs. Claire Suzanne, MA ACA *1998;* Fisher German Llp, 40 High Street, MARKET HARBOROUGH, LEICESTERSHIRE, LE16 7NX.
•HERNIMAN, Mrs. Helen Rachel, BSc FCA *1992;* The Darrington, 552E Kenilworth Road, Balsall Common, COVENTRY, CV7 7DQ.
•HERNIMAN, Miss. Joanne Clare, BA ACA *2000;* Moore Stephens LLP, 150 Aldersgate Street, LONDON, EC1A 4AB.
HERNIMAN, Mr. Stephen Robert, ACA *2011;* Flat 1, 15 Enfield Road, LONDON, N1 5EN.
HERNON, Miss. Julie Lynne, BSc ACA *1993;* Beever & Struthers, St. Georges House, 215-219 Chester Road, MANCHESTER, M15 4JE.
HEROD, Mr. Nicholas Julian, BA(Econ) ACA *1998;* Sequel Business Solutions Ltd, Peninsular House, 30 Monument Street, LONDON, EC3R 8LJ.
HERODOTOU, Miss. Chrysanthi, ACA *2009;* 24 Oakwood Crescent, Winchmore Hill, LONDON, N21 1PB.
HERON, Mr. Andrew Mark, ACA *2009;* University of Cumbria, Bowerham Road, LANCASTER, LA1 3JD.
HERON, Miss. Angela Edna, BA ACA *1992;* 17 Stanley Drive, Roundhay, LEEDS, LS8 2EZ.
HERON, Mr. Christopher, BA(Hons) ACA *2004;* 2 Avarn Road, LONDON, SW17 9HA.
HERON, Dr. Daniel Anthony Westwood, BSc ACA *1999;* 2 Astwood Cottages, Astwood Lane, Stoke Prior, BROMSGROVE, B60 4BE.
HERON, Mr. James Robert McNab, BSc ACA *1992;* 1 Northmead, Prestbury, MACCLESFIELD, SK10 4XD.
HERON, Mr. John Phillip, MA FCA *1954;* 3 The Farm, Princes Way, LONDON, SW19 6QF. (Life Member)
HERON, Mr. Mark, BSc ACA *1994;* 64 Fieldhead Road, Guiseley, LEEDS, LS20 8DU.
HERON, Mr. Miles Richard, BSc ACA *1995;* 243 Waldegrave Road, TWICKENHAM, MIDDLESEX, TW1 4SY.
HERON, Mr. Richard William, BCom FCA *1986;* 1 Nash Drive, REDHILL, RH1 1LH.
•HERON, Mr. Robert Samuel David, BSc ACA *2000;* Ernst & Young LLP, Bedford House, 16-22 Bedford Street, BELFAST, COUNTY ANTRIM, BT2 7DT. See also Ernst & Young Europe LLP
HERON, Miss. Saimah Saara, BA(Hons) ACA *2010;* 27 Lime Meadow Avenue, SOUTH CROYDON, SURREY, CR2 9AS.
HEROYS, Mr. Nicholas, MA FCA *1964;* St. Catherines, 10 London Road, Southborough, TUNBRIDGE WELLS, TN4 0RR.
HERRERA, Mr. David John Brendon, FCA *1955;* La Chiocciola 19, 22060 CARIMATE, LOMBARDIA, ITALY. (Life Member)
HERRERA, Mrs. Jennifer Elaine, BA ACA *2003;* 5 Birkdale Grove, YORK, YO26 5RW.
HERRERA, Mr. Matthew, ACA *2004;* MacIntyre Hudson Llp, 30-34 New Bridge Street, LONDON, EC4V 6BJ.

HERRICK, Mr. David John, BSc ACA *1994;* 11 Trinity Road, LONDON, SW19 8QT.
HERRICK, Mr. Simon Edward, MSc ACA *1990;* 94 Broom Road, TEDDINGTON, TW11 9PF.
HERRIDGE, Mr. Jeremy, BA(Hons) ACA *2001;* Lyndale, Sheerwater Avenue, Woodham, ADDLESTONE, SURREY, KT15 3DR.
HERRIMAN, Mrs. Sarah Louise, BA(Hons) ACA ACIM *2002;* 31 Clifton Road, NEWBURY, BERKSHIRE, RG14 5JS.
HERRING, Mr. Adrian Charles, BSc ACA *1990;* 55 Beechfields, Eccleston, CHORLEY, PR7 5RF.
HERRING, Mr. Christopher Paul, DPhil BA FCA *1977;* 108 Weir Road, LONDON, SW12 0ND.
HERRING, Mr. Lionel, BCom FCA *1975;* Alterra Capital Holdings Limited, PO Box HM 2565, HAMILTON HM KX, BERMUDA.
HERRING, Miss. Lorna Jayne, BSc ACA *2007;* Pricewaterhousecoopers, 1 Kingsway, CARDIFF, CF10 3PW.
HERRING, Mr. Matthew Alexander, BA ACA ATT *1999;* with Hollis and Co Ltd, 35 Wilkinson Street, SHEFFIELD, S10 2GB.
•**HERRING, Mr. Nigel, BA ACA** *1991;* KLS Business Consultants Limited, 21 Coniscliffe Road, DARLINGTON, COUNTY DURHAM, DL3 7EE. See also Nigel Herring & Co
HERRING, Mr. Paul John, MBA BSc FCA *1990;* 175 W. Jackson Blvd, Suite 2000, CHICAGO, IL 60603, UNITED STATES.
HERRING, Miss. Rachel, BSc(Hons) ACA *2011;* 8 Russell Close, Wilnecote, TAMWORTH, STAFFORDSHIRE, B77 5FF.
HERRING, Mr. Rhys Matthew, ACA *2008;* Flat 54, 12 Bermondsey Square, LONDON, SE1 3FD.
HERRING, Mr. Stephen Geoffrey, BA ACA *1998;* 22 Fairfax Avenue, Didsbury, MANCHESTER, M20 6AJ.
•**HERRING, Mr. Stephen John, BA(Econ) ACA CTA** *1979;* BDO LLP, 55 Baker Street, LONDON, W1U 7EU. See also BDO Stoy Hayward LLP
HERRING, Mr. Thomas, MBA BSc ACA *2007;* 30 Jersy Road Paddington, PADDINGTON, NSW 2021, AUSTRALIA.
HERRING, Mr. Timothy John Crawford, BSc ACA *1996;* The Reading Room, Barnwell, PETERBOROUGH, PE8 5PH.
HERRINGTON, Mr. David Clifton, BA ACA *1985;* 22 Kintore Street, CAMBERWELL, VIC 3124, AUSTRALIA.
HERRINGTON, Mr. Ian Michael, BA ACA *1987;* 2 Scholars Close, Great Shefford, HUNGERFORD, RG17 7EW.
HERRINGTON, Mr. Ivor Jack, FCA *1968;* P.O.Box CR-56766, Suite #788, NASSAU, BAHAMAS.
HERRINGTON, Miss. Jane Elizabeth Mary, BSc ACA *1989;* Greenacres Attleton Green, Wickhambrook, NEWMARKET, SUFFOLK, CB8 8YB.
HERRINGTON, Miss. Jemma, MSc ACA *2011;* 35 Butcher Street, LEEDS, LS11 5WF.
HERRINGTON, Miss. Louise May, BSc ACA *1993;* 6 Pankhurst Drive, BRACKNELL, RG12 9PS.
HERRINGTON, Mr. Neil David, BSc ACA *1990;* CSL Limited, Unit 501-8 5th Floor, Cyberport 3, 100 Cyberport Road, POK FU LAM, HONG KONG ISLAND HONG KONG SAR.
HERRIOTT, Mr. Charles, BA ACA *2010;* 89 Salisbury Walk, LONDON, N19 5DU.
HERRIOTT, Mr. Timothy Mark, BA ACA *1997;* 15 Briarsleigh, STAFFORD, ST17 4QP.
HERRIOTT, Mr. William Gerard, MA FCA *1966;* 7 Vincent Close, Fetcham, LEATHERHEAD, SURREY, KT22 9PB.
HERRITY, Miss. Kayte Joanna, MA ACA *1996;* Liberty Global INC, Michelin House, 81 Fulham Road, LONDON, SW3 6RD.
HERRMANN, Mr. Lucas Oliver, BSc ACA *1989;* Deutsche Bank A G (London) Ltd, Winchester House, 1 Great Winchester Street, LONDON, EC2N 2EQ.
HERRMANN, Mr. Max Stephen, BSc ACA *1994;* Royal Institution of Great Britain, 21 Albemarle Street, LONDON, W1S 4BS.
HERROD, Mrs. Julie Diane, BA FCA CTA *1985;* (Tax Fac), 51 Arlington Drive, Alvaston, DERBY, DE24 0AW.
•**HERROD, Mr. Paul David, BA FCA** *1985;* KPMG, KPMG Centre, 18 Viaduct Harbour Avenue, P.O. Box 1584, AUCKLAND 1140, NEW ZEALAND.
HERRON, Mr. Anthony Gavin, BSc FCA *1961;* Croft House, The Green, Bardwell, BURY ST. EDMUNDS, IP31 1AW. (Life Member)
HERRON, Mrs. Joanne Mary, BSc ACA *1991;* 5 Farleigh Street, ASHFIELD, NSW 2131, AUSTRALIA.
•**HERRON, Mr. Martin Steven, BA ACA** *1997;* MacIntyre Hudson LLP, Peterbridge House, The Lakes, NORTHAMPTON, NN4 7HB. See also MH & Co
HERRON, Mr. Neil Alec, ACA CA(SA) *2010;* 9 Spring Lane, Bassingbourn, ROYSTON, HERTFORDSHIRE, SG8 5HZ.
HERRTAGE, Mr. Andrew Mark, ACA *1983;* 8 Hamboro Gardens, LEIGH-ON-SEA, SS9 2NR.
HERSEY, Mrs. Claire Nadine, BSc(Hons) ACA *2003;* Flat 506, Bunyan Court, Barbican, LONDON, EC2Y 8DH.
HERSEY, Mr. Ian Charles, MSc BA ACA FCCA *2010;* 69 Heatherside Road, EPSOM, SURREY, KT19 9QS.
HERSEY, Mr. Philip James, BSc FCA *1999;* 36a Quill Lane, LONDON, SW15 1PD.
HERSH, Miss. Sandra Maxine, BSc ACA *1990;* 17 Abbotshall Avenue, LONDON, N14 7JU.
HERSHKOWITZ, Mrs. Paula Olmin, FCA *1966;* Cockhaise, Monteswood Lane, Lindfield, HAYWARDS HEATH, RH16 2QP.
•**HERSKINE, Mr. David, BSc FCA** *1982;* David Herskine & Co, 45 Hurstwood Road, Temple Fortune, LONDON, NW11 0AX.
HERSZAFT, Mr. Daniel Henri, BA ACA *1996;* 153 Berrian Road, New Rochelle, NEW YORK, NY 10804, UNITED STATES.
•**HERSZAFT, Mr. Philippe Gerard, BA ACA** *1993;* Glazers, 843 Finchley Road, LONDON, NW11 8NA. See also Glazers Ltd
•**HERTZBERG, Mr. Stuart Jay, ACA** *1979;* S.J. Hertzberg & Co, 18 Glebelands Avenue, South Woodford, LONDON, E18 2AB.
•**HERTZBERG, Mr. Warren Henry, FCA** *1967;* (Tax Fac), Helmores UK LLP, Grosvenor Gardens House, 35-37 Grosvenor Gardens, LONDON, SW1W 0BY.
HERVEY, Mr. Christopher Symes, FCA *1976;* 5 Burlington Gardens, LONDON, W4 4LT.
HERVEY-MURRAY, Mr. David Jonathan, BSc FCA *1978;* Bridgewell Consultants, 18 Chancellors Walk, CAMBRIDGE, CB4 3JG.
HERWIG, Mr. Leon Arthur, FCA *1975;* 92 Fulwood Road, LIVERPOOL, L17 9QA.
HERZ, Mr. Miles Nicholas, BA ACA *1989;* 2 Holyoake Walk, LONDON, N2 0JX.
HERZ, Mr. Robert Henry, BA FCA *1977;* 186 north woods drive, SOUTH ORANGE, NJ 07079, UNITED STATES.
HERZBERG, Mr. Francis Robin, BA FCA *1982;* 6 Connaught Gardens, BERKHAMSTED, HERTFORDSHIRE, HP4 1SF.
•**HERZENSHTEIN, Miss. Irit, ACA** *1983;* (Tax Fac), Longboat Tax Advisers LLP, St. James House, 13 Kensington Square, LONDON, W8 5HD. See also Longboat Advisers Limited and Longboat VAT Advisers LLP
HESELTINE, Miss. Katherine Kay, ACA *2009;* Flat D, 8 Florence Street, LONDON, N1 2DX.
HESELTON, Miss. Sarah, ACA *2009;* 9 Housefield Way, ST. ALBANS, HERTFORDSHIRE, AL4 0GP.
HESFORD, Mr. Michael Martin Paterson, FCA *1964;* The Squirrels School Road, Hinton Waldrist, FARINGDON, SN7 8SE. (Life Member)
HESFORD, Mr. Paul Michael, BSc ACA *1997;* Unit 94/5A Victoria Park Parade, Zetland, SYDNEY, NSW 2017, AUSTRALIA.
HESKETH, Mr. Albert Neville, FCA *1964;* Flat 4 Churchill Place, Golfview Drive, Eccles, MANCHESTER, M30 9WN. (Life Member)
HESKETH, Mr. Alex, ACA *2011;* 2 Mayflower Gardens, CHORLEY, PR7 3TR.
HESKETH, Mr. Alexander John, BSc(Hons) ACA *2004;* BHP Billiton, Neathouse Place, LONDON, SW1V 1BH.
HESKETH, Mr. Andrew, BA FCA *1978;* (Tax Fac), 334 Devizes Road, SALISBURY, SP2 7DP.
HESKETH, Ms. Carolyn Lesley, BA FCA *1988;* Vision Express UK Ltd, Abbeyfield Road, Lenton, NOTTINGHAM, NG7 2SP.
HESKETH, Mr. David, BSc ACA *2007;* 7 Evans Close, MANCHESTER, M20 2SQ.
HESKETH, Mr. Gordon, MA ACA *2003;* Homes & Communities Agency St. Georges House, Kingsway Team Valley Trading Estate, GATESHEAD, TYNE AND WEAR, NE11 0NA.
•**HESKETH, Mrs. Linda Louise, MBA BSc FCA** *1989;* (Tax Fac), 31 Tweseldown Road, Church Crookham, FLEET, GU52 8DE.
HESKETH, Mrs. Louisa Jayne, BA ACA *2005;* 7 Evans Close, Didsbury, MANCHESTER, M20 2SQ.
HESKETH, Mr. Mark James, BTech ACA *1984;* Cross Hey Cross Lanes, Oscroft Tarvin, CHESTER, CH3 8NQ.
•**HESKETH, Mr. Martin John, LLB ACA** *1990;* Brookson Limited, Brunel House, 340 Firecrest Court, Centre Park, WARRINGTON, WA1 1RG. See also Brookson Projects Ltd
HESKETH, Miss. Sara Elizabeth, BA ACA *2008;* Flat 721 Willoughby House, Barbican, LONDON, EC2Y 8BN.
HESKETH-PRICHARD, Mr. James Michael, BA ACA *1993;* 5 Queensmere Road, Wimbledon, Parkside, LONDON, SW19 5PZ.
HESKETT, Mr. John Errington, MA FCA *1971;* The Dairy House, Maresfield Park, Maresfield, UCKFIELD, TN22 2HD.
•**HESKIN, Mr. Andrew Philip, MSc FCA** *1992;* Moore Thompson, Bank House, Broad Street, SPALDING, LINCOLNSHIRE, PE11 1TB.
HESKINS, Mr. Richard Samuel, BA FCA *1977;* Glebe Cottage, Parrotts Lane, Cholesbury, TRING, HP23 6NE.
HESLEWOOD, Miss. Meryl, BA ACA *1989;* 7 Granville Gardens, Didsbury, MANCHESTER, M20 2SX.
HESLINGTON, Mr. Nigel John, BA ACA *1993;* 38 Frankland Crescent, Lower Parkstone, POOLE, DORSET, BH14 9PX.
•**HESLOP, Mr. Colin Bernard, FCA** *1969;* C.B. Heslop & Co, 1 High Street, THATCHAM, RG19 3JG.
HESLOP, Mr. James Roland, FCA *1954;* Farraline, 2 St James Close, RIDING MILL, NE44 6BS. (Life Member)
HESLOP, Mr. Julian Spenser, FCA *1977;* Oaklands, 34 Selcroft Road, PURLEY, CR8 1AD.
HESLOP, Miss. Lucy-Ann Margaret, BA ACA *2006;* 18 Kay Road, LONDON, SW9 9DE.
HESLOP, Mr. Mark William, BSc ACA *1998;* 2 Brookside Cottages, Ismays Road, Ivy Hatch, SEVENOAKS, TN15 0NY.
HESLOP, Mr. Michael Emerson, MA FCA *1967;* The Old Vicarage, 1 Church Street, SUNBURY-ON-THAMES, TW16 6RQ.
HESLOP, Mr. Michael Hugh, FCA *1973;* Hill Top, Embleton, ALNWICK, NORTHUMBERLAND, NE66 3UX.
HESLOP, Mr. Roger Edgar, BSc ACA *1980;* Dogs Trust, 17 Wakley Street, LONDON, EC1V 7RQ.
HESLOP, Mr. Thomas Ian, ACA *2008;* 11 Horne Lane, Potton, SANDY, BEDFORDSHIRE, SG19 2LS.
HESLOP, Mr. Wilfrid John Maurice, FCA *1954;* 204-2314 Oak Bay Avenue, VICTORIA V8R 1G9, BC, CANADA. (Life Member)
HESMONDHALGH, Mr. John Stephen, BCom FCA *1971;* 238 Sanderstead Road, SOUTH CROYDON, SURREY, CR2 0AJ. (Life Member)
HESNI-FATIDEH, Mr. Bijan, MBA BA ACA MSI MCMI *1993;* University of Westminster, Watford Road, Northwick Park, HARROW, HA1 3TP.
HESP, Mr. George Arthur, FCA *1955;* Dalesway, Welshmans Lane, NANTWICH, CW5 6AB. (Life Member)
HESP, Mr. Michael John, BSc ACA *1986;* Biocomposites Ltd, Science Park, Keele, NEWCASTLE, STAFFORDSHIRE, ST5 5NL.
•**HESS, Mr. Alan, FCA** *1963;* Pinfields Limited, Meryll House, 57 Worcester Road, BROMSGROVE, WORCESTERSHIRE, B61 7DN.
HESS, Mrs. Lucy Jane, MA ACA *2001;* Korenweg 26, 3190 BOORTMEERBEEK, BELGIUM.
•**HESSELWOOD, Mr. Anthony Peter, FCA** *1975;* 38 Bromley Road, SHIPLEY, BD18 4DT.
HESSEY, Miss. Julia Jane, BMus ACA *2003;* Langholm Capital, 1st Floor, Charles House, 5-11 Regent Street, LONDON, SW1Y 4LR.
HESSEY, Mrs. Thalia Lynn, BA ACA *2000;* with PricewaterhouseCoopers LLP, 1 Embankment Place, LONDON, WC2N 6RH.
HESTER, Miss. Clare Louise Maria, BA(Hons) ACA *2002;* Pricewaterhousecoopers, 1 Embankment Place, LONDON, WC2N 6RH.
•**HESTER, Mr. Paul Richard, FCA** *1983;* 38 Selwood Way, Downley, HIGH WYCOMBE, HP13 5XR.
HESTER, Mr. Raymond James, FCA *1963;* 6 Martin Close, LEE-ON-THE-SOLENT, HAMPSHIRE, PO13 8LG. (Life Member)
HESTER, Miss. Rebecca Louise, BA FCA *1997;* 1100 Peachtree Street, Suite 700, ATLANTA, GA 30317, UNITED STATES.
HESTER, Mr. Robert John, FCA *1974;* 5 Nethercroft Court, ALTRINCHAM, CHESHIRE, WA14 4BZ.
HESTER, Mr. Timothy James, BA FCA *1986;* (Tax Fac), 26 Blakeden Drive, Claygate, ESHER, KT10 0JR.
HETHERINGTON, Mr. Alan Stewart, BCom FCA *1967;* Field House, South Back Lane, Stillington, YORK, YO61 1ND.
HETHERINGTON, Mr. Christopher John, LLB FCA *1986;* The Manor, 26 Windhill, BISHOP'S STORTFORD, HERTFORDSHIRE, CM23 2NG.
HETHERINGTON, Mrs. Claire Helen, BA ACA *1987;* (Tax Fac), Dray Stables Longwater Road, Eversley, HOOK, RG27 0NW.
HETHERINGTON, Mr. David Mackenzie, MA ACA *2010;* 1208 - 1118 12 Avenue SW, CALGARY T2R 0P4, AB, CANADA.
•**HETHERINGTON, Mr. Geoffrey William, FCA** *1967;* Bristow Burrell, 4 Riverview, Walnut Tree Close, GUILDFORD, GU1 4UX.
HETHERINGTON, Mr. Ian James, FCA *1959;* 43 Trafalgar Place, 17th Avenue, FISH HOEK, 7975, SOUTH AFRICA. (Life Member)
HETHERINGTON, Mr. Ian Reid, BCom ACA *2003;* 14 Garland Way, BIRMINGHAM, B31 2BT.
HETHERINGTON, Mr. James, CBE LLB FCA *1955;* 16 Doriam Close, Pennsylvania, EXETER, EX4 4RS. (Life Member)
HETHERINGTON, Mr. John Joseph, ACA *2008;* c/o Marsh Management Services Cayman Ltd, P.O. Box 1063, Governor's Square, Bldg 4 Floor 2, 23 Lime Tree Bay Avenue, West Bay Road GEORGE TOWN GRAND CAYMAN KY1-1102 CAYMAN ISLANDS.
•**HETHERINGTON, Mr. John Reid, FCA** *1965;* John R Hetherington, 7 Seafield Road, LONDON, N11 1AR.
•**HETHERINGTON, Ms. Judith Anita, BCom ACA** *1994;* Crowe Clark Whitehill LLP, St Bride's House, 10 Salisbury Square, LONDON, EC4Y 8EH. See also Horwath Clark Whitehill LLP and Crowe Clark Whitehill
HETHERINGTON, Mrs. Julie Rachel, BCom ACA *2003;* 14 Garland Way, Northfield, BIRMINGHAM, B31 2BT.
HETHERINGTON, Mrs. Lilian Lydia, BA ACA *1982;* 55 Fairfields, ALNWICK, NORTHUMBERLAND, NE66 1BT.
HETHERINGTON, Mr. Martin Hugh, BA(Hons) ACA *2001;* Walnut Cottage, 2 New North Road, REIGATE, SURREY, RH2 8NA.
HETHERINGTON, Mr. Maurice, FCA *1954;* 12 Edgewood Close, Pine Ridge, CROWTHORNE, RG45 6TA. (Life Member)
HETHERINGTON, Miss. Nicola, BSc ACA *2007;* 203 Fishguard Way, LONDON, E16 2RX.
HETHERINGTON, Mr. Robert, BA FCA *1980;* 68 Den Bank Crescent, Crosspool, SHEFFIELD, S10 5PD.
HETHERINGTON, Mr. Robert Guy, FCA *1964;* 27 Dowhills Road, Blundellsands, LIVERPOOL, L23 8SJ.
HETHERINGTON, Mr. Robert Maxwell, FCA *1967;* 20 Menteith View, DUNBLANE, FK15 0PD. (Life Member)
HETHERINGTON, Mrs. Shelley Patricia, ACA *2008;* J Sainsbury Plc, 33 Holborn, LONDON, EC1N 2HT.
HETHERINGTON, Miss. Sophie Virginia, BSc ACA *2001;* with Deloitte Touche Tohmatsu, 505 Bourke Street, (P.O.Box 78B), MELBOURNE, VIC 3001, AUSTRALIA.
HETHERINGTON, Mr. Thomas Duncan, BSc ACA *1989;* 53 Fifth Cross Road, TWICKENHAM, TW2 5LJ.
HETHERINGTON, Mr. William Alistair, FCA *1969;* 18 Philip Godlee Lodge, 842 Wilmslow Road, Didsbury, MANCHESTER, M20 2DS. (Life Member)
HETHERTON, Mr. Bill, BA(Hons) ACA *2007;* 87 Middlecave Road, MALTON, NORTH YORKSHIRE, YO17 7NQ.
HETTERLEY, Mr. Sean Peter, ACA *2008;* 557 Mierscourt Road, Rainham, GILLINGHAM, ME8 8RB.
HETTICH, Mr. Joachim Franz Xaver, FCA FSI *1978;* 1148 Shadow Mountain Terrace, VISTA, CA 92084, UNITED STATES.
HEUBERGER, Miss. Tina, ACA *2010;* Fuchshohl 111, 60431, FRANKFURT AM MAIN, GERMANY.
HEUCK, Mr. David Charles, ACA *1985;* Heron Foods Ltd, Jackson Way, MELTON, HU14 3HJ.
HEUNG, Mr. Tsan Fai, BA ACA *1990;* 9 Boole Heights, BRACKNELL, RG12 7GG.
HEURTIER, Mr. Sylvain, ACA *2007;* 9 Allee Jean De La Croix, 77200 TORCY, ILE DE FRANCE, FRANCE.
HEUSCH, Mr. Russell Lawrence, BSc ACA *1988;* 58 Tenby Avenue, Kenton, HARROW, HA3 8RX.
HEUSTON, Miss. Katherine, ACA *2008;* Flat 4 The Custom House, Redcliff Backs, BRISTOL, BS1 6NE.
HEW, Miss. Fee Voon, BSc ACA *1998;* 166 Jalan Ara, Bukh Bandaraya, 59100 KUALA LUMPUR, FEDERAL TERRITORY, MALAYSIA.
HEW, Mr. James Osmond, FCA *1970;* James O Hew, 16 Cassandra Boulevard, TORONTO M3A 1S4, ON, CANADA.
HEW, Mrs. Tammy Suk Ping, BA ACA *1991;* 18 Lorong PJU 1/46F, Aman Suria Damansara, 47301 PETALING JAYA, SELANGOR, MALAYSIA.
HEW, Ms. Yee Voon, BSc ACA *1997;* 41 Dollis Road, LONDON, N3 1RD.
HEWARD, Mrs. Felicity Anne, BA ACA *1982;* c/o A P Heward, Petrogas E & P LLC, P.O. Box 353, Ruwi, 112 MUSCAT, OMAN.
HEWAVISENTI, Mr. Rohan, MEng ACA *2007;* British Red Cross Society, 44 Moorfields, LONDON, EC2Y 9AL.

HEWAVISENTI, Mr. Saliya Hiran, ACA *1983;* 59/5A Gregory's Road, 7 COLOMBO, SRI LANKA.
HEWENS, Mr. John David, FCA *1959;* 29 Thorn Close, PETERSFIELD, HAMPSHIRE, GU31 4HZ. (Life Member)
HEWER, Mr. Christopher John, BSc ACA *1981;* Unit W, Heating & Plumbing Supplies Ltd Unit W, Rich Industrial Estate Avis Way, NEWHAVEN, EAST SUSSEX, BN9 0DU.
•**HEWER, Mr. Douglas James Lee, BSc ACA** *1999;* PricewaterhouseCoopers LLP, Hays Galleria, 1 Hays Lane, LONDON, SE1 2RD. See also PricewaterhouseCoopers
HEWER, Mr. Gareth Paul, BA ACA *2005;* Building Design Partnership, PO Box 85, MANCHESTER, M60 3JA.
•**HEWER, Mrs. Julie Karen, BA ACA** *1987;* Julie K Hewer, 17 Arran Avenue, SALE, M33 3NQ.
HEWES, Mr. Benjamin James, BSc(Hons) ACA *2002;* 117 Harpsden Road, HENLEY-ON-THAMES, OXFORDSHIRE, RG9 1ED.
HEWES, Miss. Sorrel, ACA *2009;* 10 Ketch Road, BRISTOL, BS3 5DQ.
HEWES, Mr. Stephen Brian, BSc ACA *1988;* Wray Cottage, Doods Way, REIGATE, SURREY, RH2 0JT.
HEWES, Mr. Steven Barry, BSc ACA *1995;* Stirling Farm, Torphins, BANCHORY, KINCARDINESHIRE, AB31 4HQ.
HEWETSON, Mr. Jason John, BSc ACA *2000;* 13 Oakwell Mount, LEEDS, LS8 1RS.
HEWETSON, Mr. John Francis, FCA *1964;* 65 Brangwyn Crescent, Merton Abbey, LONDON, SW19 2UA.
HEWETSON, Mr. Michael Robert, LLB ACA *2004;* 1 Alma Road, WEST MALLING, ME19 6RP.
HEWETSON, Mr. Peter James, BA ACA *2006;* with KPMG LLP, Edward VII Quay, Navigation Way, Ashton-on-Ribble, PRESTON, PR2 2YF.
HEWETSON, Mr. Philip Richard, BSc ACA *1991;* 60 Clement Road, Marple Bridge, STOCKPORT, SK6 5AG.
HEWETT, Mr. Andrew James, BCom FCA *1982;* Specialist Schools & Academies Trust, Millbank Tower, 21-24 Millbank, LONDON, SW1P 4QP.
HEWETT, Mr. David Christopher, FCA *1970;* Garland International, 10 Alexandra Avenue, LONDON, SW11 4DZ.
HEWETT, Mr. Gareth Simon, BSc ACA *2001;* Cheddington Court, Chedington, BEAMINSTER, DORSET, DT8 3HY.
HEWETT, Mr. Guy Anthony, BEng ACA *1995;* 9 Bisenden Road, CROYDON, CR0 6UN.
HEWETT, Mr. John Carr Bell, FCA *1964;* The Old Vicarage, Ugthorpe, WHITBY, YO21 2BQ.
HEWETT, Mr. John Christopher, FCA *1966;* 44 The Grip, Linton, CAMBRIDGE, CB21 4NR.
HEWETT, Mrs. Lucille Dorothea Racine, BSc FCA *1979;* 11 Muirfield Way, WOODHALL SPA, LINCOLNSHIRE, LN10 6WB.
HEWETT, Mr. Martin Clive, FCA *1979;* The Old Fox, Fox Street, Great Gransden, SANDY, BEDFORDSHIRE, SG19 3AA.
HEWETT, Dr. Michael Paul, PhD ACA *2009;* Flat 5, 10 Holmdene Avenue, LONDON, SE24 9LF.
HEWETT, Mr. Oliver Charles, BSc ACA *2007;* Flat 63 Dunbar Wharf, 126-134 Narrow Street, LONDON, E14 8BD.
HEWETT, Mr. Paul Jonathan, BA FCA *1991;* MDA Ltd, Gillingham House, 38-44 Gillingham Street, LONDON, SW1V 1HU.
HEWETT, Mrs. Rachel Dawn, ACA MAAT *2005;* Pure Wafer Plc, Pure Wafer Mill Brook Drive, Central Business Park Swansea Vale, SWANSEA, SA7 0AB.
HEWETT, Mr. Simon Christopher Wigmore, FCA *1976;* 154 East 66th Street, NEW YORK, NY 10061, UNITED STATES.
•**HEWISH, Mr. David Andrew, BEng ACA AMSTP MIFT** *1999;* AlixPartners UK LLP, 20 North Audley Street, LONDON, W1K 6WE.
HEWISH, Ms. Sally Elizabeth, BA ACA *1993;* with Grant Thornton UK LLP, 1 Dorset Street, SOUTHAMPTON, SO15 2DP.
HEWISON, Mr. Christopher John, BSc ACA *2005;* with PricewaterhouseCoopers, 33/F Cheung Kong Center, 2 Queen's Road, CENTRAL, HONG KONG ISLAND, HONG KONG SAR.
HEWISON, Mr. Richard John Howard, BSc ACA *1998;* 18 Snowberry Close, BARNET, HERTFORDSHIRE, EN5 5FS.
HEWITSON, Mr. Bruce, ACA *2006;* Flat 28 Lavender House, 31 Melliss Avenue, RICHMOND, SURREY, TW9 4AB.
HEWITSON, Miss. Claire, ACA *2008;* 1 Bullfinch Court, Croxted Road, West Dulwich, LONDON, SE21 8RL.
HEWITSON, Mr. Geoffrey, FCA *1973;* Oakwood, Quentin Way, VIRGINIA WATER, SURREY, GU25 4PS.
•**HEWITSON, Mr. John David, FCA** *1962;* J.D. Hewitson FCA, 1 Monks Heath Hall Farm, Chelford Road, Nether Alderley, MACCLESFIELD, CHESHIRE SK10 4SY.
HEWITSON, Mr. Jonathan Ian Barker, ACA *2008;* 8 Archel Road, LONDON, W14 9QH.
HEWITSON, Mr. Kevin David, BA ACA *1993;* Aviva Investors, 1 Poultry, LONDON, EC2R 8EJ.
HEWITSON, Mr. Mark, MA(Cantab) ACA *2004;* B P P Professional Education, 137 Stamford Street, LONDON, SE1 9NN.
HEWITSON, Mr. Mark William Gary, ACA MAAT *2000;* with HW Lee Associates LLP, New Derwent House, 69-73 Theobalds Road, LONDON, WC1X 8TA.
HEWITSON, Mr. Paul Harry, BA(Hons) ACA *2002;* 4 Crown & Anchor Cottages, Horsley, NEWCASTLE UPON TYNE, NE15 0NG.
HEWITSON, Mr. Philip Charles, BA FCA *1979;* Greystones, Husthwaite, YORK, YO61 4PX.
HEWITSON, Mr. Simon Jonathan, BA(Hons) ACA *2002;* 58 Rolley Way, Dukes Meadow, PRUDHOE, NORTHUMBERLAND, NE42 5FH.
HEWITT, Mr. Adrian Peter, BSc FCA *1992;* Paseo Reina Elisenda de Montcada 13, Esc E 4° 2ª, 08034 BARCELONA, SPAIN.
HEWITT, Mr. Alan, FCA *1970;* The Corner House, 63 Main Street, South Rauceby, SLEAFORD, LINCOLNSHIRE, NG34 8QQ.
HEWITT, Mr. Alastair Nicholas, BSc ACA *2006;* 25 East Dock, The Wharf, LEIGHTON BUZZARD, BEDFORDSHIRE, LU7 2LA.
HEWITT, Mr. Anthony William, FCA *1962;* 118 West Avenue, Handsworth Wood, BIRMINGHAM, B20 2LY. (Life Member)
HEWITT, Mrs. Cara Louise, BSocSc ACA *1998;* Windmill Court, Fidelity Investments Ltd Beech Gate, Millfield Lane Lower Kingswood, TADWORTH, KT20 6RP.
HEWITT, Mr. Christopher Jan, ACA *2009;* 10 Neville Crescent, Bromham, BEDFORD, MK43 8JE.
HEWITT, Mr. Christopher Philip, MA ACA *1992;* 72 Ketts Oak, Hethersett, NORWICH, NR9 3DJ.
HEWITT, Mr. Clive William Thomas, FCA *1959;* Fairhaven, 5 Victoria Avenue, HALESOWEN, B62 9BL. (Life Member)
HEWITT, Mr. David Edward, BA(Hons) ACA *2001;* with Deloitte LLP, Hill House, 1 Little New Street, LONDON, EC4A 3TR.
HEWITT, Mr. David Stuart, FCA *1958;* Ridgewood, 41 Quarry Road East, Heswall, WIRRAL, CH60 6RB. (Life Member)
HEWITT, Mr. Dennis Frederick, FCA *1949;* 6 Rushbrooke Drive, SUTTON COLDFIELD, B73 6QS. (Life Member)
HEWITT, Mr. Derek Newbury, BA FCA *1971;* 140 Lambeth Road, LONDON, SE1 7DF. (Life Member)
HEWITT, Mr. Edwin John, FCA *1957;* Rushkin, 260 Old Bedford Rd, LUTON, LU2 7EQ. (Life Member)
HEWITT, Mrs. Elizabeth Anne, BSc FCA *1982;* Borrowa, Hook Heath Road, WOKING, SURREY, GU22 0QE.
HEWITT, Mrs. Freda Lai Fan, BSc ACA *1993;* 23 Friends Walk, Kesgrave, IPSWICH, IP5 2FH.
HEWITT, Mr. Gordon, BA ACA *2010;* 18 Vincent Terrace, LONDON, N1 8HN.
HEWITT, Mr. Guy Edward, ACA *2009;* 177 Stainburn Crescent, LEEDS, LS17 6ND.
HEWITT, Mr. Ian, DFC FCA *1948;* 131 Newland Park, HULL, HU5 2DT. (Life Member)
•**HEWITT, Mr. Ian Arthur, ACA FCCA ATII** *2009;* Taylorcocks Thames Valley LLP, Northfield House Business Centre, Northfield House, 11 Northfield End, HENLEY-ON-THAMES, OXFORDSHIRE RG9 2JG.
HEWITT, Mr. James Neil Terry, BA ACA *1983;* 24 Amner Road, LONDON, SW11 6AA.
HEWITT, Mr. Jeffrey Lindsay, MA MBA FCA *1972;* Palo Alto, 6 College Way, NORTHWOOD, HA6 2BL.
HEWITT, Mr. John, FCA *1974;* Wales Council for Voluntary Action, Baltic House, Mount Stuart Square, CARDIFF, CF10 5FH.
HEWITT, Mr. John Herbert, FCA *1951;* (Member of Council 1975 - 1983), Springwood, Woodland Drive, NOTTINGHAM, NG3 5EX. (Life Member)
HEWITT, Mr. Jonathan Audley Hughes, FCA *1957;* 15 Parsons Green Lane, Fulham, LONDON, SW6 4HL. (Life Member)
HEWITT, Mr. Jonathan Michael, BSc FCA *1991;* Hachiyamacho 4-5, Shibuya-Ku, TOKYO, 150-0035 JAPAN.
HEWITT, Mrs. Katherine Ann, BA(Hons) ACA *2001;* Maple House, Highercombe Road, HASLEMERE, SURREY, GU27 2LQ.
HEWITT, Mr. Kenneth Anthony, FCA *1960;* Abbots Hill, 46 Rupert Road, Middleton, ILKLEY, LS29 0AT. (Life Member)
HEWITT, Mr. Kevin, ACA *1989;* FTI Consulting Ltd, Midtown 322 High Holborn, LONDON, WC1V 7PB.
HEWITT, Miss. Luisa Helen, ACA DChA *2010;* 7 Little Pynchons, HARLOW, ESSEX, CM18 7DB.
•**HEWITT, Mr. Mark James, BA ACA** *1993;* 7 Foxglove Road, SOUTH OCKENDON, ESSEX, RM15 6EU.
HEWITT, Miss. Maxime, ACA *2010;* 5 Kyle Close, Renishaw, SHEFFIELD, S21 3WW.
•**HEWITT, Mr. Neil Anthony, FCA** *1981;* Rolt Harrison & Hewitt, 110/112 Lancaster Road, BARNET, EN4 8AL. See also Brennan Pearson & Co
HEWITT, Mr. Nicholas John Christopher, FCA *1975;* 18 Riverbreeze Way, KULUIN, QLD 4558, AUSTRALIA.
HEWITT, Mr. Nicholas Stephen, BA ACA *1980;* 25 Wilhelmina Ave, COULSDON, CR5 1NL.
•**HEWITT, Mrs. Nicola Ann, BSc ACA** *2005;* Hewitts, 6 The Spindles, Great Wyrley, WALSALL, WS6 6GD.
HEWITT, Miss. Nicola Jayne, BSc ACA *2003;* ISS UK Limited, I S S House, 1 Genesis Business Park, Albert Drive, WOKING, SURREY GU21 5RW.
HEWITT, Mr. Paul, ACA *1984;* B E B C Distribution Unit 15, Albion Close Newtown Business Park, POOLE, DORSET, BH12 3LL.
HEWITT, Mr. Paul Edward, MSc BCom ACA *2007;* with Whittingham Riddell LLP, Belmont House, Shrewsbury Business Park, SHREWSBURY, SY2 6LG.
HEWITT, Mr. Paul William, BA ACA *1981;* Hough Hall, Newcastle Road, Hough, CREWE, CHESHIRE, CW2 5JG.
HEWITT, Mr. Peter Edward Karl, BSc ACA *1992;* 40 Harcourt Road, BRISTOL, BS6 7RE.
•**HEWITT, Mr. Peter John, FCA** *1955;* (Tax Fac), P.J. Hewitt & Co, Crown House, High Road, LOUGHTON, ESSEX, IG10 4LG.
HEWITT, Mr. Philip Arthur, FCA *1951;* 16 Hawthorne Close, Nether Poppleton, YORK, YO26 6HP. (Life Member)
HEWITT, Mr. Richard John, LLB ACA *2001;* 2903 Wheeler Street, BERKELEY, CA 94705, UNITED STATES.
HEWITT, Mr. Richard John, BSc ACA *1989;* Group Economic Research & Corporate Devlopment, Allianz SE, 8th Floor, 60 Gracechurch Street, LONDON, EC3V 0HR.
HEWITT, Mr. Richard Martin, BA ACA *1986;* Ricoh UK Limited 4 Rushmills, NORTHAMPTON, NN4 7YB.
HEWITT, Mr. Richard Paul, FCA *1967;* 2 Alfred Street, Stanwick, WELLINGBOROUGH, NORTHAMPTONSHIRE, NN9 6QT.
•①**HEWITT, Mr. Robert David, FCA** *1980;* Gibson Hewitt & Co, 5 Park Court, Pyrford Road, WEST BYFLEET, SURREY, KT14 6SD. See also Gibson Hewitt Outsourcing Ltd
HEWITT, Mr. Robert John, BA ACA *1995;* 21 TORESSIAN PLACE, CASHMERE, QLD 4500, AUSTRALIA.
•**HEWITT, Mr. Ronald Glyn, BSc FCA** *1979;* Glyn Hewitt, Network House, St Ives Way, Sandycroft, DEESIDE, CLWYD CH5 2QS.
HEWITT, Mrs. Rukmal, BSc ACA *1993;* Dunaree, 11 Southview Road, GERRARDS CROSS, SL9 8RG.
HEWITT, Miss. Sarah Ann, BA ACA *1986;* 160 Brompton Road, LONDON, SW3 1HW.
HEWITT, Mrs. Siara, BA ACA *2005;* 42 The Lane, LONDON, SE3 9SL.
HEWITT, Mr. Stephen Arnold, FCA *1978;* 7 Pine Road, MACCLESFIELD, CHESHIRE, SK10 1QD.
HEWITT, Mr. Stephen William, ACA *1980;* Clifton House Partnership, Clifton House, Four Elms Road, CARDIFF, CF24 1LE.
HEWITT, Mr. Steven James, BA(Hons) ACA *2001;* Kellynch, Habberley Road, BEWDLEY, WORCESTERSHIRE, DY12 1JA.
HEWITT, Ms. Susan Michele, BSc ACA *1993;* Kings School Hostel House, 5 College Green, WORCESTER, WR1 2LL.
HEWITT, Mr. Tom, FCA *1959;* Care of:, 44 Lanark Walk, MACCLESFIELD, CHESHIRE, SK10 3ES. (Life Member)
•**HEWITT-BOORMAN, Mr. Miles Roderick, BEng ACA** *1996;* Chantrey Vellacott DFK LLP, Russell Square House, 10-12 Russell Square, LONDON, WC1B 5LF.
•**HEWKIN, Mr. Michael Anthony, ACA** *1993;* G K Hewkin & Co Ltd, The Croft, Water End Lane, Beeston, KING'S LYNN, NORFOLK PE32 2NL.
HEWLETT, Mr. Anthony Michael, MA FCA *1970;* Camperdown, Sycamore Road, AMERSHAM, BUCKINGHAMSHIRE, HP6 6BB. (Life Member)
HEWLETT, Mr. Julian Alexander Parry, BSc ACA *1990;* The Vicarage, Reeth, RICHMOND, NORTH YORKSHIRE, DL11 6TR.
HEWLETT, Miss. Lindsay Anne, BSc ACA *2002;* 74 Awaba Street, MOSMAN, NSW 2088, AUSTRALIA.
•**HEWLETT, Mr. Mark John, MSc ACA** *2001;* Woodward Hale, 38 Dollar Street, CIRENCESTER, GL7 2AN. See also Woodward Hale Limited
HEWLETT, Miss. Suzanne Claire, BSc ACA *1997;* 12 Gainsborough Drive, ASCOT, SL5 8TB.
HEWLETT, Miss. Victoria Marie, ACA *2002;* 13 Pelham Close, BEMBRIDGE, ISLE OF WIGHT, PO35 5TS.
HEWS, Ms. Jayne Claire, BSc ACA *1993;* Springfield, 21 Andover Road North, WINCHESTER, SO22 6NW.
HEWSON, Mr. Andrew Nicholas, MA FCA CF *1984;* 27 Tregunter Road, LONDON, SW10 9LS.
HEWSON, Mrs. Auriol Karen, FCA DChA *1979;* 80 Woodhurst Avenue, ORPINGTON, KENT, BR5 1AT.
•**HEWSON, Mrs. Christine Deborah, BA ACA** *1993;* (Tax Fac), KPMG LLP, St. James's Square, MANCHESTER, M2 6DS. See also KPMG Europe LLP
HEWSON, Mr. Christopher Charles, BA ACA *2003;* Smiths Flour Mills, PO Box 3, WORKSOP, NOTTINGHAMSHIRE, S80 1QY.
HEWSON, Mr. Christopher Edward, BA(Hons) ACA *2001;* Flat 3, 114 Lower Richmond Road, Putney, LONDON, SW15 1LN.
HEWSON, Mr. Edmund Rothay Francis, MA ACA *1986;* BPP 6th floor Weston House, 246 High Holborn, LONDON, WC1V 7EX.
•**HEWSON, Mrs. Helen, BSc ACA** *1998;* with Ernst & Young LLP, 1 More London Place, LONDON, SE1 2AF.
•**HEWSON, Mr. Ian James, BA ACA** *1989;* (Tax Fac), Hewson and Howson, 8 Shepcote Office Village, Shepcote Lane, SHEFFIELD, S9 1TG.
HEWSON, Mr. James Peter, FCA *1959;* 1 Hurst Park, Kings Drive, MIDHURST, WEST SUSSEX, GU29 0BP. (Life Member)
HEWSON, Mr. Malcolm George, BSc FCA *1990;* 1 Camelia Street, TEA TREE GULLY, SA 5091, AUSTRALIA.
HEWSON, Mr. Mark David, ACA *1987;* 15 Longhirst Drive, Southfields, CRAMLINGTON, NE23 7XL.
•**HEWSON, Mr. Nigel David, FCA DChA** *1985;* (Tax Fac), Hewsons (UK) Limited, 80 Woodhurst Avenue, Petts Wood, ORPINGTON, KENT, BR5 1AT.
HEWSON, Mr. Richard Barry, ACA *1995;* 9 Sunnyridge Avenue, PUDSEY, LS28 7PN.
•**HEWSON, Mr. Richard Charles, FCA** *1972;* (Tax Fac), Richard Hewson & Co, 21 Corner Green, LONDON, SE3 9JJ.
•①**HEWSON, Mr. Timothy, BSc FCA** *1992;* Ashperton House, 51 Tuffley Avenue, GLOUCESTER, GL1 5LU.
HEWSTON, Mrs. Fiona Louise, BA ACA *1994;* 288 Penns Lane, SUTTON COLDFIELD, B76 1LG.
•**HEWSTON, Mr. Peter Karl, BA FCA** *1993;* Rochesters LLP, 3 Caroline Court, 13 Caroline Street, St Pauls Square, BIRMINGHAM, B3 1TR. See also Rochesters Audit Services Limited
HEXTALL, Mr. Richard Anthony, BSc ACA *1992;* Cokes Barn, Westburton, PULBOROUGH, WEST SUSSEX, RH20 1HD.
HEXTALL, Mrs. Siobhan Mary, BBS ACA *1993;* 73 Oatlands Avenue, WEYBRIDGE, SURREY, KT13 9TL.
HEXTALL, Mr. Steven John, BA FCA *1984;* with Ernst & Young LLP, 1 More London Place, LONDON, SE1 2AF.
•**HEXTALL, Mr. Timothy Charles, FCA** *1973;* Hextall Meakin Limited, Argon House, Argon Mews, LONDON, SW6 1BJ.
HEXTER, Mrs. Alison, BA ACA *1983;* Armada, 2 Henley Lodge, Yatton, BRISTOL, BS49 4JQ.
HEXTER, Mr. Derek Elsworthy, FCA *1958;* Brennels Mead, 40 Highweek Village, NEWTON ABBOT, TQ12 1QQ. (Life Member)
HEXTON, Mr. John Richard, FCA *1973;* 37 Menangle Road, CAMDEN, NSW 2570, AUSTRALIA.
HEY, Mr. Andrew David, MEng ACA *2001;* 1 Maybury Street, Tooting, LONDON, SW17 0SB.
HEY, Mr. Christopher John, FCA *1972;* 3 Applefields, Leyland, PRESTON, PR25 3AZ.
HEY, Mr. John Stephen Paul, MA ACA *1982;* 8 Hopping Lane, LONDON, N1 2NU.
HEY, Mrs. Tiffany Vivien, BSc ACA *1995;* 9 Fieldfare Court, Littleover, DERBY, DE23 3XX.
HEYBURN, Mr. Adam Michael, BA ACA *1992;* HSBC Bank Middle East Building, Level 5 Building 5, EMAAR Square, DUBAI, 502601, UNITED ARAB EMIRATES.
HEYBURN, Mrs. Judith Catherine, BA ACA *1994;* PO Box 282980, DUBAI, UNITED ARAB EMIRATES.
HEYCOCK, Mrs. Elizabeth Anne, BA ACA *1995;* 22 Abbey View Road, ST. ALBANS, HERTFORDSHIRE, AL3 4QL.
HEYCOCK, Mr. John Alistair Bissill, BCom ACA *1991;* 22Abbey View Road, ST ALBANS, HERTFORDSHIRE, al34ql.

•**HEYCOCK, Mr. Lee Treharne, BSc(Econ) ACA** *2001;* Nirius Consulting Limited, D5 Culham Science Centre, ABINGDON, OXFORDSHIRE, OX14 3DB.
HEYCOCK, Mrs. Wendy Louise, BSc ACA *2001;* Foxcombe Lodge, Sunningwell, ABINGDON, OXFORDSHIRE, OX13 6RD.
•**HEYDON, Mr. Douglas William, FCA** *1970;* Heydon & Co., 6 Templar Mews, Black Jack Street, CIRENCESTER, GLOUCESTERSHIRE, GL7 2AA.
HEYER, Ms. Rajinder, BSc ACA *1993;* The Royal Bank of Scotland, 280 Bishopsgate, 1st Floor, LONDON, EC2M 4RB.
HEYES, Mr. Courtney David, BA ACA *2006;* 64 Claughton Avenue, LEYLAND, PR25 5TL.
HEYES, Mr. Derek Allan, FCA *1958;* 6 Walk Mill, Dalston, CARLISLE, CA5 7QW. (Life Member)
HEYES, Mrs. Jacqeline Marie, BA ACA *2006;* 64 Claughton Avenue, LEYLAND, PR25 5TL.
HEYES, Mr. Mark Robert, LLB ACA *2002;* September Cottage Rue de Travers, Trinity, JERSEY, JE3 5TJ.
HEYES, Mr. Matthew Christopher, ACA *2008;* 15 Ash Road, Coppull, CHORLEY, LANCASHIRE, PR7 5BQ.
HEYES, Mr. Michael, BA(Hons) ACA *2001;* Little Biggin Farm, Sandway Road, Sandway, MAIDSTONE, ME17 2LU.
•**HEYES, Mr. Neil Martin, BSc FCA** *1999;* Rayner Essex LLP, Faulkner House, Victoria Street, ST. ALBANS, HERTFORDSHIRE, AL1 3SE.
HEYL, Ms. Odile Marie Paule, BA ACA *1993;* (Tax Fac), with Mazars LLP, Tower Bridge House, St. Katharines Way, LONDON, E1W 1DD.
HEYMAN, Mr. Richard William, BA FCA *1977;* Medbourne Manor, Manor Road, Medbourne, MARKET HARBOROUGH, LE16 8DU.
HEYMANN, Mr. Bernard, BA FCA *1969;* Voleseal & Co, 5 Ranulf Road, LONDON, NW2 2BT.
•**HEYMANN, Mr. Ronald, FCA** *1995;* Finer Heymann LLP, Premier House, 112 Station Road, EDGWARE, HA8 7BJ.
HEYN, Miss. Alexandra Beatrice, ACA *2008;* P K F Accountants & Business Advisors Farringdon Place, 20 Farringdon Road, LONDON, EC1M 3AP.
HEYNES, Mrs. Helen Jayne, ACA *1996;* 50 St. James Road, BRIDLINGTON, NORTH HUMBERSIDE, YO15 3PQ.
•**HEYNS, Mr. Herman Rene, ACA CA(SA)** *2009;* KPMG LLP, 15 Canada Square, LONDON, E14 5GL. See also KPMG Europe LLP
HEYS, Mr. Christopher Richard, MSc BEng ACA *2006;* with PricewaterhouseCoopers LLP, 1 Embankment Place, LONDON, WC2N 6RH.
HEYS, Mrs. Emma, ACA *2008;* 327 Crewe Road, Willaston, NANTWICH, CHESHIRE, CW5 6NP.
•**HEYS, Mr. Ernest, FCA** *1957;* E Heys & Co., 229 Coppull Moor Lane, Coppull, CHORLEY, PR7 5JA.
HEYWARD SAUNDERS, Mrs. Nichola Louise, BA ACA *2002;* 92 Park Rise, HARPENDEN, HERTFORDSHIRE, AL5 3AN.
•**HEYWOOD, Mr. Alan, FCA** *1979;* Alan Heywood & Co, 78 Mill Lane, West Hampstead, LONDON, NW6 1JZ.
•**HEYWOOD, Mr. Alan Reginald, FCA** *1959;* A.R.Heywood, 36 West View Road, SUTTON COLDFIELD, B75 6AY.
HEYWOOD, Mrs. Angela, BA(Hons) ACA *2001;* 1 Chadbury Close, Lostock, BOLTON, BL6 4JA.
HEYWOOD, Miss. Annabel Jane Louise, ACA *1986;* 14 Trinity Street, OXFORD, OX1 1TN.
HEYWOOD, Mr. Anthony George, FCA *1972;* Harborough Hall, Harborough Hall Lane, Messing, COLCHESTER, CO5 9UA.
HEYWOOD, Mr. David Michael, BSc FCA *1976;* High Gable, Denholmegate Road, Hipperholme, HALIFAX, HX3 8HX.
HEYWOOD, Mr. David Paul, BSc ACA *1993;* Medlar Cottage, Eastbury Manor Court, Lower Broadheath, WORCESTER, WR2 6PB.
HEYWOOD, Mr. Derek Hardman, FCA *1966;* 181 Bolton Road, ROCHDALE, OL11 3LR.
HEYWOOD, Mr. Frederick Alan, FCA *1951;* Beechway, Crewkerne Road, Raymonds Hill, AXMINSTER, EX13 5TE. (Life Member)
•**HEYWOOD, Mr. Gary Anthony, BA ACA** *1989;* H W, Sterling House, 5 Buckingham Place, Bellfield Rd West, HIGH WYCOMBE, HP13 5HQ. See also Westernshare Limited and Haines Watts
HEYWOOD, Mr. Geoffrey Roger, FCA *1964;* (Tax Fac), 195 Rue Du Faubourg, St Honore, 75008 PARIS, FRANCE.
HEYWOOD, Mrs. Helen Faith, BSc ACA *1993;* 18 Sandford Crescent, CREWE, CW2 5GJ.
•**HEYWOOD, Mr. James Andrew, BSc ACA PGCE** *2005;* 20 Little Fryth, Finchampstead, WOKINGHAM, BERKSHIRE, RG40 3RN.
HEYWOOD, Miss. Jane Rosemary, ACA *1994;* 57 Lucas Street, Deptford, LONDON, SE8 4QH.
HEYWOOD, Mr. Jason Peter, BA(Hons) ACA *2009;* 44 Monks Lode, DIDCOT, OXFORDSHIRE, OX11 7UY.
HEYWOOD, Mr. John Kenneth, LLB FCA *1972;* 55 Marloes Road, LONDON, W8 6LA.
HEYWOOD, Mr. John Malcolm, FCA *1958;* Linden Cottage, Paper Mill Lane, Standon, WARE, HERTFORDSHIRE, SG11 1LD.
HEYWOOD, Mrs. Lynda Jane, BA ACA MCT *1989;* Glebe Cottage, Tunworth Road, Mapledurwell, BASINGSTOKE, RG25 2LU.
•**HEYWOOD, Mr. Matthew Cleveland, BA FCA** *1989;* with PricewaterhouseCoopers, 9 Greyfriars Road, READING, RG1 1JG.
HEYWOOD, Mr. Michael Walter, FCA *1961;* 5b March Way, Battlefield Enterprise Park, SHREWSBURY, SY1 3JE.
•**HEYWOOD, Mr. Paul Malcolm Peter, BA FCA ATII** *1996;* (Tax Fac), Knight Wheeler Limited, 54 Sun Street, WALTHAM ABBEY, ESSEX, EN9 1EJ.
HEYWOOD, Mr. Philip Joseph, BSc ACA *1993;* 39 Fowley Common Lane, Glazebury, WARRINGTON, WA3 5JJ.
HEYWOOD, Mr. Philip Steven, BA(Hons) ACA *2002;* with PricewaterhouseCoopers LLP, 300 Madison Avenue, NEW YORK, NY 10017, UNITED STATES.
HEYWOOD, Miss. Stephanie, BSc ACA *2011;* 19 White Horse Close, Hockliffe, LEIGHTON BUZZARD, BEDFORDSHIRE, LU7 9LT.
HEYWOOD, Mr. Stephen Dene, LLB FCA *1993;* Oakside Cottage Norwich Road, Hethersett, NORWICH, NR9 3DE.
HEYWOOD, Mr. Stephen Guy, BSc(Hons) ACA *2002;* 2994 Nuha Street, BALDWINSVILLE, NY 13027, UNITED STATES.
•**HEYWOOD, Mr. Steven Paul, BA ACA** *1996;* KPMG LLP, St. James's Square, MANCHESTER, M2 6DS. See also KPMG Europe LLP
HEYWOOD, Mr. Thomas Edward, FCA JDipMA *1952;* 1 Churncote, Stirchley, TELFORD, SHROPSHIRE, TF3 1YH. (Life Member)
HEYWOOD, Miss. Vanessa Louise, BA ACA *2000;* IIR Middle East Office 320, Sultan business centre, DUBAI, PO 21743, UNITED ARAB EMIRATES.
HEYWOOD-LONSDALE, Mr. Thomas Norman, FCA *1977;* The Barn, Mount Farm, Junction Road, Churchill, CHIPPING NORTON, OXFORDSHIRE OX7 6NP.
HEYWOOD-WADDINGTON, Mr. Nicholas Roger, BA ACA *1985;* White & Case Llp, 5 Old Broad Street, LONDON, EC2N 1DW.
HEYWORTH, Mr. Christopher John, BA ACA *1979;* 80 Richmond Terrace, Richmond, MELBOURNE, VIC 3121, AUSTRALIA.
HEYWORTH, Mr. Christopher Stephen, BSc ACA *2007;* 7 Barn Meadow, Staplehurst, TONBRIDGE, TN12 0SY.
HEYWORTH, Mr. Michael Collinge, FCA *1958;* Bier Bridge, Bolton by Bowland, CLITHEROE, LANCASHIRE, BB7 4NL. (Life Member)
HEYWORTH, Mr. Roger Lingard, FCA *1962;* 1 Bankhall Lane, Hale, ALTRINCHAM, WA15 0LA. (Life Member)
HEYWORTH, Mr. Stephen, BSc ACA *1978;* West L B Woolgate Exchange, 25 Basinghall Street, LONDON, EC2V 5HA.
HEYWORTH-DUNNE, Miss. Annabel, MA ACA *1998;* Hill House, Pitt Street, Southrepps, NORWICH, NR11 8UX.
HIAN-CHEONG, Mr. Jean-Jacques Kong Main, ACA *1981;* 3198 Orlando Drive, MISSISSAUGA L4V 1R5, ON, CANADA.
HIATT, Mr. Paul Andrew Charles, BSc ACA *1997;* 9 Glenridding Close, Gamston, NOTTINGHAM, NG2 6RU.
HIBBARD, Miss. Laura Clare, ACA *2009;* 8 Cote Lea Park, BRISTOL, BS9 4AQ.
HIBBARD, Mr. Matthew Lee, BA(Hons) ACA *2001;* 67 Everard Avenue, SHEFFIELD, S17 4LY.
HIBBERD, Mrs. Catherine Mary, BA ACA *1993;* 23 Voltaire Road, Clapham, LONDON, SW4 6DF.
HIBBERD, Mr. Gary Michael, BA(Hons) ACA *2010;* 11 Meadowcroft Rise, Westfield, SHEFFIELD, S20 8EP.
HIBBERD, Mr. Richard Maurice, MBA BSc FCA ATII *1979;* 48 Brian Avenue, SOUTH CROYDON, SURREY, CR2 9NE.
HIBBERD, Mr. Stephen Loxley, FCA *1963;* 7 Tarragon Close, Walnut Tree, MILTON KEYNES, MK7 7AT.
HIBBERT, Mr. Andrew William, BSc ACA ATII *1992;* Swale Cottage, Uplees Road, Oare, FAVERSHAM, KENT, ME13 0QU.
HIBBERT, Mrs. Anne, BA ACA *1987;* Styles & Wood Aspect House, Manchester Road West Timperley, ALTRINCHAM, CHESHIRE, WA14 5PG.
HIBBERT, Mr. Anthony, BA ACA *1987;* Winterstoke, Durweston, BLANDFORD FORUM, DORSET, DT11 0QA.
HIBBERT, Mrs. Diane, MBA BSc ACA *1979;* 54 Manor Grove, WORKSOP, NOTTINGHAMSHIRE, S80 3QU.
HIBBERT, Miss. Elizabeth Anne, LLB ACA *1986;* (Tax Fac), Trowers & Hamlins Sceptre Court, 40 Tower Hill, LONDON, EC3N 4DX.
HIBBERT, Mr. Harold, FCA *1957;* 39 Winchester Drive, NEWCASTLE, ST5 3JH. (Life Member)
HIBBERT, Mr. James Lambert Roger, FCA *1957;* 76 Marple Road, STOCKPORT, SK2 5QH. (Life Member)
HIBBERT, Mr. Jeremy Charles, ACA *1981;* 54 Manor Grove, WORKSOP, NOTTINGHAMSHIRE, S80 3QU.
HIBBERT, Mrs. Joanne Elisabeth, BSc ACA *1994;* 26 Wild Duck Road, WYCKOFF, NJ 07481, UNITED STATES.
•**HIBBERT, Mr. John Benjamin, BA FCA** *1987;* Marshall Smalley Accountants Limited, Unit 15, Carlton Business Centre, Station Road, NOTTINGHAM, NG4 3AA.
HIBBERT, Mrs. Karen Elizabeth, BA ACA *1993;* Malcolm Jones & Co West Hill House, Allerton Hill Chapel Allerton, LEEDS, LS7 3QB.
HIBBERT, Miss. Katherine Laura, MA MLitt ACA *1992;* Ground Floor Flat, 31 Tremlett Grove, LONDON, N19 5JY.
HIBBERT, Mr. Martin James, BA ACA *1992;* 3 Butterwick Grove, Wynyard Woods, BILLINGHAM, TS22 5RX.
HIBBERT, Mr. Matthew, BSc ACA *1993;* with Morgan Sindall Group plc, Kent House, 14-17 Market Place, LONDON, W1W 8AJ.
HIBBERT, Mr. Michael Anthony, BSc FCA *1982;* 41 Hillwood Avenue, Monkspath Shirley, SOLIHULL, B90 4XR.
HIBBERT, Mr. Nicholas James, ACA *2007;* 51 Frith View, Chapel-en-le-Frith, HIGH PEAK, DERBYSHIRE, SK23 9TT.
HIBBERT, Mrs. Pamela Mary, FCA *1966;* 19 Hammonds Green, Totton, SOUTHAMPTON, SO40 3HU.
HIBBERT, Mr. Philip Graham, BSc ACA *1994;* 26 Wild Duck Road, WYCKOFF, NJ 07481, UNITED STATES.
HIBBERT, Mr. Robert John, BEng ACA *1990;* with KPMG LLP, 15 Canada Square, LONDON, E14 5GL.
HIBBERT, Mr. Thomas Walsh, FCA *1960;* 2 Beech Close, MILNTHORPE, LA7 7RL.
•**HIBBERT, Mr. Timothy Neil, FCA** *1974;* Hibbert & Co., 480a Roundhay Road, LEEDS, LS8 2HU.
HIBBERT, Mr. William, FCA *1958;* 20 Darwen Road, Bromley Cross, BOLTON, BL7 9AA. (Life Member)
HIBBINS, Mr. Paul Henry, FCA *1965;* c/ Buenos Aires 39, Sotogrande, 11310 CADIZ, SPAIN. (Life Member)
•**HIBBIT, Mr. Michael Oliver Douglas, FCA** *1976;* (Tax Fac), Hibbit & Partners, The Tithe Barn, Lillington, SHERBORNE, DORSET, DT9 6QX.
HIBBITT, Dr. Christopher James, BA(Hons) FCA *1986;* Moulin d'Haljoux, 5590 CINEY, BELGIUM.
HIBBITT, Mr. Peter Stephen, BSc FCA *1975;* (Tax Fac), with Baker Tilly UK Audit LLP, 25 Farringdon Street, LONDON, EC4A 4AB.
HIBBITT, Mr. Raymond Arthur, FCA *1955;* Copthorne, Vicarage Lane, Water Orton, BIRMINGHAM, B46 1RX. (Life Member)
HIBBS, Miss. Caroline Rosemary, BA ACA *1991;* 88A Offord Road, Islington, LONDON, N1 1PF.
•**HIBBS, Mr. Christopher David, BSc FCA** *1993;* PricewaterhouseCoopers LLP, Donington Court, Pegasus Business Park, Castle Donington, DERBY, DE74 2UZ. See also PricewaterhouseCoopers
HIBBS, Mr. Francis James, FCA *1969;* 26 High Street, NORTH FERRIBY, HU14 3ER.
HIBBS, Mr. Jonathan Michael, MA ACA *1980;* 183 boulevard de la République, 92210 SAINT CLOUD, FRANCE.
HIBBS, Mr. Simon Charles, MA ACA *1983;* Newmarket Promotions Ltd., McMillan House, Cheam Common Road, WORCESTER PARK, KT4 8RQ.
HICHENS, Mr. James Edward, BSc ACA CF *2003;* with Grant Thornton UK LLP, 1 Whitehall Riverside, Whitehall Road, LEEDS, WEST YORKSHIRE, LS1 4BN.
HICK, Mr. Anthony Walter Sampson, FCA *1952;* 228 Staplegrove Road, TAUNTON, TA2 6AL. (Life Member)
HICK, Mr. David Anthony, LLB ACA *1983;* 1095 Avenue of the Americas, NEW YORK, NY 10036, UNITED STATES.
HICK, Mr. Ian Richard, BSc ACA *1988;* 18 Marvejols Park, COCKERMOUTH, CUMBRIA, CA13 0QR.
HICK, Mr. Karl Stephen, BSc ACA *1986;* Tricklebank, Uffington Road, STAMFORD, LINCOLNSHIRE, PE9 3AA.
HICK, Mr. Michael Andrew, BA ACA *1987;* 133 Milton Road, Hanwell, LONDON, W7 1LG.
•**HICKERTON, Mrs. Gwendoline Glenis, BSc FCA** *1992;* Aston Hughes & Co, Livingstone House, Llewelyn Avenue, LLANDUDNO, CONWY, LL30 2ER.
HICKEY, Mr. Barry, ACA *2002;* 11 Danbury Road, RAYLEIGH, ESSEX, SS6 9BQ.
HICKEY, Ms. Catherine Mary Bernedette, BA ACA *1993;* 32 The Water Gardens De Havilland Drive, Hazlemere, HIGH WYCOMBE, BUCKINGHAMSHIRE, HP15 7FN.
HICKEY, Mr. Damian Joseph, BSc FCA *1987;* Thermo Fisher Scientific, 275 Aiken Rd, ASHEVILLE, NC 28804, UNITED STATES.
HICKEY, Mr. David James, BSc ACA *2003;* Flat 11 Stockholm Apartments, 86 Chalk Farm Road, LONDON, NW1 8AR.
HICKEY, Mr. James Arthur, FCA *1955;* 3 Littlecourt Road, SEVENOAKS, KENT, TN13 2JG. (Life Member)
HICKEY, Mr. James Philip, MA BSc ACA *1999;* 21 Quaggy Walk, Blackheath, LONDON, SE3 9EJ.
HICKEY, Mrs. Jane Elizabeth, MA FCA *1983;* 4 Cambridge Road, Wimbledon, LONDON, SW20 0SH.
HICKEY, Mr. John Patrick, ACA CTA *1991;* Serco Group Plc Serco House, 16 Bartley Wood Business Park Bartley Way, HOOK, HAMPSHIRE, RG27 9UY.
HICKEY, Mrs. Julia Edwina Anne, BSc ACA *1987;* Beech Hollow, Wingrove, ROWLANDS GILL, NE39 1DT.
•**HICKEY, Mr. Loughlin Gerrard, FCA** *1980;* (Tax Fac), KPMG LLP, 15 Canada Square, LONDON, E14 5GL. See also KPMG Europe LLP
HICKEY, Mr. Patrick Matthew, FCA *1968;* 78 Constantine Road, LONDON, NW3 2LX. (Life Member)
HICKEY, Mr. Peter James, BSc ACA *1991;* 64 Beechwood Road, Sanderstead, SOUTH CROYDON, SURREY, CR2 0AA.
HICKEY, Mr. Raymond Augustine, FCA FCPA *2000;* 26 Ringwood Close, CRAWLEY, RH10 6HH.
HICKEY, Mr. Roy Stephen, BA FCA *1975;* Springfield House, Old Stone Trough Lane, Kelbrook, COLNE, BB18 6LW.
HICKEY, Ms. Susan, ACA CA(NZ) *2010;* 96 Sandy Lane, TEDDINGTON, MIDDLESEX, TW11 0DF.
HICKEY-FRY, Mr. John Roncalli, BSc ACA *1989;* 33 Handsworth Road, BLACKPOOL, FY1 2RQ.
HICKFORD, Mr. Adrian Earle, BSc ACA *2010;* 17 Dexta Way, NORTHALLERTON, NORTH YORKSHIRE, DL7 8EY.
HICKFORD, Mr. Brian Leslie, FCA *1963;* 42 Guthlaxton Avenue, LUTTERWORTH, LE17 4ET. (Life Member)
HICKIE, Mr. Adam James Saddler, ACA CTA *2008;* Lucraft Hodgson & Dawes, 2 Ash Lane Rustington, LITTLEHAMPTON, WEST SUSSEX, BN16 3BZ.
•**HICKIE, Mr. Allan Robert, BSc ACA** *2003;* UHY Kent LLP, Thames House, Roman Square, SITTINGBOURNE, KENT, ME10 4BJ.
HICKIE, Mr. Paul Daniel, MA FCA *1969;* 47 Berkeley Court, Wilmington Square, EASTBOURNE, EAST SUSSEX, BN21 4DX. (Life Member)
•**HICKIE, Mr. Richard Ashley, FCA** *1969;* Hodgson Hickie, Unit 4, Dovedale Studios, 465 Battersea Park Road, LONDON, SW11 4LR. See also H F D Professional Services Ltd
•**HICKIN, Mr. David Edward, ACA** *1965;* DEH Accounting Ltd, Charnwood, Berry Hall Road, Barton Turf, NORWICH, NR12 8BE.
HICKINBOTHAM, Mr. Richard, BSc ACA *1984;* 39 Pemberton Road, EAST MOLESEY, SURREY, KT8 9LG.
HICKINBOTTOM, Miss. Fiona Elizabeth, ACA *2011;* 21 Harberrow Close, Hagley, STOURBRIDGE, WEST MIDLANDS, DY9 0PJ.
HICKING, Mr. Robin, BSc ACA *2003;* Speedo International Ltd Speedo House Unit, 6 Enterprise Way, NOTTINGHAM, NG2 1EN.
HICKINSON, Mr. Neil Trevor, BA ACA *1979;* 2 The Chantry, Fulbourn, CAMBRIDGE, CB21 5EJ.
•**HICKLAND, Mr. Michael Roger, BA FCA AMCT** *1986;* 51 Lower Canes, YATELEY, HAMPSHIRE, GU46 6PY.
HICKLIN, Mr. Robert James, BA ACA *1993;* 4 Breckhill Road, Woodthorpe, NOTTINGHAM, NG5 4GP.
HICKLING, Mr. Barry, BA(Hons) FCA *1955;* 23 Moorgreen, Newthorpe, NOTTINGHAM, NG16 2FD. (Life Member)
•**HICKLING, Mr. Nicholas John, BSc FCA** *1990;* Sampson West, 34 Ely Place, LONDON, EC1N 6TD. See also Cowbridge Investments Limited

HICKLING, Mr. William Robert, BSc ACA *1981;* 25 Well Close, Leigh, TONBRIDGE, KENT, TN11 8RQ.
HICKMAN, Mr. Andrew Vivian, BSc ACA *1990;* Lobatse Clay Works Pty Ltd, Private Bag 5, LOBATSE, BOTSWANA.
HICKMAN, Mr. Anthony Charles James, BSc ACA *1979;* 27 Horncastle Road, LOUTH, LN11 9LH.
HICKMAN, Mr. Gary John, BA FCA *1996;* with PricewaterhouseCoopers LLP, 1 Embankment Place, LONDON, WC2N 6RH.
HICKMAN, Mr. Hugh Walter, FCA *1966;* The Stables, Leithen Road, Innerleithen, EDINBURGH, EH44 6NH. (Life Member)
HICKMAN, Mr. Ian Douglas, BSc FCA *1994;* 43 Old Farm Drive, Codsall, WOLVERHAMPTON, WV8 1GF.
HICKMAN, Ms. Janet, BSc ACA *1991;* Wyngates, Ivy Lane, Great Brickhill, MILTON KEYNES, MK17 9AH.
HICKMAN, Mrs. Joanne, BA ACA *1997;* Holly Cottage, Oakshade Road, Oxshott, LEATHERHEAD, SURREY, KT22 0LE.
HICKMAN, Mr. John Andrew, ACA *2001;* 2 Portsdown Road, HALESOWEN, B63 1HE.
HICKMAN, Mr. John Geraint William, BA ACA *1984;* Douglas House, Mynydd Llandygai, BANGOR, GWYNEDD, LL57 4LQ.
HICKMAN, Miss. Leanne Sharon, ACA *2004;* 9 Horseshoes Lane, Benson, WALLINGFORD, OXFORDSHIRE, OX10 6LB.
HICKMAN, Mr. Michael William, FCA *1964;* Kibagare, 63 Third Avenue, FRINTON-ON-SEA, CO13 9EF.
HICKMAN, Mr. Neil James, BSc FCA *1996;* with Bourne & Co, 6 Lichfield Street, BURTON-ON-TRENT, DE14 3RD.
HICKMAN, Mr. Nicholas, BSc ACA *1998;* U B S AG, 100 Liverpool Street, LONDON, EC2M 2RH.
HICKMAN, Mr. Paul Andrew, MA ACA *1979;* K B C Peel Hunt, 111 Old Broad Street, LONDON, EC2N 1PH.
HICKMAN, Mr. Peter David, BA ACA *1989;* Linklaters, 1 Silk Street, LONDON, EC2Y 8HQ.
HICKMAN, Mr. Peter David, BSc ACA *2002;* with Forrester Boyd, Waynflete House, 139 Eastgate, LOUTH, LN11 9QQ.
HICKMAN, Miss. Rebecca Laura, ACA *2011;* 79 Caraway Drive, Branston, BURTON-ON-TRENT, STAFFORDSHIRE, DE14 3FQ.
HICKMAN, Mr. Rodney, FCA *1963;* 31 Hallamgate Road, SHEFFIELD, S10 5BS. (Life Member)
•HICKMAN, Mr. Rupert Jonathan, BCom ACA *1993;* Flat 82 Belvedere Court, Upper Richmond Road, Putney, LONDON, SW15 6HZ.
HICKMAN, Mrs. Tracy Alexis, LLB ACA *2003;* 2 Portsdown Road, HALESOWEN, B63 1HE.
HICKOX, Mr. Alan John, BA FCA *1973;* 1 Duffield Lane, Woodmancote, EMSWORTH, HAMPSHIRE, PO10 8PZ.
•HICKS, Mr. Adrian Lindsay Spencer, FCA *1974;* (Tax Fac), Hicks Randles Limited, 100 High Street, MOLD, CLWYD, CH7 1BH.
HICKS, Mr. Alexander William, FCA *1960;* 24 Trinity Mews, BURY ST.EDMUNDS, IP33 3AT. (Life Member)
•HICKS, Mr. Alun George, BSc FCA *1974;* Alun G Hicks, Westways, Tintagel Road, Finchampstead, WOKINGHAM, RG40 3JJ.
HICKS, Mr. Andrew Miles, BA ACA *1989;* Ramtech Electronics Ltd, Abbeyfield Road, NOTTINGHAM, NG7 2SZ.
HICKS, Mr. Andrew William, BA(Hons) ACA *2000;* 1636 Meyerwood Circle, HIGHLANDS RANCH, CO 80129, UNITED STATES.
HICKS, Mrs. Anna, BA ACA *2004;* 42 Cranes Park Avenue, SURBITON, KT5 8BP.
HICKS, Mr. Brian, BSc FCA *1976;* Hammondswick House, Hammondswick, HARPENDEN, AL5 2NR. (Life Member)
HICKS, Mrs. Catherine Margaret, BSc ACA *1985;* 53 Hillfield Road, Oundle, PETERBOROUGH, PE8 4QR.
HICKS, Mr. Christopher, ACA *2011;* Flat 6, 10 Albert Road, TONBRIDGE, TN9 2SR.
HICKS, Mr. Christopher, BA ACA *2006;* with Deloitte LLP, 1 Woodborough Road, NOTTINGHAM, NG1 3FG.
HICKS, Mr. Christopher James, FCA *1975;* 550 Pipeline Road, GRAFTON K0K 2G0, ON, CANADA.
•HICKS, Mr. Christopher Lewis, BA FCA DChA *1991;* Francis Clark LLP, Sigma House, Oak View Close, Edginswell Park, TORQUAY, TQ2 7FF.
HICKS, Mr. Christopher Michael, BSc ACA *1982;* Lower Bowden Manor Bowden Green, Pangbourne, READING, RG8 8JL.
HICKS, Mrs. Claire Elizabeth, ACA *1992;* with Grant Thornton UK LLP, Grant Thornton House, Kettering Parkway, Kettering Venture Park, KETTERING, NORTHAMPTONSHIRE NN15 6XR.
HICKS, Mr. Colin John, BA FCA *1960;* 14 Rollswood Drive, SOLIHULL, WEST MIDLANDS, B91 1NL. (Life Member)
•HICKS, Mr. Daniel Giles, BA ACA *2002;* Hicks Randles Limited, 100 High Street, MOLD, CLWYD, CH7 1BH.
•HICKS, Mr. David Nigel, BA ACA *1999;* KPMG LLP, 15 Canada Square, LONDON, E14 5GL. See also KPMG Europe LLP
•HICKS, Mrs. Dione Renate, MSc BSc ACA *2004;* D.R. Hicks, 107 Penn Hill Road, Weston, BATH, BA1 3RU.
•HICKS, Mr. Geoffrey Kenneth, FCA DChA *1975;* (Tax Fac), Wood Hicks & Co, Units 1-2 Warrior Court, 9-11 Mumby Road, GOSPORT, HAMPSHIRE, PO12 1BS.
HICKS, Mr. Gwyn David, BSc ACA *1997;* 12, George Lane, MARLBOROUGH, WILTSHIRE, SN8 4BX.
HICKS, Mr. Harry Stephen, MA ACA CTA *1990;* Anderson & Pennington, 44a Floral Street, LONDON, WC2E 9DA.
HICKS, Miss. Heather, BCom ACA *2002;* KPMG, Level 3 100 Melville Street, HOBART, TAS 7000, AUSTRALIA.
HICKS, Mr. Ian Martin, BCom ACA CTA *2003;* 29 Baskeyfield Close, LICHFIELD, STAFFORDSHIRE, WS14 9YT.
HICKS, Dr. James Robert, DPhil ACA *1986;* 26 Maurice Road, Milton, SOUTHSEA, PO4 8HH.
HICKS, Mrs. Janette Karen, BA ACA *1991;* Rivermead House, 7 Lewis Court Thorpe Way, ENDERBY, LE19 1SU.
HICKS, Mr. Jeremy David, MA ACA *1979;* 49 Worple Road, LONDON, SW19 4LA.
HICKS, Mr. John Cedric, FCA *1955;* 47 Penfold Way, STEYNING, BN44 3PG. (Life Member)
•HICKS, Mr. John Keith, FCA *1974;* John K Hicks & Co, 81 Penn Place, Northway, RICKMANSWORTH, HERTFORDSHIRE, WD3 1QG.
HICKS, Mr. John Mitchell, FCA *1966;* GPO Box 4507, AUCKLAND 1140, NEW ZEALAND.
HICKS, Miss. Katy Lynne, BSc ACA *2006;* 16 Highdown Avenue, Poundbury, DORCHESTER, DORSET, DT1 3WF.
HICKS, Miss. Kerstin, BA ACA *2005;* 1 Myrtle Road, DORKING, SURREY, RH4 1DQ.
HICKS, Mrs. Kirsty Louise, ACA *2006;* Ainsdale, The Goggs, WATLINGTON, OXFORDSHIRE, OX49 5JX.
HICKS, Miss. Laura Joanne, ACA *2002;* 40 Nelson Street, Brightlingsea, COLCHESTER, CO7 0DZ.
HICKS, Dr. Martina, PhD BSc ACA *2011;* 56 Downs Park East, Westbury Park, BRISTOL, BS6 7QE.
•HICKS, Mr. Michael Edward, BSc FCA DChA *1985;* Crowe Clark Whitehill LLP, St Bride's House, 10 Salisbury Square, LONDON, EC4Y 8EH. See also Horwath Clark Whitehill LLP and Crowe Clark Whitehill
HICKS, Mr. Michael John, FCA *1972;* Hollybush House, 87 Cranbourne Drive, Otterbourne, WINCHESTER, HAMPSHIRE, SO21 2ES.
HICKS, Mr. Michael Paul, ACA *1985;* Respirex Int. Ltd, Unit F, Kingsfield Business Centre, Philanthropic Road, REDHILL, SURREY RH1 4DP.
HICKS, Mr. Michael Udale, FCA *1973;* Schenker Ltd, Schenker House, Great South West Road, FELTHAM, MIDDLESEX, TW14 8NT.
HICKS, Mr. Neil Francis, FCA *1968;* with Wenn Townsend, 30 St Giles', OXFORD, OX1 3LE.
HICKS, Mr. Nicholas Dugald, BCom ACA *1999;* 113 Bramfield Road, LONDON, SW11 6PZ.
HICKS, Mr. Nigel David, BA ACA *1997;* DHL Supply Chain, Solstice House, 251 Midsummer Boulevard, MILTON KEYNES, MK9 1EQ.
HICKS, Mr. Nigel David Moreton, BSc ACA *1987;* Homelands, Pharisee Green, DUNMOW, ESSEX, CM6 1JN.
HICKS, Mr. Philip Christopher, BSc ACA *1982;* 24 Pottersfield, ST. ALBANS, AL3 6LJ.
HICKS, Mrs. Rachael, BSc(Hons) ACA CTA *2003;* 29 Baskeyfield Close, LICHFIELD, STAFFORDSHIRE, WS14 9YT.
•HICKS, Mr. Richard James, BA ACA *1992;* Flat 4 Grosvenor Court, 8 Parsonage Road, STOCKPORT, SK4 4JZ.
HICKS, Mr. Roland Douglas, FCA *1957;* 75 Peterborough Road, Fulham, LONDON, SW6 3BT. (Life Member)
HICKS, Mrs. Sally Anne, BSc ACA *1991;* Park Dale, Powdermill Lane, BATTLE, EAST SUSSEX, TN33 0SP.
HICKS, Dr. Stuart, ACA *2009;* 790 Emory Valley Road, Apartment 212, OAK RIDGE, TN 37830, UNITED STATES.
HICKS, Miss. Susan Ann, BSc ACA *1984;* with Lovewell Blake LLP, The Gables, Old Market Street, THETFORD, NORFOLK, IP24 2EN.
HICKS, Mr. Timothy Mark, BSc FCA *1986;* Flat 25, 4a Rue de L'Ouest, L2273 LUXEMBOURG, LUXEMBOURG.
HICKS, Mr. Will John, MEng ACA *2005;* 42 Cranes Park Avenue, SURBITON, KT5 8BP.
HICKS, Mr. William Beverley, BSc ACA *1989;* 52 Beaconsfield Road, LONDON, SE3 7LG.
HICKSON, Mr. Andrew James, BA ACA *1992;* 121 Gainsborough Road, WARRINGTON, WA4 6BW.
HICKSON, Mr. Andrew Richard, LLB ACA *2006;* 19 Daleview Road, NOTTINGHAM, NG3 7AJ.
•HICKSON, Mr. Anthony, FCA CTA *1977;* AP Smith Atkins and Co, 18 Tewkesbury Close, MIDDLEWICH, CHESHIRE, CW10 9HT.
HICKSON, Mr. Brian Christopher, BSc FCA *1985;* Westbrook House, Vale View Drive, Beech Hill, READING, RG7 2BD.
HICKSON, Miss. Catherine, BSc ACA *2011;* 7 Gloucester Court, Lovelace Gardens, SURBITON, KT6 6SB.
HICKSON, Mr. Derek Arthur Leslie, FCA *1953;* 4 Brettingham Gate, Broome Manor, SWINDON, SN3 1NH. (Life Member)
HICKSON, Mr. Ian Stephen, FCA *1971;* 337 route de la Petite Balme, 74330 SILLINGY, FRANCE.
•HICKSON, Mrs. Miriam Rosemond, FCA CTA *1990;* Jacob Cavenagh & Skeet, 5 Robin Hood Lane, SUTTON, SURREY, SM1 2SW.
•HICKSON, Mr. Paul Ronald, FCA *1976;* Menzies LLP, 3rd Floor Kings House, 12-42 Wood Street, KINGSTON UPON THAMES, SURREY, KT1 1TG.
HICKSON, Mr. Peter Charles Fletcher, MA FCA *1970;* 12 Crescent Road, Wimbledon, LONDON, SW20 8EX.
HICKSON, Mr. Peter John, BA FCA *1989;* 5 Winterstoke Way, RAMSGATE, CT11 8AG.
HICKSON, Mr. Robin Lister, MA FCA *1984;* West Winds, 23 Meadowbrook, OXTED, RH8 9LT.
HICKSON, Mr. Timothy John, BA ACA *1979;* Tatty Devine, 7 Gibraltar Walk, LONDON, E2 7LH.
HICKSON, Mr. William Fletcher, MA ACA *1991;* 8 Sandy Hill Terrace, WESTPORT, CT 06880, UNITED STATES.
HIDAKA, Mr. Hiromasa, MA ACA *2003;* 4 Penner Close, LONDON, SW19 6QA.
HIDAYAT, Mr. Nugraha, ACA CA(AUS) *2008;* (Tax Fac), Flat 9 Tockwith Court, Bayham Road, SEVENOAKS, TN13 3XQ.
•HIDDLESTON, Miss. Kathryn Vivienne, BSc FCA *1987;* (Tax Fac), Grant Thornton UK LLP, Grant Thornton House, 22 Melton Street, Euston Square, LONDON, NW1 2EP. See also Grant Thornton LLP
HIDE, Mr. Stephen David, BSc ACA *1995;* 15 Goldney Road, CAMBERLEY, SURREY, GU15 1EZ.
HIDOVIC-ROWE, Dr. Dzena, PhD ACA *2011;* 131 Shenley Fields Road, BIRMINGHAM, B29 5BB.
HIDSON, Mrs. Susan Clare, BA ACA *1989;* (Tax Fac), Horwath Clark Whitehill Llp, 10 Palace Avenue, MAIDSTONE, ME15 6NF.
HIEB, Miss. Elvira, BA ACA *2007;* Weinbergstr. 97, 8006 ZURICH, SWITZERLAND.
HIERNAUX, Mr. James Matthew, BA ACA *2010;* Varsovia 65 Atico 1ª, 08041 BARCELONA, SPAIN.
HIEW, Mr. Kim Loong, ACA *2008;* 12-22-3 Bukit OUG Condominium, Jalan 3A/155 OUG, 58200 KUALA LUMPUR, FEDERAL TERRITORY, MALAYSIA.
HIEW, Mr. See Keong, BA ACA *1985;* S K Hiew & Associates, Locked Bag 117, 88993 KOTA KINABALU, SABAH, MALAYSIA.
HIEW, Mr. Seng, ACA *1980;* No. 559 2nd Floor Jalan Hishamuddin, 43000 KAJANG, MALAYSIA.
HIGDON, Mr. David Edward, FCA *1979;* The New Hay House Blindmans Gate, Woolton Hill, NEWBURY, RG20 9XB.
HIGENBOTTAM, Mr. Anthony William Henry, ACA *2008;* Ricardo UK Ltd Shoreham Technical Centre, Old Shoreham Road, SHOREHAM-BY-SEA, WEST SUSSEX, BN43 5FG.
•HIGGIN, Mr. Benjamin, ACA *2003;* with PricewaterhouseCoopers LLP, Hays Galleria, 1 Hays Lane, LONDON, SE1 2RD.
HIGGIN, Mr. Michael Norland, BA FCA *1978;* Lockington, 57 High Street, HAMPTON, MIDDLESEX, TW12 2SX.
HIGGINBOTHAM, Mr. Paul Andrew, BSc ACA *2006;* with KPMG LLP, St. James's Square, MANCHESTER, M2 6DS.
HIGGINBOTHAM, Mr. Stephen William, ACA *1980;* Hyde Group Holdings Ltd, Stamford House, Stamford Street, STALYBRIDGE, CHESHIRE, SK15 1QZ.
HIGGINBOTTOM, Mr. Antony, OAM FCA FCPA *1957;* 41 Perseverance Road, TEA TREE GULLY, SA 5091, AUSTRALIA. (Life Member)
HIGGINBOTTOM, Mr. John, FCA *1975;* 19 Osprey Avenue, Westhoughton, BOLTON, BL5 2SL.
HIGGINBOTTOM, Mr. Peter, FCA *1970;* 35 Hood Street, MORPETH, NE61 1JF.
HIGGINBOTTOM, Mr. Philip Edward, BSc ACA *1999;* 37 Cavendish Park, BROUGH, HU15 1AU.
HIGGINBOTTOM, Miss. Rebecca, ACA *2008;* with Clayton & Brewill, Wilne House, 10 Salisbury Street, Long Eaton, NOTTINGHAM, NG10 1BA.
HIGGINBOTTOM, Mr. Richard, ACA *2011;* Calow Close, Baslow Road, Holymoorside, CHESTERFIELD, DERBYSHIRE, S42 7BH.
HIGGINS, Mr. Alan Mitchell, FCA *1972;* Towans Barn, Church Road, Lelant, ST. IVES, CORNWALL, TR26 3DY.
HIGGINS, Mrs. Alison Sarah, BSc ACA *1984;* Pilgrims School, 3 The Close, WINCHESTER, SO23 9LT.
HIGGINS, Mr. Alistair Clive, MA FCA *1988;* 2 St. Marys Crescent, LEAMINGTON SPA, WARWICKSHIRE, CV31 1JL.
HIGGINS, Mr. Andrew, ACA *2009;* 14 Cranleigh Close, OLDHAM, OL4 2HZ.
•HIGGINS, Mr. Andrew John, MA FCA *1980;* Bridge Farm Barn, Wrexham Road, Ridley, TARPORLEY, CHESHIRE, CW6 9SA.
HIGGINS, Mr. Anthony John, FCA *1970;* Panorama, Windyridge Lane, South Hill, SOMERTON, TA11 7JG.
HIGGINS, Mr. Brian Anthony, FCA *1957;* 43 Grove Park, KNUTSFORD, WA16 8QD. (Life Member)
HIGGINS, Mr. Brian Richard, BA ACA *1999;* 31 Legh Road, Prestbury, MACCLESFIELD, CHESHIRE, SK10 4HX.
•HIGGINS, Miss. Candice Louise, BA FCA *2000;* Whitehead & Howarth, 327 Clifton Drive South, LYTHAM ST. ANNES, FY8 1HN.
HIGGINS, Mr. Christopher James, BA ACA *1989;* 24 Ennismore Avenue, GUILDFORD, GU1 1SR.
HIGGINS, Mrs. Clare Louise, BA(Hons) ACA *2000;* 80 Academy Drive, GILLINGHAM, KENT, ME7 3EJ.
HIGGINS, Mr. Colin Alan, BA ACA *1990;* Shadowgrade Developments Ltd, Wraysbury Hall Ferry Lane, Wraysbury, STAINES, MIDDLESEX, TW19 6HG.
HIGGINS, Mr. Damian James, BA ACA *2001;* Flat 13, Lantern Court, High Street, ELY, CAMBRIDGESHIRE, CB7 4JR.
HIGGINS, Mr. David Michael, BA ACA *1980;* Higgins Agriculture Ltd, Greenbank House, Finningley, DONCASTER, DN9 3BZ.
•HIGGINS, Mrs. Debbie Ann, BSc ACA CTA *1990;* Trelawne Cottage, West End Lane, Warfield, BRACKNELL, RG42 5RJ.
HIGGINS, Mrs. Deborah, BA ACA *1999;* Danescourt La Grande Route de Faldouet, St. Martin, JERSEY, JE3 6UE.
HIGGINS, Miss. Diana Mary, ACA *1981;* Lancelot's Farm, Helions Bumpstead, HAVERHILL, CB9 7AT.
HIGGINS, Mrs. Elaine Joyce, BSc ACA *1981;* Ifg International Ltd International House, Castle Hill Douglas, ISLE OF MAN, IM2 4RB.
HIGGINS, Ms. Elizabeth, BA ACA *1997;* 9 Carew Road, LONDON, W13 9QL.
HIGGINS, Mrs. Elizabeth Victoria, BA(Hons) ACA *2010;* 1 Buckie Close, Bridge of Don, ABERDEEN, AB22 8DJ.
HIGGINS, Ms. Faye, BSc ACA *2005;* 173 Kellaway Avenue, BRISTOL, BS6 7YJ.
•HIGGINS, Mr. Fenton William, FCA *1977;* (Tax Fac), Higgins Fairbairn & Co, 1st Floor, 24/25 New Bond Street, LONDON, W1S 2RR.
HIGGINS, Mr. Francis Farquhar, FCA *1956;* Rambridge Farm, Gracious Pond, Chobham, WOKING, GU24 8HJ. (Life Member)
HIGGINS, Mrs. Helen Elizabeth, MA ACA *2000;* 13 The Quadrant, HASSOCKS, BN6 8BP.
HIGGINS, Mr. James Alexander, BSc FCA *1975;* Hillview Church Road, Doynton, BRISTOL, BS30 5SU.
•HIGGINS, Mr. John, BA FCA *1991;* PricewaterhouseCoopers LLP, 7 More London Riverside, LONDON, SE1 2RT. See also PricewaterhouseCoopers
HIGGINS, Mr. John, BSc ACA *1998;* 16 Church Lane, Chapelthorpe, WAKEFIELD, WEST YORKSHIRE, WF4 3JF.
HIGGINS, Mr. John Francis, BA ACA *1982;* Bridge House Brick Hill, Hook Norton, BANBURY, OXFORDSHIRE, OX15 5PU.
HIGGINS, Mr. John Harrison, FCA *1954;* 8 Rosecroft Court, The Kings Gap, Hoylake, WIRRAL, MERSEYSIDE, CH47 1JA. (Life Member)
HIGGINS, Mr. John Patrick, FCA *1975;* Intersolar Group Ltd, Factory 3, Cock Lane, HIGH WYCOMBE, HP13 7DE.
HIGGINS, Mr. Jonathan Charles, ACA *1982;* 8 Teddington Park, TEDDINGTON, TW11 8DA.
HIGGINS, Mrs. Louise Joanne, MEng ACA *2001;* 49 Partridge Road, HAMPTON, TW12 3SB.

HIGGINS, Miss. Lucy, BSc ACA 2004; 17 Baliol Road, HITCHIN, HERTFORDSHIRE, SG5 1TT.

HIGGINS, Mr. Mark Roman, BSc ACA 1997; (Tax Fac), 39 Kings Road, LONDON, SW14 8PF.

HIGGINS, Mr. Matthew, BA ACA 2002; 6 Boxgrove Road, GUILDFORD, GU1 2LX.

•HIGGINS, Mrs. Maxine, BA FCA 1990; (Tax Fac), Maxine Higgins, Pentire, Orchard Close, East Horsley, LEATHERHEAD, KT24 5EZ. See also Citroen Wells

HIGGINS, Mrs. Nichola Jane, BSc(Econ) ACA 1996; The Croft, Straight Mile, ETCHINGHAM, EAST SUSSEX, TN19 7BA.

HIGGINS, Mr. Nicholas Ernest, FCA 1974; Sandy Cottage The Street, Regil Winford, BRISTOL, BS40 8BB.

HIGGINS, Mr. Nigel Alan, BA FCA 1981; Conifers, Cecil Avenue, HALIFAX, HX3 8SN.

•HIGGINS, Mr. Patrick Joseph, FCA 1974; P.J. Higgins & Co, 2 Cuchulainn Place, COBH, COUNTY CORK, IRELAND.

•HIGGINS, Mr. Paul Antony, BMus(Hons) ACA 1992; Higgins Harvey Ltd, 93 Long Row, Horsforth, LEEDS, LS18 5AT.

•HIGGINS, Mr. Paul Raymond, ACA 1988; (Tax Fac), Paul Higgins, 10 Ritherdon Road, Tooting, LONDON, SW17 8QD.

HIGGINS, Mr. Raymond Stanley, ACA 1978; 47 Sovereign Way, Boyatt Wood, EASTLEIGH, SO50 4SA.

HIGGINS, Miss. Rebecca Louise, ACA 2009; John Wiley & Sons Ltd The Atrium, Southern Gate Terminus Road, CHICHESTER, WEST SUSSEX, PO19 8SQ.

HIGGINS, Mr. Richard Guy, BA ACA 1996; with PricewaterhouseCoopers LLP, Cornwall Court, 19 Cornwall Street, BIRMINGHAM, B3 2DT.

HIGGINS, Mr. Robert Darren, BSc ACA 1996; Flat 22, The Metro, 216 Kennington Road, LONDON, SE11 6HR.

•HIGGINS, Mrs. Sandra Monica, BSc FCA DChA 1996; (Tax Fac), 1234 Accountancy Limited, 54 Clarendon Road, WATFORD, WD17 1DU.

HIGGINS, Mr. Sean Patrick Joseph, BA FCA 1987; Howard Kennedy, Harcourt House, 19 Cavendish Square, LONDON, W1G 0AJ.

HIGGINS, Mr. Stewart Martin, BSc ACA 1995; Oak Lodge Church End Road, Freiston, BOSTON, LINCOLNSHIRE, PE22 0LJ.

•HIGGINS, Mr. Stewart Neville, FCA 1971; (Tax Fac), Higgins Day, 19 York Rd, MAIDENHEAD, SL6 1SQ.

•HIGGINS, Mr. Stuart, BA(Hons) ACA 2001; (Tax Fac), PricewaterhouseCoopers LLP, Hays Galleria, 1 Hays Lane, LONDON, SE1 2RD. See also PricewaterhouseCoopers

HIGGINS, Mr. Tim, ACA 2011; Zolfo Cooper, 35 Newhall Street, BIRMINGHAM, B3 3PU.

HIGGINS, Mr. William Gordon, BSc ACA 1986; Premier Place, 2 1/2 Devonshire Square, LONDON, ec2m4bn.

HIGGINSON, Mr. Andrew John, BA FCA 1979; The Willows, Coles Oak Lane, Dedham, COLCHESTER, CO7 6DN.

HIGGINSON, Mr. Brian Ronald Michael, FCA 1973; 51 Strangers Way, Leagrave, LUTON, LU4 9NE.

HIGGINSON, Mr. Christopher Geoffrey, BA FCA 1976; Station House, Norton Station Road, Norton, RUNCORN, WA7 6PY.

HIGGINSON, Mr. David Andrew, BSc FCA 1999; with KPMG LLP, 15 Canada Square, LONDON, E14 5GL.

HIGGINSON, Mr. David William, BA ACA 2004; 2893 PARK MEADOW DR, APOPKA, FL 32703, UNITED STATES.

HIGGINSON, Mr. Kevin Mark, BA FCA 1985; Meadow House, Clifton Campville, TAMWORTH, STAFFORDSHIRE, B79 0BE.

HIGGINSON, Miss. Lucy Caroline, BSc ACA 2000; 35 Hawksley Road, Stoke Newington, LONDON, N16 0TL.

•HIGGINSON, Mr. Mark Alexander, BA FCA 1986; PricewaterhouseCoopers LLP, 32 Albyn Place, ABERDEEN, AB10 1YL. See also PricewaterhouseCoopers

HIGGINSON, Mr. Martin James, BSc ACA 2006; 1 Westmorland Terrace, Holmes Chapel, CREWE, CW4 7EE.

HIGGINSON, Mr. Michael, FCA 1964; Holly Cottage, 45 Peddars Lane, Stanbridge, LEIGHTON BUZZARD, BEDFORDSHIRE, LU7 9JD. (Life Member)

HIGGINSON, Mr. Peter John, BA ACA 1978; DSG, Monxton Road, ANDOVER, HAMPSHIRE, SP11 8HT.

•HIGGINSON, Mr. Richard Ian, FCA 1982; (Tax Fac), Cheney & Co, 310 Wellingborough Road, NORTHAMPTON, NN1 4EP.

HIGGINSON, Mr. Robert Charles, BA FCA 1986; Ainsworths Farm, Peover Lane, Snelson, MACCLESFIELD, SK11 9BR.

HIGGINSON, Mr. Stewart, ACA CA(AUS) 2009; with AlixPartners Ltd, 20 North Audley Street, LONDON, W1K 6WE.

•HIGGITT, Mr. Jonathan Mark, FCA 1980; Fox Evans Limited, Abbey House, 7 Manor Road, COVENTRY, CV1 2FW.

HIGGONS, Mrs. Helen Joanne, BA ACA 2007; 77 Elizabeth Avenue, NEWBURY, BERKSHIRE, RG14 6HG.

•HIGGS, Mr. Alan Bryce, FCA 1967; (Tax Fac), Alan B Higgs, 9 Redwood Mount, REIGATE, SURREY, RH2 9NB.

HIGGS, Mr. Alan Hugh, FCA 1972; The Highlands, Ribbesford, BEWDLEY, DY12 2TR.

HIGGS, Miss. Alison Clare, BA ACA 1992; Deutsche Bank, 20 Finsbury Circus, LONDON, EC2N 4DA.

HIGGS, Mr. Andrew John, BSc FCA FCSI TEP 1985; Harbour Nominees Ltd, PO Box 73, GUERNSEY, GY1 3DD.

HIGGS, Mrs. Angela Denise, BSc FCA 1995; Archway Lodge, Paddockhurst Road, Turners Hill, CRAWLEY, RH10 4SE.

HIGGS, Mr. Bryan Norman, BCom FCA 1952; 31 Selly Wick Road, Selly Park, BIRMINGHAM, B29 7JJ. (Life Member)

HIGGS, Miss. Christina Elizabeth, ACA 2008; Flat 1, 3A Formosa Street, Little Venice, LONDON, W9 1EE.

HIGGS, Mr. Christopher Raymond, BA ACA 1991; (Tax Fac), 51 Church Street, EPSOM, KT17 4PU.

HIGGS, Miss. Clare Annette, BSc ACA 1995; 28 Osler Road, Headington, OXFORD, OX3 9BJ.

HIGGS, Mr. Edward David Alexander, MA ACA 1999; 35 Wolseley Road, GODALMING, SURREY, GU7 3EA.

HIGGS, Mr. Frederick George, FCA 1959; 15 Blueberry Downs, Coastguard Road, BUDLEIGH SALTERTON, EX9 6NU. (Life Member)

HIGGS, Mr. Graham Charles, FCA 1970; 'Lakeside', 164 Chesterfield Drive, Riverhead, SEVENOAKS, KENT, TN13 2EH.

HIGGS, Mr. Jason, ACA 2011; 11 Lainson Street, LONDON, SW18 5RS.

HIGGS, Mrs. Lucia Mulian Anne, MA ACA 1990; 70 Gracechurch Street, LONDON, EC3V 0XL.

•HIGGS, Mr. Malcolm Keith, FCA 1971; Whitley Stimpson LLP, Penrose House, 67 Hightown Road, BANBURY, OXFORDSHIRE, OX16 9BE.

HIGGS, Mrs. Marie-Christine Daisy Henriette Elizabeth, BSc FCA 1980; 91 Waterslea Drive, Heaton, BOLTON, BL1 5FA.

HIGGS, Mr. Michael John, BSc FCA 1977; 2 Revesby Road, Woodthorpe, NOTTINGHAM, NG5 4LL.

•HIGGS, Mr. Peter Anthony, BA FCA 1970; (Tax Fac), Chapman Higgs, 58 Birchwood Road, LICHFIELD, STAFFORDSHIRE, WS14 9UW.

HIGGS, Mrs. Philippa Hilary, BSc ACA 1995; 3 Mandale Crescent, Cullercoats, NORTH SHIELDS, NE30 3LX.

HIGH, Mr. Desmond Charles Fitzpatrick, BA FCA CF 1979; The Gables, 556 Loose Road, MAIDSTONE, ME15 9UR.

HIGH, Mrs. Katherine, MA ACA 1982; The Gables, 556 Loose Road, MAIDSTONE, ME15 9UR.

HIGH, Mrs. Kathryn Anne, BSc ACA 2005; 24B Thrall Street, Innaloo, PERTH, WA 6018, AUSTRALIA.

•HIGH, Mr. Malcolm, BSc FCA 1964; Malcolm High, Pantiles, Braughing Friars, WARE, SG11 2NS.

HIGH, Mrs. Sarah Louise, BA ACA 1998; 1 Spen Lane, Treales, PRESTON, LANCASHIRE, PR4 3TE.

HIGH, Mr. Stephen Geoffrey, BA FCA 1973; Little Normandy, Normandy Lane, LYMINGTON, HAMPSHIRE, SO41 8AE.

HIGHAM, Miss. Brie, ACA 2011; 24 Victoria Court, Wavertree, LIVERPOOL, L15 8LZ.

HIGHAM, Mrs. Caroline Anne, LLB ACA 2002; 11 Highbury Road, Keyworth, NOTTINGHAM, NG12 5JB.

HIGHAM, Mr. David John Paul, FCA 1975; 12 Dalloway Road, ARUNDEL, BN18 9HW.

HIGHAM, Mr. David Strachan, BA ACA 1989; 39 Bushwood Road, RICHMOND, SURREY, TW9 3BG.

HIGHAM, Mrs. Fiona Catherine, BA ACA 1999; Virgin Holidays Ltd, The Galleria, Station Road, CRAWLEY, WEST SUSSEX, RH10 1WW.

HIGHAM, Miss. Jo-Ann Louise, BA ACA 1996; 27a Islington High Street, LONDON, N1 9LH.

HIGHAM, Miss. Joanne, BSc ACA 2000; with PricewaterhouseCoopers, 2 Southbank Boulevard, Southbank, MELBOURNE, VIC 3006, AUSTRALIA.

HIGHAM, Mr. John Patrick, BSc ACA 1992; Sykes Barn Higher Commons Lane, Osbaldeston, BLACKBURN, BB2 7LS.

HIGHAM, Miss. Lisa Jayne, BA ACA 1994; 3 Scarah Bank Cottages, Ripley, HARROGATE, HG3 3EE.

HIGHAM, Mr. Malcolm David, BA FCA 1989; 15 Wellington Drive, STRATFORD-UPON-AVON, WARWICKSHIRE, CV37 7HJ.

HIGHAM, Mr. Paul Edward James, BSc ACA 2002; 51 Oliver Avenue, EDISON, NJ 08820, UNITED STATES.

HIGHAM, Mr. Paul Michael, BA ACA 2005; Cairn Capital Ltd, 27 Knightsbridge, LONDON, SW1X 7LY.

HIGHAM, Mr. Peter, FCA 1961; Higher Tretharrup, Lanreath, LOOE, PL13 2NZ. (Life Member)

HIGHAM, Mrs. Rachel Marie, BA(Hons) ACA 2002; 1 Muir Terrace, Glen Road Laxey, ISLE OF MAN, IM4 7AS.

HIGHAM, Mr. Richard Andrew Cleveland, ACA 2008; 4 Cherington Close, Handforth, WILMSLOW, CHESHIRE, SK9 3AS.

HIGHAM, Miss. Stephanie, ACA 2011; 24 Shaftesbury Road, BATH, BA2 3LQ.

HIGHAM, Mr. Terence, FCA 1962; 20 Hamsland, Horsted Keynes, HAYWARDS HEATH, WEST SUSSEX, RH17 7DX. (Life Member)

HIGHET, Mr. Alistair Maxwell, BSc ACA 1992; 31e Old Mill Lane, INVERNESS, IV2 3XP.

HIGHFIELD, Miss. Dominique, BSc(Hons) ACA 2011; 7 Timbrell Place, LONDON, SE16 5HU.

HIGHFIELD, Mr. Howard John, ACA 1982; PO Box 62532, Farmers' Service Centre, ABU DHABI, UNITED ARAB EMIRATES.

•HIGHFIELD, Mr. Neil Stuart, FCA 1988; Allotts, The Old Grammar School, 13 Moorgate Road, ROTHERHAM, SOUTH YORKSHIRE, S60 2EN.

HIGHFIELD, Mr. Stephen, BSc ACA 1990; (Tax Fac), 55 Jervois Road, #08-04 Dormer Park, SINGAPORE 249047, SINGAPORE.

HIGHLEY, Mr. Ian Godfrey, FCA 1950; Skilcroft Farm, Stanford Dingley, READING, BERKSHIRE, RG7 6LU. (Life Member)

HIGHSTED, Miss. Joanne, BSc(Hons) ACA 2002; 6 Hewitt Close, Allington, MAIDSTONE, KENT, ME16 0UJ.

HIGHT, Mr. Andrew James, ACA 2005; 72a Chatham Road, LONDON, SW11 6HG.

HIGHT, Mr. Robert Alan, BSc ACA 1991; 15 Fernhill Close, WOKING, GU22 0DJ.

HIGHTON, Mrs. Catherine Jane, BSc FCA 1987; with David J Barnett, The Point, Granite Way, Mountsorrel, LOUGHBOROUGH, LEICESTERSHIRE LE12 7TZ.

HIGHTON, Mr. David Ian, BA FCA 1993; 31 Finches Park Road, Lindfield, HAYWARDS HEATH, WEST SUSSEX, RH16 2DA.

HIGHTON, Mr. David Peter, BSc FCA 1978; White Cottage, New Yatt, WITNEY, OX29 6TF.

HIGHTON, Mr. Dennis, FCA 1958; 16 Lon Howell, DENBIGH, LL16 4AN. (Life Member)

HIGHTON, Mr. Ian Willmer, FCA 1963; 50 Langley Park Road, SUTTON, SURREY, SM2 5HG. (Life Member)

HIGHTON, Mr. Lee, ACA 2009; with Deloitte Touche Tohmatsu, Grosvenor Place, 225 George Street, P.O. Box N 250, SYDNEY, NSW 2000 AUSTRALIA.

HIGINBOTHAM, Mr. John Alfred, FCA 1952; Walnut & Well Cottage, The Street, Bolney, HAYWARDS HEATH, RH17 5QW. (Life Member)

HIGMAN, Mr. Dominic John Royston, BSc ACA 2005; 149 Whitehall Road, WOODFORD GREEN, IG8 0RH.

HIGMAN, Mrs. Hayley Joanne, BSc ACA 2004; with Bromhead, Harscombe House, 1 Darklake View, Estover, PLYMOUTH, PL6 7TL.

HIGNELL, Mr. Christopher David, MChem ACA 2007; Level 15, HSBC Main Building, 1 Queens Road, CENTRAL, HONG KONG ISLAND, HONG KONG SAR.

HIGNETT, Mr. David Garth, BSc ACA 1995; Walnut Tree House, 55 Leivers Close, East Leake, LOUGHBOROUGH, LE12 6PQ.

HIGNETT, Mr. John Mulock, BA FCA 1961; Via Privata A. Bifami 3, 16038 SANTA MARGHERITA LIGURE, LIGURIA, ITALY. (Life Member)

HIGSON, Dr. Andrew William, PhD BSc FCA 1983; Loughborough University, Business School, LOUGHBOROUGH, LE11 3TU.

HIGSON, Prof. Christopher John, MSc BA FCA 1974; London Business School, Sussex Place, Regents Park, LONDON, NW1 4SA.

HIGSON, Mrs. Cicely Vaughan, BA FCA 1974; 24 Oakley Park, BOLTON, BL1 5XL.

HIGSON, Miss. Joanne Alice, BSc ACA 1998; 18 Riverview Road, CLAREVILLE, NSW 2107, AUSTRALIA.

•HIGSON, Mr. Keith, FCA 1979; (Tax Fac), Higsons, 93 Market Street, Farnworth, BOLTON, BL4 7NS.

•HIGSON, Miss. Louise, ACA 1996; Louise Higson ACA, Dean House Farm, Dean House Lane, Stainland, HALIFAX, WEST YORKSHIRE HX4 9LG.

HIGSON, Miss. Sarah, BSc ACA 2007; Avondale, School Lane, Warmingham, SANDBACH, CHESHIRE, CW11 3QN.

HIGSON, Mr. Stephen Craig, ACA 1987; Ridehalgh Ltd, Guardian House, 42 Preston New Road, BLACKBURN, BB2 6AH.

HIGSON, Mr. Stephen John, BA ACA ACT 1984; 2 Claremont Avenue, CLITHEROE, BB7 1JN.

HIGSON, Mr. William Stewart, FCA 1964; 29 Pursers Cross Road, LONDON, SW6 4QY.

HIGTON, Mr. John Anthony, FCA 1969; 14 The Chancery, Claremont Avenue, Bramcote, NOTTINGHAM, NG9 3AJ.

HII, Mr. Chester, ACA CA(AUS) 2010; Flat 223, New Providence Wharf, 1 Fairmont Avenue, LONDON, E14 9PL.

HII, Mr. Yik Nan, BSc ACA 1990; 335 Bukit Timah Road, #26-02, SINGAPORE 259718, SINGAPORE.

HIIRI, Miss. Anna Alina Kristiina, ACA 2009; 347 W Milford Street, No.109, GLENDALE, CA 91203, UNITED STATES.

HILBERT, Mr. Anthony Philip, BSc ACA 1995; 161 Hornbeam Close, Bradley Stoke, BRISTOL, BS32 8FE.

HILBERT, Mr. Keith George, MA ACA 1990; 55 Grange Road, SHREWSBURY, SY3 9DG.

HILBERT, Mrs. Kirsten, BA ACA 1995; 161 Hornbeam Close, Bradley Stoke, BRISTOL, BS32 8FE.

HILBINK, Mr. Samuel John, ACA 2009; Unit 5, 5 Churchill Road, OVINGHAM, SA 5082, AUSTRALIA.

HILBOURNE, Mr. Marc Daniel, BEng ACA 1994; 88 Olinda Road, LONDON, N16 6TP.

HILDEBRAND, Mr. Anthony Michael, BCom FCA 1975; 8 Gloucester Drive, LONDON, NW11 6BH.

•HILDER, Mr. George, FCA 1974; G. Hilder, The Alde Suite, 8 Wherry Lane, IPSWICH, SUFFOLK, IP4 1LG.

HILDER, Mr. Paul William, BSc ACA 2003; 44 Rowan Way, Angmering, LITTLEHAMPTON, WEST SUSSEX, BN16 4FW.

HILDITCH, Mr. James Robert Guy, MA FCA 1990; 18 Guildford Road, FLEET, GU51 3ES.

HILDITCH, Mr. Mark Stephen Timperley, BA ACA 2006; 2 Canons Close, BOGNOR REGIS, WEST SUSSEX, PO21 4EB.

HILDRED, Mrs. Clare Elizabeth Anne, BSc ACA 1989; 3 Beech Hill, Mobberley, KNUTSFORD, WA16 7HT.

HILDRED, Mr. Graham Edward, FCA 1974; 19 Caton Close, Talbot Village, POOLE, BH12 5EU.

•HILDRED, Mr. Mark, BA FCA 1989; Moore Thompson, Bank House, Broad Street, SPALDING, LINCOLNSHIRE, PE11 1TB.

HILDRED, Mr. Mark Andrew, ACA MAAT 1995; with Vantis Group Ltd, Stoughton House, Harborough Road, Oadby, LEICESTER, LE2 4LP.

HILDRETH, Miss. Jennifer, BA ACA 2006; Flat 4 Cecil Court, 2 Acol Road, LONDON, NW6 3AP.

HILDREY, Mr. Jonathan Edmund Charles, MA FCA 1991; 19 Kings Lane, KEENE, NH 03431, UNITED STATES.

HILDYARD, Mr. Christopher D'Arcy Thoroton, BA ACA 1993; GF Office, 69 Masbro Rd, LONDON, w14 0ls.

HILDYARD, Mr. Nicholas Alexander Cyril, DL FCA 1980; The Elms, Rectory Road, Roos, HULL, HU12 0LA.

HILES, Mrs. Gillian Maureen, BA FCA 1974; Watson Wyatt Ltd Watson House, London Road, REIGATE, RH2 9PQ.

HILES, Mr. James Jonathan Mark, BSc ACA 2004; 111 Skipton Road, ILKLEY, WEST YORKSHIRE, LS29 9BJ.

HILETIS, Mr. George, ACA 2008; 1 Franklin Roosevelt Avenue, P.O. Box 50209, 3602 LIMASSOL, CYPRUS.

•HILEY, Mr. Jason Douglas, BA ACA CF 1993; PKF (UK) LLP, 4th Floor, 3 Hardman Street, MANCHESTER, M3 3HF.

•HILEY, Mr. John Robert, FCA 1970; John H. Nixon & Co, Athena House, 35 Greek Street, STOCKPORT, SK3 8BA.

HILEY, Miss. Nicola Victoria, BSc FCA 1992; 24 Grange Park, Skircoat Moor Road, HALIFAX, HX3 0JS.

HILKENE, Ms. Lorna Jane, BA ACA 2000; 4 Barton Hey, Bishops Lydeard, TAUNTON, SOMERSET, TA4 3NL.

HILL, Mr. Adrian Michael, BA ACA 1987; Intercontinental Hotels Group Plc, 1 First Avenue, Centrum One Hundred, BURTON-ON-TRENT, STAFFORDSHIRE, DE14 2WB.

HILL, Mr. Alan Thomas, FCA 1960; 8 Sussex Ring, Woodside Park, LONDON, N12 7JA.

HILL, Mr. Alastair Pinkerton, FCA 1973; 2 St Georges Cottages, Brinkers Lane, WADHURST, EAST SUSSEX, TN5 6LT.

HILL, Mr. Alexander, ACA 2011; 26A High Street, Pirton, HITCHIN, HERTFORDSHIRE, SG5 3PT.

HILL, Mr. Alexander James, BA ACA *1998;* The Studio, The O2, Peninsula Square, LONDON, SE10 0DX.

HILL, Miss. Alexandra Emily, BSc ACA MIIA *2004;* 6/40 East Esplanade, MANLY, NSW 2095, AUSTRALIA.

HILL, Mr. Alfred Edward, MBE FCA MBA *1969;* Campfield, 55 Church Road, Abbots Leigh, BRISTOL, BS8 3QU. (Life Member)

HILL, Mrs. Alison Claire, BA ACA *2005;* 7 Mayhall Ave, East Morton, KEIGHLEY, WEST YORKSHIRE, BD20 5WF.

HILL, Mr. Alistair Duncan, BEng FCA *1994;* HSBC Bank plc, 8 Canada Square, Level 18, LONDON, E14 5HQ.

HILL, Mrs. Amanda Anne Patricia, BSc FCA *1991;* Les Magnolias, Rue du Leard, 72200 LA FLECHE, FRANCE.

HILL, Mrs. Amanda Jane, BPharm ACA *1992;* 3 St. Clair Road, Greenmount, BURY, LANCASHIRE, BL8 4EU.

HILL, Miss. Amanda Jane, BA(Hons) ACA *2000;* 119 Driftwood Street, Apt 5, MARINA DEL REY, CA 90292, UNITED STATES.

•HILL, Mr. Andrew, BA ACA *1986;* (Tax Fac), D & A Hill, 18 T8/9 Brookes Mill, Armitage Bridge, HUDDERSFIELD, HD4 7NR.

HILL, Mr. Andrew, ACA *2011;* 104 Times Square, LONDON, E1 8GE.

•HILL, Mr. Andrew David Charles, BSc FCA *1999;* Cartwrights Audit Limited, Regency House, 33 Wood Street, BARNET, HERTFORDSHIRE, EN5 4BE. See also Cartwrights Advisory Services Limited

•HILL, Mr. Andrew Grant, ACA *1991;* PricewaterhouseCoopers LLP, 7 More London Riverside, LONDON, SE1 2RT. See also PricewaterhouseCoopers

HILL, Mr. Andrew Hemming, BSc FCA *1980;* Hillside, 1 Butts Farm Lane, Bishops Waltham, SOUTHAMPTON, SO32 1PE.

•HILL, Mr. Andrew Paul, BA FCA *1990;* OBC The Accountants Limited, 2 Upperton Gardens, EASTBOURNE, EAST SUSSEX, BN21 2AH.

•HILL, Mr. Andrew Robert, BSc FCA *1982;* Hill Osborne Ltd, Tower House, Parkstone Road, POOLE, DORSET, BH15 2JH.

HILL, Mr. Andrew William Richard, BA ACA *1996;* 164 Burley Road, Bransgore, CHRISTCHURCH, DORSET, BH23 8DE.

HILL, Dr. Angela Michelle, PhD BSc ACA CTA *2005;* 31 Bradley Crescent, Shirehampton, BRISTOL, BS11 9SP.

•HILL, Mrs. Ann Louise, ACA *2003;* Maycall & Co, 4 Marchwood Close, BRIDGNORTH, SHROPSHIRE, WV16 4SA.

HILL, Mr. Anthony, MPhys ACA *2011;* Foss Field Farm Haggitt Hill Lane, East Rounton, NORTHALLERTON, NORTH YORKSHIRE, DL6 2LX.

HILL, Mr. Anthony Arthur, FCA *1966;* Trenance, Hain Walk, ST.IVES, CORNWALL, TR26 2AF.

HILL, Mr. Anthony Charles, FCA *1950;* Greenacres, Hillcrest Road, Sandyford, DUBLIN, COUNTY DUBLIN, IRELAND. (Life Member)

HILL, Mr. Anthony John, FCA *1976;* 10 Well Close, WINSCOMBE, AVON, BS25 1HG.

HILL, Mr. Anthony John, FCA *1962;* Ball Copse Hall, Brent Knoll, HIGHBRIDGE, TA9 4DF.

HILL, Mr. Barrie, BSc ACA *2007;* 36 Northway Road, LONDON, SE5 9AN.

•HILL, Mr. Barry Penryn, BA FCA *1974;* (Tax Fac), Barry Hill & Co, The Brighton Forum, 95 Ditchling Road, BRIGHTON, BN1 4ST.

HILL, Mr. Benjamin Edwin, ACA *1993;* Cedar Wood, 9 Beaumont Grove, SOLIHULL, B91 1RP.

•HILL, Mrs. Beverley Anne, BSc FCA *1998;* Lucentum Limited, Kensal House, 77 Springfield Road, CHELMSFORD, CM2 6JG.

HILL, Mr. Brian Arthur, FCA *1972;* 21 Zeus, Olympus Village, Tsada, 8540 PAPHOS, CYPRUS. (Life Member)

HILL, Mr. Brian Lionel, FCA *1961;* Northwood House, North Gorley, FORDINGBRIDGE, SP6 2PL. (Life Member)

HILL, Mr. Brian Roy, BSc ACA *1987;* 32 Bressey Grove, South Woodford, LONDON, E18 2HU.

HILL, Mrs. Bridget Clare, ACA *2009;* 159 Snowley Park, Whittlesey, PETERBOROUGH, PE7 1JH.

HILL, Mr. Carl Stephen, BSc ACA *1982;* Domein Nachtegalenhof, Jan Janssensstraat 8 b 2, Wilrijk, 2610 ANTWERP, BELGIUM.

HILL, Mrs. Carol Ann, BA ACA *1989;* Trendle House, 35 Drury Lane, NORMANTON, WEST YORKSHIRE, WF6 2JT.

HILL, Mrs. Carol Anne, BA ACA *1997;* 23 Mapledene Crescent, NOTTINGHAM, NG8 2SS.

HILL, Mrs. Caroline Margot, BSc ACA *1995;* Longcot, 169 Post Office Lane, Broad Hinton, SWINDON, SN4 9PB.

HILL, Mrs. Carolyn Mary, BSc ACA *1982;* Orchard House, 163 Nine Mile Ride, Finchampstead, WOKINGHAM, RG40 4HY.

HILL, Mrs. Catherine, BA(Hons) ACA *2002;* 14 St. Georges Manor, Mandelbrote Drive, Littlemore, OXFORD, OX4 4TN.

•HILL, Mrs. Catherine, ACA CTA *2002;* Stirk Lambert & Co, Russell Chambers, 61A North Street, KEIGHLEY, BD21 3DS.

HILL, Miss. Catherine Louise, BA ACA *1993;* Gartree, Littleton Drew, CHIPPENHAM, WILTSHIRE, SN14 7NA.

•HILL, Mr. Charles Edmund, BSc FCA *1977;* C E Hill & Co (UK) Limited, Fairacre, Chiltern Road, Ballinger, GREAT MISSENDEN, BUCKINGHAMSHIRE HP16 9LJ.

HILL, Mrs. Charlotte Natasha, BSc ACA *2006;* Flat 8, Gilberts Lodge, Farriers Road, EPSOM, SURREY, KT17 1NR.

HILL, Mr. Christopher Brian, BA ACA *1999;* #06-02 Lobby F, Pebble Bay, 132 Tanjong Rhu Road, SINGAPORE 436919, SINGAPORE.

HILL, Mr. Christopher David, ACA *2009;* 158 Derinton Road, LONDON, SW17 8HY.

HILL, Mr. Christopher Dennis, BSc ACA *1997;* Treetops Church Road Swanmore, SOUTHAMPTON, SO32 2PA.

HILL, Mr. Christopher Frederick, MA ACA AMCT *1997;* 129 Marlow Bottom, Marlow Bottom, MARLOW, BUCKINGHAMSHIRE, SL7 3PJ.

HILL, Mr. Christopher George, ACA *1991;* Clement House La Rue Du Pontlietaut, St. Clement, JERSEY, JE2 6LG.

•HILL, Mr. Christopher Ingram, BA(Hons) FCA *1996;* Hawsons, Pegasus House, 463a Glossop Road, SHEFFIELD, S10 2QD.

HILL, Mr. Christopher James, BA ACA *2004;* 4 Ilton Road, Penylan, CARDIFF, CF23 5DU.

HILL, Mr. Christopher James, MA BA(Hons) ACA *2010;* 7 Wilfred Road, Eccles, MANCHESTER, M30 7LB.

HILL, Mr. Christopher James, BA ACA *2004;* 11 Eaton Road, ST. ALBANS, HERTFORDSHIRE, AL1 4UD.

HILL, Mr. Christopher James, MSci ACA *2006;* with BDO LLP, Emerald House, East Street, EPSOM, SURREY, KT17 1HS.

•HILL, Mr. Christopher James, BA FCA *1995;* with RSM Tenon Audit Limited, Cedar House, Sandbrook Business Park Sandbrook Way, ROCHDALE, LANCASHIRE, OL11 1LQ.

HILL, Mr. Christopher James, BA(Hons) ACA *2009;* 91-91a Crystal Palace Road, LONDON, SE22 9EY.

•HILL, Mr. Christopher John, FCA *1982;* WHS Accountants Limited, Elmville House, 305 Roundhay Road, LEEDS, LS8 4HT.

HILL, Mr. Christopher John Hart, ACA *1982;* KCT Holdings Limited, 22 Hayhill Industrial Estate, Sileby Road, LOUGHBOROUGH, LE12 8LD.

•①HILL, Mr. Christopher John Wilkinson, BSc FCA *1981;* Ernst & Young Llp, 1 More London Place, LONDON, SE1 2AF.

HILL, Mr. Christopher Nigel, BA ACA *1988;* Crime Reduction Initiatives Ltd, 3rd Floor, Tower Point, 44 North Road, BRIGHTON, BN1 1YR.

•HILL, Mr. Christopher Robert, BA ACA *1984;* Hill Day, Wayside House, Bedford Road, Ravensden, BEDFORD, MK44 2RA.

HILL, Miss. Clare Suzanne, BA ACA *2010;* Basement Flat, 5 Stanwick Road, LONDON, W14 8TL.

HILL, Mr. Colin, BA ACA *2004;* Apt 401, Takanawa DuplexC's, 2-3-23 Shirokane, Minato-ku, TOKYO, JAPAN.

HILL, Mr. Colin Hewer, FCA *1965;* 70 Mill Lane, Impington, CAMBRIDGE, CB24 9HS.

HILL, Mr. Colin John Richard, FCA *1964;* PO Box 790, Saigon Central Post Office, HO CHI MINH CITY, VIETNAM.

HILL, Mr. Daniel Colin, BEng ACA *2002;* 7 Bryn Terrace, Mumbles, SWANSEA, SA3 4HD.

HILL, Mr. Darren John, ACA *2008;* Flat 3, 47 Hazlewell Road, LONDON, SW15 6UT.

HILL, Mr. Darren Richard, BSc ACA *1991;* 25 Beverley Way, West Tytherington, MACCLESFIELD, SK10 2WP.

•①HILL, Mr. David, BSc FCA *1977;* Begbies Traynor, 5th Floor, Riverside House, 31 Cathedral Road, CARDIFF, CF11 9HB. See also Begbies Traynor(Central) LLP and Begbies Traynor Limited

HILL, Mr. David Charles, BSc ACA *1982;* 5 Home Farm, Leek Wootton, WARWICK, CV35 7PU.

HILL, Mr. David Christopher, BSc FCA *1987;* (Tax Fac), Leewood, ROSLIN, MIDLOTHIAN, EH25 9PZ.

HILL, Mr. David Ernest, BA(Hons) FCA *1965;* 19b Rydens Avenue, WALTON-ON-THAMES, KT12 3JB.

•HILL, Mr. David Henry Christopher, FCA *1972;* 29 Route des Tavernes, 1072 FOREL, VAUD, SWITZERLAND.

•HILL, Mr. David John, FCA *1973;* David J. Hill & Co, Museum Buildings, Church Road, Port Erin, ISLE OF MAN, IM9 6AH.

•HILL, Mr. David Martin, BA FCA *1988;* Dendy Neville Limited, 3-4 Bower Terrace, 1 Tonbridge Road, MAIDSTONE, KENT, ME16 8RY.

HILL, Mr. David Philip, BSc ACA *1997;* Flat 2, 71 Compayne Gardens, LONDON, NW6 3RS.

HILL, Mr. David Robert, FCA *1977;* Lake Farm, Denbury, NEWTON ABBOT, DEVON, TQ12 6EQ.

HILL, Mr. David Robert Paul, BSc ACA FSI *1993;* 10 Lambourne Avenue, LONDON, SW19 7DW.

HILL, Mr. David Ronald, FCA *1952;* 8 Village Close, Bryncoch, NEATH, SA10 7TE. (Life Member)

HILL, Mr. David Thomas, BSocSc ACA *1998;* Norland Managed Services Unit 9, Kingfisher Court, NEWBURY, RG14 5SJ.

HILL, Mr. David Warham, MSc BA ACA *2006;* 25 Honorwood Close, Prestwood, GREAT MISSENDEN, HP16 9HJ.

HILL, Mrs. Deborah Jayne, BSc ACA *1985;* Rose Cottage, 41 Oldfield Road, HAMPTON, TW12 2AJ.

HILL, Mrs. Debra Sharon, BSocSc ACA *1996;* 39 Geraldine Road, LONDON, SW18 2NR.

HILL, Mr. Dennis Brian, FCA *1961;* 31 Walden Road, Keynsham, BRISTOL, BS31 1QW.

HILL, Mr. Dennis Turner, FCA *1958;* 54 Birch Road, Berry Brow, HUDDERSFIELD, WEST YORKSHIRE, HD4 7LP. (Life Member)

•HILL, Mr. Derek, FCA *1953;* Derek Hill, 38 Knowsley Road, Hazel Grove, STOCKPORT, SK7 6BW.

HILL, Mr. Derek Wilfred, FCA *1963;* 74 Broad Oaks Road, SOLIHULL, B91 1HZ.

HILL, Mr. Douglas William, BSc FCA *1987;* 3 Addison Road, LONDON, E11 2RG.

HILL, Mr. Edgar Sidney, FCA *1976;* Chylowen, The Hollow, Lower Woodford, SALISBURY, SP4 6NJ.

HILL, Mr. Edward Herbert, FCA *1953;* 1 Apple Tree Close, Edwalton, NOTTINGHAM, NG12 4DX. (Life Member)

HILL, Mr. Edward Justin, BA ACA *1996;* Augusta House, 5 King Street, Castle Hedingham, HALSTEAD, ESSEX, CO9 3ER.

HILL, Miss. Elizabeth, BSc ACA *2010;* 605/41 Refinery Drive, PYRMONT, NSW 2009, AUSTRALIA.

HILL, Miss. Elizabeth Fraser, BA FCA *1977;* 34 Stronsa Road, Shepherds Bush, LONDON, W12 9LB.

HILL, Mrs. Elizabeth Jayne, BSc ACA *1995;* 5 Shurville Close, Earls Barton, NORTHAMPTON, NN6 0JB.

HILL, Miss. Emma, BA ACA *2004;* 88 Sotheron Road, WATFORD, WD17 2QA.

HILL, Mrs. Fiona, ACA *2002;* 2 Coronet Close, Appley Bridge, WIGAN, WN6 9AY.

HILL, Mrs. Fiona Mary, LLB ACA *1992;* 14 Ashburnham Road, EASTBOURNE, EAST SUSSEX, BN21 2HU.

HILL, Mr. Gareth William, BSocSc ACA *2000;* 38 Newlands Road, Bentley Heath, SOLIHULL, B93 8AU.

HILL, Mr. Gavin Fenton, BA ACA *1993;* Synergy Health Plc Stella Building, Windmill Hill Business Park Whitehill Way, SWINDON, SN5 6NX.

HILL, Mr. Gavin McDonald, BA ACA *1983;* 19 Coppice Way, Hedgerley, SLOUGH, SL2 3YL.

•HILL, Mr. Gavin Stuart, BA ACA CF *1985;* with Deloitte Audit S.P Z.O.O, Al Jan Pawla II 19, 00 854 WARSAW, POLAND.

HILL, Mr. Geoffrey Arthur Brian, FCA *1956;* Oak Beams, Warners Hill, Cookham, MAIDENHEAD, SL6 9NU. (Life Member)

•HILL, Mr. Geoffrey Demaine, FCA *1970;* IBIS Consult Ltd, 1 Hall Drive, Bramhope, LEEDS, LS16 9JF.

•HILL, Mr. Geoffrey Stanley, FCA *1971;* (Tax Fac), Griffin Stone Moscrop & Co., 41 Welbeck Street, LONDON, W1G 8EA.

HILL, Mr. Gerald Edmond, FCA *1971;* The Dormers, Dormer Close, Rowton, CHESTER, CH3 7SA.

HILL, Mr. Gerard Antony, MA ACA *1993;* 19 Ladyhill View, Worsley, MANCHESTER, M28 7LH.

HILL, Mr. Glyn Bentley, BA ACA *1986;* 15 Teal Lane, Cypress Point, LYTHAM ST. ANNES, LANCASHIRE, FY8 4FQ.

HILL, Mr. Graham Andrew, BSc ACA *1988;* C/ Guadiaro 10 5 0-2, MALAGA, 29003, SPAIN.

HILL, Mr. Graham Denis, BSc FCA *1971;* Hameau de Gourgas, 34700 ST ETIENNE DE GOURGAS, FRANCE. (Life Member)

HILL, Mr. Graham James, BCom FCA MBA *1997;* The Old Office, Silver Street, North Clifton, NEWARK, NOTTINGHAMSHIRE, NG23 7AU.

•HILL, Mr. Graham Roland, BA FCA *1992;* Phipp & Co (Accountants) Ltd, 6 Nottingham Road, Long Eaton, NOTTINGHAM, NG10 1HP. See also Phipp & Co

HILL, Mr. Gregory Rollo, BSc ACA *2001;* with Deloitte LLP, 3 Rivergate, Temple Quay, BRISTOL, BS1 6GD.

HILL, Mr. Henry Peter, BEng FCA *1976;* Tudor Cottage, Upwick Green, Albury, WARE, SG11 2JX. (Life Member)

•HILL, Mr. Iain Alasdair, BSc FCA *1991;* (Tax Fac), PricewaterhouseCoopers LLP, Benson House, 33 Wellington Street, LEEDS, LS1 4JP. See also PricewaterhouseCoopers

•HILL, Mr. Ian, FCA *1988;* Bourne & Co, 3 Charnwood Street, DERBY, DE1 2GY.

•HILL, Mr. Ian David Morrison, BSc FCA *1988;* Premex Services Limited, Premex House, Futura Park, Horwich, BOLTON, BL6 6SX.

HILL, Miss. Iona Lindsay, MSc BA FCA *1990;* Ashes Farm, Selside, SETTLE, NORTH YORKSHIRE, BD24 0JB.

HILL, Mrs. Jacqueline, MEng ACA *2006;* Deloitte, Level 5, Grosvenor Place, 225 George Street, SYDNEY, NSW 2000 AUSTRALIA.

HILL, Mr. James Robert, BSc ACA *2004;* with PricewaterhouseCoopers LLP, 1 East Parade, SHEFFIELD, S1 2ET.

HILL, Mrs. Janet Elizabeth, BSc ACA *1994;* Mount Pleasant, Swanton Road, West Peckham, MAIDSTONE, KENT, ME18 5JY.

HILL, Miss. Janette Mary, BA ACA *1989;* Elsenwood, 4 Tregolls Drive, FARNBOROUGH, Hampshire, GU14 7BN.

•HILL, Mrs. Janice Louise, BA(Hons) ACA *2000;* Janice Hill Accounting Services, 41 Forsythia Drive, CARDIFF, CF23 7HP.

HILL, Mrs. Janis Lesley, MA FCA *1985;* 9 High Thorn Piece, Redhouse Park, MILTON KEYNES, BUCKINGHAMSHIRE, MK14 5FR.

HILL, Mrs. Jayne Louise, BCom ACA *1997;* 6 Huntley Drive, SOLIHULL, WEST MIDLANDS, B91 3FL.

HILL, Miss. Jean Elizabeth, BSS FCA *1978;* 43 Eve Road, ISLEWORTH, TW7 7HS.

HILL, Mrs. Jeanette Mary, BSc ACA *2000;* 26 Hillhouse Close, BILLERICAY, ESSEX, CM12 0BB.

HILL, Mrs. Jemma Victoria, BSc ACA *1996;* 27 Parklands Road, Tooting, LONDON, SW16 6TB.

HILL, Mrs. Jennifer, BA ACA *2001;* 57 Beechwood Avenue, ST. ALBANS, HERTFORDSHIRE, AL1 4XR.

HILL, Miss. Jennifer, BSc ACA *2011;* 19 Hurrell Close, Southway, PLYMOUTH, PL6 6NB.

•HILL, Miss. Jennifer Elizabeth, BA ACA *2009;* Leonard Bye, 80 Borough Road, MIDDLESBROUGH, TS1 2JN.

•HILL, Mrs. Jennifer Susan, BA ACA *1998;* with RSM Tenon Audit Limited, Vantage, Victoria Street, BASINGSTOKE, HAMPSHIRE, RG21 3BT.

•HILL, Mrs. Joan Colby, BSc FCA CPFA *1987;* 9 Westville Avenue, KIDDERMINSTER, DY11 6BZ.

HILL, Mr. John Graeme, BA ACA *1988;* Rose Cottages, Cross Lanes, Oscroft Tarvin, CHESTER, CH3 8NQ.

HILL, Mr. John Lansdowne, FCA *1957;* April Cottage, 2 Bourne Banks, 20 Branksome Wood Road, BOURNEMOUTH, BH4 9JX. (Life Member)

HILL, The Revd. John Michael, FCA *1956;* 25D Belchamps Way, Hawkwell, HOCKLEY, SS5 4NU. (Life Member)

HILL, Mr. John Ridgway, FCA *1952;* 160 Liverpool Road South, Maghull, LIVERPOOL, L31 7AJ. (Life Member)

HILL, Mr. John Roderick, FCA *1969;* 32 Goddington Road, BOURNE END, SL8 5TZ. (Life Member)

HILL, Mr. John Stephen, BA ACA *1984;* Park Farm Oast, Cranbrook Road, Frittenden, CRANBROOK, KENT, TN17 2AU.

HILL, Mr. John Stuart, FCA *1971;* Pickford Farm, Brickhill Lane, Allesley, COVENTRY, CV5 9BU. (Life Member)

•HILL, Mr. John Thomas, FCA *1969;* John T. Hill, Sycamore House, Church Street, Birlingham, PERSHORE, WR10 3AQ.

HILL, Mr. Jonathan, ACA *2009;* 4 Rue De Fribourg, 1201 GENEVA, SWITZERLAND.

HILL, Mr. Jonathan, BA FCA *1994;* European Credit Management Ltd, 34 Grosvenor Street, LONDON, W1K 4QU.

HILL, Mr. Jonathan Charles, BSc(Hons) ACA *2001;* 38 Silverdale Road, Gatley, CHEADLE, SK8 4QS.

HILL, Mr. Jonathan James, BA FCA *1979;* 219 Forest Road, TUNBRIDGE WELLS, KENT, TN2 5HT.

HILL, Mr. Jonathan Stanley, BSc ACA *1996;* Bovis Homes Ltd The Manor House, North Ash Road New Ash Green, LONGFIELD, DA3 8HQ.

HILL, Mr. Julian Peter Dunlop, FCA *1971;* Dawslea Barn, Hollist Lane, MIDHURST, WEST SUSSEX, GU29 9AD.

HILL, Mrs. Julie Ann, BA FCA *1975;* Whitelock, Whites Meadow, Ranton, STAFFORD, ST18 9JB.

HILL, Mrs. Julie Ann, BA ACA *1995;* (Tax Fac), 99 Westfield Drive, LEYLAND, PR25 1QY.
HILL, Ms. Katharine, MA MLitt ACA *2005;* 54 Castellain Mansions, Castellain Road, LONDON, W9 1HA.
HILL, Miss. Kathryn Lisa, BSc ACA *2007;* Willow Bank, Slack Lane, Saddleworth, OLDHAM, OL3 5TJ.
HILL, Miss. Kathryn Louise, BSc ACA *1991;* Elizabeth House The Green, Lois Weedon, TOWCESTER, NORTHAMPTONSHIRE, NN12 8PN.
HILL, Mrs. Katie Mairi, BSc ACA *1998;* 23 Bowers Way, HARPENDEN, AL5 4EP.
HILL, Mr. Keith Brian, FCA *1971;* 5 Broadfields, HARPENDEN, AL5 2HJ.
HILL, Mr. Keith Edward, BSc FCA *1978;* Zeneca Agrochemicals, Fernhurst, HASLEMERE, GU27 3JE.
HILL, Mrs. Kerrie Jane, BSc ACA *1999;* 45 West Avenue, West Finchley, LONDON, N3 1AU.
HILL, Mrs. Kim Elisabeth, BA ACA *1990;* Hartley Fowler Chartered Accountants, Pavilion View, 19 New Road, BRIGHTON, BN1 1EY.
HILL, Miss. Kirsty Elaine, BA ACA *2006;* 64 King George Avenue, Morley, LEEDS, LS27 8NL.
HILL, Mr. Laurence, BA ACA *2006;* Bunzl Plc York House, 45 Seymour Street, LONDON, W1H 7JT.
•**HILL, Mr. Lawrence David Francis, MA FCA CTA** *1969;* The Hay Group, Berkeley House, Dix's Field, EXETER, EX1 1PZ. See also Hay Tax Limited
•**HILL, Ms. Lesley Anne, BEng ACA** *1996;* 25 Willow Lane, Appleton, WARRINGTON, WA4 5EA.
HILL, Mrs. Lisa, BA(Hons) ACA *2001;* 2 Folding Close, Stewkley, LEIGHTON BUZZARD, BEDFORDSHIRE, LU7 0XE.
HILL, Miss. Lizzie, BSc ACA *2006;* 9 Ingle Mews, LONDON, EC1R 1XG.
HILL, Mrs. Lorraine, BA ACA *1995;* 81 Pheasant Way, Beeches Park, CIRENCESTER, GL7 1BJ.
HILL, Mrs. Lucy Alison, BA ACA *1997;* 12 Sanderstead Court Avenue, Sanderstead, SOUTH CROYDON, SURREY, CR2 9AG.
•**HILL, Mrs. Lucy Ruth, FCA** *1986;* Lucy R Hill, Woodlands, Falcon Lane, LEDBURY, HEREFORDSHIRE, HR8 2JW.
HILL, Mrs. Lynette Patricia, BSc FCA *1979;* 33 Park Road, Congresbury, BRISTOL, BS49 5HJ.
HILL, Mrs. Lynn Swaysland, BSc ACA *1990;* 38 Eden Road, CROYDON, CR0 1BA.
•**HILL, Mrs. Margaret Elsie, BSc ACA CTA** *1990;* (Tax Fac), Armstrong Watson, Birbeck House, Duke Street, PENRITH, CA11 7NA.
•**HILL, Mr. Mark Peter, BSc FCA** *1985;* Deloitte LLP, 3 Rivergate, Temple Quay, BRISTOL, BS1 6GD. See also Deloitte & Touche LLP
HILL, Mr. Mark Selwyn Saint George, BA FCA ATII *1985;* Freshfields Bruckhaus Deringer Llp, PO Box 561, LONDON, EC4Y 1HS.
•**HILL, Mr. Martin, BSc ACA** *1995;* Fitzgerald Power, Greyfriars, WATERFORD, COUNTY WATERFORD, IRELAND.
•**HILL, Mr. Martin Hector, FCA** *1973;* (Tax Fac), 4 The Grove, Brookmans Park, HATFIELD, HERTFORDSHIRE, AL9 7RN.
HILL, Mr. Martin Paul, BSc ACA *1993;* Compass Group UK Parklands Court, 24 Parklands Rednal, BIRMINGHAM, B45 9PZ.
HILL, Mr. Martin Peter, BSc ACA *2006;* The Grass Roots Group Plc, Penny Royal Court, Station Road, TRING, HERTFORDSHIRE, HP23 5QZ.
HILL, Mr. Martin Victor, FCA *1971;* Whitelock, Whites Meadow, Ranton, STAFFORD, ST18 9JB.
HILL, Mr. Matthew Graham, BSc ACA *1994;* 17 Hedley Road, ST. ALBANS, AL1 5JL.
HILL, Mr. Matthew John, BA ACA *2005;* 8 Woodcroft Lane, HOLYWOOD, COUNTY DOWN, BT18 0QH.
HILL, Mr. Mervyn Aubrey, BSc FCA *1984;* 2 Heathlands Rise, TEIGNMOUTH, DEVON, TQ14 9HL.
•**HILL, Mr. Michael Edward, BEng ACA** *1982;* ITICA Limited, Trinity House, Cambridge Business Park, CAMBRIDGE, CB4 0WZ.
HILL, Mr. Michael Frederick Graham, FCA *1982;* Lime Tree Cottage High Park Avenue East Horsley, LEATHERHEAD, SURREY, KT24 5DE.
HILL, Mr. Michael George Charles, FCA *1962;* 6 St. Josephs Mews, BEACONSFIELD, BUCKINGHAMSHIRE, HP9 1GA. (Life Member)
HILL, Mr. Michael Gerard, MBA FCA *1975;* 6 Larkhill Lane, Formby, LIVERPOOL, L37 1LX.
HILL, Mr. Michael John, ACA *1991;* 7 Sears Close Godmanchester, HUNTINGDON, CAMBRIDGESHIRE, PE29 2JZ.
HILL, Mr. Michael John, ACA *1990;* Flat 26, Downings House, 21 Southey Road, LONDON, SW19 1ND.
HILL, Mr. Michael Thomas Albert, BA ACA *1987;* Hereward House, Wakes Colne, COLCHESTER, CO6 2BY.
HILL, Mr. Miles Geoffrey, BSc FCA *1994;* 47a Stamford Road, Bowdon, ALTRINCHAM, WA14 2JN.
HILL, Mr. Morgan Roy, BEng ACA *2001;* 1178 Pittwater Road, NARRABEEN, NSW 2101, AUSTRALIA.
HILL, Mrs. Natalie Claire, ACA *2009;* 158 Derinton Road, LONDON, SW17 8HY.
HILL, Miss. Nerys Catherine, BSc(Hons) ACA *2004;* 27 Granville Park, LONDON, SE13 7DY.
HILL, Mr. Nicholas Alan, ACA *2005;* 9 Wigston Lane Aylestone, LEICESTER, LE2 8TH.
HILL, Mr. Nicholas Frank, MEng ACA *2000;* 57 Beechwood Avenue, ST. ALBANS, HERTFORDSHIRE, AL1 4XR.
•①**HILL, Mr. Nicholas Timothy Cornforth, BA ACA** *1987;* 11/F Greenville, 2 Glenealy, CENTRAL, HONG KONG SAR.
•**HILL, Mrs. Nicola Ann, BA ACA** *1991;* Nicola A Birch, 91 Greaves Lane, Stannington, SHEFFIELD, S6 6BD.
HILL, Miss. Nicola Louise, BA ACA *2004;* Ecofirst Ltd The Tithe Office, Preston Road, YEOVIL, SOMERSET, BA20 2FJ.
•**HILL, Mr. Paul Anthony, BSc FCA** *1977;* (Tax Fac), Paul A Hill & Co Limited, 3 Bull Lane, ST. IVES, CAMBRIDGESHIRE, PE27 5AX.
HILL, Mr. Paul Antony, BSc FCA *1985;* 12802 Woodside Drive, PROSPECT, KY 40059, UNITED STATES.
HILL, Mr. Paul Jonathan Peter, BSc ACA *1992;* 9 Ringshall Gardens, Bramley, TADLEY, HAMPSHIRE, RG26 5BW.
HILL, Mr. Paul Nicholas, BA ACA *1990;* 91 Greaves Lane, Stannington, SHEFFIELD, S6 6BD.
HILL, Mr. Paul Simon, ACA *2008;* with KPMG LLP, 15 Canada Square, LONDON, E14 5GL.
HILL, Mr. Paul William, BA FCA *1986;* The Oasis Centre Lincoln House, 75 Westminster Bridge Road, LONDON, SE1 7HS.
HILL, Mrs. Peggy Hang Ping, BSc ACA *1991;* Standard Chartered, 1 Basinghall Avenue, LONDON, EC2V 5DD.
•**HILL, Mr. Peter, BSc ACA** *1990;* Peter Hill (Accountant) Limited, 76 Holburn Park, STOCKTON-ON-TEES, CLEVELAND, TS19 8BJ.
HILL, Mr. Peter, ACA *1980;* 128 Harrogate Road, Rawdon, LEEDS, LS19 6AH.
HILL, Mr. Peter Bertram, FCA *1962;* Kendal Wood, New Hutton, KENDAL, LA8 0AQ. (Life Member)
•**HILL, Mr. Peter Dominic, FCA** *1990;* (Tax Fac), Dominic Hill Associates Ltd, Archer House, Britland Estate, Northbourne Road, EASTBOURNE, BN22 8PW. See also Southbourne Business Solutions Ltd
HILL, Mr. Peter Duncan, ACA *1980;* P. O. BOX 1382, PARKLANDS, GAUTENG, 2121, SOUTH AFRICA.
HILL, Mr. Peter Edward, ACA *2007;* 42 Duxford Street, Paddington, SYDNEY, NSW 2021, AUSTRALIA.
HILL, Mr. Peter George David, BA FCA *1983;* Genworth Financial Building 11 Chiswick Park, 566 Chiswick High Road, LONDON, W4 5XR.
HILL, Mr. Peter Gordon, FCA *1972;* 16 Highgate Lane, FARNBOROUGH, Hampshire, GU14 8AF.
HILL, Mr. Peter Martin, BEng ACA *1994;* Caring Homes Group Ltd, 830 The Crescent Colchester Business Park, COLCHESTER, CO4 9YQ.
•**HILL, Mr. Peter Simon, ACA FCCA FMAAT** *2008;* Mark Holt & Co Ltd, Marine Building, Victoria Wharf, PLYMOUTH, PL4 0RF.
•**HILL, Mr. Peter William, FCA** *1980;* Hillyates, Hill House, 27 Meadowford, Newport, SAFFRON WALDEN, CB11 3QL.
HILL, Mr. Philip Edmund James, BA ACA *1985;* Russell Cooke Solicitors, 2 Putney Hill, Putney, LONDON, SW15 6AB.
HILL, Mr. Philip James, BA ACA *1999;* 45 West Avenue, LONDON, N3 1AU.
HILL, Mr. Philip John, BA ACA *1988;* U& I Limited The Quadrant, Parkway Business Centre Ltd, 99 Parkway Avenue, SHEFFIELD, S9 4WG.
HILL, Mrs. Philippa Jane, BSc ACA *2001;* with Grant Thornton UK LLP, 30 Finsbury Square, LONDON, EC2P 2YU.
HILL, Mrs. Rachael Frances, BA FCA ACA *1996;* 5 Redgate Close, Babbacombe, TORQUAY, TQ1 3UG.
HILL, Mr. Ralph William, BSc BCom ACA *1995;* 7 Charter Place, STAINES, MIDDLESEX, TW18 2HN.
HILL, Mr. Randolph Paul, FCA *1971;* Springfield House, Old Road, SHIPSTON-ON-STOUR, WARWICKSHIRE, CV36 4HE.
HILL, Mr. Raymond, FCA *1941;* 14 Risi Road, Fish Hoek, CAPE TOWN, C.P., 7975, SOUTH AFRICA. (Life Member)
HILL, Mr. Reginald David, FCA *1964;* 6 Dol Helyg, Pembrey, BURRY PORT, DYFED, SA16 0EH. (Life Member)
HILL, Mr. Richard, FCA *1972;* 8 Glenn Crescent, Marton-in-Cleveland, MIDDLESBROUGH, CLEVELAND, TS7 8ED. (Life Member)
HILL, Mr. Richard, BA(Hons) ACA *2002;* 15 Close Corlett, Peel, ISLE OF MAN, IM5 1QH.
•**HILL, Mr. Richard Andrew, BSc FCA CTA** *2000;* (Tax Fac), 2 Marsden Terrace, Ramsey, ISLE OF MAN, IM8 3DS.
HILL, Mr. Richard Conchie, FCA *1961;* 35 Allander Road, Bearsden, GLASGOW, G61 1LT. (Life Member)
•**HILL, Mr. Richard John, BA(Hons) ACA** *2000;* Griffin Stone Moscrop & Co., 41 Welbeck Street, LONDON, W1G 8EA.
•①**HILL, Mr. Richard John, BA FCA** *1983;* KPMG LLP, 100 Temple Street, BRISTOL, BS1 6AG. See also KPMG Europe LLP
HILL, Mr. Richard Simon Peter, BA ACA *2003;* High Gables, Primrose Ridge, GODALMING, SURREY, GU7 2ND.
HILL, Mr. Richard Walter, ACA *1988;* 91 Charmouth Road, ST. ALBANS, HERTFORDSHIRE, AL1 4SF.
HILL, Mr. Robert, ACA *2010;* 1 Andrews Close, Quarry Bank, BRIERLEY HILL, WEST MIDLANDS, DY5 2XB.
HILL, Mr. Robert Anthony, BSc FCA *1983;* 6 Princes Avenue, MANCHESTER, M20 6SE.
HILL, Mr. Robert Colin, ACA *1994;* 81 Pheasant Way, CIRENCESTER, GL7 1BJ.
HILL, Mr. Robert David, FCA *1974;* 9 Primrose Drive, RICHBORO, PA 18954, UNITED STATES.
HILL, Mr. Robert David, BEng ACA *1998;* with CVC Capital Partners Limited, 111 Strand, LONDON, WC2R 0AG.
•**HILL, Mr. Robert Duncan, FCA** *1963;* (Tax Fac), R.D. Hill Associates, 5 Whinslee Drive, Lostock, BOLTON, BL6 4NB.
HILL, Mr. Robert Edward, BSc ACA *1994;* Mount Pleasant, Swanton Road, West Peckham, MAIDSTONE, KENT, ME18 5JY.
•**HILL, Mr. Robert Ivan, BSc FCA** *1991;* Robert Hill, 10 Townsway, Lostock Hall, PRESTON, PR5 5YQ.
HILL, Mr. Robert John, MSc BSc ACA *2005;* 70 Regina Road, LONDON, N4 3PP.
HILL, Mr. Robert Stanley, FCA *1972;* 18 Churchside Way, WALSALL, WS9 8XG.
HILL, Mr. Robert Stephen, BSc FCA *1983;* Chestnut Cottage, Old Gore, ROSS-ON-WYE, HR9 7QR.
HILL, Mr. Robert Victor Crosby, BCom ACA *1981;* Conquermoor Cottage, 74 Tibberton, NEWPORT, TF10 8PF.
HILL, Mr. Robin Humphry, FCA *1961;* Lower Camelot, South Cadbury, YEOVIL, SOMERSET, BA22 7HA.
HILL, Mr. Rodney Graham, BA CA ACA *1993;* with PricewaterhouseCoopers, 5700 Yonge Street, NORTH YORK M2M 4K7, ON, CANADA.
HILL, Mr. Roger John, FCA *1970;* 6 Grebe Close, Plympton, PLYMOUTH, PL7 2HQ.
HILL, Mr. Roger Philip, BA ACA *1984;* 8 Tower Mews, SALISBURY, SP1 3DJ.
•**HILL, Mr. Roger Scott, FCA** *1970;* Oakhurst House, 57 Ashbourne Road, DERBY, DE22 3FS.
HILL, Mr. Roland John, BA ACA *2005;* 1 Spindle Close, EPSOM, SURREY, KT19 8FZ.
HILL, Mr. Ronald David, FCA *1976;* 3 Hambye Close, Lacey Green, PRINCES RISBOROUGH, BUCKINGHAMSHIRE, HP27 0QZ.
HILL, Mr. Ronald James, FCA *1966;* 34 Eastbourne Road, AUCKLAND 1050, NEW ZEALAND.
HILL, Mr. Rowland Paul, ACA *1981;* 16 Ashley Mansions, Vauxhall Bridge Road, LONDON, SW1V 1BS.
HILL, Mr. Roy Thomas, FCA *1959;* 308 Loughborough Road, West Bridgford, NOTTINGHAM, NG2 7FB.
HILL, Mr. Rupert Mungo Champain, BSc ACA *2004;* Threewall House, Queens Avenue, BICESTER, OXFORDSHIRE, OX26 6TA.
HILL, Mr. Russell, ACA *2008;* 68 Green Pastures Road, Wraxall, BRISTOL, BS48 1HE.
HILL, Mr. Russell David, BPharm ACA *1989;* 3 St. Clair Road Greenmount, BURY, LANCASHIRE, BL8 4EU.
HILL, Ms. Sandra Louise, BSc ACA *1992;* Croft House Cross Haw Lane, Clapham, LANCASTER, LA2 8DZ.
HILL, Mrs. Sarah Louise, ACA *1993;* 1360 Evesham Road, Astwood Bank, REDDITCH, WORCESTERSHIRE, B96 6BD.
HILL, Mrs. Sharon, ACA *1994;* Long Meadow, Otherton Lane, Cotheridge, WORCESTER, WR6 5LS.
•**HILL, Mrs. Sian Elizabeth, BA ACA** *1988;* (Tax Fac), KPMG LLP, 15 Canada Square, LONDON, E14 5GL. See also KPMG Europe LLP
HILL, Mr. Simon, ACA *2005;* 50 Dereham Road, Easton, NORWICH, NR9 5EJ.
HILL, Mr. Simon Anthony, FCA *1964;* 23 Orchehill Avenue, GERRARDS CROSS, BUCKINGHAMSHIRE, SL9 8PT.
HILL, Mr. Simon Clive, BSc FCA *1992;* 1 Barnfield Crescent, Kemsing, SEVENOAKS, TN15 6SE.
HILL, Mr. Simon David, BSc ACA *2007;* 21 The Breech, College Town, SANDHURST, BERKSHIRE, GU47 0PN.
HILL, Mr. Simon Joel, BA FCA *1995;* with PricewaterhouseCoopers LLP, First Point, Buckingham Gate, London Gatwick Airport, GATWICK, WEST SUSSEX RH6 0NT.
HILL, Mr. Simon John, BEng ACA *1993;* Everymind Limited, 11-15 Betterton Street, Covent Garden, LONDON, WC2H 9BP.
HILL, Mr. Simon Justin Andrew, LLB ACA *1992;* (Tax Fac), 6 Heol y Coed, Rhiwbina, CARDIFF, CF14 6HP.
HILL, Mr. Simon Lee, BSc ACA *1997;* Cooper Parry Llp, 3 Centro Place, Pride Park, DERBY, DE24 8RF.
HILL, Mr. Simon Roderick, BA ACA *2002;* 27 Bulkington Avenue, WORTHING, WEST SUSSEX, BN14 7HH.
HILL, Mrs. Siobhan Fiona, BSc ACA *2003;* 15 Close Corlett, Peel, ISLE OF MAN, IM5 1QH.
HILL, Miss. Sophie Natasha, BA ACA ATII *1995;* Stonegate Cottage, Stonegate Lane, Aston by Budworth, NORTHWICH, CHESHIRE, CW9 6NE.
HILL, Mr. Spencer Michael, BSc ACA *2002;* 2 Cumber Cottages, Newtown Common, NEWBURY, BERKSHIRE, RG20 9DE.
HILL, Mr. Stephen, FCA *1960;* Wyvern, 935 Walmersley Road, BURY, BL9 5LL. (Life Member)
HILL, Mr. Stephen Bradford, ACA *1983;* 46 Marriotts Close, Felmersham, BEDFORD, MK43 7HD.
HILL, Mr. Stephen George, ACA *1985;* 47 Maes/y/Sarn, Pentyrch, CARDIFF, CF15 9QQ.
HILL, Mr. Stephen Gwillam, FCA *1972;* College Villa, College Lane, Masham, RIPON, NORTH YORKSHIRE, HG4 4HE. (Life Member)
HILL, Mr. Stephen John, BA ACA *1988;* Calle Canada Nueva 36A 1A, 28200 SAN LORENZO DE EL ESCORIAL, SPAIN.
HILL, Mr. Stephen Kenneth, FCA *1977;* 14 Great College Street, LONDON, SW1P 3RX.
HILL, Mr. Stephen Paul, BA ACA *1986;* 11 Hospital Road, Riddlesden, KEIGHLEY, BD20 5EP.
HILL, Mr. Stephen Ronald, BA ACA ACT *1992;* Oakfield House, Stoke Hill, EXETER, EX4 9JN.
HILL, Mr. Stephen Thomas, BA ACA *1988;* Frucor, PO Box 3167, NORTH STRATHFIELD, NSW 2137, AUSTRALIA.
HILL, Mr. Steven Alan, ACA *1987;* 4 Alma Road, Clifton, BRISTOL, BS8 2BY.
HILL, Mr. Steven Peter, BSc ACA *1993;* 12 Oakfields, Marshfield, CARDIFF, CF3 2EZ.
HILL, Mr. Stuart Raymond, BA ACA *1997;* 12 West End Road, Box End, BEDFORD, BEDFORDSHIRE, MK43 8RT.
HILL, Mrs. Susan Eileen, ACA *1985;* 16 Woodlea Grove, Little Eaton, DERBY, DE21 5EN.
HILL, Mrs. Susan Gopal, BA ACA *1990;* 3 King George Close, FARNBOROUGH, HAMPSHIRE, GU14 6PW.
•**HILL, Mrs. Susan Margaret, BSc FCA** *1989;* Hills, Eddystone House, Aberderfyn, Johnstown, WREXHAM, LL14 1PB.
HILL, Mrs. Susan Mary, BA ACA *1981;* Ontario Ministry of Revenue, London Tax Office, 400-130 Dufferin Ave, LONDON N6A 6G8, ON, CANADA.
HILL, Mrs. Susan Sarah, ACA *1982;* (Tax Fac), with Burton Sweet, Cornerstone House, Midland Way, Thornbury, BRISTOL, BS35 2BS.
•**HILL, Mrs. Suzanne Marie, BSc ACA** *1989;* (Tax Fac), Suzanne Hill & Co Limited, Rose Cottage, Cross Lanes, Oscroft Tarvin, CHESTER, CH3 8NQ.
HILL, Mr. Thomas Anthony, FCA *1966;* 35/125 Santa Cruz Boulevarde, CLEAR ISLAND WATERS, QLD 4226, AUSTRALIA.
HILL, Mr. Thomas Rowland, MEng ACA *2001;* Flat 123, Lauderdale Mansions, Lauderdale Road, LONDON, W9 1LY.
HILL, Mr. Timothy John, BA ACA *1993;* 24 Highcroft Lane, Horndean, WATERLOOVILLE, PO8 9NX.
HILL, Mr. Timothy John Cantrell, MEng ACA *2003;* Aviva Plc, St. Helens, 1 Undershaft, LONDON, EC3P 3DQ.
•**HILL, Mr. Timothy John Richard, MA FCA** *1978;* Jolliffe Cork LLP, 33 George Street, WAKEFIELD, WEST YORKSHIRE, WF1 1LX. See also Jolliffe Cork Consulting Limited
•**HILL, Mr. Timothy Oliver, BA FCA** *1974;* Rosebank, Kingsmills Road, WREXHAM, LL13 0NS.

HILL, Mr. Tony Allen, MA ACA *1992;* Wunmorr, Mushroom Field, Kingston, LEWES, EAST SUSSEX, BN7 3LE.

HILL, Miss. Tracey Ann, BSc ACA *2010;* 18 Pine Ridge, NEWBURY, RG14 2NQ.

HILL, Mr. Trevor James, BSc ACA *1978;* Hertz Europe Ltd, Hertz House, 11 Vine Street, UXBRIDGE, MIDDLESEX, UB8 1QE.

HILL, Mr. Tristram Robert, BSc ACA *2005;* 11 Egdean Walk, SEVENOAKS, KENT, TN13 3UQ.

•**HILL, Mrs. Vanessa, BSc ARCS ACA** *1989;* Hillyates, Hill House, 27 Meadowford, Newport, SAFFRON WALDEN, CB11 3QL.

HILL, Mrs. Vanessa Jane, MA ACA *1997;* 129 Marlow Bottom, MARLOW, BUCKINGHAMSHIRE, SL7 3PJ.

HILL, Mrs. Victoria Helen, BA ACA *2006;* 25 Braddyll Street, LONDON, SE10 9AE.

HILL, Mr. Vincent George, FCA *1964;* 4 The Ridge Way, Sanderstead, SOUTH CROYDON, SURREY, CR2 0LE. (Life Member)

HILL, Mrs. Vivien Ann, BA(Hons) ACA *2003;* Old Bent House, Bent House Lane, Off Halifax Road, LITTLEBOROUGH, LANCASHIRE, OL15 0JB.

•**HILL, Mr. William Peter Favor, FCA** *1972;* MA Partners LLP, 7 The Close, NORWICH, NORFOLK, NR1 4DJ.

HILL ABRAHAMS, Mrs. Rosalind Margaret, BA(Hons) ACA FRSA *1982;* 93 Cheyne Walk, LONDON, SW10 0DQ.

HILL-ALLEN, Mr. Geoffrey Walter, FCA *1960;* 22 Melton Road, OAKHAM, LE15 6AY. (Life Member)

HILL-COTTINGHAM, Mr. Brian Edward, FCA *1961;* 40 The Dell, Great Baddow, CHELMSFORD, CM2 7JY. (Life Member)

HILLAM, Mrs. Catherine Felicity, BSc FCA *1984;* Laurel Bank, 3 Langley Avenue, Villa Road, BINGLEY, BD16 4ET.

•**HILLAM, Mr. Keith Richard, MA FCA** *1983;* Baker Tilly Tax & Advisory Services LLP, The Waterfront, Salts Mill Road, Saltaire, SHIPLEY, WEST YORKSHIRE BD17 7EZ. See also Baker Tilly UK Audit LLP

HILLARY, Mr. Ian David, BA MCMI ACA *1995;* 3 Adderstone Court, Adderstone Crescent, NEWCASTLE UPON TYNE, NE2 2EA.

•**HILLARY LESQUERRE, Ms. Sarah Harriet, ACA** *1992;* Moore Stephens LLP, 150 Aldersgate Street, LONDON, EC1A 4AB.

HILLAS, Mr. Keith John Newland, BA ACA *1992;* Highcroft, 72 St. Andrews Road, HENLEY-ON-THAMES, OXFORDSHIRE, RG9 1JE.

HILLBOM, Mr. Olle Henrik, ACA *2010;* Olle Hillbom, Skanegatan 79, 116 35 STOCKHOLM, SWEDEN.

HILLEARD, Miss. Diane Alison, BA ACA *1993;* Floor 29, Barclays Bank Plc, 1 Churchill Place, LONDON, E14 5HP.

•**HILLEL, Mr. David, FCA** *1959;* David Hillel, Flat 2, Stanview Court, 5 Queens Road, LONDON, NW4 2TH.

HILLERBY, Mr. John Marshall, FCA *1969;* 34 Waterfront Circle, COLLINGWOOD L9Y 4Z3, ON, CANADA.

HILLGARTH, Mr. Tristan Patrick Alan, MA BA FCA *1977;* Jupiter International Group Plc, 1 Grosvenor Place, LONDON, SW1X 7JJ.

•**HILLIAM, Mr. David Peter, BSc FCA** *1979;* David Hilliam, The Lodge, Oak Lawn, Woodside, Wootton, RYDE ISLE OF WIGHT PO33 4JR.

HILLIAR, Mr. Edwin John, FCA *1951;* 15 Enfield Road, Evercreech, SHEPTON MALLET, BA4 6LJ. (Life Member)

HILLIAR, Mr. Richard John, BA ACA *1985;* 79 Cabramatta Road, Mosman, MOSMAN, NSW 2088, AUSTRALIA.

•**HILLIARD, Mr. Harry Martin, BSc FCA** *1976;* Monahans, Clarks Mill, Stallard Street, TROWBRIDGE, BA14 8HH. See also Monahans Limited

•**HILLIER, Mr. Arnold, FCA** *1965;* Arnold Hillier, Dalkeith, 82 Bridge Lane, Bramhall, STOCKPORT, SK7 3AW.

HILLIER, Mr. Benjamin Charles, BA ACA *2001;* 43a Curwen Road, LONDON, W12 9AF.

HILLIER, Mrs. Caroline, FCA *1992;* 7 Bourne Firs, Lower Bourne, FARNHAM, GU10 3QD.

HILLIER, Mr. Gordon Lawrence William, FCA *1962;* Oakroyd, Bowers Place, Crawley Down, CRAWLEY, WEST SUSSEX, RH10 4HY.

HILLIER, Mr. John Henry, MBA FCA *1964;* Greenlands, Chelsfield Lane, ORPINGTON, BR6 7RS. (Life Member)

•**HILLIER, Mr. John Michael, FCA** *1993;* Condy Mathias, Suite 26, 3 Atlas House, West Devon Business Park, TAVISTOCK, PL19 9DP.

HILLIER, Mr. Mark Andrew, MA ACA *1991;* 7 Bourne Firs, Lower Bourne, FARNHAM, GU10 3QD.

HILLIER, Mr. Mark Stephen, BCom ACA *1979;* (Tax Fac), 25 Burney Street, LONDON, SE10 8EX.

HILLIER, Mr. Martin Roy, BSc ACA *1994;* 15 Brook Lane, TONBRIDGE, KENT, TN9 1PU.

HILLIER, Mr. Piers Adrian Carlyle, MPhil BSc ACA ASIP *1996;* LV Asset Management, 80 Cheapside, LONDON, EC2V 6EE.

HILLIER, Mr. Robert Malcolm, BA FCA *1979;* 23 Water Lane, Brislington, BRISTOL, BS4 5AW.

HILLIER, Mr. Ronald David, FCA *1971;* 65a New Road, Haslingfield, CAMBRIDGE, CB23 1LP.

HILLIER, Miss. Rosie, MSc ACA MRICS *1999;* Flat 17, 56 Vincent Square, Westminster, LONDON, SW1P 2NE.

HILLIER, Mr. Timothy James, ACA *2008;* Deloitte & Touche, 2 New Street Square, LONDON, EC4A 3BZ.

HILLING, Mr. Phillip Bryant, MA FCA *1976;* Halfway House, Crayke, YORK, YO61 4TJ.

•**HILLING, Mr. Richard, ACA ACCA** *2009;* (Tax Fac), David Ridley Associates Limited, Manor House, 1 Macaulay Road, BROADSTONE, DORSET, BH18 8AS.

•**HILLMAN, Mr. Andrew George Aldridge, ACA** *1986;* Birchwood House, Birchwood Lane, Pensford, BRISTOL, BS39 4NG.

HILLMAN, Mr. Benjamin Robert, BA(Hons) ACA *2001;* 70 North Larches, DUNFERMLINE, FIFE, KY11 4NY.

HILLMAN, Mr. Charles Alexander, MA ACA *1989;* Silver Birch, Greensted Green, ONGAR, CM5 9LF.

HILLMAN, Mr. Christopher Arthur, FCA *1979;* 16 Seaford Road, ENFIELD, MIDDLESEX, EN1 1NT.

•**HILLMAN, Mr. Leslie John, BSc ACA** *1994;* KZS Limited, 60 Fallowfield, WELLINGBOROUGH, NORTHAMPTONSHIRE, NN9 5YY.

HILLMAN, Mrs. Louise Karen Michelle, BSc ACA *1998;* 42 Temple Fortune Lane, LONDON, NW11 7UE.

HILLMAN, Mr. Paul Arthur, MA ACA *1978;* Apartment 43 Hanover House, 32 Westferry Circus, LONDON, E14 8RH.

HILLMAN, Mr. Peter John, FCA *1967;* Flat 4, 39 Maresfield Gardens, LONDON, NW3 5SG.

HILLMAN, Mr. Philip Samuel, FCA *1962;* 6 Whaddon House, William Mews, LONDON, SW1X 9HG. (Life Member)

HILLMAN, Mrs. Sarah Elisabeth, ACA *1991;* 3 Thomas Lane, Finchampstead, WOKINGHAM, RG40 4RU.

•**HILLS, Mr. Adrian Philip, ACA** *1989;* Kirk Hills, 5 Barnfield Crescent, EXETER, EX1 1QT. See also Kirk Hills Insolvency Ltd

•**HILLS, Mr. Alan Jeffery, FCA** *1975;* (Tax Fac), Marks Hills & Co Limited, 52 Warwick Gardens, THAMES DITTON, SURREY, KT7 0RB.

HILLS, Mr. Alex James Marchant, BSc ACA *2007;* 4 Taybridge Road, LONDON, SW11 5PS.

HILLS, Mr. Ben, MA(Cantab) ACA *2011;* Flat 5, 1 Ferndale St, LONDON, E6 6BF.

HILLS, Mr. Christopher Charles, BSc ACA *1988;* Level 39, 2 Park Street, SYDNEY, NSW 2000, AUSTRALIA.

HILLS, Mrs. Claire, BSc FCA *1995;* 4 Grange Drive, Hartford, NORTHWICH, CHESHIRE, CW8 3AE.

HILLS, Mr. Damian Richard, BSc FCA *1993;* 7 Vanda Avenue, Orchid Village, SINGAPORE 287946, SINGAPORE.

HILLS, Mr. David Philip, BSc ACA *1995;* Northland Capital Partners Ltd, 46 Worship Street, LONDON, EC2A 2EA.

HILLS, Mr. David Richard, BSc ACA *1996;* 33 Wych Elm Road, Oadby, LEICESTER, LE2 4EF.

HILLS, Mr. Derek William, FCA *1975;* with PKF (UK) LLP, Farringdon Place, 20 Farringdon Road, LONDON, EC1M 3AP.

HILLS, Mr. Dudley Gordon, FCA *1951;* 46 Barnhill Road, DUMFRIES, DG2 9HR. (Life Member)

HILLS, Mrs. Fiona, ACA *2008;* C. Lewis and Company, 28 Lime Street, LONDON, EC3M 7HR.

HILLS, Mr. Gavin, BA(Hons) ACA *2004;* 28 Hide Gardens Rustington, LITTLEHAMPTON, WEST SUSSEX, BN16 3NP.

HILLS, Mr. Graham Andrew, BA ACA *1981;* 83 Longland Road, EASTBOURNE, BN20 8JB.

HILLS, Mrs. Helen Mary, BAcc ACA *2003;* Ubiquisys Limited, The Stella Building, Windmill Hill Business Park, Whitehill Way, SWINDON, SN5 6NX.

HILLS, Mr. Ian Andrew, BSc ACA *2007;* Rossweid 1, 5643 SINS, SWITZERLAND.

HILLS, Mr. Jeremy Coleridge, FCA *1969;* 26 Dry Hill Road, TONBRIDGE, TN9 1LX. (Life Member)

HILLS, Mrs. Joanne Lesley, BSc ACA *2005;* 70 Chastilian Road, DARTFORD, DA1 3JZ.

•**HILLS, Mr. John Leonard, BA FCA** *1981;* KPMG LLP, 15 Canada Square, LONDON, E14 5GL. See also KPMG Europe LLP

•**HILLS, Mr. Jonathan William Macleod, MA FCA CTA MCIArb** *1973;* (Tax Fac), PKF (UK) LLP, Pannell House, Park Street, GUILDFORD, SURREY, GU1 4HN.

•**HILLS, Mr. Kevin Robert, BSc FCA** *1994;* Ernst & Young LLP, 100 Barbirolli Square, MANCHESTER, M2 3EY. See also Ernst & Young Europe LLP

HILLS, Mr. Lucian Edward, BSc ACA *1996;* Tribal Education Ltd, 1-4 Portland Square, BRISTOL, BS2 8RR.

HILLS, Mr. Mark Robert, BSc ACA *1990;* Village Farmhouse, Roecliffe, YORK, YO51 9LY.

HILLS, Mr. Martin Stuart, BSc ACA *1983;* with Deloitte Touche Tohmatsu, 35/F One Pacific Place, 88 Queensway, CENTRAL, HONG KONG ISLAND, HONG KONG SAR.

HILLS, Mr. Nicholas William, MA ACA *1999;* The Old Hall High Street, Barley, ROYSTON, HERTFORDSHIRE, SG8 8JA.

HILLS, Mr. Paul David, BSc ACA *2006;* 70 Chastilian Road, DARTFORD, DA1 3JZ.

HILLS, Miss. Rachel Diana Argo, BSc ACA *2004;* Robinswood, 18b York Gardens, WALTON-ON-THAMES, SURREY, KT12 3EP.

HILLS, Mr. Richard, BA ACA *1989;* 122 Barrowby Road, GRANTHAM, LINCOLNSHIRE, NG31 8AF.

•**HILLS, Mr. Russell Stewart, LLB ACA** *1991;* (Tax Fac), KPMG LLP, Saltire Court, 20 Castle Terrace, EDINBURGH, EH1 2EG. See also KPMG Europe LLP

HILLS, Mrs. Sophie, BA ACA *1999;* 40 Runnemede Road, EGHAM, TW20 9BL.

HILLS, Mr. Steven Randall, MA MBA FCA MCMI PgDip FHEA *1973;* 11 Ackroyd Place, Shenley Lodge, MILTON KEYNES, MK5 7PA.

HILLS, Miss. Suzanne Laura, BSc ACA *2005;* Flat 1 Langdale Court, Castlebar Mews, LONDON, W5 1RS.

HILLS, Mr. William James, FCA *1953;* Forest Edge, Coppice Row, Theydon Bois, EPPING, ESSEX, CM16 7DS. (Life Member)

HILLS PEARSON, Mrs. Jean, BA ACA *1988;* 4 Westfield Avenue, Gosforth, NEWCASTLE UPON TYNE, NE3 4YH.

HILLSDON, Mr. Andrew Charles, BA FCA DChA *1993;* with Crowe Clark Whitehill LLP, St Bride's House, 10 Salisbury Square, LONDON, EC4Y 8EH.

HILLSDON, Mrs. Michelle, BSc ACA *1997;* with Baker Tilly Tax & Advisory Services LLP, Hanover House, 18 Mount Ephraim Road, TUNBRIDGE WELLS, KENT, TN1 1ED.

HILLSON, Mr. Geoffrey Brian, FCA *1954;* Bramleys Meadow, Ashdon Road, Radwinter, SAFFRON WALDEN, ESSEX, CB10 2UA. (Life Member)

•**HILLYARD, Mr. Nicholas James, BA FCA** *1991;* with KPMG LLP, 1 The Embankment, Neville Street, LEEDS, LS1 4DW.

HILLYARD, Mr. Paul William, FCA *1969;* 3 Lime Avenue, NORTHAMPTON, NN3 2HA.

HILLYARD, Miss. Stacey Anne, ACA *2003;* 43 Chander Close, FERNDOWN, DORSET, BH22 8DW.

HILLYARD, Mr. Stephen Philip, BSc ACA *1997;* with Peters Elworthy & Moore, Salisbury House, Station Road, CAMBRIDGE, CB1 2LA.

HILLYER, Mr. John Edward, FCA *1970;* 14 Chandos Close, AMERSHAM, HP6 6PJ.

HILLYER, Mrs. Leanne Louise, ACA *2005;* 29 Lindley Avenue, SUTTON-IN-ASHFIELD, NOTTINGHAMSHIRE, NG17 2SY.

HILLYER, Mr. Roger Keith, BA FCA *1988;* 21 Ormonde Road, LONDON, SW14 7BE.

HILSON, Mrs. Jane Deborah, BSc ACA *1995;* with PricewaterhouseCoopers LLP, 1 Embankment Place, LONDON, WC2N 6RH.

HILSON, Mr. Richard Robert, ACA *1993;* Oakmead, 35/37 Tanhouse Road, OXTED, RH8 9PE.

HILTON, Mrs. Ajanta, BSc ACA *2003;* (Tax Fac), 37b Forge End, ST. ALBANS, HERTFORDSHIRE, AL2 3EQ.

HILTON, Mrs. Angela, ACA *2009;* P A Hull & Co, 41 Bridgeman Terrace, WIGAN, WN1 1TT.

•**HILTON, Mr. Anthony, FCA** *1979;* John Goulding & Co Ltd, 4 Southport Road, CHORLEY, LANCASHIRE, PR7 1LD.

HILTON, Mr. Christopher Dane, ACA *2005;* 82 Barnsley Road, Wath on Dearne, ROTHERHAM, S63 6DQ.

HILTON, Mr. David, BEng ACA *2007;* with Mazars LLP, The Lexicon, Mount Street, MANCHESTER, M2 5NT.

HILTON, Mr. David Stringer, FCA *1956;* PO Box 1075, Canning Bridge, APPLECROSS, WA 6153, AUSTRALIA. (Life Member)

HILTON, Mr. Donald George, BSc ACA *1980;* 2 Thrush Close, Kempshott, BASINGSTOKE, RG22 5PZ.

HILTON, Mr. Dudley James, MA FCA *1976;* Woodland Acres, Hascombe Road, GODALMING, SURREY, GU8 4AA. (Life Member)

HILTON, Mr. Guy St John, BSc ACA *1996;* 20 Addison Road, Walthamstow, LONDON, E17 9LT.

HILTON, Mr. James, MA ACA *2003;* 37b Forge End, ST. ALBANS, HERTFORDSHIRE, AL2 3EQ.

HILTON, Mr. James Robert, ACA *2009;* 26c Coombe Lane, LONDON, SW20 8ND.

HILTON, Mr. John David, FCA *1948;* 31 Hunters Way, Kimbolton, HUNTINGDON, PE28 0JF. (Life Member)

HILTON, Mr. John Geoffrey, MSc BSc FCA *1975;* PO Box 120, TYABB, VIC 3913, AUSTRALIA.

HILTON, Mr. John Mark, BSc ACA *1990;* 55 Moorgate, LONDON, EC2R 6PA.

HILTON, Mr. John Nigel, BA ACA *1983;* MEMBER OF COUNCIL, 1 Stone Close, TAUNTON, SOMERSET, TA1 4YG.

HILTON, Mr. Kenneth James, FCA *1948;* 5 Scalby Close, Whitebridge Park, Gosforth, NEWCASTLE UPON TYNE, NE3 5LJ. (Life Member)

HILTON, Mr. Kenneth Robert, BA ACA *1987;* TDG Contract Logistics, De Montfort House, High Street, Coleshill, BIRMINGHAM, B46 3BP.

HILTON, Mrs. Lesley Jane, BA ACA *1989;* 25 Carlton Road, East Sheen, LONDON, SW14 7RJ.

HILTON, Mr. Leslie, FCA *1969;* The Lodge, Les Hougues, Rue Des Choffins, St. Saviour, GUERNSEY, GY7 9XW.

HILTON, Mr. Mark Harold, MA ACA *1989;* 47 Bulwer Road, Leytonstone, LONDON, E11 1DE.

HILTON, Mr. Mark John, BSc ACA DChA *1991;* Sheffield Galleries & Museums Trust, Leader House, Surrey Street, SHEFFIELD, S1 2LH.

•**HILTON, Mr. Mark Redvers, BSc FCA** *1992;* ALG, Brook Point, 1412-1420 High Road, LONDON, N20 9BH.

•**HILTON, Mr. Nicholas David, FCA MCIM** *1974;* Moore Stephens LLP, 150 Aldersgate Street, LONDON, EC1A 4AB. See also Moore Stephens & Co

HILTON, Mr. Norman Walter, FCA *1973;* 18 Herons Rise, ANDOVER, HAMPSHIRE, SP10 2DY. (Life Member)

•**HILTON, Mr. Paul Christopher, FCA** *1992;* Accountants-E Ltd, 2 Ashurst Close, Harwood, BOLTON, BL2 3PE.

HILTON, Mr. Peter Alan, BSc ACA *1991;* Flat 17, The Mill, Coaters Lane, Wooburn Green, HIGH WYCOMBE, BUCKINGHAMSHIRE HP10 0FN.

HILTON, Mr. Peter Brinsley, BEng FCA *1975;* 5 Wharfedale Close, Allestree, DERBY, DE22 2UQ. (Life Member)

HILTON, Mr. Richard Dominic, ACA *2003;* with Ernst & Young, Ernst & Young Building, 8 Exhibition Street, MELBOURNE, VIC 3000, AUSTRALIA.

•**HILTON, Mr. Richard John, FCA** *1976;* Richard J. Hilton, 11 Crow Park Drive, Burton Joyce, NOTTINGHAM, NG14 5AS.

HILTON, Mr. Robin David, BSc FCA MBA *1997;* 65 Overstone Road, HARPENDEN, HERTFORDSHIRE, AL5 5PN.

HILTON, Mr. Samuel George, LLB ACA *2006;* Jepsons Shippon, Jepsons Farm Moor Road, Anglezarke, CHORLEY, PR6 9DQ.

•**HILTON, Mr. Timothy James, ACA** *1991;* Avonglen Limited, 2 Venture Road, Southampton Science Park, Chilworth, SOUTHAMPTON, SO16 7NP.

HIMAN, Mr. Harry, BSc ACA *1995;* 18 Alexandra Gardens, Brincliffe, SHEFFIELD, S11 9DQ.

HIMSLEY, Mr. Andrew David, BSc ACA *2006;* with FTI Consulting Limited, 322 Midtown, High Holborn, LONDON, WC1V 7PB.

HIMSWORTH, Mr. Malcolm, BSc FCA *1980;* Barrowfield Lodge, MUCH HADHAM, SG10 6BD.

HIMSWORTH, Mr. Malcolm Wright, FCA *1958;* 6 Stonedene Park, WETHERBY, WEST YORKSHIRE, LS22 7FZ. (Life Member)

HIMSWORTH, Mr. Neil Duncan, MA FCA *1987;* 1 Alwoodley Gates, Wigton Lane, LEEDS, LS17 8FB.

HINCHCLIFFE, Mr. David, BSc ACA *2006;* Midway House, Gorsey Lane, ASHTON-UNDER-LYNE, OL6 9BT.

HINCHCLIFFE, Mr. Michael Austin, BSc FCA *1992;* 222 West 14th Street, Apt 9F, NEW YORK, NY 10011, UNITED STATES.

HINCHCLIFFE, Mr. Richard David, BEng ACA *2001;* Motors Inssurance Company Ltd Jubilee House, 5 Mid Point, BRADFORD, WEST YORKSHIRE, BD3 7AG.

HINCHLIFF, Mr. Stephen, BEng ACA *1993;* 5 Poplar Avenue, Wyre Piddle, PERSHORE, WORCESTERSHIRE, WR10 2RJ.

HINCHLIFFE, Mr. Adrian, FCA *1965;* Smithy Hollow, Rathmell, SETTLE, NORTH YORKSHIRE, BD24 0LA. (Life Member)

HINCHLIFFE, Mrs. Anna Louise, BA ACA *2004;* 37 Sturdon Road, BRISTOL, BS3 2BB.
HINCHLIFFE, Mr. Craig Andrew, MEng ACA *2009;* 28 Hawthorn Road, Gatley, CHEADLE, CHESHIRE, SK8 4NB.
HINCHLIFFE, Mr. David Nelson, FCA *1955;* Midships, 89 East Beach Road, Selsey, CHICHESTER, WEST SUSSEX, PO20 0ES. (Life Member)
HINCHLIFFE, Mr. David Robert, MBA BA ACA *1987;* Whitesmiths, Smelt Road, Coedpoeth, WREXHAM, LL11 3SH.
HINCHLIFFE, Miss. Deborah Dawn, BA ACA *2000;* 63 Landells Road, LONDON, SE22 9PQ.
HINCHLIFFE, Mr. Duncan, FCA *1974;* 21 Long Meadows, Garforth, LEEDS, LS25 2BR.
HINCHLIFFE, Mr. Gregory James, ACA *2011;* 29 Shepherds Gate Drive, Weavering, MAIDSTONE, KENT, ME14 5UU.
HINCHLIFFE, Mr. James Richard Michael, BA ACA *2003;* The Coach House Barnsley Road, Silkstone, BARNSLEY, SOUTH YORKSHIRE, S75 4NG.
HINCHLIFFE, Mr. John Philip, BA FCA *1981;* P.O. Box 2378, GABORONE, BOTSWANA.
HINCHLIFFE, Mr. Jonathan, BSc ACA *2006;* PricewaterhouseCoopers, Darling Park Tower 2, 201 Sussex Street, SYDNEY, NSW 2000, AUSTRALIA.
HINCHLIFFE, Miss. Kate Louise, MSc ACA *2009;* 64 Rockhurst Drive, EASTBOURNE, EAST SUSSEX, BN20 8XD.
HINCHLIFFE, Ms. Katherine Victoria, ACA *2009;* 9 River Walk, Braddan Douglas, ISLE OF MAN, IM4 4TJ.
HINCHLIFFE, Mrs. Lesley Ann, BA ACA *1987;* Cleggs Cottage, Dog Lane Bank End, Upper Greetland, HALIFAX, HX4 8PW.
HINCHLIFFE, Miss. Margaret Diane, BSc ACA *2004;* 21 Styles Close, Leamington Spa, WARWICK, CV31 1LS.
•HINCHLIFFE, Ms. Michelle Anne, ACA *2003;* with KPMG, 147 Collins Street, MELBOURNE, VIC 3000, AUSTRALIA.
HINCHLIFFE, Mr. Nigel Mark, BA(Hons) ACA *2006;* 1 Moncrieffe Road, SHEFFIELD, S7 1HQ.
•HINCHLIFFE, Mr. Paul, BA FCA *1989;* P Hinchliffe Limited, 1 The Villas, Blackergreen Lane, Silkstone, BARNSLEY, SOUTH YORKSHIRE S75 4NF. See also Harrisaccounts LLP
HINCHLIFFE, Mr. Richard Julian, MBA BSc ACA *1994;* 17 Grove Street, BIRCHGROVE, NSW 2041, AUSTRALIA.
HINCHLIFFE, Mr. Samuel John, BSc ACA *2006;* with PricewaterhouseCoopers, Darling Park Tower 2, 201 Sussex Street, GPO Box 2650, SYDNEY, NSW 1171 AUSTRALIA.
•HINCHLIFFE, Mrs. Susan Joy, BSc FCA *1981;* (Tax Fac), Susan Hinchliffe & Co Ltd, 4 Newton Close, Newton Ferrers, PLYMOUTH, PL8 1AL.
•HINCKLEY, Mr. Ian Michael, ACA ATII *1988;* Ian Hinckley, 3 Balfour Place, MARLOW, SL7 3TB.
HIND, Mr. Andrew Clive, BA ACA *1986;* 14 Princes Avenue, LONDON, N10 3LR.
HIND, Mr. Andrew Fleming, CB FCA *1979;* 11 Byng Road, BARNET, HERTFORDSHIRE, EN5 4NW.
HIND, Mrs. Audrey, FCA *1971;* Candle Cottage, Fishers Lane, Charlbury, CHIPPING NORTON, OXFORDSHIRE, OX7 3RX. (Life Member)
HIND, Mr. Donald Bryan, FCA *1954;* 3 Marine Parade, HARWICH, CO12 3LB. (Life Member)
HIND, Mrs. Elaine Kathryn, BA ACA MAAT *2001;* 16 Tavistock Close, HARTLEPOOL, TS27 3LB.
HIND, Miss. Gillian Patricia, ACA *1983;* 141 Providence Road, SHEFFIELD, S6 5BG.
HIND, Mrs. Joanna Marie, BSc ACA *1999;* 2 Ninfield Close, Carlton Colville, LOWESTOFT, SUFFOLK, NR33 8SD.
HIND, Mr. Neale David, FCA *1977;* The Old Orchard, 2 West Street, Easton on the Hill, STAMFORD, PE9 3LS.
HIND, Mr. Reginald Tom William, FCA *1966;* 9 Dartmeet Court, Lynmouth Crescent, NOTTINGHAM, NG7 5RD. (Life Member)
HIND, Mr. Timothy Seamus, BSc ACA *1991;* 80 Valley Road, Bramhall, STOCKPORT, CHESHIRE, SK7 2NL.
HINDE, Mr. John Stephen, BSc ACA *1990;* 5 Deane Way, RUISLIP, MIDDLESEX, HA4 8SU.
HINDE, Ms. Nicola Jane, BSc ACA *1987;* (Tax Fac), 29 Cambridge Avenue, NEW MALDEN, KT3 4LD.
HINDE, Mr. Patrick Robert, BSc ACA *1994;* Gullivers, North Road, Goudhurst, CRANBROOK, KENT, TN17 1JH.
HINDE, Mr. Stephen Victor Cecil, FCA FIIA MIIA *1971;* 80 Dudley Road, WALTON-ON-THAMES, KT12 2JX.
•HINDER, Mr. Leslie John, MBA BSc FCA *1983;* Leslie Hinder, Dairy House, 59 Cheapside Road, ASCOT, BERKSHIRE, SL5 7QR.
HINDERER, Mr. Alan Albert, FCA *1957;* Wittering Court, Bramble Crescent, BENFLEET, SS7 2XE. (Life Member)
HINDES, Mr. Mark Lewis William, BA ACA *1993;* 87 Byng Road, BARNET, HERTFORDSHIRE, EN5 4NP.
HINDESS, Mr. Ian Roland, BA FCA *1981;* Hunters Moon, Whitton Road, Alkborough, SCUNTHORPE, DN15 9JG.
HINDLE, Mr. Brian Alan, FCA *1965;* 8 Plains Farm Close, Mapperley Plains, NOTTINGHAM, NG3 5RE.
•HINDLE, Mrs. Carol Wendy, BCom ACA *1993;* Deloitte LLP, 4 Brindley Place, BIRMINGHAM, B1 2HZ. See also Deloitte & Touche LLP
•HINDLE, Mr. Christopher William, FCA DChA *1969;* Chantrey Vellacott DFK LLP, Cheviot House, 53 Sheep Street, NORTHAMPTON, NN1 2NE.
•HINDLE, Mr. Howard John, BSc FCA *1981;* 7 Stockdale Place, BIRMINGHAM, B15 3XH.
HINDLE, Mr. James Edward, BEng ACA *2000;* 17 Brighton Street, Sandringham, MELBOURNE, VIC 3191, AUSTRALIA.
HINDLE, Mr. James Thomas, BA ACA *2008;* 51 Pencarrow Close, Didsbury, MANCHESTER, M20 2PS.
HINDLE, Mr. John Robert, FCA *1942;* White Cottage, Brock, Garstang, PRESTON, PR3 0GL. (Life Member)
HINDLE, Mrs. Lynne Christine, BA FCA *1990;* B A E Systems (Operations) Ltd, Warton Aerodrome, Warton, PRESTON, PR4 1AX.
HINDLE, Miss. Margaret Hilary, FCA *1973;* 35 Barry Street, BURNLEY, BB12 6DT.
•HINDLE, Mr. Matthew John, ACA FCCA *2010;* 25 Claughton Avenue, LEYLAND, LANCASHIRE, PR25 5TJ.
HINDLE, Mr. Paul Anthony, FCA *1962;* 14 East Holme, LYTHAM ST.ANNES, FY8 4HR.
•HINDLE, Mr. Paul Gary, MA ACA ATII *1988;* Paul Hindle Limited, The Old Gamedealers, Dereham Road, Garvestone, NORWICH, NR9 4QT.
HINDLE, Dr. Richard John, BSc ACA AMCT *1993;* 6 Hintlesham Avenue, BIRMINGHAM, B15 2PH.
HINDLE, Mr. Robert Keith, MA FCA *1963;* Wrights Barn, 57 Town Street, Lound, RETFORD, DN22 8RT. (Life Member)
HINDLE, Mr. Terrence Clive, FCA *1961;* Street Farm, Wootton Lane, Wootton, CANTERBURY, CT4 6RP.
HINDLE, Mr. Tim Robert, ACA *2008;* with Deloitte LLP, 2 New Street Square, LONDON, EC4A 3BZ.
•HINDLEY, Mr. Alan John, FCA FCCA FAIA *1974;* (Tax Fac), PKB UK LLP, Beechey House, 87 Church Street, CROWTHORNE, RG45 7AW. See also PKB
•HINDLEY, Mr. Christopher Douglas, FCA *1972;* C.D. Hindley & Co, 29 Captain Lees Garden, Westhoughton, BOLTON, BL5 3YF.
HINDLEY, Mrs. Debra Bernice, BSc ACA *1990;* Beech Mount, 44 Wellhouse Road, Beech, ALTON, GU34 4AG.
•HINDLEY, Mrs. Felicity Clare, ACA CTA *2008;* Mulberry Accountancy, 40 Mill Road, Frettenham, NORWICH, NR12 2LQ.
HINDLEY, Mr. Ian Anthony, BSc ACA *1996;* Churchwick House, 5 Kirkwick Avenue, HARPENDEN, HERTFORDSHIRE, AL5 2QH.
•HINDLEY, Mr. John Stephen, FCA *1975;* (Tax Fac), Hindley & Co, 733 Manchester Road, Over Hulton, BOLTON, BL5 1BA.
•HINDLEY, Mr. Kevin, BSc ACA CTA *2001;* with Alvarez & Marsal - London Office, First Floor, One Finsbury Circus, LONDON, EC2M 7EB.
HINDLEY, Mr. Martyn John, BSc ACA *1987;* Beech Mount, 44 Wellhouse Road, Beech, ALTON, GU34 4AG.
HINDLEY, Mr. Michael Harold, FCA *1966;* 4 Pheasant Walk, High Legh, KNUTSFORD, WA16 6LU.
HINDLEY, Miss. Rebecca Sarah, BA ACA *1997;* 12 Coombe Gardens, Wimbledon, LONDON, SW20 0QU.
HINDLEY, Miss. Sarah Elizabeth, BA ACA *2005;* 53 Station Road Cholsey, WALLINGFORD, OXFORDSHIRE, OX10 9QB.
HINDLEY, Mr. William Keith, BSc FCA *1973;* Meadowcroft, Audlem Road, Woore, CREWE, CW3 9RL.
HINDMARCH, Mr. Andrew, ACA FCMA *2009;* Briarwood, 45 Bryntirion Drive, PRESTATYN, CLWYD, LL19 9NT.
HINDMARCH, Mr. Graham, BSc(Hons) ACA *2003;* 9 Butterwick Gardens, WETHERBY, WEST YORKSHIRE, LS22 6GX.
HINDMARCH, Mrs. Helen Catherine, ACA *2008;* 9 Butterwick Gardens, WETHERBY, WEST YORKSHIRE, LS22 6GX.
HINDMARCH, Mr. John Mark, ACA *2008;* 47a Wellington Road, LONDON, W5 4UJ.
HINDMARCH, Mr. Joshua Wesley Alan, BA ACA *1997;* 91 Glebe Crescent, WASHINGTON, NE38 7AF.
•HINDMARCH, Mr. Mark Thomas, BSc ACA *1992;* Duncan & Toplis, 14 All Saints Street, STAMFORD, LINCOLNSHIRE, PE9 2PA. See also Fidentia Services LLP
HINDMARCH, Mr. Michael Rutherford, FCA *1966;* Kings Lodge Manor Farm, Apethorpe, PETERBOROUGH, PE8 5DP.
HINDMARSH, Mr. Frederick Charles Reed, FCA *1970;* State Street Boston Capital Corporation, 4th Floor, 225 Franklin St, BOSTON, MA 02110, UNITED STATES.
•HINDMARSH, Mrs. Jillian Florence, BSc FCA *1993;* Allen Sykes Limited, 5 Henson Close, South Church Enterprise Park, BISHOP AUCKLAND, COUNTY DURHAM, DL14 6WA.
•HINDMARSH, Mr. Richard Charlton, BA ACA *2000;* Erftstr 18, 40219 DUSSELDORF, GERMANY.
•HINDMOOR, Mr. Tony, FCA *1995;* Gibbons, Netherall Chambers, 2 Curzon Street, MARYPORT, CUMBRIA, CA15 6LL. See also Gibbons & Company
HINDOCHA, Mr. Amit, ACA *1998;* 161 Uxbridge Road, Harrow Weald, HARROW, HA3 6DG.
•HINDOCHA, Mr. Anilkumar Damodar, FCA *1980;* Hindocha & Co., 19 Harewood Road, Deepdale, PRESTON, PR1 6XH.
•HINDOCHA, Mr. Bharatkumar Thakarshi Gokaldas, FCA *1974;* (Tax Fac), Price Mann & Co, 447 Kenton Road, HARROW, HA3 0XY.
HINDOCHA, Mr. Bhikhu Popatlal, FCA *1973;* Floriana, 20 Southmeads Road, Oadby, LEICESTER, LE2 2LS.
HINDOCHA, Mrs. Bindi, BSc ACA *2009;* Flat 16 Princess Park Manor, Royal Drive, LONDON, N11 3FL.
HINDOCHA, Mr. Krushi Vinod, BSc ACA *2011;* 5 Southside Road, LEICESTER, LE3 2YZ.
•HINDOCHA, Mr. Labhendra Virjibhai, ACA *1983;* Hindocha & Co, V16 Howitt Building, Lenton Business Park, Lenton Boulevard, NOTTINGHAM, NG7 2BY. See also Trustax Services Ltd
HINDOCHA, Miss. Neha, BSc(Hons) ACA *2011;* Flat 65 Lyttelton Court, Lyttelton Road, LONDON, N2 0ED.
HINDOCHA, Mrs. Parul, BSc ACA *1988;* Gateway House, 28 The Quadrant, RICHMOND, SURREY, TW9 1DN.
HINDOCHA, Miss. Rakhee, MA ACA *2004;* 4 Heathside Avenue, BEXLEYHEATH, DA7 4PZ.
HINDOCHA, Mr. Ravi Dipak, ACA *2009;* 12 Blankley Drive, LEICESTER, LE2 2DE.
HINDOCHA, Mrs. Vilas Y, ACA *1986;* 34 Queensbury Station Parade, EDGWARE, HA8 5NN.
•HINDOCHA, Mr. Virendra Thakarshi, FCA *1979;* (Tax Fac), Price Mann & Co, 447 Kenton Road, HARROW, HA3 0XY.
•HINDOCHA, Mr. Yashlal P, BA FCA *1980;* Hindocha & Co Limited, 34 Queensbury Station Parade, EDGWARE, MIDDLESEX, HA8 5NN.
•HINDS, Mr. Clive Peter, BSc ACA *1981;* PricewaterhouseCoopers LLP, Marlborough Court, 10 Bricket Road, ST. ALBANS, HERTFORDSHIRE, AL1 3JX. See also PricewaterhouseCoopers
HINDS, Mr. Gerald Ernest, LLB FCA *1940;* 838 Plymouth Street, Apt 227, MONTREAL H4P 1B4, QUE, CANADA. (Life Member)
HINDS, Miss. Jessica, BSc(Hons) ACA *2011;* Flat 5, 5 Little Stanhope Street, BATH, BA1 2BH.
HINDS, Mr. John Gwyn, BSc ACA *1983;* Matrix Alpha, Matrix Business Park, SWANSEA, SA6 8RE.
•HINDS, Mr. Keith, FCA *1984;* Grant Thornton UK LLP, 30 Finsbury Square, LONDON, EC2P 2YU. See also Grant Thornton LLP
HINDS, Mr. Richard John, BA ACA *2004;* Ash Lodge Cross Lane, Kermincham, CONGLETON, CHESHIRE, CW12 2LJ.
•HINDS, Mr. Stuart James, ACA MAAT *2002;* Baker Tilly UK Audit LLP, Marlborough House, Victoria Road South, CHELMSFORD, ESSEX, CM1 1LN. See also Baker Tilly Tax and Advisory Services LLP
HINDSHAW, Mrs. Jennifer Mary, TD JP DL FCA *1964;* 78 Worsley Road, Worsley, MANCHESTER, M28 2SN.
•HINDSON, Mr. Eric Howard, BA ACA *1985;* Littlejohn LLP, 1 Westferry Circus, Canary Wharf, LONDON, E14 4HD.
HINDSON, Mrs. Joy Kathleen, BA ACA *2002;* Deloitte & Touche Abbots House, Abbey Street, READING, RG1 3BD.
•HINDSON, Mrs. Moira Kathleen, BA FCA *1990;* Kingston Smith LLP, Devonshire House, 60 Goswell Road, LONDON, EC1M 7AD. See also Kingston Smith Limited Liability Partnership, Devonshire Corporate Services LLP, Kingston Smith Consulting LLP and Kingston Smith(Bangladesh) Limited
HINDSON, Mr. Paul William, ACA *2009;* 11 Coach Road, WALLSEND, TYNE AND WEAR, NE28 6JA.
HINDSON, Mr. Richard Charles, ACA ACCA *2011;* 21 Gauden Road, LONDON, SW4 6LR.
HINE, Mr. Alan Richard, LLB ACA *1989;* AR Hine Associated Ltd, 17 Jay Close, BICESTER, OXFORDSHIRE, OX26 6XN.
•HINE, Mr. Anthony, BSc FCA *1975;* Tony Hine & Co, Herne House, 68 Birchanger Lane, Birchanger, BISHOP'S STORTFORD, CM23 5QA.
•HINE, Mr. Christopher, BA FCA *1982;* RSM Tenon Limited, York House, 20 York Street, MANCHESTER, M2 3BB.
HINE, Mr. Derek John, FCA *1969;* 18 Bedford Road, West Ealing, LONDON, W13 0SP. (Life Member)
HINE, Mr. Douglas George, BSc ACA *2007;* 86 Brigsley Road, Waltham, GRIMSBY, SOUTH HUMBERSIDE, DN37 0LA.
HINE, Mr. Henry, FCA *1962;* Trethin, Advent, CAMELFORD, PL32 9QW. (Life Member)
HINE, Mrs. Jacqueline Mary, BSc ACA *1991;* The Old Manse, Muirton Road, LOSSIEMOUTH, MORAYSHIRE, IV31 6SA.
HINE, Mr. John Peter, BA FCA *1970;* 13 Bray Road, Stoke D'Abernon, COBHAM, KT11 3HZ.
HINE, Mr. John Philip, BSc ACA *1986;* Kintra, Hincheslea, BROCKENHURST, HAMPSHIRE, SO42 7UP.
•HINE, Mr. John Stanley, FCA *1958;* (Tax Fac), Langdon Gray LLP, Slade House, Kirtlington, OXFORD, OXFORDSHIRE, OX5 3JA. See also John Hine Partnership Limited and Hine John & Company
HINE, Mr. Julian David, BSc FCA *1995;* 67 Bay Road, SANDRINGHAM, VIC 3191, AUSTRALIA.
•HINE, Mrs. Lynn Margaret, BSc ACA *1992;* PricewaterhouseCoopers LLP, One Kingsway, CARDIFF, CF10 3PW. See also PricewaterhouseCoopers
•HINE, Mr. Marcus Nigel, MA ACA *1989;* PricewaterhouseCoopers LLP, Hays Galleria, 1 Hays Lane, LONDON, SE1 2RD. See also PricewaterhouseCoopers
HINE, Mrs. Maria Anne, BSc ACA *1987;* Newfield Hall Nantwich Road, Minshull Vernon, MIDDLEWICH, CHESHIRE, CW10 0LR.
HINE, Mr. Mark, BSc ACA *2007;* Flat 1, 41 Thorney Hedge Road, LONDON, W4 5SB.
HINE, Ms. Nancy Kathleen, BSS ACA *1994;* 47 Sarum Crescent, WOKINGHAM, RG40 1XF.
HINE, Mr. Peter Robert, ACA *2009;* 24 Grasmere Avenue, Tilehurst, READING, RG30 6XX.
•HINE, Mr. Philip Andrew, ACA *1979;* Newfield Consultants, Newfield Hall, Nantwich Road, Minshull Vernon, MIDDLEWICH, CHESHIRE CW10 0LR.
HINE, Mr. Philip John, FCA *1967;* Firs End, Webbs Way, KIDLINGTON, OX5 2EW.
•HINE, Mr. Raymond Leslie, FCA *1961;* (Tax Fac), R.L. Hine, 72 Yew Tree Road, Southborough, TUNBRIDGE WELLS, TN4 0BN.
HINE, Mr. Richard John, FCA *1963;* Keepers Cottage, Whiteball, WELLINGTON, SOMERSET, TA21 0LP. (Life Member)
HINE, Mr. Roy, FCA *1957;* BROOKHOUSE, 10 Parklands Way, Poynton, STOCKPORT, CHESHIRE, SK12 1AJ. (Life Member)
HINE, Mrs. Samantha Laura, ACA *2008;* Inglewood, 26 High Street, Thurleigh, BEDFORD, MK44 2DS.
HINE, Mrs. Sarah Louise, LLB ACA *1989;* 17 Jay Close, BICESTER, OX26 6XN.
HINES, Mr. Anthony Charles, MSc FCA *1984;* 35 Park Crescent, EMSWORTH, HAMPSHIRE, PO10 7NT.
HINES, Mr. Anthony James, FCA *1962;* Harwood House, Cockfield, BURY ST.EDMUNDS, IP30 0HE. (Life Member)
HINES, Mr. Jack, BA(Hons) ACA CTA *2002;* 10 Bell View, ST. ALBANS, HERTFORDSHIRE, AL4 0SQ.
•HINES, Mr. John Terence, BSc ACA FCCA *1978;* Hines Harvey Woods Limited, Queens Head House, The Street, Acle, NORWICH, NR13 3DY.
•HINES, Mr. Jonathan Philip Anthony, BA ACA *1999;* PricewaterhouseCoopers LLP, 7 More London Riverside, LONDON, SE1 2RT. See also PricewaterhouseCoopers
HINES, Mr. Justin Stephen, BSc ACA *1993;* 11 Farnborough Drive, Shirley, SOLIHULL, B90 4TB.
HINES, Mr. Neil Andrew, FCA *1976;* 92 Beanoak Road, WOKINGHAM, RG40 1RN.
HINES, Mr. Richard Adam, MA FCA *1985;* 42 Carlyle Square, LONDON, SW3 6HA.
HINES, Mr. Robert, BSc ACA *2006;* PricewaterhouseCoopers, 201 Sussex Street, SYDNEY, NSW 2000, AUSTRALIA.
HINES, Mrs. Sarah Louise, BA ACA *1994;* 44 Frankholmes Drive, Shirley, SOLIHULL, B90 4YA.

HINES, Mr. Stephen John, BSc FCA *1990;* Greene Tweed & Co Ltd Mere Way, Ruddington Fields Business Park Ruddington, NOTTINGHAM, NG11 6JS.
HINEY, Mrs. Angela Margaret, MEng ACA *2005;* with Deloitte LLP, PO Box 500, 2 Hardman Street, MANCHESTER, M60 2AT.
HING, Mr. Allen Peter, FCA *1973;* Ellendene, 69 The Stitch, Friday Bridge, WISBECH, PE14 0HY.
HING, Mr. Richard Ulric, FCA *1957;* 9594 SW 125th Terrace, MIAMI, FL 33176, UNITED STATES.
HINGE, Mr. Peter Leonard Graham, MA FCA *1975;* 11 Gamlen Road, Putney, LONDON, SW15 1AB.
HINGE, Miss. Rebecca, ACA *2008;* 3 Tyler Street, STRATFORD-UPON-AVON, CV37 6TY.
HINGLEY-WILSON, Mr. Robert David, LLB ACA *1999;* The Fuchsia Garden, Ducks Hill Road, RUISLIP, MIDDLESEX, HA4 7TP.
HINGORANI, Miss. Lolita, ACA *2008;* Flat 5 Phelps Lodge, 101 Copenhagen Street, LONDON, N1 0JN.
HINGORANI, Ms. Nina, LLB ACA *2000;* Flat 10 Abbey House, 1a Abbey Road, LONDON, NW8 9BT.
HINGORANI, Mr. Sunil Lal, ACA *1984;* c/o S.I.U. LLC, 700 N. Brand Blvd, Suite 300, GLENDALE, CA 91203, UNITED STATES.
HINGRAJIA, Mr. Khilan, LLB ACA *2009;* Flagstaff House, Flat 356, 10 St. George Wharf, LONDON, SW8 2LZ.
HINGSTON, Mr. Nicholas Charles Paul, BSc ACA *1993;* Sunnyside, 83 Leverstock Green Road, HEMEL HEMPSTEAD, HERTFORDSHIRE, HP3 8PR.
HINGSTON, Mr. Paul Anthony, LLB ACA MBA *1992;* 26 Knights Orchard, HEMEL HEMPSTEAD, HERTFORDSHIRE, HP1 3QA.
HINGSTON, Mr. Stephen Terence, FCA *1974;* 48 Effingham Road, LONDON, SE12 8NU.
HINKINS, Mr. Gerald Anthony, FCA *1960;* 23 Pegasus Court, 58 Beach Road, WESTON-SUPER-MARE, AVON, BS23 4AL. (Life Member)
•HINKINS, Mrs. Jackalyn, FCA *1980;* J. Hinkins, Acorn Cottage, Abingdon Road, Tubney, ABINGDON, OXFORDSHIRE OX13 5QQ.
•HINKINS, Mr. Michael Howard, FCA *1981;* Cox Hinkins & Co, Charterford House, 75 London Road, Headington, OXFORD, OX3 9BB.
HINKLES, Mr. John Brian, FCA *1965;* The Gardens, Kirklington, BEDALE, NORTH YORKSHIRE, DL8 2NE. (Life Member)
HINKLEY, Ms. Ida Jane, FCA *1973;* 1 Southborough Close, Southborough, SURBITON, KT6 6PU.
•HINKLEY, Mr. John Lewis, FCA *1966;* (Tax Fac), John L. Hinkley, 4 Greenacres, Ponteland, NEWCASTLE UPON TYNE, NE20 9RT.
HINKS, Mr. Christopher David, BA ACA *1990;* Ernst & Young Global, Becket House, 1 Lambeth Palace Road, LONDON, SE1 7EU.
HINKS, Mr. Duncan Andrew, BSc ACA *2001;* Doncasters Group Ltd, Millennium Court, First Avenue, Centrum 100, BURTON-ON-TRENT, STAFFORDSHIRE DE14 2WW.
•HINKS, Mrs. Gillian, BSc ACA *2001;* 37 Highfield Road, West Bridgford, NOTTINGHAM, NG2 6DR.
HINKS, Miss. Kerry, ACA *2011;* Flat 3, 18 St. Marys Close, STOCKPORT, CHESHIRE, SK1 4BT.
HINKSMAN, Mr. James Lawrence Arthur Mario, LLB ACA *2001;* 3 Albert Cottages Princes Street, BEXLEYHEATH, KENT, DA7 4BL.
HINMAN, Mr. Mark, BA FCA CTA *1990;* 118 Rossall Road, THORNTON-CLEVELEYS, LANCASHIRE, FY5 1HJ.
•HINNIGAN, Mr. Stuart William, BSc FCA *1998;* Scott & Wilkinson, Dalton House, 9 Dalton Square, LANCASTER, LA1 1WD. See also Scott & Wilkinson LLP
HINNIGHAN, Mr. Nicholas Keith, BA ACA *2000;* 3 Patterdale Road, MANCHESTER, M22 4NR.
HINSELWOOD, Mrs. Michelle Madeleine, BA ACA *1995;* 4 Glenside Drive, Woodley, STOCKPORT, CHESHIRE, SK6 1JJ.
•HINSLEY, Mr. John Stephen, FCA *1977;* Westons Business Solutions Ltd, Queens Buildings, 55 Queen Street, SHEFFIELD, S1 2DX.
HINSON, Mr. John, FCA *1961;* 237 Wakefield Road, Lightcliffe, HALIFAX, WEST YORKSHIRE, HX3 8TZ. (Life Member)
HINSON, Mr. Kenneth Jack, FCA *1970;* 2544 Deora Way, HENDERSON, NE 89052, UNITED STATES.
HINSON, Mr. Philip Anthony, BSc(Hons) ACA *2000;* 11 Bronte Avenue, Stotfold, HITCHIN, HERTFORDSHIRE, SG5 4FB.
HINSON, Mr. Richard Martin, BA ACA *1987;* Sunningdale, 103 -105 Franklin Road, HARROGATE, NORTH YORKSHIRE, HG1 5EN.
HINSON, Mrs. Susan Mary, FCA *1974;* PO Box 24906, Karen 00502, NAIROBI, KENYA.
HINSTRIDGE, Mr. Peter Dennis, FCA *1977;* 42 Tudor Manor Gardens, Garston, WATFORD, WD25 9TQ.
HINTON, Mr. Cecil Robert Hamilton, FCA *1955;* Christmas Hill, Chinthurst Lane, Shalford, GUILDFORD, GU4 8JS. (Life Member)
•HINTON, Mr. Charles William Kempthorne, FCA *1981;* (Tax Fac), William Hinton Limited, Ross House, The Square, Stow on the Wold, CHELTENHAM, GLOUCESTERSHIRE GL54 1AF. See also NCTS Limited
HINTON, Mr. Christopher David, BSc ACA *1995;* 31 Elm Road, MANCHESTER, M20 6XD.
HINTON, Mr. Dennis Hugh, FCA *1955;* 2 Fleet Close, Hughenden Valley, HIGH WYCOMBE, HP14 4LL. (Life Member)
HINTON, Mr. Donald Thomas, FCA *1955;* The Well House, Stone Road, Hill Chorlton, NEWCASTLE, ST5 5DR. (Life Member)
HINTON, Mr. Gary, BSc(Econ) ACA *2001;* 68 Maylam Gardens, SITTINGBOURNE, KENT, ME10 1GB.
HINTON, Mr. Geoffrey, FCA *1947;* 36 Alphenvale, Private Bag X 17, CONSTANTIA, 7848, SOUTH AFRICA. (Life Member)
HINTON, Mr. James Michael, BSc ACA *2005;* 3 Woodman Close, HALESOWEN, B63 3EH.
HINTON, Mr. John Cranleigh, BA ACA *2001;* (Tax Fac), 66a Fernbrook Road, Hither Green, LONDON, SE13 5NF.
HINTON, Mr. Jolyon Kirtland, MA FCA *1969;* 21 Bis Rue Du Prieure, 78600 MAISONS LAFFITTE, FRANCE. (Life Member)
•HINTON, Mr. Jonathan William, MA FCA CF *1991;* Deloitte LLP, Athene Place, 66 Shoe Lane, LONDON, EC4A 3BQ. See also Deloitte & Touche LLP
HINTON, Ms. Karen Paula, BSc ACA *1992;* 15 Chestnut Drive, LONDON, E11 2TA.
•HINTON, Mrs. Laura, BSc ACA *1997;* PricewaterhouseCoopers LLP, Pricewaterhousecoopers, 12 Plumtree Court, LONDON, EC4A 4HT. See also PricewaterhouseCoopers
HINTON, Mr. Martin, BSc ACA *1987;* 14 Matlock Avenue, West Dedsbury, MANCHESTER, M20 1JS.
•HINTON, Mr. Nigel John, FCA *1978;* (Tax Fac), Andrews Orme & Hinton Limited, 4 Darwin Court, Oxon Business Park, SHREWSBURY, SY3 5AL. See also Orme Andrew
HINTON, Mr. Peter Frank, BSc ACA *1989;* P O Box 897, GABORONE, SOUTH AFRICA.
•HINTON, Mr. Richard Martin, MA(Hons) ACA *2001;* with KPMG LLP, 15 Canada Square, LONDON, E14 5GL.
HINTON, Mr. Robert Paul, BSc ACA *1981;* Pork Farms - Palethorpes, Maer Lane, MARKET DRAYTON, SHROPSHIRE, TF9 3AL.
HINTON, Mrs. Shirley Ann, FCA *1961;* 105 Alfred Court, 53 Fortune Green Road, LONDON, NW6 1DF.
HINTON, Mr. Simon Richard, FCA *1977;* 989 Scotthall Road, LEEDS, LS17 6HJ.
HINTON, Mr. Timothy James, BA BBus ACA *2000;* 10 Kojonup Close, GWELUP, WA 6018, AUSTRALIA.
HINTON, Mr. William David Stuart, FCA *1968;* 18 Glenavon Close, Claygate, ESHER, SURREY, KT10 0HP.
HINTON-GREEN, Mr. Peter James, MA FCA *1964;* 35a Sheen Lane, LONDON, SW14 8AB. (Life Member)
HINTON-JONES, Mr. Mark James, BSc(Hons) ACA *2002;* 266 Earlsfield Road, LONDON, SW18 3DY.
HINTON-SMITH, Mr. Stephen John, ACA *1982;* Friarhill Gate, Roweltown, CARLISLE, CA6 6LN.
•HINWOOD, Mr. Colin Bertram, FCA *1969;* 14 Hatherden Avenue, Parkstone, POOLE, BH14 0PJ.
HIONA, Miss. Christina, ACA *2010;* Flat 23 Chalice Court, Deanery Close, LONDON, N2 8NU.
HIORNS, Miss. Andrea Clare, BA(Hons) ACA *2001;* Antler Ltd Pilot Works, Alfred Street, BURY, BL9 9EF.
HIORNS, Mr. Trevor John, FCA *1969;* 12 Ashwell Road, Bygrave, BALDOCK, SG7 5DT.
•HIPGRAVE, Mr. Graham James, FCA *1970;* J.R.Antoine & Partners, 75 Rickmansworth Road, AMERSHAM, HP6 5JW.
HIPKIN, Mr. Clive David, FCA *1975;* 70 Southborough Road, Bickley, BROMLEY, BR1 2EN.
HIPKIN, Mr. Jonathan Anthony David, BSc ACA *1992;* Plawhatch Corner Plawhatch Lane, Sharpthorne, EAST GRINSTEAD, WEST SUSSEX, RH19 4JL.
HIPKINS, Miss. Holly, ACA *2008;* The Dingle, West Trewirgie Road, REDRUTH, CORNWALL, TR15 2TJ.
HIPKISS, Mr. Robert Richard, FCA *1962;* 39 Bracondale, NORWICH, NR1 2AT. (Life Member)
HIPPERSON, Mrs. Berice, ACA *1985;* 21 Flordon Road, Newton Flotman, NORWICH, NR15 1QX.
HIPPERSON, Mr. Peter Leonard, FCA *1976;* Canterbury House, Barton Lane, Thrumpton, NOTTINGHAM, NG11 0AU.
HIPPISLEY-COX, Mr. Jeffrey Denis, FCA *1974;* Ciro Pearls Ltd, 15 Connaught Street, LONDON, W2 2AY.
HIPPLE, Mr. David Stewart, BSc ACA *1981;* Arden House, Houghton Road, ST.IVES, CAMBRIDGESHIRE, PE27 6RN.
HIPPOLYTE, Mr. Christopher Eric Marcel, BA ACA *2000;* Ground Floor Flat, 151 Gleneldon Road, LONDON, SW16 2BQ.
HIPPS, Mr. Paul Anthony, FCA *1958;* 2 Glebe Place, LONDON, SW3 5LB. (Life Member)
HIRA, Mr. Fanos, BSc ACA *1996;* The Old Church House, School Road, Hanbury, BROMSGROVE, WORCESTERSHIRE, B60 4BT.
HIRA, Mr. Nikhil Rustam, BSc ACA *1986;* (Tax Fac), P O Box 45992, NAIROBI, 00100, KENYA.
HIRA, Mr. Pauljit Singh, MSc BA(Hons) ACA *2003;* Quintiles Limited, Station House, Market Street, BRACKNELL, RG12 1HX.
HIRANI, Mr. Chandrakant, BSc ACA *1994;* A4.80D, British Telecom BT Centre, 81 Newgate Street, LONDON, EC1A 7AJ.
HIRANI, Mr. Dhansukh Vishram, BA ACA *2006;* 66 Woodgrange Avenue, LONDON, N12 0PS.
HIRANI, Miss. Jayna, MSc BSc ACA *2010;* 78 Bowrons Avenue, WEMBLEY, MIDDLESEX, HA0 4QP.
HIRANI, Mr. Kirti, BA(Hons) ACA *2009;* 341 Crescent Road, BOLTON, BL3 2NA.
HIRANI, Mr. Neil, ACA *2011;* 34 Sylvester Road, WEMBLEY, MIDDLESEX, HA0 3AB.
HIRANI, Miss. Pooja, ACA *2011;* 62 Beresford Avenue, LONDON, W7 3AP.
HIRANI, Miss. Sheena, BSc(Hons) ACA *2000;* 198 Camrose Avenue, EDGWARE, HA8 6BU.
HIRANI, Mrs. Sunder Dinesh, BSc ACA *1997;* 76 Queenborough Gardens, ILFORD, ESSEX, IG2 6YB.
HIRANI, Mr. Sunil Naran, BA ACA *2008;* 15 Regal Way, Kenton, HARROW, HA3 0RZ.
HIRD, Mr. Christopher John, ACA *2007;* Rowlands Chartered Accountants, Rowlands House, Portobello Road, Portobello Trading Estate, Birtley, CHESTER LE STREET COUNTY DURHAM DH3 2RY.
HIRD, Mr. Daniel Robert, BA ACA *1990;* Triodos Bank Brunel House, 11 The Promenade Clifton Down, BRISTOL, BS8 3NN.
HIRD, Mr. Gareth Mark, BA ACA *2008;* 85 South Street, COTTINGHAM, NORTH HUMBERSIDE, HU16 4AP.
HIRD, Mrs. Helen Faye Baker, MA ACA *2010;* 3 The Old Organ Works, Orange Street, Thaxted, DUNMOW, ESSEX, CM6 2RS.
HIRD, Mr. Jonathon Mark, ACA *2008;* Flat 5 The Glasshouse, 40 Malden Road, LONDON, NW5 3HH.
HIRD, Mr. Mark Stephen, BSc ACA *2004;* 8 Selworthy Road, BRISTOL, BS4 2LF.
HIRD, Mr. Matthew James Kerridge, MA ACA *1998;* 73 Riddlesdown Road, PURLEY, CR8 1DJ.
HIRD, Mrs. Michelle, BA ACA *1993;* 47 Tiverton Crescent, Kingsmead, MILTON KEYNES, MK4 4BZ.
HIRD, Mr. Peter, FCA *1981;* Neves Solicitors, 702 South Seventh Street, MILTON KEYNES, MK9 2PZ.
HIRD, Mrs. Rachael, BA(Hons) ACA *2002;* 81 Dragon Rd, HARROGATE, HG1 5DB.
HIRE, Mr. Jonathan Henry, BSc ACA *1996;* 12 The Lea, KIDDERMINSTER, WORCESTERSHIRE, DY11 6JY.
HIREMATH, Mr. Rajendra Sidhraj, ACA *1982;* 30 Boundary Road, Eastcote, PINNER, MIDDLESEX, HA5 1PN.
HIRJANI, Mr. Nooren, BA ACA *1996;* PO Box 34195, DOHA, QATAR.
HIRJI, Mr. Sameer Kassamali Merali, BSc ACA *1998;* 122 Mayflower Drive, COVENTRY, CV2 5NP.
HIRJI, Mr. Zohar Abdul Abdulla, FCA *1977;* 20 Greenshire Street, RICHMOND HILL L4B 4V2, ON, CANADA.
HIRONS, Mr. Andrew David, BCom ACA *1980;* 3 The Orchards, HatfieldNorton, WORCESTER, WR5 2PY.
HIRONS, Mrs. Beverley, BA ACA *1984;* 3 The Orchards, Hatfield Norton, WORCESTER, WR5 2PY.
HIRONS, Mr. Dick Robert, FCA *1958;* Gardener's Cottage, High Legh, KNUTSFORD, WA16 6PS.
HIRONS, Mr. Peter, FCA *1973;* 7 Waters Dr, Four Oaks, SUTTON COLDFIELD, B74 4TQ.
HIRSCH, Mr. Eli, ACA *2004;* with Cohen Arnold, New Burlington House, 1075 Finchley Road, Temple Fortune, LONDON, NW11 0PU.
HIRSCH, Mr. Glyn Vincent, LLB ACA *1985;* 15 Clare Lawn Avenue, East Sheen, LONDON, SW14 8BE.
HIRSCH, Mr. Peter Frederick Nicholas, FCA *1970;* Ashley House Roundabout Copse, West Chiltington, PULBOROUGH, WEST SUSSEX, RH20 2RN.
HIRSCH, Mr. Ronald Josef, FCA *1968;* 140 Totteridge Lane, LONDON, N20 8JJ.
HIRSCHFIELD, Mrs. Debra, BA FCA *1991;* Kitwell Consultants Ltd, Kitwell House, The Warren, RADLETT, WD7 7DU.
HIRSCHFIELD, Mr. Michael Brian Victor, BSc FCA *1989;* Kitwell House, The Warren, RADLETT, WD7 7DU.
HIRSCHFIELD, Mr. Michael Hugo, BSc FCA *1998;* Financial Services Authority, 25 North Colonnade, Canary Wharf, LONDON, E14 5HS.
HIRSCHFIELD, Mrs. Nina Borisovna, BSc(Hons) ACA *2003;* 103 Bullhead Road, BOREHAMWOOD, HERTFORDSHIRE, WD6 1HR.
HIRSHMAN, Mr. Geoffrey Robin, FCA *1962;* 3 Tanglewood Lodge, Common Road, STANMORE, HA7 3JA. (Life Member)
HIRST, Mr. Alan Frank, FCA *1948;* The Old School House, Chipstable, Wiveliscombe, TAUNTON, TA4 2PX. (Life Member)
HIRST, Mr. Andrew Patrick, BA ACA *1992;* The Meadows, 25 Ogle Road, Flamborough, BRIDLINGTON, YO15 1NT.
HIRST, Mr. Benjamin John, BA ACA *2002;* 1 Pickering Grange, BROUGH, NORTH HUMBERSIDE, HU15 1GY.
HIRST, Mr. Christopher Andrew, BA ACA *2010;* 6 Middle Hall Close, LIVERSEDGE, WEST YORKSHIRE, WF15 6ND.
HIRST, Mr. Christopher Ian, BSc ACA *1979;* Mount Brandon, 28 Chalet Gardens, Lucan, DUBLIN, COUNTY DUBLIN, IRELAND.
HIRST, Mr. Christopher James, ACA *2007;* PricewaterhouseCoopers, P.O. Box 905, Strathvale House, Grand Cayman, Cayman Islands, KY1-1103 GEORGE TOWN GRAND CAYMAN P.O.Box905 CAYMAN ISLANDS.
HIRST, Mr. Daniel, ACA *2002;* Teays River Investments LLC, 101 Congressional Boulevard, Suite 115, CARMEL, IN 46032, UNITED STATES.
HIRST, Mr. David, ACA *2010;* Stonecroft, Mowden Hall Lane, Hatfield Peverel, CHELMSFORD, CM3 2NS.
HIRST, Mr. David Brian Addis, FCA *1962;* Home Farm House, Rectory Lane, Orlingbury, KETTERING, NN14 1JH. (Life Member)
HIRST, Mr. Dion, BEng ACA *1999;* 48 Peel Hall Avenue, Tyldesley, MANCHESTER, M29 8TA.
HIRST, Mr. Frank Cawood, FCA *1953;* Pine Trees, Burtons Lane, CHALFONT ST.GILES, HP8 4BN. (Life Member)
HIRST, Mr. Gary James, ACA *2011;* 33 Harlequin Drive, Kingswood, HULL, HU7 3HB.
HIRST, Mr. Gordon William, FCA *1966;* Manor House, 1 Manor Way, Failand, BRISTOL, BS8 3UY.
HIRST, Mr. Graham Carline, LLB FCA *1974;* (Tax Fac), 11 Brownroyd Road, Honley, HOLMFIRTH, West Yorkshire, HD9 6HN.
HIRST, Mrs. Helen Louise, BA ACA *2002;* Urenco Ltd, 18 Oxford Road, MARLOW, BUCKINGHAMSHIRE, SL7 2NL.
HIRST, Mr. James Brook, FCA *1963;* Blackford Cottage, Andover Road, Highclere, NEWBURY, RG20 9PF. (Life Member)
HIRST, Mr. James Michael, FCA *1967;* 2 Meadow Bank, HOLMFIRTH, HD9 1QS.
HIRST, Miss. Joanna Elizabeth, ACA *2006;* 7 Manor Road, CARLISLE, CA2 4LH.
HIRST, Mr. John Raymond, BA FCA ACT CBIM *1977;* Thicket Brow, Bath Road, Littlewick Green, MAIDENHEAD, SL6 3QR.
•HIRST, Mr. Julian Andrew, BSc(Econ) FCA *1974;* Julian A Hirst, 13 York Road, SOUTHWOLD, SUFFOLK, IP18 6AN.
HIRST, Mrs. Julie Anne, BA ACA *1989;* 35 Ryland Road, Welton, LINCOLN, LN2 3LU.
HIRST, Mr. Mark, BA ACA *2004;* 67B Chaplin Road, LONDON, NW2 5PS.
HIRST, Mr. Matthew John, BA ACA *2007;* 51 Astonville Street, LONDON, SW18 5AW.
HIRST, Mr. Michael John, MA ACA MCT *1997;* 59 Banks Drive, SANDY, BEDFORDSHIRE, SG19 1AE.
HIRST, Mr. Neil Andrew, ACA *2006;* 12 Cornation Drive, Bolton On Dearne, ROTHERHAM, S63 8DQ.
HIRST, Mr. Nicholas, MEng(Hons) ACA *2011;* 27 Countess Road, MANCHESTER, M20 6RS.

Members - Alphabetical **HIRST - HO**

HIRST, Miss. Nicole Lisa, ACA *2010;* 21 Park Gates Drive, Cheadle Hulme, CHEADLE, CHESHIRE, SK8 7DD.

HIRST, Mrs. Patricia Ann, ACA *1979;* The Orchard, Wood Lane End, Adlington, MACCLESFIELD, CHESHIRE, SK10 4PQ.

•**HIRST, Mr. Peter Graham, FCA** *1974;* Caddick Group PLC, Castlegarth Grange, Scott Lane, WETHERBY, WEST YORKSHIRE, LS22 6LH. See also Peter Hirst & Co

HIRST, Miss. Sara Louise, BSc ACA *1997;* 7 Prospect Place, Morley, LEEDS, LS27 9BJ.

HIRST, Mr. Simon Matthew, BSc FCA *1978;* 4 Ordulf Road, TAVISTOCK, DEVON, PL19 8NE.

HIRST, Mr. Simon Paul, MChem ACA *2010;* 5 Leyfield Bank, HOLMFIRTH, HD9 1XU.

HIRST, Mr. Stephen, FCA *1974;* Building PO5 Merville Barracks, Circular Road South, COLCHESTER, CO2 7UT.

HIRST, Mr. Stephen Jeremy, BSc ACA *1995;* 157 Folds Lane, SHEFFIELD, S8 0ET.

HIRTH, Mr. Frank, LLM FCA *1973;* 10 Bell Moor, East Heath Road, LONDON, NW3 1DY. (Life Member)

HIRTH, Mr. Garry Bernard, BSc FCA *1984;* 36 Wickliffe Avenue, LONDON, N3 3EJ.

HIRTZEL, Mr. Simon George Michael, MA ACA *1992;* 5th Floor, 25-28 Old Burlington Street, LONDON, W1S 3AN.

HISCOCK, Mr. Andrew Charles, BA ACA *1998;* Flat 8 William Street House, William Street, LONDON, SW1X 9HH.

HISCOCK, Mr. David John, BSc ACA *1986;* 71 Sutherland Avenue, Petts Wood, ORPINGTON, BR5 1QY.

HISCOCK, Mr. James Albert, FCA *1983;* Beck Bridge House Becks Bridge Close, Scorton, RICHMOND, NORTH YORKSHIRE, DL10 6HA.

HISCOCK, Miss. Jenna Anne, BA ACA *2005;* 54 Smiths Lane, WINDSOR, BERKSHIRE, SL4 5PG.

HISCOCK, Mr. John Roy, FCA *1969;* Canterbury Court (Unit 3.40), 1-3 Brixton Road, LONDON, SW9 6DE.

HISCOCK, Mr. Nicholas Toby, MA FCA *1987;* 49 Burlington Avenue, RICHMOND, TW9 4DG.

•**HISCOCK, Mr. Robert Grigor Heath, FCA** *1974;* (Tax Fac), King & Taylor, 10-12 Wrotham Road, GRAVESEND, DA11 0PE.

HISCOCKS, Mr. Andrew Gordon, BA ACA *1992;* 24 Hough Lane, WILMSLOW, SK9 2LQ.

HISCOCKS, Mr. Graham Robert, BA ACA *1981;* Redbarn, 4 High Close, RICKMANSWORTH, WD3 4DZ.

HISCOCKS, Mrs. Helen Margaret, BA ACA *1988;* Copsley Mews, Gayhouse Lane, Outwood, REDHILL, RH1 5PP.

HISCOCKS, Mr. William Bryan, FCA *1953;* 29a Barrow Street, MUCH WENLOCK, SHROPSHIRE, TF13 6EN.

HISCOX, Mrs. Elizabeth Jayne, BSc FCA *1992;* 16 Angram Drive, SUNDERLAND, SR2 7RD.

HISCOX, Mr. Graham, BSc FCA *1976;* 16 Angram Drive, Newminster Park, SUNDERLAND, SR2 7RD.

HISCOX, Miss. Sharon Claire, BA FCA *1993;* 96 Northover Road, BRISTOL, BS9 3LH.

HISHIKAWA, Miss. Yoko, ACA *1998;* 4-1-1-702 Kamiohsaki, Shinagawa-ku, TOKYO, 141-0021 JAPAN.

HISLOP, Mr. Dean Evan, ACA CA(NZ) *2011;* 16 Cranleigh Gardens, KINGSTON UPON THAMES, SURREY, KT2 5TX.

HISLOP, Mr. John Samuel, FCA *1954;* Geinas House, Bodfari, DENBIGH, LL16 4BY. (Life Member)

HISLOP, Mrs. Julia Carolin, BCom FCA *1987;* Graham Latham Ltd, Hedge House 1 Hangersley Hill, RINGWOOD, BH243JW.

HISTED, Miss. Charlotte Anne, BA(Hons) ACA *2003;* 2 Terrapins, 33 Lovelace Road, SURBITON, SURREY, KT6 6NB.

•**HITCH, Mr. Adrian, BSc FCA** *1987;* (Tax Fac), Baker Fox Limited, Owl Cotes Barn, Mire Close Lane, Cowling, KEIGHLEY, WEST YORKSHIRE BD22 0LE.

HITCH, Mr. Andrew John Russell, BA ACA *1997;* Kefco Sales, 41 Progress Road, LEIGH-ON-SEA, SS9 5PR.

HITCH, Mrs. Siobhan Michele, BA ACA *2000;* 57 Burntwood Lane, LONDON, SW17 0JY.

•**HITCHCOCK, Mr. Andrew Philip, FCA** *1971;* Andrew Hitchcock, 5 Ashburnham Close, CHICHESTER, WEST SUSSEX, PO19 3NB.

•**HITCHCOCK, Mr. Barry Arthur, FCA** *1972;* Hitchcock Frank & Co, Highfield House, White Horse Road, Holly Hill, Meopham, GRAVESEND DA13 0UF.

HITCHCOCK, Mr. Carl, FCA *1992;* 3rd Floor, M T V Europe United Kingdom House, 180 Oxford Street, LONDON, W1D 1DS.

HITCHCOCK, Mr. David William Warwick, ACA *1989;* 53 Watchfield Court, Sutton Court Road, LONDON, W4 4NB.

HITCHCOCK, Mrs. Deborah Anne, BA ACA *1989;* 111 Kingsdown Crescent, DAWLISH, DEVON, EX7 0HB.

HITCHCOCK, Mrs. Elizabeth Ann, BSc ACA *1995;* Laurel Cottage, The Street, Elmsett, IPSWICH, IP7 6PE.

HITCHCOCK, Mr. Jonathan Mark, ACA *2009;* 'Silverdale', 21 Stoke Road, COBHAM, SURREY, KT11 3AR.

HITCHCOCK, Mr. Michael Paul, BA ACA *1991;* 10 Westanley Avenue, AMERSHAM, HP7 9AZ.

HITCHCOCK, Mr. Paul Martin, MA ACA *1981;* Ridge Place, Hindhead Road, HINDHEAD, GU26 6BB.

HITCHCOCK, Mr. Roland Alfred, FCA *1966;* 10 St Barnabas Street, Oroklini, 7040 LARNACA, CYPRUS.

HITCHCOCK, Mr. Simon John, BSc ACA *1999;* Lyceum Capital Partners Llp, 357 Strand, LONDON, WC2R 0HS.

HITCHEN, Mr. Anthony, BA ACA *1987;* Merrow Down House, Dungeon Lane, Dalton, WIGAN, LANCASHIRE, WN8 7RH.

HITCHEN, Mr. Gary, BSc ACA *1995;* Rocklynes, Hillside, Romiley, STOCKPORT, CHESHIRE, SK6 4AZ.

HITCHEN, Mr. Geoffrey Paul, FCA *1963;* 9 Kentrigg, KENDAL, LA9 6EE.

•**HITCHEN, Mr. John Terence, BA FCA** *1982;* Garratts Wolverhampton Limited, 29 Waterloo Road, WOLVERHAMPTON, WV1 4DJ.

HITCHEN, Miss. Louise Catherine, BA ACA CTA *2006;* 2 Hornby Drive, Newton, PRESTON, PR4 3ST.

HITCHEN, Mrs. Tanya Melanie, BA ACA *2004;* Mail Room University of Exeter, Northcote House The Queens Drive, EXETER, EX4 4QJ.

•**HITCHENOR, Mr. Robert James, FCA** *1980;* (Tax Fac), Hitchenors, School Farm, Barton Lane, Bradley, STAFFORD, ST18 9EF. See also Hitchenor T.L.

HITCHENOR, Mrs. Susan Rosalie, BA ACA *1990;* Leicestershire Partnership NHS Trust Towers Hospital, Gipsy Lane, LEICESTER, LE5 0TD.

•**HITCHENOR, Mrs. Tracey Lee, BA ACA** *1984;* Hitchenors, School Farm, Barton Lane, Bradley, STAFFORD, ST18 9EF. See also Hitchenor T.L.

HITCHENS, Mrs. Nancy, BSc FCA *1999;* 5 Thetford Place, BASILDON, ESSEX, SS15 4ED.

HITCHIN, Miss. Anne-Marie, ACA *2011;* Flat 2, Catherine House, 5 Thomas Fyre Drive, Bow, LONDON, E3 2ZG.

HITCHINGS, Mr. Charles Robin, MA ACA *1996;* 32 Canford Road, LONDON, SW11 6PD.

HITCHINGS, Mr. Malcolm Rees, BA FCA *1977;* The Coach House Beechlands, Cornwells Bank Newick, LEWES, EAST SUSSEX, BN8 4RX.

HITCHINGS, Mr. Neil James, BA FCA *1996;* 22 Larks Rise, CULLOMPTON, DEVON, EX15 1UT.

•**HITCHINS, Mr. John Charles Fortescue, BA FCA** *1979;* PricewaterhouseCoopers LLP, Hays Galleria, 1 Hays Lane, LONDON, SE1 2RD. See also PricewaterhouseCoopers

HITCHMAN, Mrs. Audrey May, FCA *1957;* 29 Aviemore Gardens, NORTHAMPTON, NN4 9XJ. (Life Member)

HITCHMAN, Miss. Emma Jane, ACA *2008;* 25 Rowner Crescent, Sherfield-on-Loddon, HOOK, RG27 0SW.

HITCHMAN, Mr. Frank Hendrick, BSc FCA *1967;* 34 Moray Place, EDINBURGH, EH3 6BX.

HITCHMAN, Mr. Robert Alexander, BSc ACA *1998;* Drivers End, 16-17 Farnham Green Farnham, BISHOP'S STORTFORD, HERTFORDSHIRE, CM23 1HN.

•**HITCHMOUGH, Mr. Gareth John, BSc ACA** *2001;* Mazars LLP, Tower Building, 22 Water Street, LIVERPOOL, L3 1PQ.

HITIHAMU, Mr. Pulastha Indika, MSc BA ACA *2008;* 27 Davenport Road, YARM, CLEVELAND, TS15 9TN.

HIVES, Mr. Andrew William Preston, ACA *2011;* Flat 3, 32 Hemstal Road, LONDON, NW6 2AL.

HIVES, Miss. Jane Elizabeth, BA FCA *1979;* 24 Grove Terrace, LONDON, NW5 1PL.

•**HIVES, Mr. Robert George, FCA** *1975;* Smith Cooper, Bermuda House, Crown Square, First Avenue, BURTON-ON-TRENT, STAFFORDSHIRE DE14 2TB. See also Smith Cooper LLP

•**HIXSON, Mr. Nicholas Vivian, FCA** *1980;* Hixsons Limited, 24 Cecil Avenue, BOURNEMOUTH, BH8 9EJ.

HJELTNES, Mr. Ken Are, BA ACA *2011;* Hoiendal 10a, 1617 FREDRIKSTAD, NORWAY.

•**HJERTZEN, Mr. Mark, BA FCA** *1980;* (Tax Fac), HW Associates, Portmill House, Portmill Lane, HITCHIN, HERTFORDSHIRE, SG5 1DJ.

HJIGEORGIOU, Mr. Stylianos, FCA *1976;* 36 Buckingham Avenue, Whetstone, LONDON, N20 9DE.

HJIIOSSIF, Mr. Christakis John, BSc ACA *1989;* 12c Ayios Maronas Street, 1010 NICOSIA, CYPRUS.

HJIYIANNADJIS, Mr. Marios Antony, BA ACA *1993;* 3 Kariotakis Street, PO Box 42102, 6531 LARNACA, CYPRUS.

•**HLA, Mr. Nay-Myo Myo, FCA** *1971;* Apt. 31B, Rattankosin View Mansion, 45/2 Bangyeekan, Bangplad, BANGKOK 10700, THAILAND.

HLADUSZ, Mr. John Michael, BSc ACA *1998;* 11 Cotefield Drive, LEIGHTON BUZZARD, BEDFORDSHIRE, LU7 3DS.

HLYNSKYY, Mr. Alexander, ACA *2008;* Flat 6, 23 Belgrave Gardens, LONDON, NW8 0QY.

HNATIW, Mr. Peter, FCA *1981;* 1 Pembroke Drive, Moorside, OLDHAM, OL4 2LU.

HO, Mr. Adrian Him-Shuen, BSc ACA *1988;* Flat D 20/f Block One, 80 Robinson Road, MID LEVELS, Hong Kong Island, HONG KONG SAR.

•**HO, Miss. Ai Lian, FCA** *1973;* Great Eastern Holdings Ltd, no 1 Pickering Street 16-01, SINGAPORE 048659, SG, SINGAPORE.

HO, Mr. Ai Ting, BSc ACA *2009;* 7 Rheidol Drive, Cwm Talwg, BARRY, SOUTH GLAMORGAN, CF62 7HA.

HO, Mr. Albert, ACA *2008;* D208 Fengnan Garden Nanguo Zhong Road, DALIANG 528300, GUANGDONG PROVINCE, CHINA.

HO, Miss. Amy Chau Ying, ACA *2010;* Flat C 15/F, 90 Broadway, MEI FOO SUN CHUEN, KOWLOON, HONG KONG SAR.

HO, Mr. Andrew Thiam Kok, BA ACA *1992;* Flat 3, 23 Carburton Street, LONDON, W1W 5AR.

HO, Mr. Andrew Kar Kin, ACA *2009;* Flat 11C Block 2 Pokfulam Gardens, 180 Pokfulam Road, POK FU LAM, HONG KONG ISLAND, HONG KONG SAR.

HO, Mr. Anthony, BA FCA *2002;* 46 Hawkins Crescent, Bradley Stoke, BRISTOL, BS32 8EH.

HO, Mr. Arthur Chun Hung, BA(Hons) ACA *2002;* T2 Flat 710, Harbourview Horizon, 12 Hung Lok Road, HUNG HOM, KOWLOON, HONG KONG SAR.

HO, Miss. Audrey Mei Lian, BSc ACA *1993;* Millward Brown, 50 Scotts Road #04-01, SINGAPORE 228242, SINGAPORE.

HO, Mr. Barry Hon Ching, BSc ACA *1989;* Great Eagle Holdings Limited, c/o Internal Audit Department, 33/F. Great Eagle Centre, 23 Harbour Road, WAN CHAI, HONG KONG ISLAND HONG KONG SAR.

•**HO, Mr. Boniface Ka-Kul, ACA** *1978;* Sichuan Neptune land Co ltd, 7/f Hi Teck, Hi Tech Debelopment Zone, CHENGDU, SICHUAN PROVINCE, HONG KONG SAR.

HO, Mr. Bonny Chu Kwan, BSS ACA *1985;* 101 Wood Vale, Highgate, LONDON, N10 3DL.

HO, Mr. Che Sun, ACA *2007;* Flat H 30/F Block 8, Royal Ascot, 1 Tsun King Road, SHA TIN, NEW TERRITORIES, HONG KONG SAR.

HO, Mr. Chee Kin, FCA *1974;* 5 Burcott Road, PURLEY, CR8 4AD.

HO, Mr. Chee Shen, BA FCA *1984;* 54 Jalan USJ 2/5H, 47610 SUBANG, SELANGOR, MALAYSIA.

HO, Mr. Cheuk Yin, ACA *2007;* Flat 3108, Block E, Kornhill, QUARRY BAY, HONG KONG SAR.

HO, Mr. Chi Sing, ACA *2006;* Unit 1509 15/F, The Center, 99 Queens Road, CENTRAL, HONG KONG ISLAND, HONG KONG SAR.

HO, Mr. Chi Wah, FCA *1978;* Flat C, 11th Floor Block 2, Pok Fu Lam Gardens, 180 Pok Fu Lam Road, POK FU LAM, HONG KONG ISLAND HONG KONG SAR.

HO, Mr. Chi Wai, ACA *2007;* Flat G 5th Floor, 10 Kwan Yick Street, KENNEDY TOWN, HONG KONG SAR.

HO, Mr. Chye Hoi, ACA *1979;* 13 Lorong Sarhad, SINGAPORE 1191 39, SINGAPORE.

HO, Miss. Clara, BSc ACA *1995;* 1B Pinecrest, 65 Repulse Bay Road, REPULSE BAY, HONG KONG ISLAND, HONG KONG SAR.

HO, Ms. Connie Man Yee, ACA *2006;* HSBC Trustee(Hong Kong) Ltd, Level 13, 1 Queen's Road, CENTRAL, HONG KONG ISLAND, HONG KONG SAR.

HO, Mr. Daniel Hong Man, BSc FCA *1989;* Finance department, Qatar Airways, PO Box 22550, DOHA, QATAR.

HO, Mr. Danny, BA ACA *2001;* KPMG, 8/F Prince's Building, 10 Chater Road, CENTRAL, HONG KONG ISLAND, HONG KONG SAR.

HO, Mr. Eleutherius Yui Pok, BA FCA *1993;* Flat B, 4th floor Sutherland Court, Villa De Cascade, 2-4 Lai Wo Lane, Fo Tan, SHA TIN NEW TERRITORIES HONG KONG SAR.

HO, Miss. Elsa Man Ching, BA FCA *1993;* 30/f Flat A3, Mount Parker Lodge, 10 Hong Pak Path, HONG KONG SAR, QUARRY BAY, HONG KONG ISLAND HONG KONG SAR.

HO, Ms. Hang Yin, ACA *2008;* Chan Chun Kwong & Co, 904 Wellborne Commercial Centre, 8 Java Road, NORTH POINT, HONG KONG SAR.

HO, Mr. Hau Cheong, MBA BCom ACA *1986;* Flat B, 6th floor, 8 Sau Chuk Yuen Road, KOWLOON CITY, KOWLOON, HONG KONG SAR.

HO, Mr. Hin, ACA *2005;* Flat E 39/F Ko Fung Court, Harbour Heights, NORTH POINT, HONG KONG ISLAND, HONG KONG SAR.

HO, Mr. Hing Cheung, ACA *2007;* 4291 Garry Street, RICHMOND V7E 2T9, BC, CANADA.

HO, Ms. Hoi Yin, ACA *2007;* Room 2308 23/F, Block Q, Luk Yeung Sun Chuen, TSUEN WAN, NEW TERRITORIES, HONG KONG SAR.

HO, Dr. Hoi Ki, ACA *2008;* 22D, Lu Shan Mansion, 5 Taikoo Shing Road, TAIKOO SHING, HONG KONG SAR.

HO, Mr. Hom Man, ACA *2009;* 57 Prospect Street, HUDDERSFIELD, HD1 2NX.

HO, Mr. Horace Man Kit, ACA *2005;* Horace Ho & Company, Unit 1608 Tower 1 Silvercord, 30 Canton Road, TSIM SHA TSUI, HONG KONG SAR.

HO, Mr. Jackson Yeong Fan, BSc ACA *1992;* No 1 Jalan Industri PBP13, Taman Industri Pusat Bandar, Sengalor, 47100 PUCHONG, MALAYSIA.

HO, Miss. Joanna, BA(Hons) ACA *2010;* 2 Loves Cottages, Church Hill Road, ORMSKIRK, LANCASHIRE, L39 3BD.

HO, Mr. John Hon Ming, BA FCA FHKSA *1986;* Flat E, 10/F Greenview Gardens, 125 Robinson Road, MID LEVELS, HONG KONG ISLAND, HONG KONG SAR.

HO, Mr. Johnny Chu Kay, ACA *2007;* Johnny Ho & Co, Suite 3108 A, Tower 2 Lippo Centre, 89 Queensway, ADMIRALTY, HONG KONG SAR.

HO, Mr. Ka Pong William, ACA *2008;* Flat E 41/F Blk 6, The Long Beach, 8 Hoi Fai Road, TAI KOK TSUI, KOWLOON, HONG KONG SAR.

HO, Miss. Ka Yen Jolene, ACA *2011;* Flat 8A, Yee Yun Mansion, Lei King Wan, SAI WAN HO, HONG KONG SAR.

HO, Ms. Kar Yan, ACA *2009;* 27A Tower 1, Sham Wan Towers, Ap Lei Chau Drive, ABERDEEN, HONG KONG ISLAND, HONG KONG SAR.

HO, Mr. Kenneth Chiu Fan, ACA *2007;* Ho Chiu Fan & Co CPA, RM 1102 11/F, Henan Building, 90 Jaffe Road, WAN CHAI, HONG KONG SAR.

HO, Mr. Kenny Keen Fung, ACA *2008;* 7 Edwards Meadow, MARLBOROUGH, SN8 1UL.

HO, Mr. Khee An, FCA *1976;* 4 Derwent Road, LIGHTWATER, SURREY, GU18 5XF.

HO, Mr. Khoon Ming, BSc FCA *1992;* KPMG, 8th Floor, Tower E2, Oriental Plaza, 1 East Chang An Avenue, BEIJING 100738 CHINA.

HO, Dr. Kim Wai, BSc FCA *1981;* 5 Elm Avenue, SINGAPORE 279781, SINGAPORE.

HO, Mr. Kin Wai, MBA BA ACA FCPA *2005;* Flat A 16/F Block 9, Discovery Park, 398 Castle Peak Road, TSUEN WAN, NEW TERRITORIES, HONG KONG SAR.

HO, Mr. King Yip, ACA *2011;* Salt Winds, Victoria Avenue, St. Helier, JERSEY, JE2 3TB.

HO, Ms. Kit Man, ACA *2008;* 7B New Town Mansion, 6 Cleveland Street, CAUSEWAY BAY, HONG KONG SAR.

HO, Mr. Kwok Keung, ACA *2007;* Orient Overseas (International) Ltd, 33/F, Harbour Centre, 25 Harbour Road, WAN CHAI, HONG KONG SAR.

HO, Mr. Kwok Pui, ACA *2006;* Flat H 14/F, Banyan Mansion, Tai Koo Shing, QUARRY BAY, HONG KONG ISLAND, HONG KONG SAR.

HO, Mr. Kwok Wah George, ACA *2008;* George K W Ho & Co, Suite 1016 10/F, Chinachem Golden Plaza, 77 Mody Road, TSIM SHA TSUI, KOWLOON HONG KONG SAR.

HO, Mr. Kwok-Cheong Paul, ACA *2007;* 13A Braemar Terrace, No.1 Pak Fuk Road, NORTH POINT, HONG KONG ISLAND, HONG KONG SAR.

HO, Ms. Lai Kuen, ACA *2008;* Flat 9, 20/F Block B, King Ming Court, Junk Bay, TSEUNG KWAN O, NEW TERRITORIES HONG KONG SAR.

HO, Ms. Lai Sheung Tracy, ACA *2008;* Flat A 30th Floor Block 13, Wonderland Villas, 9 Wah King Hill Road, KWAI CHUNG, KOWLOON, HONG KONG SAR.

HO, Mr. Lee Hong, ACA *2007;* Flat E 39/F, Tower 10, South Horizons, AP LEI CHAU, HONG KONG ISLAND, HONG KONG SAR.

HO, Mr. Lim Kong, BA ACA *2005;* 16 Jalan Ibu Kota 9, Taman Ibu Kota, 53100 KUALA LUMPUR, FEDERAL TERRITORY, MALAYSIA.
HO, Mr. Lok Ki, ACA *2004;* Lok Ki Ho & Co., Suite No 2325, 8888 Odlin Crescent, RICHMOND V6X 3Z8, BC, CANADA.
HO, Ms. Mabel, ACA *2008;* Flat C, 8/F, Blue Haven, 3 ForFar Road, KOWLOON CITY, KOWLOON HONG KONG SAR.
HO, Mr. Man Wah, ACA *2010;* 18 Sherbrooke Close, LIVERPOOL, L14 2EY.
HO, Mr. Man Yuen, ACA *2007;* 6405 Aubrey Street, BURNABY V5B 2C9, BC, CANADA.
HO, Ms. Man Kwan Christine, ACA *2007;* Flat A 3/F Block 10, 1 Hung Lam Drive, Constellation Cove, TAI PO, NEW TERRITORIES, HONG KONG SAR.
HO, Mr. Man Kwong Eddie, ACA *2007;* Lee Heng Diamond Co Ltd, 6/F Sino Plaza, 256 Gloucester Road, CAUSEWAY BAY, HONG KONG SAR.
HO, Miss. Mavis, MEng ACA *2006;* 10E Tower 6, Grand Promenade, 38 Tai Hong Street, SAI WAN HO, HONG KONG ISLAND, HONG KONG SAR.
HO, Miss. May May, MSc BSc ACA *2007;* 6 Jalan Bahasa, Singapore 299262, SINGAPORE 299262, SINGAPORE.
HO, Miss. May Yee Sum, BA ACA *2009;* with Mazars LLP, Tower Bridge House, St. Katharines Way, LONDON, E1W 1DD.
HO, Miss. Mee Yee, ACA *1997;* 299 Bedok South Avenue 3, #02-11 Bedok Court, SINGAPORE 469298, SINGAPORE.
HO, Mr. Michael Kah Peng, FCA *1977;* K.P. Ho & Associates, 80 South Bridge Road 03-01, Golden Castle Building, SINGAPORE 058710, SINGAPORE.
HO, Miss. Ming Hap, BA ACA *1982;* Jasmine Cottage, 16 Raglan Road, REIGATE, RH2 0DP.
HO, Ms. Miu Chu, ACA *2008;* 15C Tower 2, Island Harbour View, TAI KOK TSUI, KOWLOON, HONG KONG SAR.
HO, Mr. Mun Piew, FCA *1974;* 166 Coronation, Road West, SINGAPORE 269381, SINGAPORE.
HO, Ms. Mun-Wai, ACA *2003;* Flat 22 Lowry House, Cassilis Road, LONDON, E14 9LL.
HO, Mr. Norman Hau-Chong, BA ACA *1981;* 1001 Admiralty Centre Tower II, Harcourt Road, CENTRAL, HONG KONG ISLAND, HONG KONG SAR.
HO, Ms. Nyuk Chong, BA ACA CFA *1982;* GIC Real Estate Pte. Ltd., 168 Robinson Road # 37-01, Capital Tower, SINGAPORE 068912, SINGAPORE.
HO, Mr. Pak Shing, ACA *2007;* PSH & Company, 12/F, Nathan Commercial Building, 430-436 Nathan Road, YAU MA TEI, KOWLOON HONG KONG SAR.
HO, Ms. Pak Wing, ACA *2008;* Flat B 7/F, Block C, Wylie Court, 15 Wylie Path, HO MAN TIN, KOWLOON HONG KONG SAR.
•**HO, Mr. Patrick Hoo Fai, FCA** *1980;* 20th Floor, East Town Building, 41 Lockhart Road, WAN CHAI, HONG KONG ISLAND, HONG KONG SAR.
HO, Mr. Patrick Jing Kan, ACA *2007;* 4th Floor, 52 Sycamore Street, MONG KOK, KOWLOON, HONG KONG SAR.
HO, Mr. Paul Wai Chi, ACA *1979;* Paul W.C. Ho & Company, 20th Floor Golden Centre, No. 188 Des Voeux Road, CENTRAL, HONG KONG ISLAND, HONG KONG SAR.
HO, Mr. Peter Gekin, MSc ACA *2006;* 25a Lyndhurst Road, BROCKENHURST, HAMPSHIRE, SO42 7RL.
HO, Mr. Peter Kok Wai, FCA *1984;* C2-05-1 Bukit Utama 1, No. 3 Changkat Bukit Utama, PJU 6 Bandar Utama, 47800 PETALING JAYA, MALAYSIA.
HO, Mr. Po Shing Shing, ACA *2007;* Flat C, 28/F Block 1, Seaview Crescent, 8 Tung Chung Waterfront Road, TUNG CHUNG, NEW TERRITORIES HONG KONG SAR.
HO, Ms. Pui Yun Gloria, ACA *2007;* 23B Albron Court, 99 Caine Road, MID LEVELS, HONG KONG ISLAND, HONG KONG SAR.
HO, Mr. Richard, ACA *2011;* 279 Maplin Way North, SOUTHEND-ON-SEA, SS1 3NX.
HO, Ms. Sabrina Chi-Wai, BSc ACA *1989;* (Tax Fac), Stephenson Harwood, 35/F Bank of China Tower, No 1 Garden Road, CENTRAL, HONG KONG ISLAND, HONG KONG SAR.
HO, Mr. Shu Fung, ACA *2004;* House 28, Greenery Gardens, 3 Fairview Park Boulevard, YUEN LONG, HONG KONG SAR.
HO, Mr. Shu Kwun, ACA *2005;* 3101/1 Sergeants Lane, ST LEONARDS, NSW 2065, AUSTRALIA.
HO, Ms. Shuk Ching Margarita, ACA *2005;* with PricewaterhouseCoopers, 33/F Cheung Kong Center, 2 Queen's Road, CENTRAL, HONG KONG ISLAND, HONG KONG SAR.
HO, Ms. Shuk Ming, ACA *2008;* Flat F 29/F Block 4, South Horizons, AP LEI CHAU, HONG KONG SAR.
HO, Ms. Shyan Yan, ACA CA(AUS) *2010;* Ernst & Young, One Raffles Quay, North Tower Level 18, SINGAPORE 048583, SINGAPORE.
HO, Mr. Simon Siu Man, BA(Hons) ACA *2003;* 7 Champions Row, Wilbury Avenue, HOVE, BN3 6AZ.
HO, Mr. Sing Wai Raymond, ACA *2007;* ROOM D1 19/F, United Centre, 95 Queensway, CENTRAL, HONG KONG SAR.
HO, Mr. Siu Chuen, ACA *2006;* Ting Ho Kwan & Chan, 9th Floor Tung Ning Bldg, 249-253 Des Voeux Road C, CENTRAL, HONG KONG ISLAND, HONG KONG SAR.
•**HO, Mr. Siu Kau, ACA** *2006;* Ho Sneddon Chow CPA Ltd, Unit 1202 Mirror Tower, 61 Mody Road, TSIM SHA TSUI, HONG KONG SAR. See also Ho Sneddon Chow
HO, Mr. Siu Tong, ACA *2007;* Oriental Link CPA Limited, Suites 1303 - 1306A, 13/F, Asian House, 1 Hennessy Road, WAN CHAI HONG KONG SAR.
HO, Mr. Siu Lam, ACA *2007;* 14/F Shanghai Industrial Investment Building, 48 Hennessy Road, WAN CHAI, HONG KONG SAR.
HO, Mr. Siu Pang Edwin, ACA *2011;* 13G Hong Fook Court, Bedford Gardens, 153 Tin Hau Temple Road, NORTH POINT, HONG KONG SAR.
HO, Mr. Siu-Pak, MA ACA *1997;* 43 Belsize Square, LONDON, NW3 4HN.
HO, Mr. Stephen Cheuk Sun, ACA *2006;* 22nd Floor, Effectual Building, 16 Hennessy Road, WAN CHAI, HONG KONG ISLAND, HONG KONG SAR.
HO, Mr. Steve Brian, ACA *2008;* with KPMG, 27/F Alexandra House, 18-20 Chater Road, CENTRAL, HONG KONG ISLAND, HONG KONG SAR.
HO, Ms. Suk Lin, ACA *2007;* 26th Floor Yardley Commercial Building, 1-6 Connaught Road West, SHEUNG WAN, HONG KONG SAR.
HO, Mr. Sze Chung Joseph, ACA *2011;* (Tax Fac), 19c Tower 2, Bailey Garden, 23 Bailey Street, HUNG HOM, KOWLOON, HONG KONG SAR.
HO, Mr. Tak Kwong, ACA *2005;* G P O BOX 10781, CENTRAL, HONG KONG SAR.
HO, Mr. Tat Sing, ACA *2007;* C W Leung & Co, Room 403, Wing on House, 71 Des Voeux Road, CENTRAL, HONG KONG ISLAND HONG KONG SAR.
HO, Mr. Tet Shin, FCA *1974;* 68 Jalan Ampang, 50450 KUALA LUMPUR, FEDERAL TERRITORY, MALAYSIA.
HO, Mrs. Tracey Ann, BA ACA *1996;* 6 Keston Drive, Hartford Lea, CRAMLINGTON, NE23 3QA.
HO, Mr. Tze Tu, BSc ACA *1988;* Apartment 6D, 23 Repulse Bay Road, REPULSE BAY, HONG KONG ISLAND, HONG KONG SAR.
HO, Mr. Tze Kit, ACA *2005;* 3003 MEMORIAL COURT, APT # 2414, HOUSTON, TX 77007, UNITED STATES.
HO, Mr. Victor Kok Yin, ACA *1985;* 50 Draycott Park, The Draycott 16-01, SINGAPORE 259396, SINGAPORE.
HO, Miss. Victoria Kwan Yin, BSc ACA *1992;* Flat B 21st Floor, 9 Perth Street, HO MAN TIN, KOWLOON, HONG KONG SAR.
HO, Miss. Wai Leng, FCA *1977;* 182 Jalan Limau Manis, Bukit Bandaraya, Bangsar, 59000 KUALA LUMPUR, FEDERAL TERRITORY, MALAYSIA.
HO, Mr. Wai Chi, ACA *2008;* Flat C Floor 5 Block 13, Central Heights, 9 Tong Tak Street, TSEUNG KWAN O, NEW TERRITORIES, HONG KONG SAR.
HO, Mr. Wai Keung, ACA *2005;* Flat B 23rd Floor, Tower 2 Aqua Marine, 8 Sham Shing Road, Cheung Sha Wan, SHAM SHUI PO, KOWLOON HONG KONG SAR.
HO, Mr. Wai Ki, ACA *2008;* Ho Wai Ki & Co, Unit C 11th Floor, Gaylord Commercial Building, 114-118 Lockhart Road, WAN CHAI, HONG KONG SAR.
HO, Mr. Wai Ming Harry, ACA *2007;* 2/F 612 Reclamation Street, MONG KOK, KOWLOON, HONG KONG SAR.
HO, Miss. Wendy Tina, BA(Hons) ACA *2008;* 25A Lyndhurst Road, BROCKENHURST, SO42 7RL.
HO, Mr. Weng Yew, BSc ACA *1992;* 80 Lorong Setiabistari 1, Damansara Heights, 50490 KUALA LUMPUR, FEDERAL TERRITORY, MALAYSIA.
HO, Mr. William Mook Lam, ACA *2005;* William M. L. Ho & Co. Limited, Unit Nos. 301-02 3/F, New East Ocean Centre, No. 9 Science Museum Road, TSIM SHA TSIU, KOWLOON HONG KONG SAR.
HO, Mr. Wing Kai, ACA *2005;* Room 802 Wo Kwan House, Cheung Wo Court, KWUN TONG, KOWLOON, HONG KONG SAR.
HO, Miss. Yann Yann, ACA *2009;* 21 Jalan 34/38A, Taman Sri Bintang, Kepong Baru, 52100 KUALA LUMPUR, FEDERAL TERRITORY, MALAYSIA.
HO, Mr. Yau Kwong Victor, BA ACA *1996;* Hawkhurst, La Rue Du Sud, St. Ouen, JERSEY, JE3 2BF.
HO, Mr. Yau Sing, ACA *2008;* Ben Y S Ho & Co, Unit B, 20/F, Nathan Comm Building, 430 - 436 Nathan Road, YAU MA TEI KOWLOON HONG KONG SAR.
HO, Ms. Yee Ling, ACA *2008;* 2/F Block D, Peakville, 22A Peak Road, CHEUNG CHAU, HONG KONG SAR.
HO, Mr. Yew Yuen, FCA *1969;* 99 Meyer Road, The Sovereign Apt 12.02, SINGAPORE 4379 20, SINGAPORE.
HO, Mr. Yiu Cheung Jason, ACA *2008;* 5A Central Heights, 9 Tong Tak Street, TSEUNG KWAN O, NEW TERRITORIES, HONG KONG SAR.
HO, Ms. Yuk Ying, ACA *2007;* A Ho Sung & Co CPA, Room 908 9/F, 248 Queen's Road East, WAN CHAI, HONG KONG ISLAND, HONG KONG SAR.
HO, Miss. Yvonne Yuen Man, MSc ACA *2004;* 307 Chapelier House, Eastfields Avenue, LONDON, SW18 1LR.
HO FAT, Miss. Marisa Emma, ACA *2011;* 176 Princes Gardens, LONDON, W3 0LW.
HO VON, Ms. Stephanie, BA ACA *2007;* Flat 361 Eden House, Water Gardens Square, LONDON, SE16 6RH.
HO WAN KAU, Mr. Michael, BA ACA *1994;* 6B Abbe de la Caille Street, BEAU BASSIN, MAURITIUS.
HOAD, Mr. Frederic Arthur Gregory, BA FCA *1963;* Otford, Nower Rd, DORKING, RH4 3BY. (Life Member)
HOAD, Mr. Mark, BA ACA *1996;* B B A Group, 20 Balderton Street, LONDON, W1K 6TL.
•**HOAD, Mr. Reginald Victor, FCA** *1972;* (Tax Fac), R.V. Hoad & Co, Suite 11, Keynes House, Chester Park, Alfreton Road, DERBY DE21 4AS.
HOAD, Mr. Stephen Graham, FCA *1975;* Whitefoord Ltd, International House, 66 Chiltern Street, LONDON, W1U 4JT.
HOAEN, Mr. Tim, BSc ACA *2006;* Flat 3, 57 Fassett Road, KINGSTON UPON THAMES, KT1 2TE.
HOAHING, Mr. Andrew Hunter, FCA *1970;* 53 Jalan Buloh Perindu, SINGAPORE 457708, SINGAPORE.
HOAKSEY, Miss. Emma Marie, ACA *2006;* Press Association, 13 Bridgegate, Howden, GOOLE, NORTH HUMBERSIDE, DN14 7AE.
HOANG, Mrs. Hong, BSc ACA *2004;* with PKF (UK) LLP, Farringdon Place, 20 Farringdon Road, LONDON, EC1M 3AP.
HOANG, Miss. Lisa Quyen Thieu, BA(Hons) ACA *2010;* 205 Mangold Way, ERITH, KENT, DA18 4DD.
HOAR, Miss. Carina Sarah, BA(Hons) ACA *2010;* 1 May Close, Eaton Bray, DUNSTABLE, BEDFORDSHIRE, LU6 2RL.
•**HOAR, Mr. John Winlo, FCA** *1963;* John Winlo Hoar, Spinney Cottage, 68 Brattlewood, SEVENOAKS, TN13 1QU.
HOARE, Mr. Anthony Malcolm Vincent, FCA *1970;* Seven Gables, The Downs, LEATHERHEAD, KT22 8LF.
HOARE, Mr. Christopher Robin, BSc ACA *1992;* 36 Walker Road, MAIDENHEAD, SL6 2QT.
•**HOARE, Mr. Colin Bernard, FCA** *1981;* C.B. Hoare, 10b The Green, Cheddington, LEIGHTON BUZZARD, BEDFORDSHIRE, LU7 0RJ.
HOARE, Mr. David Anthony, FCA *1968;* Whitport Limited, Ashton House, 12 The Central Precinct, Chandler's Ford, EASTLEIGH, HAMPSHIRE SO53 2GB.
HOARE, Mr. Edward Gerard, MSc ACA *2003;* 123 Walcot Drive, BIRMINGHAM, B43 5TH.
HOARE, Mr. Edward Robert, FCA *1966;* Ashdown, Eastham Street, CLITHEROE, LANCASHIRE, BB7 2HY.
HOARE, Mr. Eric Angus, FCA *1955;* 14A Elgood Avenue, NORTHWOOD, MIDDLESEX, HA6 3QJ. (Life Member)
HOARE, Mr. Ernest George, MA FCA *1949;* Flat 64, Wesley Court, 1 Millbay Road, PLYMOUTH, PL1 3LB. (Life Member)
HOARE, Mrs. Frauke, ACA CTA *2001;* 60 Meadow View, CHERTSEY, KT16 8QT.
HOARE, Mr. Gavin John, BSc ACA *2005;* Qlikview Villiers House, Clarendon Avenue, LEAMINGTON SPA, CV32 5PR.
HOARE, Mrs. Jane Lindsay, BA FCA *1977;* Beech House, Newton of Mounie, Oldmeldrum, INVERURIE, ABERDEENSHIRE, AB51 0ED.
HOARE, Mr. Jeremy Alexander, BEng ACA *1999;* 8 Redditch Road, Alvechurch, BIRMINGHAM, B48 7RZ.
HOARE, Mr. John Richard, BSc FCA *1969;* 4 Meadow Terrace, Hopcott Road, Alcombe, MINEHEAD, SOMERSET, TA24 6DP. (Life Member)
HOARE, Mr. Mark Anthony, FCA *1995;* 43 Cois Chuain, Glounthaune, CORK, COUNTY CORK, IRELAND.
HOARE, Mr. Michael, BSc ACA *2003;* 77 Priory Road, West Bridgford, NOTTINGHAM, NG2 5HX.
HOARE, Mr. Michael Graham, MA FCA *1968;* 12 rue Aubriot, PARIS, FRANCE.
•**HOARE, Mr. Nicholas Charles, BSc FCA** *1980;* Watbridge Intrim Ltd, Wattbridge Farm, Ashendon, AYLESBURY, BUCKINGHAMSHIRE, HP18 0HA.
HOARE, Mr. Phillip John, FCA *1961;* 1a Old Silsoe Rd, Clophill, BEDFORD, MK45 4AR. (Life Member)
HOARE, Mr. Roger John, FCA *1963;* Ash House, 4 Beech Close, Middle Winterslow, SALISBURY, WILTSHIRE, SP5 1QH. (Life Member)
HOARE, Mr. Russell, BSc ACA *1997;* 3 Parkland Close, SEVENOAKS, KENT, TN13 1SL.
HOARE, Mr. Stephen John, FCA *1979;* Winchester House, Winchester House High Street, Angmering, LITTLEHAMPTON, WEST SUSSEX, BN16 4AE.
HOARE, Mr. Stephen John Ernest, BA ACA CTA *2002;* (Tax Fac), Heathrow Business Centre, 65 High Street, EGHAM, TW20 9EY.
•**HOARE, Mr. Stuart Edward, ACA** *1989;* (Tax Fac), Stuart Hoare, 87 London Road, Cowplain, WATERLOOVILLE, PO8 8XB.
HOATH, Mr. Andrew Martin, FCA *1974;* 48 Sherwood Avenue, POOLE, DORSET, BH14 8DL.
HOATHER, Mr. Colin James, BSc ACA *1997;* 433 Darrow Ave, EVANSTON, IL 60202, UNITED STATES.
HOBAN, Mr. John, FCA *1975;* 1 Westfields, ALTRINCHAM, CHESHIRE, WA15 0LL.
HOBAN, Mr. Mark Gerard, BSc ACA MP *1989;* 20 The Vale, Locks Heath, SOUTHAMPTON, SO31 6NL.
HOBAN, Mr. Neil Anthony, BA ACA *1999;* (Tax Fac), 6 Bigbury Close, The Crofters, Newbottle, HOUGHTON LE SPRING, DH4 4XP.
HOBART, Mr. David Ashley, BSc(Econ) ACA *1983;* with Ernst & Young LLP, 1 More London Place, LONDON, SE1 2AF.
HOBBINS, Mr. Graham Raymund, FCA *1971;* 2 Potland Cottages, Toot Baldon, OXFORD, OX44 9NH.
•**HOBBS, Mr. Alan Anthony, FCA** *1963;* (Tax Fac), Hobbs & Co, 27 Albany Road, ST. LEONARDS-ON-SEA, EAST SUSSEX, TN38 0LP. See also Sussex Taxation & Business Serv. Ltd
•**HOBBS, Mr. Andrew Robert, BCom FCA** *1979;* Andrew Hobbs Limited, 17 Suckling Green Lane, Codsall, WOLVERHAMPTON, WV8 2BL. See also Andrew Hobbs
•**HOBBS, Mr. Brian William, FCA** *1962;* R.G. Hilton & Co., 10a Bank Street, CASTLEFORD, WF10 1HZ.
HOBBS, Mrs. Caroline Louise, BSc ACA *1994;* 39 Hughes Crescent, CHEPSTOW, NP16 5DY.
HOBBS, Mr. Christopher John, FCA *1970;* Manor Cottage, Kiln Lane, Otterbourne, WINCHESTER, SO21 2EJ.
HOBBS, Mr. Christopher Terence, BSc ACA *1993;* 128a Bye Mead, Emersons Green, BRISTOL, BS16 7DQ.
HOBBS, Mr. Colin Jack, ACA *1981;* 9 Saxons Way, DIDCOT, OX11 9RA.
HOBBS, Mr. Daniel, ACA *2007;* (Tax Fac), Flat 13 Kings Quarter, 80 Orme Road, WORTHING, WEST SUSSEX, BN11 4FG.
HOBBS, Mr. David Anthony, ACA *1982;* with Hobbs The Printers Ltd, Brunel Road, Totton, SOUTHAMPTON, SO40 3WX.
HOBBS, Mr. David Brian Aubrey, BA FCA *1978;* 61 Alexandra Road, Wimbledon, LONDON, SW19 7LB.
HOBBS, Mr. David John, BSc ACA *1982;* Kongsberg Driveline Systems SAS, 650 avenue de la Republique, BP 75, 74300 CLUSES, FRANCE.
HOBBS, Mr. David Michael, BSc ACA *1993;* Hunters, Sydney Road, WOODFORD GREEN, ESSEX, IG8 0TG.
•**HOBBS, Mr. David Richard, FCA** *1979;* Johnson Tidsall, 81 Burton Road, DERBY, DE1 1TJ.
HOBBS, Mr. David Richardson, FCA *1965;* Whitecroft, 8 Nab Lane, SHIPLEY, BD18 4EH.
HOBBS, Mr. Gary Kevin, BA ACA *1993;* Ingmanthorpe Barn, Loshpot Lane, Ingmanthorpe, WETHERBY, WEST YORKSHIRE, LS22 5HL.
•**HOBBS, Mr. Ian Charles, FCA** *1966;* I C Hobbs, 51 Cambridge Road, SOUTHEND-ON-SEA, SS1 1ET.
HOBBS, Mr. James Edward, FCA *1950;* 1 Pinewoods Avenue, West Hagley, STOURBRIDGE, DY9 0JF. (Life Member)

HOBBS, Miss. Jane Margaret, BA ACA *1990;* 17 Glebe Court, The Glebe Blackheath, LONDON, SE3 9TH.
•**HOBBS, Mrs. Janet Elizabeth, FCA** *1965;* Janet Hobbs, Rush Court Nurseries, WALLINGFORD, OX10 8LJ.
HOBBS, Mr. Jason Lee, BA FCA *1995;* 21 Kenton Road, Gosforth, NEWCASTLE UPON TYNE, NE3 4NE.
HOBBS, Mr. John Frederick, MA FCA *1977;* Oaklands, Wymondham Road, Wreningham, NORWICH, NR16 1AT.
HOBBS, Mr. John William, FCA *1952;* NONE, NONE. (Life Member)
•**HOBBS, Mr. Julian Lawson, MPhil BA ACA** *2003;* (Tax Fac), JLH Financial Consultancy Ltd, 2 The Quadrangle, WELWYN GARDEN CITY, HERTFORDSHIRE, AL8 6SG.
HOBBS, Miss. Kate Elizabeth, ACA *2009;* 36 Merioneth Street, BRISTOL, BS3 4SL.
•**HOBBS, Mrs. Kathleen, FCA** *1975;* Edwards & Keeping, Unity Chambers, 34 High East Street, DORCHESTER, DT1 1HA.
HOBBS, Mrs. Margaret Anne Hartley, MA FCA MBA *1992;* St. Thomas's Vicarage, 2 Sheringham Avenue, LONDON, N14 4UE.
HOBBS, Mr. Mark, BA(Hons) ACA *2002;* 38 Caberfeigh Close, REDHILL, RH1 6BF.
HOBBS, Mr. Martin John, BSc ACA *1995;* Sigma House, Oak View Close, TORQUAY, TQ2 7FF.
HOBBS, Mr. Mathew David, BSc(Hons) ACA *2002;* 15 Viaduct Close, Bassaleg, NEWPORT, GWENT, NP10 8FT.
•**HOBBS, Mr. Michael John, BA FCA** *1986;* Rothermundt Str 18, 01277 DRESDEN, GERMANY.
HOBBS, Mr. Michael John, BA FCA *1981;* 8 Springfield Road, Wimbledon, LONDON, SW19 7AL.
HOBBS, Mr. Michael Shermar, BSc ACA *1984;* UMC: 61-01-014, American Express Europe Ltd Sussex House, Civic Way, BURGESS HILL, WEST SUSSEX, RH15 9AQ.
HOBBS, Mr. Neville Arthur Thomas, FCA *1952;* 17 Rowsley Road, EASTBOURNE, BN20 7XS. (Life Member)
HOBBS, Mrs. Patricia Marie, ACA *1981;* Headbourne Worthy Grange, School Lane, Headbourne Worthy, WINCHESTER, HAMPSHIRE, SO23 7JX.
HOBBS, Mr. Philip, ACA *1981;* 2 Crownsmead, NORTHAMPTON, NN4 9XP.
HOBBS, Mr. Philip, BA ACA *1980;* 50 Kenyon Road, North End, PORTSMOUTH, PO2 0RG.
HOBBS, Mrs. Rebecca Clare, BSc(Hons) ACA *2002;* 3 South Bank, CASTLE CARY, SOMERSET, BA7 7HF.
HOBBS, Mr. Robert William, FCA *1954;* 15 Stonelea Road, HEMEL HEMPSTEAD, HP3 9JY. (Life Member)
HOBBS, Mr. Roger Philip, BA ACA *1992;* 39 Grasmere Road, HUDDERSFIELD, HD1 4LH.
HOBBS, Mr. Ronald Michael, FCA *1967;* Claudetsceer Hoffman Architects Llp Clerkenwell House, 45-47 Clerkenwell Green, LONDON, EC1R 0EB.
HOBBS, Miss. Sally Alexandra, BA ACA *1998;* 16 Lonsdale Road, OXFORD, OX2 7EW.
HOBBS, Mrs. Susan Patricia, ACA *1985;* 21 Barley Close, Little Eaton, DERBY, DE21 5DJ.
HOBBS, Dr. Victoria, ACA *1987;* 82 Route Des Argos, 74940 ANNECY LE VIEUX, FRANCE.
HOBBS, Mr. William John, FCA *1961;* Apt 51B Urb. Lago Sol, 03186 Torrevieja, ALICANTE, SPAIN.
HOBBS, Mr. William John Mervyn, FCA *1964;* 8 Drews Court, Churchdown, GLOUCESTER, GL3 2LD.
HOBBY, Mr. Benjamin John, BA(Hons) FCA *2001;* 4 Salters Gardens, Grundisburgh, WOODBRIDGE, SUFFOLK, IP13 6XE.
HOBBY, Ms. Gillian Clare, BSc ACA *1993;* 3 St. Georges Road, SEVENOAKS, KENT, TN13 3ND.
HOBDAY, Mr. Alan Arthur, FCA *1966;* 69 Tilehouse Green Lane, Knowle, SOLIHULL, B93 9EU.
HOBDAY, Miss. Catherine Anna, ACA *2009;* 87 Windmill Drive, Croxley Green, RICKMANSWORTH, HERTFORDSHIRE, WD3 3FB.
HOBDAY, Mrs. Helen Rebecca, MEng ACA *2005;* Alvarez & Marsal, 1 Finsbury Circus, LONDON, EC2M 7EB.
•**HOBDAY, Mrs. Hong Ee, BA ACA** *1983;* Hobday & Company, 20a Plantagenet Road, BARNET, HERTFORDSHIRE, EN5 5JG.
•**HOBDAY, Mrs. Karen Louise, BSc ACA ATII** *1997;* (Tax Fac), Karen Hobday, 24 Lynwood Grove, SALE, CHESHIRE, M33 2AN.
HOBDAY, Miss. Natalie Jane, BA ACA *2004;* The Leys Church Road, Long Itchington, SOUTHAM, CV47 9PW.
•**HOBDAY, Mr. Peter Charles, FCA** *1974;* Hobday & Company, 20a Plantagenet Road, BARNET, HERTFORDSHIRE, EN5 5JG.
HOBDAY, Mr. Peter Stanley, BSc ACA *1983;* Cash Bases Group Ltd, The Drove, NEWHAVEN, EAST SUSSEX, BN9 0LA.
HOBDELL, Mr. Christopher John, MSc BSc FCA *1978;* 6 Alexander Drive, Douglas, ISLE OF MAN, IM2 3QE.
HOBDEN, Mrs. Alicia Claire, ACA *2010;* 36 The Stray, South Cave, BROUGH, NORTH HUMBERSIDE, HU15 2AL.
HOBDEN, Mr. Brian Kingsford, FCA *1977;* 12 Westfields, Hazler Road, CHURCH STRETTON, SHROPSHIRE, SY6 7AF.
HOBDEN, Miss. Sarah, ACA *2011;* 16 Napier Street, PADDINGTON, NSW 2021, AUSTRALIA.
HOBDEN, Mr. Stuart James, BSc ACA *1999;* 27 Carew Road, EASTBOURNE, EAST SUSSEX, BN21 2JN.
•**HOBDEY, Mr. David William, BSc FCA CF** *1988;* Batch Cottage, The Batch, Priddy, WELLS, SOMERSET, BA5 3BD.
HOBELL, Mr. Vitaly, BA(Hons) ACA *2011;* 39 Queens Road, Caversham, READING, RG4 8DN.
HOBEN, Mr. David, BA ACA *1980;* Mott MacDonald Group Ltd, 8 Sydenham Road, CROYDON, CR0 2EE.
HOBGEN, Mr. Jonathan Charles, ACA *2011;* 23 Wimblehurst Road, HORSHAM, WEST SUSSEX, RH12 2EA.
HOBGEN, Mr. Philip James, BSc ACA *2007;* Flat 2 Bridges Place, Denne Parade, HORSHAM, WEST SUSSEX, RH12 1PU.
HOBLEY, Mr. Charles Jeremy Stuart, BA ACA *1999;* Sycamore House, 49 Telegraph Street, Cottenham, CAMBRIDGE, CB24 8QU.
HOBLEY, Mrs. Charlotte Helen, BA ACA *2000;* Sycamore House, 49 Telegraph Street, Cottenham, CAMBRIDGE, CB24 8QU.
HOBLEY, Mr. David Charles Denholm, FCA *1969;* The Hobley Residence, 13 Ranelagh Avenue, Barnes, LONDON, SW13 0BP.
HOBLEY, Mr. Denis Harry, FCA *1953;* (Member of Council 1992 - 1997), (Tax Fac), 11 Silverthorne Drive, SOUTHPORT, PR9 9PF.
•**HOBLEY, Mr. Robert Ian, FCA** *1971;* 19, Montagu Gardens, WALLINGTON, SM6 8EP.
HOBLIN, Miss. Kathryn Ann Myra, ACA *1993;* P.O. Box 3483, ROAD TOWN, TORTOLA ISLAND, VG1110, VIRGIN ISLANDS (BRITISH).
HOBMAN, Mr. William Thomas, BA(Hons) ACA *2010;* 140 Clive Road, LONDON, SE21 8BP.
HOBOROUGH, Mrs. Tamsin Louise, MEng ACA CTA *2002;* (Tax Fac), Coca-Cola Enterprises Limited, Charter Place, UXBRIDGE, MIDDLESEX, UB8 1EZ.
HOBRO, Mr. Michael George, FCA *1975;* Unit C3, Birdineye Farm, UCKFIELD, EAST SUSSEX, TN22 5HA.
HOBROW, Mr. Anthony Gordon Piers, BSc ACA *1981;* 82 Grange Road #13-04, The Colonnade, SINGAPORE 249587, SINGAPORE.
HOBSON, Mr. Andrew John, MA ACA *1988;* Marsh Court, Bridgend, Eldersfield, GLOUCESTER, GL19 4PN.
HOBSON, Mr. Anthony John, MBA BCom FCA *1971;* Thatch End, The Warren, East Horsley, LEATHERHEAD, KT24 5RH.
HOBSON, Mr. Daniel Garry, ACA *2011;* 42 Deardon Way, Shinfield, READING, RG2 9HF.
•**HOBSON, Mr. Darren Christopher, BSc FCA** *1996;* (Tax Fac), Hobson Tax Consulting Limited, 106 Old Coppice Side, HEANOR, DERBYSHIRE, DE75 7DJ.
HOBSON, Mr. David Alan, BSc(Hons) ACA *2000;* 4 Sheridan Close, HEMEL HEMPSTEAD, HP1 1XS.
HOBSON, Mr. David Paul, BSc ACA *2007;* 14 Maybury Close, Frimley, CAMBERLEY, GU16 7HH.
HOBSON, Mrs. Deborah Anne, BA(Hons) ACA *2000;* 45 Great Elms Road, APSLEY, HERTFORDSHIRE, HP3 9TW.
HOBSON, Mrs. Emma Clare, BSc ACA *2005;* 7 Charlton Road, LONDON, SE3 7EU.
•**HOBSON, Mr. Ian Richard, BEng ACA** *1993;* Ernst & Young LLP, 1 Bridgewater Place, Water Lane, LEEDS, LS11 5QR. See also Ernst & Young Europe LLP
•**HOBSON, Mr. James Richard, BA FCA** *1991;* with Grant Thornton UK LLP, 1 Whitehall Riverside, Whitehall Road, LEEDS, WEST YORKSHIRE, LS1 4BN.
HOBSON, Miss. Lara Joan Elizabeth, BSc ACA *2011;* 82 Links Avenue, ROMFORD, RM2 6NJ.
HOBSON, Mr. Michael Rowson, FCA *1965;* Seaways, Lisle Court Road, LYMINGTON, HAMPSHIRE, SO41 5SH. (Life Member)
HOBSON, Mr. Nicholas Edward, BA ACA *1998;* Barclays Capital, 5 North Colonnade, LONDON, E14 4BB.
HOBSON, Mr. Richard Neil, BSc ACA *1993;* KPMG, 1 Stokes Place, St. Stephen's Green, DUBLIN 2, COUNTY DUBLIN, IRELAND.
HOBSON, Miss. Sarah Louise, ACA *2003;* 19 Castle Syke View, PONTEFRACT, WEST YORKSHIRE, WF8 4LX.
HOBSON, Mrs. Sarah Louise, MA ACA *1998;* 1 Murieston Road, Hale, ALTRINCHAM, CHESHIRE, WA15 9SU.
HOBSON, Mrs. Sharon Denise, BSc ACA *1996;* 10 Sylvan Close, OXTED, SURREY, RH8 0DX.
•**HOBSON, Mr. Stephen, BA FCA** *1979;* (Tax Fac), Stephen Hobson BA FCA, 84 New Street, ALTRINCHAM, CHESHIRE, WA14 2QP.
•①**HOBSON, Mr. Stephen James, BA ACA** *1984;* Francis Clark LLP, Vantage Point, Woodwater Park, Pynes Hill, EXETER, EX2 5FD.
•**HOBSON, Mr. Stephen Michael, FCA** *1981;* Stephen Hobson, 3 Sona Merg Close, Heamoor, PENZANCE, TR18 3QL.
•**HOBSON, Mr. Steven, BA FCA** *1979;* Hobson & Co Accountants Limited, 37 Wollaton Road, Beeston, NOTTINGHAM, NG9 2NG.
HOBSON, Mr. Steven, BCom ACA *2009;* Flat B, 12 Stockfield Road, LONDON, SW16 2LR.
HOBSON, Mr. William Basil, FCA *1973;* Heath Place, Ewshot, FARNHAM, GU10 5AG.
•**HOCHMUTH, Mr. Gerhard, BCom ACA** *1980;* (Tax Fac), 360 Solutions (Cambridge) Ltd, Ridgeways, 47a Lambs Lane, Cottenham, CAMBRIDGE, CB24 8TB. See also GH Business & Accountancy Services
HOCKEN, The Revd. Glen Rundle, BA ACA *1984;* 16 Farnham Avenue, HASSOCKS, WEST SUSSEX, BN6 8NS.
HOCKEN, Mrs. Helen Margaret, LLB ACA *2001;* 5 Connaught Road, HARPENDEN, HERTFORDSHIRE, AL5 4TW.
HOCKEN, Mrs. Pauline Susan Miller, ACA *1992;* Cranbourne Cottage, 3 The Chase, REIGATE, SURREY, RH2 7DJ.
HOCKEN, Mr. Philip James, BA ACA *2003;* 5 Connaught Road, HARPENDEN, HERTFORDSHIRE, AL5 4TW.
HOCKEN, Miss. Susan Ann, BA ACA *1981;* 7 The Knoll, Ealing, LONDON, W13 8HZ.
HOCKENHULL, Miss. Catherine, ACA *2011;* The Hollies Farm, High Offley Road, Woodseaves, STAFFORD, ST20 0LH.
HOCKENHULL, Mr. Neil Edgar, ACA *1993;* 5a Stafford Road, SOUTHSEA, PO5 2AD.
HOCKEY, Mr. Andrew Paul, BSc ACA *1995;* 27 Plymtree, Thorpe Bay, SOUTHEND-ON-SEA, SS1 3RA.
HOCKEY, Mr. Edward John, FCA *1968;* Sumo Investments Ltd, 10 Medburn Street, LONDON, NW1 1RJ.
HOCKEY, Mr. Graeme Alan, ACA *2005;* with Langdowns DFK, Fleming Court, Leigh Road, Eastleigh, SOUTHAMPTON, SO50 9PD.
HOCKEY, Mrs. Mandy Elizabeth Ann, MA ACA *1993;* Braehead, West Road, HADDINGTON, EAST LOTHIAN, EH41 3RH.
HOCKEY, Mr. Martin Colston, MA FCA *1972;* (Tax Fac), Ardmore, Stanton Road, OXFORD, OX2 9AY. (Life Member)
HOCKEY, Dr. Martin Shaw, DPhil BSc FCA *1976;* 20 Somerford Road, CIRENCESTER, GL7 1TW. (Life Member)
HOCKIN, Mr. John Revill Theodore, FCA *1963;* Clareville, Clareville Road, CATERHAM, CR3 6LA.
•**HOCKING, Miss. Alison Debra, BA FCA** *2001;* 74 Prestwich Hills, Prestwich, MANCHESTER, M25 9PY.
HOCKING, Mr. David Alec, ACA *1982;* 260 Nicholson Road, SUBIACO, WA 6008, AUSTRALIA.
HOCKING, Miss. Genevieve Bronwen Sara, BA ACA *2000;* 54 Bicton Street, EXMOUTH, DEVON, EX8 2RU.
HOCKING, Mr. Jonathan Michael, BA ACA *1999;* 74 Hazlewell Road, Putney, LONDON, SW15 6UR.
HOCKING, Mr. Peter Scott, ACA *2006;* 94 Centennial Avenue, Helensburgh, DUNEDIN 9010, NEW ZEALAND.
HOCKING, Mrs. Rachel Claire, BSc ACA *2009;* 241 Handside Lane, WELWYN GARDEN CITY, HERTFORDSHIRE, AL8 6TF.
HOCKING, Mrs. Sarah Louise, BA ACA *1999;* 17 Nursery Avenue Hale, ALTRINCHAM, CHESHIRE, WA15 0JP.
•**HOCKING-ROBINSON, Mr. Steven, BSc ACA** *1995;* Berg Kaprow Lewis LLP, 35 Ballards Lane, LONDON, N3 1XW. See also Steven Hocking-Robinson Limited
HOCKINGS, Mr. Hamish Neil, BSc ACA *2005;* 22 Piccadilly Court, Queens Promenade Douglas, ISLE OF MAN, IM2 4NS.
HOCKINGS, Mr. Ian Christopher, BSc FCA *1992;* c/o PricewaterhouseCoopers, GPO Box 1331L, MELBOURNE, VIC 3001, AUSTRALIA.
HOCKINGS, Mr. Timothy John, BSc ACA *1987;* Marian Lodge, The Green, Little Gaddesden, BERKHAMSTED, HP4 1PH.
HOCKLEY, Mr. Anthony Peter, FCA *1973;* 42 Pirianda Way, AVELEY, WA 6069, AUSTRALIA.
HOCKLEY, Mr. Graham Bruce, BSc ACA *1991;* 6 Cygnets Close, REDHILL, RH1 2QE.
HOCKLEY, Mr. Peter Frederick, FCA *1952;* Pine Hill House, Hagley Road, FLEET, GU51 4LH. (Life Member)
•**HOCKLEY, Mr. Wayne Richard, ACA** *2004;* Anthony Russel Ltd, Winghams House, 9 Freeport Office Village, Century Drive, BRAINTREE, ESSEX CM77 8YG. See also Kaizen Projects LLP
HOCKNELL, Mr. Brian Thomas, FCA *1960;* 1a Wilson Street, STRATHFIELD, NSW 2135, AUSTRALIA. (Life Member)
HOCKNELL, Miss. Mary Elizabeth, LLB(Hons) ACA *2010;* Cape, 9 The Square, Stockley Park, UXBRIDGE, UB11 1FW.
HOCKNEY, Mr. John Henry, FCA *1958;* 86 Countryman's Way, Shepshed, LOUGHBOROUGH, LEICESTERSHIRE, LE12 9RB. (Life Member)
HOCKNEY, Mr. Paul, FCA *1961;* Beacon House, 29 Selwick Drive, Flamborough, BRIDLINGTON, NORTH HUMBERSIDE, YO15 1AP. (Life Member)
HOCQUARD, Mr. Michael George, FCA *1970;* La Tour De Garde, Gorey, JERSEY, JE3 6DX.
HODA, Mr. Feroz, BSc ACA *1998;* 2 The Marais, Bolton Road, LONDON, W4 3TH.
HODCROFT, Mr. Derek Wilfred, FCA *1956;* Derek W.Hodcroft, 91 Oldbury Orchard, Churchdown, GLOUCESTER, GLOUCESTERSHIRE, GL3 2NX. (Life Member)
HODDER, Mrs. Caroline Penelope, BA ACA *1994;* Central House, 124 High Street, HAMPTON HILL, MIDDLESEX, TW12 1NS.
HODDER, Mrs. Deborah Jean, BA ACA *1993;* Sunnybank Farm Poundfield Lane, Plaistow, BILLINGSHURST, WEST SUSSEX, RH14 0NZ.
HODDER, Mr. Julian Paul, BSc ACA *1996;* Sunnybank Farm Poundfield Lane, Plaistow, BILLINGSHURST, WEST SUSSEX, RH14 0NZ.
HODDER, Mr. Michael John, FCA *1964;* 92 Oxford Road, Cumnor, OXFORD, OX2 9PQ. (Life Member)
HODDINOTT, Mr. Christopher Mark, BSc ACA *1985;* The Old Bakery South Street, Leigh, SHERBORNE, DORSET, DT9 6JG.
HODDINOTT, Mr. David Michael, FCA *1965;* Yew Tree Cottage, Penguithal, Llangarron, ROSS-ON-WYE, HEREFORDSHIRE, HR9 6PH.
HODDINOTT, Mrs. Julie Alexandra, BSc ACA *1985;* D C A The Old Chapel, Chapel Street Taylor Hill, HUDDERSFIELD, HD4 6HL.
HODDINOTT, Mr. Mark Maurice, BA ACA *1990;* Sol Melia sa, C/Gremio Toneleros 24, Poligono de Son Castello, 07009 PALMA, BALEARIC ISLANDS, SPAIN.
HODES, Mr. Adrian, BA(Hons) ACA *2001;* 75 Holdenhurst Avenue, Finchley, LONDON, N12 0HY.
HODES, Mrs. Allison Jane, LLB ACA *1999;* (Tax Fac), Diageo Plc Lakeside Drive, Park Royal, LONDON, NW10 7HQ.
HODES, Mr. Jonathan Andrew, BSc FCA CTA *1995;* (Tax Fac), 11 Shirehall Park, Hendon, LONDON, NW4 2QJ.
HODES, Mr. Jonathan Anson, BA ACA *1989;* Flat 81 Lauderdale Mansions, Lauderdale Road, LONDON, W9 1LX.
HODES, Mr. Michael Richard, BA ACA *1996;* 7 Brookland Hill, LONDON, NW11 6DU.
HODGE, Mr. Allan Keith, FCA *1970;* Charsley Harrison Windsor House, Victoria Street, WINDSOR, SL4 1EN.
HODGE, Mr. Andrew James, BA FCA CTA *1985;* (Tax Fac), with PricewaterhouseCoopers LLP, Marlborough Court, 10 Bricket Road, ST. ALBANS, HERTFORDSHIRE, AL1 3JX.
•**HODGE, Mr. Christopher John, BA FCA** *1992;* Easterbrook Eaton Limited, Cosmopolitan House, Old Fore Street, SIDMOUTH, DEVON, EX10 8LS.
HODGE, Mr. Christopher Michael, BSc(Hons) ACA *2004;* Tower Bridge House, St Katharines Way, LONDON, E1W 1DD.
HODGE, Mr. Daniel James, BA ACA *1998;* 20 Kenilworth Avenue, LONDON, SW19 7LW.
HODGE, Mr. Dennis Arnold Sidney, FCA *1950;* 5 Danielsfield Road, YEOVIL, SOMERSET, BA20 2LR. (Life Member)
HODGE, Mr. Eric Craig, FCA *1969;* 95 Blackpool Old Road, POULTON-LE-FYLDE, FY6 7RG. (Life Member)
HODGE, Mr. Gareth David, BSc FCA *1999;* 116 Electra House, Falcon Drive, CARDIFF, CF10 4RD.
•**HODGE, Mr. Geoffrey David, FCA** *1979;* Geoffrey Hodge, 30 Market Place, HITCHIN, SG5 1DY.

HODGE - HODGSON Members - Alphabetical

HODGE, Miss. Gillian Mary, ACA *1982;* Lynton, East Hoathly, LEWES, BN8 6DR.
HODGE, Mrs. Heather Kay, BA ACA *1993;* Flat 16 Imperial House, 9 Victory Place, Limehouse, LONDON, E14 8BQ.
HODGE, Mrs. Helen Caroline, BA ACA *1998;* 20 Kenilworth Avenue, LONDON, SW19 7LW.
HODGE, Mrs. Jane, ACA *2006;* with PricewaterhouseCoopers LLP, One Kingsway, CARDIFF, CF10 3PW.
HODGE, Ms. Jane Elizabeth, BSc ACA MBA *1979;* High Trees, Le Mont Sohier, St Brelade, JERSEY, JE3 8EA.
HODGE, Mrs. Janet Marion, BA ACA *1986;* 18 Jennifer Crescent, POINT LONSDALE, VIC 3225, AUSTRALIA.
HODGE, Dr. Judith, BSc ACA CTA *2003;* 23 Hamblin Meadow, Eddington, HUNGERFORD, RG17 0HJ.
HODGE, Miss. Lesley-Anne, BA(Hons) ACA *2009;* 10 Haversham Close, CRAWLEY, WEST SUSSEX, RH10 1LB.
HODGE, Mr. Mathew Edward, BA(Hons) ACA *2001;* 706 - 95 Bronson Avenue, OTTAWA K1R 1E2, ON, CANADA.
HODGE, Mr. Nathan Andrew, BSc ACA *1998;* 119a Altenburg Gardens, Clapham, LONDON, SW11 1JQ.
•HODGE, Mr. Neil Anthony, MA FCA *1983;* (Tax Fac), Neil Hodge & Co Limited, 106A Commercial Street, Risca, NEWPORT, NP11 6EE.
HODGE, Mr. Peter Anthony, FCA *1963;* 226 De La Lande, ROSEMERE J7A 4J1, QUE, CANADA.
HODGE, Mrs. Petrina Ruth, BSc ACA *1989;* The Barn, Rodford Elm Farm, Westerleigh, BRISTOL, BS37 8QF.
HODGE, Mr. Philip Francis David, FCA *1969;* Rua Carlos Azevedo Menezes 52, 9060-050 FUNCHAL, PORTUGAL.
•HODGE, Mr. Richard Leonard, FCA *1977;* (Tax Fac), H. Rainsbury & Co., 15 Duncan Terrace, LONDON, N1 8BZ.
HODGEKINS, Mr. Andrew Michael, MChem ACA *2007;* Assurance LTT - EP3, Pricewaterhousecoopers, 1 Embankment Place, LONDON, WC2N 6RH.
HODGEN, Mr. David Alexander, MA ACA *1989;* 20 Windhill, BISHOP'S STORTFORD, CM23 2NG.
•HODGEN, Mr. Gordon Peter, MA ACA *1996;* with RSM Tenon Limited, Salisbury House, 31 Finsbury Circus, LONDON, EC2M 5SQ.
HODGEN, Mrs. Jennifer Ann, BSc ACA *2006;* with RGL LLP, 8th Floor, Dashwood, 69 Old Broad Street, LONDON, EC2M 1QS.
HODGEON, Mr. Edmund, BSc ACA *1993;* PricewaterhouseCoopers LLP, 300 Madison Avenue, NEW YORK, NY 10017, UNITED STATES. See also PricewaterhouseCoopers
HODGES, Ms. Alison Mary, MSc ACA *1995;* Westfield, Latton, SWINDON, SN6 6DS.
HODGES, Mr. Andrew, BEng ACA *1998;* Applegarth, 19 Knoll Road, DORKING, RH4 3ES.
HODGES, Mr. Andrew John Edward, FCA *1973;* 126 London Road, GUILDFORD, GU1 1TT. (Life Member)
HODGES, Mr. Brian Martin, BSc ACA *1988;* 15 Tranby Gardens, Wollaton, NOTTINGHAM, NG8 2AB.
HODGES, Mr. Bryan Gregory, FCA *1977;* Henry Lax Ltd, 2 Devonshire Crescent, LEEDS, LS8 1EP.
HODGES, Mrs. Catherine Michele, ACA *1996;* 1 Badgers Rise, Caversham, READING, RG4 7QA.
HODGES, Mrs. Catherine Sarah, BSc ACA *2003;* with Deloitte LLP, Hill House, 1 Little New Street, LONDON, EC4A 3TR.
HODGES, Mrs. Charlotte Mary, MA ACA *1997;* Applegarth, 19 Knoll Road, DORKING, RH4 3ES.
HODGES, Miss. Clare, ACA *2009;* 43 Pelter Street, LONDON, E2 7PE.
HODGES, Mr. Clive, BA FCA *1977;* 114 London Road, CHELTENHAM, GL52 6HJ.
HODGES, Mr. Colin John, BSc ACA *1988;* 4 Kensington Close, ST. ALBANS, HERTFORDSHIRE, AL1 1JT.
HODGES, Mr. Daniel, BA ACA *2007;* Flat 9, Copperways, 80 Palatine Road, MANCHESTER, M20 3JZ.
•HODGES, Mr. David Charles, FCA *1992;* c/o Deloitte & Touche, 54 Ariapita Avenue, Woodbrook, PORT OF SPAIN, TRINIDAD AND TOBAGO.
HODGES, Mr. Elliott, ACA *2008;* 48 Fore Street, North Petherton, BRIDGWATER, SOMERSET, TA6 6PZ.
HODGES, Mr. George Nigel Robert, FCA *1975;* Lowlands, Rue De La Fontaine De Colard, Trinity, JERSEY, JE3 5DR.
HODGES, Mr. James Henry Tendekai, ACA *2001;* 9 Rue de Luxembourg, L7240 BERELDANGE, LUXEMBOURG.
HODGES, Miss. Jessica Elizabeth, BA(Hons) ACA *2010;* 7 Havers Lane, BISHOP'S STORTFORD, HERTFORDSHIRE, CM23 3PA.
HODGES, Mr. John, BA FCA *1973;* Nile Brook House, Stewarts Drive, FARNHAM COMMON, BUCKINGHAMSHIRE, SL2 3LB.
•HODGES, Mr. John Edward, FCA *1970;* Hodges & Co, 62 Norwich Street, DEREHAM, NR19 1AD.
HODGES, Mr. John Kelvin, FCA *1972;* 7 Havers Lane, BISHOP'S STORTFORD, CM23 3PA.
HODGES, Miss. Karen Julia, ACA *2004;* 177 Wollaton Road, Beeston, NOTTINGHAM, NG9 2PN.
HODGES, Mr. Kenneth Bamford, LLB FCA *1966;* 4 Rue De Monttessuy, 75007 PARIS, FRANCE. (Life Member)
HODGES, Mr. Leigh James, BSc ACA CISA *1993;* 1 Sandfield Avenue, Ravenshead, NOTTINGHAM, NG15 9AR.
HODGES, Mr. Matthew Simon, BSc ACA *2003;* 36 Springhill Road, Goring, READING, RG8 0DD.
•HODGES, Mr. Michael Gordon, LLB(Hons) ACA CTA *1989;* (Tax Fac), Mazars LLP, The Lexicon, Mount Street, MANCHESTER, M2 5NT.
HODGES, Mrs. Michelle Angela, BA ACA *1996;* 5 Beechwood Avenue, ST. ALBANS, AL1 4XP.
HODGES, Mr. Nigel Ian, FCA *1974;* 150 King Street West, TORONTO M5H 1J9, ON, CANADA.
•HODGES, Mr. Paul Andrew, FCA *1972;* P.A. Hodges, The Thatched House, 24 Bromwich Lane, Pedmore, STOURBRIDGE, DY9 0QZ.
HODGES, Mr. Paul Edward, FCA *1975;* 36 Worrin Road, Shenfield, BRENTWOOD, ESSEX, CM15 8DH.
•HODGES, Mr. Peter, BSc FCA *1990;* APL Accountants LLP, 9 St. Georges Street, CHORLEY, LANCASHIRE, PR7 2AA. See also APL Accountants Limited
HODGES, Mr. Peter Lewis, MBA BA FCA DChA *1981;* 124 Emmanuel Road, LONDON, SW12 0HS.
•HODGES, Mr. Philip John, FCA *1969;* Philip J. Hodges FCA, 123 Birchfield Road, Headless Cross, REDDITCH, WORCESTERSHIRE, B97 4LE.
HODGES, Prof. Ronald, FCA *1975;* Sheffield University, 9 Mappin Street, SHEFFIELD, S1 4DT.
HODGES, Mr. Shane Edward, BSc ACIB FCA *1996;* with KPMG LLP, 15 Canada Square, LONDON, E14 5GL.
HODGES, Mr. Simon Gregory, BA ACA *2003;* 9a Kingsgate Road, LONDON, NW6 4TD.
HODGES, Mr. Simon Robert, ACA *2000;* Capital Values Group, PO Box 121408, DUBAI, 24075, UNITED ARAB EMIRATES.
HODGES, Mrs. Sophie Jane, BSc ARCS ACA *1995;* 80 Mawson Road, CAMBRIDGE, CB1 2EA.
HODGES, Mr. Stephen, BSc ACA *1987;* News International Fleet House Cygnet Park, Cygnet Road Hampton, PETERBOROUGH, PE7 8FD.
HODGES, Mr. Stephen Neil, BA ACA *1990;* Expeditors Intl of Washington Inc, 1015 Third Avenue 12th Floor, SEATTLE, WA 98104, UNITED STATES.
HODGES, Dr. Stephen Richard, PhD MMath ACA *2006;* Axis Speciality London Ltd, 4th Floor Plantation Place South, 60 Great Tower Street, LONDON, EC3R 5AZ.
HODGES, Mr. Stephen Robert, ACA *1981;* 35 Edmonton Way, OAKHAM, LE15 6JE.
HODGES, Mr. Stuart, BSc(Hons) ACA *2001;* The Barnacles East End Road, Bradwell-on-Sea, SOUTHMINSTER, ESSEX, CM0 7PX.
HODGES, Miss. Suzanne Jane, ACA *2009;* with PricewaterhouseCoopers, Darling Park Tower 2, 201 Sussex Street, GPO Box 2650, SYDNEY, NSW 1171 AUSTRALIA.
HODGES, Mr. William Raymond, FCA *1953;* Stanton Cottage, 34 Hempstead Lane, Potten End, BERKHAMSTED, HERTFORDSHIRE, HP4 2SD. (Life Member)
HODGETT, Miss. Julie, BSc ACA *1993;* Flat 96 Ocean Wharf, 60 Westferry Road, LONDON, E14 8JS.
HODGETT, Mr. Paul Timothy, BA(Hons) ACA *2002;* 5 Tudor Close, COBHAM, SURREY, KT11 2PH.
•HODGETTS, Mr. Andrew William, BA FCA *1989;* HPCA Limited, Station House, Connaught Road, Brookwood, WOKING, SURREY GU24 0ER. See also Herbert Parnell
HODGETTS, Mr. Anthony John, FCA *1956;* 4 Long Meadows, Bramhope, LEEDS, LS16 9BZ. (Life Member)
HODGETTS, Mrs. Grace Joy, ACA *2008;* 12 Foxhill Close, CANNOCK, STAFFORDSHIRE, WS12 3XD.
HODGETTS, Mrs. Jane Elizabeth, ACA *1983;* Manor House Farm, Spon Lane, Grendon, ATHERSTONE, CV9 2EX.
HODGETTS, Mrs. Jane Margaret, BSc ACA *1986;* 66, Cranley Gardens, LONDON, N10 3AJ.
HODGETTS, Mr. Kevin, BSc ACA *2005;* 71 Francis Road, Edgbaston, BIRMINGHAM, B16 8SP.
HODGETTS, Mrs. Rebecca, MChem ACA *2006;* 111a Grandison Road, LONDON, SW11 6LT.
•HODGETTS, Mr. William Alan, FCA *1962;* W.A. Hodgetts, Berachah, 1a Laustan Close, Merrow, GUILDFORD, GU1 2TS.
HODGINS, Mr. Anthony Derek Steven, BSocSc ACA *1986;* Rose Court, Wick St. Lawrence, WESTON-SUPER-MARE, AVON, BS22 7YJ.
HODGINS, Miss. Lisa Ann, BSc(Hons) ACA *2010;* 28 Meadow Way, LEEDS, LS17 7QZ.
HODGKIN, Mr. Andrew James, BA ACA *1989;* The Knoll, Common Road, Ightham, SEVENOAKS, KENT, TN15 9DY.
HODGKIN, Mrs. Fiona Bernice, BSc FCA *1993;* with ICAEW, Metropolitan House, 321 Avebury Boulevard, MILTON KEYNES, MK9 2FZ.
HODGKIN, Mr. Jean-Marc Gordon, BSc FCA ACIS DChA FSI *1995;* 7 Berrystead, Caldecotte, MILTON KEYNES, MK7 8LT.
HODGKINS, Mr. Adam Leigh, BA FCA *1983;* 55 Moorgate, LONDON, EC2R 6PA.
HODGKINS, Mr. Anthony Albert, FCA *1964;* 10 Ilex Crescent, Locksheath, SOUTHAMPTON, SO31 6SE.
HODGKINS, Mr. Christopher James, FCA *1974;* Mann Island Finance Ltd, 30-32 Pall Mall, LIVERPOOL, L3 6AL.
•HODGKINS, Mr. Mark Nicholas, BA ACA *1983;* Morris & Co Limited, Welsh Bridge, SHREWSBURY, SY3 8LH.
HODGKINSON, Mr. Alan Robert, MA FCA *1983;* (Tax Fac), Flat 48, Anchor Brewhouse, 50 Shad Thames, LONDON, SE1 2LY.
HODGKINSON, Mr. Alexander, BA ACA *2007;* with Vantis Group Ltd, 55 Station Road, BEACONSFIELD, BUCKINGHAMSHIRE, HP9 1QL.
HODGKINSON, Mr. Brian James, MA FCA *1961;* 51 Demesne Furze, Headington, OXFORD, OX3 7XG.
HODGKINSON, Mr. Claude Peter, BA FCA *1968;* Holly Cottage, Maer, NEWCASTLE, ST5 5EF. (Life Member)
HODGKINSON, Mr. Derek John, FCA *1972;* 6 Brookvale Walk, 03-03 Grassmere Block, Brookvale Park, SINGAPORE 599954, SINGAPORE. (Life Member)
HODGKINSON, Mr. Edmund Dennis, FCA *1954;* 30 Hampton Lane, WINCHESTER, SO22 5LG. (Life Member)
•HODGKINSON, Mr. Eric, FCA *1959;* E Hodgkinson & Co, Brooklyn House, Brook Street, Shepshed, LOUGHBOROUGH, LEICESTERSHIRE LE12 9RG.
HODGKINSON, Mr. Francis Geldeard, FCA *1959;* 23 Lancaster Road, Garstang, PRESTON, PR3 1JB. (Life Member)
HODGKINSON, Mr. John Ian, BA FCA *1972;* 2 Bod Ivan, NEWTOWN, SY16 2DD. (Life Member)
HODGKINSON, Miss. Kirsty, BSc ACA *2006;* 21A Woodland Rise, LONDON, N10 3UP.
HODGKINSON, Mr. Lee Andrew, BA FCA *1989;* with KPMG LLP, 333 Bay Street, Suite 4600, TORONTO M5H 2S5, ON, CANADA.
HODGKINSON, Mr. Nicholas Richard, ACA *2009;* 38 Station Road, THAMES DITTON, KT7 0NS.
HODGKINSON, Mr. Paul Mark, MA ACA *1993;* 19 The Cloisters, ST. IVES, NSW 2075, AUSTRALIA.
HODGKINSON, Mr. Richard, BA ACA *2002;* 25 The Quadrangle, Chelsea Harbour, LONDON, SW10 0UG.
HODGKINSON, Mr. Richard, FCA *1969;* Trinity Homecare Ltd, Collingham House, Gladstone Road, Wimbledon, LONDON, SW19 1QT.
HODGKINSON, Mr. Roy Arthur, FCA *1965;* 397 Highland Terrace Avenue, KETTERING, OH 45429, UNITED STATES.
HODGKINSON, Mr. Simon Paul, BSc ACA *1999;* 30 Hudson Street, JERSEY CITY, NJ 07302, UNITED STATES.
HODGKISON, Mr. Roger Jeremy McKenzie, FCA *1967;* 31 Ashbee Gardens, HERNE BAY, KENT, CT6 6TX. (Life Member)
HODGKISS, Mr. Frank Lewis, FCA *1978;* 195 Newbrook Road, Atherton, MANCHESTER, M46 9HA.
HODGKISS, Mr. Gregory Douglas, BA ACA *1983;* 20 Herington Grove, Hutton, BRENTWOOD, CM13 2NN.
HODGKISS, Mr. James David, BA ACA *2002;* 44 Appletrees Crescent, BROMSGROVE, WORCESTERSHIRE, B61 0UA.
•HODGKISS, Mr. Jeremy Geoffrey, FCA CF *1996;* Dean Statham, Bank Passage, STAFFORD, ST16 2JS.
•HODGKISS, Mrs. Kathryn Louise, BA(Hons) ACA *2004;* (Tax Fac), J. F. Balshaw & Co, 20 Old Kiln Lane, Heaton, BOLTON, BL1 5PD.
HODGKISS, Mrs. Lynne Anne, BCom ACA *2003;* 44 Appletrees Crescent, BROMSGROVE, WORCESTERSHIRE, B61 0UA.
HODGKISS, Mrs. Marion, BSc FCA ATT CTA *1978;* MEMBER OF COUNCIL, (Tax Fac), 5 Sycamore Park, LIVERPOOL, L18 3LP.
HODGKISS, Mr. Michael Frankland, LLB FCA *1977;* 7 Rutherglen Drive, Ladybridge, BOLTON, BL3 4PN.
HODGKISS, Mr. Roger Hilton, BEng ACA *1992;* The Old Stables, Ingthorne Lane, South Milford, LEEDS, LS25 5DH.
HODGKISS, Mr. Simon Paul, BA ACA *1998;* IG Markets, 417 St Kilda Road, MELBOURNE, VIC 3004, AUSTRALIA.
HODGKISSON, Mr. Mark Andrew, ACA *1989;* 29 Pegasus Place, ST. ALBANS, HERTFORDSHIRE, AL3 5QT.
HODGSON, Mr. Alan Ernest, FCA *1953;* Winwood, 86 Oaks Road, CROYDON, CR0 5HN. (Life Member)
HODGSON, Mr. Alan Parry, FCA *1965;* 29 Runnymede, Nunthorpe, MIDDLESBROUGH, CLEVELAND, TS7 0QL.
HODGSON, Mr. Alan Peter, BA(Hons) ACA *2001;* 8 Chalks Avenue, SAWBRIDGEWORTH, HERTFORDSHIRE, CM21 0BX.
HODGSON, Mr. Alexander Peter, BA ACA *2005;* Holly Cottage Willington Road, Willington, TARPORLEY, CHESHIRE, CW6 0ND.
HODGSON, Mr. Andrew, BSc ACA *2005;* Wolseley UK Ltd, PO Box 21, RIPON, NORTH YORKSHIRE, HG4 1SL.
HODGSON, Mr. Andrew Charles, LLB ACA *1992;* Warwick Cottage, Rose Cottage Lane, Staplefield, HAYWARDS HEATH, WEST SUSSEX, RH17 6EP.
•HODGSON, Mr. Andrew Jackson, BA ACA *1994;* KPMG LLP, 100 Temple Street, BRISTOL, BS1 6AG. See also KPMG Europe LLP
HODGSON, Mr. Andrew James Thomas, BA(Hons) ACA *2010;* 32 Lebanon Court, Richmond Road, TWICKENHAM, TW1 3DA.
HODGSON, Mr. Andrew Jonathan, ACA *1989;* 16 Armistead Way, Cranage, CREWE, CW4 8FE.
•HODGSON, Mr. Anthony Edward, BSc FCA *1991;* PricewaterhouseCoopers LLP, 7 More London Riverside, LONDON, SE1 2RT. See also PricewaterhouseCoopers
HODGSON, Mr. Anthony Gordon Sutherland, FCA *1964;* 3 Carew Road, EASTBOURNE, BN21 2AU.
•HODGSON, Ms. Barbara Jane, BSc ACA *1978;* c/o Easterbrook Eaton Ltd, 8 Jesu Street, OTTERY ST. MARY, EX11 1EU.
HODGSON, Mr. Bruce, BA ACA *1984;* 2 The Recess, Boyatt Wood, EASTLEIGH, HAMPSHIRE, SO50 4GF.
HODGSON, Mr. Cedric Jerome, FCA *1959;* 5 Mill Road, EXETER, DEVON, EX2 6LH.
HODGSON, Mrs. Chantelle Marie, LLB ACA *2006;* Evolution LLP, 10 Evolution, Wynyard Park, Wynyard, BILLINGHAM, CLEVELAND TS22 5TB.
HODGSON, Mr. Charles Alexander Horsford, BA ACA *2000;* Pricewaterhousecoopers, 9 Greyfriars Road, READING, RG1 1JG.
HODGSON, Mr. Charles William, FCA *1969;* 73 The Farthings, CHORLEY, LANCASHIRE, PR7 1SH.
HODGSON, Mrs. Cheryl Louise, BA(Hons) ACA *2003;* 18 Lomond Way, STEVENAGE, HERTFORDSHIRE, SG1 6AJ.
HODGSON, Miss. Christine, BA ACA *1992;* Finance - Third Floor, UK I Partnerships The Wharf, Neville Street, LEEDS, LS1 4AZ.
HODGSON, Mrs. Christine Mary, BSc ACA *1990;* 452 Kings Road, LONDON, SW10 0LQ.
HODGSON, Mr. Christopher Alan, BCom ACA *2006;* Voyage, Garrick House, 2 Queen Street, LICHFIELD, STAFFORDSHIRE, WS13 6QD.
HODGSON, Mr. Christopher David, BA ACA *1992;* (Tax Fac), 2 Tynedale Avenue, Kings Estate, WALLSEND, NE28 9NB.
HODGSON, Mr. Christopher Frank, ACA *2009;* 3 Rogersfield, Langho, BLACKBURN, BB6 8HB.
HODGSON, Mr. Christopher Ronald, FCA *1975;* 6 Salterns Terrace, BIDEFORD, EX39 4AG.
HODGSON, Mrs. Clair Julia, BSc ACA *2000;* 48 Cirencester Road, TETBURY, GLOUCESTERSHIRE, GL8 8EQ.
HODGSON, Mrs. Claire Joanne, BA(Hons) ACA *2001;* Northern Gas Networks, 1100 Century Way, Thorpe Park Business Park, Colton, LEEDS, LS15 8TU.
HODGSON, Mr. Daniel Oliver, ACA *2011;* 19 Yew Tree Drive, CHESTERFIELD, DERBYSHIRE, S40 3NB.
HODGSON, Mr. David, FCA *1963;* 8 Victory Terrace, REDCAR, TS10 1QN.

•**HODGSON, Mr. David, FCA** *1972;* (Tax Fac), Read Milburn & Co, 71 Howard Street, NORTH SHIELDS, TYNE AND WEAR, NE30 1AF.
HODGSON, Mr. David, BSc ACA *1978;* 82 Young's Road, BASKING RIDGE, NJ 07920, UNITED STATES.
HODGSON, Mr. David Andrew, BA ACA *1997;* (Tax Fac), Universal Pictures Group (UK) Ltd Prospect House 80-110 New Oxford Street, LONDON, WC1A 1HB.
•**HODGSON, Mr. David Frank, FCA** *1977;* AIMS - David F Hodgson, 7 School Lane, Laneshawbridge, COLNE, BB8 7JB.
HODGSON, Mr. Edwin, MA FCA *1974;* 5 Eastcote View, PINNER, HA5 1AT.
HODGSON, Ms. Emma, BA ACA *1985;* Churchlands, Kirdford, BILLINGSHURST, WEST SUSSEX, RH14 0LP.
HODGSON, Mr. Ernest Malcolm, FCA *1964;* Brantwood, 7 Orchard Way, Howden, GOOLE, DN14 7DT. (Life Member)
HODGSON, Mr. Frederick John Warmingham, FCA *1950;* Cumnor, Burrator Road, Dousland, YELVERTON, PL20 6NF. (Life Member)
HODGSON, Mr. Guy St John, BA ACA *1997;* Capital Trust, 49 Mount Street, LONDON, W1K 2SD.
HODGSON, Mr. James, BA ACA *2010;* 26 Wallace Road, LONDON, N1 2PG.
HODGSON, Mr. James Mcallister, FCA *1969;* 44 Porthill Road, SHREWSBURY, SY3 8RN.
•**HODGSON, Mr. James Peter Dixon, BA FCA** *1999;* (Tax Fac), Hodgsons, 48 Arwenack Street, FALMOUTH, CORNWALL, TR11 3JH.
HODGSON, Mrs. Jayne Angela, BA ACA *1995;* Building B Ground Floor, British Petroleum Co Plc, Chertsey Road, SUNBURY-ON-THAMES, MIDDLESEX, TW16 7LN.
HODGSON, Mrs. Jill Kathryn, BA ACA *1992;* 28 Chartwell Gardens, Appleton, WARRINGTON, WA4 5HZ.
HODGSON, Mrs. Joanna, BSc ACA *2005;* 21 Blackthorn Close, Woolbrook, SIDMOUTH, DEVON, EX10 9XR.
HODGSON, Mr. John, ACA *1995;* PO Box 235, CARDIFF, CF23 6XG.
HODGSON, Mr. John Andrew, BA ACA *1979;* 14 Woodlands Close, STALYBRIDGE, CHESHIRE, SK15 2SH.
HODGSON, Mr. John Anthony, FCA *1959;* Stonecroft, 23a Hill Top Road, Newmillerdam, WAKEFIELD, WF2 6PZ. (Life Member)
HODGSON, Mr. John Anthony, MA ACA *1994;* 49 Pembroke Road, Clifton, BRISTOL, BS8 3BE.
•**HODGSON, Mr. John Benjamin, FCA** *1971;* (Tax Fac), Hodgson & Co, Lydgate Farm, Ashopton Road, Bamford, HOPE VALLEY, DERBYSHIRE S33 0AZ.
•**HODGSON, Mr. John Frederick, BSc ACA** *1984;* (Tax Fac), with BTG Tax LLP, 19 George Road, Edgbaston, BIRMINGHAM, B15 1NU.
HODGSON, Mr. John Geoffrey Sanford, FCA MBA *1969;* 147 Portland Road, LONDON, W11 4LR.
HODGSON, Mr. John Gordon, MSc BA ACA *1986;* Aviva Investors, 1 Poultry, LONDON, EC2R 8EJ.
HODGSON, Mr. John Roy, FCA *1977;* 24 Elmfield Grove, Gosforth, NEWCASTLE UPON TYNE, NE3 4XA.
•**HODGSON, Mr. Keith Trevor, FCA** *1965;* 8 Holmcliffe Ave., Bankfield ParkTaylor Hill, HUDDERSFIELD, HD4 7RJ.
HODGSON, Mr. Kevin George, MSc ACA *1998;* 98 Palmerston Crescent, SOUTH MELBOURNE, VIC 3205, AUSTRALIA.
HODGSON, Miss. Laura, ACA *2009;* with KPMG LLP, 15 Canada Square, LONDON, E14 5GL.
HODGSON, Leonard William, Esq CBE FCA *1953;* Penthouse, 23 Rozel Manor Western Road, Branksome Park, POOLE, BH13 6EX. (Life Member)
HODGSON, Mrs. Lesley Ann, BSc ACA MBA *1991;* The Willows, The Crescent, LYMM, WA13 0JY.
•**HODGSON, Mr. Leslie, BA FCA** *1985;* Next Level Financial Management Ltd, Willow House, 17 East Grange, SUNDERLAND, SR5 1NX.
•**HODGSON, Miss. Lindsay Sonya, ACA** *2001;* Financial Advisory Services and Training Limited, PO Box 4182, Boulevard de l'Umuganda, KIGALI, RWANDA.
HODGSON, Mrs. Lisa Deborah, BA(Hons) ACA *2002;* 8 Glassop Street, BALMAIN, NSW 2041, AUSTRALIA.
•**HODGSON, Mr. Martin Andrew, MA ACA** *1995;* PricewaterhouseCoopers LLP, Benson House, 33 Wellington Street, LEEDS, LS1 4JP. See also PricewaterhouseCoopers
•**HODGSON, Mr. Martin Richard, FCA** *1982;* PricewaterhouseCoopers LLP, 1 Embankment Place, LONDON, WC2N 6RH. See also PricewaterhouseCoopers
•**HODGSON, Mr. Matthew James, ACA CTA** *2005;* Romsey Capital Limited, 156 New Street, CAMBRIDGE, CB1 2QX.
HODGSON, Mr. Michael Charles Peter, MA ACA *1991;* Brand Events, 35/94 Oxford Street, Darlinghurst, SYDNEY, NSW 2010, AUSTRALIA.
HODGSON, Mr. Michael Hugh, ACA *1981;* P.O. Box 412160, CRAIGHALL, 2024, SOUTH AFRICA.
HODGSON, Mr. Michael Keith, FCA *1982;* (Tax Fac), Knowle Edge, 26 Knowle Lane, SHEFFIELD, S11 9SH.
HODGSON, Mr. Nicholas Ian, BSocSc ACA *2000;* Simmons & Simmons Citypoint, 1 Ropemaker Street, LONDON, EC2Y 9SS.
•**HODGSON, Mr. Nicholas Lee, BA ACA** *1992;* Ernst & Young, Ernst & Young Building, Harcourt Centre, Harcourt Street, DUBLIN 2, COUNTY DUBLIN IRELAND. See also Ernst & Young Business Advisors
HODGSON, Mr. Nicholas Robert, BA ACA *1986;* 350 Chemin Du Puy, Le Cheverny, 06600 ANTIBES, FRANCE.
•**HODGSON, Mr. Paul Boyd, BA FCA** *1986;* Coulsons, 2 Belgrave Crescent, SCARBOROUGH, NORTH YORKSHIRE, YO11 1UB.
HODGSON, Mr. Peter, FCA *1970;* The Old School, Church Lane, LLANSANTFFRAID, POWYS, SY22 6AP.
•**HODGSON, Peter John Dixon, Esq CBE FCA** *1970;* (Tax Fac), Hodgsons, 12 Southgate Street, LAUNCESTON, PL15 9DP.
HODGSON, Mr. Peter Robinson, MA FCA *1952;* 11 Chesterford, Southacre Park, CAMBRIDGE, CB2 7TZ. (Life Member)
HODGSON, Mr. Philip Arthur, MA ACA *1980;* 26 Elliott Road, Chiswick, LONDON, W4 1PE.
HODGSON, Mr. Philip Charles Spencer, FCA *1969;* 60 South End Bassingbourn, ROYSTON, HERTFORDSHIRE, SG8 5NL. (Life Member)
HODGSON, Mrs. Rebecca Rachel, BA ACA *2006;* 55 Hillfield Road, Comberton, CAMBRIDGE, CB23 7DB.
HODGSON, Mr. Richard George, BA ACA *1996;* 13 Gunnersbury Crescent, LONDON, W3 9AA.
HODGSON, Mr. Richard Ian Peter, BSc ACA *1996;* 10 Teviot Drive, Murieston Valley, LIVINGSTON, WEST LOTHIAN, EH54 9JW.
HODGSON, Mr. Ronald George Keith, FCA *1969;* 36 Westwick Gardens, LONDON, W14 0BS.
HODGSON, Miss. Sarah Elizabeth Joan, MSc BSc ACA *2002;* 116 Harestock Road, WINCHESTER, HAMPSHIRE, SO22 6NY.
•**HODGSON, Miss. Sarah Jane, BSc FCA** *1993;* (Tax Fac), Upper Street Accounts Ltd, 3 Tolpuddle Street, Islington, LONDON, N1 0XT.
HODGSON, Mrs. Sheila Margaret, BA FCA *1978;* 5 Eastcote View, PINNER, HA5 1AT.
HODGSON, Mr. Stephen, BSc ACA *2002;* 23 Hampton Road, BRISTOL, BS6 6HP.
HODGSON, Mr. Stephen John, BEng ACA CTA *2010;* Flat 15 Villency Court, 62 Nottingham Road, LOUGHBOROUGH, LEICESTERSHIRE, LE11 1EB.
HODGSON, Mr. Steven John, BSc ACA *1989;* Direct Group Pty Ltd, Innovations Park, 431 Warringah Road, FRENCHS FOREST, NSW 2086, AUSTRALIA.
•**HODGSON, Mr. Stuart John, ACA** *1985;* (Tax Fac), with HW, Q Court, 3 Quality Street, Davidsons Mains, EDINBURGH, EH4 5BP. See also HW Edinburgh
HODGSON, Mr. Thomas, BSc ACA *2004;* Deloitte Corporate Finance, Currency House Building 1, DIFC, DUBAI, 282056, UNITED ARAB EMIRATES.
HODGSON, Mr. Thomas Eric, FCA *1953;* 10 North Street, Anlaby, HULL, HU10 7DE. (Life Member)
HODGSON, Mr. Tom Howard, MA FCA *1979;* 13 Hogarth Way, HAMPTON, TW12 2EL.
HODGSON, Miss. Vanessa Jane, BA ACA *1997;* 9 Lincoln Avenue, COLLAROY, NSW 2097, AUSTRALIA.
•**HODGSON, Mrs. Wendy Elisabeth, BSc FCA** *1981;* (Tax Fac), David Bailey, 28 Landport Terrace, PORTSMOUTH, PO1 2RG. See also DB Payroll Services Limited and Bailey David
•**HODGSON-BARKER, Mr. Michael John, FCA** *1964;* (Tax Fac), S.G. Ripley & Co, 157 Lewisham Road, LONDON, SE13 7PZ.
HODKIN, Mrs. Beverley Ann, BA ACA *1984;* PO Box 1040 GT, GEORGE TOWN, GRAND CAYMAN, KY1-1102, CAYMAN ISLANDS.
HODKIN, Mr. Donald Henry, BA FCA *1952;* 18 Pinebank, HINDHEAD, GU26 6SR. (Life Member)
HODKIN, Mr. Jeffrey, BA ACA TEP *1983;* Schroder Cayman Bank & Trust Co Ltd, P.O.Box 1040GT, Harbour Centre, GEORGE TOWN, GRAND CAYMAN, KY1-1102 CAYMAN ISLANDS.
•**HODKINSON, Mr. Christopher Lee, BSc FCA** *1984;* 32 Millers Lane, Atherton, MANCHESTER, M46 9BW.
HODKINSON, Mr. David Sydney, BA ACA *1995;* Korec, Blundellsands House, 34-44 Mersey View, Brighton-le-Sands, LIVERPOOL, L22 6QB.
HODKINSON, Mrs. Joanne Susan, BA ACA *1996;* 7 Junction Lane, Burscough, ORMSKIRK, L40 5SN.
HODKINSON, Mr. Michael Andrew, BSc ACA *1995;* 17 Dutton Drive, Spital, WIRRAL, MERSEYSIDE, CH63 9AE.
HODKINSON, Mr. Michael John, FCA *1969;* Mount Dragon, P O Box 27, UNDERBERG, 3257, SOUTH AFRICA.
HODKINSON, Mr. Stephen Richard, BA FCA *1986;* 27 The Drive, Adel, LEEDS, LS16 6BQ.
HODKINSON, Miss. Susan, LLB ACA *2001;* Corner House Main Street, Bardsea, ULVERSTON, CUMBRIA, LA12 9QT.
HODSDEN, Mr. Richard David, BSc FCA *1991;* Oransay, Misbourne Avenue, Chalfont St. Peter, GERRARDS CROSS, BUCKINGHAMSHIRE, SL9 0PF.
HODSDON, Mr. Matthew, ACA *1992;* 12 Bailey Close, MAIDENHEAD, SL6 7YN.
HODSDON, Mr. Nicholas, BA ACA *2007;* Flat 13, 5 Strype Street, LONDON, E1 7LG.
•**HODSMAN, Miss. Claire Suzanne, BA ACA** *2005;* with Gardiners Limited, Hutton House, Dale Road, Sheriff Hutton, YORK, YO60 6RZ.
•**HODSON, Mr. Allan Raymond, BA FCA** *1983;* A. Hodson, 40 The Glades, Aldridge, WALSALL, WS9 8RN.
•**HODSON, Mr. Brian Frederick, FCA** *1957;* Hodson & Co, Wiston House, 1 Wiston Avenue, WORTHING, BN14 7QL.
HODSON, Mr. Darren, BSc ACA *2002;* 6 Ashley Mount, Tattenhall, WOLVERHAMPTON, WV6 8QD.
HODSON, Mrs. Heather Ceri, BSocSc ACA *1998;* 84a West Drive, Highfields Caldecote, CAMBRIDGE, CB23 7NY.
HODSON, Ms. Hedy Elizabeth, BSc ACA *2000;* 6 Scholars Walk, Chalfont St. Peter, GERRARDS CROSS, BUCKINGHAMSHIRE, SL9 0EJ.
HODSON, Mr. Ian Roger, FCA *1970;* P.O.Box 74480, Nairobi City Square, NAIROBI, 00200, KENYA.
HODSON, Mr. James, FCA *1972;* Strathlene, CARNOUSTIE, ANGUS, DD7 6LA.
•**HODSON, Mr. Jeffrey Richard, FCA** *1977;* (Tax Fac), Duncan & Toplis, 5 Resolution Close, Endeavour Park, BOSTON, LINCOLNSHIRE, PE21 7TT.
•**HODSON, Mr. John, FCA** *1976;* Anglian Accountancy Services Limited, 36-38 King Street, KING'S LYNN, NORFOLK, PE30 1ES.
HODSON, Mr. Jonathan, ACA *2010;* 25 Leathwaite Road, LONDON, SW11 1XG.
HODSON, Mr. Justin Timothy, FCA *1974;* Catalyst Housing Group, Ealing Gateway, 26-30 Uxbridge Road, LONDON, W5 2AU.
HODSON, Mr. Kyle Richard, ACA *2011;* PricewaterhouseCoopers LLP, 1 Embankment Place, LONDON, WC2N 6RH.
HODSON, Mr. Martin, BSc ACA *2011;* H S B C, Business & Performance Planning, Forward Trust House, 12 Calthorpe Road, Edgbaston, BIRMINGHAM B15 1QZ.
HODSON, Mr. Martin Liam, BA(Hons) ACA *2010;* 26 Woodend Avenue, Crosby, LIVERPOOL, L23 2UA.
•**HODSON, Mr. Matthew John, BSc FCA** *1993;* (Tax Fac), Hodson & Co, Wiston House, 1 Wiston Avenue, WORTHING, BN14 7QL. See also Hodsons Accountants
•**HODSON, Mr. Roy Philip, BA ACA** *1980;* PricewaterhouseCoopers LLP, 1 Embankment Place, LONDON, WC2N 6RH. See also PricewaterhouseCoopers
HODSON, Mr. Simon, BSc ACA *1991;* 9 Rue Henri Dupriez, 60300 AUMONT EN HALATTE, FRANCE.
HODSON, Mr. William Laurence, BSc ACA *1989;* 27 Belvedere Grove, Wimbledon, LONDON, SW19 7RQ.
HOE, Mr. Alan Mcintosh, BA FCA *1964;* PO Box 368, (Jordangate S.0), MACCLESFIELD, CHESHIRE, SK10 1WZ. (Life Member)
HOE, Miss. Freya, BA ACA *2007;* 11 Regency Court, Cardigan Road, LEEDS, LS6 1DW.
HOE, Mr. York Joo, ACA *2004;* No 168 Tianqiao Road, YULIN 537000, CHINA.
HOEFFLER, Mr. John Alexander, BA FCA CDir *1992;* Elm Gables, 63 Rayleigh Road, Hutton, BRENTWOOD, CM13 1AJ.
HOEFLING, Mrs. Susan Jane, BSc ACA *1981;* CEVA Animal Health Ltd, 90 The Broadway, High Street, CHESHAM, BUCKINGHAMSHIRE, HP5 1EG.
HOEKSEMA, Ms. Nicola Jane, ACA CA(SA) *2010;* 176b Elsenham Street, Southfields, LONDON, SW18 5NR.
HOEY, Mrs. Carol Lorraine, BA ACA *1986;* 22 Strawberry Mead, Fair Oak, EASTLEIGH, HAMPSHIRE, SO50 8RG.
HOEY, Mrs. Yvonne, PhD BSc ACA *1985;* Jasmine Cottage, Calver Road, Baslow, BAKEWELL, DE45 1RP.
HOFER, Mr. Julien David, BA ACA *1983;* Datascope Recruitment Ltd, 109-110 Bolsover Street, LONDON, W1W 5NT.
HOFF, Mr. Laurence Piers, BA ACA *1998;* 65, Fleet Street, LONDON, EC4Y 1HT.
HOFFMAN, Mr. Adam Guy, BA ACA *1999;* 32 Cambridge Road, LONDON, E11 2PN.
HOFFMAN, Mr. Alexander James William, BA ACA *2002;* A E A Investors UK Ltd, 78 Brook Street, LONDON, W1K 5EF.
HOFFMAN, Mrs. Amanda, BA ACA *2002;* 82 Bromfelde Road, LONDON, SW4 6PR.
HOFFMAN, Mr. Andrew Keith Philip, FCA *1978;* 105 South Drive, COVINGTON, LA 70433, UNITED STATES.
HOFFMAN, Mr. Charles Julian Gordon, FCA *1955;* Cheriton Hill House, North Cheriton, TEMPLECOMBE, BA8 0AB. (Life Member)
HOFFMAN, Mr. David Michael, BA ACA *1982;* P.O. Box 229, OXFORD B0M 1P0, NS, CANADA.
HOFFMAN, Mr. Francis David, FCA *1977;* 13 Woodlands Walk, Mannings Heath, HORSHAM, RH13 6JG.
•**HOFFMAN, Mr. Jonathan Hugh, FCA FCCA** *1973;* with RSM Tenon Audit Limited, 66 Chiltern Street, LONDON, W1U 4JT.
•**HOFFMAN, Mr. Mark Ian, BA(Hons) FCA** *2001;* with Moors Andrew McClusky & Co, Halton View Villas, 3-5 Wilson Patten Street, WARRINGTON, WA1 1PG.
HOFFMAN, Mr. Michael John, FCA CTA *1976;* 2 Leigham Drive, ISLEWORTH, TW7 5LU.
HOFFMAN, Mr. Nicholas John, LLB FCA *1981;* Nicholas Hoffman & Company, 1355 Peachtree Street, N E Suite 1450, ATLANTA, GA 30309, UNITED STATES.
•**HOFFMAN, Mr. Oliver Gideon, BSc ACA CF** *1995;* Mazars LLP, Mazars House, Gelderd Road, Gildersome, LEEDS, LS27 7JN.
HOFFMAN, Mr. Philip Michael, BA ACA *1988;* 35 Cremorne Rd, Chelsea, LONDON, SW10 0NB.
•**HOFFMAN, Mr. Richard John, BCom FCA** *1985;* 25 Stafford Road, CROYDON, SURREY, CR0 4NG.
HOFFMAN, Mr. Simon, BA ACA *2006;* 38 Copley Road, STANMORE, HA7 4PF.
•**HOFFMAN, Mr. Stephen, FCA** *1969;* with Moors Andrew McClusky & Co, Halton View Villas, 3-5 Wilson Patten Street, WARRINGTON, WA1 1PG.
HOFFMAN, Mr. Thomas Dieter Dirk, LLB FCA *1971;* Old Curteis, Biddenden, ASHFORD, TN27 8JN. (Life Member)
HOFFMANN, Mr. Alan Benjamin, BA ACA *1995;* 33 Macadam Gardens, PENRITH, CUMBRIA, CA11 9HS.
HOFFMANN, Mr. Alastair Derek, BSc ACA *1989;* 22 Pembroke Avenue, Berrylands, SURBITON, KT5 8HP.
HOFFMANN, Ms. Jennifer Mary, BA FCA *1988;* 30 Coxwell Street, CIRENCESTER, GLOUCESTERSHIRE, GL7 2BH.
HOFMAIR, Mrs. Andrea Jayne, BSc ACA *1987;* Hopewell House, University of Leeds, Woodhouse Lane, LEEDS, LS2 9JT.
HOGAN, Mrs. Jane-Anne, LLM BA(Hons) ACA *1988;* The Ranch, 5 Willow Gardens, LIPHOOK, GU30 7HY.
HOGAN, Mr. Kenneth George, FCA *1982;* The Biggin, Lincolns Hill, Chiddingfold, GODALMING, GU8 4UN.
HOGAN, Mr. Kevin, BSc ACA *2007;* Flat 3, 5 Rye Hill Park, Nunhead, LONDON, SE15 3JN.
•**HOGAN, Mr. Leslie Vincent, ACA CA(AUS)** *2010;* LV Hogan & Co Ltd, Monaleen Road, Castleroy, LIMERICK, COUNTY LIMERICK, IRELAND.
HOGAN, Mr. Liam Bernard, MSc FCA *1974;* 7 Douglas Close, DOUGLAS, COUNTY CORK, IRELAND.
HOGAN, Mr. Michael Peter, BA ACA *1995;* 15 Tall Trees, Baunton Lane, CIRENCESTER, GLOUCESTERSHIRE, GL7 2AF.
HOGAN, Ms. Michelle Louise, BA FCA CTA *1997;* 51 Elms Road, STOCKPORT, CHESHIRE, SK4 4PT.
HOGAN, Dr. Olga, ACA *2008;* 20 Webb Lane, East Melbourne, MELBOURNE, VIC 3002, AUSTRALIA.
•**HOGAN, Mr. Peter Andrew, FCA** *1982;* (Tax Fac), Clive Owen & Co LLP, 140 Coniscliffe Road, DARLINGTON, DL3 7RT.
HOGAN, Mrs. Sandra Ann, ACA *1979;* Les Touches, Concourson Sur Layon, 49700 DOUE LA FONTAINE, FRANCE.
HOGAN, Ms. Sarah, ACA *2009;* 3 Templemore Avenue, Rathgar, DUBLIN 6, COUNTY DUBLIN, IRELAND.
HOGAN, Mr. Stuart, ACA *2011;* 68 Aynsley Gardens, Church Langley, HARLOW, ESSEX, CM17 9PD.
HOGAN, Mr. Vincent Albert, FCA *1984; (FCA Ireland 1982);* P.O. Box HM 3397, HAMILTON HM PX, BERMUDA.

•**HOGAN, Mr. William Patrick, FCA** *1966;* (Tax Fac), 216 Stock Road, BILLERICAY, CM12 0SH.
HOGAN-FLEMING, Mr. Arthur Charles, BA FCA *1982;* 52 Longfellow Road, STRATFORD-UPON-AVON, CV37 7PR.
HOGARTH, Miss. Anne Macpherson, BSc FCA *1976;* 8 Leyden Grove, Clovenfords, GALASHIELS, SELKIRKSHIRE, TD1 3NF.
HOGARTH, Mr. David Arthur, BA ACA *1988;* 71 Hersham Road, WALTON-ON-THAMES, SURREY, KT12 1LL.
•**HOGARTH, Mr. Frank, BA FCA** *1979;* 23 Parsons Drive, Gnosall, STAFFORD, ST20 0QS.
•**HOGARTH, Mr. Peter, BA FCA** *1992;* PricewaterhouseCoopers LLP, 1 Embankment Place, LONDON, WC2N 6RH. See also PricewaterhouseCoopers
HOGARTH, Mrs. Sarah Elizabeth, BA ACA *1989;* 71 Hersham Road, WALTON-ON-THAMES, KT12 1LL.
HOGBEN, Mr. Andrew, ACA *2008;* 80 Kensington Church Street, LONDON, W8 4BY.
HOGBEN, Mr. Graham Antony, MA ACA *1986;* 48 Wavendon Avenue, LONDON, W4 4NS.
HOGBEN, Mr. Michael Anthony, MA FCA *1966;* 1 Shermanbury Grange, Brighton Road, Shermanbury, HORSHAM, WEST SUSSEX, RH13 8HN. (Life Member)
HOGBEN, Mrs. Rachel Lesley, BSc ACA *2003;* 10 Fox Way, Barham, CANTERBURY, CT4 6QJ.
HOGBIN, Mr. Frank Anthony, FCA *1950;* 21 Durrant Way, Sway, LYMINGTON, SO41 6DQ. (Life Member)
•**HOGG, Mr. Adrian Jeffrey, BA(Hons) FCA** *2000;* Grant Thornton (Gibraltar) Limited, 6A Queensway, PO Box 64, GIBRALTAR, GIBRALTAR.
•**HOGG, Mr. Brian Cyril, ACA** *1992;* (Tax Fac), Silfern Limited, 2 Market Lane, Selby, SELBY, NORTH YORKSHIRE, YO8 4QA. See also H R Accountancy Limited
•**HOGG, Mr. Brian Douglas, FCA** *1976;* (Tax Fac), Brian D. Hogg, Brookside, Walgrave Road, Hannington, NORTHAMPTON, NN6 9SX.
HOGG, Miss. Catherine Celia Rose, BA ACA *2005;* Peacocks Stores Ltd Capital Link, Windsor Road, CARDIFF, CF24 5NG.
HOGG, Mrs. Charlotte Anne, BSc ACA *1999;* 134 Chemin De Saule, Bernex, 1233 GENEVA, SWITZERLAND.
HOGG, Mr. Christopher, ACA *2009;* 66 Redbridge Lane West, LONDON, E11 2JU.
HOGG, Mr. Christopher David, BA ACA *1992;* Haydn House, Trent Lane, South Clifton, NEWARK, NG23 7AE.
HOGG, Mr. Cyril, FCA *1952;* 11 Eardulph Avenue, CHESTER-LE-STREET, DH3 3PR. (Life Member)
HOGG, Mr. David James, MA ACA *2004;* The Royal Bank of Scotland Plc, PO Box 1000, EDINBURGH, EH12 1HQ.
HOGG, Mr. David James, ACA *2011;* 49 Rectory Lane, SIDCUP, KENT, DA14 4QR.
HOGG, Mr. David John, BA ACA *1995;* 31 High Street, Little Shelford, CAMBRIDGE, CB22 5ES.
HOGG, Mr. David Mark, FCA *1972;* 1 Camelia Way, WOKINGHAM, RG41 3NB.
HOGG, Miss. Elise, ACA *2011;* Apartment 556, Block 11 Spectrum, Blackfriars Road, SALFORD, M3 7EE.
HOGG, Mrs. Elizabeth Jane, MA ACA *1983;* The Steading, Hardmuir of Boath, Auldearn, NAIRN, IV12 5QG.
HOGG, Mrs. Erica Anne, ACA *1993;* Johnson Controls Ltd, 19 Parrys Grove, Stoke Bishop, BRISTOL, BS9 1TT.
•**HOGG, Mr. Geoffrey Myers, FCA** *1970;* Myers Hogg & Co, 3 Lemna Road, Leytenstone, LONDON, E11 1JL.
HOGG, Mr. Graeme Thomas James, BAcc ACA *1993;* 14 Springwood Bank, KELSO, TD5 8BA.
HOGG, Mrs. Hayley, BA(Hons) ACA *2003;* 9 Canterbury Close, RAYLEIGH, ESSEX, SS6 9PS.
HOGG, Mrs. Helen Victoria, BA(Hons) ACA *2001;* with Deloitte LLP, 4 Brindley Place, BIRMINGHAM, B1 2HZ.
HOGG, Mr. Ian, BA ACA *1979;* Plaza City View - 2nd Floor, Jl. Kemang Timur 22, JAKARTA, 12510, INDONESIA.
HOGG, Mr. James Andrew, MSc BSc ACA *2005;* S S L International Plc, 1 Old Park Lane, Trafford Park, Urmston, MANCHESTER, M41 7HA.
HOGG, Miss. Joanna Louise, BSc ACA *2009;* Flat 4, 25 Ramsden Road, LONDON, SW12 8QX.
HOGG, Mr. John Michael, FCA *1957;* 4 Plovers Mead, Wyatts Green, BRENTWOOD, ESSEX, CM15 0PR. (Life Member)
•**HOGG, Mr. John Trevor, ACA** *1980;* TPA Accountancy Services, 38 Stanhope Road, SOUTH SHIELDS, NE33 4BT.
HOGG, Mr. John Vernon Albert, FCA *1975;* (Tax Fac), Mall House, The Mall, FAVERSHAM, ME13 8JL.
HOGG, Mrs. Katherine Maria, BA(Hons) ACA *2002;* 139 Town Street, Rodley, LEEDS, LS13 1HW.
HOGG, Miss. Lorna Charlotte, BSc ACA *2010;* 50 Mountfield Gardens, NEWCASTLE UPON TYNE, NE3 3DD.
HOGG, Dr. Michael James, MSci ACA *2006;* 48 Fairhazel Gardens, LONDON, NW6 3SJ.
HOGG, Mr. Michael John, BSc FCA *1977;* Oakridge, 6 Penn Close, Chorleywood, RICKMANSWORTH, WD3 5HG. (Life Member)
HOGG, Mr. Nigel Broadbery, BA ACA *1985;* Ship Cottage, The Row, Henham, BISHOP'S STORTFORD, CM22 6AT.
HOGG, Mr. Richard, BSc ACA *2010;* 66 Redbridge Lane West, LONDON, E11 2JU.
•**HOGG, Mr. Rowland Anthony Rymer, FCA** *1965;* Rowland Hogg, 11 Wood Street, WALLINGFORD, OX10 0BD.
HOGG, Miss. Sophie Emma, BSc ACA *2010;* Willow Ridge, Park Close, Fetcham, LEATHERHEAD, SURREY, KT22 9BD.
•**HOGG, Mr. Stephen Marcroft, FCA ATII** *1971;* (Tax Fac), with Moore Stephens LLP, 150 Aldersgate Street, LONDON, EC1A 4AB.
HOGG, Mrs. Suzanne Louise, BSc ACA *1993;* Discovery Pharaceuticals, The Old Vicarage, Market Street, Castle Donington, DERBY, DE74 2JB.
•**HOGG, Mrs. Zara, BA FCA** *1994;* Blue Spire South LLP, Unit E1, Cumberland Business Centre, Northumberland Road, SOUTHSEA, HAMPSHIRE PO5 1DS.
HOGGAN, Mr. Andrew Robert, ACA *2008;* Barclays Bank Plc, 1 Churchill Place, LONDON, E14 5HP.
HOGGAN, Mr. Leslie Proudfoot, FCA *1952;* Dunvegan, Fernhill Heath, WORCESTER, WR3 7TZ. (Life Member)
HOGGARD, Mr. Graham Leslie, BSc ACA *1987;* Foxgloves, 2 The Stray, South Cave, BROUGH, HU15 2AL.
HOGGART, Mrs. Joy Deborah, BA ACA *1993;* Haines Watts, Interwood House Stafford Avenue, HORNCHURCH, RM11 2ER.
HOGGARTH, Mr. Alan, FCA *1965;* Sherwood, 1C Main Road, Seaton, WORKINGTON, CA14 1EA. (Life Member)
HOGGARTH, Mr. Ian Frank, MA FCA *1967;* The Stable House, Charlecote, WARWICK, CV35 9EW.
HOGGARTH, Mr. John, MA ACA *1991;* Jones Harris & Co, 17 St. Peters Place, FLEETWOOD, FY7 6EB.
HOGGETT, Mr. Alan, FCA *1960;* Danesfield, Herington Grove, Hutton, BRENTWOOD, ESSEX, CM13 2NW. (Life Member)
HOGGINS, Mr. David John, FCA *1980;* 236 Almners Road, Lyne, CHERTSEY, KT16 0BL.
HOGHTON, Mr. Charles Anthony, FCA CTA *1973;* (Tax Fac), Fiander Tovell & Co, 63-64 The Avenue, SOUTHAMPTON, SO17 1XS.
HOGLAND, Mrs. Ruth Victoria, BSc ACA *1989;* 17 Avenue de Chavoires, 74940 ANNECY LE VIEUX, FRANCE.
HOGSDEN, Mr. Andrew Paul, BA ACA *1988;* Oak Cottage, 45 Zion Hill, Coleorton, COALVILLE, LE67 8JP.
HOGSDEN, Mrs. Juliet Elizabeth, BA ACA *1988;* (Tax Fac), Oak Cottage, 45 Zion Hill, Coleorton, COALVILLE, LE67 8JP.
HOGSFLESH, Miss. Clair Frances, BA(Hons) ACA *2010;* 29 Cavan Crescent, POOLE, DORSET, BH17 7EY.
HOGWOOD, Mr. Paul Arthur, BSc FCA *1975;* 15 Ambleside, EPPING, CM16 4PT.
HOH, Miss. Ai Wee, BSc(Hons) ACA *2003;* Flat 1D Block 1, Skyline Mansion, 51 Conduit Road, MID LEVELS, HONG KONG ISLAND, HONG KONG SAR.
HOH, Mr. Hsin-Hui, ACA *2007;* 189 Lower Road, LONDON, SE16 2LW.
HOH, Mr. Jason Weng Lung, MBA BSc ACA *2003;* 42 Whiteadder Way, Clippers Quay, LONDON, E14 9UR.
HOH, Miss. Kim Hyan, FCA *1983;* 39 Jalan Kajang Raya 3, Taman Kajang Raya, 43000 KAJANG, SELANGOR, MALAYSIA.
HOH, Miss. Kim Jin, ACA *1982;* 2 Lorong Mahir Satu, Taman Connaught, Jalan Cheras, 56000 KUALA LUMPUR, FEDERAL TERRITORY, MALAYSIA.
HOH, Mr. Ming Chee, FCA *1974;* 365 Holland Road, Apt 11-04, Allsworth Park, SINGAPORE 278639, SINGAPORE.
HOH, Mr. Yue Sheng, ACA *2010;* 3 Jalan Sri Hartamas 15, Sri Hartamas, 50480 KUALA LUMPUR, FEDERAL TERRITORY, MALAYSIA.
HOHNE, Mr. Andrew Ross, BSc ACA *1992;* Tri Star Cars Ltd, Unit 1/2, Horton Road, WEST DRAYTON, MIDDLESEX, UB7 8BQ.
•**HOHNEN, Mr. David Leslie, FCA** *1958;* Hohnen David Leslie, Cedars Lodge, Church Road, WINDLESHAM, GU20 6BL.
HOIJ, Mr. Anders Daniel, BSc ACA *2006;* 18 Carlyle Road, LONDON, W5 4BL.
HOING, Mr. Adrian Clive, BA ACA *1994;* Hassans, 57/63 Line Wall Road, GIBRALTAR, GIBRALTAR.
HOING, Mr. Roy Coote, FCA *1958;* Hilbury Lodge, 18 Devonshire Close, Devonshire Avenue, AMERSHAM, BUCKINGHAMSHIRE, HP6 5JG. (Life Member)
HOLAH, Mr. Stephen Andrew, BA ACA *1989;* 14 Pownall Road, WILMSLOW, CHESHIRE, SK9 5DR.
HOLBERTON, Mr. David Lawrence, BA ACA *1985;* Atherfield Lodge, Park View Road, Woldingham, CATERHAM, SURREY, CR3 7DJ.
HOLBOROW, Mr. Mark James Ratcliffe, BSc ACA *2010;* 331 Lyham Road, LONDON, SW2 5NS.
HOLBOROW, Mr. Paul Wrexal, BA ACA *1991;* Woodside, Kirkley, NEWCASTLE UPON TYNE, NE20 0BD.
•**HOLBOURN, Mr. Gilbert John, FCA DChA** *1973;* with Saffery Champness, Lion House, Red Lion Street, LONDON, WC1R 4GB.
HOLBOURN, Miss. Natacha Helen, BSc ACA CPA *1998;* 14G Seahorse Lane, DISCOVERY BAY, HONG KONG SAR.
HOLBROOK, Mr. Christopher Maurice, BA FCA *1979;* (Tax Fac), Photo-Me International Plc, Church Road, Bookham, LEATHERHEAD, SURREY, KT23 3EU.
HOLBROOK, Mrs. Deirdre Angela, ACA *1983;* 43a High Street, Newington, SITTINGBOURNE, ME9 7JR.
HOLBROOK, Mr. Edward Matthew, BA ACA *2003;* 204/30 The Esplanade, ST KILDA, VIC 3182, AUSTRALIA.
HOLBROOK, Mrs. Elizabeth Anne, BA ACA ATII *1989;* Mazars, 8 New Fields, 2 Stinsford Road, Nuffield, POOLE, DORSET BH17 0NF.
HOLBROOK, Mr. Ian Donald, BSc ACA *1993;* Flat C 49/F, Tower 8 Albany Cove, Carribean Coast, 1 Kin Tung Road, TUNG CHUNG, NEW TERRITORIES HONG KONG SAR.
HOLBROOK, Mr. Robert John, BA ACA *1991;* 4 Wardley Hall Lane, Worsley, MANCHESTER, M28 2RL.
HOLBROW, Mr. Timothy Bruce Warren, BSc(Hons) FCA *2000;* 171 Ambleside Road, LIGHTWATER, SURREY, GU18 5UW.
HOLBURN, Mr. Gareth Franklyn, FCA *1966;* Cottage 170, VILLAGE OF HAPPINESS, 4280, SOUTH AFRICA.
HOLBURN, Mr. Marcus Raphael, BSc ACA *1999;* Ashbrook, The Croft, Aston Tirrold, DIDCOT, OXFORDSHIRE, OX11 9DL.
HOLCOMBE, Ms. Catherine Jane, MA ACA *1991;* Boreham House Church Street, Rudgwick, HORSHAM, WEST SUSSEX, RH12 3EF.
HOLCOMBE, Mr. Richard Frederick, MA FCA *1976;* 17 Carnoustie, NORWICH, NR4 6AY.
•**HOLCOMBE, Mr. Robert Julian, FCA** *1979;* R.J. Holcombe & Co, Apple Tree Cottage, Church Street, Appleford, ABINGDON, OX14 4PA.
•**HOLCOMBE, Mr. Roger John, FCA** *1973;* (Tax Fac), William Price & Co, Westbury Court, Church Road, Westbury-on-Trym, BRISTOL, BS9 3EF.
HOLCROFT, Mr. Martin John, FCA *1973;* 901 Doncaster, Marlborough Park, Bath Road Claremont, CAPE TOWN, C.P., 7780 SOUTH AFRICA.
HOLCROFT, Mrs. Ruth Ann, BSc(Hons) ACA *2002;* Marshall of Cambridge Ltd The Airport, Newmarket Road, CAMBRIDGE, CB5 8RX.
HOLCROFT, Mr. Thomas Bernard Manning, BA FCA *1971;* 4 Duchess Court, WEYBRIDGE, SURREY, KT13 9HN.
•**HOLDAWAY, Mr. John Edward, FCA** *1973;* John Holdaway, Plum Cottage, Honeysuckle Lane, Headley Down, BORDON, GU35 8JA.
HOLDAWAY, Mr. Matthew John, BSc ACA *1999;* Airbus UK Ltd, New Filton House, Filton, BRISTOL, BS99 7AR.
HOLDAWAY, Mrs. Vanessa Clare, BSc ACA *1999;* 13 High Street, Colerne, CHIPPENHAM, WILTSHIRE, SN14 8DB.
HOLDCROFT, Mr. Adam John, ACA *1998;* 6 Mulder Close, Tokai, CAPE TOWN, WESTERN CAPE PROVINCE, SOUTH AFRICA.
HOLDCROFT, Mr. Andrew Darren, BSc ACA *1995;* 9 Samford Court, Tattingstone, IPSWICH, IP9 2NQ.
HOLDEN, Mr. Adam Christopher, MA MEng ACA *2001;* Ground Floor Building E, The Royal Bank of Scotland Plc, PO Box 1000, EDINBURGH, EH12 1HQ.
HOLDEN, Mr. Adam John, BA ACA *2007;* 134 St. Davids Road, LEYLAND, PR25 4XY.
HOLDEN, Mr. Andrew John, BSocSc ACA *1995;* 85 Wilderness Road, Earley, READING, RG6 7RF.
HOLDEN, Mr. Andrew John, BSc ACA *1994;* 6 Odinel Court, PRUDHOE, NORTHUMBERLAND, NE42 5QS.
HOLDEN, Ms. Angie Marian Carolyn, BA ACA *1996;* Middle Hill Farm Lower Road, Hinton Blewett, BRISTOL, BS39 5AT.
HOLDEN, Ms. Anne Jean, BSc ACA *1990;* Ravenstone, The Grove, BATTLE, EAST SUSSEX, TN33 0UN.
HOLDEN, Mr. Christopher Charles, BSc FCA *1974;* Harbourside, 29 Esplanade, FOWEY, CORNWALL, PL23 1HY.
HOLDEN, Mr. Christopher Ian, MEng ACA *2005;* Unit C2, Skytop Gardens, 5 Mellow Sky Lane, PAGET PG03, BERMUDA.
HOLDEN, Mr. Christopher Martin, BSc ACA *1997;* 1 Dallacre Drive, Wilbarston, MARKET HARBOROUGH, LE16 8QS.
HOLDEN, Miss. Clair Elizabeth, ACA *1998;* 18 Manor Road, Wrea Green, PRESTON, PR4 2PB.
HOLDEN, Mr. Colin David, BSc ACA *1989;* 6 Danesway, Heath Charnock, CHORLEY, PR7 4EY.
HOLDEN, Mr. Daniel Ian, LLB ACA *2005;* 39 Cedars Road, BECKENHAM, KENT, BR3 4JG.
HOLDEN, Mr. David Graham, FCA *1962;* Sunnyside, 133 Salisbury Road, WORCESTER PARK, KT4 7BU. (Life Member)
HOLDEN, Mr. David Graham, BSc ACA *1984;* Croft House, Langlea Terrace, Hipperholme, HALIFAX, HX3 8LG.
HOLDEN, Mr. David James, ACA *2008;* 21 Ashleigh Court, Henllys, CWMBRAN, GWENT, NP44 6HF.
HOLDEN, Mr. David Peter, BCom ACA *1984;* Po Box 59, CROYDON, CR9 4RN.
•①**HOLDEN, Mr. Edward George, BSc FCA** *1978;* Holden & Co, PO Box 229, LONDON, SW6 4UX.
•**HOLDEN, Miss. Erika Jane, BA(Hons) ACA** *1998;* Holden Tax Consulting Limited, 12 Spring Close, SOUTHPORT, MERSEYSIDE, PR8 2BA.
•**HOLDEN, Mrs. Fleur Tamsin, BA FCA** *2001;* Clement Keys, 39/40 Calthorpe Road, Edgbaston, BIRMINGHAM, B15 1TS.
HOLDEN, Mrs. Helen, BA ACA *2002;* with National Audit Office, 157-197 Buckingham Palace Road, Victoria, LONDON, SW1W 9SP.
HOLDEN, Mr. Henry Patrick Manfield, ACA *2010;* The Bank of England, Internal Audit, Threadneedle Street, LONDON, EC2R 8AH.
•**HOLDEN, Miss. Jacqueline Anne, MA FCA** *1999;* Deloitte LLP, 2 New Street Square, LONDON, EC4A 3BZ. See also Deloitte & Touche LLP
HOLDEN, Mr. James Paul, BSc ACA *2010;* 30 Stone Leigh, Tankersley, BARNSLEY, SOUTH YORKSHIRE, S75 3BD.
HOLDEN, Ms. Jill, BSc ACA *1993;* 5 Dovewood Court, Littleover, DERBY, DE23 3ZF.
HOLDEN, Mr. Jocelyn Basil, FCA *1961;* Dower Garden, Church Street, Crondall, FARNHAM, SURREY, GU10 5QQ. (Life Member)
HOLDEN, Mr. John David, BSc ACA *1991;* 17 Magnolia Drive, Clayton le Woods, LEYLAND, PR25 5SF.
HOLDEN, Mr. John Kevin, MBA BSc FCA *1973;* Flash House, Flash Lane, Rufford, ORMSKIRK, L40 1SW.
HOLDEN, Ms. Katherine Olivia, BA(Hons) ACA *2000;* 68 Saughtonhall Drive, EDINBURGH, EH12 5TL.
•**HOLDEN, Mr. Kenneth, FCA** *1966;* (Tax Fac), H. Graham King & Co, Southernhay Suite 7, 207 Hook Road, CHESSINGTON, KT9 1HJ.
HOLDEN, Mr. Kenneth Harold, FCA *1963;* Glyfada, Gosmore Road, HITCHIN, HERTFORDSHIRE, SG4 9BE. (Life Member)
•**HOLDEN, Mr. Kevin, ACA FCCA** *2011;* Lees Limited, The Granary, Brewer Street, Bletchingley, REDHILL, RH1 4QP. See also Lees
HOLDEN, Mr. Leslie, FCA *1965;* 31 Crossacres, Pyrford, WOKING, GU22 8QS.
HOLDEN, Mr. Leslie Walter, FCA *1960;* Flat 41, The Croft, Meadow Drive, DEVIZES, WILTSHIRE, SN10 3BJ. (Life Member)
HOLDEN, Mr. Malcolm, BCom FCA *1970;* Oaklands, 482a Burton Road, DERBY, DE23 6AL.
HOLDEN, Mr. Mark Benedict, BSc ACA *1996;* (Tax Fac), 6 Leyborne Park, RICHMOND, SURREY, TW9 3HA.
HOLDEN, Miss. Mary Eleanor, BSc ACA *2005;* with Grant Thornton UK LLP, Grant Thornton House, 22 Melton Street, Euston Square, LONDON, NW1 2EP.
HOLDEN, Mr. Matthew Jonathan, BSc ACA *2000;* 10 Balmoral Close, LICHFIELD, STAFFORDSHIRE, WS14 9SP.
HOLDEN, Miss. Michelle Annette, BSc ACA *2002;* 11 Hough Side Lane, Pudsey, LEEDS, LS28 9JH.
HOLDEN, Mr. Neil Jonathan, BSc FCA *1983;* Fishpits Cottage, Fishpits Lane, BURES, SUFFOLK, CO8 5DS.

•**HOLDEN, Mr. Paul David Richard, FCA CTA** *1970;* Moore Stephens (North West) LLP, 6th Floor, Blackfriars House, The Parsonage, MANCHESTER, M3 2JA.

HOLDEN, Mr. Paul Jonathan Ewart, BA ACA *1988;* 327 Old Bath, CHELTENHAM, GLOUCESTERSHIRE, GL53 9AJ.

HOLDEN, Mr. Paul Stephen, MSc ACA *2007;* 150 Avenue Road, LONDON, N14 4DU.

•①**HOLDEN, Mr. Paul William, BSc FCA** *1977;* Pipps Cottage, Send Marsh Green, Ripley, WOKING, SURREY, GU23 6JP.

HOLDEN, Mr. Peter Colin, FCA *1959;* 7 The Croft, Meadow Drive, DEVIZES, WILTSHIRE, SN10 3BJ. (Life Member)

•**HOLDEN, Mr. Peter Graham Dixon, BSc FCA** *1969;* Wellfield, 53 Hilton Lane, Prestwich, MANCHESTER, M25 9SA.

HOLDEN, Mr. Philip Ashley William, BSc FCA *1993;* 22 Malcolm Road, Chandler's Ford, EASTLEIGH, HAMPSHIRE, SO53 5BG.

HOLDEN, Mr. Philip James, MA ACA *2001;* 26 Elverson Road, LONDON, SE8 4JN.

HOLDEN, Mr. Ralph Burton, FCA *1953;* Quarry Bank, Billinge End Road, BLACKBURN, BB2 6PT. (Life Member)

•**HOLDEN, Mr. Richard Alexander David, MA FCA CF** *2001;* Catalyst Corporate Finance LLP, 5th Floor, 12-18 Grosvenor Gardens, LONDON, SW1W 0DH.

HOLDEN, Mr. Richard Peter, BEng ACA *1999;* 11 Sunderlands Road, HALF MOON BAY 2012, NEW ZEALAND.

•**HOLDEN, Mr. Robert, BSc FCA** *1982;* Holden & Co, Ashleigh House, 81 Birmingham Road, WEST BROMWICH, WEST MIDLANDS, B70 0PX. See also R Holden & Co Accountants Ltd

HOLDEN, Mr. Robert David, BA ACA *1980;* 5 Abbey View, RADLETT, HERTFORDSHIRE, WD7 8LT.

HOLDEN, Mr. Robert James, BA ACA *1999;* 15 Avoncroft Road, Stoke Heath, BROMSGROVE, WORCESTERSHIRE, B60 4NG.

HOLDEN, Mr. Robin John, FCA *1964;* (Member of Council 1989 - 1995), Pear Tree Cottage, Canal Bank, LYMM, CHESHIRE, WA13 9NR.

HOLDEN, Miss. Rosanna, MA BA ACA *2011;* 25 Bedford Road, HORSHAM, WEST SUSSEX, RH13 5BL.

HOLDEN, Mr. Shaun Robert, ACA *2001;* Enstar (EU) Limited, Avaya House, Cathedral Hill, GUILDFORD, SURREY, GU2 7YL.

HOLDEN, Mr. Simon Nicholas John, BEng ACA *1992;* The Grange, Heronsgate, RICKMANSWORTH, HERTFORDSHIRE, WD3 5BU.

HOLDEN, Mr. Stephen James, BA ACA *1994;* Stewarts Law LLP, 5 New Street Square, LONDON, EC4A 3BF.

HOLDEN, Mr. Stephen Jameson, BSc ACA CTA *1991;* 49 Royshaw Avenue, BLACKBURN, BB1 8RJ.

HOLDEN, Mr. Steven, BA ACA *1991;* 10 Briony Close, Royton, OLDHAM, OL2 5AL.

HOLDEN, Mr. Terence James, FCA *1970;* Ancha De San Antonio 125A Apt 23, 37700 SAN MIGUEL DE ALLENDE, MEXICO.

HOLDEN, Mr. Timothy Paul, BCom ACA *1992;* Pendragon Plc, Loxley House, 2 Oakwood Court, Little Oak Drive, Annesley, NOTTINGHAM NG15 0DR.

HOLDER, Mr. Andrew John, BSc ACA *1997;* 30 Station Road, THAMES DITTON, SURREY, KT7 0NS.

•**HOLDER, Mr. Charles Peter, BSc FCA** *1991;* with Zolfo Cooper Ltd, 10 Fleet Place, LONDON, EC4M 7RB.

•**HOLDER, Mr. Christopher James, BA FCA** *1984;* McGregors Business Network Ltd, i2 Mansfield, Office Suite 2.1, Oakham Business Park, MANSFIELD, NOTTINGHAMSHIRE NG18 5BR. See also Mcgregors Corporate (Lincoln) Ltd and McGregors (Mansfield) Ltd

HOLDER, Mr. Crispin Westwood, BA ACA *1999;* 50 Wymondley Road, HITCHIN, HERTFORDSHIRE, SG4 9PT.

HOLDER, Mr. David James, JP FCA *1968;* 15 Pleydell Road, SWINDON, SN1 4DJ.

HOLDER, Mr. Dean, MEng ACA *2006;* Level 30, 275 George Street, PO Box 3107, BRISBANE, QLD 4001, AUSTRALIA.

•**HOLDER, Mr. Ian Gerard Martin, ACA** *1991;* Mazars LLP, 45 Church Street, BIRMINGHAM, B3 2RT.

HOLDER, Mr. Ian Keith, BSc ACA PgDip *1985;* Langdale House, 11 Marshallsea Road, LONDON, SE1 1EN.

HOLDER, Mrs. Jacqueline, BA ACA *1993;* L F Europe Ltd, Lawkholme Lane, KEIGHLEY, WEST YORKSHIRE, BD21 3BB.

HOLDER, Mr. James Edward, BA(Econ) FCA *1996;* West Watch House Horsted Keynes Road, Chelwood Gate, HAYWARDS HEATH, WEST SUSSEX, RH17 7DG.

HOLDER, Mr. Jeffrey James, BA(Hons) ACA *2001;* 8 Slade Close, Boston Spa, WETHERBY, WEST YORKSHIRE, LS23 6DH.

HOLDER, Mr. John Edward Knox, FCA *1958;* 1 John Anderson Drive, Apt # 604, ORMOND BEACH, FL 32176, UNITED STATES. (Life Member)

HOLDER, Ms. Kerry Anne, MA FCA CF *1996;* 113a Chadwick Road, LONDON, SE15 4PY.

HOLDER, Mr. Mark Phillip Charles, BSc ACA *1989;* Windover House, Birch Close, HAYWARDS HEATH, RH17 7ST.

•**HOLDER, Mr. Martin, BA FCA** *1984;* (Tax Fac), Peters & Co, 1 Park Road, CATERHAM, CR3 5TB.

•**HOLDER, Mr. Michael John, FCA** *1967;* Rigbey Harrison, 4 Church Green East, REDDITCH, B98 8BT.

HOLDER, Mr. Nicholas John, BA ACA *1999;* 2 Hamlet Drive, SALE, CHESHIRE, M33 5PY.

HOLDER, Mr. Nicholas Oliver, MA MSc FCA FSI *1995;* Prudential Life Assurance, 25th Floor, 37 Ton Duc Thang Street, District 1, HO CHI MINH CITY, VIETNAM.

•**HOLDER, Mr. Oliver Patrick, MA ACA** *1999;* Deloitte LLP, Athene Place, 66 Shoe Lane, LONDON, EC4A 3BQ. See also Deloitte & Touche LLP

HOLDER, Mr. Philip Bernard, MA FCA *1974;* 29 Pilgrims Way, REIGATE, RH2 9LG.

•**HOLDER, Mr. Robert George, FCA** *1974;* (Tax Fac), R.G. Holder & Co, Whetcombe Whey, Ropers Lane, Wrington, SOMERSET, BS40 5NH. See also R G Holder & Co Limited

HOLDER, Ms. Sally Anne, BSc ACA *1993;* 24 Bruton Way, LONDON, W13 0BY.

HOLDER, Mr. Simon Edward, FCA *1974;* 19 Grange Park, Henleaze, BRISTOL, BS9 4BU.

•**HOLDER, Mr. Stephen Colin, BA FCA** *1989;* HPBS Ltd, 17 Wren Garth, Sandal, WAKEFIELD, WEST YORKSHIRE, WF2 6SL.

HOLDER, Mr. Stephen John, BSc FCA *1987;* 12 Cambridge Gardens, Winchmore Hill, LONDON, N21 2AT.

HOLDER, Mr. Timothy Christopher, BA ACA *1989;* PO Box 11487, MANAMA, BAHRAIN.

HOLDER, Mrs. Vicky Yvonne, BA ACA *1988;* 21 Silvermere Park, SHIFNAL, SHROPSHIRE, TF11 9BN.

HOLDGATE, Miss. Deborah Susan, BSc ACA *1989;* 49 Brodrick Road, LONDON, SW17 7DX.

HOLDGATE, Mr. Grahame Raymond, BA FCA *1981;* E F G Private Bank Leconfield House, Curzon Street, LONDON, W1J 5JB.

HOLDICH, Mr. Thomas Anthony White, FCA *1960;* 22 Highgate, Cherry Burton, BEVERLEY, HU17 7RR.

HOLDING, Mr. Andrew, BSc ACA *1994;* 5 chemin de la Pallanterie, 1222 VESENAZ, SWITZERLAND.

HOLDING, Mr. Edward William Valentine, OBE BA FCA *1968;* Birds Hill Farmhouse, Warren Lane, Oxshott, LEATHERHEAD, KT22 0SU.

•**HOLDING, Mr. Geoffrey Ross, FCA** *1969;* (Tax Fac), Holding & Company, Birchwood House, Shaws Lane, Southwater, HORSHAM, WEST SUSSEX RH13 9BX.

HOLDING, Ms. Juliet Claire Francesca, BA ACA *1991;* 2 Keswick House, Raymond Road, LONDON, SW19 4AJ.

HOLDITCH, Ms. Catherine Elisabeth Claire, BA ACA *1991;* Regus, 3000 Aviator Way, MANCHESTER, M22 5TG.

HOLDRIDGE, Mr. John Richard, BA FCA *1984;* 30 Peatling Road, Countesthorpe, LEICESTER, LE8 5RD.

HOLDROYD, Mr. Edward Julian, MA FCA *1969;* 2 Pleasant Pastures, New Hey RoadScammonden, HUDDERSFIELD, HD3 3FT. (Life Member)

HOLDSTOCK, Mr. George William, FCA *1963;* with McCabe Ford Williams, Bank Chambers, 1 Central Ave., SITTINGBOURNE, ME10 4AE.

HOLDSTOCK, Mr. Gerald James, FCA *1971;* Griffin, Stourton Caundle, STURMINSTER NEWTON, DORSET, DT10 2JW.

HOLDSTOCK, Mr. Harry, MA MSc ACA *2011;* Stoke End, West End Lane, Stoke Poges, SLOUGH, SL2 4NA.

HOLDSTOCK, Mr. John David, FCA *1968;* (Member of Council 2000 - 2007), (Tax Fac), Yardbase Limited, 2 Middleton Road, LUTON, BEDFORDSHIRE, LU2 8HY.

HOLDSTOCK, Mr. John Terence, MA BA CA *FCA 1971;* Grant Thornton LLP, 50 Bay Street, 12th Floor, TORONTO M5J 2Z8, ON, CANADA.

HOLDSTOCK, Mr. Stephen Mark, BA ACA *1986;* Deloitte Touche Tohmatsu, Grosvenor Place, 225 George Street, P.O. Box N 250, SYDNEY, NSW 2000 AUSTRALIA.

HOLDSWORTH, Miss. Alethea Charlotte, BSc ACA *2009;* Hutchison 3G UK Ltd, Star House, 20 Grenfell Road, MAIDENHEAD, BERKSHIRE, SL6 1EH.

HOLDSWORTH, Mr. Anthony David, FCA *1977;* 11 Connaught Avenue, East Sheen, LONDON, SW14 7RH.

HOLDSWORTH, Mr. Brian Granville, FCA *1962;* 6 Marlin Close, Daws HeathThundersley, BENFLEET, SS7 2TW. (Life Member)

HOLDSWORTH, Mrs. Catherine Anne, BSc ACA *1991;* The Neale, Lewes Road, Scaynes Hill, HAYWARDS HEATH, RH17 7NG.

HOLDSWORTH, Mr. Edward, BSc ACA *2002;* 14a Sisters Avenue, Clapham, LONDON, SW11 5SQ.

HOLDSWORTH, Mr. John, BSc ACA *1980;* April Cottage, 13 Shortway, AMERSHAM, HP6 6AQ.

HOLDSWORTH, Mr. Jonathan Michael, BA ACA *1992;* Brooks Farmhouse, Belchalwell, BLANDFORD FORUM, DORSET, DT11 0EG.

HOLDSWORTH, Mr. Julian Michael, FCA *1965;* 38 Stapper Green, Wilsden, BRADFORD, BD15 0HQ. (Life Member)

HOLDSWORTH, Mrs. Karen Louise, BSc ACA *1998;* 64 King William Drive, CHELTENHAM, GL53 7RP.

HOLDSWORTH, Mrs. Katherine Patricia, BSc ACA *1989;* 18 Fairlawn Grove, LONDON, W4 5EH.

HOLDSWORTH, Mrs. Kim Marnie, ACA AMCT *1990;* Barmouth, Badgers Mount, SEVENOAKS, KENT, TN14 7AT.

HOLDSWORTH, Miss. Kimberley Anne, BSc ACA *2004;* KPMG, 2 Harbourmaster Place, DUBLIN 1, COUNTY DUBLIN, IRELAND.

HOLDSWORTH, Mr. Michael, BA ACA *1986;* Millstone, Applewick Lane, HIGH WYCOMBE, HP12 4DS.

HOLDSWORTH, Mr. Raymond Geoffrey, MA FCA *1984;* Greatre Manchester Pension Fund Investment Group, Council Offices, Wellington Road, ASHTON-UNDER-LYNE, LANCASHIRE, OL6 6DL.

HOLDSWORTH, Mr. Robert Angus, FCA *1968;* Southern Investment Ltd, 2 Boulevard Hector Otto, MC 98000 MONACO, MONACO.

HOLDSWORTH, Mr. Roderick Antony, BSc FCA *1991;* The Neale Lewes Road, Scaynes Hill, HAYWARDS HEATH, WEST SUSSEX, RH17 7NG.

HOLDSWORTH, Mr. Simon David, ACA *1980;* c/o Consolidated Timber Holdings Ltd, Clock House Station Approach, SHEPPERTON, MIDDLESEX, TW17 8AN.

HOLDSWORTH, Mr. Timothy Richard, FCA *1969;* 3495 Upper Terrace, VICTORIA V8R 6E8, BC, CANADA.

HOLDWAY, Mrs. Alison, BA ACA *1999;* DC Leisure Mgmt Ltd, Farnham Sports Centre, Dogflud Way, FARNHAM, SURREY, GU9 7UD.

•**HOLDWAY, Mr. Darren John, BA FCA** *1992;* HW Birmingham LLP, Sterling House, 71 Francis Road, BIRMINGHAM, WEST MIDLANDS, B16 8SP. See also HW Transaction Services LLP

HOLDWAY, Mr. Derek Dutton, FCA *1954;* Maple Cottage, Hooe Common, BATTLE, TN33 9EN. (Life Member)

HOLE, Mr. David John, FCA *1977;* 481 Caerleon Rd, NEWPORT, NP19 7LX.

HOLE, Mr. David Scott, BA ACA *1989;* (Tax Fac), 19 Wolfington Road, LONDON, SE27 0JF.

HOLE, Miss. Kathryn Louise, ACA *2009;* 210 Peach Road, LONDON, W10 4DY.

•**HOLE, Mr. Roderick Carr, BA FCA** *1966;* Roderick C Hole, 28 Rouse Gardens, Alleyn Park, LONDON, SE21 8AF.

HOLE, Mr. Stephen William, BA ACA *2005;* Flat 1, 14 Crescent Lane, LONDON, SW4 9PU.

HOLE, Mr. Terry Edward, BA ACA *1996;* Sony Music Entertainment, 550 Madison Avenue, NEW YORK, NY 10022, UNITED STATES.

HOLEHOUSE, Mr. Kenneth Thomas, FCA *1956;* 6 Waterfront Court, Twin Waters, MUDJIMBA, QLD 4564, AUSTRALIA. (Life Member)

HOLEHOUSE, Mr. Simon Frederick, BA(Hons) ACA *2001;* Ashmore Group, 61 Aldwych, LONDON, WC2B 4AE.

HOLFORD, Dr. Andrew, BSc ACA *1998;* Two Gables, 37 Chalfont Road, Seer Green, BEACONSFIELD, HP9 2QP.

HOLFORD, Mr. Andrew John, FCA *1966;* 53 bis avenue des Platanes, Saint Nom La Breteche, VERSAILLES, FRANCE. (Life Member)

HOLFORD, Mr. Douglas Allan, FCA *1974;* 37 Hall Green Lane, Hutton, BRENTWOOD, ESSEX, CM13 2QU.

HOLFORD, Mr. Francis Lindsay, FCA *1965;* 46 London Road, GUILDFORD, GU1 2AL.

HOLFORD, Dr. Jeffrey, BSc ACA *2001;* 271 West 47th Street, Apt PHG, NEW YORK, NY 10036, UNITED STATES.

HOLFORD, Mr. John Anthony, TD FCA *1952;* Witchwood, Cypress Way, Crossways Road, Grayshott, HINDHEAD, SURREY GU26 6EZ. (Life Member)

HOLFORD, Mr. Miles Anthony, MA FCA *1987;* Garden House, Norton, SEAFORD, BN25 2UN.

•**HOLFORD, Mrs. Sarah Elizabeth, LLB ACA DChA** *2001;* Holford Training and Accountancy, 5 Shutford Road, North Newington, BANBURY, OXFORDSHIRE, OX15 6AL.

HOLGATE, Mr. Adam Thornton, BA ACA *2000;* 3 Brookhurst Gardens, TUNBRIDGE WELLS, TN4 0UA.

HOLGATE, Miss. Catherine Jane, BA ACA *2010;* 23 Arncliffe Crescent, Morley, LEEDS, LS27 9DU.

HOLGATE, Mr. Craig, BSc ACA *2002;* 7 Vinces Court, ELY, CAMBRIDGESHIRE, CB6 3AZ.

HOLGATE, Mr. David John, FCA *1969;* Barnes Walk, 15 Brook Road, CHEADLE, CHESHIRE, SK8 1PQ. (Life Member)

HOLGATE, Mr. Derek Godfrey, FCA *1961;* Sutherland, Roothill Lane, BETCHWORTH, SURREY, RH3 7AT. (Life Member)

•**HOLGATE, Mrs. Julia Michele, BA ACA** *1986;* (Tax Fac), with PricewaterhouseCoopers, 9 Greyfriars Road, READING, RG1 1JG.

HOLGATE, Mr. Nicholas James, MA(Hons) ACA *2001;* 14 Chalcott Gardens, Long Ditton, SURBITON, SURREY, KT6 5HJ.

HOLGATE, Mr. Paul Stevens, FCA *1973;* with Crossley & Davis, 348-350 Lytham Road, BLACKPOOL, FY4 1DW.

•**HOLGATE, Mr. Peter Alan, MSc FCA** *1974;* PricewaterhouseCoopers LLP, 1 Embankment Place, LONDON, WC2N 6RH. See also PricewaterhouseCoopers

•**HOLGATE, Mr. Peter Roy, FCA** *1965;* (Member of Council 1993 - 2007), (Tax Fac), Kingston Smith LLP, Devonshire House, 60 Goswell Road, LONDON, EC1M 7AD. See also Kingston Smith Limited Liability Partnership, Devonshire Corporate Services LLP and Kingston Smith Consulting LLP

HOLGATE, Mr. Robert Geoffrey, BA FCA *1977;* (Tax Fac), 66 Purnells Way, Knowle, SOLIHULL, B93 9EE.

•**HOLGATE, Mr. Robin Andrew, BA(Hons) ACA** *2001;* with PricewaterhouseCoopers LLP, 1 Embankment Place, LONDON, WC2N 6RH.

•①**HOLGATE, Mr. Stephen Paul, ACA** *1986;* PKF (UK) LLP, Farringdon Place, 20 Farringdon Road, LONDON, EC1M 3AP.

HOLGATE, Mr. Thomas Joseph Charles, BEng ACA *2005;* 21 Haywards Road, HAYWARDS HEATH, WEST SUSSEX, RH16 4HX.

•**HOLGATE, Mrs. Zoe Ingrey, BA ACA CTA** *1998;* Ernst & Young LLP, 1 More London Place, LONDON, SE1 2AF. See also Ernst & Young Europe LLP

HOLGREAVES, Mr. Oliver David, BSc ACA *2008;* Baxter Hall Long Drax, SELBY, NORTH YORKSHIRE, YO8 8NH.

HOLIAN, Mr. Andrew, BA(Hons) ACA *2000;* PO Box 30237, SEVEN MILE BEACH, GRAND CAYMAN, KY1-1201, CAYMAN ISLANDS.

HOLIAN, Miss. Sarah, BSc ACA *2011;* Flat 4, 550 Wilbraham Road, MANCHESTER, M21 9LB.

HOLIDAY, Mr. David, BA ACA *2007;* 42 Hookfield, EPSOM, KT19 8JG.

•**HOLIDAY, Miss. Emma Marguerite, BSc FCA** *1992;* with KPMG LLP, 3 Assembly Square, Britannia Quay, CARDIFF, CF10 4AX.

HOLIDAY, Mr. Frederick Mark, FCA *1959;* Desterre, Rocques Barrees, Vale, GUERNSEY, GY3 5LT. (Life Member)

HOLIDAY, Mr. Gilbert Richard, BSc FCA *1959;* 509 Rapallo, 292 Beach Road, Sea Point, CAPE TOWN, 8005, SOUTH AFRICA. (Life Member)

HOLIDAY, Mr. John Richard Page, BSc FCA *1974;* 51 Limerston Street, LONDON, SW10 0BL.

HOLIDAY, Mr. Martin Philip, FCA *1966;* Victoria House, Stoke Road, Blisworth, NORTHAMPTON, NN7 3BZ.

•**HOLIDAY, Mr. Peter Michael, FCA** *1978;* (Tax Fac), Peter M. Holiday, Western House, 44 Western Road, Urmston, MANCHESTER, M41 6LF. See also Holiday Gordon Limited

•**HOLL, Mr. David James, BSc FCA** *1978;* Holl Cameron & Co Ltd, Ground Floor, Beresford House, Bellozanne Road, St. Helier, JERSEY JE2 3JW.

HOLL, Mrs. Naomi Julia, ACA *2008;* 13 Cleves Way, Costessey, NORWICH, NR8 5EN.

HOLLADAY, Mr. Andrew Charles, ACA *2009;* 77 Overleigh Road, CHESTER, CH4 7HN.

HOLLADAY, Mr. Mark Richard, BSc ACA *1990;* Encinas 15, 28016 MADRID, SPAIN.

HOLLADAY, Mr. Stuart Malcolm, BA FCA *1957;* Plot 8, The Heythrop, Stump LaneSpringfield, CHELMSFORD, CM2 6BX. (Life Member)

HOLLAMBY, Mr. Charles Derek, FCA *1966;* Westwood House, Meadowcot Lane, Coleshill, AMERSHAM, BUCKINGHAMSHIRE, HP7 0LL.

HOLLAMBY, Mr. Dominic Charles, MA FCA *1990;* N.M Rothchild & Sons ltd, New Court, St Swithins Lane, LONDON, EC4N 4DU.
HOLLAMBY, Mr. Paul Gordon, ACA *1983;* 11 Wedlake Close, HORNCHURCH, RM11 1SP.
HOLLAND, Mr. Alfred James, FCA *1949;* Little Aulderwood, Hungershall Park, TUNBRIDGE WELLS, TN4 8ND. (Life Member)
HOLLAND, Mrs. Alison Mary, FCA *1971;* Tan Chin Tuan Mansion, 42 Cairnhill Road #03-01, SINGAPORE 229661, SINGAPORE.
HOLLAND, Miss. Amanda Helena, ACA *2009;* with Clayton & Brewill, Cawley House, 149-155 Canal Street, NOTTINGHAM, NG1 7HR.
HOLLAND, Ms. Amanda Kim, BA ACA *1998;* 28 Woodland Gardens, LONDON, N10 3UA.
HOLLAND, Mr. Andrew, BA ACA *2006;* with Deloitte LLP, Hill House, 1 Little New Street, LONDON, EC4A 3TR.
HOLLAND, Mrs. Angela Elizabeth, BA ACA *1980;* 94 Green Drift, ROYSTON, SG8 5BT.
HOLLAND, Mr. Carl Owen, FCA *1976;* Rhode Dene, Harcombe, LYME REGIS, DORSET, DT7 3RN.
HOLLAND, Mrs. Catherine Anne, BA ACA *1993;* 61 Badgers Gate, DUNSTABLE, LU6 2BF.
HOLLAND, Mr. Charles Grahame, FCA *1961;* 18 Springwood Drive, Rufford, ORMSKIRK, L40 1XB.
HOLLAND, Mr. Christopher George, BA ACA *1999;* 40 Cherry Tree Avenue, Kirby Muxloe, LEICESTER, LE9 2HN.
HOLLAND, Mr. Christopher Richard, BSc ACA *1986;* Sapere Forensic, Level 14 68 Pitt Street, SYDNEY, NSW 2000, AUSTRALIA.
HOLLAND, Mr. Clifford John, MSc BSc FCA *1971;* (Tax Fac), Business School, Kingston University, Kingston Hill, KINGSTON UPON THAMES, KT2 7LB.
HOLLAND, Mr. David John, BA ACA *2000;* 37 La Grange Loop, Currambine, PERTH, WA 6028, AUSTRALIA.
HOLLAND, Mr. David Stephen, FCA *1983;* 113 Park Drive, UPMINSTER, RM14 3AU.
HOLLAND, Mr. Derek, FCA *1958;* 7 The Coppice, Redwood Drive, MORECAMBE, LA4 6TS. (Life Member)
HOLLAND, Miss. Donna Michelle, LLB ACA *2009;* 1 Thamesbourne Mews, Station Road, BOURNE END, BUCKINGHAMSHIRE, SL8 5RJ.
HOLLAND, Mrs. Emma, BA ACA *1996;* 79 Barkers Lane, SALE, CHESHIRE, M33 6SH.
•**HOLLAND, Mr. Gary Paul, BSocSc FCA** *1983;* (Tax Fac), G.P. Holland, 44 Rowney Croft, Hall Green, BIRMINGHAM, B28 0PL.
HOLLAND, Mr. Geoffrey Douglas, BSc ACA *1988;* Ewell Castle School, Church Street, Ewell, EPSOM, SURREY, KT17 2AW.
•**HOLLAND, Mr. Ian David, FCA** *1973;* Ian Holland Co Limited, The Clock House, 87 Paines Lane, PINNER, MIDDLESEX, HA5 3BZ.
HOLLAND, Mr. Ian Michael, MEng ACA *2003;* 37 Ashfield Road, ALTRINCHAM, CHESHIRE, WA15 9QJ.
HOLLAND, Mrs. Jacqueline Michele, BSc ACA *1989;* 61 Lyndhurst Drive, SEVENOAKS, TN13 2HG.
HOLLAND, Mr. James Alexander, BA ACA *1996;* 2109 Broadway, Apt 6-92, NEW YORK, NY 10023, UNITED STATES.
HOLLAND, Mr. James Robert, BSc ACA *1985;* 11 Chatham Court, BELPER, DERBYSHIRE, DE56 0DX.
HOLLAND, Mrs. Jodie Louise, BSc FCA *2000;* 90 Breakspear Road South, Ickenham, UXBRIDGE, MIDDLESEX, UB10 8HF.
HOLLAND, Mr. John, CBE JP DL FCA *1962;* 1 Broom Water, TEDDINGTON, TW11 9QJ. (Life Member)
HOLLAND, Mr. John Cottrill, FCA *1955;* 37 Marlborough Avenue, HARBORD, NSW 2096, 2096, AUSTRALIA. (Life Member)
HOLLAND, Mr. John Edward, FCA *1958;* 22 Village Way, Farndon, NEWARK, NOTTINGHAMSHIRE, NG24 4SX. (Life Member)
HOLLAND, Mr. John Herbert, FCA *1951;* 14 Parry Court, Hazel Grove Mapperley, NOTTINGHAM, NG3 6DR. (Life Member)
HOLLAND, Mr. John Terence, BA ACA *1985;* Wyllie House, Upper Bridge Street, Wye, ASHFORD, KENT, TN25 5AN.
HOLLAND, Mr. Joseph, FCA *1968;* 87 Chapeltown Road, Bromley Cross, BOLTON, BL7 9LZ.
•**HOLLAND, Mr. Joseph Michael, FCA** *1974;* J M Holland, 53 Elmhurst Drive, HORNCHURCH, ESSEX, RM11 1NZ.
HOLLAND, Mrs. Julie, BA FCA ATII *1988;* 13 Lodge Close, HERTFORD, SG14 3DH.
HOLLAND, Mrs. Kathryn Lesley, BA(Hons) ACA *2001;* 10 Warwick Drive, SALE, CHESHIRE, M33 2DR.
HOLLAND, Prof. Kevin Michael Peter, BA ACA *1984;* Gilwern, Heol y Buarth, ABERYSTWYTH, SY23 1LR.
HOLLAND, Mrs. Lyndsay Rachel, MChem ACA *2003;* 37 Ashfield Road, ALTRINCHAM, CHESHIRE, WA15 9QJ.
•**HOLLAND, Mrs. Margaret Irene, BSc FCA** *1991;* Maggie Holland, 4 Church View, Moulton, NORTHAMPTON, NN3 7FZ.
HOLLAND, Mr. Mark Harry, BA ACA *1987;* David Brown Gear Systems, Park Road Lockwood, HUDDERSFIELD, WEST YORKSHIRE, HD4 5DD.
•**HOLLAND, Mr. Mark James Arthur, BA FCA** *1986;* Baker Tilly Tax & Advisory Services LLP, The Clock House, 140 London Road, GUILDFORD, SURREY, GU1 1UW. See also Baker Tilly Revas Limited
HOLLAND, Mr. Mark Philip, BSc ACA *1997;* 3 Pear Tree Close, Haddenham, ELY, CAMBRIDGESHIRE, CB6 3UU.
HOLLAND, Mr. Martin Harold, FCA *1975;* 1 Little Fryth, Finchampstead, WOKINGHAM, RG40 3RN.
HOLLAND, Mr. Martin Peter, BA ACA *2006;* 11a Methley Grove, LEEDS, LS7 3PA.
HOLLAND, Mr. Martin Ronald, MA ACA *1983;* 21 Parkgate Crescent, Hadley Wood, BARNET, EN4 0NW.
HOLLAND, Mr. Michael, BA FCA *1967;* 15 Andrewes House, Barbican, LONDON, EC2Y 8AX. (Life Member)
HOLLAND, Mr. Michael Barry, BA FCA *1981;* Infiniti Finance Plc, The Courtyard, 30 London Street, CHERTSEY, SURREY, KT16 8AA.
HOLLAND, Mr. Michael David, BSc FCA CTA *1980;* 4 Lincoln's Field, Barnham Broom, NORWICH, NR9 4BZ.
HOLLAND, Mr. Michael Edmund, FCA CTA *1968;* 23 Albany Street, EDINBURGH, EH1 3QN.
•**HOLLAND, Mr. Michael John, ACA** *1989;* 18 Green Lane, HAYLING ISLAND, PO11 0BG.
HOLLAND, Mrs. Michelle, BA ACA *1995;* 14 Mill Fold, Addingham, ILKLEY, WEST YORKSHIRE, LS29 0SY.
HOLLAND, Mr. Neal Andrew, BCom ACA *1993;* Conocophillips, 2 Portman Street, LONDON, W1H 6DU.
HOLLAND, Mr. Neil Christopher, BSc ACA *1987;* 3 Lulworth Close, West Bridgford, NOTTINGHAM, NOTTINGHAMSHIRE, NG2 7UB.
HOLLAND, Mr. Neil David, BCom(ACC) ACA *1999;* Legal & General Assurance Society Ltd The Podium, City Centre House 5 Hill Street, BIRMINGHAM, B5 4US.
•**HOLLAND, Mr. Nigel, BA FCA** *1983;* Holland & Co, 102/104 Widnes Road, WIDNES, WA8 6AX.
HOLLAND, Mr. Nigel Donald, ACA *1979;* 4a Spencer Road, Canford Cliffs, POOLE, DORSET, BH13 7EU.
HOLLAND, Mr. Nigel Francis, FCA *1951;* 35 St. Johns Road, STANSTED, ESSEX, CM24 8JR. (Life Member)
•**HOLLAND, Mr. Paul Ian, BSc ACA** *1999;* with KPMG LLP, Arlington Business Park, Theale, READING, RG7 4SD.
HOLLAND, Mr. Paul John, BA FCA *1992;* 1 Cutbush Close, Harrietsham, MAIDSTONE, KENT, ME17 1LY.
HOLLAND, Mrs. Paula, BA ACA *2003;* 13 Harper Fold Road, Radcliffe Bury, MANCHESTER, M26 3RU.
HOLLAND, Mr. Peter, FCA *1967;* The Beehive, Radwinter Road, Ashdon, SAFFRON WALDEN, ESSEX, CB10 2ET.
HOLLAND, Mr. Peter, FCA *1968;* 8 Lamorna Close, Castlecroft, WOLVERHAMPTON, WV3 8LG.
HOLLAND, Mr. Peter Brian, FCA *1960;* Wexham House, Chorleywood Bottom, RICKMANSWORTH, WD3 5JR.
HOLLAND, Mr. Peter James, FCA *1970;* Woodside House, Wynnstay Lane, Marford, WREXHAM, LL12 8LH.
HOLLAND, Mr. Philip Ernest, FCA *1956;* Highfield, Stainton, PENRITH, CA11 0ES. (Life Member)
HOLLAND, Mr. Philip John, BA ACA *1995;* 61 Badgers Close, DUNSTABLE, LU6 2BF.
HOLLAND, Mrs. Rachel Victoria Ann, BSc ACA CTA AMCT *1996;* Schneider Ltd, Stafford Park 5, TELFORD, SHROPSHIRE, TF3 3BL.
•**HOLLAND, Mr. Raymond Peter, FCA** *1975;* Holland MacLennan & Co., 115 Crockhamwell Road, Woodley, READING, RG5 3JP.
HOLLAND, Mr. Richard Alfred, MBA BSc FCA *1975;* 5 Tabor Close, Harlington, DUNSTABLE, LU5 6PF.
HOLLAND, Mr. Richard Francis, BSc ACA *1990;* 28 Broadway, WILMSLOW, SK9 1NB.
HOLLAND, Mr. Robbie Justin, BSc ACA *1998;* 12 Plantation Way, Red Lodge, BURY ST. EDMUNDS, SUFFOLK, IP28 8GF.
HOLLAND, Mr. Robert Charles, FCA *1968;* Burcott, Burton Corner Spilsby Road, BOSTON, LINCOLNSHIRE, PE21 9QR.
•**HOLLAND, Mr. Robert Charles, BSc FCA** *1986;* James Cowper LLP, Mill House, Overbridge Square, Hambridge Lane, NEWBURY, BERKSHIRE RG14 5UX. See also JC Payroll Services Ltd
•**HOLLAND, Mr. Roger Stanley, FCA** *1965;* (Tax Fac), with Porritt Rainey, 9 Pembroke Road, SEVENOAKS, KENT, TN13 1XR.
HOLLAND, Mrs. Rosemary Jane, BSc ACA *1989;* 28 Broadway, WILMSLOW, SK9 1NB.
HOLLAND, Mr. Ross, BSc ACA *1997;* Skillsactive Castlewood House, 77-79 New Oxford Street, LONDON, WC1A 1DG.
•**HOLLAND, Mr. Roy Malcolm, BSc FCA** *1990;* Holland Harper LLP, 26 High Street, BATTLE, EAST SUSSEX, TN33 0EA.
HOLLAND, Mrs. Ruth Marion, BSc FCA *1983;* Lorne House, Hampden Close, Stoke Poges, SLOUGH, SL2 4JF.
HOLLAND, Mrs. Sally, ACA *2007;* 58 Queens Avenue, Highworth, SWINDON, SN6 7BA.
HOLLAND, Mr. Samuel Charles, BA ACA *2005;* with Deloitte LLP, Hill House, 1 Little New Street, LONDON, EC4A 3TR.
HOLLAND, Mrs. Sarah Catherine, BA(Hons) ACA *2004;* with BDO Limited, PO Box 180, Place du Pre, Rue du Pre, St Peter Port, GUERNSEY GY1 3LL.
HOLLAND, Mrs. Stephanie Anne, BSc ACA *2002;* 31 Spring Gardens, NEWBURY, BERKSHIRE, RG20 0PR.
HOLLAND, Mr. Stephen Philip, FCA *1974;* 42 Stillwell Road, KINGSTON 8, JAMAICA.
HOLLAND, Mrs. Suzanne Alison, BSc ACA *1991;* Oakleigh Heath End Road, Great Kingshill, HIGH WYCOMBE, BUCKINGHAMSHIRE, HP15 6HL.
HOLLAND, Mr. Timothy Mark, BSc ACA *1988;* 61 Lyndhurst Drive, SEVENOAKS, KENT, TN13 2HG.
HOLLAND, Mr. Trevor Alan, BSc FCA *1983;* Venture Studios (HK)Limited, 2001 Sing Tao news Corporation Building, 3 Tung Wong Road, SHAU KEI WAN, HONG KONG ISLAND, HONG KONG SAR.
HOLLAND, Mrs. Valerie, FCA *1979;* Daisy Bank Barn, 246 Hoyles Lane, Cottam, PRESTON, PR4 0LD.
HOLLAND, Mr. William, FCA *1955;* Bowstones, 13 Redbrook Way, Adlington, MACCLESFIELD, SK10 4NF. (Life Member)
HOLLAND, Mr. William Angus, BA ACA *1991;* Collins Stewart Ltd, 88 Wood Street, LONDON, EC2V 7QR.
•**HOLLAND, Mr. William Edward John, BA FCA** *1991;* KPMG LLP, 15 Canada Square, LONDON, E14 5GL. See also KPMG Europe LLP
HOLLAND, Mr. William Robert, FCA *1957;* 3 Angel Cottages, Milespit Hill, Mill Hill Villages, LONDON, NW7 1RD. (Life Member)
HOLLAND-LEADER, Mr. James Stephen, BA ACA *2010;* 12 The Horseshoe, GODALMING, GU7 2LW.
HOLLAND-MARTIN, Mr. Giles Thurstan, ACA *1979;* 410 West 24th Street, Apt 16B, NEW YORK, NY 10011, UNITED STATES. (Life Member)
•**HOLLANDER, Mr. Geoffrey, FCA** *1997;* (Tax Fac), Cameron Baum Limited, 88 Crawford Street, LONDON, W1H 2EJ. See also Cameron Baum
•①**HOLLANDER, Mr. Guy Robert Thomas, BA FCA** *1990;* Mazars LLP, Tower Bridge House, St. Katharines Way, LONDON, E1W 1DD.
HOLLANDER, Mr. Paul Joseph, BSc ACA *2007;* Tredowne Church Street, Horsham St. Faith, NORWICH, NR10 3JJ.
HOLLANDER, Mr. Peter, BA FCA *1981;* 21 Mount Road, CANTERBURY, CT1 1YD.
•**HOLLANDS, Mr. Adrian, FCA** *1975;* Baker Tilly Tax & Advisory Services LLP, Lancaster House, 7 Elmfield Road, BROMLEY, BR1 1LT. See also Baker Tilly UK Audit LLP
HOLLANDS, Mr. Christopher, ACA *1979;* Orchard Cottage Mundy Bois Road, Egerton, ASHFORD, TN27 9EX.
HOLLANDS, Mrs. Denise Mary, BA ACA *1984;* 1a Commerce Park, Brunel Road, READING, RG7 4AE.
HOLLANDS, Mrs. Fiona Meg, BSc(Hons) ACA *2001;* 27 Marlborough Road, IPSWICH, SUFFOLK, IP4 5AT.
HOLLANDS, Mr. Keith Roger, BSc FCA *1971;* 57 Tarnwood Park, Eltham, LONDON, SE9 5PB. (Life Member)
•**HOLLANDS, Miss. Louise, ACA** *2006;* Louise Hollands, 1 Chapel Loke, Hargham Road, Old Buckenham, NORFOLK, NR17 1PY.
HOLLANDS, Mr. Paul Daniel, BSc ACA *1999;* Carlton, 27 Marlborough Road, IPSWICH, IP4 5AT.
HOLLANDS, Mr. Richard William, BA ACA *1990;* EMIRATES LEISURE RETAIL LLC, P.O.BOX - 122199, DUBAI, UNITED ARAB EMIRATES.
HOLLAS, Mr. Walter Andrew, BA FCA *1978;* PO Box 25174, NAIROBI, 00603, KENYA.
HOLLEBONE, Mr. Paul Stephen, BSc ACA *1980;* (Tax Fac), Old Orchard, Dog Lane, STEYNING, BN44 3GE.
HOLLENS, Mr. Nicholas, BA ACA *1990;* Somes and Cooke, 1304 Hay Street, West Perth, PERTH, WA 6872, AUSTRALIA.
•**HOLLERAN, Mr. Peter Allan, BSc ACA** *1984;* G.L. Barker & Co LLP, 45-49 Austhorpe Road, Crossgates, LEEDS, LS15 8BA.
•**HOLLES, Mr. Adrian Peter, ACA** *1997;* Wallace Crooke, Wallace House, 20 Birmingham Road, WALSALL, WS1 2LT. See also Wallace Crooke & Co
HOLLETT, Ms. Alison Dawn, MSc FCA *1992;* 98 High Storrs Road, SHEFFIELD, S11 7LE.
•**HOLLETT, Mrs. Julie Ann, ACA FCCA** *2011;* The 41GP Partnership LLP, 41 Great Portland Street, LONDON, W1W 7LA.
HOLLEY, Miss. Catherine Jayne, BA(Hons) ACA *2001;* 37 Whitlam Street, SHIPLEY, WEST YORKSHIRE, BD18 4PE.
HOLLEY, Mr. David, BA ACA *1992;* 5 Endlesham Road, LONDON, SW12 8JX.
HOLLEY, Derek Peter, Esq OBE FCA *1963;* 64 Parkside, Grammar School Walk, HUNTINGDON, CAMBRIDGESHIRE, PE29 3LF.
HOLLEY, Mrs. Julia Ann, BSc ACA *1981;* 5 Oaktree Close, Kibworth Beauchamp, LEICESTER, LE8 0RL.
HOLLEY, Miss. Kathryn Geraldine, BSc(Econ) ACA *2000;* 1 Yr Aran, Dunvant, SWANSEA, SA2 7PU.
HOLLEY, Mr. Kenneth Sidney Leonard, FCA *1949;* 138 Lower Road, Bookham, LEATHERHEAD, KT23 4AN. (Life Member)
HOLLEY, Mr. Martin John, MA ACA *1982;* 17 Ludlow Close, Oadby, LEICESTER, LE2 4SU.
HOLLEY, Mr. Michael John, MA ACA *1981;* Shadowline Ltd, Pullman Road, WIGSTON, LEICESTERSHIRE, LE18 2DB.
HOLLEY, Mr. Peter Nicholas, FCA *1974;* The Beeches St. Johns Road, Bishop Monkton, HARROGATE, NORTH YORKSHIRE, HG3 3QU.
HOLLEY, Mr. Stephen James, FCA *1981;* Midland Chromium Plating Co Ltd, 116 Aldridge Road Perry Barr, BIRMINGHAM, B42 2TP.
HOLLICK, Mrs. Claire Virginia, BA(Hons) ACA *2000;* 19 Vernham Road, WINCHESTER, SO22 6BS.
HOLLICK, Mr. David John, BA ACA *1999;* Six Continents, 1 First Avenue Centrum One Hundred, BURTON-ON-TRENT, DE14 2WB.
HOLLIDAY, Mr. Andrew Simon, BA ACA *1993;* 7 Hamilton Road, Windle, ST HELENS, MERSEYSIDE, WA10 6HH.
HOLLIDAY, Mr. Christopher, MA ACA *2005;* 3 Dudley Road, RICHMOND, SURREY, TW9 2EH.
HOLLIDAY, Mr. David Charles, MA ACA *1985;* Plumb Cottage, High Street, Wethersfield, BRAINTREE, CM7 4BZ.
HOLLIDAY, Miss. Heidi, BA(Hons) ACA *2001;* with Standard Chartered Bank, 1 Basinghall Avenue, LONDON, EC2V 5DD.
HOLLIDAY, Mrs. Jane Christine, BA(Hons) ACA *2001;* 72 Church Street, Old Catton, NORWICH, NR6 7DR.
•**HOLLIDAY, Mr. Keith Charles, FCA** *1973;* Baker Tilly Tax & Advisory Services LLP, The Clock House, 140 London Road, GUILDFORD, SURREY, GU1 1UW.
HOLLIDAY, Mr. Michael James, BA ACA *1980;* 37 Hamilton Avenue, ILFORD, IG6 1AE.
HOLLIDAY, Mr. Nathan David James, BCom ACA *2004;* G K N plc, PO Box 55, REDDITCH, WORCESTERSHIRE, B98 0TL.
HOLLIDAY, Mrs. Nisreen, BSc ACA ATII *1993;* (Tax Fac), The Bothy, Hickleton, DONCASTER, SOUTH YORKSHIRE, DN5 7BA.
HOLLIDAY, Mr. Paul Anthony, BA(Hons) ACA *2004;* (Tax Fac), 12 Holmewood Avenue, COCKERMOUTH, CA13 0BE.
HOLLIDAY, Mr. Peter John, BA ACA *1998;* 86 Hollin Lane, Styal, WILMSLOW, CHESHIRE, SK9 4JJ.
HOLLIDAY, The Revd. Peter Leslie, MA BCom FCA *1973;* 60 Needlers End Lane, Balsall Common, COVENTRY, CV7 7AB.
HOLLIDAY, Mr. Philip Joseph, MA FCA *1963;* 40 The Warren, CARSHALTON, SM5 4EH. (Life Member)
HOLLIDAY, Miss. Rebecca, BSc ACA *2010;* 55 Sturton Street, CAMBRIDGE, CB1 2QG.
HOLLIDAY, Mr. Richard Peter, BCom ACA *1979;* PO Box 242, CREMORNE, NSW 2090, AUSTRALIA. (Life Member)
HOLLIDAY, Miss. Susan Claire, BA ACA *1991;* 12 Wedderburn House, 95 Lower Sloane Street, LONDON, SW1W 8BZ.
HOLLIDAY, Mr. Thomas William, BSc ACA *2003;* Westleigh Tanners Lane, Adderbury, BANBURY, OXFORDSHIRE, OX17 3ER.

HOLLIDAY, Mrs. Victoria Penelope, BA(Hons) ACA *2003;* 331 Streetsbrook Road, SOLIHULL, B91 1RW.
HOLLIDGE, Mr. Brian William, FCA *1960;* Lower Flat, The Red House, 32 Daglands Road, FOWEY, PL23 1JN. (Life Member)
HOLLIDGE, Mr. Timothy Richard Naunton, BSc ACA *1993;* 4 Heath Ridge Green, COBHAM, SURREY, KT11 2QJ.
HOLLIER, Miss. Gillian Clare, ACA *2011;* 22 Jackson Avenue, Ponteland, NEWCASTLE UPON TYNE, NE20 9UY.
HOLLIGON, Mrs. Kate Sarah, BSc ACA *1997;* The Hoe Bosham Hoe, Bosham, CHICHESTER, WEST SUSSEX, PO18 8ES.
HOLLINGBERY, Mr. Jon Robert, BSc ACA *1999;* 7 Coniston Avenue, Westbury-on-Trym, BRISTOL, BS9 3SA.
HOLLINGBERY, Mrs. Rachel Louise, BA(Hons) ACA *2002;* 7 Coniston Avenue, Westbury-on-Trym, BRISTOL, BS9 3SA.
HOLLINGDALE, Mr. Chris Roger David, BSc ACA *2011;* Brooklands, Upper End, Shipton-under-Wychwood, CHIPPING NORTON, OXFORDSHIRE, OX7 6DP.
•HOLLINGDALE, Mr. John Anthony, FCA MCIArb *1975;* Space Engineering Services, Causeway Central, Pioneer Park, BRISTOL, BS4 3QB.
HOLLINGDALE, Mr. Stephen Charles, FCA *1973;* with Crown Agents, St. Nicholas House, St. Nicholas Road, SUTTON, SURREY, SM1 1EL.
HOLLINGHURST, Miss. Claire Louise, BSc(Hons) ACA ATII *2000;* (Tax Fac), with Davison & Shingleton, Boundary House, 91-93 Charterhouse Street, LONDON, EC1M 6HR.
HOLLINGS, Mr. Daniel Gareth, MSc ACA *2001;* 44 Bryanston Road, SOLIHULL, B91 1EN.
HOLLINGSBEE, Mr. David Paul, BA ACA *2002;* 59 Sedgwick Street, CAMBRIDGE, CB1 3AJ.
HOLLINGSHEAD, Mr. Stephan, BSc ACA *1989;* Wales Hall Farm, Church Street, Wales, SHEFFIELD, S26 5LQ.
HOLLINGSWORTH, Mr. Brian Andrew, MA ACA *1982;* 1 St Giles Road, Camberwell, LONDON, SE5 7RL.
HOLLINGSWORTH, Mr. Damian, MA ACA *2001;* 2 Government Road, MOSMAN, NSW 2088, AUSTRALIA.
HOLLINGSWORTH, Mrs. Elisabeth, ACA *2009;* 3 Derwent Close, MACCLESFIELD, CHESHIRE, SK11 7XS.
HOLLINGSWORTH, Mrs. Jane Michaela, BA ACA *1993;* Leeds Metropolitan University, Old School Board, Calverley Street, LEEDS, LS1 3ED.
•HOLLINGSWORTH, Mr. John Arthur, ACA *1983;* (Tax Fac), Hollingsworth & Co, Coppice House, Halesfield 7, TELFORD, SHROPSHIRE, TF7 4NA.
HOLLINGSWORTH, Miss. Laura, BA ACA *1991;* 60 Harcourt Road, LONDON, N22 7XW.
HOLLINGSWORTH, Mr. Mark Anthony, ACA *1984;* Greenwood, Copse Lane, Jordans, BEACONSFIELD, BUCKINGHAMSHIRE, HP9 2TA.
HOLLINGSWORTH, Miss. Natalie Rachel, MA ACA *2001;* 12AF6A Mereside, Astrazeneca Alderley House, Alderley Park, MACCLESFIELD, CHESHIRE, SK10 4TF.
HOLLINGSWORTH, Mr. Peter John, BSc ACA *1980;* PHFD Limited, 4c Denham Walk, Chalfont St Peter, GERRARDS CROSS, BUCKINGHAMSHIRE, SL9 0EN.
HOLLINGSWORTH, Mr. Rex Noel, FCA *1956;* 4 Hilary Close, Wollaton, NOTTINGHAM, NG8 2SP. (Life Member)
HOLLINGSWORTH, Mr. Stephen John, BSc ACA *1982;* Limeyard Stables, 136 Main Street, Ticknall, DERBY, DE73 7JZ.
•HOLLINGTON, Mrs. Janet Elizabeth, FCA *1977;* Fredericks 2001 Limited, Highgate Business Centre, 33 Greenwood Place, LONDON, NW5 1LB.
HOLLINGTON, Mr. John Nicholas, BSc FCA *1977;* Costware Ltd, 8 Orchard Lane, EAST MOLESEY, KT8 0BN.
HOLLINGTON, Miss. Wendy, BA ACA *1994;* 57 Newfield Gardens, MARLOW, SL7 1JR.
HOLLINGWORTH, Mrs. Angela Helen, BSc(Hons) ACA *2002;* Greenways The Green, Wessington, ALFRETON, DERBYSHIRE, DE55 6DQ.
HOLLINGWORTH, Mr. Anthony Peter, FCA *1970;* 15 Brae Hill Close, Brill, AYLESBURY, HP18 9TE. (Life Member)
•HOLLINGWORTH, Miss. Victoria Louise, BA ACA *1994;* P O Box 1215, GEORGE TOWN, GRAND CAYMAN, KY1-1108, CAYMAN ISLANDS.
•HOLLINRAKE, Mr. Derek, BCom FCA *1977;* 16 Heathfield Park, BLACKBURN, BB2 6QJ.
•HOLLINS, Mr. Philip Martin, MA FCA *1975;* MEMBER OF COUNCIL, Philip M Hollins MA FCA, Lavant Gate, Lavant, CHICHESTER, WEST SUSSEX, PO18 0BB.
HOLLINS, Dr. Thomas Ivan, MSc ACA *2003;* 79 Silver Street, Kings Heath, BIRMINGHAM, B14 7QT.
HOLLINS-GIBSON, Mr. Joseph Stephen, FCA *1970;* Churchtown House, Sebergham, CARLISLE, CA5 7HS. (Life Member)
HOLLINSHEAD, Mrs. Angela Mary, BA ACA *1985;* 4 Strawberry Fields, Bisley, WOKING, GU24 9SP.
HOLLINSHEAD, Mr. Ashley John, BSc ACA CTA *2002;* with Deloitte LLP, 4 Brindley Place, BIRMINGHAM, B1 2HZ.
•HOLLINSHEAD, Mr. Paul Gerald, FCA *1984;* Mark J Rees, Granville Hall, Granville Road, LEICESTER, LE1 7RU.
HOLLINSHEAD, Mr. Philip, FCA *1976;* 5 Hawthorn Walk, LITTLEBOROUGH, LANCASHIRE, OL15 8LG.
HOLLINSHEAD, Mr. Philip, BA ACA *2007;* with Deloitte Touche Tohmatsu, Grosvenor Place, 225 George Street, P.O. Box N 250, SYDNEY, NSW 2000 AUSTRALIA.
HOLLINSHEAD, Mr. Russell, BSc ACA *1991;* 11 Hamilton Road, Chiswick, LONDON, W4 1AL.
HOLLINSHEAD, Mr. Steven John, BSc FCA *1987;* 4 Strawberry Fields, Bisley, WOKING, GU24 9SP.
HOLLIS, Mr. Anthony John, FCA *1953;* Foxbrooke House, 25 The Green, Evenley, BRACKLEY, NN13 5SQ. (Life Member)
HOLLIS, Arthur Norman, Esq OBE DFC FCA *1948;* Court Lodge, Westwell, ASHFORD, Kent, TN25 4JX. (Life Member)
HOLLIS, Mr. Christopher William, ACA *1983;* 22 Ave Montaigne, 75008 PARIS, FRANCE.
HOLLIS, Mr. Dominic John, BSc(Hons) ACA *2001;* 15 Vicarage Hill, FARNHAM, SURREY, GU9 8HL.
•HOLLIS, Mr. Graham Terence, BSc(Econ) ACA *2001;* Deloitte LLP, Union Plaza, 1 Union Wynd, ABERDEEN, AB10 1SL. See also Deloitte & Touche LLP
HOLLIS, Mr. John David, BSc ACA *1980;* Willow Mead, Ballaughton Meadows, Douglas, ISLE OF MAN, IM2 1JG.
HOLLIS, Mr. Mark Adam, BA ACA *1987;* 48 Uphill Road, Millhill, LONDON, NW7 4PP.
•HOLLIS, Mr. Michael Andrew, BA FCA CTA *1977;* (Tax Fac), Michael Hollis, Woodland House, 24 Meadowbrook Road, Kibworth Beauchamp, LEICESTER, LE8 0HU.
HOLLIS, Mr. Michael Hugh, BSc FCA *1966;* Lower Trefaldu, Nr Dingestow, MONMOUTH, NP25 4BQ.
HOLLIS, Mr. Paul Lansdell, BA ACA *2002;* 6 Montrose Avenue, TWICKENHAM, TW2 6HB.
•HOLLIS, Mr. Peter John, FCA *1980;* (Tax Fac), Hollis and Co Ltd, 35 Wilkinson Street, SHEFFIELD, S10 2GB.
HOLLIS, Mr. Richard James, ACA *2008;* Flat 18, Oppidan Apartments, 25 Linstead Street, LONDON, NW6 2HA.
•HOLLIS, Mr. Steven Peter, FCA *1983;* (Tax Fac), KPMG LLP, One Snowhill, Snow Hill Queensway, BIRMINGHAM, B4 6GN. See also KPMG Europe LLP
HOLLISS, Mr. David Kingsley, BA ACA *1984;* Mill Brook House, Milton Road, Drayton, ABINGDON, OXFORDSHIRE, OX14 4EF.
HOLLISS, Mr. John Henry George, FCA *1972;* Beckside, 13 Woodvale Crescent, Oakwood Park, BINGLEY, BD16 4AJ.
HOLLISTER, Miss. Kirsty, BSc ACA *1995;* 41 Thorneycroft Close, WALTON-ON-THAMES, KT12 2YB.
HOLLO, Miss. Andrea, ACA *2009;* Stamford Lodge Lion Close, HASLEMERE, SURREY, GU27 1JG.
•HOLLOW, Mr. John Alan Hilary, FCA *1971;* J A Hollow & Co Ltd, 1 Ventnor Terrace, ST. IVES, CORNWALL, TR26 1DY. See also Hollow J.A.H. and Leddra Perry & Co Ltd
HOLLOWAY, Mr. Adam Stuart, BA ACA *1993;* ISIS E P LLP, 100 Wood Street, LONDON, EC2V 7AN.
•HOLLOWAY, Mr. Alan, BSc FCA *1976;* (Tax Fac), Alan Holloway, 18 Lumley Drive, Tickhill, DONCASTER, SOUTH YORKSHIRE, DN11 9QE.
HOLLOWAY, Mr. Andrew Mark, LLB ACA *2006;* 85a Klea Avenue, LONDON, SW4 9HZ.
HOLLOWAY, Mr. Clive, FCA *1966;* 1450 Camelot Road, WEST VANCOUVER V7S 2L8, BC, CANADA.
•HOLLOWAY, Mr. David, BA FCA *1995;* Ribchesters, 67 Saddler Street, DURHAM, DH1 3NP.
HOLLOWAY, Mr. David John, BSc FCA *1975;* 25 Edgar Road, St.Cross, WINCHESTER, SO23 9TN.
HOLLOWAY, Mr. David Stewart, BEng ACA *2004;* BMW Financial Services Group, Europa House, 5 Bartley Wood Business Park, Bartley Way, HOOK, HAMPSHIRE RG27 9UF.
HOLLOWAY, Mrs. Diana Wendy Louise, BA ACA *1989;* Holloways, Lower Court, Suckley, WORCESTER, WR6 5DE.
HOLLOWAY, Miss. Elizabeth Clare, ACA *2008;* Pricewaterhousecoopers, 33 Wellington Street, LEEDS, LS1 4JP.
HOLLOWAY, Mrs. Fiona Mary, BA(Hons) ACA *2002;* Montrose, Nevilles Cross Bank, DURHAM, DH1 4JP.
HOLLOWAY, Mrs. Fiona Ruth, BSc ACA *1990;* (Tax Fac), 54 Swanswell Road, SOLIHULL, WEST MIDLANDS, B92 7ET.
HOLLOWAY, Mr. Frank, FCA *1948;* 6 Kingates Court, 43 Wickham Road, BECKENHAM, KENT, BR3 6NB. (Life Member)
•HOLLOWAY, Mr. Jonathan James, BCom ACA *1990;* PricewaterhouseCoopers LLP, 7 More London Riverside, LONDON, SE1 2RT. See also PricewaterhouseCoopers
HOLLOWAY, Mr. Malcolm, BSc FCA *1983;* 24 Bishopbourne Court, NORTH SHIELDS, TYNE AND WEAR, NE29 9JE.
HOLLOWAY, Mr. Malcolm John, BSc FCA *1974;* (Tax Fac), Islington & Shoreditch Housing Association Ltd, 102 Blackstock Road, LONDON, N4 2DR.
HOLLOWAY, Mr. Matthew John, BSc ACA *2006;* 44 New Street, ROCHDALE, LANCASHIRE, OL12 6NS.
HOLLOWAY, Mr. Michael Kenneth, FCA *1951;* Whiteslea, Nursery Close, Walton on the Hill, TADWORTH, KT20 7TW. (Life Member)
HOLLOWAY, Mr. Oliver, BSc ACA *2007;* 4 Dudley Road, WALTON-ON-THAMES, KT12 2JT.
HOLLOWAY, Mr. Paul Michael, MA ACA *1996;* Watson Wyatt LLP, 21 Tothill Street, Westminster, LONDON, SW1H 9LL.
HOLLOWAY, Mr. Peter, MA ACA *1986;* Cairnryan, Bank Street, DOUNE, FK16 6DB.
HOLLOWAY, Mr. Peter Geoffrey, FCA *1967;* Ty Croeso, Vauxhall Lane, CHEPSTOW, NP16 5PZ.
HOLLOWAY, Mr. Peter George, BSc FCA *1975;* 169 Pinfold Lane, Aldridge, WALSALL, WS9 0QY.
HOLLOWAY, Mr. Richard Francis, MA ACA *1996;* Kiln Group, 106 Fenchurch Street, LONDON, EC3M 5NR.
HOLLOWAY, Mr. Robin Charles Alexander, BSc ACA *1991;* The Old Tannery, Tanners Green Lane, Wythall, BIRMINGHAM, WEST MIDLANDS, B47 6BH.
HOLLOWAY, Mr. Scott Michael, BA ACA *1992;* 28 Clements Road, Chorleywood, RICKMANSWORTH, WD3 5JT.
HOLLOWAY, Mr. Simon Russell, ACA *1979;* Robin Hood, North Elham, CANTERBURY, CT4 6UY.
HOLLOWAY, Mr. Timothy Ronald, BEng ACA *1992;* Infor, 1 Lakeside Road, FARNBOROUGH, HAMPSHIRE, GU14 6XP.
HOLLOWAY, Ms. Vicky Louise, BSc ACA *2010;* 17 Hopkin Close, GUILDFORD, SURREY, GU2 9LS.
HOLLOWOOD, Mr. Jonathan William, BA ACA *2005;* 52 Springfield Mount, Horsforth, LEEDS, LS18 5QE.
HOLLOWS, Mr. Alistair Vincent, BA FCA *1986;* MEMBER OF COUNCIL, IFA Mentor Ltd, Beechfield House, Winterton Way, Lyme Green Business Park, MACCLESFIELD, CHESHIRE SK11 0LP.
HOLLOWS, Mr. Ian James, MA FCA CISA CIA *1977;* 14 Melcombe Avenue, WEYMOUTH, DORSET, DT4 7TH.
HOLLOWS, Miss. Joanne Lesley, BA ACA *2003;* 60 Thistlecroft Road, WALTON-ON-THAMES, SURREY, KT12 5QZ.
HOLLOX, Mr. Anthony Paul, BSc ACA *1992;* Hydro International Plc, Shearwater House, Clevedon Hall Estate, CLEVEDON, AVON, BS21 7RD.
•HOLLOX, Mrs. Rachel Larissa, ACA *1995;* Rachel Hollox, Jesmond, Ridgeway, OTTERY ST. MARY, DEVON, EX11 1DT.
HOLLWAY, Mr. Kenneth Henry William, FCA *1957;* 57 East Dock, The Wharf, LEIGHTON BUZZARD, BEDFORDSHIRE, LU7 2LA. (Life Member)
HOLLY, Mr. Gareth Robert, ACA *2009;* 29 Spring Bank Lane, ROCHDALE, LANCASHIRE, OL11 5SE.
HOLLY, Mr. Martin Robert, MBA BSc FCA *1991;* Cranstoun Drug Services St. Andrews House, St. Andrews Road, SURBITON, KT6 4DT.
HOLLY, Mr. Michael Charles, MA FCA *1978;* Fir Trees, 29 Spring Bank Lane, Bamford, ROCHDALE, OL11 5SE.
HOLLY-ARCHER, Miss. Susanne Alice, BSc FCA CTA *1983;* 8 Wildcroft Drive, WOKINGHAM, RG40 3HY.
HOLLYHEAD, Miss. Catherine Jayne, BSc(Econ) ACA *1996;* 10 Gurnard Heights, COWES, PO31 8EF.
HOLLYHEAD, Mrs. Lisa Anne, BA ACA *1995;* St Andrew, Hill Lane, FRESHWATER, PO40 9TQ.
HOLLYMAN, Mr. Jack, ACA MAAT *2009;* Tamarisk, The Street, High Easter, CHELMSFORD, CM1 4QW.
HOLLYMAN, Miss. Ruth, BA ACA CTA *1998;* 10 Minster Drive, CROYDON, CR0 5UP.
HOLLYOCK, Mr. Stephen Allen, FCA *1991;* 149 Rochdale Road, MOUNT CLAREMONT, WA 6010, AUSTRALIA.
HOLLYWOOD, Mrs. Catherine Jane, ACA *1991;* Windmill Hill House, Windmill Hill, Long Melford, SUDBURY, SUFFOLK, CO10 9AD.
•HOLM, Mr. David Timothy, FCA *1972;* (Tax Fac), David Holm Ltd, Plum Cottage, Mersea Road, COLCHESTER, CO2 7SG.
•HOLMAN, Mr. Barry William, FCA *1977;* B.W. Holman & Co, First Floor Suite, Enterprise House, 10 Church Hill, LOUGHTON, IG10 1LA.
HOLMAN, Miss. Briony Sue, BA(Hons) ACA *2000;* 3/19 Bolingbroke Parade, Fairlight, SYDNEY, NSW 2094, AUSTRALIA.
HOLMAN, Mrs. Catherine Frances, BSc FCA *1977;* 8 Vine Farm Road, Talbot Village, POOLE, BH12 5EN.
HOLMAN, Mrs. Christine Elizabeth, BA ACA *1987;* Roche Audio Visual, Ainley Industrial Estate, ELLAND, WEST YORKSHIRE, HX5 9JP.
HOLMAN, Mr. David Mark, FCA *1960;* Colwyn, 12 Leafield Road, FAIRFORD, GL7 4LS. (Life Member)
HOLMAN, Mrs. Helen Claire, BA ACA *1996;* 104 Ringwood Road, VERWOOD, BH31 7AL.
HOLMAN, Mr. Henry Anthony, FCA *1960;* 214 Blue Heaven Rd., CAPE CHARLES, VA 23310, UNITED STATES. (Life Member)
•HOLMAN, Mr. John William, FCA *1971;* (Tax Fac), AbacusHouse.com LLP, Abacus House, Wickhurst Lane, Broadbridge Heath, HORSHAM, RH12 3LY.
HOLMAN, Mr. Matthew Andrew James, ACA *2008;* Whitbread Plc Whitbread Court Porz Avenue, Houghton Hall Park Houghton Regis, DUNSTABLE, BEDFORDSHIRE, LU5 5XE.
HOLMAN, Mr. Richard John Gawen, FCA *1966;* Ministry of Sound Holdings Ltd, 103 Gaunt Street, LONDON, SE1 6DP.
HOLMAN, Miss. Sarah Jane, MA ACA *1991;* 16 Crichton Road, CARSHALTON, SM5 3LS.
HOLMAN, Mr. Stephen Patrick James, BA FCA *1976;* 3 Ashdene Close, WIMBORNE, BH21 1TQ.
HOLMAN, Mr. Thomas James, MA FCA *1992;* 10 Hillside Road, Pannal, HARROGATE, NORTH YORKSHIRE, HG3 1JP.
HOLMBERG, Mr. Patrick, BSc ACA *2009;* 88 Freelands Road, OXFORD, OX4 4BT.
HOLME, Mr. David John, MEng BA(Hons) ACA *2002;* Reuters Ltd, 30 South Colonnade, Canary Wharf, LONDON, E14 5EP.
HOLME, Mr. David Nicholas, BA ACA *1994;* Flat 11, 9/10 Colville Terrace, Notting Hill Gate, LONDON, W11 2BE.
•HOLME, Mr. John David Gawain, FCA *1966;* J.D.G. Holme, 40 Littleheath Lane, COBHAM, KT11 2QN.
HOLME, Mrs. Judith Angela, BSc ACA *1992;* Tower House, Charterhall Drive, CHESTER, CH99 3AN.
HOLME, Mr. Michael Alan Holt, FCA *1969;* Lafage Haute, 24550 MAZEYROLLES, FRANCE.
HOLME, Mr. Peter John, FCA *1972;* 8 Baskervyle Road, WIRRAL, CH60 8NL.
•HOLME, Mr. Richard Henry Basden, BA FCA CTA TEP FTIHK *1980;* Creaseys LLP, 12 Lonsdale Gardens, TUNBRIDGE WELLS, KENT, TN1 1PA.
HOLME, Mr. Timothy Richard, BSc ACA *1992;* 64 Tarvin Road, Littleton, CHESTER, CH3 7DF.
HOLMES, Mr. Alan Hogarth, FCA *1953;* 52 Somersby Way, BOSTON, PE21 9PQ. (Life Member)
•HOLMES, Mr. Alfred Alan, FCA *1977;* Hillside, 36 Hill Brow, HOVE, EAST SUSSEX, BN3 6QH.
•HOLMES, Ms. Alison Susan, BA ACA *1988;* Barnbrook Sinclair Limited, 1 High Street, Knaphill, WOKING, SURREY, GU21 2PG.
HOLMES, Mr. Allan, BSc ACA *1991;* (Tax Fac), One Trinity, Dickinson Dees One Trinity Gardens, Broad Chare, NEWCASTLE UPON TYNE, NE1 2HF.
HOLMES, Mr. Andrew David, BSc ACA *1998;* 12 Redthorne Way, Up Hatherley, CHELTENHAM, GL51 3NW.
HOLMES, Mr. Andrew Gary, ACA *1980;* 23 Beaconsfield Road, SOUTHPORT, PR9 7AN.
HOLMES, Mr. Andrew John, BA FCA *1985;* 5 Nettleton Close, Tong Village, BRADFORD, BD4 0SS.
•HOLMES, Mr. Arthur, FCA *1970;* Holmes & Co, 3a Bell Street, ROMSEY, SO51 8GY.
HOLMES, Mr. Brian Robert Lathom, FCA *1954;* Ferndown, 57 Greenways, HAYWARDS HEATH, RH16 2DT. (Life Member)

•HOLMES, Mrs. Carla, BA(Hons) ACA CTA 2002; (Tax Fac), Carla Holmes, 15 Guernsey Way, Winnersh, WOKINGHAM, BERKSHIRE, RG41 5FT.
HOLMES, Miss. Caroline Tallis, BA ACA 2005; 69 MacMillan Way, Tooting Bec, LONDON, SW17 6AS.
HOLMES, Mrs. Catherine Anne Lee, BSc ACA 1992; 29 Marlborough Crescent, SEVENOAKS, TN13 2HH.
HOLMES, Mr. Charles David, BSc ACA 1989; Ashcroft Care Services, 21 Gatwick Metro Centre, Balcombe Road, HORLEY, SURREY, RH6 9GA.
HOLMES, Mrs. Charlotte Ann, FCA FMAAT 2000; 4 Ruston Court, Kiln Lane, Patrington, EAST YORK, HU12 0FD.
HOLMES, Mr. Christopher, MEng ACA 2007; 20 Bedford Crescent, BRISTOL, BS7 9PP.
•HOLMES, Mr. Christopher John, FCA 1967; Christopher J Holmes, 27 Cootes Avenue, HORSHAM, WEST SUSSEX, RH12 2AD.
HOLMES, Mr. Christopher John, FCA 1963; 45a Westlands Lane, Beanacre, MELKSHAM, SN12 7QE.
HOLMES, Mr. Christopher Simon, BSc ACA 1995; 6 Whitfield Link, CHELMSFORD, CM2 9QF.
HOLMES, Mr. Colm Joseph, BBS ACA 1992; Somerton, Hyde Park, Terenure, DUBLIN 6, COUNTY DUBLIN, IRELAND.
HOLMES, Mr. David Gerald, FCA 1958; 17 Tor Crescent, Hartley, PLYMOUTH, PL3 5TW. (Life Member)
HOLMES, Mr. David Malcolm, BSc FCA 1981; 17 Lantern Lane, BARRINGTON, RI 02806, UNITED STATES.
•HOLMES, Mr. David Paul, BSc FCA 1990; 4 Highcliffe Court, Greenfold Lane, WETHERBY, WEST YORKSHIRE, LS22 6RG.
HOLMES, Mr. David Richard, BA ACA 1989; Chromalloy United Kingdom Ltd, 1 Linkmel Road, Eastwood, NOTTINGHAM, NG16 3RZ.
HOLMES, Mr. David Richard, BSc ACA 1993; R J Kiln & Co Ltd Furness House, 106 Fenchurch Street, LONDON, EC3M 5NR.
HOLMES, Mr. David Wilson, BA ACA 2006; Providence International Ltd, 3 Leeds City Office Park Holbeck, LEEDS, LS11 5BD.
HOLMES, Mr. Dennis, BA ACA 1989; 152 Birches Lane, South Wingfield, ALFRETON, DE55 7LZ.
HOLMES, Mr. Derrick Roy, FCA 1950; 9 Hereford Drive, CLITHEROE, BB7 1JP. (Life Member)
HOLMES, Mrs. Eleanor Jane, MA ACA 1992; 84 Bulmershe Road, READING, RG1 5RJ.
•HOLMES, Ms. Elspeth Lucy, BA(Hons) ACA 2001; Ottoline Ferdinand Ltd, 38A Thompson Road, East Dulwich, LONDON, SE22 9JR.
HOLMES, Miss. Emma Jane, BA ACA 1991; S A B Miller plc, S A B Miller House, Church Street West, WOKING, SURREY, GU21 6HS.
HOLMES, Mr. Eric, FCA 1956; 177 Wythenshawe Road, Northern Moor, MANCHESTER, M23 0AD. (Life Member)
HOLMES, Miss. Frances, BSc ACA 2010; 35 Millers Rise, ST. ALBANS, HERTFORDSHIRE, AL1 1QW.
•HOLMES, Mr. Geoffrey Robert Holman, FCA 1976; (Tax Fac), Johnson Holmes & Co., Towlers Court, 30a Elm Hill, NORWICH, NR3 1HG.
•HOLMES, Mrs. Glenis Billie, FCA 1977; Worton LLP, Beauchamp House, 402/403 Stourport Road, KIDDERMINSTER, WORCESTERSHIRE, DY11 7BG.
HOLMES, Mr. Graham Leslie, BA ACA 1992; 13 Little Warren Close, GUILDFORD, SURREY, GU4 8PW.
HOLMES, Miss. Heather Carol, ACA MAAT 2008; 145 Uxendon Hill, WEMBLEY, MIDDLESEX, HA9 9SH.
HOLMES, Miss. Helen, ACA 2008; Deloitte & Touche, 2 New Street Square, LONDON, EC4A 3BZ.
HOLMES, Miss. Helen, BSc(Hons) ACA 2002; La Fosse, St. John, JERSEY, JE3 4AF.
•HOLMES, Miss. Helen Mary, BSc FCA 1991; Stables Thompson & Briscoe Ltd, Lowther House, Lowther Street, KENDAL, CUMBRIA, LA9 4DX.
HOLMES, Mrs. Jennifer Ann, BA ACA 1989; 20 Kingsbridge Way, Bramcote, NOTTINGHAM, NG9 3LW.
HOLMES, Mrs. Joanna Louise, BA ACA 1993; 16 Berkeley Road, Crouch End, LONDON, N8 8RU.
HOLMES, Miss. Joanna Lucy, ACA 2010; Claughton Grange Road, St. Peter Port, GUERNSEY, GY1 1RQ.
HOLMES, Mr. John Bernard Edgar, FCA 1962; Hameau de Salleles, 34720 CAUX, FRANCE.
HOLMES, Mr. John Hadfield, BA ACA 1985; 2 Martinsclough, Lostock, BOLTON, BL6 4PF.
HOLMES, Mr. John Michael, FCA 1972; 251 Somerville Rd, HORNSBY HEIGHTS, NSW 2077, AUSTRALIA. (Life Member)
HOLMES, Mr. John Patrick, FCA 1970; 4 Rue Ingres, 44470 CARQUEFOU, FRANCE.
•HOLMES, Mr. John Richard, FCA 1975; (Tax Fac), Holmes & Co, 10 Torrington Road, Claygate, ESHER, KT10 0SA.
HOLMES, Mr. Jonathan, BA ACA CISA 1993; 38 Chelmsford Street, Ngaio, WELLINGTON, NEW ZEALAND.
HOLMES, Mr. Jonathan Philip, BA ACA 2004; 2 Emerald Grove, Rainworth, MANSFIELD, NOTTINGHAMSHIRE, NG21 0GG.
HOLMES, Mr. Jonathan Raymond Macaulay, LLB ACA 2004; with PricewaterhouseCoopers LLP, Pricewaterhousecoopers, 12 Plumtree Court, LONDON, EC4A 4HT.
HOLMES, Mr. Jonathan Stuart, BEng ACA 1998; Maylands St. Georges Place, Hurstpierpoint, HASSOCKS, BN6 9QT.
HOLMES, Mr. Jonathan Vincent Preece, MA ACA 1991; (Tax Fac), Santander UK Plc, 2-3 Triton Square, LONDON, NW1 3AN.
•HOLMES, Mr. Joseph Francis, BSc FCA 1985; Gambit Corporate Finance LLP, 3 Assembly Square, Britannia Quay, Cardiff Bay, CARDIFF, CF10 4PL.
HOLMES, Miss. Julia Mary Smith, LLB ACA 1990; The School House, 25 High Street, Cheddington, LEIGHTON BUZZARD, LU7 0RG.
①HOLMES, Mr. Karl Christopher, LLB ACA 1992; P N C Business Credit, 72 Cannon Street, LONDON, EC4N 6AE.
HOLMES, Mr. Kenneth Edmund, CBE BCom FCA 1957; Vale House, 23 Greenway Road, Galmpton, BRIXHAM, DEVON, TQ5 0LT.
HOLMES, Mr. Kenneth Marshall, FCA 1965; 7 Bowhay, Hutton, BRENTWOOD, ESSEX, CM13 2JX.
HOLMES, Mr. Kevin John, ACA 1988; (Tax Fac), 27 Cranmere Road, PLYMOUTH, PL3 5JY.
HOLMES, Mr. Kevin John, MSc ACA 2001; 29 Cleevemount Road, CHELTENHAM, GL52 3HF.
•HOLMES, Mr. Mark, BA FCA 1990; (Tax Fac), Ashworth Moulds, 11 Nicholas Street, BURNLEY, BB11 2AL.
HOLMES, Mr. Mark Adrian, BSc ACA 1991; Credit Suisse, One Cabot Square, LONDON, E14 4QJ.
HOLMES, Mr. Mark Alexander, BA ACA 1993; with PricewaterhouseCoopers, One Spencer Dock, North Wall Quay, DUBLIN 1, COUNTY DUBLIN, IRELAND.
HOLMES, Mr. Martin David Anthony, BA ACA 1994; 29 South Drive, HARROGATE, HG2 8AT.
HOLMES, Mr. Melvyn, FCA 1971; 5 Sandhill Crescent, Alwoodley, LEEDS, LS17 8DY.
HOLMES, Mr. Michael, MA(Hons) ACA 2000; Goldman Sachs, Petershill, 1 Carter Lane, LONDON, EC4V 5ER.
HOLMES, Mr. Michael Anthony, FCA 1968; 16 Flemings Road, WOODSTOCK, OX20 1NA.
HOLMES, Mr. Michael John, FCA 1957; 14 Gorse Ridge Drive, Baslow, BAKEWELL, DERBYSHIRE, DE45 1SL. (Life Member)
HOLMES, Mr. Michael John, FCA 1971; 52 Tor Bryan, INGATESTONE, CM4 9HN.
HOLMES, Mr. Michael Patrick, BSc ACA 1992; 40 St Ronans Terrace, INNERLEITHEN, EH44 6RB.
HOLMES, Mr. Michael Squire, BSc ACA 1998; Monks Cottage, St. Marys Road, ASCOT, BERKSHIRE, SL5 9AX.
•HOLMES, Mr. Nicholas Edward, BSc(Hons) ACA 2001; Chavereys, Mall House, The Mall, FAVERSHAM, KENT, ME13 8JL.
HOLMES, Mr. Nicholas Henry, FCA 1972; Little Stroods, Whitemans Green, Cuckfield, HAYWARDS HEATH, WEST SUSSEX, RH17 5DA. (Life Member)
•HOLMES, Mr. Nicholas James, ACA FCCA 2009; Darnells, Quay House, Quay Road, NEWTON ABBOT, TQ12 2BU.
HOLMES, Mr. Nicholas Stuart, BA ACA 1999; 33 Willoughby Drive, Empingham, Rutland, OAKHAM, LEICESTERSHIRE, LE15 8PY.
HOLMES, Mr. Nigel Douglas, BA FCA CTA 1995; (Tax Fac), 26 Wolsty Close, Windsor Park, CARLISLE, CUMBRIA, CA3 0PB.
•HOLMES, Mr. Oliver Morel, FCA 1963; (Tax Fac), O.M. Holmes, Holly Cottage, Main Road, Knockholt, SEVENOAKS, TN14 7LT.
HOLMES, Mrs. Patricia Ann, MA ACA 1994; 3 Ruskin Avenue, RICHMOND, SURREY, TW9 4DR.
HOLMES, Mr. Paul Andrew, BA FCA 1992; 23 Delamere Close, Sothall, SHEFFIELD, S20 2QE.
HOLMES, Mr. Paul David Steven, BA ACA 1988; 13 Dalkeith Road, HARPENDEN, AL5 5PP.
HOLMES, Mrs. Paula Jean, BA FCA MBA 1995; 19 Jubilee Avenue, Sileby, LOUGHBOROUGH, LEICESTERSHIRE, LE12 7TH.
HOLMES, Mr. Peter David, FCA 1975; Orchard Cottage The Green, Grove, WANTAGE, OXFORDSHIRE, OX12 0AN.
HOLMES, Mr. Reginald Stanley, FCA 1973; 1 Henty Road, Ferring, WORTHING, WEST SUSSEX, BN12 5PA.
HOLMES, Mr. Richard James, BCom ACA 1993; 16 Berkeley Road, LONDON, N8 8RU.
HOLMES, Mr. Richard James Elliott, BA(Hons) FCA 2001; Idis House, Churchfield Road, WEYBRIDGE, SURREY, KT13 8DB.
HOLMES, Mr. Richard Kimberley, BA ACA 1985; 92 Kimpton Road, Wheathampstead, ST.ALBANS, AL4 8LX.
HOLMES, Mr. Robert Alan, MA FCA 1977; Magnolia Cottage, Lower Road, Peldon, COLCHESTER, CO5 7QR.
HOLMES, Mr. Robert Brian, BSc ACA 2000; Oaklands Cottage, Awbridge Hill, Awbridge, ROMSEY, HAMPSHIRE, SO51 0HF.
HOLMES, Mr. Robert Douglas, FCA 1978; 5 St. Andrews Close, Burton-on-the-Wolds, LOUGHBOROUGH, LE12 5TJ.
HOLMES, Mr. Robert John Barrie Hunter, FCA 1963; The Courtlands, Palace Gardens Terrace, LONDON, W8 4RU. (Life Member)
HOLMES, Mr. Robert Joseph, BA(Hons) ACA 2004; Hadsphaltic International Ltd, PO Box 502GT, Marquee Plaza, West Bay Road, GEORGE TOWN, GRAND CAYMAN KY1 - 1106 CAYMAN ISLANDS.
HOLMES, Mr. Roger Anthony, BSc ACA 1985; The Mill House, Frensham, FARNHAM, SURREY, GU10 3EE.
HOLMES, Mrs. Sandra Jane, FCA 1976; 17 Kymer Gardens, HASSOCKS, WEST SUSSEX, BN6 8QZ.
HOLMES, Miss. Shelley Dawn, ACA 2003; 43 Knightley Way, Kingswood, HULL, HU7 3JR.
HOLMES, Mr. Simon Matthew, BA(Hons) ACA 2011; 54 Woodseats House Road, SHEFFIELD, S8 8QF.
HOLMES, Miss. Stephanie Claire, BA(Hons) ACA 2000; Carrier Refrigeration Meridian House, Sandy Lane West Littlemore, OXFORD, OX4 6LB.
HOLMES, Mr. Stephen Philip, FCA 1962; 10 Hicks Lane, Girton, CAMBRIDGE, CB3 0JS. (Life Member)
HOLMES, Mr. Steven Christopher, BA(Hons) ACA CF 2002; 15 Guernsey Way, Winnersh, WOKINGHAM, BERKSHIRE, RG41 5FT.
HOLMES, Mr. Stewart Leslie, BA FCA CTA TEP 1980; (Tax Fac), 61 Cambridge Road, TEDDINGTON, TW11 8DT.
HOLMES, Mr. Stuart Lang, FCA 1972; Stuart Holmes, 10A Yarmouth Road, Thorpe St Andrew, NORWICH, NR7 0EF.
•HOLMES, Mr. Stuart Robert Arthur, FCA 1978; (Tax Fac), Victor Boorman & Co, Europa House, Goldstone Villas, HOVE, BN3 3RQ.
•HOLMES, Miss. Susan Elizabeth, BA ACA 2000; Deloitte LLP, 1 City Square, LEEDS, WEST YORKSHIRE, LS1 2AL. See also Deloitte & Touche LLP
HOLMES, Mrs. Susan Lynsey Mary, BA ACA 2003; 172 Forest Lane, HARROGATE, NORTH YORKSHIRE, HG2 7EE.
HOLMES, Mr. Thomas William, BCom ACA 1983; (ACA Ireland 1972); 24 St Helens Road, Booterstown, BLACKROCK, COUNTY DUBLIN, IRELAND.
•HOLMES, Mr. Trevor Warren, FCA 1970; (Tax Fac), Holmes Widlake Limited, 3 Sharrow Lane, SHEFFIELD, S11 8AE.
HOLMES, Mrs. Vanessa Mary, BA ACA 1992; 7 Union Road, LEAMINGTON SPA, CV32 5NB.
HOLMES, Miss. Verity, BSc ACA 2006; 114 Sarsfeld Road, LONDON, SW12 8HL.
HOLMES, Mr. Victor John Ralph, BA FCA MCT 1977; Stonesvale, New Road, Limpsfield Common, OXTED, RH8 0UD.
HOLMES, Mr. Warren Richard, BA ACA 1990; 10 Eaton Park, COBHAM, SURREY, KT11 2JE.
HOLMES, Mr. William Lane, BA FCA 1960; 195 Shooters Hill, LONDON, SE18 3HP. (Life Member)
HOLMES, Mr. William Richard, MA FCA 1977; Standard Chartered, 1 Basinghall Avenue, LONDON, EC2V 5DD.
HOLMES-JOHNSON, Mr. Peter Henry, FCA 1964; 98 The Heights, Foxgrove Road, BECKENHAM, BR3 5BZ. (Life Member)
HOLMEWOOD, Mr. Alan Charles, FCA 1977; Flat 14 Woodlands, 4 South Bank, SURBITON, KT6 6DB.
HOLMSTOCK, Mr. Nicholas Denis, BA FCA 1981; 8 Nightingale Close, RADLETT, WD7 8NT.
HOLNESS, Mr. David John, BA ACA 1991; Hewlett Packard Ltd, Cain Road, BRACKNELL, BERKSHIRE, RG12 1HN.
HOLROYD, Mr. Geoffrey, FCA 1953; 10 Gypsy Lane, Hunton Bridge, KINGS LANGLEY, WD4 8PR. (Life Member)
HOLROYD, Mr. Ian James Thomas, BCom ACA 1985; 26 Gascoigne Way, Bloxham, BANBURY, OX15 4TL.
HOLROYD, Mr. John, FCA 1963; 1 St. Peters Close, Brafferton, YORK, YO61 2NP.
•HOLROYD, Mr. John Carless, FCA 1979; Mazars LLP, Mazars House, Gelderd Road, Gildersome, LEEDS, LS27 7JN.
HOLROYD, Mr. Jonathan James, FCA 1972; The Oaks, Husthwaite Road, Easingwold, YORK, YO61 3QF.
•HOLROYD, Mrs. Mary, MA ACA 1985; M. Holroyd, 11 Headley Gardens, Great Shelford, CAMBRIDGE, CB22 5JZ.
HOLROYD, Mrs. Minar Katherine, BA ACA 2007; 7a Grove Hill Gardens, TUNBRIDGE WELLS, TN1 1SS.
HOLROYD, Mr. Philip, FCA 1973; 8 Jonquil Way, Braiswick, COLCHESTER, CO4 5UW.
HOLROYD, Mr. Robert John, BA(Hons) ACA 2010; 22 Whitehead Street, Rawtenstall, ROSSENDALE, LANCASHIRE, BB4 7RB.
HOLROYD, Mr. Thomas, ACA 2011; 228 Elmhurst Mansions, Elmhurst Street, LONDON, SW4 6HH.
HOLROYD-DOVETON, Mr. Benjamin John William, BCom ACA 1993; 83 Huntingdon Road, East Finchley, LONDON, N2 9DX.
HOLSTEIN, Mr. Julien, BA FCA 1975; 3 CHEMIN DE ST.JAMES, 31700 CORNEBARRIEU, FRANCE.
HOLSTEIN, Miss. Xenia, BSc ACA 2010; 11 Eddystone Close, CARDIFF, CF11 8EB.
HOLT, Mrs. Adele Kathryn, BA ACA 1990; A H Davidson Chartered Accountants, 52 Walton Road, Stockton Heath, WARRINGTON, WA4 6NL.
HOLT, Mrs. Amanda, BSc ACA 1992; Churn Cottage Churn Lane, Horsmonden, TONBRIDGE, KENT, TN12 8HL.
•HOLT, Mr. Andrew, BSc FCA 1982; Overdale, 379 Fulwood Road, SHEFFIELD, S10 3GA.
HOLT, Mr. Andrew Paul, BSc ACA 2006; 11 Compston Avenue, ROSSENDALE, BB4 8BZ.
HOLT, Mr. Andrew Robert, BA(Hons) ACA 2003; 33 Poplar Grove, SALE, CHESHIRE, M33 3AX.
HOLT, Miss. Angela Mary, BSc(Hons) ACA 2001; Belmont House, Devoran, TRURO, TR3 6PZ.
HOLT, Mr. Antony Vincent Alder, MA FCA 1984; 1 Aldgate, LONDON, EC3N 1LP.
HOLT, Mr. Benjamin, MA ACA 2009; 7E, The Barclay, 237 South 18th Street, PHILADELPHIA, PA 19103, UNITED STATES.
HOLT, Miss. Catherine Linda, BA(Hons) ACA 2001; with Baker Tilly Tax and Advisory Services LLP, 25 Farringdon Street, LONDON, EC4A 4AB.
HOLT, Mr. Christopher, BSc(Hons) ACA 2003; Flat 10 St. Josephs Court, 24 Forest View, LONDON, E4 7UA.
HOLT, Mr. Christopher John, BA ACA 2003; 39 Manor Road, Wheathampstead, ST. ALBANS, HERTFORDSHIRE, AL4 8JG.
HOLT, Mr. Christopher John, BSc ACA 1997; 6 Clive Road, TWICKENHAM, TW1 4SG.
HOLT, Mr. Christopher Stuart, ACA 2007; 16 Danesleigh Gardens, LEIGH-ON-SEA, SS9 4NL.
HOLT, Mrs. Clare Eloise, BSc ACA 2005; Zurich Financial Services, UK Life Centre, Station Road, SWINDON, SN1 1EL.
HOLT, Mr. Darren Lee, BA ACA 1993; 8 Pickering Close, Timplerley, ALTRINCHAM, WA15 6PT.
HOLT, Mr. David Charles, LLB FCA 1975; 12 Court Lane, Bratton, WESTBURY, WILTSHIRE, BA13 4RE.
HOLT, Mr. David James, FCA 1963; 71 Field Rise, Littleover, DERBY, DE23 1DF.
HOLT, Mr. David Julian, BA ACA 1989; 8 Shelley Court, 5 Makepeace Road, Wanstead, LONDON, E11 1US.
•HOLT, Mr. David Kendrick, BSc ACA 1992; with RSM Tenon Audit Limited, 160 Dundee Street, EDINBURGH, EH11 1DQ.
HOLT, Mr. David Lythgoe, FCA 1955; 38 Westbank Road, Lostock, BOLTON, BL6 4HE. (Life Member)
HOLT, Mr. Gary, BA FCA 1966; Cherry Picker Cottage, 15 Long Street, Enford, PEWSEY, WILTSHIRE, SN9 6DD.
HOLT, Mr. Gavin Robert Mauchlen, FCA 1966; 26 Beverley Road, Monkseaton, WHITLEY BAY, TYNE AND WEAR, NE25 8JH. (Life Member)
HOLT, Mr. Geoffrey Alan, FCA 1973; 97 Cotes Road, Barrow upon Soar, LOUGHBOROUGH, LEICESTERSHIRE, LE12 8JP.
HOLT, Mr. Graham John, FCA 1977; 291 Ansty Road, Wyken, COVENTRY, CV2 3FN.
HOLT, Mr. Graham John, BCom FCA 1974; 6a Whitebirk Close, Greenmount, BURY, BL8 4HE.
HOLT, Mr. Ian Richard, BSc ACA 1996; 5 Winifred Close, Arkley, BARNET, EN5 3LR.
HOLT, Mr. Jeremy Michael, MA ACA 1979; 126 Guildford Park Avenue, GUILDFORD, SURREY, GU2 7NN.

Members - Alphabetical **HOLT - HOO**

HOLT, Mr. John, FCA *1955;* 122 Woodlands Road, Bookham, LEATHERHEAD, KT23 4HJ. (Life Member)

HOLT, Mr. John, BSc ACA *1993;* Gateshead College, Quarryfield Road, GATESHEAD, TYNE AND WEAR, NE8 3BE.

HOLT, Mr. John Lennox, BSc ACA *1989;* (Tax Fac), 105 Symphony Court, BIRMINGHAM, B16 8AG.

•HOLT, Mr. Jonathan Matthew, BA FCA *1998;* KPMG LLP, St. James's Square, MANCHESTER, M2 6DS. See also KPMG Europe LLP

HOLT, Miss. Kathryn Ann, LLB ACA *2002;* 3 Withypool, Up Hatherley, CHELTENHAM, GLOUCESTERSHIRE, GL51 3PY.

HOLT, Mr. Luke Patrick, BSc ACA *2006;* B D O Stoy Hayward Kings Wharf, 20-30 Kings Road, READING, RG1 3EX.

HOLT, Mr. Malcolm Keith, FCA *1977;* Flat 3, 23 Brunswick Square, HOVE, BN3 1EJ.

HOLT, Mr. Malcolm William, FCA MBA *1974;* The Warehouse, 1 Draper Street, SOUTHBOROUGH, TN4 0PG.

HOLT, Miss. Marianne Louise Campbell, BA ACA *2007;* 39 Ryecroft, HAYWARDS HEATH, WEST SUSSEX, RH16 4NW.

HOLT, Mr. Mark James, BA FCA *2000;* H M Revenue & Customs, 1 Munroe Court, White Rose Office Park, Millshaw Park Lane, LEEDS, LS11 0EA.

•HOLT, Mr. Mark Stephen, FCA *1979;* (Tax Fac), Mark Holt & Co Ltd, Marine Building, Victoria Wharf, PLYMOUTH, PL4 0RF.

HOLT, Mr. Matthew, ACA *2011;* Heathcroft, Heath Park Road, LEIGHTON BUZZARD, BEDFORDSHIRE, LU7 3BB.

HOLT, Sir Michael, Kt CBE MA LLM FCA *1958;* The Tower House, Bildeston, IPSWICH, SUFFOLK, IP7 7ER. (Life Member)

HOLT, Mr. Michael Clement Alwyn, FCA *1957;* Whitebeams, Beech Avenue, Effingham, LEATHERHEAD, KT24 5PJ. (Life Member)

HOLT, Mr. Michael John, MBA BA FCA AMCT *1990;* Marble Arch Tower, Low & Bonar Plc Marble Arch Tower, 55 Bryanston Street, LONDON, W1H 7AA.

•HOLT, Mr. Michael John, FCA *1973;* Potter McGregor & Co., 5 Willmott Close, SUTTON COLDFIELD, WEST MIDLANDS, B75 5NP.

HOLT, Mr. Nigel, BSc FCA *1977;* 1 Willoughby Court, Norwell, NEWARK, NOTTINGHAMSHIRE, NG23 6JJ.

HOLT, Mr. Patrick, MSc ACA *1986;* Flat 16, 18 Queen's Gate, South Kensington, LONDON, SW7 5JE.

HOLT, Mrs. Paula, MA ACA *2000;* with PricewaterhouseCoopers LLP, 1 Embankment Place, LONDON, WC2N 6RH.

HOLT, Mr. Peter, FCA *1962;* Culeave Cottage, Strathcarron, ARDGAY, IV24 3BP. (Life Member)

HOLT, Mr. Peter Alexander, FCA *1978;* 39 Spring Lane, Burnbridge, HARROGATE, HG3 1NP.

HOLT, Mr. Philip James Eric, BA ACA *1986;* 68 Verran Road, CAMBERLEY, GU15 2LJ.

•HOLT, Mr. Philip James Harrison, BSc ACA *1993;* (Tax Fac), Harrison Holt, High Park Farm, Kirkbymoorside, YORK, YO62 7HS.

HOLT, Mrs. Rebekah Anne, ACA *2008;* 22 Folly Wood Drive, CHORLEY, LANCASHIRE, PR7 2FW.

HOLT, Mr. Robert David, FCA *1961;* 87 Moorsholm Drive, Wollaton, NOTTINGHAM, NG8 2EE. (Life Member)

HOLT, Mr. Russell Alexander, BA ACA *1992;* BBC World Service, British Broadcasting Corporation, PO Box 76, LONDON, WC2B 4PH.

•HOLT, Mr. Stephen John, BSc ACA *1995;* Ernst & Young LLP, 1 More London Place, LONDON, SE1 2AF. See also Ernst & Young Europe LLP

HOLT, Mr. Steven Christopher, BSc(Hons) ACA *2009;* Alix Partners Ltd, 20 North Audley Street, LONDON, W1K 6WE.

HOLT, Dr. Susan Elizabeth, ACA *1992;* Lower Hall Farm Cottage, 27 Church Road, Mellor, STOCKPORT, SK6 5LY.

HOLT, Mrs. Tara Suzanne, BSc ACA CTA *1995;* (Tax Fac), 34 Deacon Road, KINGSTON-UPON-THAMES, KT2 6LU.

HOLT, Mr. Thomas James, ACA *2009;* 21 Whitby Court, Parkhurst Road, Islington, LONDON, N7 0SU.

HOLT, Mr. Trevor John, FCA *1973;* 4 Moordown Avenue, SOLIHULL, WEST MIDLANDS, B92 8QR. (Life Member)

HOLT, Mr. William Douglas Andrew, BCom CA *2011;* with ICAEW, Metropolitan House, 321 Avebury Boulevard, MILTON KEYNES, MK9 2FZ.

HOLT, Mr. William Jeffrey, FCA *1973;* Labelon Group Ltd, Unit 10, Chilford Court, Rayne Road, BRAINTREE, ESSEX CM7 2QS.

HOLTAM, Mr. David, MMath ACA *2010;* with Deloitte LLP, 2 New Street Square, LONDON, EC4A 3BZ.

HOLTERHOFF, Mr. Jonathan Richard, BSc ACA *1992;* Apt 3058, Block C, Bangkok Garden, Naradhiwas Rajanakarinda Soi 24, Yannawa, BANGKOK 10120 THAILAND.

HOLTHAM, Miss. Katherine, BSc ACA *2007;* Flat 3, Cedar House, Gorse Court, GUILDFORD, SURREY, GU4 7EZ.

HOLTOM, Mr. John Bruce, MSc FCA *1972;* Stroud Folly, Stroud Lane, Shamley Green, GUILDFORD, GU5 0ST. (Life Member)

HOLTON, Mr. Andrew, BSc FCA *1986;* SWAT Limited, Tor View House, 3 Darklake View, Estover, PLYMOUTH, PL6 7TL.

HOLTON, Mr. David Philip, BA ACA *1984;* Oakwood, Wickhams Way, Hartley, LONGFIELD, DA3 8DH.

HOLTON, Mrs. Kara Anne, BA ACA *1997;* Treelands, Landscape Road, WARLINGHAM, SURREY, CR6 9JB.

•HOLTON, Mr. Karl James, FCA *1995;* Holton Partners Limited, Treelands, Landscape Road, WARLINGHAM, SURREY, CR6 9JB.

HOLTON, Miss. Megan Frances, BA ACA *1996;* 87 Crombie Road, SIDCUP, DA15 8AT.

HOLTON, Mr. Michael Damien, LLB ACA *2000;* 15 Garrett Road, Finchampstead, WOKINGHAM, RG40 4RX.

HOLTON, Mrs. Victoria Maria, BA ACA *2002;* 15 Garrett Road, Finchampstead, WOKINGHAM, BERKSHIRE, RG40 4RX.

HOLVERSON, Ms. Joy Mary, BSc FCA *1988;* 30 Saxon Avenue, FELTHAM, MIDDLESEX, TW13 5JN.

HOLWELL, Mr. Peter, BSc FCA *1961;* Hookers Green, Bishopsbourne, CANTERBURY, CT4 5JB. (Life Member)

HOLWELL, Mrs. Sian Elizabeth, BSc ACA *1992;* 8 Birch Close, Send, WOKING, GU23 7BZ.

HOLWELL, Mr. William Peter, BSc FCA *1991;* 4 Alvernia Close, GODALMING, GU7 1YJ.

HOLWILL, Mr. Richard Charles, FCA *1972;* 12 College Green, BIDEFORD, DEVON, EX39 3JY.

•HOLYHEAD, Mr. Christian David, BSc ACA *1997;* Financial Reporting Council, Aldwych House, 71-91 Aldwych, LONDON, WC2B 4HN.

HOLYHEAD, Mrs. Ellen, BSc ACA *1996;* 36 Hargwyne Street, Stockwell, LONDON, SW9 9RG.

HOLYHEAD, Mr. Gerald Roger, BA FCA *1977;* 40 Bowly Road, GLOUCESTER, GL1 5NW.

•HOLYLAND, Mr. David, FCA *1958;* 54 Fairfield Road, MARKET HARBOROUGH, LE16 9QJ.

HOLYOAK, Mr. Arthur Mark, FCA *1964;* 33 Knights Park, KINGSTON-UPON-THAMES, KT1 2QH.

HOLYOAK, Mr. Christopher William, FCA *1972;* Treetops, Hascombe Road, GODALMING, SURREY, GU8 4AB.

HOLYOAK, Mr. David Ivor, BA ACA *1983;* 8 Grange Rd, LONDON, SW13 9RE.

HOLYOAKE, Mr. Matthew, BA ACA *2011;* 4 Wildgoose Drive, HORSHAM, WEST SUSSEX, RH12 1TU.

•HOLYOAKE, Mr. Neil Alexander, ACA ATII MAAT *1994;* Ernst & Young LLP, 1 Bridgewater Place, Water Lane, LEEDS, LS11 5QR. See also Ernst & Young Europe LLP

HOLYOAKE, Mr. Paul, FCA *1982;* 30 Enfield Chase, GUISBOROUGH, TS14 7LT.

HOLZEM, Miss. Christine, ACA *2010;* KPMG LLP, 355 South Grand Avenue, Suite 2000, LOS ANGELES, CA 90071, UNITED STATES.

HOMA, Mr. Peter Andrew, BSc FCA *1989;* Galliford Try Plc, Cowley Business Park, Cowley, UXBRIDGE, MIDDLESEX, UB8 2AL.

•①HOMAN, Mr. Andrew Mark, BA FCA *1966;* with PricewaterhouseCoopers LLP, Pricewaterhousecoopers, 12 Plumtree Court, LONDON, EC4A 4HT.

•HOMAN, Mr. Charles Spencer, FCA *1993;* Tax Audit and Accounts Solutions Limited, Southgate Chambers, 37-39 Southgate Street, WINCHESTER, HAMPSHIRE, SO23 9EH.

HOMAN, Mr. Dan, ACA *2011;* 68 Kingfisher House, Juniper Drive, LONDON, SW18 1TY.

HOMAN, Mr. David Michael, MA ACA *2002;* Flat 5, Seymour Place, North Street, HORNCHURCH, ESSEX, RM11 1SX.

HOMAN, Mr. Geoffrey Ernest, FCA *1951;* Street Farm, Wickham Skeith, EYE, IP23 8LP. (Life Member)

HOMBURGER, Mr. Alfred Nathan, FCA *1955;* 7 The Riding, LONDON, NW11 8HL. (Life Member)

HOME, Mr. Matthew, BSc(Hons) ACA *2002;* 3 Hamilton Road, Southville, BRISTOL, BS3 1PA.

HOME, Mr. Michael Frederick, ACA *1990;* 38 The Acres, Stokesley, MIDDLESBROUGH, CLEVELAND, TS9 5QA.

•HOMENT, Mr. Brian Peter, FCA *1977;* (Tax Fac), Hardcastle Burton LLP, Lake House, Market Hill, ROYSTON, HERTFORDSHIRE, SG8 9JN.

HOMER, Mrs. Alison Jean, BA ACA *1990;* Casteras, 31160 ROUEDE, FRANCE.

HOMER, Mrs. Andrea Mary, BSc ACA *1992;* Lindenweg 19, Eppstein-Vockenhausen, 65817 EPPSTEIN, HESSEN, GERMANY.

HOMER, Mr. Anton Christian, BA ACA *2002;* 23 Stockdale Walk, KNARESBOROUGH, NORTH YORKSHIRE, HG5 8DZ.

•HOMER, Mr. Arnold John, FCA *1957;* (Tax Fac), Price Pearson Ltd, Finch House, 28-30 Wolverhampton Street, DUDLEY, DY1 1DB.

HOMER, Mr. Barry John, FCA *1960;* 5 Seaway Milford Road, Barton on Sea, NEW MILTON, BH25 5PL. (Life Member)

HOMER, Miss. Clare Amanda, BA(Hons) ACA *2004;* 60 Tadworth Road, LONDON, NW2 7UD.

HOMER, Mr. James Pierson, BSc FCA *1990;* Lindenweg 19, 65817 EPPSTEIN-VOCKENHAUSEN, GERMANY.

HOMER, Mrs. Kim Elizabeth, BA FCA *1993;* Arthog, 11 Gun Meadow Avenue, KNEBWORTH, HERTFORDSHIRE, SG3 6BS.

HOMER, Mrs. Laura Ann, MSc BSc ACA *2008;* c/o Royal Bank of Canada Trust Company (Cayman) Ltd, 4th Floor, 24 Shedden Road, GEORGE TOWN, GRAND CAYMAN, KY1-1110 CAYMAN ISLANDS.

HOMER, Mr. Michael Lawrence, FCA *1955;* 152 St Johns Avenue, KIDDERMINSTER, DY11 6AT. (Life Member)

•HOMER, Mr. Roger Frederick, FCA *1970;* F.E. Sidaway Son & Co, 5-6 Long Lane, ROWLEY REGIS, B65 0JA.

HOMER, Mr. Russell Stuart, ACA *1985;* Johnson Smith Associates Ltd, PO Box 2499, GEORGETOWN, GRAND CAYMAN, KY1-1104, CAYMAN ISLANDS.

HOMER, Mr. Thomas Edward Timothy, FCA *1986;* Rosedale, Maidenhead Road, Cookham, MAIDENHEAD, BERKSHIRE, SL6 9DF.

HOMERSHAM, Mrs. Lisa Katrina, BA(Hons) ACA *2001;* 14 Braunstone Drive, MAIDSTONE, ME16 0UG.

HOMEWOOD, Mr. Andrew Trevor, MA ACA *1987;* 8 Hildenbrook Farm, Riding Lane, Hildenborough, TONBRIDGE, TN11 9JN.

•HOMEWOOD, Mr. Jason Robert, MA ACA *1998;* PKF (UK) LLP, Farringdon Place, 20 Farringdon Road, LONDON, EC1M 3AP.

HOMEWOOD, Mr. Melvin Clive, BSc ACA *1983;* Watts Cottage, Jacobs Well Road, Jacob's Well, GUILDFORD, SURREY, GU4 7PP.

•HOMYARD, Mr. Stephen Andrew, FCA *1975;* Baker Homyard, Ingouville House, Ingouville Lane, St Helier, JERSEY, JE2 4SG.

HON, Mr. Kin Yee, FCA *1975;* Flat 21A, Tower 12, 9 Wah King Hill Road, KWAI CHUNG, NEW TERRITORIES, HONG KONG SAR.

HON, Mr. Ping Cho Terence, ACA *2005;* Flat F 17/F Block 2, Academic Terrace, Pokfulam Road, POK FU LAM, HONG KONG ISLAND, HONG KONG SAR.

HON, Mr. Tai Wai David, ACA *2005;* Flat H 25/F, Wah Fung Garden, 274 Lai King Hill Road, KWAI CHUNG, KOWLOON, HONG KONG SAR.

•HONAP, Mr. Shrinivas Madhav, BA ACA *1990;* Shrinivas Honap, 178 Kineton Green Road, SOLIHULL, B92 7ES. See also Honap & Co

HONARMAND, Mr. Alan Hossein Mehrabizadeh, ACA *1989;* C C S Media Ltd Old Birdholme House, Derby Road, CHESTERFIELD, DERBYSHIRE, S40 2EX.

•HONARMAND, Mr. Andrew Madjid Mehrabizadeh, ACA *1990;* Cooper Parry LLP, 3 Centro Place, Pride Park, DERBY, DE24 8RF.

HONE, Miss. Alexandra, BA ACA *2007;* 7 Bellamy Street, LONDON, SW12 8BT.

HONE, Mr. Angus Graham, MBA BA(Hons) ACA *1992;* Old Farm, Lower Road, Croydon, ROYSTON, HERTFORDSHIRE, SG8 0HE.

HONE, Mr. Anthony, FCA *1944;* 50 Smitham Bottom Lane, PURLEY, SURREY, CR8 3DB. (Life Member)

HONES, Mrs. Caroline, BSc ACA *2006;* 15 Withey Meadows, Hookwood, HORLEY, SURREY, RH6 0AZ.

•HONEY, Mr. Christopher John, BSc FCA *1990;* McGrathNicol, Level 31, 60 Margaret Street, SYDNEY, NSW 2000, AUSTRALIA.

HONEY, Mr. David John, BA ACA PGCE *2005;* Deloitte & Touche, 2 New Street Square, LONDON, EC4A 3BZ.

HONEY, Mr. Derek Charles, FCA *1959;* 12 Blenheim Drive, OXFORD, OX2 8DG. (Life Member)

HONEY, Mr. John Stuart, FCA *1969;* Knysna Lodge, Rue De La Blanche Pierre, ST LAWRENCE, JERSEY, JE3 1EA.

•HONEY, Mr. Kevin Mark, BA ACA *1992;* Ernst & Young LLP, 1 More London Place, LONDON, SE1 2AF. See also Ernst & Young Europe LLP

HONEY, Mr. Matthew Andrew, BSc ACA *1992;* 29 Tredcroft Road, HOVE, EAST SUSSEX, BN3 6UG.

HONEY, Mr. Robert Patrick Streak, FCA *1977;* 119/ 23-24 Moo 1, Tambon Bophut, KO SAMUI 84320, THAILAND.

HONEYBALL, Mr. Geoffrey Charles, FCA *1968;* Trotterdown, Reading Road, HOOK, RG27 9ED.

HONEYBALL, Mr. Robert Ian, BSc(Hons) ACA *2000;* Apartment 32 Berkeley Tower, 48 Westferry Circus, LONDON, E14 8RP.

HONEYBONE, Mr. David John, FCA *1968;* Lambert Hall, Crockernwell, EXETER, EX6 6NG. (Life Member)

HONEYBONE, Mr. Matthew Hurst, BA ACA *1998;* Zodiak Media Ltd, The Gloucester Building, Avonmore Road, LONDON, W14 8RF.

HONEYBORNE, Mr. Graeme Bolton, ACA *2005;* Pine Lodge, 24 Overhill Road, WILMSLOW, CHESHIRE, SK9 2BE.

HONEYBOURNE, Mrs. Helen Joanne, BSc ACA *2005;* Belmont House, Old Orchards, LYMINGTON, HAMPSHIRE, SO41 3AF.

HONEYBUN, Miss. Carolyn Jane, BSc ACA *1990;* Flat 2, 20 Palmeira Square, HOVE, EAST SUSSEX, BN3 2JN.

HONEYBUN, Miss. Clare Bessie, BSc ACA *2007;* 7 Churchways Avenue, BRISTOL, BS7 8SN.

HONEYFIELD, Mr. Richard John, FCA *1960;* Warwick House, Bromfield, LUDLOW, SY8 2JU. (Life Member)

HONEYFORD, Miss. Jane Elizabeth, BA(Hons) ACA *2010;* Apartment 17 The Kensington, 61 Palatine Road, MANCHESTER, M20 3LT.

HONEYMAN, Mr. Ian Robert, FCA *1978;* Moonfleet, Limmer Lane, BOGNOR REGIS, WEST SUSSEX, PO22 7HD.

HONEYMAN BROWN, Mr. Christopher, FCA *1973;* 31 Old Glebe, Fernhurst, HASLEMERE, SURREY, GU27 3HT.

HONEYSETT, Miss. Louise, BSc ACA *2009;* First Floor Flat, 152 Courthill Road, LONDON, SE13 6DR.

HONEYSETT, Miss. Sandra Carol, BSc ACA *1980;* 9 Maitland Road, Sydenham, LONDON, SE26 5NN.

HONEYWELL, Mr. Geoffrey Guy Bailey, FCA *1968;* 41a Uttoxeter Road, Hill Ridware, RUGELEY, STAFFORDSHIRE, WS15 3QR.

HONEYWELL, Mrs. Lucy Elizabeth, ACA CTA *2002;* 8 Wincanton Close, Downend, BRISTOL, BS16 6SW.

•HONEYWELL, Mr. Peter Royston, FCA *1970;* (Tax Fac), Honeywell (Monmouth) Limited, 9 Whitecross Street, MONMOUTH, NP25 3BY.

HONEYWOOD, Mr. Benjamin, ACA *2009;* Apartment 8 Cornucopia Court, Le Mont Pinel St. Helier, JERSEY, JE2 4RS.

HONEYWOOD, Mr. John, ACA *2011;* T C Harrison Group Ltd Milford House, Mill Street, BAKEWELL, DERBYSHIRE, DE45 1HH.

HONG, Mr. Albert, ACA *2008;* 63 St. Augustines Avenue, WEMBLEY, MIDDLESEX, HA9 7NU.

HONG, Mr. Chin Kiat, BA CA ACA *1982;* 5 Pinggir Pelangi Pagi, Sg Ramal, Country Heights, 43000 KAJANG, SELANGOR MALAYSIA.

HONG, Ms. Elaine, ACA *2007;* Apt 906-A Jasmine Towers, Jalan SS2/72, 47300 PETALING JAYA, MALAYSIA.

HONG, Mr. Hee Leong, FCA *1984;* H L Hong & Co, 1B-3 Plaza Mayang, Jalan SS26/9, 47301 PETALING JAYA, SELANGOR, MALAYSIA.

HONG, Mrs. Min-Yeok, FCA *1961;* 7 Nassim Road 01-02, Nassim Lodge, SINGAPORE 258374, SINGAPORE. (Life Member)

HONNEYMAN, Mr. David George, BCom ACA *1986;* with M A Edwards Accountants Limited, 30a The Green, Kings Norton, BIRMINGHAM, B38 8SD.

•HONNYWILL, Mr. Charles Gair, BA ACA *1988;* Ernst & Young LLP, 1 More London Place, LONDON, SE1 2AF. See also Ernst & Young Europe LLP

•HONOUR, Mr. Ronald William, FCA *1973;* R.W. Honour, Bramhope, 72 Mill Lane, Whaplode, SPALDING, LINCOLNSHIRE PE12 6TS.

HOO, Mr. Byron Kee Chye, ACA *1994;* Edexcel, 190 High Holborn, LONDON, WC1V 7BH.

HOO, Mr. Jonathan Chee Weng, ACA *2008;* Flat 18 Admiral House, Willow Place, LONDON, SW1P 1JW.

HOO, Mr. Philip See Aik, BSc ACA CFA *2002;* Credit Suisse, Eleven Madison Avenue, NEW YORK, NY 10010, UNITED STATES.

HOOD, Mrs. Alison, BSc ACA *1992;* 13 Milton Road, LONDON, W7 1LQ.
HOOD, Mr. Brian, FCA *1976;* Office Suite E345, Dean Clough Office Park, HALIFAX, WEST YORKSHIRE, HX3 5AX.
HOOD, Miss. Carla Ruth Sivyer, BSc ACA *1989;* 22 Pelham Avenue, Point Chevalier, AUCKLAND 1022, NEW ZEALAND.
•**HOOD, Mrs. Catherine, BSc ACA** *1998;* Cathy Hood, 137 Barlows Lane, LIVERPOOL, L9 9HZ.
HOOD, Mr. Christopher James William, BSc ACA ACII *1999;* 18 Kooringa, WARLINGHAM, SURREY, CR6 9JP.
HOOD, Mr. David Jeffery, ACA *1978;* 18 Yester Road, CHISLEHURST, BR7 5LT.
HOOD, Mrs. Diana Sian, BA ACA *1989;* 9 Cosmur Close, Stanford Brook, LONDON, W12 9SF.
HOOD, Mr. James Alexander Stuart Tate, BSc FCA *1993;* Flat 1, 93 Sirdar Road, Kensington, LONDON, W11 4EQ.
HOOD, Mr. Jeremy Nicholas Hamilton, BSc ACA *2002;* 21 Boyne Park, TUNBRIDGE WELLS, KENT, TN4 8EL.
HOOD, Mr. John, FCA *1978;* 21 Pear Tree Way, Crowle, WORCESTER, WR7 4SB.
HOOD, Mr. John Basil, FCA *1948;* 14 Cardiff Road, BARGOED, CF81 8NY. (Life Member)
HOOD, Mr. John Edward, BSc FCA *1996;* Johnson Matthey Plc, Blythe Park Business Base, Sandon Road, Cresswell, STOKE-ON-TRENT, STAFFORDSHIRE ST11 9RD.
HOOD, Mr. John Herbert, FCA *1967;* 54 Ranvilles Lane, FAREHAM, PO14 3EA. (Life Member)
•**HOOD, Mrs. Julia Catherine, LLB FCA ATII TEP** *1983;* (Tax Fac), Redwood Wales Limited, Redwood Court, Tawe Business Village, Swansea Enterprise Park, SWANSEA, SA7 9LA.
HOOD, Ms. Katerina Nada, BA ACA *1987;* 49 Belmore Lane, LYMINGTON, HAMPSHIRE, SO41 3NR.
HOOD, Miss. Kelly Jayne, ACA *2005;* Carstar (Leeds) Ltd, 100 Bradford Road Stanningley, PUDSEY, WEST YORKSHIRE, LS28 6UR.
•①**HOOD, Mr. Nicholas Roy, FCA** *1970;* Begbies Traynor, 32 Cornhill, LONDON, EC3V 3BT. See also Begbies Traynor(Central) LLP and Begbies Traynor Limited
•**HOOD, Mr. Peter Lynas, FCA** *1960;* Peter L Hood, 20 Neville Crescent, Bromham, BEDFORD, MK43 8JE.
•**HOOD, Mr. Roderick Michael, BSc FCA** *1993;* (Tax Fac), Hood & Co, 168 Shay Lane, Walton, WAKEFIELD, WEST YORKSHIRE, WF2 6NP. See also Hood Financial Ltd
HOOD, Mr. Stuart Vaughan, BSc ACA *1993;* Thomson Reuters Ltd Aldgate House, 33 Aldgate High Street, LONDON, EC3N 1DL.
HOOD, Dr. Susan Mary, MA ACA *2010;* 42 Coppock Close, LONDON, SW11 2LF.
HOOD, Mr. William Raymond, FCA *1965;* The Ravensworth, Ambleside Road, WINDERMERE, CUMBRIA, LA23 1BA.
•**HOODA, Mr. Rezahussein, BSc ACA** *2006;* Walji & Co (UK) LLP, Prospect House, 50 Leigh Road, EASTLEIGH, HAMPSHIRE, SO50 9DT. See also Walji & Co Private Clients Ltd
HOODBHOY, Mr. Faisel Sikander, BA FCA CF *1984;* PO Box 75186, DUBAI, UNITED ARAB EMIRATES.
HOODBHOY, Mr. Tariq, ACA *1995;* 04-44 Nassim Mansiion, 40 Nassim Hill, SINGAPORE 258474, SINGAPORE.
HOODLESS, Mr. Alain Dominique, BA ACA *1998;* 7 Kinsale Avenue, Glendowie, AUCKLAND 1071, NEW ZEALAND.
HOOGEWERF, Miss. Dawn, ACA *2009;* 24 Skirlaw Close, Glebe, WASHINGTON, TYNE AND WEAR, NE38 7RE.
•**HOOGEWERF, Mr. Francis Nicholas, FCA** *1967;* (Tax Fac), Hoogewerf & Co, PO Box 878, 19 Rue Aldringen, L-2018 LUXEMBOURG, LUXEMBOURG.
HOOGEWERF, Miss. Jill, ACA *2011;* 33 Brackenhurst Drive, Moortown, LEEDS, LS17 6WE.
HOOGEWERF, Mr. Rupert Jasper, BA ACA *1997;* acru international, 4D Block 2 Grand Plaza 568 Julu Lu, SHANGHAI 200040, CHINA.
HOOI, Dr. Den Huan, ACA *1983;* 17 Dairy Farm Road, No 07-01, SINGAPORE 679043, SINGAPORE.
HOOI, Mr. Kee Sum, FCA *1969;* 32A Jalan Oh Cheng Keat, 30250 IPOH, Perak, MALAYSIA.
HOOI, Mrs. Kwan Sim, FCA *1971;* 32A Jalan Oh Cheng Keat, 30250 IPOH, Perak, MALAYSIA.
HOOI, Miss. Lai Hoong, BSc FCA *1975;* Lot 3690 Jalan UK 2, Ukay Heights, 68000 AMPANG, Selangor, MALAYSIA. (Life Member)
HOOI, Miss. Lai Ngarn, BSc ACA *1983;* 7 Maple Lane, SINGAPORE 277551, SINGAPORE.
HOOI, Mr. Yau Ming, BSc(Hons) ACA *2000;* 32A JALAN OH CHENG KEAT, 30250 IPOH, PERAK, MALAYSIA.
•**HOOK, Mr. Alan Kenneth, BA FCA** *1985;* Cranbrook House, Histons Hill, Codsall, WOLVERHAMPTON, STAFFORDSHIRE, WV8 2EY.
HOOK, Mr. Alan William, FCA *1954;* 3 King George Gardens, CHICHESTER, WEST SUSSEX, PO19 6LB. (Life Member)
HOOK, Mrs. Alison Gay, MA ACA *1991;* 2 Cade Lane, SEVENOAKS, KENT, TN13 1QX.
HOOK, Mr. Andrew, ACA *2011;* Elmlea, Green Lane, REIGATE, RH2 8JY.
HOOK, Mr. Christopher John, BA(Hons) ACA *2000;* 41 Nutfields, Ightham, SEVENOAKS, KENT, TN15 9EA.
HOOK, Mrs. Danielle, BSc ACA *2006;* 20 Richmond Drive, SUTTON COLDFIELD, WEST MIDLANDS, B75 7NU.
HOOK, Mr. David William, FCA *1955;* 25 Glentworth Close, OSWESTRY, SY10 9PY. (Life Member)
HOOK, Mr. Ian Edward, FCA *1982;* Mulberry, 18 Belmont Road, REIGATE, SURREY, RH2 7EE.
•**HOOK, Mr. Ian Martin, BA ACA** *1982;* Deloitte LLP, 2 New Street Square, LONDON, EC4A 3BZ. See also Deloitte & Touche LLP
HOOK, Mrs. Joanna Therese, MSc BMus ACA *2006;* 486 4th Street, Apartment 1L, BROOKLIN, NY 11215, UNITED STATES.
•**HOOK, Mr. Jonathan Adam, BA ACA** *1988;* PricewaterhouseCoopers LLP, 1 Embankment Place, LONDON, WC2N 6RH. See also PricewaterhouseCoopers
HOOK, Ms. Julie Anne, BA ACA *1983;* 6 Elm Tree Avenue, Upper Poppleton, YORK, YO26 6HL.
HOOK, Mr. Kevin Lloyd Christian, BSc(Econ) FCA *2001;* Credit Suisse (Gibraltar) Ltd, 1st Floor, Neptune House, MARINA BAY, GIBRALTAR.
HOOK, Mr. Marcus Christopher, ACA *2008;* Calthorpe Estates, 76 Hagley Road, BIRMINGHAM, B16 8LU.
•**HOOK, Mr. Mark Owen, BA FCA CTA** *1991;* (Tax Fac), The Rowleys Partnership Limited, 6 Dominus Way, Meridian Business Park, LEICESTER, LE19 1RP. See also Rowleys Partnership LLP
HOOK, Mr. Paul Luke, ACA *2008;* 6 Northumberland Avenue, READING, RG2 7PN.
•①**HOOK, Mr. Stephen John, FCA** *1972;* S J Hook, 38A Ledbury Road, LONDON, W11 2AB.
HOOK, Mr. Stuart Alan, MA BA(Hons) ACA *2009;* 93 Swansea Road, READING, RG1 8HA.
HOOKE, Mrs. Helen Grace, BA ACA *1992;* 12 Wimborne Gardens, Ealing, LONDON, W13 8BZ.
HOOKE, Ms. Kathryn Anne, BA ACA *1989;* 4 Green Lane, Marden, TONBRIDGE, TN12 9RE.
HOOKE, Mr. Kelvin James, BSc ACA *1997;* Terbatas Street 13-6, RIGA LV-1011, LATVIA.
HOOKE, Mr. Richard David, FCA *1980;* (Tax Fac), 6 Fisher Close, Willerby, HULL, HU10 6HA.
HOOKE, Mr. Steven John, BSc ACA *1992;* Friends Provident Life Office, Pixham End, DORKING, RH4 1QA.
HOOKER, Mr. Adam Anthony, ACA *2008;* Chestnut Cottage, Manor Road, Lower Sundon, LUTON, LU3 3PA.
HOOKER, Mrs. Caroline Sarah Louise, BCom ACA *1996;* 2 Cardinals Terrace, Broad Street, ELY, CB7 4GE.
HOOKER, Mr. Christopher Stanley Frederick, BSc FCA *1976;* 1 The Willows, Highworth, SWINDON, SN6 7PG.
HOOKER, Mr. Colin John, FCA *1965;* 17 Elizabeth Drive, Theydon Bois, EPPING, ESSEX, CM16 7HJ. (Life Member)
HOOKER, Mr. Gavin Michael James, BSc ACA *1998;* 56 Beechway, Bebington, WIRRAL, MERSEYSIDE, CH63 3AZ.
HOOKER, Mr. James Alexander, ACA *2008;* 134 Hertford Road, LONDON, N1 4LP.
•**HOOKER, Miss. Lisa Jane, BA ACA** *1992;* PricewaterhouseCoopers LLP, 7 More London Riverside, LONDON, SE1 2RT. See also PricewaterhouseCoopers
HOOKER, Mr. Richard Alan, BA ACA *2006;* Royal Bank of Scotland, 250 Bishopsgate, LONDON, EC2M 4AA.
HOOKINGS, Mr. David William, MEng ACA *2011;* 3 Hathern Gardens, LONDON, SE9 3HW.
HOOKINS, Mr. Stuart John, BEng ACA CF *1999;* 1 Stonehill Close Appleton, WARRINGTON, WA4 5QD.
•**HOOKWAY, Mr. Alexander James, BSc(Econ) ACA** *2005;* with PricewaterhouseCoopers LLP, 1 Embankment Place, LONDON, WC2N 6RH.
•**HOOKWAY, Mr. Andrew Mark, BA FCA** *1989;* Menzies LLP, Ashcombe House, 5 The Crescent, LEATHERHEAD, KT22 8DY.
HOOL, Mr. Peter Howard, FCA *1969;* Flat 10, Grason, Westminster Road, POOLE, DORSET, BH13 6JQ.
HOOLE, Mr. Allan, FCA *1972;* 46 Beanfields, Worsley, MANCHESTER, M28 2GY.
HOOLE, Mrs. Andrea Dawn, ACA *1983;* 28 Cabramatta Road, MOSMAN, NSW 2088, AUSTRALIA.
HOOLE, Miss. Angela Joy, BSc ACA *1994;* 22 Rockingham Close, CHESTERFIELD, DERBYSHIRE, S40 1JE.
HOOLE, Mr. Donald, FCA *1961;* 110 Cusworth Lane, DONCASTER, DN5 8LB.
HOOLE, Mr. Robert Godlonton, FCA *1960;* 15 Amberfield Estate, Knelsby Avenue, HILLCREST, KWAZULU NATAL, 3610, SOUTH AFRICA.
HOOLE, Mr. Simon John, BA FCA *1985;* AMP Limited, Level 23, 33 Alfred Street, Circular Quay, SYDNEY, NSW 2000 AUSTRALIA.
•**HOOLEY, Mr. Blair Tyrone, BSc(Hons) ACA** *2006;* Dorset FD Limited, 25 Olga Road, DORCHESTER, DORSET, DT1 2LY.
HOOLEY, Mr. Iain William, BA ACA *2000;* Rensburg Sheppards Plc, Beech House, 61 Napier Street, SHEFFIELD, S11 8HA.
•**HOOLEY, Mr. Jonathan Grenfell, BSc FCA CTA** *1979;* Hooley Counsulting Limited, La Maison D'Aval, Rue Des Messuriers, St. Pierre Du Bois, GUERNSEY, GY7 9SL.
HOOLEY, Mr. Justin Ryan, BSc ACA *2001;* 2 Nimbin Street, North Balgowlah, SYDNEY, NSW 2093, AUSTRALIA.
HOOLEY, Mr. Peter, MSc FCA *1968;* Chatsworth House, Blakes Lane, West Horsley, LEATHERHEAD, SURREY, KT24 6EA.
HOOLEY, Mrs. Sophie Louise, MA ACA CTA *2000;* 21 Marsh House Road, Ecclesall, SHEFFIELD, S11 9SP.
HOOLEY, Mrs. Sylvia Aileen, BSc(Hons) ACA *2002;* 2 Nimbin Street, North Balgowlah, SYDNEY, NSW 2093, AUSTRALIA.
•**HOOLEY, Mr. Terence George Martin, BCom FCA** *1974;* Ernst & Young, Angwa City, cnr Julius Nyerere & Union Ave, Box 62, HARARE, ZIMBABWE.
HOOLIHAN, Mr. Simon John, ACA *2008;* (Member of Council 2007 - 2008), Apartment 83, 29 Duke Street, LIVERPOOL, L1 5AQ.
HOOLSY, Mr. Chanakya Kumar, MSc ACA *2002;* Flat 22 Gary Court, 189 London Road, CROYDON, CR0 2DR.
HOONG, Mr. Cheong Thard, BEng ACA *1992;* 5A Kennedy Heights, 10-18 Kennedy Road, MID LEVELS, HONG KONG ISLAND, HONG KONG SAR.
HOONG, Mr. Vincent, ACA *2008;* 20 St. Johns Terrace Road, REDHILL, RH1 6HS.
•**HOOPER, Mr. Alan William, FCA ATII** *1970;* (Tax Fac), Alan W Hooper FCA CTA, 21 Hartshill Close, Hillingdon, UXBRIDGE, UB10 9LH.
HOOPER, Mr. Alistair Gordon Kenneth, BA ACA *1988;* 25 Geraldine Road, Wandsworth, LONDON, SW18 2NR.
HOOPER, Miss. Anna May, BA ACA *1998;* 9 Penrhyn Avenue, PYMBLE, NSW 2073, AUSTRALIA.
HOOPER, Mr. Anthony James Patrick, BSc ACA *1990;* 33 Pound Hill, Great Brickhill, MILTON KEYNES, MK17 9AS.
HOOPER, Mr. Anthony John, FCA *1953;* 262 Widney Lane, SOLIHULL, B91 3JY. (Life Member)
HOOPER, Mr. Antony Menear, FCA *1962;* 4 Avenue Franklin Roosevelt, 92330 SCEAUX, FRANCE.
HOOPER, Miss. Carol, BSc FCA DChA *1991;* 38 Southlands Avenue, ORPINGTON, BR6 9NZ.
•**HOOPER, Mrs. Claire, BSc ACA ATII** *1997;* Ernst & Young LLP, 1 More London Place, LONDON, SE1 2AF. See also Ernst & Young Europe LLP
HOOPER, Mrs. Coralie Anne, BA ACA *1989;* Robinwood Brighton Road, Shermanbury, HORSHAM, WEST SUSSEX, RH13 8HQ.
HOOPER, Mr. David Anthony, BCom FCA *1990;* 128 Neville Road, Shirley, SOLIHULL, B90 2QX.
HOOPER, Mr. David Edwards, ACA *2010;* 17 Maunsell Park, Station Hill, CRAWLEY, WEST SUSSEX, RH10 7AD.
HOOPER, Mr. David Michael, BSc ACA *1989;* Maybank, 6 Moreland Drive, GERRARDS CROSS, SL9 8BB.
HOOPER, Mr. David Richard, BA ACA *1988;* 23 Gladstone Road, Dorridge, SOLIHULL, B93 8BX.
•**HOOPER, Mr. Derek William, FCA** *1971;* Hooper & Co (Financial Management) Ltd, 5 Marlowe Way, COLCHESTER, CO3 4JP.
•**HOOPER, Mr. Duncan George, MA FCA** *1978;* Kershen Fairfax Limited, Beacon House, 113 Kingsway, LONDON, WC2B 6PP. See also Kershen Fairfax
HOOPER, Mr. Glenn Griffin, BA FCA *1976;* Branscombe Lodge, Casthorpe Road, Barrowby, GRANTHAM, NG32 1DW.
•**HOOPER, Mr. Iain James Howard, BSc FCA** *1989;* (Tax Fac), Wedlake Bell, 52 Bedford Row, LONDON, WC1R 4LR. See also K.I.M. Business Services Ltd
HOOPER, Mr. James Andrew, BCom ACA *1995;* Apt 11 La Verbiere, Chemin des Montaney 5, 1936 VERBIER, SWITZERLAND.
HOOPER, Mr. James William, FCA *1960;* 36 Tudor Drive, Gidea Park, ROMFORD, RM2 5LH. (Life Member)
HOOPER, Mr. Jonathan George, MA MEng ACA *2001;* Eston Shire Lane, Chorleywood, RICKMANSWORTH, HERTFORDSHIRE, WD3 5NH.
HOOPER, Miss. Julie Sharon, BSc ACA *1997;* 26 Netherton Road, St. Margaret's, TWICKENHAM, MIDDLESEX, TW1 1LZ.
HOOPER, Mr. Keith Joseph, FCA *1969;* The Garden House, Upper Parish Ghyll Lane, ILKLEY, WEST YORKSHIRE, LS29 9NX.
HOOPER, Mr. Kenneth James William, FCA *1977;* 16 Wrde Hill, Highworth, SWINDON, SN6 7BX.
HOOPER, Mr. Kenneth Stanley, BCom FCA *1966;* Ashdown, 40 Princess Road, Allostock, KNUTSFORD, CHESHIRE, WA16 9LQ. (Life Member)
•**HOOPER, Miss. Kim Denise, BSc FCA MBA** *1984;* Kim D Hooper, 58 Knebworth Avenue, LONDON, E17 5AJ.
HOOPER, Miss. Lucy Rachel, BSc ACA CTA *2003;* 104 Briardale Road, Mossley Hil, LIVERPOOL, L18 1JS.
HOOPER, Mrs. Margaret, BSc ACA *1989;* 90 Dore Avenue, Portchester, FAREHAM, PO16 8DW.
•**HOOPER, Mrs. Margaret Rhiannon Price, BSc ACA** *1992;* Hooper & Co, Little Shipton, London Road, Charlton Kings, CHELTENHAM, GLOUCESTERSHIRE GL52 6UY. See also Rhiannon Hooper
HOOPER, Mr. Mark, BSc ACA *1992;* 14 Candlemas Mead, BEACONSFIELD, BUCKINGHAMSHIRE, HP9 1AP.
HOOPER, Mr. Mark Christopher, ACA *1988;* Firstsource Solutions UK Ltd, Space One, 1 Beadon Road, LONDON, W6 0EA.
HOOPER, Mr. Matthew, ACA *2011;* 13 Windbrook Meadow, Stratton St. Margaret, SWINDON, WILTSHIRE, SN3 4UA.
HOOPER, Mr. Michael David, MA FCA *1993;* Red Oaks Outings Lane, Doddinghurst, BRENTWOOD, ESSEX, CM15 0LS.
HOOPER, Mr. Michael Edmond Hugh, FCA *1969;* Box 2214, HERMANUS, 7200, SOUTH AFRICA.
HOOPER, Mr. Nicholas Mark, BSc ACA *2000;* 27b Britannia Square, WORCESTER, WR1 3DH.
HOOPER, Mr. Nigel Arthur, FCA *1977;* 3 Badgers Mount, HOCKLEY, SS5 4SA.
•**HOOPER, Mr. Nigel Philip, BA ACA** *1990;* Northline Business Consultants Ltd, 2nd Floor, Clarendon Centre, 38 Clarendon Road, Monton, Eccles MANCHESTER M30 9ES.
HOOPER, Mr. Paul, BSc ACA *1992;* Little Shipton London Road, Charlton Kings, CHELTENHAM, GLOUCESTERSHIRE, GL52 6UY.
HOOPER, Mr. Paul, ACA *1984;* Geraint Humphreys & Co Ltd, Beatrice Street, OSWESTRY, SHROPSHIRE, SY11 1QE.
HOOPER, Mr. Percy Arthur, FCA *1951;* 36 Long Lodge Drive, WALTON-ON-THAMES, KT12 3BY. (Life Member)
•①**HOOPER, Mr. Richard Anthony Jeffrey, FCA MCIArb** *1970;* Haslers, Old Station Road, LOUGHTON, ESSEX, IG10 4PL.
HOOPER, Mr. Richard Minard, BA ACA *1997;* with Deloitte LLP, Athene Place, 66 Shoe Lane, LONDON, EC4A 3BQ.
HOOPER, Mr. Richard Paul, MA ACA *1988;* PO Box 57046, NAIROBI, 00100, KENYA.
HOOPER, Mr. Robert Chalders, BA FCA *1978;* 23 Ter Rue Labelonye, 78400 CHATOU, FRANCE.
HOOPER, Mrs. Ruth Joyce, BA ACA *1999;* 31 Hicks Common Road, Winterbourne, BRISTOL, BS36 1EH.
HOOPER, Miss. Siobhan, ACA *2010;* 20 Biddick Lane, WASHINGTON, TYNE AND WEAR, NE38 8AE.
HOOPER, Mr. Stuart Adrian, BSc ACA *1981;* 34B Downs Park West, BRISTOL, BS6 7QL.
HOOPER, Mrs. Susan Jane, BSc ACA *1990;* Westlakes Engineering Ltd, Galemire Court, Westlakes Science Park, MOOR ROW, CUMBRIA, CA24 3HY.
HOOPER, Mr. Thomas Matthew, ACA *2009;* with Moore Stephens LLP, 150 Aldersgate Street, LONDON, EC1A 4AB.
HOOPER, Mrs. Tina Jane, BSc ACA *2003;* Johnson Matthey, Gate 2, Orchard Road, ROYSTON, HERTFORDSHIRE, SG8 5HE.

HOOPER-SMITH, Mrs. Emma Jane Louise, MA FCA *1992;* Lullington Court, Coton Road, Lullington, SWADLINCOTE, DERBYSHIRE, DE12 8EJ.
HOOPER-SMITH, Mr. Peter Leslie, BCom ACA MBA *1995;* Grangewood Lea, Lodge Road, Netherseal, SWADLINCOTE, DERBYSHIRE, DE12 8AT.
HOOSANG, Mr. Gilbert Washington, FCA *1975;* 10/F, Chun Wo Commercial Centre, 23-29 Wing Wo Street, CENTRAL, HONG KONG ISLAND, HONG KONG SAR. (Life Member)
•HOOSE, Mr. David Ronald, BA FCA *1994;* with RSM Tenon Audit Limited, The Poynt, 45 Wollaton Street, NOTTINGHAM, NG1 5FW.
HOOSON, Mr. Craig Andrew, BSc ACA *1987;* 41991 Nibuck Road, TEMECULA, CA 92591, UNITED STATES.
HOOSON, Mr. Neil Edward, BA ACA *2000;* Netherwood, 18 Willow Court, Pool in Wharfedale, OTLEY, WEST YORKSHIRE, LS21 1RX.
HOOTMAN, Mr. Jonathan Robert, BEng ACA *1997;* 72a-72b New Church Road, HOVE, EAST SUSSEX, BN3 4FN.
HOOTON, Mr. Graham Marcel, FCA *1969;* 84 Thoresby Road, Bramcote, NOTTINGHAM, NG9 3EP.
HOOTON, Mr. Ian Arthur, MEng ACA *2006;* 64 Discovery Walk, LONDON, E1W 2JG.
HOOTON, Mr. John Edward, FCA *1967;* Kinnoull, Derby Road, MANSFIELD, NOTTINGHAMSHIRE, NG18 5BJ.
HOOTON, Mr. John Nicholas, BA ACA *2003;* 55 Walcot Square, LONDON, SE11 4UB.
HOOTON, Ms. Maria, ACA *1998;* Sellars Brook, Spring Lane, Burwash, ETCHINGHAM, EAST SUSSEX, TN19 7HU.
HOOTON, Mr. Mark Anthony, BSc ACA *2007;* Gentoo Fund Services Limited, Western Suite Ground Floor, Mill Court, La Charroterie, St. Peter Port, GUERNSEY GY1 1EJ.
•HOOTON, Mr. Mark Frederick, BEng ACA *1992;* (Tax Fac), Mark Hooton, 2 Butlers Close, Lockerley, ROMSEY, HAMPSHIRE, SO51 0LY.
•HOOTON, Mr. Neil Edward, BA ACA CF *1997;* Neil Hooton Accountancy Services Limited, Suite 36 The Studio, Nortex Business Centre, 105 Chorley Old Road, BOLTON, BL1 3AS.
HOOTON, Mr. Nicholas Paul Michael, MA FCA *1986;* Pastures Farm, Hammersley Lane, Penn, HIGH WYCOMBE, HP10 8HE.
HOPCRAFT, Mr. David, FCA *1963;* 9 Victoria, LOSTWITHIEL, PL22 0AX. (Life Member)
•HOPCRAFT, Mrs. Leonie, ACA *2005;* Leonie Hopcraft, The Old Cornershop, The Green, Everdon, DAVENTRY, NORTHAMPTONSHIRE NN11 3BL.
HOPCROFT, Mrs. Judith Mary, BSc ACA *1988;* 3 High Street, Ivinghoe, LEIGHTON BUZZARD, BEDFORDSHIRE, LU7 9EP.
HOPCROFT, Mr. Martin Peter, BSc ACA *1986;* 3 High Street, Ivinghoe, LEIGHTON BUZZARD, BEDFORDSHIRE, LU7 9EP.
•HOPCROFT, Mr. Terence Vivian, BSc FCA *1978;* PricewaterhouseCoopers LLP, The Atrium, 1 Harefield Road, UXBRIDGE, UB8 1EX. See also PricewaterhouseCoopers
HOPCYN-KITCHENER, Mr. Dafydd, ACA *2011;* 24 Rackfield, HASLEMERE, GU27 1NA.
HOPE, Mr. Alan Martin, FCA *1975;* Carrickhill, Breaffy, CASTLEBAR, COUNTY MAYO, IRELAND.
HOPE, Dr. Andrew John, BSc FCA *2001;* 61-63 King Street, Potton, SANDY, BEDFORDSHIRE, SG19 2QZ.
HOPE, Mr. Barry Paul, BSc ACA *1994;* 118 Lodge Hill Road, Selly Oak, BIRMINGHAM, B29 6NG.
HOPE, Mr. Brian, FCA *1959;* 46 Spring Lane, Sprotborough, DONCASTER, DN5 7QG. (Life Member)
•HOPE, Mr. Christopher Ian, BSc FCA *1975;* Chris Hope, Roselea, 82 Cleveland Avenue, DARLINGTON, DL3 7BE.
HOPE, Mr. Christopher John, BSc FCA *1962;* Maple House, Drivers Lane, Little Compton, MORETON-IN-MARSH, GL56 0SF.
HOPE, Mr. David, BA(Hons) ACA *2002;* 5 Britton Avenue, ST. ALBANS, HERTFORDSHIRE, AL3 5EJ.
•HOPE, Mr. David Alan, BSc FCA *1985;* (Tax Fac), Clear & Lane, 340 Melton Road, LEICESTER, LE4 7SL.
HOPE, Mr. David Anthony, FCA *1963;* Ramsaustrasse 97, A5324 RAMSAU, AUSTRIA.
HOPE, Mr. David Clifford, BA ACA *1980;* Aecom Ltd, One Trinity Gardens, Broad Chare, NEWCASTLE UPON TYNE, NE1 2HF.
HOPE, Mr. David Ian, FCA *1973;* 9 Evesham Road, Middleton, MANCHESTER, M24 1PS.
HOPE, Mr. David John, FCA *1984;* Fairly, Midford, BATH, BA2 7BY.
•HOPE, Mrs. Fiona Barclay, FCA *1986;* 4th Floor, 26 Mount Row, LONDON, W1K 3SQ.
HOPE, Mrs. Helen Adele, BSc ACA *1995;* 11 Beverley Park, WHITLEY BAY, TYNE AND WEAR, NE25 8JL.
HOPE, Ms. Helen Catherine, MA ACA *1997;* Scheldestraat 31, 1078GE AMSTERDAM, NETHERLANDS.
•HOPE, Mr. Jamie Richard, BEng ACA CF *1999;* Catalyst Corporate Finance LLP, 9th Floor, Bank House, 8 Cherry Street, BIRMINGHAM, B2 5AL.
HOPE, Mr. Jeremy Leigh, BSc ACA *1989;* 1 Abbey Lane, Darley Abbey, DERBY, DE22 1DG.
HOPE, Mr. Laurence, FCA *1963;* 14 Moyleen Rise, MARLOW, SL7 2DP. (Life Member)
HOPE, Mr. Lee Edward, BA ACA *1996;* 36 Wandle Road, LONDON, SW17 7DW.
HOPE, Mrs. Madeleine Louise, MEng BA ACA *2005;* with Deloitte LLP, One Trinity Gardens, Broad Chare, NEWCASTLE UPON TYNE, NE1 2HF.
HOPE, Mr. Mark Andrew, BA ACA *1992;* 2 The Haven, Hale, ALTRINCHAM, CHESHIRE, WA15 8SA.
HOPE, Mr. Michael Graham, MSc ACA *2005;* with PricewaterhouseCoopers LLP, 101 Barbirolli Square, Lower Mosley Street, MANCHESTER, M2 3PW.
HOPE, Mr. Paul Stephen, BA ACA *2005;* One Snow Hill, Snow Hill Queensway, BIRMINGHAM, B4 6GH.
•HOPE, Miss. Penelope Fiona, BSc ACA *1990;* P.F.Hope, 17 Agatha Gardens, Fernhill Heath, WORCESTER, WR3 8PB.
HOPE, Mr. Philip Robert, BA ACA *2007;* 12 Willoughby Drive, WHITLEY BAY, NE26 3DY.
HOPE, Mr. Richard Andrew, BSc FCA *1992;* Treatt Plc, Northern Way, BURY ST. EDMUNDS, SUFFOLK, IP32 6NL.
HOPE, Mr. Richard John, FCA *1971;* 13 Days Green, Capel St. Mary, IPSWICH, IP9 2HZ.
HOPE, Mr. Roger Francis, FCA *1972;* THE VENN, 152 High Street, Chapmanslade, WESTBURY, BA13 4AP.
HOPE, Mr. Roger George, FCA *1972;* Makefeyres Barn, Roughway, TONBRIDGE, TN11 9SN.
HOPE, Mr. Simon Richard, BA ACA AMCT *1994;* 4 Whitefields Gate, SOLIHULL, B91 3GE.
HOPE, Mr. Stephen George, FCA *1970;* Quadrant Visual Solutions Ltd, Unit 1, Hawthorne Road, Castle Donington, DERBY, DE74 2QR.
HOPE, Ms. Susan Jane, BSc ACA *1992;* 36 Birchington Road, LONDON, N8 8HP.
HOPE, Mr. Terence William, ACA *1986;* 8 Crawshaw Avenue, BEVERLEY, NORTH HUMBERSIDE, HU17 7QW.
HOPE, Mr. Thomas Andrew, FCA *1972;* 45 Bawnmore Road, RUGBY, WARWICKSHIRE, CV22 7QJ. (Life Member)
•HOPE, Mr. Timothy Stuart, FCA *1981;* (Tax Fac), T.S. Hope & Co., 56a Bury Road, Edenfield, Ramsbottom, BURY, LANCASHIRE BL0 0ET.
HOPE, Mr. William Arthur, FCA *1970;* Bois Cottage, Bridle Lane, Loudwater, RICKMANSWORTH, WD3 4JA.
HOPE-BELL, Mr. Joel Francis, BSc ACA *1999;* Merrill Lynch Financial Centre, 2 King Edward Street, LONDON, EC1A 1HQ.
HOPES, Mr. Clifford Byles, FCA *1956;* 14 Westbourne Avenue, HARROGATE, HG2 9BD. (Life Member)
•HOPES, Mr. Nigel David, BA FCA *1978;* PricewaterhouseCoopers LLP, The Atrium, 1 Harefield Road, UXBRIDGE, UB8 1EX. See also PricewaterhouseCoopers
•HOPES, Mr. Richard David Ernest, FCA *1980;* Alliotts, Friary Court, 13-21 High Street, GUILDFORD, SURREY, GU1 3DL.
•HOPES, Mr. Richard James, FCA *1973;* (Tax Fac), Richard Hopes Limited, Bell House, Ashford Hill, THATCHAM, BERKSHIRE, RG19 8BB.
HOPES, Mr. Terence Jon, BA FCA *1969;* (Tax Fac), 32 Queens Gate, Stoke Bishop, BRISTOL, BS9 1TZ.
HOPEWELL, Mr. David John, BA FCA *1976;* 7 Oakwood Drive, Prestbury, MACCLESFIELD, CHESHIRE, SK10 4HG.
HOPEWELL, Mr. Jason Paul, BEng ACA *1999;* 31 Gilbert Scott Gardens, Gawcott, BUCKINGHAM, MK18 4JQ.
HOPEWELL, The Revd. Jeffery Stewart, BA ACA *1979;* The Vicarage, Church Lane, Old Dalby, MELTON MOWBRAY, LEICESTERSHIRE, LE14 3LB.
HOPEWELL, Mr. Robert Michael, BSc(Econ) ACA *1998;* 2 Wensleydale Close, NOTTINGHAM, NG8 5FY.
HOPGOOD, Mr. Darren Nigel, ACA MAAT *2003;* 36 Queens Road, THAMES DITTON, SURREY, KT7 0QX.
HOPKIN, Mr. Adam Henry, BSc(Hons) ACA *2003;* Century House, 16 Par la Ville Road, HAMILTON HM08, BERMUDA.
•HOPKIN, Mr. Michael Alan, FCA *1968;* PricewaterhouseCoopers, Rua da Candelaria 65, 20091-020 RIO DE JANEIRO, BRAZIL.
•HOPKIN, Mr. Nicholas, FCA *1979;* PricewaterhouseCoopers LLP, 1 Embankment Place, LONDON, WC2N 6RH. See also PricewaterhouseCoopers
HOPKIN, Mr. Nigel William, MA ACA *1984;* Milton Gate, 60 Chiswell Street, LONDON, EC1Y 4SA.
HOPKIN, Mr. Richard, BA FCA *1981;* 37 The Meadows, Friendly, SOWERBY BRIDGE, WEST YORKSHIRE, HX6 2UN.
HOPKIN, Mr. Richard Sandy, FCA *1969;* 166 Melton Road, West Bridgford, NOTTINGHAM, NG2 6FJ.
HOPKINS, Mr. Adam Charles, BA ACA *1992;* C Mitchinson & Co, 22 Market Place, KENDAL, CUMBRIA, LA9 4TN.
HOPKINS, Mr. Anthony Brian, FCA *1973;* Central Park, 2nd floor, Candie Road, St. Peter Port, GUERNSEY, GY1 1UQ.
HOPKINS, Mr. Anthony Keith Frank, FCA *1978;* Praesta Partners LLP, 5th Floor, Berger House, 38 Berkeley Square, LONDON, W1J 5AH.
HOPKINS, Mr. Anthony Strother, CBE BSc FCA *1966;* 19 Ranfurly Avenue, BANGOR, COUNTY DOWN, BT20 3SN.
HOPKINS, Mr. Antony John, BA ACA *1987;* Broomleaf Cottage, Church Lane, Ewshot, FARNHAM, GU10 5BD.
HOPKINS, Mr. Brendon, BSc FCA *1991;* (Tax Fac), Standard Chartered Bank, 1 Basinghall Avenue, LONDON, EC2V 5DD.
HOPKINS, Mr. Brian Wynford, BA FCA *1982;* 40 Plas Sr Pol de Leon, Portway Marina, PENARTH, CF64 1TR.
HOPKINS, Mr. Christopher Luke, BA ACA *2011;* Pricewaterhousecoopers, 89 Sandyford Road, NEWCASTLE UPON TYNE, NE1 8HW.
HOPKINS, Ms. Clare Louise, BA(Hons) ACA *2002;* 28 Thirlestane, Lemsford Road, ST. ALBANS, HERTFORDSHIRE, AL1 3PE.
HOPKINS, Mr. Colin, ACA *1989;* 74 Fallbrook Drive, West Derby, LIVERPOOL, L12 5NA.
HOPKINS, Mr. Colin, BA(Hons) ACA *2011;* 195 Crownfield Road, Leyton, LONDON, E15 2AS.
HOPKINS, Mr. Darren Mathew, BSc ACA *2005;* Flat E, 26 Goldhurst Terrace, LONDON, NW6 3HU.
HOPKINS, Mr. David, BA FCA *1975;* Flat 9 Heaton Gardens, 25 Heaton Moor Road, STOCKPORT, CHESHIRE, SK4 4LT.
•HOPKINS, Mr. David Armstrong, BSc FCA *1977;* D.A. Hopkins, 7 King Street, WREXHAM, LL11 1HF.
HOPKINS, Mr. David James, ACA *2009;* 20 Greenacres Drive, HALIFAX, WEST YORKSHIRE, HX3 7QS.
HOPKINS, Mr. David John, FCA *2011;* Ireland 1988); Baker Tilly Channel Islands Limited, PO Box 437, 13 Castle Street, St Helier, JERSEY, JE4 0ZE. See also Osiris Management Services Limited
HOPKINS, Mr. David Mathew, BA ACA *2005;* Basement flat, 40 Cheniston Gardens, LONDON, W8 6TH.
HOPKINS, Mr. Geoffrey Douty Borrough, FCA *1951;* 9 Roland Gardens, LONDON, SW7 3PE. (Life Member)
HOPKINS, Mr. George William, FCA *1952;* 5 Clonard Way, Hatch End, PINNER, HA5 4BT. (Life Member)
•HOPKINS, Mr. Jacques, BSc FCA FCIS FCMI *1973;* Innisbrook Equity Group, 6350 Lake Oconee Pkwy, Ste 102, Pmb 139, GREENSBORO, GA 30642 UNITED STATES.
HOPKINS, Miss. Jenny, BA ACA CF *2005;* with Grant Thornton UK LLP, 1 Whitehall Riverside, Whitehall Road, LEEDS, WEST YORKSHIRE, LS1 4BN.
HOPKINS, Mr. John David, BSc ACA *1994;* 11 Lubbock Road, CHISLEHURST, BR7 5JG.
HOPKINS, Mr. John Douglas, FCA *1964;* 3 Kingsway, Killams Park, TAUNTON, TA1 3YD.
•HOPKINS, Mr. John Froggatt Barry, BA(Econ) FCA MSI *1963;* Hopkins Allen Procter Limited, 4th Floor, St James House, Vicar Lane, SHEFFIELD, S1 2EX.
HOPKINS, Mr. John James, MEng ACA *1995;* 8 Birch Grove, Kingswood, TADWORTH, KT20 6QU.
HOPKINS, Mr. John Robert, ACA *2008;* Green 1, National Audit Office, 157-197 Buckingham Palace Road, LONDON, SW1W 9SP.
•HOPKINS, Mrs. Julie, BA FCA *1991;* (Tax Fac), Albert Goodman LLP, Hendford Manor, YEOVIL, BA20 1UN.
•HOPKINS, Mr. Keith, FCA TEP *1977;* EQ Accountants LLP, Westby, 64 West High Street, FORFAR, ANGUS, DD8 1BJ.
HOPKINS, Mr. Leon John, FCA *1967;* 104 Birchwood Road, Wilmington, DARTFORD, DA2 7HG.
HOPKINS, Mr. Leonard John, BSc FCA *1976;* 35 Highfield Avenue, BENFLEET, ESSEX, SS7 1RY. (Life Member)
HOPKINS, Mr. Leslie Brian, FCA *1971;* 11 Shawfield Avenue, HOLMFIRTH, West Yorkshire, HD9 2LZ.
HOPKINS, Mr. Lyn Dyer, MBA FCA *1977;* Vincent House, 5 Pembridge Square, LONDON, W2 4EG.
HOPKINS, Miss. Lynn Barbara, FCA *1974;* 123 Maplewell Road, Woodhouse Eaves, LOUGHBOROUGH, LE12 8QY.
HOPKINS, Mr. Mark David, BSc ACA *1994;* 61 Norwich Close, LICHFIELD, WS13 7SJ.
•HOPKINS, Mr. Martin Peter, FCA *1981;* (Tax Fac), Hopkins & Hopkins Limited, 8 The Square, Aspley Guise, MILTON KEYNES, MK17 8DG.
•HOPKINS, Miss. Mary Elizabeth, FCA *1984;* (Tax Fac), 4 Durcott Gardens, EVESHAM, WORCESTERSHIRE, WR11 1ET.
HOPKINS, Mr. Matthew, BA(Hons) ACA *2003;* Flat 13 Chelsea Reach Tower, World's End Estate, LONDON, SW10 0EG.
HOPKINS, Mr. Michael Anthony, FCA *1967;* 2 Carlton Drive, Guiseley, LEEDS, LS20 9NQ.
HOPKINS, Mr. Neil Allen, LLB ACA *1990;* 30 Connaught Road, TEDDINGTON, MIDDLESEX, TW11 0PS.
HOPKINS, Mr. Neil Muir, BA ACA *1987;* 9 Inverary Avenue, Epsom, AUCKLAND, NEW ZEALAND.
HOPKINS, Mr. Neil Thomas, FCA *1970;* 1 Brackley Road, Chiswick, LONDON, W4 2HW.
HOPKINS, Mr. Neville Hearne, FCA *1972;* Little Oaks, Stanville Road, OXFORD, OX2 9JF.
•HOPKINS, Mr. Nicholas Lee, ACA *1995;* (Tax Fac), The Hopkins Partnership, 1 South Newton Trading Estate, Warminster Road, South Newton, SALISBURY, SP2 0QW.
HOPKINS, Miss. Nicola Rosemary Lucy, BSc ACA *1997;* 15 Perpetual House, Station Road, HENLEY-ON-THAMES, OXFORDSHIRE, RG9 1AF.
HOPKINS, Mr. Nigel Keith, BSc ACA *1983;* 31 Little Bookham Street, Little Bookham, LEATHERHEAD, KT23 3AA.
HOPKINS, Mr. Nigel Peter, BA FCA *1982;* 18 Kings Road, ST. ALBANS, HERTFORDSHIRE, AL3 4TG.
HOPKINS, Mr. Paul Malcolm, BA ACA *1984;* 30 Hainthorpe Road, West Norwood, LONDON, SE27 0PH.
HOPKINS, Mrs. Peng Yien Lilian, BA ACA *1989;* 547-D Jalan Wee Hein Tze, 11200, Tanjung Bungah, PENANG, MALAYSIA.
HOPKINS, Mr. Philip Graham, BA ACA *1993;* 4 Portway, STEYNING, WEST SUSSEX, BN44 3QF.
•HOPKINS, Mr. Richard Arthur, BA FCA CF *1978;* Mazars LLP, 37 Frederick Place, BRIGHTON, BN1 4EA.
HOPKINS, Mr. Robert Alan, ACA *2008;* with Zolfo Cooper LLP, Toronto Square, Toronto Street, LEEDS, LS1 2HJ.
HOPKINS, Mr. Robert David Moreland, BA(Hons) ACA *2001;* 26 Bankside Road, BOURNEMOUTH, BH9 3EF.
HOPKINS, The Revd. Robert James Gardner, BSc FCA *1976;* 70 St. Thomas Road, Crookes, SHEFFIELD, S10 1UX.
HOPKINS, Mr. Robert John, BSc FCA *1974;* Flat 1 Selwyn House, 29 Selwyn Road, EASTBOURNE, EAST SUSSEX, BN21 2LF.
HOPKINS, Mr. Robin Derek, BA ACA *2004;* 14 Station Road, BRAINTREE, ESSEX, CM7 3QJ.
HOPKINS, Mr. Roger Carlyle, FCA *1974;* Green Meadows, Longfield Road, TRING, HERTFORDSHIRE, HP23 4DF. (Life Member)
•HOPKINS, Mr. Roger David, BSc FCA *1976;* (Tax Fac), Roger Hopkins, 18 Princes Street, NORWICH, NR3 1AE.
HOPKINS, Mrs. Sarah Victoria Carmen, BA ACA *1995;* Flat 14 Tudor Court, West Street, WARWICK, CV34 6AJ.
HOPKINS, Mr. Simon David William, MA ACA *1989;* British Heart Foundation Greater London House, Hampstead Road, LONDON, NW1 7AW.
•HOPKINS, Mr. Simon James, BA ACA ATII *1990;* 44 Clerkenwell Close, LONDON, EC1R 0AZ.
HOPKINS, Mr. Stephen David, BSc ACA *2003;* 18 Cunard Avenue, Shirley, SOUTHAMPTON, SO15 5GP.
HOPKINS, Mr. Steven John, BSc FCA *1981;* Joseph Ash Ltd, Alcora Building, Mucklow Hill, HALESOWEN, WEST MIDLANDS, B62 8DG.
HOPKINS, Miss. Suzanne Elizabeth, ACA *2011;* 5 Avenue Close, LIPHOOK, GU30 7QE.
HOPKINS, Mr. Thomas Edward, ACA *2004;* with Deloitte LLP, 2 New Street Square, LONDON, EC4A 3BZ.
HOPKINS, Mr. Thomas William, MA ACA MBA *2003;* 119 Coningham Road, LONDON, W12 8BU.

•**HOPKINS, Mr. Timothy Price, BA ACA** *1982;* Cross & Bowen, 11 Calvert Terrace, SWANSEA, SA1 6AT.
HOPKINS, Mr. Tom Gwyn, BSc(Hons) ACA *2010;* 50 Princes Avenue, WATFORD, WD18 7RS.
HOPKINS, Mr. Wyn Ieuan, BSc ACA *2001;* 22 Macquarie Avenue, PADBURY, WA 6025, AUSTRALIA.
HOPKINS-BURTON, Mr. Richard, MA BSc ACA *2011;* (Member of Council 2009 - 2011), Deloitte Llp, 4 Brindley Place, BIRMINGHAM, B1 2HZ.
HOPKINS-COMAN, Mr. Neil, MA FCA *1987;* 57 Allison Bank, Geoffrey Watling Way, NORWICH, NR1 1GW.
HOPKINS-POWELL, Mrs. Tamsin Melanie, BA ACA *1995;* 1 Southside Common, Wimbledon, LONDON, SW19 4TG.
HOPKINSON, Mrs. Alison, BCom ACA *1985;* The Pheasantry, Henley Road, Medmenham, MARLOW, SL7 2EU.
HOPKINSON, Mr. Andrew James, ACA *2011;* 59 Holst Crescent, Old Farm Park, MILTON KEYNES, MK7 8QN.
HOPKINSON, Mr. Arthur Morton, MA FCA *1960;* Tinnacouse, Skeoughvasteen, KILKENNY, COUNTY KILKENNY, IRELAND.
HOPKINSON, Mr. Arthur Vincent, FCA *1948;* Pantiles Weald Way, CATERHAM, CR3 6EL. (Life Member)
•**HOPKINSON, Mr. Christopher John, FCA** *1971;* (Tax Fac), Mabe Allen LLP, 3 Derby Road, RIPLEY, DERBYSHIRE, DE5 3EA.
HOPKINSON, Mr. Christopher Neil, MA ACA *1994;* 39 Timber Lane, Woburn, MILTON KEYNES, MK17 9PL.
HOPKINSON, Mr. Gareth, BSc ACA *2008;* 130 Snape Hill Crescent, DRONFIELD, DERBYSHIRE, S18 2DR.
HOPKINSON, Mr. Graham Douglas, FCA *1950;* 17 Antringham Gardens, Edgbaston, BIRMINGHAM, B15 3QL. (Life Member)
HOPKINSON, Mr. Ian Michael, BA ACA *1983;* 1 Westfield, Hyde Heath, AMERSHAM, BUCKINGHAMSHIRE, HP6 5RE.
•**HOPKINSON, Mr. Jeremy Stephen Frederick, FCA** *1966;* (Tax Fac), Jeremy Hopkinson & Co, 12 Heath Road, Great Brickhill, MILTON KEYNES, MK17 9AL.
HOPKINSON, Miss. Linda Carrie, BA ACA *1993;* 10 Riverside, 317 Southend Lane, LONDON, SE6 3NF.
HOPKINSON, Miss. Lorna, BSc ACA *2010;* Flat 1 Aston Court, 18 Lansdowne Road, LONDON, SW20 8AW.
•**HOPKINSON, Mrs. Nicola Gillian, BA ACA** *1984;* Nicola Hopkinson, 23 Leyborne Park, Kew, RICHMOND, SURREY, TW9 3HB.
HOPKINSON, Mr. Paul, BSc FCA *1987;* 120 Headland Road, NORTH CURL CURL, NSW 2099, AUSTRALIA.
HOPKINSON, Mr. Paul Martin, FCA *1983;* 17 Aspen Grove, Northowram, HALIFAX, WEST YORKSHIRE, HX3 7WN.
HOPKINSON, Mr. Richard John, FCA *1979;* 2 Stanley Street, Black Rock, MELBOURNE, VIC 3193, AUSTRALIA.
HOPKINSON, Miss. Ruth Elaine, ACA *2008;* DMGT Plc, Northcliffe House, 2 Derry Street, LONDON, W8 5TT.
HOPKINSON, Mr. Thomas Duncan, FCA *1979;* E D R Financial Management, Bank House, Sawley Road, Sawley, CLITHEROE, LANCASHIRE BB7 4RS.
HOPLA, Mr. Daryl Broderick, BSc ACA *1998;* Carisbrooke 16 St. Annes Terrace, Tower Road St. Helier, JERSEY, JE2 3HU.
HOPPE, Mr. Andrew Finley, BSc ACA *1984;* Rowecord Engineering Ltd, Neptune Works, Usk Way, NEWPORT, NP20 2SS.
HOPPE, Mr. David Mark, MA ACA *1990;* Monitor, 4 Matthew Parker Street, LONDON, SW1H 9NP.
HOPPER, Mr. Benjamin Alan, ACA *2010;* 61 Sideley, Kegworth, DERBY, DE74 2FJ.
HOPPER, Mr. Christopher, ACA *2011;* 17b Norfolk Square, BRIGHTON, BN1 2PB.
HOPPER, Mrs. Elizabeth Jane, JP BA ACA *1991;* 7A Borneo Street, LONDON, SW15 1QQ.
HOPPER, Mr. Geoffrey, FCA *1968;* with Baines Jewitt, Barrington House, 41-45 Yarm Lane, STOCKTON-ON-TEES, CLEVELAND, TS18 3EA.
HOPPER, Mrs. Jane Anne, BSc(Econ) ACA *2002;* 27 Alexandra Gardens, Knaphill, WOKING, SURREY, GU21 2DG.
•**HOPPER, Mr. Kevin Stuart, ACA** *2004;* Forrester Boyd, 26 South Saint Mary's Gate, GRIMSBY, NORTH LINCOLNSHIRE, DN31 1LW.
HOPPER, Mr. Michael Arthur, FCA *1966;* 25 Sir Christopher Court, Hythe, SOUTHAMPTON, SO45 6JR.
•**HOPPER, Mr. Paul Winfield, MA FCA** *1981;* (Tax Fac), Littlejohn LLP, 1 Westferry Circus, Canary Wharf, LONDON, E14 4HD.
•**HOPPER, Mr. Richard Frederick, BSc FCA** *1981;* Richard F. Hopper, Chinthurst, 30 St. Stephens Hill, LAUNCESTON, CORNWALL, PL15 8HN.
•**HOPPER, Mr. Richard James, BSc FCA** *1996;* with Chavereys, Mall House, The Mall, FAVERSHAM, KENT, ME13 8JL.
HOPPINS, Mr. Richard Alan Kelsey, FCA *1968;* Sycamore Cottage, 5 Village Road, West Kirby, WIRRAL, MERSEYSIDE, CH48 3JN.
HOPPS, Mr. David, BA ACA *1993;* Flat 4, Portland Gate, Brodrick Court, LEEDS, LS1 3HL.
HOPPS, Mr. Michael Antony, ACA *1992;* 36A Woodholm Road, SHEFFIELD, S11 9HT.
•**HOPSON, Mr. Edward, FCA** *1970;* E Hopson Ltd, Red Roof Cottage, 27 Sands Lane, Barmston, DRIFFIELD, NORTH HUMBERSIDE YO25 8PQ.
•**HOPSON, Mr. Keith, FCA** *1968;* Findlay Wetherfield Scott & Co, 135/137 Station Road, Chingford, LONDON, E4 6AG.
HOPSON, Mr. Martin, BSc FCA MBA *1992;* Entrepreneurs Fund Management Services Standbrook House, 2-5 Old Bond Street, LONDON, W1S 4PD.
HOPTON, Mrs. Joanna Catherine, BA ACA *1996;* 19 Hereford Way, MIDDLEWICH, CW10 9GS.
HOPTON, Mr. Mark Alan, BA ACA *1992;* 19 Hereford Way, MIDDLEWICH, CW10 9GS.
•ⒹHOPTON, Mr. Mark Timothy, FCA *1979;* KPMG LLP, One Snowhill, Snow Hill Queensway, BIRMINGHAM, B4 6GN. See also KPMG Europe LLP
HOPTON, Miss. Michelle Jayne, ACA *2005;* with Deloitte LLP, 3 Rivergate, Temple Quay, BRISTOL, BS1 6GD.
HOPWELL, Mrs. Melanie Ingrid, BA ACA *2010;* 531 Tamworth Road, Long Eaton, NOTTINGHAM, NG10 3FB.
•**HOPWOOD, Mr. Andrew Michael, BSc(Hons) FCA** *2001;* Champion Accountants LLP, Refuge House, 33-37 Watergate Row South, CHESTER, CH1 2LE. See also Champion Allwoods Limited
HOPWOOD, Mrs. Angela Louise, LLB ACA *1992;* Badgers Walk, Park Lane, Lapley, STAFFORD, ST19 9JT.
HOPWOOD, Mr. Campbell, FCA *1950;* 11 Plas Garnedd Residential Home, Ffordd Penmynydd, LLANFAIRPWLLGWYNGYLL, GWYNEDD, LL61 5EX. (Life Member)
HOPWOOD, Miss. Caroline, BSc ACA *1993;* 23 Holmfield Road, LEICESTER, LE2 1SE.
HOPWOOD, Mr. Craig William, BSc ACA *1997;* Northstar Equity Investors, Calls Wharf, 2 The Calls, LEEDS, LS2 7JU.
HOPWOOD, Miss. Emma Marguerite, BSc(Econ) ACA *2000;* 59 Tresco Road, LONDON, SE15 3PY.
•**HOPWOOD, Mr. Geoffrey Thomas, BCom ACA** *1990;* (Tax Fac), HW, Keepers Lane, The Wergs, WOLVERHAMPTON, WEST MIDLANDS, WV6 8UA. See also HW Transaction Services LLP and Haines Watts
HOPWOOD, Mrs. Julie Amanda, BA(Hons) ACA *2001;* 6 Rose Farm Meadows, Altofts, NORMANTON, WEST YORKSHIRE, WF6 2HY.
HOPWOOD, Mr. Michael Andrew, BSc ACA *1990;* 4 Stoney End, Mattishall, DEREHAM, NR20 3RY.
HOPWOOD, Mr. Paul, FCA *1984;* 9 The Driveway, SHOREHAM-BY-SEA, BN43 5GG.
HOPWOOD, Mr. Paul Andrew, MEng ACA *2003;* Ground Floor Flat, 2 Edith Villas Bective Road, LONDON, SW15 2QA.
HOPWOOD, Mrs. Rachel Jill, BA ACA *1995;* 3 Smithy Court, Clotton, TARPORLEY, CHESHIRE, CW6 0HU.
HOPWOOD, Mrs. Rekha, BA ACA *1992;* The Old Smithy, Woodplumpton Road, Woodplumpton, PRESTON, PR4 0NE.
HOPWOOD, Mr. Stuart Ernest, FCA *1971;* 22 Sutherland Drive, Westlands, NEWCASTLE, ST5 3NB.
HOPWOOD, Mrs. Sylvia Jean, BSc ACA *1990;* Langley Park, Chedgrave, NORWICH, NR14 6BJ.
HOPWOOD-BELL, Mrs. Gillian Valerie, BSc ACA *2009;* K P M G, St. James's Square, MANCHESTER, M2 6DS.
HOQUE, Mr. Fozlul, ACA *2011;* 1 Clarence Road, LONDON, E12 5BB.
HORAK, Mrs. Nicolette, BSc(Hons) ACA *2002;* 35 Mango Avenue, EIMEO, QLD 4740, AUSTRALIA.
HORAN, Mr. James Mark, ACA *2003;* 5 Hinton Street, Splott, CARDIFF, CF24 2EU.
HORAN, Mr. Neil Kevin James, BA(Econ) ACA *2006;* MCR, 35 Newhall Street, BIRMINGHAM, B3 3PU.
HORBURY, Mrs. Sara Lisabeth, BA ACA *1994;* 6 Leadhall Way, HARROGATE, NORTH YORKSHIRE, HG2 9PG.
HORCHLER-TALJAARD, Mrs. Niki Margaret, BSc ACA *1990;* 59 Crescent West, Hadley Wood, BARNET, EN4 0EQ.
•**HORDER, Mr. Charles, FCA** *1983;* (Tax Fac), Everett Horder Limited, 35 Paul Street, LONDON, EC2A 4UQ.
•**HORDER, Mr. Nigel Ian, FCA** *1971;* (Tax Fac), Horder Adey, 13 Princeton Court, 53-55 Felsham Road, Putney, LONDON, SW15 1AZ.
HORDERN, Mr. Anthony Christopher Shubra, FCA *1959;* (Member of Council 1985 - 1994), 7 Bridge Street, PERSHORE, WORCESTERSHIRE, WR10 1AJ. (Life Member)
HORDERN, Mr. John Philip Sebastian, FCA *1977;* (Tax Fac), 2B Alma Road, ORPINGTON, BR5 4PT.
HORDERN, Mrs. Sarah, BA ACA *1998;* Newbury Racecourse Plc, Newbury Racecourse, NEWBURY, BERKSHIRE, RG14 7NZ.
HORDLE, Mr. Jeffrey Gordon, FCA *1959;* The Coach House, Pembroke Vale, Clifton, BRISTOL, BS8 3DN. (Life Member)
HORE, Mr. Arthur Reginald, FCA *1938;* 2 Maidens Close, Dussindale, Thorpe St Andrew, NORWICH, NR7 0RS. (Life Member)
HORE, Mr. Joseph Michael, ACA *2008;* 88 Welwyn Drive, SALFORD, M6 7PN.
•ⒹHORE, Mr. Michael John, BA FCA *1979;* Grant Thornton UK LLP, 30 Finsbury Square, LONDON, EC2P 2YU. See also Grant Thornton LLP
HORE, Mr. Samuel John, MMath MPhys ACA *2010;* 1 Windmill Gardens, LEEDS, LS15 9HU.
•**HORESH, Mr. Philip, BA FCA** *1979;* Richard Anthony & Company, 13 Station Road, Finchley, LONDON, N3 2SB.
•**HORGAN, Mr. David Oswin, BSc FCA** *1989;* Avalon Accounting, 11 Penny Close, Longlevens, GLOUCESTER, GL2 0NP.
•**HORGAN, Miss. Helen Ruth, BSc FCA** *1992;* KPMG LLP, 15 Canada Square, LONDON, E14 5GL. See also KPMG Europe LLP
HORGAN, Miss. Joanne Elizabeth, BA ACA *1990;* National Grid Plc, National Grid House, Warwick Technology Park, Gallows Hill, WARWICK, CV34 6DA.
HORGAN, Mrs. Orla, BSc ACA *1992;* Dromoland Castle, NEWMARKET-ON-FERGUS, COUNTY CLARE, IRELAND.
HORGAN, Mr. Peter Daniel, FCA *1968;* with Harrison Beale & Owen Limited, Highdown House, 11 Highdown Road, LEAMINGTON SPA, WARWICKSHIRE, CV31 1XT.
HORGAN, Mr. Robert James, BSc ACA *2007;* 17 Burgoyne Road, SHEFFIELD, S6 3QA.
HORGAN, Mrs. Sally Anne, BCom ACA *1999;* 28 Worcester Avenue, Kings Hill, WEST MALLING, KENT, ME19 4FL.
HORGAN, Mr. Spencer Lee, BSc ACA *1999;* Cedar Cottage, Cedar Road, WOKING, GU22 0JJ.
HORLER, Miss. Elizabeth Anne, BSc FCA *1999;* 9 Lionel Avenue, Wendover, AYLESBURY, BUCKINGHAMSHIRE, HP22 6LL.
•**HORLEY, Mr. Geoffrey, BSc FCA FCCA MBA DChA** *1978;* Chittenden Horley Limited, 456 Chester Road, Old Trafford, MANCHESTER, M16 9HD. See also CHCA Limited, Chittenden Horley Consulting Limited and Horley Enterprises Limited
HORLEY, Mr. Philip John, FCA *1972;* Kerizan, Martin, FORDINGBRIDGE, SP6 3LD.
HORLICK, Mr. Timothy Piers, BA ACA *1987;* Flat 7, 47 Cadogan Gardens, LONDON, SW3 2TH.
HORLOCK, Mr. Mark James, BSc FCA *1990;* New Dimensions Group Ltd, 9-10 Commerce Park, Brunel Road, Theale, READING, RG7 4AB.
HORLOCK, Miss. Rebecca Helen, BSc(Hons) ACA *2009;* 10 Church Court, 132 Church Road Earley, READING, RG6 1HR.
HORLOCK, Mr. Stephen Howard, FCA *1972;* 40 Main Road, Tolpuddle, DORCHESTER, DT2 7EU.
HORN, Mr. Andrew Nicholas, BSc(Hons) ACA *2004;* MacQuarie Bank, Level 29, Citypoint, 1 Ropemaker Street, LONDON, EC2Y 9HD.
HORN, Mr. Christopher Murray, BA ACA *2011;* Vue de la Vallee, Rue Des Grantez, La Route Du Marais, St. Ouen, JERSEY, JE3 2GX.
HORN, Mr. Gavin Alan, BSc(Hons) ACA *2003;* Scientia Limited, C P C 1, Capital Park, Fulbourn, CAMBRIDGE, CB21 5XE.
HORN, Mr. Jonathan Robert, BA FCA *2000;* 2 Burnside Road, Broughton Astley, LEICESTER, LE9 6UD.
HORN, Mrs. Marion Suzanne, BSc FCA *1992;* Rolls-Royce Plc, PO Box 31, Moor Lane, DERBY, DE24 8BJ.
HORN, Mr. Michael Leslie, BSc ACA *1996;* Jubilee House, 19 Costock Road, East Leake, LOUGHBOROUGH, LEICESTERSHIRE, LE12 6LY.
HORN, Mr. Peter John, FCA *1961;* Orchard Place, The Village, Prestbury, MACCLESFIELD, SK10 4AL.
HORN, Mr. Richard Charles, ACA *1984;* Baxter Hart & Abraham Ltd, 141 New Bedford Road, LUTON, BEDFORDSHIRE, LU3 1LF.
HORN, Mr. Stephen Thomas, BSc FCA *1982;* Wyndhams, Mile Path West, Hook Heath, WOKING, SURREY, GU22 0JX.
HORN, Mr. Timothy Robert, BA ACA *2005;* with National Audit Office, 157-197 Buckingham Palace Road, Victoria, LONDON, SW1W 9SP.
HORNBROOK, Mr. Daniel, MPhil BA ACA *2007;* 2 Chapel Loke, Old Buckenham, ATTLEBOROUGH, NORFOLK, NR17 1PY.
HORNBROOK, Mr. Peter William, FCA *1958;* 1 Hardings Reach, BURNHAM-ON-CROUCH, CM0 8LL. (Life Member)
HORNBROOK, Mr. Richard James, BSc FCA *1977;* Mole End, 3 Shepherds Well, Rodborough Common, STROUD, GLOUCESTERSHIRE, GL5 5DD.
HORNBUCKLE, Mr. Thomas Mark, BA(Hons) ACA *2010;* 48 Dudley Road, SALE, CHESHIRE, M33 7BB.
HORNBY, Miss. Alexandra Sarah, BSc ACA *2007;* 214 South Bridge Road, HULL, HU9 1SU.
HORNBY, Mr. Andrew James, BSc(Hons) ACA *2002;* with PricewaterhouseCoopers LLP, 9 Greyfriars Road, READING, RG1 1JG.
HORNBY, Mr. Andrew Robert, BSc FCA *1981;* C D K Electronics Ltd, 17-19 Buxton Road, CONGLETON, CHESHIRE, CW12 2DW.
HORNBY, Mr. Christopher Stephen, BA ACA *1985;* c/o KPMG, TrinRe Building, 69-71 Edward Street, PORT OF SPAIN, TRINIDAD AND TOBAGO.
HORNBY, Mrs. Janette Susan, BSc ACA *1991;* 25 Buckminster Drive, Dorridge, SOLIHULL, WEST MIDLANDS, B93 8PG.
HORNBY, Miss. Jenny Belinda, ACA *1989;* 16 Tower Gardens, Claygate, ESHER, SURREY, KT10 0HB.
•**HORNBY, Mr. John Fleet, FCA** *1968;* (Tax Fac), J F Hornby & Co, The Tower, Daltongate Business Centre, Daltongate, ULVERSTON, LA12 7AJ.
HORNBY, Mr. John Mark, BA ACA *1990;* 25 Buckminster Drive, Dorridge, SOLIHULL, B93 8PG.
•**HORNBY, Mr. John Roger, BSc FCA** *1977;* The Croft, Lyndon Road, Manton, OAKHAM, LE15 8SR.
HORNBY, Mr. Jonathan Matthew, BSc(Hons) FCA *2001;* 41 Hampden Road, BECKENHAM, KENT, BR3 4HD.
HORNBY, Ms. Julia Elizabeth, BSc ACA *1992;* 10 Groom Place, LONDON, SW1X 7BA.
HORNBY, Mr. Kevin Edward John, FCA *1981;* Fairview, Low Bridge Lane, Gosberton, SPALDING, LINCOLNSHIRE, PE11 4NT.
•**HORNBY, Mr. Paul, ACA** *2008;* J F Hornby & Co, The Tower, Daltongate Business Centre, Daltongate, ULVERSTON, LA12 7AJ.
HORNBY, Mr. Richard John, MA(Oxon) ACA *1998;* 12 Browning Drive, Winwick Park, WARRINGTON, WA2 8XL.
HORNBY, Miss. Sarah Louise, ACA *2009;* 153 Longton Lane, Rainhill, PRESCOT, MERSEYSIDE, L35 8NU.
HORNCASTLE, Mr. Jeffery, BSc ACA *1980;* 10 Albert Road, Caversham Heights, READING, RG4 7PE.
HORNE, Mr. Alexander James, BSc ACA *1997;* The Football Association, Wembley National Stadium Ltd, PO Box 1966, LONDON, SW1P 9EQ.
HORNE, Mrs. Alison, BA ACA ATII *1991;* 28 Elmwood, WELWYN GARDEN CITY, AL8 6LE.
•**HORNE, Mr. Brian, BA FCA AFTA** *1984;* (Tax Fac), Lemon & Co, 221 Shoreditch High Street, LONDON, E1 6PP.
HORNE, Mr. Christopher, MSc ACA *2003;* 20 Beech Drive, SWINDON, SN5 5DQ.
HORNE, Mr. Christopher Donald, FCA *1981;* 28 Butlers Court Road, BEACONSFIELD, HP9 1SG.
HORNE, Mr. Christopher Gerard Bryan, BSc ACA *1989;* 3 Orchard Avenue, HARPENDEN, HERTFORDSHIRE, AL5 2DW.
HORNE, Mr. David Andrew, BSc ACA *2005;* 5 Thorn Lane, Roundhay, LEEDS, LS8 1HW.
•**HORNE, Mr. David John, FCA** *1973;* Derrick Newman Limited, 29 Bath Road, Old Town, SWINDON, SN1 4AS.
HORNE, Mr. David Oliver, FCA *1958;* 5 The Gardens, ESHER, KT10 8QF. (Life Member)
HORNE, Mr. David Robert Geoffrey, FCA *1976;* The Timbers, Coronation Road, Little Wick Green, MAIDENHEAD, SL6 3RA.
HORNE, Mr. Duncan James, FCA *1954;* 81 Cranston Park Avenue, UPMINSTER, RM14 3XD. (Life Member)
HORNE, Mr. Edwin Charles, BA ACA *1991;* Klesch & Company Ltd, 105 Wigmore Street, LONDON, W1U 1QY.
HORNE, Mr. Gary James, BSc(Hons) ACA *2003;* 29 Gorseway, COVENTRY, CV5 8BH.

•**HORNE, Mr. James Alexander, ACA** *2004;* Grosvenor Partners LLP, 6-7 Ludgate Square, LONDON, EC4M 7AS.
HORNE, Mr. Jeremy Philip George, BSc ACA *1994;* 22 Castlebar Park, LONDON, W5 1BX.
HORNE, Mrs. Louise Katharine, BA ACA *2003;* 5 Thorn Lane, LEEDS, LS8 1NF.
HORNE, Mr. Martin Ruthven, MBA BSc ACA *2002;* Lansdowne House, Cleves Lane, Upton Grey, BASINGSTOKE, HAMPSHIRE, RG25 2RG.
HORNE, Mr. Matthew, BSc ACA *2006;* 82 Hill Mead, HORSHAM, WEST SUSSEX, RH12 2PX.
HORNE, Mr. Nicholas John, BA ACA *1987;* 9 Bucklands Batch, Nailsea, BRISTOL, BS48 4PQ.
HORNE, Mr. Nicholas Paul Stewart, MA FCA *1969;* 4 Braemar Close, GODALMING, GU7 1SA.
HORNE, Mr. Oliver Ronald, BA ACA *2006;* Aurelian Oil & Gas Plc, eth Floor, 4 Grosvenor Place, LONDON, SW1X 7HJ.
HORNE, Miss. Rebecca Adele, BSc ACA *1997;* 15-17 Huntsworth Mews, LONDON, NW1 6DD.
HORNE, Mr. Robert Alistair, BSc ACA *2001;* Vodafone Group Services Limited, Vodafone House, The Connection, NEWBURY, BERKSHIRE, RG14 2FN.
HORNE, Mr. Robert Edwin, FCA *1957;* 4 Broadlands, Holland Road, FRINTON-ON-SEA, ESSEX, CO13 9ES. (Life Member)
HORNE, Mr. Roger David John, BSc FCA *1973;* 42 Woodway Crescent, HARROW, HA1 2NQ.
HORNE, Miss. Samantha, BA ACA *1998;* Thames Valley Housing Premier House, 52 London Road, TWICKENHAM, TW1 3RP.
HORNE, Miss. Sarah Louise, BSocSc FCA CTA *1998;* Group Taxation 1st Floor, The Co-operative Group (C W S) Ltd Old Bank Building, Hanover Street, MANCHESTER, M60 0AB.
HORNE, Mr. Simon Peter Barry, BA FCA *1988;* 28 Elmwood, WELWYN GARDEN CITY, AL8 6LE.
HORNE, Miss. Sophie Louise, ACA MAAT *2009;* Flat 2, 14 Park Street, TAUNTON, SOMERSET, TA1 4DF.
HORNE, Mr. Steven, BSc ACA *1995;* Gothic Lodge Compstall Road, Romiley, STOCKPORT, CHESHIRE, SK6 4JG.
•**HORNE, Mr. Timothy Noel, ACA** *1984;* (Tax Fac), Timothy N. Horne Ltd, Bay Villa, 40 Church Road, Otley, IPSWICH, IP6 9NP.
HORNE, Miss. Toni Ruth, ACA *2006;* 5 Burghley Crescent, LOUTH, LINCOLNSHIRE, LN11 0HT.
HORNER, Miss. Adele Dawn, BSc ACA ATII *1997;* (Tax Fac), 68 Carrington Road, Urmston, MANCHESTER, M41 6HX.
HORNER, Mrs. Alison, MMath ACA *2003;* Canons House, Canons Way, BRISTOL, BS1 5LL.
•**HORNER, Mr. Allan Nigel Francis John, FCA** *1974;* A N Horner & Co, Croft House, East Road, Oundle, PETERBOROUGH, PE8 4BZ. See also A N Horner
•**HORNER, Mr. Andrew James Duncan, FCA** *1977;* Horner Christopher, First House, Altrincham Road, Styal, WILMSLOW, SK9 4JE.
HORNER, Mr. Andrew Philip, MA ACA *2002;* Mercer Limited, Clarence House, 2 Clarence Street, MANCHESTER, M2 4DW.
HORNER, Miss. Claire Louise, ACA *2008;* 15/26-32 McElhone Street, WOOLLOOMOOLOO, NSW 2011, AUSTRALIA.
HORNER, Mrs. Clare Marie, BA ACA *1997;* 7 Waldeck Road, LONDON, W4 3NL.
HORNER, Mr. David Alistair, BA ACA *1985;* 15 Macaulay Buildings, Widcombe, BATH, BA2 6AT.
HORNER, Mr. David Lawrence, MA ACA *2003;* 16 Park Avenue, Apartment 7A, NEW YORK, NY 10016, UNITED STATES.
HORNER, Mr. David Spencer, FCA *1958;* Medlars, Dial Post, HORSHAM, RH13 8NN. (Life Member)
•**HORNER, Mr. Dennis Karl, BA FCA** *1986;* P K F Accountants & Business Advisors Farringdon Place, 20 Farringdon Road, LONDON, EC1M 3AP. See also PKF (UK) LLP
•**HORNER, Mr. Gareth, BA FCA** *1992;* KPMG LLP, 15 Canada Square, LONDON, E14 5GL. See also KPMG Europe LLP
HORNER, Mr. Giles Andrew, BA ACA *1996;* Old School House Marsh Green, Colemans Hatch, HARTFIELD, EAST SUSSEX, TN7 4ET.
HORNER, Mr. Ian Wilson, FCA *1969;* 240 Lightfoot Lane, Higher Bartle, PRESTON, PR4 0LA.
HORNER, Mr. Jeremy David Neilson, BA ACA *1988;* Davis Langdon Llp Mid City Place, 71 High Holborn, LONDON, WC1V 6QS.
HORNER, Mrs. Karen Julia, BSc ACA *1999;* 17 Drummond Way, Chellaston, DERBY, DE73 5YE.
HORNER, Miss. Karen Louise, BA ACA *2007;* Chantry Cottage, Rue Des Pres, St Peters Port, GUERNSEY, GY7 9AQ.
HORNER, Mr. Keith, FCA *1974;* 12 Lowick Drive, POULTON-LE-FYLDE, FY6 8HB.
HORNER, Mr. Kenneth Richard, BSc ACA *1992;* 36 Camelon Road, FALKIRK, FK1 5SH.
HORNER, Mr. Malcolm, BCom(Hons) ACA *2011;* Flat 4, 71 Gauden Road, LONDON, SW4 6LJ.
HORNER, Mr. Maurice, MBA FCA *1975;* 16 Marsden Avenue, Karori, WELLINGTON 6012, NEW ZEALAND.
HORNER, Mr. Michael Frank, FCA *1966;* Pilgrims, 12 Morda Close, OSWESTRY, SHROPSHIRE, SY11 2BA. (Life Member)
•**HORNER, Mr. Michael William, FCA** *1958;* M.W. Horner & Co, Cilgerran, Eglwysbach, COLWYN BAY, Clwyd, LL28 5UA.
HORNER, Mr. Paul, FCA *1968;* 1 Farndon Avenue, WALLASEY, CH45 3JX.
HORNER, Mr. Richard, BSc ACA *2001;* 2 East Priory Close, BRISTOL, BS9 4DF.
•**HORNER, Mr. Richard John, FCA** *1974;* Clark & Horner LLP, Dundee Place, 1 Adelaide Street East, Suite 2340, PO Box 181, TORONTO M5C 2V9 ON CANADA.
•**HORNER, Mr. Robert James, BA FCA** *1994;* Lithgow Perkins LLP, Crown Chambers, Princes Street, HARROGATE, HG1 1NJ. See also Crown Chambers Limited
HORNER, Mr. Roland Allan, BSc ACA CTA *1992;* Apartment 6E, Kannikbakken 6, 4005 STAVANGER, NORWAY.
HORNER, Mr. Rupert Howard Milton, BA ACA *1988;* The Georgian House Nizels Lane, Hildenborough, TONBRIDGE, TN11 8NU.
HORNER, Mr. Steven Wilfrid, FCA JDipMA *1967;* 24 High Street, Winslow, BUCKINGHAM, MK18 3HF.
HORNER, Mr. Terence Crofton, BA FCA *1974;* Little Orchard, Chorleywood Road, RICKMANSWORTH, WD3 4EP. (Life Member)
HORNER, Mr. Thomas Edmund, BSc ACA *1999;* D D D Ltd, 94 Rickmansworth Road, WATFORD, WD18 7JJ.
HORNESS, Mrs. Claire, BA(Hons) ACA *2010;* 13 St. Hildas Terrace, Loftus, SALTBURN-BY-THE-SEA, CLEVELAND, TS13 4SE.
HORNIBLOW, Mrs. Jacqueline Denise, BA ACA *1999;* 3 Watton Gardens, BRIDPORT, DORSET, DT6 3DG.
HORNIBROOK, Mrs. Rachel, BSc ACA *2010;* 59 Bostock Road, ABINGDON, OXFORDSHIRE, OX14 1DW.
HORNIK, Mr. Tony Raymond, LLB ACA *1997;* 20 Wellington Terrace, CLEVEDON, AVON, BS21 7PT.
HORNINGE, Mr. Robert Kees, BSc ACA *1982;* 8 Tasman Street, DEE WHY, NSW 2099, AUSTRALIA.
HORNOR, Mr. Harry George, FCA *1962;* High Ash, Ketteringham, WYMONDHAM, NR18 9RP. (Life Member)
HORNSBY, Mr. Alan Kenneth, FCA *1951;* 223 Hempstead Road, WATFORD, WD17 3HH. (Life Member)
HORNSBY, Mr. Brian John, MA FCA *1981;* 15 Beaconsfield Road, Claygate, ESHER, SURREY, KT10 0PN.
HORNSBY, Mr. Christopher Ian, BSc FCA *1991;* Pershing, Royal Liver Building, Pier Head, LIVERPOOL, L3 1LL.
HORNSBY, Miss. Fiona Ruth, BSc ACA *2009;* Flat 3, 1 Send Road, Caversham, READING, RG4 8EH.
HORNSBY, Mr. Graham Philip, MEng ACA *2010;* 10 Riversleigh Avenue, LYTHAM ST. ANNES, LANCASHIRE, FY8 5QZ.
HORNSBY, Mr. John, BA FCA *1987;* 6 East Close, Sad Berge, DARLINGTON, DL2 1SG.
HORNSBY, Mrs. Julie Elizabeth, BA ACA *1989;* Ernst & Young SA, 7 Parc d'activite Syrdall, Luxembourg, MUNSBACH, LUXEMBOURG.
HORNSBY, Mr. Kevin Warwick, ACA *1979;* Frögatan 6, 169 73 SOLNA, SWEDEN.
•**HORNSBY, Mr. Michael Deamster John, BSc ACA** *1990;* Ernst & Young, 7 Parc d'Activitie Syrdall, L-5365 Munsbach, B.P. 780, L-2017 LUXEMBOURG, LUXEMBOURG. See also Ernst & Young Europe LLP
HORNSBY, Miss. Mya, BSc ACA *1992;* Gatehouse, Church Gate, Burton-Upon-Stather, SCUNTHORPE, DN15 9BS.
HORNSBY, Mr. Tony, BA(Hons) ACA *2001;* Langley, Garth Road, MANSFIELD, NOTTINGHAMSHIRE, NG18 5AQ.
HORNSEY, Mrs. Anne-Louise, BSc ACA *1988;* Cooksey Green Farm, Cooksey Green, Upton Warren, BROMSGROVE, B61 9EP.
HORNSEY, Mr. David Thomas, BSc ACA CFE *1993;* Financial Services Authority, 25 North Colonnade, Canary Wharf, LONDON, E14 5HS.
•**HORNSEY, Mrs. Janet Rosemary, BSc FCA** *1983;* Nockels Hornsey, 24 Bath Street, ABINGDON, OX14 3QH.
•**HORNSHAW, Mr. Steven John, ACA** *2002;* Brown Butler, Leigh House, 28-32 St Paul's Street, LEEDS, LS1 2JT.
HOROBIN, Mr. John Andrew, BSc FCA *1974;* The Croft, Toll Bar, Great Casterton, STAMFORD, PE9 4BB.
HOROBIN, Mr. Mark, BSc ACA *1995;* 30 Lower Road, REDHILL, RH1 6NN.
•**HORRABIN, Mr. John David, BA(Hons) FCA** *1993;* Yorkshire Medical Accountants LLP, Unit 1, Milestone Court Business Park, Town Street, Stanningley, LEEDS LS28 6HE.
HORRELL, Mrs. Frances Catherine, BSc ACA *1994;* 6 Stokenchurch Street, LONDON, SW6 3TR.
HORRELL, Mr. John Michael, BSc FCA *1972;* Oaklands, La Rue Du Coin Varin, St. Peter, JERSEY, JE3 7ZG.
HORRELL, Mr. Paul John, FCA *1957;* 4 Richmond Court, Ashton Keynes, SWINDON, SN6 6PP. (Life Member)
HORRELL, Miss. Sarah Jane, BSc ACA *2001;* with Deloitte LLP, Athene Place, 66 Shoe Lane, LONDON, EC4A 3BQ.
HORREX, Mr. Richard James, ACA *2005;* 21 Birch Crescent, Lakenheath, BRANDON, SUFFOLK, IP27 9JR.
HORRIGAN, Mrs. Melanie Ann, BA ACA ATII *1988;* Ernst & Young Llp Compass House, 80 Newmarket Road, CAMBRIDGE, CB5 8DZ.
HORRIGAN, Mr. Paul Thomas, BA ACA *1988;* Little House, Radwinter Road, Ashdon, SAFFRON WALDEN, ESSEX, CB10 2ET.
•**HORRIGAN, Mr. Stephen Paul, FCA** *1981;* DHB Accountants Limited, 110 Whitchurch Road, CARDIFF, CF14 3LY.
HORRILL, Mrs. Suzanne Elizabeth, BSc ACA *1998;* Wesley House, Newcastle Road, Smallwood, SANDBACH, CW11 2UB.
HORROBIN, Mr. Stephen Alan, FCA *1975;* Windsor Life Assurance Co Ltd, Windsor House, Telford Centre, TELFORD, SHROPSHIRE, TF3 4NB.
HORROCKS, Mrs. Cassandra Mary, BA ACA *1995;* Coppers, 27 Glendale, Locks Heath, SOUTHAMPTON, SO31 6UN.
HORROCKS, Miss. Charlotte Elizabeth, BSc(Hons) ACA *2002;* 41 The West Hundreds, Elvetham Heath, FLEET, HAMPSHIRE, GU51 1ER.
HORROCKS, Mr. David James, BSc ACA *1986;* Noble Organisation Ltd, 1a Dukesway Court Team Valley Trading Estate, GATESHEAD, TYNE AND WEAR, NE11 0PJ.
HORROCKS, Mr. Harry Michael, BA ACA *2007;* Heugh Hill, Stamfordham, NEWCASTLE UPON TYNE, NE18 0PS.
HORROCKS, Mr. John Gunn, BA FCA CMI *1964;* Eastfield, 52 Brechin Road, KIRRIEMUIR, ANGUS, DD8 4DD. (Life Member)
HORROCKS, Mr. John Terence, FCA *1966;* 24 Stamford Road, Bowdon, ALTRINCHAM, WA14 2JU. (Life Member)
HORROCKS, Mr. Jonathan Chiene, MA FCA *1982;* Farndale House, 66 Penn Road, BEACONSFIELD, BUCKINGHAMSHIRE, HP9 2LS.
HORROCKS, Mr. Michael, MA ACA *1984;* 4 York Crescent, WILMSLOW, CHESHIRE, SK9 2BB.
HORROCKS, Mr. Paul John, LLB ACA *2002;* Bullock Construction Ltd Northgate, Aldridge, WALSALL, WS9 8TU.
•**HORROCKS, Mr. Paul Neil, BSc ACA CTA CertPFS** *2000;* (Tax Fac), Allens Accountants Limited, 123 Wellington Road South, STOCKPORT, SK1 3TH.
HORROCKS, Mr. Peter Edward, FCA *1969;* 56 Woodfield Avenue, ACCRINGTON, BB5 2PJ.
HORROCKS, Mr. Robert Antony, BSc FCA *1986;* 27 Glendale, Locks Heath, SOUTHAMPTON, SO31 6UN.
HORROCKS, Mr. Stephen, BA ACA *2007;* Clement Keys, 39-40 Calthorpe Road, Edgbaston, BIRMINGHAM, B15 1TS.
HORROCKS, Mr. Stephen Gregory, LLB ACA *1989;* Flat 37 Speed House, Barbican, LONDON, EC2Y 8AT.
HORROCKS, Mr. Tim, BA ACA *2006;* 17 Ullswater Road, BLACKPOOL, FY4 2BZ.
HORROCKS-TAYLOR, Mr. Richard Joseph, BA ACA *1995;* RBC Capital Market, Thames Court, 1 Queenhithe, LONDON, EC4V 3RL.
HORRY, Mr. Christopher Peter, BSc ACA *1987;* ADM International Sarl, Z.A. Vers de la Piece, Route de l'Etraz, CH-1180 ROLLE, VAUD, SWITZERLAND.
HORSBURGH, Mr. David James, BA ACA CF *1988;* Kepax House, Park View Terrace, Barbourne, WORCESTER, WR3 7AG.
•**HORSBURGH, Mr. Karl-Heinz, BA FCA** *1983;* HT Group S.A., 15-17 av Gaston Diderich, L-1420 LUXEMBOURG, LUXEMBOURG.
HORSBURGH, Mrs. Ruth Abigail, BA ACA *2005;* 32 Arnison Road, EAST MOLESEY, KT8 9JP.
HORSELL, Mr. Ronald Ian, MA FCA *1953;* 2 Egmont Park House, Walton on the Hill, TADWORTH, SURREY, KT20 7QG. (Life Member)
HORSEMAN, Mr. John Robert, BSc ACA *1980;* Flat 34 Chancellor House, Mount Ephraim, TUNBRIDGE WELLS, TN4 8BT.
HORSEY, Mrs. Alison, ACA *1994;* Fairways, West Hatch, TAUNTON, TA3 5RS.
HORSFALL, Mr. Craig, ACA *2010;* 23 Gracefield Close, NEWCASTLE UPON TYNE, NE5 1SW.
HORSFALL, Miss. Kathryn, BA ACA *2010;* 70 Dronsfield Road, FLEETWOOD, LANCASHIRE, FY7 7BN.
HORSFALL, Mrs. Rebecca Elizabeth, BSc ACA *1997;* Broadcroft, Berrington Road, TENBURY WELLS, WORCESTERSHIRE, WR15 8EN.
HORSFALL, Mr. Renwick, BSc ACA *1992;* 29 Redstone Manor, REDHILL, RH1 4BS.
•**HORSFIELD, Mr. Anthony William, BA ACA** *1993;* Aims, 16 New Street, STOURPORT-ON-SEVERN, WORCESTERSHIRE, DY13 8UW.
HORSFIELD, Mr. George Herbert Nicholas, OBE FCA *1952;* Willowbank, Stonestreet Road, Ivy Hatch, SEVENOAKS, TN15 0PQ. (Life Member)
•**HORSFIELD, Mr. Gordon Christopher, BA FCA** *1972;* Intake Lodge, Yearsley, Brandsby, YORK, YO61 4SW.
HORSFIELD, Miss. Stephanie Victoria Kay, BSc ACA *1991;* 3 Camel Grove, KINGSTON UPON THAMES, KT2 5GR.
HORSFIELD, Mr. William Jasper, FCA *1957;* 14 Saxon Court, Tettenhall, WOLVERHAMPTON, WV6 8SA. (Life Member)
HORSLER, Mr. Steven, MMath ACA *2010;* 15a Healey Street, LONDON, NW1 8SR.
•**HORSLEY, Mr. Christopher, BA FCA** *1992;* Barber & Co, 2 Jardine House, The Harrovian Bus' Village, Bessborough Road, HARROW, HA1 3EX. See also PC Accounting Services Limited
HORSLEY, Mr. David Stephen, BA ACA *1997;* 66 Kimpton Road, Wheathampstead, ST. ALBANS, HERTFORDSHIRE, AL4 8LH.
•**HORSLEY, Mrs. Deborah Jane, ACA** *2007;* Weatherer Bailey Bragg LLP, Victoria Chambers, 100 Boldmere Road, SUTTON COLDFIELD, WEST MIDLANDS, B73 5UB.
•**HORSLEY, Mrs. Elaine, ACA** *1982;* Elaine Horsley & Co, Ivy House, 687 Ormskirk Road, Pemberton, WIGAN, WN5 8AQ.
HORSLEY, Mr. James Ralph, BA ACA *1997;* 109 Selby Road West Bridgford, NOTTINGHAM, NG2 7BB.
HORSLEY, Mrs. Joan Mary, BSc ACA *1992;* Leventis Overseas Ltd, Hanger Lane, Ealing, LONDON, W5 3QR.
•**HORSLEY, Mr. John Leslie, FCA** *1968;* (Tax Fac), Horsley Spry, 3 Heath Road, Gamlingay, SANDY, BEDFORDSHIRE, SG19 2JD.
•**HORSLEY, Mr. John Michael Palmer, MA FCA** *1975;* Horsley & Co, 4 Palmerston House, 60 Kensington Place, LONDON, W8 7PU.
HORSLEY, Mr. Leigh, BSc(Econ) FCA *1968;* 4 Hermitage Meadow, Clare, SUDBURY, SUFFOLK, CO10 8QQ. (Life Member)
HORSLEY, Mr. Leslie Dean, BSc ACA *1993;* 38 Church Road, Owlsmoor, SANDHURST, GU47 0TP.
HORSLEY, Mr. Richard Andrew, MA BA ACA *2005;* Sanne Trust Co Ltd, PO Box 539, JERSEY, JE4 5UT.
•**HORSLEY, Mr. Richard Geoffrey Courtenay, MA FCA** *1973;* Richard Horsley & Co Ltd, Acorn House, 395d Midsummer Boulevard, MILTON KEYNES, MK9 3HP.
HORSLEY, Miss. Sarah, BA ACA *2009;* 25 Greystoke Road, YORK, YO30 5FD.
HORSMAN, Mr. Alan Buckley Llewellyn, FCA *1960;* 30 Purbeck Drive, Lostock, BOLTON, LANCASHIRE, BL6 4JF. (Life Member)
•**HORSMAN, Mrs. Joanne Elizabeth, FCA** *1989;* Horsmans Limited, Stoney Down Farm, Rushall Lane, Corfe Mullen, WIMBORNE, DORSET BH21 3RS.
HORSMAN, Mrs. Michelle Louise, BA ACA *2006;* with Ernst & Young LLP, 400 Capability Green, LUTON, LU1 3LU.
HORSMAN, Mr. Neil Richard, BA ACA *1988;* 30 Belmont Rise, Baildon, SHIPLEY, BD17 5AW.
HORSMAN, Mr. Nigel Anthony, BSc ACA *1989;* Stoney Down Farm Rushall Lane, Corfe Mullen, WIMBORNE, DORSET, BH21 3RS.
HORSMAN, Mr. Peter Brian, BSc ACA *1980;* 23 The Spinney, KNARESBOROUGH, HG5 0TD.
•**HORSMAN, Mr. Peter James, FCA ATT CTA** *1979;* (Tax Fac), Saffery Champness, Lion House, Red Lion Street, LONDON, WC1R 4GB.

HORSMAN, Mr. Simon John Llewellyn, BA FCA MBA *1975;* Barron & Co, 175 Cole Valley Road, BIRMINGHAM, B28 0DG.
HORSNALL, Mr. James, ACA *2011;* Ernst & Young Llp The Paragon, Counterslip, BRISTOL, BS1 6BX.
•**HORSNELL, Mr. Mark Philip, BA FCA** *1989;* (Tax Fac), Elliot Woolfe & Rose, Equity House, 128-136 High Street, EDGWARE, MIDDLESEX, HA8 7TT. See also Lentongate Ltd
HORSTEAD, Mr. Ian Michael, FCA *1956;* Heron's Ghyll, 6 Greywaters Linersh Wood, Bramley, GUILDFORD, GU5 0EE. (Life Member)
HORSTHUIS, Mr. Peter Nicholas, MA FCA *1983;* H Richmond Limited, Robinsons, Ballapaddag Farm, Cooil Road, Douglas, ISLE OF MAN IM4 2AF.
HORSTMANN, Mr. Martin Daniel, BCom ACA *2006;* Fritz-Vomfelde-Str. 2-4, 40547 DUSSELDORF, GERMANY.
HORTH, Mrs. Louisa Joy, LLB ACA *2004;* Davis Langdon, Colmore Plaza, Colmore Circus Queensway, BIRMINGHAM, B4 6AT.
HORTIN, Miss. Nicola Jane, PhD BSc ACA *2002;* 4 Dukes Avenue, North Harrow, HARROW, HA2 7NZ.
•**HORTON, Mr. Andrew Leonard, MA FCA** *1981;* (Tax Fac), M R Salvage Limited, 7-8 Eghams Court, Boston Drive, BOURNE END, BUCKINGHAMSHIRE, SL8 5YS.
•**HORTON, Miss. Ann, FCA** *1988;* Hammett Associates Ltd, 8-10 Queen Street, SEATON, DEVON, EX12 2NY.
HORTON, Mr. Christopher Charles, FCA *1962;* Apartment 2, Devere Gardens, 49 South Promenade, LYTHAM ST. ANNES, LANCASHIRE, FY8 1LZ.
HORTON, Mr. Clive Fielding, FCA *1954;* (Member of Council 1973 - 1977), c/o 4 Threshers Drive, Weavering, MAIDSTONE, KENT, ME14 5UA. (Life Member)
•**HORTON, Mr. Darren, BA(Hons) ACA** *2002;* Williamson West, 10 Langdale Gate, WITNEY, OX28 6EX.
HORTON, Mr. David Andrew, BA ACA *1988;* BeazleyGroup Plc, Plantation Place South, 60 Great Tower Street, LONDON, EC3R 5AD.
HORTON, Mr. David Edmund, FCA *1973;* 53 Stonnall Rd, WALSALL, WS9 8JZ.
HORTON, Mr. David Michael, BSc ACA *1990;* 3 Howgill Close, Bolton Low Houses, WIGTON, CUMBRIA, CA7 8PG.
HORTON, Mr. David William John, BSc FCA *1987;* Alcoa Europe Flat Rolled Products, PO Box 383, Kitts Green Road, Kitts Green, BIRMINGHAM, B33 9QR.
HORTON, Mrs. Dawn Elizabeth, BA ACA *1991;* 4 The Wold, Claverley, WOLVERHAMPTON, WV5 7BD.
HORTON, Mr. Dominic, FCA *1961;* 1a Rosecroft Avenue, LONDON, NW3 7QA.
•**HORTON, Mrs. Ellen, BA ACA** *1999;* EH Consulting Limited, 30 Castle Lane, Chandlers Ford, EASTLEIGH, HAMPSHIRE, SO53 4AG.
HORTON, Mr. George Harold, LLB ACA *2007;* Yew Trees, Pilgrims Way, Hollingbourne, MAIDSTONE, ME17 1UR.
HORTON, Mr. Ian Charles, FCA *1977;* 18 Millwood, Lisvane, CARDIFF, CF14 0TL.
HORTON, Miss. Jacqueline, BA FCA *1986;* 40 Greswolde Road, SOLIHULL, WEST MIDLANDS, B91 1DY.
HORTON, Mr. James Richard, PhD MChem ACA *2009;* 12 Stamford Avenue, ROYSTON, HERTFORDSHIRE, SG8 7DD.
HORTON, Mrs. Janet Susan, BA FCA *1976;* 111 Green End Road, Boxmoor, HEMEL HEMPSTEAD, HP1 1RT.
HORTON, Mr. John Anderson, FCA *1970;* 3 Coucy Close, Framlingham, WOODBRIDGE, SUFFOLK, IP13 9AX.
•**HORTON, Mr. John Pannell, FCA** *1964;* John Horton Ltd, 15 Malham Drive, LINCOLN, LINCOLNSHIRE, LN6 0XD.
HORTON, Mr. John Rolfe, FCA *1958;* 55 Lanchester Road, Highgate, LONDON, N6 4SX. (Life Member)
•**HORTON, Mr. John Thomas, FCA** *1974;* John Horton FCA, PO Box 52020, 4060 LIMASSOL, CYPRUS.
HORTON, Mr. Jonathan Paul, BSc ACA *1991;* 33 High Street, Sutton Courtenay, ABINGDON, OX14 4AW.
HORTON, Mrs. Karen Lynda, BSc ACA *1989;* Retrak Landmark House, Station Road Cheadle Hulme, CHEADLE, CHESHIRE, SK8 7BS.
HORTON, Mrs. Kathryn Helen, BSc(Hons) ACA *2001;* 53 Meadowcroft, Hagley, STOURBRIDGE, WEST MIDLANDS, DY9 0LJ.
•**HORTON, Mr. Malcolm Charles, FCA** *1967;* Malcolm Horton & Co Limited, 57 Windmill Street, GRAVESEND, KENT, DA12 1BB.
HORTON, Mr. Martin Clifford, FCA *1969;* 27 Barley Croft, Westbury-on-Trym, BRISTOL, BS9 3TG.
HORTON, Mr. Michael John, BSc FCA *1989;* 10 Granville Road, SEVENOAKS, TN13 1ER.
HORTON, Mr. Nigel Thomas, BSc ACA *1982;* 139 Westfield Avenue, WATFORD, WD24 7HF.
•**HORTON, Mr. Paul Almon, BSc(Hons) ACA** *2002;* Paul Horton and Associates Limited, 86 Stannington View Road, Crookes, SHEFFIELD, S10 1SR.
HORTON, Mr. Paul John, BSc ACA *1992;* Green Acres, Rashwood Hill, Rashwood, DROITWICH, WR9 0BJ.
HORTON, Mr. Peter, FCA *1956;* 11 Horseshoe Walk, BATH, BA2 6DE. (Life Member)
HORTON, Mr. Peter Robert, FCA *1975;* 17 Sweyn Place, LONDON, SE3 0EZ.
HORTON, Mrs. Rachel Elizabeth, BSc ACA *1997;* Lauriston, Dalefords Lane, Whitegate, NORTHWICH, CHESHIRE, CW8 2BW.
HORTON, Ms. Rachel Elizabeth, BA(Hons) ACA *2006;* 72b Wimbledon Park Road, LONDON, SW18 5SH.
HORTON, Miss. Rachelle, BSc(Hons) ACA *2011;* 36 Redbourn Road, WALSALL, WS3 3XT.
HORTON, Mr. Richard Glyn, FCA *1981;* (Tax Fac), with Baker Tilly Tax & Advisory Services LLP, 3rd Floor Preece House, Davigdor Road, HOVE, EAST SUSSEX, BN3 1RE.
HORTON, Mr. Richard Paul, MA FCA *1976;* 31 Furze Lane, PURLEY, SURREY, CR8 3EJ.
HORTON, Mr. Rodney Christopher, FCA *1980;* 2 Southfield Drive, LEEDS, LS17 6RP.
HORTON, Mrs. Ruth Elizabeth, BA ACA *1998;* 1 Oaklands, Bunce Common Road, Leigh, REIGATE, SURREY, RH2 8NS.
HORTON, Mrs. Samantha, BA ACA *1992;* Oakhanger, Newnham Road, HOOK, HAMPSHIRE, RG27 9NQ.
HORTON, Miss. Sarah, BSc ACA *2010;* Flat 30 Casper House, 100 Charlotte Street, BIRMINGHAM, B3 1PW.
HORTON, Mrs. Sarah Louise, ACA *2011;* 222 Tempest Road, Lostock, BOLTON, BL6 4ES.
•**HORTON, Mr. Stephen Paul, FCA** *1983;* Milsted Langdon LLP, Winchester House, Deane Gate Avenue, TAUNTON, SOMERSET, TA1 2UH.
HORTON, Mr. Timothy James, BA ACA *2004;* with Deloitte LLP, 3 Rivergate, Temple Quay, BRISTOL, BS1 6GD.
HORTON, Miss. Victoria Ann, BSc ACA *1995;* 2 Lilly Hill, OLNEY, BUCKINGHAMSHIRE, MK46 5EZ.
•**HORTON-TURNER, Mr. Paul Nicholas, FCA** *1975;* (Tax Fac), Ling Phipp, Cliffe Hill House, 22-26 Nottingham Road, Stapleford, NOTTINGHAM, NG9 8AA.
HORTOP, Mr. Scott, BSc ACA *1985;* 50, Lower Bevendean Avenue, BRIGHTON, BN2 4FE.
HORTOPP, Mr. Robert Ashley, BA FCA *1995;* 20 Badgers Walk, Shiplake, HENLEY-ON-THAMES, OXFORDSHIRE, RG9 3JQ.
•**HORVATH, Mr. Andreas Peter, BA ACA** *1993;* Malcolm Piper & Company Limited, Business Services Centre, 446-450 Kingstanding Road, BIRMINGHAM, WEST MIDLANDS, B44 9SA. See also Horvath Accountants and Malcolm Piper & Co Ltd
HORVATH, Mrs. Rhiannon Elizabeth, BA ACA *1993;* 100 Elsenham Street, LONDON, SW18 5NT.
HORWATH, Mr. Colin John, BSc ACA *1982;* 23 St. Johns Road, STAFFORD, ST17 9AS.
HORWELL, Mr. Mark David, BSc ACA *2005;* 9 Cunliffe Avenue, PLYMOUTH, PL9 9TL.
HORWICH, Mr. Brian Philip, BSc FCA *1985;* Pant Glas Bach, Axton, HOLYWELL, CH8 9DH.
HORWICH, Mr. Leonard Simon, FCA *1981;* Hayasmin 77, Romat Poleg, 42650 NETANYA, ISRAEL. (Life Member)
HORWILL, Miss. Ceridwen Ann, BA(Hons) ACA *2002;* with KPMG, KPMG Centre, 18 Viaduct Harbour Avenue, P.O. Box 1584, AUCKLAND 1140, NEW ZEALAND.
•**HORWOOD, Mr. Adam Robson, BA(Hons) ACA** *1999;* A2B Accounting Services, Holly House, Diss Road, Burston, DISS, NORFOLK IP22 5TS.
•**HORWOOD, Mr. Colin George, FCA** *1959;* Colin G. Horwood, The Bungalow, Glebelands, Mildenhall, MARLBOROUGH, SN8 2LR.
HORWOOD, Mr. Ian Albert, FCA FCMA *1961;* 18 Ashwood Court, Highgate Road, FOREST ROW, EAST SUSSEX, RH18 5BT. (Life Member)
HORWOOD, Mrs. Karen Anne, BSc FCA *1990;* The Bothy, Cleevelands Avenue, CHELTENHAM, GLOUCESTERSHIRE, GL50 4PY.
HORWOOD, Mr. Mark Stephen, BA ACA *1990;* The Bothy, Cleevelands Avenue, CHELTENHAM, GLOUCESTERSHIRE, GL50 4PY.
HORWOOD, Mr. Martin Charles, FCA *1965;* 114 Allaway Avenue, PORTSMOUTH, PO6 4HF.
•**HORWOOD, Mr. Philip Osborne, FCA** *1972;* Griffith Williams & Co, 36 Stryd Fawr, PWLLHELI, LL53 5RT.
HORWOOD, Mr. Roger Ian, BA FCA *1994;* with Deloitte LLP, 2 New Street Square, LONDON, EC4A 3BZ.
HOSANGADY, Mr. Rammohan Manohar Raghavendra, FCA *1968;* 10 Northey Avenue, SUTTON, SURREY, SM2 7HR.
HOSE, Mrs. Angela Catherine, BSc ACA *1996;* 19 The Firs, Chester Road, WHITCHURCH, Shropshire, SY13 1NL.
HOSEIN, Mr. Azim, BCom ACA *2006;* 67 Riverview Park, LONDON, SE6 4PL.
HOSEIN, Mr. Paul Edward, BSc ACA *1992;* 39 Vanbrugh Park, Blackheath, LONDON, SE3 7AA.
•**HOSEMANN, Mr. Graham Neil, FCA** *1988;* 4 Stephyns Drive, FLEET, HAMPSHIRE, GU51 1GN.
HOSEMANN, Mr. Paul John, FCA *1984;* (Tax Fac), Ardwick Cottage, 176 Sycamore Road, FARNBOROUGH, Hampshire, GU14 6RG.
HOSIE, Mrs. Helen Joyce, BSc ACA *1985;* Woodbine Cottage, The Long Road, Rowledge, FARNHAM, GU10 4DL.
HOSIE, Mr. Michael Douglas, ACA *1983;* Woodbine Cottage, The Long Road, Rowledge, FARNHAM, GU10 4DL.
•**HOSIER, Mr. Brian Michael, FCA** *1966;* 109 Derwent Road, Palmers Green, LONDON, N13 4QA.
HOSIER, Mr. David James, BSc ACA *1994;* Ariel Holdings Ltd, 5th Floor, Victoria Place, 31 Victoria Street, HAMILTON HM 10, BERMUDA.
HOSIER, Mr. David John, FCA *1961;* 110 Leverstock Green Road, HEMEL HEMPSTEAD, HERTFORDSHIRE, HP3 8QA.
HOSIER, Miss. Kelly, ACA *2010;* 40 Harthall Lane, KINGS LANGLEY, HERTFORDSHIRE, WD4 8JH.
HOSIER, Mr. Peter James, ACA *2010;* 4 Collingwood Avenue, SURBITON, SURREY, KT5 9PT.
HOSKEN, Dr. Gladys Daphne, PhD MSc BSc(Hons) FCA *2000;* A O N Group Ltd, 8 Devonshire Square, LONDON, EC2M 4PL.
HOSKEN, Mr. Nick James, BA(Hons) ACA *2003;* 32 Claremont Drive, Aughton, ORMSKIRK, L39 4SP.
HOSKEN, Mr. Simon William Harvey, BSc ACA *1987;* 57 Park Road, LONDON, W4 3EY.
HOSKER, Mr. Peter Benjamin, MEng ACA *2008;* 10 Ambrose Drive, MANCHESTER, M20 2YE.
•**HOSKER, Mr. Steven Clifford, BA ACA** *1983;* S C Hosker & Co Limited, Endeavour House, 98 Waters Meeting Road, Navigation Business Park, The Valley, BOLTON BL1 8SW.
HOSKIN, Miss. Alison Ruth, BA ACA *2004;* 5 Cropston Close, CHESTERFIELD, DERBYSHIRE, S41 0YD.
HOSKIN, Mr. Gareth John, BSc ACA *1987;* Beltring House, Maidstone Road, TONBRIDGE, TN12 6PY.
•**HOSKIN, Mr. John Hugo, BSc ACA** *1999;* Saxon House, Staithe Street, Bubwith, SELBY, NORTH YORKSHIRE, YO8 6LS.
HOSKIN, Mr. Mark Andrew John, BA ACA CFP *1997;* Holden & Partners Ltd, 4th Floor, Piano Factory, 117 Farringdon Road, LONDON, EC1R 3BX.
HOSKIN, Mr. Peter William, FCA *1951;* Flat 2 Woodcrest, Christchurch Park, SUTTON, SURREY, SM2 5TU. (Life Member)
HOSKIN, Mr. Richard Tremaine, FCA *1975;* St.Pirans, 4 Brownhill Lane, Wembury, PLYMOUTH, PL9 0JH.
HOSKIN, Mr. Spencer, FCA *1960;* 3 Pine View, Ashgate, CHESTERFIELD, S40 4DN. (Life Member)
HOSKIN, Miss. Thea, MA(Cantab) ACA *2011;* Flat 20 Primrose Mansions, Prince of Wales Drive, LONDON, SW11 4ED.
HOSKIN, Mrs. Victoria, BSc ACA *1986;* Beltring House, Maidstone Road, Beltring, TONBRIDGE, TN12 6PY.
HOSKING, Mrs. Alicia Louise, BA ACA *1991;* Collinwood House, Pickhurst Road, Chiddingfold, GODALMING, SURREY, GU8 4YD.
HOSKING, Mr. John Alexander, BSc ACA AMCT *1993;* Barclays Capital, 5 North Colonnade, LONDON, E14 4BB.
HOSKING, Miss. Lindsay, BSc ACA *2003;* 227 Mill Lane, Dorridge, SOLIHULL, WEST MIDLANDS, B93 8NU.
HOSKING, Mr. Simon Christopher Duncan, BSc ACA *1991;* British Car Auctions Ltd Headway House, Crosby Way, FARNHAM, GU9 7XG.
HOSKINS, Mr. Alan Stanley, FCA *1964;* 23 Dove Park, Chorleywood, RICKMANSWORTH, WD3 5NY. (Life Member)
•**HOSKINS, Mr. David Paul, FCA** *1985;* (Tax Fac), 757 Ltd, 123 Priests Lane, Shenfield, BRENTWOOD, ESSEX, CM15 8HJ.
HOSKINS, Mr. Gary Richard, BA ACA *1998;* Cleves Windmill Lane, Ashurst Wood, EAST GRINSTEAD, WEST SUSSEX, RH19 3SZ.
HOSKINS, Mr. Geoffrey Mark, FCA *1957;* 44 Peninsula Square, WINCHESTER, HAMPSHIRE, SO23 8GJ. (Life Member)
HOSKINS, Mr. Jonathan Anthony, ACA *1984;* 1 Southfield Road, TUNBRIDGE WELLS, KENT, TN4 9UH.
HOSKINS, Mrs. Julia Ruth, BA ACA CTA *1987;* Barclays Bank Plc, 1 Churchill Place, LONDON, E14 5HP.
HOSKINS, Mr. Malcolm Geoffrey Ronald, FCA *1963;* (Member of Council 1988 - 1993 1996 - 1999), Higher Crossings, Crossings Road, Chapel-En-Le-Frith, HIGH PEAK, SK23 9RX. (Life Member)
HOSKINS, Mr. Nicholas, FCA *1972;* Wyvern, Cote, BAMPTON, OX18 2EG.
HOSKINS, Mr. Nigel David, BA FCA *1984;* 51 Heath Court, LEIGHTON BUZZARD, BEDFORDSHIRE, LU7 3JR.
HOSKINS, Mr. Richard, BA ACA *1989;* 945 Eastwood Road, GLENCOE, IL 60022, UNITED STATES.
HOSKINS, Mr. Ronald Stanley, FCA *1962;* 40 North End, Meldreth, ROYSTON, SG8 6NT.
HOSKINS, Mr. Toby Edwin, BA ACA *1988;* 12 Box Ridge Avenue, PURLEY, CR8 3AP.
HOSKINS, Mr. William John, BA FCA *1977;* 11 Grange Court Road, HARPENDEN, HERTFORDSHIRE, AL5 1BY.
HOSKINSON, Miss. Julia Helen, MA BA ACA *2011;* 8 Le Clos de Gouray, La Rue Horman, Grouville, JERSEY, JE3 9EN.
HOSKISON, Mr. Thomas Peter, BSc ACA *2004;* 32 Stumperlowe Hall Road, SHEFFIELD, S10 3QS.
HOSKYNS-ABRAHALL, Mrs. Fiona Jane, BSc ACA *1992;* Millburn House, 42 Canaan Lane, EDINBURGH, EH10 4SU.
•**HOSKYNS-ABRAHALL, Mr. Mark Egerton Wren, BSc ACA** *1993;* PricewaterhouseCoopers LLP, 141 Bothwell Street, GLASGOW, G2 7EQ. See also PricewaterhouseCoopers
•**HOSMER, Mr. Michael John, BA FCA** *1962;* (Tax Fac), M.J.Hosmer, Barfords, Standford Hill, Standford, BORDON, HAMPSHIRE GU35 8QU.
HOSP, Mr. Philip Julius, BSc ACA *1992;* with Ernst & Young LLP, 1 More London Place, LONDON, SE1 2AF.
•**HOSSAIN, Mr. Abul Kalam Md Mosharraf, FCA** *1964;* M.Huque & Co, 70/C Purana Paltan Line, 3rd Floor, DHAKA 1000, BANGLADESH.
•**HOSSAIN, Mr. Mohammad Modashar, FCA** *1976;* Kamal Hossain & Co, Suite 24, Fitzroy House, Lynwood Drive, WORCESTER PARK, KT4 7AT.
HOSSAIN, Mr. Shaikh Mohamed Akkas, FCA *1963;* 5 Green Pastures, Heaton Mersey, STOCKPORT, SK4 3RB.
HOSSAIN, Mr. Sufi Akbar, FCA *1970;* 17 Avenue Road, PINNER, MIDDLESEX, HA5 3EZ.
HOSSEIN, Mr. Mohammad Sowkat, FCA *1972;* 39 Conway Road, LONDON, N15 3BB.
HOSSEINI-SOHI, Mr. Mojtaba, FCA *1975;* Elahieh, Khazar Street, Hossein Street No. 9, TEHRAN, 19149, IRAN.
HOSSICK, Miss. Ceridwen, ACA *2009;* 25 Aspen Road, HERNE BAY, CT6 7JS.
HOSTAD, Mr. Brian David, BSc ACA *1993;* 179 Humberston Road, CLEETHORPES, SOUTH HUMBERSIDE, DN35 0PH.
HOSTAD, Mrs. Teresa Inez, BA ACA *1995;* 179 Humberston Road, CLEETHORPES, SOUTH HUMBERSIDE, DN35 0PH.
HOSTOMBE, Mr. Roger Eric, FCA *1968;* Hostombe Group Ltd., Minalloy House, Regent Street, SHEFFIELD, S1 3NJ.
•**HOSZOWSKYJ, Mr. Pawlo, BSc ACA** *1993;* (Tax Fac), Armitt & Company Limited, Marsland Chambers, 1a Marsland Road, Sale Moor, SALE, M33 3HP. See also Armitt & Company and PJH & Company
HOTCHEN, Mr. Graham Peter, ACA *1983;* Thorn Villa, Kings Thorn, HEREFORD, HR2 8AN.
HOTCHEN, Mr. Ian Derek, MA FCA *1954;* Markwood, 30 Dean Lane, WINCHESTER, SO22 5LL. (Life Member)
HOTCHEN, Miss. Wendy Marie Catherine, BA ACA *1989;* Rydes Hill Lodge, Aldershot Road, GUILDFORD, GU3 3AG.
HOTCHIN, Mr. Mark Richard, MA FCA *1991;* Chamberlin & Hill Castings Ltd, Chuckery Road, WALSALL, WS1 2DU.
HOTCHIN, Mrs. Nicola Joanne, BA FCA MCT *1990;* Uniq Plc, 1 Chalfont Park, GERRARDS CROSS, BUCKINGHAMSHIRE, SL9 0UN.
HOTCHKIN, Mrs. Caroline Louise, BA ACA *1993;* 61 Welhome Avenue, GRIMSBY, DN32 0PL.
•**HOTCHKISS, Mr. Anthony John, FCA** *1968;* Browning Hotchkiss & Partners, Buckhurst Chambers, Coppid Beech Hill, London Road, WOKINGHAM, RG40 1PD.

•**HOTHERSALL, Mrs. Catharine Mary, BA FCA** *2000;* (Tax Fac), P A Hull & Co, Beech House, 23 Ladies Lane, Hindley, WIGAN, WN2 2QA.

HOTHERSALL, Mr. Martin John, BA FCA *1978;* Park View, 79 Royalty Lane, New Longton, PRESTON, PR4 4JE.

•**HOTHERSALL, Mr. Matthew Thomas, BSc(Econ) FCA** *2000;* P A Hull & Co, Beech House, 23 Ladies Lane, Hindley, WIGAN, WN2 2QA.

HOTHI, Mrs. Amarjit Kaur, BSc FCA *1995;* 12 Willow Drive, MAIDENHEAD, SL6 2JX.

HOTHI, Miss. Kamaldip Kaur, BSc ACA *2004;* The Cottage Willey Lane, Chaldon, CATERHAM, CR3 6AR.

HOTOPF, Mr. Arnold William, BSocSc ACA *2003;* The Princes Trust, 18 Park Square East, LONDON, NW1 4LH.

•**HOTSON, Mr. Carl Anthony, FCA** *1971;* Plan For Success, 4 Murray Road, HUDDERSFIELD, HD2 2AD.

HOTSON, Mrs. Dorothy Louann, FCA *1980;* Home Farm, Wadenhoe, PETERBOROUGH, PE8 5SX.

HOTSTON, Mrs. Pauline, ACA *1983;* 53 Calder Road, MAIDSTONE, ME14 2QG.

•**HOTSTON MOORE, Mrs. Fiona Catriona, BSc FCA** *1991;* (Tax Fac), Crowe Clark Whitehill LLP, St Bride's House, 10 Salisbury Square, LONDON, EC4Y 8EH. See also Horwath Clark Whitehill LLP

HOTTEN, Mr. Adrian Michael, FCA *1977;* 8 Halstead Road, Wanstead, LONDON, E11 2AZ. (Life Member)

HOUCKHAM, Miss. Rebecca, ACA *2008;* 10B Nelson Street, BALACLAVA, VIC 3183, AUSTRALIA.

HOUGH, Mr. Alex, BA(Hons) ACA *2010;* 51 Gregory Street, SUDBURY, SUFFOLK, CO10 1BA.

HOUGH, Miss. Alexa Jane, BA(Hons) ACA *2002;* C/O 89 Parkhead Road, SHEFFIELD, S11 9RA.

•**HOUGH, Mr. Alexander George, FCA** *1972;* (Tax Fac), Shelvoke Pickering Janney & Co, 57-61 Market Place, CANNOCK, WS11 1BP.

HOUGH, Mr. Andrew Paul, BA ACA *2005;* 1/ 208 Bridge Road, GLEBE, NSW 2037, AUSTRALIA.

HOUGH, Miss. Anna, BSc(Hons) ACA *2003;* British Energy, Barnett Way, Barnwood, GLOUCESTER, GL4 3RS.

HOUGH, Mr. David, BA(Hons) ACA *2010;* Upper Floor Flat, 134 Portnall Road, LONDON, W9 3BQ.

HOUGH, Mr. David Ashley, LLB ACA *1988;* 8 Dogwood Hill, UPPER SADDLE RIVER, NJ 07458, UNITED STATES.

HOUGH, Mr. David Peter Thomas, BSc ACA *2010;* 20D Westbourne Terrace Road, LONDON, W2 6NF.

HOUGH, Mr. David Richard, BSc ACA *1996;* Level 30, Swiss RE Properties Ltd, 30 St. Mary Axe, LONDON, EC3A 8EP.

HOUGH, Mr. Dermot Patrick, BSc ACA *1999;* with BDO LLP, 55 Baker Street, LONDON, W1U 7EU.

HOUGH, Mr. Frederick John, FCA CTA *1961;* 29 Water Drive, Standish, WIGAN, LANCASHIRE, WN6 0EH.

HOUGH, Mr. John David, BSc ACA *1992;* 5 Kettlewell Close, WOKING, SURREY, GU21 4HY.

HOUGH, Miss. Laura, MA(Cantab) ACA *2011;* 14 Egerton Drive, LONDON, SE10 8JS.

HOUGH, Miss. Margaret Irene, BA ACA *1983;* 48 Linden Avenue, SHEFFIELD, S8 0GA.

HOUGH, Mr. Mark Ian, BSc ACA *1995;* (Tax Fac), 173 Ham Park Road, LONDON, E7 9LG.

HOUGH, Mr. Matthew Jason, ACA MAAT *2006;* 25 Clevedon Crescent, LEICESTER, LE4 9BT.

•**HOUGH, Mr. Nigel Christopher, BSc ACA** *1989;* Helmores UK LLP, Grosvenor Gardens House, 35-37 Grosvenor Gardens, LONDON, SW1W 0BY.

HOUGH, Miss. Rebecca Charlotte, BA(Hons) ACA *2010;* Top floor flat, 11 Strathblaine Road, LONDON, SW11 1RG.

•**HOUGH, Mr. Richard Geoffrey, BSc ACA** *2001;* Deseret Accountants Ltd, 4 Thorpe Court, Thorpe Waterville, KETTERING, NORTHAMPTONSHIRE, NN14 3DE.

HOUGH, Mr. Richard Stuart, BA ACA *1988;* 14 Coniston Close, CAMBERLEY, SURREY, GU15 1BE.

•**HOUGH, Mrs. Sarah Jane, ACA FCCA DChA** *2008;* with Edwards & Keeping, Unity Chambers, 34 High East Street, DORCHESTER, DT1 1HA.

HOUGH, Mr. Scott William, BSc ACA *1998;* Flat 93, The Edge, Clowes Street, MANCHESTER, M3 5ND.

HOUGH, Mr. Timothy James, ACA *2009;* with Dyke Ruscoe & Hayes Limited, 110 Corve Street, LUDLOW, SHROPSHIRE, SY8 1DJ.

HOUGH, Mr. Timothy John Denham, ACA *1982;* Animal Animal House, Vanguard Road, POOLE, DORSET, BH15 1PH.

HOUGHAM, Mr. Dominic Paul, BSc ACA *1992;* 1205 E. Loma Alta Drive, ALTADENA, CA 91001, UNITED STATES.

HOUGHT, Mr. Derek Edward, BSc FCA *1972;* 318 Crystal Springs Road, BRADFORDWOODS, PA 15015, UNITED STATES.

HOUGHTON, Mr. Alan David, FCA *1973;* 1a Tynewydd Road, RHYL, CLWYD, LL18 3BA.

HOUGHTON, Mr. Andrew Philip, MBA BSc ACA *1992;* 4545 Airport Way, DENVER, CO 80239, UNITED STATES.

HOUGHTON, Mr. Bernard, BSc ACA *1997;* Hilliadum Ltd Unit 16, Merton Industrial Park Lee Road, LONDON, SW19 3HX.

HOUGHTON, Mrs. Catherine Elizabeth, BA ACA *1999;* 1 The Tudors, Kennford, EXETER, EX6 7TX.

HOUGHTON, Miss. Catherine Laura Jane, BSc ACA *1997;* 6a Chorlton Green, MANCHESTER, M21 9HS.

HOUGHTON, Miss. Charlotte Louise, BSc(Hons) ACA *2010;* Flat 13 Greenhill Court, Windmill Close, BANBURY, OXFORDSHIRE, OX16 9DE.

HOUGHTON, Mr. Christopher, ACA *2006;* 6 Parkway, Westhoughton, BOLTON, BL5 2RY.

•**HOUGHTON, Mr. Clifford Leicester, LLB FCA** *1975;* with Ernst & Young LLP, 1 More London Place, LONDON, SE1 2AF.

HOUGHTON, Mr. David James, ACA *2000;* 1 The Tudors, Kennford, EXETER, EX6 7TX.

HOUGHTON, Mr. David Lee, BA ACA *1993;* Brabners Chaffe Street Llp Horton House, Exchange Flags, LIVERPOOL, L2 3YL.

HOUGHTON, Mr. David Patrick, BSc ACA *1978;* 17 Yuille Street, BRIGHTON, VIC 3186, AUSTRALIA.

•**HOUGHTON, Mrs. Dawn Louise, ACA** *2003;* Aurora, 26 Netherwood Grove, Winstanley Wigan, WIGAN, LANCASHIRE, WN3 6NF.

HOUGHTON, Ms. Deborah Jocelyn, BA ACA *1994;* 2 Tyning End, BATH, BA2 6AN.

HOUGHTON, Mr. Edward Peter, BA ACA *2007;* 7 Mountain View, Peel, ISLE OF MAN, IM5 1QD.

•①**HOUGHTON, Mr. Gary, BA ACA** *1988;* Baker Tilly Tax & Advisory Services LLP, 3 Hardman Street, MANCHESTER, M3 3HF. See also Baker Tilly Corporate Finance LLP

HOUGHTON, Mr. George Arthur, FCA *1959;* 2 Springfield Close, SHIPSTON-ON-STOUR, CV36 4EZ. (Life Member)

HOUGHTON, Mr. Henry Hector, MA FCA *1966;* 37 Whitehaven Close, BROMLEY, BR2 0YA. (Life Member)

HOUGHTON, Mr. Ian, BA ACA *1988;* Sunnyside Clay Lake, Endon, STOKE-ON-TRENT, ST9 9DE.

HOUGHTON, Mr. James, ACA *2008;* K P M G Llp, 15 Canada Square, LONDON, E14 5GL.

HOUGHTON, Mr. James, BSc ACA *2010;* 66 Castle Street, FARNHAM, GU9 7LN.

HOUGHTON, Mr. James Stephen, BA ACA *1996;* 106 Weydon Hill Road, FARNHAM, SURREY, GU9 8NZ.

•**HOUGHTON, Mrs. Jennifer Kim, FCA** *1983;* Jefferys Houghton & Co, The Commercial Centre, 6 Green End, Comberton, CAMBRIDGE, CB23 7DY.

HOUGHTON, Miss. Joanne Linda, BA ACA *1991;* (Tax Fac), 47 Gardner Road, Prestwich, MANCHESTER, M25 3HX.

HOUGHTON, Miss. Louise Mary, FCA CTA *1981;* C R Jones & Co, 45 Staplegrove Road, TAUNTON, SOMERSET, TA1 1DG.

•①**HOUGHTON, Miss. Lynn Margaret, FCA MIPA MABRP** *1980;* Houghton & Co, 86 Holme Park Avenue, Upper Newbold, CHESTERFIELD, DERBYSHIRE, S41 8XB. See also Lynn M Houghton

HOUGHTON, Mr. Matthew Peter, MA ACA PGCE *2001;* 4 Darwin Close, Medbourne, MILTON KEYNES, MK5 6FF.

HOUGHTON, Mr. Michael Colin, FCA *1964;* Dell Farm, Painswick, STROUD, GLOUCESTERSHIRE, GL6 6SQ.

HOUGHTON, Mr. Neill Robert Lyons, BSc FCA *1974;* 30 Stanley Point Road, Devonport, AUCKLAND 0624, NEW ZEALAND.

HOUGHTON, Miss. Nicola Margaret, BA ACA *1997;* 19 Portmore Park Road, WEYBRIDGE, KT13 8ET.

HOUGHTON, Mr. Paul, MA ACA *2004;* with PricewaterhouseCoopers LLP, 1 Embankment Place, LONDON, WC2N 6RH.

•**HOUGHTON, Mr. Paul Richard, BSc FCA** *1997;* Grant Thornton UK LLP, Unit 2, Broadfield Court, SHEFFIELD, S8 0XF. See also Grant Thornton LLP

HOUGHTON, Mr. Richard David, BA FCA *1992;* Aspen RE Plantation Place, 30 Fenchurch Street, LONDON, EC3M 3BD.

HOUGHTON, Mr. Richard Philip, BSc ACA *1980;* 9 Boydell Avenue, Latchford, WARRINGTON, CHESHIRE, WA4 1XQ.

HOUGHTON, Mr. Robert David, ACA *2009;* 136 Moss Bank Road, ST.HELENS, MERSEYSIDE, WA11 7DH.

HOUGHTON, Mr. Rodger Clifford, BSc ACA *1992;* 9 Cardigan Road, BRISTOL, BS9 4DY.

HOUGHTON, Mr. Russell Anthony, BSc ACA *1992;* Rose Neath, 52 Reading Road, Blackwater, CAMBERLEY, HAMPSHIRE, GU17 0AZ.

HOUGHTON, Ms. Shirley Ann, BA ACA *1996;* Flat 53, Slipway House, 2 Burrells Wharf Square, LONDON, E14 3TD.

HOUGHTON, Mr. Stephen Noel, FCA *1961;* 25 Cassia Drive, SINGAPORE 289718, SINGAPORE. (Life Member)

HOUGHTON, Mr. Steven Brett, BSc FCA *1985;* 2 Brent Moor Road, Bramhall, STOCKPORT, SK7 3PT.

HOUGHTON, Ms. Susan Wendy, BA ACA *1990;* 19 McCartney Avenue, Chatswood, SYDNEY, NSW 2063, AUSTRALIA.

HOUGHTON, Mr. Thomas Steven, ACA *2009;* 44 Cygnet Gardens, ST. HELENS, MERSEYSIDE, WA9 1SE.

HOUGHTON, Mrs. Wendy, BEng FCA *1996;* 138 Old Vicarage, Westhoughton, BOLTON, BL5 2EG.

HOUGHTON, Mr. William Neil, FCA *1964;* 177a Green Lane, Wylde Green, SUTTON COLDFIELD, B73 5LX.

HOUGHTON-BROWN, Mr. Nicholas Alexander, MBA BA FCA *1981;* 2 Main Street, Nether Poppleton, YORK, YO26 6HS.

HOUILLON, Mr. Peter Martin, ACA FCCA *2011;* 24 Glenlyon Road, Eltham, LONDON, SE9 1AJ.

HOULAHAN, Mr. Kevin John, BSc ACA *1986;* 145 Hawley Road, DARTFORD, DA1 1PB.

HOULBERG, Mr. Torben, FCA *1975;* Church View, 13 Rodden Row, Abbotsbury, WEYMOUTH, DORSET, DT3 4JL.

HOULDEN, Mr. Eric Henry, BA(Hons) FCA CTA *1999;* 2-12-47 TAKANAWA, MINATO KU, TOKYO, 108-0074 JAPAN.

•**HOULDEN, Mr. John Alexander, BSc ACA MBA** *1995;* Ernst & Young LLP, 1 Colmore Square, BIRMINGHAM, B4 6HQ. See also Ernst & Young Europe LLP

HOULDEN, Mr. Neale Anthony, BSc ACA *1981;* 4 Tower Place, Greatpark, WARLINGHAM, CR6 9PW.

HOULDEN, Mrs. Rachel Catherine, BA ACA *1999;* 50 Gurney Court Road, ST. ALBANS, AL1 4RL.

HOULDEN - SOAN, Mrs. Joslyn Ann, BSc ACA *1995;* Meadow Cheese Co Ltd, Hazel Park, Dymock Road, LEDBURY, HEREFORDSHIRE, HR8 2JQ.

HOULDER, Mr. James William, BSc ACA *2005;* Flat 2, 219 Bedford Hill, LONDON, SW12 9HH.

HOULDGREAVES, Mr. Stephen William, BSc ACA *1979;* 72 Larkfield, Eccleston, CHORLEY, LANCASHIRE, PR7 5RN.

HOULDING, Mr. Robert George, FCA *1959;* 8 McCallum Court, BINNINGUP, WA 6233, AUSTRALIA. (Life Member)

HOULDSWORTH, Mr. Andrew Michael, MEng ACA *2006;* 22 Ravensmede Way, LONDON, W4 1TD.

HOULDSWORTH, Mr. Daniel, BA ACA *2002;* 7 Avenue Gardens, LONDON, W3 8HA.

•**HOULDSWORTH, Mrs. Kate Josephine, BSc ACA** *1999;* Deloitte LLP, 2 New Street Square, LONDON, EC4A 3BZ. See also Deloitte & Touche LLP

HOULDSWORTH, Mrs. Lucinda, BA ACA *1995;* Smith & Williamson, 21 Chipper Lane, SALISBURY, SP1 1BG.

HOULDSWORTH, Mr. Raymond, BSc FCA *1989;* 41 Pole Hill Road, Chingford, LONDON, E4 7LZ.

•**HOULDSWORTH, Mr. Vaughan Martyn, FCA** *1981;* (Tax Fac), Naylor Wintersgill Ltd, Carlton House, Grammar School Street, BRADFORD, WEST YORKSHIRE, BD1 4NS.

HOULIHAN, Mr. Edward Thomas, BSc FCA *1991;* 6 Christian Fields, Norbury, LONDON, SW16 3JZ.

HOULISTON, Mr. Stuart Duncan, MSc BA(Hons) ACA *2001;* with KPMG, KPMG Centre, 18 Viaduct Harbour Avenue, P.O. Box 1584, AUCKLAND 1140, NEW ZEALAND.

•**HOULSTON, Mr. Philip Leslie, FCA** *1972;* (Tax Fac), Sephton & Company LLP, Marston House, 5 Elmdon Lane, Marston Green, BIRMINGHAM, B37 7DL.

HOULT, Mr. Christopher, BSc FCA *1988;* Michin House, Aylesbeare, EXETER, EX5 2BY.

HOULT, Mr. Christopher Michael John, BSc ACA *1988;* 9 St Margarets Lane, Backwell, BRISTOL, BS48 3JR.

HOULT, Mr. Edward Wilson, MA FCA *1961;* 14 Layton Place, RICHMOND, TW9 3PP. (Life Member)

HOULT, Mrs. Helen Grace, BSc ACA *1988;* Field View Cottage, Petersfield Road, Ropley, ALRESFORD, HAMPSHIRE, SO24 0EG.

HOULT, Mr. Kevin David, BA FCA *2000;* with Sagars LLP, Gresham House, 5-7 St. Pauls Street, LEEDS, LS1 2JG.

HOULT, Mr. Mark James Norton, BA ACA *1991;* 3-4 West Pallant, CHICHESTER, WEST SUSSEX, PO19 1TD.

HOULT, Mr. Richard Philip Vear, BA ACA *2005;* Apartment 9 Oriel Court, Newsom Place Manor Road, ST. ALBANS, HERTFORDSHIRE, AL1 3FN.

HOULTON, Miss. Emma Jane, ACA *1991;* Tecalemit Garage Equipment Company Ltd, Eagle Road Langage Business Park, PLYMOUTH, DEVON, PL7 5JH.

HOULTON, Mr. John, BA FCA *1978;* Houlton & Co, Hill House, Pomper Lane, Hurstpierpoint, HASSOCKS, BN6 9LJ.

HOULTON, Mr. Jonathan Charles Bennett, BSc ACA *1987;* 2 Corney Reach Way, Chiswick, LONDON, W4 2TU.

•**HOULTON, Mr. Paul Adrian, BA FCA** *1992;* CTA (Leeds) Ltd, 20b Main Street, Barwick in Elmet, LEEDS, LS15 4JQ. See also Certax Accounting (Leeds & Wetherby)

HOUNAM, Miss. Jayne Maria, BA ACA *2003;* 1 Overdene, NEWCASTLE UPON TYNE, NE15 7TS.

HOUNSELL, Mr. Christopher John, FCA FCT *1968;* 6 Westminster Close, HIGH WYCOMBE, BUCKINGHAMSHIRE, HP11 1QR.

HOUNSELL, Miss. Sarah Lisa, BSc ACA *1994;* 36 Courthouse Close, Winslow, BUCKINGHAM, MK18 3QH.

HOUNSELL, Mrs. Susan Davison, MBA BA FCA *1975;* 217 High Street, DALBEATTIE, KIRKCUDBRIGHTSHIRE, DG5 4DW.

HOUNSFIELD, Mrs. Sarah Frances Clare, BSc ACA *1993;* 258 Waterside, CHESHAM, HP5 1PY.

HOUNSLOW, Miss. Frances Ann, BSc(Hons) ACA *2003;* Hillmoor, Station Road, Wakes Colne, COLCHESTER, CO6 2DS.

HOUNSLOW, Mr. Peter George Stephen, FCA *1975;* (Tax Fac), Newlands Cottage, Guildford Lane, Albury, GUILDFORD, SURREY, GU5 9BG.

HOUNSOME, Miss. Marjory Elizabeth, BSc ACA *2011;* 52 Derwent Road, LEIGHTON BUZZARD, BEDFORDSHIRE, LU7 2QW.

HOUPS, Mr. Craig Edward, BEng ACA *1996;* 54 Holmhead Road, Cathcart, GLASGOW, G44 3AG.

HOURIGAN, Miss. Tammy, BSc ACA *2005;* Tesco Stores Ltd Tesco House, Delamare Road Cheshunt, WALTHAM CROSS, HERTFORDSHIRE, EN8 9SL.

•**HOURIHAN, Mrs. Amanda, BA FCA** *1992;* Hourihan Limited, 21 Millbrook Road, DINAS POWYS, SOUTH GLAMORGAN, CF64 4BZ.

HOURSTON, Mrs. Beverly, BA ACA *1990;* 2 Manse Road, LINLITHGOW, EH49 6AL.

HOUSDEN, Mr. Antoine Charles, ACA *2008;* 15 Kings Tower, Marconi Plaza, CHELMSFORD, CM1 1GS.

HOUSDEN, Mr. Michael Richard, BSc ACA *1979;* 8 Southside, Wimbledon, LONDON, SW19 7SZ.

HOUSDEN, Mr. Paul, BA ACA *2002;* 24 Hazelwood Drive, VERWOOD, DORSET, BH31 6YQ.

HOUSDEN, Mr. Philip James, FCA *1958;* 21 Bownham Mead, Rodborough Common, STROUD, GL5 5DZ. (Life Member)

HOUSDEN, Mr. Steven John, BSc FCA *1986;* 19 The Paddocks, MARKET DRAYTON, SHROPSHIRE, TF9 3UE.

HOUSDEN, Mrs. Valerie Ruth, BA FCA *1977;* (Tax Fac), 319 Lordship Lane, Dulwich, LONDON, SE22 8JH.

HOUSE, Mr. Anthony William, FCA *1966;* 43 St. Stephens Road, LONDON, W13 8HJ.

HOUSE, Mr. Charles William, FCA *1968;* 9 Higglers Close, Buxted, UCKFIELD, EAST SUSSEX, TN22 4HE.

HOUSE, Mr. David Ian, ACA *1987;* 1 Stonehouse Drive, Queensbury, BRADFORD, BD13 2FB.

•**HOUSE, Mr. David John, FCA** *1974;* (Tax Fac), David J House Limited, 21 Barton Court Avenue, Barton on Sea, NEW MILTON, HAMPSHIRE, BH25 7EP.

HOUSE, Mr. Frederick Albert, MA FCA *1964;* 14 Roper Place, KILLARA, NSW 2071, AUSTRALIA.

HOUSE, Miss. Jessica, ACA *2011;* 2d Love Lane, ANDOVER, SP10 2AF.

HOUSE, Mr. John Peter, BA ACA *1993;* 39 Underhill, Moulsford, WALLINGFORD, OX10 9JH.

•**HOUSE, Mr. Jonathan Charles, FCA** *1983;* (Tax Fac), Simpkins Edwards LLP, 12 The Square, HOLSWORTHY, DEVON, EX22 6DL.

HOUSE, Mrs. Julia Diane, BSc ACA *1993;* 1 Elm Lodge Road, Wraxall, BRISTOL, BS48 1JG.

HOUSE, Mr. Michael Marshall, FCA *1956;* Merrywood, 3 The Maltings, OXTED, SURREY, RH8 9DZ. (Life Member)
HOUSE, Mrs. Nicola Michelle, BA ACA *1996;* 39 Underhill, Moulsford, WALLINGFORD, OX10 9JH.
•**HOUSE, Mr. Nigel Melville Douglas, BSc ACA** *1980;* (Tax Fac), Nigel House Limited, 1 Westminster Close, SHAFTESBURY, DORSET, SP7 9JY.
HOUSE, Mr. Robert Lawrence, FCA *1970;* 31 Bodsham Crescent, Bearsted, MAIDSTONE, KENT, ME15 8NL.
HOUSE, Miss. Rosie Clare, BA(Hons) ACA *2010;* 73 Mountain Wood, Bathford, BATH, BA1 7SA.
HOUSEAGO, Mrs. Sian Miriam, BA ACA PGCE *1984;* Sutton Training Office, Sutton College of Further Education, Lichfield Road, SUTTON COLDFIELD, B74 2NW.
HOUSECHILD, Mr. Roger John, BSc FCA *1967;* 24 Goodyers Avenue, RADLETT, WD7 8BA. (Life Member)
HOUSEMAN, Mrs. Kerri Louise, BSc ACA *2003;* 76 Loddon Bridge Road, Woodley, READING, RG5 4AN.
HOUSEMAN, Mr. Michael, FCA *1964;* 7 Sandall Park Drive, DONCASTER, SOUTH YORKSHIRE, DN2 5RS.
HOUSLEY, Miss. Joanne Louise, ACA *2009;* 23 Church Lane, Meanwood, LEEDS, LS6 4NP.
HOUSTON, Mr. Graham Anthony Christopher Dashwood, MA FCA *1967;* 5 Girton House, Manor Fields Putney, LONDON, SW15 3LN. (Life Member)
HOUSTON, Mr. James, ACA *2011;* 56 Forge Place, LONDON, NW1 8DQ.
HOUSTON, Mr. James Alexander, ACA *2008;* 15 Wentworth Mews, Ackworth, PONTEFRACT, WF7 7EN.
HOUSTON, Miss. Katherine Eloise Dashwood, BSc ACA *1994;* 1612 North Curson Ave, LOS ANGELES, CA 90046, UNITED STATES.
HOUSTON, Mrs. Nicolette Ann, ACA *1985;* 41 Eastwood Rd, LEIGH-ON-SEA, SS9 3AJ.
HOUSTON, Miss. Patricia, BA ACA *2006;* 6 Thirsk Road, LONDON, SW11 5SX.
HOUSTON, Mr. Peter Richard Vivian, FCA *1977;* Fair Dawn, Southstoke, BATH, BA2 7DL.
•**HOUSTOUN, Mr. Adrian James, FCA** *1982;* (Tax Fac), Kingston Smith & Partners LLP, Devonshire House, 60 Goswell Road, LONDON, EC1M 7AD. See also Kingston Smith Limited Liability Partnership, Kingston Smith LLP, Devonshire Corporate Services LLP and Kingston Smith Consulting LLP
HOUSTOUN, Mr. Paul Keith, BSc ACA *1995;* 59 Ballyholme Road, BANGOR, COUNTY DOWN, BT20 5JR.
HOUSTOUN, Mr. Timothy Edward, BA FCA *1990;* Glebe House, Timoleague, CORK, COUNTY CORK, IRELAND.
HOUZE, Mrs. Joanna Ruth, ACA *2000;* PO Box 786190, SANDTON, GAUTENG, 2146, SOUTH AFRICA.
HOVARD, Mr. Martin John, BSc ACA *1986;* Eldred House, High Street, Deddington, BANBURY, OX15 0SL.
HOVEY, Mr. Frederick James, FCA *1971;* 19 Dean Close, Littleover, DERBY, DE23 4EF.
HOVEY, Mr. Kenneth Philip Blandford, FCA *1951;* 45 The Gateway, Woodham, WOKING, GU21 5SL. (Life Member)
HOVEY, Miss. Lucy, BA(Hons) ACA *2009;* Flat 48 Albert Palace Mansions, Lurline Gardens, LONDON, SW11 4DQ.
HOVEY, Miss. Samantha Jane, BSc ACA *1999;* Cooper Gay & Co Ltd, 52 Leadenhall Street, LONDON, EC3A 2EB.
•**HOW, Miss. Ai Tee, ACA** *1987;* (Tax Fac), Armstrong & Co, Pegaxis House, Suite 8, 61 Victoria Road, SURBITON, SURREY KT6 4JX.
HOW, Mr. Alan, BSc FCA DChA *1983;* 3 Lynsted Close, BROMLEY, KENT, BR1 3UE.
HOW, Mr. Alan Thomas, FCA *1952;* Apartment 7, 99 Warwick Park, TUNBRIDGE WELLS, KENT, TN2 5FD. (Life Member)
HOW, Miss. Catherine Marie, ACA *2007;* 91 Hassett Road, LONDON, E9 5SL.
HOW, Mrs. Elizabeth Mary, BSc FCA *1976;* 47 Battlefield Road, ST. ALBANS, HERTFORDSHIRE, AL1 4DB.
HOW, Mr. Eng Keat, BA(Hons) ACA *2001;* 21 Rufus Isaacs Road, Caversham, READING, RG4 6DD.
HOW, Mr. Kevin Kow, FCA *1976;* Kevin How & Co, PO Box 11209, KOTA KINABALU, SABAH, MALAYSIA.
HOW, Mrs. Martha Mary, MA FCA MCIM *1987;* 16 Hill Row, Haddenham, ELY, CB6 3TH.
HOW, Mr. Nicholas Martin, LLB ACA *1998;* Oriel Securities Ltd, 125 Wood Street, LONDON, EC2V 7AN.
HOW, Mrs. Sarah Caroline Louise, BSc ACA *1997;* 9 Crabtree Lane, LONDON, SW6 6LP.
HOW, Miss. Wei Thing, ACA *1982;* Block E7-1, Hijauan Kiara, No.6 Jalan Kiara 5, Mont Kiara, 50480 KUALA LUMPUR, FEDERAL TERRITORY MALAYSIA.
HOW CHIAP KIN, Miss. Kwee Hane Carline, BSc ACA *2010;* 54 Labourdonais Street, ROSE HILL, MAURITIUS.
HOW KIN SANG, Mr. Paul Cyril, ACA *1989;* Mount Ory, Moka, PORT LOUIS, MAURITIUS.
HOW YOUNG CHEN, Mr. Yow Wen, ACA *1991;* 22 Bagatelle Estates, Villa Road, MOKA, MAURITIUS.
HOWARD, Mr. Adrian John, BA ACA *1987;* Lake Financial Systems Stable Mews, Beechwoods Estate Elmete Lane, LEEDS, LS8 2LQ.
HOWARD, Mr. Alan Edward, FCA *1973;* with Wilkins Kennedy, Cecil House, 52 St Andrew Street, HERTFORD, SG14 1JA.
HOWARD, Mr. Alan Roger, FCA *1969;* 3 Parade Walk, Shoeburyness, SOUTHEND-ON-SEA, SS3 9GE.
•**HOWARD, Mr. Albert Larry, FCA** *1970;* A.L. Howard, Highlands, 15 Vernon Road, LEIGH-ON-SEA, SS9 2NG.
HOWARD, Mr. Alexander Daniel, BA ACA *1998;* 3 The Cloisters, RICKMANSWORTH, HERTFORDSHIRE, WD3 1HL.
HOWARD, Miss. Alice Theresa, BSc ACA *2009;* 36 Priory Wharf, BIRKENHEAD, MERSEYSIDE, CH41 5LB.
HOWARD, Miss. Alison, BSc ACA *2005;* Schroder Investment Management Ltd Garrard House, 31-45 Gresham Street, LONDON, EC2V 7QA.
HOWARD, Mr. Alun Morgan, BSc(Econ) ACA *2000;* Orchard Block Finance dept, Sun Valley Foods Ltd, Grandstand Road, HEREFORD, HR4 9PB.
HOWARD, Mrs. Andrea, BA ACA *1997;* 11 Park Crescent, Appleton, WARRINGTON, WA4 5JJ.
HOWARD, Mr. Andrew James, BSc ACA *2006;* 37 Bellamy Farm Road, Shirley, SOLIHULL, B90 3DH.
HOWARD, Mr. Andrew Percival, FCA *1984;* The Old Shambles, 41 Park Street, Kings Cliffe, PETERBOROUGH, PE8 6XN.
HOWARD, Miss. Anna Katharine, MA ACA *1995;* 45 Quakers Court, ABINGDON, OXFORDSHIRE, OX14 3PY.
HOWARD, Mr. Bernard Maurice, BA ACA *1993;* Flat 8, Europa House, 79a Randolph Avenue, LONDON, W9 1DW.
•**HOWARD, Mr. Brian William, FCA** *1967;* Brian W. Howard, Argel Vean, Parknoweth, Churchtown Cury, HELSTON, CORNWALL TR12 7BW.
HOWARD, Mrs. Caroline Sarah, BA(Hons) ACA *2001;* Flat 78 Antrim Mansions, Antrim Road, LONDON, NW3 4XL.
•**HOWARD, Mr. Christopher Leonard, FCA** *1973;* 111 London Road, BRAINTREE, CM7 2AS.
HOWARD, Mr. Christopher Mervyn, FCA *1973;* 88 Knightlow Road, BIRMINGHAM, B17 8QA.
HOWARD, Mr. Christopher Michael, ACA *2009;* Anglo American Plc, Anglo American House, 20 Carlton House Terrace, LONDON, SW1Y 5AN.
HOWARD, Mr. Christy John, BA(Hons) ACA *2001;* 18 Beaver Road, Allington, MAIDSTONE, KENT, ME16 0FN.
•**HOWARD, Miss. Claire Louise, BA FCA** *1999;* (Tax Fac), Lings, Provident House, 51 Wardwick, DERBY, DE1 1HN.
HOWARD, Mr. Crispian Michael Pitt, BSc ACA *1988;* 69 Burrell Road, Compton, NEWBURY, RG20 6QX.
HOWARD, Mr. David Brian, FCA *1966;* 12 The Picknalls, UTTOXETER, ST14 7QN.
•**HOWARD, Mr. David Crawford, BSc FCA** *1974;* Stoneygate Consulting Ltd, 16 Morland Avenue, Stoneygate, LEICESTER, LE2 2PE.
HOWARD, Mr. David Keith, BSc ACA *1989;* Warren Lodge, Beech Drive, Kingswood, TADWORTH, KT20 6PJ.
HOWARD, Mr. David Norman, FCA *1962;* 8 Honeysuckle Close, Whittle-Le-Woods, CHORLEY, PR6 7RF.
HOWARD, Mr. David Stewart, MA ACA *1979;* Daglingworth House, CIRENCESTER, GL7 7AG.
HOWARD, Mrs. Deborah Jayne, BSc ACA *1994;* 1 Catley Close, Whittle-le-Woods, CHORLEY, LANCASHIRE, PR6 7GZ.
HOWARD, Mr. Edward Christopher William, BA ACA *1991;* Blackbaud Europe Ltd The Tower Building, 11 York Road, LONDON, SE1 7NX.
HOWARD, Mrs. Elizabeth Ann, BSc ACA *2002;* 35 Merestones Drive, CHELTENHAM, GLOUCESTERSHIRE, GL50 2SU.
HOWARD, Miss. Elizabeth Anne, MA ACA *1986;* Home Wards, Chapel Road, Weston Colville, CAMBRIDGE, CB21 5NX.
HOWARD, Mrs. Elizabeth Frances, BSc(Hons) ACA *2000;* 3 The Cloisters, RICKMANSWORTH, HERTFORDSHIRE, WD3 1HL.
HOWARD, Miss. Fiona Maria, ACA MAAT *2010;* Burns Waring, Roper Yard, Roper Road, CANTERBURY, CT2 7EX.
•**HOWARD, Mr. Gary John, FCA** *1985;* Howard Wilson, 36 Crown Rise, WATFORD, WD25 0NE.
•**HOWARD, Mr. Gary Michael, FCA** *1982;* (Tax Fac), G M Howard & Company Ltd, Unit 17, Park Farm Business Centre, Fornham St. Genevieve, BURY ST. EDMUNDS, SUFFOLK IP28 6TS.
HOWARD, Miss. Gemma, BSc ACA *2007;* 16 Hallam Grange Road, SHEFFIELD, S10 4BJ.
HOWARD, Mr. Geoffrey Frank, MA FCA *1969;* 27 Shannon, TAMWORTH, STAFFORDSHIRE, B77 2NZ. (Life Member)
HOWARD, Mr. George, BCom FCA *1960;* Dale Croft, 1 Moorland Close, Embsay, SKIPTON, NORTH YORKSHIRE, BD23 6SG. (Life Member)
HOWARD, Mr. George Simon, BSc ACA *1989;* Gower Furniture Ltd Holmfield Industrial Estate, Holmfield, HALIFAX, WEST YORKSHIRE, HX2 9TN.
HOWARD, Ms. Grace Katharine Alethea, BA FCA *1984;* Grace Howard Consulting Ltd, Motty's, Frith End, BORDON, HAMPSHIRE, GU35 0RA.
HOWARD, Mr. Graeme Alexander, ACA *2009;* Flat 6, 100 Rope Street, LONDON, SE16 7TQ.
HOWARD, Mr. Graeme Anthony, BSc ACA *1992;* Woodside 12 Saxon Walk, LICHFIELD, STAFFORDSHIRE, WS13 8AJ.
•**HOWARD, Mr. Grant McKechnie, ACA** *1986;* Burgis & Bullock Corporate Finance Ltd, 2 Chapel Court, Holly Walk, LEAMINGTON SPA, CV32 4YS. See also Burgis & Bullock
HOWARD, Miss. Hannah Jane, BSc(Hons) ACA *2010;* 32 Albert Road, ASHFORD, KENT, TN24 8NX.
HOWARD, Mrs. Helen Jane, BA FCA *1989;* with ICAEW, Metropolitan House, 321 Avebury Boulevard, MILTON KEYNES, MK9 2FZ.
HOWARD, Dr. Ian, PhD BA(Hons) FCA *1968;* 18 Firs Crescent, Freshfield Formby, LIVERPOOL, L37 1PT. (Life Member)
HOWARD, Mr. Ian John William, ACA *2008;* Flat 17, Peregrine House, Sullivan Close, LONDON, SW11 2NL.
HOWARD, Mr. Ivor John, BA FCA *1989;* 4 Warners Close, Great Brickhill, MILTON KEYNES, MK17 9BJ.
HOWARD, Mrs. Jacqueline Sarah, BSc ACA *1991;* with Deloitte LLP, The Pinnacle, 150 Midsummer Boulevard, MILTON KEYNES, MK9 1FD.
HOWARD, Mr. James Henry, MA ACA *1995;* U B S AG, 100 Liverpool Street, LONDON, EC2M 2RH.
HOWARD, Mrs. Jane Louise, MA ACA ATII *1986;* 12 Maypole Close, SAFFRON WALDEN, CB11 4DB.
HOWARD, Mrs. Janet Adele, MA(Hons) ACA *2001;* 9 Mortimer Road, BRISTOL, BS8 4EX.
HOWARD, Mrs. Jean Jillian, FCA *1987;* 36 Crown Rise, Garston, WATFORD, WD25 0NE.
HOWARD, Mrs. Jennifer Anne, BA(Hons) ACA *2001;* 11 Stephenson Drive, EAST GRINSTEAD, WEST SUSSEX, RH19 4AP.
HOWARD, Miss. Jessica Anne, BSc ACA *2007;* with Mazars LLP, Tower Bridge House, St. Katharines Way, LONDON, E1W 1DD.
HOWARD, Mr. John, FCA *1968;* Narrowboat 'Nero 2', St. Marys Marina, Manor House Farm, Diamond Jubilee Road, Rufford, ORMSKIRK LANCASHIRE L40 1TD.
HOWARD, Mr. John, FCA *1962;* The Old Hall, Old Hall Square, Hadfield, GLOSSOP, DERBYSHIRE, SK13 1AZ.
•**HOWARD, Mr. John, BA FCA** *1994;* Wilkins Kennedy, Bridge House, London Bridge, LONDON, SE1 9QR.
HOWARD, Mr. John James Emerton, MA FCA *1975;* Rue Pierre Géruzet 17, 1160 BRUSSELS, BELGIUM. (Life Member)
HOWARD, Mr. John Michael, BSc ACA *1997;* John W. Lovell Building, Suite 100, Lower Collymore Rock, ST MICHAEL, 11115, BARBADOS.
HOWARD, Mr. John Paul, ACA *1983;* (Tax Fac), 30 Avondale Road, Hoylake, WIRRAL, CH47 3AS.
HOWARD, Mr. John Schofield, FCA *1976;* The Willows, Longton Road, Barlaston, STOKE-ON-TRENT, ST12 9AU.
HOWARD, Mr. John Spencer Zachary, FCA *1977;* 14D Chemin de Panlievre, 1266 DUILLIER, SWITZERLAND.
HOWARD, Mr. Jonathan Paul, BA ACA *1988;* Inexus Group Limited, Ocean Park House, East Tyndall Street, CARDIFF, CF24 5GT.
HOWARD, Mr. Joseph, LLB ACA *2003;* Providence House High Street, Whixley, YORK, YO26 8AW.
HOWARD, Mrs. Karen Jane, BSc(Hons) ACA *2001;* Flat 6 Sandown House, 1 High Street, ESHER, KT10 9SL.
HOWARD, Ms. Katharine Ann, BA ACA *2005;* 8 The Courtyard, Southam Road Prestbury, CHELTENHAM, GLOUCESTERSHIRE, GL52 3NQ.
HOWARD, Mrs. Katherine, BSc(Hons) ACA *2003;* 11 Dunmore Road, MARKET HARBOROUGH, LEICESTERSHIRE, LE16 8AZ.
HOWARD, Mrs. Kathy Louise, BSc ACA *2006;* Hazelwoods Staverton Court, Staverton, CHELTENHAM, GLOUCESTERSHIRE, GL51 0UX.
HOWARD, Mr. Keith, FCA *1960;* 3 St. Michael's Close, SOUTHPORT, PR9 9QY. (Life Member)
HOWARD, Mr. Kevin Ashley, BA ACA *1987;* Potash Cottage, Blacksmith Green, Wetheringsett, STOWMARKET, IP14 5PY.
HOWARD, Mrs. Kirstie June, MA ACA *1995;* 6 Hillier Road, LONDON, SW11 6AU.
HOWARD, Miss. Laura, BSc ACA *2011;* 95-97 Chatham Road, LONDON, SW11 6HJ.
HOWARD, Miss. Laura Anne, ACA *2007;* 53 Ritherdon Road, LONDON, SW17 8QE.
HOWARD, Mr. Leslie Reginald, MBA FCA *1951;* Blk 2 B7, 25 Tai Hang Drive, CAUSEWAY BAY, HONG KONG ISLAND, HONG KONG SAR. (Life Member)
HOWARD, Mrs. Linda Denise, BSc ACA *1996;* 61 Pewterspear Green Road, Appleton, WARRINGTON, WA4 5FE.
HOWARD, Miss. Lisa-Jayne, ACA *2010;* 9 Westcott Way, SUTTON, SURREY, SM2 7JY.
HOWARD, Mrs. Lynda Jane, BSc ACA *1985;* Fairways, 50 St Botolphs Road, SEVENOAKS, TN13 3AG.
•**HOWARD, Mr. Marc Robert, BA(Hons) ACA** *2008;* Howard + Co Accountants LLP, 6 Market Street, Birstall, BATLEY, WEST YORKSHIRE, WF17 9EN.
HOWARD, Mr. Mark, BSc ACA *1994;* 25 Malyons Road, Hextable, SWANLEY, KENT, BR8 7RE.
•**HOWARD, Mr. Mark Alexander, FCA** *1981;* (Tax Fac), Creaseys LLP, 12 Lonsdale Gardens, TUNBRIDGE WELLS, KENT, TN1 1PA.
HOWARD, Mr. Mark Gordon, BSc ACA *1984;* 14 Queens Road, KINGSTON UPON THAMES, SURREY, KT2 7SN.
•**HOWARD, Mr. Martin John, BA ACA** *2001;* Hazlewoods LLP, Windsor House, Barnett Way, Barnwood, GLOUCESTER, GL4 3RT.
HOWARD, Mr. Matthew, ACA *2011;* 52 Betjeman Close, Larkfield, AYLESFORD, ME20 6TQ.
•**HOWARD, Mr. Michael John, MA FCA** *1981;* Albert Goodman CBH Limited, The Lupins Business Centre, 1-3 Greenhill, WEYMOUTH, DORSET, DT4 7SP. See also Coyne Butterworth Hardwicke Limited
HOWARD, Mr. Monty Bernard, FCA *1950;* 68 Pinner Court, Pinner Road, Harrow, PINNER, MIDDLESEX, HA5 5RN. (Life Member)
HOWARD, Mr. Nathan, BSc ACA *2011;* Flat 11, Corelli Court, 316 Lynton Road, LONDON, SE1 5DD.
HOWARD, Mr. Neil Albert Nicholas, BA ACA *1990;* 27a Portmore Park Road, WEYBRIDGE, KT13 8ET.
•**HOWARD, Mr. Neil John, FCA** *1983;* Howard & Co, 10-12 Wellington Street, (St Johns), BLACKBURN, BB1 8AG.
HOWARD, Mr. Nicholas Charles, MSc ACA *1990;* 101 Couzens Close, Chipping Sodbury, BRISTOL, BS37 6BS.
HOWARD, Miss. Nicola Caitlin, ACA *2008;* with Ernst & Young LLP, 1 More London Place, LONDON, SE1 2AF.
HOWARD, Mr. Nigel, FCA *1974;* Talland Fernbrae Close, Rowledge, FARNHAM, SURREY, GU10 4ED.
HOWARD, Mr. Nigel Peter, BSc FCA *1979;* 86 Rewley Road, OXFORD, OX1 2RQ.
•**HOWARD, Mr. Nigel Robert, BA ACA ATII** *1987;* Armitages Limited, 9 Archbell Avenue, BRIGHOUSE, WEST YORKSHIRE, HD6 3SU.
HOWARD, Mr. Patrick Valentine Eliot, MA FCA *1967;* The Old Farmhouse, Osterley Park, ISLEWORTH, MIDDLESEX, TW7 4RB.
HOWARD, Mr. Patrick William, BA ACA *2005;* 2 Parsonage Barn Lane, RINGWOOD, BH24 1PZ.
HOWARD, Mr. Paul, BA FCA CTA *1986;* (Tax Fac), Gabelle LLP, 33 Cavendish Square, LONDON, W1G 0PW.
HOWARD, Mr. Paul Arthur, BSc ACA *1995;* Tudor Grange, Camp End Road, WEYBRIDGE, KT13 0NW.
•**HOWARD, Mr. Peter, ACA** *1979;* Booth Ainsworth LLP, Alpha House, 4 Greek Street, STOCKPORT, CHESHIRE, SK3 8AB.

HOWARD, Mr. Peter Alfred, FCA *1961;* 5 Keighley Mews, North ShoeburyEssex, SOUTHEND-ON-SEA, SS3 8YD. (Life Member)
HOWARD, Mr. Peter Anderson, FCA *1972;* 1325 West Morningside Drive, BURBANK, CA 91506, UNITED STATES.
•HOWARD, Mr. Peter Ashley Bruce, BA ACA *1983;* Baker Tilly Tax & Advisory Services LLP, Abbotsgate House, Hollow Road, BURY ST. EDMUNDS, SUFFOLK, IP32 7FA. See also Baker Tilly UK Audit LLP
•HOWARD, Mr. Philip Vardon, FCA *1971;* (Tax Fac), Philip Howard Accounting Services, 10 Manston Drive, Crossgates, LEEDS, LS15 8RA.
HOWARD, Mrs. Rebecca Joanne, BSc ACA *1993;* Australia Farmhouse, Twentypence Road, Wilburton, ELY, CB6 3PX.
HOWARD, Mrs. Rhiannon Sarah, BSc ACA *1992;* Ty Sarn, Rudry, CAERPHILLY, CF83 3DF.
HOWARD, Mr. Richard Daniel, BA ACA *2004;* 12 Picknalls Avenue, UTTOXETER, STAFFORDSHIRE, ST14 7QN.
HOWARD, Mr. Richard Ian Ashton, FCA *1966;* 7 Cheveley Gardens, Burnham, SLOUGH, SL1 8AX. (Life Member)
•HOWARD, Mr. Robert, FCA *1974;* Wilkins Kennedy, 1-5 Nelson St, SOUTHEND-ON-SEA, SS1 1EG.
HOWARD, Mr. Robert Ian, FCA *1972;* 1 Cavalier Court, Watford Road, ST ALBANS, HERTFORDSHIRE, AL1 2AE.
HOWARD, Mr. Robert John, BSc ACA *1997;* 7 Lenham Close, Winnersh, WOKINGHAM, RG41 1HR.
HOWARD, Mr. Robert Michael, BCom FCA CTA *1976;* (Tax Fac), York House, York Street, Crawshawbooth, ROSSENDALE, LANCASHIRE, BB4 8NL.
•HOWARD, Mr. Robert Paul, BSc ACA *1987;* Crouch Chapman, 62 Wilson Street, LONDON, EC2A 2BU.
HOWARD, Mr. Robin David, BEng ACA *1991;* Ty Sarn, Rudry, CAERPHILLY, CF83 3DF.
HOWARD, Mr. Robin Ivan, ACA *1981;* (Tax Fac), Dawson Howard Int, Broadacre House, Coningsby Lane, Fifield, MAIDENHEAD, BERKSHIRE SL6 2PF.
HOWARD, Mr. Ronald William, BA ACA CIA *1985;* Number 34, Block 20, Park Place Village, Anabu, CAVITE, PHILIPPINES.
•HOWARD, Mr. Ross Iain, BSc FCA *1996;* Deloitte LLP, 2 New Street Square, LONDON, EC4A 3BZ. See also Deloitte & Touche LLP
HOWARD, Mr. Royston Bernard, FCA *1949;* 63 Millers Green Close, Old Park Road, ENFIELD, EN2 7BD. (Life Member)
HOWARD, Mr. Russell Barry, BSc FCA *1972;* Winterbourne, Church Lane, Tathwell, LOUTH, LN11 9SR.
HOWARD, Mrs. Sacha Belinda, ACA *2001;* 18 Beaver Road, Allington, MAIDSTONE, ME16 0FN.
HOWARD, Miss. Samantha Jo, ACA MAAT *2009;* 50 Audley Drive, MAIDENHEAD, SL6 4QP.
HOWARD, Miss. Sarah, BA ACA *2007;* 3-3 De Genestetstraat, 1054 AW AMSTERDAM, NETHERLANDS.
HOWARD, Mrs. Sarah Alison, BSc ACA *1990;* 27a Portmore Park Road, WEYBRIDGE, KT13 8ET.
HOWARD, Ms. Sarah Jane, BA ACA *1992;* Jersey General Hospital, Health and Social Services, 3rd Floor, Peter Crill House, JERSEY, JE1 3QS.
HOWARD, Mrs. Shona Mary, BSc ACA *1999;* B P P Bristol Ltd B P P House, Grove Avenue, BRISTOL, BS1 4QY.
HOWARD, Mr. Simon Anthony, BA(Hons) ACA *2001;* Deloitte, Plaza Pablo Ruiz Picasso 1, Torre Picasso, 28020 MADRID, SPAIN.
HOWARD, Mrs. Sophie Jane, BA ACA *2007;* 2 Avoncrest Drive, TEWKESBURY, GLOUCESTERSHIRE, GL20 5FY.
HOWARD, Mrs. Stacey Ann, BA ACA *1999;* 19 The Dreel, Edgbaston, BIRMINGHAM, B15 3NS.
HOWARD, Mr. Steven, BA ACA *1990;* 9 Oak Road, Healing, GRIMSBY, SOUTH HUMBERSIDE, DN41 7RJ.
HOWARD, Mr. Stuart John, BSc(Econ) ACA *1999;* 26 Camp Road, ST. ALBANS, HERTFORDSHIRE, AL1 5DY.
HOWARD, Mr. Stuart Michael, BA FCA *1987;* Vines, Vines Lane, Hildenborough, TONBRIDGE, KENT, TN11 9LT.
HOWARD, Mr. Sydney, FCA *1954;* 1 Martlet Avenue, Disley, STOCKPORT, SK12 2JH. (Life Member)
HOWARD, Mr. Terence Reuben, FCA *1967;* 84 Brunswick Road, IPSWICH, IP4 4BP.
HOWARD, Mr. Thomas Malcolm, BA ACA *1998;* 6 Fulwith Gate, HARROGATE, HG2 8HS.
HOWARD, Mr. Tim Mark, BA ACA *2010;* 4 Dorrells Orchard, Bishampton, PERSHORE, WORCESTERSHIRE, WR10 2NS.
•HOWARD, Mr. Timothy David, MA FCA *1982;* 12 Maypole Close, SAFFRON WALDEN, CB11 4DB.
HOWARD, Mr. Timothy David, MSc ACA MCT *1995;* Heatherdene, Brackley Avenue, Hartley Wintney, HOOK, HAMPSHIRE, RG27 8QU.
•HOWARD, Mr. Tone Vincent, BSc FCA *1977;* EYOP LLP, 1 More London Place, LONDON, SE1 2AF.
HOWARD, Miss. Tracey Jane, BSc FCA *1992;* High Chase, Alders Lane, Tansley, MATLOCK, DERBYSHIRE, DE4 5FB.
•HOWARD, Mr. William, FCA *1957;* W. Howard, 102 Bluehouse Lane, Limpsfield, OXTED, RH8 0AJ.
HOWARD, Mr. William James, FCA *1968;* The Old Barn, Albert Street, Kibworth Harcourt, LEICESTER, LE8 0NA. (Life Member)
•HOWARD DAVIES, Mr. Timothy James, BA FCA *1987;* John Davies & Co, St Andrews House, Yale Business Village, Ellice Way, WREXHAM, CLWYD LL13 7YL.
HOWARD-HARWOOD, Miss. Sarah Elizabeth, BSc ACA *1996;* Room 1302, Building 6, Lane 1599 Dingxiang Road, Pudong New District, SHANGHAI 200135, CHINA.
•HOWARD-JONES, Mr. Peter Nicholas, MA FCA CF *1984;* (Tax Fac), Peter Howard-Jones Ltd, 8 Quy Court, Colliers Lane, Stow-cum-Quy, CAMBRIDGE, CB25 9AU.
•HOWARD-JONES, Mr. Robert Francis, BSc FCA *1978;* Regents Well House, Chapman Lane, BOURNE END, BUCKINGHAMSHIRE, SL8 5PA.
HOWARD-VYSE, Mrs. Clare Elizabeth, BSc ACA *1988;* 80 Lees Gardens, MAIDENHEAD, BERKSHIRE, SL6 4NT.
•HOWARTH, Mr. Alex, BA ACA *1996;* P&A Accountants Ltd, North Barn, Broughton Hall, SKIPTON, BD23 3AE.
HOWARTH, Mr. Alexander George, BSc ACA *1995;* Moksha8, 1550 Liberty Ridge drive, Suite 300, WAYNE, PA 19087, UNITED STATES.
HOWARTH, Mr. Andrew David, BSc FCA *1995;* 47 Hawthorne Way, Shelley, HUDDERSFIELD, HD8 8PX.
HOWARTH, Mrs. Anne Marie, BA ACA *2007;* 1 Westville Avenue, ILKLEY, WEST YORKSHIRE, LS29 9AH.
HOWARTH, Mrs. Barbara Carol, BSc ACA *1984;* 10 Church Road, LEATHERHEAD, KT22 8AY.
HOWARTH, Mr. Brian Jeffrey, FCA *1967;* 1 Pinewood Park, Langton Rd Norton, MALTON, YO17 9JT.
•HOWARTH, Mr. Bryan, BSc ACA *2003;* BH Accountancy Limited, Design Works, William Street, Felling, GATESHEAD, TYNE AND WEAR NE10 0JP.
HOWARTH, Mrs. Catherine Margaret Quayle, BSc ACA *1996;* Moss Farm Cottage, Moss Lane, Churchtown, SOUTHPORT, PR9 8AF.
HOWARTH, Mrs. Christine Elaine, BA FCA *1991;* 2 Dene Garth, Ovingham, PRUDHOE, NORTHUMBERLAND, NE42 6AW.
•HOWARTH, Ms. Claire Marie, ACA FCCA CTA *2006;* Novis Howarth Limited, 1 Victoria Court, Bank Square, Morley, LEEDS, LS27 9SE. See also Novis Business Servicess LLP
HOWARTH, Mr. Daniel James, ACA *2008;* 54a Wellington Road, ENFIELD, MIDDLESEX, EN1 2PH.
HOWARTH, Mr. David, FCA *1956;* 7 Bishop Burton Road, Cherry Burton, BEVERLEY, NORTH HUMBERSIDE, HU17 7RW. (Life Member)
HOWARTH, Mr. David Christopher, BA FCA *1983;* Zahid Group, PO Box 8928, JEDDAH, 21492, SAUDI ARABIA.
HOWARTH, Mr. David Edward, BA ACA *2005;* 75 Wymundsley, CHORLEY, LANCASHIRE, PR7 1US.
HOWARTH, Miss. Debra, BSc ACA *1993;* 6 Hilton Court, Bramhope, LEEDS, LS16 9LG.
HOWARTH, Miss. Elizabeth Anne, BSc ACA *1993;* PO Box 421, ROLLINSVILLE, CO 80474, UNITED STATES.
HOWARTH, Mr. Geoffrey Garth, FCA *1953;* 27 The Poplars, Leconfield, BEVERLEY, NORTH HUMBERSIDE, HU17 7NB. (Life Member)
HOWARTH, Mr. John Philip, MA FCA *1973;* (Tax Fac), 17 Quarlton Drive, Hawkshaw, BURY, BL8 4JY. (Life Member)
HOWARTH, Mr. John Stephen, FCA *1962;* 4 St. Lawrence Way, Bricket Wood, ST. ALBANS, HERTFORDSHIRE, AL2 3XN. (Life Member)
HOWARTH, Mr. Jonathan, ACA *2010;* Brotherton Esseco Ltd, Calder Vale Road, WAKEFIELD, WF1 5PH.
HOWARTH, Miss. Kathleen Ann, BA ACA *1989;* 238 Bradshaw Meadows, Bradshaw, BOLTON, BL2 4NE.
HOWARTH, Mr. Kieron Francis, FCA *1977;* PO Box 37055, PARNELL 1151, NEW ZEALAND.
HOWARTH, Mr. Leigh James, BA ACA *1989;* Ladyhill, Bieldside, ABERDEEN, AB15 9BR.
HOWARTH, Mr. Mark William, FCA *1982;* with Howarth Associates, 31 Chapel Brow, LEYLAND, PR25 3NH.
HOWARTH, Mrs. Megan Elizabeth, MA(Hons) ACA *2002;* Cranleigh, 22 Park Avenue, SALE, CHESHIRE, M33 6HE.
•HOWARTH, Mr. Michael, ACA *1980;* (Tax Fac), Howarth & Co, 49 Fields Road, Haslingden, ROSSENDALE, BB4 6QA.
HOWARTH, Mr. Michael Frank, FCA *1975;* with Whitehead & Howarth, 327 Clifton Drive South, LYTHAM ST. ANNES, FY8 1HN.
HOWARTH, Mr. Paul Arthur, BSc ACA *1994;* 12 Woodlands Park Road, MAIDENHEAD, SL6 3NW.
HOWARTH, Mr. Peter, FCA *1972;* Barclays Bank Plc, Radbroke Hall, KNUTSFORD, CHESHIRE, WA16 9EU.
HOWARTH, Mr. Peter, FCA *1963;* 26 Ashfield Road, SHIPLEY, BD18 4LE. (Life Member)
HOWARTH, Mr. Peter Dennis, BSc ACA *1997;* 13-15 Mallow Street, LONDON, EC1Y 8RD.
HOWARTH, Mr. Peter Ian, FCA *1971;* 1 West Avenue, EXETER, EX4 4SD.
HOWARTH, Mr. Raymond, FCA *1957;* 7 Greenroyd Close, HALIFAX, HX3 0JX. (Life Member)
HOWARTH, Mr. Richard John, ACA FCCA *2010;* 182 Preston Road, Whittle-le-Woods, CHORLEY, PR6 7HL.
HOWARTH, Mr. Samuel Kenneth, FCA *1951;* 9 Singleton Avenue, St Annes on Sea, LYTHAM ST. ANNES, LANCASHIRE, FY8 3JT. (Life Member)
HOWARTH, Mrs. Sharon Michelle, ACA *1988;* 14 Armistead Way, Cranage, CREWE, CW4 8FE.
HOWARTH, Mr. Simon David, BSocSc ACA *1992;* 7504 Lashley Court, GREENSBORO, NC 27455, UNITED STATES.
•HOWARTH, Mr. Steven Barry, FCA *1972;* Leonard Gold, 24 Landport Terrace, PORTSMOUTH, PO1 2RG. See also Carter Gold Ltd
HOWAT, Mr. Alan John, BA ACA *1993;* KeyPoint Technologies Ltd, 1 Ainslie Road, Hillington Industrial Estate, GLASGOW, G52 4RU.
HOWAT, Mr. Peter Alan, BA ACA *1986;* Alington, 10 Blundellsands Road West, Blundellsands, LIVERPOOL, L23 6TF.
HOWATSON, Mr. Peter Frederick, ACA *1985;* 9 Northfield Close, HENLEY-ON-THAMES, OXFORDSHIRE, RG9 2LH.
HOWCROFT, Mr. Adrian John, BA ACA *1990;* 24 Wakehurst Road, LONDON, SW11 6BY.
HOWCROFT, Mr. Alastair Graeme, BA ACA *2006;* with PricewaterhouseCoopers LLP, 101 Barbirolli Square, Lower Mosley Street, MANCHESTER, M2 3PW.
HOWDEN, Mr. Graham Paul, FCA *1963;* 5 Cookridge Drive, LEEDS, LS16 7LS. (Life Member)
HOWDEN, Miss. Ruth Angela, ACA *2003;* 23 Little Meadows, Haxby, YORK, YO32 3YY.
HOWDLE, Miss. Charlotte Louise, BSc ACA *1996;* 208 13 Avenue NE, CALGARY T2E 1B7, AB, CANADA.
HOWDLE, Mrs. Michelle Claire, ACA *2003;* 95 Crabtree Lane, BROMSGROVE, WORCESTERSHIRE, B61 8PA.
HOWE, Mr. Adrian Trevor, BA ACA *1986;* 12 St Albans Road, KINGSTON UPON THAMES, KT2 5HQ.
HOWE, Ms. Alison, BA ACA *1990;* 2d Gillsland Road, EDINBURGH, EH10 5BW.
HOWE, Mr. Anthony James, ACA *2010;* 23 Julian Road, IVYBRIDGE, DEVON, PL21 9BU.
HOWE, Mr. Benjamin James, FCA *1963;* Home Lea, 57 Maydowns Road, Chestfield, WHITSTABLE, KENT, CT5 3LN. (Life Member)
HOWE, Mr. Brian William, BA FCA *1968;* 34 Lukin Avenue, DARLINGTON, WA 6070, AUSTRALIA.
HOWE, Ms. Carol Anne, BSc FCA ATII TEP *1981;* 1 Denbigh Close, HEMEL HEMPSTEAD, HERTFORDSHIRE, HP2 4JY. (Life Member)
HOWE, Mr. Christopher, MA ACA *1993;* 7 Northmead, Prestbury, MACCLESFIELD, SK10 4XD.
•HOWE, Mr. Christopher Leonard, BA FCA *1987;* (Tax Fac), FKCA Limited, Prospero House, 46-48 Rothesay Road, LUTON, LU1 1QZ. See also Foxley Kingham Medical LLP
•HOWE, Miss. Clare Julia, BA ACA *2003;* 37 Hawthorndene Road, Hayes, BROMLEY, BR2 7DY.
HOWE, Mr. Colin James, BA ACA *1986;* 51 Shrubland Avenue, IPSWICH, IP1 5EB.
•HOWE, Mr. Colin John, FCA *1980;* Colin J Howe Limited, Charter Court, Midland Road, HEMEL HEMPSTEAD, HERTFORDSHIRE, HP2 5GE. See also HH Accounting & Tax Solutions Limited
HOWE, Mr. Colin Sutherland, BA FCA *1972;* Red Tiles, Harlequin Lane, CROWBOROUGH, TN6 1HT.
HOWE, Mr. David, FCA *1969;* 3 Benty Farm Grove, Irby, WIRRAL, CH61 3YB. (Life Member)
HOWE, Mr. David Patrick Leonard, FCA *1961;* 7 Christchurch Road, Clifton, BRISTOL, BS8 4EE.
•HOWE, Mr. Duncan Nicholas, MA FCA *1975;* Willowhayne, 37 Bulstrode Way, GERRARDS CROSS, BUCKINGHAMSHIRE, SL9 7QT.
HOWE, Mr. Gary Ian, BSc FCA *1992;* 24 Hartford Road, HUNTINGDON, PE29 3QE.
HOWE, Miss. Georgina, BCom ACA *1979;* 49 Shaftesbury Drive, MAIDSTONE, ME16 0JR.
HOWE, Mr. Graham Edward, BCom ACA *1987;* Limbrick Hall, Limbrick Road, HARPENDEN, HERTFORDSHIRE, AL5 1DE.
HOWE, Mr. Graham Lawrence, FCA *1979;* Woodruff, Deane Road, Stokinteignhead, NEWTON ABBOT, TQ12 4QF.
HOWE, Mrs. Hannah, BA ACA *2006;* The School House, 5 Gaulby Road, Billesdon, LEICESTER, LE7 9AG.
HOWE, Mr. James Duncan, ACA *2008;* 3/69 Fletcher Street, TAMARAMA, NSW 2026, AUSTRALIA.
HOWE, Mrs. Jane Evelyn, BSc ACA *1985;* Epsilon House, University of Southampton Science Park, SOUTHAMPTON, SO16 7NS.
HOWE, Mr. John, FCA *1968;* Kensington, Croft Drive East, Caldy, WIRRAL, CH48 1LS. (Life Member)
•HOWE, Mr. Jonathan Paul, BA ACA *1997;* (Tax Fac), PricewaterhouseCoopers LLP, Hays Galleria, 1 Hays Lane, LONDON, SE1 2RD. See also PricewaterhouseCoopers
HOWE, Mr. Kevin John, BSc FCA *1987;* 35 Flamingo Crescent, THORNLANDS, QLD 4164, AUSTRALIA.
HOWE, Miss. Kirsty, BSc ACA *2006;* BP Group, Chertsey Road, SUNBURY-ON-THAMES, MIDDLESEX, TW16 7BP.
•HOWE, Mrs. Lesley Jane, BA FCA *1984;* Mall & Co, PO Box 433, MANCHESTER, M28 8AT.
HOWE, Mr. Malcolm Sutherland, FCA *1972;* 6 Garden End, Melbourn, ROYSTON, SG8 6HD. (Life Member)
HOWE, Mr. Marcus David, BA ACA *2004;* Unit 2 The Business Centre, Molly Millars Lane, WOKINGHAM, BERKSHIRE, RG41 2QZ.
•HOWE, Mr. Matthew Robert, BA ACA *2006;* M Howe Accountancy Services, 6 Henders, Stony Stratford, MILTON KEYNES, MK11 1RB.
HOWE, Mr. Norman Herbert Frederick, FCA *1948;* 13 Maplehurst Close, ST. LEONARDS-ON-SEA, EAST SUSSEX, TN37 7NB. (Life Member)
HOWE, Mr. Paul Andrew, BA ACA *1989;* 8 Groby Road, ALTRINCHAM, WA14 1RS.
HOWE, Mr. Peter John, BSc ACA *1988;* 27 Osbaldeston Gardens, NEWCASTLE UPON TYNE, NE3 4JE.
HOWE, Mr. Peter Ward, FCA *1966;* North Barn, Sowerby, PRESTON, LANCASHIRE, PR3 0TU.
HOWE, Ms. Philippa Mary, ACA *1991;* Kilvington Leith Marketing Ltd, 8 Wake Green Road, BIRMINGHAM, B13 9EZ.
HOWE, Mr. Reece Kirkwood, BSc ACA *2006;* Kirkwood Care, 77 Walnut Tree Close, GUILDFORD, SURREY, GU1 4UH.
HOWE, Mr. Richard Oliver Charles, BMus ACA *2005;* 6 Warren Close Hartley Wintney, HOOK, HAMPSHIRE, RG27 8DS.
HOWE, Mr. Robert John, FCA *1978;* (Tax Fac), L' Assemblage Ltd, Flat A West Pallant House, 12 West Pallant, CHICHESTER, WEST SUSSEX, PO19 1TB.
HOWE, Mr. Robert William, BEng ACA *2002;* 128 Main Road, Hawkwell, HOCKLEY, ESSEX, SS5 4EN.
HOWE, Mrs. Samantha Jane, BSc ACA *1997;* 2 Parkland Avenue, Parkland Village, CARLISLE, CA1 3GN.
HOWE, Mrs. Samantha Michelle, BSc ACA *2001;* 22 Hawkes Leap, WINDLESHAM, SURREY, GU20 6JL.
HOWE, Mrs. Sarah Louise, BA ACA *1997;* 59 Heronway, Hutton, BRENTWOOD, ESSEX, CM13 2LQ.
HOWE, Mrs. Sharon Heather, ACA *2009;* Pricewaterhousecoopers, 89 Sandyford Road, NEWCASTLE UPON TYNE, NE1 8HW.
HOWE, Mr. Stephen Richard, ACA *1988;* 364 Galley Hill, HEMEL HEMPSTEAD, HP1 3LA.
HOWE, Mr. Thomas John, MA FCA *1996;* Conran Ltd Conran Building, 22 Shad Thames, LONDON, SE1 2YU.

HOWE, Mr. Trevor Bruce, BSc FCA *1982;* Absolute Invoice Finance Ltd, St. James House, 7 Charlotte Street, MANCHESTER, M1 4DZ.
HOWE, Mr. William Webster, FCA *1965;* The Vinery, Claverton, BATH, BA2 7BG. (Life Member)
•**HOWELL, Mr. Alan William, FCA** *1969;* Alan Howell, 4 South View Road, ASHTEAD, SURREY, KT21 2NB.
•**HOWELL, Mrs. Alicia Clair, BSc ACA** *1999;* Alicia Howell BSc (Hons) ACA, 13 Ipswich Grove, NORWICH, NR2 2LU.
•**HOWELL, Mr. Andrew Griffith, FCA** *1976;* (Tax Fac), Brian Bell Meyer & Co Limited, Plymouth Chambers, 23 Bartlett Street, CAERPHILLY, MID GLAMORGAN, CF83 1JS.
HOWELL, Mr. Anthony, FCA *1969;* 2 Cardales Close, Findern, DERBY, DE65 6QN.
HOWELL, Mr. Anthony Edward, FCA *1960;* 1 Belvoir Close, Market Deeping, PETERBOROUGH, PE6 8SS. (Life Member)
HOWELL, Mr. Anthony James, BA ACA *1996;* Multiserv Plc, Harsco House, 299 Kingston Road, LEATHERHEAD, SURREY, KT22 7SG.
HOWELL, Miss. Bethan Alice, ACA *2008;* Flat 4, 182 Sutherland Avenue, LONDON, W9 1HR.
HOWELL, Mrs. Christine Emma, BSc ACA CTA *1994;* 41 Maple Hatch Close, GODALMING, SURREY, GU7 1TH.
•**HOWELL, Mr. Christopher James, ACA** *2009;* Flat D, 167 Picardy Road, BELVEDERE, KENT, DA17 5QL.
HOWELL, Mr. Christopher John, BA ACA *2006;* 86 Argyle Street, CAMBRIDGE, CB1 3LS.
HOWELL, Mr. Christopher Piers, BSc FCA *1973;* 2 Pynes Close, Cheriton Fitzpaine, CREDITON, DEVON, EX17 4HT.
HOWELL, Mr. David, FCA *1974;* Flat 10 (Isabella), Hatchford Park, Ockham Lane, Hatchford, COBHAM, SURREY KT11 1LH.
HOWELL, Mr. David Charles Wilfred, BSc FCA *1988;* House 64C, Sheung Sze Wan, SAI KUNG, NEW TERRITORIES, HONG KONG SAR.
HOWELL, Mr. David Harcourt, FCA *1965;* 11 Wollaston Court, Wollaston, STOURBRIDGE, WEST MIDLANDS, DY8 4SQ.
•①**HOWELL, Mr. Derek Anthony, BSc FCA** *1979;* PricewaterhouseCoopers LLP, One Kingsway, CARDIFF, CF10 3PW. See also PricewaterhouseCoopers
HOWELL, Mr. Derek Charles Patrick, FCA *1962;* 37 Muraban Road, DURAL, NSW 2158, AUSTRALIA. (Life Member)
•**HOWELL, Mr. Derek Pryce, FCA** *1975;* D P Howell, 33 Grove Road, Coombe Dingle, BRISTOL, BS9 2RJ. See also Howell
HOWELL, Mr. Donald Trevor, BSc FCA *1968;* Longbow Cottage, Off Neston Road, Burton, NESTON, CH64 5SZ.
HOWELL, Mrs. Emma Louise, ACA *2006;* Park Cottage, Park Lane, Audley, STOKE-ON-TRENT, ST7 8HP.
HOWELL, Mr. Geoffrey Martin, BSc FCA *1972;* 12 Penydarren Park, MERTHYR TYDFIL, MID GLAMORGAN, CF47 8YW. (Life Member)
HOWELL, Mr. George Denis, BCom FCA *1965;* Crosskeys Cottage, 3 Northorpe, Thurlby, BOURNE, LINCOLNSHIRE, PE10 0HH. (Life Member)
HOWELL, Mr. George Stuart, BA ACA *2010;* 59 Dalmeny Road, CARSHALTON, SURREY, SM5 4PW.
HOWELL, Mr. Gerald, FCA *1953;* Pillerton House, Pillerton Hersey, WARWICK, CV35 0QJ. (Life Member)
HOWELL, Mr. James Clifford, MA ACA *2000;* Millward Brown UK, 24-28 Bloomsbury Way, LONDON, WC1A 2PX.
HOWELL, Mr. James Emlyn, BSc ACA *1979;* 31 Brookway Road, Charlton Kings, CHELTENHAM, GLOUCESTERSHIRE, GL53 8HF.
HOWELL, Mrs. Jennifer Jane, ACA *2008;* 40 Poplar Avenue, WINDLESHAM, GU20 6PW.
HOWELL, Miss. Joanna Clare, BEng ACA *1999;* 29 Cambridge Road, Wadesmill, WARE, HERTFORDSHIRE, SG12 0TJ.
HOWELL, Mr. John Michael, MBA LLB FCA *1977;* 11a De Wet Road, CAPE TOWN, 8005, SOUTH AFRICA.
HOWELL, Mr. Jonathan Anton George, BCom ACA *1987;* Glebe Barn Church Street, Ashley, NEWMARKET, SUFFOLK, CB8 9DU.
HOWELL, Miss. Laura, ACA *2010;* 4 Beckets Place, Otford, SEVENOAKS, KENT, TN14 5QA.
•**HOWELL, Mr. Mark Andrew, ACA** *1998;* with Nicklin LLP, Church Court, Stourbridge Road, HALESOWEN, WEST MIDLANDS, B63 3TT.
•**HOWELL, Mr. Mark Iain Anthony, LLB ACA** *1992;* Kentwell Corporation Limited, 86 Musters Road, West Bridgford, NOTTINGHAM, NG2 7PS.
HOWELL, Mr. Mark John, ACA *1979;* Burnside, Avonwick, SOUTH BRENT, DEVON, TQ10 9EZ.
HOWELL, Mr. Martyn Thomas, ACA *2008;* 40 Poplar Avenue, WINDLESHAM, GU20 6PW.
•**HOWELL, Mr. Matthew James, BSc ACA** *1999;* Deloitte LLP, Athene Place, 66 Shoe Lane, LONDON, EC4A 3BQ. See also Deloitte & Touche LLP
HOWELL, Mr. Miles Richard Alastair, FCA *1969;* 22 Nelson Close, EMSWORTH, HAMPSHIRE, PO10 8JW.
HOWELL, Miss. Naomi, BSc ACA *2011;* 39 Manningtree Road, RUISLIP, MIDDLESEX, HA4 0ER.
HOWELL, Mr. Nigel Charles, BA FCA CTA *1992;* (Tax Fac), with ICAEW, Metropolitan House, 321 Avebury Boulevard, MILTON KEYNES, MK9 2FZ.
HOWELL, Mr. Owain Morgan Rhys, MA FCA *1962;* Caegwyn, Bro Waldo, CLYNDERWEN, PEMBROKESHIRE, SA66 7NQ. (Life Member)
HOWELL, Mr. Peter Cartwright Mccallum, MA FCA *1974;* 15289 Russell Road, CHAGRIN FALLS, OH 44022, UNITED STATES.
HOWELL, Mr. Peter Jonathan, BSc ACA *1988;* Azlan House, Mulberry Business Park, Fishponds Road, WOKINGHAM, BERKSHIRE, RG41 2GY.
HOWELL, Mr. Philip Adrian, BA ACA *1988;* 36 Springfield Road, LONDON, NW8 0QN.
HOWELL, Miss. Rebecca Jane Harcourt, BA(Hons) ACA *2009;* Flat A, 12 Inman Road, LONDON, SW18 3BB.
HOWELL, Mr. Richard, BA ACA *1991;* Flat 7 Kilment House, 36 Arterberry Road, Wimbldon, LONDON, SW20 8AQ.
HOWELL, Mr. Richard Edward, BSc FCA *1978;* White House Farm, Great Broughton, MIDDLESBROUGH, CLEVELAND, TS9 7HN.
HOWELL, Mr. Richard John, BSc ACA *1996;* 32A Mona Road, Darling Point, SYDNEY, NSW 2027, AUSTRALIA.
HOWELL, Mr. Robert Richard, FCA *1965;* 5 Pine Grove, Brookmans Park, HATFIELD, AL9 7BP. (Life Member)
•**HOWELL, Mr. Roger Melville, BSc FCA** *1972;* Great Life Limited, Shoreston Cottage, Shoreston, SEAHOUSES, NORTHUMBERLAND, NE68 7SX.
HOWELL, Mr. Ronald Victor, FCA *1954;* 7 Monmouth Drive, SUTTON COLDFIELD, B73 6JQ. (Life Member)
•**HOWELL, Mr. Samuel Robert, FCA** *1961;* Suite F Jollife House, 32 West Street, POOLE, DORSET, BH15 1LD.
HOWELL, Ms. Sarah Louise, ACA *2004;* 6 Downlea, TAVISTOCK, DEVON, PL19 9AW.
HOWELL, Mr. Simon Benedict, BSc(Econ) ACA *1979;* The Barn Oast, Nickle Farm, Ashford Road, Chartham, CANTERBURY, KENT CT4 7PE.
HOWELL, Mr. Simon Paul, BSc ACA *1993;* 5 Coxs Road, Shrivenham, SWINDON, SN6 8EL.
HOWELL, Mr. Stephen Alexander, BSc ACA *2004;* 128 Kingsway, WOKING, GU21 6NR.
•**HOWELL, Mr. Stephen Arthur, BSc ACA** *1984;* (Tax Fac), Stephen A Howell, Pant Y Fedwen, Gelli'r Haidd, Tonyrefail, PORTH, MID GLAMORGAN CF39 8AP.
HOWELL, Mr. Stephen Harcourt, MSc BSc FCA *1974;* (Tax Fac), 5 Bramshall Drive, Dorridge, SOLIHULL, B93 8TG.
HOWELL, Mr. Stuart Christopher, BSc ACA *1986;* 109 High Street, Wargrave, READING, RG10 8DD.
HOWELL, Mrs. Terri Georgina, BA ACA *1995;* 19 Ranvilles Lane, FAREHAM, HAMPSHIRE, PO14 3DX.
HOWELL, Mr. Timothy John, BCom ACA *1985;* The Old Vicarage, High Street, Cuckfield, HAYWARDS HEATH, WEST SUSSEX, RH17 5JX.
•**HOWELL, Mr. William George, FCA** *1971;* William Howell & Co, 2 Seabrook Drive, WEST WICKHAM, BR4 9AJ. See also Walshe & Co Ltd
HOWELLS, Mr. Adrian Phillip, BA ACA *2010;* 56 Lillymill Chine, Chineham, BASINGSTOKE, RG24 8JT.
•**HOWELLS, Miss. Beverley, BA ACA** *2000;* (Tax Fac), UHY Torgersens, Somerford Buildings, Norfolk Street, SUNDERLAND, SR1 1EE.
HOWELLS, Mrs. Claire Louise, BSc ACA *1997;* with PricewaterhouseCoopers LLP, 1 Embankment Place, LONDON, WC2N 6RH.
HOWELLS, Mr. David, BSocSc ACA *1992;* 21 Torcross Close, HARTLEPOOL, CLEVELAND, TS27 3ND.
HOWELLS, Mr. David Michael, BSc FCA *1984;* (Tax Fac), with KPMG LLP, 15 Canada Square, LONDON, E14 5GL.
HOWELLS, Mr. David Richard, BSc ACA *2000;* 19 Llwyn Coch, Broadlands, BRIDGEND, MID GLAMORGAN, CF31 5BJ.
HOWELLS, Mr. Dorian Wyn, BA FCA *1993;* Steris Ltd, Steris House, Jays Close, Viables, BASINGSTOKE, HAMPSHIRE RG22 4AX.
•**HOWELLS, Mr. Edward James, BA(Hons) ACA FCCA** *1992;* Howells Cook Associates Limited, 20a High Street, GLASTONBURY, SOMERSET, BA6 9DU. See also Edward Howells Associates Limited
•**HOWELLS, Mr. Geraint Wynne, BSc ACA** *1985;* Howells & Co Limited, 39 Glenferrie Road, ST. ALBANS, HERTFORDSHIRE, AL1 4JT.
HOWELLS, Mr. Ian, BSc ACA *1987;* Honda Motor Europe Ltd, 470 London Road, SLOUGH, SL3 8QY.
HOWELLS, Mrs. Jayne Mary, BSc ACA *1990;* Highwood, Lowden Hill, CHIPPENHAM, SN15 2BT.
HOWELLS, Ms. Jennifer Christine, BA ACA *1995;* Trust Offices, Nuffield Orthopaedic Centre Old Road, Headington, OXFORD, OX3 7LD.
HOWELLS, Mr. John Stuart, FCA *1964;* Well Cottage, 4 Vicarage Lane, Frampton on Severn, GLOUCESTER, GL2 7EE.
HOWELLS, Mr. Mark Henry, BSc ACA *1999;* 123 Worthington Road, LICHFIELD, STAFFORDSHIRE, WS13 8PG.
HOWELLS, Mr. Nigel David, FCA *1975;* 4 Merganser Drive, BICESTER, OX26 6UQ.
HOWELLS, Mr. Peter Glynne, BSc FCA *1980;* (Tax Fac), 55 Lakewood Road, Chandlers Ford, EASTLEIGH, SO53 1EU.
HOWELLS, Mr. Robert Anthony, ACA *2007;* Oak Lea Moss Lane, Mobberley, KNUTSFORD, CHESHIRE, WA16 7BU.
HOWELLS, Mrs. Sally Joanna, BSc ACA *1992;* 29 Woodruff Way, Thornhill, CARDIFF, CF14 9FP.
HOWELLS, Mr. Thomas Andrew, BSc ACA *1985;* The Silvers, Maendy, COWBRIDGE, CF71 7TG.
HOWELLS, Mr. Thomas Brinley, MBA BSc ACA *1987;* Euroventures Kft, Martonhegyi ut 61/a., H-1121 BUDAPEST, HUNGARY.
•**HOWES, Mr. Andrew Stephen, BA ACA** *1989;* A S Howes & Co Limited, Unit 3a, Minton Place, Victoria Road, BICESTER, OXFORDSHIRE OX26 6QB.
HOWES, Mr. Brian, BSc FCA *1975;* Sundial Group, Highgate House, Creaton, NORTHAMPTON, NN6 8NN.
•**HOWES, Mr. Craig Harrison, FCA** *1990;* Old Mill, Number One, Goldcroft, YEOVIL, SOMERSET, BA21 4DX.
HOWES, Mr. David Alan, BSc ACA *1991;* 27 Woodend Drive, ASCOT, BERKSHIRE, SL5 9BD.
HOWES, Mr. David George Luke, FCA *1968;* 7 Rookery Lane, Great Totham, MALDON, ESSEX, CM9 8DF.
HOWES, Mr. David Robert, BSc ACA *2007;* 30 Wheatcroft Way, DEREHAM, NORFOLK, NR20 3SS.
HOWES, Mrs. Elizabeth Ann, BA FCA *1990;* MAHLE Industries UK Limited, 2 Central Park Drive, RUGBY, CV23 0WE.
HOWES, Mr. Glyn Anthony, MPhil BSc ACA *1989;* Halliwell Jones (Warrington) Ltd, Winwick Road, WARRINGTON, WA2 8HY.
•**HOWES, Mr. Ian David, BA(Hons) ACA** *1996;* Woodlands Bourne Lane, Hamstreet, ASHFORD, KENT, TN26 2HH. See also HMN Accountants Ltd
•**HOWES, Mr. James, MA FCA CTA** *1979;* James Howes & Co Selas, 54-56 Avenue Hoche, 75008 PARIS, FRANCE.
HOWES, Mr. James Philip, FCA *1939;* Low Box Tree, Levens, KENDAL, LA8 8NZ. (Life Member)
HOWES, Mr. John Kenneth, BSc ACA *1983;* Inhowes Computer Solutions Amherst House, 22 London Road Riverhead, SEVENOAKS, TN13 2BT.
HOWES, Mrs. Laura Michelle, BSc ACA *2007;* 30 Wheatcroft Way, DEREHAM, NORFOLK, NR20 3SS.
HOWES, Mr. Leslie Walter, FCA *1951;* Flat 40, Waverley Court, Verulum Place, ST. LEONARDS-ON-SEA, EAST SUSSEX, TN37 6QR. (Life Member)
HOWES, Mr. Luke Sebastian John, BA ACA *2005;* 59 Roydon Court, Mayfield Road, Hersham, WALTON-ON-THAMES, SURREY, KT12 5HZ.
•**HOWES, Mr. Marc Karl, ACA FCCA** *2010;* Ballams, Crane Court, 302 London Road, IPSWICH, IP2 0AJ.
HOWES, Mr. Michael Denis, FCA *1960;* 7 Market Street, CHIPPING NORTON, OX7 5NQ. (Life Member)
HOWES, Mr. Nigel Guy, LLB FCA *1975;* Hill Top Hall, Pannal, HARROGATE, HG3 1PA.
HOWES, Mr. Peter Brian, BA FCA *1993;* 23 Kabanbay Batyr Avenue, ASTANA 010000, KAZAKHSTAN.
•**HOWES, Mr. Peter Kenneth, BSc FCA ATII** *1991;* Peter Howes Associates, 6 Abbey Hill Close, WINCHESTER, SO23 7AZ.
•**HOWES, Mr. Philip Charles Frederick, FCA** *1973;* Philip Howes, 37 Heather Lea Avenue, SHEFFIELD, S17 3DL. See also CHF Accountancy Limited
HOWES, Mr. Richard David, BSc ACA *1995;* 17 Knossington Road, Braunston, OAKHAM, RUTLAND, LE15 8QX.
HOWES, Mr. Robert John, FCA *1961;* 21 Wedgewood Court, North Park Avenue, LEEDS, LS8 1DD. (Life Member)
•**HOWES, Mr. Robert Mark, MA FCA** *1979;* (Tax Fac), Robert M Howes, Catochil Farm, Glenfarg, PERTH, PH2 9PX.
HOWES, Mr. Rupert Spencer, MSc BA DIC ACA *1991;* Marine House, 1-3 Snow Hill, LONDON, EC1A 2DH.
HOWES, Mrs. Sandra Dawn, BSc FCA *1989;* 1 Argyle Road, BARNET, EN5 4DX.
HOWES, Mr. Stephen Andrew, BA FCA *1989;* 12 Rowe Close, RUGBY, WARWICKSHIRE, CV21 4DL.
HOWES, Mr. Timothy Mark, BSc ACA *1990;* 38 Howard Close, Avenue GreenThorpe St Andrew, NORWICH, NR7 0LE.
HOWES, Mrs. Tracey, BA ACA *1989;* 9 Knowle Cottages, Wadhurst Rd Frant, TUNBRIDGE WELLS, TN3 9EJ.
HOWES, Mr. Trevor James, BSc FCA *1979;* with PKF (UK) LLP, Farringdon Place, 20 Farringdon Road, LONDON, EC1M 3AP.
HOWES, Mrs. Victoria Jayne, BSc ACA *2002;* R Bennett & Co Ltd, Constitution Hill, DUDLEY, WEST MIDLANDS, DY2 8RZ.
HOWESON, Mr. Anthony Clive, FCA *1970;* Ashenden, Plaxtol, SEVENOAKS, TN15 0QA.
HOWESON, Mrs. Claire Suzanne, BSc(Hons) ACA *2002;* 53 Firwood Avenue, ST. ALBANS, HERTFORDSHIRE, AL4 0TD.
HOWESON, Mr. Richard John, BSc ACA *1978;* Woodbine Cottage, Cakeham Road, West Wittering, CHICHESTER, PO20 8AD.
HOWEY, Mrs. Carole Lynne, BA ACA *1985;* (Tax Fac), Stratford House, 49 St. Bernards Road, Olton, SOLIHULL, B92 7AX.
HOWFORD, Mr. Dean Ashley, BA ACA *1999;* 17 Brookfield, Oxspring, SHEFFIELD, S36 8WG.
HOWGATE, Mr. John Matthew, BCom FCA *1964;* 1 Jubilee Court, Bridewell Lane, TENTERDEN, KENT, TN30 6EY. (Life Member)
HOWGATE, Mr. Rodney Denton, FCA *1960;* Silverdale, Sand Lane, Nether Alderley, MACCLESFIELD, CHESHIRE, SK10 4TS. (Life Member)
HOWGEGO, Mr. James Alfred Lloyd, BA ACA *1996;* H M L Holdings plc, 9-11 The Quadrant, RICHMOND, TW9 1BP.
HOWIE, Mrs. Diane, FCA *1985;* Stratford House, 15 The Plantations, Wynyard Woods Wynyard, STOCKTON-ON-TEES, TS22 5SN.
HOWIE, Mr. Guy Alexander, BSc ACA *1998;* 34 Spring Woods, FLEET, GU52 7SX.
HOWIE, Mr. Iain Campbell, MA ACA *1989;* Zurich Insurance Company, Level 6East Wing, The Gate, DIFC, PO Box 50389, DUBAI UNITED ARAB EMIRATES.
HOWIE, Mr. Stuart John, BSc ACA *1996;* 43 Creskeld Lane, Bramhope, LEEDS, LS16 9EP.
HOWITT, Mr. Anthony Wentworth, MA FCA *1948;* 17 Basing Hill, Golders Green, LONDON, NW11 8TE. (Life Member)
HOWITT, Mr. Brian Kevin, BA ACA *1998;* 6 Thirlmere Close, Killingworth, NEWCASTLE UPON TYNE, NE12 6GZ.
•**HOWITT, Mr. Christopher, ACA** *2004;* Henton & Co LLP, St. Andrews House, St. Andrews Street, LEEDS, LS3 1LF.
HOWITT, Mr. Ian Howard, BCom FCA *1969;* The Spinney, Mill Lane, Rainhill, PRESCOT, MERSEYSIDE, L35 6NG.
•**HOWITT, Mr. John Norman George, FCA** *1965;* John N.G. Howitt, 2 The Paddock Attenborough, Beeston, NOTTINGHAM, NG9 6AR.
•**HOWITT, Mrs. Penelope Anne, ACA** *1983;* Penny Howitt, 4 Canvey Close, WIGSTON, LE18 3WS.
HOWKINS, Mrs. Caroline Sophie Jane, BA ACA *1989;* Rabley Park, Packhorse Lane, Ridge, POTTERS BAR, HERTFORDSHIRE, EN6 3LX.
HOWKINS, Mr. Jamie, MA ACA *2007;* with Deloitte LLP, Abbots House, Abbey Street, READING, RG1 3BD.
•**HOWKINS, Mr. Paul Anthony, FCA** *1976;* (Tax Fac), Keens Shay Keens Limited, Christchurch House, Upper George Street, LUTON, LU1 2RS.
HOWKINS, Mr. Timothy Alexander, BSc ACA *1988;* Rabley Park, Ridge, POTTERS BAR, HERTFORDSHIRE, EN6 3LX.
•**HOWL, Mrs. Andrea Clare, BSc FCA** *1991;* Oak Grange, 7a Hermitage Road, Edgbaston, BIRMINGHAM, B15 3UP.
HOWL, Mr. James, BA ACA *2007;* Flat 7 Citadel Court, 1-9 Ronalds Road, LONDON, N5 1XH.

HOWL, Mr. Oliver Jonathan Dyke, BSc ACA *1988;* House 10, Three bays, 7 Stanley Beach Road, Tai Tam Bay, STANLEY, HONG KONG SAR.
HOWL, Mr. Robert Russell, FCA *1967;* Wychwood, 23 Huntingdon, Cradley, MALVERN, WR13 5JZ.
•**HOWLADER, Mr. Hasib Reza, MEng ACA CTA MCSI** *2007;* Howlader & Associates Ltd, 56 Leman Street, LONDON, E1 8EU. See also Howlader & Company Ltd
HOWLAND, Mr. Adrian James, BSc ACA *1985;* 32 Highlands Road, BUCKINGHAM, MK18 1PL.
•**HOWLAND, Mr. Jeremy Richard, FCA** *1970;* J.R. Howland, 15 Bear Lane, North Moreton, DIDCOT, OX11 9AS.
HOWLAND, Mr. Kevin, FCA *1986;* 40 Deerstone Ridge, WETHERBY, LS22 7XN.
HOWLAND, Mr. Vernon Maxwell, ACA *1990;* 5 Davidson Avenue, WARRAWEE, NSW 2074, AUSTRALIA.
HOWLES, Mr. Craig Francis, MBA LLB FCA *1993;* National Air Traffic Services Ltd, 4000 Parkway, Whiteley, FAREHAM, HAMPSHIRE, PO15 7FL.
HOWLETT, Mr. Ben, BSc ACA *2010;* Clare Cottage, Green End Road, Radnage, HIGH WYCOMBE, BUCKINGHAMSHIRE, HP14 4BZ.
•**HOWLETT, Mr. Brendon Ashley, BA FCA** *1993;* (Tax Fac), B A Howlett, Aleys Barn, Swan Chase, Swan Street, Sible Hedingham, HALSTEAD ESSEX CO9 3RB.
HOWLETT, Mr. Desmond, FCA *1970;* 1 Grosvenor Crescent, GRIMSBY, DN32 0QJ.
HOWLETT, Miss. Jennifer, BSc ACA *2006;* Ferrier Hodgson, Level 13 225 George Street, SYDNEY, NSW 2000, AUSTRALIA.
HOWLETT, Mr. John Charles, FCA *1961;* Komoka, 12 Fawkham Avenue, New Barn, LONGFIELD, DA3 7HF.
HOWLETT, Mr. Michael John, BA FCA *1977;* 35 Harwater Drive, LOUGHTON, ESSEX, IG10 1LP.
HOWLETT, Mr. Michael Robert, FCA *1972;* 45 Kendal Close, NORTHAMPTON, NN3 6WJ.
HOWLETT, Mr. Neville Philip, BSc ACA CTA *1985;* Five Oaks, 18A Thorn Road, Boundstone, FARNHAM, GU10 4TU.
•**HOWLETT, Mr. Nigel John, BEng ACA** *1993;* PricewaterhouseCoopers LLP, 1 Embankment Place, LONDON, WC2N 6RH. See also PricewaterhouseCoopers
HOWLETT, Mr. Paul James, BSc ACA *1985;* 42 Wainwright Gardens, Hedge End, SOUTHAMPTON, SO30 2NF.
HOWLETT, Mr. Peter William, FCA *1990;* 9 Birchwood Road, Petts Wood, ORPINGTON, KENT, BR5 1NX.
HOWLETT, Mr. Rex, FCA *1961;* 91 Fircroft Road, IPSWICH, IP1 6PU.
HOWLETT, Mr. Robert Leslie, FCA *1962;* 23 Poppys Lane, Pulham St. Mary, DISS, NORFOLK, IP21 4QW.
HOWLETT, Mr. Stephen, ACA *2011;* 11 Croeso'r Gwanwyn, Llansamlet, SWANSEA, SA7 9WP.
HOWLETT, Mr. Stuart Neil, ACA *2006;* Rowans, Wells Road, Hindringham, FAKENHAM, NR21 0PL.
•**HOWLETT, Mrs. Suzanne Odette, BA(Hons) ACA** *2000;* Howlett Accounts Limited, Mistletoe Corner, 4 Oatlands, Elmstead, COLCHESTER, CO7 7EN. See also Howlett's
HOWLETT, Mrs. Victoria Jayne, MA BSc ACA *2005;* 206 New Road, Stoke Gifford, BRISTOL, BS34 8TG.
HOWLETT, Mr. William, MEng ACA *2007;* Level 7 Ropemaker Place, 28 Ropemaker Street, LONDON, EC2Y 9HD.
HOWLETT-BOLTON, Mr. Andrew John, BSc ACA *2006;* 1 Bell Road, ENFIELD, MIDDLESEX, EN1 3JZ.
HOWLEY, Mr. Christopher Stephen, BA ACA *1995;* 54 Salisbury Street, Calverley, PUDSEY, WEST YORKSHIRE, LS28 5PY.
HOWLEY, Mrs. Julie Ann, MA FCA *1986;* 193 Queens Road, LONDON, SW19 8NX.
HOWLEY, Mr. Matthew Paul, BSc ACA *2004;* DHL Global Forwarding (UK) Limited, Magna House, 18-32 London Road, STAINES, MIDDLESEX, TW18 4BP.
•**HOWLEY, Mrs. Olivia Mary, BSc ACA** *1996;* Bell Howley LLP, 1 Laurel Road, Chalfont St. Peter, GERRARDS CROSS, BUCKINGHAMSHIRE, SL9 9SL.
HOWLEY, Mrs. Sarah Joanne, BSc ACA *1998;* 42 Doolan Court, NOOSAVILLE, QLD 4566, AUSTRALIA.
HOWLING, Mr. James Robert, MA ACA *1997;* 47 Barnfield Crescent, SALE, CHESHIRE, M33 6WJ.
HOWLISON, Mr. James David, BSc ACA *1993;* Adam Phones Ltd, 2-3 Dolphin Square, Edensor Road, LONDON, W4 2ST.
HOWORTH, Mr. Derek Paul, FCA *1963;* Copseham Rise, Pine Walk, East Horsley, LEATHERHEAD, KT24 5AG.
HOWSE, Mrs. Anna Elizabeth, MA ACA *1998;* The Beeches, 279 High Street, Boston Spa, WETHERBY, WEST YORKSHIRE, LS23 6AL.
HOWSE, Mr. Christopher John, BSc FCA *1986;* 52 Gregories Road, BEACONSFIELD, BUCKINGHAMSHIRE, HP9 1HQ.
HOWSE, Mrs. Jayne, MA ACA *1998;* 91 Woodville Street, HENDRA, QLD 4011, AUSTRALIA.
HOWSE, Mr. Richard, BSc ACA ATII *1996;* 91 Woodville Street, HENDRA, QLD 4011, AUSTRALIA.
HOWSE, Mr. Stuart Edward, BSc ACA *1995;* 27 Meadow Rise, Blackmore, INGATESTONE, ESSEX, CM4 0QY.
•**HOWSON, Mr. Andrew, BSc ACA** *1989;* Hewson and Howson, 8 Shepcote Office Village, Shepcote Lane, SHEFFIELD, S9 1TG.
HOWSON, Mr. Andrew John, MA(Hons) ACA *2000;* 15 Merton Hall Gardens, LONDON, SW20 8SN.
HOWSON, Mr. Barry Kelvin, FCA *1976;* 45 Passmore, Tinkers Bridge, MILTON KEYNES, MK6 3DY.
HOWSON, Mr. James Robert, BA ACA *2003;* 1387 East 14th Avenue, VANCOUVER V5N 2C7, BC, CANADA.
HOWSON, Miss. Jayne Elizabeth, BA ACA *1990;* 3 The Glen, Redland, BRISTOL, BS6 7JH.
HOWSON, Mr. Lloyd Anthony Joseph, BSc ACA *1993;* Lindens Hangerwood, Shermanbury, HORSHAM, WEST SUSSEX, RH13 8HJ.
HOWSON, Mr. Michael Roxburgh, FCA *1968;* 28 Parsley Close, Walnut Tree, MILTON KEYNES, MK7 7DA.
HOWSON, Mrs. Tracey Jane, ACA *1991;* Lint Croft, Sloade Lane, Ridgeway, SHEFFIELD, S12 3YA.
•**HOWSON-GREEN, Mr. Michael, FCA** *1950;* Secretarial Law Ltd, Ashton House, 12 The Precinct, Winchester Road, Chandler's Ford, EASTLEIGH HAMPSHIRE SO53 2GB.
HOXLEY, Miss. Rachel Elise, ACA *2008;* 56 Portland Street, NORWICH, NR2 3LF.
HOY, Miss. Caroline Elizabeth Louise, ACA *2007;* 49 Ridings Avenue Great Notley, BRAINTREE, ESSEX, CM77 7ZP.
•**HOY, Mr. Colin William, FCA** *1959;* Colin W. Hoy, 12 Millfield, Wadesmill, WARE, SG12 0TU.
HOY, Mr. David John, BSc FCA *1973;* with Benten & Co., Abbey House, 51 High Street, SAFFRON WALDEN, ESSEX, CB10 1AF.
HOY, Miss. Emily Rachel, ACA *2009;* 28.G13.6, Barclays Bank Plc, 1 Churchill Place, LONDON, E14 5HP.
HOY, Mrs. Judith Anne, BSc ACA ATII *1993;* Clive Cottage, Back Lane, Clive, SHREWSBURY, SY4 3LA.
HOY, Mrs. Karen Ann, BSc ACA *1981;* Headington School, Headington Road, Headington, OXFORD, OX3 7BL.
HOY, Mr. Michael John, BA ACA *1997;* 17-19 Maddox Street, LONDON, W1S 2QH.
HOY, Mr. Michael Neil, FCA *1955;* 9 Raylands Mead, Bull Lane, GERRARDS CROSS, BUCKINGHAMSHIRE, SL9 8SJ. (Life Member)
HOY, Mr. Stephen Michael, FCA *1979;* Layters Cottage, 5 Layters Way, GERRARDS CROSS, SL9 7QZ.
HOY, Mr. William James, BCom ACA *1995;* G K N plc, Ipsley Church Lane, Ipsley, REDDITCH, WORCESTERSHIRE, B98 0TL.
HOYE, Miss. Lucille, BMus ACA *2007;* 22 Northfield Way, BRIGHTON, BN1 8EH.
HOYER MILLAR, Mr. Christian James Charles, BSc ACA *1991;* Inchyra House, Glencarse, PERTH, PH2 7LU.
HOYES, Mr. Stephen Anthony, BA ACA *1994;* 13 Parkwood Road, Wimbledon, LONDON, SW19 7AQ.
HOYLE, Mr. Alexis Paul, ACA *2010;* Flat 42 Woodside House, Woodside, LONDON, SW19 7QN.
HOYLE, Mrs. Andrea, BSc ACA *1993;* 9 Thrum Fold, Shawclough, ROCHDALE, OL12 6DG.
HOYLE, Mr. Andrew John, ACA *2008;* Flat B, 168 Lower Richmond Road, LONDON, SW15 1LY.
HOYLE, Mr. Charles David, FCA *1974;* 98/408 Moo 10 Pruklada, Bangrakyai Banmai Road, Bangmaenang, NONTHABURI 11140, THAILAND.
HOYLE, Mr. Christopher, BA ACA *2011;* 5 Sandwich Crescent, HUDDERSFIELD, HD2 2NQ.
HOYLE, Mr. David, BA ACA *1986;* 478 Holcombe Road, Greenmount, BURY, BL8 4HB.
HOYLE, Mr. David Stuart, BA FCA *1991;* Cherry Tree House, 2 The Meade, Garforth, LEEDS, LS25 1QL.
HOYLE, Miss. Ellen, LLB(Hons) ACA *2010;* Flat 12, 133 Larkhall Lane, LONDON, SW4 6RD.
•**HOYLE, Mr. James Brendan, FCA** *1979;* Wyatt Morris Golland & Co, Park House, 200 Drake Street, ROCHDALE, OL16 1PJ.
HOYLE, Mr. James Shaw, ACA *1980;* 7 Brecon Rd, Henleaze, BRISTOL, BS9 4DT.
•**HOYLE, Mr. John Roger Horrocks, BSc FCA** *1972;* Fraser Campbell LLP, Direct House, Lancaster House, Wingates Inds Est, Westhoughton, BOLTON BL5 3XD.
HOYLE, Mr. Jonathan James Austin, BA ACA *1996;* Morris Lane, 31/33 Commercial Road, POOLE, DORSET, BH14 0HU.
•**HOYLE, Mrs. Joy Angela, FCA CTA** *1983;* (Tax Fac), Hoyle & Co, Wootton Farm, Pencombe, BROMYARD, HR7 4RR.
HOYLE, Miss. Lindsay Joanne, BA ACA *2007;* 7 College Road, Ash Vale, ALDERSHOT, GU12 5BT.
HOYLE, Mr. Matthew George, BSc ACA *2005;* Stonecroft Tems Side, Giggleswick, SETTLE, NORTH YORKSHIRE, BD24 0BS.
HOYLE, Mr. Michael Robert, BSc ACA *2009;* with PKF (UK) LLP, 4th Floor, 3 Hardman Street, MANCHESTER, M3 3HF.
HOYLE, Mr. Peter John Harrison, BSc FCA *1978;* 2 Marsh Hall Barn, Thurstonland, HUDDERSFIELD, HD4 6XB.
HOYLE, Mr. Richard John, BSc FCA *1985;* Millstones, Milner Lane, Greetland, HALIFAX, HX4 8HP.
•**HOYLE, Mr. Ronald, FCA** *1964;* (Tax Fac), R Hoyle, 51 Oakwood Avenue, BECKENHAM, BR3 6PT.
HOYLE, Mr. Rupert Felix, FCA *1964;* 4 Princes Drive, Oxshott, LEATHERHEAD, KT22 0UF.
HOYLE, Mrs. Sally Elizabeth, BA ACA *1988;* Millstones, Milner Lane, Greetland, HALIFAX, HX4 8HW.
HOYLE, Miss. Sara Ann, ACA *1999;* 6 Freshwood Close, BECKENHAM, BR3 5JX.
HOYLE, Mr. Stephen William, FCA *1974;* White Beck, Crosthwaite, KENDAL, CUMBRIA, LA8 8HX.
HOYLE, Miss. Suzanne Elizabeth, BSc ACA *1996;* 1009 Great North Road, Point Chevalier, AUCKLAND 1022, NEW ZEALAND.
HOYLE, Mr. Timothy John, MA BA BSc(Hons) ACA *1983;* 2 Starling Road, St. Athan, BARRY, SOUTH GLAMORGAN, CF62 4NJ.
HOYLE, Mrs. Valerie Jane, FCA *1974;* 8 Domaine des Pins, Route d'Albas, 11360 DURBAN CORBIERES, FRANCE.
HOYLES, Mr. Raymond William, FCA *1951;* 11 St. Helens Drive, HOVE, EAST SUSSEX, BN3 8EA. (Life Member)
HOYOW, Mr. Mark Andre, BSc FCA *1983;* The Acorns, 1 Oakmore Drive, Les Camps Du Moulin, St. Martin, GUERNSEY, GY4 6DY.
HOZIER, Mr. Barrie Clifford, FCA *1969;* 16 Danesbury Park, HERTFORD, SG14 3HX.
HREMIAKO, Mr. Leonard, BSc ACA *1990;* 40 Reynolds Street, CREMORNE, NSW 2090, AUSTRALIA.
HRYNCYSZYN, Miss. Katherine, ACA *2008;* Tudor Lodge, Denham Avenue, Denham, UXBRIDGE, MIDDLESEX, UB9 5ER.
HSIANG, Ms. Yuet Ming, ACA *2008;* Grant Thornton, 6th Floor, Nexus Building, 41 Conaught Road, CENTRAL, HONG KONG ISLAND HONG KONG SAR.
HSIEH, Miss. Chia Chieh, ACA *2009;* The Pines, Brookside, Headington, OXFORD, OX3 7PJ.
HSU, Mr. Hok Kin Kenneth, ACA *2009;* Block C 4/F, Evelyn Towers, 38 Cloud View Road, NORTH POINT, HONG KONG ISLAND, HONG KONG SAR.
HSU, Mr. Joseph Kar Hing, MSc ACA *1991;* Flat 5A Block One, Scenic Garden, 9 Kotewall Road, MID LEVELS, HONG KONG SAR.
HSU, Mr. Kelvin Tsun Yiu, BSc ACA *1997;* Flat 1 18/F Block A, Ventris Place, 19-23 Ventris Road, HAPPY VALLEY, HONG KONG ISLAND, HONG KONG SAR.
HSU, Miss. Ya Ting, ACA CA(SA) *2009;* Flat 2, Caernarvon House, 8 Audley Drive, LONDON, E16 1TP.
HSUEN, Mr. Kei, ACA *2008;* Flat C 35/F Block 1, 8 Oi King Street, HUNG HOM, KOWLOON, HONG KONG SAR.
HU, Mr. Bo, ACA *2009;* Room 902, No 8 Lane, 1288 Lianhua Road(S), Minhang District, SHANGHAI 201100, CHINA.
HU FOUYE, Mr. Louis Edmond Kim Fen, FCA *1975;* Unit 5, 14 The Boulevarde, BRIGHTON-LE-SANDS, NSW 2216, AUSTRALIA.
HUAH, Mr. Kenny San Loong, BEng ACA *2001;* 54 Jalan Cengal Pasir, Sierramas, 47000 SUNGAI BULOH, SELANGOR, MALAYSIA.
HUANG, Mr. Anthony Yick Kin, BSc FCA *1976;* Bond Capital Partners (UK) Ltd, 21 Arlington Street, LONDON, SW1A 1RN.
HUANG, Mr. Aobo, ACA *2011;* UBS Investment Bank, 50/F, Two International Finance Center, CENTRAL, HONG KONG SAR.
•**HUANG, Miss. Pae-Ling, ACA CA(NZ)** *2009;* (Tax Fac), A B Accounting and Consulting Limited, 34 Langbourne Place, LONDON, E14 3WN.
HUANG, Mr. Shi Chin, ACA *1985;* 1 Jalan Emas 5, Taman Megah Emas, 47301 PETALING JAYA, SELANGOR, MALAYSIA.
HUANG, Mrs. Suwen, BE ACA *2010;* 3-3-602 Jin Du Hua Yuan, No 570 Wen San Xi Lu, HANGZHOU 310012, ZHEJIANG PROVINCE, CHINA.
HUANG, Mr. Xue Qing, MPhil BSc ACA *2011;* Internal Audit Department, PengFeng Automobile (Group) Ltd, East Side of FuTian Bus Station, Shen Nan Zhong Road, SHENZHEN 518000, GUANGDONG PROVINCE CHINA.
HUANG, Miss. Yanfei, MSc ACA *2011;* BlackRock, 12 Throgmorton Avenue, LONDON, EC2N 2DL.
HUANG, Ms. Yanyao, ACA *2011;* Flat 1503, Building 36-5, Yu Quan Xi Li Er Qu, Shi Jing Shan District, BEIJING 100040, CHINA.
HUANG, Mrs. Yunjie, ACA *2010;* 3-103 Xiziyuan, Xianjia xincun, Tongzipo Road, Yuelu District, CHANGSHA 410205, CHINA.
HUANG WAN YAN, Miss. Winnie, BSc ACA *2002;* Blk922c, Parc Palais, 18 wylie Road, KOWLOON TONG, KOWLOON, HONG KONG SAR.
HUBBARD, Mr. Adam, BA(Hons) ACA *2009;* 174 Cumberland Avenue, BENFLEET, SS7 1DY.
HUBBARD, Mr. Adrian Alan, BSc(Hons) ACA *2010;* 12 Pit Lane, SWAFFHAM, NORFOLK, PE37 7DA.
HUBBARD, Mr. Alistair, BSc ACA *2006;* 92 John Archer Way, LONDON, SW18 2TT.
•**HUBBARD, Mr. Andrew John, FCA** *1973;* Mazars LLP, Tower Bridge House, St. Katharines Way, LONDON, E1W 1DD.
HUBBARD, Mr. Cedric George, BA ACA *1999;* Hutchison 3 G UK Ltd Star House, 20 Grenfell Road, MAIDENHEAD, SL6 1EH.
HUBBARD, Mr. Christopher Richard, ACA *2007;* 34 Bobbin Lane, LINCOLN, LINCOLNSHIRE, LN2 4ZB.
HUBBARD, Mrs. Clair, BSc ACA *2006;* AXA Liabilities Managers Suffolk House, Civic Drive, IPSWICH, SUFFOLK, IP1 2AN.
•**HUBBARD, Mr. David Stuart, FCA** *1983;* (Tax Fac), Hubbard Lloyd, 8 The Courtyard, Wyncolls Road, Severalls Industrial Park, COLCHESTER, ESSEX CO4 9PE.
HUBBARD, Mr. David Vernon, FCA *1966;* 43 Church View, Laleston, BRIDGEND, MID GLAMORGAN, CF32 0HF. (Life Member)
HUBBARD, Mr. Harold Dennis, FCA *1962;* Flat 5, 36 Victoria Park Road, LEICESTER, LE2 1XB. (Life Member)
•**HUBBARD, Mrs. Helen Samantha, ACA MAAT** *2009;* 62 Sydney Road, HAYWARDS HEATH, WEST SUSSEX, RH16 1QA.
HUBBARD, Mr. James Leigh, BSc ACA *2010;* The Studio, 13 Middle Lane, TEDDINGTON, MIDDLESEX, TW11 0HQ.
HUBBARD, Mrs. Joanne, MA BSc ACA *2007;* with Ernst & Young LLP, Compass House, 80 Newmarket Road, CAMBRIDGE, CB5 8DZ.
HUBBARD, Mr. John Aubrey, BSc FCA *1980;* 30 Oleander Close, CROWTHORNE, RG45 6TU.
HUBBARD, Mr. John Barton, FCA *1984;* 48 Whites Road, Bitterne, SOUTHAMPTON, SO19 7NQ.
HUBBARD, Mr. John Christopher, BA FCA *1957;* 89 Selborne Road, LONDON, N14 7DE. (Life Member)
•**HUBBARD, Mr. John Michael, FCA** *1968;* (Tax Fac), John Hubbard Ltd, 3 St. Marys Street, WORCESTER, WR1 1HA.
HUBBARD, Mrs. Lynne Elisabeth Clarissa, LLB ACA *1988;* 53 Skeena Hill, LONDON, SW18 5PW.
HUBBARD, Mr. Mark Alan, MA ACA *2000;* Flat 4, 9 Dorset Square, LONDON, NW1 6QB.
HUBBARD, Mr. Nathan, BSc ACA *2006;* 1 Tower House Stables, Cheveley Park Cheveley, NEWMARKET, SUFFOLK, CB8 9DE.
HUBBARD, Mr. Nicholas Raymond, FCA *1982;* BAE Systems PLC, 6 Carlton Gardens, LONDON, SW1Y 5AD.
HUBBARD, Mr. Paul Charles, BA FCA *1979;* (Member of Council 1999 - 2005), with KPMG Deutsche Treuhand-Gesellschaft, Wirtschaftsprüfungsgesellschaft, Ganghoferstrasse 29, 80339 MUNICH, GERMANY.
HUBBARD, Mr. Paul Mark, BA ACA *1995;* 25 Walcott Avenue, CHRISTCHURCH, BH23 2NQ.
•**HUBBARD, Mr. Peter Harold, FCA** *1971;* Peter H. Hubbard, 5 Broadway Market, Fencepiece Road, Barkingside, ILFORD, ESSEX IG6 2JT.
HUBBARD, Mr. Peter John, BSc FCA *1980;* Huddaknoll House Seven Leaze Lane, Edge, STROUD, GLOUCESTERSHIRE, GL6 6NL.
HUBBARD, Mr. Piers John Sherlock, FCA *1958;* 44 Court Hill, Sanderstead, SOUTH CROYDON, Surrey, CR2 9NA. (Life Member)

HUBBARD, Mr. Raymond Aubrey, FCA *1948;* 9 Kelmscott Close, Caversham, READING, RG4 7DG. (Life Member)
HUBBARD, Mr. Ronald Leslie, BA FCA *1975;* Old Mutual Group Services Limited, PO Box HM3085, HAMILTON HM NX, BERMUDA.
HUBBARD, Miss. Sarah, LLB ACA *2010;* 2 Shaftesbury Mount, Blackwater, CAMBERLEY, SURREY, GU17 9JR.
HUBBARD, Miss. Sarah Elizabeth, MA ACA *1988;* with PricewaterhouseCoopers LLP, 1 Embankment Place, LONDON, WC2N 6RH.
HUBBARD, Mr. Stephen, BSc ACA *1996;* with KPMG LLP, 1-2 Dorset Rise, LONDON, EC4Y 8EN.
HUBBARD-BROWN, Mr. Keith, BSc FCA *1972;* (Tax Fac), 24 Beckett Avenue, KENLEY, CR8 5LT.
HUBBARD-FORD, Mr. Jonathan Louis, MA FCA *1969;* Flat 8, 1 Uxbridge Street, LONDON, W8 7TQ. (Life Member)
•**HUBBLE, Mr. Barry Royston, FCA CMI** *1971;* 5 Parsons Street, DUDLEY, WEST MIDLANDS, DY1 1JJ.
HUBBLE, Miss. Elizabeth Ann, LLB ACA *2002;* Poundland Plc, Wellmans Road, WILLENHALL, WV13 2QT.
HUBBLE, Mr. Nicholas Peter, BA(Hons) ACA *2000;* 127 Annandale Road, LONDON, SE10 0JY.
HUBBLE, Mr. Robert John, BSc FCA *1975;* Dippers, Shaugh Prior, PLYMOUTH, PL7 5HA.
HUBBLE, Mr. Robert John, FCA *1964;* 77 Oxford Road, Old Marston, OXFORD, OX3 0PH.
HUBBLE, Mr. Robert John Lloyd, FCA FCT *1975;* 17 Ouseley Road, LONDON, SW12 8ED.
HUBBLE, Mr. Simon James, BA(Hons) ACA *2001;* 1 Westmead, PRINCES RISBOROUGH, BUCKINGHAMSHIRE, HP27 9HP.
•**HUBBOCKS, Mr. Mark Roger, BA ACA** *2001;* Wags LLP, Richmond House, Walkern Road, STEVENAGE, HERTFORDSHIRE, SG1 3QP.
HUBER, Mr. John Christopher, FCA *1965;* 1, Birling CloseBearsted, MAIDSTONE, ME14 4AZ. (Life Member)
HUBERMAN, Mr. Paul Laurence, BA FCA *1986;* Tufton Properties Ltd, 11 Bruton Place, LONDON, W1J 6LT.
HUBERT, Mr. Daniel, BSc ACA *1984;* Post House La Moye Road, Vale, GUERNSEY, GY3 5BZ.
HUBRIG, Mr. Gary Peter, BSc ACA *1999;* British Petroleum Co Plc, 20 Canada Square, LONDON, E14 5NJ.
HUBSCHMID, Mr. Martin, BA ACA *1992;* 24 Scott Walk, Bridgeyate, BRISTOL, BS30 5WB.
HUBY, Mr. Kevin Neil Turner, BSc ACA *1988;* with Ernst & Young LLP, 1 Bridgewater Place, Water Lane, LEEDS, LS11 5QR.
HUCKER, Mr. Bryan Herbert, BSc FCA *1974;* Northlew, Lansdown Road, BATH, BA1 5TD.
HUCKER, Mr. Gavin James, BSc ACA *1993;* PO Box 99679, NEWMARKET 1149, NEW ZEALAND.
HUCKER, Mr. Mark, BA FCA *1995;* South House, La Grande Rue, St. Mary, JERSEY, JE3 3BD.
HUCKERBY, Mr. Dale, BA ACA *1993;* 224 Loxley Road, STRATFORD-UPON-AVON, WARWICKSHIRE, CV37 7DU.
HUCKERBY, Mrs. Lisa Nicole, ACA *2009;* 1 Bromyard Drive, Chellaston, DERBY, DE73 6PF.
HUCKERBY, Mr. Stephen Allen, BA ACA *1993;* La Fantasie Le Vieux Beaumont, St. Peter, JERSEY, JE3 7EZ.
HUCKETT, Mr. Michael Alexander, ACA *2010;* Lucraft Hodgson & Dawes, 2 Ash Lane Rustington, LITTLEHAMPTON, WEST SUSSEX, BN16 3BZ.
HUCKLE, Mr. Gethin John, ACA *2008;* Ernst & Young, 62 Forum Lane, CAMANA BAY, GRAND CAYMAN, KY1 1106, CAYMAN ISLANDS.
HUCKLE, Mr. Ian James, FCA *1985;* Business & Decision Ltd 8th Floor, 55 Old Broad Street, LONDON, EC2M 1RX.
HUCKLE, Mr. James William, MA ACA *2002;* NBGI Private Equity Limited, Old Change House, 128 Queen Victoria Street, LONDON, EC4V 4BJ.
HUCKLE, Mr. John George, FCA *1966;* Farr Farm, Newcastle, MONMOUTH, GWENT, NP25 5NF. (Life Member)
HUCKLE, Mr. John Richard William, BSc FCA *1977;* 12 Homefield Road, Wimbledon, LONDON, SW19 4QE.
HUCKNALL, Mr. Andrew David, BSc FCA *1992;* with PKF(UK)LLP, Farringdon Place, 20 Farringdon Road, LONDON, EC1M 3AP.
•**HUCKRIDGE, Mr. Robert Adair, FCA** *1974;* Mace And Partners, 52 Talbot Road, Talbot Green, PONTYCLUN, MID GLAMORGAN, CF72 8AF.
HUCKSTEP, Mr. Mark, BA ACA *1998;* 55, Hunting Gate, BIRCHINGTON, CT7 9JB.
HUCQ, Mr. Brandon Jay, ACA CA(SA) *2011;* 43 Baldock Road, LETCHWORTH GARDEN CITY, HERTFORDSHIRE, SG6 3JX.
HUDA, Mr. Khayrul, BSc ACA *2004;* 73 Heathcroft Avenue, SUNBURY-ON-THAMES, MIDDLESEX, TW16 7SR.
HUDA, Mr. Khizerul, BSc ACA *2004;* 35 Parkland Grove, ASHFORD, MIDDLESEX, TW15 2JB.
HUDANI, Mr. Sirazali Gulamali Merali, FCA *1974;* Alfarover Ltd, PO Box 33710, KAMPALA, UGANDA.
•**HUDD, Mr. David John, BA ACA** *1991;* Livesey Spottiswood Holding Ltd, 17 George Street, ST. HELENS, MERSEYSIDE, WA10 1DB. See also Livesey Spottiswood Limited
HUDD, Mr. David Leslie, BA FCA *1969;* 97 Gunterstone Road, LONDON, W14 9BT.
HUDD, Mrs. Jayne Clare, FCA *2000;* 3 Rose Lea Close, WIDNES, WA8 9JA.
HUDD, Mr. John Peter, FCA *1965;* 71390 SASSANGY, FRANCE.
HUDDART, Mr. Ian Bruce Charles, BSc ACA *1991;* (Tax Fac), 20 Ely Gardens, TONBRIDGE, TN10 4NZ.
•**HUDDART, Mr. Jeffrey Alan, FCA** *1968;* (Tax Fac), Jeffrey A Huddart, 164 Walkden Road, Worsley, MANCHESTER, M28 7DP.
HUDDART, Mr. Steven John, BSc FCA *2000;* G E Capital Fleet Services, Old Hall Road, SALE, CHESHIRE, M33 2GZ.
•**HUDDLESTON, Mr. Andrew Jeremy, MA(Oxon) ACA** *2001;* PKF (UK) LLP, Farringdon Place, 20 Farringdon Road, LONDON, EC1M 3AP.
HUDDLESTON, Mr. Jonathan, BSc ACA *1991;* Flat 3, 5 Hillcrest Road, LONDON, W5 2AY.
HUDDLESTON, Mrs. Karen Jean Helen Christian, ACA *2000;* 4 Grange Close, Bletchingley, REDHILL, RH1 4LW.
•**HUDDLESTON, Mr. Matthew Everett, BSc ACA** *2003;* with Charterhouse Group International Limited, Viking House, St. Pauls Square, Ramsey, ISLE OF MAN, IM8 1FF.
HUDDLESTONE, Mr. Paul Ivan Michael, BA FCA *1975;* Royal Bank of Canada (C.I) Ltd, 19-21 Broad Street, St Helier, JERSEY, JE1 3PB.
HUDDY, Mr. David George, MA FCA *1958;* 22 Inglis Road, Ealing, LONDON, W5 3RN. (Life Member)
HUDSON, Miss. Amy Louise, ACA *2009;* Grillparzerstrasse 43, 81675, MUNICH, GERMANY.
HUDSON, Mr. Andrew Colin, BA MSt ACA *2010;* 83 Deakin Road, Erdington, BIRMINGHAM, B24 9AL.
•**HUDSON, Mrs. Anne Elizabeth, MA ACA** *1980;* John & Anne Hudson, 15 Neville Close, BASINGSTOKE, RG21 3HG.
HUDSON, Miss. Belinda Jane, LLB ACA *1984;* 34 Cambridge Road, East Twickenham, TWICKENHAM, TW1 2HL.
HUDSON, Ms. Catherine Clare, MA ACA *1995;* 16a Burlington Avenue, RICHMOND, TW9 4DQ.
HUDSON, Miss. Catherine Gayle, ACA *2009;* 21 Cliffe Terrace, Baildon, SHIPLEY, WEST YORKSHIRE, BD17 5LA.
HUDSON, Mr. Christopher James, ACA *2010;* Macquarie, Level 18, Corner of Salaam & Electra St, PO Box 939, ABU DHABI, UNITED ARAB EMIRATES.
HUDSON, Mr. Christopher John Gerard, FCA MSI *1979;* 209 Linnet Drive, CHELMSFORD, CM2 8AH.
HUDSON, Mr. Christopher Mark, ACA *1983;* 8 Ivy Road, SHIPLEY, BD18 4JY.
HUDSON, Miss. Claire, ACA *2011;* 9 Preston Street, SHREWSBURY, SY2 5PG.
HUDSON, Mrs. Clare Elizabeth, BA ACA *1998;* Furzewood Barden Road, Speldhurst, TUNBRIDGE WELLS, KENT, TN3 0LE.
•**HUDSON, Mr. Colin George, BCom FCA** *1983;* Deloitte LLP, 2 New Street Square, LONDON, EC4A 3BZ. See also Deloitte & Touche LLP
HUDSON, Mr. David Anthony, BA ACA *1987;* 25 Johnson Way, Chilwell, Beeston, NOTTINGHAM, NG9 6RJ.
HUDSON, Mr. David Brian, BSc FCA *1986;* The Orchard, 12 Burford Lane, LYMM, WA13 0SE.
HUDSON, Mr. David Charles Wesley, BA FCA *1977;* 7 Setley Way, Martins Heron, BRACKNELL, RG12 9FF. (Life Member)
HUDSON, Mr. David Christopher, ACA *2006;* with Grant Thornton UK LLP, 30 Finsbury Square, LONDON, EC2P 2YU.
HUDSON, Mr. David William, FCA *1972;* 28 Greenfield Road, Brunton Park, Gosforth, NEWCASTLE UPON TYNE, NE3 5TP.
•**HUDSON, Mrs. Della Louise, BSc FCA** *1995;* Hudson Accountants, 14 West Town Road, Backwell, BRISTOL, BS48 3HH.
•**HUDSON, Mr. Derek Ernest, FCA** *1951;* (Tax Fac), Hudson & Co, Sterling House, 20 Station Road, GERRARDS CROSS, SL9 8EL.
HUDSON, Mr. Dimond John, BA FCA *1973;* Bradley Fold, Woodford Lane, Newton, MACCLESFIELD, SK10 4LH. (Life Member)
HUDSON, Mrs. Elizabeth, BA ACA *1983;* Bradley Fold, Woodford Lane, Newton, MACCLESFIELD, SK10 4LH.
•**HUDSON, Mr. Francis John Bernard, MA ACA ATII** *2002;* Wilder Coe LLP, 233-237 Old Marylebone Road, LONDON, NW1 5QT.
HUDSON, Mr. Frank Russell, BSc FCA *1980;* 3 Woodlands, Pickwick, CORSHAM, WILTSHIRE, SN13 0DA.
HUDSON, Mrs. Genevieve Retha, BSc ACA *2002;* with Clear Channel - Internal Audit, 33 Golden Square, LONDON, W1F 9JT.
HUDSON, Mr. Geoffrey Miles, FCA *1953;* 25 The Avenue, HALIFAX, WEST YORKSHIRE, HX3 8NP. (Life Member)
HUDSON, Mrs. Georgina Wanda, MA ACA *1998;* with PricewaterhouseCoopers LLP, 7 More London Riverside, LONDON, SE1 2RT.
HUDSON, Mr. Gerard, BSc FCA *1990;* 69 Rimu Road, Raumati Beach, PARAPARAUMU 5032, NEW ZEALAND.
HUDSON, Mr. Giles Matthew, BSc ACA *1997;* 27 Wentworth Grange, WINCHESTER, HAMPSHIRE, SO22 4HZ.
HUDSON, Mr. Glen Jeffery, ACA *2009;* 14B Rocha Street, San Lorenzo Village, MAKATI CITY 1223, PHILIPPINES.
HUDSON, Mrs. Helen Louise, BA ACA *2001;* with Baker Tilly Corporate Finance LLP, 25 Farringdon Street, LONDON, EC4A 4AB.
•**HUDSON, Mrs. Hemione Rajni Anne, BSc ACA** *1999;* PricewaterhouseCoopers LLP, 1 Embankment Place, LONDON, WC2N 6RH. See also PricewaterhouseCoopers
HUDSON, Mr. Ian, LLB ACA *2002;* 526 UVEDALE ROAD, RIVERSIDE, IL 60546, UNITED STATES.
HUDSON, Mr. Ian David, BA ACA *1990;* 52 Lewes Road, Ditchling, HASSOCKS, WEST SUSSEX, BN6 8TU.
•**HUDSON, Mr. Ian John, FCA** *1969;* 87 Alzey Gardens, HARPENDEN, AL5 5SZ.
HUDSON, Mr. Ian Robert, BSc FCA *1974;* 14 Farnleys Mead, Belmore Lane, LYMINGTON, SO41 3TJ.
HUDSON, Mr. Ian William, FCA *1961;* (Tax Fac), 19 Downsview Gardens, DORKING, RH4 2DX.
HUDSON, Mr. James Alexander, BA ACA *1988;* 71 Collingwood Avenue, LONDON, N10 3EE.
HUDSON, Mr. James Andrew David, BSc ACA *2004;* 76 Discovery Walk, LONDON, E1W 2JG.
HUDSON, Mrs. Jennifer Louise, ACA *1982;* 12 Museum Street, IPSWICH, SUFFOLK, IP1 1HF.
HUDSON, Mrs. Jennifer Ruth, BSSc ACA *1991;* 24 Keswick Gardens, RUISLIP, MIDDLESEX, HA4 7XN.
HUDSON, Mr. John Charles, BA ACA *1985;* Oakmere, North Weirs, BROCKENHURST, HAMPSHIRE, SO42 7QA.
•**HUDSON, Mr. John Christopher Mozeen, MBA ACA** *1981;* John & Anne Hudson, 15 Neville Close, BASINGSTOKE, RG21 3HG.
HUDSON, Mr. John Gerard, BA ACA *1990;* 6 Fielding Lane, Ratby, LEICESTER, LE6 0AS.
•**HUDSON, Mr. John Henry, LLB ACA** *2001;* with FTI Forensic Accounting Limited, 322 High Holborn, LONDON, WC1V 7PB.
HUDSON, Dr. John Matthew, BSc ACA *1999;* 61 The Rise, Darras Hall, Ponteland, NEWCASTLE UPON TYNE, NE20 9LQ.
HUDSON, Mr. John Michael, BSc ACA *1997;* The Garden House, Hollington, Woolton Hill, NEWBURY, RG20 9XT.
•**HUDSON, Mr. John Michael William, FCA** *1976;* Baker Tilly UK Audit LLP, 25 Farringdon Street, LONDON, EC4A 4AB.
HUDSON, Mr. John Robin Laverack, FCA *1962;* Ashness, 81 Boroughbridge Road, YORK, YO26 5ST.
HUDSON, Mr. John Stewart, FCA *1977;* 1/ 81A Union Street, MCMAHONS POINT, NSW 2060, AUSTRALIA.
HUDSON, Mr. Jonathan Paul, BSc ACA *1991;* Royal London Royal London House, Alderley Road, WILMSLOW, CHESHIRE, SK9 1PF.
•**HUDSON, Ms. Julia Mary, BSc ACA** *1990;* Accountancy Business Support Ltd, 2 Rawcliffe Grove, YORK, YO30 6NR.
HUDSON, Mr. Keith Maurice, FCA *1975;* Brock House, 6 Lemsford Road, ST. ALBANS, HERTFORDSHIRE, AL1 3PB.
HUDSON, Mr. Kelvin Mark, MA ACA *1986;* with Saffery Champness, P O Box 141, La Tonnelle House, Les Banques, St. Sampson, GUERNSEY GY1 3HS.
•**HUDSON, Mr. Kevin James, BSc FCA** *1998;* with CW Fellowes Limited, Carnac Place, Cams Hall Estate, Fareham, PORTSMOUTH, PO16 8UY.
HUDSON, Mr. Kevin Michael, FCA *1984;* 14 West Avenue, Clarendon Park, LEICESTER, LE2 1TR.
HUDSON, Mr. Kevin Robert, BSc FCA *1988;* 4 Dean Drive, Bowdon, ALTRINCHAM, WA14 3NE.
HUDSON, Miss. Leigh Eleanor, BSc(Hons) ACA *2011;* Flat K, Windsor Court, 14 Winn Road, SOUTHAMPTON, SO17 1EN.
HUDSON, Mr. Leslie George, FCA *1970;* P.O. Box 1983, RIVONIA, GAUTENG, 2128, SOUTH AFRICA.
HUDSON, Mr. Lester Thompson, MA ACA *1990;* 128 Capel Road, Forest Gate, LONDON, E7 0JT.
HUDSON, Mrs. Lisa Marie, BA ACA *2003;* 36 Subiaco Road, SUBIACO, WA 6008, AUSTRALIA.
HUDSON, Mrs. Margaret Mary Patricia, BSc ACA *1992;* XI Communications Ltd, Genesis House Sanbeck Way, WETHERBY, WEST YORKSHIRE, LS22 7DN.
HUDSON, Mr. Mark Andrew, BSc FCA *1998;* Novae Group Plc, 71 Fenchurch Street, LONDON, EC3M 4HH.
HUDSON, Mr. Mark Edward Charles, BSc ACA *1989;* 10 Dew Lane, NEW CANAAN, CT 06840, UNITED STATES.
HUDSON, Mr. Martin Arthur, FCA *1971;* 40 Bowling Green Lane, LONDON, EC1R 0NE.
HUDSON, Mr. Matthew Charles, BA ACA *1998;* Transport for London, Windsor House, 42-50 Victoria Street, LONDON, SW1H 0TL.
HUDSON, Mrs. Melanie Ann, BSc(Hons) ACA *2002;* Tamerton, College Rise, MAIDENHEAD, BERKSHIRE, SL6 6BP.
HUDSON, Mr. Michael, FCA *1974;* Le Moulin des Brosses, 16500 ST MAURICE DES LIONS, FRANCE. (Life Member)
HUDSON, Mrs. Natalie, ACA *2003;* 6b Lincoln Road, Skellingthorpe, LINCOLN, LN6 5UT.
•**HUDSON, Mr. Neil Alan, BA FCA ATII** *1991;* Deloitte LLP, 2 New Street Square, LONDON, EC4A 3BZ. See also Deloitte & Touche LLP
HUDSON, Mr. Nicholas Edward, BSc ACA *1999;* 37 Copse Wood Way, NORTHWOOD, HA6 2TZ.
HUDSON, Mr. Nicholas John, BA ACA *1993;* Orchard House, Latton, SWINDON, WILTSHIRE, SN6 6DS.
HUDSON, Mr. Nicholas John, ACA *1985;* 102 Duncastle Park, Newbuildings, LONDONDERRY, BT47 2QL.
HUDSON, Ms. Nicola Jane, ACA *1984;* 143A Queens Road, Wimbledon, LONDON, SW19 8NS.
•**HUDSON, Mrs. Nicola Louise, ACA FCCA** *2008;* Walkers Accountants Limited, 16-18 Devonshire Street, KEIGHLEY, WEST YORKSHIRE, BD21 2DG.
HUDSON, Mr. Nigel Charles, BA ACA *1990;* Seabourne Express Courier International Distribution Centre, Crabtree Road Thorpe, EGHAM, TW20 8RS.
HUDSON, Mr. Paul Andrew, BSc ACA *1990;* XI Communications Ltd, Genesys House Sanbeck Way, WETHERBY, WEST YORKSHIRE, LS22 7DN.
HUDSON, Mr. Paul Michael, BSc FCA CTA *1992;* H P H Chartered Accountants, 54 Bootham, YORK, YO30 7XZ.
•**HUDSON, Mr. Peter David, BA FCA** *1984;* (Tax Fac), Reeves & Co LLP, Third Floor, 24 Chiswell Street, LONDON, EC1Y 4YX.
•**HUDSON, Mr. Peter Edwin, FCA** *1968;* Proactax Ltd, 361 Rayleigh Road, LEIGH-ON-SEA, SS9 5PS.
HUDSON, Mr. Peter Evason, ACA CTA *1984;* 16 Sugden Road, LONDON, SW11 5EF.
HUDSON, Mr. Peter Malcolm, BSc ACA *2003;* 1 Burnell Road Admaston, TELFORD, SHROPSHIRE, TF5 0BQ.
HUDSON, Mr. Peter Mervyn, FCA *1965;* 27 Glencairn Crescent, EDINBURGH, EH12 5BT. (Life Member)
•**HUDSON, Mr. Philip John, FCA** *1974;* (Tax Fac), Philip Hudson & Co, 454-458 Chiswick High Road, LONDON, W4 5TT. See also Hadlow & Harborow Ltd
HUDSON, Mrs. Rachel Elizabeth, BA ACA *2005;* OMG Plc, 14 Minns Business Park, West way, OXFORD, OXFORDSHIRE, OX20JB.
HUDSON, Miss. Rebecca Anne, BA ACA *1990;* Tenon, Tenon House, Ferryboat Lane, SUNDERLAND, SR5 3JN.
HUDSON, Mr. Richard Andrew, MA ACA *1991;* 90 Constable Road, IPSWICH, IP4 2UZ.
•①**HUDSON, Mr. Richard Hayward, FCA MBA** *1980;* Richard H. Hudson, Lilyhurst House, Lilyhurst, SHIFNAL, TF11 8RL.
HUDSON, Mr. Richard James, BSc ACA *2000;* 113 St. James's Drive, LONDON, SW17 7RP.
•**HUDSON, Mr. Richard Jonathan, FCA** *1993;* (Tax Fac), Stirk Lambert & Co, Russell Chambers, 61A North Street, KEIGHLEY, BD21 3DS.
•**HUDSON, Mr. Richard Lawrence, FCA** *1968;* Richard L Hudson FCA, The Elms, 29 North Bar Without, BEVERLEY, HU17 7AG.

HUDSON, Mr. Richard Lewis, MA FCA *1974;* 8 Laurel Gardens, BROADSTONE, BH18 8LT.
HUDSON, Mr. Robert, BA FCA ALCM *1970;* 11A Worcester Road, Woodthorpe, NOTTINGHAM, NG5 4HW.
HUDSON, Mr. Robert Jan, BSc ACA *1998;* Flat 10 Parkview House 1-13 Miller Street, LONDON, NW1 7DN.
•HUDSON, Mr. Robert Lionel Frederick, BSc FCA *1976;* PKF (UK) LLP, New Guild House, 45 Great Charles Street, BIRMINGHAM, B3 2LX.
HUDSON, Mr. Robert Michael, FCA *1981;* Brigadoon 19, PO Box CR 56766-860, NASSAU, BAHAMAS.
HUDSON, Mr. Robin Andrew, BA FCA *1989;* 11 Talbot Way, NANTWICH, CHESHIRE, CW5 7RR.
HUDSON, Mr. Roger Stuart, FCA *1971;* 41 Tudor Hill, SUTTON COLDFIELD, B73 6BE.
HUDSON, Mrs. Sally, BA ACA *1993;* The Grange High Street, Otford, SEVENOAKS, TN14 5PL.
HUDSON, Miss. Sarah Jane, BSc FCA *1976;* 192 Shakespeare Tower, Barbican, LONDON, EC2Y 8DR.
HUDSON, Mr. Scott Gregory, ACA CA(AUS) *2008;* 13 Fernbank Mews, LONDON, SW12 9NJ.
HUDSON, Mr. Simon Dean, BSc ACA *1994;* The Grange High Street, Otford, SEVENOAKS, TN14 5PL.
HUDSON, Mrs. Sonia Fay, ACA *2009;* RSM, Bentley Jennison Charter House, Legge Street, BIRMINGHAM, B4 7EU.
HUDSON, Mr. Stanley Herbert, FCA *1951;* 10 Holt Lane, LEEDS, LS16 7NX. (Life Member)
•HUDSON, Mr. Stephen Charles, BA FCA *1982;* Stephen C Hudson, 24 Westfield Close, Brampton, CHESTERFIELD, S40 3RS.
HUDSON, Mr. Stephen James, BA(Hons) ACA *2001;* 62 Heol Y Bont, Rhiwbina, CARDIFF, CF14 6AL.
HUDSON, Mr. Stephen Paul, BSc ACA *1989;* 143 Charlton Road, Keynsham, BRISTOL, BS31 2LH.
•HUDSON, Mrs. Susan Jane, BMus FCA *1992;* Firth Parish, 1 Airport West, Lancaster Way, Yeadon, LEEDS, LS19 7ZA.
HUDSON, Mrs. Tamar Taylor, BA ACA *1989;* Oakmere, North Weirs, BROCKENHURST, HAMPSHIRE, SO42 7QA.
•HUDSON, Mr. Thomas Francis, BSc FCA CTA *1983;* Stephenson Nuttall & Co, Ossington Chambers, 6-8 Castle Gate, NEWARK, NG24 1AX.
•HUDSON, Mr. Timothy William, BSc FCA *1989;* Mazars LLP, The Lexicon, Mount Street, MANCHESTER, M2 5NT.
HUDSON, Mr. Trevor, FCA *1976;* 29 Stanton Avenue, BELPER, DERBYSHIRE, DE56 1EE.
HUDSON, Mr. William David, BA ACA *1990;* I T E Group Plc, 105-109 Salusbury Road, LONDON, NW6 6RG.
HUDSON-DAVIES, Mr. Bernt Hugh Reinhardt, CVO FCA *1959;* 21 Woodhall Drive, Dulwich, LONDON, SE21 7HJ. (Life Member)
HUDSON-DAVIES, Mr. Michael James, BA ACA *1995;* 55 Ongar Road, Fulham, LONDON, SW6 1SH.
HUDSWELL, Mr. Ronald Frank, FCA *1962;* 32 St. Augustine Avenue, LUTON, LU3 1QB.
HUELIN, Mrs. Anne Elizabeth, BSc ACA *1984;* 6 Warwick Close, CAMBERLEY, SURREY, GU15 1ES.
HUELIN, Mr. Colin Andrew, BSc ACA *1990;* Caleh Le Mont Gras D'Eau, St. Brelade, JERSEY, JE3 8ED.
HUELIN, Mr. Graham Arthur, BSc ACA TEP *1985;* Les Rochettes La Rue Militaire, St. John, JERSEY, JE3 4DP.
•HUELIN, Mr. Michael Charles, BSc FCA CTA *1985;* Michael Huelin, 6 Warwick Close, CAMBERLEY, SURREY, GU15 1ES.
HUEN, Mr. Alfred Hon Kwong, ACA *2006;* Alfred HK Yuen & Company, 14/F Wing On Cheong Building, 5 Wink Lok Street, CENTRAL, KOWLOON, HONG KONG SAR. See also Alfred HK Huen & Company
HUETSON, Mr. Adrian Stephen, BA ACA *1995;* 95 Gowthorpe, SELBY, NORTH YORKSHIRE, YO8 4HD.
HUFF, Mr. David Andrew, BSocSc FCA *1983;* (Tax Fac), with 3i Group plc, 16 Palace Street, LONDON, SW1E 5JD.
HUFF, Mrs. Winnie Sau Man, BA ACA *1984;* Tryfan, 23 Woodlands Road, BROMLEY, BR1 2AD.
HUFFADINE, Mr. David Stuart, FCA *1974;* The Meadows Lower Road, Hinton Blewett, BRISTOL, BS39 5AT.
HUFFEE, Ms. Carole Ann, BA FCA CTA *1999;* 170 Knighton Church Road, LEICESTER, LE2 3JL.
•HUFFEN, Mrs. Sharon, ACA *1991;* Sharon Huffen, Woodman House, 18 Main Street, Ryther, TADCASTER, LS24 9EE.
HUFFORD, Mr. Horace Gordon, FCA ATII *1953;* 10 Marlborough House, Graemesdyke Road, BERKHAMSTED, HERTFORDSHIRE, HP4 3YE. (Life Member)
HUFFORD, Mrs. Jayne Frances, BSc ACA *1993;* with MILES cmc, Stanley House, 33-35 West Hill, Portishead, BRISTOL, BS20 6LG.
HUFTON, Mr. Michael Stuart, MBA BSc ACA *1985;* 14 Manor Fields Drive, ILKESTON, DE7 5FA.
HUFTON, Ms. Tina, LLM ACA *2004;* with PricewaterhouseCoopers LLP, 101 Barbirolli Square, Lower Mosley Street, MANCHESTER, M2 3PW.
HUGEL, Miss. Terri, ACA *2007;* 21 Forum Court, BURY ST. EDMUNDS, SUFFOLK, IP32 6BP.
HUGGETT, Mr. Dennis George, FCA *1951;* 125 Goldstone Crescent, HOVE, BN3 6BB. (Life Member)
HUGGETT, Mr. Derek William Crease, FCA *1960;* 61 Amberley Road, LONDON, N13 4BH. (Life Member)
HUGGETT, Miss. Frances Monica, MA FCA *1975;* Fistic Ltd, 51 Main Street, EGREMONT, CUMBRIA, CA22 2DB.
•HUGGETT, Mr. Ian Alan, BSc FCA *1989;* (Tax Fac), Simpkins Edwards LLP, 21 Boutport Street, BARNSTAPLE, DEVON, EX31 1RP.
HUGGETT, Mr. John Ward, FCA *1975;* 33B ALDERHURST CRESCENT, BAYSWATER, WA 6053, AUSTRALIA.
HUGGETT, Dr. Kate Elizabeth, PhD MA(Hons) ACA *2001;* (Tax Fac), 15 Pipistrelle Way, Charvil, READING, RG10 9WA.
HUGGETT, Mr. Stephen Philip, BA FCA *1985;* Sunny Dene, East End, WITNEY, OXFORDSHIRE, OX29 6PY.
HUGGINS, Mr. David John, MA FCA *1986;* 4 Victoria Grove, Brimington, CHESTERFIELD, S43 1QR.
•HUGGINS, Mr. David Paul, FCA *1974;* Bird Luckin limited, Aquila House, Waterloo Lane, CHELMSFORD, CM1 1BN.
HUGGINS, Miss. Emma Jane Elizabeth, ACA *2008;* 83 Mayford Road, LONDON, SW12 8SH.
•HUGGINS, Mrs. Jacqueline Ann, BA ACA *1989;* Hadrian Fulready, Ettington, STRATFORD-UPON-AVON, CV37 7PE.
HUGGINS, Mr. Jeffrey Michael, BA(Econ) FCA *1999;* with Mazars LLP, 37 Frederick Place, BRIGHTON, BN1 4EA.
•HUGGINS, Mr. Michael Alec, BA FCA DChA *1988;* Baker Tilly UK Audit LLP, St Philips Point, Temple Row, BIRMINGHAM, B2 5AF. See also Baker Tilly Corporate Finance LLP
HUGGINS, Mr. Nicholas John, MA ACA *1992;* Apt 1201 Sapphire Building, Tiara Residence, Palm Jumeriah, DUBAI, UNITED ARAB EMIRATES.
HUGGINS, Mr. Norman Edward, ACA *1984;* Ketts House, Queen's Street, Spooner Row, WYMONDHAM, NR18 9JU.
HUGGINS, Mr. Paul, BA BSc ACA *2010;* Apartment 311 Astra House, 23-25 Arklow Road, LONDON, SE14 6BY.
HUGGINS, Mr. Peter James, FCA *1958;* 'Woodleigh', 6 Robin Lane, SANDHURST, BERKSHIRE, GU47 9AU. (Life Member)
HUGGINS, Mr. Ronald, FCA *1948;* 132 Scalby Road, SCARBOROUGH, NORTH YORKSHIRE, YO12 5QP. (Life Member)
HUGGINS, Mr. William Robert, BA FCA *1983;* Bournville Place, Cadbury Ltd PO Box 12, Bournville, BIRMINGHAM, B30 2LU.
HUGGON, Miss. Deborah Jane, BSc ACA *1993;* 127 Columbus Ravine, SCARBOROUGH, NORTH YORKSHIRE, YO12 7QZ.
HUGH, Mr. Alexander, LLB ACA *2002;* 6 Chessington Avenue, LONDON, N3 3DP.
HUGH, Mr. Jonathan Laurence, MA ACA *1996;* 8 Tudor Well Close, STANMORE, MIDDLESEX, HA7 2SD.
•HUGH, Mr. Robert, BSc FCA *1981;* (Tax Fac), Robert Hugh Limited, 15 Dan-y-Bryn Avenue, Radyr, CARDIFF, CF15 8DD.
HUGH-SMITH, Mr. David, MA ACA *1996;* Bathealton Court, Bathealton, TAUNTON, SOMERSET, TA4 2AJ.
HUGHES, Mr. Adam Douglas, BSc ACA *2004;* 9 Cross Oak Road, BERKHAMSTED, HERTFORDSHIRE, HP4 3EH.
HUGHES, Mr. Adam Talfan, BA ACA *2004;* Rutland The Street, Steeple, SOUTHMINSTER, ESSEX, CM0 7RJ.
•HUGHES, Mr. Adrian Francis, BSc FCA *1989;* Batten Hughes & Co Ltd, 173 College Road, Crosby, LIVERPOOL, L23 3AT. See also Batten Hughes & Co
HUGHES, Mr. Adrian Neil, BSc ACA *2000;* with PricewaterhouseCoopers LLP, 1 Embankment Place, LONDON, WC2N 6RH.
HUGHES, Mrs. Adrienne Jane, BA ACA *1998;* Huttenstrasse 40, 8006 ZURICH, SWITZERLAND.
HUGHES, Mr. Aidan John, BSc ACA *1987;* The Crest, Smallburn, NEWCASTLE UPON TYNE, NE20 0AD.
HUGHES, Mr. Alan Brereton, FCA *1975;* 10 Elm Lane, EXMOUTH, DEVON, EX8 2RR.
HUGHES, Mr. Alan Tapscott, FCA *1954;* 27 Seaforth Gardens, Ewell, EPSOM, KT19 0LR. (Life Member)
HUGHES, Mr. Alexander James, ACA *2009;* 42 Westfield Drive, Aldridge, WALSALL, WS9 8ZA.
HUGHES, Mr. Alexander Paul, ACA *2008;* 6 Ravenoak Park Road, Cheadle Hulme, CHEADLE, CHESHIRE, SK8 7EH.
HUGHES, Mrs. Alison Mary, BSc ACA ATII *1993;* (Tax Fac), 39 Clonmel Road, Fulham, LONDON, SW6 5BL.
HUGHES, Mrs. Amanda, MA ACA *1991;* Keepers Lodge, Star, GAERWEN, GWYNEDD, LL60 6AS.
HUGHES, Mr. Andrew, BSc ACA *1999;* Heals, 196 Tottenham Court Road, LONDON, W1T 7LQ.
•HUGHES, Mrs. Angela June, MA FCA *1984;* Money Manager At Home, 3 Guernsey Farm Drive, Horsell, WOKING, SURREY, GU21 4BE.
HUGHES, Mr. Angus Leslie, BSc ACA *1995;* 20 Heath House Drive, Wombourne, WOLVERHAMPTON, WV5 8EZ.
•①HUGHES, Mrs. Anita Jane, BSc FCA *1985;* Baker Tilly, 1 St. James Gate, NEWCASTLE UPON TYNE, NE1 4AD.
HUGHES, Mrs. Anna Louise, BA ACA *1991;* Brook Farm Days Road, Capel St. Mary, IPSWICH, IP9 2LB.
HUGHES, Mr. Anthony, BSc ACA *1982;* 20 Dudley Road, Wimbledon, LONDON, SW19 8PN.
HUGHES, Mr. Anthony Bevan, FCA *1970;* 174 Tyntyla Road, Llwynypia, TONYPANDY, MID GLAMORGAN, CF40 2SP.
•HUGHES, Mr. Anthony David, FCA *1982;* Gary Sargeant + Company, 5 White Oak Square, London Road, SWANLEY, BR8 7AG.
•HUGHES, Mr. Anthony Miles, BA ACA ATII *1993;* (Tax Fac), Anthony M Hughes & Co Central Chambers, 83A High Street, CRADLEY HEATH, B64 5HA.
HUGHES, Mr. Anthony Roland, FCA *1958;* Fanns Cottage, Canfield Road, Takeley, BISHOP'S STORTFORD, CM22 6SX. (Life Member)
HUGHES, Mr. Anthony Trevor, FCA *1955;* 2 Manor Lodge, Park Road, Cheadle Hulme, CHEADLE, CHESHIRE, SK8 7DA. (Life Member)
HUGHES, Mr. Aubrey Daniel Bedford, BA FCA *1961;* 36 Eldon Road, Marsh, HUDDERSFIELD, HD1 4NE. (Life Member)
HUGHES, Mr. Barry Anthony, BA FCA *1987;* 1 Pinehurst Glen, Saddlestone, Douglas, ISLE OF MAN, IM2 1PP.
HUGHES, Mr. Barry James, FCA DChA *1977;* Aristo Argaka Villae 1, No 35 grigori Auxentiou, Argaka, 8873 PAPHOS, CYPRUS.
HUGHES, Mr. Benjamin Alexander Gross, BSc ACA *2006;* Flat 35, Eagle Wharf Court, Lafone Street, LONDON, SE1 2LZ.
HUGHES, Mr. Benjamin John, BSc ACA *1999;* Brays Cottage Chalk Lane, Hyde Heath, AMERSHAM, BUCKINGHAMSHIRE, HP6 5SA.
HUGHES, Mr. Bernard John, FCA *1969;* Glenburn Mill Lane, Taplow, MAIDENHEAD, SL6 0AG.
HUGHES, Miss. Bethan Marie, BSc ACA *2009;* 12 Egerton Road, BERKHAMSTED, HERTFORDSHIRE, HP4 1DT.
HUGHES, Mr. Brendan James, BSc ACA *1997;* Expert Training Systems Plc, 123 New Zealand Avenue, WALTON-ON-THAMES, KT12 1QA.
•HUGHES, Mr. Brian, BA ACA *1994;* (Tax Fac), A. Hughes-Jones Dyson & Co, Bryn Afon, Segontium Terrace, CAERNARFON, LL55 2PN.
HUGHES, Mr. Brian Leslie, FCA *1974;* (Tax Fac), Culzean, Hyde Heath, AMERSHAM, BUCKINGHAMSHIRE, HP6 5RW.
HUGHES, Mr. Byron Paull, BSc ACA *2011;* Laurel Cottage, Alpraham, TARPORLEY, CHESHIRE, CW6 9JE.
HUGHES, Mrs. Cara, MSc BSc ACA *2005;* Rutland, The Street, Steeple, SOUTHMINSTER, ESSEX, CM0 7RJ.
•HUGHES, Mr. Carl David, MA FCA *1987;* Deloitte LLP, 2 New Street Square, LONDON, EC4A 3BZ. See also Deloitte & Touche LLP
HUGHES, Miss. Caroline Denise, BA ACA *1995;* Zurich Financial Services, 126 Hagley Road, BIRMINGHAM, B169PF.
HUGHES, Mrs. Caron Margaret, BSc ACA *2000;* 23-01 Block 74 Bamboo Grove, 74-86 Kennedy Road, WAN CHAI, HONG KONG SAR.
HUGHES, Miss. Carys Wyn, BSc ACA *2007;* Brynawelon, Capel Bangor, ABERYSTWYTH, DYFED, SY23 3LR.
HUGHES, Mrs. Catharine Anne, BSc ACA *1999;* 11 Clifford Road, Poynton, STOCKPORT, CHESHIRE, SK12 1HY.
HUGHES, Mr. Christopher, ACA *2009;* R P M Ltd, 24-40 Goodwin Road, LONDON, W12 9JW.
•HUGHES, Mr. Christopher Charles, BA ACA *1992;* (Tax Fac), Kingston Smith LLP, Devonshire House, 60 Goswell Road, LONDON, EC1M 7AD. See also Kingston Smith Limited Liability Partnership, Devonshire Corporate Services LLP and Kingston Smith Consulting LLP
HUGHES, Mr. Christopher John, BA ACA *1992;* 4 The Quadrangle, WELWYN GARDEN CITY, HERTFORDSHIRE, AL8 6SG.
•①HUGHES, Mr. Christopher John, MA FCA *1973;* with Talbot Hughes McKillop LLP, 6 Snow Hill, LONDON, EC1A 2AY.
HUGHES, Mr. Christopher Trevor, BA ACA *1991;* 78 Park Road, Keynsham, BRISTOL, BS31 1DE.
HUGHES, Mrs. Claire Elizabeth, BSc ACA *1994;* 5 Priory Road, West Bridgford, NOTTINGHAM, NG2 5HU. (Life Member)
HUGHES, Miss. Claire Jacqueline, BSc(Hons) ACA *2003;* 16 Lorne Gardens, LONDON, E11 2BZ.
HUGHES, Mr. Colin Benedict, BSc ACA *1994;* 27 Chaucer Road, BATH, BA2 4QX.
•HUGHES, Mr. Colin Harry John, FCA ACMA *1970;* (Tax Fac), Coppins-Hughes, The Croft, Pit Lane, Treflach, OSWESTRY, SY10 9HB. See also Coppin-Hughes Limited
HUGHES, Mr. Colin Pickering, FCA *1966;* 13 Canadian Bay Road, MOUNT ELIZA, VIC 3930, AUSTRALIA.
•HUGHES, Mr. Craig William Owen, BSc ACA *1997;* Ernst & Young LLP, 1 More London Place, LONDON, SE1 2AF. See also Ernst & Young Europe LLP
HUGHES, Mr. Daniel James, BA ACA *2004;* with KPMG LLP, St. James's Square, MANCHESTER, M2 6DS.
HUGHES, Mr. Daniel James, MSc MSci ACA *2006;* Flat 7, 8c Penrith Street, LONDON, SW16 6DW.
HUGHES, Mr. Darren David, ACA *1992;* Copper Cable Co Ltd Interlink Way East, Bardon Hill, COALVILLE, LEICESTERSHIRE, LE67 1LA.
HUGHES, Mr. David, BCom FCA *1969;* 55 Seven Star Road, SOLIHULL, B91 2BZ.
HUGHES, Mr. David, FCA *1968;* 81 Hastings Road, BATTLE, EAST SUSSEX, TN33 0TF.
•HUGHES, Mr. David, BA FCA *1984;* (Tax Fac), Saffery Champness, Edinburgh Quay, 133 Fountainbridge, EDINBURGH, EH3 9BA.
HUGHES, Mr. David Alun, BA ACA *1989;* High View House, Kingsthorne, HEREFORD, HR2 8AH.
HUGHES, Mr. David Anthony Reginald, BBS ACA FTII AITI *1991;* Hazlems Fenton Palladium House, 1-4 Argyll Street, LONDON, W1F 7LD.
•HUGHES, Mr. David Clewin, MA FCA *1979;* David Clewin Hughes, Silverleigh House, 3 Silver Lane, PURLEY, SURREY, CR8 3HJ.
•HUGHES, Mr. David Edwards, FCA *1964;* (Tax Fac), Laud Meredith & Co, 94 High Street, PORTHMADOG, LL49 9NW.
HUGHES, Mr. David Elwyn, FCA *1970;* Macara, 09100 UNZENT, FRANCE. (Life Member)
HUGHES, Mr. David Frank, FCA *1971;* Abbotsbury, 53 The Broadway, DUDLEY, DY1 4AP.
HUGHES, Mr. David George, BA FCA *1977;* Spindrift, 65 Pipers Lane, Heswall, WIRRAL, MERSEYSIDE, CH60 9HY.
HUGHES, Mr. David James, BSc ACA *1987;* The Midland News Association Ltd, 51-53 Queen Street, WOLVERHAMPTON, WV1 1ES.
HUGHES, Mr. David John, BSc ACA *1992;* 2 Sheepridge, Ogbourne St. Andrew, MARLBOROUGH, WILTSHIRE, SN8 1UJ.
HUGHES, Mr. David John, BSc ACA *1994;* Krones UK Ltd, Westregen House, Great Bank Road, Wingates Industrial Estate, Westhoughton, BOLTON BL5 3XB.
HUGHES, Mr. David Kenneth, FCA *1936;* Flat 45, Montrose Court 1a Market St, Hoylake, WIRRAL, CH48 2AP. (Life Member)
HUGHES, Mr. David Kenneth Anthony Paul, FCA *1968;* The Querns, 130 Pinkneys Road, MAIDENHEAD, BERKSHIRE, SL6 5DN.
HUGHES, Mr. David Martin, BSc(Hons) ACA *2001;* 16 Gladiator Close, Wootton, NORTHAMPTON, NN4 6LS.
HUGHES, Mr. David Michael, BA FCA *1980;* 75 Rydes Hill Road, GUILDFORD, GU2 9SP.
HUGHES, Mr. David Michael, BSc(Econ) ACA *1998;* Melverley, Halcog, Brymbo, WREXHAM, CLWYD, LL11 5DQ.

HULL, Mr. Anthony Grove Horton, FCA *1961;* C/O Mrs A Duncan, 12 Kinmundy Avenue, WESTHILL, ABERDEENSHIRE, AB32 6TG. (Life Member)
HULL, Mr. Christopher George, MA ACA *1987;* Network Rail Ltd, Queen Ann Road, BRISTOL, BS5 9TX.
HULL, Mr. Christopher John, BSc ACA *1992;* Birchfield Church Lane, Grappenhall, WARRINGTON, WA4 3EP.
•**HULL, Mr. Colin Christopher, BA ACA** *1986;* CCH & Co, PO Box 827, London Colney, ST. ALBANS, HERTFORDSHIRE, AL1 9AB.
HULL, Mr. Daniel James, ACA *2008;* 39 Trent Avenue, Flitwick, BEDFORD, MK45 1SH.
HULL, Mr. David Victor Michael, BSc FCA *1972;* Vorosmarty utca 13, 8228 LOVAS, HUNGARY. (Life Member)
HULL, Mrs. Elizabeth Jill, MA ACA *1994;* Birchfield, Church Lane, Grappenhall, WARRINGTON, WA4 3EP.
HULL, Mrs. Emma, BSc(Hons) ACA *2010;* 12 Broughton Road, LONDON, SW6 2LA.
HULL, Miss. Emma Louise, BA ACA *2007;* Apartment 4, 67 Palatine Road, MANCHESTER, M20 3AP.
HULL, Mr. George Julian Candon, BA FCA *1962;* 10 Ogilvie Court, West Ferry, DUNDEE, DD5 1LR. (Life Member)
HULL, Mr. George Stephen, BSc FCA *1994;* with PKF (Isle of Man) LLC, PO Box 16, Analyst House, Douglas, ISLE OF MAN, IM99 1AP.
•**HULL, Mr. Gerard Anthony, BA FCA** *1991;* (Tax Fac), P A Hull & Co, 41 Bridgeman Terrace, WIGAN, LANCASHIRE, WN1 1TT.
•**HULL, Mrs. Jane Elizabeth, BSc ACA** *1991;* CCH & Co, PO Box 827, London Colney, ST. ALBANS, HERTFORDSHIRE, AL1 9AB.
HULL, Mr. Jonathan, BSc ACA *1991;* Old Post Office, Boxford, NEWBURY, RG20 8DH.
HULL, Mr. Jonathon Philip, BA ACA ATII *1999;* BDO, 38 Station Street, SUBIACO, WA 6008, AUSTRALIA.
HULL, Mrs. Mary Louise, BA ACA *2009;* 7 Boscombe Road, Tooting, LONDON, SW17 9JL.
HULL, Mr. Matthew James Robert, BA(Hons) ACA *2003;* 4 North Parade, West Park, LEEDS, LS16 5AY.
HULL, Mr. Michael David, FCA *1975;* Brisal House, 36 Main Road, Holme, HUNSTANTON, NORFOLK, PE36 6LA.
HULL, Mr. Nicholas James, BSc ACA *2000;* 9 Melfort Close, Cherry Tree, BLACKBURN, BB2 5BL.
HULL, Mr. Peter Cowan, FCA *1961;* 28 Naseby Road, SOLIHULL, B91 2DR.
HULL, Mr. Peter Robert, ACA *1983;* 14 Robinwood Court, Park Villas, LEEDS, LS8 1DZ.
HULL, Ms. Rebecca Paige, ACA *2009;* 1 Mariners Wharf, Quayside, NEWCASTLE UPON TYNE, NE1 2BJ.
HULL, Dr. Roger Steven, PhD FCA *2000;* with PricewaterhouseCoopers LLP, 1 Embankment Place, LONDON, WC2N 6RH.
•**HULL, Mr. Roy Bernard, BSc FCA** *1978;* Hanson Heidelberg Cement, Hanson House, 14 Castle Hill, MAIDENHEAD, BERKSHIRE, SL6 4JJ.
HULL, Mr. Stephen James, BSc FCA *1975;* 22 Charlotte Square, CARDIFF, CF14 6NE.
HULL, Mr. Stuart, BSc ACA *2006;* Flat 7 The Lab Building, 177 Roseberry Avenue, LONDON, EC1R 4TW.
HULL, Ms. Teresa Jane, BSc ACA *1992;* University of Bradford, Richmond Road, BRADFORD, WEST YORKSHIRE, BD7 1DP.
HULL, Miss. Tracey Caroline, BSc ACA *2009;* 173 Park Hill Road, Harborne, BIRMINGHAM, B17 9HE.
HULL, Mr. William Robert, FCA *1971;* Lyttleton House, Lye Green, Claverdon, WARWICK, CV35 8LP. (Life Member)
HULLAH, Mr. Nicholas Peter, FCA *1967;* 15 Taunton Street, PYMBLE, NSW 2073, AUSTRALIA.
HULLAIT, Mr. Gurinder Singh, BSc ACA *2004;* 249 Singlewell Road, GRAVESEND, DA11 7RN.
HULLAIT, Mr. Rashpal Singh, BA FCA *1991;* Samovar West End Lane, Stoke Poges, SLOUGH, SL2 4NA.
HULLAND, Mr. Christopher James Snow, BCom FCA *1977;* 47 Swinton Lane, WORCESTER, WR2 4JP.
HULLAND, Mr. David John, ACA *1979;* 13019 Signature Point, Apt 241, SAN DIEGO, CA 92130, UNITED STATES.
HULLAND, Mr. Terence James, FCA *1970;* Fields House, 15 Littlemead, Box, CORSHAM, WILTSHIRE, SN13 8AH.
HULLEY, Mr. Mark, BA ACA *1991;* 5 Compass Court, Tower House Piazza, Shad Thames, LONDON, SE1 2NJ.
HULLEY, Mr. Timothy John, BA ACA *1986;* 22 Greenlands Close, BURGESS HILL, WEST SUSSEX, RH15 0AR.
HULLIN, Mr. Chris John, BA ACA *2005;* 35 Westfield Road, SURBITON, SURREY, KT6 4EL.
HULLIN, Mrs. Joanne Lyndsay, BSc ACA *2003;* 35 Westfield Road, SURBITON, KT6 4EL.
HULLIS, Mrs. Jennie Louise, BA ACA *1996;* 4 Laughton Avenue, West Bridgford, NOTTINGHAM, NOTTINGHAMSHIRE, NG2 7GJ.
HULLIS, Mrs. Karen, BA ACA *1990;* Nutwood, Emmets Nest, Binfield, BRACKNELL, RG42 4HH.
HULLS, Ms. Elizabeth Jane, BSc ACA *1994;* 2 The Nursery, Sutton Courtenay, ABINGDON, OX14 4UA.
HULLY, Mr. Desmond Hooton, FCA *1959;* 403 Ashford Forest Drive, HOUSTON, TX 77079, UNITED STATES. (Life Member)
HULLY, Mr. Ronald Erwin, BSc ACA *2006;* 30 Gillott Road, BIRMINGHAM, B16 0EZ.
HULME, Mr. Adrian Harry, ACA *1997;* (Tax Fac), with Barber Harrison & Platt, 2 Rutland Park, SHEFFIELD, S10 2PD.
HULME, Mrs. Alison Julie, BSc ACA *1995;* 3 Bishopdale Close, Feniscowles, BLACKBURN, BB2 5EB.
•**HULME, Mr. Andrew John, FCA** *1970;* Andrew Hulme, 12 Tunbridge Lane, Bottisham, CAMBRIDGE, CB25 9DU.
HULME, Mr. Andrew Philip, BSc FCA *1988;* 46 Tudor Gardens, Stony Stratford, MILTON KEYNES, MK11 1HX.
HULME, Mrs. Ann Louise, BSc ACA *1997;* 2 Chattaway Drive, Balsall Common, COVENTRY, CV7 7QH.
HULME, Dr. Ashley, PhD MChem ACA *2011;* 4 Harmsworth Street, Kennington, LONDON, SE17 3TJ.
HULME, Miss. Cate Anne, BSc ACA *1999;* 42 Mauldeth Road, MANCHESTER, M20 4WD.
HULME, Mrs. Catherine Margaret, BA ACA *1993;* 10 Broadway, Atherton, MANCHESTER, M46 9HW.
HULME, Mr. Colin Stuart, ACA *2009;* Pricewaterhousecoopers, 9 Greyfriars Road, READING, RG1 1JG.
HULME, Mr. David, FCA *1967;* David Hulme, Martlets, 4 Ashdene Crescent, Ash, ALDERSHOT, SURREY GU12 6TA.
HULME, Mr. Douglas James Morley, FCA *1967;* Fortchamp, 10 Fort Road, St. Peter Port, GUERNSEY, GY1 1ZU.
HULME, Mr. Edward Thomas, BA ACA *2004;* XL Group Plc, XL House, One Bermudiana Road, HAMILTON HM 08, BERMUDA.
HULME, Mr. Gary Michael, BA ACA *1992;* 9 Standen Park House, LANCASTER, LA1 3FF.
•**HULME, Mr. Graham, FCA** *1972;* Reece Hulme & Co, 1 Wilson Patten Street, WARRINGTON, WA1 1PG.
HULME, Mrs. Hana, MPhys ACA *2007;* Flat 2, Warwick House, Windsor Way, Brook Green, LONDON, W14 0UQ.
HULME, Miss. Janette Anna, BSc ACA *2007;* 2 St. Johns Court, WAKEFIELD, WEST YORKSHIRE, WF1 2RY.
HULME, Mr. Martin, FCA *1964;* La Brossardinre, Chateau Bordin, 79310 SAINT PARDOUX, FRANCE. (Life Member)
•**HULME, Mr. Nicholas Andrew, BA ACA** *1989;* Nick Hulme Corporate Finance, Atria, Spa Road, BOLTON, BL1 4AG.
HULME, Mr. Richard Brian, BSc FCA *1976;* 5 St. Anthonys Court, Burkes Road, BEACONSFIELD, BUCKINGHAMSHIRE, HP9 1ER.
•**HULME, Mrs. Rosalind Sarah, ACA** *1985;* Wheelhouse Hulme, Westfield House, Woodhouse Lane, Biddulph, STOKE-ON-TRENT, ST8 7DR.
HULME, Mr. Simon David, BSc ACA *1992;* 1 Lavinia Court, Knutsford Road, ALDERLEY EDGE, CHESHIRE, SK9 7SD.
HULME, Mr. Stephen Jon, BA ACA *1996;* The Cottage, 13 Leahurst Road, West Bridgford, NOTTINGHAM, NG2 6JD.
HULME, Mr. Wayne Marshall, BA ACA *1999;* 4923 Dunmore Lane, KISSIMMEE, FL 34746, UNITED STATES.
HULMES, Mr. David, FCA *1961;* 14 Mayfield Road, Timperley, ALTRINCHAM, WA15 7SZ. (Life Member)
HULSE, Mr. Andrew, ACA *2010;* 45 Naples Drive, NEWCASTLE, STAFFORDSHIRE, ST5 2QD.
HULSE, Mr. Andrew David, BA FCA *1997;* Four Gables, 11 Chestnut Avenue, Walton, WAKEFIELD, WF2 6TE.
•**HULSE, Mr. Anthony Philip, MA FCA** *1978;* 48 Platts Lane, LONDON, NW3 7NT.
HULSE, Mr. Christopher David, BSc ACA *2002;* c/o BG Group: US Houston, BG Group Plc, 100 Thames Valley Park Drive, READING, BERKSHIRE, RG6 1PT.
HULSE, Mr. Christopher Thomas, BA ACA *1988;* 6 Manor Park Drive, Great Sutton, ELLESMERE PORT, CH66 2ET.
HULSE, Mr. David, FCA *1977;* Woodview Farm, Wood Lane Cadeby, Market Bosworth, NUNEATON, CV13 0AU. (Life Member)
HULSE, Mrs. Deborah Jane, BSc ACA *1984;* Bacardi International Limited, P.O. Box HM720, HAMILTON, BERMUDA.
•**HULSE, Mrs. Elaine Marie, BA ACA** *1987;* (Tax Fac), Elaine M Hulse, 6 Manor Park Drive, Great Sutton, ELLESMERE PORT, CH66 2ET.
HULSE, Mr. John Michael, FCA *1966;* (Tax Fac), 27 Widney Road, Knowle, SOLIHULL, B93 9DX.
HULSE, Mr. Jonathan, MA(Oxon) BA(Hons) ACA *2010;* Flat 2, 1-4 Hillbrow Court, Hillbrow Road, ESHER, KT10 9UA.
HULSE, Ms. Louise, BA(Hons) ACA *2010;* 816 North Row, MILTON KEYNES, MK9 3BL.
HULSE, Mr. Timothy, BSc ACA *1985;* Ariel Ltd, 18 Queen street, HAMILTON, BERMUDA.
HULSEN, Mrs. Sian Elizabeth, BSc ACA *1999;* 7 Heath Park Drive, BROMLEY, KENT, BR1 2WQ.
HULSEY, Mrs. Tracey Ann, BSc ACA *1995;* Haigh House, Cinderhills Road, HOLMFIRTH, HD9 1EH.
•**HULSON, Mr. Nicholas John, BSc FCA** *1989;* (Tax Fac), Harold Smith, Unit 32, Llys Edmund Prys, St. Asaph Business Park, ST. ASAPH, LL17 0JA.
HULSTON, Mr. Ben John Thomas, BSc(Hons) ACA *2010;* 41 Jepson Lane, ELLAND, WEST YORKSHIRE, HX5 0PY.
HULSTROM, Mr. Anthony Guy Julius, BA ACA *1984;* 18 Caddington Road, Cricklewood, LONDON, NW2 1RS.
HUMAYUN, Mr. Asad, ACA *2008;* A B N Amro Bank NV, 250 Bishopsgate, LONDON, EC2M 4AA.
HUMBER, Mr. Paul Edmund, BTech ACA *1978;* The Old Vicarage, Orleton, LUDLOW, SY8 4HN.
HUMBERSTON, Mr. John Denniss, ACA *1979;* The Elms Gretton Road, Harringworth, CORBY, NORTHAMPTONSHIRE, NN17 3AD.
HUMBERSTONE, Ms. Kim Elizabeth, BA ACA FCIPD *1988;* Hung Maau GA, Trowley Rise, ABBOTS LANGLEY, HERTFORDSHIRE, WD5 0LN.
HUMBERSTONE, Mrs. Mary Ann Patricia, BSc ACA *1989;* Shepherds Bush Housing Association Ltd, Mulliner House, Flanders Road, LONDON, W4 1NN.
HUMBERSTONE, Mr. Quentin Charles Triscott, BSc FCA CF *1977;* Tree Tops, 22 Courtlands Avenue, ESHER, KT10 9HZ.
HUMBLE, Mr. Anthony John, FCA *1955;* 2 North Ridge, Red House Farm, WHITLEY BAY, NE25 9XT. (Life Member)
HUMBLE, Mr. Lee, BA(Hons) ACA *2010;* 298 Hexham Road, NEWCASTLE UPON TYNE, NE15 9QX.
HUMBLE, Mr. Mark Francis William, BSc ACA *1993;* 68 Church Hill, Cheddington, LEIGHTON BUZZARD, LU7 0SY.
HUMBLE, Mr. Miles Jonathan, BA FCA *1990;* Fenwick Ltd, 39 Northumberland Street, NEWCASTLE UPON TYNE, NE99 1AR.
HUMBY, Mr. Christopher John, ACA *1985;* Lime Tree Cottage, The Green, Old Knebworth, KNEBWORTH, SG3 6QN.
•**HUMBY, Mrs. Jane Marie, ACA** *1992;* (Tax Fac), Knipe Whiting Heath & Associates Limited, 1 Blackfriars Street, HEREFORD, HR4 9HS.
HUMBY, Mrs. Laura Jane, BA ACA *1998;* 46 Woodland Drive, HOVE, BN3 6DL.
HUMBY, Mr. Michael James, FCA *1963;* Ridge House, Queensberry Road, SALISBURY, SP1 3PJ.
HUMBY, Mr. Nicholas Wayne, BCom ACA *1982;* The Manor House, 6 Manor House Court, Heath Road, READING, RG6 1NA.
HUMBY, Mr. Reginald Herbert George, FCA *1951;* 17 Avenue Gardens, Cliftonville, MARGATE, KENT, CT9 3BD. (Life Member)
HUME, Mr. Andrew Charles, BSc ACA *1988;* 27 Holland Green, SINGAPORE 276150, SINGAPORE.
HUME, Mr. Barry William, FCA *1966;* The MidgeBliby Wood, Bilsington Mersham ASHFORD, Kent, TN25 7JB.
HUME, Mr. Benjamin James, BA(Hons) ACA *2001;* Deloitte & Touche LLP, 550 S. Tryon St, CHARLOTTE, NC 28202, UNITED STATES.
HUME, Mr. Charles Robert, FCA *1975;* Pitfold, Hurtmore Road, GODALMING, GU7 2RB.
HUME, Mr. Christopher David, FCA *1959;* 7 Fell View, Embsay, SKIPTON, NORTH YORKSHIRE, BD23 6RX. (Life Member)
•**HUME, Mr. David Jonathan, BA ACA** *1990;* Deloitte LLP, 2 New Street Square, LONDON, EC4A 3BZ. See also Deloitte & Touche LLP
HUME, Mr. David Peter, MA MBA ACA *1993;* Flat 8 Raven Wharf Apartments, 14 Lafone Street, LONDON, SE1 2LR.
HUME, Mr. Iain Robert, FCA *1977;* Cairngorm, La Rue Des Naftiaux, St. Andrew, GUERNSEY, GY6 8RD.
HUME, Mrs. Jeannette Ann, BSc FCA *1992;* 6 The Boltons, South Wootton, KING'S LYNN, NORFOLK, PE30 3NQ.
HUME, Mr. Jeffrey, FCA *1977;* 38 Burdon Lane, SUTTON, SM2 7PT.
HUME, Mrs. Jennifer May, FCA *1975;* 38 Burdon Lane, Cheam, SUTTON, SM2 7PT.
HUME, Dr. Joanne, ACA *2008;* Medimmune Ltd Milstein Building, Granta Park Great Abington, CAMBRIDGE, CB21 6GH.
HUME, Mr. Kevin, BSc ACA *1989;* 2 Russell Way, BOURNE, LINCOLNSHIRE, PE10 0FP.
HUME, Ms. Lindsey, BA(Hons) ACA *2002;* 15 Talbot Crescent, Roundhay, LEEDS, LS8 1AL.
HUME, Mrs. Lynne Tracy, ACA *2002;* 14 Dulverton Road, MELTON MOWBRAY, LEICESTERSHIRE, LE13 0SF.
HUME, Mr. Martin Jeffrey, BSc ACA *2002;* 15 Talbot Crescent, Roundhay, LEEDS, LS8 1AL.
HUME, Mrs. Michelle Anne, ACA FCCA *2010;* 15 Porters Close, BUNTINGFORD, HERTFORDSHIRE, SG9 9BW.
•**HUME, Mr. Nicholas Mark, FCA** *1988;* Calcutt Matthews Ltd, 19 North Street, ASHFORD, KENT, TN24 8LF.
HUME, Miss. Sarah Myfanwy Rebecca, BSc(Hons) ACA *2001;* PO Box 1452, MARGARET RIVER, WA 6285, AUSTRALIA.
HUME, Mrs. Shirley Harriet, BSc ACA *1986;* 11 Bellhouse Walk, Kingsweston Road, BRISTOL, BS11 0UE.
HUME, Dr. Stephen Christopher, BSc ACA *2003;* 1 Bridgewater Place, Water Lane, LEEDS, LS11 5RU.
HUME SMITH, Mr. Robert, FCA *1953;* Weathervane, Sarum Road, WINCHESTER, SO22 5QE. (Life Member)
HUMES, Mrs. Jennifer Margaret, BA ACA *1990;* Castle Hill House, Church Street, MALPAS, CHESHIRE, SY14 8PW.
HUMES, Mr. Stephen, BA ACA *1990;* 12th Floor NCH, The Co-operative Group (C W S) Ltd New Century House, Corporation Street, MANCHESTER, M60 4ES.
HUMM, Mr. Andrew Mark, ACA *2008;* I M I Kynoch Plc Lakeside Unit 4040, Solihull Parkway Birmingham Business Park, BIRMINGHAM, B37 7XZ.
HUMM, Mr. Roger James, MBA BSc FCA *1984;* Westfield Orchard, Dinghurst Road, Churchill, WINSCOMBE, AVON, BS25 5PJ.
HUMMEL, Mr. John Duncan, BSc ACA *1994;* Dunkelman & Son Manor House, Gold Street Desborough, KETTERING, NORTHAMPTONSHIRE, NN14 2PF.
•**HUMMITZSCH, Mr. Erik, ACA** *2002;* PricewaterhouseCoopers GmbH, Elsenheimerstrasse 31-33, D-80687 MUNICH, GERMANY.
HUMPAGE, Mr. Anthony Carlyle, FCA *1978;* 11075 E Beck Ln, SCOTTSDALE, AZ 85255, UNITED STATES.
•**HUMPAGE, Mr. Christopher James, FCA** *1996;* RDP Newmans LLP, 457 Southchurch Road, SOUTHEND-ON-SEA, SS1 2PH.
HUMPAGE, Mr. Colin John, FCA *1968;* 11 Kendall Close, BURY ST. EDMUNDS, SUFFOLK, IP32 7PQ.
HUMPAGE, Mr. David Thomas, BA FCA *1967;* 22 St Andrews Rd, Heaton moor, STOCKPORT, SK4 4BD.
HUMPAGE, Mrs. Emma Jane, BA ACA *2004;* 72B Cliffsea Grove, LEIGH-ON-SEA, SS9 1NQ.
HUMPAGE, Mr. Peter Leslie Patrick, MA FCA *1969;* Newlands, Higher Gardens, Corfe Castle, WAREHAM, DORSET, BH20 5ES. (Life Member)
HUMPHERSON, Mr. Edward Allen, MA ACA *1996;* 114 Elm Road, KINGSTON UPON THAMES, SURREY, KT2 6HU.
HUMPHRAY, Mr. Kenneth Samuel, ACA *2010;* 90 Fulbeck Avenue, Hawkley Hall, WIGAN, LANCASHIRE, WN3 5QL.
HUMPHREY, Mr. Brian Curtis, FCA *1960;* 5 Mounton Close, CHEPSTOW, GWENT, NP16 5EG. (Life Member)
HUMPHREY, Miss. Ceri Suzanne, MA ACA *1998;* Little Shepherds Cottage, Colemans Hatch, HARTFIELD, EAST SUSSEX, TN7 4HF.
HUMPHREY, Prof. Christopher Graham, PhD MA(Econ) BCom ACA *1984;* (Member of Council 2004 - 2011), 138 Ivy Road, BOLTON, BL1 6EF.
•**HUMPHREY, Mr. Colin Joseph, BCom FCA** *1982;* Baker Tilly Tax & Advisory Services LLP, 1210 Centre Park Square, WARRINGTON, WA1 1RU.
HUMPHREY, Mrs. Colina Mary Campbell, ACA *1993;* Wood Farm, Newtown Road, Awbridge, ROMSEY, HAMPSHIRE, SO51 0GG.
HUMPHREY, Mr. Craig, ACA *2011;* 42 Barnard Avenue, Whitefield, MANCHESTER, M45 6TY.
•**HUMPHREY, Mr. Derek Graham, BA ACA** *1988;* Littlestone Martin Glenton, 73 Wimpole Street, LONDON, W1G 8AZ.

HUMPHREY, Mr. Grant Edward, BSc(Hons) FCA *2001;* 1 Windsor Place, Windsor Drive, Houghton Regis, DUNSTABLE, BEDFORDSHIRE, LU5 5SQ.
HUMPHREY, Mr. Jamie, BA ACA *1995;* Evidens Consult SA, 15 rue du Cendrier, CP 1456 GENEVA, SWITZERLAND.
HUMPHREY, Ms. Jill, BA ACA *1991;* Deutsche Bank, 1 Appold Street, LONDON, EC2A 2HE.
HUMPHREY, Mr. John Charles, FCA *1961;* 15a Barton Court Avenue, Barton on Sea, NEW MILTON, HAMPSHIRE, BH25 7EP.
HUMPHREY, Mr. Jonathan Paul, BSc ACA *2002;* Woolgate Exchange, 25 Basinghall Street, LONDON, EC2V 5HA.
HUMPHREY, Mr. Matthew Robert, ACA *2002;* 6 Curie Drive, Gorleston, GREAT YARMOUTH, NORFOLK, NR31 7RH.
HUMPHREY, Mr. Norman Ian, BSc ACA *1982;* Garden Flat, 39 Norland Square, LONDON, W11 4PZ.
HUMPHREY, Miss. Sarah Blanche, BA ACA *2010;* 31 Brighton Grove, WHITLEY BAY, TYNE AND WEAR, NE26 1QH.
HUMPHREY, Mr. Simon David, BSc ACA *2000;* 29 Nelson Street, Rozelle, SYDNEY, NSW 2039, AUSTRALIA.
HUMPHREY, Mr. Stephen William, BSc FCA *1991;* 200 Buryfield Road, SOLIHULL, B91 2AR.
HUMPHREY, Mrs. Susan Louise, BSc ACA *1996;* Napp Cambridge Science Park, Milton Road, CAMBRIDGE, CB4 0AB.
HUMPHREY, Mr. Terry, FCA *1965;* Browfield House, Manchester Road, Baxenden, ACCRINGTON, BB5 2RG.
•HUMPHREY, Mrs. Veronica, FCA *1982;* Littlestone Golding Limited, 29 Hawthorn Crescent, Hazlemere, HIGH WYCOMBE, HP15 7PL.
HUMPHREY-EVANS, Dr. Diane Pamela, BSc ACA *1995;* 1 Hawkes Close, WOKINGHAM, RG41 2SZ.
HUMPHREYS, Mr. Andrew Michael, BA ACA *1988;* 133-135 Westminster Bridge Road, LONDON, SE1 7HR.
HUMPHREYS, Mr. Anthony Cecil James, FCA *1953;* Anthony C J Humphreys, 25 Crestwood Drive, SCARBOROUGH M1E 1E6, ON, CANADA.
•HUMPHREYS, Mr. Antony Edward, BA(Hons) ACA *2003;* Crowfoot and Company Limited, Lonsdale House, High Street, LUTTERWORTH, LEICESTERSHIRE, LE17 4AD.
HUMPHREYS, Mr. Antony John, FCA *1967;* Gotenyama Heights # 609, 5-6-16 Kita Shinagawa, Shinagawa-Ku, TOKYO, 141-0001 JAPAN. (Life Member)
HUMPHREYS, Mr. Brian Joseph, BSc FCA *1962;* with Caldwell & Braham, 1st Floor, 5 Breams Buildings, LONDON, EC4A 1DY.
HUMPHREYS, Miss. Christa Alexandra Zoe, BA(Hons) ACA *2003;* (Tax Fac), 44 Lady Lane, CHELMSFORD, CM2 0TQ.
HUMPHREYS, Mr. Christopher Andrew, BSc ACA *1991;* Addlestone Manor Stanley Pool, Stanley, STOKE-ON-TRENT, ST9 9LS.
•HUMPHREYS, Mr. Christopher John, FCA *1982;* (Tax Fac), Philip Barnes & Co Ltd, The Old Council Chambers, Halford Street, TAMWORTH, B79 7RB.
•HUMPHREYS, Mr. Christopher Paul, BA ACA *1992;* (Tax Fac), PKF (UK) LLP, 2nd Floor, Fountain Precinct, Balm Green, SHEFFIELD, S1 2JA.
HUMPHREYS, Mr. David Christopher, BSc(Hons) ACA *2002;* 18 Vale Road, Hartford, NORTHWICH, CHESHIRE, CW8 1PL.
•HUMPHREYS, Mr. David Eirian, ACA ACCA *2010;* L.H. Phillips & Co, 29/30 Quay St., CARMARTHEN, SA31 3JT.
HUMPHREYS, Mr. David James, BA FCA *2001;* with PricewaterhouseCoopers LLP, 300 Madison Avenue, NEW YORK, NY 10017, UNITED STATES.
HUMPHREYS, Mr. David John, ACA *1989;* 15 Woodstone Avenue, Stoneleigh, EPSOM, KT17 2JS.
HUMPHREYS, Mr. Derek Edward, FCA *1957;* 7 Broxfield Close, Oadby, LEICESTER, LE2 5WJ. (Life Member)
HUMPHREYS, Mr. Edward William, MA BA BLitt BA(Hons) FCA ACMA *1954;* PO Box 11, MOUNT ELIZA, VIC 3930, AUSTRALIA. (Life Member)
HUMPHREYS, Mr. George Oliver, MSc ACA CFA *2000;* Flat 43, 8 Selsdon Way, LONDON, E14 9GR.
•HUMPHREYS, Mr. Geraint, FCA *1973;* (Tax Fac), Geraint Humphreys & Co, 5-7 Beatrice Street, OSWESTRY, SY11 1QE.
HUMPHREYS, Mr. Graeme, ACA *2009;* 25-98 36th St Apt 3F, ASTORIA, 11103, UNITED STATES.
HUMPHREYS, Mr. Jason Mark, BSc ACA *1997;* Neue Allmendstrasse 37, 8703 ERLENBACH, SWITZERLAND.
HUMPHREYS, Mr. John, BA FCA *1990;* Tenon, York House, 20 York Street, MANCHESTER, M2 3BB.
HUMPHREYS, Mr. John David, FCA *1971;* 26 Chemin des Messes 26, 1380 LASNE, BELGIUM.
HUMPHREYS, Mr. John Foster, FCA *1963;* 82 Lutterworth Road, NUNEATON, CV11 6PH. (Life Member)
HUMPHREYS, Mr. John Gareth, BA FCA *1969;* P.O. Box 53705, 3317 LIMASSOL, CYPRUS.
HUMPHREYS, Mr. Leighton, BSc ACA *2001;* 5 Samuels Crescent, CARDIFF, CF14 2TH.
HUMPHREYS, Mr. Leonard, FCA *1953;* Schiehallion, Manse Road, KILLIN, FK21 8UY. (Life Member)
HUMPHREYS, Mrs. Lorraine Elizabeth, BSc ACA *2007;* 39 Hunters Close, TRING, HERTFORDSHIRE, HP23 5PQ.
HUMPHREYS, Mr. Mark Charles, BSc ACA *1985;* (Tax Fac), 14 Greenway Gardens, Shirley, CROYDON, CR0 8QG.
HUMPHREYS, Mr. Michael Brendan Stephan, BSc FCA *1972;* 128 Avenue de Tervuren, B-1150 BRUSSELS, BELGIUM.
HUMPHREYS, Mr. Paul Clifford, FCA *1974;* 24 Grange Road, SHANKLIN, PO37 6NN.
HUMPHREYS, Mr. Paul Justin, BA ACA *1983;* Care UK Ltd, 21 Great Winchester Street, LONDON, EC2N 2JA.
HUMPHREYS, Mr. Peter, FCA *1967;* Firs Farmhouse, Hill Road North, Helsby, FRODSHAM, WA6 9AQ.
HUMPHREYS, Mr. Peter Kenneth Charles, MA FCA *1979;* Little Hayes Bay Road, GILLINGHAM, DORSET, SP8 4EW.
•HUMPHREYS, Miss. Philippa Margaret, FCA *1980;* P.M. Humphreys & Co, 82a Whitchurch Road, CARDIFF, CF14 3LX.
HUMPHREYS, Mr. Raoul, ACA *1995;* 7 Penrose Terrace, PENZANCE, CORNWALL, TR18 2HQ.
HUMPHREYS, Mr. Robert Aled, BA FCA *1993;* Pathway Care Ltd, Unit 10, Village Way, Tongwynlais, CARDIFF, CF15 7NE.
HUMPHREYS, Mr. Robert Griffith, BSc ACA DChA *1986;* Oxfam House, John Smith Drive, OXFORD, OX4 2JY.
•HUMPHREYS, Mr. Robert James, BEng ACA *2004;* with Turner Peachey, Column House, London Road, SHREWSBURY, SY2 6NN.
HUMPHREYS, Mr. Robert Leonard, FCA *1956;* 18 Lewes Road, Friern Barnet, LONDON, N12 9NL. (Life Member)
HUMPHREYS, Mr. Roger Owen, ACA *1985;* Kirkstile Inn, Loweswater, COCKERMOUTH, CA13 0RU.
HUMPHREYS, Mr. Ronald John, FCA *1950;* Farthings, Blythburgh, HALESWORTH, IP19 9LN. (Life Member)
HUMPHREYS, Mrs. Sarah Ann Beslee, MA ACA *2004;* with Deloitte LLP, Athene Place, 66 Shoe Lane, LONDON, EC4A 3BQ.
•HUMPHREYS, Mr. Stephen Edward, ACA *1987;* Morgan Rose, 37 Marlowes, HEMEL HEMPSTEAD, HERTFORDSHIRE, HP1 1LD.
HUMPHREYS, Mr. Stuart Calvin, BA ACA *1988;* Woodbine Cottage, Old Forge Lane, Granby, NOTTINGHAM, NG13 9PS.
HUMPHREYS, Mrs. Vida Kim, ACA *2001;* 1 Quad Villas, 188 North Road, Combe Down, BATH, BA2 5DN.
HUMPHREYS, Mr. Wayne Stuart, BSc ACA *1986;* Glebe Barn, Drayton, BANBURY, OX15 6EG.
•HUMPHREYS, Mr. William Charles, DipPFS FCA TEP *1982;* (Tax Fac), Libra Wealth Manangement Limited, 18 Mitchell Road, WEST MALLING, KENT, ME19 4RF.
HUMPHREYS-EVANS, Mrs. Eve, BSc(Hons) ACA *2001;* 46 Papist Way, Cholsey, WALLINGFORD, OXFORDSHIRE, OX10 9QH.
HUMPHREYS-EVANS, Mr. Giles William, BA(Hons) ACA *2002;* 46 Papist Way, Cholsey, WALLINGFORD, OXFORDSHIRE, OX10 9QH.
HUMPHREYS-JONES, Miss. Penny Rhiannon, ACA *2010;* 9 Shirragh Way, Port Erin, ISLE OF MAN, IM9 6FB.
HUMPHRIES, Mr. Andrew John, BSc ACA *1992;* Hachette Filipacchi, 64 North Row, LONDON, W1K 7LL.
HUMPHRIES, Mr. Brian Bernard, FCA *1956;* 21 Tanglewood Close, WOKING, SURREY, GU22 8LG. (Life Member)
HUMPHRIES, Ms. Claire, ACA *2008;* 79 Dixon Close, REDDITCH, WORCESTERSHIRE, B97 6AP.
HUMPHRIES, Mr. David Ian, MA(Oxon) FCA *1992;* (Tax Fac), The White House, 7 Ennismore Avenue, GUILDFORD, GU1 1SP.
HUMPHRIES, Mr. David John, BSc ACA *1994;* 9 Knole Way, SEVENOAKS, TN13 3RS.
HUMPHRIES, Mr. Edward James, BSc(Hons) ACA *2002;* 207 Stourbridge Road, KIDDERMINSTER, WORCESTERSHIRE, DY10 2UY.
HUMPHRIES, Mrs. Eve, BSc ACA *2001;* 30 Lancut Hill, RUGBY, WARWICKSHIRE, CV23 0JR.
HUMPHRIES, Mr. James Colin, BA(Hons) ACA *2009;* Pricewaterhousecoopers Abacus House, Castle Park, CAMBRIDGE, CB3 0AN.
•HUMPHRIES, Mr. Julian John, MA FCA *1982;* Baker Tilly Tax and Advisory Services LLP, Charter House, The Square, Lower Bristol Road, BATH, BA2 3BH.
•HUMPHRIES, Mr. Mark Stephen, BSc FCA *1995;* Catalyst Corporate Finance LLP, 5th Floor, 12-18 Grosvenor Gardens, LONDON, SW1W 0DH.
HUMPHRIES, Mr. Michael James, FCA *1975;* 22 Arden Cl, Bradley Stoke, BRISTOL, BS32 8AX.
HUMPHRIES, Mr. Michael John, FCA *1966;* Mar Y SOL Local 6/12, Sotogrande, San Roque, CADIZ, SPAIN. (Life Member)
HUMPHRIES, Mr. Michael Rodney, FCA *1965;* 82 Boyers Orchard, Harby, MELTON MOWBRAY, LEICESTERSHIRE, LE14 4BA. (Life Member)
•HUMPHRIES, Mr. Philip Mervyn, BSc FCA *1979;* (Tax Fac), King & Taylor, 10-12 Wrotham Road, GRAVESEND, DA11 0PE.
HUMPHRIES, Mr. Robert Cameron, FCA *1950;* 29 Mark Way Manor, Upper Mark Way, KINGSTON 8, JAMAICA. (Life Member)
HUMPHRIES, Mr. Robert John, FCA CTA *1980;* (Tax Fac), 1 The Crest, Berrylands, SURBITON, KT5 8JZ.
HUMPHRIES, Mr. Simon Richard, ACA *1997;* Flat 20B, 2 Park Road, MID LEVELS, HONG KONG SAR.
HUMPHRIES, Mrs. Stella, ACA *2003;* with Woodward Hale, 38 Dollar Street, CIRENCESTER, GL7 2AN.
•HUMPHRIES, Mr. Stephen Dominic, BSc FCA *1986;* (Tax Fac), Clarke Nicklin LLP, Clarke Nicklin House, Brooks Drive, Cheadle Royal Business Park, CHEADLE, CHESHIRE SK8 3TD.
•HUMPHRIES, Mr. Stephen James, ACA *1995;* Griffiths Marshall, Beaumont House, 172 Southgate Street, GLOUCESTER, GL1 2EZ.
HUMPHRIES, Mr. Stephen James Donald, BSc ACA *1985;* PricewaterhouseCoopers, Darling Park Tower 2, 201 Sussex Street, GPO Box 2650, SYDNEY, NSW 1171 AUSTRALIA.
HUMPHRIES, Mr. Stephen Paul, BA ACA *1993;* 22 Ashbourne Gardens, HERTFORD, SG13 8BQ.
HUMPHRIES, Mr. Stephen William, BA ACA *2005;* with PricewaterhouseCoopers LLP, First Point, Buckingham Gate, London Gatwick Airport, GATWICK, WEST SUSSEX RH6 0NT.
•HUMPHRIES, Mr. Thomas Grant, ACA ACCA *2010;* Chisnall Comer Ismail & Co, Maria House, 35 Millers Road, BRIGHTON, BN1 5NP.
•HUMPHRY, Mr. Robert Murchison, FCA *1972;* (Tax Fac), Robert M Humphry Limited, 2 East Street, OKEHAMPTON, DEVON, EX20 1AS.
HUMPHRY-BAKER, Mr. Guy Neville, FCA *1977;* Fuerst Day Lawson Ltd Devon House, 58-60 St. Katharines Way, LONDON, E1W 1JP.
HUMPHRYES, Mr. Adam Salusbury, FCA *1970;* Eleanor House, Gilbert Street, Ropley, ALRESFORD, HAMPSHIRE, SO24 0BY.
HUMPHRYS, Mr. David Richard, BA ACA CTA *1993;* (Tax Fac), 97 Fulford Grove, WATFORD, WD19 7QJ.
HUMPHRYS, Mr. John William, BSc FCA *1981;* Paul Crowdy Partnership Ltd Redmayne House, 4 Whiteladies Road, BRISTOL, BS8 1PD.
HUMPHRYS, Mr. Steven Lee, BA(Hons) ACA *2001;* 6 Padstow Close, ORPINGTON, BR6 9XL.
HUNDAL, Mr. Ameet Singh, ACA *2009;* 107 Marlborough Road, SLOUGH, SL3 7JS.
HUNDAL, Mr. Sanjivan Singh, BA(Hons) ACA *2000;* 77 Villiers Avenue, SURBITON, KT5 8BE.
HUNG, Mr. Andrew George, BA FCA *1988;* 6A Arcadia Gardens, 10 Ede Road, KOWLOON TONG, KOWLOON, HONG KONG SAR.
HUNG, Ms. Che Wan GiGi, ACA *2006;* Flat H 26/F Tower 22, South Horizons, AP LEI CHAU, HONG KONG SAR.
HUNG, Mr. Clement Ka Hai, BA ACA *1985;* Deloitte Touche Tohmatsu, 35/F One Pacific Place, 88 Queensway, CENTRAL, HONG KONG ISLAND, HONG KONG SAR.
HUNG, Mr. Fan Kwan, ACA *2007;* Flat F44/F, Block 1, Metro Harbour View, 8 Fuk Lee Street, TAI KOK TSUI, KOWLOON HONG KONG SAR.
HUNG, Mr. Hak-Hip, FCA *1969;* Flat A/5F, Twin Brook, 43 Repulse Bay Road, REPULSE BAY, HONG KONG ISLAND, HONG KONG SAR.
HUNG, Mr. John Ting-On, FCA MBA *1992;* with Deloitte Touche Tohmatsu, 30th Floor, Bund Centre, 222 Yan An Road East, SHANGHAI 20002, CHINA.
HUNG, Mr. Jun Fai, BA ACA *1994;* HSBC Level 6 The Metropolitan, 235 Dong Khoi Street District 1, HO CHI MINH CITY, VIETNAM.
HUNG, Mr. Ka Wai, ACA CF *2005;* Flat C 15/F, Wah Fai Court, 1-6 Ying Wah Terrace, SHEK TONG TSUI, HONG KONG ISLAND, HONG KONG SAR.
HUNG, Mr. Kai Tung, ACA *2006;* Unit 102 No 13 Lane 263 Huan Long Road, (Yi Dong Garden), PUDONG 200127, CHINA.
HUNG, Mr. Kam Wing Timmy, ACA *2008;* Flat E 6/F Tower 6, Le Point, 8 King Ling Road, TSEUNG KWAN O, HONG KONG SAR.
HUNG, Mr. Kwang Hou, ACA *1982;* 60 Lorong 6/30D, 46000 PETALING JAYA, SELANGOR, MALAYSIA.
HUNG, Ms. Lap, ACA *2010;* (Tax Fac), 17/F Flat G, Evergreen Towers, 32 Fei Fung Street, WONG TAI SIN, KOWLOON, HONG KONG SAR.
HUNG, Miss. Liza Yu Man, MA ACA *2005;* JP Morgan, 25th Chater house, Connaught Road, CENTRAL, HONG KONG SAR.
HUNG, Ms. Sau Hing, ACA *2005;* Unit 7B China Overseas Building, 139 Hennessy Road, WAN CHAI, HONG KONG SAR.
HUNG, Mr. Sing Chun Peter, BSc ACA CPA *2005;* 1362 Nanton Avenue, VANCOUVER V6H 2C9, BC, CANADA.
HUNG JUT YU, Miss. Angela, BA ACA *2004;* Rossmore Court, Flat 104 Rossmore Court, LONDON, NW1 6XZ.
HUNJAN, Miss. Sonea Kaur, BA ACA *2011;* 4 Dalmeny Road, CARSHALTON, SURREY, SM5 4PP.
HUNKIN, Mr. John Llewellyn, FCA *1950;* 20 Maes Yr Hafod, Cadoxton, NEATH, SA10 8AZ. (Life Member)
•HUNKIN, Mr. Philip Llewellyn, BSc FCA *1980;* (Tax Fac), WBV Limited, Woodfield House, Castle Walk, NEATH, SA11 3LN. See also PLH Limited
•HUNN, Mr. Graham Maurice George, FCA *1964;* (Tax Fac), Graham Hunn & Company, Field Walls, The Avenue, SHERBORNE, DORSET, DT9 3AH.
HUNN, Mr. Richard George, BCom FCA *1951;* The Willows, Culford, BURY ST. EDMUNDS, IP28 6TZ. (Life Member)
•HUNOT, Mr. George Andrew, FCA *1971;* Hunot & Co Limited, The Gate House, Underhill, Maresfield, UCKFIELD, TN22 3AX. See also Hunot & Co
HUNSTON, Mr. John Richard, LLB FCA *1983;* with Armstrong Watson, 15 Victoria Place, CARLISLE, CA1 1EW.
HUNT, Mr. Adam, MEng ACA *2011;* 21 Daphne Street, LONDON, SW18 2BJ.
HUNT, Mr. Adrian Manuel, BA ACA *1993;* 46 Belvedere Court, Alwoodley, LEEDS, LS17 8NF.
HUNT, Mr. Adrian Piers, MBiochem ACA *2009;* Flat 1, 70 Marylands Road, LONDON, W9 2DR.
HUNT, Mr. Alan William, FCA *1977;* Devonia, 513 Woodham Lane, WOKING, GU21 5SR.
HUNT, Mr. Alex James, BA(Hons) ACA *2010;* 47 Highbank Drive, MANCHESTER, M20 5QR.
•HUNT, Mr. Alistair John, BSc FCA *1992;* RSM Tenon Audit Limited, The Poynt, 45 Wollaton Street, NOTTINGHAM, NG1 5FW. See also Tenon Audit Limited
HUNT, Miss. Amanda Jayne, BSc ACA *1993;* 6 Ranelagh Grove, Wollaton, NOTTINGHAM, NG8 1HT.
HUNT, Mrs. Aminta Jane, BSc ACA AMCT *1998;* 19 Orbel Street, LONDON, SW11 3NX.
HUNT, Mr. Andrew Douglas, MSc BA ACA *1991;* Inspectorate International Ltd, 2 Perry Road, WITHAM, ESSEX, CM8 3TU.
•HUNT, Mr. Andrew Graham, BA FCA *1993;* with Ormerod Rutter Limited, The Oakley, Kidderminster Road, DROITWICH, WORCESTERSHIRE, WR9 9AY.
•HUNT, Mr. Andrew Rudland, BA FCA *1982;* A. R. Hunt & Co, 50 Ridge Crest, ENFIELD, EN2 8JX.
•HUNT, Mr. Andrew Wymark, MA FCA *1983;* (Tax Fac), Andrew W. Hunt & Co, 13 Lowthian Terrace, WASHINGTON, TYNE AND WEAR, NE38 7BA.
HUNT, Mr. Anthony John, FCA *1978;* Compton House, 29 Spur Hill Avenue, POOLE, BH14 9PH.
HUNT, Mr. Anthony Nettleship, FCA *1962;* Lanterns, 27 Bois Avenue, AMERSHAM, HP6 5NU. (Life Member)
HUNT, Mr. Arthur Thomas, FCA *1958;* 12 Saxon Road, LONDON, N22 5EB. (Life Member)
HUNT, Mr. Arthur Walter, BSc FCA *1964;* 609 Gray Fox Lane, ROCKY HILL, CT 06067, UNITED STATES. (Life Member)
HUNT, Mr. Barry Thomas, FCA *1970;* Barmadel Farming Co, 5 The Paddocks, Leverington, WISBECH, CAMBRIDGESHIRE, PE13 5DZ.

HUNT, Mr. Ben, BSc ACA *2006;* 1 Chub Close, WORCESTER, WR5 3FG.
HUNT, Mr. Brian David, FCA *1964;* 11A Delmar Road, KNUTSFORD, WA16 8BG. (Life Member)
•**HUNT, Mr. Brian David, FCA** *1965;* John Crook & Partners, 255 Green Lanes, Palmers Green, LONDON, N13 4XE.
HUNT, Mrs. Bridget Elizabeth, BA ACA *1985;* 7 The Street, Wallington, BALDOCK, HERTFORDSHIRE, SG7 6SW.
HUNT, Mrs. Carole Anne, BA ACA *1988;* Brae Wood, 11 Pine Ridge Drive, Lower Bourne, FARNHAM, SURREY, GU10 3JP.
•**HUNT, Mrs. Caroline, BSc ACA ATII** *1987;* Verulam Business Services, Willow Cottage, 19 Pancake Lane, Leverstock Green, HEMEL HEMPSTEAD, HERTFORDSHIRE HP2 4NB.
•**HUNT, Mr. Charles Arthur, FCA** *1976;* Blue Spire South LLP, Cawley Priory, South Pallant, CHICHESTER, WEST SUSSEX, PO19 1SY.
•**HUNT, Mr. Charles David, MA FCA** *1977;* C.D. Hunt & Co, Unit 3.07, Q West, Great West Road, BRENTFORD, MIDDLESEX TW8 0GP.
HUNT, Mrs. Cheryl Elizabeth, BSc ACA *1989;* Dunster, Jacobean Lane, Knowle, SOLIHULL, B93 9LP.
HUNT, Mr. Christian John, MA FCA *2000;* 4a Sutherland Row, LONDON, SW1V 4JT.
HUNT, Mr. Christopher, MEd BSc ACA *1990;* 9 Burleigh Road, West Bridgford, NOTTINGHAM, NG2 6FP.
•**HUNT, Mr. Christopher Brian, FCA** *1994;* Pelham, Pelham Business Centre, 16 Dudley Street, GRIMSBY, DN31 2AB. See also Johnson Hunt (UK) Ltd
•**HUNT, Mr. Christopher Bruce, FCA** *1970;* C B Hunt, 52 Roundway, CAMBERLEY, SURREY, GU15 1NU.
HUNT, Mr. Christopher Edward John, ACA *1990;* 104 Oakfield Road, BENFLEET, SS7 5NN.
HUNT, Mr. Christopher Edwin, BA FCA *1992;* The Mill House, The Hollow, West Chiltington, PULBOROUGH, RH20 2QA.
HUNT, Mr. Christopher John William, BA ACA *1985;* Macmillan Cancer Support, 89 Albert Embankment, LONDON, SE1 9UQ.
HUNT, Mr. Christopher Paul, BA ACA *1994;* Astra Zeneca Ltd, 2 Kingdom Street, LONDON, W2 6BD.
•**HUNT, Mr. Christopher Philip, FCA ATII** *1993;* (Tax Fac), Forrester Boyd, Waynflete House, 139 Eastgate, LOUTH, LN11 9QQ.
HUNT, Mr. Colin John, BA ACA *1983;* 10 Regent Close, KINGS LANGLEY, WD4 8TP.
•**HUNT, Mr. David Charles, FCA** *1972;* Poplar Cottage, The Common, Compton, GUILDFORD, SURREY, GU3 1JF.
HUNT, Mr. David Edward, BA ACA *1993;* 25 Monks Orchard, PETERSFIELD, HAMPSHIRE, GU32 2JD.
HUNT, Mr. David John Guy, BA ACA *1990;* The Drillies, Pinfarthings, Amberley, STROUD, GL5 5JQ.
HUNT, Mr. David Lindsay, MA FCA *1980;* KC Maritime Ltd, 15/F South China Building, 1 Wyndham Street, CENTRAL, HONG KONG ISLAND, HONG KONG SAR.
HUNT, Prof. David Malcolm, MSc FCA FFA FMAAT FRSA CPFA FCIPD FSCMA *1966;* (Member of Council 1989 - 2009), 28 Elm Close, NOTTINGHAM, NG3 5AH.
HUNT, Mr. David Paul, BSc FCA *1995;* 19 Wootton Green Lane, Balsall Common, COVENTRY, CV7 7EZ.
HUNT, Mr. Dennis Paul, FCA FCCA *1961;* 7 Brunel Avenue, Rogerstone, NEWPORT, GWENT, NP10 0DN. (Life Member)
HUNT, Mr. Derek Roy, FCA *1969;* Flat 3, 9 Gloucester Road, TEDDINGTON, MIDDLESEX, TW11 0NS. (Life Member)
HUNT, Mr. Dominic John, BSc ACA *1998;* 5 Duck End Close, Houghton Conquest, BEDFORD, MK45 3NP.
HUNT, Mrs. Elaine Joan, BA ACA *1996;* The Mill House, The Hollow, West Chiltington, PULBOROUGH, RH20 2QA.
HUNT, Mrs. Elisabeth Jane, BSc(Hons) ACA *2003;* (Tax Fac), 6 Saltcoats Road, LONDON, W4 1AR.
HUNT, Miss. Elizabeth Doreena, BA(Hons) ACA *2009;* 4 Paddox Court, Rugby Road Kilsby, RUGBY, CV23 8XX.
HUNT, Mrs. Fiona Suzanne, BEng ACA *2005;* 32 Seacrest Avenue, NORTH SHIELDS, NE30 3DP.
HUNT, Mr. Gareth, BSc ACA *2005;* 27 Murray Road, SHEFFIELD, S11 7GF.
HUNT, Mr. Geoffrey Alan, FCA *1975;* Somers Farm, Ramsey, ISLE OF MAN, IM7 3HH.
HUNT, Mr. Geoffrey Robert, BSc FCA *1973;* The House By The Lake, Beeston Saint Lawrence, NORWICH, NR12 8YS.
HUNT, Mr. Giles Antony, BA ACA *1997;* Flat 8, Russell Court, 108 Hammersmith Grove, LONDON, W6 7HB.
HUNT, Mrs. Gillian, BA ACA *1998;* N V Q Training & Consultancy Egerton House, 2 Tower Road, BIRKENHEAD, MERSEYSIDE, CH41 1FN.
HUNT, Mr. Glynn Frederick, FCA *1977;* 9 Hunters Croft, Haxey, DONCASTER, SOUTH YORKSHIRE, DN9 2NX.
HUNT, Mr. Graham, BSc ACA *1981;* 23 Parkwood Road, HUDDERSFIELD, HD3 4TT.
•**HUNT, Mr. Graham Anthony, BSc FCA** *1990;* (Tax Fac), Graham Hunt & Co, Unit 15, Hockliffe Business Park, Watling Street Hockliffe, LEIGHTON BUZZARD, LU7 9NB.
HUNT, Mr. Graham Ashley, BA ACA *1990;* Stapleton, Oak Way, REIGATE, RH2 7ES.
HUNT, Mr. Graham Mark, BA FCA *1993;* Twin Oaks, 36 Moreland Drive, GERRARDS CROSS, SO9 8BD.
HUNT, Ms. Helen, ACA *2008;* 143 Rutland Drive, MORDEN, SM4 5QQ.
HUNT, Mrs. Helen Jane, BSc ACA *1995;* 19 Wootton Green Lane, Balsall Common, COVENTRY, CV7 7EZ.
HUNT, Mr. Henry Jeffrey, FCA *1967;* 6 Meadow Close, LEIGH, WN7 3LR. (Life Member)
HUNT, Mr. Ian, MBA BSc ACA *1981;* 4th Floor, Lloyds, 10 Gresham Street, LONDON, EC2V 7AE.
•**HUNT, Mr. Ian, FCA** *1983;* Clear & Lane, 340 Melton Road, LEICESTER, LE4 7SL.
•**HUNT, Mr. Ian Andrew, FCA** *1991;* John Crook & Partners, 255 Green Lanes, Palmers Green, LONDON, N13 4XE.
HUNT, Mr. James, MMath ACA *2011;* Apartment 52, Queens College Chambers, 38 Paradise Street, BIRMINGHAM, B1 2AF.
HUNT, Mr. James Sinclair, BCom ACA *1987;* 13 Rue Louis Lambert, 41100 NAVEIL, FRANCE.
HUNT, Miss. Jane Elizabeth, BCom ACA *1984;* 16 Aintree Drive, Cowplain, WATERLOOVILLE, PO7 8NG.
HUNT, Mr. Jeremy, MSci ACA *2010;* Flat 15 Horselydown Mansions, Lafone Street, LONDON, SE1 2NA.
HUNT, Miss. Joanna Clare, BSc ACA *2010;* 13 Sorrell Grove, GUISBOROUGH, CLEVELAND, TS14 8DP.
•**HUNT, Mr. John Addison, BA ACA** *1987;* Military House Limited, Military House, 24 Castle Street, CHESTER, CH1 2DS. See also Chester Accounting Services
HUNT, Mr. John Brian, FCA *1956;* 4 Baytree Cottage, Newnham Green, Crowmarsh Gifford, WALLINGFORD, OX10 8EW. (Life Member)
HUNT, Mr. John Marshall, FCA *1953;* St Giles Mede, Auden Close, LINCOLN, LN2 4BS. (Life Member)
HUNT, Mr. John Robert, BSc ACA *1997;* 8 The Wern, LECHLADE, GL7 3FF.
HUNT, Mr. John Simon, MA ACA *1989;* Tweede Weteringplantsoen 21, P.O Box 28, 1000 AA AMSTERDAM, NETHERLANDS.
HUNT, Mr. Jonathan Douglas Fletcher, ACA *1980;* with ICAEW, Chartered Accountants' Hall, Moorgate Place, LONDON, EC2P 2BJ.
HUNT, Mr. Joseph James, MA ACA *2006;* 21 Lindley Avenue, SOUTHSEA, HAMPSHIRE, PO4 9NT.
HUNT, Mrs. Judith Alison, BA ACA *1996;* 153 Grove Lane, Cheadle Hulme, CHEADLE, CHESHIRE, SK8 7NG.
HUNT, Mrs. Julia Anne, BA ACA *1991;* c/o Peter Hunt, Sun Microsystems, PO Box 50769, DUBAI, UNITED ARAB EMIRATES.
HUNT, Mr. Julian Michael, BA ACA *2000;* with Deloitte LLP, 1 City Square, LEEDS, WEST YORKSHIRE, LS1 2AL.
HUNT, Mrs. Karen Stella, BSc ACA *2009;* 23 Inkpen Gardens, Lychpit, BASINGSTOKE, HAMPSHIRE, RG24 8YQ.
HUNT, Mr. Keith, BSc ACA *1984;* Results Business Consulting, 24-25 New Bond Street, LONDON, W1S 2RR.
HUNT, Mr. Kenneth, ACA *1974; (ACA Ireland 1955);* Apartado de Correos No 21, Ugijar, 18480 GRANADA, SPAIN. (Life Member)
HUNT, Mr. Kenneth Grant, ACA CA(SA) *2008;* 116 Sandy Lane, Cheam, SUTTON, SURREY, SM2 7ES.
HUNT, Mr. Kieron Anthony, MSc FCA *1979;* Heights House, Heights Road, Fence, BURNLEY, LANCASHIRE, BB12 9JF.
•**HUNT, Miss. Kim Anne, BA FCA** *1987;* J.K. Research Ltd, 6-8 The Wash, HERTFORD, SG14 1PX.
HUNT, Miss. Laurina Mary, BA ACA *1993;* 79 Whitehall Road, Terenure, DUBLIN 12, COUNTY DUBLIN, IRELAND.
HUNT, Mrs. Linda, MA ACA *1990;* 22 Murrayfield Road, EDINBURGH, EH12 6ER.
HUNT, Mrs. Lindy Ann, ACA *1991;* 11 Thimble Drive, SUTTON COLDFIELD, WEST MIDLANDS, B76 2TL.
HUNT, Miss. Lyn Carol, MA ACA *1996;* 1a Chesterfield Avenue, GLENDOWIE, AUCKLAND, NEW ZEALAND.
HUNT, Mrs. Lynn, MA ACA *1986;* Audit Commission, Nickalls House, Metro Centre, GATESHEAD, NE11 9NH.
HUNT, Mrs. Lynne, FCA *1986;* 8 Lebanon Drive, COBHAM, KT11 2PR.
HUNT, Mrs. Margaret Gillian, BSc ACA *1990;* 14 Fishers Lane, Orwell, ROYSTON, HERTFORDSHIRE, SG8 5QX.
•**HUNT, Mr. Mark Adrian, FCA CTA** *1979;* (Tax Fac), Crowe Clark Whitehill LLP, Carrick House, Lypiatt Road, CHELTENHAM, GLOUCESTERSHIRE, GL50 2QJ. See also Horwath Clark Whitehill LLP and Crowe Clark Whitehill
HUNT, Mr. Mark Allan, MEng ACA *2003;* Hampson Industries Plc, 7 Harbour Buildings, Waterfront West, Dudley Road, BRIERLEY HILL, WEST MIDLANDS DY5 1LN.
•**HUNT, Mr. Mark Edward, BSc FCA** *1988;* BDO LLP, 55 Baker Street, LONDON, W1U 7EU. See also BDO Stoy Hayward LLP
•**HUNT, Mr. Matthew, FCA** *1963;* Hunt Blake Ltd, Jubilee House, The Oaks, RUISLIP, MIDDLESEX, HA4 7LF.
HUNT, Mr. Melvyn William Benoit, FCA *1970;* The Old Barn, 1 Grange Court, High Grange, CROOK, DL15 8AZ.
HUNT, Mr. Michael Elliott, BSc ACA *1989;* Brae Wood, Pine Ridge Drive, Lower Bourne, FARNHAM, SURREY, GU10 3JP.
HUNT, Mr. Michael Glyn Thomas, BA ACA *1993;* 52 Albert Street, WINDSOR, BERKSHIRE, SL4 5BU.
HUNT, Mr. Michael Gordon, BSc ACA *1984;* Balgristrasse 70, 8008 ZURICH, SWITZERLAND.
HUNT, Mr. Michael James, BA ACA *1996;* 17 Torrington Road, BERKHAMSTED, HP4 3DB.
HUNT, Mr. Michael Wood, BA ACA *2001;* (Tax Fac), 113 Gowan Avenue, LONDON, SW6 6RQ.
HUNT, Mrs. Michelle Louise, BSc ACA *1999;* 27 Long West Croft, Calverton, NOTTINGHAM, NG14 6PY.
HUNT, Mrs. Natalie Elizabeth, BA ACA *1997;* 13 Purssell Close, MAIDENHEAD, BERKSHIRE, SL6 3XU.
HUNT, Mr. Neil Andrew, BSc ACA *1984;* Mizuho Corporate Bank Ltd, River Plate House, 9-11 Finsbury Circus, LONDON, EC2M 7DH.
HUNT, Mrs. Nicola Dawn, BA ACA *1995;* 8 The Rydings, Langho, BLACKBURN, BB6 8BQ.
HUNT, Mrs. Nicola-Jane, ACA *2009;* 36 Derwent, TAMWORTH, STAFFORDSHIRE, B77 2LD.
HUNT, Mr. Nicolas John Farrant, FCA *1960;* 147 Teg Down Meads, WINCHESTER, SO22 5NP. (Life Member)
HUNT, Mr. Nigel Andrew, FCA *1973;* 60 Sandringham Road, MAIDENHEAD, SL6 7PN.
•**HUNT, Mr. Nigel Martin, FCA** *1977;* Nigel M Hunt FCA, 4 Millburgh Hall, Selham Road, Graffham, PETWORTH, WEST SUSSEX GU28 0QH.
HUNT, Mr. Noel David, BA ACA *1992;* 8 The Rydings, Langho, BLACKBURN, BB6 8BQ.
HUNT, Mr. Norman Thornley, FCA *1950;* 111 Belgrave Road, DARWEN, BB3 2SF. (Life Member)
HUNT, Miss. Patricia Virginia, BA ACA *2006;* PO Box 30681, SEVEN MILE BEACH, GRAND CAYMAN, KY1-1203, CAYMAN ISLANDS.
HUNT, Mr. Patrick Seager, MA ACA *1997;* Church House, Sandhutton, THIRSK, NORTH YORKSHIRE, YO7 4RW.
HUNT, Mr. Paul Neville, BSc ACA *1998;* Euromoney Institutional Investor Plc, Nestor House, 4 Playhouse Yard, LONDON, EC4V 5EX.
HUNT, Mr. Paul Richard, MSc BA ACA *1989;* Zur Muhle, Muhlestalden 1, 8824 SCHONENBERG, SWITZERLAND.
•**HUNT, Mr. Peter Charles Patrick, FCA** *1973;* Peter Hunt & Co Limited, Argon House, Argon Mews, Fulham Broadway, LONDON, SW6 1BJ.
HUNT, Mr. Peter Julian Frederick, BA ACA *1989;* Sun Microsystems, PO Box 50769, DUBAI, UNITED ARAB EMIRATES.
HUNT, Mr. Peter Thomas, FCA *1961;* 15 Anworth Close, WOODFORD GREEN, IG8 0DR. (Life Member)
HUNT, Mr. Philip John, BA ACA *2007;* 8 Riverside Gardens, Auckley, DONCASTER, DN9 3QE.
HUNT, Miss. Rachel Mary, BA ACA *1998;* 9 Miles Close, St. Katherines Park, Ham Green, Pill, BRISTOL, BS20 0LH.
HUNT, Mr. Ralph James, FCA *1952;* 249 Hillbury Road, WARLINGHAM, SURREY, CR6 9TL. (Life Member)
HUNT, Mr. Richard, FCA *1970;* 38 Town Street, Birkenshaw, BRADFORD, BD11 2HX.
HUNT, Mr. Richard, BSc ACA *2006;* 120 Mallinson Road, LONDON, SW11 1BJ.
HUNT, Mr. Richard Michael, BA FCA *1999;* 6 Church Bank, Kelsall, TARPORLEY, CHESHIRE, CW6 0TL.
HUNT, Mr. Richard Peter, ACA *2009;* The Farthings, Clifford Road, Chafford Hundred, GRAYS, RM16 6QL.
HUNT, Mr. Richard Pierson, BSc FCA *1970;* Windmill Cottage Crowborough Road Nutley, UCKFIELD, EAST SUSSEX, TN22 3HY.
HUNT, Mr. Robert Edward Notley, MA ACA *2006;* with KPMG LLP, 15 Canada Square, LONDON, E14 5GL.
•①**HUNT, Mr. Robert Jonathan, BA FCA** *1988;* PricewaterhouseCoopers LLP, Pricewaterhousecoopers, 12 Plumtree Court, LONDON, EC4A 4HT. See also PricewaterhouseCoopers
HUNT, Mr. Robert William, FCA *1958;* 16 Gardenia Drive, COVENTRY, CV5 9BN. (Life Member)
HUNT, Mrs. Roberta Gail, FCA *1970;* Rissick, Crows-an-Wra, St. Buryan, PENZANCE, TR19 6HS.
HUNT, Mr. Roger, FCA *1952;* 106 Berkeley Avenue, READING, RG1 6HY. (Life Member)
•**HUNT, Mr. Roger Stanford, FCA** *1990;* RSH Accounting, Waters Edge, 4 Sydney Loader Place, Darby Green, CAMBERLEY, SURREY GU17 0AF.
HUNT, Mr. Roy Malcolm, FCA *1960;* 29 Dickens Lodge, Wealdhurst Park, BROADSTAIRS, KENT, CT10 2DY. (Life Member)
HUNT, Mr. Russell James, BSc ACA *1991;* The Hawthorns, 11 Field Lane, Tarvin, CHESTER, CH3 8LF.
HUNT, Mrs. Ruth Elaina, BSc ACA ACT *2003;* Shell International, Shell Centre, LONDON, SE1 7NA.
HUNT, Miss. Sarah, ACA *2007;* with KPMG LLP, Dukes Keep, Marsh Lane, SOUTHAMPTON, HAMPSHIRE, SO14 3EX.
HUNT, Mrs. Sarah Ellen, BSc ACA *1992;* 237 Eastwood Road North, LEIGH-ON-SEA, SS9 4ND.
HUNT, Mrs. Sarah Jane, ACA *1990;* 38 Upton Lane, Upton, CHESTER, CH2 1EE.
HUNT, Mr. Simon, ACA *2011;* Ground Floor Flat, 33 Lancaster Road, LONDON, SW19 5DF.
HUNT, Dr. Simon Anthony, DPhil BA ACA *2000;* FLO International eV, Bonner Talweg 177, 53129 BONN, GERMANY.
•**HUNT, Mr. Simon David, BA ACA** *2001;* PricewaterhouseCoopers LLP, Hays Galleria, 1 Hays Lane, LONDON, SE1 2RD. See also PricewaterhouseCoopers
HUNT, Mr. Simon Lindsay Rattcliff, BA ACA *1999;* 114 Burnt Hill Road, Lower Bourne, FARNHAM, GU10 3LJ.
HUNT, Mr. Stephen Alexander, BA ACA *2000;* Lamorna, 7 Keswick Road, ORPINGTON, KENT, BR6 0EU.
HUNT, Mr. Stephen Andrew Robert, BSc ACA *1992;* The Dormers, Crown East, Rushwick, WORCESTER, WR2 5TU.
•**HUNT, Mr. Stephen Arthur, FCA** *1975;* Hunt Johnston Stokes Ltd, 12-14 Carlton Place, SOUTHAMPTON, SO15 2EA.
HUNT, Mr. Stephen David, BSc ACA *1992;* 48 Round Hill, Darton, BARNSLEY, S75 5QJ.
HUNT, Mr. Stephen John, MBA BSc FCA *1978;* 4 Paddox Court, Kilsby, RUGBY, WARWICKSHIRE, CV23 8XX.
•**HUNT, Mr. Stephen Richard, FCA** *1995;* (Tax Fac), NA Associates LLP, 1st Floor, Woodgate Studios, 2-8 Games Road, Cockfosters, BARNET HERTFORDSHIRE EN4 9HN.
•**HUNT, Mr. Steven Dean, BA ACA** *2000;* KPMG Channel Islands Limited, 5 St. Andrew's Place, Charing Cross, St. Helier, JERSEY, JE4 8WQ.
HUNT, Miss. Susan Elizabeth, ACA *2001;* 18 Sycamore Court, Henllys, CWMBRAN, GWENT, NP44 6HN.
HUNT, Mrs. Susan Jane, MA ACA *1983;* 31 Morden Road, Blackheath, LONDON, SE3 0AD.
HUNT, Mrs. Susan Margaret, BA ACA *1993;* 3 Conisboro Avenue, Caversham Heights, READING, BERKSHIRE, RG4 7JB.
HUNT, Mr. Timo Anthony, BSc ACA *1999;* Flat 2a York Mansions 215, Earls Court Road, LONDON, SW5 9AF.
HUNT, Mr. Timothy James, MA ACA *1992;* 67A Hall Carr Lane, Longton, PRESTON, PR4 5JL.
HUNT, Mr. Timothy William, BA ACA *1990;* (Tax Fac), 38 Upton Lane, Upton, CHESTER, CH2 1EE.
HUNT, Mr. Trevor John, FCA *1978;* 47 Bishops Drive, WOKINGHAM, RG40 1WA.
HUNT, Miss. Victoria Taylor, MEng ACA CTA *2001;* 10 Te Ruru Way, Stanmore Bay, WHANGAPARAOA 0932, NEW ZEALAND.

Members - Alphabetical HUNT - HUQ

HUNT, Mr. Warwick Ean, ACA CA(SA) CA(NZ) *2009;* PricewaterhouseCoopers, Emirates Towers Offices, PO Box 11987, Level 40, Sheikh Zayed Road, PO Box 11987 DUBAI UNITED ARAB EMIRATES.
HUNT, Mr. William George, TD BA FCA *1973;* with Windsor Herald of Arms, College of Arms, 130 Queen Victoria Street, LONDON, EC4V 4BT. (Life Member)
HUNT, Mr. William Richard, BA ACA *1999;* with KPMG Deutsche Treuhand Group, Ganghoferstrasse 29, 80339 MUNICH, GERMANY.
HUNT, Mrs. Zoe Burdett, BA ACA *1992;* Stapleton, Oak Way, REIGATE, SURREY, RH2 7ES.
•**HUNT, Miss. Zoe Louise, BSc ACA** *2007;* with The Taylor Cocks Partnership Limited, Arena Business Centre, 9 Nimrod Way, WIMBORNE, DORSET, BH21 7SH.
HUNT COOKE, Mr. Christopher, FCA *1968;* 15 Mardley Dell, WELWYN, HERTFORDSHIRE, AL6 0UR. (Life Member)
HUNTE, Mr. Rupert Gregory, FCA *1973;* Bellavista, 156A Greys Road, HENLEY-ON-THAMES, RG9 1QR.
HUNTER, Mr. Adam, ACA *2008;* 44 Osprey Way, CHELMSFORD, CM2 8XU.
HUNTER, Mr. Adrian Philip, BSc ACA *1991;* 40 Upper Packington Road, ASHBY-DE-LA-ZOUCH, LEICESTERSHIRE, LE65 1EF.
HUNTER, Mr. Alan Thomas Ferguson, BSc FCA *1977;* High Birks Farm, Crosthwaite, KENDAL, LA8 8BX.
•**HUNTER, Mr. Alastair James, MA FCA** *1982;* KPMG LLP, 15 Canada Square, LONDON, E14 5GL. See also KPMG Europe LLP
HUNTER, Mr. Alastair Martin Wardrop, FCA *1975;* Cottenden Oast, Stonegate, WADHURST, EAST SUSSEX, TN5 7DT.
HUNTER, Mr. Alex Rayleigh, BA FCA CFA *1995;* 30 Thornhill Square, LONDON, N1 1BQ.
HUNTER, Mr. Alexander Beaufort De Marigny, FCA *1972;* Institute of Practitioners in Advertising, 44 Belgrave Square, LONDON, SW1X 8QS.
HUNTER, Mr. Alexander Peter, BSc FCA *1981;* North Gates, 23 New Road, Bignall End, STOKE-ON-TRENT, ST7 8QF.
HUNTER, Miss. Alison, BSc ACA *1991;* 6 Phyllis Street, ROCHDALE, LANCASHIRE, OL12 7NA.
HUNTER, Dr. Alison Deborah, PhD BSc ACA *1995;* 23c Winchester Road, LONDON, NW3 3NR.
HUNTER, Mr. Andrew Douglas Hope, BA ACA *1984;* Ladyrig Farmhouse, KELSO, ROXBURGHSHIRE, TD5 8JP.
HUNTER, Mrs. Angela Michele, ACA *1994;* 816 Broad Street (Upper), ST JOSEPH, MI 49085, UNITED STATES.
HUNTER, Mr. Barry Randolph, FCA *1973;* 68 Windmill Street, Brill, AYLESBURY, HP18 9TG.
HUNTER, Mr. Barry Robert, BA ACA *1999;* 132 Florence Road, LONDON, SW19 8TN.
HUNTER, Mr. Bernard Eliot Osborn, BSc ACA *1991;* Loft 14, 1-10 Summers Street, Clerkenwell, LONDON, EC1R 5BD.
HUNTER, Mrs. Beverley, BA ACA *1992;* 44 Lisadell Road, MEDOWIE, NSW 2318, AUSTRALIA.
HUNTER, Ms. Caroline Judith, BEng ACA *1993;* 34 Guildford Street, STAINES, TW18 2EQ.
HUNTER, Mr. Charles David, FCA *1962;* 6 Mowbray Garth, Boroughbridge, YORK, YO51 9NT. (Life Member)
•**HUNTER, Mrs. Christine Lesley, ACA** *1982;* (Tax Fac), with Finrob Limited, Suite 5b, Brook House, 77 Fountain Street, MANCHESTER, M2 2EE.
HUNTER, Mr. Christopher Alan, BA FCA *1988;* Boot Farm Cottage, Lichfield Road, Whittington, LICHFIELD, WS14 9JZ.
HUNTER, Miss. Clare Marie, ACA *2009;* 10 Denehurst Way, NUNEATON, CV10 7DD.
HUNTER, Mr. Clifford Crosby, MSc FCA *1977;* Hurst House, High Street, RIPLEY, SURREY, GU23 6AY.
HUNTER, Mr. Colin Terry, FCA *1969;* The Cottage White Hermitage, Church Road Old Windsor, WINDSOR, SL4 2JX.
HUNTER, Mr. Craig Richard, BA ACA *2001;* 21 North Parade, YORK, YO30 7AB.
HUNTER, Mr. David Edgar, BSc FCA *1980;* 32 Sydney Road, RICHMOND, TW9 1UB.
•**HUNTER, Mr. David Ian Harper, FCA** *1973;* (Tax Fac), Pennington Hunter Limited, Stanhope House, Mark Rake, Bromborough, WIRRAL, MERSEYSIDE CH62 2DN. See also Pennington Williams
•**HUNTER, Mr. David James, FCA** *1970;* Hunter Marshall & Co Ltd, Suite C, 1st Floor, Hinksey Court, West Way, Botley OXFORD OX2 9JU.
•**HUNTER, Mr. David Mark, BSc FCA DChA** *1989;* Hunter Accountants Limited, 3 Kings Court, Little King Street, BRISTOL, BS1 4HW.
HUNTER, Mr. David Morris, ACA *1980;* 31 Burley Road, LEEDS, LS3 1JT.
•**HUNTER, Mr. David Nigel, BSc FCA** *1986;* Beever and Struthers, St George's House, 215-219 Chester Road, MANCHESTER, M15 4JE.
HUNTER, Mr. Derek John, ACA *1993;* Steel Industries, P O Box 1249, BOROKO, PAPUA NEW GUINEA.
HUNTER, Mr. Derek Ronald, BCom ACA *2004;* 49 Maidenstone Hill, LONDON, SE10 8SY.
HUNTER, Mrs. Diana Mary, FCA *1968;* 20 The Strand, Steeple Ashton, TROWBRIDGE, BA14 6EP.
HUNTER, Mr. Duncan, BSc(Econ) ACA *1998;* Flat 45, Ormsby Lodge, The Avenue, LONDON, W4 1HS.
HUNTER, Mr. Edward Atta, BSc(Hons) ACA *2010;* 3 The Grove, Twyford, READING, RG10 9DT.
HUNTER, Miss. Eleanor Jane, BA ACA *1996;* (Tax Fac), with Dixon Wilson, 22 Chancery Lane, LONDON, WC2A 1LS.
HUNTER, Mrs. Emma Louise, BA ACA *2003;* 90 Willow Road, Barrow upon Soar, LOUGHBOROUGH, LEICESTERSHIRE, LE12 8GQ.
•**HUNTER, Mr. Geoffrey Matthew, MA FCA ACIS** *1983;* 1 Nelson's Yard, Beatty Street, LONDON, NW1 7RN.
HUNTER, Mr. George Hedley, FCA *1960;* 10 Noss Mayo, PLYMOUTH, PL8 1EW. (Life Member)
HUNTER, Miss. Georgina, BSc ACA *2005;* Bisley Farm Cheltenham Road, Bisley, STROUD, GL6 7BJ.
HUNTER, Mr. Graham George, BCom FCA *1989;* Pullman Fleet Services Middle Bank House, Middle Bank, DONCASTER, SOUTH YORKSHIRE, DN4 5PF.
HUNTER, Mr. Grant Gordon, BA ACA *2007;* 27 Edgehill, Ponteland, NEWCASTLE UPON TYNE, NE20 9RW.
HUNTER, Mrs. Helen Frances, BA ACA *1991;* 2 The Ridgway, SUTTON, SURREY, SM2 5JY.
HUNTER, Mr. Hugh, BSc FCA *1991;* Balfour Beatty Ltd, 130 Wilton Road, LONDON, SW1V 1LQ.
HUNTER, Mr. Ian John, FCA *1977;* HDR Marne Plant Ltd, The Old Forge, Priory Farm Lane, Inkberrow, WORCESTER, WR7 4HT.
•**HUNTER, Mr. Ian Mark Suffield, FCA** *1978;* Hunter & Co., 415 Blackburn Road, BOLTON, BL1 8NJ.
HUNTER, Mrs. Jacqueline Louise, BA ACA *1988;* Norwood Cottage, Norwood Lane, Meopham, GRAVESEND, DA13 0YE.
HUNTER, Mr. James, MA FCA *1976;* 40 Kingsway Crescent, TORONTO M8X 2R4, ON, CANADA.
HUNTER, Mr. James Edward, BA ACA *1997;* 21 Lyndon Drive, EAST BOLDON, TYNE AND WEAR, NE36 0NU.
HUNTER, Mr. James Stephen, ACA *2008;* Flat 25 Hunsaker, Alfred Street, READING, RG1 7AU.
HUNTER, Mrs. Joanna Catherine, BA ACA *1987;* 47 Yeomans Row, LONDON, SW3 2AL.
HUNTER, Mr. John, FCA *1959;* Watergate, Bainton, BICESTER, OX27 8RW. (Life Member)
HUNTER, Mr. John Campbell, MA FCA *1958;* 9 Ennismore Avenue, GUILDFORD, GU1 1SP. (Life Member)
HUNTER, Mr. John Duncanson, BA(Hons) ACA *2001;* 30 Inman Road, LONDON, SW18 3BB.
HUNTER, Mr. John Patrick, BA ACA *1994;* Stable House, Hill Farm Lane, CHALFONT ST. GILES, BUCKINGHAMSHIRE, HP8 4NT.
•**HUNTER, Mr. John Richard, FCA** *1978;* J.R. Hunter F.C.A, 12 Church Meadow, Sherburn in Elmet, LEEDS, LS25 6NX. See also J.R. Hunter
•**HUNTER, Mr. John Robert, BTech FCA DChA** *1978;* Kites Abbey, Snelsmore, NEWBURY, RG14 3BU.
HUNTER, Mr. Jonathan James, BSc ACA *1999;* 34 The Stray, South Cave, BROUGH, NORTH HUMBERSIDE, HU15 2AL.
HUNTER, Miss. Louise, ACA *2011;* Bryleen, Holmpton, WITHERNSEA, NORTH HUMBERSIDE, HU19 2RB.
HUNTER, Miss. Louise Elizabeth Anderson, ACA *2008;* 4 Plantation Avenue, Shadwell, LEEDS, LS17 8TB.
HUNTER, Mr. Malcolm Christopher George, BSc FCA *1987;* 53 Quickley Lane, Chorleywood, RICKMANSWORTH, WD3 5AE.
•**HUNTER, Mrs. Marilyn Diana, FCA** *1980;* Hunters, 10 Catlin Gardens, GODSTONE, SURREY, RH9 8NT.
HUNTER, Mr. Mark, BA ACA *1987;* N G Bailey & Co Ltd, Heathcote, 31 Kings Road, ILKLEY, WEST YORKSHIRE, LS29 9AS.
•**HUNTER, Mr. Mark Alexander Francis, BSc ACA** *1990;* PricewaterhouseCoopers LLP, Pricewaterhousecoopers, 12 Plumtree Court, LONDON, EC4A 4HT. See also PricewaterhouseCoopers
HUNTER, Mr. Mark Andrew Renz, MA ACA *1993;* 3 Claremont Gardens, EDINBURGH, EH6 7NF.
HUNTER, Mr. Mark David, MA(Hons) ACA *2011;* Unit 3 Brooklyn Close, La Rue Des Pres St. Saviour, JERSEY, JE2 7QL.
•**HUNTER, Mr. Mark James, BA FCA** *1995;* Saffery Champness, Sovereign House, 6 Windsor Court, Clarence Drive, HARROGATE, NORTH YORKSHIRE HG1 2PE.
HUNTER, Mr. Martin David, BA ACA *1983;* Garden Flat, 40 Cavendish Road, LONDON, NW6 7XP.
HUNTER, Miss. Mia, BA ACA *2006;* 33 Downs Road, SUTTON, SURREY, SM2 5NR.
HUNTER, Mr. Michael Lafayette, MA FCA *1965;* 135 Kenilworth Court, Lower Richmond Road, Putney, LONDON, SW15 1HB. (Life Member)
HUNTER, Mrs. Michelle Marie, BSc(Hons) ACA *2001;* 34 The Stray, South Cave, BROUGH, NORTH HUMBERSIDE, HU15 2AL.
HUNTER, Mr. Nicholas James, BA ACA *1989;* Hillview, 1031 Oxford Road, Tilehurst, READING, RG31 6TL.
HUNTER, Mrs. Nicola Jane, BSc ACA *1988;* 2 Latham Close, TWICKENHAM, TW1 1BP.
HUNTER, Mrs. Patricia Ann, BSc ACA *1990;* Hillview, 1031 Oxford Road, Tilehurst, READING, RG31 6TL.
HUNTER, Mr. Patrick Alexander Cowan, ACA *2008;* Aon Risk Solutions, Level 33, Aon Tower, 201 Kent Street, SYDNEY, NSW 2000 AUSTRALIA.
HUNTER, Mr. Paul Anthony, BA ACA *1989;* Newsquest Media Group Ltd, 58 Church Street, WEYBRIDGE, SURREY, KT13 8DP.
HUNTER, Miss. Pauline, BA FCA *1988;* 47 Holcroft Lane, Culcheth, WARRINGTON, WA3 5AQ.
HUNTER, Mr. Peter Colin Cavendish, FCA *1964;* Maheno, Bluett Avenue, SEAVIEW, PO34 5HE. (Life Member)
HUNTER, Mr. Philip John Danby, FCA *1971;* Hale Hamilton (Valves) Ltd Frays Mill Works, Cowley Road, UXBRIDGE, UB8 2AF.
HUNTER, Mr. Phillip Hans Renold, ACA *1979;* 3 Cedar Walk Claygate, ESHER, SURREY, KT10 0RN.
HUNTER, Mr. Ralph Edward, BA ACA *1991;* 17 Kirk Farm Road, GROTON, MA 01450, UNITED STATES.
HUNTER, Mr. Raymond Arthur, FCA *1967;* Wales House, Wales, Queen Camel, YEOVIL, BA22 7PA.
HUNTER, Mr. Richard, BSc ACA *1995;* Mokum, Suite 1-2, Ensign House, Admirals Way, LONDON, E14 9XQ.
HUNTER, Mr. Richard James, BA ACA *2005;* Apartment 66 Mere House, 62 Ellesmere Street, MANCHESTER, M15 4QR.
•**HUNTER, Mr. Ross Andrew, BSc ACA** *1986;* PricewaterhouseCoopers LLP, 1 Embankment Place, LONDON, WC2N 6RH. See also PricewaterhouseCoopers
HUNTER, Mr. Scott Anthony, ACA *2007;* Townends Chartered Accountants, 7-9 Cornmarket, PONTEFRACT, WEST YORKSHIRE, WF8 1AN.
•**HUNTER, Mr. Simon Francis, FCA** *1973;* Atkinson Hunter & Co., Weir Bank, Monkey Island Lane, Bray, MAIDENHEAD, BERKSHIRE SL6 2EA.
HUNTER, Mr. Simon Ian, BEng ACA *1997;* 48 Wildern Lane, NORTHAMPTON, NN4 0SN.
HUNTER, Miss. Stephanie, BA ACA *2011;* Lynton, Cotherstone, BARNARD CASTLE, COUNTY DURHAM, DL12 9PG.
•**HUNTER, Mr. Stephen, BA ACA** *1983;* (Tax Fac), KPMG LLP, Edward VII Quay, Navigation Way, Ashton-on-Ribble, PRESTON, PR2 2YF. See also KPMG Europe LLP
HUNTER, Mr. Steven Andrew, BSc ACA *1988;* Prospect House, Newport Road, Emberton, OLNEY, MK46 5JG.
HUNTER, Ms. Susan Elizabeth, BA ACA *1983;* Apartment 29, 8 Bluelion Place, LONDON, SE1 4PU.
HUNTER, Miss. Suzanne, BSc ACA *2002;* with PricewaterhouseCoopers LLP, Cornwall Court, 19 Cornwall Street, BIRMINGHAM, B3 2DT.
HUNTER, Miss. Tracey, ACA *2008;* 1 St. Martins Close, HYDE, CHESHIRE, SK14 2SS.
HUNTER, Mrs. Tracy Anne, ACA CA(SA) *2009;* 62 Minster Way, BATH, BA2 6RL.
HUNTER, Mr. William John, FCA *1952;* 4 Ridge Court, Westhall Road, WARLINGHAM, CR6 9BH. (Life Member)
•**HUNTER, Mr. William Stewart Andrew, FCA** *1975;* (Tax Fac), Thompson & Hunter, 43/45 High Street, SEVENOAKS, TN13 1JF.
HUNTER GORDON, Miss. Alisa Carolyn, BSc ACA *1993;* Hartmoor Farm Sandley, GILLINGHAM, DORSET, SP8 5EB.
HUNTER GORDON, Mr. Nigel, MA FCA *1973;* Killearnan House, Killearnan, Muir of Ord, INVERNESS, IV6 7SQ.
HUNTER JOHNSTON, Mr. Andrew Malcolm, MA FCA *1980;* BlackRock, 33 King William Street, LONDON, EC4R 9DU.
HUNTER SMART, Mr. Edward Charles, BA(Hons) ACA *2003;* Belvedere House, 3 The Belvederes, 23 Chaddesley Glen, POOLE, DORSET, BH13 7PB.
HUNTING, Mr. Gordon Robert, BSc FCA *1978;* 15 Cottesmore Gardens, LONDON, W8 5PR.
HUNTINGFIELD, Lord Joshua Charles, MA ACA *1993;* 69 Barrons Way, Comberton, CAMBRIDGE, CB23 7EQ.
HUNTINGFORD, Mr. Donald Roy, FCA *1949;* Hedgefield, Splash Lane, Wyton, HUNTINGDON, CAMBRIDGESHIRE, PE28 2AF. (Life Member)
HUNTINGFORD, Mr. John Rodney, MA FCA *1975;* Bryces Farm, Derrybrook Lane, Debenham, STOWMARKET, SUFFOLK, IP14 6PU.
HUNTINGFORD, Mr. Michael David Legh, BSc ACA *1988;* Farm Energy Ltd, The Tannery, East Street, SOUTH MOLTON, DEVON, EX36 3DQ.
HUNTINGFORD, Mr. Richard Norman Leigh, FCA *1979;* 11 Baronsmead Road, LONDON, SW13 9RR.
HUNTINGTON, Mr. Colin Eric, ACA *2008;* Coppenhall, Alvanley Road, Helsby, FRODSHAM, WA6 9QF.
HUNTINGTON, Mr. David, BA ACA *1986;* 10 Westway, Eldwick, BINGLEY, BD16 3LZ.
HUNTINGTON, Mr. John Michael, FCA *1975;* 7 Granby Road, HARROGATE, NORTH YORKSHIRE, HG1 4ST.
HUNTINGTON, Miss. Kathleen, BSc ACA *2010;* 34 Brookmead Avenue, BROMLEY, BR1 2LA.
HUNTINGTON, Miss. Sarah Louise, ACA *2009;* 6 West End Close, Oulton, WIGTON, CUMBRIA, CA7 0NQ.
HUNTINGTON-WHITELEY, Sir Hugo Baldwin, Bt FCA *1954;* Ripple Hall, TEWKESBURY, GLOUCESTERSHIRE, GL20 6EY. (Life Member)
HUNTLEY, Mrs. Helen Elizabeth, ACA *2010;* 16 Bridges View, GATESHEAD, TYNE AND WEAR, NE8 1NZ.
HUNTLEY, Miss. Karen Louise, BSc ACA *2007;* 21 Orchard Road, Fair Oak, EASTLEIGH, HAMPSHIRE, SO50 7AS.
•**HUNTLEY, Mr. Neil Ryan, ACA FCCA** *2008;* Mark Holt & Co Ltd, Marine Building, Victoria Wharf, PLYMOUTH, PL4 0RF.
•**HUNTLEY, Mr. Richard Bernard, FCA** *1973;* (Tax Fac), TTR Barnes Limited, 3-5 Grange Terrace, Stockton Road, SUNDERLAND, SR2 7DG.
HUNTON, Mr. Barry Robert Kirk, FCA *1957;* Wychwood, 54 Dowhills Road, LIVERPOOL, L23 8SP. (Life Member)
•**HUNTON, Mr. Dale, BA ACA** *1995;* Hunton Bros Ltd, 23 Rossway, DARLINGTON, DL1 3RD.
HUNTRISS, Mr. Geoffrey Norman, BA FCA *1976;* 11 Aspen Close, WIRRAL, CH60 1YJ.
HUNTRISS, Mr. Roger Keith, FCA *1977;* The Garden Flat, 57 Overleigh Road, Handbridge, CHESTER, CH4 7HN.
•**HUNWICK, Mr. Nicholas Graham, FCA** *1975;* with Simpson Wreford & Partners, Suffolk House, George Street, CROYDON, CR0 0YN.
HUNWICKS, Mrs. Bhanita, BSc ACA *2002;* Flat 17 Axis Court, Woodland Crescent, LONDON, SE10 9UD.
HUNWICKS, Mr. William George, BA(Hons) ACA *2001;* Flat 17 Axis Court, Woodland Crescent, LONDON, SE10 9UD.
HUNZIKER, Mr. Robert Andrew, MBA BA ACA *1990;* 19 Rue du Rhone, CP 5141, 1211 GENEVA, SWITZERLAND.
•**HUNZIKER, Mr. Roger Francis, FCA** *1960;* Hunziker Associates SA, 100 rue du Rhone, PO Box 1624, 1204 GENEVA, SWITZERLAND.
HUO, Mr. Jupeng, ACA *2011;* Room 706, Tower E1, Oriental Plaza, No1 East Chang An Avenue, Dougcheng District, BEIJING 100738 CHINA.
•**HUPJE, Mr. Hans, ACA** *2009;* (Tax Fac), One 4 Tax and Accounts Ltd, 20 Woodmere Avenue, WATFORD, WD24 7LN. See also One Company Formation Ltd
HUPTON, Mr. David John, ACA *1984;* Beech House, Norwich Rd, New Buckenham, NORWICH, NR16 2AS.
•**HUQ, Mr. Rizwan-Ul, ACA FCCA** *2011;* with RCi (Peterborough) Limited, First Floor, 254-256 Lincoln Road, PETERBOROUGH, CAMBRIDGESHIRE, PE1 2ND.
HUQ, Mr. Tahmur Al, BSc(Hons) ACA *2001;* 4 Gibbon Road, KINGSTON UPON THAMES, KT2 6AB.

HUQUE, Mr. Kazi Aminul, FCA *1966;* House 4, Road 12, Dhanmandi R/A, DHAKA, BANGLADESH.
HUQUE, Mr. Mujibul, FCA *1974;* M.Huque & Co, 70/C Purana Paltan Line, 3rd Floor, DHAKA 1000, BANGLADESH.
HUR, Mr. Steven David Isaac, BSc ACA *1979;* 16 Lumiere Court, 209 Balham High Road, LONDON, SW17 7BQ.
HURCOMB, Mr. David Stuart, BSc ACA *1991;* Sandlands, Roman Road, DORKING, RH4 3EU.
HURCOMBE, Mr. Alan James David, BA FCA *1993;* Scholastic Ltd, Westfield Road, SOUTHAM, WARWICKSHIRE, CV47 0RA.
HURD, Mr. Christopher John, FCA *1970;* 2 Forest Close, WOODFORD GREEN, IG8 0QD.
HURD, Mr. Christopher John Wycombe, FCA *1977;* P O Box 351, MALINDI, 80200, KENYA.
HURD, Mr. Daniel Christopher, BSS ACA *2000;* 17 Kingscote Road, Dorridge, SOLIHULL, B93 8RB.
HURD, Mrs. Janette Anne, FCA *1975;* Levisham Hall, Levisham, PICKERING, YO18 7NL.
HURD, Mr. Richard Brian, BA ACA *1999;* 56 Shakespeare Avenue, BATH, SOMERSET, BA2 4RG.
HURD, Mr. Robin Hugh Wycombe, FCA *1975;* Levisham Hall, Levisham, PICKERING, YO18 7NL.
HURDEN, Mr. Martin Philip, BSc ACA *1999;* 4511 Old Course Drive, CHARLOTTE, NC 28277, UNITED STATES.
HURDLE, Mr. Timothy James, BA ACA *1993;* 8 Rosehill, Claygate, ESHER, KT10 0HL.
•**HURDMAN, Mr. Mark John, BA ACA** *2002;* (Tax Fac), Levicks, Station Gates, 3 Lloyd Road, BROADSTAIRS, CT10 1HY. See also Somerfield Consultants Limited
•**HURER, Mr. Ertan, BSc FCA** *1988;* (Tax Fac), HSCA Limited, 291-293 Green Lanes, Palmers Green, LONDON, N13 4XS.
HURER, Mr. Hasan, BSc ACA *2011;* 4 Griffins Close, Winchmore Hill, LONDON, N21 2EW.
•**HURFORD, Mr. Angus John, FCA** *1980;* Kinnaird Hill, Montagu House, 81 High Street, HUNTINGDON, CAMBRIDGESHIRE, PE29 3NY.
HURFORD, Mr. Jonathan Andrew, LLB ACA *2004;* 50 Biddlestone Road, NEWCASTLE UPON TYNE, NE6 5SL.
HURFORD, Mr. Michael Scott, BA ACA *1981;* Orchard House, 32A Church End, Biddenham, BEDFORD, MK40 4AR.
HURFURT, Mr. Gareth John, BSc FCA *1993;* 6 Hazelwood Close, Godley, HYDE, SK14 3SP.
HURL-HODGES, Mrs. Mary Monina, BEng FCA *1993;* Furlong View, Bridge Road, UTTOXETER, STAFFORDSHIRE, ST14 8BA.
HURLBUT, Mr. John Dennis, FCA *1973;* 15 Fulwith Road, HARROGATE, HG2 8HL. (Life Member)
•**HURLEY, Mr. Anthony, FCA** *1973;* A. Hurley, 4 Friars Crescent, NEWPORT, NP20 4EY.
HURLEY, Ms. Chloe Lynne, BA ACA *2004;* Room 302, No. 147, 288 Long, Shuang Yuang Bei Road, SHANGHAI 200433, CHINA.
HURLEY, Mr. Christopher Richard, BSc ACA *1998;* 5 Newent Road, Northfield, BIRMINGHAM, B31 2ED.
HURLEY, Mrs. Fiona Jane, BSc ACA *1991;* 12 Oakland Vineries, La Rue Du Presbytere, St. Clement, JERSEY, JE2 6RB.
HURLEY, Mr. John David, FCA *1975;* 9 Firbank Road, ST. ALBANS, AL3 6NA.
HURLEY, Miss. Katherine Mary, BA ACA *2008;* with KPMG LLP, St. James's Square, MANCHESTER, M2 6DS.
HURLEY, Mr. Keith William Walter, FCA *1967;* Wargrave House, School Lane, Wargrave, READING, RG10 8AA.
HURLEY, Mrs. Lindsay Fiona, BSc ACA *2003;* with BDO LLP, 55 Baker Street, LONDON, W1U 7EU.
HURLEY, Mr. Matthew Rhys, BSc ACA *1999;* 47 Fields Road, NEWPORT, NP20 5BP.
HURLEY, Mrs. Patricia, BSc ACA *1982;* O'Connell Street, Ballymote, SLIGO, COUNTY SLIGO, IRELAND.
HURLEY, Mr. Patrick Aloysius, MBA BCom FCA *1978;* Santa Maria, Seapoint Avenue, Monkstown, DUBLIN, COUNTY DUBLIN, IRELAND.
HURLEY, Mr. Patrick William, FCA *1963;* 4 Fairbourne, COBHAM, SURREY, KT11 2BT.
HURLEY, Mr. Paul Anthony John, BSc FCA *1971;* Broadham Care Ltd Vector House, Merle Common Road, OXTED, SURREY, RH8 0RP.
HURLEY, Mr. Paul Barrington Andrew, BSc FCA *1978;* Flat 1, Brockwell Grange, 47 Brockwell Lane, CHESTERFIELD, DERBYSHIRE, S40 4EA.
HURLEY, Mr. Peter Laurence, FCA *1967;* 25 Waldgrooms, DUNMOW, ESSEX, CM6 1DZ.
HURLEY, Mr. Roger, FCA *1968;* 25 Teazel Avenue, Bournville, BIRMINGHAM, B30 1LZ.
HURLEY, Mr. Stephen Mark, ACA *1983;* Flat 14 Edencroft, Wheeleys Road, BIRMINGHAM, B15 2LW.
•**HURLEY, Mr. Thomas Edward, ACA** *2007;* Catalyst Corporate Finance LLP, 5th Floor, 12-18 Grosvenor Gardens, LONDON, SW1W 0DH.
HURLSTONE, Mrs. Angela Jill, BA ACA *1996;* 25 Claremont Gardens, UPMINSTER, ESSEX, RM14 1DW.
HURLSTONE, Mr. Daniel John, BSc ACA *2004;* 75 Avonleigh Road, Bedminster, BRISTOL, BS3 3JA.
HURLSTONE, Mr. Fredric George, FCA *1967;* 5 Briar Lane, WEST WICKHAM, BR4 9RA. (Life Member)
HURLSTONE, Mr. Toby Oliver Matthew, BSc ACA MBA *1996;* 4th Floor, 101 Euston Road, LONDON, NW1 2RA.
HURMAN-FEUILLERAT, Mrs. Claudine, ACA *1992;* 12 Rue de Seine, 78230 LE PECQ, FRANCE.
HURN, Mrs. Rachel Louise, BSc ACA *1998;* 5 Carlile Gardens, Twyford, READING, RG10 9BU.
HURN, Mr. Robert Peter, FCA *1969;* 29 Kent Road, LONDON, W4 5EY.
HURN, Mrs. Sally-Anne, ACA *2009;* Rochester House, Little Steeping, SPILSBY, LINCOLNSHIRE, PE23 5BL.
HURRAN, Mr. Anthony Robert, BA ACA *2001;* 41 Dove Park, Chorleywood, RICKMANSWORTH, HERTFORDSHIRE, WD3 5NY.
•**HURRELL, Mrs. Claire Louise, ACA** *2001;* Claire Hurrell ACA, Oaktree Cottage, The Street, Swanton Abbott, NORWICH, NR10 5DU.
HURRELL, Dr. Esther Victoria, PhD MA ACA *2005;* with PricewaterhouseCoopers LLP, Erskine House, 68-73 Queen Street, EDINBURGH, EH2 4NH.
•**HURRELL, Mr. James Stephen, BSc ACA CTA** *1992;* (Tax Fac), Moore Stephens LLP, 150 Aldersgate Street, LONDON, EC1A 4AB. See also Moore Stephens & Co
HURRELL, Mrs. Janina, ACA *1994;* 2 Sutton Mead, CHELMSFORD, CM2 6QB.
HURREN, Mrs. Celia Helen, BA ACA *1999;* 2 The Crescent, HORSHAM, WEST SUSSEX, RH12 1NB.
•**HURREN, Mr. Christopher Ian, BA ACA** *1996;* Baker Tilly Tax & Advisory Services LLP, The Clock House, 140 London Road, GUILDFORD, SURREY, GU1 1UW. See also Baker Tilly UK Audit LLP
HURREN, Mr. Mark Ashley, MMath ACA *2010;* 48 Nicholson Drive, BECCLES, SUFFOLK, NR34 9UX.
•**HURREN, Mr. Martin David, FCA** *1973;* Bennett & Co, 16 Upland Road, Dulwich, LONDON, SE22 9GG.
HURST, Mr. Adam Howard, BA FCA *1993;* Entertainment One Ltd., 120 New Cavendish St, LONDON, W1W 6XX.
HURST, Mr. Andrew Patrick, FCA *1974;* Wendover Investments Ltd, 19 Ebury Street, LONDON, SW1W 0LD.
HURST, Mr. Brian Charles, BA FCA *1975;* Georgian House, 20 Church Street, Storrington, PULBOROUGH, RH20 4LA.
HURST, Miss. Charlotte, BA(Hons) ACA *2011;* 15 Berkeley Court, WEYBRIDGE, KT13 9HX.
HURST, Mrs. Christine Hazel, BSc FCA *1984;* Birchwood House Shaws Lane, Southwater, HORSHAM, WEST SUSSEX, RH13 9BX.
HURST, Mr. Clifford Graham, BA FCA MCT *1987;* (Tax Fac), Mullions, 10 Crossways, BERKHAMSTED, HP4 3NH.
HURST, Mr. David Berkeley, MA FCA *1966;* 32 Kenway Road, LONDON, SW5 0RR.
•**HURST, Mr. David Ian, LLB FCA** *1985;* HMT Assurance LLP, 5 Fairmile, HENLEY-ON-THAMES, OXFORDSHIRE, RG9 2JR.
•①**HURST, Mr. David Peter, BCom FCA** *1999;* 12 Edgeworth Avenue, LONDON, NW4 4EY.
HURST, Mr. David Vivian, FCA *1964;* Varandas, Rua Sacadura Cabral Bloco B-3A, 5. Pedro Do Estoril, 2765553 ESTORIL, PORTUGAL.
HURST, Mr. Dennis Grahame, FCA *1966;* The Hermitage, Longville in the Dale, MUCH WENLOCK, SHROPSHIRE, TF13 6DS.
HURST, Miss. Elizabeth Mary, BSc ACA *1987;* 27 Applecroft, Park Street, ST. ALBANS, AL2 2AP.
HURST, Mrs. Esther Mary, MA MBA FCA *1988;* General Motors, Griffin House, Osborne Road, LUTON, LU1 3YT.
HURST, Mr. Gordon Mark, BSc ACA *1987;* Luckdon Farm, North Bovey, NEWTON ABBOT, DEVON, TQ13 8QX.
HURST, Mr. Graeme Andrew, ACA *2007;* 83 Springbank Road, Gildersome, Morley, LEEDS, WEST YORKSHIRE, LS27 7DL.
•**HURST, Mr. Graham, ACA** *1979;* Hurst & Co, 74/76 High St, WINSFORD, CW7 2AP.
•**HURST, Mr. Graham Barry, FCA** *1984;* HMT Assurance LLP, 5 Fairmile, HENLEY-ON-THAMES, OXFORDSHIRE, RG9 2JR.
HURST, Mr. Graham David, FCA *1969;* 15 Tendring Drive, WIGSTON, LE18 3WR.
•**HURST, Mr. Harry Malcolm Guy, BA FCA** *1977;* 7 Lansdown Close, Cheadle Hulme, CHEADLE, CHESHIRE, SK8 7HF.
HURST, Miss. Jane Ellen, BSc ACA *2004;* 188 Southstand Apartments, Highbury Stadium Square, LONDON, N5 1FD.
HURST, Mr. Jason Mark, BCom ACA *1995;* 7 Sequoia Gardens, ORPINGTON, KENT, BR6 0TZ.
HURST, Mrs. Jennifer Anne, BSc FCA *1997;* 7 Kenwell Drive, Bradway, SHEFFIELD, S17 4PJ.
HURST, Mr. John, FCA *1948;* 19 Kilwardby St, ASHBY-DE-LA-ZOUCH, LE65 2FR. (Life Member)
HURST, Mr. John Ayton, FCA *1973;* Bee Cottage, Terras Hill, LOSTWITHIEL, CORNWALL, PL22 0AP. (Life Member)
HURST, Mr. Jonathan David, BSc FCA *1990;* 2 Wells Close, TONBRIDGE, TN10 4NW.
•**HURST, Mr. Jonathan Paul Fenton, BSc ACA** *1984;* KPMG LLP, St. James's Square, MANCHESTER, M2 6DS. See also KPMG Europe LLP
•**HURST, Ms. Kim Barbara, BA FCA** *1982;* Mazars LLP, Tower Bridge House, St. Katharines Way, LONDON, E1W 1DD. See also Mazars Corporate Finance Limited
HURST, Mr. Laurence, MEng ACA *2009;* Flat B, 190 Bedford Hill, LONDON, SW12 9HL.
•**HURST, Mr. Lawrence David, FCA** *1971;* Lawrence Hurst & Co, 2nd Floor Morritt House, 10/12 Love Lane, PINNER, HA5 3EF.
HURST, Mrs. Lianne, BSc ACA *2005;* 2 Wheeldale, WIGSTON, LEICESTERSHIRE, LE18 3XN.
•**HURST, Mr. Martin, BSc ACA** *1990;* Ernst & Young GmbH, Merghentalerallee 10-12, 65760 ESCHBORN, GERMANY. See also Ernst & Young Europe LLP
•**HURST, Mr. Martin Gary, FCA** *1990;* RHP Partnership, Lancaster House, 87 Yarmouth Road, NORWICH, NORFOLK, NR7 0HF.
HURST, Mr. Matthew, MSci ARCS ACA *2011;* 47 Little Ealing Lane, LONDON, W5 4ED.
HURST, Mr. Michael Robert, FCA *1968;* 6 Akamas Street, Aphrodite Hills, Kouilica, 8509 PAPHOS, CYPRUS.
•**HURST, Mr. Patrick John, FCA** *1972;* (Tax Fac), 2 Manor Crescent, Tytherington, MACCLESFIELD, SK10 2EN.
HURST, Mr. Paul Stuart, ACA *1983;* 68 Abbot Meadow, Penwortham, PRESTON, PR1 9JX.
HURST, Mr. Peter Anthony, FCA *1973;* 26 Park Crescent, Finchley, LONDON, N3 2NJ.
HURST, Mr. Peter William, BA FCA *1964;* 7 Chapel Drive, Aston Clinton, AYLESBURY, HP22 5EN.
HURST, Mr. Phillip James, ACA *2006;* 29 Sperling Drive, HAVERHILL, SUFFOLK, CB9 9SG.
•**HURST, Mr. Richard Andrew, FCA** *1988;* Hopper Williams & Bell Limited, Highland House, Mayflower Close, Chandler's Ford, SOUTHAMPTON, HAMPSHIRE SO53 4AR. See also HWB Holdings Limited
HURST, Mr. Robert Andrew, FCA *1971;* Hilltop Farm, Rusper, HORSHAM, RH12 4QS.
HURST, Mr. Robert Ashley, BSc ACA *1989;* Audio Network Plc, 61 Holywell Hill, ST. ALBANS, AL1 1HF.
HURST, Mr. Simon John, BA *1984;* (Member of Council 2002 - 2005), The Knowledge Base, Birchfield, Winterpit Lane, Mannings Heath, HORSHAM, WEST SUSSEX RH13 6LZ.
HURST, Miss. Stephanie, BA ACA *2007;* John Hurst Hocke Design, 200 Beech Road, ST. ALBANS, HERTFORDSHIRE, AL3 5AX.
HURST, Mr. Stephen John, BA(Hons) ACA *2001;* 104 Woolton Road, Wavertree, LIVERPOOL, L15 6TH.
HURST, Mrs. Susan Margaret, BA FCA CTA *1993;* (Tax Fac), 8 Hamilton Road, Whitefield, MANCHESTER, M45 6QW.
HURST, Mrs. Tammy Anne, BA(Hons) ACA *2010;* Yew Hedge House, Upper Street, Child Okeford, BLANDFORD FORUM, DORSET, DT11 8EF.
HURST, Mr. Terence James, BPhil FCA *1966;* The Lodge, Gayton Lane, Heswall, WIRRAL, CH60 3RE.
HURST-BROWN, Mr. Christopher Nigel, BSc FCA *1977;* Hotchkis and Wiley (UK) Ltd, 26 Cresswell Place, LONDON, SW10 9RB.
•**HURSTHOUSE, Mr. Michael Lawrence, BA ACA** *1985;* M L Hursthouse BA ACA, 85 Derwent Close, Alsager, STOKE-ON-TRENT, ST7 2EL.
HURT, Mr. Douglas Malcolm, MA ACA *1981;* I M I Kynoch plc, Lakeside, Unit 4040, Solihull Parkway, Birmingham Business Park, BIRMINGHAM B37 7XZ.
HURWITZ, Mrs. Maria Christina, ACA *2008;* 424 West End Avenue 12B, NEW YORK, NY 10024, UNITED STATES.
HURWORTH, Mrs. Christine, FCA *1962;* 8 Holyrood Avenue, DARLINGTON, DL3 8AZ.
HURWORTH, Mrs. Claire Katherine, BSc ACA *1993;* 24 Swinburne Road, DARLINGTON, DL3 7TD.
HURWORTH, Mr. David Martin, BSc ACA *1993;* 8 Holyrood Avenue, DARLINGTON, DL3 8AZ.
HURWORTH, Mr. Graeme Richard, BSc ACA *1993;* 24 Swinburne Road, DARLINGTON, COUNTY DURHAM, DL3 7TD.
HURWORTH, Mrs. Jane, BA ACA AMCT *1995;* 19 Stroud Road, LONDON, SW19 8DQ.
HURWORTH, Mr. John Maitland, FCA *1963;* 8 Holyrood Avenue, DARLINGTON, DL3 8AZ.
HURYNAG, Mr. Rajdipaksingh, MBA ACA ACCA ACMA *2008;* 7 Merlin Crescent, EDGWARE, MIDDLESEX, HA8 6JL.
•**HUSAIN, Mr. Arif, FCA** *1971;* Lincoln house, 137-143 Hammersmith Road, LONDON, W14 0GL.
HUSAIN, Miss. Farah, MA ACA *2005;* House No 4/1 23rd Street, Off Khayaban-e-Tanzeem, DHA Phase 5, KARACHI, PAKISTAN.
HUSAIN, Mrs. Lisa Ferguson, MA ACA *2004;* Garden Flat, 63 Shepherds Hill, LONDON, N6 5RE.
HUSAIN, Mr. Maqsood Amer, BSc ACA *1990;* 5269 Creditview Road, MISSISSAUGA L5V 1T6, ON, CANADA.
•**HUSAIN, Mr. Qazi Matlub, FCA** *1970;* Q M Husain & Co Limited, 37 Grove Avenue, Muswell Hill, LONDON, N10 2AS.
HUSAIN, Mr. Saiyed Enayet, FCA *1963;* House No 15, Street No 6, F-8/3, ISLAMABAD 44000, PAKISTAN.
HUSAIN, Mr. Saleem, FCA *1972;* 60 Raleigh Drive, Whetstone, LONDON, N20 0UU.
HUSAIN, Mr. Shairan Huzani, BA FCA *1993;* 2 Jalan Teratak U8/96D, Bukit Jelutong, 40150 SHAH ALAM, MALAYSIA.
•**HUSAIN, Mr. Syed, FCA** *1975;* S. Husain & Co, 83 Corbins Lane, South Harrow, HARROW, HA2 8EN. See also Shears & Dube and S. Syedain & Co
HUSAIN, Mr. Syed Khurshid, LLB ACA *1986;* Mount Pleasant Farm, Nutt Lane, Prestwich, MANCHESTER, M25 2SJ.
HUSAIN, Mr. Syed Tariq, ACA *1981;* 80 Faran Society, Ahmed Barrister Road, off Haider Ali Road, KARACHI 74800, PAKISTAN.
HUSBAND, Mrs. Christine Elizabeth, BSc ACA *1982;* Apple Porch, Overdale Road, Willaston, NESTON, CH64 1SX.
•**HUSBAND, Mr. Ian Simon, MA FCA** *1983;* Richardsons Financial Group Limited, 30 Upper High Street, THAME, OXFORDSHIRE, OX9 3EZ.
•**HUSBAND, Mr. James Henry, BSc ACA** *1990;* 52 Marmont Road, LONDON, SE15 5TE.
•**HUSBAND, Mr. John, BA FCA** *1986;* (Tax Fac), John F Harvey Limited, Dynevor House, 5-6 De la Beche Street, SWANSEA, SA1 3HA.
HUSBAND, Mr. Richard Radclyffe, FCA *1971;* 44 Fendon Road, CAMBRIDGE, CB1 7RT.
•**HUSBAND, Mr. Robert, ACA FCCA** *2009;* HW Lee Associates LLP, New Derwent House, 69-73 Theobalds Road, LONDON, WC1X 8TA.
HUSBAND, Mr. Thomas, FCA *1967;* Oak Field, 1 School Green Lane, SHEFFIELD, S10 4GP. (Life Member)
HUSBANDS, Mr. Benjamin Edward, LLB ACA *2000;* Blackhorse Cottage, 189 Woodside Road, AMERSHAM, BUCKINGHAMSHIRE, HP6 6NU.
•**HUSBANDS, Mr. Charles Martin Wilson, BA FCA** *1978;* Husbands & Co, Forge House, Forge Road, Osbaston, MONMOUTH, GWENT NP25 3AZ.
HUSBANDS, Mrs. Rachel Alexandra, BSc FCA *1999;* Pres Du Phare La Rue de la Corbiere, St. Brelade, JERSEY, JE3 8HN.
HUSE, Mr. Derek Graham, BSc ACA *2000;* Oakley Capital Limited, 3 Cadogan Gate, Chelsea, LONDON, SW1X 0AS.
•**HUSEIN, Mr. Zaki Sayed Kaiser, ACA FCCA** *2007;* (Tax Fac), Kaiser Yamawaki LLP, Unit 4, 17 Plumbers Row, LONDON, E1 1EQ.
HUSK, Mrs. Joanne Elizabeth, BSc ACA *1982;* 37 Graburn Road, Formby, LIVERPOOL, L37 3PA.
HUSK, Mr. Richard Antony, ACA *2010;* 37 Graburn Road, LIVERPOOL, L37 3PA.
HUSKINSON, Mrs. Deborah Rachel Elizabeth, BA ACA *2000;* Whitbread Plc, Whitbread Court, Porz Avenue, Houghton Hall Park, Houghton Regis, DUNSTABLE BEDFORDSHIRE LU5 5XE.
HUSKINSON, Mr. Timothy James, MEng ACA *2010;* Flat 1 The Courtyard, 3 Besson Street, LONDON, SE14 5AE.

•HUSLER, Mr. Mark Charles, FCA *1974;* (Tax Fac), Wyatt & Co (Scarborough) Limited, 50-51 Albemarle Crescent, SCARBOROUGH, NORTH YORKSHIRE, YO11 1XX. See also Wyatt Husler Cook(Accountants) Limited and Wyatt & Co
HUSON, Miss. Elizabeth Joy, FCA *1982;* (Tax Fac), 23 Conyers Close, Hersham, WALTON-ON-THAMES, KT12 4NG.
HUSON, Mrs. Julia Anne, ACA *2002;* 22 Barnes Wallis Avenue, Christs Hospital, HORSHAM, WEST SUSSEX, RH13 0TL.
HUSON, Mr. Malcolm Keith, BA ACA *1982;* Arlington, Upper Verran Road, CAMBERLEY, SURREY, GU15 2JL.
HUSON, Mr. Thomas Patrick, BSc ACA *2004;* 22 Barnes Wallis Avenue, Christs Hospital, HORSHAM, WEST SUSSEX, RH13 0TL.
HUSSAIN, Mr. Amir, LLM LLB ACA *2002;* 154 Hainault Road, Leytonstone, LONDON, E11 1EW.
HUSSAIN, Mr. Amir, BA(Hons) ACA *2010;* 9 High Street, Brierfield, NELSON, LANCASHIRE, BB9 5AP.
•HUSSAIN, Mr. Amjad, BSc ACA *2000;* Amjad Hussain BSc ACA, 74 Hazelwood Road, Walthamstow, LONDON, E17 7AL.
•HUSSAIN, Mr. Amtaz, BSc ACA *2007;* 2 Lancaster House, 16 Lancaster Road, LONDON, E11 3FD.
HUSSAIN, Mr. Aqeel, ACA *2011;* Flat 16 Lane End, 196 West Hill, LONDON, SW15 3SH.
HUSSAIN, Mr. Arif, MPhil BSc ACA *1996;* P O Box 413951, Craighall, JOHANNESBURG, GAUTENG, 2024, SOUTH AFRICA.
HUSSAIN, Mr. Ayaz Mahmud, ACA *1982;* IATA, Iata Centre, Route De L'Aeroport 33, P.O. Box 416, CH 1215 GENEVA, SWITZERLAND.
HUSSAIN, Miss. Ayesha Somee, BSc ACA *2003;* 15 Rookery Way, Lower Kingswood, TADWORTH, KT20 7DT.
HUSSAIN, Mr. Azhar, BA ACA *2000;* 28 Dunsham Lane, AYLESBURY, BUCKINGHAMSHIRE, HP20 2EG.
HUSSAIN, Mr. Azhar Mahmood, LLB ACA *2003;* 39 Springfield Road, KEIGHLEY, WEST YORKSHIRE, BD20 6JR.
HUSSAIN, Mr. Faraz, BSc ACA *2010;* 54 Elborough Street, Southfields, LONDON, SW18 5DN.
HUSSAIN, Mr. Fida, MSc BA ACA *1998;* 278 Stoke Poges Lane, SLOUGH, SL1 3LL.
HUSSAIN, Mr. Gumuri Bin, FCA *1975;* with PricewaterhouseCoopers, P.O.Box 10192, Level 10 1 Sentral, Jalan Travers, 50470 KUALA LUMPUR, FEDERAL TERRITORY MALAYSIA.
HUSSAIN, Miss. Habiba, BSc(Hons) ACA *2010;* Athene Place, Deloitte & Touche Llp, 66 Shoe Lane, LONDON, EC4A 3BQ.
HUSSAIN, Mr. Hamayou Akbar, BA ACA *1999;* (Tax Fac), The Prudential Assurance Co Ltd Minster House, 12 Arthur Street, LONDON, EC4R 9AQ.
HUSSAIN, Mrs. Helen Rachel, BA FCA *1998;* 55 Courtfield Avenue, HARROW, HA1 2LB.
•HUSSAIN, Mr. Imtiaz, FCA *1981;* I. Hussain & Company, 11 George Street West, LUTON, LU1 2BJ.
HUSSAIN, Mr. Iqbal, FCA *1975;* 273 Abid Majeed Road, RAWALPINDI 46000, PAKISTAN.
•HUSSAIN, Mr. Irfan, BSc FCA *1997;* ASL Partners Ltd, 14 Honister Gardens, STANMORE, MIDDLESEX, HA7 2EH. See also Knav UK Limited
HUSSAIN, Mr. Ishaat, FCA *1973;* Tata Sons Ltd, Bombay House, Homi Mody Street, MUMBAI 400001, MAHARASHTRA, INDIA.
HUSSAIN, Mr. Karim Aly, BSc ACA *2010;* 16 Chyngton Gardens, SEAFORD, EAST SUSSEX, BN25 3RP.
HUSSAIN, Mr. Khashrul, BA ACA *2008;* 11 Ripon Gardens, ILFORD, IG1 3SL.
HUSSAIN, Mr. Mahmood Ahmed, MA(Hons) ACA *2002;* 15 Drake Street, KEIGHLEY, BD21 3AY.
HUSSAIN, Mr. Mahmudul, ACA *2008;* 66 Aldborough Road South, ILFORD, IG3 8EX.
•HUSSAIN, Mr. Mohamed Kamal Bin, FCA *1975;* M.K.B. Hussain, Unit 1003 Level 10 Block A, Pusat Perdagangan Phileo, Damansara 2, No 15 Jalan 16/11, Off Jalan Damansara 46350 PETALING JAYA SELANGOR MALAYSIA.
HUSSAIN, Mr. Mohammad Abrar, ACA ACMA *2009;* Occidental Petroleum of Qatar Ltd, PO Box 22611, Navigation Plaza, C Ring Road, DOHA, QATAR.
HUSSAIN, Mr. Mohammed Shahryer, MEng ACA *2001;* with National Audit Office, 157-197 Buckingham Palace Road, Victoria, LONDON, SW1W 9SP.
HUSSAIN, Mr. Mokbul, ACA *2008;* 8 Folgate Street, LONDON, E1 6BX.
HUSSAIN, Mr. Nadeem, MSc BSc(Hons) ACA *2011;* 37 Broadway, WALSALL, WS1 3EZ.
HUSSAIN, Miss. Naheed Kousar, BSc(Hons) ACA *2001;* 28 Whitchurch Road, CARDIFF, CF14 3LW.
HUSSAIN, Mr. Naiem, BSc DipEd ACA *1997;* Flat 3, 12 Philbeach Gardens, LONDON, SW5 9DY.
HUSSAIN, Mr. Nazir, BCom ACA CFA *1992;* 28 Kinnaird Avenue, LONDON, W4 3SH.
HUSSAIN, Mr. Raza, BA(Hons) ACA *2010;* 119 Kimbolton Road, BEDFORD, MK41 8DT.
HUSSAIN, Mr. Reza, BA ACA *2006;* 5 Stanton Avenue, Didsbury, MANCHESTER, M20 2PG.
HUSSAIN, Mr. Sabbir, BSc ACA *2007;* 1 Birchen Grove, LUTON, LU2 7TJ.
HUSSAIN, Mr. Saieem, BSc ACA *1992;* 63 Broadwalk, LONDON, E18 2DN.
HUSSAIN, Miss. Samrin Arif, ACA *2008;* 56 Lansdowne Road, MANCHESTER, M8 5SH.
HUSSAIN, Mr. Saqib, ACA *2009;* 16 Shetland Close, Wilpshire, BLACKBURN, BB1 9NQ.
HUSSAIN, Mr. Sayed Shahzad, BSc ACA *2005;* 33 Bradenham Road, Grange Park, SWINDON, SN5 6EB.
•HUSSAIN, Mr. Shahbaz, BSc ACA *2006;* I. Hussain & Company, 11 George Street West, LUTON, LU1 2BJ.
HUSSAIN, Mr. Shahzad, ACA *1981;* A.F. Ferguson & Co, Al-Falah Building, PO Box39, Shahrah-e-Quaid-e-Azam, LAHORE, PAKISTAN.
HUSSAIN, Miss. Shajeda, LLB ACA *2005;* Flat 2, 16 Melrose Avenue, LONDON, SW19 8BY.
HUSSAIN, Mr. Sharif Mohammed Kamal, MSc ACA *1992;* 79 Sotheby Road, Islington, LONDON, N5 2UT.
HUSSAIN, Mr. Sulman, BA(Hons) ACA *2010;* 23 Hamilton Road, ILFORD, ESSEX, IG1 2EU.
HUSSAIN, Mr. Sushovan Tareque, BA ACA *1991;* Cade House, 2 Chipstead Lane, Riverhead, SEVENOAKS, TN13 2AG.
HUSSAIN, Mr. Syed Qalandar, ACA *1980;* 108/1 Fazil Road, St. John's Park, Lahore Cantt, LAHORE, PAKISTAN.
HUSSAIN, Mr. Syed Sajid, BCom FCA *1968;* Karachi Development Authority, C/121 K.D.A., Scheme No 1, KARACHI 75350, PAKISTAN. (Life Member)
HUSSAIN, Mr. Syedul, BSc ACA *1999;* with PricewaterhouseCoopers LLP, 101 Barbirolli Square, Lower Mosley Street, MANCHESTER, M2 3PW.
•HUSSAIN, Mr. Tahir, ACA FCCA *2009;* Tahir & Co, 96 Boundary Road, Plaistow, LONDON, E13 9QG.
•HUSSAIN, Mr. Tajammal, MPhil BSc FCA *1987;* T Hussain & Co, 123-E/1, Unit B, Hali Road, Gulberg III, LAHORE PAKISTAN.
HUSSAIN, Mr. Zeeshan, BSc ACA *2009;* 87 Montrose Avenue, LUTON, LU3 1HP.
•①HUSSAIN, Mr. Zelf, BCom FCA *1995;* PricewaterhouseCoopers, 7 More London Riverside, LONDON, SE1 2RT. See also PricewaterhouseCoopers LLP
HUSSAINI, Miss. Nora Junita, BSc(Econ) ACA *2004;* Level 8 Axiata Centre 9 Jalan Stesen Sentral 5, 50470 KUALA LUMPUR, FEDERAL TERRITORY, MALAYSIA.
HUSSEIN, Mr. Baber, BEng ACA *1998;* (Tax Fac), 19 Regis Park Road, READING, RG6 7AD.
HUSSEIN, Mr. Mehmet, ACA *2008;* 7 Holyrood Road, New Barnet, BARNET, HERTFORDSHIRE, EN5 1DQ.
HUSSEIN, Mrs. Melike Sule, MSc ACA *2006;* Flat 510 California Building, Deals Gateway, LONDON, SE13 7SF.
•HUSSEIN, Mr. Shaukat, FCA *1979;* Haines Watts Wimbledon LLP, 158-160 Arthur Road, LONDON, SW19 8AQ.
HUSSEIN, Mr. Zahid, ACA *2008;* 13 Preston Road, Wimbledon, LONDON, SW20 0SS.
HUSSELL, Miss. Karen Maria, BSc FCA ATII *1990;* 1 Alexander Terrace, Liverpool Gardens, WORTHING, BN11 1YH.
HUSSELL, Miss. Laura, BA ACA *2005;* Top Floor Flat, 62 Heathfield Road, CROYDON, CR0 1EW.
•HUSSEY, Mr. Alan, FCA *1987;* Alan Hussey Accountants, Unit 4, Parsonage Business Centre, Church Street, Ticehurst, WADHURST EAST SUSSEX TN5 7DL.
•HUSSEY, Mrs. Anne Catherine, BA ACA *1985;* Catherine Hussey, 3 O'Rahilly Row, Fermoy, CORK, COUNTY CORK, IRELAND.
HUSSEY, Mr. Duncan Robert, BSc ACA *1991;* 6 Moat Close, Green Street Green, ORPINGTON, BR6 6ET.
HUSSEY, Mrs. Emma Jane, BSc ACA *2004;* St. Peters Hospice Charlton Road, Brentry, BRISTOL, BS10 6NL.
HUSSEY, Mr. Frederick Joseph, MA BCom FCA *1959;* 30 Hawth Crescent, SEAFORD, BN25 2RR. (Life Member)
HUSSEY, Mr. James Richard, BEng ACA *2000;* 16 The Crescent, WEYBRIDGE, SURREY, KT13 8EL.
HUSSEY, Mr. Jeremy Michael, BSc ACA *1995;* 78 Cowper Road, HARPENDEN, AL5 5NH.
HUSSEY, Mr. Lascelles Charles, MBA BA ACA *1985;* HB Consulting, Po Box 21660, LONDON, SW16 1WJ.
HUSSEY, Mr. Michael, BA(Econ) ACA *2007;* 22 Crosbies Yard, Ossorry Road, DUBLIN 3, COUNTY DUBLIN, IRELAND.
HUSSEY, Miss. Nicola Jane, BA ACA *1995;* 2 Bunbury Street, STIRLING, ACT 2611, AUSTRALIA.
•HUSSEY, Mr. Peter James Waltham, FCA *1979;* Spofforths LLP, A2 Yeoman Gate, Yeoman Way, WORTHING, WEST SUSSEX, BN13 3QZ.
•HUSSEY, Mr. Richard John, BSc FCA *1980;* (Tax Fac), Francis Clark, Francis Clark LLP, Sigma House, Oak View Close, Edginswell Park, TORQUAY TQ2 7FF. See also Francis Clark LLP
HUSSEY, Mr. Robert James, BSc ACA *1986;* 54 Rylands Heath, LUTON, LU2 8TZ.
HUSSEY, Mr. Shaun Anthony, ACA *1997;* 1250 Sunset Road, WINNETKA, IL 60093, UNITED STATES.
HUSSEY, Mr. Stephen James, MA ACA *1991;* 7 Princes Riverside, Rotherhithe, LONDON, SE16 5RD.
•HUSSEY, Mr. Terence John, FCA *1970;* (Tax Fac), T.J. Hussey, Andrew Hill Cottage, Andrew Hill Lane, Hedgerley, SLOUGH, SL2 3UL.
HUSSEY, Miss. Victoria Joanna Louise, BEng ACA *2000;* Stanley House, Camden Road, BATH, BA1 5JE.
HUSTHWAITE, Mr. William, BA ACA *1984;* Shell Eastern Petroleum (Pte) Ltd, Shell House, 4 Floor East, 83 Clemenceau Avenue, SINGAPORE 239920, SINGAPORE.
HUSTLER, Mr. John Randolph, FCA CF *1969;* (Member of Council 1997 - 2000), Hustler Venture Partners Ltd, Ripsley House, Portsmouth Rd, LIPHOOK, GU30 7JH.
HUSTLER, Mrs. Karolyn Jane, BA ACA *1995;* HWCA Limited, 120-124 Towngate, LEYLAND, LANCASHIRE, PR25 2LQ.
HUSTON, Mr. Michael Andrew, BA ACA *2005;* 8 West Drive, Upton, WIRRAL, MERSEYSIDE, CH49 6JX.
HUSTWICK, Miss. Ruth, BSc(Hons) ACA *2010;* 63 Juniper Way, GAINSBOROUGH, LINCOLNSHIRE, DN21 1GW.
HUTCHEON, Mr. Ian Maxwell Byres, MA FCA *1975;* 55 Basuto Road, LONDON, SW6 4BL.
HUTCHESON, Mrs. Francesca Katy, BA(Hons) ACA *2003;* 136 Radcliffe New Road, Whitefield, MANCHESTER, M45 7RW.
HUTCHFIELD, Mr. Robert Anthony, BSocSc ACA *1984;* Flat 4, 2a Darley Street, Darlinghurst, SYDNEY, NSW 2010, AUSTRALIA.
HUTCHIESON, Mrs. Elizabeth, BA ACA CPFA *1992;* 1 Preedys Close, Abbots Bromley, RUGELEY, STAFFORDSHIRE, WS15 3EE.
HUTCHINGS, Mrs. Angela, BA ACA *2002;* 39 Kylemore Avenue, Mossley Hill, LIVERPOOL, L18 4PZ.
HUTCHINGS, Mr. Carl Anthony, ACA *2008;* 12 Hadfield Street, Wombwell, BARNSLEY, SOUTH YORKSHIRE, S73 0JR.
HUTCHINGS, Mr. David Graham, BSc ACA *1992;* 17 Caewal Road, CARDIFF, CF5 2BT.
HUTCHINGS, Mr. David Mark, ACA *2010;* 4 Turnpike Lane, SUTTON, SM1 4ET.
HUTCHINGS, Miss. Elizabeth Kathryn, BSc ACA *2000;* 10 Carrick Road, CHESTER, CH4 8AW.
HUTCHINGS, Mr. Ian Stewart, BA ACA *1991;* Plastal, Alders Way, PAIGNTON, DEVON, TQ4 7QE.
HUTCHINGS, Mr. Keith, FCA *1971;* 5 Shillingridge Park, Frieth Road, MARLOW, SL7 2QX. (Life Member)
HUTCHINGS, Mr. Leon Derek, BEng ACA *1981;* MOOG Components Group Ltd, 30 Sutton Park Avenue, Earley, READING, RG6 1AW.
HUTCHINGS, Mr. Mark, ACA *1985;* 54 Smithbarn, HORSHAM, RH13 6DX.
HUTCHINGS, Mr. Mark Alexander, BSc ACA *1992;* Abbotswick, Gretton, CHELTENHAM, GLOUCESTERSHIRE, GL54 5EY.
HUTCHINGS, Mr. Mark Terry, BA ACA *1991;* 8 Southampton Road, ROMSEY, HAMPSHIRE, SO51 8AF.
•HUTCHINGS, Mrs. Michelle, ACA CTA FMAAT *2002;* with Apsleys, 21 Bampton St, TIVERTON, EX16 6AA.
HUTCHINGS, Mr. Neil Raymond, BSc ACA *2002;* with Albert Goodman LLP, Mary Street House, Mary Street, TAUNTON, TA1 3NW.
•HUTCHINGS, Mrs. Nicola Wendy, ACA *2010;* Heywood Shepherd, 1 Park Street, MACCLESFIELD, CHESHIRE, SK11 6SR.
HUTCHINGS, Mr. Norman Frank, FCA CPA *1953;* 31 Manstone Lane, SIDMOUTH, EX10 9TU. (Life Member)
HUTCHINGS, Mr. Paul Derek, FCA *1976;* 32 North Down, Sanderstead, SOUTH CROYDON, Surrey, CR2 9PA.
HUTCHINGS, Mr. Paul Derek, BTech CEng ACA *1995;* 155a Curzon Street, Long Eaton, NOTTINGHAM, NG10 4FH.
HUTCHINGS, Mr. Paul Edward, BSc ACA *1999;* with Hawsons, Pegasus House, 463a Glossop Road, SHEFFIELD, S10 2QD.
HUTCHINGS, Mr. Philip John, ACA *1981;* 2 Newlands Close, Chandler's Ford, EASTLEIGH, HAMPSHIRE, SO53 4PD.
HUTCHINGS, Mr. Richard Edward Keith, BA ACA *1990;* Camomile Associates, 11 The Green, RICHMOND, TW9 1PX.
HUTCHINGS, Mr. Robert Leroy, BSc FCA *1974;* Charnwood House, 52 Tring Avenue, Ealing, LONDON, W5 3QB.
HUTCHINGS, Mr. Robin Mark, BA ACA *1997;* 19 Lynwood Road, THAMES DITTON, KT7 0DN.
•HUTCHINGS, Mr. Roy John, FCA *1964;* Roy J. Hutchings, Brenacre, Ford Street, WELLINGTON, TA21 9PE.
HUTCHINGS, Ms. Sally Patricia, BSc ACA *1991;* Mercia Group Ltd, Best House, Grange Business Park, Whetstone, LEICESTER, LE8 6EP.
HUTCHINGS, Mrs. Victoria, BSc(Hons) ACA *2000;* 1 Clifford Manor Road, GUILDFORD, GU4 8AG.
HUTCHINS, Mr. Colin George, FCA *1961;* 29 Arundel Avenue, East Ewell, EPSOM, KT17 2RF. (Life Member)
HUTCHINS, Mr. David Victor, FCA *1969;* Forest View, Harpford, SIDMOUTH, EX10 0NJ.
HUTCHINS, Mr. James Michael Jesse, FCA *1962;* 17 Littlepark Road, PAIGNTON, TQ3 3QP. (Life Member)
•HUTCHINS, Miss. Kate Evelyn May, BSc ACA *2003;* Kate Hutchins ACA, 4 Brixton Terrace, HELSTON, CORNWALL, TR13 8TW.
HUTCHINS, Mr. Kenneth, FCA *1977;* 16 Little Heath, St. Marys Road, SWANLEY, KENT, BR8 7BU.
HUTCHINS, Mr. Michael Charles, BA ACA *2001;* Flat 4, Carburton House, Carburton Street, LONDON, W1W 5AN.
HUTCHINS, Mr. Neil, ACA *2007;* 1 Tumut Court, Keilor, MELBOURNE, VIC 3036, AUSTRALIA.
HUTCHINS, Mr. Robert William, FCA *1957;* Chromis, St Michael's Hill, Milverton, TAUNTON, TA4 1JT. (Life Member)
HUTCHINS, Mr. Robin Charles Neville, BA ACA *1986;* (Tax Fac), Clifford Chance, 10 Upper Bank Street, LONDON, E14 5JJ.
HUTCHINS, Mr. Simon John, BSc(Hons) ACA *2001;* 4060 Whispering Pines Court, SUWANEE, GA 30024, UNITED STATES.
•HUTCHINS, Mr. Trevor, BSc FCA ATII *1976;* Hutchins and Co Limited, 371 Wood Lane, Stannington, SHEFFIELD, S6 5LR.
HUTCHINSON, Mr. Alexander James, BA ACA *1999;* 10 Western Avenue, Easton On The Hill, STAMFORD, NORTHAMPTONSHIRE, PE9 3NB.
HUTCHINSON, Mr. Andrew, BSc(Hons) ACA *2001;* 3 Maple Fold, New Farnley, LEEDS, LS12 5RX.
HUTCHINSON, Mr. Andrew James, MA FCA *1975;* Bursars Office, Sutton Valence School, North Street, Sutton Valence, MAIDSTONE, KENT ME17 3HN.
HUTCHINSON, Mr. Andrew Thomas, BA ACA *2005;* 6 Lime Grove, Cherry Tree Hill, DERBY, DE21 6WN.
HUTCHINSON, Mr. Anthony Peter, MA FCA *1974;* Flintway, Slines Oak Road, Woldingham, CATERHAM, CR3 7BH.
HUTCHINSON, Mr. Arnold, MBE FCA *1952;* 9 Oak Avenue, Walton-on-the-Hill, STAFFORD, ST17 0LX. (Life Member)
HUTCHINSON, Mr. Arthur Francis, FCA *1969;* Hereford House, Sutton Street, TENBY, SA70 7DX. (Life Member)
HUTCHINSON, Mrs. Brenda Julia, BSc ACA *1992;* 43 Leamington Close, Great Sankey, WARRINGTON, WA5 3PY.
•HUTCHINSON, Mr. Brian Peter, FCA *1973;* Mazars LLP, 8 New Fields, 2 Stinsford Road, Nuffield, POOLE, DORSET BH17 0NF.
HUTCHINSON, Mr. Charles Eric, BA ACA MSI *1984;* 31 Rue Principale, Waldbredinus, L5465 LUXEMBOURG, LUXEMBOURG.
HUTCHINSON, Mr. Cornelius Nicholas, FCA *1967;* Marvean, Eastcliff Avenue Number 1, Porthtowan, TRURO, TR4 8AL. (Life Member)
HUTCHINSON, Mr. David Antony, BA ACA *1987;* H.L. Hutchinson Ltd, Weasenham Lane, WISBECH, PE13 2RN.
•HUTCHINSON, Mr. David John, BSc FCA *1977;* with KPMG LLP, 1 The Embankment, Neville Street, LEEDS, LS1 4DW.
HUTCHINSON, Mr. David William, ACA *1979;* 5 Thompsons Close, Wolviston Village, BILLINGHAM, TS22 5LR.
HUTCHINSON, Miss. Deborah Jane, BSc ACA *1991;* 6 Platinum House 103 St. John Street, LONDON, EC1M 4AS.
HUTCHINSON, Mrs. Eleanor Mary, FCA *1971;* Kilsall Hall, SHIFNAL, TF11 8PL. (Life Member)

HUTCHINSON, Mr. Gareth Stanley, MA ACA *1987;* 24 Grassington Road, SKIPTON, NORTH YORKSHIRE, BD23 1LL.
HUTCHINSON, Mr. Gavin, BSc ACA *2003;* 35 Willowdale, LEEDS, LS10 4FN.
HUTCHINSON, Mr. Geoffrey Allan, FCA *1973;* 23 Ulverston Road, Swarthmoor, ULVERSTON, LA12 0JB.
HUTCHINSON, Mr. Gregory William Scott, BSc ACA *1993;* Tigh Na Coille 16 Hollybush Lane Flamstead, ST. ALBANS, HERTFORDSHIRE, AL3 8DG.
HUTCHINSON, Mr. Iain James, BA ACA *1993;* 36 Highlands Road, BARNET, HERTFORDSHIRE, EN5 5AB.
HUTCHINSON, Mr. Ian David, FCA *1970;* 2 Moorlands Road, Skelton, YORK, YO30 1XZ.
HUTCHINSON, Mr. Ian David, MA FCA *1979;* 22 Old Millmeads, HORSHAM, WEST SUSSEX, RH12 2LZ.
HUTCHINSON, Mr. Ian Hay, FCA *1956;* 3 Birch Grove, SPALDING, PE11 2HL. (Life Member)
HUTCHINSON, Mr. Ivan John, FCA *1953;* 1 Grasmere Avenue, Linton Park, WETHERBY, LS22 6YT. (Life Member)
HUTCHINSON, Mr. James Alexander, FCA *1959;* 23 Parravano Court, WILLOWDALE M2R 3S8, ON, CANADA. (Life Member)
•HUTCHINSON, Mr. James Martin, BSc FCA *1992;* (Tax Fac), The Hutchinson Partnership Limited, The Bull Pen, Amberley Court, Sutton St. Nicholas, HEREFORD, HR1 3BX.
HUTCHINSON, Mrs. Janine, BSc ACA *2002;* 3 Maple Fold, New Farnley, LEEDS, LS12 5RX.
HUTCHINSON, Miss. Jayne Elizabeth, BA ACA *2004;* U B S Warburg, 100 Liverpool Street, LONDON, EC2M 2RH.
HUTCHINSON, Mr. Jeffrey, FCA *1981;* Jones Cooper Ltd, Suite 2, Hedley Court, 76 Boothferry Road, GOOLE, NORTH HUMBERSIDE DN14 6AA.
HUTCHINSON, Miss. Joanne, BA ACA *1999;* 21 Alma Street, Melbourne, DERBY, DE73 8GA.
HUTCHINSON, Mr. John, BA FCA *1990;* The Tax Stop (Bolton) Ltd, 52 Market Street, Farnworth, BOLTON, BL4 7NY.
HUTCHINSON, Mr. John Villiers, MA FCA *1972;* P.O. Box 89, SURRY HILLS, NSW 2010, AUSTRALIA.
HUTCHINSON, Mr. Joseph Kenneth, FCA *1956;* 8 Hillview Crescent, Baldwins Gate, NEWCASTLE, STAFFORDSHIRE, ST5 5DE. (Life Member)
•HUTCHINSON, Mrs. Julianne, BA FCA *1991;* The Hutchinson Partnership Limited, The Bull Pen, Amberley Court, Sutton St. Nicholas, HEREFORD, HR1 3BX.
HUTCHINSON, Miss. Katie, ACA *2011;* 27 Bridge Drive, Christleton, CHESTER, CH3 6AW.
HUTCHINSON, Mr. Kenneth Ernest, BA FCA *1949;* Llanra, 6 Birkdale Avenue, Stoneygate, LEICESTER, LE2 3HA. (Life Member)
HUTCHINSON, Mrs. Kerrie Elizabeth, ACA *2006;* 69 Woodbine Road, NEWCASTLE UPON TYNE, NE3 1DE.
HUTCHINSON, Mr. Leon Leslie, ACA *2003;* 31 Mountbatten Drive, Burncross, SHEFFIELD, S35 1WF.
HUTCHINSON, Mrs. Linda Christine, FCA *1977;* Flat 3, Carlekemp, De la Warr Parade, BEXHILL-ON-SEA, TN40 1NR.
HUTCHINSON, Miss. Lynsey Ann, BA ACA *2009;* 9 Low Shops Lane, Rothwell, LEEDS, LS26 0RH.
HUTCHINSON, Mr. Mark, BA ACA *2011;* 56 Allestree Drive, GRIMSBY, SOUTH HUMBERSIDE, DN33 3DX.
HUTCHINSON, Mr. Mark Douglas, FCA *1976;* 24 Shaftesbury Avenue, HORNSEA, NORTH HUMBERSIDE, HU18 1LX.
HUTCHINSON, Mr. Mark Edward Benedict, MA ACA *2000;* 135 Bishopsgate, LONDON, EC2M 3UR.
•HUTCHINSON, Mr. Mark Edward John, MA ACA *1994;* KPMG LLP, 15 Canada Square, LONDON, E14 5GL. See also KPMG Europe LLP
HUTCHINSON, Mr. Mark Rodham, BSc ACA *2002;* Flat 1 Chatham Lodge, 148 Barlow Moor Road, MANCHESTER, M20 2UT.
HUTCHINSON, Mr. Mathew James Edward, BA ACA *1998;* C B P E Capital, 2 George Yard, LONDON, EC3V 9DH.
•HUTCHINSON, Mr. Michael David, BA ACA *1989;* Kelsall Steele Limited, Woodlands Court, Truro Business Park, TRURO, CORNWALL, TR4 9NH.
HUTCHINSON, Mr. Michael Ian, BA FCA *1979;* The Arches Barn, 11 Lower Road, Woolavington, BRIDGWATER, TA7 8EQ.
HUTCHINSON, Mr. Neville Bainbridge, BSc FCA *1973;* Zelgenweg 4, CH 8424 EMBRACH, SWITZERLAND.
HUTCHINSON, Mr. Nicholas Mark, BA *1986;* La Saulire, La Rue De La Presse, St Peter, JERSEY, JE3 7YG.
•HUTCHINSON, Mrs. Nicola Anne, FCA *1992;* 8 Station Road, Helmsley, YORK, YO62 5BZ.
•HUTCHINSON, Mr. Paul Anthony, FCA *1980;* P A Hutchinson & Co Ltd, Old Courts Road, BRIGG, LINCOLNSHIRE, DN20 8JD.
HUTCHINSON, Mr. Paul Anthony, FCA *1970;* 25461 Mulholland HWY, CALABASAS, CA 91302, UNITED STATES.
•HUTCHINSON, Mr. Paul Stanley, BSc FCA *1988;* (Tax Fac), Harrison Hutchinson Ltd, 246 Park View, WHITLEY BAY, TYNE AND WEAR, NE26 3QX.
HUTCHINSON, Mrs. Penelope Florence Evans, BA ACA *1982;* Arts Victoria, 2 Kavanagh Street, SOUTH BANK, VIC 3205, AUSTRALIA.
HUTCHINSON, Mr. Peter Anthony, BA FCA *1988;* 7 Cooper Lane, Potto, NORTHALLERTON, DL6 3HG.
HUTCHINSON, Mr. Peter Ronald, BA FCA *1976;* Hutchinson & Co, 5 Priory Court, Tuscam Way, CAMBERLEY, GU15 3YX.
HUTCHINSON, Mr. Philip Alexander, BA ACA *2010;* Apartment 79, The Citadel, 15 Ludgate Hill, MANCHESTER, M4 4AP.
HUTCHINSON, Mr. Richard Eugene, BA FCA *1977;* Wheatcroft, Roseacre Barns, Bedmond Road Pimlico, HEMEL HEMPSTEAD, HP3 8SF.
•HUTCHINSON, Mr. Robert Anthony, BA FCA *1990;* KPMG Channel Islands Limited, 20 New Street, St Peter Port, GUERNSEY, GY1 4AN.
HUTCHINSON, Mr. Robert Keith, BA ACA *1990;* 43 Leamington Close, Great Sankey, WARRINGTON, WA5 3PY.
HUTCHINSON, Mr. Robert William, FCA *1968;* 4 Waldie Griffiths Drive, KELSO, ROXBURGHSHIRE, TD5 7UH.
HUTCHINSON, Mrs. Sally Elizabeth, ACA *1983;* Badgers, Salters Lane, Lower Moor, PERSHORE, WORCESTERSHIRE, WR10 2PE.
HUTCHINSON, Miss. Sarah Jane, BSc FCA *1981;* B A Pensions, Whitelocke House, 2-4 Lampton Road, HOUNSLOW, TW3 1HU.
HUTCHINSON, Mrs. Shirleyanne, BA ACA *1992;* Ischebeck Titan Ltd, John Dean House, Wellington Road, BURTON-ON-TRENT, STAFFORDSHIRE, DE14 2TG.
HUTCHINSON, Mr. Terrence Gordon, FCA *1967;* 16 Millholme Close, SOUTHAM, CV47 1FQ. (Life Member)
HUTCHINSON, Mr. Vincent Alan, FCA *1972;* Meadow View, Wood Lane, Cadeby, NUNEATON, WARWICKSHIRE, CV13 0AU. (Life Member)
HUTCHINSON, Mr. Wilford, BSc FCA *1975;* 11 Cape Gardens, Shaw, OLDHAM, OL2 8PD.
•HUTCHINSON, Mr. William James, FCA *1975;* Hutchinson & Co, 3 Scot Grove, PINNER, HA5 4RT.
HUTCHISON, Mr. Andrew, MSc ACA *2011;* Flat 114 Melmerby Court, Eccles New Road, SALFORD, M5 4UQ.
HUTCHISON, Mr. Bruce Donald, BA ACA *1995;* Scoresoft S.A.M, Le Michelangelo, 7 Avenue Des Papalins, Fontvielle, 98000 MONTE CARLO, MONACO.
•HUTCHISON, Mr. David Graham Michael, FCA *1968;* Banda School, Magadi Road, P.O. Box 24722, NAIROBI, 00502, KENYA.
HUTCHISON, Mr. Derek, FCA *1959;* 79 Elmfield Crescent, Moseley, BIRMINGHAM, B13 9TL. (Life Member)
HUTCHISON, Mr. Donald, MA FCA *1980;* 35 Judith Gardens, Potton, SANDY, SG19 2RJ.
HUTCHISON, Mrs. Emma, BSc ACA *1999;* Route de Chailly 7A, CH-1807, BLONAY, SWITZERLAND.
HUTCHISON, Miss. Fiona Lesley Brough, BD ACA CTA *2001;* Carillion Plc, 24 Birch Street, WOLVERHAMPTON, WV1 4HY.
HUTCHISON, Mrs. Joanna Maria, BSc ACA *2004;* 21 Weybourne Street, LONDON, SW18 4HG.
HUTCHISON, Mr. John, BA ACA *1980;* 17 Hazel Gardens, Sonning Common, READING, RG4 9TF.
HUTCHISON, Mr. Jonathan George, BSc ACA *2004;* 21 Weybourne Street, LONDON, SW18 4HG.
HUTCHISON, Mr. Mark Andrew, MA ACA *1996;* Route de Chailly 7A, 1807 BLONAY, VAUD, SWITZERLAND.
HUTCHISON, Mr. Michael John, FCA *1975;* Copperfields Dilly Lane, Hartley Wintney, HOOK, HAMPSHIRE, RG27 8EQ.
HUTCHISON, Mr. Paul Stewart, BSc ACA *1999;* 6 Heriot Way, HERIOT, EH38 5YN.
HUTCHISON, Mr. Peter, FCA *1974;* Le Payssel, Chemin De Marbriere, Faugeres, 34600 HERAULT, FRANCE.
HUTCHISON, Mr. Richard Anderson, BSc FCA *1977;* 25 Palace Court, Adams Close, SURBITON, KT5 8LB.
HUTCHISON, Mrs. Ruth, BSc ACA CTA *2004;* 51 Kings Croft, Long Ashton, BRISTOL, BS41 9ED.
HUTHWAITE, Mr. Charles Brian, FCA *1963;* 11 Grange Road, Woodthorpe, NOTTINGHAM, NG5 4FU. (Life Member)
•HUTSON, Mr. Colin, BA FCA *1985;* (Tax Fac), Kenneth Easby LLP, Oak House, Market Place, 35 North End, BEDALE, NORTH YORKSHIRE DL8 1AQ.
HUTSON, Mr. Daniel James David, LLB ACA *2007;* 22 Milner Drive, Whitton, TWICKENHAM, TW2 7PJ.
HUTSON, Mr. John Alexander, FCA *1948;* 1 Marathon Drive, MOUNT ELIZA, VIC 3930, AUSTRALIA. (Life Member)
HUTSON, Mr. John Wyatt, FCA *1963;* P O Box 628, MCLAREN VALE, SA 5171, AUSTRALIA.
HUTSON, Mr. Julius John Herd, FCA *1992;* 36 Arundel Avenue, SITTINGBOURNE, ME10 4RG.
HUTT, Mr. Gregory Dale, ACA CA(SA) *2008;* 7 Lincoln Street, LONDON, SW3 2TS.
HUTT, Mrs. Letitia, BSc ACA *2006;* 10 Park Street, HATFIELD, HERTFORDSHIRE, AL9 5AX.
•HUTT, Mr. Neil John, BSc ACA *1996;* Ernst & Young LLP, Apex Plaza, Forbury Road, READING, RG1 1YE. See also Ernst & Young Europe LLP
HUTT, Mr. Paul Raymond, BSc ACA *2006;* 10 Park Street, HATFIELD, HERTFORDSHIRE, AL9 5AX.
•HUTTER, Mrs. Susan Frances, FCA *1980;* Shelley Stock Hutter LLP, 7-10 Chandos Street, LONDON, W1G 9DQ.
HUTTNER, Mr. Michael Igor, MA ACA CFA *1985;* 47 Fletcher Road, LONDON, W4 5AT.
HUTTON, Mr. Andrew Kilpatrick, BA FCA *1970;* Barn Court, Park Lane, Swalcliffe, BANBURY, OXFORDSHIRE, OX15 5ET.
HUTTON, Mrs. Catherine, MSc BSc ACA *2011;* Pricewaterhousecoopers, Donington Court, Herald Way, East Midlands Airport, Castle Donington, DERBY DE74 2UZ.
HUTTON, Mr. Christopher Nigel, ACA *1993;* Pear Tree House, Rye Road, Hawkhurst, CRANBROOK, KENT, TN18 5DA.
HUTTON, Mr. Clive, FCA *1971;* Mary Ward Centre, 42 Queen Square, LONDON, WC1N 3AQ.
HUTTON, Mr. David, BA ACA *1994;* Springfield Farmhouse, Whitwell Lane, Stocksbridge, SHEFFIELD, S36 1GB.
•HUTTON, Mr. David Robin, BSc FCA *1985;* (Tax Fac), Loxley, 6 Goldsmid Road, TONBRIDGE, KENT, TN9 2BT.
HUTTON, Mr. Edward Fleming Kilpatrick, MA FCA *1978;* White Friars, Bishops Sutton, ALRESFORD, SO24 0AL.
HUTTON, Mr. Edward Norman Clift, BSc ACA *1994;* H S B C Metropolitan House, 321 Avebury Boulevard, MILTON KEYNES, MK9 2GA.
HUTTON, Mrs. Eugenie, BA ACA *2004;* 50 Flossmore Way, Gildersome, LEEDS, LS27 7UE.
HUTTON, Mr. Gary Ernest, BA ACA *1985;* Priory House, 1 Church Street, LEAMINGTON SPA, CV31 1EG.
HUTTON, Mr. Gregory John, ACA CA(AUS) *2010;* Flat 12, 39 Courtfield Gardens, South Kensington, LONDON, SW5 0PJ.
HUTTON, Mr. Harold Lyell, ACA *2008;* Flat B 9/F, Ficus Garden, 11 Lok King Street, Fo Tan, SHA TIN, NEW TERRITORIES HONG KONG SAR.
HUTTON, Mr. Jason, BCom ACA *1996;* 50 Flossmore Way, Gildersome, Morley, LEEDS, LS27 7UE.
•HUTTON, Mr. John Nigel, BA FCA *1978;* Grange Lodge, Off Belmont Road, Belmont, BOLTON, BL7 8BA.
HUTTON, Mr. Michael, MSc BA FCA ACII *1984;* 40 The Locks, BINGLEY, WEST YORKSHIRE, BD16 4BG.
HUTTON, Mr. Michael John Charles, BSc ACA *1981;* (Tax Fac), West Gables, Singleton Road, Great Chart, ASHFORD, KENT, TN23 3BA.
HUTTON, Mr. Michael William, FCA *1968;* 1 Church Walk, Thurlaston, RUGBY, WARWICKSHIRE, CV23 9JX.
HUTTON, Mr. Peter McBean, ACA CA(SA) *2010;* 6 Alexandra Road, TWICKENHAM, TW1 2HE.
HUTTON, Mr. Richard Anthony, MA FCA *1968;* R. Hutton Inv Research, Garden Cottage, Ribston Park, WETHERBY, LS22 4EZ.
HUTTON, Mr. Richard James Haslam, BSc(Hons) ACA *2002;* 2 Entertain Ltd, 33 Foley Street, LONDON, W1W 7TL.
•HUTTON, Mr. Richard John, FCA FCCA *1968;* (Tax Fac), Harwood Hutton Limited, 22 Wycombe End, BEACONSFIELD, BUCKINGHAMSHIRE, HP9 1NB. See also Harwood Hutton Tax Advisory LLP
HUTTON, Mr. Richard John, BA FCA *1992;* Greggs plc, Fernwood House, Clayton Road, Jesmond, NEWCASTLE UPON TYNE, NE2 1TL.
HUTTON, Mrs. Sarah Jane, BSc ACA *1998;* Chemin de la Paudeze 10, 1092 BELMONT-SUR-LAUSANNE, SWITZERLAND.
•HUTTON, Mr. Stephen Kenneth, BA ACA *1981;* Willis Scott Group, 5 Kensington, Cockton Hill Road, BISHOP AUCKLAND, COUNTY DURHAM, DL14 6HX.
HUTTON, Mr. Thomas Andrew, ACA *2009;* 29 Station Road, Desford, LEICESTER, LE9 9FN.
HUTTON, Mr. Thomas Graham, FCA *1959;* 57 Springfield Road, Millhouses, SHEFFIELD, S7 2GE. (Life Member)
HUTTON, Mr. Timothy Horace, FCA *1965;* Chestnut House, High Street, Hallaton, MARKET HARBOROUGH, LEICESTERSHIRE, LE16 8UD.
HUTTON, Mr. Wayne, BA ACA *1985;* 11 Ouse Walk, HUNTINGDON, CAMBRIDGESHIRE, PE29 3QL.
HUTTON, Mr. William, BA FCA *1955;* 2 Coombe Close, Bovey Tracey, NEWTON ABBOT, DEVON, TQ13 9ER. (Life Member)
HUTTON-ASHKENNY, Miss. Gail Louise, ACA *2008;* 33 Comyn Road, LONDON, SW11 1QB.
HUTTON-PENMAN, Mr. Nicholas Ian, BSc ACA *1992;* Woodstock, Sunningdale Road, Althorne, CHELMSFORD, CM3 6HW.
•HUTTON-POTTS, Mr. Orlando Charles, BSc FCA *1991;* Grant Thornton UK LLP, Grant Thornton House, 22 Melton Street, Euston Square, LONDON, NW1 2EP. See also Grant Thornton LLP
HUTTY, Mr. Richard Vernon, FCA *1969;* 6 Park Road, BURGESS HILL, WEST SUSSEX, RH15 8ET.
HUWS, Mr. Owain Gwynedd, BSc ACA *2000;* Bryn Awel, St. Meugans, RUTHIN, CLWYD, LL15 1RD.
HUXHAM, Mr. Matthew David, MA MA(Oxon) ACA *2010;* Top Flat, 9 Jerningham Road, LONDON, SE14 5NQ.
HUXHAM, Mrs. Pia, BSc ACA *1991;* 6 Bretland Road, Rusthall, TUNBRIDGE WELLS, KENT, TN4 8PB.
•HUXLEY, Mr. Dominic James, BSc ACA *1995;* Wrigley Partington, Sterling House, 501 Middleton Road, Chadderton, OLDHAM, OL9 9LY.
HUXLEY, Miss. Emma Rachel, ACA *2005;* Flat 5 Bridgers House, Balcombe Road, HAYWARDS HEATH, WEST SUSSEX, RH16 1NR.
HUXLEY, Mr. Graham Roland, BSc FCA *1982;* 16 Trevalyn Way Harwoods Lane, Rossett, WREXHAM, LL12 0EJ.
HUXLEY, Mrs. Jacqueline, BA ACA *1985;* 4 Victoria Close, Aspull, WIGAN, WN2 1YD.
HUXLEY, Miss. Jodanna, MChem ACA *2010;* Flat 3, 61 Clyde Road, MANCHESTER, M20 2WW.
HUXLEY, Mr. Peter Charles, MA ACA *2004;* The Coach House, Haywards Heath Road, Balcombe, HAYWARDS HEATH, WEST SUSSEX, RH17 6PG.
HUXSTER, Mr. Robert Francis, FCA *1968;* Lavender Cottage, 5 Station Road, THAMES DITTON, KT7 0NU. (Life Member)
HUXTABLE, Mr. Frederick William, BSc FCA ATII *1981;* (Tax Fac), 16 Granville Gardens, LONDON, W5 3PA.
HUXTABLE, Mr. Ian Richard, MA FCA *1984;* 27 Hook Hill, Sanderstead, SOUTH CROYDON, SURREY, CR2 0LB.
HUXTABLE, Mr. James David, BA(Hons) ACA *2009;* 8 Mills Bakery, 4 Royal William Yard, PLYMOUTH, PL1 3GD.
HUXTABLE, Mrs. Joanna Felicity, BA ACA ACCA *1995;* La Cherterie Rue Des Fontenelles, Forest, GUERNSEY, GY8 0BL.
HUXTABLE, Ms. Zoe Avis, BSc ACA *1998;* 2 Hazeleigh Avenue, Woolston, SOUTHAMPTON, SO19 9DF.
HUYNH, Miss. Ai Hoan, BA(Hons) ACA CTA *2002;* (Tax Fac), 7 Tilkey Road, Coggeshall, COLCHESTER, CO6 1PG.
HUYNH, Mr. Chan Giang, ACA *2004;* KCG & Co., Rooms 1401-2, 253-261 Hennessy Road, WAN CHAI, HONG KONG ISLAND, HONG KONG SAR.
HUYNH, Miss. Khiet Doanh, BA(Hons) ACA *2002;* Flat 10, Tavistock Tower, Russell Place, LONDON, SE16 7PQ.
HUYTON, Mr. Stephen John, BCom ACA *1984;* 168 Victoria Road, Wargrave, READING, RG10 8AJ.
•HUYTON, Mr. Stephen Stanley, BA ACA *1985;* (Member of Council 2008 - 2011), Thermopatch, Draaibrugweg 14, 1332 AD ALMERE, NETHERLANDS.
HUZAL, Mr. Christopher Jon, BA ACA *2005;* Yew Tree Barn, West Horrington, WELLS, SOMERSET, BA5 3ED.
•HUZAL, Mrs. Nicola Jane, BSc ACA *2005;* Sutcliffe & Co Ltd, Old Bank House, STURMINSTER NEWTON, DT10 1AN.
HVASS, Mr. Carl, BA ACA *2000;* Curtis House, Kidmore End, READING, RG4 9AY.
HWANG, Mr. Chin Guan, BA ACA *1986;* RBS Group, 1 Princes Street, LONDON, EC2R 4BP.

HWANG, Miss. Da Un Amy, BSc ACA *2007;* 27 Colwell Road, LONDON, SE22 8QP.
HWANG, Miss. Min-Jen, BSc ACA *2003;* 22 Coriander Crescent, GUILDFORD, GU2 9YU.
HYAM, Mr. Aaron Lee, BSc ACA *1998;* Flat 7, 17 Dock Street, LONDON, E1 8LJ.
HYAM, Mr. Gerald Sidney, FCA *1966;* Audley House, 9 North Audley Street, LONDON, W1K 6WF.
HYAM, Mr. Saul, FCA *1967;* 48 Hollickwood Avenue, Finchley, LONDON, N12 0LT.
HYAMS, Mr. Alan Jack, BSc FCA CF *1976;* 22 The Carriages, Booth Road, ALTRINCHAM, CHESHIRE, WA14 4AF.
•**HYAMS, Mr. Christopher John, BA ACA** *1993;* Deloitte LLP, Athene Place, 66 Shoe Lane, LONDON, EC4A 3BQ. See also Deloitte & Touche LLP
HYAMS, Mr. John Graham, BA ACA *1981;* 64 Heath View, LONDON, N2 0QB.
•**HYAMS, Mrs. Rolanda Gail, FCA** *1979;* (Tax Fac), Stein Richards Limited, 10 London Mews, LONDON, W2 1HY.
•**HYATT, Mr. Henry Alan, FCA** *1971;* (Tax Fac), H A Hyatt & Co Limited, 4-5 King Street, RICHMOND, SURREY, TW9 1ND.
HYATT, Mr. Ibrahim Abbas, FCA *1964;* Case Postale 367, 1215 GENEVA, SWITZERLAND. (Life Member)
HYATT, Mr. Matthew Thomas, BSc ACA *2006;* 12 Townsend Road, Tiddington, STRATFORD-UPON-AVON, CV37 7DE.
HYATT, Mr. Peter Robin, FCA *1971;* Pippins, Vicarage Road, Potten End, BERKHAMSTED, HERTFORDSHIRE, HP4 2QZ. (Life Member)
HYATT, Mr. Richard Michael, BSc ACA *1981;* 39 Coupland Close, Old Whittington, CHESTERFIELD, S41 9TB.
HYDARI, Mr. Imtiaz Hussain, FCA *1970;* HBG Holdings Limited, PO Box 113341, DUBAI, 113341, UNITED ARAB EMIRATES.
HYDE, Mr. Alexander Samuel, BA(Hons) FCA *2000;* with Grant Thornton UK LLP, Enterprise House, 115 Edmund Street, BIRMINGHAM, B3 2HJ.
HYDE, Mrs. Caroline Helen, BA ACA *1997;* Kinswood, Hatch Lane, Chapel Row, READING, RG7 6NX.
HYDE, Mr. Charles Adam, FCA *1977;* 20 Warwick Road, Hale, ALTRINCHAM, WA15 9NP.
HYDE, Mr. Christopher Matthew, BSc ACA *1978;* 16 Old Park Avenue, LONDON, SW12 8RH.
HYDE, Mr. David Philip, BSc ACA *2009;* Flat 49, The Greenwich, Gloucester Square, SOUTHAMPTON, SO14 2GJ.
HYDE, Mr. Duncan Robert, MA ACA *1992;* 48 Milner Road, KINGSTON UPON THAMES, KT1 2AU.
HYDE, Mr. Geoffrey Rocliffe, FCA *1955;* 25 Fellbrook, Ham, RICHMOND, TW10 7UN. (Life Member)
HYDE, Mr. Ian Michael, BA ACA *1994;* North Somerset Housing, 40 Martingale Way Portishead, BRISTOL, BS20 7AW.
•**HYDE, Mrs. Jacqueline Ann, BA FCA** *1990;* JPH Ltd, 112-114 Whitegate Drive, BLACKPOOL, FY3 9XH.
•**HYDE, Mr. Jeremy Laurence, ACA FCCA** *2007;* CG Lee Ltd, Ingram House, Meridian Way, NORWICH, NR7 0TA.
HYDE, Mr. John, FCA *1974;* 121 Berry Head Road, BRIXHAM, DEVON, TQ5 9AH.
HYDE, Mr. John-Derek Gregory, BSc FCA *1985;* 19 Norton Road, LETCHWORTH GARDEN CITY, HERTFORDSHIRE, SG6 1AA.
HYDE, Mr. Julian Roderic Nigel, MBA MSc FCA *1975;* Areva Risk Management Consulting Ltd, 7 Hitching Court, Blacklands Way, ABINGDON, OXFORDSHIRE, OX14 1RA.
HYDE, Mr. Kenneth, FCA *1956;* 7 Moseley Wood View, Cookridge, LEEDS, LS16 7ES. (Life Member)
•**HYDE, Mrs. Maria Angela, BA FCA** *1983;* 2 Masons Close, Sandilands, MABLETHORPE, LINCOLNSHIRE, LN12 2SE.
HYDE, Miss. Mary Helen, ACA MAAT *2003;* Bravington House, 2 Bravington Walk, LONDON, N1 9AF.
HYDE, Miss. Merryleas Jane, BA ACA *2005;* 15 rue Eugene Carriere, 75018 PARIS, FRANCE.
HYDE, Mr. Michael Edwin, ACA *2009;* 58 Queens Road, Caversham, READING, RG4 8DL.
HYDE, Mr. Michael Robertson, FCA *1967;* 3 Capell Road, Chorleywood, RICKMANSWORTH, HERTFORDSHIRE, WD3 5HY.
HYDE, Mr. Nigel Colin, BA FCA ACA *1986;* 5a Mountfield Road, LUTON, LU2 7JN.
HYDE, Mr. Peter Alexander, MSci ACA DChA *2007;* 14 Lathkill Court, Hayne Road, BECKENHAM, BR3 4JH.
HYDE, Mr. Peter James, FCA *1959;* 4 Bluebell Walk, HARROGATE, NORTH YORKSHIRE, HG3 2SJ. (Life Member)
HYDE, Mr. Richard Glyn, BSc ACA *1993;* 2977 Talinga Ct, LIVERMORE, CA 94550, UNITED STATES.
HYDE, Mr. Richard Oliver Hamilton, BSc FCA *1988;* Fern Bank, Kissing Tree Lane, Alveston, STRATFORD-UPON-AVON, CV37 7QS.
HYDE, Mr. Robert James, BA ACA *2006;* 37 Empire Square East, Empire Square, LONDON, SE1 4NB.
HYDE, Mr. Roderick, BCom ACA *2003;* 3 The Maltings, Wetmore Road, BURTON-ON-TRENT, STAFFORDSHIRE, DE14 1SE.
•**HYDE, Mrs. Stephanie Tricia, BA ACA** *1999;* PricewaterhouseCoopers LLP, 9 Greyfriars Road, READING, RG1 1JG. See also PricewaterhouseCoopers
HYDE, Mr. Stephen, BSc FCA CFA *1989;* Abu Dhabi Investment Authority, PO Box 3600, ABU DHABI, UNITED ARAB EMIRATES.
HYDE, Mr. Stephen, BA FCA *1981;* 39 Sherrardspark Road, WELWYN GARDEN CITY, HERTFORDSHIRE, AL8 7JY.
HYDE, Mr. Thomas Nigel, BA ACA *2003;* 54 Courtenay Street, LONDON, SE11 5PQ.
HYDE, Ms. Zoe Georgina, ACA CTA *2006;* 101a/1 St. Stephen Street, EDINBURGH, EH3 5AB.
•**HYDE-COOPER, Mr. Christopher, FCA** *1975;* (Tax Fac), Christopher Hyde-Cooper, 74 Claverton Street, LONDON, SW1V 3AX.
HYDE-HARRISON, Mr. Colin Pitman, BSc ACA *1988;* 101 Marlow Rd, Anerley, LONDON, SE20 7XW.
HYDE-THOMSON, Mr. Paul Cater, CBE MA FCA *1954;* The Stable House, North Kilworth, LUTTERWORTH, LE17 6JE. (Life Member)
•**HYDES, Mr. Anthony Duncan, BSc FCA** *1984;* Jolliffe Cork LLP, 33 George Street, WAKEFIELD, WEST YORKSHIRE, WF1 1LX. See also Jolliffe Cork Consulting Limited
HYEM, Mr. Gary John, BSc FCA CF *1992;* 108 Park Hill, BIRMINGHAM, B13 8DS.
HYEM, Mrs. Lisa Caroline, BSc ACA *1992;* Beck House, Main Street, Keyworth, NOTTINGHAM, NG12 5PY.
HYETT, Mr. Peter, FCA *1976;* 23 Iverley Road, HALESOWEN, B63 3EP.
HYETT, Mr. Phillip Justin, ACA *2008;* Flat 16 Chester House, 17 Eccleston Place, LONDON, SW1W 9NF.
HYGATE, Mrs. Pauline Stephenson, BA ACA *1993;* 9 Ashfield Avenue, Kings Heath, BIRMINGHAM, B14 7AT.
HYLAND, Mr. Christopher James, BSc ACA *1986;* 45 St Georges Road, FARNHAM, SURREY, GU9 8NA.
HYLAND, Miss. Jane, BSc ACA *1995;* Minney & Co, 59 Union Street, DUNSTABLE, BEDFORDSHIRE, LU6 1EX.
HYLAND, Mrs. Jane Elizabeth, BA ACA *2003;* Level 2, 82 Pitt Street, SYDNEY, NSW 2000, AUSTRALIA.
•**HYLAND, Mr. John Gerard, ACA** *1978;* Hadley & Co, Adelphi Chambers, 30 Hoghton Street, SOUTHPORT, PR9 0NZ.
•**HYLAND, Mr. Paul, BA FCA** *1992;* 44 The Pantiles, TUNBRIDGE WELLS, TN2 5TN.
•**HYLAND, Mr. Paul Francis, MA BSc FCA** *1981;* (Tax Fac), Duncan Sheard Glass, Castle Chambers, 43 Castle St, LIVERPOOL, L2 9TL. See also DSG Accountancy and Taxation Services Limited
HYLAND, Mr. Richard William, BA ACA *1992;* Flat 25D Tower 2 Illumination Terrace, 7 Tai Hang Road, TAI HANG, HONG KONG ISLAND, HONG KONG SAR.
HYLAND, Mr. Shaun Leslie, BSc ACA *1990;* HSBC Invoice Finance, 3 Rivergate, BRISTOL, BS1 6ER.
HYLDON, Miss. Charlotte Isabel Catherine, BSc ACA *1999;* (Tax Fac), 17 Lakewood Road, Chandler's Ford, EASTLEIGH, HAMPSHIRE, SO53 1ER.
HYLTON, Mr. Christopher, BA(Hons) ACA *2004;* K P M G, St. James's Square, MANCHESTER, M2 6DS.
•**HYLTON, Mr. Eric Walter, BA FCA** *1975;* Humphrey & Co, 7-9 The Avenue, EASTBOURNE, EAST SUSSEX, BN21 3YA.
HYLTON, Miss. Joanna Frances, ACA *2009;* 17 St. Olaf's Road, LONDON, SW6 7DL.
HYLTON, Mr. Richard, DSC FCA *1947;* 10 St Magnus Court, HARROGATE, HG2 0HN. (Life Member)
HYLTON, Mr. Thomas Eric, BSc ACA *2007;* 53a Hambalt Road, LONDON, SW4 9EQ.
•**HYMAN, Mr. Clive Mark, MA FCA** *1987;* Hyman Capital Services Limited, 33 West Common Way, HARPENDEN, HERTFORDSHIRE, AL5 2LH.
HYMAN, Mr. Cyril, FCA *1949;* 18 Highwood, WOODFORD GREEN, IG8 0SZ. (Life Member)
HYMAN, Mr. Harry Abraham, MA FCA CF *1982;* Flat 201, Carrington House, Hertford Street, LONDON, W1J 7RG.
•**HYMAN, Mr. Howard Jonathan, BA FCA** *1976;* Hyman Associates, 1 Cato Street, LONDON, W1H 5HG.
HYMAN, Mrs. Janice Susan, ACA *1981;* 5 Hereford Drive, Prestwich, MANCHESTER, M25 0JY.
HYMAN, Mr. Jonathan David, ACA *1981;* 17 Brittany Road, HOVE, BN3 4PA.
HYMAN, Mr. Jonathan Mark, BSc(Hons) ACA *2009;* HCA International Ltd, The Wellington Hospital, Wellington Place, LONDON, NW8 9LE.
HYMAN, Mr. Leslie Michael, FCA *1970;* 4 Pollicott Close, Sandringham Crescent, ST. ALBANS, HERTFORDSHIRE, AL4 9YL.
•**HYMAN, Mr. Martin Barry, BSc BEng FCA** *1990;* Rosh FD Ltd, 33 Richmond Hill Road, CHEADLE, CHESHIRE, SK8 1QF.
HYMAN, Mr. Maurice John, BA(Econ) FCA CPA *1971;* 12 Denya Street, HAIFA, 34980, ISRAEL.
HYMAN, Mr. Paul, BSc ACA *1981;* 31 Main Street, Hoby, MELTON MOWBRAY, LE14 3DT.
HYMAN, Mr. Philip Andrew, BSc ACA *1997;* 60 St Andrews Gardens, COBHAM, KT11 1HQ.
HYMAN, Mr. Philip James, BA ACA *1996;* 1 Brooklands Crescent, SALE, CHESHIRE, M33 3NB.
HYMAS, Mr. Christopher Andrew, BA(Hons) ACA *2000;* 264 Vale Road, Ash Vale, ALDERSHOT, HAMPSHIRE, GU12 5JQ.
HYMAS, Mr. Peter David, FCA *1956;* Woodlawn, Grange Court, Brixworth, NORTHAMPTON, NN6 9NN. (Life Member)
•**HYMAS, Mr. Robert John, BA FCA** *1988;* Manana, Church Street, Rudgwick, HORSHAM, RH12 3ET.
HYMERS, Mr. John Paul, BA ACA PGCE *2005;* Room 1104 Radisson Blu, Dubai Marina, PO Box 73029, DUBAI, UNITED ARAB EMIRATES.
HYMERS, Mr. Martin John, FCA *1988;* (Tax Fac), 21 The Quantocks, Flitwick, BEDFORD, MK45 1TG.
HYNAN, Mr. John Gerald, FCA *1972;* FirstCity Partnership Ltd, 13-15 Folgate Street, LONDON, E1 6BX.
•**HYND, Mr. Alistair Stewart Ronald, BSc FCA CF MCT** *1996;* Baker Tilly Tax and Advisory Services LLP, 25 Farringdon Street, LONDON, EC4A 4AB. See also Baker Tilly Corporate Finance LLP
HYND, Mr. Francis Faulds, FCA *1974;* P.O. Box 456, GEORGETOWN, GRAND CAYMAN, CAYMAN ISLANDS, GEORGETOWN, KY1-1107 CAYMAN ISLANDS.
HYND, Miss. Jennie Louise, BA(Hons) ACA *2001;* Disney Channel Unit 12 Chiswick Park, 566 Chiswick High Road, LONDON, W4 5AN.
HYND, Mr. Michael Robert, BA ACA *1992;* 6 Roebuck Close, ASHTEAD, KT21 2DN.
HYNDMAN, Mr. Peter, ACA *1986;* House in the Wood Arford Common, Headley, BORDON, HAMPSHIRE, GU35 8AF.
HYNDMAN, Mrs. Vivienne Lesley, BSc ACA *1982;* Broadmead Stack Lane, Hartley, LONGFIELD, DA3 8BL.
HYNE, Mr. Nicholas Geoffrey, BA ACA *1989;* 50 Hall Lane, Hagley, STOURBRIDGE, DY9 9LH.
HYNER, Mr. Andrew Leslie, FCA *1973;* Mangligot-Hyner Residence, Santiago-Diffun Highway, (Near old PNP outpost), Purok 6, Patul, SANTIAGO CITY 3311 PHILIPPINES.
•**HYNES, Mr. Gerald Thomas, BA FCA** *1982;* Hynes & Company (Newbury) Limited, Anstell House, Donnington Square, NEWBURY, BERKSHIRE, RG14 1PP.
HYNES, Miss. Geraldine Ann, BA ACA *1995;* 21 Duchy Avenue, HARROGATE, NORTH YORKSHIRE, HG2 0NB.
HYNES, Mr. Martin Christopher, ACA *1981;* 1320 Autos Five Acres, Moor Road Great Staughton, ST. NEOTS, CAMBRIDGESHIRE, PE19 5BJ.
HYNES, Mr. Michael Anthony, FCA *1954;* 4 Mortimer Road, Ealing, LONDON, W13 8NG. (Life Member)
HYNES, Mr. Sean, BSc ACA *2010;* 107 Wolsey Road, NORTHWOOD, MIDDLESEX, HA6 2EB.
HYNES, Mr. Thomas Patrick, BA(Hons) ACA *2003;* 19 Lattimore Road, ST. ALBANS, HERTFORDSHIRE, AL1 3XL.
HYOMS, Mr. Mark Colin, BSc(Hons) ACA *2004;* 401/88 Beach Street, PORT MELBOURNE, VIC 3207, AUSTRALIA.
HYON, Miss. Young, BSc(Hons) ACA *2010;* Flat 918, New Providence Wharf, 1 Fairmont Avenue, LONDON, E14 9PJ.
HYSLOP, Mr. Alan, BSc ACA FRSA *1981;* Crown Agents, St Nicholas House, St Nicholas Road, SUTTON, SM1 1EL.
HYSLOP, Miss. Gillian Margaret, BA FCA *1982;* with BDO LLP, Emerald House, East Street, EPSOM, SURREY, KT17 1HS.
•**HYSON, Mr. Mark Edmund Keedwell, FCA** *1972;* (Tax Fac), Hysons, 14 London Street, ANDOVER, SP10 2PA.
HYSTED, Mrs. Pamela Anne, FCA *1966;* 76 Pickhurst Rise, WEST WICKHAM, BR4 0AN.
HYYPIA, Mr. Marko, BA MSt ACA *2008;* 10 Kingston Square, LONDON, SE19 1JE.
•**I'ANSON, Mr. David Charles, BSc ACA** *1996;* with PricewaterhouseCoopers LLP, Savannah House, 3 Ocean Way, Ocean Village, SOUTHAMPTON, SO14 3TJ.
I'ANSON, Mrs. Helen Mary, BA ACA *1993;* House 23a, Street 302, Boeung Keng Kang I, Khan Chamcar Mon, PHNOM PENN, CAMBODIA.
I'ANSON, Mr. Peter, FCA *1961;* 23 Victoria Avenue, Brierfield, NELSON, BB9 5RH.
IACOLINO, Miss. Maria Concetta, LLB ACA *2001;* 45 Corser Street, STOURBRIDGE, WEST MIDLANDS, DY8 2DE.
IACOLINO, Miss. Tiziana, BSc ACA *2002;* Coors Brewers Ltd, 137 High Street, BURTON-ON-TRENT, STAFFORDSHIRE, DE14 1JZ.
IACOVIDES, Mr. Pantelakis, BSc ACA *1998;* 3 Chrysanthou Mylona Street, CY 1085 NICOSIA, CYPRUS.
IACOVOU, Mr. Alexis, BA(Econ) ACA *2002;* (Tax Fac), 5 Eptalophou Street, 3086 LIMASSOL, CYPRUS.
IACOVOU, Mr. Barry Andrew, BA ACA *2005;* Cosma Aitolou 10, Flat 101 Malvina Court, Mesa Geitonia, 4004 LIMASSOL, CYPRUS.
•**IACOVOU, Mr. Michael Stavrou, FCA** *1963;* M.S. Iacovou & Co, 6 Thyra Grove, North Finchley, LONDON, N12 8HB.
IAKOVIDIS, Mr. Spyridon, MSc BSc ACA *2011;* 5 IRODOTOU STREET, KOLONAKI, 106 74 ATHENS, GREECE.
IAKOVIDOU, Miss. Ekaterini, BSc ACA *2006;* Chrysanthou Mylona 3, Ayii Omoloyites, 1085 NICOSIA, CYPRUS.
IANNETTA, Miss. Angela Suzanne, BA ACA *1994;* Astra Zeneca Ltd, 2 Kingdom Street, LONDON, W2 6BD.
IASONOS, Mrs. Antonia, BSc ACA *2000;* 8A Egkomis Street, 2224 Latsia, NICOSIA, CYPRUS.
IBBESON, Mrs. Louise Sarah, BA ACA *1998;* 3 White Hill Close, CHESHAM, BUCKINGHAMSHIRE, HP5 1AS.
IBBETSON, Mrs. Diana Heather, BA ACA *1985;* Atlas House Ltd, Tyler Way, WHITSTABLE, CT5 2RS.
IBBETSON, Mr. Stephen John, BSc ACA *1984;* Vivimed Labs Europe Ltd, PO Box B3, HUDDERSFIELD, HD1 6BU.
IBBETT, Mr. Richard Michael Allan, BSc(Hons) ACA *2004;* 17 Reeves Road, MANCHESTER, M21 8BU.
•**IBBITSON, Mrs. Claire, BSc FCA** *1997;* Claire Ibbitson BSc(Hons) FCA, 24 Bryn Dreinog, Capel Hendre, AMMANFORD, DYFED, SA18 3RJ.
IBBOTSON, Mr. Alan, BA ACA *1995;* 14 Swincliffe Gardens Gomersal, CLECKHEATON, WEST YORKSHIRE, BD19 4BR.
IBBOTSON, Mrs. Beverley Jane, LLB ACA *1997;* 23 Ventnor Close, Gomersal, CLECKHEATON, BD19 4AQ.
IBBOTSON, Mrs. Cara Denise, BSc ACA *1992;* 3 Badgers Way, MARLOW, SL7 3QU.
IBBOTSON, Mr. Ian Ronald, BSc ACA *1983;* Lupofresh Ltd Benover Road, Yalding, MAIDSTONE, ME18 6ET.
IBBOTSON, Ms. Kate Louise, BSc ACA *2007;* 7 Rough Meadow, Long Meadow, WORCESTER, WR4 0JN.
•**IBBOTSON, Mr. Mark, BSc ACA** *2002;* Barnes Roffe LLP, Leytonstone House, Leytonstone, LONDON, E11 1GA.
IBBOTSON, Mr. Martin, BSc ACA *1988;* Unit 1 Maidenbower Office Park, Balconbe Road, CRAWLEY, RH10 7NN.
•**IBBOTSON, Mr. Nicholas John, BA ACA** *1985;* Ibboco Contracting Limited, 66 Jordan Road, Four Oaks, SUTTON COLDFIELD, WEST MIDLANDS, B75 5AD.
IBBOTSON, Mr. Stephen Duncan Julian, BCom ACA *1983;* 3 Honey Hill, Emberton, OLNEY, MK46 5LT.
IBBOTSON, Mr. Timothy, ACA *1997;* Brick Kiln Farmhouse, Mundesley Road, Trunch, NORTH WALSHAM, NORFOLK, NR28 0QB.
IBRAHIM, Mr. Arshad Akber Haji, ACA *2008;* 1a Whinbrook Gardens, LEEDS, LS17 6AE.
IBRAHIM, Mr. Bishr Ibrahim Baker, BSc ACA *1992;* P.O. Box 6981, AMMAN, JORDAN.
•**IBRAHIM, Mr. Farouk, FCA** *1969;* Farouk Ibrahim, 12 North Crescent, Finchley, LONDON, N3 3LL.
IBRAHIM, Mr. Hani Ahmed, MSc ACA *2004;* QInvest, PO Box 26222, DOHA, QATAR.
IBRAHIM, Mr. Ibrahim Mussa Cassam, BSc ACA *2011;* 5 Bridge Close, BIRMINGHAM, B11 4JF.
IBRAHIM, Mr. Ibrahim Omer, BSc(Hons) ACA MBA *2001;* Masdar(Abu Dhabi Future Energy Company), Saf II Building, Masdar City, ABU DHABI, POBOX54115, UNITED ARAB EMIRATES.

•**IBRAHIM, Mr. Ibrahim Tahir, MBA BEng ACA** *1999;* CAS, 69-71 High Street, CHATHAM, KENT, ME4 4EE. See also CAS House Limited
IBRAHIM, Mr. Kamalshah, BA BSc ACA *1987;* 31 Goldbeaters Grove, EDGWARE, HA8 0QE.
•**IBRAHIM, Mr. Mohamed Sheikh Idris, BSc ACA** *1991;* (Tax Fac), Sheikh & Co, Aboulela New Building, Gamhoria Street, P O Box 1608, KHARTOUM, 1111 SUDAN.
IBRAHIM, Mr. Sultanali Abdulla, FCA *1970;* 18427 95A Avenue, EDMONTON T5T 3V7, AB, CANADA.
IBRAHIM, Mr. Zahir Mohammed, BA ACA *1996;* 78 Muirfield Drive, Mickleover, DERBY, DE3 9YF.
ICETON, Mr. Kevin, ACA *2001;* 15 Violet Grove, DARLINGTON, DL1 1GR.
ICETON, Mrs. Natalie Gayle, MA ACA *2000;* (Tax Fac), 127 Woodcote Avenue, KENILWORTH, CV8 1BE.
ICHINOHE, Ms. Sachiko, BA ACA *2008;* Flat 24 Weatherbury, 90 Talbot Road, LONDON, W2 5LF.
•**ICKE, Mrs. Katie Joanne, BA FCA** *1996;* Icke & Co Limited, The Old Barn, Avoncroft Farm, Gibbs Lane, Offenham, EVESHAM WORCESTERSHIRE WR11 8RR.
IDALIA, Miss. Ioanna, BSc ACA *1996;* 8 Finea Str, Strovolos, 2036 NICOSIA, CYPRUS.
IDDON, Mr. Michael, MA(Oxon) ACA CTA *1990;* 1 Wentworth Gardens, Toddington, DUNSTABLE, BEDFORDSHIRE, LU5 6DN.
IDE, Mr. Alan David, MA BA ACA *2006;* 22 Glyndon Court, BRIGHOUSE, HD6 3UB.
IDE, Mr. Norman Sydney, FCA *1961;* 22 Cardinal Close, Caversham, READING, RG4 8BZ. (Life Member)
IDLE, Mr. Christopher John, FCA *1977;* 251 Bilton Road, RUGBY, CV22 7EQ.
•**IDNANI, Mr. Deepak, BSc(Hons) FCA** *1996;* (Tax Fac), Deepak Idnani Accountancy Services, 83 Selwood Road, CROYDON, CR0 7JW.
IDNANI, Mr. Manoj Anil, BSc ACA *1991;* 44 Woodside Road, PURLEY, CR8 4LP.
IDRIS, Mr. Amaar, BSc ACA *2010;* 307 Fullwell Avenue, ILFORD, ESSEX, IG5 0RG.
IDRIS, Miss. Hezlinn Fariss, BSc ACA *2000;* 201 Jalan Sundang, 54100 KUALA LUMPUR, FEDERAL TERRITORY, MALAYSIA.
IE, Miss. Hwie Wendy, BCom ACA *1994;* Flat 1902, Fortress Metro Tower Block D, 238 King's RoadNORTH POINT, Hong Kong Island, HONG KONG SAR.
IENT, Mr. James Alasdair, MEng ACA *2003;* Tradition Group, 63 Market Street, Level 7, SINGAPORE 048942, SINGAPORE.
IEONG, Mr. Cheng Va, ACA *2005;* P.O. Box No. 23406, Wan Chai Post Office, WAN CHAI, HONG KONG ISLAND, HONG KONG SAR.
IERODIACONOU, Miss. Marilena, BSc ACA *1996;* P.O. Box 5556, NICOSIA, CYPRUS.
•**IERODIAKONOU, Mr. Christos, BSc ACA** *2006;* Ekkeshis Ierodiakonou Ltd, 39 Themistocles Dervis Street, Office 102, CY-1066 NICOSIA, CYPRUS.
IERONYMIDES, Mr. Leonidas, BSc ACA *2002;* PO BOX 58052, 3730 LIMASSOL, CYPRUS.
•**IERSTON, Mr. John Godfrey, FCA CTA** *1974;* UHY Hacker Young, St John's Chambers, Love Street, CHESTER, CH1 1QN.
IEVERS, Mr. Michael John Eyre, FCA *1974;* Amaryllis House, Montrose Road, CHELMSFORD, cm2 6te.
•**IFIELD, Mr. Stuart Jerrold, FCA** *1969;* Ifield Keene Associates, 11 Whitchurch Parade, Whitchurch Lane, EDGWARE, MIDDLESEX, HA8 6LR.
IFILL, Mrs. Patricia, FCA *1964;* 58 Bowness Avenue, DIDCOT, OX11 8NE.
IFOULD, Mr. Martyn, BA FCA *1985;* Cliffe House, 35 East Street, Lindley, HUDDERSFIELD, HD3 3ND.
IFTIKHAR, Mr. Asim, ACA *1982;* Anjum Asim Shahid Rahman, 1 Inter-Floor Eden Centre, 43 Jail Road, LAHORE 54000, PAKISTAN.
IFTIKHAR, Mr. Uqba Jamshaid, ACA *2008;* 344-23A-1 Vista Damai Condominium Jalan Tun Razak, 50450 KUALA LUMPUR, FEDERAL TERRITORY, MALAYSIA.
IGBINADOLOR, Miss. Elsie Anatasia, BA ACA *1994;* Flat 1 Grice Court, Alwyne Square, LONDON, N1 2JY.
IGBOKWE, Mr. Kenneth Uche, BSc ACA *1985;* PricewaterhouseCoopers, Plot 252E Muri Okunola Street, Victoria Island, P O Box 2419, LAGOS, NIGERIA.
IGHODARO, Mrs. Olufunke, BSc FCA *1990;* PO Box 651511, BENMORE, GAUTENG, 2010, SOUTH AFRICA.
•**IGNATIUS, Mr. Rishanthan Jude, ACA ACMA ATII** *1990;* (Tax Fac), 15 Friary Way, North Finchley, LONDON, N12 9PE.
IGNATOW, Mr. Alexej, ACA *2010;* 20 Ersham Road, CANTERBURY, CT1 3AR.
IGNATOWICZ, Mr. Christopher Antoni, MA FCA *1977;* 6 Handleys Lane, Wickham Bishops, WITHAM, CM8 3NJ.
IGNEA, Mr. Ciprian, BA ACA *2004;* Neudorfstrasse 45, 8810 HORGEN, SWITZERLAND.
IGOE, Mr. Nicholas, BA ACA *1981;* 2 The Meadow, CHISLEHURST, BR7 6AA.
IGOE, Mr. Stephen James, LLB ACA *1988;* 5 Cheviot Close Ledsham Park, Little Sutton, ELLESMERE PORT, CH66 4YS.
•**IJAZ, Mr. Hassan, ACA ACCA** *2009;* Exalter Limited, Second Floor, Berkeley Square House, Berkeley Square, LONDON, W1J 6BD.
IKEL, Mr. Terence John, FCA *1974;* Newfee Ltd, The Old Vicarage, Church Lane, Shinfield, READING, RG2 9BY.
•**IKOMI, Ms. Esigbemi, BA ACA** *1993;* 11502 Wickersham Lane, HOUSTON, TX 77077, UNITED STATES.
ILAHI, Mr. Khwaja Mahboob, BSc FCA *1963;* c/o Khwaja Group of Industries, 267 Block A, Kamal Road, PO Box No 452, RAWALPINDI 46000, PAKISTAN.
ILAKO, Mr. Charles Francis, MSc FCA *1990;* 2c Kensington Court Gardens, LONDON, W8 5QE.
ILES, Mr. Ben Thomas, BSc ACA *2004;* (Tax Fac), 9 Kings Mill, Newmarket Road, Great Chesterford, SAFFRON WALDEN, ESSEX, CB10 1PE.
ILES, Miss. Charlotte Elizabeth, BA(Hons) ACA *2011;* 16 Beaurevoir Way, WARWICK, CV34 4NY.
ILES, Mr. Colin William, BSc ACA *2000;* Postnet Suite 222, Private Bag X51, BRYANSTON, 2021, SOUTH AFRICA.
ILES, Miss. Jennifer, BA(Hons) ACA *2011;* 2 Beech Close, Effingham, LEATHERHEAD, SURREY, KT24 5PQ.
ILES, Mrs. Juliette Brigitte Joelle, PhD BSc ACA *2000;* 605 Route De Crozet, 01710 THOIRY, FRANCE.
ILES, Mr. Martin David, BSc ACA *1992;* 3 Milburn Walk, EPSOM, SURREY, KT18 5JN.
ILES, Mr. Michael Victor Stanton, ACA *1983;* Poplars Oast, Churn Lane, Horsmonden, TONBRIDGE, TN12 8HN.
ILES, Mr. Stephen David, BSc ACA *1990;* Dalby Holdings Ltd, Gloucester Crescent, WIGSTON, LE18 4YQ.
ILETT, Mr. Andrew David, ACA *2008;* with Deloitte Touche Tohmatsu, 180 Lonsdale Street, MELBOURNE, VIC 3000, AUSTRALIA.
•**ILETT, Mr. Franklyn Leonard, FCA** *1987;* Deloitte LLP, Athene Place, 66 Shoe Lane, LONDON, EC4A 3BQ. See also Deloitte & Touche LLP
ILETT, Mr. Stephen Kenneth, BSc FCA *1980;* 10 Sycamore Way, TEDDINGTON, TW11 9QQ.
ILEY, Mr. Gareth Geraint Matthew, BSc ACA *1998;* 126 Northfield Road, Kings Norton, BIRMINGHAM, B30 1DX.
ILEY, Miss. Suzanne Jeanette, BSc ACA *2001;* 133 Duke Road, LONDON, W4 2BX.
ILIEVE, Mrs. Helen Elizabeth, MA FCA *1978;* Aldiecroft, Fossoway, KINROSS, KY13 0QH.
•**ILIFF, Mr. Anthony, FCA** *1958;* Anthony Iliff, Westgate, 55 Milestone Drive, Hagley, STOURBRIDGE, DY9 0LH.
•**ILIFFE, Mr. Graham Charles, FCA** *1971;* (Tax Fac), G.Iliffe, 6 Greystoke Court, 29 Albemarle Road, BECKENHAM, BR3 5HL.
ILIFFE, Mr. Jeffrey Michael, BSc ACA *1986;* Randalls, 30 Greenhill Road, Otford, SEVENOAKS, TN14 5RS.
ILIFFE, Mr. Stuart Ronald, ACA *1981;* 90 Ralph Street, OTTAWA K1S 5J4, ON, CANADA.
•**ILIFFE, Mr. Timothy John, FCA** *1973;* Iliffe Poulter & Co., 1A Bonnington Road, Mapperley, NOTTINGHAM, NG3 5JR.
ILIFFE MOON, Mr. Leon Edouard, MSc ACA *1995;* Bank Cottage, Brook End, Luckington, CHIPPENHAM, SN14 6PJ.
ILKHANY, Mr. Nariman, BSc FCA *1977;* 4- 8 Motahary Avenue, TEHRAN, 14, IRAN.
ILLES, Mr. Joseph Peter, ACA *2008;* Flat 2 Forest Heights, Epping New Road, BUCKHURST HILL, IG9 5TE.
•**ILLINGSWORTH, Mr. Mark, BA FCA** *1991;* Versant Associates LLP, The Old Mill, 9 Soar Lane, LEICESTER, LE3 5DE.
ILLINGWORTH, Mr. David, MA ACA *1979;* Business in the Community, 44-60 Richardshaw Lane, PUDSEY, WEST YORKSHIRE, LS28 7UR.
ILLINGWORTH, Mr. David Brian, BA ACA *1995;* Garden Cottage Station Road, Yaxham, DEREHAM, NORFOLK, NR19 1RD.
ILLINGWORTH, Mr. David Jeremy, BA FCA *1972;* (President 2003 - 2004) (Member of Council 1997 - 2006), 7 Park Lane, Greenfield, OLDHAM, OL3 7DX.
ILLINGWORTH, Mr. Derek, FCA *1956;* 17 Stonemead, Romiley, STOCKPORT, SK6 4LP. (Life Member)
ILLINGWORTH, Mr. John Mark, BA FCA *1981;* Sackville House, 143 - 149 Fenchurch Street, LONDON, EC3 6BN.
ILLINGWORTH, Mr. Mark Clafton, MBA BA FCA *1983;* 57 Weetwood Lane, LEEDS, LS16 5NP.
•**ILLINGWORTH, Mr. Michael David Holden, FCA** *1974;* Account 2 Grow Limited, 36 Ormiston Grove, LONDON, W12 0JT. See also Illingworth Michael
ILLINGWORTH, Mr. Nicholas Mark, MBA BSc ACA *1985;* Horsefall Fold, 6 Whiddon Croft, Menston, ILKLEY, LS29 6QQ.
ILLINGWORTH, Miss. Rebecca Michelle, BA ACA *2007;* 149 Westfield Road, HARPENDEN, HERTFORDSHIRE, AL5 4LU.
•**ILLINGWORTH, Mr. Richard Julian, BA ACA** *1995;* RJI Consulting Ltd, 18 White Oak Drive, Bishops Wood, STAFFORD, ST19 9AH.
ILLINGWORTH, Mrs. Sarah, BSc ACA *2003;* 57 Houseman Crescent, MANCHESTER, M20 2JD.
ILLINGWORTH, Mr. Stephen Robert, BA ACA *1983;* Blue Ridges House, Vann Lake Road, Ockley, DORKING, SURREY, RH5 5NS.
ILLIUS, Mr. Robert Warwick, BSc FCA *1935;* Pitts Garden, Fittleworth, PULBOROUGH, RH20 1JH. (Life Member)
ILLMAN, Mr. Robert James, FCA *1973;* Wyck Manor Farm, Wyck, ALTON, GU34 3AH.
ILLSLEY, Mr. Nicholas John, MA BA ACA *2003;* Blue Crest Capital Management Ltd, 40 Grosvenor Place, LONDON, SW1X 7AW.
ILLSTON, Mr. Peter Adrian, BA ACA *1995;* The Old Malt House, Malting Lane, MUCH HADHAM, HERTFORDSHIRE, SG10 6AW.
ILOTT, Mrs. Judith Anne, BSc ACA *1992;* Kingshott School, St Ippolyts, HITCHIN, HERTFORDSHIRE, SG4 7JX.
ILSLEY, Mr. Gary John, BA ACA *1987;* 14508 Greenleaf St, SHERMAN OAKS, CA 91403, UNITED STATES.
ILSLEY, Mr. Martin, FCA *1961;* Starboard Cottage, Long Park, East Portlemouth, SALCOMBE, TQ8 8PA. (Life Member)
ILUBE, Mr. Roland Alexander, BSc ACA *1995;* Room 1613B, Freeman House, 21/22 Marina, Lagos Island, LAGOS, NIGERIA.
ILYAS, Mr. Mohammed Ahtesham, ACA *2008;* Alfriston, Chalfont Avenue, AMERSHAM, BUCKINGHAMSHIRE, HP6 6RF.
ILYAS, Mr. Mustafa, MEng ACA *2011;* 213 Wexham Road, SLOUGH, SL2 5JT.
ILYAS, Mr. Nadeem, ACA *2010;* Flat 9, Augustine Bell Tower, 7 Pancras Way, LONDON, E3 2SU.
ILYAS, Mr. Osman, BSc(Hons) ACA *2002;* 2 Beales Lane, Walton Park, MILTON KEYNES, MK7 7HB.
ILYASOVA, Miss. Ksenia, MSc ACA *2010;* K P M G Llp, 15 Canada Square, LONDON, E14 5GL.
IM, Miss. Grace Ng May, BSc ACA *2007;* Flat 201 Windsor House, Cumberland Market, LONDON, NW1 4DE.
IMAI, Mr. Natsuo, MA ACA *1998;* Room 1102, Famile Hisakata, 5-24-21 Koishikawa, Bunkyoku, TOKYO, 107 6122 JAPAN.
IMAKI, Mr. Keita, MSc BA ACA *2006;* Prager & Fenton Llp Imperial House, 15-19 Kingsway, LONDON, WC2B 6UN.
IMBER, Mrs. Fiona Ann, BSc ACA *1989;* The Firs Lamb Lane, Sible Hedingham, HALSTEAD, CO9 3RS.
IMBER, Mr. Neil Raymond, FCA *1995;* 33 Bridge Meadow Drive, Knowle, SOLIHULL, B93 9QG.
IMELLOS, Mr. Michael Nicholas, ACA *1994;* NIKIS 10E, LAGONISSI, KALYVIA THORIKOU, 19010 ATHENS, GREECE.
IMER, Mrs. Ceyda Sedef, MSc ACA *2000;* 9 GRAPEVINE LANE, MCLAREN VALE, SA 5171, AUSTRALIA.
IMISON, Mr. Philip, FCA *1968;* 115 Gotch Road, Barton Seagrave, KETTERING, NN15 6UG.
•**IMMS, Mr. Michael Ian, BA FCA** *1991;* Immovation Ltd, 2 Greywethers Avenue, SWINDON, SN3 1QF.
•**IMPEY, Mr. Alistair Geoffrey, BSc FCA** *1976;* PricewaterhouseCoopers, Largo Saydi Mingas, Predio BPC 16th floor, LUANDA, CP 5957, ANGOLA.
IMPEY, Mr. John Donovan, FCA *1974;* Woodlands, Coopers Hill, Alvechurch, BIRMINGHAM, B48 7BX.
IMPEY, Mr. Kenneth William, FCA *1949;* The Byre, Old Durham Farm, Bent House Lane, DURHAM, DH1 2RY. (Life Member)
IMRAN, Mr. Shahrin, ACA *2008;* 87 Colegrave Road, LONDON, E15 1DZ.
•**IMRAY, Mr. Robert Peter, MA FCA** *1973;* (Tax Fac), R P Imray, 6 The Old Maltings, Ditton Walk, CAMBRIDGE, CB5 8PY.
IMRIE, Mr. Andrew John, BA(Hons) ACA *2001;* 20 Prince Edward Way, Stotfold, HITCHIN, HERTFORDSHIRE, SG5 4PU.
IMRIE, Mr. Douglas Fisackerly, BSc ACA *1999;* 50 Bective Road, LONDON, SW15 2QA.
IMRIE, Mr. Duncan Robert, ACA *2008;* 17b Treport Street, LONDON, SW18 2BW.
IMRIE, Mr. Ian Richard, ACA MAAT *2001;* 30 Hartest Way, Great Cornard, SUDBURY, SUFFOLK, CO10 0LA.
IMRIE, Mr. James William, MEng ACA *2009;* Sheiling Cottage, Cromhall, WOTTON-UNDER-EDGE, GL12 8AT.
IMRIT, Mr. Nadim Muhammad, BSc ACA *2006;* 29 Chestnut Grove, ILFORD, IG6 3AS.
IMTIAZI, Mrs. Shazia Tanveer, BSc ACA *1998;* 4a Peaks Hill, PURLEY, SURREY, cr8 3je.
INAYAT, Miss. Roxanna, BA(Hons) ACA *2011;* 35 Kingsley Avenue, BRADFORD, WEST YORKSHIRE, BD2 1DP.
•**INCE, Ms. Debbie, BA ACA ATII** *1997;* (Tax Fac), Chantrey Vellacott DFK LLP, Russell Square House, 10-12 Russell Square, LONDON, WC1B 5LF.
INCE, Mr. Derren, BA(Hons) ACA *2001;* 1 Dukeries Crescent, Edwinstowe, MANSFIELD, NG21 9AR.
INCE, Mr. Gary Anthony, BA FCA *1980;* 21 Sextant Avenue, Compass Point, Isle Of Dogs, LONDON, E14 3DX.
INCE, Miss. Janice Catherine, BSc ACA *1992;* 58 Warren Road, Wanstead, LONDON, E11 2NA.
INCE, Mr. Kenneth George, FCA *1958;* 21 Trienna, Orton Longueville, PETERBOROUGH, PE2 7ZW. (Life Member)
INCE, Mr. Michael Julian, MBA FCA *1970;* PO Box 23, NJORO, 20107, KENYA. (Life Member)
INCE, Mr. Nicholas, ACA *2008;* 81 Vincent Close, Old Hall, WARRINGTON, WA5 8TB.
INCE, Mr. Peter Geoffrey David, BA ACA *1989;* 14 Cliff Way, Radcliffe-on-Trent, NOTTINGHAM, NG12 1AQ.
INCE, Mr. Stanley Racine Norman, MA BSc FCA ACT *1993;* 124 West 79th Street Apt 12C, NEW YORK, NY 10024, UNITED STATES.
INCH, Mr. Christopher Michael, BA FCA *1985;* 10 Great Riding, Norton, RUNCORN, CHESHIRE, WA7 6SL.
INCH, Miss. Victoria Jayne, BSc ACA *2006;* 24 Torquay Avenue, SOUTHAMPTON, SO15 5HB.
INCHAUSTI-NAYLOR, Mr. Michael Alexander, MBA BA FCA *1980;* PO Box 125036, St Heliers, AUCKLAND, NEW ZEALAND.
INCHBALD, Mr. Charles Edward Elliot, BA ACA *1998;* 8 Moss Way, BEACONSFIELD, BUCKINGHAMSHIRE, HP9 1TG.
INCHLEY, Mr. Edward Arthur, FCA *1960;* 12 Dunholme Road, Welton, LINCOLN, LN2 3RS. (Life Member)
INCHLEY, Mr. Simon Nicholas, BA ACA *1988;* Parkers Barn Farm, The Fosse Way, Eathorpe, LEAMINGTON SPA, WARWICKSHIRE, CV33 9DF.
IND, Mr. Ronald Christopher, BA FCA *1961;* 72 Eccleston Square, LONDON, SW1V 1PJ. (Life Member)
IND, Mr. Stephen Bernard, BA ACA *1979;* BP Group, Chertsey Road, SUNBURY-ON-THAMES, MIDDLESEX, TW16 7BP.
IND, Ms. Sue-Ann, BSc ACA *2007;* 1 Sycamore Way, TEDDINGTON, MIDDLESEX, TW11 9QQ.
•**INDGE, Mr. Richard Kenneth, BSc FCA** *1989;* Ernst & Young LLP, 1 More London Place, LONDON, SE1 2AF. See also Ernst & Young Europe LLP
•**INESON, Mr. Ernest, FCA** *1963;* (Tax Fac), Greenwood Barton & Co, Barclays Bank Chambers, 2 Northgate, CLECKHEATON, WEST YORKSHIRE, BD19 5AA.
INESON, Mrs. Patricia Ann, ACA *1985;* 11 Scott Lane, Gomersal, CLECKHEATON, WEST YORKSHIRE, BD19 4JY.
ING, Mrs. Sarah Lucy, BSc ACA *1991;* 57 Rusholme Road, LONDON, SW15 3LF.
•**INGALL, Mr. David Andrew, FCA** *1968;* David Ingall, 40 Garth Lane, Hambleton, SELBY, NORTH YORKSHIRE, YO8 9QA.
INGALL, Mr. David James, MBA BEng FCA *1993;* 15b Wentworth Avenue, SHEFFIELD, S11 9QX.
INGALL, Mr. James Peter Henniker, BA ACA *1999;* 15 Redan Street, LONDON, W14 0AB.
INGALL, Mr. Simon Mark, BSc ACA *1979;* 1 Walham Rise, Wimbledon Hill Road, LONDON, SW19 7QY.
INGALL-TOMBS, Mr. Stuart Michael, BA ACA *1992;* The Oaklands, Honiley Road, Beausale, WARWICK, CV35 7NX.
INGAMELLS, Mr. Matthew James, ACA *2009;* Apartment 112 College House, Huddersfield Road, BARNSLEY, SOUTH YORKSHIRE, S75 1DS.
INGATE, Mr. Barry Roger, FCA *1965;* 14 South Walk, BOGNOR REGIS, WEST SUSSEX, PO22 7RW. (Life Member)
INGE, Miss. Nicola, BSc ACA *2011;* 29 Watling Place, SITTINGBOURNE, KENT, ME10 4ST.

•INGHAM, Mr. Antony William, BSc FCA CTA 1993; Ingham & Co, George Stanley House, 2 West Parade Road, SCARBOROUGH, NORTH YORKSHIRE, YO12 5ED. See also Charles A Wood & Co Ltd and Harrison Ingham & Co
INGHAM, Mrs. Carol Anne, BA ACA 1999; 16 Lawrence Way, LICHFIELD, STAFFORDSHIRE, WS13 6RD.
INGHAM, Miss. Caroline Louise, ACA 2008; Flat 3, 3 Netherwood Road, LONDON, W14 0BL.
INGHAM, Mrs. Catherine Ann, BSc ACA 2004; with Deloitte LLP, Abbots House, Abbey Street, READING, RG1 3BD.
INGHAM, Mr. David, MChem ACA 2006; Travelex UK Ltd, 65 Kingsway, LONDON, WC2B 6TD.
INGHAM, Mr. David Edward, BSc ACA 1982; 1 Old Camp Road, EASTBOURNE, BN20 8DH.
INGHAM, Mr. David Mark, BSc ACA 2005; 4 Highlands, LIVERSEDGE, WEST YORKSHIRE, WF15 8DS.
INGHAM, Mr. David William, MA ACA 1992; 30/9 Eyre Crescent, EDINBURGH, EH3 5EU.
INGHAM, Mr. Frederick Roy, BA ACA 2002; Neuberger Berman Asia Limited, Suites 2010-20, 20th Floor Jardine House, 1 Connaught Road, CENTRAL, HONG KONG ISLAND HONG KONG SAR.
INGHAM, Mrs. Helen, BEng ACA 2000; 34 Tudor Road, BARNET, HERTFORDSHIRE, EN5 5NP.
INGHAM, Mr. Ian Mark, BA ACA 1995; 16 Lawrence Way, LICHFIELD, STAFFORDSHIRE, WS13 6RD.
•INGHAM, Mr. John, FCA 1960; John Ingham, 5 Victoria Street, GLOSSOP, SK13 8HT.
INGHAM, Mr. John Serjeant, LLB FCA 1966; 10 Monks Close, Dorchester on Thames, WALLINGFORD, OX10 7JA.
INGHAM, Miss. Judith Caroline, BA ACA 1987; (Tax Fac), with PricewaterhouseCoopers LLP, Cornwall Court, 19 Cornwall Street, BIRMINGHAM, B3 2DT.
INGHAM, Mr. Kevin Thomas, ACA 1979; 153 Upper Welland Road, Upper Welland Malvern Wells, MALVERN, WR14 4LB.
INGHAM, Mr. Lee, BSc FCA 1976; 1090 Seale Drive, ALPHARETTA, GA 30022, UNITED STATES.
INGHAM, Miss. Louise, BA ACA 2006; 6 The Grove, SHIPLEY, WEST YORKSHIRE, BD18 4LD.
INGHAM, Mr. Mark Howard, ACA 1980; Thermogenics Inc., 6 Scanlon Court, AURORA L4G 7B2, ON, CANADA.
INGHAM, Mr. Martin Gordon, BSc FCA 1975; 6 The Grove, Moorhead, SHIPLEY, BD18 4LD.
INGHAM, Mr. Michael Harry Peter, FCA 1978; Rotch Property Group Ltd, Leconfield House, Curzon Street, LONDON, W1J 5JA.
INGHAM, Mrs. Morag Gail, ACA 2008; Grant Thornton, GPO Box 1008, BRISBANE, QLD 4001, AUSTRALIA.
INGHAM, Mr. Nicholas, BEng ACA 2010; Flat 63 Watermans Quay, William Morris Way, LONDON, SW6 2UU.
INGHAM, Mrs. Nicola Jane, ACA 1997; Nicton House, Crossgates, SCARBOROUGH, NORTH YORKSHIRE, YO12 4ND.
INGHAM, Mrs. Nicola Jayne, BA ACA 1989; 7 Willow Grove, BUCKLEY, CLWYD, CH7 3NR.
INGHAM, Mr. Nigel John, FCA 1982; 6 Route de la Scie, 1271, GIVRINS, VAUD, SWITZERLAND.
INGHAM, Mr. Norman Leonard, BSc ACA 1991; 52 Gwaelodygarth, MERTHYR TYDFIL, CF47 8YY.
•INGHAM, Mr. Peter, FCA 1967; (Tax Fac), Ingham & Co, George Stanley House, 2 West Parade Road, SCARBOROUGH, NORTH YORKSHIRE, YO12 5ED. See also Charles A Wood & Co Ltd
INGHAM, Mr. Quentin Clifford, BA(Hons) ACA 2000; 34 Tudor Road, BARNET, HERTFORDSHIRE, EN5 5NP.
INGHAM, Mr. Robert Benjamin Fuller, MA FCA 1963; 39 Binswood Avenue, LEAMINGTON SPA, CV32 5SE.
INGHAM, Mrs. Sara Amanda, BA ACA 2005; Proctor & Gamble UK, Cobalt 12A, Silver Fox Way, Cobalt Business Park, NEWCASTLE UPON TYNE, NE27 0QW.
INGHAM, Miss. Sharon Julia, BA ACA 2006; Catlin Holdings Ltd, 6th Floor, 3 Minster Court, LONDON, EC3R 7DD.
INGHAM, Miss. Suzanna Jane, BSc(Hons) ACA 2006; with PricewaterhouseCoopers LLP, 101 Barbirolli Square, Lower Mosley Street, MANCHESTER, M2 3PW.
INGHAM CLARK, Mr. Robert James, FCA 1987; 26 Parkside, LONDON, NW7 2LH.
INGLE, Mr. Brian Charles, FCA 1968; 14 Oakway, Southgate, LONDON, N14 5NN.
INGLE, Mr. Charles Frederick, BSc FCA 1976; 1 The Park, Park LaneSowood, HALIFAX, HX4 9LE. (Life Member)
INGLE, Mr. Christopher John, ACA 1989; 19 St. Oswalds Close, Wilberfoss, YORK, YO41 5LT.
INGLE, Miss. Clare, BSc ACA 2005; with PricewaterhouseCoopers LLP, 89 Sandyford Road, NEWCASTLE UPON TYNE, NE1 8HW.
INGLE, Mr. Derek Richard, BSc ACA 1985; 7 Osprey Walk, BUCKINGHAM, MK18 7JA.
INGLE, Mrs. Elizabeth Jane, BA FCA 1977; Park Cottage, Holloway, MATLOCK, DERBYSHIRE, DE4 5AR.
INGLE, Mrs. Laura Elizabeth, ACA 2008; 31 Denbigh Avenue, SUNDERLAND, SR6 8HQ.
•INGLE, Mr. Mark, ACA 2004; (Tax Fac), Sedley Richard Laurence Voulters, Fifth Floor, 89 New Bond Street, LONDON, W1S 1DA.
INGLE, Miss. Rachael Cassandra, BSc ACA 2007; ASX, 20 Bridge Street, SYDNEY, NSW 2000, AUSTRALIA.
•INGLE, Mr. Richard George, BA FCA 1980; Ashworth Treasure Limited, 17-19 Park Street, LYTHAM ST. ANNES, LANCASHIRE, FY8 5LU.
•INGLEBY, Mr. Bryan Sidney, MA ACA 2004; National Audit Office, 157-197 Buckingham Palace Road, Victoria, LONDON, SW1W 9SP. See also B S Ingleby
INGLEBY, Mr. Dennis Sinclair, FCA 1958; 34 Cavendish Drive, West Hagley, STOURBRIDGE, DY9 0LS. (Life Member)
INGLEBY, Mr. John Mungo, MA FCA 1970; Malling Farm, Port Of Menteith, STIRLING, FK8 3RD.
INGLEDEW, Miss. Georgina Jane, BSc ACA 2005; Flat 2, Picking Court, 10 Gordon Road, LONDON, N11 2PN.
INGLEDEW, Mr. John Frazer, FCA 1960; Great Killough, Llantilio Crossenny, ABERGAVENNY, NP7 8SR. (Life Member)
•INGLEFIELD, Mr. Peter Roberts, FCA 1976; 16 Golf Course Drive, Moka Heights, Maraval, PORT OF SPAIN, TRINIDAD AND TOBAGO.
INGLEFIELD, Mr. Timothy John Urquhart, BSc FCA 1972; McLellan and Partners Ltd, Sheer House, WEST BYFLEET, KT14 6NL.
INGLES, Mrs. Claire Tracy, BA ACA 2006; 92 Burnside Way, Winnington, NORTHWICH, CHESHIRE, CW8 4XS.
INGLES, Mr. George Robert Grant, BA ACA 2005; Everton Football Club Co Ltd, Goodison Park, LIVERPOOL, L4 4EL.
INGLES, Mr. Lees Justin, BSc ACA 2010; 4 Rockford Lodge, KNUTSFORD, CHESHIRE, WA16 8AH.
•INGLES, Mr. Martyn Raymond, BSc FCA CTA 1984; (Tax Fac), Martyn Ingles & Co, 50 High Street, Stoke Goldington, NEWPORT PAGNELL, MK16 8NR. See also Ingles Martyn
INGLES, Mr. Richard Darren, BSc ACA 2008; 92 Burnside Way, Winnington, NORTHWICH, CHESHIRE, CW8 4XS.
INGLES, Mr. Roger Rex, BSc ACA 1979; 10 School Hill, Merstham, REDHILL, RH1 3EG.
INGLES, Mr. Stephen Robert, BA FCA 1984; La Cheneau 7, CH 1276 GINGINS, SWITZERLAND.
INGLESENT, Mr. David Anthony, FCA 1962; 32 West Walk, West Bay, BRIDPORT, DORSET, DT6 4HT. (Life Member)
INGLESON, Mr. Malcolm, FCA 1960; 19 Carrbottom Road, Greengates, BRADFORD, BD10 0BB. (Life Member)
•INGLETON, Mr. Adrian, FCA 1985; RNS, The Poplars, Bridge Street, BRIGG, NORTH LINCOLNSHIRE, DN20 8NQ.
INGLIS, Mr. Alan James, BA ACA 1986; The Willows, Thame Road, Longwick, PRINCES RISBOROUGH, HP27 9QU.
INGLIS, Mr. Andrew David, ACA 2009; 88 Bronallt Road, Hendy, Pontarddulais, SWANSEA, SA4 0UE.
INGLIS, Mr. Colin Graham, FCA 1973; 24 Stambourne Way, WEST WICKHAM, BR4 9NF.
INGLIS, Mr. Geoffrey Neil, BA FCA 1971; 10 Aldersyde Way, Guiseley, LEEDS, LS20 8QS.
INGLIS, Mr. Graham Marchbank, LLB ACA 1989; 7 Curzon St, LONDON, W1J 7HN.
INGLIS, Mr. Ian Robert, FCA 1952; Travel Africa, Rycote Lane Farm, Rycote Lane, Milton Common, THAME, OXFORDSHIRE OX9 2NZ. (Life Member)
INGLIS, Mr. James Richard, BA ACA 1995; 3 Buckmaster Road, LONDON, SW11 1EN.
INGLIS, Miss. Lindsey Jayne, ACA 2011; 38 Richmond Road, YEOVIL, SOMERSET, BA20 1BA.
•INGLIS, Dr. Louise, PhD BSc(Hons) ACA 2008; Inglis Accountancy Services, Craike View, 3 The Terrace, Kirby Hill, Boroughbridge, YORK YO51 9DQ.
INGLIS, Mr. Murray Robert Hamilton, FCA 1974; Old Bilsham Farmhouse Bilsham Lane, Yapton, ARUNDEL, WEST SUSSEX, BN18 0JX.
INGLIS, Mr. Paul Nigel John, BA ACA 1995; with FTI Consulting Limited, 322 Midtown, High Holborn, LONDON, WC1V 7PB.
INGLIS, Mr. Richard Jeremy George, BA ACA 1987; 79 Chart Lane, REIGATE, RH2 7EB.
INGLIS, Mr. Richard John, MA ACA 2007; 14 Keppel Bay Drive, Caribbean at Keppel Bay, #02-18, SINGAPORE 098642, SINGAPORE.
INGLIS, Mr. Rob Devonsher, FCA 1969; Thornton, Edinburgh Road, LINLITHGOW, EH49 6AA.
INGLIS, Mr. Robert Sinclair, FCA 1961; 21 Willow Close, BISHOP'S STORTFORD, CM23 2RY.
INGLIS, Mr. Thomas George Mathison, BA ACA 1984; Javelin Wealth Management Pte Ltd, 77A Amoy Street, SINGAPORE 069896, SINGAPORE.
INGLIS, Mr. William Devonsher, MA ACA 2000; 61 Bickley Street, LONDON, SW17 9NF.
•INGLIS, Mr. William Robert Hamilton, MA FCA 1981; Deloitte LLP, Athene Place, 66 Shoe Lane, LONDON, EC4A 3BQ. See also Deloitte & Touche LLP
INGMAN, Miss. Nia, BSc ACA 1995; 12 Stanhope Terrace, LONDON, W2 2UB.
INGMIRE, Mr. David Richard Bonner, BA FCA 1966; (Tax Fac), Rugby Football Union, Conference Centre, 200 Whitton Road, TWICKENHAM, TW2 7BA.
INGMIRE, Mr. Michael David, ACA 2002; 2 Dunelm Close, CHELTENHAM, GLOUCESTERSHIRE, GL51 0QU.
INGOLD, Mr. John Christopher, BSc FCA 1976; 11 The Fennings, AMERSHAM, BUCKINGHAMSHIRE, HP6 5LE. (Life Member)
INGRAM, Mr. Andrew John, BSc(Hons) ACA MMus 2010; 74 Parkside Avenue, BEXLEYHEATH, DA7 6NL.
INGRAM, Mrs. Anne, BSc FCA 1978; Hambleton, 7 Belgrave Drive, SHEFFIELD, S10 3LQ.
INGRAM, Mr. Anthony Lionel, FCA ACMA 1948; 52 Rue De Moillebeau, 1209 GENEVA, SWITZERLAND. (Life Member)
INGRAM, Mr. Anthony Patrick, BSc ACA 1990; Club La Costa Executive Offices, Urbanizacion Marina del Sol, Ctra de Cadiz, KM 206 Mijas Costa, 29650 MALAGA, SPAIN.
INGRAM, Mr. Bruce Guy, FCA 1965; 1075 Governor Dempsey Drive, SANTA FE, NM 87501, UNITED STATES. (Life Member)
INGRAM, Miss. Claire Louise, ACA 2008; Rixons Farm, 91 High Street, Weston Favell, NORTHAMPTON, NN3 3JX.
INGRAM, Mr. Daniel David, BSc ACA 2006; 24a Brackenbury Road, LONDON, W6 0BA.
•INGRAM, Mr. David Anthony, ACA 1987; Grant Thornton UK LLP, 30 Finsbury Square, LONDON, EC2P 2YU. See also Grant Thornton LLP
INGRAM, Mr. David Colin, BSc ACA 1982; Matrix Group, The Coach House, The Green, Marston Moretaine, BEDFORD, MK43 0NF.
•INGRAM, Mr. David Michael, BA ACA 1990; Moore and Smalley LLP, Richard House, 9 Winckley Square, PRESTON, PR1 3HP.
INGRAM, Mrs. Elaine, BSc FCA 1976; Woodfield, Quarry Road, OXTED, RH8 9HE.
INGRAM, Mr. Geoffrey Gordon, FCA 1952; 17 Rue Flandres Dunkerque, 53400 CRAON, FRANCE. (Life Member)
INGRAM, Mr. Gerald Vaughan, BSc ACA 1982; 3 Monterey Drive, Locks Heath, SOUTHAMPTON, SO31 6NW.
INGRAM, Mrs. Helen Joanne, BA(Hons) ACA 2002; 10 Avon Close, Pontllanfraith, BLACKWOOD, NP12 2GB.
•INGRAM, Mrs. Jean Pamela, ACA 1981; (Tax Fac), Jean Ingram Limited, 106a High Street, CHESHAM, BUCKINGHAMSHIRE, HP5 1EB.
INGRAM, Mr. John Charles Beresford, BSc FCA 1975; Clark County Auditors Office, 1300 Franklin St, VANCOUVER, WA 98666, UNITED STATES.
INGRAM, Mr. John Keith, FCA 1958; 51 Alexandra Road, PETERBOROUGH, PE1 3DE. (Life Member)
INGRAM, Mrs. Josephine Beatrice, ACA 2011; 74 Parkside Avenue, Barnehurst, BEXLEYHEATH, KENT, DA7 6NL.
INGRAM, Miss. Kate, BSc ACA 2007; with PricewaterhouseCoopers LLP, 1 Embankment Place, LONDON, WC2N 6RH.
•INGRAM, Mr. Kevin, BSc FCA 1979; 22 Postmill Close, Shirley, CROYDON, CR0 5DY.
INGRAM, Mr. Kevin John, BSc ACA 1992; Environment Agency Wales Cambria House, 29 Newport Road, CARDIFF, CF24 0TP.
INGRAM, Mrs. Leslie Ann, MSc ACA 1993; 8 The Beeches, Hope, WREXHAM, LL12 9NX.
INGRAM, Mr. Marc, BSc ACA 2008; Flat 3 59, Priory Road, LONDON, NW6 3NH.
INGRAM, Mr. Mark Philip, MSc FCA AMCT 1986; 30 Reigate Road, REIGATE, SURREY, RH2 0QN.
INGRAM, Mr. Matthew Philip, BA ACA 2007; Floor 19, 56 Pitt Street, SYDNEY, NSW 2000, AUSTRALIA.
INGRAM, Mr. Michael Vincent, LLB ACA 2007; Morton Cottage, The Street, Mortimer, READING, RG7 3DW.
•INGRAM, Mr. Miles, BA FCA 1969; M. Ingram, Teal Cottage, 5 Holt View, Great Easton, MARKET HARBOROUGH, LEICESTERSHIRE LE16 8TN.
INGRAM, Mr. Nathan, BA ACA 2011; 56 Crocus Drive, SITTINGBOURNE, ME10 4ES.
INGRAM, Miss. Nicola Clare, ACA 2009; 22 Postmill Close, CROYDON, CR0 5DY.
INGRAM, Mr. Patrick Daniel Williams, BA ACA 1987; The Laurels, 282 The Common, Holt, TROWBRIDGE, BA14 6QJ.
INGRAM, Mr. Peter Jonathan Stuart, FCA 1968; Thomas Edge House Tunnell Street, St. Helier, JERSEY, JE2 4LU.
INGRAM, Mr. Peter Michael, BSc ACA 2001; 27 Queens Road, TEDDINGTON, MIDDLESEX, TW11 0LX.
INGRAM, Mr. Reginald Charles, FCA 1950; Lime Trees Farm, Compass Road, Silfield, WYMONDHAM, NORFOLK, NR18 9NN. (Life Member)
INGRAM, Mr. Richard, BSc ACA 2002; Flat 191, Compass House, Smugglers Way, LONDON, SW18 1DJ.
INGRAM, Mr. Richard Michael, BSc ACA 1991; Deans Croft, 3 St. Leonards Road, Claygate, ESHER, SURREY, KT10 0EL.
INGRAM, Mr. Robert Alfred, FCA 1971; 11 Sunnybank Road, Wylde Green, SUTTON COLDFIELD, B73 5RE.
INGRAM, Mr. Robert John, BSc FCA 1978; Thomson Snell & Passmore, 3 Lonsdale Gardens, TUNBRIDGE WELLS, KENT, TN1 1NX.
INGRAM, Mr. Robert Michael, MA MSc FCA 1973; Little Vale, Rue Du Vieux Menage, St Saviour, JERSEY, JE2 7XG.
•INGRAM, Mr. Roger Andrew, BSc FCA 1971; Ingram Accountancy Services Ltd, 29 Wellesley Road, COLCHESTER, CO3 3HE.
INGRAM, Mr. Rowland Nicholas Harper, FCA 1973; 4 Solent Avenue, LYMINGTON, SO41 3SD.
•INGRAM, Mr. Stephen, BA(Econ) FCA CF 1973; Ingram Forrest Corporate Finance LLP, 2 Rutland Park, SHEFFIELD, S10 2PD. See also Barber Harrison & Platt
•INGRAM, Mr. Trevor John, BSc FCA 1979; 56 Crocus Drive, SITTINGBOURNE, ME10 4ES.
INGREY, Miss. Hannah Elizabeth Leigh, ACA 2009; 9 Hadleigh Court, High Road, BROXBOURNE, HERTFORDSHIRE, EN10 6PS.
•INGS, Mr. David John, FCA 1976; (Tax Fac), Langdowns DFK Limited, Fleming Court, Leigh Road, EASTLEIGH, HAMPSHIRE, SO50 9PD.
INGS, Miss. Joanne Marie, BSc ACA 2009; 29 Elms Drive, Marston, OXFORD, OX3 0NN.
INIGHT, Mrs. Gwenda May, BSc FCA 1980; The Summerhouse, 182 Ashbourne Road, Turnditch, BELPER, DERBYSHIRE, DE56 2LH.
INIGO-JONES, Mr. Charles Henry, MA FCA 1989; Farthings Stapley Lane, Ropley, ALRESFORD, SO24 0EN.
INIONS, Mr. Edward Charles, MA FCA ACIS 1985; 6 Fitzgerald Road, Mortlake, LONDON, SW14 8HA.
INKPEN, Mr. James Martin, FCA 1961; Wisegain LTD, Birchwood, 1/B Welch Road, SOUTHSEA, PO4 0QD. (Life Member)
INKSON, Mr. Jonathan Allen, MA ACA MBA 1997; 18 Bareena Avenue, WAHROONGA, NSW 2076, AUSTRALIA.
INMAN, Mr. Christopher, BSc(Econ) ACA 1980; Southside, Marsh Lane, Laughterton, LINCOLN, LN1 2JX.
INMAN, Mr. David, BA ACA 2006; N V M Private Equity Ltd, Northumberland House, Princess Square, NEWCASTLE UPON TYNE, NE1 8ER.
•INMAN, Mr. Ian, FCA 1991; Inman & Co, 17 Abinger Court, Ealing, LONDON, W5 2AF. See also Inman Business Advisors Limited
•INMAN, Mr. John James, BA FCA 1977; (Tax Fac), Inman Waverley Ltd, 36 New Road, Milford, GODALMING, GU8 5BE. See also Waverley Inman
•INMAN, Mr. Paul John, BSc ACA 1991; with PricewaterhouseCoopers, BusinessCommunityCenter, Katerinska 40/466, 120 00 PRAGUE, CZECH REPUBLIC.
INMAN, Mr. Peter Bradwell, MA FCA 1976; 4 Bleriot Crescent, Whiteley, FAREHAM, HAMPSHIRE, PO15 7JD.

IRWIN, Mr. Clifford Edward, BSc ACA *1987;* South Haining, Brockenhurst Road, ASCOT, SL5 9HB.
•**IRWIN, Mr. David, BA ACA CF** *1991;* BTG Financial Consulting LLP, 340 Deansgate, MANCHESTER, M3 4LY. See also BTG McInnes Corporate Finance LLP
IRWIN, Mrs. Donna Lesley, BA ACA *1983;* 9 Seath Avenue, Langbank, PORT GLASGOW, PA14 6PD.
IRWIN, Mrs. Fiona Mary, BSc FCA *1993;* with Hamlyns LLP, Sundial House, 98 High Street, Horsell, WOKING, SURREY GU21 4SU.
IRWIN, Mrs. Janine, BA(Hons) ACA *2003;* 6 Windsor Terrace, WHITLEY BAY, TYNE AND WEAR, NE26 2NS.
IRWIN, Mr. John Henry, FCA *1992;* 619a Roman Road, LONDON, E3 2RN.
IRWIN, Miss. Juliette Francesca, BA ACA *2010;* Deloitte & Touche, 2 New Street Square, LONDON, EC4A 3BZ.
IRWIN, Mr. Kingsley Stuart, BA FCA *1969;* 18 Colley Wood, Kennington, OXFORD, OX1 5NF.
IRWIN, Mr. Mark Joseph, BSc ACA *1990;* 28 Upper Main Street, BUNCRANA, COUNTY DONEGAL, IRELAND.
IRWIN, Mr. Michael Alan, FCA *1976;* 8 Wartling Close, ST LEONARDS-ON-SEA, EAST SUSSEX, TN38 9QX.
IRWIN, Miss. Michelle Louise, ACA *2003;* 10 Salem Walk, RAYLEIGH, ESSEX, SS6 9SS.
•**IRWIN, Mrs. Monica Sarah, FCA** *1983;* (Tax Fac), Monica Irwin, 1 Barn Close, Cumnor Hill, OXFORD, OX2 9JP.
•**IRWIN, Mr. Nathan Luke, BA(Hons) ACA** *2003;* with PricewaterhouseCoopers LLP, 31 Great George Street, BRISTOL, BS1 5QD.
IRWIN, Mr. Oliver John, FCA *1951;* Kyindu Ranch, Postnet 180 Kabulonga, Private Bag E 835, LUSAKA, ZAMBIA. (Life Member)
IRWIN, Mr. Patrick James, BA ACA *1993;* Well Cottage Farhill, Llanishen, CHEPSTOW, GWENT, NP16 6QY.
IRWIN, Mr. Patrick Staples, FCA *1964;* 51 Ashford Way, HASTINGS, TN34 2HG. (Life Member)
IRWIN, Ms. Penelope Regina Joanna, BA ACA *1990;* 13 Beechfield Road, HEMEL HEMPSTEAD, HP1 1PP.
IRWIN, Mr. Richard James, BA FCA *1993;* PricewaterhouseCoopers (Vietnam) Ltd, 4th Floor Saigon Tower, 29 Le Duan Boulevard, District 1, HO CHI MINH CITY, VIETNAM.
IRWIN, Mr. Stephen Richard, BA FCA *1980;* Token House, 11-12 Tokenhouse Yard, LONDON, EC2R 7AS.
IRWIN, Mrs. Susan Claire, BA FCA *1979;* 23 Home Close, Pound Hill, CRAWLEY, WEST SUSSEX, RH10 3AF.
IRWING, Miss. Lorraine, BSc ACA *1992;* Oxford Radcliffe Hospitals Charitable Funds Department, Manor House Headley Way Headington, OXFORD, OX3 9DZ.
ISAAC, Mr. Carl, LLB ACA *2002;* 2 Mill Cottages, Frouds Lane Aldermaston, READING, RG7 4LQ.
ISAAC, Mr. David Glyn, BA ACA *1983;* 36 Avon Road, Hale, ALTRINCHAM, CHESHIRE, WA15 0LB.
ISAAC, Mr. Duncan Robert, ACA *2009;* 88 Purves Road, LONDON, NW10 5TB.
ISAAC, Mr. Gareth Roger, BA ACA *1998;* Flat 4 Palace Place Mansions, 36 Kensington Court, LONDON, W8 5BB.
ISAAC, Mr. Hywel Glyn, FCA *1955;* Rawdon 6, Woodway, GUILDFORD, SURREY, GU1 2TF. (Life Member)
ISAAC, Mr. James Victor Stanford, FCA *1960;* 12 Leigh Rodd, Carpenders Park, WATFORD, WD19 5BJ. (Life Member)
ISAAC, Miss. Joleen, MA ACA *2006;* Funac Services Ltd, 16 Charles II Street, LONDON, SW1Y 4QU.
ISAAC, Mr. Keith Shelby, FCA *1969;* Clare Cottage, Fir Tree Road, LEATHERHEAD, KT22 8RF.
ISAAC, Mr. Michael James, BSc ACA *1988;* 259 Morley Road, DERBY, DE21 4TD.
ISAAC, Mr. Peter Edward, BSc ACA *2004;* Brook House, Brookfield Drive, Hoveringham, NOTTINGHAM, NG14 7JW.
ISAAC, Mr. Stephen John Neil, BA ACA *2005;* 8/262 Pittwater Road, MANLY, NSW 2095, AUSTRALIA.
ISAAC, Miss. Tracy Ann, BA(Hons) ACA *2010;* 10 Kerrocoar Close, Onchan, ISLE OF MAN, IM3 1JA.
ISAAC-SAUL, Mr. Isaac Benjamin, BSc ACA *2008;* F&C Reit Asset Management, 5 Wigmore Street, LONDON, W1U 1PB.
ISAACS, Mr. Anthony, BSc ACA *1992;* 32 Nightingale Road, GUILDFORD, SURREY, GU1 1ER.
ISAACS, Bryan Eric, Esq OBE FCA *1961;* 80915 Weiskopf, LA QUINTA, CA 92253, UNITED STATES. (Life Member)
•**ISAACS, Mr. David, BSc FCA** *1982;* David Isaacs & Company, 2nd Floor, Walsingham House, 1331-1337 High Road, Whetstone, LONDON N20 9HR.
ISAACS, Mrs. Joanne, BCom ACA *1987;* 136 Mill Lane, Bentley Heath, SOLIHULL, B93 8NZ.
•**ISAACS, Mr. Jonathan, BSc ACA CF** *2000;* Jeffreys Henry LLP, Finsgate, 5-7 Cranwood Street, LONDON, EC1V 9EE. See also Alfred Henry Corporate Finance Limited
ISAACS, Mrs. Kate Frances, BSc ACA *2003;* Weapon7 Ltd, 196 Tottenham Court Road, LONDON, W1T 7LQ.
ISAACS, Mr. Michael, MA FCA *1976;* 18 Rythe Road, Claygate, ESHER, KT10 9DF.
ISAACS, Mr. Michael, FCA *1957;* 2 Nicholl Road, EPPING, CM16 4HX. (Life Member)
•**ISAACS, Mr. Michael David, FCA** *1971;* (Tax Fac), Harold Everett Wreford LLP, 1st Floor, 44-46 Whitfield Street, LONDON, W1T 2RJ.
ISAACS, Mr. Michael Reuben, BA ACA *1994;* Ernst & Young, Kost Forer Gabbay & Kasierer, 3 Aminadav Street, 67067 TEL AVIV, ISRAEL.
•①**ISAACS, Mr. Roger Anthony Stanford, BSc FCA** *1992;* Milsted Langdon LLP, 1 Redcliff Street, BRISTOL, BS1 6NP.
ISAACS, Mr. Roger Edwin, BSc ACA *1984;* with PricewaterhouseCoopers, 63 rue de Villiers, 92208 NEUILLY SUR SEINE CEDEX, FRANCE.
ISAACS, Mrs. Rosalyn Sue, BSc ACA *1999;* 60 Jellicoe Gardens, STANMORE, MIDDLESEX, HA7 3NS.
ISAACS, Mr. Samuel Leonard, FCA *1950;* 21 Royston Park Road, PINNER, HA5 4AA. (Life Member)
ISAACS, Mr. Simon Lewis, BSc ACA *1993;* Enjo Elstree Business Centre, Elstree Way, BOREHAMWOOD, HERTFORDSHIRE, WD6 1RX.
ISAACS, Mr. Stanley Irvyn, FCA *1957;* 47 The Droveway, HOVE, BN3 6PR. (Life Member)
ISAACS, Mr. Timothy Keith, BSc ACA *1993;* 4 Raeburn Close, LONDON, NW11 6UE.
•**ISAACSON, Mr. Robert Eric, FCA** *1995;* with Silver Levene LLP, 37 Warren Street, LONDON, W1T 6AD.
ISAIA, Mrs. Mihaela Diana, BSc ACA *2008;* 17BGIORGI DIMITROF, PALLOURIOTISSA, 1048 NICOSIA, CYPRUS.
ISAILOVIC, Mr. Nenad, ACA *2008;* Flat 2D, Felicity Building, 38 Peel Street, SHEUNG WAN, HONG KONG ISLAND, HONG KONG SAR.
•**ISARD, Mr. Grahame Ronald Harold, MA FCA** *1982;* (Tax Fac), Grahame Isard, 129 Southgate Street, BURY ST. EDMUNDS, SUFFOLK, IP33 2AF.
ISBELL, Mr. Clive Robert, FCA *1959;* Trewint House, Chelmsford Road, Causeway End, Felsted, DUNMOW, ESSEX CM6 3LS. (Life Member)
ISBELL, Mr. George John Robert, FCA *1960;* Holme View, 3 Smugglers Close, HUNSTANTON, NORFOLK, PE36 6JU. (Life Member)
•**ISEMAN, Mr. Stephen Michael, BSc FCA** *1981;* Stephen Iseman & Co., 30 Oakridge Avenue, RADLETT, HERTFORDSHIRE, WD7 8ER.
ISEMANN, Mr. William George, BSc ACA *1998;* 2 Franche Court Road, Earlsfield, LONDON, SW17 0JU.
ISENBERG, Mr. Brett, ACA CA(SA) *2009;* 9 Clarence Crescent, SIDCUP, KENT, DA14 4DG.
ISENWATER, Mr. Harvey Victor, FCA *1971;* 3 Chartwell Road, Ainsdale, SOUTHPORT, PR8 2QP.
ISGAR, Mr. Wayne Mark, BSc ACA *2003;* 142 Ryeworth Road, Charlton Kings, CHELTENHAM, GLOUCESTERSHIRE, GL52 6LY.
ISHAK, Mr. Harris, BA ACA *2004;* CIMB Investment Bank Berhad, 10th Floor Bangunan CIMB, Jalan Semantan, Damansara Heights, 50490 KUALA LUMPUR, FEDERAL TERRITORY MALAYSIA.
•**ISHAM, Mr. Andrew Paul, BA FCA** *1999;* with Deloitte LLP, PO Box 403, Lord Coutanche House, 66-68 Esplanade, St Helier, JERSEY JE4 8WA.
ISHANI, Mrs. Marilyn Elizabeth, MA FCA *1977;* Papillon, Steels Lane, Oxshott, LEATHERHEAD, SURREY, KT22 0QH. (Life Member)
ISHANI, Mr. Rafik, BA ACA *2006;* with Deloitte LLP, 2 New Street Square, LONDON, EC4A 3BZ.
ISHAQ, Mr. Majid, BA ACA *1996;* 22 St. Mary's Avenue, Wanstead, LONDON, E11 2NP.
ISHERWOOD, Mrs. Alison Margaret, ACA *1988;* 3 College Road, Ealing, LONDON, W13 8LQ.
ISHERWOOD, Mrs. Amanda Patricia, ACA *1985;* 1 Rarewood House, Marple Road Chisworth, GLOSSOP, DERBYSHIRE, SK13 5DL.
ISHERWOOD, Mr. Anthony Vincent De Paul, FCA *1961;* 21 Hillcrest Gardens, Hinchley Wood, ESHER, SURREY, KT10 0BU. (Life Member)
ISHERWOOD, Mrs. Caroline Stephanie Elizabeth, BA ACA *1995;* Volkswagen Group UK Ltd Yeomans Drive, Blakelands, MILTON KEYNES, MK14 5AN.
ISHERWOOD, Mrs. Clarissa Amelia, BA(Hons) ACA *2002;* 3 Elmores, LOUGHTON, ESSEX, IG10 1NS.
•**ISHERWOOD, Mr. David, BSc FCA** *1996;* BDO LLP, 55 Baker Street, LONDON, W1U 7EU. See also BDO Stoy Hayward LLP
ISHERWOOD, Mr. Derek Browett, FCA *1962;* The Willows, 2A Clarendon Road North, St Annes, LYTHAM ST.ANNES, FY8 3EF. (Life Member)
ISHERWOOD, Mr. Graham, BA ACA *1995;* 09-29 River Place, 60 Havelock Road, SINGAPORE 169658, SINGAPORE.
ISHERWOOD, Mr. James, ACA *2011;* 40 Albion Terrace, London Road, READING, RG1 5BG.
ISHERWOOD, Mr. John Gordon, FCA *1964;* 25 Cornwallis Drive, SHIFNAL, SHROPSHIRE, TF11 8UB.
ISHERWOOD, Mrs. Kristina Maria, BSc ACA *1994;* 4 The Ridgeway, GUILDFORD, SURREY, GU1 2DG.
ISHERWOOD, Mr. Luke, BA ACA *2002;* Deutsche Bank AG Dubai, DIFC Branch, The Gate West Wing 3rd Floor, Dubai International Financial Centre, PO Box 504902, DUBAI UNITED ARAB EMIRATES.
ISHERWOOD, Mr. Michael, FCA *1972;* 21 Rudgwick Drive, Brandesholme, BURY, BL8 1YA.
ISHERWOOD, Mr. Michael Slater, FCA *1953;* Dean Cottage, Monsal Dale, BUXTON, SK17 8SZ. (Life Member)
ISHERWOOD, Mr. Robert Glyn, BA ACA *1994;* 208 Camberwell Grove, LONDON, SE5 8RJ.
•**ISHERWOOD, Mr. Roland John, FCA** *1973;* (Tax Fac), Isherwood & Co, 15 London Road, Stockton Heath, WARRINGTON, WA4 6SG.
ISHTIAQ, Mr. Nohman, ACA ACMA *2008;* 216-A, Street 13, Gulzar-e-Quaid, RAWALPINDI 44000, PAKISTAN.
ISICHEI, Mr. Eustace Anthony, FCA *1966;* Eami Associates Limited, P.O.Box 50439, Ikoyi, LAGOS, NIGERIA.
•**ISICHEI, Mr. Innocent Thomas, FCA** *1973;* GT3 Stallion Estate, Lobito Crescent, Wuise 2, PO Box 3337, Garki, ABUJA NIGERIA. See also Akintola Williams Adetona Isichei & Co
•**ISLAM, Mr. Abu Layes Mohammad Anwarul, MCom(Bangl) FCA** *1973;* Anwar Islam & Co, 12 Cheyne Walk, LONDON, NW4 3QJ.
ISLAM, Mr. Aminul, ACA *1980;* Merit Partners, 2nd Floor, 9-11 Cavenagh Street, DARWIN, NT 0800, AUSTRALIA. See also Ernst & Young
ISLAM, Mr. Arif-Ul, ACA *1983;* 77B Kh-Shahbaz, PH VI, Defence Housing Authority, KARACHI 75500, PAKISTAN.
ISLAM, Mr. Azizul, BSc ACA *2007;* 2 Lower City Road, Tividale, OLDBURY, WEST MIDLANDS, B69 2HA.
•**ISLAM, Mr. Farrukh Jamal, FCA** *1980;* (Tax Fac), Salman Ross, 141 Woodlands Road, ILFORD, IG1 1JR.
•**ISLAM, Mr. Iftikharul, BA ACA** *2002;* Saleha and Co, 40 Cranley Drive, ILFORD, ESSEX, IG2 6AH.
ISLAM, Mr. Kamal Ziaul, BCom FCA *1963;* Nirman International Ltd, 199 Tejgaon Industrial Area, DHAKA -1208, BANGLADESH.
ISLAM, Mr. Kazi Fauzan, ACA *1980;* 158 Wilton Road, SOUTHAMPTON, SO15 5JT.
•**ISLAM, Mr. Md Nurul, FCA** *1970;* Islam & Ahmed Ltd, 68 Seymour Grove, Old Trafford, MANCHESTER, M16 0LN.
•**ISLAM, Mr. Mohamed Azharul, FCA** *1970;* 15a Whiteknights Road, READING, RG6 7BY.
ISLAM, Mr. Mohammad Rafiqul, ACA *2009;* 5 Warminster Gardens, LONDON, SE25 4DN.
ISLAM, Mr. Mohammed Monzurul, BA(Hons) ACA *2004;* 64 Hampton Road, LONDON, E7 0NU.
ISLAM, Mr. Mohammed Tawhidul, BA ACA *2009;* 4 Martin Close, LIVERPOOL, L18 4RL.
ISLAM, Mr. Moynul, BSc ACA *2006;* 43 Eccleston Crescent, ROMFORD, RM6 4QX.
ISLAM, Mr. Rejaul, ACA *2009;* Mecom, 70 Jermyn Street, LONDON, SW1Y 6NY.
ISLAM, Mr. Sabin, BA(Hons) ACA *2004;* Moda Furniture Limited, Junction House, Junction Business Park, Rake Lane, Clifton, Swinton MANCHESTER M27 8LU.
ISLAM, Mr. Shahid Muzaffar-Ul, FCA *1977;* 76 Grove Way, ESHER, SURREY, KT10 8HW.
ISLAM, Mr. Sheikh Mohammed Shohel, ACA CPFA *2011;* with KPMG LLP, One Snowhill, Snow Hill Queensway, BIRMINGHAM, B4 6GN.
ISLAM, Miss. Tahiya, MSc BSc ACA *2011;* 81 Glenwood Gardens, ILFORD, ESSEX, IG2 6XU.
ISLAM, Mr. Zahidul, ACA *2010;* 40 Princelet Street, LONDON, E1 5LP.
ISLES, Mrs. Rachael, BSc ACA *2004;* 4 Dennison Road, Cheadle Hulme, CHEADLE, CHESHIRE, SK8 6LW.
ISMAIL, Mr. Abid, BSc ACA *2004;* 51a Coldershaw Road, West Ealing, LONDON, W13 9EA.
ISMAIL, Mr. Anwarali Hassanali, FCA *1975;* #62-8760 FOREST GROVE DRIVE, BURNABY V5A 4C9, BC, CANADA. (Life Member)
ISMAIL, Mr. Azhan, BA ACA *2006;* 5 Jalan SS19/3C, 47500 SUBANG, SELANGOR, MALAYSIA.
ISMAIL, Miss. Dahlia, BA(Hons) ACA *2001;* 21 Rufus Isaacs Road, Caversham, READING, RG4 6DD.
ISMAIL, Mr. Faisal Bin, ACA *1987;* 27 Pinggiran Golf, Saujana Resort U2, 40150 SHAH ALAM, MALAYSIA.
ISMAIL, Mr. Inayat Ali, FCA *1973;* B-1, K.D.A. Scheme No 1, KARACHI, 75350, PAKISTAN. (Life Member)
ISMAIL, Mr. Mohammed Afzal, MSc ACA *1997;* Barclays Bank Plc, Barclays Internal Audit, Floor No 10, 1 Churchill Place, LONDON, E14 5HP.
ISMAIL, Mr. Sheik Adam, ACA *2007;* Flat A4, 18F Block A, Elizabeth House, 250 Gloucester Road, CAUSEWAY BAY, HONG KONG ISLAND HONG KONG SAR.
ISMAR, Miss. Ismarita, BSc ACA *2002;* No. 6 Jalan Suasana 5/3A, Bandar Tun Hussein Onn Jalan Cheras, 43200 KUALA LUMPUR, FEDERAL TERRITORY, MALAYSIA.
ISMAY, Mr. Roderick Mark, BA FCA *1995;* 74 Silverdale Road, SHEFFIELD, S11 9JL.
ISOLA, Mr. Francis Anthony, FCA *1964;* Villa Lourdes, 21 South Barrack Road, PO Box 215, GIBRALTAR, GIBRALTAR.
ISOLA, Mr. James, BA ACA *2004;* 21 Varden Street, LONDON, E1 2AW.
ISON, Mr. David John, MA ACA *1999;* 62 Esperance Road, GLENDOWIE 1071, NEW ZEALAND.
ISON, Mr. Paul Leslie, BSc ACA *1979;* (Tax Fac), Hawkins & Co, Yorkshire House, 9-11 Stratford Road, Shirley, SOLIHULL, WEST MIDLANDS B90 3LU.
•**ISON, Mr. Peter Kevin, BA FCA** *1982;* (Tax Fac), Four Fifty Partnership Limited, 34 Boulevard, WESTON-SUPER-MARE, AVON, BS23 1NF. See also T P Lewis & Partners (WSM) Limited
ISRAEL, Mr. Benjamin, BSc ACA *2009;* 5 St. Peters Court, LONDON, NW4 2HG.
ISRAEL, Mrs. Evelyn Rachel Hazel, FCA *1977;* 22 Tenterden Drive, LONDON, NW4 1ED.
ISRAEL, Mr. Jeremy Mark, ACA *2008;* 22 Tenterden Drive, LONDON, NW4 1ED.
ISRAEL, Ms. Marion, BA(Hons) ACA *2002;* Warner Bros Entertainment UK Ltd, Warner Bros, 98 Theobalds Road, LONDON, WC1X 8WB.
•**ISRAEL, Mr. Martin Anthony Brenner, FCA** *1979;* Crowe Clark Whitehill LLP, St Bride's House, 10 Salisbury Square, LONDON, EC4Y 8EH. See also Horwath Clark Whitehill LLP and Crowe Clark Whitehill
•**ISRAEL, Mr. Michael Abraham, FCA** *1975;* Michael Israel FCA, 22 Tenterden Drive, LONDON, NW4 1ED.
ISRAEL, Mr. Michael David, ACA *2009;* 2 / 47 Johnston Street, PORT MELBOURNE, VIC 3207, AUSTRALIA.
ISRAEL, Mr. Paul, BA FCA MBA *1999;* 15 Beech Drive, LONDON, N2 9NX.
ISRAELSOHN, Mr. Joel Wulf, FCA *1995;* 60 Compayne Gardens, LONDON, NW6 3RY.
ISSA, Mr. Ali Hassan, BA ACA *1985;* Ernst & Young, Level 28, AL Attar Bus Tower, Sheikh Zayed Road, P.O. Box 9267, DUBAI UNITED ARAB EMIRATES.
•**ISSACHAROFF, Mr. Lawrence Jeffery, FCA** *1984;* 3 Queens Avenue, LONDON, N20 0HZ.
ISSADEEN, Mr. Sheikh Siraj, BSc ACA *2011;* Flat 22, Warren House, Beckford Close, Warwick Road, LONDON, W14 8TT.
ISSAEVA, Miss. Ekaterina, ACA *2008;* Apartment 227, Romney House, 47 Marsham Street, LONDON, SW1P 3DR.
ISSAIAS, Mr. Michael Demetrios, BSc FCA *1986;* 29 Granville Road, COWES, ISLE OF WIGHT, PO31 7JF.
ISSAJI, Ms. Munira, BA ACA *2003;* 1208 Sutter Creek Trail, AUSTIN, TX 78717, UNITED STATES.
ISSAR, Mr. Arun Paul Singh, BA ACA *1999;* 50 Friary Road, LONDON, N12 9PB.
ISSOTT, Mr. Christopher, BA FCA *1993;* 10 Heritage Way Oakworth, KEIGHLEY, BD22 7SW.
ISTED, Mrs. Joanne Lesley, BSc ACA *2000;* 4 Moreton End Close, HARPENDEN, AL5 2EZ.
ISTED, Mr. Richard William, BSc ACA *2000;* Astrazeneca, Horizon Place, 600 Capability Green, LUTON, LU1 3LU.

•**ISTED, Mrs. Sarah Teresa, BA ACA** *2000;* PricewaterhouseCoopers LLP, 80 Strand, LONDON, WC2R 0AF. See also PricewaterhouseCoopers
ISTRATESCU, Mr. Alexandru Bogdan, ACA MAAT *2010;* 110 Kingsley Road, MAIDSTONE, ME15 7UP.
ITALIA, Mrs. Dolly, BA ACA MBA *2000;* 17 Avenue Mansions, Finchley Road, LONDON, NW3 7AX.
ITALIA, Mr. Dynshaw, ACA *1997;* Flat 17 Avenue Mansions, Finchley Road, LONDON, NW3 7AX.
IU, Ms. Man Ying Maggie, ACA *2007;* 17/F Worldwide House 19 Des Voeux Road, CENTRAL, HONG KONG SAR.
IVANOV, Mr. Dimitre, BA(Econ) ACA *2002;* 3 Bromfield Street, LONDON, N1 0QA.
IVANOVA, Miss. Iva, MA ACA *2004;* 10 Demetri Mavrogeni Street, 8201 PAPHOS, CYPRUS.
IVANOVA, Miss. Marina, ACA *2011;* Novokosinskaya Street, Bldg 14/6, Apt 204, 111672 MOSCOW, RUSSIAN FEDERATION.
•**IVE, Mr. Stephen Leonard, FCA** *1992;* Lawfords Consulting Limited, Union House, Walton Lodge, Bridge Street, WALTON-ON-THAMES, SURREY KT12 1BT.
IVELAW-CHAPMAN, Ms. Emma Jane, LLB ACA ATII *1992;* 54 Stanhope Road, ST. ALBANS, HERTFORDSHIRE, AL1 5BL.
•**IVERMEE, Mr. Stephen George, BA ACA** *1994;* Ernst & Young Europe LLP, 1 More London Place, LONDON, SE1 2AF. See also Ernst & Young LLP
IVERS, Mr. Michael Anthony, FCA *1975;* 183 Old Limekiln Road, CHALFONT, PA 18914, UNITED STATES.
IVERSEN, Mrs. Barbara Anne, BSc FCA *1979;* The Grange, Beverley Road, North Newbald, YORK, YO43 4SQ.
IVES, Mr. David Jonathan, ACA *1979;* Flat 24, Regal House, Lensbury Avenue, Imperial Wharf, LONDON, SW6 2GZ.
•**IVES, Mr. Gary Burl, FCA** *1980;* MacIntyre Hudson LLP, Moorgate House, 201 Silbury Boulevard, MILTON KEYNES, MK9 1LZ.
IVES, Mrs. Helen Rebecca, ACA *1995;* 80 Bladindon Drive, BEXLEY, DA5 3BN.
IVESON, Miss. Ann Marie, BSc ACA *1984;* Kenbrook, Fitzroy Park, Highgate, LONDON, N6 6HT.
IVESON, Mr. Jonathan Mark, BSc ACA *1993;* 13 Cavendish Avenue, SEVENOAKS, TN13 3HP.
IVESON, Mr. Thomas Michael, BA ACA *1982;* Glencoe, Summerbridge, HARROGATE, NORTH YORKSHIRE, HG3 4HR.
IVESON, Mrs. Victoria Catherine, ACA *1998;* Redwood House, Pocklington Road, Huggate, YORK, YO42 1YJ.
IVEY, Mrs. Annemarie, BSc ACA *1990;* 1 Dylan Close, Hawarden, DEESIDE, CH5 3TT.
IVEY, Ms. Elizabeth Clare, BSc ACA *1992;* 75 The Shearers, BISHOP'S STORTFORD, CM23 4AZ.
IVEY, Mr. Gavin Edward, BSc ACA *2001;* 4 Hunters Close, Bovingdon, HEMEL HEMPSTEAD, HERTFORDSHIRE, HP3 0NF.
IVEY, Mr. Grahame, BA ACA *1985;* 48 Grosvenor Street, LONDON, W1K 3HW.
IVEY, Mrs. Laura Nell, BCom ACA *1980;* Furzehill House, 46 Preston Down Road, PAIGNTON, DEVON, TQ3 2RN.
IVEY, Mr. Rodney Guy, ACA *1982;* The Boatshed, Robert Owen Communities Unit C, Dart Marine Park Steamer Quay Road, TOTNES, DEVON, TQ9 5AL.
IVIMEY-COOK, Mr. Richard Charles, BSc FCA *1989;* 10 The Chestnuts, ABINGDON, OX14 3YN.
IVISON, Mr. David Brian, FCA *1967;* 8 Manor Road, HARTLEPOOL, CLEVELAND, TS26 0EH.
IVISON, Miss. Helen Rachael, BA ACA *2007;* 9 Egglestone Drive, Eaglescliffe, STOCKTON-ON-TEES, TS16 0GF.
IVISON, Mr. Kenneth, FCA *1955;* Flat 4 Devington Court, Cliff Road, FALMOUTH, TR11 4PD. (Life Member)
•**IVORY, Mr. Gregory, FCA** *1978;* G P Ivory & Co Ltd, 344 Croydon Road, BECKENHAM, KENT, BR3 4EX.
IVORY, Miss. Michele, BSc ACA ATII *2002;* La Niche 7 Le Clos Du Bourg, La Grande Route de la Cote St. Clement, JERSEY, JE2 6SL.
IWANAGA, Ms. Ayako, BSc ACA *1997;* Via Belvedere 8-1, 50019 SESTO FIORENTINO, ITALY.
IWASAKI, Ms. Jo Kiyoko, MSc BSc ACA *2002;* with ICAEW, Chartered Accountants' Hall, Moorgate Place, LONDON, EC2P 2BJ.
IXER, Mr. Christopher Rowe, FCA *1967;* C/O Mark Stretch, 90 High Street, EVESHAM, WORCESTERSHIRE, WR11 4EU. (Life Member)
IXER, Mr. Dean, BSc ACA *2005;* 44/20 Eve Street, ERSKINEVILLE, NSW 2043, AUSTRALIA.
IYADURAI, Mr. Gnana Chandran, FCA *1984;* MACC, Block D6 Complex D, Federal Govt. Admin Centre, 62002 PUTRAJAYA, WILAYAH PERSEKUTUAN, MALAYSIA.
IYENGAR, Mr. Carl Raju, BCom ACA *1992;* Merrill Lynch Financial Centre, 2 King Edward Street, LONDON, EC1A 1HQ.
•**IYENGAR, Mr. Gopal Sheshadri, ACA** *1985;* Gopal & Co, 349 Hagley Rd, Edgbaston, BIRMINGHAM, B17 8DL.
IYENGAR, Mr. Narahari Ranga, MSc ACA *1992;* 2/3 Edward Road, BANGALORE 560052, INDIA.
IYENGAR, Mr. Sridar Arvamudhan, FCA *1973;* 85 Fair Oaks Lane, ATHERTON, CA 94027, UNITED STATES.
IYER, Ms. Meenakshi, BSc ACA *2007;* Flat 27 Nova Building, 3 Newton Place, LONDON, E14 3TT.
IYER, Mr. Nigel Krishna, BSc ACA *1989;* Ansgar Sorlies Vei 53, 0576 OSLO, NORWAY.
IYER, Mr. Ramakrishna Raghunatha, FCA *1971;* 13 Ramsbury Drive, Earley, READING, RG6 7RT.
IYER, Mr. Shanker, OBE FCA *1974;* Shanker Iyer & Co, 3 Phillip Street, Unit 18-00, Commerce Point, SINGAPORE 048693, SINGAPORE.
IYER, Mr. Sunder, FCA *1974;* 2 John Jay Place, RYE, NY 10580, UNITED STATES.
IYER, Mr. Sunil, ACA *2008;* Flat 48, 1 Chepstow Place, LONDON, W2 4TE.
IZABY-WHITE, Mr. William Michael, FCA *1964;* Applecroft Wootton Courtenay, MINEHEAD, SOMERSET, TA24 8RD. (Life Member)
•**IZOD, Mr. Adrian Howard, BA FCA** *1986;* (Tax Fac), Izod Bassett, 105 High Street, Needham Market, IPSWICH, IP6 8DQ.
•**IZQUIERDO, Mrs. Michaela Faith Sarah, BA FCA** *1996;* with Wilkins Kennedy, Gladstone House, 77-79 High Street, EGHAM, TW20 9HY.
IZZA, Mrs. Gillian Anne, BA ACA *1990;* (Tax Fac), with PricewaterhouseCoopers LLP, The Atrium, 1 Harefield Road, UXBRIDGE, UB8 1EX.
IZZA, Mr. Michael Donald McCartney, BA FCA *1987;* with ICAEW, Chartered Accountants' Hall, Moorgate Place, LONDON, EC2P 2BJ.
IZZARD, Mr. James William Francis, MMath ACA *2010;* 30 Edwin Avenue, Guiseley, LEEDS, LS20 8QJ.
IZZARD, Mr. Raymond John, FCA *1971;* 95 North Franklin Road, INDIANAPOLIS, IN 46219, UNITED STATES. (Life Member)
IZZO, Mrs. Alison Louise, BA ACA *1993;* 11 Oakdale Road, WEYBRIDGE, SURREY, KT13 8EJ.
IZZO, Mrs. Alison Sara, BA ACA *1992;* Berkley Homes (Oxford & Chiltern) Ltd, Berkley House, Abingdon Science Park, Barton Lane, ABINGDON, OXFORDSHIRE OX14 3NB.
J'AFARI-PAK, Mrs. Lindsay Clare, BA ACA *1998;* (Tax Fac), Flat J, 66 St. John Street, LONDON, EC1M 4DT.
JAAFAR, Miss. Azizah Binti Mohd, FCA *1970;* 15 Cemerlang Heights, Jalan TC 2B/3A, 53100 GOMBAK, SELANGOR, MALAYSIA. (Life Member)
JABAR, Mr. Khalil Abdul, BSc ACA *1995;* Karvela Consulting Limited 2nd Floor, 145-157 St John Street, LONDON, EC1V 4PY.
JABBOUR, Miss. Dominique Mary Catherine, BSc ACA *1989;* 37 Gloucester Road, HAMPTON, TW12 2UQ.
JABEEN, Miss. Nazish Akram, ACA *2010;* 14 Blenheim Crescent, LUTON, LU3 1HA.
JABLONOWSKI, Mr. Alexander David, BA ACA *1999;* 15 Sylvandale, WELWYN GARDEN CITY, HERTFORDSHIRE, AL7 2HP.
JABLONOWSKI, Mr. Richard Andrew, BA ACA *1999;* H S B C Private Bank Ltd, 78 St. James's Street, LONDON, SW1A 1JB.
JACCARINI, Mr. Edward Anthony, MBA BA FCA AMCT *1990;* Mediterranean Bank PLC, 10 St Barbara Bastion, VALLETTA VLT 1000, MALTA.
JACK, Mr. Cameron James, MA ACA *2000;* Copper Beeches West Hill, Dormans Park, EAST GRINSTEAD, WEST SUSSEX, RH19 2ND.
JACK, Mr. David Barry, FCA *1960;* Jasmine, Tixall Mews, Tixall, STAFFORD, ST18 0XT. (Life Member)
JACK, Mr. David William Ralph, FCA *1975;* 24 rue Principale, L-5240 SANDWEILER, LUXEMBOURG.
JACK, Mrs. Farah, BSc ACA CTA *1991;* (Tax Fac), 59 Barrow Road, Quorn, LOUGHBOROUGH, LE12 8DH.
JACK, Miss. Fiona Caroline, BSc ACA *2001;* 18 The Hall Close, Dunchurch, RUGBY, WARWICKSHIRE, CV22 6NP.
JACK, Mr. James, BSc ACA *1997;* Lower Farm, Icomb, CHELTENHAM, GLOUCESTERSHIRE, GL54 1JG.
JACK, Mr. John William, BSc FCA *1992;* 47 Canonbury Park North, LONDON, N1 2JU.
JACK, Miss. Nicola, BSc(Hons) ACA *2009;* Flat 28 Groveside Court, 4 Lombard Road, LONDON, SW11 3RQ.
JACK, Mr. Paul William Francis, BA ACA *2009;* 27 Hart Road, Byfleet, WEST BYFLEET, KT14 7NH.
JACK, Mr. Robert, MBE FCA *1957;* Woodville, 14 Treesdale Close, Birkdale, SOUTHPORT, MERSEYSIDE, PR8 2EL. (Life Member)
JACK, Mr. Simon, MA(Hons) ACA MBA *2001;* 11 Maidencraig Crescent, EDINBURGH, EH4 2BH.
JACK, Mr. Stephen Andrew, BA ACA *1984;* 1 Hunter Road, West Wimbledon, LONDON, SW20 8NZ.
•①**JACK, Mr. Thomas Andrew, BA ACA MABRP** *1999;* Ernst & Young LLP, 100 Barbirolli Square, MANCHESTER, M2 3EY. See also Ernst & Young Europe LLP
JACK, Mr. Thomas Edward, BSc FCA FCT *1989;* Kraft Foods Finance Europe AG, Chollerstrasse 4, 6301 ZUG, SWITZERLAND.
JACKAMAN, Mr. Paul Alan, BSc ACA *1998;* 10 Warren Road, SIDCUP, DA14 4NH.
JACKETS, Miss. Mary Ann, BA ACA *1994;* The Coach House, 235 Upper Richmond Road, LONDON, SW15 6SN.
JACKIEWICZ, Miss. Michelle Anne, ACA *2009;* 3 Wordsworth Mead, REDHILL, RH1 1AH.
JACKLIN, Mr. Benjamin Mark, BSc ACA *2006;* 144c Putney Bridge Road, LONDON, SW15 2NQ.
JACKLIN, Mr. Bernard Charles, FCA *1969;* Mole Cottage, Carrside, Great Ouseburn, YORK, YO26 9RW.
JACKLIN, Mr. John Nicholas, BCom FCA *1964;* Gorse Barn, Rock Lane, Tockholes, DARWEN, BB3 0LX. (Life Member)
JACKLIN, Mrs. Susan Elizabeth, BSc ACA *1999;* 78 Lady Acre Close, LYMM, CHESHIRE, WA13 0SR.
JACKLIN, Mr. Tony Rowson, FCA *1966;* 4 Summerfields, Kings Road, CLEETHORPES, SOUTH HUMBERSIDE, DN35 0AF. (Life Member)
JACKMAN, Mr. Andrew Alfred, BSc FCA *1982;* 23 Blenheim Avenue, SOUTHAMPTON, SO17 1DW.
JACKMAN, Mrs. Ann Veronica, BA ACA *1981;* 6 Brookside Court, CRANBURY, NJ 08512, UNITED STATES.
JACKMAN, Mrs. Bernardine, ACA *1985;* 27 Chelwood Gardens, Kew, RICHMOND, TW9 4JG.
JACKMAN, Mr. Christopher John, MA FCA *1963;* 8 St James Lane, TURRAMURRA, NSW 2074, AUSTRALIA. (Life Member)
•**JACKMAN, Mr. John Frederick, FCA** *1965;* J.F. Jackman, Tilthams Farm, Tilthams Corner Road, GODALMING, GU7 3DE.
•**JACKMAN, Mr. Keith, BA FCA CF** *1978;* Smith & Williamson Ltd, 25 Moorgate, LONDON, EC2R 6AY. See also Nexia Audit Limited
JACKS, Mr. David Michael, BSc ACA *1987;* 174 Meadvale Road, Ealing, LONDON, W5 1LT.
JACKS, Mr. Graham Thomas, BA ACA *1983;* RMD Kwikform Ltd, Brickyard Road, Aldridge, WALSALL, WS9 8BW.
JACKS, Mrs. Sharon Ann, BSc ACA *1986;* 502 Streetsbrook Road, SOLIHULL, WEST MIDLANDS, B91 1RH.
JACKSON, Mr. Alan Crispin, FCA *1969;* Butler Jackson Partners LLP, Brookfield House, Green Lane, Ivinghoe, LEIGHTON BUZZARD, BEDFORDSHIRE LU7 9ES.
JACKSON, Mr. Alan Frederick, BSS FCA *1986;* 11 Nicholii Loop, JERRABOMBERRA, NSW 2619, AUSTRALIA.
•**JACKSON, Mr. Alan Keith, FCA** *1977;* Alan K. Jackson, 63 Church Hill Road, East Barnet, BARNET, EN4 8SY.
JACKSON, Mr. Alan Raymond, FCA *1966;* 56 London Road North, Poynton, STOCKPORT, SK12 1BY. (Life Member)
JACKSON, Mr. Albert Wallace, FCA *1954;* 10 Draycott Avenue, HORNSEA, HU18 1HH. (Life Member)
JACKSON, Mr. Alexander Ridley Mackwood, BSc(Hons) ACA *2002;* 107a Sulgrave Road, LONDON, W6 7QH.
JACKSON, Miss. Alison Margaret, BA(Hons) ACA *2003;* 21 Bassano Street, LONDON, SE22 8RU.
JACKSON, Mr. Alwyn Dudley, FCA *1961;* 'Chez Tigger', Liversenq, 12270 LUNAC, FRANCE. (Life Member)
JACKSON, Miss. Andrea Suzanne, BA ACA *1995;* The Mistal, Pool Crook Farm Arthington Lane, Pool in Wharfedale, OTLEY, WEST YORKSHIRE, LS21 1NH.
JACKSON, Mr. Andrew, ACA CA(AUS) *2008;* 65 Walsingham Road, HOVE, EAST SUSSEX, BN3 4FE.
JACKSON, Mr. Andrew, BSc ACA *1993;* 15 Cumberland Avenue, EMSWORTH, PO10 7UH.
JACKSON, Mr. Andrew, BA ACA *1999;* 49 Banquo Approach, Heathcote, WARWICK, CV34 6GB.
JACKSON, Mr. Andrew Colin, ACA *1988;* 8 Coombe Rise, Shenfield, BRENTWOOD, CM15 8JJ.
JACKSON, Mr. Andrew John, BA ACA *1993;* 54 Popes Grove, Strawberry Hill, TWICKENHAM, TW1 4JY.
JACKSON, Mr. Andrew Kenneth Peter, FCA *1966;* Hogshatch, Poundsbridge, Penshurst, TONBRIDGE, TN11 8AS. (Life Member)
JACKSON, Mr. Andrew Paul, ACA *2011;* Overdale, Middleham Road, LEYBURN, NORTH YORKSHIRE, DL8 5EY.
•**JACKSON, Mr. Andrew Philip, FCA** *1989;* Haywood & Co., 24-26 Mansfield Road, ROTHERHAM, S60 2DR.
JACKSON, Mr. Andrew Richard, BA FCA *1995;* with National Audit Office, 1st Floor, 89 Sandyford Road, NEWCASTLE UPON TYNE, NE1 8HW.
JACKSON, Mr. Andrew Robert, BSc ACA *1982;* E A R T H Co Unit 5, The Dock, ELY, CAMBRIDGESHIRE, CB7 4GS.
JACKSON, Mr. Andrew Stuart, BSc ACA *1994;* Old Bakehouse, Parbrook, GLASTONBURY, SOMERSET, BA6 8PD.
JACKSON, Mr. Andrew Terrence John, BA ACA *1996;* 13 Beresford Road, LONDON, N2 8AT.
•**JACKSON, Mr. Andrew Thomas Peter, BSc FCA** *1992;* KPMG Al Fozan & Al Sadhan, 13th Floor, Al Subeaei Towers, King Abdulaziz Street, PO Box 4803, AL KHOBAR 31952 SAUDI ARABIA. See also KPMG Europe LLP
JACKSON, Mr. Andrew Timothy, MA ACA *1992;* Flat 5, Cedar Court, Colney Hatch Lane, Muswell Lane, LONDON, N10 1EE.
JACKSON, Mrs. Anne Elizabeth, ACA *2003;* 43 The Fairways Low Utley, KEIGHLEY, WEST YORKSHIRE, BD20 6UJ.
•**JACKSON, Mr. Anthony Coburn, FCA** *1969;* (Tax Fac), F.W. Smith Riches & Co, 15 Whitehall, LONDON, SW1A 2DD.
•**JACKSON, Mr. Anthony David, FCA** *1976;* BTG Tax, 19 George Road, Edgbaston, BIRMINGHAM, B15 1NU.
JACKSON, Mr. Anthony Grahame, FCA *1962;* 8 Eton Walk, Shoeburyness, SOUTHEND-ON-SEA, SS3 8TB. (Life Member)
JACKSON, Mr. Anthony Maurice, BA FCA *1966;* 26 Willifield Way, LONDON, NW11 7XT.
JACKSON, Mr. Anthony Thomas, FCA *1972;* Chelwood, Green Lane, South Chailey, LEWES, BN8 4BT.
JACKSON, Mr. Arthur Kenneth, FCA *1949;* c/o Mr R Jackson, 14 Higherfield, Langho, BLACKBURN, BB6 8HQ. (Life Member)
JACKSON, Mrs. Assunta Luisa, BA ACA *2000;* Flat E, 1 Parkland Drive, DISCOVERY BAY, NEW TERRITORIES, HONG KONG SAR.
JACKSON, Mr. Barry, BSc ACA *2006;* 3 Old Lane, Bramhope, LEEDS, LS16 9AY.
JACKSON, Mr. Barry Kingsley, FCA *1966;* 31 Reayrt Carnane, Tromode, ISLE OF MAN, IM2 5LN.
JACKSON, Mr. Barry Neville, BA ACA *2005;* 78 Stickleback Road, CALNE, WILTSHIRE, SN11 9RB.
JACKSON, Mr. Ben, BA ACA *2003;* 53 Lakeside Drive, Chobham, WOKING, SURREY, GU24 8BD.
JACKSON, Mr. Ben, ACA *2009;* Flat 22 Academy Court, 34 Glengall Road, LONDON, NW6 7FB.
•**JACKSON, Mr. Brian, BA FCA** *1980;* Warnford Court, 29 Throgmorton Street, LONDON, SE17 2JX.
JACKSON, Mr. Brian, BA ACA *1998;* 46 Whirlow Lane, SHEFFIELD, S11 9QF.
JACKSON, Mr. Brian David, BA ACA *1979;* 29 Half Moon Lane, LONDON, SE24 9JX.
•**JACKSON, Mr. Brian Leslie, FCA** *1968;* Torringtons Limited, Hillside House, 2-6 Friern Park, North Finchley, LONDON, N12 9FB.
JACKSON, Mr. Brian Malcolm, FCA *1954;* 15 Clarkson Court, Ipswich Road, WOODBRIDGE, SUFFOLK, IP12 4BF. (Life Member)
JACKSON, Ms. Bridget, ACA *2007;* Flat 11 Parliament Court, Parliament Hill, LONDON, NW3 2TS.
JACKSON, Mr. Carl, BA FCA *1995;* 35 Longcroft Gardens, WELWYN GARDEN CITY, HERTFORDSHIRE, AL8 6JR.
•①**JACKSON, Mr. Carl Stuart, BSc ACA** *1989;* RSM Tenon Limited, Highfield Court, Tollgate, Chandler's Ford, EASTLEIGH, HAMPSHIRE SO53 3TY. See also Premier Strategies Limited
JACKSON, Miss. Carly, ACA *2007;* 22 Kingfisher House, Juniper Drive, LONDON, SW18 1TX.
JACKSON, Ms. Carol Ann, MA ACA *1981;* Refugee Council, 240-250 Ferndale Road, LONDON, SW9 8BB.

JACKSON, Miss. Carol Ann, MA FCA *1990;* 8 Beldesert Close, HENLEY-IN-ARDEN, WARWICKSHIRE, B95 5JU.
JACKSON, Mrs. Carole Anne, BA ACA *2005;* 13 Cranborne Avenue, SURBITON, KT6 7JP.
JACKSON, Mrs. Caroline Fay, BA(Hons) ACA *2000;* 13 Redhoods Way East, LETCHWORTH GARDEN CITY, HERTFORDSHIRE, SG6 4DF.
JACKSON, Mrs. Caroline Louise, BCom ACA ATII *2001;* 17 Brockenhurst Road, BRACKNELL, BERKSHIRE, RG12 9FJ.
JACKSON, Mrs. Catharine Ann, ACA *1985;* 18 Newtown, Kelvedon, COLCHESTER, CO5 9PB.
JACKSON, Mrs. Catherine Anne, BCom ACA *1989;* 6 Welbeck Close, HALESOWEN, B62 8PX.
•JACKSON, Mr. Christopher Andrew, BA FCA *1997;* Mazars LLP, The Pinnacle, 160 Midsummer Boulevard, MILTON KEYNES, MK9 1FF.
JACKSON, Mr. Christopher David, BA FCA *1980;* with ICAEW, Chartered Accountants' Hall, Moorgate Place, LONDON, EC2P 2BJ.
JACKSON, Mr. Christopher Francis, ACA *2007;* K P M G, 1 The Embankment, LEEDS, LS1 4DW.
JACKSON, Mr. Christopher Henry, BA ACA *1993;* 63b Queens Road, ALTON, HAMPSHIRE, GU34 1JG.
•JACKSON, Mr. Christopher John, BA ACA *1994;* PricewaterhouseCoopers LLP, 1 Embankment Place, LONDON, WC2N 6RH. See also PricewaterhouseCoopers
JACKSON, Mr. Christopher John, BSc ACA *2010;* with Maxwells, 4 King Square, BRIDGWATER, SOMERSET, TA6 3YF.
JACKSON, Mr. Christopher Joseph, BSocSc ACA *2000;* Eastwood Cottage Milken Lane, Far Hill Ashover, CHESTERFIELD, DERBYSHIRE, S45 0BA.
•JACKSON, Mr. Christopher Keith, BSc FCA *1994;* MacIntyre Hudson LLP, Euro House, 1394 High Road, Whetstone, LONDON, N20 9YZ.
•JACKSON, Mr. Christopher Nigel, BSc FCA *1981;* De La Wyche Baker Limited, 7 St. Petersgate, STOCKPORT, CHESHIRE, SK1 1EB.
JACKSON, Mrs. Claire Charlotte, ACA *2004;* Sagars Llp Gresham House, 5-7 St. Pauls Street, LEEDS, LS1 2JG.
JACKSON, Mrs. Clare, MA ACA *2002;* 40 Sheldon Avenue, LONDON, N6 4JR.
JACKSON, Mr. Clive, FCA *1966;* 46 Digswell Rise, WELWYN GARDEN CITY, AL8 7PW. (Life Member)
JACKSON, Mrs. Colette Teresa, BSc ACA *1999;* Heathview, 15 Gloucester Road, Thornbury, BRISTOL, BS35 1DJ.
JACKSON, Mr. Colin Stuart, ACA *2002;* Tiffany & Co, 25 Old Bond Street, LONDON, W1S 4QB.
JACKSON, Mr. Daniel Barry, BA(Hons) ACA *2002;* 284 Carlton Road, WORKSOP, NOTTINGHAMSHIRE, S81 7LL.
•JACKSON, Mr. Daniel Scott, ACA *2007;* Blythe Squires Wilson, 1-2 Vernon Street, DERBY, DE1 1FR.
•JACKSON, Mr. Daniel Thomas, BA ACA CF *1999;* Langtons, The Plaza, 100 Old Hall Street, LIVERPOOL, L3 9QJ.
JACKSON, Mr. Danny Robert, FCA *1975;* 10 Greville Lodge, Broadhurst Avenue, EDGWARE, HA8 8TL.
JACKSON, Mr. David, BA ACA *1987;* Flat 1, 8 Wharfedale Street, LONDON, SW10 9AL.
JACKSON, Mr. David, MSc ACA *1986;* Institute Cottage, Church Road, Great Milton, OXFORD, OX44 7PD.
JACKSON, Mr. David, FCA *1961;* 141 Argyle Road, Ealing, LONDON, W13 0DB. (Life Member)
JACKSON, Mr. David Andrew, BA ACA *1996;* Blue Crest Capital Management Ltd, 40 Grosvenor Place, LONDON, SW1X 7AW.
JACKSON, Mr. David Charles, BSc FCA CTA *1977;* (Tax Fac), Whispers, Blackdown Avenue, WOKING, SURREY, GU22 8QH.
JACKSON, Mr. David Cooper, MA FCA *1973;* Melverley, 15 Brownswood Road, BEACONSFIELD, HP9 2NU.
JACKSON, Mr. David Gilfoy, FCA *1963;* Lynwood, 19 Station Road, Scalby, SCARBOROUGH, YO13 0PU.
JACKSON, Mr. David James, FCA MCT *1968;* 82 Horseshoe Lane, Bromley Cross, BOLTON, BL7 9RR. (Life Member)
JACKSON, Mr. David James, ACA *1980;* 10 Stone Rings Close, HARROGATE, NORTH YORKSHIRE, HG2 9HZ.
JACKSON, Mr. David John, FCA *1955;* 28 Castle Crescent, St. Briavels, LYDNEY, GL15 6UA. (Life Member)
JACKSON, Mr. David Martin, BSc FCA *1973;* 10 Cranford Avenue, EXMOUTH, EX8 2HT.
JACKSON, Mr. David Robert, BSc ACA *2007;* 21/1-11 Murray Street, WATERLOO, NSW 2017, AUSTRALIA.
JACKSON, Mr. David Samuel, BSc ACA *2005;* 7 Wood Road, Ashurst, SOUTHAMPTON, SO40 7BD.
JACKSON, Mr. David Thomas, ACA *1989;* 67 Codmore Crescent, CHESHAM, BUCKINGHAMSHIRE, HP5 3LZ.
JACKSON, Mr. David William, BSc ACA *2000;* with KPMG LLP, 15 Canada Square, LONDON, E14 5GL.
JACKSON, Mrs. Denise Angela, BSc ACA *1992;* Unit 2, 257 Boundary Street, SPRING HILL, QLD 4000, AUSTRALIA.
JACKSON, Mr. Donald Frederick, FCA *1964;* 2 Swinburn Court, Masham, RIPON, HG4 4HJ.
JACKSON, Mr. Duncan John, MSc BA ACA *1999;* 11 Clifton Holm, Delph, OLDHAM, OL3 5EZ.
JACKSON, Mr. Edward, ACA *2011;* 2b Eliot Park, Lewisham, LONDON, SE13 7EG.
JACKSON, Mr. Edward George, BA ACA *1978;* Pennon Group Plc, Peninsula House, Rydon Lane, EXETER, EX2 7HR.
JACKSON, Mr. Edward Norman, FCA *1974;* Spreckley Ltd, 79 Arnold Road, NOTTINGHAM, NG6 0EZ.
JACKSON, Mr. Edward Paul, BSc ACA CPA *1995;* with PricewaterhouseCoopers LLP, 488 Almaden Boulevard, SAN JOSE, CA 95110, UNITED STATES.
JACKSON, Mr. Edward Peter, BSc FCA *1964;* 17 Hartley Road, Birkdale, SOUTHPORT, PR8 4SA. (Life Member)
JACKSON, Mr. Edward Rollo, ACA *2008;* 7 Mount Ararat Road, RICHMOND, TW10 6PQ.
JACKSON, Mrs. Elaine Margaret, BSc ACA *1997;* 33 Sedburgh Close, SALE, M33 5SR.
JACKSON, Mrs. Eleanor, FCA *1961;* 2 Admiral's Croft, Wellington Street West, The Anchorage, Hull Marina, HULL, HU1 2DR. (Life Member)
JACKSON, Mrs. Elizabeth Warmington, BA ACA *1990;* 10 Stone Rings Close, HARROGATE, NORTH YORKSHIRE, HG2 9HZ.
JACKSON, Mrs. Ellaine, BSc FCA *1980;* 98 Grimshaw Lane, ORMSKIRK, LANCASHIRE, L39 1PE.
JACKSON, Mrs. Emma Louise, BSc ACA *1996;* 43 Alesmore Meadow, LICHFIELD, STAFFORDSHIRE, WS13 8FD.
JACKSON, Mr. Eric Arthur, FCA FRSA *1979;* The Garden House, Melton Road, Rearsby, LEICESTER, LE7 4YS.
JACKSON, Mrs. Fiona Kathryn, BA ACA *1997;* 1 Kingsbury Close, Appleton, WARRINGTON, WA4 5FF.
JACKSON, Miss. Fionnuala Jane, BA ACA *2006;* Ground Floor, 15 Cromwell Grove, LONDON, W6 7RQ.
JACKSON, The Venerable Frances Anne, MA FCA *1976;* The Rectory, Llancarfan, BARRY, SOUTH GLAMORGAN, CF62 3AJ.
JACKSON, Mr. Frederick Edward Hugh, FCA *1962;* 80 Lawn Road, LONDON, NW3 2XB.
•JACKSON, Mr. Gary, FCA *1980;* Arram Berlyn Gardner, 30 City Road, LONDON, EC1Y 2AB. See also ABG Business Support Services Ltd
•JACKSON, Mr. Gary Joseph, FCA *1991;* G J Jackson Accountants Limited, 5 Victoria Avenue, BISHOP AUCKLAND, COUNTY DURHAM, DL14 7JH.
JACKSON, Mr. Gavin David, BA ACA *1994;* Orchard Lodge, Pinfold Lane, Fishlake, DONCASTER, SOUTH YORKSHIRE, DN7 5JT.
JACKSON, Mr. Geoffrey Harold, FCA *1973;* Dyers, Willow Vale, FROME, BA11 1BG. (Life Member)
JACKSON, Mr. Geoffrey Sear, FCA *1960;* Quartier Grand Combe, 30200 VENEJAN, FRANCE. (Life Member)
JACKSON, Mrs. Gillian Lesley, BA ACA *1986;* 87 Beswick Gardens, RUGBY, CV22 7PR.
JACKSON, Mr. Glenn Anthony, ACA *2008;* Flat A, 37 Avenell Road, LONDON, N5 1DN.
JACKSON, Mr. Graham Mark, ACA *1989;* 88 Popham Road, SCARSDALE, NY 10583, UNITED STATES.
JACKSON, Mr. Graham Stewart, BA ACA *2009;* 7 Long Royd Drive, Baildon, SHIPLEY, BD17 6TS.
•JACKSON, Mr. Hartley Rowland, FCA DChA *1975;* Jackson & Jackson Accountants Limited, 33 Chingford Mount Road, LONDON, E4 8LU.
JACKSON, Miss. Hazel, BSc ACA *1991;* Wirral Borough Council, Treasury Building, Cleveland Street, BIRKENHEAD, MERSEYSIDE, CH41 6ND.
JACKSON, Miss. Helen Louise, MA BA ACA *2009;* Flat 6, 99a Westminster Bridge Road, LONDON, SE1 7HR.
•JACKSON, Miss. Helen Margaret, BA ACA *1999;* Jackson Stephen LLP, James House, Stonecross Business Park, 5 Yew Tree Way, Golborne, WARRINGTON CHESHIRE WA3 3JD.
JACKSON, Miss. Helen Mary, BSc ACA *2005;* Flat 34 Wimbledon Close, The Downs, LONDON, SW20 8HL.
JACKSON, Mr. Henry, FCA *1957;* 36 Fairholme Gardens, LONDON, N3 3EB. (Life Member)
JACKSON, Mr. Howard, BSc FCA *1986;* 40 Barham Avenue, Elstree, BOREHAMWOOD, WD6 3PN.
•JACKSON, Mr. Hugh, BA ACA *1988;* (Tax Fac), Jacksons, The Old Bakehouse, Course Road, ASCOT, SL5 7HL.
JACKSON, Mr. Ian, BA ACA *1992;* 24 Clandon Avenue, EGHAM, TW20 8LP.
JACKSON, Mr. Ian, BSc(Hons) ACA *2004;* 87 Park Road, Wath-upon-Dearne, ROTHERHAM, SOUTH YORKSHIRE, S63 7LE.
JACKSON, Mr. Ian Clive, MA ACA *1988;* 88 Woodlands Park Road, Bournville, BIRMINGHAM, B30 1RX.
JACKSON, Mr. Ian Ronald, ACA *1982;* Broomfield View, 76 High Street, Stonebroom, ALFRETON, DE55 6JY.
JACKSON, Mr. Ian Stewart, BA ACA *1997;* 58 Elm Park Road, Finchley, LONDON, N3 1EB.
JACKSON, Mr. Ian Walter, FCA *1969;* 57 Armistead Way, Cranage, CREWE, CW4 8FE.
•JACKSON, Mrs. Jacqueline, BA FCA *2000;* 9 Thomas Road, Balderton, NEWARK, NOTTINGHAMSHIRE, NG24 3FU.
JACKSON, Mr. James, BA(Hons) ACA *2011;* Fraerwood, Long Grove, Upper Bucklebury, READING, RG7 6QS.
•JACKSON, Mr. James Gordon, LLB FCA *1964;* (Tax Fac), James Jackson & Co., Barberry Cottage, Waterhouse Lane, Kingswood, TADWORTH, KT20 6DT.
JACKSON, Mr. James Ian, MA ACA *1995;* Cannon Dell, West Tisted, ALRESFORD, HAMPSHIRE, SO24 0HH.
JACKSON, Mr. James Lee, BSc ACA *1998;* 3rd Floor Ambler Mill, Cape Street, BRADFORD, BD1 4RP.
JACKSON, Mr. James Neal Brindley, BA ACA *2007;* Bockenwood, Private Road, Balcombe, HAYWARDS HEATH, RH17 6PS.
JACKSON, Mrs. Jane Louise, BSc ACA *1998;* 1 Woodpack Avenue, Whickham, NEWCASTLE UPON TYNE, NE16 5YX.
JACKSON, Miss. Jane Tamsin Kate, BSc(Hons) ACA *2001;* 11 Moorfield Close, Penwortham, PRESTON, LANCASHIRE, PR1 0NW.
JACKSON, Miss. Jennifer Marie, BSc ACA *1999;* 121 How Wood, Park Street, ST. ALBANS, HERTFORDSHIRE, AL2 2SA.
•JACKSON, Mr. Jeremy Richard, BA ACA CTA *1985;* AGM Partners LLP, Suite 9, Innovation Centre, 23 Cambridge Science Park, CAMBRIDGE, CB4 0EY.
JACKSON, Miss. Joan Shirley Margaret, BSc ACA *1980;* 20 Eastmont Road, Hinchley Wood, ESHER, KT10 9AZ.
JACKSON, Mr. John Andrew, BSc FCA *1975;* Flat 7, Hill Court, 34 Highgate West Hill, LONDON, N6 6NJ.
JACKSON, Mr. John Anthony, BSc ACA FCT *1985;* Clydesdale Bank Exchange, Weir Group Plc, 20 Waterloo Street, GLASGOW, G2 6DB.
JACKSON, Mr. John Edward, BA FCA *1977;* 3 Potomac Mews, Clumber Road East, The Park, NOTTINGHAM, NG7 1LF.
•JACKSON, Mr. John Haydon, FCA *1968;* Old Mill Accountancy LLP, The Old Mill, Park Road, SHEPTON MALLET, SOMERSET, BA4 5BS. See also Old Mill Audit LLP
JACKSON, Mr. John Paul, BSc ACA *1991;* Brady Corporation Ltd, Wildmere Industrial Estate, BANBURY, OXFORDSHIRE, OX16 3JU.
JACKSON, Mr. John Robert, BA ACA *1995;* Ivy Lodge, Main Road, Pentrich, RIPLEY, DE5 3RE.
•JACKSON, Mr. John Stephen, FCA *1964;* (Tax Fac), Jackson Stephen LLP, James House, Stonecross Business Park, 5 Yew Tree Way, Golborne, WARRINGTON CHESHIRE WA3 3JD.
JACKSON, Mr. Jonathan George, BSc ACA *1993;* Zurich Financial Services UK Life Centre, Station Road, SWINDON, SN1 1EL.
JACKSON, Ms. Josephine Karinann, BA ACA *1998;* Grant Thornton LLP, Grant Thornton House, 22 Melton Street, LONDON, NW1 2EP.
JACKSON, Mrs. Julie Ann, BSc ACA *1989;* 19 Whale Cove, Red Beach, OREWA 0932, NEW ZEALAND.
•JACKSON, Mrs. Karen Lesley, ACA *1993;* Rowmic, 3 Meadway, Harrold, BEDFORD, MK43 7DP.
JACKSON, Mrs. Karen Louise, BSc ACA *1992;* 123 Laughton Road, Thurcroft, ROTHERHAM, S66 9BP.
JACKSON, Mrs. Karin, ACA *2005;* with KPMG LLP, 15 Canada Square, LONDON, E14 5GL.
JACKSON, Mr. Karl, BSc ACA *1993;* 56 Anderby Drive, GRIMSBY, DN37 9HB.
JACKSON, Mrs. Katharine Mary, BA ACA *1990;* 24 Kyrle Road, LONDON, SW11 6AZ.
JACKSON, Mrs. Kathryn, BA ACA *2004;* 4 Elms Road, BURTON-ON-TRENT, STAFFORDSHIRE, DE15 9AG.
JACKSON, Ms. Kathryn, BA ACA *2007;* 69 Mitcham Lane, LONDON, SW16 6LW.
JACKSON, Miss. Kathryn Anne, BSc(Hons) ACA *2010;* 3rd Floor, Deloitte & Touche Abbots House, Abbey Street, READING, RG1 3BD.
JACKSON, Mrs. Kathryn Helen, BSc ACA *1991;* 15 Woodstock Gardens Appleton, WARRINGTON, WA4 5HN.
JACKSON, Mrs. Katie, BA ACA *2003;* 4 Homerfield, WELWYN GARDEN CITY, HERTFORDSHIRE, AL8 6QZ.
JACKSON, Miss. Katie Louise, ACA *2008;* 63 Oxclose Park Rise, Halfway, SHEFFIELD, S20 8GW.
JACKSON, Mr. Keith Austin, FCA *1972;* 31 Four Winds Court, HARTLEPOOL, CLEVELAND, TS26 0LP.
JACKSON, Mrs. Kelly, BSc ACA *2001;* The Forge, Wilsthorpe, STAMFORD, LINCOLNSHIRE, PE9 4PE.
JACKSON, Mrs. Kelly Elizabeth, MSc ACA *2008;* 39 Feltham Close, ROMSEY, SO51 8PB.
JACKSON, Mr. Kenneth, FCA *1953;* 57 Estcourt Road, GLOUCESTER, GL1 3LX. (Life Member)
JACKSON, Mr. Kenneth Peter, FCA *1957;* 16 Beacon Road, Rolleston, BURTON-ON-TRENT, DE13 9EF. (Life Member)
JACKSON, Miss. Kerry Joanne, BA FCA *1992;* 26 Gledhow Wood Grove, LEEDS, LS8 1NZ.
JACKSON, Mrs. Kerry Louise, BSc(Hons) ACA *2001;* 257 Worsley Bridge Road, BECKENHAM, BR3 1RW.
JACKSON, Mr. Kevin, FCA *1973;* 163 Sunnybank Rd, MIRFIELD, WF14 0JG.
JACKSON, Mr. Kevin Joseph, BSc ACA *1990;* Independent Inspections Ltd, Unit 6, Fulwood Park, Caxton Road, Fulwood, PRESTON PR2 9NZ.
JACKSON, Miss. Laura, BA ACA *2006;* 59 Garfield Road, LONDON, SW19 8RZ.
JACKSON, Miss. Lauren Elizabeth, ACA *2009;* 8 Blakeney Avenue, BECKENHAM, KENT, BR3 1HH.
JACKSON, Mrs. Lesley, MBA BA FCA *1989;* Meadow House Lyne, PEEBLES, EH45 8NP.
JACKSON, Mr. Leslie, FCA *1947;* 12 Charlbury Road, OXFORD, OX2 6UT. (Life Member)
JACKSON, Mr. Leslie William, FCA *1980;* Tenon House, Tenon Accountants Tenon House, Ferryboat Lane, SUNDERLAND, SR5 3JN.
JACKSON, Miss. Lindsey Ann, BA ACA *2007;* Masion du Soleil, 17 Port Vase, Burnt Lane, St Peter Port, GUERNSEY, GY1 2PP.
JACKSON, Mrs. Louise Marie, BA ACA *1991;* Tree Tops, Greendale Lane, Mottram St. Andrew, MACCLESFIELD, CHESHIRE, SK10 4AY.
JACKSON, Mr. Malcolm Eric, BA FCA *1970;* 6 Medow Mead, RADLETT, WD7 8ES.
JACKSON, Mr. Marcus, BSc ACA *1990;* 98 Dunstable Road, Redbourn, ST. ALBANS, AL3 7QB.
•JACKSON, Mr. Mark, BA FCA *1990;* (Tax Fac), Jacksons, 1 The Pathway, Alfred Gelder Street, HULL, HU1 1XJ.
JACKSON, Mr. Mark Adam, ACA *2009;* 21 Maxwelton Avenue, LONDON, NW7 3NB.
•JACKSON, Mr. Mark Andrew, FCA DChA *1994;* Rawlinsons, Ruthlyn House, 90 Lincoln Road, PETERBOROUGH, PE1 2SP.
JACKSON, Mr. Mark Brian, FCA *1973;* 8325 East Via Del Sol Drive, SCOTTSDALE, AZ 85255, UNITED STATES.
JACKSON, Mr. Mark Nicholas Allan, BSc ACA *1987;* Buckle Lane Farm, Buckle Lane, Warfield, BRACKNELL, RG42 5SA.
•JACKSON, Mr. Martin, FCA *1974;* (Tax Fac), Jackson Calvert, 33 Coleshill Street, SUTTON COLDFIELD, WEST MIDLANDS, B72 1SD. See also Martin Jackson FCA, ACIArb, MAE and M J One Limited
JACKSON, Mr. Martin Andrew, MA FCA *1995;* 6 Bergamot Close, Manton, MARLBOROUGH, SN8 4HT.
JACKSON, Mr. Martin Francis Leslie, BSc ACA *1982;* 247 FISHER AVE, BROOKLINE, MA 02445, UNITED STATES.
JACKSON, Mr. Martin James, BA ACA *1992;* Tree Tops, Greendale Lane, Mottram St. Andrew, MACCLESFIELD, CHESHIRE, SK10 4AY.
JACKSON, Mr. Martyn Dean, BA ACA *1988;* 198 Rugby Road, LEAMINGTON SPA, CV32 6DU.
JACKSON, Mr. Matthew, ACA *2011;* 18 Warwick Close, Chandler's Ford, EASTLEIGH, HAMPSHIRE, SO53 4PH.
JACKSON, Mr. Maurice Trevor, FCA *1956;* 2 Admirals Croft, Wellington Street West, HULL, HU1 2DR. (Life Member)

•**JACKSON, Mr. Michael Anthony, FCA DChA** *1983;* Baker Tilly UK Audit LLP, 2 Whitehall Quay, LEEDS, LS1 4HG. See also Baker Tilly Tax and Advisory Services LLP
JACKSON, Mr. Michael Ian, BA ACA *1990;* 4 Oak Hill Close, Whitley, WIGAN, WN1 2QL.
JACKSON, Mr. Michael James, BSc ACA *2003;* Hogg Robinson Plc Global House, Victoria Street, BASINGSTOKE, RG21 3BT.
JACKSON, Mr. Michael James, BA(Hons) ACA *2010;* Chinley House, Orchard Road, Pratts Bottom, ORPINGTON, KENT, BR6 7NS.
•**JACKSON, Mr. Michael Paul, BSc FCA** *1982;* Champion Accountants LLP, Refuge House, 33-37 Watergate Row South, CHESTER, CH1 2LE. See also Champion Allwoods Limited
JACKSON, Mr. Michael Ralph, FCA *1966;* N11, 2 Deanery Cl, Abbots Park, CHESTER, CH1 4AU.
•**JACKSON, Mr. Mike Thomas, BSc ACA** *2004;* with Hurst & Company Accountants LLP, Lancashire Gate, 21 Tiviot Dale, STOCKPORT, CHESHIRE, SK1 1TD.
JACKSON, Mr. Miles James, BSc ACA *1991;* 3 Marsworth Avenue, PINNER, MIDDLESEX, HA5 4UD.
JACKSON, Mr. Neil, ACA *2009;* 36 Church Road, MANCHESTER, M22 4NW.
JACKSON, Mr. Neil David, ACA *2010;* 15 Rosa Street, SOUTH SHIELDS, TYNE AND WEAR, NE33 3LN.
JACKSON, Mr. Neil Kenneth, ACA *2009;* 33 Worwood Drive, West Bridgford, NOTTINGHAM, NG2 7LY.
JACKSON, Mr. Nicholas Christopher, BA ACA DChA *1992;* 14 Richmond Road, EXMOUTH, DEVON, EX8 2NB.
JACKSON, Mr. Nick Richard, BA ACA *2005;* 76a Santos Road, LONDON, SW18 1NS.
JACKSON, Mrs. Nicola Susan, FCA *1982;* 2 Middleton Boulevard, Wollaton Park, NOTTINGHAM, NG8 1BH.
•**JACKSON, Mr. Nicolas Paul Dryden, FCA** *1977;* N P D Jackson FCA, 14 Gronant Road, PRESTATYN, CLWYD, LL19 9DS.
JACKSON, Mr. Nigel Keith, FCA FPC *1978;* Newton Grange, Newton Lane, Newton-by-Tattenhall, Tattenhall, CHESTER, CH3 9NE.
JACKSON, Mr. Nigel Scott, BSc ACA *1995;* Lucite International UK Ltd, PO Box 34, DARWEN, LANCASHIRE, BB3 1QB.
JACKSON, Mr. Oliver Mark, BA ACA *1989;* Walt Disney Studios Motion, Pictures Germany GmbH, Kronstadterstrasse 9, 81677 MUNICH, GERMANY.
JACKSON, Dr. Owen David, BA ACA *2006;* 7 Ty Draw Place, Penylan, CARDIFF, CF23 5HF.
•**JACKSON, Miss. Pamela, FCA** *1981;* PricewaterhouseCoopers LLP, 7 More London Riverside, LONDON, SE1 2RT. See also PricewaterhouseCoopers
JACKSON, Mrs. Pamela Jane Cochrane, ACA *1998;* 2020 Perfect Vision Ltd, Unit 12 Millshaw Park Avenue, LEEDS, WEST YORKSHIRE, LS11 0LR.
JACKSON, Mr. Paul, ACA *2011;* 76 Eleanor Road, WALTHAM CROSS, HERTFORDSHIRE, EN8 7DL.
•**JACKSON, Mr. Paul, FCA** *1978;* (Tax Fac), P Jackson Ltd, Avtech House, Bird Hall Lane, Cheadle Heath, STOCKPORT, SK3 0XX.
•**JACKSON, Mr. Paul David, BSc FCA** *1989;* Bowker Stevens & Co, Suite No. 2, Centre Court, Vine Lane, HALESOWEN, B63 3EB. See also Jackson Paul
•**JACKSON, Mr. Paul Francis, FCA** *1974;* Beavis Morgan LLP, 82 St. John Street, LONDON, EC1M 4JN.
JACKSON, Mr. Paul Howard, BA ACA *1996;* 27a Luton Road, Wilstead, BEDFORD, MK45 3ER.
JACKSON, Mr. Paul Rodney, FCA *1966;* Lilac Cottage, Cross Lane, Stocksmoor, HUDDERSFIELD, HD4 6XH.
•**JACKSON, Mr. Peter, FCA** *1974;* J. Humphrey Jones & Co, Suite 3C, St Christopher House, Wellington Road South, STOCKPORT, SK2 6NG.
JACKSON, Mr. Peter, BSc FCA *1978;* 35 Stanley Road, Heaton Moor, STOCKPORT, SK4 4HW.
JACKSON, Mr. Peter, FCA *1984;* Hall Jackson Pty Ltd, 505/39 East Esplanade, P.O. Box 404, MANLY, NSW 2095, AUSTRALIA.
JACKSON, Mr. Peter Edward, BA ACA *1992;* 17 Thistledown, Highwoods, COLCHESTER, CO4 9UH.
JACKSON, Mr. Peter Garth Andrew, FCA *1974;* (Tax Fac), 17A Courtfield Rise, WEST WICKHAM, BR4 9BD.
JACKSON, Mr. Peter James, MSci ACA *2005;* 5 St. Laurence Way, Bidford-on-Avon, ALCESTER, WARWICKSHIRE, B50 4FG.
JACKSON, Mr. Peter James, BA FCA *1984;* Flat 5 Upper Tooting Park Mansions, Marius Road, LONDON, SW17 7QR.
JACKSON, Mr. Peter Michael Gregory, FCA *1974;* 41a Palmerston Street, Bollington, MACCLESFIELD, CHESHIRE, SK10 5PX.
JACKSON, Mr. Peter Norman, FCA *1961;* 122 Kingsley Road, Bishops Tachbrook, LEAMINGTON SPA, CV33 9RZ.
•**JACKSON, Mr. Philip, BA FCA** *1980;* 101 Turker Lane, NORTHALLERTON, NORTH YORKSHIRE, DL6 1QJ.
JACKSON, Mr. Philip, BSc FCA *1992;* 206 Eden Way, BECKENHAM, BR3 3DT.
JACKSON, Mr. Philip, FCA *1978;* 4 Timberhurst, BURY, BL9 7NZ.
JACKSON, Mr. Philip David, ACA *2008;* 2 MILLCROFT, MILLHOUSE GREEN, SHEFFIELD, SOUTH YORKSHIRE, S36 9AR.
JACKSON, Mr. Philip George, MA FCA *1978;* 24 Rectory Farm Road Sompting, LANCING, WEST SUSSEX, BN15 0ED.
JACKSON, Mr. Philip Michael, BSc ACA CF *1987;* 1 The Orchard, Bozeat, WELLINGBOROUGH, NN29 7NW.
JACKSON, Mrs. Rachel Louise, BSc ACA *1998;* 2 Gunnersbury Way, Nuthall, NOTTINGHAM, NG16 1QD.
JACKSON, Mrs. Rachel Mary, BSc ACA *1992;* Jl Kemang Dalam 10 D15c, JAKARTA, 12730, INDONESIA.
JACKSON, Mr. Raymond Siva, BSc ACA *1998;* 134 Maywood Way, SAN RAFAEL, CA 94901, UNITED STATES.
JACKSON, Mr. Richard Alastair, BSc ACA *2002;* Lloyds TSB, Canons House, Canons Way, BRISTOL, BS99 7LB.
JACKSON, Mr. Richard Andrew, BA ACA *1997;* 97 Lower Richmond Road, Mortlake, LONDON, SW14 7HU.
JACKSON, Mr. Richard Arthur, ACA *1992;* 40 Birchill Gardens, HARTLEPOOL, TS26 0JT.
JACKSON, Mr. Richard Charles Edward, MA ACA *1982;* 7 Alan Road, LONDON, SW19 7PT.
JACKSON, Mr. Richard Charles William, FCA *1974;* 38 Long Road, Framingham Earl, NORWICH, NR14 7RY.
JACKSON, Mr. Richard Henry George, MBA BSc FCA *1991;* The Old Stables, Prispen Drive, Silverton, EXETER, EX5 4DP.
JACKSON, Mr. Richard Ian, BA ACA *1996;* 2 Gunnersbury Way, Nuthall, NOTTINGHAM, NG16 1QD.
JACKSON, Mr. Richard John, BA ACA *1998;* Ernst & Young LLP, 303 Almaden Blvd, SAN JOSE, CA 95110, UNITED STATES.
•**JACKSON, Mr. Richard Mackwood, FCA** *1966;* (Tax Fac), with haysmacintyre, Fairfax House, 15 Fulwood Place, LONDON, WC1V 6AY.
•**JACKSON, Mr. Richard Paul, BSc FCA CTA** *1999;* BDO Limited, PO Box 180, Place du Pre, Rue du Pre, St Peter Port, GUERNSEY GY1 3LL.
JACKSON, Mr. Ricky Martyn, BA ACA *1995;* London Southend Airport Co Ltd, Southend Airport, SOUTHEND-ON-SEA, SS2 6YF.
JACKSON, Mr. Robert Anthony, BA ACA *1988;* Barham, 3 Lyttelton Road, DROITWICH, WORCESTERSHIRE, WR9 7AA.
•**JACKSON, Mr. Robert Hodges, FCA** *1974;* R H Jackson and Co, 1 Wroth Tyes Cottage, Upper Hartfield, HARTFIELD, EAST SUSSEX, TN7 4DY.
•**JACKSON, Mr. Robert Ian, MBA BA ACA** *1989;* Robert Jackson Management Limited, 41 Avondale Avenue, Woodside Pk, Finchley, LONDON, N12 8ER.
JACKSON, The Hon. Robert Ward, BA ACA *1981;* The Coach House, Nutcombe Lane, HINDHEAD, SURREY, GU26 6BP.
JACKSON, Mr. Robert William Edward, FCA *1959;* Oakash, Golf Links Lane, Selsey, CHICHESTER, PO20 9DP. (Life Member)
JACKSON, Mr. Robin, BA FCA *1977;* P.O. Box, 64012, 8071 PAPHOS, CYPRUS.
JACKSON, Mr. Robin Arthur, BSc ACA *1989;* Agrimin Limited, Arlanda Way, Humberside Airport, Kirmington, ULCEBY, NORTH LINCOLNSHIRE DN39 6YH.
•**JACKSON, Mr. Robin Brian, BA DipPFS ACA CTA** *1988;* (Tax Fac), Churchgate Accountants Limited, 18 Langton Place, BURY ST. EDMUNDS, SUFFOLK, IP33 1NE.
JACKSON, Mr. Robin Nigel, BSc ACA *1998;* Sunnybank, Lynn Road, MULLINGAR, COUNTY WESTMEATH, IRELAND.
•**JACKSON, Mr. Rodney, BSc ACA** *1981;* R. Jackson, 18 Plane Tree Croft, LEEDS, LS17 8UQ.
JACKSON, Mr. Roger Ian, JP FCA FCIS *1964;* 28 Everard Drive, SHEFFIELD, S17 4NE.
JACKSON, Mrs. Rosalind Parkinson, BCom FCA *1968;* Holly House, 24 High Street, Caistor, MARKET RASEN, LINCOLNSHIRE, LN7 6QF. (Life Member)
JACKSON, Ms. Ruth Margaret, ACA *1984;* 27 Cranmere Road, Higher Compton, PLYMOUTH, PL3 5JY.
JACKSON, Mrs. Sally Anne, BSc ACA *1991;* Eastview, Nettleton Shrub, Nettleton, CHIPPENHAM, SN14 7NN.
•**JACKSON, Mrs. Sara Louise, BA FCA** *1992;* Hale Jackson Knight, Montague House, 4 St. Marys Street, ROSS-ON-WYE, HEREFORDSHIRE, HR9 5HT.
JACKSON, Miss. Sarah, ACA MAAT *2010;* 68 Woodstock Road, Beeston, NOTTINGHAM, NG9 6JQ.
JACKSON, Mr. Scott Andrew, BSc(Hons) ACA *2001;* 12 Crondall Terrace, BASINGSTOKE, RG24 9GA.
JACKSON, Mrs. Sheila Jean, FCA *1955;* 8 Woodlands Road, SURBITON, KT6 6PS. (Life Member)
JACKSON, Mr. Simon, BSc ACA *1992;* 910 8th Avenue, Apt 1215, SEATTLE, WA 98104, UNITED STATES.
JACKSON, Mr. Simon, FCA *1981;* 115 Wirksworth Road, Duffield, BELPER, DE56 4GY.
JACKSON, Mr. Simon James, ACA *1988;* Bridge Farmhouse, Appleford on Thames, ABINGDON, OX14 4NU.
JACKSON, Mr. Simon John, BA ACA *1989;* Charnwood Borough Council, Southfield Road, LOUGHBOROUGH, LEICESTERSHIRE, LE11 2TN.
JACKSON, Mr. Simon John, BA ACA *1986;* 181 Highbury Quadrant, Highbury, LONDON, N5 2TG.
JACKSON, Mr. Simon Paul, Meng ACA *2009;* 37 Shepherds Leaze, WOTTON-UNDER-EDGE, GLOUCESTERSHIRE, GL12 7LJ.
JACKSON, Mr. Stephen, BA ACA *2006;* with PKF (Isle of Man) LLC, PO Box 16, Analyst House, Douglas, ISLE OF MAN, IM99 1AP.
JACKSON, Mr. Stephen Charles, ACA *1993;* 5 Newport Drive, Winterton, SCUNTHORPE, DN15 9RG.
JACKSON, Mr. Stephen Douglas, BA FCA *1983;* 13 Hinckley Court, AUCKLAND 2016, NEW ZEALAND.
JACKSON, Mr. Stephen Martin Rowan, FCA *1988;* Masters Legal Costs Services Benllan House, 3-4 New Street, LONDON, EC2M 4HD.
•**JACKSON, Mrs. Susan Sarah, BA ACA** *1987;* Sheridan Brooks Limited, Sheridan Brooks Ltd, 176 Brighton Road, COULSDON, SURREY, CR5 2NF.
JACKSON, Miss. Suzanne Marie, MA ACA *2004;* 14 Southfield Road, Westbury-on-Trym, BRISTOL, BS9 3BH.
JACKSON, Mr. Terence Guy, BSc ACA *2001;* with Baker Tilly Tax & Advisory Services LLP, The Clock House, 140 London Road, GUILDFORD, SURREY, GU1 1UW.
JACKSON, Mr. Terence Leslie, BA ACA *1979;* 14 Down Barn's Road, South, RUISLIP, HA4 0LY.
JACKSON, Mr. Thomas David, BA(Hons) ACA *2002;* School House Church Lane, Langar, NOTTINGHAM, NG13 9HG.
JACKSON, Mr. Thompson William, FCA *1965;* 34 Russell Av, High Lane, STOCKPORT, SK6 8DT. (Life Member)
JACKSON, Mr. Timothy, MA ACA *2010;* Flat 17, 4 Orsett Terrace, LONDON, W2 6AZ.
JACKSON, Mr. Timothy Christopher, BSc FCA *1989;* Green Square Group, Stonehill Green, SWINDON, WILTSHIRE, SN5 7HB.
JACKSON, Mr. Timothy David, BA ACA *1986;* 4 Meadow Road, Mountsorrel, LOUGHBOROUGH, LEICESTERSHIRE, LE12 7HN.
JACKSON, Mr. Timothy Neill, BA ACA *1992;* 80 Kingsley Road, NORTHAMPTON, NN2 7BL.
JACKSON, Mr. Timothy Roger, BSc ACA *2002;* Flat 3, 1 New Village Way Morley, LEEDS, LS27 7NU.
JACKSON, Mr. Timothy Roy, MA ACA *1997;* 22 Alfred Street Pinxton, NOTTINGHAM, DERBYSHIRE, NG16 6NQ.
JACKSON, Mrs. Vanessa Lorraine, MPhil BA(Hons) ACA *2002;* Sulzer (UK) Pumps Ltd, Manor Mill Lane, LEEDS, LS11 8BR.
JACKSON, Mrs. Vanessa May, BA ACA *1994;* Audit Commission, Littlemoor House, Littlemoor, Eckington, SHEFFIELD, S21 4EF.
JACKSON, Mrs. Victoria Emma Louise, BSc(Hons) ACA *2000;* 46 Whirlow Lane, SHEFFIELD, S11 9QF.
JACKSON, Mrs. Victoria Louise, ACA *2009;* 2 Millcroft, SHEFFIELD, S36 9AR.
JACKSON, Miss. Victoria Marie, MSc BSc FCA *1987;* 39 Albion Road, ST. ALBANS, HERTFORDSHIRE, AL1 5EB.
JACKSON, Mrs. Wendy Louise, BSc ACA CTA *1995;* 4 Clover Lay, Rainham, GILLINGHAM, KENT, ME8 8LY.
JACKSON, Mr. William Joseph, BMus ACA *2005;* with KPMG LLP, 15 Canada Square, LONDON, E14 5GL.
•**JACKSON, Mr. William Shaun, FCA** *1982;* 1495 The Links Drive, OAKVILLE L6M 2P2, ON, CANADA.
JACKSON, Mrs. Yolanda Catherine, BSc(Hons) ACA *2010;* 98 Fromond Road, WINCHESTER, HAMPSHIRE, SO22 6EF.
•**JACKSON, Mrs. Yvonne June, BSc FCA** *1999;* Clayton & Brewill, Cawley House, 149-155 Canal Street, NOTTINGHAM, NG1 7HR.
•**JACKSON, Mrs. Zara Charlene, ACA** *2009;* with Complete Audit and Accounting Solutions Ltd, Unit 203, China House, 401 Edgware Road, LONDON, NW2 6GY.
JACKSON - DOOLEY, Mr. Rory, BSc ACA *2011;* 32 Tuffley Road, BRISTOL, BS10 5EG.
JACKSON-BAKER, Mrs. Bethan Elizabeth, BA ACA *1999;* 9 Dengate Drive, Balsall Common, COVENTRY, CV7 7UL.
JACKSON COUSIN, Mrs. Ann Susan, BBS ACA *1992;* 37 Southfields Road, LONDON, SW18 1QW.
JACKSON COUSIN, Mr. Rupert Charles, BA ACA *1993;* 37 Southfields Road, LONDON, SW18 1QW.
JACKSON-COX, Mrs. Jacquelinee, BSc FCA *1965;* 38 Tile Kiln Hill, Blean, CANTERBURY, CT2 9EE.
JACKSON-DOOLEY, Mrs. Joanna, ACA *2011;* 32 Tuffley Road, BRISTOL, BS10 5EG.
•**JACKSON-JAKUBOWSKI, Mr. Andrew, BCom FCA** *1956;* A. Jackson-Jakubowski, 5 Lowfield Road, Acton, LONDON, W3 0AY.
•**JACKSON-MOORE, Mr. William, BA ACA** *1993;* PricewaterhouseCoopers, 7 More London Riverside, LONDON, SE1 2RT. See also PricewaterhouseCoopers LLP
JACKSON-PROES, Mrs. Sarah Elizabeth, BA ACA *1994;* The Willows, Hill Close, Wonersh, GUILDFORD, SURREY, GU5 0QP.
JACKSON-SPILLMAN, Mrs. Janie Danielle, BSc ACA *2002;* Moat House, The Warren, RADLETT, HERTFORDSHIRE, WD7 7DU.
JACOB, Mr. Andrew Byrt, FCA *1974;* 35 Pollards Hill North, LONDON, SW16 4NJ.
JACOB, Mr. Carey John Howard, BSc ACA *1993;* 143 - 145 Franklin Street, ELTHAM, VIC 3095, AUSTRALIA.
JACOB, Ms. Christina Marie, BSc ACA *1996;* 1 St Arilds Road, Didmarton, BADMINTON, GLOUCESTERSHIRE, GL9 1DP.
JACOB, Mr. Christopher, BSc FCA *1976;* 6 Meakin Close, CONGLETON, CHESHIRE, CW12 3TG. (Life Member)
JACOB, Mr. Christopher Horton, FCA *1969;* Netherwood Cottage, Arbour Tree Lane, Chadwick End, SOLIHULL, B93 0AZ.
•**JACOB, Mr. Graham Keith, FCA** *1971;* Brindley Millen Limited, 167 Turners Hill, Cheshunt, WALTHAM CROSS, HERTFORDSHIRE, EN8 9BH.
JACOB, Mr. Ian Theodorus, LLB ACA *2010;* 43 Arthur Road, FARNHAM, GU9 8PD.
•**JACOB, Mr. Ipe, FCA** *1976;* Flat 9 Dorset House, Gloucester Place, LONDON, NW1 5AB.
JACOB, Miss. Katherine Rebecca, BSc ACA *2003;* 12 Flat, 75 Winchester Street, LONDON, SW1V 4NU.
JACOB, Miss. Leanne, BCom ACA *2010;* Grant Thornton Enterprise House, 115 Edmund Street, BIRMINGHAM, B3 2HJ.
JACOB, Mr. Michael Clive, BA ACA *1980;* 54 Wharfedale Avenue, HARROGATE, NORTH YORKSHIRE, HG2 0AU.
JACOB, Miss. Penelope Anne, BSc ACA *2003;* The Laurels, Buckley Green, HENLEY-IN-ARDEN, WEST MIDLANDS, B95 5QE.
JACOB, Mr. Peter Doraisingham, FCA *1986;* 261 River Valley Road, #05-10 Aspen Heights, SINGAPORE 238307, SINGAPORE.
•**JACOB, Mr. Ronald Ian, FCA** *1983;* (Tax Fac), Lachman Livingstone, 136 Pinner Road, NORTHWOOD, MIDDLESEX, HA6 1BP. See also Northwood Registrars Ltd
•**JACOB, Mr. Simon Raymond, FCA** *1970;* (Tax Fac), Jacob Ting & Co, 40 Homer Street, LONDON, W1H 4NL.
JACOB, Mr. Stephen John, BA FCA *1999;* The Masters House, High Street, Elham, CANTERBURY, CT4 6TB.
JACOBI, Miss. Nicola Sarah, BA ACA *1995;* 22 Beaumont Road, Flitwick, BEDFORD, MK45 1WD.
JACOBMEYER, Mrs. Brenda Lillian, BA ACA *1981;* (Tax Fac), Sun Life of Canada Matrix House, Basing View, BASINGSTOKE, RG21 4DZ.
•**JACOBS, Mr. Adrian Mark, BSc FCA** *1989;* 13 Beaufort Gardens, Hendon, LONDON, NW4 3QN.
•**JACOBS, Mr. Alvin Harris, FCA** *1977;* Jacobs & Co, Credcoll House, 96 Marsh Lane, LEEDS, LS9 8SR.
•**JACOBS, Mr. Austin Kingsley, BSc FCA** *1997;* Prager and Fenton LLP, 8th Floor, Imperial House, 15-19 Kingsway, LONDON, WC2B 6UN.
JACOBS, Mr. Bernard Joseph, FCA *1971;* Dove Cottage, 1 Pigeonhouse Lane, Rustington, LITTLEHAMPTON, WEST SUSSEX, BN16 2AY.
JACOBS, Mr. Brian David, MA ACA *1988;* 12 Silverdale, HASSOCKS, BN6 8RD.
JACOBS, Mr. Daniel Jacobus, ACA CA(SA) *2009;* 48, Reeds Meadow, REDHILL, RH1 2FJ.
JACOBS, Lord David Anthony, FCA *1956;* 90 Eaton Square, LONDON, SW1W 9AG. (Life Member)
•**JACOBS, Mr. David Steven, BA FCA** *1986;* Milsted Langdon LLP, 1 Redcliff Street, BRISTOL, BS1 6NP.
JACOBS, Miss. Deborah Jane, BA ACA *1991;* 37 Mountfield Road, LONDON, W5 2NQ.

•**JACOBS, Mr. Dennis, FCA** *1974;* (Tax Fac), DJM Accountants LLP, Fourth Floor, Brook Point, 1412 High Road, LONDON, N20 9BH.

JACOBS, Mr. Dennis Eli, FCA FCMA *1946;* 1 Redington Road, Hampstead, LONDON, NW3 7QX. (Life Member)

JACOBS, Mr. Denzil Henry, FCA *1948;* 54 Chester Close South, Regents Park, LONDON, NW1 4JG. (Life Member)

JACOBS, Mr. Elliott Leslie, BA ACA *2007;* Flat 11 Highlands, Oakleigh Road North, LONDON, N20 9HA.

JACOBS, Mr. Gaskell Edward, FCA *1973;* Seal House, 34 Pottery Lane, LONDON, W11 4LZ.

ⒾJACOBS, Mr. George David Jeremy, BA ACA** *1985;* 9 Heton Gardens, Hendon, LONDON, NW4 4XS.

•**JACOBS, Mr. Harvey, FCA CPA** *1954;* J.S. Management Ltd, 87 Westfield, Kidderpore Avenue, Hampstead, LONDON, NW3 7SG.

JACOBS, Mr. Harvey Steven, BA ACA *1985;* 5 Sandy Meade, MANCHESTER, M25 9PR.

•**JACOBS, Mr. Ian Gordon, BA FCA** *1991;* MacIntyre Hudson LLP, 8-12 Priestgate, PETERBOROUGH, PE1 1JA.

JACOBS, Mrs. Janet Eileen, ACA *1980;* The Barn, Fulford Dale, Fulford, STOKE-ON-TRENT, ST11 9QR.

JACOBS, Mrs. Karen Elizabeth, BA(Hons) ACA *2001;* 3 Pink Green Lane, Brockhill, REDDITCH, WORCESTERSHIRE, B97 6GU.

JACOBS, Mrs. Kathleen Teresa, BSc ACA *1993;* 4 Prince Arthur Terrace, Rathmines, DUBLIN 6, COUNTY DUBLIN, IRELAND.

JACOBS, Mr. Keith Michael, FCA *1974;* 13 Oakhill Avenue, PINNER, MIDDLESEX, HA5 3DL.

•**JACOBS, Mr. Laurence Anthony, FCA** *1977;* Haslers, Old Station Road, LOUGHTON, ESSEX, IG10 4PL.

JACOBS, Mr. Leslie Henry, FCA *1961;* Flat 1, Sommerville Court, Park Lane, SALFORD, M7 4HU.

•**JACOBS, Mr. Mark George, BSc FCA** *1988;* (Tax Fac), Scodie Deyong LLP, 85 Frampton Street, LONDON, NW8 8NQ.

JACOBS, Mr. Mark Stephen, BA FCA *1985;* 10 Northcliffe Drive, Totteridge, LONDON, N20 8JZ.

JACOBS, Mrs. Mary Elizabeth, BSc ACA *1991;* Heatherslade, 27 Ryhill Way, Lower Earley, READING, RG6 4AZ.

JACOBS, Mr. Nicholas Oliver William, LLB ACA *2004;* with Deloitte LLP, Hill House, 1 Little New Street, LONDON, EC4A 3TR.

JACOBS, Mr. Nyall Stephen, BA ACA *1991;* (Tax Fac), 15 Brockley Avenue, STANMORE, HA7 4LX.

JACOBS, Mr. Paul, BA FCA *1993;* Transvaal Cottage, New Barn Road, SWANLEY, BR8 7PW.

JACOBS, Mr. Paul Andrew, FCA *1980;* Darlstone House, 1b Grange Cliffe Close, Ecclesall, SHEFFIELD, S11 9JE.

JACOBS, Mr. Paul Lewis Arthur, BSc ACA *1979;* 19 Welclose Street, ST. ALBANS, HERTFORDSHIRE, AL3 4QD.

JACOBS, Mr. Peter Jonathan, BA FCA *1978;* 6 Perceval Avenue, Belsize Park, LONDON, NW3 4PY.

JACOBS, Mr. Robert Michael, BA FCA *1970;* 21 Halfway Close, TROWBRIDGE, BA14 7HQ.

JACOBS, Mr. Robert Sebastian, BA FCA *1983;* 7 Mountbatten Close, NEWBURY, RG14 2HT.

•**JACOBS, Mr. Robert Sydney, ACA** *1983;* Jacobs & Company, 152-154 Coles Green Road, LONDON, NW2 7HD.

JACOBS, Mr. Russell, BA *2005;* 59 Garfield Road, LONDON, SW19 8RZ.

JACOBS, Mrs. Ruth Elizabeth, BSc ACA *1995;* with Goodband Viner Taylor, Ellin House, 42 Kingfield Road, SHEFFIELD, S11 9AS.

•**JACOBS, Mr. Stephen Colin, FCA** *1980;* Rayner Essex LLP, Tavistock House South, Tavistock Square, LONDON, WC1H 9LG.

JACOBS, Mr. Steven Michael, BA FCA *1993;* BTG Pactual LLP, Berkeley Square House, 4-19 Berkeley Square, LONDON, W1J 6BR.

JACOBS, Mrs. Susan Mary, ACA *1980;* 6 Perceval Avenue, Belsize Park, LONDON, NW3 4PY.

JACOBS, Dr. Tom, PhD ACA *2011;* 18 Rose Hill Park West, SUTTON, SURREY, SM1 3LB.

JACOBS, Mr. Warren Howard, BSc(Hons) FCA *1993;* 65 Brim Hill, LONDON, N2 0HA.

JACOBSON, Mr. Derek John, BEng ACA *1990;* PO Box 31426, Seven Mile Beach, SEVEN MILE BEACH, GRAND CAYMAN, KY1-1206, CAYMAN ISLANDS.

JACOBSON, Mr. Mark Lloyd, BSc ACA *2008;* (Tax Fac), 18 West Meade, Prestwich, MANCHESTER, M25 0JD.

•**JACOBSON, Mr. Philip Ronald, FCA** *1971;* Philip Jacobson, Sheldon House, 904-908 High Road, LONDON, N12 9RW.

JACOBSON, Mr. Ryan Benjamin, BA ACA *2004;* 35 Johns Avenue, LONDON, NW4 4EN.

JACOBSSON, Mr. Ian Martin, BSc ACA *1981;* Au Bourg, 82120 MONTGAILLARD, TARN ET GARONNE, FRANCE.

JACOBSSON, Mr. Per Stefan, BSc ACA *1986;* The Griffin, Knipp Hill, COBHAM, KT112PE.

JACOBY, Mr. Michael Roland, ACA *2009;* Hillier Hopkins LLP 3rd Floor North, 32 Duke Street, LONDON, SW1Y 6DF.

JACOURIS, Mr. Anthony John, FCA *1973;* Alkistis Street 16, Appt.401, Strovolos, CY-2007 NICOSIA, CYPRUS.

JACOURIS, Mr. Antonis, BA ACA *1990;* Warren Farm Barn Fordcombe Road, Penshurst, TONBRIDGE, TN11 8DL.

JACOVIDES, Mr. Haris, BSc ACA *1989;* 78 Tolmers Road, Cuffley, POTTERS BAR, EN6 4JY.

JACOVOU, Mr. Jacovos George, BSc(Hons) ACA *2002;* 115 Westpole Avenue, Cockfosters, BARNET, HERTFORDSHIRE, EN4 0BB.

JACQUES, Mr. Christopher Michael, BSc ACA *2007;* 68 Hollyshaw Lane, LEEDS, LS15 7AG.

JACQUES, Miss. Claire Alison, BA(Hons) ACA *2001;* 9 Samwell Way, NORTHAMPTON, NN4 9QJ.

JACQUES, Mr. Guy Martin, MBA FCA *1968;* 48 Seacliffe Avenue, Belmont, NORTH SHORE CITY 0622, AUCKLAND, NEW ZEALAND.

JACQUES, Mr. Ivan Mark, ACA *1990;* 70 Myrtle Road, SEACLIFF, SA 5049, AUSTRALIA.

JACQUES, Mr. Nicholas Charles, MA FCA MBA *2000;* with Deloitte LLP, Hill House, 1 Little New Street, LONDON, EC4A 3TR.

JACQUES, Mr. Nicholas John, BSocSc ACA *2000;* 97 Chadwick Place, SURBITON, SURREY, KT6 5RG.

JACQUES, Mr. Robert Keith, BSc ACA *1985;* 64 Stapleton Road, Formby, LIVERPOOL, L37 2YT.

JACQUES, Miss. Suzy Marie, BSc ACA *2000;* 215 Euston Road, The Wellcome Trust, LONDON, NW1 2BE.

JADAVJI, Mr. Ismat Didarali Hadi, ACA *1979;* 84 Leigh Gardens, LONDON, NW10 5HP.

JADCZYSZYN, Ms. Ewa, MSc ACA *2011;* with PricewaterhouseCoopers AG, Birchstrasse 160, 8050 ZURICH, SWITZERLAND.

JADESIMI, Mr. Oladipupo Adedeji, MA FCA *1970;* Penthouse 2, 65 Harbour Sq, TORONTO M5J 2G4, ON, CANADA.

•**JADY, Miss. Clare Heather, BSc FCA** *1992;* P A Hull & Co, 41 Bridgeman Terrace, WIGAN, LANCASHIRE, WN1 1TT.

JAFAR, Mr. Junaid, ACA *1997;* Tadhamon Capital, 12th Floor GB Corp Tower, Bahrain Financial Harbour, P.O. Box 75511, MANAMA, BAHRAIN.

JAFFE, Mr. Isaac Philip, FCA *1954;* (Tax Fac), 8 High Grove Road, CHEADLE, SK8 1NR.

JAFFE, Mr. Michael Ian, MA ACA *1991;* Henderson Global Investors, 201 Bishopsgate, LONDON, EC2M 3AE.

•**JAFFE, Mr. Steven Harold, BSc FCA** *1976;* (Tax Fac), Hazlems Fenton LLP, Palladium House, 1-4 Argyll Street, LONDON, W1F 7LD. See also Argyll Street Management Services Ltd

JAFFER, Miss. Anfaal, LLB ACA *2007;* Glaxo Smithkline, 980 Great West Road, BRENTFORD, MIDDLESEX, TW8 9GS.

JAFFER, Mr. Bashir Abdulrasul, FCA *1970;* 1617 Page Road, NORTH VANCOUVER V7K 1R9, BC, CANADA.

•**JAFFER, Mr. Makbul Mohamed Kassamali, FCA** *1985;* Jaffery's, 113 Devonshire Road, Mill Hill, LONDON, NW7 1EA.

JAFFER, Mr. Navshir, BSc ACA ATII *1993;* (Tax Fac), 38 Lloyd Park Avenue, CROYDON, CR0 5SB.

JAFFER, Mr. Nazim, FCA *1963;* Prevention & Detection, (Holdings) Ltd., Unit 1, 2 Southlands Road, BROMLEY, BR2 9QP.

JAFFERJEE, Mr. Aziz Tayabali, FCA *1963;* 11262 NW 46th Drive, CORAL SPRINGS, FL 33076, UNITED STATES.

JAFFERJEE, Mr. Husein Asger, BSc FCA *1978;* 31 Hamilton Avenue, WEEHAWKEN, NJ 07086, UNITED STATES.

JAFFERY, Mr. Mohamed Razi, FCA *1960;* 345 A/3, Gulberg III, LAHORE, PAKISTAN. (Life Member)

JAFFRAY, Mr. Benjamin Paul, BA ACA *2010;* Flat 4, 133 Lapwing Lane, MANCHESTER, M20 6US.

JAFFREY, Mr. Sameem Islam, BA ACA *1993;* UBS AG, 1 Broadgate, LONDON, EC2M 2PP.

JAFRANI, Mr. Humayun, BSc(Econ) CA ACA *2000;* 37 Routliffe Lane, TORONTO M2N 0A5, ON, CANADA.

JAGANNATHAN, Mr. Venkatarama, FCA *1973;* Flat C First Floor, 101 First Main Road, Gandhinagar, Adyar, MADRAS 600020, INDIA.

JAGARNATH, Mr. Ashish Dooriodhun, FCA *1993;* International Proximity, 608 St James Court, St Denis Street, PORT LOUIS, MAURITIUS.

JAGGER, Mr. Charles William, FCA *1976;* Linfit, Henley Mount, Rawdon, LEEDS, LS19 6PX.

JAGGER, Mr. Eric, FCA *1950;* 9 Partridge Close, Moor Park Bamford, ROCHDALE, OL11 5SP. (Life Member)

JAGGER, Mr. Gordon David, BA ACA *1979;* The Royal Bank Of Scotland Plc(Australia Branch), Level 22R135 Tower, 88 Phillip Street, SYDNEY, NSW 2000, AUSTRALIA.

JAGGER, Mr. Ian Richard, BA ACA *1996;* 3C/99 Anzac Avenue, AUCKLAND 1010, NEW ZEALAND.

•**JAGGER, Mr. Jon Richard, BA FCA** *1989;* Menzies LLP, Woking Office, Midas House, 62 Goldsworth Road, WOKING, SURREY GU21 6LQ.

JAGGER, Mr. Simon Andrew, BSc(Hons) ACA *2003;* with PKF (UK) LLP, Farringdon Place, 20 Farringdon Road, LONDON, EC1M 3AP.

JAGGER, Mr. Timothy Andrew, MA FCA *1977;* Wickhurst, Fulking Rd, Poynings, BRIGHTON, BN45 7AB.

JAGGERS, Mrs. Claire Jane, BA ACA *2003;* Summer Hill, Wilderness Road, OXTED, RH8 9HS.

JAGO, Mr. Bryan Francis, FCA *1966;* (Tax Fac), Windyridge, 2 Ashbourne Croft, CLECKHEATON, WEST YORKSHIRE, BD19 5JF. (Life Member)

JAGO, Mrs. Carolyn Jane Siobhan, BSc ACA *1993;* White Hart House, The Street, Ewhurst, CRANLEIGH, GU6 7QD.

JAGO, Mr. Gavin Andrew, MA BA ACA *2006;* 29 Weston Road, THAMES DITTON, KT7 0HN.

JAGO, Mr. Stephen, BSc ACA *1981;* 9 Hoober Avenue, SHEFFIELD, S11 9SG.

JAGOT, Ms. Julie Sandra, ACA *1985;* 100 Knights Track, WINCHELSEA, VIC 3241, AUSTRALIA.

JAGOTA, Mr. Rahul, BSc ACA *1998;* Prem Nivas New Road, Terling, CHELMSFORD, CM3 2PN.

•**JAGPAL, Mrs. Rajni Kanta, FCA** *1973;* (Tax Fac), R. Jagpal & Co, 51 Harrowdene Road, WEMBLEY, HA0 2JQ.

JAGPAL, Mr. Shamit, BSc ACA *1990;* 19 The Glade, LONDON, N21 1QG.

JAGUCKA, Mrs. Anna Zofia, ACA *2008;* ul. WENUS 17, 83-010 STRASZYN, POLAND.

JAGUS, Mr. Marek Antoni, BSc(Hons) ACA *1990;* T W G Services Ltd Aspen Building, Vantage Point Business Village, MITCHELDEAN, GLOUCESTERSHIRE, GL17 0AF.

JAHANBANI, Mr. Shahram, BSc ACA *1990;* BG Group, Thames Valley Park, READING, BERKSHIRE, RG6 1PT.

•**JAHANGIR, Mr. Hammad, BSc ACA** *2006;* BBG Professionals, 13 Nevill Lodge, Ferndale Close, TUNBRIDGE WELLS, KENT, TN2 3RP.

JAHED, Mr. Parviz, BSc FCA *1973;* 1077 Fleet Street, MISSISSAUGA L5H 3P4, ON, CANADA.

JAHN, Mrs. Alison, BA(Hons) ACA *2004;* with Royal Sun Alliance plc, Nw Hall Place, Old Hall Street, LIVERPOOL, L69 3EN.

JAHN, Mr. Philip, BSc ACA *2009;* 50 A Thane Villas, Holloway, LONDON, N7 7PG.

JAHNKE, Miss. Holly Elizabeth, BEng ACA CTA *2001;* (Tax Fac), 14 Lee Terrace, Blackheath, LONDON, SE3 9TZ.

JAIJEE, Miss. Anjali, ACA *2009;* 12 High Ridge Way, Radbrook Green, SHREWSBURY, SY3 6DJ.

JAIN, Mr. Anand Jagdish, BSc(Hons) ACA CF *2001;* CBPE Capital LLP, 2 George Yard, LONDON, EC3V 9DH.

JAIN, Mr. Gautam Jagdish, MA ACA *2000;* Flat 16 Anchorage Point, 42 Cuba Street, LONDON, E14 8NE.

•**JAIN, Ms. Geetika, ACA** *2005;* (Tax Fac), Geetika Jain Accountancy Services, 123 Thornbury Road, 15 Leworth, ISLEWORTH, MIDDLESEX, TW7 4ND.

JAIN, Mr. Krishna, ACA *1993;* Gazprom House, Gazprom Marketing & Trading Ltd, 60 Marina Place Hampton Wick, KINGSTON UPON THAMES, KT1 4BH.

JAIN, Mr. Maneesh, MA ACA *1996;* Ground Floor, 68 Redcliffe Square, LONDON, SW10 9BN.

JAIN, Mr. Manish, BSc ACA *1997;* 35 Chemin De La Prairie, 1296 COPPET, VAUD, SWITZERLAND.

JAIN, Mr. Mitthu, BSc FCA *1995;* PO Box 391323, MOUNTAIN VIEW, CA 94039, UNITED STATES.

JAIN, Mr. Mohit Omprakash, BSc ACA *1997;* 2 Weymouth Avenue, LONDON, W5 4SA.

JAIN, Mr. Rohit, BSc ACA *2005;* 28 Angus Drive, RUISLIP, MIDDLESEX, HA4 0SB.

JAIN, Mrs. Salina, ACA *2007;* 101 Hurworth Avenue, SLOUGH, SL3 7FG.

JAIN, Mr. Sharad Prasad, FCA *1983;* with PricewaterhouseCoopers, 1 Seagate, Suite 1800, TOLEDO, OH 43604-1574, UNITED STATES.

•**JAITLY, Mr. Ashvani Kumar, FCA** *1975;* (Tax Fac), Leat Thorn & Partners, 64 High View, PINNER, MIDDLESEX, HA5 3PB.

•Ⓘ**JAITLY, Mr. Rajiv, MSc FCA FABRP** *1988;* 5 Wighton Mews, London Road, ISLEWORTH, MIDDLESEX, TW7 4DZ.

•**JAKARA, Mr. Anthony Stephen, BA FCA** *1981;* Clarke Nicklin LLP, Clarke Nicklin House, Brooks Drive, Cheadle Royal Business Park, CHEADLE, CHESHIRE SK8 3TD.

JAKEMAN, Mr. Leonard John, ACA *1983;* 32 Gardens Walk, Upton-Upon-Severn, WORCESTER, WR8 0LL.

JAKES, Mr. Clifford Duncan, FCA *1965;* Deeracres, Lisle Court Road, LYMINGTON, SO41 5SH.

JAKES, Miss. Donna Suzanne, ACA *2010;* 86a Shortmead Street, BIGGLESWADE, BEDFORDSHIRE, SG18 0AP.

JAKES, Ms. Sarah Frances, BSc ACA *2009;* 8 Orchidhurst, TUNBRIDGE WELLS, KENT, TN2 3BZ.

JAKEWAYS, Mr. Mike, ACA *2009;* 72 Elderwood Place, LONDON, SE27 0HL.

JAKOB, Mr. Nicholas Francis, BSc ACA *1982;* Custom House Annexe 2nd floor, 32 St Mary at Hill, LONDON, EC3R 8DY.

JAKOB, Mr. Peter Murray, ACA *1985;* 41 Greenhill Road, Otford, SEVENOAKS, TN14 5RR.

JAKOBSEN, Mrs. Susan Anne, BSc(Hons) ACA *2002;* 3 Pembrook Mews, Wandsworth, LONDON, SW11 2UJ.

JAKOVLEVS, Mr. Sergejs, MSc ACA *2010;* 44 Matcham Road, LONDON, E11 3LF.

JAKOWYSZYN, Mrs. Natalie Elizabeth, ACA *2009;* Unit 4/5, Telewest Communications Communications House, Broad Lane, BRADFORD, WEST YORKSHIRE, BD4 8PW.

JALAF, Mr. Jaswant Singh, MA ACA *1995;* 25 Syon Park Gardens, Osterley, ISLEWORTH, MIDDLESEX, TW7 5NE.

•**JALAF, Mr. Sandeep, MSc BSc ACA CTA** *2005;* Finite, 88 Burnley Road, Dollis Hill, LONDON, NW10 1EH.

JALAL, Mr. Anjam, ACA *2008;* with Deloitte Corporate Finance Limited, Level 5, Currency House, Dubai International Financial Centre, DUBAI, UNITED ARAB EMIRATES.

JALAL, Mr. Malik Ahmad, BSc ACA *2003;* c/o Dr Sabra Jalal, House 27 National Park Road, General Officers Colony, RAWALPINDI, PAKISTAN.

JALES, Dr. Andrew Robert, PhD BSc ACA *2005;* 13 Wodeland Avenue, GUILDFORD, GU2 4JX.

•**JALIF, Mr. Avtar, BA ACA** *1994;* with KPMG LLP, 15 Canada Square, LONDON, E14 5GL.

JALIL, Mr. Muhammad Saqib, ACA *2010;* 3rd Floor, Finance Department, Pakistan Petroleum Limited, PIDC House, Dr. Ziauddin Ahmad Road, KARACHI SINDH PAKISTAN.

JALLANDS, Mr. Stephen, MA ACA *1995;* 10 Elswick Avenue, Bramhall, STOCKPORT, SK7 2PN.

JALLOH, Miss. Mariama Elaine, BA(Hons) ACA *2002;* 51 Oakwood Hill, LOUGHTON, IG10 3EW.

JAM, Mr. Ali Reza, FCA *1975;* KPMG Bayat Rayan, 3rd Floor, 239 Motahari Ave, TEHRAN, 15876, IRAN.

•**JAMAL, Mr. Abdulali Abdulmalek, BSc FCA** *1972;* (Tax Fac), A A Jamal Tax Consultants Limited, 28 Fairlop Road, LONDON, E11 1BN.

JAMAL, Mr. Alaudin Alibhai, BSc FCA *1972;* 7100 Woodbine Avenue, Suite 305, MARKHAM L3R 5J2, ON, CANADA.

JAMAL, Mr. Asad, BSc ACA *1985;* 5300 Stevens Creek Boulevard, Suite 500, SAN JOSE, CA 95129, UNITED STATES.

JAMAL, Mr. Imshan, BSc ACA *1993;* 3 Cumberland House, Clifton Gardens, LONDON, W9 1DX.

JAMAL, Mr. Karim Mohamed Kassam, BA ACA *1996;* 75 Highland Road, NORTHWOOD, MIDDLESEX, HA6 1JS.

JAMAL, Mr. Liaquatali Ramzanali Shariff, FCA *1974;* 1215 Saginaw Crescent, MISSISSAUGA L5H 3W4, ON, CANADA.

JAMAL, Mr. Mohamed, FCA *1973;* 1001 918 Cooperage Way, VANCOUVER V6B 0A7, BC, CANADA.

JAMAL, Mr. Nizar Ahmed, BSc FCA *1976;* 8 St. Margarets Crescent, LONDON, SW15 6HL. (Life Member)

JAMAL, Mr. Samir, ACA *2011;* Flat 212, Raphael House, 250 High Road, ILFORD, ESSEX, IG1 1YS.

•**JAMAL, Mr. Vazirali Mohamed, FCA** *1967;* DSJ Partners LLP, 2nd Floor, 1 Bell Street, LONDON, NW1 5BY.

JAMAL, Mrs. Yasmin, ACA *2011;* 87 Queniborough Road, LEICESTER, LE4 6GX.

JAMEEL, Mr. Mohammad Ali, BSc ACA *1994;* TPL Trakker Ltd., 39-K Block 6 P.E.C.H.S., KARACHI 74400, PAKISTAN.
JAMES, Mr. Adam Michael, BSc(Hons) ACA *2011;* 1 Clydesdale Close, DROITWICH, WORCESTERSHIRE, WR9 7SB.
•JAMES, Mr. Alan Graham, FCA *1982;* (Tax Fac), Alan James & Co, Quantum House, 59-61 Guildford Street, CHERTSEY, SURREY, KT16 9AX.
JAMES, Mr. Alan Hudson, BSc ACA *1987;* 14 Whalton Park, Gallowhill, MORPETH, NORTHUMBERLAND, NE61 3TU.
JAMES, Mr. Albert Edward, BSc FCA *1972;* Loughrigg, The Crescent, WYLAM, NE41 8HU.
JAMES, Mr. Alexander William, BSc(Hons) ACA *2003;* Flat 7 Kingsdown Point, 136 Palace Road, LONDON, SW2 3JZ.
•JAMES, Mrs. Alison Jane, BSc ACA *1991;* 11 Lauriston Park, The Park, CHELTENHAM, GLOUCESTERSHIRE, GL50 2QL.
JAMES, Mrs. Alison Rodger, BA ACA *1990;* 20 Garrick St, LONDON, WC2E 9BT.
JAMES, Mr. Alva Elliott, BA FCA *1974;* 99 High Street, KNARESBOROUGH, NORTH YORKSHIRE, HG5 0HL. (Life Member)
JAMES, Mrs. Amanda Jean, BSc ACA *1994;* 50 Gayville Road, LONDON, SW11 6JP.
•JAMES, Mr. Andrew Alan, FCA *1978;* James & Co, The Old Vineyard, 52 Stevenage Road, KNEBWORTH, SG3 6NN.
•JAMES, Mr. Andrew Christopher, BA FCA *1992;* (Tax Fac), Priors Little Cottage, 7 Church Street, Old Heathfield, HEATHFIELD, EAST SUSSEX, TN21 9AH.
•JAMES, Mr. Andrew Eric Stephen, BCom ACA *1983;* James Stanley & Co, 1733 Coventry Road, South Yardley, BIRMINGHAM, B26 1DT.
•JAMES, Mr. Andrew Ewart Harvey, FCA *1963;* 20 Alford Gardens, Myddle, SHREWSBURY, SY4 3RG.
JAMES, Mr. Andrew Keith, BSc ACA *1989;* The Old Pond House Morgans Vale Road Redlynch, SALISBURY, SP5 2HU.
JAMES, Mr. Andrew Mark, BSc FCA *1991;* First Great Western, 1 Milford Street, SWINDON, SN1 1HL.
JAMES, Mr. Andrew Thurstan Trewartha, MSc ACA *1992;* Vodafone, 1 Kingdom Street, LONDON, W2 6BY.
JAMES, Mr. Andrew William, BA ACA *2001;* Mask Cottage, East Garston, HUNGERFORD, RG17 7EU.
•JAMES, Miss. Anouska Ann, BA(Hons) ACA ACII *2002;* A & N Accountancy Solutions Limited, Willowbend, Dunwood Hill, East Wellow, ROMSEY, HAMPSHIRE SO51 6FD.
JAMES, Mr. Anthony, MA MBA FCA *1975;* The Lodge Ty Llangenny, Llangenny, CRICKHOWELL, POWYS, NP8 1TB.
JAMES, Mr. Anthony Clive, BSc FCA *1974;* 117 Wavertree Road, LONDON, SW2 3SN.
•JAMES, Mr. Anthony Edward, BSc FCA *1977;* (Tax Fac), James & Uzzell Limited, Axis 15, Axis Court, Mallard Way, Riverside Business Park, Swansea Vale SWANSEA SA7 0AJ. See also James & Uzzell
JAMES, Mr. Anthony John, BA ACA *1987;* 44 Alderney Street, LONDON, SW1V 4EU.
•JAMES, Mr. Anthony Ronald, FCA *1971;* James & Company, 15 Queens Walk, Thornbury, BRISTOL, BS35 1SR.
JAMES, Mr. Anthony William Searson, BSc ACA *1995;* Grosvenor, 70 Grosvenor Street, LONDON, W1K 3JP.
JAMES, Mr. Antony Ronald, FCA *1962;* Old Wall House, The Close, Tattingstone, IPSWICH, IP9 2PD. (Life Member)
JAMES, Mr. Barry Christopher, BA ACA *1990;* 51 Lambton Road, MANCHESTER, M21 0ZJ.
JAMES, Ms. Brenda Margaret, BA ACA *1995;* 24 Bloomfield Road, HARPENDEN, HERTFORDSHIRE, AL5 4DB.
•JAMES, Mr. Brian Richard, FCA *1975;* (Tax Fac), Brian James, 45 Wide Bargate, BOSTON, PE21 6SH.
JAMES, Mr. Carl Anthony Mark, BSc ACA *2009;* 76 Buxton Road, LONDON, E15 1QU.
JAMES, Ms. Caroline Philippa, BA ACA *2004;* 29 Albany Road, LONDON, W13 8PQ.
•JAMES, Mr. Carwyn Llyr, BA FCA *1981;* (Tax Fac), Llyr James, 25 Bridge Street, CARMARTHEN, SA31 3JS.
JAMES, Mr. Charles Barrie, FCA *1968;* Little Calartha, Higher Downgate, CALLINGTON, PL17 8HL. (Life Member)
•JAMES, Mr. Charles David, BSc FCA *1977;* (Tax Fac), Chantrey Vellacott DFK LLP, Russell Square House, 10-12 Russell Square, LONDON, WC1B 5LF.
JAMES, Miss. Christina, BSc ACA *2005;* Flat B 103 Tollington Way, LONDON, N7 6RE.
JAMES, Mr. Christopher, BSc ACA *1995;* 52 Abbotswood Road, LONDON, SW16 1AW.
JAMES, Mr. Christopher, BA ACA *2010;* Sunrise Medical Ltd Sunrise Business Park, High Street Wollaston, STOURBRIDGE, DY8 4PS.
•JAMES, Mr. Christopher Chesnaye, FCA *1971;* (Tax Fac), Richard Place & Co, 25 Springdale Way, Walkington, BEVERLEY, NORTH HUMBERSIDE, HU17 8NU.
JAMES, Mr. Christopher Howard, BSc ACA *2003;* 10 Little How Croft, ABBOTS LANGLEY, HERTFORDSHIRE, WD5 0BR.
JAMES, Mr. Christopher Ian, BEng ACA *2004;* Apartment 14 Trinity Court, 53 Wake Green Road, BIRMINGHAM, B13 9HW.
JAMES, Mr. Christopher Martin, BSc ACA *2003;* 24 Friars Gardens, Hughenden Valley, HIGH WYCOMBE, BUCKINGHAMSHIRE, HP14 4LU.
JAMES, Mr. Christopher Richard, FCA *1984;* Flat 3, 26 Draycott Place, LONDON, SW3 2SB.
•JAMES, Mr. Christopher Stephen, BSc ACA *1980;* (Tax Fac), C S James & Co Limited, 88 New Road, Skewen, NEATH, WEST GLAMORGAN, SA10 6HG.
JAMES, Mrs. Claire, BA ACA *1990;* Sidlow Barn, Sidlow, REIGATE, RH2 8PP.
JAMES, Miss. Claire Elizabeth, BSc ACA *1979;* Park Lodge, 55 Parkside Drive, Cassiobury, WATFORD, WD17 3AU.
JAMES, Mrs. Clare, BA ACA *2007;* Virgin Media Shared Services Organisation, Mayfair Business Park, Broad Lane, BRADFORD, WEST YORKSHIRE, BD4 8PW.
JAMES, Mr. Clement Peter, FCA *1962;* Le Fougueyra, 33350 FLAUJAGUES, FRANCE. (Life Member)
JAMES, Mr. Colin Charles, BSc ACA *1982;* Atlantic Security Ltd, Windsor Place, 18 Queen Street, HAMILTON HM11, BERMUDA.
JAMES, Mr. Colin John Richard, BA ACA *1987;* 39a Straight Bit, Flackwell Heath, HIGH WYCOMBE, HP10 9LT.
JAMES, Mr. Daniel Peter, ACA *2007;* 11 College Rise, MAIDENHEAD, SL6 6BP.
JAMES, Mr. Darren, BA ACA *1996;* 30 Wellington Street West, PO Box 400, Stn Commerce Court, TORONTO M5L 1B1, ON, CANADA.
JAMES, Mr. Darryl, BSc ACA *2001;* 24 Heol Nant, North Cornelly, BRIDGEND, MID GLAMORGAN, CF33 4DG.
•JAMES, Mr. David Adrian, FCA *1975;* James de Frias Limited, Llanover House, Llanover Road, PONTYPRIDD, CF37 4DY.
JAMES, Mr. David Anthony, FCA *1972;* Charleston House, Hawk Plant Hire & Sales Cruckmoor Lane, Prees Green, WHITCHURCH, SHROPSHIRE, SY13 2BS.
JAMES, The Venerable David Brian, BA FCA *1953;* 1 Llys Ger-y-Llan, Pontarddulais, SWANSEA, SA4 8HJ. (Life Member)
JAMES, Mr. David Ian, LLB ACA *1983;* 120 Ely Road, Llandaff, CARDIFF, CF5 2DA.
JAMES, Mr. David John, MA ACA *1992;* Strategia Horwath Sp. z o.o., ul Wiejska 12a, 00-490 WARSAW, POLAND.
JAMES, Mr. David Kenneth, BSc ACA *1980;* 20 Holywell Rise, LICHFIELD, WS14 9SW.
JAMES, Mr. David Mark, MA ACA *1989;* HEFCE, Northavon House, Coldharbour Lane, BRISTOL, BS16 1QD.
JAMES, Mr. David Martin, BA ACA *1988;* Sidlow Barn, Sidlow, REIGATE, RH2 8PP.
JAMES, Mr. David Martin, FCA *1962;* The Barn, 6 west Lane, SEATON, LE15 9BA.
JAMES, Mr. David Powell Randall, FCA *1959;* Sark Cottage, Crest Hill, Peaslake, GUILDFORD, GU5 9PE. (Life Member)
JAMES, Mr. David Pryce, BSc ACA *1987;* 63 Malvern Road, ENFIELD, MIDDLESEX, EN3 6DB.
JAMES, Mr. David Richard, BA ACA *2001;* University of Sussex, Arts Building B, Arts Road, Falmer, BRIGHTON, BN1 9QN.
JAMES, Mr. David Roy, ACA *2003;* 23 Saxon Grove, Willington, DERBY, DE65 6YD.
JAMES, Mr. David Thomas Edward, BSS FCA *1995;* 2a Highfield Road, WALTON-ON-THAMES, SURREY, KT12 2RJ.
JAMES, Mrs. Dawn Mary, ACA CA(SA) *2009;* Flat 9 Amber Court, 4-6 Bagshot Road, ASCOT, SL5 9NZ.
JAMES, Ms. Dawn Wendy, FCA *1991;* Unit D Prospect House, Hyde Business Park, BRIGHTON, EAST SUSSEX, BN2 4JE.
JAMES, Mrs. Deborah Anne, BA ACA *2004;* 10 Radcliffe Road, SALISBURY, SP2 8EH.
JAMES, Mrs. Deborah May, BSc ACA CTA *2000;* (Tax Fac), 28 Waun Ganol, PENARTH, SOUTH GLAMORGAN, CF64 3RH.
JAMES, Mr. Derek Albert, FCA *1953;* Ashridge, Chichester Road, DORKING, SURREY, RH4 1LR. (Life Member)
JAMES, Mr. Derek John, FCA *1954;* Bees Lane Barn, Shipton Oliffe, CHELTENHAM, GLOUCESTERSHIRE, GL54 4JF. (Life Member)
•JAMES, Mr. Derek Richard, FCA *1954;* (Tax Fac), Ickenham Property Services, 10 Hercies Road, Hillingdon, UXBRIDGE, MIDDLESEX, UB10 9NA. See also James Derek R & Co
JAMES, Mr. Derek William, FCA *1966;* Frog Hollow, Letcombe Bassett, WANTAGE, OXFORDSHIRE, OX12 9LP. (Life Member)
•JAMES, Mr. Duncan Ross, BA ACA *1995;* Deloitte LLP, Athene Place, 66 Shoe Lane, LONDON, EC4A 3BQ. See also Deloitte & Touche LLP
JAMES, Mr. Edward, BA FCA *1993;* 23 North Parade, YORK, YO30 7AB.
•JAMES, Mr. Edward Grenfell Davy, FCA *1963;* Grenfell James, 2 Shottery Brook Office Park, Timothys Bridge Road, Stratford Enterprise Park, STRATFORD-UPON-AVON, WARWICKSHIRE CV37 9NR. See also Grenfell James Limited
JAMES, Mr. Edward Morgan, BSc ACA *1990;* 297 Bloomfield Road, BATH, BA2 2NU.
JAMES, Miss. Elspeth Louise, BSc ACA *2000;* Johnston Carmichael, 7-11 Melville Street, EDINBURGH, EH3 7PE.
JAMES, Miss. Emma, BA ACA *2011;* 349 Tachbrook Road, LEAMINGTON SPA, CV31 3DE.
JAMES, Miss. Felicity Elizabeth, ACA CA(AUS) *2011;* 29 The Chase, LONDON, SW4 0NP.
•JAMES, Mrs. Frances Catherine, BSc FCA *1988;* Haines Watts Kent LLP, 4-5 Kings Row, Armstrong Road, MAIDSTONE, KENT, ME15 6AQ.
JAMES, Mrs. Gail, FCA *1981;* 36 High Street, Bozeat, WELLINGBOROUGH, NORTHAMPTONSHIRE, NN29 7NF.
JAMES, Mr. Gareth Francis, BSc ACA *1997;* 20 Ullswater Crescent, Morriston, SWANSEA, SA6 7QF.
JAMES, Mr. Gareth Russell, MEng ACA *2001;* Ladderbanks, 17 Ladderbanks Lane, Baildon, SHIPLEY, WEST YORKSHIRE, BD17 6RX.
JAMES, Mr. Garrod Alexander, MA(Hons) ACA *2000;* Wren House, Park Lane, Ashurst Wood, EAST GRINSTEAD, WEST SUSSEX, RH19 3TF.
JAMES, Mr. Gary Terence, BA FCA *1992;* with Grant Thornton, 6th Floor, Nexus Building, 41 Conaught Road, CENTRAL, HONG KONG ISLAND HONG KONG SAR.
JAMES, Mr. Gavin Keith, BSc FCA *1987;* Camelford, Bradcutts Lane, Cookham Dean, MAIDENHEAD, BERKSHIRE, SL6 9AA.
JAMES, Miss. Gemma, BSc ACA *2009;* with KPMG LLP, One Snowhill, Snow Hill Queensway, BIRMINGHAM, B4 6GN.
JAMES, Mr. Geraint, BSc ACA *1993;* Fagwr Ganol, Craig Cefn Parc, SWANSEA, SA6 5RW.
JAMES, Mr. Gerwyn, BSc ACA *2011;* 26 Dairyman Close, LONDON, NW2 1EP.
JAMES, Mr. Graham Douglas, BSc FCA *1977;* 1 Gavin Close, Thorpe Astley, Braunstone, LEICESTER, LE3 3UG.
JAMES, Mr. Guy Michael, ACA *1992;* 11 Lauriston Park, The Park, CHELTENHAM, GLOUCESTERSHIRE, GL50 2QL.
JAMES, Mrs. Helen Leigh, BA ACA *2005;* with H W Fisher & Company, Acre House, 11-15 William Road, LONDON, NW1 3ER.
JAMES, Ms. Helen Louise, ACA *2005;* 28 John Street, HINCKLEY, LE10 1UY.
JAMES, Mrs. Helen Mary, BSc ACA *1981;* Aylesford, 9 Long Lane, Tuckers Town, ST. GEORGES HS02, BERMUDA.
JAMES, Mrs. Helen Ophelia, BSc ACA *1991;* 9 Townsend Road, HARPENDEN, AL5 4BQ.
JAMES, Mrs. Helen Sarah, MA ACA ATII *1986;* Dixons Stores Group Plc, Maylands Avenue, Hemel Hempstead Industrial Estate, HEMEL HEMPSTEAD, HERTFORDSHIRE, HP2 7TG.
JAMES, Mrs. Hester, ACA *2009;* 2 Mellington Close, SHEFFIELD, S8 8JZ.
JAMES, Mr. Howard Trevelyan, BSc FCA *1981;* Green Ways, Llysworney, COWBRIDGE, SOUTH GLAMORGAN, CF71 7NQ.
JAMES, Mr. Huw David, BSc ACA *2005;* 3 Gellideg Road, Maes-y-coed, PONTYPRIDD, CF37 1EJ.
JAMES, Mr. Hywel Morgan Cledwyn, MA FCA *1961;* Canton House, New Street, Painswick, STROUD, GL6 6XH.
JAMES, Mr. Ian Andrew, ACA *2010;* K P M G Edward VII Quay, Navigation Way Ashton-on-Ribble, PRESTON, PR2 2YF.
JAMES, Mr. Ian Humphries, BSc FCA *1977;* 6 Stranks Close, Highworth, SWINDON, SN6 7DQ.
JAMES, Mr. James Henry Lander, FCA *1962;* 17 Gateways, Off Epsom Road, GUILDFORD, GU1 2LF.
JAMES, Mrs. Janet, BSc ACA *1991;* 2 Fielders Green, GUILDFORD, GU1 2JY.
JAMES, Mrs. Jayne Elizabeth, BA ACA *1992;* City & County of Swansea, 11b St. Marys Square, SWANSEA, SA1 3LP.
JAMES, Mrs. Jennifer, ACA *1993;* Oak Timbers, 84 The Maultway, CAMBERLEY, SURREY, GU15 1QF.
JAMES, Mr. Jeremy Gordon Douglas, BA ACA *1987;* Owenbeg, Kiltimon, Ashford, WICKLOW, COUNTY WICKLOW, IRELAND.
JAMES, Miss. Joanne Clare, BSc ACA *2001;* 3H16 1-310A, Postbus 10.000, 1951 CA IJMUIDEN, NETHERLANDS.
JAMES, Miss. Jocelyn Ann, BA ACA *1986;* 3rd Floor, 185 Park Street, LONDON, SE1 9BL.
JAMES, Mr. John, BA FCA *1975;* 9 Duncombe Grove, BIRMINGHAM, B17 8SJ.
JAMES, Mr. John Jesse, BSc FCA *1965;* 3 Wharf Road, Longueville, SYDNEY, NSW 2066, AUSTRALIA. (Life Member)
JAMES, Mr. John Leslie, FCA *1962;* Gladholm, 15 The Grove, MERTHYR TYDFIL, CF47 8YR. (Life Member)
JAMES, Mr. John Mansel, BA FCA *1963;* 35 Heol y Delyn, Lisvane, CARDIFF, CF14 0SR.
•JAMES, Mr. John Martin, BA FCA *1974;* (Tax Fac), J.Martin James, 101A High Street, YARM, TS15 9BB.
•JAMES, Mr. John Michael, FCA *1968;* 16 Clevedon Road, Tilehurst, READING, RG31 6RL.
•JAMES, Mr. John Paul, FCA *1972;* (Tax Fac), Paul James Associates, Turnstile Cottage, Firle Road, SEAFORD, BN25 2JD.
JAMES, Mr. John Peter Richard, ACA *1980;* Rua Nascimento Silva 538-301, Ipanema, RIO DE JANEIRO, 22421-020, BRAZIL.
JAMES, Miss. Josephine Ann, BSc ACA *1993;* (Tax Fac), Earlswood, Earls Road, TUNBRIDGE WELLS, KENT, TN4 8EA.
JAMES, Mrs. Julie Ann, LLB ACA *2002;* McCann Medical Communications Ltd, 19-21 King Edward Street, MACCLESFIELD, CHESHIRE, SK10 1AQ.
JAMES, Mrs. Juliet Anne, BA ACA *2002;* Fairholme, 12 Millway, REIGATE, SURREY, RH2 0RH.
JAMES, Miss. Kathryn, BSc ACA *1992;* Apartment 1, The Rock Mill, Rock Mill Lane, LEAMINGTON SPA, WARWICKSHIRE, CV32 6AZ.
JAMES, Mrs. Kathryn, FCA *1970;* 43 Chancery Lane, Debenham, STOWMARKET, IP14 6PH.
JAMES, Mrs. Kathryn Melanie, BSc ACA *1989;* 117 Walton Road, SIDCUP, DA14 4LL.
JAMES, Miss. Katie Alexandra, BSc ACA *2005;* Flat D, 11 Compton Road, LONDON, N1 2PA.
JAMES, Mr. Keith, FCA *1966;* Grange House, 76 Upton Park, Upton, CHESTER, CH2 1DQ.
JAMES, Mr. Kenneth Dudley, FCA *1962;* 50 The Green, Southwick, BRIGHTON, BN42 4FS.
JAMES, Mr. Kenneth Eric, FCA *1960;* Old Orchard Croft, 1A Highfield Grove, Carlton-In-Lindrick, WORKSOP, NOTTINGHAMSHIRE, S81 9ET. (Life Member)
JAMES, Miss. Keri Joanne, BSc ACA *1998;* 27 Portmore Park Road, WEYBRIDGE, KT13 8ET.
JAMES, Mr. Kevin, ACA *2011;* 116 Southmoor Road, OXFORD, OX2 6RB.
JAMES, Mr. Kevin Lloyd, BSc FCA *1980;* Brookwood House, Holcot Road, Moulton, NORTHAMPTON, NN3 7NW.
JAMES, Mr. Kingsley, BSc ACA *1993;* Emperor Design Zetland House, 5-25 Scrutton Street, LONDON, EC2A 4HJ.
JAMES, Mr. Lea Morris, BSc ACA *1993;* 44 Lincoln Hill, Ironbridge, TELFORD, SHROPSHIRE, TF8 7NY.
JAMES, Mr. Lee, ACA *2008;* 31 Crawford Drive, FAREHAM, PO16 7RW.
JAMES, Mrs. Linda Jane, ACA *1991;* 26 New Road, BRENTFORD, MIDDLESEX, TW8 0NX.
•JAMES, Mrs. Lisa Ann, BA ACA *1999;* (Tax Fac), Lisa James, 20 Gander Green, HAYWARDS HEATH, WEST SUSSEX, RH16 1RB.
JAMES, Mrs. Lorraine Evelyn, BSc ACA *1987;* St. Georges Bristol, Great George Street, off Park Street, BRISTOL, BS1 5RR.
JAMES, Mrs. Lyndsey Joy, ACA *2004;* 51 Holyoake Street, WELLINGTON, TA21 8LE.
JAMES, Mr. Malcolm David, BA ACA *1988;* 11 Dalton Street, CARDIFF, CF24 4HB.
JAMES, Miss. Margaret Eleri, BA ACA *1987;* (Tax Fac), 10 Cae Mawr, Penrhyncoch, ABERYSTWYTH, DYFED, SY23 3EJ.
JAMES, Mr. Mark, ACA *2009;* Old Post Office Cottage, Great Salkeld, PENRITH, CUMBRIA, CA11 9LW.
JAMES, Mr. Mark David, BEng FCA *1991;* Smugglers, Belmont Lane, HASSOCKS, BN6 9EP.
JAMES, Mr. Mark Jonathan Clipsham, BSc ACA *1991;* 31 St Botolphs Road, SEVENOAKS, TN13 3AQ.
JAMES, Mr. Mark Litten, BA ACA *1990;* 8 The Paddocks, Church Farm Court, Middle Tysoe, WARWICK, CV34 4LH.
JAMES, Mr. Mark Owen, BA ACA *1993;* (Tax Fac), 12 Millway, REIGATE, SURREY, RH2 0RH.
•JAMES, Mr. Mark William, BA FCA *1985;* PricewaterhouseCoopers CI LLP, Twenty Two Colomberie, St Helier, JERSEY, JE1 4XA.

JAMES - JANGIR Members - Alphabetical

JAMES, Mr. Martin David, BA ACA *1986;* Chantrey Vellacott DFK LLP, Russell Square House, 10-12 Russell Square, LONDON, WC1B 5LF.
JAMES, Mr. Martin Norman, FCA *1972;* 84 Heol-y-Deri, Rhiwbina, CARDIFF, CF14 6HJ.
JAMES, Mr. Martin Paul, LLB ACA *1989;* with PricewaterhouseCoopers SA, Birchstrasse 160, 8050 ZURICH, SWITZERLAND.
JAMES, Mrs. Mary Elizabeth, LLB ACA *2004;* 39 Trenton Drive, Long Eaton, NOTTINGHAM, NG10 2EG.
JAMES, Mrs. Maya Patricia, BSc ACA *1993;* Aviva Plc, Rougier Street, YORK, YO1 6HZ.
JAMES, Mr. Michael, BSc(Hons) ACA *2003;* 18/20 Benelong Street, SEAFORTH, NSW 2092, AUSTRALIA.
JAMES, Mr. Michael, FCA *1965;* 9 Leathercote, Garstang, PRESTON, PR3 1QT.
JAMES, Mr. Michael Joseph, MBA BSc ACA *1992;* Flat 16 Greenhill, Prince Arthur Road, LONDON, NW3 5UB.
JAMES, Mr. Michael Kenneth, FCA *1976;* 56a Killarney Street, Takapuna, AUCKLAND 0622, NEW ZEALAND.
JAMES, Mr. Michael Richard, BA ACA *1990;* 9 Underwood Road, SOUTHAMPTON, SO16 7BZ.
•JAMES, Mrs. Monica Christine Anne, BA ACA *1980;* (Tax Fac), Monica C.A. James, 2 Scots Cottages, Kington, Thornbury, BRISTOL, BS35 1NF.
JAMES, Mrs. Natasha Marita, MSci ACA *2003;* 10 Little How Croft, ABBOTS LANGLEY, HERTFORDSHIRE, WD5 0BR.
JAMES, Mr. Neil, BSc ACA *1994;* Petrochem Carless Ltd, Cedar Court, Guildford Road, Fetcham, LEATHERHEAD, SURREY KT22 9RX.
JAMES, Mr. Neil Philip, FCA *1989;* Princes Foods Ltd Royal Liver Building, Pier Head, LIVERPOOL, L3 1NX.
•JAMES, Mr. Neville Meirion, ACA *1981;* Marchwoods, 3 Berry Lane, Blewbury, DIDCOT, OX11 9QJ.
•JAMES, Mr. Nicholas Charles, FCA *1971;* James Accounting Limited, 6 Blenheim Mews, MINEHEAD, TA24 5QZ.
JAMES, Mr. Nicholas David, BA ACA *1985;* B N P Paribas Lease Group Plc Northern Cross, Basing View, BASINGSTOKE, HAMPSHIRE, RG21 4HL.
JAMES, Mr. Nicholas Michael Edward, FCA *1983;* Millbrook, 90 Royal Avenue, Onchan, ISLE OF MAN, IM3 1LE.
•JAMES, Mr. Nickolas Charles, BA ACA *1990;* (Tax Fac), Nick James, Yew Tree Cottage, Scot Lane, Chew Stoke, BRISTOL, BS40 8UW.
JAMES, Miss. Nicola Anne, BSc ACA *2011;* Flat 15, Fairheathe, 43 Putney Hill, LONDON, SW15 6QP.
JAMES, Mrs. Nicola Louise, LLB ACA *2001;* 31 Oxford Street, Caversham, READING, RG4 8HN.
JAMES, Mr. Nigel Rodney, BSc ACA *1981;* 24 Rosevale, Heald Green, CHEADLE, SK8 3RN.
JAMES, Mr. Norman Charles, BA FCA *1961;* 29 Rue des Peupliers, 93140 BONDY, FRANCE. (Life Member)
JAMES, Mr. Owen Rhys, BA ACA *2004;* 51 Links Road, LONDON, SW17 9EE.
JAMES, Mr. Paul Anthony, BSc FCA MBA *1995;* Valley View Lane 2, Prokovsky Hills, Beregovaya Street 3, 125367 MOSCOW, RUSSIAN FEDERATION.
JAMES, Mr. Paul James, BSc FCA *1978;* 96 Wakehurst Road, LONDON, SW11 6BT.
JAMES, Mr. Paul Leonard, FCA *1961;* 25 Ellenbridge Way, Sanderstead, SOUTH CROYDON, CR2 0EW.
JAMES, Mr. Paul Michael, BCom FCA *1986;* The Foodservice Centre, Cheddar Business Park, Wedmore Road, CHEDDAR, SOMERSET, BS27 3EB.
•JAMES, Mr. Paul Sewell, FCA *1976;* Sigma (Accounting Tax & Business Advice) LLP, Vale House, Over Compton, SHERBORNE, DORSET, DT9 4QS.
JAMES, Mrs. Penelope Jane, BSc ACA *1995;* Knoll House, North End, Broughton, STOCKBRIDGE, HAMPSHIRE, SO20 8AN.
JAMES, Mr. Peter Glenn, MA FCA *1980;* 14 Tofts Close, Titchmarsh, KETTERING, NN14 3DW.
JAMES, Mr. Peter Nicholas, MA ACA *1995;* 99 Hadlow Road, TONBRIDGE, KENT, TN9 1QE.
JAMES, Mr. Peter Owen, BSc ACA *2004;* with PricewaterhouseCoopers LLP, 31 Great George Street, BRISTOL, BS1 5QD.
•JAMES, Mr. Peter Richard, BCom FCA *1973;* Peter James, 71 Washford Road, SHREWSBURY, SHROPSHIRE, SY3 9HW.
JAMES, Mr. Peter Stoyle, BSc FCA *1961;* 7 Vicarage Close, Wrea Green, PRESTON, PR4 2PQ.
JAMES, Mrs. Phyllida Mary, MA FCA *1985;* Flat 17, Aspen Lodge, 61-63 Wimbledon Hill Road, LONDON, SW19 7QP.
JAMES, Mr. Richard, BSc ACA *2006;* 795 Columbus Avenue, Suite 10N, NEW YORK, NY 10025, UNITED STATES.
JAMES, Mr. Richard Andrew, BSc ACA *1992;* The Old Rectory, 2 Walkern Road, Benington, STEVENAGE, HERTFORDSHIRE, SG2 7LP.
•JAMES, Mr. Richard David, BA FCA *1986;* Four J's, 46 Chester Road, Stockton Heath, WARRINGTON, WA4 2RX.
JAMES, Mr. Richard David, BSc ACA *1989;* Alfa Finance Group, 25 Park Lane, LONDON, W1K 1RA.
JAMES, Mr. Richard Howell, FCA *1972;* Genrich, 4 Chemin Le Grenier, Commugny, 1291 GENEVA, SWITZERLAND.
JAMES, Mr. Robert Angus, BSc ACA *2002;* Flat 8 Langton Court, 1 Portinscale Road, LONDON, SW15 2HR.
JAMES, Mr. Robert Anthony, FCA *1964;* Rushbrook, Westbourne Crescent, Whitchurch, CARDIFF, CF14 2BL. (Life Member)
JAMES, Mr. Robert Joseph, ACA *2008;* 3 Fairfield Road, CHESTER, CH2 3RN.
JAMES, Mr. Robert Simon Glendon, BA ACA *2002;* 10 Glen Orchy Court, Cumbernauld, GLASGOW, G68 0DH.
JAMES, Mr. Robert William, BSc FCA *1980;* Business Complex 'Legion 1', 4 FloorBolshaya Ordynka Str., 40 Bldg 4, 119017 MOSCOW, RUSSIAN FEDERATION.
JAMES, Mr. Roger Lidington, FCA *1965;* Old Mill Hey, Mill Lane, Willaston, NESTON, CH64 1RQ. (Life Member)
JAMES, Mr. Roger Michael, FCA *1963;* Canfield, Lambridge Wood Road, HENLEY-ON-THAMES, RG9 3BP.
JAMES, Mr. Ronald Charles, FCA *1954;* The Hawthorns, Lodge Lane, Nailsea, BRISTOL, BS48 2BB. (Life Member)
JAMES, Mr. Russell Thomas, BSc ACA *1995;* Briar Cottage, Hawley Road, Blackwater, CAMBERLEY, GU17 9EU.
•JAMES, Mrs. Ruth Hazel, BSc FCA *1992;* Nolan James Limited, Suite 1, Armcon Business Park, London Road South, Poynton, STOCKPORT CHESHIRE SK12 1LQ.
JAMES, Mrs. Samantha Marie, BSc(Econ) ACA *1997;* Pippins, Trerhyngyll, COWBRIDGE, SOUTH GLAMORGAN, CF71 7TN.
JAMES, Mrs. Sarah, BA ACA *1991;* 89 Hertford Road, ALCESTER, B49 6AS.
JAMES, Mrs. Sarah Elizabeth, ACA *2009;* 17 Selston Road, Jacksdale, NOTTINGHAM, NG16 5LF.
JAMES, Miss. Sarah Kathleen, BSc ACA *1985;* 11 Oakley Gardens, MAIDENHEAD, BERKSHIRE, SL6 2FN.
JAMES, Mr. Simon Andrew, BSc ACA *1997;* Level 6 9 Help Street, Chatswood, SYDNEY, NSW 2067, AUSTRALIA.
•JAMES, Mr. Simon Andrew, FCA *1995;* Rawlinson & Hunter Limited, Trafalgar Court, 3rd Floor, West Wing, St Peter Port, GUERNSEY GY1 2JA.
•JAMES, Mr. Simon Noel, BA ACA *1986;* Carlton Haines Ltd, Carlton House, 28/29 Carlton Terrace, Portslade, BRIGHTON, BN41 1XF.
JAMES, Mr. Simon Powell, BA ACA *1997;* with Ernst & Young, The Ernst & Young Building, 680 George Street, SYDNEY, NSW 2000, AUSTRALIA.
JAMES, Mr. Simon Thomas, ACA *2011;* 115 Lavender Hill, TONBRIDGE, KENT, TN9 2AY.
JAMES, Mrs. Siobhan, BSc FCA *1985;* (Tax Fac), 12 Castle Street, St. Helier, JERSEY, JE2 3RT.
JAMES, Mrs. Stephanie, BSc ACA *1991;* Smugglers, Belmont Lane, HASSOCKS, BN6 9EP.
•JAMES, Mrs. Stephanie Sandra, BCom ACA *1993;* Stephanie James, 44 Lincoln Hill, Ironbridge, TELFORD, SHROPSHIRE, TF8 7NY.
JAMES, Mr. Stephen, FCA *1981;* Debt Lifeboat Limited Floor 12, Centre City Tower, 7 Hill Street, BIRMINGHAM, B5 4UU.
JAMES, Mr. Steven John, BSc ACA *1991;* 46 Ulleswater Road, Southgate, LONDON, N14 7BS.
JAMES, Mr. Stuart Allan, BSc FCA *1984;* 19 Highfield Road, CHELMSFORD, CM1 2NF.
JAMES, Mrs. Susan, BSc(Hons) ACA *2001;* 30 Ynyslyn Road, Hawthorn, PONTYPRIDD, CF37 5AS.
JAMES, Mrs. Susannah Jane, BA(Hons) ACA *2002;* (Tax Fac), 67 Oaken Lane, Claygate, Esher, ESHER, SURREY, KT10 0RQ.
JAMES, Miss. Tessa Patricia, BSc ACA *1991;* Flat F, 25 Russell Road, LONDON, W14 8HU.
JAMES, Mr. Thomas Harold, BSc FCA *1992;* euNetworks, 15 Old Bailey, LONDON, EC4M 7EF.
JAMES, Mr. Timothy Bidewell, MBA FCA *1971;* Independent Energy Solutions srl., Viale Liegi 41, 00198 ROME, LAZIO, ITALY.
JAMES, Mr. Timothy Richard, FCA *1971;* 2 Romsley Road, Daimler Green, COVENTRY, CV6 3LG.
•JAMES, Mrs. Tracey Dawn, BA ACA *1988;* Grant Thornton UK LLP, 3140 Rowan Place, John Smith Drive, Oxford Business Park South, OXFORD, OX4 2WB. See also Grant Thornton LLP
•JAMES, Miss. Tracey Denise, FCA *1991;* Holder Blackthorn, Blackthorn House, St Pauls Square, BIRMINGHAM, B3 1RL.
JAMES, Mr. Trevor Alan, BSc FCA *1984;* 18 Dawes Close, CLEVEDON, BS21 5HA.
•JAMES, Mr. Trevor Ernest, FCA DChA *1972;* Sheen Stickland LLP, 7 East Pallant, CHICHESTER, WEST SUSSEX, PO19 1TR.
JAMES, Mr. William Barron, FCA *1957;* 2 Hanbury Gardens, Braunston-in-Rutland, OAKHAM, LE15 8QN. (Life Member)
JAMES, Mr. William John, FCA *1956;* Rosewenna, 28 Church Street, St. Columb Minor, NEWQUAY, TR7 3EX. (Life Member)
JAMES, Mr. William Stirling, MA FCA *1968;* Champions Farm, Thakeham, PULBOROUGH, RH20 3EF.
JAMES, Mr. William Thomas, MA ACA *1991;* Kuwait Petroleum International Aviation Co Ltd Dukes Court, Duke Street, WOKING, GU21 5BH.
JAMES-LEE, Mr. Ewan, ACA *2004;* Bank of America Merrill Lynch, 5 Paternoster Square, LONDON, EC4M 7AG.
JAMES-MOORE, Mr. Rufus Cholmondeley, BSc FCA *1966;* 8 Newey Drive, KENILWORTH, WARWICKSHIRE, CV8 1QS. (Life Member)
JAMES-RENDLEMAN, Mrs. Helena Lucy Annette, BA ACA *1995;* 3745 Canterbury Court, Woodfield Hunt Club, BOCA RATON, FL 33434, UNITED STATES.
JAMESON, Mr. Alexander Raymond, FCA *1960;* 53 Hill Road, Portchester, FAREHAM, PO16 8LA. (Life Member)
JAMESON, Mr. Andrew David, BSc ACA *1999;* Orchard Homes and Developments Limited, Orchard House, 51-67 Commercial Road, SOUTHAMPTON, SO15 1GG.
JAMESON, Mr. Christopher, BSc ACA *2003;* 777 Dunsmuir Street, PO Box 10426, VANCOUVER V7Y 1K3, BC, CANADA.
JAMESON, Mrs. Helen Jane, MA ACA *1984;* Department of Transport, Great Minster House, 76 Marsham Street, LONDON, SW1P 4DR.
JAMESON, Mr. Ian, BSc FCA *1998;* N C C Education Services Ltd The Towers, Towers Business Park Wilmslow Road, MANCHESTER, M20 2EZ.
JAMESON, Mrs. Joanna Claire, BA ACA *2000;* The Gables, 87 Hillesden Avenue, Elstow, BEDFORD, MK42 9AJ.
JAMESON, Mr. Paul Andrew, BSc ACA *1983;* 42 Priory Avenue, LONDON, W4 1TY.
JAMESON, Mr. Paul Richard, BSc ACA *1996;* The Gables, 87 Hillesden Avenue, Elstow, BEDFORD, MK42 9AJ.
JAMESON, Mr. Richard Morpeth, BA ACA *1989;* TAG Worldwide, 29 Clerkenwell Road, LONDON, EC1M 5TA.
JAMIESON, Mr. Alan Rae Dalziel, BSc FCA *1979;* Underwood, Wildernesse Avenue, SEVENOAKS, TN15 0EA.
JAMIESON, Mrs. Aleida Laura, ACA *1981;* 8 The Chanonry, ABERDEEN, AB24 1RN.
JAMIESON, Miss. Angela Rosemary, BA ACA *2001;* PO Box 23464, CLAREMONT, 7735, SOUTH AFRICA.
JAMIESON, Ms. Ann Marie, ACA CA(AUS) *2009;* 36 Trewint Street, LONDON, SW18 4HB.
JAMIESON, Mr. Charles James Guy Auldjo, MA FCA *1972;* Dipley Farm, Dipley Common, Hartley Wintney, HOOK, RG27 8JS.
JAMIESON, Mrs. Christine, BSc ACA *2004;* 33 Riverdale Gardens, TWICKENHAM, TW1 2BX.
JAMIESON, Mr. David Matthew, ACA *2008;* Apartment 118, 50 Sherborne Street, BIRMINGHAM, B16 8FN.
JAMIESON, Mrs. Diane Elaine, BSc FCA *1988;* 10 Kingfisher Grove, WAKEFIELD, WEST YORKSHIRE, WF2 6SD.
JAMIESON, Mrs. Doris Anne, BA ACA *1987;* Pond Farm, 40 Greengate, Swanton Morley, DEREHAM, NORFOLK, NR20 4ND.
JAMIESON, Mr. Edward Robert Francis, MA ACA *2004;* Diageo Plc Lakeside Drive, Park Royal, LONDON, NW10 7HQ.
JAMIESON, Mrs. Eilish, BSc ACA *2002;* 6 The Gallops, More Lane, ESHER, SURREY, KT10 8AB.
JAMIESON, Mr. Iain Alexander, MA ACA *1991;* C A S Services Ltd Scott House, Alencon Link, BASINGSTOKE, HAMPSHIRE, RG21 7PP.
JAMIESON, Mr. Ian, FCA *1983;* Jamieson Corporate Finance LLP, 7th Floor, Manfield House, 1 Southampton Street, LONDON, WC2R 0LR.
JAMIESON, Mr. James William, FCA *1972;* 4 Valence Court, Aston Road, BAMPTON, OXFORDSHIRE, OX18 2AF. (Life Member)
JAMIESON, Miss. Joanna Clare, BSc ACA *1998;* 75 York Road, TEDDINGTON, TW11 8SL.
JAMIESON, Mr. Keith Roderick, BA ACA *1990;* (Tax Fac), 6 Cherry Leys, Steeple Claydon, BUCKINGHAM, MK18 2RL.
JAMIESON, Mr. Lindsay Stuart Napier, FCA *1973;* 5 Dunstan Street, SHERBORNE, DORSET, DT9 3SE.
JAMIESON, Mrs. Maureen Janice, FCA MAAT *1996;* 12 Atkinson Gardens, Royal Quays, NORTH SHIELDS, TYNE AND WEAR, NE29 6YJ.
JAMIESON, Mr. Michael Douglas Alister, FCA *1966;* Kingcraig, Westwell, ASHFORD, Kent, TN25 4LQ.
JAMIESON, Mr. Nicholas Alister, BA ACA *1997;* Lenthalls, 76 Church Lane, Dry Sandford, ABINGDON, OXFORDSHIRE, OX13 6JP.
JAMIESON, Mr. Parviz Homayounfar, BA FCA *1986;* 39 High Street, Datchet, SLOUGH, SL3 9EQ.
JAMIESON, Mr. Peter Ralph, BCom ACA *1989;* 57 Effra Road, LONDON, SW19 8PS.
•JAMIESON, Mr. Robert Ian, MA FCA CTA(Fellow) *1973;* (Tax Fac), Mercer & Hole, 76 Shoe Lane, LONDON, EC4A 3JB.
JAMIESON, Mr. Stephen Johan, BA ACA *1981;* Management Revisions Ltd, 9th Flooor, New Zealand High Commission, New Zealand House, 80 Haymarket, LONDON SW1Y 4TQ.
JAMIESON, Mr. Steven Mark, BSc ACA *2004;* Unit 414, 320 Harris Street, PYRMONT, NSW 2009, AUSTRALIA.
JAMIESON, Mr. Tom Grant, BSc FCA *1981;* Paterson.Jamieson.Associates, 1200-1199 West Hastings Street, VANCOUVER V6E 3T5, BC, CANADA.
JAMIESON, Mr. William Brian Ian, FCA *1951;* Wembridge House, Chithurst, Rogate, PETERSFIELD, GU31 5EU. (Life Member)
JAMIL, Mr. Aftab, FCA *1994;* 1327 Hearst Drive, PLEASANTON, CA 94566, UNITED STATES.
JAMIL, Mr. Salman, ACA *2001;* (Tax Fac), 24 Central Way, CARSHALTON, SM5 3NF.
JAMIL, Mr. Shahid, FCA *1967;* 41 Alfreton Close, LONDON, SW19 5NS.
JAMIL-O'NEILL, Ms. Seema, BSc(Econ) ACA *2001;* 5 Llanaway Road, GODALMING, GU7 3EB.
JAMISON, Miss. Abigail Waller Grace, BA(Econ) ACA *2001;* Hemming Group Ltd, 32 Vauxhall Bridge Road, LONDON, SW1V 2SS.
JAMISON, Mr. Mark Paul, BSc ACA *1980;* Ashling, 3 Sycamore Close, Fetcham, LEATHERHEAD, SURREY, KT22 9EX.
JAMSHED, Mr. Agha, ACA *1979;* 43/II Khayaban-E-Muslim, Phase VI Defence Housing Auth, KARACHI, PAKISTAN.
JAMSON, Mr. Andrew Peter, BSc ACA *1982;* 141 Nelson Street, WOOLOOWIN, QLD 4030, AUSTRALIA.
JAN, Mr. Philip, BA(Hons) ACA *2002;* Flat 1, 7 Trouville Road, LONDON, SW4 8QL.
JANE, Mr. Frederick Martin, FCA *1970;* Wheelbarrow Farm, Cornwells Bank, Newick, LEWES, BN8 4RX.
JANES, Mr. Daniel Paul, MA ACA *2004;* Barclays Capital, Level 42, 225 George Street, SYDNEY, NSW 2001, AUSTRALIA.
JANES, Mr. Denys Henry, MA ACA *1984;* Haukeveien 39, 1357 BEKKESTUA, NORWAY.
JANES, Mr. Gavin Christopher David, BSc ACA *2003;* The Phoenix, Central Boulevard, Blythe Valley Park, Shirley, SOLIHULL, WEST MIDLANDS B90 8BG.
JANES, Miss. Helen Clare, BA ACA *2001;* PO Box 3042, ROAD TOWN, TORTOLA ISLAND, VG1110, VIRGIN ISLANDS (BRITISH).
•JANES, Mr. Justin Paul, FCA *1970;* (Tax Fac), Flat 4C, 35 High Street, Sandridge, ST. ALBANS, HERTFORDSHIRE, AL4 9DD. See also The Janes Partnership
JANES, Miss. Mandy Elaine, ACA *2009;* H W Fisher & Co Acre House, 11-15 William Road, LONDON, NW1 3ER.
JANES, Mr. Paul Nicholas, BA ACA *1988;* 12 Lister Drive, NORTHAMPTON, NN4 9XE.
JANES, Mr. Peter Robin, BSc FCA *1995;* 24 Hatherleigh Close, MORDEN, SURREY, SM4 5AD.
JANES, Mr. Simon, BSc FCA *1982;* Dominion Insurance Co Ltd Midas House, 2 Knoll Rise, ORPINGTON, BR6 0NX.
JANES, Mr. Stuart Anthony Roland, ACA *2008;* 21 Woodville Court, LEEDS, LS8 1JA.
JANES, Mrs. Suzanne Marie, BA ACA *2001;* Hammond McNulty, Bank House Market Square, CONGLETON, CHESHIRE, CW12 1ET.
JANGIR, Mr. Saqab, BA(Econ) ACA *2004;* with BDO Binder, Level 19, 2 Market Street, SYDNEY, NSW 2000, AUSTRALIA.

JANI, Mr. Harish Girjashanker, FCA *1973;* Crystal Palace Football Club 1986 Ltd Selhurst Park Stadium, Holmesdale Road, LONDON, SE25 6PU.
•**JANI, Mr. Rajnikant Champaklal, BSc FCA** *1984;* (Tax Fac), Jani Taylor Associates Limited, Office 6A, Popin Business Centre, South Way, WEMBLEY, HA9 0HF.
JANJUA, Ms. Rohila Reshid, BA ACA *1996;* 35 Conygre Grove, BRISTOL, BS34 7DN.
JANKEL, Mr. Anthony Louis Harry, FCA *1973;* PO Box 1, WEYBRIDGE, KT13 8XR.
JANKEL, Miss. Zoe Sarah, BA ACA *2005;* Arup, 13 Fitzroy Street, LONDON, W1T 4BQ.
JANKUNAITE, Miss. Viktorija, BA ACA CTA *2006;* (Tax Fac), Research in Motion UK Ltd, 200 Bath Road, SLOUGH, SL1 3XE.
JANMOHAMED, Mr. Abdulraheman Mohamedali Ismaili, MBA BSc ACA *1981;* 38 Arundel Avenue, Sanderstead, SOUTH CROYDON, SURREY, CR2 8BB.
JANMOHAMED, Mr. Mehdi Abdulsultan Rahemtulla, FCA *1977;* P O Box 72630, NAIROBI, KENYA.
•**JANMOHAMED, Mr. Shabir Hassanali Moledina, FCA** *1989;* 92 Barrowgate Road, Chiswick, LONDON, W4 4QP.
•**JANMOHAMED, Mr. Shafiq Dawood Hassan, FCA** *1975;* S.D. Janmohamed, 235-2903 Rabbit Hill Road, EDMONTON T6R 3A3, AB, CANADA.
JANSE VAN RENSBURG, Mr. Francois Johannes, ACA CA(SA) *2010;* 25 Wilton Crescent, HERTFORD, SG13 8JS.
•**JANSEN, Mr. Wilhelmus Hendericus, FCA** *1994;* Prinses Margriet Plantsoen 46, PO Box 30715, 2500 GS THE HAGUE, NETHERLANDS.
JANSON, Mr. Edward Victor, BA FCA *1987;* with Deloitte & Touche GmbH, Franklinstrasse 50, 60486 FRANKFURT AM MAIN, GERMANY.
JANSON, Mr. Hamish Timothy Warren, BA FCA *1967;* Longhope, Newton Valence, ALTON, HAMPSHIRE, GU34 3RB.
JANSON, Mrs. Joyce, BA ACA *1989;* Zeller Strasse 37, 64753 BROMBACHTAL, GERMANY.
JANSSEN, Mr. Frits Cornelius, BSc FCA *1969;* Dymoke House, Easton, WINCHESTER, SO21 1EH.
JANSSEN, Mr. Luke, BSc ACA *2002;* TigerSpike, 448 W16th Street, 5th Floor Suite 10, NEW YORK, NY 10011, UNITED STATES.
JANSSENS, Mr. Peter Anthony, FCA *1962;* 3 Rue Mondefaire, 94440 VILLECRESNES, FRANCE.
JANSZE, Miss. Louise Barbara Elise, BA ACA *1996;* with Davison & Shingleton, Boundary House, 91-93 Charterhouse Street, LONDON, EC1M 6HR.
JANTA-LIPINSKI, Mr. Robert Gerhard, BSc FCA FCT *1978;* Pipers Cottage, Collapit, KINGSBRIDGE, DEVON, TQ7 3BB.
JANTET, Mr. Sebastien Guillaume Bernard, BA ACA *1996;* 9 Waldemar Avenue, LONDON, SW6 5LB.
JANTZEN, Mr. Marc Uwe, BA ACA *1995;* Tree Tops, 27 Birtley Rise, Bramley, GUILDFORD, SURREY, GU5 0HZ.
JANUARY, Mrs. Karen Theresa, BA FCA *1993;* 27 Oakapple Close, Willowbridge, BEDLINGTON, NE22 7LL.
•**JANUARY, Mr. Michael, BA FCA** *1982;* Michael January, 7 Birklands Park, London Road, ST. ALBANS, HERTFORDSHIRE, AL1 1TS.
JANUARY, Mr. Robert Paul, BA ACA *1993;* 27 Oakapple Close, Willowbridge, BEDLINGTON, NE22 7LL.
JANUSZEWSKI, Mr. Adam Josef, BSc ACA *1996;* 15 Woodstock Road South, ST. ALBANS, HERTFORDSHIRE, AL1 4QH.
JANUSZEWSKI, Mr. Justin John, BSc(Hons) ACA *2010;* 18 Brandling Court, Akenside Terrace, NEWCASTLE UPON TYNE, NE2 1TN.
JAQUES, Mr. Matthew David, BSc(Hons) ACA *2001;* 52 Borrowdale Croft, Yeadon, LEEDS, LS19 7FN.
JAQUES, Mr. Richard Charles, BA FCA *1990;* 14 Kershaw Grove, MACCLESFIELD, CHESHIRE, SK11 8TN.
JAQUES, Mr. Richard David, BSc ACA *1993;* 8 Craw Park, BRAMPTON, CA8 1UZ.
•**JAQUEST, Mr. Gordon Nicholas, FCA CTA** *1969;* (Tax Fac), Jaquest & Co, 29 Little Meadow, Loughton, MILTON KEYNES, MK5 8EH.
JARDINE, Mr. Andrew James, MBA BA FCA *1987;* 8 Shorland House, Beaufort RoadClifton, BRISTOL, BS8 2JT.
JARDINE, Mr. Christopher Douglas, MSc FCA *1971;* Pound House, 65 Updown Hill, WINDLESHAM, GU20 6DW.
JARDINE, Mr. Colin Ernest, BA FCA *1980;* 64 Churchill Crescent, Sonning Common, READING, RG4 9RX.
•**JARDINE, Mr. David, BA FCA** *1989;* Cragness, 44 New Platt Lane, Goostrey, CREWE, CW4 8NJ.
JARDINE, Mr. Paul Daniel, BCom FCA *2000;* 3 Wincanton Road, LONDON, SW18 5TZ.
JARDINE-PATERSON, Mr. David Henry, ACA *2009;* David Jardine-Patterson Balgray Ltd, Balgray, LOCKERBIE, DUMFRIESSHIRE, DG11 2JT.
JARMAN, Mr. David, LLB ACA *2006;* 37 Royal Victoria Park, BRISTOL, BS10 6TD.
•**JARMAN, Mr. David Neil, BSc FCA** *2000;* Buzzacott LLP, 130 Wood Street, LONDON, EC2V 6DL.
JARMAN, Mr. Graham Owen, FCA *1970;* 12 Craft Way, Steeple Morden, ROYSTON, SG8 0PF.
•**JARMAN, Mrs. Joanne, FCA** *1988;* Webb House Limited, 11 Duncan Close, Moulton Park Industrial Estate, NORTHAMPTON, NN3 6WL.
JARMAN, Mr. Martin Philip, BSc FCA *1993;* Little Copse, Starrock Lane, Chipstead, COULSDON, SURREY, CR5 3QD.
JARMAN, Mr. Matthew Richard, BSc ACA MSI *1994;* Morgan Stanley, 20 Bank Street, LONDON, E14 4AD.
JARMAN, Mr. Michael Charles, FCA *1963;* Castle Fields, BUCKINGHAM, MK18 6AA.
JARMAN, Mr. Michael Roger, FCA *1967;* Little Barn, Harby Lane, Colston Bassett, NOTTINGHAM, NG12 3FH.
JARMAN, Mr. Philip Austin, FCA *1949;* 2 Birkenholme Close, Headley Down, BORDON, GU35 8HJ. (Life Member)
JARMAN, Mrs. Richa, LLM LLB ACA *2001;* 8 Burkes Close, BEACONSFIELD, BUCKINGHAMSHIRE, HP9 1ES.
JARRAD, Mr. Mark Julian Donne, FCA *1966;* The Tile House, The Street, Chipperfield, KINGS LANGLEY, WD4 9BH. (Life Member)
JARRARD, Mr. Jonathan, MSc ACA *2009;* 19 Mossbury Road, LONDON, SW11 2PA.
•**JARRARD, Mr. Raymond Frederick, FCA** *1971;* (Tax Fac), CBHC LLP, Riverside House, 1-5 Como Street, ROMFORD, RM7 7DN.
JARRATT, Miss. Alison Alison Louise, BA ACA *1998;* Centurion Power Cleaning Ltd, 3 Stocks Lane, Steventon, ABINGDON, OXFORDSHIRE, OX13 6SG.
JARRATT, Mr. Andrew Christopher, BSc ACA *2000;* 50 Lycett Road, YORK, YO24 1NB.
•**JARRATT, Mr. Christopher Howard, BA(Hons) ACA** *2001;* Andrews & Palmer Limited, 32 The Square, GILLINGHAM, DORSET, SP8 4AR.
JARRATT, Mr. Mark Leslie, BA ACA *1997;* Whitechurch House, Winterborne Whitechurch, BLANDFORD FORUM, DORSET, DT11 0AP.
JARRATT, Mr. Peter Glynne, BA FCA *1957;* Nordmere House, Northumberland Avenue, HORNSEA, NORTH HUMBERSIDE, HU18 1EQ. (Life Member)
JARRED, Mr. Roy William, FCA *1953;* 53 Galleywood Road, Great Baddow, CHELMSFORD, CM2 8DJ. (Life Member)
JARRETT, Mr. Brian Leslie, BSc ACA *1992;* 7 Vale Cottages, Kingston Vale, LONDON, SW15 3RW.
JARRETT, Mr. Christopher John, FCA *1974;* Lakin Clark Financial Planning Ltd, 1 Union Crescent, MARGATE, KENT, CT9 1NR.
JARRETT, Miss. Kathleen Mary, ACA *1990;* Shell Information Technology International BV, PO Box162, 2501 AN DEN HAAG, NETHERLANDS.
JARRETT, Mr. Kenneth Richard, FCA *1959;* Claycross, 23 Windermere Way, Wray Common, REIGATE, RH2 0LW. (Life Member)
JARRETT, Mr. Lee, BSc ACA *2006;* with PricewaterhouseCoopers, West London Office, The Atrium, 1 Harefield Road, UXBRIDGE, UB8 1EX.
JARRETT, Mr. Leslie John, FCA *1948;* Resthaven, 123 Grand Drive, HERNE BAY, KENT, CT6 8HS. (Life Member)
JARRETT, Mr. Michael Andrew, FCA *1955;* 72 Parkhouse Road, MINEHEAD, SOMERSET, TA24 8AF. (Life Member)
JARRETT, Mr. Michael Richard, FCA *1953;* 2057 Touraine Lane, HALF MOON BAY, CA 94019-1444, UNITED STATES. (Life Member)
JARRETT, Miss. Susan Lynne, BSc ACA ACIS *1982;* 83 Saxon Way, Willingham, CAMBRIDGE, CB24 5UR.
JARROLD, Mr. Charles John, BSc ACA *1991;* Broomhill House, Broomhill, WIMBORNE, DORSET, BH21 7AR.
•**JARROLD, Mr. Roy Herbert, ACA FCCA** *2007;* Banham Graham, Windsor Terrace, 76-80 Thorpe Road, NORWICH, NR1 1BA. See also Banham Graham Corporate Limited
JARROLD, Mr. Stuart Anthony, BA ACA *1995;* 15 Great Groves, Goffs Oak, WALTHAM CROSS, HERTFORDSHIRE, EN7 6SX.
JARVIE, Miss. Marie, BA ACA *1991;* 8 Burnet Avenue, GUILDFORD, GU1 1YD.
•**JARVIE, Miss. Susan Christina, BSc FCA** *1980;* Whitelaw Wells, 9 Ainslie Place, EDINBURGH, EH3 6AT.
JARVIE, Mr. Thomas Frederick, BSc(Hons) ACA *2009;* Apartment 268 The Crescent, Hannover Quay, BRISTOL, BS1 5JR.
JARVILL, Mr. Christopher Mark, BSc ACA *1989;* with Ernst & Young LLP, 1 More London Place, LONDON, SE1 2AF.
JARVIS, Mr. Alistair Kenton, BSc ACA *1992;* 22 Douglas Road, HARPENDEN, HERTFORDSHIRE, AL5 2EW.
•**JARVIS, Mr. Andrew Douglas, BSc ACA** *2009;* AJ, 6a Deacon Road, LONDON, NW2 5QH.
•**JARVIS, Mr. Andrew Philip, BSc ACA** *2004;* with HAT Group of Accountants, 12 Cock Lane, LONDON, EC1A 9BU.
JARVIS, Mr. Andrew Russell, FCA *1991;* 12 West Avenue, ST. ALBANS, AL2 3HF.
•**JARVIS, Mr. Anthony Henry, FCA** *1978;* The Rowleys Partnership LLP, 6 Dominus Way, Meridian Business Park, LEICESTER, LE19 1RP. See also The Rowleys Partnership Limited
JARVIS, Mr. Antony Graham, BSc ACA *1995;* 5 Loch Avenue, ST KILDA EAST, VIC 3183, AUSTRALIA.
•**JARVIS, Mr. Brian John, FCA** *1964;* B J Jarvis & Co Limited, 109 Churchill Road, Earls Barton, NORTHAMPTON, NN6 0RE.
JARVIS, Mr. Charles Richard, MBA BA FCA *1974;* 2a Saffron Close, FOWEY, CORNWALL, PL23 1EU. (Life Member)
JARVIS, Mr. Christopher Paul, BSc ACA *2005;* 43 Fortescue Road, WEYBRIDGE, SURREY, KT13 8XG. See also Numerosity
JARVIS, Miss. Clare Margaret, BA(Hons) ACA *2002;* First Floor Flat, 41 Heythorp Street, LONDON, SW18 5BS.
JARVIS, Mr. Clive, BA ACA *1991;* Chemin du Marais 12, 1297 FOUNEX, VAUD, SWITZERLAND.
JARVIS, Mr. Darren, BSc ACA *1997;* Goldman Sachs Peterborough Court, 133 Fleet Street, LONDON, EC4A 2BB.
JARVIS, Mrs. Diane, BA ACA *1988;* 53B Mazlin Close, Edge Hill, CAIRNS, QLD 4870, AUSTRALIA.
JARVIS, Mr. Dudley Reginald, FCA *1958;* The Lilacs, 4 Orchard Close, Charmouth, BRIDPORT, DT6 6RS. (Life Member)
•**JARVIS, Mr. Elfed Wyn, BSc ACA** *1979;* Baker Tilly Tax & Advisory Services LLP, 12 Gleneagles Court, Brighton Road, CRAWLEY, WEST SUSSEX, RH10 6AD. See also Baker Tilly UK Audit LLP
JARVIS, Mr. George Baldwin, FCA *1959;* 14 Lodge Close, Stoke D'Abernon, COBHAM, KT11 2SG. (Life Member)
JARVIS, Mrs. Helen Mary, BA ACA *1991;* 9 Mortimer Close, Orleton, LUDLOW, SHROPSHIRE, SY8 4PG.
JARVIS, Mr. Ian Edward, BCom FCA MIoD *1997;* Brooklands, 8 The Green, Mickleover, DERBY, DE3 0DE.
JARVIS, Mr. Ian Ernest, MBA ACA *1992;* 11 Powderham Avenue, WORCESTER, WR4 0DN.
JARVIS, Mr. Ian Neville, ACA *1984;* 14 Skylark Rise, Woolwell, PLYMOUTH, PL6 7SN.
JARVIS, Mr. Ian Nicholas Helge, MA ACA *1987;* Man Group Plc, Sugar Quay, Lower Thames Street, LONDON, EC3R 6DU.
JARVIS, Mr. Ian Robert John, BSc ACA *2010;* 65 Erica Road, ST. IVES, CAMBRIDGESHIRE, PE27 3AG.
JARVIS, Mr. Ian Stuart, ACA *1992;* 35 Samson Road, Hellesdon, NORWICH, NR6 5HG.
JARVIS, Miss. Jacqueline Anne, ACA *1988;* 65 Streathbourne Road, LONDON, SW17 8RA.
JARVIS, Mr. John, FCA *1955;* Flat 1, Lansdown Lea, 48 Christ Church Road, CHELTENHAM, GLOUCESTERSHIRE, GL50 2PP. (Life Member)
JARVIS, Mr. John Edward, FCA *1955;* 71 Victoria Road, LONDON, E4 6BZ. (Life Member)
JARVIS, Mr. John Michael, FCA *1968;* 2 Greystone Park, Sundridge, SEVENOAKS, KENT, TN14 6EB.
JARVIS, Mr. Jon, BSc ACA *2009;* 10 Long Walk, NEW MALDEN, KT3 3EJ.
•**JARVIS, Mr. Kevin Leonard, FCA** *1975;* Jarvis & Co Business Services Ltd, 75 Main Road, ROMFORD, RM2 5EL.
JARVIS, Miss. Lisa Carole, ACA *2010;* 292 West Point, Wellington Street, LEEDS, LS1 4JT.
JARVIS, Mr. Mark Edwin, BSc ACA *1991;* 4 Donnington Place, Winnersh, WOKINGHAM, RG41 5TN.
JARVIS, Mr. Mark Gilbert, BSc ACA *1992;* 23 Kelsey Close, LISS, HAMPSHIRE, GU33 7HR.
JARVIS, Mr. Martyn, BA ACA *1992;* 22 Priory Way, Langstone, NEWPORT, GWENT, NP18 2JE.
JARVIS, Mrs. Mary Ann, ACA *1979;* Rowleys Partnership Ltd, 6 Dominus Way, Meridian Business Park, LEICESTER, LE19 1RP.
•**JARVIS, Mr. Michael Alan, FCA** *1973;* (Tax Fac), Michael A. Jarvis & Co, Edenthorpe, Grove Road, ROTHERHAM, S60 2ER.
JARVIS, Mr. Michael William, FCA *1974;* 13 College Lane, LONDON, NW5 1BJ.
JARVIS, Mr. Nicholas David Alexander, BSc ACA *2004;* Walpole cottage, 88 Walpole Avenue, COULSDON, CR5 3PN.
JARVIS, Mr. Nicky, ACA *2011;* 79 Malgraves Place, Pitsea, BASILDON, ESSEX, SS13 3QA.
JARVIS, Miss. Nicola Ann, LLB ACA *1996;* Yennadon Lodge, Burrator Road, Dousland, YELVERTON, PL20 6LU.
•**JARVIS, Mr. Paul, FCA** *1977;* Milby Associates Ltd, 11 Changebrook Close, NUNEATON, CV11 6XJ.
JARVIS, Mr. Paul Havelock Ernest, FCA *1965;* 3 The Heights, Cotman Road, NORWICH, NR1 4BZ.
JARVIS, Miss. Rachel Yoonshen, BA ACA *2005;* (Tax Fac), 27 Appleby Gardens, DUNSTABLE, BEDFORDSHIRE, LU6 3DB.
JARVIS, Mr. Richard, BSc ACA *2010;* 12 Norman Snow Way, NORTHAMPTON, NN5 6FH.
JARVIS, Mr. Richard Haydon, FCA *1981;* 18 Beaurevoir Way, Emscote Lawns, WARWICK, CV34 4NY.
JARVIS, Mr. Robert Payne, FCA *1973;* Northgate House, Northgate Drive, CAMBERLEY, GU15 2AP.
•**JARVIS, Mrs. Terri, FCA** *1998;* Ash Shaw LLP, 180 Piccadilly, LONDON, W1J 9HF.
JARVIS, Mrs. Tina Christine, ACA *1998;* 30 Carew Close, COULSDON, SURREY, CR5 1QS.
JARVIS, Mrs. Victoria, ACA *2010;* 12 Norman Snow Way, Duston, NORTHAMPTON, NN5 6FH.
JARVIS, Mr. William Alexander, FCA *1968;* 1 Rue du Pre Chauvin, 22550 MATIGNON, FRANCE. (Life Member)
JARY, Miss. Katherine Helen, BA ACA *1993;* 4 Forge Cottages, High Street, Flimwell, WADHURST, TN5 7PA.
JARZYNKOWSKA, Ms. Elzbieta, BSc(Hons) ACA *2002;* European Bank for Reconstruction & Development, 1 Exchange Square Primrose Street, LONDON, EC2A 2JN.
•**JASANI, Mr. Ashok, ACA** *1981;* Jasani & Co, 23 Wetherby Close, Queniborough, LEICESTER, LE7 3FR.
•**JASANI, Mr. Mazharhusein Abdulmalek Mohamed, FCA** *1972;* Jasani & Co, 380 Cherry Hinton Road, CAMBRIDGE, CB1 8BA.
JASANI, Mr. Narendra Kumar, FCA CF *1974;* SJ Grant Thornton, No 11, Faber Imperial Court, Jalan Sultan Ismail, 50250 KUALA LUMPUR, FEDERAL TERRITORY MALAYSIA.
JASANI, Mr. Nirmal, ACA *2009;* 46 Stainforth Road, ILFORD, ESSEX, IG2 7EH.
JASPAL, Mr. Kanwardeep, ACA *2011;* #1765/1 Sector 39-B, CHANDIGARH 160036, INDIA.
JASPER, Mr. Darren, ACA *2011;* 2 Upper Crooked Meadow, OKEHAMPTON, DEVON, EX20 1WW.
JASPER, Mr. Stephen Gary, ACA *2005;* 02 UK Ltd, 260 Bath Road, SLOUGH, SL1 4DX. See also Stephen Jasper
JASSAL, Mr. Amar Deep, BA(Hons) ACA *2004;* with PricewaterhouseCoopers, Darling Park Tower 2, 201 Sussex Street, GPO Box 2650, SYDNEY, NSW 1171 AUSTRALIA.
JASSAL, Mrs. Clare Patricia, BSc(Hons) ACA *2004;* with PricewaterhouseCoopers, Darling Park Tower 2, 201 Sussex Street, GPO Box 2650, SYDNEY, NSW 1171 AUSTRALIA.
JASSAL, Mr. Jaswinder, BSc ACA *2004;* 21 Gerrard Avenue, ROCHESTER, ME1 2RN.
•**JASSAL, Mr. Rajinder Kumar, BA FCA DChA** *1995;* (Tax Fac), Jassal & Company, 829 Stratford Road, Springfield, BIRMINGHAM, B11 4DA.
JASSAT, Miss. Bilkees, ACA *2009;* 21 Studley Road, LONDON, E7 9LU.
JASSI, Mrs. Sundash Kumari, BCom ACA *1998;* 101 Ivybridge Road, COVENTRY, CV3 5PG.
JAUFURALLY, Mr. Adam Surriff, BSc ACA *2004;* Lafarge Plasterboard, Gordano House, Marsh Lane, Easton in Gordano, BRISTOL, BS20 0NF.
•**JAUFURAULLY, Mr. Swadick Mohammud, FCA** *1978;* S.M. Jaufuraully, 122 Northover Road, Westbury On Trym, BRISTOL, BS9 3LG.
JAVAHERI, Mr. Iman, ACA CA(SA) *2009;* c/o PricewaterhouseCoopers, Prinses Margrietplantsoen 46, 2595 BR, DEN HAAG, NETHERLANDS.
JAVAHERY, Mr. Parviz Eftekhar, FCA *1968;* 1730 Garden Ave, NORTH VANCOUVER V7P 3A7, BC, CANADA.
JAVAID, Mr. Furkan Haider, BA ACA *1993;* 5 Bostock House, 14 Biscoe Close, HOUNSLOW, TW5 0UW.

JAVED, Mr. Kashif Irfan, BSc ACA *2000;* (Tax Fac), 20 Stepney City Apartments, 49 Clark Street, LONDON, E1 3HS.
JAVED, Mr. Khuram, MSc BSc (Hons) ACA *2011;* 21 Pound Road, WEDNESBURY, WEST MIDLANDS, WS10 9HJ.
JAVED, Mr. M Aslam, FCA *1976;* 32 Alla Ud Din Road, Cantt, LAHORE 54810, PAKISTAN. (Life Member)
•**JAVED, Mr. Rizwan, MPhil BSc FCA** *1997;* (Tax Fac), Javed & Co, 109 Hagley Road, Edgbaston, BIRMINGHAM, B16 8LA.
JAVED, Mrs. Susan Jennifer, BSc ACA *2004;* 76 Prince Thorpe Road, Scholars Heath, WILLENHALL, WEST MIDLANDS, WV13 2LD.
JAVERI, Mr. Rustom Naval, FCA *1967;* Apartment 128, Eustace Building, 372 Queenstown Road, LONDON, SW8 4PP. (Life Member)
JAWA, Mr. Sanjay, BA FCA *1989;* 54 Woodstock Road, LONDON, W4 1UF.
JAWAD, Mr. Aasim Wajid, BSc(Hons) FCA *2001;* 1/2 Khyayabane Mujahid, OffSaba Avenue, D.H.A Phase 5, KARACHI, SINDH, PAKISTAN.
JAWAID, Mr. Jamshaid Ahmed, FCA *1973;* 67/ B Block 5, Gulshan-E-Iqbal, KARACHI 47, PAKISTAN.
JAWANMARDI, Mr. Jehangir, FCA *1975;* Arab Banking Corporation, P.O. Box 5698, MANAMA, BAHRAIN.
JAWARA, Mrs. Victoria, BSc ACA *2011;* 38 Bachelor Road, HARROGATE, NORTH YORKSHIRE, HG1 3EQ.
JAWED, Mr. Omar, ACA *2008;* 97 Brockhurst Road, BIRMINGHAM, WEST MIDLANDS, B36 8JE.
JAWED, Mr. Yasir, BSc(Hons) ACA *2011;* Pricewaterhousecoopers Cornwall Court, 19 Cornwall Street, BIRMINGHAM, B3 2DT.
•**JAY, Mr. Antony Jonathan, BSc FCA** *1974;* Jay & Co, 28 Fishpool Street, ST. ALBANS, HERTFORDSHIRE, AL3 4RT.
JAY, Mrs. Catherine Anne, MA ACA *1986;* 6 Polyanthus Way, Kings Copse, CROWTHORNE, BERKSHIRE, RG45 6UZ.
JAY, Mr. Christopher John, BSc ACA *1992;* 19 The Old College, Wilkinson Court, RIPON, NORTH YORKSHIRE, HG4 2TW.
JAY, Mr. Christopher William, BSc ACA *1991;* 31 Foxleigh Meadows, Handsacre, RUGELEY, STAFFORDSHIRE, WS15 4TG.
JAY, Mr. David, FCA *1976;* Mulberry House Pinfold Lane, Kirk Smeaton, PONTEFRACT, WEST YORKSHIRE, WF8 3JT.
JAY, Mrs. Deborah Jane, BSc ACA *1985;* 54 Broadwells Crescent, Westwood Heath, COVENTRY, CV4 8JD.
•**JAY, Mrs. Lesley Ann Shaw, BA ACA** *1996;* Stanley House Consulting Limited, Stanley House, Trevellance Lane, PERRANPORTH, CORNWALL, TR6 0AX.
•**JAY, Mr. Michael John, FCA** *1987;* (Tax Fac), Mapus-Smith & Lemmon LLP, 48 King Street, KING'S LYNN, NORFOLK, PE30 1HE.
JAY, Mr. Michael Paul Johnson, FCA *1961;* 3 Gordon Road, SHEPPERTON, TW17 8JY.
JAY, Mr. Peter Arnold, FCA *1959;* Corner Lodge, Kennedy Close, PINNER, MIDDLESEX, HA5 4HL. (Life Member)
JAY, Mr. Peter Bernard, FCA *1979;* (Tax Fac), 16 Gorse Walk, Hazlemere, HIGH WYCOMBE, HP15 7UN.
•**JAY, Mrs. Rachel Elizabeth, BSc ACA** *1998;* Rachel Sykes, The Old Church, West Allerdean, BERWICK-UPON-TWEED, TD15 2TD.
•**JAY, Mr. Stephen John, MA FCA ATII** *1976;* (Tax Fac), Stephen Jay, 17 Geraldine Road, Wandsworth, LONDON, SW18 2NR.
•**JAYAKAR, Mr. Antony Wilder, FCA** *1961;* Wilder Jayakar & Company, 15 Heathermount Gardens, CROWTHORNE, RG45 6HW.
•**JAYAKUMAR, Mr. Nagaraj Murthy, BSc(Hons) FCA CTA** *1994;* Jaya Accountancy, 283a Turf Lane, Royton, OLDHAM, OL2 6ET.
JAYANTILAL, Miss. Roshni, BA(Hons) ACA *2003;* Block 3-9-2 Pantai Panorama Condo, Jalan 112H, Off Jalan Kerinchi, Kg Kerinchi, 59200 KUALA LUMPUR, FEDERAL TERRITORY MALAYSIA.
JAYAPRAKASH, Mr. Deepak, BA ACA *2000;* 28 Pincroft Wood, LONGFIELD, DA3 7HB.
JAYARAJ, Mrs. Charlotte Hope, BSc ACA *1998;* Toys Hill House, Toys Hill, WESTERHAM, KENT, TN16 1QG.
JAYARAJ, Mr. Sandy John Marikili, MA ACA *1999;* Morgan Stanley, 20 Bank Street, LONDON, E14 4AD.
JAYARATNE, Mr. Merenna Ajit Mahendra De Silva, BSc FCA *1967;* 80/5 Layards Road, 5 COLOMBO, SRI LANKA. (Life Member)
JAYASEELAN, Mr. David Roshan, BSc ACA *1991;* Pricewaterhouse Coopers, PO Box 21144, 9th Floor BMB Centre, MANAMA, BAHRAIN.
JAYASEGARAM, Miss. Nyssa Jane Patricia, ACA *2009;* (Tax Fac), 3 Fryerns Terrace, BASILDON, ESSEX, SS14 3QD.
JAYASEKERA, Mr. Arthur Ranjit, FCA *1967;* 43/74 Poorwarama Mawatha, 05 COLOMBO, SRI LANKA.
JAYASENA, Mr. Yehen Bimalroy Lebunahewa, MSc ACA *1995;* 3 Gatesden Close, Fetcham, LEATHERHEAD, KT22 9QX.
JAYASINGHE, Mr. Mark Anthony, ACA *2002;* 11/64 Perfect Park, Moo 3 Ramkumheng, 164 Ratpattana Road, BANGKOK 10520, THAILAND.
JAYASINGHE, Mr. Prasan Keith, MPhil BSc FCA *1994;* 3 Hemmings Close, SIDCUP, DA14 4JR.
JAYASURIYA, Mr. Gayan, BSc ACA *2009;* 4 Morden Way, SUTTON, SURREY, SM3 9PH.
•**JAYAWARDENE, Mr. Peter Christopher Nihaler, FCA** *1968;* Gardezi Jay & Co, Hamilton House, 4a The Avenue, LONDON, E4 9LD.
•**JAYAWEERASINGHAM, Mr. Vadivelupillai, ACA FCCA** *2008;* Dharun & Co Accountants & Auditors Limited, 19 Tintern Avenue, LONDON, NW9 0RH. See also City Wise Accountants Limited
JAYCOCK, Mr. Martin Nicholas, BA ACA *1979;* with Deloitte LLP, 3 New Street Square, LONDON, EC4A 3BT.
•**JAYE, Mr. David Anthony, FCA** *1973;* (Tax Fac), Dodd Harris, 35/37 Brent Street, Hendon, LONDON, NW4 2FF
JAYES, Mr. Anthony Peter, LLB FCA *1962;* Pennycroft, The Orchard, Coley LaneLittle Haywood, STAFFORD, ST18 0UJ.
•**JAYES, Mr. Harold Robert, FCA** *1966;* Jayes Freed, C P House, Otterspool Way, WATFORD, WD25 8HP.
•**JAYSON, Mr. Geoffrey Russell, FCA** *1968;* Jayson Business Consultants Limited, Hillsdown House, 32 Hampstead High Street, LONDON, NW3 1QD.
•**JAYSON, Mr. Michael John Hugo, BSc FCA** *1997;* Crowe Clark Whitehill LLP, Arkwright House, Parsonage Gardens, MANCHESTER, M3 2HP. See also Horwath Clark Whitehill LLP and Crowe Clark Whitehill
JAYSON, Mr. Raymond Victor, MA FCA *1964;* Flat 2, 28 Radak Street, 92186 JERUSALEM, ISRAEL. (Life Member)
JAYSON, Mr. Richard Andrew, BEng FCA *1995;* 3 The Ridgeway, RADLETT, HERTFORDSHIRE, WD7 8PZ.
•**JAZAYERI, Mr. Amir Mohsen, FCA** *1973;* Amir M. Jazayeri, 15 Fleming Street, Vari, 16672 ATHENS, GREECE.
JEACOCK, Mr. David George, FCA *1958;* 21 The Parchments, LICHFIELD, WS13 7NA. (Life Member)
JEAFFRESON, Mr. Daniel Howard Henry, MA ACA *1992;* 22 avenue Madame Laffitte, 78600 MAISONS LAFFITTE, FRANCE.
JEAL, Mr. Derek Anthony, FCA MABRP *1974;* 3 Higher Lidden Road, PENZANCE, CORNWALL, TR18 4NZ.
•**JEAL, Mr. Ian Richard, BSc ACA** *1992;* Jeal & Co Limited, Sovereign House, 51 High Street, WETHERBY, LS22 6LR.
•**JEAL, Mr. Nicholas James, BSc ACA** *1996;* Deloitte LLP, Athene Place, 66 Shoe Lane, LONDON, EC4A 3BQ. See also Deloitte & Touche LLP
JEAN-LOUIS, Mrs. Marie Jennifer, ACA FCCA CA(AUS) *2003;* c/o Afrasia Bank Limited, 10 Dr Ferriere Street, PORT LOUIS, MAURITIUS.
JEANES, Mr. Colin, FCA *1976;* 15 Bracken Hall, Bracken Place, Chilworth, SOUTHAMPTON, HAMPSHIRE, SO16 3ET.
•**JEANROY, Mrs. Laragh Ann, FCA** *2001;* Peters Elworthy & Moore, Salisbury House, Station Road, CAMBRIDGE, CB1 2LA.
JEANS, Mr. Anthony Edgar, FCA *1972;* 19 Derby Road, Cheam, SUTTON, SM1 2BL.
JEANS, Miss. Gwen, BA(Hons) ACA *2001;* 5 Richmond Avenue, LONDON, SW20 8LA.
JEANS, Mr. Michael Anthony, BSc ACA *1982;* Zoggs Europe Ltd Courtyard House, The Square, LIGHTWATER, GU18 5SS.
JEANS, Mr. Michael Henry Vickery, MBE BA FCA *1967;* Flat 512 Balmoral Apartments, 2 Praed Street, LONDON, W2 1AL.
JEARY, Mr. Iain Kenneth, BA ACA *1998;* 10 Torwoodlee, PERTH, PH1 1SY.
JEATER, Mr. Martin Sidney Lockington, BSc ACA *1984;* 15 Burchett Coppice, WOKINGHAM, BERKSHIRE, RG40 4YA.
JEAVONS, Mr. Andrew, BA ACA *2007;* 58 Portland Road, West Bridgford, NOTTINGHAM, NG2 6DL.
JEAVONS, Mr. Michael John, BA ACA *1998;* Wulston, Droitwich Road, Claines, WORCESTER, WR3 7SR.
JEAVONS, Mr. Michael John, BSc ACA *1995;* 30 Kingfisher Close, Wheathampstead, ST. ALBANS, HERTFORDSHIRE, AL4 8JJ.
JEAVONS, Mr. Stephen, BA ACA *1999;* 40 Armstrong Road, NORWICH, NR7 9LJ.
JEAYS, Mr. Benjamin Edwin, BSc ACA *2005;* 85 Leyton Crescent, Beeston, NOTTINGHAM, NG9 1PS.
JEBARETNAM, Mr. Selvarajah, ACA CA(NZ) *2010;* Omar Arif & Co (Af0786), Suite 1610-1611, 16th Floor, Plaza Pengkalan, Batu 3 Jalan Ipoh, 51200 KUALA LUMPUR FEDERAL TERRITORY MALAYSIA.
•**JEBB, Mr. Roger, FCA** *1972;* Howell Davies Limited, 37a Birmingham New Road, WOLVERHAMPTON, WV4 6BL.
JEBSON, Mr. Alan Wayne, FCA *1971;* 8033 Nicklaus North Boulevard, WHISTLER V0N 1B8, BC, CANADA.
JEBSON, Miss. Claire Melanie, BSc ACA *1991;* 70 Glasslyn Road, LONDON, N8 8RH.
JEBSON, Mrs. Elspeth Ann Helen, BCom ACA *1996;* 28 Vicarage Road, Kings Heath, BIRMINGHAM, B14 7RA.
JEBSON, Miss. Laura Marie, BA ACA *2005;* Brown Butler, Apsley House, 78 Wellington Street, LEEDS, LS1 2JT.
JEBSON, Mr. Lawrence Ian, FCA *1977;* 138 Cravells Road, HARPENDEN, HERTFORDSHIRE, AL5 1BQ.
JEBSON, Mr. Michael John, FCA *1967;* 11 Barrow Hall Farm, Village Road Great Barrow, CHESTER, CH3 7JH.
JEBSON, Mr. Simon John, BCom ACA *1996;* Wolseley Plc Parkview, 1220 Arlington Business Park Theale, READING, RG7 4GA.
•**JEDRZEJEWSKI, Mr. Wladyslaw Mieczyslaw Michael, FCA** *1972;* (Tax Fac), W M M Jed & Co, 6 Old Barn Close, Hempstead, GILLINGHAM, KENT, ME7 3PJ.
JEDSMO, Miss. Sandra Liselott Victoria, BA ACA *2003;* 12 Kendall Road, BECKENHAM, KENT, BR3 4PZ.
JEE, Mr. John Frederic, FCA *1953;* Peckleton Hall, Church Road, Peckleton, LEICESTER, LE9 7RA. (Life Member)
JEE, Miss. Siew Yong, FCA *1974;* 1 Fei Ngo Shan Road, NGAU CHI WAN, KOWLOON, HONG KONG SAR. (Life Member)
JEE, Mrs. Susan, BSc FCA *1990;* The Poplars, 301 Crow Lane East, NEWTON-LE-WILLOWS, MERSEYSIDE, WA12 9TS.
JEEBAN, Mrs. Shirley Jean, BA ACA *1992;* c/o Musanada, PO Box 33700, Bainuna Street, ABU DHABI, UNITED ARAB EMIRATES.
JEENS, Mr. Robert Charles Hubert, MA FCA *1979;* 7 Cambridge Road, LONDON, SW20 0SQ.
JEEVAN, Miss. Mohini, BA ACA *2011;* 10 Sheraton Close, Elstree, BOREHAMWOOD, HERTFORDSHIRE, WD6 3PZ.
JEEVES, Mr. Andrew Michael Spencer, BEng FCA *1996;* with Deloitte LLP, 2 New Street Square, LONDON, EC4A 3BZ.
•**JEFF, Mr. Raymond George, FCA** *1972;* Howell Davies Limited, 37a Birmingham New Road, WOLVERHAMPTON, WV4 6BL.
JEFFAY, Mr. Cedric Bernard, FCA *1960;* 2 College House, South Downs Road, Bowdon, ALTRINCHAM, WA14 3DZ. (Life Member)
JEFFCOATE, Mr. Matthew Daniel, BA ACA *1994;* Royal London, Royal London House, Alderley Road, WILMSLOW, CHESHIRE, SK9 1PF.
•**JEFFCOTT, Mr. Alastair John, BA FCA** *1986;* (Tax Fac), McLintocks, 2 Hilliards Court, Chester Business Park, CHESTER, CH4 9PX. See also McLintocks Ltd and McLintocks Partnership
•**JEFFCOTT, Mr. Steven John, BA FCA** *1982;* Shipleys LLP, 10 Orange Street, Haymarket, LONDON, WC2H 7DQ. See also Abacus Fiscal Solutions Ltd
JEFFELS, Mr. Stephen Leonard, MA MBA ACA ATII *1992;* 4 Redbourne Drive, Wychwood Park, Weston, CREWE, CW2 5GH.
•**JEFFERD, Mr. Barry David, FCA CTA TEP** *1985;* (Tax Fac), George Hay, St George's House, George Street, HUNTINGDON, PE29 3GH. See also GH Online Accounting Ltd
JEFFERIES, Miss. Amy, BSc(Hons) ACA *2011;* 23 Lawson Road, Broomhill, SHEFFIELD, S10 5BU.
•**JEFFERIES, Mr. Anthony, FCA** *1986;* (Tax Fac), D E Ball & Co Ltd, 15 Bridge Road, Wellington, TELFORD, SHROPSHIRE, TF1 1EB.
JEFFERIES, Mr. Anthony Roger, MBA LLB FCA *1960;* Moorside, 2 Laurel Drive, BROADSTONE, BH18 8LJ. (Life Member)
JEFFERIES, Miss. Claire Elizabeth, ACA *2011;* Potash Farm Potash Road, Wyverstone, STOWMARKET, SUFFOLK, IP14 4SN.
JEFFERIES, Mr. David Myles, BA FCA *1993;* 1 Thorpe Road, HOCKLEY, SS5 4EP.
•**JEFFERIES, Mr. Ian Stewart, BEng ACA** *1991;* (Tax Fac), Jeffers & Stock Ltd, The Orchard, Mithian, ST. AGNES, CORNWALL, TR5 0QF.
•**JEFFERIES, Miss. Jemma, BSc(Hons) ACA** *2004;* Clarke Jefferies, 105 Duke Street, BARROW-IN-FURNESS, CUMBRIA, LA14 1RH.
JEFFERIES, Miss. Katharine Louise, MEng ACA *2007;* Grant Thornton, Hartwell House, 55-61 Victoria Street, BRISTOL, BS1 6FT.
JEFFERIES, Mrs. Lisa Ann, ACA *1998;* (Tax Fac), 27 Shepherds Hey Road, Totton, SOUTHAMPTON, SO40 2RD.
JEFFERIES, Mr. Michael Stuart, FCA *1972;* Church Avenue House, Lamerton, TAVISTOCK, PL19 8RN.
JEFFERIES, Mr. Neil, BSc ACA *2007;* 19 Alexandra Road, ST. ALBANS, HERTFORDSHIRE, AL1 3AU.
JEFFERIES, Mr. Paul Coningby, FCA *1958;* 2 Woodbridge Park, East Preston, LITTLEHAMPTON, WEST SUSSEX, BN16 1NL. (Life Member)
JEFFERIES, Mrs. Roberta, BA FCA *1978;* Field Fare Old End, Padbury, BUCKINGHAM, MK18 2BD.
JEFFERIES-CLARK, Mrs. Jody, ACA *2001;* Retrac Productions Ltd, Unit 3-4, Bramble Road, Techno Trading Estate, SWINDON, SN2 8HB.
•**JEFFERIS, Mrs. Carol Ruth, BA FCA** *1976;* Carol Jefferis, 3 Upper Station Road, RADLETT, WD7 8BY.
JEFFERIS, Mr. Simon Peter, BSc ACA *1985;* Imperial Tobacco Ltd, PO Box 244, BRISTOL, BS99 7UJ.
JEFFERIS, Miss. Wendy Jane, BA ACA *1992;* Knowles & Son (Oxford) Ltd, Holywell House, Osney Mead, OXFORD, OX2 0EA.
JEFFERSON, Mr. Andrew Michael, FCA *1982;* Felderland House, Felderland Lane, Worth, DEAL, CT14 0BT.
JEFFERSON, Miss. Catherine Anne, ACA *2009;* Grant Thornton UK Llp, 1 Whitehall Riverside, LEEDS, LS1 4BN.
•**JEFFERSON, Mr. Colin Peter, FCA** *1975;* C Jefferson FCA, 20 The Paddocks, WEYBRIDGE, SURREY, KT13 9RJ.
JEFFERSON, Mr. David John, ACA *1980;* 3 Mander Grove, WARWICK, WARWICKSHIRE, CV34 6RY.
JEFFERSON, Mr. George Kenneth, BSc ACA *1991;* P.O. Box 595, GEORGETOWN, GRAND CAYMAN, KY1-1107, CAYMAN ISLANDS.
•**JEFFERSON, Mr. Ian Andrew, FCA** *1991;* Wilkins Kennedy, Bridge House, London Bridge, LONDON, SE1 9QR.
JEFFERSON, Mr. Ian David, MSc ACA *1997;* Rose Cottage, 5 Backhouse Lane, Woolley, WAKEFIELD, WEST YORKSHIRE, WF4 2LB.
JEFFERSON, Mr. John Anthony, FCA *1966;* Binton Grange, Binton, STRATFORD-UPON-AVON, CV37 9TN.
•**JEFFERSON, Mr. Lee Spencer, MSc BEng ACA** *1998;* (Tax Fac), BDO LLP, 55 Baker Street, LONDON, W1U 7EU. See also BDO Stoy Hayward LLP
JEFFERSON, Miss. Nicola Mary, LLB ACA *1999;* Rose Cottage, 5 Backhouse Lane, Woolley, WAKEFIELD, WEST YORKSHIRE, WF4 2LB.
JEFFERSON, Mr. Paul Michael, BSc ACA *2010;* 22 Pingles Road, North Wootton, KING'S LYNN, NORFOLK, PE30 3RW.
JEFFERSON, Mr. Robert William, FCA *1975;* 19 Castlereagh, Wynyard, BILLINGHAM, CLEVELAND, TS22 5QF.
JEFFERSON, Mrs. Susan Margaret, BA ACA *1984;* 44 Netherwitton Way, NEWCASTLE UPON TYNE, NE3 5RP.
JEFFERY, Mr. Brian Trelogan, BSc FCA *1973;* 76 Avenue Du General Leclerc, 94100 ST-MAUR-DES-FOSSES, FRANCE.
JEFFERY, Mr. David John, BA ACA *1989;* Camelia Tree Cottage, Carbery Lane, ASCOT, BERKSHIRE, SL5 7EJ.
JEFFERY, Mrs. Deborah Jayne, BSc ACA *1998;* 61 Seventh Avenue, KEDRON, QLD 4031, AUSTRALIA.
JEFFERY, Mr. Derek Robert, FCA *1969;* 28212 Foothill Drive, AGOURA HILLS, CA 91301, UNITED STATES. (Life Member)
JEFFERY, Mrs. Diana Mary, BA ACA *1989;* 8 Eaves Close, ADDLESTONE, SURREY, KT15 2BF.
•**JEFFERY, Mr. Harry Ernest, BSc FCA** *1973;* (Tax Fac), Harry Jeffery & Co Ltd, St Lawrence, 28 Station Road, Bardney, LINCOLN, LINCOLNSHIRE LN3 5UD.
JEFFERY, Miss. Helen Margaret, ACA *2008;* 3 Avonmore Gardens, LONDON, W14 8RU.
JEFFERY, Mr. Ian Stuart, BA(Hons) FCA DChA *1980;* The Dyers Co Dyers Hall, 10 Dowgate Hill, LONDON, EC4R 2ST.
JEFFERY, Mrs. Jessica Meta, BSc ACA *2009;* with Winter Rule, Lowin House, Tregolls Road, TRURO, TR1 2NA.
JEFFERY, Mr. Peter, FCA *1954;* 11 Stoneacre Gardens, Appleton, WARRINGTON, WA4 5ET. (Life Member)
•**JEFFERY, Mr. Peter Graham, FCA** *1966;* (Tax Fac), P.G.Jeffery, 84 Townside, Haddenham, AYLESBURY, BUCKINGHAMSHIRE, HP17 8AW.
JEFFERY, Mr. Robert Alan, FCA *1975;* Teras, Clintmains, St. Boswells, MELROSE, ROXBURGHSHIRE, TD6 0DY. (Life Member)

JEFFERY, Mr. Robert James, ACA *2008;* 323 Maidstone Road, GILLINGHAM, KENT, ME8 0HS.
JEFFERY, Mr. Robin Adrian Rexworthy, FCA *1972;* Grinterley Ltd, 2 Lancer House, Hussar Court, WATERLOOVILLE, HAMPSHIRE, PO7 7SE.
•**JEFFERY, Mrs. Rosemary Jane, BSc FCA** *1988;* (Tax Fac), Rosy Jeffery Ltd, Highdown, Lime Kiln Lane, Uplyme, LYME REGIS, DT7 3XG.
•**JEFFERY, Mr. Stephen Peter, BSc ACA** *1987;* SRLV, 89 New Bond Street, LONDON, W1S 1DA.
JEFFERY, Miss. Victoria Anne Westcott, MA BSc ACA *2005;* 201 Talgarth Road, LONDON, W6 8BJ.
JEFFERYS, Mr. Alan Guy, FCA *1972;* 3 Stafford Close, Chafford Hundred, GRAYS, RM16 6ND.
JEFFORD, Mrs. Caroline, BSc ACA *1990;* 42 Woodland Drive, Thorpe End, NORWICH, NR13 5BH.
•**JEFFORD, Mr. David, MA FCA** *1981;* (Tax Fac), Larking Gowen, King Street House, 15 Upper King Street, NORWICH, NR3 1RB.
JEFFORD, Mr. Graeme Robert, BA(Hons) ACA *2003;* 87b Crookham Road, Church Crookham, FLEET, HAMPSHIRE, GU51 5NP.
JEFFORD, Mr. Stuart George, MA(Hons) MSci ACA *2010;* with PricewaterhouseCoopers LLP, 80 Strand, LONDON, WC2R 0AF.
JEFFREY, Mrs. Alison Elizabeth, BSc ACA *1992;* 29 Calderwood, GRAVESEND, DA12 4QH.
JEFFREY, Mr. David Frederick, BCom FCA *1955;* 16 Longfield Drive, AMERSHAM, HP6 5HD. (Life Member)
JEFFREY, Mr. David George De Mowbray, FCA *1965;* The Downs, Hurdle Way, Compton Down, WINCHESTER, SO21 2AN. (Life Member)
JEFFREY, Mr. David Michael, FCA *1991;* 2 East Causeway Close, Adel, LEEDS, LS16 8LN.
JEFFREY, Mr. Dennis, MSc FCA *1970;* 5 Parkside, MAIDENHEAD, SL6 6JP.
•**JEFFREY, Mr. James Stuart, FCA** *1975;* SME Corporate Finance Limited, Suite 6, 43 Bedford Street, LONDON, WC2E 9HA.
JEFFREY, Mr. Leonard, FCA *1954;* 7 The Hawthorns, Holly Lodge, LUTTERWORTH, LE17 4UL. (Life Member)
•**JEFFREY, Mr. Michael, BSocSc ACA** *2000;* with PricewaterhouseCoopers LLP, 89 Sandyford Road, NEWCASTLE UPON TYNE, NE1 8HW.
JEFFREY, Mr. Nicholas John, BSc ACA *1997;* with Grant Thornton UK LLP, Grant Thornton House, 22 Melton Street, Euston Square, LONDON, NW1 2EP.
JEFFREY, Mrs. Nicola Dianne, BA ACA CTA *1987;* Northumbrian Water Ltd, Abbey Road, DURHAM, DH1 5FJ.
•**JEFFREY, Mr. Peter Charles, BSc FCA** *1981;* PricewaterhouseCoopers LLP, Hays Galleria, 1 Hays Lane, LONDON, SE1 2RD. See also PricewaterhouseCoopers
JEFFREY, Mr. Peter Dudley, FCA *1972;* 318 Woodcrest Court, KELOWNA V1V 2L3, BC, CANADA.
JEFFREY, Mr. Richard, ACA *2007;* 318 Woodcrest Court, KELOWNA V1V 2L3, BC, CANADA.
•**JEFFREY, Mr. Simon John, BA ACA** *1999;* Hall Livesey Brown, 68 High Street, TARPORLEY, CW6 0AT.
JEFFREY, Miss. Zoe Eloise, ACA *2010;* The Downs, Hurdle Way, Compton, WINCHESTER, HAMPSHIRE, SO21 2AN.
JEFFREYS, Mrs. Daphne Mary, ACA *1990;* Rochelle, Four Crosses, Llandysilio, LLANYMYNECH, SY22 6RB.
•**JEFFREYS, Mr. David, BSc FCA** *1986;* Jeffreys Livemore, 112 The Lindens, LOUGHTON, ESSEX, IG10 3HU.
JEFFREYS, Mr. David Charles, BSc FCA *1985;* Canon Hall, La Turquie, Bordeaux, GUERNSEY, GY3 5EB.
•**JEFFREYS, Mr. David Christopher, MA ACA CTA** *1989;* David Jeffreys Ltd, First Floor, 4 Princes Street, HUNTINGDON, PE29 3PA.
JEFFREYS, Mr. John Evan, BSc ACA *1988;* 8 Ogmore Drive, Nottage, PORTHCAWL, CF36 3HR.
JEFFREYS, Mr. Mark William, BSc ACA *2002;* 5 Ravensworth Terrace, Sunniside, NEWCASTLE UPON TYNE, NE16 5LW.
JEFFREYS, Mr. Nicholas Richard, MA FCA MCT *1991;* World Health Organisation, Av Appia, 1211 GENEVA, SWITZERLAND.
JEFFREYS, Mr. Peter, BSc FCA *1978;* Ashlea Ltd, Scotland Road, CARNFORTH, LANCASHIRE, LA5 9RE.
JEFFREYS, Mr. Peter Edward, MA ACA *2003;* 16 Treherne Road, NEWCASTLE UPON TYNE, NE2 3NP.
JEFFREYS, Mr. Richard Benjamin, BA ACA *1981;* 40 Copse Close, Oadby, LEICESTER, LE2 4FB.
JEFFREYS, Mr. Richard Edwin John, BSc ACA *1989;* Chartis International, 175 Water Street, NEW YORK, NY 10038, UNITED STATES.
JEFFREYS, Mr. Robert Alan, FCA *1971;* Brook Cottage, Blakeney Road, BECKENHAM, BR3 1HA.
JEFFREYS, Mr. Rodney, FCA *1971;* 5 Kingsway, Blakeney, HOLT, NORFOLK, NR25 7PL.
JEFFREYS, Mr. Simon John Lewis, FCA *1995;* Broadmark House, 26 Meadway, ESHER, SURREY, KT10 9HF.
JEFFREYS, Mr. Simon Robert, BSc FCA *1981;* Appleton Manor Eaton Road, Appleton, ABINGDON, OXFORDSHIRE, OX13 5JR.
•**JEFFRIES, Mr. Alan, FCA** *1977;* (Tax Fac), Masons, 337 Bath Road, SLOUGH, SL1 5PR. See also Masons Forensic Accounting Services Limited
JEFFRIES, Mr. Brian John, BA FCA *1964;* 75 Ormond Crescent, HAMPTON, TW12 2TQ. (Life Member)
JEFFRIES, Mr. Christopher Graham, BA FCA *1981;* 1 Queens Rd, Cheadle Hulme, CHEADLE, SK8 5HG.
JEFFRIES, Mrs. Clare Lindsay, BA(Hons) ACA *2002;* Unit 11, 12 Broughton Road, ARTARMON, NSW 2064, AUSTRALIA.
JEFFRIES, Mr. David Lewis, FCA *1976;* J+S Limited, Riverside Road Pottington Business Park, BARNSTAPLE, DEVON, EX31 1LY.
JEFFRIES, Ms. Deborah Ann, BA ACA *1989;* Sundale Main Street, Tysoe, WARWICK, CV35 0SE.
JEFFRIES, Mr. Francis David, FCA *1949;* 4 The Marsh, Crick, NORTHAMPTON, NORTHAMPTONSHIRE, NN6 7TN. (Life Member)
JEFFRIES, Mr. Graham Alan, BA ACA *1993;* 59 Rosewood Avenue, Tottington, BURY, BL8 3HG.
JEFFRIES, Miss. Joanna Caroline, ACA ATII *1989;* 6A High Street, Willingham By Stow, GAINSBOROUGH, DN21 5JZ.
JEFFRIES, Miss. Kirstyn, BA(Hons) ACA *2004;* 29 Greenways, Standish, WIGAN, LANCASHIRE, WN6 0AF.
JEFFRIES, Mr. Mark Richard, ACA *1984;* 10 Lucy Lane, Loughton, MILTON KEYNES, MK5 8EP.
•**JEFFRIES, Mr. Michael William, FCA** *1969;* Wootton & Co, 29 Tidmarsh Road, Leek Wootton, WARWICK, CV35 7QP.
JEFFRIES, Mr. Paul, BA ACA *2001;* 6 The Ridge, SHEFFIELD, S10 4LL.
JEFFRIES, Mr. Peter Jocelyn, FCA *1963;* Brownings House, Ide Hill, SEVENOAKS, TN14 6JT. (Life Member)
JEFFRIES, Mr. Robert Anthony, FCA *1977;* (Tax Fac), Innovis House, A S B Law, 108 High Street, CRAWLEY, WEST SUSSEX, RH10 1AS.
JEFFRIES, Mr. Roger Ian, ACA *1979;* 40 Station Road, EPPING, CM16 4HN.
•**JEFFRIES, Ms. Sally-Anne, BA FCA** *1985;* (Tax Fac), K.A.Jeffries & Company, 18 Melbourne Grove, LONDON, SE22 8RA.
•**JEFFRIES, Miss. Sandra Lynn, BSc FCA** *1992;* APL Accountants LLP, 9 St. Georges Street, CHORLEY, LANCASHIRE, PR7 2AA. See also APL Accountants Limited
JEFFRIES, Mr. Stephen John, LLB FCA *2001;* 23 Laburnum Way, LOUGHBOROUGH, LEICESTERSHIRE, LE11 2FB.
JEFFRIES, Mr. Stephen Paul, FCA *1973;* 8 The Bowls, Vicarage Lane, CHIGWELL, ESSEX, IG7 6NB.
JEFFS, Mr. Alan, ACA *1982;* Lawrence David Ltd, Morley Way, Woodston Industy, PETERBOROUGH, PE2 7BW.
JEFFS, Mr. Christopher Richard, FCA *1958;* Ingleborough, 10 Lister Avenue, HITCHIN, SG4 9ES. (Life Member)
JEFFS, Mr. David Gareth, BSc ACA *1995;* Deutsche Bank, One Raffles Quay, SINGAPORE, SINGAPORE.
•**JEFFS, Mr. Graham Alan, FCA** *1970;* Jeffs Bishop & Partners (Consultants) Ltd, Grayswood, Crossways Park, West Chiltington, PULBOROUGH, WEST SUSSEX RH20 2QZ.
•**JEFFS, Mr. Harry, FCA** *1967;* AIMS - Harry Jeffs, 1 Beacon Buildings, Yard 23 Stramongate, KENDAL, LA9 4BH.
JEFFS, Mr. Neal, BSc(Econ) ACA *2000;* Brooklands, Forest Road, ASCOT, BERKSHIRE, SL5 8QF.
JEFFS, Miss. Sonya, BA ACA *2004;* 38 Ash Hill Drive, LEEDS, LS17 8JP.
JEFFS, Mr. Terence Paul Sheridan, BSc FCA *1974;* 509 Roselawn Avenue, TORONTO M5N 1K2, ON, CANADA.
JEHAN, Mr. John, BSc ACA *2005;* with Moore Stephens LLP, 150 Aldersgate Street, LONDON, EC1A 4AB.
•**JEHAN, Mr. Neale David, BSc ACA** *1998;* KPMG Channel Islands Limited, 20 New Street, St Peter Port, GUERNSEY, GY1 4AN.
•**JEHAN, Mr. Terence Ahier, FCA** *1976;* T.A. Jehan & Co, Ingouville House, Ingouville Lane, St Helier, JERSEY, JE4 8SP.
JEHRING, Mr. Peter John Yarington, FCA *1951;* 10 Metamorphoseos Str, Kissonerga, 8574 PAPHOS, CYPRUS. (Life Member)
JELBART, Mr. Grahame Rolfe, BSc FCA *1976;* 3 Columbus Court, 153 Rotherhithe Street, LONDON, SE16 5QN.
JELFS, Mr. Peter David, MChem ACA CTA *2004;* with Mazars LLP, 45 Church Street, BIRMINGHAM, B3 2RT.
JELICIC, Mrs. Elaine Ann, BSc ACA *1990;* 19 Downs Side, SUTTON, SURREY, SM2 7EH.
JELKS, Mr. Ronald Percy, FCA *1950;* Yew Tree HouseAbbey Green, Whixall WHITCHURCH, Shropshire, SY13 2PT. (Life Member)
•**JELL, Mr. Graham Edward, FCA** *1974;* Ridge House Associates Limited, Ridge House, Over Old Road, Hartpury, GLOUCESTER, GL19 3DH.
•**JELL, Mr. Stewart Alexander Edward, BA(Hons) ACA** *2002;* Shipleys LLP, 10 Orange Street, Haymarket, LONDON, WC2H 7DQ.
JELLEY, Mr. Glyn Paul, BA(Hons) ACA MAAT *2010;* (Tax Fac), 23 Ffordd Pennant, MOLD, CLWYD, CH7 1RP.
JELLEY, Mr. Keith, ACA CA(SA) *2008;* Flat 3, 23 Roland Gardens, LONDON, SW7 3PF.
JELLEY, Mr. Nicholas Duncan, MA ACA *2002;* 25 Hare Bridge Crescent, INGATESTONE, ESSEX, CM4 9DR.
•**JELLEY, Mr. Paul Alan, FCA** *1982;* Ford House, Lower Street, Chewton Mendip, RADSTOCK, BA3 4PD.
JELLEY, Mr. Richard Alan, FCA *1971;* Lockheed Martin Insys Ltd, Reddings Wood, Ampthill, BEDFORD, MK45 2HD.
JELLICOE, Mr. Andrew Raymond, BA ACA *1994;* 102 Brookhurst Avenue, Bromborough, WIRRAL, MERSEYSIDE, CH63 0PR.
JELLICOE, Mrs. Julia Louise, BSc ACA *1995;* 17 Blackwater Lane, CRAWLEY, WEST SUSSEX, RH107RL.
•**JELLICOE, Mr. Michael John, BSc FCA DChA** *1976;* (Tax Fac), Michael Jellicoe, 59 Knowle Wood Road, Dorridge, SOLIHULL, B93 8JP.
JELLICOE, Mr. Paul Martin, BA ACA *1986;* Miles Smith Reinsurance Ltd Birchin Court, 20 Birchin Lane, LONDON, EC3V 9DU.
JELLIS-BALDOCK, Mr. Douglas Roland Edward, FCA *1955;* 18A Abingdon Road, Dorchester on Thames, WALLINGFORD, OX10 7JY. (Life Member)
JELLYMAN, Mrs. Suzanne Jean, BSc ACA PGCE *2000;* Workmates Ltd, Hadwyn House, Field Road, READING, RG1 6AP.
JELMAN, Miss. Helene Sakina Nedjma, BSc ACA *1994;* Flat 9, 4 Elm Park Gardens, LONDON, SW10 9NY.
•**JEMMETT, Mr. David Ian, FCA** *1976;* Parker Business Services Ltd, Cornelius House, 178-180 Church Road, HOVE, EAST SUSSEX, BN3 2DJ.
•**JEMMETT, Mr. Richard John, FCA** *1972;* Carr Jemmett Limited, 66 St. Peters Avenue, CLEETHORPES, SOUTH HUMBERSIDE, DN35 8HP. See also Carr Jemmett (Cleethorpes) Ltd
JEMMETT-PAGE, Mrs. Shonaid Christina Ross, MA FCA *1985;* Spanyards Farm, Adams Lane, Northiam, RYE, EAST SUSSEX, TN31 6JR.
JENKIN, Mr. David Lawrence, FCA *1964;* 21 Churchfield Road, POOLE, DORSET, BH15 2QL.
JENKIN, Mr. David Robert, BSc ACA *2006;* with KPMG, Montague Sterling Centre, East Bay Street, PO Box N123, NASSAU, BAHAMAS.
JENKIN, Mr. Frederick Maurice, FCA *1968;* 3 Franklyn Close, ST AUSTELL, CORNWALL, PL25 3UP.
JENKIN, Mr. Nicholas Paul, ACA *1993;* 2 Trevean Way, NEWQUAY, CORNWALL, TR7 1TW.
•**JENKIN, Mr. Robert, FCA** *1966;* Jenkin & Co, 28 Waterloo Street, WESTON-SUPER-MARE, AVON, BS23 1LN.
JENKIN, Mr. Toby, BSc ACA *2006;* Apartment 6 Trinity Court, Newsom Place Manor Road, ST. ALBANS, HERTFORDSHIRE, AL1 3FT.
JENKING, Mr. Simon Douglas, BCom ACA *1980;* 94 Radford Park Road, PLYMOUTH, PL9 9DX.
•**JENKINS, Mr. Adrian Leslie Tilsley, BA ACA** *1996;* Financial Progression Limited, 16 Marlin Court, MARLOW, BUCKINGHAMSHIRE, SL7 2AJ.
JENKINS, Mrs. Agnieszka, PhD ACA *2000;* The Wood, Park Drive, Hale, ALTRINCHAM, CHESHIRE, WA15 9DH.
JENKINS, Mr. Alan David, BA FCA *1988;* Kaplan Terminal House, 52 Grosvenor Gardens, LONDON, SW1W 0AU.
JENKINS, Mr. Alexander Andraeas, BA ACA *2008;* 23 Nimrod Close, Woodley, READING, RG5 4UW.
JENKINS, Mr. Alexander Picton, BSc(Hons) ACA *2002;* Aneirin, Capel Dewi, CARMARTHEN, DYFED, SA32 8AD.
JENKINS, Mr. Alistair Hilary, BA(Hons) FCA *2001;* First Floor Flat, 145 Windsor Road, PENARTH, SOUTH GLAMORGAN, CF64 1JF.
JENKINS, Miss. Amanda Helen, BA ACA *1999;* 10 Hillside Avenue, Mutley, PLYMOUTH, PL4 6PR.
JENKINS, Mr. Andrew, BSc FCA *1982;* M7 Real Estate LLP, Kings Scholars House, 230 Vauxhall Bridge Road, LONDON, SW1V 1AU.
JENKINS, Mrs. Angela Jane, BA ACA *1991;* Down Lane Cottage, 4 Down Lane, Frant, TUNBRIDGE WELLS, EAST SUSSEX, TN3 9HW.
JENKINS, Mrs. Anita Helen, BA ACA *1992;* 10 Cleevelands Drive, CHELTENHAM, GLOUCESTERSHIRE, GL50 4QF.
JENKINS, Mrs. Anne, BA FCA *1984;* (Member of Council 1993 - 2003), 50 Beaconsfield Road, St. Margarets, TWICKENHAM, TW1 3HU.
JENKINS, Mr. Anthony, BA ACA *1992;* Espolsa-Sacs No 4, 08002 BARCELONA, SPAIN.
JENKINS, Mr. Arthur Bryan, FCA *1954;* 10 Beechwood Road, Portishead, BRISTOL, BS20 8EP. (Life Member)
JENKINS, Mr. Arwyn Meurig, BSc ACA *1989;* 54 Carisbrooke Way, Cyncoed, CARDIFF, CF23 9HW.
JENKINS, Sir Brian Garton, GBE MA FCA *1963;* (President 1985 - 1986) (Member of Council 1976 - 1995), Vine Cottage, 4 Park Gate, LONDON, SE3 9XE. (Life Member)
JENKINS, Mr. Brian Stuart, FCA *1959;* Beeston House Moss Lane, Beeston, TARPORLEY, CHESHIRE, CW6 9SQ. (Life Member)
JENKINS, Mr. Carey Blaise David, BSc ACA *1993;* 165 West 91st Street, Apt 11E, NEW YORK, NY 10024, UNITED STATES.
JENKINS, Miss. Carol Anne, BA ACA *1998;* 19 Eleanor Close, Hithe Point, LONDON, SE16 6PE.
JENKINS, Miss. Catherine, ACA *2010;* 27 Vernon Road, Poynton, STOCKPORT, CHESHIRE, SK12 1LP.
JENKINS, Mrs. Catherine Elizabeth, BSc ACA *2004;* 39 Bridgend Road, PORTHCAWL, MID GLAMORGAN, CF36 5RL.
•**JENKINS, Mr. Christopher Carter, BSc ACA** *1982;* Christopher C Jenkins & Co, Birchden Corner, Station Road, Groombridge, TUNBRIDGE WELLS, KENT TN3 9NG.
•**JENKINS, Mr. Christopher Crozier, BA FCA** *1979;* Wingrave Yeats Partnership LLP, 101 Wigmore Street, LONDON, W1U 1QU. See also Wingrave Yeats Limited
JENKINS, Mr. Christopher James, LLB BA(Econ) FCA *1972;* 118 Cambridge Road, Crosby, LIVERPOOL, L23 7UA.
JENKINS, Mr. Christopher James Richard, FCA *1968;* 3 Chapmans End, Puckeridge, WARE, SG11 1SR.
•**JENKINS, Mr. Christopher John, BA FCA** *1986;* with KPMG LLP, 15 Canada Square, LONDON, E14 5GL.
JENKINS, Mr. Clive Damian Alwyn, BA ACA *1995;* 12 Lamb Street, NORTH LAKES, QLD 4509, AUSTRALIA.
JENKINS, Mr. Darren, BA ACA *1992;* 7 Chatsworth Close, WEST WICKHAM, KENT, BR4 9QS.
JENKINS, Mr. David, MA ACA *1998;* The Prudential Assurance Co Ltd Minster House, 12 Arthur Street, LONDON, EC4R 9AQ.
JENKINS, Mr. David Charles, BSc ACA *1989;* Fitzgerald & Law, 8 Lincoln's Inn Fields, LONDON, WC2A 3BP.
JENKINS, Mr. David Geoffrey, FCA *1958;* 5 Pendean, BURGESS HILL, WEST SUSSEX, RH15 0DW. (Life Member)
•**JENKINS, Mr. David Geraint, BA FCA** *1968;* 24a Tennyson Road, HARPENDEN, AL5 4BB.
JENKINS, Mr. David Howard, FCA *1960;* Gilfachgam, Cilrhedyn, LLANFYRNACH, PEMBROKESHIRE, SA35 0AD. (Life Member)
JENKINS, Mr. David Lewis Rosser, ACA *1981;* 58 Heol Pentre Bach, Westmead Court, Gorseinon, SWANSEA, SA4 4ZA.
JENKINS, Mr. David Rhys, BSc ACA *1987;* 14 Courtlands Road, Shipton-under-Wychwood, CHIPPING NORTON, OXFORDSHIRE, OX7 6DF.
JENKINS, Mr. David Robert, BA(Hons) ACA *2001;* Lloyds TSB Bank Plc Tredegar Park, Pencarn Way Duffryn, NEWPORT, GWENT, NP10 8SB.
JENKINS, Mr. David Roy, BSc(Hons) ACA *1992;* 20 Kingsmead, Nailsea, BRISTOL, BS48 2XH.
JENKINS, Mr. David Stannard, FCA *1968;* 15 Hurlingham Gardens, LONDON, SW6 3PL.
JENKINS, Mr. David Ward, BEng FCA *1973;* Lanby, 16 White House, BARRY, SOUTH GLAMORGAN, CF62 6FB. (Life Member)
JENKINS, Mrs. Debby, ACA *2011;* 6 Selby Street, WALLASEY, MERSEYSIDE, CH45 7LN.

JENKINS, Mr. Derek Charles, FCA *1976;* Greenacres Cottage, Church Lane, Oving, CHICHESTER, WEST SUSSEX, PO20 2DG.
JENKINS, Mr. Derek Edmund, FCA *1976;* 1 Dukefield Houses, Dukefield Three Crosses, SWANSEA, SA4 3PT.
JENKINS, Mr. Derek William, FCA *1958;* The Pines, Springfield Road, CAMBERLEY, GU15 1AB. (Life Member)
JENKINS, Mrs. Dorothy, MSc ACA *1987;* 8 Paragon Court Flats, The Paragon, TENBY, DYFED, SA70 7HP.
JENKINS, Mr. Edward, BA ACA *2007;* 6 Dolby Road, LONDON, SW6 3NE.
JENKINS, Mr. Edward Horace Jarvis, FCA *1973;* Wilderton Grange, 4 Wilderton Road West, Branksome Park, POOLE, DORSET, BH13 6EF.
JENKINS, Mr. Edward James, MA ACA *1999;* 31 Jeffreys Street, LONDON, NW1 9PS.
JENKINS, Mr. Eifion Wynn, FCA *1970;* 11 Hayfield Drive, Gresford, WREXHAM, CLWYD, LL12 8YJ.
JENKINS, Mr. Eric Peter, FCA *1970;* Springfield, Gay Street Lane, North Heath, PULBOROUGH, RH20 2HN.
•JENKINS, Mr. Eric Richard, FCA *1971;* (Tax Fac), Eric R. Jenkins, 104 Southover, LONDON, N12 7HD.
JENKINS, Mrs. Fiona Catherine, BSc(Hons) ACA *2002;* 17 Oak Close, Yate, BRISTOL, BS37 5TN.
JENKINS, Mr. Frank Charles, CBE FCA *1961;* 1 Jacobs Close, TETBURY, GLOUCESTERSHIRE, GL8 8RE.
JENKINS, Mr. Gavin Allan Murray, BSc ACA *2000;* 61 Orchard Crescent, ENFIELD, MIDDLESEX, EN1 3NS.
JENKINS, Mrs. Gemma Louise, ACA *2003;* with Menzies LLP, Victoria House, 50-58 Victoria Road, FARNBOROUGH, HAMPSHIRE, GU14 7PG.
JENKINS, Mr. George Brian, FCA *1968;* 10 Bisum Street, DAMASCUS, SYRIAN ARAB REPUBLIC.
JENKINS, Mr. Glyn Alfred Lloyd, BSc FCA *1958;* White Ladies, Montagu Road, Datchet, SLOUGH, SL3 9DJ. (Life Member)
JENKINS, Mr. Glyn Alva, FCA *1955;* 2 Bruton Close, CHISLEHURST, KENT, BR7 5SF. (Life Member)
JENKINS, Mr. Graham Nicholas Vellacott, FCA *1969;* Huntercombe Golf Club Huntercombe, Nuffield, HENLEY-ON-THAMES, OXFORDSHIRE, RG9 5SL.
JENKINS, Mrs. Helen Jane, BSc ACA *1991;* 14 Courtlands Road, Shipton-under-Wychwood, CHIPPING NORTON, OXFORDSHIRE, OX7 6DF.
JENKINS, Mr. Henry Gardiner Ernest, BA FCA *1978;* Flat 10, 39 Queen's Gate, LONDON, SW7 5HR.
JENKINS, Mrs. Hilary Alexandra, BSc ACA *1992;* 10 The Avenue, Llandaff, CARDIFF, CF5 2LQ.
JENKINS, Mr. Huw David, MA FCA *1980;* 23 Woodfield Lane, ASHTEAD, SURREY, KT21 2BQ.
JENKINS, Mr. Huw William Howell, BSc FCA *1990;* 14 Blackwell Road, Barnt Green, BIRMINGHAM, B45 8BU.
•JENKINS, Mr. Ian Keith, BSc FCA *1991;* Swindells LLP, 20-21 Clinton Place, SEAFORD, EAST SUSSEX, BN25 1NP.
JENKINS, Mr. Ian Philip, BA ACA *1996;* Building 3125, Thorpe Park Century Way, LEEDS, WEST YORKSHIRE, LS15 8ZB.
JENKINS, Mr. Ian Simon, MEng ACA *1990;* 95 Castelnau, Barnes, LONDON, SW13 9EL.
JENKINS, Mr. Ifor Wynn, FCA *1970;* Ty Newydd Lon Cilan, Cilcain, MOLD, CLWYD, CH7 5PL.
JENKINS, Mrs. Jacqueline Elizabeth, BSc ACA *1990;* 54 Carisbrooke Way, Cyncoed, CARDIFF, CF23 9HW.
JENKINS, Mr. Jayson, BSc ACA *1990;* 12 Groveland Court, LONDON, EC4M 9EH.
JENKINS, Mr. Jean-Paul Michael, BA ACA *1991;* M+W Group GmbH, Lotterbergstr. 30, 70499 STUTTGART, GERMANY.
JENKINS, Mrs. Joanna Louise, ACA *1996;* Bromford Housing Group Exchange Court, Bradbourne Avenue Wolverhampton Business Park, WOLVERHAMPTON, WV10 6AU.
JENKINS, Mr. John David, BA FCA *1978;* St Anne's Vineyard, Wain House, Oxenhall, NEWENT, GL18 1RW.
•JENKINS, Mr. John Michael, FCA *1973;* (Tax Fac), John Jenkins & Co, Seal Lodge, Simms Lane, Mortimer, READING, RG7 2JP.
•JENKINS, Mr. John Richard, MA FCA *1989;* Trewen Consultancy, Trewen, Lon ty Llwyd, Llanfarian, ABERYSTWYTH, DYFED SY23 4UH.
JENKINS, Mr. John Robert, BSc FCA *1975;* The Redhouse, Chilbolton, STOCKBRIDGE, SO20 6BE.
JENKINS, Mr. Joseph Patrick, BA ACA *1992;* 23 Latch Burn Wynd, Dunning, PERTH, PH2 0SP.
•JENKINS, Mr. Julian Stuart, BSc FCA *1990;* PricewaterhouseCoopers LLP, 1 Embankment Place, LONDON, WC2N 6RH. See also PricewaterhouseCoopers
JENKINS, Mrs. Julie Elizabeth, BSc ACA *1992;* 23 Latch Burn Wynd, Dunning, PERTH, PH2 0SP.
JENKINS, Miss. Karen Elizabeth, BSc(Hons) ACA *2001;* 7 Grovelands Close, HARROW, MIDDLESEX, HA2 8PA.
JENKINS, Mrs. Karen Louise, BSocSc ACA *1996;* 34 Whitefields Gate, SOLIHULL, WEST MIDLANDS, B91 3GE.
JENKINS, Miss. Kate Harriet, ACA *2009;* Primary Capital Ltd, Augustine House, 6a Austin Friars, LONDON, EC2N 2HA.
JENKINS, Mr. Keith, BA FCA *1969;* 10 Haversham Court, Middleton Road, MANCHESTER, M8 4JY.
JENKINS, Mr. Keith Anthony, FCA *1969;* Maison de Bas, La Rue de la Ville Au Bas, St. Lawrence, JERSEY, JE3 1EW.
JENKINS, Mrs. Kim Rebecca, BSc(Hons) ACA *2001;* 3 Chestnut Close, Machen, CAERPHILLY, MID GLAMORGAN, CF83 8LF.
JENKINS, Mrs. Kirsty Louise, BSc(Econ) ACA *2001;* Cwm Ywen, Penrhyncoch, ABERYSTWYTH, CEREDIGION, SY23 3EW.
JENKINS, Mr. Lloyd Daniel, MEng ACA ACGI *2001;* 43 Casterton Road, STAMFORD, LINCOLNSHIRE, PE9 2UA.
JENKINS, Miss. Lucy Megan, BSc ACA *2007;* with Baker Tilly UK Audit LLP, 2 Whitehall Quay, LEEDS, LS1 4HG.
JENKINS, Ms. Lynne Maria, BSc FCA *1979;* Flat 6 The Sycamores, Devisdale Road, ALTRINCHAM, CHESHIRE, WA14 2BD.
JENKINS, Mr. Mark, BA ACA *2011;* 26 Oakfield Road, LONDON, N3 2HT.
JENKINS, Mr. Mark David, BA ACA *1989;* Shoaibi Group, P O Box 1280, AL KHOBAR, 31952, SAUDI ARABIA.
JENKINS, Mr. Mark James, BA ACA *1991;* 82 Thornhill Road, SUTTON COLDFIELD, WEST MIDLANDS, B74 3EW.
JENKINS, Mr. Mark Radclyffe, BA FCA *1989;* North Brook House, Sutton Lane, Sutton, WITNEY, OXFORDSHIRE, OX29 5RU.
•JENKINS, Mr. Martin Alexander, BA FCA CF *1993;* Deloitte LLP, 1 City Square, LEEDS, WEST YORKSHIRE, LS1 2AL. See also Deloitte & Touche LLP
JENKINS, Mr. Michael, BSc ACA *1996;* 34 Whitefields Gate, SOLIHULL, B91 3GE.
JENKINS, Mr. Michael Burton, BCom FCA *1954;* Hawthorns, Baskerville Lane, Shiplake, HENLEY-ON-THAMES, RG9 3JY. (Life Member)
JENKINS, Mr. Michael Ian, BA ACA *1999;* 4 Down Lane Cottage, Down Lane, Frant, TUNBRIDGE WELLS, KENT, TN3 9HW.
JENKINS, Mr. Michael John, BA FCA *1976;* 171 Denmark Hill, LONDON, SE5 8DX. (Life Member)
JENKINS, Ms. Navkiran Jit Kaur, BSc FCA MSI *1991;* Meadowside, Costock Road, Wysall, NOTTINGHAM, NG12 5QT.
JENKINS, Mr. Neil Richard, ACA *2008;* 59 Whitegate Close, Swavesey, CAMBRIDGE, CB24 4TT.
JENKINS, Miss. Nicola Jane, BA ACA *1999;* Post Office The Moor, Hawkhurst, CRANBROOK, TN18 4NX.
•JENKINS, Mr. Nicolaus Stuart, MA FCA *1987;* UHY Hacker Young, St John's Chambers, Love Street, CHESTER, CH1 1QN.
JENKINS, Mr. Owen David, BSc ACA *2007;* 1 Ashleigh Mews, LONDON, SE15 4BF.
JENKINS, Mrs. Patricia Anne, BSc FCA *1977;* Darbyns Brook, Littleford Lane, Shamley Green, GUILDFORD, GU5 0RH.
JENKINS, Mr. Paul Anthony Burton, BA ACA *1987;* True Digital, First Floor, Royal London, 42-46 Baldwin Street, BRISTOL, BS1 1PN.
•JENKINS, Mr. Paul Klauzner, BSc FCA *1979;* Jenkins & Co 2004 Limited, 86 Mildred Avenue, WATFORD, WD18 7DX.
JENKINS, Mr. Paul Richard, BA ACA *1989;* 10 Cleevelands Drive, CHELTENHAM, GLOUCESTERSHIRE, GL50 4QF.
•JENKINS, Mr. Paul Wayne, BSc ACA *1981;* Old Vicarage, 32 Higher Lane, Langland, SWANSEA, SA3 4NT.
JENKINS, Mr. Peter George, FCA *1974;* 24 School Lane, Weston Turville, AYLESBURY, HP22 5SE.
JENKINS, Mr. Peter Lewis, BSc FCA *1982;* MEMBER OF COUNCIL, 50 Beaconsfield Road, St Margarets, TWICKENHAM, TW1 3HU.
JENKINS, Mr. Peter William Sidney Kenwood, FCA *1960;* The Jays, 19 Lethbridge Park, Bishops Lydeard, TAUNTON, TA4 3QU. (Life Member)
JENKINS, Mr. Philip, BA ACA *1978;* 19 The Rise, Llanishen, CARDIFF, CF14 0RB.
JENKINS, Mr. Philip David, BSocSc FCA *1983;* 'Tre-Grar', 4 Lanelay Crescent, PONTYPRIDD, MID GLAMORGAN, CF37 1JB.
JENKINS, Mr. Philip John, BA ACA *1993;* Lyncroft, Wey Road, WEYBRIDGE, SURREY, KT13 8HN.
•JENKINS, Mr. Phillip, BA FCA *1992;* Phillip Jenkins Limited, 16 Parkfields, Pen-Y-Fai, BRIDGEND, MID GLAMORGAN, CF31 4NQ.
JENKINS, Mrs. Rachael Katie, MSc BSc ACA *2006;* 124 Essex Road, SOUTHSEA, HAMPSHIRE, PO4 8DJ.
JENKINS, Miss. Rachel Clare, BSc ACA *2005;* Flat 9, The Royal, Queens Road, PENARTH, SOUTH GLAMORGAN, CF64 1BQ.
JENKINS, Miss. Rhiannon Sarah, BSc(Hons) ACA PGCE *2001;* 8 Beech Lane, Spofforth, HARROGATE, NORTH YORKSHIRE, HG3 1AN.
JENKINS, Mr. Rhodri Huw, ACA FCMA *2010;* 76 Galleon Way, CARDIFF, CF10 4JB.
JENKINS, Mr. Richard, BA FCA *1978;* (Tax Fac), BPP, Bolton House, Chorlton Street, MANCHESTER, M1 3HY.
JENKINS, Mr. Richard David, BA(Hons) ACA *2002;* 47 Raymond Avenue, LONDON, W13 9UY.
JENKINS, Mr. Richard Frank, BA ACA *1982;* The Grange, Crabhill Lane, South Nutfield, REDHILL, RH1 5NR.
JENKINS, Mr. Richard Thomas, FCA *1970;* The Paddock, Wixoe, Stoke by Clare, SUDBURY, SUFFOLK, CO10 8UD. (Life Member)
JENKINS, Mr. Richard William, FCA *1960;* 101 Pettits Lane, ROMFORD, RM1 4ER. (Life Member)
JENKINS, Mr. Robert Henry, BA FCA *1988;* with Stryker UK Limited, Stryker UK Ltd, Stryker House, Hambridge Road, NEWBURY, BERKSHIRE RG14 5EG.
JENKINS, Mr. Robert John Garton, MA ACA *1979;* 22 Devereux Lane, LONDON, SW13 8DA.
•JENKINS, Mr. Roger Graham, FCA *1974;* Roger Jenkins & Co, Skyburriowe Vean, Skyburriowe Lane, Garras, HELSTON, CORNWALL TR12 6LR.
JENKINS, Miss. Rosalind Karen, BSc ACA *1989;* 40 Fairfax Road, TEDDINGTON, MIDDLESEX, TW11 9BZ.
JENKINS, Miss. Rosemary, BA ACA *2005;* 8 Dartmouth Road, ANNANDALE, NJ 08801, UNITED STATES.
JENKINS, Miss. Roxine Angelique, BSc ACA *2004;* 51 Chelsfield Grove, MANCHESTER, M21 7SU.
•JENKINS, Mr. Russell John, LLB FCA ACIArb MEWI *1990;* KTS Owens Thomas Limited, The Counting House, Dunleavy Drive, CARDIFF, CF11 0SN.
JENKINS, Miss. Ruth Gudrun, ACA DChA *2008;* 124 Lea Bridge Road, LONDON, E5 9RB.
•JENKINS, Miss. Sarah Price, BSc ACA *1988;* Price Jenkins & Co, 14 Plas y Ddol, Johnstown, CARMARTHEN, DYFED, SA31 3PL.
•JENKINS, Mrs. Sarah Rebecca, BSc ACA ATII *1991;* Milsted Langdon LLP, 1 Redcliff Street, BRISTOL, BS1 6NP.
JENKINS, Mrs. Sharon Vanessa, BSc FCA *1996;* Flat 60 Horsley Court, Montaigne Close, LONDON, SW1P 4BF.
•JENKINS, Mrs. Sheelagh Ann, BSc ACA *1995;* Amalveor Cottage, Amalveor, ST. IVES, CORNWALL, TR26 3AG.
JENKINS, Mrs. Sheila Katharine, BA ACA CTA *1989;* North Brook House, Sutton Lane, Sutton, WITNEY, OXFORDSHIRE, OX29 5RU.
JENKINS, Mrs. Sophie Elizabeth, BA ACA *2000;* with PricewaterhouseCoopers LLP, 1 Embankment Place, LONDON, WC2N 6RH.
JENKINS, Mrs. Sophie Helen, ACA *2008;* with KPMG LLP, One Snowhill, Snow Hill Queensway, BIRMINGHAM, B4 6GN.
JENKINS, Mr. Stanley Robert, FCA *1959;* Blatchington Lodge House, Firle Road, SEAFORD, EAST SUSSEX, BN25 2HJ. (Life Member)
JENKINS, Mr. Stephen Adrian, BSc ACA *1992;* Kings View Manor Road, Penn, HIGH WYCOMBE, HP10 8JA.
•JENKINS, Mr. Terence Paul, BSc FCA *1975;* Paul Jenkins, 39 High Street, PERSHORE, WR10 1EU.
JENKINS, Mr. Thomas, BSc ACA *2011;* 125 Endlesham Road, LONDON, SW12 8JP.
JENKINS, Mr. Thomas Arthur John, MA ACA *1999;* 24 Balham Park Road, LONDON, SW12 8DU.
JENKINS, Mr. Thomas Ian, MA(Oxon) ACA *2002;* with KPMG, 8th Floor, Tower E2, Oriental Plaza, 1 East Chang An Avenue, BEIJING 100738 CHINA.
JENKINS, Mr. Thomas Stephen, FCA *1973;* 61 Farley Road, SOUTH CROYDON, Surrey, CR2 7NG. (Life Member)
JENKINS, Mr. Tyssul Llewellyn, FCA *1966;* Tyssul Li Jenkins, 50 St. Mary Street, CARDIGAN, DYFED, SA43 1HA.
JENKINS, Mr. William Charles, BSc(Econ) FCA *2000;* Flat 60 Horsley Court, Montaigne Close, LONDON, SW1P 4BF.
JENKINS, Mr. William David Cleaton, BA ACA *1998;* 69 Eggbuckland Road, PLYMOUTH, PL3 5JR.
JENKINS, Mr. William John, FCA *1976;* Albion Ventures LLP, 1 King's Arms Yard, LONDON, EC2R 7AF.
JENKINSON, Mr. Adam Clifford, BA ACA *1993;* 33 Pentridge Way, Totton, SOUTHAMPTON, SO40 7QF.
JENKINSON, Mr. Andrew Timothy, BSc FCA *1977;* 16 Rosebery Avenue, HARPENDEN, AL5 2QP.
JENKINSON, Mr. Barry, BA FCA *1983;* Woodlands, Rue Du Friquet, Vale, GUERNSEY, GY6 8AN.
JENKINSON, Miss. Emma, BSc ACA *2004;* 11 Bell Drive, LONDON, SW18 5PZ.
•JENKINSON, Mr. Gordon William David, FCA *1984;* Thomas Coombs & Son, Century House, 29 Clarendon Road, LEEDS, LS2 9PG.
JENKINSON, Mr. John Andrew, BSc ACA *1993;* 96 Billington Gardens, Hedge End, SOUTHAMPTON, SO30 2RT.
JENKINSON, Miss. Kerry, BA ACA *1997;* 2 Cairnmore Road, Mossley Hill, LIVERPOOL, L18 4QW.
JENKINSON, Mr. Kevin John, MA ACA CTA *1989;* (Tax Fac), with PricewaterhouseCoopers LLP, Abacus House, Castle Park, CAMBRIDGE, CB3 0AN.
JENKINSON, Dr. Lynsey Suzanne, BSc ACA *2007;* 3400, 666 Burrard Street, VANCOUVER V6C 2X8, BC, CANADA.
JENKINSON, Miss. Nicola, BSc ACA *2000;* 5 Kings Park, LEIGH, LANCASHIRE, WN7 1UE.
•JENKINSON, Mr. Paul Niall, BSc ACA *1995;* (Tax Fac), Jenson Solutions Limited, Communications House, 26 York Street, LONDON, W1U 6PZ. See also Cornel Partners Limited
JENKINSON, Mr. Peter, FCA *1970;* Highfield, Florendine Street, Amington, TAMWORTH, B77 3DD.
JENKINSON, Mr. Philip Anthony, FCA *1973;* Iona, The Villas, Miltonhill, Kinloss, FORRES, MORAYSHIRE IV36 2UA.
•JENKINSON, Mr. Robert Charles, BA FCA *1980;* PricewaterhouseCoopers, Strathvale House, PO Box 258, GEORGE TOWN, GRAND CAYMAN, KY1-1104 CAYMAN ISLANDS.
JENKINSON, Mrs. Sharon Eugenie, BA ACA *2003;* 61 Halsey Drive, HITCHIN, HERTFORDSHIRE, SG4 9PZ.
•JENKINSON, Mr. Stephen Philip, BSc FCA *1987;* The cba Partnership, 72 Lairgate, BEVERLEY, HU17 8EU. See also CBA Financial Services Limited
JENKINSON, Mr. Stuart Camille, BA FCA CFE ACIL *1997;* Calyon Broadwalk House, 5 Appold Street, LONDON, EC2A 2DA.
JENKINSON, Mr. Timothy Simon, BSc ACA *1992;* Brunelcare, 3 Redcliffe Parade West, BRISTOL, BS1 6SL.
JENKINSON, Mrs. Valerie Carol, BSc FCA *1983;* Briery Hall Farm, Chevet Lane, Chevet Sandal, WAKEFIELD, WF2 6PT.
JENKS, Mr. Anthony Stephen, BCom ACA *1996;* EOS Solutions UK PLC, 2 Birchwood Office Park, Crab Lane, Fearnhead, WARRINGTON, WA2 0XS.
JENKS, Mr. Graham Christopher, BA FCA *1971;* 36 Copland Meadow, TOTNES, TQ9 6ES.
JENKS, Mrs. Jo, BA FCA *1996;* 4a Winnipeg Way, Kingston, WELLINGTON 6021, NEW ZEALAND.
•JENKS, Mr. Martyn Nigel, FCA *1975;* (Tax Fac), M N Jenks & Co Limited, 72 Commercial Road, Paddock Wood, TONBRIDGE, KENT, TN12 6DP.
JENKS, Mrs. Nicola Jane, BSc ACA *1996;* Pryors Mead, Weetwood, TARPORLEY, CHESHIRE, CW6 0NQ.
JENKS, Mr. Richard Albert Benedict, BA ACA *1993;* with RGL LLP, 8th Floor, Dashwood, 69 Old Broad Street, LONDON, EC2M 1QS.
JENKS, Sir Richard John Peter, Bt FCA *1959;* 81 Onslow Square, LONDON, SW7 3LT. (Life Member)
JENKYN-JONES, Mr. William Arthur, MA FCA *1963;* The Bryn, Redwick, Magor, CALDICOT, GWENT, NP26 3DE.
•JENMAN, Mr. Eric Howard, FCA *1966;* (Tax Fac), A R Raymond & Co Limited, 67 London Road, ST. LEONARDS-ON-SEA, EAST SUSSEX, TN37 6AR.
•JENNER, Mr. Andrew Keith, FCA *1971;* 18 Briarleas Gardens, UPMINSTER, ESSEX, RM14 1LP.
JENNER, Mr. Andrew Mark, BSc ACA *1993;* Deers Hill, Sutton Lane, Abinger Hammer, DORKING, SURREY, RH5 6PS.

•**JENNER, Mr. Christopher John, FCA** *1972;* Christopher Jenner & Co Ltd, 4 Walcote Place, High Street, WINCHESTER, HAMPSHIRE, SO23 9AP.
JENNER, Mr. Christopher Paul, FCA *1969;* 57a rue John Grun, Mondorf les Bains, L5619 LUXEMBOURG, LUXEMBOURG.
JENNER, Mr. Edward Reece, BSc ACA *2002;* Chesterton Farm, CIRENCESTER, GLOUCESTERSHIRE, GL7 6JP.
JENNER, Mrs. Elizabeth, BSc FCA MCT *1987;* Lloyds TSB Bank Plc Canons House, Canons Way, BRISTOL, BS1 5LL.
•**JENNER, Mrs. Fiona Jane, BSc ACA CTA** *1989;* (Tax Fac), JJ Accounts Limited, Redroofs, Berrington Road, TENBURY WELLS, WORCESTERSHIRE, WR15 8EN.
•**JENNER, Mr. Graham Richard, ACA** *1984;* Jenner Accountants Ltd, 245 Queensway, Bletchley, MILTON KEYNES, MK2 2EH. See also Jenner & Co
JENNER, Mr. Jason Adam, ACA *1997;* (Tax Fac), 4 Mandeville Road, SAFFRON WALDEN, CB11 4AQ.
•**JENNER, Mr. John Christopher, FCA** *1973;* J.C. Jenner, 4 Timberling Gardens, Sanderstead, SOUTH CROYDON, SURREY, CR2 0AW.
JENNER, Mr. John Edward, BA ACA *1991;* Cunningham Lindsey, Apex Plaza, Forbury Road, READING, RG1 1AX.
JENNER, Mr. John Openshaw, FCA *1963;* 47 Spring Lane, Bassingbourn, ROYSTON, SG8 5HT. (Life Member)
JENNER, Mrs. Julia, BSc ACA *1997;* Casa Las Rodrigass/n, 23685 SABARIEGO, JAEN, SPAIN.
JENNER, Mr. Keith Tony, ACA *1994;* 1 Hall Cross Avenue, Wombwell, BARNSLEY, SOUTH YORKSHIRE, S73 0NN.
JENNER, Mrs. Kim-Elizabeth, BA FCA *2000;* 56 Beech Avenue, SWANLEY, KENT, BR8 8AU.
JENNER, Mr. Malcolm, BA FCA *1981;* with RSM Tenon Audit Limited, Arkwright House, Parsonage Gardens, MANCHESTER, M3 3BB.
•**JENNER, Mr. Mark Andrew, BSc FCA** *1993;* Mark Jenner & Co, PO Box 628, YORK, YO1 0EQ.
JENNER, Mr. Neil Stuart, BSc ACA *2009;* 38 Garland Road, COLCHESTER, CO2 7GD.
•①**JENNER, Mr. Nicholas, FCA** *1970;* (Tax Fac), Nicholas Jenner & Co, PO Box 4001, Pangbourne, READING, RG8 7FN.
JENNER, Miss. Sarah Louise, BSc ACA *1993;* Ormiston Lodge, Bunch Lane, HASLEMERE, SURREY, GU27 1AJ.
•**JENNER, Mrs. Sheila Katherine, BSc FCA** *1980;* (Tax Fac), Archie Jenner Consultants, The Old Post Office, 109 Northampton Road, Brixworth, NORTHAMPTON, NN6 9BU.
JENNER, Mr. Simon Ashley, BA ACA *1997;* 2 Wilton Castle, Wilton Village, REDCAR, CLEVELAND, TS10 4FB.
JENNESON, Mr. Neil, BSc FCA *1974;* The Moorings, 17 Station Road, NORTH FERRIBY, HU14 3DG.
JENNI, Mr. Anthony Patrick, BA ACA *1979;* 42 Mereway Road, TWICKENHAM, TW2 6RG.
JENNINGS, Miss. Adele Marie, BSc ACA *2004;* 18b Marjorie Grove, LONDON, SW11 5SJ.
JENNINGS, Mr. Adrian Mark, BA FCA *1990;* Cripps Harries Hall LLP, Wallside House, 12 Mount Ephraim Road, TUNBRIDGE WELLS, KENT, TN1 1EG.
JENNINGS, Mr. Andrew Geoffrey, MA FCA *1977;* 19 St. Martins Avenue, EPSOM, KT18 5HZ.
JENNINGS, Mr. Andrew Hubert Gwyn, FCA *1974;* Ince & Co, International House, 1 St. Katharines Way, LONDON, E1W 1AY.
JENNINGS, Mr. Andrew Rayner, BA FCA *1996;* 3 Green Gables, Eaton Ford, ST. NEOTS, CAMBRIDGESHIRE, PE19 7SL.
JENNINGS, Mr. Anthony, FCA *1975;* Bilfinger Berger Enviromental Ltd, 75 Guildford Street, CHERTSEY, KT16 9AS.
JENNINGS, Mrs. Arlette Rose, BA ACA *1997;* 129 Friern Barnet Lane, Whetstone, LONDON, N20 0XZ.
JENNINGS, Mr. Brian Charles, ACA *1978;* 8 Blackberry Way, Clayton, BRADFORD, BD14 6NB.
JENNINGS, Mr. Christopher Anthony, ACA CA(SA) *2011;* 21 Jeavons Lane, Great Cambourne, CAMBRIDGE, CB23 6AF.
JENNINGS, Mr. Christopher Geoffrey, BCom FCA *1974;* Simpson Carpenter Ltd, Tuition House, 27-37 St Georges Road, Wimbledon, LONDON, SW19 4EU.
JENNINGS, Mr. Christopher Martin, BA FCA *1982;* Lions Den, 100 Welsford Road, Eaton Rise, NORWICH, NR4 6QH.
JENNINGS, Mr. Christopher Michael, BSc ACA *1989;* MJF Group Ltd, River House, Riverside Way, UXBRIDGE, UB8 2YF.
JENNINGS, Mrs. Churni, BA(Hons) ACA *2002;* 85 Langham Road, LONDON, N15 3LR.
JENNINGS, Miss. Clare Louisa Minnie, BA ACA *2002;* Cadbury Plc, Cadbury House, Sanderson Road, UXBRIDGE, MIDDLESEX, UB8 1DH.
JENNINGS, Mr. Clive Adrian Roynon, BSc ACA *1984;* 54 Forge End, Chiswell Green, ST. ALBANS, AL2 3EQ.
JENNINGS, Mr. Daniel Hamilton, BA ACA *1981;* 25 Pigeon House Lane, Freeland, WITNEY, OXFORDSHIRE, OX29 8AG.
JENNINGS, Mr. Daniel Owen, BEng ACA *2004;* 57 Westfields, ST. ALBANS, HERTFORDSHIRE, AL3 4LS.
•**JENNINGS, Mr. David Heron, FCA** *1968;* (Tax Fac), Newton & Co., Ranmore House, 19 Ranmore Road, DORKING, SURREY, RH4 1HE.
JENNINGS, Mr. David John Gregory, BA ACA *1987;* 8 Magnus Dr, Hatch Warden, BASINGSTOKE, RG22 4TX.
JENNINGS, Mr. David Nevill, FCA *1972;* Afton Manor, FRESHWATER, PO40 9TW.
JENNINGS, Mr. Derek John, FCA *1953;* Ivydene Ox Lane, St. Michaels, TENTERDEN, TN30 6NG. (Life Member)
JENNINGS, Mr. Edwin Leslie, FCA *1971;* Barnfield, Smith Lane, Mobberley, KNUTSFORD, WA16 6JY. (Life Member)
JENNINGS, Ms. Elaine, BSc ACA *1995;* 99 Louth Road, GRIMSBY, DN33 2JH.
JENNINGS, Mrs. Emma, BSc ACA *2007;* Constellation Europe Ltd Constellation Park, Kings Weston Lane Avonmouth, BRISTOL, BS11 9FG.
•**JENNINGS, Mrs. Frances Jane, BA ACA** *1992;* (Tax Fac), Rawlinson & Hunter, Lower Mill, Kingston Road, Ewell, EPSOM, KT17 2AE.
JENNINGS, Mr. George Bryan Frederick, BCom FCA *1969;* 121 Hambalt Road, Clapham, LONDON, SW4 9EL. (Life Member)
JENNINGS, Ms. Geraldine Yvette, ACA CA(SA) *2010;* Obere Heslibachstrasse 87b, 8700 KUSNACHT, SWITZERLAND.
JENNINGS, Mr. Henry Alderson, FCA *1952;* Sunny Cote, Sunnyside, KENDAL, LA9 7DJ. (Life Member)
JENNINGS, Mr. Ian Andrew, BSc FCA *1980;* PO Box SS 5541, Commonwealth Bank, Head Office, The Plaza, Mackey Street, NASSAU PO SS5541 BAHAMAS.
•**JENNINGS, Mr. Ian Paul, BSc FCA** *1978;* Jennings & Co, 6 New Laithe Close, SKIPTON, BD23 6AZ.
JENNINGS, Mr. Ian Stewart, FCA *1974;* 17 Woodcote, MAIDENHEAD, SL6 4DU.
JENNINGS, Mrs. Jacqueline Elizabeth, BSc ACA *1987;* 14 FELGATE PARADE, VERMONT SOUTH, VIC 3133, AUSTRALIA.
JENNINGS, Mr. James Scott, BA ACA *1986;* Highfield House, Highfield House Peover Lane, Snelson, MACCLESFIELD, CHESHIRE, SK11 9AW.
•**JENNINGS, Mrs. Jane Andrea, BSc ACA** *1989;* (Tax Fac), Jane Jennings ACA, 28 Barbaras Meadow, Tilehurst, READING, RG31 6YF.
•**JENNINGS, Mrs. Jean, BSc FCA** *1978;* Jennings & Co, 6 New Laithe Close, SKIPTON, BD23 6AZ.
JENNINGS, Mrs. Jeannette Hanne, MA ACA *1988;* 17 Woodcote, MAIDENHEAD, SL6 4DU.
JENNINGS, Mr. Jeremy Allan, FCA *1973;* Holy Trinity Brompton, Brompton Road, LONDON, SW7 1JA.
•**JENNINGS, Mr. Jeremy Nicholas Wayne, OBE ACA** *1981;* MEMBER OF COUNCIL, Ernst & Young, 2 De Kleetlann, B-1831 DIEGEM, BELGIUM. See also Ernst & Young Europe LLP
JENNINGS, Miss. Jessica, MA(Cantab) ACA *2011;* Upper Flat, 32 Freegrove Road, LONDON, N7 9RQ.
JENNINGS, Mr. John Charles, FCA *1955;* Greenacres Farm Horsted Lane, Danehill, HAYWARDS HEATH, WEST SUSSEX, RH17 7HP. (Life Member)
JENNINGS, Mr. John Michael, BSc FCA *1974;* 53 Langley Road, WATFORD, WD17 4PB.
JENNINGS, Mr. John Paul, BA FCA *1999;* Business School, The University of Winchester, Sparkford Road, WINCHESTER, SO22 4NR.
JENNINGS, Mr. John Philip, BA ACA *2005;* 24 Tyne Road, BRISTOL, BS7 8EE.
JENNINGS, Mrs. Julie Amanda, MA ACA *1997;* 20 Shaftesbury Drive, Stotfold, HITCHIN, HERTFORDSHIRE, SG5 4FS.
JENNINGS, Mrs. Kirsty Jane, BA ACA *1999;* 86 Wodeland Avenue, GUILDFORD, SURREY, GU2 4LD.
JENNINGS, Mr. Lawrence David, FCA *1970;* MacMillan Publishers, Brunel Road, BASINGSTOKE, RG21 6XT.
JENNINGS, Miss. Lisa, ACA *2003;* 205/32 Warayama Place, ROZELLE, NSW 2039, AUSTRALIA.
JENNINGS, Mrs. Lynn, BA(Hons) ACA *2000;* 54 Hazelhurst Road, Worsley, MANCHESTER, M28 2SQ.
JENNINGS, Mr. Marcus Henry Charles, BA ACA *2007;* 39 Windsor Drive, WALLINGFORD, OXFORDSHIRE, OX10 9GG.
JENNINGS, Mr. Mark Eric, MSci ACA *2009;* Flat A 164 Maygrove Road, LONDON, NW6 2EP.
JENNINGS, Mr. Mark John William, BSc ACA *1995;* 3 Grove Road, OLDBURY, B68 9JL.
JENNINGS, Mr. Martin, FCA *1965;* 9 Redlake Road, Pedmore, STOURBRIDGE, DY9 0RZ. (Life Member)
JENNINGS, Mr. Martin Alexander, BA ACA *1983;* 68 Woodlea Drive, SOLIHULL, B91 1PJ.
JENNINGS, Mr. Michael David, BSc ACA *1982;* Jennings of Garsington Ltd, Hampden House, Monument Business Park, Warpsgrove Lane, Chalgrove, OXFORD OX44 7RW.
•**JENNINGS, Mr. Michael John, BA ACA MCIM DipM** *1998;* Deloitte & Touche, Nile House, karolinska 654/2, Karlin, 18600 PRAGUE, CZECH REPUBLIC.
JENNINGS, Mrs. Natalie Jayne, ACA *1996;* 10 Heathside Place, EPSOM, SURREY, KT18 5TX.
JENNINGS, Mr. Neil, BSc FCA *1975;* Orpington House, The Derry, Ashton Keynes, SWINDON, SN6 6PW.
JENNINGS, Mr. Neil Daniel Gillespie, BA FCA *1991;* Maza Skolas iela 2-1, RIGA LV-1050, LATVIA.
JENNINGS, Mr. Nicholas David De Burgh, MA FCA *1986;* Daily Mail & General Trust plc, Northcliffe House Room 671, 2 Derry Street, Kensington, LONDON, W8 5TT.
JENNINGS, Mr. Nicky Martin, ACA *2003;* Kent Frozen Foods, 5 Priory Park, Mills Road, AYLESFORD, KENT, ME20 7PP.
JENNINGS, Mrs. Nina Victoria, BA FCA *1980;* 5 Mansfield House, Manor Fields, LONDON, SW15 3NQ.
JENNINGS, Mr. Paul William, MA ACA *1980;* 65 Station Road, AMERSHAM, BUCKINGHAMSHIRE, HP7 0BB.
JENNINGS, Mr. Peter James, BSc ACA *2007;* with Grant Thornton UK LLP, 30 Finsbury Square, LONDON, EC2P 2YU.
JENNINGS, Mr. Peter John Francis, BA ACA *1991;* 39 Dublin Croft, Great Sutton, ELLESMERE PORT, CH66 2TD.
•**JENNINGS, Mr. Peter Morrison Nevill, FCA** *1970;* Peter M N Jennings FCA, Mariners, Longs Wharf, YARMOUTH, ISLE OF WIGHT, PO41 0PW.
JENNINGS, Mr. Peter William, BSc(Hons) ACA *2004;* 32 The Sanctuary, WESTLEIGH, NSW 2120, AUSTRALIA.
•**JENNINGS, Mr. Peter Wolfgang, BA ACA** *1989;* (Tax Fac), Jennings & Co, The Sharman Law Building, 1 Harpur Street, BEDFORD, MK40 1PF.
JENNINGS, Mrs. Rachel Elizabeth, BSc ACA *1990;* 6 Ely Gardens, TONBRIDGE, TN10 4NZ.
JENNINGS, Mr. Richard Charles, MBA BA ACA *1992;* 2 Parkers Cottages, Milley Road, Waltham St. Lawrence, READING, BERKSHIRE, RG10 0JS.
JENNINGS, Mr. Ricky James, ACA MAAT *2004;* 32 Campbell Road, CATERHAM, SURREY, CR3 5JL.
JENNINGS, Mr. Roy Leonard, BSc FCA FTII MBA *1961;* Orchard House, 8 Fairbourne, COBHAM, KT11 2BT. (Life Member)
JENNINGS, Miss. Sandra, BA ACA *1989;* 127 Frimley Green Road, Frimley Green, CAMBERLEY, GU16 6JX.
JENNINGS, Mrs. Sarah Elizabeth, BSc ACA *2003;* 30 Brockenhurst Avenue, MAIDSTONE, KENT, ME15 7ED.
JENNINGS, Miss. Sarah Jemma, ACA *2009;* 103/27 Waruda Street, Kirribilli, SYDNEY, NSW 2061, AUSTRALIA.
JENNINGS, Mr. Scott Peter, BA ACA *2008;* Apt 4 43 Strand Rd Sandymount, DUBLIN 4, COUNTY DUBLIN, IRELAND.
JENNINGS, Mr. Simon David, BA ACA *1993;* Ferrier Hodgson, Level 29, 600 Bourke Street, MELBOURNE, VIC 3000, AUSTRALIA.
•**JENNINGS, Mr. Simon Paul, MA FCA** *1979;* (Tax Fac), Rawlinson & Hunter, Eighth Floor, 6 New Street Square, New Fetter Lane, LONDON, EC4A 3AQ. See also Rawlinson & Hunter Limited
•**JENNINGS, Mr. Stephen Clive Hedley, MA FCA** *1976;* (Tax Fac), EKAS, Link Asia House, Penthouse Suite, 127- 129 Commercial Road, LONDON, E1 1PX.
•**JENNINGS, Mr. Stephen Michael, BSc FCA** *1995;* Simmons Gainsford LLP, 5th Floor, 7-10 Chandos Street, Cavendish Square, LONDON, W1G 9DQ.
•**JENNINGS, Mr. Steven Martin, FCA** *1984;* PricewaterhouseCoopers LLP, 1 Embankment Place, LONDON, WC2N 6RH. See also PricewaterhouseCoopers
JENNINGS, Mr. Stuart Charles, BA ACA *1992;* September Cottage, 11 Denmark Road, Wimbledon, LONDON, SW19 4PG.
JENNINGS, Dr. Susan Jane, BSc ACA *1984;* Flat 19, Seven Dials Court, 3 Shorts Gardens, Covent Garden, LONDON, WC2H 9AT.
JENNINGS, Mr. Thomas John, BSc ACA *1984;* Wandlebury House, Hare Lane, Broadway, ILMINSTER, TA19 9LN.
JENNINGS, Mr. Timothy John William, BSc ACA *1983;* Apt 6E/6F, 103-25 68th Avenue, Forest Hills, NEW YORK, NY 11375, UNITED STATES.
JENNINGS, Mr. Timothy Michael, BA FCA *1988;* 8 Beaumaris Grove, Shenley Church End, MILTON KEYNES, MK5 6EN.
JENNINGS, Mr. Wilson Whitehead, BA FCA *1986;* Wilsden House, Goldsmiths Avenue, CROWBOROUGH, EAST SUSSEX, TN6 1RH.
JENNINS, Mr. Christopher Robert, BCom FCA *1966;* 24 Upland Road, Upton, WIRRAL, CH49 6LP.
JENNIS, Mrs. Elena, BA(Hons) ACA *2003;* 34 Kinsey View, Kesgrave, IPSWICH, SUFFOLK, IP5 2HD.
JENNISON, Mr. Timothy Martin Clifton, BSc FCA *1989;* 180 Remuera Road, Remuera, AUCKLAND 1050, NEW ZEALAND.
JENNS, Mr. Darren Antony, BA(Hons) ACA *2000;* 74 Voltri Street, MENTONE, VIC 3194, AUSTRALIA.
JENSEN, Mr. Garry Brame, FCA *1959;* Spindlebrook, Bell Road, HASLEMERE, GU27 3SF. (Life Member)
JENSEN, Mr. Jeremy Michael Jorgen Malherbe, BSc ACA *1984;* 25 Chiswick Quay, LONDON, W4 3UR.
•**JENSEN, Mr. Jeremy Ralph, MA ACA** *1995;* PricewaterhouseCoopers LLP, Hays Galleria, 1 Hays Lane, LONDON, SE1 2RD. See also PricewaterhouseCoopers
JENSEN, Mr. Michael Charles, BA FCA *1975;* 13 St James Gardens, Holland Park, LONDON, W11 4RD.
•**JENSEN, Mr. Peter Arthur, FCA** *1972;* (Tax Fac), Peter Jensen, 5 Bridge Street, BISHOP'S STORTFORD, HERTFORDSHIRE, CM23 2JU.
JENSEN, Mr. Richard Martin Dyson, MA FCA *1968;* Queensberry Viagens, Av Sao Luiz 165, 2nd Floor, SAO PAULO, 01046-911, BRAZIL.
•**JENSEN, Ms. Stella, BSc ACA** *1991;* Jensen & Co, 15 Water Wheel Close, Quedgeley, GLOUCESTER, GL2 4XH.
JENSEN, Miss. Suzanne, BA ACA CFA *2000;* Northview Services Ltd., PO Box 10741, GEORGE TOWN, GRAND CAYMAN, KY1-1007, CAYMAN ISLANDS.
JENSEN, Miss. Victoria Jacqueline, BSc(Econ) ACA *2001;* Flat 3, 39 Regents Park Road, LONDON, NW1 7SY.
JENSEN-HUMPHREYS, Mr. Julien Jensen, FCA *1973;* Reigate Grammar School, Reigate Road, REIGATE, SURREY, RH2 0QS.
JENVEY, Mr. Andrew Charles, ACA *1993;* Mudpie Designs Unit 21-23 Home Farm Rural Industries, East Tytherley Road Lockerley, ROMSEY, SO51 0JT.
JENVEY, Mr. David Ralph, FCA *1961;* 3 The Purrocks, PETERSFIELD, GU32 2HU. (Life Member)
JENVEY, Mr. Robert Dennis, BTech FCA CPA *1982;* 112-01 Queens Boulevard, Apartment 19-G, Forest Hills, NEW YORK, NY 11375, UNITED STATES.
•**JENYNS, Mr. Roger Gambier, MA FCA** *1967;* (Tax Fac), R.G. Jenyns, Bottisham Hall, Bottisham, CAMBRIDGE, CB5 9ED.
JENYNS, Mr. Roger George Edward, BA ACA *2006;* Ernst & Young Llp Compass House, 80 Newmarket Road, CAMBRIDGE, CB5 8DZ.
JEPHCOTT, Mr. Dominic Gregory Mark, BSc ACA *1997;* UBS AG, 1285 Avenue of Americas, NEW YORK, NY 10019, UNITED STATES.
JEPHCOTT, Mr. Paul Francis, BSc FCA ATII *1981;* Algonquin, 5 Oundle Road, Polebrook, PETERBOROUGH, PE8 5LQ.
JEPHSON, Mr. Wayne Andrew, LLB ACA *2000;* with Ernst & Young LLP, 1 Colmore Square, BIRMINGHAM, B4 6HQ.
JEPPE, Mr. Alexander Walter, ACA CA(SA) *2010;* 45 Lingfield Avenue, KINGSTON UPON THAMES, KT1 2TL.
JEPSON, Mr. Carl, MSc ACA *1998;* Flat 9 Mavery Court, Grasmere Road, BROMLEY, BR1 4BE.
JEPSON, Miss. Clare Melanie, ACA *2008;* 72 Merton Road, Bearsted, MAIDSTONE, ME15 8LL.
JEPSON, Mr. George Michael Alastair, BA FCA *1977;* Tarkett Ltd Dickley Lane, Lenham, MAIDSTONE, ME17 2QX.
•**JEPSON, Mr. James Leonard, BSc FCA** *1980;* J.L. Jepson, 5 Valley Way, STALYBRIDGE, SK15 2QZ.
JEPSON, Mr. James Roland, BCom FCA *1963;* Moor Park, 67 Manor Road, DARWEN, BB3 2SN.

JEPSON, Mr. Jonathan Fraser, ACA *1988;* 95 Woodcote Grove Road, COULSDON, SURREY, CR5 2AN.
JEPSON-RANDALL, Mr. Christopher John, BSc ACA *1995;* 47 Myrddin Crescent, CARMARTHEN, DYFED, SA31 1DX.
JERAM, Mr. Satish Ambram, BA ACA *1983;* 20 Harrowes Meade, EDGWARE, MIDDLESEX, HA8 8RP.
JEREMIAH, Mr. Andrew Thomas, BEng ACA *1995;* 431 St. Leonards Road, WINDSOR, SL4 3DT.
JEREMIAH, Miss. Deborah Sian, BA ACA *1996;* 16 New Drive, HIGH WYCOMBE, BUCKINGHAMSHIRE, HP13 6JS.
JEREMY, Mr. John David Sydney, BA FCA *1961;* 29 East Cliff, Southgate, SWANSEA, SA3 2AS.
JERICHOWER, Mr. Allan Samuel, FCA *1976;* P.O.Box 29037, 91290 JERUSALEM, ISRAEL.
•**JERMY, Mr. Martin Paul, FCA** *1984;* Martin Jermy Accountants, 14 Royalist Drive, Thorpe St Andrew, NORWICH, NR7 0YN.
JERMYN, Mr. Christopher Michael, ACA *2009;* 88 Greenwich Street, Apartment 3203, NEW YORK, NY 10006, UNITED STATES.
•**JERMYN, Mr. Karl, FCA** *1997;* Karl Jermyn, 10a Whitlingham Hall, NORWICH, NORFOLK, NR14 8QH.
JEROME, Mr. Mark Edward, BA FCA *1992;* KPMG Limited, 16th Floor Pacific Place, 83B Ly Thuong Kiet Street, Hoan Kiem District, HANOI, VIETNAM.
JERRAM, Mr. David Justin, BSc FCA *1981;* 3 Boyle Farm Road, THAMES DITTON, KT7 0TS.
JERRAM, Mrs. Gemma, BSc ACA *2003;* David LLoyd Leisure, Mosquito Way, Hatfield Bus Park, HATFIELD, AL109AX.
JERRAM, Mr. Mark Richard, BSc ACA *1997;* R T C Europe Ltd Eurolink Industrial Centre, Castle Road, SITTINGBOURNE, ME10 3RN.
JERRAM, Mr. Peter Anthony, FCA *1970;* Treguth, Poyle Lane, Burnham, SLOUGH, SL1 8LA.
•**JERRETT, Mr. Colin Harold, ACA** *1980;* (Tax Fac), Accountants You Can Talk With Limited, 38 Worple Road, STAINES, TW18 1EA.
•**JERROM, Mr. Michael George Lindsay, MA FCA** *1968;* Heather Bank, Platt Common, Platt, SEVENOAKS, KENT, TN15 8JU.
•**JERROM, Mr. Richard Michael, FCA** *1970;* (Tax Fac), Barnfield, Lye Green, Claverdon, WARWICK, CV35 8LP.
JERVIS, Mrs. Beverley, BSc ACA *1997;* 2 Haydens, High Street, Wrington, BRISTOL, BS40 5QD.
JERVIS, Mr. Christopher Clive Bentley, FCA *1965;* 48 Knowsley Road, Cressington Park, LIVERPOOL, L19 0PG. (Life Member)
JERVIS, Mr. Edward John, BSc ACA *1995;* Long Copse, The Street, West Clandon, GUILDFORD, SURREY, GU4 7ST.
JERVIS, Miss. Elizabeth, MA ACA *2003;* Cogent Breeding Ltd, Lea Lane, Aldford, CHESTER, CH3 6JQ.
JERVIS, Miss. Emma Marie, BSc(Hons) ACA *2004;* 13 Ocean Way, PORT TALBOT, WEST GLAMORGAN, SA12 7NP.
JERVIS, Mr. James Gordon, BA FCA *1957;* 1 Stubden Grove, Clifton Moor, YORK, YO30 4UY. (Life Member)
JERVIS, Mrs. Karen Jane, BSc ACA *1988;* 31 Sandy Lodge Road, Moor Park, RICKMANSWORTH, WD3 1LP.
•①**JERVIS, Mr. Michael John Andrew, BA ACA** *1988;* PricewaterhouseCoopers LLP, Pricewaterhousecoopers, 12 Plumtree Court, LONDON, EC4A 4HT. See also PricewaterhouseCoopers
•**JERVIS, Mr. Roger David, FCA** *1965;* 4 Home Acre, Little Houghton, NORTHAMPTON, NN7 1AG.
JERVIS, Mr. Roland Martin, BA ACA *1979;* Roundabout, 5 Sea Close, BOGNOR REGIS, PO22 7RU.
JERVIS, Mr. Simon, BA FCA CTA *1984;* (Tax Fac), 51 Goose Green Lane, Shirland, ALFRETON, DE55 6BR.
JERVIS, Mrs. Susan Janice, BA ACA *1988;* 16 Skipton Avenue, Crossens, SOUTHPORT, PR9 8JP.
JERVOISE, Mr. Anthony Richard Loveys, BSc ACA *1991;* Rowden Manor Farm, Sampford Courtenay, OKEHAMPTON, EX20 2SJ.
JERVOISE, Mr. John Tristram Loveys, BA ACA *1987;* Herriard Park, BASINGSTOKE, RG25 2PL.
JESINGER, Mr. Paul Martin, BA ACA *2000;* 5 Barngate Road, Gatley, CHEADLE, SK8 4EH.
JESKINES, Mr. Thomas, BSc ACA *2010;* 5 Foxley Grove, Bicton Heath, SHREWSBURY, SY3 5DF.
JESKY, Ms. Amanda Rosemary, BSc ACA *1993;* Sinai Primary School, Shakespeare Drive, HARROW, MIDDLESEX, HA3 9UD.
•**JESPER, Mr. Martin Guy, BSc ACA** *1989;* Rootcorz Limited, 21 Washington Terrace, NORTH SHIELDS, TYNE AND WEAR, NE30 2HG.
•**JESS, Miss. Elaine Elizabeth, MA FCA** *1981;* (Tax Fac), Milner Boardman Limited, MBL House, 16 Edward Court, Altrincham Business Park, George Richards Way, ALTRINCHAM CHESHIRE WA14 5GL.
JESS, Mr. Peter, BSc ACA *1999;* Frito Lay Russia, CityDel Business Centre, 9 Zemlyanoy Val, MOSCOW, RUSSIAN FEDERATION.
JESSA, Mr. Aminmohamed Abdulali Mitha, FCA *1967;* 60 Penshurst Gardens, EDGWARE, MIDDLESEX, HA8 9TU.
•**JESSA, Mr. Murtaza Fidahussein, FCA DChA** *1986;* (Tax Fac), haysmacintyre, Fairfax House, 15 Fulwood Place, LONDON, WC1V 6AY.
JESSANI, Mr. Mohamedali GulamhusKurji, FCA *1968;* P O Box 156, LONDON, SW7 4XZ. (Life Member)
JESSE, Miss. Emma Louise, BSc ACA *2004;* One Exchange Square, European Bank for Reconstruction & Development, 1 Exchange Square Primrose Street, LONDON, EC2A 2JN.
•**JESSE, Mr. Harold Joseph, BCom ACA** *1980;* Livesey Spottiswood Holding Ltd, 17 George Street, ST. HELENS, MERSEYSIDE, WA10 1DB. See also Livesey Spottiswood Limited
JESSEN, Mr. Timothy Peter, BSc ACA *1996;* 24 Angelica Way, Thornhill, CARDIFF, CF14 9FJ.
JESSETT, Mr. Peter George, FCA *1957;* 4 Seale Hill, REIGATE, RH2 8HZ. (Life Member)
JESSETT, Mr. Robert James, BSc ACA *2009;* Flat 12, 71e Drayton Park, LONDON, N5 1DH.
JESSEY, Mr. Timothy Michael, BA(Hons) ACA *2002;* Flat D 43 Floor, Shining Heights, 83 Sycamore Street, KOWLOON CITY, HONG KONG SAR.
JESSON, Mr. Gary, FCA *1985;* 1 Virginia Close, LUTON, LU2 7LX.
JESSON, Miss. Helen Margaret, BSc FCA *1989;* (Member of Council 2005 - 2007), (Tax Fac), 9 Chuters Grove, EPSOM, KT17 4AS.
•**JESSON, Mrs. Janet Caroline, BSc ACA** *1997;* Janet Jesson, 31 Withenfield Road, MANCHESTER, M23 9BT.
JESSON, Mr. Paul, ACA *1997;* Fir Tree Cottage, 17 High Street, Stoke Goldington, NEWPORT PAGNELL, BUCKINGHAMSHIRE, MK16 8NP.
JESSON, Mr. Peter Kenneth, BA FCA *1972;* 1725 Queens Avenue, WEST VANCOUVER V7V 2X6, BC, CANADA. (Life Member)
JESSOP, Mr. David Graham, FCA *1968;* 8 Helmsley Road, LEEDS, LS16 5JA. (Life Member)
JESSOP, Mr. Edward Mark, BA ACA *1987;* Flat 8F Juniper Mansion, TAIKOO SHING, HONG KONG ISLAND, HONG KONG SAR.
JESSOP, Miss. Emma Victoria, BA ACA *2001;* 28a Shop Lane, HUDDERSFIELD, HD5 0DB.
JESSOP, Mrs. Jacqueline, BA ACA *1993;* 108 Worrin Road, Shenfield, BRENTWOOD, ESSEX, CM15 8JN.
JESSOP, Mr. John William, FCA *1962;* Linden Lea, 6 Linden Road, ELLAND, HX5 0QL.
•**JESSOP, Mrs. Lorna Catherine, BSc ACA** *2000;* Jellybean Accounts, White House Farm, Church Lane, East Cottingwith, YORK, YO42 4TL.
JESSOP, Mr. Malcolm George, FCA *1974;* 21 Drovers Way, BISHOP'S STORTFORD, HERTFORDSHIRE, CM23 4GF.
•**JESSOP, Mr. Marcus Nathan, BA(Hons) ACA** *2000;* 32 Coppin Hall Lane, MIRFIELD, WF14 0EJ. See also Jessop & Barnes Business Adviser Ltd
•**JESSOP, Mr. Michael Edward, BA FCA** *1977;* 36 Endcliffe Grove Avenue, SHEFFIELD, S10 3EJ.
JESSOP, Ms. Ruth, MMath MSc BA ACA *2007;* 31 Murillo Road, LONDON, SE13 5QF.
•**JESSOP, Mr. Stuart Patrick, FCA** *1975;* PKF (UK) LLP, Pannell House, 6 Queen Street, LEEDS, LS1 2TW.
JESSUP, Mr. Alan, FCA *1955;* Smithy House, Station Road, Burnham Market, KING'S LYNN, NORFOLK, PE31 8HA. (Life Member)
JESSUP, Mr. Alex, BA(Hons) ACA *2004;* Practice Plan Kempthorne House, Park Avenue, OSWESTRY, SHROPSHIRE, SY11 1AY.
JESSUP, Mr. Anthony, BSc ACA *2003;* 4 Flora Thompson Drive, NEWPORT PAGNELL, BUCKINGHAMSHIRE, MK16 8ST.
•**JESSUP, Mr. Brian Edwin, FCA** *1972;* Jessup & Co, 44 Athol Street, Douglas, ISLE OF MAN, IM1 1JB.
•**JESSUP, Mr. David Michael John, BSc FCA** *1979;* PricewaterhouseCoopers LLP, Hays Galleria, 1 Hays Lane, LONDON, SE1 2RD. See also PricewaterhouseCoopers
•**JESSUP, Mrs. Edith Elizabeth, BA FCA** *1988;* Lunson Mitchenall Ltd, 33 Cork Street, LONDON, W1X 1HB. See also Jessup Edith
JESSUP, Mr. Paul, BSc ACA *1991;* (Tax Fac), 7 Golf Links Road, BROADSTONE, BH18 8BE.
JESSUP, Mr. Paul Henry, FCA *1977;* Croftriver Limited, 14 Southend Road, BECKENHAM, BR3 1SD.
JESSUP, Mr. Ronald, FCA *1971;* 2a Elmer Close, Elmer Sands, BOGNOR REGIS, PO22 6JU. (Life Member)
JESSUP, Miss. Wendy Elaine, BSc ACA *2007;* with PricewaterhouseCoopers LLP, 1 Embankment Place, LONDON, WC2N 6RH.
JESSUP, Mr. William, FCA *1974;* Slade House, Hinwick, WELLINGBOROUGH, NN29 7JB.
JESTER, Miss. Lucy Jade, ACA *2008;* Level 3 Grosvenor Place, 225 George Street, SYDNEY, NSW 2027, AUSTRALIA.
JESTER, Mr. Peter Michael Harper, FCA *1975;* The Old Kings Head, Berden, BISHOP'S STORTFORD, CM23 1AN.
JESTICO, Mrs. Alison Jean, MA ACA DChA *1980;* Oxfam GB, Oxfam House, John Smith Drive, OXFORD, OX4 2JY.
JESTICO, Mr. William Richard, FCA *1980;* 18 Donnington Place, WANTAGE, OX12 9YE.
JESTY, Mr. Jonathan Robert, MA ACA *1984;* Schroder Investment Management Ltd Garrard House, 31-45 Gresham Street, LONDON, EC2V 7QA.
JESUDASEN, Mr. Vikram, FCA *1972;* Flat F1 2nd Floor Ashiwn Apartments - Keerthana, 70/34 2nd Main Road R.A. Puram, CHENNAI 600028, INDIA.
JESUDASON, Miss. Carol Sharmini, BA ACA *1995;* 317 Banbury Road, OXFORD, OX2 7JH.
JETHA, Mr. Nigel Karim, MSc FCA *1989;* 9 Clarendon Road, BRISTOL, BS6 7EX.
JETHANI, Mr. Ramesh, ACA *1991;* Video Duplicating Co Ltd, Unit 3/4, Nucleus Business Centre, Central Way, Park Royal, LONDON NW10 7XT.
JETHWA, Mr. Dinesh, FCA *1975;* 17 Douglas Close, CARDIFF, CF5 2QT.
•**JETHWA, Mr. Pravin Gowardhandas, FCA** *1974;* (Tax Fac), J M Pitman & Co, Dometo House, Molesey Road, Hersham, WALTON-ON-THAMES, KT12 3PW.
JETHWA, Miss. Sheena, ACA *2008;* 10 South Esk Road, LONDON, E7 8EY.
JETUAH, Mrs. Hannah Morven, ACA *2010;* 89 College Gardens, LONDON, SW17 7UQ.
JEUDA, Mr. Basil Simon, BA FCA *1961;* 47 Sandringham Road, Higher Holdsfield, MACCLESFIELD, CHESHIRE, SK10 1QB.
JEVONS, Mr. Harold, FCA *1961;* 3 Holt Park Avenue, LEEDS, LS16 7RA.
JEVONS, Ms. Jane Helen, BA ACA *2002;* Glebelands, Main Road, Dibden, SOUTHAMPTON, SO45 5TD.
JEWEL-CLARK, Mr. Christopher, BA ACA *2007;* Ground Floor Flat, 5 Clifton Avenue, LONDON, W12 9DR.
JEWELL, Mr. Adam, MSc BSc ACA *2009;* 139 Valley Road, KENLEY, CR8 5BZ.
•**JEWELL, Mr. Christopher Adrian, MA ACA** *1991;* Christopher Jewell, Torvista, Heathfield Road, Sands, HIGH WYCOMBE, BUCKINGHAMSHIRE HP12 4DG.
JEWELL, Mr. Guy Charles, BA FCA *1990;* 34 Queensgate, NORTHWICH, CHESHIRE, CW8 1DU.
•**JEWELL, Mr. Michael John, FCA** *1976;* Deacon Jewell Limited, 7 West Street, LISKEARD, CORNWALL, PL14 6BW.
JEWELL, Mr. Michael John, FCA *1972;* Dixon Walsh St. Marys House, Magdalene Street, TAUNTON, SOMERSET, TA1 1SB.
JEWELL, Mrs. Susan Carol, MPhys ACA *2010;* 139 Valley Road, KENLEY, CR8 5BZ.
JEWISS, Mrs. Judith Ann, FCA *1986;* with King & Taylor, 10-12 Wrotham Road, GRAVESEND, DA11 0PE.
JEWITT, Mr. Alexander Mark James, MA ACA *2009;* Flat 10, Salisbury House, 23 Highbury Corner, LONDON, N5 1RB.
•**JEWITT, Mr. Andrew Keith, ACA FCCA** *2008;* 3 Coltman Close, BROUGH, NORTH HUMBERSIDE, HU15 1GS.
JEWITT, Mr. John Peter, BSc ACA *1979;* Spittleborough Farmhouse, Swindon Road, Wootton Bassett, SWINDON, SN4 8ET.
JEWITT, Mr. Keith William, MA ACA *1986;* with Ernst & Young LLP, Citygate, St James' Boulevard, NEWCASTLE UPON TYNE, NE1 4JD.
JEWITT-WILKERSON, Mrs. Marie Julia Ann, BSc FCA MCT *1986;* Hedree, 3 Fircroft, Bagshot Road, Englefield Green, EGHAM, SURREY TW20 0RS.
JEWKES, Miss. Amy Angharad, ACA *2011;* Flat 24, Oxford Court, Queens Drive, LONDON, W3 0HH.
•**JEWKES, Mr. David William, FCA** *1983;* Jewkes Consulting Limited, Red Lodge, The Village, Kingswinford, DUDLEY, WEST MIDLANDS DY6 8AY.
JEWKES, Mrs. Lucy Marie, BA FCA *1986;* Roundton House, Chirbury, MONTGOMERY, POWYS, SY15 6DD.
JEWKES, Mr. Simon, BSc ACA *2010;* 70 Bushwood Road, RICHMOND, SURREY, TW9 3BQ.
JEWSBURY, Miss. Hannah, BSc(Hons) ACA *2009;* Flat 13 Caistor House, Caistor Road, LONDON, SW12 8PY.
•**JEWSON, Mr. John William, FCA** *1972;* Blanche & Co., The Lanterns, 16 Melbourn Street, ROYSTON, HERTFORDSHIRE, SG8 7BX.
JEX, Mrs. Anna Claire, MA ACA ATII *2000;* 12 Brampton Road, ST. ALBANS, AL1 4PW.
JEYANANDHAN, Mr. Jayantha, MSci ACA *2002;* 30 Paul Gardens, CROYDON, CR0 5QL.
JEYANANDHAN, Mr. Prasaanna, ACA *2009;* 9 Birdhurst Avenue, SOUTH CROYDON, CR2 7DX.
JEYARATNAM, Mr. Tamotharam Pillai, ACA *1984;* 3 Lorong Tempinis Kanan 2, Lucky Garden, Bangsar, 59000 KUALA LUMPUR, FEDERAL TERRITORY, MALAYSIA.
JEYASEELANAYAGAM, Mr. Romesh Fabian, BSc ACA *2001;* 161 Pen-Y-Dre, Rhiwbina, CARDIFF, CF14 6EN.
•**JEYES, Mr. Daniel John, BA(Hons) ACA** *2001;* (Tax Fac), Daniel Jeyes, 23 Abington Park Crescent, NORTHAMPTON, NN3 3AD.
JEYES, Mr. Peter Martin, FCA *1970;* Lime Tree Lodge, Church Lane, Owermoigne, DORCHESTER, DT2 8HS.
JEYNES, Mrs. Sarah Jane, BA(Hons) ACA *2002;* 35 St. Nicholas Drive, GRIMSBY, SOUTH HUMBERSIDE, DN37 9QD.
•**JEZIERSKI, Mr. Robert Marek, BA FCA** *1981;* Landau Morley LLP, Lanmor House, 370-386 High Road, WEMBLEY, MIDDLESEX, HA9 6AX.
JHALA, Mr. Nikesh, ACA *2010;* 7 Ducie Avenue, BOLTON, BL1 4RJ.
JHAMNA, Miss. Preetee, BA ACA *1999;* Morcellement, PANORAMA COROMANDEL, MAURITIUS.
JHANGIANI, Mr. Anil Lachman, BSc ACA *2007;* Royal Bank of Scotland, 135 Bishopsgate, LONDON, EC2M 3UR.
JHANGIANI, Mr. Sanjay Jairam, BA ACA *2001;* 1 Raffles Link, 03/04-01 South Lobby, SINGAPORE 039393, SINGAPORE.
JHANJI, Mr. Suneel, BSc ACA *1986;* 3195/17-29 Rama IV Road, Klong Ton, Klong Toey District, BANGKOK 10110, THAILAND.
JHAVERI, Miss. Kitu, BSc ACA *2000;* 3A Creffield Road, LONDON, W5 3HP.
JHAVERI, Mr. Noormahomed Omar, ACA CA(SA) *2010;* (Tax Fac), 1 Custom House Reach, Odessa Street, LONDON, SE16 7LX.
JHEENGOOR, Mr. Belaid Abdessalam, BSc ACA *1999;* with PricewaterhouseCoopers, Dorchester House, 7 Church Street West, PO Box HM1171, HAMILTON HM EX, BERMUDA.
•**JHUGROO, Mr. Priyaved, FCA** *1994;* C/O Lancasters Chartered Accountants, 14 Lancaster Court, Lavoquer Street, PORT LOUIS, MAURITIUS.
JHUGROO, Miss. Shirin, BA ACA *2006;* 13 Brookside Road, FRODSHAM, WA6 7BL.
JIANG, Mr. Hu, MSc ACA *1999;* Azko Nobel Deco China (ICI), 3rd Floor K. Wah Centre, 1010 Huai Hai Rd., SHANGHAI, CHINA.
JIANG, Ms. Li Yue, ACA CA(NZ) *2010;* 103A Mead Street, Avondale, AUCKLAND 1026, NEW ZEALAND.
JIANG, Ms. Lu, MSc ACA *2001;* Flat M, Pampas Court, 13 Waterway Avenue, LONDON, SE13 7GB.
•**JIANG, Miss. Suwei, MBA BA ACA** *2001;* MEMBER OF COUNCIL, PricewaterhouseCoopers LLP, 1 Embankment Place, LONDON, WC2N 6RH. See also PricewaterhouseCoopers
JIANG, Mr. Weike, ACA *2011;* 13/F China Resources Building, 5001 Shennan Road East, SHENZHEN 518010, CHINA.
JIANG, Miss. Xiaohong, MSc BA ACA *2006;* 3 Frederick Square, LONDON, SE16 5XR.
JIANG, Mr. Ziyuan, ACA *2011;* 11th floor, K P M G Llp, 15 Canada Square, LONDON, E14 5GL.
JIBRIL, Mr. Ahmed Rashid, ACA *1991;* 255 Duncan Mills Road Suite 308, TORONTO M3B 3H9, ON, CANADA.
JIGGINS, Mr. Matthew Francis, BA ACA *1999;* Deloitte Finance TS, 185 Avenue Charles de Gaulle, 92524 NEUILLY-SUR-SEINE, FRANCE.
JIGGINS, Mrs. Ruth Louise, BSc ACA *2001;* 4 Impasse Beauséjour, 78600 LE MESNIL LE ROI, FRANCE.
•**JILANI, Mr. Mohammad Wasif Sirtaj, FCA** *1968;* Pearlman Rose, 2 St. Georges Mews, 43 Westminster Bridge Road, LONDON, SE1 7JB.
JILLARD, Mr. Keith Ralph, FCA *1972;* Candara, Church Park Road, Newton Ferrers, PLYMOUTH, PL8 1AZ. (Life Member)
JILLINGS, Mr. Christopher Howard, BA ACA *1988;* The Panel on Takeovers & Mergers, 10 Paternoster Square, LONDON, EC4M 7DY.

JIM, Mr. Sammy Kwok Wah, BSc ACA *1992;* C/o MTR Corporation Ltd, Corporate Finance Department, 18th Floor, MTR Headquarters Building, Telford Plaza, 33 Wai Yip Street KOWLOON BAY KOWLOON HONG KONG SAR.
JIN, Mr. Hassan Noorali, MSc BSc ACA *2006;* 579 Uxbridge Road, Hatchend, PINNER, HA5 4RB.
JIN, Mr. Lawrence Lingyun, BAcc FCA *1999;* with Deloitte Touche Tohmatsu, 30/F Bund Center, 222 Yan An Road East, SHANGHAI 200002, CHINA.
JIN, Miss. Linlin, BSc ACA *2010;* Deloitte & Touche, 2 New Street Square, LONDON, EC4A 3BZ.
JIN, Miss. Meitong, MSc ACA *2003;* 55 Marylands Road, LONDON, W9 2DU.
JINA, Mr. Dilip, BEng ACA *1992;* 9 Excalibur Close, Leicester Forest East, LEICESTER, LE3 3ET.
JINDAL, Mr. Ian Krishna, MA(Oxon) BA ACA CITP *1990;* 32 Quilter Street, LONDON, E2 7BT.
JINKS, Mr. Alan Michael, FCA *1959;* 2 Ferneley Rise, Thrussington, LEICESTER, LE7 4UA. (Life Member)
JINKS, Mr. David Alan, BSc FCA *1990;* The Boots Company plc, 1 Thane Road, NOTTINGHAM, NG90 1BS.
JINKS, Mr. Donald Richard, FCA *1954;* Whitegates, 92 West Street, Selsey, CHICHESTER, PO20 9AG. (Life Member)
JINKS, Mr. Gareth Martin, BSc ACA *1998;* 216 Raeburne Street, TE AWAMUTU 2400, NEW ZEALAND.
•JINKS, Mr. Martin Philip, FCA *1987;* Somerbys Limited, 30 Nelson Street, LEICESTER, LE1 7BA.
JINKS, Mr. Peter James, ACA *1988;* 23 Glen Rock Drive, KINNELON, NJ 07405, UNITED STATES.
JINKS, Mr. Philip Michael, BSc ACA *1990;* 27 Eastwood Road, LEIGH-ON-SEA, SS9 3AJ.
JINKS, Mrs. Rosalind Kay, BSc FCA FCIS *1995;* 16 Clos de Priaulx, Brock Road, St Sampsons, GUERNSEY, GY2 4PW.
JIRKAS, Mr. Nicolas Andreas, BSc ACA *1999;* 5 Irodotou Street, CYBC Area, 2121 NICOSIA, CYPRUS.
JIVA, Mr. Mohamed Taiyeb, BA(Hons) ACA *2002;* 52 Marlborough Drive, ILFORD, IG5 0JW.
JIVANI-HEMANI, Mrs. Nasim, FCA *1980;* 4th Floor, 32 St James's Street, LONDON, SW1A 1HD.
•JIVANJEE, Mr. Mustaali Kassamali, FCA *1975;* HLB Jivanjee & Company, P.O. Box 3401, ABU DHABI, UNITED ARAB EMIRATES.
JIVRAJ, Mr. Salim Badrudin, ACA *1982;* Cityscape Developments Ltd, 1711 College Lane SW, CALGARY T2S 2G9, AB, CANADA.
JIWA, Mrs. Izzat, FCA *1980;* In transition and will notify of new address, TORONTO, ON, CANADA.
JIWA, Mr. Sajeed Kamrudin, BA ACA *1992;* 41 The Woodlands, 651 High Road, LONDON, N12 0DU.
JIWAJI, Ms. Nabila, MSc BA(Hons) ACA *2010;* 1 Old Dairy Mews, Kentish Town Road, LONDON, NW5 2JW.
JIWANI, Miss. Fahrah Firoz, ACA *2008;* 94 West End Road, RUISLIP, MIDDLESEX, HA4 6DS.
JIWANI, Miss. Soriya, ACA *2011;* Cloverdale, Cannon Lane, MAIDENHEAD, BERKSHIRE, SL6 3NR.
JOACHIM, Mr. Stephane Walter, ACA CA(AUS) *2011;* 61 Church Street, CASTLE HILL, NSW 2154, AUSTRALIA.
JOANES, Miss. Katherine, BSc ACA *1997;* Newburn, Limes Road, Kemble, CIRENCESTER, GLOUCESTERSHIRE, GL7 6FS.
JOANNIDES, Miss. Artemis, BSc ACA *1986;* Evelpidon 6, Strovolos, 2057 NICOSIA, CYPRUS.
JOANNIDES, Mr. Marios, BA FCA *1981;* PO Box 21660, NICOSIA, CYPRUS.
•JOANNIDI, Mrs. Sarah, BSc ACA *1999;* 22 Stanbury Road, BRISTOL, BS3 4QG.
JOANNOU, Ms. Katerina Nan, BA ACA *1994;* with ICAEW, Chartered Accountants' Hall, Moorgate Place, LONDON, EC2P 2BJ.
JOARDER, Mr. Peter, BSc FCA *1997;* Chapman Freeborn Holdings Ltd, 6th Floor, Astral Towers, Betts Way, CRAWLEY, WEST SUSSEX RH10 9XY.
JOB, Mr. Derek Charles, FCA *1973;* Apartment 71, Rue Froissart, 1040 BRUSSELS, BELGIUM.
JOB, Mr. Jonathan George Alexander, BSc ACA *1995;* 8, Downsedge Terrace Epsom Road, GUILDFORD, GU1 2SS.
JOB, Mr. Michael Nicholas, BSc ACA *1979;* North View House, Main Street, Kirkby Malzeard, RIPON, HG4 3RY.
•JOBANPUTRA, Mr. Anilkumar Chhotalal, FCA *1971;* Anil & Co, 220 Maplin Way North, Thrope Bay, SOUTHEND-ON-SEA, SS1 3NT.
JOBANPUTRA, Mr. Avinash Chhotalal, FCA *1972;* (Tax Fac), 163 Chantry Road, CHESSINGTON, KT9 1XD.
•JOBANPUTRA, Mr. Chandrakant Tulsidas, FCA *1969;* API Partnership Limited, 75 Westow Hill, Crystal Palace, LONDON, SE19 1TX.
JOBANPUTRA, Mrs. Manorama, BSc ACA *1981;* 24 Swanswell Road, Olton, SOLIHULL, B92 7ET.
JOBANPUTRA, Mr. Rishi Ramesh, BA ACA *1996;* with PricewaterhouseCoopers LLP, 488 Almaden Boulevard, SAN JOSE, CA 95110, UNITED STATES.
JOBANPUTRA, Miss. Sejal Sureshchandra, BA ACA *1992;* 6 Carlton Gardens, LONDON, SW1Y 5AD.
JOBANPUTRA, Mr. Vijaykumar Harjivan, BSc ACA *1979;* 315 Calvington Place, WATERLOO N2T 1P9, ON, CANADA.
JOBBINS, Mr. Stuart, BSc FCA *1988;* Evans Property Group, Millshaw, LEEDS, LS11 8EG.
•JOBERNS, Mr. Stephen Lewis, LLM FCA *1996;* Shipleys LLP, 10 Orange Street, Haymarket, LONDON, WC2H 7DQ.
JOBLING, Mr. David Robert, BA ACA *2005;* 113 Melanesia Road, Kohimarama, AUCKLAND 1071, NEW ZEALAND.
JOBLING, Mr. Nicholas Andrew, BSc ACA *1990;* Winklern Wiggaton, OTTERY ST. MARY, DEVON, EX11 1PU.
JOBLING, Mr. Paul Alistair Willan, ACA *1982;* PO BOX 603, PROVIDENCIALES, TURKS AND CAICOS ISLANDS.
JOBLING, Miss. Rachael Victoria, BSc ACA *2010;* 85 Woodleigh Drive, Sutton-on-Hull, HULL, HU7 4YY.
JOBLING, Mr. Richard Ernest Crosbie, FCA *1938;* 208 Helderberg Village, Private Bag X19, SOMERSET WEST, C.P., 7129, SOUTH AFRICA. (Life Member)
JOBLING, Mr. Timothy, FCA *1972;* Owslebury House, Owslebury, WINCHESTER, SO21 1LU.
•JOBSEY, Mr. Gary Nicholas John, FCA ACMA *1976;* Gary Jobsey, 3 Barnsway, Love Lane, KINGS LANGLEY, WD4 9PW. See also Gary Jobsey & Co
JOBSON, Mr. Adam William, BA(Hons) ACA CTA *2002;* Flat C 80 Fairhazel Gardens, LONDON, NW6 3SR.
JOBSON, Mrs. Joanna Elizabeth Darracott, BA FCA *1991;* 15 Birdwood Road, MAIDENHEAD, BERKSHIRE, SL6 5AP.
JOBSON, Mr. John, BA ACA *1995;* Northern Rock (Asset Management) Plc, Northern Rock House, Regent Centre, Gosforth, NEWCASTLE UPON TYNE, NE3 4PL.
JOBSON, Mr. Simon Paul, BA ACA *2005;* Flat 33, Candelmakers, 112 York road, LONDON, SW11 3RS.
JOCE, Mr. Nicholas John, ACA *1979;* Royal Automobile Club, 89-91 Pall Mall, LONDON, SW1Y 5HS.
JOCELYN, Miss. Caragh Clodagh, BA ACA *2001;* (Tax Fac), Kyo Close, WYLAM, NORTHUMBERLAND, NE41 8JW.
JOCHEMS, Mr. Mark, ACA CA(SA) *2009;* 142 Ennerdale Road, RICHMOND, SURREY, TW9 2DG.
JOCKELSON, Mr. Bruce Lionel Marsden, FCA *1971;* Waverley, Battledown Approach, CHELTENHAM, GLOUCESTERSHIRE, GL52 6RE. (Life Member)
JODIYAWALLA, Mr. Aziz Mohamedhusein, BCom ACA *1993;* 12 Mentmore Close, HARROW, HA3 0EA.
JODLOWSKI, Mr. Peter, ACA *1982;* pobox 500124, DUBAI, UNITED ARAB EMIRATES.
JOEL, Miss. Amy Louise, BSc ACA *2010;* 6 Lambourne Grove, Milnrow, ROCHDALE, LANCASHIRE, OL16 4YA.
JOELS, Mr. Jonathan, BA ACA *1980;* 191 South Woodland Street, ENGLEWOOD, NJ 07631, UNITED STATES.
JOELS, Mr. Nicholas Emanuel, BA FCA *1984;* 20 Copse Wood Way, NORTHWOOD, HA6 2UF.
JOERGENSEN, Mr. Kjetil, MA ACA *2011;* 136 Seren Park Gardens, LONDON, SE3 7RR.
JOFFREY, Mr. Waheed, FCA *1963;* 46 Evesham Road, Bounds Green, LONDON, N11 2RN. (Life Member)
JOGLEKAR, Ms. Ashvini Monica, BSc ACA *1997;* CFS, Internal Audit, 5th Floor, 1 Balloon Street, MANCHESTER, M60 4EP.
JOHAL, Mr. Akbal Singh, BA ACA *1995;* 12 Lancing Road, Newbury Park, ILFORD, IG2 7DR.
JOHAL, Mr. Avtar Singh, LLB ACA *2001;* 15 Broxbourne Avenue, South Woodford, LONDON, E18 1QG.
JOHAL, Mr. Billie, BSc(Eng) ACA *2006;* 2N Kingsbridge Apartments, 72 Wellesley Street West, AUCKLAND 1010, NEW ZEALAND.
•JOHAL, Mr. Gurpal, BA FCA *1979;* 317 Aspley Lane, NOTTINGHAM, NG8 5GA.
JOHAL, Mr. Gurvinder Singh, BSc ACA *1995;* Caparo Plc Caparo House, Popes Lane, OLDBURY, B69 4PJ.
JOHAL, Mr. Jagdeep Singh, BSc ACA *2008;* 17 Gladstone Street, Hadley, TELFORD, SHROPSHIRE, TF1 5NW.
JOHAL, Mr. Kean, BA ACA *1990;* Flat 80, St. Williams Court, 1 Gifford Street, LONDON, N1 0GJ.
JOHAL, Miss. Kiren Kaur, BA ACA *2006;* 57 Widney Lane, SOLIHULL, B91 3LL.
JOHAL, Miss. Manjinder, BSc ACA *1995;* 47 St. James Close, LONDON, NW8 7LQ.
JOHAL, Mr. Mukhvinder, BA ACA *2007;* 23 Ringers Spinney, Oadby, LEICESTER, LE2 2HB.
JOHAL, Miss. Parminder, LLB ACA *1999;* 21 Manorgate Road, KINGSTON UPON THAMES, SURREY, KT2 7AW.
JOHAL, Mr. Parminderjit, BSc(Hons) ACA *2011;* 2 Finchfield Road, WOLVERHAMPTON, WV3 9LU.
JOHAL, Mr. Parmjit Singh, BSc(Hons) ACA CTA *2001;* (Tax Fac), 6 Crawford Gardens, Palmers Green, LONDON, N13 5TD.
•JOHAL, Mr. Ranjit Singh, BCom ACA *1998;* Accounting Policy Advisory Limited, 15b Addington Close, WINDSOR, BERKSHIRE, SL4 4BP.
JOHAL, Mr. Sandip Singh, BSc ACA ACII *2004;* 9 Laburnum Grove, RUISLIP, MIDDLESEX, HA4 7XF.
JOHAL, Ms. Sharonjit Kaur, BA ACA *2000;* Ernst & Young Llp, 1 More London Place, LONDON, SE1 2AF.
JOHAL, Mrs. Sukhvinder, BA ACA *1999;* 22 Oakland Close, SOLIHULL, B91 2QB.
JOHAN ARIEF JOTHI, Miss. Shahira-Zaireen, BSc ACA *2009;* 469 Jalan Warisan Puteri A16, Bandar Warisan Puteri, 71770 SEREMBAN, NEGERI SEMBILAN, MALAYSIA.
JOHANAN, Miss. Georgina Sarah, BSc ACA *2006;* Flat E, 119 Bedford Hill, LONDON, SW12 9HE.
JOHANSEN, Mr. Peter Andre, BA FCA *1967;* Le Plati, 51 Bis Rue Plati, 98000 MONTE CARLO, MONACO.
JOHANSEN, Mr. Peter John Sverre, MBA BSc FCA *1982;* Brintons Ltd, PO Box 16, Exchange Street, KIDDERMINSTER, WORCESTERSHIRE, DY10 1AG.
JOHANSON, Mrs. Catherine Margaret, BA ACA *1993;* 3 Orchard Avenue, RAYLEIGH, SS6 7SQ.
JOHANSON, Mr. Matthew John, BEng ACA *1993;* 3 Orchard Avenue, RAYLEIGH, SS6 7SQ.
JOHANSSON, Mr. Jeremy Patrick, BSc ACA *1990;* 6/63 Stawell Street, RICHMOND, VIC 3121, AUSTRALIA.
•JOHN, Mr. Adrian Kenneth, FCA CTA *1973;* Adrian John, Belvedere, 20 Priestley Drive, Larkfield, AYLESFORD, ME20 6TX.
JOHN, Mr. Adrian Michael, BSc ACA *1988;* Quantas Airways Limited, Level 6 Qantas Centre Building F, 203 Coward Street, MASCOT, NSW 2020, AUSTRALIA.
JOHN, Mr. Albert, ACA *1953;* 14 Lloyd Road, HOVE, BN3 6NL. (Life Member)
JOHN, Mr. Alfred Howe, FCA *1953;* 5 Adenfield Way, Rhoose, BARRY, CF62 3EA. (Life Member)
JOHN, Mrs. Alison Joy, BSc ACA *1986;* 107 Blunts Wood Road, HAYWARDS HEATH, RH16 1ND.
JOHN, Miss. Amanda Jane, BA ACA *1994;* 35 Ruden Way, EPSOM, KT17 3LL.
JOHN, Mr. Andrew Lee, BA ACA *2006;* 4 Woodside Place, Wildhill Road, HATFIELD, HERTFORDSHIRE, AL9 6DN.
JOHN, Mr. Andrew Richard, BSc(Hons) ACA *2009;* Foxway Rise, Avenue Road, FLEET, HAMPSHIRE, GU51 4NG.
JOHN, Mrs. Ann-Marie Josephine, BEng BCom ACA *1999;* 64 Meadway, HARPENDEN, HERTFORDSHIRE, AL5 1JQ.
JOHN, Mrs. Carolyn Jane, BA ACA *1988;* 2 Chatsworth Place, Oxshott, LEATHERHEAD, KT22 0SS.
JOHN, Miss. Cerith, BSc ACA *1991;* Tan y Ffrith, Loggerheads Road, Cilcain, MOLD, CH7 5PG.
JOHN, Mrs. Christine Anne, BSc(Hons) ACA *2004;* Flat 1 Avondowns Court, 7-9 Alma Vale Road, BRISTOL, BS8 2HL.
JOHN, Mr. Christopher Llewellyn, FCA *1963;* 56 Hill Rise, RICHMOND, TW10 6UB. (Life Member)
JOHN, Mrs. Claire, MSc ACA *2003;* Mulberry House, Gwehelog, USK, GWENT, NP15 1RB.
JOHN, Mr. Clive Alan, FCA *1976;* Foxway Rise, Avenue Road, FLEET, HAMPSHIRE, GU51 4NG.
JOHN, Mr. Colin Neil, BA ACA CF *1985;* 61 Hill View, Henleaze, BRISTOL, BS9 4QF.
•JOHN, Mr. Colin Richard, ACA ACCA *2009;* (Tax Fac), Llewelyn Davies, Bank House, St.James Street, NARBERTH, PEMBROKESHIRE, SA67 7BX.
JOHN, Mr. Dafydd Rhys, BSc(Econ) ACA *1999;* Mulberry House, Gwehelog, USK, GWENT, NP15 1RB.
•JOHN, Mr. David Charles, BA ACA *1988;* PricewaterhouseCoopers LLP, Cornwall Court, 19 Cornwall Street, BIRMINGHAM, B3 2DT. See also PricewaterhouseCoopers
•JOHN, Mr. David Robert, BSc FCA *1980;* (Tax Fac), Butterworth Jones, 80 Oxford Street, BURNHAM-ON-SEA, SOMERSET, TA8 1EF. See also Chedzoy Butterworth Limited
JOHN, Mrs. Dawn Elizabeth, BSc ACA *1999;* Bache Commodities Ltd, 9 Devonshire Square, LONDON, EC2M 4HP.
JOHN, Miss. Emma, BA ACA *1998;* 82 Cranmer Avenue, LONDON, W13 9XU.
JOHN, Mrs. Emma Claire, BA(Hons) ACA *2003;* The Boathouse, 43 Green End, Fen Ditton, CAMBRIDGE, CB5 8SX.
JOHN, Mr. Gareth George, MSc FCA CPA *1976;* 7520 113th Street, Apartment 5E, FOREST HILLS, NY 11375, UNITED STATES.
JOHN, Mr. Gareth Glyn Edward, BA ACA *1997;* 43 Green End, Fen Ditton, CAMBRIDGE, CB5 8SX.
•JOHN, Mr. Gareth Ivor, BSc FCA *1979;* (Tax Fac), Accountants Plus Limited, 18 Coychurch Road, Pencoed, BRIDGEND, MID GLAMORGAN, CF35 5NG.
•JOHN, Mr. Graham Maldwyn, BSc FCA *1996;* Young & Co, Bewell House, Bewell Street, HEREFORD, HR4 0BA.
JOHN, Mrs. Helen Sarah Louise, MA ACA FRSA *1990;* 84 Bluehouse Lane, OXTED, RH8 0AD.
•JOHN, Mr. Huw Stradling, BA FCA *1967;* (Tax Fac), Huw John & Co Ltd, Upper Floor, 5-7 Mill Street, PONTYPRIDD, MID GLAMORGAN, CF37 2SN.
JOHN, Mr. Hywel Rhys Richard, MA ACA *1989;* 84 Bluehouse Lane, OXTED, SURREY, RH8 0AD.
JOHN, Mr. Iain Martyn, MA ACA *1999;* 64 Meadway, HARPENDEN, HERTFORDSHIRE, AL5 1JQ.
JOHN, Mr. Ivan Douglas, FCA *1961;* 2005 San Ramon Av Apt F 802, MOUNTAIN VIEW, CA 94043-5129, UNITED STATES.
JOHN, Mr. Llewellyn, BA ACA *2003;* 1st Floor Cayzer House, 30 Buckingham Gate, LONDON, SW1E 6NN.
•JOHN, Miss. Mandy, BA ACA *2003;* 19 Beechlands Park, Haverfordwest, PEMBROKE, SA61 1EN.
•JOHN, Mr. Michael, FCA *1977;* (Tax Fac), Hatfield & John Ltd, 2 Market Street, ABERAERON, DYFED, SA46 0AS.
JOHN, Miss. Nicola, BSc ACA *1991;* 19 Poplar Grove, LONDON, W6 7RF.
JOHN, Mrs. Patricia Clare, BA FCA *1981;* Care & Repair Cymru, 4-5 Norbury House Norbury Road, CARDIFF, CF5 3AS.
JOHN, Mr. Philip David, BSc ACA *1987;* Unicorn Asset Management Ltd, Preachers Court, The Charterhouse, Charterhouse Square, LONDON, EC1M 6AU.
JOHN, Mrs. Rachel Ann, BA(Hons) ACA *2001;* 3 Fairfax Crescent, PORTHCAWL, MID GLAMORGAN, CF36 3EN.
JOHN, Mr. Richard David Nathan, BSc ACA *2004;* 3 Belgrave Gardens, Walter Road, SWANSEA, SA1 4QF.
•JOHN, Mr. Robert Francis, FCA *1968;* (Tax Fac), Clarkson Hyde LLP, 2nd Floor, Mutual House, 70 Conduit Street, LONDON, W1S 2GF. See also Business Matters (UK) Ltd
•JOHN, Mr. Robin Wayne, FCA CTA *1978;* Wellden Turnbull LLP, 78 Portsmouth Road, COBHAM, SURREY, KT11 1PP. See also WT Accountants Ltd
JOHN, Mrs. Sarah Anne, BA ACA *1994;* Westbury, Harvest Hill, BOURNE END, BUCKINGHAMSHIRE, SL8 5JJ.
JOHN, Mr. Simon, MSci ACA *2011;* 23 Oxford Close, NEWCASTLE UPON TYNE, NE12 8TN.
JOHN, Mr. Stanley Kenneth, FCA *1968;* 22 Colcokes Road, BANSTEAD, SM7 2EW.
JOHN, Mr. Stephen Mark, BA FCA *1998;* Waxman International Ltd Grove Mills, Elland Lane, ELLAND, WEST YORKSHIRE, HX5 9DZ.
JOHN, Mr. Trevor Thomas, MA FCA *1970;* Southstoke Hall, Southstoke, BATH, BA2 7DL. (Life Member)
JOHN, Mr. William David, BSc ACA *1987;* Securon (Amersham) Ltd, Winchmore Hill, AMERSHAM, BUCKINGHAMSHIRE, HP7 0NZ.
JOHNS, Mr. Benjamin Richard, BSc ACA *2000;* 17 Bennerley Road, LONDON, SW11 6DR.
JOHNS, Mr. Brooke Elliot Mackelcan, FCA *1964;* The Laundry Cottage, Gowran Grange, Punchestown, NAAS, COUNTY KILDARE, IRELAND.
JOHNS, Mrs. Catherine Ann, BCom ACA *1987;* Dundas House, Follaton, Plymouth Road, TOTNES, TQ9 5NB.
JOHNS, Mr. Christopher Ian, BSc ACA *1996;* 92 Bolling Road, Ben Rhydding, ILKLEY, WEST YORKSHIRE, LS29 8QQ.

•**JOHNS, Mrs. Clare Esther, BSc ACA** *1994;* (Tax Fac), Clare E Johns, 13 Banks Way, GUILDFORD, SURREY, GU4 7NL.

JOHNS, Mr. David Hugh, MA ACA *1983;* 15 Holmead Road, LONDON, SW6 2JE.

JOHNS, Mr. David Kenneth, BA ACA *1983;* 3 Oak Corner, Beare Green, DORKING, RH5 4SG.

JOHNS, Mr. David Rees, FCA *1959;* Cornerways, 2 The Whimbrels, PORTHCAWL, CF36 3TR. (Life Member)

JOHNS, Mr. David Sidney, FCA *1966;* Flat 219, Lyle Court, Lilleshall Road, MORDEN, SURREY, SM4 6DT.

JOHNS, Mr. Edward, ACA *2008;* Pricewaterhousecoopers, 7 More London Riverside, LONDON, SE1 2RT.

JOHNS, Mr. Frank Timothy, MSc BA FCA *1973;* Mundipharma Pte Ltd, 10 Hoe Chiang Road, Apt 20-04/05 Keppel Towers, SINGAPORE 089315, SINGAPORE.

JOHNS, Mr. Fraser, ACA *2009;* 5 Middle Farm Close, Dauntsey, CHIPPENHAM, SN15 4GY.

JOHNS, Miss. Hayley, BSc ACA MAAT *2010;* 25 Wells Square, RADSTOCK, BA3 3UF.

JOHNS, Mr. Ian Peter, FCA *1970;* 73 Millrace Close, Lisvane, CARDIFF, CF14 0UQ.

JOHNS, Mrs. Jane, ACA DChA *1994;* with Francis Clark, 23 Devon Square, NEWTON ABBOT, DEVON, TQ12 2HU.

•**JOHNS, Mr. Jonathan Henry, FCA CF** *1982;* Jonathan Johns Consulting, Bellenden, Wrefords Lane, EXETER, EX4 5BR.

•**JOHNS, Mr. Kevin Hugh, BSc FCA** *1992;* Prime Accountants & Business Advisers Limited, Marlborough House, 679 Warwick Road, SOLIHULL, WEST MIDLANDS, B91 3DA. See also Prime Pilleys, Prime Accountants Group Limited and Prime Coventry Ltd

•**JOHNS, Mr. Lewis David, FCA** *1974;* Geoffrey W Pillar & Co, Erme House, Station Road, PLYMOUTH, PL7 2AU.

•**JOHNS, Mr. Mark Andrew, ACA FCCA** *2008;* Princecroft Willis LLP, Towngate House, 2-8 Parkstone Road, POOLE, DORSET, BH15 2PW. See also PW Business Solutions

JOHNS, Mr. Matthew, BA ACA *1995;* 41 Mount Drive, Park Street, ST. ALBANS, AL2 2NP.

JOHNS, Mr. Michael Alan, BA ACA *1987;* ShelterBox Unit 1A, Water-ma-Trout, HELSTON, CORNWALL, TR13 0LW.

JOHNS, Mrs. Nicola Kate, BSc ACA *2005;* Tutukaka, La Villette, St. Martin, GUERNSEY, GY4 6QA.

JOHNS, Mrs. Patricia Margaret, BA ACA *1989;* Crane House, 28 Church Road, Mylor, FALMOUTH, TR11 5NL.

JOHNS, Mr. Peter Michael, FCA *1966;* APA Associates Ltd, Robsons Orchard, Lavant, CHICHESTER, WEST SUSSEX, PO18 0BG.

JOHNS, Mr. Philip Shane, FCA *1959;* 10 George Street, Bathwick Hill, BATH, BA2 6BP. (Life Member)

JOHNS, Mr. Richard Anthony, BA(Econ) ACA *1997;* 1101 Safa Street, HERNDON, VA 20170, UNITED STATES.

JOHNS, Mr. Richard Trevor Morris, MA FCA *1966;* 54 Racton Road, Fulham, LONDON, SW6 1LP. (Life Member)

JOHNS, Ms. Sandra Jane, BSc ACA *1996;* 92 Bolling Road, Ben Rhydding, ILKLEY, LS29 8QQ.

JOHNS, Mr. Simon Beresford, BA ACA *2003;* Tutukaka, Rue De La Villette, St. Martin, GUERNSEY, GY4 6QA.

JOHNS, Mr. Simon Christopher, MA FCA MBA *1995;* 19 Richmond Avenue, Wimbledon, LONDON, SW20 8LA.

•**JOHNS, Mr. Simon Roger, FCA** *1973;* Davies Williams, 21 St. Andrews Crescent, CARDIFF, CF10 3DB. See also DW Consultancy Services Ltd

JOHNS, Mr. Stewart, BSc FCA *1987;* 11 Ladymead Lane, Langford, BRISTOL, BS40 5EG.

JOHNS, Mr. Thomas Trevor, BSc ACA *1995;* Unisys Australia Pty Limited, 1G Homebush Bay, RHODES, NSW 2138, AUSTRALIA.

JOHNS, Mr. Trevor Edward, BSc FCA *1975;* 35 Woodburn Square, Douglas, ISLE OF MAN, IM1 4DD. (Life Member)

JOHNSEN, Mr. Ben Finn, BA ACA *2005;* 16 Broad View, Thorpe End, NORWICH, NR13 5DZ.

JOHNSON, Mr. Adrian, FCA *1972;* 25 Venton Close, WOKING, GU21 3BX.

JOHNSON, Mr. Alan, FCA *1953;* 26 Trafalgar Park, New Waltham, GRIMSBY, DN36 4YP. (Life Member)

JOHNSON, Mr. Alan Beverley, FCA *1955;* Fletchers, Pembury, TUNBRIDGE WELLS, TN2 4BL. (Life Member)

•**JOHNSON, Mr. Alan Samuel, FCA** *1969;* Alan S Johnson, 173 College Road, LIVERPOOL, L23 3AT.

JOHNSON, Mr. Alex, MA ACA *1999;* STG, Equity Jubilee House, 1 Jubilee Street, BRIGHTON, BN1 1GE.

JOHNSON, Mr. Alexander, BEng ACA *1995;* Sky High, 10 High Street, TADCASTER, NORTH YORKSHIRE, LS24 9AT.

JOHNSON, Mr. Alexander James, BCom FCA *1962;* Toad Cottage, Carr Lane, Scalby, SCARBOROUGH, YO13 0SB.

JOHNSON, Mrs. Andrea, BA ACA *1996;* 8 Pakenham Road, BIRMINGHAM, B15 2NE.

JOHNSON, Mr. Andrew, ACA *2005;* 24 Melrose Drive, STOCKTON-ON-TEES, CLEVELAND, TS18 3UE.

•**JOHNSON, Mr. Andrew Anthony Mark, BA FCA** *1995;* Johnson & Co, 239 Moor End Lane, BIRMINGHAM, B24 9DS. See also J2U Consulting Ltd

JOHNSON, Mr. Andrew David, BA ACA *1989;* Wishanger, 78 Middle Bourne Lane, Lower Bourne, FARNHAM, GU10 3NJ.

JOHNSON, Mr. Andrew Edward, BSc ACA *2004;* Flat 21 Lochbie, Crouch Hill, LONDON, N4 4SB.

JOHNSON, Mr. Andrew James, BSc(Hons) ACA *2003;* 14 The Causeway, Carlton, BEDFORD, MK43 7LT.

JOHNSON, Mr. Andrew James, ACA *2008;* with Ernst & Young LLP, 1 Colmore Square, BIRMINGHAM, B4 6HQ.

JOHNSON, Mr. Andrew Kevin, BA FCA *1983;* 112 Beech Road, Elloughton, BROUGH, NORTH HUMBERSIDE, HU15 1JZ.

JOHNSON, Mr. Andrew Mark, BA(Hons) ACA *2002;* EXXON MOBIL, Ermyn Way, LEATHERHEAD, SURREY, KT22 8UX.

JOHNSON, Mr. Andrew Stuart, ACA *2006;* 3 Armscot Place, LIVERPOOL, L25 0PD.

JOHNSON, Mrs. Angela, BEng ACA *1992;* Room 4W57 Quarry House, Quarry Hill, LEEDS, LS2 7UE.

JOHNSON, Mrs. Angela Mary, BSc ACA *1992;* 18 Lady Housty Avenue, Newton, SWANSEA, SA3 4TS.

•**JOHNSON, Miss. Angela Mary, BCom FCA** *1986;* 1 Fairhurst Drive, Parbold, WIGAN, LANCASHIRE, WN8 7DJ.

JOHNSON, Miss. Ann Elizabeth, BSc ACA *1989;* Flat 5, 69 Hartfield Road, Wimbledon, LONDON, SW19 3TJ.

JOHNSON, Dr. Anna Karina, PhD BA ACA *2005;* 1 Hazeldene Drive, PINNER, MIDDLESEX, HA5 3NJ.

JOHNSON, Mrs. Anna-Maria, BSc ACA *1990;* 7 The Holt, Washington, PULBOROUGH, WEST SUSSEX, RH20 4AN.

JOHNSON, Mrs. Anne Marie, BSc ACA *1990;* 3321 Marquette St, DALLAS, TX 75225, UNITED STATES.

JOHNSON, Mr. Anthony Ian, MBA BA FCA *1971;* 3 Cedar Close, Kingston Vale, LONDON, SW15 3SD.

•**JOHNSON, Mr. Anthony Roland, BSc(Econ) FCA CTA** *1992;* ARJ Accountancy Limited, 9 Loreille Gardens, Rownhams, SOUTHAMPTON, SO16 8LP.

JOHNSON, Mr. Arawn Andrew, BEng ACA *1993;* (Tax Fac), Arawn Johnson, PO Box 14574, RAS AL-KHAIMAH, UNITED ARAB EMIRATES.

JOHNSON, Mr. Arthur Beaumont, ACA *1979;* 25 Oakleigh Crescent Rushington, Totton, SOUTHAMPTON, SO40 9AR.

JOHNSON, Mr. Arthur David, BCom FCA *1962;* Johnsons Veterinary Products, Ltd., Reddicap Trading Est., SUTTON COLDFIELD, B75 7DF.

JOHNSON, Mr. Arthur Hewitt, LLB FCA *1966;* Sanderling, 23 Baskervyle Road, Heswall, WIRRAL, CH60 8NJ.

JOHNSON, Mr. Barry Cooper, FCA *1972;* 14 Garland, Rothley, LEICESTER, LE7 7RF.

•**JOHNSON, Mr. Barry Martin, FCA** *1977;* with PricewaterhouseCoopers LLP, 1 Embankment Place, LONDON, WC2N 6RH.

•**JOHNSON, Mr. Brian, BCom FCA** *1975;* Brian Johnson B.Com FCA, 9 Shrublands Road, BERKHAMSTED, HERTFORDSHIRE, HP4 3HY.

JOHNSON, Mr. Brian George, FCA *1955;* 5 Denleigh Gardens, THAMES DITTON, SURREY, KT7 0YL. (Life Member)

JOHNSON, Mr. Brian Keyworth, FCA *1959;* Cribyn, Court Gardens, St Arvans, CHEPSTOW, NP16 6DZ. (Life Member)

JOHNSON, Mr. Brian Mark, ACA CA(SA) *2011;* 22 Grange Road, WINCHESTER, SO23 9RT.

JOHNSON, Mr. Brian Richard, FCA *1975;* 26 Park Road, Swarland, MORPETH, NE65 9JD.

JOHNSON, Mr. Brian Richard, BSc FCA *1977;* 4 Trevone Way, DARLINGTON, COUNTY DURHAM, DL3 0ZX.

JOHNSON, Mr. Carl Eric, BA ACA *2005;* 3 Organsdale Cottages Organsdale Kelsall, TARPORLEY, CHESHIRE, CW6 0SR.

JOHNSON, Mrs. Carol Amanda Ann, BSc ACA *1998;* 29 Abbey Court, London Road South, Poynton, STOCKPORT, CHESHIRE, SK12 1WW.

•**JOHNSON, Mrs. Caroline Elizabeth, BA FCA** *1998;* AIC Accountancy, 97 Normandy Avenue, BEVERLEY, HU17 8PR.

JOHNSON, Miss. Carolyn Elizabeth, BA ACA *1986;* 1 Kirkby Garth, Scarcroft, LEEDS, LS14 3LF.

JOHNSON, Miss. Catherine Barbara, MSc ACA *2008;* with Deloitte LLP, PO Box 403, Lord Coutanche House, 66-68 Esplanade, St Helier, JERSEY JE4 8WA.

JOHNSON, Mrs. Catriona Anne, BA ACA *1995;* 6 Heather Close, St Leonards, RINGWOOD, BH24 2QJ.

JOHNSON, Mrs. Celia Mary, MA FCA *1979;* 55 Kings Road, RICHMOND, SURREY, TW10 6EG.

JOHNSON, Mr. Christian Glyn, BSc ACA *2006;* G4S Regional Management (UK&I) Limited, Farncombe House, BROADWAY, WORCESTERSHIRE, WR12 7LJ.

JOHNSON, Mrs. Christine, BSc ACA *1984;* Alburgh Hall, Church Road, Alburgh, HARLESTON, IP20 0DB.

•**JOHNSON, Mrs. Christine Elizabeth, BSc FCA** *1984;* (Tax Fac), Gardner Steward Limited, Charwell House, Wilsom Road, ALTON, HAMPSHIRE, GU34 2PP. See also Audit & Compliance Solutions Limited

JOHNSON, Mr. Christopher, ACA *2009;* 10 Derwent Court, DARWEN, LANCASHIRE, BB3 3SJ.

JOHNSON, Mr. Christopher, BA FCA *1982;* PricewaterhouseCoopers, Riverside Centre, 123 Eagle Street, GPO Box 150, BRISBANE, QLD 4001 AUSTRALIA.

JOHNSON, Mr. Christopher Alan, BA ACA *2005;* 14 Harlesden Road, ST. ALBANS, HERTFORDSHIRE, AL1 4LF.

JOHNSON, Mr. Christopher Bruce, BSc ACA *1981;* Moore Stephens, 10 Anson Road, Apt 29-15, International Plaza, SINGAPORE 079903, SINGAPORE.

•**JOHNSON, Mr. Christopher David, FCA** *1973;* THP Limited, 34-40 High Street, Wanstead, LONDON, E11 2RJ. See also THP Company Secretarial LLP

JOHNSON, Mr. Christopher David, BA ACA *1991;* 24 Onslow Gardens, LONDON, N10 3JU.

JOHNSON, Mr. Christopher David, BSc ACA *1995;* 36 St. James's Avenue, BECKENHAM, KENT, BR3 4HG.

JOHNSON, Mr. Christopher Denis, FCA *1970;* 21 Cherry Grove, HUNGERFORD, RG17 0HP.

•**JOHNSON, Mr. Christopher Dorrien, FCA** *1968;* Johnson Smith Associates Ltd, PO Box 2499, Elizabethan Square, 80 Shedden Road, GEORGE TOWN, GRAND CAYMAN KY1-1104 CAYMAN ISLANDS. See also Chris Johnson Associates Ltd

JOHNSON, Mr. Christopher Matthew Leverne, BA ACA MBA *1990;* Rua Das Betulas 335, Alphaville Graciosa, PINHAIS, 83.327-126, BRAZIL.

JOHNSON, Mr. Christopher Nigel, FCA *1972;* Banque Audi (Suisse) SA, 18 cours des Bastions, 1211 GENEVA, SWITZERLAND.

JOHNSON, Mrs. Clair Patricia Maria, BA(Hons) ACA *2004;* 6 Church Farm Close, Bierton, AYLESBURY, BUCKINGHAMSHIRE, HP22 5EL.

JOHNSON, Miss. Claire Ann, BA ACA *1998;* 83 Curzon Terrace, YORK, YO23 1EZ.

JOHNSON, Miss. Claire Louise, BSc ACA *2000;* 25 Kelmore Grove, East Dulwich, LONDON, SE22 9BH.

JOHNSON, Miss. Clare, BA ACA *2009;* 14 McCrone Mews, Belsize Lane, LONDON, NW3 5BG.

•**JOHNSON, Mr. Clive Etheridge, FCA** *1968;* C.E. Johnson, 2 Friary Gardens, LICHFIELD, WS13 6QU.

JOHNSON, Mr. Colin James, MA FCA *1981;* 35 Jubilee Road, FORDINGBRIDGE, SP6 1DP.

JOHNSON, Mr. Colin Stuart, FCA *1959;* 95 Old Park Ridings, Old Park Ridings, LONDON, N21 2EJ. (Life Member)

JOHNSON, Mr. Daniel, MEng ACA *2002;* 24 College Crescent, WINDSOR, SL4 3PG.

JOHNSON, Mr. David, ACA CPA *2011;* Flat 32, Seacon Tower, 5 Hutchings Street, LONDON, E14 8JX.

•**JOHNSON, Mr. David, BSc(Hons) FCA** *1991;* Strathmore Accountants Limited, 3rd Floor, Ivy Mill, Crown Street, Failsworth, MANCHESTER M35 9BG. See also Strathmore Audit Limited

JOHNSON, Mr. David, BA FCA *1989;* The Production Centre Unit 1, 191a Askew Road, LONDON, W12 9AX.

JOHNSON, Mr. David Andrew, BA ACA *1989;* 15 Upton Lane, Upton, CHESTER, CH2 1EB.

JOHNSON, Mr. David Anthony, BA ACA *1990;* 7 The Holt, Washington, PULBOROUGH, WEST SUSSEX, RH20 4AN.

JOHNSON, Mr. David Anthony, JP BSc FCA *1971;* Cold Knowle Farm, Stanbury, KEIGHLEY, WEST YORKSHIRE, BD22 0HH. (Life Member)

JOHNSON, Mr. David Arthur, FCA *1966;* 21 Wanderdown Road, BRIGHTON, BN2 7BT. (Life Member)

JOHNSON, Mr. David Brian, BSc ACA *2003;* 25 Little Mill Close, Barlestone, NUNEATON, WARWICKSHIRE, CV13 0HW.

•①**JOHNSON, Mr. David Edward, FCA** *1977;* Saint & Co., Unit 3, Lakeland Business Park, Lamplugh Road, COCKERMOUTH, CA13 0QT.

JOHNSON, Mr. David Edward, BCom FCA *1971;* Madacas, 11 Birch Way, Charlton Down, DORCHESTER, DORSET, DT2 9XX. (Life Member)

JOHNSON, Mr. David Frank, BSc ACA *1992;* with BJ Dixon Walsh Limited, St. Marys House, Magdalene Street, TAUNTON, SOMERSET, TA1 1SB.

JOHNSON, Mr. David John Crump, FCA *1962;* Wychwood House, 136 Comberton Road, KIDDERMINSTER, WORCESTERSHIRE, DY10 3DS.

JOHNSON, Mr. David Joseph, BCom FCA *1970;* Meadow Barn, Hardwick, WITNEY, OXFORDSHIRE, OX29 7QE. (Life Member)

JOHNSON, Mr. David Martin, BEng ACA *1982;* The Cedar Barn, Home Farm, Buckland, FARINGDON, OXFORDSHIRE, SN7 8RG.

•**JOHNSON, Mr. David Martin, BA FCA** *1985;* UHY Torgersens, Somerford Buildings, Norfolk Street, SUNDERLAND, SR1 1EE. See also UHY Torgersens Limited

•**JOHNSON, Mr. David Michael, BA FCA** *1999;* Deloitte LLP, 1 City Square, LEEDS, WEST YORKSHIRE, LS1 2AL. See also Deloitte & Touche LLP

JOHNSON, Mr. David Noel, LLB ACA *1984;* 19 Hawes Road, BROMLEY, BR1 3JS.

•**JOHNSON, Mr. David Reginald, BA ACA** *1987;* Johnson & Co, Hawthorne House, 28 Cowgate, Welton, BROUGH, NORTH HUMBERSIDE HU15 1NB.

JOHNSON, Mr. David Richard, FCA *1959;* 23 Roman Way, CARSHALTON, SM5 4EF. (Life Member)

JOHNSON, Mr. David Richard, ACA *1979;* 41 Station Lane, Lapworth, SOLIHULL, B94 6LW.

•**JOHNSON, Mr. David Victor, FCA** *1969;* Johnson & Co, 5 Lothian Wood, TADWORTH, SURREY, KT20 5DQ.

JOHNSON, Miss. Dawn, ACA *2010;* 24 Clamp Drive, SWADLINCOTE, DERBYSHIRE, DE11 9BP.

JOHNSON, Mrs. Deborah Jane, BSc ACA *2002;* 17 Grayling Road, GATESHEAD, NE11 9ND.

JOHNSON, Mrs. Debra Kate, BCom FCA *1986;* 11 Woodbourne Road, Edgbaston, BIRMINGHAM, B15 3QJ.

JOHNSON, Mr. Denis Alfred, FCA *1953;* 332 Hillmorton Road, RUGBY, WARWICKSHIRE, CV22 5EY. (Life Member)

JOHNSON, Mr. Derek Strafford, FCA *1968;* 63 Ryder Crescent, Hillside, SOUTHPORT, PR8 3AE.

JOHNSON, Miss. Diane Margaret, BA FCA DChA *1991;* 41 Allington Garden, BOSTON, PE21 9DW.

JOHNSON, Miss. Dione Germaine, BSc(Hons) ACA *2001;* 87 Earls Hall Avenue, SOUTHEND-ON-SEA, SS2 6NT.

JOHNSON, Mrs. Donna Louise, ACA *2009;* 35 Draycott Drive, Mickleover, DERBY, DE3 0QE.

JOHNSON, Mr. Douglas George, BSc ACA *2006;* JMH Group, 40a Dover Street, LONDON, W1S 4NW.

JOHNSON, Mr. Duncan Edward, MA ACA AMSI *1995;* Baigens, Winchester Road, Chawton, ALTON, HAMPSHIRE, GU34 1SL.

JOHNSON, Mr. Edward, BSc ACA *1997;* 33 Meadow Avenue, Wetley Rocks, STOKE-ON-TRENT, ST9 0BD.

JOHNSON, Mr. Edward, MSci ACA *2004;* 32 Marmet Avenue, LETCHWORTH GARDEN CITY, HERTFORDSHIRE, SG6 4QE.

JOHNSON, Mr. Edward Alexander Martin, BSc ACA *2005;* 33 Pretoria Road, WATFORD, WD18 0RL.

JOHNSON, Mr. Edward Arthur George, FCA *1968;* The Old Rectory, Town Lane, Garvestone, NORWICH, NR9 4QR.

JOHNSON, Mr. Edward Herbert, FCA *1953;* 3 Woodlands Road, Parkgate, NESTON, CH64 6RT. (Life Member)

JOHNSON, Mr. Edward Stewart, BA(Hons) ACA *2003;* U B S AG, 100 Liverpool Street, LONDON, EC2M 2RH.

•**JOHNSON, Mr. Edwin Colin, BA FCA** *1962;* Briston Johnson & Co, 8 Carrington Avenue, COTTINGHAM, HU16 4DU.

JOHNSON, Mr. Edwin Howard Russell, BSc ACA *1992;* 4 Carthew Road, Hammersmith, LONDON, W6 0DX.

•**JOHNSON, Mrs. Elizabeth Anne, FCA** *1976;* Elizabeth A. Johnson, 5 Lee Road, Hollywood, BIRMINGHAM, B47 5NY.

JOHNSON, Miss. Elizabeth Georgina, MA ACA *1988;* Bridge Cottage Castle Grove Road, Chobham, WOKING, GU24 8EG.
•**JOHNSON, Mrs. Emma, BEng ACA** *1998;* Oury Clark, PO Box 150, Herschel House, 58 Herschel Street, SLOUGH, SL1 1HD.
JOHNSON, Miss. Emma Louise, ACA *2008;* P D Ports Logistics & Shipping, 17-27 Queens Square, MIDDLESBROUGH, CLEVELAND, TS2 1AH.
JOHNSON, Miss. Erica Jane, BA ACA *2005;* 8 Hopwood Close, LONDON, SW17 0AG.
JOHNSON, Mrs. Fiona Clare, BA ACA *1992;* The Red House, 44 Boxgrove Avenue, GUILDFORD, GU1 1XQ.
JOHNSON, Mrs. Frances Mary Clare, BSc ACA *2000;* 1 Warren Lane, Hartford, NORTHWICH, CHESHIRE, CW8 1RQ.
JOHNSON, Mr. Frank Cyril, BCom ACA *1983;* RPMI Railpen Investments, Camomile Court, 23 Camomile Street, LONDON, EC3A 7LL.
•**JOHNSON, Mr. Frank Paul, FCA** *1973;* (Tax Fac), F.P. Johnson, Suite 75, 24 St Leonards Road, WINDSOR, BERKSHIRE, SL4 3BB.
JOHNSON, Mr. Fraser Adrian, BA(Hons) ACA *1998;* Shell Centre, York Road, LONDON, SE17NA.
•**JOHNSON, Mr. Frederick Andrew, FCA** *1980;* (Tax Fac), JWPCreers, 20-24 Park Street, SELBY, NORTH YORKSHIRE, YO8 4PW.
JOHNSON, Ms. Gabrielle, BSc ACA *1993;* 24 Onslow Gardens, LONDON, N10 3JU.
JOHNSON, Mrs. Gail Elizabeth, MVO MA FCA *1979;* 8 West Road, BERKHAMSTED, HP4 3HT.
JOHNSON, Mr. Gary Michael, ACA *1983;* 37 Burbo Bank Roa, Blundellsands, LIVERPOOL, L23 6TQ.
JOHNSON, Mr. Gavin Anthony, BSc ACA *2000;* 14 Hambalt Road, LONDON, SW4 9EF.
JOHNSON, Mr. Geoffrey Alan, BEng ACA *2008;* BDO, PO Box 31118, 2nd Floor Building 3, Governors Square, 23 Lime Tree Bay Avenue, SEVEN MILE BEACH GRAND CAYMAN KY1-1205 CAYMAN ISLANDS.
•**JOHNSON, Mr. Geoffrey Edwin, BA FCA** *1972;* PricewaterhouseCoopers LLP, 300 Madison Avenue, NEW YORK, NY 10017, UNITED STATES. See also PricewaterhouseCoopers
JOHNSON, Mr. Geoffrey Leonard, FCA *1951;* 15 Kingsland Garden Close, Mannamead, PLYMOUTH, PL3 5NR. (Life Member)
•**JOHNSON, Mr. Geoffrey Thomas, FCA** *1967;* 33 Park Brook Lane, Shevington, WIGAN, LANCASHIRE, WN6 8AF.
JOHNSON, Mr. George Lee, BA FCA *1975;* 50 Oakwood Avenue, BECKENHAM, KENT, BR3 6PJ.
JOHNSON, Mr. Gerald Clive Frederick, FCA *1953;* 32 Park Farm Road, BROMLEY, BR1 2PE. (Life Member)
JOHNSON, Mr. Giles, MA ACA *1997;* Groveside, Glasbury, HEREFORD, HR3 5NR.
•**JOHNSON, Mrs. Gillian Anne, ACA CTA** *1987;* (Tax Fac), Johnson & Co, Hawthorne House, 28 Cowgate, Welton, BROUGH, NORTH HUMBERSIDE HU15 1NB.
JOHNSON, Mrs. Gillian Margaret, FCA *1984;* Fieldhead, Fieldhead Lane, Oxenhope, KEIGHLEY, WEST YORKSHIRE, BD22 0EJ.
JOHNSON, Mrs. Gillian Patricia, FCA *1970;* York Cottage, 10 Sidlands, SIDMOUTH, DEVON, EX10 8UE.
JOHNSON, Mr. Graham Edward, MEng&Man ACA *1997;* 26 Summit Way, Southgate, LONDON, N14 7NL.
JOHNSON, Mr. Graham Kenneth, BA FCA *1974;* 588 Chorley New Road, Lostock, BOLTON, BL6 4DW.
JOHNSON, Mr. Gregory, MChem ACA *2011;* Flat 10, 74 Holland Park, LONDON, W11 3SL.
JOHNSON, Mrs. Hannah Leigh, BSc(Hons) ACA *2004;* 27 Sudeley, TAMWORTH, STAFFORDSHIRE, B77 1JR.
JOHNSON, Dr. Hannah Yik Siew, ACA *2011;* 59 Fernhill Road, FARNBOROUGH, GU14 9SA.
JOHNSON, Miss. Harriet, BSc(Hons) ACA *2010;* Middle Farm London Road, Shrewton, SALISBURY, SP3 4DR.
JOHNSON, Mrs. Heather, LLB ACA *2011;* 29 Breary Lane East, Bramhope, LEEDS, WEST YORKSHIRE, LS16 9EU.
JOHNSON, Mrs. Heather Joy, BSc ACA *1991;* 23 Bemersyde Drive, Jesmond, NEWCASTLE UPON TYNE, NE2 2HL.
JOHNSON, Miss. Helen, BSc ACA *1994;* 47 Sims Close, Ramsbottom, BURY, LANCASHIRE, BL0 9NT.
JOHNSON, Mrs. Helen Elizabeth, BSc ACA ATII *1996;* Holm Oak Barn, Watnall, NOTTINGHAM, NG16 1HU.
JOHNSON, Mrs. Helena Jane Hartley, BA ACA *1994;* Kaplan Financial, Kaplan City Campus, 51 Cuppage Road 04-07, SINGAPORE 229469, SINGAPORE.
•**JOHNSON, Mr. Herbert Ronald, FCA** *1955;* Charles Wakeling & Co, 72-73 Wilton Road, Victoria, LONDON, SW1V 1DE.
JOHNSON, Ms. Hilary, BSc FCA *1983;* 28 Kimberley, Teal Farm, WASHINGTON, NE38 8TT.
JOHNSON, Mr. Howard James, FCA *1972;* 16a St. John Street, LEWES, EAST SUSSEX, BN7 2QE.
•**JOHNSON, Mr. Humphrey, FCA** *1968;* Humphrey Johnson FCA, 53 Edisford Road, CLITHEROE, LANCASHIRE, BB7 3LA.
JOHNSON, Mr. Iain, BA(Hons) ACA ACIM DipM *2002;* Wellands Farmhouse, Moor Bottom, CLECKHEATON, BD19 6AL.
JOHNSON, Mr. Iain Barrington, BSc ACA *1992;* 6 Kingsdown Road, EPSOM, KT17 3PU.
JOHNSON, Mr. Ian, BSc ACA *2003;* 101 Nelson Road, LONDON, SW19 1HU.
JOHNSON, Mr. Ian, MA FCA *1979;* Rowan House, Bricklehampton Lane, PERSHORE, WR10 3JT.
JOHNSON, Mr. Ian Alfred, FCA *1983;* The Watch Hospital Ltd, 12 Bond Street, WAKEFIELD, WEST YORKSHIRE, WF1 2QP.
JOHNSON, Mr. Ian Barry, BSc ACA *1992;* Block 31 Westwood Green, Lane 500 Xingle Road, Minhang District, SHANGHAI 201107, CHINA.
•**JOHNSON, Mr. Ian Brook, FCA** *1976;* Chantrey Vellacott DFK LLP, Prospect House, 58 Queens Road, READING, BERKSHIRE, RG1 4RP.
JOHNSON, Mr. Ian Edward, BSc ACA MCT *1983;* MSD, 338 Euston Road, LONDON, NW1 3BH.
JOHNSON, Mr. Ian James, BSc ACA *1989;* 1/3 Wiston Gardens, Double Bay, SYDNEY, NSW 2028, AUSTRALIA.
•**JOHNSON, Mr. Ian Kenneth, FCA** *1975;* Moulton Johnson, Lutidine House, Newark Lane, Ripley, WOKING, SURREY GU23 6BS. See also MJ Results Ltd, Moulton Johnson Limited
JOHNSON, Mr. Ian Paul, BSc FCA *1980;* Islington House, Q A Ltd, 17 Gelderd Trading Estate West Vale, LEEDS, LS12 6BD.
JOHNSON, Mr. Ian Paul, BSc ACA *1984;* Jacques Vert Plc, 46 Colebrooke Row, LONDON, N1 8AF.
•**JOHNSON, Mr. Ian Richards, BA FCA** *1981;* (Tax Fac), Grant Thornton UK LLP, Regent House, 80 Regent Road, LEICESTER, LE1 7NH. See also Grant Thornton LLP
JOHNSON, Mr. Ian Robert, ACA *2003;* (Tax Fac), Manchester Airport Plc Olympic House, Manchester Airport, MANCHESTER, M90 1QX.
JOHNSON, Mr. Ian Roderick, BCom ACA *1995;* Haresbottom House Lower Norcote Barns, Lower Norcote, CIRENCESTER, GLOUCESTERSHIRE, GL7 5RJ.
JOHNSON, Mr. Ian Spencer, FCA *1961;* 48 Union Road, Bridge, CANTERBURY, KENT, CT4 5LW.
JOHNSON, Miss. Jackie, BSc ACA *2006;* Verdala, Frimley Road, Ash Vale, ALDERSHOT, HAMPSHIRE, GU12 5NN.
JOHNSON, Mrs. Jacquelin Amanda, LLB ACA *1991;* Tilecroft, Lewes Road, Lindfield, HAYWARDS HEATH, RH16 2LF.
JOHNSON, Mrs. Jacqueline Anne, BA ACA *1992;* 15 Upton Lane, Upton, CHESTER, CH2 1EB.
JOHNSON, Mr. James, BSc ACA *2011;* Flat 3, Crispin Court, 17-19 Freemantle Street, LONDON, SE17 2JP.
JOHNSON, Mr. James Alfred Earlam, FCA *1970;* The Coach House, Kirkandrews-on-Eden, CARLISLE, CA5 6DU.
•**JOHNSON, Mr. James Andrew, BA(Hons) ACA** *2002;* J Johnson BA(Hons) ACA, 6 Church Farm Close, Bierton, AYLESBURY, BUCKINGHAMSHIRE, HP22 5EL. See also C & J Accountancy
JOHNSON, Mr. James Charles, BA(Hons) ACA *2003;* 6 Coopers Meadow, Redbourn, ST. ALBANS, HERTFORDSHIRE, AL3 7EY.
JOHNSON, Mr. James Dominic, BSc ACA *1983;* 5 Tyndale Terrace, LONDON, N1 2AT.
JOHNSON, Mr. James Douglas, BSc FCA *1978;* 26 Hackness Road, Newby, SCARBOROUGH, YO12 5RY.
JOHNSON, Mr. James Lee, ACA *1995;* 81a Warrington Crescent, LONDON, W9 1EH.
JOHNSON, Mr. James Richard, FCA *1959;* Acorn Cottage, 26 Gosforth Lane, DRONFIELD, DERBYSHIRE, S18 1PR. (Life Member)
JOHNSON, Mr. James Valentine, FCA *1972;* La Teranga, 65700 CASTELNAU RIVIERE BASSE, FRANCE.
JOHNSON, Miss. Jane Suzanne, BA ACA *1992;* Mulberry House, Henwood, LISKEARD, PL14 5BP.
JOHNSON, Mrs. Janice, MA ACA *1985;* Dollar Academy, DOLLAR, CLACKMANNANSHIRE, FK14 7DU.
JOHNSON, Mr. Jeffrey Nicholas, FCA *1977;* 47 Lionel Road North, BRENTFORD, TW8 9QZ.
JOHNSON, Mrs. Jennifer, BSc ACA *2007;* 48 Merivale Way, ELY, CAMBRIDGESHIRE, CB7 4GQ.
JOHNSON, Miss. Jennifer Anne, BSc ACA *1993;* 108 Alwyn Court Maple Road, SURBITON, SURREY, KT6 4DR.
JOHNSON, Mr. Jeremy Guyutt, MA FCA *1971;* 18 Grasmere Close, Merrow, GUILDFORD, GU1 2TG.
JOHNSON, Miss. Jessica, LLB ACA *2006;* 1 Beech House, Weetwood Lane, LEEDS, LS16 5TZ.
JOHNSON, Mr. John Joseph, BSc FCA *1978;* 10 Collingham Drive, Nunthorpe, MIDDLESBROUGH, CLEVELAND, TS7 0GB.
JOHNSON, Mr. John Michael, FCA *1967;* Officenote LTD, 16 Unwin Close, LETCHWORTH GARDEN CITY, HERTFORDSHIRE, SG6 3RS.
JOHNSON, Mrs. Joy Hoi Ying, BA ACA *2006;* Flat 2, Northfleet Lodge, 6 Claremont Avenue, WOKING, SURREY, GU22 7RL.
JOHNSON, Miss. Julia, BSc ACA *2006;* 147 Tranmere Road, LONDON, SW18 3QX.
JOHNSON, Mrs. Julia Elizabeth, MA ACA *2004;* with Deloitte LLP, PO Box 500, 2 Hardman Street, MANCHESTER, M60 2AT.
•**JOHNSON, Mrs. Julie Ann, FCA** *1991;* 36 2nd Avenue, QIPCO, West Bay, DOHA, QATAR.
JOHNSON, Mrs. Julie Patricia, BSc ACA *1997;* Messier Dowty Ltd, Cheltenham Road East, GLOUCESTER, GL2 9QH.
JOHNSON, Mrs. Juliette Martine, BSc(Hons) ACA *2002;* 13 Limes Avenue, LONDON, NW7 3NY.
JOHNSON, Miss. Karen Anne, BA(Hons) ACA *2003;* 6 Coopers Meadow, Redbourn, ST. ALBANS, HERTFORDSHIRE, AL3 7EY.
JOHNSON, Mrs. Karen Louise, BA(Hons) FCA MBA DChA *1991;* St. Leonards Hospice, 185 Tadcaster Road, Dringhouses, YORK, YO24 1GL.
JOHNSON, Mrs. Karen Louise, BA ACA *1995;* 18 Colwyn Road, Bramhall, STOCKPORT, SK7 2JQ.
JOHNSON, Miss. Katey, ACA *2010;* 33 Church Lane, Clayton le Moors, ACCRINGTON, LANCASHIRE, BB5 4DE.
JOHNSON, Miss. Katharine Louise, ACA *2010;* Flat 64, 64 St. Georges Way, LONDON, SE15 6QW.
JOHNSON, Ms. Katharine Ruth, BSc ACA *1998;* (Tax Fac), Hilltop Barn, Hindringham Road, WALSINGHAM, NR22 6DR.
JOHNSON, Mrs. Katherine Jane, BSc ACA *1987;* 78 Middle Bourne Lane, Lower Bourne, FARNHAM, GU10 3NJ.
•**JOHNSON, Mr. Keith Albert, FCA** *1971;* K.A. Johnson, Norfolk House, Norfolk Rd, RICKMANSWORTH, WD3 1RD.
•**JOHNSON, Mr. Keith Henry, FCA** *1967;* The Pastures, 3 Old Hall Spinney, Honington, GRANTHAM, LINCOLNSHIRE, NG32 2PU.
JOHNSON, Mr. Keith James, FCA *1956;* Tall Trees, 12 Tylers Close, KINGS LANGLEY, WD4 9QA. (Life Member)
JOHNSON, Mr. Keith Osmond, FCA *1967;* 18 Raglan Close, Chandler's Ford, EASTLEIGH, HAMPSHIRE, SO53 4NH.
JOHNSON, Mr. Keith Patrick, FCA *1982;* Pippins High Street Great Sampford, SAFFRON WALDEN, ESSEX, CB10 2RG.
•**JOHNSON, Mr. Keith Stewart, FCA** *1975;* Keith S Johnson Consulting Ltd, Brookside, Smiddyhill, ALFORD, ABERDEENSHIRE, AB33 8NA.
JOHNSON, Mr. Keith William, FCA *1974;* Deutsche Bank International Limited, PO Box 424, Lefebvre Court, Lefebvre Street, St Peterport, GUERNSEY GY1 3WT.
JOHNSON, Mrs. Kelly, BA(Hons) ACA *2002;* 9 Fenwick Close, Backworth, NEWCASTLE UPON TYNE, NE27 0RL.
JOHNSON, Mr. Kenneth Carter, FCA *1931;* c/o Barclays National Bank, Ltd., P.O. Box 189, EAST LONDON, C.P., 5200 SOUTH AFRICA. (Life Member)
JOHNSON, Mr. Kenneth Claude, FCA *1951;* 32 Carden Hill, BRIGHTON, BN1 8AB. (Life Member)
JOHNSON, Mr. Kenneth James, FCA *1953;* Fairfield, London Road, Adlington, MACCLESFIELD, SK10 4NA. (Life Member)
JOHNSON, Mr. Kenneth Richard, FCA *1970;* Ashurst Business Services, 5 Appold Street, LONDON, EC2A 2HA.
JOHNSON, Mr. Kenneth Wallace, FCA *1948;* Rosscote, School Lane, Little Neston, NESTON, CH64 4DG. (Life Member)
JOHNSON, Miss. Kerry Ann, BA(Hons) ACA *2002;* Siemens Sir William Siemens Square, Frimley, CAMBERLEY, GU16 8QD.
JOHNSON, Mr. Kevin Andrew, BA ACA CF *1995;* 79 Morris Drive, BILLINGSHURST, WEST SUSSEX, RH14 9ST.
JOHNSON, Mr. Kevin Mark, BSc ACA *1998;* 52 Prospect Road, ST. ALBANS, HERTFORDSHIRE, AL1 2AX.
JOHNSON, Mr. Kieran James, BA ACA *2003;* Aura Minerals Inc, PO Box 10434, Pacific Centre Suite 1950, 777 Dunsmuir Street, VANCOUVER V7Y 1K4, BC CANADA.
JOHNSON, Mr. Kieran Roy Darren, BSc ACA *1995;* GSK Plc, 980 Great West Road, BRENTFORD, MIDDLESEX, TW8 9GS.
JOHNSON, Mr. Kingsley Stephen, BA(Hons) ACA *2001;* 10 Wheatley Avenue, ILKLEY, WEST YORKSHIRE, LS29 8PT.
JOHNSON, Miss. Laura, ACA *2011;* 708 North Point Street, Unit No.2, SAN FRANCISCO, CA 94109, UNITED STATES.
JOHNSON, Mr. Lawrence, LLB ACA *2011;* Gun Wharf, Flat 3, 130 Wapping High Street, LONDON, E1W 2NH.
JOHNSON, Mr. Lawrence Stanley, FCA JDipMA *1954;* Tanglemead, 5 Lavender Close, COULSDON, CR5 3EU. (Life Member)
JOHNSON, Mr. Lee James, BA(Hons) ACA *2001;* 53 Habershon Drive, Frimley, CAMBERLEY, GU16 9TW.
JOHNSON, Miss. Leigh Anne, ACA *2007;* 11 The Mount, MIDDLESBROUGH, CLEVELAND, TS6 0HG.
JOHNSON, Mrs. Lesley, FCA *1981;* with Condy Mathias, Suite 26, 3 Atlas House, West Devon Business Park, TAVISTOCK, PL19 9DP.
JOHNSON, Mrs. Linda Maree, ACA CA(NZ) *2009;* KPMG Channel Islands Ltd, PO Box 20, 20 New Street, St Peter Port, GUERNSEY, GY1 4AN.
•**JOHNSON, Mr. Lindsay Peter, MA(Oxon) FCA AITI CFE** *1986;* Hyland Johnson Keane, Library House, 18 Dyke Parade, Mardyke, CORK, COUNTY CORK IRELAND.
JOHNSON, Mrs. Lorraine Ann, FCA *1978;* 16B Crescent Road, LEIGH-ON-SEA, SS9 2PF.
JOHNSON, Miss. Lucinda Mary, MA FCA *1982;* 2 Blyth's Wharf, Narrow Street, LONDON, E14 8BF.
JOHNSON, Mr. Mark, BA ACA *2009;* Flat 13 Springboard Urban, 89-91 West End Lane, LONDON, NW6 4SY.
JOHNSON, Mr. Mark Andrew, FCA *1979;* Hampton Steel Ltd, London Road, WELLINGBOROUGH, NORTHAMPTONSHIRE, NN8 2DJ.
JOHNSON, Mr. Mark Edward, BSc ACA *2000;* Unit 29, 44 Bent Street, Neutral Bay, SYDNEY, NSW 2089, AUSTRALIA.
JOHNSON, Mr. Mark Edward, ACA *2007;* 2 Greenbank Close, Whitwood, CASTLEFORD, WEST YORKSHIRE, WF10 5TP.
JOHNSON, Mr. Mark Edward, BA(Hons) ACA *2010;* 2 Keats Lane, Wincham, NORTHWICH, CHESHIRE, CW9 6PP.
JOHNSON, Mr. Mark Leonard, BSc ACA *1989;* 7 Willow Drive, Send Marsh, Ripley, WOKING, GU23 6LF.
JOHNSON, Mr. Mark Nicholas, LLB FCA MSI *2000;* (Tax Fac), Gogland Cottage, Nomansland, TIVERTON, DEVON, EX16 8NJ.
JOHNSON, Mr. Mark Stephen, LLB ACA *2010;* Flat 57 Terrace Apartments, 40 Drayton Park, LONDON, N5 1PW.
JOHNSON, Mr. Martin Graham, MA BSc ACA *1997;* (Tax Fac), 65 Middlewood Close, SOLIHULL, WEST MIDLANDS, B91 2TZ.
JOHNSON, Mr. Martin Graham, BA ACA *1995;* Great Rail Journeys, Saviour House, 9 St. Saviourgate, YORK, YO1 8NL.
•**JOHNSON, Mr. Martin John, BSc ACA** *1986;* KJA Huque Chaudhry Limited, 199 Roundhay Road, LEEDS, LS8 5AN. See also Qaisar Johnson Associates Limited
JOHNSON, Mr. Martin Kenneth, FCA *1972;* 64 Tycehurst Hill, LOUGHTON, IG10 1DA.
•**JOHNSON, Mr. Martin Peter, ACA** *1991;* Saffery Champness, Lion House, Red Lion Street, LONDON, WC1R 4GB.
JOHNSON, Mr. Matthew James, BSc ACA *2010;* 18 Endsleigh Park Road, PLYMOUTH, PL3 4NH.
JOHNSON, Mr. Matthew Paul, BSc ACA *2009;* 5 Newcastle Close, GRANTHAM, LINCOLNSHIRE, NG31 8SG.
JOHNSON, Mrs. Melissa, BSc ACA *2002;* Broad Close Villa, Kineton Road, Pillerton Hersey, WARWICK, CV35 0QF.
•**JOHNSON, Mr. Michael, FCA** *1959;* Hunters Green, Short Lane, Goosnargh, PRESTON, PR3 2JN.
JOHNSON, Mr. Michael, BA FCA *1954;* Michael Johnson, Charlton House, Queen Charlton, Keynsham, BRISTOL, BS31 2SJ. (Life Member)
JOHNSON, Mr. Michael Gordon Dixon, FCA *1950;* Peartwater Cottage, Spaxton, BRIDGWATER, TA5 1DG. (Life Member)
JOHNSON, Mr. Michael Henry Trevor, FCA *1959;* Hardrigg, Frizington Road, Wath Brow, CLEATOR MOOR, CA25 5EP. (Life Member)

JOHNSON, Mr. Michael John, BSc ACA *1992;* 15 Korytsas Street, Ayios Andreas, 1107 NICOSIA, CYPRUS.

JOHNSON, Mr. Michael John, FCA *1967;* The Elms, Talls Lane, Fenstanton, HUNTINGDON, PE28 9JJ. (Life Member)

JOHNSON, Mr. Michael Joseph, FCA *1954;* 12842 173rd Court N.E., REDMOND, WA 98052, UNITED STATES. (Life Member)

JOHNSON, Mr. Michael Kevin, BA ACA *1988;* Penally, Plough Road, Tibberton, DROITWICH, WR9 7NN.

JOHNSON, Mr. Michael Percival Klaus, BCom CA FCA *1966;* P O Box 246, Rondebosch, CAPE TOWN, WESTERN CAPE PROVINCE, 7701, SOUTH AFRICA.

JOHNSON, Mr. Michael Philip, BA ACA *2000;* 51 Mostyn Road, LONDON, SW19 3LL.

•JOHNSON, Mr. Michael Prior, FCA *1977;* Morris Owen, 43-45 Devizes Road, SWINDON, SN1 4BG.

JOHNSON, Mr. Michael T, BA ACA *2005;* 21 Lyric Road, LONDON, SW13 9QA.

JOHNSON, Mrs. Michelle Antoinette Angela, MBA BA ACA *1995;* 29 Croft Drive East, Caldy, WIRRAL, MERSEYSIDE, CH48 1LU.

•JOHNSON, Mrs. Michelle Sharon-Loye, BA ACA *1989;* Audition Accounting & Tax Services, 11 Sutherland House, Royal Herbert Pavilions, Gilbert Close, LONDON, SE18 4PS.

JOHNSON, Mr. Myles Anthony, BSocSc ACA *1998;* 68 Oakley Road, LONDON, N1 3LR.

JOHNSON, Miss. Natalie, ACA *2011;* 9 Church Street, Bignall End, STOKE-ON-TRENT, ST7 8PE.

JOHNSON, Mr. Neil Andrew, MA FCA *1991;* 23 Bemersyde Drive, NEWCASTLE UPON TYNE, NE2 2HL.

JOHNSON, Mr. Neil Anthony, BA ACA *1996;* The Malden Group Plc, 171 Selsdon Park Road, SOUTH CROYDON, SURREY, CR2 8JJ.

JOHNSON, Mr. Neil Austin, BEng ACA *1995;* 34 Lakeside Road, LYMM, CHESHIRE, WA13 0QE.

•JOHNSON, Mr. Neil Francis Keith, MA FCA *1986;* BRYDEN JOHNSON, Kings Parade, Lower Coombe Street, CROYDON, CR0 1AA. See also Bryden Johnson Payroll Services Limited

JOHNSON, Mrs. Nerise Dawn, BA ACA *1999;* 26 Ashton Drive, WIRRAL, MERSEYSIDE, CH48 0RQ.

JOHNSON, Mr. Neville Christopher, MA BSc ACA *1983;* 48 Cedarbrook Close, S.W., CALGARY T2W 5B8, AB, CANADA.

JOHNSON, Mr. Neville George, FCA *1979;* 2 Rue de la Ree, La Grande Rue, St Saviour, GUERNSEY, GY7 9PW.

JOHNSON, Mrs. Nichola Margaret, BSc ACA *1992;* 13 Biddulph Road, SOUTH CROYDON, CR2 6QA.

•JOHNSON, Mr. Nicholas Ainsley, BEng ACA CF *1996;* Atticus Corporate Finance LLP, 8 Pakenham Road, BIRMINGHAM, B15 2NE. See also Mazars LLP

JOHNSON, Mr. Nicholas Christian, MEng BA ACA *2000;* 1144 Beaufort Road, NORTH VANCOUVER V7G 1R7, BC, CANADA.

JOHNSON, Mr. Nicholas Eric William, MA FCA *1975;* (Tax Fac), 44 Belsize Avenue, Springfield, MILTON KEYNES, MK6 3LW.

JOHNSON, Mr. Nicholas Norman Bartlett, ACA *1989;* 59/34 Saiyuan Soi 16, Mu 7, Rawai, PHUKET 83130, THAILAND.

JOHNSON, Mrs. Nicola Ann, MA ACA *1996;* Caggy Pole Farm, Buckhorn Weston, GILLINGHAM, Dorset, SP8 5HN.

JOHNSON, Mrs. Nicola Jane, BSc ACA *2002;* 52 Danebower Road, STOKE-ON-TRENT, ST4 8TJ.

JOHNSON, Miss. Nicola Louise, MSc ACA CTA *2003;* 89 Fairhurst Drive, Parbold, WIGAN, WN8 7DP.

JOHNSON, Mr. Nigel Derrick Marson, FCA *1966;* Summerhill, Fairfield Road, Shawford, WINCHESTER, HAMPSHIRE, SO21 2DA.

•JOHNSON, Mr. Nigel Ralph, BA FCA *1978;* Deloitte LLP, 3 Victoria Square, Victoria Street, ST. ALBANS, HERTFORDSHIRE, AL1 3TF. See also Deloitte & Touche LLP

JOHNSON, Mr. Oluseye Olufunmilayo, BCom FCA *1958;* Oluseye Johnson & Co, 16 Modupe Johnson Crecent, SurulereP.O. Box 6206, LAGOS, NIGERIA. See also Adefeso O.A. & Co and Temple Gothard Johnson Abioye & Co

JOHNSON, Mr. Patrick, ACA *1983;* 21 High Street, Great Gonerby, GRANTHAM, LINCOLNSHIRE, NG31 8JS.

JOHNSON, Mr. Patrick Ralph, MA ACA *1988;* 2/ Floor, 28D O Pui Village, Mang Kung UK, SAI KUNG, NEW TERRITORIES, HONG KONG SAR.

JOHNSON, Mr. Paul, MEng ACA *2010;* 102 St. Olaf's Road, LONDON, SW6 7DW.

JOHNSON, Mr. Paul Andrew, BA FCA *1986;* 101 North Street, Crowland, PETERBOROUGH, PE6 0EG.

•JOHNSON, Mr. Paul David, BA FCA *1993;* 12 Cross Hedge, Rothley, LEICESTER, LE7 7RR.

JOHNSON, Mr. Paul Frederick, BA FCA *1983;* Drovers Cottage, Groombridge, TUNBRIDGE WELLS, KENT, TN3 9NR.

JOHNSON, Mr. Paul George, BSc ACA *2010;* 15 Swarland Avenue, NEWCASTLE UPON TYNE, NE7 7TE.

JOHNSON, Mr. Paul James, MA FCA *1985;* 31 Oakdene Road, Brockham, BETCHWORTH, RH3 7JU.

JOHNSON, Mr. Paul John, BSc(Hons) ACA ACII ACILA MBCI *1996;* 3rd Floor Ivy Mill, Crown Street, MANCHESTER, M359BG.

•JOHNSON, Mr. Paul Robert, BA FCA CF *1987;* Baker Tilly Tax & Advisory Services LLP, St Philips Point, Temple Row, BIRMINGHAM, B2 5AF. See also Baker Tilly Corporate Finance LLP

•JOHNSON, Mr. Paul Robert, BSc FCA *1978;* KPMG LLP, 15 Canada Square, LONDON, E14 5GL. See also KPMG Europe LLP

JOHNSON, Mr. Paul Timothy, BSocSc FCA *1983;* The Spanish House, 63 Beeston Fields Drive, Bramcote, NOTTINGHAM, NG9 3TD.

JOHNSON, Mr. Peter, FCA *1970;* 5 Tegdown, PETERSFIELD, GU31 4PE. (Life Member)

JOHNSON, Mr. Peter, MA MSci BA ACA *2011;* 11 Glenlyn Avenue, ST. ALBANS, HERTFORDSHIRE, AL1 5PF.

JOHNSON, Mr. Peter, FCA *1967;* (Tax Fac), with Percy Westhead & Company, Greg's Buildings, 1 Booth Street, MANCHESTER, M2 4AD.

JOHNSON, Mr. Peter Andrew Charles, FCA *1984;* with Baker Tilly UK Audit LLP, Elgar House, Holmer Road, HEREFORD, HR4 9SF.

•①JOHNSON, Mr. Peter Anthony, FCA *1978;* Johnson Holmes & Co., Towlers Court, 30a Elm Hill, NORWICH, NR3 1HG.

JOHNSON, Mr. Peter David, FCA *1956;* Unit 11, Princeton Apartments, 1 Brigid Road, SUBIACO, WA 6008, AUSTRALIA. (Life Member)

JOHNSON, Mr. Peter Geoffrey Nevil, MA ACA *1986;* 39 Grosvenor Park, LONDON, SE5 0NH.

JOHNSON, Dr. Peter Graham, PhD BSc FCA *1986;* Hollybush House Crawley, WINCHESTER, HAMPSHIRE, SO21 2QB.

JOHNSON, Mr. Peter Luckman, FCA *1957;* Magpie Farm, Magpie Lane, Balsall Common, COVENTRY, CV7 7AW. (Life Member)

JOHNSON, Mr. Peter Martin Russell, BSc FCA *1976;* 281 Alexandra Park Road, Wood Green, LONDON, N22 7BJ.

•JOHNSON, Mr. Peter Medwell, FCA *1971;* PM Johnson, Tarag', 48 Rectory Road, Gosforth, NEWCASTLE UPON TYNE, NE3 1XP.

JOHNSON, Mr. Peter Thomas, BA ACA *1980;* 34 Homewood Road, ST. ALBANS, AL1 4BQ.

JOHNSON, Mr. Philip Charles, BSc ACA *1982;* 52 Harts Grove, WOODFORD GREEN, IG8 0BN.

JOHNSON, Mr. Philip Michael, MA ACA *1997;* 62 Tavistock Road, LONDON, W11 1AW.

JOHNSON, Mr. Philip Michael, FCA *1971;* 9 Pitshouse Lane, Norden, ROCHDALE, OL12 7RA.

•JOHNSON, Mr. Philip Robert, FCA *1970;* Arden House, Coppice Lane, Disley, STOCKPORT, SK12 2LT.

JOHNSON, Miss. Philippa Helen, ACA *2008;* (Tax Fac), Network Rail Infrastructure Ltd Kings Place, 90 York Way, LONDON, N1 9AG.

JOHNSON, Mr. Phillip Robert, FCA *1962;* Badgers, Cartmel, GRANGE-OVER-SANDS, CUMBRIA, LA11 7NR. (Life Member)

JOHNSON, Mrs. Rachael, BA ACA *1992;* 110 Clifton, YORK, YO30 6BA.

•JOHNSON, Mrs. Rachael Louise, ACA *2009;* (Tax Fac), G Foxwell & Co, Foxwell House, Libanus Road, EBBW VALE, GWENT, NP23 6YY.

JOHNSON, Miss. Rebecca Louise, BSc(Hons) ACA *2004;* 12 Stretton Road, Great Glen, LEICESTER, LE8 9GN.

•JOHNSON, Mr. Rex Michael, FCA *1975;* (Tax Fac), Alco Audit Limited, 12-14 Percy Street, ROTHERHAM, SOUTH YORKSHIRE, S65 1ED. See also Terence Houghton & Co Ltd

JOHNSON, Mr. Rhys Alan, BA ACA *1992;* 123 Greenwood Avenue, SINGAPORE 287042, SINGAPORE.

JOHNSON, Mr. Richard, BSc ACA *2007;* 18 Shandon Road, LONDON, SW4 9HR.

JOHNSON, Mr. Richard Arthur, BA ACA *1987;* 47 Nevern Square, LONDON, SW5 9PF.

JOHNSON, Mr. Richard Henry, FCA *1959;* 8 Ashwood Drive, BROADSTONE, BH18 8LN. (Life Member)

JOHNSON, Mr. Richard Keith, BA ACA *1993;* H L Hutchinson Ltd, Weasenham Lane, WISBECH, CAMBRIDGESHIRE, PE13 2RN.

JOHNSON, Mr. Richard Mark, BSc FCA *1990;* 60 Gordon Street, CLONTARF, NSW 2093, AUSTRALIA.

JOHNSON, Mr. Richard Mark, BEng ACA *1996;* Oil Spill Response Ltd, Lower William Street, SOUTHAMPTON, SO14 5QE.

•JOHNSON, Mr. Richard William, BSc FCA *2001;* Mitchell Charlesworth, 5 Temple Square, Temple Street, LIVERPOOL, L2 5RH.

JOHNSON, Mrs. Rita June, FCA *1961;* 18 St Marys Park, LOUTH, LN11 0EF.

JOHNSON, Mr. Robert Edward, FCA *1980;* The Chase, 15 Warning Tongue Lane, DONCASTER, SOUTH YORKSHIRE, DN4 6TB.

JOHNSON, Mr. Robert Fitzhugh, BA ACA *2005;* 91 Woodbank Drive, NOTTINGHAM, NG8 2QW.

JOHNSON, Mr. Robert George, FCA *1970;* 12 Crescent Grove, LONDON, SW4 7AH.

JOHNSON, Mr. Robert Gregory, BA ACA *2010;* Smith & Nephew Plc, 15 Adam Street, LONDON, WC2N 6LA.

JOHNSON, Mr. Robert Leslie, FCA *1971;* c/o 57 Scarisbrick Road, Rainford, ST. HELENS, MERSEYSIDE, WA11 8JN.

JOHNSON, Mr. Robert Lynn, FCA *1969;* (Tax Fac), 7 The Hall, Foxes Dale, LONDON, SE3 9BE.

•JOHNSON, Mr. Robert Norman George, FCA *1975;* Wilkins Kennedy, Bridge House, London Bridge, LONDON, SE1 9QR.

JOHNSON, Miss. Roberta, BA(Hons) ACA *2009;* 123 Long Road, CAMBRIDGE, CB2 8HE.

•JOHNSON, Mr. Roderick Michael, FCA *1970;* R.M. Johnson, 36 Wolds Rise, MATLOCK, DE4 3HJ.

•JOHNSON, Mr. Rodney Howard, FCA *1970;* Proudler Hiser & Co, 46/48 Coatham Road, REDCAR, TS10 1RS.

•JOHNSON, Mrs. Rosemary Anne, FCA *1978;* AIMS Accountants for Business, 3 Grindleford Close, Desborough, KETTERING, NORTHAMPTONSHIRE, NN14 2FG. See also AIMS - Rosemary Johnson

•JOHNSON, Mrs. Roxanne, BSc(Hons) ACA *2001;* (Tax Fac), RMJ Accounting, Top Barn, Greensforge Lane, Stourton, STOURBRIDGE, WEST MIDLANDS DY7 5BD.

JOHNSON, Mr. Roy William, FCA *1964;* 1 The Rosery, BOURNE END, BUCKINGHAMSHIRE, SL8 5TB. (Life Member)

JOHNSON, Mr. Royston Arthur, FCA *1953;* 62 Croft Court, TENBY, PEMBROKESHIRE, SA70 8AR. (Life Member)

JOHNSON, Mr. Russell Alan, BSc ACA *1981;* Homes in Havering, London Borough of Havering District Housing Manager, Chippenham Road Harold Hill, ROMFORD, RM3 8YQ.

JOHNSON, Miss. Sally, BSc(Hons) ACA *2004;* 40 Sandhurst Avenue, STOURBRIDGE, DY9 0XL.

JOHNSON, Miss. Sally Jane, ACA *2008;* Flat 3, 22 Denmark Avenue, LONDON, SW19 4HF.

JOHNSON, Mrs. Sally Kate Miranda, BA ACA *1999;* Penguin Group (UK), 80 Strand, LONDON, WC2R 0DT.

•JOHNSON, Mrs. Sarah Caroline, ACA *2009;* Gibson Appleby, 1-3 Ship Street, SHOREHAM-BY-SEA, WEST SUSSEX, BN43 5DH.

JOHNSON, Miss. Sarah Jane, ACA *2008;* Flat C, 143 Bedford Road, LONDON, SW4 7RA.

JOHNSON, Mrs. Sarah Julia, BA ACA *2000;* 10 Lynwood, GUILDFORD, SURREY, GU2 7NY.

JOHNSON, Mrs. Sarah Louise, BA ACA *2000;* 103 Bell Common, EPPING, CM16 4DZ.

JOHNSON, Mrs. Sarah Louise, BA ACA CTA *1999;* A O N Ltd, 8 Devonshire Square, LONDON, EC2M 4PL.

JOHNSON, Mr. Seth Adam, BSc ACA *1998;* Credit Suisse, 1 Cabot Square, LONDON, E14 4QJ.

JOHNSON, Mrs. Sheila Mary, BSc ACA *1979;* Hasty Leys Farm, Brailes, BANBURY, OX15 5AF.

JOHNSON, Mr. Simon, BA FCA *1986;* 5 Pinehurst, Sunninghill, ASCOT, SL5 0TN.

JOHNSON, Mr. Simon Christopher, BA ACA *1990;* 3 Coppins Close, BERKHAMSTED, HERTFORDSHIRE, HP4 3NZ.

JOHNSON, Mr. Simon Mark, BA ACA *1999;* Hillfoot Steel Group Ltd, Herries Road, SHEFFIELD, S6 1HP.

JOHNSON, Mr. Simon Peter Jarmain, BA ACA *1990;* 2 Woods Court, HARROGATE, NORTH YORKSHIRE, HG2 9QP.

JOHNSON, Mr. Simon William, BEng ACA *1997;* 23 Faraday Gardens, Stotfold, HITCHIN, HERTFORDSHIRE, SG5 4FW.

JOHNSON, Miss. Sophie Claire, ACA *2008;* 50 Longridge Avenue, NEWCASTLE UPON TYNE, NE7 7LB.

JOHNSON, Mr. Stanley, FCA *1956;* 50 Tandlewood Park, Royton, OLDHAM, OL2 5UZ. (Life Member)

JOHNSON, Mr. Stephen Arthur, BA FCA *1978;* 10 Eldon Court, Brondesbury Road, LONDON, NW6 6AX.

•JOHNSON, Mr. Stephen Charles, BSc FCA *1977;* S Johnson & Co, 100 Overstone Road, Sywell, NORTHAMPTON, NN6 0AW.

JOHNSON, Mr. Stephen David, BA(Hons) ACA *2001;* 16 Ernest Road, Emerson Park, HORNCHURCH, RM11 3JF.

JOHNSON, Mr. Stephen Garry, BSc ACA *1986;* 3 Hutton Place, Hutton, BRENTWOOD, Essex, CM13 1HE.

JOHNSON, Mr. Stephen Geoffrey, BSc ACA *1980;* 103 Chapel Road, West End, SOUTHAMPTON, SO30 3GQ.

JOHNSON, Mr. Stephen James, BCom ACA *1982;* 3 Leominster Drive, Oakwood, DERBY, DE21 2RE.

•JOHNSON, Mr. Stephen Lee, ACA *2009;* Goldhaven, 5 White Pillars, Holly Bank Road, WOKING, SURREY, GU22 0LL.

•JOHNSON, Mr. Stephen William, FCA *1978;* Parker Gradwell & Co, 17 Chapel Street, HYDE, SK14 1LF.

JOHNSON, Mr. Steven Robert, BA(Hons) ACA *2006;* 65 Lavington Road, WORTHING, WEST SUSSEX, BN14 7SH.

JOHNSON, Mr. Stuart Gordon Lea, LLB ACA *1989;* Davidson Holdings Ltd, Unit 1, Woodley Park Estate, Woodley, READING BERKSHIRE RG5 3AN.

JOHNSON, Mrs. Tarryn, ACA *2009;* 75 Surbiton Hill Park, SURBITON, KT5 8EH.

•JOHNSON, Mr. Timothy Andrew Arie, MA MBA ACA *1991;* (Tax Fac), Timothy Johnson Limited, 8 Rhodesia Road, LONDON, SW9 9EL.

JOHNSON, Mr. Timothy Clive, MA ACA *1979;* Nut Hedges, Jeremys Lane, Bolney, HAYWARDS HEATH, WEST SUSSEX, RH17 5QE.

•JOHNSON, Mr. Timothy Phillip, FCA *1974;* Kinnaird Hill, Montagu House, 81 High Street, HUNTINGDON, CAMBRIDGESHIRE, PE29 3NY.

JOHNSON, Mr. Timothy Robert, BSc FCA *1973;* 5 Belper Close, Oadby, LEICESTER, LE2 5WB.

JOHNSON, Mr. Timothy Robin Ian, BA ACA *1990;* 27 Grand Drive, Raynes Park, LONDON, SW20 0JB.

•JOHNSON, Mrs. Tracey Nicole, BA ACA DChA *1988;* Moore and Smalley LLP, Richard House, 9 Winckley Square, PRESTON, PR1 3HP.

JOHNSON, Miss. Valerie Elizabeth, MA ACA *1989;* 8 Brimstone Walk, BERKHAMSTED, HERTFORDSHIRE, HP4 1TJ.

•JOHNSON, Mrs. Vicki Clare, BA ACA *1990;* (Tax Fac), Vicki Johnson, 86 Sywell Road, Overstone, NORTHAMPTON, NN6 0AQ.

JOHNSON, Ms. Victoria Alice, ACA *2009;* 18 Binley Close, Shirley, SOLIHULL, B90 2RB.

JOHNSON, Miss. Victoria Karen, LLB ACA *1996;* with PKF (UK) LLP, 4th Floor, 3 Hardman Street, MANCHESTER, M3 3HF.

JOHNSON, Mr. William, ACA *2011;* 14 Joseph Trotter Close, Finsbury Estate, LONDON, EC1R 1UB.

JOHNSON, Mr. William, BA ACA *2006;* 8 St. Georges Mews, FARNHAM, GU9 7LX.

JOHNSON, Mr. William Henry, BSc FCA *1975;* 56 Dene Bank, BOLTON, BL2 3EA.

JOHNSON, Mrs. Yvonne, BA ACA *1989;* 70 Foxbourne Road, LONDON, SW17 8EW.

JOHNSON FERGUSON, Miss. Laura Rose, BA ACA *1993;* 26A Webb's Road, LONDON, SW11 6SF.

JOHNSON-FERGUSON, Mr. Paul Duncan, BA ACA *1992;* 22 Rue Puebla, 78600 MAISONS LAFFITTE, FRANCE.

JOHNSON-FERGUSON, Miss. Sarah Catherine, BSc ACA *1989;* 205 Victoria Rise, LONDON, SW4 0PF.

JOHNSON-RANDLES, Mr. Ronald, BSc ACA *1988;* 1 Wesley Close, Parkgate, NESTON, CH64 6TW.

JOHNSON-STOTT, Mr. Steven Ronald, MEng ACA *1995;* PO Box 828, WHISTLER V0N 1B0, BC, CANADA.

JOHNSON-TREHERNE, Mr. Peter Miles, BA FCA *1996;* 10 The Old Quarry, LIVERPOOL, L25 6LF.

JOHNSTON, Mr. Alan Christopher, BTech ACA *1980;* Hartlea House High Drive, Woldingham, CATERHAM, CR3 7EL.

•JOHNSTON, Mr. Alan James, BA FCA *1985;* Armstrong Watson, Fairview House, Victoria Place, CARLISLE, CA1 1HP.

JOHNSTON, Mr. Alan Patrick Lorrain, FCA *1963;* Hulme Johnston & Co, 38 York Road, NORTHAMPTON, NN1 5QJ.

JOHNSTON, Mr. Alasdair Keith, MA FCA *1973;* Springbank, Gattonside, MELROSE, ROXBURGHSHIRE, TD6 9NH.

•**JOHNSTON, Mrs. Alison Margaret, FCA** *1993;* Dodd & Co., Fifteen Rosehill, Montgomery Way, Rosehill Estate, CARLISLE, CA1 2RW.
•**JOHNSTON, Mr. Alistair Dewar Kerr, CMG BSc FCA** *1976;* 4 Phene Street, Chelsea, LONDON, SW3 5NZ.
JOHNSTON, Mr. Alistair Howard McKenzie, BSc ACA *1987;* Fishers Hollow, Fishers Lane, Cold Ash, THATCHAM, BERKSHIRE, RG18 9NG.
JOHNSTON, Mr. Allan, BSc ACA *1981;* Rollstud Ltd, Unit 5 Denmore Industrial Est, Denmore Road, Bridge Of Don, ABERDEEN, AB23 8JW.
JOHNSTON, Mr. Arthur Morley, ACA *1982;* 23 Crossfield Road, LONDON, N17 6AY.
JOHNSTON, Mrs. Audrey, BA ACA *1992;* 21 Moonbeam View, Holland Gardens, SINGAPORE 277275, SINGAPORE.
JOHNSTON, Mrs. Audrey Elizabeth Anne, BAcc ACA *1996;* JAJ Consulting Ltd, 15 Eggleton Drive, TRING, HERTFORDSHIRE, HP23 5AJ.
JOHNSTON, Mr. Benjamin Monk, BSc ACA *2002;* 34 Perth Road, LONDON, N4 3HB.
JOHNSTON, Mrs. Choo San Audrey, BSc ACA *1987;* House 71, Palm Drive, 18 Pak Pat Shan Road, Redhill, TAI TAM, HONG KONG ISLAND HONG KONG SAR.
JOHNSTON, Ms. Claire Denise, MA ACA *1994;* 22 Moraga Via, ORINDA, CA 94563, UNITED STATES.
JOHNSTON, Mr. Colin Shearer, MA ACA *1982;* Deloitte & Touche SpA, Galleria San Federico 54, I-10121 TORINO, ITALY.
JOHNSTON, Mr. Colin Stuart, FCA *1982;* 1 Hillhead Cottages, Gibside, Burnopfield, NEWCASTLE UPON TYNE, NE16 6AB.
JOHNSTON, Mr. Daniel Bernard, FCA *1970;* 150 Route de Ferney, P.O. Box 2100, CH1211 GENEVA, SWITZERLAND.
JOHNSTON, Mr. David Alexander, MA ACA *1993;* 29 Courtenay Street, Kennington, LONDON, SE11 5PH.
JOHNSTON, Mr. David Horn Sharp, FCA *1954;* 36 Oakfield Road, ASHTEAD, KT21 2RD. (Life Member)
JOHNSTON, Mr. David Lewis Hardy, BA FCA *1986;* 4835 Longchamps Drive NE, ATLANTA, GA 30319, UNITED STATES.
•**JOHNSTON, Mr. Dean, BSc FCA CTA** *1991;* (Tax Fac), Dodd & Co., Fifteen Rosehill, Montgomery Way, Rosehill Estate, CARLISLE, CA1 2RW.
•**JOHNSTON, Mr. Duncan, MA ACA** *1989;* Deloitte LLP, Athene Place, 66 Shoe Lane, LONDON, EC4A 3BQ. See also Deloitte & Touche LLP
JOHNSTON, Mrs. Edwina Jane, BSc ACA *1987;* Fishers Hollow, Fishers Lane, Cold Ash, THATCHAM, BERKSHIRE, RG18 9NG.
•**JOHNSTON, Mrs. Elaine, FCA** *1979;* E Johnston & Co, 17 Crowhill, Godmanchester, HUNTINGDON, PE29 2LP.
JOHNSTON, Mrs. Elizabeth Ann, BA ACA *1986;* Tonbridge Mill, Mill Lane, TONBRIDGE, TN9 1PJ.
JOHNSTON, Miss. Emma Katherine, ACA *2009;* 11 Tirnascobe Road, ARMAGH, BT61 9HT.
JOHNSTON, Mr. Eoghan, BA(Hons) ACA *2011;* with PricewaterhouseCoopers LLP, 89 Sandyford Road, NEWCASTLE UPON TYNE, NE1 8HW.
JOHNSTON, Mr. Ewan, BSc ACA *2004;* 72 Lincoln Road, LONDON, N2 9DL.
JOHNSTON, Miss. Fiona, BA ACA *2009;* Bessler Hendrie Ltd Albury Mill, Mill Lane Chilworth, GUILDFORD, GU4 8RU.
•**JOHNSTON, Mr. Francis William, BA FCA** *1977;* ST Hampden Limited, 57 London Road, HIGH WYCOMBE, BUCKINGHAMSHIRE, HP11 1BS. See also Seymour Taylor Audit Ltd
JOHNSTON, Mr. Fraser Stuart, ACA *2009;* 12 Smiles Place, WOKING, GU22 8BJ.
JOHNSTON, Mr. Gavin Henry Robert, MA ACA *1992;* 21 Albany Road, LONDON, W13 8PQ.
JOHNSTON, Mr. George Kenneth Charles, FCA *1951;* 39 Heron Island, Caversham, READING, RG4 8DQ. (Life Member)
JOHNSTON, Miss. Gillian, BSc ACA *1996;* 19 Cranley Park, BANGOR, COUNTY DOWN, BT19 7HF.
JOHNSTON, Mrs. Gillian, MA ACA *1999;* 77 Moffats Lane, Brookmans Park, HATFIELD, HERTFORDSHIRE, AL9 7RT.
JOHNSTON, Mr. Gordon James, MA ACA *1999;* Allianz, 27 Knightsbridge, LONDON, SW1X 7LY.
•①**JOHNSTON, Mr. Gordon John, BA ACA** *1993;* Hunt Johnston Stokes Ltd, 12-14 Carlton Place, SOUTHAMPTON, SO15 2EA. See also HJS Recovery LLP
JOHNSTON, Mr. Graeme Cairncross, BA FCA *1990;* 4 Netherbank View, EDINBURGH, EH16 6YY.
JOHNSTON, Mr. Henry Barrie Galloway, MA FCA *1968;* 39 Mimosa Lane, MOGGILL, QLD 4070, AUSTRALIA.
•**JOHNSTON, Mr. Howard William, BSocSc FCA** *1980;* Silvertribe Limited, 7 Manor Farm Way, Seer Green, BEACONSFIELD, HP9 2YD.
JOHNSTON, Mr. Iain, FCA *1976;* 3 Scholes Park Road, SCARBOROUGH, YO12 6RE.
JOHNSTON, Mr. Iain Rory Chetwynd, ACA *2006;* 30 Roberts Avenue, RANDWICK, NSW 2031, AUSTRALIA.
JOHNSTON, Mr. James Edmund Mitchell, BSc ACA *1990;* Corporate Mosaic Ltd, 2 Piries Place, HORSHAM, WEST SUSSEX, RH12 1EH.
JOHNSTON, Mrs. Janet, BA ACA *1988;* Abbots Lodge, The Street, Mortimer, READING, RG7 3PE.
JOHNSTON, Mrs. Joanna Claire, MA ACA *2002;* with Begbies Chettle Agar, Epworth House, 25 City Road, LONDON, EC1Y 1AR.
JOHNSTON, Mrs. Karen Linda, BA ACA *1990;* Weedon Cottage, 23 Weedon Lane, AMERSHAM, BUCKINGHAMSHIRE, HP6 5QT.
JOHNSTON, Mr. Keith Joseph, BA ACA *1994;* Nelson Hill Farm, Plumpton, PENRITH, CA11 9NP.
JOHNSTON, Mrs. Lisa, BA ACA *2006;* 19 Clares Green Road, Spencers Wood, READING, RG7 1DY.
JOHNSTON, Miss. Lisa Jane, BA(Hons) ACA *2009;* 277 Derby Road, Bramcote, NOTTINGHAM, NG9 3JA.
JOHNSTON, Mrs. Luisa Jane, BSc(Econ) ACA *2002;* 13 Alexandra Road, Kingsdown, DEAL, KENT, CT14 8DS.
JOHNSTON, Miss. Lynn Patricia, BA ACA *1982;* P.O.Box 3000, ROAD TOWN, TORTOLA ISLAND, VG 1110, VIRGIN ISLANDS (BRITISH).
JOHNSTON, Mr. Mark Daniel, BA ACA *1998;* 10th Floor, Thomson Reuters Thomson Reuters Building, 30 South Colonnade, LONDON, E14 5EP.
JOHNSTON, Mr. Martin James Hardy, MA FCA *1977;* Cawdor House, Knowle Park, MAYFIELD, TN20 6DY.
JOHNSTON, Mr. Matthew, ACA *2011;* Flat 1, 14 Caedmon Road, LONDON, N7 6DH.
JOHNSTON, Mr. Matthew Ian, BSc ACA *2001;* Alix Partners Ltd, 20 North Audley Street, LONDON, W1K 6WE.
JOHNSTON, Mr. Michael John, ACA *2010;* 7 Red House Close, WARE, HERTFORDSHIRE, SG12 9NW.
JOHNSTON, Mr. Neil, ACA *2010;* 19 Clares Green Road, Spencers Wood, READING, RG7 1DY.
JOHNSTON, Dr. Neil Gerard, PhD ACA *1995;* Durrbergstrasse 28, 4132 Muttenz, Basel Landschaft, MUTTENZ, SWITZERLAND.
JOHNSTON, Mr. Neil Richard, BA ACA *1993;* 67a Larkfield Road, Rawdon, LEEDS, LS19 6DZ.
JOHNSTON, Mr. Nicholas Anthony, BA ACA *1996;* The Park Residences at the Ritz-Carlton, Tokyo #403, 9-7-7 Akasaka, Minato-ku, TOKYO, 107-0052 JAPAN.
JOHNSTON, Mr. Nicholas James, BA ACA *1985;* Chaplains House, 4 Honeypot Lane, HusbandsBosworth, LUTTERWORTH, LE17 6LY.
JOHNSTON, Mr. Oliver, BSc ACA *1989;* 53 Forester Crescent, CHERRYBROOK, NSW 2126, AUSTRALIA.
JOHNSTON, Mr. Paul Robert, BSc ACA *1991;* Ellis & Co, 114-120 Northgate Street, CHESTER, CHESHIRE, CH1 2HT.
JOHNSTON, Mr. Paul Thomas, BA ACA *1991;* 24 Belgrave Street, CREMORNE, NSW 2090, AUSTRALIA.
•**JOHNSTON, Mr. Paul Thomas, FCA** *1978;* dhjh LLP, Springhill House, 94-98 Kidderminster Road, BEWDLEY, WORCESTERSHIRE, DY12 1DQ.
JOHNSTON, Mr. Paul William, BA ACA *1998;* Croyle & Associates PC, 220 Broadway, Suite 204, LYNNFIELD, MA 01904, UNITED STATES.
JOHNSTON, Ms. Pauline Susan Cornelia, BSc ACA *2007;* 51 Carminia Road, LONDON, SW17 8AJ.
JOHNSTON, Mr. Peter, MA(Hons) ACA *2010;* Flat 4, 55 Buckley Road, LONDON, NW6 7LX.
JOHNSTON, Mr. Peter Douglas, BA ACA *1990;* Polestar UK Print Unit 1, Apex Business Centre Boscombe Road, DUNSTABLE, BEDFORDSHIRE, LU5 4SB.
JOHNSTON, Mr. Peter Ian, FCA *1965;* Silvana, 86 Camp Road, GERRARDS CROSS, BUCKINGHAMSHIRE, SL9 7PB. (Life Member)
JOHNSTON, Mr. Richard, BA ACA *1994;* 73 Lavender Sweep, LONDON, SW11 1EA.
JOHNSTON, Mr. Richard Andrew, MSci ACA *2009;* Flat 810 Landmark East Tower, 24 Marsh Wall, LONDON, E14 9BT.
JOHNSTON, Mr. Richard Johnston, BA ACA CTA *2002;* with PricewaterhouseCoopers LLP, 1 Embankment Place, LONDON, WC2N 6RH.
JOHNSTON, Mr. Richard William, BSc ACA *1985;* House 71 Palm Drive, 18 Pak Pat Shan Road, Redhill, TAI TAM, HONG KONG ISLAND, HONG KONG SAR.
JOHNSTON, Mr. Robert Alexander, LLB ACA *2002;* with PricewaterhouseCoopers LLP, 1 Embankment Place, LONDON, WC2N 6RH.
JOHNSTON, Mr. Ronald Hugh, FCA *1963;* 59 Wellington Road, Bush Hill Park, ENFIELD, EN1 2PH. (Life Member)
JOHNSTON, Mr. Rory William Ramsay, BA ACA *1994;* Grove Farm House, Grove Lane, Little Wenham, COLCHESTER, SUFFOLK, CO7 6QB.
JOHNSTON, Mrs. Rose Mary, BSc ACA *1987;* 4 Dickens Close, Harrold, BEDFORD, MK43 7ER.
JOHNSTON, Mr. Scot James, ACA *1990;* 4th Floor Old Change House, 128 Queen Victoria street, LONDON, EC4V 4HR.
JOHNSTON, Mr. Shane, ACA *2003;* Hillcrest, 155 Exwick Road, EXETER, EX4 2BB.
JOHNSTON, Mr. Simon Paul, BA ACA *2008;* Flat 18, 61 Victoria Road, NEWPORT, ISLE OF WIGHT, PO30 2DW.
JOHNSTON, Mr. Stephen Henry, BA FCA *1964;* 56 Fairlawn Grove, Chiswick, LONDON, W4 5EH. (Life Member)
•**JOHNSTON, Mr. Stephen Mark, FCA** *1982;* S. Johnston & Co Limited, 24 Picton House, Hussar Court, WATERLOOVILLE, HAMPSHIRE, PO7 7SQ.
JOHNSTON, Mr. Steven John Fischer, BA ACA *2005;* Lloyds TSB Bank Plc, Canons House, Canons Way, BRISTOL, BS1 5LL.
JOHNSTON, Mrs. Suzanne Louise, BA ACA *1999;* 62 Bourneys Manor Close, Willingham, CAMBRIDGE, CB24 5GX.
JOHNSTON, Mr. Terence Paul, FCA *1977;* 24 Derby Road, Beeston, NOTTINGHAM, NG9 2TJ.
JOHNSTON, Mr. Theunis Ian Boyd, MEng ACA *1998;* 75a High Street, INGATESTONE, ESSEX, CM4 9EU.
JOHNSTON, Mr. Timothy Courtenay, FCA *1967;* PO Box 2116, BOMADERRY, NSW 2541, AUSTRALIA.
•**JOHNSTON, Mr. Timothy Kevin, BSc FCA** *1977;* Amion Consulting Ltd, Horton House, Exchange Flags, LIVERPOOL, L2 3YL.
JOHNSTON, Mr. Timothy Paul, MA ACA CFA *2002;* 7 Clare Court, Woldingham, CATERHAM, CR3 7ER.
JOHNSTON, Mr. Wilfred Mark, LLB ACA *1986;* Beechcroft School Lane, Baslow, BAKEWELL, DERBYSHIRE, DE45 1RZ.
JOHNSTON, Mr. William Peter, FCA *1968;* Copyhold, Church Lane, Playford, IPSWICH, IP6 9DR.
JOHNSTON, Mrs. Yvonne, MA ACA *1984;* The Hermitage, Chapel Loke, The Green, Surlingham, NORWICH, NR14 7AQ.
JOHNSTONE, Mrs. Alison Elizabeth, BSc FCA *1977;* with Booth Ainsworth LLP, Alpha House, 4 Greek Street, STOCKPORT, CHESHIRE, SK3 8AB.
JOHNSTONE, Mrs. Anna-Maree, BA ACA *1993;* 56 Well Road, Otford, SEVENOAKS, TN14 5PT.
•**JOHNSTONE, Mr. Brian Robert, BA FCA** *1982;* B.R. Johnstone & Co, Errwood House, 212 Moss Lane, Bramhall, STOCKPORT, CHESHIRE SK7 1BD.
JOHNSTONE, Mr. Charles Anthony Carlyle, MA ACA *2000;* Little Dale, Horsell Park, WOKING, SURREY, GU21 4LY.
JOHNSTONE, Miss. Christine Lesley, BA FCA *2000;* 59 Shelley Way, LONDON, SW19 1TH.
JOHNSTONE, Mr. Christopher, ACA *2009;* 35 Kendal Road, BOLTON, BL1 4DS.
JOHNSTONE, Mr. Christopher Charles, ACA *1982;* Shaws House Shaws Lane Top, Triangle, SOWERBY BRIDGE, WEST YORKSHIRE, HX6 3EZ.
JOHNSTONE, Mr. David Andrew, BCom ACA *1987;* The Tensar Group Ltd, Unit 2/4, Cunningham Court, Shadsworth Business Park, BLACKBURN, BB1 2QX.
JOHNSTONE, Mr. David Graham, BSc ACA *1989;* 70 Western Way, Ponteland, NEWCASTLE UPON TYNE, NE20 9AP.
JOHNSTONE, Mr. David William Robert, MA FCA *1964;* 5 West End, Somerset Street, Kingsdown, BRISTOL, BS2 8NE.
JOHNSTONE, Mr. Edward Richard Melville, FCA *1995;* PO Box 114, Karen, NAIROBI, NAIROBI PROVINCE, 00502, KENYA.
JOHNSTONE, Mr. Edwin, BA FCA *1968;* A-6 L'Aspra, Urb El Bosquet, Anyos, LA MASSANA, ANDORRA. (Life Member)
•**JOHNSTONE, Mrs. Fiona Vanessa Helen, BSc ACA** *1998;* 11 Bainbridge Close, Grange Park, SWINDON, SN5 6BD.
JOHNSTONE, Mr. Francis, ACA *2010;* 2 Foxglove Way, Springfield, CHELMSFORD, CM1 6QS.
•**JOHNSTONE, Mr. George Alexander, BA FCA** *1979;* PricewaterhouseCoopers KFT, Wesselenyi u 16, BUDAPEST, H-1077, HUNGARY.
•**JOHNSTONE, Mr. Iain James Masson, FCA** *1983;* CK, No 4 Castle Court 2, Castlegate Way, DUDLEY, WEST MIDLANDS, DY1 4RH.
JOHNSTONE, Mr. John Barrie, BA FCA *1978;* Johnson Service Group, Abbots House, Monks Way, Preston Brook, RUNCORN, CHESHIRE WA7 3GH.
JOHNSTONE, John Mill Nelson, Esq OBE BCom FCA *1953;* 16 West Castle Road, EDINBURGH, EH10 5AU. (Life Member)
JOHNSTONE, Mr. Lee, BSc(Hons) ACA *2002;* 16 Mulberry Way, Northowram, HALIFAX, WEST YORKSHIRE, HX3 7WJ.
JOHNSTONE, Mrs. Lynne Denise, ACA *2005;* 16 Mill Brow Armathwaite, CARLISLE, CA4 9PJ.
JOHNSTONE, Mr. Mark Alexander Talbot, BA FCA *1981;* Studio House, School Lane, Cookham, MAIDENHEAD, BERKSHIRE, SL6 9QJ.
•**JOHNSTONE, Mr. Mark Andrew, MA FCA** *1996;* Argents, 15 Palace Street, NORWICH, NR3 1RT.
JOHNSTONE, Mr. Mark Robert, BA ACA *1995;* 1 Harberton Mead, Headington, OXFORD, OX3 0DB.
JOHNSTONE, Mr. Mark Robin, BSc ACA *1992;* 201 S. Orange Avenue, Suite 1100, ORLANDO, FL 32801, UNITED STATES.
JOHNSTONE, Miss. Rebecca, BA ACA *2007;* 11c Church Terrace, LONDON, SE13 5BT.
JOHNSTONE, Mr. Robert Sutherland, BEng ACA *1994;* 201 South Lady Slipper Lane, GREER, SC 29650, UNITED STATES.
JOHNSTONE, Mr. Robin, FCA *1977;* Path of Thyme, Legion Lane, Kings Worthy, WINCHESTER, HAMPSHIRE, SO23 7RA.
JOHNSTONE, Mr. Steven Francis, BA ACA *1991;* 568 Green Lanes, LONDON, N13 5RZ.
JOHRI, Mr. Tej Bahadur, MCom FCA *1953;* 16A Deshapriya Park East, CALCUTTA 700029, INDIA. (Life Member)
JOICEY-CECIL, Mr. James David Edward, FCA *1970;* Flat 24 Clapham Mansions, Nightingale Lane, LONDON, SW4 9AQ.
JOINER, Mrs. Katherine Ann, BSc ACA *2006;* 64 Muncaster Road, LONDON, SW11 6NU.
•**JOINER, Mr. Keith Raymond, FCA** *1969;* South East Accountancy Services Ltd, 34 Wells Way, FAVERSHAM, KENT, ME13 7QP.
JOINER, Mr. Kenneth George, FCA *1958;* 36 Grange Gardens, PINNER, HA5 5QE. (Life Member)
JOINER, Mr. Mark Andrew, ACA *1982;* Pier 3 Level 3 (UB3350), 800 Bourke Street, DOCKLANDS, VIC 3008, AUSTRALIA.
•**JOINER, Mr. Raymond George, FCA** *1972;* PO Box 491, LONEHILL, 2062, SOUTH AFRICA.
JOINT, Mr. Christopher, FCA *1971;* 8 Rue de Remparts, 28220 MONTIGNY LE GANNELON, EURE ET LOIR, FRANCE.
JOKHOO, Mr. Harrysh Chandrasingh, ACA *2009;* 1 Garth Close, MORDEN, SM4 4NN.
JOLLEY, Mr. Derrick Adrian, BSc ACA *1989;* 13 Longfellow Avenue, BATH, BA2 4SJ.
•**JOLLEY, Mr. Stephen, BA FCA** *1985;* Alexander & Co, 17 St Ann's Square, MANCHESTER, M2 7PW.
JOLLIE, Mr. Peter Edward John, FCA *1962;* Currawinya, 94 Elliott Street, BALMAIN, NSW 2041, AUSTRALIA.
JOLLIFFE, Mr. Andrew Kenneth, BSc FCA *1976;* Manor Beeches, Maids Moreton, BUCKINGHAM, MK18 1QA.
JOLLIFFE, Mrs. Bryony Elizabeth, BSc ACA *1988;* The Yeld, Clee St. Margaret, CRAVEN ARMS, SY7 9DT.
JOLLIFFE, Mr. David Roy, BA ACA *1979;* 715 Acacia Drive, BURLINGAME, CA 94010, UNITED STATES.
JOLLIFFE, Mr. Nicholas William, BSc ACA *1983;* 34 Galveston Rd, Putney, LONDON, SW15 2SA.
JOLLIFFE, Mr. Robert St John, FCA *1971;* Cobblers, Rooks Hill, Loudwater, RICKMANSWORTH, WD3 4HZ.
JOLLIFFE, Mr. William Orlando, FCA CPFA *1956;* 12 The Leylands, LYTHAM ST.ANNES, FY8 5QS. (Life Member)
•**JOLLY, Mr. Barkit Singh, FCA** *1970;* Jolly & Co, Aashiana, Broomfield Close, GREAT MISSENDEN, HP16 9HX.
JOLLY, Miss. Bethan Lewis, BA ACA *2009;* Liongate Capital Management LLP, 103 Mount Street, LONDON, W1K 2TJ.
JOLLY, Mrs. Claire Louise, MA(Oxon) ACA *2005;* with Deloitte LLP, Stonecutter Court, 1 Stonecutter Street, LONDON, EC4A 4TR.
JOLLY, Mr. David Anderton, FCA *1959;* The Orchard, 2A Vicarage Road, Coopersale, EPPING, CM16 7RB. (Life Member)
JOLLY, Mr. Edward, BSc ACA *2007;* Flat 7, 66 Gloucester Street, LONDON, SW1V 4EF.

JOLLY - JONES

Members - Alphabetical

JOLLY, Mr. Peter Stanley, MA FCA CTA *1966;* 167 Hadleigh Road, LEIGH-ON-SEA, SS9 2LR. (Life Member)
JOLLY, Mr. Robert Miles, FCA *1963;* Essex House, Burton, LINCOLN, LN1 2RD.
JOLLY, Mrs. Robina, ACA *1987;* A B B Ltd, Hanover Place, SUNDERLAND, SR4 6BY.
JOLLY, Mrs. Sarah, ACA *2009;* 32 Nuneham Grove Westcroft, MILTON KEYNES, BUCKINGHAMSHIRE, MK4 4DH.
•**JOLLY, Mr. Trevor Alan, BA ACA** *1982;* Bennett Jolly, 4 Hollies Way, Thurnby, LEICESTER, LE7 9RJ. See also Bennett Jolly Ltd
JOLLYE, Miss. Helen, BSc ACA *2009;* 22 Southview Drive, UPMINSTER, RM14 2LA.
JOLY, Miss. Kirsten Louise, BA ACA *1998;* Flat 1 Milford Court, Gale Moor Avenue, GOSPORT, PO12 2TN.
•**JONAH, Mr. Celestine Babafunlayo, FCA** *1966;* C.Babs-Jonah & Co, Central House, 1 Ballards Lane, Finchley, LONDON, N3 1LQ.
JONAH, Mr. Ephraim Sassoon, FCA *1958;* 34/10 Efrata Street, JERUSALEM, 93384, ISRAEL. (Life Member)
JONAS, Mr. Adam Mark, BA ACA *1990;* Isram Israel, 40 Aliyat Hanoar St, 67540 TEL AVIV, ISRAEL.
JONAS, Miss. Karen Elizabeth, ACA *1997;* 57 Canterbury Drive, RAMSEY, NJ 07446, UNITED STATES.
JONDORF, Mrs. Janet May, MSc BSc(Hons) FCA *1964;* 33 Oldhill Wood, Studham, DUNSTABLE, BEDFORDSHIRE, LU6 2NE. (Life Member)
JONES, Mr. Aaron Justin, BA ACA *1990;* Level 27 101 Collins St, MELBOURNE, VIC 3000, AUSTRALIA.
JONES, Mr. Adam, MA BA ACA *2006;* 8 The Drive, Roundhay, LEEDS, LS8 1JF.
JONES, Mr. Adam Mark, BSc ACA *2005;* 59 Mill Lane, Stockton Heath, WARRINGTON, WA4 2DE.
JONES, Mr. Adam Maxwell, BCom ACA *1993;* 32b Arkwright Road, LONDON, NW3 6BH.
JONES, Mr. Adam Ross, BA ACA *2006;* 9 Spibey Lane, Rothwell, LEEDS, LS26 0NW.
•**JONES, Mr. Adrian, FCA** *1978;* (Tax Fac), A & S Associates Limited, P O Box 3310, 126 Fairlie Road, SLOUGH, BERKSHIRE, SL1 0AG.
JONES, Mr. Adrian Christopher, MA ACA *1991;* Penny Lane Foods Ltd, 1 Yeo Road, BRIDGWATER, TA6 5NA.
JONES, Mr. Adrian Ford, MA ACA *1980;* Andrew Weir, Dexter House, 2 Royal Mint Court, LONDON, EC3N 4XX.
JONES, Mr. Adrian Holyman, ACA *1982;* The Old Cottage, Winterbourne, NEWBURY, RG20 8BB.
•**JONES, Mr. Adrian Lawrence, BA FCA** *1982;* with Smith Cooper, Livery Place, 35 Livery Street, BIRMINGHAM, WEST MIDLANDS, B3 2PB.
•**JONES, Mr. Adrian Lee, BA ACA** *1999;* Gambit Corporate Finance LLP, 3 Assembly Square, Britannia Quay, Cardiff Bay, CARDIFF, CF10 4PL.
JONES, Mr. Adrian Robert, BA ACA DipM *1999;* 84 Sutton Road, MANSFIELD, NG18 5EU.
JONES, Mr. Alan, FCA *1969;* PO Box 731595, Fairland, JOHANNESBURG, 2030, SOUTH AFRICA.
JONES, Mr. Alan, FCA *1963;* 27 Aldersleigh Crescent, Hoghton, PRESTON, PR5 0BB.
•**JONES, Mr. Alan, FCA** *1966;* Alan Jones & Co., 15 Killegland Street, ASHBOURNE, COUNTY MEATH, IRELAND.
JONES, Mr. Alan, FCA *1950;* 36 Brabyns Road, HYDE, SK14 5EE. (Life Member)
JONES, Mr. Alan Craig, BSc FCA *1994;* PO Box 39048, DOHA, QATAR.
•**JONES, Mr. Alan David, BSc FCA** *1974;* (Tax Fac), Pine Grove, Chiltern Road, Chesham Bois, AMERSHAM, BUCKINGHAMSHIRE, HP6 5PG.
JONES, Mr. Alan David, BSc ACA *1986;* 32 Falcondale Road, Westbury-on-Trym, BRISTOL, BS9 3JU.
JONES, Mr. Alan Norman, MA FCA *1975;* May Cottage, Grubwood Lane, Cookham, MAIDENHEAD, BERKSHIRE, SL6 9UD.
JONES, Mr. Alan Philip Hampton, MA ACA *1988;* (Tax Fac), 109 Philbeach Gardens, LONDON, SW5 9ET.
JONES, Mr. Alan Raymond, FCA FCCA *1993;* National Grid Plc, N G T House, Warwick Technology Park, Gallows Hill, WARWICK, CV34 6DA.
•**JONES, Mr. Alan Victor, BSc FCA** *1975;* Alan Jones & Co, 59 Meadow Road, Kingswood, WATFORD, WD25 0JB.
•**JONES, Mr. Alan William, BSc ACA** *1988;* Financial Project Consulting, Egerton House, Chilton Business Park, Chilton, AYLESBURY, BUCKINGHAMSHIRE HP18 9LS.
JONES, Mr. Alastair Francis, FCA *1966;* Sgynlas House, Glasbury, HEREFORD, HR3 5NZ.
JONES, Mr. Alec, FCA *1963;* 53 Park Road, Barton under Needwood, BURTON-ON-TRENT, STAFFORDSHIRE, DE13 8DB.
•**JONES, Mr. Alec Norman, BA FCA** *1975;* Woodgate, 37 Hartopp Road, Four Oaks, SUTTON COLDFIELD, WEST MIDLANDS, B74 2QR.
JONES, Mr. Aled, BSc ACA *1996;* Flat 17, 1-3 Seward Street, LONDON, EC1V 3NY.
JONES, Dr. Alexa, PhD ACA *2011;* 11 Ponsonby Terrace, DERBY, DE1 1DT.
JONES, Ms. Alexandra Emma, BA ACA *2000;* Hodder & Stoughton Publishers, 338 Euston Road, LONDON, NW1 3BH.
•**JONES, Mrs. Alison Elizabeth, BA(Hons) ACA** *1994;* A.E. Jones, 51 Kelston Road, Whitchurch, CARDIFF, CF14 2AH.
JONES, Mrs. Alison Emmeline, BA ACA *1995;* 44 Ffynnon Dawel, Aberdulais, NEATH, WEST GLAMORGAN, SA10 8EQ.
JONES, Mrs. Alison Jane, BA ACA *1981;* 11 Cardigan Road, Henleaze, BRISTOL, BS9 4DY.
JONES, Mrs. Alison Jane, BSc ACA *1991;* Highfure Cottage, Marringdean Road, BILLINGSHURST, RH14 9EL.
JONES, Mrs. Alison Jane, BA ACA *1994;* Ash Lodge, Patrick Road, St Johns, ISLE OF MAN, IM4 3BR.
•**JONES, Miss. Alison Jane Francis, FCA** *1988;* Spofforths LLP, One Jubilee Street, BRIGHTON, BN1 1GE.
JONES, Ms. Alison Margaret, BA FCA *1995;* New Hall Farm, Colne Road, Cowling, KEIGHLEY, NORTH YORKSHIRE, BD22 0JQ.
JONES, Miss. Alison Mary, MA ACA *1981;* Flat 3, 23 Pembridge Crescent, LONDON, W11 3DS.
JONES, Miss. Alison Pamela, BSc(Hons) ACA *2001;* 65 Amethyst Drive, SITTINGBOURNE, ME10 5LE.
JONES, Mr. Alistair Paul, BEng ACA *1997;* Sygenta Asia Pacific Pte. Ltd, N0. 1 Harbour Front Avenue, #03-03 Keppel Bay Tower, SINGAPORE 098632, SINGAPORE.
JONES, Mr. Allan Gerald, BA(Hons) ACA *2004;* with Ernst & Young LLP, 1 More London Place, LONDON, SE1 2AF.
JONES, Mr. Allan Leslie David, FCA *1960;* Ty Madoc, Kenfig, BRIDGEND, Mid Glamorgan, CF33 4PT. (Life Member)
JONES, Mr. Allen Frederick, FCA *1963;* 197 Greys Road, HENLEY-ON-THAMES, OXFORDSHIRE, RG9 1QU. (Life Member)
JONES, Mr. Alun Huw, MA ACA *1989;* 23 Strangeways Road, CAMBRIDGE, CB1 8PR.
JONES, Mr. Alun Richard, MA FCA *1973;* Brookfield, 23 Oxshott Rise, COBHAM, KT11 2RW.
JONES, Miss. Alwine, ACA *1984;* Bishop's Croft, 46 Main Road, Wetley Rocks, STOKE-ON-TRENT, STAFFORDSHIRE, ST9 0BG.
JONES, Mrs. Amanda Jane, BSc ACA *1998;* Wood Cottage, 30 Green Lane, COBHAM, SURREY, KT11 2NN.
JONES, Mrs. Amanda Jane, BSc ACA *2001;* 106 Hardy Road, LONDON, SW19 1HZ.
JONES, Mrs. Andrea Louise, BSc ACA *1988;* Godolphin House, Broom Way, WEYBRIDGE, KT13 9TG.
JONES, Miss. Andrea Mary, BSc ACA *1993;* Marriott Hotel International Ltd Barnards Inn, 86 Fetter Lane, LONDON, EC4A 1EN.
JONES, Mr. Andrew Brian, BA ACA *1993;* 6 Springfield Road, Wimbledon, LONDON, SW19 7AL.
JONES, Mr. Andrew Callis, BSc FCA *1992;* 11 Leadhall Crescent, HARROGATE, NORTH YORKSHIRE, HG2 9NG.
•**JONES, Mr. Andrew Charles, FCA** *1977;* (Tax Fac), Dafferns Llp, 1 Eastwood Business Village, Harry Weston Road, COVENTRY, CV3 2UB.
•**JONES, Mr. Andrew Charles, ACA CA(AUS)** *2008;* James Cowper LLP, Willow Court, 7 West Way, OXFORD, OX2 0JB.
•**JONES, Mr. Andrew Charles, BSc FCA** *1980;* (Tax Fac), Andrew Jones & Co, The Old Surgery, Spa Road, LLANDRINDOD WELLS, POWYS, LD1 5EY. See also AJ Accountancy
JONES, Mr. Andrew Christopher, BSc ACA *2003;* with KPMG LLP, 1 The Embankment, Neville Street, LEEDS, LS1 4DW.
JONES, Mr. Andrew Christopher, BSc ACA *1989;* 6 Monks Hollow, MARLOW, SL7 3SY.
JONES, Mr. Andrew Cresswell, MA FCA CFA *1992;* 23 Granville Park, LEWISHAM, SE13 7DY.
JONES, Mr. Andrew David, BSc ACA *1997;* Virgin Media Matrix Court, Siemens Way Swansea Enterprise Park, SWANSEA, SA7 9BB.
•**JONES, Mr. Andrew David Gaunt, ACA** *1984;* A.D.G. Jones & Co, Osmunda, Wells Road, Hallatrow, BRISTOL, BS39 6EJ.
•**JONES, Mr. Andrew David Willis, BSc ACA** *1987;* Willis Jones, 64 Walter Road, SWANSEA, SA1 4PT.
JONES, Mr. Andrew John, BSc ACA *1996;* 47 Carless Avenue, Harborne, BIRMINGHAM, B17 9BN.
JONES, Mr. Andrew John Michael, LLB ACA *1997;* Flat 4 Jowitt Court, 27 Tudor Way, LONDON, N14 6PS.
JONES, Mr. Andrew Keith, BA ACA *1997;* AGCO Corporation, 4205 River Green Parkway, DULUTH, GA 30096, UNITED STATES.
JONES, Mr. Andrew Keith, BSc FCA CTA *1984;* 14 Welford Place, LONDON, SW19 5AJ.
JONES, Mr. Andrew Lloyd, BSc ACA *1991;* Fidelity International Windmill Court (XTW43), Kingswood Fields, TADWORTH, KT206RY.
JONES, Mr. Andrew Mark, BA ACA *1993;* 2 Stanley Street South, BRISTOL, BS3 3PG.
JONES, Mr. Andrew Mark, BSc ACA *1995;* Milford Haven Port Authority, PO Box 14, Hakin, MILFORD HAVEN, DYFED, SA73 3ER.
JONES, Mr. Andrew Mark, BA ACA *2010;* 88 Cedar Glade, Dunnington, YORK, YO19 5PL.
JONES, Mr. Andrew Neil, ACA *1987;* 17 Elswick Gardens, Mellor, BLACKBURN, BB2 7JD.
•**JONES, Mr. Andrew Nicholas, BCom FCA** *1987;* Jones & Co Business Performance Solutions, 333 Station Road, Dorridge, SOLIHULL, B93 8EY.
JONES, Mr. Andrew Norman, BSc ACA *1983;* 67 Spetchley Road, WORCESTER, WR5 2LR.
JONES, Mr. Andrew Norman, BSc ACA *1985;* 5 Ryland Park, Thingwall, WIRRAL, MERSEYSIDE, CH61 9QJ.
•**JONES, Mr. Andrew Peter Mitchell, BSc ACA** *1991;* Deloitte LLP, 3 Rivergate, Temple Quay, BRISTOL, BS1 6GD. See also Deloitte & Touche LLP
JONES, Mr. Andrew Philip, ACA *2008;* Abcam Inc., Building 200, Suite B2304, One Kendall Square, CAMBRIDGE, MA 02139 UNITED STATES.
JONES, Mr. Andrew Richard, BSc ACA *2004;* B P P Financial Education, 3 London Wall Buildings, LONDON, EC2M 5PD.
JONES, Mr. Andrew Richard, BSc ACA *1991;* 12904 Buckeye Drive, GAITHERSBURG, MD 20878, UNITED STATES.
JONES, Mr. Andrew Robert, BSc ACA *2005;* 3 The Croft, HENLEY-IN-ARDEN, B95 5DY.
JONES, Mr. Andrew Rodney, BSc(Hons) ACA *2001;* 38 Priory Walk, Leicester Forest East, LEICESTER, LE3 3PP.
JONES, Mr. Andrew Simon, BA FCA *1979;* with Audit Inspection Unit, Financial Reporting Council, 5th Floor, Aldwych House, 71-91 Aldwych, LONDON WC2B 4HN.
JONES, Mr. Andrew Timothy, MA ACA *1991;* 5 Vesey Place, DUN LAOGHAIRE, COUNTY DUBLIN, IRELAND.
JONES, Mr. Andrew William, BSc ACA *1995;* Spencer House, 27 St James's Place, LONDON, SW1A 1NR.
JONES, Mr. Andrew Wilson Neale, MA ACA *1987;* Kraft Foods UK Ltd, St Georges House, Bayshill Road, CHELTENHAM, GL50 3AE.
JONES, Miss. Angela, BA ACA *2006;* 59 Towers Way, Corfe Mullen, WIMBORNE, BH21 3UA.
JONES, Ms. Angela Heide, BA ACA *1993;* 35 Church Road, WATFORD, WD17 4PY.
JONES, Mrs. Angela Mary, LLB FCA *1989;* 6 Hill Burn, Henleaze, BRISTOL, BS9 4RH.
JONES, Mrs. Angeline, BA ACA *1999;* 52 Sherifoot Lane, SUTTON COLDFIELD, B75 5DT.
•**JONES, Miss. Angharad Elizabeth Morgan, FCA** *1970;* (Tax Fac), A.E.M. Jones, Tai Cochion, Brynsiencyn, LLANFAIRPWLLGWYNGYLL, LL61 6TQ.
JONES, Miss. Angharad Haf, BSc ACA *2004;* 36 Orient Close, ST. ALBANS, HERTFORDSHIRE, AL1 1AJ.
JONES, Mrs. Anita, BAcc ACA *1996;* 17 Honeycroft Drive, ST. ALBANS, AL4 0GF.
JONES, Miss. Anna Kathryn, LLM ACA *1999;* with Kilsby & Williams LLP, Cedar House, Hazell Drive, NEWPORT, GWENT, NP10 8FY.
JONES, Miss. Anna Louise, BSc ACA *2005;* 2 Purley Close, Maidenbower, CRAWLEY, WEST SUSSEX, RH10 7QR.
JONES, Miss. Anna Louise, BSc(Hons) ACA *2009;* 79 Bromedale Avenue, Mulbarton, NORWICH, NR14 8GG.
JONES, Miss. Anna Louise, LLB(Hons) ACA *2010;* Flat 3 14 Camphill Avenue, GLASGOW, G41 3AY.
JONES, Ms. Annabel, BSc(Econ) ACA *1999;* 34 Sutton Lane South, LONDON, W4 3JT.
•**JONES, Mrs. Anne, BSc ACA** *1982;* Andon Freres, Cavendish House, St Andrew's Court, Burley Street, LEEDS, LS3 1JY.
JONES, Mrs. Anne Margaret Alice, BA ACA *1998;* 16 Stanmore Chase, ST. ALBANS, HERTFORDSHIRE, AL4 0EZ.
JONES, Mrs. Anne Randmael, MSc ACA *1998;* Gruvemyra 85, 1354 BAERUMS VERK, NORWAY.
•**JONES, Mrs. Annette Carol, BSc ACA** *1990;* GJCA Limited, 15 The South Street Centre, 16-20 South Street, Hythe, SOUTHAMPTON, SO45 6EB.
JONES, Mr. Anthony, FCA *1948;* 29 Horsell Moor, Horsell, WOKING, GU21 4NH. (Life Member)
JONES, Mr. Anthony, LLB ACA *2000;* 5 Milk Hall Barns, Latimer Road, CHESHAM, BUCKINGHAMSHIRE, HP5 1QH.
JONES, Mr. Anthony Campbell, FCA *1970;* 11 Gander Green, HAYWARDS HEATH, WEST SUSSEX, RH16 1RB.
•**JONES, Mr. Anthony David, BA ACA** *1993;* Monkspath Financial Management Limited, 25 Horton Grove, Shirley, SOLIHULL, WEST MIDLANDS, B90 4UZ.
JONES, Mr. Anthony David, BA FCA *1983;* 25 Chaveney Walk, Quorn, LOUGHBOROUGH, LEICESTERSHIRE, LE12 8FH.
•**JONES, Mr. Anthony Patrick, FCA** *1977;* A.P. Jones, 19 Tekels Avenue, CAMBERLEY, GU15 2LA.
JONES, Mr. Anthony Paul, BSc BCom ACA *1987;* 36 Upton Park, SLOUGH, SL1 2DE.
JONES, Mr. Anthony Peter Beverley, FCA *1958;* Windsong, Frogmore, KINGSBRIDGE, DEVON, TQ7 2NR. (Life Member)
JONES, Mr. Arthur Edward Morgan, BSc ACA *1984;* P.O Box HM 2257, HAMILTON HMJX, BERMUDA.
JONES, Mr. Arwel Clwyd, BA ACA *1996;* Evadx Ltd Unit 9, Tir Llwyd Enterprise Park Kinmel Bay, RHYL, CLWYD, LL18 5JZ.
JONES, Mr. Ashley, BA(Hons) ACA *2011;* Flat 25 Bennets Courtyard, Watermill Way, LONDON, SW19 2RW.
JONES, Mrs. Avril Jane, BA ACA *1991;* Loxboro Cottage, Chinnor Road, Bledlow Ridge, HIGH WYCOMBE, BUCKINGHAMSHIRE, HP14 4AA.
JONES, Miss. Barbara, BSc ACA *1980;* 21 Sandpiper Close, STRATFORD-UPON-AVON, CV37 9EY.
JONES, Mrs. Barbara Ellen, ACA *1981;* Sovereign Housing Woodlands, 90 Bartholomew Street, NEWBURY, BERKSHIRE, RG14 5EE.
JONES, Mrs. Barbara Jane, BA ACA *1984;* Daval House, Spa Fields Industrial Estate, New Street, Slaithwaite, HUDDERSFIELD, HD7 5BB.
JONES, Mr. Barrie Howard, BSc ACA *1981;* (Tax Fac), Southcott, South Chard, CHARD, TA20 2SA.
JONES, Mr. Barrie Ian, BSc FCA *1972;* Moor Lane Cottage, Kirk Langley, ASHBOURNE, DE6 4LQ.
JONES, Mr. Barrie Michael, FCA *1974;* 9 Linden Court, EDGEMEAD, 7441, SOUTH AFRICA.
JONES, Mr. Barry, FCA *1964;* 7 Barker Close, Stanley Common, ILKESTON, DERBYSHIRE, DE7 6FN.
JONES, Mr. Barry Cave, FCA *1959;* 30 Park Lane, BEWDLEY, WORCESTERSHIRE, DY12 2EU. (Life Member)
JONES, Mr. Barry Howard, BA ACA *1997;* 17F Comfort Court, 52 Third Street, SAI YING PUN, HONG KONG SAR.
JONES, Mr. Barry Michael, BA ACA *1984;* 22 Limewood Close, BECKENHAM, KENT, BR3 3XW.
JONES, Mr. Barry Robert, BSc(Econ) ACA *2001;* 25 Chester Road, WREXHAM, LL11 2SF.
JONES, Mr. Barry Stewart, FCA *1969;* 30 Woodhall Close, Cuckfield, HAYWARDS HEATH, RH17 5HJ.
JONES, Mr. Barry William, FCA *1957;* 57 Ivy Lane, MACCLESFIELD, SK11 8NU. (Life Member)
JONES, Mr. Ben Philip, BA ACA *2006;* Athene Place, 66 Shoe Lane, LONDON, EC4A 3BQ.
JONES, Mr. Benjamin Dudley, MSc ACA *2003;* 108 Red Square, LONDON, N16 9AG.
JONES, Mr. Benjamin Geoffrey, FCA *1955;* 4 Wood Grove, Whitefield, MANCHESTER, M45 7ST. (Life Member)
JONES, Miss. Bethan Lloyd, BA ACA *1990;* Faenol, Gellifor, RUTHIN, LL15 1SG.
JONES, Mrs. Bethan Mair, BSc ACA *2005;* 19 Llewelyn Goch, St. Fagans, CARDIFF, CF5 6HR.
JONES, Miss. Beverley Mary, BA ACA *1996;* 2 Lumley Way, NEWCASTLE UPON TYNE, NE3 5RR.
•①**JONES, Ms. Beverly Karen, MA FCA** *1984;* Hawkesbury, Rawson Avenue, Skircoat Green, HALIFAX, WEST YORKSHIRE, HX3 0JP.
JONES, Ms. Bonnie, ACA *2011;* K P M G Llp, 15 Canada Square, LONDON, E14 5GL.

•JONES, Mr. Brian David, LLB FCA FCCA 1966; (Tax Fac), Brian D Jones, 59 Little Sutton Lane, SUTTON COLDFIELD, WEST MIDLANDS, B75 6SJ.
JONES, Mr. Brian Edward, FCA 1957; The Ides, Church Road, Shedfield, SOUTHAMPTON, SO32 2HY. (Life Member)
JONES, Mr. Brian Hugh, FCA 1972; 1 The Pound, BOGNOR REGIS, WEST SUSSEX, PO21 3SR.
JONES, Mr. Brian Martin, BA FCA 1972; 7 Acacia Road, HAMPTON, TW12 3DP.
•JONES, Mr. Brian Moelwyn, FCA 1970; (Tax Fac), Simson Jones, Calle Ostrero, Posthouse Suite 88, Chiclana, 11130 CADIZ, SPAIN.
JONES, Mr. Brian Norman, BSc FCA 1982; Ahead for Business Pty Ltd, Level 10, 420 St Kilda Road, MELBOURNE, VIC 3004, AUSTRALIA.
JONES, Mr. Brian Peter, FCA 1966; The Studio Staple Cross, Hockworthy, WELLINGTON, SOMERSET, TA21 0NH.
•JONES, Mr. Brian Peter, FCA 1977; Cooper Paul, Abacus House, 14-18 Forest Road, LOUGHTON, IG10 1DX.
JONES, Mr. Brian Philip, MA FCA 1976; 26 Nash Drive, REDHILL, RH1 1LH.
JONES, Mr. Brian Stewart, FCA 1957; 11 Heather Bank, HAYWARDS HEATH, RH16 1HY. (Life Member)
JONES, Mr. Brian Wallace, BCom FCA 1956; 5 Kaigh Avenue, Great Crosby, LIVERPOOL, L23 7YH. (Life Member)
JONES, Mrs. Bridget Yvonne, MSc ACA 1993; Brecken Ridge, The Fairway, WEYBRIDGE, KT13 0RZ.
JONES, Mrs. Bronwen Elizabeth Stuart, BA ACA APMI 1988; 81 Nevill Road, LONDON, N16 0SU.
•JONES, Mr. Bruce Frank, FCA 1983; Ramon Lee & Partners, Kemp House, 152-160 City Road, LONDON, EC1V 2DW. See also RLP Accounting Limited
•JONES, Mr. Bryan, BSc FCA 1978; Bryan Jones, 5 Longmans Lane, COTTINGHAM, NORTH HUMBERSIDE, HU16 4EA.
JONES, Mr. Bryan Johnson, BA FCA 1954; Glennydd, Bontnewydd, CAERNARFON, LL54 7YG. (Life Member)
JONES, Mr. Bryan William, FCA 1964; 59 Parkside, NOTTINGHAM, NG8 2NQ. (Life Member)
JONES, Mr. Bryn, ACA 2008; 109 Southview Rise, ALTON, GU34 2AR.
•JONES, Mr. Bryn Owen, BSc ACA 1993; W.J. Matthews & Son, 11 - 15 Bridge Street, CAERNARFON, LL55 1AB.
JONES, Mr. Bryn Parry, BSc ACA 1993; 50 Bull Street, Aston, BAMPTON, OXFORDSHIRE, OX18 2DT.
•JONES, Mrs. Carol, BSc ACA 1987; Carol Jones FCA, 35 Dean Close, Rhosnesni, WREXHAM, LL13 9EP.
JONES, Mrs. Carol, BSc 2001; 9 Cranford Gardens, Chandler's Ford, EASTLEIGH, HAMPSHIRE, SO53 1PU.
JONES, Miss. Carol, BA ACA 2010; Ernst & Young, 11th Floor, Al Ghaith Tower, Hamdan Street, ABU DHABI, UNITED ARAB EMIRATES.
JONES, Mrs. Carole Ann, BA FCA 1990; NDA, Herdus House, Ingwell Drive, Westlakes Science & Technology Park, MOOR ROW, CUMBRIA CA24 3HU.
JONES, Mrs. Caroline, BA FCA CTA 1998; (Tax Fac), 6 Orchard Avenue, THAMES DITTON, SURREY, KT7 0BD.
JONES, Mrs. Caroline Frampton, BSc FCA 1989; 169 Bourn View Road, Netherton, HUDDERSFIELD, HD4 7JS.
JONES, Ms. Caroline Mary, BSc ACA 1991; Protective Packaging Ltd, Dane Road Industrial Estate, Dane Road, SALE, CHESHIRE, M33 7BH.
JONES, Ms. Caroline Patricia, BA ACA 1993; 1 Woodburn Drive, West Cross, SWANSEA, SA3 5TZ.
JONES, Mrs. Carolyn Louise, BCom ACA 2007; 8 East O' Hills Close, Heswall, WIRRAL, MERSEYSIDE, CH60 5SZ.
JONES, Mrs. Carolyn Marie, BSc ACA 1993; 59 Llwyn-Y-Grant Road, Penylan, CARDIFF, CF23 9HL.
JONES, Mr. Carwyn Alan, BA ACA 2000; 6 Butterfly Close, Church Village, Rhondda-Cynon-Taff, PONTYPRIDD, MID GLAMORGAN, CF38 1AZ.
JONES, Miss. Carys Ann, BSc ACA ATII 1996; 10 Orchard Gardens, Effingham, LEATHERHEAD, SURREY, KT24 5NR.
JONES, Mrs. Catherine Ann, BSc FCA 1977; 17 Queen Annes Gate, LONDON, SW1H 9BU.
JONES, Mrs. Catherine Ann, BSc ARCS ACA 1986; Bryn Ceirch, 1 Pen y Coed, DOLGELLAU, GWYNEDD, LL40 2YP.
JONES, Mrs. Catherine Helen, MA ACA 2003; HMT Corporate Finance LLP The Hub, Station Road, HENLEY-ON-THAMES, OXFORDSHIRE, RG9 1AY.
JONES, Miss. Catherine Helena, BA ACA 1991; Athene Place, Deloitte & Touche Llp, 66 Shoe Lane, LONDON, EC4A 3BQ.
JONES, Miss. Catherine Sarah, ACA 2010; 4 Shepperds Green, Shenley Church End, MILTON KEYNES, MK5 6DA.
JONES, Miss. Catrin Mira Rees, MSc LLB ACA 2004; West Park House La Route de St. Aubin, St. Helier, JERSEY, JE2 3SF.
JONES, Mr. Ceredig Ifan, BSc ACA 2009; 16 Fairmile, HENLEY-ON-THAMES, OXFORDSHIRE, RG9 2JZ.
JONES, Miss. Ceri, BSc ACA 2001; 12 L'Arbre Crescent, Whickham, NEWCASTLE UPON TYNE, NE16 5YF.
JONES, Miss. Ceri Louise, ACA 2008; 36 Park Road, SALFORD, M6 8JP.
JONES, Mr. Ceri Marc, BSc ACA 1984; Camtronics Vale Ltd The Gateway Building, Tredegar Business Park, TREDEGAR, GWENT, NP22 3EL.
JONES, Mr. Charles Edward, MA ACA 1988; 16 Westmoreland Terrace, LONDON, SW1V 4AL.
JONES, Mr. Charles John, BA ACA 2007; 100 Gould Road, TWICKENHAM, TW2 6RW.
JONES, Mr. Charles Thompson, FCA 1958; Partida Alguasta 4 Buzón 10/009, 03688 HONDON DE LAS NIEVES, ALICANTE, SPAIN. (Life Member)
JONES, Miss. Charlotte Claire, BA ACA 1994; 9 Belvedere Drive, Wimbledon, LONDON, SW19 7BX.
JONES, Mrs. Christine, BA ACA 1988; Health Intelligence Saxon House, Moston Road, SANDBACH, CHESHIRE, CW11 3HL.
JONES, Mrs. Christine Lucy, BSc ACA 1983; 82 Ashby Road, BURTON-ON-TRENT, DE15 0NX.
JONES, Mr. Christopher Allan, FCA 1969; Jones C. Allen, Dormy Cottage, Middle Drive, Maresfield Park, Maresfield, UCKFIELD EAST SUSSEX TN22 2HG.
JONES, Mr. Christopher Bryan, BSc ACA 1979; 23 Blacka Moor Crescent, Dore, SHEFFIELD, S17 3GL.
JONES, Mr. Christopher Carl Whitmore, MA ACA 1998; 25 Ashlyns Road, BERKHAMSTED, HERTFORDSHIRE, HP4 3BN.
JONES, Mr. Christopher David, LLB ACA 1999; S A P (UK) Ltd, Clockhouse Place, Bedfont Road, FELTHAM, MIDDLESEX, TW14 8HD.
•JONES, Mr. Christopher David, BEng ACA 2004; Harries Watkins & Jones Ltd, First Floor, 85 Taff Street, PONTYPRIDD, MID GLAMORGAN, CF37 4SL.
•JONES, Mr. Christopher Derek, FCA 1975; (Tax Fac), Christopher D Jones, Strawberry Cottage, Strawberry Lane, Mollington, CHESTER, CH1 6LL.
•JONES, Mr. Christopher Dominic, BA ACA 1996; Richardson Jones Limited, Mercury House, 19/21 Chapel Street, MARLOW, BUCKINGHAMSHIRE, SL7 3HN.
•JONES, Mr. Christopher Edward, FCA 1974; Pride, Polymer Court, Hope Street, DUDLEY, DY2 8RS.
JONES, Mr. Christopher Edward Meynell, MSci ACA 2004; Deutsche Bank, One Raffles Quay, South Tower #17-00, SINGAPORE 048583, SINGAPORE.
•JONES, Mr. Christopher Glanville, BA ACA 1992; Bates Weston LLP, The Mills, Canal Street, DERBY, DE1 2RJ.
JONES, Mr. Christopher Howard, FCA 1971; Serenus, Cross Lane, Brancaster, KING'S LYNN, NORFOLK, PE31 8AE. (Life Member)
•JONES, Mr. Christopher Ian, BSc ACA 1989; Harold Smith, Unit 32, Llys Edmund Prys, St. Asaph Business Park, ST. ASAPH, LL17 0JA.
JONES, Mr. Christopher Ian, BSc ACA 1984; 16 Sowood Street, LEEDS, LS4 2JZ.
JONES, Mr. Christopher John, BA ACA 1985; 85 Butterfield Road, Wheathampstead, ST.ALBANS, AL4 8PX.
JONES, Mr. Christopher Lloyd, MSc BSc ACA 1991; 3 Redvers Gate, Bolbeck Park, MILTON KEYNES, BUCKINGHAMSHIRE, MK15 8QJ.
JONES, Mr. Christopher Mark, BSc ACA 1997; 35 St. Johns Crescent, Whitchurch, CARDIFF, CF14 7AF.
JONES, Mr. Christopher Melland, BA ACA ACCA 1998; 70 Jalan Mat Jambol, SPRINGWOOD 119543, SINGAPORE.
JONES, Mr. Christopher Michael, MSc ACA 1980; 92 Gidley Way, Horspath, OXFORD, OX33 1TG.
JONES, Mr. Christopher Paul, MSt BA(Hons) ACA 2002; 70 Blenheim Close, Upper Cambourne, CAMBRIDGE, CB23 6AP.
•JONES, Mr. Christopher Paul, MA FCA 1999; Deloitte LLP, 20 route de Pre-Bois, ICC Building H, 1215 GENEVA, SWITZERLAND. See also Deloitte & Touche LLP
•JONES, Mr. Christopher Philip, BA FCA 1980; PricewaterhouseCoopers LLP, Hays Galleria, 1 Hays Lane, LONDON, SE1 2RD. See also PricewaterhouseCoopers
JONES, Mr. Christopher Philip, BSc(Hons) ACA 2001; 6/10 Ronald Avenue, HARBORD, NSW 2096, AUSTRALIA.
•JONES, Mr. Christopher Robin, FCA 1963; C.R. Jones & Co Limited, 45 Staplegrove Road, TAUNTON, TA1 1DG.
•JONES, Mr. Christopher Stuart, FCA 1990; Daw White Murrall, 1 George Street, WOLVERHAMPTON, WV2 4DG.
•JONES, Mr. Christopher Tom, FCA 1972; C T Jones & Co, Suite 108A, Glenfield Park, Philips Road, BLACKBURN, BB1 5PF.
•JONES, Mr. Christopher Winston, BA FCA 1990; Sagars LLP, Gresham House, 5-7 St. Pauls Street, LEEDS, LS1 2JG.
JONES, Miss. Clair, MA ACA 1990; 212 East 47th Street, Apt 35J, NEW YORK, NY 10022, UNITED STATES.
JONES, Miss. Claire, BSc ACA 1998; Sanderling House, Flitton Hill, Flitton, BEDFORD, MK45 5EA.
JONES, Mrs. Claire Katharine, ACA 2002; with Deloitte LLP, 2 New Street Square, LONDON, EC4A 3BZ.
JONES, Mrs. Clare, BSc FCA MIIA 1998; 27 Penland Road, HAYWARDS HEATH, WEST SUSSEX, RH16 1PP.
JONES, Mrs. Clare, BSc ACA 1989; 6 Monks Hollow, Marlow Bottom, MARLOW, SL7 3SY.
JONES, Mrs. Clare Alison, BA ACA 1997; 32 Derby Avenue, LONDON, N12 8DD.
JONES, Mrs. Clare Christine, BA(Hons) ACA 2004; 104 St. Austell Avenue, MACCLESFIELD, CHESHIRE, SK10 3NY.
JONES, Mrs. Clare Mary, BSc ACA 1984; 3 Pant Glas Court, Bassaleg, NEWPORT, NP10 8JE.
JONES, Mr. Clinton Bernard Ashton, FCA 1974; 42 Driftwood Avenue, Chiswell Green, ST. ALBANS, AL2 3DE. (Life Member)
JONES, Mr. Clive, FCA 1970; Millfield, Beaufort Road, Llangattock, CRICKHOWELL, NP8 1LD. (Life Member)
JONES, Mr. Clive, FCA 1966; Penybont, LLANFYRNACH, PEMBROKESHIRE, SA35 0BZ.
•JONES, Mr. Clive James, FCA 1974; C.J.Jones, 45 Cwm Cwddy Drive, Rhiwderin Heights, NEWPORT, NP10 8JN.
JONES, Mr. Clive Martin, BSc ACA 1993; 8 Sovereign Crescent, LONDON, SE16 5XH.
JONES, Mr. Clive Murray, FCA 1952; 53 St Marks Close, EVESHAM, WR11 2EU. (Life Member)
JONES, Mr. Colin, FCA 1965; 11 Wind Street, BRIDGEND, Mid Glamorgan, CF32 0HU. (Life Member)
•JONES, Mr. Colin Elsmore, FCA 1971; (Tax Fac), Colin E Jones, Fernwood, Christchurch Rd, VIRGINIA WATER, GU25 4QB.
•JONES, Mr. Colin Martin, FCA 1982; The Mudd Partnership, Lakeview House, 4 Woodbrook Crescent, BILLERICAY, ESSEX, CM12 0EQ. See also Moore Emmerson Accountants Ltd
•JONES, Mr. Colin Neal, BSc FCA 1992; UHY Hacker Young LLP, Quadrant House, 4 Thomas More Square, LONDON, E1W 1YW.
•JONES, Mr. Colin Osborne, FCA 1974; (Tax Fac), A R Raymond & Co Limited, 67 London Road, ST. LEONARDS-ON-SEA, EAST SUSSEX, TN37 6AR.
JONES, Mr. Colin Paul, FCA 1961; Church Cottage, Carmans Lane, Compton, WINCHESTER, SO21 2AR.
JONES, Mr. Colin Richard, BSc FCA 1984; Brabners Chaffe Street, Horton House, Atlantic Court, Exchange Flags, LIVERPOOL, L2 3YL.
JONES, Mr. Colin Robert, BSc ACA 1985; Nestor House, Playhouse Yard, LONDON, EC4V 5EX.
JONES, Mr. Colin Stephen, FCA 1957; 6 Shannon Close, LITTLEHAMPTON, WEST SUSSEX, BN17 6PR. (Life Member)
JONES, Miss. Colleen Tracy, BA ACA CTA 1992; Half Moon House, Jevington Place, BEACONSFIELD, BUCKINGHAMSHIRE, HP9 2TN.
JONES, Mr. Conrad Austin, BA ACA 1997; Deutsche Bank 2nd Floor Mail Stop 208, 175 Bishopsgate, LONDON, EC2A 2JN.
JONES, Mr. Curtis, BA(Hons) ACA 2003; York Court Properties Ltd, 1 Red Hall Crescent, WAKEFIELD, WEST YORKSHIRE, WF1 2DF.
JONES, Mr. Dafydd Glyn, LLB ACA 2004; O'Brien & Partners, Highdale House, 7 Centre Court, Treforest Industrial Estate, PONTYPRIDD, MID GLAMORGAN CF37 5YR.
•JONES, Mr. Dafydd Llewelyn, BSc FCA 1982; I.G. Jones & Co, Cefni Chambers, 10a High Street, LLANGEFNI, LL77 7LT.
JONES, Mr. Dafydd Rowland, MSc ACA 1999; 16 Howard Place, Reigate Hill, REIGATE, SURREY, RH2 9NP.
JONES, Mr. Damien, BA ACA 2003; Flat 1, 1-7 Kendall Street, SURRY HILLS, NSW 2010, AUSTRALIA.
JONES, Mr. Daniel, ACA 2006; Gwithian, Chelmsford Road, Rawreth, WICKFORD, ESSEX, SS11 8SY.
JONES, Mr. Daniel, ACA 2011; 53 Frankton Close, SOLIHULL, B92 8LX.
JONES, Mr. Daniel, MSc BSc(Econ) ACA 2011; Flat 4 Gardenhurst, 45 Cardigan Road, LEEDS, LS6 1WD.
•JONES, Mr. Daniel Charles Rhys, BSc ACA 1997; Deloitte LLP, PO Box 500, 2 Hardman Street, MANCHESTER, M60 2AT. See also Deloitte & Touche LLP
JONES, Mr. Daniel Edward, BA ACA 1995; Lenovo Technology Uk Ltd, Discovery House 240 Bartley Wood Business Park, HOOK, HAMPSHIRE, RG27 9UP.
JONES, Mr. Daniel Glyn, MMath ACA 2002; 16 Rainham Gardens, Ruddington, NOTTINGHAM, NG11 6HX.
JONES, Mr. Daniel Martin, ACA 1996; The British Land Company Ltd, York House, 45 Seymour Street, LONDON, W1H 7LX.
JONES, Mr. Daniel Matthew Allan, ACA 1999; 4th Floor, Ul Marszalkowska 89, 00-693 WARSAW, POLAND.
JONES, Mr. Daniel Rhys, BA ACA 2004; 11 Vyne Road, BASINGSTOKE, HAMPSHIRE, RG21 5NU.
JONES, Mr. Danny Louis, ACA 2010; 111 Moscow Drive, LIVERPOOL, L13 7DG.
JONES, Mr. Darren, ACA 2003; 3c Lebanon Gardens, Biggin Hill, WESTERHAM, KENT, TN16 3HB.
JONES, Mr. Darren, BA ACA 1992; 168 Park Close, WALTON-ON-THAMES, SURREY, KT12 1EW.
JONES, Mr. Darren, BSc ACA 1993; Home Farm Hyde Road, Denchworth, WANTAGE, OXFORDSHIRE, OX12 0DP.
JONES, Mr. Darren William, BA ACA 2007; 1a Palmer Avenue, SUTTON, SM3 8EF.
JONES, Mr. David, BA FCA 1987; with UNW LLP, Citygate, St. James Boulevard, NEWCASTLE UPON TYNE, NE1 4JE.
JONES, Mr. David, BSc FCA 1961; 19 Sheen Common Drive, RICHMOND, TW10 5BW. (Life Member)
JONES, Mr. David Andrew, BA ACA 1984; 24/1 Heriot Row, EDINBURGH, EH3 6EN.
JONES, Mr. David Andrew, BA ACA 1985; Merley Cottage, 6 Cullwood Lane, NEW MILTON, HAMPSHIRE, BH25 5QJ.
JONES, Mr. David Anthony, FCA 1965; 7522 Weeping Willow Boulevard, SARASOTA, FL 34241, UNITED STATES.
JONES, Mr. David Anthony, FCA 1971; 28 Chadwicke Close, Stapeley, NANTWICH, CHESHIRE, CW5 7NF.
JONES, Mr. David Barrington, FCA 1967; Corngrave House, Four Lane Ends, Upleatham, REDCAR, CLEVELAND, TS11 8AD. (Life Member)
•JONES, Mr. David Buckley, FCA 1977; D.B. Jones & Co, 14 Providence Street, Earlsdon, COVENTRY, WEST MIDLANDS, CV5 6ED. See also D B Jones & Co Limited
JONES, Mr. David Charles, FCA 1969; Civitas Law Global Reach, Dunleavy Drive, CARDIFF, CF11 0SN.
•JONES, Mr. David Charles, FCA CTA 1980; 70 Wintringham Way, Purley on Thames, READING, RG8 8BG.
JONES, Mr. David Colin, MEng ACA 2007; 98 Buckhurst Way, BUCKHURST HILL, IG9 6HP.
JONES, Mr. David Edward, BSc FCA 1991; Briar Hill, Goodworth Clatford, ANDOVER, HAMPSHIRE, SP11 7QX.
JONES, Mr. David Edward, BSc ACA 1999; 15 Ullswater Crescent, LONDON, SW15 3RG.
•JONES, Mr. David Edward, BA FCA 1990; Harwood Hutton Limited, 22 Wycombe End, BEACONSFIELD, BUCKINGHAMSHIRE, HP9 1NB. See also Jones D.E.
JONES, Mr. David Frank, FCA 1964; Chiltern Business Assistance Limited, 3 Moor End, Eaton Bray, DUNSTABLE, LU6 2HN.
JONES, Mr. David Gareth, FCA 1971; Hill House Farm, Misbrooks Green Road, Beare Green, DORKING, RH5 4QQ.
JONES, Mr. David Gareth, MA ACA 1990; 80 Thompson Avenue, RICHMOND, SURREY, TW9 4JW.
JONES, Mr. David Gethin, BA FCA 1982; Heathercliffe, Draughton Road, Maidwell, NORTHAMPTON, NN6 9JF.
JONES, Mr. David Gordon, FCA 1962; 28 Bracken Close, Tittensor, STOKE-ON-TRENT, ST12 9JD.
•JONES, Mr. David Gordon, FCA 1974; Hill Top, 44 Bloomfield Road, HARPENDEN, AL5 4DB.
JONES, Mr. David Gwyn, BA ACA 2002; 26 Lowside Avenue, BOLTON, BL1 5XQ.
JONES, Mr. David Gwynne, BA FCA 1988; Monsoon Monsoon Building, 1 Nicholas Road, LONDON, W11 4AN.
JONES, Mr. David Harold, BSc FCA 1958; The Old Stables, Eastergate House, Church Lane Eastergate, CHICHESTER, PO20 3UT. (Life Member)

•**JONES, Mr. David Havard, FCA** *1971;* Rushton Osborne & Co Limited, Ringley Park House, 59 Reigate Road, REIGATE, SURREY, RH2 0QJ.

JONES, Mr. David Ian, BA FCA *1993;* 46 Meadow Way, BRACKNELL, RG42 1UF.

JONES, Mr. David Ieuan, FCA *1956;* 49 Maesceinion, Waunfawr, ABERYSTWYTH, SY23 3QQ. (Life Member)

•**JONES, Mr. David James, FCA** *1967;* (Tax Fac), D.J. Jones, 10 Beacon Court, Southcote Road, READING, RG30 2ER.

JONES, Mr. David Jonathan Hadley, BA ACA *1985;* Pricewaterhousecoopers, 1 Embankment Place, LONDON, WC2N 6RH.

•**JONES, Mr. David Jones Francis, BSc ACA** *2006;* David Jones & Co, Spring Mill, 2 Main Street, Wilsden, BRADFORD, WEST YORKSHIRE BD15 0DX. See also Binary Accounting Limited

JONES, Mr. David Llewelyn Edwards, FCA *1967;* Houghton House, Houghton, ARUNDEL, BN18 9LW. (Life Member)

JONES, Mr. David Lloyd, FCA MBA *1982;* Axon Centre, Church Road, EGHAM, TW20 9QB.

JONES, Mr. David Mansel, FCA *1962;* Heath House, Eastgate, COWBRIDGE, CF71 7AB. (Life Member)

JONES, Mr. David Mark, ACA *2003;* 51 Watt Road, Edington, BIRMINGHAM, B23 6EU.

JONES, Mr. David Mason, BA FCA CF *1986;* Orchard House, 5 Church Farm Way, Arthingworth, MARKET HARBOROUGH, LE16 8NP.

JONES, Mr. David Mervyn, FCA *1948;* 48 Llys Pegasus, Ty-Glas Road, CARDIFF, CF14 5ER. (Life Member)

JONES, Mr. David Mervyn Hinds, FCA *1955;* Craignybaa, Llangunnor Road, CARMARTHEN, SA31 2PB. (Life Member)

•**JONES, Mr. David Michael, FCA** *1966;* D M Jones, 2 Burnside Road, Gatley, CHEADLE, CHESHIRE, SK8 4NA.

JONES, Mr. David Neil, BA ACA *1991;* 38 Kingsway, Chandlers Ford, EASTLEIGH, SO53 1EN.

JONES, Mr. David Nigel Tunstall, BA FCA *1965;* (Member of Council 1985 - 1999), Webbsbrook Cottage, Silver Street, Wrington, BRISTOL, BS40 5QL. (Life Member)

JONES, Mr. David Paul, BSc ACA *2001;* 14 Oak Road, Ballawattleworth Estate Peel, ISLE OF MAN, IM5 1WN.

JONES, Mr. David Peter Gwynne, BA ACA *1999;* Ashwood Aspley Heath Lane, Tanworth-in-Arden, SOLIHULL, B94 5HU.

•**JONES, Mr. David Richard, BSc ACA** *1982;* Midicorp Corporate Finance Ltd, New Bond House, 124 New Bond Street, LONDON, W1S 1DX.

•**JONES, Mr. David Richard, ACA** *1981;* Hirons & Co, 2 Corfton Drive, WOLVERHAMPTON, WV6 8NR.

•**JONES, Mr. David Robert, FCA** *1988;* Day Smith & Hunter, Batchworth House, Batchworth Place, Church Street, RICKMANSWORTH, HERTFORDSHIRE WD3 1JE.

JONES, Mr. David Ronald, BSc FCA *1984;* 70 Les Champs-Blancs, 1279 CHAVANNES-DE-BOGIS, SWITZERLAND.

JONES, Mr. David Ronald Henry, FCA *1972;* Pine Trees, 51 Terrington Hill, MARLOW, SL7 2RE.

JONES, Mr. David Simon Tudor, BA ACA *2007;* 23 Mackeson Road, LONDON, NW3 2LU.

JONES, Mr. David Simon Vaughan, BSc FCA *1983;* 3405 Wentworth Way, LEWISVILLE, TX 75077, UNITED STATES.

JONES, Mr. David Stephen, FCA *1973;* 6 Murrell Close, ST. NEOTS, CAMBRIDGESHIRE, PE19 1LN.

JONES, Mr. David Thomas Grant, BA ACA CF *1983;* with Smith & Williamson Ltd, 25 Moorgate, LONDON, EC2R 6AY.

•**JONES, Mr. David Timothy, FCA** *1972;* Morgan Griffiths LLP, Cross Chambers, 9 High Street, NEWTOWN, POWYS, SY16 2NY.

JONES, Mr. David Vaughan, ACA *1979;* Flat 4 Craddoc Court, 30 Bodenham Road, Tupsley, HEREFORD, HR1 2TS.

JONES, Mrs. Debbie Jane, BA ACA *1996;* 37 Oversley Road, Minworth, SUTTON COLDFIELD, B76 1XB.

JONES, Mrs. Deborah, BA ACA *1996;* Micro Librarian Systems, Arden House, Shepley Lane, Hawk Green, Marple, STOCKPORT CHESHIRE SK6 7JW.

JONES, Mrs. Deborah Helen, BA(Hons) ACA *2001;* with Lings, Provident House, 51 Wardwick, DERBY, DE1 1HN.

JONES, Mrs. Deborah Jane, MA ACA *1987;* 15 Wellington Road, NEWPORT, TF10 7HF.

JONES, Mrs. Deborah Mary, BA ACA *1992;* 45 The Cloisters, South Gosforth, NEWCASTLE UPON TYNE, NE7 7LS.

JONES, Miss. Debra Louise, BA ACA *2005;* with Armstrong Watson, First Floor East, Bridge Mills, Stramongate, KENDAL, CUMBRIA LA9 4UB.

JONES, Mrs. Debra Lynne, BSc ACA *1988;* 26 Smithies Avenue, Sully, PENARTH, CF64 5SS.

JONES, Mr. Deian Lewis, BSc ACA *2000;* 14 Llewelyn Goch St. Fagans, CARDIFF, CF5 6HR.

JONES, Miss. Delyth, BA ACA *2010;* 13 Maes Meddyg, CAERNARFON, GWYNEDD, LL55 2SF.

JONES, Miss. Delyth Wyn, BSc ACA *2006;* 50 Aldsworth Road, Victoria Park, CARDIFF, CF5 1AB.

JONES, Mr. Dennis, FCA *1972;* 21 B WESTENRA TERRACE, CASHMERE, CHRISTCHURCH 8022, NEW ZEALAND.

JONES, Mr. Dennis Charles, FCA *1957;* 1 Drew Road, Pedmore, STOURBRIDGE, WEST MIDLANDS, DY9 0UZ. (Life Member)

JONES, Mr. Dennis Gareth, BSc ACA *1992;* Briar House, Spinfield Lane, MARLOW, BUCKINGHAMSHIRE, SL7 2JT.

JONES, Mr. Derek, FCA *1956;* 1 Burnham Court, Fairford Road, MAIDENHEAD, BERKSHIRE, SL6 7AB. (Life Member)

JONES, Mr. Derek, FCA *1965;* 8 Trimpley Gardens, Penn, WOLVERHAMPTON, WV4 5PG. (Life Member)

JONES, Mr. Derrek Layton, FCA *1960;* 6 Rosewood Close, Lisvane, CARDIFF, CF14 0EU. (Life Member)

JONES, Mr. Donald Philip, FCA *1944;* 33 Hugo Road, LONDON, N19 5EU. (Life Member)

JONES, Mrs. Donna Maria, BSc ACA *1999;* 1 Kentsford Drive, Radcliffe, MANCHESTER, M26 3XX.

JONES, Mr. Duncan Andrew, BA ACA *1998;* Pretoria Cottage, 28-30 Crown Street, Banham, NORWICH, NR16 2EX.

JONES, Mr. Duncan William, BA ACA *1985;* Ashlawn, Forest Drive, Kirby Muxloe, LEICESTER, LE9 2EA.

JONES, Mr. Dyfan Rhodri Glanville, BA FCA *2000;* Gelligron, 12 East Cliff, Pennard, SWANSEA, SA3 2AS.

•**JONES, Mr. Dylan, BSc(Econ) ACA** *1990;* J Gareth Morgan & Co, Clun House, 11 Morgan Street, TREDEGAR, GWENT, NP22 3NA. See also J Gareth Morgan & Co Ltd

JONES, Mr. Edmund William, FCA *1954;* 12 Fleet Close, Littleport, ELY, CAMBRIDGESHIRE, CB6 1PG. (Life Member)

JONES, Mr. Edward Anthony, BSc ACA *1997;* Hunters Estate Agents, 18-19 Colliergate, YORK, YO1 8BN.

JONES, Mr. Edward John, BSc ACA *1989;* 16 Brunswick Court, Henry Road, BARNET, HERTFORDSHIRE, EN4 8BQ.

JONES, Mr. Edward Simon, BSc FCA *1980;* 30 Warrington Road, DANBURY, CT 06810, UNITED STATES.

JONES, Mrs. Elaine, BA ACA *1997;* Orchard House Weedon Hill, Hyde Heath, AMERSHAM, BUCKINGHAMSHIRE, HP6 5RH.

JONES, Miss. Elaine, BSc ACA *2006;* Weston Kay, 73 Mortimer Street, LONDON, W1W 7SQ.

•**JONES, Mrs. Elaine, BSc ACA** *1989;* Elaine Jones Book-Keeping, 8 Fusilier Way, Weedon, NORTHAMPTON, NN7 4TH.

•**JONES, Mrs. Elaine Gillian, FCA** *1979;* E.G. Jones & Co, 2 Colwyn Avenue, Rhos-on-Sea, COLWYN BAY, LL28 4RB.

JONES, Mrs. Elaine Helen, BA ACA *1995;* Woodlands, Forest Road, East Horsley, LEATHERHEAD, SURREY, KT24 5BX.

JONES, Miss. Elen Prys, BSc ACA *2003;* with KPMG LLP, 3 Assembly Square, Britannia Quay, CARDIFF, CF10 4AX.

JONES, Mrs. Elen Wyn, BSc ACA *2003;* 60 St. Johns Crescent, Whitchurch, CARDIFF, CF14 7AG.

JONES, Miss. Elizabeth, BA(Hons) ACA *2002;* 21 Birchtree Drive, LIVERPOOL, L31 1DE.

JONES, Mrs. Elizabeth, BSc ACA ATII *1985;* 82A St. Marks Road, HENLEY-ON-THAMES, OXFORDSHIRE, RG9 1LW.

JONES, Mrs. Elizabeth Alice, BSc ACA *2010;* 42 Westcots Drive, WINKLEIGH, DEVON, EX19 8JP.

JONES, Miss. Elizabeth Ann, BSc FCA *1977;* Flat 4 Ridgmont House, 29 Ridgmont Road, ST. ALBANS, AL1 3AG.

JONES, Miss. Elizabeth Ruth, ACA *2009;* 3 Fairfield Road, CHESTER, CH2 3RN.

JONES, Mr. Elwyn Tudor, FCA *1958;* Lea House, Sutton Park, Bishop Sutton, BRISTOL, BS39 5UQ. (Life Member)

•**JONES, Miss. Emma Caroline, ACA** *2008;* Jones & Petty LLP, 21 Kelvedon Close, RAYLEIGH, ESSEX, SS6 9SQ.

JONES, Mrs. Emma Elizabeth, BSc ACA *2005;* Green Oaks Dunraven Terrace, TREORCHY, CF42 6EL.

JONES, Miss. Emma Frances, BA(Hons) ACA *2009;* 18 Felden Street, LONDON, SW6 5AF.

JONES, Mrs. Emma Jane, BSc ACA *2002;* 158 Oxford Road, MACCLESFIELD, CHESHIRE, SK11 8JY.

JONES, Miss. Emma-Jane, BSc ACA *1996;* SPS Print Group, 1 Nimrod Way, Ferndown Ind Est, WIMBORNE, BH21 7SH.

JONES, Mr. Emyr Gwyn, FCA *1955;* 15 Glan Towy, CARMARTHEN, SA31 2HE. (Life Member)

JONES, Mr. Emyr Wyn, BA FCA *1973;* 42 Hudson Parade, CLAREVILLE, NSW 2107, AUSTRALIA.

JONES, Mr. Eric, FCA *1972;* Froome House, Bridgnorth Road, Stourton, STOURBRIDGE, WEST MIDLANDS, DY7 5BG.

•**JONES, Mr. Eric Malcolm, BSc ACA** *2000;* J&S Accountants Limited, 6 Northlands Road, SOUTHAMPTON, HAMPSHIRE, SO15 2FL.

JONES, Mr. Eric Neil, BSc ACA *1989;* 1 Fairview Close, Marple, STOCKPORT, CHESHIRE, SK6 6LX.

JONES, Mr. Ernest Arnold, FCA *1953;* 8 Hazeldene, Wendover, AYLESBURY, BUCKINGHAMSHIRE, HP22 6NG. (Life Member)

JONES, Mrs. Esme Rebecca Tarasewicz, ACA *2008;* 22 The Croft, Park Hill, LONDON, W5 2JW.

JONES, Mrs. Esther Amelia, MA ACA *2004;* 18 Grove Street, LEAMINGTON SPA, WARWICKSHIRE, CV32 5AJ.

JONES, Miss. Esyllt Lloyd, BSc ACA *2007;* 19 Hall Avenue, Timperley, ALTRINCHAM, CHESHIRE, WA15 6SD.

JONES, Mrs. Felicity Jane, BA ACA *1983;* Systems Biology Laboratory UK, Unit 7, 127 Milton Park, Milton, ABINGDON, OXFORDSHIRE OX14 4SA.

JONES, Mrs. Frances, BSc ACA *1994;* Thales Research & Technology (UK) Ltd, Worton Drive, Worton Grange, Business Park, READING, BERKSHIRE RG2 0SB.

JONES, Mrs. Frances Louise, ACA *2009;* 43 Turls Hill Road, DUDLEY, WEST MIDLANDS, DY3 1HQ.

JONES, Mr. Francis Gary, BSc ACA *1993;* Shepherd Widnes Ltd, Moss Bank Road, WIDNES, WA8 0RU.

JONES, Mr. Frank, FCA *1977;* 1394 Junction Road West, Lostock, BOLTON, BL6 4EQ.

JONES, Mr. Frederick Stanley, FCA *1951;* 62 Trinity Crescent, LLANDUDNO, GWYNEDD, LL30 2PQ. (Life Member)

JONES, Mrs. Gail Tracey, BA ACA *1994;* Sevenoaks School, High Street, SEVENOAKS, TN13 1HU.

•**JONES, Mr. Gareth, FCA** *1969;* (Tax Fac), Gareth Jones, Ger-y-garth, Tyddyngwyn, Manod, BLAENAU FFESTINIOG, LL41 4AL.

JONES, Mr. Gareth, BSc FCA DChA *1974;* 63 Church Road, Whitchurch, CARDIFF, CF14 2DY.

JONES, Mr. Gareth, BA ACA ATII *1999;* 37 Soke Road, Newborough, PETERBOROUGH, PE6 7QT.

JONES, Mr. Gareth Brynmor, BSc(Hons) ACA *2004;* 2 Wards Closes, WIGSTON, LEICESTERSHIRE, LE18 3TS.

JONES, Mr. Gareth David, BA ACA *1979;* 2 Rosemont Road, RICHMOND, SURREY, TW10 6QL.

JONES, Mr. Gareth David, BSc(Econ) ACA *1996;* 12721 Longstock Ct, HUNTERSVILLE, NC 28078, UNITED STATES.

JONES, Mr. Gareth Edward, FCA *1973;* 18 Thread Mill Lane, Pymore, BRIDPORT, DORSET, DT6 5QT. (Life Member)

JONES, Mr. Gareth Evan Lloyd, BSc ACA *2004;* Mazars Llp The Atrium, Park Street West, LUTON, LU1 3BE.

JONES, Mr. Gareth Everett, FCA *1973;* Woodland Cottage, Eyton, WREXHAM, LL13 0YB.

JONES, Mr. Gareth Hywel, BEng ACA *1993;* 5 Hamilton Avenue, HARROGATE, NORTH YORKSHIRE, HG2 8JB.

JONES, Mr. Gareth Mark, BSc ACA *1999;* 8 Pine Grove, WEYBRIDGE, KT13 9AX.

JONES, Mr. Gareth Michael, MA ACA *1996;* 21 Braemar Avenue, Wimbledon Park, LONDON, SW19 8AY.

•**JONES, Mr. Gareth Morgan, BSc FCA** *1996;* Chantrey Vellacott DFK LLP, 23-28 Great Russell Street, LONDON, WC1B 3NG.

•**JONES, Mr. Gareth Picton Gwyn, BSc FCA** *1983;* (Tax Fac), Donald Owen Ltd, 34 Quay Street, CARMARTHEN, CARMARTHENSHIRE, SA31 3JT.

JONES, Mr. Gareth Robert Lynton, BA(Econ) ACA CF *2003;* with Fitzgerald and Law LLP, 8 Lincoln's Inn Fields, LONDON, WC2A 3BP.

JONES, Mr. Garry, BSc FCA *1982;* RSM Tenon, Charter House legge St, BIRMINGHAM, B4 7EU.

JONES, Mr. Garry Mason Cleaver, BCom ACA *1992;* 37 St. Kingsmark Avenue, CHEPSTOW, GWENT, NP16 5LY.

JONES, Mr. Gary Martin, FCA *1970;* 10 Queens Close, ROMSEY, SO51 5EG.

JONES, Mr. Gary Stanley, FCA *1980;* 27 Ellis Way, UCKFIELD, EAST SUSSEX, TN22 2BT.

JONES, Mr. Gary Timothy, BSc ACA *1989;* 35 Dean Close, Rhosnesni, WREXHAM, LL13 9EP.

JONES, Mr. Gary Wayne, FCA *1983;* 2 Heston Close, Portskewett, CALDICOT, GWENT, NP26 5RU.

JONES, Mr. Gavin Richard, BSc ACA MSI *2002;* 19 Links Avenue, FELIXSTOWE, SUFFOLK, IP11 9HD.

JONES, Mr. Gavin Stewart, BSc ACA *1996;* 25 The Drive, Henleaze, BRISTOL, BS9 4LD.

JONES, Miss. Gaynor Ann, ACA *2008;* 79 Cornhill Terrace, EDINBURGH, EH6 8EJ.

JONES, Miss. Gemma, ACA *2008;* 32 Camargue Drive, MARCH, CAMBRIDGESHIRE, PE15 9PD.

JONES, Miss. Gemma Louise, ACA *2008;* Flat, 10 Englands Lane, LONDON, NW3 4TG.

JONES, Mr. Geoffrey Brinley, FCA *1972;* 3 Rectory Court, Llanmaes, LLANTWIT MAJOR, SOUTH GLAMORGAN, CF61 2WJ.

JONES, Mr. Geoffrey John Charles, BA FCA FCT *1952;* 21 Verte Prairie B, Route De Fontanivent 39, CH-1817 BRENT, SWITZERLAND. (Life Member)

JONES, Mr. Geoffrey Trevor, BSc FCA *1988;* 8 The Hermitage, STAMFORD, PE9 2RF.

JONES, Mr. Geoffrey William, FCA *1970;* 47 Roumania Crescent, LLANDUDNO, LL30 1UP.

JONES, Mr. George Arthur, FCA *1940;* 87 Hunts Cross Avenue, Woolton, LIVERPOOL, L25 5NU. (Life Member)

JONES, Mr. Geraint Allan, BSc FCA *2000;* 17 Llwyn y Pia Road, Lisvane, CARDIFF, CF14 0SX.

•**JONES, Mr. Geraint Hywel, BA FCA** *1997;* BDO LLP, 55 Baker Street, LONDON, W1U 7EU. See also BDO Stoy Hayward LLP

JONES, Mr. Gerwyn Maybery, FCA *1961;* West Town Lodge, Llangennith, SWANSEA, SA3 1JE.

•**JONES, Mrs. Ghislaine Mary, FCA** *1980;* with Ellacotts LLP, Countrywide House, 23 West Bar Street, BANBURY, OXFORDSHIRE, OX16 9SA.

JONES, Mr. Gilbert Arthur, FCA *1953;* Highfield, Joan Lane, Bamford, HOPE VALLEY, S33 0AW. (Life Member)

•**JONES, Mrs. Gillian, BA(Hons) ACA** *2001;* Gillian Jones & Company, Ballykeane, GEASHILL, COUNTY OFFALY, IRELAND.

JONES, Mrs. Gillian Lisa, BA ACA *1993;* Brownhills, Leebotwood, CHURCH STRETTON, SY6 6LU.

•**JONES, Mr. Glen Brian, BA FCA** *1986;* Mazars LLP, 45 Church Street, BIRMINGHAM, B3 2RT.

JONES, Mrs. Glenys, FCA *1970;* 1 Balmoral Road, WREXHAM, CLWYD, LL11 2RW.

JONES, Mr. Glyn, FCA *1987;* with KPMG LLP, 15 Canada Square, LONDON, E14 5GL.

JONES, Mr. Glyn Carl Evan, FCA *1968;* 51 Ferriby High Road, NORTH FERRIBY, HU14 3LD. (Life Member)

JONES, Mr. Glyn Parry, MA FCA *1977;* 17 Queen Annes Gate, LONDON, SW1H 9BU.

JONES, Mr. Glyn William, BA ACA *2006;* K M Business Solutions Ltd, 6 Grimshaw Street, BURNLEY, BB11 2AZ.

JONES, Mr. Gordon, ACA CA(AUS) *2009;* Kilve, Park Copse, DORKING, SURREY, RH5 4BL.

JONES, Mr. Gordon David Spencer, FCA *1971;* The Paddocks, 32 Heycroft Way, Nayland, COLCHESTER, CO6 4LF.

JONES, Mr. Gordon George, FCA *1965;* 4 Osborne Road, DUNSTABLE, LU6 3JS. (Life Member)

•**JONES, Mr. Gordon Howard, BSc ACA** *1990;* (Tax Fac), Reeves & Co LLP, Montague Place, Quayside, Chatham Maritime, CHATHAM, KENT ME4 4QU.

JONES, Mr. Gordon William, FCA *1955;* 2 Ashleigh Court, 304b New Road, Newton, PORTHCAWL, MID GLAMORGAN, CF36 5PL. (Life Member)

JONES, Mr. Graeme Alistair, BSc ACA *2006;* 16 Bramston Road, LONDON, SW17 0JR.

JONES, Mr. Graeme Wallace, FCA *1973;* 92 Egham Crescent, Cheam, SUTTON, SM3 9AW.

•**JONES, Mr. Graham, BSc ACA** *1990;* GJCA Limited, 15 The South Street Centre, 16-20 South Street, Hythe, SOUTHAMPTON, SO45 6EB.

•**JONES, Mr. Graham, BA FCA** *1977;* GJ Consultancy Services Ltd, 55 Siskin Road, Offerton, STOCKPORT, CHESHIRE, SK2 5JX.

JONES, Mr. Graham Becket, FCA *1965;* 7 Brierley Avenue, West Mersea, COLCHESTER, ESSEX, CO5 8HG. (Life Member)

JONES, Mr. Graham Beverley, FCA *1970;* 30 Hartopp Road, Four Oaks, SUTTON COLDFIELD, B74 2QY.

JONES, Mr. Graham Charles, BSc FCA *1981;* 111 Blackbrook Lane, BROMLEY, BR1 2LP.

JONES, Mr. Graham Douglas, MSc BSc FCA *1977;* 20 Ridgeway, Wargrave, READING, RG10 8AS. (Life Member)
•**JONES, Mr. Graham Howard, BA FCA** *1987;* Rawlinsons, Ruthlyn House, 90 Lincoln Road, PETERBOROUGH, PE1 2SP.
JONES, Mr. Graham Ian Lennox, MBA BSc ACA *1993;* 39 Braikenridge Close, CLEVEDON, BS21 5LA.
JONES, Mr. Graham Radclift, FCA *1955;* 7 Bramblewood Close, Thornhill, CARDIFF, CF14 9DN. (Life Member)
JONES, Mr. Graham Thomas John, BSc FCA *1969;* 80 Gabalfa Road, Sketty, SWANSEA, SA2 8NA. (Life Member)
•**JONES, Prof. Grant Meredith, LLM FCA FCIArb MIPA FABRP** *1986;* (Member of Council 2007 - 2011), Cooper Parry LLP, Tower 42, 25 Old Broad Street, LONDON, EC2N 1HN.
JONES, Mr. Gregg, ACA *2010;* 17 The Refinery, Jacob Street, BRISTOL, BS2 0HS.
JONES, Mr. Gregory Kenneth William, MSc BSc(Econ) LLB ACA CPA *1988;* 696 Torrens Road, PENNINGTON, SA 5013, AUSTRALIA.
JONES, Miss. Gwendolyn Anne Niven, BA(Hons) ACA *2000;* 6 Hopefield Green, Rothwell, LEEDS, LS26 0YB.
JONES, Mr. Gwilym Athelstan, MSci ACA *2010;* Fferm Pwll Iwrch, Darowen, MACHYNLLETH, POWYS, SY20 8NS.
JONES, Mr. Gwyn, MSc(Econ) BSc(Econ) ACA *2011;* 55 Parc Alafowlia, DENBIGH, CLWYD, LL16 3HZ.
JONES, Miss. Hannah Rose, ACA *2010;* 20 Stan Petersen Close, NORWICH, NR1 4QJ.
JONES, Miss. Hannah Sophie, BSc ACA *2009;* 149a Putney High Street, LONDON, SW15 1SU.
JONES, Mr. Harold Chave, FCA *1935;* 24 Rockwell Court, Albert Street, Stapleford, NOTTINGHAM, NG9 8BZ. (Life Member)
JONES, Miss. Harriet Kathryn, BSc ACA *1992;* University College School, Frognal, Hampstead, LONDON, NW3 6XH.
JONES, Mr. Harvey Lloyd, MA FCA MBA *1995;* ETSA Utilities, 1 Anzac Highway, KESWICK, SA 5066, AUSTRALIA.
JONES, Mr. Haydn, FCA *1954;* 20 Pointfields Crescent, Hakin, MILFORD HAVEN, SA73 3DA. (Life Member)
JONES, Mr. Haydn, BSc ACA *2010;* 10 Corn Avill Close, ABINGDON, OXFORDSHIRE, OX14 2ND.
JONES, Miss. Hayley, BSc ACA *2008;* 12 Springwood Drive, Mansfield Woodhouse, MANSFIELD, NOTTINGHAMSHIRE, NG19 9EB.
•**JONES, Mrs. Heather, BCom ACA** *1987;* Jones & Co Business Performance Solutions, 333 Station Road, Dorridge, SOLIHULL, B93 8EY.
JONES, Miss. Heather Ann, BSc ACA *1992;* E Conversions Ltd Galatix House, 9 Dallington Street, LONDON, EC1V 0BQ.
JONES, Miss. Helen Amanda, MEng ACA *2004;* 28 Turner Avenue, CRANBROOK, KENT, TN17 3DD.
•**JONES, Mrs. Helen Angela, FCA** *1987;* Gregory Wildman, The Granary, Crowhill Farm, Ravensden Road, Wilden, BEDFORD MK44 2QS.
JONES, Miss. Helen Audrey, BA ACA *1989;* Glaxo Smithkline Plc G S K House, 980 Great West Road, BRENTFORD, MIDDLESEX, TW8 9GS.
•**JONES, Miss. Helen Louise, BA ACA** *2005;* 35 Kingsman Road, STANFORD-LE-HOPE, ESSEX, SS17 0JP.
JONES, Mrs. Helen Mary Kinsey, BA ACA *2004;* Corus, Reporting & Control, PO Box 30, Orb Works, Stephen Street, NEWPORT GWENT NP19 0XT.
JONES, Mrs. Helen Sandra, BSc ACA *1983;* 3405 Wentworth Way, LEWISVILLE, TX 75077, UNITED STATES.
JONES, Mr. Henry John Foster, FCA *1954;* Squirrels Leap, Spinney Lane, Tabley Road, KNUTSFORD, WA16 0NQ. (Life Member)
JONES, Mr. Henry Willoughby Llewellyn, BA FCA *1954;* 5 Ardwell Close, CROWTHORNE, BERKSHIRE, RG45 6BA. (Life Member)
JONES, Miss. Hilary, ACA *2011;* Flat 31, Delaware Mansions, Delaware Road, LONDON, W9 2LH.
JONES, Miss. Holly, ACA *2009;* 63 Tranmere Road, LONDON, SW18 3QH.
JONES, Mr. Howard Derwyn Newton, FCA *1965;* 37 Earl Street, ROSEVILLE, NSW 2069, AUSTRALIA.
JONES, Mr. Howard Maurice, MBA BSc FCA *1971;* 33 St. Augustines Road, BEDFORD, MK40 2NA. (Life Member)
JONES, Mr. Howard Ralph, BSc FCA *1989;* Floor 4, Norfolk County Council Corporate Finance, County Hall Martineau Lane, NORWICH, NR1 2DW.
JONES, Mr. Howard Roland, BCom ACA *1995;* 17 Honeycroft Drive, ST. ALBANS, HERTFORDSHIRE, AL4 0GF.
JONES, Mr. Howard Ronald, FCA *1976;* Grand Buildings, Star Energy Group Ltd 1-3 Strand, LONDON, WC2N 5EJ.
•**JONES, Mr. Hugh, FCA** *1966;* Pritchard Jones Accountancy Services Limited, 3 Quay Street, CARMARTHEN, DYFED, SA31 3JT. See also Pritchard Jones & Co
•**JONES, Mr. Hugh Arthur Prys, BA FCA** *1980;* Williams Denton Cyf, Glaslyn, Ffordd y Parc, Parc Menai, BANGOR, GWYNEDD LL57 4FE.
JONES, Mr. Hugh David, FCA *1982;* Trevescan Farm, Sennen, PENZANCE, CORNWALL, TR19 7AQ.
JONES, Mr. Hugh Robert Trevor, BA ACA *1983;* 111 Stephens Road, TUNBRIDGE WELLS, KENT, TN4 9QB.
•**JONES, Mr. Hugh Thomas Wilfred, BSc FCA** *1975;* R.H. Jeffs & Rowe, 27-28 Gelliwastad Road, PONTYPRIDD, CF37 2BW. See also RH Jeffs & Rowe Ltd
JONES, Mr. Huw, BA ACA *2007;* Stowe School, Stowe, BUCKINGHAM, MK18 5EH.
JONES, Mr. Huw Emlyn, MMath(Hons) ACA *2004;* 12 Ashwell Place, WATFORD, WD24 5JX.
JONES, Mr. Huw Lloyd, MBA BSc FCA *1990;* Charlemagne Capital (IOM) Limited, St. Marys Court Hill Street, Douglas, ISLE OF MAN, IM1 1EU.
•**JONES, Mr. Huw Wyndham Lloyd, ACA** *1981;* Huw Jones & Co, Larchfield, Pregge Lane, CRICKHOWELL, POWYS, NP8 1SE.
JONES, Mr. Hywel, BA ACA *1979;* Calshot House, Kelmscott Place, ASHTEAD, SURREY, KT212HD.
JONES, Mr. Hywel Eifion, BA FCA *1973;* Bella Vista, Bryn Eryl Mold Road, RUTHIN, LL15 1DT.
JONES, Hywel Gwyn, Esq CBE FCA *1968;* Penllaen, 114 Heol Isaf, Radyr, CARDIFF, CF15 8EA.
•**JONES, Mr. Hywel Puleston, BA FCA CTA** *1985;* with KPMG LLP, 8 Princes Parade, LIVERPOOL, L3 1QH.
JONES, Mr. Ian, BSc ACA *1993;* 8 Oakley Rise, Wilstead, BEDFORD, MK45 3FD.
JONES, Mr. Ian, BA ACA *1986;* 23 Loughborough Road, Hoton, LOUGHBOROUGH, LEICESTERSHIRE, LE12 5SF.
•**JONES, Mr. Ian, MA FCA** *1985;* Ian Jones MA (Cantab) FCA, 17 Long Street, DEVIZES, WILTSHIRE, SN10 1NN.
JONES, Mr. Ian, BA ACA *2005;* 46 Churchfield Avenue, LONDON, N12 0NT.
JONES, Mr. Ian Andrew, FCA MBA *1975;* Homewood, Meadway, BERKHAMSTED, HERTFORDSHIRE, HP4 2PL.
JONES, Mr. Ian David, BA ACA *1989;* c/o Delmas (UK) Limited, 52 Charlotte Street, BIRMINGHAM, B3 1AR.
JONES, Mr. Ian Gary, BSc ACA *1990;* Avocet Hardware Ltd Brookfoot Industrial Estate, Brookfoot, BRIGHOUSE, WEST YORKSHIRE, HD6 2RW.
JONES, Mr. Ian George, ACA *1981;* 24 Gardeners Walk, Elmswell, BURY ST. EDMUNDS, SUFFOLK, IP30 9ET.
JONES, Mr. Ian Hugh, MA ACA *1992;* Lloyds International, Level 26, 45 Clarence Street, SYDNEY, NSW 2000, AUSTRALIA.
JONES, Mr. Ian Mark, BA ACA *1989;* with James Fisher & Son PLC, Fisher House, PO Box 4, BARROW-IN-FURNESS, CUMBRIA, LA14 1HR.
JONES, Mr. Ian Martin, BSc FCA *1978;* with Baker Tilly UK Audit LLP, 1210 Centre Park Square, WARRINGTON, CHESHIRE, WA1 1RU.
JONES, Mr. Ian Martin Lloyd, MA ACA *1987;* Hewlands House Farm, Rawden Hill, Arthington, OTLEY, WEST YORKSHIRE, LS21 1PS.
JONES, Mr. Ian Paul, ACA *2006;* Medreich Plc, 9 Royal Parade, RICHMOND, TW9 3QD.
JONES, Mr. Ian Peter, ACA *1988;* Patheon UK Ltd Patheon Building, Kingfisher Drive, SWINDON, SN3 5BZ.
JONES, Mr. Ian Philip, FCA *1981;* 11 Brading Close, HASTINGS, TN34 2HT.
JONES, Mr. Ian Philip, BSc ACA *2007;* 26 De Clare Drive, Radyr, CARDIFF, CF15 8FW.
JONES, Mr. Ian Stephen, BA ACA *1991;* 12 The Foxwood, Charnock Richard, CHORLEY, LANCASHIRE, PR7 5JQ.
•**JONES, Mr. Ian Wynne, BA ACA** *1993;* Cairn Business Solutions Limited, Ground Floor, 24 Hill Street, St. Helier, JERSEY, JE2 4UA.
JONES, Mr. Ieuan Arfon, BSc FCA *1986;* Steel Supply Co (Western) Ltd, 10 St James Crescent, Uplands, SWANSEA, SA1 6DZ.
JONES, Mr. Ivor Lloyd, FCA *1959;* 19 Central Avenue, BEVERLEY, HU17 8LL. (Life Member)
JONES, Mr. Iwan Gwynedd, PhD BSc ACA *2005;* 13 Glyn Teg, Upper Bryn Coch, MOLD, CLWYD, CH7 1XH.
JONES, Mr. Iwan John, BSc ACA *1993;* Firstplus Financial Group Plc The Avenue Industrial Park, Croescadarn Close, CARDIFF, CF23 8FF.
JONES, Mr. Iwan Lloyd, BSc ACA *2011;* 46 Judkin Court, Heol Tredwen, CARDIFF, CF10 5AU.
JONES, Ms. Jacqueline Ann, BA ACA *1983;* Ballathie, The Green, St Boswells, MELROSE, TD6 0ET.
JONES, Ms. Jacqueline Anne, BSc ACA *1989;* Clovelly, Greensward Lane, Arborfield, READING, RG2 9JN.
JONES, Mr. James Anthony, BA ACA *1991;* I P Access Ltd, 2020 Cambourne Business Park, Cambourne, CAMBRIDGE, CB23 6DW.
JONES, Mr. James Kenneth Rees, FCA *1954;* 17 Birch House Little Aston Hall Drive, Little Aston, SUTTON COLDFIELD, WEST MIDLANDS, B74 3BF. (Life Member)
JONES, Mr. James Peter Henry, BSc ACA *2010;* 40 Jacobs Court, 19 Plumbers Row, LONDON, E1 1AE.
JONES, Mr. James Richard, BA ACA *2003;* 19 Llewelyn Goch, St. Fagans, CARDIFF, CF5 6HR.
JONES, Mr. Jamieson Ronald, FCA *1987;* 45 Whitecotes Park, Walton, CHESTERFIELD, S40 3RT.
JONES, Mrs. Jane Louise Morgan, BSc ACA *1991;* Lancaster University Students Union, Slaidburn House Bailrigg, LANCASTER, LA1 4YA.
JONES, Mrs. Jane Margaret, FCA *1975;* Traviss & Co, Newtown House, Newtown Road, LIPHOOK, HAMPSHIRE, GU30 7DT.
JONES, Dr. Jane Marie, BSc(Hons) ACA *2002;* with PricewaterhouseCoopers LLP, Donington Court, Pegasus Business Park, Castle Donington, DERBY, DE74 2UZ.
•**JONES, Mrs. Janet, FCA** *1975;* 9 Radway Close, Church Hill, REDDITCH, B98 8RZ.
JONES, Mrs. Janet, BSc ACA *1992;* 3 Chapel Street, Warmington, PETERBOROUGH, PE8 6TR.
JONES, Mrs. Janet Susan, ACA *1985;* 18 Orchard Grove, Croyde, BRAUNTON, EX33 1NF.
JONES, Mr. Jason Sebastian, BSc ACA *1998;* 31 Rodway Road, BROMLEY, BR1 3JP.
JONES, Mr. Jeffrey Mark, MSc ACA *1984;* Corporate Assist Ltd, Otley House, 2 Arthurs Avenue, HARROGATE, NORTH YORKSHIRE, HG2 0DX.
JONES, Miss. Jemima Julie, ACA *2009;* 3 Chertsey House, Bridge Wharf, CHERTSEY, SURREY, KT16 8JD.
JONES, Mrs. Jennifer Anne, ACA *1989;* Plas Y Bryn, Penrallt, PWLLHELI, LL53 5UE.
•**JONES, Ms. Jennifer Elspeth, BA FCA** *1994;* Elspeth Consulting, 50 Denton Avenue, LEEDS, LS8 1LE.
•**JONES, Mrs. Jennifer Lyn, BSc ACA** *1994;* Jennifer Jones ACA, 2 Sandholes, Farnsfield, NEWARK, NOTTINGHAMSHIRE, NG22 8HQ.
JONES, Mrs. Jennifer Rose, ACA *2009;* 5 Andrews Close, Tarvin, CHESTER, CH3 8LN.
JONES, Mr. Jeremy, BSc ACA *2006;* 133 Athenlay Road, LONDON, SE15 3EJ.
JONES, Mrs. Jessica Mary, BSc ACA *2006;* Flat 2, 85 Lillie Road, LONDON, SW6 1UD.
•**JONES, Mrs. Jillian Margaret, BA FCA** *1987;* Baker Tilly Tax & Advisory Services LLP, Steam Mill, Steam Mill Street, CHESTER, CH3 5AN. See also Baker Tilly UK Audit LLP
JONES, Mrs. Joanna, BA(Hons) ACA *2009;* Woodcourt Pooks Green, Marchwood, SOUTHAMPTON, SO40 4WQ.
JONES, Mrs. Joanna, BSc ACA *1994;* 86 The Mount, SHREWSBURY, SY3 8PL.
JONES, Mrs. Joanna Claire, BA ACA *1996;* c/o Time Projects (Botswana) (PTY) Limited, PO Box 1395, GABORONE, BOTSWANA.
JONES, Mrs. Joanna Elizabeth, BSc ACA *1994;* with PricewaterhouseCoopers LLP, Cornwall Court, 19 Cornwall Street, BIRMINGHAM, B3 2DT.
JONES, Mrs. Joanna Lydia, BA ACA *1992;* (Tax Fac), 255 El Alamein Way, Bradwell, GREAT YARMOUTH, NORFOLK, NR31 8TX.
JONES, Mrs. Joanne Denise, BSc ACA *2007;* Bron Afon Community Housing William Brown Close, Llantarnam Industrial Park, CWMBRAN, GWENT, NP44 3AB.
JONES, Mrs. Joanne Jennifer, BSc ACA *1990;* Tyrrells Potato Crisps Ltd, Tyrrells Court, Stretford Bridge, LEOMINSTER, HEREFORDSHIRE, HR6 9DQ.
JONES, Mrs. Joanne Louise, ACA *1994;* 2 Fell Close, Saddington Grange, Fleckney, LEICESTER, LE8 8DG.
JONES, Mrs. Joanne Louise, BA(Hons) ACA *2009;* with Whittingham Riddell LLP, Belmont House, Shrewsbury Business Park, SHREWSBURY, SY2 6LG.
JONES, Mrs. Jocelyn Mary, FCA *1950;* Parsons Gift, Bettiscombe, BRIDPORT, DT6 5NT. (Life Member)
JONES, Mr. John Alan, MBA BEng ACA *1993;* The Willows, 2 Lightfoot Close, Heswall, WIRRAL, CH60 2TR.
JONES, Mr. John Alun Lewis, FCA *1974;* Kingswood, Parc Henry Lane, Bonllwyn, AMMANFORD, SA18 2EH.
JONES, Mr. John Bernard, MA FCA *1964;* J Bernard Jones, 40 Redwood Glade, LEIGHTON BUZZARD, BEDFORDSHIRE, LU7 3JT.
JONES, Mr. John Colin, FCA *1953;* 31 Clos Nant Y Cwm, CARDIFF, CF23 8LG. (Life Member)
JONES, Mr. John David, FCA *1963;* 74 Fairfield Crescent, LIVERPOOL, L6 8PJ.
•**JONES, Mr. John Duncan, MA ACA** *1987;* Knox Cropper, 8-9 Well Court, LONDON, EC4M 9DN.
JONES, Mr. John Francis, ACA *1993;* 191 Priests Lane, Shenfield, BRENTWOOD, ESSEX, CM15 8LF.
JONES, Mr. John Graham, BA FCA *1974;* Lowick House, 41 Creskeld Lane, Bramhope, LEEDS, LS16 9EP. (Life Member)
•**JONES, Mr. John Gregory, FCA** *1972;* John G. Jones, 8 Briars Close, COVENTRY, CV2 5JR.
JONES, Mr. John Humphrey, FCA *1950;* 9 Dalebrook Road, SALE, M33 3LD. (Life Member)
JONES, Mr. John Hywelfryn, BSc ACA *1991;* 18 Brian Avenue, Stockton Heath, WARRINGTON, WA4 2BG.
JONES, Mr. John Ivor, LLB FCA *1963;* 19 Hammonds Ridge, BURGESS HILL, RH15 9QW.
JONES, Mr. John Mark, BEng ACA *2008;* I M I Kynoch Plc Lakeside Unit 4040, Solihull Parkway Birmingham Business Park, BIRMINGHAM, B37 7XZ.
JONES, Mr. John Michael, BSc ACA FCT *1996;* Imperial Tobacco Group PLC, PO Box 244, Southville, BRISTOL, BS99 7UJ.
JONES, Mr. John Michael, FCA *1964;* 4 Stillions Close, Windmill Hill, ALTON, GU34 2RX.
JONES, Mr. John Morgan, FCA *1966;* Hines Farm, Earl Stonham, STOWMARKET, IP14 5HQ.
JONES, Mr. John Peter Morris, FCA *1965;* Esgairarth, Pennant, LLANON, SY23 5JL.
•**JONES, Mr. John Ralph, FCA** *1971;* John Jones, 30 Woodvale Avenue, Cyncoed, CARDIFF, CF23 6SQ.
•**JONES, Mr. John Richard, BA FCA CF** *1990;* Beever and Struthers, St George's House, 215-219 Chester Road, MANCHESTER, M15 4JE.
JONES, Mr. John Robert, BSc FCA *1979;* Stornoway, Harestone Hill, CATERHAM, CR3 6BG.
JONES, Mr. John Trevor, FCA *1958;* 45 Mellor Brow, Mellor, BLACKBURN, BB2 7EX. (Life Member)
JONES, Mr. John William, FCA *1974;* 12 Little Walton, Eastry, SANDWICH, CT13 0DW.
JONES, Mr. Johnathan, BSc ACA *2005;* 1 Castle Road, WELLINGBOROUGH, NORTHAMPTONSHIRE, NN8 1LL.
JONES, Mr. Jonathan, ACA *2008;* Flat 5, Talbot House, 10 Ladbroke Crescent, LONDON, W11 1PS.
JONES, Mr. Jonathan, ACA *2010;* 21a Clarendon Street, Pimlico, LONDON, SW1V 2EN.
JONES, Mr. Jonathan Berwyn, BA ACA *2006;* with Hill & Roberts, 50 High Street, MOLD, CH7 1BH.
JONES, Mr. Jonathan Peter, BSc ACA *1992;* Nemo Personal Finance, Trafalgar House, 5 Fitzalan Place, CARDIFF, CF24 0ED.
JONES, Mr. Jonathan Philip, BSc ACA *1999;* 34 Erkenbrechtstr, Neustadt/Weinstrasse, 67434 RHEINLAND PFAIZ, GERMANY.
JONES, Mr. Jonathan Robert, BCom ACA *1991;* 45 The Cloisters, South Gosforth, NEWCASTLE UPON TYNE, NE7 7LS.
•**JONES, Mr. Julian Edward, BEng ACA** *1995;* Alvarez & Marsal, 1 Finsbury Circus, LONDON, EC2M 7EB.
•**JONES, Mrs. Julie, BCom ACA** *1998;* 109 Wells Green Road, Olton, SOLIHULL, B92 7PQ.
JONES, Mrs. Julie, BA ACA *1982;* N M Rothschild & Sons Ltd, New Court, 19 St. Swithin's Lane, LONDON, EC4N 8AD.
JONES, Mr. Justin Charles, BSc ACA *1992;* 88 Ditton Road, SURBITON, SURREY, KT6 6RH.
JONES, Mrs. Justine Emma, BSc ACA *1995;* Bedlam Barn, 3 Bridgeford Hall Barns, Cherry Lane Great Bridgeford, STAFFORD, ST18 9SL.
JONES, Miss. Karen, BA ACA *1996;* 7 Eastfield Avenue, BASINGSTOKE, HAMPSHIRE, RG21 4BQ.
•**JONES, Mrs. Karen Amanda, BSc FCA** *1991;* with Lanham & Francis, Church House, Church Street, YEOVIL, BA20 1HB.
JONES, Mrs. Karen Ann, BA ACA *1991;* 94 rue du Joran, 01210 VERSONNEX, FRANCE.

JONES, Mrs. Karen Anne, BA ACA *1989;* Warren Partners Ltd, Warren House, Rudheath Way, Gadbrook Park, NORTHWICH, CHESHIRE CW9 7LT.
JONES, Mrs. Karen Jean, BSc ACA *1990;* 106 St Albans Avenue, Chiswick, LONDON, W4 5JR.
JONES, Ms. Karen Lynne, BSc ACA *1996;* 28 Springfield Road, Old Town, SWINDON, WILTSHIRE, SN1 4EP.
JONES, Mrs. Karen Michelle, BA ACA *1992;* Burwood, Hare Lane, Kingshill, GREAT MISSENDEN, HP16 0EF.
JONES, Mrs. Karen Ruby, BAcc ACA *2000;* 1 Lindisfarne Terrace, NORTH SHIELDS, TYNE AND WEAR, NE30 2DB.
JONES, Mrs. Karen Susan, BSc ACA *1996;* 17 Llwyn y Pia Road, Lisvane, CARDIFF, CF14 0SX.
JONES, Mrs. Katharine Alice, FCA *1972;* 32 Squirrel Chase, HEMEL HEMPSTEAD, HERTFORDSHIRE, HP1 2TL.
•**JONES, Miss. Katherine, ACA FCCA** *2009;* David Cutter & Co, 2 Lyttleton Court, Birmingham Street, HALESOWEN, WEST MIDLANDS, B63 3HN. See also Cutter & Co Limited
JONES, Miss. Katherine Anne, BSocSc ACA *2004;* 6 Cherrytree Close, Holmer Green, HIGH WYCOMBE, BUCKINGHAMSHIRE, HP15 6RP.
JONES, Miss. Katherine Elizabeth, BA ACA *1999;* Foxhollows, Bishton, NEWPORT, GWENT, NP18 2DZ.
JONES, Miss. Kathryn, BA ACA *1989;* Cysgod yr Efail, 8 Cavan Row, MAESTEG, CF34 0AN.
JONES, Miss. Kathryn, BSc ACA *2009;* 102 Stansfield Drive, Grappenhall, WARRINGTON, WA4 3EA.
JONES, Miss. Kathryn Ada, BSc ACA *1999;* 1st Floor, Cayzer House, 30 Buckingham Gate, LONDON, SW1E 6NN.
JONES, Miss. Kathryn Margaret, BA FCA *1984;* (Tax Fac), 3 Stainburn Terrace, LEEDS, LS17 6NJ.
JONES, Mr. Keith, BSc FCA *1975;* 34 Orchard Way, Acocks Green, BIRMINGHAM, B27 6QE.
JONES, Mr. Keith, FCA *1960;* 3 Laustan Close, GUILDFORD, GU1 2TS. (Life Member)
JONES, Mr. Keith, BA ACA *1984;* 40 Shrewsbury Road, REDHILL, RH1 6BH.
JONES, Mr. Keith Alfred, FCA *1974;* 5 Tilford Road, Lovedean, WATERLOOVILLE, PO8 9SX.
JONES, Mr. Keith Gareth Lloyd, BSc FCA *1970;* 7 The Boulevard, WORTHING, BN13 1JZ.
•**JONES, Mr. Keith James, FCA** *1976;* (Tax Fac), Keith Jones, 3 Tudor Grove, Church Crescent, LONDON, N20 0JW.
JONES, Mr. Keith Lewis, BSc ACA *1991;* Lower Castlebythe, Castlebythe, HAVERFORDWEST, DYFED, SA62 5DN.
JONES, Mr. Keith Martyn, BSc ACA *1983;* 8 Oak Tree Avenue, ScholesHolmfirth, HUDDERSFIELD, HD9 1SD.
JONES, Mr. Keith Morris, BSc ACA *1991;* 23 Victoria Grove, Heaton Chapel, STOCKPORT, CHESHIRE, SK4 5BU.
JONES, Mr. Keith Richard, BCom FCA *1991;* with HW Lee Associates LLP, New Derwent House, 69-73 Theobalds Road, LONDON, WC1X 8TA.
JONES, Mr. Keith Sydney, FCA *1962;* 14 Beanhay Close, Liverton, NEWTON ABBOT, DEVON, TQ12 6YY.
•**JONES, Mr. Keith Wilson, FCA** *1979;* Williams Ross Ltd, 4 Ynys Bridge Court, Gwaelod Y Garth, CARDIFF, CF15 9SS. See also Epiphany Business Solutions Limited
JONES, Mr. Kell, BA ACA *1995;* 69 Deanery Road, BRISTOL, BS1 5QH.
JONES, Mrs. Kelly Louise, BA ACA *2009;* 91 Ruby Street, BRISTOL, BS3 3DW.
•**JONES, Mr. Kenneth, FCA** *1982;* (Tax Fac), Burgess Hodgson, Camburgh House, 27 New Dover Road, CANTERBURY, CT1 3DN.
JONES, Mr. Kenneth Ankers, FCA *1960;* Eastwood, Canny Hill, Newby Bridge, ULVERSTON, CUMBRIA, LA12 8NT. (Life Member)
•**JONES, Mr. Kenneth David Alun, BSc ACA** *1989;* A.C.O.L. Business Matters Limited, 27 Heol-y-Bryn, Rhiwbina, CARDIFF, CF14 6HX.
•**JONES, Mr. Kenneth Edwin, FCA** *1973;* Kenneth Jones & Co Ltd, 8 Church Avenue, Clent, STOURBRIDGE, WEST MIDLANDS, DY9 9QT.
JONES, Mr. Kenneth Graham, BSc ACA *2006;* 2 Salisbury Close, WORCESTER, WR5 1QY.
JONES, Mr. Kenneth Maelor, FCA *1959;* White Thorns, East Street, Hambledon, WATERLOOVILLE, PO7 4SA. (Life Member)
JONES, Mr. Kenneth Richard, FCA *1963;* St.Kilda Hotel, Central Promenade, LLANDUDNO, Clwyd, LL30 2XS.
JONES, Mr. Kenneth Watts, FCA *1953;* 25 Kirkland Avenue, Clayhall, ILFORD, IG5 0TH. (Life Member)
•**JONES, Mr. Keri Cosslett, FCA** *1969;* Ellis Lloyd Jones LLP, Alan House, 2 Risca Road, NEWPORT, GWENT, NP20 4JW.
JONES, Mrs. Kerry Melissa, BSc ACA *2008;* 11 Eyam Close, Bramcote, NOTTINGHAM, NG9 3GQ.
JONES, Mr. Kevin Bryan, BSc ACA *1987;* 1 Pen y Coed, DOLGELLAU, GWYNEDD, LL40 2YP.
JONES, Mr. Kevin David, BA FCA CTA *1993;* 16 Milton Street, IPSWICH, IP4 4PP.
JONES, Mr. Kevin Gareth Brown, BA ACA *1989;* 67 Ellis Road, CROWTHORNE, RG45 6PP.
•**JONES, Mr. Kevin Leslie, ACA ATT MAAT** *1996;* Cqs (Gobal Services) Ltd, 2 Hill Street St. Helier, JERSEY, JE2 4UA.
JONES, Mr. Kevin Patrick, BA ACA CISA *1995;* One Hanson Place #24B, BROOKLYN, NY 11243, UNITED STATES.
JONES, The Revd. Kevin Philip, BSc ACA *1988;* 108 The Keep, KINGSTON UPON THAMES, SURREY, KT2 5UD.
•**JONES, Mr. Kim Beachcroft, MA FCA** *1972;* (Tax Fac), K.B. Jones, 6 Strathmore Close, Holmes Chapel, CREWE, CW4 7PP.
JONES, Mrs. Kirsten Louise, MA ACA *1986;* Gowanbank, 3 Botham Hall Road, HUDDERSFIELD, HD3 4RJ.
JONES, Mrs. Laura, BSc ACA *2002;* 5 Cefn Bychan, Pentyrch, CARDIFF, CF15 9PG.
JONES, Mr. Laurence Jonathan, BSc ACA *1987;* Leicester Grange Cottage, Wolvey Road, HINCKLEY, LEICESTERSHIRE, LE10 3JB.
•**JONES, Mr. Lawrence Barry, FCA** *1969;* 43 Broadlands Drive, MALVERN, WORCESTERSHIRE, WR14 1PW.
JONES, Mr. Leonard Edward, BA FCA *1982;* Wardle Bank, Calveley Hall Lane, Wardle, NANTWICH, CHESHIRE, CW5 6BS.
JONES, Mrs. Lesley Ann, BSc ACA *1993;* 24 Belland Drive, Charlton Kings, CHELTENHAM, GLOUCESTERSHIRE, GL53 9HU.
JONES, Miss. Lesley-Anne, BSc ACA CTA *1995;* (Tax Fac), with Crowe Clark Whitehill LLP, Arkwright House, Parsonage Gardens, MANCHESTER, M3 2HP.
JONES, Mr. Leslie David, FCA *1968;* 19 Links Avenue, FELIXSTOWE, IP11 9HD.
JONES, Mrs. Lisa Jane, BSc(Hons) ACA *2001;* 3 Churchlea, Old Rhosrobin, Rhosrobin, WREXHAM, CLWYD, LL11 4RB.
JONES, Mrs. Louise, BSc ACA *1999;* Stourbridge College, Hagley Road, STOURBRIDGE, WEST MIDLANDS, DY8 1QU.
JONES, Miss. Louise Claire, BSc ACA *2001;* 64 Gloucester Gardens, LONDON, W2 6BN.
JONES, Mrs. Louise Sarah, BA ACA *2004;* 8 The Drive, Roundhay, LEEDS, LS8 1JF.
JONES, Mrs. Lucy Caroline, BA ACA *1983;* 20 Brunswick Road, KINGSTON-UPON-THAMES, KT2 6SA.
JONES, Mrs. Lucy Clare, BA ACA *2007;* 11 Emlyn Buildings, Brocas Street, Eton, WINDSOR, BERKSHIRE, SL4 6BP.
•**JONES, Mrs. Lucy Jo, ACA** *2003;* Lucy Jones, First Floor, Pier House, Pier Road, Hobbs Point, PEMBROKE DOCK DYFED SA72 6TR. See also Lucy Jones Ltd
JONES, Mr. Luke Daniel, BSc(Hons) ACA *2003;* Mezzanine Management UK Ltd Grand Buildings, 1-3 Strand, LONDON, WC2N 5HR.
JONES, Mr. Luke Evan, BA ACA *2000;* C/O Halo Asia Limited, 17 Gough Street, CENTRAL, HONG KONG ISLAND, HONG KONG SAR.
JONES, Mr. Luke Wayne, ACA *2006;* Grant Thornton Hartwell House, 55-61 Victoria Street, BRISTOL, BS1 6FT.
•**JONES, Mr. Lyndon Hughes, BSc ACA** *1987;* (Tax Fac), Barlow Mendham & Co, Glandover House, 67 Bute Street, ABERDARE, SOUTH GLAMORGAN, CF44 7LD.
JONES, Mrs. Lynn, BSc ACA CTA *1987;* The Paddocks, Silverbirches Lane, Aspley Heath, MILTON KEYNES, MK17 8TL.
•**JONES, Mrs. Lynn Ann, FCA** *1977;* (Tax Fac), L J Accountancy, 7 Newman Lane, Drayton, ABINGDON, OXFORDSHIRE, OX14 4LP.
JONES, Mrs. Lynne Kathryn, BA ACA *1991;* 28 Malting Lane, Aldbury, TRING, HERTFORDSHIRE, HP23 5RH.
JONES, Ms. Lynsey Ann, BA ACA *2001;* 12 Sandale Close, Gamston, NOTTINGHAM, NG2 6QG.
JONES, Mr. Malcolm David, FCA *1967;* 93 Rigby Drive, WIRRAL, MERSEYSIDE, CH49 1RE.
JONES, Mr. Malcolm Edward Garnsey, FCA *1958;* 7 Ashdale Grove, STANMORE, HA7 3SB. (Life Member)
•**JONES, Mr. Malcolm Philip, FCA** *1977;* (Tax Fac), Malcolm Jones & Co LLP, West Hill House, Allerton Hill, Chapel Allerton, LEEDS, LS7 3QB.
JONES, Mr. Malcolm Vaughan, BEng ACA *1991;* 1 Albany Close, REIGATE, SURREY, RH2 9PP.
JONES, Miss. Mandy, ACA *2007;* Beech Road, ARKLOW, COUNTY WICKLOW, IRELAND.
JONES, Mr. Marc Jonathan Oliver, ACA *2008;* with Deloitte LLP, Athene Place, 66 Shoe Lane, LONDON, EC4A 3BQ.
•**JONES, Mrs. Margaret Elizabeth, BSc FCA** *1978;* Gerald Thomas & Co, Furze Bank, 34 Hanover Street, SWANSEA, SA1 6BA.
•**JONES, Mrs. Margaret Helen, FCA** *1976;* Magnes Accountants, 52 Fruitlands, MALVERN, WR14 4XA.
JONES, Mrs. Margaret Julia, BSc FCA *1988;* Hillbrow, Winters Hill, Durley, SOUTHAMPTON, SO32 2AH.
JONES, Mrs. Margaret Lynne, MA ACA *1995;* 278 Rainbow Street, COOGEE, NSW 2034, AUSTRALIA.
JONES, Miss. Marianne Rosalind, BA ACA *1989;* Telesis Eagle Ltd, Dolphin Street, COLYTON, DEVON, EX24 6LU.
•**JONES, Mr. Mark, FCA** *1983;* Cook & Partners Limited, Manufactory House, Bell Lane, HERTFORD, SG14 1BP. See also Cook & Partners
JONES, Mr. Mark, MBA BA CA FCA CPA *1988;* 281 Union Road, BALWYN, VIC 3103, AUSTRALIA.
JONES, Mr. Mark Adrian, M.Ed BSc FCA *1988;* 35 The Verlands, COWBRIDGE, SOUTH GLAMORGAN, CF71 7BY.
•**JONES, Mr. Mark Anthony, BSc ACA** *1996;* Jones Kinsey Limited, 86 The Mount, SHREWSBURY, SY3 8PL.
JONES, Mr. Mark Anthony, BSc ACA *1990;* Redhill House, Hazeley Heath, HOOK, HAMPSHIRE, RG27 8NA.
JONES, Mr. Mark Christopher, BSc ACA *2008;* with Clay Shaw Butler Ltd, 24 Lammas Street, CARMARTHEN, DYFED, SA31 3AL.
JONES, Mr. Mark David, MEng ACA *1999;* Jardine Lloyd Thompson PLC, Jardine House, 6 Crutched Friars, LONDON, EC3N 2PH.
JONES, Mr. Mark Duncan Mitchell, MA ACA *1989;* Armstrong Richardson & Co Ltd 1 Mount Pleasant Way, Stokesley Business Park Stokesley, MIDDLESBROUGH, CLEVELAND, TS9 5NZ.
JONES, Mr. Mark Francis, BSc ACA *2003;* 50 Fort Austin Avenue, PLYMOUTH, PL6 5JW.
•**JONES, Mr. Mark Francis, FCA** *1974;* (Tax Fac), Ernst & Young LLP, 100 Barbirolli Square, MANCHESTER, M2 3EY. See also Ernst & Young Europe LLP
•**JONES, Mr. Mark Gordon, FCA** *1979;* Broomfield & Alexander Limited, Ty Derw, Lime Tree Court, Cardiff Gate Business Park, CARDIFF, CF23 8AB. See also B & A Associates
JONES, Mr. Mark Greville, ACA *1985;* 6 Woodfalls Manor, Bucks Green, Rudgwick, HORSHAM, RH12 3DW.
JONES, Mr. Mark Ian, BSc ACA *1992;* Hatherleigh, Tite Hill, Englefield Green, EGHAM, SURREY, TW20 0NH.
•**JONES, Mr. Mark Peter, BA FCA MIPA** *1992;* Mark Jones & Co, 9a Southside Common, LONDON, SW19 4TL.
JONES, Mr. Mark Robert, BA ACA *2000;* 4855 PROSPECT STREET, BOW MAR, LITTLETON, CO 80123-2768, UNITED STATES.
JONES, Mr. Mark Roger, BA ACA *1990;* Crest Nicholson Plc Crest House, Pyrcroft Road, CHERTSEY, SURREY, KT16 9GN.
•**JONES, Mr. Mark Terence, BSc FCA** *1993;* Oakwoods Accountancy Limited, 8 Morston Court, Kingswood Lakeside, CANNOCK, STAFFORDSHIRE, WS11 8JB.
JONES, Mr. Mark Trevennan, BA ACA *1993;* Parker Hannifin Europe SARL, La Tuilière 6, 1163 ETOY, VAUD, SWITZERLAND.
JONES, Mr. Martin, FCA *1970;* 40 Branksome Road, NORWICH, NR4 6SW.
JONES, Mr. Martin Arthur Llewelyn, BSc ACA *1991;* Guildford College, Stoke Park Campus, GUILDFORD, SURREY, GU1 1EZ.
•**JONES, Mr. Martin Christopher, FCA** *1970;* 3 Sawyers Crescent, Copmanthorpe, YORK, YO23 3YA.
JONES, Mr. Martin Hayland, BSc ACA *1987;* JEMMETTS, 4 Oxford Road, THAME, OXFORDSHIRE, OX9 2AH.
•**JONES, Mr. Martin Hugh, ACA** *1980;* M.H. Jones & Co, Stuart House, Valepits Road, Garretts Green, BIRMINGHAM, B33 0TD.
•**JONES, Mr. Martin Lee, BA ACA** *1988;* Wingrave Yeats Partnership LLP, 101 Wigmore Street, LONDON, W1U 1QU. See also Wingrave Yeats Limited
JONES, Mr. Martin Lloyd, BSc FCA *1979;* Jakmart Ltd, The Old Cottage, Shepperton Road, STAINES, MIDDLESEX, TW18 1SE.
•**JONES, Mr. Martin Neil, BA FCA** *1989;* (Tax Fac), Kingly Brookes LLP, 415 Linen Hall, 162-168 Regent Street, LONDON, W1B 5TE. See also Kingly Brookes
•**JONES, Mr. Martin Oliver, FCA** *1973;* Martin Jones, 10 Seggs Lane, ALCESTER, B49 5HJ.
JONES, Mr. Martin Philip, BA ACA *1999;* Hudson's Bay Co, 11th Floor 401 Bay Street, TORONTO M5H 2Y4, ON, CANADA.
•**JONES, Mr. Martin Philip Henry, FCA** *1977;* (Tax Fac), Wallace Crooke & Co, College House, St. Leonards Close, BRIDGNORTH, SHROPSHIRE, WV16 4EJ. See also Wallace Crooke
JONES, Mr. Martin William, BA(Hons) ACA *2001;* Capital International Ltd, Capital House, Circular Road, Douglas, ISLE OF MAN, IM1 1AG.
•**JONES, Mr. Martin Wyndham, FCA** *1975;* 10 Regency House Flats, Regent Road, St. Helier, JERSEY, JE2 4UZ.
•**JONES, Mr. Martyn Eynon, BSc FCA FRSA** *1976;* VICE-PRESIDENT MEMBER OF COUNCIL, Deloitte LLP, 2 New Street Square, LONDON, EC4A 3BZ. See also Deloitte & Touche LLP
JONES, Mr. Matthew, ACA *2008;* Flat 3 Warren House Court, 17 St. Peters Avenue Caversham, READING, RG4 7RG.
JONES, Mr. Matthew, BA ACA *2009;* 4 Scholars Lane, STRATFORD-UPON-AVON, CV37 6HE.
JONES, Mr. Matthew Anthony, BA(Hons) ACA *2001;* c/o Prophecy L31 Six Battery Road, SINGAPORE 049909, SINGAPORE.
JONES, Mr. Matthew Brian, BA ACA *1996;* 168 Niemietz Cove, CIBOLO, TX 78108, UNITED STATES.
•**JONES, Mr. Matthew Cook, FCA** *1975;* (Tax Fac), Jones Boyd, 103 Station Road, ASHINGTON, NORTHUMBERLAND, NE63 8RS.
JONES, Mr. Matthew Leonard, BA ACA *1997;* Wood Cottage, 30 Green Lane, COBHAM, SURREY, KT11 2NN.
JONES, Mr. Matthew Neville, BA ACA *1996;* with Deloitte LLP, Abbots House, Abbey Street, READING, RG1 3BD.
JONES, Mr. Matthew Thomas, ACA *1998;* Bryn Villa, Hall Street, Penycae, WREXHAM, CLWYD, LL14 2RT.
JONES, Mr. Matthew Thomas, BA(Econ) ACA *1999;* 19, Broom Road, TEDDINGTON, MIDDLESEX, TW11 9PG.
JONES, Miss. Mayrid Laura, MSc BSc ACA *2007;* 49 Bangor Street, CARDIFF, CF24 3LQ.
•**JONES, Miss. Megan Andrea, FCA** *1995;* Morris Cook, 3-5 Watergate Street, ELLESMERE, SHROPSHIRE, SY12 0EX.
JONES, Mr. Meirion Richard, BA ACA *1994;* 22 Kendal Meadow, Chestfield, WHITSTABLE, KENT, CT5 3PZ.
JONES, Miss. Melanie Jane, BSc ACA *1992;* 13 Aspen Walk, RHYL, LL18 4GH.
JONES, Mr. Melvyn Rees, ACA *1980;* 7 Ffrwd-Y-Felin, Aberlash Road, Bonllwyn, AMMANFORD, SA18 3NP.
JONES, Mr. Michael, BEng ACA *1992;* The Hermitage Coach House, 32 Fishpond Drive, The Park, NOTTINGHAM, NG7 1DG.
JONES, Mr. Michael, BA ACA *1998;* DJ Property, 114 Wyke Road, WEYMOUTH, DT4 9QP.
•**JONES, Mr. Michael, FCA** *1978;* (Tax Fac), Jones Hunt & Company, Ickleford Manor, Turnpike Lane, Ickleford, HITCHIN, SG5 3XE.
•**JONES, Mr. Michael, BA FCA** *1968;* Michael Jones, St Bernards, 28 The Ridgeway, Rothley, LEICESTER, LE7 7LE.
JONES, Mr. Michael Adrian, BSc ACA *1987;* Minos, 3 Shaftesbury Drove, West Harnham, SALISBURY, SP2 8QH.
•**JONES, Mr. Michael Andrew, BSc ACA** *1998;* ASE Group Ltd, Rowan Court, Concord Business Park Threapwood Road, MANCHESTER, M22 0RR. See also ASE Audit LLP
•**JONES, Mr. Michael Anthony, FCA** *1970;* (Tax Fac), Naunton, 4 Park Road, PENARTH, SOUTH GLAMORGAN, CF64 3BD.
JONES, Mr. Michael Anthony, BSc FCA *1977;* 4 Kingsway, STOCKPORT, SK7 3BG.
JONES, Mr. Michael Anthony, FCA *1969;* 2 April Gardens, Lavant, CHICHESTER, WEST SUSSEX, PO18 0FD.
•**JONES, Mr. Michael David, FCA** *1971;* M D Jones, 96 Skip Lane, WALSALL, WS5 3LR.
•**JONES, Mr. Michael Denis, ACA** *1985;* Michael D. Jones, Chelwood, Carrhouse Road, Belton, DONCASTER, DN9 1PG.
JONES, Mr. Michael Desmond, FCA *1981;* The Hawthorns, 286 Bristol Road, Quedgeley, GLOUCESTER, GL2 4QW.
JONES, Mr. Michael Elfyn, BCom FCA *1964;* 6 Stray Walk, HARROGATE, HG2 8HU.

JONES, Mr. Michael Frank, FCA *1962;* 4 The Elms, Maidenhead Road, STRATFORD-UPON-AVON, CV37 6YB.
JONES, Mr. Michael George, FCA *1964;* 15 Brockenhurst Close, WOKING, GU21 4DS.
JONES, Mr. Michael Howlett, MSc BSc FCA *1974;* with thewealthworks Limited, The Flour Mill, High Beeches Lane, Handcross, HAYWARDS HEATH, WEST SUSSEX RH17 6HQ.
•**JONES, Mr. Michael James Morgan, BSc FCA** *1981;* Murray Smith LLP, Darland House, 44 Winnington Hill, NORTHWICH, CHESHIRE, CW8 1AU.
JONES, Mr. Michael John, BSc FCA *1975;* 9 Norman Avenue, TWICKENHAM, TW1 2LY.
JONES, Mr. Michael John, BA FCA *1980;* 1 Belle Vue Terrace, PENARTH, SOUTH GLAMORGAN, CF64 1DB.
JONES, Mr. Michael Laurence, BSc ACA *1996;* 31 Broad Lane, HAMPTON, TW12 3AL.
•**JONES, Mr. Michael Nicholas, BA ACA** *1997;* PricewaterhouseCoopers LLP, First Point, Buckingham Gate, London Gatwick Airport, GATWICK, WEST SUSSEX RH6 0NT. See also PricewaterhouseCoopers
•**JONES, Mr. Michael Peter, FCA** *1986;* Easterbrook Eaton Limited, 8 Jesu Street, OTTERY ST. MARY, DEVON, EX11 1EU.
JONES, Mr. Michael Purcell, FCA *1970;* 57 Allt-Yr-Yn Close, NEWPORT, NP20 5EE.
JONES, Mr. Michael Sonny, BSc FCA MBCS *1995;* 3 The Crescent, Daracombe Park Mile End Road, NEWTON ABBOT, DEVON, TQ12 1RW.
JONES, Mr. Michael Thomas George, BA ACA *1991;* with Saffery Champness, Stuart House, City Road, PETERBOROUGH, PE1 1QF.
JONES, Mr. Michael William, BSc FCA *1996;* 2 Willowdene Court, Warley, BRENTWOOD, ESSEX, CM14 5ET.
•**JONES, Mr. Michael William, BSc ACA** *1989;* Deloitte LLP, 4 Brindley Place, BIRMINGHAM, B1 2HZ. See also Deloitte & Touche LLP
JONES, Mrs. Michelle Jayne, ACA *2008;* 4 Hanover Street Mossley, ASHTON-UNDER-LYNE, LANCASHIRE, OL5 0HJ.
JONES, Mr. Morris David, BA FCA *1987;* Rosemount, Wicken Road, Leckhampstead, BUCKINGHAM, MK18 5NZ.
JONES, Ms. Natalie, BA(Hons) ACA *2004;* Flat 41, 20 Palmers Road, LONDON, E2 0SZ.
JONES, Miss. Natalie Claire, BSc ACA *2010;* 5 Blackacre Road, Theydon Bois, EPPING, CM16 7LT.
JONES, Mrs. Natalie Louise, BA ACA *2007;* 59 Mill Lane, Stockton Heath, WARRINGTON, WA4 2DE.
•**JONES, Mrs. Natasha Jane, BSc ACA** *2000;* with PricewaterhouseCoopers LLP, Savannah House, 3 Ocean Way, Ocean Village, SOUTHAMPTON, SO14 3TJ.
•①**JONES, Mr. Nathan Malet, BA FCA** *1998;* with FRP Advisory, Castle Acres, Everard Way, Narborough, LEICESTER, LEICESTERSHIRE LE19 BY.
JONES, Mr. Neil, ACA MAAT *2004;* 30 Shelfield Close, Hockley Heath, SOLIHULL, B94 6NG.
JONES, Mr. Neil Andrew, BEng ACA *1992;* 33 Woodlands Park, GUILDFORD, GU1 2TJ.
JONES, Mr. Neil Booth, FCA *1964;* P.O.Box 24536, Karen 00502, NAIROBI, KENYA.
JONES, Mr. Neil Gareth, BA ACA *2002;* 2 Finsbury Road, LUTON, LU4 9AH.
JONES, Mr. Neil Garth, BA ACA *1991;* 28 Malting Lane, Aldbury, TRING, HERTFORDSHIRE, HP23 5RH.
•**JONES, Mr. Neil Gregory, BSc FCA** *1994;* Deloitte LLP, 4 Brindley Place, BIRMINGHAM, B1 2HZ. See also Deloitte & Touche LLP
JONES, Mr. Neil Grenville, BSc ACA *1987;* Equitrek Ltd Bent Ley Mill, Bent Ley Road Meltham, HOLMFIRTH, HD9 4AP.
JONES, Mr. Neil Matthew, MA LLM ACA *2002;* 23 Compton Avenue, Gidea Park, ROMFORD, RM2 6ET.
•**JONES, Mr. Neil Richard, FCA** *1990;* Meyer Williams, Queen Alexandra House, 2 Bluecoats Avenue, HERTFORD, HERTFORDSHIRE, SG14 1PB.
JONES, Mr. Neil Robert, BSc ACA *1998;* 9 Goosehill Court, Balby, DONCASTER, SOUTH YORKSHIRE, DN4 8SX.
JONES, Mr. Neil Steven, BSc FCA *1992;* Astex Therapeutics Ltd, 436 Cambridge Science Park, Milton Road, CAMBRIDGE, CB4 0QA.
JONES, Mr. Niall Edward, BA ACA *2011;* 40 St. Margarets, London Road, GUILDFORD, GU1 1TL.
JONES, Mr. Nicholas, BSc(Hons) ACA *2011;* Flat B, 62 Cavendish Road, LONDON, NW6 7XP.
JONES, Mr. Nicholas Darren, BA FCA *1992;* Brownhills, Leebotwood, CHURCH STRETTON, SY6 6LU.
JONES, Mr. Nicholas David, BSc ACA *1989;* 94 Vaughan Williams Way, Warley, BRENTWOOD, CM14 5WT.
JONES, Mr. Nicholas Donne, BSc(Hons) ACA *2009;* 5 Rhee Spring, BALDOCK, HERTFORDSHIRE, SG7 6TD.
JONES, Mr. Nicholas Humphrey, FCA *1972;* Society of Operations Engineers, 22 Greencoat Place, LONDON, SW1P 1PR.
JONES, Mr. Nicholas Lee, BA ACA *2003;* 15 Tetney Road, Ranmoor, SHEFFIELD, S10 3GZ.
JONES, Mr. Nicholas Owen, BSc ACA *2002;* Dover Harbour Board, Harbour House, Marine Parade, DOVER, KENT, CT17 9BU.
JONES, Mr. Nicholas Paul, BSc ACA *1983;* 9 Orchard Springs, Newmarket Road, Nailsworth, STROUD, GL6 0FB.
•**JONES, Mr. Nicholas Robert, BA ACA** *1982;* Trelawnes, 7 Uplands Road, KENLEY, CR8 5EE.
JONES, Mr. Nicholas Roger John, BSc ACA *2009;* with PricewaterhouseCoopers, Darling Park Tower 2, 201 Sussex Street, GPO Box 2650, SYDNEY, NSW 1171 AUSTRALIA.
JONES, Mr. Nicholas Stuart, BA ACA *2010;* 52 Lydiard Way, TROWBRIDGE, WILTSHIRE, BA14 0UJ.
JONES, Mr. Nicholas Thomas, BA(Hons) ACA *2001;* Wates Group, Wates House, Station Approach, LEATHERHEAD, SURREY, KT22 7SW.
JONES, Mr. Nicholas Vaughan, BSc ACA *2000;* Aesica Pharmaceuticals Ltd, Balliol Business Park East, Benton Lane, NEWCASTLE UPON TYNE, NE12 8BS.
JONES, Mr. Nicholas William, FCA *1970;* Higham House, 19 Higham Road, WOODFORD GREEN, IG8 9JN.
JONES, Miss. Nicola, BA ACA *2007;* 21 Padstow Close, MANSFIELD, NOTTINGHAMSHIRE, NG18 4QY.
•**JONES, Mrs. Nicola, BSc ACA** *2002;* Nicola Jones, 30 Tamar Close, Whitefield, MANCHESTER, M45 8SJ.
JONES, Miss. Nicola Gail, BA ACA *2008;* Longstraw Barn, 10 Ickham Court Farm, The Street Ickham, CANTERBURY, CT3 1QQ.
JONES, Mrs. Nicola Jane, BA ACA *1997;* 69 Deanery Road, BRISTOL, BS1 5QH.
JONES, Mrs. Nicola Janet, BA ACA *1984;* 6 London Road, BUCKINGHAM, MK18 1AS.
JONES, Miss. Nicola Suzanne, BSc ACA *1997;* 31 Manor Court, High Street Southgate, LONDON, N14 6NG.
JONES, Mr. Nigel, BSc ACA *1985;* Nationwide Bldg Soc, Nationwide House, Pipers Way, SWINDON, SN3 1TA.
•**JONES, Mr. Nigel, FCA** *1982;* Jones & Co of York Limited, Prospect House, 148 Lawrence Street, YORK, YO10 3EB.
•**JONES, Mr. Nigel Glanville Ollerton, ACA** *1983;* Ernst & Young LLP, 1 More London Place, LONDON, SE1 2AF. See also Ernst & Young Europe LLP
JONES, Mr. Nigel Lawrence, FCA *1973;* Renaissance Habitat Ltd, 116 Bartholomew Street, NEWBURY, BERKSHIRE, RG14 5DT.
JONES, Mr. Nigel Layton, BSc ACA *1995;* 21 Bylanes Close, Cuckfield, HAYWARDS HEATH, WEST SUSSEX, RH17 5HB.
JONES, Mr. Nigel Peter, BA ACA *1990;* 4 Hollies Avenue, CANNOCK, WS11 1DW.
JONES, Mr. Nigel Philip, MA ACA *1991;* International Power plc Senator House, 85 Queen Victoria Street, LONDON, EC4V 4DP.
JONES, Mr. Nigel Richard, BA FCA *1983;* PO Box 64605, CY-8077 PAPHOS, CYPRUS.
JONES, Mrs. Nooshin, BEng ACA *1992;* 47 Thorney Hedge Road, LONDON, W4.
JONES, Mr. Norman, FCA *1954;* 18 Pownall Avenue, Bramhall, STOCKPORT, SK7 2HE. (Life Member)
•**JONES, Mr. Norman Glyn, FCA** *1977;* (Tax Fac), Forty-Two Consulting LLP, Percivals Barn, Fairfield Farm, Upper Weald, MILTON KEYNES, MK19 6EL. See also Silverstone Audit Limited
JONES, Mr. Oliver John Tudor, BA ACA *2002;* Rectory Close Church Lane, Arborfield, READING, RG2 9HZ.
JONES, Mr. Omodele Robert Nicholas, MSc BA FCA(SL) ACA ACMI *1991;* PO Box 3099, Serrekunda Post Office, SERREKUNDA, KSMD, GAMBIA.
•**JONES, Mrs. Patricia Ann, FCA** *1967;* Patricia A Jones, 316 Bristol Road, Edgbaston, BIRMINGHAM, B5 7SN.
JONES, Ms. Patricia Anne, MA ACA *1983;* The Cedars, Miller Place, GERRARDS CROSS, SL9 7QQ.
•**JONES, Mr. Patrick Alan, FCA** *1968;* (Tax Fac), C Wiltshire & Co Stratford Limited, 17 Greenhill Street, STRATFORD-UPON-AVON, WARWICKSHIRE, CV37 6LF.
•**JONES, Mr. Paul, BA ACA CF** *1995;* Clearwater Corporate Finance LLP, 7th Floor, Chancery Place, 50 Brown Street, MANCHESTER, M2 2JT.
JONES, Mr. Paul David, BA ACA *2006;* with Deloitte LLP, Athene Place, 66 Shoe Lane, LONDON, EC4A 3BQ.
JONES, Mr. Paul Ian, FCA *1969;* 53 Mimosa Avenue, Merley, WIMBORNE, BH21 1TU. (Life Member)
JONES, Mr. Paul James, BSc ACA *1989;* 11 Bridgewater Drive, Wombourne, WOLVERHAMPTON, WV5 8EN.
•**JONES, Mr. Paul Oliver Hadley, BA FCA** *1979;* J W Hinks, 19 Highfield Road, Edgbaston, BIRMINGHAM, B15 3BH.
JONES, Mr. Paul Robert, BSc ACA *1999;* 52 Sherifoot Lane, SUTTON COLDFIELD, B75 5DT.
JONES, Mr. Paul Robin Huson, BA ACA *1992;* 89 Shepherds Leaze, WOTTON-UNDER-EDGE, GLOUCESTERSHIRE, GL12 7LJ.
JONES, Mrs. Pauline, BSc FCA *1980;* 42 Coronation Road West, #03-04 Astrid Meadows, SINGAPORE 269259, SINGAPORE.
JONES, Mrs. Penelope Julia, BA FCA AMCT *1995;* 3 The Crescent, Daracombe Park, Mile End Road, Highweek, NEWTON ABBOT, DEVON TQ12 1RW.
JONES, Mrs. Penelope Sarah Ann, PhD MA ACA *1989;* Department for Education, Mowden Hall, Staindrop Road, DARLINGTON, DL3 9BG.
JONES, Mr. Peter, BA ACA *1988;* 33 Sims Close, ROMFORD, RM1 3QT.
JONES, Mr. Peter, FCA *1974;* 21 Crowe Lane, Freshford, BATH, BA2 7WB.
•**JONES, Mr. Peter Bernard, FCA** *1975;* 22 Browns Coppice Avenue, SOLIHULL, B91 1PL.
JONES, Mr. Peter Brandon, FCA *1978;* P.O Box 130, SAN PEDRO, BELIZE.
JONES, Mr. Peter Brian, BSc ACA *1993;* 9 Kinloch Drive, Earls Keep, DUDLEY, WEST MIDLANDS, DY1 3DB.
•**JONES, Mr. Peter Charles, BA FCA** *1982;* Cromack & Co, 29 High Street, Morley, LEEDS, LS27 9AL.
JONES, Mr. Peter Duniam, BCom FCA *1955;* 4 Blue Bridge Road, Brookmans Park, HATFIELD, AL9 7SB. (Life Member)
JONES, Mr. Peter Griffith, BA ACA *1995;* 20 Jarvis Fields, Bursledon, SOUTHAMPTON, HAMPSHIRE, SO31 8AF.
JONES, Mr. Peter John, FCA *1973;* c/o Moss & Williamson, 32 Booth Street, ASHTON-UNDER-LYNE, LANCASHIRE, OL6 7LQ.
JONES, Mr. Peter Kingsley, BA ACA *1990;* 3 Chapel Street, Warmington, PETERBOROUGH, PE8 6TR.
JONES, Mr. Peter Norman, BSc FCA *1981;* (Tax Fac), 91 Augustus Road, Edgbaston, BIRMINGHAM, B15 3LT.
JONES, Mr. Peter Richard, ACA *1983;* 28 Sir Christopher Court, Hythe, SOUTHAMPTON, SO45 6JR.
JONES, Mr. Peter Richard, FCA *1972;* with Thomas Westcott, Queens House, New Street, HONITON, DEVON, EX14 1BJ.
JONES, Mr. Peter Stuart, FCA *1960;* 40 Woolacombe Road, Childwall, LIVERPOOL, L16 9JQ. (Life Member)
JONES, Mr. Peter William Lewis, FCA *1972;* 3 Millfield Park, Undy, CALDICOT, GWENT, NP26 3LF.
JONES, Mr. Peter Wingfield, FCA *1961;* 27 Beeston Fields Drive, Beeston, NOTTINGHAM, NG9 3DB.
JONES, Mr. Philip, BA ACA *1990;* T Jolly Services Ltd, 2 Wyder Court, Millenium City Park, Bluebell Way, Ribbleton, PRESTON PR2 5BW.
JONES, Mr. Philip Arthur, BA ACA *1983;* 33 Brook Road South, BRENTFORD, MIDDLESEX, TW8 0NN.
•**JONES, Mr. Philip David, ACA ATII** *1987;* Orchard House, Walton, BRAMPTON, CUMBRIA, CA8 2DJ.
JONES, Mr. Philip Hugh, FCA *1976;* Three Ways, Kemberton, SHIFNAL, SHROPSHIRE, TF11 9LH.
JONES, Mr. Philip Ian, FCA *1976;* 6 Hunters Park, BERKHAMSTED, HP4 2PT.
JONES, Mr. Philip Justin, MA ACA *1985;* N C I Systems, 2 Rydens Road, WALTON-ON-THAMES, SURREY, KT12 3BS.
JONES, Mr. Philip Laurence, BSc(Econ) FCA *1979;* Park House, 11 Cardigan Road, Henleaze, BRISTOL, BS9 4DY.
•**JONES, Mr. Philip Mark, FCA** *1983;* Barber & Co LLP, Level 5, City Tower, 40 Basinghall Street, LONDON, EC2V 5DE.
JONES, Mr. Philip Richard, BSc FCA CTA *1971;* 5 Melindwr, Draethen, NEWPORT, GWENT, NP10 8GL.
JONES, Mr. Philip William, FCA *1967;* 26 Daleside, Upton-by-, CHESTER, CH2 1EP.
JONES, Miss. Philippa, BSc ACA *1995;* H M Prison Armley Jail, Gloucester Terrace Armley, LEEDS, LS12 2TJ.
JONES, Miss. Philippa Lucie, BSc ACA *2003;* 35 Tewkesbury Avenue, LONDON, SE23 3DG.
JONES, Mr. Phillip Elfed, BSc ACA *1980;* 39 Westbourne Road, PENARTH, CF64 3HA.
JONES, Miss. Rachel, ACA *2009;* Pricewaterhousecoopers Llp, 80 Strand, LONDON, WC2R 0AF.
JONES, Miss. Rachel Louise, ACA *2009;* 5 Sudlow Road, LONDON, SW18 1HP.
JONES, Mr. Raymond, FCA *1950;* 7 Oakdene Road, Marple, STOCKPORT, SK6 6PJ. (Life Member)
JONES, Mr. Raymond Thomas, BSc FCA DChA *1979;* Charity Commissioners for England & Wales, South West Regional Office Woodfield House Castle Street, TAUNTON, SOMERSET, TA1 4BL.
JONES, Ms. Rebecca, MEng ACA *2004;* 19 Pochard Place, OXFORD, OX4 7GT.
JONES, Mrs. Rebecca, MChem ACA *2010;* 30 Shelfield Close, Hockley Heath, SOLIHULL, B94 6NG.
JONES, Mrs. Rebecca Clair, ACA *2010;* 14 Norwich Way, JARROW, TYNE AND WEAR, NE32 4UX.
JONES, Mr. Reginald Edward, FCA *1962;* Lower Holywich House, Hartfield Road, Cowden, EDENBRIDGE, TN8 7DY.
JONES, Mr. Reginald Sydney, FCA *1970;* D R B Engineering Ltd, 71-75 New Summer Street, BIRMINGHAM, B19 3TE.
JONES, Miss. Rhiannon Sarah, BSc ACA *2004;* Torex Retail The XN Centre, Houghton Hall Park Houghton Regis, DUNSTABLE, BEDFORDSHIRE, LU5 5YG.
JONES, Mr. Rhys, ACA *2009;* 156 Eswyn Road, LONDON, SW17 8TN.
•**JONES, Mr. Richard, ACA** *1995;* Cooper Parry LLP, 14 Park Row, NOTTINGHAM, NG1 6GR.
JONES, Mr. Richard Adrian, BSc ACA *1992;* 7 Eastcott Close, Littledown, BOURNEMOUTH, BH7 7EQ.
•**JONES, Mr. Richard Alan, FCA** *1959;* Jones R.A., Tynycoed, Penybontfawr, OSWESTRY, SY10 0PB.
JONES, Mr. Richard Alexander, CA ACA *1992;* 4a Baslow Road, EASTBOURNE, EAST SUSSEX, BN20 7UJ.
JONES, Mr. Richard Allan, BA ACA *2004;* B P P, marcello house, Pentonville Road, LONDON, N1 9JY.
JONES, Mr. Richard Andrew, BA ACA *1989;* 78 Addison Road, HOVE, BN3 1TR.
JONES, Mr. Richard Anthony, BA ACA *1997;* 91 West Road, BOURNE, LINCOLNSHIRE, PE10 9PX.
JONES, Mr. Richard Anthony, BA ACA *1990;* McArthurGlen UK Ltd, Nations House, 3rd Floor, 103 Wigmore Street, LONDON, W1U 1WH.
JONES, Mr. Richard Brian, BA ACA *2000;* with PricewaterhouseCoopers, BusinessCommunityCenter, Katerinska 40/466, 120 00 PRAGUE, CZECH REPUBLIC.
JONES, Mr. Richard Charles, BA ACA *1995;* Garenne House, Garenne Park, Rue de la Cache, St. Sampson, GUERNSEY, GY2 4AF.
JONES, Mr. Richard Crispin Morgan, BEng ACA *1992;* North View House, Hedley, STOCKSFIELD, NORTHUMBERLAND, NE43 7SW.
JONES, Mr. Richard David, BSc ACA *1988;* Cineworld Cinemas Power Road Studios, 114 Power Road, LONDON, W4 5PY.
JONES, Mr. Richard Dennis, BSc ACA *1994;* Ash Lodge, Patrick Road, St. Johns, ISLE OF MAN, IM4 3BR.
•**JONES, Mr. Richard Gareth, BSc(Hons) ACA** *2006;* 36 Stukeley Road, BASINGSTOKE, RG21 8XE.
JONES, Mr. Richard Henry, BA FCA *1976;* (Tax Fac), Rhiwle, 26 Allum Lane, Elstree, BOREHAMWOOD, WD6 3NP.
•①**JONES, Mr. Richard Ivor Bartlett, FCA** *1974;* JonesGiles Limited, 11 Coopers Yard, Curran Road, CARDIFF, CF10 5NB.
JONES, Mr. Richard James, BCom ACA *1998;* Stockeld Grange Farm, Harrogate Road, WETHERBY, LS22 4AN.
JONES, Mr. Richard James, BA ACA *1989;* 14 Audric Close, KINGSTON UPON THAMES, SURREY, KT2 6BP.
JONES, Mr. Richard James Chapman, BSc FCA *1969;* 5 Bickenhall Mansions, Bickenhall Street, LONDON, W1U 6BP.
JONES, Mr. Richard Lionel, BSc ACA *1978;* Brinley Morris Rees & Jones Solicitors, 3 John Street, LLANELLI, SA15 1UN.
JONES, Mr. Richard Mark, BSc ACA *2002;* Flat 5, 7 Woodchurch Road, LONDON, NW6 3PL.
JONES, Mr. Richard Mark Lea, BA FCA *1988;* Leycester Cottage, Middlewich Road, Toft, KNUTSFORD, WA16 9PG.
JONES, Mr. Richard Martin, BA(Hons) ACA *2000;* 163 Manor Road, Abersychan, PONTYPOOL, GWENT, NP4 7DN.
JONES, Mr. Richard Mervyn, FCA *1975;* 2 Greville Avenue, SOUTH CROYDON, SURREY, CR2 8NL.
JONES, Mr. Richard Michael, BSocSc ACA *2002;* (Tax Fac), The Boundary, 14 Cameron Road, BROMLEY, BR2 9AR.
JONES, Mr. Richard Neal, BA ACA *1990;* 16 Foxdown, WADEBRIDGE, PL27 6BD.

•**JONES, Mr. Richard Parry, BSc ACA** *1984;* Ernst & Young LLP, The Paragon, Counterslip, BRISTOL, BS1 6BX. See also Ernst & Young Europe LLP

JONES, Mr. Richard Perryman, BSc ACA *1991;* 81 Cloonmore Avenue, ORPINGTON, BR6 9LG.

•**JONES, Mr. Richard Philip, BSc FCA** *1995;* Cornel Partners Limited, 115 Alexandra Park Road, LONDON, N10 2DP.

JONES, Mr. Richard Thomas, BA ACA *1994;* 7 Abbey Gardens, CHERTSEY, KT16 8RQ.

JONES, Mr. Richard Wendell, FCA *1955;* Meadow House, Meadow Lane, Fulbrook, BURFORD, OXFORDSHIRE, OX18 4BS. (Life Member)

JONES, Mr. Richard William Alexander, BA ACA *1999;* N M Rothschild & Sons, New Court, 19 St. Swithin's Lane, LONDON, EC4N 8AD.

JONES, Mr. Richard Wyn, BSc ACA *2005;* with PricewaterhouseCoopers LLP, 101 Barbirolli Square, Lower Mosley Street, MANCHESTER, M2 3PW.

•**JONES, Mr. Richard Wynne, FCA** *1972;* (Tax Fac), Accountancy & Tax Advisers Limited, Fetcham Park House, Lower Road, Fetcham, LEATHERHEAD, SURREY KT22 9HD.

JONES, Mr. Robert, MA FCA *1969;* Arden, 33 Church Walk, ATHERSTONE, WARWICKSHIRE, CV9 1AJ.

•**JONES, Mr. Robert Anthony, BA ACA** *2000;* ASE Audit LLP, Rowan Court, Concord Business Park, MANCHESTER, M22 0RR.

JONES, Mr. Robert Anthony, BSc ACA *2010;* 15 Kilnshaw Place, NEWCASTLE UPON TYNE, NE3 5QQ.

JONES, Mr. Robert Bryan, FCA *1955;* 5 The Retreat, Kingsbury, LONDON, NW9 0QB. (Life Member)

JONES, Mr. Robert Charles, FCA *1974;* 9 Brookside Close, CAERPHILLY, MID GLAMORGAN, CF83 2RR.

JONES, Mr. Robert Crawford, BSc FCA ACII *1983;* 15 Warmington Gardens, Downhead Park, MILTON KEYNES, MK15 9BP.

JONES, Mr. Robert Cyril, FCA *1957;* The Cottage, Harrison Drive, Goostrey, CREWE, CW4 8NP. (Life Member)

•**JONES, Mr. Robert David Philip, BSc ACA** *1992;* Fountain Accountancy Limited, Great Western House, The Sidings, Chester Street, Saltney, CHESTERFIELD CH4 8RD. See also Robert Jones Accountants Limited

•**JONES, Mr. Robert Eric Robertshaw, FCA** *1975;* 38 Alrewas Road, Kings Bromley, BURTON-ON-TRENT, DE13 7HW.

•**JONES, Mr. Robert Francis Glyn, BSc FCA ATII MBA** *1994;* (Tax Fac), Robert Jones (Wales) Limited, The Forge, Glanusk Park, CRICKHOWELL, POWYS, NP8 1LP.

JONES, Mr. Robert Gordon, BSc ACA *1984;* Mitre hall and Letts, Goat Mill Road, Dowlais, MERTHYR TYDFIL, MID GLAMORGAN, CF48 3TD.

JONES, Mr. Robert Hugh, FCA *1969;* 27 Catterick Road, Didsbury, MANCHESTER, M20 6HF.

JONES, Mr. Robert John, BSc ACA *2004;* 27 Peveril Crescent, West Hallam, ILKESTON, DE7 6JF.

JONES, Mr. Robert Leonard, BSc ACA CIA *2003;* 7 Saunders Close, Twyford, READING, RG10 0XT.

JONES, Mr. Robert Michael, BA ACA *2003;* 14a Chemin de Muguets, 1234 VESSY, SWITZERLAND.

•**JONES, Mr. Robert Michael, BA FCA** *1969;* (Tax Fac), with Butterworth Jones, Sansom House, Bow Street, LANGPORT, TA10 9PR.

•**JONES, Mr. Robert Richard, FCA** *1972;* Jones & Co, Analyst House, Penthouse Suite, Peel Road, Douglas, ISLE OF MAN IM1 4LZ.

•**JONES, Mr. Robert Stanley, FCA** *1970;* with Ellacotts LLP, Countrywide House, 23 West Bar Street, BANBURY, OXFORDSHIRE, OX16 9SA.

JONES, Mr. Robert Stephen, ACA *2009;* 67 Blenkinsop Way, LEEDS, LS10 4GG.

JONES, Mr. Robert Stuart Glynne, FCA *1968;* Cole Jones & Co, 41 Royal Crescent, LONDON, W11 4SN.

JONES, Mr. Robert William, FCA *1951;* Rowanden, Eghams Wood Road, BEACONSFIELD, HP9 1JP. (Life Member)

JONES, Mr. Robin Edward, FCA *1963;* 14 Roots Lane, Wickham Bishops, WITHAM, CM8 3LS.

JONES, Mr. Robin Geoffrey, MSc ACA *2000;* 5 Lodge Close, Yatton, BRISTOL, BS49 4DX.

JONES, Mr. Robin Jeffrey Llewellyn, BA FCA *1967;* Ivydene, 2 Stone Cottages, Newlands, Brixworth, NORTHAMPTON, NN6 9DN.

JONES, Mr. Robin John, FCA *1974;* 6 Mickle Mead, Highnam, GLOUCESTER, GL2 8NF.

•**JONES, Mr. Roderick Julian, MA ACA MIPA FABRP** *1989;* (Tax Fac), Glaister Jones & Co, 1a The Wool Market, Dyer Street, CIRENCESTER, GLOUCESTERSHIRE, GL7 2PR.

JONES, Mr. Roger Wyn, BA FCA *1969;* 4 The Rummers, CHICHESTER, WEST SUSSEX, PO19 5RT.

JONES, Mr. Roland Edmund, FCA *1958;* 4 Sandhurst Court, South Promenade, LYTHAM ST.ANNES, FY8 1LS. (Life Member)

JONES, Mr. Ron, BA ACA *1995;* Liverpool Football Club, 10th Floor Unity Building, 20 Chapel Street, LIVERPOOL, L3 9AG.

JONES, Mr. Ronald Francis, FCA *1957;* PO Box 262, BUNDANOON, NSW 2578, AUSTRALIA. (Life Member)

JONES, Mr. Ross Anthony, ACA *2011;* 16 Plimsoll Road, LONDON, N4 2EW.

•**JONES, Mr. Roy Anthony, BSc FCA ATII** *1979;* (Tax Fac), R A Jones & Co, 38 Rumbridge Street, Totton, SOUTHAMPTON, SO40 9DS.

•**JONES, Mr. Roy Michael, FCA** *1973;* (Tax Fac), Williams & Co, 4 Cambridge Gardens, HASTINGS, TN34 1EH. See also B.A. Khan & Co

JONES, Mr. Royston Antonio, MSc ACA *1985;* PO Box N-9653, NASSAU, BAHAMAS.

JONES, Mr. Rupert Rodric Maynard, MA ACA *1998;* 21 Dulka Road, LONDON, SW11 6SB.

JONES, Mr. Russell Treharne, BA ACA *1995;* Woodlands, Forest Road, East Horsley, LEATHERHEAD, SURREY, KT24 5BX.

JONES, Mrs. Ruth Marion, BA ACA *1988;* 10 Fairfield Close, EXMOUTH, DEVON, EX8 2BN.

•**JONES, Miss. Ruth Mary Spencer, BEng ACA** *1992;* (Tax Fac), with Whittingham Riddell LLP, 3-4 The Business Quarter, Eco Park Road, LUDLOW, SHROPSHIRE, SY8 1FD.

JONES, Mr. Ryal Barry, FCA *1953;* 10 Hetty Ave, Fairland, JOHANNESBURG, GAUTENG, 2195, SOUTH AFRICA. (Life Member)

JONES, Mr. Ryan Francis, BA(Hons) ACA *2001;* 13/52-54 McEvoy Street, WATERLOO, NSW 2017, AUSTRALIA.

JONES, Mr. Ryan Marc, BSc ACA *2005;* Upper Flat, 34 Sarre Road, LONDON, NW2 3SL.

JONES, Mrs. Sally Frances Lyne, BA ACA *1988;* ExecuJet Aviation Centre, Zurich Flughafen, CH 8058 ZURICH, SWITZERLAND.

JONES, Mr. Sam, BSc ACA *2011;* 73 Union Street, BARNET, HERTFORDSHIRE, EN5 4HY.

JONES, Miss. Samantha Louise, BSc(Econ) ACA *2004;* with BDO Alto Limited, Windward House, La Route de la Liberation, St Helier, JERSEY, JE1 1BG.

JONES, Mrs. Sarah, BSc ACA *2010;* 1 Clos Treventy, Cefneithin, LLANELLI, DYFED, SA14 7DH.

JONES, Mrs. Sarah Ann, ACA *1991;* Audit Commission, 1st Floor, King Edward Building, 205-213 Corporation Street, BIRMINGHAM, B4 6FE.

JONES, Mrs. Sarah Anne, ACA *1998;* 6 Springfield Road, LONDON, SW19 7AL.

JONES, Miss. Sarah Catherine Evans, BA(Hons) ACA *2010;* Flat 35, Charter House, 85 Canute Road, SOUTHAMPTON, SO14 3FY.

JONES, Miss. Sarah Frances, ACA *2011;* 23 Blacka Moor Crescent, SHEFFIELD, S17 3GL.

JONES, Mrs. Sarah Louise, ACA *2008;* Providence International Ltd, 3 Leeds City Office Park Holbeck, LEEDS, LS11 5BD.

•**JONES, Mrs. Sarah Louise, BA ACA** *1994;* The Farmhouse Mewith Head, Mewith Bentham, LANCASTER, LA2 7AP.

JONES, Mrs. Sarah Nancy, BA ACA *1992;* University of Plymouth, Finance Department, Drake Circus, PLYMOUTH, PL4 8AA.

JONES, Mr. Saul Brendan, BA(Hons) ACA *2001;* 104 Rouncil Lane, KENILWORTH, WARWICKSHIRE, CV8 1FQ.

JONES, Mr. Scott, BSc ACA *2011;* 199 Oldfield Road, COVENTRY, CV5 8FQ.

JONES, Mrs. Seema, BSc ACA *1998;* 19 Broom Road, TEDDINGTON, TW11 9pg.

JONES, Miss. Sharon Lindsey, BA ACA ACII *2001;* Collingwood Insurance, 3/1 Waterpoint Place, GIBRALTAR, GIBRALTAR.

JONES, Mrs. Shirley Ann, BSc ACA *1990;* Hillview, Beech Avenue, FRODSHAM, WA6 6PS.

JONES, Miss. Sian Angharad, BSc ACA *2003;* wesley Manse, Cliff Street, CHEDDAR, bs27 3pl.

JONES, Mrs. Sian Elizabeth, BSc ACA *1989;* Presentable Ltd, 46 Cardiff Road, Llandaff, CARDIFF, CF5 2DT.

JONES, Miss. Sian Mererid, BSc ACA *2003;* Mudiad Ysgolion Meithrin, Boulevard St. Briuec, ABERYSTWYTH, DYFED, SY23 1PD.

JONES, Mr. Simon, BSc ACA *2001;* 29 Barfield Road, LONDON, E11 3AF.

JONES, Mr. Simon, BSc ACA *1993;* 24 Lowbury Gardens, Compton, NEWBURY, RG20 6NN.

JONES, Mr. Simon, ACA *2008;* Ground Floor Flat, 132 Cavendish Road, LONDON, SW12 0DE.

JONES, Mr. Simon, BSc(Hons) ACA *2001;* 106 Hardy Road, Wimbledon, LONDON, SW19 1HZ.

JONES, Mr. Simon, ACA *2011;* Flat 5, 13 Cranes Drive, SURBITON, KT5 8AJ.

JONES, Mr. Simon Charles, MA ACA *1983;* 15 Wellington Road, NEWPORT, TF10 7HF.

JONES, Mr. Simon Christopher, ACA *2008;* 12 Rosecroft Road, IPSWICH, IP1 6AP.

JONES, Mr. Simon David Ainslie, BSc FCA MBA *1995;* Dane Close, 9 Hall Park Gate, BERKHAMSTED, HP4 2NL.

JONES, Mr. Simon Dominic, MBA LLB FCA *1980;* 42 Holland Green, SINGAPORE 276165, SINGAPORE.

JONES, Mr. Simon Edward, ACA MAAT *2011;* 45 Amersham Road, HIGH WYCOMBE, BUCKINGHAMSHIRE, HP13 5AA.

JONES, Mr. Simon Francis, MA FCA *1988;* with Crown Agents, St. Nicholas House, St. Nicholas Road, SUTTON, SURREY, SM1 1EL.

JONES, Mr. Simon Glyndon, BA(Hons) ACA *2002;* Aegis Group Plc, 180 Great Portland Street, LONDON, W1W 5QZ.

•**JONES, Mr. Simon Jonathan, FCA** *1992;* Grant Thornton UK LLP, Grant Thornton House, 202 Silbury Boulevard, MILTON KEYNES, BUCKINGHAMSHIRE, MK9 1LW. See also Grant Thornton LLP

JONES, Mr. Simon Matthew Hinton, BSc ACA *1994;* The Village Farmhouse, Hanchurch Lane, Hanchurch, STOKE-ON-TRENT, ST4 8RY.

JONES, Mr. Simon Maxwell, MA BSc ACA *2005;* 16 Dawson Road, KINGSTON UPON THAMES, SURREY, KT1 3AT.

JONES, Mr. Simon Melvyn, BA ACA *1993;* 14 Rockliffe Avenue, BATH, BA2 6QP.

JONES, Mr. Simon Newcombe, BA ACA *2003;* Unit 3, 130 - 140 Mitchell Road, ALEXANDRIA, NSW 2015, AUSTRALIA.

JONES, Mr. Simon Paul, BSc ACA *1992;* 59 Llwyn-y-Grant Road, Penylan, CARDIFF, CF23 9HL.

•**JONES, Mr. Simon Richard, BA ACA** *1991;* Zero Two Twenty Limited, 7 Beaumont Avenue, RICHMOND, SURREY, TW9 2HE.

JONES, Mr. Simon Robert, BA FCA *1992;* Autumn House, 97 Lower Road, Fetcham, LEATHERHEAD, SURREY, KT22 9NQ.

•**JONES, Mr. Simon Ronald, BA FCA** *1989;* (Tax Fac), KPMG LLP, 3 Assembly Square, Britannia Quay, CARDIFF, CF10 4AX. See also KPMG Europe LLP

JONES, Mr. Spencer Raymond Arthur, BA ACA *1999;* 42 Bishops Meadow, SUTTON COLDFIELD, WEST MIDLANDS, B75 5PQ.

JONES, Mr. Stanley Vaughan, ACA *1979;* 93 The Street, Boughton-under-Blean, FAVERSHAM, ME13 9BG.

JONES, Mr. Stephen, FCA *1976;* 31 Beech Road, Bournville, BIRMINGHAM, B30 1LL.

•**JONES, Mr. Stephen, ACA** *1984;* (Tax Fac), Jones Harper, 25 Roseberry Road, BILLINGHAM, CLEVELAND, TS23 2SD.

JONES, Mr. Stephen, ACA *1980;* Dormy House, Baffam Lane, Brayton, SELBY, NORTH YORKSHIRE, YO8 9AX.

JONES, Dr. Stephen, ACA *2010;* 14 Wath Road, SHEFFIELD, S7 1HE.

•**JONES, Mr. Stephen Alan, FCA** *1983;* Myrus Smith, Norman House, 8 Burnell Road, SUTTON, SURREY, SM1 4BW.

JONES, Mr. Stephen Charles, BA FCA *1977;* U C B Celltech, 208 Bath Road, SLOUGH, BERKSHIRE, SL1 3WE.

JONES, Mr. Stephen Christopher, BSc ACA *1982;* 21 The Dell, LICHFIELD, STAFFORDSHIRE, WS13 8AZ.

JONES, Mr. Stephen Douglas, MSc FCA *1979;* Rugby Estates Plc, 4 Farm Street, LONDON, W1J 5RD.

•**JONES, Mr. Stephen Edward William, ACA ACCA** *2009;* R.E.Jones & Co, 132 Burnt Ash Road, Lee, LONDON, SE12 8PU.

JONES, Mr. Stephen Francis, BEng ACA *1992;* 60 Littleton Street, Earlsfield, LONDON, SW18 3SY.

JONES, Mr. Stephen Glyn, FCA *1977;* 25 Ynys y Mond Road, Alltwen, Pontardawe, SWANSEA, SA8 3BA.

JONES, Mr. Stephen Graham, BSc ACA *2006;* Flat 3, Sprucefield Court, 130 Ifield Road, CRAWLEY, WEST SUSSEX, RH11 7BF.

JONES, Mr. Stephen Ian, ACA *1985;* Langham Hall UK Llp, Amadeus House, 27b Floral Street, LONDON, WC2E 9DP.

JONES, Mr. Stephen James, BSc ACA *1988;* 4 Harrier Way, Morley, LEEDS, LS27 8TG.

JONES, Mr. Stephen James, BA ACA *1989;* 89 Bournville Road, Blaina, ABERTILLERY, GWENT, NP13 3EN.

JONES, Mr. Stephen James, BSc ACA *1992;* 7a Park Road, TWICKENHAM, TW1 2QD.

JONES, Mr. Stephen Llewellyn, BSc ACA *2004;* with PricewaterhouseCoopers LLP, 1 Embankment Place, LONDON, WC2N 6RH.

JONES, Mr. Stephen Michael, BA ACA *1996;* 9 Silver Crescent, Chiswick, LONDON, W4 5SF.

JONES, Mr. Stephen Paul, BA(Hons) ACA *2003;* 16 Holden Gardens, SELBY, NORTH YORKSHIRE, YO8 4JR.

JONES, Mr. Stephen Paul, FCA *1982;* 74 Victoria Avenue, Princes Avenue, HULL, HU5 3DS.

JONES, Mr. Stephen Philip, BSc ACA *1982;* 11 Pownall Avenue, Bramhall, STOCKPORT, SK7 2HE.

JONES, Mr. Stephen Rimmer, FCA *1971;* 21 Upton Bridle Path, WIDNES, WA8 9HB.

JONES, Mr. Stephen Robert, BCom FCA *1985;* 12 Oakdale, Oakwood Pk, BINGLEY, BD16 4AN.

•**JONES, Mr. Stephen William, FCA** *1983;* (Tax Fac), Stephen W. Jones, King Edward House, 82 Stourbridge Road, HALESOWEN, B63 3UP.

JONES, Mr. Steven, BSc FCA MBA *1990;* 15 Cavendish Road, Tean, STOKE-ON-TRENT, STAFFORDSHIRE, ST10 4RH.

•**JONES, Mr. Steven Llystyn, BSc ACA** *1985;* Steve Jones (Bath) Limited, 74 Newbridge Road, BATH, BA1 3LA.

JONES, Mr. Steven Paul, BSc ACA *1991;* 40 Ivy Road, Gosforth, NEWCASTLE UPON TYNE, NE3 1DB.

•**JONES, Mr. Steven Russell, FCA** *1977;* S.R. Jones, Middle Lane Ends Farm, Lane Ends Lane, Cowling, KEIGHLEY, BD22 0LD.

•**JONES, Mr. Steven Wayne, BA ACA** *1992;* (Tax Fac), Craig Callum Associates Ltd, 51 Sandhills Lane, LIVERPOOL, L5 9XJ.

JONES, Mr. Stuart Graham, BSc FCA *1997;* Birchwood Lodge, Mount Pleasant Kings Worthy, WINCHESTER, HAMPSHIRE, SO23 7QU.

•**JONES, Mr. Stuart John, FCA** *1977;* (Tax Fac), 3CA Limited, Kent Cottage, Bridge Lane, KENDAL, CUMBRIA, LA9 7DD.

•**JONES, Mr. Stuart Keith, FCA** *1980;* Stuart K Jones FCA, 56-58 Warwick Road, KENILWORTH, WARWICKSHIRE, CV8 1HH.

•**JONES, Mrs. Susan, BSc FCA** *1994;* (Tax Fac), Vista Partners Limited, Chancery House, 3 Hatchlands Road, REDHILL, RH1 6AA. See also Vista Audit LLP

JONES, Miss. Susan, BA FCA *1993;* Silversands Ltd, Unit 3/5, Albany Park, Cabot Lane, POOLE, DORSET BH17 7BX.

JONES, Mrs. Susan Clare, BA ACA *2009;* with LB Group Ltd, 82 East Hill, COLCHESTER, CO1 2QW.

JONES, Mrs. Susan Deborah, BA ACA *1996;* Hanson Building Products Ltd, Stewartby, BEDFORD, MK43 9LZ.

JONES, Mrs. Susan Glenys, BA ACA *1989;* (Tax Fac), with Crowe Clark Whitehill LLP, St Bride's House, 10 Salisbury Square, LONDON, EC4Y 8EH.

JONES, Miss. Susan Lorraine, BA ACA *1997;* PO BOX 30753 SMB, SEVEN MILE BEACH, GRAND CAYMAN, KY1-1204, CAYMAN ISLANDS.

JONES, Mrs. Susan Louise, BSc ACA MCT *1998;* 10 Clifden Road, TWICKENHAM, MIDDLESEX, TW1 4LX.

JONES, Miss. Susan Mary, BA ACA *1993;* 1 Cloudbridge Drive, SOLIHULL, WEST MIDLANDS, B92 0PY.

•**JONES, Mrs. Suzanna Clelia, FCA** *1984;* (Tax Fac), A & S Associates Limited, P O Box 3310, 126 Fairlie Road, SLOUGH, BERKSHIRE, SL1 0AG.

JONES, Miss. Suzanne Elizabeth, BSc ACA *2002;* 72 Cronk Coar, Douglas, ISLE OF MAN, IM2 5LY.

JONES, Mrs. Suzanne Elizabeth, BSc(Hons) ACA *2000;* Millennium House, 46 Athol Street, Douglas, ISLE OF MAN, IM1 1JB.

•**JONES, Mrs. Tania Elizabeth, ACA** *1995;* Decorative Panels Holdings Ltd Century House, Premier Way Lowfields Business Park, ELLAND, WEST YORKSHIRE, HX5 9HF.

JONES, Mr. Tarquin Samuel, BSc(Hons) FCA *2000;* Health Protection Agency, Seacroft Hospital Site, Bridle Path, LEEDS, LS15 7TR.

JONES, Mr. Terence Mark, BSc FCA *1992;* 39 Overlea Avenue, Deganwy, CONWY, LL31 9TA.

JONES, Mr. Terence Oliver, FCA *1959;* Kringloop 23, 1186 GR AMSTELVEEN, NETHERLANDS. (Life Member)

JONES, Mr. Terence Percy, FCA *1965;* 8 North Drive, Littleton, WINCHESTER, SO22 6QA.

JONES, Mrs. Teresa Jane, BA ACA *1986;* Sewell Moorhouse Ltd, Omega Court, 364 Cemetery Road, SHEFFIELD, S11 8FT.

JONES, Mrs. Theresa Mary, BSc ACA *1992;* 1 Lower Court, Kinsham, PRESTEIGNE, POWYS, LD8 2HP.

JONES, Mr. Thomas Edgar, FCA *1963;* First Floor 30 Cannon Street, International Accounting Standards Board, 30 Cannon Street, LONDON, EC4M 6XH.

JONES, Mr. Thomas Henry, ACA *2011;* 2 Sherman Place, READING, RG1 2PL.

JONES, Mr. Thomas Stephen, BA FCA *1973;* Greengates, St.Brides Hill, SAUNDERSFOOT, SA69 9NP.

JONES, Mr. Tim Paul Howorth, MSc ACA *2009;* Matrix-Securities Limited, 1 Vine Street, LONDON, W1J 0AH.

•**JONES, Mr. Timothy Adrian, FCA** *1992;* Ashby Berry & Co, 48/49 Albemarle Crescent, SCARBOROUGH, YO11 1XU.

JONES, Mr. Timothy Charles, MA ACA *1990;* Godolphin House, Broom Way, WEYBRIDGE, KT13 9TG.

JONES, Mr. Timothy Francis, BSc ACA *2010;* Flat 15 Tanner House, Pincott Road, LONDON, SW19 2NW.

JONES, Mr. Timothy Harry, BA(Hons) ACA *2003;* with PricewaterhouseCoopers LLP, The Atrium, 1 Harefield Road, UXBRIDGE, UB8 1EX.

•**JONES, Mr. Timothy Jay, BSc FCA** *1989;* T J Jones Limited, Belmont House, Shrewsbury Business Park, SHREWSBURY, SY2 6LG.

JONES, Mr. Timothy John, BSc ACA *1985;* Wyfold Farm, Wyfold, READING, RG4 9HU.

JONES, Mr. Timothy John Alexander, ACA *2004;* 1 Browning Close, Whiteley, FAREHAM, HAMPSHIRE, PO15 7LX.

JONES, Mr. Timothy John Nigel, BSc FCA *1975;* W.C.V.A., Baltic House, Mount Stuart Square, CARDIFF, CF10 5FH.

JONES, Mr. Timothy John Tovell, BSc ACA *1989;* (Tax Fac), 12 Wychwood Crescent, Earley, READING, RG6 5RA.

JONES, Mr. Timothy Michael, BSc ACA *1985;* IBM China/HK Ltd, 10/F Pccw Tower, QUARRY BAY, HONG KONG ISLAND, HONG KONG SAR.

JONES, Mr. Timothy Peter, MA ACA *1989;* 15 Grove Park Road, LONDON, SE9 4NP.

•**JONES, Mr. Timothy Raymond, BSc FCA** *1972;* Two Ashes, Radford, Inkberrow, WORCESTER, WR7 4LS.

•**JONES, Mr. Timothy Stephen, MA FCA** *1974;* (Tax Fac), Timothy Jones & Co, 1 Arbrook Lane, ESHER, SURREY, KT10 9EG.

JONES, Mr. Timothy William, MSc ACA *1999;* The Haven Priestlands Lane, Pennington, LYMINGTON, HAMPSHIRE, SO41 8HZ.

JONES, Mr. Timothy William, MA ACA *1997;* 96 Foley Road, Claygate, ESHER, SURREY, KT10 0NB.

JONES, Mr. Tobin Neill, BA FCA *1995;* Infraco Management Services Ltd, Eastgate House, 16-19 Eastcastle Street, LONDON, W1W 8DA.

JONES, Mr. Toby Allan, BA ACA ACCA *1998;* 5 Prospero Road, LONDON, N19 3QX.

JONES, Mr. Tony Robert, BSc ACA *1981;* 79 Stradella Road, LONDON, SE24 9HL.

•**JONES, Mrs. Tracey, ACA FCCA** *2009;* (Tax Fac), KB Ferugson Limited, 95 High Street, Gorseinon, SWANSEA, SA4 4BL.

JONES, Miss. Tracey Lea, MA ACA *2002;* 945 Europort, Europort Avenue, GIBRALTAR, GIBRALTAR.

JONES, Mrs. Tracy, ACA CA(SA) *2008;* 4 Grove Avenue, SUTTON, SURREY, SM1 2DP.

JONES, Miss. Tracy, BA ACA *2006;* 6B / 90 Mount Street, Coogee, SYDNEY, NSW 2034, AUSTRALIA.

JONES, Mr. Trevor Alexander, BCom FCA CF *1974;* Flat 8 Worplesdon Hill House, Heath House Road, WOKING, GU22 0QX.

JONES, Mr. Trevor Andrew, FCA *1968;* Swaythorne, Bullocks Lane, Sutton, MACCLESFIELD, SK11 0HE.

JONES, Mr. Trevor Anthony Carden, FCA *1972;* 178 Beech Road, ST. ALBANS, AL3 5AX.

JONES, Mr. Trevor John Mansel, BA ACA *1992;* 30 Richmond Road, LONDON, SW20 0PQ.

JONES, Ms. Vanessa Gay, BSc ACA *1993;* 29 Woburn Close, Caversham, READING, RG4 7HB.

JONES, Mrs. Vanessa Jane, BA(Hons) ACA *2003;* with PricewaterhouseCoopers LLP, 101 Barbirolli Square, Lower Mosley Street, MANCHESTER, M2 3PW.

JONES, Mrs. Victoria Louise, BA ACA *2005;* 14 Llewelyn Goch, St. Fagans, CARDIFF, CF5 6HR.

JONES, Mr. Vincent, ACA *2002;* Turner & Townsend, Low Hall, Calverley Lane, Horsforth, LEEDS, LS18 4GH.

•**JONES, Mr. Vincent Hugh Kevin, FCA** *1981;* (Tax Fac), Baker Chapman & Bussey, Magnet House, 3 North Hill, COLCHESTER, CO1 1DZ.

•**JONES, Mr. Vivian Eyton, BA FCA** *1980;* (Tax Fac), Gittins Limited, 28 Salop Road, OSWESTRY, SHROPSHIRE, SY11 2NZ.

JONES, Mr. Warwick Richard, MA FCA *1976;* White Gables, 16 The Ridge, PURLEY, CR8 3PE.

JONES, Mrs. Wendy, BA ACA *1993;* Murmar Phipps, 21 Rothersthorpe Crescent Rothersthorpe Avenue Ind Estate, NORTHAMPTON, NN4 8JD.

JONES, Mrs. Wendy Sarah, BSc ACA *2006;* 1 Browning Close, Whiteley, FAREHAM, HAMPSHIRE, PO15 7LX.

JONES, Mr. Wilfred, BA LLB FCA *1958;* 13 The Coppice, ENFIELD, EN2 7BY. (Life Member)

JONES, Mr. Wilfred Henry, BCom FCA *1951;* 10 Dylan Road, Killay, SWANSEA, SA2 7BN. (Life Member)

•①**JONES, Mr. Wilfred Vaughan, BA FCA** *1983;* with JonesGiles Limited, 11 Coopers Yard, Curran Road, CARDIFF, CF10 5NB.

JONES, Mr. William, BA FCA *1974;* Shady Brook, Crowsnest Lane, Comberbach, NORTHWICH, CW9 6HY.

•**JONES, Mr. William Charles David, FCA ACMA** *1981;* Cheshire PB5, Unit 3B County Design Centre, TARPORLEY, CHESHIRE, CW6 9DY.

JONES, Mr. William Edward, ACA *1978;* 7 Bradford Close, Lansdown Park, CLEVEDON, BS21 5ES.

JONES, Mr. William Huw, FCA *1973;* 60 Villiers Street, NUNEATON, CV11 5PJ.

JONES, Mr. William Nigel Henry, FCA *1977;* 10 Quindell Place, Kings Hill, WEST MALLING, KENT, ME19 4GQ.

JONES, Mr. William Rhodri, FCA *1973;* 28 Burnham Road, Knaphill, WOKING, GU21 2AE.

JONES, Mr. William Russell, FCA *1958;* 34 Merchants Quay, SALFORD, M50 3XR. (Life Member)

JONES, Mr. William Thomas, BA FCA *1972;* 33 Manor Road, SALFORD, M6 8QN. (Life Member)

JONES, Mrs. Zoe Caroline Jane, BSc FCA *1987;* Teva Pharmaceuticals Ltd, The Gatehouse, Gatehouse Way, AYLESBURY, BUCKINGHAMSHIRE HP19 8DB.

JONES, Miss. Zoe Louise, ACA *2009;* 30 Upland Drive, Trevethin, PONTYPOOL, GWENT, NP4 8HS.

JONES, Miss. Zoe Miranda, MMath ACA *2009;* (Tax Fac), 80 Eton Avenue, BARNET, HERTFORDSHIRE, EN4 8TY.

•**JONES, Dr. Zoe Sarah, BSc ACA** *2003;* 18 Sandpiper Crescent, MALVERN, WORCESTERSHIRE, WR14 1UY.

JONES-BAK, Mrs. Helen R, BSc ACA *1997;* Birchwood, 8 Compton Avenue, Hutton, BRENTWOOD, ESSEX, CM13 2HH.

JONES-FERGUSON, Mrs. Sarah Louise, BA FCA *1999;* Briar Knoll Chapel Lane, Sissinghurst, CRANBROOK, TN17 2JN.

JONES-OWEN, Mr. David, BSc ACA *2005;* 94 North View, PINNER, MIDDLESEX, HA5 1PF.

JONES-PRITCHARD, Mr. Keith, FCA *1971;* 5B-805 Silver Maple Garden, 6 Caihong Road, Dashanzi, Chaoyang District, BEIJING 100015, CHINA.

JONES-PRITCHARD, Mr. Mark Anthony, BA(Hons) ACA *2002;* Flat 178 Viridian Apartments, 75 Battersea Park Road, LONDON, SW8 4DG.

JONES-SMYTHE, Mr. Glen, BA ACA *2007;* Flat 2, Albany Court, Richmond Road, KINGSTON UPON THAMES, SURREY, KT2 5DF.

JONKER, Mr. Abraham Hendrik, ACA CA(SA) *2009;* 825 Elveden Row, WEST VANCOUVER V7 1Y7, BC, CANADA.

JONSSON, Mr. Ian Kenneth, BA ACA *1981;* Mediterranean Shipping Co Medite House, 10 The Havens Ransomes Europark, IPSWICH, IP3 9SJ.

•**JONSSON, Mr. Simon Lars, BA ACA** *1992;* (Tax Fac), KPMG LLP, One Snowhill, Snow Hill Queensway, BIRMINGHAM, B4 6GN. See also KPMG Europe LLP

JOOMA, Mr. Ali, FCA *1961;* 20/1-23rd Street, Khayaban-e-Tanzeem, Phase-V, Defence Housing Authority, KARACHI, PAKISTAN. (Life Member)

•**JOOMA, Mr. Murtaza Yusuf, FCA CTA** *1981;* (Tax Fac), BRAAMS LLP, First Floor, Allied Sainif House, 412 Greenford Road, GREENFORD, UB6 9AH.

JOOMA, Mr. Nawshad Yusuf, BSc ACA *1984;* 2 Moss Close, PINNER, HA5 3AY.

JOORY, Mr. Kapildev, FCA *1974;* (Tax Fac), International Financial Services Limited, IFS Court, TwentyEight, Cybercity, Ebene, REDUIT MAURITIUS.

•**JOOSTE, Mrs. Karen Lisa, BSc ACA** *1996;* KJ Accounting Services, Dragons Lye, Tollgate Lane, Whitemans Green, Cuckfield, HAYWARDS HEATH WEST SUSSEX RH17 5DJ.

JOPLING, Mr. David William, FCA *1964;* 137 Darlington Road, DARLINGTON, WA 6070, AUSTRALIA. (Life Member)

JOPLING, Mr. Douglas Noble, BSc ACA *1998;* 246 Bobbin Head Road, NORTH TURRAMURRA, NSW 2074, AUSTRALIA.

•**JOPSON, Mr. Anthony Paul, BSc FCA** *1989;* Tony Jopson & Co Limited, 246 Peverell Park Road, Peverell, PLYMOUTH, PL3 4QG.

JOPSON, Mr. Wayne Alan, BSc(Hons) ACA *2001;* 82 Hammersmith Bridge Road, LONDON, W6 9DB.

JOR, Mr. Hon Ming, BA ACA *2002;* 199 Old Hall Lane, MANCHESTER, M14 6HJ.

•**JORDAN, Mr. Alan Michael, FCA DChA** *1994;* with The Taylor Cocks Partnership Limited, Abbey House, Hickleys Court, South Street, FARNHAM, GU9 7QQ.

JORDAN, Mr. Andrew David, BSc ACA *2007;* 48 Curlew Close, LICHFIELD, STAFFORDSHIRE, WS14 9UL.

JORDAN, Mr. Andrew Derek, ACA *2008;* 514 Becket House, New Road, BRENTWOOD, ESSEX, CM14 4GB.

JORDAN, Mr. Andrew James, ACA *2004;* Flat 16 The Custom House, Redcliff Backs, BRISTOL, BS1 6NE.

JORDAN, Miss. Annabel Lucy, BA ACA *2006;* 12A Hopetoun Street, SOUTH PERTH, WA 6151, AUSTRALIA.

JORDAN, Mr. Anthony Graham, BSc ACA *2005;* Flat 50, Albany Mansions, Albert Bridge Road, LONDON, SW11 4PQ.

JORDAN, Mrs. Beverley Ann, BA ACA *1991;* Laneside, Coldalhurst Lane, Astley, Tyldesley, MANCHESTER, M29 7BS.

JORDAN, Mr. Brian Clifford, FCA *1967;* 17 Royal Close, Henbury, BRISTOL, BS10 7XF.

JORDAN, Mrs. Claire Louise, LLB ACA *1999;* Manor Court, Lees Hill, South Warnborough, HOOK, HAMPSHIRE, RG29 1RQ.

•**JORDAN, Mr. Darren Glyn, FCA** *1996;* Blick Rothenberg, 12 York Gate, Regent's Park, LONDON, NW1 4QS.

JORDAN, Mr. Darren James, MA ACA *1995;* 5 Barons Hurst, EPSOM, SURREY, KT18 7DU.

•**JORDAN, Mrs. Elizabeth Mary, FCA** *1976;* (Tax Fac), UHY Kent LLP, Thames House, Roman Square, SITTINGBOURNE, KENT, ME10 4BJ.

JORDAN, Mr. Eric Richard, FCA *1941;* 1 Sycamore House, Woodland Court Partridge Drive, BRISTOL, BS16 2RD. (Life Member)

JORDAN, Mr. Gavin, ACA *2011;* 10 Liberty Street, Apartment 7C, NEW YORK, NY 10005, UNITED STATES.

JORDAN, Mrs. Gillian, BA ACA *1991;* 19 Upper Oldfield Park, BATH, BA2 3JX.

JORDAN, Mr. James Dominic, BSc(Hons) ACA *2002;* 4 Brand Street, LONDON, SE10 8SR.

•**JORDAN, Mr. John Edwin, FCA** *1968;* with HW, Bridge House, Ashley Road, Hale, ALTRINCHAM, WA14 2UT.

JORDAN, Mr. John Oliver Philip, FCA CTA *1958;* Beech Lodge, Back Lane, MALVERN, WORCESTERSHIRE, WR14 2HJ. (Life Member)

JORDAN, Mr. John Philip, BA FCA FCCA *1962;* 36 Park Lane, BEWDLEY, WORCESTERSHIRE, DY12 2EU. (Life Member)

JORDAN, Mrs. Julia Anne, BA ACA *1991;* 72 Valley Drive, ILKLEY, LS29 8PA.

•**JORDAN, Mr. Keith Barry, FCA** *1973;* (Tax Fac), Victor Boorman & Co, Europa House, Goldstone Villas, HOVE, BN3 3RQ.

JORDAN, Miss. Kim Rowan, MA FCA *2001;* The Prudential Assurance Co Ltd, 121 Kings Road, READING, RG1 3ES.

JORDAN, Mrs. Laura Ann, ACA *2008;* 3/86 St Pauls Street, RANDWICK, NSW 2031, AUSTRALIA.

JORDAN, Mrs. Laura Jane, MA BA ACA *2005;* 10 Ransom Yard, Bancroft, HITCHIN, HERTFORDSHIRE, SG5 1NB.

JORDAN, Mr. Mark, BA ACA *1992;* Highclere, Bighton Lane, Gundleton, ALRESFORD, SO24 9SW.

•**JORDAN, Mr. Mark, BA(Hons) ACA** *2001;* PricewaterhouseCoopers LLP, 1 Embankment Place, LONDON, WC2N 6RH. See also PricewaterhouseCoopers

•**JORDAN, Mr. Mark Adrian, FCA** *1988;* Jordan & Company, Knighton House, 62 Hagley Road, STOURBRIDGE, DY8 1QD.

JORDAN, Mr. Mark Andrew, ACA *2008;* Flat 4 Dryburgh Court, 1 Dryburgh Road, LONDON, SW15 1BN.

•**JORDAN, Mr. Mark David, BA FCA** *1994;* MDJ Accountancy Limited, Timaru, Corseley Road, Groombridge, TUNBRIDGE WELLS, KENT TN3 9SG.

JORDAN, Mr. Michael Anthony, FCA *1957;* Ballinger Farm, Ballinger, GREAT MISSENDEN, BUCKINGHAMSHIRE, HP16 9LQ. (Life Member)

JORDAN, Mr. Michael Terence, BSc ACA *1990;* Barclays Wealth, 1 Churchill Place, Canary Wharf, LONDON, E14 5HP.

JORDAN, Mr. Nicholas, BSc ACA *2002;* 1 Manor Crescent, SURBITON, SURREY, KT5 8LG.

JORDAN, Mr. Oliver, BSc(Hons) ACA *2009;* 10 Hitchen Hatch Lane, SEVENOAKS, TN13 3AT.

JORDAN, Mr. Paul Edward, BA(Hons) ACA *2001;* 10 Frenchs Forest Road, SEAFORTH, NSW 2092, AUSTRALIA.

JORDAN, Mr. Peter Edward, BA ACA *2010;* 69 Sheepfold Road, GUILDFORD, SURREY, GU2 9TU.

JORDAN, Mr. Peter Kenneth, BA FCA *1973;* Limetree Lodge Thorpe Road, Mattersey, DONCASTER, SOUTH YORKSHIRE, DN10 5ED.

JORDAN, Mr. Philip Rodney, FCA *1965;* 40 Thirlmere Drive, LOUGHBOROUGH, LE11 3SY. (Life Member)

JORDAN, Mr. Philip Thomas Deverill, BSc FCA *1978;* 13 Locke Road, LIPHOOK, GU30 7DQ.

JORDAN, Mrs. Rachael, BA(Hons) ACA *2010;* 14 Upper Carlisle Road, EASTBOURNE, EAST SUSSEX, BN20 7TH.

JORDAN, Mr. Richard Lawrence, MA ACA *2001;* 45 Scotts Road, #11-03, Scotts HighPark, SINGAPORE 228232, SINGAPORE.

JORDAN, Mr. Rob, BSc ACA *2003;* 93 Franciscan Road, LONDON, SW17 8DZ.

JORDAN, Miss. Rosalind Lucy, MEng ACA *1998;* Flat 6, 23 Madeley Road, Ealing, LONDON, W5 2LS.

JORDAN, Mr. Stephen James, BSc ACA *1982;* 11 Thornton Road, LONDON, SW19 4NE.

JORDAN, Mr. Stephen Thomas, BSc FCA *1979;* Mulberry House, Lucas Road, HIGH WYCOMBE, HP13 6QE.

JORDAN, Mrs. Susan Elaine, BA ACA *1995;* 67 Mount Pleasant, NORWICH, NR2 2DQ.

JORDAN, Mr. Timothy Mark, MBA BA ACA *2008;* 179 Lower Road, FAVERSHAM, ME13 7NE.

•**JORDANOU, Mr. Kypros, BSc ACA** *1982;* (Tax Fac), AJ & S Associates Ltd, 289a High Street, WEST BROMWICH, WEST MIDLANDS, B70 8ND. See also AJ & Associates

JORDEN, Mr. George Brian, BSc FCA CTA *1976;* (Tax Fac), 5 Rishworth Avenue, HUDDERSFIELD, HD8 9SB.

JORDEN, Miss. Shelagh Margaret, BSc ACA *1982;* 10 Easenby Close, Swanland, NORTH FERRIBY, NORTH HUMBERSIDE, HU14 3NP.

JORDISON, Mrs. Louisa Elizabeth, BA ACA *2004;* 10 Dere Croft, Borrowash, DERBY, DERBYSHIRE, DE72 3WG.

JORGENSEN, Mr. Daniel Bandholtz, BA ACA *2005;* Flat 27 Premier House, Waterloo Terrace, LONDON, N1 1TG.

JORGENSEN, Mrs. Seona Jane, MA ACA *2004;* 3 St. Marks Road, HENLEY-ON-THAMES, OXFORDSHIRE, RG9 1LN.

JORIO, Mr. Christopher Marc, BSc(Hons) ACA *2002;* 10 Bonchurch Road, LONDON, W13 9JE.

JORY, Mr. Richard James, BSc ACA *1993;* Lloyds, 10 Gresham Street, LONDON, EC2V 7AE.

JORYSZ, Mrs. Maria Tessa, BSc ACA *1987;* The VicarageWigley Bush Lane, South Weald BRENTWOOD, Essex, CM14 5QP.

JOSCELYNE, Mr. Paul Michael, MSc FCA *2000;* 22 Foxglove Close, BUCKINGHAM, BUCKINGHAMSHIRE, MK18 1FU.

JOSCELYNE, Mr. Richard Hugh Verney, BSc FCA *1973;* The Lodge, Egerton Road, WEYBRIDGE, KT13 0PR.

JOSE, Mr. Michael Anthony, FCA *1961;* 9 Carter Walk, Tylers GreenPenn, HIGH WYCOMBE, HP10 8ER.

JOSE, Miss. Nicola Suzanne, BSc ACA *1994;* 1 Buttermel Close, Godmanchester, HUNTINGDON, PE29 2JU.

•**JOSELAND, Mr. Charles Lansley, MA ACA** *1989;* PricewaterhouseCoopers LLP, 1 Embankment Place, LONDON, WC2N 6RH. See also PricewaterhouseCoopers

JOSEPH, Mr. Aaron Dov, BA ACA *2007;* 7 Hurstwood Road, LONDON, NW11 0AS.

•**JOSEPH, Mr. Bernard Michael, FCA** *1975;* (Tax Fac), Bernard Joseph, PO Box 199, EDGWARE, MIDDLESEX, HA8 7FG.

JOSEPH, Miss. Carly, BA ACA *2006;* 2 Hartley Place, Vicarage Road, Edgbaston, BIRMINGHAM, B15 3HS.

JOSEPH, Ms. Chantal Lara, ACA CA(SA) *2009;* 76 Melbourne Road, LONDON, SW19 3BA.

JOSEPH, Mrs. Claire, MA ACA *2001;* with PKF (UK) LLP, Farringdon Place, 20 Farringdon Road, LONDON, EC1M 3AP.

JOSEPH, Miss. Dalia Grace, BA ACA *1996;* 26 Station Road, AMERSHAM, BUCKINGHAMSHIRE, HP7 0BE.

JOSEPH, Mr. David, LLB ACA *1992;* The Cottage, Home Farm Leicester Road, Thornhaugh, PETERBOROUGH, PE8 6NL.

JOSEPH, Mrs. Denise Nicole, BSc FCA *1987;* 32 Elsworthy Road, LONDON, NW3 3DL.

JOSEPH, Miss. Eleanor, ACA *2009;* 3 Alms Mews, Almshouse Lane Ilchester, YEOVIL, SOMERSET, BA22 8NJ.

JOSEPH, Mr. Gnanapragasam Edward, BA FCA *1973;* 8 Oakington Avenue, WEMBLEY, HA9 8JA. (Life Member)

•**JOSEPH, Mr. Godfrey Marcus Anthony, MSc FCA** *1974;* 27 Wordsworth Place, LONDON, NW5 4HG.

JOSEPH, Mrs. Jennifer Emma, BSc ACA *2006;* Building B, British Petroleum Co Plc, Chertsey Road, SUNBURY-ON-THAMES, MIDDLESEX, TW16 7LN.
•**JOSEPH, Mr. Joey Jizchak, FCA** *1982;* (Tax Fac), Joseph Kahan Associates LLP, 923 Finchley Road, LONDON, NW11 7PE. See also Joseph Kahan Associates Taxation Services ltd, Jody Associates Limited and Joseph Kahan Associates Payroll Services Ltd
JOSEPH, Mr. Jonathan Gareth, BSc FCA *1997;* 20 Hazelwood, Elstead, GODALMING, SURREY, GU8 6HJ.
JOSEPH, Mrs. Lara, BSc ACA *2003;* with PricewaterhouseCoopers LLP, 1 Embankment Place, LONDON, WC2N 6RH.
JOSEPH, Miss. Laura Amy, BA ACA *2010;* 93 Brockman Rise, Downham, BROMLEY, KENT, BR1 5RE.
JOSEPH, Mr. Leon, FCA *1956;* 19 Collingridge House, 5 Old Park Road, ENFIELD, MIDDLESEX, EN2 7BE. (Life Member)
JOSEPH, Mr. Manoj, ACA *2010;* PO Box 185958, DUBAI, UNITED ARAB EMIRATES.
JOSEPH, Mr. Mario Christy, BSc ACA *1997;* 5 rue de acacias, 68220 HESINGUE, FRANCE.
JOSEPH, Mr. Mark William, BA ACA *1993;* 6 Langford Place, LONDON, NW8 0LL.
•**JOSEPH, Mr. Martin Ian, BA FCA** *1983;* (Tax Fac), Whittingtons Business Services Ltd, 1 High Street, GUILDFORD, SURREY, GU2 4HP.
JOSEPH, Mr. Maurice Ian, BA ACA *2007;* 30 Westfields Avenue, LONDON, SW13 0AU.
JOSEPH, Mr. Michael Adam, ACA *1987;* 13 Grayling Road, LONDON, N16 0BL.
•**JOSEPH, Mr. Neville Anthony, FCA** *1959;* Neville A. Joseph, Marlowe House, Hale Road, Wendover, AYLESBURY, HP22 6NE.
JOSEPH, Mr. Paul, BSc ACA MAAT *2011;* 7 Adams Mews, LONDON, SW17 7RD.
JOSEPH, Mrs. Pauline Alix, BA ACA *1994;* (Tax Fac), 36 Rushington Avenue, MAIDENHEAD, BERKSHIRE, SL6 1BZ.
JOSEPH, Mr. Ramon, FCA *1959;* 17 Riviera, 63 Grove Road, BOURNEMOUTH, BH1 3AE. (Life Member)
•**JOSEPH, Mr. Richard Lewis, FCA** *1972;* Richard Joseph & Co, 2nd Floor, 65 Station Road, EDGWARE, HA8 7HX. See also Richard L. Joseph
JOSEPH, Mr. Robin Lewis, FCA *1967;* 53 Malham Road, STOURPORT-ON-SEVERN, DY13 8NT.
JOSEPH, Mrs. Sarojini Marie Angela, LLB FCA *1972;* 35 Northside, Streatham Common North, LONDON, SW16 3HR.
•**JOSEPH, Mr. Stephen Michael Basil, FCA** *1974;* Stephen M. Joseph, 29 Bentley Way, STANMORE, HA7 3RR.
JOSEPH, Mr. Stephen Zev, BSc ACA *2008;* with BDO LLP, 55 Baker Street, LONDON, W1U 7EU.
JOSEPH, Mr. Steven, ACA *1987;* 26 Southerndown Avenue, Mayals, SWANSEA, SA3 5EL.
•**JOSEPHS, Mr. Anthony Alan, BCom FCA** *1976;* RMT Accountants and Business Advisors Limited, Unit 2, Gosforth Park Avenue, NEWCASTLE UPON TYNE, NE12 8EG. See also RMT Accountants and Business Advisors
•**JOSEPHS, Mr. David Leslie Mayer, FCA** *1971;* (Tax Fac), David Josephs, 2 Queens Avenue, Whetstone, LONDON, N20 0JE.
JOSEPHS, Mr. John Irving, BA FCA *1969;* 55 Moor Court, Westfield, NEWCASTLE UPON TYNE, NE3 4YD.
JOSEPHS, Mr. Michael Stanley, FCA *1946;* 33 York Terrace West, LONDON, NW1 4QA.
JOSEPHS, Mr. Paul Ian, MBA ACA *1994;* 25 Granville Road, BOURNEMOUTH, BH5 2AH.
JOSEPHY, Mr. Albert Wrightson, FCA *1938;* Hillcrest, The Heads, KESWICK, CUMBRIA, CA12 5ER. (Life Member)
JOSEY, Mrs. Julie Katherine, BA FCA *1989;* Linfield Cottage, 1b Lovel Road, CHALFONT ST. PETER, BUCKINGHAMSHIRE, SL9 9NW.
JOSEY, Mrs. Susan Caroline, BSc ACA *1988;* 4 Rufford Gardens, BOURNEMOUTH, BH6 3HX.
JOSH, Mrs. Linda, BSc ACA *1990;* UBC Advancement Services, 500-5950 University Boulevard, VANCOUVER V6T 1Z3, BC, CANADA.
JOSHI, Miss. Aarti, MA(Oxon) ACA *2010;* 46 St. Pauls Avenue, HARROW, MIDDLESEX, HA3 9PS.
JOSHI, Mr. Anil, BSc ACA *1995;* 38 Hazlewell Road, LONDON, SW15 6LR.
•**JOSHI, Mr. Arvind Liladhar, FCA DChA** *1974;* (Tax Fac), Levy + Partners Limited, 86-88 South Ealing Road, LONDON, W5 4QB.
JOSHI, Mr. Dilipkumar Shantilal, ACA *1986;* Orion House, 5 Upper St. Martin's Lane, LONDON, WC2H 9EA.
JOSHI, Mr. Hamal, ACA *2008;* 54 Becmead Avenue, HARROW, MIDDLESEX, HA3 8EY.
JOSHI, Miss. Jyoti, FCA *1984;* Apartment 221, 21-33 Worple Road, LONDON, SW19 4BH.
•**JOSHI, Mr. Kishorkumar Narsinh Vishram, FCA** *1967;* (Tax Fac), Joshi & Co, 3A Upgate, Poringland, NORWICH, NR14 7SH.
JOSHI, Mr. Manish Vinayakrai, BEng ACA *1993;* 13 DALEBURY ROAD, LONDON, SW17 7HQ.
JOSHI, Mr. Nikhil, ACA *2004;* First Floor Flat, 295 Eversleigh Road, LONDON, SW11 5XS.
JOSHI, Miss. Purvi, BA ACA *2005;* 4 Osbourne Croft, Shirley, SOLIHULL, B90 4SP.
•**JOSHI, Mr. Rashesh, BSc FCA** *1998;* Alexander Rosse Limited, 10 Linford Forum, Rockingham Drive, Linford Wood, MILTON KEYNES, MK14 6LY.
JOSHI, Mr. Ronak Dayaram, BSc ACA *2001;* Deutsche Bank, Winchester House, 1 Great Winchester Street, LONDON, EC2N 2DB.
JOSHI, Mr. Sandip Kantilal, BSc FCA AMCT *1996;* RBS Global Banking and Markets, 135 Bishops Gate, LONDON, EC2M 3UR.
JOSHI, Mr. Sunder Devshankar, FCA *1974;* 3108 Vermillion Drive, PLANO, TX 75093, UNITED STATES.
JOSHI, Mr. Sunil Dutt, BEng ACA *1996;* 59 Masefield Avenue, BOREHAMWOOD, HERTFORDSHIRE, WD6 2HH.
JOSHUA, Mrs. Beverley Jane, BA ACA *2004;* I F E S, 319-321 Banbury Road, OXFORD, OX2 7JZ.
JOSHUA, Mrs. Janet Clare, ACA *2001;* The Croft, 5 Well Lane, Mollington, CHESTER, CHESHIRE, CH1 6LD.
JOSLIN, Mrs. Caroline Patricia, BA ACA *1987;* Wyndbourne, Prey Heath Close, Mayford, WOKING, GU22 0SP.
JOSLIN, Mr. Cyril John, FCA *1961;* 4 Hearsall Avenue, Broomfield, CHELMSFORD, CM1 7DD. (Life Member)
•**JOSLIN, Mr. Mark Francis, FCA** *1982;* Davisons Ltd, Lime Court, Pathfields Business Park, SOUTH MOLTON, DEVON, EX36 3LH.
JOSLIN, Mrs. Sarah Jane, BSc ACA *1988;* Finance Department, University of Brighton Mithras House, Lewes Road, BRIGHTON, BN2 4AT.
•**JOSLIN, Mr. Stephen Robert, LLB FCA** *1989;* Joslin & Co Limited, 30 Milton Road, WESTCLIFF-ON-SEA, ESSEX, SS0 7JX.
JOSLING, Mr. Michael Laurence, FCA *1963;* 26 Barrowfield, Cuckfield, HAYWARDS HEATH, RH17 5ER. (Life Member)
JOST, Mr. Christopher Joseph, BA ACA *2005;* 82 Cavendish Road, LONDON, N4 1RS.
JOTHAM, Miss. Barbara Helen, BA FCA DChA *1990;* The Landmark Trust, Shottesbrooke Park, Broadmoor Road, White Waltham, MAIDENHEAD, BERKSHIRE SL6 3SW.
JOUBERT, Mrs. Frances Verity Anderson, MA ACA *1978;* 18a Greenside, Waterbeach, CAMBRIDGE, CB25 9HP.
JOUJOU, Mr. Edgard, MA FCA *1990;* KPMG, Beirut Central District, Lazarieh Building - Bloc A3, 6th Floor, BO Box 11-8270, BEIRUT LEBANON.
JOURDIER, Mr. Anthony Maxwell Kirkpatrick, MA FCA *1970;* Shrubbery House, Stanford Bridge, WORCESTER, WR6 6SG.
JOURDIER, Mr. Peter G K, ACA *2010;* Shrubbery House, Stanford Bridge, WORCESTER, WR6 6SG.
JOURES, Mr. Thomas, BCom FCA *1956;* 15 Camilla Road, Heddon-on-the-Wall, NEWCASTLE UPON TYNE, NE15 0ED. (Life Member)
•**JOURNEAUX, Mr. Graham Edward, PhD BTech ACA** *1981;* PO Box 18206, MANAMA, BAHRAIN.
JOURNEAUX, Mrs. Vivien Elizabeth, FCA *1971;* 69 West Street, Welford, NORTHAMPTON, NN6 6HU.
JOVANOVIC, Miss. Jasminka, BA BSc ACA *2004;* Ernst & Young Llp, 1 More London Place, LONDON, SE1 2AF.
JOW-JENG, Mrs. Kumba, MSc BA(Hons) ACA *2003;* 24 Canterbury Close, BIRMINGHAM, B23 7QL.
JOWETT, Mr. Anthony Hurt, MA ACA *1986;* Route de Buchillon 6F, St Prex, 1162 VAUD, SWITZERLAND.
JOWETT, Mr. Daniel, BA FCA *2000;* Shaw Stockbroking Limited, Level 15, 60 Castlereagh Street, SYDNEY, NSW 2000, AUSTRALIA.
JOWETT, Mr. David Ian, BSc ACA *1982;* Manor Farm, Aike, DRIFFIELD, YO25 9BG.
JOWETT, Mr. Graham, BSc FCA *1977;* Worcester College, Walton Street, OXFORD, OX1 2HB.
JOWETT, Mr. Graham Richard, BA FCA *1986;* 101 Ashley Street, ROSEVILLE, NSW 2069, AUSTRALIA.
JOWETT, Mr. James, BSc FCA *1979;* Eversden, 24 Woodcote Avenue, WALLINGTON, SM6 0QY.
JOWETT, Mr. James Andrew, BSc ACA *1991;* 13038 Pebblebrooke Drive, HOUSTON, TX 77079, UNITED STATES.
JOWETT, Miss. Jocelyn Sarah, BA ACA *1993;* 12 Brendon Street, Marylebone, LONDON, W1H 5HE.
JOWETT, Mr. Kenneth, FCA *1961;* 30 The Wayside, Hurworth, DARLINGTON, COUNTY DURHAM, DL2 2EE. (Life Member)
•**JOWHAL, Mr. Jagdish Singh, BA FCA** *1980;* (Tax Fac), Abacus Business Strategies Limited, 13 Fairway Heights, CAMBERLEY, SURREY, GU15 1NJ.
JOWICZ, Mr. John Peter, MBA BSc ACA *1978;* 5 Rushes Mill, Pelsall, WALSALL, WS3 4QU.
•**JOWITT, Mr. Robin David, BA ACA** *1990;* Ernst & Young LLP, 1 More London Place, LONDON, SE1 2AF. See also Ernst & Young Europe LLP
JOY, Mr. Christopher Henry, LLB FCA *1983;* Hong Kong Institute of CPAs, 37th Floor Wu Chung House, 213 Queens Road East, WAN CHAI, HONG KONG ISLAND, HONG KONG SAR.
JOY, Mrs. Elaine Danielle, ACA *1999;* First Actuarial, 4 Woodside Court Clayton Wood Rise, LEEDS, LS16 6RF.
•**JOY, Mr. Malcolm, BA ACA CTA** *1994;* BDO LLP, Kings Wharf, 20-30 Kings Road, READING, RG1 3EX. See also BDO Stoy Hayward LLP
•**JOY, Mr. Michael Gilbert, FCA** *1979;* Mercer & Hole, Silbury Court, 420 Silbury Boulevard, MILTON KEYNES, BUCKINGHAMSHIRE, MK9 2AF.
JOY, Mrs. Pauline, BA ACA *1990;* 2 Cassiobury Park Avenue, WATFORD, WD18 7LB.
JOY, Mr. Peter, FCA *1985;* Les Sommeilleuses, Hougue Des Doreys, Vale, GUERNSEY, GY6 8ND.
JOY, Mr. Peter Colin Murray, BSc ACA *1982;* Deercopse Guildford Road, Clemsfold, HORSHAM, WEST SUSSEX, RH12 3PW.
JOYCE, Mr. Andrew Robert, BA ACA *1992;* 57 Wishaw Loop, KINROSS, WA 6028, AUSTRALIA.
JOYCE, Mrs. Ann Julie, BA ACA *1983;* Cherry Trees, Menith Wood, WORCESTER, WR6 6UG.
JOYCE, Mr. David John, BA ACA *1985;* Priory Place The Street, Wilmington, POLEGATE, EAST SUSSEX, BN26 5SL.
JOYCE, Mr. David Phillip, BA ACA *1997;* 6 Mons Street, Russell Lea, SYDNEY, NSW 2046, AUSTRALIA.
•**JOYCE, Mr. Duncan Neil, ACA** *1992;* Duncan Joyce & Associates, 36-38 Cross Hayes, MALMESBURY, WILTSHIRE, SN16 9BG. See also Hazell Minshall LLP
JOYCE, Mr. Gary Raymond, ACA *2008;* with Kingston Smith & Partners LLP, Devonshire House, 60 Goswell Road, LONDON, EC1M 7AD.
JOYCE, Mr. Ian Malcolm, FCA *1963;* Flat 7 Latimer Place, 40 Eastbury Avenue, NORTHWOOD, HA6 3FD.
JOYCE, Mrs. Janette Lisa, BA(Hons) ACA DChA *2001;* with Crowe Clark Whitehill LLP, Aquis House, 49-51 Blagrave Street, READING, RG1 1PL.
JOYCE, Ms. Jo Lois, ACA *2008;* K P M G, 1 The Embankment, LEEDS, LS1 4DW.
JOYCE, Mr. Jonathan Mark, BA ACA *2000;* Bowman House, 49 Mabgate, LEEDS, LS9 7DR.
JOYCE, Mr. Kevin, ACA *1983;* 2 Harland Close, BROMSGROVE, WORCESTERSHIRE, B61 8QR.
JOYCE, Mr. Malcolm Howard, BA ACA *1990;* Ash Villa Pipers Ash, Hare Lane Guilden Sutton, CHESTER, CH3 7ED.
JOYCE, Mr. Martin Joseph, BSc ACA *1989;* A S D Metal Services, Valley Farm Road, Stourton, LEEDS, LS10 1SD.
JOYCE, Mr. Matthew, BA ACA *2010;* 9 Langham Gardens, LONDON, W13 8PY.
JOYCE, Mr. Matthew Owen, ACA *2009;* 19 Perrett Way, Ham Green Pill, BRISTOL, BS20 0HX.
JOYCE, Mr. Michael Robert Sean, BSc ACA *1993;* Interquest Group PLC, 16-18 Kirby Street, LONDON, EC1N 8TS.
JOYCE, Mr. Paul Andrew, BSc ACA *2006;* 93 Ivydale Road, LONDON, SE15 3DS.
•**JOYCE, Mr. Philip Clive, FCA ACIS** *1992;* The Orange Partnership Ltd, 17 Crane Mews, Gould Road, TWICKENHAM, TW2 6RS.
JOYCE, Mrs. Rachael Louise, BA ACA *2010;* Pricewaterhousecoopers, 101 Barbirolli Square, MANCHESTER, M2 3PW.
JOYCE, Miss. Rebecca Katherine, BA ACA ACIS *1985;* 7 Seaton Road, WIGSTON, LEICESTERSHIRE, LE18 2BY.
JOYCE, Mr. Richard William, BA FCA *1981;* Avebury, Argos Ltd, 489-499 Avebury Boulevard, MILTON KEYNES, MK9 2NW.
JOYCE, Mr. Ruairi, BSc ACA *2011;* 40 Rathcoole Avenue, Hornsey, LONDON, N8 9NA.
JOYCE, Mr. Shaun William, LLB(Hons) ACA *1993;* Addele Smithies Valley Farm, Parkside Road, LEEDS, LS16 8EZ.
JOYCE, Mrs. Tania, BA ACA *1999;* Angel Wells Farmhouse, Castle Bytham, GRANTHAM, LINCOLNSHIRE, NG33 4SW.
JOYCE, Mr. Timothy John, BA ACA *1984;* High Beech, Sion Road, BATH, BA1 5SG.
JOYCE, Miss. Wendy Annette, BCom ACA *1993;* Laurel Bank, 9 Weaste Lane, Thelwall, WARRINGTON, WA4 3JT.
JOYES, Mr. David, BSc ACA *2005;* with Deloitte LLP, Hill House, 1 Little New Street, LONDON, EC4A 3TR.
JOYNER, Mr. Kevin Charles, ACA *1982;* Magpies, 254 Nine Ashes Road, Blackmore, INGATESTONE, CM4 0JZ.
JOYNER, Dr. Louise, PhD BSc ACA *2011;* 109 Drope Road, St. George's-super-Ely, CARDIFF, CF5 6EP.
JOYNER, Mr. Philip, BSc(Hons) ACA *2004;* 17 Micklefield Lane, Rawdon, LEEDS, LS19 6AZ.
JOYNER, Miss. Rebecca Jane, BA ACA *1991;* 320 East 46th Street, Apt 8A, NEW YORK, NY 10017, UNITED STATES.
JOYNER, Mrs. Sharon Jane, BSc(Hons) ACA *2001;* 3024 Oxford Road, OXFORD 7430, NEW ZEALAND.
JOYNES, Mr. Barry, FCA *1959;* Flat 4 Westbrook Court, 8 West Park Crescent, LEEDS, LS8 2HF. (Life Member)
JOYNSON, Mr. David, FCA *1964;* 12 Spinner Crescent, Comberbach, NORTHWICH, CHESHIRE, CW9 6BB.
JOYNSON, Ms. Juliet Alice Cecilia, BSc ACA *1991;* 11 Pentland Street, LONDON, SW18 2AW.
JOYNSON, Mr. Neil Robert, BA ACA *1999;* Unit 901, 73 Victoria Street, POTTS POINT, NSW 2011, AUSTRALIA.
JOYNSON, Mr. Richard Anthony Paul, BSc ACA *1992;* 35 Bramley Road, Bramhall, STOCKPORT, SK7 2DW.
JOYNT, Mr. Frank Gordon, FCA *1956;* 5 Holme Fauld, Scotby, CARLISLE, CA4 8BL. (Life Member)
JOYNT, Mr. Richard Mark, MA FCA MBA *1998;* Crossland Private Office, 3rd Floor Sir Walter Raleigh House, 48-50 Esplanade, St Helier, JERSEY, JE2 3QB.
•**JUBB, Mr. Christopher Geoffrey Harrold, FCA** *1975;* Slaney & Co, Portland House, 3 Queen Street, WORKSOP, NOTTINGHAMSHIRE, S80 2AW.
JUBB, Mr. David Anthony, BSc ACA *1981;* 24 Ashdale Park, WOKINGHAM, RG40 3QS.
JUBB, Mr. Duncan David Howard, MA ACA *1989;* Squirrels Lodge, Naunton Beauchamp, PERSHORE, WORCESTERSHIRE, WR10 2LQ.
JUBB, Mr. Matthew Richard, BA ACA *2010;* Pricewaterhousecoopers, 9 Greyfriars Road, READING, RG1 1JG.
JUBB, Mr. Matthew Robert, BA(Hons) ACA *2010;* 75 Sandwath Drive, Church Fenton, TADCASTER, NORTH YORKSHIRE, LS24 9US.
JUBB, Mr. Paul David, ACA *1993;* 116 Tranby Lane, Anlaby, HULL, HU10 7EA.
JUBB, Mr. William Thornton, FCA *1969;* 4 Woodlands Road, STALYBRIDGE, SK15 2SQ.
JUBERT, Miss. Natasha Victoria, BA ACA *2005;* 173 Lower Road, Bookham, LEATHERHEAD, SURREY, KT23 4AU.
JUCKES, Mr. Daniel, ACA *2009;* 18a Mildmay Grove South, LONDON, N1 4RL.
JUDD, Mr. Alan Frederick, FCA *1968;* Apartment 93, Commodore House, Juniper Drive, LONDON, SW18 1TZ.
•**JUDD, Mrs. Carole Elizabeth, BSc FCA** *1989;* Carole Judd, 82a Winchester Road, ANDOVER, SP10 2ER.
JUDD, Ms. Catherine Mary, BA ACA *1990;* 8 Park Avenue, East Sheen, LONDON, SW14 8AT.
JUDD, Mr. Charles Owen Matthews, MA FCA *1968;* Granville Court Residents Co Ltd, 33 Granville Court, Cheney Lane, Headington, OXFORD, OX3 0HS.
JUDD, Mr. Colin, ACA *1979;* Grand Buildings 1st Floor, 1-3 Strand, LONDON, WC2N 5EJ.
JUDD, Mr. David Harry, FCA *1964;* 237 Robin Hood Lane, Hall Green, BIRMINGHAM, B28 0DH. (Life Member)
JUDD, Bishop Derek John, FCA *1965;* 47 Swansea Road, Penllergaer, SWANSEA, SA4 9AQ.
•**JUDD, Mr. Edward James, BSc(Hons) ACA** *2000;* Sensible Finance, 15 Lower Evingar Road, WHITCHURCH, HAMPSHIRE, RG28 7BX.
JUDD, Mr. Jasper Rayner Augusto, MA ACA *1988;* 1 Tabalum Road, BALGOWLAH HEIGHTS, NSW 2093, AUSTRALIA.
•**JUDD, Mr. Neal Anthony, BA FCA FSI** *1996;* NA Judd Limited, Milton Keynes Business Centre, Foxhunter Drive, Linford Wood, MILTON KEYNES, MK14 6GD.
JUDD, Mr. Nicholas Ian Campbell, BSc ACA *2006;* Flat 2 Queens Court, Kelburne Road, OXFORD, OXFORDSHIRE, OX4 3SH.

Members - Alphabetical JUDD - KAHN

JUDD, Mr. Norman Douglas, ACA CA(SA) *2008;* 2 Bramblewood Place, FLEET, HAMPSHIRE, GU51 4EF.
JUDD, Mr. Paul Stewart, ACA *1985;* 90B Hebron Road, Torbay, AUCKLAND, NEW ZEALAND.
JUDD, Mrs. Penelope Ruth, BSc ACA *1988;* Fanns Farm House, Canfield Road, Takeley, BISHOP'S STORTFORD, HERTFORDSHIRE, CM22 6SX.
JUDD, Mr. Ronald Leslie, BA FCA *1975;* 25-36 Mayflower Street, Timog Park, ANGELES CITY 2009, PHILIPPINES.
JUDD, Miss. Susan Elizabeth, MA BSc ACA *1980;* 16 Bepton Down, PETERSFIELD, GU31 4PR.
JUDE, Mrs. Clare, BA(Hons) ACA *2001;* 6 Statters Street, COBURG, VIC 3058, AUSTRALIA.
JUDE, Mr. Duncan Jeremy, BA ACA *1993;* Broadways, 63 Ballanard Road, Douglas, ISLE OF MAN, IM2 5HD.
JUDE, Mr. Simon Mark, MEng ACA *2010;* Apartment 4 The Mayfair, 59 Palatine Road, MANCHESTER, M20 3LS.
JUDES, Mr. Alan Marc, FCA *1999;* Strategic Remuneration, 2 Hampstead Heights, LONDON, N2 0PX.
JUDGE, Mr. Andrew James, BA ACA *1995;* 175 Elms Crescent, LONDON, SW4 8QQ.
JUDGE, Mr. Christopher Richard, BA ACA *2004;* Flat 4, Chelsea House, 4 Cavendish Road, MANCHESTER, M20 1JG.
JUDGE, Mr. David Fraser, ACA CA(SA) *2010;* 50 Pensford Avenue, RICHMOND, SURREY, TW9 4AP.
JUDGE, Mr. David James, BA ACA *1983;* Old Vicarage, Manchester Road, Hapton, BURNLEY, BB11 5RF.
JUDGE, Mrs. Hazel Anne, BSc ACA *2004;* 1 Leamington Gate, Coxwell Road, FARINGDON, OXFORDSHIRE, SN7 7FP.
JUDGE, Mrs. Louise Claire, BSc ACA *1994;* Suffolk Life, 153 Princes Street, IPSWICH, IP1 1QJ.
JUDGE, Mr. Matthew Edward, ACA *2000;* 90 Wavendon Avenue, LONDON, W4 4NS.
JUDGE, Mr. Robert David, FCA *1973;* 4 Hayfield Close, Greenmount, BURY, BL8 4QE.
•JUDGES, Mr. Paul Ian, FCA *1975;* W J van, Ghentstraat 23, 3223 RH HELLEVOETSUIS, NETHERLANDS.
JUDKINS, Mr. James Matthew, MMath ACA *2011;* 86 Green Oak Avenue, SHEFFIELD, S17 4FT.
JUDSON, Mr. Christopher William, BSc ACA *1990;* God's Promise, Shap, PENRITH, CA10 3NJ.
JUDSON, Mr. John Michael, FCA *1972;* (Member of Council 1995 - 1999), Croft Head Farm, Ryecroft Road, Glusburn, KEIGHLEY, BD20 8RT.
JUDSON, Mr. Martin Brian, BSc ACA *1992;* Field House, 80 Tollerton Lane, Tollerton, NOTTINGHAM, NG12 4FR.
•JUDSON, Mrs. Rebecca Louise, BA(Hons) ACA *2004;* JL Advisory LLP, 48 Chester Road, Poynton, STOCKPORT, CHESHIRE, SK12 1HA.
JUDSON, Mrs. Sarah Jane, BSc(Hons) ACA *2002;* Laing Investment Management Services Ltd Allington House, 150 Victoria Street, LONDON, SW1E 5LB.
JUDSON, Mr. Stephen Donald, MA FCA *1970;* 2/13 Huntly Road, Campbells Bay, AUCKLAND, NEW ZEALAND.
•JUDSON SMITH, Mrs. Julia Margaret, BSc FCA TEP *1981;* (Tax Fac), UHY Calvert Smith, 31 St Saviourgate, YORK, YO1 8NQ.
JUDT, Mr. Andrew Thomas, BSc FCA *1992;* 135 Wades Hill, LONDON, N21 1EQ.
•JUETT, Mr. Richard Anthony, BSc ACA CTA *1989;* Richard Juett, 2 St Mary's Road, Bishopstoke, EASTLEIGH, SO50 6BP.
JUFFS, Mr. Raymond Stuart, FCA *1968;* Wheatfields, 2 Park Palings Walk, Haynes, BEDFORD, MK45 3PY.
JUGGESSUR, Mr. Ashley, BA(Hons) ACA *2011;* 155 Colin Crescent, LONDON, NW9 6ET.
JUGGINS, Mrs. Janine Claire, BA ACA CTA AMCT *1988;* 33 Crocket Lane, Empingham, OAKHAM, LEICESTERSHIRE, LE15 8PW.
JUGGINS, Mr. John Kenneth, FCA *1975;* Sherbourne, Old Forge Gardens Inn Lane, Hartlebury, KIDDERMINSTER, DY11 7TA.
JUGOO, Mr. Al Jai Shaun Krishna, MSci ARCS FCA MInstP FSI *2001;* L C H.Clearnet Ltd, Aldgate House, 33 Aldgate High Street, LONDON, EC3N 1EA.
JUGURNAUTH, Miss. Sabrina, MSci ACA *2011;* Flat A, 105 St. Georges Road, LONDON, SE1 6HY.
JUHASZ, Miss. Eve Marion, BSc ACA *1995;* Diageo Plc Lakeside Drive, Park Royal, LONDON, NW10 7HQ.
JUHASZ, Mr. Karoly Sandor, MSci ACA *2001;* with National Audit Office, 157-197 Buckingham Palace Road, Victoria, LONDON, SW1W 9SP.
JUKES, Mr. Adam Paul, BSc(Hons) ACA *2001;* #05-06 The Belvedere, 53 Meyer Road, SINGAPORE 437876, SINGAPORE.
•JUKES, Mr. Brian Charles, BSc ACA CTA *1993;* (Tax Fac), Dafferns Resource LLP, 1 Eastwood Business Village, Harry Weston Road, Binley Business Park, COVENTRY, CV3 2UB.
JUKES, Mr. Christopher, BSc ACA *2005;* 16 Valley Drive, SEVENOAKS, TN13 1EG.
•JUKES, Mr. Darren, BCom ACA *1996;* PricewaterhouseCoopers LLP, 7 More London Riverside, LONDON, SE1 2RT. See also PricewaterhouseCoopers
JUKES, Mrs. Heidi, BSc ACA *1995;* 1 Comice Grove, Crowle, WORCESTER, WR7 4SE.
JUKES, Mr. Murray, BSc ACA *1993;* 11 Dolly Bridge Road, RANDOLPH, NJ 07869, UNITED STATES.
JUKES, Mr. Neil Martin, LLB ACA *1999;* 82 Middle Gordon Road, CAMBERLEY, GU15 2HT.
JUKES, Mr. Paul Francis, FCA *1975;* 6 Woodend Park, COBHAM, KT11 3BX.
JUKES, Miss. Tracey Avril, BA ACA *1997;* 17 Hopwood Bank, Horsforth, LEEDS, LS18 5AW.
•JUKES, Mr. William David, FCA *1961;* William Jukes, 30 Parkway, Meols, WIRRAL, MERSEYSIDE, CH47 7BT. See also AIMS - William Jukes
JULER, Mr. Trevor, BSc ACA *1982;* 2 Marlborough Crescent Long Hanborough, WITNEY, OXFORDSHIRE, OX29 8JP.
JULIAN, Mr. David Alistair, BA FCA *1994;* 21 Bluebell Green, CHELMSFORD, CM1 6XF.
•JULIAN, Miss. Hilary Jane, BA FCA DChA *1988;* Carpenter Box LLP, Amelia House, WORTHING, WEST SUSSEX, BN11 1QR.
JULIAN, Mr. John Terence, FCA *1974;* (Tax Fac), 14 Cotswold Gardens, Weavers Rise Otham, MAIDSTONE, ME15 8TB.
JULIAN, Miss. Suzanne Margaret, LLB FCA *1981;* (Tax Fac), 25 Quick Road, LONDON, W4 2BU.
JULIEN, Mr. Michael Frederick, FCA *1964;* (Member of Council 1984 - 1985), 1 Beechwood Avenue, WEYBRIDGE, KT13 9TF. (Life Member)
JULIER, Mr. Peter James, BSc ACA *1995;* Danaway Farm, Maidstone Road, SITTINGBOURNE, ME9 7PY.
JULIO, Mr. Mark Steven, ACA CA(SA) *2008;* Flat 6, 4-6 Oxford Road, LONDON, SW15 2LF.
JULIUS, Mr. Anthony Colin, BA FCA *1996;* 92 Gainsborough Road, Kew, RICHMOND, TW9 2EA.
JULIUS, Mr. Cyril, FCA *1953;* 16 Pavillion Court, Mount Vernon Frognal Rise, LONDON, NW3 6PZ. (Life Member)
JULIUS, Mr. Laurence Jeffrey, BSc FCA *1979;* 30 Bina Gardens, LONDON, SW5 0LA.
•JULLEEKEEA, Mr. Rajesh Kumar, BCom ACA ATII *1995;* (Tax Fac), PricewaterhouseCoopers LLP, The Atrium, 1 Harefield Road, UXBRIDGE, UB8 1EX. See also PricewaterhouseCoopers
JULLIENNE, Mr. Jean France Mario, FCA *1970;* Corona Clothing (H.K.) Co Ltd, La Brasserie Road, FOREST SIDE, MAURITIUS.
JUMA, Mr. Zaherali Amirali Hasan, FCA *1972;* 59 - 151 Townsgate Drive, THORNHILL L4J 8J7, ON, CANADA.
JUMABHOY, Mr. Rafiq, BA(Hons) FCA *1976;* 27 Jalan Pakat Ukay Heights, 68000 AMPANG, SELANGOR, MALAYSIA.
JUMANI, Mr. Aftab Ahmed, BA ACA *1996;* 52 Selborne Road, ILFORD, IG1 3AJ.
•JUMP, Mr. Roger, FCA *1973;* (Tax Fac), Waters & Atkinson, The Old Court House, Clark Street, MORECAMBE, LA4 5HR.
JUNAID, Mr. Mohammed, FCA FCCA *1991;* Ernst & Young Ford Rhodes Sidat Hyder, Mall View Building, 4 Bank Square, LAHORE 54000, PAKISTAN.
JUNEJA, Mr. Manoj Kumar, MSc FCA *1986;* FAO United Nations, CP 64169, 00153 ROME, ITALY.
•JUNEMAN, Mr. Richard John, BSc FCA *1982;* (Tax Fac), Richard Juneman Limited, 8 Great James Street, LONDON, WC1N 3DF.
JUNER, Mr. Richard, MBA ACA ATII *2002;* 11 Albert Road, FALKIRK, FK1 5LS.
JUNG, Mr. Syed Mahin Mahmud, BA FCA *1968;* 137-143, High Street, SUTTON, SM1 1JH.
JUNIPER, Mr. Barry Derek, FCA *1968;* 7 Gainsborough Road, Ashley Heath, RINGWOOD, HAMPSHIRE, BH24 2HY.
JUNIPER, Mr. Brett Robert, ACA *2008;* 54 Ravenslea Road, LONDON, SW12 8RX.
JUNIPER, Mr. Paul Frederick John, FCA *1973;* 47 Dulsie Road, BOURNEMOUTH, BH3 7DZ.
JUNOR, Mr. Neville Keith, FCA *1948;* 7 Fulmar Drive, KENDAL, LA9 7RN. (Life Member)
JUPP, Mrs. Amy Victoria, BSc ACA *2005;* 14 Holmecroft Chase, Westhoughton, BOLTON, BL5 3ZN.
•JUPP, Dr. Andrew Peter, FCA *1991;* (Tax Fac), haysmacintyre, Fairfax House, 15 Fulwood Place, LONDON, WC1V 6AY.
JUPP, Mrs. Jane Elizabeth, BSc FCA ATII *1978;* (Tax Fac), Charlotte Cottage, Kilmington Common, Kilmington, WARMINSTER, BA12 6QY.
JUPP, Mr. Nigel, BSc ACA *1991;* Logica Australia Pty Ltd, level 13, 100 Pacific Highway, SYDNEY, NSW 2060, AUSTRALIA.
•JUPP, Mr. Nigel Graeme Anthony, BSc FCA *1989;* Jupps Limited, County House, 3 Shelley Road, WORTHING, WEST SUSSEX, BN11 1TT.
JUPP, Dr. Sonia, PhD BSc ACA CTA AIIT *1988;* (Tax Fac), Basement Flat, 18 Southborough Road, LONDON, E9 7EF.
JUPP, Mrs. Susan Kathleen, ACA *1993;* Southview, 5 St Martin's Park, Marshfield, CHIPPENHAM, SN14 8PQ.
JUPP, Dr. Tara Louise, PhD ACA *2009;* 4 Wether Road, Great Cambourne, CAMBRIDGE, CB23 5DT.
•JURD, Mrs. Rachael Kerry, ACA FCCA *2009;* AM-PM Accounting Solutions Limited, Building 6000, Langstone Technology Park, Langstone Road, HAVANT, HAMPSHIRE PO9 1SA.
JURENKO, Mr. Andrew Tadeusz, FCA *1974;* Copley Dene, 15 Briar Hill, PURLEY, CR8 3LF.
JURKOWSKI, Mrs. Alison Frances, BSc ACA *1989;* 112 Park Road, Timperley, ALTRINCHAM, WA15 6TQ.
JURY, Mr. Simon Peter, BSc FCA *1984;* Liverpool Victoria, County Gates House, County Gates, BOURNEMOUTH, BH1 2NF.
•JURY, Mr. Timothy Denis Hoyle, FCA *1979;* 5 Saddlers Mews, CLITHEROE, BB7 1AF.
JUSKIW, Miss. Emma Louise, ACA *2010;* 45 Stewart Close, ABBOTS LANGLEY, HERTFORDSHIRE, WD5 0LU.
JUST, Mr. Richard Charles, BA ACA *2006;* 118 North Street, Burwell, CAMBRIDGE, CB5 0BB.
JUSTESEN, Mr. Mark Christian, BA ACA *1994;* Summerfield House, Brook Street, Fovant, SALISBURY, SP3 5JB.
•JUSTICE, Ms. Hannah Elizabeth, ACA FCCA *2010;* BSN Associates Limited, 3b Swallowfield Courtyard, Wolverhampton Road, OLDBURY, WEST MIDLANDS, B69 2JG. See also BSN Associates Holdings Limited
JUSTICE, Mrs. Jennifer Margaret, BA ACA *1999;* The Laurels Sandy Lane, Kingswood, TADWORTH, KT20 6NQ.
JUSTICE, Mr. Kevin Thomas, BA ACA *2006;* Davis Langdon Llp Colmore Plaza, 20 Colmore Circus Queensway, BIRMINGHAM, B4 6AT.
JUSTICE, Miss. Lisa, ACA *2008;* 53 Stansted Road, SOUTHSEA, PO5 1RZ.
•JUSTICE, Mr. Robert George, FCA *1973;* (Tax Fac), R.G. Justice & Co, 36 Heath Street, STOURBRIDGE, WEST MIDLANDS, DY8 1SB.
JUSTICE, Mrs. Ruth, BA ACA *2005;* 48 Anchor Lane, SOLIHULL, B91 2LA.
JUSTICE, Mr. Warren Henry, MBA BSc ACA *1994;* 35 St. Michaels Road, CARDIFF, CF5 2AL.
JUSTICE, Mr. William David Alexander, FCA *1964;* 51 Gwendwr Road, LONDON, W14 9BG.
JUSTIN, Miss. Helen Louise, BSc ACA *2002;* Flat 31, Solar Court, Etchingham Park Road, LONDON, N3 2DZ.
•JUTHANI, Mr. Kanak Kumar Rugnath, ACA *1981;* (Tax Fac), Kanak Juthani, 209A Headstone Lane, HARROW, MIDDLESEX, HA2 6ND.
JUTSON, Mr. Kevin Trevor, BA ACA *2002;* Hendford Manor, Hendford, YEOVIL, SOMERSET, BA20 1UN.
JUTSUM, Mr. John Alfred, BA FCA *1975;* Little Acre, The Park, Minchinhampton, STROUD, GL6 9BS.
JUUL, Mr. Peter Neil, BSc ACA *1979;* 10 Cotham Lawn Road, Cotham, BRISTOL, BS6 6DU.
KA, Mr. Andy Francis, BA ACA *2002;* with Grant Thornton UK LLP, Grant Thornton House, 22 Melton Street, Euston Square, LONDON, NW1 2EP.
KAARS SIJPESTEIJN, Mr. Casper Hendrik, BA ACA *2009;* George IV House, Main Street, Scotton, KNARESBOROUGH, NORTH YORKSHIRE, HG5 9HY.
•KABAN, Mr. Tugrul, BA FCA *1985;* (Tax Fac), Percepture Ltd, Marquis House, 68 Great North Road, HATFIELD, HERTFORDSHIRE, AL9 5ER.
•KABEL, Mr. Michael, FCA *1971;* Clayman & Co, 189 Bickenhall Mansions, Bickenhall StreetBaker Street, LONDON, W1U 6BX.
KABERRY, Mr. Andrew Murdoch, BA FCA *1972;* Thorp Arch Hall, WETHERBY, LS23 7AW.
KABERRY, Sir Christopher Donald, Bt FCA *1967;* London & Continental Stations & Property Ltd, 183 Eversholt Street, LONDON, NW1 1AY.
•KABINI, Mr. Alfred Freddy, ACA *1995;* (Tax Fac), A F Kabini & Co, 14 Conlan Street, LONDON, W10 5AR.
KABWE, Mr. George Mubanga, BEng FCA *1995;* 6114 Nevada Avenue NW, WASHINGTON, DC 20015, UNITED STATES.
KACHALA, Mrs. Angeli, BAcc ACA *1999;* 105 Heath Road, BEACONSFIELD, BUCKINGHAMSHIRE, HP9 1DJ.
•①KACHANI, Mr. Alex, FCA *1979;* Crawfords Accountants LLP, Stanton House, 41 Blackfriars Road, SALFORD, M3 7DB.
•KACHHELA, Miss. Trusha, BSc ACA ATII *1996;* (Tax Fac), PricewaterhouseCoopers LLP, Donington Court, Pegasus Business Park, Castle Donington, DERBY, DE74 2UZ. See also PricewaterhouseCoopers
•KACHWALLA, Mrs. Nafisa, BSc FCA *1991;* (Tax Fac), Ashings Limited, Northside House, Mount Pleasent, BARNET, HERTFORDSHIRE, EN4 9EB.
KACZMAR, Mr. Paul, BA FCA *1988;* 11 The Beeches, Uppingham, OAKHAM, LE15 9PG.
KADAR, Mr. Aqib, ACA *2011;* 8 Daws Hill Lane, HIGH WYCOMBE, BUCKINGHAMSHIRE, HP11 1PW.
KADHIM, Mr. Simon, FCA *1966;* PO BOX 31303, DUBAI, UNITED ARAB EMIRATES. (Life Member)
KADIFACHI, Mr. Ali Sadiq Patrick, MEng BEng ACA *2000;* Flat 7, Lilliput Hall, 9 Old Jamaica Road, LONDON, SE16 4TE.
KADIR ISMAIL, Ms. Noor Nahar, BA(Hons) ACA *2002;* 149A Villa Laman Tasik, Bandar SR1, Permaisuri, Cheras, 56000 KUALA LUMPUR, FEDERAL TERRITORY MALAYSIA.
KADIRI, Mrs. Tasneem, BSc ACA *2006;* (Tax Fac), Akzo Nobel, Portland House, Bressenden Place, LONDON, SW1E 5BH.
KADRI, Mr. Mohammed Rafik, ACA *1984;* 69 Nield Road, HAYES, MIDDLESEX, UB3 1SG.
KADWANI, Mr. Mohammed, ACA *2010;* 73 Hartfield Avenue, Elstree, BOREHAMWOOD, HERTFORDSHIRE, WD6 3JJ.
KAFFAS, Mr. Antonios Kyriakos, FCA *1977;* THISEOS 2, 19013 SARONIDA, GREECE.
•KAFFEL, Mr. Lawrence, FCA *1965;* L. Kaffel, Helmsdale, Green Lane, STANMORE, HA7 3AH.
KAGAN, Mr. Howard Alan, BA ACA *2001;* Audley Capital Advisors, 11-14 Grafton Street, LONDON, W1S 4EW.
•KAGDADIA, Mr. Ashwin Govindji, BSc FCA *1990;* (Tax Fac), AGK Limited, 246 Narborough Road, LEICESTER, LE3 2AP.
KAGZI, Mrs. Emma Jane, BA(Hons) ACA *2001;* 15 Naseby Rise, NEWBURY, BERKSHIRE, RG14 2SF.
•KAHAN, Mr. Akiva, FCA *1992;* Joseph Kahan Associates LLP, 923 Finchley Road, LONDON, NW11 7PE. See also Joseph Kahan Associates Taxation Services ltd, Jody Associates Limited and Joseph Kahan Associates Payroll Services Ltd
KAHAN, Mrs. Emma Louise, ACA *2008;* Deloitte Llp, 5 Callaghan Square, CARDIFF, CF10 5BT.
KAHAN, Mr. James, BSc ACA *2011;* 68 Cranbourne Gardens, LONDON, NW11 0JD.
•KAHAN, Mr. Jeffrey Herman, FCA *1974;* Jeffrey H. Kahan, 5 Aprey Gardens, LONDON, NW4 2RH.
KAHAN, Mr. Keith Raymond, BA FCA *1982;* 1628 Royal Palm Way, BOCA RATON, FL 33432, UNITED STATES.
KAHAN, Mr. Naftali Hertz, BA ACA *1982;* Zurenborgstraat 38, 2018 ANTWERP, BELGIUM.
•KAHAN, Mr. Shlomo Alex, LLB ACA *1984;* (Tax Fac), Lopian Gross Barnett & Co, 6th Floor, Cardinal House, 20 St. Marys Parsonage, MANCHESTER, M3 2LG. See also Harvester Consultants Limited
KAHAN, Mr. Steven, ACA *2008;* 46 St. Georges Road, Golders Green, LONDON, NW11 0LR.
KAHAN, Mr. Thomas Alfred, ACA *2008;* 22 Deri Road, CARDIFF, CF23 5AJ.
KAHER, Mr. Amit, BEng ACA *2010;* 38 Cambridge Avenue, GREENFORD, MIDDLESEX, UB6 0PJ.
KAHLER, Miss. Jane Elizabeth, BSc ACA *2002;* Unit 4, 10 Crathern Close, Edge Hill, CAIRNS, QLD 4870, AUSTRALIA.
KAHLON, Miss. Charanjit, BSc ACA *1999;* 3 Elwin Drive, Bramcote, NOTTINGHAM, NG9 3LT.
KAHLON, Mr. Himmet Singh, ACA *1982;* House 59, Sector 5, CHANDIGARH, INDIA.
KAHLON, Miss. Rajwinder, ACA *2008;* Flat 7, 30 Belsize Park, LONDON, NW3 4DX.
KAHN, Mr. Clive Ian, ACA *1982;* 1 Bickenhall st, LONDON, w1u6bn.

KAHN, Mr. John Emmanuel, BSc FCA CITP CPA *1988;* 3156 East Addison, ALPHARETTA, GA 30022, UNITED STATES.

•①**KAHN, Mr. Neville Barry, BA FCA** *1987;* Deloitte LLP, Athene Place, 66 Shoe Lane, LONDON, EC4A 3BQ. See also Deloitte & Touche LLP

KAICKER, Mr. Raman, FCA *1985;* BUSINESS CLINIC, 107 Cumballa Crest, 42 Pedder road, MUMBAI 400026, MAHARASHTRA, INDIA.

•**KAIL, Mr. Andrew, BA ACA** *1994;* PricewaterhouseCoopers LLP, Hays Galleria, 1 Hays Lane, LONDON, SE1 2RD. See also PricewaterhouseCoopers

KAIMAKAMIS, Mr. Frixos, BSc ACA *2010;* 7 Elm Avenue, LONDON, W5 3XA.

•**KAINTH, Mr. Sanjev, BA ACA CTA** *2004;* (Tax Fac), S Kainth & Co Limited, 34 Belvedere Avenue, Clayhall, ILFORD, ESSEX, IG5 0UE. See also S Kainth & Co

KAINTH, Miss. Sarita, ACA *2008;* 25 Albert Road, Merstham, REDHILL, RH1 3LU.

•**KAISER, Mrs. Julie Caroline, ACA** *1997;* (Tax Fac), Baker Tilly Tax & Advisory Services LLP, 2 Humber Quays, Wellington Street West, HULL, HU1 2BN.

KAISSIDES, Mr. Athos, BSc ACA *1993;* Eurobank EFG Cyprus Ltd, 41 Arch Makarios Avenue, 1065 NICOSIA, CYPRUS.

KAJEE, Mr. Shoaib Mahmed, BAEcon(Hons) ACA *2011;* 8 Roland Road, BOLTON, BL3 4DG.

KAKAD, Mr. Ronak, BSc(Hons) ACA *2001;* 10 Trillium Close, West Hamilton, LEICESTER, LE5 1UQ.

KAKAWAND, Mr. Mohsen, BSc FCA *1978;* Triftenstr. 78, 32547 BAD OEYNHAUSEN, GERMANY.

•**KAKKAD, Mr. Dilip Tulsidas, BSc FCA CTA** *1979;* (Tax Fac), Saffery Champness, Lion House, Red Lion Street, LONDON, WC1R 4GB.

KAKKAD, Miss. Shikha, BSc ACA *2007;* 42 Bethune Avenue, LONDON, N11 3LE.

KAKKAD, Mr. Snehal, BSc ACA *1995;* 20 St. Marys Road, WATFORD, WD18 0EF.

KAKKOU, Mr. Yiannakis, BA ACA *2008;* 4 Markou Drakou Flat 301, 2012 Strovolos, 2012 NICOSIA, CYPRUS.

•**KAKOFENGITIS, Mr. Athos, BSc FCA** *1994;* SCI Kakofengitis & Co Ltd, Zinas Kanther 4, 3035 LIMASSOL, CYPRUS.

•**KAKOULLIS, Mr. Panos Koulis, MA FCA** *1992;* Deloitte LLP, 2 New Street Square, LONDON, EC4A 3BZ. See also Deloitte & Touche LLP

KALA, Mr. Haffiz, BEcons(Hons) ACA *2011;* 65 Wincanton Crescent, NORTHOLT, MIDDLESEX, UB5 4HQ.

•**KALABALIKI, Miss. Maria, MSc FCA** *2001;* 790 Boylston Street, Apt 7B, BOSTON, MA 02199, UNITED STATES.

KALACHAND, Mr. Aakash, ACA *2011;* Apartment 48, Annes Court, 3 Palgrave Gardens, Rossmore Road, LONDON, NW1 6EN.

KALACHAND, Mr. Ashok Kumar Jai Krishen, BSc ACA *1979;* J.Kalachand & Company Limited, Anse Courtois, PAILLES, MAURITIUS.

KALADEEN, Mr. Christopher, BEng ACA *1996;* 31, 31 Hereford Square, LONDON, SW7 4NB.

KALADEEN, Mr. Mike, MEng ACA *2007;* Morgan Stanley, 20 Bank Street, LONDON, E14 4AD.

KALADEEN, Miss. Nalini, BSc(Econ) ACA *2001;* 16 Shirley Avenue, Cheam, SUTTON, SM2 7QR.

KALATZI, Mrs. Siwan Elizabeth, BA ACA *2005;* 55 Shelgate Walk, Woodley, READING, RG5 3DP.

KALAWADH, Mr. Hadi Abdulnabi Abedali, ACA *2002;* PO Box 26772, MANAMA, BAHRAIN.

KALB, Mr. Nigel David, BA ACA *1989;* Flat 17, Ryalls Court, 430 Oakleigh Road North, LONDON, N20 0RY.

KALBFELL, Miss. Cathrin, ACA *2011;* Apartment 24, Cityview, Lansdowne Lane, LONDON, SE7 8JE.

KALDERON, Mrs. Susan Mary Radford, MA FCA *1979;* 9 Burghley Road, Wimbledon, LONDON, SW19 5BG.

KALE, Mr. Yashodhan Madhusudan, FCA *1971;* (Tax Fac), 2 Sumit, 31 Carmichael Road, MUMBAI 400026, MAHARASHTRA, INDIA.

KALER, Mr. Izmar Suhail, BA ACA *2002;* 39 Heathfield Road, Penenden Heath, MAIDSTONE, ME14 2AD.

•**KALEY, Mrs. Andrea Suzanne, ACA FCCA** *2010;* Fisher Michael, Boundary House, 4 County Place, New London Road, CHELMSFORD, CM2 0RE.

KALI, Mr. Raffik, FCA *1982;* Comet Ltd, P.O. Box 51146, LIMBE, MALAWI.

KALIA, Mr. Ajai, BA ACA *2004;* 14 Spring Gardens, NOTTINGHAM, NG8 4JN.

•**KALIAS, Mr. Costas A, ACA** *2009;* KPMG, 14 Esperidon Street, 1087 NICOSIA, CYPRUS.

•**KALIRAI, Mr. Surrinder Singh, BSc ACA** *1988;* AIMS - Accountants for Business, 2 Pinfold Lane, Penn, WOLVERHAMPTON, WV4 4EE.

KALISPERAS, Mrs. Paola, BSc ACA *1994;* 167 Portland Road, Notting Hill, LONDON, W11 4LR.

KALLAWAY, Mrs. Claire Fiona, MA(Hons) ACA *2004;* Leigh Farm, Leigh, CHARD, TA20 4HT.

KALLENBERG, Mr. Michael Howard, FCA *1972;* 73 Richmond Road, New Barnet, BARNET, HERTFORDSHIRE, EN5 1SF.

KALLENOS, Mr. Emilios Georgalli, FCA *1974;* 3Charalambou Mouskou Street, Dasoupolis, 2015 NICOSIA, CYPRUS.

KALLER, Mrs. Amanprit Kaur, ACA CISA *2004;* 20 Yateley Avenue, BIRMINGHAM, B42 1JN.

•**KALLI, Mr. Constantinos, BSc(Hons) ACA** *2002;* KPMG Limited, P O Box 21121, 1502 NICOSIA, CYPRUS. See also KPMG Metaxas Loizides Syrimis

•**KALLIAS, Mr. Marios, MSc FCA ATII** *1998;* M Kallias & Co Ltd, Office 202, 10 Gregoriou Xenapoulou Street, 1061 NICOSIA, CYPRUS.

KALLINIKOU, Mr. Michael Antoniou, FCA *1982;* Central Bank of Cyprus, 80 Kennedy Avenue, 1076 NICOSIA, CYPRUS.

KALLIS, Mr. Jacovos, FCA *1980;* ERECHTHIOU 20, 2121 NICOSIA, CYPRUS.

KALLIS, Mr. Marinos, BCom ACA *1997;* P.O.Box 21750, 1512 NICOSIA, CYPRUS.

•**KALLU, Mr. Simon Richard, ACA** *2010;* SRK Accounting Limited, 27 Holmes Court, Paradise Road, LONDON, SW4 6QJ.

KALMAKRIAN, Mr. Leon, BSc ACA *2006;* Flat 1 159 Lewisham Road, LONDON, SE13 7PZ.

KALMAN, Mr. Jeffrey Philip, FCA *1967;* Highcroft, 241 Hale Lane, EDGWARE, HA8 9QF.

KALMAN, Mrs. Karen Muriel, FCA *1976;* White Gables, Beauport Estate, St. Brelade, JERSEY, JE3 8DG.

KALMAN, Mr. Melvyn, FCA *1975;* BKS Family Office Limited, 22 Colomberie, St Helier, JERSEY, JE1 4XA.

KALMS, Mr. Daniel Julian, BA FCA *2001;* 38 Furham Feild, PINNER, MIDDLESEX, HA5 4DZ.

KALONA, Mr. Patrick, BSc ACA *2010;* Flat 3, Leeside Court, 169 Rotherhithe Street, LONDON, SE16 5SZ.

KALOTHEOU, Mr. Andreas, ACA *2011;* 25a Priory Terrace, LONDON, NW6 4DG.

KALOYEROS, Mr. Constantinos Stephanou, BSc ACA *1993;* 3 Michalakis Zambas Street, Strovolos, 2057 NICOSIA, CYPRUS.

KALOYIROU, Ms. Eleni Stefanou, MA FCA *1989;* P O Box 24774, NICOSIA, 1303, CYPRUS.

•**KALRA, Mr. Anil, BSc ACA** *1993;* (Tax Fac), 38 Cissbury Ring South, LONDON, N12 7BE.

KALRA, Mr. Kunal, ACA *2008;* 11 Tudor Close, LONDON, NW3 4AB.

KALRA, Mr. Manmohan Singh, FCA *1979;* The Oxford, 422 East 72nd Street, Apt #26D, NEW YORK, NY 10021, UNITED STATES.

KALRA, Mr. Vinod Kumar, FCA *1963;* 3/12 Shanti Niketan, NEW DELHI 110 021, INDIA.

KALSI, Mrs. Balvinder, BSc ACA *1993;* Select Enterprises, Crown House 227 Aldborough Road South, ILFORD, IG3 8HZ.

KALSI, Mr. Gurminder Singh, BA(Hons) ACA *2003;* 1 Devonshire Close, RUGBY, WARWICKSHIRE, CV22 7EE.

KALSI, Mrs. Jenney Kaur, MSc BA ACA *2005;* with KPMG LLP, 15 Canada Square, LONDON, E14 5GL.

KALSI, Mr. Kamaljit Singh, BSc ACA *1991;* BT Global Services, PP A2-1, Leavesden Park, Hercules Way, Leavesden, WATFORD WD25 7GR.

KALSI, Mr. Manmeet, ACA *2010;* 34 Pippin Grove, ROYSTON, HERTFORDSHIRE, SG8 5HP.

KALSI, Mr. Neil, ACA *2008;* CBRE Investors, Consolidated Property Group, 21 Bryanston Street, LONDON, W1H 7PR.

KALSI, Mr. Tom, BSc(Hons) ACA *2009;* 14 Keble Drive, Syston, LEICESTER, LE7 2AN.

KALTZ, Mr. Michael Jonathan, BSc FCA *1981;* 43 Wieland Road, NORTHWOOD, MIDDLESEX, HA6 3QX.

KALU, Mr. Kalu Uke, BA FCA *1965;* 3 Idemili Drive, Independence Layout, P.O. Box 107, ENUGU, NIGERIA. (Life Member)

KALUS, Mr. Henry, BA ACA *1980;* 8 Morland Avenue, LEICESTER, LE2 2PE.

KALYAN, Miss. Janice, BA ACA *2002;* 71 Deeds Grove, HIGH WYCOMBE, HP12 3NT.

KAM, Mr. Adrian Thiam Yew, ACA *2011;* E-2656 Taman Zurina, Jalan Wong Ah Jang, 25100 KUANTAN, PAHANG, MALAYSIA.

KAM, Mr. Alex Kwong Fai, ACA *1982;* 25 Moorsom Road, JARDINE'S LOOKOUT, HONG KONG ISLAND, HONG KONG SAR.

KAM, Mr. Anthony Chi Chiu, MA FCA *1987;* 1701 Shui On Centre, 6-8 Harbour Road, WAN CHAI, HONG KONG ISLAND, HONG KONG SAR.

KAM, Miss. Connie Sin Yu, ACA *2008;* 5 Scholars Walk, CAMBRIDGE, CAMBRIDGESHIRE, CB4 1DW.

KAM, Mr. Hau Choi Anthony, ACA *2005;* Anthony Kam & Associates Ltd, 2105 Wing On Centre, 111 Connaught Road, CENTRAL, HONG KONG ISLAND, HONG KONG SAR.

KAM, Miss. Ka Woo Annie, BSc ACA *1993;* 10/F, Chun Wo Commercial Centre, 23-29 Wing Wo Street, SHEUNG WAN, HONG KONG ISLAND, HONG KONG SAR.

KAM, Mr. Leung Ming, ACA *2007;* Room B3 19/F Kin Lee Building Tower B, No. 130-146 Jaffe Road, WAN CHAI, HONG KONG ISLAND, HONG KONG SAR.

KAM, Ms. Miu Han Shirley, ACA *2008;* 17H, Block 14, Chi Fu Fa Yuen, POK FU LAM, HONG KONG SAR.

KAM, Mr. Philip Yuen Kirk, BA ACA *1996;* 125 Chanctonbury Way, LONDON, N12 7AE.

KAM, Mr. Pok Man, ACA *2007;* Flat A, 16/F Kenyon Court, 50 Bonham Road, MID LEVELS, HONG KONG ISLAND, HONG KONG SAR.

KAM, Mrs. Suk-Han Astor, ACA *1983;* 25 Moorsom Road, JARDINE'S LOOKOUT, HONG KONG ISLAND, HONG KONG SAR.

KAM, Mr. Wilfred Yiu-Ming, ACA *1987;* 1B Block 1, Joy Garden, 3 Alnwick Road, KOWLOON TONG, KOWLOON, HONG KONG SAR.

KAM, Mr. Yiu Kwok, ACA *2005;* Flat A 26/F. Tower 7 Discovery Park, 398 Castle Peak Road, TSUEN WAN, NEW TERRITORIES, HONG KONG SAR.

KAM, Mr. Yiu Shing Tony, ACA *2008;* Kam & Cheung, Room 401 4th Floor, Wah Yuen Building, 149 Queen's Road, CENTRAL, HONG KONG SAR.

•**KAM CHEONG, Mr. Stewart Kien Lo, FCA** *1991;* MAS, 6C Parc D'Activites Syrdall, 5365 MUNSBACH, LUXEMBOURG.

KAMAL, Mr. Ismet, BA ACA *1986;* KPMG Croatia D O O, Eurtower 17 Kat, Ivana Lucica 2A, ZAGREB, CROATIA.

•①**KAMAL, Mr. Javed, FCA FABRP** *1978;* (Tax Fac), Ferguson Maidment & Co, Sardinia House, Sardinia Street, Lincolns Inn Fields, LONDON, WC2A 3LZ.

KAMAL, Mrs. Linda, BA ACA *1990;* 15 Cotswold View, BATH, BA2 1HA.

KAMAL, Miss. Samra, BSc ACA *2011;* 7 Church Avenue, PINNER, MIDDLESEX, HA5 5HZ.

KAMAL, Mr. Shahid, BSc(Hons) ACA *2004;* 42 Amberwood Rise, NEW MALDEN, KT3 5JF.

KAMAL, Mr. Tarif Burhan, FCA *1971;* 19 Durrels House, Warwick Gardens, LONDON, W14 8QB. (Life Member)

KAMALARAJAH, Mr. Ganesar, BSc ACA *1992;* 64 The Ride, BRENTFORD, MIDDLESEX, TW8 9LA.

KAMALUDDIN, Mr. Jonathan Damian, BEng FCA *1999;* 134 Wakehurst Road, LONDON, SW11 6BS.

KAMARAJ, Miss. Kardhika, BSc ACA *2011;* 53 Rosebery Avenue, LONDON, E12 6PY.

KAMARALZAMAN, Mr. Suhaimi, BA ACA *1995;* 18 Jalan PJU3/18J, Damansara Indah Resort Homes, 47410 PETALING JAYA, SELANGOR, MALAYSIA.

KAMARIS, Mr. Christopher George Michael, BSc ACA *1984;* with PricewaterhouseCoopers LLP, 1 Embankment Place, LONDON, WC2N 6RH.

•**KAMARUDDIN, Mr. Tengku Yunus, BA FCA** *1971;* 14 Jalan Maktab Lima, 54000 KUALA LUMPUR, FEDERAL TERRITORY, MALAYSIA.

KAMARUZZAMAN, Miss. Iza Mazrini, BSc ACA *2000;* 25 Jalan PJU1A/28C, Ara Damansara, 47301 PETALING JAYA, SELANGOR, MALAYSIA.

KAMAU, Mr. Benson Ngari, ACA *1994;* P.O. Box 4097, (GPO), NAIROBI, 00100, KENYA.

KAMAU, Mr. Philip Ojwang, MBA BCom ACIB FCA FFA CPA AMCT *1991;* AFRICAN EXPORT-IMPORT BANK, 72B EL-MAAHAD EL-ESHTERAKY STREET, P.O BOX 613 HELIOPOLIS, CAIRO 11757, EGYPT, CAIRO EGYPT.

KAMBERIS, Mr. Alexios Theodoros, BA ACA *2003;* 19 Parthenonos Street, Engomi, CY2413 NICOSIA, CYPRUS.

KAMBLI, Mr. Sunil Mangesh, MBA LLB ACA CTA *2001;* Premier Solicitors, Mayfair House, 11 Lurke Street, BEDFORD, MK40 3HZ.

KAMBO, Mr. Gurjit Singh, BSc ACA *2000;* 16 Langham Drive, ROMFORD, RM6 4TD.

KAMBO, Mr. Gursharan Singh, MSc ACA *2004;* 15 St. Thomas Drive, PINNER, HA5 4SX.

•**KAMBO, Mr. Harjinder Singh, BSc FCA** *1990;* (Tax Fac), Kambo & Co, 109-111 Malling Road, SNODLAND, KENT, ME6 5AB.

•**KAMBOJ, Mr. Harjinder Pal, ACA** *1980;* Kamboj Associates Ltd, 29 New Broadway, UXBRIDGE, UB10 0LL.

KAMDAR, Mr. Divyesh M, BSc ACA *1986;* Comline Trade Ltd Unit B1, Luton Enterprise Park Sundon Park Road, LUTON, LU3 3GU.

KAMEEN, Miss. Caroline Elizabeth, BSc ACA *2007;* 3d Shooters Hill Road, LONDON, SE3 7AR.

KAMENOVA, Miss. Elena, BSc ACA *2010;* Apt 201, 41 Essex Street, BIRMINGHAM, B5 4TR.

KAMERI, Ms. Maria, BA ACA *2005;* Flat 1, Thetidos Street, AP. Petrou & Pavlou Area, 3086 LIMASSOL, CYPRUS.

•**KAMHAWI, Mr. Nabil Walid, FCA** *1975;* Allied Business Advisors, P O Box 347, Al-Orman Giza, CAIRO, 12612, EGYPT.

KAMIL, Mr. Nik Rizal, ACA *2001;* 1079 Jalan Damansara, Taman Tun Dr. Ismail, 60000 KUALA LUMPUR, FEDERAL TERRITORY, MALAYSIA.

KAMINSKI, Mr. Daniel Joseph, BSc ACA *1979;* The Neos Company Limited, 12 Russell Road, LONDON, W14 8JA.

KAMPING, Mr. Arend Vaughan William Alfred, FCA ACCA *1975;* Merivale, Duffield Bank, Duffield, BELPER, DERBYSHIRE, DE56 4BG.

KAMRA, Mr. Jatinder, BA ACA *2005;* Michael Page, 5 Aldermanbury Square, LONDON, EC2V 7HR.

KAMRAN, Mr. Mohammed, BA ACA *2008;* 5 Kiniths Crescent, WEST BROMWICH, WEST MIDLANDS, B71 4BX.

KAMTE, Mr. Anil Anand, ACA *1981;* 10 Fermanagh Road, CAMBERWELL, VIC 3124, AUSTRALIA.

KAN, Mr. Billy Albert Che Kin, BSc ACA *1979;* 18/F, Flat B2, Elm Tree Towers, 10 Chun Fai Rd, JARDINE'S LOOKOUT, HONG KONG ISLAND HONG KONG SAR.

KAN, Mr. Chi-Keung, MBA BSc FCA *1990;* Flat B 11/F, Cornell Court, 56 Kings Road, NORTH POINT, HONG KONG ISLAND, HONG KONG SAR.

KAN, Mr. Edward Siew Cheng, FCA *1974;* 800 Reece Court, MILTON L9T 0M9, ON, CANADA.

KAN, Dr. Ernest Yaw-Kiong, BA FCA *1986;* Deloitte & Touche, 6 Shenton Way, 32-00, DBS Building Tower Two, SINGAPORE 068809, SINGAPORE.

KAN, Mr. Gavin, ACA *2008;* Flat 7 Oak Tree Court, 40 Overton Road, SUTTON, SM2 6DN.

KAN, Mr. Ho Wan Andrew, ACA *2008;* 20th Floor, Henley Building, 5 Queen's Road, CENTRAL, HONG KONG ISLAND, HONG KONG SAR.

KAN, Mr. Joe Yat Cho, BEng ACA *1992;* 19 Princess Margaret Road 8/F, HO MAN TIN, Kowloon, HONG KONG SAR.

KAN, Mr. Patrick Mun Gneen, FCA *1973;* Patrick Kan & Co, 80 Marine Parade Road, #16-09, Parkway Parade, SINGAPORE 449269, SINGAPORE.

KAN, Mr. Peng Yim, FCA *1989;* 14 Alexandra Road, LONDON, N8 0PP.

KAN, Mr. Peter Yu Leung, FCA *1992;* KPMG, 8/F Prince's Building, 10 Chater Road, CENTRAL, HONG KONG ISLAND, HONG KONG SAR.

KAN, Miss. Shen, BSc ACA *2011;* 7 Bywater Place, LONDON, SE16 5ND.

KAN, Mr. Shun Ming, BSc FCA *1985;* 19th Floor Massmutual Tower, 38 Gloucester Road, WAN CHAI, HONG KONG ISLAND, HONG KONG SAR.

KAN, Mr. Tak Kwong, ACA *2008;* 18B, Tower 5, Dynasty Court, 23 Old Peak Road, MID LEVELS, HONG KONG SAR.

KAN, Miss. Wing Yan Grace, BSc ACA *2010;* Apartment 73, Metro Central Heights, 119 Newington Causeway, LONDON, SE1 6BA.

KAN, Miss. Winnie Wing-Yin, BSc ACA *1997;* Flat J2, 11/F Beverly Hill, 6 Broadwood Road, HAPPY VALLEY, HONG KONG ISLAND, HONG KONG SAR.

KAN, Mr. Yuet Yun Michael, FCA *1967;* 373 Onan Rd., #05-07 Malvern Springs, SINGAPORE 424775, SINGAPORE.

KAN, Mr. Yut Keong, BSc ACA *1983;* PricewaterhouseCoopers LLP, 17-00 PWC Building, 8 Cross Street, SINGAPORE 048424, SINGAPORE.

•**KANAAN, Mr. Joseph Nagib, FCA** *1964;* Amin G Chaktoura Building, El-Ayoun, BRUMMANA, LEBANON.

KANAGARAJAH, Mr. Sutharman, BSc ACA *2003;* (Tax Fac), 6 Derwent Avenue, BARNET, EN4 8LX.

Members - Alphabetical KANAKIA - KAR

KANAKIA, Mr. Pradip Manilal, ACA *1985;* PricewaterhouseCoopers Pvt. Ltd, 5th Floor Tower D The Millenia, 1 & 2 Murphy Road, Ulsoor, BANGALORE 560008, KARNATAKA INDIA. See also PricewaterhouseCoopers Ltd
KANANI, Miss. Nisha, ACA *2009;* 25 Wyvern Avenue, LEICESTER, LE4 7HJ.
•KANANI, Mr. Shams Mohamedtaqui, FCA *1975;* 1604 Twin Towers, Baniyas Road, Deira Creek, P.O. Box 42509, DUBAI, UNITED ARAB EMIRATES.
KANARIS, Mr. Efthymios, BSc ACA *2006;* 6 Lamias Street, Kaimakli, 1021 NICOSIA, CYPRUS.
KANARIS, Mr. Soteris, BA ACA *2005;* 6 Lamias st, Kaimakli, 1021 NICOSIA, CYPRUS.
•KANAS, Mr. Philip Ellis, FCA *1959;* (Tax Fac), Philip E Kanas, Downs Court, 29 The Downs, ALTRINCHAM, WA14 2QD.
KANASAR, Ms. Sivarogini, ACA *1993;* Usaha Tegas Sdn Bhd, L29 Menara Maxis, Kuala Lumpur City Centre, 50088 KUALA LUMPUR, FEDERAL TERRITORY, MALAYSIA.
KANCZULA, Miss. Helena, BA(Hons) ACA *2001;* (Tax Fac), 46 Westbeech Road, LONDON, N22 6HT.
KANDAPPU, Miss. Shirley Anne, ACA *1979;* 1 Valleywood Drive, Unit 4&5, MARKHAM L3R 5L9, ON, CANADA.
KANDAVANAM, Mr. Sivam, ACA *1985;* Usata Tegas Sdn Bhd, Level 44, Menara Maxis, Kuala Lumpur City Centre, 50088 KUALA LUMPUR, FEDERAL TERRITORY MALAYSIA.
KANDAWALLA, Mr. Darius, FCA *1967;* Kandawalla's (PVT) Ltd, Corner M.A. Jinnah and, Abdullah Haroon Road, KARACHI 74400, PAKISTAN.
KANDHARI, Mr. Jasjeev Singh, BA(Econ) ACA *1997;* Al Dobowi Ltd, P O Box 61348, Jebel Ali, DUBAI, UNITED ARAB EMIRATES.
KANDHARI, Mr. Pravin, BSc ACA *1993;* RBS, LEVEL 18 PARK PLACE, SZR, PO BOX 191474, DUBAI, UNITED ARAB EMIRATES.
KANDIAH, Mr. Pulendran, FCA *1973;* 36 Jalan 5/15, 46000 PETALING JAYA, Selangor, MALAYSIA.
KANDIAH, Mr. Subramaniam, FCA *1978;* 9Jalan 19/19, 46300 PETALING JAYA, SELANGOR, MALAYSIA.
KANDIAH, Mr. Thevakumar, BSc ACA *1979;* 8A Jalan Seputeh, 58000 KUALA LUMPUR, FEDERAL TERRITORY, MALAYSIA.
KANDLER, Mr. Joel Mark, BA FCA *1983;* 32 Heriot Road, LONDON, NW4 2DG.
KANE, Mr. Adrian, BA ACA *2000;* 2 Lucerne Close, WOKING, SURREY, GU22 7SH.
KANE, Mr. Andrew Stephen, OBE BSc FCA CPA *1978;* 13470 Firth Drive, BEVERLY HILLS, CA 90210, UNITED STATES.
KANE, Miss. Anthea Julia, BA ACA *1993;* 31 Bateman Street, HAMPTON, VIC 3188, AUSTRALIA.
KANE, Mr. Charles Martin, BSc ACA *1991;* Kraft Foods Middle East and Africa, P.O.Box 261983, Level 4 The Galleries No.3, Downtown Jebel Ali, DUBAI, UNITED ARAB EMIRATES.
•KANE, Mr. Christopher, ACA *1979;* (Tax Fac), DPC Accountants Limited, Vernon Road, STOKE-ON-TRENT, ST4 2QY. See also The DPC Group Limited
KANE, Mr. Dean Stephen, BSc ACA *2004;* 41 Hardy Way, Stotfold, HITCHIN, HERTFORDSHIRE, SG5 4GL.
•KANE, Mr. Edward John, BA FCA *1994;* Libris Accounting Limited, 25 Nursery Close, Potton, SANDY, BEDFORDSHIRE, SG19 2QE.
KANE, Mrs. Gabrielle Maria, BSc ACA *1992;* Deutsche Bank AG, Dubai International Financial Centre, The Gate West Wing Level 3, P O Box 504902, DUBAI, UNITED ARAB EMIRATES.
KANE, Mr. James Robert, LLB ACA *2004;* 11 Brantwood Road, STOCKPORT, CHESHIRE, SK4 2RL.
KANE, Mrs. Maxine Amanda, BSc ACA *1999;* 7 Fairpoint Gardens, Fairyland Road, PEMBROKE HM 05, BERMUDA.
KANE, Mrs. Nicola Jane, BSc ACA *2003;* 13 Farne Avenue, Gosforth, NEWCASTLE UPON TYNE, NE3 2BJ.
KANE, Mrs. Nicola Suzanne, BSc ACA *1991;* Goldman Sachs, 1 Carter Lane, LONDON, EC4V 5ER.
•KANE, Mr. Peter Martin, BA ACA *1999;* Kane Consultancy, 5 Parkgate Crescent, Hadley Wood, BARNET, HERTFORDSHIRE, EN4 0NW.
•KANE, Mr. Philip James, BA ACA *1988;* The Old Bakery, 9 Church Road, Almondsbury, BRISTOL, BS32 4ED.
KANE, Mr. Richard Anthony, FCA *1972;* Lakelands, Furzen Lane, Ellens GreenNr Rudgwick, HORSHAM, RH12 3AP.
KANE, Miss. Sasha Suzanne-Louise, MSc ACA *2009;* Panoramic Lower, 13 Cloverdale Road, DEVONSHIRE FL01, BERMUDA.
KANE, Mr. Thomas Christopher, ACA *1992;* LAMCO Services Ltd 6th Floor, 111 Old Broad Street, LONDON, EC2N 1FP.
KANE, Mr. William John, BA ACA *1990;* DEMCO Europe ltd., Grange House Geddings Road, HODDESDON, HERTFORDSHIRE, EN11 0NT.
KANENGISSER, Mrs. Anat, BA ACA *2005;* 4 Elmwood Road, Streetly, SUTTON COLDFIELD, WEST MIDLANDS, B74 2DQ.
KANERIA, Mr. Amit, BA(Hons) ACA *2011;* (Tax Fac), Nava Blossom, Allum Lane, Elstree, BOREHAMWOOD, HERTFORDSHIRE, WD6 3NE.
KANESALINGAM, Mr. Sabapathipillai, BSc FCA *1962;* 57 Cotswold Road, STRATHFIELD, NSW 2135, AUSTRALIA. (Life Member)
KANESU, Mr. Bahirathan, BSc ACA *2004;* 128, Goodenough College London House, Mecklenburgh Square, LONDON, WC1N 2AB.
KANEY, Mr. Arnold Edward, FCA *1963;* 6 Charles Norris Gardens, SAUNDERSFOOT, SA69 9DF. (Life Member)
KANG, Mr. Amrik Singh, BSc FCA *1993;* 6 Shaggy Calf Lane, SLOUGH, SL2 5HJ.
KANG, Mr. Anoop, BCom ACA *2001;* 107 St. Marys Road, WEYBRIDGE, KT13 9QA.
KANG, Mr. Eng Beng, ACA *1981;* 28 Jalan Ambar, ALOR STAR, KEDAH, MALAYSIA.
KANG, Mr. Jagdeep Singh, BCom FCA *2001;* 71 Richmond Hill Road, Edgbaston, BIRMINGHAM, B15 3SA.
KANG, Miss. Karendeep, BSc ACA *2010;* 61 St. Lukes Road, Old Windsor, WINDSOR, SL4 2QL.
KANG, Miss. Lay Choo, BSc ACA *1980;* 57 BURGUNDY DRIVE, SINGAPORE 658846, SINGAPORE.
KANG, Mr. Paul Choon Wai, LLB ACA *1992;* Flat 1 30/F Block A Ventris Place, 19-23 Ventris Road, HAPPY VALLEY, HONG KONG ISLAND, HONG KONG SAR.
KANG, Miss. Ria Ranjit Kaur, BSc ACA *2002;* 35 Kingsway, LEAMINGTON SPA, WARWICKSHIRE, CV31 3LW.
KANG, Miss. Samneet, BSc ACA *2011;* 38 Woodcroft Avenue, BIRMINGHAM, B20 1AS.
KANG, Mr. Shing Leung, ACA *2007;* Flat A, 12/F, Cypress Court, Ocean Gardens, Taipa, MACAU CHINA.
KANG, Miss. Vivian Bee Lin, ACA *1981;* 15A Sunlight Gardens, 2 Man Wan Road, HO MAN TIN, Kowloon, HONG KONG SAR.
KANG, Mrs. Yongwen, ACA *2009;* Flat 301, Block 13, No. 2993 Dongfang Road, Pudong District, SHANGHAI 200215, CHINA.
KANGA, Mr. Mayank, ACA *2009;* 25 Lincoln Park, AMERSHAM, BUCKINGHAMSHIRE, HP7 9EZ.
KANGA, Miss. Panayiota, MBA MBS BA ACA *2009;* 15 Elia Venezi Street, 2401 ENGOMI, CYPRUS.
KANGA, Mr. Rustom Bejon, FCA *1982;* Boulevard Helvetique 18, 1207 GENEVA, SWITZERLAND.
KANGAYAN, Mr. Fabienne, MEng ACA *2004;* 35 Manor Park, Histon, CAMBRIDGE, CB4 9JT.
KANGESON, Miss. Hema, BSc(Hons) ACA *2002;* Unit 15 9A Cook Street, GLEBE, NSW 2037, AUSTRALIA.
KANISH, Mr. Parikshat, LLB ACA *2005;* Flat 1, Collection Point, 73 Crouch Hall Road, Crouchend, LONDON, N8 8HF.
KANJA, Mr. David Muchoki, BCom FCA *1987;* 11 Grant Avenue, CLIFFSIDE PARK, NJ 07010, UNITED STATES.
KANJI, Mr. Al-Noor Subzali Ratansi, FCA *1975;* KPMG LLP, Box 10426 Pacific Centre, 777 Dunsmuir Street, VANCOUVER V7Y 1K3, BC, CANADA.
KANJI, Mr. Muntazir, BCom ACA *2006;* 26 The Chase, Eastcote, PINNER, MIDDLESEX, HA5 1SN.
•KANJI, Mr. Muslim Roshanali, FCA *1975;* 49 Grove Farm Park, NORTHWOOD, MIDDLESEX, HA6 2BQ.
KANJI, Mr. Nizar Esmail, FCA *1965;* 51 German Mills Road, THORNHILL L3T 4H6, ON, CANADA.
•KANJI, Mr. Nizar Tajuddin, FCA *1978;* (Tax Fac), Nizar Kanji & Co, 18 The Fairway, NORTHWOOD, HA6 3DY.
KANJI, Mr. Riz, MSc ACA FCCA FMAAT CPA *2010;* 6 Hobart Court, 29 Roxborough Avenue, Harrow on the Hill, HARROW, HA1 3DW.
KANJI, Mrs. Samira Hassanali, BSc FCA *1980;* 11447 Kennedy Road, MARKHAM L6C 1P2, ON, CANADA.
KANJI, Mr. Zeeshan Hussein, BSc FCA *1996;* 103 Mount Street, LONDON, W1K 2TJ.
KANKAI, Mrs. Jasbir Kaur, BA ACA *2004;* 146 Leamington Road, COVENTRY, CV3 6JY.
KANKALIL, Mr. John Zachariah, BSc ACA *2007;* 19 Wensleydale, WALLSEND, TYNE AND WEAR, NE28 8TW.
KANNAVIAS, Mr. Charalambos, ACA FCCA *2009;* 15 Agaristis Street, Kato Polemidia, 4154, LIMASSOL, CYPRUS.
KANNENBERG, Ms. Marga Helena, ACA CA(SA) *2008;* 29 Clarendon Drive, LONDON, SW15 1AW.
KANOUI, Mrs. Valerie Claude, BA ACA *1991;* 27 Boulevard Michelet, 44300 NANTES, FRANCE.
KANSAL, Mr. Sunil Kumar, ACA *2011;* Ernst & Young Llp, 1 More London Place, LONDON, SE1 2AF.
KANTARI, Miss. Loukia, BSc ACA *2005;* Avenue Brugmann 186 Bt6, 1050 BRUSSELS, BELGIUM.
KANTARIA, Mr. Arun Chhotalal, FCA *1976;* Arunkumar Chhotalal, Kantaria, PO Box 49925, NAIROBI, 00100GPO, KENYA.
KANTARIA, Mr. Kamalesh Himatlal, BSc ACA *1995;* 4 Churchill Court, 58, Station Road, North Harrow, HARROW, HA2 7SA.
KANTARIA, Mr. Mehul, ACA *2008;* 102 The Drive, RICKMANSWORTH, HERTFORDSHIRE, WD3 4DU.
KANTER, Mr. Cyril, FCA *1962;* Flat 10 Hambleden Place, 32 Gills Hill, RADLETT, HERTFORDSHIRE, WD7 8BT. (Life Member)
KANTER, Mr. Edward Frank, FCA *1965;* 36 Linden Road, LONDON, N10 3DH. (Life Member)
KANTER, Mr. Jonathan Paul, BA ACA *1997;* 442 Main Street, HINGHAM, MA 02043, UNITED STATES.
KANTOR, Miss. Kazimiera Teresa, BSc FCA *1975;* 27 Springhill Road, Begbroke, KIDLINGTON, OXFORDSHIRE, OX5 1RX.
KANUNGO, Mr. Tushar, BSc ACA *2006;* Booz & Company N.A., 101 Park Avenue, NEW YORK, NY 10178, UNITED STATES.
KANWAL, Mr. Manjinder, ACA *2009;* 18 Carroll Crescent, COVENTRY, CV2 3PX.
KANWAR, Mrs. Kamal, ACA FCCA *2010;* 90 Clarence Road, WINDSOR, BERKSHIRE, SL4 5AT.
•KAOURIS, Mr. Panayiotis Yiangou, BA FCA *1987;* PricewaterhouseCoopers Limited, Julia House, 3 Themistocles Dervis Street, CY-1066 NICOSIA, CYPRUS.
KAPADIA, Mr. Abdus Sattar, FCA *1974;* 2078 Rose Villa Street, PASADENA, CA 91107, UNITED STATES.
KAPADIA, Mrs. Anaheita Keki, ACA *1993;* 3421 N.E.Madison Way, ISSAQUAH, WA 98029-3509, UNITED STATES.
KAPADIA, Mr. Cyrus N, BSc ACA *1997;* Great House, Parrotts Lane, Buckland Common, TRING, HERTFORDSHIRE, HP23 6NX.
KAPADIA, Miss. Minoti, BCom ACA *2001;* Flat 3 Lime House, 33 Melliss Avenue, RICHMOND, TW9 4AE.
KAPADIA, Mr. Pesi Jamshedji, FCA *1952;* 8 The Beacon, 140 Madam Cama Road, MUMBAI 400021, INDIA. (Life Member)
•KAPADIA, Mr. Ramesh Anilkant, ACA FCCA *2011;* West Wake Price LLP, 4 Chiswell Street, LONDON, EC1Y 4UP.
KAPADIA, Dr. Robin, BSc ACA *1993;* Kesslerplatz 9, 90489 NUERNBERG, GERMANY.
KAPADIA, Mr. Samir Satish, MBBS ACA *1993;* 17 Derby Avenue, LONDON, N12 8DD.
•KAPADIA, Mr. Vijay Vissonji, FCA *1973;* (Tax Fac), V Kapadia & Co, 53 Sheen Lane, LONDON, SW14 8AB. See also V Kapadia & Co Limited
KAPASHI, Miss. Raxita, BEng ACA *1991;* 3 Uxendon Crescent, WEMBLEY, HA9 9TW.
•KAPASI, Mr. Enayathusein Akbarali, BSc FCA *1991;* (Tax Fac), Kapasi & Co, 20 Highland Avenue, LONDON, W7 3RF. See also Dauman & Co Limited
•KAPAYA, Dr. George, ACA *1988;* George & Co, 16 Berberis Close, Walnut Tree, MILTON KEYNES, MK7 7DZ.
•KAPETANIOS, Mr. Yiannis, BSc(Econ) ACA *2004;* BDO Limited, Antonis Zenios Tower, 1 Erehthiou Street Engomi, PO Box 25277, 2413 NICOSIA, CYPRUS. See also BDO Philippides Limited
KAPICA, Mrs. Joanne Michelle, BSc(Hons) ACA *2001;* 89 Bathurst Walk, IVER, BUCKINGHAMSHIRE, SL0 9EF.
KAPICA, Mr. Julian Richard, BSc(Hons) ACA *2001;* 89 Bathurst Walk, IVER, BUCKINGHAMSHIRE, SL0 9EF.
•KAPILA, Mr. Rakesh, BSc FCA *1983;* Sim Kapila, St. George's House, 14-17 Wells Street, LONDON, W1T 3PD.
KAPIRI, Mr. Avraam Michael, BSc ACA *1993;* 57 Steliou Mavrommati St., Ayios Dhometios, 2364 NICOSIA, CYPRUS.
KAPIRIAL, Mr. Jebtha, ACA MAAT *2011;* 120 Caulfield Road, LONDON, E6 2DG.
KAPLAN, Mr. Basil, FCA *1960;* 20/42 Diamond Bay Road, VAUCLUSE, NSW 2030, AUSTRALIA. (Life Member)
KAPLAN, Mr. Gavin Andre, BA ACA *1982;* 128 Francklyn Gardens, EDGWARE, HA8 8SA.
KAPLAN, Mr. Ian, ACA CA(SA) *2010;* 51 St Georges Crescent, HEATHERTON, VIC 3202, AUSTRALIA.
KAPLAN, Mrs. Zoe Mary, BA ACA *1986;* 112 Chestnut Lane, AMERSHAM, BUCKINGHAMSHIRE, HP6 6DZ.
KAPLANSKI, Mr. Peter Paul, FCA *1972;* The Oaks, Simons Lane, WOKINGHAM, RG41 3HH.
KAPNISSI, Miss. Panayiota, BA ACA *2004;* 9 Trikallon, Lakatamia, 2313 NICOSIA, CYPRUS.
KAPONI, Mr. Andrew, MSc BA(Hons) ACA *2003;* 24 Oakleigh Crescent, LONDON, N20 0BS.
•KAPONIDES, Mr. Yiangos Aristides, BA FCA *1996;* PricewaterhouseCoopers Limited, City House, 6 Karaiskakis Street, CY-3032 LIMASSOL, CYPRUS.
KAPOOR, Mr. Amrit, FCA *1973;* D3 WESTEND COLONY, NEW DELHI 110021, INDIA.
•KAPOOR, Mr. Anil, BA(Econ) ACA *2002;* with BDO LLP, 55 Baker Street, LONDON, W1U 7EU.
KAPOOR, Mr. Anish, BSc ACA *1998;* 1 Wingate Drive, MANCHESTER, M20 2RT.
KAPOOR, Mr. Bhisham, ACA *1980;* K & K Enterprises Inc, PO Box 5309, BASKING RIDGE, NJ 07920, UNITED STATES.
KAPOOR, Miss. Meenakshi, BSc ACA *2007;* (Tax Fac), 42 Rosemont Road, LONDON, NW3 6NE.
KAPOOR, Mr. Naval, BSc ACA *2000;* 42 Rosemont Road, LONDON, NW3 6NE.
KAPOOR, Mr. Nitan, FCA *1975;* c/o Eastone Exports Pvt Ltd, W-20 Sector XI, NOIDA UP 201301, INDIA.
KAPOOR, Mr. Pavan, MSc ACA MBA *1999;* KPMG Al Fozan & Al Sadhan, Al Subeaie Towers 13th Floor, King Abdulaziz Road, P.O. Box 4803, AL KHOBAR, 31952 SAUDI ARABIA.
KAPOOR, Mr. Rajan, FCA *1976;* Pinegables, 12 Sylvan Gardens, SURBITON, KT6 6PP.
KAPOOR, Mr. Rajesh, ACA *1982;* with Mazars LLP, Tower Bridge House, St. Katharines Way, LONDON, E1W 1DD.
KAPOOR, Mr. Randhir, FCA *1978;* 156 Kings Drive, EDGWARE, MIDDLESEX, HA8 8EQ.
KAPOOR, Miss. Reema, BCom ACA *2002;* 193 Spring Street, Apt 2R, NEW YORK, NY 10012, UNITED STATES.
KAPOOR, Mr. Sanjay, ACA *1995;* 7 Ulundi Road, LONDON, SE3 7UQ.
KAPOOR, Mr. Shiv, BSc ACA *1999;* 12 Temple Gardens, RICKMANSWORTH, HERTFORDSHIRE, WD3 1QJ.
KAPOOR, Mr. Shiv Pratap, FCA *1992;* A163 Sector 40, NOIDA 201302, INDIA.
•KAPOOR, Mr. Shub Chander Pal, FCA *1974;* Benjamin Kay & Brummer, York House, Empire Way, WEMBLEY, HA9 0QL.
KAPOOR, Miss. Sujata, BSc ACA *1998;* 2 Rebecca Road, SINGAPORE 266715, SINGAPORE.
•KAPOOR, Mr. Vivek, FCA *1999;* Ferguson Maidment & Co, Sardinia House, Sardinia Street, Lincolns Inn Fields, LONDON, WC2A 3LZ.
KAPUR, Mr. Anil, FCA *1970;* 1922 Burnside Ct, CONCORD, CA 94521, UNITED STATES.
KAPUR, Mr. Arvind Michael, BSc ACA *1990;* The Laurels, 7 Knighton Rise, LEICESTER, LE2 2RF.
KAPUR, Mr. Bankim Krishan, ACA *2008;* (Tax Fac), 19 Jacobs Court, 19 Plumbers Row, LONDON, E1 1AE.
KAPUR, Mr. Chander Shekhar, FCA *1971;* A5 Beach House, Ghandigram Road, Juhu, MUMBAI 49, INDIA.
KAPUR, Mr. Gunveer, ACA *1978;* B-61 Greater Kailash 1, NEW DELHI 110048, INDIA.
•KAPUR, Mr. Neeraj, BEng CF *1993;* MEMBER OF COUNCIL, The Old Granary, Hillside Road, Frensham, FARNHAM, SURREY, GU10 3AJ.
KAPUR, Mr. Rohit Kumar, BPharm ACA *2002;* 8 High Firs Crescent, HARPENDEN, HERTFORDSHIRE, AL5 1NA.
•KAPUR, Mr. Sheetal, ACA *1981;* S. Kapur & Co, 6 Hartfield Close, Elstree, BOREHAMWOOD, WD6 3JD. See also Aaron Chadha & Evans Ltd
KAPUR, Mrs. Sophie Alexandra, BA(Hons) ACA *2002;* 8 High Firs Crescent, HARPENDEN, HERTFORDSHIRE, AL5 1NA.
KAPUR, Mr. Sumant, FCA *1977;* Prime Land Real Estates(Pvt) Ltd, 7th Floor, Meridien Corporate Tower, One Windsor Place, NEW DELHI 110001, CAPITAL TERRITORY OF DELHI INDIA.
KAPUR, Mr. Sunil, FCA *1974;* 159 Citadel Acres Close NW, CALGARY T3G 5A8, AB, CANADA.
KAPUTIN, Mr. Anton, ACA *2010;* 14 Georgiou Avenue, Lordos Andrea Court, f.10, CY-4047 LIMASSOL, CYPRUS.
KAR, Mr. Arjun, MA ACA *1997;* Flat 20, Jetty Court, Old Bellgate Place, LONDON, E14 3SX.

KAR, Mr. Subrata, FCA *1974;* Gee Kar & Co, 22 Kohinoor, 105 Park Street, CALCUTTA 700 016, INDIA.
KARACHIWALLA, Mr. Aameer Mustaal, ACA *1984;* United Bank Limited, 8th Floor State Life Bldg # 1, I. I. Chundrigar Road, KARACHI, PAKISTAN.
KARADIMITRIS, Mr. Ioannis, ACA *2009;* 284 Muswell Hill Broadway, LONDON, N10 2QR.
•**KARAFISTAN, Ms. Nursen, BSc FCA** *1993;* Nursen Karafistan, Flat 3, Christchurch Place, Christ Church Mount, EPSOM, SURREY KT19 8RS. See also Nursen Davies
•**KARAGEORGHIS, Mr. Panayiotis, FCA** *1987;* (Tax Fac), PCK Accounting Ltd, 11 Dove Lane, POTTERS BAR, EN6 2SG. See also PCK & Co
•**KARAGEORGHIS, Mr. Panos, MSc BSc ACA** *2005;* API Partnership Limited, 75 Westow Hill, Crystal Palace, LONDON, SE19 1TX.
KARAISKOS, Mr. Michael, BSc ACA *2006;* 56 Sandy Lodge Way, NORTHWOOD, MIDDLESEX, HA6 2AS.
KARAKATSANI, Miss. Yianna, ACA *2011;* 3 Scopelou Street, St Athanasios, 4105 LIMASSOL, CYPRUS.
KARAMATULLAH, Mr. Vaiz, BSc FCA *1971;* C/o National Prawn Company, PO Box 42082, JEDDAH, 21541, SAUDI ARABIA.
KARAMCHANDANI, Mr. Dilip Kumar, ACA *1992;* 71 Portland Crescent, STANMORE, HA7 1LZ.
KARAME, Mr. David Marwan, ACA *2008;* Save the Children Fund, 1 St. John's Lane, LONDON, EC1M 4AR.
KARANDAWALA, Mr. Asoka Panduka Bandara, BA FCA *1984;* 124 Buckingham Road, HAMPTON, MIDDLESEX, TW12 3JR.
KARANI, Mr. Mark James, BA ACA *2010;* 7 Harrod Drive, SOUTHPORT, MERSEYSIDE, PR8 2HA.
KARANTONI, Miss. Kyproulla, BSc ACA *2006;* Fiducitrust Services Limited, 2nd Floor, 66 Acropolis Avenue, Strovolos, 2012 NICOSIA, CYPRUS.
•**KARANTONI, Miss. Maria, BSc ACA** *2002;* KPMG Limited, P O Box 21121, 1502 NICOSIA, CYPRUS. See also KPMG Metaxas Loizides Syrimis
KARANTONIS, Mr. Antonios, MA BA ACA *2011;* Pricewaterhousecoopers, 7 More London Riverside, LONDON, SE1 2RT.
KARAOLIS, Mr. Kyriakos, BA(Hons) ACA *2011;* PO Box 28089, 2090 NICOSIA, CYPRUS.
KARASIEWICZ, Miss. Irena Mary, BA ACA *1981;* 95 Union Street, MELBOURNE, VIC 3056, AUSTRALIA.
KARATSIS, Mr. Dionysios, MSc BSc ACA *2002;* Filoxtiti 18, Strovolos, 2036 NICOSIA, CYPRUS.
KARAVADRA, Mr. Kailesh, MEng ACA *1994;* with Ernst & Young, 303 Almaden Boulevard, SAN JOSE, CA 95110, UNITED STATES.
KARAYIANNIS, Mr. Costas, BA ACA *1994;* 23 Pump Hill, LOUGHTON, ESSEX, IG10 1RU.
•**KARBANI, Mr. Faizal Abdul Gafar, BSc ACA** *1998;* Integra Accounting Solutions Limited, The Station Masters House, 168 Thornbury Road, Osterley Village, ISLEWORTH, MIDDLESEX TW7 4QE.
KARBASSI, Mr. Reza, BSc ACA *1993;* Flat 29 Hanover House, St John's Wood High Street, LONDON, NW8 7DY.
KARDAR, Mr. Shahid Hafiz, BA ACA *1980;* 46 B/3 Gulberg 111, LAHORE, PAKISTAN.
KARDOONI, Mrs. Kate Elizabeth, MA FCA *1996;* UBS Investment Bank, 100 Liverpool Street, LONDON, EC2M 2RH.
KARIA, Mrs. Anuja, BSc ACA *1993;* Glenhayes, Chorleywood Road, RICKMANSWORTH, HERTFORDSHIRE, WD3 4EP.
KARIA, Miss. Asha, ACA *2008;* 69 Devenay Road, LONDON, E15 4AZ.
KARIA, Mr. Jatin, BSc ACA *1994;* 11 Copley Way, TADWORTH, SURREY, KT20 5QS.
KARIA, Miss. Shilpa, MA FCA *1998;* 31 Lorong Chuan, #14-03 The Chuan, SINGAPORE 556820, SINGAPORE.
KARIA, Mr. Vinesh Mahendra, BSc ACA *2004;* 43 Oxford Drive, Eastcote, PINNER, HA4 9EY.
•**KARIM, Mr. Abu Zahed Fazlul, FCA** *1971;* Karim & Co, 142 Edgware Way, EDGWARE, HA8 8JY.
KARIM, Mr. Aftab Hussain, FCA *1991;* 60 Raymond Road, Upton Park, LONDON, E13 0SW.
KARIM, Mr. Amir Aly, FCA *1960;* Flat 75 Meadowside, Cambridge Park, TWICKENHAM, TW1 2JQ. (Life Member)
KARIM, Mr. Areful, FCA *1979;* Nirala, Golf Club Road, WEYBRIDGE, SURREY, KT13 0NN.
KARIM, Mr. Fazal, ACA *2009;* Internal Audit, 12th Floor NSH Tower, Dammam Khobar Highway P.O. Box 151, AL KHOBAR, 31952, SAUDI ARABIA.
KARIM, Mr. Fazal Iqbal Mahmood, BA ACA *1992;* New Bungalow, Yew Tree Farm, Shirehall Road, Hawley, DARTFORD, DA2 7SE.
KARIM, Mr. Khalid Rashid, FCA *1979;* Gulf Navigation Holding PJSC, P.O. Box 49651, Saba Tower 1 Jumeirah Lake Towers, DUBAI, UNITED ARAB EMIRATES.
KARIM, Mr. Mohammed Tariq, FCA *1975;* 12 Netherwood Road, MANCHESTER, M22 4BQ.
KARIM, Mr. Muqarrab Bin, BSc ACA *1998;* 50 Murray Street, Apt 412, NEW YORK, NY 10007, UNITED STATES.
•**KARIM, Mr. Shiraz Habib Kassam, FCA** *1975;* 12 Lancaster Road, HARROW, MIDDLESEX, HA2 7NL.
KARIM, Mr. Sulaiman Abdul, FCA *1987;* c/o Taher Group, Head Office, P.O. Box 1178, JEDDAH, 21431, SAUDI ARABIA.
KARIMBEIK, Mrs. Pamela Anne, ACA *1987;* Maarse & Kroonhof 4, 1431PB AALSMEER, NORD HOLLAND, NETHERLANDS.
KARIMJEE, Mr. Arif, BTech ACA *1992;* 8 South Farm Lane, BAGSHOT, SURREY, GU19 5NT.
KARIMJEE, Mr. Nazim Alibhai, BA FCA *1975;* Sennen, Rancliffe Avenue, Keyworth, NOTTINGHAM, NG12 5HY.
KARIMJEE, Mr. Zaffer Ebrahim Tayabali, FCA *1974;* P.O.Box 55797, DUBAI, UNITED ARAB EMIRATES. (Life Member)
KARIPAT, Mr. Santhosh Jacob, MSc ACA *1982;* VENTURE CAPITAL BANK BSC (C), VENTURE CAPITAL BUILDING, P O Box 11755, Diplomatic Area, MANAMA, BAHRAIN.
KARIR, Mr. Attul, BA(Hons) ACA *2004;* 24 Central Avenue, HOUNSLOW, TW3 2QH.
KARIR-TAKHAR, Mrs. Anita, BA ACA *1996;* 4 Turnstone Close, Winnersh, WOKINGHAM, RG41 5LQ.
KARIUKI, Ms. Elizabeth Nyawira, BSc FCA *1992;* P O Box 30680, NAIROBI, KENYA.
KARIUKI, Mr. Martin Ndatha, ACA CA(SA) *2009;* Number 13 La Carmague, 20 Benmore Road, BENMORE GARDENS, GAUTENG, 2196, SOUTH AFRICA.
•**KARIYA, Mr. Niranjan Jivraj, FCA** *1963;* Clayton Stark & Co, 5th Floor Charles House, 108-110 Finchley Road, LONDON, NW3 5JJ.
KARKI, Mrs. Amanda Jane, BSc ACA *1999;* The Laurels Nursery Lane, Wivelsfield Green, HAYWARDS HEATH, WEST SUSSEX, RH17 7RB.
KARLEKAR, Mr. Vikas Vasant, BSc ACA *1996;* 87a Fitzjohn Avenue, BARNET, HERTFORDSHIRE, EN5 2HR.
KARLSSON, Miss. Caroline, ACA *2009;* Neuberggata 6F, 0367 OSLO, NORWAY.
KARMARKAR, Mr. Neel Rahul, BA ACA *1998;* 99 John Street Apt 1602, NEW YORK, NY 10038, UNITED STATES.
•**KARMEL, Mr. Richard Anthony, BA FCA** *1992;* Mazars LLP, Tower Bridge House, St. Katharines Way, LONDON, E1W 1DD. See also Mazars Corporate Finance Limited
KARMY, Mr. Anthony Douglas, FCA *1965;* 7 Lynn Way, FARNBOROUGH, HAMPSHIRE, GU14 8RT.
•**KARN, Mr. Lawrence William, FCA** *1981;* (Tax Fac), Lawrence W. Karn & Co, Rosebank House, Shripney Road, BOGNOR REGIS, PO22 9PA.
KARNICKI, Mr. Edward Alexander George, FCA *1972;* P.O. Box BW 21, Borrowdale, HARARE, ZIMBABWE.
KARNIK, Mr. Deven, ACA *1994;* Flat 8b, Tegunter Tower 1, 14 Tegunter Path, MID LEVELS, HONG KONG SAR.
KAROLIA, Mr. Ebrahim Bashir, BA(Hons) FCA *2001;* (Tax Fac), with PricewaterhouseCoopers, PO Box 21144, BMB Centre 9th Floor, Diplomatic Area, MANAMA, BAHRAIN.
KAROLY, Mr. Jeffrey Laszlo, BSc ACA *1995;* The Old School House, School Lane, DIDCOT, OXFORDSHIRE, OX11 0ES.
KARONIAS, Mr. Nicolas Peter, BSc ACA *1980;* 66 Palewell Park, East Sheen, LONDON, SW14 8JH.
•**KARP, Mr. Michael Benjamin, MA FCA** *1982;* PricewaterhouseCoopers LLP, 1 Embankment Place, LONDON, WC2N 6RH. See also PricewaterhouseCoopers
KARPAL, Mr. Anil Chand Ralph, BSc ACA *1995;* Goldman Sachs, Peterborough Court, 133 Fleet Street, LONDON, EC4A 2BB.
KARPINSKI, Mrs. Jane Bronwyn, ACA *1989;* 5 Katherine Close, Penn, HIGH WYCOMBE, BUCKINGHAMSHIRE, HP10 8ET.
KARPOV, Mr. Kirill, ACA *2008;* 8th March street, 13-126, 125319 MOSCOW, RUSSIAN FEDERATION.
KARPUSHEFF, Mr. Nicholas Anthony, BSc ACA *1990;* Le Schuylkill, 19 Boulevard de Suisse, MC 98000 MONTE CARLO, MONACO.
KARRAN, Mr. Andrew, MMath ACA *2010;* E on UK Plc Westwood Way, Westwood Business Park, COVENTRY, CV4 8LG.
KARRAN, Mr. James Andrew Geoffrey, ACA *2009;* Flat 76, 384 Deansgate, MANCHESTER, M3 4LA.
•**KARSAN, Mr. Hassan Popat, MSc ACA FCCA** *2008;* (Tax Fac), Karsan Consulting Limited, Karsan Business Centre, 15 Thrale Road, (Entrance Penwortham Road), Streatham, LONDON SW16 1NS. See also Maurice G. Wood Partnership
•**KARSAN, Mr. Husein Popat, ACA FCCA** *2010;* 7 Woodcote Park Avenue, PURLEY, SURREY, CR8 3ND.
•**KARSAS, Mrs. Constandina, ACA** *1996;* Deloitte Hadjipavlou Sofianos & Cambanis S.A, 3a Fragoklissias & Granikou Str, Maroussi, 15125 ATHENS, GREECE.
KARSKI, Mr. Alexander John, MSc ACA *2004;* with BDO LLP, 55 Baker Street, LONDON, W1U 7EU.
KARSTEN, Mr. Peter Robert Anthony, FCA *1975;* The Coach House, Hunsdonbury, WARE, SG12 8PW.
KARTHIKEYAN, Miss. Sivaranjani, BSc(Hons) ACA *2010;* 10 Montacute Road, MORDEN, SURREY, SM4 6RL.
KARTOUDES, Mr. Charalambos, BA ACA *2006;* Fiducenter (Cyprus) Limited, Vashiotis Business Center, 1 Iakovou Tompazi Street, CY-3017 LIMASSOL, CYPRUS.
KARUNAKARAN, Mrs. Mee Yeong, ACA *1992;* 42 Jalan Rahim Kajai, Taman Tun Dr Ismail, 60000 KUALA LUMPUR, FEDERAL TERRITORY, MALAYSIA.
•**KARUNARATNE, Mr. Deshan Sanjaya, BSc ACA** *2001;* with PricewaterhouseCoopers LLP, Marlborough Court, 10 Bricket Road, ST. ALBANS, HERTFORDSHIRE, AL1 3JX.
KARUNARATNE, Mr. Waidya Kulatilake, FCA *1970;* 104 Golf Links Drive, AURORA L4G 3V3, ON, CANADA.
KARUNATHILAKE, Miss. Niluka Chrishani, BA ACA *2007;* 46 Cumberland Mills Square, LONDON, E14 3BJ.
KARUPIAH, Mr. Segar, ACA *1986;* 42 Whitgift House, 61 Westbridge Road, LONDON, SW11 3TH.
KARYDAS, Mr. Nicolaos Theodosiou, MSc ACA *1986;* 17 Acropoleos Street, Pano Dheftera, 2460 NICOSIA, CYPRUS.
KASARI, Mr. Philip Reginald, BSc FCA *1981;* 4 Linja 18, 30100 FORSSA, FINLAND.
KASBEKAR, Mr. Ajit Bhawanishankar, FCA *1970;* 5 Lalit Apartments, Survey No. 131/ 1+2Aundh, PUNE 411007, INDIA.
•**KASEM, Mr. Akhtar Sohel, FCA** *1981;* A Qasem & Co, Gulshan Pink City, Suites 01-03 Level 7, Plot No. 15 Road No. 103, Gulshan Avenue, DHAKA 1212 BANGLADESH.
KASHIOURIS, Mr. Markos Andreas, MSc BA(Econ) ACA ACIM *1999;* Terra Investments, PO Box 35496, LONDON, NW8 9WJ.
KASHOULIS, Mr. Marios, BSc ACA *1993;* 3 Diagorou Street, Fessas R Kashoulis, Tower, CY1097 NICOSIA, CYPRUS.
KASIMOV, Mr. Arthur, ACA *2010;* Kinnis Court 11 flat 101, Christaki Kranou, 4041 LIMASSOL, CYPRUS.
KASIR, Mr. Ameen, BA FCA *1999;* Al Salaam Compound Villa 42, PO Box 41599, JEDDAH, 21531, SAUDI ARABIA.
KASKANTANIS, Mr. Dimitrios, ACA *2011;* Lereos Dousi 63, 15126 ATHENS, GREECE.
KASMANI, Mr. Anverali Alimohamed Essa, ACA *1979;* Stamford Risk Analytics, Maple House, High Street, POTTERS BAR, HERTFORDSHIRE, EN6 5BS.
KASMANI, Mr. Firoz Eqbal, ACA *2011;* with Ernst & Young, Al Faisaliah Office Tower, Level 14, PO Box 2732, RIYADH, 11461 SAUDI ARABIA.
KASMANI, Mrs. Zaeda, BSc ACA *1988;* 99 Pulborough Road, Southfields, LONDON, SW18 5UL.
•**KASMIR, Mr. Alan David, FCA** *1976;* KWG Ltd, Millstream House, 39a East Street, WIMBORNE, DORSET, BH21 1DX.
KASPARIAN, Mr. Andre Edouard, BA FCA *1988;* Ernst & Young, PO Box 136, ABU DHABI, UNITED ARAB EMIRATES.
KASPARIAN, Mr. George John, BA ACA *2006;* 45 Edgwarebury Lane, EDGWARE, HA8 8LJ.
KASSAM, Mr. Alykhan Shiraz, BA ACA *1995;* 12 Russell Road, Moor Park, NORTHWOOD, MIDDLESEX, HA6 2LL.
KASSAM, Mr. Amirali Abdulrasul Ahmed, FCA *1973;* Amir Kassam, Suite 207, 1911 Kennedy Road, SCARBOROUGH M1P 2L9, ON, CANADA.
KASSAM, Mr. Ashif Aziz, BA ACA *1990;* 4 Saddlers Close, Arkley, BARNET, HERTFORDSHIRE, EN5 3LU.
KASSAM, Mr. Inqilab, BSc ACA *2010;* 118 Eastcroft House, 86 Northolt Road, HARROW, HA2 0ES.
KASSAM, Mr. Issa Dewsi, FCA *1973;* 9045 Easterling Drive, ORLANDO, FL 32819, UNITED STATES.
KASSAM, Mr. Masumali Noorali, BSc FCA *1976;* 157 Upper Selsdon Road, SOUTH CROYDON, Surrey, CR2 0DU. (Life Member)
KASSAM, Mr. Mohamed Hassanali, FCA *1978;* 327 Harvet Grove Place N E, CALGARY T3K 5C4, AB, CANADA.
KASSAM, Mr. Nizar Abdulrasul Ahmed, ACA *1979;* 411 West 28th Street, NORTH VANCOUVER V7N2J4, BC, CANADA.
KASSAM, Mr. Nizarali Mohamedali, FCA *1977;* 5330 Schou Street, BURNABY V5G 4L1, BC, CANADA.
•**KASSAM, Mr. Noordin Jaffer, FCA** *1967;* N K Consultancy, 37 Clarence Gate Gardens, Glentworth Street, LONDON, NW1 6BA.
KASSAM, Miss. Nosrat Bibi, BA FCA CTA *1980;* 7 Pine Lodge, 1 Whitefield Close, LONDON, SW15 3SS.
KASSAM, Miss. Salimah, ACA *2010;* 16 Brocket Close, CHIGWELL, ESSEX, IG7 4ET.
KASSAM, Miss. Shelina, BSc ACA *1988;* 159 Maplin Park, SLOUGH, SL3 8YD.
KASSAMALI, Mr. Nazir Pyarali Rajabali, ACA *1979;* 11724-41 Avenue, EDMONTON T6J 0V3, AB, CANADA.
•**KASSAMALI, Mr. Rizwan, ACA** *1984;* (Tax Fac), Jaffer & Co, 7 Hazlitt Mews, Hazlitt Road, LONDON, W14 0JZ.
KASSAMALI, Mr. Sajjad, BA(Hons) ACA *2010;* 110 Hillside Gardens, EDGWARE, HA8 8HD.
•**KASSANI, Mrs. Pinelopi, ACA** *2008;* with Ernst & Young, 11Klm National Road, Athens-Lamia, Metamorphosi, 14451 ATHENS, GREECE.
•**KASSAPIS, Mr. Antonis Elia, BSc FCA** *1984;* UHY Antonis Kassapis Ltd, 89 Kennedy Avenue, Off 201, Floor 2, P O Box 26624, 1640 NICOSIA CYPRUS.
KASSAPIS, Mr. Charalambos, BA ACA *2005;* 4A Nikia Street, Strovolos, 2045 NICOSIA, CYPRUS.
•**KASSAPIS, Mr. Erodotos, BSc ACA** *1993;* Ledra Audit Services Limited, Kyrenia House, 5 Skra Street, Agios Andreas, 1100 NICOSIA, CYPRUS.
KASSAPIS, Mr. George Elia, BSc ACA *1991;* UHY Antonis Kassapis Ltd, 89 Kennedy Avenue, Off 201, Floor 2, P O Box 26624, 1640 NICOSIA CYPRUS.
KASSAPIS, Mr. Marios Gheorgiou, BSc ACA *1984;* 17 karolou Koun, Ayios Athanasios, 4108 LIMASSOL, CYPRUS.
KASSIM, Mrs. Emma, BA ACA *1998;* 34 Kenley Road, LONDON, SW19 3JQ.
KASSIM-LAKHA, Mr. Ameerally Rahemtulla, FCA ACIArb CPA(K) *1957;* Arkle Management Consultants Ltd, Kalamu House, Waiyaki Way, P O Box 40130-00100, NAIROBI, KENYA.
KASSINOPOULLOS, Mr. Polydoros Andreou, BSc ACA *1991;* Kinyra 3, Gloria House, Off 203, PAPHOS, CYPRUS.
KASSIR, Mr. Wathiq Asad, BSc ACA *1998;* 3 Moor Park Gardens, Coombe Lane West, KINGSTON UPON THAMES, KT2 7UD.
KASSIRAM, Mr. Phillip John, BSc(Hons) ACA *2000;* 46 Grasmere, HUNTINGDON, CAMBRIDGESHIRE, PE29 6UR.
•**KASTELLANIS, Mr. Nicolas, ACA** *2003;* KPSA, 15 Themistokli Dervi Street, 1st Floor, Margarita House, PO Box 27040, 1641 NICOSIA CYPRUS.
•**KASUMU-OLALEYE, Mr. Folorunso Abdullatif, BSc FCA** *1973;* Folorunso Olaleye & Co, 17th Floor(Right Wing), Western House, 8-10 Broad Street, LAGOS, NIGERIA.
KATARI, Mr. Gunninder Singh, FCA *1975;* 3 Bega Road, NORTHBRIDGE, NSW 2063, AUSTRALIA.
KATARIA, Mr. Amar Bhikhu, BA ACA *1990;* 8 Westwick Place, WATFORD, WD25 0FD.
•**KATARIA, Mr. Ashok, ACA** *1980;* (Tax Fac), DeMontfort Solutions Ltd, 32 De Montfort Street, LEICESTER, LE1 7GD.
KATARIA, Mr. Shyamal, BSc ACA *2010;* 130 Preston Hill, HARROW, MIDDLESEX, HA3 9XF.
KATARIA, Miss. Trishna, ACA *2011;* Flat 4 Woodside Grange, 77 Holden Road, LONDON, N12 7DP.
KATELI, Mr. Cyrus, BCom ACA MCT *1992;* Cairn Capital Limited, 27 Knightbridge, LONDON, SW1X 7LY.
KATES, Miss. Melanie, BSc(Hons) ACA *2009;* Tomkins Plc, East Putney House, 84 Upper Richmond Road, LONDON, SW15 2ST.
KATESMARK, Mr. Michael Edward William, FCA *1968;* 4 Chapel Drive, Little Waltham, CHELMSFORD, CM3 3LW. (Life Member)
KATHAWALA, Mr. Abdul Karim, BSc ACA *2009;* 71 Wright Street, COVENTRY, CV1 5HL.
KATHIR VELU, Mr. Chander, MPhil BSc ACA *1993;* 14 Amhurst Court, CAMBRIDGE, CB3 9BH.
KATHIRGAMANATHAN, Mr. Shahilan, ACA *2009;* 23 Elmbridge Lane, WOKING, SURREY, GU22 9AN.

Members - Alphabetical KATHOKE - KAYE

KATHOKE, Mr. Rustom Kaikhushroo, FCA *1975;* PO Box 28830, Sunridge Park, PORT ELIZABETH, 6008, SOUTH AFRICA.
KATHORIA, Mr. Mathra Das, FCA *1969;* 61 Allcroft Road, READING, RG1 5HN.
KATHPALIA, Mr. Surinder Dev Raj, ACA *1982;* 5 Holland Grove View, SINGAPORE 276179, SINGAPORE.
KATHURIA, Mr. Dalbir Singh, BSc ACA *2006;* 28 Grange Crescent, CHIGWELL, IG7 5JB.
KATIMBO-MUGWANYA, Mr. Edward, ACA *1980;* Centenery Bank, Plot 7, Entebbe Road, PO Box 1892, KAMPALA, UGANDA.
KATON, Mr. Alexander Crutchley, BA ACA *1994;* International Power, Senator House, 85 Queen Victoria Street, LONDON, EC4V 4DP.
KATSAOUNI, Miss. Pelagia, MSc BSc ACA *2007;* 40 Lancaster Drive, LONDON, E14 9PT.
KATSICADELLIS, Ms. Argyro, ACA *2004;* Ethniki Insurance Co, 103 - 105 Sygrou Avenue, 11745 ATHENS, GREECE.
KATSINA, Ms. Dimitra, ACA MBA *2010;* 7 Limnou Street, Melissia, 15127 ATHENS, GREECE.
KATSOULIERIS, Mr. Eleftherios, MSc ACA *2010;* Messinios 40, Halandri, 15234 ATHENS, GREECE.
KATSOURIS, Mr. Andrew Paul, BSc ACA *1996;* Foxes Lair, 25 Llanrwst Road, COLWYN BAY, CLWYD, LL29 7YT.
KATSOURIS, Mrs. Jessica Shimona Sophy, BA ACA *2002;* with KPMG LLP, St. James's Square, MANCHESTER, M2 6DS.
KATSOURIS, Miss. Sofia Louisa, BA ACA *2007;* Apartment 2.11, 12 Leftbank, MANCHESTER, M3 3AG.
KATTAN, Mr. James Michael, MEng ACA *2010;* KPMG, PO Box 493, Century Yard, Cricket Square, GEORGE TOWN, KY1-1106 CAYMAN ISLANDS.
KATTAU, Mr. Arthur, FCA *1956;* 62 Gallys Road, WINDSOR, SL4 5RA. (Life Member)
•**KATTE, Mr. Ian Paul, BSc FCA** *1981;* (Tax Fac), Ian Katte & Co, Lyndale House, 24 High Street, ADDLESTONE, SURREY, KT15 1TN.
•**KATTEN, Mr. Adam Simon, BA ACA** *1992;* Nyman Libson Paul, Regina House, 124 Finchley Road, LONDON, NW3 5JS.
KATUNGU, Mrs. Myrna Jane, LLB ACA *1986;* 26 Granville Street, KETTERING, NN16 0TA. (Life Member)
KATZ, Mr. Alan Jacob, BSc FCA *1969;* Woodcroft, Middle Entrance Drive, Bowness-on-Windermere, WINDERMERE, CUMBRIA, LA23 3JY.
KATZ, Mr. Andre Avi, BA ACA *2002;* 14 Beechwood Avenue, Little Chalfont, AMERSHAM, BUCKINGHAMSHIRE, HP6 6PL.
•**KATZ, Mr. Ian David, FCA** *1977;* 6 Coppice Walk, Totteridge, LONDON, N20 8BZ.
•**KATZ, Mr. John Harvey, FCA** *1970;* Rhodes & Rhodes, 42 Doughty Street, LONDON, WC1N 2LY.
•**KATZ, Mr. Matthew Elliott Ferrand, BA(Hons) ACA** *2000;* Roffe Swayne, Ashcombe Court, Woolsack Way, GODALMING, GU7 1LQ.
•**KATZ, Mr. Peter David, FCA** *1974;* (Tax Fac), P.D. Katz, Apartment 8, Alexandra House, Richmond Drive, Repton Park, WOODFORD GREEN ESSEX IG8 8RF.
KATZ, Mrs. Sarah Jane, BCom ACA *1995;* 60 Loom Lane, RADLETT, HERTFORDSHIRE, WD7 8PA.
•ⒹKATZ, **Mr. Stephen Mark, BA FCA FABRP** *1988;* David Rubin & Partners LLP, Pearl Assurance House, 319 Ballards Lane, North Finchley, LONDON, N12 8LY. See also David Rubin & Partners
•**KATZ, Mr. Stewart Alan, FCA FCCA** *1973;* Katz & Co, 135 Notting Hill Gate, LONDON, W11 3LB.
KATZ, Mr. William, FCA *1950;* 32 Bowwood Road, CLAREMONT, C.P., 7708, SOUTH AFRICA. (Life Member)
KATZEN, Mr. David Mark, ACA *1981;* 4811 Sandestin Drive, DALLAS, TX 75287, UNITED STATES.
•**KATZENBERG, Mr. Isaac, FCA** *1971;* Mount Katten & Co., 35 Temple Gardens, LONDON, NW11 0LP.
KAUFFMAN, Mr. Ivor Alan, FCA *1966;* Intertax Consulting Ltd, 33/6 Trumpeldor Street, PETACH TIKVA, 49403, ISRAEL.
•**KAUFMAN, Miss. Rachelle Esther, BSc ACA ATII** *1985;* (Tax Fac), R Kaufman, 7 Mayfield Gardens, LONDON, NW4 2PY.
KAUFMAN, Mr. Raymond, BSc FCA *1974;* Oldham Metropolitan Borough Council, Civic Centre, West Street, PO Box 160, OLDHAM, OL1 1UG.
•**KAUL, Mr. Navin, BSc ACA** *1993;* Ernst & Young LLP, 1 More London Place, LONDON, SE1 2AF. See also Ernst & Young Europe LLP
KAUL, Mrs. Rita, BSc ACA *1995;* Willowtrees, 19 Kewferry Drive, NORTHWOOD, MIDDLESEX, HA6 2NT.
•**KAUL, Mr. Surinder Nath, BA FCA ACIS** *1970;* (Member of Council 2004 - 2007), Wular Kaul & Co, 61 Colin Crescent, LONDON, NW9 6EU.
KAULA, Mr. Nigel William Meredith, FCA *1973;* Lingwood, Eglinton Road, Rushmoor, FARNHAM, GU10 2DH.
KAUR, Miss. Harminder, BSc(Hons) ACA *2009;* 86 Cherry Avenue, SLOUGH, SL3 7BX.
KAUR, Miss. Ivneet, MSc ACA *2009;* Flat G/1 Pulse Apartments, 52 Lymington Road, LONDON, NW6 1HQ.
KAUR, Miss. Jaspreet, BA ACA *1992;* 35 North Common, Redbourn, ST. ALBANS, HERTFORDSHIRE, AL3 7BU.
KAUR, Miss. Karmjit, MSc BSocSc ACA *1998;* Flat 1, 87 Anson Road, LONDON, NW2 4AB.
KAUR, Miss. Lakhvir, ACA *2008;* Flat D, 61b-61e Bedford Road, LONDON, SW4 7RH.
KAUR, Miss. Pam Manveen, BCom *1990;* 51 Lower Belgrave Street, LONDON, SW1W 0LP.
KAUR, Miss. Pavandeep, ACA *2011;* 57 West Avenue, PINNER, HA5 5DA.
KAUR, Miss. Sharanjit, BSc ACA *2005;* Flat 7, 24-26 Parkhill Road, LONDON, NW3 2YP.
KAUR, Miss. Tejinder, ACA *2009;* 35 Quinn Way, LETCHWORTH GARDEN CITY, HERTFORDSHIRE, SG6 2TX.
KAUR DEGUN, Mrs. Rajpal, BA ACA *2004;* 84 Malmesbury Road, LONDON, E18 2NN.
•**KAUR HAIRE, Mrs. Ramenpreet, BSc ACA** *2007;* 44 West Royd Crescent, SHIPLEY, WEST YORKSHIRE, BD18 1HW.
KAURA, Mr. Ajay Kumar, BSc ACA *2003;* 1 Uffcott Close, Lower Earley, READING, RG6 4BQ.
KAURA, Mr. Rajiv, BSc ACA *2005;* Foster Wheeler Energy Ltd Shinfield Park, Shinfield, READING, RG2 9FW.
KAURA, Mrs. Vibha, ACA *2009;* Flat 8 Godfree Court, 35 Long Lane, LONDON, SE1 4PS.
KAUSAR, Miss. Romana, BA ACA *2008;* 19 Bamford Way, ROCHDALE, LANCASHIRE, OL11 5NA.
KAUSHAL, Mrs. Asokamala, BSc(Hons) ACA *1993;* Alchemy Partners Llp, 25 Bedford Street, LONDON, WC2E 9ES.
KAUSHAL, Mr. Krishan, MBA BSc ACA *1992;* London Clubs International Limited, 10 Brick Street, LONDON, W1J 7HQ.
KAUSHAL, Miss. Rutchi, BA ACA *2008;* Unit 25/1 Brigid Road, SUBIACO, WA 6008, AUSTRALIA.
KAUSHIK, Mr. Ajay, FCA *1979;* Ajay Kaushik, Chrysalia Court, 206 Makarios Avenue, P O Box 50465, 3605 LIMASSOL, CYPRUS.
KAUTH, Mr. Christopher Robin, FCA *1975;* Farriers, 30 Burwood Park Road, WALTON-ON-THAMES, KT12 5LH.
KAUTH, Miss. Katharine, BSc(Hons) ACA *2011;* 9 Rembrandt Way, WALTON-ON-THAMES, SURREY, KT12 3SH.
KAUTH, Mr. Peter Martin, FCA *1967;* Mill Cottage, Windmill Hill, Ashill, ILMINSTER, TA19 9NT. (Life Member)
•**KAVANAGH, Mr. Anthony Charles, BA FCA** *1973;* Via Monte Cristallo 33, 30027 SAN DONA DI PIAVE, ITALY.
KAVANAGH, Mr. Chris John, BA(Hons) ACA *2009;* 17 Saxe Coburg Street, EDINBURGH, EH3 5BW.
KAVANAGH, Mr. David Paul, BSc(Hons) ACA *2001;* 15 Delta Road, WORCESTER PARK, SURREY, KT4 7HP.
KAVANAGH, Mrs. Dawn Ann, BA ACA *1991;* 9 Hambledon Hill, EPSOM, KT18 7BZ.
KAVANAGH, Miss. Emma, ACA *2009;* Flat 6 Fir Tree Lodge, 97 Barrowell Green, LONDON, N21 3AU.
KAVANAGH, Miss. Emma Jayne, BSc ACA *2009;* 3 Bexhill Drive, Amington, TAMWORTH, STAFFORDSHIRE, B77 3AL.
•**KAVANAGH, Mrs. Janette Sheila, BA ACA** *1980;* Accounting Centre Eynsham Ltd, 7-14 Station Point, Old Station Way, Eynsham Road, WITNEY, OXFORDSHIRE OX29 4DL.
•**KAVANAGH, Mr. Kevin Sean, FCA** *1978;* Accounting Centre Eynsham Ltd, 7-14 Station Point, Old Station Way, Eynsham Road, WITNEY, OXFORDSHIRE OX29 4DL.
KAVANAGH, Mr. Michael, ACA CPA *2003;* IAASA, Willow House, Millenium Park, NAAS, COUNTY KILDARE, IRELAND.
KAVANAGH, Mr. Nicholas, FCA DChA *1978;* 66 Birchdene Drive, Thamesmead, LONDON, SE28 8RP.
•**KAVANAGH, Mr. Peter John, FCA** *1973;* (Tax Fac), kavanagh Ltd, Battlefield House, Kidderminster Road, Dodford, BROMSGROVE, B61 9AD. See also Kavanagh PJ & Co Limited
•**KAVANAGH, Mr. Steven Paul, FCA** *1982;* (Tax Fac), Cowbridge Finance Ltd, Aeolian House, Piccadilly, Llanblethian, COWBRIDGE, SOUTH GLAMORGAN CF71 7JL. See also AIMS - Steven Kavanagh
KAVANAGH, Mr. Thomas, BSc ACA *2009;* 1 Bideford Drive, Sunnyhill, DERBY, DE23 1LT.
•**KAVANAGH-BROWN, Mr. Nigel Quentin, BA FCA** *1976;* Kavanagh Brown & Co, 30 Wentworth Close, WATFORD, WD17 4LW.
•**KAVANAGH-BROWN, Mrs. Patricia, BA FCA** *1980;* Kavanagh Brown & Co, 30 Wentworth Close, WATFORD, WD17 4LW.
KAVARANA, Mr. Farrokh Kaikhushru, FCA *1968;* Tata International AG, Gotthardstrasse 3, Ch-6300, ZUG, SWITZERLAND.
KAVAZY, Mr. Gregory Charles George, BA FCA *1992;* 3 Hoober Road, SHEFFIELD, S11 9SF.
KAVENEY, Mr. Raymond Alan, FCA *1976;* Age UK West Sussex, Suite 2 Anchor Springs, LITTLEHAMPTON, WEST SUSSEX, BN17 6BP.
KAWA, Mr. Tamer Ramsey, BA(Hons) ACA *2002;* Villa 32 Wasmiya Gardens, AL-QURAYYA, 0545, BAHRAIN.
KAY, Mr. Adam Michael, BA(Hons) ACA CTA *2003;* (Tax Fac), with Saffery Champness, Lion House, Red Lion Street, LONDON, WC1R 4GB.
KAY, Mr. Adrian Charles Donald, BA FCA *1977;* (Tax Fac), 20 Telegraph La, Claygate, ESHER, KT10 0DU.
KAY, Mr. Alan Martin Jeremy, FCA *1981;* Laurel Cottage, Kingsway, IVER, BUCKINGHAMSHIRE, SL0 9PL.
KAY, Mr. Alan William, FCA *1962;* 54 Blenheim Drive, Bredon, TEWKESBURY, GLOUCESTERSHIRE, GL20 7QQ.
KAY, Mr. Andrew John Benjamin, BCom ACA CF *1997;* 3 Hayfield Gardens, BIRMINGHAM, B13 9LE.
•**KAY, Mr. Brian Richard, FCA** *1976;* (Tax Fac), KBDR, The Old Tannery, Hensington Road, WOODSTOCK, OXFORDSHIRE, OX20 1JL.
•**KAY, Mr. Christopher David, BSc ACA** *1990;* Thorne Lancaster Parker, 8th Floor, Aldwych House, 81 Aldwych, LONDON, WC2B 4HN.
•**KAY, Mr. David Andrew, BA ACA** *1990;* Barlow Andrews LLP, Carlyle House, 78 Chorley New Road, BOLTON, BL1 4BY. See also Beech Business Services Limited
KAY, Mr. David Haviland, FCA *1965;* 8b Coxwell Court, CIRENCESTER, GLOUCESTERSHIRE, GL7 2BZ.
KAY, Mr. David John, BSc CA *1985;* c/o Superclubs, ICWI Building, 2 St Lucia Avenue, KINGSTON, JAMAICA.
KAY, Mr. David Michael, BSc FCA *1979;* c/o CEO Office, GO plc, Spencer Hill, MARSA MRS 1950, MALTA.
KAY, Mr. David Moburn, FCA *1968;* 31 St Andrews Wharf, Shad Thames, LONDON, SE1 2YN. (Life Member)
KAY, Mr. David Murray, BA ACA *2007;* 67 Clissold Crescent, LONDON, N16 9AR.
KAY, Ms. Deborah Anne, BA ACA *1994;* 3 Shepherds Well, Little Wold Lane, South Cave, BROUGH, NORTH HUMBERSIDE, HU15 2GE.
KAY, Mrs. Debra Elaine, ACA *1985;* Nasza Chatka, Crampmoor Lane, Crampmoor, ROMSEY, SO51 9AJ.
•**KAY, Mr. Donald George Frederick, BCom FCA** *1961;* with Barker Hibbert & Co, 133 Cherry Orchard Road, CROYDON, CR0 6BE.
KAY, Mrs. Emma, BA ACA *1992;* 2 Laurel Bank, Luddendenfoot, HALIFAX, WEST YORKSHIRE, HX2 6PS.
KAY, Mr. Gordon Thomas, FCA *1972;* 16 Ribbleton Close, BURY, BL8 2TH.
•**KAY, Mrs. Helen Belinda, BA ACA** *1993;* Roffe Swayne Ashcombe Court, Woolsack Way, GODALMING, GU7 1LQ.
•**KAY, Miss. Helena Clare Diane, BSc FCA** *1998;* Helena Kay, North Lodge, Ironsbottom, Sidlow, REIGATE, SURREY RH2 8PU.
KAY, Mr. Ian Andrew, MA ACA *1985;* 35 Pacific Parade, MANLY, NSW 2095, AUSTRALIA.
KAY, Mrs. Jennifer, BSc ACA *1999;* 3 Stockmar Grange, Heaton, BOLTON, BL1 5GQ.
KAY, Mrs. Joanne, ACA *2005;* Prospect House, Prospect Hill, STOURBRIDGE, WEST MIDLANDS, DY8 1PN.
KAY, Mr. John Clement, BSc FCA *1979;* Gleadhill Dawbers Lane, Euxton, CHORLEY, PR7 6EA.
KAY, Mr. John Winder, FCA *1944;* 3 Avalon, Sandbanks Road, POOLE, BH14 8HT. (Life Member)
KAY, Mr. Jonathan Francis, LLB ACA *2001;* Richmond Green Group, Lion House, Red Lion Street, RICHMOND, SURREY, TW9 1RE.
KAY, Mr. Jonathan Paul Malcolm, BA ACA FSI *1994;* Investec Wealth & Investment Ltd Quayside House, Canal Wharf Holbeck, LEEDS, LS11 5PU.
KAY, Miss. Katherine Ann, BSc ACA *1994;* The Hawthorns, Harbour Lane, Wheelton, CHORLEY, LANCASHIRE, PR6 8JS.
KAY, Mrs. Keely Joanne, BSc(Hons) ACA *2002;* 103 Pewterspear Green Road, Appleton, WARRINGTON, WA4 5FR.
KAY, Mr. Kevin Joseph, FCA *1965;* 15 Melbourne Road, Bramhall, STOCKPORT, SK7 1LR. (Life Member)
KAY, Mrs. Lisa Fiona, BA ACA *1989;* Lisa Kay Shoes, Unit D, Penfold Ind Est, WATFORD, WD24 4YY.
KAY, Mr. Mathew Gregory, ACA *1988;* High Meadows, Preston Road, Gosmore, HITCHIN, SG4 7QS.
KAY, Mr. Matthew James, ACA *2008;* Flat 5, 12 Abbeville Road, LONDON, SW4 9NJ.
KAY, Mr. Matthew Martin, BA ACA *1992;* 2 Laurel Bank, Stocks Lane, Luddenden, HALIFAX, HX2 6PS.
KAY, Mr. Matthew Roy, ACA *2009;* 37 Fownes Street, LONDON, SW11 2TJ.
•**KAY, Mr. Melvin Clifford, BA FCA** *1979;* (Tax Fac), Weston Kay, 73/75 Mortimer Street, LONDON, W1W 7SQ.
•**KAY, Mr. Michael, FCA** *1966;* (Tax Fac), Michael Kay & Company, 2 Water Court, Water Street, BIRMINGHAM, B3 1HP.
KAY, Mr. Michael John, BA ACA *1994;* Abbeyfield Society Wey Valley House, Mike Hawthorn Drive, FARNHAM, GU9 7UQ.
•**KAY, Mr. Michael John, BSc ACA CF** *1995;* MacIntyre Hudson LLP, Boundary House, 4 County Place, CHELMSFORD, CM2 0RE.
•**KAY, Mr. Peter, FCA** *1975;* (Tax Fac), Peter Kay, 14 Hamond Close, SOUTH CROYDON, SURREY, CR2 6BZ.
KAY, Mr. Peter Laurence, FCA *1966;* 36 The Avenue, Muswell Hill, LONDON, N10 2QL. (Life Member)
KAY, Mr. Peter Stuart, BSc FCA *1975;* Old School, Arley, NORTHWICH, CHESHIRE, CW9 6LZ. (Life Member)
KAY, Mr. Richard John, BSc FCA *1998;* 16 Carisbrooke Drive, MAIDSTONE, KENT, ME16 0HY.
KAY, Mr. Richard Michael, BSc ACA *1989;* McDermott Development Ltd 1 Mercury Rise, Altham Business Park Altham, ACCRINGTON, BB5 5BY.
KAY, Mr. Richard Tony, FCA *1978;* Seager House, 2 The Grange, STEVENAGE, HERTFORDSHIRE, SG1 3WA.
KAY, Mr. Robert Frank, FCA *1969;* 25 Shepherds Way, RICKMANSWORTH, HERTFORDSHIRE, WD3 7NN.
•**KAY, Mr. Robert Gerald Charles, FCA** *1974;* (Tax Fac), Buckinghams (Accountants) Ltd, 7 The Cottages, Biddlesden, BRACKLEY, NORTHAMPTONSHIRE, NN13 5TR.
KAY, Mr. Robert Henry, MA ACA *1980;* Hambrook Cottage, Hambrook, Hereford Road, LEDBURY, HR8 2PX.
KAY, Mr. Roy Hamilton, BA FCA *1958;* Brent House, High Street, LLANTWIT MAJOR, SOUTH GLAMORGAN, CF61 1SS. (Life Member)
KAY, Mr. Simeon, BA(Hons) ACA *2002;* Complinet Ltd Vintners Place, 68 Upper Thames Street, LONDON, EC4V 3BJ.
KAY, Mr. Simon, BA ACA *1989;* Nasza Chatka, Crampmoor Lane, Crampmoor, ROMSEY, SO51 9AJ.
KAY, Mrs. Sinead Mary, BSocSc ACA *2002;* 7 Burton Road, KENDAL, CUMBRIA, LA9 7LJ.
KAY, Mr. Stephen David, FCA *1965;* 15 Linfield Close, LONDON, NW4 1BZ.
KAY, Mr. Stephen Paul, BSc ACA *1988;* 1354 East Avenue, Suite R #381, CHICO, CA 95926, UNITED STATES.
KAY, Mr. Stephen William, BCom FCA *1978;* 3 Cumberland Road, SALE, M33 3FR.
•**KAY, Mr. Stewart Jeffrey, FCA** *1969;* (Tax Fac), Everetts, 86 Bury Old Road, Cheetham Village, MANCHESTER, M8 5BW.
•**KAY, Mr. Stuart James, FCA** *1968;* (Tax Fac), Stuart Kay, Elmdene, Ridgley Road, Chiddingfold, GODALMING, GU8 4QN.
KAY, Mr. Thomas, FCA *1963;* A. Conway Ltd, 114-116 Curtain Road, LONDON, EC2A 3AH.
KAY, Mr. Thomas William, ACA *2010;* 21a Quinton Street, LONDON, SW18 3QR.
KAY, Mr. Timothy Mark, LLB ACA *2001;* The Old Schoolhouse, Muiravonside, LINLITHGOW, WEST LOTHIAN, EH49 6LN.
KAY, Mr. Trevor Nigel, FCA *1961;* 22 Shipton Road, YORK, YO30 5RF.
KAYAT, Mr. Omar Adam, ACA *2008;* Flat 2, 14 Royal Crescent, LONDON, W11 4SL.
•**KAYE, Mr. Alan David, FCA** *1977;* BBK Partnership, 1 Beauchamp Court, Victors Way, BARNET, HERTFORDSHIRE, EN5 5TZ.
•**KAYE, Mr. Andrew Charles, BSc FCA CF** *1985;* with Deloitte LLP, Athene Place, 66 Shoe Lane, LONDON, EC4A 3BQ.
•**KAYE, Mr. Andrew Jonathan, BA FCA** *1991;* Harford Michaels Kaye Limited, 250 Hendon Way, LONDON, NW4 3NL.
•**KAYE, Mr. Andrew Mark, FCA** *1969;* 12 Culverlands Close, STANMORE, HA7 3AG.

KAYE, Mrs. Carolyn Mary Naomi, BA ACA *1990;* 24 Sydney Road, GUILDFORD, GU1 3LL.
KAYE, Mr. Christopher John, FCA *1975;* 6 Lindsey Crescent, KENILWORTH, WARWICKSHIRE, CV8 1FL.
•①**KAYE, Mr. David Norman, BCom FCA** *1974;* Crawfords Accountants LLP, Stanton House, 41 Blackfriars Road, SALFORD, M3 7DB.
KAYE, Mr. David Wolf, MA ACA *1980;* 15 Priory Avenue, LONDON, W4 1TZ.
•**KAYE, Mr. Denis Stanley, BA FCA** *1977;* Firm Ideas Ltd, 32 Malthouse Lane, Burn Bridge, HARROGATE, NORTH YORKSHIRE, HG3 1PD.
KAYE, Mr. Elliot Saul, BA ACA *1996;* 21 King George Avenue, BUSHEY, WD23 4NT.
•**KAYE, Mr. Farley Dene, BSc ACA** *2007;* Farley Kaye Limited, Caradene, Gills Hill Lane, RADLETT, HERTFORDSHIRE, WD7 8DB.
KAYE, Mr. Gary Phillip, FCA *1977;* Ernst & Young, 175 Commerce Valley Drive West, Suite 600, THORNHILL L3T 7P6, ON, CANADA.
•**KAYE, Mr. Gavin Mark, BSc ACA** *1988;* Opus Health Capital Limited, Ground Floor, 17 Red Lion Square, LONDON, WC1R 4QH. See also Optima Corporate Finance LLP
KAYE, Mr. Ian Hamilton, FCA *1957;* 17 Main Street, Bishopthorpe, YORK, YO23 2RA. (Life Member)
KAYE, Mr. James Maxwell, FCA *1959;* Hill Cottage, 3 Cock-A-Dobby, SANDHURST, BERKSHIRE, GU47 8LB. (Life Member)
•**KAYE, Mr. Jeffrey, BA ACA** *1988;* Jeffrey James, First Floor, 421A Finchley Road, Hampstead, LONDON, NW3 6HJ.
KAYE, Mr. John David, FCA *1964;* 25 River Holme View, Brockholes, HOLMFIRTH, HD9 7BP. (Life Member)
KAYE, Mr. John Neville, FCA *1957;* 17 Newton Park, Hove Edge, BRIGHOUSE, HD6 2LW. (Life Member)
•**KAYE, Mr. Jonathan Mark, BA FCA** *1988;* (Tax Fac), J M Kaye, 12 Embry Way, STANMORE, HA7 3AZ.
KAYE, Mr. Jonathan Russell, BA ACA *1998;* Darwin Private Equity, 15 Bedford Street, LONDON, WC2E 9HE.
KAYE, Mrs. Julia Marie, ACA *1995;* 13 Freyer Street, WILLIAMSTOWN, VIC 3016, AUSTRALIA.
KAYE, Mrs. Karen Sarah, BA(Hons) ACA *2003;* 15 Tonsley Hill, LONDON, SW18 1BE.
KAYE, Mr. Kevin Richard, BSc ACA *1993;* 6 Fowlers Garth, Longacres, Haworth, KEIGHLEY, WEST YORKSHIRE, BD22 0TH.
KAYE, Mr. Leslie John, FCA *1978;* Couchmans Farm, Harvest Hill Lane, Allesley, COVENTRY, CV5 9DE.
KAYE, Miss. Linda, ACA *1987;* Mothercare UK Ltd, Cherry Tree Road, WATFORD, WD24 6SH.
•**KAYE, Mr. Martin Wallace, FCA** *1978;* (Tax Fac), 23 All Saints Avenue, MAIDENHEAD, SL6 6EL.
KAYE, Mrs. Melva Dorothy, FCA *1961;* 2 Lowgate Lane, Bicker, BOSTON, LINCOLNSHIRE, PE20 3DG. (Life Member)
•**KAYE, Mr. Nicholas Simon, FCA** *1981;* AEL Partners LLP, 2nd Floor, 201 Haverstock Hill, LONDON, NW3 4QG.
KAYE, Mr. Paul, BSc FCA *1973;* Old Market Place Market Lane, Greet, CHELTENHAM, GLOUCESTERSHIRE, GL54 5BJ.
•**KAYE, Mr. Peter David, FCA** *1974;* Rooke Holt Limited, Giffords Farm, Giffords Cross, Bampton, TIVERTON, DEVON EX16 9DR.
KAYE, Mr. Philip Matthew, BA ACA *1996;* 20 Rue des Pres, 68220 KNOERINGUE, FRANCE.
KAYE, Mr. Philip Michael, BA ACA *1980;* Infini, 29 Harley Street, LONDON, W1G 9QR.
•**KAYE, Dr. Philip Roger, MA DPhil FCA ATII** *1991;* Deloitte LLP, Abbots House, Abbey Street, READING, RG1 3BD. See also Deloitte & Touche LLP
KAYE, Mrs. Rachel, BA FCA *1978;* 32 Malthouse Lane, Burn Bridge, HARROGATE, NORTH YORKSHIRE, HG3 1PD.
•**KAYE, Mr. Rodney Alan Charles, FCA** *1978;* Rose Cottage, Mop End, AMERSHAM, BUCKINGHAMSHIRE, HP7 0QP.
KAYE, Mr. Simon, ACA *2008;* 8 Ravens Close, Prestwich, MANCHESTER, M25 0FU.
KAYE, Miss. Stephanie Margaret, BCom ACA *2002;* 122 Swaby Road, Earlsfield, LONDON, SW18 3QZ.
•**KAYE, Mr. Stephen Alan, FCA FCCA** *1972;* Thornton Springer LLP, 67 Westow Street, Upper Norwood, LONDON, SE19 3RW.
KAYE, Mr. Stephen David, BSc(Eng) ACA *1989;* Hay Group, The Wanamaker Building, 100 Penn Square East, PHILADELPHIA, PA 19107-3388, UNITED STATES.
KAYLL, Mr. Simon James, MBA BA(Hons) FCA *1991;* Medical Protection Society Ltd, Granary Wharf House, LEEDS, LS11 5PY.
•**KAYNE, Mr. Stephen Warren, FCA** *1971;* Sloan & Co, Granite Buildings, 6 Stanley Street, LIVERPOOL, L1 6AF.
KAYONDO, Mr. David Kateregga, ACA *2009;* 20 Lockhart Avenue, Oxley Park, MILTON KEYNES, MK4 4TY.
•**KAYSER, Mr. Michael Ian, FCA** *1971;* Michael I. Kayser, 12A Belsize Park Gardens, LONDON, NW3 4LD.
KAZA, Ms. Pelagia, ACA *2011;* Apartment 927, 245E Regency Towers, 63rd Street, NEW YORK, NY 10065, UNITED STATES.
•**KAZAMIA, Mr. Stelios, ACA FCCA** *2007;* SNK, 13 Machera Street, 2650 NICOSIA, CYPRUS.
KAZAMIAS, Miss. Androulla, BCom ACA *1997;* with Baker Tilly & Co Limited, 25 Farringdon Street, LONDON, EC4A 4AB.
KAZAMIAS, Mr. Costas, BA(Hons) ACA *2002;* 143 Walsall Road, SUTTON COLDFIELD, B74 4NR.
•**KAZAMIAS, Mr. George, BSc ACA** *2002;* PricewaterhouseCoopers Limited, Julia House, 3 Themistocles Dervis Street, CY-1066 NICOSIA, CYPRUS.
KAZANTZIS, Mr. Christophoros, MSc BSc ACA *2009;* Skra 11, Agios Andreas, 1100 NICOSIA, CYPRUS.
KAZDOVA, Miss. Martina, ACA *2008;* Lukavecka 1732, 193 00 PRAGUE, CZECH REPUBLIC.
KAZEMI, Mr. Abi Abdollah, FCA *1978;* 22287 Stevens Creek Blvd, CUPERTINO, CA 95014, UNITED STATES.
KAZEMI, Mr. Bijan, ACA CPA *1980;* 4104 Cheswick Ln, VIRGINIA BEACH, VA 23455, UNITED STATES.
KAZI, Mr. Abdul Jabbar, FCA *1969;* J.3/II 7th Gizri Street, Off Gizri Avenue, DHA Phase IV, KARACHI 75500, PAKISTAN. (Life Member)
KAZI, Mr. Abdur Raoof, FCA *1970;* 50 Windermere Avenue, WEMBLEY, HA9 8SF.
•**KAZI, Mr. Mohammed Aamir, FCA** *1992;* (Tax Fac), Civvals Ltd, 50 Seymour Street, LONDON, W1H 7JG. See also Civvals Ellam Ltd and Civvals
KAZI, Mr. Nazrul, BSc ACA *2005;* GE Money Home Lending Building 4, Hatters Lane Croxley Business Park, WATFORD, WD18 8YF.
KAZI, Mr. Sohail, FCA CFA *1979;* The West Of England Ship Owner, Mutual Assurance Assoc, (Luxemb, 33 Boulevard Prince Henri, B P 841 LUXEMBOURG, LUXEMBOURG.
KAZI, Mr. Tariq, BSc ACA *1998;* Flat 7 Waterford Court, 20 Daventry Street, LONDON, NW1 6TD.
KAZIKAS, Mr. Marios, BA(Hons) ACA *2011;* 10 B Antonis Papadopoulos street, 6053 LARNACA, CYPRUS.
KAZIMI, Mr. Ali Hasan, BSc ACA *1997;* with Deloitte LLP, Hill House, 1 Little New Street, LONDON, EC4A 3TR.
KAZIMIEROWICZ, Mr. Jan, BSc ACA *1999;* 13 Hartley Road, EXMOUTH, EX8 2SG.
KAZMI, Mr. Ali, MSc ACA *1999;* Fleet House, Beckenham Place Park, BECKENHAM, BR3 5BS.
KAZMI, Mr. Amir Ali, BSc ACA *1989;* Oilspace Ltd Castlewood House, 77-91 New Oxford Street, LONDON, WC1A 1DG.
KAZMI, Mrs. Shermeen, MBA ACA *2006;* 1 Laurino Place, Hartsbourne Avenue, BUSHEY, HERTFORDSHIRE, WD23 1QP.
•**KAZMI, Mr. Syed Humayun, ACA** *1989;* (Tax Fac), Seymour King, 3 Accommodation Road, LONDON, NW11 8ED.
KAZMI, Mr. Syed Sameer Abbas, ACA *2011;* Flat 10, Centurion House, 69 Station Road, EDGWARE, MIDDLESEX, HA8 7JQ.
KAZNOWSKI, Mr. Lee John, ACA *2005;* 60 Baildon Wood Court, Baildon, SHIPLEY, WEST YORKSHIRE, BD17 5QG.
KEABLE, Mr. Alan James, FCA *1976;* Yorkshire Technology Ltd, 5 Guy Street, BRADFORD, WEST YORKSHIRE, BD4 7BB.
KEAL, Mr. David, LLB ACA *1997;* 18 Hervey Road, SLEAFORD, LINCOLNSHIRE, NG34 7LT.
KEALEY, Mrs. Clare, BA ACA *1997;* 44 Grange Road, Dorridge, SOLIHULL, WEST MIDLANDS, B93 8QS.
KEAM, Mrs. Elisabeth Angela Caroline, BA ACA *1989;* Horseshoe Wood Farm, Therfield Road, Kelshall, ROYSTON, SG8 9SS.
KEAN, Mr. Andrew James, BSc ACA *1991;* 19 Austral Avenue, NORTH MANLY, NSW 2100, AUSTRALIA.
KEAN, Mr. Christopher, FCA *1970;* Wynngates, Cowpitts Lane, RINGWOOD, HAMPSHIRE, BH24 3JX. (Life Member)
KEAN, Mr. Robert, FCA *1975;* 9411 Glenallan Drive, RICHMOND V7A 2S9, BC, CANADA. (Life Member)
KEAN, Mr. Stuart William, FCA *1972;* Hayward House, 18 Pelhams Walk, ESHER, KT10 8QD.
KEAN, Ms. Susan Patricia, BA ACA *1986;* Old Mutual Plc Millennium Bridge House, 2 Lambeth Hill, LONDON, EC4V 4GG.
KEAN, Mr. Timothy James, FCA *1978;* 616 Burton Drive, LAFAYETTE, CA, 94549, UNITED STATES.
KEANE, Mr. Adrian Spencer, BSc FCA *1989;* 7 Main Street, Lockington, DERBY, DE74 2RH.
KEANE, Mr. Conor John Francis, BBS FCA *1989;* 10294 E Sheri Lane, ENGLEWOOD, CO 80111, UNITED STATES.
KEANE, Miss. Helen, BSc ACA *1995;* #7B 225 West 83 Street, NEW YORK, NY 10024, UNITED STATES.
KEANE, Mr. Henry Oliver, ACA *2010;* Cedar Cottage, Slaugham, HAYWARDS HEATH, WEST SUSSEX, RH17 6AQ.
KEANE, Mr. James Francis, FCA *1965;* 3 Banstead Road, CARSHALTON, SURREY, SM5 3NS.
KEANE, Mr. John Michael, FCA *1958;* c/o Saltrates International SA, 17 Rue des Pierres-du-Niton, CH 1207 GENEVA, SWITZERLAND.
KEANE, Mr. Justin Stanley Takeshi, ACA *2001;* 305 East 40th Street, Apt 3J, NEW YORK, NY 10016, UNITED STATES.
•**KEANE, Miss. Maura Josephine Bernadette, MBA BA FCA** *1980;* 149 Coombe Road, CROYDON, CR0 5SQ.
KEANE, Mr. Maurice, FCA *1960;* 11 Clockhouse Lane, ASHFORD, MIDDLESEX, TW15 2EP.
KEANE, Mr. Nigel Patrick, BSc ARCS ACA *1986;* Wales Social Partners Unit Limited, Room 208 Titan House, Titan Road, CARDIFF, CF24 5BS.
KEANE, Mr. Philip Michael, FCA *1970;* Regus, 54 Clarendon Road, WATFORD, WD17 1DU.
•**KEANE, Miss. Philippa Mary, BA ACA DChA** *1983;* with Carston & Co Limited, First Floor, Tudor House, 16 Cathedral Road, CARDIFF, CF11 9LJ.
•**KEANE, Mr. Richard Hilton, FCA** *1973;* Oak Lodge, Ash Close, YELVERTON, PL20 6HT.
KEANE, Mr. Robert Simon, BA ACA *2001;* 2nd Floor, 19 South Audley Street, LONDON, W1K 2NU.
•**KEANE, Mrs. Susan Mary, BEng FCA** *1995;* Fuller Harvey Ltd, Mill House, 58 Guildford Street, CHERTSEY, SURREY, KT16 9BE.
KEANEY, Mr. Dale, BSc(Hons) ACA *2000;* Wentworth Club, Wentworth Drive, VIRGINIA WATER, GU25 4LS.
KEANEY, Miss. Joanna Therese, FCA *1993;* 35D Onslow Road, RICHMOND, SURREY, TW10 6QH.
KEANY, Mr. Anthony, BSc ACA *2002;* PricewaterhouseCoopers, 91 King William Streeet, ADELAIDE, SA SA 5022, AUSTRALIA.
KEANY, Mrs. Sarah, BA ACA *2001;* 16 Lathkill Drive, RIPLEY, DERBYSHIRE, DE5 8HW.
KEAR, Mrs. Ceri Patricia, ACA *2003;* Castle View House, 4 Castle Street, USK, GWENT, NP15 1BU.
•**KEAREY, Mr. Martyn Edward, BTech ACA** *1982;* with Hobday & Company, 20a Plantagenet Road, BARNET, HERTFORDSHIRE, EN5 5JG.
KEARLEY, Mr. Andrew Paul, FCA *1974;* Shortlands, 12 Fiddicroft Avenue, BANSTEAD, SM7 3AD.
KEARNEY, Mrs. Bridin, ACA *2008;* 3 Lady Anne Court, Queen Mary Avenue, LONDON, E18 2FR.
KEARNEY, Mrs. Elizabeth Jane Parlane, BA ACA *1995;* 2 Cadogan Grove, Backwell, BRISTOL, BS48 3QN.
•**KEARNEY, Mr. Kevin Gerard, FCA** *1974;* (Tax Fac), Kevin Kearney Associates Ltd, Suite 3, Weybridge Business Centre, 66 York Road, WEYBRIDGE, KT13 9DY.
KEARNEY, Mr. Kevin John, ACA *2011;* 6 Elgin Drive, WALLASEY, MERSEYSIDE, CH45 7PR.
KEARNEY, Mr. Martyn James, FCA *1975;* Argyll Business Centre Gefinor House, 18b Charles Street, LONDON, W1J 5DU.
KEARNEY, Ms. Mary Catherine, BA ACA *2002;* 114 St. Cross Road, WINCHESTER, HAMPSHIRE, SO23 9RE.
KEARNEY, Mr. Michael Anthony, FCA *1972;* 28 Chartwell, 80 Parkside, LONDON, SW19 5LN. (Life Member)
KEARNEY, Mr. Paul Anthony, BA ACA *2003;* with RSM Tenon Audit Limited, 66 Chiltern Street, LONDON, W1U 4JT.
KEARNEY, Mr. Paul Leonard, BA ACA *1991;* Long Common, Scatterdells Lane, Chipperfield, KINGS LANGLEY, WD4 9EX.
KEARNEY, Miss. Rachel, BSc ACA *2006;* 19d Shepherds Bush Road, LONDON, W6 7LX.
KEARNEY, Mrs. Sally Ann, MA ACA *1989;* The Dormies, Epsom Road, GUILDFORD, GU4 7AB.
KEARNS, Miss. Amanda, ACA *2011;* Watling House, Old Watling Street, Markyate, ST. ALBANS, HERTFORDSHIRE, AL3 8LT.
KEARNS, Mr. David Thomas, BSc ACA *1995;* GRI Group, 5 Acorn Business Park Woodseats Close, SHEFFIELD, S8 0TB.
KEARNS, Mr. Hubert Joseph Bartholomew, FCA *1958;* 68 The Rise, MOUNT MERRION 2, COUNTY DUBLIN, IRELAND. (Life Member)
KEARNS, Mr. Lawrence Albert, FCA *1974;* Highton, Ballanard Road, Douglas, ISLE OF MAN, IM2 5PP.
KEARNS, Mrs. Sarah Louise, ACA *1995;* 70 Christ Church Mount, EPSOM, KT19 8LP.
KEARNS, Mr. Timothy Augustine, BSc ACA *1986;* Greenlane Farmhouse, Green Lane Farm Sinderland Lane, Dunham Massey, ALTRINCHAM, CHESHIRE, WA14 5SX.
KEARSEY, Mr. James Edward, BEng ACA *1995;* Walnut Tree House, 20b Old Lincoln Road, Caythorpe, GRANTHAM, LINCOLNSHIRE, NG32 3DF.
KEARSEY, Miss. Rachel, MEng ACA *2004;* 32 Fox Hill, LONDON, SE19 2XE.
•**KEARSEY, Mr. Richard Michael, FCA** *1987;* Charter Place, Ifm Trust, JERSEY, JE1 1JY.
KEARSEY, Mr. Richard Peter, BA ACA *1990;* Willowside, 13A Albury Road, GUILDFORD, GU1 2BZ.
•**KEARSLEY, Mr. Alan, FCA** *1973;* 47 The Courtyard, Southwell Park Road, CAMBERLEY, GU15 3GL.
KEARSLEY, Mr. Derek Robert, BA ACA *1979;* 22 Havenwood Road, Whitley, WIGAN, WN1 2PA.
KEARTON, Mr. Richard Michael Wooff, BSc ACA *1994;* Bank Cottage, High Street, Little Chesterford, SAFFRON WALDEN, CB10 1TS.
KEARVELL, Mr. Nicholas Paul, ACA *2009;* Flat 3 Camden Place, 106-110 Kentish Town Road, LONDON, NW1 9PX.
KEARVELL-WHITE, Mr. Brian Richard, BA(Hons) FCA CISA *1979;* 4 Bluebell Lane, Glooston, MARKET HARBOROUGH, LE16 7SQ.
KEAST, Mr. Alexander William John, BA ACA *2005;* Building 3, Plymouth Hospitals NHS Trust Finance Directorate, 3 Derriford Park Derriford Business Park, PLYMOUTH, PL6 5QZ.
KEAST, Mr. Andrew, BSc ACA *1995;* Ellacoombe Perrancoombe, PERRANPORTH, CORNWALL, TR6 0HX.
KEAST, Ms. Lorna June, FCA *1976;* 5 Cranbrook Drive, MAIDENHEAD, BERKSHIRE, SL6 6SA.
KEAST, Mr. Timothy Peter, BSc ACA *2006;* 34 Sunnyhill Road, LONDON, SW16 2UH.
KEAST, Mr. Wayne Bruce, ACA CA(SA) *2010;* (Tax Fac), 4 Royal Close, Wimbledon Village, LONDON, SW19 5RS.
KEAT, Miss. Deborah Claire, ACA *2009;* Flat 34, Goodhart Place, Limehouse, LONDON, E14 8EG.
KEATES, Mr. Anthony William George, BSc ACA *2005;* Mall House, The Mall, FAVERSHAM, ME13 8JL.
•**KEATES, Mr. Brian Edward, FCA FIFP CFP** *1973;* (Tax Fac), Financial Planners Co UK Limited, Studio 3, Waterside Court, Third Avenue Centrum 100, BURTON-ON-TRENT, DE14 2WQ.
•**KEATES, Mr. Martyn Paul, ACA FCCA** *2011;* Action Business Consultants Limited, 58 Watchetts Drive, CAMBERLEY, SURREY, GU15 2PQ.
•**KEATES-PORTER, Mr. Christopher John, FCA** *1988;* R.S. Porter & Co, 77/81 Alma Rd, Clifton, BRISTOL, BS8 2DP.
KEATING, Mr. Anthony John, FCA *1973;* 86 Greenhayes Avenue, BANSTEAD, SM7 2JQ.
KEATING, Mr. Daire, ACA *2008;* DCC House, Brewery Road, Stillorgan, BLACKROCK, COUNTY DUBLIN, IRELAND.
KEATING, Mr. Daniel Alexander, BA(Econ) ACA *2003;* 31 Cassell Road, BRISTOL, BS16 5DE.
KEATING, Mr. Dominic Paul, ACA *1995;* 45 Maplefield, Park Street, ST. ALBANS, HERTFORDSHIRE, AL2 2BE.
•**KEATING, Mr. Emmet James, MPhys ACA CF** *2006;* Catalyst Corporate Finance LLP, 9th Floor, Bank House, 8 Cherry Street, BIRMINGHAM, B2 5AL.
KEATING, Mr. Francis Alexander, BA FCA *1978;* Elizabeth Fitzroy Support Fitzroy House, 8 Hylton Road, PETERSFIELD, GU32 3JY.
KEATING, Mrs. Janette Christine, BSc ACA *1993;* Pyne Lodge, Sparks Lane, Cuckfield, HAYWARDS HEATH, RH17 5JP.
•**KEATING, Mr. John Arthur, FCA** *1973;* (Tax Fac), Chantrey Vellacott DFK LLP, Russell Square House, 10-12 Russell Square, LONDON, WC1B 5LF.
•①**KEATING, Mr. Stephen Charles, MA ACA** *1992;* Privet Capital LLP, 18b Charles Street, LONDON, W1J 5DU.
KEATINGS, Mrs. Beverly, BSc ACA *1981;* 1 Eversley Gardens, Leasgill, MILNTHORPE, LA7 7EY.

KEATLEY, Mr. Ian Stuart, FCA *1976;* Covidien Ltd Ashwood Crockford Lane, Chineham Business Park Chineham, BASINGSTOKE, RG24 8EH.
•**KEATS, Mr. Robert David, ACA** *1983;* Robert Keats, 29 Lyndhurst, SKELMERSDALE, LANCASHIRE, WN8 6UH.
KEAY, Miss. Lucy Dawn, ACA *2009;* 13 Macaulay Road, RUGBY, WARWICKSHIRE, CV22 6HE.
KEAYS, Mr. Douglas Louis Frederick, FCA *1954;* Apartment 208, The Hawthorns Retirement Residence Hotel, 18-19 Elton Road, CLEVEDON, AVON, BS21 7EH. (Life Member)
KECK, Mr. Oliver Alexander, MEng ACA *2009;* 24 Bloemfontein Road, LONDON, W12 7BX.
KECK, Miss. Rebekah, ACA *2011;* 14 Angelica Close, Littleover, DERBY, DE23 1NJ.
KEDDIE, Mr. David William, BSc ACA *1998;* Handlow House, Churcham, GLOUCESTER, GL2 8BB.
KEDDIE, Mr. Iain, BSc ACA *1991;* 103 Awaba Street, MOSMAN, NSW 2088, AUSTRALIA.
KEDDIE, Mrs. Jane, BSc ACA *1990;* Deloitte LLP Union Plaza, 1 Union Wynd, ABERDEEN, AB10 1SL.
KEDDY, Mrs. Joanne Clare, BSc ACA *1998;* 63 High Street, Kimpton, HITCHIN, HERTFORDSHIRE, SG4 8PU.
KEDIA, Miss. Ritu Nawal, MSc ACA *2004;* 129 London Road, ST. ALBANS, AL1 1TA.
KEDRACKA, Miss. Malgorzata, BSc ACA *2007;* 23 Chaucer Road, LONDON, W3 6DR.
KEDWARD, Mr. Paul David, BSc ACA *2001;* 24 Dunnydeer View, INSCH, ABERDEENSHIRE, AB52 6HW.
KEE, Mr. Yang Khiaw, BA ACA *1993;* 19 Jalan Sutera 3, Taman Sentosa 80150, JOHOR BAHRU, JOHOR, MALAYSIA.
KEEBLE, Mr. Christopher Murray, BSc FCA *1987;* The Barn, Main Road, Wormingford, COLCHESTER, CO6 3AX.
•**KEEBLE, Mr. Daniel Kenneth, BSc ACA** *1999;* Deloitte LLP, Hill House, 1 Little New Street, LONDON, EC4A 3TR. See also Deloitte & Touche LLP
•**KEEBLE, Mr. Graham Charles, FCA** *1982;* (Tax Fac), Graham Keeble Partnership LLP, First Floor, 5 Doolittle Yard, Froghall Road, Ampthill, BEDFORD MK45 2NW.
KEEBLE, Mr. Michael Philip, ACA *1987;* The Cottage, Lower Street, Shere, GUILDFORD, GU5 9HX.
•**KEEBLE, Mrs. Nicola Catherine, FCA** *1986;* Keebles, Ivanhoe, Maitland Close, WEST BYFLEET, SURREY, KT14 6RF. See also Aries Consultants LLP
KEEBLE, Mr. Paul Richard, BSc ACA *2006;* Draft F C B, 84 Eccleston Square, LONDON, SW1V 1PX.
•**KEEBLE, Mr. Richard Francis, FCA** *1977;* (Tax Fac), Gilberts, Pendragon House, 65 London Road, ST. ALBANS, AL1 1LJ.
•**KEEBLE, Mrs. Sarah Louise, ACA CTA** *2000;* Mrs Sarah Keeble BA(Hons) ACA CTA, 51 Pembury Road, BEXLEYHEATH, KENT, DA7 5LN.
•**KEEBLE, Mr. Simon John, FCA** *1982;* Ivanhoe, Maitland Close, WEST BYFLEET, SURREY, KT14 6RF. See also Aries Consultants LLP
KEEBLE, Mrs. Tracey, ACA *1990;* B D O Stoy Hayward Llp Kreston House, 66 Broomfield Road, CHELMSFORD, CM1 1SW.
KEEBLE-CARTER, Mrs. Samantha Anne, BSc ACA *1993;* 62 Hawthorn Crescent, Yatton, BRISTOL, BS49 4BF.
KEECH, Mr. Andrew Michael, BA ACA *1991;* 16 Stratford Way, Lower Shelton, BEDFORD, MK43 0LJ.
KEECH, Miss. Lucy, BSc ACA *1998;* 65a Burlington Road, LONDON, SW6 4NH.
KEECH, Mr. Trevor Leslie, BSc ACA *1984;* PricewaterCoopers, Slovensko s r o, Namestie, Maja 18, 81532 BRATISLAVA, SLOVAK REPUBLIC.
KEEFE, Mr. Andrew, ACA *1982;* 95 Harptree Drive, Walderslade, CHATHAM, ME5 0TF.
KEEFE, Mr. Donald George, FCA *1961;* 3 Heatherslade Road, Southgate, SWANSEA, SA3 2DD. (Life Member)
•**KEEFE, Mr. Joseph James, FCA** *1974;* J.J. Keefe, 77 The Wheel House, Burrells Wharf, Westferry Road, LONDON, E14 3TB.
KEEFE, Mr. Simon Russell, BSc ACA *1985;* 20 Smithbarn, HORSHAM, WEST SUSSEX, RH13 6EB.
KEEGAN, Dame Elizabeth Mary, DBE MA FCA *1977;* (Member of Council 1994 - 1997), Old Matthews Farm, Kerswell, CULLOMPTON, DEVON, EX15 2EL.
KEEGAN, Mr. Jason Michael, BSc ACA *1998;* 37 Alford Grove, Sprowston, NORWICH, NR7 8XB.
KEEGAN, Mr. Mark Anthony, BA(Hons) ACA *2004;* 11 Cornhill, Allestree, DERBY, DE22 2GG.
KEEGAN, Mr. Matthew James, BA ACA *1998;* Henmans LLP, 5000 John Smith Drive, Oxford Business Park South, OXFORD, OX4 2BH.
KEEGAN, Mr. Michael Anthony, BA ACA *1979;* 25 Grange Road, Hedge End, SOUTHAMPTON, SO30 2FL.
KEEGAN, Mr. Nicholas Francis, MA FCA *1982;* Alderminster Lodge, Alderminster, STRATFORD-UPON-AVON, CV37 8NY.
KEEGAN, Mrs. Susan Amanda, MA ACA *1989;* 23 Cedar Road, TEDDINGTON, TW11 9AN.
KEEHAN, Miss. Claire Margaret, ACA *2011;* 33 Grimwade Avenue, CROYDON, SURREY, CR0 5DJ.
•**KEEHAN, Mrs. Jill, ACA** *1978;* (Tax Fac), Britt & Keehan, 33 Grimwade Avenue, CROYDON, CR0 5DJ.
KEEHAN, Mr. John Patrick, ACA *1979;* 33 Grimwade Avenue, CROYDON, CR0 5RD.
KEEHNER, Mr. Arnold, FCA *1952;* 143 Patterson Crescent, CARLETON PLACE K7C 4P3, ON, CANADA. (Life Member)
•**KEEL, Mr. Brett Matthew, ACA** *2010;* 44 Upton Road, POOLE, DORSET, BH17 7AH.
•**KEEL, Mr. Douglas Vincent, MA FCA** *1973;* (Tax Fac), 21 Dover Park Drive, Putney Heath, LONDON, SW15 5BD.
KEEL, Mr. Reginald Oscar Arnold, FCA *1948;* (Member of Council 1963 - 1977), Warren End, 126 Coombe Lane West, KINGSTON-UPON-THAMES, KT2 7DD. (Life Member)
KEELE, Mr. Stephen Clare Kennedy, BA FCA *1958;* 11 Belmont Crescent, GLASGOW, G12 8EU. (Life Member)
KEELER, Mr. Brian Robert, FCA *1959;* The Hawthorns, Swan Street, Chappel, COLCHESTER, CO6 2EE. (Life Member)
KEELER, Mr. John Arthur, FCA *1966;* Calle Roma 4 Bajos, 08023 BARCELONA, SPAIN.
KEELER, Mr. Robert Michael, BA ACA *1983;* 55 Baker Street, LONDON, W1U 7EU.
KEELEY, Mr. Christopher Arthur, FCA *1967;* 33 Pegasus Way, EAST GRINSTEAD, WEST SUSSEX, RH19 3NP.
KEELEY, Mr. David Christopher, BA ACA *1991;* 40 Gorsey Croft, Eccleston Park, PRESCOT, L34 2RT.
•**KEELEY, Mrs. Indrani, BSc ACA CPA** *1992;* Houghton Stone, The Conifers, Filton Road, Hambrook, BRISTOL, BS16 1QG.
•**KEELEY, Mr. John, FCA** *1974;* (Tax Fac), Hollows & Hesketh, 9 Sandy Lane, SKELMERSDALE, WN8 8LA.
KEELEY, Mr. Mark Daniel, BA(Hons) ACA *2003;* E C I Colchester House, 38-40 Peter Street, MANCHESTER, M2 5GP.
KEELEY, Mr. Stephen Robert, BSc(Econ) FCA CertPFS *1992;* with Isle of Man Creamery Ltd, Ballafletcher Farm Road, Cronkbourne, ISLE OF MAN, IM4 4QE.
KEELING, Mr. Andrew Colin, BSc ACA *1999;* with KPMG LLP, 15 Canada Square, LONDON, E14 5GL.
KEELING, Mr. Damian John, BA ACA *1982;* Juniper Holdings Limited, 182 Ashley Road, HALE, CHESHIRE, WA15 9SF.
KEELING, Mr. David John, FCA *1972;* Happmount Limited, 26 Lloyd Road, HOVE, EAST SUSSEX, BN3 6NL.
KEELING, Mr. James Septimus, BA ACA *1990;* MEMBER OF COUNCIL, with Corbett Keeling Ltd, 13 St Swithins Lane, LONDON, EC4N 8AL.
KEELING, Mr. Max Warren, BA ACA *2004;* Floor 25, Barclays Bank Plc, 1 Churchill Place, LONDON, E14 5HP.
KEELING, Mr. Michael Edward Allis, MA FCA *1953;* Jacobs Farm, Sedlescombe, BATTLE, TN33 0PL. (Life Member)
KEELING, Mr. Peter Charles, ACA *1980;* 3 The Peppers, LYMM, CHESHIRE, WA13 0JA.
KEELING, Mr. Peter James, BSc FCA *1980;* 11 The Dairyground, Shutford, BANBURY, OXFORDSHIRE, OX15 6PN.
KEELING, Mr. Stephen, BA ACA ATII *1986;* No.1 Godwin Street, BRADFORD, BD1 2SU.
KEELTY, Miss. Alexandra Karen, LLB ACA *2006;* K P M G Quayside House, 110 Quayside, NEWCASTLE UPON TYNE, NE1 3DX.
KEELTY, Mr. Michael Patrick, BA ACA *1998;* 32 Dominion Road, Addiscombe, CROYDON, CR0 6JP.
KEELY, Miss. Fay, BSc ACA *1997;* Holly Tree Farm, Main Road, Higham, ALFRETON, DE55 6EF.
KEELY, Mrs. Julie Elizabeth, BSc ACA *1991;* 119 Kenningknowes Road, STIRLING, FK7 9JF.
KEELY, Mr. Paul, BA ACA *2005;* Apartamento 1601 Torre 2, Edificio Balcones del Parque, C99a-52-160, BARRANQUILLA, COLOMBIA.
KEELY, Miss. Sharon, BA ACA *1987;* 239 W. 10th St, SAN PEDRO, CA 90731, UNITED STATES.
KEELY, Mr. Terence, FCA *1970;* Bellfield Furnishings Ltd Unit 1, Furnace Road, ILKESTON, DERBYSHIRE, DE7 5EP.
KEEMER, Mr. Simon Mark, BA ACA CPA *1998;* 4005 W. Highway 22, CRESTWOOD, KY 40014, UNITED STATES.
KEEN, Mr. Adrian Peter, BSc ACA *2007;* 41a Sutton Wick Lane, Drayton, ABINGDON, OXFORDSHIRE, OX14 4HH.
KEEN, Mr. Allan Roy, BA FCA *1967;* 21 Cherwell Road, Keynsham, BRISTOL, BS31 1QT.
KEEN, Mr. Christian, BSc ACA MBA *1990;* 56 Beverley Crescent, BEDFORD, MK40 4BY.
KEEN, Mr. David, ACA *2009;* Murco Petroleum Ltd, 4 Beaconsfield Road, ST. ALBANS, HERTFORDSHIRE, AL1 3RH.
KEEN, Mr. David Dorian Oliver, BA ACA *1987;* 20 Waldegrave Park, TWICKENHAM, MIDDLESEX, TW1 4TQ.
KEEN, Mr. David George, FCA *1955;* 3 Furze View, Chorleywood, RICKMANSWORTH, HERTFORDSHIRE, WD3 5HT. (Life Member)
KEEN, Dr. David James, ACA *1992;* N D S Ltd, 1 London Road, STAINES, MIDDLESEX, TW18 4EX.
KEEN, Miss. Joanna Louise, BSc ACA *2001;* 69 Alexander Road, Rhyddings, NEATH, SA10 8EG.
•**KEEN, Mr. John Samuel, BSc ACA** *1997;* Alvarez & Marsal Europe, 10th Floor, 1 Canada Square, Canary Wharf, LONDON, E14 5AA.
KEEN, Mrs. Katherine Anne, BA ACA *1993;* 13 Warwick Close, HAMPTON, TW12 2TY.
KEEN, Mrs. Laura Margaret, BSc FCA *1990;* 56 Beverley Crescent, BEDFORD, MK40 4BY.
KEEN, Mr. Laurence Brian, BSc ACA *2001;* 1 Almond Way, BOREHAMWOOD, HERTFORDSHIRE, WD6 1HF.
•**KEEN, Mr. Malcolm Fraser, BSc FCA** *1988;* (Tax Fac), Carpenter Keen LLP, Grand Prix House, 102-104 Sheen Road, RICHMOND, SURREY, TW9 1UF.
KEEN, Mr. Mark Andrew, BA FCA CF *1988;* 36 Selkirk Road, Curzon Park, CHESTER, CH4 8AH.
KEEN, Mr. Matthew Bryan, BSc ACA *2003;* 24 Trevor Road, LONDON, SW19 3PW.
KEEN, Mr. Melvyn, MA FCA *1979;* Middlesex University Business School, The Burroughs, LONDON, NW4 4BT.
KEEN, Mr. Neil Gordon, FCA *1968;* Edmont Joinery Limited, Hyde Road, Upper Stratton, SWINDON, SN2 7RB.
•**KEEN, Mr. Nigel John, MA FCA** *1972;* 19 Pembroke Square, LONDON, W8 6PA.
KEEN, Mr. Paul Andrew, MA ACA *1995;* 155 Carshalton Park Road, CARSHALTON, SM5 3SF.
KEEN, Mr. Peter Stephen, BSc ACA *1981;* 26 Manor Road, Hemingford Grey, HUNTINGDON, PE28 9BX.
KEEN, Miss. Sally Virginia, BSc FCA *1992;* Chris Sedgeman Scaffolding Ltd Unit 2b, Long Rock Industrial Estate Long Rock, PENZANCE, CORNWALL, TR20 8HX.
•**KEEN, Mrs. Samantha Jane, BSc FCA** *1994;* Ernst & Young LLP, 1 More London Place, LONDON, SE1 2AF. See also Ernst & Young Europe LLP
KEEN, Mr. Simon Lloyd, BSc ACA *2004;* Babcock Airports Unit 2, Radius Park Faggs Road, FELTHAM, TW14 0NG.
KEEN, Mr. Thomas William, FCA *1954;* 27 Chapel Farm Road, LONDON, SE9 3NJ. (Life Member)
KEEN, Mr. Timothy William Patrick, FCA *1973;* Flat 7, Jackson & Joseph Building, 8 Princelet Street, LONDON, E1 6QJ.
KEEN, Mr. William Howard, FCA *1972;* North Shore Credit Union, 1112 Lonsdale Avenue, NORTH VANCOUVER V7M 2H2, BC, CANADA.
•**KEENAN, Mr. Anthony William, BSc ACA ATII** *1992;* (Tax Fac), Keenan, 89-91 Marsden Road, BLACKPOOL, FY4 3BY. See also Hark Grimley & Co
KEENAN, Mr. Gerard Anthony Mathieson, BSc FCA *1993;* 172 Singlewell Road, GRAVESEND, KENT, DA11 7RB.
•**KEENAN, Ms. Mary Caroline, BSc FCA** *1993;* 29 Cuttyshane Road, Crossgar, DOWNPATRICK, COUNTY DOWN, BT30 9EX.
KEENAN, Mr. Michael John, FCA *1972;* St Lawrence House, 16 High Street, Winslow, BUCKINGHAM, MK18 3HF.
KEENAN, Mr. Peter Charles, LLB ACA *1994;* Saffrons, Rucklers Lane, KINGS LANGLEY, HERTFORDSHIRE, WD4 9NQ.
•**KEENAN, Mrs. Rachel Jane, BEng ACA** *2001;* Rachel Keenan & Co Ltd, 16 Thornfield Hey, Spital, WIRRAL, MERSEYSIDE, CH63 9JT.
KEENAN, Mr. Scott, ACA *1994;* 6 Falkner Street, LIVERPOOL, L8 7PZ.
KEENAN, Mr. Sean Patrick, BSc ACA *1995;* 21 The Paddock, Oswaldtwistle, ACCRINGTON, BB5 3AB.
KEENAN, Dr. William Laurence, ACA *1984;* 78 Russia Lane, LONDON, E2 9LU.
KEENE, Mr. Adrian Charles, MA MSc FCA *1977;* (Member of Council 2000 - 2009), (Tax Fac), Mutual Clothing & Supply Co Ltd, 39 Bedford Street South, LEICESTER, LE1 3JN.
•**KEENE, Mr. Charles John, FCA** *1977;* Continuum Limited, Gild House, 66 Norwich Avenue West, BOURNEMOUTH, BH2 6AW.
KEENE, Mr. Colin Bernard William, FCA *1967;* 43 St. James Avenue, SUTTON, SURREY, SM1 2TQ.
KEENE, Mr. David William, FCA *1973;* Union Bank UK Plc, P O Box 148, 14-18 Copthall Avenue, LONDON, EC2R 7BN.
KEENE, Mr. Kevin Robert, BSc ACA *1991;* Flat 8 Floor 12, Alley 18 Lane 397, Ming Shui Road, TAIPEI, 104, TAIWAN.
KEENE, Mr. Stephen Paul, BSc ACA *1990;* 45 Derby Road, Heaton Moor, STOCKPORT, SK4 4NF.
KEENEY, Mr. Philip, FCA *1974;* 865 Mendakota Court, MENDOTA HEIGHTS, MN 55120, UNITED STATES.
KEENOY, Mrs. Andrea Jane, BA ACA *2001;* 47 Guildersfield Road, LONDON, SW16 5LS.
KEENS, Mr. Christopher Paul, MSci ACA *2010;* 21 Mickleden Avenue, Fulwood, PRESTON, PR2 9TA.
KEENS, Mr. Peter Philip, JP FCA *1960;* 9 St Pauls Court, Stony Stratford, MILTON KEYNES, MK11 1LJ. (Life Member)
KEENS, Mr. Warren David, BSc ACA *1995;* P.O. Box 1034, GEORGETOWN, GRAND CAYMAN, KY1-1102, CAYMAN ISLANDS.
KEEP, Mr. Antony Frank William, FCA *1952;* 7 Franklin Avenue, Hartley Wintney, HOOK, HAMPSHIRE, RG27 8RB. (Life Member)
KEEP, Mr. Robert Michael Howard, ACA *2004;* Two Financial Center, 60 South Street, BOSTON, MA 02111, UNITED STATES.
KEEP, Mrs. Sheena Louise, BA ACA *1987;* Weldmar Hospicecare Trust, Hammick House, Bridport Road, Poundbury, DORCHESTER, DT1 3SD.
KEEP, Mr. Terence Stephen, BSc FCA *1993;* with Griffins, Griffins Court, 24-32 London Road, NEWBURY, RG14 1JX.
KEEP, Mr. Timothy Thomas, BSc ACA *1999;* with Ernst & Young LLP, City Gate West, Toll House Hill, NOTTINGHAM, NG1 5FY.
KEEPAX, Mr. Stephen John, BSc ACA PGCE *1999;* Gothic Cottage, Holywell Road, MALVERN, WORCESTERSHIRE, WR14 4LE.
KEEPING, Mr. Benjamin James, BA(Hons) ACA *2001;* Tempus, Chinnor Road, Bledlow Ridge, HIGH WYCOMBE, BUCKINGHAMSHIRE, HP14 4AE.
KEEPING, Mrs. Christine Denise, BSc FCA *1991;* Spinney Farm, Duns Tew, BICESTER, OXFORDSHIRE, OX25 6JT.
KEEPING, Mr. Jason Guy, BA ACA *1996;* 12 Anisa Close, Kings Hill, WEST MALLING, ME19 4EW.
KEEPING, Mr. Norman Albert Leslie, FCA *1952;* 74 Barnham Broom Road, Ketts Meadow, WYMONDHAM, NR18 0EB. (Life Member)
KEEPING, Mr. Roy George, FCA *1965;* 44 Cook Terrace, MONA VALE, NSW 2103, AUSTRALIA.
KEERS, Mrs. Nicola Anne, MA BSc ACA *2001;* GB Building Solution Ltd, Grosvenor House, 4-7 Station Road, SUNBURY-ON-THAMES, MIDDLESEX, TW16 6SB.
•**KEERS, Mr. Richard John, BSc ACA** *1989;* PricewaterhouseCoopers LLP, Hays Galleria, 1 Hays Lane, LONDON, SE1 2RD. See also PricewaterhouseCoopers
KEERS, Mr. Robert, BSc ACA *2002;* 33 Delta Road, WORCESTER PARK, KT4 7HP.
KEETCH, Mr. Eric Peter, BA FCA *1975;* 3 Chiswick Quay, Chiswick, LONDON, W4 3UR.
KEETCH, Mr. Wilfred, FCA *1952;* Flat 1, Arborfield, Landscore Road, TEIGNMOUTH, TQ14 9JJ. (Life Member)
KEETLEY, Mr. Paul, BSc FCA *1998;* 7300 Oakbury Lane, MCKINNEY, TX 75071, UNITED STATES.
KEETLEY, Mrs. Samantha Louise, BSc FCA *1999;* 7300 Oakbury Ln, MCKINNEY, TX 75071, UNITED STATES.
•**KEETON, Mr. James Peter, BA ACA** *1999;* with BDO LLP, Fourth Floor, One Victoria Street, BRISTOL, BS1 6AA.
KEEVIL, Mr. David John, FCA *1965;* Villa Lascombes, La Rue Du Hocq, St. Clement, JERSEY, JE2 6LF.
•**KEEVIL, Mr. Michael Frederick, FCA** *1975;* Michael F Keevil, Park House, 10 Osborne Road, POTTERS BAR, EN6 1RZ.
•**KEFFLER, Mr. David Paul, BA FCA FCCA MIPPM** *1987;* David Keffler & Co, 30 Greenway Lane, Charlton Kings, CHELTENHAM, GLOUCESTERSHIRE, GL52 6LB. See also David Keffler
KEFFLER, Mr. Paul John Leon George, FCA *1959;* 11 Ambleside Road, Allerton, LIVERPOOL, L18 9US. (Life Member)
KEFFORD, Mr. Adam Nigel, ACA *2009;* 89 Round Table Meet, EXETER, EX4 8LG.
KEFFORD, Miss. Jennifer May, BA ACA *1995;* (Tax Fac), 17 Glenfield Drive, Great Doddington, WELLINGBOROUGH, NN29 7TE.

KEHOE, Mr. Aidan Paul, BSc ACA DipHSM *1993;* 5 Allandale, BLACKPOOL, FY4 1RH.
•**KEHOE, Mrs. Barbara Ruth, BSc ACA** *1992;* The Workhouse, Allstone Cottage, Cold Bath Road, Caerleon, NEWPORT, GWENT NP18 1NF.
•**KEHOE, Mrs. Caron Marie, BA ACA** *1993;* Caron M Kehoe, 53 Brabourne Rise, Park Langley, BECKENHAM, KENT, BR3 6SD. See also Lamond Caron M
KEHOE, Mr. Christopher Michael, BA FCA AMCT *1988;* 11 Shelwick Grove, Dorridge, SOLIHULL, B93 8UH.
KEHOE, Mrs. Kate Melanie, BSc ACA *2001;* 9 Corner Farm Close, TADWORTH, KT20 5SJ.
KEHOE, Mr. Michael Geoffrey, BA ACA *1987;* The Old Parsonage, Church Street, Rudgwick, HORSHAM, RH12 3EB.
KEHOE, Mr. Rowan Alexander, ACA *2011;* 364a Finchley Road, LONDON, NW3 7AJ.
KEHOE, Mrs. Stella Muriel, FCA *1968;* 111 Park Lane, Whitefield, MANCHESTER, M45 7GT. (Life Member)
KEIG, Miss. Jeanette, BA(Hons) ACA *2003;* 48 Ridgetor Road, Woolton Village, LIVERPOOL, L25 6DQ.
KEIGHER, Mr. Stewart James, BSc FCA *1978;* Courtenay House, Courtenay Road, WINCHESTER, SO23 7ER.
KEIGHLEY, Mr. John, FCA *1965;* Drinkers End Farm, Corse Lawn, GLOUCESTER, GL19 4NE. (Life Member)
KEIGHLEY, Mr. John Archibald, FCA *1966;* Ambrose Hill, Higher Clatcombe, SHERBORNE, DORSET, DT9 4RN. (Life Member)
KEIGHLEY, Mr. John Wilson, BCom ACA *1990;* HSBC, 12 Calthorpe Road, Edgbaston, BIRMINGHAM, B15 1QZ.
KEIGHLEY, Miss. Philippa Theresa, ACA *2007;* Mill Hill Cottage The Slade, Fenny Compton, SOUTHAM, CV47 2YB.
KEIGHLEY, Mrs. Ruth Helen, BCom ACA *1988;* Farcroft, 3 Woodland Avenue, Hagley, STOURBRIDGE, DY8 2XQ.
KEIGHT, Mr. Gavin Wynne, ACA *2008;* 14a Whirlow Grove, SHEFFIELD, S11 9NR.
KEIGHTLEY, Miss. Janet Rosalyn, BSc FCA *1975;* Orchard Cottage Jockey End, Gaddesden Row, HEMEL HEMPSTEAD, HERTFORDSHIRE, HP2 6HR.
KEILLER, Mr. Dudley George, BEng ACA *1998;* woestduinstraat 50-2, 1058TG AMSTERDAM, NETHERLANDS.
KEILTHY, Mr. Dermot John, BSc ACA *1982;* 40 Floor PCCW Tower, Taikoo Place, QUARRY BAY, HONG KONG SAR.
KEILTHY, Mrs. Victoria Charlotte LeHuray, MA ACA *2000;* National Audit Office, 157-197 Buckingham Palace Road, LONDON, SW1W 9SP.
KEIR, Mr. Thomas Joseph David, MSc BA FCA ASIP *1997;* 13 Rotherwood Road, LONDON, SW15 1LA.
KEISNER, Mr. Michael Anthony, ACA *1979;* 2 Shiremead, Elstree, BOREHAMWOOD, HERTFORDSHIRE, WD6 3JZ.
•**KEITES, Mr. Andrew James, FCA** *1991;* Thomas Edge House Tunnell Street, St. Helier, JERSEY, JE2 4LU.
KEITH, Mr. James Angus, FCA *1965;* The Willows, Sidney Road, Theydon Bois, EPPING, ESSEX, CM16 7DT.
KEITH, Miss. Joanna, BSc(Hons) ACA *2006;* Apartment 14, 29 Laycock Street, LONDON, N1 1UR.
KEITH, Mrs. Lisa Mary Elizabeth, ACA *2008;* 3 Hampton Court, HOCKLEY, SS5 4XE.
KEITH, Mrs. Lizanne Jayne, BA ACA *1998;* (Tax Fac), 68 Russell Road, Toddington, DUNSTABLE, LU5 6QF.
KEITH, Mr. Richard Anthony, BA(Hons) FCA *2000;* (Tax Fac), 3 Hampton Court, HOCKLEY, ESSEX, SS5 4XE.
KEITH, Mr. Roger Graham, BSc ACA *1980;* Rowan House, 48 Banbury Road, BRACKLEY, NN13 6AT.
KEIZER, Mr. Melvin John, FCA *1980;* M.J. Keizer, 2113 Castle View Road, MANSFIELD, TX 76063, UNITED STATES.
KEJRIWAL, Mr. Ajay Kumar, BSc ACA *1995;* 70 Dalkeith Grove, STANMORE, HA7 4SF.
KEJRIWAL, Mr. Ashutosh, BSc ACA *1990;* 10 Alwyn Close, Elstree, BOREHAMWOOD, HERTFORDSHIRE, WD6 3LF.
KEJRIWAL, Mrs. Sangita, BSc ACA *1995;* 70 Dalkeith Grove, STANMORE, HA7 4SF.
KEKI, Miss. Aimie Rebecca, BA ACA *2005;* 80 Rushton Road, Rothwell, KETTERING, NORTHAMPTONSHIRE, NN14 6HQ.
•**KEKOVSKA, Ms. Ana, ACA CA(AUS)** *2011;* Montais House, 9 Tudor Close, Les Quennevais Drive, St. Brelade, JERSEY, JE3 8GX.
KEKULAWALA, Mr. Joseph Dacius Nihal, FCA *1983;* 4 Castle Street, 8 COLOMBO, SRI LANKA.
KELCEY, Mrs. Elaine Meriel, ACA *1996;* 3 The Paddock, Claverley, WOLVERHAMPTON, WV5 7DW.
KELEY, Mr. Richard Brian, BCom ACA *2003;* with Deloitte Touche Tohmatsu, 505 Bourke Street, (P.O.Box 78B), MELBOURNE, VIC 3001, AUSTRALIA.
KELEY, Mr. Steven Mark, ACA *2008;* 65b Barnard Mews, LONDON, SW11 1QU.
KELHAM, Mr. David William, BA FCA *1982;* Chastilian, Gough Road, FLEET, GU51 4LJ.
KELJIK, Mr. Christopher Avedis, OBE BA FCA *1973;* 62a Flood Street, LONDON, SW3 5TE.
KELK, Mr. Graham Howard, FCA *1962;* 8 Dalebrook Court, Belgrave Road, Ranmoor, SHEFFIELD, S10 3JJ.
KELK, Mr. Terence Michael, BA FCA *1984;* Pinsent Masons, 3 Colmore Circus, BIRMINGHAM, B4 6BH.
•**KELK, Mrs. Tracey Amanda, BSc FCA** *1993;* Lucentum Limited, Kensal House, 77 Springfield Road, CHELMSFORD, CM2 6JG.
KELL, Mr. Arthur Edward James, FCA *1950;* 49 Hillcrest Avenue, Nether Poppleton, YORK, YO26 6LD. (Life Member)
KELL, Mr. Christopher Raymond, MA FCA CTA *1984;* 6 Gorse Close, DROITWICH, WR9 7SG.
KELL, Mr. Douglas William, FCA *1957;* 8 Henry Ralph Avenue, Beaumont Park, HUDDERSFIELD, HD4 7AJ. (Life Member)
KELL, Mr. Ronald Wilson, FCA *1953;* Hillcrest, St Chloe Mead, Amberley, STROUD, GL5 5AR. (Life Member)
•**KELL, Mr. Steven Paul, ACA** *2005;* SP Kell, Clwyd House, 3c Clwyd Street, RUTHIN, CLWYD, LL15 1HF.
KELL, Mrs. Susan Mary, BA ACA *1986;* Willow House, Hill Green, Clavering, SAFFRON WALDEN, CB11 4QS.
KELLAGHER, Mr. James Nicholas Bannerman, MA ACA *1983;* Rest Harrow Green Lane, Exton, EXETER, EX3 0PW.
KELLAGHER, Mrs. Sarah Louise, BSc ACA DChA *1985;* Rest Harrow, Green Lane, Exton, EXETER, EX3 0PW.
KELLALI, Mr. Samir, BSc ACA *2009;* 33 Tudor Avenue, Chadderton, OLDHAM, OL9 9PG.
KELLAND, Dr. David, BSc ARCS ACA *1992;* 16 Esher Place Avenue, ESHER, SURREY, KT10 8PY.
•**KELLAND, Mr. David Hugh, FCA** *1987;* Meadows & Co, 1 Kings Court, Kettering Parkway, KETTERING, NORTHAMPTONSHIRE, NN15 6WJ.
•**KELLAND, Mr. Ian Michael, FCA** *1978;* (Tax Fac), Lentells Limited, 17-18, Leach Road, Chard Business Park, CHARD, SOMERSET TA20 1FA.
KELLAND, Mr. John Frederick, FCA *1957;* The Moorings, Bronshill Road, TORQUAY, TQ1 3HA. (Life Member)
KELLAND, Mr. Percy Harold, BA FCA *1984;* 36 Wellington Walk, Henleaze, BRISTOL, BS10 5ET.
KELLAS, Miss. Beatrice Louise, BSc ACA *1982;* 168 Elizabeth Avenue, Little Chalfont, AMERSHAM, HP6 6RS.
KELLAS, Mr. John Farquhar, BSc ACA *1982;* Office for Public Management, 252b Gray's Inn Road, LONDON, WC1X 8XG.
KELLAS, Mr. John Henry, CBE MA FCA *1975;* 4 Croham Park Avenue, SOUTH CROYDON, SURREY, CR2 7HH.
KELLAWAY, Mr. Paul James David, ACA *2008;* Flat 6, Seville House 11 & A Half, Wapping High Street, LONDON, E1W 1NX.
KELLAWAY, Mr. Simon Daniel, BA(Hons) ACA *2001;* 47 Delph Drive, Burscough, ORMSKIRK, L40 5BD.
•**KELLEDY, Mrs. Deborah Ann, ACA** *1994;* (Tax Fac), Kelledy & Co, 4 Cecil Way, Hayes, BROMLEY, BR2 7JU.
•**KELLEHER, Ms. Julie Diane, BSc ACA** *2002;* Matthew Craig Associates Limited, 10 Riversdale, Llandaff, CARDIFF, CF5 2QL.
KELLEHER, Mr. Thomas Colm, MA FCA *1984;* Morgan Stanley, 20 Bank Street, LONDON, E14 4AD.
KELLEN, Mr. Sebastien, ACA *2011;* 1 Place du Lieutenant Callemeyn-Boite 45, 6700 ARLON, BELGIUM.
KELLER, Mrs. Emily Harriet, BA ACA *1999;* Competition Commission, Victoria House, Southampton Row, LONDON, WC1B 4AD.
KELLER, Ms. Ilana Deborah, BCom ACA *2000;* 29 Clare Close, Elstree, BOREHAMWOOD, WD6 3NJ.
KELLER, Mr. John David, BA ACA *2006;* 9 Mornington Road, WOODFORD GREEN, IG8 0TS.
KELLER, Mr. Jonathan Lewis, FCA *1975;* 24 Rehov Grinberg, RA'ANANA, ISRAEL.
•**KELLER, Mr. Kenneth Calman, FCA** *1970;* N & P Accounting Solutions Limited, Lynwood House, 373-375 Station Road, HARROW, MIDDLESEX, HA1 2AW.
KELLER, Mr. Philip Henry, BA ACA *1991;* I C G Plc, Juxon House, 100 St. Paul's Churchyard, LONDON, EC4M 8BU.
KELLER, Miss. Rachel Clare, MA ACA *1992;* 98 Star Street, LONDON, W2 1QF.
KELLER, Mr. Richard Henry, FCA *1958;* A Keller & Sons (Holdings) Ltd, Trianon House, 181 The Broadway, West Hendon, LONDON, NW9 7DD.
•**KELLER, Mr. Robert Franz, ACA** *1984;* Keller Accountancy Services Limited, 367b Church Road, Frampton Cotterell, BRISTOL, BS36 2AQ.
KELLETT, Mr. Andrew, BSc ACA *1992;* 32 Grove Road, WINDSOR, SL4 1JQ.
KELLETT, Mrs. Angela Marie, BSc ACA *2000;* 2 Lower Dunsley Cottage, London Road, TRING, HERTFORDSHIRE, HP23 5ND.
KELLETT, Mr. Christopher John, BSc ACA *2006;* Flat 45 Velocity West, 5 City Walk, LEEDS, WEST YORKSHIRE, LS119BG.
KELLETT, Mrs. Helen Marie, BSc ACA FCSI *1996;* Steetley Dolomite Ltd, Whitwell Works, Whitwell, WORKSOP, NOTTINGHAMSHIRE, S80 3LJ.
KELLETT, Mr. Howard Lyndon, BA ACA *1993;* MTL Group Limited, Grange Lane, Brinsworth, ROTHERHAM, SOUTH YORKSHIRE, S60 5AE.
KELLETT, Mr. Ian Michael, BA ACA *1988;* 3 Sandlebridge Farm, Mill Lane, ALDERLEY EDGE, CHESHIRE, SK9 7TD.
KELLETT, Mrs. Jane Charlotte, BA ACA *1991;* B G Group Plc, 100 Thames Valley Park Drive, READING, RG6 1PT.
KELLETT, Mr. John Neville, BSc ACA *1988;* 41 Lower Hill Road, EPSOM, KT19 8LS.
KELLETT, Miss. Laura Megan, BSc ACA *2009;* 10 Redwood, Burnham, SLOUGH, SL1 8JN.
KELLETT, Miss. Lauren Elizabeth, BSc(Hons) ACA *2009;* Flat 7 Russell Quay, West Street, GRAVESEND, DA11 0BP.
KELLETT, Mrs. Margaret Anne, BA ACA *1984;* 5 Woodham Gate, Woodham Village, NEWTON AYCLIFFE, DL5 4UB.
KELLETT, Mr. Neil, FCA *1967;* 1 Dryden Avenue, CHEADLE, SK8 2AW.
KELLETT, Mr. Neil Christopher, BA(Hons) ACA *2001;* Flat 20 Andrew Reed Court, Keele Close, WATFORD, WD24 4RU.
KELLETT, Mr. Peter Henry, FCA *1965;* The Laurels Nursery, Benenden, CRANBROOK, TN17 4JU.
KELLETT, Mrs. Rachel, BA ACA *1991;* Edge Foundation, 4 Millbank, LONDON, SW1P 3JA.
•**KELLEWAY, Mr. Noel Christopher, FCA** *1976;* (Tax Fac), Rickard Keen LLP, Glenny House, Fenton Way, Southfields Business Park, BASILDON, ESSEX SS15 6TD. See also MGI Rickard Keen LLP
KELLEWAY, Miss. Rachel Elizabeth, BA ACA *2010;* 22 Theobalds Road, LEIGH-ON-SEA, ESSEX, SS9 2NE.
KELLEY, Mr. Anthony Leonard, BSc ACA ATII *1988;* (Tax Fac), National Grid, National Grid House, Warwick Technology Park, WARWICK, CV34 6DA.
•**KELLEY, Mrs. Beverley Eileen, ACA** *1995;* Kelley & Lowe Limited, Gwynfa House, 677 Princes Road, DARTFORD, KENT, DA2 6EF.
KELLEY, Mr. Paul, BA ACA *2006;* 21 Bryanston Street, LONDON, W1H 7PR.
KELLEY, Mr. Richard Scott, BSc ACA *1995;* Beazley Group Plc, Plantantion Place South, 60 Great Tower Street, LONDON, EC3R 5AD.
KELLEY, Mr. Steven John, ACIB ACA *2000;* 36 Warboys Crescent, Highams Park, LONDON, E4 9HR.
•**KELLIE-SMITH, Mr. David Anthony, FCA** *1964;* (Tax Fac), David Kellie-Smith, 50 Peterborough Road, LONDON, SW6 3EB.
•**KELLIHER, Mrs. Tracy Ann, ACA** *1993;* Lindley Adams Limited, 28 Prescott Street, HALIFAX, WEST YORKSHIRE, HX1 2LG.
KELLITT, Mr. Ian David, FCA *1974;* 61 Rue de la Fausse Acre, 27470 FONTAINE L'ABBE, FRANCE.
KELLMAN, Mrs. Debra Elizabeth, BSc ACA *1996;* 28 Badgers Bank, Lychpit, BASINGSTOKE, HAMPSHIRE, RG24 8RT.
•**KELLNER, Mr. Stuart David, BEng FCA** *1993;* Dufton Kellner Limited, Barnston House, Beacon Lane, Heswall, WIRRAL, CH60 0EE.
KELLOND, Mr. Peter Michael, FCA *1975;* Half Moon Bay Limited, Box 80, MONTEGO BAY, JAMAICA.
KELLOW, Miss. Michelle Kathryn, BA(Hons) ACA *2002;* Cornwall County Council, Room 404, New County Hall, TRURO, CORNWALL, TR7 3AY.
KELLY, Mr. Aidan, ACA *2010;* 3 Landells Road, LONDON, SE22 9PG.
KELLY, Mr. Alan, BSc FCA *1973;* 4601 Piper Glen Drive, CHARLOTTE, NC 28277, UNITED STATES.
KELLY, Mr. Alan Spencer, FCA *1974;* Peart Hall Church Road, Spaxton, BRIDGWATER, SOMERSET, TA5 1DA. (Life Member)
KELLY, Mr. Alexander John, BA ACA *2006;* with Crowe Clark Whitehill LLP, Aquis House, 49-51 Blagrave Street, READING, RG1 1PL.
KELLY, Mrs. Amy Kate, BSc ACA *1999;* 4 Southview Road, HARPENDEN, HERTFORDSHIRE, AL5 5AP.
KELLY, Mr. Andrew John, MA ACA *2003;* Anglo American Plc, Anglo American House, 20 Carlton House Terrace, LONDON, SW1Y 5AN.
•**KELLY, Mr. Andrew John, MA FCA** *1990;* Deloitte LLP, 2 New Street Square, LONDON, EC4A 3BZ. See also Deloitte & Touche LLP
KELLY, Miss. Anne Marie, BSc ACA *1991;* 22 Eglamour Way, Heathcote, WARWICK, CV34 6GE.
•**KELLY, Mr. Anthony, BSc FCA** *1985;* Roffe Swayne, Ashcombe Court, Woolsack Way, GODALMING, GU7 1LQ.
KELLY, Mrs. Beverley Ann, BA ACA *2007;* 3 Ingleborough Close, Mayfield, WASHINGTON, NE37 1RZ.
KELLY, Mr. Brian Dominic Arthur, BSc ACA *1990;* 35 Spencer Road, LONDON, W4 3SS.
KELLY, Mr. Brian Frederick, FCA *1958;* 3 Kendal Close, Wray Common, REIGATE, RH2 0LR. (Life Member)
KELLY, Mr. Brian Gabriel, MSc BA ACA MCT *1994;* B A A Airports Ltd The Compass Centre, Nelson Road London Heathrow Airport, HOUNSLOW, TW6 2GW.
KELLY, Mrs. Carla Jane, BSc ACA *2004;* 47 Appledore Drive, COVENTRY, CV5 7PQ.
KELLY, Mrs. Catherine Victoria, ACA *2008;* Cooper Parry Llp, 14 Park Row, NOTTINGHAM, NG1 6GR.
KELLY, Mr. Charles, MEng ACA *1999;* 128 Mayfield Road, EDINBURGH, EH9 3AH.
KELLY, Mr. Christopher Anthony, BEng ACA *2002;* 5 Beauclere House, South Bank, SURBITON, SURREY, KT6 6DN.
KELLY, Mr. Christopher Charles Cannan, BSc(Econ) FCA *1984;* Royal Bank of Scotland, 1 Princes Street, LONDON, EC2R 8BP.
KELLY, Mr. Christopher Hugh, BSc ACA *1994;* Home Farm, High Street, Hinton Charterhouse, BATH, BA2 7SW.
•**KELLY, Mr. Christopher John, BA ACA** *1987;* 6 Fulton Place, LEEDS, LS16 5RS.
•**KELLY, Mr. Christopher Patrick, FCA** *1990;* Whiting & Partners, Garland House, Garland Street, BURY ST. EDMUNDS, SUFFOLK, IP33 1EZ.
KELLY, Mr. Christopher Rayner, BSc ACA *1987;* Pioneer, Tokyo Electron Europe Ltd Crawley Business Quarter, Fleming Way, CRAWLEY, WEST SUSSEX, RH10 9QL.
KELLY, Mrs. Claire Emma, BA ACA *2003;* Bella Vista, Longfield Avenue, La Route Des Genets, St. Brelade, JERSEY, JE3 8EB.
KELLY, Miss. Clare Elizabeth, ACA *2009;* Slieau Chairn Blackberry Lane, Onchan, ISLE OF MAN, IM3 1NR.
KELLY, Mrs. Colette, BA ACA *2002;* 15 Upper Meadow, Hedgerley Lane, GERRARDS CROSS, BUCKINGHAMSHIRE, SL9 7EY.
KELLY, Mr. Daniel, BSc ACA *2010;* Mondrian Investment Partners Ltd, 10 Gresham Street, LONDON, EC2V 7JD.
KELLY, Mr. David, FCA *1976;* 16 Pentland Court, GLEN WAVERLEY, VIC 3150, AUSTRALIA.
KELLY, Mr. David, FCA *1967;* 56 Joyce Close, CRANBROOK, KENT, TN17 3LZ.
KELLY, Mr. David Anthony, BA FCA *1974;* Alipore, Alipore Close, Lower Parkstone, POOLE, BH14 9NS.
•**KELLY, Mr. David James, ACA** *1993;* Kelly Accounting Limited, 42 Comrie Street, CRIEFF, PERTHSHIRE, PH7 4AX.
KELLY, Mr. David Jonathan, BSc ACA *2005;* with KPMG LLP, 15 Canada Square, LONDON, E14 5GL.
KELLY, Mr. David Raymond, BA(Hons) FCA *2001;* Liberty Syndicate Management Ltd, 60 Great Tower Street, LONDON, EC3R 5AZ.
KELLY, Mr. David Rodney Stuart, FCA *1964;* 2742 Harbormaster Drive SE, SOUTHPORT, NC 28461-8000, UNITED STATES. (Life Member)
KELLY, Mrs. Denise Marie, BSc ACA *1993;* 6 Fulton Place, Headingley, LEEDS, LS16 8RS.
KELLY, Mr. Derek Alan, BSc ACA *2006;* Apt 6 House 8, Linden Square, Grove Avenue, BLACKROCK, COUNTY DUBLIN, IRELAND.
KELLY, Mr. Derek Kevin, FCA *1969;* 7 Longstaff Court, Bankfoot, HEBDEN BRIDGE, WEST YORKSHIRE, HX7 6AB. (Life Member)
KELLY, Mrs. Donna Elizabeth, BSc ACA *1990;* 49 Meadow Road, DAGENHAM, RM9 5PR.
KELLY, Mr. Eamonn Martin, BCom ACA *1991;* 1131 Steeles Avenue West, TORONTO M2R 3W8, ON, CANADA.
KELLY, Miss. Eleanor Jane, BA ACA *2003;* 10420 Highland Manor Drive, TAMPA, FL 33610, UNITED STATES.
KELLY, Mrs. Emma, ACA *2008;* 50 Wandle Road, LONDON, SW17 7DW.
•**KELLY, Mrs. Fiona Alison, FCA** *1987;* F Kelly & Co, 43 Carpenters Wood Drive, Chorleywood, RICKMANSWORTH, HERTFORDSHIRE, WD3 5RN.

KELLY, Mrs. Fiona Jemima, BA ACA *1984;* 40 Mavelstone Road, BROMLEY, BR1 2PB.
KELLY, Mr. Francis Alan, BSc ACA *1993;* 102 Wentworth Crescent, Hatch Warren, BASINGSTOKE, HAMPSHIRE, RG22 4WX.
KELLY, Mr. Gary Peter Hearn, BSc(Hons) ACA *2000;* 13 Honeyeater Close, BUDERIM, QLD 4556, AUSTRALIA.
KELLY, Mr. Geoffrey Burdon, FCA *1975;* 26 Kilham Lane, WINCHESTER, SO22 5PT.
KELLY, Mr. George Bryan, FCA *1959;* 502 Lia Way, EASLEY, SC 29642, UNITED STATES. (Life Member)
KELLY, Mr. Gerard, BA ACA *1997;* 5th Floor, Union House Union Street, JERSEY, JE2 3RF.
KELLY, Mr. Gerard Martin, BSc FCA FFB *1986;* 3 Famet Walk, PURLEY, CR8 2DY.
KELLY, Mr. Gerard Patrick, BA ACA *1981;* 3 Beechcroft Avenue, KENLEY, CR8 5JZ.
KELLY, Miss. Gillian Elizabeth, ACA *2008;* 75 Byrne Road, Balham, LONDON, SW12 9HZ.
KELLY, Mrs. Giuseppina, BA ACA *2006;* 9 Treasury Court, Cross Street, WINCHESTER, HAMPSHIRE, SO23 8EJ.
KELLY, Mr. Graham, BA ACA *2007;* Flat 3, 112 Mill Lane, LONDON, NW6 1NF.
KELLY, Mr. Henry Cannell, MA ACA *1979;* KellyConsult Sarl, 4 rue Jean-Pierre Lanter, Itzig, L-5943 LUXEMBOURG, LUXEMBOURG.
KELLY, Mr. Hugh Morris, BA ACA *1988;* Canberra, Cranston Road, EAST GRINSTEAD, WEST SUSSEX, RH19 3HQ.
KELLY, Mr. Ian Philip, BSc ACA *2000;* Flat 6, 20 South Park Road, Wimbledon, LONDON, SW19 8SX.
KELLY, Mr. James, BA ACA *1987;* 40 Mavelstone Rd, BROMLEY, BR1 2PB.
•**KELLY, Mr. James Cameron, FCA** *1985;* Science Ltd, 13-14 Welbeck Street, LONDON, W1G 9XU.
KELLY, Mr. James Edward Trutch, BA(Hons) ACA *2004;* 50 Wandle Road, LONDON, SW17 7DW.
KELLY, Mr. James Tod, MA(Econ) ACA *2006;* 1 Tower Hill, HORSHAM, WEST SUSSEX, RH13 0AE.
KELLY, Mr. James Vincent, MA(Cantab) ACA *2010;* Flat 3, 76-78 Gloucester Avenue, LONDON, NW1 8JD.
KELLY, Mr. James William, BEng ACA *2006;* Glendinning Management Consultants Glendinning House, 1 Station Road, ADDLESTONE, KT15 2AG.
KELLY, Mr. Jamie Stephen, BSc ACA *2008;* Flat 6, 37 Burton Road, MANCHESTER, M20 3GB.
KELLY, Mrs. Jane Elizabeth, BSc ACA *2000;* Amber House Church Street, Ashover, CHESTERFIELD, DERBYSHIRE, S45 0AB.
KELLY, Mrs. Jane Elizabeth, BSc(Hons) FCA *2001;* 4 Woodland Way, Petts Wood, ORPINGTON, KENT, BR5 1ND.
•**KELLY, Mrs. Jane Rosemary, FCA** *1988;* (Tax Fac), Sully & Co, 75 South Street, SOUTH MOLTON, DEVON, EX36 4AG.
KELLY, Mrs. Janice, BA ACA CTA *1987;* 62 Duthie's Track, PO Box 84, WOOMELANG, VIC 3485, AUSTRALIA.
KELLY, Mrs. Jayne Elizabeth, BA ACA *1995;* Higher Holcombe House, Higher Holcombe Road, TEIGNMOUTH, DEVON, TQ14 9NP.
KELLY, Miss. Jayne Frances, BSc ACA *1994;* 11 Floris Place, Clapham, LONDON, SW4 0HH.
•**KELLY, Mr. Jeffrey Neil, ACA** *1987;* (Tax Fac), Coveney Nicholls Limited, The Old Wheel House, 31/37 Church Street, REIGATE, RH2 0AD. See also Coveney Nicholls
•**KELLY, Mrs. Jillian Diane, BSc FCA** *1994;* Ernst & Young LLC, Rose House, 51-59 Circular Road, Douglas, ISLE OF MAN, IM1 1AZ. See also Ernst & Young Europe LLP
KELLY, Mr. John, MA MEng ACA *2010;* Honeysuckle House, 2a Green Lane, COBHAM, SURREY, KT11 2NN.
KELLY, Mr. John Antony Brian, RD LLB FCA *1967;* Cherry Trees, 49 Penn Road, BEACONSFIELD, HP9 2LW.
KELLY, Mr. John Brian, BSc ACA *1991;* 41 High Street, Port St. Mary, ISLE OF MAN, IM9 5DN.
KELLY, Mr. John Dennis, FCA *1963;* 21 Broadwaters Road, LOWESTOFT, NR33 9HU.
KELLY, Mr. John Edward, BA ACA *1990;* 61 Windmill Lane, ASHBOURNE, DERBYSHIRE, DE6 1EY.
•**KELLY, Mr. John Howard, BA ACA** *1989;* KPMG LLP, 15 Canada Square, LONDON, E14 5GL. See also KPMG Europe LLP
KELLY, Mr. John Joseph Wolff, BA ACA *2004;* Lombard Corporate Finance, 5th Floor, 1 Spinningfields Square, MANCHESTER, M3 3AP.
KELLY, Mr. John Patrick Anthony, BA FCA FPC *1984;* Hangar 4, Fast Helicopters Ltd, Shoreham Airport, SHOREHAM-BY-SEA, WEST SUSSEX, BN43 5FF.
KELLY, Mr. John Peter, BSc ACA CFA *1992;* 3139 Shillington Place, CHARLOTTE, NC 28210, UNITED STATES.
KELLY, Mr. John Peter, FCA *1982;* J Marr Property Ltd 18 Langthwaite Road, Langthwaite Grange Ind Estate South Kirkby, PONTEFRACT, WEST YORKSHIRE, WF9 3AP.
KELLY, Mr. John Terence, FCA *1962;* 2 Turnberry Place, Alwoodley, LEEDS, LS17 7TH.
KELLY, Mr. Jonathan Paul, BSc FCA *1975;* British Institute of Learning Disabilities Campion House, Green Street, KIDDERMINSTER, WORCESTERSHIRE, DY10 1JL.
KELLY, Mr. Joseph Patrick, BA ACA *1990;* Field End House, Holly Bush Lane, Bendish, HITCHIN, HERTFORDSHIRE, SG4 8JB.
KELLY, Mr. Julian Robert, MA ACA *1999;* ASPone Ltd, Sutherland House 3 Lloyds Avenue, LONDON, EC3N 3DS.
KELLY, Miss. Julie Ann, ACA *2008;* 27A Rata Street, HAMILTON 3200, NEW ZEALAND.
KELLY, Miss. Julie Dawn, BA ACA *1985;* (Tax Fac), P.O. Box 844, St Helier, JERSEY, JE4 0UU.
KELLY, Mrs. Katherine Sian, MA ACA *1999;* 3/47 Anstey Street, SOUTH PERTH, WA 6151, AUSTRALIA.
KELLY, Mrs. Kathleen Frances, BSc FCA *1980;* 16 Rockwood Drive, SKIPTON, NORTH YORKSHIRE, BD23 1NF.
KELLY, Miss. Laura Marie, ACA *2011;* Flat 5, 6 River Terrace, HENLEY-ON-THAMES, OXFORDSHIRE, RG9 1BG.
•**KELLY, Mr. Lee Martin, MA ACA CTA** *1993;* (Tax Fac), McEllin Kelly, Abacus House, 35 Cumberland Street, MACCLESFIELD, CHESHIRE, SK10 1DD.
KELLY, Mr. Leonard Robert, FCA *1960;* 62 Leas Road, WARLINGHAM, SURREY, CR6 9LL. (Life Member)
KELLY, Mr. Liam John, BSc ACA *1992;* 1150 West Bradley Ave., EL CAJON, CA 92020, UNITED STATES.
KELLY, Mrs. Lynn Catherine, BSc ACA *1995;* The Old Barn Church Lane, Seaton, OAKHAM, LE15 9HR.
KELLY, Mr. Mark Peter, BA ACA MCT *1985;* 20 Duchy Road, HARROGATE, NORTH YORKSHIRE, HG1 2ER.
•**KELLY, Mr. Mark Russell, BA FCA** *1997;* KPMG LLC, Heritage Court, 41 Athol Street, Douglas, ISLE OF MAN, IM99 1HN. See also KPMG Audit LLC
KELLY, Mr. Martin Thomas, BA ACA *1999;* Hambleton House, Minskip, YORK, NORTH YORKSHIRE, YO51 9HZ.
•**KELLY, Mr. Martyn Paul, BA FCA** *1979;* Triquetra Limited, 3 Meadow Close, SEVENOAKS, TN13 3HZ.
•**KELLY, Ms. Mary Ellen, BA FCA ATII** *1996;* (Tax Fac), HearnKelly Consulting, 67 Ebery Grove, PORTSMOUTH, HAMPSHIRE, PO3 6HG.
KELLY, Mr. Matthew John Scott, BSc ACA *1995;* 281 Hamersley Road, SUBIACO, WA 6008, AUSTRALIA.
KELLY, Mr. Matthew Robert, BA(Hons) FCA *2001;* 4 Woodland Way, Petts Wood, ORPINGTON, KENT, BR5 1ND.
•**KELLY, Mr. Michael, BA ACA** *1989;* Northern Alliance Limited, 47 White Rose Lane, WOKING, GU22 7CB.
KELLY, Mr. Michael David, BSc FCA *1996;* Holly Lodge, 21a Farmhill Park, Douglas, ISLE OF MAN, IM2 2EE.
KELLY, Mr. Michael Finbarr, FCA *1975;* Dunmore House, Flat 7 Dunmore House, 1 Dunmore Road, LONDON, SW20 8TN.
KELLY, Mr. Michael James, BSc ACA *1998;* White House, Kingston, RINGWOOD, HAMPSHIRE, BH24 3BQ.
KELLY, Mr. Michael Joseph, FCA *1983;* Birmingham International Airport Ltd Diamond House, Birmingham International Airport, BIRMINGHAM, B26 3QJ.
KELLY, Mr. Michael Robert, FCA *1973;* White Lodge Ballamodha Straight, Ballamodha Ballasalla, ISLE OF MAN, IM9 3AZ.
KELLY, Mrs. Mitali, BSc ACA *2001;* 16 East Park Farm Drive, Charvil, READING, RG10 9UJ.
KELLY, Miss. Monica Patricia, ACA *2009;* 51 Sutton Road, Erdington, BIRMINGHAM, B23 6QJ.
KELLY, Miss. Natalie-Jane Sarah, ACA *2009;* Flat 105 Bolonachi Building, Enid Street, LONDON, SE16 3EX.
KELLY, Mr. Neil David, BA(Hons) ACA *2002;* with Mazars LLP, Tower Building, 22 Water Street, LIVERPOOL, L3 1PQ.
KELLY, Mr. Neil James, BA(Hons) ACA *2006;* 24 Ballabrooie Way, Douglas, ISLE OF MAN, IM1 4EN.
KELLY, Mr. Neil Thomas, BA FCA *1981;* 1 Glastonbury Close, ORPINGTON, BR5 4LF.
KELLY, Mrs. Nicola Jayne, BSc ACA *1998;* 78 Sandgate Road, Hall Green, BIRMINGHAM, B28 0UL.
KELLY, Mr. Noel Anthony, BA ACA *1993;* 27 The Heath, LEIGHTON BUZZARD, BEDFORDSHIRE, LU7 3HL.
KELLY, Mr. Oliver Godefroi, FCA *1969;* 3206 Main Street, VANCOUVER V5V 3M5, BC, CANADA. (Life Member)
KELLY, Mr. Paul Anthony, ACA *2008;* (Tax Fac), 51 Byrne Avenue, BIRKENHEAD, MERSEYSIDE, CH42 4PG.
KELLY, Mr. Paul Brian John, BSc ACA *2005;* 35 Tanyfarteg, Ystradgynlais, SWANSEA, SA9 2JU.
KELLY, Mr. Paul Martin, BSc ACA *1992;* 12 West Drive, Gatley, CHEADLE, CHESHIRE, SK8 4JJ.
KELLY, Mr. Paul Raymond, FCA *1977;* Quarry Hill Farm, Church Lane, Bardsey, LEEDS, LS17 9DP.
•**KELLY, Mr. Peter, BSc FCA** *1978;* (Tax Fac), Kelly Williams, 135/137 Queen Street, Morley, LEEDS, LS27 8HE.
KELLY, Mr. Peter Mitchell, BA ACA *1981;* 26 Castle View Terrace, SKIPTON, NORTH YORKSHIRE, BD23 1NT.
KELLY, Miss. Philippa Jane, LLB(Hons) ACA *2011;* Elmlea, Green Lane, REIGATE, RH2 8JY.
KELLY, Mr. Phillip James, BA ACA *1998;* Northrop Grumman, 1840 Century Park East, LOS ANGELES, CA 90067-2199, UNITED STATES.
KELLY, Mr. Richard Charles, BA ACA *1993;* 26 Henleaze Gardens, Henleaze, BRISTOL, BS9 4HJ.
KELLY, Mr. Richard Darragh, BA ACA *1988;* Apt 35, Hanover Riverside (Block K), Sir John Rogerson Quay, DUBLIN 2, COUNTY DUBLIN, IRELAND.
•**KELLY, Mr. Richard Nicholas, BSc FCA** *1993;* BDO LLP, Prospect Place, 85 Great North Road, HATFIELD, HERTFORDSHIRE, AL9 5BS. See also BDO Stoy Hayward LLP
KELLY, Mr. Robert Andrew, BA FCA *1969;* Cruachan, 8 Matty Lonning, Thursby, CARLISLE, CA5 6PQ. (Life Member)
KELLY, Mr. Robert Benjamin, BSc ACA *2011;* 129 Gloucester Avenue, LONDON, NW1 8LA.
KELLY, Mr. Robert Daniel, MA FCA *1987;* Stafford House, 33 Stafford Hill Lane, Kirkheaton, HUDDERSFIELD, HD5 0EE.
KELLY, Mr. Sam Paul, BSc ACA *2005;* Flat 4, 208 Kingsland Road, LONDON, E2 8AJ.
•**KELLY, Mrs. Samantha, BA ACA** *1993;* Samantha Kelly ACA, 10 Ferniefields, HIGH WYCOMBE, BUCKINGHAMSHIRE, HP12 4SP.
KELLY, Ms. Sandra Claire, ACA MSI *1985;* Cop Close, 112 High Street, Long Crendon, AYLESBURY, BUCKINGHAMSHIRE, HP18 9AN.
KELLY, Mr. Sean Antony, BA FCA *1982;* 133 Sterling Place, #4B, NEW YORK, NY 11217, UNITED STATES.
•**KELLY, Mr. Sean Patrick, FCA** *1976;* 30 Ardglas, Sandyford Road, Dundrum, DUBLIN 16, COUNTY DUBLIN, IRELAND.
KELLY, Mr. Shane Roger, BSc ACA AMCT *1995;* 12 South Western Road, TWICKENHAM, TW1 1LQ.
KELLY, Mr. Simon Columb Mark, BA FCA *1989;* 16 Bullecourt Avenue, MOSMAN, NSW 2088, AUSTRALIA.
•**KELLY, Mr. Stephen, FCA** *1974;* (Tax Fac), Kelly Associates, 4 Club Lane, Rodley, LEEDS, LS13 1JG.
•**KELLY, Mr. Stephen John, BSc ACA** *1994;* (Tax Fac), 2020 CA Ltd, 1 St. Andrew's Hill, LONDON, EC4V 5BY.
KELLY, Mr. Stephen Mark, ACA *1993;* Archbishop Thurstan C of E School, Hopewell Road, HULL, HU9 4HD.
KELLY, Mr. Stuart Dennis, FCA *1963;* 18 Felton Lea, SIDCUP, DA14 6BA. (Life Member)
KELLY, Mrs. Susan Elizabeth, BA ACA *1997;* 27 Parrs Wood Avenue, MANCHESTER, M20 5WB.
KELLY, Ms. Suzanne, BCom ACA *1997;* 3 Beresford Avenue, Drumcondra, DUBLIN 9, COUNTY DUBLIN, IRELAND.
KELLY, Mr. Thomas Graham, FCA *1971;* 106 Old Station Road, Hampton-in-Arden, SOLIHULL, WEST MIDLANDS, B92 0HF.
KELLY, Miss. Victoria Ann, BA ACA *2010;* 18 Somerford Way, LONDON, SE16 6QW.
KELLY, Mr. William David, FCA *1984;* Brantwood, Keepers Lane, The Wergs, WOLVERHAMPTON, WV6 8UA.
•①**KELLY, Mr. William John, FCA** *1977;* Begbies Traynor, 10th Floor, Temple Point, 1 Temple Row, BIRMINGHAM, B2 5YB. See also Begbies Traynor(Central) LLP and Begbies Traynor Limited
KELLY-SMITH, Mrs. Angela Susan Elizabeth, ACA *1996;* 160 Nevay Road, Karaka Bay, WELLINGTON 6022, NEW ZEALAND.
KELMAN, Mr. Richard Francis, BSc ACA *2007;* 9 Solent Drive, Hatch Warren, BASINGSTOKE, RG22 4XS.
KELMAN, Mr. Thomas, CA FMAAT MCT *2011;* Scotland 1986); AAT, 140 Aldersgate Street, LONDON, EC1A 4HY.
KELMAN-MCCONNACHIE, Miss. Jane Caroline, BSc ACA *1994;* 3 Korte Meijerkamplaan, 1406sv BUSSUM, NETHERLANDS.
KELMANSON, Miss. Claire Emma, ACA *2008;* 118 Offord Road, LONDON, N1 1PF.
KELPI HADJILOUCAS, Mrs. Ioanna, BSc ACA *2002;* 10 Tobin Close, LONDON, NW3 3DY.
KELSALL, Mr. Angus Jameson, BA ACA *1994;* 246 Ravenscliff Road, Saint Davids, ST DAVIDS, PA 19087, UNITED STATES.
KELSALL, Mr. Christopher John, BA ACA *1992;* 13 Woodlands Parkway, Timperley, ALTRINCHAM, WA15 7QT.
KELSALL, Mr. Daniel Joseph, BA(Hons) ACA *2009;* Zolfo Cooper Toronto Square, Toronto Street, LEEDS, LS1 2HJ.
•**KELSALL, Mrs. Deborah Jayne, FCA** *1994;* Stubbs Parkin South, The Manse, Dodington, WHITCHURCH, SHROPSHIRE, SY13 1DZ. See also Stubbs Parkin & South
KELSALL, Mr. Ernest Peter Birkenhead, BSc FCA *1971;* Flat 2 Trevethan Court, Mitchell Road, FALMOUTH, CORNWALL, TR11 2UQ. (Life Member)
KELSALL, Mr. Ian Gordon, BA(Hons) ACA *2001;* with Ernst & Young, Citygate, St James' Boulevard, NEWCASTLE UPON TYNE, NE1 4JD.
KELSALL, Mrs. Jane Mary, BA ACA *1998;* Hays FZ LLC, PO Box 500340, Block 19 1st Floor F-02, Knowledge Village, DUBAI, UNITED ARAB EMIRATES.
KELSALL, Mr. Matthew David Charles, BSc ACA *2005;* 1 Clarence Drive, CAMBERLEY, GU15 1JT.
KELSALL, Mr. Matthew John, BA(Hons) ACA *2001;* Clyde & Co, City Tower 2, Sheikh Zayed Road, P O Box 31645, DUBAI, UNITED ARAB EMIRATES.
KELSALL, Mr. Nicholas Paul, BA ACA *1982;* 7 Dunnockswood, Alsager, STOKE-ON-TRENT, ST7 2XU.
KELSALL, Mrs. Sarah Louise, BSc ACA *1998;* (Tax Fac), with KPMG LLP, St. James's Square, MANCHESTER, M2 6DS.
KELSALL, Mrs. Sarah Victoria, BA ACA *2004;* with KPMG LLP, Edward VII Quay, Navigation Way, Ashton-on-Ribble, PRESTON, PR2 2YF.
KELSALL, Mr. Simon James, BA ACA *1998;* 33 Pentire Road, LICHFIELD, STAFFORDSHIRE, WS14 9SG.
KELSEY, Mr. Alistair Peter, BA ACA *1999;* with PKF (UK) LLP, Farringdon Place, 20 Farringdon Road, LONDON, EC1M 3AP.
•**KELSEY, Mr. Brian, BA FCA** *1959;* Brian Kelsey & Co Limited, 7a Court Street, FAVERSHAM, KENT, ME13 7AN.
•**KELSEY, Mrs. Fiona Elizabeth, BSc ACA** *1988;* PricewaterhouseCoopers LLP, 1 Embankment Place, LONDON, WC2N 6RH. See also PricewaterhouseCoopers
KELSEY, Mrs. Frances Lucy, BA(Hons) ACA *2002;* Corporate Services Finance, Worcestershire County Council County Hall, Spetchley Road, WORCESTER, WR5 2NP.
KELSEY, Mr. James Andrew, ACA *1994;* 10 Queensway, LINCOLN, LN2 4AH.
KELSEY, Mr. Jeremy Paul, BSc ACA *2004;* Garden Flat, 12 Frederick Place, BRISTOL, BS8 1AS.
•**KELSEY, Mr. John Peter Lloyd, FCA** *1974;* 102 High Street, Hook, GOOLE, NORTH HUMBERSIDE, DN14 5PQ.
•**KELSEY, Mr. Mark Andrew, ACA** *1994;* 9 Station Road, SLOUGH, SL1 6JJ.
•**KELSEY, Mr. Nicholas James, ACA** *1980;* Saffery Champness, Lion House, Red Lion Street, LONDON, WC1R 4GB.
KELSEY, Mr. Richard, FCA *1968;* 9 Wood Road, HYTHE, KENT, CT21 6BJ. (Life Member)
KELSEY, Mr. Richard Heneage Morton, FCA *1968;* 1 Rectory Close, Littlebury, SAFFRON WALDEN, CB11 4TJ.
KELSEY, Mr. Richard Peter, MA ACA CFA *2000;* Kaiserstrasse 67-69331, 1070 VIENNA, AUSTRIA.
KELSEY, Miss. Sarah Jane, BSc ACA *2006;* 57 Bownham Park Rodborough Common, STROUD, GLOUCESTERSHIRE, GL5 5BZ.
KELSEY, Mr. Timothy George, FCA *1963;* 9a Greetwell Road, LINCOLN, LN2 4AQ.
KELSEY BURGE, Mr. Julian Douglas, MSc ACA *1997;* 16 Bourne Street, LONDON, SW1W 8JR.
KELSEY-WILSON, Mrs. Karen Elizabeth, ACA *2002;* with PricewaterhouseCoopers LLP, 2 Humber Quays, Wellington Street West, HULL, HU1 2BN.
KELSH, Miss. Emma Christina, BSc ACA *2002;* 39 Village Way, BECKENHAM, KENT, BR3 3NA.
KELSO, Mr. Martin Allardyce, FCA MBA *1985;* 3 Edderston Ridge View, PEEBLES, EH45 9NB.

KELSO, Mr. Russell Longwell, BA(Hons) ACA *2003;* 53 Highdown Road, HOVE, EAST SUSSEX, BN3 6EA.
KELTY, Mr. Neil Gareth, BA ACA *2008;* Holly Grove, 9 Brearley Close, Bidston, PRENTON, MERSEYSIDE, CH43 7XW.
KELWAY, Mrs. Angela, BSc(Hons) ACA CTA *2003;* with Coutts & Co, 440 Strand, LONDON, WC2R 0QS.
•KEMAL, Mr. Altan, ACA FCCA *2009;* (Tax Fac), Alton & Co, 237 Kennington Lane, LONDON, SE11 5QU.
KEMBALL-COOK, Mr. Julian Richard, FCA *1973;* Highfield House, Summer Hill, Harbledown, CANTERBURY, KENT, CT2 8NH.
KEMBALL PRICE, Mr. Anthony, FCA MSI *1958;* Earlsmead, 42 Dyke Road Avenue, BRIGHTON, BN1 5LE. (Life Member)
KEMBER, Mr. Matthew William, ACA *1992;* (Tax Fac), Anglia Circuits (Holdings) Ltd, Burrell Road, ST.IVES, CAMBRIDGESHIRE, PE27 3LB.
KEMBER, Mr. William Percy, FCA *1956;* 83 Hillway, Highgate, LONDON, N6 6AB. (Life Member)
KEMBERY, Mrs. Christina Margaret, BSc ACA *1989;* Maison Cambrai, La Rue de la Presse, St. Peter, JERSEY, JE3 7YG.
KEMKERS, Mr. Peter Edward, BSc ACA *1998;* Hillside Guildford Road, Westcott, DORKING, RH4 3LF.
KEMM, Mr. Michael John, FCA *1966;* 8 The Green, Old Dalby, MELTON MOWBRAY, LE14 3LL.
KEMMENOE, Mr. John Harold, FCA *1977;* Brambles, 6 Millbank, Headcorn, ASHFORD, KENT, TN27 9RD.
KEMMETT, Mr. Simon William, BSc ACA *1996;* 38 Meadow Drive, East Herrington, SUNDERLAND, SR3 3RD.
KEMMIS, Miss. Anna Clare, BA ACA *2004;* 36 rue Jean de la Fontaire, 78000 VERSAILLES, FRANCE.
KEMP, Mr. Adrian Gordon, BA ACA *1998;* One Raffles Quay, #12-00 South Tower, SINGAPORE 048583, SINGAPORE.
KEMP, Mr. Alan Harry Robert, FCA *1969;* Luscombe House, 1 The Drive, Brudenell Avenue, Canford Cliffs, POOLE, DORSET BH13 7NW. (Life Member)
•KEMP, Mr. Andrew Charles, BA ACA *1986;* PricewaterhouseCoopers LLP, 1 Embankment Place, LONDON, WC2N 6RH. See also PricewaterhouseCoopers
•KEMP, Miss. Barbara Ann, FCA *1958;* Elm Cottage, Elm Park Road, PINNER, MIDDLESEX, HA5 3LA.
KEMP, Miss. Carly Rose, ACA *2008;* Flat 3, 20 Avenue Elmers, SURBITON, KT6 4SE.
KEMP, Miss. Cathryn Anne, BA ACA *1996;* 21 Clifton Drive, Gatley, CHEADLE, CHESHIRE, SK8 4EQ.
KEMP, Mr. Charles William, BA ACA *1986;* 8 Hillhead, BONNYRIGG, EH19 2AH.
KEMP, Miss. Charlotte Amie, ACA *2003;* Apartment 7, 6 North Road, RICHMOND, TW9 4HA.
KEMP, Mr. Christopher Malcolm Henry, FCA *1974;* Netherwood Farm, Bromley Wood, Abbots Bromley, RUGELEY, WS15 3AG.
KEMP, Mr. Christopher Simon Guy, BSc ACA *1991;* Hilltop, 12 Shackstead Lane, Busbridge, GODALMING, GU7 1RW.
KEMP, Mrs. Corinna, BA(Hons) ACA *2002;* Liverpool Daily Post & Echo Ltd, PO Box 48, LIVERPOOL, L69 3EB.
KEMP, Mr. David Anthony, BSc ACA AMCT *1988;* Gleneagles Hotels Limited, The Gleneagles Hotel, AUCHTERARDER, PERTHSHIRE, PH3 1NF.
KEMP, Mr. Edward Alexander, BA ACA *1997;* Heiderweg 3, 40489 DUSSELDORF, GERMANY.
KEMP, Mr. Graham Charles Richard, BA FCA *1985;* 26 Conger Lane, Toddington, DUNSTABLE, BEDFORDSHIRE, LU5 6BT.
•KEMP, Mr. Harry Charles, BSc FCA *1994;* (Tax Fac), Kemps Accounting Solutions Limited, 84 High Street, BROADSTAIRS, KENT, CT10 1JJ.
KEMP, Mrs. Helen Anne, BA FCA DChA *1987;* St. Gemmas Hospice, 329 Harrogate Road, LEEDS, LS17 6QD.
KEMP, Mrs. Jane, BA ACA *2000;* 300 East 56, 12A, NEW YORK, NY 10022, UNITED STATES.
KEMP, Miss. Jane Mary, BSc ACA *1992;* with KPMG LLP, Management Services Centre, 58 Clarendon Road, WATFORD, WD17 1DE.
KEMP, Miss. Jodie Luena, BA ACA *2006;* 4th Floor, Warner Bros, 98 Theobalds Road, LONDON, WC1X 8WB.
KEMP, Mr. John Ogilvie, BSc ACA *1979;* 53 Limefield Road, Smithills, BOLTON, BL1 6LA.
KEMP, Mr. John Peter, ACA *2009;* 3 Langold Drive, Norton, DONCASTER, SOUTH YORKSHIRE, DN6 9GE.
KEMP, Mr. John Robert Andrew, BA ACA *1986;* TFE, Old London Road, PENRITH, CUMBRIA, CA11 8GU.
KEMP, Mr. Mark Andrew, ACA *1992;* 6 Ibworth Lane, FLEET, GU51 1AU.
KEMP, Mr. Martin Lindley, FCA *1955;* 2A Arnside Road, Oxton, Birken Head, PRENTON, MERSEYSIDE, CH43 2JU.
KEMP, Mr. Martin Thomas, BSocSc FCA *1999;* Sanctuary Housing Association Chamber Court, Castle Street, WORCESTER, WR1 3ZQ.
KEMP, Mr. Michael Graeme Dominic, BSc ACA *1991;* 60 Loxwood, Earley, READING, RG6 5QZ.
KEMP, Mr. Michael Paul, LLB ACA *1992;* 30 Carr Manor Parade, Moortown, LEEDS, LS17 5AF.
KEMP, Mr. Nicholas Walle, BEng ACA *1992;* 12 St. Francis Road, LONDON, SE22 8DE.
KEMP, Mr. Peter John, BA FCA *1969;* Wiltshire & Swindon Learning Resources, Libraries & Heritage Building, County Hall East, By The Sea Road, TROWBRIDGE, WILTSHIRE BA14 8BS.
•KEMP, Mr. Peter John, BSc FCA *1986;* Critchleys, Avalon House, Marcham Road, ABINGDON, OX14 1UD. See also Peter Kemp Ltd
KEMP, Mr. Philip, ACA *1998;* 300 E 56th Street, Apartment 7M, NEW YORK, NY 10022, UNITED STATES.
KEMP, Mr. Philip George, BSc ACA *2007;* 62 Boyn Hill Road, MAIDENHEAD, SL6 4HJ.
KEMP, Mr. Philip James, BA(Hons) ACA *2001;* 8 Bulkeley Avenue, WINDSOR, BERKSHIRE, SL4 3LP.
•KEMP, Mr. Richard George, FCA *1973;* Richard Kemp & Co, 33a Crook Log, BEXLEYHEATH, DA6 8EB.
KEMP, Mr. Roger Clifford, FCA *1964;* 85 Woodlands Drive, Offerton, STOCKPORT, SK2 5AP. (Life Member)
KEMP, Mr. Roger John, FCA *1969;* 1884 John St, THORNHILL L3T 1Z1, ON, CANADA.
KEMP, Mr. Roy Peter, FCA FCCA CTA FCMI *1968;* Ridgmont, Northfield Avenue, PINNER, MIDDLESEX, HA5 1AR.
KEMP, Mr. Russell Philip Dean, BA(Hons) ACA *2003;* Gibbons & Mannington, 20-22 Eversley Road, BEXHILL-ON-SEA, EAST SUSSEX, TN40 1HE.
KEMP, Miss. Samantha Jane, ACA *2008;* 42 Tiber Road, North Hykeham, LINCOLN, LN6 9TY.
KEMP, Mr. Samuel, BA ACA *1995;* Citibank Plc, 25 Canada Square, LONDON, E14 5LQ.
KEMP, Miss. Sarah, BA(Hons) ACA *2011;* 3 Garmondsway Court, West Cornforth, FERRYHILL, COUNTY DURHAM, DL17 9HE.
KEMP, Mrs. Stephanie Claire, MA ACA *1985;* 123 Cremorne Road, CREMORNE POINT, NSW 2090, AUSTRALIA.
KEMP, Mr. Stephen Brian, BSc ACA *1996;* 27 Elm Road, WINDSOR, SL4 3NB.
•KEMP, Mr. Stephen Charles, BSc FCA *1994;* Bramble Cottage, James Road, ST HELIER, JE2 4QY.
KEMP, Mr. Stephen John, LLB FCA *1986;* 125 Higher Meadow, LEYLAND, PR25 5RP.
KEMP, Mr. Stephen Richard, BA FCA *1976;* Hopedene, 4 Ranelagh Avenue, Barnes, LONDON, SW13 0BY.
•KEMP, Ms. Susan, ACA *1983;* Ms Susan Kemp ACA, 100 Welsford Road, NORWICH, NR4 6QH.
•KEMP, Mrs. Susan Margaret, ACA *1989;* (Tax Fac), Kemp Accountants, Little Compton, Rannoch Road, CROWBOROUGH, EAST SUSSEX, TN6 1RB.
KEMP, Mr. Terence Robert William, BSc FCA *1962;* 15 Southgate Park, Spittal, HAVERFORDWEST, SA62 5QQ.
•KEMP, Mr. Timothy John, BA FCA *1981;* Tim Kemp Accountancy Services Ltd, Top Barn, Rectory Road, Steppingley, BEDFORD, MK45 5AT. See also AIMS - Timothy Kemp
KEMP, Mr. Timothy William, BA ACA *1990;* The Manse Station Road, Heighington, LINCOLN, LN4 1QJ. (Life Member)
KEMP, Mr. William David, BSc(Econ) FCA *1967;* 10 Brampton Road, Bramhall, STOCKPORT, SK7 3BS. (Life Member)
KEMP-GEE, Mr. David Marquis, MBA FCA *1969;* Sandwell, Harberton, TOTNES, TQ9 7LN. (Life Member)
KEMP HARPER, Mr. Robert Lindsay, FCA *1967;* Dinmore House, Hastings Pool, Poolbrook Road, MALVERN, WORCESTERSHIRE, WR14 3QL. (Life Member)
KEMP-POTTER, Mr. Michael Peter, FCA *1967;* Church House, The Street, Clapham, WORTHING, BN13 3UU. (Life Member)
KEMP-WELCH, Mr. Peter John, MA ACA *1995;* 94 Brook Green, LONDON, W6 7BD.
KEMPEN, Miss. Anna, BSc(Hons) ACA *2011;* 88 Prince of Wales Avenue, SOUTHAMPTON, SO15 4LU.
KEMPEN, Mr. Ian Robin, BA FCA *1996;* The Old Eagle, Plains Road Little Totham, MALDON, ESSEX, CM9 8JG.
KEMPENAAR, Miss. Linda Melanie, BA ACA *2005;* with PricewaterhouseCoopers, Prince's Building, 22/F, 10 Chater Road, CENTRAL, HONG KONG ISLAND HONG KONG SAR.
KEMPNER, Mr. Michael Alfred, FCA *1976;* 29 Windsor Road, Kew, RICHMOND, TW9 2EJ.
KEMPSELL, Mr. John Baron, FCA *1964;* 3 All Saints Drive, Limpsfield Rd, Sanderstead, SOUTH CROYDON, SURREY, CR2 9ES. (Life Member)
KEMPSON, Mr. Derek Chown, FCA *1950;* Rogate, Arkley Drive, Arkley, BARNET, EN5 3LN. (Life Member)
•KEMPSTER, Mr. Jeffrey Paul, FCA *1977;* Kempsters, Prospect House, 20 High Street, WESTERHAM, KENT, TN16 1RG. See also Kempster & Dale Partnership
KEMPSTER, Mr. Jonathan, BA ACA *1991;* Glaston Hill Lodge, Church Road, Eversley, HOOK, HAMPSHIRE, RG27 0PX.
KEMPSTER, Mr. Peter, BA FCA *1982;* (Tax Fac), Amberley, Ockham Road South, East Horsley, LEATHERHEAD, KT24 6SN.
KEMPTON, Mrs. Bethan Lea, BA ACA *2007;* 38 Briary Avenue, High Green, SHEFFIELD, S35 4FY.
•KEMPTON, Mrs. Briony Ruth, BSc ACA *1990;* with Ernst & Young LLP, The Paragon, Counterslip, BRISTOL, BS1 6BX.
KEMPTON, Mr. James Daniel, BA ACA *2000;* Saxton Bampfylde Hever, 35 Old Queen Street, LONDON, SW1H 9JA.
KEMPTON, Mr. Peter Albert, FCA *1960;* 35 Chichester Drive West, Saltdean, BRIGHTON, BN2 8SH.
KEMSHALL, Mr. Adrian Philip, FCA *1975;* 135 Post Office Road, Seisdon, WOLVERHAMPTON, WV5 7HA.
KEMSHALL, Mr. Graeme, FCA *1971;* 7 Westcliff Gardens, SCUNTHORPE, DN17 1DT.
KEMSLEY, Ms. Alexis Natasha, BA ACA *2003;* 7 Humberstone Road, SOUTHWELL, NOTTINGHAMSHIRE, NG25 0FE.
KEMSLEY, Mrs. Antoinette Patricia, BA ACA *1983;* 5 Oakdene Road, SEVENOAKS, TN13 3HH.
•KEMSLEY, Mr. Craig, ACA CA(AUS) *2008;* Grant Thornton UK LLP, Grant Thornton House, 22 Melton Street, Euston Square, LONDON, NW1 2EP. See also Grant Thornton LLP
KEMSLEY, Mr. Kenneth Jack Zeital, FCA *1961;* 6 Dewlands Court, Turnberry Close, LONDON, NW4 1JL.
•KEMSLEY, Mr. Michael, FCA *1980;* Kemsley and Company, 12 Heathfield South, TWICKENHAM, TW2 7SS.
KEMSLEY, Mrs. Rachel Clare, ACA *1994;* 15 Nunn Close, Martlesham, WOODBRIDGE, SUFFOLK, IP12 4UL.
•KEMSLEY, Mr. Robin William, ACA *1982;* Kemsley & Co., Upper North Court, Bullens Farm Business Centre, Bullens Lane, East Peckham, TONBRIDGE KENT TN12 5LX.
KENBER, Mr. Anthony Patrick Michael, FCA FCMI *1970;* Dolphin House, 38 Church Road, Magdalen, KING'S LYNN, NORFOLK, PE34 3DG.
•KENCH, Mr. Eric Arthur, FCA *1977;* (Member of Council 2004 - 2008), (Tax Fac), Kench & Co Ltd, 10 Station Road, HENLEY-ON-THAMES, OXFORDSHIRE, RG9 1AY.
KENCH, Mr. Ronald Stuart, FCA *1952;* 33 High View Road, South Woodford, LONDON, E18 2HL. (Life Member)
KENDAL, Mr. Clive Timothy, ACA *1984;* 15 Craigour Avenue, Torphins, BANCHORY, AB31 4JA.
•KENDAL, Mr. Jonathan David, BCom ACA CTA *1984;* (Tax Fac), Jonathan Kendal & Co, 4 Holt Close, LONDON, N10 3HW.
KENDAL, Mrs. Margaret Ann Eleanor, BSc FCA *1978;* 28 George Lane, Read, BURNLEY, BB12 7RH.
KENDAL, Mr. Martin, FCA *1952;* 376 Wokingham Road, Earley, READING, RG6 7HX. (Life Member)
KENDALL, Mr. Adam James, ACA *2005;* The Doctors House, High Street, BURES, SUFFOLK, CO8 5HZ.
KENDALL, Mrs. Alison Elisabeth, LLB ACA *1991;* Stafford Borough Council Civic Centre, Riverside, STAFFORD, ST16 3AQ.
KENDALL, Mr. Andrew, BSc ACA *1994;* 2 Faraday Road, WEST MOLESEY, KT8 2TQ.
KENDALL, Mr. Andrew Edward, BSc ACA *1993;* Whiteladyes, Sandy Way, COBHAM, KT11 2EY.
KENDALL, Mrs. Angela Rosemary, FCA *1968;* 177 South Road, SMITHS HS 01, BERMUDA.
KENDALL, Mrs. Averill Ellen, ACA *1981;* 24 Penhale Gardens, FAREHAM, PO14 4NL.
KENDALL, Mr. Clive Peter, FCA *1968;* 25 Osborne Court, Park View Road, LONDON, W5 2JE.
•KENDALL, Mr. David James, BSc FCA *1977;* McCabe Ford Williams, Invicta Business Centre, Monument Way, Orbital Park, ASHFORD, KENT TN24 0HB.
KENDALL, Mr. David John, OBE BEng FCA *1977;* Derwen College, Whittington Road, Gobowen, OSWESTRY, SHROPSHIRE, SY11 3JA.
KENDALL, Mr. David William, FCA *1962;* 41 Albion St, LONDON, W2 2AU. (Life Member)
KENDALL, Mr. Donald, FCA *1957;* 16 Kilby Avenue, Birstall, LEICESTER, LE4 4AR. (Life Member)
KENDALL, Mr. Geoffrey Marris, FCA *1957;* 33 Rectory Lane, Kibworth Beauchamp, LEICESTER, LE8 0NW. (Life Member)
KENDALL, Mrs. Gillian Rosemary, MEng ACA *2004;* 27 Arran Way, Rothwell, LEEDS, LS26 0WB.
KENDALL, Mr. Guy Francis, PhD MA MSc FCA *1993;* 66 Church Hill, Penn, WOLVERHAMPTON, WV4 5JD.
KENDALL, Mr. Ian Alistair, BA ACA *1985;* Elgfaret 29, 1453 BJORNEMYR, NORWAY.
KENDALL, Miss. Jody Anne, BSc ACA *1998;* 8 Craiglands Park, ILKLEY, WEST YORKSHIRE, LS29 8SX.
KENDALL, Mr. Jonathan Mark, BA ACA *1994;* Povoas Packaging Ltd Stoke Albany Road, Desborough, KETTERING, NORTHAMPTONSHIRE, NN14 2SR.
KENDALL, Mrs. Kathryn Sylvia, BSc ACA *1993;* Hawthorn House, 182 Long Street, Easingwold, YORK, YO61 3JD.
KENDALL, Mrs. Lynda, BSc ACA *1985;* (Tax Fac), Oakwood, Plymouth Drive, Radyr, CARDIFF, CF15 8BL.
KENDALL, Mr. Matthew Paul, BSc ACA *1999;* 27 Arran Way, Rothwell, LEEDS, LS26 0WB.
KENDALL, Mr. Matthew Stephen, ACA *2011;* 53 Ellerker Rise, Willerby, HULL, HU10 6EU.
KENDALL, Mr. Maximillian Adrian Peter, ACA *2007;* 26 Osborne Court, Park View Road, LONDON, W5 2JE.
KENDALL, Mrs. Nicola Susan, BA ACA *2002;* 2 Budges Cottages, Keephatch Road, WOKINGHAM, BERKSHIRE, RG40 5PY.
KENDALL, Mr. Nigel Francis Herrick, FCA *1968;* Tangley House, Tangley Lane, GUILDFORD, SURREY, GU3 3JZ.
•KENDALL, Mr. Paul Francis, BSc FCA *1987;* Corner Barn, High Bank Hill, PENRITH, CUMBRIA, CA10 1EZ.
KENDALL, Mr. Philip James, MEng ACA *1991;* Simons Group Ltd, 991 Doddington Road, LINCOLN, LN6 3AA.
•KENDALL, Mr. Richard John, MA ACA *1978;* (Tax Fac), Richard Kendall & Co Ltd, 15 Victoria Road, TEDDINGTON, MIDDLESEX, TW11 0BB.
•KENDALL, Mr. Robert Frederick, FCA *1974;* 80 Harpenden Lane, Redbourn, ST. ALBANS, HERTFORDSHIRE, AL3 7PB.
KENDALL, Mr. Robert Mark, BSc ACA *1998;* 80 Ridley Park, SINGAPORE 248506, SINGAPORE.
•KENDALL, Mr. Robert Norman, FCA *1978;* (Tax Fac), Harrison Beale & Owen Limited, Highdown House, 11 Highdown Road, LEAMINGTON SPA, WARWICKSHIRE, CV31 1XT. See also Harrison Beale & Owen Management Services
KENDALL, Mr. Robert William, BSc FCA *1978;* 44 Moreland Drive, GERRARDS CROSS, SL9 8BD.
KENDALL, Mr. Simon Christopher Edward, FCA *1974;* Cumbers Farm, LISS, HAMPSHIRE, GU33 7LL.
KENDALL, Mr. Simon James, BA ACA *1983;* 18 Mount Ephraim Road, LONDON, SW16 1NG.
KENDALL, Mr. Stephen Michael, FCA *1968;* Random Stones, 49 Sandygate Park Road, SHEFFIELD, S10 5TX.
KENDALL, Ms. Susan, MA ACA *2011;* 15 Hampden Road, Caversham, READING, RG4 5ED.
KENDALL, Mr. Thomas Joseph, FCA *1958;* 6 Leigh Hill Road, COBHAM, SURREY, KT11 2HX. (Life Member)
KENDALL, Mr. William Henry, BSc ACA *1990;* Vollman Brothers, 1 Cornhill, LONDON, EC3V 3NB.
KENDALL-SMITH, Mr. Michael Andrew, BSc ACA *1984;* 42 Spofforth Hill, WETHERBY, LS22 6SE.
•KENDELL, Mr. Philip John, BSc FCA ATII *1988;* (Tax Fac), Philip Kendell, 4 Wheelwrights Corner, Nailsworth, STROUD, GL6 0DB.
KENDREW, Mr. Geoffrey Birchall, FCA *1970;* 8 Chapel Drive, Halebarns, ALTRINCHAM, WA15 0BL.
•KENDREW, Mrs. Lesley Anne, BSc FCA *1989;* Clough & Company LLP, New Chartford House, Centurion Way, CLECKHEATON, WEST YORKSHIRE, BD19 3QB. See also Clough Taxation Solutions LLP and Clough Management Services LLP

KENDRICK, Mr. Ian, BA ACA *1996;* 1 Cheviot Close, Shaw, SWINDON, SN5 9QD.
KENDRICK, Mr. John Edward, BEng ACA *1992;* Elan Homes Limited, Oak House, Lloyd Drive, ELLESMERE PORT, CHESHIRE, ch65 9hq.
KENDRICK, Mr. Robert Neil, BSc ACA *1985;* 7 Sunningdale Close, STOURBRIDGE, DY8 2LS.
•KENDRICK, Mr. Timothy Michael Joseph, ACA *1986;* Iden Business Services Limited, 2 Garden Close, Staplehurst, TONBRIDGE, TN12 0EW.
KENEE, Mr. Steven Michael, BA ACA *2005;* Downing Corporate Finance Ltd, 10 Lower Grosvenor Place, LONDON, SW1W 0EN.
KENINGTON, Mr. John Stephen, BSc ACA *2004;* 13 Lawn Avenue, Burley in Wharfedale, ILKLEY, WEST YORKSHIRE, LS29 7ET.
•KENMARE, Mr. Robert Andrew, BSc ACA CF *1997;* Moore and Smalley LLP, Richard House, 9 Winckley Square, PRESTON, PR1 3HP.
•KENMIR, Mr. David Forbes, BSc ACA *1988;* PricewaterhouseCoopers LLP, 7 More London Riverside, LONDON, SE1 2RT. See also PricewaterhouseCoopers
KENMIR, Mr. Edward Cawthorne, FCA *1958;* 2 Cedar Drive, Farewall Hall, DURHAM, DH1 3TF.
KENMIR, Miss. Rebecca Jane, ACA *2009;* 26 Burgess Close, Woodley, READING, RG5 3LJ.
KENMUIR, Mr. Ian Alexander, BSc ACA *1979;* 1 Cherrington Road, NANTWICH, CHESHIRE, CW5 7AW.
KENN, Mr. Robert William, BCom ACA *1989;* 32 Curban Street, Balgowlah Heights, SYDNEY, NSW 2093, AUSTRALIA.
KENNA, Mrs. Michelle Denise, BA(Hons) ACA *2000;* Westland Horticulture Ltd, Alconbury Hill, Alconbury Weston, HUNTINGDON, CAMBRIDGESHIRE, PE28 4HY.
KENNA, Mr. Raymond Douglas, BA FCA *1977;* 3 Nursery Gardens, Codsall, WOLVERHAMPTON, WV8 1AT.
•KENNAN, Mr. Peter John, BA FCA ATII *1983;* (Tax Fac), Hawsons, Pegasus House, 463a Glossop Road, SHEFFIELD, S10 2QD.
•KENNARD, Mr. Andrew Marc Julian, BA FCA *1990;* (Tax Fac), Kelevra Ltd, 1 Queens Mews, Queens Road, BUCKHURST HILL, ESSEX, IG9 5AZ.
•KENNARD, Mr. Andrew Maurice, BA ACA *1992;* HK- Consultores de Gestão Lda, Av. Miguel Bombarda N° 21 3 Esq., 1050-161 LISBON, PORTUGAL. See also Horwath & Associados SROC Lda
KENNARD, Mr. Christopher William, MA FCA *1983;* Shadwell Estate Co Ltd Nunnery Stud, Euston, THETFORD, NORFOLK, IP24 2QE.
KENNARD, Mr. David Arthur, BSc ACA *1983;* Deaks Mead, Staplefield Road, Cuckfield, HAYWARDS HEATH, RH17 5JD.
•KENNARD, Mr. David Nigel, FCA *1982;* JDK Accounting, 16 Crown Acres, East Peckham, TONBRIDGE, KENT, TN12 5HB.
KENNARD, Mr. David Vaughan, BSc ACA *1991;* Jl Palbatu I/41, RT007/ RW04, JAKARTA, 12870, INDONESIA.
KENNARD, Mr. Harry Alan, MBE FCA *1965;* c/o ICAEW, Chartered Accountants Hall, PO Box 433, Moorgate Place, LONDON, EC2P 2BT.
•KENNARD, Mrs. Janis, BSc ACA ATII *1987;* Janis Webster, Tannery Cottage, Style Loke, Barford, NORWICH, NR9 4BE.
KENNARD, Mr. Martin Ronald, ACA MAAT *1996;* Neunbrunnenstrasse 132, 8050 ZURICH, SWITZERLAND.
KENNARD, Mr. Nigel Robert, FCA *1968;* Instead Manor, Weybread, DISS, NORFOLK, IP21 5UH.
KENNARD, Mr. Stephen Astley Martyn, FCA *1966;* Marden Cottage, Rhinefield Road, BROCKENHURST, SO42 7SQ. (Life Member)
KENNARD, Mr. Stephen Michael James, BSc ACIB FCA ATII *1992;* (Tax Fac), 48 Oakwood Avenue, PURLEY, CR8 1AQ.
•KENNAUGH, Mr. Graham Leigh, BA ACA *2004;* Evolution Accounting Limited, West Suite, Ragnall House, 18 Peel Road, Douglas, ISLE OF MAN IM1 4LZ.
KENNAWAY, Mr. Ian, MEng ACA *2006;* 13 Quarrington Road, BRISTOL, BS7 9PJ.
KENNEALLY, Mrs. Jane Anne, ACA *1989;* Apartment 12 Hirst Court, 20 Gatliff Road, LONDON, SW1W 8QD.
•KENNEDY, Mr. Alan John, BSc FCA *1986;* Smith Kennedy Limited, 14 Stanton Harcourt Road, WITNEY, OXFORDSHIRE, OX28 3LD.
•KENNEDY, Mr. Alastair Crawford, MA FCA *1971;* Howsons, 50 Broad Street, LEEK, ST13 5NS. See also Howsons Accountants Limited
KENNEDY, Mr. Alastair John, MEng ACA *1990;* 102 East Sheen Avenue, LONDON, SW14 8AU.
KENNEDY, Mr. Andrew James, BA ACA *2004;* 44 Tamar Way, WOKINGHAM, BERKSHIRE, RG41 3UB.
KENNEDY, Mr. Andrew Neilson, FCA *1975;* West Hill, Easton, WINCHESTER, SO21 1ER.
KENNEDY, Mr. Andrew William, MA(Hons) ACA MBA *2001;* 107 Gilmore Place, EDINBURGH, EH3 9PP.
•KENNEDY, Mr. Anthony Francis, BSc ACA *1998;* with KPMG LLP, 15 Canada Square, LONDON, E14 5GL.
KENNEDY, Miss. Bridget Mary, MA ACA *1990;* Citigroup, Citigroup Centre, 33 Canada Square, Canary Wharf, LONDON, E14 5LB.
KENNEDY, Mr. Cedric, MA FCA *1976;* Confederation of British Industry, Centre Point, 103 New Oxford Street, LONDON, WC1A 1DU.
KENNEDY, Mrs. Cerie Louise, BA ACA *1999;* Reed Business Information Ltd Quadrant House, The Quadrant Brighton Road, SUTTON, SM2 5AS.
KENNEDY, Miss. Christine, BA ACA *1999;* 27 Springfield Drive, CHESTER, CH2 3QF.
KENNEDY, Mr. Christopher John, BA ACA *1988;* Hangar 89, Easyjet Airline Co Ltd, Airport Approach Road, LUTON, LU2 9PF.
•KENNEDY, Mrs. Claire Louise, BSc ACA *2000;* CL Finance Associates, 3 Dodford Lane, Christian Malford, CHIPPENHAM, WILTSHIRE, SN15 4DE.
•KENNEDY, Mrs. Claire Margaret, BSc FCA *1984;* Beever and Struthers, St George's House, 215-219 Chester Road, MANCHESTER, M15 4JE.
KENNEDY, Ms. Clare Elizabeth, BA ACA *1996;* 67 Yarmouth Road, NORWICH, NR7 0EW.
KENNEDY, Ms. Clare Louise, BA ACA *1999;* 12 Manor Lane, LONDON, SE13 5QP.
KENNEDY, Clive John, Esq OBE FCA *1959;* Schefflerweg 6, 22605 HAMBURG, GERMANY. (Life Member)
KENNEDY, Mr. Daniel James, MA ACA *1998;* (Tax Fac), 9 Christ Church Road, FOLKESTONE, KENT, CT20 2SJ.
KENNEDY, Mrs. Deborah Ann, BA ACA *1999;* 2 Vue de Charriere, La Grande Route de St. Jean St. Helier, JERSEY, JE2 3FL.
KENNEDY, Mr. Duncan, BSc(Hons) ACA *2000;* 13 Grafton Close, ST. ALBANS, HERTFORDSHIRE, AL4 0ES.
KENNEDY, Mrs. Emily Elizabeth Lyons, MA(Oxon) ACA *2006;* 8 Wexford Road, PRENTON, MERSEYSIDE, CH43 9TB.
•KENNEDY, Mr. Euan Stewart, FCA *1970;* Kennedy & Co, 5 Gauden Road, LONDON, SW4 6LR.
KENNEDY, Mr. Fintan Michael, BBS FCA *1998;* 2 Vue de Charriere, La Grande Route de St Jean, St Helier, JERSEY, JE2 3FL.
KENNEDY, Mr. Frank, FCA *1966;* 256 Newton Drive, BLACKPOOL, FY3 8PZ.
KENNEDY, Mr. Fraser James, LLB ACA *2002;* 32 Ramsden Road, LONDON, SW12 8QY.
KENNEDY, Mr. Ian Marshall, BSc ACA *1991;* B N P Paribas, 5 Aldermanbury Square, LONDON, EC2V 7BP.
KENNEDY, Mr. James Alexander, BSc ACA *1996;* Electra Partners LLP, Paternoster House, 65 St. Paul's Churchyard, LONDON, EC4M 8AB.
KENNEDY, Mr. James English, FCA *1958;* 12 Crofters Close, The Wyndings Annitsford, CRAMLINGTON, NE23 7RJ. (Life Member)
KENNEDY, Miss. Jane Myra, BSc ACA *1988;* New Hall School, Boreham, CHELMSFORD, CM3 3HS.
KENNEDY, Ms. Jessica, BA ACA *1998;* 4 Gladstone Street, LONDON, SE1 6EY.
KENNEDY, Mrs. Joanna, BA ACA *2007;* 32 Ramsden Road, Balham, LONDON, SW12 8QY.
KENNEDY, Miss. Joanne, BA(Hons) ACA *2011;* 10 Byron Terrace, Greenhead, BRAMPTON, CUMBRIA, CA8 7JG.
•KENNEDY, Mr. John, BSc FCA *1971;* John F. Kennedy, Fiteco - Sevres, 25 Avenue De L Europe, BP 56, 92312 SEVRES, FRANCE.
KENNEDY, Mr. John, BSc ACA *2006;* 48 Clarendon Road, ASHFORD, MIDDLESEX, TW15 2QE.
KENNEDY, Mr. John Anthony, BA FCA *1973;* Po Box 3101, RINGWOOD, BH24 1GF.
KENNEDY, Mr. John Bryan, FCA *1983;* North East Lincolnshire PCT, Informatics Directorate, 1 Prince Albert Gardens, GRIMSBY, SOUTH HUMBERSIDE, DN31 3HT.
KENNEDY, Mr. John Dominic, BEng ACA *1992;* 10 Wightman Close, LICHFIELD, WS14 9RR.
•KENNEDY, Mr. John Francis Martin, FCA *1977;* Woolmer & Kennedy, 30 Star Hill, ROCHESTER, ME1 1XB.
KENNEDY, Mr. John Leslie, BA FCA *1980;* 17 Alsthorpe Road, OAKHAM, LEICESTERSHIRE, LE15 6FD.
KENNEDY, Mr. John Neil, FCA *1977;* 26 Radnor Walk, LONDON, SW3 4BN.
KENNEDY, Mr. John Robert Clifford, BSc FCA *1997;* 145 Holland Gardens, BRENTFORD, MIDDLESEX, TW8 0AY.
KENNEDY, Mr. Jonathan Andrew, MA ACA *1998;* 19 Lady Somerset Drive, LEDBURY, HR8 2FF.
KENNEDY, Mr. Jonathan Robert Samuel, BEng ACA *1999;* Silverdale Park Lane, Harefield, UXBRIDGE, MIDDLESEX, UB9 6HR.
KENNEDY, Mrs. Katie, BA ACA *2000;* 1 Cote Park, BRISTOL, BS9 2AE.
KENNEDY, Mr. Mark, BA(Hons) ACA *2011;* 6 Hollyridge, HASLEMERE, SURREY, GU27 2NP.
KENNEDY, Mr. Mark Oscar Henley, ACA *2010;* 2 York Close, Southwater, HORSHAM, WEST SUSSEX, RH13 9XJ.
KENNEDY, Mr. Mark Patrick, MA(Hons) ACA *2001;* 30 Beaconsfield Road, ST. ALBANS, HERTFORDSHIRE, AL1 3RB.
KENNEDY, Mr. Martin Philip Bannerman, BA ACA *1980;* 64 Sloane Street, LONDON, SW1X 9SH.
•KENNEDY, Mr. Michael Andrew, BA FCA *1979;* (Tax Fac), Smallfield Cody & Co., 5 Harley Place, Harley Street, LONDON, W1G 8QD.
KENNEDY, Mr. Michael James, FCA *1974;* Wildfell, Blackburn Road, BRIGHOUSE, HD6 2ET.
•KENNEDY, Mr. Michael John, FCA *1962;* The Gables, Canon Hill Close, Bray, MAIDENHEAD, BERKSHIRE, SL6 2DH.
KENNEDY, Mr. Millar, FCA *1962;* 15 East Street, OAKVILLE L6L 3K3, ON, CANADA. (Life Member)
KENNEDY, Mr. Nicholas, BSc FCA *1981;* 56 Clive Avenue, IPSWICH, IP1 4LU.
KENNEDY, Mr. Nicholas Benson, BA ACA *2006;* B Global Plc, Arkwright House, 2 Arkwright Court, Commercial Road, DARWEN, LANCASHIRE BB3 0FG.
KENNEDY, Miss. Nicola Jane, ACA *2009;* 8 Weavers Close, BILLERICAY, CM11 2AS.
KENNEDY, Mr. Nicolas Charles, MA FCA *1968;* 3 The Mount, Dukes Brow, BLACKBURN, BB2 6EX.
KENNEDY, Mrs. Pamela Hamilton, BA ACA CTA *1995;* 1 Homeston Avenue, Bothwell, GLASGOW, G71 8PL.
•KENNEDY, Mr. Patrick William, MA FCA *1984;* PK Audit LLP, 22 The Quadrant, RICHMOND, SURREY, TW9 1BP. See also PK Partners LLP
KENNEDY, The Revd. Paul Alan, ACA *1992;* The Rectory, Petersfield Road, WINCHESTER, HAMPSHIRE, SO23 0JD.
KENNEDY, Mr. Paul Michael, BA FCA *1983;* Level 26 HSBC Main Building, 1 Queen's Road, CENTRAL, HONG KONG SAR.
•KENNEDY, Mr. Paul Michael, ACA *1987;* (Tax Fac), O'Byrne & Kennedy LLP, East Wing, Goffs Oak House, Goffs Lane, Goffs Oak, WALTHAM CROSS HERTFORDSHIRE EN7 5BW.
KENNEDY, Mrs. Peggy Pui Ki, BA ACA *1993;* 8B Second Floor, Borrett Mansions, 8 Bowen Road, MID LEVELS, HONG KONG ISLAND, HONG KONG SAR.
KENNEDY, Miss. Rebecca Jayne, BSc ACA *1993;* Oak House, Coombe Park, KINGSTON UPON THAMES, KT2 7JD.
•KENNEDY, Mr. Richard Ian, LLB FCA *1982;* Francis Clark, 9 The Crescent, TAUNTON, SOMERSET, TA1 4EA. See also Francis Clark LLP
KENNEDY, Mr. Robert William, BA ACA *1999;* 8 Monks Road, BANSTEAD, SM7 2EP.
KENNEDY, Mrs. Rosie Ann, MEng ACA *1998;* 127 Carrs Mill, DONABATE, COUNTY DUBLIN, IRELAND.
KENNEDY, Miss. Sarah, BA(Hons) ACA *2011;* Flat 10, Warren House, 17 St. Peters Avenue, Caversham, READING, RG4 7RW.
•KENNEDY, Miss. Shan Mary, MA FCA *1983;* Shan Kennedy Limited, 71 Palewell Park, LONDON, SW14 8JJ.
KENNEDY, Mr. Simon Ralph, BSc ACA *1980;* 18 School Lane, Islip, KETTERING, NN14 3LQ.
KENNEDY, Mr. Stephen James, ACA *1979;* 10 Woodbank Road, Sedgley, DUDLEY, DY3 3NW.
•KENNEDY, Mr. Stephen John David, FCA *1984;* Kennedy & Co, ul Godebskiego 65, RASZYN, 05 090, POLAND.
KENNEDY, Mr. Stephen Joseph, BSc ACA *1985;* Hersilia, 33 rue du Portier, 98000 MONTE CARLO, MONACO.
KENNEDY, Miss. Susan Helen, BA ACA *1993;* Flat 5, 31 Kempsford Gardens, LONDON, SW5 9LA.
KENNEDY, Mr. Thomas, BSc MEB ACA *2010;* Flat 11, The Quays, Cumberland Road, BRISTOL, BS1 6UQ.
KENNEDY, Mr. Thomas Brendan, BCom FCA *1968;* 21 Knocklyon Heights, Knocklyon, DUBLIN 16, COUNTY DUBLIN, IRELAND. (Life Member)
KENNEDY, Mr. Wayne Norman Timothy, BEng ACA *2000;* with KPMG LLP, 15 Canada Square, LONDON, E14 5GL.
KENNEDY, Mr. William, ACA *2005;* 2 Temple Close, Banbury Road Bloxham, BANBURY, OXFORDSHIRE, OX15 4FW.
KENNEDY, Mr. William Alexander, BA ACA *1994;* 1 Homeston Avenue, Bothwell, GLASGOW, G71 8PL.
KENNEDY-ALEXANDER, Mr. Rupert Julian Stanley, ACA *2009;* 12 Brooks Road, LONDON, W4 3BH.
KENNER, Mr. Paul Martin, ACA *1978;* The Old Poor House, Selmeston, POLEGATE, EAST SUSSEX, BN26 6TX.
•KENNER, Mr. Stanley Trevor, ACA *1979;* Stanley Kenner & Co Limited, 3 Walbrook, Woodford Road, South Woodford, LONDON, E18 2EG.
KENNERLEY, Mr. David John Christopher, BA ACA AMCT *2001;* 52 Wilton Drive East, RIDGEFIELD, CT 06877, UNITED STATES.
KENNERLEY, Mr. Jeremy Francis Edgar, FCA *1990;* 551 Broadway, Miramar, WELLINGTON 6022, NEW ZEALAND.
KENNERLEY, Mr. Stephen, BSc ACA *2006;* 3 The Old Dairy, Ansell Road, DORKING, SURREY, RH4 1QQ.
KENNETT, Mr. Alan, FCA *1971;* Northfields, 27 The Street, North Nibley, DURSLEY, GLOUCESTERSHIRE, GL11 6DW.
KENNETT, Mrs. Christina Mary, BSc ACA *1992;* Soestdijkerstraatweg 63, 1213VS HILVERSUM, NETHERLANDS.
•KENNETT, Mr. Mark, ACA *1985;* Mark Kennett & Co Limited, Market Gate, Salop Road, OSWESTRY, SHROPSHIRE, SY11 2NR.
KENNETT, Mr. Mark William, BSc ACA *1991;* Henry Ling Ltd, 23 High East Street, DORCHESTER, DORSET, DT1 1HD.
KENNETT, Mrs. Melanie Anne, BA ACA *1997;* (Tax Fac), 1 Cavendish Drive, Claygate, ESHER, KT10 0QE.
KENNETT, Mr. Michael Henry, BA FCA *1963;* Jaspers, Bury Lane, WOKING, GU21 4RR. (Life Member)
KENNETT, Mr. Richard Luckham, BSc FCA *1976;* 9 Ruxley Ridge, Claygate, ESHER, KT10 0HZ.
KENNETT, Miss. Sally Anne, BA ACA *2004;* 68 Tanfield Road, CROYDON, CR0 1AL.
KENNETT, Mr. Timothy Robert, LLB ACA *2001;* 32 Carlton Road, LONDON, SW14 7RJ.
KENNEWELL, Mr. Brian Eric, BSc FCA *1974;* Little Oaks, 82 Maldon Road, Danbury, CHELMSFORD, CM3 4QW.
•KENNEY, Mr. James, FCA *1966;* James Kenney & Co, 202-204 Swan Lane, COVENTRY, CV2 4GD.
KENNEY, Mr. William Ernest, FCA *1968;* 86 New House Park, ST. ALBANS, AL1 1UP.
KENNING, Mr. Christopher, MA ACA *2011;* Dennington, 1 The Ride, Tubney Wood, ABINGDON, OXFORDSHIRE, OX13 5QF.
KENNING, Mr. David Berkeley Buchanan, MA FCA *1977;* G.K. Group Ltd., Chatsworth Rd, CHESTERFIELD, DERBYSHIRE, S40 2BJ.
KENNING, Mr. George Robert John, FCA *1972;* G K Group Ltd, Chatsworth Road, CHESTERFIELD, DERBYSHIRE, S40 2BJ.
KENNING, Mr. Richard Thomas, MA ACA *1979;* GKL Leasing, Lisle Road, Hughenden Avenue, HIGH WYCOMBE, BUCKINGHAMSHIRE, HP13 5SH.
KENNINGHAM, Mr. Alan David, FCA *1969;* with Grosvenor Partners LLP, 6-7 Ludgate Square, LONDON, EC4M 7AS. (Life Member)
KENNINGTON, Mr. Ivor Gordon, MA FCA *1960;* 19 Deepdale, LONDON, SW19 5EZ. (Life Member)
•KENNINGTON, Mr. Neil Anthony, BSc FCA *1990;* Heywood Shepherd, 1 Park Street, MACCLESFIELD, CHESHIRE, SK11 6SR.
KENNINGTON, Mr. Owen, MA MEng ACA *2004;* 54 Weavers Field, Girton, CAMBRIDGE, CB3 0XB.
KENNINGTON, Mrs. Penelope Jane, BA ACA *1994;* Apt 5F, Pearl Gardens, 7 Conduit Road, MID LEVELS, HONG KONG ISLAND, HONG KONG SAR.
KENNINGTON, Mr. Peter Frank, FCA *1958;* 6 Burbage Way, 97 Macclesfield Road, BUXTON, DERBYSHIRE, SK17 9GB. (Life Member)
KENNINGTON, Miss. Rebecca Ann, BSc ACA *1995;* APH Industries Limited, Anderson Works, Tongue Lane, Fairfield, BUXTON, DERBYSHIRE SK17 7LG.
•KENNISH, Mr. Richard William, FCA *1964;* Andrews & Associe CA SENC, 151 Boulevard Hymus, POINTE CLAIRE H9R 1E9, QC, CANADA.
KENNON, Mr. Andrew George, ACA *2006;* 28 Smithy Croft, Houghton, CARLISLE, CA3 0NS.
KENNY, Mr. Alexander, BEng ACA *1994;* 6th & 7th Floors, 120 Holborn, LONDON, EC1N 2TD.

KENNY, Mr. Anthony Edward, BA ACA *1989;* 30 Druid Stoke Avenue, Stoke Bishop, BRISTOL, BS9 1DD.
•KENNY, Mr. Bernard Augustine, BSc ACA *1991;* 5 Ringley Park Avenue, REIGATE, RH2 7DW.
KENNY, Mr. Charles Michael, FCA *1969;* 2 Glaston Court, Grange Road, LONDON, W5 5QR.
KENNY, Mr. Derek Joseph, BA ACA *1987;* The Kloof, Valley Road, Fawkham, LONGFIELD, DA3 8NA.
KENNY, Miss. Eileen Frances, BCom ACA *2000;* 7 Limes Road, WEYBRIDGE, SURREY, KT13 8DH.
KENNY, Miss. Emma Marie, BSc ACA *2003;* with Deloitte LLP, Hill House, 1 Little New Street, LONDON, EC4A 3TR.
KENNY, Mr. Eoin Michael Edmond Denis, MA MPhil ACA *2000;* 71 Carroll Street, Apt 3B, BROOKLYN, NY 11231, UNITED STATES.
KENNY, Mrs. Gaynor Anne, BA ACA *1987;* The Kloof, Valley Road, Fawkham, LONGFIELD, DA3 8NA.
KENNY, Mr. James Francis Lawrence, FCA *1976;* Sarnia Group, 953 Islington Street, Suite 24, PORTSMOUTH, NH 03801, UNITED STATES.
KENNY, Mr. John Louis, MA FCA *1982;* Partnerships for Schools, 33 Greycoat Street, LONDON, SW1P 2QF.
KENNY, Mr. Jonathan Michael, BSc ACA *2007;* 80 Stanway Road, Shirley, SOLIHULL, B90 3JG.
KENNY, Mr. Kevin John, FCA *1978;* 2 Le Grand Closin, 1380 OHAIN, BELGIUM.
KENNY, Mrs. Linda Michelle, FCA *1975;* Apartado 1147, Vilamoura, 8125 QUARTEIRA, ALGARVE, PORTUGAL.
•KENNY, Miss. Marion Frances, BSc ACA *1980;* Kenny & Co, 39 Wallace Fields, Ewell, EPSOM, KT17 3AX.
KENNY, Mr. Matthew Christopher David, BSc ACA *1995;* 8 Ripon Hall Avenue, Ramsbottom, BURY, LANCASHIRE, BL0 9RE.
KENNY, Mr. Matthew Joseph, BSc ACA *2004;* Flat 93 Dolphin House, Smugglers Way, LONDON, SW18 1DG.
KENNY, Mr. Paul Joseph, BA ACA *1987;* 22 Holmesdale Road, TEDDINGTON, TW11 9LF.
KENNY, Mr. Peter Nigel, PhD BSc FCA *1977;* Chemin Sous-Bois 7, 1172 BOUGY-VILLARS, VAUD, SWITZERLAND.
KENNY, Mr. Sacha, BSc FCA *1997;* 138 Graham Road, LONDON, SW19 3SJ.
KENNY, Miss. Sarah Louise, BEng ACA *2002;* Bauhaus, Gazprom Marketing & Trading Retail Ltd, 27 Quay Street, MANCHESTER, M3 3GY.
KENNY, Mr. Stephen Edward, BA ACA *2009;* Woodside, 3 Hellwood Lane, Scarcroft, LEEDS, LS14 3BP.
KENNY, Mr. Stephen Phillip, LLM LLB ACA *2010;* (Tax Fac), 7 Wakeham Street, LONDON, N1 3HP.
KENRICK, Mr. Robert James, MA FCA *1978;* 5 Goldsack Street, GLEN OSMOND, SA 5064, AUSTRALIA.
KENSALL, Mr. Graham John, BSc(Hons) ACA *2010;* 5 Ellens Bank, Lightmoor Green, TELFORD, SHROPSHIRE, TF4 3QP.
KENSINGTON, Mr. Esmond Nikolai Marc-ange Julian, BSc ACA *1992;* 62 Kempe Road, LONDON, NW6 6SL.
KENSINGTON, Mr. Julian Alfred Ivan St Vincent, MA FCA *1961;* 27 Chemin Du Tirage, 1299 VD CRANS, SWITZERLAND.
KENT, Mr. Alexander David, BA(Hons) ACA *2011;* Flat 3, Vassali House, 20 Central Road, LEEDS, LS1 6DE.
KENT, Miss. Angela, BA(Hons) ACA *2011;* 3 Sherburn Grove, Birkenshaw, BRADFORD, WEST YORKSHIRE, BD11 2JH.
•KENT, Mr. Anthony Thomas, FCA *1984;* Highgrove Accountants, 1st Floor, Unit 13, Victoria Way, Pride Park, DERBY DE24 8AN.
KENT, Mr. Antony Richard, BSc(Hons) ACA *2004;* 69 Kimberwick Crescent, OTTAWA K1V 0W7, ON, CANADA.
KENT, Mr. Benjamin David Jemphrey, MA ACA *1992;* BUPA, BUPA House, 15-19 Bloomsbury Way, LONDON, WC1A 2BA.
KENT, Mrs. Carol Anne, BSc ACA *1993;* 12 Fordington Avenue, WINCHESTER, HAMPSHIRE, SO22 5AW.
KENT, Mrs. Caroline Margaret, BA ACA *2005;* 77 Sumatra Road, LONDON, NW6 1PT.
KENT, Mr. Charles Michael, BSc FCA *1981;* Lemara, Trewince Lane, Grampound Road, TRURO, TR2 4DX.
KENT, Mrs. Cheryl, BA ACA *1994;* 91 King Georges Avenue, WATFORD, WD18 7QE.
KENT, Mr. Christopher, BA(Hons) ACA *2006;* 14 Hill Top, Earl Shilton, LEICESTER, LE9 7DP.
KENT, Mr. Christopher Kenneth, FCA *1994;* The Stables Upton Road, Clevelode, MALVERN, WORCESTERSHIRE, WR13 6PB.
KENT, Mr. Christopher Mark, BSc ACA *1987;* 53 Saddleback Drive, DAYBORO, QLD 4521, AUSTRALIA.
•KENT, Mr. Christopher Thomas, BA FCA *1970;* Christopher Kent, 23 Rivergreen Crescent, Bramcote, NOTTINGHAM, NG9 3ET.
KENT, Mr. David, BA ACA *1992;* Bures Cottage, Church Lane, Great Kimble, AYLESBURY, BUCKINGHAMSHIRE, HP17 9TH.
KENT, Mr. David Bellworthy, FCA *1963;* 101 Old Hall Lane, Fallowfield, MANCHESTER, M14 6HL. (Life Member)
KENT, Mr. David James, FCA *1968;* 1 The Yews, Nether End, Great Dalby, MELTON MOWBRAY, LEICESTERSHIRE, LE14 2EH.
KENT, Mr. David Trevor, FCA *1959;* Yamal, Keswick Road, Witley, GODALMING, SURREY, GU8 5QF.
KENT, Mr. Douglas Goodman, FCA *1949;* 29 Caraway Road, Fulbourn, CAMBRIDGE, CB21 5DU. (Life Member)
KENT, Mrs. Fiona, BSc ACA *1990;* Bures, Church Lane, Great Kimble, AYLESBURY, BUCKINGHAMSHIRE, HP17 9TH.
KENT, Mr. Frederick Kenneth, FCA *1956;* 1 Alder Street, ORANGEVILLE L9W 5A3, ON, CANADA. (Life Member)
KENT, Mr. Graham John, BSc FCA *1977;* 32 Cranley Gardens, Muswell Hill, LONDON, N10 3AP.
KENT, Mr. Ian Matthew, MEng ACA *2004;* 33 rue de la Forêt, L-5320 CONTERN, LUXEMBOURG.
KENT, Mrs. Imogen Christine, ACA *2009;* 37 Raglan Road, Knaphill, WOKING, SURREY, GU21 2AR.
KENT, Mrs. Joanna Edwina, BA ACA *1983;* House 278, Road 3503 Area 935, East Riffa, MANAMA, BAHRAIN.
KENT, Mrs. Jodi, MSci ACA *2006;* 2 Beech Court, Long Stratton, NORWICH, NR15 2WY.
KENT, Mr. John Beaumont, FCA *1958;* 101 Parkstone Avenue, HORNCHURCH, RM11 3LP. (Life Member)
KENT, Mr. John Frederick, FCA *1974;* Unit 1402, 70 Lorimer Street, DOCKLANDS, VIC 3008, AUSTRALIA.
•KENT, Mr. John Richard, BSc ACA *1997;* Chestnut Corner, 27A Montague Road, BERKHAMSTED, HERTFORDSHIRE, HP4 3DS.
KENT, Ms. Judith Amanda, MA ACA ATII *1989;* (Tax Fac), 26 Kingsway, GERRARDS CROSS, SL9 8NT.
KENT, Miss. Louisa Beatrice, BSc ACA *2007;* 46 Bruton Place, LONDON, W1J 6PD.
KENT, Mrs. Lucinda Anne, BA ACA *1996;* 27a Montague Road, BERKHAMSTED, HERTFORDSHIRE, HP4 3DS.
•KENT, Mr. Martyn Robert, ACA CTA *2008;* (Tax Fac), DRE & Co, 7 Lower Brook Street, OSWESTRY, SY11 2HG. See also DRE & Co (Knighton) Limited, D R E & Co (Audit) Limited
•KENT, Mr. Michael Alan, FCA *1972;* (Tax Fac), 10 Friars Walk, DUNSTABLE, BEDFORDSHIRE, LU6 3JA.
KENT, Mr. Michael William Bates, ACA *1985;* 36 Moorside Lane, Holbrook, BELPER, DE56 0TW.
KENT, Mr. Patrick Anthony, BSc(Hons) ACA *1991;* Simons Group Ltd, 991 Doddington Road, LINCOLN, LN6 3AA.
KENT, Mr. Peter, FCA *1971;* (Tax Fac), 75 Glenholt Road, PLYMOUTH, PL6 7JD.
KENT, Mr. Richard Gordon, FCA *1973;* PO Box 22707, DUBAI, UNITED ARAB EMIRATES.
KENT, Mr. Richard John, BA ACA *1990;* 1 Roopers, Speldhurst, TUNBRIDGE WELLS, TN3 0QL.
KENT, Mr. Robert Arthur, FCA *1967;* 21 Pyle Rd, Bishopston, SWANSEA, SA3 3HH.
•KENT, Mr. Ronald Victor, FCA *1961;* (Tax Fac), R.V. Kent, Philpot House, Station Road, RAYLEIGH, SS6 7HH.
KENT, Mr. Russell Peter, BEng ACA *2000;* Bay House Bay View Road, Port St. Mary, ISLE OF MAN, IM9 5AQ.
KENT, Mr. Sean Mark, MBA FCA CTA *1988;* 10 Cleves Way, Old Costessey, NORWICH, NR8 5EN.
•KENT, Mr. Simon Andrew David, FCA *1968;* (Tax Fac), Kent & Co Ltd, Evans House, 107 Marsh Road, PINNER, MIDDLESEX, HA5 5PA.
KENT, Mr. Simon Mark, BA CA FCA CPA *1994;* with PricewaterhouseCoopers, Brunswick House, Suite 300, 44 Chipman Hill, SAINT JOHN E2L 4B9, NB CANADA.
•KENT, Mr. Stephen Michael, BA ACA *1988;* (Tax Fac), Stephen Kent & Company Ltd, 456 Gower Road, Killay, SWANSEA, SA2 7AL.
KENT, Miss. Susan Catherine, BA ACA *1990;* 18 Portmore Park Road, WEYBRIDGE, KT13 8ES.
KENT, Ms. Susan Hazel, ACA *1992;* Lautze & Lautze, 303 Second Street, Suite 950, SAN FRANCISCO, CA 94107, UNITED STATES.
KENT, Miss. Tara Claire, BSc ACA *1996;* 77 Beaconsfield Road, SURBITON, SURREY, KT5 9AW.
KENT-PHILLIPS, Mrs. Lynne, LLB ACA *1985;* 87 Manchuria Road, LONDON, SW11 6AF.
KENT-TAYLOR, Mr. Stephen John, BSc ACA *2000;* University of Cambridge Research Accounting, 16 Mill Lane, CAMBRIDGE, CB2 1SB.
KENT-WOOLSEY, Miss. Helen Elizabeth, ACA CTA *2002;* with Stacey & Partners, 87 Whiting Street, BURY ST. EDMUNDS, SUFFOLK, IP33 1PD.
•KENTAS, Mr. Michael, FCA *1986;* (Tax Fac), Michael Kentas & Co Ltd, 72 Wimpole Street, LONDON, W1G 9RP.
KENTH, Mrs. Smita, BA ACA *2007;* 25 Artemis Close, GRAVESEND, DA12 2QW.
KENTISBEER, Mr. Mark Richard, BSc ACA *1992;* 27 Alexandra Road, South Woodford, LONDON, E18 1PZ.
•KENTISH, Mr. Alan Roy, BSc ACA *1992;* Montagu Pavilion, 8-10 Queenway, PO Box 1188, GIBRALTAR, GIBRALTAR.
KENTISH, Mr. Micheal James, BA ACA *1993;* Flat 401 Royle Building, 31 Wenlock Road, LONDON, N1 7SH.
KENTISH, Ms. Pamela Louise, BA ACA *2005;* 9 The Withies, LEATHERHEAD, SURREY, KT22 7EY.
•KENTISH, Mr. Steven, BA FCA *1993;* PricewaterhouseCoopers LLP, Cornwall Court, 19 Cornwall Street, BIRMINGHAM, B3 2DT. See also PricewaterhouseCoopers
•KENTON, Mr. Howard Neil, FCA FCCA FTII *1968;* (Tax Fac), Howard N. Kenton, 79 College Road, HARROW, MIDDLESEX, HA1 1BD.
KENWARD, Mr. James Tristan, BCom ACA *1997;* 8 Valley Road, WELLINGTON POINT, QLD 4160, AUSTRALIA.
KENWARD, Mr. Michael Charles, BSc ACA *1995;* 17 Valenciennes Road, SITTINGBOURNE, ME10 1EN.
KENWAY-SMITH, Miss. Wendy Alison, BA FCA *1983;* 4 Southfield, Rennington, ALNWICK, NORTHUMBERLAND, NE66 3SH.
•KENWELL, Mr. Robert, BSc FCA CTA *1981;* (Tax Fac), Pritchett & Co Limited, 16 Wynnstay Road, COLWYN BAY, CONWY, LL29 8NB.
KENWORTHY, Mr. Bradley, ACA CA(AUS) *2008;* Flat 3 Beckhaven House, 68 Gilbert Road, LONDON, SE11 4NL.
KENWORTHY, Mr. Eric, FCA *1954;* 46 Lane Head Lane, Kirkburton, HUDDERSFIELD, HD8 0SQ. (Life Member)
KENWORTHY, Mr. Glenn Nigel, BSc FCA *1976;* Grey Gables, 44 South St., Middleton-On-The-Wolds, DRIFFIELD, YO25 9UB.
KENWORTHY, Mr. Lawrence James, BSc ACA *1994;* Lloyds TSB Bank Plc, 10 Gresham Street, LONDON, EC2V 7AE.
KENWORTHY, Mr. Robert, FCA *1971;* Homewood, Carlton Rd, South Park, GODSTONE, RH9 8LE.
KENWORTHY, Mr. Roger Ashley, MA FCA *1974;* 8 Crodingley, Thongsbridge, HOLMFIRTH, HD9 3TZ.
KENWRIGHT, Mr. Joseph Arthur, FCA *1951;* 12 Eastmoor Close, Foley Road East, Streetly, SUTTON COLDFIELD, WEST MIDLANDS, B74 3JS. (Life Member)
KENYON, Mr. Alan, FCA *1965;* 2 Dunedin Rd, Greenmount, BURY, BL8 4EX. (Life Member)
KENYON, Mr. Andrew, BSc(Hons) ACA *2011;* 27a The Links, HYDE, CHESHIRE, SK14 4GR.
KENYON, Mr. Andrew Graham, BSc ACA *1991;* 16 Paddock Close, Bidford-on-Avon, ALCESTER, B50 4PJ.
KENYON, Mr. Christopher Anthony, BSc FCA *1974;* Hopyards Cottage, Flat Lane, Kelsall, TARPORLEY, CW6 0PU.
KENYON, Mrs. Clare Louise, BSc FCA *1992;* Ashlish, 127 Cronk Liauyr, Douglas, ISLE OF MAN, IM2 5LT.
KENYON, Mr. David Richard, MA ACA *2001;* 12 Southville Road, THAMES DITTON, KT7 0UL.
KENYON, Mr. Henry James, MSc FCA *1976;* Myrtle Cottage, Harris Lane, Abbots Leigh, BRISTOL, BS8 3RZ.
KENYON, Mr. Ian Peter, BSc ACA *1987;* 44 Warren Road, GUILDFORD, GU1 2HE.
KENYON, Mr. Ian Stuart, ACA *1995;* 23 Picton Close, CAMBERLEY, GU15 1QT.
KENYON, Mr. John Leonard, FCA *1963;* 25 Rossway, NORTHWOOD, MIDDLESEX, HA6 3HU.
•KENYON, Mrs. Laura Mary, BA ACA *2001;* Laura Kenyon Associates, 12 Southville Road, THAMES DITTON, SURREY, KT7 0UL. See also Laura Kenyon & Associates
KENYON, Mr. Michael Adrian O'Brien, FCA *1975;* 9 Gloucester Mews, BRIGHTON, BN1 4BW.
•KENYON, Mr. Michael James, FCA *1971;* (Tax Fac), Michael James Kenyon, Ashview, 88A Knutsford Road, WILMSLOW, SK9 6JD. See also CLK Payrolls Limited
KENYON, Mr. Michael John, FCA *1971;* 298 Wigan Lane, WIGAN, WN1 2RW.
KENYON, Mr. Michael John, BA FCA *1995;* Ashlish, 127 Cronk Liauyr, Tromode Park, Douglas, ISLE OF MAN, IM2 5LT.
KENYON, Mr. Neil James, BSc(Econ) ACA *2000;* British Museum Co Ltd, 38 Russell Square, LONDON, WC1B 3QQ.
KENYON, Mr. Paul, BA ACA *2005;* 42 Warwick Close, BURY, BL8 1RT.
KENYON, Mr. Peter Graham, FCA *1973;* 9 Alder Grove, The Park, BUXTON, SK17 6TJ.
KENYON, Mr. Peter Wood, BSc FCA *1972;* 17 Holt Park Avenue, LEEDS, LS16 7RA. (Life Member)
KENYON, Mr. Raymond John, FCA *1953;* Honeywood, Middlewich Road, Lower Peover, KNUTSFORD, WA16 9PU. (Life Member)
KENYON, Mr. Richard David, BSc ACA *1989;* 191 Moor Green Lane, Moseley, BIRMINGHAM, B13 8NT.
•KENYON, Mr. Richard James, BA FCA *1998;* Auker Rhodes Professional Services LLP, Sapphire House, Albion Road, Greengates, BRADFORD, WEST YORKSHIRE BD10 9TQ. See also Auker Rhodes Tax & Financial Planning Ltd
•KENYON, Mr. Ronald James, FCA *1975;* (Tax Fac), 30 Wordsworth Street, PENRITH, CUMBRIA, CA11 7QY.
KENYON, Mrs. Sarah Ann, BA ACA *1994;* 44 Clarence Road, ST. ALBANS, AL1 4NG.
KENYON, Mr. Simon Philip, WP FCA *1981;* Heckenkirschenweg 6, Kirchheim, 85551 MUNICH, GERMANY.
KENYON, Mr. Stephen Bernard, MBA ACA *1991;* 6 Steadings Rise, Mere, KNUTSFORD, CHESHIRE, WA16 0WB.
•KENYON, Mr. William, BA ACA *1993;* 44 Clarence Road, ST. ALBANS, AL1 4NG. See also PricewaterhouseCoopers LLP
KEOGAN, Mr. Andrew, ACA CISA MIIA *1998;* 289 Perrysfield Road Cheshunt, WALTHAM CROSS, HERTFORDSHIRE, EN8 0TP.
KEOGAN, Mr. Anthony Gerard, BA ACA *1988;* (Tax Fac), 10 Parkgate, LONDON, SE3 9XB.
KEOGH, Mrs. Angela Jeanette, MA ACA *1999;* Bird & Bird Llp, 15 Fetter Lane, LONDON, EC4A 1JP.
KEOGH, Miss. Anna Kathryn, BA ACA *2000;* 47 Brownside Road, BURNLEY, BB10 3JS.
KEOGH, Mr. Anthony James, FCA *1970;* 9 Acadia Street, DOLLARD DES ORMEAUX H9A 1T5, QUE, CANADA.
KEOGH, Mr. Jason Mark, BSc ACA *2001;* Syfer Technology Limited, Old Stoke Road, Arminghall, NORWICH, NORFOLK, NR14 8SQ.
KEOGH, Mr. John Francis, FCA FCMA *1954;* 2 St Margarets Close, Castle Park Road, DALKEY, COUNTY DUBLIN, IRELAND. (Life Member)
KEOGH, Mr. Mark William, BEng ACA *1991;* Norfolk House, 28 Kidmore Road, Caversham, READING, RG4 7LU.
KEOGH, Mr. Simon Neil David, FCA *1973;* The Old Well House, The Coombe, BETCHWORTH, RH3 7BT.
KEOHANE, Mr. Timothy Thomas, MA FCA *1977;* 33 Waverley Avenue, TWICKENHAM, TW2 6DQ.
KEONG, Mr. Choon Keat, FCA *1969;* 6 Jalan Mihrab Empat U8/12D Bukit Jelutong, 40150 SHAH ALAM, MALAYSIA.
KEONG, Miss. Chwee Lyn, ACA CA(AUS) *2009;* 114 MacMillan Way, LONDON, SW17 6AU.
KEOUGH, Mr. Raymond Guy Gervase, BA ACA *2000;* 122 Whalley Road, Langho, BLACKBURN, BB6 8DD.
KEOWN, Mrs. Linda Margaret, BA ACA *1983;* 1 Tudor Road, New Barnet, BARNET, EN5 5NL.
•KEOWN, Mr. Philip Robert, BA ACA *1983;* 30 Finsbury Square, LONDON, EC2P 2YU.
KER, Mr. Ah Ann, FCA *1985;* 13 Blamey Street, Bentleigh East, MELBOURNE, VIC 3165, AUSTRALIA.
KER, Mr. Charles Philip Robert, ACA *2011;* Flat 3, Honeysuckle Court, Buckhurst Way, BUCKHURST HILL, ESSEX, IG9 6HD.
KER, Miss. Jane Lucy, BA FCA *1986;* Littlecote, Petworth Road, Wormley, GODALMING, GU8 5TR.
KERAI, Mr. Anil Naran, BA ACA *2005;* 107 Portland Crescent, STANMORE, MIDDLESEX, HA7 1LY.
KERAI, Mr. Harish Devji, BA(Hons) ACA *2002;* 39 Ledway Drive, WEMBLEY, MIDDLESEX, HA9 9TH.
KERAI, Mr. Yameen, BSc ACA *1983;* 180-B Shabbirabad, KARACHI 00000, PAKISTAN.
KERBY, Mr. Christopher David, FCA *1984;* 80 Park Road, BURGESS HILL, RH15 8HG.

KERBY, Mr. Michael Hugh, FCA *1975;* Bernina, Northbrook Avenue, WINCHESTER, HAMPSHIRE, SO23 0JW.
KERBY, Mr. Nigel Paul, BSc FCA *1982;* European Bank for, Reconstruction & Development, One Exchange Square, LONDON, EC2A 2JN.
•KERBY, Mr. Stephen Michael, FCA *1981;* (Tax Fac), Nicholsons, Newland House, The Point, Weaver Road, LINCOLN, LN6 3QN.
KEREMIDJIAN, Mr. Andricos-Antranic, ACA *1986;* 10 Lycimachou Street, 2328 LAKATAMIA, CYPRUS.
KEREVAN, Mr. Austin James, FCA *1959;* Eastfield Lodge, Eastfield Lane, Whitchurch on Thames, READING, RG8 7EJ. (Life Member)
KERFOOT, Mr. Mark Jonathan, BSc ACA *1997;* 27 Mossdale Avenue, BOLTON, BL1 5YA.
KERFOOT, Mr. Matthew John, BSc(Hons) ACA *2003;* Baker Hughes, Via Di Vittorio 41, 20068 PESCHIERA BORROMEO, ITALY.
KERIGAN, Mr. Stephen Paul, BA ACA *1990;* Thomson Reuters Thomson Reuters Building, 30 South Colonnade, LONDON, E14 5EP.
KERIN, Mrs. Fiona Ann, ACA *1991; (ACA Ireland 1986);* (Tax Fac), F A Kerin, 92 Woodgrange Avenue, North Finchley, LONDON, N12 0PS.
KERKHAM, Mr. Giles William Robin, MSc ACA DChA *2004;* with Larking Gowen, King Street House, 15 Upper King Street, NORWICH, NR3 1RB.
KERLEY, Miss. Annabel Kay, BA ACA *2005;* 9 Trelawn Road, LONDON, SW2 1DH.
KERLEY, Mrs. Fiona Jane, BA ACA *2006;* Les Pres, La Verte Rue, Trinity, JERSEY, JE3 5EA.
KERLEY, Mr. Giles Hayden, BSc(Hons) ACA *2005;* Amboise Kingsley Avenue, La Grande Route de la Cote St. Clement, JERSEY, JE2 6PH.
KERMALLI, Mr. Arif, BSc ACA *1997;* 19 Fairmead Close, Heston, HOUNSLOW, TW5 9JB.
KERMATH, Mr. Brian, BCom ACA *2000;* 7 Hillview Court, Halbeath, DUNFERMLINE, FIFE, KY12 0WP.
KERMER, Mr. Michael, BA ACA *1982;* 20 Malwood Road, LONDON, SW12 8EN.
KERMODE, Mr. Andrew James, BSc ACA *2001;* 7 Third Avenue, Douglas, ISLE OF MAN, IM2 6AL.
KERMODE, Mr. Neil William, FCA *1954;* 4 Westcombe, Alphington, EXETER, EX2 8GH. (Life Member)
KERNAGHAN, Mr. Paul Stephen, BA FCA *1988;* L9 2 Market Street, SYDNEY, NSW 2000, AUSTRALIA.
KERNAN, Mr. Michael Patrick, FCA *1976;* 49 The Lloyds, Kesgrave, IPSWICH, IP5 2WH.
KERNER, Mr. Stuart Melvyn, FCA *1971;* 3 St Hildas Mount, 82 Marsh Lane, Mill Hill, LONDON, NW7 4NX.
KERNICK, Mr. Stephen Milward, FCA *1966;* 26 Longstomps Avenue, CHELMSFORD, CM2 9LA.
KERNON, Mr. Arthur Pat, FCA *1947;* Urbanisation Sansofe, Puerto 82, Calle La Honduria, Puerto de Santiago, 38683 TENERIFE, CANARY ISLANDS SPAIN. (Life Member)
•KERNON, Mr. Barry Patrick Waring, FCA *1971;* (Tax Fac), with H W Fisher & Company Limited, Acre House, 11/15 William Road, LONDON, NW1 3ER.
KERNOT, Mrs. Pauline Margaret, BA FCA *1994;* Mill House Hotel, 4 Dean Street Stewarton, KILMARNOCK, AYRSHIRE, KA3 5EQ.
KERNTHALER, Mr. Jeremy, MA BA ACA *2004;* 32 Falcon Way, LONDON, E14 9UP.
KERR, Mr. Alastair John, FCA *1968;* 22 Threlfall Drive, Habberley Coppice, BEWDLEY, DY12 1HU.
•KERR, Mrs. Alison Jane, BSc FCA *1991;* Albert Goodman LLP, Mary Street House, Mary Street, TAUNTON, TA1 3NW.
KERR, Mr. Andrew, BA ACA *1992;* 42 Beaumont Avenue, ST. ALBANS, HERTFORDSHIRE, AL1 4TJ.
KERR, Mr. Andrew James, ACA *2009;* 48 Flax House, Navigation Walk, LEEDS, LS10 1JH.
KERR, Mr. Andrew Stewart, MA ACA *2005;* 31 Grosvenor Drive, WHITLEY BAY, TYNE AND WEAR, NE26 2JR.
•KERR, Mr. Andrew Thomas, FCA *1975;* (Tax Fac), with Pearson May, 5 Wicker Hill, TROWBRIDGE, BA14 8JS.
KERR, Mr. Andrew Warren, ACA FMAAT *2002;* 114 Southwood Road, LONDON, SE9 3QS.
KERR, Mr. Anthony Robert, FCA *1970;* 7 Papeley Meadow, Barrow, BURY ST.EDMUNDS, IP29 5DL.
KERR, Mr. Brian Joseph, FCA *1958;* 1241 Mathers Ave, WEST VANCOUVER V7T 2G4, BC, CANADA. (Life Member)
KERR, Mr. Charles, ACA *2001;* 5 Brooks Road, LONDON, W4 3BJ.
KERR, Mrs. Clare Elizabeth, BA(Hons) ACA *2000;* Portlands Cudham Lane South, Knockholt, SEVENOAKS, KENT, TN14 7PA.
KERR, Mr. Colin Aubrey, BA ACA *1992;* Level 23, 9 Castlereagh Street, SYDNEY, NSW 2000, AUSTRALIA.
KERR, Mr. Derek Johnstone, ACA *2009;* 25c Osborne Avenue, NEWCASTLE UPON TYNE, NE2 1JR.
KERR, Mr. Donald Macaulay, FCA *1973;* Woolhampton Court, Woolhampton Hill, Woolhampton, READING, RG7 5ST.
KERR, Mrs. Elizabeth Mary, LLB FCA *1989;* The Limes, 10 Front Street, Gaulby, LEICESTER, LE7 9BW.
KERR, Ms. Fiona Mary, BSc ACA *2008;* Suite 3.1.4 Universal Square, Devonshire Street, MANCHESTER, M12 6JH.
KERR, Mr. Giles Francis Bertram, BSc ACA *1985;* The Old Vicarage, Lower Green, Towersey, THAME, OXFORDSHIRE, OX9 3QW.
KERR, Mr. Henry, BSc ACA *1986;* Avalon Investment Services Ltd, 2 Market Place, TETBURY, GLOUCESTERSHIRE, GL8 8DA.
KERR, Mr. Ian Nigel, MA ACA *1981;* Apoquindo 3650, Piso 5, Las Condes, SANTIAGO, CHILE.
•KERR, Mr. James Fergus, LLB ACA *1991;* Springfords LLP, Dundas House, Westfield Park, Eskbank, DALKEITH, MIDLOTHIAN EH22 3FB.
KERR, Mr. James Matthew, BSc ACA *2005;* 153 Park Street, BRIDGEND, MID GLAMORGAN, CF31 4BB.
KERR, Miss. Jenni Louise, ACA *2009;* 6 Martindale Close, BRADFORD, WEST YORKSHIRE, BD2 3SR.
KERR, Miss. Jennifer Susan Victoria, BEng ACA *2001;* Flat 216 Waterman Building, 14 Westferry Road, LONDON, E14 8NG.
KERR, Mr. John, FCA *1974;* Conjuncto Latina 46, Dona Pepe 2, 03170, ROJALES, ALICANTE, SPAIN.
•KERR, Mr. John Francis Edward, FCA *1958;* (Tax Fac), JKCA Business Support Ltd, 375 Eaton Road, West Derby, LIVERPOOL, L12 2AH.
•KERR, Mr. John Malcolm Robert Sinclair, FCA CTA *1964;* J.M. Kerr & Co, 26 Spencer Avenue, LEEK, STAFFORDSHIRE, ST13 5PA.
KERR, Mr. John Walter, FCA *1972;* 839 Oak Drive, Kyalami Estate, Kyalami, MIDRAND, GAUTENG, SOUTH AFRICA.
KERR, Mr. Kenneth Scott, LLB ACA *1993;* KHI, Parkview Square, 600 North Bridge Road, 13-09, SINGAPORE 188778, SINGAPORE.
KERR, Mrs. Lisa Martine, BCom ACA MSI *2002;* 162 Church Green, SHOREHAM-BY-SEA, WEST SUSSEX, BN43 6JW.
•KERR, Mrs. Lorraine, BA ACA *1992;* Lorraine Kerr ACA, 2 Tompkins Close, Aston Clinton, AYLESBURY, BUCKINGHAMSHIRE, HP22 5WH.
KERR, Mr. Luke Barnaby, BA(Hons) ACA CFA *2001;* Portlands Cudham Lane South, Knockholt, SEVENOAKS, KENT, TN14 7PA.
KERR, Mr. Malcolm Alastair, BA FCA *1974;* Churerstrasse 120, CH-8808 PFAFFIKON, SWITZERLAND.
KERR, Mr. Michael John, FCA *1955;* Lisangle, 72 West Street, STOKE-SUB-HAMDON, TA14 6QL. (Life Member)
KERR, Mr. Michael Walter, FCA *1972;* PO Box 554 High Road, KINGS LANGLEY, HERTFORDSHIRE, WD4 4AY.
KERR, Mr. Milo John, MA FCA *1974;* The Culver House, Dean Road, NEWNHAM, GL14 1HH.
KERR, Miss. Nicola Claire, MSc BSc ACA *2004;* 122 Crestway, LONDON, SW15 5DD.
•KERR, Miss. Nicola Jane, BSc ACA *1987;* Deloitte LLP, Athene Place, 66 Shoe Lane, LONDON, EC4A 3BQ. See also Deloitte & Touche LLP
KERR, Mr. Paul Jonathan, ACA *1981;* 3rd Floor Portland House, Bressenden Place, LONDON, SW1E 5BH.
KERR, Mr. Peter Dennis, ACA CA(NZ) *2010;* 27 Fraser Street, LONDON, W4 2DA.
KERR, Mr. Peter James Keen, BSc ACA *1980;* 12 The Furrows, WALTON-ON-THAMES, KT12 3JG.
KERR, Mrs. Rachel Agnes Sarah, LLB ACA *2003;* 121 Carrick Knowe Drive, EDINBURGH, EH12 7EL.
KERR, Mr. Raymond Alexander, FCA *1970;* Fern Bank, Croft Road, Goring, READING, BERKSHIRE, RG8 9ES. (Life Member)
•KERR, Mr. Robert, BSc FCA *1981;* Robert Kerr, Doonane, Ingleby Road, Stanton-by-Bridge, DERBY, DE73 7HT.
KERR, Mr. Robert Andrew, BSc FCA *1976;* Dalkey, Bellingdon, CHESHAM, HP5 2XU.
KERR, Mr. Robert Gwilym, FCA *1970;* c/o PT Consulting Svs Indonesia, 35th Floor Wisma GKBI, 28 Jl Jend Sudirman, JAKARTA, 10210, INDONESIA.
KERR, Mr. Tim, ACA CA(NZ) *2009;* 20 Burntwood Lane, LONDON, SW17 0JZ.
•KERR, Mr. William John Everitt, BSc ACA *1989;* Everitt Kerr & Co, 2 Crossways Business Centre, Bicester Road, Kingswood, AYLESBURY, BUCKINGHAMSHIRE HP18 0RA.
KERR, Mr. William Lancelot, BSc FCA *1985;* Vitec Group Plc, 1 Wheatfield Way, KINGSTON UPON THAMES, SURREY, KT1 2TU.
KERR, Mr. William Walter Raleigh, MA ACA *1979;* Lloyd George Management, 3808 One Exchange Square, CENTRAL, Hong Kong Island, HONG KONG SAR.
KERRANE, Mr. James Patrick, BA ACA *2004;* 12 Sudbury Court Road, HARROW, HA1 3SH.
KERRICH, Mr. Jeremy Adrian Ambrose, MA FCA *1961;* Cheriton, Viggory Lane, Horsell, WOKING, GU21 4XH. (Life Member)
KERRIDGE, Mr. Ian, BSc FCA *1975;* 5 Kirk Brae, Tarves, ELLON, AB41 7JU.
KERRIDGE, Mr. Michael, BA ACA *1991;* with PricewaterhouseCoopers LLP, 1 Embankment Place, LONDON, WC2N 6RH.
•KERRIDGE, Mr. Michael John, BSc FCA *1975;* (Tax Fac), M J Kerridge & Co, Unit 8, Midshires House, Midshires Business Park, Smeaton Close, AYLESBURY BUCKINGHAMSHIRE HP19 8HL.
•KERRIDGE, Mr. Richard, FCA *1972;* R.Kerridge, 32 Queens Road, READING, RG1 4AU.
KERRIGAN, Mrs. Joanne Margaret, BA ACA *1994;* Avenue de Beaulieu 4, 1180 ROLLE, SWITZERLAND.
KERRIGAN, Mr. Michael, MA ACA *1981;* The Haberdashers Company, 18 West Smithfield, LONDON, EC1A 9HQ.
KERRIGAN, Mr. Michael, FCA *1957;* Willow Lake, Tathwell, LOUTH, LINCOLNSHIRE, LN11 9SR. (Life Member)
•KERRIGAN, Miss. Victoria Ann, BA ACA *1994;* PricewaterhouseCoopers LLP, 7 More London Riverside, LONDON, SE1 2RT. See also PricewaterhouseCoopers
KERRISON, Mr. David Martin, BA ACA *1991;* 9 Aylmer Drive, Courtown Park, KILCOCK, COUNTY KILDARE, IRELAND. (Life Member)
KERRISON, Mr. Ian, BA ACA *2000;* C N A Insurance Co Ltd, 2 Minster Court, LONDON, EC3R 7BB.
KERRISON, Miss. Jacky, BSc ACA *2001;* Little Prospect Farmhouse, Monxton, ANDOVER, SP11 7DA.
KERRISON, Mr. Michael Arthur, BSc ACA *1988;* Beechbank, Mount Park Avenue, Harrow On The Hill, HARROW, HA1 3JN.
KERRISON, Mr. Michael John, BSc ACA *1991;* Rockport Financial Services Ltd, 6 Durlings Orchard, Ightham, SEVENOAKS, TN15 9HW.
KERRISON, Mrs. Sophie Elizabeth, BA(Hons) ACA *2001;* 11 Whittington Chase, Kingsmead, MILTON KEYNES, MK4 4HL.
KERRUISH, Mr. Mark, Msc BA ACA *2011;* 81 Farndale Drive, GUISBOROUGH, CLEVELAND, TS14 8JX.
•KERRY, Mrs. Adrienne Mary, BSc FCA ATII *1982;* (Tax Fac), PKF (UK) LLP, St Hughs, 23 Newport, LINCOLN, LN1 3DN.
KERRY, Mr. Daniel Bernard, MA BA ACA *2008;* 3 Trenchard Street, LONDON, SE10 9PA.
KERRY, Mr. Jonathan James, BSc(Hons) ACA *2002;* with Wright Vigar Limited, 15 Newland, LINCOLN, LN1 1XG.
KERRY, Mrs. Margaret Joan, MA MSc ACA *1984;* 66 Newmarket Road, Burwell, CAMBRIDGE, CB25 0AE.
KERRY, Mr. Norman Ernest, FCA *1952;* Le Patela, Southlands Grove, BROMLEY, BR1 2DQ. (Life Member)
•KERRY, Mr. Robert, ACA FCCA *2009;* The Jamesons Partnership Limited, 92 Station Road, CLACTON-ON-SEA, CO15 1SG.
•KERRY, Mr. Stephen John, BA FCA *1987;* (Tax Fac), Stephen J. Kerry, 90 Hilltop, TONBRIDGE, TN9 2UP.
•KERRY, Mrs. Susan Margaret, BA FCA *1987;* Pendeford Metal Spinnings Ltd, Neachells Lane, WILLENHALL, WEST MIDLANDS, WV13 3SF.
KERRY, Mr. Timothy James, BA ACA *2003;* 9 Twilley Street, Earlsfield, LONDON, SW18 4NU.
KERSE, Mr. Robert William, MA ACA *2003;* Arcadia Housing Group, Station Road, Worle, WESTON-SUPER-MARE, AVON, BS22 6AP.
KERSE, Mr. Scott McKenzie, ACA *1994;* Private Bag 92 162, AUCKLAND, NEW ZEALAND.
KERSEY, Mrs. Lindsey Claire, BSc ACA ATT *1991;* Carter Dutton, 65-66 St. Mary Street, CHIPPENHAM, SN15 3JF.
KERSEY, Mr. Michael Alexander, BA ACA *2005;* 17 Hazeley Close, Hartley Wintney, HOOK, RG27 8QR.
KERSEY, Mr. Simon Mark, BA(Hons) ACA *2001;* Standard Bank Plc, 20 Gresham Street, LONDON, EC2V 7JE.
KERSHAW, Mr. Adrian, BSc ACA *1999;* P.O. Box 29478, ABU DHABI, UNITED ARAB EMIRATES.
KERSHAW, Mr. Alan Mark, BA ACA *1992;* 59 Kylemore Avenue, LIVERPOOL, L18 4PZ.
KERSHAW, Miss. Angela Jane, ACA *1991;* 1 Priesthouse Lane, Formby, LIVERPOOL, L37 8BB.
KERSHAW, Mr. Brian, FCA *1959;* 144 Seacoast Road, LIMAVADY, COUNTY LONDONDERRY, BT49 9EG. (Life Member)
KERSHAW, Mr. Christopher Graham, ACA *1985;* 53 Ellar Gardens, Menston, ILKLEY, WEST YORKSHIRE, LS29 6QA.
KERSHAW, Mr. Christopher Sydney Sagar, FCA *1980;* LF Europe Ltd, Aire Valley Business Centre, Lawkholme Lane, KEIGHLEY, WEST YORKSHIRE, BD21 3BB.
KERSHAW, Mr. David Wallace, BSc FCA *1980;* Littlewoods Shop Direct Home Shopping Ltd Skyways House, Speke Road Speke, LIVERPOOL, L70 1AB.
KERSHAW, Mrs. Emma, BSc ACA *2001;* with PricewaterhouseCoopers LLP, Hays Galleria, 1 Hays Lane, LONDON, SE1 2RD.
KERSHAW, Mrs. Emma, BSc(Hons) ACA *2001;* 17A Jubilee Avenue, Penketh, WARRINGTON, WA5 2PU.
•KERSHAW, Mr. Francis Edward, ACA *2009;* Whins Associates LLP, 12 Draycott Place, LONDON, SW3 2SB.
KERSHAW, Mr. George, FCA *1954;* Quinta, 8 Audley Crescent, Belgrave Park, CHESTER, CH4 7ET. (Life Member)
KERSHAW, Mrs. Glenda Winifred, BSc ACA ATII *1992;* Glyndhurst, Birmingham Road, Henley In Arden, SOLIHULL, B95 5QD.
KERSHAW, Mr. Ian, FCA *1973;* 18 Mill Gap Road, EASTBOURNE, BN21 2JE.
KERSHAW, Mr. James Allan, MSc BSc ACA *2002;* 9 Downham View, DURSLEY, GLOUCESTERSHIRE, GL11 5GB.
•KERSHAW, Lord John, FCA *1964;* John Kershaw, 38 High View, Hempsted, GLOUCESTER, GL2 5LN.
KERSHAW, Mr. John Nicholas, BSc ACA *1998;* 31 Bucharest Road, LONDON, SW18 3AS.
KERSHAW, Mr. John Philip, FCA *1969;* 34 Oatlands Drive, HARROGATE, HG2 8JR.
KERSHAW, Mr. Jonathan David, BSc ACA *1996;* Derceto Limited, PO Box 6114, AUCKLAND 1141, NEW ZEALAND.
KERSHAW, Mrs. Kim Julia, BA ACA *1992;* 59 Kylemore Avenue, Mossley Hill, LIVERPOOL, L18 4PZ.
•KERSHAW, Mr. Lawrence Simon, FCA *1977;* Brody Lee Kershaw & Co, 2nd Floor, Hanover House, 30-32 Charlotte Street, MANCHESTER, M1 4EX. See also Brody Lee Kershaw Ltd
•KERSHAW, Mr. Michael, ACA *1984;* PKW LLP, Cloth Hall, 150 Drake Street, ROCHDALE, LANCASHIRE, OL16 1PX.
KERSHAW, Mr. Michael John, MBA BSc FCA *1973;* The Shaw Group Inc, 4171 Essen Lane, BATON ROUGE, LA 70809, UNITED STATES.
KERSHAW, Mr. Michael Joseph, MA MSc ACA *1982;* Flat 609 Spice Quay Heights, 32 Shad Thames, LONDON, SE1 2YL.
KERSHAW, Miss. Natalie Jane, BA ACA *2001;* Lucky Hill #4, Farmers Lane, Burnt House Hill, WARWICK WK04, BERMUDA.
KERSHAW, Miss. Natasha Neomi, BEng ACA *2002;* 3 Maltings Court, Alne, YORK, YO61 1RW.
KERSHAW, Mr. Neil, FCA *1977;* Magnesium Elektron, P.O.Box 23, Swinton, MANCHESTER, M27 8DD.
KERSHAW, Mr. Nicolas Paul, BSc ACA *1995;* 67 Wentworth Road, High Barnet, BARNET, EN5 4NZ.
•KERSHAW, Mrs. Patricia Anne, BA ACA *1982;* P.A. Kershaw, Meadowbank, Willington Road, Willington, TARPORLEY, CW6 0ND.
KERSHAW, Mr. Paul, BSc ACA *1980;* Glyndhurst, Birmingham Road, Henley In Arden, SOLIHULL, B95 5QD.
KERSHAW, Mr. Paul Richard, ACA *1980;* Meadowbank, Willington Road, Willington, TARPORLEY, CHESHIRE, CW6 0ND. (Life Member)
KERSHAW, Mrs. Rebecca Elizabeth, BSc ACA *1999;* 9/6 Connaught Place, EDINBURGH, EH6 4RQ.
KERSHAW, Mr. Richard James, BA ACA *2000;* Foxhill House, 10b Foxhill Close, HIGH WYCOMBE, BUCKINGHAMSHIRE, HP13 5BL.
KERSHAW, Mrs. Susan, BA ACA *1992;* Offices of the Vice Chancellor Richmond Building, University of Bradford, Richmond Road, BRADFORD, BD7 1DP.
KERSHEN, Mr. Martin Bernard, FCA *1961;* Gander Beach Hemford, Minsterley, SHREWSBURY, SY5 0HJ.

KHAN, Miss. Shazia, ACA *2008;* 28 Station Crescent, LONDON, N15 5BE.
KHAN, Mr. Sheeraz, ACA *2010;* 95 Studland Road, BIRMINGHAM, B28 8NP.
KHAN, Mrs. Shezba, ACA MAAT *2007;* 119A Connaught Road, LUTON, BEDFORDSHIRE, LU4 8ER.
KHAN, Mr. Shoib Ali, BA ACA *2005;* 38 Leyfield, WORCESTER PARK, KT4 7LR.
KHAN, Mr. Shokat Noor, FCA *1972;* 15411 Lanswick Drive, HOUSTON, TX 77062-3306, UNITED STATES. (Life Member)
KHAN, Mr. Shuja Mohammed, BSc ACA *2004;* Flat 3 Challoner Mansions, Challoner Street, LONDON, W14 9LD.
KHAN, Mr. Sikander Hayat, FCA *1974;* Flat 64, 55 Ebury Street, LONDON, SW1W 0PB.
KHAN, Mr. Sirfraz Mohammed, BA(Hons) FCA *1994;* 35 De Vere Gardens, ILFORD, IG1 3EB.
KHAN, Miss. Sophia, BSc ACA *2002;* 12 St. Abbs Court, Tattenhoe, MILTON KEYNES, MK4 3FW.
KHAN, Mr. Sulman Zafar, BA ACA *2006;* 75 Selsdon Park Road, SOUTH CROYDON, SURREY, CR2 8JG.
KHAN, Mr. Tamoor, BCom ACA MBA *2001;* Land Rover, Banbury Road, Gaydon, WARWICK, CV35 0RR.
KHAN, Mr. Tariq Ahmad, ACA *1983;* BOQUIVAL MANAGEMENT CONSULTANCY, P.O. BOX 124405, DUBAI, UNITED ARAB EMIRATES.
•**KHAN, Mr. Tariq Said, FCA** *1987;* Tarima Consulting Limited, 1a Becket Gardens, WELWYN, HERTFORDSHIRE, AL6 9JE.
KHAN, Miss. Tehmeena Anis, ACA *2005;* 93/II 19th Street, Off Khayaban-e-Rahat, Phase VI DHA, KARACHI 00000, SINDH, PAKISTAN.
KHAN, Mr. Umar, LLB ACA *2004;* 24 Broadlands, KEIGHLEY, BD20 6HX.
KHAN, Mr. Umar Ihtishamul Haq, BCom ACA *2004;* M 62 Phase 1, Defence Housing Authority, LAHORE 54792, PAKISTAN.
KHAN, Miss. Wahida, BSc ACA *2005;* Flat 12 The Grange, 18 Games Road, BARNET, HERTFORDSHIRE, EN4 9HR.
•**KHAN, Mr. Yasar Usman, MA ACA** *1995;* (Tax Fac), Abacus 36 Limited, Cantium House, Railway Approach, WALLINGTON, SURREY, SM6 0DZ.
KHAN, Mr. Yousuf Mohamad, LLB BCom FCA *1952;* 3 Tara Court, DONCASTER EAST, VIC 3108, AUSTRALIA. (Life Member)
KHAN, Mr. Zafar Ali, FCA *1973;* House No 678, Main Double Road, National Police Foundation, Sector E-11/4, ISLAMABAD, PAKISTAN.
KHAN, Mr. Zafar Iqbal, BSc FCA *1995;* Flat 25, Yarrell Mansions, Queen's Club Gardens, LONDON, W14 9TB.
KHAN, Mr. Zafar Mahmud, FCA *1975;* 8707 Westwind Lane, HIGHLANDS RANCH, CO 80126-2604, UNITED STATES.
KHAN, Mr. Zahid, BSc(Hons) ACA *2011;* 24 Collington Avenue, BEXHILL-ON-SEA, EAST SUSSEX, TN39 3QA.
KHAN, Mr. Zahoor Ali, ACA *1980;* Gulf Investment Corporation, PO Box 3402, SAFAT, 13035, KUWAIT.
•**KHAN, Mr. Zia Ullah, BA LLB ACA FCCA CTA** *2007;* Brown & Batts LLP, 25-29 Harper Road, LONDON, SE1 6AW.
KHAN, Mr. Zuhaib Niaz, ACA *2011;* KPMG (Transaction Services), Level 17, 1706 Saba Tower 1, Jumeirah Lakes Towers, Shaikh Zayed Road, DUBAI POB 346038 UNITED ARAB EMIRATES.
•**KHAN-AHMED, Mrs. Saba Mahjabeen, BA(Hons) ACA** *2007;* (Tax Fac), C A Pitts & Co, Omnibus Business Centre, 39-41 North Road, LONDON, N7 9DP.
KHAN-GHAURI, Mr. Abdul Aziz, ACA *2009;* 230 Harrow Road, WEMBLEY, MIDDLESEX, HA9 6QL.
KHAN-JACKSON, Mr. Andrew David, MA ACA *2000;* 136 Westcott Crescent, Ealing, LONDON, W7 1PD.
KHAN-ROKADIA, Mrs. Nazia Anwar, BSc ACA *2006;* 26 Prebendal Drive, Slip End, LUTON, LU1 4JW.
KHANAM, Miss. Sitha, ACA *2010;* Apartment 7, 1 Jubilee Drive, BIRMINGHAM, B20 2SU.
KHANBABI, Miss. Fariyal, BA ACA *1992;* Richmond House, Great North Road, Bell Bar, HATFIELD, HERTFORDSHIRE, AL9 6DA.
KHANDAKER, Mr. Imdad, BSc ACA *2008;* 19 Beechwood Avenue, RUISLIP, HA4 6EG.
•**KHANDERIA, Mr. Kishor Devji, ACA** *1981;* Agutter-Khanderia, First Floor, 85a Great Portland Street, LONDON, W1W 7LT.
•**KHANDERIA, Mr. Vinodray Savchand Narbheram, FCA** *1970;* (Tax Fac), Patel Khanderia & Co, 9 Hitherwood Drive, LONDON, SE19 1XA.
KHANDKE, Mrs. Juliette Kaye, BSc ACA *1992;* 34 Dovehouse Close, Bromham, BEDFORD, MK43 8PS.
KHANDWALA, Mr. Majid A, ACA *1979;* Ernst & Young Ford Rhodes Sidat Hyder, 601 Progressive Plaza, Beaumont Road, KARACHI 75530, SINDH, PAKISTAN.
KHANDWALA, Mr. Mustafa, FCA *1975;* Ernst & Young Ford Rhodes Sidat Hyder, 601 Progressive Plaza, Beaumont Road, KARACHI 75530, SINDH, PAKISTAN.
KHANGURA, Mr. Hardeep, BCom ACA *1998;* British American Tobacco Plc Globe House, 4 Temple Place, LONDON, WC2R 2PG.
KHANGURA, Mrs. Sukhbinder, BA ACA *2004;* 12 Harefield Park, Birkby, HUDDERSFIELD, HD2 2AS.
KHANNA, Mr. Anil Kumar, FCA *1977;* R.K. Khanna & Co, D-41, NDSE Dart II, NEW DELHI 110049, INDIA.
KHANNA, Mr. Anish, ACA *1996;* Portable Components LLC, One Quality Place, EDISON, NJ 08820, UNITED STATES.
KHANNA, Mr. Ashok, BSc FCA *1968;* 60 Pinto Lane, NOVATO, CA 94947, UNITED STATES. (Life Member)
KHANNA, Mr. Ashok Chand, FCA *1971;* 20 Driscoll Drive, FRAMINGHAM, MA 01701-3401, UNITED STATES.
KHANNA, Mr. Atul, ACA *1991;* 131 Pik Uk, CLEARWATER BAY, HONG KONG SAR.
•**KHANNA, Mr. Atul, MA FCA CTA** *1981;* (Tax Fac), Khanna & Co Limited, 6 Vicarage Road, Edgbaston, BIRMINGHAM, B15 3ES.
KHANNA, Mr. Dinesh, BSc ACA *2006;* 1 Wyatt Close, HAYES, UB4 0BT.
KHANNA, Mrs. Dipali, BA ACA *2006;* Woodland, Meadow Close, WILMSLOW, CHESHIRE, SK9 6JN.
KHANNA, Mr. Kanti Chand, BA FCA *1963;* Commonwealth 8/2, Madame Cama Road, MUMBAI 400 020, INDIA.
KHANNA, Mr. Lakshmi Chand, FCA *1965;* Torre Uno Strada Anulare San Felice, 20090 SEGRATE, ITALY.
KHANNA, Mr. Pavan, BSc ACA *1993;* Holmfield House, 17 Knighton Drive, LEICESTER, LE2 3HD.
KHANNA, Mr. Pradeep Chand, FCA *1964;* C/O Qatar Jet Fuel Co, PO Box 22244, DOHA, QATAR.
KHANNA, Mr. Ramesh Kumar, ACA *1980;* 9 Pine Court, 63 Aspen Lane, NORTHOLT, UB5 6XF.
KHANNA, Mr. Romesh Chandra, BCom FCA *1949;* with A.F. Ferguson & Co, Hansalaya, Barakhamba Road, NEW DELHI 110 001, INDIA. (Life Member)
KHANNA, Mr. Subash Chandra, BA BCom FCA *1953;* 7 Rockdale, 16 L.D Ruparel Marg, MUMBAI 400 006, INDIA. (Life Member)
KHANNAK, Mr. Ala Abdul Hamid, FCA *1981;* c/o Abu Dhabi Ports Company, Finance Division, PO Box 54477, ABU DHABI, UNITED ARAB EMIRATES.
KHANOM, Miss. Lippe, MSci ACA *2011;* 619 Bristol Road South, Northfield, BIRMINGHAM, B31 2JS.
KHANOM, Miss. Muhsima, BSc ACA *2009;* 27 Hampton Road, Forest Gate, LONDON, E7 0PD.
KHAO, Ms. Soo Lan, ACA *2005;* Room 1901, World Wide House, 19 Des Voeux Road Central, CENTRAL, HONG KONG ISLAND, HONG KONG SAR.
•**KHAREGAT, Mr. Rustom Shapoor, BSc(Econ) ACA** *1989;* KPMG LLP, 15 Canada Square, LONDON, E14 5GL. See also KPMG Europe LLP
KHARINA, Mrs. Ekaterina, ACA *2009;* 302 Kennet Side, READING, RG1 3DW.
KHASRU, Mr. Mohammed Ameer, FCA *1968;* 235 Walworth Road, LONDON, SE17 1RL.
KHATANI, Miss. Neeta, BSc ACA *2006;* 24 Heming Road, EDGWARE, MIDDLESEX, HA8 9AE.
KHATCHIROVA, Miss. Alana, BA ACA *2011;* Flat 7, 39 Netherhall Gardens, LONDON, NW3 5RL.
KHATIB, Mr. Louay Hamid, BSc ACA *1999;* ARAMARK, 1101 Market Street, PHILADELPHIA, PA 19107, UNITED STATES.
KHATIB, Mr. Zoubeir, ACA *2009;* 4 Volcy Pougnet street, PORT LOUIS, MAURITIUS.
•**KHATIBI, Dr. Iraj, BA(Hons) ACA DIPFM** *2003;* (Tax Fac), Khatibi & Associates, 57 Hemstal Road, West Hampstead, LONDON, NW6 2AD.
KHATKAR, Mr. Charandeep Singh, BA ACA *2006;* Oyster Cottage Elm Close, Farnham Common, SLOUGH, SL2 3NA.
KHATKAR, Mr. Gurinder Singh, MSc ACA *2010;* 25 Sherwood Street, WOLVERHAMPTON, WV1 4RG.
KHATKAR, Mr. Jagdeep Singh, BA ACA *1995;* Oakview, 14 - 20 Overfield Road, BIRMINGHAM, B32 3BA.
KHATRI, Mr. Goind Ram, ACA *2010;* 62 Adamstown Avenue, Lucan Co. Dublin, DUBLIN, COUNTY DUBLIN, IRELAND.
KHATRI, Mr. Issack Abdulla, FCA *1971;* 20 Headstone Gardens, HARROW, HA2 6PR.
KHATRI, Mr. Mehboob Husein, BA ACA *1985;* 49 Old Park Road, LONDON, N13 4RG.
•**KHATRI, Mr. Mukesh Vallabh, BA FCA DChA** *1988;* (Tax Fac), Barcant Beardon LLP, 8 Blackstock Mews, Islington, LONDON, N4 2BT. See also Genial Systems Ltd
KHATRI, Mr. Sameer Osman, BSc ACA *1999;* 276 Chase Side, LONDON, N14 4PR.
KHATTAB, Mr. Basim, BA ACA *1998;* (Tax Fac), 10 Bamford Road, MANCHESTER, M20 2GW.
KHATTAK, Ms. Shireen, ACA *2007;* Flat 4 Cumberland Court, Cumberland Street, LONDON, SW1V 4LR.
KHATTAU, Mr. Nikhil Nirvan, ACA *1991;* 2nd Floor, Kermani Building, Sir P. M. Road Fort, MUMBAI 400001, MAHARASHTRA, INDIA.
KHATUN, Miss. Parbin, BSc ACA *2004;* 13 Royston Gardens, ILFORD, ESSEX, IG1 3SX.
KHATWANI, Mrs. Bina, BSc ACA *2004;* 92 Chamberlayne Avenue, WEMBLEY, MIDDLESEX, HA9 8SS.
KHATWANI, Mr. Lalit, ACA *2008;* 306 Trafalgar House, Rosia Road, GIBRALTAR, GIBRALTAR.
KHAW, Mr. Boon Thong, ACA *1981;* 22 Adrian Crescent, MARKHAM L3P 6Z7, ON, CANADA.
KHAW, Mr. Kenneth Jin Teck, LLB FCA *1997;* 15B Balmoral Road, #05-10 Belmond Green, SINGAPORE 259817, SINGAPORE.
KHAW, Mr. Leonard Teik Gin, BA ACA *1984;* Deloitte Touche Tohmatsu, 35/F One Pacific Place, 88 Queensway, CENTRAL, HONG KONG ISLAND, HONG KONG SAR.
KHAWAJA, Miss. Farida Rashid, ACA *2009;* 124 Harehills Avenue, LEEDS, LS8 4EX.
KHAWAJA, Mr. Haroon, FCA *1993;* P O Box 691777, ORLANDO, FL 32869, UNITED STATES.
KHAWAJA, Mr. Haroun Ahmed, BSc(Econ) ACA *1998;* 3A Third North Street, DHA, Phase 1, KARACHI, PAKISTAN.
KHAWAJA, Mr. Moazzam Raza, ACA FCCA *2010;* 2 Alderley Way, STOCKPORT, CHESHIRE, SK3 8XL.
KHAWAJA, Mr. Mohammad Fasih-Ullisan, FCA *1964;* 69 17th Street, Khyaban e Badban Defene Housing Authority Phase 5, KARACHI 75500, SINDH, PAKISTAN.
KHAWAJA, Mr. Mohammad Naveed, BSc ACA *2005;* P O Box 8827, DUBAI, UNITED ARAB EMIRATES.
KHAWAJA, Mr. Muhammad Sabeeh, FCA *1982;* MODERN PHARMACEUTICAL CO. P.O.BOX 1586, DUBAI, UNITED ARAB EMIRATES.
KHAWAJA, Mr. Zahoor-Ud-Din, BCom FCA *1965;* 4-A /2/1, 13th South Street, DHA Phase 2, KARACHI, PAKISTAN.
KHAWAJA AHMED, Mr. Farhan, ACA FCCA *2009;* HQ2-12B-309, Control Unit - Finance, International Monetary Fund, 1900 Pennsylvania Ave NW, Washington DC, WASHINGTON DC 20006 UNITED STATES.
KHAWAR, Mr. Muhammad Anis, FCA *1966;* PO Box 72571, DUBAI, UNITED ARAB EMIRATES. (Life Member)
KHAYAT, Mr. Anthony Elias, BCom ACA *2003;* 36 Yeomans Way, SUTTON COLDFIELD, WEST MIDLANDS, B75 7TZ.
KHAZOVA, Miss. Katherine, ACA *2010;* Flat 2, Cliffsend House, Cowley Road, LONDON, SW9 6HE.
KHEDERIAN, Mr. Ara-Jean, BSc ACA *1995;* PO Box 94133, Khalidiya, ABU DHABI, UNITED ARAB EMIRATES.
•**KHEDOORY, Mr. Joseph, BCom FCA** *1967;* Joseph Khedoory, Office 110, 250 York Road, Battersea, LONDON, SW11 3SJ.
•**KHELA, Mr. Jasbir Singh, BA(Hons) FCA** *1995;* with PricewaterhouseCoopers LLP, Cornwall Court, 19 Cornwall Street, BIRMINGHAM, B3 2DT.
KHERA, Mr. Mandeep Singh, ACA *2009;* 57 Glencoe Road, COVENTRY, CV3 1GJ.
KHERA, Mr. Meetul, ACA *2009;* 12 Aldridge Avenue, RUISLIP, MIDDLESEX, HA4 9JU.
KHERATI, Mr. Mohammed Fahd, BSc ACA *2008;* Flat 1 2 Collage Terrace, The Grange, St. Peter Port, GUERNSEY, GY1 2PX.
KHETANI, Mr. Anil, ACA *2011;* 43 Tiverton Road, EDGWARE, MIDDLESEX, HA8 6BQ.
KHETANI, Ms. Rakhi, BA ACA *2004;* Ritec International Limited Innova Science Park (Enfield) Ltd 4 Kinetic Crescent, ENFIELD, MIDDLESEX, EN3 7XH.
KHILJI, Mr. Faizullah, FCA *1970;* 23 School Road, Sector F-6/1, ISLAMABAD, PAKISTAN.
KHIMASIA, Mrs. Hema, BA ACA *1999;* 17 Cranbourne Drive, PINNER, MIDDLESEX, HA5 1BX.
KHIMASIA, Mr. Nishil, BCom ACA *1996;* 17 Cranbourne Drive, PINNER, MIDDLESEX, HA5 1BX.
•**KHIMASIA, Mr. Satish Raichand, FCA** *1973;* Satish R. Khimasia, P.O. Box 40214, NAIROBI, KENYA.
KHIMJI, Mrs. Rashmita, BSc ACA *2010;* 274 Tokyngton Avenue, WEMBLEY, MIDDLESEX, HA9 6HH.
KHINDA, Mr. Navdip Singh, BA ACA *1994;* 107 Louisville Road, LONDON, SW17 8RN.
KHINDA, Mr. Ranbir Singh, BA ACA *1992;* 1 Ackers Barn Courtyard, Carrington Lane, MANCHESTER, M31 4AE.
KHIROYA, Mr. Parag, BA ACA *1990;* Dime Ltd, Unit 4, Wintonlea, Monument Way West, WOKING, SURREY GU21 5EN.
KHIYTANI, Dr. Deborah Jane, PhD BSc ACA *2005;* 112 Tudor Drive, KINGSTON UPON THAMES, SURREY, KT2 5QF.
KHO, Mr. Yaw Huat, ACA *1979;* P.O. Box No. 73031, Kowloon Central Post Office, 405 Nathan Road, YAU MA TEI, KOWLOON, HONG KONG SAR.
KHOBOTOV, Mr. Alexander, MS ACA *2011;* Iacovou Patatsou 4 flat 32, CY-2000 NICOSIA, CYPRUS.
KHOKHAR, Mrs. Beate Simone, ACA *2010;* Flat 29 Projection East, Merchants Place, READING, RG1 1EG.
•**KHOKHAR, Mr. Khurshid Alam, FCA** *1975;* (Tax Fac), Khokar Moughal & Jackson, 2 Fitzroy Place, Sauciehall Street, GLASGOW, G3 7RH. See also AKC Limited
•**KHOKHAR, Mr. Mohammad Irshad, FCA** *1971;* (Tax Fac), Khokhar & Co, 85 Shepherds Hill, Highgate, LONDON, N6 5RG.
KHOKHAR, Mr. Nadeem Irshad, BSc ACA *1992;* 67 Topaz Lane, TRUMBULL, CT 06611, UNITED STATES.
KHOKHAR, Mr. Saleem Irshad, BSc ACA *1993;* 85 Shepherds Hill, Highgate, LONDON, N6 5RG.
KHOKHAR, Mr. Sultan Mehmood, ACA *2011;* 29 Projection East House, Merchant's Place, READING, BERKSHIRE, RG1 1EG.
KHONA, Mr. Sachin, ACA *2009;* 9 Northumberland Road, NORTH HARROW, HA27RA.
•**KHONG, Ms. Yee Voon, FCA** *1985;* (Tax Fac), KC Partners, 1st Floor, 76 New Bond Street, LONDON, W1S 1RX.
KHOO, Mr. Beng, MSc FCA *1988; (ACA Ireland 1984);* UBS AG, One Raffles Quay, #50-01 North Tower, SINGAPORE 048583, SINGAPORE.
KHOO, Mrs. Betty, MA ACA *1979;* 9 Bukit Ayer Molek, SINGAPORE 589704, SINGAPORE.
KHOO, Mr. Chee Hong, BSc ACA *1981;* Flat 9th f 11 Jalan Lambak, Wisma Bunga, 86000 KLUANG, Johor, MALAYSIA.
KHOO, Miss. Chuan Ai, ACA *1989;* 3 Jalan 21/29, Taman S.E.A, 46300 PETALING JAYA, Selangor, MALAYSIA.
KHOO, Mr. Chuan Keat, ACA *1978;* with PricewaterhouseCoopers, P.O.Box 10192, Level 10 1 Sentral, Jalan Travers, 50470 KUALA LUMPUR, FEDERAL TERRITORY MALAYSIA.
KHOO, Mr. Chung Wei, ACA *2011;* 25, Jalan Sepah Puteri 5/3, Seri Utama, Kota Damansara, 47810 PETALING JAYA, SELANGOR MALAYSIA.
KHOO, Miss. Daisy Lee Jin, BA ACA *1989;* 4 Hillcrest Road, SINGAPORE 288895, SINGAPORE.
KHOO, Mr. Ee Bin, BA FCA *1986;* Hamworthy Combustion Engineering Ltd, Fleets Corner, POOLE, DORSET, BH17 0LA.
KHOO, Miss. Eileen Ai Yin, BSc ACA *2005;* Morgan Stanley Equity Research, 20 Bank Street Canary Wharf, LONDON, E14 4AD.
KHOO, Mr. Eng Lee, ACA *1983;* Khoo & Associates, 51 Jalan Alpha SS 20/1, Damansara Utama, 47400 PETALING JAYA, Selangor, MALAYSIA.
KHOO, Mr. Glenn Litt Mun, MSc BEng ACA *2002;* 38 Warley Close, BRAINTREE, ESSEX, CM7 9EE.
KHOO, Miss. Irene Gaik Suan, ACA *1982;* 103 Jalan U Thant, 55000 KUALA LUMPUR, FEDERAL TERRITORY, MALAYSIA.
KHOO, Mr. Ken-Min, BA ACA *1998;* Flat 1933 Floor 19 Tower 4, HONG KONG SAR Parkview, 88 Tai Tam Reservoir Road, TAI TAM, HONG KONG ISLAND, HONG KONG SAR.
KHOO, Mr. Kevin Teng Hoe, BCom ACA *2004;* 2 Lanark Place, LONDON, W9 1BS.
KHOO, Mr. Kum Wing, FCA *1967;* 11A Mount Rosie Road, SINGAPORE 308048, SINGAPORE. (Life Member)
KHOO, Miss. Ling Lin, BA ACA *2005;* Room B 8/F Rosedale Garden, 133 Castle Peak Road, TUEN MUN, NEW TERRITORIES, HONG KONG SAR.
KHOO, Mr. Nigel Teng Guan, BA ACA *1998;* 16 Jalan 17/1, Seksyen 17, 46400 Petaling Jaya, PETALING JAYA, SELANGOR, MALAYSIA.
KHOO, Mr. Paul Ghee Leng, ACA *1980;* 15A CITRUS AVENUE, HORNSBY, NSW 2077, AUSTRALIA.

KHOO, Miss. Pek Ling, FCA *1977;* Folks DFK & Co, 12th Floor, Wisma Tun Sambanthan, No. 2 Jalan Sultan Sulaiman, 50000 KUALA LUMPUR, FEDERAL TERRITORY MALAYSIA.
KHOO, Ms. Peng Ean, BA ACA *1997;* 20 Wilby Road, #08-02, The Tessarina, SINGAPORE 276305, SINGAPORE.
KHOO, Mr. Puay Tek, BSc FCA *1984;* Alan Khoo & Co, Lot 15-3 3rd Floor, Block B, Lintas Square, Jalan Lintas, PO Box 12196 88824 KOTA KINABALU SABAH MALAYSIA.
KHOO, Mr. Sai Woon, BA ACA *1986;* 2 Jalan Dato Tahir Dua, 42200 Kapar, KLANG, Selangor, MALAYSIA.
KHOO, Mr. Soo Peng, FCA *1971;* Latour, 15 Jalan 20/11, 46300 PETALING JAYA, Selangor, MALAYSIA. (Life Member)
KHOO, Mr. Swee Hock, ACA *1982;* 3A-01-04 Bungaraya Condo, Saujana ResortSection U2, 40150 SHAH ALAMSelangor, MALAYSIA.
KHOO, Mr. Teng Chuan, BA ACA *1993;* 37 Jalan Wangsa Budi 5, Wangsa Melawati, 53300 KUALA LUMPUR, FEDERAL TERRITORY, MALAYSIA.
KHOO, Mr. Teng Hai, ACA *1980;* 88 Persiaran Wangsa, Baiduri Dua, 47500 SUBANG, SELANGOR, MALAYSIA.
KHOO KAY KIM, Mr. Jeremy, BSc(Hons) ACA *2004;* 45 Jalan ss2/22, Selangor Darul Ehsan, 47300 PETALING JAYA, SELANGOR, MALAYSIA.
KHOR, Miss. Sim Lee, FCA *1977;* 288 Jalan Manggis, 31200, CR0604 CHEMOR, PERAK, MALAYSIA.
KHOR, Mr. Sunny Kang Wei, ACA *2011;* 166A Lower Road, LONDON, SE16 2UN.
KHOR, Miss. Wyn Nee, ACA *2010;* Flat 22, Knowles Wharf, 38 St. Pancras Way, LONDON, NW1 0QW.
KHOR, Mr. Yew Teik, BSc(Econ) ACA *1992;* 112A Jalan Terasek Satu, Bangsar Baru, 59100 KUALA LUMPUR, FEDERAL TERRITORY, MALAYSIA.
•KHOSHABA, Mr. Robert Kambar, BCom FCA *1971;* Khoshaba & Co., 15 Harefield Road, MAIDENHEAD, SL6 5EA.
KHOSLA, Mr. Adarsh Mohanlal, FCA *1980;* 153 Borrows Street, THORNHILL L4J 2W5, ON, CANADA.
•KHOSLA, Mr. Anil, BA ACA *1992;* AKK Consultants Limited, 45 Mymms Drive, Brookmans Park, HATFIELD, AL9 7AE.
KHOSLA, Mr. Anup Singh, MBA FCA *1974;* E-35 Sector 30, NOIDA 201 301, UTTAR PRADESH, INDIA.
KHOSLA, Mr. Chandra Mohan, FCA *1973;* 33 Beechwood Rise, CHISLEHURST, KENT, BR7 6TF.
KHOSLA, Mr. Deepak, BSc ACA *1995;* BG Group, 100 Thames Valley Park Drive, READING, RG6 1PT.
KHOSLA, Mr. Naresh, FCA *1963;* 606 Merton Street, TORONTO M4S 1B3, ON, CANADA.
KHOSLA, Mr. Rakesh Kumur, BSc ACA *1982;* 4 Arlington Drive, NOTTINGHAM, NG3 5EN.
KHOSLA, Mr. Somendra, FCA *1970;* Atma Ram House, C-37 Connaught Place, NEW DELHI 110001, INDIA.
KHOSLA, Ms. Superna, BA ACA *1999;* Flat B, 6 Wedderburn Road, LONDON, NW3 5QE.
KHOSLA, Mr. Vijay, FCA *1968;* D.P. Khosla & Co, Atma Ram House, C-37 Connaught Place, NEW DELHI 110001, INDIA.
KHOSLA, Mr. Vishal, BSc ACA *1994;* 1 Elder Close, SIDCUP, KENT, DA15 8HQ.
KHOURY, Miss. Emma Jane, BA ACA *2010;* 18 Exeter Close, CHIPPENHAM, WILTSHIRE, SN14 0YG.
KHOURY, Mr. Fouad Adib, ACA *1980;* C/O CCC, P.O.Box 11-2254 Riad El-Solh, BEIRUT, 1107-2100, LEBANON.
KHOURY, Mr. Michael Georges, FCA *1965;* Al Noor Co Ltd, PO Box 54607, MANAMA, BAHRAIN.
KHOW, Mr. Teik Wang, ACA *2010;* 8 Springwell Court, Springwell Avenue, Mill End, RICKMANSWORTH, HERTFORDSHIRE, WD3 8DL.
KHOW, Mr. Teik-Fong, MEng ACA *2006;* 98 Merton Avenue, Hillingdon, UXBRIDGE, UB10 9BL.
KHRABROV, Mr. Alexey, ACA *2009;* Building 613, Flat 261, Zelenograd, 124489 MOSCOW, RUSSIAN FEDERATION.
KHRISTOFOROV, Mr. Leonid, BSc ACA CTA *2004;* 10 Dovercourt Gardens, STANMORE, MIDDLESEX, HA7 4SH.
KHROUD, Miss. Pardip Kaur, BA ACA *2007;* Flat 7, 4 Archie Street, LONDON, SE1 3JT.
•KHUBCHANDANI, Mr. Girish, ACA *1982;* 4 The Avenue, WEMBLEY, MIDDLESEX, HA9 9QJ.
KHULLAR, Mr. Ashim, BSc ACA *1994;* 23 Braithwaite Gardens, STANMORE, MIDDLESEX, HA7 2QG.
KHULLAR, Mr. Haqiqat Rai, FCA *1965;* 23 Braithwaite Gardens, STANMORE, HA7 2QG. (Life Member)
•KHULLAR, Mr. Sanjay Kumar, BA FCA *1986;* HWCA Limited, Hamilton Office Park, 31 High View Close, LEICESTER, LEICESTERSHIRE, LE4 9LJ. See also HW Leicester LLP
KHULLAR, Mr. Sumeet, BSc ACA *2004;* 29 Woodford Crescent, PINNER, MIDDLESEX, HA5 3TZ.
•KHUNDKAR, Mr. Fazle Hasan, FCA ATII *1967;* BSS Associates Limited, Gresham House, 116 Sussex Gardens, LONDON, W2 1UA.
KHURANA, Mr. Micky Rajpal Singh, BSc(Econ) ACA *1999;* Second Floor, Diageo Plc Lakeside Drive, Park Royal, LONDON, NW10 7HQ.
KHURANA, Mr. Praveen, FCA *1975;* N-91 Panchshila Park, NEW DELHI 110017, INDIA. (Life Member)
KHURANA, Mr. Rishi, BSc ACA *2010;* 40 The Ridgeway, Kenton, HARROW, MIDDLESEX, HA3 0LL.
•KHURMI, Mr. Hari Nandan, BEng ACA *1995;* 3 Torvill Heights, Wollaton, NOTTINGHAM, NG8 2AU.
KHURMI, Mrs. Reema, LLB ACA *2001;* 106 Buryfield Road, SOLIHULL, WEST MIDLANDS, B91 2DP.
KHUSHAL, Mr. Paresh, BSc ACA *1997;* Calle Aligustre 24, Piso 3 Izquierda, 28039 MADRID, SPAIN.
KHWAJA, Mr. Iqbal Ahmad, FCA *1976;* 214A St.13 Gulzar-E-Quaid, Airport Road, RAWALPINDI, PAKISTAN. (Life Member)
KI YUEN, Mr. Choy-Sien, ACA *1982;* 79 Albert Road, STRATHFIELD, NSW 2135, AUSTRALIA.
KIAIE, Mrs. Erica Jane, ACA *2009;* 31 Strawberrry Dale Avenue, HARROGATE, HG1 5EA.
KIANI, Ms. Asma, BSc ACA *2004;* Global Radio, The Chase, Calcot, READING, RG31 7RB.
KIBBLE, Mr. Christopher John William, BA FCA *1981;* 3888 West 23rd Avenue, VANCOUVER V6S 1K9, BC, CANADA.
KIBBLE, Mrs. Helen Louise, BSc(Hons) ACA *2002;* The Willows, Back Street, Garboldisham, DISS, NORFOLK, IP22 2SD.
KIBBLE, Miss. Josephine Judy, BSc ACA *1990;* 85 Beche Road, CAMBRIDGE, CB5 8HX.
KIBBLE-WHITE, Mr. Roger Duncan, BSc ACA AMCT *1993;* Meadham House, 1 Churchgate Street, HARLOW, ESSEX, CM17 0JS.
KIBBLEWHITE, Miss. Sarah Jean, MA ACA *1989;* Torgyle, 10 Afton Terrace, EDINBURGH, EH5 3NG.
KIBE, Miss. Doris Wanjiku, BA ACA *2001;* 32 Mill Road, TWICKENHAM, TW2 5HA.
KIBEL, Mr. Jonathan, BSc ACA *2008;* 9 Oakwood Avenue, BOREHAMWOOD, HERTFORDSHIRE, WD6 1SP.
•KIBEL, Mr. Simon David, BSc FCA *1968;* (Tax Fac), with Lawrence Grant, 2nd Floor, Hygeia House, 66 College Road, HARROW, MIDDLESEX HA1 1BE.
KIBRIA, Mr. Abu Haider Mohammed, ACA *2011;* KPMG, 18 Smith Street, DARWIN, NT 0800, AUSTRALIA.
KIBUI, Mrs. Phyllis Susan, ACA *1985;* 1925 Brightleaf Court, SILVER SPRING, MD 20902, UNITED STATES.
KICK, Miss. Jennifer Marie, BSc(Hons) ACA *2006;* 401/88 Beach Street Port Melbourne, MELBOURNE, VIC 3207, AUSTRALIA.
KICKS, Mr. Jonathan, BSc ACA CTA *2006;* RSM Tenon, The Poynt Building, 45 Wollaton Street, NOTTINGHAM, NG1 5FW.
KIDD, Mr. Brian John, FCA *1965;* Tangletrees, Chelmsford Road, Hatfield Heath, BISHOP'S STORTFORD, CM22 7BD.
•KIDD, Mr. David John Bohun, BA FCA CTA *1982;* Citroen Wells, Devonshire House, 1 Devonshire Street, LONDON, W1W 5DR.
KIDD, Mrs. Elizabeth Abigail, BSc FCA *1998;* Burford House, 171 Victoria Road, Wargrave, READING, RG10 8AH.
KIDD, Miss. Fiona, BA ACA *1988;* A2 La Sauvagine, Route Des Ardoisieres, 74110 MORZINE, SAVOIE, FRANCE.
KIDD, Mr. Frank, FCA *1937;* c/o Mr & Mrs Pritchard, Socks Orchard, Smallridge, AXMINSTER, DEVON, EX13 7JN. (Life Member)
KIDD, Mr. James Lister, BSc ACA *1991;* Green Tree Barn, Faraday Road, KIRKBY STEPHEN, CUMBRIA, CA17 4QL.
KIDD, Mr. John Christopher Norman, BA ACA *1992;* Cumberland Building Society, Cumberland House, Castle Street, CARLISLE, CA3 8RX.
KIDD, Mr. John Mcauslan, FCA *1966;* Garden Flat, 37 Esplanade Gardens, SCARBOROUGH, NORTH YORKSHIRE, YO11 2AW.
•KIDD, Ms. Linda, MA FCA *1993;* LK Tax & Accountancy Services Ltd, 27 St. Ternans Road, Newtonhill, STONEHAVEN, KINCARDINESHIRE, AB39 3PF.
KIDD, Mr. Michael Herbert, FCA *1962;* Farthings, Woods Lane, Flintham, NEWARK, NG23 5LR. (Life Member)
KIDD, Mr. Michael Robert, BSc ACA *1990;* 28 Rue Puert, L5433 NIEDERDONVEN, LUXEMBOURG.
KIDD, Mr. Reginald Alexander Graeme, FCA *1958;* 33 Maidstone Drive, Wollaton, NOTTINGHAM, NG8 2RF. (Life Member)
•KIDD, Mr. Robert Howard, FCA *1982;* 7 Lucerne Road, BRIGHTON, BN1 6GH.
KIDD, Dr. Robert Thorin, PhD FCA *2000;* Burford House, 171 Victoria Road, Wargrave, READING, RG10 8AH.
•KIDD, Mrs. Sarah Catherine, ACA *1991;* 2 Badinton Lane, Bainton, STAMFORD, PE9 3AU.
KIDD, Mr. Steven James, BSc ACA *1992;* 1 Brooke End, Redbourn, ST. ALBANS, HERTFORDSHIRE, AL3 7GA.
KIDD, Mrs. Susan Caroline, BSc ACA *1988;* 32 Henleaze Avenue, Henleaze, BRISTOL, BS9 4ET.
KIDD, Mr. Timothy Charles, BA ACA *1991;* Wolmer Cottage, Frieth Road, MARLOW, BUCKINGHAMSHIRE, SL7 2JQ.
KIDDELL, Mr. John Edward, FCA *1964;* C/ Arturo Soria 263 B, 28033 MADRID, SPAIN.
KIDDLE, Miss. Annabel, ACA *2010;* Flat H/65 Du Cane Court Balham High Road, LONDON, SW17 7JT.
•KIDDLE, Mr. Arthur David, FCA *1958;* A.D. Kiddle, Newlands Farm, Wickham Bishops, WITHAM, ESSEX, CM8 3JH.
KIDDLE, Mr. George Charles Oliver, FCA *1967;* Flintwood House, Burpham, ARUNDEL, WEST SUSSEX, BN18 9RR.
KIDDLE, Mr. John Patrick, BSc ACA CTA *1998;* 2 Stockbridge Road, Elvetham Heath, FLEET, HAMPSHIRE, GU51 1AR.
KIDDLE, Mr. Peter Michael, BSc ACA *1991;* Unit 01-11 The Grand Duchess, St Patricks Road, SINGAPORE, SINGAPORE.
•KIDDY, Mr. Amin, BSc ACA *1982;* Kiddy & Co, 61 Cowbridge Road East, CARDIFF, CF11 9AE.
KIDDY, Mr. John Patrick, BA ACA *1978;* Chace House, Coopers Lane, POTTERS BAR, EN6 4AG.
KIDDY, Mr. Timothy Olmsted, BSc ACA *1992;* 24 Coulsdon Road, COULSDON, SURREY, CR5 2LA.
•KIDGELL, Mr. James Kenneth, BSc ACA *2001;* Dixon Wilson, 22 Chancery Lane, LONDON, WC2A 1LS.
•KIDGER, Mr. Julian, BA ACA *1993;* AKA Consulting Limited, 6 Esplanade Crescent, SCARBOROUGH, NORTH YORKSHIRE, YO11 2XB.
KIDMAN, Miss. Ann Elizabeth, ACA *1984;* 19 Countess Avenue, WHITLEY BAY, TYNE AND WEAR, NE26 3PN.
KIDMAN, Mr. Arthur Clive, FCA *1965;* The Flying Engine, Fletching, UCKFIELD, TN22 3PY.
KIDMAN, Ms. Lydia Madelyn, ACA *2009;* National Audit Office, 157-197 Buckingham Palace Road, LONDON, SW1W 9SP.
KIDNER, Mr. Bruce Anthony, BSc(Econ) ACA *1997;* Namibia Breweries limited, PO Box 206, Iscor Street, WINDHOEK, NAMIBIA.
KIDNEY, Mr. Alexander Nicholas, LLB ACA *1992;* c/o Fine & Rare Wines Ltd, Woolyard 54 Bermondsey Street, LONDON, SE1 3UD.
KIDNEY, Mr. John Ernest Henry, FCA *1960;* 39A Sandy Lane, WOKINGHAM, RG41 4SS. (Life Member)
•KIDSON, Mr. Charles Graham Douglas, MA FCA *1972;* (Tax Fac), Kidson, The Harrop, 19 Anglesey Drive, Poynton, STOCKPORT, CHESHIRE SK12 1BT.
KIDSON, Mr. Christopher Paul, BSc(Hons) ACA CIA *2003;* 3 Lumbley Close, Great Cambourne, CAMBRIDGE, CAMBRIDGESHIRE, CB23 6HA.
KIDSON, Mr. Jonathan Peter Braithwaite, FCA *1980;* Terrace Farm, Blymhill, Brineton, SHIFNAL, SHROPSHIRE, TF11 8NQ.
KIDSON, Mrs. Patricia Mary, FCA *1974;* The White House, Eastbourne Road, Halland, LEWES, EAST SUSSEX, BN8 6PS.
KIDWAI, Mr. Faraz Ur Rahman, BSc ACA *2005;* 28 Pates Manor Drive, FELTHAM, MIDDLESEX, TW14 8JJ.
KIDWAI, Mr. Zafar Ahmad, BSc(Econ) ACA *1997;* 24 Seafield Road, LONDON, N11 1AS.
KIDWELL, Mr. James Richard de Villeneuve, BA FCA *1988;* 5 Cloncurry Street, LONDON, SW6 6DR.
KIDWELL, Miss. Sandra Clare, BSc ACA *1988;* Sunny Clough, 243 Bass Lane, Summerseat, BURY, BL9 5NS.
KIDWELL, Mrs. Tamsin Jane, BSc ACA *1994;* The New Barn, 2 Batts Farmyard, Wilton, MARLBOROUGH, WILTSHIRE, SN8 3SS.
KIDY, Ms. Fiona, ACA *1995;* 81 Oxford St, LONDON, W1D 2EU.
•KIEDISH, Mr. Mark James, BSc ACA *2006;* (Tax Fac), M J Kiedish, 24 Rosebery Road, CHELMSFORD, ESSEX, CM2 0TU.
KIEFT, Mr. Andrew Thomas, FCA *1967;* Hayburn, 10 Crooksbury Road, FARNHAM, SURREY, GU10 1QE.
•KIEL, Mr. Eric Stanley, FCA CTA *1967;* (Tax Fac), Eric Kiel & Co, 49 Ravenscroft Avenue, WEMBLEY, MIDDLESEX, HA9 9TE.
KIELTHY, Mrs. Sarah Bethan, BA ACA *2003;* H C UK Unit 39-40, Rassau Industrial Estate Rassau, EBBW VALE, GWENT, NP23 5SD.
KIELY, Mr. Paul, ACA *2011;* 17 Hawthorn Lane, Ashton-on-Mersey, SALE, CHESHIRE, M33 5WW.
KIELY, Mr. Peter George Stewart, FCA *1952;* 2 Kensington Court, 9 Burton Road, POOLE, BH13 6DT. (Life Member)
KIENLEN, Mr. Robert Edward, ACA *1997;* 1 Kings Hill, WEST MALLING, KENT, ME19 4AE.
KIERAN, Mr. Gerard Paul, FCA *1971;* Flat 6, Bracknell Lodge, 5 Frognal Lane, LONDON, NW3 7DL.
•KIERNAN, Miss. Anne Maria, MSc FCA *1982;* (Tax Fac), Anne Kiernan, Apt 1, 9 Otley Road, HARROGATE, NORTH YORKSHIRE, HG2 0DJ.
KIERNAN, Mr. Edward Paul, MEng ACA *1999;* 12 Cranwells Park, BATH, BA1 2YD.
KIERNAN, Mr. Mark, BSc ACA *2004;* 1a Plantagenet Road, BARNET, HERTFORDSHIRE, EN5 5JG.
KIERNAN, Mr. Paul Roger, BSc ACA *1992;* 10 Roman Close, Mountnessing, BRENTWOOD, ESSEX, CM15 0UT.
KIERNAN, Mr. Peter Anthony, MA ACA *1986;* 2 Larpent Avenue, LONDON, SW15 6UP.
KIERNAN, Mrs. Wendy, FCA *1969;* Island Treasurer, Office of the Treasurer, La Chasse Marette, Sark, GUERNSEY, GY9 0SF.
KIERNAN, Mr. William St John, FCA *1978;* 94 Wistaston Road, Willaston, NANTWICH, CW5 6QU.
•KIERNANDER, Mr. John Anthony, FCA *1968;* (Tax Fac), Neill & Co, 26 New Broadway, Ealing, LONDON, W5 2XA.
KIERNEY, Mr. Andrew Christopher, BA(Hons) ACA *2009;* with KPMG, 10 Shelley Street, SYDNEY, NSW 2000, AUSTRALIA.
•KIERSE, Mr. Eoin Patrick, BCom FCA *1988;* Kierse, 8a Convent Hill Centre, Convent Hill, KILLALOE, COUNTY CLARE, IRELAND.
•KIEW, Mr. Richard Jiat Fong, FCA *1982;* Richard Kiew & Co, 1st Floor No. 10 A, Lorong 4, Jalan Nanas, PO Box 2536, 93750 KUCHING SARAWAK MALAYSIA.
KIFF, Mr. Andrew, MSc ACA *2005;* 12 Bulmer Close, Broughton, MILTON KEYNES, MK10 9LG.
KIFF, Mr. Matthew David, BA ACA *2002;* 11 Somerville Lea, ALDEBURGH, SUFFOLK, IP15 5LH.
KIFT, Ms. Clair Louise, BA ACA *2002;* 5 Sunnybank, MARLOW, BUCKINGHAMSHIRE, SL7 3BL.
KIGGINS, Mr. David William, BSc ACA *1994;* 46 Cawston Road, ATTADALE, WA 6156, AUSTRALIA.
KIGHTLEY, Mrs. Jocelyn Anne, BCom ACA *1984;* 9 Bulldog Lane, LICHFIELD, WS13 7LN.
KIGHTLEY, Mr. Mark John, BA ACA *1996;* 31 Claymoor Park Booker, MARLOW, BUCKINGHAMSHIRE, SL7 3DL.
•KILBANE, Miss. Sharon Anne, FCA *1993;* Sharon Kilbane, 87 How Wood, Park Street, ST. ALBANS, HERTFORDSHIRE, AL2 2RW.
KILBEE, Mr. John Richard, MA FCA *1972;* Downsview, Goatacre, CALNE, WILTSHIRE, SN11 9HY.
KILBEY, Mr. Dennis Ernest, FCA *1973;* Brookway, Hamperden End, NR. Debden Green, SAFFRON WALDEN, CB11 3NA.
KILBEY, Miss. Gemma Sinead, MEng ACA *2005;* with BDO LLP, 55 Baker Street, LONDON, W1U 7EU.
KILBEY, Mr. Graham John, FCA *1975;* 20 Brookmans Avenue, Brookmans Park, HATFIELD, AL9 7QJ.
KILBORN, Miss. Emma Jane, BSc(Hons) ACA *2001;* 155 May Lane, Kings Heath, BIRMINGHAM, B14 4AQ.
KILBORN, Mr. Neil Gurney, MA ACA *1980;* with Grant Thornton UK LLP, Grant Thornton House, 22 Melton Street, Euston Square, LONDON, NW1 2EP.
KILBORN, Mr. Robert Anthony, MA FCA *1970;* 58 St. Mary's Mansions, St. Mary's Terrace, LONDON, W2 1SX. (Life Member)
•KILBORN, Mr. Wayne, FCA *1983;* WK Accountants, 5 Welland Court, Desborough, KETTERING, NN14 2PQ.
KILBRIDE, Mrs. Elizabeth Ann, BSc ACA *1985;* The Old Vicarage Upper Stanton, Stanton Drew, BRISTOL, BS39 4EG.
KILBRIDE, Mr. John Peter, BA(Hons) ACA *2002;* Homeserve Claims Management Ltd Unit 7 Fulwood Park, Caxton Road Fulwood, PRESTON, PR2 9NZ.

KILBRIDE, Mrs. Kathryn Susan, BA ACA *2004;* 39 Warwick Gardens, BOLTON, BL3 3SP.
KILBRIDE, Mr. Timothy Lawrence, BSc ACA *1985;* Amcor UK Group Management Ltd, 83 Tower Road North, BRISTOL, BS30 8XP.
KILBRIDE-NEWMAN, Ms. Marie Aoife, BSc FCA *1999;* 228b London Road, ST. ALBANS, HERTFORDSHIRE, AL1 1JQ.
KILBURN, Mr. Alan Godfrey, FCA *1958;* 133 Alma Avenue, HORNCHURCH, RM12 6BS. (Life Member)
•KILBURN, Mr. Martin Graham, BSc FCA *1982;* (Tax Fac), Mistal Barn, Lower Castle Hill, Almondbury, HUDDERSFIELD, HD4 6TA.
KILBY, Mr. David Alexander, BSc ACA *1989;* 1181 Britton Avenue, SAN JOSE, CA 95125, UNITED STATES.
KILBY, Mr. David Leslie, LLB ACA *1992;* 108 Barnstaple Road, SOUTHEND-ON-SEA, SS1 3PW.
KILBY, Mr. Eric Melvyn, BA FCA *1968;* Scriven House Richmond Road, Bowdon, ALTRINCHAM, CHESHIRE, WA14 2TT.
KILBY, Mr. Ian, BSc ACA *2004;* 8 Weavers Lane, MILTON KEYNES, MK14 6FQ.
KILBY, Mr. John Andrew, MA FCA *1985;* 19 Burstead Close, COBHAM, SURREY, KT11 2NL.
•KILBY, Mr. John David, FCA *1970;* (Tax Fac), John D Kilby & Co, Mutfords, Hare Street, BUNTINGFORD, HERTFORDSHIRE, SG9 0ED. See also John D Kilby & Co Limited
KILBY, Mr. Lee Charles, BA ACA *1998;* MBDA UK Limited (PB110), SixHills Way, STEVENAGE, HERTFORDSHIRE, SG1 2DA.
KILBY, Mr. Stuart Peter, BA ACA *1999;* 2 Wetearth Green, Pendlebury, MANCHESTER, M27 8AL.
KILBY, Mrs. Susan Edith, BBS FCA *1980;* 19 Burstead Close, COBHAM, SURREY, KT11 2NL.
KILCOYNE, Mrs. Elizabeth Ann, BA ACA *2005;* 80 Sycamore Way, Littlethorpe, LEICESTER, LE19 2HU.
KILCZEWSKI, Ms. Natasha Marion, BSc(Econ) ACA *1999;* (Tax Fac), 24 Leopold Avenue, FARNBOROUGH, HAMPSHIRE, GU14 8NJ.
KILDEA, Mrs. Gayna Ruth, BSc ACA *1991;* Highfields, Norwood Lane, Graffham, PETWORTH, WEST SUSSEX, GU28 0QG.
KILDUFF, Mr. Paul Anthony Nicolas, BSc ACA *1982;* Tidmarsh Manor, Tidmarsh Lane, Tidmarsh, READING, RG8 8HD.
KILFORD, Mr. Brian Peter, FCA *1982;* 33 Gloucester Avenue, Oultonbroad, LOWESTOFT, SUFFOLK, NR32 4SQ.
KILGALLON, Mr. Andrew John, BA ACA *2004;* 15 Pinero Place, Bucklands Beach, AUCKLAND 2014, NEW ZEALAND.
KILGALLON, Mrs. Catharine Jane, BA ACA *1999;* Piccadilly Radio Unit 1, Castle Quay, MANCHESTER, M15 4PR.
KILGOUR, Mr. Andrew, BSc ACA *2010;* Alan r Grey & Co Old Forge, Beck Place Gosforth, SEASCALE, CUMBRIA, CA20 1AT.
KILGOUR, Mr. David John, BSc FCA *1987;* 2 Dean Drive, Bowdon, ALTRINCHAM, CHESHIRE, WA14 3NE.
KILGOUR, Mr. Peter Alan, BA ACA *1982;* 5 Helene Court, 14 Shouson Hill Road, REPULSE BAY, HONG KONG ISLAND, HONG KONG SAR.
KILILIS, Mr. Panayiotis, BSc ACA *2011;* Alkaiou 2, 2323 LAKATAMIA, CYPRUS.
KILKENNY, Miss. Margaret Mary, FCA *1949;* 4 Copeland Drive, Lower Parkstone, POOLE, BH14 8NW. (Life Member)
KILKENNY, Miss. Sian Louise, BSc ACA *2010;* 3 Biskra, Langley Road, WATFORD, WD17 4PF.
KILLBERY, Mrs. Tracey Gillian, BA ACA *1995;* 3 Longford Close, Stapenhill, BURTON-ON-TRENT, DE15 9FZ.
KILLEEN, Mr. David, FCA *1976;* 781 Curramore Road, WITTA, QLD 4552, AUSTRALIA.
KILLEEN, Mr. Michael Joseph, BA ACA *1986;* 11 Digby Mansions, Hammersmith Bridge Road, LONDON, W6 9DE.
KILLEEN, Mr. Nicholas Mark, MA ACA *1997;* 16 Oakwood Avenue, Otterbourne, WINCHESTER, SO21 2ED.
KILLEN, Mrs. Nicola Louise, BA ACA *2003;* 9 Chesterfield Grove, LONDON, SE22 8RP.
KILLEN, Miss. Sara Nicole, BA(Hons) ACA *2009;* 33 Ilford Avenue, CRAMLINGTON, NORTHUMBERLAND, NE23 3LE.
KILLEN, Miss. Sheelagh Margaret, MA LLM MBA FCA CTA ADIT ACIS MCT MCSI *1996;* 13 Kings Grove, Barton, CAMBRIDGE, CB23 7AZ.
KILLER, Mr. Martin David, MA ACA *1999;* Havenswood, 4a Waldens Park Road, WOKING, SURREY, GU21 4RN.
KILLEY, Mr. Jonathan Martyn, ACA *2011;* 18 Meadow Crescent, Saddlestone, Douglas, ISLE OF MAN, IM2 1NJ.
KILLICK, Mr. Brian Neil Edward, FCA *1952;* Flat 6 Trent House, 24 Ormonde Gate, LONDON, SW3 4EX. (Life Member)
•KILLICK, Mr. Ian Christopher, FCA *1973;* with Plummer Parsons, 5 North Street, HAILSHAM, EAST SUSSEX, BN27 1DQ.
•KILLICK, Mr. James Andrew Hugh, BSc FCA CF *1992;* Baker Tilly Tax & Advisory Services LLP, 3rd Floor Preece House, Davigdor Road, HOVE, EAST SUSSEX, BN3 1RE. See also Baker Tilly Corporate Finance LLP
KILLICK, Mrs. Janice, BA ACA *1991;* 11 Clifton Wood Road, BRISTOL, BS8 4TN.
KILLICK, Mr. Michael James, FCA *2000;* with Bird Luckin limited, Aquila House, Waterloo Lane, CHELMSFORD, CM1 1BN.
KILLIGREW, Mr. John Daniel, BSc ACA *2000;* West Barn, Lower Honor End, Little Hampden, GREAT MISSENDEN, BUCKINGHAMSHIRE, HP16 9PR.
KILLIGREW, Mr. Paul Robert, BSc ACA *2002;* 29 Philip Street, BONDI, NSW 2026, AUSTRALIA.
KILLING, Mr. James, BSc ACA *1998;* Manor Cottage, Worldham Hill, East Worldham, ALTON, GU34 3AX.
KILLINGLEY, Mr. John Herbert, FCA *1954;* Hartington Hotel, Hartington Road, West Ealing, LONDON, W13 3QL. (Life Member)
KILLINGLEY, Mr. Michael Sedley, MA FCA *1974;* Woodlands, Southdown Road, Shawford, WINCHESTER, SO21 2BY.
KILLIP, Miss. Jenny Elizabeth, BA(Hons) ACA MBA *2001;* Flat 4, 15-19 Bedford Hill, LONDON, SW12 9DS.
KILLORAN, Mr. Michael Hugh, BA ACA *1985;* Upwood, Woodlands Drive, Rawdon, LEEDS, LS19 6JZ.
KILLOUGHERY, Mr. Paul Gerard, BSc ACA *1989;* George Killoughery Ltd, 1st Floor, Herald House, 17 Throwley Way, SUTTON, SURREY SM1 4AF.
KILLOURY, Mr. Dominic Martin, ACA *1992;* Pullan & Barnes Stephenson House, Richard Street Hetton-le-Hole, HOUGHTON LE SPRING, TYNE AND WEAR, DH5 9HW.
KILLWORTH, Mr. Adrian Peter Allen, BSc ACA *1992;* R C I Europe Ltd, Kettering Parkway, KETTERING, NORTHAMPTONSHIRE, NN15 6EY.
KILMARTIN, Mr. Adrian Robert, BA FCA *1966;* Church Farm, Old Sodbury Road, Acton Turville, BADMINTON, GL9 1HD.
KILMARTIN, Mrs. Sarah Margaret, MPhil BA ACA *2001;* Novo Nordisk Ltd Broadfield Park, Brighton Road Pease Pottage, CRAWLEY, WEST SUSSEX, RH11 9RT.
•KILMARTIN, Mr. Steven John, FCA *1980;* (Tax Fac), Forster Stott & Co, Langton House, 124 Acomb Road, Holgate, YORK, NORTH YORKSHIRE YO24 4EY.
KILNER, Mr. Anthony Thomas Pomfret, MA MSc ACA *1997;* Finance Directorate, The Castle, JAMESTOWN, STHL 1ZZ, SAINT HELENA.
KILNER, Mrs. Beverley Marcella, MA ACA *1999;* PO Box 109, JAMESTOWN, STHL 1ZZ, SAINT HELENA.
KILNER, Mr. Brian, FCA *1968;* 34 Wilmar Drive, Salendine Nook, HUDDERSFIELD, HD3 3XQ.
KILNER, Ms. Daryl, BA(Hons) ACA *2003;* 43 North Road, SOUTH OCKENDON, RM15 6PT.
•KILNER, Mr. David Leonard, FCA *1964;* (Tax Fac), David L. Kilner, 7 Eldon Square, NEWCASTLE UPON TYNE, NE1 7JG.
KILNER, Ms. Elizabeth, BA ACA *1987;* 5 Dene Park, Highburton, HUDDERSFIELD, HD8 0XJ.
•KILNER, Mr. James Ritchie, BSc FCA *1984;* KJA Kilner Johnson Limited, Network House, Stubs Beck Lane, Bradford, CLECKHEATON, WEST YORKSHIRE BD19 4TT.
KILNER, Mr. Peter Geoffrey, BA ACA *1995;* Bristol & West Plc, PO Box 27, BRISTOL, BS99 7AX.
KILNER, Mr. Thomas Anthony Alistair, FCA *1958;* Oakhanger Cottage, Oakhanger, BORDON, GU35 9JU. (Life Member)
KILPATRICK, Mrs. Annabel Margaret, BA ACA *1996;* 5 Grafton Road, WINCHESTER, HAMPSHIRE, SO23 9SX.
KILPATRICK, Mr. Benjamin, MA(Hons) ACA *2011;* 54 Allestree Road, LONDON, SW6 6AE.
KILPATRICK, Mr. Jeffery Paul, FCA *1976;* 9 Green Close, Springfield, CHELMSFORD, CM1 7SL.
KILPATRICK, Mr. Kenneth Watt, MSc BCom ACA *2002;* Civil Nuclear Constabulary, Building F6, 1st Floor, Culham Science Centre, ABINGDON, OXFORDSHIRE OX14 3DB.
KILPATRICK, Mr. Seumas, BEng ACA *1996;* 14 Woodlands Avenue, EMSWORTH, PO10 7QE.
KILPATRICK, Mr. Stuart Charles, BSc ACA *1989;* 59 Priory Road, RICHMOND, SURREY, TW9 3DQ.
KILPATRICK, Mr. William Gordon, FCA *1976;* Anton van Duinkerkenlaan 40, 1187WC AMSTELVEEN, NETHERLANDS.
KILROY, Mrs. Tina Arleene, ACA *2001;* (Tax Fac), Ranfurly, Stoke Hill, Chew Stoke, BRISTOL, BS40 8XF.
•KILSBY, Mr. Andrew James, BA ACA *1979;* (Tax Fac), Kilsby & Williams LLP, Cedar House, Hazell Drive, NEWPORT, GWENT, NP10 8FY.
KILSBY, Mrs. Helen Alexandra Catherine, MA ACA *1994;* 43 Alwyn Avenue, LONDON, W4 4PA.
KILSBY, Mr. Michael David Grant, BSc ACA *1992;* 43 Alwyn Avenue, Chiswick, LONDON, W4 4PA.
KILSBY, Mr. Richard Philip, LLB FCA *1976;* 16 Elnathan Mews, LONDON, W9 2JE.
•KILSHAW, Mr. Andrew Donald, FCA *1969;* (Tax Fac), Andrew D. Kilshaw, 99 Stanley Road, BOOTLE, MERSEYSIDE, L20 7DA.
•KILSHAW, Mr. Samuel James, BA(Hons) ACA *2004;* (Tax Fac), Stanes Rand LLP, 10 Jesus Lane, CAMBRIDGE, CB5 8BA.
KILTIE, Mr. David Robert Stewart, BA ACA *1992;* 65 Cedar Avenue, Whitton, TWICKENHAM, TW2 7HD.
KILVINGTON, Mr. Stanley, FCA *1958;* 11a Hartington Road, High Lane, STOCKPORT, SK6 8BY. (Life Member)
KIM, Mr. Bong Kwan David, ACA *2010;* Deloitte & Touche, 2 New Street Square, LONDON, EC4A 3BZ.
KIM, Ms. Hana, ACA CA(NZ) *2009;* PO Box 305 239, Triton Plaza, North Shore City, AUCKLAND 0757, NEW ZEALAND.
KIM, Mr. Sun-Ho, BSc ACA *2011;* Dobonggu Chang-5-Dong, 825Bunji, Bookhansan I-PARK 513 Dong 1203 Ho, SEOUL, 132-738, KOREA REPUBLIC OF.
KIM, Miss. Sunmi, MA ACA *2004;* 44 Harold Road, LONDON, E11 4QY.
KIM TIAM FOOK CHONG, Mr. Tsiung-Siong, BA ACA *2009;* Flat 144, Salamanca Square, 9 Albert Embankment, LONDON, SE1 7HG.
KIMACIA, Mrs. Bernice, ACA *1993;* c/o PricewaterhouseCoopers Rwanda Limited, PO Box 1495, KIGALI, RWANDA.
KIMBER, Mr. David Edward, FCA *1962;* Water View, Broad Street, ALRESFORD, SO24 9AN. (Life Member)
KIMBER, Mr. David Jonathan, BA ACA *2002;* 65 Underdown Road, Southwick, BRIGHTON, BN42 4HN.
KIMBER, Mrs. Emma, ACA MAAT *2011;* David Lloyd Leisure, PO Box 439, HATFIELD, HERTFORDSHIRE, AL10 1EF.
KIMBER, Mrs. Evelyn Ai Siang, FCA *1974;* 15 Abbottsleigh Gardens Caversham, READING, RG4 6LA.
KIMBER, Mr. John Robert, ACA *1981;* Laterna Cresta Drive, Woodham, ADDLESTONE, SURREY, KT15 3SW.
•KIMBER, Mr. Malcolm Denison, FCA *1972;* Kimbers, 20 Scillonian Road, GUILDFORD, SURREY, GU2 7PS.
KIMBER, Mr. Nicholas, BA ACA *2005;* Land Lease Europe Ltd, PO Box 67914, 20 Triton Street, Regents Place, LONDON, NW1 3BF.
•KIMBER, Mr. Nigel Philip, BSc FCA CF *1995;* McBrides Accountants LLP, Nexus House, 2 Cray Road, SIDCUP, KENT, DA14 5DA. See also McBrides Corporate Finance Limited
KIMBER, Mr. Paul Stephen, BA ACA *2003;* Flat 4, 48 York Street, LONDON, W1H 1GD.
KIMBER, Mrs. Rachel Natasha, BA ACA *2002;* 24 Hart Road, ST. ALBANS, HERTFORDSHIRE, AL1 1NF.
•KIMBER, Mr. Richard George, FCA *1966;* 6 Tremola Avenue, Saltdean, BRIGHTON, BN2 8AT.
KIMBER, Mr. Richard John, FCA *1963;* Platavagen 30 2tr, S19136 SOLLENTUNA, SWEDEN.
KIMBER, Mr. Robert Charles, BSc FCA *1984;* 8 Beauchamp Road, EAST MOLESEY, KT8 0PA.
KIMBER, Mrs. Tracey Elizabeth, BSc ACA *1996;* 64 Thornbury Wood, Chandler's Ford, EASTLEIGH, HAMPSHIRE, SO53 5DQ.
•KIMBERLEE, Mr. Nicholas Ian, ACA *1986;* Kimberlee Limited, Hunt House Farm, Frith Common, Eardiston, TENBURY WELLS, WORCESTERSHIRE WR15 8JY.
KIMBERLEY, Mr. David Oliver, MA ACA *1982;* (Tax Fac), 51 Finlay Street, LONDON, SW6 6HF.
KIMBERLEY, Mr. Howard, BA FCA *1991;* 8 Lyttelton Road, DROITWICH, WORCESTERSHIRE, WR9 7AA.
KIMBERLEY, Mrs. Kay Elizabeth, BA ACA *1991;* Falaise, 8 Lyttelton Road, DROITWICH, WR9 7AA.
KIMBERLEY, Mr. Mark, BSc ACA *1985;* 17 Maple Grove, Masters Close, PRUDHOE, NE42 6PU.
KIMBERLEY, Mr. Neil James, BA ACA *1997;* BlueBay Asset Management plc, 77 Grosvenor Street, LONDON, W1K 3JR.
•KIMBERLIN, Mrs. Catherine Anne, BA FCA *1986;* Rees Pollock, 35 New Bridge Street, LONDON, EC4V 6BW.
•KIMBERY, Mr. Mark Andrew, BA ACA *1990;* The Mak Practice, Chiltlee Manor, Haslemere Road, LIPHOOK, HAMPSHIRE, GU30 7AZ.
KIMCHE, Mr. James, FCA *1950;* 41 Bayit Vegan Street, JERUSALEM, 96425, ISRAEL. (Life Member)
•KIME, Mr. Geoffrey Harry, FCA *1974;* Kime O'Brien Limited, 1 Church Mews, Churchill Way, MACCLESFIELD, CHESHIRE, SK11 6AY.
KIMEZE, Miss. Clare, BA(Oxon) ACA *2010;* 26 Birkbeck Avenue, LONDON, W3 6HX.
KIMISHIS, Mr. Andreas Thomas, BSc ACA *2009;* Doiranis 3 Flat 103, Strovolos, 2012 NICOSIA, CYPRUS.
KIMPTON, Mr. James Eric Clive, FCA *1968;* 121 Kingsway, Chandler's Ford, EASTLEIGH, HAMPSHIRE, SO53 5DU.
KIMPTON, Mr. Reginald Ralph, FCA *1963;* Hunters Lodge, Mill Lane, Churchgate St, HARLOW, ESSEX, CM17 0LN.
KIMPTON-SMITH, Mr. Matthew James Kimpton, MA ACA *1993;* The Cygnet Group Swan House New Cheshire Business Park, Wincham Lane Wincham, NORTHWICH, CHESHIRE, CW9 6GG.
KIMURA, Miss. Kaoru, ACA *1994;* 39A Ormonde Terrace, LONDON, NW8 7LR.
KIN, Mr. Andrew Nicholas, BSc ACA *1987;* 48 Skeena Hill, LONDON, SW18 5PL.
•KINAHAN, Ms. Patricia Ann, ACA *2000;* Hazlewoods LLP, Windsor House, Bayshill Road, CHELTENHAM, GLOUCESTERSHIRE, GL50 3AT.
KINAL, Mr. Paul Stefan, FCA *1975;* 1 Gaulby Lane, Houghton-On-The-Hill, LEICESTER, LE7 9HB.
KINANE, Miss. Katy Veronique, BSc ACA *2010;* 73 Cleasby Road, Menston, ILKLEY, WEST YORKSHIRE, LS29 6HW.
•KINAST, Mr. Andrzej Wojciech, BSc FCA *1985;* Andrzej Kinast Biegly Rewident, ul Zielona 31, 33-380 KRYNICA ZDROJ, POLAND.
KINCH, Mr. Alan, BSc ACA *2004;* Birch Tree House, 350 Barkham Road, WOKINGHAM, RG41 4DE.
KINCH, Mr. Stephen Paul, BA ACA *1993;* Townsend Farm, Littleton Drew, CHIPPENHAM, WILTSHIRE, SN14 7NA.
KINCHIN, Mr. David James, BSc ACA *1998;* House 10, 9 3/4 Riverside Drive, NAIROBI, KENYA.
KINCHUCK, Mr. Stuart Michael, FCA *1961;* 33 Dukes Avenue, EDGWARE, HA8 7RZ.
KIND, Mrs. Alison Jane, ACA *1987;* Staunton House, Littleworth Lane, Belton in Rutland, OAKHAM, LEICESTERSHIRE, LE15 9JZ.
KIND, Miss. Rosemary Jane, LLB ACA *1990;* Schilde Lodge, Tholthorpe, YORK, YO61 1SN.
KIND, Mr. Terrence Bernard, FCA *1960;* Windrush House, Main Street, Bruntingthorpe, LUTTERWORTH, LE17 5QE. (Life Member)
KINDER, Mr. Anthony John, BSc ACA *1993;* Hill House, 2 Exchange Road, ASCOT, SL5 7AW.
KINDER, Mr. Christopher James, BA ACA *2001;* 8 Bennerley Road, LONDON, SW11 6DS.
KINDER, Mr. Christopher William, MA ACA *1983;* Accenture, 20 Old Bailey, LONDON, EC4M 7AN.
KINDER, Mr. John Michael, FCA *1970;* Go Skills Ltd, Concorde House, Trinity Park, SOLIHULL, WEST MIDLANDS, B37 7UQ.
KINDER, Mr. John Russell, MA FCA *1964;* 23 Woodville Gardens, Ealing, LONDON, W5 2LL.
KINDER, Mr. Richard John, BSc FCA *1980;* Juniper House, The Gables Paddock, Eastrington, GOOLE, NORTH HUMBERSIDE, DN14 7GF.
KINDERSLEY, Mr. Dickon Michael, ACA *1992;* Woodham Hall, Rye Road, Hawkhurst, CRANBROOK, KENT, TN18 5DA.
•KINDLON, Mr. Rory Thomas, BA ACA *1999;* Flat 6, 2 St. Stephens Crescent, LONDON, W2 5QT.
KINDNESS, Miss. Fiona Jane, BSc FCA *1990;* Flat 9 Cedar Court, The Drive, LONDON, N3 1AE.
•KINDRED, Mr. Alan Stuart, ACA *1985;* (Tax Fac), Alan S. Kindred, Normans Corner, 41 Church Lane, Fulbourn, CAMBRIDGE, CB21 5EP.
KING, Mr. Adam, BSc(Hons) ACA *2004;* 19 Hill Crescent, SURBITON, KT5 8DP.
KING, Mr. Adam David, BSc ACA *2007;* 7 Beaconsfield Place, NEWPORT PAGNELL, BUCKINGHAMSHIRE, MK16 0DX.
KING, Mr. Adrian, BA(Hons) ACA *2000;* Hook Lane House Hook Lane, Hadleigh, IPSWICH, IP7 5JP.
•KING, Mr. Adrian Paul, FCA *1985;* (Tax Fac), 130 High Street, MARLBOROUGH, WILTSHIRE, SN8 1LZ. See also Bew & Co Limited

KING, Mr. Adrian Vincent, BSc FCA *1993;* 27 Illawong Drive, DONVALE, VIC 3111, AUSTRALIA.
KING, Mr. Alan, FCA *1973;* 18 Lune Way, Bingham, NOTTINGHAM, NG13 8YX.
KING, Mr. Alan David, BA FCA *1966;* 6 Brockhurst Park, Marldon, PAIGNTON, DEVON, TQ3 1LB.
KING, Mr. Alan David, FCA *1966;* 2 Hallam Gardens, Hatch End, PINNER, HA5 4PR. (Life Member)
KING, Mr. Alan Ross, FCA *1995;* 53 Derby Road, Douglas, ISLE OF MAN, IM2 3EW.
KING, Mr. Albert Aubrey Benjamin, JP FCA *1970;* Hillfoot, 25 Ben Rhydding Drive, ILKLEY, WEST YORKSHIRE, LS29 8AY.
•**KING, Mr. Albert James, MA FCA** *1981;* A.J. King & Co, Scanda House, Main Street, Rathcoole, DUBLIN, COUNTY DUBLIN IRELAND.
KING, Mr. Alex, BA(Hons) ACA *2001;* Flat 9, Victoria House, Park Heights, St. Johns Road, St. Helier, JERSEY JE2 3TG.
KING, Mr. Alexander James Edward, ACA *2009;* c/o Deloitte & Touche (M.E.), Bin Ghanim Tower, Hamdan Street, PO Box 990, ABU DHABI, UNITED ARAB EMIRATES.
KING, Mrs. Alison Judith, BA ACA *1998;* 43 Greenhill Road, Otford, SEVENOAKS, TN14 5RR.
•**KING, Mr. Alistair John, FCA** *1984;* AJK Commercial Consultancy Limited, Yew Tree Cottage, Bredons Norton, TEWKESBURY, GLOUCESTERSHIRE, GL20 7EZ.
KING, Mr. Alwyn, FCA *1960;* 6 Somerleigh Road, DORCHESTER, DORSET, DT1 3GX. (Life Member)
KING, Ms. Amanda Jane, BA ACA *1996;* 22 Grange Road, LONDON, W4 4DA.
KING, Mr. Andrew, BCom ACA FCILA *1982;* 1 Castille Gardens, KINGS LANGLEY, WD4 9PT.
KING, Mr. Andrew, FCA *1966;* 11 Bank End Close, Bolton-On-Dearne, ROTHERHAM, S63 8NR.
KING, Mr. Andrew Charles, MA ACA *1998;* with KPMG, 10 Shelley Street, SYDNEY, NSW 2000, AUSTRALIA.
KING, Mr. Andrew McNeill, BSc ACA *1993;* 145 Franklin Street, ELTHAM, VIC 3095, AUSTRALIA.
KING, Mr. Andrew Paul, BA FCA *1982;* 12 Princess Mead, Goldsborough, KNARESBOROUGH, HG5 8NP.
KING, Mr. Andrew Peter, LLB ACA *1992;* 24 The Chase, LONDON, SW4 0NH.
•**KING, Mr. Andrew Richard, BSc FCA** *1978;* Richardsons Financial Group Limited, 30 Upper High Street, THAME, OXFORDSHIRE, OX9 3EZ.
KING, Ms. Anna Ruth, BA ACA *1998;* 30 Herondale Avenue, LONDON, SW18 3JL.
KING, Mrs. Annabel, BSc ACA *1999;* 1375 Pineway Court, OAKVILLE L6M 2H3, ON, CANADA.
KING, Mr. Antoine Kon-Kam, BA FCA *1981;* PO Box 67553, NAIROBI, 00200, KENYA.
KING, Mr. Barry Andrew, FCA *1981;* with Amari Metals Limited, 25 High Street, COBHAM, SURREY, KT11 3DH.
KING, Mr. Basil Richard, FCA *1952;* 9 Summerfield Close, IPSWICH, IP4 3NS. (Life Member)
•**KING, Mrs. Bernadette Anne Elizabeth, BSc ACA** *2000;* haysmacintyre, Fairfax House, 15 Fulwood Place, LONDON, WC1V 6AY.
KING, Mrs. Bina Jane, MA ACA *2003;* 7 Elm Walk, LONDON, SW20 9ED.
•**KING, Mr. Brian Andrew, BSc ACA CTA** *1990;* Dafferns Resource LLP, 1 Eastwood Business Village, Harry Weston Road, Binley Business Park, COVENTRY, CV3 2UB.
KING, Ms. Brigitte Isabelle, BSc ACA *1992;* 53 Woodside, Wimbledon, LONDON, SW19 7AF.
KING, Ms. Carole, MBiochem ACA *2011;* 34 Valley Road, Burghfield Common, READING, RG7 3NF.
KING, Mrs. Caroline Jayne, FCA *1989;* 13 Primrose Way, The Foxgloves, Rogerstone, NEWPORT, NP10 9BB.
KING, Mr. Casimir Alexis Maher, MMath ACA *2003;* Floor 4, 1 Cavendish Place, LONDON, W1G 0QF.
KING, Mrs. Catherine Margaret, BA ACA *1989;* 6 Highgate Avenue, Fulwood, PRESTON, PR2 8LL.
KING, Mr. Charles Duncan, FCA *1974;* CD King Chatered Accountant, 6 Wexford Place, KILLARNEY HEIGHTS, NSW 2087, AUSTRALIA.
•ⓓ**KING, Mr. Charles Graham John, BSc FCA** *1991;* with Ernst & Young LLP, 1 Bridgewater Place, Water Lane, LEEDS, LS11 5QR.
KING, Miss. Charlotte, ACA *2010;* Ensors, 285 Milton Road, CAMBRIDGE, CB4 1XQ.
KING, Mr. Christopher Gordon, BEng ACA *2001;* 6 Maple Avenue, MANCHESTER, M21 8BD.
KING, Mr. Christopher John, BA ACA *1981;* Druces LLP Salisbury House, London Wall, LONDON, EC2M 5PS.
KING, Mr. Christopher Paul, FCA *1961;* Dunelm, Duck Lane, Welford on Avon, STRATFORD-UPON-AVON, WARWICKSHIRE, CV37 8QD.
KING, Miss. Claire, BA(Hons) ACA *2011;* 15 St. Gabriels Court, Horsforth, LEEDS, LS18 5WN.
KING, Mrs. Claire Louise, BSc(Hons) ACA *2000;* Hook Lane House Hook Lane, Hadleigh, IPSWICH, IP7 5JP.
KING, Mrs. Clare Elizabeth, BSc FCA *2001;* 32 Havelock Road, BEXHILL-ON-SEA, EAST SUSSEX, TN40 2BZ.
KING, Mrs. Clare Louise, BA ACA *1999;* 121 Church Farm Road, Emersons Green, BRISTOL, BS16 7BE.
•**KING, Mr. Colin Andrew, FCA** *1973;* (Tax Fac), 2 Sale Hill, Broomhill, SHEFFIELD, S10 5BX.
KING, Mr. Colin Forbes, BSc FCA *1978;* Oak Barn, MONTGOMERY, POWYS, SY15 6SZ.
KING, Mr. David, ACA *1987;* (Tax Fac), Garbutt & Elliott, Arabesque House, Monks Cross Drive, Huntington, YORK, YO32 9GW.
KING, Mr. David, BSc ACA *1999;* 45 Atbara Road, TEDDINGTON, MIDDLESEX, TW11 9PA.
KING, Mr. David Anthony, FCA *1969;* 17 Armour Avenue, Mount Victoria, WELLINGTON, NEW ZEALAND.
•**KING, Mr. David Clifford, FCA** *1970;* David King, The Old King William, Nettleton, CHIPPENHAM, SN14 7NW.
KING, Mr. David Edward, ACA *2004;* Ward Security Limited, A9 & A10 Spectrum Business Centre, Medway City Estate, ROCHESTER, KENT, ME2 4NP.
KING, Mr. David George Robert, ACA *2009;* KPMG, KPMG Centre, 18 Viaduct Harbour Avenue, AUCKLAND 1140, NEW ZEALAND.
KING, Mr. David Harold, BSc FCA *1976;* The Dell, Old Farm Road, HAMPTON, TW12 3RJ.
KING, Mr. David John, BSc ACA *1993;* Aldar, Altwood Close, MAIDENHEAD, SL6 4PP.
KING, Mr. David John, BA FCA *1984;* Time Out Universal House, 251 Tottenham Court Road, LONDON, W1T 7AB.
KING, Mr. David Philip, BSc ACA *1993;* Kinetic Partners Llp, 1 London Wall, LONDON, EC2Y 5HB.
KING, Mr. David Raymond, BSc FCA *1983;* Eastern Credit Ltd, Beacon Innovation Centre, Camelot Road, Beacon Park, Gorleston, GREAT YARMOUTH NORFOLK NR31 7RA.
KING, Mr. David Richard, BA FCA *1983;* Standard Bank Offshore, 47-49 La Motte Street, St Helier, JERSEY, JE4 8XR.
KING, Mr. David William, ACA *1987;* (Tax Fac), Prudential Capital Plc, Laurence Pountney Hill, LONDON, EC4R 0HH.
KING, Mrs. Debbie, BSc ACA *2005;* 9 Duart Place, GLENROTHES, FIFE, KY7 4RZ.
KING, Miss. Deborah, BSc(Hons) ACA *2001;* 5 Maple Dell Lower Dene, EAST GRINSTEAD, WEST SUSSEX, RH19 3NG.
KING, Mrs. Deborah Ann, BA ACA *1983;* Rowbarns Manor, Green Dene, East Horsley, LEATHERHEAD, KT24 5RQ.
KING, Mrs. Deborah Anne, BSc ACA *1989;* The Kings at Ivy House Newhaven, BUXTON, DERBYSHIRE, SK17 0DT.
•**KING, Miss. Deborah Janet, BA(Hons) ACA** *2000;* with Zolfo Cooper Ltd, 10 Fleet Place, LONDON, EC4M 7RB.
KING, Mrs. Deborah Jayne, ACA *1998;* 1 Charlecote Road, Whitmore Park, COVENTRY, CV6 2HZ.
KING, Mr. Denis Philip, BSc FCA *1976;* 2 Magnolia Close, KINGSTON UPON THAMES, KT2 7JF.
KING, The Revd. Dennis, FCA *1953;* Hillcrest, Stubben Edge, Ashover, CHESTERFIELD, S45 0EU. (Life Member)
KING, Mrs. Diane Jennifer, BSc ACA *1989;* West Barn, Rull Lane, CULLOMPTON, DEVON, EX15 1NG.
KING, Mr. Dick Anthony, FCA *1950;* 11 Byefields, Kempsey, WORCESTER, WR5 3NN. (Life Member)
KING, Mr. Donald, FCA *1959;* 439 Balmy Beach Road, RR 2, OWEN SOUND N4K 5N4, ON, CANADA. (Life Member)
•**KING, Mr. Douglas John, MA FCA** *1983;* Deloitte LLP, 2 New Street Square, LONDON, EC4A 3BZ. See also Deloitte & Touche LLP
KING, Mr. Douglas Robert Hunter, ACA *2010;* 13 Princes Road, Broadheath, ALTRINCHAM, CHESHIRE, WA14 4EX.
KING, Mr. Douglas Robert John, BSc ACA *2003;* 81 Ashmole Street, LONDON, SW8 1NF.
•**KING, Mr. Duncan, BA FCA** *1984;* (Tax Fac), Duncan King, 2 Macneice Drive, Barton Park, MARLBOROUGH, SN8 1TR.
KING, Mr. Edwin Arthur, FCA *1951;* The Coach House, Forest Green Road, Holyport, MAIDENHEAD, BERKSHIRE, SL6 3LQ. (Life Member)
KING, Mrs. Elizabeth Ann, FCA CTA *1997;* (Tax Fac), 4 Evans Drift, Kesgrave, IPSWICH, IP5 2BD.
KING, Mrs. Elizabeth Catherine, ACA MAAT *1997;* Berries, 35 Chalfont Road, Seer Green, BEACONSFIELD, BUCKINGHAMSHIRE, HP9 2QP.
KING, Ms. Elizabeth Jane, BSc FCA *1996;* Mulberry Cottage, Kemishford, WOKING, GU22 0RP.
KING, Miss. Emma Jane, BA ACA *1993;* Byways, Rye Lane, Otford, SEVENOAKS, KENT, TN14 5JF.
KING, Mrs. Eshani Malika, BSc FCA ATII *1988;* (Tax Fac), Yew Tree Cottage, Bredons Norton, TEWKESBURY, GLOUCESTERSHIRE, GL20 7EZ.
KING, Mrs. Estella Lu, ACA *2009;* Flat 7 Empire Court, Charlwood Street, BOGNOR REGIS, WEST SUSSEX, PO21 2PQ.
•**KING, Mrs. Eva Maggie, FCA** *1980;* Brent King Limited, 18 Gosport Business Centre, Frater Gate, GOSPORT, HAMPSHIRE, PO13 0FQ.
KING, Miss. Felicity, BA ACA *1988;* The Guinness Trust Hillfields House, Sigford Road Marsh Barton Trading Estate, EXETER, EX2 8NL.
KING, Miss. Francesca Diana, BA ACA *2006;* Top floor flat, 233B Garratt Lane, LONDON, SW18 4DT.
KING, Mr. Francis Holden, FCA *1978;* 14 Spring Park Road, Wilsden, BRADFORD, BD15 0EA.
KING, Mr. George Ernest, FCA *1961;* Far Oakfield, 22 Redhills Road, Arnside, CARNFORTH, LANCASHIRE, LA5 0AU.
KING, Mr. George William, BA ACA *1997;* Flat B 28/F Tower 2, Dynasty Court, 23 Old Peak Road, MID LEVELS, HONG KONG ISLAND, HONG KONG SAR.
KING, Mr. Gerald James, FCA *1952;* 14 Gestridge Road, Kingsteignton, NEWTON ABBOT, TQ12 3HB. (Life Member)
KING, Mr. Gervase Benjamin, BSc ACA *1996;* 14 Lisle Close, Heritage Road, Tooting Bec Common, LONDON, SW17 6LA.
KING, Ms. Gillian Marie, BA(Hons) FCA *2000;* Duncan Lawrie Ltd, Hobart Place, LONDON, SW1W 0HU.
KING, Mr. Gordon Anthony, FCA *1966;* 12 Ashmole Close, LICHFIELD, WS14 9RS.
•**KING, Mr. Graham David, FCA** *1975;* King Freeman, 1st Floor, Kimberley House, Vaughan Way, LEICESTER, LE1 4SG.
•**KING, Mr. Graham Geoffrey, FCA** *1969;* Kings Accountancy Services Ltd, 23 Porters Wood, ST. ALBANS, HERTFORDSHIRE, AL3 6PQ.
KING, Mr. Graham John, FCA *1979;* 14 Neponset Road, QUINCY, MA 02169, UNITED STATES.
KING, Mr. Graham Reginald, FCA *1972;* Tufton Oceanic (IOM) Ltd, St Georges Court 2nd Floor, Upper Church Street, Douglas, ISLE OF MAN, IM1 1EE.
KING, Mr. Gregor Hoffmann, MA ACA *2001;* 71 Proctors Road, WOKINGHAM, BERKSHIRE, RG40 1RP.
KING, Mrs. Gwendoline Margaret, BSc FCA *1976;* The Great Generation, 18 Spring Street, LONDON, W2 3RA.
KING, Mrs. Hannah Frances, BA ACA *1992;* with PricewaterhouseCoopers LLP, 1 Embankment Place, LONDON, WC2N 6RH.
KING, Mr. Harold Anthony Halloran, FCA *1949;* Faircroft, Fenni Fach Road, BRECON, POWYS, LD3 9LL. (Life Member)
KING, Mrs. Hazel Joan, BSc ACA *1999;* 45 Atbara Road, TEDDINGTON, MIDDLESEX, TW11 9PA.
•ⓓ**KING, Mrs. Heather, BSc ACA** *1988;* with PricewaterhouseCoopers LLP, Pricewaterhousecoopers, 12 Plumtree Court, LONDON, EC4A 4HT.
KING, Mrs. Helen, BSc ACA *1993;* Red Roof, Flecknoe, RUGBY, CV23 8AT.
KING, Mr. Henry George John, MA ACA *1997;* Fountain Court Chambers, Fountain Court, Temple, LONDON, EC4Y 9DH.
KING, Miss. Hollie Roxanne, BSc ACA *2009;* Canon Australia, 1 Thomas Holt Drive, NORTH RYDE, NSW 2113, AUSTRALIA.
KING, Mrs. Holly, BEng ACA *2004;* Pathside, Palmers Lane, Burghfield Common, READING, RG7 3DY.
KING, Mr. Iain Alexander, BSc ACA DChA *2006;* 12 Park Hill, HARPENDEN, HERTFORDSHIRE, AL5 3AT.
KING, Mr. Ian Ayliffe, FCA *1962;* 2 Beoley Hall, Icknield Street, Beoley, REDDITCH, WORCESTERSHIRE, B98 9AL.
KING, Mr. Ian Norman, FCA *1970;* 22 Cheddleton Park Avenue, Cheddleton, LEEK, ST13 7NS.
KING, Mr. James, BA ACA *2004;* 4 Landseer Road, HOVE, EAST SUSSEX, BN3 7AF.
KING, Mr. James, ACA *2011;* Hampden Dale, Spurlands End Road, Great Kingshill, HIGH WYCOMBE, BUCKINGHAMSHIRE, HP15 6HX.
KING, Mr. James Alan, FCA *1969;* 15 Crown Mill, Elmswell, BURY ST. EDMUNDS, IP30 9GF.
KING, Mr. James Daniel, ACA *2009;* Oaklands, 2 Burland Green Lane, Weston Underwood, ASHBOURNE, DERBYSHIRE, DE6 4PF.
KING, Mr. James Francis, FCA *1955;* Rua Angra Dos Reis 346, 04643 060 SAO PAULO, BRAZIL. (Life Member)
•**KING, Mr. James Frederick, MSc BA FCA** *1982;* James King, 5 Ashmore Avenue, Eckington, SHEFFIELD, S21 4AH.
KING, Mr. James Matthew, BA ACA *2006;* 53 Bolton Road, Abbey Village, CHORLEY, LANCASHIRE, PR6 8DP.
KING, Mrs. Jane, BSocSc FCA *1983;* Oxford Brookes University Wheatley Campus, Wheatley, OXFORD, OX33 1HX.
KING, Mr. Jason, BA ACA *1997;* (Tax Fac), 92 Elm Road, KINGSTON UPON THAMES, SURREY, KT2 6HU.
KING, Mr. Jason James, FCA *1995;* Watling JCB Ltd, Dog & Gun Lane, Whetstone, LEICESTER, LE8 6LJ.
KING, Miss. Jemima Felicity-Anne, BA ACA *2010;* Library Farm, 9 Oxford Road, Garsington, OXFORD, OX44 9DA.
KING, Miss. Jenny, BSc ACA *1998;* Carlynne, Childerditch Lane, Little Warley, BRENTWOOD, ESSEX, CM13 3EE.
KING, Mr. Jeremy Stephen Pearce, BA ACA *2007;* 48 Cotford Road, BIRMINGHAM, B14 5JP.
•**KING, Mr. Jeremy Stuart, BA FCA** *1983;* PricewaterhouseCoopers LLP, 1 Embankment Place, LONDON, WC2N 6RH. See also PricewaterhouseCoopers
KING, Miss. Jillian, BSc ACA *1998;* Old Smithy Lanton, JEDBURGH, ROXBURGHSHIRE, TD8 6SX.
KING, Mrs. Joanne, LLB ACA *2001;* Appleyard Lees, 15 Clare Road, HALIFAX, WEST YORKSHIRE, HX1 2HY.
•**KING, Mrs. Joanne Louise, ACA** *2000;* with RSM Tenon Audit Limited, Highfield Court, Tollgate, Chandlers Ford, EASTLEIGH, SO53 3TY.
KING, Mr. John Bryan, BA ACA *1989;* Green Shutters, Summerhill Lane, Lindfield, HAYWARDS HEATH, WEST SUSSEX RH16 1RP.
KING, Mr. John David, BSc ACA *1989;* 7 Newbury Gardens, EPSOM, KT19 0NS.
KING, Mr. John Ernest, FCA *1970;* 1 Blades Close, LEATHERHEAD, KT22 7JY.
KING, Mr. John Francis, BSc FCA *1983;* 9 Stratford Road, Middleton, MANCHESTER, M24 1PT.
KING, Mr. John Howard, FCA *1966;* 14 The Empire, Grand Parade, BATH, BA2 4DF. (Life Member)
KING, Mr. John Michael, FCA *1955;* 10 Blyton Close, BEACONSFIELD, HP9 2LX. (Life Member)
KING, Mr. John Michael Ewen, FCA *1951;* 4 Groby Court, Groby Road, ALTRINCHAM, WA14 2BH. (Life Member)
•**KING, Mr. John Richard, FCA** *1977;* Cound & Co LLP, 27 Granby Street, LOUGHBOROUGH, LE11 3DU.
•**KING, Mr. John Rupert Charles, FCA** *1973;* (Tax Fac), Rupert King & Company Limited, Stanton House, 31 Westgate, GRANTHAM, LINCOLNSHIRE, NG31 6LX.
KING, Mr. Jonathan David, BA ACA *1990;* 7 Devonport Lane, St.Albans, CHRISTCHURCH 8014, NEW ZEALAND.
KING, Mr. Jonathan Simon, BA ACA *1986;* Deutsche Bank, Winchester House, 1 Great Winchester Street, LONDON, EC1N 2DG.
KING, Miss. Katharine Mary, BSocSc ACA *1997;* 56 Berkeley Court, WEYBRIDGE, SURREY, KT13 9HY.
KING, Mr. Kristan James, BA ACA *2003;* with KPMG LLP, St. James's Square, MANCHESTER, M2 6DS.
KING, Mr. Laurence, BA FCA *1988;* Conifers, 6 Highgate Avenue, Fulwood, PRESTON, PR2 8LL.
KING, Mr. Leslie, FCA *1960;* 1B Moor Lane, Murton, YORK, YO19 5UH.
KING, Mrs. Linda Margaret, FCA *1981;* Barclays Capital, 5 The North Colonnade, Canary Wharf, LONDON, E14 4BB.
KING, Mr. Lionel, BSc ACA *1990;* (Tax Fac), 6 Vicarage Close, Hackleton, NORTHAMPTON, NN7 2BY.
KING, Miss. Louisa, MA ACA *2006;* Flat 2, 13 Oakfield Road, LONDON, N4 4NH.
KING, Mrs. Luana Veronica, BSc ACA *1981;* 8 Decker Place, FADDEN, ACT 2904, AUSTRALIA.
KING, Mr. Malcolm Robert, BA ACA *1981;* 34 Haslemere Road, LONDON, N8 9RB.
•**KING, Mrs. Marion Patricia, FCA** *1973;* Marion King, 13 Pinecroft, HEMEL HEMPSTEAD, HP3 8AW.

•KING, Mr. Mark Anthony, BSc ACA *1992;* PricewaterhouseCoopers LLP, 1 Embankment Place, LONDON, WC2N 6RH. See also PricewaterhouseCoopers
•KING, Mrs. Mary Clare Augusta, BA FCA *1978;* (Tax Fac), King & Co, The Dell, Old Farm Road, HAMPTON, TW12 3RJ.
KING, Miss. Mary-Anne, BSc ACA *1993;* Europa House, Midland Way, Thornbury, BRISTOL, BS35 2JX.
KING, Mr. Mathew James, ACA *2008;* Healthcare Homes Lodge Lane, Langham, COLCHESTER, CO4 5NE.
•KING, Mr. Matthew, BSc FCA *1997;* PricewaterhouseCoopers LLP, Hays Galleria, 1 Hays Lane, LONDON, SE1 2RD. See also PricewaterhouseCoopers
KING, Mr. Matthew, BSc ACA *1998;* 5 Candlemas Lane, BEACONSFIELD, BUCKINGHAMSHIRE, HP9 1AH.
KING, Mr. Matthew, BA ACA *2005;* 14 Friendly Avenue, SOWERBY BRIDGE, WEST YORKSHIRE, HX6 2TY.
KING, Mr. Matthew John, BSc FCA FCSI *1996;* 16 Mayflower Road, Chafford Hundred, GRAYS, RM16 6BE.
KING, Mr. Matthew John, BA(Hons) ACA *2001;* TCI Fund Management (UK) LLP, 7 Clifford Street, LONDON, W1S 2WE.
KING, Miss. Melanie Anne, MSc BA ACA *2005;* Flat 20, Building 36, Marlborough Road, LONDON, SE18 6XD.
KING, Mr. Michael, BSc ACA *1999;* 18 Fountains Road, NORTHALLERTON, DL6 1QR.
KING, Mr. Michael David, BSc FCA *1992;* 61 Hamilton Avenue, SURBITON, KT6 7PW.
KING, Mr. Michael Henry, BA ACA ACII *1987;* Chestnuts Church Road, Great Barton, BURY ST. EDMUNDS, SUFFOLK, IP31 2QR.
KING, Mr. Michael John, FCA *1954;* 24 Gilbert Scott Court, Whielden Street, AMERSHAM, BUCKINGHAMSHIRE, HP7 0AP. (Life Member)
KING, Mr. Michael John Cape, FCA *1970;* Upper Farm House, Walterstone, HEREFORD, HR2 8ED.
KING, Mr. Michael Peter, FCA *1956;* 3 King William Drive, Charlton Park, CHELTENHAM, GL53 7RP. (Life Member)
KING, Mr. Michael Robert, FCA *1976;* with Honey Barrett Limited, The Clock House, High Street, WADHURST, EAST SUSSEX, TN5 6AA.
•KING, Mr. Michael Sidney, FCA *1956;* (Tax Fac), Michael King & Co, Suite 4, Stanmore Towers, 8-14 Church Road, STANMORE, MIDDLESEX HA7 4AW.
KING, Mr. Michael Wallis, FCA *1960;* Bagatelle, 21 Killarney Road, Sandhurst, SANDTON, 2196, SOUTH AFRICA.
KING, Mr. Neale George, BSc ACA *1989;* 9 Woodville Street, HALIFAX, WEST YORKSHIRE, HX3 5BY.
KING, Mr. Neil Ian, BSc ACA *1992;* 89 Beatty Avenue, CARDIFF, CF23 5QS.
KING, Mr. Nicholas Geoffrey, FCA *1974;* 11 Park Grove, Penn Road, Knotty Green, BEACONSFIELD, BUCKINGHAMSHIRE, HP9 2EN.
KING, Mr. Nicholas James, LLB FCA *1984;* (Tax Fac), 5 Shaftesbury Close, Purton, SWINDON, SN5 4FD.
•KING, Mr. Nicholas James Vincent, FCA *1978;* Moore Stephens, 150 Aldersgate Street, LONDON, EC1A 4AB.
KING, Mr. Nicholas Michael, BEng ACA *1992;* 54 St. Andrews Crescent, WINDSOR, BERKSHIRE, SL4 4EL.
KING, Mr. Nicholas Stephen, FCA *1970;* 4 Cowlins, HARLOW, ESSEX, CM17 0FZ. (Life Member)
•KING, Mrs. Nicola, BA(Hons) ACA FCCA *2007;* David Howard, 1 Park Road, Hampton Wick, KINGSTON UPON THAMES, KT1 4AS.
KING, Mr. Norman Stanley, FCA *1958;* 3D Court Road, Ickenham, UXBRIDGE, UB10 8TE. (Life Member)
KING, Miss. Pamela Gibb, MA ACA *1988;* 7 Orchard Drive, Wooburn Green, HIGH WYCOMBE, HP10 0QN.
KING, Mr. Patrick David Charles, ACA *2008;* 71 Alleyn Park, LONDON, SE21 8AT.
KING, Mr. Patrick Michael, FCA *1970;* 7 Kingston Lane, Southwick, BRIGHTON, BN42 4SJ. (Life Member)
KING, Mr. Paul Daniel, BSc ACA *2006;* Flat 22, Princes House, North Street, BRIGHTON, BN1 1EA.
KING, Mr. Paul James, BA(Hons) ACA *2004;* Flat 9 Empire Court, 56 Plaistow Lane, BROMLEY, BR1 3JE.
KING, Mr. Paul Stephen, BCom ACA *1985;* BT Global Services, Guidion House, Site 500 Harvest Crescent, Ansells Business Park, FLEET, HAMPSHIRE GU51 2QP.
KING, Miss. Paula Louise, MSc ACA *2001;* The Elms, Lower Village, Blunsdon, SWINDON, SN26 7BJ.
KING, Mr. Peter, BA ACA *1986;* I P Wireless UK Ltd, Unit 7, Greenways Business Park, Bellinger Close, CHIPPENHAM, WILTSHIRE SN15 1BN.
KING, Mr. Peter David, MBA BA FCA FCIS *1979;* Chase, Loseley Park, GUILDFORD, SURREY, GU3 1HS.
KING, Mr. Peter Derek, BCom ACA *1999;* 14 Chads Green Wybunbury, NANTWICH, CHESHIRE, CW5 7NL.
KING, Mr. Peter Douglas, FCA *1959;* New Winterton, Farley Lane, WESTERHAM, KENT, TN16 1UD. (Life Member)
KING, Mr. Peter Robert, BSc ACA *1993;* 141 Centurion Square, Skeldergate, YORK, YO1 6DE.
•KING, Mr. Philip, FCA *1979;* Menzies LLP, Lynton House, 7-12 Tavistock Square, LONDON, WC1H 9LT.
KING, Mr. Philip Edward, MA MBA FCA *1976;* Hall Cottage, Park Lane. Ashtree Corner, Hamstead Marshall, NEWBURY, RG20 0HL.
KING, Mr. Philip George Maitland, FCA *1965;* 5 Cornish Close, GreenacresSontley Road, WREXHAM, LL13 7JE.
KING, Mrs. Rachel Elizabeth, BA ACA *1998;* Flat B 28/F, Tower 2 Dynasty Court, 23 Old Peak Road, MID LEVELS, HONG KONG ISLAND, HONG KONG SAR.
KING, Miss. Rachel Rose, ACA *2008;* with PricewaterhouseCoopers LLP, 1 Embankment Place, LONDON, WC2N 6RH.
KING, Mr. Raymond, BSc FCA *1977;* Bupa House, 15-19 Bloomsbury Way, LONDON, WC1A 2BA.
KING, Miss. Rebecca Anne, MA ACA *1991;* 4 Globe Ley, Globefields, Topsham, EXETER, EX3 0EZ.
KING, Mrs. Rhiannon Sarah, BA(Hons) ACA *2011;* 69 Thomas Street, WELLINGBOROUGH, NORTHAMPTONSHIRE, NN8 1DU.
•KING, Mr. Richard, FCA *1976;* J.R.Antoine & Partners, 75 Rickmansworth Road, AMERSHAM, HP6 5JW.
•KING, Mr. Richard, FCA *1980;* Mark J Rees, Granville Hall, Granville Road, LEICESTER, LE1 7RU.
KING, Mr. Richard Anthony, BSc FCA *1976;* Wren Corporate Finance Ltd, The Cross, John's Lane, Blackley, ELLAND, WEST YORKSHIRE HX5 0TQ.
•KING, Mr. Richard Hamilton, BA ACA *1995;* Baker Tilly Tax & Advisory Services LLP, 2 Whitehall Quay, LEEDS, LS1 4HG. See also Baker Tilly UK Audit LLP
KING, Mr. Richard Henry Donald, FCA *1963;* 10198N. 105th Way, SCOTTSDALE, AZ 85258, UNITED STATES.
KING, Mr. Richard Jon, BSc(Hons) ACA *2004;* 58 Falmer Road, LONDON, N15 5BA.
KING, Mr. Richard Philip, FCA *1978;* CAE Aircrew Training Services plc MSHATF, Royal Air Force, Benson, WALLINGFORD, OXFORDSHIRE, OX10 6AA.
KING, Mr. Richard Thomas, BA ACA *2005;* 3 Grove Court, LEEDS, LS6 4AE.
KING, Mr. Richard Walter, FCA *1980;* Paddock Lodge, Kimpton, HITCHIN, HERTFORDSHIRE, SG4 8ER.
KING, Mr. Robert, BA ACA *1992;* 18 Newlands Drive, Lowton, WARRINGTON, WA3 2RY.
•KING, Mr. Robert Forbes, FCA *1968;* (Tax Fac), Wallace Williams & Co, 4 Island Farm Close, BRIDGEND, CF31 3LY.
KING, Mr. Robert Gordon, FCA *1950;* 22 St Johns Close, BEVERLEY, HU17 8FD. (Life Member)
•KING, Mr. Robert Harvey Leeder, FCA *1981;* (Tax Fac), Kings Accounting House Limited, 37 Gayfere Road, EPSOM, SURREY, KT17 2JY.
KING, Mr. Robert James, ACA *1990;* Woodhouse, Bettiscombe, BRIDPORT, DT6 5NS.
KING, Mr. Robert Stuart, ACA *1990;* Strategic Procurement Health Support, Dept of Health, Level 3, 73 Miller Street, NORTH SYDNEY, NSW 2060 AUSTRALIA.
KING, Mr. Robin Horsley, FCA *1957;* 1 Beeches Close, Rednal, BIRMINGHAM, B45 9HD. (Life Member)
KING, Mr. Roger David, FCA *1967;* 6 Highcroft, Cherry Burton, BEVERLEY, HU17 7SG.
•KING, Mr. Roger Grenville, MA FCA *1972;* Roger King S.R.L, Via Amilcare Ponchielli 3, 20129 MILAN, ITALY. See also Roger Grenville King
KING, Roland Edouard Vincent Michel, Esq OBE FCA *1962;* 123 Av. Jean-Francois Debecker, B1200 BRUSSELS, BELGIUM. (Life Member)
KING, Ms. Ruth Margaret, BSc FCA *1980;* 48 King Street, Seagrave, LOUGHBOROUGH, LEICESTERSHIRE, LE12 7LY.
KING, Ms. Samantha Jane, BA ACA ATII *1999;* 50D St. Gabriels Road, Willesden Green, LONDON, NW2 4SA.
KING, Mrs. Samantha Jane, BA FCA *1998;* with Shipleys LLP, 10 Orange Street, Haymarket, LONDON, WC2H 7DQ.
KING, Mrs. Sara Rachel, BMus ACA *1992;* Two Tias, Greenacres Close, RINGWOOD, BH24 2AP.
KING, Miss. Sarah, BA ACA *2011;* 111a, Englefield Road, LONDON, N1 3LH.
KING, Mrs. Sarah Bridget, MA ACA *1983;* 8 Kingswood Drive, LONDON, SE19 1UR.
KING, Mrs. Sarah Emma, BSc ACA *1999;* 23 Osborne Road, POTTERS BAR, HERTFORDSHIRE, EN6 1RZ.
KING, Miss. Sarah Louise, BSc ACA *2010;* 15 Filby Gardens, ST. HELENS, MERSEYSIDE, WA9 5WF.
KING, Mr. Sean Anthony, BSc ACA *1993;* 33 Sawmill Road, DANVILLE, NH 03819, UNITED STATES.
KING, Mr. Sean Julian, ACA *1987;* Eastdene, High Street, Colne, HUNTINGDON, PE28 3ND.
KING, Mr. Seth, BSocSc ACA *1997;* 6 Kingsway, HARROGATE, NORTH YORKSHIRE, HG1 5NQ.
KING, Mr. Simon Alexander Brewer, BSc ACA *2002;* 34 Tanner Close, RADSTOCK, SOMERSET, BA3 3BT.
KING, Mr. Simon Andrew Walter, BA FCA *1994;* 15 Crane Way, TWICKENHAM, TW2 7NH.
KING, Mr. Simon Mark, ACA *1997;* 42 Compton Way, WINCHESTER, HAMPSHIRE, SO22 4HW.
KING, Mr. Simon Paul, FCA FSI *1994;* 2 Jubilee Terrace, Burlington Road, LONDON, SW6 4NT.
KING, Mr. Simon Thomas, BSc(Hons) ACA *1991;* Gordon Ellis & Co Trent Lane, Trent Lane Industrial Estate Castle Donington, DERBY, DE74 2PY.
KING, Mr. Simon Yorke, BEng ACA *1999;* 16 The Avenue, Rowledge, FARNHAM, GU10 4BD.
KING, Mr. Spencer John, BSc ACA *1999;* 23 Osborne Road, POTTERS BAR, HERTFORDSHIRE, EN6 1RZ.
•KING, Mr. Stephen, BEd FCA *1991;* PKF (UK) LLP, Pannell House, 159 Charles Street, LEICESTER, LE1 1LD.
KING, Mr. Stephen Anthony, MBA BA FCA *1986;* 24 Bernard Gardens, Wimbledon, LONDON, SW19 7BE.
KING, Mr. Stephen James, MSc BSc ACA *1992;* Farriers Cottage, Ilmington Road, Blackwell, SHIPSTON-ON-STOUR, WARWICKSHIRE, CV36 4PE.
•KING, Mr. Stephen Mark, MBA BA ACA *1989;* Churchside House, Stanton Drew, BRISTOL, BS39 4EW.
KING, Mr. Stephen Maurice, FCA *1976;* 22 Lounsbury Road, Croton-On-Hudson, NEW YORK, NY 10520, UNITED STATES.
KING, Mr. Stephen Michael, BEng ACA *1992;* The Cottage Gibsmere, Bleasby, NOTTINGHAM, NG14 7FS.
KING, Mr. Stephen Noel, BSc ACA *1993;* South Cot, Wayside, Chipperfield, KINGS LANGLEY, HERTFORDSHIRE, WD4 9JJ.
KING, Mr. Stephen Roy, BSc ACA *1997;* 1 Jacqueline Road, MARKFIELD, LE67 9RD.
KING, Mr. Steven, BSc ACA *1995;* Conquest House, Church Street, WALTHAM ABBEY, ESSEX, EN9 1DX.
KING, Mr. Stuart, MChem ACA *2011;* 51 Eden Road, West End, SOUTHAMPTON, SO18 3QW.
KING, Mr. Stuart Alan, BSc ACA *1996;* 80 Burntmeadow Road, RINGWOOD, NJ 07456, UNITED STATES.
KING, Mr. Stuart John, MSc ACA *2003;* Tangerine Group, Docklands, Dock Road, LYTHAM ST. ANNES, LANCASHIRE, FY8 5AQ.
KING, Mr. Stuart Wilfred, FCA *1964;* 11 Carroll Avenue, FERNDOWN, BH22 8BW.
•KING, Mrs. Susan Wendy, ACA *1985;* Susan King ACA, Hazlemere, 115 London Road, Temple Ewell, DOVER, CT16 3BY.
KING, Mrs. Suzanne Georgina, BA ACA *1987;* Beech Croft, 29 Stock Lane, Wybunbury, CREWE, CW2 5ED.
KING, Miss. Suzanne Jane, BSc ACA *1989;* 114 Ramillies Road, LONDON, W4 1JA.
KING, Miss. Tamasine Lisa, BSocSc ACA *1995;* The White House, Lower Padworth, READING, RG7 4JU.
•KING, Mr. Terry, FCA *1968;* T. King & Co Ltd, 72 Mill Road, ERITH, DA8 1HN.
KING, Mr. Thomas Edward, BSc ACA *2004;* 169 Penwith Road, LONDON, SW18 4PZ.
KING, Mr. Timothy Charles Fredric, BA ACA *1991;* 28 Sebert Road, BURY ST. EDMUNDS, IP32 7EG.
KING, Mr. Toby, BA(Hons) ACA *2003;* 7 Elm Walk, LONDON, SW20 9ED.
KING, Mrs. Tracey Jane, ACA *1998;* 17 Fern Ley Close, MARKET HARBOROUGH, LEICESTERSHIRE, LE16 8FY.
KING, Miss. Tracy, BSc ACA *1993;* 29 Tarikaka Street, Ngaio, WELLINGTON, NEW ZEALAND.
KING, Ms. Vanessa Ann, BSc ACA *1991;* 62 Devonshire Road, Ealing, LONDON, W5 4TP.
KING, Miss. Victoria, ACA *2010;* 63 Cloudeseley Close, SIDCUP, DA14 6TF.
KING, Mr. Vincent, BSc ACA *2006;* Omnium LLC, 131 South Dearborn Street, CHICAGO, IL 60614, UNITED STATES.
KING, Mr. Wayne Geoffrey, BA ACA *2007;* 35 Ashby Close, WELLINGBOROUGH, NORTHAMPTONSHIRE, NN8 5FH.
•KING, Mr. Wayne Thomas, FCA *1976;* (Tax Fac), Wayne T. King & Co, 2 High Street, MENAI BRIDGE, GWYNEDD, LL59 5EE.
KING, Mr. William David Graeme, FCA *1974;* 16 Jessica Road, Wandsworth, LONDON, SW18 2QN.
KING, Mr. William Roger, FCA *1977;* (Tax Fac), Anglo Saxon trust Limited, PO Box 264, St Helier, JERSEY, JE4 8TQ.
KING-BRITTON, Mr. Peter John, FCA *1954;* Chapel House, Menith Wood, WORCESTER, WR6 6UG. (Life Member)
KING-CLARKE, Mrs. Vanessa Ann, ACA *1999;* 7 Pits Avenue, Braunstone, LEICESTER, LE3 2XL.
KING YIU, Mr. Kong, ACA *2005;* Flat A 19/F Nelly Heights, Belair Garden, 52 Tai Chung Kiu Road, SHA TIN, NEW TERRITORIES, HONG KONG SAR.
KINGDOM, Mrs. Catherine Elizabeth, BA ACA *1994;* 8 Roxton Gardens, CROYDON, CR0 5AL.
•KINGDOM, Mr. Paul Anthony, BA FCA *1986;* (Tax Fac), A.C. Mole & Sons, Riverside House, Riverside Business Park, Wylds Road, BRIDGWATER, TA6 4BH.
KINGDOM, Mr. Philip John, BSc ACA *1992;* with PricewaterhouseCoopers LLP, 1 Embankment Place, LONDON, WC2N 6RH.
KINGDOM, Mr. Robert Frederick, BSc ACA *1986;* with PricewaterhouseCoopers LLP, Pricewaterhousecoopers, 12 Plumtree Court, LONDON, EC4A 4HT.
KINGDON, Mr. David Rhys, BSc ACA *2007;* 58 Parc-y-Coed, Creigiau, CARDIFF, CF15 9LY.
KINGDON, Mr. Simon Charles, FCA *1979;* Flint Meadow, Hockley Lane, Stoke Poges, SLOUGH, SL2 4QE.
KINGE, Mrs. Kathryn Mary, ACA *2006;* 6 Haseley Close, LEAMINGTON SPA, WARWICKSHIRE, CV31 2PD.
•KINGETT, Mr. Ian Nicholas, FCA *1983;* (Tax Fac), Kingett's, Carolyn House, 5 Dudley Road, HALESOWEN, B63 3LS.
KINGHAM, Miss. Emma, BA(Hons) ACA *2011;* 5 Peggles Lane, Stotfold, HITCHIN, HERTFORDSHIRE, SG5 4GF.
KINGHAM, Mr. John Dyson, FCA *1966;* 338 Old Bedford Road, LUTON, LU2 7EJ. (Life Member)
•KINGHAM, Mr. Paul, FCA *1980;* Team Audit LLP, Kingham House, 161 College Street, ST. HELENS, MERSEYSIDE, WA10 1TY. See also Kingham Accountancy Ltd
KINGHAM, Miss. Sheila Jane, BA ACA *1999;* 76 Chipstead Park, SEVENOAKS, KENT, TN13 2SH.
KINGHORN, Miss. Myra Anne, FCA CDir *1978;* 10 Courtenay Drive, Oakwood Avenue, BECKENHAM, BR3 6YE.
KINGMA, Mr. Bruce Anthony, BSc(Hons) ACA *2011;* 16 Brackley, WEYBRIDGE, SURREY, KT13 0BJ.
KINGMAN, Mrs. Jane Elizabeth, BA ACA *1991;* 317 Cromwell Lane, Burton Green, KENILWORTH, CV8 1PG.
•KINGON, Mr. Neil Bernard, MSc FCA *1972;* Kingon & Co, Green Pastures, Bullocks Farm Lane, Wheeler End, HIGH WYCOMBE, HP14 3NQ.
•KINGON, Mrs. Wendy Margaret, FCA *1974;* (Tax Fac), Kingon & Co, Green Pastures, Bullocks Farm Lane, Wheeler End, HIGH WYCOMBE, HP14 3NQ.
KINGS, Mr. Andrew Francis, ACA *1987;* 7 Reedmace, TAMWORTH, B77 1BH.
•KINGS, Mrs. Christine Emily, BSc ACA *1983;* 40 Highgate, Penwortham, PRESTON, PR1 0DU.
KINGS, Mr. Clement George, FCA *1959;* Flat 17, Meadwood, St. Marks Road, TORQUAY, TQ1 2EH. (Life Member)
•KINGS, Mr. Hylton, FCA *1953;* H. Kings, 18 Birchfield Gdns, Harlow Green, GATESHEAD, NE9 7TJ.
•ⒹKINGS, Mr. Ian William, BA ACA *1984;* with RSM Tenon Limited, Ferryboat Lane, SUNDERLAND, SR5 3JN.
KINGS, Mrs. Michelle, BSc ACA *2004;* Hale Jackson Knight, Montague House, 4 St Marys Street, ROSS-ON-WYE, HEREFORDSHIRE, HR9 5HT.
KINGSBURY, Mr. Mark William, BSc ACA *1989;* 9 Ralliwood Road, ASHTEAD, SURREY, KT21 1DD.
KINGSBURY, Mr. Michael Trevor, BSc FCA *1985;* High Bank House, Barbon, CARNFORTH, LANCASHIRE, LA6 2LG.

•**KINGSBURY, Mr. William Howard, MA ACA** *1981;* Apt 402, 15 Halkokondyli Street, NICOSIA, CYPRUS.
KINGSCOTT, Mrs. Jill, BA ACA *2003;* Woodhurst, Horsham Lane, Ewhurst, CRANLEIGH, SURREY, GU6 7SW.
KINGSHOTT, Ms. Deirdre Ann, BSc ACA *1993;* 14 Thorley Drive, Timperley, ALTRINCHAM, CHESHIRE, WA15 7AP.
KINGSHOTT, Mr. Graeme Paul, BSc ACA *1996;* Calle Cristofol Mestres 82, 08810 SANT PERE DE RIBES, SPAIN.
KINGSHOTT, Mr. Paul Martin, BSc ACA *1994;* Elmstead, Meon Road, Titchfield, FAREHAM, HAMPSHIRE, PO14 4HJ.
KINGSLEY, Mr. Alan, FCA *1970;* Sandalwood, 2 Woodcote, GUILDFORD, GU2 4HQ.
KINGSLEY, Mr. Daniel Jon, MA ACA *1996;* Efraim 28, MODI'IN, ISRAEL.
KINGSLEY, Miss. Hannah Gillam, ACA *2009;* 38 Braemar Avenue, LONDON, N22 7BY.
KINGSLEY, Mr. John Edwin, FCA *1950;* 40 East Drive, Angmering, LITTLEHAMPTON, WEST SUSSEX, BN16 4JH. (Life Member)
KINGSLEY, Mr. John Howard Cleeve, FCA *1972;* 108 Cranbrook Road, LONDON, W4 2LJ.
KINGSLEY, Miss. Martine Clare, BSc ACA *1990;* (Tax Fac), General Healthcare Group, 4 Thameside Centre Kew Bridge Road, BRENTFORD, MIDDLESEX, TW8 0HF.
KINGSLEY, Mr. Michael John, BSc ACA *2008;* (Tax Fac), Flat 26 Tavistock Court, Tavistock Square, LONDON, WC1H 9HE.
KINGSLEY, Mrs. Miriam Janet, BA ACA *1990;* 4 Winnington Road, LONDON, N2 0UB.
KINGSLEY, Miss. Muriel Jayne, BSc ACA *2008;* 83 Wells Crescent, Viaduct Road, CHELMSFORD, ESSEX, CM1 1GR.
KINGSLEY, Mr. Niall Andrew, ACA *2009;* 24 Main Street, Redmile, NOTTINGHAM, NG13 0GA.
KINGSLEY, Mr. Nigel, FCA *1975;* (Tax Fac), Europa House, Goldstone Villas, HOVE, BN3 3RQ.
KINGSLEY, Mrs. Nina, ACA *2008;* 11A Etloe Road, Westbury Park, BRISTOL, BS6 7NZ.
•**KINGSLEY, Mr. Simon Patrick Dominic St John, BSc ACA** *1993;* Simon Kingsley, 58 Montague Road, Hackney, LONDON, E8 2HW.
•**KINGSLEY, Mr. Stephen Michael, BSc FCA** *1976;* 23 Gloucester Walk, Kensington, LONDON, W8 4HZ.
KINGSLEY, Mr. Walter, BA FCA *1956;* 30 Ashley Lane, LONDON, NW4 1HG. (Life Member)
KINGSLEY-TOMKINS, Mr. Damien, ACA *2009;* City Harbour, Flat 42, 8 Selsdon Way, LONDON, E14 9GR.
KINGSMELL, Mr. John Christopher, FCA *1962;* 34 Park Avenue, BROMLEY, BR1 4EE. (Life Member)
KINGSMILL, Mr. Charles Robert, MA ACA *1984;* 45 Whitehall Park Road, LONDON, W4 3NB.
KINGSMILL, Mr. David Gordon, BSc FCA *1971;* Addaction Central Office, 67-69 Cowcross Street, LONDON, EC1M 6PU.
KINGSMILL, Mr. Gordon Harold, MM FCA *1949;* (Member of Council 1972 - 1985), The Grove, Hinton Parva, SWINDON, SN4 0DH. (Life Member)
KINGSMILL, Mr. Patrick Major, FCA *1970;* 104 Cambridge Road, TEDDINGTON, MIDDLESEX, TW11 8DJ. (Life Member)
KINGSNORTH, Mr. David Anthony, BSc ACA *1986;* 15 Langton Drive, Two Mile Ash, MILTON KEYNES, MK8 8PD.
KINGSNORTH, Mrs. Hayley Louise, ACA *2005;* with Day Smith & Hunter, Globe House, Eclipse Park, Sittingbourne Road, MAIDSTONE, KENT ME14 3EN.
KINGSNORTH, Miss. Jacqueline Dawn, BSc FCA ATII *1996;* 18 William James Way, HENLEY-IN-ARDEN, B95 5GB.
KINGSNORTH, Mrs. Joanne, ACA *2007;* 126 Sheerstock, Haddenham, AYLESBURY, BUCKINGHAMSHIRE, HP17 8EX.
KINGSTON, Mr. Andrew Eric, FCA *1973;* Swift Cottage, 3 The Green, Standlake, WITNEY, OXFORDSHIRE, OX29 7SD.
•**KINGSTON, Mr. Anthony John, FCA** *1971;* (Tax Fac), Kingston & Co, Rush Lane End, Sudthorpe Hill, Fulbeck, GRANTHAM, LINCOLNSHIRE NG32 3LE.
KINGSTON, Mr. Daniel, BSc ACA *2011;* 16 Pelham Gardens, FOLKESTONE, KENT, CT20 2LF.
KINGSTON, Mr. David Timothy, BSc FCA *1996;* 25 Roestock Gardens, Colney Heath, ST. ALBANS, HERTFORDSHIRE, AL4 0QJ.
KINGSTON, Mrs. Gaynor Elizabeth Verna, FCA *1968;* (Tax Fac), Bryngarth Lodge, Much Birch, HEREFORD, HR2 8HJ.
KINGSTON, Mr. John Paul, BA ACA *2009;* Pricewaterhousecoopers, 7 More London Riverside, LONDON, SE1 2RT.
•**KINGSTON, Mrs. Judith Christine, ACA** *1981;* Judith Kingston, 7 The Manor, Potton, SANDY, SG19 2RN.
KINGSTON, Mrs. Maria Helena Louise, MA ACA *2006;* Plymouth House, Dimlands Road, LLANTWIT MAJOR, SOUTH GLAMORGAN, CF61 1SJ.
KINGSTON, Mr. Mark Andrew, BA ACA *1990;* 14 Rectory Close, Woodchurch, ASHFORD, KENT, TN26 3QD.
KINGSTON, Mr. Martin Lawrence, BA ACA *1983;* PO Box 411332, CRAIGHALL, GAUTENG, 2024, SOUTH AFRICA.
KINGSTON, Mr. Neil Brian, BA FCA *1976;* 3 Broom Hollow, Loggerheads, MARKET DRAYTON, SHROPSHIRE, TF9 4NT.
•**KINGSTON, Mr. Neil Mccallum, FCA** *1982;* Burton Sweet Limited, Prospect House, 5 May Lane, DURSLEY, GLOUCESTERSHIRE, GL11 4JH. See also Burton Sweet
KINGSTON, Mr. Peter James, MA ACA *1978;* 1111 McDonald Avenue, SANTA ROSA, CA 95404, UNITED STATES.
KINGSTON, Mr. Peter Richard, MA FCA *1972;* 5720 Walton Road, RICHMOND V7C 2L9, BC, CANADA.
KINGSTON, Miss. Philippa Rachel, BSc ACA *2007;* 33 Cong Burn View, Pelton Fell, CHESTER LE STREET, COUNTY DURHAM, DH2 2BN.
KINGSTON, Mr. Richard Michael, BA ACA *1989;* 70 Woodland Rise, LONDON, N10 3UJ.
KINGSTON, Mrs. Sarah Louise, BA ACA *2001;* 2f Lidgett Park Road, LEEDS, LS8 1EQ.
KINGSTON, Mr. Stephen Alan Andrew, BA ACA *2001;* 2f Lidgett Park Road, LEEDS, LS8 1EQ.
KINGSTON, Dr. Stephen Paul, MA BA ACA *2006;* 69 Phyllis Avenue, NEW MALDEN, SURREY, KT3 6LA.
KINGSTON, Mr. Tom John, ACA *2009;* with Francis Clark LLP, North Quay House, Sutton Harbour, North Quay, PLYMOUTH, PL4 0RA.
•**KINGSTON, Mr. Wayne Rogers, FCA** *1981;* Keens Shay Keens Limited, Victoria House, 42-44 Shortmead Street, BIGGLESWADE, BEDFORDSHIRE, SG18 0AP.
KININMONTH, Miss. Lauren, BSc ACA *2006;* Flat 1, Park House, Highbury Park, LONDON, N5 1TJ.
KINIRONS, Mr. Peter, BA ACA *1989;* Am Rosskamp 17, 40668 MEERBUSCH, GERMANY.
KINISU, Mr. Philip Kundu Buyai, FCA *1983;* PricewaterhouseCoopers, Rahimtulla Tower, Upper Hill Road, PO Box 43963, NAIROBI, 00100 KENYA.
KINLEN, The Revd. Robert John, FCA *1972;* 292 Cowpen Road, BLYTH, NORTHUMBERLAND, NE24 5JN.
KINLEY, Miss. Alison Jean, BBA ACA *2005;* 7 Ridge Crescent, Marple, STOCKPORT, CHESHIRE, SK6 7JA.
KINLOCH, Mr. Andrew Gordon, BSc FCA *1981;* Apartment 9B, Magazine Gap Towers, 15 Magazine Gap Road, MID LEVELS, HONG KONG ISLAND, HONG KONG SAR.
KINLOCH, Mr. James Jeffrey, MA ACA *1990;* 6 Pentland Drive, EDINBURGH, EH10 6PX.
KINMOND, Miss. Elinor Jane, ACA *2010;* 10 Mondrian Road, BROMSGROVE, WORCESTERSHIRE, B60 2DP.
KINNAIR, Mr. Peter Lock, FCA *1951;* The Bungalow, 33 Plessey Avenue, BLYTH, NORTHUMBERLAND, NE24 3JR. (Life Member)
KINNARD, Mrs. Cathryn Lucy, BSc ACA *1991;* 23 Concorde Way, Woodley, READING, RG5 4NF.
KINNARD, Mr. John Derek, BSc FCA *1991;* 9 Lordswood Gardens, SOUTHAMPTON, SO16 6RY.
KINNEAR, Mr. Alexander, FCA *1974;* 34 Wellhouse Road, BECKENHAM, BR3 3JR. (Life Member)
KINNEAR, Mrs. Catherine, ACA *1992;* Stapley House, Stapley Lane, Ropley, ALRESFORD, HAMPSHIRE, SO24 0EN.
KINNEAR, Mr. Kenneth Francis, FCA *1954;* 33 Orwell Road, WALSALL, WS1 2PJ. (Life Member)
KINNEEN, Mr. Gerard Michael Andrew, BSc ACA *1985;* 19 Theydon Grove, WOODFORD GREEN, IG8 7HQ. (Life Member)
KINNEY, Mr. Martin, FCA *1962;* Markin Finance Ltd, South Broom, Westover Road, Milford on Sea, LYMINGTON, HAMPSHIRE SO41 0PW.
KINNIBURGH, Miss. Jane Elizabeth, MA(Hons) ACA *2006;* 445 The Ridgeway, ST. ALBANS, HERTFORDSHIRE, AL4 9TY.
KINNINGS-SMITH, Mrs. Joan Rachel, BSc FCA *1987;* Southwold Pier Ltd, North Parade, SOUTHWOLD, SUFFOLK, IP18 6BN.
•**KINNISON, Mrs. Julie Anne, FCA** *1990;* with FRP Advisory LLP, Southfield House, 11 Liverpool Gardens, WORTHING, WEST SUSSEX, BN11 1RY.
KINNISON, Mr. Robert Clive Andrew, BA ACA *1992;* Roffey Park Institute, Forest Road, HORSHAM, WEST SUSSEX, RH12 4TB.
KINNON, Mrs. Alison, MEng ACA *1993;* Karibu, Fernhill Lane, WOKING, SURREY, GU22 0DR.
KINNON, Mr. David John, LLB ACA *2005;* 100a Broughton Road, LONDON, SW6 2LB.
KINO, Mr. Andrew William, FCA *1974;* Beeches, Westminster Villas, ILFRACOMBE, DEVON, EX34 9NX.
KINSELLA, Mr. Andrew Jason Lee, MSc BA ACA *1997;* 18 Ardgowan Road, LONDON, SE6 1AJ.
KINSELLA, Miss. Clare Elizabeth, BA(Hons) ACA *2001;* 39 Holmes Road, TWICKENHAM, TW1 4RF.
KINSELLA, Miss. Clare Jayne, BSc ACA *1998;* Flat 15 George Gillett Court, 70 Banner Street, LONDON, EC1Y 8QH.
KINSELLA, Mr. John, FCA *1961;* 3 Argyle Road, Southborough, TUNBRIDGE WELLS, TN4 0SU.
•**KINSELLA, Mr. Kenneth Joseph, MA BBS ACA** *1995;* Apt 3003, 301 Fayetteville Street, RALEIGH, NC 27601, UNITED STATES.
•**KINSELLA, Mr. Michael Thomas, FCA** *1972;* Ridgefield Cottage, Palatine Road, Birkdale, SOUTHPORT, PR8 2BS.
KINSEY, Mr. Christopher John, ACA *2008;* Railway Cottage, 1 Station Approach, Bekesbourne, CANTERBURY, KENT, CT4 5DT.
•**KINSEY, Mr. Douglas Stawart, FCA** *1975;* Learchild Limited, 4 Lansdowne Terrace, Gosforth, NEWCASTLE UPON TYNE, NE3 1HN.
KINSEY, Mrs. Jacqueline Vera, BSc ACA *1988;* 7 Lakeside Drive, Littleover, DERBY, DE23 7US.
KINSEY, Mr. Keith Michael, BSc ACA *1987;* G L W Feeds Ltd, Ashby Road, Shepshed, LOUGHBOROUGH, LEICESTERSHIRE, LE12 9BS.
KINSEY, Mr. Martin Lowther, FCA *1973;* (Tax Fac), 25 Paxford Place, WILMSLOW, SK9 1NL.
KINSEY, Mr. Peter John, BSc ACA *1984;* 38 Eversley Road, Sketty, SWANSEA, SA2 9DA.
KINSEY, Mr. Richard, BA(Hons) ACA *2009;* 17 Bullrush Lane, Great Cambourne, CAMBRIDGE, CB23 6BG.
KINSEY, Mrs. Suzanne Jane, BSc ACA *1990;* 12 Oakhurst, LICHFIELD, WS14 9AJ.
KINSEY, Miss. Tessa Frances, ACA *2009;* 6 Gable Lodge, 334-338 Essex Road, LONDON, N1 3PB.
KINSLEY, Mr. Adam, BA ACA *1998;* Tudor Cottage, 13 Elm Park Road, PINNER, MIDDLESEX, HA5 3LE.
KINSLEY, Mr. David Jeremy, BSc FCA *1974;* VIA TRISTANO CALCO 2, 20125 MILAN, ITALY.
•**KINSLEY, Mr. John Terence, FCA** *1959;* J.T. Kinsley, 28 Harfield Road, SUNBURY-ON-THAMES, TW16 5PT.
KINSMAN, Mr. Barry Bromiley Purvis, FCA *1958;* 67 Lingdale Road, PRENTON, MERSEYSIDE, CH43 8TF. (Life Member)
KINSMAN, Mrs. Caroline Noelle, BA ACA *1990;* 58 John Street, Heyrod, STALYBRIDGE, CHESHIRE, SK15 3BS.
KINSMAN, Miss. Hannah Rachel, ACA *2009;* Cranmere, Chollacott Lane, TAVISTOCK, DEVON, PL19 9DD.
•**KINSON, Mr. Michael John, FCA** *1976;* UK Accounting Limited, 5 Saxon Close, Breedon-on-the-Hill, DERBY, DE73 8LS. See also Inspired Accountants (UK) Limited and Underwood Kinson
KINTISH, Mr. William, FCA *1971;* Kintish Ltd, Network House, 7 Scholes Lane, Prestwich, MANCHESTER, M25 0PD.
•**KINTON, Mr. Joseph, MA ACA** *2004;* Shipleys LLP, 10 Orange Street, Haymarket, LONDON, WC2H 7DQ.
KINVIG, Mr. Mark Joseph, BSc ACA *1993;* House A, 90 Peak Road, CENTRAL, HONG KONG ISLAND, HONG KONG SAR.
KIPLING, Mr. David, BCom ACA *1983;* Rose Bank, 28 Queens Road, CONSETT, DH8 0BL.
•**KIPLING, Mr. David Garrie, BSc FCA** *1989;* NWHI Limited, 194a Ferry Road, EDINBURGH, EH6 4NW. See also NWH International limited
KIPLING, Mr. Geoffrey Paul, FCA *1975;* (Tax Fac), 6 The Furrows, ST. IVES, CAMBRIDGESHIRE, PE27 5WG.
KIPLING, Mr. Jonathan Mark, FCA DChA *1975;* Cranberry, North Street, Westbourne, EMSWORTH, HAMPSHIRE, PO10 8SP.
KIPLING, Miss. Lisa Victoria, BSc ACA *1997;* 1 Barnacre Drive, Parkgate, Swirral, NESTON, CHESHIRE, CH64 6RJ.
KIPLING, Mrs. Paula, BA ACA *1989;* 194 Ferry Road, EDINBURGH, EH6 4NW.
KIPPAX, Mr. Andrew Philip Mackintosh, BA ACA *1995;* Partner Capital Ltd, 23 Grafton Street, LONDON, W1S 4EY.
KIPPING, Mr. Frederic Nigel, ACA *1981;* 5925 RFD, LONG GROVE, IL 60047, UNITED STATES.
KIR-ON, Mr. Pinhas Joseph, FCA *1970;* P.J. Kir-on, 3 Shatner Centre, 95461 JERUSALEM, ISRAEL.
•**KIRALFY, Mr. Roger, BSc ACA** *1990;* (Tax Fac), Arkadia Limited, 159 Rochester Road, Burham, ROCHESTER, KENT, ME1 3SF.
KIRBY, Mr. Adrian Paul, MA FCA *1976;* 19 Westwood Park Road, PETERBOROUGH, PE3 6JL.
KIRBY, Mr. Andrew Mark, BSc ACA *1992;* Alexander Dennis Ltd, 2-3 Dennis Way, GUILDFORD, SURREY, GU1 1AF.
KIRBY, Mr. Andrew Roger, BCom ACA *1999;* 9 The Pasture, Somersham, HUNTINGDON, CAMBRIDGESHIRE, PE28 3YX.
KIRBY, Mrs. Anna Victoria, LLB ACA *2002;* 11 Woolgreaves Close, WAKEFIELD, WF2 6DZ.
KIRBY, Mr. Benjamin James Richmond, ACA *2008;* GCP Capital Partners, Lansdowne House, 57 Berkeley Square, LONDON, W1J 6ER.
KIRBY, Miss. Cecilia Ann, MA ACA *1991;* (Tax Fac), Overfields Farm, Long Hill End Lane, Cowling, KEIGHLEY, BD22 0NR.
KIRBY, Mr. Christopher Charles, MA ACA *1987;* 2565 164 Street, SURREY V3S 0E2, BC, CANADA.
KIRBY, Mr. Christopher Mansfield, BSc ACA *1979;* 15 Fryerning Lane, INGATESTONE, CM4 0DD.
KIRBY, Miss. Clare, BSc ACA *2011;* Flat 2, 56 Dafforne Road, LONDON, SW17 8TZ.
•**KIRBY, Mr. David John, BSc(Hons) ACA** *1991;* Wilson Henry LLP, 145 Edge Lane, Edge Hill, LIVERPOOL, L7 2PF.
KIRBY, Mr. George William, LLB ACA *1981;* Willowbridge House, Green Lane, HYTHE, CT21 4DY.
KIRBY, Mrs. Helen Julie, ACA *2007;* with Larking Gowen, Summerhill House, 1 Sculthorpe Road, FAKENHAM, NORFOLK, NR21 9HA.
KIRBY, Mr. Hugh Anthony, MA ACA *1981;* Applehill Cottage, Saleshurst Park Farm, ROBERTSBRIDGE, EAST SUSSEX, TN32 5NG.
KIRBY, Mr. Ian Michael, BA ACA *2007;* 82 Swaby Road, LONDON, SW18 3QZ.
KIRBY, Mr. John Peter, FCA *1964;* The Folly, High Street, Pavenham, BEDFORD, MK43 7PE. (Life Member)
KIRBY, Miss. Lara Elizabeth, BA ACA *2011;* 38 Lakewood Crescent, BRISTOL, BS10 5HN.
KIRBY, Miss. Lisa Alexandra, ACA *2008;* 5 Jersey Way, Littleport, ELY, CAMBRIDGESHIRE, CB6 1GF.
•**KIRBY, Mr. Martin Andrew, BA FCA** *1979;* with RSM Tenon Limited, Sumner House, St Thomas's Rd, CHORLEY, PR7 1HP.
•**KIRBY, Mr. Michael Francis, BSc FCA** *1978;* (Tax Fac), Antrobus Accountants Limited, Antrobus House, 18 College Street, PETERSFIELD, HAMPSHIRE, GU31 4AD.
KIRBY, Mr. Neil Arnold, BA FCA *1990;* 39 Barleycroft Road, WELWYN GARDEN CITY, AL8 6JX.
•**KIRBY, Mr. Neil Gordon, FCA** *1979;* (Tax Fac), Kirby and Haslam, 11 King Street, KING'S LYNN, NORFOLK, PE30 1ET. See also Kirby and Haslam Limited
KIRBY, Mrs. Nichola Joan, FCA *1980;* 26 Ditchbury, LYMINGTON, SO41 9FJ.
•**KIRBY, Mr. Paul, BA FCA** *1983;* Paul Kirby & Company Ltd, Davenport House, Bawtry Road, Everton, DONCASTER, SOUTH YORKSHIRE DN10 5BP.
KIRBY, Mr. Peter Robert, MA ACA CTA *1983;* 32 St. Monica Grove, Crossgate Moor, DURHAM, DH1 4AT.
KIRBY, Mr. Philip Lewis Charles, BA ACA *2010;* 13 Howard Close, Terrington St. Clement, KING'S LYNN, NORFOLK, PE34 4JT.
KIRBY, Mr. Phillip, ACA *2008;* Brew Tea Bar, 25 Bold Street, LIVERPOOL, MERSEYSIDE, L1 4DN.
KIRBY, Mr. Raymond Arthur, FCA *1966;* 17 St. Marthas Avenue, Westfield, WOKING, SURREY, GU22 9BN.
KIRBY, Mr. Raymond Philip, BSc ACA *2006;* 17 Toddington Road, Tebworth, LEIGHTON BUZZARD, BEDFORDSHIRE, LU7 9QD.
KIRBY, Mr. Richard Alan, FCA *1969;* Roseberry House, 33a Levenside, Stokesley, MIDDLESBROUGH, NORTH YORKSHIRE, TS9 5BH.
KIRBY, Mr. Richard Graham, FCA *1968;* 9 Clare Road, BEDFORD, MK41 8QX.
KIRBY, Mr. Robert Anthony, BA ACA *1988;* 16 Southend Avenue, DARLINGTON, COUNTY DURHAM, DL3 7HL.
•**KIRBY, Miss. Sally Jane, BA FCA DChA** *1995;* Crowe Clark Whitehill LLP, St Bride's House, 10 Salisbury Square, LONDON, EC4Y 8EH. See also Horwath Clark Whitehill LLP and Crowe Clark Whitehill

KIRBY, Miss. Samantha, BSc ACA *1997;* 81c Osbaldeston Road, Stoke Newington, LONDON, N16 6NP.

KIRBY, Mrs. Samantha Louise, ACA CTA *1994;* 88 Pevensey Way, Frimley, CAMBERLEY, GU16 9UX.

•KIRBY, Mr. Shaun, BSc ACA *2000;* with KPMG LLP, 15 Canada Square, LONDON, E14 5GL.

KIRBY, Mr. Steven, MA(Oxon) ACA *2005;* 8 Edwards Lane, LONDON, N16 0JJ.

KIRBY, Mr. Terence Colin, FCA *1958;* 91 Harland Way, COTTINGHAM, HU16 5PT. (Life Member)

KIRBY, Miss. Treasa Maria, BEng ACA *1995;* 23 Spencer Road, LONDON, SW18 2SP.

•KIRBY, Mr. Victor George, FCA *1975;* Victor Kirby & Co Limited, Business & Technology Centre, Shire Hill, SAFFRON WALDEN, ESSEX, CB11 3AQ.

KIRBY, Miss. Victoria Margaret, LLB(Hons) ACA *2010;* 11 Weston Road, RUNCORN, CHESHIRE, WA7 4JX.

KIRBY, Mr. William Henry, FCA *1976;* 8 Pickles Lane, Skelmanthorpe, HUDDERSFIELD, HD8 9EJ.

KIRBY-WELCH, Mr. David Hamilton, FCA *1973;* 12 Nursery Lane, WILMSLOW, CHESHIRE, SK9 5JQ.

KIRCHEM, Mrs. Jean Miriam, FCA *1960;* 8 The Courtyard, Sudbourne Park, WOODBRIDGE, IP12 2AJ. (Life Member)

KIRCHIN, Mrs. Helen Elizabeth, BSc ACA *2001;* 16 Dove Lane, Harrold, BEDFORD, MK43 7DF.

KIRIELLA, Mrs. Malkanthi, FCA *1981;* 456 North Rocks Road, CARLINGFORD, NSW 2118, AUSTRALIA.

KIRK, Mr. Adrian Christopher, BA ACA *1992;* 8 Mardale Avenue, Urmston, MANCHESTER, M41 5SA.

KIRK, Mr. Andrew, LLB ACA *2009;* 15 The Granary, Scotter, GAINSBOROUGH, LINCOLNSHIRE, DN21 3RQ.

KIRK, Mr. Andrew Ross, ACA *2004;* 52 Nene Place, NORTHAMPTON, NN5 7PR.

KIRK, Mr. Anthony James, MA FCA *1974;* 14 Kersey Drive, Selsdon, SOUTH CROYDON, SURREY, CR2 8SX. (Life Member)

•KIRK, Mr. Bruce Anthony, BSc FCA *1978;* (Tax Fac), B.A. Kirk & Co, 21A Ulundi Road, Blackheath, LONDON, SE3 7UQ.

KIRK, Miss. Charlotte, BA ACA *2007;* Bahrain Mumtalakat Holding Company, PO Box 820, MANAMA, BAHRAIN.

KIRK, Mr. Christopher William, BSc FCA *1980;* 2 Kingscourt Cottages, Cooksmill Green, CHELMSFORD, CM1 3SJ.

KIRK, Mr. Clive Bernard, FCA *1953;* Millbrook House, Murcot, BROADWAY, WR12 7HS. (Life Member)

•KIRK, Mr. David Andrew, BSc FCA *1981;* Auker Hutton, The Stables, Little Coldharbour Farm, Tong Lane, Lamberhurst, TUNBRIDGE WELLS KENT TN3 8AD. See also Auker Hutton Limited

KIRK, Mr. David Francis, BSc FCA *1978;* Oakcroft, 34 Main Avenue, NORTHWOOD, HA6 2LQ.

•KIRK, Mr. David Geoffrey, FCA *1964;* David Kirk, 91 Bawtry Road, Bessacarr, DONCASTER, SOUTH YORKSHIRE, DN4 7AG. See also David Kirk & Company

•①KIRK, Mr. David Gerard, ACA *1990;* Kirk Hills, 5 Barnfield Crescent, EXETER, EX1 1QT. See also Kirk Hills Insolvency Ltd

•KIRK, Mr. David Kirk, MA FCA ATII *1980;* (Tax Fac), David Kirk & Co, 183 Fraser Road, SHEFFIELD, S8 0JP.

KIRK, Mr. Derek Richard, BSc FCA *1986;* 28 Salisbury Street, Beeston, NOTTINGHAM, NG9 2EQ.

KIRK, Mr. Eric Ronald, FCA *1957;* 1 Chestnut Grove, Upper Westwood, BRADFORD-ON-AVON, WILTSHIRE, BA15 2DQ. (Life Member)

•①KIRK, Mr. Geoffrey John, LLB ACA *2000;* G J Kirk LIP, 6 The Crescent, PLYMOUTH, PL1 3AB.

•KIRK, Mr. Graham, BEng FCA *1986;* (Tax Fac), Kirk Newsholme Ltd, 4315 Park Approach, Thorpe Park, LEEDS, LS15 8GB.

KIRK, Mr. Ian David, BSc ACA *1990;* 52 Aberdeen Park, LONDON, N5 2BL.

KIRK, Mr. Jeremy George, BSc FCA *1980;* 304 Hotwell Road, BRISTOL, BS8 4NN.

KIRK, Mr. Joseph Charles, FCA *1987;* 15 Trent Close, Sompting, LANCING, WEST SUSSEX, BN15 0EJ.

•KIRK, Mr. Kenneth Stanley, FCA *1959;* with Page Kirk LLP, Sherwood House, 7 Gregory Boulevard, NOTTINGHAM, NG7 6LB.

KIRK, Ms. Lesley, MA ACA PGCE *1989;* Marwell Wildlife, Owslebury, WINCHESTER, SO21 1JH.

KIRK, Mr. Martin Frederick, BSc FCA *1985;* (Tax Fac), St. Hughs, 23 Newport, LINCOLN, LN1 3DN.

KIRK, Mr. Martin Patrick, BA ACA *1986;* 6 Cannon Close, NEWARK, NG24 2LS.

KIRK, Mr. Mathew Owen, BSc CF *1994;* Talk Talk Group, 11 Evesham Street, LONDON, W11 4AR.

KIRK, Mr. Michael David, OBE FCA *1961;* 46 Shirley Road, LEICESTER, LE2 3LJ.

KIRK, Mr. Neil Philip, BA ACA *2005;* 10a Lowther Close, Langham, OAKHAM, LE15 7JJ.

KIRK, Mr. Neil Simon, BEng ACA *2001;* 54 Field Lane, TEDDINGTON, MIDDLESEX, TW11 9AS.

KIRK, Mr. Nicholas George, BSc(Hons) ACA *2001;* 3 Queens Road, EGHAM, TW20 9RT.

KIRK, Mr. Nicholas John, FCA *1970;* Vallum House, Church Lane, LINCOLN, LN2 1QJ.

KIRK, Mr. Nicholas John, MA FCA MCT *1980;* Silver Greys, 24 Onslow Road, Burwood Park, WALTON-ON-THAMES, KT12 5BB.

KIRK, Mrs. Nicola Patrice, FCA *1983;* The Wickets, 35 Barton Road, Barton Seagrave, KETTERING, NN15 6RS.

KIRK, Mr. Philip Andrew, BSc ACA *1991;* 178 Kew Road, RICHMOND, SURREY, TW9 2AS.

KIRK, Mr. Philip Anthony, BSc FCA *1982;* Aysgarth, Greenroyd Avenue, HALIFAX, WEST YORKSHIRE, HX3 0LP.

KIRK, Miss. Rebecca, BSc ACA *2005;* 3 Grosvenor Mews, Grosvenor Road, EPSOM, KT18 6JL.

•KIRK, Mr. Ronald Derek, FCA *1969;* (Tax Fac), Draycott & Kirk, Cleveland House, 92 Westgate, GUISBOROUGH, CLEVELAND, TS14 6AP.

KIRK, Mr. Ronald Leslie James, FCA *1969;* LOT A 203 RESIDENCE, 19 rue Nicolas Bouvier, 35400 SAINT MALO, FRANCE.

KIRK, Mrs. Sarah Jane, PhD MPhil BA(Hons) ACA *2010;* 61 Buccleuch Road, STOKE-ON-TRENT, ST3 4RJ.

KIRK, Miss. Sarah Victoria, BA(Hons) ACA *2010;* KPMG, PO Box 493, Century Yard Cricket Square, GEORGE TOWN, GRAND CAYMAN, ky1 1106 CAYMAN ISLANDS.

KIRK, Mr. Scott Kenneth, ACA *2001;* Clairwood, 106 Bluehouse Lane, OXTED, SURREY, RH8 0AR.

KIRK, Mr. Stephen John, MEng ACA *2002;* 11 Gleneagles Drive, Blackwell, BROMSGROVE, WORCESTERSHIRE, B60 1BD.

KIRK, Mr. Stuart, ACA *2008;* G09/279 Wellington Parade South, MELBOURNE, VIC 3002, AUSTRALIA.

KIRK, Mr. Terence Gilliland, BSc ACA *1985;* Whitston House, Woodstock Road, Charlbury, CHIPPING NORTON, OX7 3ET.

KIRK, Mr. Thomas Cyril, FCA *1953;* Hill House, 7 Temple Gardens, Moor Park, RICKMANSWORTH, WD3 1QJ. (Life Member)

•KIRK, Mr. Timothy David, FCA *1980;* (Tax Fac), P. Willson & Co, Carlton House, High Street, Higham Ferrers, RUSHDEN, NN10 8BW.

KIRKALDY, Mr. John, FCA *1965;* PO Box 323, KRIEL, MPUMULANGA PROVINCE, 2271, SOUTH AFRICA.

KIRKBRIDE, Mr. Jason, BA(Hons) ACA *2011;* 43 Alwinton Terrace, NEWCASTLE UPON TYNE, NE3 1UD.

•KIRKBRIDE, Mr. Mark Major Bowes, BA FCA CTA *1985;* (Tax Fac), Mark Kirkbride & Co Limited, Greenbanks, Hoo Lane, CHIPPING CAMPDEN, GL55 6AZ.

KIRKBRIGHT, Mr. David, FCA *1975;* 17 Thetford Close, Brandlesholme, BURY, BL8 1XB.

•KIRKBRIGHT, Mr. Paul Allan, FCA *1995;* KPMG LLP, 15 Canada Square, LONDON, E14 5GL. See also KPMG Europe LLP

KIRKBY, Mrs. Azra Nisar, BSc FCA *1993;* 66 South Lambeth Road, Vauxhall, LONDON, E16 3NN.

KIRKBY, Mr. David Ashley, FCA *1966;* Tarnok Utca 3, 1014 BUDAPEST, HUNGARY. (Life Member)

KIRKBY, Mr. Donald, MSc FCA *1962;* 9 Church Lane, MIRFIELD, WF14 9HU. (Life Member)

KIRKBY, Mrs. Florence, BSc FCA *1999;* Le Coin La Rue Du Coin, St. Ouen, JERSEY, JE3 2LJ.

KIRKBY, Mr. Gareth, BSc ACA *2004;* WorleyParsons, Level 12, 141 Walker Street, NORTH SYDNEY, NSW 2060, AUSTRALIA.

KIRKBY, Mr. Michael Robin, BSc ACA *1991;* 12 Briar Grove, Penistone, SHEFFIELD, S36 6UJ.

KIRKBY, Mr. Neil Robert Ernest, BA ACA *1992;* Gordon House Sceptre Way, Bamber Bridge, PRESTON, PR5 6AW.

KIRKBY, Mr. Peter William Ragg, FCA *1970;* Willowcroft, The Bent, Curbar, HOPE VALLEY, S32 3YD.

•KIRKBY, Mr. Robert James, BA ACA *1999;* KPMG Channel Islands Limited, 5 St. Andrew's Place, Charing Cross, St. Helier, JERSEY, JE4 8WQ.

KIRKBY, Miss. Sarah Elizabeth, LLB ACA *2002;* 29 Glenfield Road, LONDON, SW12 0HQ.

•KIRKCALDY, Miss. Victoria Jan, ACA CTA *2003;* Kirkcaldy Accountancy Ltd, 5 Hazel Close, Chandler's Ford, EASTLEIGH, HAMPSHIRE, SO53 5RF.

•KIRKE-SMITH, Mr. David Mackenzie, FCA *1972;* D.M. Kirke-Smith, Springhill House, Pilgrims Way, WESTERHAM, TN16 2DU.

KIRKE-SMITH, Mr. Douglas, ACA *2008;* Save the Children Rwanda Programme, Kacyiru - below US Embassy, PO Box 2953, KIGALI, RWANDA.

KIRKHAM, Mrs. Ann Linda, BA ACA *1996;* 6 The Green, Cutnall Green, DROITWICH, WORCESTERSHIRE, WR9 0PW.

KIRKHAM, Mrs. Carolyn Jill, BA FCA *1982;* (Tax Fac), 1 Alderwood Drive, HOOK, HAMPSHIRE, RG27 9RE.

KIRKHAM, Mrs. Christine Margaret, BA ACA *1984;* 45 Charlecote Road, Poynton, STOCKPORT, SK12 1DJ.

KIRKHAM, Mr. Darren James, BA ACA *1992;* 6 Warwick Gate, Aston, NANTWICH, CHESHIRE, CW5 8DY.

KIRKHAM, Mr. David Michael, BA(Hons) ACA *2002;* 17 Goodwood Road, Wollaton, NOTTINGHAM, NG8 2FT.

KIRKHAM, Dr. Deborah Anne, MA BA BSc ACA *1987;* 57 Goulden Road, MANCHESTER, M20 4YF.

•KIRKHAM, Mrs. Fiona Jane, BA(Hons) ACA *2001;* Baker Tilly Isle of Man LLC, PO Box 95, 2a Lord Street, Douglas, ISLE OF MAN, IM99 1HP. See also Baker Tilly Bennett Roy LLC

•KIRKHAM, Mr. Frank David, FCA *1959;* (Tax Fac), Frank Kirkham, Greetwell Place, 2 Limekiln Way, LINCOLN, LN2 4US.

KIRKHAM, Mr. Gavin Alan, ACA *2008;* Basement Flat, 5 Stanwick Road, LONDON, W14 8TL.

KIRKHAM, Mrs. Jayne Louise, BA ACA *2002;* Daniel Thwaites Plc, PO Box 50, Star Brewery, BLACKBURN, BB1 5BU.

KIRKHAM, Mrs. Jeanette Mary, BSc FCA *1976;* 29 Elvington Road, Hightown, LIVERPOOL, L38 9AN.

•KIRKHAM, Mr. Jeffery Allen, FCA *1980;* (Tax Fac), PKF (UK) LLP, St Hughs, 23 Newport, LINCOLN, LN1 3DN.

KIRKHAM, Mr. Jeffrey Alan, BSc(Econ) ACA *1992;* 54 Stafford Road, WESTON-SUPER-MARE, AVON, BS23 3BW.

KIRKHAM, Mrs. Jessica Mary, LLB ACA *1989;* 4 Richmond Close, Honingham, NORWICH, NR9 5BP.

KIRKHAM, Mr. John David, FCA *1966;* 437A Sandygate Road, SHEFFIELD, S10 5UD.

KIRKHAM, Mr. John Peter, FCA *1966;* 3 Lowlands Crescent, Great Kingshill, HIGH WYCOMBE, HP15 6EG.

KIRKHAM, Mr. Lee, OBE BSc ACA *1983;* PO Box 62084, City Square, NAIROBI, 00200, KENYA.

KIRKHAM, Mr. Leonard Jeffrey, FCA *1973;* Pinecroft, 79 Updown Hill, WINDLESHAM, GU20 6DS.

KIRKHAM, Mr. Martin Alan, BSc ARCS ACA *1986;* 25 The Meadows, Milltimber, ABERDEEN, AB13 0JT.

KIRKHAM, Mr. Michael Robert, FCA *1958;* Quedgeley, 12 Eldon Drive, ABERGELE, LL22 7BY. (Life Member)

KIRKHAM, Mrs. Rebecca Ann, BSc ACA *1982;* 8 Bishops Road, HOVE, BN3 6PQ.

•KIRKHAM, Mr. Robert James, BCom ACA *2002;* Baker Tilly Isle of Man LLC, PO Box 95, 2a Lord Street, Douglas, ISLE OF MAN, IM99 1HP. See also Baker Tilly Bennett Roy LLC

KIRKHAM, Ms. Selina, BA(Hons) ACA *2011;* Delamere, Buxton Road, Chinley, HIGH PEAK, DERBYSHIRE, SK23 6DR.

•KIRKHAM, Mr. Stephen Paul John, FCA *1982;* (Tax Fac), Spofforths LLP, One Jubilee Street, BRIGHTON, BN1 1GE. See also Spofforths Private Client Services LLP

KIRKHAM, Mrs. Susan Claire, BSc FCA *1986;* Newbiggin House, Carleton, CARLISLE, CA4 0AJ.

•KIRKHAM PARRY, Mr. Jeremy Patrick, BSc ACA *1989;* (Tax Fac), Kirkham Parry Limited, Stoneybridge House, Twardreath, PAR, CORNWALL, PL24 2TY.

KIRKHAM-SANDY, Mr. Christopher, BA FCA *1974;* QwertyWord Limited, 5 The Quadrant, EXETER, EX2 4LE.

KIRKHOPE, Mr. David Alexander, MEng ACA *1998;* 12 Elm Bank Gardens, LONDON, SW13 0NT.

KIRKHOPE, Mrs. Louisa Mary, BA ACA *1999;* Brookside Farm, Broadway Road, WINDLESHAM, SURREY, GU20 6BU.

•①KIRKHOPE, Mr. Simon Ian, BEng FCA MABRP *1997;* with Deloitte LLP, Athene Place, 66 Shoe Lane, LONDON, EC4A 3BQ.

KIRKIN, Mr. Richard William, FCA *1969;* 2 Redwood Close, Woolston, WARRINGTON, WA1 4EH.

KIRKLAND, Mr. Andrew John, ACA *1984;* 90 Eastern Road, SUTTON COLDFIELD, B73 5NX.

KIRKLAND, Mr. Charles William, FCA *1961;* Peacock Barn, Birlingham, PERSHORE, WR10 3AD.

KIRKLAND, Mr. George Smith, FCA *1954;* 71 Freeman Avenue, Hampden Park, EASTBOURNE, BN22 9NX. (Life Member)

KIRKLAND, Mr. Mark Adrian, BSc ACA *1995;* Raven Russia Ltd, 21 Knightsbridge, LONDON, SW1X 7LY.

KIRKLAND, Mrs. Natalie Suk Yin, BSc ACA *2011;* 68 Cotswold Way, WORCESTER PARK, SURREY, KT4 8LN.

KIRKLAND, Mr. Paul John, BSc ACA *1996;* 79 Westfields Avenue, LONDON, SW13 0AY.

KIRKLAND, Mr. Peter Robert, FCA *1973;* 23 Ellenborough Place, LONDON, SW15 5LZ. (Life Member)

•KIRKLAND, Mr. Peter Sydney, FCA *1966;* Peter S Kirkland, 30 Sunningdale Drive, Woodborough, NOTTINGHAM, NG14 6EQ.

KIRKLAND, Miss. Shelagh, BSc ACA *1985;* (Tax Fac), 1 King Stairs Close, Off Elephant Lane, LONDON, SE16 4JF.

KIRKLEY, Miss. Julie Marie, MMath ACA *2003;* 29 Hallamgate Road, SHEFFIELD, S10 5BS.

KIRKMAN, Mr. Andrew Michael David, MA ACA *1997;* 1 Sheep Walk Mews, LONDON, SW19 4QL.

KIRKMAN, Mr. Brian, FCA *1967;* 13 Lingmoor Road, Heaton, BOLTON, BL1 5EA.

KIRKMAN, Mr. David John, MA FCA *1959;* 35 Newfield Crescent, Dore, SHEFFIELD, S17 3DE. (Life Member)

KIRKMAN, Mr. Michael Christopher, BSc ACA *2000;* 27 Bowes Road, WALTON-ON-THAMES, SURREY, KT12 3HT.

KIRKMAN, Mr. Peter John, MA FCA *1970;* Acorn House, 114 Mitton Road, Whalley, CLITHEROE, BB7 9JN. (Life Member)

KIRKMAN, Mr. Stephen Alan, BA ACA *1989;* 11 Etive Place, Woodthorpe, YORK, YO24 2XG.

KIRKNESS, Mr. Christopher Desmond, ACA *1979;* Korn Ferry Whitehead Mann, Ryder Court, 14 Ryder Street, LONDON, SW1Y 6QB.

•KIRKNESS, Mr. David John, FCA *1970;* (Tax Fac), Kirkness & Co., 21 Silver Street, OTTERY ST. MARY, EX11 1DB.

KIRKNESS, Mr. Edward Carl, BSc ACA *2004;* Flat 304, Maritime House, Old Town, LONDON, SW4 0JW.

KIRKNESS, Mr. James Henry Magnusen, FCA *1971;* 41 impasse des Muriers, 30000 NIMES, FRANCE.

KIRKNESS, Mr. Roraigh David McCall, ACA *2008;* 334 Wandsworth Bridge Road, LONDON, SW6 2TZ.

KIRKNESS, Mr. William, ACA *2009;* 11 Homemead Road, BROMLEY, BR2 8BB.

KIRKOS, Mr. Christos, BEng ACA *2006;* 21 St. Marks Avenue, ALTRINCHAM, CHESHIRE, WA14 4JB.

KIRKOS, Mr. Costas, BA ACA *1985;* 4 Boumboulivas Street, 1060 NICOSIA, CYPRUS.

KIRKPATRICK, Mr. Brian Robert, MA FCA *1972;* Dove House, Hurtmore Road, GODALMING, GU7 2RA. (Life Member)

KIRKPATRICK, Mr. David, BSc ACA *2010;* 63a St. Philip Street, LONDON, SW8 3SS.

KIRKPATRICK, Mr. Donald Bruce, FCA *1947;* 100 Pentecost Avenue, PYMBLE, NSW 2073, AUSTRALIA. (Life Member)

KIRKPATRICK, Mrs. Emma Jayne, BSc ACA *2010;* Flat 8 Alveston Court, 85-87 Holland Road, HOVE, EAST SUSSEX, BN3 1JP.

•KIRKPATRICK, Mr. John Edward, FCA *1976;* 502 Lickey Road Cofton, BIRMINGHAM, B45 8UU.

KIRKPATRICK, Mrs. Kathryn Louise, BSc ACA *2006;* 156 Westley Road, BURY ST. EDMUNDS, SUFFOLK, IP33 3SD.

KIRKPATRICK, Mr. Keith, BA ACA *1999;* 73 Cranford Gardens, West Bridgford, NOTTINGHAM, NOTTINGHAMSHIRE, NG2 7SE.

KIRKPATRICK, Miss. Laura, ACA *2008;* 8 Roseland Avenue, MANCHESTER, M20 3QY.

KIRKPATRICK, Mr. Roger James, FCA *1963;* Society of St. Francis, The Friary, Hilfield, DORCHESTER, DORSET, DT2 7BE.

KIRKPATRICK, Mr. Thomas, MA ACA *1987;* Globe OP Financial Servcies Ltd, Grand Buildings, 1-3 Strand, LONDON, WC2N 5HR.

KIRKUP, Mr. David, MA BSc FCA *1978;* M S I Forks, Carr Hill, DONCASTER, SOUTH YORKSHIRE, DN4 8DH.

KIRKUP, Mr. Frederick William, FCA *1965;* Rua Dos Ingleses 222-131, Bela Vista, SAO PAULO, BRAZIL.

KIRKUP, Mr. Michael James, FCA *1962;* Shepherds House, Shepherds Lane, Hurley, MAIDENHEAD, SL6 5NG. (Life Member)

KIRKUP, Mr. Michael Richard, BA ACA CTA *1984;* 20 Belle Vue Avenue, Gosforth, NEWCASTLE UPON TYNE, NE3 1AH.

KIRKWOOD, Mr. Allan Steven, BSc(Hons) ACA *2010;* 32 Salisbury Road, EXETER, EX4 6LU.
•**KIRKWOOD, Mr. David Ian, FCA** *1972;* (Tax Fac), Alwyns LLP, Crown House, 151 High Road, LOUGHTON, ESSEX, IG10 4LG.
•①**KIRKWOOD, Mr. Edwin James, BA FCA** *1979;* Bridgewood Financial Solutions Ltd, Bridgewood Financial Solutions, 23-24 Westminster Buildings, Theatre Square, NOTTINGHAM, NG1 6LG. See also EJK Associates Limited
KIRKWOOD, Mrs. Isobel Jennifer, BSc ACA *2000;* Northern Rock (Asset Management) Plc Prudhoe Building, Regent Centre Gosforth, NEWCASTLE UPON TYNE, NE3 4AW.
•**KIRKWOOD, Mr. John, FCA** *1960;* (Tax Fac), J.Kirkwood & Co, School End, Rowton Bridge Road, Christleton, CHESTER, CH3 7BD.
KIRKWOOD, Mrs. Karen Natasha, BA ACA *1999;* with PricewaterhouseCoopers, 1 Embankment Place, LONDON, WC2N 6RH.
KIRKWOOD, Mr. Paul, BEng ACA *1999;* 15 Anzio Gardens, CATERHAM, SURREY, CR3 5GE.
KIRKWOOD, Mr. Scott, BA ACA *2007;* Flat 7, 65 Putney Bridge Road, LONDON, SW18 1NP.
•**KIRKWOOD-WILSON, Mrs. Caroline Elizabeth, BA FCA** *1982;* Caroline Wilson, 45 Kensington Road, SOUTHPORT, MERSEYSIDE, PR9 0RT.
KIRMAN, Mr. John Ernest, FCA *1972;* Old Vicarage, Market Place, Easingwold, YORK, YO61 3AL.
KIRPALANI, Mr. Heeranand Lachiram, MBE BCom FCA *1964;* Swymmers Farm, Broad Road, Blagdon, BRISTOL, BS40 7XJ.
KIRPALANI, Mr. Shankar Tuljaram, FCA *1975;* 33 Ocean Crest, 85 Warden Rd, MUMBAI 4000036, MAHARASHTRA, INDIA.
KIRRAGE, Mr. John Kenneth, BA ACA *1989;* 24 Southernhay, LEIGH-ON-SEA, SS9 5PF.
KIRRANE, Mr. Christopher John, FCA *1969;* 2 Newton Drive, Greenmount, BURY, BL8 4DH.
•**KIRSHEN, Mr. Andrew Simon, FCA** *1975;* Kershen Fairfax Limited, Beacon House, 113 Kingsway, LONDON, WC2B 6PP. See also Kershen Fairfax
KIRSOP, Mrs. Hannah Rachel Irene, BA ACA *2006;* 46 Worlingham Road, LONDON, SE22 9HD.
KIRSOPP, Mr. Michael, BA ACA *1999;* Ash View Station Road, Cumwhinton, CARLISLE, CA4 8DJ.
KIRSTEIN, Mr. Ivor Malcolm, FCA *1960;* I.M. Kirstein F.C.A., 26 Wensley Avenue, WOODFORD GREEN, IG8 9HE. (Life Member)
KIRSZANEK, Mr. Paul James, BA(Hons) ACA *2001;* Tote, Douglas House, Tote Park, Chapel Lane, WIGAN, LANCASHIRE WN3 4HS.
KIRTHI-SINGHA, Mr. Astrapani Chittranjan, MA FCA *1963;* By-the-Wey, Tannery Lane, Send, WOKING, GU23 7EF. (Life Member)
KIRTHISINGHA, Mr. Arjan Vishan, BSc ACA *1998;* Anglo American Luxembourg, 48 Rue de Bragance, 1-1255, LUXEMBOURG, LUXEMBOURG.
KIRTLAND, Mrs. Alison Margaret, BA ACA *1998;* 48 Church Lane, Dry Sandford, ABINGDON, OX13 6JP.
•**KIRTLAND, Mr. Robert Maurice, BSc FCA** *1992;* Critchleys LLP, Greyfriars Court, Paradise Square, OXFORD, OX1 1BE. See also Landtax LLP
KIRTLEY, Mr. Ian Simpson, BSc ACA *1987;* 11 Baronswood, Gosforth, NEWCASTLE UPON TYNE, NE3 3UB.
•**KIRTON, Mr. Christopher Hedley, FCA ATII** *1981;* with BDO LLP, 2 City Place, Beehive Ring Road, GATWICK, WEST SUSSEX, RH6 0PA.
KIRTON, Mrs. Emma Helen, BSc(Hons) ACA *2009;* Severn Bunkers Hill Close, Tetney, GRIMSBY, SOUTH HUMBERSIDE, DN36 5PF.
KIRTON, Mr. John Robert, FCA *1967;* Pool Tree Farm, Hamsterley, BISHOP AUCKLAND, COUNTY DURHAM, DL13 3QW.
•**KIRTON, Mr. Shane Edward, BA FCA** *1987;* (Tax Fac), Kirton & Co, 3 Primrose Close, HEMEL HEMPSTEAD, HP1 2DL.
KIRVELL, Mr. Paul Richard, BA ACA *1988;* 62 Inverness Mews, LONDON, E16 2SP.
KIRVEN, Mr. David, BSc ACA *1991;* 20 Derrymore Road, Willerby, HULL, HU10 6ES.
•**KIRWAN, Mr. Edward Oliver, FCA** *1962;* Edward O Kirwan, 3 Pine Tree Garden, Oadby, LEICESTER, LE2 5UT.
KIRWAN, Mr. Michael Ralph, FCA *1964;* 18 Greenhill Gardens, EDINBURGH, EH10 4BW. (Life Member)
KIRWAN, Mr. Patrick Anthony, BA ACA *1995;* 2a St Giles Road, LONDON, SE5 7RL.
KIRWAN, Mr. Peter Andrew Charles, MSci ACA *2007;* 15 Beaker Close, Smeeton Westerby, LEICESTER, LE8 0RT.
KIRWIN, Mr. David Charles, BSc ACA CTA *2002;* 7 Hornby Chase, Maghull, LIVERPOOL, MERSEYSIDE, L31 5PP.
KISBY, Mr. Edward John, BA FCA *1980;* (Tax Fac), MacFarlanes Solicitors, 20 Cursitor Street, LONDON, EC4A 1LT.
KISBY, Mr. Joseph John, ACA *2009;* 9 Mulberry Close, Heald Green, CHEADLE, CHESHIRE, SK8 3NJ.
KISBY, Mr. Michael, FCA *1973;* 5 Main Street, Peatling Magna, LEICESTER, LE8 5UQ.
KISIC, Mr. Marco, ACA *2010;* Flat 40, Clifton House, Club Row, LONDON, E2 7HB.
KISILU, Mr. Japheth Musembi, ACA *1994;* P.O. Box 57637, NAIROBI, 00200, KENYA.
KISSACH, Mr. Mark Andrew, BA ACA *2004;* Henkel Ltd, 2 Apollo Court Bishops Square Business Park, HATFIELD, HERTFORDSHIRE, AL10 9EY.
KISSACK, Mr. Mark, BA ACA *1992;* Ch. du Bon 3, 1134 VUFFLENS-LE-CHATEAU, SWITZERLAND.
•**KISSANE, Mr. Patrick John, LLB FCA** *1965;* Unit 1, 8 Musgrave Crescent 0810, DARWIN, NT 0810, AUSTRALIA.
•**KISSUN, Miss. Nicole Yvette, BSc ACA** *1988;* PKF (UK) LLP, Farringdon Place, 20 Farringdon Road, LONDON, EC1M 3AP.
KITABI, Miss. Farrah, ACA DChA *2009;* flat 13, 3 Cottage Road, LONDON, N7 8TP.
KITANOVA, Ms. Petya, ACA *2008;* H J Heinz Co Ltd Hayes Park South Building, Hayes End Road, HAYES, MIDDLESEX, UB4 8AL.
KITCATT, Mr. Martin David, BSc ACA CF *1988;* 5 Aldford Street, LONDON, W1K 2AF.
KITCHEN, Mrs. Alison Mary, BA ACA *1987;* 5 Myrnong Crescent, TOORAK, VIC 3142, AUSTRALIA.
KITCHEN, Mr. Geoffrey Lambert, FCA *1953;* Fieldhead, 22 Goose Cote Lane, Oakworth, KEIGHLEY, WEST YORKSHIRE, BD22 7NG. (Life Member)
KITCHEN, Mr. Graham Morton, FCA *1963;* Vicarage Cottage, East Kennett, MARLBOROUGH, SN8 4EY.
KITCHEN, Mrs. Jacqueline Elizabeth, LLB ACA *1980;* 2 Woodlands Park Avenue, Woodlands Park, MAIDENHEAD, SL6 3LS.
KITCHEN, Mr. John Martin, FCA *1956;* 14 Westfield Road, MIRFIELD, WF14 9PW. (Life Member)
KITCHEN, Mr. Perry Duncan Crispin Newent, MA FCA *1979;* Chelsea Financial Services Plc St. James Hall, Moore Park Road, LONDON, SW6 2JS.
KITCHEN, Mr. Peter Keith, BA ACA *1991;* with BDO LLP, Emerald House, East Street, EPSOM, SURREY, KT17 1HS.
•**KITCHEN, Mr. Philip Thomas, BA(Hons) ACA** *2009;* with PCLG Limited, Equinox House, Clifton Park Avenue, Shipton Road, YORK, YO30 5PA.
KITCHEN, Mr. Robert George Christopher, FCA *1972;* Boskessy, Cargreen, SALTASH, PL12 6PA.
KITCHEN, Miss. Sarah, BA ACA *1999;* (Tax Fac), Flat 8, Elm House, 8 Allerton Park, LEEDS, LS7 4ND.
KITCHEN, Mrs. Tracy, BA FCA *1989;* 36 Stradella Road, LONDON, SE24 9HA.
•**KITCHEN, Mr. William Vernon, BSc ACA** *1978;* (Tax Fac), 6 Brookfield Avenue, Fulwood, PRESTON, PR2 6XR.
KITCHENER, Mr. Ellis, MA ACA *2002;* 18a St. Georges Square, LONDON, SW1V 2HP.
KITCHENER, Mr. John Charles, MEng ACA CISA *1992;* 19 Theobalds Road, LEIGH-ON-SEA, ESSEX, SS9 2NE.
•**KITCHER, Mr. George Albert, FCA** *1976;* George A. Kitcher & Company, 1 Cyncoed Crescent, Cyncoed, CARDIFF, CF23 6SW.
KITCHIN, Mr. Stephen Adrian, BEng ACA *2003;* 16 Minden Close, WOKINGHAM, BERKSHIRE, RG41 3UG.
KITCHING, Mr. Graham Edward, BSc ACA *1990;* 326 Eastgaste Drive, MONMOUTH JUNCTION, NJ 08852, UNITED STATES.
KITCHING, Mr. Neil Cameron, MA ACA *1992;* 13 Drummond Rise, DUNBLANE, FK15 0EX.
KITCHING, Mr. St John, ACA MAAT *1995;* 91 Tunstall Road, CROYDON, CR0 6TZ.
KITCHING, Mr. Stephen Mark, BSc ACA *1989;* Stirk Lambert & Co Russell Chambers, 61a North Street, KEIGHLEY, BD21 3DS.
KITCHINGMAN, Mr. Andrew James, BSc FCA *1989;* 2 wellington place, LEEDS, ls14af.
KITE, Miss. Alice Elizabeth, ACA *2010;* 45 Whitton Walk, LONDON, E3 2AF.
•**KITE, Mrs. Barbara Patricia, FCA ATII** *1986;* (Tax Fac), 4 The Waldrons, OXTED, SURREY, RH8 9DY.
KITE, Mr. Edward, MEng ACA *2002;* 291 Pedro de Valdivia, Providencia, SANTIAGO CP 7500524, CHILE.
KITE, Mrs. Pamela Jane, MA ACA *1987;* Cheriton Rowton Lane Rowton, CHESTER, CH3 6AT.
KITE, Mr. Philip John, BA FCA *1985;* Flat 5, Eastfield House, 15 Moor Road South, NEWCASTLE UPON TYNE, NE3 1NP.
•**KITE, Mr. Raymond John, FCA DChA** *1975;* with Helmores UK LLP, Grosvenor Gardens House, 35-37 Grosvenor Gardens, LONDON, SW1W 0BY.
•**KITE, Mr. Simon Rollo, BSc FCA** *1995;* Saffery Champness, City Tower, Piccadilly Plaza, MANCHESTER, M1 4BT.
KITE, Mr. Timothy James, BSc ACA *1984;* (Tax Fac), Arisaig, Reading Road North, FLEET, GU51 4HP.
KITELEY, Mr. Timothy John, BSc(Hons) ACA ATII PGCE *2001;* Dow France SAS, 8 Route De Herrlisheim, 67410 DRUSENHEIM, FRANCE.
KITHORAY, Mr. Tej Paul Singh, MA ACA *1998;* 15 Beaulieu Gardens, West Bridgford, NOTTINGHAM, NG2 7TL.
KITIBOS, Mrs. Martha, ACA *2009;* 69 Vera Avenue, LONDON, N21 1RJ.
KITLEY, Mr. Robert Gowan, BSc ACA *1990;* 1 Holywell Terrace, Holywell Street, SHREWSBURY, SY2 5DF.
KITNEY, Mr. Stephen James, ACA *1991;* Stenball Construction Ltd St. Martins House Business Centre, Ockham Road South East Horsley, LEATHERHEAD, KT24 6RX.
KITSBERG, Mr. Jonathan Stuart, BA ACA *1991;* 69 Reuben Street, 99544 BET SHEMESH, ISRAEL.
•**KITSON, Mr. Alan Phillip, FCA** *1974;* Alan Kitson & Company Limited, 65 Kingswood Chase, LEIGH-ON-SEA, SS9 3BB.
KITSON, Mr. Arran, MA BA ACA *2003;* RWE Supply & Trading Switzerland SA, 1 Rue de Jargonnant, CH-1207 GENEVA, SWITZERLAND.
KITSON, Mr. David, LLB ACA *2005;* Flat 9 Norman House, St. Saviours Estate, LONDON, SE1 3DH.
•**KITSON, Mr. James Buller, FCA** *1975;* Metherell Gard, Old Memorial Hall, Morval, LOOE, CORNWALL, PL13 1PN.
KITSON, Mr. James Jordan Heyworth, BEng FCA *1992;* The Manor House, 9 Worships Hill, Riverhead, SEVENOAKS, TN13 2AS.
KITSON, Mr. Jeremy Paul, BA ACA *2004;* 44 Lugtrout Lane, SOLIHULL, B91 2SB.
KITSON, Mrs. Leanne Clare, BSc ACA *2004;* 37 Bevington Close, Patchway, BRISTOL, BS34 5NW.
KITSON, Mr. Peter, ACA *1986;* Killgerm Group Limited, Wakefield Road, OSSETT, WEST YORKSHIRE, WF5 9AJ.
KITTERICK, Mr. Martin Joseph, BA FCA CF *1989;* 45 Waterloo Lane, Ballsbridge, DUBLIN 4, COUNTY DUBLIN, IRELAND.
KITTLE, Mr. Robert Lewis, FCA *1969;* 918 Shabona Lane, Wilmette, CHICAGO, IL 60091, UNITED STATES. (Life Member)
KITTO, Mr. John Wesley, BSc FCA *1978;* Charity Farm, Birchley Heath, NUNEATON, WARWICKSHIRE, CV10 0QX.
KITTO, Mr. Michael, BA ACA CF *1990;* 25 Riceyman House, Lloyd Baker Street, LONDON, WC1X 9BH.
KITTO, Mr. Nicholas John, FCA *1977;* 3 Ocean Court, 21 H.H. Wing Lung Road, CLEARWATER BAY, KOWLOON, HONG KONG SAR.
KITTO, Miss. Sasha, LLB ACA *2001;* PricewaterhouseCoopers, 91 King William Street, ADELAIDE, SA 5000, AUSTRALIA.
KITTOE, Mr. Stephen Maurice, FCA *1974;* Lavender House, 255 Southbourne Road, EASTBOURNE, EAST SUSSEX, BN22 8RE.
•**KITTS, Mr. Alan Raymond, BA FCA** *1963;* Doron, Hazel Avenue, Redland, BRISTOL, BS6 6UD.
KIVERSTEIN, Mr. Ivor, FCA *1968;* Tullens Toat, Pickhurst Lane, PULBOROUGH, WEST SUSSEX, RH20 1DA.
KIYANI, Mr. Nadeem, BCom ACA *1996;* 4 Wordsworth Avenue, LONDON, E18 2HE.
KIZILBASH, Mr. Sohail Alam, FCA *1974;* 6183 Teal Lane NW, ROCHESTER, MN 55901, UNITED STATES.
KIZILIS, Mrs. Mary Elizabeth, BA ACA *2005;* 67 Hazell Close, CLEVEDON, AVON, BS21 5DW.
KLAHR, Mr. Harry Tobias, BSc FCA *1967;* 20 Chessington Court, Charter Way, LONDON, N3 3DT. (Life Member)
KLANG, Miss. Camilla Gudrun Ulrika, BA ACA *2007;* Flat 3, 14 Belsize Park, LONDON, NW3 4ES.
KLANGA, Miss. Andre, BSc ACA *2002;* 55 Wynchgate, Southgate, LONDON, N14 6RH.
KLANTE, Mrs. Pauline, BSc ACA *2002;* 5/36 Cranbrook Avenue, CREMORNE, NSW 2090, AUSTRALIA.
KLASS, Mr. Julian Nicholas, BSc ACA *1996;* 70 Court Way, TWICKENHAM, TW2 7SW.
KLAUBER, Mr. Peter Arthur, BA FCA *1982;* 4 Gloucester Gardens, LONDON, NW11 9AB.
KLEANTHOUS, Mr. Akis Stelios, MBA BSc ACA *1999;* 6 Onisillos street, 3075 LIMASSOL, CYPRUS.
KLEANTHOUS, Mr. Christos Stelios, BSc ACA *2004;* 6 Onisillou, 3075 LIMASSOL, CYPRUS.
KLEBOE, Miss. Victoria Joanne, ACA *2009;* 8 Tudor Hall, Branksome Park Road, CAMBERLEY, GU15 2AE.
KLECHTCHEV, Mr. Vladimir, BA FCA *2000;* 170D Muswell Hill Road, LONDON, N10 3NG.
KLEE, Mr. Robert Graham Patrick, BSc(Hons) FCA *1987;* The Firs, 9 Stilemans Wood, Cressing, BRAINTREE, CM77 8GR.
•**KLEIN, Mr. Anthony Philip, FCA FCCA** *1974;* (Tax Fac), Gross Klein, 6 Breams Buildings, LONDON, EC4A 1QL. See also Gross, Klein & Partners
KLEIN, Miss. Kelly, BSc ACA *2006;* with PricewaterhouseCoopers LLP, 300 Madison Avenue, NEW YORK, NY 10017, UNITED STATES.
KLEIN, Mrs. Louise, BA ACA *1989;* 53 Hawthorn Lane, WILMSLOW, CHESHIRE, SK9 5DQ.
•**KLEIN, Mr. Nicholas Jeffrey, FCA FCCA** *1983;* (Tax Fac), Klein Evangelou, 368 Forest Road, LONDON, E17 5JF.
KLEIN, Mrs. Sheela, BCom ACA *1995;* 5 Ridley Park, 02-03 Tanglin Park, SINGAPORE 248476, SINGAPORE.
•**KLEINBERG, Mr. Marcus David, FCA** *1974;* M.D. Kleinberg & Co, 12 Gill's Hill Lane, RADLETT, WD7 8DF.
KLEINBERG, Mr. Sidney Alexander, FCA *1941;* Flat 24, Lutyens Lodge, 523 Uxbridge Road, Hatch End, PINNER, MIDDLESEX HA5 4JX. (Life Member)
•**KLEINER, Mr. Richard Howard, FCA** *1983;* Richard Kleiner LLP, 25 Harley Street, LONDON, W1G 9BR. See also Gerald Edelman Transaction Services Ltd
•**KLEINFELD, Mr. Nigel Peter, FCA** *1974;* MWS, Kingsridge House, 601 London Road, WESTCLIFF-ON-SEA, ESSEX, SS0 9PE.
KLEINMAN, Miss. Lisa Jayne, BA ACA *2006;* with PricewaterhouseCoopers LLP, Hays Galleria, 1 Hays Lane, LONDON, SE1 2RD.
•**KLEINMAN, Mr. Paul Raymond, BA FCA** *1983;* (Tax Fac), Kleinman Graham, Turnberry House, 1404 -1410 High Road, Whetstone, LONDON, N20 9BH. See also Howard Frank Limited and Graham Kleinman
KLEINMAN, Mr. Robert, BA(Hons) ACA *2010;* Flat 23 Monarchs Court, 10 Grenville Place, LONDON, NW7 3SF.
KLEINWORT, Mrs. Sarah Elizabeth, BA ACA *1998;* 5 Scarsdale Villas, LONDON, W8 6PT.
KLEMEN, Mr. Alexander Peter, BSc FCA *1971;* Le Gres Bas, 12270 NAJAC, FRANCE.
•①**KLEMPKA, Mr. Edward, FCA** *1979;* Begbies Traynor (Central) LLP, 340 Deansgate, MANCHESTER, M3 4LY.
KLENK, Mrs. Margaret Mary, BA ACA *1990;* 2 Henacre Wood Court, Queensbury, BRADFORD, BD13 2LJ.
KLEOVOULOU, Miss. Despo, BA ACA *2011;* 10 Ayias Zonis, 3027 LIMASSOL, CYPRUS.
KLEOVOULOU, Mr. Zenon, BA ACA *2007;* Flat 4/H, Oxford & Cambridge Mansions, Old Marylebone Road, LONDON, NW1 5EE.
KLEPPEN, Mr. Douglas James, BSc ACA *1995;* Eversley House, 8 Alexandra Place, ILKLEY, WEST YORKSHIRE, LS29 9ES.
KLEPPEN, Mr. Stephen John, BSc ACA *1991;* 55 High Street North, Stewkley, LEIGHTON BUZZARD, BEDFORDSHIRE, LU7 0EZ.
•**KLEPZIG, Mr. Roland Peter, MA FCA** *1987;* (Tax Fac), Roland Klepzig Limited, 42 Copperfield Street, LONDON, SE1 0DY.
KLERIDES, Mr. Mark, BA ACA *2007;* CMK Eurofinance Consultants Ltd, P.O. Box 28681, 2081 NICOSIA, CYPRUS.
KLETZ, Mr. Anthony Michael, BCom FCA *1986;* 16 Hill Rise View, Aughton, ORMSKIRK, L39 3RG.
KLEYMAN, Mr. Emanuel David, FCA *1964;* Mail Box 176, Ctra Cabo La Nao (Pla) 124-6, Javea, 03730 ALICANTE, SPAIN.
KLEYN, Mr. Warren Learoy Anthony, MBA BSc ACA *1985;* 11 Princes Close, SOUTH CROYDON, SURREY, CR2 9BP.
KLEYNHANS, Ms. Nicola Maria, ACA CA(SA) *2009;* 127 Ashmore Road, LONDON, W9 3DA.
KLIMCZAK, Miss. Anna Elise, BA(Hons) ACA *2010;* Cross Hill House, Tidenham, CHEPSTOW, GWENT, NP16 7JF.
•**KLINGAMAN, Ms. Elizabeth Klingaman, MA FCA** *1992;* HWEA Ltd, 8 Hopper Way, Diss Business Park, DISS, NORFOLK, IP22 4GT.
•**KLINGER, Mr. Philip David, BSc FCA** *1972;* Westbury, 145/157 St John Street, LONDON, EC1V 4PY.
KLINKENBERG, Mr. Michael Anthony, BA ACA *1994;* 80 Southern Cross Circle, Ocean Reef, PERTH, WA 6027, AUSTRALIA.
KLIPPEL, Mr. John, FCA *1956;* The Garden Bungalow, 62a High Oak Road, WARE, HERTFORDSHIRE, SG12 7PD. (Life Member)

KLITOU, Mr. Marios Aristotelous, BA FCA *1991;* with Baker Tilly Klitou and Partners Ltd, 11 Bouboulinas Street, 1060 NICOSIA, CYPRUS.
KLOER, Mr. John Parsons, FCA *1968;* 78 Painswick Road, CHELTENHAM, GL50 2EU.
KLOKKOS, Mr. George, BA ACA *1982;* 117 Brindley Close, WEMBLEY, MIDDLESEX, HA0 1BT.
KLUGER, Mrs. Heather Louise, FCA *1972;* 51 Granville Road, BARNET, EN5 4DS.
KLUGER, Mr. John William, FCA *1975;* 51 Granville Road, BARNET, EN5 4DS.
KLUTSE, Mr. Paul Kojo, BSc ACA *2005;* 20 Highwood Park, CRAWLEY, RH11 9PP.
•KLUYVER, Mrs. Fiona Gaye, BCom FCA *1983;* F.G. Kluyver, Moor End, Bridge Street, Lower Moor, PERSHORE, WORCESTERSHIRE WR10 2PL.
KLYHN, Mr. Richard Derek, MBA BSc ACA *1982;* 26 Lexham Gardens, AMERSHAM, HP6 5JP.
•KNAGGS, Mr. Colin, FCA *1980;* (Tax Fac), Sadofskys, Princes House, Wright Street, HULL, HU2 8HX. See also Procuro Payroll Services Ltd
KNAGGS, Mr. Keith Anthony, MA MSc FCA *1975;* Felbridge Normanby, Sinnington, YORK, YO62 6RH.
KNAPMAN, Mr. David John, FCA *1973;* with Baker Tilly Tax & Advisory Services LLP, The Pinnacle, 170 Midsummer Boulevard, MILTON KEYNES, MK9 1BP.
KNAPMAN, Mr. Jonathan Paul, ACA *1992;* Brend Hotels Park Hotel, New Road, BARNSTAPLE, DEVON, EX32 9AE.
KNAPMAN, Mr. Peter John, FCA *1973;* 3 Downlands, New Town Road, Storrington, PULBOROUGH, WEST SUSSEX, RH20 4LZ.
•KNAPP, Mr. Alan John, FCA *1975;* Littlejohn LLP, 1 Westferry Circus, Canary Wharf, LONDON, E14 4HD.
•KNAPP, Mr. Daniel Bernard, FCA CF *1975;* Baker Tilly Tax & Advisory Services LLP, 3rd Floor Preece House, Davigdor Road, HOVE, EAST SUSSEX, BN3 1RE. See also Baker Tilly Corporate Finance LLP
•KNAPP, Mr. John Emerson, BSc FCA *1978;* 10 Heath Gardens, Manor Heath Road, HALIFAX, HX3 0BD.
KNAPP, Mr. Richard Philip, BA ACA *2000;* 18 Bradgate Road, HINCKLEY, LEICESTERSHIRE, LE10 1LA.
•KNAPP, Mrs. Sally Ann, ACA *1982;* JMBt Limited, The Old Studio, High Street, West Wycombe, HIGH WYCOMBE, HP14 3AB.
KNAPP, Mr. Simon, BA(Hons) ACA *2002;* The International Institute for Strategic Studies, 13-15 Arundel Street, LONDON, WC2R 3DX.
•KNAPPER, Mrs. Alison, BSc ACA *2003;* Tax - Easy, Mayfield Cottage, Eastham Street, CLITHEROE, LANCASHIRE, BB7 2HY.
KNAPPER, Mr. Andrew Mark, BA(Hons) ACA *2010;* 37 Vincent Street, CREWE, CW1 4AA.
•KNAPTON, Mr. Anthony John, FCA *1967;* (Tax Fac), Anthony J. Knapton, 6 St. Johns Close, Bovey Tracey, NEWTON ABBOT, DEVON, TQ13 9BU.
KNAPTON, Mr. Anthony William, FCA *1960;* 62 Shaftesbury Avenue, DONCASTER, DN2 6EQ. (Life Member)
KNAPTON, Mr. Kevin, MA BSc ACA *2005;* 2 The Homestead, 19 Crescent East, Hadley Wood, BARNET, HERTFORDSHIRE, EN4 0EY.
KNAPTON, Mr. Mark Christopher David, ACA *1987;* Lloyds Banking Group, Trinity Road, HALIFAX, HX1 2RG.
KNATCHBULL, Mr. Andrew James, BCom FCA *1993;* R A B Capital, 1 Adam Street, LONDON, WC2N 6LE.
KNATCHBULL, Miss. Melinda Lu San, BA ACA *2001;* 6 Kilmington Close, Hutton, BRENTWOOD, ESSEX, CM13 2JZ.
KNEAFSEY, Ms. Hannah Mary, ACA *2009;* West Croft Farm, Skirpenbeck, YORK, YO41 1HF.
KNEALE, Mr. John, FCA *1954;* 42 Meadow Road, WOKINGHAM, RG41 2TD. (Life Member)
•KNEALE, Mr. Martin James, BA ACA *2001;* PKF (Isle of Man) LLC, PO Box 16, Analyst House, Douglas, ISLE OF MAN, IM99 1AP.
KNEALE, Mr. Peter Charles Williams, FCA *1983;* 5 Blackthorne Road, LICHFIELD, STAFFORDSHIRE, WS14 9YJ.
KNEE, Mr. Gareth David, BA ACA *1997;* 20 Sturges Road, WOKINGHAM, BERKSHIRE, RG40 2HD.
KNEE, Mr. Peter Lawrence Charles, ACA *1979;* SmartCast Solutions Ltd, 5 Laggan Gardens, BATH, BA1 5RX.
KNEE, Miss. Rachel Joanne, ACA *2007;* Queens House, Thomas Westcott, 44 New Street, HONITON, DEVON, EX14 1BJ.
•KNEE, Mr. Simon David, BA FCA *1993;* (Tax Fac), SD Knee Ltd, 10 Bath Road, Old Town, SWINDON, SN1 4BA. See also S D K Educational Consultancy Limited
KNEE, Mr. Stuart Daniel, BSc FCA *1998;* Data Connection Ltd, 100 Church Street, ENFIELD, EN2 6BQ.
KNEE, Mr. Stuart Ronald, FCA *1972;* Evendine, Hardwick Close, Oxshott, LEATHERHEAD, KT22 0HZ.
KNEEBONE, Mr. Stephen Mark, BA ACA *1986;* Minton, Burtons Lane, CHALFONT ST.GILES, HP8 4BB.
KNEESHAW, Mr. William Peter, FCA *1965;* 6 Sallow Avenue, Berrydale, NORTHAMPTON, NN3 5HP.
•KNEILL, Mr. Michael Anthony, FCA *1968;* Kneill & Co, Mayfield, Back Gate, Ingleton, CARNFORTH, LANCASHIRE LA6 3BT.
KNELLER, Mr. Godfrey Meinrad, FCA *1956;* 113 Pine, HUDSON J0P 1H0, QUE, CANADA. (Life Member)
KNELLER, Mr. Richard Dudley, FCA *1967;* 50 Danbury Vale, Danbury, CHELMSFORD, ESSEX, CM3 4LA. (Life Member)
KNELLER, Mr. Ross, ACA *2009;* Tonga Whare 7 Farnborough House, Damouettes Lane St. Peter Port, GUERNSEY, GY1 1ZN.
KNEPLER, Mr. Gerald Henry, BSc(Econ) FCA *1961;* 83 Uxendon Hill, WEMBLEY, HA9 9SH.
KNIBB, Mr. Richard Trevor, BA ACA *1989;* Cameron Mackintosh Ltd, 1 Bedford Square, LONDON, WC1B 3RB.
KNIBB, Mr. Ronald Derek, FCA *1961;* 31 Ashcroft Road, Ashdown Park, Paddock Wood, TONBRIDGE, TN12 6LQ. (Life Member)
KNIBBS, Mr. Colin Richard, FCA *1968;* 11 Kingsnorth Place, Meir Park, STOKE-ON-TRENT, ST3 7ST.
KNIBBS, Mr. Simon Andrew Vivian, MA ACA *2007;* with MacIntyre Hudson LLP, Peterbridge House, The Lakes, NORTHAMPTON, NN4 7HB.
KNIFTON, Mr. Kevin, BA ACA *1996;* Dole Thailand, Panjathani Tower, 10th Floor, 127/11 Nonsee Road, Chongnonsee, YANNAWA 10120 THAILAND.
KNIGHT, Mr. Adam James, ACA *2008;* 137 Holford Road, BRIDGWATER, SOMERSET, TA6 7NZ.
KNIGHT, Mr. Adrian Timothy, FCA CTA *1973;* Elmlea, Taddyforde, St Davids, EXETER, EX4 4AT.
KNIGHT, Mr. Alan Roy, FCA *1952;* 11 Cleeve Lawns, Downend, BRISTOL, BS16 6HH. (Life Member)
KNIGHT, Mr. Alexander William, BA ACA *2004;* Creston plc, 16 Charles II Street, LONDON, SW1Y 4QU.
KNIGHT, Miss. Alexandra Fiona, BA ACA *1999;* with Reeves & Co LLP, 37 St. Margarets Street, CANTERBURY, KENT, CT1 2TU.
KNIGHT, Mrs. Amanda Louise, BSc ACA CTA *1999;* Tui Travel Plc, Crawley Business Quarter, Fleming Way, CRAWLEY, WEST SUSSEX, RH10 9QL.
KNIGHT, Mr. Andrew John, BSocSc FCA *1998;* Waterdale Associates, 111-113 Fort Dunlop Fort Parkway, BIRMINGHAM, B24 9FD.
KNIGHT, Mr. Andrew Richard, BSc ACA *1994;* 3 Ty Pucca Close, Machen, CAERPHILLY, CF83 8LE.
KNIGHT, Mr. Anthony James, BA ACA *1990;* 78 Toms Lane, KINGS LANGLEY, HERTFORDSHIRE, WD4 8NB.
•KNIGHT, Mr. Ashley Thomas, ACA *1980;* (Tax Fac), 80K Limited, 45 Days Lane, Biddenham, BEDFORD, MK40 4AE.
KNIGHT, Mr. Barnaby St John, BA ACA *1995;* 10 Clare Park, AMERSHAM, BUCKINGHAMSHIRE, HP7 9HW.
KNIGHT, Mr. Barry Kenneth, BSc FCA *1978;* Langdale, 8 Shenfield Gardens, Hutton, BRENTWOOD, CM13 1DT.
•KNIGHT, Mr. Barry Scott, MA FCA MCT *1987;* 32 Weston Park, LONDON, N8 9TJ.
KNIGHT, Mr. Bruce David, BA ACA *1994;* Credit Suisse, One Raffles Link, SINGAPORE 039393, SINGAPORE.
KNIGHT, Miss. Catherine Florence, BSc ACA *2010;* 27 Tonbridge Walk, GRIMSBY, SOUTH HUMBERSIDE, DN33 3AT.
•KNIGHT, Mrs. Christina Frances, FCA CTA *1975;* (Tax Fac), Robert Knight, 34A Station Road, Cuffley, POTTERS BAR, HERTFORDSHIRE, EN6 4HE.
KNIGHT, Mr. Christopher, ACA *1981;* 19 Runswick Drive, Wollaton, NOTTINGHAM, NG8 1JE.
KNIGHT, Mr. Christopher James, BA ACA *1987;* Ardex UK Ltd, Homefield Road, HAVERHILL, SUFFOLK, CB9 8QP.
KNIGHT, Mr. Christopher John, MA FCA *1972;* 26 Highbury Place, LONDON, N5 1QP.
KNIGHT, Mr. Christopher John, BSc ACA *1992;* 8 Cornwall Avenue, LONDON, N3 1LD.
KNIGHT, Mr. Colin Clifford, ACA *1979;* (Tax Fac), 6 Brunwyn Close, BURY ST. EDMUNDS, SUFFOLK, IP32 7LL.
KNIGHT, Mr. Colin David, BSc FCA *1980;* 15 Orchard Way, Horringer, BURY ST. EDMUNDS, IP29 5SF.
KNIGHT, Mr. Daniel, ACA *2011;* Little Pulleys, Wambrook, CHARD, SOMERSET, TA20 3DF.
KNIGHT, Mr. Dave, BA ACA *2011;* 87 High Street, Tarvin, CHESTER, CH3 8JA.
KNIGHT, Mr. David Andrew, BA ACA *1993;* 156 Clonmore Street, Southfields, LONDON, SW18 5HB.
KNIGHT, Mr. David Andrew, ACA *2009;* 5 Brooks Lane, Bosham, CHICHESTER, WEST SUSSEX, PO18 8JT.
KNIGHT, Mr. David Frank, BSc ACA *2009;* 10 The Mount, EPSOM, KT17 1LZ.
KNIGHT, Mr. David Harper, FCA *1977;* Castle Furlong, Heath House, WEDMORE, SOMERSET, BS28 4UJ.
KNIGHT, Mr. David James, BA ACA *2005;* 13 Clare Road, WHITSTABLE, CT5 2EL.
•KNIGHT, Mr. David John, FCA *1991;* (Tax Fac), 4 St. Helier Court Flats, Val Plaisant, St. Helier, JERSEY, JE2 4TB.
KNIGHT, Mr. David John, ACA *1982;* (Tax Fac), Agincourt, 23 Douglas Avenue, Airth Castle, Airth, FALKIRK, FK2 8GF.
KNIGHT, Mr. David John, BSc ACA *1986;* 124 Maple Road, SURBITON, KT6 4AU.
KNIGHT, Mrs. Deborah Jane, BSc FCA *1990;* Fairmount Cottage, Belmer Drive, DEVONSHIRE, BERMUDA.
KNIGHT, Mr. Dennis Arthur, FCA *1948;* 19 Grangethorpe Road, Urmston, MANCHESTER, M41 9HX. (Life Member)
KNIGHT, Mr. Derek Graham Blundell, FCA *1960;* Pound Hill House, Frittenden, CRANBROOK, TN17 2EL. (Life Member)
KNIGHT, Mr. Donald, FCA *1968;* 2 Rudyard Close, STONE, STAFFORDSHIRE, ST15 8ZJ. (Life Member)
KNIGHT, Mr. Douglas Malcolm, FCA *1961;* 85 Avondale Avenue, STAINES, TW18 2NG. (Life Member)
KNIGHT, Mr. Edward Malyn, MA ACA *1995;* Chambers of Mann Q C & Steinfeld Q C, 24 Old Buildings, LONDON, WC2A 3UP.
•KNIGHT, Mrs. Elizabeth, ACA *2007;* (Tax Fac), Brooking Ruse & Co Limited, 3 Beaconsfield Road, WESTON-SUPER-MARE, SOMERSET, BS23 1YE.
KNIGHT, Mr. Eric William, FCA *1968;* The Willows, 1a Station Road, New Longton, PRESTON, PR4 4LL.
•KNIGHT, Mr. Francis John, FCA *1974;* The Print Partner Practice, 4 Denning Close, MAIDSTONE, KENT, ME16 0WT.
KNIGHT, Mr. Gareth, ACA *2011;* 14 Byron Close, Twyford, READING, RG10 0BG.
KNIGHT, Mr. Gary Brian, BSc FCA *1990;* PO Box DV 295, DEVONSHIRE DV BX, BERMUDA.
KNIGHT, Mrs. Gemma Kathleen, ACA *2011;* 6 Dudley Green, LEAMINGTON SPA, WARWICKSHIRE, CV32 7QU.
KNIGHT, Mr. Geoffrey Norman, FCA *1970;* Croxton Lodge, The Street, Croxton, THETFORD, IP24 1LN.
•KNIGHT, Mr. Geoffrey William, FCA *1975;* (Tax Fac), Knight & Company, 11 Castle Hill, MAIDENHEAD, BERKSHIRE, SL6 4AA.
KNIGHT, Mr. Giles Richard, BA(Hons) ACA *2000;* Frazione Castel Sant Angelo C. S. 2, 62022 MC CASTELRAIMONDO, ITALY.
KNIGHT, Mrs. Gillian Brenda, BA FCA *1975;* with Rimmer & May, 19 Murray Street, LLANELLI, DYFED, SA15 1AQ.
KNIGHT, Mr. Graham John, BA ACA *1999;* 68 Lashmere, Copthorne, CRAWLEY, WEST SUSSEX, RH10 3RT.
KNIGHT, Miss. Helen, ACA *2010;* 4 Reading Court, Stable Road, BICESTER, OXFORDSHIRE, OX26 3HX.
KNIGHT, Mrs. Helen Margaret Anne, BSc FCA *1991;* Vernon Cottage, Weston Road, Lewknor, WATLINGTON, OX49 5TU.
KNIGHT, Mrs. Ing Hua, ACA *1991;* Springs 14, Street 6, Villa 16, DUBAI, UNITED ARAB EMIRATES.
KNIGHT, Mr. Jacob Thomas, ACA *2009;* 109 St. James Lane, LONDON, N10 3RJ.
KNIGHT, Mr. James, ACA *2008;* PricewaterhouseCoopers, Royal Trust Tower TD Centre, Suite 3000, TORONTO M5K 1G8, ON, CANADA.
KNIGHT, Mr. James Capel, BSc ACA *2000;* 22 Chapman Avenue, MAIDSTONE, KENT, ME15 8EN.
KNIGHT, Mrs. Jane Suzanne, BA ACA *1986;* CLM Fleet Management Plc, Jenna Way, Interchange Park, Newport Pagnell, MILTON KEYNES, BUCKINGHAMSHIRE MK16 9QB.
KNIGHT, Mrs. Janet Elizabeth, BSc ACA *1989;* 16 Musgrave Close, SUTTON COLDFIELD, B76 1LA.
KNIGHT, Mr. Jeffrey Russell, MA FCA *1966;* Lordsmeade, Hurtmore Road, GODALMING, GU7 2DY. (Life Member)
KNIGHT, Mr. Jeremy Rupert, FCA *1967;* 1 Lutyens Close, Stapleton, BRISTOL, BS16 1WL. (Life Member)
KNIGHT, Mr. John, FCA *1972;* Kittiwake Developments, 3-6 Thorgate Road, LITTLEHAMPTON, WEST SUSSEX, BN17 7LU.
KNIGHT, Mr. John Austin, FCA *1968;* 5 Sandypits Lane, Etwall, DERBY, DE65 6JA.
KNIGHT, Mr. John Charles, ACA MCMI *1978;* 49 Quinn Way, LETCHWORTH GARDEN CITY, HERTFORDSHIRE, SG6 2TX.
KNIGHT, Mr. John David, BSc ACA *1989;* 16 Musgrave Close, SUTTON COLDFIELD, B76 1LA.
KNIGHT, Mr. John Oliver, FCA *1951;* 184 Howbeck Road, Arnold, NOTTINGHAM, NG5 8QE. (Life Member)
KNIGHT, Mr. John Richard, FCA *1955;* 4 Beechwood Avenue, Chorleywood, RICKMANSWORTH, HERTFORDSHIRE, WD3 5RL. (Life Member)
KNIGHT, Mr. Jon, ACA *2007;* 61 Sedgefield Drive, Syston, LEICESTER, LE7 1YU.
KNIGHT, Mr. Jonathan Peter, BSc ACA *2003;* 67 Church Road, NORTHWICH, CHESHIRE, CW9 5PB.
KNIGHT, Miss. Julie, BA ACA *1994;* GE Money Home Lending, Sherbourne House (unit 5) Hatters Lane Coxley Business Park, WATFORD, HERTFORDSHIRE, WD18 8YF.
KNIGHT, Miss. Katie Rose, ACA *2009;* 9 Whiphill Close, DONCASTER, SOUTH YORKSHIRE, DN4 6DX.
KNIGHT, The Revd. Keith, BA FCA *1960;* 5 Northedge Meadow, BRADFORD, BD10 8SF. (Life Member)
KNIGHT, Mr. Kevin John, BSc ACA *1988;* 10011 BAYOU GLEN ROAD, HOUSTON, TX 77042, UNITED STATES.
KNIGHT, Mrs. Krystyna Maria, BA ACA CTA *1993;* (Tax Fac), 33 Blythwood Road, PINNER, HA5 3QD.
KNIGHT, Miss. Laura Jessica Jane, BA ACA *2008;* 11 Houghton Square, LONDON, SW9 9AN.
KNIGHT, Miss. Lisa Joan, BA ACA *1993;* 5 Marlborough Crescent, WIDNES, CHESHIRE, WA8 9EJ.
KNIGHT, Mr. Marcus, BA ACA *2010;* 69 Felden Street, LONDON, SW6 5AE.
KNIGHT, Mr. Martyn Drysdale, BSc ACA *1987;* 5 Woodside, Wimbledon, LONDON, SW19 7AR.
KNIGHT, Mr. Matthew, BEng ACA *1997;* Lyndhurst, Rutland Road, MAIDENHEAD, SL6 4HY.
KNIGHT, Mr. Matthew David, LLM ACA *1999;* Stockland, Level 29, 133 Castlereagh Street, SYDNEY, NSW 2000, AUSTRALIA.
KNIGHT, Mr. Michael Alan, FCA *1957;* No. 2, The Paddock, Happisburgh, NORWICH, NR12 0PU. (Life Member)
KNIGHT, Mr. Michael Anthony, BA FCA *1977;* The Haven, Bridgend, Noss Mayo, PLYMOUTH, PL8 1DX.
KNIGHT, Mr. Michael Burt, MA ACA *1979;* 40 Howard Road, DORKING, RH4 3HP.
•KNIGHT, Mr. Michael George, MSc BA FCA *1972;* 50 Lydney Close, LONDON, SW19 6JN.
KNIGHT, Mr. Michael James, BCom ACA *1984;* Claremont, School Road, Pentlow, SUDBURY, CO10 7JP.
KNIGHT, Mr. Michael John, BA ACA MCT *1986;* Triolgy Communications Limited, 26 Focus Way, ANDOVER, HAMPSHIRE, SP10 5NY.
KNIGHT, Mr. Michael Norman, FCA *1963;* 846 Coventry Road, DAVENPORT, FL 33897, UNITED STATES.
KNIGHT, Mr. Murray Edward Miller, FCA *1978;* Company Registrars Ltd, Aldwych House, 71-91 Aldwych, LONDON, WC2B 4HN.
KNIGHT, Mr. Nicholas David, FCA MAAT *1998;* 27 Harwood Road, Old Lakenham, NORWICH, NR1 2NG.
•KNIGHT, Mr. Patrick Jennison, FCA *1962;* Patrick J Knight FCA, Marlow, Manorial Road, Parkgate, NESTON, CH64 6QW.
•KNIGHT, Mr. Paul Arthur John, FCA *1983;* Honey Barrett Limited, 53 Gildredge Road, EASTBOURNE, EAST SUSSEX, BN21 4SF.
•KNIGHT, Mrs. Paula Elizabeth, BSc FCA *1989;* Hale Jackson Knight, Montague House, 4 St. Marys Street, ROSS-ON-WYE, HEREFORDSHIRE, HR9 5HT.
KNIGHT, Mr. Peter, FCA *1957;* 9 Alder Walk, Stanborough Park, WATFORD, WD25 0RT. (Life Member)
KNIGHT, Mr. Peter, BSc FCA *1970;* 5 Melville Avenue, SOUTH CROYDON, SURREY, CR2 7HZ.
KNIGHT, Mr. Philip Gregory, BSc ACA *1992;* 87 Barnsbury Street, LONDON, N1 1EJ.
•KNIGHT, Mr. Philip Ivan, BSc FCA *1989;* (Tax Fac), Knight Goodhead Limited, 7 Bournemouth Road, Chandler's Ford, EASTLEIGH, HAMPSHIRE, SO53 3DA.
KNIGHT, Mr. Philip Justin, BA FCA *1982;* 16 Victoria Drive, Horsforth, LEEDS, LS18 4PW.

KNIGHT, Miss. Rachel Debra, BSc ACA *2005;* 194b New Kings Road, LONDON, SW6 4NF.
KNIGHT, Miss. Rachel Elizabeth, BSc ACA *2002;* 9 Penny Croft, HARPENDEN, HERTFORDSHIRE, AL5 2PD.
KNIGHT, Mrs. Rachel Louise, BSc ACA *2002;* Reef One Ltd, F1 Abbey Farm Business Park, Horsham St. Faith, NORWICH, NR10 3JU.
KNIGHT, Miss. Rebecca Anne, BSc(Hons) ACA *2006;* 147 Amyand Park Road, TWICKENHAM, TW1 3HN.
KNIGHT, Mr. Richard James, BSc ACA *1996;* 25, Wakehurst Road, LONDON, SW11 6DB.
•**KNIGHT, Mr. Robert Iain, FCA** *1975;* Robert Knight, 34A Station Road, Cuffley, POTTERS BAR, HERTFORDSHIRE, EN6 4HE.
•**KNIGHT, Mr. Robert John, BA(Hons) ACA** *2001;* Deloitte LLP, 3 Victoria Square, Victoria Street, ST. ALBANS, HERTFORDSHIRE, AL1 3TF. See also Deloitte & Touche LLP
KNIGHT, Mr. Robert John, BSc FCA *1980;* Howicks, Nonnington Lane, Graffham, PETWORTH, GU28 0PX.
•ⒹKNIGHT, Mr. Robert Leonard Harry, BSc FCA MIPA FABRP** *1975;* Buchlers LLP, Global House, 1 Ashley Avenue, EPSOM, SURREY, KT18 5AD.
KNIGHT, Mr. Robert Patrick Graham, BSc(Hons) ACA *2002;* 12 Ballantine Street, LONDON, SW18 1AL.
KNIGHT, Mr. Roger John, FCA *1961;* Carisbrooke, 1 St. Marys Way, Chalfont St. Peter, GERRARDS CROSS, BUCKINGHAMSHIRE, SL9 9BL.
KNIGHT, Mr. Roger John, MA FCA *1979;* PricewaterhouseCoopers, 33/F Cheung Kong Center, 2 Queen's Road, CENTRAL, HONG KONG ISLAND, HONG KONG SAR.
KNIGHT, Mr. Ronald George Thomas, FCA *1960;* 5 Arnolds Close, Kingston, KINGSBRIDGE, TQ7 4QF. (Life Member)
KNIGHT, Mr. Roy Basil, FCA *1953;* The Downs, Bully's Hill, Brading, SANDOWN, PO36 0ER. (Life Member)
KNIGHT, Mr. Russell Alexander Roy, BSc ACA *1992;* PT Karma Bali, Karma Building, Sunset Road, Kuta, BALI, 80361 INDONESIA.
KNIGHT, Miss. Sarah Jane, BSc ACA *1993;* 27 Flemish Place, Warfield, BRACKNELL, RG42 2FG.
KNIGHT, Miss. Sarah Marsha, MA ACA *2004;* Flat 3, 63 Carlton Hill, LONDON, NW8 0EN.
KNIGHT, Miss. Sarah Verity, BA ACA *2004;* 32 Woodlands, LONDON, SW20 9JF.
•**KNIGHT, Mr. Scott William, BSc ACA** *1998;* BDO LLP, 55 Baker Street, LONDON, W1U 7EU. See also BDO Stoy Hayward LLP
KNIGHT, Mr. Stanley William, FCA *1952;* Flat 3, Mountier Court, Homesdale Close, New Wanstead, LONDON, E11 2TL. (Life Member)
KNIGHT, Mrs. Stephanie Melissa Margaret, ACA *2001;* Hafod Lon, Trerhyngyll, COWBRIDGE, SOUTH GLAMORGAN, CF71 7TN.
•**KNIGHT, Mr. Stephen Charles, BA FCA** *1986;* 11 rue Charles de Gaulle, 78860 ST NOM LA BRETECHE, FRANCE.
•**KNIGHT, Mr. Stephen Richard, BSc ACA** *1988;* Deloitte LLP, Athene Place, 66 Shoe Lane, LONDON, EC4A 3BQ. See also Deloitte & Touche LLP
KNIGHT, Mr. Steven, ACA *2011;* 13 South View, Woodley, STOCKPORT, CHESHIRE, SK6 1PD.
•**KNIGHT, Mr. Steven Andrew, FCA TEP** *1985;* (Tax Fac), Knights, Europort 932, GIBRALTAR, GIBRALTAR.
•**KNIGHT, Mr. Terence, ACA** *1983;* Knights, Baxter House, 48 Church Road, ASCOT, SL5 8RR.
KNIGHT, Mr. Terence John, BA FCA *1979;* Carrine Farm, Sparnock, TRURO, CORNWALL, TR3 6EB.
•**KNIGHT, Mr. Terence Mark, BA FCA** *1988;* with BDO Canada LLP, 600 Cathedral Place, 925 West Georgia Street, VANCOUVER V6C 3L2, BC, CANADA.
KNIGHT, Mr. Thomas Henry, ACA *2009;* 49 St. Stephens Place, CAMBRIDGE, CB3 0JE.
KNIGHT, Mr. Timothy Gregory, FCA *1970;* Quarry House, Salterns Road, LEE-ON-THE-SOLENT, HAMPSHIRE, PO13 9NL. (Life Member)
KNIGHT, Mr. Victor Paul Martin, MA MBA FCA *1977;* 20 Varney Close, Cheshunt, WALTHAM CROSS, HERTFORDSHIRE, EN7 6LU.
KNIGHT, Mr. Warburton James, BSc ACA *1990;* 17 North Grove Mount, WETHERBY, LS22 7GD.
•**KNIGHT, Mr. William Jeremy Jonathan, FCA** *1975;* (Member of Council 1995 - 2005), Jeremy Knight & Co LLP, 68 Ship Street, BRIGHTON, BN1 1AE. See also Richard Floyd & Co
KNIGHT-EVANS, Mr. Carlyon John, MEng ACA *1993;* with Ernst & Young, 18/F, Two International Finance Centre, 8 Finance Street, CENTRAL, HONG KONG ISLAND HONG KONG SAR.
•**KNIGHT-EVANS, Mr. Nigel David, FCA** *1975;* (Tax Fac), Knight Evans Limited, 11 Church Street, GODALMING, SURREY, GU7 1EQ.
•**KNIGHT-GREGSON, Mr. Michael Douglas, BA ACA** *1979;* Knight-Gregson, 40 Kingsmere Close, BIRMINGHAM, B24 8QL.
KNIGHT-JONES, Mr. Godfrey, FCA *1964;* 135 Lower Kirklington Road, SOUTHWELL, NG25 0DR.
KNIGHTLEY, Mr. Brian James, FCA *1952;* 32 Abbotsbury House, 139 Abbotsbury Road, LONDON, W14 8EN. (Life Member)
KNIGHTON, Mr. Edward Myles, BA FCA *1987;* 40 Southmoor Road, OXFORD, OX2 6RD.
KNIGHTON, Mr. John Christopher, ACA *1990;* 46 Repton Avenue, Gidea Park, ROMFORD, RM2 5LT.
KNIGHTON, Miss. Louise, ACA *2011;* Flat B, 91 Tooting Bec Road, LONDON, SW17 8BW.
KNIGHTS, Mr. Adam, BA ACA *2008;* 251B Hackney Road, LONDON, E2 8NA.
KNIGHTS, Mr. Alan John, FCA *1948;* Cottarson Farm, Awliscombe, HONITON, DEVON, EX14 3NR. (Life Member)
KNIGHTS, Mr. Andrew Lewis, FCA *1994;* 22 Crofters Walk, BRAINTREE, ESSEX, CM77 7GP.
KNIGHTS, Mr. Graham Robert, BA ACA *1997;* 33 Firgrove Hill, FARNHAM, GU9 8LN.
KNIGHTS, Mr. James, BSc ACA *2010;* 53a St. Johns Street, BURY ST. EDMUNDS, SUFFOLK, IP33 1SP.
KNIGHTS, Mrs. Jane Christine, BSc ACA *1985;* The Royal High School, Lansdown Road, BATH, BA1 5SZ.
KNIGHTS, Mr. Keith William, BSc FCA *1979;* Geo Houlton & Sons Ltd, Hyperion Street, HULL, HU9 1BD.
KNIGHTS, Mr. Lewis John, ACA *2008;* 8 Shakespeare Road, ST. IVES, CAMBRIDGESHIRE, PE27 6TR.
KNIGHTS, Mr. Martin William, BSc ACA *1982;* Amberley High Street Calver, HOPE VALLEY, DERBYSHIRE, S32 3XP.
KNIGHTS, Mr. Michael Timothy, FCA *1969;* (Tax Fac), Springside Farm, Tismans Common, Rudgwick, HORSHAM, RH12 3DU.
•**KNIGHTS, Mr. Paul Andrew, FCA** *1983;* (Tax Fac), Knights Lowe, Eldo House, Kempson Way, Suffolk Business Park, BURY ST. EDMUNDS, IP32 7AR. See also Knights Lowe Limited
•**KNIGHTS, Mr. Richard Charles, BA ACA** *1988;* Deloitte LLP, City House, 126-130 Hills Road, CAMBRIDGE, CB2 1RY. See also Deloitte & Touche LLP
•**KNIGHTS, Mr. Shaun Russell Macartan, FCA** *1966;* RM Professional Practice Ltd, Forge House, Ansell Road, DORKING, RH4 1UN.
KNILL, Mr. Bruce Thomas Hicks, FCA *1955;* PO Box 308, Clayton, NEW YORK, NY 13624, UNITED STATES. (Life Member)
KNIPE, Mr. Frederick Robin, BA ACA *1993;* 147 Mallinson Road, LONDON, SW11 1BH.
KNIPE, Mr. James Francis, BSc FCA *1974;* Bluff View, Hungerstone, Allensmore, HEREFORD, HR2 9BE.
KNIPE, Mr. Philip Andrew, BSc FCA *1978;* Adcock Financial Ltd, 10 Milton Court Ravenshead, NOTTINGHAM, NG15 9BD.
KNIPPEL, Mr. Nolton James, ACA *2003;* 83 Clarence Road, EAST COWES, PO32 6ET.
KNOCK, Mr. John Edwin, FCA *1959;* 12 Lealands Av, Leigh, TONBRIDGE, TN11 8QU. (Life Member)
KNOCK, Miss. Sarah, BSc ACA *1993;* Centrica Plc Millstream, Maidenhead Road, WINDSOR, BERKSHIRE, SL4 5GD.
KNOPE, Mr. Leonard Charles Sidney, FCA *1955;* 4 Lark Valley Court, Lark Valley Drive, Fornham St Martin, BURY ST.EDMUNDS, IP28 6UQ. (Life Member)
KNOPF, Miss. Elaine Julia, ACA *2008;* Flat 6 Guildown Court, Stoke Road, GUILDFORD, GU1 4HQ.
KNOTH, Mrs. Kathryn Jane, BA ACA *1992;* Ernst-Sievers-Str 67, 49078 OSNABRUCK, GERMANY.
KNOTT, Miss. Andrea Jane, BSc ACA *1993;* Applewhite Cottage, Green End Farm Hope Road, Broughton, CHESTER, CH4 0RU.
KNOTT, Mr. Andrew David, ACA *1987;* Atlantic House, 50 Holborn Viaduct, LONDON, EC1A 2FG.
KNOTT, Mr. Andrew James, ACA ACMA *2009;* 27 Yew Tree Court, Chy Hwel, TRURO, CORNWALL, TR1 1AF.
•**KNOTT, Mrs. Christina Jayne, FCA** *1987;* Homer Knott & Co, Hawthorne House, Charlotte Street, DUDLEY, DY1 1TD.
•**KNOTT, Mrs. Deborah, BA ACA** *2002;* Deborah Knott BA (Hons) ACA, 3 Oakfield Lane, Hemingbrough, SELBY, NORTH YORKSHIRE, YO8 6RH.
KNOTT, Mr. Gary James, BSc ACA *1993;* Schwannstraße 6, 40476 DUSSELDORF, GERMANY.
KNOTT, Mr. Ian Alexander, BA(Hons) ACA *2002;* 1 Don View, Monymusk, INVERURIE, AB51 7JE.
KNOTT, Mr. John Alan, FCA *1958;* The Oast House, Spinney Close, Warmington, PETERBOROUGH, PE8 6TF.
KNOTT, Mr. Kevin John Selwyn, CVO BA ACA *1982;* Trinity College, Broad Street, OXFORD, OX1 3BH.
KNOTT, Mr. Paul, PhD BSc FCA *1983;* The Gables Elvendon Road, Goring, READING, RG8 0DT.
KNOTT, Mr. Peter Douglas, BSc(Hons) ACA *2004;* 31 Bradford Street, BALMAIN, NSW 2041, AUSTRALIA.
KNOTT, Mr. Peter Richard Andrew, BA FCA CF *1989;* 10 Baring Crescent, EXETER, EX1 1TL.
KNOTT, Mr. Samuel Wensley, BA ACA *2010;* Geibelstrasse 47 a, 22303 HAMBURG, GERMANY.
KNOTT, Mr. Trevor Leonard, BA(Hons) ACA *2000;* 803 Willow Avenue, Apt 1S, HOBOKEN, NJ 07030, UNITED STATES.
KNOTT, Miss. Valerie Elizabeth, BCom ACA *1989;* 16 Cleveland Road, Barnes, LONDON, SW13 0AB.
KNOWELDEN, Mrs. Laura Emma, BSc ACA *2003;* 59 Hamilton Road, Wimbledon, LONDON, SW19 1JG.
KNOWLES, Mr. Adrian Robert, BSc ACA *1991;* 12 Forum Close, SWINDON, SN3 4BU.
KNOWLES, Mr. Alan James, BA FCA *1989;* Flat 20 Regents Court, St. Georges Avenue, WEYBRIDGE, KT13 0DQ.
KNOWLES, Miss. Amanda Jane, BA ACA *2004;* V P Plc Beckwith Knowle, Otley Road Beckwithshaw, HARROGATE, NORTH YORKSHIRE, HG3 1UD.
•**KNOWLES, Mr. Anthony, MA FCA** *1985;* (Tax Fac), Hanleys Limited, Spring Court, Spring Road, Hale, ALTRINCHAM, CHESHIRE WA14 2UQ. See also Hale Financial Limited
KNOWLES, Mrs. Christine Ann, BSc ACA *1982;* James Cowper, 3 Wesley Gate Queens Road, READING, RG1 4AP.
KNOWLES, Mr. Christopher Peter, BSc ACA *2004;* 23 Ludlow Street, Floor 2, NEW YORK, NY 10002, UNITED STATES.
KNOWLES, Mr. Clifford John, FCA *1972;* 16 Trinity Close, Pound Hill, CRAWLEY, RH10 3TN.
KNOWLES, Miss. Cynthia, BSc(Hons) ACA *2001;* 116 St. Josephs Vale, LONDON, SE3 0XQ.
KNOWLES, Mr. Cyril Alan, FCA *1955;* 3 Yattendon Court, Yattendon, THATCHAM, BERKSHIRE, RG18 0UT. (Life Member)
•**KNOWLES, Mr. Damian Thomas, BA ACA** *1996;* 110 Sutherland Avenue, LONDON, W9 2QP.
KNOWLES, Mr. David Roger, MA FCA *1968;* 1 Gainsborough Road, LONDON, W4 1NJ. (Life Member)
KNOWLES, Mrs. Deborah Jane, BSc ACA *1997;* Ernst & Young Llp, 1 More London Place, LONDON, SE1 2AF.
KNOWLES, Mr. Edwin John, FCA *1974;* Apartment 201, Kavouri Court No 16, Panagioti Symeou Street, 3105 LIMASSOL, CYPRUS.
KNOWLES, Ms. Elizabeth, ACA *2011;* 5 Cranford Avenue, Whitefield, MANCHESTER, M45 7SJ.
KNOWLES, Miss. Faye Elizabeth, ACA *2008;* 135 Bury & Bolton Road, Radcliffe, MANCHESTER, M26 4JY.
KNOWLES, Mr. Francis Vincent, BA ACA *1996;* Ipsley House, G K N Group Services Ltd, PO Box 55, REDDITCH, WORCESTERSHIRE, B98 0TL.
KNOWLES, Mr. Frank John, FCA *1957;* 42 Fairview Road, Katikati, TAURANGA 3129, NEW ZEALAND. (Life Member)
KNOWLES, Mr. Gary Stephen, ACA *2011;* 82 Kingston Road, Willerby, HULL, HU10 6BH.
KNOWLES, Mr. Godfrey Nelson, FCA *1956;* 4 Field Close, Compton Down, WINCHESTER, SO21 2AE. (Life Member)
KNOWLES, Mr. Graeme Paul, BA ACA *1985;* 10 Chantry Avenue, Hartford, NORTHWICH, CW8 1LZ.
KNOWLES, Mr. Graham Malcolm, FCA *1962;* 3 Fairfields, The Street, Blo Norton, DISS, NORFOLK, IP22 2JB.
KNOWLES, Mr. Gregory Paul, FCA *1972;* 50 Hillcroft Avenue, PINNER, MIDDLESEX, HA5 5AS.
KNOWLES, Miss. Helen, LLB ACA *2005;* 4 Fairman Drive, Hindley, WIGAN, LANCASHIRE, WN2 2RT.
KNOWLES, Miss. Helen Claire, BA(Hons) ACA *2010;* 188 Quay Street, Private Bag 92162, AUCKLAND 1142, NEW ZEALAND.
KNOWLES, Mr. Hugh Stanley Keith, BA ACA *1989;* 51 Britannia Road, LONDON, SW6 2HJ.
KNOWLES, Mrs. Jennifer Dawn, BSc ACA *2008;* 30 New Rowley Road, DUDLEY, DY2 8AS.
KNOWLES, Mrs. Jessica Ann, BA ACA *2000;* IBM UK Ltd, 76 Upper Ground, LONDON, SE1 9PZ.
KNOWLES, Mr. John Charles, BSc FCA *1972;* 15 High Chase Rise, Little Haywood, STAFFORD, ST18 0TY. (Life Member)
KNOWLES, Mr. John Richard, FCA *1974;* 106 Hightown Road, LIVERSEDGE, WEST YORKSHIRE, WF15 8BZ.
KNOWLES, Miss. Kathryn Elizabeth, ACA *2008;* 112 Carr Manor Road, LEEDS, LS17 5AL.
KNOWLES, Miss. Kerri Michelle, ACA *2009;* Pricewaterhousecoopers, 8 Princes Parade, LIVERPOOL, L3 1QJ.
KNOWLES, Mr. Kevin Mark, BSc(Hons) ACA *2002;* 116 St. Josephs Vale, LONDON, SE3 0XQ.
KNOWLES, Miss. Laura Frances Bennett, ACA *2010;* 122a Balham High Road, LONDON, SW12 9AA.
•**KNOWLES, Mr. Nigel Mark, ACA** *1989;* (Tax Fac), Williams Knowles & Co, Lloyd Chambers, 139 Carlton Road, WORKSOP, S81 7AD.
KNOWLES, Mr. Patrick John, BA ACA *1987;* 1 Turnberry Close, LYMM, WA13 9LY.
KNOWLES, Mr. Philip David, BA ACA *1993;* 18 Parkfield Road South, Didsbury, MANCHESTER, M20 6DH.
KNOWLES, Mrs. Rachel Anne, BSc ACA *1989;* 28 Sunnyside Road, WEYMOUTH, DORSET, DT4 9BL.
KNOWLES, Mr. Richard, BA ACA *2006;* 21 Beauval Road, LONDON, SE22 8UG.
KNOWLES, Mr. Richard, BSc FCA *1973;* 51 East Busk Lane, OTLEY, LS21 1SZ.
•**KNOWLES, Mr. Roy Anthony, ACA** *1986;* 1 Sandringham Grove, Haslingden, ROSSENDALE, LANCASHIRE, BB4 4BX.
KNOWLES, Mr. Simon Nelson, FCA *1982;* La Lombardie, 12350 DRULHE, FRANCE.
KNOWLES, Miss. Sophie Rebecca, BA(Hons) ACA *2011;* 9 Somerset Avenue, Wilpshire, BLACKBURN, LANCASHIRE, BB1 9JD.
KNOWLES, Mrs. Stephanie Jane, BSc ACA *2005;* 21 Sefton Park Road, BRISTOL, BS7 9AN.
•**KNOWLES, Mr. Stephen Frank, BSc FCA** *1976;* Appleby & Wood, Bolton Enterprise Centre, Washington Street, BOLTON, BL3 5EY. See also Appleby & Wood Ltd
•**KNOWLES, Mr. Steven Dudley, FCA** *1981;* (Tax Fac), Knowles Warwick Group Limited, 183 Fraser Road, SHEFFIELD, S8 0JP. See also Knowles Warwick Limited
•**KNOWLES, Miss. Susan Elizabeth, BA ACA** *1992;* Susan Knowles ACA, 210 Rockingham Road, KETTERING, NORTHAMPTONSHIRE, NN16 9AH.
KNOWLES, Mr. Terence Peter, FCA *1973;* 29 St. Peters Road, Radstock, BATH, BA3 4BJ.
KNOWLES, Mr. Timothy, FCA *1960;* Cae Ffynnon, 12 Ger-y-Llan, St. Nicholas, CARDIFF, CF5 6SY. (Life Member)
KNOWLES, Mr. Timothy David, BA ACA *1990;* M B N A International Bank Ltd, Chester Business Park, CHESTER, CH4 9FB.
KNOWLES, Mr. Timothy Richard Edward, BSc ACA *2000;* 21 Sefton Park Road, BRISTOL, BS7 9AN.
•**KNOWLES, Mr. Tracy Eugene, FCA** *1977;* KPMG Peat Marwick, PO Box N123, Montague Sterling Centre, East Bay Street, NASSAU, BAHAMAS.
KNOWLES, Mr. Trevor, FCA *1961;* 45 Cromwell Road, CLEETHORPES, DN35 0AU.
KNOWLSON, Mr. Albert Denton, FCA *1949;* Hillcroft, Motherby, PENRITH, CA11 0RJ. (Life Member)
KNOX, Mrs. Alexandra Christian, BA ACA *2000;* 127 Rosendale Road, LONDON, SE21 8HE.
KNOX, Mr. Alistair James, BSc ACA *2000;* 4 Mount Holme Thorkhill Road, THAMES DITTON, SURREY, KT7 0UB.
KNOX, Mr. Andrew James, BSc(Hons) ACA *2003;* 18 Mill Road, Caversham, READING, RG4 8DP.
KNOX, Mr. Chris, MEng ACA *2006;* 25a Dickens Boulevard, Stotfold, HITCHIN, HERTFORDSHIRE, SG5 4FD.
KNOX, Mr. Colin Graham, MA ACA *1996;* Fulmer Hall Windmill Road, Fulmer, SLOUGH, SL3 6HD.
KNOX, Mr. David Geoffrey, BA FCA *1972;* 7 Darland Close, Lavister, WREXHAM, LL12 0EN. (Life Member)
KNOX, Mr. Ian Malcolm, FCA *1977;* Knox Accounting, Waterside House, Bridge Approach, BARROW-IN-FURNESS, CUMBRIA, LA14 2HE.

KNOX - KONFORTION Members - Alphabetical

KNOX, Mr. John Andrew, MA FCA *1964;* 103 Wickham Way, BECKENHAM, KENT, BR3 3AP.
KNOX, Mr. John Dyne, BSc FCA *1972;* Crowsley Grange, Crowsley, HENLEY-ON-THAMES, RG9 4JP.
KNOX, Mr. Malcolm Robert, BA ACA *1992;* 75 Rathgullion, Chapel Road, MEIGH, COUNTY DOWN, BT35 8GW.
KNOX, Mr. Peter Dennis, FCA *1955;* Tall Timbers, The Avenue, South Nutfield, REDHILL, RH1 5RY. (Life Member)
KNOX, Mr. Robert William, FCA *1966;* 14 Elm Tree Avenue, ESHER, KT10 8JG.
KNOX, Mrs. Sally Theresa, BSc ACA *1994;* Old Walls, Woodland Rise, Seal, SEVENOAKS, KENT, TN15 0JB.
KNOX, Mrs. Sian Alison, BSc ACA *1994;* 1 Baygrove Mews, Hampton Wick, KINGSTON UPON THAMES, KT1 4HD.
KNUBLEY, Ms. Rachel Joanne, BA ACA *1998;* 4 Lucien Road, LONDON, SW17 8HN.
KNUCKEY, Mr. Robert Andrew, ACA *1984;* Flybe, Jack Walker House, Exeter Airport, Clyst Honiton, EXETER, EX5 2HL.
KNUDSEN, Mrs. Wendy, BSc ACA *1980;* College Barn, High Street, Ilchester, YEOVIL, SOMERSET, BA22 8NQ.
KNUDSON, Mr. Paul Spencer, BSc ACA *1992;* Key Travel, 28-32 Britannia Street, LONDON, WC1X 9JF.
KNUDSSEN, Miss. Abigail Helen Jane, BSc ACA *1999;* 40 High Street, MACCLESFIELD, CHESHIRE, SK11 8BR.
KNUST, Mr. John Frederick Dover, LLM FCA *1969;* 31 Main Avenue, Moor Park, NORTHWOOD, HA6 2LH. (Life Member)
KNUTSON, Mr. Christian Michael, ACA *2003;* Flat B, 130 Camden Street, LONDON, NW1 0HY.
KNUTSON, Mrs. Emma Louise, BSc ACA *2003;* 130b Camden Street, LONDON, NW1 0HY.
KNYCHALA, Mrs. Debra, BA ACA *1983;* Beck House Water Lane, Ancaster, GRANTHAM, LINCOLNSHIRE, NG32 3QS.
KO, Mr. Boon Leong, BSc ACA *1981;* Francis Lee & Co, 48 Jalan Che Wan, Off Jalan Chung Thye Phin, 30250 IPOH, PERAK, MALAYSIA.
KO, Mr. Chee Wai David, ACA *2005;* KPMG, 8/F Prince's Building, 10 Chater Road, CENTRAL, HONG KONG ISLAND, HONG KONG SAR.
KO, Mr. Chi Keung, ACA *2007;* 5/F Dah Sing Life Building, 99-105 Des Voeux Road, CENTRAL, HONG KONG SAR.
KO, Mr. Desmond Tak Fai, MSc ACA *1994;* A2 4/F Villa Monte Rosa, 41A Stubbs Road, WAN CHAI, HONG KONG ISLAND, HONG KONG SAR.
KO, Mr. Felix Tak Shing, BA ACA *2006;* Flat 19, Cresta House, 133 Finchley Road, LONDON, NW3 6HT.
KO, Ms. Fiona Tze-Fun, BEng ACA *1996;* Flat 1605 Block E, Kornhill, QUARRY BAY, HONG KONG ISLAND, HONG KONG SAR.
KO, Mr. Jenva, ACA *2007;* 12th Floor, 358 Yan He Da Dao, Qiaokou, WUHAN CITY 430033, CHINA.
KO, Ms. Ka Mei Sabine, ACA *2008;* 14A, Yee Ga Court, 62 Bonham Road, MID LEVELS, HONG KONG ISLAND, HONG KONG SAR.
KO, Miss. Ka Yan Karen, ACA *2008;* 2A Sunrise House, 21-27 Old Bailey Street, CENTRAL, HONG KONG SAR.
KO, Miss. Karen Wai Yee, MA ACA *2011;* 41 Brindles Field, TONBRIDGE, KENT, TN9 2YR.
KO, Mr. Kwai Yi, ACA *2008;* 2/F Warwick House, Taikoo Place, 979 King's Road, QUARRY BAY, HONG KONG SAR.
KO, Mr. Kwok Fai Dennis, ACA *2007;* Room 5, 9/F, KA Kit House, Ka Lung Court, ABERDEEN, HONG KONG ISLAND HONG KONG SAR.
KO, Ms. Lee Lee, ACA *2007;* Flat 3, 16/F Block 34, Heng Fa Chuen, 100 Shing Tai Road, CHAI WAN, HONG KONG ISLAND HONG KONG SAR.
KO, Mr. Man Lut, ACA *2004;* 16C, Block 1, Academic Terrace, 101 Pokfulam Road, POK FU LAM, HONG KONG ISLAND HONG KONG SAR.
KO, Mr. Ming Kin, ACA *2007;* Flat F 12 Floor Ko Fung Court Harbour Heights 5 Fook Yum Road, NORTH POINT, HONG KONG SAR.
KO, Mr. Peter Chung Ting, BA ACA *1982;* Flat B, 17 Floor Cheong Wan Mansion, 55 Hill Road, WESTERN DISTRICT, NT, HONG KONG SAR.
KO, Ms. Pui Ching, ACA *2007;* 11A, Hing On Mansion, TAIKOO SHING, HONG KONG SAR.
•KO, Mr. Robert Siu Wah, BSc ACA *1982;* Robert Ko & Company, 33 Crofton Avenue, LONDON, W4 3EW. See also Robert Ko
KO, Mr. Sai Leung, ACA *2007;* Room D 38/F., Tower One Phase One, 20 Lung Wah Street, KENNEDY TOWN, HONG KONG SAR.
KO, Mr. Tak Wing, ACA *2007;* JBL & Co, Room 1301-2, CRE Bldg, 303 Hennessy Road, WAN CHAI, HONG KONG SAR.
KO, Ms. Victoria Miu Ha, MBA BSc ACA *1984;* 3 Pandan Valley, Chemdaka Court, Apt 03-301, SINGAPORE 597627, SINGAPORE.
KO, Mr. Wai Fung Ronald, ACA *2005;* Ronald W.F. Ko & Co, 4th Floor Winbase Centre, 208 Queen's Road Central, CENTRAL, HONG KONG ISLAND, HONG KONG SAR.
KO, Mr. Yat Wing Wallace, ACA *2005;* Wallace Ko & Co., 19th Floor, Kam Chung Commercial Building, 19-21 Hennessy Road, WAN CHAI, HONG KONG ISLAND HONG KONG SAR.
KO, Ms. Yee Kuen Yvette, ACA *2008;* Flat E, 21/F, 9 Wing Fong Road, Hang King Garden, KWAI CHUNG, HONG KONG SAR.
KOAY, Mr. Chniah Chniah, ACA *1982;* No 11 Jalan 5/128A, Taman Bukit Aman, 58200 KUALA LUMPUR, FEDERAL TERRITORY, MALAYSIA.
KOAY, Mr. Swee Teik, MSc BA ACA *1990;* Block 2 Tanjong Pagar Plaza, Apt 11-38, Tanjong Pagar Road, SINGAPORE 082002, SINGAPORE.
KOAY, Mr. Timothy Chung Tinn, ACA *2010;* B5 5/F, 32 Broadcast Drive, KOWLOON TONG, KOWLOON, HONG KONG SAR.
KOBER, Mr. Stephen Walter, FCA *1972;* 17 Whirlow Park Road, SHEFFIELD, S11 9NN.
KOCH, Mrs. Helen, BSc ACA *1995;* Birch Tree House, Bourne Lane, Hook Norton, BANBURY, OXFORDSHIRE, OX15 5PG.
KOCHANSKI, Mrs. Laura, MA FCA ATII *1984;* (Tax Fac), K P M G, 100 Temple Street, BRISTOL, BS1 6AG.
KOCHHAR, Mrs. Ashvinder, BSc ACA *2001;* White House, Denbridge Road, BROMLEY, BR1 2AG.
KOCK, Mr. Egmont Stephanus, BA ACA *1979;* 21 Church Road, Barnes, LONDON, SW13 9HE.
KOCK, Mrs. Kathryn Elizabeth, BSc ACA *1980;* 21 Church Road, Barnes, LONDON, SW13 9HE.
•KOCKELBERGH, Mr. Mark Charles, BA FCA *1992;* (Tax Fac), Marlowe & Co, 22 Shawe Avenue, NUNEATON, WARWICKSHIRE, CV10 0EL.
KOCYLO, Mrs. Adriana Grazyna, BSc ACA *2010;* 30 Windmill Heights, BILLERICAY, ESSEX, CM12 9QY.
KOECH, Mr. Mathew Kipkirui, ACA *1992;* BISHOPS GARDEN TOWERS, BISHOPS ROAD, PO Box 44584, NAIROBI, 0100 GPO, KENYA.
KOELMEYER, Mr. Paul Christopher, FCA *1985;* PO Box 12635, A Beckett Street, MELBOURNE, VIC 8006, AUSTRALIA.
KOFFLER-SLUIJTER, Mrs. Susan Mary, ACA *1990;* 30 Glenham Road, THAME, OXFORDSHIRE, OX9 3WD.
KOGAN, Ms. Inna, ACA *2009;* Deloitte & Touche, Business Center, White Square, 5 Lesnaya St, Building B, 125047 MOSCOW RUSSIAN FEDERATION.
KOGAN, Mr. Leigh Howard, BSc FCA *1981;* 58 Lord Avenue, Clayhall, ILFORD, IG5 0HN.
KOGER, Mr. Przemyslaw, ACA *2010;* Flat 2, 84 Alderney Street, LONDON, SW1V 4EY.
KOH, Mr. Alvin, ACA *2008;* Block 521 Hougang Avenue, 6#06-39, SINGAPORE 530521, SINGAPORE.
KOH, Mr. Bruce Yap Ming, ACA *1979;* 456 Jalan 17/13, 46400 PETALING JAYA, SELANGOR, MALAYSIA.
KOH, Mr. Choon Heong, ACA *1982;* Heng Long Leather Co Pte Ltd, SINGAPORE 539356, SINGAPORE.
KOH, Mr. Chuan Seng, BSc ACA *1994;* 25 Jalan 5/3, 46000 PETALING JAYA, SELANGOR, MALAYSIA.
KOH, Mr. Darren Ngiap Thiam, LLB(Hons) FCA CTA CPA *1992;* Apt 06-04 Sherwood Towers, 1 Jalan Anak Bukit, SINGAPORE 588996, SINGAPORE.
KOH, Mr. Derek Thong-Hean, BSc FCA *1993;* 11B Mount Sinai Lane, #01-10 Glentrees, SINGAPORE 277051, SINGAPORE.
KOH, Mr. Foo Weng, BSc FCA *1989;* 28/181-185 Pacific Highway, ROSEVILLE, NSW 2069, AUSTRALIA.
KOH, Mr. Hin Choi, ACA *1994;* 30-2-1 (block A), Jalan 5/101C, Cheras Business Centre, Batu 5, Jalan Cheras, 56100 KUALA LUMPUR FEDERAL TERRITORY MALAYSIA.
KOH, Mr. Hock Joo Rupert, FCA *1979;* 14 Jalan 20/18, 46300, PETALING JAYA, SELANGOR, MALAYSIA.
KOH, Miss. Huei Wearn, ACA *2010;* Flat 10, Velocity North, 3 City Walk, LEEDS, LS11 9BE.
•KOH, Mr. Hui Chang, FCA *1973;* H.C.Koh & Co, 190 Middle Road, 14-02 Fortune Centre, SINGAPORE 188979, SINGAPORE.
KOH, Miss. Karen Kay Mun, BA ACA *1994;* 5925 NE Alder St, HILLSBORO, OR 97124, UNITED STATES.
KOH, Mr. Kek Sin, BSc ACA *1991;* Yum! Restaurants International, 99 Bukit Timah Road, No. 06-00, SINGAPORE 229835, SINGAPORE.
KOH, Mr. Kok Wee Adrian, LLB ACA *2006;* 9 Amber Gardens, #14-27, One Amber, SINGAPORE 439958, SINGAPORE.
KOH, Miss. Kwai Yim, LLB ACA *1993;* Flat 204 2/F Block C, Westlands Garden, 4 Westlands Road, QUARRY BAY, HONG KONG SAR.
KOH, Mrs. Lavinia, BSc FCA *1993;* 11B Mount Sinai Lane, No. 1-10, Glentrees, SINGAPORE 277051, SINGAPORE.
KOH, Mr. Lay Kian, ACA *1979;* Stephen Koh & Co, 90 Cecil Street #08-03, RHB Bank Building, SINGAPORE 069531, SINGAPORE.
KOH, Miss. Li-Tze, ACA *2009;* 19 Jalan Haji Abdul Hamid, 70200 SEREMBAN, NEGERI SEMBILAN, MALAYSIA.
KOH, Ms. Nadia, ACA CA(AUS) *2010;* Ineum Consulting, 2nd Floor, 10 Fleet Place, LONDON, EC4M 7RB.
KOH, Miss. Phaik Heah, FCA *1980;* 53 Jalan SS 5A/16, Kelana Jaya, 47301 PETALING JAYA, Selangor, MALAYSIA.
KOH, Miss. Poh-Chan, FCA *1973;* c/o Harbour Plaza Hotels & Resorts, 8/F Two Harbourfront, 22 Tak Fung Street, HUNG HOM, Kowloon, HONG KONG SAR.
KOH, Miss. Poy Yong, ACA *1983;* with Genting Malaysia Berhad, Finance Department, 18th Floor Wisma Genting, 28 Jalan Sultan Ismail, 50250 KUALA LUMPUR, FEDERAL TERRITORY MALAYSIA.
KOH, Mrs. Puay San, FCA *1971;* 33 Oxley Rise, 05-03, Vision Crest, SINGAPORE 238710, SINGAPORE.
KOH, Mr. Soo Eng, ACA *1988;* 21 Jalan Kelapa Jaya, Taman Soga, 83000 BATU PAHAT, JOHOR, MALAYSIA.
KOH, Mr. Yu Soon, BA FCA *1986;* 635 Kathleen Place, Westbury, NEW YORK, NY 11590, UNITED STATES.
KOHER, Mr. Abu, Bsc ACA *2011;* 8 Whitehouse Close, FARNBOROUGH, HAMPSHIRE, GU14 8JJ.
KOHLER, Mr. Anthony John, FCA *1958;* P O BOX 218, PLETTENBERG BAY, 6600, SOUTH AFRICA. (Life Member)
KOHLER, Mr. Michael Bruce, ACA CA(SA) *2011;* 1 Watersfield Lane, TONBRIDGE, KENT, TN10 3BE.
KOHLER, Mrs. Susan Marian, BSc ACA *1985;* 10 Newmills Grove, BALERNO, MIDLOTHIAN, EH14 5SY.
KOHLER, Mr. Thomas George, BA ACA *2010;* 3 Mathews Yard, LONDON, WC2H 9AR.
•KOHLI, Mr. Chander, BSc ACA *1984;* PricewaterhouseCoopers, One Spencer Dock, North Wall Quay, DUBLIN 1, COUNTY DUBLIN, IRELAND.
KOHLI, Mrs. Meera, BA ACA *2005;* PO Box 113467, DUBAI, UNITED ARAB EMIRATES.
KOHLI, Mr. Mohan, BSc FCA *1984;* PricewaterhouseCoopers, Prince's Building, 22/F, 10 Chater Road, CENTRAL, HONG KONG ISLAND HONG KONG SAR.
KOHLI, Mrs. Parveen, ACA *2009;* 94 Greenock Crescent, WOLVERHAMPTON, WV4 6BJ.
•KOHLI, Mr. Rajesh Paul, BSc FCA *2000;* Power Accountax Limited, 8c High Street, SOUTHAMPTON, SO14 2DH.
KOHLI, Mr. Sanjiv, BSc ACA *1992;* 4 Newbold Road, Kirkby Mallory, LEICESTER, LE9 7QG.
KOHLI, Mr. Vivek, ACA *2008;* 126 Marshall Square, SOUTHAMPTON, SO15 2PQ.
KOHN, Mr. Alfred, MSc FCA *1974;* 2 West 46th. Street, Suite 609, NEW YORK, NY 10036, UNITED STATES.
KOHYA, Mr. Sajid Suleiman, BSc(Econ) ACA *2005;* Merrill Lynch, 2 King Edward Street, LONDON, EC1A 1HQ.
KOID, Miss. Phei Yinn, BSc ACA *2005;* 45 G-H Tower 2, The Pacifica, 9 Sham Shing Road, CHEUNG SHA WAN, KOWLOON, HONG KONG SAR.
KOIZIA, Mrs. Desiree, ACA *1985;* Kwality Garment Services Ltd, Unit 30/35, Lake Business Centre, Tariff Road, LONDON, N17 0YX.
KOIZOU, Mr. Terry Nicholas, BSc(Hons) ACA *2001;* 5 Woodside Avenue, EASTLEIGH, HAMPSHIRE, SO50 9ER.
KOJIC, Miss. Jovana, ACA *2010;* with PricewaterhouseCoopers LLP, Hays Galleria, 1 Hays Lane, LONDON, SE1 2RD.
KOK, Mr. Eugene Siu Kong, BSc ACA *1994;* 4291 Bonavista Drive, RICHMOND V7E 5BI, BC, CANADA.
KOK, Miss. Helen Lai Fong, BA FCA *1994;* 900 DUNEARN ROAD, #06-22 THE BLOSSOMVALE, SINGAPORE 589473, SINGAPORE.
KOK, Mr. Joseph, ACA *1986;* 25 Wilton Road, Muswell Hill, LONDON, N10 1LX.
KOK, Mr. Nam Soon, FCA *1980;* 26 Jalan Athinahapan 3, Taman Tun Dr Ismail, 60000 KUALA LUMPUR, FEDERAL TERRITORY, MALAYSIA. (Life Member)
KOK, Mr. Peter Peet Teck, FCA MBA *1979;* 11 Hill Street, ARNCLIFFE, NSW 2205, AUSTRALIA.
KOK, Mr. Robbie, ACA *2009;* 38 Broughville Drive, MANCHESTER, M20 5WH.
KOKACH OSEI, Mrs. Christine, ACA *2008;* 53 High Street, Stretham, ELY, CAMBRIDGESHIRE, CB6 3LD.
•KOKKINOS, Mr. Joseph Antoniou, ACA *1984;* Joseph Kokkinos & Co Ltd, 22 Ajax Street, Ayioi Omoloyites, 1082 NICOSIA, CYPRUS. See also Joseph Kokkinos & Co and A.K. Limited
KOKKINOS, Miss. Melina Loui, LLB ACA *1990;* 8 Armenias Street, 2003 NICOSIA, CYPRUS.
•KOKKINOS, Mr. Michael, FCA *1981;* KPMG Certified Auditors AE, 3 Stratigou Tombra Street, Aghia Paraskevi, GR 153 42 ATHENS, GREECE.
KOKKINOU, Mrs. Maria, BSc ACA *2010;* 117 A Aigaioy, Lakatamia, NICOSIA, CYPRUS.
KOL, Mr. Eric, BSc ACA *1999;* 4 Beech Walk, Ewell, EPSOM, KT17 1PU.
KOLADE, Mrs. Kerry Suzanne, BSc ACA *1993;* Bolney Lodge, Foxhole Lane, Bolney, HAYWARDS HEATH, WEST SUSSEX, RH17 5RS.
KOLANDAVELU, Mr. Shunmuga Velu, ACA *1983;* 62 Mount Sinai Avenue, SINGAPORE 277200, SINGAPORE.
KOLBERT, Mrs. Carolyn Teresa, BSc ACA *2004;* 9 Saunders Close, Twyford, READING, RG10 0XT.
KOLKMAN, Mrs. Sarah Louise, BSc ACA *1991;* 61 Norfolk Street, KILLARA, NSW 2071, AUSTRALIA.
KOLLER, Mr. Warner Thomas, BSc FCA *1980;* Mercator Trust Co. Ltd, PO Box 336, GUERNSEY, GY1 3UQ.
KOLLI, Miss. Laura Priya, MA ACA *2010;* Flat 43 Chantry Court, Woods Avenue, HATFIELD, HERTFORDSHIRE, AL10 8NB.
KOLOCASSIDES, Mr. Kyriacos, BSc ACA *1993;* 122 Strovolos Avenue, Apt. 801, Strovolos, 2042 NICOSIA, CYPRUS.
KOLOKOTRONI, Miss. Marina, ACA *1994;* PO Box 52689, Drosia, 14565 ATHENS, ATTICA, GREECE.
KOLOKOTRONI, Miss. Rea, BA FCA *1986;* 23 Korniliou, 2333 NICOSIA, CYPRUS.
KOLOKOTRONIS, Mr. Loizos Evangelou, FCA *1973;* 16 Metsovou Street, 175 63 Palaion Faliron, ATHENS, GREECE.
KOLOMYITSEVA, Miss. Ekaterina, BSc ACA *2011;* 32 rue des Cévennes, Apt 14, 75015 PARIS, FRANCE.
•KOLSTERS, Mr. Jasper Geert, ACA *2010;* with Ernst & Young LLP, 1 More London Place, LONDON, SE1 2AF.
KOMEDERA, Mr. Anthony Peter, FCA *1978;* 42 Mount Avenue, Ealing, LONDON, W5 2QJ.
•KOMODROMOS, Mr. Panicos, BSc FCA *1990;* V. Komodromos & Co Accountants & Consultants Ltd, PO Box 27162, 1642 NICOSIA, CYPRUS. See also Panicos Y Komodromos & Co
•KOMODROMOS, Mr. Vassos, ACA *1991;* V. Komodromos & Co Accountants & Consultants Ltd, PO Box 27162, 1642 NICOSIA, CYPRUS.
KON, Miss. Cze Yan, BSc ACA *1990;* 27 Jalan BU 11/12, Bandar Utama, 47800 PETALING JAYA, SELANGOR, MALAYSIA.
KON, Mr. Jeremy Michael, ACA *1979;* 21 Parkway, LONDON, NW11 0EX.
KON, Mr. Wui Seng, BSc ACA *1989;* 27 Canadiana Drive, THORNHILL L3T 2Y7, ON, CANADA.
KON, Mr. Yin Thiam, MBA BSc(Econ) FCA CFA *1997;* 95 Penni Lane, NORTH ANDOVER, MA 01845, UNITED STATES.
KON, Mr. Yin Tong, BSc FCA *1991;* 15 Jalan Ketumbit, SINGAPORE 808867, SINGAPORE.
KON, Mr. Yuen Kong, FCA *1960;* 370 C Lorong Chuan, SINGAPORE 556794, SINGAPORE. (Life Member)
•KONCZYK, Miss. Julie Margaret, ACA FCCA *2010;* Farrar Smith Limited, 2 Woodside Mews, Clayton Wood Close, LEEDS, LS16 6QE. See also Ambler & Co Limited
KONDO, Mrs. Elizabeth Anne, BSc ACA *1996;* Mulberry House, Heather Drive, ASCOT, SL5 0HP.
KONFORTION, Miss. Martine Stephanie, BSc ACA *2004;* Financial Consulting Services, 3rd Floor Cerne House, La Chaussee, PORT LOUIS, MAURITIUS.
KONFORTION, Miss. Sarah Christine, BA ACA *2011;* 26 Park Mansions, Knightsbridge, LONDON, SW1X 7QS.

KONFORTION, Mr. Stephen Robert, FCA *1973;* Kemp Chatteris Deloitte, 7th. Floor, Raffles Tower, 19 Cybercity, EBENE, MAURITIUS. See also Kemp Chatteris Associates Ltd

KONG, Miss. Barbara Cheng Chee, FCA *1963;* 35 Cornwall Gardens, SINGAPORE 269661, SINGAPORE. (Life Member)

KONG, Mr. Chi Kin, ACA *2005;* Flat C 5/F Block 10, Vista Paradiso, 2 Hang Ming Street, Ma On Shan, SHA TIN, NT HONG KONG SAR.

KONG, Mr. Chi-Nang, BA ACA *2005;* Halifax Plc, 33 Old Broad Street, LONDON, EC2N 1HZ.

KONG, Ms. Flora Wai Fong, BA FCA *1982;* 46 St Barnabas Road, WOODFORD GREEN, IG8 7DA.

•KONG, Mr. Han Seng, FCA *1973;* H.S. Kong & Co, Sovereign Manor, Gover View, Gover Hill, TONBRIDGE, TN11 9SQ.

KONG, Mr. James Tze Wing, ACA *2004;* James T. W. Kong & Co., Room 1901 19/F C C Wu Building, 302-308 Hennessy Road, WAN CHAI, HONG KONG ISLAND, HONG KONG SAR.

KONG, Mr. Johnson Chi-How, BA ACA *1987;* with BDO Limited, 25/F Wing On Centre, 111 Connaught Road, CENTRAL, HONG KONG ISLAND, HONG KONG SAR.

KONG, Mr. Kam-Yu, BEng ACA *1995;* Flat H 19/F, Yiu Sing Mansion, Tai Koo Shing, QUARRY BAY, HONG KONG ISLAND, HONG KONG SAR.

•KONG, Mr. Kwet Liong, FCA *1973;* Liong Kong, 2195 Westhill Wynd, VANCOUVER V7S 2Z3, BC, CANADA.

KONG, Miss. Lee Kin, ACA *1984;* 12 Fairmeads, COBHAM, KT11 2JD.

KONG, Mr. Patrick Fui Kiong, FCA *1970;* Patrick Kong & Associates, 2nd Floor Lot 19, Luyang Phase 8 Kota Kinabalu, Specialist Ctr POB 11835, 88830 KOTA KINABALU, SABAH MALAYSIA.

KONG, Mrs. Rebecca, BSc ACA *1994;* 65 Lyndhurst Grove, LONDON, SE15 5AW.

KONG, Mr. Robert Patrick, BSc ACA *1992;* 77 Upper Changi Road East Summer Gardens, SINGAPORE 486176, SINGAPORE.

KONG, Mr. Shau Choong, ACA *2007;* 16/F AIA Central, 1 Connaught Road, CENTRAL, HONG KONG ISLAND, HONG KONG SAR.

KONG, Mr. Siew Cheong, LLB ACA *1991;* 2 Sunset Avenue, Ruffles Park, SINGAPORE 288244, SINGAPORE.

KONG, Mr. Sik Hung, FCA *1962;* 2 Sunset Avenue, Raffles Park, SINGAPORE 288244, SINGAPORE. (Life Member)

KONG, Mr. Sin Seng Daniel, BA ACA *1982;* 10-8-5 Kiaramas Cendana Condominium, 10 Jalan Desa Kiara, Bukit Kiara, 50480 KUALA LUMPUR, FEDERAL TERRITORY, MALAYSIA.

KONG, Mr. Tin Lok, ACA *2009;* Flat G 1st Floor, Block 2, Bayview Garden, TSUEN WAN, NEW TERRITORIES, HONG KONG SAR.

KONG, Mr. Tzu-Chiang, BA FCA *1988;* 3 Little Wood Close, ORPINGTON, KENT, BR5 2LA.

KONG, Ms. Wai Lam Maggie, ACA *2007;* Room 2208, Block A, Perfect Mount Gardens, 1 Po Man Street, SHAU KEI WAN, HONG KONG ISLAND HONG KONG SAR.

KONG, Mr. Wan Ho, ACA *2008;* Flat 430th Floor, Hong King House, Hong Yat Court, Kai Tin Road, LAM TIN, KOWLOON HONG KONG SAR.

KONG, Miss. Yen Nee, BSc ACA *2005;* 3 Jalan Sulaiman, 43000 KAJANG, SELANGOR, MALAYSIA.

KONG TSIN CHAN, Mr. Ah Kwun, MBA BSc ACA *1983;* 28 Illiliwa Street, CREMORNE, NSW 2090, AUSTRALIA.

KONG WIN CHANG, Miss. Jenna, ACA *2010;* Flat 268, Bromyard House, Bromyard Avenue, LONDON, W3 7BS.

KONG YAO FAH, Mr. Jean-Marc Miow Lim, BSc ACA *1994;* 7140 Henri Bourassa O, SAINT-LAURENT H4S 2B2, QUE, CANADA.

KONG YAO FAH, Miss. Marie-Anne Sew Youne, BSc ACA *1995;* Pricewaterhousecoopers, 33/F Cheung Kong Center, 2 Queens Road, CENTRAL, HONG KONG ISLAND, HONG KONG SAR.

•KONII, Dr. Yuki, DPhil FCA ATII *1994;* Deloitte LLP, 2 New Street Square, LONDON, EC4A 3BZ. See also Deloitte & Touche LLP

•KONINGS, Mr. Frederik Jan, BA FCA *1979;* PricewaterhouseCoopers, Princes Margrietplantsoen 46, PO Box 30715, 2500 THE HAGUE, NETHERLANDS.

KONOMANYI, Mr. Andrew Aiah, MSc BA ACA *2004;* The Global Fund, Chemin de Blandonnet 8, 1214 Vernier, GENEVA, SWITZERLAND.

KONOPLIANIKOVA, Miss. Anna, MSc ACA *2005;* Athinas 6B, Melissia, 15127 ATHENS, ATTICA, GREECE.

KONRAD, Dr. Jonathan Paul, PhD ACA MCT *2002;* 22 King's College Court, Primrose Hill Road, LONDON, NW3 3EA.

•KONRAD, Mr. Tony, FCA *1968;* 13C Wedderburn Road, Hampstead, LONDON, NW3 5QS.

KONRATH, Mr. Ian David Charles, BA ACA *1990;* 5 Coltsfoot Crescent, Drovers Mead, BURY ST.EDMUNDS, IP32 7NN.

KONSTANTINOU, Ms. Rodia, BSc ACA *2011;* 20 Dositheou Eiconomou, Mesa Geitonia, 4001 LIMASSOL, CYPRUS.

KONU, Mr. Adebayo Kwashie, BSc ACA *1988;* 12 Cochrane Mews, LONDON, NW8 6NY.

KONU, Ms. Selasi Esi, ACA *2009;* Flat 18 Solomons Court, 451 High Road, LONDON, N12 0AW.

KOO, Mr. Cheuk On Timmie, ACA *2005;* Flat G 16/F, Kwun King Mansion, Lei King Wan, SAI WAN HO, HONG KONG ISLAND, HONG KONG SAR.

KOO, Mr. Hock Fee, FCA *1976;* No. 15 Jalan USJ 2/5K, UEP Subang Jaya, 47600 SUBANG, SELANGOR, MALAYSIA.

KOO, Mr. Wing Kei Keith, ACA *2010;* Flat B 8/FBlock 2, Oak Mansions, 7 Tak Fung Street, Whampoa Garden, Site 5, HUNG HOM KOWLOON HONG KONG SAR.

KOO, Miss. Yuen Sum, FCA *1976;* 456 Jalan 17/13, 46400 PETALING JAYA, SELANGOR, MALAYSIA.

KOO SIN LIN, Mrs. Christine Choo Hoon, FCA *1973;* IPOH Omnibus Co. SDN. BHD., Bus Station Jalan Kidd., 30200 IPOH, PERAK, MALAYSIA.

KOO TEE FONG, Miss. Dolly Liew Yoong, ACA *2009;* 257 Kennington Lane, LONDON, SE11 5QU.

KOOI, Mr. Richard Tock Lim, BBS ACA *1992;* 15 Gerrard Road, LONDON, N1 8AY.

KOOK, Mr. Nicholas Jonathan, ACA *1989;* with Deloitte & Touche, P.O.Box HM 1556, Corner House, Church & Parliament Streets, HAMILTON HM FX, BERMUDA.

KOOL, Mr. Hans Lourens, BSc ACA *1986;* 12 Hyde Green South, STEVENAGE, HERTFORDSHIRE, SG2 9XU.

KOOMEN, Mr. Joshua James, ACA CA(AUS) *2009;* BT Pension Scheme Management Ltd, 1 Portsoken Street, LONDON, E1 8HZ.

KOOMEN, Miss. Petra, ACA *2010;* Bilderdijkkade 66-2, 1053VN AMSTERDAM, NETHERLANDS.

KOON, Mr. Fung Sing Thomson, ACA *2005;* Koon Fung Sing, Flat H 13/F Hong Fai Court, Healthy Village Hsg. Estate, 190 Tsat Tsz Mui Road, NORTH POINT, HONG KONG ISLAND HONG KONG SAR.

KOON, Ms. Toi Nei, ACA *2008;* 148 Cypress Drive, Palm Springs, YUEN LONG, NEW TERRITORIES, HONG KONG SAR.

KOON KAM KING, Mr. David, BSc ACA *2008;* (Tax Fac), KPMG, 1st floor, 31 Cybercity, EBENE, MAURITIUS.

•KOON KAM KING, Mr. Wilfrid, FCA *1971;* 8 SEVREMONT STREET, BEAU BASSIN, MAURITIUS.

KOON SIW, Mr. Piang Cheong Chin, ACA *2008;* Barclays Capital, B Z W, 10 South Colonnade, LONDON, E14 4PU.

•KOONER, Miss. Sukhbinder, BSc ACA *1999;* with Deloitte LLP, 2 New Street Square, LONDON, EC4A 3BZ.

KOONER, Mr. Surjit Singh, MA BSc ACA *2002;* Midven Limited, 39-41 Waterloo Street, BIRMINGHAM, B2 5PP.

KOOPMAN, Mr. George Arthur, BSc FCA *1967;* Xtrac Limited, Gables Way, Kenner Park, THATCHAM, BERKSHIRE, RG19 4ZA.

KOOROS, Miss. Zohreh, MA ACA *1996;* 9 Berridge Mews, LONDON, NW6 1RF.

KOOSEENLIN, Mr. Nick, BA ACA *2006;* 51 Willowdale, LEEDS, LS10 4FN.

KOPEC, Mr. Mieczyslaw Karol, MA FCA *1979;* Fichtenweg 10, D-76547 SINZHEIM, GERMANY.

•KOPPA, Mr. Ravi, BSc ACA *1992;* CK Partnership Limited, 1 Old Court Mews, 311a Chase Road, LONDON, N14 6JS.

KOPPEL, Miss. Lanie Vivienne, BA FCA *1979;* Sucden Financial Ltd 3rd Floor, Plantation Place South 60 Great Tower Street, LONDON, EC3R 5AZ.

KORAL, Mr. Gregory David, BSc ACA *1990;* 39 St. Bernards Road, SOLIHULL, WEST MIDLANDS, B92 7AX.

KORAM, Mr. Emmanuel Offei, FCA *1960;* NONE, NONE, GHANA. (Life Member)

KORANTENG, Mr. Francis Solace Oduro, BSc FCA *1988;* E33 SEQUOIA LANE D.T.D, COMMUNITY 18, LASHIBI, TEMA, GHANA.

•KOREK, Mr. Julian Witold, BSc FCA *1982;* Kinetic Partners, 1 London Wall, Level 10, LONDON, EC2Y 5HB. See also Kinetic Partners Audits LLP

KOREL, Mr. Brian Maurice, FCA *1983;* 9 Sheraton Close, Elstree, BOREHAMWOOD, HERTFORDSHIRE, WD6 3PZ.

KORELLIS, Mr. Georgios, BSc(Econ) ACA *1997;* 1 Michalaki Kousoulides, Dasoupolis, Strovolos, 2024 NICOSIA, CYPRUS.

KORICAN, Mr. Bruce Thomas, BSc ACA *1989;* The Manor House, Nutshell Lane, FARNHAM, GU9 0HG.

KORINOS, Mr. Panayiotis Kyriacou, BSc DIC ACA MBA *1997;* 6 Valaoritis Street, Engomi, 2411 NICOSIA, CYPRUS.

KORKUSHKO, Ms. Irina, ACA *2009;* with Ernst & Young Moscow LLC, Sadovnieskaya Nab 77, Building 1, 115035 MOSCOW, RUSSIAN FEDERATION.

•KORMAN, Mr. Victor, BSc FCA *1984;* (Tax Fac), CMEASY Limited, Anglo Dal House, 5 Spring Villa Park, EDGWARE, MIDDLESEX, HA8 7EB.

•KORN, Mr. Martin Geoffrey, FCA *1969;* 2 Golders Close, EDGWARE, MIDDLESEX, HA8 9QD.

•KOROLKIEWICZ, Mr. Paul Alexander, BA FCA *1993;* KPMG LLP, 15 Canada Square, LONDON, E14 5GL. See also KPMG Europe LLP

KORONIS, Miss. Christina, ACA *2008;* 3A Promitheos Street, Makedonitissa, Engomi, 2413 NICOSIA, CYPRUS.

•KORONIS, Mr. Costas, FCA *1976;* 3a Prometheos Street, Makedonitissa Engomi, 2413 NICOSIA, CYPRUS.

KORONIS, Mr. Nicholas, BA ACA *2008;* 3A Promitheos Street, Makedonitissa, 2413 Engomi, NICOSIA, CYPRUS.

KOROYE, Mr. Poweide, ACA *1998;* The World Bank, 1818 H Street NW, Mail Stop MC5-518, WASHINGTON, DC 20433, UNITED STATES.

KORTLANDT, Miss. Jane Elizabeth, BA ACA *2005;* Finance B1, Lewisham College, Breakspears Road, LONDON, SE4 1UT.

KORTZ, Mrs. Julia Laura, BSc ACA *1998;* 108 Malthouse Lane, Earlswood, SOLIHULL, WEST MIDLANDS, B94 5SA.

KORWASER, Mr. Mieczyslaw Henryck Andrzej, BCom FCA *1961;* 24 Thorpe Hall, Eaton Rise, LONDON, W5 2HB. (Life Member)

KOSCICA, Mr. Alexander, BSc ACA *1978;* 2 Hatfield Close, Matchborough East, REDDITCH, B98 0AD.

•KOSHAL, Mr. Deepak, FCA *1974;* G & Co Molesey Ltd, Gautam House, 1-3 Shenley Avenue, Ruislip Manor, RUISLIP, MIDDLESEX HA4 6BP. See also WAB Grove Ltd, Timecount Ltd and Koshal Associates

KOSHY, Miss. Rahel, ACA *2008;* 44 First Avenue, LONDON, SW14 8SR.

KOSKUBA, Miss. Karla Eva, BSc ACA *2001;* 8 Vicarage Gardens, East Sheen, LONDON, SW14 8RT.

•KOSLOVER, Mr. Hugh Paul, BA FCA *1988;* Ashton Hart David Lee, Sterling House, Langston Road, LOUGHTON, ESSEX, IG10 3FA.

KOSLOVER, Mr. Jonathan Jacob, BSc ACA MCT *1987;* Chart House, 33 Bow Green Road, Bowdon, ALTRINCHAM, WA14 3LF.

KOSMIDER, Mr. Christopher Zbigniew Andrzej, BSc ACA *1988;* Bank Pekao SA, Head Office, 53/57 Grzybowska Street, 00-950 WARSAW, POLAND.

KOSNOWSKI, Mr. Stephen Eugene, BSc FCA *1975;* Prevoj 73, 10000 ZAGREB, CROATIA.

KOSS, Mr. Andrew Robert, BSc ACA MCT *1996;* 46 Scarcroft Hill, YORK, YO24 1DE.

KOSSIFOS, Mr. Alex, ACA FCCA *2009;* The Old Rectory, 8 Shirburn Road, TORQUAY, TQ1 3JH.

KOSTER, Mr. Pieter, FCA *1950;* 17 Airlie Road, CAPE TOWN, 7945, SOUTH AFRICA. (Life Member)

KOSTICK, Mrs. Marjorie Phyllis, BA FCA CTA *1980;* 20 Magdalene Court, Magdalene Street, TAUNTON, SOMERSET, TA1 1QY. (Life Member)

KOSTKA, Mr. Edward, BSc FCA *1979;* Interaudit, 119 Avenue de la Faiencerie, L-1511 LUXEMBOURG, LUXEMBOURG.

KOSTYN, Mr. Michael Neil, BA(Econ) ACA *1996;* Flat 14/H, Portman Mansions, Chiltern Street, LONDON, W1U 6NX.

KOTA, Mr. Kartik, ACA *2011;* 26 Gabrielle House, 332-336 Perth Road, ILFORD, ESSEX, IG2 6FF.

KOTA, Mr. Navnit, ACA *1983;* 15 Mountview, NORTHWOOD, MIDDLESEX, HA6 3NZ.

•KOTAK, Mr. Dinesh, FCA *1979;* High Thurney Farm, Ridgemere Lane, South Croxton, LEICESTER, LE7 3RR.

KOTAK, Mr. Nishit, BSc ACA *1993;* Execellence Ltd, 8a Silverwood Close, CAMBRIDGE, CB1 3HA.

KOTECHA, Mr. Anil Purshottam, FCA *1972;* 1590 Kelvinway Lane, PICKERING L1V 5X5, ON, CANADA.

KOTECHA, Mrs. Baldeep, ACA *2011;* Flat 42, Kirk House, Hirst Crescent, WEMBLEY, MIDDLESEX, HA9 7HF.

KOTECHA, Mr. Bhagirath, BA ACA *1986;* 66 Oakleigh Avenue, EDGWARE, HA8 5DS.

KOTECHA, Mr. Bhavesh, MSc BSc ACA *2007;* 60 Mount Grove, EDGWARE, HA8 9SX.

•KOTECHA, Mrs. Bindu, FCA *1991;* (Tax Fac), Browne Jacobson Llp, 44 Castle Gate, NOTTINGHAM, NG1 7BJ.

•KOTECHA, Mr. Bipin, BSc(Econ) FCA *1986;* (Tax Fac), Bipin Kotecha, 123 Queen Alexandra Mansions, Tonbridge Street, LONDON, WC1H 9DW.

KOTECHA, Mr. Chetendra, BA ACA *1995;* Scancom Distribution, 264 - 266 Leicester Road, WIGSTON, LEICESTERSHIRE, LE18 1HQ.

•KOTECHA, Mr. Dharmesh, BSc ACA *2002;* Coppersun Accountants Limited, 7 Wynlie Gardens, PINNER, MIDDLESEX, HA5 3TN.

KOTECHA, Mr. Dilip Dullabhji, FCA *1972;* 5561 Whirlaway Lane, RACINE, WI 53402, UNITED STATES. (Life Member)

KOTECHA, Mr. Harish Chhaganlal, BA ACA *1983;* 128 Berry Lane, RICKMANSWORTH, WD3 4BT.

•KOTECHA, Mr. Jay, BSc FCA *1983;* Linkca Ltd, 1 Admiral House, Cardinal Way, HARROW, MIDDLESEX, HA3 5TE.

KOTECHA, Mrs. Manorama, ACA ATII *1978;* High Elms House, High Elms, HARPENDEN, HERTFORDSHIRE, AL5 2JU.

KOTECHA, Mr. Mitesh, BA ACA *1992;* A B N Amro Bank NV, 250 Bishopsgate, LONDON, EC2M 4AA.

•KOTECHA, Mr. Mukundrai Kanjibhai, FCA CFP *1977;* (Tax Fac), Mac Kotecha & Co., Lichfield House, 2 Lichfield Grove, LONDON, N3 2JP.

KOTECHA, Mr. Pritesh Dharshi, BA ACA *1997;* (Tax Fac), with BDO LLP, 55 Baker Street, LONDON, W1U 7EU.

•KOTECHA, Miss. Priya, ACA *2004;* Mac Kotecha & Co., Lichfield House, 2 Lichfield Grove, LONDON, N3 2JP.

KOTECHA, Mr. Rajesh B, BSc(Econ) ACA *1997;* 20 Howberry Road, EDGWARE, MIDDLESEX, HA8 6ST.

KOTECHA, Mr. Rakesh Rasik, BSc ACA *1995;* PricewaterhouseCoopers, 1 North Wacker Drive, CHICAGO, IL 60606, UNITED STATES.

KOTECHA, Miss. Reena, LLB ACA *2003;* 37b Cygnet Close, NORTHWOOD, MIDDLESEX, HA6 2TA.

KOTECHA, Mr. Rupen Premji, BSc ACA *1994;* 4 Gemmell Way, HILLARYS, WA 6025, AUSTRALIA.

KOTECHA, Mr. Rupin, BSc ACA *1992;* Elsevier Ltd, 32 Jamestown Road, Camden, LONDON, NW1 7BY.

KOTECHA, Miss. Shenai, BSc FCA *1998;* (Tax Fac), 18 Rockingham Close, LEICESTER, LE5 4EG.

•KOTECHA, Mr. Viren, BA(Hons) ACA *2003;* Alacrity Accountancy Ltd, 21 High View Close, Hamilton, LEICESTER, LE4 9LJ.

•KOTEN, Mr. Barry, FCA *1974;* Koten & Co, Suite 7, Essex House, Station Road, UPMINSTER, RM14 2SJ. See also Koten B. & Co

KOTHARI, Mr. Atul, ACA FCCA *2011;* 51 Rowlands Avenue, Hatch End, PINNER, MIDDLESEX, HA5 4DF.

KOTHARI, Mr. Bipinchandra N, ACA *1983;* 12 Paulhan Road, HARROW, HA3 9AR.

KOTHARI, Mr. Jagdish Chandra Popatlal Hemchand, FCA *1966;* Via Cottalorda 27, 21022 AZZATE, ITALY.

•KOTHARI, Mr. Jayesh Jamnadas Dayalji, FCA FCCA CTA *1976;* Kothari & Co, Unit 1, Acton Hill Mews Business Centre, 310/328 Uxbridge Road, LONDON, W3 9QN.

•KOTHARI, Mr. Nalinkant Nanalal, FCA *1973;* N.N. Kothari & Co, 19 Collins Avenue, STANMORE, HA7 1DL.

KOTHARI, Mr. Rajendra Khupchand, MBA ACA *1983;* with PricewaterhouseCoopers, Royal Trust Tower, Suite 3000 TD Centre, Box 82, 77 King Street West, TORONTO M5K 1G8 ON CANADA.

•KOTLARZEWSKI, Mr. Roman Blaise, BA ACA *1983;* Confin Interim Management Ltd, 95 Crofters Way, DROITWICH, WORCESTERSHIRE, WR9 9HU.

•KOTSAPAS, Mr. Michael, BSc ACA *2005;* Moore Stephens LLP, 150 Aldersgate Street, LONDON, EC1A 4AB.

KOTSIOPOULOS, Mrs. Akaterine, ACA *2000;* 5 Austin Avenue, ELWOOD, VIC 3184, AUSTRALIA.

KOTSOMITIS, Mr. Aristedes, BSc ACA *1996;* (Tax Fac), POBOX 22784, CY 1524, CY 1524 NICOSIA, CYPRUS.

KOTT, Mr. Alexander, BSc ACA *1999;* 67 Oakwood Drive, ST. ALBANS, HERTFORDSHIRE, AL4 0UL.

KOTTEGODA, Mr. Siraj Naomal, BSocSc ACA *1984;* Embers, Kirkdale Road, HARPENDEN, AL5 2PT.

KOTTLER, Mr. James Richard, BA ACA *1998;* 87 Lion Road, TWICKENHAM, TW1 4HT.

KOTTWITZ, Mr. Sven Dennis, MSc BA(Hons) ACA *2001;* Meridiam Infrastructure, 28 Boulevard Haussmann, 75009 PARIS, FRANCE.

KOTWAL, Mr. Mahiyar, FCA *1978;* with Grant Thornton UK LLP, Royal Liver Building, Pier Head, LIVERPOOL, L3 1PS.
KOTWINSKI, Mr. David Peter, MEng ACA *2003;* 103a Penwith Road, LONDON, SW18 4PY.
KOTZE, Mr. Johann Christopher, ACA CA(SA) *2011;* 3 Stanmore Chase, ST ALBANS, AL4 0EZ.
KOTZE, Mrs. Michelle, BA(Hons) ACA *2001;* The Haven Church Lane, Sompting, LANCING, WEST SUSSEX, BN15 0BA.
KOUFARI, Miss. Bobbi, ACA *2008;* Thrasyvoulou 13, Mesa Geitonia, 4003 LIMASSOL, CYPRUS.
KOUFARIS, Mr. Christopher Vassou, BSc ACA *1979;* Iris House, 840A John Kennedy Street, P.O.Box 53510, Enaerios, CY 3300 LIMASSOL, CYPRUS.
KOUFARIS, Mr. George, ACA *1978;* 3 Menelaos Fragkoudes, Strovolos, 2055 NICOSIA, CYPRUS.
KOUFARIS, Mr. Vasilis, BA ACA *2005;* melinas merkouri 46 engomi, 2411 NICOSIA, CYPRUS.
KOUKLOVA, Miss. Petia, ACA *2011;* 15 Karchiddonos Street, 2413 NICOSIA, CYPRUS.
•**KOUKOUMAS, Mr. George Andrea, BA FCA** *1996;* PKF/ATCO Limited, 2 Limassol Avenue, Aluminium Tower, Floors 3 & 4, Strovolos, 2003 NICOSIA CYPRUS. See also PKF Savvides & Co Ltd
KOULLAS, Mr. Panayiotis, BCom ACA *2001;* 2 Dyke Road Avenue, BRIGHTON, BN1 5LA.
KOULOUMBRI, Miss. Margarita, ACA *2008;* 11 Karaiskaki Street, Flat 301, Acropolis, 2012 NICOSIA, CYPRUS.
KOUMERA, Miss. Charitini, MPhil BSc ACA *2007;* Flat 3, 100 Elgin Avenue, LONDON, W9 2HD.
KOUMETTOU, Mr. Christakis, BA ACA *1990;* 8 Constantinoupoleos Str, Makedonitissa, NICOSIA, CYPRUS.
•**KOUMETTOU, Mr. Ninos Ioannou, FCA FCCA** *1976;* Alexander Lawson Jacobs Ltd, 1 Kings Avenue, LONDON, N21 3NA. See also Koumettou Tackoushis & Ioannou
•**KOUMETTOU, Mr. Yiannis, ACA** *2008;* Alexander Lawson Jacobs Ltd, 1 Kings Avenue, LONDON, N21 3NA.
KOUMI, Mr. Iacovos, BSc FCA *1981;* 66 Brookdale, LONDON, N11 1BN.
KOUMIS, Mr. Andreas, BSc FCA *1997;* 14 Yp. Nicolaou Georgiou, Opalia Hill, Mesa Yitonia, 4008 LIMASSOL, CYPRUS.
KOUMIS, Mr. George, BA ACA *1992;* 3 DEDALOS STREET, 3017 LIMASSOL, CYPRUS.
KOUMPAROS, Mr. Alex Simon, LLB ACA *2005;* 103 Tuscany Springs Landing NW, CALGARY T3L 3B9, AB, CANADA.
KOUNNAMAS, Mr. Iakovos, BSc ACA *2007;* 8c Charalambou Mouskou, Lakatamia, 2310 NICOSIA, CYPRUS.
KOUNNAMAS, Mr. Iakovos, BSc ACA *2010;* 3 Miltiadis Stylianou Street, Akropolis, NICOSIA, CYPRUS.
•**KOUNNIS, Mr. Constantinos, ACA** *2008;* C Kounnis Ltd, 100 Yiannis Kranidiotis Avenue, Office 102, Latsia, 2235 NICOSIA, CYPRUS.
KOUNTOURIS, Mr. Nicos, BA FCA *2000;* 3 George Lapithis Street, Engomi, 2407 NICOSIA, CYPRUS.
KOUPPARIS, Mr. Antonis, BSc ACA *1995;* Philip Morris International Management, Avenue de Rhodanie 50, 1001 LAUSANNE, SWITZERLAND.
KOUROUFEXI, Miss. Maria, ACA *2011;* Kreontos 8, Strovolos, 2021 NICOSIA, CYPRUS.
•**KOURRIS, Mr. George, BSc FCA** *1983;* MEMBER OF COUNCIL, Ernst & Young Cyprus Limited, Nicosia Tower Centre, 36 Byron Avenue, P.O Box 21656, 1511 NICOSIA, CYPRUS. See also Ernst & Young Europe LLP
KOURSARI, Miss. Margarita, LLB(Hons) ACA *2011;* 10 Klementos street, 1061 NICOSIA, CYPRUS.
KOURSAROU, Miss. Elena, BA ACA *2011;* Kosta Georgiou 6A, 3080 LIMASSOL, CYPRUS.
KOURTIS, Mr. Timos, MEng ACA *2010;* 86 Belsize Road, LONDON, NW6 4TG.
KOUSELINIS, Mr. Demetrios Nicolaou, BSc FCA *1988;* c/o Central Bank of Cyprus, 80 Kennedy Avenue, PO Box 25529, 1395 NICOSIA, CYPRUS.
KOUSHIAPPAS, Mr. Christophoros, MSc BA ACA *2010;* 15 Parthenonos Street, Aglanjia, 2101 NICOSIA, CYPRUS.
KOUSSA, Mrs. Shahana, BSc ACA *2006;* 57 Hinchley Road, MANCHESTER, M9 7FG.
KOUTALIS, Mr. Demetris, BA ACA *2006;* 10 Bellini Street, Petrou And Pavlou, 3081 LIMASSOL, CYPRUS.
KOUTSAKOU, Ms. Victoria, BSc ACA *2001;* P.O.BOX 62750, 8068 PAFOS, CYPRUS.
KOUTSIOUNDAS, Mr. Vassos, BA ACA *1999;* Odos Oniron 2, Aradippou, 7102 LARNACA, CYPRUS.
KOUTSOFTAS, Mr. Demetris, ACA *2009;* POB 33391, 5313 PARALIMNI, FAMAGUSTA DISTRICT, CYPRUS.
•**KOUTSOFTAS, Mr. Petros Andreou, BA(Econ) FCA** *2000;* K&S Quality Audit Ltd, PO Box 23404, CY 1683 NICOSIA, CYPRUS.
KOUVAROS, Mr. Nikos, BSc ACA *2010;* 19B ASPROU POTAMOU STR AGIOS GEORGIOS PEGEIAS, 8570 PAPHOS, CYPRUS.
KOUWENHOVEN, Miss. Adrienne Louise Beatrice, ACA *2001;* c/o Jebsen Asset Management, 4.Obergeschoss, Brandschenkestrasse 6, CH-8001 ZURICH, SWITZERLAND.
KOUYOUMJIAN, Mr. Vicken Alain, BA ACA *1995;* 11 Westpoint, 49 Putney Hill, LONDON, SW15 6RU.
KOUZALIS, Mr. Charalambos Demetriou, FCA *1982;* 81 Arch Makarios Avenue, 2671 Ayii Trimithias, NICOSIA, CYPRUS.
KOUZARI, Miss. Annita, BSc ACA *2008;* Ioanni Ntinan 12, Theodorou Court 5, Flat 202, 6042 LARNACA, CYPRUS.
KOUZNITSYNA, Ms. Natalia, MA BA ACA *2006;* Ground Floor Flat 41 Midhurst Avenue, LONDON, N10 3EP.
KOVACS, Ms. Susan, BSc ACA *1992;* 60 Hillpark Grove, EDINBURGH, MIDLOTHIAN, EH4 7AP.
KOW, Mr. Dew Lim, ACA *1979;* C/O Melaka Tong Bee Sdn Bhd, 87 Jalan Kampong Hulu, 75200 MALACCA CITY, MALACCA STATE, MALAYSIA.
KOWALCZYK, Miss. Anna, BEng ACA *2009;* Neoss Ltd Windsor House, Cornwall Road, HARROGATE, NORTH YORKSHIRE, HG1 2PW.
KOWALENKO, Mrs. Hannah, ACA *2008;* 54 Terrace Lane, Pleasley, MANSFIELD, NOTTINGHAMSHIRE, NG19 7PU.
KOWALSKI, Mr. Adam Richard, BA ACA *1999;* Axa Investment Managers 4th Floor, 7 Newgate Street, LONDON, W5 4EP.
KOWALSKI, Mr. Jerzy Zenon, BCom FCA *1959;* 63 Hartswood Road, LONDON, W12 9NE. (Life Member)
KOWALSKI, Mr. Timothy John, BSc FCA *1986;* Findel Plc, 2 Gregory Street, HYDE, CHESHIRE, SK14 4TH.
•**KOWENICKI, Mr. Richard Alexander, ACA** *1979;* Normandie House Rue A Chiens, St. Sampson, GUERNSEY, GY2 4AE.
KOWSZUN, Mr. James Stephen Peregrine, MA ACA *1993;* Bibendum Wine Ltd, 113 Regents Park Road, LONDON, NW1 8UR.
KOWSZUN, Mrs. Susan Ann, BA ACA DChA *1989;* The Counting House, Christs Hospital, HORSHAM, WEST SUSSEX, RH13 0YP.
KOY, Mr. Andy Kwan Loong, LLB ACA *2003;* Shalimar, Westbury Road, BROMLEY, BR1 2QB.
KOZAKIS, Mr. Costas, ACA *2010;* 14 Demonikou Street, 1086 NICOSIA, CYPRUS.
KOZIARSKI, Mrs. Sophie Margaret, BCom ACA *2002;* 27 College Road, Ardingly, HAYWARDS HEATH, WEST SUSSEX, RH17 6TU.
KOZIOL, Mr. Michael Walter, BA ACA *1982;* 18 Tryhorn Drive, Bishopdown, SALISBURY, SP1 3WA.
KOZLOWSKI, Ms. Katrina, ACA ACMA *2010;* 155 Westfield Road, HARPENDEN, HERTFORDSHIRE, AL5 4ND.
•**KOZUBA-KOZUBSKA, Miss. Danuta Ann, FCA** *1971;* (Tax Fac), The Stables Pains Hill, Donhead St. Andrew, SHAFTESBURY, SP7 9EA.
KRAFCHIK, Mr. Laurence Raphael, BA FCA *1995;* 72 Lodge Lane, North Fincley, LONDON, N12 8JJ.
KRAFT, Mr. Jeremy David, BA ACA *1990;* 27 Avenue Gardens, TEDDINGTON, MIDDLESEX, TW11 0BH.
KRAFT, Mr. Sidney Raymond, FCA *1957;* 67 Compayne Gardens, LONDON, NW6 3DB. (Life Member)
KRAG, Mr. Stephen Rosenstjerne, MA ACA *1984;* 3 Lovelace Close, Hurley, MAIDENHEAD, SL6 5NF.
KRAILING, Mr. John Kenneth Blois, FCA *1969;* Haylocks, 48 High Street, West Wratting, CAMBRIDGE, CB21 5LU.
KRAILING, Mr. Thomas Tyrrell Blois, BA ACA *2005;* Flat 23 Elsfield, 42 Highgate Road, Kentish Town, LONDON, NW5 1NT.
KRAINES, Mr. Eldred Hyman, ACA CA(SA) *2010;* 9a Orchard Close, Bushey Heath, BUSHEY, WD23 1LW.
KRAIS, Mr. Ashley Simon, BSc ACA *1989;* Lavenham, 74 Marsh Lane, Mill Hill, LONDON, NW7 4NT.
•**KRAITT, Mr. Michael Stanley, FCA ATII** *1966;* (Tax Fac), Addison Beyer Green & Co, 233-237 Old Marylebone Road, LONDON, NW1 5QT.
KRAJEWSKI, Mr. Richard Mark, BSc ACA *1990;* Croft Cottage, Pound Lane, MARLOW, BUCKINGHAMSHIRE, SL7 2AQ.
KRAKOWIAN, Miss. Sophia Claire, BSc ACA *1986;* 6 Charlbury Road, OXFORD, OX2 6UT.
KRAMER, Mrs. Anna Frederika Margriete, MA ACA *2000;* 12 Rue Grande Duchesse Charlotte, Fischbach, L 7430 LUXEMBOURG, LUXEMBOURG.
•**KRAMER, Mr. David Philip, FCA** *1980;* Carter Backer Winter LLP, Enterprise House, 21 Buckle Street, LONDON, E1 8NN.
KRAMER, Mr. Howard Geoffrey, FCA *1971;* 2 Brightwen Grove, STANMORE, MIDDLESEX, HA7 4WH. (Life Member)
KRAMER, Mr. Kenneth, FCA *1972;* 26 Main Road, Stanton Harcourt, WITNEY, OXFORDSHIRE, OX29 5RP.
KRAMER, Mr. Nicholas Martin, BA ACA *1993;* 25 Dukes Avenue, EDGWARE, MIDDLESEX, HA8 7RZ.
KRAMER, Mr. Paul, ACA *1998;* 69 Sumatra Road, LONDON, NW6 1PT.
KRAMER, Mrs. Rachel Elizabeth, BSc ACA *1997;* 69 Sumatra Road, LONDON, NW6 1PT.
KRAMER, Mr. Robert Paul, BA(Hons) ACA *2010;* Flat A, 94 Maygrove Road, LONDON, NW6 2ED.
KRAMERS, Mr. Edmund Anthony William, BA FCA *1979;* 31 Cedars Avenue, RICKMANSWORTH, WD3 7AW.
•**KRAMRISCH, Mr. Gary Stuart, BA FCA** *1989;* Alexander & Co, 17 St Ann's Square, MANCHESTER, M2 7PW.
KRANIDIOTOU GREGORIOU, Mrs. Athena, MBA BA ACA *1994;* 12 Kikas & Frosos, Sountia Street, 6016 LARNACA, CYPRUS.
•**KRANTZ, Mr. Martyn Ralph, BA(Hons) ACA FCCA CTA** *2007;* (Tax Fac), 49 Hillside Gardens, EDGWARE, MIDDLESEX, HA8 8HB.
KRASE, Mr. Alexander John, BA ACA *2007;* with Citroen Wells, Devonshire House, 1 Devonshire Street, LONDON, W1W 5DR.
KRASHIAS, Mr. Constantinos, BSc ACA *1983;* 50 Kronos Street, Strovolos, 2048 NICOSIA, CYPRUS.
•①**KRASNER, Mr. Gerald Maurice, FCA** *1971;* Begbies Traynor (Central) LLP, Glendevon House, Hawthorn Park, Coal Road, LEEDS, LS14 1PQ.
•**KRAUS, Mr. Edward Stuart, BSc ACA** *1986;* Northend House, 110 North End, BATH, BA1 7HA.
•**KRAUS, Mr. Michael James, BSc FCA** *1977;* Stephen Daniel & Co., 138 Pinner Road, HARROW, HA1 4JE.
KRAUSE, Mr. David Michael, FCA *1955;* 6 Corrance Road, Wyke, BRADFORD, BD12 9LH.
KRAUSE, Mr. Julian Antony, FCA *1991;* 14 Walnut Lane, Hartford, NORTHWICH, CW8 1QN.
KRAVCHENKO, Mr. Valentin, BA ACA *2004;* Flat 92 Trentham Court, Victoria Road, LONDON, W3 6BF.
•①**KRAVETZ, Mr. Richard Simon, BSc FCA** *1979;* with BBK Partnership, 1 Beauchamp Court, Victors Way, BARNET, HERTFORDSHIRE, EN5 5TZ.
KRAWIECKA, Mrs. Margaret Louise, ACA *1990;* 17 Troed Y Garth, Pentyrch, CARDIFF, CF15 9AB.
KREFTING, Mr. James Rupert Howard, BA ACA *1994;* Numis Securities Ltd, 10 Paternoster Square, LONDON, EC4M 7LT.
KREMPEL, Mr. Mark, FCA *1975;* 45 Abbeygate Street, BURY ST. EDMUNDS, SUFFOLK, IP33 1LB.
KRENITSKAYA, Miss. Elena, MS BSc ACA *2010;* 27 Byron Hill Road, HARROW, MIDDLESEX, HA2 0JD.
KREPA, Mr. Leslie Andrew, BA ACA *1984;* 37 Whitford Drive, Monkspath Shirley, SOLIHULL, B90 4YG.
KRESOVIC, Ms. Louise Albina, ACA *1993;* Les Mezieres Cottage, La Rue Du Friquet, Castel, GUERNSEY, GY5 7SU.
KRETCHETOV, Mr. Evgueni, MSc BSc ACA *2009;* 41 Norwich Road, HOLT, NORFOLK, NR25 6SE.
KRETSCHMER, Miss. Susanne, ACA *2011;* 50 D, Brondesbury Villas, LONDON, NW6 6AB.
KREY, Miss. Claudia, MPhil ACA *2000;* Eidelstedter, Weg No 94, 25469 HALSTENBEK, GERMANY.
KRIEFMAN, Mr. Barry Eli, BA FCA *1974;* St Michaels Cheshire, Home, AXBRIDGE, BS26 2DW. (Life Member)
•**KRIEGER, Mr. Ian Stephen, BA FCA** *1976;* Deloitte LLP, 2 New Street Square, LONDON, EC4A 3BZ. See also Deloitte & Touche LLP
KRIEGER, Mr. John, FCA *1956;* c/o 5 Prospect Terrace, Constantia, CAPE TOWN, 7800, SOUTH AFRICA. (Life Member)
•**KRIEGER, Mr. Michael Maurice, BSc FCA** *1984;* Hazlems Fenton LLP, Palladium House, 1-4 Argyll Street, LONDON, W1F 7LD. See also Argyll Street Management Services Ltd
KRINKS, Mrs. Claudia Anne, BA ACA *1999;* 57 Bangalore Street, LONDON, SW15 1QF.
•**KRIPALANI, Mr. Mohan, BA ACA ATII** *1992;* (Tax Fac), Penningtons, Wellington House, 209-217 High Street, Hampton Hill, HAMPTON, MIDDLESEX TW12 1NP.
KRISHANTHAN, Mr. Jogeesvaran Chris, LLM ACA *1999;* 28 Abbey Gardens, LONDON, NW8 9AT.
KRISHNA, Mr. Gautam, BSc ACA *2001;* Credit Suisse, 5 Cabot Square, LONDON, E14 4QR.
KRISHNA, Mr. Vikram, BA ACA *2002;* G M T Communications Partners, Sackville House, 40 Piccadilly, LONDON, W1J 0DR.
KRISHNAMOORTHY, Mr. Bangalore, FCA *1941;* 2B Sahjeevan Apts., 219 Rajamahal VilasExtension, BANGALORE 560 080, INDIA. (Life Member)
KRISHNAMOORTHY, Mr. Rajesh, FCA *1991;* Deloitte & Touche LLP, Suite 1400, 181 Bay Street, TORONTO M5J 2V1, ON, CANADA.
KRISHNAMRA, Mr. Somkrit, BSc ACA *2005;* 10 Sukhumvit soi 7, BANGKOK 10110, THAILAND.
KRISHNAMRA, Mr. Somroek, FCA *1974;* Deloitte Touche Tohmatsu Jaiyos Co Ltd, Rajanakarn Building, 25 Floor 183 South Sathorn Rd, Yannawa, BANGKOK 10120, THAILAND. See also Deloitte Touche Tohmatsu Jaiyos
KRISHNAMRA, Mr. Toemsakdi, BA FCA *1955;* Deloitte Touche Tohmatsu Jiyios Co Ltd, 25th floor Rajanakarn Building, 183 South Sathorn Road, Yannawa, BANGKOK 10120, THAILAND.
KRISHNAMURTHY, Mr. Balaji, BSc ACA *2005;* 6 Richmond Gardens, Hendon Central, LONDON, NW4 4RT.
KRISHNAN, Mr. Arjun, ACA *1978;* 7427 W Via Montoya Drive, GLENDALE, AZ 85310, UNITED STATES.
KRISHNAN, Mr. Ratnagiri Sivaram, ACA *1992;* Flat 1601, 16th Floor Kritika Towers, Chembur, MUMBAI 400071, INDIA.
KRISHNAN, Mr. Sundar Sivarama, BSc ACA *1995;* 36B Star Sky The Cullinan 1 Austin Rd West, TSIM SHA TSUI, HONG KONG SAR.
KRISHNAREDDIGARI, Mr. Deepak, BSc ACA *2011;* 19 Chatteris Drive, Oakwood, DERBY, DE21 4SF.
KRISHNASAMY, Miss. Radica Ruby Crystal, ACA *2009;* 26 St. Marks Crescent, MAIDENHEAD, BERKSHIRE, SL6 5DB.
KRISHNASWAMY, Mr. Swaminathan, FCA *1969;* 9 Howard Street, KEW, VIC 3101, AUSTRALIA.
KRISMAN, Mr. William David, FCA *1980;* KPMG Somekh Chaikin, P O Box 212, 91001 JERUSALEM, ISRAEL.
KRISTIANSEN, Mrs. Laura Jayne Dorrington Smithson, BA(Hons) ACA *2004;* Toyota Motor Manufacturing (UK) Ltd, Burnaston, DERBY, DE1 9TA.
KRITEMAN, Mr. Grant Antony, FCA *1970;* 55 Southway, LONDON, NW11 6SB.
KRITEMAN, Mr. Michael John, BSc FCA *1969;* with Sinclairs Carston Ltd, 32 Queen Anne Street, LONDON, W1G 8HD.
•**KRITICOS, Mr. Marios Aristou, FCA** *1977;* Marios Aristou Kriticos & Co, The Box Works, Loft 201, 4 Worsley Street, Castlefield, MANCHESTER M15 4NU.
KRNIC, Mrs. Jo-Anne Louise, BSc ACA *2000;* Langton, 21 Surrey Gardens, Effingham Junction, LEATHERHEAD, SURREY, KT24 5HH.
KRNIC, Mr. Sinisha, BA ACA *1999;* Providence Equity Llp, 28 St. George Street, LONDON, W1S 2FA.
KROGER, Mrs. Karen Linda, BA(Hons) ACA *2001;* First Floor Flat, 1 Belmont Street, LONDON, NW1 8HJ.
•**KROGH PETERSEN, Mr. Per, ACA** *1995;* Krogh & Partners Ltd, 823 Salisbury House, 29 Finsbury Circus, LONDON, EC2M 5QQ.
•**KROL, Mr. Christopher Jan, FCA** *1978;* (Tax Fac), Craufurd Hale Audit Services Ltd, Ground Floor, Belmont Place, Belmont Road, MAIDENHEAD, BERKSHIRE SL6 6TB. See also Hale & Company
KROLL, Mr. David, FCA *1959;* 19 Elliott Square, LONDON, NW3 3SU. (Life Member)
KROLL, Mr. Joachim Ulrich, FCA *1952;* C/o 91 Mendelssohn Road, Roosevelt Park, JOHANNESBURG, 2195, SOUTH AFRICA. (Life Member)
KRONBERGS, Mr. Zigurds Guntis, MA BSc ACA *1978;* (Tax Fac), Rotselaarlaan 51, 3080 TERVUREN, BELGIUM.
KRONE, Mrs. Judith Linda, ACA *1982;* St. Bernards High School, Milton Road, WESTCLIFF-ON-SEA, SS0 7JS.

KRONSON, Mr. Peter David, ACA *2006;* PO Box 29629 Sandringham, JOHANNESBURG, GAUTENG, 2131, SOUTH AFRICA.
KROON, Mrs. Mary-Clare, BSc ACA *1991;* 38 Darlow Drive, Biddenham, BEDFORD, MK40 4AY.
KROUSTIS, Mr. Sotiris, BSc ACA *2002;* 18 Waynflete Street, LONDON, SW18 3QE.
KRUCHKOV, Mr. Alexander, MA ACA *2009;* ZAO Deloitte & Touche CIS, 5 Lesnaya Street, Building 'B', 125047 MOSCOW, RUSSIAN FEDERATION.
KRUDY, Mr. Elemer Arpad, BSc FCA *1980;* Harting Ltd, Caswell Road, Brackmills Industrial Estate, NORTHAMPTON, NN4 7PW.
KRUEGER, Mr. David Christian, ACA *1996;* Kreuzwiesenstr. 3b, 82065 BAIERBRUNN, GERMANY.
KRUEGER, Mrs. Lucy Kate, BCom ACA *1997;* Kreuzwiesenstr. 3b, 82065 BAIERBRUNN, GERMANY.
KRUEGER, Mr. Stefan Michael, ACA *2007;* Hubco Automotive, 46 Parkhouse Road, PO Box 11-017, CHRISTCHURCH 8443, NEW ZEALAND.
KRUGER, Mr. John Peter, FCA *1971;* 2 Kewhurst Manor Cottages, Little Common Road, BEXHILL-ON-SEA, EAST SUSSEX, TN39 4LF.
KRUPPA, Mr. Peter Robert, MA FCA *1997;* 21 Cowper Road, HARPENDEN, HERTFORDSHIRE, AL5 5NF.
KRUPPA, Mr. Robert, BA(Hons) ACA *2009;* 20 Salet Way, WATERLOOVILLE, HAMPSHIRE, PO7 8QS.
KRUPSKI, Mr. Adam, BA(Hons) ACA *2010;* 1 Edgbaston Drive, STOKE-ON-TRENT, STAFFORDSHIRE, ST4 8FJ.
KRUPSKI, Mr. Christopher Peter, BA ACA *1980;* House No.35 Esmat Muslim Street, PO Box 700, Shar-E-Naw, KABUL, AFGHANISTAN.
•**KRUPSKI, Mrs. Gina May, BSc ACA** *1980;* Krupski & Krupski, The Maples, Almshouse Croft, Bradley, STAFFORD, ST18 9DF.
KRUPSKI, Mr. Marian Stanislaw Andrew, ACA *1981;* 9 Elms Road, LEICESTER, LE2 3JE.
•**KRYCLER, Mr. Michael John, FCA** *1974;* Krycler Ervin Taubman & Walheim, 15303 Ventura Boulevard, Suite 1040, SHERMAN OAKS, CA 91403, UNITED STATES.
KRZYSICA, Ms. Marie-Claire, ACA *2008;* Zenteum, The Dovecote Crewe Hall Farm, Old Park Road, CREWE, CW1 5UE.
KSHIRSAGAR, Mr. Eknath Atmaram, FCA *1968;* 19 Tarangini Apts, Twin Towers Road, Prabhadevi, MUMBAI 400025, MAHARASHTRA, INDIA.
KSHIRSAGAR, Mr. Yogesh Sadashiv, ACA *1998;* 15 Joothica, Makarand Society, V.S. Marg Mahim, MUMBAI 400016, INDIA.
KTORI, Mr. Nicholas George Andreas, BA ACA *1994;* Craegmoor Healthcare, Craegmoor House, Perdiswell Park, WORCESTER, WR3 7NW.
KTORI, Mrs. Sarah Jane, BSc ACA *1999;* with Ernst & Young LLP, 1 Colmore Square, BIRMINGHAM, B4 6HQ.
KTORIDES, Mr. Andreas, ACA *2010;* 12 Theofilou Georgiadi, Egomi, 2411 NICOSIA, CYPRUS.
KU, Miss. Mary Mei Li, ACA *1989;* Borneo Samudera SDN BHD, Jalan Kelapa Sawit, Off KM 4 Jalan, Tuaran, 88300 KOTA KINABALU, SABAH MALAYSIA.
KUAH, Mr. Boon Wee, BEng ACA *1993;* 182 Pandan Loop, SINGAPORE 128373, SINGAPORE.
KUAN, Mrs. Ching Poh, ACA *1978;* 15 Tiberius Gardens, WITHAM, CM8 1HJ.
KUAN, Miss. Tammy Ah Mooi Mooi, BA ACA *1987;* Morgan Stanley Asia Singapore, 23 Church Street, #16-01 Capital Square, SINGAPORE 049481, SINGAPORE.
KUBAIR, Mrs. Gouri, MCom BCom ACA *2008;* 14 Oaklands Wood, HATFIELD, HERTFORDSHIRE, AL10 8LU.
KUBBA, Mr. Ahmed Bassam, BEng ACA MBA *1995;* Royal Capital PJSC, PO Box 53883, Khalifa Street, 6F Tawam Tower 1, ABU DHABI, UNITED ARAB EMIRATES.
•**KUBINSKI, Mr. Antos Kazimierz, BSc ACA** *1984;* Kubinski, Eldon House, 201 Penistone Road, Kirkburton, HUDDERSFIELD, HD8 0PE.
•**KUBINSKI, Mr. Jurek Andrew, BSc FCA** *1979;* Kubinski, Eldon House, 201 Penistone Road, Kirkburton, HUDDERSFIELD, HD8 0PE.
KUBITZA, Mr. Loic, ACA *1996;* with PricewaterhouseCoopers S.a.r.l., 400 route d'Esch, B P 1443, L-1014 LUXEMBOURG, LUXEMBOURG.
KUCI, Mr. Bledar, BSc ACA *2009;* 11 Strathblaine Road, LONDON, SW11 1RG.
KUCK, Mr. Wee Kiat, ACA *1976;* 2 Lorong Jarak, Damansara Heights, 50490 KUALA LUMPUR, FEDERAL TERRITORY, MALAYSIA.
KUDERBUX, Mr. Amanulla, ACA ACCA *2008;* Hunderenveldlaan 1, Sint-Agatha-Berchem, 1082 BRUSSELS, BELGIUM.
KUDHAIL, Mrs. Jatinder, ACA *2007;* 8 Pulborough Gardens, Littleover, DERBY, DE23 3UE.
KUDLICK, Mr. Martin, FCA *1956;* 36 Paines Lane, PINNER, HA5 3DB. (Life Member)
KUEH, Miss. Geok Lian, BCom ACA *1982;* 24 Marymount Terrace, SINGAPORE 576367, SINGAPORE.
•**KUEHLING, Mr. Harry George, FCA** *1976;* 97 King George V Drive North, CARDIFF, CF14 4EH.
KUEK, Mr. Christopher Chai Eng, ACA *1991;* 34 Selkirk Drive, KINROSS, WA 6028, AUSTRALIA.
KUENZEL, Mr. Gregory, ACA CA(AUS) *2008;* 47 Charles Street, LONDON, W1J 5EL.
KUFORIJI-OLUBI, Her Highness Bola, MON BSc FCA *1968;* Phoenix Ocean Line Ltd, 13-15 Wharf Road, Apapa, LAGOS, NIGERIA.
KUGATHAS, Miss. Anushiya, BSc ACA *2007;* K B R Hill Park Court, Springfield Drive, LEATHERHEAD, KT22 7NL.
KUGATHASAN, Miss. Kugajini, ACA *2011;* 18 Comet Street, LONDON, SE8 4AN.
KUI, Mr. Jee Yeng, FCA *1982;* Yeng & Co, 53B Jalan SS 15/4, 47500 SUBANG, SELANGOR, MALAYSIA.
KUIPA, Mr. Tineyi, MSc BSc ACA *2011;* 42 Westbourne Terrace, LONDON, W2 3UH.
KUIT, Miss. Candy Fung Sim, BSc ACA *2004;* 9 Peggs Way, BASINGSTOKE, HAMPSHIRE, RG24 9FX.
KUJUR, Miss. Sama, BA ACA *1994;* 27 Repton Road, HARROW, MIDDLESEX, HA3 9QD.
KUKHNIN, Mr. Ivan, ACA *2011;* Flat 1, Knot House, 3 Brewery Square, LONDON, SE1 2LF.
KULANAYAGAM, Mr. John Arjunan, FCA *1983;* 34 Keswick Avenue, LONDON, SW19 3JE.
KULAR, Mr. Boota, BCom ACA *2001;* Oxford Aviation Academy, Fleming Way, CRAWLEY, WEST SUSSEX, RH10 9UH.
KULASEGARAM, Miss. Priyanka Sharmini, LLB ACA *2003;* 15 Craiglea Drive, EDINBURGH, EH10 5PB.
KULATHUNGA SINGHAM, Mr. Sri Rangan, BSc(Hons) ACA *2003;* 56 Hazelwood Avenue, MORDEN, SURREY, SM4 5RR.
•**KULCZYCKI, Mrs. Elizabeth Karen, BSc ACA** *2003;* BDO LLP, Emerald House, East Street, EPSOM, SURREY, KT17 1HS. See also BDO Stoy Hayward LLP
KULCZYCKI, Mr. Peter Simon, BSc ACA *2003;* 2 Stompond Lane, WALTON-ON-THAMES, KT12 1HB.
KULKARNI, Mrs. Namrata Sanjaya, MSc BA ACA *2011;* Flat 33 Edison Building, 20 Westferry Road, LONDON, E14 8LU.
KULKARNI, Mrs. Prachi, ACA *2011;* 70 Holly Bank, WHITEHAVEN, CUMBRIA, CA28 6SA.
KULKARNI, Mr. Sanjay, ACA *2009;* New Loom House, 101 Back Church Lane, LONDON, E1 1LU.
KULVANICH, Mr. Chai, ACA *1980;* 999/79 Kesineeville 9, Pracha-Utid Road, Huay Kwang District, BANGKOK 10320, THAILAND.
KUMAR, Mr. Akshay, BSc ACA *2006;* Netplay TV Plc, 80 Silverthorne Road, LONDON, SW8 3HE.
KUMAR, Mrs. Alison Judith, BSc ACA *1987;* Kimball Smith, Kings Worthy House, Court Road, Kings Worthy, WINCHESTER, HAMPSHIRE SO23 7QA.
KUMAR, Mr. Anil, FCA *1973;* 40 Wheatfield Way, Langshott, HORLEY, SURREY, RH6 9DA.
KUMAR, Mr. Anu, BSc ACA *1997;* 22 Grangeway, Handforth, WILMSLOW, CHESHIRE, SK9 3HZ.
KUMAR, Mr. Arun, ACA *1993;* DII 313 Vinay Marg, Chanakyapuri, NEW DELHI PIN 110021, INDIA.
KUMAR, Mr. Ashish, ACA *2007;* 14 Daiseyfield Crescent, VAUGHAN L4H 2T9, ON, CANADA.
KUMAR, Mr. Deepak, BA(Hons) ACA *2004;* Vedanta Resources Plc, 16 Berkeley Street, LONDON, W1J 8DZ.
KUMAR, Miss. Divya, ACA *2011;* 32 Corve Dale Walk, West Bridgford, NOTTINGHAM, NG2 6TY.
KUMAR, Mr. Karan, MPhil ACA *2010;* K P M G Llp, 15 Canada Square, LONDON, E14 5GL.
KUMAR, Mr. Kiran, BSc ACA *1999;* L45 Australia Square, 264-278 George Street, SYDNEY, NSW 2000, AUSTRALIA.
KUMAR, Mr. Makesh, BSc FCA *1990;* 3 Paddock Gardens, WALSALL, WS5 3NZ.
KUMAR, Miss. Malini, MA MPhil BSc ACA *2001;* 4533 Forest Cove Road, BELMONT, NC NC 28012, UNITED STATES.
KUMAR, Mr. Narendra, FCA *1972;* N. Kumar & Co, J-14 Hauz Khas, Yusaf Sarai, Mehrauli Road, NEW DELHI 16, INDIA.
KUMAR, Mr. Parvathaneni Santhosh, FCA *1973;* Brahmayya & Co, 48 Masilamani Road, Balaji Nagar, Royapettah, CHENNAI 600 014, INDIA.
KUMAR, Mr. Raja Prem, BA FCA *1967;* 3 Palace Road, BUXTON, SK17 6AF. (Life Member)
KUMAR, Mr. Ranjan, BSc ACA *1995;* (Tax Fac), Monsoon Cottage Fairway Avenue, Tilehurst, READING, RG30 4QB.
KUMAR, Mr. Shailendra, BSc ACA *1995;* Ground Floor Flat, 1 Gledhow Gardens, LONDON, SW5 0BL.
KUMAR, Mr. Shavil, MSc BSc(Hons) ACA *2010;* 9 Kilpatrick Way, HAYES, MIDDLESEX, UB4 9SX.
KUMAR, Mr. Sundip, ACA *1991;* 56 Elgin Road, CROYDON, CR0 6XA.
•**KUMAR, Ms. Susan, BA ACA** *1995;* (Tax Fac), Kumar & Co Tax & Business Accountants, 85 Rydens Road, WALTON-ON-THAMES, SURREY, KT12 3AN.
KUMARANAYAKAM, Mr. Sanjeev, ACA *2009;* 172 Twyford Road, HARROW, MIDDLESEX, HA2 0SN.
KUMARASINGHE, Mr. Kelum, ACA CA(AUS) *2011;* Flat 25, Rodin Court, 25 Essex Road, LONDON, N1 2SD.
KUMARIA, Mr. Shyam Krishna, FCA *1974;* 22327 BROKEN TWIG RD, DIAMOND BAR, CA 91765, UNITED STATES.
KUMETA, Mr. Bernard John, ACA *1986;* The Webb Group Limited, Queensbridge Works, Queen street, BURTON-ON-TRENT, DE14 3LP.
KUMORDZIE BROUN, Ms. Griselda, ACA *2010;* 22 Beeston Way, Allerton Bywater, CASTLEFORD, WEST YORKSHIRE, WF10 2AG.
KUMRA, Mr. Nalin, BSc ACA *1992;* 201 Long Hill Drive, SHORT HILLS, NJ 07078, UNITED STATES.
KUMRA, Mr. Rajesh, BA ACA *1983;* 31a Syke Cluan, IVER, SL0 9EP.
KUMSI, Mr. Nitin, ACA *2011;* 34 Jade House, 325 South Row, MILTON KEYNES, MK92FG.
KUN, Ms. Mo Kit Jenny, ACA *2005;* Jenny Kun & Co. CPA, Room 1112, 11/F, Hollywood Plaza, 610 Nathan Road, MONG KOK KOWLOON HONG KONG SAR.
•**KUNDU, Mr. Sudipta Basudev, MA FCA CTA** *1991;* PricewaterhouseCoopers LLP, Hays Galleria, 1 Hays Lane, LONDON, SE1 2RD. See also PricewaterhouseCoopers
KUNERT, Mr. Paul, BSc ACA *1995;* Globeleq, 7th floor 2 More London, LONDON, SE1 2JT.
KUNG, Mr. Daniel, BA FCA *1981;* G.P.O. Box 4675, CENTRAL, HONG KONG ISLAND, HONG KONG SAR.
KUNG, Miss. Hing See Ruth, ACA *2005;* TOKYO, JAPAN.
KUNG, Mr. Lok Lam, ACA *2008;* Kung Lok Lam & Co, Office G2, 17/F Legend Tower, No 7 Shing Yip Street, KWUN TONG, KOWLOON HONG KONG SAR.
KUNG, Mr. Peter Wing-Tak, BA ACA *1987;* KPMG, 8/F Prince's Building, 10 Chater Road, CENTRAL, HONG KONG ISLAND, HONG KONG SAR.
KUNJAPPY, Mr. Philip, FCA *1983;* Unit No 56-1 Seri Duta Condominium 1, Jalan Gallagher, Taman Duta, 50480 KUALA LUMPUR, FEDERAL TERRITORY, MALAYSIA.
KUNORUBWE, Mr. Peter Tendai, BSc(Hons) ACA *2010;* 166 Wightman Road, LONDON, N8 0BD.
KUNZ, Mr. Colin James, MBA BSc FCA *1991;* 2 Nobold Court, Gold Street, Clipston, MARKET HARBOROUGH, LEICESTERSHIRE, LE16 9RR.
KUNZER, Mr. David Alexander, BSc FCA *1994;* M+W Group, Methuen South Bath Road, CHIPPENHAM, SN14 0GT.
KUNZMANN, Mr. Manfred Albert, FCA *1974;* 50 Somerset Drive, Glenfield, LEICESTER, LE3 8QW.
KUOK, Mr. David Khoon Hin, FCA *1966;* 28 Jalan Delima, 55100 KUALA LUMPUR, FEDERAL TERRITORY, MALAYSIA.
KURCHENKO, Mrs. Anna, BSc(Hons) ACA *2004;* (Tax Fac), RSA House, Sandyford Road, Dundrum Town Centre, DUBLIN 16, COUNTY DUBLIN, IRELAND.
•**KURESHI, Mr. Kamal Ahmed, ACA** *1982;* (Tax Fac), K K Associates, 5 Perivale Lodge, Perivale Lane, GREENFORD, MIDDLESEX, UB6 8TW.
KURODA, Ms. Kaori, ACA *2009;* 10 Montagu Mansions, LONDON, W1U 6LB.
KUROWSKA, Miss. Anna, ACA *2010;* 11 Nascot Street, WATFORD, WD17 4YB.
KURTZ, Miss. Catherine Elizabeth Strathmore, BSc ACA *1994;* 6 Berkeley Road, TUNBRIDGE WELLS, TN1 1YR.
KURUKULASURIYA, Miss. Shyantika Dilukshini, BSc ACA *1996;* OnePath Australia, Level 20, 347 Kent Street, SYDNEY, NSW 2089, AUSTRALIA.
•**KURUP, Mr. Prakash Divaker, FCA** *1983;* Harris Lipman LLP, 2 Mountview Court, 310 Friern Barnet Lane, LONDON, N20 0YZ.
KURUPPU, Miss. Lashini Mevanthi, ACA *2010;* 19f Upper Richmond Road, LONDON, SW15 2RF.
KURWIE, Mrs. Rosemary Margaret, BSc ACA *1983;* 6 Kensington Road, St Johns, WAKEFIELD, WF1 3JX.
KURWIE, Mr. Tiessir Shhab, BSc ACA *1983;* 6 Kensington Road, St John's, WAKEFIELD, WF1 3JX.
•**KURZ, Mr. Stuart Leon, FCA** *1974;* (Tax Fac), Somers Baker Prince Kurz LLP, 45 Ealing Road, WEMBLEY, HA0 4BA.
KURZMANN, Ms. Annett, MBA ACA *2001;* Schermer 118, 8244 AR LELYSTAD, NETHERLANDS.
KURZON, Miss. Nicole, BA ACA *2004;* 55 The Priory, Priory Park, LONDON, SE3 9UZ.
KUSHNER, Mr. Bennett Harold, BSc FCA *1976;* Cotswold Care Hospice, Burleigh Lane, Minchinhampton, STROUD, GLOUCESTERSHIRE, GL5 2PQ.
KUSHNIR, Miss. Olga, MSc ACA *2006;* Prospect Mira 97, kv. 263, 129085 MOSCOW, RUSSIAN FEDERATION.
KUSI-YEBOAH, Mr. Christian, MSc ACA *2004;* 30 CANNON STREET, International Accounting Standards Board, 30 Cannon Street, LONDON, EC4M 6XH.
KUSMIRAK, Mr. Michael Solomon, LLB FCA *1962;* 10 Landseer Road, SUTTON, SM1 2DE. (Life Member)
KUSNERAITIS, Mr. Christian Neil, BSc ACA *1995;* 7th Floor Kings Place, 90 York Way, LONDON, N1 9AG.
KUSTNER, Mrs. Jane Lesley, BA FCA *1979;* 191 Hither Green Lane, LONDON, SE13 6QE.
KUTCHINSKY, Mr. Roger Nicholas, FCA *1967;* Rivendell, Greenacres Hive Road, Bushey Heath, BUSHEY, WD23 1RF.
KUTCHUKIAN, Mr. Alan Vahe, FCA *1974;* Tower International Consultants, Tekeyan Centre, 50 Khnajyan Street, YEREVAN 0025, ARMENIA.
KUTNER, Mr. John Michael, FCA *1963;* 34 The Fairway, New Barnet, BARNET, HERTFORDSHIRE, EN5 1HN.
KUTNER, Mr. Matthew, BA ACA *2011;* 140 Barrier Point Road, LONDON, E16 2SE.
KUTNER, Mr. Michael, FCA *1964;* 11 Appledore, SOUTHEND-ON-SEA, SS3 8UW.
•**KUTNER, Mr. Paul Louis, FCA** *1977;* Landau Morley LLP, Lanmor House, 370-386 High Road, WEMBLEY, MIDDLESEX, HA9 6AX.
KUTTEN, Mr. David, MBA BA ACA *2006;* 57 Broughton Avenue, LONDON, N3 3EN.
KUTTEN, Mrs. Lindsey Lee, BA ACA *1999;* (Tax Fac), 57 Broughton Avenue, LONDON, N3 3EN.
KUWAN, Mr. Thiery Dinla, ACA MBA *2011;* Flat 7, 14 Marriott Street, Semilong, NORTHAMPTON, NN2 6AW.
KVELLO, Miss. Michelle, BA(Hons) ACA *2001;* 286a Rainbow Street, COOGEE, NSW 2034, AUSTRALIA.
KWAN, Mr. Alex Ching Sing, BSc ACA *1990;* Villa Monte Rosa, Flat F2 8th Floor, 41A Stubbs Road, WAN CHAI, HONG KONG SAR.
KWAN, Mr. Andrew Chun Wai, BA FCA *1981;* 66 Lyndwood Court, Stoughton Road, Stoneygate, LEICESTER, LE2 2EJ.
•**KWAN, Mr. Bing Hung, BSc ACA** *1986;* B.H. Kwan, 16 Pontinscale Close, Leigh Lane Walshaw, BURY, BL8 1RL.
KWAN, Mr. Bo Ren, BSc ACA *1991;* KBR Management Limited, Suite 3306 Exchange Square Two, No 8 Connaught Road Central, CENTRAL, HONG KONG SAR.
KWAN, Mr. Chi Keung, ACA *2007;* Flat 10, 13th Floor, Block H, Chun Man Court, 66 Chung Hau Street, HO MAN TIN KOWLOON HONG KONG SAR.
KWAN, Miss. Corinna, ACA *2006;* Block C 6/F, Mong Kok House, 122 Argyle Street, MONG KOK, KOWLOON, HONG KONG SAR.
KWAN, Miss. Deborah Shuk Yee, BSc(Hons) FCA CTA *1986;* with HSBC, 8-14 Canada Square, LONDON, E14 5HQ.
KWAN, Miss. Eliza Kit Hing, BA FCA *1979;* PO Box 759, RONDEBOSCH, 7701, SOUTH AFRICA.
KWAN, Mr. Esmond Shui Cheung, BSc FCA *1996;* with PricewaterhouseCoopers, 11//F, PricewaterhouseCoopers Center, 2 Corporate Avenue, 202 Hu Bin Road, SHANGHAI 200021 CHINA.
KWAN, Mr. Kam Shing, ACA *2006;* Unit F 1st Floor Block 2, Villa Concerto, Symphony Bay, 530 Sai Sha Road, SAI KUNG, NEW TERRITORIES HONG KONG SAR.
KWAN, Mr. Kie Yip, ACA *2004;* Eton Properties Ltd, 21/F Eton Tower, 8 Hysan Avenue, CAUSEWAY BAY, HONG KONG ISLAND, HONG KONG SAR.

KWAN, Mr. King Nam, ACA *2005;* Flat B 25/F Block 12, Laguna City, LAM TIN, KOWLOON, HONG KONG SAR.

KWAN, Ms. Mariana Kar Yee, BSc ACA *1991;* 5 Northcote Close 1/F, Sassoon Road, Pokfulam, POK FU LAM, HONG KONG ISLAND, HONG KONG SAR.

KWAN, Ms. Nga Chee, ACA *2007;* 22 E Tower 1 Univerity Heights, 23 Pokfield Road, MID LEVELS, HONG KONG SAR.

KWAN, Mr. Pak Kong, ACA *2008;* AIP Partners CPA Ltd, Room 1304, C C Wu Building, 302-308 Hennessy Road, WAN CHAI, HONG KONG SAR.

KWAN, Miss. Pek Sin, FCA *1976;* P.O. Box 13283, 88837 KOTA KINABALU, Sabah, MALAYSIA.

KWAN, Mr. Po Man Ray, ACA *2008;* Flat A, 18/F, Lotus Mansion, 6 Taikoo Wan Road, TAIKOO SHING, HONG KONG SAR.

KWAN, Mr. Robert Chiu Yin, MA FCA *1962;* Flat 4A, 4A MacDonnell House, 6-8 MacDonnell Road, MID LEVELS, HONG KONG ISLAND, HONG KONG SAR. (Life Member)

•**KWAN, Mr. Sai Leung, ACA** *2006;* (Tax Fac), Kwan Accounting Services Limited, 352a Carlton Hill, Carlton, NOTTINGHAM, NG4 1JB. See also Kwan Chan Accounting Services Limited

KWAN, Mr. Vincent Po Chuen, ACA *2008;* Flat E, 1st Floor, Blessings Garden I, 95 Robinson Road, MID LEVELS, HONG KONG SAR.

KWAN, Mr. Vun Pau, BSc ACA *2005;* 15B Tower 6, Sorrento, 1 Austin Road West, TSIM SHA TSUI, KOWLOON, HONG KONG SAR.

KWAN, Mr. Yiu Ming Patrick, ACA *2008;* 9/F Yue Wong Building, 9 Fa Yuen Street, MONG KOK, KOWLOON, HONG KONG SAR.

KWAN, Ms. Yuen Ling, ACA *2005;* Flat A, 10/F, Hang Po Building, 6-8 Mercury Street, NORTH POINT, HONG KONG ISLAND HONG KONG SAR.

KWANG, Mr. Yoong Chen, ACA CA(AUS) *2008;* 114 MacMillan Way, LONDON, SW17 6AU.

KWAPONG, Mr. Edward, BA ACA *2004;* 43 Tockley Road, Burham, SLOUGH, SL1 7DQ.

KWIATKOWSKI, Mr. Stefan Marek, ACA *2008;* 75 Valerie Street, Dianella, PERTH, WA 6059, AUSTRALIA.

KWIK, Mr. Stephen Siong Han, FCA *1971;* 20 Willowie Road, CASTLE COVE, NSW 2069, AUSTRALIA.

KWOK, Mr. Alexander Wing-Kai, BA ACA *1993;* 19 Winfield Gardens, 38 Shan Kwong Road, HAPPY VALLEY, HONG KONG ISLAND, HONG KONG SAR.

KWOK, Miss. Anita May-Ling, MBA BSc FCA *1992;* Flat 19 Winfield Gardens, 38 Shan Kwong Road, HAPPY VALLEY, HONG KONG ISLAND, HONG KONG SAR.

•**KWOK, Mr. Bennie Kai Bun, MBA BSc FCA MRICS CFE FCPA** *1991;* B Kwok & Co, Units 2003 & 2004, 20/F Hua Qin, International Building, 340 Queens Road, CENTRAL HONG KONG SAR.

KWOK, Mr. Chee Hoh, ACA *1985;* Arrow Electrical, Discount Centre, 245-247 Cricklewood Broadway, LONDON, NW2 6NY.

KWOK, Mr. Chi Fai, ACA *2008;* Flat A 4/F, Block 37, Laguna City, Cha Kwo Ling Road, KWUN TONG, KOWLOON HONG KONG SAR.

KWOK, Mr. Chi Kwong, ACA *2005;* Flat F 25/F Block 10, Sea Crest Villa Phase 3, TSING LUNG TAU, NEW TERRITORIES, HONG KONG SAR.

KWOK, Mr. Chi Shan, ACA *2005;* Flat 867, Tai On Building, 57-87 Shaukeiwan Road, SHAU KEI WAN, HONG KONG ISLAND, HONG KONG SAR.

KWOK, Mr. Clement King Man, BSc ACA *1983;* Hong Kong & Shanghai Hotels Ltd, 8/F St George's Building, 2 Ice House Street, CENTRAL, Hong Kong Island, HONG KONG SAR.

KWOK, Mr. Edward Ho Lai, ACA *2009;* 46/F Sun Hung Kai Centre, 30 Harbour Road, WAN CHAI, HONG KONG SAR.

KWOK, Mr. Harrison Wai-Ching, ACA *2005;* Methanex Asia Pacific Ltd, 3117-3112 Two Pacific Place, 88 Queensway, ADMIRALTY, HONG KONG ISLAND, HONG KONG SAR.

KWOK, Ms. Hung Kwan Edith, ACA *2008;* Crowe Horwath (HK) CPA Ltd, 34/F The Lee Gardens, 33 Hysan Avenue, CAUSEWAY BAY, HONG KONG SAR.

KWOK, Mrs. Jessica Onn Yee, BSc ACA *1992;* 36 Applecroft Road, WELWYN GARDEN CITY, AL8 6LA.

KWOK, Mr. Jimmy, BCom ACA *2004;* with Ernst & Young LLP, 1 More London Place, LONDON, SE1 2AF.

KWOK, Miss. Joanna Wai-Hei, BA ACA *2001;* Flat B 12th Floor, DragonView, 39 Macdonnell Road, MID LEVELS, HONG KONG ISLAND, HONG KONG SAR.

KWOK, Mr. Khien Kevin, BA ACA *1980;* Ernst & Young, One Raffles Quay, North Tower, Level 18, SINGAPORE 048583, SINGAPORE. See also Evan Wong & Co and Ee Peng Liang & Co

KWOK, Dr. Kim Kwong Samuel, ACA *2007;* Flat 701, Block G, Shimao Lakeside Garden, Pudong, SHANGHAI 200135, CHINA.

KWOK, Mr. Kin Wah Clive, ACA *2007;* Flat a 5/f Tower 11, Phase 3 Ocean Shores, 88 O King Road, TSEUNG KWAN O, NEW TERRITORIES, HONG KONG SAR.

KWOK, Mr. Kwan Hung, ACA *2008;* Kwok & Partners, Room 4101, 41st Floor, Tower Two Lippo Centre, 89 Queensway, ADMIRALTY HONG KONG SAR.

KWOK, Mr. Larry Lam Kwong, ACA *2007;* 79 Palm Drive, Redhill Peninsula, TAI TAM, HONG KONG ISLAND, HONG KONG SAR.

KWOK, Mr. Man Chung, ACA *2007;* Flat D 20/F Tower 2, The Orchards, 3 Greig Road, QUARRY BAY, HONG KONG SAR.

KWOK, Miss. Mei-Sze Macy, BSc ACA *1993;* Flat A 13/F Block 6 Cavendish Heights, 33 Perkins Road, JARDINE'S LOOKOUT, HONG KONG SAR.

KWOK, Miss. Mui Ping Marinde, BA ACA *1990;* 11 Thunderbird Court, MARKHAM L6C 2T2, ON, CANADA.

KWOK, Mr. Patrick Po-Wah, ACA *2008;* 33 Amery Road, HARROW, MIDDLESEX, HA1 3UH.

KWOK, Ms. Po Yi, ACA *2008;* Flat F 34/F Tower 3, Phase 1 Belvedere Garden, 530-590 Castle Peak Road, TSUEN WAN, NEW TERRITORIES, HONG KONG SAR.

KWOK, Ms. Pui Ha, ACA *2008;* 17B, Block 3, Hampton Place, 11 Hoi Fan Road, TAI KOK TSUI, KOWLOON HONG KONG SAR.

KWOK, Mr. Raymond, BSc ACA *1994;* Flat 40D Block 1, Le Sommet, 28 Fortress Hill Road, NORTH POINT, HONG KONG ISLAND, HONG KONG SAR.

KWOK, Miss. Renee, MSc BSc ACA *2001;* Flat 27C Kingsford Height, 17-19 Babington Path, MID LEVELS, HONG KONG ISLAND, HONG KONG SAR.

KWOK, Ms. Sau Fan, ACA *2008;* S F Kwok & Co, Room 1609-11, 16/F Tai Yau Building, 181Johnston Road, WAN CHAI, HONG KONG SAR.

KWOK, Mr. Shiu Lun Clarence, ACA *2005;* Flat B 56/F Tower 8, Caribbean Coast, 1 Kin Tung Road, TUNG CHUNG, NEW TERRITORIES, HONG KONG SAR.

•**KWOK, Mr. Sin Kui Jerry, ACA** *2004;* Chui & Kwok, Room 705 & 706, 7th Floor, China Insurance Group Building, No 141 Des Voeux Road Central, CENTRAL HONG KONG ISLAND HONG KONG SAR.

KWOK, Mr. Siu Kai Dennis, ACA *2006;* Octopus Holdings Ltd, 36/f 148 Electric Road, NORTH POINT, HONG KONG SAR.

KWOK, Mr. Siu Ki Edmond, ACA *2007;* Flat 2009, 20/F, Kam Wan House, Choi Hung Estate, SAN PO KONG, KOWLOON HONG KONG SAR.

KWOK, Mr. Siu Nam Dave, ACA *2005;* Dave Kwok & Co, Room 902, General Commercial Building, 156-164 Des Voeux Road, CENTRAL, HONG KONG ISLAND HONG KONG SAR.

KWOK, Mr. Wai-Meng, BSc ACA *1985;* 4 Elm Park, Filton, BRISTOL, BS34 7PS.

KWOK, Ms. Wun Pik Jalan, ACA *2007;* AIF Capital Limited, Suite 3401Jardine House, 1 Connaught Place, CENTRAL, HONG KONG ISLAND, HONG KONG SAR.

KWOK, Mr. Ying Tung, ACA *2005;* Flat F 39/F Tower 19, South Horizons, SOUTH HORIZONS, HONG KONG SAR.

KWOK, Mr. Yiu Wai David, ACA *2009;* Flat C3 6th floor, Block C, Central Mansion, Wan Tau Square, TAI PO, NEW TERRITORIES HONG KONG SAR.

KWOK, Mr. Yu Shun, ACA *2011;* 2907 Block F, Luk Yeung Sun Chuen, TSUEN WAN, NEW TERRITORIES, HONG KONG SAR.

KWOK, Ms. Yuen Man, ACA *2008;* Mazars CPA Limited, 42nd Floor, Central Plaza, 18 Harbour Road, WAN CHAI, HONG KONG ISLAND HONG KONG SAR.

KWOK, Ms. Yuk Sim Betty, ACA *2008;* Flat H 39/F, Block 8, Royal Ascot, Fotan, SHA TIN, NEW TERRITORIES HONG KONG SAR.

KWON, Mr. Hyuk Jin, BA ACA *2000;* 44 Raymond Road, LONDON, SW19 4AP.

KWONG, Mr. Andrew Kam Chan, ACA *2007;* Business Vantage Point, Level 10, 32 Martin Place, SYDNEY, NSW 2000, AUSTRALIA.

KWONG, Mr. Chi Choi Oliver, ACA *2005;* C.C. Kwong & Co, Room 601 6/F, Tai Tung Building, No 8 Fleming Road, WAN CHAI, HONG KONG ISLAND HONG KONG SAR.

KWONG, Mr. Choong Yew, BSc FCA MBA *1982;* 301B/640 SWANSTON STREET, CARLTON, VIC 3053, AUSTRALIA.

KWONG, Mr. Chun Man, ACA *2007;* Flat F 32/F Block 28, Park Island, MA WAN, HONG KONG SAR.

KWONG, Ms. Frances, ACA *2006;* Sagefield Management Services Inc., 18 Wynford Drive, Unit 109, DON MILLS M3C 3S2, ON, CANADA.

KWONG, Mr. Gordon Che Keung, FCA *1977;* 2 Palm Cove Villas, 28 Ng Fai Tin, CLEARWATER BAY, KOWLOON, HONG KONG SAR.

KWONG, Ms. Hang Fong Janet, ACA *2008;* 5A Central Heights, 9 Tong Tak Street, TSEUNG KWAN O, NEW TERRITORIES, HONG KONG SAR.

KWONG, Ms. Hiu Hung Jowie, ACA *2007;* Flat C, 38/F, Tower 7, Banyan Garden, 863 Lai Chi Kok Road, CHEUNG SHA WAN KOWLOON HONG KONG SAR.

KWONG, Mr. Kenny Kam Yong, ACA *1980;* Waters Dace Partners Pty Ltd PO Box 447, DANDENONG, VIC 3175, AUSTRALIA.

KWONG, Ms. Kit Ping, ACA *2008;* Flat E 24/F, Block 10, City Garden, NORTH POINT, HONG KONG SAR.

KWONG, Mr. Lok Wah, BA FCA *1975;* Kwong & Co, 260 Lorong Maarof, Bukit Bandaraya, 59100 KUALA LUMPUR, FEDERAL TERRITORY, MALAYSIA.

KWONG, Mr. Man Fai Eric, ACA *2008;* with Deloitte Touche Tohmatsu, 8-F Tower W2, The Towers, Oriental Plaza, 1 East Chang An Avenue, BEIJING 100738 CHINA.

KWONG, Mr. Patrick, BSc ACA *1994;* 8 Ballingdon Road, Battersea, LONDON, SW11 6AJ.

KWONG, Mr. Pui Kei, ACA *2007;* PK Kwong & Co, Unit 2011, 20/F Hopewell Centre, 183 Queens Road East, WAN CHAI, HONG KONG ISLAND HONG KONG SAR.

KWONG, Mr. Roland Ho Lun, ACA *2010;* Henderson Equity Partners Level 9, Henderson Global Investors, 201 Bishopsgate, LONDON, EC2M 3AE.

•**KWONG, Mr. S Yoon, FCA** *1969;* S Y Kwong Foong & Co, 4/F 108 Jalan Tun H.S. Lee, 50000 KUALA LUMPUR, FEDERAL TERRITORY, MALAYSIA.

KWONG, Ms. Suk Yee Renita, ACA *2005;* 11/F Flat D Tower One, Les Saisons, 28 Tai On Street, SAI WAN HO, HONG KONG ISLAND, HONG KONG SAR.

KWONG, Mr. Tin Lap, ACA *2008;* Flat C, 16/F, Tower 2, Tsing Yung Terrace, TUEN MUN, NEW TERRITORIES HONG KONG SAR.

KWONG, Ms. Wai Chi, ACA *2008;* Flat 4, 3/F, Hoi Tin Court, Aberdeen Center, ABERDEEN, HONG KONG SAR.

KWONG, Mr. Wilson Wai Sun, BA ACA *1990;* Gushan Enviromental Energy Ltd, Unit 908China Merchants Tower, 168-200 Connaught Road, SHEUNG WAN, HONG KONG ISLAND, HONG KONG SAR.

KWONG, Mr. Yau Shing Vincent, BSc ACA *1987;* 25G Nam Hoi Mansion, Kwun Hoi Terrace, 2 tai Wing Avenue, TAIKOO SHING, HONG KONG SAR.

KWONG CHEUNG, Mrs. Eliza Mo Yin, ACA *2005;* 172 Leigh Hunt Drive, LONDON, N14 6DQ.

KWONG YIN, Mr. David Andrew, BSc ACA *2010;* Flat B, 108 Argyle Street, LONDON, WC1H 8EB.

KYBETT, Mrs. Claire Anne, BSc ACA *2005;* Kandy Park Estate, La Route Des Genets St. Brelade, JERSEY, JE3 8EQ.

KYBIRD, Mr. Seth, BA ACA *2004;* 6 Palm Court, 11-13 Fellows Road, LONDON, NW3 3LT.

KYDD, Mr. Clive Barry, FCA *1972;* 17 Sanford Road, STOCKTON, NJ 08559-1204, UNITED STATES.

KYE THIAM, Miss. Marie Veronique, BSc ACA *2003;* The Bank of England, Threadneedle Street, LONDON, EC2R 8AH.

KYI, Mr. Maung Aung, FCA *1965;* 12 Woodlands Road, TAREN POINT, NSW 2229, AUSTRALIA. (Life Member)

KYLE, Miss. Alyson, BSc(Hons) ACA CTA *2003;* 8 Clumber Street, MELTON MOWBRAY, LEICESTERSHIRE, LE13 0ND.

KYLE, Mr. Christopher Douglas, FCA *1961;* (Member of Council 1982 - 1985), Bourne House, Milbourne Street, CARLISLE, CA2 5XF.

KYLE, Mrs. Helen Michelle, BSc ACA *1992;* Rose Cottage, 5 Green Street, Lower Sunbury, SUNBURY-ON-THAMES, TW16 6RE.

KYLE, Miss. Jennifer Anne, ACA *2008;* RGF, 12 Bolingbroke Road, LONDON, W14 0AL.

KYLE, Mr. Kenneth Murray, BA ACA *1996;* D90 Head Office, Boots the Chemists Ltd, Thane Road, NOTTINGHAM, NG90 1BS.

KYLE, Mr. Peter, BSc ACA *1991;* The Cottage Hunts Hill, Blunsdon, SWINDON, SN26 7BN.

KYLE, Miss. Renee Sheffield, BSc ACA ATII *1993;* (Tax Fac), Hill View, 63 Wells Road, GLASTONBURY, BA6 9BY.

KYLE, The Revd. Steven Warnock, FCA *1973;* 9 Flemingate House, Flemingate, BEVERLEY, NORTH HUMBERSIDE, HU17 0LL.

KYLE-HENNEY, Mrs. Alison Virginia, BSc FCA *1990;* Hill View, Common Hill Road, Braishfield, ROMSEY, SO51 0QF.

KYMM, Mr. Chang-Won, BSc ACA *2000;* Flat 2 9F Bamboo Grove, 76 Kennedy Road, MID LEVELS, HONG KONG SAR.

KYNASTON, Mrs. Anne Mary, BSc FCA ACII *1979;* I CAN, 8 Wakley Street, LONDON, EC1V 7QE.

KYNASTON, Mr. Frederick James Russell, FCA *1950;* 1 St Chad Road, BRIDLINGTON, YO16 4DY. (Life Member)

KYNASTON, Mr. Gordon Irwin, BSc FCA *1980;* 1 Saxon Close, AMERSHAM, HP6 5QA.

KYNASTON, Mrs. Rachael Susan, BSc ACA CTA *1997;* Glenlyn, 59 Moor Lane, WILMSLOW, SK9 6BQ.

KYNASTON, Mr. Richard, BA ACA *2007;* 52 Vancouver Quay, SALFORD, M50 3TU.

KYNASTON, Mr. Robin John, BSc FCA *1976;* Flat 2 Cwrt Peris, Colwyn Crescent Rhos on Sea, COLWYN BAY, CLWYD, LL28 4RR.

KYNASTON, Mr. Timothy, BSc ACA *1994;* 59 Moor Lane, WILMSLOW, SK9 6BQ.

KYNE, Mrs. Jill, BSc ACA CTA *1990;* E M I Group Plc Kensley House, 27 Wrights Lane, LONDON, W8 5SW.

•**KYNE, Mr. William John, BA ACA** *1990;* Proactive Accounting (South East) Limited, 31 Oakwood Avenue, PURLEY, SURREY, CR8 1AR.

KYPREOS, Mr. Constantinos, BSc ACA *1998;* 3 Michael Kassialou, 2036 NICOSIA, CYPRUS.

KYPREOU, Ms. Elli, ACA *2011;* P.O.Box 28571, 2080 NICOSIA, CYPRUS.

•**KYPRI, Mr. Soteris, BSc ACA** *2009;* Flat 301, 14 Agamemnonos Street, Strovolos, 2000 NICOSIA, CYPRUS.

KYPRI, Mr. Yiannis Soteri, BSc FCA CF *1978;* c/o Bank of Cyprus Ltd, P.O.Box 1472, NICOSIA, CYPRUS.

•**KYPRIANIDES, Miss. Pola Kypros, BSc FCA** *1989;* 48 THEMISTOCLIS DERVIS AVENUE, OFFICE 401, 1066 NICOSIA, CYPRUS. See also Kyprianides, Nicolaou & Economides and Kyprianides, Nicolaou & Associates

KYPRIANOU, Mr. Alexis Eou, BA ACA *1995;* 21 Rue Louis Gandillet, 78420 CARRIERES SUR SEINE, FRANCE.

KYPRIANOU, Miss. Anne, BSc ACA *2000;* 145 West 67 Street, Apartment 21H, NEW YORK, NY 10023, UNITED STATES.

KYPRIANOU, Mr. Anthony Haralambos, MBA BSc FCA CF *1989;* Gulf Connect Capital, 28th/29th Floor Arraya Center, Sharq, KUWAIT CITY, KUWAIT.

•**KYPRIANOU, Mr. Chrysostomos, BA FCA** *1984;* (Tax Fac), TKG Partnership Limited, Unit 3, Gateway Mews, Ringway, Bounds Green, LONDON N11 2UT.

•**KYPRIANOU, Mr. Kypros, BA ACA** *1981;* 7 Belgrave Gardens, LONDON, N14 4TS.

KYPRIANOU, Mr. Marios Kyprou, FCA *1973;* PO Box 56319, CY-3306 LIMASSOL, CYPRUS.

KYPRIANOU, Mr. Vassos, BSc ACA *2002;* Andrea Kariou 4, Pareklisia, 4520 LIMASSOL, CYPRUS.

KYRANIDES, Mr. Stelios, BSc ACA *2009;* 19 Theodosi Pieridi Street, Oroklini, 7040 LARNACA, CYPRUS.

KYRIACOU, Mr. Ioannis, BA ACA *2005;* Kavallas 9, Lakatamia, 2311 NICOSIA, CYPRUS.

KYRIACOU, Mr. Kyriacos, BA ACA *1991;* 7 Frinis Str., Lakatamia, 2304 NICOSIA, CYPRUS.

KYRIACOU, Mr. Kyriacos, BEng ACA *2007;* Cooperative Central Bank, 8 Gregoris Afxentiou Steet, P.O. Box 24537, 1389 NICOSIA, CYPRUS.

KYRIACOU, Mrs. Marianna, BA ACA *2008;* 9 Kavallas Steet, Lakatamia, 2311 NICOSIA, CYPRUS.

KYRIACOU, Mr. Marios, ACA *2005;* 10A Alamanas Street, CY-2415 NICOSIA, CYPRUS.

•**KYRIACOU, Mr. Marios Telemahou, FCA** *1968;* KPMG Certified Auditors AE, 3 Stratigou Tombra Street, Aghia Paraskevi, GR 153 42 ATHENS, GREECE.

KYRIACOU, Mr. Nicos, ACA *1998;* Tasou Isaak 5, Paradisos Amarousiou, 15125 MAROUSI, GREECE.

KYRIAKIDES, Mr. Christakis Nicolaou, FCA *1980;* (Tax Fac), 16 Theodose Pieride, Engomi, 2411 NICOSIA, CYPRUS.

KYRIAKIDES, Mr. Lambros, LLM BSc ACA *2009;* P.O. Box 70761, 3802 LIMASSOL, CYPRUS.

•**KYRIAKIDES, Mr. Michael, MSc ACA** *2000;* (Tax Fac), Michael K, 7 Forest Road, SUTTON, SURREY, SM3 9NT.

KYRIAKIDES, Mr. Nicos Stelios, BSc ACA *1986;* Deloitte Limited, Maximos Plaza, Tower 1 3rd Floor, 214 Arch Makarios III Avenue, CY 3105 LIMASSOL, CYPRUS.
•**KYRIAKIDIS, Mr. Argiris, BSc FCA** *1977;* with Deloitte LLP, Hill House, 1 Little New Street, LONDON, EC4A 3TR.
KYRIAKIDOU, Miss. Stephanie, BSc ACA *2008;* Flat 101, Pecora Kimonos Court, 16 Kimonos Street, 3095 LIMASSOL, CYPRUS.
KYRIAKIDOU MARKARI, Mrs. Angelina, BSc(Hons) ACA *2002;* 25 Polytechniou Street Kapsalos, 3083 LIMASSOL, CYPRUS.
KYRIAKOU, Mrs. Joanna, ACA *2011;* 200 Frangilinou Rousvelt, Zakaki, 3045 LIMASSOL, CYPRUS.
KYRIAKOU, Ms. Theodora, BA ACA *2010;* 58 28th October Street, Palechori, 2740 NICOSIA, CYPRUS.
KYRIAKOYDES, Mr. Georgios, BA ACA *2009;* Flat 1, 14 Vasilissis Amalias Street, 1101 NICOSIA, CYPRUS.
KYRRIS, Mr. Roghiros Leonidas, BSc FCA *1968;* 9A Hermes Street, Strovolos, 2062 NICOSIA, CYPRUS.
KYSELA, Mrs. Jennifer Ann, BA ACA *2004;* The Gala Coral Group, New Castle House, Castle Boulevard, NOTTINGHAM, NG7 1FT.
KYTE, Mr. Donald William George, FCA *1955;* 122 Low Road, Burwell, CAMBRIDGE, CB5 0EJ. (Life Member)
KYTE, Mrs. Laura Jane, ACA CTA *2008;* Morgan Cameron Ltd Wittas House, Two Rivers Industrial Estate Station Lane, WITNEY, OXFORDSHIRE, OX28 4BH.
KYTHREOTIS, Mr. Michalis, BA ACA *2011;* 3 Pavlou Kalliga Street, Ayios Andreas, 1100 NICOSIA, CYPRUS.
KYTHREOTIS, Mr. Nicholas Alexander, BSc ACA *1992;* P.O.Box 27491, 1645 NICOSIA, CYPRUS.
L'AIMABLE, Mr. Gerard Christian, LLB ACA *1990;* Hillside, Woodlands Road, Bickley, BROMLEY, BR1 2AR.
L'ESTRANGE, Mr. John Scholles, FCA *1960;* 7 The Mullions, BILLERICAY, ESSEX, CM12 9XG. (Life Member)
L'ESTRANGE, Miss. Katharine, BA ACA *2004;* with KPMG LLP, 15 Canada Square, LONDON, E14 5GL.
L'HEUREUX, Mr. Brendan J, ACA *2011;* University of London, College Hall, Malet Street, LONDON, WC1E 7HZ.
LA BROOY, Mr. Peter William, BA ACA *1982;* 34 Nevill Road, Rottingdean, BRIGHTON, BN2 7HG.
LA FRANCA, Mr. Fabio, ACA MBA *2009;* Flat 16 Chilworth Court, Windlesham Grove, LONDON, SW19 6AL.
LA NIECE, Mr. David John, FCA *1957;* Ivy Cottage, Reigate Heath, REIGATE, RH2 8QR. (Life Member)
LA PLAIN, Mr. Jeremy Charles Anthony, BA(Hons) ACA *2001;* 45 Grenville Way, STEVENAGE, HERTFORDSHIRE, SG2 8XZ.
LA RIVIERE, Miss. Michele, BSc ARCS ACA *1992;* 8 Courageous Place, Beachlands, MANUKAU 2018, NEW ZEALAND.
LA VIA, Miss. Alessandra, ACA *2011;* 190 Elgar Road, READING, RG2 0BN.
LABAN, Miss. Christine Inga, ACA *2011;* 9 Gordon Avenue, LONDON, E4 9QT.
LABATON, Mr. Adrian, FCA *1975;* (Tax Fac), 170 Squirrel Walk, Fforest, Pontarddulais, SWANSEA, SA4 0UG.
LABBE, Miss. Helene Andree Paule Fernande, MSc ACA *2000;* 10 Ashbourne Grove, LONDON, W4 2JH.
LABBETT, Mr. John Edgar, FCA *1972;* 80 Stagecoach Road, BELL CANYON, CA 91307, UNITED STATES.
LABBETT, Mr. Keith Lawrence, BCom FCA *1975;* 17 Millside, BOURNE END, SL8 5UN.
LABI, Mr. Robert, BA FCA *1970;* 26 Parklands Drive, LONDON, N3 3HA.
LABISI, Mr. Michael Olawunmi, BSc(Hons) ACA *2009;* 10 Brymay Close, LONDON, E3 2SY.
LABOVSKAYA, Miss. Polina, ACA *2011;* Raised Ground Floor, 136 Tufnell Park Road, LONDON, N7 0DU.
LABRAM, Mr. Dominic Henry, MA(Hons) ACA *2009;* 40 Grandison Road, LONDON, SW11 6LW.
LABREY, Mr. John Gordon, FCA *1958;* Ladyshawe Barn, Bridge Street, New Mills, HIGH PEAK, SK22 4DN. (Life Member)
LABROSS, Mr. Peter Vincent, MA ACA CTA *1983;* 6 Bleaberry Close, West Bridgford, NOTTINGHAM, NG2 6RQ.
LABRUM, Mr. Michael George, MA FCA *1979;* LDR Medical, Technopole de l'Aube, BP2, CEDEX 9, 10902 TROYES, FRANCE.
LABRUM, Mrs. Susan Alison, BSc ACA *1992;* 23 Knole Way, SEVENOAKS, KENT, TN13 3RS.
LABUSCHAGNE, Mr. Robbert, ACA CA(SA) *2010;* 301 St. Davids Square, LONDON, E14 3WF.
LACCOHEE-DUFFIELD, Mrs. Jennifer Ella, BSc ACA *2011;* 24 Rose Avenue, Queens Hill, Costessey, NORWICH, NORFOLK, NR8 5EX.
LACE, Mr. David, FCA *1970;* 61 Wessenden Head Road, Meltham, HOLMFIRTH, West Yorkshire, HD9 4ET.
LACE, Mr. Peter Charles, LLB ACA *1984;* 97 Queens Road, Wimbledon, LONDON, SW19 8NR.
•**LACE, Mr. Peter Dennis, BSc ACA** *1981;* Peter D. Lace, First Floor, 18 Hope Street, Douglas, ISLE OF MAN, IM1 1AQ.
LACEY, Mr. Andrew, BA ACA *2006;* 117 Midhurst Gardens, UXBRIDGE, MIDDLESEX, UB10 9DP.
LACEY, Mrs. Bridget Amanda Jane, BSc ACA *1991;* Chiltern House Chiltern Road, AMERSHAM, BUCKINGHAMSHIRE, HP6 5PH.
LACEY, Mrs. Caroline Susan, BSc ACA *1990;* 4 High Street, NORTH FERRIBY, HU14 3JP.
LACEY, Mr. Derek Oliver, FCA *1961;* Wood Cote, 14 Orchard Way, ESHER, SURREY, KT10 9DY. (Life Member)
LACEY, Mr. Donald Robert, FCA *1957;* 16 Drovers Rise, Elloughton, BROUGH, HU15 1LN. (Life Member)
LACEY, Miss. Emma Claire, BSc ACA *1999;* 37 Carolyn Place, FERNY GROVE, QLD 4055, AUSTRALIA.
•**LACEY, Mr. Gregory James, LLB FCA** *1996;* 20 Hooley Range, Heaton Moor, STOCKPORT, CHESHIRE, SK4 4HU.
LACEY, Mr. Ian John, FCA *1974;* (Tax Fac), Geodrill Limited, 20b Aviation Road, Airport Residentail Area, ACCRA, GHANA.
LACEY, Mrs. Jennifer Mary, BA ACA *1981;* 16 Hamilton Avenue, HENLEY-ON-THAMES, RG9 1SH.
LACEY, Mr. John Robert, ACA *1985;* Kemira Chemicals (UK) Limited, Bowling Park Drive, BRADFORD, WEST YORKSHIRE, BD4 7TT.
LACEY, Mr. Jonathan, BA(Hons) ACA *2000;* with Monahans Limited, Lennox House, 3 Pierrepont Street, BATH, BA1 1LB.
LACEY, Mr. Jonathan David, BSc FCA CTA *1995;* 83 Lyncombe Hill, BATH, BA2 4PJ.
LACEY, Mr. Martin James, FCA *1974;* with National Audit Office, 157-197 Buckingham Palace Road, Victoria, LONDON, SW1W 9SP.
LACEY, Mr. Matthew James, BA ACA MSI *1999;* Egg Plc, Riverside Road Pride Park, DERBY, DE99 3GG.
LACEY, Mr. Maurice Raymond, FCA *1962;* 37 Humberston Road, Wollaton, NOTTINGHAM, NG8 2SU.
LACEY, Mr. Michael Francis, BA ACA *1988;* 193 Woolton Road, Wavertree, LIVERPOOL, L15 6XW.
LACEY, Mr. Michael John, BA ACA *1990;* 2 Elm Barns, Cottenham, CAMBRIDGE, CB24 8DB.
LACEY, Mr. Michael John, FCA *1963;* Oakbanks, Wellbrook Hill, MAYFIELD, EAST SUSSEX, TN20 6EA.
•**LACEY, Mr. Neville Denis, BSc FCA FRSA** *1980;* (Tax Fac), Jones Avens Limited, Piper House, 4 Dukes Court, Bognor Road, CHICHESTER, PO19 8FX.
LACEY, Mr. Nigel Mark, BSc ACA *1986;* Galaunia Farms Limited, P.O. Box 30089, LUSAKA, ZAMBIA.
LACEY, Mr. Patrick William, FCA *1961;* 4950 Ivy Ridge Dr. SE, Unit 106, SMYRNA, GA 30080, UNITED STATES.
LACEY, Mr. Paul Anthony, BA ACA DipCII *1997;* Willis Group, 51 Lime Street, LONDON, EC3M 7DQ.
LACEY, Mr. Peter Edward, FCA *1968;* Broadside Boatyard Ltd, 1 St. Martins, High Street, Bosham, CHICHESTER, WEST SUSSEX PO18 8LT.
•**LACEY, Mr. Peter William, FCA** *1969;* Peter W. Lacey, The Old Forge, West Buckland, WELLINGTON, TA21 9JS.
•**LACEY, Mr. Richard Donald, BA FCA** *1988;* (Tax Fac), Harris Lacey and Swain, 8 Waterside Business Park, Livingstone Road, HESSLE, NORTH HUMBERSIDE, HU13 0EN.
LACEY, Mr. Richard James, BSc ACA *1993;* Desarollos Canacosta, PO Box 18-5159, VILLAREAL, GUANACASTE PROVINCE, COSTA RICA.
•**LACEY, Mrs. Sarah Louise, BSc(Hons) ACA** *2003;* SLL Accounts, Burnside, Station Road, EDENBRIDGE, KENT, TN8 5NB.
LACEY, Mr. Stephen, BA ACA *1981;* The Coach House, Hungershall Park, TUNBRIDGE WELLS, KENT, TN4 8ND.
LACEY, Mr. Stuart James, LLB ACA *2002;* 15614 East Atlantic Circle, AURORA, CO 80013, UNITED STATES.
LACEY, Mrs. Yolanda Mellissa Yun-Ling, BSc ACA *1992;* Tricor Services Ltd, 7 Hill Street, Douglas, ISLE OF MAN, IM1 1EF.
LACEY-SMITH, Miss. Penny Ann, BSc ACA *1999;* Old Woodhill Cottage Woodhill, Send, WOKING, SURREY, GU23 7JP.
LACHAMBRE, Mr. Vincent, ACA MBA *2001;* Petit Forester UK Ltd Watling Street, Dordon, TAMWORTH, STAFFORDSHIRE, B78 1TS.
•**LACHMAN, Mr. Frank Simon, FCA** *1977;* Frank S Lachman, Nachal Sorek 33-16, Remat Beit, SHEMESH-ALEPH, ISRAEL.
•**LACHMAN, Mr. Neville Garfield, MSc FCA** *1986;* Lachman Livingstone, 136 Pinner Road, NORTHWOOD, MIDDLESEX, HA6 1BP. See also Northwood Registrars Ltd
LACK, Mr. Ian David, BEng ACA *1999;* Spectris Plc, Station Road, EGHAM, SURREY, TW20 9NP.
LACK, Mrs. Juliet Alexandra, BSc ACA *1992;* 3 Jennings Close, SURBITON, SURREY, KT6 5RB.
LACK, Mr. Thomas, MA ACA *1993;* 3 Jennings Close, SURBITON, SURREY, KT6 5RB.
LACKEY, Mr. David Andrew, BSc FCA *1986;* Gilead Sciences (Finance Dept), Flowers Building, Granta Park, Great Abington, CAMBRIDGE, CAMBRIDGESHIRE CB21 6GT.
•**LACKEY, Mrs. Lynette, BA FCA** *1987;* Sycamore House Vicarage Close, Waterbeach, CAMBRIDGE, CB25 9QG.
•**LACKMAKER, Mr. David Harry, FCA** *1975;* Lackmaker & Co, 10 Bradden Lane, Gaddesden Row, HEMEL HEMPSTEAD, HP2 6HZ.
•**LACOME, Mr. Gerald Anthony, BSc FCA** *1980;* (Tax Fac), Lacome & Co Limited, Sapphire House, 73 St Margarets Avenue, LONDON, N20 9LD.
LACY, Miss. Christina, ACA *2008;* 2 School Street, Morley, LEEDS, LS27 8BW.
LACY, Miss. Penelope Jane, BA ACA *1988;* 11 Mallison Hill Drive Easingwold, YORK, YO61 3RY.
LACY SCOTT, Mr. David Geffrey, BA FCA *1952;* Scotma Ltd, 5 Haygate, EYE, IP23 7BN. (Life Member)
LAD, Mr. Bipin, BA ACA *1994;* with PKF (UK) LLP, Farringdon Place, 20 Farringdon Road, LONDON, EC1M 3AP.
LAD, Mrs. Jasneet Kaur, BSc(Hons) ACA *2010;* Flat 16 Ravensbourne Court, 1 Amias Drive, EDGWARE, HA8 8EY.
LAD, Mr. Manoj, BSc ACA *1997;* First Floor Flat, 103 Culford Road, LONDON, N1 4HL.
LAD, Mrs. Nila Ishwarlal, BSc ACA *2002;* 6 Alverstone Road, WEMBLEY, HA9 9SB.
LAD, Mr. Nilesh, BSc FCA *1992;* PricewaterhouseCoopers, 75 Zhylyanska Street, 01032 KIEV, UKRAINE.
LADAK, Mr. Rizwan, BA(Hons) ACA *2010;* 24 Newhaven Road, LEICESTER, LE5 6JG.
LADAK, Mr. Zulfikarali Jusab, FCA *1977;* 306 836 - 15th Avenue S.W, CALGARY T2R 1S2, AB, CANADA.
•**LADANOWSKI, Miss. Kathryn, BA ACA** *2002;* (Tax Fac), Aster Accountants, 7 Aster Crescent, Beechwood, RUNCORN, CHESHIRE, WA7 3HS.
LADBROOK, Mr. Charles Bertram Valentine, FCA *1952;* 1 Manor Road, Collingham, NEWARK, NG23 7PL. (Life Member)
LADBROOK, Mr. Roger Gerrard, FCA *1973;* 8 Wilkes Court, TINBEERWAH, QLD 4563, AUSTRALIA.
LADBURY, Mrs. Annabel, BSc ACA *1998;* 24 Horsley Road, LONDON, E4 7HX.
LADD, Mr. David Mark, FCA *1963;* Michaelmass Meadows, Penfold Lane, Little Missenden, AMERSHAM, HP7 0QU. (Life Member)
LADD, Mrs. Justine Maria, BA ACA *1996;* 59 Barmoor Drive, NEWCASTLE UPON TYNE, NE3 5RE.
LADD, Mr. Kenneth Peter, FCA *1952;* 62 Eastbury Road, NORTHWOOD, HA6 3AR. (Life Member)
LADD, Mrs. Victoria Hays, BA ACA *2004;* 4 Norborne Road, Broad Hinton, SWINDON, SN4 9PT.
LADDIN, Mr. Phillip, FCA *1961;* Dunham Mews, 7 Edgemoor Park Road, Bowdon, ALTRINCHAM, WA14 3JN.
•**LADDS, Mr. Graham Ian, FCA** *1973;* Accountancy (East Notts) Limited, Spinners, Old Great North Road, Sutton-on-Trent, NEWARK, NOTTINGHAMSHIRE NG23 6QL.
LADE, Mr. William Matthew, BA ACA *2007;* 117 High Street, NORTHWOOD, MIDDLESEX, HA6 1ED.
•**LADEJOBI, Mr. Ibikunle Adeoye, FCA** *1969;* Kunle Ladejobi & Co, G.P.O. Box 6816, LAGOS, NIGERIA.
LADELL, Mr. Mark Richard Bailey, ACA *1992;* 42 Tadorne Road, TADWORTH, SURREY, KT20 5TF.
•**LADEN, Mrs. Karen Virginia, FCA** *1979;* K.V. Laden, 7 St. Marys Road, BENFLEET, SS7 1NR.
•**LADENHEIM, Mr. Lawrence Bernard, ACA** *1984;* Lawrence B Ladenheim, 5 Yehuda Halevi Street, 43555 RA'ANANA, ISRAEL.
LADER, Mr. Jeffrey, MA FCA ACIS *1988;* Group Compliance Office, T.D Waterhouse, Exchange Court, Duncombe Street, LEEDS, LS1 4AX.
LADEVEZE, Mr. Jack Edward, FCA *1956;* Scypens Marksbury, BATH, BA2 9HP. (Life Member)
LADHA, Mr. Ashfaq Farooq Mohammad, MBA BA ACA *2006;* 1002 Mesk Tower Marina Walk Dubai Marina, PO Box 48748, DUBAI, 48748, UNITED ARAB EMIRATES.
LADHA, Miss. Azmina Allaudin, MEng ACA *2002;* 13 Clauson Avenue, NORTHOLT, UB5 4PR.
LADHA, Mr. Zaheer Ali, BSc ACA *2010;* 102 Mortlake Road, ILFORD, ESSEX, IG1 2SY.
LADHANI, Mr. Barkatali Amarshi, ACA *1981;* 152 West Hill, LONDON, SW15 3SR.
•**LADIMEJI, Mr. Oladapo Alani, MA FCA MBA** *1982;* (Tax Fac), Ladimeji & Co, Five Kings House, 1 Queen Street Place, LONDON, EC4R 1QS.
LADIPO, Miss. Omowunmi Adebisi Kafayat, BSc FCA *1989;* The World Bank Group, MSN KGLWB, Kigali, PO Box 27839, WASHINGTON, DC 20038-7839 UNITED STATES.
LADKIN, Miss. Penelope Anne, BA ACA *2005;* 29 Langham House Close, RICHMOND, SURREY, TW10 7JE.
LADVA, Mr. Dhiresh Lalji, ACA *1992;* 2 Priory Hill, Sudbury, WEMBLEY, HA0 2QF.
LAFFERTY, Miss. Anais Nathalie, MSc BSc ACA *2010;* Conde Nast International, 25 Maddox Street, LONDON, W1S 2QN.
LAFFERTY, Ms. Isabella Maria Caroline, BSc ACA *2006;* 392 Goldhawk Road, Chiswick, LONDON, W6 0SB.
LAFFERTY, Mr. Michael Joseph, FCA *1972;* Lafferty Group, 1 Lyric Square, LONDON, W6 0NB.
LAFLIN, Mr. John Hammond, BA FCA *1967;* The White Cottage, Great Wymondley, HITCHIN, SG4 7ET. (Life Member)
LAFUENTE, Ms. Nena Patricia, MSc ACA *1998;* c/o CARE Vietnam, 66 Xuan Dieu Road, Tay Ho, HANOI, VIETNAM.
LAGANOWSKA, Ms. Katarzyna Karolina, MA ACA *1999;* 7 Shaftesbury Road, BATH, BA2 3LQ.
LAGER, Mr. Michael Charles Moore, BA FCA *1966;* 45 Chipping Hill, WITHAM, CM8 2JT.
•**LAGERBERG, Mrs. Francesca Clare, LLB FCA CTA** *1992;* (Member of Council 2005 - 2007), (Tax Fac), Grant Thornton UK LLP, Grant Thornton House, 22 Melton Street, Euston Square, LONDON, NW1 2EP. See also Grant Thornton LLP
•**LAGERBERG, Mr. Gerard John, LLB FCA** *1987;* PricewaterhouseCoopers LLP, Pricewaterhousecoopers, 12 Plumtree Court, LONDON, EC4A 4HT. See also PricewaterhouseCoopers
LAGGAN, Mr. Neil William, BA ACA *2002;* with Audit Inspection Unit, Financial Reporting Council, 5th Floor, Aldwych House, 71-91 Aldwych, LONDON WC2B 4HN.
•**LAHAN, Mrs. Karen, FCA** *1976;* Unifurn Interiors Limited, 73-87 Lower Hillgate, STOCKPORT, CHESHIRE, SK1 3AW.
LAHDENPERA, Mr. Juho Matti, BA ACA *2007;* 15 Whittell Gardens, LONDON, SE26 4LN.
LAHELMA-BARNSLEY, Mrs. Marja Tuulikki, BA ACA *2004;* Hawkslee House, Bosley, MACCLESFIELD, CHESHIRE, SK11 0NZ.
LAHIRI, Mr. Pranab Kumar, FCA *1958;* 1742 Ridgecrest Court N.E., ATLANTA, GA 30307, UNITED STATES. (Life Member)
LAI, Miss. Amy Ying Yen, BA ACA *2002;* 11 Deedman Close, Ash, ALDERSHOT, HAMPSHIRE, GU12 6RQ.
LAI, Ms. Chi Kam, ACA *2005;* GPO Box 9321, CENTRAL, HONG KONG ISLAND, HONG KONG SAR.
LAI, Mr. Chuck Y Andy, ACA *2007;* Flat 505 5/F Block 28, Heng Fa Chuen 100 Shing Tai Road, CHAI WAN, HONG KONG SAR.
LAI, Mr. Chun Yu, BA ACA *2007;* Room 3906, Hoi Kin House, Hoi Lai Estate, LAI CHI KOK, KOWLOON, HONG KONG SAR.
LAI, Mr. David Chee On, ACA *1980;* B5 19/F Elizabeth House, 252 Gloucester Road, CAUSEWAY BAY, Hong Kong Island, HONG KONG SAR.
LAI, Mr. David Shin Fah, BSc FCA *1995;* B-G-3A Uthant Residence, 28 Jalan Taman Uthant, 550000 KUALA LUMPUR, FEDERAL TERRITORY, MALAYSIA.
LAI, Mr. Gavin Gregory, ACA CA(SA) *2010;* 5 Hutton Mews, Pleasance Road, Putney, LONDON, SW15 5HZ.
LAI, Ms. Hau Wan, ACA *2008;* with CIG CPA Limited, Unit 702 7th Floor, Tung Hip Commercial Building, 244 Des Voeux Road, CENTRAL, HONG KONG SAR.
LAI, Mr. Hee Guang, BSc ACA *1986;* P.O Box 56499, Dominion Road, Mt Eden, AUCKLAND 1446, NEW ZEALAND.

LAI, Ms. Hon Man Judy, ACA *2008;* Flat 137A, 2nd Basement, Golden Valley Mansion, 135-137 Caine Road, MID LEVELS, HONG KONG SAR.

LAI, Ms. Hong Yee, ACA *2008;* Room 2903, Kam Chun House, Tung Chun Court, SHAU KEI WAN, HONG KONG ISLAND, HONG KONG SAR.

LAI, Mr. Jay Yat Kean, ACA *2010;* 134 Plover Way, LONDON, SE16 7TZ.

LAI, Miss. Jenny Sock Ching, FCA *1970;* 8 Dover Rise No., 10-04 Heritage View Tower A, SINGAPORE 138679, SINGAPORE.

LAI, Mr. Jeremy Simon, BA FCA *1992;* 70 Clarkegrove Road, SHEFFIELD, S10 2NJ.

LAI, Mr. Jonathan Tak Shing, BCom FCA *1998;* HLB Hodgson Impey Cheng, 31/F Gloucester Tower, The Landmark, 11 Pedder Street, CENTRAL, HONG KONG ISLAND HONG KONG SAR.

LAI, Mr. Ka Cheung Andrew, ACA *2005;* Andrew K.C. Lai & Company, Room 1901-1902 Hong Kong Trade Centre, 161-167 Des Voeux Road, CENTRAL, HONG KONG ISLAND, HONG KONG SAR.

LAI, Mr. Kam Yu, BA ACA *1991;* 878/155 Narasiri Pattanakarn, Sri Nakarindra Road, Suanluang, BANGKOK 10250, THAILAND.

LAI, Mr. Kar Wai, ACA *2007;* 23A Block 1, Braemar Hill Mansion, 15 Braemar Hill Road, NORTH POINT, HONG KONG ISLAND, HONG KONG SAR.

LAI, Ms. Kar Bik, ACA *2008;* Flat 3, 21/F, Block B, Yat Fai House, Yue Fai Court, 45 Yue Kwong Road ABERDEEN HONG KONG SAR.

LAI, Mr. Ki Shing, ACA *2008;* Room 514, Yin Shui House, Shui Pin Wai Estate, YUEN LONG, NEW TERRITORIES, HONG KONG SAR.

LAI, Mr. Kwok Wai Vincent, ACA *2007;* Flat C, 28/F Block 2, Tivoli Garden, 75 Tsing King Road, TSING YI, NEW TERRITORIES HONG KONG SAR.

LAI, Mr. Ling Muk, BSc FCA *1990;* BP China 19F Taikang Financial Tower, No 38 East 3rd Ring Road, North Road, Chaoyang District, BEIJING 100026, CHINA.

LAI, Ms. Lisa Wai Fong, BA(Hons) ACA *2002;* Vodafone UK, The Connection, NEWBURY, BERKSHIRE, RG14 2FN.

LAI, Ms. Man Ling, ACA *2007;* Flat A, 4/F Block 4, City One Sha Tin, SHA TIN, NEW TERRITORIES, HONG KONG SAR.

LAI, Dr. Mei Ling, FCA *1970;* 7 Jalan 14/55, 46100 PETALING JAYA, Selangor, MALAYSIA.

•LAI, Miss. Mei Sim, OBE DL FCA FCCA DChA *1976;* LaiPeters & Co, New Broad Street House, 35 New Broad Street, LONDON, EC2M 1NH. See also LaiPeters Limited

LAI, Ms. Miu Shan Michelle, ACA *2007;* Flat G8/F La Rossa A Coastal Skyline, Tung Chung, LANTAU ISLAND, NEW TERRITORIES, HONG KONG SAR.

LAI, Ms. Pik Chi Peggy, ACA *2007;* Flat D, 6/F Block 11, Serenity Park, TAI PO, NEW TERRITORIES, HONG KONG SAR.

LAI, Mr. Po Sing, ACA *2007;* Unit A, 24/F Tower 1, Cayman Rise, 29 Ka Wai Man Road, KENNEDY TOWN, HONG KONG ISLAND HONG KONG SAR.

LAI, Mr. Poon Ken, ACA *1980;* 44 Jalan Kampong Pantai, 75200 MALACCA CITY, MALACCA STATE, MALAYSIA.

LAI, Mr. Sai Kwong, BSc ACA *1989;* Flat A, 26/F Block 2, Lyttelton Garden, 17-29 Lyttelton Road, Western Mid-Level, CENTRAL HONG KONG ISLAND HONG KONG SAR.

LAI, Mr. Shi Hong Edward, ACA *2008;* Flat C3, 5/F Block C, Phoenix Court, 8-10 Marconi Road, KOWLOON TONG, KOWLOON HONG KONG SAR.

LAI, Mr. Sin Tong Thomas, ACA *2007;* Chan Lai Pang & Co, 28/F Times Tower, 393 Jaffe Road, WAN CHAI, HONG KONG ISLAND, HONG KONG SAR.

LAI, Mr. Steve Chi Wai, MSc BA ACA MIMgt *1990;* 3 Craybury End, LONDON, SE9 3SL.

LAI, Miss. Sum Yee Rachel, BA ACA *2004;* Flat C 8th Floor, 57 Beacon Hill Road, KOWLOON TONG, KOWLOON, HONG KONG SAR.

LAI, Miss. Voon Huey, BSc ACA *1992;* Ireka Corporation Berhad Level 18 Wisma Mont' Kiara No. 1 Jalan Kiara Mont' Kiara, 50480 KUALA LUMPUR, MALAYSIA.

LAI, Miss. Wing-Man, BSc ACA *2006;* Flat 5 Middleton House, 1 Grenard Close, LONDON, SE15 5GZ.

LAI, Mr. Winston Kam Wah, BEng ACA *1993;* Flat C, 55/F Tower 6, Bellagio, 33 Castle Peak Road, SHAM TSENG, NEW TERRITORIES HONG KONG SAR.

LAI, Mr. Wui Wing Patrick, ACA *2004;* Patrick Lai & Co., Room 1106, Capitol Centre, 5-19 Jardine's Bazaar, CAUSEWAY BAY, HONG KONG SAR.

LAI, Miss. Wut-Yu Eileen, BSc FCA *1992;* Flat B, 43/F, Tower 6, Bel-Air, 68 Bel-Air Peak Avenue, POK FU LAM HONG KONG ISLAND HONG KONG SAR.

LAI, Mr. Yau Fai, BSc FCA *1988;* WAH Tong Group, Room 2721-2722 27th Floor, 1 Hung To Road, KWUN TONG, KOWLOON, HONG KONG SAR.

LAI, Miss. Yuen Yun, ACA *1987;* 49 Tong Min Tsuen, Lam Tsuen, TAI PO, NEW TERRITORIES, HONG KONG SAR.

LAI, Miss. Yuet Ming Mary, MSc BSc ACA *2005;* 20 Grendon Gardens, WEMBLEY, MIDDLESEX, HA9 9NE.

LAI, Mr. Yuk Kwong, ACA *2005;* 37/F The World Trade Centre, 280 Gloucester Road, CAUSEWAY BAY, HONG KONG ISLAND, HONG KONG SAR.

LAI, Mr. Yun Hung, ACA *2005;* Lai & Wong, Unit B 8th Floor, Success Commercial Building, 245-251 Hennessy Road, WAN CHAI, HONG KONG ISLAND HONG KONG SAR.

•LAI CHEONG, Mrs. Florise Brigitte Margaret, FCA *1980;* Nicholson & Co., Monument House, 215 Marsh Road, PINNER, HA5 5NE.

LAI-KIN-FOO, Mr. Max, BSc ACA *2003;* Parkhill (Internal Audit), Aneurin Bevan House, 81-91 Commercial Road, LONDON, E1 2RD.

LAI MIN, Miss. Vanessa Suie Lan, BSc ACA *2005;* Royal Road Telfair, MOKA, MAURITIUS.

LAI PAT FONG, Miss. Josee, LLB FCA *1992;* 14B Blk 5 Pacific View, 38 Tai Tam Rd, TAI TAM, HONG KONG SAR.

LAI-PAT-FONG, Miss. Suzanne, BSc ACA *1993;* (Tax Fac), National Car Parks Ltd, Whitgift Centre, CROYDON, CR0 1LP.

LAI WAI, Miss. Beatrice Lai Shoye Mee, ACA *2008;* Flat 6 Quilting Court, Garter Way, LONDON, SE16 6XF.

LAI WAN LOONG, Mr. Andre Young, BSc ACA *1993;* Ernst & Young, 9th Floor, Tower 1, NextTeracom, Cybercity, EBENE MAURITIUS.

LAIDLAW, Mr. Christopher Walter, BSc ACA *1978;* 5 The Coach House, Northwick Park Blockley, MORETON-IN-MARSH, GLOUCESTERSHIRE, GL56 9RJ.

LAIDLAW, Miss. Claire Anne, MA ACA *1997;* 87 Huia Rd, Point Chevalier, AUCKLAND 1022, NEW ZEALAND.

•LAIDLAW, Mr. Daren Paul Philip, BA ACA *1997;* Rothman Pantall LLP, 88 Northern Road, Cosham, PORTSMOUTH, PO6 3ER.

LAIDLAW, Mr. James Robin, BSc ACA *1993;* The Coach House, 235 Upper Richmond Road, LONDON, SW15 6SN.

LAIDLER, Mr. John, FCA *1960;* 16 Elmfield Park, NEWCASTLE UPON TYNE, NE3 4UX. (Life Member)

LAIDLER, Ms. Sarah, BSc ACA *1999;* 44 Witherford Way, Selly Oak, BIRMINGHAM, B29 4AX.

LAIDLER, Mr. William, FCA FCA(Honorary) *1954;* Brigadoon, Nine Ashes Road, Blackmore, INGATESTONE, CM4 0QW. (Life Member)

LAIDLOW, Mr. Jonathan David, MA BA ACA *1999;* Insparo Asset Management Ltd, 55 Blandford Street, LONDON, W1U 7HW.

LAIGHT, Miss. Carol Linda, BA FCA *1982;* 38 Cranesfield, Sherborne St. John, BASINGSTOKE, RG24 9LN.

LAIKIN, Mr. David Bernard, BSc ACA *1992;* 43 Wayside Avenue, BUSHEY, WD23 4SH.

LAIKIN, Mr. Mark Alan, BSc ACA *1992;* 58 Bushey Grove Road, BUSHEY, WD23 2JJ.

LAIN, Mr. David Adam, BSc ACA PGCE *2002;* 5 Woodlands Road, TONBRIDGE, TN9 2NE.

LAINCHBURY, Mr. Stanley Ernest, DFM FCA *1957;* 115 Dereham Road, Mattishall, DEREHAM, NORFOLK, NR20 3NU. (Life Member)

LAINE, Mr. Christopher Norman, FCA *1967;* (President 1997 - 1998) (Member of Council 1990 - 2000), Woodlands Cottage, Lower Common Road, West Wellow, ROMSEY, SO51 6BT. (Life Member)

•LAING, Ms. Anne-Marie, FCA *1999;* Zolfo Cooper LLP, 10 Fleet Place, LONDON, EC4M 7RB.

LAING, Mr. Cameron, BSc ACA *1996;* Rosemead Weedon Hill, Hyde Heath, AMERSHAM, BUCKINGHAMSHIRE, HP6 5RN.

LAING, Mr. David, BSc ACA *1994;* 23 Pickford Road, Markyate, ST. ALBANS, HERTFORDSHIRE, AL3 8RS.

LAING, Mr. David, FCA *1959;* Kemps Cottage, Clatterbury Lane, Clavering, SAFFRON WALDEN, CB11 4QU. (Life Member)

LAING, Mr. David Ian, FCA *1987;* 2 Pitter Close, Littleton, WINCHESTER, HAMPSHIRE, SO22 6PD.

LAING, Mrs. Deborah Ann, FCA *1994;* 3 Westfield Close, Horton Heath, EASTLEIGH, HAMPSHIRE, SO50 7PR.

LAING, Miss. Evelyn Mary, BSc ACA *1995;* Wolfson Medical School Building, University Avenue, GLASGOW, G12 8QQ.

LAING, Mr. Hamish, BA ACA *2006;* One Raffles Quay #34-03 North Tower, SINGAPORE 048583, SINGAPORE.

LAING, Mrs. Hilary Anne, BA ACA *1996;* 23 Pickford Road, Markyate, ST. ALBANS, HERTFORDSHIRE, AL3 8RS.

LAING, Mrs. Janet, BSc ACA *1988;* 15 Rugby Road, BRIGHTON, BN1 6EB.

LAING, Mr. John Bernard Gordon, BA ACA FRSS *1987;* Home Farm, Remenham Lane, Remenham, HENLEY-ON-THAMES, OXFORDSHIRE, RG9 2LS.

LAING, Mr. Richard George, MA FCA *1980;* Great Lywood Farmhouse Lindfield Road, Ardingly, HAYWARDS HEATH, WEST SUSSEX, RH17 6SW.

LAING, Mrs. Susan Judith, BCom ACA *1988;* Home Farm Remenham Lane, Remenham, HENLEY-ON-THAMES, OXFORDSHIRE, RG9 2LS.

•LAING-WILLIAMS, Mr. Kelvin Stuart, FCA *1979;* PricewaterhouseCoopers LLP, Hays Galleria, 1 Hays Lane, LONDON, SE1 2RD. See also PricewaterhouseCoopers

LAIRD, Miss. Alison, MA ACA *2004;* Franklin Templeton Investments, 5 Morrison Street, EDINBURGH, EH3 8BH.

LAIRD, Mrs. Helen, BSc ACA *1992;* 20 Rowena Cade Avenue, CHELTENHAM, GLOUCESTERSHIRE, GL50 2LA.

•LAIRD, Mr. Ian Stanley, FCA *1978;* Clay Ratnage Stevens & Hills, Construction House, Runwell Road, WICKFORD, ESSEX, SS11 7HQ. See also Clay Ratnage Daffin & Co Ltd

LAIRD, Mrs. Lesley-Ann, BSc ACA *1994;* Gatehead Farm, KILMARNOCK, AYRSHIRE, KA1 5JP.

LAIRD, Mrs. Monique Florence, BA ACA *1991;* 62 Alphington Avenue, Frimley, CAMBERLEY, GU16 8LR.

LAIRD, Mr. Neil John Duncan, MA FCA *1977;* 132 Silverwood Drive, SCOTTS VALLEY, CA 95066, UNITED STATES.

LAIRD, Miss. Paula Karen Julie, BSc(Hons) ACA *2003;* Wateraid, 47-49 Durham Street, LONDON, SE11 5JD.

LAIRD, Mr. Robert James, BSc ACA *1999;* 23 Ullswater House, 203 Mossley Hill Drive, LIVERPOOL, L17 0EL.

LAIRD, Mr. Tom, ACA MAAT *2010;* 16 Clayspring Close, HOCKLEY, SS5 5AW.

LAIRD, Ms. Yvonne, BSc(Hons) ACA *2004;* Serco Learning, Winchester House, Wyvern Business Park, Stanier Way, Chaddesden, DERBY DE21 6BF.

LAISTER, Mr. Ian, BA(Hons) ACA *2000;* 26 The Balk Staincross, BARNSLEY, SOUTH YORKSHIRE, S75 6JJ.

LAISTER, Mr. John Robert, FCA *1975;* 22 Burne Crescent, Glenashly, DURBAN, KWAZULU NATAL, 4051, SOUTH AFRICA.

LAIT, Mr. Brian Havelock, FCA *1964;* 8 Ayios Minas Street, Maroni, 7737 LARNACA, CYPRUS. (Life Member)

LAITHWAITE, Mrs. Andrea Dawn, BSc(Hons) ACA *2002;* 12 Church Meadows, BOLTON, BL2 3PB.

LAITHWAITE, The Hon. Jessica Mary Clare, BA ACA *1996;* 41 Buckingham Rd, Killara, SYDNEY, NSW 2071, AUSTRALIA.

LAITHWAITE, Mr. Marcus Jonathon Anderson, BSc ACA *1996;* PricewaterhouseCoopers, Darling Park Tower 2, 201 Sussex Street, GPO Box 2650, SYDNEY, NSW 1171 AUSTRALIA.

LAITHWAITE, Mr. Richard Croston, BSc ACA *1997;* 9 Gatcombe Crescent, ASCOT, BERKSHIRE, SL5 7HA.

•LAITNER, Mr. Stewart Anthony, FCA *1967;* (Tax Fac), Stewart Laitner & Co, 17 Bancroft Avenue, East Finchley, LONDON, N2 0AR.

•LAITY, Mr. Jason Scott, ACA *1994;* (Tax Fac), KPMG Channel Islands Limited, 5 St. Andrew's Place, Charing Cross, St. Helier, JERSEY, JE4 8WQ.

LAITY, Mrs. Lynn, BA ACA *1997;* Le Petit Coin, Parcq de L'Oeilliere, Le Mont de la Pulente, St. Brelade, JERSEY, JE3 8HF.

LAJMI, Mr. Vinay, MA ACA *1995;* Shell International Eastern Trading Company, Shell House, 83 Clemenceau Avenue, SINGAPORE 239920, SINGAPORE.

LAKE, Mr. Andrew Stephen, BSc ACA *1983;* 32 Connaught Way, Brickhill, BEDFORD, MK41 7LB.

LAKE, Miss. Claire Alexandra, ACA *2010;* Moss Rose Cottage, Court Road, Rollesby, GREAT YARMOUTH, NORFOLK, NR29 5HQ.

LAKE, Mrs. Clare Louise, BA(Hons) ACA *2002;* 18 Upper Green Road, Tewin, WELWYN, HERTFORDSHIRE, AL6 0LG.

LAKE, Mr. David, BA ACA *2010;* Chequers Inn, The Street, Roxwell, CHELMSFORD, CM1 4PD.

LAKE, Mr. David Anthony, FCA *1975;* 66 Elm Park Road, LONDON, SW3 6AU.

LAKE, Mr. David Howard, MSc BA FCA *1979;* Bungalow # 91 Palm City Residences Zanzour, TRIPOLI, LIBYAN ARAB JAMAHIRIYA.

LAKE, Mr. David John, FCA *1969;* Bluebay Asset Management Plc, 77 Grosvenor Street, LONDON, W1K 3JR.

LAKE, Mr. Dean Lee, BSc ACA *2002;* 6, Sultan Street, BECKENHAM, BR3 4QS.

LAKE, Mrs. Gillian Patricia, BSc FCA *1982;* (Tax Fac), 32 Connaught Way, Brickhill, BEDFORD, MK41 7LB.

LAKE, Miss. Helen Clare, ACA *1993;* 4 Windermere Close, Gamston, NOTTINGHAM, NG2 6PQ.

LAKE, Ms. Jane Anne, BA(Hons) FCA CTA *1989;* (Tax Fac), Card Protection Plan Holgate Park, Holgate Road, YORK, YO26 4GA.

LAKE, Mr. Jeffrey Richard, BA ACA *1982;* 33 Green Close, Mayals, SWANSEA, SA3 5DN.

LAKE, Miss. Joanna, BSc ACA *1993;* 12 Hunter Road, Wimbledon, LONDON, SW20 8NZ.

LAKE, Miss. Joanne Carolyn, BA ACA CF *1990;* Evolution Securities Ltd Kings House, 1 King Street, LEEDS, LS1 2HH.

LAKE, Mr. John Rex, FCA *1966;* 9 Ashcroft Close, HARPENDEN, HERTFORDSHIRE, AL5 1JJ. (Life Member)

LAKE, Mr. Jonathan Robert, BSc ACA *1994;* The Gables, 135 Hale Road, Hale, ALTRINCHAM, CHESHIRE, WA15 9HQ.

LAKE, Miss. Marianne, BSc ACA *1995;* 525 East 11th Street, Apt 3B, NEW YORK, NY 10009, UNITED STATES.

LAKE, Mr. Martin James, BSc ACA *1991;* 3 Orchard Close, Welford on Avon, STRATFORD-UPON-AVON, WARWICKSHIRE, CV37 8HA.

LAKE, Mrs. Melanie Jane, BA(Hons) ACA *2000;* Ground Floor Flat, 13 Vyvyan Terrace, BRISTOL, BS8 3DG.

•LAKE, Mr. Michael Edward, FCA *1962;* LB Group Ltd, 82 East Hill, COLCHESTER, CO1 2QW.

LAKE, Mr. Nicholas William Givan, MA FCA *1978;* The Coach House, Wild Oak Lane, Trull, TAUNTON, SOMERSET, TA3 7JS.

LAKE, Mrs. Nicola Louise, BSc ACA *2000;* 5 Greensand Ridge, Lidlington, BEDFORD, MK43 0PB.

LAKE, Mr. Nigel Timothy Johnson, MA ACA *1993;* Pottinger, Level 35 AMP Centre, 50 Bridge Street, SYDNEY, NSW 2000, AUSTRALIA.

LAKE, Mr. Oliver James, ACA *2008;* Straight Plc, 1 Whitehall Riverside, LEEDS, LS1 4BN.

LAKE, Mr. Paul Edward, BA ACA *1990;* PO Box 989, Seeb Airport CPO, 111 SEEB, OMAN.

LAKE, Mr. Robert Hamilton, FCA *1968;* Red Oaks, Tye Common Road, BILLERICAY, CM12 9NX. (Life Member)

LAKE, Mr. Robert John, BA ACA *2004;* Flat 72 White House, Vicarage Crescent, LONDON, SW11 3LH.

LAKE, Miss. Robyn, BSc ACA *2009;* Flat 6, Lyon House, 53 Riding House Street, LONDON, W1W 7ED.

LAKE, Mrs. Samantha Maria, BSc ACA *1998;* 111 Grantham Avenue, Great Notley, BRAINTREE, ESSEX, CM77 7FP.

•LAKE, Mr. Simon Geoffrey, FCA *1983;* 8 Church Croft, Edlesborough, DUNSTABLE, BEDFORDSHIRE, LU6 2HU.

LAKE, Mr. Simon Neville, MA FCA *1981;* (Tax Fac), Westgate Farmhouse, 43 West Green, Barrington, CAMBRIDGE, CB22 7RZ.

LAKE, Mr. Stephen Clyde, MBA BA ACA *1984;* Highfields, Cleeve Hill, CHELTENHAM, GLOUCESTERSHIRE, GL52 3PX.

LAKE, Mr. Steven Richard, BSc ACA *1989;* Associated British Ports Ocean Gate, Atlantic Way Eastern Docks, SOUTHAMPTON, SO14 3QN.

LAKE, Miss. Tammy Anne, BA(Hons) ACA *2002;* Onslow Capital Management Limited, 2 Babmaes Street, LONDON, SW1Y 6HD.

LAKE, Ms. Tania Claire, BSc ACA *1992;* 7 Dowry Square, BRISTOL, BS8 4SH.

LAKE, Mr. Timothy William Crompton, FCA *1965;* Stone Cottage Rayne Hatch, Stisted, BRAINTREE, ESSEX, CM77 8BY. (Life Member)

•LAKE, Mr. Trevor Michael, FCA *1995;* LB Group Limited, 1 Vicarage Lane, Stratford, LONDON, E15 4HF.

LAKE, Miss. Victoria Elizabeth, BA ACA *2005;* Accenture Plantation Place, 30 Fenchurch Street, LONDON, EC3M 3BD.

LAKEMAN, Mr. Ceri Boon, FCA *1959;* Briar Cottage, Meadow Lane, West Wittering, CHICHESTER, PO20 8LR. (Life Member)

LAKEMAN, Mrs. Helen, BA ACA *2007;* 96 Alwyn Street, Aigburth, LIVERPOOL, L17 7DY.

LAKEMAN, Miss. Peggy Patricia Violet, FCA *1967;* Mildenhall, 36 Houghton Road South, CARLISLE, CA3 0LA. (Life Member)

•LAKEMAN, Mr. Richard Andrew, FCA *1968;* Cheriton House Cottage, South Cheriton, TEMPLECOMBE, SOMERSET, BA8 0BS.

Members - Alphabetical LAKER - LAM

LAKER, Mr. Richard Stephen, BSc(Hons) ACA *2001;* Northgate Plc, Norflex House, 20 Allington Way, DARLINGTON, COUNTY DURHAM, DL1 4DY.

•**LAKHA, Mr. Azim Mohamedali Sunderji, FCA** *1979;* (Tax Fac), Hamsun & Hogate, 2 Bramber Court, 2 Bramber Road, LONDON, W14 9PA.

LAKHANI, Mr. Arun Ashok, BSc ACA *2005;* Apt. 2804 Al Murjan Towers, Dubai Marina, PO Box 48748, DUBAI, UNITED ARAB EMIRATES.

•**LAKHANI, Mr. Atulkumar G, BSc FCA** *1986;* Lakhani & Co, 25 Station Road, Desford, LEICESTER, LE9 9FN. See also Baker Consultancy Ltd

LAKHANI, Mr. Bimal Chandrakant, BSc(Hons) ACA *2001;* 27 Gloucester Road, BARNET, HERTFORDSHIRE, EN5 1RT.

LAKHANI, Mrs. Bindi, BSc ACA *1996;* 55 Kew Crescent, SUTTON, SM3 9RU.

LAKHANI, Mr. Bipinchandra Jadavji Jivandas, FCA *1970;* Maxwells (Kensington) & Co, 148 Gloucester Road, LONDON, SW7 4SZ.

•**LAKHANI, Mrs. Daksha, FCA** *1986;* Robert Clow & Co Ltd, 40-44 High Street, NORTHWOOD, MIDDLESEX, HA6 1BN.

LAKHANI, Mr. Himanshurai Chhagalal Liladhar, ACA *1979;* 2 Elliot Close, DONVALE, VIC 3111, AUSTRALIA.

•**LAKHANI, Mr. Jayendra Sunderji, ACA FCCA** *1980;* (Tax Fac), Nagle Jay Ltd, 100 College Road, HARROW, HA1 1BQ.

LAKHANI, Miss. Kashmira, BA ACA *1993;* 251 Kings Road, Rayners Lane, HARROW, HA2 9LF.

•**LAKHANI, Mr. Kaushik Jagjivan, FCA** *1978;* (Tax Fac), Lakers, 3 Galley House, Moon Lane, BARNET, HERTFORDSHIRE, EN5 5YL.

LAKHANI, Mr. Kinner Ratilal, BSc ACA *1998;* 41 Gyles Park, STANMORE, MIDDLESEX, HA7 1AN.

LAKHANI, Mr. Mahesh Mohanlal, BA ACA *1991;* 12 Grayrigg Road, Maidenbower, CRAWLEY, WEST SUSSEX, RH10 7AB.

LAKHANI, Mrs. Mayuri, BA ACA *1996;* Leewood, Kingswood Avenue, Tylers Green, Penn, HIGH WYCOMBE, BUCKINGHAMSHIRE HP10 8DR.

LAKHANI, Mr. Nimish Natvarlal, BSc ACA *1993;* 22 Campden Crescent, WEMBLEY, MIDDLESEX, HA0 3JQ.

LAKHANI, Miss. Nisha Jayendra, ACA *2009;* Sunder Nivas, Park View Road, PINNER, MIDDLESEX, HA5 3YF.

•**LAKHANI, Mr. Pankaj Bhuralal, BSc FCA** *1987;* MapleWoods Partnership, 74 The Drive, North Harrow, HARROW, MIDDLESEX, HA2 7EJ.

LAKHANI, Mr. Raees, BCom FCA *1983;* 2 Chiltern Park Thornbury, BRISTOL, BS35 2HX.

LAKHANI, Miss. Rakhee, BSc ACA *2005;* 59 Sheringham Avenue, LONDON, N14 4UH.

•**LAKHANI, Mr. Satish, BA FCA** *1983;* (Tax Fac), Lake & Co, 25a Kenton Park Parade, Kenton RoadKenton, HARROW, HA3 8DN.

LAKHANI, Mr. Shelein, BA ACA *2007;* with Ernst & Young LLP, 1 More London Place, LONDON, SE1 2AF.

LAKHANI, Miss. Sonal, ACA *2008;* (Tax Fac), 12 The Drive, EDGWARE, MIDDLESEX, HA8 8PT.

•**LAKHANI, Mr. Subhash Kanjibhai, FCA** *1978;* Templetons (UK) Ltd, 309 Hoe Street, LONDON, E17 9BG.

LAKHANI, Mr. Tulan, BSc ACA *1994;* Level 7 Exchange Square, Bangunan Bursa Malaysia, Bukit Kewangan, 50200 KUALA LUMPUR, FEDERAL TERRITORY, MALAYSIA.

LAKHI, Mr. Aboobakar Ismail, BSc ACA *2001;* with British American Investment Co. (MTIUS) Ltd, BAI Building, 25 Pope Hennessy Street, PO Box 331, PORT LOUIS, MAURITIUS.

LAKHOTIA, Mr. Shashikant, BSc ACA *2006;* Anand Associates, 10 Glentworth Street, Berkeley Court, LONDON, NW1 5PG.

LAKHUMALANI, Mr. Bhagvan Divanising, FCA *1939;* 84 Mira Housing Society, Salisbury Park Road, PUNE 1-411001, INDIA. (Life Member)

LAKIN, Mr. Andrew David, BSc ACA *1991;* Cherry Cottage, Broughton Crescent, Barlaston, STOKE-ON-TRENT, ST12 9DD.

•**LAKIN, Miss. Anne, BA ACA** *1989;* Baker Tilly Tax & Advisory Services LLP, Festival Way, Festival Park, STOKE-ON-TRENT, ST1 5BB. See also Baker Tilly UK Audit LLP

LAKIN, Mr. Bruce Ivan Lawrence, BA FCA *1987;* Sanyo Europe Ltd, 18 Colonial Way, WATFORD, WD24 4PT.

•**LAKIN, Mr. David, ACA** *1984;* Lakin Accounting Services Limited, Manor Lodge, Teeton, NORTHAMPTON, NN6 8LH.

LAKIN, Mrs. Elizabeth Mary, ACA *2008;* Suite 411, 1321 Kensington Close NW, CALGARY T2N 3J6, AL, CANADA.

•**LAKIN, Mr. Keith, BSc FCA** *1980;* (Tax Fac), Lakin & Co, The Neuk, 46 Caryl Road, LYTHAM ST. ANNES, FY8 2QB.

•**LAKIN, Mr. Mark Philip, FCA** *1968;* Lakin & Co., Rest Hill House, Over Worton, CHIPPING NORTON, OXFORDSHIRE, OX7 7EN.

LAKIN, Mr. Ronald John, FCA *1959;* 96 Central Avenue, HERNE BAY, CT6 8RR. (Life Member)

LAKKOTRIPIS, Mr. Giorgos, BA ACA *2010;* 22 Orthodoxias Street, Anthoupoli, 2304 NICOSIA, CYPRUS.

LAKOUFI JOHNSON, Mrs. Aliki, BSc ACA *1992;* 15 KORYTSAS STREET, AGIOS ANDREAS, 1107 NICOSIA, CYPRUS.

LAKOUFIS, Mr. Nicholas Neophytou, FCA *1960;* P. O. Box 21381, 1507 NICOSIA, CYPRUS.

LAKRA, Mr. Homi, FCA *1967;* 382 Elgin Mills Road West, RICHMOND HILL L4C 4M2, ON, CANADA.

•**LAKSHMAN, Mr. Vir, MBA ACA** *1984;* KPMG AG Wirtschaftsprufungsgesellschaft, Tersteegenstrasse19-31, 40474 DUSSELDORF, GERMANY.

LAKSHMANAN, Ms. Chithra Olagu, ACA *2001;* 92 Watling Street, ST. ALBANS, HERTFORDSHIRE, AL1 2QG.

LAL, Mr. Ajay, BSc ACA ACT *1993;* 20 Halland Way, NORTHWOOD, MIDDLESEX, HA6 2AG.

LAL, Mr. Brij, FCA *1966;* Strand V 43, 1545 HVITSTEN, NORWAY. (Life Member)

LAL, Mr. Harry Krishna, BSc ACA *1995;* 85 Hornsey Road, Holloway, LONDON, N7 6DJ.

LALA, Mr. Aslam Hashim, BA ACA *1989;* 12 Lancelot Close, Windsor Meadows, SLOUGH, SL1 9DX.

LALA, Mr. Pharok Soli, ACA *1983;* Rajesh Mansion, M.Karve Road, Churchgate, MUMBAI 400020, MAHARASHTRA, INDIA.

LALANI, Mr. Azim, BA ACA *1990;* 9 Clarence Road, WINDSOR, SL4 5AE.

LALANI, Mr. Barkatali Jumabhai, FCA *1974;* 144 B WEST 16TH STREET, NORTH VANCOUVER V7M1T5, BC, CANADA.

LALEK, Miss. Emma Marie, BSc ACA *2010;* 28 Forest Drive, Broughton, CHESTER, CH4 0QJ.

LALJI, Mr. Amirali Rashid, FCA *1967;* AMIR R-Lalji, 3964 Ruby Avenue, NORTH VANCOUVER V7R 4B2, BC, CANADA.

LALJI, Mr. Mustafa, BSc(Hons) ACA *2002;* Honey Pot Cosmetics (Wholesale) Ltd, Unit 4A Parr Road, STANMORE, MIDDLESEX, HA7 1NL.

LALL, Mr. Dharam Bir, FCA ACMA *1964;* 17 Stradbroke Drive, CHIGWELL, IG7 5QU. (Life Member)

LALL, Mrs. Nikita, BSc ACA *2010;* 33 Raymere Gardens, LONDON, SE18 2LB.

LALLEMAND, Mr. Christopher John, BSc FCA CTA *1991;* (Tax Fac), 4 Jasons Drive, GUILDFORD, SURREY, GU4 7XG.

LALLI, Mr. Sukhjit Singh, BSc(Hons) ACA *2001;* 2528 Woodpark Place, ABBOTSFORD V2S 0A5, BC, CANADA.

LALLOO, Mr. Abdur Raouf, MSc ACA *1992;* Villa 1, Shaker Village, P.O. Box 10994, JEDDAH, 21443, SAUDI ARABIA.

LALLOO, Mr. Abdur Rashid, MSc ACA *1996;* Sunny View, Causeway Close, POTTERS BAR, HERTFORDSHIRE, EN6 5HW.

LALLY, Miss. Alison Mary, BA FCA CPFA *1993;* 20 Flinchwell Road, SHEFFIELD, S13 9AS.

•**LALLY, Mr. Daniel Brendan, BA ACA** *2005;* Daniel Lally, Flat 3, 76 Shooters Hill Road, Blackheath, LONDON, SE3 7BG.

•**LALLY, Mr. Kevin Patrick, BA ACA DChA** *1984;* Knox Cropper, 8-9 Well Court, LONDON, EC4M 9DN.

LALLY, Mr. Kevin William, MEng ACA CISA *1999;* Mitford House Station Road, Gilling East, YORK, YO62 4JL.

•**LALOR, Mr. Edward, BCL FCA** *1975;* Lalor Holohan & Company, Church Street, WICKLOW, COUNTY WICKLOW, IRELAND. See also Lalor Holsman & Company

LALOR, Mrs. Lucinda Jane Lancaster, BSc ACA *1993;* Windgarth, Mark Way, GODALMING, SURREY, GU7 2BL.

LALOR, Ms. Sarah, BEng ACA *2009;* 3/297 Edgecliff Road, Woollahra, WOOLLAHRA, NSW 2025, AUSTRALIA.

LALRIA, Miss. Gursharn, ACA *2011;* 35 Sevenlands Drive, Boulton Moor, DERBY, DE24 5AD.

LALRIA, Mr. Rajinder Singh, BA ACA *2000;* 296 Leigh Hunt Drive, LONDON, N14 6BZ.

LALSING, Mr. Anthony, ACA *2009;* 7 Parklawn Avenue, EPSOM, SURREY, KT18 7SQ.

LALSODAGAR, Mr. Dipak Mahendra, ACA *1986;* 20 Gallows Hill Lane, ABBOTS LANGLEY, HERTFORDSHIRE, WD5 0DA.

LALVANI, Mr. Ranjit Tolaram, BSc FCA *1967;* 9 Oval View, 150 M Karve Road, Churchgate, MUMBAI 400020, INDIA. (Life Member)

LALWANI, Mr. Kamal, BSc ACA *1991;* 59 Yeldham Road, LONDON, W6 8JQ.

LAM, Mr. Andrew, BSc(Hons) ACA *2000;* Flat 23C, 1 Tai Hang Road, WAN CHAI, HONG KONG ISLAND, HONG KONG SAR.

•**LAM, Mr. Andrew Hung-Yun, BA FCA** *1990;* 10 FL Harbour View Terrace, 112 Tin Hau Temple Road, NORTH POINT, HONG KONG ISLAND, HONG KONG SAR.

LAM, Mr. Anthony Robert, BA(Hons) ACA *2003;* Level 11 Angel Place, 123 Pitt Street, SYDNEY, NSW 2000, AUSTRALIA.

LAM, Mr. Cheuk Ming, FCA *1975;* P O Box 73021, Kowloon Central Post Office, YAU MA TEI, KOWLOON, HONG KONG SAR. (Life Member)

LAM, Mr. Cheung, ACA *2007;* The Wittgensteins, 1003 10/F, Silvercord Tower 1, 30 Canton Road, TSIM SHA TSUI, KOWLOON HONG KONG SAR.

LAM, Mr. Cheung Shing, ACA *2008;* Room D 31/F. Block 12 Tierra Verde, TSING YI, HONG KONG SAR.

LAM, Mr. Chi Keung, BSc ACA *2005;* Flat 80 Studley Court, 4 Jamestown Way, LONDON, E14 2DA.

LAM, Mr. Chi Ming, ACA *2008;* Flat 9 4/F, Cheong Tai Building, 120 Tseuk Luk Street, SAN PO KONG, HONG KONG SAR.

LAM, Mr. Chi Sun Jason, ACA *2005;* Units 1103-4 Chinachem, Johnston Plaza, 178-186 Johnston Road, WAN CHAI, HONG KONG ISLAND, HONG KONG SAR.

LAM, Mr. Chi Yuen, ACA *2004;* Nelson and Company CPA, Room 304 3/F Tung Wah Mansion, 199 - 203 Hennessy Road, WAN CHAI, HONG KONG ISLAND, HONG KONG SAR.

LAM, Mr. Chi Yung, ACA *2008;* Flat E, 33/F, Block 5, Royal Ascot, SHA TIN, NEW TERRITORIES HONG KONG SAR.

LAM, Mr. Chin Chiu, ACA *2007;* Gary C.C. Lam & Co, Room 1501 15th Floor, Shanghai Industrial Investment Building 48-62 Hennessy Road, WAN CHAI, HONG KONG ISLAND, HONG KONG SAR.

LAM, Ms. Ching Chi, ACA *2007;* ICICI Bank UK Plc, Frankfurt Branch, Mainzer Landstr. 69 - 71, 60329 FRANKFURT AM MAIN, GERMANY.

LAM, Mr. Ching Hing, MSc ACA *1984;* 25E Tai Shan Mansion, Tai Koo Shing, Tai Koo Shing Road, QUARRY BAY, HONG KONG SAR.

LAM, Ms. Ching Quen Queenie, ACA *2005;* Flat B 1/F Mantin Court, 6 Homantin Hill Road, HO MAN TIN, KOWLOON, HONG KONG SAR.

LAM, Ms. Choi Kam Miranda, ACA *2008;* C K Lam & Co, Unit 704, Fourseas Building, 208-212 Nathan Road, KOWLOON CITY, KOWLOON HONG KONG SAR.

LAM, Ms. Chui Kwan, ACA *2007;* Duplex 3, Dynasty Villa 12, Dynasty Heights, Beacon Hill, KOWLOON TONG, KOWLOON HONG KONG SAR.

LAM, Mr. David, ACA *2009;* 49 Manor Drive North, NEW MALDEN, SURREY, KT3 5NY.

LAM, Mr. Firoz Maneckshaw, FCA *1958;* Keki Court, 3rd Floor, Cumballa Hill Road, MUMBAI 400036, MAHARASHTRA, INDIA. (Life Member)

LAM, Mr. Framsy Dinshaw, FCA *1963;* 51 Wilmington Avenue, Chiswick, LONDON, W4 3HA.

LAM, Ms. Fung Ha, ACA *2011;* Flat 10B Jenny's Court, 241-243 Sai Yee Street, MONG KOK, KOWLOON, HONG KONG SAR.

LAM, Ms. Fung Ming Sandra, ACA *2008;* Room 212, Block M, Kornhill, QUARRY BAY, HONG KONG SAR.

LAM, Ms. Fung Ying Sara, ACA *2005;* 7 Harris Street, ROSEBERY, NSW 2018, AUSTRALIA.

LAM, Mr. Gee Chiu, BSc ACA *2010;* 1 Baron Close, Friern Barnet, LONDON, N11 3PS.

LAM, Mr. Hin Chi, ACA *2008;* Flat G, 19/F Orchid Court, New Town Plaza 3, SHA TIN, NEW TERRITORIES, HONG KONG SAR.

LAM, Mr. Hing Chau Leon, ACA *2004;* 7/F Blk B Eastern Sea Ind Bldg., 48-56 Tai Lin Pai Road, KWAI CHUNG, NEW TERRITORIES, HONG KONG SAR.

LAM, Miss. Hiu Ling, ACA *2004;* Flat 7 21/F Tower 1, The Metropolis Residence, 8 Metropolis Drive, HUNG HOM, KOWLOON, HONG KONG SAR.

•**LAM, Mr. Hoi Ham, FCA** *1970;* H.H.Lam & Co, Yu To Sang Bldg 9/F, 37 Queens Road, CENTRAL, Hong Kong Island, HONG KONG SAR.

LAM, Mr. Hoi Yiu, ACA *2007;* FLAT B 15/F JADE SUITES 600 CANTON ROAD, YAU MA TEI, HONG KONG SAR.

LAM, Mr. Hok Wai, ACA *2008;* Flat 4, 13/F Treasury Tower, Shatin Plaza, SHA TIN, NT, HONG KONG SAR.

LAM, Ms. Hon Ying Gloria, ACA *2007;* Flat 10, 9/F, Rondall Bldg, 168 Tai Po Road, SHAM SHUI PO, KOWLOON HONG KONG SAR.

LAM, Miss. Hu Fan Rita, BSc ACA *1990;* House 30, Price Road, 2-32 Jardine Terrace, JARDINE'S LOOKOUT, HONG KONG ISLAND, HONG KONG SAR.

LAM, Miss. Ivy A W, BSc ACA *2007;* 161 Stoke Road, GOSPORT, HAMPSHIRE, PO12 1SE.

LAM, Mr. J Fung Edward, ACA *2008;* Flat 2A, 8 Ede Road, KOWLOON TONG, HONG KONG SAR.

LAM, Ms. Judy Ming Wai, ACA *2006;* Room 1803, Block 29, Heng Fa Chuen, CHAI WAN, HONG KONG ISLAND, HONG KONG SAR.

LAM, Mr. Ka Cheong, ACA *2008;* Flat D, 3/F Hyde Park Masion 53, Paterson St, CAUSEWAY BAY, HONG KONG SAR.

LAM, Mr. Ka Lun, ACA FCCA CPA *2008;* Ka Lun Lam & Co, Unit F 15th Floor, Seabright Plaza, 9 -23 Shell Street, NORTH POINT, HONG KONG SAR.

LAM, Mr. Ka Ning, ACA *2008;* Flat E 28/F, Tower 3 Manhattan Hill, 1 Po Lun Street, LAI CHI KOK, KOWLOON, HONG KONG SAR.

LAM, Mrs. Kathy Pui Yee, MSci ACA *2009;* 6 Watchet Court, Furzton, MILTON KEYNES, MK4 1HE.

LAM, Mr. Kenneth, ACA *2004;* Airbus China Limited, Tianwei Erjie, Tian Zhu Airport Industrial Zone, Shunyi District, P.O. Box 3420, BEIJING 101312 CHINA.

LAM, Mr. Kenneth Gee Kin, MSci ACA *2006;* 18 Blossom Drive, ORPINGTON, BR6 0AS.

LAM, Mr. Kim Yuen, ACA *2007;* 4th Floor, No.104 Wing Kwong Street, TO KWA WAN, KOWLOON, HONG KONG SAR.

LAM, Mr. Kin Kau Mark, ACA *2005;* Mark K. Lam & Co, Room A3 13th Floor, Wing Chzong Commercial Building, 19-25 Jervis Street, CENTRAL, HONG KONG ISLAND HONG KONG SAR. See also Mark K. Lam

LAM, Mr. Kin Kwok, ACA *2005;* Room D 11/F, 99 Caine Road, CENTRAL, HONG KONG ISLAND, HONG KONG SAR.

LAM, Mr. Kin Leung, ACA *2005;* K. L. Lam & Co., 2/F Xiu Ping Commercial Building, 104 Jervois Street, SHEUNG WAN, HONG KONG ISLAND, HONG KONG SAR.

LAM, Mr. Kin Wo, ACA *2007;* Grand Dynasty View, Blk. 29 7E No. 9, Ma Wo Road, TAI PO, NEW TERRITORIES, HONG KONG SAR.

LAM, Ms. Kit Wah, ACA *2008;* Flat F 7/F Block 3, Site 1, Whampoa Garden, HUNG HOM, KOWLOON, HONG KONG SAR.

LAM, Miss. Kit-Lai, BA ACA DChA *2001;* 30 Erskine Crescent, Ferry Lane, LONDON, N17 9PA.

LAM, Mr. Kwok Ming, ACA *2008;* Flat 3 6/F, Block A, Kwong Chiu Terrace, 4 Fortress Hill Road, NORTH POINT, HONG KONG SAR.

LAM, Mr. Lap Wai, ACA *2008;* Flat 9, 10/F Block A, Kornhill, QUARRY BAY, HONG KONG ISLAND, HONG KONG SAR.

LAM, Ms. Lin Chu, ACA *2008;* Flat F 55/F, Tower 9, Island Resort, CHAI WAN, HONG KONG SAR.

•**LAM, Mrs. Linda Chay Leng, BSc FCA** *1990;* (Tax Fac), Lam & Co, 94 Orchard Gate, GREENFORD, UB6 0QP.

LAM, Ms. Lu Na Luna, ACA *2008;* Luna Lam & Co, Room 801, The Centre Mark, 287-299 Queen's Road Central, CENTRAL, HONG KONG SAR.

LAM, Mr. Man Chi, ACA *2009;* Room 1009, Lung Fung House, Lower Wong Tai Sin Estate, KOWLOON PEAK, HONG KONG SAR.

LAM, Mr. Man Ho, ACA *2011;* Flat 1709, Block G, Kornhill, QUARRY BAY, HONG KONG SAR.

LAM, Miss. May-Ling, ACA *2009;* 35 Birchmead Avenue, PINNER, MIDDLESEX, HA5 2BQ.

LAM, Ms. Mei Lan, ACA *2007;* Flat E 11/F Block 11, Laguna City, CHA KWO LING, KOWLOON, HONG KONG SAR.

LAM, Ms. Nga Lai Alice, ACA *2008;* Flat F 30th Floor, Fu Bon Court, Fortress Garden, 32 Fortress Hill Road, NORTH POINT, HONG KONG SAR.

LAM, Mr. Nicholas, LLM ACA *2011;* 32 Ruskin, Henley Road, Caversham, READING, RG4 6LE.

LAM, Ms. Oi Man Vivian, ACA *2008;* HH Lam & Co, Room 905-909 Yu To Sang Building, 37 Queens Road, CENTRAL, HONG KONG SAR.

LAM, Ms. Oi Yan Fiona, ACA *2005;* Room 905-909, Yu To Sang Building, Ka Ning Path, CAUSEWAY BAY, HONG KONG ISLAND, HONG KONG SAR.

LAM, Ms. On Na Anna, ACA *2008;* Flat E, 32/F, Fullview Court, 32 Fortress Hill Road, NORTH POINT, HONG KONG ISLAND HONG KONG SAR.

LAM - LAMB
Members - Alphabetical

LAM, Mr. Pak Hay, ACA *2005;* P.H.Lam & Company, Room 1602, Tung Hip Commercial Building, 244-252 Des Voeux Road, CENTRAL, HONG KONG ISLAND HONG KONG SAR.
LAM, Mr. Patrick Shu Yan, ACA *1983;* 72 Caravan Head Road, OYSTER BAY, NSW 2225, AUSTRALIA.
LAM, Mr. Patrick Wai-Hon, FCA MBA *1989;* NWS Holdings Ltd, 28 Floor New World Tower, 18 Queen's Road, CENTRAL, HONG KONG ISLAND, HONG KONG SAR.
LAM, Mr. Peter Kwai Choi, ACA *2005;* Peter Lam & co., Suite 1807 The Gateway, Tower II Harbour City, 25 Canton Road, TSIM SHA TSIU, KOWLOON HONG KONG SAR.
LAM, Ms. Pik Wah, ACA *2007;* 2407, High Block, Shek Chun House, Shek Lei Est, KWAI CHUNG, NEW TERRITORIES HONG KONG SAR.
LAM, Ms. Pik Kwan, ACA *2011;* (Tax Fac), 16A Yae Lam Court, Lucky Plaza, SHA TIN, HONG KONG SAR.
LAM, Mr. Ping Shan, BA(Hons) FCA *1988;* Flat 3C Amber Garden, 110 Blue Pool Road, HAPPY VALLEY, HONG KONG ISLAND, HONG KONG SAR.
LAM, Mr. Pui Sum, ACA *2009;* Flat 26H Block 4, Chi Fu Fa Yuen, POK FU LAM, HONG KONG SAR.
LAM, Ms. Pui Yin, ACA *2010;* Flat F 32/F Block 28, Park Island, MA WAN, NEW TERRITORIES, HONG KONG SAR.
LAM, Miss. Rachel Yee Man, BA(Hons) ACA *2003;* Flat 546, 6 St. George Wharf, LONDON, SW8 2JE.
LAM, Mr. Rainier Hok Chung, BA LLB ACA *1982;* 555 Victoria Road, Block 20 11th Floor Flat C, Baguio Villa, POK FU LAM, HONG KONG ISLAND, HONG KONG SAR.
LAM, Mr. Robert Hu Yang, BA ACA *1994;* 30 Price Road, JARDINE'S LOOKOUT, HONG KONG SAR.
LAM, Miss. Selina, ACA *2011;* 59 Fernwood Crescent, LONDON, N20 0RP.
LAM, Miss. Sheena Fung Sang, BSc ACA *2007;* 530 South Hewitt Street, Unit 527, LOS ANGELES, CA 90013, UNITED STATES.
LAM, Ms. Shu Man, ACA *2008;* Flat C, 26/F, Block 3, Hanford Garden, Castle Peak Bay, TUEN MUN NEW TERRITORIES HONG KONG SAR.
LAM, Ms. Shuk Kwan, ACA *2008;* with PricewaterhouseCoopers, 19/F Tower A, Manulife Financial Centre, 223-231 Wai Yip Street, KWUN TONG, KOWLOON HONG KONG SAR.
LAM, Ms. Shuk Man, ACA *2008;* Flat H, 31/F, Block two, The Belcher's, 89 Pok Fu Lam Road, POK FU LAM HONG KONG SAR.
LAM, Mr. Sik On, ACA *2008;* Unit H 8/F Block 2, Villa Esplanada, 8 Nga Ying Chau Street, TSING YI, NT, HONG KONG SAR.
•**LAM, Mr. Simon Siu Lun, ACA** *1979;* S.L. Lam & Company, Rooms 1804-5, The Centre Mark, 287-299 Queen's Road, CENTRAL, HONG KONG ISLAND HONG KONG SAR.
LAM, Mr. Siu Hung, ACA *2007;* Lam Siu Hung & Co, Room 1602, Chit Lee Commercial Building, 30-36 Shau Kei Wan Road, SHAU KEI WAN, HONG KONG ISLAND HONG KONG SAR.
LAM, Ms. Siu Wai, BA ACA *1994;* Flat B, 8/F Block 1, Victoria Garden, 301 Victoria Road, POK FU LAM, HONG KONG ISLAND HONG KONG SAR.
LAM, Ms. Siu Yin, BA ACA TEP *1996;* Flat A 20/F, Kelford Mansion, 168 Hollywood Road, SHEUNG WAN, HONG KONG ISLAND, HONG KONG SAR.
LAM, Mr. Son Gia, BA ACA *2006;* 230 Grange Road, LONDON, E13 0HB.
LAM, Miss. Soo Li Joyce, ACA *1993;* 75E Koon Seng Road, SINGAPORE 427018, SINGAPORE.
LAM, Mr. Stephen Sou Wing, BSc FCA *1966;* Block B Flat 4, 7th Floor, Ventris Place, 19-23b Ventris Road, HAPPY VALLEY, HONG KONG ISLAND HONG KONG SAR.
LAM, Mr. Steven Foong-Sin, BSc ACA *1992;* 22 St Johns Road, SUTTON, SM1 3JA.
LAM, Mr. Steven Kai Bong, BSc ACA *1997;* Barclays Capital, 5 North Colonnade, LONDON, E14 4BB.
LAM, Mr. Steven Wai-Chung, BSc ACA *1997;* Flat 42G Tower 5, The Belchers, 89 Pokfulam Road, POK FU LAM, HONG KONG ISLAND, HONG KONG SAR.
LAM, Mr. Teck Yeow Leonard, BA(Econ) ACA *2000;* 1003 Bukit Timah Road, #10-07, SINGAPORE 596289, SINGAPORE.
LAM, Mr. Thomas Wing Kin, BSc ACA *1984;* Unit E5 Commerce Park, Southgate, FROME, SOMERSET, BA11 2RY.
LAM, Mr. Tim, BS ACA *2011;* Apartment 306, Marshall Building, 3 Hermitage Street, LONDON, W2 1PB.
LAM, Dr. Tin Yan, ACA *2006;* Flat 14C, Block 4, Whampoa Garden, Site 5, HUNG HOM, KOWLOON HONG KONG SAR.
LAM, Mr. Tin Faat, ACA *2008;* TF Lam & Company, Unit 2105, 21/F Exchange Tower, 33 Wang Chiu Road, KOWLOON BAY, HONG KONG SAR. See also Lam & Company
LAM, Mr. Ting Chung Wilfred, ACA *2009;* KPMG, 8/F Princes Building, 10 Chater Road, CENTRAL, HONG KONG SAR.
LAM, Mr. To Ming, ACA *2008;* House 25, 26th Street, Hong Lok Yuen, TAI PO, NEW TERRITORIES, HONG KONG SAR.
LAM, Mr. Toby Chun Hoong, BSc FCA *1961;* c/o Lot 10 The Highway Centre, Jalan 51/205, 46050 PETALING JAYA, SELANGOR, MALAYSIA. (Life Member)
LAM, Mr. Victor Chee Peng, BA ACA *1992;* 2A Jalan PJU 1A/27, Ara Damansara, 47301 PETALING JAYA, SELANGOR, MALAYSIA.
LAM, Miss. Virginia Wai Man, MSc ACA *1988;* 6c Evergreen Gardens, 18 Shouson Hill Road, SHOUSON HILL, HONG KONG ISLAND, HONG KONG SAR.
LAM, Mr. Wai Hon, BA FCA *1981;* Apt E-1 16th Floor, Villa Monte Rosa, 41A Stubbs Road, HAPPY VALLEY, HONG KONG ISLAND, HONG KONG SAR.
LAM, Ms. Wai Man Vera, ACA *2005;* 3728 Nightstar Drive, MISSISSAUGA L5M 7Z7, ON, CANADA.
LAM, Mr. Wai Ming Calvin, ACA *2008;* Deloitte Touche Tohmatsu, 35/F One Pacific Place, 88 Queensway, CENTRAL, HONG KONG ISLAND, HONG KONG SAR.
LAM, Mr. Wai Nang William, ACA *2008;* with PricewaterhouseCoopers, 26/F Office Tower A, Beijing Fortune Plaza, 23 Dongsanhuan North Road, Chaoyang District, BEIJING 100020 CHINA.
LAM, Mr. Wai Shing Canvas, ACA *2010;* Flat H 9/F. Tower 1 Greenwood Terrace, 2 Tai Man Street, WAN CHAI, HONG KONG SAR.
LAM, Ms. Wai Sze, ACA *2006;* Flat B 12/F Block 1, Provident Centre, 21 Wharf Road, NORTH POINT, HONG KONG ISLAND, HONG KONG SAR.
LAM, Mr. Weng Liong, FCA *1981;* B2-08 Pangsapuri Seri Jati, Jalan PH4, Taman Puchong Hartamas, PUCHONG, MALAYSIA.
LAM, Mr. William Michael, MSc BA ACA *2002;* 36 Vicarage Road, HENLEY-ON-THAMES, OXFORDSHIRE, RG9 1HW.
LAM, Miss. Wing Chi Wincy, BSc ACA *1993;* KPMG, 8/F Prince's Building, 10 Chater Road, CENTRAL, HONG KONG SAR.
LAM, Mr. Wing-Keung Vincent, ACA *2007;* Flat D, 16/F, Block one, Coymon Rise, 29 Ka Wai Man Road, KENNEDY TOWN HONG KONG SAR.
LAM, Mr. Woon Cheung Desmond, ACA *2007;* 17 Babington Path, Flat C 5/F, Kingsford Height, MID LEVELS, HONG KONG SAR.
LAM, Mr. Wye Keong, ACA *1984;* Scanhouse UK Limited, Kinetic Centre, Theobald Street, BOREHAMWOOD, WD6 4PJ.
LAM, Mr. Yat Chung Paul, ACA *2005;* 2/F Kong Ling Building, 102 Jervois Street, SHEUNG WAN, HONG KONG ISLAND, HONG KONG SAR.
LAM, Mr. Yat Ngok, ACA *2009;* Flat 6B Sung Ling Mansion, 1A Babington Path, MID LEVELS, HONG KONG ISLAND, HONG KONG SAR.
LAM, Mr. Yick Wah Kalvin, ACA *2008;* Room 1524, Chung Chun House, Chung Nga Court, TAI PO, NEW TERRITORIES, HONG KONG SAR.
LAM, Mr. Yik Yin, ACA *2008;* Lam Yik Yin & Co, Room 802, 8/F, Lee Kiu Building, 51 Jordan Road, YAU MA TEI KOWLOON HONG KONG SAR.
LAM, Mr. Yiu Kwong, ACA *2008;* Flat B 30/F, Cornwall Court, 54 King's Road, NORTH POINT, HONG KONG ISLAND, HONG KONG SAR.
LAM, Mr. Yiu-Kin, ACA *1981;* PricewaterhouseCoopers, Prince's Building, 22/F, 10 Chater Road, CENTRAL, HONG KONG ISLAND HONG KONG SAR.
LAM, Mr. Yu Leung Tony, ACA *2004;* 4515 Painters Mill Road, Mail Code: OM-3450, OWINGS MILLS, MD 21117, UNITED STATES.
LAM, Mr. Yu Lung, ACA *2005;* Tse & Lam, Unit A, 5F China Overseas Building, 139 Hennessy Road, WAN CHAI, HONG KONG ISLAND HONG KONG SAR. See also Tse, Robert
LAM, Ms. Yuet Ling Karen, ACA *2005;* Flat 7 15/F, Fung Yan House, Fung Lai Court, Diamond Hill, WONG TAI SIN, KOWLOON HONG KONG SAR.
LAM, Mr. Yuk Lau, ACA *2007;* Flat H 17/ Floor, Block 6, Laguna City, Cha Kwo Ling, LAM TIN, HONG KONG SAR.
LAM HAU CHING, Miss. Doreen Lam Ka Li, BSc ACA *2003;* Splendid View, Flamboyant Crescent Avenue, ALBION, MAURITIUS.
LAM HUNG, Miss. Esthel Patty Kiune Yin, ACA *2010;* 89A Sir Seewoosagur Ramgoolam Avenue, QUATRE-BORNES, MAURITIUS.
•**LAM HUNG, Mr. Kune Foo Jean-Claude, BA(Hons) ACA** *2002;* Mazars LLP, The Atrium, Park Street West, LUTON, LU1 3BE.
LAM HUNG, Mr. Kune Kwee Mervyn, BSc ACA *2010;* 22 Sophia Square, LONDON, SE16 5XL.
LAM KIN TENG, Mr. Dean Allen, BSc FCA *1995;* 9 Charles De Gaulle Street, ROSE HILL, MAURITIUS.
LAM MAN CHUN, Miss. Julie, ACA *2008;* 423 Uxbridge Road, SOUTHALL, MIDDLESEX, UB1 3EW.
LAM PO TANG, Miss. Emma Kimfa, BSc ACA *2010;* with KPMG LLP, 15 Canada Square, LONDON, E14 5GL.
•**LAM THUON MINE, Mr. Lam Fat Kwong, BA ACA** *1983;* LAM & PARTNERS S.àr.l., 30 Grand-Rue, L1660 LUXEMBOURG, LUXEMBOURG.
LAM THUON MINE, Mr. Lim Siong Kwong, BSc ACA *1993;* with Deloitte, 560 rue de Neudorf, L2220 LUXEMBOURG, LUXEMBOURG.
LAM WING CHEUNG, Mrs. Tracy Lee Lin, BSc ACA *2009;* 1 Molyneux Drive, LONDON, SW17 6BA.
LAM YAN FOON, Mr. Patrick Eric Ronald, MA ACA *1999;* 61 Fleetwood Court, Evelyn Denington Road, Beckton, LONDON, E6 5XZ.
LAM YEW FONG, Miss. Youn-Moy, BSc ACA *2009;* Apartment 193 Woods House, 7 Gatliff Road, LONDON, SW1W 8DF.
LAM YUI, Miss. Christine, BA ACA *2000;* 8 Haredon Close, LONDON, SE23 3TG.
LAMACRAFT, Mr. Paul Alan, BSc ACA CF *1999;* 4 Baileys Barn, BRADFORD-ON-AVON, BA15 1BX.
LAMAISON, Mr. Martin, BA FCA *1968;* Aston Court, 6 Aston Gardens, Aston Rowant, WATLINGTON, OXFORDSHIRE, OX49 5SY.
LAMAISON, Mr. Peter Laurens, FCA *1965;* Longwood House, 21 Westmead, LONDON, SW15 5BH.
LAMAN-TRIP, Mr. Michael Scato, BSc FCA *1977;* 77 Boulevard Vauban, 59000 LILLE, FRANCE.
LAMARCHE, Dr. Vanessa, ACA *2011;* 93 Melody Road, LONDON, SW18 2QQ.
LAMARE, Mr. Andrew James Anthony, ACA *2009;* 66 Camberwell New Road, LONDON, SE5 0RS.
LAMB, Mr. Adrian Frank, FCA *1966;* Lynbury House, Burtons Way, CHALFONT ST.GILES, HP8 4BP.
LAMB, Mr. Adrian Geoffrey, BSc FCA *1986;* Woodlands, Birdcage Walk, OTLEY, LS21 3HB.
LAMB, Mr. Andrew Christopher, BA ACA *1990;* Thorntons Plc, Thornton Park, Somercotes, ALFRETON, DERBYSHIRE, DE55 4XJ.
LAMB, Mr. Andrew William Fraser, MA FCA *1969;* 314 Centennial Road, WEST HILL M1C 2A3, ON, CANADA. (Life Member)
LAMB, Mrs. Annette Louise, DBA BSc ACA *2001;* 33 Nottingham Road, LONDON, SW17 7EA.
•**LAMB, Mr. Anthony Noel, BSc ACA** *1978;* (Tax Fac), Finance Directors Ltd, 14 The Droveway, Lucastes Lane, HAYWARDS HEATH, RH16 1LL. See also Lamb A.N.
•**LAMB, Mrs. Bernadette, MA ACA** *1981;* Lamb & Co., 18 South Close, LONDON, N6 5UQ.
LAMB, Ms. Caroline Sarah, BA ACA *1990;* N H S Education for Scotland, Hanover Buildings, 66 Rose Street, EDINBURGH, EH2 2NN.
•**LAMB, Mr. Charles Sebastian, MA ACA** *1988;* (Tax Fac), Charles Lamb Professional Services Ltd, 3 Blacklands Crescent, FOREST ROW, EAST SUSSEX, RH18 5NN.
•**LAMB, Mr. Christopher Michael, BSc FCA** *1982;* Rowan Business Solutions Limited, 4 Craig Meadows, Ringmer, LEWES, EAST SUSSEX, BN8 5FB.
LAMB, Mrs. Clare Lynn, ACA *1998;* Oak Cottage, Bow Street, Great Ellingham, ATTLEBOROUGH, NORFOLK, NR17 1JB.
LAMB, Mr. David John, BSc ACA *2001;* 33 Nottingham Road, LONDON, SW17 7EA.
LAMB, Ms. Deborah Elizabeth Stewart, MA FCA *1981;* Fairport, Port Arthur, Scalloway, SHETLAND, ZE1 0UN.
•**LAMB, Mr. Duncan Alexander, BA ACA CF** *1999;* Grant Thornton UK LLP, Pinnacle Building, 20 Tudor Road, READING, RG1 1NH. See also Grant Thornton LLP
LAMB, Ms. Frances Josephine, BA ACA *1990;* 15 Silver Street, MALDON, CM9 4QE.
LAMB, Miss. Gail Evelyn, MEng ACA *1997;* 12 Oakleigh Gardens, EDGWARE, MIDDLESEX, HA8 8EA.
•**LAMB, Mr. Gavin, ACA MAAT** *2003;* Naylor Wintersgill Ltd, Carlton House, Grammar School Street, BRADFORD, WEST YORKSHIRE, BD1 4NS.
LAMB, Mr. Graham Martin, BCom ACA *1996;* CTC Insurance Management (Bermuda) Ltd, Burnaby House 16 Burnaby Street, HAMILTON, BERMUDA.
•**LAMB, Mr. Ian Robert, FCA CF** *1981;* (Tax Fac), Smailes Goldie, Regents Court, Princess Street, HULL, HU2 8BA.
LAMB, Mr. James Andrew, BA ACA *1997;* 171 Amyand Park Road, St Margarets, TWICKENHAM, TW1 3HN.
LAMB, Mr. James Nicholas, FCA *1980;* 74 Regency Gardens, WALTON-ON-THAMES, KT12 2BE.
LAMB, Mr. John Peter, BSc ACA *1994;* Promatic International Ltd, Station Works, Hooton Road, Hooton, ELLESMERE PORT, CH66 7NF.
LAMB, Mr. John Telfer Walker, FCA *1967;* 11 Town Ing Mills, Stainland, HALIFAX, WEST YORKSHIRE, HX4 9EF. (Life Member)
LAMB, Miss. Kathryn Susan, BSc ACA *1990;* 18 Woodham Close, Hartford, NORTHWICH, CW8 1SG.
LAMB, Mr. Keith, FCA *1971;* Manor House, Trafford Hill, Eaglescliffe, STOCKTON-ON-TEES, TS16 0QT.
LAMB, Dr. Margaret Anne, FCA *1983;* 65 Timber Drive, STORRS, CT 06268, UNITED STATES.
•**LAMB, Mr. Mark Edward, FCA** *1989;* Chantrey Vellacott DFK LLP, Russell Square House, 10-12 Russell Square, LONDON, WC1B 5LF.
LAMB, Mr. Maurice Ernest, FCA *1959;* 187 Reading Road, WOKINGHAM, RG41 1LJ. (Life Member)
LAMB, Mr. Michael James, BA(Hons) ACA *1996;* 152 Watten Estate Road, SINGAPORE 287606, SINGAPORE.
LAMB, Mr. Michael Mackenzie, BSc ACA *1992;* 13 Herondale Avenue, Wandsworth, LONDON, SW18 3JN.
•**LAMB, Ms. Michaela Simone, BSc ACA ATT** *2006;* Everett & Son, 35 Paul Street, LONDON, EC2A 4UQ.
LAMB, Mr. Neil Alistair, BA ACA *1990;* 3 Hunter Street, CARNEGIE, VIC 3163, AUSTRALIA.
LAMB, Mr. Nicholas Jason, ACA *1998;* Oak Cottage, Bow Street, Great Ellingham, ATTLEBOROUGH, NORFOLK, NR17 1JB.
LAMB, Mr. Peter, BA FCA *1984;* Liverpool Victoria, County Gates, BOURNEMOUTH, BH1 2NF.
LAMB, Mr. Peter, PhD MEc BA ACA *1981;* 38 Birchgrove Road, Balmain, SYDNEY, NSW 2041, AUSTRALIA.
LAMB, Mr. Peter John, FCA *1974;* 19 Dalfaber Park, Aviemore, INVERNESS, PH22 1QF.
•**LAMB, Mr. Philip William, BSc ACA** *1995;* Allen Sykes Limited, 5 Henson Close, South Church Enterprise Park, BISHOP AUCKLAND, COUNTY DURHAM, DL14 6WA.
•**LAMB, Mr. Richard Charles, ACA** *1980;* Charles Lamb ACA, 3 Queen Street, Dorchester-on-Thames, WALLINGFORD, OXFORDSHIRE, OX10 7HR.
LAMB, Mr. Robert, MSc BSc ACA *2010;* 5 Chiddingfold, LONDON, N12 7EX.
LAMB, Mr. Robert Jonathan, BSc ACA *2000;* Fly53 Ltd, 11 Lowesmoor Wharf Lowesmoor, WORCESTER, WR1 2RS.
LAMB, Mr. Roger Paul, BSc ACA *2001;* 3 The Tyleshades, ROMSEY, SO51 5RJ.
LAMB, Mr. Ronald, FCA ACMA *1951;* 18 Brudenell, St. Leonards Hill, WINDSOR, SL4 4UR. (Life Member)
LAMB, Mr. Ryan, BSc(Hons) ACA *2010;* 40 West Stockwell Street, COLCHESTER, CO1 1HS.
•**LAMB, Mrs. Sarah Elizabeth, BSc ACA** *2002;* Sarah E Lamb BSc ACA, 23 Park Drive, Midgey, WHITEHAVEN, CUMBRIA, CA28 7RY.
LAMB, Mr. Simon Martyn, BA ACA *1983;* 40 East 52nd Street, NEW YORK, NY 10022, UNITED STATES.
•**LAMB, Miss. Stephanie Clare, MA(Hons) ACA CIOT** *2003;* Ernst & Young LLP, 1 More London Place, LONDON, SE1 2AF. See also Ernst & Young Europe LLP
•**LAMB, Mr. Stephen, FCA** *1983;* (Tax Fac), Murray & Lamb Accountants Ltd, 25-27 Medomsley Road, CONSETT, COUNTY DURHAM, DH8 5HE.
LAMB, Mr. Stephen, BA ACA *1999;* Dalvey, Glen Road, NEWTONMORE, INVERNESS-SHIRE, PH20 1EA.
LAMB, Mr. Stephen James, FCA *1981;* (Tax Fac), 6 Sunray Avenue, LONDON, SE24 9PY.
LAMB, Mr. Stephen Richard, FCA *1979;* 32 Penn Drive, Frenchay, BRISTOL, BS16 1NN.
LAMB, Mr. Thomas Sutton, BSc ACA *1984;* 11 Walpole Road, SURBITON, KT6 6BU.

LAMB, Mr. Timothy Alan, FCA *1977;* 24 Coniston Close, Hartington Road Chiswick, LONDON, W4 3UG.
•**LAMBA, Mr. Ravinder Singh, BSc(Hons) ACA** *2002;* 16 Ross Way, NORTHWOOD, HA6 3HU.
LAMBARTH, Miss. Pamela, FCA *1974;* 3400 N El Camino, Rinconado, TUCSON, AZ 85749, UNITED STATES. (Life Member)
•**LAMBDEN, Mr. James Percival, BSc ACA** *1991;* (Tax Fac), with Beever and Struthers, 3rd Floor, Alperton House, Bridgewater Road, WEMBLEY, MIDDLESEX HA0 1EH.
LAMBE, Mr. Brian Anthony, FCA *1962;* Orchard End, Southwood, WOKINGHAM, BERKSHIRE, RG40 2HF.
LAMBE, Mr. William Anthony, MA ACA *2000;* 15 Goddard Way, Warfield, BRACKNELL, RG42 2JR.
LAMBELL, Miss. Melissa, ACA *2010;* 337 Copperfield, CHIGWELL, ESSEX, IG7 5NP.
LAMBERT, Mr. Alastair James, BA ACA *1992;* 8 Vernon Park Road, St John's, WORCESTER, WR2 4NF.
•**LAMBERT, Mrs. Alison Jane, BSc ACA** *1992;* 108 Elsenham Street, LONDON, SW18 5NP.
LAMBERT, Miss. Alison Judith, BSc ACA *2003;* 129 Route De Choulex, Choulex, 1244 GENEVA, SWITZERLAND.
LAMBERT, Mrs. Amanda Jane, BA ACA *1985;* Conocophillips, 2 Portman Street, LONDON, W1H 6DU.
LAMBERT, Mr. Andrew, BEng ACA *2011;* 50B Queenstown Road, Battersea, LONDON, SW8 3RY.
LAMBERT, Mr. Andrew Graham, BSc ACA *1992;* Unit B, Methuen Park Methuenm South, CHIPPENHAM, WILTSHIRE, SN140GT.
LAMBERT, Mr. Andrew Kenneth Robert, BSc ACA *1991;* 74 Styal Road, WILMSLOW, CHESHIRE, SK9 4AQ.
LAMBERT, Mr. Andrew Paul, BSc ACA *1989;* 98 Ramsden Street, Clifton Hill, MELBOURNE, VIC 3068, AUSTRALIA.
LAMBERT, Mr. Anthony Jack Martin, FCA *1966;* 30 College Lane, STRATFORD-UPON-AVON, WARWICKSHIRE, CV37 6BS.
LAMBERT, Mr. Anthony John, FCA *1969;* 5 Newhall Rd, Kirk Sandall, DONCASTER, DN3 1QQ.
LAMBERT, Mr. Antony Ian, BA ACA *2005;* 34 Hillside Court, LEEDS, LS7 4NJ.
LAMBERT, Mr. Brian Michael, BA FCA *1970;* Grove House, Icknield Road, Goring, READING, RG8 0LT.
•**LAMBERT, Mrs. Brona, BA FCA** *1991;* Moore Stephens, P O Box 236, First Island House, Peter Street, St. Helier, JERSEY JE4 8SG.
LAMBERT, Mr. Charles Roger, MA ACA *1984;* 2028 Cadenza Lane, RALEIGH, NC 27614, UNITED STATES.
LAMBERT, Mrs. Charlotte, BA ACA *2007;* 14 Yale Court, Honeybourne Road, LONDON, NW6 1JF.
LAMBERT, Mr. Christopher James, BSc FCA *1979;* (Tax Fac), 31 Elmside, Onslow Village, GUILDFORD, GU2 7SH.
LAMBERT, Mr. Christopher Robert, FCA *1972;* 49 Syke Ings, IVER, BUCKINGHAMSHIRE, SL0 9ES.
LAMBERT, Mrs. Claire Michelle, BSc ACA *2002;* 80 Bramwoods Road, CHELMSFORD, ESSEX, CM2 7LT.
LAMBERT, Mr. Damon Mark, BA ACA *1997;* 7th Floor, Swiss RE Properties Ltd, 30 St. Mary Axe, LONDON, EC3A 8EP.
LAMBERT, Mr. David John, BSc ACA *1982;* School Lane Farm House School Lane, Colston Bassett, NOTTINGHAM, NG12 3FD.
LAMBERT, Mr. David Peter, BA FCA *1988;* 10 Rydal Drive, Maldon, CHELMSFORD, ESSEX, CM9 5LG.
•**LAMBERT, Mr. David William, BA ACA** *1995;* Ernst & Young LLP, 1 More London Place, LONDON, SE1 2AF. See also Ernst & Young Europe LLP
LAMBERT, Mr. Derek Alan, BA ACA *1986;* 5 Grove End, Paddock Wood, HARPENDEN, AL5 1JU.
LAMBERT, Mr. Donald Herbert, FCA *1952;* 202 Thornhill Road, SUTTON COLDFIELD, B74 2EP. (Life Member)
LAMBERT, Mr. Francis John, FCA *1971;* Beechings, Station Road, SAFFRON WALDEN, ESSEX, CB11 3HQ.
LAMBERT, Mr. Glenn Stephen, BA ACA *1993;* P.O. Box 21646, NICOSIA, CYPRUS.
•**LAMBERT, Mr. Graham John, BSc ACA** *1990;* PricewaterhouseCoopers LLP, First Point, Buckingham Gate, London Gatwick Airport, GATWICK, WEST SUSSEX RH6 0NT. See also PricewaterhouseCoopers
LAMBERT, Mr. Ian, FCA *1969;* The Chalfont, St. Mary's Way, Brownshill, STROUD, GLOUCESTERSHIRE, GL6 8SW. (Life Member)
LAMBERT, Mr. Ian, BA ACA *1991;* Mourant Services Ltd, PO Box 87, JERSEY, JE4 8PX.
LAMBERT, Mr. Ian Robin, MA MPhil ACA *1985;* Grove Cottage The Frenches, East Wellow, ROMSEY, SO51 6FE.
LAMBERT, Mr. James Mark, BA(Hons) ACA *2002;* John George & Sons Ltd, 2-4 Deacon Way, Tilehurst, READING, RG30 6AZ.
LAMBERT, Mrs. Janet Elizabeth, BSc ACA *1980;* 41 Majestic Road, BASINGSTOKE, RG22 4XD.
LAMBERT, Mr. John David, FCA *1966;* 27 Island Close, STAINES, TW18 4YZ.
LAMBERT, Mr. John Ewart, FCA *1959;* 18 Lea Mount Close, DAWLISH, EX7 9EP. (Life Member)
LAMBERT, Mr. John Rodney, FCA *1967;* Larks Hill, Clopton Road, Tuddenham, IPSWICH, IP6 9BY.
LAMBERT, Mr. Jonathan Mark, BA ACA *1991;* 27 Duncan Road, RICHMOND, SURREY, TW9 2JD.
•**LAMBERT, Mr. Jonathan Wyndham, BA ACA** *2001;* PricewaterhouseCoopers LLP, 1 Embankment Place, LONDON, WC2N 6RH. See also PricewaterhouseCoopers
LAMBERT, Miss. Kathryn Louise, BA ACA *1999;* 18 Brecon Avenue, HUDDERSFIELD, HD3 3QF.
LAMBERT, Mrs. Kathryn Ruth, LLB ACA *2003;* (Tax Fac), 72 Queens Court, Queens Road, RICHMOND, SURREY, TW10 6LB.
LAMBERT, Mr. Kevin Paul, BA ACA *1990;* Arnolds, 36 Prince of Wales Road, NORWICH, NR1 1LH.
LAMBERT, Mrs. Louise Alice, BSc ACA *1995;* 9 Park Rise Close, HARPENDEN, HERTFORDSHIRE, AL5 3AW.
LAMBERT, Mrs. Lynn, BSc ACA *1990;* The Stationery Office St. Crispins House, Duke Street, NORWICH, NR3 1PD.
LAMBERT, Mr. Malcolm Robert, ACA *2008;* Spooners Cottage, 1 The Green, Sandon, CHELMSFORD, CM2 7SH.
LAMBERT, Mrs. Marie Clare, MSc BA(Hons) ACA *2001;* Aisling, Pyrford Road, WOKING, SURREY, GU22 8UF.
LAMBERT, Mr. Mark Andrew, MA ACA *1991;* Owls Castle Cottage Hoghole Lane, Lamberhurst, TUNBRIDGE WELLS, TN3 8BN.
LAMBERT, Mr. Mark Kenway, BSocSc ACA *1996;* 19 Oakleigh Close, Backwell, BRISTOL, BS48 3JX.
LAMBERT, Mr. Martin Lee, MBA BA ACA *1992;* 12 Sherwood Close, Eldwick, BINGLEY, WEST YORKSHIRE, BD16 3EL.
LAMBERT, Mr. Michael, ACA *1979;* 16 Rutland Avenue, Toton, NOTTINGHAM, NG9 6EP.
LAMBERT, Mr. Michael Anthony, CBE FCA *1959;* (Tax Fac), Over Hall, Colne Engaine, COLCHESTER, CO6 2HW.
LAMBERT, Mr. Michael Leonard, FCA *1964;* Acorns, 10a Hogarth Close, West Mersea, COLCHESTER, CO5 8PT.
LAMBERT, Mr. Neil Andrew, ACA *1993;* Kerscheck Str 57, Vasoldsberg, A - 8071, HAUSMANNSTATTEN, AUSTRIA.
LAMBERT, Mr. Nicholas John, LLB FCA *1979;* Orchard Information Systems, Limited, Newcastle Technopole, Kings Manor, NEWCASTLE UPON TYNE, NE1 6PA.
LAMBERT, Ms. Nicole, BA ACA *2002;* 100 William Street, BIRMINGHAM, B15 1LH.
LAMBERT, Mr. Owen James, ACA *2008;* W H Smith Ltd, PO Box 1, SWINDON, SN3 3LD.
LAMBERT, Mr. Owen Reginald, ACA CA(SA) *2010;* Flat A, 43 Avalon Road, LONDON, SW6 2EX.
LAMBERT, Mr. Paul, BSc ACA *1999;* 12 Bellflower Way, Chandler's Ford, EASTLEIGH, HAMPSHIRE, SO53 4HN.
LAMBERT, Mr. Paul Gregory, BSc ACA *1987;* 26 Gertrude Road, West Bridgford, NOTTINGHAM, NG2 5BY.
LAMBERT, Mr. Peter Douglas, MA ACA *1985;* B A E Systems Plc, 1st floor York House, FARNBOROUGH, HAMPSHIRE, GU14 6YU.
LAMBERT, Mr. Peter Robert, BA FCA *1973;* Old Rectory, Great Asby, APPLEBY-IN-WESTMORLAND, CUMBRIA, CA16 6EX.
LAMBERT, Miss. Rhiannon Jane, ACA *2008;* 50b-50c Queenstown Road, LONDON, SW8 3RY.
LAMBERT, Mr. Richard Arthur, BSc FCA MCT *1969;* 6 Fitzhardinge House, 4 Kemerton Road, BECKENHAM, BR3 6NJ.
•**LAMBERT, Mr. Richard John, BCom ACA** *1985;* (Tax Fac), Lambert & Co, The Malt House, Mortimer Hill, Cleobury Mortimer, KIDDERMINSTER, WORCESTERSHIRE DY14 8QQ.
LAMBERT, Mr. Robert, BA FCA *1965;* Red Roof Tithe Barn Lane, Bardsey, LEEDS, LS17 9DX. (Life Member)
LAMBERT, Mr. Rodney Edward, FCA FSI *1968;* EFG Harris Allday, Stock Exchange Buildings, 33 Great Charles Street, BIRMINGHAM, B3 3JN.
LAMBERT, Mr. Ross John, BA ACA *2011;* 123 Blackburn Avenue, BROUGH, NORTH HUMBERSIDE, HU15 1EU.
LAMBERT, Mrs. Sarah, ACA *2008;* 1 Curlew Grove, Heysham, MORECAMBE, LANCASHIRE, LA3 2SN.
LAMBERT, Mrs. Sarah Le Messurier, BA ACA *1988;* Dunsgate, Plaistow Road, Dunsfold, GODALMING, SURREY, GU8 4PJ.
LAMBERT, Mrs. Shaila, BSc ACA *1986;* 63 Heritage Park, BASINGSTOKE, HAMPSHIRE, RG22 4XT.
LAMBERT, Mr. Simon Christopher, BSc ACA *1992;* 5 Jalan Tanah Puteh, SINGAPORE 457331, SINGAPORE.
LAMBERT, Mr. Simon William, MA ACA *1996;* 108 Elsenham Street, LONDON, SW18 5NP.
LAMBERT, Mr. Stephen David, BA ACA *1991;* J X Nippon Exploration & Production UK Ltd Milbank House, 1 Finsbury Square, LONDON, EC2A 1AE.
•**LAMBERT, Mr. Stewart Alexander, BSc ACA** *1994;* James Cowper Corporate Finance LLP, 3 Wesley Gate, Queens Road, READING, RG1 4AP.
LAMBERT, Mr. Thierry Betrand, ACA *2005;* Résidence Fontaine St Antoine, 768 Chemin de Rigaulte, Apartement 30, 84800 L'ISLE SUR LA SOURGE, FRANCE.
LAMBERT, Mr. Thomas George Ludlow, ACA *2009;* 101 Ravensbury Road, LONDON, SW18 4RY.
LAMBERT, Mr. William John, BSc ACA *1986;* Standard Life Investments, 1 George Street, EDINBURGH, EH2 2LL.
LAMBERTH, Ms. Elizabeth Anne, BSc ACA *1990;* British Airways London Eye Riverside Building, County Hall Westminster Bridge Road, LONDON, SE1 7PB.
LAMBERTH, Mrs. Joanne Elizabeth, BSc ACA *2000;* (Tax Fac), 6 Roper Place, EAST KILLARA, NSW 2071, AUSTRALIA.
LAMBERTON, Mr. Peter Alexander, FCA *1970;* 28 Snaithing Lane, SHEFFIELD, S10 3LG.
LAMBETH, Mr. Trevor, ACA *1988;* 44 Highlands Road, Finchfeld, WOLVERHAMPTON, WV3 8AH.
LAMBIS, Mr. George, BA FCA MIMgt *1984;* Asra Greater London Housing Association Asra House, 1 Long Lane, LONDON, SE1 4PG.
LAMBLEY, Mr. John Robert Nelson, FCA *1962;* Stanley House, Oxford Street, Ramsbury, MARLBOROUGH, SN8 2PS. (Life Member)
LAMBOURN, Mr. John Paul, BA ACA *1989;* Sealed Air Ltd, Fleets Lane, POOLE, DORSET, BH15 3BT.
•**LAMBOURNE, Mr. John Horace, BA FCA** *1986;* (Tax Fac), Latham Lambourne, First Floor, Priory Buildings, Church Hill, ORPINGTON, KENT BR6 0HH.
LAMBOURNE, Mr. Robert Ernest, MA FCA *1977;* Merry Gardens Ltd, Merry Gardens, Church Lane, Burley, RINGWOOD, HAMPSHIRE BH24 4AP.
LAMBRECHTS, Mrs. Carien, ACA CA(SA) *2010;* 500 West 56th Street, Apartment 2208, NEW YORK, NY 10019, UNITED STATES.
LAMBROU, Ms. Chrystalla, BSc ACA *2006;* 13A Metsobou Street, Aglontzia, Strovolos, 2103 NICOSIA, CYPRUS.
•**LAMBROU, Mr. George Constantinos, MA ACA MBA** *1995;* PricewaterhouseCoopers Limited, Julia House, 3 Themistocles Dervis Street, CY-1066 NICOSIA, CYPRUS.
•**LAMBROU, Mr. Lambros, BA ACA** *1989;* Lambrou & Co, 223 Cavendish Avenue, Ealing, LONDON, W13 0JZ.
LAMBROU, Ms. Maria, BA ACA *2004;* 5 Kyriakou Kolokasi Street Aglantzia, 2108 NICOSIA, CYPRUS.
•**LAMBROU, Miss. Maria Constantinos, BA ACA** *1997;* Deloitte Limited, 24 Spyrou Kyprianou Avenue, P.O.Box 21675 CY-1512, 1075 NICOSIA, CYPRUS.
LAMBROU, Mrs. Martha, BSc ACA *2003;* P.O. Box 54464, CY 3724 LIMASSOL, CYPRUS.
•**LAMBSON, Mr. Andrew Charles, BSc FCA** *1985;* 2 Raikes Avenue, SKIPTON, NORTH YORKSHIRE, BD23 1LP.
LAMBSON, Mrs. Margaret Elizabeth, BA ACA CTA *1989;* (Tax Fac), 7 Crutchfield Lane, WALTON-ON-THAMES, KT12 2QY.
•**LAMBURN, Mr. David John, BA ACA** *1986;* 25 Tuffnells Way, HARPENDEN, AL5 3HJ.
•**LAMBURN, Mrs. Maureen Dunlop, MA FCA ATII** *1986;* MEMBER OF COUNCIL, Lamburn & Turner, Riverside House, 1 Place Farm, Place Farm, Wheathampstead, ST. ALBANS AL4 8SB. See also The Accounts Factory Ltd
LAMDIN, Mr. Ian David, BA ACA CPA CFE *1985;* 1499 Mt Diablo Avenue, MILPITAS, CA 95035, UNITED STATES.
LAMDIN, Mr. Stephen John, BA FCA *1980;* Wackland Farm, Wackland Lane, Newchurch, SANDOWN, ISLE OF WIGHT, PO36 0NB.
LAMERS, Miss. Pascale Maria, BA ACA *2000;* 31 Tawney Street, OXFORD, OX4 1NJ.
•**LAMEY, Mr. David Robert, FCA** *1971;* Lamey & Co Limited, Ridge Cottage, Speldhurst, TUNBRIDGE WELLS, KENT, TN3 0LE.
LAMMERT, Mrs. Karen, BA ACA *2000;* 35 Western Road, RAYLEIGH, SS6 7AY.
LAMMIE, Mr. Colin Andrew, BSc ACA *1993;* Downlands, The Crescent, STEYNING, WEST SUSSEX, BN44 3GD.
LAMMIN, Mr. Aynsley, MPhil BSc ACA *1998;* 27 Leicester Road, LONDON, E11 2DW.
LAMMING, Mr. Guy Richard Daniel, BA ACA *1991;* 2 Holland Park Road, LONDON, W14 8LZ.
LAMOND, Miss. Anne Elizabeth, BA ACA *1980;* 1625 N Taylor St, ARLINGTON, VA 22207-3158, UNITED STATES.
LAMOND, Mrs. Nicola Rose, BSc ACA *1992;* 16 Penrith Close, VERWOOD, BH31 6XE.
LAMOND, Mr. Peter Geoffrey, MBA BSc FCA *1992;* June Cottage, Church Road, Chelsfield, ORPINGTON, KENT, BR6 7RE.
LAMOND, Mr. Robert Anthony Wilson, ACA *1983;* 17 Queens Road, Sunninghill, ASCOT, SL5 9AF.
LAMONT, Mr. Christopher, BSc ACA *1989;* The Yews, Murcott, KIDLINGTON, OX5 2RE.
•**LAMONT, Mr. Christopher Ian, BSc ACA** *2008;* Lamont Pridmore Limited, Arkle House, 31 Lonsdale Street, CARLISLE, CA1 1BJ. See also Lamont Pridmore (South Cumbria) Limited
LAMONT, Ms. Grace, BA ACA *1992;* 450 E83rd street, Apt 8e, NEW YORK, NY 10028, UNITED STATES.
•**LAMONT, Mr. Graham William, FCA FCCA AIMC ACIS FRSA MCMI** *1978;* (Tax Fac), Lamont Pridmore, Milburn House, 3 Oxford Street, WORKINGTON, CA14 2AL. See also Lamont Pridmore (South Cumbria) Limited, Lamont Pridmore Limited, Lamont Pridmore Limited, E.J. Williams & Co
LAMONT, Ms. Heather Robb, MA FCA DChA *1992;* 1 Gate Cottages, Old Common Road, CHORLEYWOOD, HERTFORDSHIRE, WD3 5LW.
•**LAMPARD, Mr. Anthony, ACA** *1980;* (Tax Fac), 28 Woodbastwick Road, LONDON, SE26 5LH.
LAMPARD, Mr. Daniel Malachi, BA ACA *2006;* 12 Bunting Mews, Worsley, MANCHESTER, M28 7XG.
LAMPARD, Mrs. Helen Claire, BSc FCA *1989;* 11 Springfield Park Road, HORSHAM, RH12 2PW.
LAMPERT, Mr. James Andrew, ACA *2009;* Flat 9 Haute Chapelle, Victoria Road St. Peter Port, GUERNSEY, GY1 1JB.
•**LAMPERT, Mr. Richard, FCA** *1971;* Landau Morley LLP, Lanmor House, 370-386 High Road, WEMBLEY, MIDDLESEX, HA9 6AX.
•**LAMPING, Mr. Richard Alan, FCA** *1975;* 63 Margravine Gardens, LONDON, W6 8RN.
LAMPIT, Mr. David Howell, FCA *1973;* Abergwaun, 9 Tribe Road No 1, DEVONSHIRE DV06, BERMUDA.
LAMPITT, Mr. David, BA ACA *2001;* Greenboughs, Coach Road, Ivy Hatch, SEVENOAKS, KENT, TN15 0PF.
LAMPITT, Miss. Fiona Maria, BSc ACA *2005;* 60 Clayfield Road, MEXBOROUGH, S64 0HW.
LAMPKIN, Mr. Malcolm William, BA FCA *1975;* Glendale, Farm Lane, Shurdington, CHELTENHAM, GL51 4XN.
LAMPTEY, Mr. Jonathan, MSc ACA *2003;* 53 Howland Way, LONDON, SE16 6HW.
LAMSTAES, Mr. Pierre Gaetan, FCA *1982;* (Tax Fac), 99 Solefields Road, SEVENOAKS, TN13 1PJ.
LAMUSSE, Mr. Marie Joseph Raymond, FCA *1959;* La Casa Bleue, Coastal Road, MELVILLE, MAURITIUS. (Life Member)
•①**LAN, Mr. Henry Kam, FCA** *1975;* David Rubin & Partners LLP, Pearl Assurance House, 319 Ballards Lane, North Finchley, LONDON, N12 8LY. See also David Rubin & Partners
LAN, Mr. Nigel, BA ACA *2009;* 512 Wharfside Point South, 4 Prestons Road, LONDON, E149RL.
•**LAN CHEONG WAH, Mr. Desire, BSc FCA** *2000;* Kross Border, St Louis Business Centre, Cnr St Louis/Desroches Streets, PORT LOUIS, MAURITIUS.
LAN HUN KUEN, Mr. Jean Marie Gaetan, FCA *1977;* 12 Gladstone Avenue, QUATRE-BORNES, MAURITIUS.
LANAWAY, Mr. Christopher James, ACA *2007;* 51 Boundary Road, LONDON, SW19 2AW.
LANC, Mrs. Anne Elizabeth, BA ACA *1989;* 5 Netherbank View, Alnwickhill, EDINBURGH, EH16 6YY.
LANCASHIRE, Mr. Elliot Christopher, ACA *2009;* 9 Winterdown Road, ESHER, KT10 8LJ.
•**LANCASHIRE, Mrs. Jane Elizabeth-Anne, BA(Hons) ACA** *2000;* Lancashire Accountants Ltd, 3 Osborne Street, Bredbury, STOCKPORT, CHESHIRE, SK6 2BT.

LANCASHIRE, Mr. Jeffrey Howard, FCA *1969;* 62 Mossley Road, Grasscroft, OLDHAM, OL4 4HA. (Life Member)
LANCASHIRE, Mr. John Christopher, BSc ACA *1979;* 20 Kenwood Drive, Burwood Park, WALTON-ON-THAMES, KT12 5AU.
LANCASHIRE, Mr. Jonathan Michael, MA FCA *1994;* 1 Drury Lane House, Drury Lane, Redmarley, GLOUCESTER, GL19 3JX.
LANCASHIRE, Mr. Matthew Paul, LLB ACA *2005;* with PricewaterhouseCoopers LLP, 1 Embankment Place, LONDON, WC2N 6RH.
LANCASHIRE, Mr. William John, FCA *1959;* 34 Highfield Road, Corfe Mullen, WIMBORNE, BH21 3PF. (Life Member)
LANCASTER, Mr. Andrew James, MSc ACA *1999;* 22b Parker Lane, MIRFIELD, WF14 9PF.
•**LANCASTER, Mr. Arthur John, BA FCA CTA** *1989;* (Tax Fac), Cronk Urleigh House, Douglas Road, Kirk Michael, ISLE OF MAN, IM6 1AU.
•**LANCASTER, Mrs. Carolyn Jane, MSc ACA ATII** *1985;* (Tax Fac), Dan y Rallt, Llanynis, BUILTH WELLS, POWYS, LD2 3HN.
LANCASTER, Mr. David, FCA *1967;* Vauvert Manor, Vauvert, St. Peter Port, GUERNSEY, GY1 1NJ. (Life Member)
LANCASTER, Mr. David Michael, BA FCA *1974;* (Tax Fac), 42 Hayden Lane, Hucknall, NOTTINGHAM, NG15 8BJ.
LANCASTER, Ms. Emma, BA ACA *2000;* Foxes Den Sutton Green Road, Sutton Green, GUILDFORD, GU4 7QD.
LANCASTER, Ms. Emma Voirrey, BA ACA *1995;* S H L, The Pavilion, 1 Atwell Place, THAMES DITTON, SURREY, KT7 0NE.
LANCASTER, Mrs. Emma-Jane, BA ACA *1999;* 288 Ansty Road, Wyken, COVENTRY, CV2 3FB.
LANCASTER, Miss. Gillian, BSc ACA *1992;* Fairlawn, 55 Kidbrooke Grove, Blackheath, LONDON, SE3 0LJ.
LANCASTER, Miss. Gillian Mary, BA ACA *1992;* 3410 La Sombra Drive, LOS ANGELES, CA 90068, UNITED STATES.
LANCASTER, Mr. Gordon, FCA *1958;* 33 Fearnville View, LEEDS, LS8 3DJ. (Life Member)
LANCASTER, Mr. Graham John, BA FCA *1971;* Westlands Alresford Road, Cheriton, ALRESFORD, SO24 0QB.
LANCASTER, Mr. Graham Richard, BSc FCA *1979;* Belton, Pembroke Road, WOKING, GU22 7EB.
•**LANCASTER, Mr. Ian, FCA** *1974;* Ian Lancaster Limited, 108 Needingworth Road, ST. IVES, CAMBRIDGESHIRE, PE27 5JY.
•**LANCASTER, Mr. Ian Callander, FCA** *1979;* (Tax Fac), N.B. Lancaster & Co, 6 Brunswick Street, CARLISLE, CA1 1PN.
LANCASTER, Mr. James, FCA *1971;* Upper Childown, Accommodation Road, Longcross, CHERTSEY, KT16 0EJ.
LANCASTER, Mr. James Edmund, FCA *1968;* Bridge House, Templebridge, Temple Cloud, BRISTOL, BS39 5AA.
LANCASTER, Mrs. Jane Elizabeth, MA ACA ATII *1992;* Cronk Urleigh House, Douglas Road, Kirk Michael, ISLE OF MAN, IM6 1AU.
LANCASTER, Mrs. Jo-Anne, FCA *1975;* Morgan Hemp, 104 Walter Road, SWANSEA, SA1 5QF.
LANCASTER, Mr. John Barry, FCA *1970;* 13 Banbury Road, STRATFORD-UPON-AVON, CV37 7HN.
LANCASTER, Mr. John Barry, FCA *1966;* 14 Arbutus Street, MOSMAN, NSW 2088, AUSTRALIA. (Life Member)
•**LANCASTER, Mr. John David, FCA** *1966;* John D Lancaster, Tenpenny House, Colchester Main Road, Alresford, COLCHESTER, CO7 8DJ.
LANCASTER, Mr. John Lewis, BA FCA *1974;* 38A Bellagio One, 1 Forbes Town Road, Bonifacio Global City, TAGUIG CITY 1634, PHILIPPINES. (Life Member)
LANCASTER, Mrs. Kathryn Anne, BA ACA *1999;* JP Morgan, Canberra House, Lydiard Fields, SWINDON, SN5 8UB.
LANCASTER, Mr. Keith David, BSc ACA *2001;* Unit 2802 No.7, Lane 2 West Wei Fang Road, Pudong District, SHANGHAI 200120, CHINA.
•**LANCASTER, Mr. Kenneth Alan, FCA** *1974;* 10160 St. Vincent's Place, RICHMOND V7E 5R8, BC, CANADA.
•**LANCASTER, Mr. Malcolm Higham, FCA** *1976;* 3 Lefkes Gardens, Kyriakou Adamou, Chlorakas, 8220 PAPHOS, CYPRUS.
LANCASTER, Mrs. Margaret Eileen, FCA *1974;* Westlands, Cheriton, ALRESFORD, SO24 0QB.
LANCASTER, Mr. Mark John, BSc ACA *1993;* 1 Sycamore Road, Latchbrook, SALTASH, PL12 4XS.
LANCASTER, Mr. Martin, BA FCA *1982;* P.O. Box 10221, GEORGE TOWN, GRAND CAYMAN, KY1-1002, CAYMAN ISLANDS.
LANCASTER, Mr. Matthew Thomas, BSc ACA *2006;* Lubbock Fine Unit 9-10 City Forum, 250 City Road, LONDON, EC1V 2QQ.
LANCASTER, Mr. Michael Andrew, BSc ACA *1985;* 20 Balland Way, Wootton Park, Wootton Fields, NORTHAMPTON, NN4 6AU.
•**LANCASTER, Mr. Neil, FCA** *1994;* Adams Moore Audit Limited, 38-39 Albert Road, TAMWORTH, STAFFORDSHIRE, B79 7JS. See also Adams Moore Ltd
LANCASTER, Mr. Neil Felton, BSS ACA *1991;* Unit 64, 127 Gooding Drive, MERRIMAC, QLD 4226, AUSTRALIA.
LANCASTER, Mrs. Nicola Anne, BSc ACA *1993;* 1 Sycamore Road, Latchbrook, SALTASH, PL12 4XS.
LANCASTER, Mrs. Nicola Mary, BA ACA *1995;* 15 Flint Close, ATHERSTONE, CV9 3AN.
LANCASTER, Mr. Nigel Phillip, BA ACA *1988;* 36 Ashley Road, FARNBOROUGH, HAMPSHIRE, GU14 7HA.
•**LANCASTER, Mr. Noel Brownrigg, FCA** *1958;* Little Drawdyke, 4 Whiteclose Gate, CARLISLE, CA3 0JD.
LANCASTER, Mr. Paul Stuart, BA FCA *1983;* G O'Briens & Sons, Cleadon House, Cleadon Lane, EAST BOLDON, TYNE AND WEAR, NE36 0AJ.
LANCASTER, Miss. Sarah Helen, MA ACA *2003;* with GE Capital Europe Limited, 3rd Floor, 1 Trevelyan Square, LEEDS, LS1 6HP.
LANCASTER, Miss. Sonya Dawn, ACA *1990;* TABS, 28 Victoria Street, PAIGNTON, DEVON, TQ4 5DN.
LANCASTER, Mr. Stephen, ACA *2008;* 42 Victoria Road, WHITEHAVEN, CUMBRIA, CA28 6JB.
LANCASTER, Mrs. Theodora Janet, FCA *1954;* 1 Willow Cottages, New Forest Lane, Old Wives Lees, CANTERBURY, CT4 8BG. (Life Member)
LANCASTER, Miss. Victoria Helen, BA ACA *2006;* 4 The Chesils, COVENTRY, CV3 5BN.
LANCE, Mr. Christopher John, FCA *1975;* 52 Kidmore Road, Caversham, READING, RG4 7LX.
LANCE, Mr. Nicholas Owen, FCA *1959;* Furzy Lea, Bowesden Lane, Shorne, GRAVESEND, DA12 3LA. (Life Member)
LANCEFIELD, Mr. Robert, BSc FCA *1979;* with Chantrey Vellacott DFK LLP, Russell Square House, 10-12 Russell Square, LONDON, WC1B 5LF.
LANCELEY, Mr. Nigel Stuart, FCA *1972;* RENSBERG SHEPPARDS PLC, Rensburg, 100 Old Hall Street, LIVERPOOL, L3 9AB.
LANCELOTT, Mr. Anthony Robert, BCom FCA *1984;* 68 Hoodcote Gardens, LONDON, N21 2NE.
LANCET, Mr. Howard Jonathan, BA ACA *1985;* 38 Dunstan Road, LONDON, NW11 8AA.
LANCEY, Mr. Roger Keith, MSc FCA *1962;* 23 Caspian Close, Whiteley, FAREHAM, HAMPSHIRE, PO15 7BP.
LANCH, Mr. David, MA MLitt FCA *1969;* Langdale, Regal Way, Kenton, HARROW, HA3 0RX. (Life Member)
•**LANCHBURY, Mr. Keith, FCA** *1958;* Keith Lanchbury, 6 West Street, Moulton, NORTHAMPTON, NN3 7SB.
LAND, Mr. Christopher, ACA *2009;* 15 Hatton Place, LONDON, EC1N 8RU.
LAND, Mr. Christopher John, MSc ACA AMCT *1999;* (Tax Fac), 42 Westcott Road, LONDON, SE17 3QY.
LAND, Mr. Ian, BSc ACA *1988;* Express Gifts Ltd Church Bridge House, Henry Street Church, ACCRINGTON, BB5 4EE.
LAND, James Gordon Murray, Esq OBE FCA *1955;* Rosa de Lima 44, Las Matas, 28290 MADRID, SPAIN. (Life Member)
LAND, Mr. James William, ACA *1982;* Amalgamated Metal Trading Ltd, 55 Bishopsgate, LONDON, EC2N 3AH.
LAND, Ms. Julia Margaret, BSc FCA *1986;* 62 Talbot Road, Highgate, LONDON, N6 4RA.
LAND, Mrs. Kirsten, BA(Hons) ACA *2001;* 10 Kermode Road, Eyreton Lea, Crosby, ISLE OF MAN, IM4 4BZ.
LAND, Mr. Maurice Jack, BA FCA *1976;* (Tax Fac), 41A High Green, Brooke, NORWICH, NR15 1JA.
LAND, Mr. Nicholas Charles Edward, FCA *1971;* 10 Homefield Road, LONDON, W4 2LN.
LAND, Mr. Nigel Magnus, BA ACA *1997;* Qube, 90 Whitfield Street, LONDON, W1T 4EZ.
•**LAND, Mr. Paul Douglas, BSc ACA** *1998;* (Tax Fac), TLP, 3 Greengate, Cardale Park, HARROGATE, NORTH YORKSHIRE, HG3 1GY. See also TLP Audit Limited, TLP Consulting LLP
LAND, Mr. Peter Anthony, FCA *1950;* 41 Harwood Road, MARLOW, SL7 2AR. (Life Member)
LAND, Ms. Sian Louise, BSc ACA *1995;* 11 Clover Drive, Pickmere, KNUTSFORD, WA16 0WF.
•**LANDAU, Mr. David Mark Bernard, BA FCA** *1991;* Berg Kaprow Lewis LLP, 35 Ballards Lane, LONDON, N3 1XW.
LANDAU, Mrs. Emily Henrietta, BSc ACA *1992;* 33 Pattison Road, LONDON, NW2 2HL.
•**LANDAU, Mr. Julian, BSc FCA** *1990;* The KBSP Partnership, Harben House, Harben Parade, Finchley Road, LONDON, NW3 6LH. See also Stardata Business Services Limited
LANDAU, Mr. Martin Richard, FCA *1960;* Le Schuylkill, 19 Boulevard de Suisse, MC 98000, MONTE CARLO, MONACO. (Life Member)
LANDAU, Mr. Michael Lindsay, BA ACA *1990;* Lycamobile Ltd, Wallbrook Buildings, 195 Marsh Wall, LONDON, E14 9SG.
LANDAUER, Mr. Robert, MA ACA *1996;* Mill House, Rookery Way, HAYWARDS HEATH, WEST SUSSEX, RH16 4RE.
LANDE, Mr. Paul Charles, BSc ACA *1989;* 14 Harford Walk, LONDON, N2 0JB.
LANDELL-MILLS, Mr. Nicholas, MA ACA CFA *1993;* 22 Abercorn Place, LONDON, NW8 9XP.
LANDELLS, Mrs. Karen, BSc ACA CTA *2003;* 2 Scholes Lodge Lane, Scholes, LEEDS, LS15 4BZ.
LANDER, Mrs. Jacqueline, BSc ACA *1979;* 33 Midfield Way, St.Pauls Cray, ORPINGTON, BR5 2QH.
LANDER, Mr. Jonathan Michael, BSc FCA *1982;* Holly Cottage, Old Milverton, LEAMINGTON SPA, CV32 6SA.
LANDER, Mr. Mark Philip, BSc ACA *1997;* 3 Cambisgate, 109 Church Road, Wimbledon, LONDON, SW19 5AL.
•**LANDER, Mr. Roger Francis, FCA** *1959;* R F Lander, Spinney Corner, Green Lane, Aspley Guise, MILTON KEYNES, MK17 8EN.
LANDER, Mr. Timothy John, BSc(Hons) ACA *1992;* White House, Sparsholt, WINCHESTER, SO21 2NJ.
•**LANDERGAN, Mr. Philip Martin, BA FCA** *1987;* (Tax Fac), Landergan & Co, 42 Whetstone Road, LONDON, SE3 8PX.
LANDERS, Mr. Gerard Francis, FCA *1978;* Tragalee, Tuosist, KILLARNEY, COUNTY KERRY, IRELAND.
LANDERS, Mrs. Sarah Catherine, BA ACA *1986;* Briarbank House, 12a Childs Hall Road, Bookham, LEATHERHEAD, KT23 3QG.
LANDERS, Mr. Thomas Michael, BA ACA *2006;* Morgan Griffiths, Cross Chambers, 9 High Street, NEWTOWN, POWYS, SY16 2NY.
LANDES, Mr. Anthony Joseph, BSc FCA *1972;* Quill Computer Systems Barclay House, 35 Whitworth Street West, MANCHESTER, M1 5NG.
•**LANDES, Mr. Steven Harry, BA FCA** *1985;* (Tax Fac), S H Landes LLP, 3rd Floor, Fairgate House, 78 New Oxford Street, LONDON, WC1A 1HB.
LANDGRAF, Miss. Sheena Maureen, BSc FCA *1989;* 2 Longsdon Way, CATERHAM, SURREY, CR3 6BN.
LANDIS, Mr. Arnold, FCA *1958;* 2 Forest Laneway 2503, TORONTO M2N 5X7, ON, CANADA. (Life Member)
LANDMAN, Mr. Anton, ACA CA(SA) *2008;* Casa 70, Clayton Village, PANAMA CITY, PANAMA.
LANDMAN, Mr. Martin, BCom FCA *1981;* Intrust Ltd, 38 Wigmore Street, LONDON, W1U 2HA.
LANDON, Mr. Anthony Edward, BCom FCA *1972;* 14 Hogarth Drive, Barton Seagrave, KETTERING, NORTHAMPTONSHIRE, NN15 5UQ.
LANDON, Miss. Arabella Elizabeth Suzette, BSc ACA *2009;* Pricewaterhousecoopers Llp, 1 Hays Lane, LONDON, SE1 2RD.
LANDON, Mrs. Elena, ACA *1997;* The Coach House, 48a Wolsey Road, EAST MOLESEY, KT8 9EN.
LANDON, Mr. James Frederic, FCA *1970;* (Tax Fac), Baxter Healthcare Ltd, Wallingford Road, Compton, NEWBURY, BERKSHIRE, RG20 7QW.
LANDON, Mrs. Katherine Elizabeth, MEng ACA *2003;* KPMG, 10 Shelley Street, SYDNEY, NSW 2000, AUSTRALIA.
LANDON, Mr. Marc Charles Anthony, ACA *2009;* 17 The Quays, Castle Quay Close, NOTTINGHAM, NG7 1HR.
LANDON, Mr. Peter Lawrence, FCA CTA *1967;* (Tax Fac), 40, Queen Street, LONDON, EC4R 1DD.
LANDON, Mr. Richard David, BA ACA *2000;* 51 Alexander Street, MANLY, NSW 2095, AUSTRALIA.
LANDON, Mr. Robin Edward, BA FCA *1972;* (Tax Fac), 7 Sibella Road, LONDON, SW4 6JA.
LANDOW-LEVY, Ms. Paula Lenore, ACA *1981;* 3 Calder Avenue, Brookmans Park, HATFIELD, AL9 7AH.
LANDSBERG, Mr. Kenneth William, BSc ACA *1984;* with E C I Partners, Brettenham House, Lancaster Place, LONDON, WC2E 7EN.
LANDSBERG, Mr. Richard Mark, BA ACA *2007;* 40 Heywood Boulevard, Thingwall, WIRRAL, CH61 3XF.
LANDSBERT, Mr. Terence Carl, FCA *1960;* West Manor, Church Street, WEYMOUTH, DORSET, DT3 5QB. (Life Member)
LANDSHOFF, Miss. Rebecca, BA ACA *2006;* 58 Addison Drive, STRATFORD-UPON-AVON, WARWICKSHIRE, CV37 7PL.
LANDSMAN, Mr. Arnold Charles, FCA *1958;* 8 River Drive, UPMINSTER, RM14 1AS. (Life Member)
•①**LANDSMAN, Mr. Marc Justin, BSc ACA** *1993;* Carmichaels Insolvency Ltd, 2nd Floor, Portland Tower, Portland Street, MANCHESTER, M1 3LF. See also Management of Personal Insolvencies Ltd
LANDSMAN, Mr. Martin, FCA *1955;* 116 Leeside Crescent, LONDON, NW11 0JY. (Life Member)
LANDSMAN, Mr. Paul Stewart, BA ACA *2005;* LGV Capital Ltd, One Coleman Street, LONDON, EC2R 5AA.
•**LANDSMAN, Mrs. Rachel Rosanne, BSc FCA DChA** *1995;* Landsman, 43 Broadway, CHEADLE, CHESHIRE, SK8 1LB. See also Rachel Landsman
LANDY, Mr. Simon Philip, ACA *2010;* 15 Arabella Street, CARDIFF, CF24 4SW.
•**LANDY, Mr. Stephen Simon, FCA** *1971;* Wilder Coe LLP, 233-237 Old Marylebone Road, LONDON, NW1 5QT. See also Addison, Beyer, Green & Co and Wilder Coe
LANE, Mrs. Adele Christine, BSc FCA *1980;* 81 Broad Road, SALE, M33 2EU.
LANE, Mr. Adrian David, MA MPhil ACA *2002;* Fairlea, La Grande Route de la Cote, ST CLEMENT, JE2 6SD.
LANE, Mr. Andrew Charles, MA ACA *1995;* (Tax Fac), 23 North Croft, East Hagbourne, DIDCOT, OX11 9LT.
LANE, Mr. Andrew Charles, BSc ACA *1992;* 2 Piper Close, LOUGHBOROUGH, LEICESTERSHIRE, LE11 3LG.
LANE, Mr. Andrew John, FCA *1974;* 56b Motor Main Road Wilberforce, FREETOWN, SIERRA LEONE.
•**LANE, Mr. Andrew Mark, FCA** *1974;* Clear & Lane, 340 Melton Road, LEICESTER, LE4 7SL.
LANE, Mr. Andrew Peter, BSc ACA *1992;* 11a Coniston Way, BEWDLEY, WORCESTERSHIRE, DY12 2QA.
LANE, Mrs. Angela Claire, BA ACA *1988;* Old Manor Farm House, Avon, CHRISTCHURCH, DORSET, BH23 7BL.
LANE, Ms. Anita, BSc ACA *1994;* Varian Medical Systems UK Ltd, Gatwick Road, CRAWLEY, WEST SUSSEX, RH10 9RG.
•**LANE, Mr. Anthony Edward Stuart, BA FCA** *1977;* Syngenta Bioline, Telstar Nurseries, Holland Road, Little Clacton, CLACTON-ON-SEA, ESSEX CO16 9QG.
•**LANE, Mr. Anthony John, BCom FCA** *1979;* Harold Sharp, Holland House, 1-5 Oakfield, SALE, M33 6TT.
•**LANE, Mr. Bobby, BA(Hons) FCA** *1998;* Shelley Stock Hutter LLP, 7-10 Chandos Street, LONDON, W1G 9DQ.
LANE, Mrs. Catherine, BA ACA *2000;* 4 Pelham Road, BECKENHAM, KENT, BR3 4SG.
LANE, Ms. Catherine Margaret Anne, BSc(Econ) ACA *1996;* 5 St. Margarets Close, CARDIFF, CF14 7AE.
LANE, Mr. Christopher David, BA ACA *1992;* Long Meadow, Harvest Hill, BOURNE END, BUCKINGHAMSHIRE, SL8 5JJ.
LANE, Mr. Christopher George, FCA *1972;* 2 Place du Commerce, Domaine de Grandchamp, 78230 LE PECQ, FRANCE.
•**LANE, Mr. Christopher John, FCA** *1983;* (Tax Fac), Kingston Smith LLP, Devonshire House, 60 Goswell Road, LONDON, EC1M 7AD. See also Kingston Smith Limited Liability Partnership, Devonshire Corporate Services LLP and Kingston Smith Consulting LLP
LANE, Mr. Christopher John, BA ACA *1989;* 18 Palmerston Road, TWICKENHAM, TW2 7QX.
LANE, Mrs. Claire Marie, BA ACA *2000;* 29 Goldsmith Way, ST. ALBANS, HERTFORDSHIRE, AL3 5LH.
LANE, Mr. Daevid Anthony, BSc ACA CISA *1988;* CMC S.L., Calle Caleruega 81 - 3°, 28033 MADRID, SPAIN.
•**LANE, Mr. Derek Henry, BA ACA** *2000;* DHL Accountancy Services, 30 Willowbank Gardens, TADWORTH, SURREY, KT20 5DS.
LANE, Miss. Erin Alexis, ACA *2009;* Deloitte, 1 City Square, LEEDS, LS1 2AL.

LANE, Mrs. Galina, BA(Hons) ACA *2002;* 25 Wansford Close, Owington Farm, BILLINGHAM, TS23 3LB.
LANE, Mr. Gareth Alan, BSc ACA *2010;* 9 Hillside Court, Llantwit Fardre, PONTYPRIDD, MID GLAMORGAN, CF38 2PE.
LANE, Mr. Gareth William, BA ACA *1995;* 153 Cyncoed Road, CARDIFF, CF23 6AG.
•LANE, Mr. Geoffrey Charles, BA FCA *1979;* (Tax Fac), The MGroup Partnership, Cranbrook House, 287/291 Banbury Road, OXFORD, OX2 7JQ. See also The MGroup Corporate Finance LLP, The MGroup Secretarial Services Limited
•LANE, Mr. Geoffrey Newton, BSc FCA *1975;* with Chantrey Vellacott DFK LLP, Russell Square House, 10-12 Russell Square, LONDON, WC1B 5LF.
•LANE, Mr. Gordon Douglas, BA FCA *1989;* BDO LLP, 6th Floor, 3 Hardman Street, Spinningfields, MANCHESTER, M3 3AT. See also BDO Stoy Hayward LLP
LANE, Mr. Graham Richard, FCA *1974;* 43 Tyrone Road, Thorpe Bay, SOUTHEND-ON-SEA, SS1 3HE.
LANE, Mrs. Helen Mary, FCA *1985;* Sandhills House, Lichfield Rd Sandhills, Walsall Wood, WALSALL, WS9 9DJ.
LANE, Mr. Henry John Noxon, FCA *1953;* Parkside, 32 The Avenue, SANDY, SG19 1ER. (Life Member)
LANE, Miss. Jacqueline Bernadette, BCom ACA *1990;* 28 Eade Road, NORWICH, NR3 3EJ.
LANE, Mrs. Jacqueline Maria, BA ACA *1988;* Wealdridge, Top Road, Sharpthorne, EAST GRINSTEAD, RH19 4NT.
LANE, Mrs. Janet Christine, BA ACA *1983;* 21 Elmhurst Road, LYTHAM ST.ANNES, FY8 3JH.
LANE, Mr. John Francis, ACA *1987;* with PricewaterhouseCoopers LLP, 1 Embankment Place, LONDON, WC2N 6RH.
LANE, Mr. John Godfrey, FCA *1955;* Flat 5, The Grange, Grange Avenue, LONDON, N20 8AB. (Life Member)
LANE, Mr. Julian Dai, FCA *1986;* (Tax Fac), Le Houmet, Houmet Lane, Vale, GUERNSEY, GY6 8JQ.
LANE, Mr. Karl, BA ACA *1996;* 165 Birkenshaw Road, BIRMINGHAM, B44 8UN.
LANE, Mr. Kenneth William West, MA FCA *1972;* Lea House, Villiers Mead, WOKINGHAM, RG41 2UB.
LANE, Miss. Kerry Michelle, BA(Hons) ACA *2001;* with RSM Tenon Limited, Charter House, Legge Street, BIRMINGHAM, B4 7EU.
•LANE, Mr. Kevin Eslin, ACA *1995;* Kevin Lane, 7 Yew Tree Close, Silsoe, BEDFORD, MK45 4EQ.
LANE, Mrs. Louise Anne, BA ACA CTA *2003;* with Wright Vigar Limited, 15 Newland, LINCOLN, LN1 1XG.
•LANE, Mr. Mark Anthony, FCA *1991;* LMW Limited, Riverside View, Basing Road, Basing, BASINGSTOKE, HAMPSHIRE RG24 7AL.
LANE, Mr. Mark John, BSc ACA *1996;* 15 Minorca Road, WEYBRIDGE, KT13 8DU.
LANE, Mrs. Melissa Jane, BSc ARCS ACA *1999;* 7 South View, EPSOM, KT19 7LA.
LANE, Mr. Michael John David, BA ACA *1982;* 20 Meadowcourt Road, Oadby, LEICESTER, LE2 2PB.
LANE, Mr. Michael John Reginald, MA FCA *1954;* Mill Court, 23 Fulwith Mill Lane, HARROGATE, HG2 8HJ. (Life Member)
LANE, Miss. Miranda Sophia, BA ACA *1985;* Copt Hill Farm Launde Road, Launde, LEICESTER, LE7 9XB.
LANE, Mr. Nicholas, MSc ACA *2007;* Flat 12, Knebworth House, Union Grove, LONDON, SW8 2RS.
LANE, Mr. Nicholas David Jeremy, MA FCA *1964;* 146 N Bellefield Ave, Apt 1101, PITTSBURGH, PA 15213, UNITED STATES. (Life Member)
LANE, Mr. Nicholas Patrick, ACA *2008;* 85 Long Lane, WALSALL, WS6 6AT.
LANE, Mr. Nicholas Reginald, ACA *2004;* 24 St. Anthony's Close, LONDON, E1W 1LT.
•LANE, Mr. Norman Arnold, BA FCA *1964;* (Tax Fac), N.A. Lane, 17394 N 77th Street, SCOTTSDALE, AZ 85255, UNITED STATES.
LANE, Mr. Paul Edward, BSc ACA *1991;* 3 Hornbeam Close, WOKINGHAM, RG41 4UR.
LANE, Mr. Paul James, BA ACA *1984;* R C I Financial Services Ltd Egale House, 78 St. Albans Road, WATFORD, WD17 1AF.
LANE, Mr. Peter Geoffrey, FCA *1952;* 9 The Street, Hoole Bank, CHESTER, CH2 4ES. (Life Member)
LANE, Mr. Peter John, FCA *1955;* 11 Ryknild Drive, SUTTON COLDFIELD, WEST MIDLANDS, B74 2AZ. (Life Member)
LANE, Mr. Peter William, FCA *1953;* with The Trevor Jones Partnership LLP, Springfield House, 99-101 Crossbrook Street, Cheshunt, WALTHAM CROSS, HERTFORDSHIRE EN8 8JR. (Life Member)
•LANE, Mr. Phillip Ivor, BCom FCA *1982;* Whittingham Riddell LLP, Belmont House, Shrewsbury Business Park, SHREWSBURY, SY2 6LG.
LANE, Mr. Phillip John, BSc ACA *2000;* 63 Redgrove Park, CHELTENHAM, GLOUCESTERSHIRE, GL51 6QY.
LANE, Mrs. Renee Janet, BSc ACA *1991;* AVC Productions Ltd, 242 Gresham Road, SLOUGH, SL1 4PH.
LANE, Mr. Richard, BA(Hons) ACA *2009;* 6 Ducaine Apartments, Merchant Street, LONDON, E3 4PG.
LANE, Mr. Richard Ernest, OBE FCA *1968;* 13 St. Michaels Close, BROMLEY, BR1 2DX.
•LANE, Mr. Richard James, BA ACA *1993;* Lane & Co, 4 Saville Grove, KENILWORTH, WARWICKSHIRE, CV8 2PR.
•LANE, Mr. Richard William, FCA *1983;* The Trevor Jones Partnership LLP, Springfield House, 99-101 Crossbrook Street, Cheshunt, WALTHAM CROSS, HERTFORDSHIRE EN8 8JR. See also Colesgrove Trustees Ltd and Springfield Tax Services Ltd
•LANE, Mr. Richard William, BSc ACA *1995;* Leonard Brown Ltd, Thornbury House, 16 Woodlands, GERRARDS CROSS, SL9 8DD. See also Lane Accounting Limited and Brown, Leonard Ltd
LANE, Mr. Ricky Thomas, BA ACA *2007;* 3 Milestone Close, Stokenchurch, HIGH WYCOMBE, BUCKINGHAMSHIRE, HP14 3RH.
LANE, Mr. Robert David, ACA *1985;* 42 Bridgnorth Road, Wombourne, WOLVERHAMPTON, WV5 0AA.
LANE, Mr. Robert Michael, BA ACA *2000;* 29 Goldsmith Way, ST. ALBANS, HERTFORDSHIRE, AL3 5LH.
LANE, Mr. Robin Spencer Norman, BSc FCA *1962;* 151 Banstead Road, BANSTEAD, SM7 1QH. (Life Member)
LANE, Mr. Ronald William, FCA *1940;* Flat 11 Moresby Court, Westbury Road, FAREHAM, PO16 7US. (Life Member)
LANE, Mrs. Sandra Catherine Margaret, BA ACA DChA *1981;* 20 Meadowcourt Road, LEICESTER, LE2 2PB.
LANE, Miss. Sarah Denise, ACA *2007;* 94 Africa Drive, Marchwood, SOUTHAMPTON, SO40 4WF.
LANE, Mrs. Sarah Louise, ACA *1995;* Godwyn, Dean Lane, Stoke Orchard, CHELTENHAM, GLOUCESTERSHIRE, GL52 7RX.
LANE, Mr. Simon Paul, BA ACA *1988;* Dreams Plc 14 Knaves Beech Business Centre, Davies Way Loudwater, HIGH WYCOMBE, BUCKINGHAMSHIRE, HP10 9YU.
LANE, Mr. Stephen Bryan, BSc ACA *1995;* Mostyn Group Ltd Avon Works, Bridge Street, CHRISTCHURCH, DORSET, BH23 1DY.
LANE, Mr. Stephen John Roger, BA ACA *1992;* 55 Matlock Road, Caversham, READING, RG4 7BP.
LANE, Mr. Stephen Waddington, MA FCA *1959;* 26 Nursery Lane, LEEDS, LS17 7HN. (Life Member)
LANE, Mr. Stuart Christopher, BA ACA *2006;* Flat 13, Centurion Court, 83 Camp Road, ST. ALBANS, HERTFORDSHIRE, AL1 5JN.
LANE, Ms. Susan Marina, MA ACA *1987;* 2a Rochester Terrace, EDINBURGH, EH10 5AA.
LANE, Ms. Susan Patricia, BA ACA *1991;* 10 The Grove, SHIPLEY, WEST YORKSHIRE, BD18 4LD.
LANE, Miss. Tammy-Michelle Sa'Adiah, ACA *2009;* Flat 9, 4 Rosecroft Avenue, LONDON, NW3 7QB.
•LANE, Mr. Thomas Arthur, FCA *1965;* Thomas Lane, Little Hill Cottage, Buckland St Mary, CHARD, TA20 3SS.
•LANE, Mr. Trevor, BSc FCA *1982;* M N Jenks & Co Limited, 72 Commercial Road, Paddock Wood, TONBRIDGE, KENT, TN12 6DP.
LANE, Mr. William Albert, FCA *1954;* Lindum, 177 Burley Lane, Quarndon, DERBY, DE22 5JS. (Life Member)
LANE, Mr. William Frederick Charles, BSc ACA *2006;* Flat 161 Defoe House, Barbican, LONDON, EC2Y 8ND.
LANE, Miss. Zara, BA ACA *2005;* with UNW LLP, Citygate, St. James Boulevard, NEWCASTLE UPON TYNE, NE1 4JE.
LANES, Mr. Jonathan James Alan, ACA *2009;* with BDO LLP, 125 Colmore Row, BIRMINGHAM, B3 3SD.
LANES, Mr. Stephen Alec, BSc FCA *1979;* Thorpe House, 105 Mycenae Road, Blackheath, LONDON, SE3 7RX.
LANEY, Mrs. Joanne Katharine, BSc FCA *1989;* 17 Fishbourne Road East, CHICHESTER, WEST SUSSEX, PO19 3HS.
LANFEAR, Mr. Matthew George, MBA BSc FCA *1996;* Mugerenmatt 31, CH-6330 CHAM, SWITZERLAND.
•LANG, Mr. Andrew Charles D'arcy, FCA *1973;* (Tax Fac), Sandison Lang & Co, 2 St.Mary's Road, TONBRIDGE, TN9 2LB.
•LANG, Miss. Catriona Margaret, BSc ACA *2004;* Dow Schofield Watts Transaction Services LLP, 7700 Daresbury Park, Daresbury, WARRINGTON, WA4 4BS.
LANG, Mr. Christopher John Gordon, FCA *1973;* Robin Hill, 23 Hill Road, HASLEMERE, GU27 2JN.
LANG, Mr. David, BSc FCA *1977;* Styria, Borrans Road, AMBLESIDE, LA22 0EN.
LANG, Mr. Edward Nicholas, BA ACA *1983;* Posterns Court, Henfold Lane, Holmwood, DORKING, RH5 4NX.
LANG, Mr. Giles, BA ACA *2007;* Deloitte & Touche Hill House, 1 Little New Street, LONDON, EC4A 3TR.
LANG, Mr. Graham Ronald, BSc FCA *1980;* 12 Curzon Way, CHELMSFORD, CM2 6PF.
LANG, Mrs. Joanne Lucy, LLB ACA *2000;* with PricewaterhouseCoopers, 101 Barbirolli Square, Lower Mosley Street, MANCHESTER, M2 3PW.
LANG, Mr. Jonathan David, BA(Hons) ACA *2000;* P Z Cussons (UK) Ltd, 3500 Aviator Way, MANCHESTER, M22 5TG.
LANG, Mrs. Joy Elaine, ACA *2004;* 63 St. James's Avenue, BECKENHAM, KENT, BR3 4HE.
LANG, Mr. Julian Charles Vaughan, FCA *1964;* Headborough, Tey Road, Aldham, COLCHESTER, CO6 3RX. (Life Member)
LANG, Mr. Justin Robert Charles Reynolds, BA ACA *1993;* Serco Thomson House Faraday Street, Birchwood Park Birchwood, WARRINGTON, WA3 6GA.
LANG, Mrs. Liza Maria, BA ACA *2002;* 18 Highfield Road, Hale, ALTRINCHAM, CHESHIRE, WA15 8BX.
•LANG, Mrs. Marie Louise, BA FCA *1995;* G B A C Ltd, 83-85 Shambles Street, BARNSLEY, SOUTH YORKSHIRE, S70 2SB.
LANG, Mr. Martin John, ACA *1991;* PO Box 61, GEORGETOWN, GRAND CAYMAN, CAYMAN ISLANDS.
LANG, Mr. Paul, ACA *2009;* 134a Stroud Green Road, LONDON, N4 3RZ.
LANG, Mr. Peter William, FCA *1955;* Charters, Nantderry, ABERGAVENNY, NP7 9DN. (Life Member)
LANG, Mr. Richard Edwin, BA ACA *1999;* 1 Treetops, Kemsing, SEVENOAKS, KENT, TN15 6SP.
LANG, Mr. Robert John, BSc ACA *1989;* Homeleigh, 57 Dyffryn Rd, Gorseinon, SWANSEA, SA4 6BA.
•LANG, Mr. Ruediger, ACA *2011;* with Mazars LLP, Tower Bridge House, St. Katharines Way, LONDON, E1W 1DD.
LANG, Miss. Sarah Jane, BA ACA *2007;* with Deloitte LLP, Athene Place, 66 Shoe Lane, LONDON, EC4A 3BQ.
•LANG, Mr. Steven Craig, BA ACA *1996;* Ernst & Young LLP, 1 More London Place, LONDON, SE1 2AF. See also Ernst & Young Europe LLP
LANG, Mrs. Tracey Wynne, LLB ACA *1983;* Lang Software Ltd, 31 Clifton Road, POOLE, BH14 9PW.
•LANG, Mrs. Yvonne Jane, BSc FCA *1985;* Smith & Williamson Ltd, 25 Moorgate, LONDON, EC2R 6AY. See also Nexia Audit Limited
LANGAN, Mrs. Deborah Elaine, ACA *1986;* Affiniti, Technology House, Maylands Avenue, HEMEL HEMPSTEAD, HERTFORDSHIRE, HP2 7DF.
•LANGAN, Ms. Marie Claire, MA FCA *1993;* 34 Raglan Road, BRISTOL, BS7 8EG.
LANGAN, Ms. Rita Mary, PhD BSc ACA *2001;* 8 Dane Drive, CAMBRIDGE, CB3 9LP.
LANGAN, Mrs. Tracey, BA(Hons) ACA *2002;* 63 Elmbank Way, LONDON, W7 3DF.
LANGARD, Mr. Paul Attwood, BSc ACA *1997;* Blythe Valley Innovation Centre, Central Boulevard, SOLIHULL, WEST MIDLANDS, B90 8AJ.
LANGDALE, Mr. Roger Gaimster, FCA *1958;* 28 Leonie Hill 03-28, SINGAPORE 239227, SINGAPORE. (Life Member)
•LANGDON, Mr. Jonathan Charles, BSc FCA *1982;* Milsted Langdon LLP, Winchester House, Deane Gate Avenue, TAUNTON, SOMERSET, TA1 2UH.
LANGDON, Mrs. Kate, MA ACA *2004;* 9 Napier Road, EDINBURGH, EH10 5AZ.
LANGDON, Mr. Martin Howard, FCA *1958;* 6 Hereford Road, LONDON, W2 4AA. (Life Member)
LANGDON, Mr. Michael Robert Finch, MA FCA *1974;* Rutland Partners LLP, Cunard House, 15 Regent Street, LONDON, SW1Y 4LR.
•LANGDON, Mr. Patrick John, FCA *1973;* (Tax Fac), Manningtons, 7-9 Wellington Square, HASTINGS, EAST SUSSEX, TN34 1PD.
•LANGDON, Mr. Paul Frederick, BA FCA FPC TEP *1990;* (Tax Fac), Saffery Champness, Lion House, Red Lion Street, LONDON, WC1R 4GB.
•LANGDON, Mr. Peter Michael, ACA CA(AUS) *2010;* Captus, Flat G104, Gilbert Scott Building, Scott Avenue, LONDON, SW15 3SG.
LANGDON, Miss. Philippa, BSc(Hons) ACA *2010;* 2 St. Johns Road, SIDCUP, DA14 4HB.
LANGDON, Mr. Robert Martin, FCA *1966;* 18/19 Harcourt Street, DUBLIN 2, COUNTY DUBLIN, IRELAND.
•LANGDON, Mr. Rowland John, FCA *1967;* Langdon Gray LLP, PO Box 447, Stone Court, Helmdon Road, Sulgrave, BANBURY OXFORDSHIRE OX17 2EF. See also Langdons and L G Accountants Limited
LANGDOWN, Mr. Paul, BSc ACA *2007;* 12 Purdown Road, BRISTOL, BS7 9PG.
LANGE, Mr. Matthew Thomas, BSc ACA *2009;* Beech Mount, Trimpley Lane, BEWDLEY, WORCESTERSHIRE, DY12 1JJ.
LANGEN, Miss. Sabine Elisabeth, ACA *2009;* 24 Trafalgar Road, Moseley, BIRMINGHAM, B13 8BH.
•LANGER, Mr. Eric Graham, BSc FCA *1976;* (Tax Fac), Langer & Co Limited, 8-10 Gatley Road, CHEADLE, CHESHIRE, SK8 1PY. See also Langer & Co
LANGER, Mr. Henry David, FCA *1967;* Pultec Ltd, Pultec House, Southway Drive, Warmley, BRISTOL, BS30 5LW.
•LANGFIELD, Mr. Gregory William, FCA *1963;* G W Langfield, 55 Seaburn Road, Toton, Beeston, NOTTINGHAM, NG9 6HN.
LANGFIELD, Mr. John Michael, BA FCA CTA *1990;* (Tax Fac), 14 Oldfield, Honley, HOLMFIRTH, HD9 6RL.
LANGFIELD, Mr. Paul Michael, BA(Hons) ACA *2004;* 14 Henrys Grant, Riverside Road, ST. ALBANS, HERTFORDSHIRE, AL1 1RY.
LANGFORD, Mr. Andrew George Simon, MChem ACA *2006;* 4 Vaughan Road, THAMES DITTON, SURREY, KT7 0UF.
LANGFORD, Mr. Angus John Roper, MBA BA FCA *1990;* Intellect, Russell Square House, 10-12 Russell Square, LONDON, WC1B 5EH.
LANGFORD, Mr. Benjamin Ross, BA(Hons) ACA *2003;* with Grant Thornton UK LLP, Grant Thornton House, 22 Melton Street, Euston Square, LONDON, NW1 2EP.
•LANGFORD, Mr. Christopher John, FCA *1969;* Langford & Co, 93 Western Road, TRING, HP23 4BN.
LANGFORD, Mrs. Felicity Abigail, BSc ACA *2004;* 6 The Landings, Haxby, YORK, YO32 2SJ.
LANGFORD, Mr. Francis, FCA *1961;* Holly Oaks, 16 Clos y Deri, Llanedi, Pontarddulais, SWANSEA, SA4 0XW.
LANGFORD, Mr. Jonathan Neil, LLB ACA *1999;* 77 Cardross Street, LONDON, W6 0DP.
LANGFORD, Mrs. Marie Teresa, FCA *1982;* 16 Woodthorpe Avenue, Woodthorpe, NOTTINGHAM, NG5 4FD.
LANGFORD, Mr. Mark David, BA(Hons) ACA *2001;* 6 The Landings, Haxby, YORK, NORTH YORKSHIRE, YO32 2SJ.
LANGFORD, Mr. Michael Alan Sussex, ACA *1982;* 38 Nigel Fisher Way, CHESSINGTON, KT9 2SN.
LANGFORD, Mrs. Michelle, BA ACA *2006;* with PricewaterhouseCoopers LLP, Donington Court, Pegasus Business Park, Castle Donington, DERBY, DE74 2UZ.
LANGFORD, Mr. Norman, FCA *1954;* 86 Elm Hall Drive, LIVERPOOL, L18 5JA. (Life Member)
LANGFORD, Mr. Peter Michael, MA ACA *1983;* Asset Risk Consultants Limited, 7 New Street St. Peter Port, GUERNSEY, GY1 2PF.
LANGFORD, Mr. Philip Graham, FCA *1953;* Cobo Cottage, West Ashling Road, Hambrook, CHICHESTER, PO18 8UF. (Life Member)
LANGFORD, Mr. Reginald, BSc ACA *1987;* (Tax Fac), 5 Claridge Court, Hempstead, GILLINGHAM, Kent, ME7 3NE.
LANGFORD, Mr. Robert, FCA *1963;* 22 Pinewood Road, STOCKTON-ON-TEES, TS16 0AJ.
LANGFORD, Mr. Robert Endean, MA FCA *1972;* South Ridge, The Avenue, TADWORTH, KT20 5AY. (Life Member)
LANGFORD, Mr. Robert Francis, BA(Hons) ACA *2000;* 39 Danescourt Crescent, SUTTON, SURREY, SM1 3DZ.
LANGFORD, Mr. Roger William, FCA *1960;* The Coinings, East Farm, Humshaugh, HEXHAM, NE46 4DF. (Life Member)
LANGFORD, Mr. Ronan Laurence, ACA CA(SA) *2011;* 60b Sandpit Lane, ST. ALBANS, HERTFORDSHIRE, AL1 4BW.
LANGFORD, Mrs. Sarah Jane, BSc ACA *1982;* 44 Eastmont Road, Hinchley Wood, ESHER, KT10 9AZ.

LANGFORD, Mr. Simon, ACA *2004;* Garden Flat, 61 Gwendwr Road, West Kensington, LONDON, W14 9BG.
LANGFORD, Miss. Vivien Elizabeth, BA ACA *1987;* 11 George Street, BATH, BA1 2EH.
•**LANGHAM, Mr. Christopher Roy David, MA FCA** *1991;* Chris Langham Consulting, 17 Springs Road, KESWICK, CUMBRIA, CA12 4AQ.
•**LANGHAM, Mr. Dale Martin, ACA** *1984;* Langham & Co, 54 Westmorland Drive, Desborough, KETTERING, NORTHAMPTONSHIRE, NN14 2XB.
LANGHAM, Mrs. Donna Louise, BSc ACA *1997;* Bennett Gibson Group, 126 Jellicoe Street, TE PUKE 3185, NEW ZEALAND.
LANGHAM, Mr. Stephen John, LLB ACA *1990;* 2450 Granada Boulevard, KISSIMMEE, FL 34746, UNITED STATES.
•**LANGHELT, Mr. Mitchell, FCA** *1981;* Sutcliffe & Co Ltd, Old Bank House, STURMINSTER NEWTON, DT10 1AN.
LANGHORN, Mr. Michael David, MA ACA *1987;* Itochu Europe Plc Broadgate Tower, 20 Primrose Street, LONDON, EC2A 2EW.
•**LANGHORN, Mr. Paul Rodney, BA FCA** *1984;* with RSM Tenon Audit Limited, 66 Chiltern Street, LONDON, W1U 4JT.
LANGHORN, Mr. Russell Martin, BSc ACA *1993;* Cobwebs, The Green, Green Hammerton, YORK, YO26 8BQ.
LANGLANDS, Mrs. Alexandra Helen, BSc ACA *2006;* 50 Whoberley Avenue, COVENTRY, CV5 8EP.
LANGLANDS, Mr. David Robin, BSc ACA *1992;* 7 School Lane, Elton, PETERBOROUGH, PE8 6RS.
LANGLANDS, Mr. Mark Colin, BA ACA *1999;* 15 Campion Grove, HARROGATE, HG3 2UG.
LANGLANDS, Mr. Robert, BA ACA *1984;* (Tax Fac), Roddis Taylor Robinson, Unit 6, Acorn Business Park, Woodseats Close, SHEFFIELD, S8 0TB.
LANGLANDS, Mr. Steven, BA ACA *1992;* 2 Middlefields, Cheadle Hulme, CHEADLE, SK8 5RL.
LANGLAY-SMITH, Mr. Graham Michael, BA ACA ACT *1986;* Waller Hill Farmhouse, Grandshore Lane, Frittenden, CRANBROOK, TN17 2DB.
LANGLEY, Mr. Alan, FCA *1978;* 5 Mimosa Close, LOUGHBOROUGH, LE11 2DJ.
•**LANGLEY, Mr. Alex, ACA** *2009;* Grant Thornton Limited, Kensington Chambers, 46/50 Kensington Place, JERSEY, JE1 1ET.
LANGLEY, Mrs. Alice Caroline, BA ACA *2005;* 38 Muncaster Road, LONDON, SW11 6NU.
LANGLEY, Miss. Caroline Moira, MA MSc ACA *2002;* Cheviot Asset Management, 2nd Floor, 90 Long Acre, LONDON, WC2E 9RA.
LANGLEY, Mr. Daniel Robert, BA ACA *2001;* 18 Dresden Road, LONDON, N19 3BD.
•**LANGLEY, Mr. David John, FCA** *1962;* David Langley, 82 Marine Crescent, Goring-by-Sea, WORTHING, WEST SUSSEX, BN12 4JH.
LANGLEY, Mr. David John, BA ACA *2005;* Qubic Tax 5th Floor Central Square South, Orchard Street, NEWCASTLE UPON TYNE, NE1 3AZ.
LANGLEY, Mr. David Thomas, ACA *1988;* 8 Dover Close, Winklebury, BASINGSTOKE, RG23 8EG.
LANGLEY, Mrs. Helen Elizabeth, BSc ACA *1989;* 3 Rectory Road, NEWCASTLE UPON TYNE, NE3 1XR.
LANGLEY, Mr. Jason, BEng ACA *2004;* 12 Bockhampton Road, KINGSTON UPON THAMES, SURREY, KT2 5JU.
LANGLEY, Mrs. Jennifer Ann, FCA *1977;* Heber Ltd, Belvedere Mill, Chalford, STROUD, GLOUCESTERSHIRE, GL6 8NT.
LANGLEY, Mr. John Antony, BSc FCA *1990;* 10 STEEP HOLLOW LANE, COS COB, CT 06807, UNITED STATES.
LANGLEY, Mr. John Paul, BSc ACA *1990;* 42 Clarence Road, Harborne, BIRMINGHAM, B17 9LG.
LANGLEY, Mr. John Peter, FCA *1970;* 65 Goldbrook, Hoxne, EYE, SUFFOLK, IP21 5AN.
LANGLEY, Mr. Martyn, ACA MAAT *2005;* with Smith Craven, 18 South Street, CHESTERFIELD, DERBYSHIRE, S40 1QX.
LANGLEY, Mr. Michael Gordon, MA FCA *1974;* Riverside House, Chiswick Mall, LONDON, W4 2PR.
LANGLEY, Mrs. Natalie Jane, BA ACA CTA *2001;* 18 Dresden Road, LONDON, N19 3BD.
LANGLEY, Mr. Nigel Mark, MA FCA *1993;* Ribbonswood, Rowsells Lane, TOTNES, DEVON, TQ9 5AG.
LANGLEY, Mr. Roger Christopher, FCA *1957;* The Firefly Trust, 14 Sergison Close, HAYWARDS HEATH, WEST SUSSEX, RH16 1HU. (Life Member)
LANGLEY, Mrs. Sheila Estelle, FCA *1962;* 715 Kenton Lane, HARROW, HA3 6AR.
LANGLEY, Mr. Simon Andrew, BSc ACA *1993;* 36 St. James Road, ILKLEY, WEST YORKSHIRE, LS29 9PY.
LANGLEY, Mr. Steven David, BA ACA *1989;* 33 Fletching Avenue, Essexwold, BEDFORDVIEW, 2007, SOUTH AFRICA.
LANGLEY, Mr. Steven Harald, FCA *1983;* with Pitt Godden & Taylor, Brunel House, George Street, GLOUCESTER, GL1 1BZ.
LANGLEY, Mrs. Suzanne Patricia, ACA *1992;* 8 Greenway, HARPENDEN, AL5 1NQ.
LANGLEY, Mr. Toby, BSc ACA *2006;* 74 Orbel Street, LONDON, SW11 3NY.
LANGLEY, Mr. William, BA(Hons) ACA *2011;* Deloitte & Touche, Floor 3, Hill House, 1 Little New Street, LONDON, EC4A 3TR.
LANGMAID, Mr. Peter Anthony, FCA *1957;* The Grange, 5 Dormy Avenue, Mannamead, PLYMOUTH, PL3 5BE.
LANGMAID, Mr. Stephen Peter, BSc FCA *1992;* Marina Bar, Vauxhall Quay, Sutton Harbour, PLYMOUTH, PL4 0DN.
LANGMAN, Dr. Adam Boyd, PhD FCA *1992;* Storeys S S P, Higham House, New Bridge Street West, NEWCASTLE UPON TYNE, NE1 8AU.
•**LANGMAN, Mr. David Thomas, FCA** *1970;* with Somerbys Limited, 30 Nelson Street, LEICESTER, LE1 7BA.
LANGMEAD, Mrs. Rosalie May, ACA *2006;* 15 Greenmeadow Drive, BARNSTAPLE, DEVON, EX31 4HT.
•**LANGRICK, Mr. Christopher John, ACA** *2002;* Langrick Accounting Limited, Suite 9C, Caledonian House, Tatton Street, KNUTSFORD, CHESHIRE WA16 6AG. See also Langrick Consulting Limited
LANGRICK, Mr. John Nigel, BSc FCA *1982;* Unit 23, Lane 418, Jin Xiu East Road, Jan Qiao EPZ, PUDONG 201206, CHINA.
LANGRIDGE, Miss. Alison Louise, ACA *2007;* 19 Stanley Road, HALSTEAD, ESSEX, CO9 1LA.
LANGRIDGE, Mr. Christopher Timothy, ACA *1979;* Pebbles Court, Holyport, MAIDENHEAD, SL6 2JL.
•**LANGRIDGE, Mr. David Henry, FCA** *1972;* (Tax Fac), David Langridge, 77A High Street, Lindfield, HAYWARDS HEATH, RH16 2HN.
LANGRIDGE, Mr. Gary Tony, BA ACA *1983;* The Old Coach House, Walton Road, Kimcote, LUTTERWORTH, LEICESTERSHIRE, LE17 5RU.
LANGRIDGE, Mrs. Linda Ann, BSc ACA *1988;* 5 Oldean Close, Tilehurst, READING, RG31 5QA.
LANGRIDGE, Mr. Martin Andrew, BSc ACA *1988;* Toshiba Tec UK Imaging Systems Ltd, Abbey Cloisters, Abbey Green, CHERTSEY, SURREY, KT16 8RF.
LANGRIDGE, Mr. Neil James, MSc BA ACA *1981;* 38 Lower Hill Road, EPSOM, SURREY, KT19 8LT.
LANGRIDGE, Mr. Robert Edward, ACA *1983;* 55 Woodfield Drive, WINCHESTER, HAMPSHIRE, SO22 5PY.
LANGRISH, Mr. Richard Michael John, MA ACA *1999;* Avenue de l'Aigle 12, Woluwe St Pierre, B-1150 BRUSSELS, BELGIUM.
LANGSHAW, Mr. Andrew George Ashbrook, ACA CA(AUS) *2008;* with David Rubin & Partners LLP, 26-28 Bedford Row, LONDON, WC1R 4HE.
LANGSTAFF, Miss. Clare Elizabeth, BSc ACA *2003;* 29 Hermon Hill, LONDON, E11 2AR.
LANGSTAFF, Ms. Kerry Anne, BSc ACA *2006;* 150 West 82nd Street Apt 3F, NEW YORK, NY 10024, UNITED STATES.
LANGSTAFF, Mr. Nigel Jeremy, BA ACA *1996;* 21 Townshend Road, RICHMOND, TW9 1XH.
LANGSTON, Ms. Doreen Julie, BSc FCA *1980;* Roundwood Cottage Green Dene, East Horsley, LEATHERHEAD, KT24 5RE.
LANGSTON, Mr. Edward, ACA *1978;* 23 Manilla Road, BRISTOL, BS8 4EB.
LANGSTON, Mr. John, BA FCA *1977;* 11a Esher Park Avenue, ESHER, KT10 9NX.
LANGSTONE-BOLT, Mrs. Alison Jane, BSc(Econ) ACA *1995;* 6 Cope Place, Kensington, LONDON, W8 6AA.
LANGTON, Mrs. Anne Gillian, BCom FCA *1979;* Woodside Cottage, Cogshall Lane, Little Leigh, NORTHWICH, CHESHIRE, CW9 6BN.
•①**LANGTON, Mr. David John, BA FCA MABRP** *1988;* with Deloitte LLP, 4 Brindley Place, BIRMINGHAM, B1 2HZ.
LANGTON, Mrs. Diane Shirley, BSc ACA *1989;* 2 Wellfield Close, Balsall Common, COVENTRY, CV7 7SZ.
LANGTON, Mr. John, FCA *1966;* Bozzarisstrasse 7, 81545 MUNICH, GERMANY. (Life Member)
LANGTON, Mr. Mark Robert, BSc(Hons) ACA *2002;* 6 Wallis Field, Corseley Road Groombridge, TUNBRIDGE WELLS, TN3 9SQ.
LANGTON, Mr. Paul Frederick Thomas, BSc ACA *1992;* Shropshire Gate Manor, Old Woodhouses, WHITCHURCH, SHROPSHIRE, SY13 4EH.
LANGTON, Mr. Peter John, BSc FCA *1979;* Promart Manufacturing Ltd, Caddick Road, Knowsley Business Park, PRESCOT, MERSEYSIDE, L34 9HP.
LANGTON, Mr. Richard David Neil, BSc ACA *1996;* 4 Derby Road, Caversham, READING, RG4 5EY.
LANGTON, Mr. Robert Neil, BSc FCA *1965;* Woodside Cottage, Cogshall Lane, Little Leigh, NORTHWICH, CHESHIRE, CW9 6BN.
LANGTON, Mr. Stephen Paget, FCA *1963;* 25 Gloucester Street, CIRENCESTER, GLOUCESTERSHIRE, GL7 2DJ. (Life Member)
LANGTON, Mr. Will, ACA *2010;* The Red House, Vowchurch, HEREFORD, HR2 0RB.
•**LANGTON-DAVIES, Mrs. Melanie Jane, ACA FCCA** *2008;* (Tax Fac), Gardners Accountants Ltd, Brynford House, Brynford Street, HOLYWELL, CLWYD, CH8 7RD. See also Gardner Salisbury Limited
LANGTRY, Mr. Richard Beresford, FCA *1969;* High Barn, Lynx Hill, East Horsley, LEATHERHEAD, KT24 5AX. (Life Member)
LANGWORTHY, Mr. Simon Richard Briscoe, BA ACA *1995;* Thompsons House, Taylors Hill, Chilham, CANTERBURY, KENT, CT4 8BZ.
LANHAM, Mr. Craig Berkeley, BA ACA *1991;* 609 Clover Hill Road, SOMERSET, PA 15501, UNITED STATES.
•**LANHAM, Mr. Hugh Christopher, FCA** *1978;* Lanham and Company Limited, 9 Great Chesterford Court, London Road, Gt Chesterford, SAFFRON WALDEN, CB10 1PF.
LANIADO, Ms. Beverley Regina, BA ACA *1996;* 12 Brooklands Drive, Goostrey, CREWE, CW4 8JB.
LANIGAN, Mr. Gerard, FCA *1958;* with Jack Ross, Barnfield House, The Approach, MANCHESTER, M3 7BX. (Life Member)
LANIGAN, Mr. Philip Nicholas, BA ACA *1989;* 120 Buckingham Road, Heaton Moor, STOCKPORT, SK4 4RG.
•**LANKESTER, Mr. Clive Arthur, ACA** *1987;* (Tax Fac), Janelle Lankester, The Foundry, 9 Park Lane, Puckeridge, WARE, SG11 1RL.
LANKESTER, Mr. Robert George, BSc FCA *1967;* Merrydown, 6 Fountain Hill, BUDLEIGH SALTERTON, EX9 6BX.
LANKESTER, Mr. Toby Elliott, BA ACA *1995;* 69 Drummond Way, MACCLESFIELD, CHESHIRE, SK10 4XJ.
LANKFER, Mr. Robert William, BSc ACA *1987;* 44 Elm Road, Folksworth, PETERBOROUGH, PE7 3SX.
LANMAN, Mr. James Alexander, ACA *2009;* 71 Abbots Gardens, LONDON, N2 0JG.
•①**LANNAGAN, Mr. Patrick Alexander, BCom ACA** *1999;* BDO LLP, 6th Floor, 3 Hardman Street, Spinningfields, MANCHESTER, M3 3AT. See also BDO Stoy Hayward LLP
LANNI, Mr. Peter Anthony, FCA *1982;* 25 Rosafield Avenue, HALESOWEN, B62 9BU.
LANNIN, Mr. Timothy Charles, BSc FCA *1994;* with Francis Clark LLP, Sigma House, Oak View Close, Edginswell Park, TORQUAY, TQ2 7FF.
•**LANNING, Mr. Leonard Samuel, FCA** *1973;* L.S. Lanning, 2 Eton Court, STAINES, TW18 2AF.
LANNING, Miss. Ruth, BSc ACA *2009;* Flat 25 Sidney House, Old Ford Road, LONDON, E2 9QB.
LANNON, Miss. Claire, MA ACA *1996;* House 12A, Bella Vista, 15 Silver Terrace Road, Silver Strand, SAI KUNG, NEW TERRITORIES HONG KONG SAR.
•**LANNON, Mr. Damian Edward, BA(Hons) ACA CTA** *2001;* Francis Clark LLP, Sigma House, Oak View Close, Edginswell Park, TORQUAY, TQ2 7FF.
•**LANSBERRY, Mr. Peter Robert, FCA ATII CF** *1979;* Spofforths Private Client Services LLP, Comewell House, North Street, HORSHAM, WEST SUSSEX, RH12 1RL.
LANSDALE, Mr. Barrie, FCA *1965;* Thackra's Cottage, 231 Cumberworth Lane, Denby Dale, HUDDERSFIELD, HD8 8PR.
LANSDELL, Mr. Michael Roy, ACA CA(SA) *2010;* (Tax Fac), 44 Abingdon Road, LONDON, W8 6AR.
LANSDELL, Mr. Paul Michael, BSc ACA *1991;* 9213 Talisman Drive, VIENNA, VA 22182, UNITED STATES.
•**LANSDOWN, Mr. Alan John Christopher, FCA** *1968;* Newton Lodge, Cynwyl Elfed, CARMARTHEN, DYFED, SA33 6SP.
•**LANSDOWN, Mr. Christopher John, BSc FCA** *1969;* C.J. Lansdown & Co Limited, 7 Terrey Road, SHEFFIELD, S17 4DD. See also Lansdown C.J. Limited
LANSDOWN, Mrs. Claire Jane, BA ACA *1998;* with Smith & Williamson Ltd, 25 Moorgate, LONDON, EC2R 6AY.
•**LANSDOWN, Mr. Ian Gregory, BSc ACA** *1991;* (Tax Fac), 53 Cranwells Park, Weston, BATH, BA1 2YE.
LANSDOWN, Mr. Michael William, BSc ACA *1992;* Serco Group Plc, Enterprise House, 11 Bartley Wood Business Park, Bartley Way, HOOK, HAMPSHIRE RG27 9XB.
LANSDOWN, Mr. Stephen Philip, FCA *1975;* Jolivet Village de Putron, St. Peter Port, GUERNSEY, GY1 2TF.
LANSDOWN, Mrs. Wendy Pamela, FCA *1958;* Spin Hill House, Market Lavington, DEVIZES, SN10 4NR. (Life Member)
LANSDOWN-DAVIS, Mr. Norman Stanley, FCA *1956;* Stoneleigh, 2 Highfield Place, EPPING, CM16 4DB. (Life Member)
LANSDOWNE, Mr. Richard Edgar, BSc FCA *1975;* Wanborough Manor, Wanborough, GUILDFORD, SURREY, GU3 2JR. (Life Member)
LANSER, Mr. Andre Marcel, Bcom ACA CA(SA) *2010;* 88 Ladbroke Road, LONDON, W11 3NU.
LANSLEY, Mr. Anthony Philip, BA FCA *1987;* West Port, Rotten Row, LEWES, BN7 1LJ.
LANSTON, Mr. Michael, BA ACA *1991;* Two 12th Street, Apt 807, HOBOKEN, NJ 07030, UNITED STATES.
LANT, Mr. Alexander, BA(Hons) ACA *2011;* 37 Roberts Road, POOLE, DORSET, BH17 7HE.
•**LANT, Mrs. Marcia, BA FCA AMCT** *1990;* 18 Haldane Terrace, Jesmond, NEWCASTLE UPON TYNE, NE2 3AN.
•**LANT, Mr. Stephen, MA ACA CF CTA** *1990;* (Tax Fac), UNW LLP, Citygate, St. James Boulevard, NEWCASTLE UPON TYNE, NE1 4JE.
LANTSBURY, Mr. Paul James, BCom ACA *2000;* 2 West Hill Place, BRIGHTON, BN1 3RU.
LANYON, Mr. Christopher Barry, BA ACA *1981;* 5 Dukes Lane, LONDON, W8 4JL.
LANYON, Mr. Phillip, BSc ACA *1992;* 65 Stathern Lane, Harby, MELTON MOWBRAY, LE14 4DA.
LANYON, Mrs. Victoria Marianne, MA ACA *1996;* 65 Stathern Lane, Harby, MELTON MOWBRAY, LE14 4DA.
LAO, Mr. Shi Chun, ACA *2008;* Flat E, 8/F Block 9, Belvedere Garden Phase 2, TSUEN WAN, NEW TERRITORIES, HONG KONG SAR.
LAO, Miss. Shui Fung, ACA *1984;* Flat F 10/F Block 10, Cherry Mansions, Whampoa Garden, HUNG HOM, KOWLOON, HONG KONG SAR.
LAO, Ms. Veng Chao Anita, ACA *2008;* 4C Walton Mansion, 306 - 308 Prince Edward Road West, KWUN TONG, KOWLOON, HONG KONG SAR.
LAO, Mr. Wai Keung, ACA *2008;* Flat C, 3/F, Imperial Heights, Belair Gardens, SHA TIN, HONG KONG SAR.
LAOYE, Mrs. Folashade, ACA *1995;* Bank of Industry Building (5th floor), 23 Marina, LAGOS, NIGERIA.
LAPAGE, Mr. Nigel James, ACA *1980;* Burry & Knight Ltd, 261 Lymington Road, Highcliffe, CHRISTCHURCH, DORSET, BH23 5EE.
LAPHAM, Mr. Derek Ronald, FCA *1965;* 1 The Old Walled Garden, Whitney Wood, STEVENAGE, SG1 4TN.
LAPHAM, Mr. Keith Patrick, BSc ACA *1991;* 14 Rookery Close, ST.IVES, CAMBRIDGESHIRE, PE27 5FX.
LAPINSKA, Ms. Christina Mary, BSc FCA *1979;* 4922 Windward Way, FORT LAUDERDALE, FL 33312, UNITED STATES.
LAPPAS, Miss. Mary, LLB ACA *2007;* Flat 126, 1 Prescot Street, LONDON, E1 8RL.
LAPPER, Mr. Simon John, BA ACA *1979;* P.O. Box 6902, KIGALI, RWANDA.
LAPPIN, Mr. John, BSc FCA *1981;* Care Quality Commission, Healthcare Commission Finsbury Tower, 103-105 Bunhill Row, LONDON, EC1Y 8TG.
LAPPIN, Mr. Ralph Edward Rodger, FCA *1955;* 20 Gorselands, Andover Road, NEWBURY, RG14 6PX. (Life Member)
LAPRAIK, Mr. Ian James, BSc ACA PGCE *2001;* HBOS Plc, 10 Canons Way, BRISTOL, BS1 5LF.
LAPSA, Mr. Colin Richard, BCom MSt FRAeS FCA *1983;* Am Friedrichshain 26, 10407 BERLIN, GERMANY.
LAPSLEY, Mr. Adrian James, BA ACA *2005;* 5 Bridge Court, WELWYN GARDEN CITY, HERTFORDSHIRE, AL7 1GY.
LAPSLEY, Miss. Margaret Katherine, BSc ACA *2011;* 17 Brookfield Avenue, MANCHESTER, M21 8TX.
•**LAPTHORN, Mr. David Edwin Richard, BSc ACA CTA TEP** *1986;* (Tax Fac), Ward Goodman Limited, 4 Cedar Park, Cobham Road, Ferndown Industrial Estate, WIMBORNE, DORSET BH21 7SF. See also Ward Goodman
LAPWORTH, Mr. Richard Andrew, FCA *1979;* Boslowen, School Lane, MARAZION, TR17 0DG.

LARARD, Miss. Victoria Kate, BA ACA *2004;* Royal Bank of Scotland 6th Floor, 250 Bishopsgate, LONDON, EC2M 3UR.
LARAWAY, Mrs. Janice Patricia, FCA *1978;* 2 Nesfield Grove, Hampton In Arden, SOLIHULL, B92 0BQ.
LARBY, Mr. Paul Martin, FCA *1977;* 4 Eulalie Avenue, RANDWICK, NSW 2031, AUSTRALIA.
LARCHE, Mr. Jean-Paul, ACA *2009;* 76 Yeading Lane, HAYES, MIDDLESEX, UB4 0EY.
LARCOMBE, Mr. Antony Stuart, FCA *1951;* 74 Eastwood Old Road, LEIGH-ON-SEA, SS9 4RS. (Life Member)
LARCOMBE, Mr. Christopher Paul, FCA *1977;* Ground Floor, 9 St Clare Street, LONDON, EC3N 1LQ.
LARCOMBE, Mr. Raymond Peter, FCA *1970;* 19 Redrock Road, ROTHERHAM, S60 3JP.
LARCOMBE, Mr. Shaun Phillip, BSc ACA *1991;* 6 Kirtle Drive, Four Marks, ALTON, GU34 5HF.
LARDER, Mr. Derek, FCA *1966;* 22 Waterleaze, TAUNTON, SOMERSET, TA2 8PX.
LARDNER, Mr. William John, FCA *1979;* Meadow Farm House Bathingbourne Lane, Bathingbourne, SANDOWN, ISLE OF WIGHT, PO36 0LU.
LARGE, Mr. Andrew Neil, BA ACA *2006;* The Glebe House Martins Lane Hargrave, CHESTER, CH3 7RX.
LARGE, Charles Graeme, Esq MBE ED FCA *1955;* Chun Fai Yuen, 2nd Floor, 15 Consort Rise, POK FU LAM, HONG KONG ISLAND, HONG KONG SAR. (Life Member)
•**LARGE, Mr. David John, FCA** *1974;* (Tax Fac), LCA Services Ltd, 13 Silver Street, BARNSTAPLE, DEVON, EX32 8HR. See also Devon Finance Director LLP
LARGE, Mr. Derek John, FCA *1958;* Linden House, Manor Road, Barrowby, GRANTHAM, NG32 1BB. (Life Member)
LARGE, Mr. Eric Charles Stanley, FCA *1941;* High Barn, The Green, AMBLESIDE, LA22 9AU. (Life Member)
•**LARGE, Mrs. Margaret Anne, FCA** *1977;* LCA Services Ltd, 13 Silver Street, BARNSTAPLE, DEVON, EX32 8HR. See also Devon Finance Director LLP
LARGE, Mr. Michael, ACA CA(AUS) *2011;* Extract House, Princes House, 1C, 38 Jermyn Street, LONDON, SW1Y 6DN.
LARGE, Mr. Nicholas Stephen, FCA *1977;* with Deloitte LLP, Hill House, 1 Little New Street, LONDON, EC4A 3TR.
LARGE, Miss. Nicola Jayne, BA ACA *2007;* 40 Telfords Yard, LONDON, E1W 2BQ.
LARGE, Mr. Peter Robert, FCA *1969;* 21 Court Meadow, Stone, BERKELEY, GL13 9LR.
LARGE, Mr. Robert Hedley Grierson, BSc ACA *1991;* 32 Sutherland Gardens, LONDON, SW14 8DB.
LARGE, Mrs. Ruth Elizabeth, BA(Hons) ACA *2002;* West House, Avenue Road, CRANLEIGH, GU67LL.
LARGE, Mr. Simon George, BA ACA *1990;* 9 Hailsham Close, Owlsmoor, SANDHURST, BERKSHIRE, GU47 0YN.
LARGE, Mrs. Simone Louise, BSc ACA *2005;* 32 Home Close Road, Houghton-on-the-Hill, LEICESTER, LE7 9GT.
LARGE, Mrs. Susan, BA ACA *1983;* 5 Barbers Lane, Catherine-de-Barnes, SOLIHULL, WEST MIDLANDS, B92 0DH.
LARIVE, Mr. Ian, BSc ACA *2006;* 4 Pottery Street, LONDON, SE16 4PH.
LARK, Mr. Graham Robert Starling, BA ACA *1985;* Gorsley House, Pett Bottom, CANTERBURY, CT4 6EH.
LARKHAM, Miss. Rowena Jane, BA ACA *1989;* 3 Western Road, TRING, HERTFORDSHIRE, HP23 4BE.
LARKIN, Mr. John Douglas Edward, MA FCA MBA *1978;* 54 Fox Dene, GODALMING, SURREY, GU7 1YQ.
LARKIN, Miss. Julie, BSc ACA *2000;* Sodexho The Merchant Centre, 1 New Street Square, LONDON, EC4A 3BF.
LARKIN, Mr. Matthew, BA ACA *1999;* 42 Hillside Road, FRODSHAM, WA6 6AQ.
LARKIN, Mrs. Michelle Marie, BA ACA *2000;* 29 Wood Street, STRATFORD-UPON-AVON, WARWICKSHIRE, CV37 6JG.
LARKIN, Miss. Sarah, ACA *2000;* 36 Beechwood Drive, Thorpe St Andrew, NORWICH, NORFOLK, NR7 0LP.
LARKIN-BRAMLEY, Ms. Kathryn Anne, MBA BA FCA PGCE *1985;* Hickory Place, 5 Dickens Wynd, Elvet Moor, DURHAM, DH1 3QR.
LARKING, Mr. Peter Charles Gordon, FCA *1954;* Apple Tree Cottage, Heath Road, Linton, MAIDSTONE, ME17 4NT. (Life Member)
LARKINS, Mr. Brian Hunter, FCA *1951;* Gattigues, 30700 AIGALIERS, FRANCE. (Life Member)
LARKMAN, Mrs. Catherine Ann, BSc ACA *1990;* 11 Ipswich Grove, NORWICH, NR2 2LU.
LARKMAN, Mr. Robert Anthony, MA ACA *1983;* 70 Love Lane, PINNER, HA5 3EX.
LARKMAN, Mr. Stephen, ACA *2005;* Flat 11 John Bell Tower West, 5 Pancras Way, LONDON, E3 2ST.
•**LARKOS, Mr. Michael, BEng FCA** *1993;* Auditpro Services Ltd, 28th October Avenue No. 1, Engomi Business Centre Block B, Office 104, Engomi Nicosia, CYPRUS 2413 NICOSIA CYPRUS.
LARKOS, Mr. Philip Xenis, BSc ACA FCCA *1987;* SFS Group Public Company Limited, P.O Box 22379, CY 1521 NICOSIA, CYPRUS.
LARKWORTHY, Mr. Richard John, BA ACA CPA *1987;* with Deloitte & Touche LLP, 1750 Tysons Boulevard, MCLEAN, VA 22101, UNITED STATES.
LARMAN, Mr. Peter Desmond Morris, FCA *1965;* Butterfly Cottage, 18 Pyecombe Street, Pyecombe, BRIGHTON, BN45 7EE.
LARMER, Mr. Nicholas Mark, MMath ACA *2006;* with Place Campbell, Wilmington House, High Street, EAST GRINSTEAD, RH19 3AU.
LARMOND, Mrs. Patricia Marie, BA ACA *1996;* 23 Stanton Road, SOUTHAMPTON, SO15 4HF.
•**LARNDER, Miss. Denise Janet, BA ACA** *1989;* Ernst & Young LLP, 1 More London Place, LONDON, SE1 2AF. See also Ernst & Young Europe LLP
•**LARNER, Mrs. Elisabeth, BSc ACA** *2002;* Elisabeth Larner Limited, Meadow Croft, Pouk Lane, Hilton, LICHFIELD, STAFFORDSHIRE WS14 0ET.
LARNER, Mr. James David, BCom ACA *2002;* Meadow Croft, Pouk Lane, LICHFIELD, STAFFORDSHIRE, WS14 0ET.
LARNER, Mr. Luke, ACA *2011;* 7 Amberley Gardens, WOKINGHAM, RG41 1LN.
•**LARQUETOUX, Mrs. Claire Louise, BSc ACA** *2005;* with Mazars LLP, Tower Bridge House, St. Katharines Way, LONDON, E1W 1DD.
LARQUETOUX, Mr. Frederic, ACA *2004;* 1st Floor Flat, 10 Upper Park Road, LONDON, NW3 2UP.
LARRAGA, Miss. Margarita, BA(Hons) ACA *2009;* Apartment 196 Centenary Plaza, 18 Holliday Street, BIRMINGHAM, B1 1TH.
LARROQUE, Mr. Pierre-Christophe Herve Marie, ACA *2003;* 7 Impasse, St Ouen, 75017 PARIS, FRANCE.
LARSEN, Mr. Alan, MA ACA *1983;* 35 Kilgour Road, LONDON, SE23 1PG.
LARSEN, Mr. Andrew Gordon, ACA CA(SA) *2008;* 67 Godley Road, LONDON, SW18 3HB.
LARSEN, Miss. Anne Catherine, BA FCA *1985;* with Wilding Hudson & Co, Saxon House, 17 Lewis Road, SUTTON, SM1 4BR.
LARSEN, Mr. David Brinsley, BSc FCA *1978;* (Tax Fac), 12 Chiltern Place, 96 Harestone Valley Road, CATERHAM, CR3 6HZ.
LARSEN, Miss. Joanna, BSc ACA *2009;* 3 Keynsham Street, CHELTENHAM, GL52 6EJ.
LARSEN, Miss. Mary Caroline, BSc ACA *1993;* with Ingle Bhatti & Co, RAB House, 102-104 Park Lane, CROYDON, CR0 1JB.
LARSEN, Mr. Michael Joseph, ACA CA(NZ) *2009;* (Tax Fac), Flat 59 Melville Court, Goldhawk Road, LONDON, W12 9NY.
•**LARSEN, Mrs. Rachel Ann, BSc ACA CTA** *1998;* Larsens Accountants Limited, 2 High Brighton Street, WITHERNSEA, NORTH HUMBERSIDE, HU19 2HL. See also Larsen and Co
LARSON, Mr. Mark Elliott, MA ACA *1998;* 52 Cleveland Road, LONDON, W13 8AL.
LARTER, Miss. Rose Sarah Ann, BCom ACA *2006;* First Floor Flat, 41 Shandon Road, LONDON, SW4 9HS.
LARTHWELL, Mrs. Fiona Kirkpatrick, MA ACA *2004;* 700 N Coronado St, Apt #2138 Coronado Crossing, CHANDLER, AZ 85224, UNITED STATES.
LASCHETTI, Miss. Rebecca, BA ACA *1989;* 9 York Mansions, Prince of Wales Drive, LONDON, SW11 4DN.
LASEBIKAN, Mr. Abimbola Oluwole, BCom FCA *1969;* PO Box 9213, Marina, LAGOS, NIGERIA.
LASETTA, Ms. Eleni, ACA *2008;* 3 Profiti Elia, Tseri, 2480 NICOSIA, CYPRUS.
LASHAM, Mr. Nicholas Brian, ACA *1984;* Meadow Rest, 3 Lovell Close, Thruxton, ANDOVER, HAMPSHIRE, SP11 8NH.
LASHER, Mrs. Cathy, ACA *1988;* 21 Longfield Avenue, LONDON, NW7 2EH.
LASHMAR, Mr. Dudley Stewart, BA FCA *1978;* 76 Kingsway, Petts Wood, ORPINGTON, BR5 1PT.
LASHMAR, Mr. James Robert, ACA *1991;* 12 Cherry Tree Grove, WOKINGHAM, BERKSHIRE, RG41 4UZ.
LASHMAR, Mr. Michael William, BSc ACA *2004;* Alverstone Barrow Hill Road, Copythorne, SOUTHAMPTON, SO40 2PJ.
•**LASI, Mr. Behzad, ACA** *2008;* Lasi Associates, 7 Vernon Drive, STANMORE, MIDDLESEX, HA7 2BP.
LASIK, Mr. Mateusz, BA ACA *2003;* with Deloitte LLP, 2 New Street Square, LONDON, EC4A 3BZ.
LASK, Mr. Howard Andrew, BA ACA *1992;* 23 Donovan Avenue, LONDON, N10 2JU.
•**LASK, Mr. Hugh Michael, BA FCA** *1981;* (Tax Fac), Harris & Trotter LLP, 65 New Cavendish Street, LONDON, W1G 7LS.
LASKEY, Miss. Donna, ACA *2003;* 47 Intwood Road, Cringleford, NORWICH, NR4 6AA.
LASKOWICZ, Mr. Sammy Neil, BA ACA *2008;* 21 Ranelagh Drive, EDGWARE, HA8 8HJ.
LASKY, Mr. Brian Lawrence, BSc FCA *1972;* 34 Purcells Avenue, EDGWARE, HA8 8DZ.
LASORE, Miss. Victoria Morolayo, ACA *2009;* National Audit Office, 157-197 Buckingham Palace Road, LONDON, SW1W 9SP.
LASSETER, Mr. Ronald Sydney Gaston, BSc FCA *1971;* 4 Palm Court, Coastguard Road, BUDLEIGH SALTERTON, EX9 6NU.
LASSETTER, Mr. James John, MEng ACA *2000;* 5 Chakola Avenue, HORNSBY HEIGHTS, NSW 2077, AUSTRALIA.
LAST, Miss. Amanda, BA ACA *1990;* 54 London Street, Godmanchester, HUNTINGDON, CAMBRIDGESHIRE, PE29 2HX.
LAST, Mr. Andrew, BA ACA *2006;* 1 Ryle Road, FARNHAM, GU9 8RW.
LAST, Mr. Andrew John, BA ACA *1999;* 26 Meadow Lane, NEWMARKET, SUFFOLK, CB8 8FZ.
•**LAST, Mr. Jon Edward, BA ACA** *2005;* Warrener Stewart Limited, Harwood House, 43 Harwood Road, LONDON, SW6 4QP.
LAST, Mrs. Karine Eliane, BA ACA *2005;* Manor Farm House Pixey Green, Stradbroke, EYE, SUFFOLK, IP21 5NJ.
•**LAST, Mrs. Kay Barbara, FCA** *1986;* (Tax Fac), T and C Services Ltd, 76 Townsend Lane, HARPENDEN, AL5 2RQ.
LAST, Mr. Martin John, BSc ACA *1987;* Hoehenring 63, CH-8052 ZURICH, SWITZERLAND.
LAST, Mr. Michael David, ACA MAAT *1998;* 26 Grove Road, HAVANT, PO9 1AR.
LAST, Miss. Natalie Claire, BSc ACA *2006;* with Deloitte LLP, Abbots House, Abbey Street, READING, RG1 3BD.
•**LAST, Mr. Peter Frank, FCA** *1968;* Last & Co, 269 Newmarket Road, CAMBRIDGE, CB5 8JE.
LAST, Mr. Peter James, BSc FCA *1983;* 35 Eversden Road, Harlton, CAMBRIDGE, CB23 1ET.
LAST, Mr. Richard, BA FCA *1982;* Hobbs Hole Farm, Ledwell Road, Great Tew, CHIPPING NORTON, OXFORDSHIRE, OX7 4DN.
LAST, Mr. Stewart, BA FCA *1971;* Longden & Cook Commercial, 32 Crescent, SALFORD, M5 4PF.
LATARCHE, Mr. Simon John, BA ACA *2001;* Sherwood, 172 Newmarket Road, NORWICH, NR4 6AR.
LATCH, Miss. Jennifer Ruth, BA ACA *2003;* 63 St. Ronans Crescent, WOODFORD GREEN, ESSEX, IG8 9DQ.
LATCH, Mrs. Teresa, LLB ACA *2003;* 44 Oak Tree Road, READING, BERKSHIRE, RG31 6JX.
LATCHFORD, Mr. James Frederick, MA FCA *1961;* Catherine Cottage, Main Street, Wick, PERSHORE, WR10 3NZ.
LATCHFORD, Mr. John, BSc ACA *1981;* 6 Barnfield Close, HODDESDON, EN11 9EP.
LATEF, Mr. Javed Anver, MSc FCA *1975;* 25 East Allendale Road, SADDLE RIVER, NJ 07458, UNITED STATES. (Life Member)
LATER, Miss. Frances, BSc ACA *2007;* with Kingston Smith LLP, Devonshire House, 60 Goswell Road, LONDON, EC1M 7AD.
LATHAM, Mr. Alan Richard, BSc ACA *1987;* Laurel House, West Lilling, YORK, YO60 6RP.
LATHAM, Mrs. Amanda Elizabeth, BA ACA *1991;* 17 Keats Way, Cottam, PRESTON, PR4 0NL.
•**LATHAM, Mr. Andrew Philip, BA ACA** *1993;* PricewaterhouseCoopers LLP, Marlborough Court, 10 Bricket Road, ST. ALBANS, HERTFORDSHIRE, AL1 3JX. See also PricewaterhouseCoopers
LATHAM, Mr. Anthony Edward, MA(Hons) ACA *2001;* 37 Marler Road, Forest Hill, LONDON, SE23 2AE.
LATHAM, Mr. Anthony Robert, BSc FCA *1975;* 46 Victoria Road, ABINGDON, OXFORDSHIRE, OX14 1DQ.
LATHAM, Mr. Brian Albert, FCA *1971;* 28 Queens Avenue, BROADSTAIRS, KENT, CT10 1EH. (Life Member)
LATHAM, Mr. Charles Joseph, BSc CA ACA *1979;* Bio Innovation SA, Level 15, 33 King William Street, ADELAIDE, SA 5000, AUSTRALIA.
LATHAM, Mr. Christopher George Arnot, MA FCA *1959;* Quarry Court, Quarry Wood, MARLOW, SL7 1RF. (Life Member)
LATHAM, Mr. Christopher Valleton Mere, MA FCA *1955;* Long Close, Prior Park Road, ASHBY-DE-LA-ZOUCH, LE65 1BL. (Life Member)
LATHAM, Mrs. Dorothy, ACA *1981;* Stubton Hill Farm, Fenton Road, Stubton, NEWARK, NG23 5DB.
LATHAM, Mrs. Elizabeth Ruth, BSc ACA *1999;* 15 Whitehead Grove, Balsall Common, COVENTRY, CV7 7US.
LATHAM, Mr. Geoffrey Anthony, FCA *1959;* Flat 23, Sandown House, 1 High Street, ESHER, SURREY, KT10 9SL. (Life Member)
•**LATHAM, Mr. Graham William, MA FCA** *1983;* (Tax Fac), Graham Latham Limited, Hedge House, Hangersley Hill, Hangersley, RINGWOOD, HAMPSHIRE BH24 3JW.
LATHAM, Miss. Harriet Clare, BA ACA *1998;* 81 Southernhay Road, LEICESTER, LE2 3TP.
LATHAM, Mr. Harry, FCA *1953;* Dunloe, Church Lane, Stoke Poges, SLOUGH, SL2 4PB. (Life Member)
LATHAM, Mrs. Heather Jayne, BA ACA *2001;* 33 Ramsbury Road, ST. ALBANS, HERTFORDSHIRE, AL1 1SN.
LATHAM, Miss. Helen Philippa, BSc ACA *2005;* 4 Lessar Avenue, LONDON, SW4 9HJ.
•**LATHAM, Mr. Ian, BSc ACA CF** *1990;* Baker Tilly Tax & Advisory Services LLP, 1 Old Hall Street, LIVERPOOL, L3 9SX. See also Baker Tilly Corporate Finance LLP
•**LATHAM, Mr. Ian Michael Wilkinson, FCA** *1973;* Wilkinson Latham, 5 College Mews, Saint Ann's Hill, LONDON, SW18 2SJ. See also Pembroke Accountancy Services
LATHAM, Mr. Ian Peter, BA(Hons) ACA *2002;* 55 Kendal Road, LONDON, NW10 1JG.
LATHAM, Mrs. Jacqueline Anne, BSc ACA CTA *1989;* Rolls-Royce Plc, PO Box 31, DERBY, DE24 8BJ.
LATHAM, Miss. Joanne Claire, BSc ACA *2001;* 9 Byrom Street, ALTRINCHAM, CHESHIRE, WA14 2EN.
LATHAM, Mr. John Martin, MA FCA *1969;* 53 Abbotsbury Close, LONDON, W14 8EQ. (Life Member)
LATHAM, Mrs. Madeline Louise, MA ACA *1987;* WMT LLP, 47 Holywell Hill, ST. ALBANS, HERTFORDSHIRE, AL1 1HD.
LATHAM, Mr. Michael John, FCA *1969;* 22 Elmsleigh Road, WESTON-SUPER-MARE, AVON, BS23 4JN.
LATHAM, Mr. Neil, BSc ACA *1999;* 15 Whitehead Grove, Balsall Common, COVENTRY, CV7 7US.
•**LATHAM, Mr. Neil Andrew, FCA** *1978;* (Tax Fac), Harrison Latham & Company, 97 Tulketh Street, SOUTHPORT, PR8 1AW.
LATHAM, Mr. Nicholas, BSc ACA *1981;* 14 Churchill Road, ST. ALBANS, HERTFORDSHIRE, AL1 4HQ.
LATHAM, Mr. Nicholas Hugh James, BEng ACA *2001;* 29 Hill Meadows, High Shincliffe, DURHAM, DH1 2PE.
LATHAM, Mrs. Nicola Pauline, BSc ACA *1997;* 11 Chudleigh Road, EXETER, EX2 8TS.
LATHAM, Mr. Patrick, FCA *1968;* Littledene, 2 Guildown Avenue, GUILDFORD, SURREY, GU2 4HB.
LATHAM, Mr. Paul Alan, BSc FCA *1983;* The Old Hall, Eaves Green Lane, Goosnargh, PRESTON, LANCASHIRE, PR3 2FE.
LATHAM, Mrs. Paula Jane, BA ACA *1992;* Motorpoint of Derby Ltd, Chartwell Drive, West Meadows, DERBY, DE21 6BZ.
•**LATHAM, Mr. Peter David, MSc ACA** *2000;* 40 Glebe Hyrst, SOUTH CROYDON, CR2 9JF.
LATHAM, Mr. Roger Kenneth, FCA *1968;* Mount Royd, 8 Vicarage Road, LLANDUDNO, Clwyd, LL30 1PT.
•**LATHAM, Mr. William Anthony, BA FCA** *1975;* Salisbury & Co, Irish Square, Upper Denbigh Road, ST. ASAPH, CLWYD, LL17 0RN.
LATHAM-BOAL, Mrs. Helena Frances Elizabeth, LLB ACA *2000;* Norbury Manor, Norbury, ASHBOURNE, DERBYSHIRE, DE6 2ED.
LATHOM-SHARP, Ivanhoe Nigel Stuart, Esq OBE FCA *1949;* North Hill House, 46 Ivry Street, IPSWICH, IP1 3QW. (Life Member)
LATHOM-SHARP, Mr. Martin Stephen Jeremy, BEng ACA *1992;* Lyndhurst Cecil Avenue, HALIFAX, WEST YORKSHIRE, HX3 8SN.
LATIF, Mr. Haris Bilal, BSc(Hons) ACA *2009;* BP Pakistan Exploration and Production Inc. 4th Floor Bahria Complex-I 24 M.T. Khan Road PO Box, KARACHI, PAKISTAN.
LATIF, Mr. Mohammed Fatehul Mubin, BSc ACA *1996;* 38 Murray Crescent, PINNER, MIDDLESEX, HA5 3QE.
•**LATIF, Mr. Quazi Abdul, FCA** *1971;* (Tax Fac), Latif & Company, Chestnut House, 101A High Street, Old Town, STEVENAGE, SG1 3HR.
LATIF, Miss. Sabina Yasmin, BSc ACA *1999;* Flat 6, 9 Highbury Hill, LONDON, N5 1SU.
LATIF, Mr. Shahed Khalid, BSc ACA *1992;* with KPMG LLP, 500 East Middlefield Road, MOUNTAIN VIEW, CA 94043, UNITED STATES.
LATIF, Miss. Shaheen, FCA *1986;* 30 Simper Street, WEMBLEY, WA 6014, AUSTRALIA.

LATIF, Miss. Shahida, BSc ACA *1997;* 367 Wellington Road North, Heaton Chapel, STOCKPORT, SK4 5AQ.
LATIF, Mr. Zahed Khalid, BA ACA *1995;* 3 Nobs Crook, HOOK, HAMPSHIRE, RG27 9UB.
LATIMER, Miss. Ann, BA ACA *1983;* 9 Alexandra Road, WINDSOR, SL4 1JH.
LATIMER, Mrs. Clare Frances Louise, BSc ACA *2005;* 7 Hordle Gardens, ST. ALBANS, HERTFORDSHIRE, AL1 1JW.
LATIMER, Mr. Dennis George, FCA *1954;* 8 Pulford Close, NORTHWICH, CHESHIRE, CW9 8FS. (Life Member)
LATIMER, Mrs. Gillian Valerie, BA FCA *1968;* (Tax Fac), 4 Stanley Street, BEDFORD, MK41 7RF.
•LATIMER, Mr. John Adrian Gordon, FCA *1970;* with JWPCreers, 20-24 Park Street, SELBY, NORTH YORKSHIRE, YO8 4PW.
LATIMER, Mr. Jonathan Mannin, BA FCA *1978;* Naworth, Maine Road, Port Erin, ISLE OF MAN, IM9 6LQ.
LATIMER, Mr. Nicholas John, BSc(Hons) ACA *2002;* (Tax Fac), 3 Godolphin Road, Seer Green, BEACONSFIELD, BUCKINGHAMSHIRE, HP9 2XQ.
LATIMER, Mr. Nicholas William, BA ACA *2000;* Credit Suisse, Izumi Garden Tower, 6-1 Roppongi 1-Chome, Minato-Ku, TOKYO, 106-6024 JAPAN.
•LATIMIR, Mr. Gordon, BSc FCA *1984;* PricewaterhouseCoopers, White Square Office Center, 10 Butyrsky Val, 125047 MOSCOW, RUSSIAN FEDERATION.
LATNER, Mr. Nicholas Edward, BSc ACA *2005;* 19 Limes Avenue, LONDON, NW7 3NY.
LATNER, Mr. Richard Daniel, ACA *2009;* Flat 1, 61 Redington Road, LONDON, NW3 7RP.
LATTER, Miss. Eleanor Ursula, BSc ACA *2010;* Flat 115 Goulden House, Bullen Street, LONDON, SW11 3HH.
LATTER, Mr. Ian George, BA FCA *1980;* 156 Basin Approach, LONDON, E14 7JG.
LATTER, Mrs. Olivia Melanie, BSc ACA *1995;* 18 Cranborne Road, HATFIELD, AL10 8AP.
LATTER, Mr. Philip James, BSc ACA *1980;* 170 Whyteleaf Road, CATERHAM, CR3 5ED.
LATTER, Mrs. Rosemary Helen, BA ACA *1993;* The Old Barn, Sarson, Amport, ANDOVER, SP11 8AE.
LATTER, Mr. Thomas James, MA ACA *2004;* 149 Gassiot Road, LONDON, SW17 8LF.
LATTIMER, Mrs. Carol Elizabeth, MSc FCA *1971;* 24 Springcroft Avenue, East Finchley, LONDON, N2 9JE. (Life Member)
LATTO, Miss. Clare, MA ACA *2010;* Flat 5, 34 Clephane Road, LONDON, N1 2FT.
LATTO, Mr. Gavin Fyall, BSc ACA *1988;* 37 Picton Way, Caversham, READING, RG4 8NJ.
LAU, Mr. Adam, ACA *2011;* 1 Pippin Close, CROYDON, CR0 7QT.
LAU, Mr. Alan Cheuk Lun, ACA *2005;* Flat C 26/F, Block 8, City Garden 233 Electric Road, NORTH POINT, HONG KONG SAR.
LAU, Mr. Alex, BSc ACA CF *1988;* Flat E 7/F Block 1, Royal Ascot, 1 Tsun King Road, SHA TIN, NEW TERRITORIES, HONG KONG SAR.
LAU, Miss. Angela, BSc(Hons) ACA *2010;* 112 Javelin Avenue, BIRMINGHAM, B35 7LW.
LAU, Mr. Arthur Kwok Kwong, FCA *1972;* Room 806 Tung Ming Building, 42 Des Voeux Road, CENTRAL, HONG KONG ISLAND, HONG KONG SAR.
LAU, Mr. Butt Farn, BSc FCA *1978;* 11th Floor LiFung Tower, 868-888 Cheung Sha Wan Road, LAI CHI KOK, KOWLOON, HONG KONG SAR.
LAU, Miss. Catherine Yim Ling, BSc ACA *1995;* Central Provident Fund Board, 79 Robinson Road, CPF Building, SINGAPORE 068897, SINGAPORE.
LAU, Mr. Chak Keung, ACA *2007;* Flat D, 6/F Block 7, 69 Siu Lek Yuen Road, Castello, SHA TIN, NEW TERRITORIES HONG KONG SAR.
LAU, Mr. Chau Wing, BSc ACA *1998;* 12 Sai O Village Sub Sze Heung, North Yerk, SAI KUNG, NEW TERRITORIES, HONG KONG SAR.
LAU, Mr. Che Yan Kenneth, ACA *2005;* 2A/F Block 19, Baguio Villa, POK FU LAM, HONG KONG ISLAND, HONG KONG SAR.
LAU, Mr. Cheong Koon, ACA *1984;* MBF Leasing SDN.BHD, Lot 6.03, 6th Floor Plaza Prima, 4 1/2 Miles Old Klang Road, 58200 KUALA LUMPUR, FEDERAL TERRITORY MALAYSIA.
•LAU, Mr. Cheong Seng, FCA *1979;* (Tax Fac), Bajaria Gibbs & Co, 72 Plumstead High Street, LONDON, SE18 1SL.
LAU, Miss. Cheryl, ACA *2011;* K P M G Salisbury Square House, 8 Salisbury Square, LONDON, EC4Y 8BB.
LAU, Mr. Chi Hung, ACA *2007;* Flat D 5/F, Block 38, Laguna City, LAM TIN, KOWLOON, HONG KONG SAR.
LAU, Mr. Chi Keung Sammy, ACA *2007;* Flat D 33 Floor, Tower 12, Ocean Shores, 88 OKing Road, TSEUNG KWAN O, KOWLOON HONG KONG SAR.
LAU, Mr. Chi Ming, ACA *2005;* Expeditors Int'l Of Wash Inc., 38/F Enterprise Square Three, 39 Wong Chiu Road, KOWLOON BAY, KOWLOON, HONG KONG SAR.
LAU, Mr. Chi Wai, ACA *2008;* Poon Mak & Wan, Room 2210, C C Wu Building, 302 Hennessy Road, WAN CHAI, HONG KONG ISLAND HONG KONG SAR.
LAU, Miss. Ching Fun Amy, BA ACA *1994;* A3 4/Fl, 90 Kennedy Road, WAN CHAI, HONG KONG ISLAND, HONG KONG SAR.
LAU, Mrs. Cho Yee, BA ACA *1989;* Flat C, 10/F Mercantile House, 186 Nathan Road, TSIM SHA TSUI, KOWLOON, HONG KONG SAR.
LAU, Mr. Choy On David, ACA *2005;* 56 Waterbridge Lane, UNIONVILLE L3R 8V9, ON, CANADA.
LAU, Mrs. Christine Ah Yee, BCom ACA *2003;* 27 Laxton Way, BEDFORD, MK41 7FH.
LAU, Mr. Chun Tuck Philip, BA ACA *1992;* 5 Lorong Taman Pantai Enam, 59100 KUALA LUMPUR, FEDERAL TERRITORY, MALAYSIA.
LAU, Ms. Chung Lo Selina, ACA *2006;* 12/F Flat D, 94 Prince Edward Road, MONG KOK, KOWLOON, HONG KONG SAR.
LAU, Mr. Danny Wai-Kit, BA ACA *1984;* Deloitte Touche Tohmatsu, 35/F One Pacific Place, 88 Queensway, CENTRAL, HONG KONG ISLAND, HONG KONG SAR.
LAU, Mr. Douglas Chun Fai, ACA CA(AUS) *2010;* ICAEW China, Room 706A Tower E1, Oriental Plaza, No 1 East Chang An Avenue, Dong Cheng District, BEIJING 100738 CHINA.
LAU, Mr. Fai Lawrence, ACA *2008;* Flat E 47/F Tower 1, Grand Waterfront, 38 San Ma Tau Street, TO KWA WAN, KOWLOON, HONG KONG SAR.
LAU, Mr. Fook Meng, FCA *1978;* 44 Jalan Setia Jaya, Bukit Damansara, 50490 KUALA LUMPUR, FEDERAL TERRITORY, MALAYSIA.
LAU, Mr. Franky Ka Wai, BSc ACA *2005;* 87 Chadbourn Street, LONDON, E14 6QP.
LAU, Mr. Gavin, BSc ACA *2010;* Flat 24 Parkview Apartments, 122 Chrisp Street, LONDON, E14 6ET.
LAU, Miss. Ginny Aun Shih, ACA *2003;* 33 Aveley House, Iliffe Close, READING, RG1 2QF.
LAU, Miss. Gladys Aun Nee, BA(Econ) ACA *1999;* 17 Hollym Close, Lower Earley, READING, RG6 3XW.
LAU, Mr. Hendry Yinon, ACA *2005;* Hendry Lau & Co., Room 704, 7/F Landwide Commercial Building, 118-120 Austin Road, TSIM SHA TSIU, KOWLOON HONG KONG SAR.
LAU, Mr. Herald Ling Fai, FCA *1971;* No. 6 11th Street, Hong Lok Yuen Tai Po, TAI PO, NEW TERRITORIES, HONG KONG SAR. (Life Member)
LAU, Mr. Hin Ming, ACA *2008;* Renolit Hong Kong Limited, Room 1103-05, Tins Enterprises Centre, 777 Lai Chi Kok Road, LAI CHI KOK, KOWLOON HONG KONG SAR.
LAU, Mr. Ho Kit Ivan, ACA *2007;* A303, 1029 King's Road, QUARRY BAY, HONG KONG ISLAND, HONG KONG SAR.
LAU, Mr. Ho Man Edward, ACA *2005;* Edward Lau & Co., 16A Eib Centre, 40 Bonham Strand, SHEUNG WAN, HONG KONG ISLAND, HONG KONG SAR.
LAU, Mr. Hui Sie, ACA *1978;* P.O. Box 657, SIBU, Sarawak, MALAYSIA.
LAU, Miss. Jennifer, BSc ACA *2011;* 25 Brixfield Way, Shirley, SOLIHULL, WEST MIDLANDS, B90 1RQ.
LAU, Miss. Jennifer Chi-On, LLB ACA *2004;* Shell Eastern Petroleum (Private) Ltd, Shell House, 83 Clemenceau Avenue, SINGAPORE 239920, SINGAPORE.
LAU, Mr. Ka Wing, ACA *2010;* 3/F Room G, Block 15, Yuet Wu Villa, TUEN MUN, HONG KONG SAR.
LAU, Ms. Ka Yi, ACA *2008;* Room 3607, Kwun Hei Court, HO MAN TIN, KOWLOON, HONG KONG SAR.
LAU, Mr. Kam Kuen, BEng ACA *1994;* Flat D 21/F Block 2, Coastal Skyline, TUNG CHUNG, HONG KONG SAR.
LAU, Miss. Kei Kwan, ACA *2010;* Room 916, 9F Heng Yu House, Fu Heng Estate, TAI PO, NEW TERRITORIES, HONG KONG SAR.
LAU, Mrs. Kim Gek-Kim, BSc ACA *1996;* 85 Priory Gardens, LONDON, N6 5QU.
LAU, Mr. Kim Wan, ACA *2008;* K W Lau CPA Limited, 9th Floor, Chiyu Bank Building, 78 Des Voeux Road Central, CENTRAL, HONG KONG SAR.
LAU, Mr. Kin Chun, ACA *2006;* KPMG Advisory (China)Limited, 4/F Inter Royal Building, 15 Donghai West Road Shinan District, QINGDAO 266071, CHINA.
LAU, Mr. King Lok, ACA *2005;* Flat B 23F, Block 9, City Garden, NORTH POINT, HONG KONG ISLAND, HONG KONG SAR.
LAU, Mrs. Kit-Yee, BSc ACA *2003;* 27 Tersha Street, RICHMOND, SURREY, TW9 2LY.
LAU, Ms. Koon Kwan Doris, ACA *2007;* Flat B, 23rd Floor, No 1 Ho Man Tin Hill, 1 Ho Man Tin Hill Road, MONG KOK, KOWLOON HONG KONG SAR.
LAU, Mr. Koon Sing, ACA *2008;* 18 Loweswater Avenue, MARKHAM L3R7W4, ON, CANADA.
•LAU, Mr. Kung Ngieng, ACA *1988;* 04-76, Blk 236, Lorong 1, SINGAPORE 310236, SINGAPORE.
•LAU, Mr. Kwan Fai Barry, MSc BA(Hons) ACA ATII *2000;* Barrette Limited, 144 Thatto Heath Road, Thatto Heath, ST. HELENS, MERSEYSIDE, WA9 5PE.
•LAU, Miss. Kwan Wai Yvette, BA ACA *2000;* Barrette Limited, 144 Thatto Heath Road, Thatto Heath, ST. HELENS, MERSEYSIDE, WA9 5PE.
LAU, Mr. Kwok Wa, ACA *2007;* Ernst & Young Hua Ming Shanghai Branch, 50th Floor, Shanghai World Financial Center, 100 Century Avenue, Pudong New Area, SHANGHAI 200120 CHINA. See also Ernst & Young
LAU, Ms. Lai Kuen, ACA *2008;* 14 Ground Floor, Wong Chuk Wan, SAI KUNG, NEW TERRITORIES, HONG KONG SAR.
LAU, Mr. Lawrence Cho-Ming, BA ACA *2001;* Flat 30F Tower 2, Sorrento, 1 Austin Road West, TSIM SHA TSUI, KOWLOON, HONG KONG SAR.
LAU, Miss. Lesley, ACA *2008;* Hewitt New Bridge Street, Hewitt Associates, 6 More London Place, LONDON, SE1 2DA.
LAU, Ms. Lye Kum, FCA *1979;* 92 Jalan Rahim Kajai, Taman Tun Dr Ismail, 60000 KUALA LUMPUR, FEDERAL TERRITORY, MALAYSIA.
•LAU, Mr. Man Yiu Edward, ACA *1986;* Messrs W Edwards & Co, 15 Cedar Drive, PINNER, HA5 4BY.
LAU, Mr. Marty Siu Bong, BSc ACA *2001;* with Crowe Clark Whitehill LLP, St Bride's House, 10 Salisbury Square, LONDON, EC4Y 8EH.
LAU, Mr. Ming Fai Eddy, ACA *2008;* Flat E, 7/F Block 4, Site 4 Palm Mansions, Whampoa Garden, HUNG HOM, KOWLOON HONG KONG SAR.
LAU, Mr. Peter King Ching, FCA *1975;* 2 Bruang Road, P O Box 71, 96000 SIBU, SARAWAK, MALAYSIA.
LAU, Mr. Peter Wing Wing, BA ACA *1982;* (Tax Fac), L & M Partners Limited, 454 Ewell Road, SURBITON, SURREY, KT6 7EL.
LAU, Mr. Philip Chu Sing, BSc FCA *1985;* with PricewaterhouseCoopers, 26/F Office Tower A, Beijing Fortune Plaza, 23 Dongsanhuan North Road, Chaoyang District, BEIJING 100020 CHINA.
LAU, Ms. Po Yee Mirai, ACA *2008;* U B S AG, 100 Liverpool Street, LONDON, EC2M 2RH.
LAU, Mr. Po Shan, ACA *2006;* Flat D, 6th Floor, 36 Sung Kit Street, HUNG HOM, KOWLOON, HONG KONG SAR.
LAU, Mr. Pok Lam Lawrence, ACA *2005;* Lau Tsui & Company, 22/F HONG KONG SAR Trade Centre, 161 Des Voeux Road, CENTRAL, HONG KONG SAR.
LAU, Mr. Richard Kin Hung, ACA *2005;* Flat A4 13th Floor, No. 21 Hyde Towers, Kung Lok Road, KWUN TONG, KOWLOON, HONG KONG SAR.
LAU, Miss. Rowena, BSc ACA *2007;* 4 Treeview Close, LONDON, SE19 2QT.
LAU, Mr. Sai Lap David, ACA CA(SA) *2010;* 71 Hidden Creek Point NW, CALGARY T3A 6J7, AL, CANADA.
LAU, Mr. Sai Yung, ACA *2005;* Union Alpha CPA Limited, 19/F No. 3 Lockhart Road, WAN CHAI, HONG KONG ISLAND, HONG KONG SAR. See also Lau SY & Co.
LAU, Mr. Shui Ming Paulus, ACA *2007;* 10D, Cheung Pak Mansion, Parkvale, QUARRY BAY, HONG KONG ISLAND, HONG KONG SAR.
LAU, Ms. Shuk Yin, ACA *2008;* Flat F18/ FTower 4, Jubilant Place, 99 Pau Chung Street, TO KWA WAN, KOWLOON, HONG KONG SAR.
LAU, Mr. Sin Sang, ACA *2004;* S. S. Lau & Co., Unit A, 13/F, Empire Land Commercial Centre, 81-85 Lockhart Road, WAN CHAI HONG KONG ISLAND HONG KONG SAR.
LAU, Mr. Sing Ho, MPA ACA ACCA CPA *2004;* P.O. Box 1437, Sha Tin Central Post Office, SHA TIN, NEW TERRITORIES, HONG KONG SAR.
LAU, Mr. Siu Kay Frankie, BSc FCA *1991;* Shatin Central Post Office, Box No 1642, SHA TIN, NEW TERRITORIES, HONG KONG SAR.
LAU, Ms. Siu Mui, ACA *2007;* 16E Fou Wah Centre, 210 Castle Peak Road, TSUEN WAN, NEW TERRITORIES, HONG KONG SAR.
LAU, Mr. Siu Wai, ACA *2008;* Wong Chan Lau CPA Co Ltd, Rooms 805-6, 8/F, Tai Yau Building, 181 Johnston Road, WAN CHAI HONG KONG SAR.
LAU, Mr. Stephen Buong Lik, BA ACA *1984;* 21 Peel Road, SINGAPORE 248623, SINGAPORE.
•LAU, Mr. Stephen Sing-Hung, FCA *1976;* China Timber Resources Group Ltd, Suite 1606 Office Tower, Convention Plaza, 1 Harbour Road, WAN CHAI, HONG KONG ISLAND HONG KONG SAR.
LAU, Miss. Susanna, BA ACA *1993;* House 34 Lychee Road South Fairview Park, YUEN LONG, HONG KONG SAR.
LAU, Miss. Sze Min, BA ACA *1994;* A-22-7 Vista Kiara Condominium, 7 Jalan Kiara 3, Bukit Kiara, 50480 KUALA LUMPUR, FEDERAL TERRITORY, MALAYSIA.
LAU, Ms. Sze Man, ACA *2008;* P.O Box No. 3485, General Post Office, CENTRAL, HONG KONG ISLAND, HONG KONG SAR.
LAU, Mr. Tak Shing, ACA *2005;* 1/F 60 Po Hing Fong, SHEUNG WAN, HONG KONG ISLAND, HONG KONG SAR.
LAU, Mr. Tat Hong Andrew, ACA *2005;* Unit 4, Kellett Heights, 61B Mount Kellett Road, THE PEAK, HONG KONG ISLAND, HONG KONG SAR.
LAU, Miss. Teresa Shuk-Yee, ACA *2009;* 16 Browns Road, LONDON, E17 4RW.
LAU, Mr. Titan Tze Fai, ACA *2007;* Flat G 19th Floor, Block 9, Tung Chung Crescent, 2 Mei Tung Street, TUNG CHUNG, NEW TERRITORIES HONG KONG SAR.
LAU, Dr. Tommy Sing Chiu, BSc ACA *1980;* 109 Kau Pui Lung Road, 4/F, TO KWA WAN, KOWLOON, HONG KONG SAR.
LAU, Mr. Tony Ho Wing, ACA *1982;* Flat 11A, Block 9, South Horizons, AP LEI CHAU, HONG KONG ISLAND, HONG KONG SAR.
LAU, Ms. Vanessa Bik-Yun, BA ACA *1998;* Flat 30F Tower 2, Sorrento, 1 Austin Road West, TSIM SHA TSUI, KOWLOON, HONG KONG SAR.
LAU, Mr. Vishaal, MSc ACA MBA *2002;* 33 Melbourne Road, ILFORD, IG1 4LF.
LAU, Mr. Wai Ming, ACA *2005;* Edmund Lau & Co, Unit 1403, President Commercial Centre, 608 Nathan Road, MONG KOK, KOWLOON HONG KONG SAR.
LAU, Mr. Wai Tat, MA ACA *2003;* Flat 22 Fairweather House, Parkhurst Road, LONDON, N7 0NS.
LAU, Ms. Wai Fong Teresa, ACA *2008;* Flat H, 5/F, Goldwin Heights, 2 Seymour Road, MID LEVELS, HONG KONG SAR.
LAU, Ms. Wai Fun, ACA *2008;* Jardine Matheson Limited, 48/F Jardine House, Connaught Road, CENTRAL, HONG KONG SAR.
LAU, Mr. Wai Kai, ACA *2007;* Flat E 32nd Floor Fullview Court 32 Fortress Hill Road, NORTH POINT, HONG KONG SAR.
LAU, Mr. Wai Kuen, ACA *2005;* 18/F Bank of East Asia Harbour, View Centre, 56 Gloucester Road, WAN CHAI, HONG KONG ISLAND, HONG KONG SAR.
LAU, Mr. Wai Shun, ACA *2006;* PO Box 2891, Carlingford Court, CARLINGFORD, NSW 2118, AUSTRALIA.
LAU, Ms. Wai Yin Susanna, ACA *2007;* c/o Securities and Futures Commission, 8/F Chater House, 8 Connaught Road Central, CENTRAL, HONG KONG ISLAND, HONG KONG SAR.
LAU, Miss. Wai-Ka Larissa, BSc ACA *2009;* U B S AG, 100 Liverpool Street, LONDON, EC2M 2RH.
LAU, Mr. William Tze Hau, ACA *2007;* Blk 788 Choa Chu Kang Nth6 #03-220, Singapore, SINGAPORE 680788, SINGAPORE.
LAU, Ms. Yin Mei, ACA *2007;* Flat F, 30/F, Block 7, Full View Garden, CHAI WAN, HONG KONG ISLAND HONG KONG SAR.
LAU, Mr. Yip Leung, ACA *2005;* Fung Lau & Co., Room 2604 26/F, C. C. Wu Building, 302-308 Hennessy Road, WAN CHAI, HONG KONG ISLAND HONG KONG SAR.
LAU, Mr. Yiu Kit, ACA *2007;* Room 803, Tung Hip Comm. Blog, 248 Des Voeux Road, CENTRAL, HONG KONG ISLAND, HONG KONG SAR.
LAU, Mr. Yuen Yee, ACA *2008;* S L Lee & Lau CPA Limited, Room 1702, 17/F, Tung Hip Commercial Building, 248 Des Voeux Road, CENTRAL HONG KONG SAR.
LAU, Mr. Yun Wa, ACA *2009;* Flat 112, On Tin House, Pak Tin Estate, SHAM SHUI PO, KOWLOON, HONG KONG SAR.

LAU KUEN WING, Mr. Lau Niow Chong, BSc FCA *1975;* 6 Chaseley Drive, Sanderstead, SOUTH CROYDON, Surrey, CR2 0DN. (Life Member)
LAU MOON LIN, Mr. Kiat Fah, ACA *1978;* 15 Waterfield Drive, SCARBOROUGH M1P 3W4, ON, CANADA.
LAUCHLAN, Mr. Stephen Robert, BA ACA *2000;* Flat 2C, Kam Yuen Mansion, 3 Old Peak Road, MID LEVELS, HONG KONG ISLAND, HONG KONG SAR.
LAUD, Mr. Christopher James, BSc FCA *1990;* Haldane House, Unit 3, Ruston Road, GRANTHAM, LINCOLNSHIRE, NG31 9SW.
LAUDER, Mr. Chris, BSocSc FCA *1989;* 7 Gill Burn, Sherburn Towers, ROWLANDS GILL, NE39 2PT.
LAUER, Ms. Felicity, BSc ACA *2006;* 8 High Bank Close, HASTINGS, EAST SUSSEX, TN35 5LS.
LAUFFER, Mr. Adam, ACA *2008;* with Deloitte LLP, Athene Place, 66 Shoe Lane, LONDON, EC4A 3BQ.
LAUGHARNE, Mr. Alun Edward William, BA FCA *1957;* 26 Sunningdale Avenue, KENILWORTH, CV8 2BZ. (Life Member)
LAUGHER, Mr. Nicholas David, MA ACA *2004;* with PricewaterhouseCoopers LLP, 1 Embankment Place, LONDON, WC2N 6RH.
LAUGHLAND, Mr. Ian Michael, FCA *1969;* 236 Singlewell Road, GRAVESEND, DA11 7RE. (Life Member)
LAUGHLIN, Miss. Claire Marie, BA FCA *1992;* 2 Edwards Road, SUTTON COLDFIELD, B75 5NG.
•**LAUGHLIN, Ms. Fiona Elizabeth, BSc ACA** *1988;* FE Laughlin Ltd, 23 The Crescent, WHITLEY BAY, TYNE AND WEAR, NE26 2JG.
LAUGHLIN, Ms. Gillian Anette, BA(Hons) ACA *2001;* 372, British Nuclear Fuels Plc Springfield Works, Salwick, PRESTON, PR4 0XJ.
LAUGHLIN, Mr. Herbert Desmond Blakeley, FCA *1939;* 16 Castle Gate, ILKLEY, WEST YORKSHIRE, LS29 8DF. (Life Member)
LAUGHLIN, Prof. Richard Charles, PhD FCA *1969;* 3 Savill Mews, Armstrong Road, Englefield Green, EGHAM, SURREY, TW20 0SN. (Life Member)
LAUGHLIN, Mrs. Wendy Jane, BA FCA *1985;* Kings Cottage, Main Road, Somersham, IPSWICH, IP8 4QA.
LAUGHTON, Mr. Anthony, ACA *2008;* with PricewaterhouseCoopers LLP, 1 Embankment Place, LONDON, WC2N 6RH.
•①**LAUGHTON, Mr. Christopher, BSc FCA FIPA FABRP** *1984;* Mercer & Hole, 76 Shoe Lane, LONDON, EC4A 3JB.
LAUGHTON, Mr. David George, FCA *1972;* Makinson Cowell Ltd Cheapside House, 138 Cheapside, LONDON, EC2V 6LQ.
•**LAUGHTON, Mr. Gene Melvin, FCA** *1966;* Haines Watts Corporate Finance, 211 Regent Street, LONDON, W1B 4NF.
LAUGHTON, Mr. Harold, FCA *1956;* PO Box 2477, Mt Edgecombe Country Club, MOUNT EDGECOMBE, 4301, SOUTH AFRICA. (Life Member)
LAUGHTON, Mr. Humphrey Montague, BCom FCA *1979;* 10 Sartfell Road, Douglas, ISLE OF MAN, IM2 3LZ.
LAUGHTON, Mr. Jonathan Michael, BA ACA *1999;* Green Drove House, Green Drove, PEWSEY, SN9 5JD.
LAUGHTON, Mrs. Maria Frances, BA ACA *1992;* Nesfield, Andertons Lane, Henbury, MACCLESFIELD, SK11 9PB.
LAUGHTON, Mr. Mark Timothy, BA FCA *1990;* Nesfield Andertons Lane, Henbury, MACCLESFIELD, SK11 9PB.
LAUGHTON, Mr. Richard Antony Daniel, BSc ACA *1998;* 17 Hightree Drive, Henbury, MACCLESFIELD, CHESHIRE, SK11 9PD.
LAUGHTON-SCOTT, Mr. Oliver Edward, BA ACA *1985;* with IMAS Corporate Advisors Limited, 11-12 Bury Street, LONDON, EC3A 5AT.
LAUGIER, Mrs. Alison, ACA *2011;* Flat 3, 12 Westville Road, LONDON, W12 9BD.
LAUNDERS, Mr. James Edward, MEng ACA *2009;* 14 Richmount Gardens, LONDON, SE3 9AE.
LAUNDERS, Mr. Robin Peter, BSc FCA *1976;* Mas Des Vignes, 81140 CAHUZAC SUR VERE, FRANCE.
LAUREL, Mr. Stephen Anthony, MA ACA *1992;* 80 Forest House Lane, Leicester Forest East, LEICESTER, LE3 3NU.
LAURENCE, Mr. Charles Winston, BA FCA *1990;* 214 East 9th Street #2B, NEW YORK, NY 10003, UNITED STATES.
LAURENCE, Mr. John Gilbert, FCA *1952;* 2 Hope Cottages, Little Shore Lane, Bishops Waltham, SOUTHAMPTON, SO32 1ED. (Life Member)
LAURENSON, Mr. James Tait, MA FCA *1967;* Woodhill House, 38 Kaipara View Road, RD2, HELENSVILLE 0875, NEW ZEALAND. (Life Member)
LAURIE, Mr. Donald Lansbury, FCA *1958;* 60 Millersgate, Cottam, PRESTON, PR4 0AZ. (Life Member)
LAURIE, Mr. Ian Cameron, MA FCA *1972;* Mayfields, 67 Scatterdells Lane, Chipperfield, KINGS LANGLEY, WD4 9EU. (Life Member)
LAURIE, Mr. John William, FCA *1949;* Briar Wood, Blackhall Lane, SEVENOAKS, TN15 0HN. (Life Member)
LAURIE, Miss. Victoria Emma, BSc ACA *2000;* Old Hall Cottage, The Common, DISS, NORFOLK, IP21 4AH.
LAURIE-WILSON, Mrs. Adele Sandra, BA ACA *1996;* Nursery Cottage, 76 Bachelor Gardens, HARROGATE, NORTH YORKSHIRE, HG1 3EA.
LAURISTON, Mr. Ian David, BSc(Econ) FCA *1974;* 69 Hackwood Park, HEXHAM, NORTHUMBERLAND, NE46 1AZ.
LAURSEN, Mrs. Sara Christina Johansson, ACA *2002;* Vikan A/S, Rævevej 1, 7800 SKIVE, DENMARK.
LAVAN, Mr. Nicholas, BA ACA *2006;* 14 Scrubbitts Park Road, RADLETT, HERTFORDSHIRE, WD7 8JP.
•**LAVARELLO, Mr. Edgar Charles Andrew, BSc FCA** *1990;* PricewaterhouseCoopers, Intnl Commercial Centre, Casemates Square, GIBRALTAR, GIBRALTAR.
•**LAVELLE, Miss. Alison Jayne, BA FCA** *1995;* Mitchell Charlesworth, 5 Temple Square, Temple Street, LIVERPOOL, L2 5RH.
LAVELLE, Mr. Dominic Joseph, BEng ACA *1990;* Flat 3, 2 West Grove, LONDON, SE10 8QT.
LAVELLE, Mr. James Patrick, BA(Econ) ACA *2001;* Fitzpatricks, Walsh Island, TULLAMORE, COUNTY OFFALY, IRELAND.
LAVELLE, Miss. Jennifer Anne, BA ACA *2007;* 43 Charlestown Road, MANCHESTER, M9 7AB.
LAVELLE, Ms. Patricia Ann, BA ACA *1990;* 3 Ingleby Drive, TADCASTER, NORTH YORKSHIRE, LS24 8HW.
LAVELLE, Mr. Peter John, ACA *1983;* 15 Crummer Street, PORT MACQUARIE, NSW 2444, AUSTRALIA.
LAVELLE, Mr. Simon James, BA ACA *1994;* 30 Shirley Avenue, COULSDON, CR5 1QW.
LAVELLE, Mrs. Susan Jane, BSc FCA *1992;* 27 Champagne Avenue, THORNTON-CLEVELEYS, FY5 3UD.
LAVELLI, Mr. John Stephen, BA FCA *1979;* Oak Hse, 2 Nathans Cl, WELWYN, AL6 9QB.
LAVENDER, Miss. Alison Ruth, BA ACA *1986;* 6 Haaptstrooss, L8525 CALMUS, LUXEMBOURG.
LAVENDER, Miss. Catherine Jane, BA(Hons) ACA *2002;* The Clock House, 6 St. Mongahs Court, Copgrove, HARROGATE, NORTH YORKSHIRE, HG3 3TY.
LAVENDER, Mr. John Charles, FCA *1955;* Lochaber, Start Lane, Whaley Bridge, HIGH PEAK, SK23 7BP. (Life Member)
LAVENDER, Mr. John Dilworth, FCA *1965;* 16/18 High Street, Wighton, WELLS-NEXT-THE-SEA, NR23 1AL. (Life Member)
•**LAVENDER, Mr. John Ernest, FCA** *1967;* John E. Lavender, 4 Fox Lane, BROMSGROVE, WORCESTERSHIRE, B61 7NL.
LAVENDER, Miss. Karen Elizabeth, BEng FCA *1991;* 45 Walcote Drive, West Bridgford, NOTTINGHAM, NG2 7JQ.
LAVENDER, Mr. Paul Anthony, FCA CF *1979;* Olantigh, Pudding Lane, CHIGWELL, IG7 6BY.
LAVENDER, Mr. Richard Andrew, FCA *1966;* 105A La Cumbre del Sol, 03726 BENITACHELL, ALICANTE, SPAIN. (Life Member)
LAVENDER, Mr. Roger Ian, FCA *1965;* KPMG Somekh Chaikin, 17 Ha'arba'a Street, TEL AVIV, 64739, ISRAEL. (Life Member)
LAVENDER, Mr. Samuel, BA(Hons) ACA *2010;* 97 Burdon Lane, SUTTON, SURREY, SM2 7BZ.
LAVENDER, Mrs. Sarah, BSc ACA *1995;* Ensus Ltd The Granary, 17a High Street, YARM, CLEVELAND, TS15 9BW.
•**LAVENTURE, Mr. Brian George, MA FCA** *1971;* (Tax Fac), B G Laventure FCA, Monard, High Lane, HASLEMERE, SURREY, GU27 1BD.
LAVER, Mr. Andrew David, BSc ACA *1990;* with Sage (UK) Limited, Building 3, Exchange Quay, Salford Quays, MANCHESTER, M5 3ED.
LAVER, Mr. Andrew James, BSc ACA *1992;* Hill Top Hall Farm, Kirkby Overblow, HARROGATE, HG3 1EZ.
LAVER, Mr. Anthony Edward, BSc FCA *1975;* 2 Tithe Orchard, Felbridge, EAST GRINSTEAD, WEST SUSSEX, RH19 2PH.
LAVER, Mrs. Dorothy Joyce, BA ACA *1984;* 2 Lanchester Gardens, Brockhall Village, Old Langho, BLACKBURN, BB6 8DE.
LAVER, Mr. Douglas Lindsay Hay, BA ACA *1990;* 21 Victoria Avenue, Didsbury, MANCHESTER, M20 2GY.
LAVER, Ms. Fiona Alison, BA ACA *1992;* 50 Cluny Gardens, EDINBURGH, EH10 6BN.
LAVER, Mr. Timothy James, BA(Hons) ACA *2001;* 79 Bradford Road, Atworth, MELKSHAM, WILTSHIRE, SN12 8HY.
LAVERACK, Miss. Jennifer Anne, MSc ACA *2000;* 29 Clayton Crescent, BRENTFORD, MIDDLESEX, TW8 9PT.
LAVERCOMBE, Mrs. Elizabeth Jane, MA ACA CTA *1998;* Ten Acre House, Cat Street, Upper Hartfield, HARTFIELD, TN7 4DT.
•**LAVERCOMBE, Mr. Paul Richard, MEng ACA** *1996;* BDO LLP, 2 City Place, Beehive Ring Road, GATWICK, WEST SUSSEX, RH6 0PA. See also BDO Stoy Hayward LLP
LAVERICK, Ms. Celia Joan, BA ACA *1990;* Suffolk College, Rope Walk, IPSWICH, IP4 1LT.
LAVERICK, Mr. David, BSc ACA *1995;* Belmore, Foundry Lane, SANDBACH, CHESHIRE, CW11 3JP.
LAVERICK, Mrs. Joanne, BSc ACA *1994;* 2 Benty Farm Grove, WIRRAL, MERSEYSIDE, CH61 3YB.
LAVERICK, Miss. Katherine Victoria, MPhys ACA *2010;* Flat 13 Plymouth House, Devonshire Drive, LONDON, SE10 8LE.
•**LAVERICK, Mr. Richard, BA ACA** *1988;* Ernst & Young LLP, Ten George Street, EDINBURGH, EH2 2DZ. See also Ernst & Young Europe LLP
LAVERS, Mr. Roger John, FCA *1968;* Polhill Properties Ltd, North Downs Business Park, Limepit Lane, Dunton Green, SEVENOAKS, TN13 2TL.
LAVERS, Mr. Stephen Frank, BA ACA *1980;* 6 Glyn Avenue, Hale, ALTRINCHAM, WA15 9DG.
LAVERTY, Mr. Bernard Robert Sinclair, BA FCA *1984;* David Whitehead & Sons Ltd, 2a The Common Parbold, WIGAN, WN8 7DA.
LAVERTY, Miss. Donna Louisa, MA ACA *1999;* Du Heaume Cottage Mount Bingham, St. Helier, JERSEY, JE2 4XY.
LAVERTY, Mrs. Fiona, LLB ACA *1998;* PO Box 434, BUNGENDORE, NSW 2621, AUSTRALIA.
LAVERTY, Miss. Hailey Viven, BSc ACA *2005;* Rolls-Royce Plc, PO Box 31, DERBY, DE24 8BJ.
LAVERTY, Mr. Mark James, BA(Hons) ACA *2003;* Armajaro Trading Limited 6th Floor Nightingale House, 65 Curzon Street, LONDON, W1J 8PE.
LAVERTY, Mr. Neil James, BA ACA *2002;* 425 Massachusetts Ave NW, Apt 920, WASHINGTON, DC 20001, UNITED STATES.
•**LAVERTY, Mr. Patrick John, FCA** *1965;* (Tax Fac), Laverty & Co, Rectory Cottage, Church Road, Hascombe, GODALMING, SURREY GU8 4JD.
LAVERY, Mr. Andrew Charles, BSc FCA *1988;* Forestside Cottage, Boundary Road, Rowledge, FARNHAM, GU10 4EP.
LAVERY, Miss. Anne Marie, BSc FCA *1992;* 11 Whitebeam Close, Colden Common, WINCHESTER, HAMPSHIRE, SO21 1AJ.
LAVERY, Miss. Elizabeth Irene, BA ACA *1982;* Cala Group Ltd, Adam House, 5 Mid New Cultins, EDINBURGH, EH11 4DU.
•**LAVERY, Mr. Patrick John, BSc FCA** *1977;* P.Lavery & Company Limited, 64 Grosvenor Road, Muswell Hill, LONDON, N10 2DS.
LAVILLE, Mr. Julian Michael Alexander, BSc(Econ) ACA *2002;* 28 Chesterfield Grove, LONDON, SE22 8RW.
LAVILLE, Mr. Louis Victor Ralph, BSc ACA *1985;* Pennington House, 27a Marryat Road, Wimbledon, LONDON, SW19 5BE.
LAVILLE, Mrs. Sarah Helena Christina, MA ACA *1993;* 54 Canonbury Park North, LONDON, N1 2JT.
LAVIN, Mr. Andrew, BSc ACA *2009;* Aggreko, PO BOX 17576, JEBEL ALI, UNITED ARAB EMIRATES.
LAVIN, Mrs. Clare Gemma Blaise, BSc(Hons) ACA *2006;* 19, Kelly Gardens Oxley Park, MILTON KEYNES, MK4 4HY.
LAVIN, Mrs. Helena Sarah, BSc(Hons) ACA *2001;* 35 South Grove, MORECAMBE, LANCASHIRE, LA4 5RL.
LAVIN, Mr. John Brendan, FCA *1960;* Homewood, Shawes Drive, Anderton, CHORLEY, PR6 9HR. (Life Member)
LAVIN, Mr. Michael Anthony, BA ACA *1990;* 50 Denham Lane, Chalfont St. Peter, GERRARDS CROSS, BUCKINGHAMSHIRE, SL9 0ET.
LAVIN, Mr. Stephen James, BA ACA *1998;* 15 Coombe Gardens, BERKHAMSTED, HERTFORDSHIRE, HP4 3PA.
LAVINGTON, Mr. Mark, FCA *1968;* Selva, Upperton, PETWORTH, GU28 9BE.
•**LAVIS, Mr. Christopher Alan, FCA** *1983;* Chris Lavis & Co., Pineapple Business Park, Salway Ash, BRIDPORT, DORSET, DT6 5DB. See also Chris Lavis & Co Ltd
LAVY, Mr. Jonathan Samuel, FCA *1971;* Flat 138, Chiltern Court, Baker Street, LONDON, NW1 5SF.
LAW, Mr. Alan Kwok Fai, ACA *2007;* Flat 12E, Block 7, City Garden, 233 Electric Road, NORTH POINT, HONG KONG ISLAND HONG KONG SAR.
LAW, Mr. Alastair Gibbon, FCA *1980;* 51 Woodfield Lane, ASHTEAD, SURREY, KT21 2BT.
•**LAW, Mr. Alastair Hudson, FCA** *1984;* Fitzgerald and Law LLP, 8 Lincoln's Inn Fields, LONDON, WC2A 3BP.
LAW, Mr. Alex, BSc ACA *2006;* Deloitte & Touche (M.E.), Currency House Building 1 5th Floor, DIFC, Dubai International Financial Centre, PO Box 282056, DUBAI, UNITED ARAB EMIRATES.
LAW, Miss. Amy Sarah, BSc ACA *2005;* U H Y George Hay, St. Georges House, 14 George Street, HUNTINGDON, CAMBRIDGESHIRE, PE29 3GH.
•**LAW, Mrs. Andrea Louise, BSc ACA** *2003;* Andrea Law, Sandrock Farmhouse, Limes Lane, Buxted, UCKFIELD, EAST SUSSEX TN22 4PE.
LAW, Mrs. Ann-Louise, MA ACA *2003;* Orchard Barn Elm Tree Farm, Portskewett, CALDICOT, GWENT, NP26 5TT.
LAW, Mr. Arden Sang, FCA *1978;* 1804 Nottingham Lane, SAN DIMAS, CA 91773, UNITED STATES. (Life Member)
LAW, Mr. Brian, FCA *1960;* 14 Oaks Road, Shiplake, HENLEY-ON-THAMES, RG9 3JH. (Life Member)
LAW, Mr. Bruce Marcus Alexander, FCA *1970;* 106 Ashley Road, WALTON-ON-THAMES, KT12 1HP.
LAW, Mrs. Catherine Ruth, MA ACA *1993;* 1 Portman Mews, Fairford Leys, AYLESBURY, BUCKINGHAMSHIRE, HP19 7AX.
LAW, Mrs. Ceris, BSc ACA ATII *1990;* 69 Chatsworth Road, Worsley, MANCHESTER, M28 2WS.
LAW, Mr. Charles Howard, BA ACA *1981;* Oak Bank, London Road East, AMERSHAM, BUCKINGHAMSHIRE, HP7 9DP.
LAW, Mr. Cheuk Shing, ACA *2008;* F S Law & Co, Room 1315, Leighton Centre, 77 Leighton Road, CAUSEWAY BAY, HONG KONG SAR.
LAW, Mr. Chi Shing, ACA *2007;* Philip Lee & Co., Office B, 22nd floor, Guangdong Investment Tower, 148 Connaught Road, CENTRAL HONG KONG ISLAND HONG KONG SAR.
LAW, Mr. Chi Kin, ACA *2008;* Flat B, 10th Floor, Rialto Building, 2 Landale Street, WAN CHAI, HONG KONG SAR.
LAW, Mr. Chi Shing, ACA *2008;* Flat E 19F Block 11, Sea Crest Villa, 44 Castle Peak Road, SHAM TSENG, NEW TERRITORIES, HONG KONG SAR.
LAW, Mr. Chi Yuen, ACA *2008;* Flat G, 17th Floor, Block 1, Park Island, MA WAN, NEW TERRITORIES HONG KONG SAR.
LAW, Mrs. Christine Margaret, ACA *1981;* Johnson Tidsall, 81 Burton Road, DERBY, DE1 1TJ.
LAW, Mr. Chun Kuen, ACA *2004;* CK Law & Co., 1101 Bank Centre, 630-636 Nathan Road, MONG KOK, KOWLOON, HONG KONG SAR.
LAW, Mr. Chung Wing, ACA *2011;* Flat 43, 187 East India Dock Road, LONDON, E14 0EF.
LAW, Mr. Conrad Yue Kwong, BSc FCA *1996;* 3 Ashfield Road, East Acton, LONDON, W3 7JE.
•**LAW, Mr. David John Alexander, MA ACA** *1987;* PricewaterhouseCoopers LLP, 7 More London Riverside, LONDON, SE1 2RT. See also PricewaterhouseCoopers
LAW, Miss. Davina Hoi Ling, BSc ACA *2009;* 6/2 Cowper Street, RANDWICK, NSW 2031, AUSTRALIA.
LAW, Mr. Edward Jeremy, FCA *1969;* Bishopslough, BENNETTSBRIDGE, COUNTY KILKENNY, IRELAND.
LAW, Ms. Elizabeth, ACA *2006;* Law & Partners CPA Limited, 8/F Chinachem Tower, 34-37 Connaught Road, CENTRAL, HONG KONG ISLAND, HONG KONG SAR. See also Stephen Law & Company
LAW, Mrs. Elizabeth Marie-Claire, BA ACA *1997;* 8 Bowland Drive, CHESTERFIELD, DERBYSHIRE, S42 7LZ.
LAW, Mr. Eric Hon Dick, MA(Hons) ACA *2002;* Flat 34D, Royal Tower, Hillsborough Court, 18 Old Peak Road, THE PEAK, HONG KONG ISLAND HONG KONG SAR.
LAW, Miss. Eva Chi Wah, BSc ACA *1994;* 1 Ardmore Park, No. 20-02 Ardmore II, SINGAPORE 259962, SINGAPORE.
LAW, Mr. Glenn Darren, MSc ACA *1997;* Tithefield, Dark Lane, Chearsley, AYLESBURY, HP18 0DA.
LAW, Miss. Helen Jean, ACA *1990;* Llewellyn Ryland Ltd, Haden Street, BIRMINGHAM, B12 9DB.
LAW, Miss. Helen Margaret, BSc ACA *1993;* Wieslerstrasse 11, CH-8702 Zollikon, ZOLLIKON, SWITZERLAND.

LAW, Mr. Hoi Ching, ACA 2011; Rm 2508 25/F, Yiu Shun House, Yiu On Est, SHA TIN, NEW TERRITORIES, HONG KONG SAR.
LAW, Mr. Hon Hing Henry, ACA FCCA 2004; Henry Law & Company, Room 301-2, Hang Seng Wanchai Building 3rd Floor, No. 200 Hennessy Road, WAN CHAI, HONG KONG ISLAND HONG KONG SAR.
LAW, Mr. Hon Man Thomas, ACA 2008; Rolex(Hong Kong) Ltd, 12/F, Jardine House, CENTRAL, HONG KONG SAR.
LAW, Mr. Howard Duncan Clive, BA(Hons) ACA 2002; 58 Crail Close, WOKINGHAM, RG41 2PZ.
LAW, Mr. Ian Richard Macleod, FCA 1968; P O Box 434, SIMONS TOWN, 7995, SOUTH AFRICA. (Life Member)
LAW, Miss. Idy Wai Man, ACA 2008; Flat 15 City Tower, 3 Limeharbour, LONDON, E14 9LS.
LAW, Ms. Iris Wai Han, ACA 2008; Flat D, 10th Floor, Hoi Ming Mansion, Riviera Gardens, TSUEN WAN, NEW TERRITORIES HONG KONG SAR.
•LAW, Mr. Jack Wing Tak, BA ACA 1984; Ribchester Smith & Law, Sutherland House, 5-7 The Friars, NEWCASTLE UPON TYNE, NE1 5XE. See also Ribchesters
•LAW, Mr. James Hermon, FCA 1976; Edwards Veeder LLP, Alex House, 260-268 Chapel Street, SALFORD, M3 5JZ.
LAW, Mrs. Jane Elizabeth, MA FCA 1996; Institute of Chartered Accountants, Metropolitan House, 321 Avebury Boulevard, MILTON KEYNES, MK9 2GA.
•LAW, Mrs. Jennifer Monique, LLB ACA 1989; Monique Law, 129 Randolph Avenue, LONDON, W9 1DN.
LAW, Mrs. Joanne Catherine, BSc ACA 2002; 11 Middle Avenue, FARNHAM, GU9 8JL.
LAW, Mr. John Derek, BSc ACA 1983; 44 Camlet Way, ST. ALBANS, AL3 4TL.
LAW, Mr. Joseph Shu Sang, BSc ACA 1987; 24/F Prosperous Commercial Buildings, 54-58 Jardines Bazaar, CAUSEWAY BAY, HONG KONG ISLAND, HONG KONG SAR.
LAW, Ms. Ka Man, ACA 2007; Flat B 10/F Block 5, Grand Promenade, SAI WAN HO, HONG KONG ISLAND, HONG KONG SAR.
LAW, Mr. Kam Wing, ACA 2005; Law Kam Wing & Company, 9th Floor, Full View Commercial Bldg, 140-142 Des Voeux Road, CENTRAL, HONG KONG ISLAND HONG KONG SAR.
LAW, Mr. Kee, BSc(Hons) ACA 2002; 3 Clifton Park Avenue, Raynes Park, LONDON, SW20 8BB.
LAW, Mr. Kian Huat, ACA 2008; 24 Jalan Suria U5/104, Taman Subang Idaman, Seksyen U5, 40150 SHAH ALAM, SELANGOR, MALAYSIA.
LAW, Mrs. Kirsty Jayne, BSc ACA 2003; 58 Crail Close, WOKINGHAM, RG41 2PZ.
LAW, Mr. Kwok Wai, ACA 2007; Flt E 30/F Tower 10, Royal Ascot, Tsun King Road, Fo Tan, SHA TIN, NEW TERRITORIES HONG KONG SAR.
LAW, Mr. Kwok Chung, ACA 2005; Flat A First Floor, 37 Parkes Street, YAU MA TEI, KOWLOON, HONG KONG SAR.
LAW, Ms. Lorraine Nicola, PhD BSc ACA 2001; (Tax Fac), 14 Cameron Road, BROMLEY, BR2 9AR.
LAW, Mrs. Louise Marie, BSc ACA 1998; (Tax Fac), 77 Ridgeway, Wargrave, READING, RG10 8AS.
•LAW, Mr. Mark Philip, BA FCA DChA 1987; with Baker Tilly Tax & Advisory Services LLP, Lancaster House, 7 Elmfield Road, BROMLEY, BR1 1LT.
LAW, Mr. Mark Sebastian, BA(Hons) ACA 2003; Yoyogi Duplex A, 5-34-1 Yoyogi, Shibuya-Ku, TOKYO, 151-0053 JAPAN.
LAW, Mr. Martin, BA ACA 1993; J P MORGAN, 60 VICTORIA EMBANKMENT, LONDON, EC4Y 0JP.
•LAW, Mr. Martin John, ACA 1981; Hardcastle Burton LLP, Lake House, Market Hill, ROYSTON, HERTFORDSHIRE, SG8 9JN.
LAW, Mr. Michael John, BA ACA 1980; 29 Kent Road, EAST MOLESEY, KT8 9JZ.
LAW, Ms. Mun Yee, ACA 2008; Flat C, 27/F Tower 2, The Pacifica, 9 Sham Shing Road, LAI CHI KOK, KOWLOON HONG KONG SAR.
LAW, Miss. Nancy Rae, MA ACA 1991; La Hanniere Farm, La Rue Du Rat, St. Martin, JERSEY, JE3 6AE.
LAW, Mr. Nim Keung, ACA 2007; Flat G, 7/F, Block 1, Ravana Garden, 1 - 3 On King Street, SHA TIN NEW TERRITORIES HONG KONG SAR.
LAW, Mr. Pak Ying Raymond, ACA 2005; Richie Villa, 59 Kan Tau Tsuen, FANLING, NEW TERRITORIES, HONG KONG SAR.
LAW, Mr. Patrick Fu Yuen, MSc ACA 1992; 33A Tower 2, Phase III, Bel-Air On The Peak, POK FU LAM, HONG KONG ISLAND, HONG KONG SAR.
LAW, Mr. Peter David, BA ACA 1989; 171 Warton Terrace, Heaton, NEWCASTLE UPON TYNE, NE6 5DX.
LAW, Ms. Pik Shan, ACA 2008; Unit E, 29/F, Tower 3, Tai Hing Gardens, Phase 1, Tsun Wen Road No 11 TUEN MUN NEW TERRITORIES HONG KONG SAR.
LAW, Mr. Ping Kwan, ACA 2007; 1 Little Overwood, West Timperley, ALTRINCHAM, CHESHIRE, WA14 5UE.
LAW, Mr. Ping Wah, ACA 2008; Celestial Asia Securites Holdings Ltd, 28/F Manhattan Place, 23 Wang Tai Road, KOWLOON BAY, KOWLOON, HONG KONG SAR.
LAW, Mr. Pui Cheung, ACA 2005; Li Tang Chen & Co., 10/F Sun Hung Kai Centre, 30 Harbour Road, WAN CHAI, HONG KONG ISLAND, HONG KONG SAR.
•LAW, Mr. Richard Alastair, MA FCA 1979; Gunn Cottage Station Road, South Leigh, WITNEY, OXFORDSHIRE, OX29 6XJ.
LAW, Mr. Richard Anthony, BSc ACA 1991; 69 Chatsworth Road, Worsley, MANCHESTER, M28 2WS.
LAW, Mr. Richard Michael, BSc(Hons) ACA 2010; 38 Trefoil Gardens, Amblecote, STOURBRIDGE, DY8 4DB.
LAW, Mr. Richard William, BSc ACA 1989; 84 Upper Tollington Park, LONDON, N4 4NB.
LAW, Mr. Robert David, BSc FCA 1985; 1 Chatsworth Grove, Folly Hill, FARNHAM, GU9 0DJ.
•LAW, Mr. Robert Edward, FCA 1972; Mason Law LLP, 9 Frederick Road, Edgbaston, BIRMINGHAM, B15 1TW.
•LAW, Mr. Robert Philip, FCA 1977; Langdowns DFK Limited, Fleming Court, Leigh Road, EASTLEIGH, HAMPSHIRE, SO50 9PD.
LAW, Miss. Sarah, MA(Oxon) ACA 2011; Flat 32, 9 Moreton Street, LONDON, SW1V 2PW.
•LAW, Mrs. Sarah Elizabeth, FCA 1993; Bloomer Heaven Limited, Rutland House, 148 Edmund Street, BIRMINGHAM, B3 2FD.
LAW, Mr. Shiu Wing, ACA 2008; Flat 9, 2/F, Po Yiu House, Po Pui Court, KWUN TONG, KOWLOON HONG KONG SAR.
LAW, Mr. Sidney George, FCA 1948; 29 Holland Park, CLACTON-ON-SEA, CO15 6LS. (Life Member)
LAW, Mr. Simon David Kelway, BA FCA 1997; 11 Middle Avenue, FARNHAM, GU9 8JL.
•LAW, Mr. Simon John, BSc ACA 1996; Mark Holt & Co Ltd, Marine Building, Victoria Wharf, PLYMOUTH, PL4 0RF.
LAW, Mr. Simon John, BSc ACA 2001; Orchard Barn Elm Tree Farm, Portskewett, CALDICOT, GWENT, NP26 5TT.
LAW, Mr. Stephen Cheuk Kin, MBA BSc ACA CPA 1989; Flat C 6/F. Block 1, Ronsdale Garden, 25 Tai Hang Drive, TAI HANG, HONG KONG SAR.
•①LAW, Mr. Steven Mark, FCA 1984; Ensors, Cardinal House, 46 St Nicholas Street, IPSWICH, IP1 1TT.
LAW, Mrs. Suzanne Lesley, BSc(Hons) ACA 2001; Cambrian Homes Ltd, Unit 7b, Birchwood One Business Park, Dewhurst Road, Birchwood, WARRINGTON WA3 7GB.
LAW, Mr. Tak Wing, ACA 2007; 18 Sommerset Way, Suite 2303, TORONTO M2N 6X5, ON, CANADA.
LAW, Mr. Timothy William, MA ACA 1998; 5 The Slade, Newton Longville, MILTON KEYNES, MK17 0DR.
LAW, Mr. Tin-Kin, MSc ACA 2011; Flat 121, 14 New Crane Place, LONDON, E1W 3TU.
LAW, Dr. Trevor Anthony, ACA 1988; 67 Stoney Lane, Spondon, DERBY, DE21 7QG.
LAW, Ms. Tsz Han, ACA 2010; Flat C 15/F Blk 5, Nan Fung Plaza, 8 Pui SHing Road, Junk Bay, TSEUNG KWAN O, NEW TERRITORIES HONG KONG SAR.
LAW, Mr. Wai Fai, ACA 2007; Room 904, Wah Ying Cheong Central Building, 158-164 Queen's Road, CENTRAL, HONG KONG ISLAND, HONG KONG SAR.
LAW, Mr. Wang Chak Waltery, ACA 2007; Flat C, 17/F, Block 7, Braemar Hill Mansions, 27 Braemar Hill Road, NORTH POINT HONG KONG SAR.
•LAW, Mr. William John, BSc FCA 1981; Princecroft Willis LLP, Towngate House, 2-8 Parkstone Road, POOLE, DORSET, BH15 2PW. See also PW Business Solutions
LAW, Mr. Wing Kin, ACA 2004; P.O. BOX NO. 62729, KWUN TONG POST OFFICE, KWUN TONG, KOWLOON, HONG KONG SAR.
LAW, Mr. Wing Tak, ACA 2008; Flat C, 12/F, Albron Court, 99 Caine Road, CENTRAL, HONG KONG SAR.
LAW, Miss. Yee Man, ACA CTA MAAT 2002; (Tax Fac), 3 Bodill Gardens, Hucknall, NOTTINGHAM, NG15 7SQ.
LAW, Miss. Yen Hua, BA(Hons) ACA 2002; No. 39 Jalan Pekaka 8/14 Kota Damansara, 47810 PETALING JAYA, SELANGOR, MALAYSIA.
LAW, Mr. Yu Kwan Albert, ACA 2006; Flat B 15/Floor, Prosperous Height, 62 Conduit Road, MID LEVELS, HONG KONG ISLAND, HONG KONG SAR.
LAW, Mr. Yui Lun, ACA 2005; Y.L. Law and Company, Room 502 5/F, Prosperous Building, 48-52 Des Voeux Road, CENTRAL, HONG KONG ISLAND HONG KONG SAR.
LAW-GISIKO, Mr. Peter, FCA 1979; 285 Madison Avenue, NEW YORK, NY 10017, UNITED STATES.
LAW MIN, Mr. Jean Alain, MBA BA ACA 1986; 9-15 Sir William Newton Street, PORT LOUIS, MAURITIUS.
•LAW PAK CHONG, Mr. Nicholas Laval, BSc(Hons) ACA 2002; Clarke & Co, Acorn House, 33 Churchfield Road, Acton, LONDON, W3 6AY.
LAWAL, Miss. Omotunde Olayemi, BSc(Hons) ACA 2004; 21 Woodstock Drive, Ickenham, UXBRIDGE, UB10 8EG.
•LAWES, Mr. Andrew David, MA MSc FCA 1991; Baker Tilly Tax & Advisory Services LLP, The Pinnacle, 170 Midsummer Boulevard, MILTON KEYNES, MK9 1BP. See also Baker Tilly UK Audit LLP
•LAWES, Mr. Christopher William, BSc ACA 1989; (Tax Fac), with Banks Cooper Associates Ltd, 17 Marina Court, Castle Street, HULL, HU1 1TJ.
LAWES, Mr. Graham William, MA ACA 2003; Yew Tree House, Haultwick, WARE, HERTFORDSHIRE, SG11 1JQ.
•LAWES, Mr. Kevin Leslie, FCA 1968; Lawes & Co UK Limited, Boyces Building, 42 Regent Street, Clifton, BRISTOL, BS8 4HU.
LAWES, Mr. Paul Raymond, BA ACA 1999; No.1 Traveller Ltd, Cameron Robey Ltd Suite 3a, 44 Carnaby Street, LONDON, W1F 9PP.
LAWES, Mr. Richard James, ACA 1998; 94 Dene Road, Didsbury, MANCHESTER, M20 2GU.
LAWES, Mr. Stephen Finlay Heron, BA ACA 1980; 10 Ernle Road, LONDON, SW20 0HJ.
•LAWES, Mr. Stephen Mark, BA ACA 1994; DPR Accountancy Limited, 3 Station Road, HAVERHILL, SUFFOLK, CB9 0EU.
•LAWES, Mrs. Susan Jacqueline, BAcc ACA 1993; (Tax Fac), DPR Accountancy Limited, 3 Station Road, HAVERHILL, SUFFOLK, CB9 0EU.
LAWES, Mrs. Tanja, BA(Hons) ACA 2004; 17 Grassy Glade, Hempstead, GILLINGHAM, KENT, ME7 3RR.
LAWES, Mr. Timothy Robin, FCA 1978; Blakeney Lodge, 2 Green Street, SUNBURY-ON-THAMES, MIDDLESEX, TW16 6RN.
LAWFORD, Mr. David Allan, FCA 1967; 7 Manorial Road, Roughley, SUTTON COLDFIELD, B75 5UD.
LAWFORD, Miss. Eleanor Rosalind, BA ACA 2004; Credit Suisse, 1 Cabot Square, LONDON, E14 4QJ.
LAWFORD, Mr. Jason, BSc ACA 2001; Flat 44, 11 Point Pleasant, LONDON, SW18 1PT.
LAWFORD, Mr. Nigel Philip Charles, LLB FCA 1974; Elsdon, 10 Lancaster Av, FARNHAM, GU9 8JY.
LAWFORD, Mr. Roderick Charles, FCA 1993; 6 Sarsen Close, SWINDON, SN1 4LA.
•LAWLAN, Mr. John Ross Binks, FCA 1974; (Tax Fac), G.T. Grant & Co, 79 High Street, Gosforth, NEWCASTLE UPON TYNE, NE3 4AA.
LAWLER, Miss. Beverley Ann, BSc ACA 1988; 6 Rue St Joseph, 1227 Carouge, GENEVA, SWITZERLAND.
LAWLER, Mr. David Andrew, MBA FCA 1989; The Limes, Grenfell Road, MAIDENHEAD, SL6 1HA.
•LAWLER, Mr. David Mark, PhD FCA 1991; Forensic Risk Alliance, 3rd floor, Audrey House, 16-20 Ely Place, LONDON, EC1N 6SN.
LAWLER, Mr. Geoffrey James, BA ACA 1995; 6 Bloomfield Way, Sawtry, HUNTINGDON, CAMBRIDGESHIRE, PE28 5RH.
LAWLER, Mr. Michael Anthony, BA ACA 1992; 8 Damson Close, Walkwood, REDDITCH, B97 5WA.
LAWLER, Mr. Michael Philip, MSc ACA 2003; 8 West Way, SHIPLEY, WEST YORKSHIRE, BD18 4HW.
LAWLER, Mr. Thomas Philip, BA(Hons) FCA 1966; Woodby, 20 Park Wood Close, SKIPTON, NORTH YORKSHIRE, BD23 1QW. (Life Member)
LAWLESS, Mr. Ian Michael, BSc ACA 1994; 44 Wood Street, Mow Cop, STOKE-ON-TRENT, ST7 3PF.
LAWLESS, Mrs. Joanna, BEng ACA 2007; 10 St Elvan Crescent, Porthleven, HELSTON, TR13 9NA.
LAWLESS, Mr. Stuart Ian, BEng ACA 1994; Nuffield Health Cannons House, 40-44 Coombe Road, NEW MALDEN, KT3 4QF.
LAWLEY, Miss. Anne Katharine, MA FCA 1977; 25 Parkside, 17 Hamilton Road, LONDON, W5 2EG.
LAWLEY, Mr. Barry William, FCA 1957; 26 Keytes Lane, Barford, WARWICK, CV35 8EP. (Life Member)
LAWLEY, Mr. David John, MSc FCA 1986; 11 Appian Way, Cheswick Green, SOLIHULL, B90 4HD.
LAWLEY, Mr. John Daniel, BMus ACA 2005; Flat 5 Tavistock Hall, 53 Balaclava Road Long Ditton, SURBITON, SURREY, KT6 5RU.
LAWLEY, Mr. Keith David, BA FCA 1980; Bird Group of Companies, The Mill, Bestholey, NEWPORT, NP15 1LR.
LAWLEY, Miss. Rebecca Louise, BA ACA 2010; Flat 35 Heritage Court, 15 Warstone Lane, BIRMINGHAM, B18 6HP.
LAWLEY, Miss. Rosamond Alice, ACA 2009; 9 Fernwood Avenue, NEWCASTLE UPON TYNE, NE3 5DJ.
LAWLOR, Mr. Ciaran Michael, BA ACA 1993; 18 Woodbourne Square, Douglas, ISLE OF MAN, IM1 4DE.
LAWLOR, Mr. Joseph Ronan, BA ACA 1999; 28 The Watermill, Raheny, DUBLIN 5, COUNTY DUBLIN, IRELAND.
LAWLOR, Miss. Kate, BA ACA 2008; 8 Dalston Drive, Bramhall, STOCKPORT, CHESHIRE, SK7 1DW.
•LAWLOR, Mr. Paul Joseph, ACA CPA 1993; (Tax Fac), Donal Lucey Lawlor, 43 Highfield Road, DARTFORD, DA1 2JS.
LAWLOR, Mr. Stephen John, BSc ACA 1989; 65 Madeira Croft, Chapelfields, COVENTRY, CV5 8NX.
LAWLOR, Mr. Timothy Charles, BA ACA 1995; Elcombe, Malthouse Lane, Fox Corner, Worplesdon, GUILDFORD, SURREY GU3 3PS.
LAWMAN, Mr. Christopher James, BSc ACA 2005; 11 Redgrave Rise, WIGAN, LANCASHIRE, WN3 6HG.
•LAWMAN, Mr. Christopher John, FCA 1970; Deblaw Limited, 44 Hall Orchard Lane, Frisby-On-The-Wreake, MELTON MOWBRAY, LE14 2NH.
LAWN, Mr. David, FCA 1974; 1 Burwell Walk, HARTLEPOOL, TS25 2JF.
LAWN, Miss. Sharon Denise, BA ACA 1994; 51 Welling Road, Orsett, GRAYS, RM16 3DW.
LAWN, Mr. Timothy David, LLB ACA 2000; 32 Belvoir Road, Bottesford, NOTTINGHAM, NG13 0BG.
LAWNE, Mr. Peter George, BA ACA 1980; Shell Chemicals Ltd, Shell Centre, LONDON, SE1 7NA.
•LAWRANCE, Mr. Benjamin George, BSc(Hons) FCA 2001; Baker Tillly Tax & Advisory Services LLP, St Philips Point, Temple Row, BIRMINGHAM, B2 5AF. See also Baker Tilly UK Audit LLP
LAWRANCE, Miss. Jane Elizabeth, BSc ACA 1998; 224 8th Avenue, Apt 11, NEW YORK, NY 10011, UNITED STATES.
•LAWRANCE, Mr. John, FCA 1970; 112 The Welkin, Lindfield, HAYWARDS HEATH, WEST SUSSEX, RH16 2PL.
LAWRANCE, Mr. Maurice Roy, FCA 1962; Rose Cottage, Pond Lane, Hatfield Heath, BISHOP'S STORTFORD, CM22 7AB. (Life Member)
LAWRANCE, Mr. Peter Richard, BA FCA 1975; 50 Brewery Road, Horsell, WOKING, GU21 4NA.
LAWRENCE, Mr. Adrian, BSc FCA 1994; 9 Stoneleigh Grove, Muxton, TELFORD, TF2 8SU.
LAWRENCE, Mr. Alan Steven James, ACA 2009; 74 Tothill Street, Minster, RAMSGATE, CT12 4AJ.
LAWRENCE, Mr. Andrew March, BSc FCA 1990; BBC World Service Trust, 3rd Floor Bush House, The Strand, LONDON, WC2B 4PH.
LAWRENCE, Miss. Annabel Jane, MA MSci ACA CTA 2006; 47 Whitton Road, TWICKENHAM, TW1 1BH.
LAWRENCE, Miss. Anne, BSc(Hons) ACA 2002; 15 Field Way, RUISLIP, HA4 7LY.
LAWRENCE, Mr. Benjamin John Charles, BA ACA 2000; Woodyers Cranleigh Road, Wonersh, GUILDFORD, GU5 0PB.
LAWRENCE, Mr. Brian Paul, BSc FCA 1984; PricewaterhouseCoopers, Darling Park Tower 2, 201 Sussex Street, GPO Box 2650, SYDNEY, NSW 1171 AUSTRALIA.
LAWRENCE, Mrs. Carol, BA FCA 1992; Diocese of Shrewsbury, Curial Offices, 2 Park Road South, PRENTON, MERSEYSIDE, CH43 4UX.
LAWRENCE, Mr. Charles Edward, BA FCA 1972; 40 South Road, SOUTHAMPTON SN 01, BERMUDA.
LAWRENCE, Mr. Christer Shaun, BSc FCA 1999; Pear Tree House The Turnpike, Bunwell, NORWICH, NR16 1SP.

•**LAWRENCE, Mrs. Christine Pamela, FCA** *1986;* with ICAEW, Metropolitan House, 321 Avebury Boulevard, MILTON KEYNES, MK9 2FZ.
LAWRENCE, Mr. Christopher Edward Arthur, MA MPhil ACA *1994;* 12a Sutton Court, Fauconberg Road, LONDON, W4 3JG.
LAWRENCE, Mr. Christopher Hugh, BA ACA *1987;* 32 The Close, NORWICH, NR1 4DZ.
LAWRENCE, Mrs. Claire Louisa, BA(Hons) ACA *2001;* 56 Queens Road, CHELMSFORD, ESSEX, CM2 6HB.
LAWRENCE, Mrs. Claire Louise, LLB ACA *2003;* 2 Tennyson Street, Pudsey, LEEDS, WEST YORKSHIRE, LS28 9HA.
LAWRENCE, Mrs. Corinne Elaine, ACA *1994;* 1 Seymour Way, Leicester Forest East, LEICESTER, LE3 3LY.
LAWRENCE, Mr. David, BSc(Hons) ACA *2011;* 8 Mulberry Court, South Road, BISHOP'S STORTFORD, HERTFORDSHIRE, CM23 3JW.
LAWRENCE, Mr. David George, FCA *1970;* 1 Edge Hill Road, SUTTON COLDFIELD, B74 4NU.
•**LAWRENCE, Mr. David Ivor, FCA** *1972;* Cavendish, 4th Floor, Centre Heights, 137 Finchley Road, LONDON, NW3 6JG.
LAWRENCE, Mr. David James, BA(Hons) ACA *2001;* 2 Cowper Road, CAMBRIDGE, CB1 3SN.
LAWRENCE, Mr. David James, BSc FCA *1977;* Flat 181 Lauderdale Tower, Barbican, LONDON, EC2Y 8BY.
LAWRENCE, Mr. David John, BA ACA *1984;* 21 Hall Close, Kislingbury, NORTHAMPTON, NN7 4BQ.
LAWRENCE, Mr. David John, FCA *1951;* (Member of Council 1977 - 1985), Flintwell, Iford, LEWES, BN7 3EU. (Life Member)
LAWRENCE, Miss. Donna Ruth, MA ACA *1989;* 28 Hollywood Avenue, Gosforth, NEWCASTLE UPON TYNE, NE3 5BP.
LAWRENCE, Miss. Elaine, BBA ACA *2007;* with PricewaterhouseCoopers LLP, 31 Great George Street, BRISTOL, BS1 5QD.
LAWRENCE, Mrs. Elaine Louise, BSc ACA *1990;* Kennet Equipment Leasing Ltd, Kennet House, 2 Temple Court, Temple Way, Coleshill, BIRMINGHAM B46 1HH.
LAWRENCE, Mrs. Emma Louise, ACA MAAT *2009;* 27 Wheatsheaf Close, Sindlesham, WOKINGHAM, RG41 5PT.
LAWRENCE, Mr. Eric Alexander, BA FCA *1987;* 35B Pitt Road, NORTH CURL CURL, NSW 2099, AUSTRALIA.
LAWRENCE, Mrs. Frances Margaret, BEng ACA *1997;* 5 Dalby Close, Hurst, READING, RG10 0BZ.
LAWRENCE, Mr. Geoffrey Charles, FCA *1961;* Pinewood, 83 Purley Downs Road, Sanderstead, SOUTH CROYDON, SURREY, CR2 0RJ. (Life Member)
•**LAWRENCE, Mr. George Ashlin, BA FCA** *1970;* Lawrence & Co Professional Limited, 2 Albany Park, Cabot Lane, POOLE, DORSET, BH17 7BX.
LAWRENCE, Mrs. Gillian, BA FCA *1989;* 35b Pitt Road, NORTH CURL CURL, NSW 2099, AUSTRALIA.
LAWRENCE, Miss. Gillian Jane, BSc ACA CTA *1990;* with Rawlinson & Hunter, Lower Mill, Kingston Road, Ewell, EPSOM, KT17 2AE.
LAWRENCE, Mr. Gordon Charles, FCA JDipMA *1955;* 30 The Pound, Bromham, CHIPPENHAM, WILTSHIRE, SN15 2HE. (Life Member)
LAWRENCE, Mr. Graham Neil, BA ACA *1992;* WHP Facilities Ltd, Staithes 2 The Waterpark, GATESHEAD, TYNE AND WEAR, NE11 9SN.
LAWRENCE, Mr. Greg Frederick Rene, BSc FCA *1975;* Rusland, Leatherhead Rd, Fetcham, LEATHERHEAD, KT23 4RR.
LAWRENCE, Mr. Harold Brian, MA FCA *1967;* 8 Greenfield Crescent, BIRMINGHAM, B15 3BE.
•**LAWRENCE, Mr. Harvey Neil, FCA** *1973;* The Lawrence Woolfson Partnership, 1 Bentinck Street, LONDON, W1U 2ED.
•**LAWRENCE, Miss. Helen Louise, BA(Hons) ACA** *2000;* M Lawrence & Co, 213 Station Road, Stechford, BIRMINGHAM, B33 8BB.
LAWRENCE, Mr. Ian Christopher, BCom ACA *1983;* 239 Broyhill Road, MORAVIAN FALLS, NC 28654, UNITED STATES.
LAWRENCE, Mr. Ian Michael, BA ACA *1988;* 40 Parklands Avenue, Dinnington, SHEFFIELD, SOUTH YORKSHIRE, S25 2XW.
•**LAWRENCE, Mr. Ian Robert, BSc ACA** *1993;* Lawrence Rose Limited, 53 Basepoint Business Centre, Rivermead Drive, SWINDON, WILTSHIRE, SN5 7EX.
LAWRENCE, Mrs. Isabel Marion, BSc FCA *1993;* Ballachrink, 14 Peveril Avenue, Peel, ISLE OF MAN, IM5 1QB.
LAWRENCE, Mrs. Jacqueline, ACA *1996;* Merrywood, 22 Birds Hill Drive, Oxshott, LEATHERHEAD, SURREY, KT22 0SP.
LAWRENCE, Mr. James Howard, BSc ACA *2009;* Brookfield House Church Eaton Road, Haughton, STAFFORD, ST18 9JG.
LAWRENCE, Mr. James Wyndham Stuart, BA ACA *1996;* 169 Oatlands Drive, WEYBRIDGE, SURREY, KT13 9JY.
LAWRENCE, Mr. Jason Paul, BA(Hons) ACA *2002;* 22 Grange Road, SEVENOAKS, KENT, TN13 2PQ.
LAWRENCE, Mr. Jeremy Oliver John, BA FCA *1978;* 33 London Road, STROUD, GL5 2AJ.
LAWRENCE, Mrs. Jessica, ACA *2005;* 1 Glebe Field Croft, WETHERBY, LS22 6WQ.
LAWRENCE, Mrs. Jessica Elizabeth, BSc ACA *1993;* Upper Grange Farm, Gibsons Lane, Old Dalby, MELTON MOWBRAY, LEICESTERSHIRE, LE14 3LH.
LAWRENCE, Mr. John Alan, BA FCA *1974;* 2 Baulks Lane, Aldwincle, KETTERING, NN14 3EW.
•**LAWRENCE, Mr. John Daniel, FCA** *1966;* Lawrence Nudds & Co, Alpha House, 176a High Street, BARNET, HERTFORDSHIRE, EN5 5SZ.
LAWRENCE, Mr. John Patrick, BA FCA *1969;* Ewhurst, 42 Main Road, Radcliffe-on-Trent, NOTTINGHAM, NG12 2AA.
LAWRENCE, Mr. John Robert, ACA *2008;* (Tax Fac), Parlane Purkiss, 177 London Road, SOUTHEND-ON-SEA, SS1 1PW.
•**LAWRENCE, Mr. John Thomas Charles, BSc FCA** *1972;* Broad Acre, 11 Upgate, Poringland, NORWICH, NR14 7SH.
LAWRENCE, Mr. Jonathan Timothy, BA ACA *1997;* 6 Old Derry Hill, CALNE, WILTSHIRE, SN11 9PJ.
LAWRENCE, Mrs. Julia Rachel, BSc ACA *1997;* 96 South Parade, PUDSEY, WEST YORKSHIRE, LS28 8NX.
•**LAWRENCE, Mr. Keith Barry, FCA CTA** *1967;* Keith Lawrence, Haven Court, 5 Library Ramp, PO Box 900, GIBRALTAR, GIBRALTAR.
LAWRENCE, Mr. Kevin Brian, ACA *1988;* Kingsbury House, Arlington, Bibury, CIRENCESTER, GLOUCESTERSHIRE, GL7 5ND.
LAWRENCE, Mrs. Kirsten Lucy, ACA *2008;* Apartment 303, 50374 Uptown Avenue, CANTON, MI 48187, UNITED STATES.
LAWRENCE, Mr. Mark, BA ACA *1995;* 41 Highbury Lane, Campbell Heights, MILTON KEYNES, MK9 4AQ.
LAWRENCE, Mr. Mark, ACA CA(NZ) *2009;* with KPMG LLP, 16 Raffles Quay, # 22-00, Hong Leong Building, SINGAPORE 048581, SINGAPORE.
LAWRENCE, Mr. Mark Henry, BA ACA *1992;* Ferndale, Tower-House Lane, Wraxall, BRISTOL, BS48 1JS.
•**LAWRENCE, Mr. Martin, FCA** *1969;* (Tax Fac), M Lawrence & Co, 213 Station Road, Stechford, BIRMINGHAM, B33 8BB.
LAWRENCE, Mr. Martin Allan, BA ACA CTA *1997;* 6 Glendale Avenue, Whickham, NEWCASTLE UPON TYNE, NE16 5JA.
LAWRENCE, Ms. Mary Josephine, BSc ACA *1981;* 11 Saddlebrook Park, SUNBURY-ON-THAMES, TW16 7NG.
•**LAWRENCE, Mr. Matthew Edward, BSc ACA** *2002;* with KPMG, 8/F Prince's Building, 10 Chater Road, CENTRAL, HONG KONG ISLAND, HONG KONG SAR.
LAWRENCE, Mr. Matthew John, BA ACA *2000;* The Homestead, Penn Street, AMERSHAM, BUCKINGHAMSHIRE, HP7 0PY.
LAWRENCE, Mr. Michael Alexander, BSc ACA *1982;* 2 Arnold Drive, CHESSINGTON, SURREY, KT9 2GD.
LAWRENCE, Mr. Michael James, MA ACA *1983;* 50 Woodberry Avenue, Winchmore Hill, LONDON, N21 3LD.
LAWRENCE, Mr. Paul Michael, BA ACA *1991;* Valley View, Mountain Hare, MERTHYR TYDFIL, MID GLAMORGAN, CF47 0LH.
•**LAWRENCE, Mr. Peter Anthony, BA FCA** *1984;* GLK Financial Services S.L., Cl. Imaculada Conception 7, Edif Europa of 1, Arroyo De La Hiel, 29631 MALAGA, SPAIN.
LAWRENCE, Mr. Peter Anthony, MA ACA *1990;* Council of the Isles of Scilly, Town Hall, St. Mary's, ISLES OF SCILLY, TR21 0LW.
LAWRENCE, Mr. Peter Geoffrey, FCA *1958;* 487 Tavistock Road, Roborough, PLYMOUTH, PL6 7AA. (Life Member)
LAWRENCE, Mr. Peter March, FCA *1957;* Hampton House, Chase Close, Coleshill, AMERSHAM, HP7 0LX. (Life Member)
LAWRENCE, Mr. Philip, BSc(Hons) ACA *2004;* 170 Reading Road, HENLEY-ON-THAMES, OXFORDSHIRE, RG9 1EA.
•**LAWRENCE, Mr. Philip, FCA** *1978;* Baverstocks Limited, Dickens House, 3-7 Guithavon Street, WITHAM, ESSEX, CM8 1BJ.
LAWRENCE, Mr. Philip Graham, BA ACA *1989;* 4 Van Dyck Rise, MACKENZIE, QLD 4156, AUSTRALIA.
LAWRENCE, Mr. Philip James, BSc ACA *1994;* The Coal Authority, 200 Lichfield Lane, MANSFIELD, NOTTINGHAMSHIRE, NG18 4RG.
LAWRENCE, Mr. Philip John, ACA *1978;* 17 Farnleys Mead, LYMINGTON, SO41 3TJ.
LAWRENCE, Mrs. Rachel Marie, BA ACA *2005;* with Ernst & Young LLP, Broadwalk House, Southernhay West, EXETER, EX1 1LF.
LAWRENCE, Mrs. Rhiannon Katherine, BA ACA *2001;* The Homestead, Penn Street, AMERSHAM, BUCKINGHAMSHIRE, HP7 0PY.
LAWRENCE, Mr. Richard John, BA ACA *1998;* 9 Long Grove, Seer Green, BEACONSFIELD, BUCKINGHAMSHIRE, HP9 2YN.
LAWRENCE, Mr. Richard Loveland, FCA *1971;* PO BOX 60156, MAIL BOX 455, 8101 PAFOS, CYPRUS.
•**LAWRENCE, Mr. Richard Simon, BA FCA** *1986;* 30 Sorrin Close, Idle, BRADFORD, BD10 8QF.
LAWRENCE, Mr. Robert Thomas, BSc ACA *1993;* 2 Stainburn Avenue, LEEDS, LS17 6PQ.
•**LAWRENCE, Mr. Rodney Kevin, FCA** *1968;* R.K. Lawrence & Co, 94 Brook Street, ERITH, DA8 1JF.
LAWRENCE, Mr. Roy, FCA *1947;* Rowden Mill, Winslow, BROMYARD, HR7 4LS. (Life Member)
LAWRENCE, Mr. Roy Donald, FCA *1956;* 8 Cavendish Place, Avenue Road, LYMINGTON, HAMPSHIRE, SO41 9ET. (Life Member)
LAWRENCE, Mrs. Sally, BA ACA *2000;* (Tax Fac), 169 Oatlands Drive, WEYBRIDGE, SURREY, KT13 9JY.
LAWRENCE, Mrs. Sally Dianne, BSc ACA *1991;* Clyptos, The Forest, LONDON, E11 1PJ.
LAWRENCE, Miss. Sally Ellen, ACA *2008;* 7 Mountain View, Peel, ISLE OF MAN, IM5 1QD.
LAWRENCE, Miss. Sarah, BA ACA *2010;* 38B Norfolk House Road, LONDON, SW16 1JH.
•**LAWRENCE, Mr. Scott Michael, BSc FCA** *1997;* Hazlewoods LLP, Windsor House, Bayshill Road, CHELTENHAM, GLOUCESTERSHIRE, GL50 3AT.
LAWRENCE, Mrs. Sheryl Arlene Frances, MBA BSc ACA *1990;* 12 Squirrel Close, Grange Park, NORTHAMPTON, NN4 5DL.
LAWRENCE, Mrs. Sian Elizabeth, BA ACA *1993;* J E Lawrence and Son Ltd, Willow Wood, Clarbeston Road, HAVERFORDWEST, SA63 4UN.
LAWRENCE, Mr. Simon David, BA ACA *1989;* Peugeot Citroen Automobiles UK Ltd Pinley House, 2 Sunbeam Way, COVENTRY, CV3 1ND.
LAWRENCE, Mr. Simon Roland Stuart, BSc FCA *2001;* 6 Westlake Drive, Mt Ommaney, BRISBANE, QLD 4074, AUSTRALIA.
LAWRENCE, Mr. Stephen Francis, BSc ACA *1985;* Galloway House, High Street, AMERSHAM, BUCKINGHAMSHIRE, HP7 0ED.
•**LAWRENCE, Mr. Stephen Geoffrey, BA FCA** *1981;* Stonebridge Stewart, Daryl House, 76a Pensby Road, Heswall, WIRRAL, CH60 7RF.
LAWRENCE, Mr. Stephen Howard, BA ACA *1992;* 4 Main Street, Willoughby Waterleys, LEICESTER, LE8 6UF.
LAWRENCE, Mr. Stephen Kenneth, BSc FCA *1978;* Micklefield Green House Sarratt Road, Sarratt, RICKMANSWORTH, HERTFORDSHIRE, WD3 6AH.
LAWRENCE, Mrs. Susan Elizabeth, BSc ACA *1992;* Jubilee House, Marton, WELSHPOOL, SY21 8UP.
LAWRENCE, Miss. Susannah, BA(Hons) ACA *2011;* 83 Mayola Road, LONDON, E5 0RF.
•**LAWRENCE, Mr. Timothy Gordon Roland, FCA** *1958;* Tim Lawrence, Whitethorn, Collinswood Road, Farnham Common, SLOUGH, SL2 3LH.
LAWRENCE, Mr. Timothy John, ACA *2008;* Apt _5#303, 50374 Uptown Avenue, CANTON, MI 48187, UNITED STATES.
LAWRENCE, Mr. Tyrone Patrick, BA ACA *1998;* 222a Park Road, KINGSTON UPON THAMES, KT2 5LS.
LAWRENCE, Miss. Victoria Louise, ACA *2009;* Flat 62 Coopers Court, Church Road, LONDON, W3 8PN.
LAWRENCE, Mr. William James, FCA *1961;* 5 Rock Close, PAIGNTON, DEVON, TQ4 6LA. (Life Member)
LAWRENCE, Mrs. Yewande Omolara, BSc ACA *1995;* 12 Grove Road, ISLEWORTH, MIDDLESEX, TW7 4JH.
•**LAWRENCE-ARCHER, Mr. Jonathan Charles Richard, FCA** *1970;* Bruton Charles, The Coach House, Greys Green Business Centre, Rotherfield Greys, HENLEY-ON-THAMES, OXFORDSHIRE RG9 4QG.
LAWRENSON, Mrs. Helen Jane, BA(Hons) ACA *2003;* 4 Ebers Grove, NOTTINGHAM, NG3 5EA.
LAWRENSON, Mr. John Allen, FCA *1964;* 4 Beamsley Street, MALVERN, VIC 3144, AUSTRALIA.
LAWRENSON, Mr. Mark Stephen, BSc ACA *2003;* 4 Ebers Grove, NOTTINGHAM, NG3 5EA.
LAWRENSON, Mr. Michael Anthony, BCom ACA *1980;* 31 Balmoral Road, WIDNES, WA8 9HH.
LAWRENSON, Mr. Paul, MBA MEng ACA AMCT *2007;* 10 Larne Court, WIDNES, CHESHIRE, WA8 9SG.
LAWRENSON, Mrs. Wendy, BA ACA *1998;* 47 Brookthorpe Close, WALLASEY, MERSEYSIDE, CH45 7SH.
LAWREY, Mr. Andrew Charles Keith, BA ACA *2002;* ThyssenKrupp Allee 1, 45143 ESSEN, GERMANY.
LAWREY, Mr. Stephen, ACA *2011;* 94 Norreys Road, Cumnor, OXFORD, OX2 9PU.
LAWRIE, Mrs. Belinda Letitia, BSc ACA *1999;* The Old Malthouse, Lower Westwood, BRADFORD-ON-AVON, WILTSHIRE, BA15 2AG.
LAWRIE, Mrs. Clare Michelle, BSc ACA *2005;* 11 Vulcan Drive, BRACKNELL, BERKSHIRE, RG12 9GN.
LAWRIE, Mr. James Stuart, BA ACA *1990;* Woodthorpe, 1 Padley Hill, Nether Padley, Grindleford, HOPE VALLEY, DERBYSHIRE S32 2HQ.
LAWRIE, Mr. John Graham, FCA *1971;* Essex & London Wine Services, Flat 39 Binbrook House, Sutton Way, LONDON, W10 5HF. (Life Member)
•**LAWRIE, Mr. John Linton, BSc ACA** *1987;* L & J Lawrie, 23 Buckingham Terrace, West End, EDINBURGH, EH4 3AE.
LAWRIE, Mrs. Laura-Jane, ACA *2003;* 67 Brookside, East Barnet, BARNET, HERTFORDSHIRE, EN4 8TS.
LAWRIE, Miss. Tamsyn Jane, MSc ACA *2007;* Rosenun Cottage, Horningtops, LISKEARD, CORNWALL, PL14 3QE.
LAWRINSON, Mr. Anthony James, BA ACA MCT *1994;* The Hawthorns, Lower End, Thornborough, BUCKINGHAM, MK18 2DA.
LAWRINSON, Mr. Neil, BSc ACA *1999;* 21 Woolston Avenue, LETCHWORTH GARDEN CITY, HERTFORDSHIRE, SG6 2ED.
LAWS, Mr. Christopher Fredric, BA ACA *1990;* Plaza Rafael Salgado 28.3.d, 41013 SEVILLE, SPAIN.
LAWS, Mr. David John, BSc ACA *1993;* 78 Metcalfe Ct, John Harrison Way, LONDON, SE10 0BZ.
LAWS, Mr. Edward Charles Alexander William, BSocSc ACA *1997;* Flat 3, The Glass House, 175 Shaftesbury Avenue, LONDON, WC2H 8AN.
LAWS, Mrs. Hannah Harriet, BSc ACA *2005;* U H Y Hacker Young LLP, 4 Thomas More Square, LONDON, E1W 1YW.
LAWS, Mr. Ian, BA ACA *2007;* 39 Halifax Road, ENFIELD, MIDDLESEX, EN2 0PR.
LAWS, Mr. John Charles, FCA *1976;* with Laws Associates Limited, 4 Chesterment Way, Lower Earley, READING, RG6 4HW.
LAWS, Miss. Kathryn Janet, BSc ACA *1992;* 7 Poppy Close, Brooklands, MANCHESTER, M23 9TF.
LAWS, Mr. Kenneth, FCA *1954;* The Orchards, Seven Star Green, Eight Ash Green, COLCHESTER, CO6 3QB. (Life Member)
LAWS, Mr. Michael Lutener, FCA *1951;* 37 Constantia Place, Southern Cross Drive, CONSTANTIA, 7806, SOUTH AFRICA. (Life Member)
LAWS, Mrs. Pamela Mary, MA FCA *1954;* 47 High Street, WATLINGTON, OXFORDSHIRE, OX49 5PZ. (Life Member)
LAWS, Mr. Peter John Daughton, BSc FCA ATII *1978;* Old Ditch Farm, Lynch Lane, Westbury Sub Mendip, WELLS, BA5 1HW.
LAWS, Dr. Peter Michael, ACA *2005;* Oxygen Insurance Brokers Ltd, 33 Harbour Exchange Square, LONDON, E14 9GG.
LAWS, Mr. Robert Alfred, ACA *1981;* with Frank Brown & Walford, 314 Linthorpe Road, MIDDLESBROUGH, TS1 3QX.
LAWS, Miss. Sarah Caroline, BSc ACA MCT *1983;* Hanbury House, The Berrells, TETBURY, GLOUCESTERSHIRE, GL8 8ED.
LAWS, Mr. Simon James, BA ACA *1986;* Flat 13, Windsor Court, Vicarage Crescent, LONDON, SW11 3LA.
LAWS, Mrs. Victoria Kate, ACA *2007;* C R A International UK, 99 Bishopsgate, LONDON, EC2M 3XD.
LAWS, Mr. William, BA ACA *2006;* Far Barn, St. Maughans, MONMOUTH, GWENT, NP25 5QQ.
LAWSON, Mr. Andrew Stewart, FCA *1973;* 6 Binalong Court, WRIGHTS MOUNTAIN, QLD 4520, AUSTRALIA.
LAWSON, Mr. Antony William, FCA *1965;* 55 Halkingcroft, Langley, SLOUGH, SL3 7BB.
LAWSON, Miss. Ashleigh, ACA *2009;* 1st Floor 2 Savour Court, Strand, LONDON, WC2R0EZ.

LAWSON, Ms. Beverley Elizabeth, BA ACA *1988;* 41 Rook Lane, CATERHAM, CR3 5AP.
LAWSON, Mrs. Catherine Jane, MA ACA *1995;* Harpington Hill, Mordon, Sedgefield, STOCKTON-ON-TEES, CLEVELAND, TS21 2HA.
•LAWSON, Mr. Charles Bruce Farquharson, FCA *1969;* (Tax Fac), Montgomery Tax Services Ltd, Hendomen Farmhouse, Hendomen, MONTGOMERY, SY15 6HB. See also Pubtax Limited
LAWSON, Mr. Charles Robert, FCA *1974;* 9 H Hilltop, 60 Cloudview Road, NORTH POINT, HONG KONG ISLAND, HONG KONG SAR.
LAWSON, Mr. David Bruce, BA ACA *1990;* c/- PricewaterhouseCoopers, 101 Hudson Street, JERSEY CITY, NJ 07302, UNITED STATES.
LAWSON, Mr. David Neil, ACA *1992;* 79 Beech Grove, Stanwix, CARLISLE, CA3 9BN.
LAWSON, Mr. David Sydney, BSc FCA *1992;* P & M M Ltd Rockingham Drive, Linford Wood, MILTON KEYNES, MK14 6LY.
LAWSON, Mr. Duncan, BA ACA *1985;* 13 Regent Avenue, MACCLESFIELD, SK11 8JP.
•LAWSON, Mr. Geoffrey, BA ACA *1981;* 24 Cleveleys Road, SOUTHPORT, MERSEYSIDE, PR9 9SP.
LAWSON, Mr. Graeme, MSc ACA *1995;* 19 Marrow Meade, FLEET, HAMPSHIRE, GU51 1HH.
LAWSON, Mr. James Douglas, FCA *1959;* Beechwood, Colliers Close, Moorhead Lane, SHIPLEY, BD18 4LL. (Life Member)
LAWSON, Mrs. Jane Louise, BSc ACA *2000;* 197 Dentons Green Lane, Dentons Green, ST. HELENS, MERSEYSIDE, WA10 6RU.
LAWSON, Mr. Jarrod, BSc(Hons) ACA *2011;* 14 Pipit Green, BRACKNELL, BERKSHIRE, RG12 8BY.
LAWSON, Mr. Jayson Arron, ACA MAAT *1998;* 19 Bulrush Crescent, BURY ST. EDMUNDS, SUFFOLK, IP33 3ZE.
•LAWSON, Mrs. Jean Denise, BA FCA CTA *1986;* Westdale Associates Limited, 44 Dale Lee, Captain Lees Road, Westhoughton, BOLTON, BL5 3YE. See also AIMS - Jean Lawson
LAWSON, Mr. John, MEng ACA *2010;* Nissan Motor Manufacturing (UK) Ltd, Washington Road, SUNDERLAND, SR5 3NS.
LAWSON, Mr. John Hadrian, FCA *1970;* 14 The Willow Chase, Longnewton, STOCKTON-ON-TEES, CLEVELAND, TS21 1PD. (Life Member)
•LAWSON, Mr. John Ian, BSc FCA *1984;* Lawson & Co, FPCI Group Building, Ellerbeck Way, Stokesley Ind Park, Stokesley, MIDDLESBROUGH TS9 5JZ.
LAWSON, Mr. John Mcpherson, FCA *1975;* C M S Sanitary Systems Ltd, Edlington Lane, Warmsworth, DONCASTER, SOUTH YORKSHIRE, DN4 9LS.
LAWSON, Mr. John William, FCA *1967;* 14 Munnion Road, Ardingly, HAYWARDS HEATH, WEST SUSSEX, RH17 6RP.
LAWSON, Mr. Jonathan Ian, BA ACA *2002;* 47 William Coltman Way, STOKE-ON-TRENT, ST6 5XB.
LAWSON, Mrs. Karen Elizabeth, BA ACA *1993;* 17 Tapton Crescent Road, Broomhill, SHEFFIELD, S10 5DA.
LAWSON, Mrs. Katherine Moyra, BSc ACA *2001;* 51 East 78th Street, Apt 1B, NEW YORK, NY 10075, UNITED STATES.
LAWSON, Mrs. Katrina Nancy, BSc ACA *1985;* The Ridings Federation Winterbourne International Academy, High Street Winterbourne, BRISTOL, BS36 1JL.
LAWSON, Mr. Kenneth, FCA *1961;* Oban House, 1a Queen's Drive, HUNSTANTON, PE36 6EX. (Life Member)
LAWSON, Mr. Kolapo Adesola, BSc FCA *1975;* HIGHTREES, THE COMMON, STANMORE, MIDDLESEX, HA7 3HP.
LAWSON, Mrs. Laura Chryse, BA FCA ATII *1990;* Measurement Technology, 910 Butterfield Great Marlings, LUTON, LU2 8DL.
LAWSON, Miss. Lucy Anne, BA ACA *2007;* (Tax Fac), 77 Littlewood Street Rothwell, KETTERING, NORTHAMPTONSHIRE, NN14 6DU.
•LAWSON, Mr. Marc, FCA ATII *1981;* (Tax Fac), Marc Lawson & Co Limited, Unit 7, Brooklands, Budshead Road, PLYMOUTH, PL6 5XR.
•LAWSON, Mrs. Margaret Anne, BSc ACA *1979;* 57 Fairway Avenue, WOORIM, QLD 4507, AUSTRALIA.
LAWSON, Mr. Mark Frederick, BA ACA *1987;* 30 Rudston Road, Childwall, LIVERPOOL, L16 4PH.
LAWSON, Mr. Mark Peter, BA(Hons) ACA *2001;* Sealy of Australia, 1299 Boundary Road, WACOL, QLD 4076, AUSTRALIA.
LAWSON, Mr. Matthew Jeremy, BSc ACA *1987;* with London Fancy Box Co Ltd, Unit 11, Poulton Business Park, Poulton Close, DOVER, KENT CT17 0XB.
LAWSON, Mr. Michael John, BSc ACA *1987;* 15 rue des Erables, 78150 ROCQUENCOURT, FRANCE.
•LAWSON, Mr. Michael Keith, MA ACA *1983;* Hendford Care Home, 166 Hendford Hill, YEOVIL, SOMERSET, BA20 2RG.
LAWSON, Mr. Nicholas, BSc ACA *2007;* with KPMG LLP, 15 Canada Square, LONDON, E14 5GL.
LAWSON, Mr. Nicholas Benjamin, BA(Hons) ACA *2004;* 7/80 Tinning Street, BRUNSWICK, VIC 3056, AUSTRALIA.
LAWSON, Mr. Nicholas St John, MA ACA *1987;* Ashton, Hillbrow Road, ESHER, KT10 9UD.
LAWSON, Mrs. Nicola Ellen, ACA *2009;* 40 Hunters Road, LEYLAND, PR25 5TT.
•LAWSON, Mrs. Paula Jane, FCA *1993;* Stephenson Smart & Co, Stephenson House, 15 Church Walk, PETERBOROUGH, PE1 2TP.
LAWSON, Mr. Peter Bryan, FCA *1970;* Arcadia, 19 Woodlands Road, BUSHEY, WD23 2LS.
•LAWSON, Mr. Richard Shaun, BSc ACA *2000;* with PricewaterhouseCoopers, 1 Embankment Place, LONDON, WC2N 6RH.
LAWSON, Mr. Robert Ian, FCA *1967;* 15 St Georges Avenue, HARROGATE, NORTH YORKSHIRE, HG2 9DP.
LAWSON, Mr. Roger Hardman, FCA *1967;* (President 1994 - 1995) (Member of Council 1987 - 1998), 62 Thurleigh Road, LONDON, SW12 8UD.
•LAWSON, Mrs. Sarah, ACA *2002;* Lawson Accounting Limited, 34 Feldspar Close, SITTINGBOURNE, KENT, ME10 5FE.
LAWSON, Mr. Stephen, BSc FCA *1969;* 6 Prince Arthur Mews, Perrins Lane, LONDON, NW3 1RD.
•LAWSON, Mr. Stephen James, FCA *1978;* UHY Hacker Young Manchester LLP, St. James Buildings, 79 Oxford Street, MANCHESTER, M1 6HT.
LAWSON, Mr. Steven James, BA ACA *1993;* 5 Tathams Orchard, SOUTHWELL, NOTTINGHAMSHIRE, NG25 0FL.
LAWSON, Mr. Stuart John, BA ACA *1993;* Beech Hurst Stonehurst Lane, Five Ashes, MAYFIELD, EAST SUSSEX, TN20 6LJ.
•LAWSON, Mr. Tony Harold, BSc FCA *1982;* (Tax Fac), Lawson & Co, Little Hide, 18 The Lagger, CHALFONT ST. GILES, HP8 4DG. See also Lawsons Accountants Limited
•LAWSON, Mrs. Vanessa Maria Eleonora, MA(Oxon) ACA CTA *1997;* Avonhurst Accountancy Services Limited, Severn View Villa, Gloucester Road, Tutshill, CHEPSTOW, GWENT NP16 7DH. See also Lawson Vanessa
LAWSON, Miss. Victoria Jane, BSc(Hons) ACA *2000;* 28 McHardy Street, HAVELOCK NORTH 4130, NEW ZEALAND.
LAWSON, Miss. Vivien Mary, LLB ACA *1986;* The Rookery, East Dundry Lane, Dundry, BRISTOL, BS41 8NJ.
LAWSON, Mr. William, FCA *1956;* 45 The General's Wood, Harraton, WASHINGTON, NE38 9BN. (Life Member)
LAWSON-BROWN, Mr. Jamie, BA ACA *2003;* H S B C, 8-16 Canada Square, LONDON, E14 5HQ.
LAWTEY, Mrs. Sara Rebekah, MMath ACA *2007;* 12 Lindley Street, SCUNTHORPE, SOUTH HUMBERSIDE, DN16 2SG.
LAWTHER, Mr. Samuel David, BSc ACA *1983;* 41 Earl's Court Square, LONDON, SW5 9BY.
LAWTHER, Mr. William Michael, BA ACA *1983;* Le Marais, Rue Du Marais, Vale, GUERNSEY, GY3 5AQ.
•LAWTON, Mr. Alasdair Richard, BA ACA *1993;* MacWilliams Consulting Limited, 2 Ardival East, STRATHPEFFER, ROSS-SHIRE, IV14 9DY.
LAWTON, Mr. Andrew Charles, BEng ACA *1989;* 38 Woodcote Park Road, EPSOM, KT18 7EX.
LAWTON, Mr. Andrew Francis, BA FCA *1977;* 18 Walker Close, HAMPTON, TW12 3XT.
LAWTON, Mrs. Anne Marie, BA(Econ) ACA *1998;* 2 Sutton Park, Bishop Sutton, BRISTOL, BS39 5UQ.
LAWTON, Mr. Brian Craig, BSc ACA *2003;* Worlds Apart Ltd, Unit 3, Hurling Way, St. Columb Major Business Park, ST COLUMB, CORNWALL TR9 6SX.
LAWTON, Mrs. Christina Marie-France, BA FCA *1975;* Redgarth, 2 Barrymore Road, Grappenhall, WARRINGTON, WA4 2PZ.
LAWTON, Mr. Christopher Erskine, BSc ACA *1989;* 11 Strettit Gardens, East Peckham, TONBRIDGE, TN12 5ES.
•LAWTON, Ms. Claire Louise, FCA *1991;* Jolliffe Cork LLP, 33 George Street, WAKEFIELD, WEST YORKSHIRE, WF1 1LX. See also Jolliffe Cork Consulting Limited
LAWTON, Mr. David John, BSc(Hons) ACA *2001;* K P M G Llp, 15 Canada Square, LONDON, E14 5GL.
LAWTON, Mr. David William Patrick, FCA *1970;* Maison Gure Egoitza, Route D'Arneguy, 64220 UHART CIZE, FRANCE.
LAWTON, Mr. Jamie Matthew, BSc(Hons) ACA *2004;* CLP Envirogas Ltd, 6 Deben Mill Business Centre, Old Maltings Approach, WOODBRIDGE, SUFFOLK, IP12 1BL.
LAWTON, Mrs. Joanne, BSc ACA *2002;* 152 Trinity Road, LONDON, SW17 7HT.
LAWTON, Mrs. Katherine Jane, BA ACA *1990;* Long Ash, Woodbridge Lane, Withington, CHELTENHAM, GLOUCESTERSHIRE, GL54 4BP.
LAWTON, Miss. Katrina Bernadette, ACA AMCT *2002;* 6 Fence Street, Greatmoor, STOCKPORT, SK2 7HP.
LAWTON, Mr. Kieran Anthony, BA ACA *2006;* with BDO LLP, 6th Floor, 3 Hardman Street, Spinningfields, MANCHESTER, M3 3AT.
LAWTON, Ms. Lindsey, MEd BA ACA *1983;* P O Box 8016, Symonds Street, AUCKLAND, NEW ZEALAND.
•LAWTON, Miss. Lynn Christine, BA FCA FIIA CITP FBCS CISA *1982;* Flat 3, 35 Hyde Park Square, LONDON, W2 2NW.
LAWTON, Mr. Mark David, MBA BSc ACA *1998;* 2 Sutton Park, Bishop Sutton, BRISTOL, BS39 5UQ.
LAWTON, Mr. Paul Stephen, BSc FCA *1989;* with BDO LLP, Arcadia House, Maritime Walk, Ocean Village, SOUTHAMPTON, SO14 3TL.
LAWTON, Mr. Peter Lines, FCA *1951;* 10 Kirk Mews, Burnham Road, Althorne, CHELMSFORD, CM3 6GL. (Life Member)
LAWTON, Miss. Rachel Anne, BSc FCA *1993;* 30 Willersley Avenue, SIDCUP, DA15 9EW.
LAWTON, Mr. Richard Ernest, BSc ACA *1991;* 19 St. Chads Avenue, Headingley, LEEDS, LS6 3QF.
LAWTON, Mr. Roger Timothy, FCA *1968;* 16 Blenheim Road, Ainsdale, SOUTHPORT, PR8 2RX.
LAWTON, Mrs. Sarah Patricia, BSc ACA *1992;* with Ernst & Young LLP, 1 Bridgewater Place, Water Lane, LEEDS, LS11 5QR.
LAWTON, Mrs. Shenaz, BPharm ACA *2005;* with GlaxoSmithKline plc, 980 Great West Road, BRENTFORD, MIDDLESEX, TW8 9GS.
LAWTON, Mr. Simon Marcus, BA FCA *1985;* Long Ash, Woodbridge Lane, Withington, CHELTENHAM, GLOUCESTERSHIRE, GL54 4BP.
•LAWTON, Mr. Thomas William, FCA *1980;* BDO LLP, 125 Colmore Row, BIRMINGHAM, B3 3SD. See also BDO Stoy Hayward LLP
LAWTON, Mr. Tom, FCA *1956;* Strathmore, 12 Green Lane, Poynton, STOCKPORT, SK12 1TJ.
LAWTON, Mr. Vernon Charles, FCA *1964;* Oakwood, Lillington Avenue, LEAMINGTON SPA, CV32 5UE. (Life Member)
LAWTON, Mr. William, FCA *1954;* 73 Hillside Road, Cheddleton, LEEK, STAFFORDSHIRE, ST13 7JQ. (Life Member)
LAWTON, Mrs. Zena Maria, BSc ACA *1993;* 81 Sur Credette, 01170 CESSY, FRANCE.
LAX, Mr. David William, BA ACA *1984;* Grant Thornton Grant Thornton House, Kettering Parkway Kettering Venture Park, KETTERING, NORTHAMPTONSHIRE, NN15 6XR.
•LAX, Mr. Jacky Chaim, LLB ACA *1980;* Jacob Charles & Co, Sentinel House, Sentinel Square, Brent Street, LONDON, NW4 2EP.
LAX, Mr. Jason, ACA *2009;* 104 Beresford Avenue, SURBITON, SURREY, KT5 9LW.
LAX, Mr. Noel Geoffrey, BA ACA *1984;* 5 Haweswater Close, WETHERBY, LS22 6FG.
LAX, Miss. Sarah Michelle, BA ACA *2010;* Flat 14, 2 Berryfield Gardens West Timperley, ALTRINCHAM, CHESHIRE, WA14 5GQ.
LAX, Mr. Simon Keith, BA ACA *1984;* 2 Satterley Close, Witham St. Hughs, LINCOLN, LN6 9QB.
LAX, Mr. William Henry, FCA *1956;* Henry Lax Ltd, 2 Devonshire Crescent, LEEDS, LS8 1EP. (Life Member)
LAX, Mr. William John, MA FCA *1976;* 1 Century Row, Middle Way, Summertown, OXFORD, OX2 7LP.
LAXTON, Mr. David, MBA BA FCA *1976;* 11 Armstrong House, Manor Fields, LONDON, SW15 3NF.
LAXTON, Mr. David, BA ACA *1986;* North House, 9, Brock Hollow, SANDBACH, CW11 3WA.
LAXTON, Mr. Kevin Edward, BSc ACA *1992;* 7 Mortimer Hall, The Street, Mortimer, READING, RG7 3NS.
LAXTON, Mr. Russell, BSc FCA *1976;* 2A Sheringham Way, Orton Longueville, PETERBOROUGH, PE2 7AH.
LAXTON, Mr. Timothy Raymond Wentworth, MA ACA *1985;* 7 Milton Road, LONDON, SE24 0NL.
LAY, Mr. Brian William, FCA *1956;* 15 Highridge Close, EPSOM, KT18 5HF. (Life Member)
LAY, Mrs. Georgia, LLB FCA *1992;* Caple Farm, Caple Lane, Chew Stoke, BRISTOL, BS40 8YE.
LAY, Mr. Ian Stuart, BA ACA *1989;* The Dene, Forest Way, TUNBRIDGE WELLS, TN2 5HA.
LAY, Mr. James Christopher, LLB ACA *2000;* 49a Fernbank Road, Redland, BRISTOL, BS6 6PX.
LAY, Mr. James Edward George, BSc ACA *2004;* with Larking Gowen, King Street House, 15 Upper King Street, NORWICH, NR3 1RB.
LAY, Mrs. Jennifer Vivian, ACA *1984;* 208 Cascade Road, STAMFORD, CT 06903, UNITED STATES.
LAY, Mr. Peter Richard, BSc(Hons) ACA *2003;* 15 Anding Close, OLNEY, BUCKINGHAMSHIRE, MK46 5QL.
LAY, Mrs. Rachel Julia, BSc ACA *1999;* First Floor, 49a Fernbank Road, BRISTOL, BS6 6PX.
•LAY, Mr. Richard John, ACA *1990;* (Tax Fac), Sheards Accountancy Limited, Vernon House, 40 New North Road, HUDDERSFIELD, HD1 5LS. See also Sheards
•LAY-FLURRIE, Mrs. Dawn Teresa, BSc ACA *1990;* Chantrey Vellacott DFK LLP, Town Wall House, Balkerne Hill, COLCHESTER, CO3 3AD.
LAYBOURN, Mr. David Anthony, FCA *1974;* 8 Swan Lane, Stock, INGATESTONE, CM4 9BQ. (Life Member)
LAYBURN, Ms. Sally Jayne, MA ACA DChA *2000;* St. Johns College, OXFORD, OX1 3JP.
LAYCOCK, Mrs. Claire, BA(Hons) ACA *2002;* Transaction Network Services (UK) Ltd, Sheffield Airport Business Park, Europa Link, SHEFFIELD, S9 1XU.
LAYCOCK, Mrs. Gail Rowena, BEng ACA *1998;* 28 Fishermans Close, Winterley, SANDBACH, CW11 4SW.
•LAYCOCK, Mr. Graham John, BA FCA *1983;* Graham Laycock Associates, 152 Eastern Road, BRIGHTON, BN2 0AE. See also Graham Laycock & Associates
LAYCOCK, Miss. Jennifer, ACA *2011;* Flat A, 19 Sheen Lane, LONDON, SW14 8HY.
LAYCOCK, Mr. Michael Peter Latham, LLB FCA CTA *1963;* 33 Wheatlands Road East, HARROGATE, HG2 8QS. (Life Member)
LAYCOCK, Mr. Nicholas Charles, BA ACA *2000;* Barclays Capital, 5 North Colonnade, Canary Wharf, LONDON, E14 4BB.
LAYCOCK, Mr. Richard John, BSc FCA *1998;* 36 Oakdene Drive, LEEDS, LS17 8XW.
LAYCOCK, Mr. Richard Tempest, MA FCA *1957;* 10 Bishops Avenue, NORTHWOOD, HA6 3DG. (Life Member)
LAYCOCK, Mr. Rob Anthony, MEng ACA *2010;* 43 Chandos Street, Netherfield, NOTTINGHAM, NG4 2LP.
LAYCOCK, Mr. Trevor Smith, FCA *1970;* 14 Bennetts Close, Cippenham, SLOUGH, SL1 5AS.
LAYER, Mrs. Jacqueline, BSc ACA *1982;* Roque Brune, La Route De La Cote, Gorey St Martin, JERSEY, JE3 6DR.
LAYER, Mr. Simon Andrew, BA FCA *1985;* 1 Beldams Gate, Beldams Lane, BISHOP'S STORTFORD, CM23 5RN.
LAYFIELD, Mrs. Elizabeth Helen, ACIB ACA ATII *2001;* Wash Beck Farm, Hamsterley, BISHOP AUCKLAND, COUNTY DURHAM, DL13 3QZ.
•LAYFIELD, Mr. Peter Richard, BSc *1984;* Layfield & Co Ltd, The Lodge, Whitehouse Lane, NANTWICH, CHESHIRE, CW5 6HQ.
LAYLAND, Mr. Ernest James, MA ACA *1995;* The Cedars, 1 Haddon Road, MANSFIELD, NOTTINGHAMSHIRE, NG19 7BS.
LAYLAND, Miss. Katherine Sarah, BSc ACA *2001;* Skandia Life Assurance Co Ltd, PO Box 37, SOUTHAMPTON, SO14 7AY.
•LAYLAND, Miss. Tracy-Lee, ACA *1996;* (Tax Fac), Young & Company, Church Farm House, Lodge Lane, Tendring, CLACTON-ON-SEA, ESSEX CO16 0BS.
LAYLEE, Mr. Graham Alexander, BSc ACA *1982;* 12 Dorchester Drive, LONDON, SE24 0DQ.
LAYTE, Mr. Paul Owen, BSc ACA *2006;* 6 McDougall Road, BERKHAMSTED, HERTFORDSHIRE, HP4 2WQ.
LAYTHORPE, Mr. Andrew Mcewan, BCom FCA *1968;* 85 Brownhill Road, Chandler's Ford, EASTLEIGH, HAMPSHIRE, SO53 2FJ. (Life Member)
LAYTON, Mr. John, FCA CPFA *1969;* 34 Millers Way, Milford, BELPER, DERBYSHIRE, DE56 0RZ.
LAYTON, Mrs. Margarita Maria, ACA CA(NZ) *2009;* 2 Bernadine Close, Warfield, BRACKNELL, BERKSHIRE, RG42 3DU.

LAYTON, Mr. Richard Andrew, BA ACA *2003;* 3 Sheendale Road, RICHMOND, TW9 2JJ.

•**LAYTON, Mr. Richard William, BSc ACA** *1979;* 5824 Falcon Road, WEST VANCOUVER V7W 1S3, BC, CANADA.

•**LAYTON, Mr. Robert Anthony, BSc FCA** *1992;* Layton Lee LLP, 6 Manchester Road, BUXTON, DERBYSHIRE, SK17 6SB.

LAYTON, Miss. Victoria Mary, BSc ACA *1988;* Villa Claude, 5 Ave St Michel, 98000 MONTE CARLO, MONACO.

LAYZELL, Mr. David Richard Huw, MA FCA *1975;* 17170 NW Brugger Road, PORTLAND, OR 97229, UNITED STATES.

LAYZELL, Mr. Dennis John, FCA *1962;* Nutscale, Chorleywood Road, Chorleywood, RICKMANSWORTH, WD3 4EU. (Life Member)

LAYZELL, Mr. Erik Francis, BSc ACA *1989;* Subsea 7, Kanalsetta 9, 4052 ROYNEBERG, NORWAY.

•**LAYZELL, Miss. Jacqueline Ann, BA FCA** *1992;* Wenn Townsend, Victoria House, 10 Broad Street, ABINGDON, OX14 3LH. See also Wenn Townsend Accountants Limited

LAYZELL, Mr. Mark Christopher, BA FCA *1987;* Whitehall, La Grande Route Des Sablons, Grouville, JERSEY, JE3 9FE.

LAYZELL, Mr. Norman, FCA *1958;* 6 Orlestone Gardens, ORPINGTON, BR6 6HB. (Life Member)

•**LAYZELL, Mr. Thomas Richard, BSc FCA FCMA** *1962;* (Tax Fac), Thomas R. Layzell & Co, 185 Winchester Road, Chandlers Ford, EASTLEIGH, SO53 2DU.

LAZAR, Mr. Wilfred Jeyaraj, BSc FCA *1982;* 11 Sanctuary Point Road, WEST PENNANT HILLS, NSW 2125, AUSTRALIA.

•**LAZAREVIC, Mr. Charles, MBA BSc FCA** *1980;* Moore Stephens LLP, 150 Aldersgate Street, LONDON, EC1A 4AB. See also Moore Stephens & Co

LAZAREVS, Mr. Vladimirs, BA(Hons) ACA *2010;* Basement Flat, 36 Tavistock Place, LONDON, WC1H 9RE.

LAZARIDES, Mr. Vassilios, FCA *1982;* 14 OTHELLOS STREET, AYIOS ATHANASIOS, 4105 LIMASSOL, CYPRUS.

LAZAROU, Mr. Christakis Stavrou, ACA *1992;* Flat 1 Hadjidaki 1, PO Box 16169, NICOSIA, 2086, CYPRUS.

LAZAROU, Mr. Lazarus, BSc ACA *1998;* Flat 9, Ripon Court, 119 Ribblesdale Avenue, LONDON, N11 3BE.

LAZAROU, Mr. Marios G, BSc ACA MBA *2003;* 2 Nikis Street, Aglantzia, 2102 NICOSIA, CYPRUS.

•**LAZAROU, Mr. Yiannakis Phidia, MBA BA FCA** *1993;* (Tax Fac), Y P Lazarou, 79 Ellados Avenue, 8020 PAPHOS, CYPRUS.

LAZARUS, Mr. Alex, ACA *2011;* Flat 3, 32 Alderney Street, LONDON, SW1V 4EU.

LAZARUS, Mr. Barrie Jack, JP FCA *1962;* 1 Seymour Mews, SAWBRIDGEWORTH, HERTFORDSHIRE, CM21 0BD.

LAZARUS, Mr. Benjamin James, BA ACA *2000;* with PricewatherhouseCoopers, Trade Tower, 25 Hamered Street, 68125 TEL AVIV, ISRAEL.

LAZARUS, Mr. David Michael, BA FCA *1986;* 49 Southway, Totteridge, LONDON, N20 8DD.

LAZARUS, Mr. Ebenezer John, ACA *2010;* Block 260B, No 04-444, Sengkang East Way, SINGAPORE 542260, SINGAPORE.

LAZARUS, Mr. Eric Carl, BA ACA *1986;* with PKF (UK) LLP, Farringdon Place, 20 Farringdon Road, LONDON, EC1M 3AP.

•**LAZARUS, Mr. Lennard Stewart, FCA** *1967;* L.S.Lazarus and Co., 9 Northwick Circle, Kenton, HARROW, HA3 0EJ.

LAZARUS, Mr. Norman Arthur, FCA *1954;* 22c Elm Tree Road, LONDON, NW8 9JP. (Life Member)

LAZARUS, Mr. Ralph Leonard, FCA *1952;* 15/444 Pacific Highway, Lindfield, SYDNEY, NSW 2070, AUSTRALIA. (Life Member)

LAZARUS, Mr. Roger Alan, BA ACA *1983;* with Ernst & Young, 560 Mission Street, Suite 1600, SAN FRANCISCO, CA 94105-2907, UNITED STATES.

LAZARUS, Mr. Simon Eliot, MA ACA *1994;* Finance Department, John Radcliffe Hospital, Headley Way, Headington, OXFORD, OX3 9DU.

LAZARUS, Mr. William Ian David, FCA *1975;* Radbrook House, Binfield Heath, HENLEY-ON-THAMES, RG9 4LL.

•**LAZDA, Mrs. Angela Christine, FCA** *1976;* (Tax Fac), Crowe Clark Whitehill LLP, Aquis House, 49-51 Blagrave Street, READING, RG1 1PL. See also Horwath Clark Whitehill LLP and Crowe Clark Whitehill

LAZELL, Mr. Michael Alan, FCA *1983;* 18 Church Lane, Great Warley, BRENTWOOD, Essex, CM13 3EP.

LAZENBY, Mr. Martin Anthony, FCA *1971;* Hazel Cottage, 19 Hazel Avenue, FARNBOROUGH, Hampshire, GU14 0HA. (Life Member)

LAZENBY, Mrs. Sabrina Mohd Ismail, BA ACA *2002;* 7 Bulbourne Close, BERKHAMSTED, HERTFORDSHIRE, HP4 3QA.

LAZERIS, Mr. Kevin, BA ACA *1987;* Amberleigh, Halifax Road, Heronsgate, RICKMANSWORTH, HERTFORDSHIRE, WD3 5DF.

LAZO, Mrs. Marusya Kris, MA ACA *2003;* 5914 Barbados Place, Apt 202, ROCKVILLE, MD 20852, UNITED STATES.

LAZONBY, Mr. Norman Anderson, BSc FCA *1983;* 51 Musters Road, Ruddington, NOTTINGHAM, NG11 6JB.

LE, Ms. Giang Huong, BSc ACA *2004;* 157 Randlesdown Road, LONDON, SE6 3SR.

LE, Mr. Hien Thanh, ACA DChA *2010;* 8 Dumbarton Avenue, WALTHAM CROSS, HERTFORDSHIRE, EN8 8BY.

LE, Miss. Rosalind, BSc ACA *2009;* 42 Sandringham Way, MARKET HARBOROUGH, LE16 8EP.

LE, Miss. Thao Thanh Thi, BSc ACA *2002;* Cargill Financial Markets Plc Knowle Hill Park, Fairmile Lane, COBHAM, KT11 2PD.

LE, Miss. Truc Thanh Thi, BSc ACA CTA *2002;* AES Electric Ltd, 37-39 Kew Foot Road, RICHMOND, SURREY, TW9 2SS.

LE BAILLY, Mr. James Alexander, ACA *2011;* (Le Bailly), La Villaise, La Route de la Villaise, St. Ouen, JERSEY, JE3 2AP.

LE BAS, Mrs. Nichola Anne, BA(Hons) ACA *2003;* B D O Stoy Hayward Llp, Arcadia House, Maritime Walk, SOUTHAMPTON, SO14 3TL.

LE BAS, Mr. Nigel Alan, BA(Hons) ACA *2003;* with Grant Thornton UK LLP, 1 Dorset Street, SOUTHAMPTON, SO15 2DP.

•**LE BAS, Mr. Stephen Hedley, BA FCA** *1996;* with BDO LLP, Arcadia House, Maritime Walk, Ocean Village, SOUTHAMPTON, SO14 3TL.

LE BAS, Miss. Yvonne Josephine, ACA *1990;* 40 Reynolds Street, CREMORNE, NSW 2090, AUSTRALIA.

LE BIHAN, Mrs. Nicola Catherine, BSc FCA *1994;* Monalto Investments Limited, P O box 239, 17 Hilary Street, St Helier, JERSEY, JE2 4SX.

LE BLAN, Mrs. Julia, BA FCA *1980;* 2 Snowbury Road, LONDON, SW6 2NR.

LE BOSQUET, Mr. Peter, BSc ACA *1985;* 32 Beckenham Road, WEST WICKHAM, KENT, BR4 0QT.

•**LE BRAS, Mr. Stephen Jean Armand James, FCA** *1975;* (Tax Fac), Stephen Le Bras, 6 Queen Anne's Court, Peascod Street, WINDSOR, SL4 1DG.

LE BRETON, Mrs. Aurelia Julie, BA ACA *2000;* 74a Upper Tulse Hill, LONDON, SW2 2RW.

LE BROCQ, Mr. Edward Martin, FCA *1957;* 4 Woodlands Road, SURBITON, KT6 6PS. (Life Member)

LE BRUN, Mr. Andrew Martin, ACA *1990;* Jersey Financial Services Commission, 14-18 Castle Street, St Helier, JERSEY, JE4 8TP.

•**LE BRUN, Ms. Aynslie Colette, BSc(Econ) FCA** *1986;* Clive Tomes & Co, PO Box 771, Ground Floor, Colomberie Close, St. Helier, JERSEY JE4 0RX.

•**LE CHEMINANT, Mr. Andrew David, FCA TEP** *1986;* Alex Picot, 95-97 Halkett Place, St. Helier, JERSEY, JE1 1BX. See also Alex Picot Ltd

•**LE CLAIRE, Mr. Bernard Michael, FCA** *1984;* (Tax Fac), Baker Tilly Channel Islands Limited, PO Box 437, 13 Castle Street, St Helier, JERSEY, JE4 0ZE. See also Osiris Management Services Limited

LE CONTE, Mr. Anthony Lloyd, FCA *1979;* Briarwood, La Turquie, Grande Rue, Vale, GUERNSEY, GY3 5EB.

LE CONTE, Mr. Christopher David, ACA *1993;* Entre Deux Mers La Garenne, Vale, GUERNSEY, GY3 5SQ.

LE CORNU, Mr. Aaron Dene, BSc ACA *1996;* Ogier, Ogier House, The Esplanade, JERSEY, JE4 9WG.

LE CORNU, Mr. Charles Harvie, BSc ACA *2007;* Ogier Fiduciary Services Limited, Whiteley Chambers, Don Street, St Helier, JERSEY, JE4 9WG.

LE CORNU, Mr. David Mallet, FCA *1951;* Flat 16, Chateau Royale, La Rue Vardon, Grouville, JERSEY, JE3 9HT. (Life Member)

LE CORNU, Mrs. Katie Georgina, BSc ACA *2007;* Meadow Land, 22 La Belle Vallette, La Route de la Hougue Bie, St. Saviour, JERSEY, JE2 7BP.

LE COUILLIARD, Mr. James, BSc ACA *1992;* 24 Station Road, Welham Green North Mymms, HATFIELD, HERTFORDSHIRE, AL9 7PG.

LE COUILLIARD, Miss. Joanna Susan, MA ACA *1989;* Rake House Crossways Road, Grayshott, HINDHEAD, GU26 6HE.

LE COUTEUR, Miss. Emily, BSc ACA *2010;* c/o KPMG, P.O. Box 493, GEORGETOWN, GRAND CAYMAN, KY1-1106, CAYMAN ISLANDS.

LE COZ, Mrs. Kathryn Olive Elizabeth, BMus ACA *2004;* with PricewaterhouseCoopers LLP, 1 Embankment Place, LONDON, WC2N 6RH.

LE DIEU, Mrs. Caroline Mary, BA ACA *2004;* 11a Castle Road, RAYLEIGH, SS6 7QD.

LE DOEUIL, Mr. Dominique Daniel Jean, ACA *1992;* Cargill International SA, 14 chemin de Normandie, 1206 GENEVA, SWITZERLAND.

LE DOEUIL, Mrs. Siu Mei Christine, BSc ACA *1995;* GAVI Alliance Secretariat, 2 Chemin des Mines, 1202 GENEVA, SWITZERLAND.

LE DRUILLENEC, Mr. Paul Vincent, MA ACA *1979;* 7 Thornhill Bridge Wharf Caledonian Road, LONDON, N1 0RU.

LE-FAYE, Mr. Nicholas Charles, BA ACA *1989;* 9 Tamerton Square, WOKING, GU22 7SZ.

LE FEUVRE, Mr. Darren Edward, MA ACA *1999;* Calle Altamira 16, Pueblo, Nuevo De Guadiaro, 11311 SOTOGRANDE, SPAIN.

LE FEUVRE, Mr. John Arthur, FCA *1969;* 3 Clos Du Moulin, La Rue Du Pont, St. Ouen, JERSEY, JE3 2DX.

LE FEVRE, Mr. Andrew Paul, BA ACA *2008;* 42 Penfold Road, Broadwater, WORTHING, WEST SUSSEX, BN14 8PH.

LE FLEM, Mr. Andrew John, ACA *2000;* Capelles Building Stores Les Petites Capelles Road, St. Sampson, GUERNSEY, GY2 4GR.

•**LE FLEMING, Mrs. Barbara Maria, MA ACA** *1998;* (Tax Fac), Barbara le Fleming, 14 Cliveden Mead, MAIDENHEAD, BERKSHIRE, SL6 8HE.

LE FLEMING, Mr. Daniel James, BSc ACA *1989;* Metlife Insurance Ltd, 1 Canada Square, LONDON, E14 5AA.

LE FLEMING SHEPHERD, Mr. Tom, BSc ACA *2007;* Flat 2, 21 Bevenden Street, LONDON, N1 6BH.

LE FLUFY, Mr. Patrick James, MA ACA *2011;* College Farm, Queen Street, Tintinhull, YEOVIL, SOMERSET, BA22 8PQ.

LE FONDRE, Mr. John Alexander, BA ACA *1994;* 3 Avenue le Petit Felard, Le Mont Felard, St. Lawrence, JERSEY, JE3 1JE.

•**LE FORT, Mr. Alan Roger, FCA** *1970;* Le Forts, Britannia House, Roberts Mews, ORPINGTON, BR6 0JP.

•**LE FORT, Mr. Justin Jacques, ACA** *2008;* Navitas Advisors Limited, Albany House, 4th Floor Office 404, 324-326 Regent Street, LONDON, W1B 3HH.

LE FORT, Mr. Nicholas, BSc ACA *2008;* Le Fort & Co Britannia House, Roberts Mews, ORPINGTON, BR6 0JP.

LE FRIANT, Miss. Alison Marie, BA ACA *2005;* 210 Terrace Road, WALTON-ON-THAMES, KT12 2ED.

LE FRIEC, Mrs. Karen Anne, FCA *1983;* Springhurst House, Le Bourg, Forest, GUERNSEY, GY8 0AN.

LE GASSICKE, Mr. Simon John, BSc ACA *1985;* Box 382, HONIARA, SOLOMON ISLANDS.

LE GEYT, Mr. Michael Andrew, BSc FCA ACII *1994;* 9 Hoddle Crescent, DAVIDSON, NSW 2085, AUSTRALIA.

LE GRESLEY, Miss. Lisa Ann, BA ACA CMCSI MBA *2006;* 430 Le Capelain House, Castle Quay Waterfront, St Helier, JERSEY, JE2 3EB.

•**LE GRYS, Mrs. Carol Annn, FCA** *1966;* (Tax Fac), Carol Le Grys, 19 Amberley Road, Bush Hill Park, ENFIELD, EN1 2QX.

LE GRYS, Mr. James Robert, BSc ACA *1995;* West Way Nissan, Spon End, COVENTRY, CV1 3HF.

LE HEGARAT, Mr. Roy Frank, MA ACA *1992;* Intertrust, PO Box 119, Matello Court, Admiral Park, GUERNSEY, GY1 3HB.

LE LORRAIN, Mr. Michael Robert, BSc FCA *1980;* 8a Castle Terrace, EDINBURGH, EH1 2DP.

LE MAIN, Mrs. Emma Clare, BSc ACA MAAT *2002;* L'Ecurie, Rue de la Pointe, St. Ouen, JERSEY, JE3 2AF.

LE MAIN, Mr. Helier James, ACA MAAT *2004;* L'Ecurie, La Rue de la Pointe, St. Ouen, JERSEY, JE3 2AF.

LE MAISTRE, Miss. Amy Joanne, BSc(Hons) ACA *2009;* 1 Bel Royal Gardens, La Route de St. Aubin, St. Lawrence, JERSEY, JE3 1JU.

LE MAISTRE, Mr. Geoffrey Francis, BSc FCA *1969;* Spindrift, 16 Le Clos le Geyt, Deloraine Road, St. Saviour, JERSEY, JE2 7NY. (Life Member)

LE MAISTRE, Mr. Jonathan James, BA ACA *1995;* Les Martinnais, La Grande Route Des Sablons, Grouville, JERSEY, JE3 9FQ.

LE MAISTRE, Mr. Simon Peter, BSc ACA *1995;* 24a Moffat Street, BRIGHTON, VIC 3186, AUSTRALIA.

•**LE MAITRE, Mrs. Jane Anne, FCA CTA TEP** *1989;* (Tax Fac), Martello Court, Admiral Park, St Peter Port, GUERNSEY, GY1 3HB.

LE MAITRE, Mr. Neil Wallace Hartley, FCA *1963;* 127 Kingshayes Road, Aldridge, WALSALL, WS9 8SN. (Life Member)

•**LE MARQUAND, Mr. Clive Robert, BSc FCA** *1991;* BBA Limited, Beachside Business Centre, La Rue du Hocq, St Clement, JERSEY, JE2 6LF.

LE MARREC, Mr. Paul, ACA *1990;* Rose Cottage La Rue Du Huquet, St. Martin, JERSEY, JE3 6HE.

•**LE MASURIER, Mr. David Paul, FCA** *1974;* Naunton Jones Le Masurier, 3 Herbert Terrace, PENARTH, CF64 2AH.

LE MASURIER, Mr. Nigel George, BEng ACA *1995;* 32 chemin du Foron, 1226 THONEX, SWITZERLAND.

LE MAY, Mrs. Catherine Sarah, LLB ACA *1982;* Upham House, Church Street, Upham, SOUTHAMPTON, SO32 1JH.

LE MAY, Mr. Malcolm John, BA ACA *1983;* Upham House, Church Street, Upham, SOUTHAMPTON, SO32 1JH.

LE MIERE, Mr. Raulin Paul Edouard, ACA *2005;* with Deloitte LLP, Hill House, 1 Little New Street, LONDON, EC4A 3TR.

LE MOTTEE, Mr. Matthew, BA ACA *2008;* Flat 2 4 Roseville Terrace, Roseville Street, ST HELIER, JE2 4PL.

LE NEVE FOSTER, Mr. Patrick Vivian, BA FCA *1959;* 14 Trafalgar Gate, Brighton Marina, BRIGHTON, BN2 5UY. (Life Member)

LE NOC, Mr. Julien, ACA *2009;* Flat 36 The Circle, Queen Elizabeth Street, LONDON, SE1 2JG.

LE NOURY, Miss. Michelle, BSc ACA *2001;* 12 College Gardens, Wandsworth Common, LONDON, SW17 7UG.

LE NOURY, Mrs. Nadia Maria, BA ACA *2004;* Pentland, 15 Clos Des Pecqueries, La Rue Des Cottes, St. Sampson, GUERNSEY, GY2 4TU.

LE NOURY, Mr. Peter John, BSc ACA *1993;* O T R Tyres Ltd 8 Bluebell Close, Clover Nook Industrial Park Somercotes, ALFRETON, DERBYSHIRE, DE55 4RD.

LE NOURY, Mr. Stephen David, BSc ACA *2003;* 15 Clos Des Pecqueries, La Rue Des Cottes St. Sampson, GUERNSEY, GY2 4TU.

LE PAGE, Mrs. Carole Maxine, BSc ACA CTA *1998;* with PricewaterhouseCoopers LLP, 1 Embankment Place, LONDON, WC2N 6RH.

•**LE PAGE, Mr. Stephen John, FCA** *1985;* PricewaterhouseCoopers CI LLP, PO Box 321, Royal Bank Place, 1 Glategny Esplanade, St Peter Port, GUERNSEY GY1 4ND.

LE PAGE, Mrs. Susan Patricia, MA ACA *1979;* Cumbrae, 50 High Road, Cookham Rise, MAIDENHEAD, SL6 9HR.

LE PATOUREL, Ms. Kim Zia, BA ACA *2005;* Carillion plc, 24 Birch Street, WOLVERHAMPTON, WV1 4HY.

LE PELLEY, Mr. Martin Thomas, BA FCA *1995;* Heritage Insurance Brokers Ltd, PO Box 225, GUERNSEY, GY1 4HY.

LE POIDEVIN, Miss. Fiona Louise Amy, BSc(Hons) ACA *2002;* (Tax Fac), Guernsey Finance, PO Box 655, North Plantation, St Peter Port, GUERNSEY, GY1 3PN.

•**LE POIDEVIN, Mr. John, MA FCA** *1995;* BDO LLP, 55 Baker Street, LONDON, W1U 7EU. See also BDO Stoy Hayward LLP

LE POIDEVIN, Mrs. Victoria Jayne, ACA *2004;* Petit Mullot Cottages, Sandy Lane, St. Sampson, GUERNSEY, GY2 4RT.

LE PREVOST, Mr. Dean Alan, BSc ACA *2004;* 57A Crown Road, Queenscliff, SYDNEY, NSW 2096, AUSTRALIA.

LE PREVOST, Mr. Keith Lloyd, ACA *1979;* Lince Salisbury, Avenue House, St. Julians Avenue, St. Peter Port, GUERNSEY, GY1 1WA.

LE PREVOST, Mr. Roy Johnn, FCA *1955;* La Vieille Orange, Les Pieces, Forest, GUERNSEY, GY8 0AY. (Life Member)

LE PREVOST, Mr. Steven Philip Reginald, BA ACA *2007;* Gentoo Fund Services Limited, Western Suite Ground Floor, Mill Court, La Charroterie, St. Peter Port, GUERNSEY GY1 1EJ.

LE QUESNE, Mr. Charles Richard De Faye, FCA *1974;* PO Box 285, JERSEY, JE4 8TA.

LE QUESNE, Mr. Stephen Graeme, BA ACA *1996;* 2e2 Jersey Limited La Rue A la Dame, St. Saviour, JERSEY, JE2 7NH.

LE RAY, Mr. Stephen, BA ACA *1995;* (Tax Fac), Regency Court, Glategny Esplanade, St. Peter Port, GUERNSEY, GY1 1WW.

LE ROSSIGNOL, Mr. Graeme, FCA *1964;* Beau Soleil, Le Mont Vibert, St. Ouen, JERSEY, JE3 2DS. (Life Member)

LE ROSSIGNOL, Miss. Lisa Gemma, BSc ACA *2003;* 5 Vicq Farm, Le Rue Maraval, La Grande Route Des Sablons, JERSEY, JE3 9FL.

LE ROUX, Mr. Egbertus, ACA CA(SA) *2010;* 121 Val Ste Croix, L-1371 LUXEMBOURG, LUXEMBOURG.

LE ROUX, Mr. Liam George, BSc ACA *2007;* MGPA, 60 Sloane Avenue, LONDON, SW3 3XB.

LE ROUX, Mrs. Linda Theresa, BSc FCA *1996;* Blenheim Management Services Ltd, First Floor, Tudor House, Le Bordage, St. Peter Port, GUERNSEY GY1 1DB.

LE ROUX, Mr. Rudolph Fairbairn, ACA CA(SA) *2008;* 4 Belmont Gardens, Les Croutes St. Peter Port, GUERNSEY, GY1 1PZ.

LE ROY, Mr. Philip Edwin, BSc FCA *1976;* Granite Le Pelley, Garenne House, Rue De La Cache, St. Sampson, GUERNSEY, GY2 4AF.

LE SCELLEUR, Miss. Karin, MA ACA *1991;* Cherry Tree Barn, Kington St. Michael, CHIPPENHAM, WILTSHIRE, SN14 6HX.

LE SEELLEUR, Mr. Andrew James, BEng FCA *2000;* 8th Floor, Union House, Union Street, St. Helier, JERSEY, JE2 3RF.

•LE SEELLEUR, Mr. Peter David, BA FCA ACIM *1988;* RTA Limited, PO Box 851, 2nd Floor, 24-26 Broad Street, JERSEY, JE4 0XE.

•LE STRANGE MEAKIN, Mr. Charles Henry William, BSc ACA *1993;* KPMG Europe LLP, 15 Canada Square, LONDON, E14 5GL. See also KPMG LLP

LE SUEUR, Mr. James Leicester, ACA *1989;* Tower Capital Ltd, 3 St Andrews Place, St. Helier, JERSEY, JE2 3RP.

LE SUEUR, Ms. Judith Louise, BA ACA *1999;* Les- Favieres, La Grande Route de Mont A L'Abbe, St. Helier, JERSEY, JE2 3HA.

LE SUEUR, Mr. Terence Augustine, MA FCA *1970;* La Porte, La Rue de la Porte, St. John, JERSEY, JE3 4DE.

•LE TISSIER, Mrs. Chantelle, BA ACA *1998;* Kemp Le Tissier Limited, Suite 2 Houmet House, Rue Des Houmets, Castel, GUERNSEY, GY5 7XZ.

LE TISSIER, Mr. Martin Richard, BA ACA *2000;* State Street Trust and Banking Co Ltd, Midtown Tower 9-7-1 Akasaka Minato-ku, TOKYO, 107-6329 JAPAN.

LE VALLOIS, Ms. Sarah Isabel, BSc ACA *1991;* P O Box 86340, Eros, WINDHOEK, NAMIBIA.

LE VAN, Mrs. Kerry, BA ACA *1993;* 9 Forest Road, Dorridge, SOLIHULL, WEST MIDLANDS, B93 8HA.

LE VAVASSEUR DIT DURELL, Mr. Edward Hugh Kelway, BA ACA *2009;* with PricewaterhouseCoopers LLP, Hays Galleria, 1 Hays Lane, LONDON, SE1 2RD.

LE VAVASSEUR DIT DURELL, Mr. Hugh Alan, FCA *1976;* 1st Floor, 17 Bond Street, St Helier, JERSEY, JE2 3NP.

LE VESCONTE, Mrs. Katrina Bernadette, BA ACA CTA *1994;* Les Hiboux La Rue Des Servais, St. John, JERSEY, JE3 4FQ.

LE VESCONTE, Mr. Philip James Jackman, FCA *1992;* Les Hiboux, Sion, St John, JERSEY, JE3 4FQ.

•LEA, Mr. Adrian Kenneth, BSc FCA *1990;* West Hill Tax Services Limited, Cedar Haven, Toadpit Lane, West Hill, OTTERY ST. MARY, DEVON EX11 1TR.

LEA, Mr. Barry Gordon, BSc FCA *1978;* Advanced Engineering Ltd, Guardian House, Stroudley House, BASINGSTOKE, HAMPSHIRE, RG24 8NL.

LEA, Miss. Carey Gail, BA ACA *2005;* The Royal Bank of Scotland Plc, 280 Bishopsgate, LONDON, EC2M 4RB.

LEA, Mr. Christopher Paul, BSc ACA *1992;* Aviagen Ltd, 11 Lochend Road, Ratho Station, NEWBRIDGE, MIDLOTHIAN, EH28 8SZ.

LEA, Mrs. Claire Louise, ACA *2009;* Flat 20 High Point, North Hill, LONDON, N6 4BA.

LEA, Miss. Daphne Selina, BEng ACA *1996;* 59 Popes Grove, TWICKENHAM, TW1 4JZ.

LEA, Mr. David Andrew, LLB ACA *1998;* 14 Higher Lane, Kerridge, MACCLESFIELD, SK10 5AR.

LEA, Ms. Deborah Ann, BSc ACA *1997;* Spring Grove Junior Infant & Nursery School, Bow Street, HUDDERSFIELD, HD1 4BJ.

•LEA, Mrs. Desirie Dolores, ACA ACCA *2007;* (Tax Fac), Morris & Co (2011) Limited, Chester House, Lloyd Drive, Chesire Oaks Business Park, ELLESMERE PORT, CHESHIRE CH65 9HQ.

LEA, Mr. Edward William, FCA *1966;* 24 Waddling Lane, Wheathampstead, ST.ALBANS, AL4 8SD.

•LEA, Mr. Francis William Peter, FCA *1975;* FWPL Accounting Ltd, 58 Manor Road, WOODSTOCK, OXFORDSHIRE, OX20 1XJ. See also Lea F.W.P. & Co

LEA, Mr. Gareth John, BSc ACA CPA CFE *1997;* 66 Glenbrook Road, Apt 3424, STAMFORD, CT 06902, UNITED STATES.

LEA, Mr. Gary Frayn, BSc FCA CA(SA) *1990;* PO Box 44451, Claremont, CAPE TOWN, 7735, SOUTH AFRICA.

LEA, Mr. George William, FCA *1957;* 5 St. Brannocks Road, Cheadle Hulme, CHEADLE, CHESHIRE, SK8 7LA. (Life Member)

LEA, Mrs. Helen Rosemary Elizabeth, BSc(Hons) ACA CTA *2002;* Cannons Rouse, Steel Lane, Catcott, BRIDGWATER, SOMERSET, TA7 9HW.

LEA, Mr. James John, MA ACA *2008;* The Old Vicarage, Alpraham Green, Alpraham, TARPORLEY, CHESHIRE, CW6 9LJ.

LEA, Miss. Jennifer Ann, ACA *2010;* with PricewaterhouseCoopers LLP, 8 Princes Parade, St Nicholas Place, LIVERPOOL, L3 1QJ.

LEA, Miss. Jo-Ann Brenda, BA ACA *1991;* 7 Wakefield Mews, Eagley Brook, BOLTON, BL7 9DR.

LEA, Mr. John Edward, MA FCA *1971;* The Old Vicarage, Alpraham Green, TARPORLEY, CW6 9LJ.

•LEA, Mr. John Edward, FCA *1966;* John Lea & Co, Naldretts Tower House, Mill Lane, Hurstpierpoint, HASSOCKS, WEST SUSSEX BN6 9HL.

LEA, Ms. Julia Kaye, BA ACA *1993;* with KPMG LLP, 1 The Embankment, Neville Street, LEEDS, LS1 4DW.

•LEA, Mr. Michael David, BA FCA ATII *1988;* (Tax Fac), Smith & Williamson (Bristol) LLP, Portwall Place, Portwall Lane, BRISTOL, BS1 6NA. See also Smith & Williamson Ltd

•LEA, Mr. Peter Evans, FCA *1973;* Dorrell Oliver Ltd, 26 Monk Street, ABERGAVENNY, GWENT, NP7 5NF.

LEA, Mr. Richard Arthur, FCA *1968;* 9 Jacobean Lane, Knowle, SOLIHULL, B93 9LP. (Life Member)

•LEA, Mr. Robert Charles, FCA *1972;* Robert C. Lea, 20 Hawthorn Road, SHREWSBURY, SY3 7NB.

LEA, Mr. Robert Michael, BEng ACA *2000;* UBS AG, 2 International Finance Centre, 52/F 8 Finance Street, CENTRAL, HONG KONG SAR.

LEA, Mrs. Sally Elizabeth, BA ACA *2003;* (Tax Fac), Grant Thornton UK Llp, 4 Hardman Square, MANCHESTER, M3 3EB.

LEA, Mrs. Stacey, ACA *2008;* Manor Cottage Common Wood, Wem, SHREWSBURY, SY4 5SJ.

LEA-WILSON, Mr. Philip James, FCA *1970;* Woodlands, Gorelands Lane, CHALFONT ST. GILES, BUCKINGHAMSHIRE, HP8 4HQ.

LEACH, Mr. Adrian Paul, ACA *1984;* 12 Hawthorn Way, Stoke Gifford, BRISTOL, BS34 8UP. (Life Member)

LEACH, Mr. Andrew Keith, MBA FCA *1982;* 4 Linwood Road, SOLIHULL, B91 1HL.

LEACH, Mr. Andrew William, BA ACA *1982;* Gorsecot, Booth Road, ALTRINCHAM, WA14 4AU.

LEACH, Mr. Anthony John, FCA *1950;* The Old Rectory, Weston under Penyard, ROSS-ON-WYE, HEREFORDSHIRE, HR9 7PF.

LEACH, Mr. Anthony Raymond, FCA *1963;* 2716 Via Pacheco, PALOS VERDES ESTATES, CA 90274, UNITED STATES.

•LEACH, Mrs. Catharine, FCA DChA *1992;* Hillier Hopkins LLP, 64 Clarendon Road, WATFORD, WD17 1DA.

LEACH, Mr. David Andrew, BSc ACA *1992;* TWG Services Limited Integra House Floor 2, Vicarage Road, EGHAM, SURREY, TW20 9JZ.

LEACH, Mr. David John Edgar, FCA *1966;* 48 Fitzroy Street, KIRRIBILLI, NSW 2061, AUSTRALIA. (Life Member)

LEACH, Miss. Elaine, LLB ACA *1998;* with PricewaterhouseCoopers, 1 Embankment Place, LONDON, WC2N 6RH.

LEACH, Mrs. Elizabeth Josephine, BSc ACA *1986;* Canons Garth, Main Street, Gilling East, YORK, YO62 4JH.

LEACH, Miss. Elizabeth Rebecca, BA ACA *2007;* ING Real Estate Investment Management 1st Floor, I N G Bank, 60 London Wall, LONDON, EC2M 5TQ.

LEACH, Mrs. Gillian Margaret, BA ACA *1993;* 14 Burnmoor Meadow, Finchampstead, WOKINGHAM, BERKSHIRE, RG40 3TX.

LEACH, Mr. Graham, MBA BA FCA *1979;* Costain House, Costain Group Plc, Vanwall Road, MAIDENHEAD, SL6 4UB.

LEACH, Mr. Guy William, BA ACA *1988;* 28 Westmoreland Terrace, LONDON, SW1V 4AL.

LEACH, Mrs. Harriet Kate, MA ACA *2000;* 81 Langdon Park, TEDDINGTON, MIDDLESEX, TW11 9PR.

LEACH, Miss. Helen Louise, ACA *2007;* 8 Granville Street, MARKET HARBOROUGH, LE16 9EX.

LEACH, Mr. Huw Mostyn, LLB ACA *1990;* (Tax Fac), Knox & Wells Limited, Creswell House, Fieldway, Heath, CARDIFF, CF14 4UH.

•LEACH, Miss. Jane Susannah, BSc FCA *1991;* KPMG LLP, 15 Canada Square, LONDON, E14 5GL. See also KPMG Europe LLP

•LEACH, Mr. Jason Edward, BA ACA *1996;* with PricewaterhouseCoopers LLP, 8 Princes Parade, St Nicholas Place, LIVERPOOL, L3 1QJ.

LEACH, Mrs. Jemima Elizabeth, BA(Hons) ACA *2004;* Westward House Tower Road, St. Helier, JERSEY, JE2 3HR.

LEACH, Mr. John Leslie, FCA FCT *1971;* Hill House, 3 Parkfields, Oxshott, LEATHERHEAD, KT22 0PW.

LEACH, Mr. John Vincent, FCA *1962;* 19a Lake Avenue, BROMLEY, BR1 4EN. (Life Member)

LEACH, Mrs. Karen Elizabeth, BSc ACA *1986;* Gorsecot, Booth Road, ALTRINCHAM, WA14 4AU.

LEACH, Mrs. Katherine Louise, BSc ACA *1981;* 4 Linwood Road, SOLIHULL, B91 1HL.

LEACH, Mr. Patrick, BA(Hons) ACA *2009;* Halcyon, Ormond Avenue, RICHMOND, TW10 6TN.

•LEACH, Mr. Paul Anthony Priestley, FCA *1965;* P.A.P. Leach, 14 Manilla Rd, Clifton, BRISTOL, BS8 4ED.

LEACH, Mr. Peter Clifford, FCA *1976;* 2 Dartmouth Park Road, LONDON, NW5 1SY.

LEACH, Mr. Peter Timothy Lionel, FCA *1969;* The Old Dairy, Benington Park Farm, Benington, STEVENAGE, SG2 7BU.

•LEACH, Mr. Richard Andrew, BSc ACA *1990;* Kuhrt Leach LLP, 81-82 Akeman Street, TRING, HERTFORDSHIRE, HP23 6AF.

LEACH, Mr. Robert, ACA *2006;* (Tax Fac), 19 Chestnut Avenue, EPSOM, SURREY, KT19 0SY.

LEACH, Mr. Simon, BA(Hons) ACA *2001;* (Tax Fac), Half Acre Lightlands Lane, Cookham, MAIDENHEAD, BERKSHIRE, SL6 9DH.

LEACH, Mr. Stephen Edward, BSc ACA *1988;* Longfield, Coulsdon Lane, Chipstead, COULSDON, SURREY, CR5 3QG.

LEACH, Mr. Stuart Lawson, ACA *2001;* with THS Accountants Limited, The Old School House, Leckhampton Road, CHELTENHAM, GLOUCESTERSHIRE, GL53 0AX.

LEACH, Mr. Thomas Edward, LLB ACA *2006;* 32 Moy Road, CARDIFF, CF24 4TF.

•LEACH, Mr. Trevor, FCA *1968;* Trevor Leach & Co, Bradda House, Bradda Road, Port Erin, ISLE OF MAN, IM9 6PQ.

LEACOCK, Mr. Albert Ellison, BSc FCA *1967;* 8715 Stony Falls Way, LOUISVILLE, KY 40299, UNITED STATES.

LEACY, Mrs. Susan, MSc ACA *1988;* 18 Sycamore Terrace, Bootham, YORK, YO30 7DN.

LEADBEATER, Mr. David, FCA *1978;* (Tax Fac), 7 Mansion Drive, TRING, HERTFORDSHIRE, HP23 5BD.

LEADBEATER, Mr. Kenneth Frank Martin, BA ACA *1985;* 46 Water Mill Way, South Darenth, DARTFORD, DA4 9BE.

LEADBEATER, Mr. Kenneth John, FCA *1958;* The Tower, 42A Merrin Street, AVONHEAD, NEW ZEALAND. (Life Member)

LEADBEATER, Mrs. Mary Dolores, BA FCA *1978;* 7 Mansion Drive, TRING, HP23 5BD.

LEADBEATER, Mr. Roger Brian, BA ACA *1992;* 5 Duncombe Close, AMERSHAM, HP6 6NS.

LEADBEATER, Mr. Stephen Paul, ACA *1986;* Allt-Nam-Breac, Mill Lane, Legbourne, LOUTH, LN11 8LT.

LEADBETTER, Mr. Andrew John, BSc ACA *2010;* Basement Flat, 9 Devonport Road, LONDON, W12 8NZ.

LEADBETTER, Miss. Athene Zoe, MA ACA *2010;* High Walls, Ashprington, TOTNES, DEVON, TQ9 7UW.

LEADBETTER, Mrs. Diana Justine, BA ACA *1990;* SDL Imports Ltd, 2 Windham Road, BOURNEMOUTH, BH1 4RW.

LEADBETTER, Mr. Martin John, BA FCA *1976;* Red House Farm, HINTLESHAM, SUFFOLK, IP8 3PW.

LEADBETTER, Mr. Peter, BA ACA *2009;* 59 Grasmere Way, LEIGHTON BUZZARD, BEDFORDSHIRE, LU7 2QL.

•LEADBETTER, Mr. Raymond Michael, FCA *1977;* 47 Broadwater Road, Twyford, READING, RG10 0EU.

LEADER, Mrs. Amanda Dawn, BA ACA *2000;* Innovia Films Ltd, Station Road, WIGTON, CUMBRIA, CA7 9BG.

LEADER, Mr. Andrew Gabriel, BA ACA *1998;* Budget Directorate-General, European Commission, BUDG D3, BRU-BREY 12/42, B-1049, B-1049 BRUSSELS BELGIUM.

LEADER, Mr. David Michael, FCA *1969;* 34 Elizabeth Drive, Oadby, LEICESTER, LE2 4RD. (Life Member)

LEADER, Mr. Ian Trevor, FCA *1966;* Adelaide Cottage, Templewood Lane, Stoke Poges, SLOUGH, SL2 4BG. (Life Member)

LEADER, Mr. Peter William, FCA *1969;* Flat 1, Odun Hall, Odun Road, Appledore, BIDEFORD, DEVON EX39 1PT.

LEADER, Mr. Thomas William, BSc ACA *1990;* Cayzer House, 30 Buckingham Gate, LONDON, SW1E 6NN.

LEADILL, Mrs. Ann Marlene, BA ACA *1981;* 34 Bedford Road, NORTHWOOD, HA6 2AZ.

LEADILL, Mr. Stuart Kenneth, BA FCA *1980;* 34 Bedford Road, NORTHWOOD, HA6 2AZ.

LEADLEY, Mr. Herbert James, FCA *1948;* Apartment 23, Coachman Court, 35 Ashingdon Road, ROCHFORD, ESSEX, SS4 1FF. (Life Member)

LEADLEY, Mrs. Rebekah Susan, MA ACA *1991;* Long Acre The Blundells, KENILWORTH, CV8 2PE.

LEAF, Mr. Alan Stanley, FCA *1955;* 9 Marlowe House, Portsmouth Road, KINGSTON-UPON-THAMES, KT1 2NY. (Life Member)

LEAF, Mr. Geoffrey, BSc FCA *1977;* 12 Oak Close, FILEY, NORTH YORKSHIRE, YO14 9NP.

LEAF, Mr. John William, FCA *1976;* PO Box 399, GPO Toodyay, TOODYAY, WA 6566, AUSTRALIA.

•LEAF, Mr. Michael John, FCA *1969;* (Tax Fac), M J Leaf & Co, Melville House, 8-12 Woodhouse Road, Finchley, LONDON, N12 0RG.

LEAF, Mrs. Noelle Christine, ACA *1992;* PO Box 970, MORNINGSIDE, GAUTENG, 2057, SOUTH AFRICA.

LEAFE, Mr. David Edward, BA FCA *1975;* 14 Linen Street, WARWICK, CV34 4DS.

LEAFE, Mr. Martin Peter, BSc ACA *2002;* 5 Alabama Way, ST.IVES, CAMBRIDGESHIRE, PE27 6SH.

LEAGAS, Mr. Gavin David, ACA *2003;* 27 Strawberry Close, BRAINTREE, CM7 1EG.

LEAH, Mr. Anthony John, FCA *1965;* Leah & Warhurst, Lowfield House, 222 Wellington Road South, STOCKPORT, CHESHIRE, SK2 6RS.

LEAH, Mrs. Jennifer Helen, ACA *2008;* 46 Alan Road, STOCKPORT, CHESHIRE, SK4 4LE.

LEAH, Mr. Mark, BA(Hons) ACA *2003;* 14 Pellatt Road, LONDON, SE22 9JA.

•LEAH, Mr. Philip Geoffrey, FCA *1972;* Allens Accountants Limited, 123 Wellington Road South, STOCKPORT, SK1 3TH.

LEAHY, Mr. Christopher John, BSc ACA *1985;* 521 Shackamaxon Drive, WESTFIELD, NJ 07090, UNITED STATES.

LEAHY, Mr. Christopher Michael, BSc ACA *1997;* Piramal Healthcare UK Ltd, Whalton Road, MORPETH, NORTHUMBERLAND, NE61 3YA.

LEAHY, Mr. Edward, ACA *2011;* 36 Merioneth Street, BRISTOL, BS3 4SL.

•LEAHY, Miss. Eileen Maria, FCA *1992;* Hilson Moran Partnership Ltd, 1 Columbus Drive Southwood Business Park, FARNBOROUGH, GU14 0NZ.

LEAHY, Miss. Elizabeth, BSc ACA *2000;* Penauille Servisair Inc, 100 Alexis Nihon (Suite 400), Ville St Laurent, QUEBEC CITY H4M 2N9, QC, CANADA.

LEAHY, Mr. Gerald, BA(Hons) ACA *2009;* 50 Crofton Avenue, Timperley, ALTRINCHAM, CHESHIRE, WA15 6DA.

•LEAHY, Mr. Michael, BA ACA FABRP *1998;* Talbot Hughes McKillop LLP, 6 Snow Hill, LONDON, EC1A 2AY.

•LEAHY, Mr. Michael Joseph, BA FCA *1979;* Michael J. Leahy, 47 Vicars Road, Chorlton-Cum-Hardy, MANCHESTER, M21 9JB.

LEAHY, Miss. Patricia Anne, BA ACA *1983;* 25 Woodcombe, MELKSHAM, SN12 7SD.

LEAHY, Mr. Shaun Laurence, BSc FCA *1990;* 29 Berkeley Road, NEWBURY, BERKSHIRE, RG14 5JE.

LEAHY, Mr. Ultan Francis, BA ACA *1993;* 17 Tavistock Mews, HIGH WYCOMBE, BUCKINGHAMSHIRE, HP12 3DG.

LEAK, Mr. Martin Paul, FCA *1979;* Glebe House, Lower Street, Doveridge, ASHBOURNE, DE6 5NS.

LEAK, Mr. Paul James, BSc ACA *1991;* Woodend Cottage, Bunloit, Drumnadrochit, INVERNESS, IV63 6XF.

LEAK, Mr. Robert, BA FCA *1978;* 17 Manor Road, BARNET, EN5 2LH.

LEAKE, Mr. Gavin, ACA CA(AUS) *2008;* 12 Lower Sawley Wood, BANSTEAD, SUR, BANSTEAD, SURREY, SM7 2DB.

LEAKE, Mr. John David, BCom FCA *1962;* (Tax Fac), Berrington Mill, Station Road, CHIPPING CAMPDEN, GL55 6HY.

•LEAKE, Mr. Julian Ian, MA ACA *1996;* Deloitte LLP, Stonecutter Court, 1 Stonecutter Street, LONDON, EC4A 4TR. See also Deloitte & Touche LLP

•LEAKE, Mrs. Rabea Iris, MSc BA ACA *2005;* Buchhaltungsburo Rabea Leake, Kleinburgwedeler Str. 6B, 30938 BURGWEDEL, GERMANY.

LEAKE, Mr. Scott Reginald, BA ACA *2000;* White Horse Inn White Horse Lane, Meopham, GRAVESEND, DA13 0UE.

LEAKEY, Mr. Graham Peter, BSc ACA *1995;* 16 Nea Close, CHRISTCHURCH, DORSET, BH23 4QQ.

•LEAL, Mr. Andrew Robert John, BA FCA *1986;* Percy Gore & Co, 39 Hawley Square, MARGATE, KENT, CT9 1NZ.

LEAL, Miss. Angela Maria Constance, BSc ACA *2003;* 7 Pinewood Close, Station Road, Preston Park, BRIGHTON, BN1 6TA.

LEAL, Mrs. Bianca Campelo, mm ACA *2007;* Conniexpress, Alameda Madeira 222, Andar 1, Alphaville, BARUERI, 06454-010 BRAZIL.

LEAMAN, Mr. Daniel Maxwell, BA(Econ) ACA *2003;* 141 Clayhall Avenue, ILFORD, ESSEX, IG5 0PN.

•**LEAMAN, Mr. Ian David, BA FCA CF** *1988;* Buckingham Corporate Finance Limited, 57A Catherine Place, LONDON, SW1E 6DY.
LEAMON, Mrs. Vanessa Katharine, BA(Hons) ACA *2002;* 49 Eton Wick Road, Eton Wick, WINDSOR, SL4 6LX.
LEAMY, Mr. Stuart Nigel, MA FCA *1976;* St James House, 9 - 15 St James Road, SURBITON, KT6 4QH.
LEAN, Mr. Tai Huat, FCA *1981;* 44 Watten View, SINGAPORE 287173, SINGAPORE.
LEANAGE, Mr. John Sunil Raymond, FCA *1971;* 86 Jerome Park Drive, DUNDAS L9H 6H3, ON, CANADA.
LEANDRO, Mr. Benjamin James, BA ACA *2010;* 115 Plimsoll Road, LONDON, N4 2ED.
LEANE, Mr. David Christopher, BA ACA *2006;* Newlyn St. Johns Hill Road, WOKING, SURREY, GU21 7QY.
LEANEY, Mr. Andrew Robert, BA ACA *1994;* West View, Bolton, APPLEBY-IN-WESTMORLAND, CUMBRIA, CA16 6AL.
•**LEAPMAN, Mr. Henry Jonathan, BSc FCA** *1982;* Leapman Weiss, Hillside House, 2-6 Friern Park, North Finchley, LONDON, N12 9BT.
LEAR, Miss. Amanda Toril, LLB ACA *2006;* 83 Park Road, CAMBERLEY, GU15 2SW.
•**LEAR, Mr. Andrew Nicholas, FCA** *1977;* (Tax Fac), Hawes Richards & Co, 17 The Terrace, TORQUAY, TQ1 1BN.
LEAR, Mr. Christopher Martin, BA ACA *1992;* (Tax Fac), E D & F Man Holdings Ltd, The Cottons Centre, Hays Lane, LONDON, SE1 2QE.
LEAR, Mr. Daniel Richard, BSc ACA *2010;* 41 Golwg y Coed, Birchgrove, SWANSEA, SA7 0HY.
•**LEAR, Mr. David Alan, BA ACA** *1981;* (Tax Fac), DG Accounting & Business Administration Ltd, Orchard House, Three Elm Lane, Golden Green, TONBRIDGE, KENT TN11 0BE.
LEARED, Mr. Adrian Boxwell, FCA *1988;* Avenida de Gran Canaria 66, Goya 5, 35100 PLAYA DEL INGLES, GRAN CANARIA, SPAIN.
•**LEARER, Mr. Adrian David, FCA** *1983;* PlanIT Services Limited, Lansdowne House, City Forum, 250 City Road, LONDON, EC1V 2QZ.
LEARMONT, Mr. David Murray, BEng ACA *2003;* Tallow House, 23 Whitecroft, Forest Green Nailsworth, STROUD, GLOUCESTERSHIRE, GL6 0NS.
LEARMONT, Mr. John Malcolm, FCA *1961;* 24 Swann Lane, Cheadle Hulme, CHEADLE, CHESHIRE, SK8 7HR.
LEARMONTH, Ms. Caroline Diane Mary, BA ACA *1989;* P O Box 781527, SANDTON, GAUTENG, 2146, SOUTH AFRICA.
•**LEARMONTH, Mr. Christopher James, BA ACA** *1992;* (Tax Fac), Learmonth & Co Limited, The Granary, 39 Bell Street, SAWBRIDGEWORTH, HERTFORDSHIRE, CM21 9AR.
LEARMONTH, Mr. John Mark, MA ACA *1991;* P O Box 781527, SANDTON, GAUTENG, 2146, SOUTH AFRICA.
LEARMOUTH, Mr. Duncan, BSc ACA *1992;* (Member of Council 2001 - 2004), Crowhill, Christmas Lane, Farnham Common, SLOUGH, SL2 3JF.
LEARMOUTH, The Revd. Michael Walter, FCA *1975;* 10 Thornhill Square, Islington, LONDON, N1 1BQ.
LEARNER, Mr. Mark, BA ACA *1997;* Nomura International Plc, 1 Angel Lane, LONDON, EC4R 3AB.
LEAROYD, Mrs. Alison Louise, BA ACA *2003;* 57 Camlet Way, ST. ALBANS, HERTFORDSHIRE, AL3 4TL.
•**LEARY, Mr. Michael David, BSc ACA** *1994;* Mazars LLP, The Lexicon, Mount Street, MANCHESTER, M2 5NT.
LEARY, Mr. Paul Allen, BA ACA *1988;* 27 Gartmoor Gardens, Southfields, LONDON, SW19 6NX.
LEARY, Mr. Paul Ian, BA(Hons) ACA *2001;* 155 Kirkby View, SHEFFIELD, S12 2NQ.
LEARY, Mr. Stewart Robert, BEd ACA DChA *2001;* 24 Clement Close, PURLEY, SURREY, CR8 4BY.
LEARY, Mr. Trevor Andrew Falcon, BSc FCA *1977;* Hilbre House, 14 Macdona Drive, West Kirby, WIRRAL, CH48 3JD. (Life Member)
LEASK, Mr. Edward Peter Shephard, FCA ATII *1970;* Fast Track, One Boyd, The Admirals, Gunwharf Quays, PORTSMOUTH, HAMPSHIRE PO1 3TW.
LEASK, Mrs. Frances May, BSc ACA *1981;* 5 Home Stead Gardens, Claygate, ESHER, KT10 0QF.
LEASK, Mr. Graeme Wallace, MA ACA *1993;* 6 Bellflower Way, Chandler'S Ford, EASTLEIGH, SO53 4HN.
•**LEASK, Mr. Graham Peter, ACA ATII ASI TEP** *1980;* 9 Copperkins Lane, AMERSHAM, BUCKINGHAMSHIRE, HP6 5QB.
LEATES, Mr. Timothy Philip, BSc FCA *1976;* Crofton Farm, 161 Crofton Lane, Petts Wood, ORPINGTON, BR6 0BP.
LEATHAM, Mr. Christopher John, BSc ACA *2001;* with PricewaterhouseCoopers, 113-119 The Terrace, PO Box 243, WELLINGTON 6011, NEW ZEALAND.
•**LEATHAM, Mr. Daniel, ACA FCCA** *2009;* Schofields Partnership LLP, 6th Floor, Dean Park House, Dean Park Crescent, BOURNEMOUTH, BH1 1HP.
LEATHAM, Mr. Nicholas, BA ACA *2007;* Flat 114 Southfleet, Malden Road, LONDON, NW5 4DH.
LEATHAM, Mr. Simon Anthony Michael, FCA *1974;* 23 Southside Quarter, 38 Burns Road, LONDON, SW11 5GY.
•**LEATHEM, Mrs. Susan Elizabeth, ACA** *1980;* (Tax Fac), J.R. Watson & Co, Eastgate House, 11 Cheyne Walk, NORTHAMPTON, NN1 5PT. See also Eastgate Accounts Office Limited
LEATHER, Mr. David Richard, BA FCA *1979;* 14 Oakfields Road, KNEBWORTH, SG3 6NS.
•**LEATHER, Mr. David William, BA ACA** *1990;* Ernst & Young LLP, 100 Barbirolli Square, MANCHESTER, M2 3EY. See also Ernst & Young Europe LLP
LEATHER, Mr. Edward Ross, BA(Hons) ACA *2003;* 4 Grammar School Place, BRIGHOUSE, WEST YORKSHIRE, HD6 3HJ.
LEATHER, Mr. Jonathan Nelson, BSc ACA *2005;* 2 Hazelbourne Road, LONDON, SW12 9NS.
•**LEATHER, Mr. Michael Robert, BA ACA** *1987;* (Tax Fac), Leathers LLP, 17th Floor, Cale Cross House, 156 Pilgrim Street, NEWCASTLE UPON TYNE, NE1 6SU.
LEATHER, Mr. Paul Michael, ACA *2010;* Flat 10, Central 5, Wharf Road, SALE, CHESHIRE, M33 2ZJ.
LEATHER, Mr. Stuart Bruce, FCA *1969;* 10 Coach Road, Hove Edge, BRIGHOUSE, HD6 2LX.
LEATHERDALE, Mr. Paul Henry Francis, BA ACA *1984;* Cramond Cottage Aldershot Road, Pirbright, WOKING, GU24 0BY.
LEATHERLAND, Mrs. Alison, MEng ACA *2006;* 19 Long Hassocks, RUGBY, WARWICKSHIRE, CV23 0JS.
LEATHERLAND, Mr. Simon James, BSc ACA *2001;* Deutsche Bank, PO Box 135, LONDON, EC2A 2HE.
LEATHERS, Mr. David Frederick James, FCA *1966;* Eastcotehouse Church Lane, Dogmersfield, HOOK, RG27 8TB.
LEATHERS, Mr. Simon Michael, BEng ACA *2000;* Fox Davis Capital Ltd, 1 Tudor Street, LONDON, EC4Y 0AH.
LEATHES, Mr. Gregor Ben Edward, ACA *2008;* Flat 6, 20 Pelham Road, LONDON, SW19 1SX.
LEATHES, Mr. Simon William De Mussenden, MA FCA *1973;* 19 Lauriston Road, Wimbledon, LONDON, SW19 4TJ.
LEATHLEY, Mr. Christopher Mark, BSc ACA *1992;* Berrycombe, Gwealfolds, HELSTON, CORNWALL, TR13 8LN.
LEATHLEY, Miss. Katie, BSc(Hons) ACA *2002;* 14 Norfolk Terrace, LEEDS, LS7 4QW.
LEATHLEY, Mr. Stephen Grant, BSc ACA *1986;* 89 Hough top, Bramley, LEEDS, LS13 4QN.
LEATHWOOD, Mr. Martin Robert, FCA *1966;* Thatched Wells, Duckhole, Lower Morton Thornbury, BRISTOL, BS35 1LD.
LEATT, Mr. Gary John, BA ACA *1997;* Le Bouchon, La Route Des Genets, St Brelade, JERSEY, JE3 8LF.
LEAU, Miss. Chin Ching, BA ACA *1993;* Flat B 20/F Tower 2, Jupiter Terrace, 18 Jupiter Street, NORTH POINT, HONG KONG ISLAND, HONG KONG SAR.
LEAVER, Mr. Antony Michael, FCA *1964;* Springhurst, The Quarries, Mannings Heath, HORSHAM, WEST SUSSEX, RH13 6SW. (Life Member)
LEAVER, Mr. Christopher John, BA ACA *1998;* 18 High Street, Pulloxhill, BEDFORD, MK45 5HA.
LEAVER, Mr. David Anthony, BSc FCA *1988;* KPMG LLP, 16 Raffles Quay, # 22-00, Hong Leong Building, SINGAPORE 048581, SINGAPORE.
LEAVER, Mr. Guy Cameron, MBA BA ACA *1991;* Neoss Ltd Windsor House, Cornwall Road, HARROGATE, NORTH YORKSHIRE, HG1 2PW.
LEAVER, Mrs. Joanne Nicola, BA ACA *1998;* 18 High Street, Pulloxhill, BEDFORD, MK45 5HA.
LEAVER, Mr. John David, FCA *1966;* 6 Hazelfields, Worsley, MANCHESTER, M28 2LS.
LEAVER, Mr. Kevin John, FCA *1982;* (Tax Fac), with PricewaterhouseCoopers LLP, 1 Embankment Place, LONDON, WC2N 6RH.
LEAVER, Mr. Marc Daniel, BA ACA *2000;* Standard Chartered Bank, Marina Bay Financial Centre (Tower 1), 8 Marina Boulevard, Level 21, SINGAPORE 018981, SINGAPORE.
LEAVER, Mr. Timothy, MA FCA *1995;* 10 Broomfield Avenue, Palmers Green, LONDON, N13 4JN.
LEAVITT, Mrs. Helen, BSc ACA *2006;* Birmingham & Solihull Mental Health Trust, Unit 1, 50 Summer Hill Road, BIRMINGHAM, B1 3RB.
LEAVOLD, Miss. Tracey Jayne, BA ACA *2001;* 5 Church Street, Fenstanton, HUNTINGDON, CAMBRIDGESHIRE, PE28 9JL.
LEAVY, Mr. Nigel Edward, FCA *1970;* Boot Cottage, Boot Street, Stonesfield, WITNEY, OX29 8PX.
LEAW, Mr. Kok Yin, FCA *1968;* 31 Jalan Sempadan, #04-06 Tower 2, Villa Marina, SINGAPORE 457403, SINGAPORE. (Life Member)
LEBBELL, Mr. David, FCA *1953;* 3305 Argyle Place, VICTORIA V8P 5R8, BC, CANADA. (Life Member)
LEBBON, Mr. Timothy Owen, FCA FCPA FSIA *1971;* Leadenhall Australia Ltd, Level 1, 31 Franklin Street, ADELAIDE, SA 5000, AUSTRALIA.
LEBENTZ, Mr. Derek, FCA *1965;* 9 Providence Park, Bassett, SOUTHAMPTON, SO16 7QN. (Life Member)
LEBON, Miss. Sylviane Lili Ghislaine, BSc ACA MBA *2001;* 9/29 Waiapu Road, Kelburn, WELLINGTON 6012, NEW ZEALAND.
LEBUS, Mr. Richard Michael, BSc FCA *1974;* 238 St. Margarets Road, TWICKENHAM, TW1 1NL.
•**LECHARPENTIER, Mrs. Karen Elizabeth, BSc ACA** *2002;* 32 Lancock Street, Rockwell Green, WELLINGTON, SOMERSET, TA21 9RS.
LECI, Mr. Jonathan Ilan, BSc(Econ) ACA *1999;* Primo Levi 7, Apartment 5, 93783 JERUSALEM, ISRAEL.
•**LECK, Mr. Christopher David, MA FCA** *1981;* Le Chalenet, Le Vier Mont, Grouville, JERSEY, JE3 9GF.
LECK, Ms. Fiona Jane, BSc ACA *1995;* Leicestershire & Rutland Probation Area, 2 St. John Street, LEICESTER, LE1 3WL.
LECKIE, Mr. Stephen Peter, ACA *1987;* Grant Thornton UK LLP, 30 Finsbury Square, LONDON, EC2P 2YU.
LECKY, Mrs. Helen Elizabeth, ACA *2009;* 35 Smithy Close, Brindle, CHORLEY, PR6 8NW.
LECOUTRE, Mr. Paul Florent, FCA *1969;* Oak Lodge, Slines Oak Road, Woldingham, CATERHAM, CR3 7HL.
LECRIVAIN, Mrs. Julia Heidi, ACA *1993;* Le Picachon, La Grande Rue, St. Mary, JERSEY, JE3 3BD.
LECROY, Mr. David Aaron, BA ACA *1999;* 5 Westgate Park, Hough, CREWE, CW2 5GY.
LEDBURY, Mrs. Angela Jane, BSc ACA *1988;* Fir Grange Lodge, 2 Grange Avenue, WEYBRIDGE, SURREY, KT13 9AR.
LEDBURY, Mr. Gordon Herbert, FCA *1954;* Weavers House, 15B Horse Road, Hilperton Marsh, TROWBRIDGE, BA14 7PE. (Life Member)
LEDDEN, Mr. Graham Nicholas, BA FCA *1981;* Cherry Orchard, Weston Under Penyard, ROSS-ON-WYE, HR9 7PH.
LEDDINGTON, Mr. Robert, FCA *1978;* 36 Shaftesbury Street, WEST BROMWICH, WEST MIDLANDS, B71 1LP.
•**LEDERER, Mr. David Anthony, BSc ACA** *1980;* David Lederer, Riverdale, 32 Kings Road, Pownall Park, WILMSLOW, SK9 5PZ.
LEDERER, Mrs. Marian Adele, FCA *1970;* Oberer Reisberg 22, 61350 BAD-HOMBURG-DORNHOLZHAUSEN, GERMANY.
LEDERMAN, Mr. Colin Stuart, FCA FFA *1962;* 52-23 King Solomon Street, 42265 NETANYA, ISRAEL.
•**LEDERMAN, Mr. Paul, DMS FCA** *1968;* Paul Lederman, 18 Wheatley Close, LONDON, NW4 4LG.
LEDESMA, Miss. Simone Ann, ACA *2007;* 6 Treport Street, LONDON, SW18 2BP.
LEDGARD, Mr. Christopher William, BSc FCA *1988;* Willow House, 3 Hazelwood Court, HALIFAX, WEST YORKSHIRE, HX1 2PY.
•**LEDGARD, Mr. Nicholas Arthur, BA FCA** *1995;* Walker & Sutcliffe, 12 Greenhead Road, HUDDERSFIELD, HD1 4EN. See also Walker & Sutcliffe (Bookkeeping Services) Limited
LEDGARD, Mr. Phillip Neil, BSc(Hons) ACA *2001;* 107 Aston Cantlow Road, Wilmcote, STRATFORD-UPON-AVON, WARWICKSHIRE, CV37 9XW.
LEDGER, Mr. Charles Stanley, FCA *1960;* The Birches, Braithwaite, KESWICK, CA12 5RY. (Life Member)
LEDGER, Mr. Curtis Lee, MA ACA *1999;* 4 Turnberry Fold, LEEDS, LS17 7WB.
LEDGER, Mr. David Anthony, FCA *1972;* 6 Doddington Drive, Longthorpe, PETERBOROUGH, PE3 9NN.
LEDGER, Mr. David Graham, BSc FCA ACILA *1991;* 38 Myddelton Park, LONDON, N20 0JL.
LEDGER, Mr. Howard, FCA *1957;* 68 Chatsworth Drive, MANSFIELD, NG18 4QX. (Life Member)
LEDGER, Miss. Jennifer Louise, BSc ACA *2004;* 51B Rodney Street, HOWICK 2014, NEW ZEALAND.
•**LEDGER, Mr. Mark, BA ACA** *1980;* Ledger & Co, Brackendene, Lower Daggons, FORDINGBRIDGE, SP6 3EE.
LEDGER, Mr. Robert Charles, ACA *2010;* Flat 101 Dolphin House, Smugglers Way, LONDON, SW18 1DG.
LEDGER, Mr. Robert Mark, BA ACA *1982;* 10 Blackhurst Lane, TUNBRIDGE WELLS, KENT, TN2 4QB.
LEDGER, Mr. Simon Paul, BA(Hons) ACA *2002;* House 16, Chikankata Mission Hospital, MAZABUKA, SOUTHERN PROVINCE, ZAMBIA.
•**LEDGER, Mr. Stephen John, ACA** *1980;* Reeves & Co LLP, 37 St. Margarets Street, CANTERBURY, KENT, CT1 2TU.
LEDGER, Mr. Steven John, BA ACA *1999;* 67 Aughton Lane, Aston, SHEFFIELD, S26 2AN.
•**LEDGER-BEADELL, Mr. Mark David, BSc FCA CF** *1988;* Meta Corporate Finance Limited, Hop House, Lower Green Road, Pembury, TUNBRIDGE WELLS, TN2 4HS.
LEDIARD, Mr. Alan Colin, BA FCA *1988;* 107 Manor Abbey Road, Lapal, HALESOWEN, B62 0AA.
LEDIGO, Mr. Martin, BSc FCA *1983;* 56 Aberdeen Road, LONDON, N5 2XB.
•**LEDINGHAM, Mr. Nicholas Orme, BSc FCA** *1985;* (Tax Fac), Morris & Co (2011) Limited, Chester House, Lloyd Drive, Chesire Oaks Business Park, ELLESMERE PORT, CHESHIRE CH65 9HQ.
LEDNOR, Mrs. Amy Louise, BA ACA *2004;* 27 Mount Drive, Park Street, ST. ALBANS, HERTFORDSHIRE, AL2 2NP.
LEDSHAM, Mr. David, FCA *1975;* Ministry of Defence: 2sl-Cnh Headquarter, Centurion Building, Grange Road, GOSPORT, HAMPSHIRE, PO13 9XA.
LEDSHAM, Mr. David Anthony, PhD ACA *1980;* Saxobank, 40 Bank Street, LONDON, E14 5DA.
LEDSHAM, Mr. Geoffrey, FCA *1974;* Bryn Glas, 7 Glyn Avenue, PRESTATYN, LL19 9NN. (Life Member)
LEDSHAM, Mr. Mark Stephen, BA ACA *2006;* 4 West Avenue, DARLINGHURST, NSW 2010, AUSTRALIA.
LEDSON, Mr. Thomas Paul Johnson, BSc(Hons) ACA *2002;* 10 McKinley Way, WIDNES, CHESHIRE, WA8 9QH.
LEDSTER, Mr. David Graham, FCA *1971;* Half Acre, 28 St. Peters Way, Chorleywood, RICKMANSWORTH, HERTFORDSHIRE, WD3 5QE.
LEDWARD, Mr. Andrew, FCA DChA *1989;* 47 Roman Way, UCKFIELD, EAST SUSSEX, TN22 1UY.
LEDWARD, Mr. James Richard, BSc ACA *2002;* 71 Fennel Road, Portishead, BRISTOL, BS20 7AR.
LEDWITH, Mr. Lee Christopher, BSc ACA *1990;* 40 Primrose Lane, GLOSSOP, DERBYSHIRE, SK13 8EW.
LEE, Mr. Aaron Kong Tzung, BSc ACA *2010;* Flat 918 New Providence Wharf, 1 Fairmont Avenue, LONDON, E14 9PJ.
•**LEE, Mr. Adrian John, FCA** *1978;* Wheawill & Sudworth, P.O. Box B30, 35 Westgate, HUDDERSFIELD, HD1 1PA.
LEE, Mr. Adrian Lye Wang, BSc(Econ) ACA *1998;* KPMG, Level 10, KPMG Tower, 8 First Avenue, Bandar Utama, 47800 PETALING JAYA MALAYSIA.
LEE, Mr. Adrian Peter, BSc(Hons) ACA *2003;* The Cottage, Station Road, Bleasby, NOTTINGHAM, NG14 7GD.
LEE, Miss. Ai Vin, ACA *2010;* Flat 35 Settlers Court, 17 Newport Avenue, LONDON, E14 2DG.
LEE, Miss. Ai-Ling, LLB ACA *1997;* 14 British Grove, LONDON, W4 2NL.
LEE, Mr. Alfred, ACA *2008;* BDO Limited, 25/F Wing On Centre, 111 Connaught Road, CENTRAL, HONG KONG ISLAND, HONG KONG SAR. See also BDO McCabe Lo & Limited
LEE, Miss. Alison Fung Ying, BA FCA *1988;* 8b Kenville Building, 32 Kennedy Road, CENTRAL, HONG KONG ISLAND, HONG KONG SAR.
LEE, Mrs. Amanda, BSc ACA *1995;* 52 Rectory Close, NEWBURY, BERKSHIRE, RG14 6DD.
LEE, Mr. Andrew, MSc LLB ACA *2007;* 121 Felsham Road, LONDON, SW15 1BA.
LEE, Mr. Andrew, BSc ACA *1996;* 23 Riverside Crescent, OTLEY, WEST YORKSHIRE, LS21 2RS.

LEE, Mr. Andrew, BA ACA *1987;* 47 Hamdown Court, Picts Hill, LANGPORT, SOMERSET, TA10 9EB.
LEE, Mr. Andrew Chiu Man, BA ACA ATII *1989;* (Tax Fac), 27 Banks Way, GUILDFORD, SURREY, GU4 7NL.
LEE, Mr. Andrew George Arthur, ACA MAAT *2009;* 4 Churchfields, Fawley, SOUTHAMPTON, HAMPSHIRE, SO45 1FY.
LEE, Mr. Andrew Heng Wan, BEng ACA *1993;* 1 Jalan Dato Amar 1, Off Persiaran Raja Muda Musa, 41100 KLANG, MALAYSIA.
LEE, Mr. Andrew Lawrence, BCom FCA *1975;* 10 Brunswick Road, KINGSTON-UPON-THAMES, KT2 6SA.
LEE, Mr. Andrew Michael, ACA *1987;* Bulwell Precision Engineers Limited, Wharf Road Industrial Estate, Pinxton, NOTTINGHAM, NG16 6LE.
LEE, Mr. Andrew Paul, BA ACA *1999;* 44 Jessica Road, LONDON, SW18 2QN.
LEE, Mr. Andrew Philip, BA ACA *1988;* 29 Alder Lane, Balsall Common, COVENTRY, CV7 7DZ.
•LEE, Mr. Andrew Simon, BSc ACA *1988;* Graham Paul Limited, 372-374 Cyncoed Road, CARDIFF, CF23 6SA.
LEE, Mr. Andrew William, MA FCA *1983;* Good Energies (UK) LLP, 2-5 Old Bond Street, LONDON, W1S 4PD.
LEE, Mrs. Angelina Pui Ling, LLB FCA *1974;* 26th Floor, Jardine House, 1 Connaught Place, CENTRAL, HONG KONG SAR.
LEE, Ms. Anne Keat Chiew, FCA *1983;* 72 Hougang Avenue 7, #02-09, SINGAPORE 538805, SINGAPORE.
LEE, Mr. Anthony Mark, BSc ACA *1997;* Global Aerospace Underwriting Managers Ltd Fitzwilliam Hous 10 St. Mary Axe, LONDON, EC3A 8EQ.
•LEE, Mr. Antoine Yim Ok, FCA *1970;* (Tax Fac), 27 Exeter Gardens, ILFORD, ESSEX, IG1 3LA.
LEE, Mr. Antony Richard, BA FCA *1992;* 12 St. Elizabeth Drive, EPSOM, SURREY, KT18 7LA.
LEE, Mr. Arthur Philip, FCA *1953;* 4 Essex Avenue, BURNLEY, BB12 6DE. (Life Member)
LEE, Mr. Barry, MSc BEng ACA *2007;* 6 Hillview Close, PINNER, MIDDLESEX, HA5 4PD.
LEE, Mr. Benjamin, MChem ACA *2011;* Flat 19, Beddington Manor, 45 Eaton Road, SUTTON, SURREY, SM2 5ED.
LEE, The Revd Canon Brian Ernest, FCA *1959;* Saint Fursey House, Belsey Bridge Road, Ditchingham, BUNGAY, NR35 2DZ. (Life Member)
LEE, Mr. Brian Martin, BSc ACA *1984;* (Tax Fac), Ifg International Ltd International House, Castle Hill Douglas, ISLE OF MAN, IM2 4RB.
LEE, Mr. Brian William, FCA *1960;* 24 Calstock Road, Woodthorpe, NOTTINGHAM, NG5 4FH.
LEE, Miss. Carol Alexandra, ACA *2008;* Flat 43 Streatleigh Court, Streatham High Road, LONDON, SW16 1EG.
LEE, Miss. Catherine Elizabeth, BA(Hons) ACA *2002;* 4th Floor, Hays Personnel Services Ltd, 250 Euston Road, LONDON, NW1 2AF.
LEE, Miss. Catherine Yuet Ming, BSc ACA *1994;* 14061 Indigo Bunting Court, GAINESVILLE, VA 20155, UNITED STATES.
LEE, Mr. Cecil Gek Hian, BSc ACA *1988;* 103 Gallop Park Road, SINGAPORE 258997, SINGAPORE.
LEE, Mr. Cecil Stephen, FCA *1951;* 2 Earlsdon Way, Highcliffe, CHRISTCHURCH, BH23 5AU. (Life Member)
LEE, Mr. Chan Beng, FCA *1986;* P.O.Box 108, BOROKO, NATIONAL CAPITAL DISTRICT, 111, PAPUA NEW GUINEA.
LEE, Mr. Chan Vun, FCA *1984;* C V Lee & Co, P.O. Box 14288, 88849 KOTA KINABALU, Sabah, MALAYSIA.
•LEE, Mr. Charles Robert, FCA *1970;* (Tax Fac), Robert Lee, 18 The Village, West Hallam, ILKESTON, DERBYSHIRE, DE7 6GR.
LEE, Mrs. Charlotte Laura, BA ACA *2004;* 10 Oaklands, Leavenheath, COLCHESTER, SUFFOLK, CO6 4UH.
LEE, Mr. Chee Kai, ACA *1983;* 39 Jalan SS26/3, Taman Mayang Jaya, 47301 PETALING JAYA, Selangor, MALAYSIA.
LEE, Mr. Chee Kuen, ACA *2006;* Barry Lee & Co, Unit C, 8th Floor, Charmhill Centre, 50 Hillwood Road, TSIM SHA TSUI KOWLOON HONG KONG SAR.
LEE, Mr. Chee Man, ACA *2007;* Flat 1, 7/F, Block E, Beverly Hill, 6 Broadwood Road, HAPPY VALLEY HONG KONG SAR.
LEE, Ms. Cherie, ACA *2008;* 4203, Two Exchange Square, 8 Connaught Place, CENTRAL, HONG KONG SAR.
LEE, Miss. Cheryl Anne, BSc ACA *2009;* 19 Cranleigh Gardens, CHATHAM, KENT, ME4 6UN.
LEE, Mrs. Chi, BA ACA *1989;* 39 Ormond Crescent, HAMPTON, TW12 2TJ.
LEE, Mr. Chi Keung, ACA *2007;* Room 13 10/F, Shun Hong House, Shun Chi Court, KWUN TONG, KOWLOON, HONG KONG SAR.
LEE, Mr. Chi Kin, ACA *2007;* c/o Sheraton Shenyang Lido Hotel, 386 Qingnian Street, Heping District, SHENYANG 110004, LIAONING PROVINCE, CHINA.
LEE, Mr. Chi Hang, ACA *2008;* David Yim & Co, Room 9-1027/F, Seapower Tower, Concordia Plaza, 1 Science Museum Road, TSIM SHA TSUI KOWLOON HONG KONG SAR.
LEE, Mr. Chi Hung, ACA *2005;* Flat B 13/F Tower 5, Manhattan Hill, 1 Po Lun Street, LAI CHI KOK, KOWLOON, HONG KONG SAR.
LEE, Mr. Chi Yan, ACA *2005;* P.O. Box No. 23406, Wanchai Post Office, WAN CHAI, HONG KONG ISLAND, HONG KONG SAR.
LEE, Mr. Chi-Man, MBA ACA *1990;* c/o Birdsnest, 4 Barley Market St, TAVISTOCK, PL19 0JF.
LEE, Mr. Chin Yin, ACA *1982;* 31 Mugliston Park, SINGAPORE 798545, SINGAPORE.
LEE, Miss. Ching Kit, ACA *1980;* KHK Advertising Sdn Bhd, 6 Jalan Wan Kadir, Taman Tun Dr Ismail, 60000 KUALA LUMPUR, FEDERAL TERRITORY, MALAYSIA.
•LEE, Mr. Chiu Tsun Philip, ACA *2005;* Philip Lee & Co., Office B, 22nd floor, Guangdong Investment Tower, 148 Connaught Road, CENTRAL HONG KONG ISLAND HONG KONG SAR.
LEE, Mr. Choo Hock, ACA *1980;* 93 Jalan Leboh Bagor, Taman Petaling, 41200 KLANG, SELANGOR, MALAYSIA.
LEE, Mr. Choon Kyung, BA FCA *1964;* 102 - 1001 Kwangjin Houstory, 813 Jayangdong Kwangjingu, SEOUL, 143 - 190, KOREA REPUBLIC OF. (Life Member)
LEE, Mr. Choong Yan, BSc ACA *1988;* Genting Malaysia Berhad, 23rd floor Wisma Genting, Jalan Sultan Ismail, 50250 KUALA LUMPUR, FEDERAL TERRITORY, MALAYSIA.
LEE, Mr. Christopher Jonathan, BEng ACA *2000;* 52 Dorset Road, LONDON, E7 8PS.
LEE, Mr. Christopher Norman, ACA *1986;* Wicketts, Stoke Row, HENLEY-ON-THAMES, OXFORDSHIRE, RG9 5PL.
LEE, Mr. Chuen Kei, ACA *2007;* Flat 3806, 38/F Block E, Hong Ting House, Hong Yat Court, LAM TIN, KOWLOON HONG KONG SAR.
LEE, Mr. Chun Ho, ACA *2008;* with Ernst & Young, 62/F, One Island East, 18 Westlands Road, QUARRY BAY, HONG KONG ISLAND HONG KONG SAR.
LEE, Mr. Chung Hei Jonathan, ACA *2004;* China Travel Service (Holdings) Hong Kong Ltd, 17/F. CTS House, 78-83 Connaught Road Central, CENTRAL, HONG KONG SAR.
LEE, Mrs. Claire, ACA *2008;* 14 Oxcroft Estate, Mansfield Road Creswell, WORKSOP, NOTTINGHAMSHIRE, S80 4NA.
LEE, Mr. Clement Siew Loon, LLB ACA *2002;* 1 Rhu Cross, #12-03 Costa Rhu, SINGAPORE 437431, SINGAPORE.
LEE, Mr. Clive John, BSc FCA *1976;* 347 Evesham Road, Crabbs Cross, REDDITCH, B97 5JA.
LEE, Mr. Clive Youn-Wen, BSc ACA *1994;* 73 Tanjong Bungah Park, 11200 PENANG, MALAYSIA.
LEE, Mrs. Colette Joanne, ACA *1991;* 48 Beckhall, Welton, LINCOLN, LN2 3LJ.
LEE, Mr. Colin Victor Lionel, FCA *1962;* Orchards Cottage, 202 Kent Street, Mereworth, MAIDSTONE, ME18 5QW. (Life Member)
LEE, Mr. Colin Youn-Tze, BSc ACA *1994;* 73 Tanjong Bungah Park, 11200 PENANG, MALAYSIA.
LEE, Mrs. Connie, BSc ACA *2002;* 110 Southam Road, BIRMINGHAM, B28 0AD.
LEE, Mr. Cyril Alfred, BCom FCA *1962;* 117 Chiltern Avenue, BUSHEY, WD23 4QE.
LEE, Mr. David, BSc ACA *1996;* Incisive Media, Haymarket House, 28-29 Haymarket, LONDON, SW1Y 4RX.
LEE, Mr. David, BSc(Hons) ACA *2003;* PWC, 188 Quay Street, AUCKLAND 1142, NEW ZEALAND.
•LEE, Mr. David Alan, FCA BEng(Hons) *1999;* Layton Lee LLP, 6 Manchester Road, BUXTON, DERBYSHIRE, SK17 6SB.
LEE, Mr. David Chung Hong, FCA *1973;* 8A Block 2, Grand Garden, 61 South Bay Road, REPULSE BAY, HONG KONG ISLAND, HONG KONG SAR.
•LEE, Mr. David Eric, BA ACA *1979;* David Lee, 26 Old London Road, HYTHE, KENT, CT21 4DQ.
LEE, Mr. David Gordon, FCA *1970;* 9 Rectory Farm Road, Little Wilbraham, CAMBRIDGE, CB21 5LB.
LEE, Mr. David Lawrence Chartres, FCA *1965;* Corner Cottage, 15 Old Street, Hill Head, FAREHAM, PO14 3HT.
•LEE, Mr. David Leslie, BA FCA *1982;* (Tax Fac), BSG Valentine, Lynton House, 7/12 Tavistock Square, LONDON, WC1H 9BQ.
LEE, Mr. David William, BEng ACA AKC *1992;* 20 Melody Road, LONDON, SW18 2QF.
•LEE, Mr. Derek John, FCA *1972;* (Tax Fac), Lees Limited, The Granary, Brewer Street, Bletchingley, REDHILL, RH1 4QP. See also Lees
LEE, Mr. Derence Brian, ACA *2010;* K P M G, St. James's Square, MANCHESTER, M2 6DS.
LEE, Mr. Douglas John, BSc ARCS ACA *1992;* 189 Cyncoed Road, Cyncoed, CARDIFF, CF23 6AJ.
LEE, Mr. Douglas Norfolk, FCA *1967;* Liss House, Cold Ash Hill, Cold Ash, THATCHAM, RG18 9PS.
LEE, Mr. Ean Lean, ACA *1981;* B-12-5. Strauss Tower, Mont'Kiara Sophia, No 2 Jalan Kiara 1, 50480 KUALA LUMPUR, FEDERAL TERRITORY, MALAYSIA.
LEE, Mr. Eddie, ACA *1981;* La Roseraie. Batiment N, 10 Rue Des Violettes, 78750 MAREIL MARLY, FRANCE.
LEE, Mr. Eddy Chi Kwong, MSc BSc ACA *2010;* 11 Clematis Gardens, WOODFORD GREEN, ESSEX, IG8 0BU.
LEE, Mr. Edward James Rothwell, ACA *2010;* Basement Rear, 4 Southwell Gardens, LONDON, SW7 4SB.
LEE, Mr. Edward Rowland, FCA *1979;* 6 Green Balk Lane, Lepton, HUDDERSFIELD, HD8 0EW.
LEE, Miss. Elaine Caroline, ACA *2010;* Hightrees, Stroud Lane, Blackwater, CAMBERLEY, SURREY, GU17 0BL.
LEE, Ms. Elizabeth Byrne, BCom ACA *1989;* Glendon, 9 Harrington Sound Road, HAMILTON HS02, BERMUDA.
LEE, Mr. Felix Kwo Hang, BSc FCA *1993;* KPMG, 8/F Prince's Building, 10 Chater Road, CENTRAL, HONG KONG ISLAND, HONG KONG SAR.
LEE, Mr. Fook Kiong, FCA FCMA FHKSA *1983;* 1701 St George's Building, 2 Ice House Street, CENTRAL, HONG KONG SAR.
LEE, Mr. Francis Kwong Shing, MA ACA *1988;* Flat G, 5th Floor The Hilltop, 60 Cloudview Road, NORTH POINT, HONG KONG ISLAND, HONG KONG SAR.
LEE, Mr. Francois Paul, ACA *1980;* Flat 1, 39 Nevern Square, LONDON, SW5 9PE.
LEE, Mr. Frank, BEng ACA *1997;* Hersham Place Technology Park Mail drop H25, Air Products Plc Hersham Place, 41-61 Molesey Road Hersham, WALTON-ON-THAMES, KT12 4RZ.
LEE, Mr. Frank David, MA FCA *1969;* 40 Newgate Lane, Whitestake, PRESTON, PR4 4JU.
LEE, Mr. Franklin Yong Kwee, LLM ACA MBA *1985;* 1510 Silver Tower, 933 Zhongshan West Road, Hongqiao, SHANGHAI S200051, CHINA.
LEE, Ms. Fung Ling, ACA *2005;* Flat G, 27/F, Block 6, Verbena Heights, Mau Tai Road, Tseung Kwan O SAI KUNG NEW TERRITORIES HONG KONG SAR.
LEE, Mrs. Gail Hosie, BA ACA *1991;* 47 Castle Terrace, BERWICK-UPON-TWEED, TD15 1NZ.
LEE, Mr. Gareth Edgar, BSc ACA *2005;* Suite 2000, 335 South Grand Avenue, LOS ANGELES, CA 90071-1568, UNITED STATES.
•LEE, Mr. Gary David, BA FCA *1978;* Brody Lee Kershaw & Co, 2nd Floor, Hanover House, 30-32 Charlotte Street, MANCHESTER, M1 4EX. See also Brody Lee Kershaw Ltd
•LEE, Mr. Gary Norton, BA FCA *1995;* Begbies Traynor, 340 Deansgate, MANCHESTER, M3 4LY. See also Begbies Traynor Limited
LEE, Mr. Geoffrey Alan, PhD BSc FCA *1951;* Hazleford Care Home, Boat Lane, Bleasby, NOTTINGHAM, NG14 7FT. (Life Member)
LEE, Mr. Geoffrey Charles, BA FCA *1966;* 8 Hazlitt Drive, MAIDSTONE, ME16 0EG.
LEE, Mr. Geoffrey Roland, BSc(Hons) ARCS FCA *1981;* Whitefields, Mill Hill, EDENBRIDGE, TN8 5DB.
LEE, Miss. Geok Cheng, BSc ACA *1998;* Ventris House, La Brigade Road, St. Andrew, GUERNSEY, GY6 8RG.
LEE, Miss. Geok Hiang, BA FCA *1990;* 70 Mei Hwan Drive, #06-17 Goldenhill Park, SINGAPORE 568431, SINGAPORE.
LEE, Mr. Geok Ling, BSc FCA *1982;* with PricewaterhouseCoopers, P.O.Box 10192, Level 10 1 Sentral, Jalan Travers, 50470 KUALA LUMPUR, FEDERAL TERRITORY MALAYSIA.
LEE, Mrs. Gillian Elizabeth, BA ACA *1999;* 17 High Meadow, Walton-le-Dale, PRESTON, PR5 4WR.
•LEE, Mr. Grant Sebastian, BSc ACA *2003;* with PricewaterhouseCoopers LLP, 7 More London Riverside, LONDON, SE1 2RT.
LEE, Mr. Haifeng Nicolas, BEng ACA *1997;* Apt 1101 No.1 Building, No.3201 Hong Mei Road, SHANGHAI 201103, CHINA.
LEE, Miss. Hannah Katherine, BA ACA *2004;* Flat 3, 24 Hervey Road, Blackheath, LONDON, SE3 8BS.
LEE, Mr. Harold Pembroke, BSc LLB FCA *1961;* Merrileas, Old Road, Monkland, LEOMINSTER, HR6 9DB. (Life Member)
LEE, Mr. Hayden Philip, BA(Hons) ACA *2004;* MGPA, 8 Shenton Way, #15-02, SINGAPORE 068811, SINGAPORE.
•LEE, Mrs. Helen Margaret Louise, MA FCA *1992;* Helen Lee, 55 Wodeland Avenue, GUILDFORD, SURREY, GU2 4LA.
LEE, Mr. Heng Keng, BEng ACA CF *1992;* No.11 Jalan Setiakasih 8, Damansara Heights, 50490 KUALA LUMPUR, FEDERAL TERRITORY, MALAYSIA.
LEE, Mr. Hing Tai Ronald, ACA *2004;* Ronald H. T. Lee & Co., Room 1002, 10/F, Malaysia Building, 50 Gloucester Road, WAN CHAI HONG KONG ISLAND HONG KONG SAR.
LEE, Mr. Ho Yin, ACA *2007;* Block 7, 22/F, Room D, Fullview Garden, 18 Siu Sai Wan Road, CHAI WAN HONG KONG SAR.
LEE, Mr. Hock Khoon, ACA *1982;* 9 Jalan 5/37, 46000 PETALING JAYA, SELANGOR, MALAYSIA.
LEE, Mr. Howard Graham, FCA *1976;* 20 Hill Hall, Theydon Mount, EPPING, ESSEX, CM16 7QQ.
•LEE, Mr. Howard Patrick, FCA *1973;* (Tax Fac), Howard Lee Fellows & Co, 11-13 First Floor, The Meads Business Centre, 19 Kingsmead, FARNBOROUGH, HAMPSHIRE GU14 7SR.
LEE, Miss. Hsin Ye, BA ACA *2003;* 63 Jalan BU7/1, 47800 BANDAR UTAMA, SELANGOR, MALAYSIA.
LEE, Miss. Hung, ACA *2006;* Flat E, 28/F Tower 8, The Belchers, 89 Pokfulam Road, POK FU LAM, HONG KONG ISLAND HONG KONG SAR.
LEE, Mr. Hung Hoi, FCA *1977;* 2541 West King Edward Av, VANCOUVER V6L 1T5, BC, CANADA.
LEE, Mr. Hyman Wai Kam, ACA *2006;* Flat E 6/F, Loong Shan Mansion, Taikoo Shing, 21 Taikoo Shing Road, TAIKOO SHING, HONG KONG ISLAND HONG KONG SAR.
LEE, Mr. Ian, MA FCA *1999;* 85 Church Lane, LONDON, SW19 3NY.
LEE, Mr. Ian Philip, ACA *2008;* Flat 2 6/F Block B, Dragon Court, 6 Dragon Terrace, NORTH POINT, HONG KONG ISLAND, HONG KONG SAR.
LEE, Mr. Jacky Kai Leung, ACA *2006;* LanZhou HuangHe Enterprise Co. Ltd, 22/F Jin Yun Mansion, 219 Qing Yang Road, LANZHOU 730030, CHINA.
LEE, Mr. Jacob Chun Keung, ACA *2006;* Financial Management Division, 11th Floor Wing Hang Bank Bldg, 161 Queen Road Central, CENTRAL, HONG KONG ISLAND, HONG KONG SAR.
LEE, Mr. James, BA ACA *2004;* Wood House, Grove Terrace, Burnopfield, NEWCASTLE UPON TYNE, NE16 6NP.
LEE, Mr. James, ACA CA(AUS) *2009;* Flat 132 Regents Court, Sopwith Way, KINGSTON UPON THAMES, KT2 5AQ.
LEE, Mr. James Denis, BSc(Hons) ACA MCT *2001;* Babbage House, Vodafone Group Plc Vodafone House, The Connection, NEWBURY, RG14 2FN.
•LEE, Mr. James Kingtan, ACA *1978;* James K. Lee, 22 Dorian Place, THORNHILL L4J 2M3, ON, CANADA.
LEE, Mr. James Michael Maconchy, BSc ACA *2009;* The Farm, Northington, ALRESFORD, HAMPSHIRE, SO24 9TH.
LEE, Mr. James Richard Francis, BEng ACA *2003;* Flat 50, Sullivan House, Churchill Gardens, LONDON, SW1V 3BP.
LEE, Miss. Janet Bui See, MSc BSc ACA *2006;* Flat 100, Paramount Court, 41 University Street, LONDON, WC1E 6JW.
LEE, Mrs. Janet Mary, BA ACA *1997;* 9 Matthew Street, GRANGE, SA 5022, AUSTRALIA.
LEE, Miss. Jennifer, ACA *2010;* Apartment 98, Britannia Mills, 11 Hulme Hall Road, MANCHESTER, M15 4LB.
LEE, Miss. Jennifer Chow Chiw, BA ACA *2003;* 19 Rosedale Road, LONDON, E7 8AU.
LEE, Mrs. Jennifer Louise, BA ACA *2005;* 28 Old Dover Road, LIVERPOOL, L36 4PZ.
LEE, Ms. Jennifer Yuan-Ching, ACA *2007;* Sapientnitro, 8 Spital Square, LONDON, E1 6DU.
LEE, Mrs. Jennifer Yuet Ying, BSc ACA *1993;* Sumitomo Trust & Banking Co Ltd, 155 Bishopsgate, LONDON, EC2M 3XU.
LEE, Mr. Jeremy Stephen William, MA ACA *1988;* 10 Hodge Fold, Moss LaneBroadbottom, HYDE, SK14 6BL.

LEE, Mr. Jick Seng Jason, ACA *2007;* 17th Floor, Flat C, Tower 2 Jupiter Terrace, 18 Jupiter Street, NORTH POINT, HONG KONG ISLAND HONG KONG SAR.

LEE, Mr. Jit Tong, BA ACA *1987;* 2 Marina Boulevard, No.41-03 The Sail at Marina Bay, SINGAPORE 018987, SINGAPORE.

LEE, Mrs. Joanna, BSc(Hons) ACA *2002;* Kent County Council Sessions House, County Road, MAIDSTONE, ME14 1XQ.

LEE, Mr. Joey Joseph, BSc ACA *2001;* Flat A8, 277 Prince Edward Road, MONG KOK, KOWLOON, HONG KONG SAR.

LEE, Mr. Johann Sze-Tchian, LLB ACA *1999;* 17 Sandover House, 124 Spa Road, LONDON, SE16 3FD.

LEE, Mr. John, ACA *2010;* Flat 408, Sidney Webb House, 159 Great Dover Street, LONDON, SE1 4WW.

•LEE, Mr. John David, BA FCA *1983;* (Tax Fac), Lee Accounting Services Limited, 26 High Street, RICKMANSWORTH, HERTFORDSHIRE, WD3 1ER.

LEE, Mr. John Graham, BA FCA *1979;* Quintiles Ltd, Station House, Market Street, BRACKNELL, BERKSHIRE, RG12 1HX.

•LEE, Mr. John Hendrik Chadwick, FCA *1978;* Horsfields, Belgrave Place, 8 Manchester Rd, BURY, BL9 0ED.

LEE, Mr. John Philip Macarthur, LLB FCA *1971;* Howard de Walden Estates Ltd, 23 Queen Anne Street, LONDON, W1G 9DL.

LEE, Lord John Robert Louis, DL FCA *1964;* House of Lords, Houses of Parliament, LONDON, SW1A 0PW.

LEE, Mr. Jonathan, BA ACA *2007;* 6 Ravensbury Terrace, LONDON, SW18 4RL.

LEE, Mr. Jonathan Charles Elliott, MA ACA *1996;* Uppingham School West Bank, 1 Stockerston Road Uppingham, OAKHAM, LE15 9UF.

LEE, Mr. Jonathan Howard Redvers, BA ACA *1990;* 23 East Sheen Avenue, LONDON, SW14 8AR.

LEE, Mr. Jonathan Pheng Kiang, BA FCA *1980;* 7 Ascot Rise, SINGAPORE 289819, SINGAPORE.

LEE, Mr. Jonathon Glyn, BSc ACA *2006;* KPMG, 8th floor, Princes Building, 10 Chater Road, CENTRAL, HONG KONG ISLAND HONG KONG SAR.

LEE, Mr. Jonathon Marcus, BSc ACA *1992;* Cooper Fulleon Llp, Llantar Park, CWMBRAN, NP44 3AW.

LEE, Mrs. Josephine Claire, BA ACA *2004;* 1 Langar Cottages, Main Street, Langar, NOTTINGHAM, NG13 9HE.

LEE, Miss. Julia Li Choo, ACA FCCA *1994;* Sherwood Towers, 3 Jalan Anak Bukit, No. 03-07, SINGAPORE 588998, SINGAPORE.

LEE, Mr. Julian, MA(Cantab) BA ACA *2011;* Flat 90, Amelia House, 11 Boulevard Drive, LONDON, NW9 5JQ.

LEE, Mr. Julian, MA ACA *1996;* 17 Hanover Sqare, Hanover Square, LONDON, W1S 1HU.

LEE, Mr. Julian Francis Kaines, FCA *1970;* 8 Aspen Court, Fairfield Road, EAST GRINSTEAD, WEST SUSSEX, RH19 4HG.

LEE, Mr. Julian Philip Nigel, BA ACA *1995;* Flat 25.03, Aragon Tower, George Beard Road, LONDON, SE8 3AL.

LEE, Mrs. Julie Lisa, BA ACA CTA *1999;* 44 Wellfield Road, Lindley, HUDDERSFIELD, HD3 4BJ.

LEE, Mrs. Juliet Emma, BSc ACA *1998;* Airlie, Lovel Road, Winkfield, WINDSOR, BERKSHIRE, SL4 2EU.

LEE, Mr. Ka Po, BA FCA *1987;* 18 Burlington Road, ALTRINCHAM, CHESHIRE, WA14 1HR.

LEE, Mr. Ka Yue Samuel, BA FCA *1986;* Flat A 53/F Tower 2, The Belchers, 89 Pokfulam Road, POK FU LAM, HONG KONG SAR.

LEE, Mr. Ka Fai, ACA *2007;* Allan Lee Professional solutions Limited, Flat B 10F Block 5, Grand Promenade, 38 Tai Wong Street, SAI WAN HO, HONG KONG SAR.

LEE, Ms. Ka Man, ACA *2008;* Lee Ka Man & Co, 10/F Hang Seng Wan chai Building, 200 Hennessy Road, WAN CHAI, HONG KONG SAR.

LEE, Dr. Ka Yam Danny, ACA *2007;* Flat G, 56th Floor Block One, The Belchers, 89 Po Fu Lam Road, POK FU LAM, HONG KONG ISLAND HONG KONG SAR.

LEE, Mr. Kam Kau, ACA *2007;* Flat A 59/F Tower 9, 8 King Ling Road Le Point, TSEUNG KWAN O, KOWLOON, HONG KONG SAR.

LEE, Mr. Kam Wah Edward, ACA *2007;* Flat 7, 22/F Block D, New Kwai Fong Gardens, 14 Kwai Yi Road, KWAI CHUNG, NEW TERRITORIES HONG KONG SAR.

LEE, Ms. Kam Fung Candi, ACA *2005;* Flat F 18/F, Tower One Sky Tower, 38 Sung Wong Toi Road, TO KWA WAN, KOWLOON, HONG KONG SAR.

LEE, Mr. Kan Fatt, ACA *1983;* 9 Brookgreene Crescent, RICHMOND HILL L4C 0M1, ON, CANADA.

LEE, Miss. Karen Frances, BA ACA *1984;* 7 Montagu Gardens, CHELMSFORD, CM1 6EB.

•LEE, Mrs. Karen Jane, BSc(Hons) ACA *2001;* Wilkins Kennedy, Globe Offices, Philomel Street, STANLEY, FALKLAND ISLANDS.

LEE, Miss. Katherine Anne Francis, BSc FCA *2000;* 27 Vale Road, LONDON, N4 1QA.

LEE, Miss. Kathryn Jane, ACA *1988;* W H Marriage & Sons Ltd Chelmer Mills, New Street, CHELMSFORD, CM1 1PN.

LEE, Mrs. Katy, BA ACA *2003;* Red Cottage, Branksome Park Road, CAMBERLEY, GU15 2AE.

LEE, Mrs. Kaye, BA ACA CTA *2006;* 23 Jamestown Way, LONDON, E14 2DE.

LEE, Mr. Kee Hang, ACA *2007;* Flat 14B, Way Man Court, 50-52 Village Road, HAPPY VALLEY, HONG KONG ISLAND, HONG KONG SAR.

LEE, Mr. Keen Pong, ACA *2010;* No 1 Jalan Aman Perdana, 7J/KU5 Taman Aman Perdana, 41050 KLANG, SELANGOR, MALAYSIA.

LEE, Ms. Kei Fong Jennifer, ACA *2007;* 9D Hilltop, 60 Cloud View Road, NORTH POINT, HONG KONG ISLAND, HONG KONG SAR.

LEE, Mr. Kenneth Arthur, FCA *1949;* 12 Whitland Avenue, Heaton, BOLTON, BL1 5FB. (Life Member)

LEE, Mr. Kenneth Hon Leong, ACA *1985;* Lee Financial Management P/L, 18 Grevillea Cresent, HORNSBY, NSW 2077, AUSTRALIA.

•LEE, Mr. Kevin Howard, FCA *1984;* with RSM Tenon Limited, Vantage, Victoria Street, BASINGSTOKE, RG21 3BT.

LEE, Mr. Khai Fatt Kyle, MBA BA DIC ACA *1980;* Flat 38, Central Building, 3 Matthew Parker Street, LONDON, SW1H 9NE.

LEE, Mr. Khim Sin, FCA *1969;* Ground Floor Lot 2764 Block 10 Lorong Tun Ahmad Zaidi Adruce 12, 93150 KUCHING, SARAWAK, MALAYSIA.

LEE, Mr. Kim Sun, FCA *1980;* 2-19A Penthouse-Rembia, Faber Ria Jalan Desa, Sentosa, Taman Desa, 58100 KUALA LUMPUR, FEDERAL TERRITORY MALAYSIA.

LEE, Mr. Kim Yan, BSc FCA *1985;* Lee Corporatehouse Associates, No 11, 1st Floor, Regent Square, Simpang 150, BANDAR SERI BEGAWAN BRUNEI DARUSSALAM.

LEE, Miss. Kimberley Jane, ACA *2008;* Adlestrop Goose Lane, Lower Quinton, STRATFORD-UPON-AVON, CV37 8SZ.

LEE, Mr. Kin Arthur, ACA *2004;* Meiya Power Company Limited, 15/F Harbour Centre, 25 Harbour Road, WAN CHAI, HONG KONG ISLAND, HONG KONG SAR.

LEE, Mr. Kin Fat, ACA *2008;* GPO Box 7621, General Post Office, CENTRAL, HONG KONG ISLAND, HONG KONG SAR.

LEE, Mr. King Chaw, ACA *1981;* 54 Keightley Road, Shenton Park, PERTH, WA 6008, AUSTRALIA.

LEE, Mr. King Chung Roger, ACA *2008;* Roger K C Lee & Co, Room 1109, 11/F, 118 Connaught Road West, SAI YING POON, HONG KONG ISLAND HONG KONG SAR.

LEE, Mr. King Lam, ACA *2005;* Unit 22, 1-5 Linda Street, HORNSBY, NSW 2077, AUSTRALIA.

LEE, Ms. Kit Ying, BA FCA *1982;* Room 801, Yue Shing Commerical Building, 15-16 Queen Victoria Street, CENTRAL, HONG KONG ISLAND, HONG KONG SAR.

LEE, Mr. Kit Wah, ACA *2007;* Katon CPA Limited, Office B, 21st Floor, Legend Tower, 7 Shing Yip Street, KWUN TONG KOWLOON HONG KONG SAR.

LEE, Mr. Kok Hooi, FCA *1992;* 50 University Walk, University Park, SINGAPORE 297757, SINGAPORE.

LEE, Mr. Kok Keong Peter, FCA *1983;* 9 Fellowship Link, ATWELL, WA 6164, AUSTRALIA.

LEE, Mr. Kong Beng, BSc FCA *1978;* 1G Jalan Ru 3, Bandar Baru Air Itam, 11500 PENANG, MALAYSIA.

LEE, Mr. Kong Eng, BA ACA *1985;* 20 Lorong Utara, 46200 PETALING JAYA, SELANGOR, MALAYSIA.

LEE, Mr. Kong Wai Conway, ACA *2007;* A9 Europa Garden, 48 Kwu Tung Rd, SHEUNG SHUI, NEW TERRITORIES, HONG KONG SAR.

LEE, Mr. Koon Yan, ACA *2008;* Flat C 40/F, Block 11, Royal Ascot, SHA TIN, NEW TERRITORIES, HONG KONG SAR.

LEE, Mr. Kuan-Yong, BSc ACA *1981;* 34 Jalan BU 11/8, Bandar Utama, 47800 PETALING JAYA, SELANGOR, MALAYSIA.

LEE, Mr. Kwan Ho Jason, BA ACA *2006;* Flat E, 18/F Wilton Place, 18 Park Road, MID LEVELS, HONG KONG ISLAND, HONG KONG SAR.

LEE, Mr. Kwan Por, BSc FCA *1991;* 12-1 Jalan Sri Hartamas 8, Taman Sri Hartamas, 50480 KUALA LUMPUR, FEDERAL TERRITORY, MALAYSIA.

LEE, Mr. Kwok Keung, BSc ACA *1991;* Flat F 1/F, Tower 22 Parc Oasis, 28 Grandeur Road, YAU YAT TSUEN, KOWLOON, HONG KONG SAR.

LEE, Mr. Kwok Ming, ACA *2008;* Room 212, Block M, Kornhill, QUARRY BAY, HONG KONG SAR.

LEE, Mr. Kwok Wai, ACA *2008;* Flat A 2nd Floor, Golden Block, 12 Cassia Road, YAU YAT TSUEN, KOWLOON, HONG KONG SAR.

LEE, Ms. Lai Lan, ACA *2007;* 17A Block 15, Laguna City, Cha Kwo Ling, KWUN TONG, KOWLOON, HONG KONG SAR.

LEE, Miss. Lai Leng, BA ACA *2000;* 55 Pinggir Zaaba, Taman Tun Dr Ismail, 60000 KUALA LUMPUR, FEDERAL TERRITORY, MALAYSIA.

LEE, Ms. Lai Ngor, ACA *2007;* Unit 9 45-47 Cornelia Road, TOONGABBIE, NSW 2146, AUSTRALIA.

LEE, Ms. Lai Chu, ACA *2005;* Flat 9 A&B, Block 6 The Premier, Chianti, DISCOVERY BAY, NEW TERRITORIES, HONG KONG SAR.

LEE, Ms. Lai Mui Kimmy, ACA *2007;* 3811 Kwong Sui House, Kwong Ming Court, TSEUNG KWAN O, NEW TERRITORIES, HONG KONG SAR.

LEE, Ms. Lai Ping Lillian, ACA *2008;* Room 802, Block E Healthy Gardens, 560 Kings Road, NORTH POINT, HONG KONG ISLAND, HONG KONG SAR.

LEE, Mr. Lap Bong Albert, ACA *2008;* Flat 2 6/F, Block B, YY Mansions, 96 Pokfulam Road, POK FU LAM, HONG KONG ISLAND HONG KONG SAR.

LEE, Mr. Laurence John, MA ACA *1997;* 2 Sanders Close, STANSTED, ESSEX, CM24 8GY.

LEE, Mr. Lawrence, BA ACA *1994;* Flat G21st Floor Block 6, Serenity Park TAI PO, New Territories, HONG KONG SAR.

LEE, Mr. Lawrence Cheow Hock, FCA *1976;* 35 Mount Sinai Rise, #04-03 Village Tower, SINGAPORE 276955, SINGAPORE.

LEE, Mr. Lawrence Chun Wo, BSc ACA *1990;* Flat 11 B, Woodbury Court, 137 Pokfulam Road, POK FU LAM, HONG KONG ISLAND, HONG KONG SAR.

LEE, Mr. Lee King, ACA *1980;* Mazars LLP, 133 Cecil Street, Apt.15-02 Keck Seng Tower, SINGAPORE 048545, SINGAPORE.

LEE, Miss. Li Ming, BSc ACA *1992;* 30 Jalan Bentara 6, Taman Iskandar, Johor Malaysia, 80050 JOHOR BAHRU, MALAYSIA.

LEE, Miss. Lisa Yin San, BA ACA *2011;* 39 Jacklin Drive, Finham, COVENTRY, CV3 6QG.

LEE, Mr. Lok, BSc(Econ) FCA *1974;* 9 - 48 Montreal Street, VICTORIA V8V 1Y5, BC, CANADA.

LEE, Miss. Lucy, BSc(Hons) ACA *2010;* 9 Nightingale Gardens, RUGBY, WARWICKSHIRE, CV23 0WT.

LEE, Mr. Luen Wai John, ACA *2005;* 70 Tai Hang Road, Flat 29B Trafalgar Court, TAI HANG, HONG KONG ISLAND, HONG KONG SAR.

LEE, Mrs. Lynda, ACA *1992;* with Dyke Yaxley Limited, 1 Brassey Road, Old Potts Way, SHREWSBURY, SY3 7FA.

LEE, Mr. Malcolm Stuart, FCA *1970;* Hook Cottage, Askett, PRINCES RISBOROUGH, BUCKINGHAMSHIRE, HP27 9LT. (Life Member)

LEE, Mr. Man Po, ACA *2004;* CLL CPA Limited, Suite A, 8/F Ritz Plaza, 122 Austin Road, TSIM SHA TSUI, KOWLOON HONG KONG SAR.

LEE, Miss. Man-Ching, ACA *2011;* 8 Village Close, SKELMERSDALE, LANCASHIRE, WN8 8BF.

LEE, Miss. Margaret, ACA *2011;* 7 The Edge Apartments, Glenville Grove, LONDON, SE8 4AJ.

LEE, Mr. Mark Nigel, FCA CTA MMC *1982;* (Member of Council 2003 - 2005), (Tax Fac), Upper Gallilee, 6 Oakleigh Road, PINNER, MIDDLESEX, HA5 4HB.

LEE, Mr. Mark Samuel Wilton, BSc FCA *1988;* 31 Shreres Dyche, WARWICK, CV34 6BX.

LEE, Mr. Martin, BSc ACA MCT *1990;* 106 South Norwood Hill, LONDON, SE25 6AQ.

LEE, Mr. Martin Bernard, BA ACA *1984;* Crown Eyeglass plc, Glenfield Park, Blakewater Rd, BLACKBURN, BB1 5QH.

LEE, Mr. Martin John, FCA *1975;* Fillis Cottage, The Street, Kingston, LEWES, BN7 3NT.

LEE, Mr. Martin Richard, BSc FCA *1975;* Colston Lodge Langar Lane, Langar, NOTTINGHAM, NG13 9HA.

LEE, Mr. Matthew, ACA *2009;* Roseacre, Kingsdown Park, WHITSTABLE, KENT, CT5 2DT.

•LEE, Mr. Matthew Duncan, FCA *1986;* Bishop Fleming, 16 Queen Square, BRISTOL, BS1 4NT.

LEE, Ms. May Lun Janice, ACA *2006;* Flat F 29/F, Tower 32 South Horizons, AP LEI CHAU, HONG KONG SAR.

LEE, Ms. May Yee, ACA *2008;* Flat 50B, Tower 12, Park Central, TSEUNG KWAN O, KOWLOON, HONG KONG SAR.

LEE, Ms. Mee Kwan Helena, ACA *2008;* Ernst & Young, 18/F, Two International Finance Centre, 8 Finance Street, CENTRAL, HONG KONG ISLAND HONG KONG SAR.

LEE, Miss. Mei, BSc ACA *2001;* 171 Stanhope Street, LONDON, NW1 3LR.

LEE, Ms. Mei Mei Linda, ACA *2007;* 18 H Block 2, Flora Plaza, 88 Pak Wo Road, FANLING, NEW TERRITORIES, HONG KONG SAR.

LEE, Mr. Melvin Hong Teik, FCA *1977;* Filtrona Plc, Avebury House, 201-249 Avebury Boulevard, MILTON KEYNES, MK9 1AU.

LEE, Mr. Meng Seong, ACA *2009;* Flat 11 Melville Court, Croft Street, LONDON, SE8 5DR.

LEE, Mr. Michael Ashton, LLB FCA *1997;* Airlie, Lovel Road, Winkfield, WINDSOR, BERKSHIRE, SL4 2EU.

LEE, Mr. Michael Chun Wai, BSc ACA *1992;* Meggitt Unit 19, Eyncourt Road Woodside Estate, DUNSTABLE, BEDFORDSHIRE, LU5 4TS.

LEE, Mr. Michael George, FCA *1953;* Ave. du Moulin 3, 1110 MORGES, SWITZERLAND. (Life Member)

•LEE, Mr. Michael John, FCA *1977;* (Tax Fac), Certax Accounting, Charwell House Business Centre, Wilsom Road, ALTON, HAMPSHIRE, GU34 2PP.

LEE, Miss. Millie Mui Huang, BA ACA *1990;* 335 Bukit Timah Road, 26-02 Wing on Life Garden, SINGAPORE 259718, SINGAPORE.

LEE, Datin Millie Siew Kim, FCA *1976;* Kenanga Investment Bank Berhad, Kenanga International, Jalan Sultan Ismail, 50250 KUALA LUMPUR, FEDERAL TERRITORY, MALAYSIA.

LEE, Miss. Min Joo, ACA *2009;* Junggu Sindang3dong Namsan town Apt 17-1302, SEOUL, 100-754, KOREA REPUBLIC OF.

LEE, Mr. Ming Peter, BSc ACA *1996;* Finance Transformation B523, Land Rover Banbury Road, Gaydon, WARWICK, CV35 0RR.

LEE, Mr. Ming San, MA BA ACA *1990;* 81 Kheam Hock Road, SINGAPORE 298838, SINGAPORE.

LEE, Miss. Ming-Li, ACA *2010;* Flat 1/A Foundling Court, Brunswick Centre, LONDON, WC1N 1AN.

LEE, Miss. Moon Yin, BSc(Hons) ACA *2004;* 41 Jalan Batai, Damansara Heights, 50490 KUALA LUMPUR, FEDERAL TERRITORY, MALAYSIA.

•LEE, Miss. Natasha, BA(Hons) ACA CF *2002;* Nexia Smith & Williamson Audit Limited, Portwall Place, Portwall Lane, BRISTOL, BS1 6NA. See also Smith & Williamson Ltd and Nexia Audit Limited

LEE, Mr. Nicholas, BA ACA *1988;* Stables Mayfield Road, Frant, TUNBRIDGE WELLS, TN3 9HS.

LEE, Mr. Nicholas James, BA ACA *1995;* 5 Garratts Lane, BANSTEAD, SM7 2DZ.

LEE, Mr. Nicholas John, FCA *1965;* 31 St. Clairs Road, St. Osyth, CLACTON-ON-SEA, CO16 8QQ.

LEE, Mr. Nicholas Patrick, BA ACA *1998;* 9 Matthew Street, GRANGE, SA 5022, AUSTRALIA.

LEE, Mr. Nicholas Richard Wilton, BA ACA *1985;* 15 Half Moon Court, Bartholomew Close, LONDON, EC1A 7HF.

LEE, Mrs. Nicole Shun-Li, BA FCA *1990;* H S B C, 8-16 Canada Square, LONDON, E14 5HQ.

LEE, Mr. Nigel Bruce, BSc ACA *2003;* 181 Tanjong Rhu Road, #05-18 Sanctuary Green, SINGAPORE 436922, SINGAPORE.

LEE, Mr. Nigel Jeffrey, BA ACA *1978;* 28 Dunkeld Road, Talbot Woods, BOURNEMOUTH, BH3 7EW.

•LEE, Mr. Nigel Ronald, BA FCA *1988;* CFO Solutions Limited, 47 Maplehurst Road, CHICHESTER, WEST SUSSEX, PO19 6QL.

LEE, Ms. Nim Mui Virginia, ACA *2008;* Unit 105, 19-23 Herbert Street, ST LEONARDS, NSW 2065, AUSTRALIA.

LEE, Mr. Nixon Kok Fai, MA ACA *1997;* 34 Gospel Lane, Manor Park, Acocks Green, BIRMINGHAM, B27 7AA.

LEE, Miss. Pamela, BA(Hons) ACA *2002;* 19 North Weald Close, HORNCHURCH, ESSEX, RM12 5AQ.

•LEE, Mr. Patrick William, FCA *1980;* (Tax Fac), Ashdown Hurrey LLP, 20 Havelock Road, HASTINGS, EAST SUSSEX, TN34 1BP.

•LEE, Mrs. Patsy, BA ACA *1988;* Lee Accounting Services Limited, 26 High Street, RICKMANSWORTH, HERTFORDSHIRE, WD3 1ER.

LEE, Mr. Paul Allan, BSc ACA *1989;* Domestic & General Services Ltd Swan Court, 11 Worple Road, LONDON, SW19 4JS.
LEE, Mr. Paul Anthony, BSc FCA *1985;* (Tax Fac), 10 Kent Folly, Warfield, BRACKNELL, RG42 3UB.
LEE, Mr. Paul Francis, BSc FCA *1982;* 7 Heol Y Coed, Rhiwbina, CARDIFF, CF14 6HP.
LEE, Mr. Paul John, BA ACA *2004;* George Hammond Plc, Aycliffe Business Centre, Archcliffe Road, DOVER, KENT, CT17 9EL.
LEE, Mr. Peng Khoon, FCA *1978;* Integrated Petroleum Services Sdn Bhd, Suite E Level 9, Tower 2 Etiqa Twins, 11 Jalan Pinang, 50450 KUALA LUMPUR, FEDERAL TERRITORY MALAYSIA.
LEE, Mr. Peng Ling, FCA *1977;* 74 Jalan Ping Pong 13/19, 40100 SHAH ALAM, SELANGOR, MALAYSIA.
LEE, Mr. Peter, FCA *1955;* 1 Grey Turrett, Manor Road, SIDMOUTH, DEVON, EX10 8RP. (Life Member)
LEE, Mr. Peter Andrew, BA FCA *1980;* 16 St. Andrews Park Road, Southborough, TUNBRIDGE WELLS, TN4 0NL.
•LEE, Mr. Peter John, FCA *1962;* (Tax Fac), Musket Lane Enterprises Limited, Autumn Cottage, Musket Lane, Hollingbourne, MAIDSTONE, KENT ME17 1UY.
LEE, Mr. Peter Ting-Pong, BA ACA *1994;* A1/ 19F Dragon Court, Dragon Terrace, Tin Hau, CAUSEWAY BAY, HONG KONG ISLAND, HONG KONG SAR.
•ⒹLEE, Mr. Philip, FCA *1972;* Lee & Company, Crown House, Armley Road, LEEDS, LS12 2EJ.
•LEE, Mr. Phillip, ACA *1978;* (Tax Fac), Moss & Williamson, 11 Stamford Street, STALYBRIDGE, SK15 1JP. See also Moss & Williamson Ltd
LEE, Ms. Ping Ping, BSc ACA *1994;* Apartment 704 Block B, Queens Garden, 9 Old Peak Road, MID LEVELS, HONG KONG SAR.
LEE, Mr. Ping Shih, FCA *1974;* 8A Orange Grove Road, #19-01 D'Grove Villas, SINGAPORE 258343, SINGAPORE.
LEE, Mr. Ping Kai, ACA *2005;* Flat B 31/F Tower 2, Tierra Verde, 33 Tsing King Road, TSING YI, NEW TERRITORIES, HONG KONG SAR.
LEE, Mr. Po On, ACA *2006;* Flat 12, 2nd Floor, Peak Gardens, 18 Mount Austin Road, THE PEAK, HONG KONG SAR.
LEE, Miss. Polly-Bo Yee, BSc ACA *1991;* Flat B 14th Floor, Tower 4, Hillsborough Court, 18 Old Peak Road, MID LEVELS, HONG KONG ISLAND HONG KONG SAR.
LEE, Mrs. Rachel Christine, BSc(Hons) ACA *2000;* 12 Wenlock Road, SALE, CHESHIRE, M33 3TR.
LEE, Mr. Raymond, FCA *1974;* 7C Woodland Heights, 2 Wong Nei Chung Gap Road, WONG NAI CHUNG GAP, Hong Kong Island, HONG KONG SAR.
LEE, Mr. Raymond Allan, FCA *1956;* 12 Cove Drive, Silverdale, CARNFORTH, LANCASHIRE, LA5 0SD. (Life Member)
LEE, Mr. Raymond Leonard Hoi Him, BCom FCA *1981;* Flat 2, 12th Floor, Block E., Villa Monte Rosa, 41A Stubbs Road, HAPPY VALLEY HONG KONG ISLAND HONG KONG SAR.
LEE, Mr. Redmond John, FCA *1974;* 2 South View Cottages, Newchapel Road, LINGFIELD, SURREY, RH7 6BG.
LEE, Mr. Richard, FCA *1979;* Northbound Management Consultants, 2 Dunkirk Terrace, CORBRIDGE, NORTHUMBERLAND, NE45 5AQ.
LEE, Mr. Richard Anthony, BSc FCA *1980;* with Deloitte & Touche LLP, 30 Wellington Street West, PO Box 400, Stn Commerce Court, TORONTO M5L 1B1, ON CANADA.
LEE, Mr. Richard John, BSc ACA *1987;* Glyn Iddens, Leddington, LEDBURY, HEREFORDSHIRE, HR8 2LG.
LEE, Mr. Richard Michael, BA ACA *1992;* Nations House, 103 Wigmore Street, LONDON, W1U 1WH.
LEE, Mr. Richard Philip, BA ACA *2006;* Morden Estates Co, The Estate Office, Charborough Park, WAREHAM, DORSET, BH20 7EN.
LEE, Mr. Robert Christopher, BSc ACA *1996;* 20 Wellington Street, Edgbaston, BIRMINGHAM, B15 2EQ.
LEE, Mr. Robert Edward, ACA *1997;* 111 Castle Rock Drive, RICHMOND HILL L4C5W4, ON, CANADA.
LEE, Mr. Robert James, ACA *2011;* 18 Cowper Road, WORTHING, WEST SUSSEX, BN11 4PD.
LEE, Mr. Robert James, BSc ACA *2006;* 18 Earlsfield Road, LIVERPOOL, L15 5BZ.
LEE, Mr. Robert John, ACA *2009;* 28 Vernon Avenue, BIRMINGHAM, B20 1DF.
LEE, Mr. Robert Jon, BSc(Hons) ACA *2001;* 34 Golden Hind Drive, STOURPORT-ON-SEVERN, WORCESTERSHIRE, DY13 9RJ.
LEE, Mr. Robert Poi Keong, FCA MIIA CMIIA *1984;* 10 Jalan Matahari, Off Jalan Raya Barat, 41100 KLANG, SELANGOR, MALAYSIA.
LEE, Mr. Robert William, ACA *2008;* 21 Ramsey House, St. Johns Walk, YORK, YO31 7SG.
•LEE, Mr. Robin, FCA *1969;* (Tax Fac), Pearson Jones plc, Clayton Wood Close, West Park Ring Road, LEEDS, LS16 6QE.
•LEE, Mr. Robin Charles, BSc FCA *1992;* Streets, Suite 27, The Quadrant, 99 Parkway Avenue, Parkway Business Park, SHEFFIELD S9 4WG. See also Streets LLP
LEE, Mr. Robin Win-Suern, BSc ACA *2001;* 233 St. Davids Square, LONDON, E14 3WE.
LEE, Mr. Roger Barry, FCA *1984;* Bourne Leisure Group Ltd, 1 Park Lane, HEMEL HEMPSTEAD, HERTFORDSHIRE, HP2 4YL.
•LEE, Mr. Roger David, FCA *1975;* (Tax Fac), Lees Limited, The Granary, Brewer Street, Bletchingley, REDHILL, RH1 4QP. See also Lees
LEE, Mr. Roger Douglas, MA FCA *1979;* 62 Bedgrove, AYLESBURY, HP21 7BD.
LEE, Mr. Roger Francis, MSc FCA *1977;* 48 Champion Street, BRIGHTON, VIC 3186, AUSTRALIA.
LEE, Mr. Roger John Medley, FCA *1972;* 9 Grasmere Road, SALE, M33 3QU.
LEE, Mr. Roger Leonard, BSc FCA *1992;* 21F Branksome Crest, 3a Tregunter Path, MID LEVELS, HONG KONG SAR.
LEE, Mr. Roger Murray, MA ACA *2001;* 14 Elms Road, LONDON, SW4 9EX.
LEE, Mr. Ronald Ernest, FCA *1948;* 15 Brandy Hole Lane, CHICHESTER, WEST SUSSEX, PO19 5RL. (Life Member)
LEE, Mr. Rupert, BCom ACA *2007;* Flat 8 Christchurch Court, Willesden Lane, LONDON, NW6 7XF.
LEE, Mr. Ryan Matthew, BA(Hons) ACA *2003;* 109 Acorn Walk, LONDON, SE16 5DX.
LEE, Mrs. Sally Yoon Ping, FCA *1976;* 11/F EastSavoy Court, 101 Robinson Road MID LEVELS, Hong Kong Island, HONG KONG SAR.
LEE, Mr. Samuel Byung Jin, BSc(Econ) FCA *1998;* 7 Marshalswick Lane, ST. ALBANS, HERTFORDSHIRE, AL1 4UR.
LEE, Mrs. San Hem, FCA *1977;* 2 Jalan Setiabakti 3, Damansara Heights, 50490 KUALA LUMPUR, FEDERAL TERRITORY, MALAYSIA.
LEE, Mrs. Sandra Elizabeth, BSc ACA *1986;* Highwood, Duddenhoe End, SAFFRON WALDEN, CB11 4UT.
LEE, Mr. Sandy Shei Lam, MSc BSc ACA *2009;* Cherry House, The Avenue, LYMM, CHESHIRE, WA13 0SU.
LEE, Miss. Sarah Elizabeth, BA ACA *2005;* 30 Spencer Road, WELLINGBOROUGH, NORTHAMPTONSHIRE, NN8 2QB.
LEE, Ms. Sau Kuen Doris, ACA *2008;* Flat C, 21/F Tower 2, Hampton Place, 11 Hoi Fan Road, TAI KOK TSUI, KOWLOON HONG KONG SAR.
LEE, Mr. Seang Seng, FCA *1982;* 2 Jalan 16/16, 46350, PETALING JAYA, Selangor, MALAYSIA.
LEE, Mr. See Ho, BSc ACA *2009;* Cae Hir, Bryn y Bia Road, LLANDUDNO, GWYNEDD, LL30 3AY.
LEE, Mr. Sen-Choon, FCA *1980;* 371 Beach Road #09-06, KeyPoint, SINGAPORE 199597, SINGAPORE.
LEE, Mr. Seng Cheong, FCA *1973;* 41 Lucky View, SINGAPORE 467473, SINGAPORE.
LEE, Mr. Seng Chow, BA ACA *1993;* 8F Block 1Scenic Villas, 18 Scenic Villa Drive, POK FU LAM, HONG KONG ISLAND, HONG KONG SAR.
LEE, Mr. Seng-Chee, BSc ACA *2001;* 2 UPPER BUKIT TIMAH VIEW, SINGAPORE 588138, SINGAPORE.
LEE, Miss. Shall Hui, ACA *2008;* Blk 172 Gangsa Road unit 10 -18, Singapore 670172, SINGAPORE, SINGAPORE.
LEE, Miss. Sheila, MSc BSc ACA *2008;* 20 Buile Drive, Blackley, MANCHESTER, M9 6BD.
LEE, Mr. Sheung Wah, ACA *2006;* Flat C 15/F, 75 Broadway, MEI FOO SUN CHUEN, KOWLOON, HONG KONG SAR.
LEE, Mr. Sheung Yiu, ACA *2008;* Flat H, 31/F, Block two, The Belcher's, 89 Pok Fu Lam Road, POK FU LAM HONG KONG ISLAND HONG KONG SAR.
LEE, Miss. Shi Ruh, BSc FCA *1993;* 98 SURIN AVENUE, SINGAPORE 535666, SINGAPORE.
LEE, Mr. Siang Chin, FCA *1973;* 31-1-1 Intan Kenny, Persiaran Bukit Tunku, Bukit Tunku, 50480 KUALA LUMPUR, FEDERAL TERRITORY, MALAYSIA.
LEE, Mrs. Siew Choo, FCA *1966;* 1-3-2 Horizon Towers, 1 Tanjong Bungah Park, 11200 PENANG, MALAYSIA.
LEE, Mr. Sik Nin Sydney, ACA *2004;* The Royal Bank of Scotland N.V. (Canada Branch), 79 Wellington Street West, Suite 1610, TORONTO M5K 1G8, ON, CANADA.
LEE, Mr. Sik Wai Benjamin, ACA *2005;* Lee Sik Wai & Co, Offices 1612-17, Hollywood Plaza, 610 Nathan Road, Kowloon, MONG KOK HONG KONG SAR.
LEE, Mr. Simon, ACA *2007;* H S B C, 62-76 Park Street, LONDON, SE1 9DZ.
LEE, Mr. Simon Andrew, ACA *1990;* 66 Highland Road, EMSWORTH, PO10 7JN.
LEE, Mr. Simon Christopher, BA ACA *1989;* Moorlands, Harrow Road West, DORKING, RH4 3BH.
LEE, Mr. Simon Edward Redvers, BA FCA *1992;* 17 High Ridge Way, SHREWSBURY, SY3 6DJ.
LEE, Mr. Simon Kuan Chieh, LLB ACA *2004;* 7/ 6-8 Ross Street, GLADESVILLE, NSW 2111, AUSTRALIA.
LEE, Mr. Simon Nicholas, FCA *1968;* Cueva Pagan 32, La Pinilla, Fuente Alamo, 30335 MURCIA, SPAIN.
LEE, Mr. Simon Philip, BA ACA *1996;* 9 Woodfield Road, SOLIHULL, B91 2DW.
LEE, Ms. Sin Chi, ACA *2008;* 5 D Garve Court, Perth Garden, 9 Perth Street, HO MAN TIN, HONG KONG SAR.
LEE, Mr. Sing Fung, ACA *2007;* Whampoa Garden, Site 2 Cherry Mansions, Block 7 Flat 9/c, HUNG HOM, KOWLOON, HONG KONG SAR.
LEE, Ms. Siu Mei, ACA *2007;* Flat 9G, Block 13A, South Horizons, AP LEI CHAU, HONG KONG ISLAND, HONG KONG SAR.
LEE, Mr. Siu Leung, ACA *2008;* S L Lee & Lau CPA Limited, Room 1702, 17/F, Tung Hip Commercial Building, 248 Des Voeux Road, CENTRAL HONG KONG SAR.
LEE, Mr. Siu Wai Patrick, ACA *2005;* Flat B 11/F Block 5, Majestic Park, 11 Farm Road, TO KWA WAN, KOWLOON, HONG KONG SAR.
LEE, Ms. Siu Yin, ACA *2007;* Room H 28/F. Block 5, Sceneway Garden, LAM TIN, KOWLOON, HONG KONG SAR.
LEE, Mr. Soo Hoon, FCA *1969;* Phillip Lee Management Consultants Pte Ltd, Blk 166 Woodlands St 13, Apartment 02-521, SINGAPORE 730166, SINGAPORE. See also Evan Wong & Co, Ee Peng Liang & Co (Life Member)
LEE, Mr. Spencer Tien-Chye, FCA *1975;* No 6 Greenleaf Drive, SINGAPORE 1027, SINGAPORE.
LEE, Mr. Stephen Hoi Yin, BA ACA *1987;* KPMG, 8/F Prince's Building, 10 Chater Road, CENTRAL, HONG KONG ISLAND, HONG KONG SAR.
LEE, Mr. Stephen Michael, BA ACA *1990;* 2 James Terrace, Church Path, Mortlake, LONDON, SW14 8HB.
LEE, Mr. Stephen Richard, BA ACA *1982;* Capstone Mortgage Services Ltd, 4th floor, Royal London House, 22-25 Finsbury Square, LONDON, EC2A 1DX.
LEE, Mr. Steve Wing Kin, BA ACA *1997;* 140 Park Avenue, ORPINGTON, KENT, BR6 9EE.
LEE, Mr. Stuart Anthony, BSc FCA *1983;* Trudy Lee Ltd Unit 3, Devonshire Business Centre Cranborne Road, POTTERS BAR, HERTFORDSHIRE, EN6 3JR.
LEE, Miss. Su Shyan Jeanette, BSc ACA *1994;* 4 Derbyshire Road, Apt 13-06 Ultra Mansion, SINGAPORE, SINGAPORE.
LEE, Ms. Suk Kan, ACA *2006;* Treasury HK Government, Room 3113, 31/F Immigration Tower, Gloucester Road, WAN CHAI, HONG KONG SAR.
LEE, Miss. Susan Elizabeth, BA ACA *1992;* 3 Robotham Close, Narborough, LEICESTER, LE19 2RH.
LEE, Ms. Susanna Yuk Wan, ACA *2007;* Flat 706, 7/F, Block D, Healthy Gardens, 560 King's Road, NORTH POINT HONG KONG SAR.
LEE, Mrs. Tania Anne, BSc ACA *1991;* The Old Post Office, Alderley, WOTTON-UNDER-EDGE, GL12 7QT.
LEE, Mr. Tat Cheung Vincent, ACA *2004;* Vincent Lee & Co., 1/F Xiu Ping Commercial Building, 104 Jervois Street, SHEUNG WAN, HONG KONG ISLAND, HONG KONG SAR.
•LEE, Mr. Teck Leong, FCA *1986;* Lee Teck Leong & Co, 47 Jalan Batai Laut 5, Kawasan 16, Taman Intan, 41300 KLANG, SELANGOR MALAYSIA.
ⒹLEE, Miss. Teresa Ellen, ACA *2010;* with Sanderlings LLP, Sanderling House, 1071 Warwick Road, Acocks Green, BIRMINGHAM, B27 6QT.
LEE, Mrs. Theresa Choe Choe, BA ACA *2000;* 3 Beech Avenue, Northenden, MANCHESTER, M22 4JE.
LEE, Mr. Thomas Cheuk Hang, BSc ACA *1992;* 30A 9th Floor Broadway Street, Mei Foo Sun Cheun, MEI FOO SUN CHUEN, KOWLOON, HONG KONG SAR.
LEE, Mr. Tian Seng, FCA *1973;* Flat 4, 47 Redington Rd, Hampstead, LONDON, NW3 7RA.
LEE, Mr. Timothy John, BSc FCA *1980;* 18 Great Molewood, HERTFORD, SG14 2PN.
LEE, Mr. Toby Siu Hang, BSc ACA *2010;* Flat 7 7 Blackthorn Avenue, Islington, LONDON, N7 8AJ.
LEE, Ms. Tsui Wa, ACA *2008;* Flat B, 19/F, Block 5, Verbena Heights, 8 Mau Tai Road, TSEUNG KWAN O KOWLOON HONG KONG SAR.
LEE, Mr. Tze Leung, ACA *2007;* 10/F, 378, Lai Chi Kok Road, LAI CHI KOK, KOWLOON, HONG KONG SAR.
LEE, Mr. Tze Leung, ACA *2008;* 23H, Block 2, Lai Bo Garden, 38 Cheung Wah Street, CHEUNG SHA WAN, KOWLOON HONG KONG SAR.
LEE, Miss. Valerie Margaret, BPharm ACA *1994;* 3 Lower Blakemere Road, Poundbury, DORCHESTER, DORSET, DT1 3RZ.
LEE, Miss. Velencia, BSc ACA *1991;* Flat 26a block 2, The Grand Panorama, 10 Robinson Road, MID LEVELS, HONG KONG ISLAND, HONG KONG SAR.
LEE, Mr. Victor Edmund, BSc ACA *1994;* Cleeveside, Hill Lane, Upper Brailes, BANBURY, OXFORDSHIRE, OX15 5AX.
LEE, Mrs. Victoria Louise, BSc FCA *1980;* K E Mathers & Co, Nethercroft, Upper Batley Lane, BATLEY, WEST YORKSHIRE, WF17 0AR.
LEE, Mr. Vincent Wei Gia, BSc FCA MBA AMCT *1992;* Block A 1201 Prima 16, 1 Jalan 16/18, 46350 PETALING JAYA, MALAYSIA.
LEE, Mr. Vivian, BSc ACIB FCA *1974;* C1 10/F Kingsford Gardens, 210 Tin Hau Temple Road, NORTH POINT, HONG KONG ISLAND, HONG KONG SAR.
LEE, Ms. Vivian Wai-Hang, BSc ACA *1992;* Flat 3D, Delite Court, Pictorial Garden Phase 2, 23 On King Street, SHA TIN, HONG KONG SAR.
LEE, Mr. Wah Ming, ACA *2011;* No. 513- A, Taman Sungai Ujong, Jalan Rasah, 70300, Seremban, 70300 SEREMBAN NEGERI SEMBILAN MALAYSIA.
LEE, Ms. Wai King Starry, ACA *2008;* Crowe Horwath(HK) CPA Limited, 34/F The Lee Gardens, 33 Hysan Avenue, CAUSEWAY BAY, HONG KONG SAR.
LEE, Ms. Wai Ling, ACA *2008;* Flat 01, 3/F, Block 23, Heng Fa Chuen, CHAI WAN, HONG KONG SAR.
LEE, Mr. Wai Lun, ACA *2008;* with Ernst & Young, 18/F, Two International Finance Centre, 8 Finance Street, CENTRAL, HONG KONG ISLAND HONG KONG SAR.
LEE, Mr. Wai Ming, ACA *2007;* Linkpath CPA Limited, 4/F HONG KONG SAR Trade Centre, 161-167 Des Voeux Road, CENTRAL, HONG KONG SAR.
LEE, Mr. Wai Ming Klampar, ACA *2008;* Unit 2706, 113 Argyle Street, MONG KOK, KOWLOON, HONG KONG SAR.
LEE, Ms. Wai Yee, ACA *2008;* 9H, Tower 2, Queen's Terrace, 1 Queen Street, SHEUNG WAN, HONG KONG SAR.
LEE, Ms. Wai Yee, ACA *2008;* Flat A 25/F, Tower 2, Aria Kowloon Peak, 51 Fung Shing Street, NGAU CHI WAN, HONG KONG ISLAND HONG KONG SAR.
LEE, Miss. Wanmone, BA(Hons) ACA *2001;* 27 Jalan Batai Barat, Damansara Heights, 50490 KUALA LUMPUR, FEDERAL TERRITORY, MALAYSIA.
LEE, Mr. Wayne Hung Wing, BSc(Hons) ACA MAAT *2010;* 15 Glentworth Drive, OSWESTRY, SHROPSHIRE, SY10 9JB.
LEE, Mr. William, BA ACA *1990;* 27 Holyrood Avenue, HARROW, MIDDLESEX, HA2 8UD.
LEE, Mr. William Meadowcroft, FCA *1954;* 24 Westwood Mews, LYTHAM ST. ANNES, LANCASHIRE, FY8 5QE. (Life Member)
LEE, Mr. Wing Yiu, ACA *2008;* Flat D, 26/F, Ko On Mansion, TAIKOO SHING, HONG KONG SAR.
LEE, Ms. Woon Ching Teresa, ACA *2008;* Flat A 14/F, Yen Men Building, 98-108 Jaffe Road, WAN CHAI, HONG KONG SAR.
LEE, Mr. Yat Kit Eric, ACA *2011;* with PricewaterhouseCoopers, 21/F Edinburgh Tower, 15 Queen's Road Central, CENTRAL, HONG KONG ISLAND, HONG KONG SAR.
LEE, Mr. Yee Kian, BA(Econ) ACA *2000;* 11F, BLOCK 2, TUNG CHUNG CRESCENT, TUNG CHUNG, HONG KONG SAR.
LEE, Mr. Yee Lam, BCom ACA *1984;* Great Eastern Life Assurance (M)Berhad, Level 7 Menara Great Eastern, 303 Jalan Ampang, 50450 KUALA LUMPUR, FEDERAL TERRITORY, MALAYSIA.

Members - Alphabetical LEE - LEES

LEE, Ms. Yee Lun, ACA *2008;* Flat H 9/F, Block 13, Chi Fu Fa Yuen, POK FU LAM, HONG KONG SAR.
LEE, Ms. Yee Min Helen, ACA *2005;* 893 King's Road, 14/F Flat C, QUARRY BAY, HONG KONG ISLAND, HONG KONG SAR.
LEE, Ms. Yee Wah, ACA *2005;* Flat B 13/F, Tower 5, Manhattan Hill, Lai Chi Kok, LAI CHI KOK, KOWLOON HONG KONG SAR.
LEE, Ms. Yeuk Lui Rosa, ACA *2007;* Flat 4B Woodbury Court, 137 Pok Fu Lam Road, POK FU LAM, HONG KONG ISLAND, HONG KONG SAR.
LEE, Ms. Yin Ming Rosanna, ACA *2007;* Rm J 17th Floor BLock 17, Charming Garden, MONG KOK, KOWLOON, HONG KONG SAR.
LEE, Mr. Ying Leong, BA ACA *2002;* 2C Duke Garden, 2 Duke Street, MONG KOK, KOWLOON, HONG KONG SAR.
LEE, Mr. Yiu Ming, ACA *2008;* Flat E 10/F, Gallant Court, 240-246 Prince Edward Road West, MONG KOK, KOWLOON, HONG KONG SAR.
•LEE, Mr. Yoke Hing, ACA *1979;* (Tax Fac), Lee Associates, 30 Malpas Drive, PINNER, MIDDLESEX, HA5 1DQ.
LEE, Mr. Yong Jay, BSc ACA *1993;* Yongsan-Gu Ichon 1-Dong Rex Apt. 16-405, SEOUL, 140-722, KOREA REPUBLIC OF.
LEE, Miss. Yoon Ling, BSc ACA *1980;* Lot 7 H10 Lorong Sri Pulutan 2, Taman Sri Pulutan Phase 2, Off Mile 8 Jalan Tuaran Menggatal, 88450 KOTA KINABALU, SABAH, MALAYSIA.
LEE, Mr. Yu-Jin, BA ACA *1992;* 4465 Lee Hin Neo 3, Ukay Heights, 68000 AMPANG, SELANGOR, MALAYSIA.
LEE, Mr. Yuen Kwong, ACA *2008;* Lee Yuen Kwong & Company, Unit 1301 13/F, Lemmi Centre, 50 Hoi Yuen Road, KWUN TONG, KOWLOON HONG KONG SAR.
LEE, Mr. Yuk Kong, BA ACA *1990;* Block E3 Floor 15, Plover Cove Garden, Tai Po Market TAI PO, New Territories, HONG KONG SAR.
LEE, Ms. Yuk Kun Vivian, ACA *2008;* LVMH Fashion Group Pacific Limited, 22/F Dorset House, 979 Kings Road, QUARRY BAY, HONG KONG ISLAND, HONG KONG SAR.
LEE, Miss. Yung Yung, ACA *2011;* 81 Burr Close, LONDON, E1W 1ND.
LEE, Mr. Zin Keat, ACA *2010;* 56A, 56 Harleyford Road, LONDON, SE11 5AY.
LEE-AMIES, Mrs. Charlotte Catherine, ACA *1994;* 24 Exeter Close, TONBRIDGE, TN10 4NT.
•LEE-AMIES, Mr. Mark Robert, BA FCA *1990;* Deloitte LLP, 2 New Street Square, LONDON, EC4A 3BZ. See also Deloitte & Touche LLP
LEE CHAN KAM, Mr. Kee Sen, FCA *1974;* 270 Beauchamp Road, MATRAVILLE, NSW 2036, AUSTRALIA.
LEE-DAVEY, Mr. Robert, BA(Hons) ACA *2005;* Flat 9, 1 Culverden Park, TUNBRIDGE WELLS, TN4 9QZ.
LEE-EMERY, Mr. Adrian John Carnac, FCA *1970;* P.O. Box HM 2025, HAMILTON HM HX, BERMUDA.
LEE-GERRISH, Mrs. Kwan-Yee, BSc(Hons) ACA *2004;* 38 Davenwood, SWINDON, SN2 7LL.
LEE-MOHAN, Mrs. Caroline Mary, BA ACA *1990;* Beech Hill Farmhouse, The Walled Garden, Beech Hill, READING, RG7 2LA.
LEE-MOORE, Mrs. Debra Ann, BSc FCA *1986;* 2, Eastway, MORDEN, SM4 4HW.
LEE-RICHARDS, Mr. Gareth Maurice, FCA *1972;* 20 Holmesdale Road, TEDDINGTON, MIDDLESEX, TW11 9LF.
LEE SIN CHEONG, Mr. Lee Choong Fo, BA FCA *1976;* Royal Road, Pointe Aux Feuilles, GRAND RIVER SOUTH EAST, MAURITIUS.
LEE-SMITH, Mr. Bryan Griffith, FCA *1973;* Cobetstraat 36, 2313 KC LEIDEN, NETHERLANDS.
LEE-SMITH, Mr. Dennis Walter, FCA *1949;* 18 The Cedars, St. Stephens RoadEaling, LONDON, W13 8JF. (Life Member)
LEE-SMITH, Mr. Percy Thomas Willson, FCA *1960;* 4 Bayview Road, WHITSTABLE, CT5 4NP.
LEE SOW FONG, Miss. Christine Audrey, BA ACA *2005;* 43 Leasway, WESTCLIFF-ON-SEA, ESSEX, SS0 8PA.
LEE-STEERE, Mr. James, MA ACA *2003;* Jayes Park, Ockley, DORKING, RH5 5RR.
LEE TO, Mrs. Estella Hon Ping, ACA *2007;* Ernst & Young, 18/F, Two International Finance Centre, 8 Finance Street, CENTRAL, HONG KONG ISLAND HONG KONG SAR.
LEE YIM OK, Mr. Louis Lindsay Francois, FCA *1976;* 18 Airlie Gardens, ILFORD, IG1 4LB.
•LEECE, Mrs. Claire, BA ACA *1998;* Baker Tilly Tax & Advisory Services LLP, 1 St. James Gate, NEWCASTLE UPON TYNE, NE1 4AD. See also Baker Tilly UK Audit LLP
LEECE, Mr. Colin Andrew, BA ACA *1990;* Burnsall, 10 Gainsborough Road, Birkdale, SOUTHPORT, PR8 2EY.
LEECE, Mr. Geoffrey Robert, FCA *1954;* Thornhill, Briardale Road, Willaston, NESTON, CH64 1TD.
LEECE, Mr. Ian, FCA *1979;* Kelda Group Plc, Western Way, Halifax Road, BRADFORD, BD6 2SZ.
LEECE, Mr. John Henry, BA ACA *1988;* Bell Pottinger Corporate & Financial Holborn Gate, 330 High Holborn, LONDON, WC1V 7QD.
LEECE, Mr. Steven Alan Charles, BSc(Hons) ACA *2009;* 6 Cronk Cullyn, Colby, ISLE OF MAN, IM9 4NQ.
LEECE, Mr. Terence David, FCA *1960;* 22 Compton Hill Drive, Compton, WOLVERHAMPTON, WV3 9DL. (Life Member)
LEECH, Mr. Andrew James, BA ACA *2001;* 13 McHardy Street, HAVELOCK NORTH 4130, NEW ZEALAND.
LEECH, Mr. Anthony, FCA *1974;* Easter House, Bacons Green Road, Westhall, HALESWORTH, SUFFOLK, IP19 8RA.
LEECH, Miss. Catherine Mary, BSc ACA *1992;* 66 Sandringham Road, SWINDON, SN3 1HX.
•LEECH, Mr. Christopher John, FCA *1972;* (Tax Fac), C.J. Leech & Company, 88 Sheep Street, BICESTER, OX26 6LP.
LEECH, Mrs. Emma, BSc ACA *2002;* 3 Arden Glade, Kington Lane Claverdon, WARWICK, CV35 8PP.
LEECH, Mr. Frank Denis, FCA *1952;* 56 The Walk, POTTERS BAR, HERTFORDSHIRE, EN6 1QE. (Life Member)
LEECH, Mr. Graham Charles, BA ACA *1989;* 430 Tukituki Road, RD 2, HASTINGS, NEW ZEALAND.
LEECH, Mr. Graham Louis, FCA *1975;* Hollihurst Hollihurst Road Lodsworth, PETWORTH, WEST SUSSEX, GU28 9BT.
LEECH, Mr. Ian Robert, BA FCA *1985;* Drift House, First Drift, Wothorpe, STAMFORD, PE9 3JL.
LEECH, Mr. John Clive Boulton, FCA *1960;* Four Winds, 9 Highland Road, KENILWORTH, CV8 2EU. (Life Member)
•LEECH, Mr. John David, BA ACA *1995;* KPMG LLP, One Snowhill, Snow Hill Queensway, BIRMINGHAM, B4 6GN. See also KPMG Europe LLP
LEECH, Mr. John Richard, BA FCA *1995;* West Woodlands Main Road, St. Johns, ISLE OF MAN, IM4 3LU.
LEECH, Mr. John Stuart, BSc ACA *1989;* 30 Alford Close, Beeston, NOTTINGHAM, NG9 1QP.
LEECH, Miss. Lynne Elizabeth, BSc ACA *2005;* Knox House, 16-18 Finch Road Douglas, ISLE OF MAN, IM1 2PT.
LEECH, Mr. Marc Thomas, BSc ACA *2010;* Level 9, 1 Margaret Street, SYDNEY, NSW 2000, AUSTRALIA.
LEECH, Mr. Martin, MA ACA *1992;* Riverside Centre, Level 26 123 Eagle Street, BRISBANE, QLD 4000, AUSTRALIA.
LEECH, Mr. Martin Richard, FCA *1955;* 119 Lache Lane, CHESTER, CH4 7LU. (Life Member)
LEECH, Mr. Matthew Raymond, BSc ACA *2007;* 35 Newfield Drive, KINGSWINFORD, DY6 8HY.
LEECH, Mr. Melvin Allan, BA FCA *1984;* 13b Beck Road, CARLISLE, CA2 7QL.
LEECH, Mr. Paul Nigel, BA FCA *1979;* with Deloitte LLP, Hill House, 1 Little New Street, LONDON, EC4A 3TR.
LEECH, Mr. Robert, FCA *1975;* 11 Laneside, Kirkheaton, HUDDERSFIELD, HD5 0EP.
LEECH, Mr. Steven Joseph, BA(Hons) ACA *2004;* Zurich International Life Ltd, DIFC Gate Village Building 7 Floor 3, DUBAI, 50389, UNITED ARAB EMIRATES.
LEECH, Miss. Susan, BA ACA *1982;* 806 Bay Club Lane West, BEACH HAVEN, NJ 08008, UNITED STATES.
LEEDER, Mrs. Cherry Janette Mary, BA ACA *1983;* 35 Hall Orchards, Middleton, KING'S LYNN, NORFOLK, PE32 1RY.
LEEDER, Mr. Colin William, FCA *1973;* 35 Hall Orchards, Middleton, KING'S LYNN, PE32 1RY.
LEEDER, Mr. David John, ACA *1981;* Lowlands, Bardwell Road, Stanton, BURY ST.EDMUNDS, IP31 2EA.
LEEDER, Mr. Mark Joseph, BSc ACA *1994;* 26 Lorna Avenue, NORTH RYDE, NSW 2113, AUSTRALIA.
LEEDHAM, Mr. David John, BA ACA *1996;* Park Gate, Maidensgrove, HENLEY-ON-THAMES, OXFORDSHIRE, RG9 6HA.
LEEDHAM, Mrs. Heather Jane, BSc ACA *1996;* Park Gate, Maidensgrove, HENLEY-ON-THAMES, OXFORDSHIRE, RG9 6HA.
LEEDHAM, Miss. Sarah Alison, BSc ACA CPFA *1992;* 5 Keats Terrace, CAMBRIDGE, NEW ZEALAND.
LEEDS, Mrs. Sarah Ann, BSc ACA PGCE *1995;* 14 Hinton Road, Childswickham, BROADWAY, WR12 7HY.
LEEFE, Mr. Peter Andrew, BSc FCA *1984;* 10 Royal Avenue, WORCESTER PARK, SURREY, KT4 7JE.
LEEFE, Mr. Simon Neville Arden, BA ACA *1991;* Candover Investments Plc, 20 Old Bailey, LONDON, EC4M 7LN.
LEEK, Mr. Christopher John Henry, BSc(Hons) ACA *2001;* Limburger Strasse 26C, D-61462 KOENIGSTEIN, GERMANY.
LEEK, Mr. Edward Jonathan Salter, BA ACA *1997;* KPMG, Av 9 De Julho, 5109 7 Andar, SAO PAULO, 01407 905, BRAZIL.
LEEK, Mr. James Anthony, FCA *1967;* 11 Parkside Gardens, Wimbledon, LONDON, SW19 5EU.
LEEK, Mr. Julian Martyn, ACA *1993;* Cullen Building Products Ltd, 1 Wheatstone Place, Southfield Industrial Estate, GLENROTHES, FIFE, KY6 2SW.
LEEK, Mr. Marcus, BSc ACA *2001;* Apartment 9 Clement House, The Blundells, KENILWORTH, CV8 2PE.
LEEK, Mr. Nigel Elmer, BSc FCA *1974;* 11 Walnut Road, Mere, WARMINSTER, BA12 6FG.
LEEK, Mrs. Sarah Ann, ACA *2008;* with Shipleys LLP, 10 Orange Street, Haymarket, LONDON, WC2H 7DQ.
LEEKE, Mr. Gerald Llewellyn, FCA *1966;* Hensol Mill, Hensol, PONTYCLUN, CF72 8JX.
LEEKE, Mrs. Jeanette Louise, FCA *1967;* White Lodge, Ystradowen, COWBRIDGE, CF71 7SZ.
LEEKE, Mr. Timothy David, BSc ACA *1999;* 14 The Verlands, COWBRIDGE, SOUTH GLAMORGAN, CF71 7BY.
LEEKS, Mr. Peter Norman, BSc ACA *1995;* 38 Cavendish Road, WOKING, GU22 0EP.
•LEEMAN, Mr. Timothy Guy, BA FCA *1987;* (Tax Fac), MCABA Limited, 91-97 Saltergate, CHESTERFIELD, DERBYSHIRE, S40 1LA. See also Mitchells
LEEMING, Mr. Adrian Paul, FCA *1968;* St Mary's House, Churchgate, Glemsford, SUDBURY, CO10 7QE.
LEEMING, Mr. Arthur Stuart, FCA CTA *1965;* The Gables, Cecil Avenue, Lightcliffe, HALIFAX, WEST YORKSHIRE, HX3 8SN. (Life Member)
LEEMING, Mr. David Alan, FCA *1968;* 57 Flats Lane, Barwick-in-Elmet, LEEDS, LS15 4LJ.
LEEMING, Mr. David William, ACA *1983;* TMDP LTD, 10/11 Gladman Business Quater, WREXHAM, LL13 7YT.
LEEMING, Mr. Gary Edward, BA ACA *1988;* High Trees, Ballabrooie Drive, Douglas, ISLE OF MAN, IM1 4HF.
LEEMING, Mr. Graham David, BA ACA *1994;* Babcock International Group Plc, 33 Wigmore Street, LONDON, W1U 1QX.
LEEMING, Miss. Helene, BA ACA *2007;* 23 Mayfield Way, Great Cambourne, CAMBRIDGE, CB23 5JA.
LEEMING, Mr. Robert, BSc ACA *1990;* Shandon, Monteith Close, Langton Green, TUNBRIDGE WELLS, TN3 0AD.
LEEMING, Mr. Thomas Edward, FCA *1955;* 8 Third Avenue, Douglas, ISLE OF MAN, IM2 6AL. (Life Member)
LEEN, Mr. David Sean, BSc ACA *1992;* St Marys University College, Waldegrave Road, TWICKENHAM, TW1 4SX.
LEEN, Mr. Denis Joseph, FCA *1975;* 1 Lyon Close, ABINGDON, OXFORDSHIRE, OX14 1PT. (Life Member)
LEENANE, Mr. John Michael, BCom ACA *1991;* 106 Stillorgan Heath, Stillorgan, DUBLIN, COUNTY DUBLIN, IRELAND.
LEEPINGSANG, Mr. Neville, ACA *2008;* 61 Devonshire Road, HARROW, MIDDLESEX, HA1 4LS.
•LEES, Mr. Alan, BA FCA *1983;* Grant Thornton UK LLP, 30 Finsbury Square, LONDON, EC2P 2YU. See also Grant Thornton LLP
•LEES, Mrs. Alison, ACA *1981;* PricewaterhouseCoopers LLP, 1 Embankment Place, LONDON, WC2N 6RH. See also PricewaterhouseCoopers
LEES, Mr. Andrew David, BSc ACA *1993;* 12 Beverley Terrace, Cullercoats, NORTH SHIELDS, TYNE AND WEAR, NE30 4NT.
LEES, Mr. Andrew John, BA ACA *1990;* Barclays Capital, 1st Floor, 3 Hardman Street, Spinningfields, MANCHESTER, M3 3HF.
LEES, Mr. Cameron Morgan, BA ACA *1988;* 56 Minster Court, Hillcrest Road, LONDON, W5 1HH.
LEES, Mrs. Charlotte Kate, BA(Hons) ACA *2000;* 6 Sunny Bank Road, Helmshore, ROSSENDALE, LANCASHIRE, BB4 4PF.
LEES, Mr. Christopher, BA ACA *1990;* Oak House, High Street, Church Eaton, STAFFORD, ST20 0AG.
LEES, Mr. Christopher James Burnett, BA ACA *2003;* 8 Zinnia Drive, Bisley, WOKING, SURREY, GU24 9RY.
LEES, Mr. Clifford Rowland, FCA *1955;* 40 Ellerton Road, Hartburn, STOCKTON-ON-TEES, TS18 5PU. (Life Member)
LEES, Mr. Colin Alan, BSc(Econ) ACA *2010;* 268 Roundthorn Road, OLDHAM, OL4 5LJ.
LEES, Mr. Darren Mark, BSc(Hons) ACA *2000;* 18 Haven Lane, LONDON, W5 2HN.
•LEES, Mr. David Arthur, BA FCA *1967;* (Tax Fac), David A Lees, 8 Fosters Grove, WINDLESHAM, GU20 6JZ.
LEES, Sir David Bryan, Kt FCA *1963;* Oakhurst, Uffington, SHREWSBURY, SY4 4SN.
LEES, Mr. David William, FCA *1978;* 43 Finstall Road, Finstall, BROMSGROVE, WORCESTERSHIRE, B60 3DF.
LEES, Mr. Edmund Campbell D'Olier, FCA *1955;* Wheelwrights, The Street, Coaley, DURSLEY, GLOUCESTERSHIRE, GL11 5EB. (Life Member)
LEES, Miss. Eleanor, BA ACA *2010;* 1st Floor Flat, 54 South Ealing Road, LONDON, W5 4QA.
LEES, Mrs. Elizabeth Mary, BA(Hons) ACA *2000;* 48 Midsummer Meadow, Inkberrow, WORCESTER, WR7 4HD.
LEES, Mr. Eric Liberman, BA FCA *1951;* 17 Atwater Court, Faversham Road, Lenham, MAIDSTONE, KENT, ME17 2PW. (Life Member)
LEES, Mr. Fraser, LLB ACA *2003;* Flat 4, 28 Rowantree Road, ENFIELD, EN2 8PY.
LEES, Mr. Frederick William, FCA *1947;* Prestbury Court, Residential Home, Brimley Lane, Bovey Tracey, NEWTON ABBOT TQ13 9JS. (Life Member)
LEES, Mrs. Gaynor Anne, BA ACA *1995;* Thie Ny Chibbyr, Eairy, ISLE OF MAN, IM4 3HU.
LEES, Mr. Geoffrey, FCA *1951;* 107 Lyndale Avenue, Edenthorpe, DONCASTER, DN3 2LB. (Life Member)
LEES, Mr. Geoffrey William Henderson, BA FCA *1993;* Accounts Commission for Scotland Osborne House, 1 Osborne Terrace, EDINBURGH, EH12 5HG.
LEES, Mr. Howard, BA ACA *1987;* 3rd Floor Federation Building, The Co-operative Group (C W S) Ltd New Century House, Corporation Street, MANCHESTER, M60 4ES.
LEES, Mr. Iain Fraser, BSc ACA *1991;* 7 Glenmore Manor, Lambeg Road, LISBURN, COUNTY ANTRIM, BT27 4BZ.
LEES, Mr. Iain Roger, BA FCA *1986;* Church Farm, School Lane, Pickmere, KNUTSFORD, WA16 0JF.
•①LEES, Mr. Ian Peter, LLB FCA *1984;* 15 Shoreditch Close, Heaton Moor, STOCKPORT, CHESHIRE, SK4 4RW.
LEES, Mr. James Cooper, FCA *1950;* Hillfield, 4 Wentworth Road, SUTTON COLDFIELD, B74 2SG. (Life Member)
LEES, Mrs. Jane, ACA *1995;* 421 Milnrow Road, Shaw, OLDHAM, OL2 8BU.
LEES, Mrs. Joanne Lindsay, BSc ACA *2003;* 8 Zinnia Drive, Bisley, WOKING, GU24 9RY.
LEES, Mr. John Michael, FCA *1970;* 3 Clysbarton Court, Bramhall Park Road, Bramhall, STOCKPORT, CHESHIRE, SK7 3NP.
LEES, Mr. John Robin Middleton, FCA *1961;* 2 Quarry Gardens, Waterloo Road, TONBRIDGE, TN9 2SG.
LEES, Mr. Jonathan Charles, BA ACA *1982;* Magnolia Cottage, Earleydene, ASCOT, SL5 9JY.
LEES, Mr. Jonathan David Alexander, ACA *2009;* 34 Longfield Drive, LEEDS, LS13 1JX.
LEES, Mr. Keith Albert, FCA *1975;* 20 Windermere Road, BLACKPOOL, FY4 2BX.
LEES, Mr. Keith Edmond Coulthard, FCA *1955;* Flat 2 Broughton Mews, 139 Marsland Road, SALE, M33 3NX. (Life Member)
LEES, Mr. Leslie Paul, BSc ACA *1987;* ThyssenKrupp Tallent Ltd., Wolverhampton Road, CANNOCK, STAFFORDSHIRE, WS11 1LY.
LEES, Mrs. Margaret Julia, BSc ACA *1988;* 19 Cant Crescent, ST ANDREWS, KY16 8NF.
LEES, Mr. Marshall Cobbold, BSc FCA *1961;* 28 Cardinal's Walk, HAMPTON, TW12 2TS. (Life Member)
LEES, Mr. Matthew, LLB ACA *1999;* 15 High Ash Road, Wheathampstead, ST. ALBANS, HERTFORDSHIRE, AL4 8DY.
LEES, Mr. Richard Frederic Archdale, FCA *1972;* Kelburnfoot, Kelburn Estate, Fairlie, LARGS, AYRSHIRE, KA29 0BD.
LEES, Mr. Roger Alan, LLB ACA *1987;* Flat 32 Tamarind Court, 18 Gainsford Street, LONDON, SE1 2NE.
LEES, Mrs. Ruth Helen, BA ACA *1994;* Hbos Plc, West Bank, LEEDS, LS98 3HX.
LEES, Miss. Sadie, ACA *2007;* 4 Fludger Close, WALLINGFORD, OXFORDSHIRE, OX10 9BP.

LEES, Miss. Sarah Elizabeth Anne, BA ACA *2000;* 3 Iris Drive, PETERBOROUGH, PE2 9SS.
•**LEES, Mr. Stuart, BA FCA** *1981;* Signia Corporate Finance Limited, Springfield, Macclesfield Road, ALDERLEY EDGE, CHESHIRE, SK9 7BW.
LEES, Miss. Susan, BSc ACA *1987;* Woodhill Farm, Pick Hill, WALTHAM ABBEY, ESSEX, EN9 3LE.
LEES, Mr. William John, FCA *1955;* Suite 3319, Two Pacific Place, 88 Queensway, ADMIRALTY, HONG KONG ISLAND, HONG KONG SAR. (Life Member)
•**LEES-BUCKLEY, Mr. Lewis Gary, FCA** *1978;* (Tax Fac), LBCo Ltd, 16 Northfields Prospect Business Centre, Putney Bridge Road, LONDON, SW18 1PE.
LEES-COBB, Miss. Rachel Elsa May, ACA *2008;* with KPMG LLP, 15 Canada Square, LONDON, E14 5GL.
•**LEESE, Mr. David Brian, ACA** *1982;* (Tax Fac), The Davison Partnership, Reliance House, Moorland Road, Burslem, STOKE-ON-TRENT, ST6 1DP.
LEESE, Mrs. Frances Catherine, BA ACA *2008;* 30 Chaldon Way, COULSDON, SURREY, CR5 1DB.
LEESE, Mr. John David, BA ACA *1993;* 3 Kelham Gardens, MARLBOROUGH, SN8 1PW.
LEESE, Mr. Kristian, ACA *2008;* 30 Chaldon Way, COULSDON, SURREY, CR5 1DB.
LEESE, Mr. Vivian Andrew, BSc ACA *1999;* Garban-Intercapital Plc, 2 Broadgate, LONDON, EC2M 7UR.
LEESING, Mr. Brian, FCA *1957;* Limestones, Back Lane, Old Edlington, DONCASTER, SOUTH YORKSHIRE, DN12 1QA.
LEESMITH, Mr. Alan Eustace, FCA *1969;* Bavelaw House, Copyhold Lane, Cuckfield, HAYWARDS HEATH, RH17 5EB.
LEESON, Mr. Anthony Eric, BSc FCA *1979;* Harpersheldon, The Old School House, Leckhampton Road, CHELTENHAM, GLOUCESTERSHIRE, GL53 0AX.
LEESON, Mr. Ian Arthur, MA FCA *1964;* Eaton House, 7 Eaton Park, COBHAM, KT11 2JF. (Life Member)
LEESON, Mr. James Andrew Michael, BSc ACA *1980;* 136 Hawthorne Way, Shelley, HUDDERSFIELD, HD8 8PX.
•**LEESON, Mrs. Joanne Louise, BA ACA** *1998;* PricewaterhouseCoopers LLP, 31 Great George Street, BRISTOL, BS1 5QD. See also PricewaterhouseCoopers
LEESON, Mrs. Linda Kathryn, LLB ACA *1989;* 84 Albert Drive, Deganwy, CONWY, LL31 9RL.
LEESON, Mr. Peter Harvey, FCA *1968;* The Manor House, Mellbecks, KIRKBY STEPHEN, CA17 4AB.
LEEVES, Mr. James Peter, BSc ACA *2010;* Burgess Hodgson, 27 New Dover Road, CANTERBURY, CT1 3DN.
LEFEVRE, Mr. Bernard Marie Anne Georges, BSc FCA *1963;* 51 Rue Du President Wilson, 78230 LE PECQ, FRANCE. (Life Member)
LEFEVRE, Mr. David Andrew, BA ACA *2005;* 2 The Heights, Cotman Road, NORWICH, NR1 4BZ.
•**LEFEVRE, Mrs. Ellen Margaret, FCA CTA** *1993;* (Tax Fac), Lefevres Limited, 4 Huddington Glade, YATELEY, HAMPSHIRE, GU46 6FG.
LEFEVRE, Miss. Julie, MA ACA *2005;* with Ernst & Young, Ernst & Young House, 34 - 36 Cranmer Square, CHRISTCHURCH, NEW ZEALAND.
LEFEVRE, Mr. Oscar Joseph, FCA *1964;* PO Box 702, LINK HILLS, 3652, SOUTH AFRICA. (Life Member)
LEFEVRE, Mrs. Sylvie, BSc ACA *2005;* Reckitt Benckiser Plc, 103-105 Bath Road, SLOUGH, SL1 3UH.
LEFF, Mr. Norman Nathan, FCA *1952;* 34 Waterfall Road, New Southgate, LONDON, N11 1BU. (Life Member)
LEFKATIS, Mr. Theodoulos, BA ACA *2004;* 84 Kleisthenous Road, Archangelos, Lakatamia, 2335 NICOSIA, CYPRUS.
LEFORT, Mrs. Kay Emily, BA ACA *1998;* Vencap International Plc King Charles House, Park End Street, OXFORD, OX1 1JD.
LEFORT, Mr. Paul Albert, BSc ACA *1982;* 105 Henley Road, IPSWICH, IP1 4NG.
LEFROY, Mr. Jeremy John Elton, MA ACA *1985;* 9 Highway Lane, Keele, NEWCASTLE, ST5 5AN.
LEFROY BROOKS, Mrs. Alison Sally, BA ACA MCT *1987;* Aggreko Plc, 8th Floor, 120 Bothwell Street, GLASGOW, G2 7JS.
LEFTLEY, Mr. Brian Douglas, FCA *1972;* 44 Spareleaze Hill, LOUGHTON, IG10 1BT.
LEFTLEY, Mrs. Joanna Jane, BSc ACA *1995;* Priory Cottage Rectory Road, Taplow, MAIDENHEAD, SL6 0ET.
LEFTLEY, Mr. Malcolm George, FCA *1965;* 44 Sweetcroft Lane, UXBRIDGE, UB10 9LE.
LEFTWICH, Mr. Peter James, BA FCA *1977;* 414 East Glenhaven Drive, PHOENIX, AZ 85048, UNITED STATES.
LEFTWICH, Mr. Robert James, BCom ACA *1995;* Ambers, 212 Amersham Road, Hazlemere, HIGH WYCOMBE, BUCKINGHAMSHIRE, HP15 7QT.
LEGARD, Mr. Christopher John Charles, ACA *1989;* Scampston Hall, Scampston, MALTON, NORTH YORKSHIRE, YO17 8NG.
LEGENHAUSEN, Mr. Dirk, BSc ACA *2000;* 19 Trapani Ave, POINT COOK, VIC 3030, AUSTRALIA.
LEGG, Mrs. Alison Mary, BSc FCA *1982;* Grange Farm House, Doncaster Road, Hickleton, DONCASTER, SOUTH YORKSHIRE, DN5 7BG.
LEGG, Mrs. Catherine Ruth, BA ACA *1990;* 8 Tyler Drive, Arborfield, READING, RG2 9NG.
LEGG, Mr. Charles Stanley, CertEd FCA FMAAT *1970;* Wells Cottage, 12 Copthorne Road, Croxley Green, RICKMANSWORTH, WD3 4AE.
LEGG, Mr. David Charles, FCA *1957;* 13 Rushmoor Grove, Backwell, BRISTOL, BS48 3BW. (Life Member)
LEGG, Mr. Guy Philip, FCA *1950;* P.O. Box 138, KLOOF, KWAZULU NATAL, 3640, SOUTH AFRICA. (Life Member)
LEGG, Miss. Helen Catherine, BSc ACA *2007;* Penny Pot Cottage, Charlton Musgrove, WINCANTON, SOMERSET, BA9 8HN.
LEGG, Mr. James William Sidney, BA ACA *1998;* 93 Salisbury Road, GREAT YARMOUTH, NR30 4LS.
LEGG, Mr. Leslie Harry James, FCA *1959;* Conerways, 7 Lower Neatham Mill Lane, Holybourne, ALTON, HAMPSHIRE, GU34 4ET. (Life Member)
LEGG, Ms. Louise, MA(Hons) FIA ACA *2002;* Actuary Platinum Underwriters Bermuda Ltd, The Belvedere Building, 69 Pitts Bay Road, PEMBROKE HM08, BERMUDA.
LEGG, Mr. Michael John, BA FCA *1973;* Doric House, 1a Wraylands Drive, REIGATE, RH2 0LG.
LEGG, Miss. Monica Jane, BEng ACA *1997;* Building D, British Petroleum Co Plc, Chertsey Road, SUNBURY-ON-THAMES, MIDDLESEX, TW16 7LN.
•**LEGG, Mr. Murray John, BSc FCA** *1983;* PricewaterhouseCoopers LLP, 1 Embankment Place, LONDON, WC2N 6RH. See also PricewaterhouseCoopers
•**LEGG, Mrs. Pamela June, FCA** *1964;* Pamela J Legg, Doric House, Wraylands Drive, REIGATE, SURREY, RH2 0LG.
LEGG, Miss. Rebecca Mary, BSc ACA *2005;* 1 Fuchsia Close, Reayrt Ny Keylley Peel, ISLE OF MAN, IM5 1GL.
LEGG, Mr. Simon, BA ACA *2007;* Flat 303 Madison Building, 38 Blackheath Road, LONDON, SE10 8EE.
LEGG, Mr. Simon Gregory, FCA *1975;* Pennypot Cottage, Barrow Lane, Charlton Musgrove, WINCANTON, BA9 8HN.
LEGG, Mr. Stephen Robert, BSc FCA CPA *1994;* Grant Thornton, 1 California Street, Suite 2300, SAN FRANCISCO, CA 94115, UNITED STATES.
LEGG, Mrs. Suzanne Marie, BSc ACA *1996;* 590 Dartington Way, ALPHARETTA, GA 30022, UNITED STATES.
•**LEGG, Mr. Terence, ACA** *1979;* Legg & Co., 589 Marton Road, MIDDLESBROUGH, CLEVELAND, TS4 3SD.
LEGG, Mr. Victor John, FCA *1958;* The Dene, 7 Harrop Road, Hale, ALTRINCHAM, WA15 9BU. (Life Member)
LEGGAT, Mr. Duncan Angus, BA FCA *1993;* 70 Barrow Road, Shippon, ABINGDON, OX13 6JQ.
•**LEGGATE, Mr. Andrew, LLB ACA FCMA** *2008;* Leggate Associates Limited, Bencroft Dassels, Braughing, WARE, HERTFORDSHIRE, SG11 2RW.
•**LEGGATE, Mr. Christopher Jonathan, BA ACA** *1989;* C.J. Leggate & Associates, 15 New Road, HIGH WYCOMBE, HP12 4LH.
LEGGATE MCLAUGHLIN, Dr. Heather Kathleen, PhD MSc BA FCA *1990;* Faculty of Business and Management, Canterbury Christ Church University, North Holmes Road, CANTERBURY, CT1 1QU.
•**LEGGATT, Mrs. Lisa, ACA FCCA** *2011;* Kingsmead Accounting Ltd, 3 North Street, Oadby, LEICESTER, LE2 5AH.
LEGGATT, Mr. Stephen, FCA *1972;* Postnet Suite 387, Private Bag x 75, BRYANSTON, GAUTENG, 2021, SOUTH AFRICA.
LEGGE, Mrs. Allison Christina, BSc ACA CA(SA) *1995;* with PricewaterhouseCoopers Inc, PO Box 2799, CAPE TOWN, C.P., 8000, SOUTH AFRICA.
LEGGE, Mrs. Catherine Laura Joanne, BA ACA *2002;* The Nook Dean Street, ILKLEY, WEST YORKSHIRE, LS29 8JR.
•**LEGGE, Mr. Christopher Fawcus Lovell, BA FCA** *1980;* De Beauvoir House Fermain Road, St. Peter Port, GUERNSEY, GY1 2TB.
LEGGE, Mr. David Andrew, BSc(Hons) ACA CPA *2002;* 1129 Ashton Road, WYNNEWOOD, PA 19096, UNITED STATES.
LEGGE, Mr. Ingram Alistair Thomson, FCA *1960;* Ingram Legge & Co, 2nd Floor, 56 Hamilton Square, BIRKENHEAD, MERSEYSIDE, CH41 5AS.
LEGGE, Mr. Richard Hildebrand, FCA *1960;* Baskerville Farm, Stour Row, SHAFTESBURY, SP7 0QH. (Life Member)
LEGGE, Mr. Sam Richard, BA ACA *2004;* 4 Hapsford Close, Birchwood, WARRINGTON, WA3 6NA.
LEGGE, Miss. Sarah Louise, ACA *2009;* 39 Grizedale Court, SUNDERLAND, SR6 8JP.
LEGGE, The Earl of Dartmout William, BA FCA *1975;* 16 Westbourne Terrace, LONDON, W2 3UW.
LEGGETT, Miss. Amanda Kay, MMath ACA *2007;* 86 Quebec Drive, Kesgrave, IPSWICH, IP5 1HU.
LEGGETT, Mrs. Anne, BA ACA *1993;* Hillfoot Cottage, Chapel Row, READING, BERKSHIRE, RG7 6PG.
LEGGETT, Mr. Duncan, BSc ACA *2006;* 59 Upper Culver Road, ST. ALBANS, HERTFORDSHIRE, AL1 4EE.
LEGGETT, Mr. Frank Ian, FCA *1962;* Grevel Croft, Grevel Lane, CHIPPING CAMPDEN, GL55 6HS. (Life Member)
LEGGETT, Miss. Hayley Jayne, BSc ACA *2003;* 54 Millers Croft, BATLEY, WEST YORKSHIRE, WF17 0RN.
LEGGETT, Mr. Kevan Paul, BSc ACA *1990;* Hillfoot Cottage, Chapel Row, READING, RG7 6PG.
LEGGETT, Mr. Matthew David, ACA *2008;* with Lovewell Blake LLP, Sixty Six, North Quay, GREAT YARMOUTH, NORFOLK, NR30 1HE.
•**LEGGETT, Mr. Michael Antony, BSc FCA** *1981;* The Southill Partnership Limited, Southill Business Park, Cornbury Park, Charlbury, CHIPPING NORTON, OXFORDSHIRE OX7 3EW.
LEGGETT, Mr. Paul James, BSc ACA *2003;* Deloitte Corporate Finance Limited, DIFC, Dubai International Financial Centre, Currency House Building 1 Level 5, P.O. Box 282056, DUBAI, UNITED ARAB EMIRATES.
•**LEGGETT, Mr. Robert David, ACA CTA** *2002;* (Tax Fac), Ensors, Cardinal House, 46 St Nicholas Street, IPSWICH, IP1 1TT.
•**LEGGETT, Mr. Russell Alan, FCA TEP** *1978;* (Tax Fac), Lovewell Blake LLP, Sixty Six, North Quay, GREAT YARMOUTH, NORFOLK, NR30 1HE.
LEGGETT, Mrs. Susan Mary, BA ACA *1986;* Fountain Ridge, Montreal Road, Riverhead, SEVENOAKS, TN13 2EP.
•**LEGGETT, Mr. Timothy James, BA FCA** *1977;* Ernst & Young LLP, 1 More London Place, LONDON, SE1 2AF. See also Ernst & Young Europe LLP
•**LEGGOTT, Mr. John Edward, FCA** *1961;* Leggott J.E., Wayside Cottage, Cross Street, Great Hatfield, HULL, HU11 4UR.
LEGGOTT, Mrs. Mary Margaret, FCA *1963;* 4 Forgeway Close, TORQUAY, TQ2 6SH.
•**LEGON, Mr. Richard John Alex, BA FCA** *1980;* Deloitte & Associes, 185 avenue Charles de Gaulle, 92524 NEUILLY SUR SEINE CEDEX, FRANCE. See also Constantin
LEGOOD, Mr. Christopher John, FCA *1972;* 6 Bruce Grove, Tottenham, LONDON, N17 6RA.
LEGOOD, Mr. Simon Vaughan, FCA *1982;* 10 Honeysuckle Square, WYMONDHAM, NORFOLK, NR18 0FH.
LEGOUAIS, Mr. Geoff, MSc ACA *2004;* Calle Almagro 5 1A, Getafe, 28904 MADRID, SPAIN.
LEGRICE, Mr. Paul Matthew, BSc(Hons) ACA *2004;* Bramble Cottage, Woodgate Lane, Swanton Morley, DEREHAM, NORFOLK, NR20 4NS.
•**LEGRIS, Mr. Fabrice Jean-Marc, BEng FCA** *1993;* Westlake Clark, Nat West Bank Chambers, 55 Station Road, NEW MILTON, HAMPSHIRE, BH25 6JA.
LEGROVE, Mr. Robert, FCA *1971;* Morgana House, Davy Avenue, Knowlhill, MILTON KEYNES, MK5 8HJ.
LEHANE, Ms. Fiona Maria, BSc ACA *2002;* 4 Park Hall Milltown Avenue, Mount St Annes, Milltown, DUBLIN 6, COUNTY DUBLIN, IRELAND.
LEHL, Mr. Navtej Singh, BSc ACA *1998;* 80 The Shearers, BISHOP'S STORTFORD, HERTFORDSHIRE, CM23 4AZ.
LEHMAN, Mr. John Lloyd, BSc ACA *1998;* The Pines Cranhill Farm, Harborough Road Billesdon, LEICESTER, LE7 9EL.
•**LEHMANN, Mr. Colin Ivor, FCA** *1980;* Blick Rothenberg, 12 York Gate, Regent's Park, LONDON, NW1 4QS.
LEHMANN, Mrs. Helen Mary Louise, BSc ACA *1987;* 20 Pumicestone Place, GOLDEN BEACH, QLD 4551, AUSTRALIA.
LEHMANN, Mr. Nicholas Roy, MSc FCA *1982;* P.O. Box 74285, DUBAI, 74285, UNITED ARAB EMIRATES.
LEHMBERG, Ms. Tanya Elizabeth, ACA CA(SA) *2010;* Flat 8, Deborah Court, Victoria Road, LONDON, E18 1LF.
LEHRER, Mr. Keith, BA FCA *1967;* York University, 256 Atkinson College, 4700 Keele Street, NORTH YORK M3J 1P3, ON, CANADA.
LEHRER, Mr. Michael Alex, BA(Hons) ACA *2001;* 518 South Forest Drive, TEANECK, NJ 07666, UNITED STATES.
LEI, Miss. Ada Karman, MA ACA *2004;* Flat 10 Coliseum Court, 200 Regents Park Road, LONDON, N3 3HF.
LEI, Mr. Francis, BSc ACA *2007;* Ousebank Cottage, 5 Church Passage, NEWPORT PAGNELL, BUCKINGHAMSHIRE, MK16 8AW.
LEIBOVITCH, Mr. Andrew, ACA *1991;* 70 Excelsior Street, SHENTON PARK, WA 6008, AUSTRALIA.
•**LEIBOVITCH, Mr. Barry, FCA** *1987;* (Tax Fac), Tish Leibovitch, 249 Cranbrook Road, ILFORD, IG1 4TG. See also Leibovitch & Co
LEICESTER, Mr. Alexander, BA ACA *2006;* with Alchemy Partners LLP, 25 Bedford Street, LONDON, WC2E 9ES.
LEICOS, Mr. Jimmy, ACA *2006;* SIS Chartered Accountants INPACT International, PO BOX 58352, 3733 LIMASSOL, CYPRUS.
LEIGH, Mr. Alfred Lea, FCA *1950;* 91 Macaulay Drive, Craigiebuckler, ABERDEEN, AB15 8FL. (Life Member)
LEIGH, Mr. Anthony Edwin, FCA *1979;* 8 School Road, Hampton Hill, HAMPTON, MIDDLESEX, TW12 1QL.
•**LEIGH, Mr. Barry, BA(Hons) ACA CTA** *2004;* (Tax Fac), Cohen Arnold, New Burlington House, 1075 Finchley Road, Temple Fortune, LONDON, NW11 0PU. See also Cohen Arnold & Co
•**LEIGH, Mr. Barry Malcolm, BSc ACA** *1983;* (Tax Fac), Leigh Marx, 11 Kensington Place, BRIGHTON, BN1 4EJ.
LEIGH, Mr. Brandon Howard, BSocSc ACA *1996;* 216 Outwood Road, Heald Green, CHEADLE, CHESHIRE, SK8 3JL.
LEIGH, Mr. Christopher David, LLB FCA *1971;* Chapel Barn, St. Breward, BODMIN, PL30 4NA.
LEIGH, Mr. Christopher Michael, BA FCA *1984;* Arranmoor, 11 Hillwood Close, Hutton, BRENTWOOD, CM13 2PE.
LEIGH, Mr. Christopher Paul, BA ACA *1992;* Glasson Grain Ltd West Quay, Glasson Dock, LANCASTER, LA2 0DB.
LEIGH, Mr. Christopher Peter, BSc ACA *2010;* 8 Lammas Road, Cheddington, LEIGHTON BUZZARD, BEDFORDSHIRE, LU7 0RY.
LEIGH, Mr. Clive Howard, BA ACA *1987;* Outback Steakhouse Restaurants, 3390 Peachtree Road Ne, ATLANTA, GA 30326, UNITED STATES.
LEIGH, Mr. David, FCA *1951;* Flat 9 Farthing Court, 33 Langstone Way, LONDON, NW7 1GQ. (Life Member)
•**LEIGH, Mr. David Richard, FCA** *1982;* Leigh Saxton Green, Clearwater House, 4-7 Manchester Street, LONDON, W1U 3AE.
LEIGH, Ms. Deborah Joan, BA FCA *1984;* 15 Elton Road, DARLINGTON, DL3 8HU.
LEIGH, Ms. Emma Jane, MA ACA *1999;* 4 Teneriffe Close, Bloubergstrand, CAPE TOWN, 7441, SOUTH AFRICA.
LEIGH, Mrs. Emma Louise, BSc(Hons) ACA *2004;* 18 Gilbert Road, LONDON, SW19 1BP.
LEIGH, Mr. Emmanuel Harold, FCA *1953;* 1 Freston Park, Finchley, LONDON, N3 1UP. (Life Member)
LEIGH, Mr. Gareth John, BA FCA *1980;* (Tax Fac), 306 Cyncoed Road, CARDIFF, CF23 6RX.
•**LEIGH, Mr. Gordon William, BA FCA** *1979;* Barlow Andrews LLP, Carlyle House, 78 Chorley New Road, BOLTON, BL1 4BY. See also Beech Business Services Limited
LEIGH, Mr. Graham Charles, FCA *1974;* (Tax Fac), Swan Cottage, Hulme Lane, Lower Peover, KNUTSFORD, CHESHIRE, WA16 9QE.
LEIGH, Mr. Gregory Joseph, BA FCA *1976;* Tulip Tree House, Donhead St. Mary, SHAFTESBURY, DORSET, SP7 9DL.
LEIGH, Mrs. Hannah, BA ACA *2005;* 19 Quakers Road, DEVIZES, SN10 2FH.
LEIGH, Mr. Howard Darryl, BSc FCA ATII CF *1984;* (Member of Council 2000 - 2004), with Cavendish Corporate Finance, 40 Portland Place, LONDON, W1B 1NB.
•**LEIGH, Mr. Ian, BA ACA** *1989;* (Tax Fac), Ian Leigh Limited, 16 Cyprus Avenue, LONDON, N3 1ST.
LEIGH, Miss. Jacqueline, ACA *2009;* 120/149-197 Pyrmont Street, PYRMONT, NSW 2009, AUSTRALIA.
•**LEIGH, Mr. James Alaric, LLB FCA** *1990;* Deloitte LLP, 2 New Street Square, LONDON, EC4A 3BZ. See also Deloitte & Touche LLP

LEIGH, Mr. James Bernard, FCA *1968;* Stretton Hall, Stretton, Tilston, MALPAS, SY14 7JA.

LEIGH, Mr. James David, ACA *2008;* 52 Marshall Street, MIRFIELD, WF14 8PG.

LEIGH, Mr. James Richard, BA FCA *2001;* 14 Fairway Close, LIPHOOK, HAMPSHIRE, GU30 7XD.

LEIGH, Mrs. Janet, BA ACA *1991;* 4 Russell Street, Compstall, STOCKPORT, SK6 5JY.

LEIGH, Mr. John, BSc(Econ) FCA *1968;* 14 Brookfield Avenue, Ealing, LONDON, W5 1LA. (Life Member)

LEIGH, Mr. John Owen, BSc FCA *1987;* 53 South Park Gardens, BERKHAMSTED, HERTFORDSHIRE, HP4 1HZ.

•LEIGH, Mr. John Raymond, FCA *1959;* (Tax Fac), 8 Harford Walk, East Finchley, LONDON, N2 0JB.

LEIGH, Mr. Jonathan Allister Heywood, BSc ACA *1992;* Ind Group KFT, Oktagon, Aradi Utca, BUDAPEST, HUNGARY.

LEIGH, Mr. Julian Grant Beresford, BA ACA *2000;* 2nd floor Regal House, 3 Queensway, GIBRALTAR, GIBRALTAR.

LEIGH, Mr. Kenneth Bruce, FCA CA(SA) *1956;* 74 Cheltenham Road East, Churchdown, GLOUCESTER, GL3 1JN. (Life Member)

LEIGH, Mrs. Laura, BCom ACA *1991; (ACA Ireland 1990);* 37 Park Avenue North, HARPENDEN, HERTFORDSHIRE, AL5 2EE.

•LEIGH, Mrs. Leanne, BA ACA *1997;* Grunberg & Co., 10-14 Accommodation Road, Golders Green, LONDON, NW11 8ED.

LEIGH, Mr. Man Sung Camballaw, ACA *2008;* Apex CPA Limited, Units 2205-07, 22/F China Merchants Building, 303-307 Des Voeux Road Central, SHEUNG WAN, HONG KONG SAR.

•LEIGH, Mr. Mark Stephen, BA FCA CF *1987;* Roffe Swayne, Ashcombe Court, Woolsack Way, GODALMING, GU7 1LQ.

•LEIGH, Mr. Michael Arnold, BA FCA *1975;* (Tax Fac), Leigh & Co, 3 Shelbourne Close, PINNER, HA5 3AF.

LEIGH, Mr. Michael Paul Vernon, JP FCA *1953;* Laurel Cottage, 2 Bowmont Close, Hutton, BRENTWOOD, CM13 1EB. (Life Member)

•LEIGH, Mr. Michael Richard, MA FCA ATII *1977;* (Tax Fac), Citadel Tax Consultants LLP, 3 The Glen, BOLTON, BL1 5DB.

LEIGH, Mrs. Miriam, FCA *1981;* Bradleigh, High Bank Lane, BOLTON, BL6 4DT.

LEIGH, Miss. Rachel Elizabeth, BSc ACA *1997;* 360 E57th Street, 9A, NEW YORK, NY 10022, UNITED STATES.

LEIGH, Mr. Richard Ian, FCA *1992;* 6 Raeburn Close, LONDON, NW11 6UG.

LEIGH, Mr. Richard Steven, BSc FCA *1990;* 322 Flamingo Road, THORNHILL L4J 8L4, ON, CANADA.

LEIGH, Mr. Robin Adamson Lennox, BA ACA *1987;* Princess Kitchens & Bedrooms, The Showroom, Wilkie Road, BARROW-IN-FURNESS, LA14 5UT.

•LEIGH, Mr. Simon John, BA FCA FPC *1995;* Allens Accountants Limited, 123 Wellington Road South, STOCKPORT, SK1 3TH.

LEIGH, Mr. Thomas William Elliott, BA ACA *1999;* 19 Cardinal Crescent, NEW MALDEN, SURREY, KT3 3EF.

LEIGH, Mr. Timothy Nicholas, FCA *1977;* 21 Beaconsfield Road, Knowle, BRISTOL, BS4 2JE.

LEIGH, Mr. Timothy Roy, FCA *1962;* Care Focus Ltd, Capital House, 18 Bury Street, STOWMARKET, SUFFOLK, IP14 1HH.

LEIGH, Miss. Tracy, ACA *2003;* 6 Myrtle Grove, 42 St. Johns Road, St. Helier, JERSEY, JE2 3LD.

LEIGH, Mr. William Rowland Llewellyn, FCA *1969;* Chancel House Church Street, Hadlow, TONBRIDGE, TN11 0DB. (Life Member)

•LEIGH-POLLITT, Mr. Guy Anthony Piers, FCA *1962;* G.A.P. Leigh-Pollitt Ltd, The Old Post Office, Polstead Street, STOKE BY NAYLAND, SUFFOLK, CO6 4SA.

LEIGH-POLLITT, Mr. Iain Lucien, BSc ACA *1995;* Royal Bank of Scotland, 135 Bishopsgate, LONDON, EC2M 3UR.

LEIGHS, Mr. Anthony Mark, BSocSc ACA *1992;* AM Leighs, Duckpool Barn, Rouse Lane, Oxhill, WARWICK, CV35 0NZ.

LEIGHTON, Mr. Andrew David, ACA *2000;* Rose Cottage Broomfield, Yatton Keynell, CHIPPENHAM, SN14 7JY.

LEIGHTON, Mr. Andrew Philip, BA(Hons) ACA *2011;* 28 Bracken Green, East Ardsley, WAKEFIELD, WF3 2LT.

LEIGHTON, Mr. Barry Miles, MA ACA *1987;* 57 Highbury Hill, LONDON, N5 1SU.

LEIGHTON, Mr. David William, BA ACA *1986;* TaxAssist Accountants, 73 Lowther Street, WHITEHAVEN, CUMBRIA, CA28 7AH.

•LEIGHTON, Mr. Edward Michael, BA ACA *1988;* 7 Prince Arthur Road, LONDON, NW3 6AX.

•LEIGHTON, Mr. Henry Gerard Mather, MA FCA *1957;* The West of England Trust Ltd, 21 St. Thomas Street, BRISTOL, BS1 6JS. See also Jordans International Limited

LEIGHTON, Mr. James Philip, ACA *1984;* Chemin du Vieux Bois 10B, Chambesy 1292, GENEVA, SWITZERLAND.

LEIGHTON, Mrs. Joanne, BA ACA CTA *1990;* with Deloitte LLP, PO Box 500, 2 Hardman Street, MANCHESTER, M60 2AT.

LEIGHTON, Mr. John, MPhys ACA *2006;* Flat 2, 1 Thirlmere Road, LONDON, SW16 1QW.

LEIGHTON, Mrs. Katherine Jennifer, BA ACA *1999;* Kirk House, 19 Victoria Terrace, Kemnay, INVERURIE, ABERDEENSHIRE, AB51 5RL.

LEIGHTON, Mrs. Kathryn Emma, BA ACA *2001;* with PricewaterhouseCoopers LLP, 1 Embankment Place, LONDON, WC2N 6RH.

LEIGHTON, Mr. Keith, BA ACA *1994;* Kirk House, Victoria Terrace, Kemnay, INVERURIE, AB51 5RL.

LEIGHTON, Mr. Kevin Anthony, BSc FCA *1989;* 21 Waterfall Avenue, FORESTVILLE, NSW 2087, AUSTRALIA.

•LEIGHTON, Mrs. Lisa Ann, BA FCA CF *1999;* Barber Harrison & Platt, 2 Rutland Park, SHEFFIELD, S10 2PD.

LEIGHTON, Mr. Martin Jonathan Robert, LLB ACA *1997;* Great Portland Estates Plc, 33 Cavendish Square, LONDON, W1G 0PW.

LEIGHTON, Mrs. Nicola Jane, BA(Hons) ACA *2000;* 53 Manor House, Flockton, WAKEFIELD, WEST YORKSHIRE, WF4 4AN.

•LEIGHTON, Mr. Norman, BA FCA *1978;* Norman Leighton, 4 Rue Des Orchidees, MC98000 MONACO, MONACO.

LEIGHTON, Mr. Paul Stuart, BSc ACA *1998;* 53 Manor House, Flockton, WAKEFIELD, WEST YORKSHIRE, WF4 4AN.

•LEIGHTON, Mr. Richard Martin, BA FCA *1982;* (Tax Fac), Leighton & Co, 40 Alexandra Road, WISBECH, PE13 1HQ.

LEIGHTON, Mr. Russell Eric, BA ACA *1998;* 4 Kensington Chase, SHEFFIELD, S10 4NN.

LEIGHTON, Mr. Steven Mark, BSc ACA *1982;* Cilonnen, Brimaston, Hayscastle, HAVERFORDWEST, DYFED, SA62 5PW.

LEIGHTON, Mr. Stuart, BA ACA *1994;* 98 Monifieth Road, Broughty Ferry, DUNDEE, DD5 2SJ.

LEIGHTON, Miss. Vicki Joanne, BA ACA *2005;* 62 Falcon Road, STOKE-ON-TRENT, ST3 7FQ.

LEIGHTON-DAVIES, Mr. Christopher John, BSc ACA *2005;* 5 Beaulieu Place, LONDON, W4 5SY.

LEIGHTON-YOUNG, Mrs. Sarah Louise, BSc ACA *1991;* 32 Wargrave Road, Twyford, READING, BERKSHIRE, RG10 9PQ.

•LEINHARDT, Mr. Geoffrey, BA FCA *1969;* Edwards Veeder (Oldham) LLP, Block E, Brunswick Square, Union Street, OLDHAM, OL1 1DE.

LEINSTER, Mr. Norman Kennedy, BA ACA *1992;* 42 Boundary Road, ST. ALBANS, HERTFORDSHIRE, AL1 4DW.

LEIPER, Mr. David Alan, MA FCA *1973;* 3 The Beeches, TRING, HP23 5NP.

LEIPER, Mr. Donald Alan, BA ACA *1989;* 3 Orton Fields Bramcote, NOTTINGHAM, NOTTINGHAMSHIRE, NG9 3NL.

LEIPER, Mr. Julian Guthrie, MA ACA *1979;* 55 Great King Street, EDINBURGH, EH3 6RP.

LEISHMAN, Mr. James Chisholm, FCA *1962;* Daniel De La Vega 1381, La Reina, SANTIAGO 6871420, CHILE. (Life Member)

LEITAO, Mr. Eduardo Francisco Felipe Read, LLB FCA *1963;* Rua Joao Antonio Gaspar, Lote 11 (No 180), Sao Joao do Estoril, 2765-296 ESTORIL, PORTUGAL.

LEITAO, Mr. Robert Mark, BSc ACA *1988;* 1 Scarsdale Villas, LONDON, W8 6PT.

LEITCH, Mr. Alexander Walker, FCA JDipMA *1958;* Ellerslie House, Ribchester Road, Clayton-le-dale, BLACKBURN, BB1 9EE. (Life Member)

LEITCH, Mr. Glenn Stuart, BA FCA *1974;* 4 Ashleigh, Orton Wistow, PETERBOROUGH, PE2 6FR.

LEITCH, Mr. James Robert, BSc ACA *1979;* P.O. Box HM 1475, HAMILTON HM FX, BERMUDA.

LEITCH, Mr. Matthew, BSc ACA *1995;* 29 Ridgeway, EPSOM, KT19 8LD.

LEITCH, The Revd. Peter William, FCA *1958;* 104 St. Andrews Road, FELIXSTOWE, IP11 7ED. (Life Member)

LEITCH, Ms. Susan Claire, ACA *2008;* 39 Western Road, OXFORD, OX1 4LF.

•LEITCH, Mrs. Suzanne Jane, ACA MAAT *2005;* Bay Tree Bookkeeping, 2 Minnis Green, Stelling Minnis, CANTERBURY, KENT, CT4 6AA.

LEITCH, Mrs. Tracey Lynne, BSc ACA *1989;* 7 The Promenade, PEACEHAVEN, EAST SUSSEX, BN10 8QF.

LEITE, Mr. Marc Jorge, BA ACA *2011;* 310 Woolston Warehouse, Grattan Road, BRADFORD, BD1 2NG.

LEITH, Miss. Sarah, ACA *2009;* 13 Woodlands Road, Heaton Mersey, STOCKPORT, CHESHIRE, SK4 3AF.

LEITHEAD, Mr. Iain Charles Hunter, BA ACA *1986;* 31 Westbourne Gardens, HOVE, EAST SUSSEX, BN3 5PL.

LEIVERS, Miss. Deborah Ann, BSc(Econ) ACA *2004;* 15 Maes Cadwgan, Creigiau, CARDIFF, CF15 9TQ.

•LEIWY, Mr. Daniel Harry Abram, MA FCA *1976;* Leiwy Sherman & Co, 19 Downalong, BUSHEY, WD23 1HZ.

•LEIWY, Mr. Philip, BA FCA ATII *1985;* P Leiwy & Co Ltd, 74 Salisbury Road, HARROW, HA1 1NZ.

LEJEUNE, Mr. Elias Sadi, BA FCA *1962;* 79 Kenilworth Avenue, READING, RG30 3EH.

LEKHYANANDA, Mr. Suvit, FCA *1964;* 150 Areesamphan, BANGKOK, 10400, THAILAND. (Life Member)

LELEAN, Miss. Rachel Margaret, ACA *1985;* 8th Floor, Standard Chartered, 1 Basinghall Avenue, LONDON, EC2V 5DD.

LELEU, Mr. Shaun, BSc ACA *1991;* Calle Margarita 33, Urb. El Paraiso Bajo, Estepona 29680, MALAGA, SPAIN.

•LELLIOTT, Mr. Timothy John, BA FCA *1989;* (Tax Fac), TJ Lelliott FCA, 7 The Lilacs, Barkham, WOKINGHAM, RG41 4UT.

LEMANS, Mrs. Natalie Dawn, ACA *2001;* 14 Purley Bury Close, PURLEY, SURREY, CR8 1HU.

LEMANS, Mr. Nicholas James, BEng ACA *1993;* Villa Sonne, Corfe Lodge Road, BROADSTONE, BH18 9NQ.

LEMANSKI, Mrs. Helena, BA ACA *2006;* with Deloitte LLP, Hill House, 1 Little New Street, LONDON, EC4A 3TR.

LEMANSKI, Mr. Philip Robert, MA FCA *1975;* Hill House Farm, Upper Weare, AXBRIDGE, SOMERSET, BS26 2LN.

LEMAR, Mr. Andrew Gordon, BSc ACA *1987;* Envy Retail Ltd, Ullswater House, Kendal Avenue, LONDON, W3 0XA.

LEMAR, Mr. Christopher John, MA FCA *1977;* 26 West Common Way, HARPENDEN, AL5 2LG.

LEMAR, Mrs. Suzannah Maria, BA ACA *1991;* 63 Eastbury Road, NORTHWOOD, HA6 3AP.

LEMEE, Mr. Darren Paul, ACA *1996;* Latchmere Rue Maze, St. Martin, GUERNSEY, GY4 6LW.

LEMESSIOU, Miss. Lina Apostolia, BSc ACA *1993;* 11 Byron Avenue, 1096 NICOSIA, CYPRUS.

LEMIN, Mrs. Sian, BSc ACA *2003;* Woodcroft Clydesdale Road, Box, CORSHAM, WILTSHIRE, SN13 8EN.

LEMLIN, Mr. Stephen Charles, BA ACA *1988;* TP3 Pty Ltd, Level 21, 580 George Street, SYDNEY, NSW 2000, AUSTRALIA.

LEMMON, Mr. David George, BA ACA *2008;* K P M G, 1 Canada Square, LONDON, E14 5AG.

LEMMON, Mr. Kenneth Stephen, FCA *1960;* Eastfield Farm, Chapel Haddlesey, SELBY, YO8 8QQ. (Life Member)

LEMMON, Mr. Mark Benjamin, MSc BA FCA *1978;* 11 Crescent Road, Wimbledon, LONDON, SW20 8EX.

LEMMON, Mr. Robert James, BA ACA *2009;* 1 Tablerock Avenue, PEMBROKE HM04, BERMUDA.

LEMON, Mr. Andrew James, ACA CA(NZ) *2010;* 64 Woodfield Lodge, Woodfield Road, CRAWLEY, WEST SUSSEX, RH10 8AH.

LEMON, Mr. Andrew Mark, BA ACA *1993;* 163 Stanley Hill, AMERSHAM, BUCKINGHAMSHIRE, HP7 9EY.

LEMON, Mr. Christopher Andrew, MA BA ACA *2010;* 10 Lyth Close, BRIDLINGTON, NORTH HUMBERSIDE, YO16 6YJ.

•LEMON, Mr. David, BA ACA *1997;* (Tax Fac), Saffery Champness, Beaufort House, 2 Beaufort Road, Clifton, BRISTOL, BS8 2AE.

LEMON, Mr. George Arthur, FCA *1947;* 61 Windarra Drive, City Beach, PERTH, WA 6015, AUSTRALIA. (Life Member)

LEMON, Mr. Julian Mark, MA ACA *1993;* 42 Bois Lane, AMERSHAM, BUCKINGHAMSHIRE, HP6 6BX.

LEMON, Mr. Mark Alexander Sebastian, MA ACA *2002;* LTQ Engineering Pty Limited, 70-90 Garden Drive, TULLAMARINE, VIC 3043, AUSTRALIA.

LEMPRIERE, Mr. Paul John, ACA *1979;* Riva Foods Ltd, 32 Copenhagen Road, Sutton Fields Industrial Estate, HULL, HU7 0XQ.

LEMPRIERE, Mr. Simon John, BA ACA *1993;* 36 Rickard Street, Balgowlah, SYDNEY, NSW 2093, AUSTRALIA.

LENARD, Mr. Andrew James Pyne, BA ACA *1999;* The Gables D/13, Triq Piscopo Macedonia, Xemxija, ST PAULS BAY SPB 4233, MALTA.

LENCH, Miss. Michelle, BA(Hons) ACA *2003;* 6 Bolney Green, LUTON, BEDFORDSHIRE, LU2 8RT.

LENDERING, Ms. Elizabeth Antonia, BA FCA *1996;* 72 Pwllmelin Road, CARDIFF, CF5 2NH.

LENDON, Mr. Gavin John, BA ACA *1992;* 9 Lords Meadow, Redbourn, ST. ALBANS, HERTFORDSHIRE, AL3 7BX.

LENEHAN, Mr. Benjamin, BA(Hons) ACA *2010;* Flat B, 80 Landor Road, LONDON, SW9 9PE.

LENEHAN, Mr. Peter, MA ACA *1996;* 6 Whinston Close, Naisberry Park, HARTLEPOOL, TS26 0PF.

LENETTE, Mr. Louis, BCom ACA *2000;* 21 Laurinda Crescent, SPRINGWOOD, QLD 4127, AUSTRALIA.

LENG, Mr. Ronald, FCA *1956;* Triton, Oakhurst Drive, CROWBOROUGH, TN6 2TA. (Life Member)

LENHAM, Miss. Lucy, BSc(Hons) ACA *2002;* 85 Albert Park Road, MALVERN, WORCESTERSHIRE, WR14 1RR.

LENIHAN, Mr. Richard Denis, ACA *2011;* 22 Hurland Road, TRURO, CORNWALL, TR1 2BU.

LENK, Mr. Karl Eugene, BA(Hons) ACA *2000;* 45 Sandhurst Road, CROWTHORNE, BERKSHIRE, RG45 7HY.

LENNARD, Mr. Andrew Charles, MA FCA *1980;* Financial Reporting Council Aldwych House, 71-91 Aldwych, LONDON, WC2B 4HN.

LENNARD, Mr. Andrew Dacre, ACA *1978;* Pheasant Hill House, Windmill Road, Kemble, CIRENCESTER, GL7 6AW.

LENNARD, Mr. Geoffrey, FCA *1962;* 5 Queensborough House South, 18 Oatlands Chase, WEYBRIDGE, SURREY, KT13 9SF.

•LENNARD, Mr. Mark John, FCA *1983;* Lennard Dakin, 88 Great King Street, MACCLESFIELD, CHESHIRE, SK11 6PW.

LENNARD, Mr. Stephen Charles, FCA *1974;* 17 Brookview Drive, Keyworth, NOTTINGHAM, NG12 5JN.

LENNARD, Mr. Timothy Andrew, BA ACA *1988;* The Farm, Berrylodge Farm, Blackmore Park Road, Welland, MALVERN, WORCESTERSHIRE WR13 6NL.

LENNARK, Mr. Jason Ian, ACA CTA *1994;* 24c Clifton Gardens, LONDON, NW11 7EL.

•LENNEY, Mrs. Susanna Loretta, BA FCA *1979;* (Tax Fac), Watson Lenney, Pendell Court Farmhouse, Pendell Road, Bletchingley, REDHILL, RH1 4QH.

LENNIE, Ms. Vanessa Jane, ACA CA(NZ) *2009;* Flat 1, 89 Crescent Lane, LONDON, SW4 9AW.

•LENNON, Mr. Anthony, BA FCA *1976;* Rigby Lennon & Co, 20 Winmarleigh Street, WARRINGTON, WA1 1JY.

LENNON, Mr. Geoffrey Peter, FCA *1979;* Access House, 16a Lenten Street, ALTON, GU34 1HG.

•LENNON, Mr. Hugh Edward, FCA *1975;* Hugh Lennon & Associates, 8-10 Church View, CAVAN, COUNTY CAVAN, IRELAND.

LENNON, Mr. John William, BA FCA *1952;* 15 Moultrie Road, RUGBY, CV21 3BD. (Life Member)

LENNON, Mr. Mark Alexander, MSc ACA *1982;* Singer & Friedlander Ltd, 21 New Street, LONDON, EC2M 4HR.

•LENNON, Mr. Peter John, MA FCA *1983;* PricewaterhouseCoopers LLP, 1 Embankment Place, LONDON, WC2N 6RH. See also PricewaterhouseCoopers

LENNOX, Mrs. Elizabeth May Turner, BTech ACA *1982;* Blazefield House Farm, Blazefield, Pateley Bridge, HARROGATE, HG3 5DR.

LENNOX, Mr. Eric Gordon Angus, BA ACA *1982;* 183 Dunkirk Avenue, Desborough, KETTERING, NN14 2PR.

LENNOX, Mr. Ian, FCA *1979;* 30 The Ryde, HATFIELD, AL9 5DL.

LENNOX, Mr. Ian William, ACA *1980;* Rose Cottage, The Dhoor, Ramsey, ISLE OF MAN, IM7 4ED.

LENNOX, Mrs. Linda Ann, BSc ACA *1980;* Joseph Rochford Gardens Ltd, Pipers End, Letty Green, HERTFORD, SG14 2PB.

LENNOX, Mr. Michael James Madill, FCA *1967;* 59 Top End, Renhold, BEDFORD, MK41 0LS.

LENNOX, Mr. Norman Barrington, BA ACA *1991;* 92 Dunmail Drive, CARLISLE, CA2 6DQ.

LENNOX, Mrs. Rachel Tegwen, BSc(Hons) ACA CTA *2002;* 45 Woodlands Drive, Groby, LEICESTER, LE6 0BR.

LENNOX, Miss. Sarah Louise, ACA *2011;* 74 Bramley Road, LONDON, N14 4HS.

LENON, Mr. Philip Hugh, BA ACA *1987;* 1 Highbury Road, LONDON, SW19 7PR.

LENOX-SMITH, Mr. Geoffrey Martin, ACA *1984;* 27 Alacross Road, Ealing, LONDON, W5 4HT.

•LENT, Mr. Jeffrey Alan, FCA *1968;* Hogarth House, 6 North End, LONDON, NW3 7HL.

LENT, Mr. Martin Victor, FCA *1977;* Oakmayne Properties Ltd, The Factory, Winchester Wharf, Clink Street, LONDON, SE1 9DG.

LENTHALL, Mrs. Nicola Louise, ACA *1987;* Easter Management Ltd, 18 Buckingham Gate, LONDON, SW1E 6LB.

•①**LENTHALL, Mr. Richard, BA FCA** *1987;* Marshmallow, Sally Deards Lane, WELWYN, HERTFORDSHIRE, AL6 9UE.

LENTIN, Mr. Andrew Cavis, BSc ACA *1996;* Management Consulting Group Plc, 10 Fleet Place, LONDON, EC4M 7RB.

LENTIN, Mrs. Susannah Jane, BSc ACA *1992;* 198 The Hill, BURFORD, OXFORDSHIRE, OX18 4HX.

•**LENTON, Mr. James Alan, BSc(Hons) ACA** *2001;* Ernst & Young LLP, 1 More London Place, LONDON, SE1 2AF. See also Ernst & Young Europe LLP

LENTON, Mr. Paul Richard, BSc ACA *1988;* 13-21 Curtain Road, LONDON, EC2A 3LU.

LENTON, Mr. Philip John, LLB ACA *2001;* with Deloitte LLP, 2 New Street Square, LONDON, EC4A 3BZ.

LENTON, Ms. Sarah Jane, MA ACA *1995;* 1 Wike Ridge View, LEEDS, LS17 9NS.

LENTON-SMITH, Mr. Colin Edward, FCA *1979;* Top House, Middle Hill, Englefield Green, EGHAM, TW20 0JG.

LENZ, Mr. Maurice Anthony, FCA *1968;* 9 Priory Close, Totteridge, LONDON, N20 8BB.

LENZAN, Mr. Jack Adam, BSc(Hons) ACA *2010;* 5 Granville Road, WELLING, DA16 1SG.

LEO, Mrs. Carol, BSc ACA *1987;* 38 Farndale Road, KNARESBOROUGH, NORTH YORKSHIRE, HG5 0NY.

LEOFFELER, Mr. Harold Victor, FCA *1960;* 10 The Lindens, Well Lane, Stock, INGATESTONE, CM4 9NH.

LEON, Mr. Anthony Jack, DL FCA *1960;* 4 Westfields, Hale, ALTRINCHAM, CHESHIRE, WA15 0LL.

LEON, Mr. Anthony Michael, BA ACA *2005;* Flat 12, Lyncroft Mansions, Lyncroft Gardens, LONDON, NW6 1JX.

LEON, Mr. Farrell Stanley, FCA *1962;* 6 Eme Etage, 31 Avenue Bugeaud, 75116 PARIS, FRANCE.

LEON, Miss. Natalie Joanne, BSc ACA *2001;* 2 Bloomsbury Close, LONDON, NW7 2DT.

LEON, Mr. William Rupert Emil Henry, BA(Hons) FCA *1958;* Le Chateau Du Monastere, 9 Rue Bourlon-Clauzel, 92410 VILLE D'AVRAY, FRANCE. (Life Member)

LEONARD, Mr. Andrew Peter, FCA *1976;* with ICAEW, Metropolitan House, 321 Avebury Boulevard, MILTON KEYNES, MK9 2FZ.

LEONARD, Mr. Anthony, BA ACA *2003;* 68 Windsor Road, RICHMOND, SURREY, TW9 2EL.

LEONARD, Mr. Brian, FCA *1951;* 7 St. Bernards Road, Knott End-On-Sea, POULTON-LE-FYLDE, FY6 0AW. (Life Member)

LEONARD, Miss. Charlotte, BA ACA *1989;* 51 Whellock Road, Chiswick, LONDON, W4 1DY.

LEONARD, Mr. Christopher Paul, BSc ACA *2006;* 67b Lavender Sweep, LONDON, SW11 1DY.

LEONARD, Mr. David James, BA ACA *2002;* 120 Dane Road, SALE, CHESHIRE, M33 2BX.

•**LEONARD, Mr. Duncan Michael, ACA** *2001;* DL Accountancy Limited, 2 Brunel Way, Church Gresley, SWADLINCOTE, DERBYSHIRE, DE11 9LE.

LEONARD, Mr. Edmund James, LLB ACA *1995;* 9 Lincoln Close, Wellesbourne, WARWICK, CV35 9JE.

LEONARD, Miss. Emer, BSc ACA *2010;* 3 Larchwood Avenue, BANBRIDGE, COUNTY DOWN, BT32 3XH.

LEONARD, Mr. Gary Harvey, ACA MAAT *2002;* 51 Winns Terrace, Walthamstow, LONDON, E17 5EJ.

LEONARD, Miss. Gillian Claire, ACA *2008;* 5 Bairns Ford Court, New Carron, FALKIRK, FK2 7LZ.

LEONARD, Mr. Gordon Lawrence, FCA *1960;* 35 Timber Lane, OAKVILLE L6L 2Z4, ON, CANADA. (Life Member)

LEONARD, Miss. Helen Anne, BSc ACA *2002;* 29 Lumiere Court, 209 Balham High Road, LONDON, SW17 7BQ.

LEONARD, Mrs. Janice Carole, BSc ACA *1985;* 176 Portsmouth Road, Horndean, WATERLOOVILLE, PO8 9HP.

LEONARD, Miss. Joanne Pearl, BA ACA *1996;* 6 Peppercorn Way, Hedge End, SOUTHAMPTON, SO30 2NA.

LEONARD, Mr. John Bell, FCA *1957;* 15 Nicholas Avenue, Whitburn, SUNDERLAND, SR6 7DB. (Life Member)

•**LEONARD, Mr. John Douglas, FCA** *1980;* (Tax Fac), Brennan Neil & Leonard, 32 Brenkley Way, Blezard Business Park, Seaton Burn, NEWCASTLE UPON TYNE, NE13 6DS.

LEONARD, Mr. Martin Simon, BEng ACA *1991;* 35 Kathleen Street, CORINDA, QLD 4075, AUSTRALIA.

LEONARD, Mr. Michael, FCA *1972;* 35 York Drive, Flagstaff Hill, ADELAIDE, SA 5159, AUSTRALIA.

LEONARD, Miss. Michelle Louise, ACA *1998;* Francis Clark Chartered Accountants Sigma House, Oak View Close, TORQUAY, TQ2 7FF.

LEONARD, Mr. Neil Trevor, BSc ACA *1983;* Windrush House, Fortune Hill, KNARESBOROUGH, HG5 9DG.

LEONARD, Mr. Patrick, BSc ACA *1994;* 20 Colehill Gardens, Fulham Palace Road, LONDON, SW6 6SZ.

LEONARD, Mr. Peter Charles, BSc FCA *1978;* Scrafton, 24a Lyons Lane, Appleton, WARRINGTON, WA4 5JG.

LEONARD, Mr. Peter Michael, ACA *2007;* 32 Mercer Road, BILLERICAY, CM11 1EP.

LEONARD, Mr. Richard John, MA FCA *1973;* (Tax Fac), with Dixon Wilson, 22 Chancery Lane, LONDON, WC2A 1LS.

LEONARD, Mrs. Sarah Amanda, ACA *2002;* Westcote, 29 The Cotes, Soham, ELY, CAMBRIDGESHIRE, CB7 5EP.

LEONARD, Mr. Stephen, BSc ACA *1985;* Ferndale Benn Lane, Farley, SALISBURY, SP5 1AF.

LEONARD, Mr. Steven Charles, BA FCA *1977;* Financial Reporting Council, 5th Floor, Aldwych House, 71-91 Aldwych, LONDON, WC2B 4HN.

LEONARD, Mr. Steven James, MSc BSc ACA *2011;* 43 Northwick Road, EVESHAM, WORCESTERSHIRE, WR11 3AL.

LEONARD, Mr. Steven John, BA ACA *1998;* Hogg Robinson Plc Global House, Victoria Street, BASINGSTOKE, RG21 3BT.

LEONARD, Mr. Stuart John, BSc ACA *1984;* 3 Pak Tam Chung, NT, SAI KUNG, HONG KONG SAR.

LEONARD, Mr. Timothy, FCA *1969;* Rua Dona Mara 394, Vila de sao Fernando, Cotia, SAO PAULO, 06705 520, BRAZIL. (Life Member)

LEONARDI, Mr. Clarence William Joseph, FCA *1951;* 27 Kirby's Way, HUNTSVILLE P1H 2M6, ON, CANADA. (Life Member)

LEONG, Miss. Alethea, BEng ACA *2003;* 12 Kensington Court Place, LONDON, W8 5BJ.

LEONG, Mr. Andrew, ACA *2009;* 32 Park Avenue, RUISLIP, MIDDLESEX, HA4 7UQ.

LEONG, Mr. Benjamin Wye Hoong, BSc ACA *1999;* Desa Bistari Condo, Unit 2A-2-11 Jalan Setiabistari, Damansara Heights, 50490 KUALA LUMPUR, FEDERAL TERRITORY, MALAYSIA.

•**LEONG, Miss. Choi Har, FCA** *1975;* Wandle House Associates, Wandle House, 47 Wandle Road, CROYDON, SURREY, CR0 1DF.

LEONG, Miss. Choy Ying, BA FCA *1994;* 25 Jalan Goh Boon Hiong, Taynton View, Cheras, 56000 KUALA LUMPUR, FEDERAL TERRITORY, MALAYSIA.

LEONG, Mr. Colin Yeen Luen, ACA *2010;* Flat 1/A Foundling Court, Brunswick Centre, LONDON, WC1N 1AN.

LEONG, Mr. David, ACA *2008;* 59 Bucknalls Drive, Bricket Wood, ST. ALBANS, HERTFORDSHIRE, AL2 3XJ.

LEONG, Mr. David Ting Kwok, BSc ACA *1992;* 26/F Citicorp Centre, 18 Whitfield Road, CAUSEWAY BAY, HONG KONG ISLAND, HONG KONG SAR.

LEONG, Miss. Elaine Chui Ling, BSc(Econ) ACA *2004;* Maverick Elm Grove, Wivenhoe, COLCHESTER, CO7 9AY.

LEONG, Miss. Eva, ACA *1988;* Flat 3B Block 5, Phoenix Court, 39 Kennedy Road, WAN CHAI, HONG KONG SAR.

LEONG, Mr. Frank Yee Yew, MBA ACA *1979;* 808 Thomson Road, Apartment 07-19, Thomson 800, SINGAPORE 298190, SINGAPORE.

LEONG, Mr. Herman Soon Lee, ACA *1979;* 16 Silver Springs Mews N.W., CALGARY T3B 3R3, AB, CANADA.

LEONG, Mrs. Jacqueline, ACA CA(SA) *2010;* 5 Hutton Mews, Pleasance Road, LONDON, SW15 5HZ.

LEONG, Miss. Julia, ACA *2004;* 10 Tanglin Road #03-04, SINGAPORE 247908, SINGAPORE.

LEONG, Mrs. Katherine Sii Har, ACA *1979;* Bara Shipping Agencies Co.Ltd, U Chu Liang Building, 968 Rama 4 Road, BANGKOK, 10500, THAILAND.

LEONG, Mr. Khian Kiee, ACA *1980;* K K Leong & Partners, 7500A Beach Road, 12-313 The Plaza, SINGAPORE 199591, SINGAPORE.

LEONG, Mr. Kin Bong, ACA *2008;* PricewaterhouseCoopers, 26/F Office Tower A, Beijing Fortune Plaza, 23 Dongsanhuan North Road, Chaoyang District, BEIJING 100020 CHINA.

LEONG, Mr. Kong Sang, ACA *2008;* Flat 7, 7/F Whampoa Estate Block R, 6 Tak Man Street, HUNG HOM, KOWLOON, HONG KONG SAR.

LEONG, Mr. Kwok Hung, BSc ACA *1984;* B2-11-3A Forest Green Condo, 43000 KAJANG, SELANGOR, MALAYSIA.

LEONG, Mr. Lincoln Kwok Kuen, BA ACA *1985;* House 31 Manderly Garden, 48 Deep Water Bay Road, DEEP WATER BAY, HONG KONG ISLAND, HONG KONG SAR.

LEONG, Mr. Lipp San, BSc ACA *1994;* P O Box 696, KUALA BELAIT, 6006, BRUNEI DARUSSALAM.

•**LEONG, Mr. Michael Chee Loke, FCA** *1982;* (Tax Fac), Michael Leong and Company Limited, 43 Overstone Road, LONDON, W6 0AD. See also Michael Leong & Company

LEONG, Miss. Miew Chih, FCA *1980;* 12 First Avenue, SINGAPORE 268748, SINGAPORE.

LEONG, Miss. Mun Sean, BSc ACA *2003;* 152-5-6 Villa Flora Condo, Jalan Burhanuddin Helmi, Taman Tun Dr Ismail, 60000 KUALA LUMPUR, FEDERAL TERRITORY, MALAYSIA.

LEONG, Mr. Mun Seng, FCA *1979;* 25 Japonica Road, EPPING, NSW 2121, AUSTRALIA.

LEONG, Miss. Oi Ling, FCA *1970;* AA-16-01., Mont' Kiara 10, Jalan Kiara 1, Mont' Kiara, 50480 KUALA LUMPUR, FEDERAL TERRITORY MALAYSIA.

LEONG, Miss. Onnwah, ACA *1988;* 11 Chestnut Grove, NEW MALDEN, KT3 3JJ.

LEONG, Mr. Pooi Wah, BA ACA *1997;* A-3-1 3rd Floor 8 Avenue, Jalan Sungai Jerneh 8/1, 46050 PETALING JAYA, MALAYSIA.

LEONG, Mr. Ronald Wai Mun, ACA *1983;* 35 Garrick Avenue, Golders Green, LONDON, NW11 9AR.

LEONG, Mr. Shin Hyun, FCA *1977;* S H Leong & Co, 138-2 Jalan Radin Anum 1, Bandar Baru Sri Petaling, 57000 KUALA LUMPUR, FEDERAL TERRITORY, MALAYSIA.

LEONG, Mr. Siew Meng, ACA CISA FRM *1994;* Flat H 12th Floor Tower 23A, Mei Ka Court No 23A South, Horizons Drive, AP LEI CHAU, HONG KONG ISLAND, HONG KONG SAR.

LEONG, Miss. Sing Tze, BSc(Hons) ACA *2011;* Flat 13, Levyne Court, Pine Street, LONDON, EC1R 0JQ.

LEONG, Miss. Sou Wan, FCA *1973;* Tina Leong, 21 Blandford Close, LONDON, N2 0DH.

LEONG, Ms. Swee Leng, BSc ACA *1991;* 55 Jalan BU2/3, Bandar Utama, 47800 PETALING JAYA, MALAYSIA.

•**LEONG, Mr. Sylvester, ACA** *1993;* Foo Kon & Tan, 1st FloorUnit No 15, Lot 7191Bgn Haji Hassa, Hj Abd. Ghani Dan Anak-anak, Jalan Jaya Negara, Kg Pandan KUALA BELAIT KA 1931 BRUNEI DARUSSALAM.

LEONG, Ms. Wai Kuan, BA ACA *1995;* 9 Jalan SS22/16, 47400 PETALING JAYA, SELANGOR, MALAYSIA.

LEONG, Miss. Wai Ling Mishell, BSc ACA *2005;* 130 Thomson Road, Unit 04-01 Birmingham Mansions, SINGAPORE 307682, SINGAPORE.

LEONG, Mr. Wing Pun, BA ACA *1983;* 22 Lonicera Place, CHERRYBROOK, NSW 2126, AUSTRALIA.

LEONG, Miss. Winifred Nyok Fan, FCA *1993;* 94 Guibal Road, LONDON, SE12 9LZ.

LEONG, Mr. Yoon Siang, MA ACA *1993;* Lafata (Far East) Limited, Room 2104C Tower 1, Admiralty Centre, 18 Harcourt Road, ADMIRALTY, HONG KONG ISLAND HONG KONG SAR.

LEONG-CHUNG, Mr. Herve, BA ACA *1990;* with Smythe Ratcliffe CA, 7th Floor Marine Building, 355 Burrard Street, VANCOUVER V6C 2G8, BC, CANADA.

LEONG-SON, Mr. Louis Raymond, FCA *1974;* 12 Ayleswater, AYLESBURY, BUCKINGHAMSHIRE, HP19 0FB.

•**LEONIDOU, Mr. Leonidas Anastasis, FCA** *1979;* (Tax Fac), Lyons Leonidou, Galla House, 695 High Rd, North Finchley, LONDON, N12 0BT.

LEONTIOU, Mr. Harris, BSc ACA MSI *1993;* P.O. Box 62155, 152 10 HALANDRI, GREECE.

•**LEOPARD, Mr. Adrian John, FCA** *1973;* Adrian Leopard & Co, PO Box 27, Alderney, GUERNSEY, GY9 3AS. See also Alderney Offshore Ltd

LEOPARD, Mr. Roger Anthony, FCA *1966;* 168 Sentier de La Roche, Logras, 01630 PERON, FRANCE.

LEOW, Mr. Brian Poh Kak, FCA *1974;* Ridgemont 19/95A Ridge Street, NORTH SYDNEY, NSW 2060, AUSTRALIA.

LEOW, Miss. Kar Ping, BA ACA *2002;* 3 Persiaran Kuantan, Setapak, 53200 KUALA LUMPUR, FEDERAL TERRITORY, MALAYSIA.

LEOW, Mr. Min Fong, FCA *1973;* Kurnia Insurance (Malaysia), Berhad Menara Kurnia, 9 Jalan PJS 8/9, 46150 PETALING JAYA, MALAYSIA.

LEOW, Miss. Siok Ling, BA ACA *1993;* 8/F Block 1, Scenic Villas, 18 Scenic Villa Drive, Pokfulam, POK FU LAM, HONG KONG ISLAND HONG KONG SAR.

LEOW, Mr. Thang Fong, FCA *1976;* c/o South Malaysia Industries Bhd, 15th Floor Lorong P.Ramlee, Menara SMI, KUALA LUMPUR, FEDERAL TERRITORY, MALAYSIA.

LEOW, Mr. Wayne Tze Waye, BSc ACA *2006;* 240A West End Lane, West Hampstead, LONDON, NW6 1LG.

LEOW, Miss. Wee Yean, ACA *2011;* 40 ss25/39, Taman Mayang, 47301 PETALING JAYA, MALAYSIA.

•**LEPPARD, Mrs. Josephine Sara, BA FCA** *1983;* with Harrison Beale & Owen Management Services, Highdown House, 11 Highdown Road, Sydenham, LEAMINGTON SPA, WARWICKSHIRE CV31 1XT.

LEPPARD, Mr. Neil Alexander, BSc ACA *1996;* with PricewaterhouseCoopers LLP, 1 Embankment Place, LONDON, WC2N 6RH.

•**LEPPARD, Mrs. Suzanne, BA ACA** *2006;* Azumba, 43 De Paul Way, Weald Park, BRENTWOOD, ESSEX, CM14 4FT.

LEPPINGTON, Mr. Peter Edward, BA ACA *1995;* 17 Chiswell Road, POOLE, BH17 9FB.

LEPPINGTON, Mr. William Neil, ACA *1969;* 1 Carlton Croft, Streetly, SUTTON COLDFIELD, B74 3JT.

LEPTOS-BOURGI, Mr. Socratis, BSc ACA *1998;* with PricewaterhouseCoopers, 268-270 Kifissias Avenue, Halandri, 15232 ATHENS, GREECE.

LER, Mr. Beng Teck, ACA *1980;* 726 Jalan Rasah, 70300 SEREMBAN, MALAYSIA. (Life Member)

LERAT-DEWAVRIN, Miss. Cecile, ACA *2002;* Park House Ward Williams Limited, 25-27 Monument Hill, WEYBRIDGE, KT13 8RT.

•**LERMAN, Mr. Michael, FCA** *1984;* (Tax Fac), Starplayer Limited, 510 Centennial Park, Centennial Avenue, Elstree, BOREHAMWOOD, HERTFORDSHIRE WD6 3FG.

LERMER, Mr. David, ACA *1985;* with PricewaterhouseCoopers Inc, PO Box 2799, CAPE TOWN, C.P., 8000, SOUTH AFRICA.

•**LERMER, Mr. Jeffrey Ian, BSc** *1989;* (Tax Fac), Jeff Lermer & Associates LLP, 42 Lytton Road, New Barnet, BARNET, HERTFORDSHIRE, EN5 5BY. See also Jeff Lermer and Associates and New Thinking Leaders Limited

•**LERMIT, Mr. Michael Jonathan, MA ACA** *1982;* MJ Lermit, 9 Tennyson Mansions, Queen's Club Gardens, LONDON, W14 9TJ.

LERMON, Mr. David Nicholas, MA FCA *1970;* (Tax Fac), Beech House, Cotswold Avenue, Lisvane, CARDIFF, CF14 0TA.

LERNER, Mr. Damon Russell, BSc(Econ) ACA *1999;* 22 St. Albans Road, WOODFORD GREEN, ESSEX, IG8 9EQ.

LERNER, Mr. Howard Stephen, FCA *1975;* SBLR LLP, 2345 Yonge Street, Suite 300, TORONTO M4P 2E5, ON, CANADA.

•**LERNER, Mr. Leonard, FCA** *1975;* 2L Cara House, 339 Seven Sisters Road, LONDON, N15 6RD.

•**LERNER, Mr. Michael Anthony, FCA** *1975;* (Tax Fac), Wilson Wright LLP, First Floor, Thavies Inn House, 3-4 Holborn Circus, LONDON, EC1N 2HA.

LERNER, Mr. Neil Joseph, MA FCA *1972;* (Member of Council 2001 - 2006), 2 Priory Close, Totteridge, LONDON, N20 8BB.

LERNER, Mr. Stanley Jack, FCA *1957;* 37 Hove Park Way, HOVE, EAST SUSSEX, BN3 6PW. (Life Member)

•**LERNER, Mr. Stephen Ian, FCA ATII** *1983;* (Tax Fac), Bartrum Lerner, 39A Welbeck Street, LONDON, W1G 8DH.

LERONI, Mrs. Joanna Louise, BSc ACA *1989;* Trellick, Laurel Bank, TUNBRIDGE WELLS, TN4 0DG.

LERWILL, Mr. Robert Earl, BA FCA *1977;* Old Rectory, Runwell Road, WICKFORD, SS11 7HW.

•**LERWILL, Mr. Timothy Lynden, BSc FCA** *1999;* Baker Tilly UK Audit LLP, Hartwell House, 55-61 Victoria Street, BRISTOL, BS1 6AD. See also Baker Tilly Tax and Advisory Services LLP

LESH, Mr. John, FCA *1959;* The Towan House, Politmore, EXETER, EX4 0AW. (Life Member)

LESIAK, Mr. Jerzy Stanislaw, BA FCA *1990;* with Heaton Lumb Lisle, Thorpe House, 61 Richardshaw Lane, PUDSEY, LS28 7EL.

LESJONGARD, Mr. Alain Paul, BSc ACA *1993;* Bank of New York, 1 Canada Square, LONDON, E14 5AL.

LESKIN, Mr. Bernard, FCA *1954;* 5 Ashcombe Gardens, EDGWARE, HA8 8HR.

LESLIE, Mrs. Christine Eleanor Ann, ACA *2008;* with BDO LLP, 1 Bridgewater Place, Water Lane, LEEDS, LS11 5RU.

•**LESLIE, Mr. Duncan, BSc ACA** *1999;* with Deloitte LLP, Abbots House, Abbey Street, READING, RG1 3BD.

•**LESLIE, Ms. Janet, MSc BA ACA** *1998;* with Ernst & Young LLP, 1 More London Place, LONDON, SE1 2AF.

LESLIE, Mr. Jason Ricky, ACA CA(SA) *2011;* 17 St. Marys Road, LONDON, NW11 9UE.

LESLIE, Mrs. Maria, BSc ACA *1990;* 39 Orchard Way, Horsmonden, TONBRIDGE, TN12 8LA.

LESLIE, Dr. Mark, ACA *2009;* 12 Westminster Terrace, Douglas, ISLE OF MAN, IM1 4ED.

LESLIE, Mrs. Nadine Lucy, MA(Oxon) ACA *2005;* (Tax Fac), 24 Beauchamp Road, BRISTOL, BS7 8LQ.

LESLIE, Mr. Niall Malcolm, BA FCA *1977;* 69 Speldhurst Road, LONDON, W4 1BY.

LESLIE, Miss. Paula Scott, BCom ACA *2000;* 12 Denoon Terrace, DUNDEE, DD2 2EL.

LESLIE, Mrs. Rachel Mary, BA(Hons) ACA *2001;* 117 Moss Lane, Timperley, ALTRINCHAM, CHESHIRE, WA15 6JG.

•**LESLIE, Mr. Richard Andrew, MBA FCA FCCA FCMI** *1977;* (Tax Fac), R.A. Leslie & Co LLP, Gowran House, 56 Broad Street, Chipping Sodbury, BRISTOL, BS37 6AG. See also R.A. Leslie & Co

LESLIE, Mr. Richard Paterson, ACA *2008;* Flat 8, 320c Earlsfield Road, LONDON, SW18 3EJ.

LESLIE, Mr. Richard Stephen, FCA *1964;* Charterhouse Simon Ltd, 52 Alston Road, BARNET, HERTFORDSHIRE, EN5 4EY. (Life Member)

LESLIE, Mr. Spencer Adam, BA ACA *1994;* 6 Abbey View, Mill Hill, LONDON, NW7 4PB.

LESLIE, Mr. Stephen Douglas, BSc ACA *1993;* Mirabaud Securities, 33 Grosvenor Place, LONDON, SW1X 7HY.

LESNAJA, Ms. Ana, ACA *2008;* A B N Amro Bank NV, 250 Bishopsgate, LONDON, EC2M 4AA.

LESNIAK, Mrs. Alicja Barbara, BSc FCA *1976;* Flat 6, 28 Chesham Place, LONDON, SW1X 8HG.

LESOURD, Mrs. Alison Vivien, BSc ACA *1987;* Clos Des Ecossais II, 1410 WATERLOO, BELGIUM.

LESSELS, Mr. Bruce William, BA ACA *1994;* Apt. 26, Avalon, West Street, BRIGHTON, BN1 2RP.

LESSER, Mr. Henry Alan, BSc ACA *1981;* 34 Middleway, Hampstead Garden Suburb, LONDON, NW11 6SG.

LESSER, Mr. Simon, FCA *1979;* McGladrey & Pullen Llp, 1 South Wacker Drive, CHICAGO, IL 60606, UNITED STATES.

•**LESSER, Mr. Stephen Morris, BA FCA** *1977;* (Tax Fac), Lesser & Co, 147 Station Road, North Chingford, LONDON, E4 6AG. See also Lesser Business Services Ltd

LESTER, Mr. Adam Paul, BA ACA *1999;* Flat 4 Tavistock Chambers, 40 Bloomsbury Way, LONDON, WC1A 2SE.

•**LESTER, Mr. Alan Keith, FCA** *1975;* H W Fisher & Company, Acre House, 11-15 William Road, LONDON, NW1 3ER. See also H W Fisher & Company Limited

•**LESTER, Mr. Alan Terence, FCA** *1973;* Association of Optometrists, 61 Southwark Street, LONDON, SE1 0HL.

LESTER, Mr. Andrew Lawrence, MA ACA *1996;* 11 Alfriston Grove, Kings Hill, WEST MALLING, KENT, ME19 4AS.

LESTER, Mr. Brian, FCA *1966;* 168 Southchurch Boulevard, SOUTHEND-ON-SEA, SS2 4UX.

•**LESTER, Miss. Catherine Anna, BA ACA** *2006;* with PricewaterhouseCoopers LLP, 1 Embankment Place, LONDON, WC2N 6RH.

LESTER, Mr. David Frederick, FCA *1962;* 25 Beech Way, Blackmore End, Wheathampstead, ST. ALBANS, HERTFORDSHIRE, AL4 8LY.

LESTER, Mr. Edmund Alfred Keith, BSc FCA FCCA *1968;* 28 Birds Hill Drive, Oxshott, LEATHERHEAD, SURREY, KT22 0SP.

•**LESTER, Mr. Graham Charles, BSc ACA** *1979;* 42 Luke Avenue, BURWOOD, NSW 2134, AUSTRALIA.

LESTER, Mr. Guy Anthony, MA MEng ACA *1989;* Ministry of Defence ; 02.F.17, Main Building Horse Guards Avenue Whitehall, LONDON, SW1A 2HB.

LESTER, Mr. Huw Edgar Thomas, BSc ACA *2002;* PricewaterhouseCoopers Riverside Centre 123 Eagle Street GPO Box 150, BRISBANE, QLD QLD4001, AUSTRALIA.

①**LESTER, Mr. Ian David, ACA** *1979;* with PricewaterhouseCoopers LLP, 89 Sandyford Road, NEWCASTLE UPON TYNE, NE1 8HW.

•**LESTER, Mr. Jason Roy, BA ACA** *1998;* Ernst & Young LLP, 1 Colmore Square, BIRMINGHAM, B4 6HQ. See also Ernst & Young Europe LLP

•**LESTER, Mr. Jeremy, FCA** *1984;* Baines Jewitt, Barrington House, 41-45 Yarm Lane, STOCKTON-ON-TEES, CLEVELAND, TS18 3EA. See also Barrington House Solutions Limited

LESTER, Mr. Jonathan Adrian David, BSc ACA *1990;* The Old Rectory, Milton Abbas, BLANDFORD FORUM, DORSET, DT11 0BW.

LESTER, Mr. Jonathan Robert, FCA *1969;* The Old School House, Church Lane, Brook, GODALMING, SURREY, GU8 5UQ.

LESTER, Mr. Justin Lawrence, BA(Hons) ACA *2002;* 58 Cambourne Close, Adwick-le-Street, DONCASTER, SOUTH YORKSHIRE, DN6 7DB.

LESTER, Mr. Lawrence, FCA *1961;* with Lester & Co, 25 Station Road, HINCKLEY, LEICESTERSHIRE, LE10 1AP. (Life Member)

•**LESTER, Mr. Mark Adrian, FCA** *1982;* (Tax Fac), Lester & Co, 25 Station Road, HINCKLEY, LEICESTERSHIRE, LE10 1AP.

•**LESTER, Mr. Martin, FCA** *1968;* 8 Beaconsfield Road, SUTTON COLDFIELD, WEST MIDLANDS, B74 2NX.

LESTER, Mr. Martin, FCA *1968;* Church House, 47 Church Street, Dunnington, YORK, YO19 5PP.

LESTER, Mr. Matthew John, BA ACA *1988;* 13 Pond Road, Blackheath, LONDON, SE3 0SL.

LESTER, Mrs. Megan Howell, BA(Hons) ACA *2001;* Little Putlands, Fairwarp, UCKFIELD, EAST SUSSEX, TN22 3BJ.

LESTER, Mr. Michael, FCA *1961;* 5 Avon Mews, Devonshire Road, PINNER, HA5 4ND. (Life Member)

LESTER, Mr. Michael David, BA(Hons) ACA *2001;* Little Putlands, Fairwarp, UCKFIELD, EAST SUSSEX, TN22 3BJ.

•**LESTER, Mr. Michael Patrick, BSc FCA** *1989;* (Tax Fac), Lester & Co, 25 Station Road, HINCKLEY, LEICESTERSHIRE, LE10 1AP.

LESTER, Mr. Richard, FCA *1980;* 16 Ferney Road, Cheshunt, WALTHAM CROSS, EN7 6XP.

LESTER, Miss. Sarah Louise, BSc ACA *2004;* 9 Green Close, Epping Green, EPPING, ESSEX, CM16 6PS.

LESTER, Mrs. Sinead Anna, BA ACA *2005;* 73 Chudleigh Road, TWICKENHAM, TW2 7QP.

LESTER, Mr. Stuart, FCA *1971;* 65 Cotswold Gardens, LONDON, NW2 1QT.

LESTER, Miss. Vicky Rosemary, ACA *1994;* 18 pucknells close, SWANLEY, br8 7th.

LESTER-SWINDELL, Miss. Clare, BSc ACA *1993;* 12 Landrock Road, LONDON, N8 9HL.

LESTNER, Mrs. Joanne Francine, BA ACA *1995;* 16 Windermere Drive, LEEDS, LS17 7UZ.

LESZCZYSZYN, Mr. Oleh Jurij, BSc ACA *1992;* Bank of Montreal, Financial Strategy T&O, 55 Bloor Street West, 12th Floor, TORONTO M4W 3N5, ON CANADA.

LETCH, Mr. Frank William, FCA *1952;* Knightwood Lodge, Knightwood Avenue, LYNDHURST, SO43 7DQ. (Life Member)

LETCHET, Mr. Nicholas Hugh, BA ACA *1981;* Swindon College, North Star Avenue, SWINDON, SN2 1DY.

LETCHFIELD, Mr. Jonathan Mark, BA ACA *1987;* 13 Collins Street, Blackheath, LONDON, SE3 0UG.

LETCHFORD, Mr. Grahame Howard, FCA *1975;* Anchorage, Links Road, LONGNIDDRY, EAST LOTHIAN, EH32 0NJ.

LETCHFORD, Miss. Sally, ACA *2010;* 3/30 LeFevre Terrace, NORTH ADELAIDE, SA 5006, AUSTRALIA.

LETCHUMANAN, Mr. Narayanan, ACA *1991;* Block 207 Petir Road, #05-561, SINGAPORE 670207, SINGAPORE.

LETEVE, Mrs. Lindsay Elisabeth, ACA *2003;* 15 Birkdale Drive, Walton, CHESTERFIELD, S40 3JL.

LETHABY, Mrs. Julia, BA ACA *1995;* Chartfield, Seal Chart, SEVENOAKS, KENT, TN15 0HA.

LETHABY, Mr. Michael, BSc ACA *1990;* Chartfield, Church Road, Seal, Chart, SEVENOAKS, KENT TN15 0HA.

LETHAM, Mr. Ian Ritchie, LLB FCA *1964;* 45 Palin Wood Road, Delph, OLDHAM, OL3 5UW. (Life Member)

LETHAM, Mr. Richard John, MA ACA *1990;* 21/2f East Claremont Street, EDINBURGH, EH7 4HT.

LETHAM, Mr. Robert, ACA *2008;* 2f1 75 Morningside Road, EDINBURGH, EH10 4AY.

LETHBRIDGE, Mr. David Ernest, BSc FCA *1963;* 69 Fern Road, Aller Park, NEWTON ABBOT, TQ12 4NZ.

LETHBRIDGE, Mr. Edward Christopher Wroth, BA ACA *2004;* with Lincoln International, 16 Garrick Street, Covent Garden, LONDON, WC2E 9BA.

LETHBRIDGE, Mr. Ian, FCA *1976;* Lower Wat Ing, London Road, Norland, SOWERBY BRIDGE, HX6 3QY.

LETHBRIDGE, Mr. Jeremy Mark, MEng ACA *2004;* with PricewaterhouseCoopers LLP, 31 Great George Street, BRISTOL, BS1 5QD.

LETHBRIDGE, Mr. John Berkeley Christian, MA FCA *1956;* The Old Bakery, Thames Street, Charlbury, CHIPPING NORTON, OX7 3QQ. (Life Member)

LETHBY, Mr. Neil Hamilton, MSc FCA *1981;* Granary Ventures Ltd, The Granary, Middle Twinhoe, BATH, BA2 8QX.

•**LETHEREN, Mr. Nigel David, FCA** *1981;* Martin & Company (Bridport) Limited, 2 Victoria Grove, BRIDPORT, DORSET, DT6 3AA.

LETOREY, Mrs. Paula Zoe, BA ACA CTA *1999;* with BDO LLP, 1 Bridgewater Place, Water Lane, LEEDS, LS11 5RU.

•**LETT, Mr. James William, BA ACA** *2000;* 102 Park Road, KINGSTON UPON THAMES, KT2 5JZ.

LETT, Mr. Kenneth Robert, FCA *1962;* 28 Dos Encinas, ORINDA, CA 94563, UNITED STATES. (Life Member)

LETT, Miss. Laura, MSc BA ACA *2009;* 26 Rowan Rise, Barnton, NORTHWICH, CHESHIRE, CW8 4NZ.

LETT, Mr. Simon John Read, BCom ACA *1985;* Boston Mayflower Ltd Friars House, Quaker Lane, BOSTON, LINCOLNSHIRE, PE21 6BZ.

•**LETTICE, Mr. James Alfred, BA FCA MIPA MABRP** *1987;* Peters Elworthy & Moore, Salisbury House, Station Road, CAMBRIDGE, CB1 2LA. See also PEM VAT Services LLP, PEM Corporate Finance LLP

LETTIN, Mr. John Martin, FCA *1957;* Conifers, 5 Acorn Close, EAST GRINSTEAD, WEST SUSSEX, RH19 4BY. (Life Member)

LETTS, Mr. Charles Adam, FCA *1977;* 6812 Dickinson Terrace, PORT ST LUCIE, FL 34952, UNITED STATES.

LETTS, Mrs. Monica Edna, BSc ACA *1993;* Pennyfarthings, Hop Gardens, Fairwarp, UCKFIELD, EAST SUSSEX, TN22 3BT.

•**LETTS, Mr. Simon Duncan, BA FCA** *1988;* Deloitte LLP, 2 New Street Square, LONDON, EC4A 3BZ. See also Deloitte & Touche LLP

LETTS, Miss. Victoria Karen, BA ACA *2009;* Flat 1, 57-60 Royal Mint Street, LONDON, E1 8LG.

LEUNG, Mr. Alan Kwan Tao, MA ACA *1989;* Flat 16 Leighton House, Oak Hill Road, SURBITON, KT6 6EJ.

LEUNG, Mr. Alex Raymond, ACA *2001;* 66 Hanson Road, ABINGDON, OXFORDSHIRE, OX14 1YL.

LEUNG, Mr. Alfred, ACA *2007;* Flat 18D Tower 5 The Waterfront, 1 Austin Road West, TSIM SHA TSUI, KOWLOON, HONG KONG SAR.

LEUNG, Mr. Brian See Lim, BSc ACA *1992;* Flat 8B Block 3, King's Park Villa, 1 King's Park Rise, KINGS PARK, KOWLOON, HONG KONG SAR.

LEUNG, Mr. Charles Tai Tsan, ACA *1979;* 3/F Caltex House, 258 Hennessy Road, WAN CHAI, HONG KONG ISLAND, HONG KONG SAR.

LEUNG, Mr. Chau Yuen, ACA *2007;* Fung Leung & Co, Room 1606, Nan Fung Centre, 264-298 Castle Peak Road, TSEUNG KWAN O, NEW TERRITORIES HONG KONG SAR.

LEUNG, Mrs. Cheung Fong Winnie, BSc ACA *1991;* 2 Harris Avenue, Davyhulme, MANCHESTER, M41 7FT.

LEUNG, Mr. Chi Kin, ACA FCCA *2007;* Chang Leung Hiu & Li CPA Limited, 12th Floor, No 3, Lockhart Road, WAN CHAI, HONG KONG ISLAND HONG KONG SAR.

LEUNG, Ms. Chi Ying, ACA *2008;* Ernst & Young, 18/F, Two International Finance Centre, 8 Finance Street, CENTRAL, HONG KONG ISLAND HONG KONG SAR.

LEUNG, Mr. Chin Ming, ACA *2007;* Flat A 8/F, On Hiu Mansion, Lei King Wan, SAI WAN HO, HONG KONG SAR.

LEUNG, Mr. Cho Woo Julian, ACA *2008;* Flat A Block 1 7th Floor, Pristine Villa, 18 Pak Lok Path, Tung Lo Wan Hill Road, TAI WAI, NEW TERRITORIES HONG KONG SAR.

LEUNG, Mr. Christian Herve, BSc CA ACA *1980;* Royal Bank Plaza, 13th Flr South Tower, TORONTO M5J 2J5, ON, CANADA.

LEUNG, Mr. Chuen Fai, ACA *2008;* Room 2217, Block H, Lok Man Estate, TO KWA WAN, KOWLOON, HONG KONG SAR.

LEUNG, Mr. Chun Shing, MA FCA *1968;* Flat 1 Block E 2nd Floor, 41A Stubbs Road, Villa Monte Rosa, MID LEVELS, HONG KONG ISLAND, HONG KONG SAR. (Life Member)

LEUNG, Mr. Chung Kan, ACA *2007;* 13A Block 2, Flora Garden, 7 Chun Fai Road, JARDINE'S LOOKOUT, HONG KONG ISLAND, HONG KONG SAR.

LEUNG, Miss. Dawn Lucy, ACA *2008;* Flat 1 4 Eagling Close, LONDON, E3 4EE.

LEUNG, Mr. Eldridge Wai Hung, ACA *2005;* 641 Elgar Road, Box Hill North, MELBOURNE, VIC 3129, AUSTRALIA.

LEUNG, Miss. Eunice Man Yin, BA ACA CTA AMCT *1995;* 1377 Lincoln Road, Werrington, PETERBOROUGH, PE4 6LT.

LEUNG, Mr. Fat Pui Raymond, ACA *2008;* 9 Beehive Lane, MARKHAM L6E 0K6, ON, CANADA.

•**LEUNG, Mr. Felix Chun Ning, BA ACA** *1992;* Felix Chun Ning Leung, 16027 Ventura Boulevard, Suite 400, ENCINO, CA 91436, UNITED STATES.

LEUNG, Miss. Hebe, BSc ACA *2007;* Flat 21B, Block 5, Monte Vista, Ma On Shan, SHA TIN, NEW TERRITORIES HONG KONG SAR.

LEUNG, Mr. Heung Ying, MSc LLB FCA *1991;* Flat A, 13th Floor, Block 7, 7 Nassau Street, MEI FOO SUN CHUEN, KOWLOON HONG KONG SAR.

LEUNG, Mr. Ho Ming Danny, ACA *2010;* 23B The Montbello, 155 Argyle Street, KOWLOON BAY, KOWLOON, HONG KONG SAR.

LEUNG, Ms. Hoi Yan Sylvia, ACA *2008;* Room 1709, Hong Ying Court, LAM TIN, KOWLOON, HONG KONG SAR.

LEUNG, Mrs. Jennifer Chong Kan, ACA *2005;* JCK Shum Leung Luk & Co., 2nd Floor, Jonsim Place, 228 Queen's Road East, WAN CHAI, HONG KONG ISLAND HONG KONG SAR.

•**LEUNG, Mr. Jesse Nai-Chau, FCA** *1977;* Leung & Puen CPA Ltd, 6th Floor, Kwan Chart Tower, 6 Tonnochy Road, WAN CHAI, HONG KONG ISLAND HONG KONG SAR.

LEUNG, Mr. John Wai Man, ACA *1999;* 96 Arundel Avenue, East Ewell, EPSOM, KT17 2RL.

LEUNG, Mr. Joseph Kan-Sang, BSc ACA *1980;* Flat 7B The Leighton Hill Tower 2, 2B Broadwood Road, CAUSEWAY BAY, HONG KONG ISLAND, HONG KONG SAR.

LEUNG, Mr. Jupiter, ACA *2005;* Lehman Brown, 6/F Dong Wai Diplomatic, Office Bldg, 23 Dongzhimen Wai Dajie, BEIJING 10060, CHINA.

LEUNG, Mr. Ka Fai, BEng ACA *1995;* 183 Parnell Road, LONDON, E3 2JW.

LEUNG, Mr. Ka Ki, ACA *1981;* 801/11 Railway Street, CHATSWOOD, NSW 2067, AUSTRALIA.

LEUNG, Ms. Ka Lai, ACA *2006;* Flat D, 3rd Floor, Full Yau Court, 51G Yau San Street, YUEN LONG, NEW TERRITORIES HONG KONG SAR.

LEUNG, Mr. Ka Man, ACA *2007;* Flat G, 25/F, Tower 8, Park Avenue, 18 Hoi Ting Road, MONG KOK KOWLOON HONG KONG SAR.

LEUNG, Ms. Ka Wa, ACA *2007;* Unit C, 32/F Ocean Court, Tower 1, 3 Aberdeen Praya Road, ABERDEEN, HONG KONG ISLAND HONG KONG SAR.

LEUNG, Mr. Ka Cheung, ACA *2004;* KCG & Co., Rooms 1401-2, 253-261 Hennessy Road, WAN CHAI, HONG KONG ISLAND, HONG KONG SAR.

LEUNG, Mr. Kam Hong, BSc(Econ) FCA MCT *1988;* 48 Somerford Way, LONDON, SE16 6QW.

LEUNG, Mr. Kam Lung, ACA *2008;* Flat F, 14/F, Tsui Kung Mansion, TAIKOO SHING, QUARRY BAY, HONG KONG ISLAND HONG KONG SAR.

LEUNG, Mr. Kam Yuen, ACA *2005;* 72 Ma Tseuk Leng San Uk Ha, SHA TAU KOK, NEW TERRITORIES, HONG KONG SAR.

LEUNG, Mr. Kenneth Kai Cheong, BSc FCA *1990;* 29/F, Jardine House, One Connaught Place, CENTRAL, HONG KONG ISLAND, HONG KONG SAR.

LEUNG, Mr. Kent Ning Louis, ACA *2008;* 10/F, 23A Broadway, MEI FOO SUN CHUEN, KOWLOON, HONG KONG SAR.

LEUNG, Ms. Kim Lan Frances, ACA *2006;* 7E Maple Mansion, Tai Koo Shing, QUARRY BAY, HONG KONG ISLAND, HONG KONG SAR.

LEUNG, Mr. Kin Hei, MEng MSc ACA *2010;* 21 Gardner Street, MANCHESTER, M12 5PH.

LEUNG, Mr. Kin Sang, ACA *2007;* Flat A 8/F, Cheong Ning Building, Tsuen Cheong Centre, Sai Lau Kok Road, TSUEN WAN, NEW TERRITORIES HONG KONG SAR.

LEUNG, Mr. King Chak, ACA *2004;* 88 Shek Po Road, House A5 G/F. Hung Shui Kiu, YUEN LONG, HONG KONG SAR.

LEUNG, Mr. King Chiu Patrick, ACA *2008;* 31/F Millenium City 2, 378 Kwun Tong Road, KWUN TONG, KOWLOON, HONG KONG SAR.

LEWIS, Mr. Andrew Maurice, BSc ACA *1979;* Cardiff & Vale UHB Headquarters, Whitchurch Hospital Park Road, Whitchurch, CARDIFF, CF14 7XB.

LEWIS, Mr. Andrew Reveley, FCA *1973;* 7 Richter Crescent, DAVIDSON, NSW 2085, AUSTRALIA.

LEWIS, Mrs. Ann, FCA *1965;* 93 Five Ashes Road, Westminster Park, CHESTER, CH4 7QA.

LEWIS, Mrs. Anne Victoria, BSc ACA *1991;* Orchard Vale, 8 Sherenden Park, Golden Green, TONBRIDGE, KENT, TN11 0LQ.

LEWIS, Mr. Anthony, BA FCA *1980;* 39 Edward Street, MACLEOD, VIC 3085, AUSTRALIA.

LEWIS, Mr. Anthony, FCA *1974;* 4 Sir Johns Road, Selly Park, BIRMINGHAM, B29 7ER.

LEWIS, Mr. Anthony George, FCA *1963;* Turkey Lodge, Knowsley Park, PRESCOT, MERSEYSIDE, L34 4AQ.

LEWIS, Mr. Anthony John Bowen, BSc FCA *1985;* 1 The Greenways, Paddock Wood, TONBRIDGE, TN12 6LS.

LEWIS, Mr. Ashley Martin, BSc ACA *1980;* The Spinney Bollinway, Hale, ALTRINCHAM, CHESHIRE, WA15 0NZ.

LEWIS, Miss. Audrey Jane, BCom ACA *1994;* 25 Rue du Schlammeste, L-5770 WEILER LA TOUR, LUXEMBOURG.

•**LEWIS, Mr. Barnaby James, FCA** *1971;* (Tax Fac), B J Lewis & Co Ltd, 134 London Road, Southborough, TUNBRIDGE WELLS, TN4 0PL.

LEWIS, Mr. Barrington, BCom FCA *1964;* 30 Woodrow Park, Scartho, GRIMSBY, DN33 2EF.

LEWIS, Mr. Barry, FCA *1970;* 12 Trefusis Way, East Budleigh, BUDLEIGH SALTERTON, EX9 7EP.

•①**LEWIS, Mr. Barry David, FCA** *1972;* (Tax Fac), Harris Lipman LLP, 2 Mountview Court, 310 Friern Barnet Lane, LONDON, N20 0YZ.

LEWIS, Mr. Barry John, FCA *1973;* 16 Inglewood Court, 9 Oaklands Road, BROMLEY, BR1 3SJ.

LEWIS, Mr. Ben Joseph, MSc FCA *1970;* 84 Green Lane, EDGWARE, MIDDLESEX, HA8 7QD.

LEWIS, Mr. Benjamin John, BSc ACA *1998;* Qinetiq Cody Technology Park, Old Ively Road, FARNBOROUGH, HAMPSHIRE, GU14 0LX.

LEWIS, Mr. Benjamin William, BSc ACA *1999;* Dreams Plc Knaves Beech Industrial Estate, Knaves Beech Way Loudwater, HIGH WYCOMBE, BUCKINGHAMSHIRE, HP10 9QY.

•**LEWIS, Mr. Brian, FCA** *1988;* Shaddick Smith LLP, Bank Chambers, 7 Market Street, LEIGH, LANCASHIRE, WN7 1ED.

•**LEWIS, Mr. Brian Edward, FCA** *1967;* BRIAN LEWIS AND COMPANY CPAS APC, 10900 WILSHIRE BOULEVARD SUITE 610, LOS ANGELES, CA 90024, UNITED STATES.

•**LEWIS, Mr. Brian Jeffrey, FCA** *1975;* Brian Lewis FCA, 146 Queens Road, WATFORD, WD17 2NX.

•**LEWIS, Mrs. Carol, BSc ACA** *2005;* Bainbridge Lewis Limited, 13 Kingsway House, 134-140 Church Road, HOVE, EAST SUSSEX, BN3 2DL.

LEWIS, Miss. Carol Denise, BCom ACA *1986;* Tate & Lyle PLC, Thames Refinery, Factory Road, Silvertown, LONDON, E16 2EW.

LEWIS, Mr. Chesney Alan, FCA *1969;* Flat 3, Stangate, 1 The Leas, WESTCLIFF-ON-SEA, SS0 7SZ. (Life Member)

LEWIS, Mr. Chris, ACA *2011;* Flat 3 Faroe, Gotts Road, LEEDS, LS12 1DF.

LEWIS, Mrs. Christine, BSc ACA *1992;* Cobble Hall, Commondale, WHITBY, NORTH YORKSHIRE, YO21 2HS.

•**LEWIS, Mr. Christopher, FCA** *1970;* (Tax Fac), The Tax & Accountancy Practice, 1 The Old School, The Square, Pennington, LYMINGTON, HAMPSHIRE SO41 8GN. See also Underwood Barron Associates Limited

LEWIS, Mr. Christopher John, BSc ACA *2003;* 12 Tavy Close, Chandler's Ford, EASTLEIGH, HAMPSHIRE, SO53 4SN.

LEWIS, Mr. Christopher John, BA ACA *2009;* 18 Florence Avenue, SUTTON COLDFIELD, B73 5NQ.

LEWIS, Mr. Christopher Simon, BSc ACA *2001;* 23 Bewley Street, LONDON, SW19 1XF.

LEWIS, Mr. Christopher Wickham, FCA *1970;* VisitBritain - 9th floor, Department for International Development, 1 Palace Street, LONDON, SW1E 5HE.

LEWIS, Mrs. Claire, BA ACA *2004;* 11 The Mount, Alwoodley, LEEDS, LS17 7RH.

LEWIS, Ms. Claire Elizabeth, LLB ACA CTA *2002;* 48 Middleton Drive, PINNER, HA5 2PG.

LEWIS, Miss. Clare Alison, ACA *1992;* 2/35 Fairlight Crescent, FAIRLIGHT, NSW 2094, AUSTRALIA.

LEWIS, Mrs. Clare Elizabeth, BA ACA *2007;* 117 Skylark Way, Shinfield, READING, RG2 9AD.

•**LEWIS, Mr. Clifton Lambert, BSc FCA** *1976;* Lambert Lewis, 401 Cowbridge Road East, Canton, CARDIFF, CF5 1JG.

LEWIS, Mr. Clive, BSc FCA *1984;* 16 Rue du Village, L-6183 GONDERANGE, LUXEMBOURG.

LEWIS, Mr. Clive Ivor, ACA *1981;* 32 Barons Court Road, Penylan, CARDIFF, CF23 9DF.

LEWIS, Mr. Colin Michael, FCA *1962;* 3 Maycroft House, Park Avenue, LIVERPOOL, L18 8BT.

LEWIS, Mr. Colmar Aitken, FCA *1973;* Bromley Mind Anchor House, 5 Station Road, ORPINGTON, BR6 0RZ.

•①**LEWIS, Mr. Craig Anthony, BSc ACA** *1996;* 18 Hoof Close, Littleport, ELY, CAMBRIDGESHIRE, CB6 1HU.

LEWIS, Mr. Dan, ACA *2008;* Flat 4 Heathway House, Church Terrace, LONDON, SE13 5BT.

LEWIS, Mr. Darren Mathew, BSc(Econ) ACA *2001;* 1 Woodford Close, DEVIZES, WILTSHIRE, SN10 5LQ.

•**LEWIS, Mr. David, BA FCA** *1975;* Baker Tilly Tax & Advisory Services LLP, 1st Floor, 46 Clarendon Road, WATFORD, WD17 1JJ.

LEWIS, Mr. David Andrew, BSc ACA *2006;* 105 Streathbourne Road, LONDON, SW17 8RA.

LEWIS, Mr. David Arthur, FCA *1965;* 1 Howfield Green, HODDESDON, EN11 9AL. (Life Member)

LEWIS, Mr. David Byron, FCA *1968;* Bryn Newydd House, 1 Derwen Fawr Road, Sketty, SWANSEA, SA2 8AA.

LEWIS, Mr. David Gareth, BSc(Hons) ACA *2003;* RBS Insurance, Decision Support, 3rd Floor, Green Flag House, Cote Lane, PUDSEY LS28 5GF.

LEWIS, Mr. David Geoffrey, BSc FCA *1976;* 22 Tring Court, 60 Waldegrave Park, TWICKENHAM, TW1 4TH.

LEWIS, Dr. David Glynne, PhD MA BSc ACA *1981;* 5 Gloucester Place, WINDSOR, SL4 2AJ.

•**LEWIS, Mr. David Gordon, BSc FCA** *1979;* Twobuoys, 60a Links Lane, ROWLAND'S CASTLE, PO9 6AF.

LEWIS, Mr. David Harold, FCA *1962;* 7 Idsworth Close, Horndean, WATERLOOVILLE, PO8 0DW. (Life Member)

LEWIS, Mr. David Howard, MBA BSc FCA *1992;* Fairways, Bordyke, TONBRIDGE, KENT, TN9 1NW.

LEWIS, Mr. David Isaac Heath, FCA FCMA *1954;* Little Coniston, The Fence, St Briavels, LYDNEY, GL15 6QG.

LEWIS, Mr. David James, FCA *1974;* 13 Chandas, 33860 MARCILLAC, FRANCE.

•**LEWIS, Mr. David Jeffrey, FCA** *1971;* D.J. Lewis, 23 Heol Eglwys, Ystradgynlais, SWANSEA, SA9 1EY.

LEWIS, Mr. David John, ACA *1985;* 194b rue de la Victoire Box 1, St Gilles, B-1060 BRUSSELS, BELGIUM.

LEWIS, Mr. David John, BTech ACA *1984;* 151 Huddersfield Road, HOLMFIRTH, HD9 3TP.

LEWIS, Mr. David John, BSc FCA *1994;* 17 Coleherne Mews, LONDON, SW10 9DZ.

LEWIS, Mr. David John, FCA *1966;* 3 Taverngate, Main Street, Hawksworth, LEEDS, LS20 8NX.

LEWIS, Mr. David John, FCA *1961;* 16 Green Curve, BANSTEAD, SM7 1NX. (Life Member)

LEWIS, Mr. David John, BCom FCA *1977;* Pepsi Cola International, 800 Fairway Drive, Suite 400, DEERFIELD BEACH, FL 33441-1830, UNITED STATES.

LEWIS, Mr. David John Rhystyd, FCA *1969;* 39 Earlsway, CHESTER, CH4 8AY.

LEWIS, Mr. David John Wildsmith, BSc MCMI ACIB FCA *1974;* Deri Grove, Bowood Lane, Wendover Dean, AYLESBURY, HP22 6PX.

•**LEWIS, Mr. David Michael, FCA** *1982;* Camrose Consulting Limited, 61 St. Margarets Road, EDGWARE, MIDDLESEX, HA8 9UT.

LEWIS, Mr. David Michael, LLB FCA *1977;* 124 Columbia Heights, BROOKLYN, NY 11201, UNITED STATES.

•**LEWIS, Mr. David Michael, BA FCA** *1965;* (Tax Fac), David Lewis & Co, Flat 1, 16 Lindfield Gardens, Hampstead, LONDON, NW3 6PU.

•**LEWIS, Mr. David Peter, FCA** *1978;* Heaton Lumb Lisle, Thorpe House, 61 Richardshaw Lane, PUDSEY, LS28 7EL.

LEWIS, Mr. David Richard, BSc ACA *1979;* Wildwood House, Sway Road, BROCKENHURST, SO42 7SG.

LEWIS, Mr. David Rodney, AE FCA *1959;* Fairlane, Bywood Close, KENLEY, CR8 5LS. (Life Member)

LEWIS, Mr. David Rohan, BSc ACA *1988;* 12 Barrowden Road, Ketton, STAMFORD, PE9 3RJ.

LEWIS, Mr. David Ronald, FCA FinstMC *1969;* 59 Old Lodge Lane, PURLEY, CR8 4DN. (Life Member)

LEWIS, Mr. David Winston, FCA *1979;* 3 Fair Field, Waltham On The Wolds, MELTON MOWBRAY, LE14 4AX.

LEWIS, Mrs. Deborah Clare, MSci ACA *2006;* with PricewaterhouseCoopers LLP, 31 Great George Street, BRISTOL, BS1 5QD.

LEWIS, Mrs. Deborah Stewart, MBA BA ACA *1988;* 1a Mayals Farm Cottage, Mayals Green, Mayals, SWANSEA, SA3 5JR.

LEWIS, Miss. Debra Ruth, LLB FCA *1988;* Gladsmuir, Lyndhurst Gardens, LONDON, N3 1TB.

LEWIS, Mr. Dennis Stanley, FCA *1951;* 51 Arnison Road, EAST MOLESEY, KT8 9JR. (Life Member)

LEWIS, Mr. Donald James, FCA *1949;* 24 Copes Crescent, WOLVERHAMPTON, WV10 0SL. (Life Member)

LEWIS, Mrs. Donnah Kerry Elayne, ACA *2006;* Treallex, Chilsworthy, HOLSWORTHY, DEVON, EX22 7BQ.

LEWIS, Mr. Duncan, ACA *2008;* 11A Jindabyne Street, FRENCHS FOREST, NSW 2086, AUSTRALIA.

LEWIS, Mr. Duncan Simon, BA(Hons) ACA *2001;* Flat 5 Faircourt, 113 Haverstock Hill, LONDON, NW3 4RY.

•**LEWIS, Mr. Edward Greville, FCA** *1961;* 218 Ridgeway Road, Rumney, CARDIFF, CF3 4AG.

LEWIS, Miss. Elaine Margaret, MA BSc(Econ) ACA *2001;* Garden Flat 180 Camden Road, LONDON, NW1 9HG.

LEWIS, Ms. Eleonore, BSc ACA *2006;* 9 Meadow Road, GUILDFORD, SURREY, GU4 7LW.

•**LEWIS, Miss. Elizabeth Jayne, BSc FCA** *1990;* (Tax Fac), Pritchard Evans & Co Ltd, 21 Carmarthen Street, LLANDEILO, CARMARTHENSHIRE, SA19 6AN.

LEWIS, Mrs. Elizabeth Margaret, BA ACA *1993;* with Leonard Gold, 24 Landport Terrace, PORTSMOUTH, PO1 2RG.

LEWIS, Miss. Emma, ACA *2004;* 7 Leinster Mews, LONDON, W2 3EY.

LEWIS, Miss. Emma Joanne, LLB ACA *2011;* 102 Anglesey Avenue, Smiths Wood, BIRMINGHAM, B36 0NX.

LEWIS, Miss. Enid Mair, BSc ACA *1988;* Welsh Language Board, Market Chambers, 5-7 St. Mary Street, CARDIFF, CF10 1AT.

LEWIS, Mr. Eric Bowes, FCA *1949;* Carabel, 20 Wadham Close, SHEPPERTON, TW17 9HT. (Life Member)

LEWIS, Mr. Eric Keith, FCA *1955;* 16 Daryngton Drive, Perivale Park, GREENFORD, UB6 8BN. (Life Member)

LEWIS, Mrs. Erica Mary, ACA *2009;* 70 Meadow Close, LONDON, SW20 9JD.

LEWIS, Mr. Evan Richard Charles, FCA *1966;* The Monks Barn, Carr Lane, Watton, DRIFFIELD, NORTH HUMBERSIDE, YO25 9AH.

LEWIS, Mr. Frank, FCA *1995;* 14 Franklin Close, Whetstone, LONDON, N20 9QG.

LEWIS, Mr. Gareth David, BSc(Hons) ACA *2001;* The Lawn, Webbington Road, Compton Bishop, AXBRIDGE, SOMERSET, BS26 2EU.

LEWIS, Mr. Gareth Glyndwr, MA ACA *1982;* 86 Cruickshank Grove, Crownhill, MILTON KEYNES, MK8 0HG.

LEWIS, Mr. Garnet Wade, DPh BSc FCA *1976;* Domaine De La Valette, La Rue De Sorel, St. John, JERSEY, JE3 4AA. (Life Member)

LEWIS, Mr. Gavin Andrew, MA ACA CTA AMCT *1999;* 38 Victoria Avenue, SURBITON, KT6 5DW.

LEWIS, Mr. Gavin John, BA(Hons) ACA *2000;* 6 Blays Lane, Englefield Green, EGHAM, SURREY, TW20 0PH.

LEWIS, Mr. Gavin John, ACA *1997;* 10 Alvaston Way, Rivermead, Monkmoor, SHREWSBURY, SY2 5TT.

•**LEWIS, Mr. Gavin Mark, BEng ACA** *2000;* Lewis & Son Accountants Limited, 37 Stoke Road, Blisworth, NORTHAMPTON, NN7 3BZ.

LEWIS, Miss. Gemma, ACA *2011;* 15 Ryburn Close, TAUNTON, SOMERSET, TA1 2RH.

LEWIS, Mr. Geoffrey Thomas, ACA *1981;* 11 Chells Lane, Chells Manor, STEVENAGE, SG2 7AA.

LEWIS, Mr. George Brooke, FCA *1972;* Brooke House, 2 Poplars Farm Close, Hannington, NORTHAMPTON, NN6 9GL.

LEWIS, Mrs. Georgina, BA ACA *1995;* 10 Cherry Tree Road, East Finchley, LONDON, N2 9QL.

•**LEWIS, Mr. Gethin William, BSc FCA CTA** *1974;* (Tax Fac), Gethin Lewis FCA CTA, 24 Chiltern Drive, Royton, OLDHAM, OL2 5TD.

LEWIS, Mr. Gordon John, FCA *1972;* 53 Wellington Road, BIRMINGHAM, B15 2ER.

LEWIS, Mr. Graeme Robert, MA ACA *1987;* Calle Yerupaja 19, Ciudalcampo, San Sebastian de los Reyes, 28707 MADRID, SPAIN.

•**LEWIS, Mr. Graham, MA FCA CTA** *1986;* (Tax Fac), Lurie & Associates LLP, 2nd Floor, 7 Newcombe Park, LONDON, NW7 3QN.

LEWIS, Mr. Graham Alan, BA ACA *1989;* Cloverdale, 10 Westbourne Road, Coltishall, NORWICH, NORFOLK, NR12 7HT.

LEWIS, Mr. Graham Kelvin, FCA *1976;* Lottery West, PO Box 1113, OSBORNE PARK, WA 6017, AUSTRALIA.

LEWIS, Mr. Grahame John, MBA FCA *1973;* 2a Peatling Road, Countesthorpe, LEICESTER, LE8 5RD.

LEWIS, Mr. Grant Emery, ACA CA(SA) *2011;* 26a White Rose Lane, WOKING, SURREY, GU22 7JY.

LEWIS, Mr. Greg, ACA *2010;* Darwin House, Palmers Flat, Coalway, COLEFORD, GLOUCESTERSHIRE, GL16 7HT.

•**LEWIS, Mr. Gwynfor, FCA** *1969;* 9 Ullswater Crescent, Brynrock, SWANSEA, SA6 7QF.

LEWIS, Mrs. Hannah Elizabeth, BMus ACA *1995;* Claremont Hospital, 401 Sandygate Road, SHEFFIELD, S10 5UB.

LEWIS, Mr. Harry Frederick, FCA *1951;* 9 Croft Road, Edwalton, NOTTINGHAM, NG12 4BW. (Life Member)

LEWIS, Mrs. Hayley May, BA FCA *1990;* 11 Briargrove Drive, Nine Oaks, INVERNESS, IV2 5AF.

LEWIS, Mrs. Heather Josafine Yvonne, BSc ACA *1990;* 10 St Georges Crescent, Queens Park, CHESTER, CH4 7AR.

LEWIS, Miss. Helen Louise, BA ACA CTA *2004;* (Tax Fac), 45 Linnet Close, Pennsylvania, EXETER, EX4 5HF.

LEWIS, Mr. Herbert John, FCA *1955;* Strath Isla, First Drift, Wothorpe, STAMFORD, PE9 3JL. (Life Member)

•**LEWIS, Mr. Howard Keith, FCA** *1973;* MacIntyre Hudson LLP, New Bridge Street House, 30-34 New Bridge Street, LONDON, EC4V 6BJ.

•**LEWIS, Mr. Hugh Richard Clive, FCA ACMA** *1970;* H R C Lewis & Co, 54 Amersham Hill Drive, HIGH WYCOMBE, HP13 6QY.

LEWIS, Mr. Huw Martin, BSc ACA *1999;* G E Healthcare Ltd, The Maynard Centre, Londwood Drive, Whitchurch, CARDIFF, CF14 7YT.

LEWIS, Mr. Huw Roderic, BSc FCA *1973;* 26 Chattaway Drive, Balsall Common, COVENTRY, CV7 7QH.

•**LEWIS, Mr. Ian Macintyre, BA ACA** *1988;* (Tax Fac), Johnston Carmichael, Bishops Court, 29 Albyn Place, ABERDEEN, AB10 1YL.

•**LEWIS, Mr. Ian Martin, BA ACA** *1998;* Rodl & Partner Limited, Concorde House, Trinity Park, Solihull, BIRMINGHAM, B37 7UQ.

•**LEWIS, Mr. Ian Robert, ACA** *1989;* Lewis Accounting Ltd, 26 Brookfields Way, East Leake, LOUGHBOROUGH, LEICESTERSHIRE, LE12 6HD.

LEWIS, Mr. Ian Thomas, BSc FCA *1975;* 82 Berkeley Rd, Bishopston, BRISTOL, BS7 8HG.

LEWIS, Mr. Ivan Keith, BSc ACA *1998;* Finance Department, South Manchester University Hospitals N H S Trust, Wythenshawe Hospital Southmoor Road, MANCHESTER, M23 9LT.

LEWIS, Mr. Jack, FCA *1961;* The Nook9 Hillcrest Road, Redcliffe BayPortishead, BRISTOL, BS20 8HS.

LEWIS, Dr. James, BSc ACA *2007;* 3 Gloucester Mews West, LONDON, W2 6DY.

•**LEWIS, Mr. James Barrow, BA FCA** *1991;* (Tax Fac), BJ Dixon Walsh Limited, St. Marys House, Magdalene Street, TAUNTON, SOMERSET, TA1 1SB.

LEWIS, Mr. James Christian, BA ACA *2001;* with Deloitte LLP, Athene Place, 66 Shoe Lane, LONDON, EC4A 3BQ.

LEWIS, Mr. James Creyke Hulton, ACA *2009;* Pepsi Cola International Ltd, 63 Kew Road, RICHMOND, TW9 2QL.

LEWIS, Mr. James Robert, ACA *2009;* 41 Narbonne Avenue, LONDON, SW4 9JP.

LEWIS, Mr. James William, BA ACA *1996;* Flat 6, Andover Court, Hampton Road, WORCESTER PARK, SURREY, KT4 8EX.

LEWIS, Mr. James William, FCA *1957;* Woodstock Windmill Hill, Brenchley, TONBRIDGE, TN12 7NP. (Life Member)

LEWIS, Ms. Janet Elizabeth, MSc BSc FCA *1972;* 5 Hepworth Drive, ETOBICOKE M9R 3W1, ON, CANADA.

LEWIS, Mr. Jason Alan, ACA MAAT *1998;* 10 Cae Ffynnon, Church Village, PONTYPRIDD, MID GLAMORGAN, CF38 1UB.

LEWIS, Miss. Jean Clare, BSc FCA *1990;* 14 The Paddock, Upton, WIRRAL, MERSEYSIDE, CH49 6NP.

LEWIS, Mr. Jeffrey David, FCA *1964;* 39 Malmains Drive, Frenchay, BRISTOL, BS16 1PJ.

LEWIS, Mr. Jenkin Robert Glanna, FCA *1971;* Homefield, Cote Drive, Westbury-On-Trym, BRISTOL, BS9 3UP. (Life Member)

LEWIS, Mrs. Jennie Elizabeth, BSc ACA *2001;* 41 Gladwyn Road, LONDON, SW15 1JY.
LEWIS, Mr. Jeremy John, MSc FCA *1993;* 8 Craiglands Park, ILKLEY, LS29 8SX.
LEWIS, Mr. Jeremy Michael James, BSc ACA *1988;* 5 Ruvigny Gardens, LONDON, SW15 1JR.
LEWIS, Mr. Jeremy Neil, ACA *1985;* 13 Minton Mews, Lymington Road, LONDON, NW6 1XX.
LEWIS, Mrs. Joanna Alexandra, BSc ACA *1994;* 2 Northgate, LINCOLN, LN2 1QS.
LEWIS, Mr. John, FCA *1972;* 15 The Spring, Long Eaton, NOTTINGHAM, NG10 1PJ.
LEWIS, Mr. John Anthony Llewelyn, FCA *1968;* Woodlands, 16 Grove Road, Shawford, WINCHESTER, SO21 2DD. (Life Member)
LEWIS, Mr. John Arthur, ACA *1982;* 8 Brimhill Rise, Chapmanslade, WESTBURY, WILTSHIRE, BA13 4AX.
LEWIS, Mr. John Brian, FCA *1956;* 14 Holyrood Avenue, Old Colwyn, COLWYN BAY, CLWYD, LL29 8BA. (Life Member)
LEWIS, Mr. John Christopher, BA FCA *1990;* 18 Brightlingsea Place, Limehouse, LONDON, E14 8DB.
LEWIS, Mr. John Clive, BSc FCA *1989;* DirectorsPlus Limited, P.O. Box 31855, GEORGE TOWN, GRAND CAYMAN, KY1-1207, CAYMAN ISLANDS.
•LEWIS, Mr. John Ernest, FCA *1971;* (Tax Fac), ATTS Ltd, 42-48 Charlbert Street, St Johns Wood, LONDON, NW8 7BU. See also John Lewis
LEWIS, Mr. John Hywel, FCA *1973;* Sisial Y Nant, 33 Millbrook Close, DINAS POWYS, CF64 4DD.
LEWIS, Mr. John Martin, BSc FCA *1983;* 73 Bulstrode Way, GERRARDS CROSS, BUCKINGHAMSHIRE, SL9 7RB.
LEWIS, Mr. John Paul Edward, ACA *1985;* PricewaterhouseCoopers, PO Box 569, MBABANE, SWAZILAND.
LEWIS, Mr. John Richard Simon, FCA *1965;* Stonecrop Rectory Lane, Buckland, BETCHWORTH, RH3 7BL.
LEWIS, Mr. John Robert, BA FCA *1980;* Vista Society for the Blind, Margaret Road, LEICESTER, LE5 5FU.
LEWIS, Mr. John Trevor, FCA *1962;* 14 Woodside Road, BEACONSFIELD, HP9 1JW. (Life Member)
LEWIS, Mr. Jonathan, MSc ACA *2011;* 10 Lacey Street, Horbury, WAKEFIELD, WEST YORKSHIRE, WF4 5HP.
•LEWIS, Mr. Jonathan Edward, BA FCA *1995;* Reid & Co Corporate Services Limited, Witan Court, 305 Upper Fourth Street, Central, MILTON KEYNES, MK9 1EH.
LEWIS, Mr. Jonathan Wayne, BSc ACA *1993;* Casenove, Clenches Farm Road, SEVENOAKS, KENT, TN13 2LU.
LEWIS, Mr. Jonathan Wyndham, BSc ACA *1980;* 2 Chacombe Place, BEACONSFIELD, HP9 2WS.
•LEWIS, Mr. Julian Michael, FCA *1973;* Simmons Gainford, 7-10 Chandos Street, LONDON, W1G 9DQ.
LEWIS, Mrs. Julie, BCom ACA *1989;* Le Grenier a Pomme, La Rue de la Prairie, St. Mary, JERSEY, JE3 3BY.
•LEWIS, Mrs. Julie, BA ACA *1985;* Windrush AEC Limited, The Cottage, Fordwells, WITNEY, OXFORDSHIRE, OX29 9PP.
LEWIS, Mrs. Karen Sandra, BA ACA *1995;* Briar House West End, Foxham, CHIPPENHAM, SN15 4NB.
LEWIS, Mrs. Kate Elizabeth, BSc ACA *1995;* Tudor Farm, Battlesea Green, Stradbroke, EYE, IP21 5NE.
LEWIS, Mrs. Kate Louise, BA ACA *1997;* 45 Lower Oxford Road, Basford, NEWCASTLE, STAFFORDSHIRE, ST5 0PB.
LEWIS, Miss. Katherine Mary, BSc ACA *1995;* 30 Latham Road, TWICKENHAM, TW1 1BN.
LEWIS, Miss. Katherine Sarah, ACA MAAT *2010;* 45 Broadlands, Thundersley, BENFLEET, ESSEX, SS7 3BD.
LEWIS, Mrs. Katie, ACA *2008;* 31 Sandcross Lane, REIGATE, RH2 8EX.
LEWIS, Mr. Keith John, FCA *1972;* Harold G Walker & Co, 21 Oxford Road, BOURNEMOUTH, BH8 8ET.
LEWIS, Mr. Kenneth John, FCA *1972;* Poplars Farmhouse, Mollington, BANBURY, OX17 1BN.
•LEWIS, Mr. Kenneth Raymond, FCA *1968;* (Tax Fac), Kenneth Lewis & Co, 22 Gelliwastad Rd, PONTYPRIDD, CF37 2BW. See also Business and Tax Cures Limited
LEWIS, Mr. Kevin John Nicholas, BA ACA *1980;* Sparrow Cottage, Iwerne Minster, BLANDFORD FORUM, DORSET, DT11 8LW.
LEWIS, Mr. Kevin Michael, BCom FCA *1974;* 56 Singing Oaks Drive, WESTON, CT 06883, UNITED STATES.
LEWIS, Mrs. Kirsty Ann, MSc ACA *2000;* 2 Beech Drive, Shipham, WINSCOMBE, AVON, BS25 1SH.
LEWIS, Mr. Leonard, FCA *1957;* 39 The Warren Drive, Wanstead, LONDON, E11 2LR. (Life Member)
LEWIS, Mr. Leonard Sidney, BSc ACA *1981;* 67 New Church Road, HOVE, BN3 4BA.
LEWIS, Mrs. Linda Christine, BSc ACA *1991;* The Old Chapel Chapel Lane, Bishopstone, SALISBURY, SP5 4BT.
LEWIS, Mrs. Lisl Bettina, BEng FCA *1994;* #93 Mango Close, Bakers Woods, ST PETER, BARBADOS.
LEWIS, Mrs. Lois Marie, BA(Hons) ACA *2000;* 13 Boxgrove Avenue, GUILDFORD, SURREY, GU1 1XG.
LEWIS, Mrs. Lorraine Margaret, BA ACA *1983;* 5 Nathan Close, SUTTON COLDFIELD, B75 6SR.
LEWIS, Mrs. Louise Margaret, MA FCA *1986;* 97 School Cottages, Old Worthing Road, Dial Post, HORSHAM, RH13 8NQ.
LEWIS, Mr. Malcolm Derek, BSc ACA *1986;* Incommunities Group Limited, 5 New Augustus Street, BRADFORD, WEST YORKSHIRE, BD1 5LL.
•LEWIS, Mr. Malcolm Elvet, MSc BSc FCA *1986;* 10 Southfield Road, Westbury-on-Trym, BRISTOL, BS9 3BH.
LEWIS, Mr. Malcolm Evan, BSc ACA *1983;* 14 West Road, Histon, CAMBRIDGE, CB24 9LH.
LEWIS, Mr. Malcolm Stephen, FCA *1976;* La Grenier A Pomme La Rue de la Prairie, St. Mary, JERSEY, JE3 3EH.
LEWIS, Mrs. Margaret Jill, FCA *1973;* Homefield, Cote Drive, Westbury-On-Trym, BRISTOL, BS9 3UP. (Life Member)
LEWIS, Mrs. Marie Annabelle, BA ACA *1997;* 309 Kent Street, SYDNEY, NSW 2000, AUSTRALIA.
LEWIS, Mr. Mark Andrew, BA ACA *1997;* Penn Fields, 169 Longdon Road, Knowle, SOLIHULL, WEST MIDLANDS, B93 9HY.
LEWIS, Mr. Mark Charles Drury, ACA *2008;* Flat 2, 9 Marlborough Road, LONDON, N19 4NA.
LEWIS, Mr. Mark Christopher, BSc ACA *1989;* PO Box 369, North Sydney Post Office, NORTH SYDNEY, NSW 2059, AUSTRALIA.
LEWIS, Mr. Mark Simon, BSc ACA *2001;* Cap Gemini UK Plc, 1 Forge End, WOKING, SURREY, GU21 6DB.
LEWIS, Mr. Mark Talbot, FCA *1983;* Alchornes, Bell Lane, Nutley, UCKFIELD, TN22 3PD.
•LEWIS, Mr. Martin Allen, BA ACA *1990;* (Tax Fac), Lewis Dyson LLP, 10 Fleet Place, LONDON, EC4M 7RB. See also Kroll Ltd
LEWIS, Mr. Martin Chris, ACA CA(SA) *2011;* 9 Regent Way, Kings Hill, WEST MALLING, KENT, ME19 4EB.
•LEWIS, Mr. Martin Lawrence, FCA *1962;* Foster Lewis Stone, 302-308 Preston Road, HARROW, HA3 0QP.
LEWIS, Mr. Martin Llewellyn, FCA *1975;* 10 Bridge Road, WEYBRIDGE, KT13 8XT.
LEWIS, Mr. Martin Pierce, BSc ACA *1988;* Pinfold Cottage, Pinfold Lane, Northop Hall, MOLD, CH7 6HE.
LEWIS, Mr. Martin Sean, BA ACA *1989;* CB Richard Ellis, St. Martins Court, 10 Paternoster Row, LONDON, EC4M 7HP.
•LEWIS, Mr. Martyn Leslie, BA FCA *1987;* Martyn Lewis, 1 Brewery House, Brook Street, Wivenhoe, COLCHESTER, CO7 9DS.
•LEWIS, Mr. Matthew John, MA FCA *1985;* (Tax Fac), KPMG LLP, 15 Canada Square, LONDON, E14 5GL. See also KPMG Europe LLP
LEWIS, Mr. Maxim, BA(Hons) ACA *2011;* 329 Cavendish Road, Balham, LONDON, SW12 0PQ.
LEWIS, Mrs. Melanie Courtenay, BSc ACA *1996;* 20 Detillens Lane, OXTED, RH8 0DJ.
LEWIS, Mr. Melvin Yong, BSc ACA *2008;* 10 Simpson Close, LONDON, N21 1SR.
LEWIS, Dr. Michael, MBChB ACA *2011;* KPMG, 1 The Embankment, Neville Street, LEEDS, LS1 4DW.
•LEWIS, Mr. Michael, BSc FCA *1982;* Michael Lewis Audit Limited, William James House, Cowley Road, CAMBRIDGE, CB4 0WX. See also Michael Lewis Ltd
LEWIS, Mr. Michael Anthony, BA FCA *1976;* 23 Chalkland Rise, BRIGHTON, BN2 6RJ.
LEWIS, Mr. Michael Ernest George, BA FCA *1962;* 32 Wheatland Close, Oadby, LEICESTER, LE2 4SY.
•LEWIS, Mr. Michael Ian, FCA *1984;* First Class Accounting Limited, Suite 15, 20 Churchill Square, Kings Hill, WEST MALLING, KENT ME19 4YU. See also First Place Accounting Limited
•LEWIS, Mr. Michael Victor, BSc CEng ACA FCCA ACMA MIET MBA *2010;* (Tax Fac), Ghiaci Goodhand Smith Limited, 12a Marlborough Place, BRIGHTON, EAST SUSSEX, BN1 1WN. See also GGS Consulting Limited
LEWIS, Mr. Michael William Lister, FCA *1966;* 15b Nower Hill, PINNER, MIDDLESEX, HA5 5QR.
LEWIS, Mrs. Michelle, BSc ACA *2000;* R P S Planning & Development, 85d Milton Park Milton, ABINGDON, OXFORDSHIRE, OX14 4RY.
LEWIS, Mr. Mostyn, BSc ACA *2003;* 76a Main Street, Alrewas, BURTON-ON-TRENT, STAFFORDSHIRE, DE13 7AE.
LEWIS, Mr. Murray, BSc FCA *1980;* 11 Clevedon Road, Tilehurst, READING, RG31 6RL.
LEWIS, Mr. Neil, BSc ACA *1989;* 14 Windmill Field, Denmead, WATERLOOVILLE, PO7 6PL.
•LEWIS, Mr. Nicholas Charles, ACIB FCA *1971;* (Tax Fac), Nicholas Charles Lewis & Co, 5 Leycroft Close, CANTERBURY, KENT, CT2 7LD.
LEWIS, Mr. Nicholas David, FCA *1965;* 12 Glenhurst Avenue, LONDON, NW5 1PS.
•LEWIS, Mr. Nicholas Howard, MA MSc ACA *1981;* with Lewis & Co, Walden, Widcombe Hill, BATH, BA2 6ED.
LEWIS, Mr. Nicholas John, MA FCA *1982;* Lower Living, Shobrooke, CREDITON, EX17 1AH.
LEWIS, Mr. Nicholas Tudor Pendrill, MA FCA *1978;* Goscar, 1 Clyne Drive, Mayals, SWANSEA, SA3 5BU.
LEWIS, Mr. Nigel James, BSc ACA *1993;* Les Charmilles, Grand Douit Road, St. Sampson, GUERNSEY, GY2 4WG.
LEWIS, Mr. Owen, MA(Cantab) ACA *2011;* 43 Humphreys Road, CAMBRIDGE, CB4 2JR.
•LEWIS, Mr. Owen, FCA *1967;* O. Lewis, Cefni Chambers, 10A High Street, LLANGEFNI, LL77 7LT.
LEWIS, Mr. Owen Peter, BEng ACA *1999;* PWC, Dronning Eufemiasgate 8, Pb 748 Sentrum, N-0106 OSLO, NORWAY.
•LEWIS, Miss. Patricia, FCA *1961;* (Tax Fac), Miss Patricia Lewis FCA, 207 Clevedon Road, Tickenham, CLEVEDON, AVON, BS21 6RX.
LEWIS, Mr. Patrick, BA ACA *2011;* 21 Avon Rise, Flitwick, BEDFORD, MK45 1SQ.
LEWIS, Mr. Patrick Anthony Proctor, BA FCA *1970;* 1 Stoneleigh, SAWBRIDGEWORTH, CM21 0BT.
LEWIS, Mr. Paul Alexander, BSc ACA *1991;* 14 Stephen Street, Redfield, BRISTOL, BS5 9DY.
•LEWIS, Mr. Paul Graham, FCA *1971;* Paul G. Lewis, 2 Le Clos de la Vallee, La Vallee de St. Pierre, St. Lawrence, JERSEY, JE3 1LF.
LEWIS, Mr. Paul James, ACA *1996;* Roof Top View, 16 Castle Road, Lavendon, OLNEY, BUCKINGHAMSHIRE, MK46 4JE.
LEWIS, Mr. Paul John, ACA *2008;* 65 Blackthorn Close, CAMBRIDGE, CB4 1FZ.
LEWIS, Mr. Paul Roger, BA(Hons) ACA *2000;* 2 Ferndale Close, Attenborough Beeston, NOTTINGHAM, NG9 6AQ.
LEWIS, Mr. Paul Scott, FCA *1959;* 119 Cliveden Gages, Taplow, MAIDENHEAD, BERKSHIRE, SL6 0GB. (Life Member)
LEWIS, Mr. Paul Stephen, BSc ACA *1988;* Cooper Safety Limited Jephson Court, Tancred Close, LEAMINGTON SPA, CV31 3RZ.
LEWIS, Mr. Paul William, BA(Hons) ACA *2004;* (Tax Fac), 2 Park Road, EXMOUTH, DEVON, EX8 1TN.
LEWIS, Mr. Perry Rufus, FCA CF *1977;* Moor House, Little Humby, GRANTHAM, LINCOLNSHIRE, NG33 4HW.
LEWIS, Mr. Peter Cyril Robert, BCom FCA *1971;* Abbey House, Moorland Road, Bramhope, LEEDS, LS16 9HW.
•LEWIS, Mr. Peter Grosvenor, FCA *1971;* Thorne Widgery Accountancy Ltd, 33 Bridge Street, HEREFORD, HR4 9DQ. See also TW Business Solutions LLP and Thorne Widgery & Jones LLP
LEWIS, Mr. Peter Howard, FCA *1960;* 24 Cooper Avenue North, LIVERPOOL, L18 4PG.
•LEWIS, Mr. Peter John, ACA *1984;* Lewis & Co (Financial Management) Ltd, 2 Doughty Buildings, Crow Arch Lane, RINGWOOD, HAMPSHIRE, BH24 1NZ.
LEWIS, Mr. Peter Michael, BSc FCA FSI *1979;* 8 Springfield Close, Cropwell Bishop, NOTTINGHAM, NG12 3GJ.
LEWIS, Mr. Peter Morgan, BA FCA *1979;* Morgan Lewis Consulting Ltd, 28 Neath Road, MAESTEG, MID GLAMORGAN, CF34 9PG.
LEWIS, Mr. Peter Ross, BSc ACA *2000;* B D O Stoy Hayward, Emerald House, East Street, EPSOM, SURREY, KT17 1HS.
LEWIS, Mr. Philip Andrew John, MA ACA *1988;* (Tax Fac), with KPMG LLP, 15 Canada Square, LONDON, E14 5GL.
LEWIS, Mr. Philip Leslie, ACA *1986;* 62 The Avenue, SALE, M33 4WA.
LEWIS, Mr. Philip Simon, BA ACA *1997;* Dunbury Lodge, Dunbury Lane, Winterborne Stickland, BLANDFORD FORUM, DORSET, DT11 0NN.
LEWIS, Mrs. Rachel Victoria, MChem ACA *2006;* 22nd Floor, Finance Department, EUI Limited, Capital Tower, Greyfriars Road, CARDIFF CF10 3AZ.
LEWIS, Mr. Randy, ACA FCCA *2011;* PO Box 753, Mattingley Heights, BASSETERRE, SAINT KITTS AND NEVIS.
LEWIS, Miss. Rebecca Anne, BSc ACA *1995;* Oakhill House, Fil Investments Ltd, 130 Tonbridge Road Hildenborough, TONBRIDGE, TN11 9DZ.
LEWIS, Mr. Reginald Harvey, FCA *1958;* 4 Firs Crescent, Freshfield, Formby, LIVERPOOL, L37 1PT. (Life Member)
LEWIS, Mr. Richard, BSc ACA *1995;* House 1, The Green Villa, Ta Ku Ling San Pseun, Clear Water Bay Road, SAI KUNG, NEW TERRITORIES HONG KONG SAR.
LEWIS, Dr. Richard, ACA *2011;* Flat 3, Parkgate Mansions, Leslie Road, East Finchley, LONDON, N2 8BL.
LEWIS, Mr. Richard, BSc ACA *2005;* 1 Summerville Terrace, Harborne Park Road, BIRMINGHAM, B17 0DQ.
LEWIS, Mr. Richard Andrew, LLB ACA *2002;* 95 College Road, EPSOM, KT17 4HY.
LEWIS, Mr. Richard George, ACA *2011;* PO BOX 905, GEORGETOWN, KY1 1103, CAYMAN ISLANDS.
•LEWIS, Mr. Richard Paul, MA ACA *1990;* Ernst & Young (CIS) B.V., Sadovnicheskaya Naberezhnaya 77/1, 115035 MOSCOW, RUSSIAN FEDERATION. See also Ernst & Young Europe LLP
•LEWIS, Mr. Richard Peter Gwynne, FCA *1970;* Richard P G Lewis, Brick Kiln Cottage, 20 Comfort Road, Mylor Bridge, FALMOUTH, CORNWALL TR11 5SE.
LEWIS, Mr. Richard Reginald, BSc FCA *1973;* 19 Woodsford Square, LONDON, W14 8DP.
•LEWIS, Mr. Richard Wayne, MSc FCA *1965;* (Tax Fac), Lewis & Co, 19 Goodge Street, LONDON, W1T 2PH.
•LEWIS, Mr. Robert, BSc FCA *1986;* Berkeley Hamilton LLP, 5 Pullman Court, Great Western Road, GLOUCESTER, GL1 3ND.
•LEWIS, Mr. Robert Andrew, FCA *1970;* Robert A. Lewis & Co, Manor Farm, West End, Ashton, CHESTER, CH3 8DG.
LEWIS, Mr. Robert David, BSc ACA *1997;* Grofftydd, Carno, CAERSWS, POWYS, SY17 5JR.
LEWIS, Mr. Robert John, BSc(Econ) ACA *1998;* 28 Moorland Avenue, Newton, SWANSEA, SA3 4UA.
•LEWIS, Mr. Robert Leonard, BSc FCA *1975;* Wildin & Co, Kings Buildings, Hill Street, LYDNEY, GLOUCESTERSHIRE, GL15 5HE.
•ⒹLEWIS, Mr. Robert Nicholas, BA FCA *1995;* PricewaterhouseCoopers LLP, 31 Great George Street, BRISTOL, BS1 5QD. See also PricewaterhouseCoopers
•LEWIS, Mr. Robert Niven, FCA *1975;* Summers Accountancy and Book Keeping Services, 70 New Road, Skewen, NEATH, WEST GLAMORGAN, SA10 6HA.
•LEWIS, Mr. Robert Philip, BSc FCA *1987;* KPMG LLP, 15 Canada Square, LONDON, E14 5GL. See also KPMG Europe LLP
LEWIS, Mr. Robert Price, FCA *1971;* (Tax Fac), Measteg, Whitton, KNIGHTON, POWYS, LD7 1NP.
LEWIS, Mr. Robert Stephen, BSc(Hons) ACA *2001;* 17 Granby Crescent, WIRRAL, CH63 9NY.
LEWIS, Mr. Robert William Gerald, BSc FCA *1965;* The Tumble, Gillotts Lane, Harpsden, HENLEY-ON-THAMES, RG9 4AY. (Life Member)
LEWIS, Mr. Roger, FCA *1962;* Dawkins Lewis & Soar, 4 Portelant Barns, Cowdown Barn, Micheldever, WINCHESTER, HAMPSHIRE SO21 3DN.
LEWIS, Mr. Roger Graham, FCA *1970;* 51 Greenmeadow Drive, Parc Seymour Penhow, CALDICOT, GWENT, NP26 3AW. (Life Member)
LEWIS, Mr. Roger St John Hulton, FCA *1972;* Le Bocage, La Rue Du Bocage, St. Brelade, JERSEY, JE3 8BP.
LEWIS, Mr. Ronald Horace, FCA *1953;* Flat 1, Jeanette Court, 49 Chaucer Road, ASHFORD, MIDDLESEX, TW15 2QW. (Life Member)
LEWIS, Mr. Rory James, BSc ACA *2003;* Flat 6, 192 Bedford Hill, LONDON, SW12 9HL.
LEWIS, Mrs. Rosalind Susan, BSc ACA *1999;* 3 Highlands, HATFIELD, HERTFORDSHIRE, AL9 5DW.
LEWIS, Miss. Rosemary Elaine, BA(Hons) ACA *2002;* Flat 3, 182 Lewisham Way, Brockley, LONDON, SE4 1UU.
LEWIS, Mrs. Samantha, BA ACA *1995;* 12 Fewing Street, CLOVELLY, NSW 2031, AUSTRALIA.
LEWIS, Miss. Sarah Amanda, LLB ACA *2010;* 4 Worcester Crescent, WOODFORD GREEN, ESSEX, IG8 0LU.
LEWIS, Mrs. Sarah Elizabeth, BA ACA *1992;* Thetford Town Council, Kings House, King Street, THETFORD, NORFOLK, IP24 2AP.

LEWIS, Mrs. Sarah Margaret, MA ACA *1991;* 10 Cow Brook Lane, Papworth Everard, CAMBRIDGE, CB23 3GP.
LEWIS, Mrs. Sasha Elizabeth, BSc ACA *2000;* Pricewaterhousecoopers Savannah House, 3 Ocean Way, SOUTHAMPTON, SO14 3TJ.
LEWIS, Mr. Simon, ACA *2011;* 43 Kenwyn Road, LONDON, SW4 7LJ.
LEWIS, Mr. Simon Anthony, BA ACA *1987;* Highbridge Westcott House, 35 Portland Place, LONDON, W1B 1AE.
LEWIS, Mr. Simon Archer, BA ACA *2007;* 7 Franklin Close, Colney Heath, ST. ALBANS, HERTFORDSHIRE, AL4 0QL.
LEWIS, Mr. Simon Avrom, BSc FCA *1982;* Harmony House, Savile Close, THAMES DITTON, KT7 0BU.
LEWIS, Mr. Simon David, BA ACA *2007;* 2 Bude Road, WALSALL, WS5 3EX.
LEWIS, Mr. Simon David, BA ACA *1985;* 101 Crawfords Road, MAYLANDS, WA 6051, AUSTRALIA.
•LEWIS, Mr. Simon James, BA(Hons) ACA *2003;* Thompson Jenner LLP, 28 Alexandra Terrace, EXMOUTH, DEVON, EX8 1BD.
•LEWIS, Mr. Simon Mark Henry, BA ACA *1989;* (Tax Fac), DFC, First Floor Unit 4C, Village Way, GreenMeadow Springs Business Park, CARDIFF, CF15 7NE. See also Dennis, Freedman, Clayton & Co
LEWIS, Mr. Stephen, MA FCA *1990;* 1, Cobblers cross lane, TARPORLEY, CHESHIRE, Cw6 0du.
•LEWIS, Mr. Stephen, BA FCA FPC *1976;* Morgan Griffiths LLP, Cross Chambers, 9 High Street, NEWTOWN, POWYS, SY16 2NY.
LEWIS, Mr. Stephen David, MA FCA *1967;* Wood End Farm, Hall Lane, Bickerstaffe, ORMSKIRK, LANCASHIRE, L39 0ES.
LEWIS, Mr. Stephen Howard, BCom ACA *1989;* Brimingham Heartlands & Solihull NHS Trust, Bordesley Green, BIRMINGHAM, B9 5SS.
•LEWIS, Mr. Stephen John, LLB FCA *1992;* Mazars LLP, 45 Church Street, BIRMINGHAM, B3 2RT.
LEWIS, Dr. Stephen John, MBBS ACA *2000;* 70 Gosden Hill Road, Burpham, GUILDFORD, GU4 7JD.
•LEWIS, Mr. Stephen Mark, BSc FCA *1996;* Trevor Jones & Co., Old Bank Chambers, 582-586 Kingsbury Road, Erdington, BIRMINGHAM, B24 9ND.
•LEWIS, Mr. Stewart Malcolm, BSc FCA *1979;* Wine & Co, 20-22 Bridge End, LEEDS, LS1 4DJ.
•ⓁLEWIS, Miss. Susan Anne, BSc ACA *1983;* with Deloitte LLP, 1 Woodborough Road, NOTTINGHAM, NG1 3FG.
LEWIS, Mrs. Susan Jane, BA(Hons) ACA *2003;* Leadership Development Ltd, 495 Fulham Road, LONDON, SW6 1HH.
•LEWIS, Mrs. Susan Joanne, LLB ACA *1994;* Sue Lewis Accountancy Services, Dove Cottage, 18 Style Road, Wiveliscombe, TAUNTON, SOMERSET TA4 2LN.
LEWIS, Mrs. Suzanne Jane, MBA BA ACA *1994;* La Vignette 7 Santa Rosa, Patier Lane, St. Saviour, JERSEY, JE2 7LQ.
LEWIS, Mr. Sven Evan, MSt BA(Hons) ACA *2001;* Pricewaterhousecoopers, 9 Greyfriars Road, READING, RG1 1JG.
•LEWIS, Mr. Terence Paul, FCA *1968;* T P Lewis & Partners (BOS) Limited, 3/5 College Street, BURNHAM-ON-SEA, SOMERSET, TA8 1AR.
LEWIS, Mrs. Teresa Lynn, BA FCA *1984;* Fossedene Manor Fosse Way, Combrook, WARWICK, CV35 9HS. (Life Member)
LEWIS, Mr. Terrence Ronald, BSc FCA *1982;* 93 Edgell Road, STAINES, MIDDLESEX, TW18 2EN.
•LEWIS, Mr. Thomas Edward, MA ACA *1996;* PricewaterhouseCoopers LLP, Pricewaterhousecoopers, 12 Plumtree Court, LONDON, EC4A 4HT. See also PricewaterhouseCoopers
LEWIS, Mr. Thomas Geraint John, BA FCA *1999;* 4 St. Barnabas Court, St. Barnabas Road, CAMBRIDGE, CB1 2BZ.
LEWIS, Mr. Thomas Michael, BSc ACA *2002;* 20 Crescent Rise, LONDON, N22 7AW.
LEWIS, Mr. Tim Richard Gwynne, MSci ACA *2005;* 69 Lyric Road, LONDON, SW13 9QA.
LEWIS, Mr. Timothy, MA ACA *1988;* 100 Avenue Vanderbilt, 78955 CARRIERES-SOUS-POISSY, FRANCE.
LEWIS, Mr. Timothy Richard, BSc ACA *1992;* 9 Warburton Close, Hale Barns, ALTRINCHAM, CHESHIRE, WA15 0SJ.
LEWIS, Mr. Timothy William Hunt, MA FCA *1980;* Durran House, Beckhampton, MARLBOROUGH, SN8 1QJ.
LEWIS, Mr. Tomos, BA ACA *1991;* G M P T E, 2 Picadilly Place, MANCHESTER, M1 3BG.
LEWIS, Mrs. Tonia, LLB ACA *2001;* Wales & West Utilities, Wales & West House, Spooner Close, Coedkernew, NEWPORT, GWENT NP10 8FZ.
LEWIS, Miss. Tracy, ACA *2008;* 54 Trevithick Road, TRURO, CORNWALL, TR1 1NS.
LEWIS, Mr. Tristan, MA(Oxon) ACA *2006;* Domaine De La Valette, Rue De Sorel, St John, JERSEY, JE3 4AA.
LEWIS, Mrs. Valerie, BSc ACA *1984;* Dulux Decorator Centre, Manchester Road, West Timperley, ALTRINCHAM, CHESHIRE, WA14 5PG.
LEWIS, Mrs. Victoria Ann, BA ACA *1999;* 14 Harland Road, LONDON, SE12 0JA.
LEWIS, Miss. Victoria Jane, BSc ACA *2009;* 3 Uplands Drive, St Johns Road, ST HELIER, JE2 3UD.
LEWIS, Mr. Vivian Wheaton, BA FCA *1959;* 18 Heol y Ffynnon, Efail Isaf, PONTYPRIDD, CF38 1AU. (Life Member)
LEWIS, Mr. Walter Alan, FCA *1960;* Flat 402, 2360 James White Boulevard, SIDNEY V8L 1Z7, BC, CANADA. (Life Member)
LEWIS, Mr. Wayne, BA ACA *1983;* 58 Lyndhurst Drive, SEVENOAKS, KENT, TN13 2HQ.
LEWIS, Mr. William Llewelyn, BSc FCA *1972;* Eden House, 1 Eden Road, TUNBRIDGE WELLS, TN1 1TS.
LEWIS, Mr. William Rowland Andrew, BA ACA *2010;* Homefield, Cote Drive, Westbury-on-Trym, BRISTOL, BS9 3UP.
LEWIS, Mr. Wyn Parry, MA FCA *1976;* PO Box 30030, SMB Post Office, GEORGETOWN, GRAND CAYMAN, CAYMAN ISLANDS.
•LEWIS - JAMES, Mrs. Rhian, BSc FCA *1995;* (Tax Fac), RLJ & Co Limited, Chapel Cottage, Michaelston-y-Fedw, CARDIFF, CF3 6XT.
LEWIS-BAKER, Mrs. Celine Estelle Charlotte, BSc ACA *1996;* 13 Eastbrook Terrace, Trull, TAUNTON, SOMERSET, TA3 7LJ.
LEWIS-CROSBY, Mr. John Cornwalll, BA FCA *1972;* Oxford Instruments Ltd Research Instruments, Tubney Wood, ABINGDON, OXFORDSHIRE, OX13 5QX.
LEWIS-DAVIES, Mr. Philip Alun, BA FCA *1982;* Brynawel, Brynberian, CRYMYCH, PEMBROKESHIRE, SA41 3UB.
LEWIS-GOW, Mrs. Annette Mary, FCA *1986;* Two Saints Ltd, 35 Waterside Gardens, FAREHAM, HAMPSHIRE, PO16 8SD.
•LEWIS-JONES, Mr. Christopher, BA FCA *1985;* The Smithy Monks Lane, Acton, NANTWICH, CHESHIRE, CW5 8LE.
LEWIS-JONES, Mr. Clive Richard, MA MSc FCA *1974;* 50 Westhall Road, WARLINGHAM, SURREY, CR6 9BH.
LEWIS-WILLIAMS, Miss. Laura Clare, ACA *2009;* Quintin Kynaston School, Marlborough Hill, LONDON, NW8 0NL.
LEWITT, Mr. Frank Malcolm, BSc FCA *1978;* Rowley Lodge, Forty Acre Lane, Kermincham, CREWE, CW4 8DX.
LEWORTHY, Mr. Roger Gerald Harrison, FCA *1971;* 15967 Viney Creek Drive, HOUSTON, TX 77095, UNITED STATES.
LEWSLEY, Mrs. Daphne Winifred, BSc ACA *1984;* Sandwell & West Birmingham Hospitals NHS Trust, Management Block, City Hospital, Dudley Road, BIRMINGHAM, B18 7QH.
•LEWSLEY, Mr. David Martin, FCA *1983;* Gregory Wildman, The Granary, Crowhill Farm, Ravensden Road, Wilden, BEDFORD MK44 2QS.
LEWTAS, Miss. Carolyn, ACA *2010;* 37 Westgate Drive, Swinton, MANCHESTER, M27 5QB.
LEWTHWAITE, Miss. Claire Ellen, BSocSc ACA *2002;* Npower, 2 Princes Way, SOLIHULL, B91 3ES.
LEWTHWAITE, Mr. Mark, BSc ACA *1980;* Highfields, Tokers Green Lane, Kidmore End, READING, RG4 9AY.
LEWTHWAITE, Miss. Mellissa Kim, BSc(Hons) ACA *2005;* 69 Frosthole Crescent, FAREHAM, PO15 6AH.
•LEWTHWAITE, Mr. Thomas Owen, MA FCA *1989;* Deloitte LLP, Hill House, 1 Little New Street, LONDON, EC4A 3TR. See also Deloitte & Touche LLP
LEWTY, Miss. Claire Louise, BEng ACA *1996;* 11a West Park Road, RICHMOND, SURREY, TW9 4DB.
LEWYCKYJ, Mr. Bohdan, BSc ACA *1995;* Harris & Trotter, 65 New Cavendish Street, LONDON, W1G 7LS.
LEWYS-LLOYD, Mr. John Cadwaladrr, MA FCA *1967;* Manor Farm, 100 Caldy Road, WIRRAL, CH48 2HZ.
LEWZEY, Miss. Elizabeth Honor, BSc FCA *1984;* Somerled, 8 Kings Warren, Oxshott, LEATHERHEAD, SURREY, KT22 0PE.
LEY, Mrs. Clare Suzanne, BA ACA *1999;* 14/522 New South Head Road, DOUBLE BAY, NSW 2028, AUSTRALIA.
LEY, Mr. Gordon Chaunter, FCA *1955;* 13 Lime Tree Gardens, Lowdham, NOTTINGHAM, NG14 7DJ. (Life Member)
•LEY, Mr. John, FCA *1973;* Wadlan Ley, 119 Battersea Business Centre, Lavender Hill, LONDON, SW11 5QL.
LEY, Mrs. Lindsay, BA ACA *1995;* 60 Burnedge Fold Road, Grasscroft, OLDHAM, OL4 4EE.
LEY, Mr. Martin Nigel, BA ACA *1997;* Calle Cruces 8 - 2 - C, Las Rozas, 28231 MADRID, SPAIN.
•LEY, Mr. Stephen Geraint, BSc ACA *1997;* Deloitte LLP, 2 New Street Square, LONDON, EC4A 3BZ. See also Deloitte & Touche LLP
LEY, Mr. Thomas Henry, MA MSc ACA *1995;* Flat 161, Andrewes House, Barbican, LONDON, EC2Y 8BA.
LEY GREAVES, Mr. John Bruce, FCA *1970;* 34 Wendell Road, LONDON, W12 9RS.
•LEYBOURNE, Mr. Stephen, FCA *1974;* Leybourne & Co, 25 Crossley Hill, HALIFAX, HX3 0PL.
LEYDEN, Mr. Michael David, BA ACA ACIM *1984;* Heathrow Express, 50 Eastbourne Terrace, LONDON, W2 6LG.
LEYDEN, Mrs. Sonja Catriona, BA ACA ATII *1988;* Marsh Ltd, 1 Tower Place West, LONDON, EC3R 5BU.
•LEYHANE, Mr. Dennis Frederick, FCA *1975;* (Tax Fac), Dennis Leyhane, Greenleaf, 46 The Gables, ONGAR, ESSEX, CM5 0GA.
LEYHANE, Mr. Robert Charles, FCA *1964;* Suite 302, Morrison House, 390 Upper Middle Road East, OAKVILLE L6H 0A5, ON, CANADA.
LEYLAND, Mr. Andrew Paul, BA(Hons) ACA *2001;* with M J Riley & Co, 22 Church Street, KIDDERMINSTER, DY10 2AW.
LEYLAND, Mr. Bernard John, FCA *1969;* Marlborough Fund Managers Ltd Marlborough House, 59 Chorley New Road, BOLTON, BL1 4QP.
LEYLAND, Miss. Lucy Emma, ACA *2008;* 11 Orchard Close, FRODSHAM, WA6 6DS.
LEYLAND, Mr. Mark, ACA *2010;* 36 Maxim Tower, Mercury Gardens, ROMFORD, RM1 3HE.
LEYLAND, Mr. Michael Stuart, BSc FCA *1973;* 5 Garners Close, Chalfont St. Peter, GERRARDS CROSS, SL9 0HB.
LEYSHON, Miss. Alison, BA ACA *1994;* 30 Foster Road, Chiswick, LONDON, W4 4NY.
LEYSHON, Mr. Richard Hugh Clifford, FCA *1974;* 18 Meadow Sweet Drive, St Mellons, CARDIFF, CF3 0RD.
LEYTON, Mr. John William, BA FCA *1977;* 46 Forest Way, WOODFORD GREEN, ESSEX, IG8 0QB.
LI, Mr. Alain Jacques Gilbert, BSc FCA *1987;* Richemont Asia Pacific Ltd, 6/F Jardine House, 1 Connaught Place, CENTRAL, HONG KONG SAR.
LI, Mr. Alan, BA(Hons) ACA *2002;* 8 Marwood Close, Furzton, MILTON KEYNES, MK4 1LP.
LI, Mr. Alvin Ngai, BSc ACA *1992;* Flat A 8/F, Royal Garden, 27 Repulse Bay Road, REPULSE BAY, HONG KONG ISLAND, HONG KONG SAR.
LI, Mr. Andy Wai Kwan, ACA *2008;* 17A Evelyn Towers, 38 Cloud View Road, NORTH POINT, HONG KONG ISLAND, HONG KONG SAR.
LI, Miss. Angela, BSc ACA *2008;* 14 Holmefield, SALE, CHESHIRE, M33 3AN.
LI, Mr. Brian Man Bun, BA FCA *1999;* The Bank of East Asia Limited, 11/F. The Bank of East Asia Building, 10 Des Voeux Road, CENTRAL, HONG KONG ISLAND, HONG KONG SAR.
•LI, Mr. Bruce Wing, BA ACA *1993;* 9 Enys Road, EASTBOURNE, BN21 2DG.
LI, Ms. Catherine Yan Ying, ACA *2009;* 21A Kennedy Heights, 18 Kennedy Road, MID LEVELS, HONG KONG SAR.
LI, Mr. Charles Yourui, ACA *2010;* 124 TAMPINES ST 11, #08-418, SINGAPORE 521124, SINGAPORE.
LI, Miss. Chen, BA ACA *2009;* 25 Elm Road, CHESSINGTON, SURREY, KT9 1AF.
LI, Miss. Chen, BEng ACA *2002;* 16/F Maxdo Centre 8 Xingyi Road Chang Ning District, SHANGHAI 200336, CHINA.
LI, Miss. Choi-Ling, BSc(Hons) ACA *2009;* Flat 506, Holly Court, John Harrison Way, LONDON, SE10 0BL.
LI, Mr. Chris Siu Hung, BEng FCA *1995;* 2203 Tower B, Queens Garden, 9 Old Peak Road, MID LEVELS, HONG KONG ISLAND, HONG KONG SAR.
LI, Mr. Christian, ACA FCMA *2009;* C/o CKLB Financial Services Group, PO Box 80 Felix House, 24 Dr Joseph Riviere Str., PORT LOUIS, MAURITIUS.
LI, Mr. Chung Kwong Andrew, ACA *2008;* c/o Shanghai Electric Group Co. Ltd, 30/F. Shanghai Maxdo Center, 8 Xing Yi Road, SHANGHAI 200336, CHINA.
LI, Ms. Cynthia Seung Kiu, ACA *2007;* Flat A 22/F Tower 6, Ocean Shores, 88 O King Road, TSEUNG KWAN O, NEW TERRITORIES, HONG KONG SAR.
LI, Sir David Kwok Po, OBE MA FCA *1966;* The Bank of East Asia Limited, 21st Floor, Bank of East Asia Building, 10 Des Voeux Road, CENTRAL, HONG KONG ISLAND HONG KONG SAR.
LI, Miss. Diana Shiu May, BSc ACA *1987;* 15A Tung Tze Terrace, 6 Aberdeen Street, CENTRAL, HONG KONG ISLAND, HONG KONG SAR.
LI, Mr. Dominic Kam Fai, ACA *1981;* Dominic K.F. Li & Co, Room 2107-821/F, Kai Tak Commercial Building, 317-319 Des Voeux Road, CENTRAL, HONG KONG ISLAND HONG KONG SAR.
LI, Mr. Douglas, BSc ACA *1981;* SmarTone Mobile Communications Limited, 31/F Millennium City 2, 378 Kwun Tong Road, KWUN TONG, KOWLOON, HONG KONG SAR.
LI, Miss. Edwina Shuk Yin, BA FCA *1990;* KPMG, 8/F Prince's Building, 10 Chater Road, CENTRAL, HONG KONG ISLAND, HONG KONG SAR.
LI, Miss. Emily Wai Han, BSc ACA *1993;* 4th Floor, K.Y. Mansion, 4A Shiu Fai Terrace, WAN CHAI, HONG KONG SAR.
LI, Mr. Eric Ka-Cheung, BA FCA *1978;* Li Tang Chen & Co., 10/F Sun Hung Kai Centre, 30 Harbour Road, WAN CHAI, HONG KONG ISLAND, HONG KONG SAR.
LI, Mr. Eric Kwok Yeung, MSc BA ACA *2005;* Flat 56D, Tower 2, Florient Rise, 38 Cherry Street, TAI KOK TSUI, KOWLOON HONG KONG SAR.
LI, Mr. Fat Chung, ACA *2007;* Chan Li Law & Co, Unit 402, 4/F Malaysia Building, 50 Gloucester Road, WAN CHAI, HONG KONG ISLAND HONG KONG SAR.
LI, Mr. George Wing Chung, BSc FCA CTA *1980;* (Tax Fac), Flat C 3rd Floor, Ewan Court, 54-56 Kennedy Road, WAN CHAI, HONG KONG SAR.
LI, Miss. Helen Siu Lai, BSc ACA *1984;* 22 High Garth, ESHER, KT10 9DN.
LI, Mr. Hon Kuen, ACA *2007;* Flat D, 7th Floor, Ko On Mansion, 9 Tai Yue Avenue, Taikoo Shing, QUARRY BAY HONG KONG ISLAND HONG KONG SAR.
LI, Mr. Jeremy Yuen Lim, MA(Cantab) ACA *2011;* Flat 1A Tregunter Building Tower 2, 14 Tregunter Path, Old Peak Road, MID LEVELS, HONG KONG ISLAND, HONG KONG SAR.
LI, Miss. Jia, ACA *2010;* Apartment 6, Ashfield House, 19 Claremont Road, SALE, CHESHIRE, M33 7LN.
LI, Ms. Jiarui, BSc ACA *2010;* Flat 8 Studley Court, 4 Jamestown Way, LONDON, E14 2DA.
LI, Ms. Jingyu, ACA CICPA *2010;* Room 401, Unit 2, Building 3 Huanglong, Yayuan, 143 Xixi Road, HANGZHOU 310007 ZHEJIANG PROVINCE CHINA.
LI, Mr. John Kwok Heem, BSc FCA *1979;* B-6 Carolina Gardens, 24 Coombe Road, THE PEAK, HONG KONG ISLAND, HONG KONG SAR.
LI, Mr. Jonathan Chong Hing, BA ACA *2000;* Flat A 10/F, Block 2 Aquamarine, 8 Sham Shing Road, CHEUNG SHA WAN, KOWLOON, HONG KONG SAR.
LI, Mr. Joseph Jeremy Kachu, BA ACA *1993;* 5M Edificio Bela Vista, No4C Ave da Republica, Sai Van, MACAU, MACAO.
LI, Mr. Ka Fai, ACA *2007;* 15E Block 8, Laguna City, LAM TIN, KOWLOON, HONG KONG SAR.
LI, Mr. Ka Fai, ACA *2008;* 20H Block 16 Laguna City, KWUN TONG, HONG KONG SAR.
LI, Mr. Ka Fai David, ACA *2005;* Li Tang Chen & Co., 10/F Sun Hung Kai Centre, 30 Harbour Road, WAN CHAI, HONG KONG ISLAND, HONG KONG SAR.
LI, Mr. Ka Hong, BA ACA *2004;* 3 Porchester Road, Bingham, NOTTINGHAM, NG13 8ES.
LI, Mr. Kar Lok Bruce, MPA BSc ACA ACIS CPA *2005;* Flat A 4/F, 27 Broadway, MEI FOO SUN CHUEN, KOWLOON, HONG KONG SAR.
LI, Ms. Kar Wai Agnes, ACA *2008;* 15D Two Robinson Place, 70 Robinson Road, MID LEVELS, HONG KONG SAR.
LI, Miss. Katherine Ah Yan, ACA *2010;* with Cookson Group plc, 165 Fleet Street, LONDON, EC4A 2AE.
LI, Mr. Ken Tom, ACA *2009;* 16 Peterborough Close, GRANTHAM, LINCOLNSHIRE, NG31 8SH.
LI, Dr. Kevin Ka Wing, PhD ACA *2009;* 42 Railway Street, CHELMSFORD, CM1 1QS.
LI, Mr. Kwan Hung, BEng ACA CTA *1988;* (Tax Fac), 5 Maxfield Close, Whetstone, LONDON, N20 9DF.
LI, Mr. Kwan Chuen, ACA *2007;* Flat 2110, 21/F. Kwai Kin House, Kwai Fong Estate, TSUEN WAN, NEW TERRITORIES, HONG KONG SAR.
LI, Mr. Kwok Ting, BSc FCA *1962;* 11686 Palm Spring Court, CUPERTINO, CA 95014, UNITED STATES. (Life Member)
LI, Mr. Larry, BA(Hons) ACA *2001;* Rm 4001 Plaza 66 Phase 1, Nanjing Xi Lu, SHANGHAI 200040, CHINA.

LI, Ms. Liang, ACA CA(NZ) *2010;* H106 / 2 Quay Street, SYDNEY, NSW 2000, AUSTRALIA.
LI, Mr. Ling, ACA *2011;* Flat 86, Park West, Edgware Road, LONDON, W2 2QJ.
LI, Miss. Lolita Kwok Wei, BSc ACA *1980;* Flat 47/F Block C, Imperial Court, 62G Conduit Road, MID LEVELS, HONG KONG ISLAND, HONG KONG SAR.
LI, Mrs. Louise, BA FCA *1991;* 23 Cope Place, Kensington, LONDON, W8 6AA.
LI, Mr. Man Choi, ACA *2005;* 30/D Block 3, Hilltop Garden, Hammer Hill, 33 Fung Shing Street, SAN PO KONG, KOWLOON HONG KONG SAR.
LI, Mr. Man Kei, ACA *2008;* Deloitte Touche Tohmatsu, 35/F One Pacific Place, 88 Queensway, CENTRAL, HONG KONG ISLAND, HONG KONG SAR.
LI, Mr. Man Shing, ACA *2008;* Room 8A, Lomond Court, 16 Lomond Road, KOWLOON CITY, KOWLOON, HONG KONG SAR.
LI, Mr. Man Wai, BSc ACA *1996;* 1C Medallion Heights, 45 Conduit Road, MID LEVELS, HONG KONG ISLAND, HONG KONG SAR.
LI, Mr. Mann-Kee, BSc ACA *1988;* 97 Northgate Street, GLOUCESTER, GL1 2AA.
LI, Mrs. Maria Suzanne, BA ACA *1995;* Durbin Metal Industries Ltd Unit O, Lawrence Drive Yate, BRISTOL, BS37 5PG.
LI, Miss. Mei Ching, BSc ACA *2000;* 9 Queen Annes Gate, Caversham, READING, RG4 5DU.
LI, Mrs. Mei Lee, FCA *1962;* Flat D1, Seacliff Mansions, 19 Repulse Bay Road, REPULSE BAY, HONG KONG ISLAND, HONG KONG SAR. (Life Member)
LI, Mr. Michael, BSc ACA *2011;* B-6 Carolina Gardens, 24 Coombe Road, THE PEAK, HONG KONG ISLAND, HONG KONG SAR.
LI, Miss. Ming, ACA *2010;* Flat 9, Burrage Court, Worgan Street, LONDON, SE16 7WA.
LI, Mr. Nicholas, BSc ACA *2003;* 2496 Waterbury Lane, BUFFALO GROVE, IL 60089, UNITED STATES.
LI, Miss. Ou, ACA *2011;* 42 Finland Street, LONDON, SE16 7TP.
LI, Mr. Pak Ki, ACA *2008;* 25th Floor Wing On Centre, 111 Connaught Road, CENTRAL, HONG KONG ISLAND, HONG KONG SAR. See also Horwath Hong Kong CPA Limited
LI, Mr. Philip Sau Yan, BSc ACA *1986;* 60A Begonia Rd Ground Floor, YAU YAT TSUEN, Kowloon, HONG KONG SAR.
LI, Miss. Ran, MA ACA *2010;* Flat 37, Paper Mill Wharf, 50 Narrow Street, LONDON, E14 8BZ.
LI, Mr. Rui, MSc ACA *2009;* 57 Langbourne Place, LONDON, E14 3WN.
LI, Mr. Sai Yue Peter, ACA *2005;* Tower 3, Unut G, 20/F Manhattan Hill, LAI CHI KOK, KOWLOON, HONG KONG SAR.
LI, Ms. Sau Wan, ACA *2008;* A Chow & Partners, 17/F, Amtel Building, 144-148 Des Voeux Road Central, CENTRAL, HONG KONG SAR.
LI, Ms. Sheung Mei, ACA *2005;* Barclays Capital Asia Limited, 41/F Cheung Kong Center, 2 Queens Road, CENTRAL, HONG KONG SAR.
LI, Mr. Sheung Ki Lawrence, ACA *2005;* 18D Block 11, Sea Crest Villa Phase 4, TSING LUNG TAU, NEW TERRITORIES, HONG KONG SAR.
LI, Miss. Shi-Han, BSc ACA *2009;* 3 Batesquire, Sothall, SHEFFIELD, S20 2GS.
LI, Mr. Shu Pui, MSc FCA *1992;* 55/F Two International Finance Centre, 8 Finance Street, CENTRAL, HONG KONG ISLAND, HONG KONG SAR.
LI, Mr. Shu Tak, ACA *2004;* Flat 3312 Yu Cheong House, Yu Ming Court, TSEUNG KWAN O, NEW TERRITORIES, HONG KONG SAR.
LI, Miss. Shu-Ming Teresa, BA ACA *1984;* The Victoria Towers, Tower 2 40G, 188 Canton Road, TSIM SHA TSUI, KOWLOON, HONG KONG SAR.
LI, Mr. Shujun, ACA *2010;* Manshi Group, No.2 Xiaoyuanlu, Dongsheng District, ORDOS 017000, INNER MONGOLIA, CHINA.
LI, Mrs. Siu Yu Doris, BSc ACA *1993;* St. Marys Court Hill Street, Douglas, ISLE OF MAN, IM1 1EU.
LI, Mr. Siu Ping, ACA *2005;* Flat H 19th Floor Tower 1, Nan Fung Plaza, 8 Pui Shing Road, TSEUNG KWAN O, HONG KONG SAR.
LI, Ms. Siu Sun Cindy, ACA *2006;* 3rd Floor King Inn Mansion, 13-15 Yik Yam Street, HAPPY VALLEY, HONG KONG SAR.
LI, Mr. Stephen Charles, BSc ACA *1985;* 35D Estoril Court, 55 Garden Road, CENTRAL, HONG KONG ISLAND, HONG KONG SAR.
LI, Ms. Suet Lai, ACA *2008;* Unit 1908, Izumi Garden Residence, 1-5-3 Roppongi, Minato-ku, TOKYO, 106-0032 JAPAN.
LI, Ms. Suk Han Jenny, ACA *2007;* Room 2122, Yiu Him House, Yiu On Estate, Ma On Shan, SHA TIN, NEW TERRITORIES HONG KONG SAR.
LI, Ms. Susana Kit Chuen, BA FCA *1989;* Legal & General Investment Management, 1 Coleman Street, LONDON, EC2R 5AA.
LI, Mr. Sze Tang, ACA CF *2005;* Room 2912 Shell Tower, Times Square 1 Matheson Street, CAUSEWAY BAY, HONG KONG SAR.
LI, Mr. Tak Man, ACA *2008;* 16A, Block 1, Maritime Bay, 18 Pui Shing Road, TSEUNG KWAN O, KOWLOON HONG KONG SAR.
LI, Mr. Tak Wai, ACA *2008;* Flat E 37/F, Block 3 Prima Villa, No 8 Chui Yan Street, SHA TIN, NEW TERRITORIES, HONG KONG SAR.
LI, Miss. Tammy Tim Ling, BA ACA *2009;* 15 Garden Road, TUNBRIDGE WELLS, TN1 2XJ.
LI, Mr. Tao, ACA *2010;* 14 Culloden Close, LONDON, SE16 3JH.
LI, Mr. Terance, ACA *2009;* Apartment 304, Astra House, 23-25 Arklow Road, LONDON, SE14 6BY.
LI, Miss. Vivienne Wei-Mung, ACA *2009;* Flat 41 Edge Hill Court, Edge Hill, LONDON, SW19 4LW.
LI, Miss. Wai Chee, BSc ACA *1994;* 239 Jalan 5/50, Off Jalan Gasing, 46000 PETALING JAYA, Selangor, MALAYSIA.
LI, Mr. Wai See, ACA *2010;* Flat B 29th Floor Block 10, Monte Vista, 9 Sha On Street, Ma On Shan, SHA TIN, NEW TERRITORIES HONG KONG SAR.
LI, Miss. Wai Yi, BSc ACA *2000;* 43 Langdale Road, Bramhall, STOCKPORT, CHESHIRE, SK7 1DL.
LI, Mr. Wai Chung, ACA *2007;* Flat D 47/F Block 6, Rambler Crest, TSING YI, HONG KONG SAR.
LI, Ms. Wei, ACA *2007;* 12 Ashlake Road, LONDON, SW16 2BB.
LI, Mr. Wing Kwong Benjamin, ACA CPA *2008;* 9B Block 1, Cayman Rise, 29 Ka Wai Man Road, KENNEDY TOWN, HONG KONG SAR.
LI, Mr. Wing Yin, ACA *2008;* with Grant Thornton, 6th Floor, Nexus Building, 41 Conaught Road, CENTRAL, HONG KONG ISLAND HONG KONG SAR.
LI, Miss. Xiao, BSc ACA *2009;* Room 302, No 415, Yu Tian Road, Hongkou District, SHANGHAI 200083, CHINA.
LI, Miss. Xiuzhen, ACA *2011;* 45/F Shanghai world Financial Center 100 Century Avenue Pudong New Area, SHANGHAI 200120, CHINA.
LI, Mr. Yin-Hong, MA ACA *2004;* 68/F Cheung Kong Center, 2 Queens Road, CENTRAL, HONG KONG ISLAND, HONG KONG SAR.
LI, Miss. Ying, BE ACA *2009;* Room 802, Building 2, 736 YingChun Road, SHANGHAI 200135, CHINA.
LI, Miss. YingWen, ACA *2011;* F6-09H; North Zone Building F 6th Floor;, Lenovo, ShangDi Road West;, HaiDian District, ?????????6?????????F?6?F6-09H, BEIJING CHINA.
LI, Mr. Yu, ACA *2008;* Flat 8B Block 1, Florient Rise, 38 Cherry Street, TAI KOK TSUI, KOWLOON, HONG KONG SAR.
LI, Miss. Yu Jiao, ACA *2008;* Apartment 0389, HONG KONG SAR Parkview, Tower 16, 88 Tai Tam Reservior Road, WAN CHAI, HONG KONG ISLAND HONG KONG SAR.
LI, Miss. Yuanqi, ACA *2009;* Flat 273 Ability Place, 37 Millharbour, LONDON, E14 9DL.
LI, Ms. Yuet Ching Agnes, ACA *2008;* Flat C 7/F Block 1, The Parcville, 33 Kau Hui Road, YUEN LONG, NEW TERRITORIES, HONG KONG SAR.
LI, Mr. Zhancheng, MSc ACA *2010;* GuangzhouPanYu Shiqiao, Qing He Dong Lu251 Dong Xin Hua Ting 1 Ti 1802, GUANGZHOU 511400, CHINA.
LI, Miss. Zhen, ACA *2010;* Flat 802 Washington Building, Deals Gateway, LONDON, SE13 7SE.
LI CHAY CHUNG, Mr. Robert Chin Lip, MA ACA *1991;* 22 Greenstead Gardens, WOODFORD GREEN, IG8 7EX.
LI CHEONG MAN, Mrs. Marie Laurence Pin Lan, ACA *1980;* Ministry of Education, Mowat Block 21st Floor, 900 Bay Street, TORONTO M7A 1L2, ON, CANADA.
•LI HOW CHEONG, Mr. John Eng Heon, FCA *1985;* KPMG Audit, 9 Allee Scheffer, 2520 LUXEMBOURG, LUXEMBOURG. See also KPMG Europe LLP
LI LIONG, Mr. Ah Kiung, ACA *1985;* Export Plus Ltd, 16 De Speville Street, BEAU BASSIN, MAURITIUS.
LI SUNG SANG, Mr. Kenneth Youne Fong, ACA *2011;* 6 Oakfield Gardens, LONDON, SE19 1HF.
LI-TIN-PO, Mr. Georges Huing Sen, FCA *1974;* G.H.S. Li-Tin-Po, 7 Mallaby Road, WILLOWDALE M2H 1P3, ON, CANADA.
LI WAI SUEN, Mr. James Cheng Tai, FCA *1974;* 16 Surrey Court, UNIONVILLE L3R 0G2, ON, CANADA.
LI-YAN-HUI, Mrs. Xiao Rong Winny, MPhil BA ACA *2003;* 3 Brunswick Court, Fulbourn, CAMBRIDGE, CB21 5XN.
LIAN, Mr. David Chee Wai, MA BA ACA *2007;* 10 Gloucester Avenue, CHELMSFORD, CM2 9LD.
LIAN, Miss. Sui-Sim, BSc FCA *1973;* 11 Ardmore Park, Apt 15-03, SINGAPORE 259957, SINGAPORE. (Life Member)
LIAN STEVENS, Mrs. Cheng, ACA *1987;* 16 Copse Wood Way, NORTHWOOD, MIDDLESEX, HA6 2UE.
LIANDU, Mr. Namasiku Donald, MEd BSc ACA *1991;* CENTER FOR ACCOUNTING & IT, BAHRAIN INSTITUTE OF BANKING & FINANCE, PO BOX 20525, MANAMA, BAHRAIN.
LIANG, Ms. Fung Cheung, ACA *2007;* Flat 1601Block E, Sun Tung House, Yu Tung Court, Tung Chung, LANTAU ISLAND, NEW TERRITORIES HONG KONG SAR.
LIANG, Ms. Jing, ACA *2010;* Flat 16, 119 Haverstock Hill, LONDON, NW3 4RS.
LIANG, Mr. Jingfeng, MSc ACA *2010;* FAS Department, Deloitte & Touche, Financial Advisory Services Limited Beijing Branch 8F Deloitte Tower The Towers Oriental Plaza 1, BEIJING 100738, CHINA.
LIANG, Miss. Xiuying, MA ACA *2010;* 1 Monkton Road, YORK, YO31 9AJ.
LIAO, Mr. Weinan, BSc ACA *2000;* Mesotron Corporation, Room 1901, L19 Tower E2, The Towers Oriental Plaza, No. 1 East Chang An Avenue, Dong Cheng District BEIJING 100738 CHINA.
LIAO, Mr. Yoon Kian, FCA *1977;* Seal Mart (M) Sdn Bhd, 47 Jalan Segambut Selatan, 51200 KUALA LUMPUR, FEDERAL TERRITORY, MALAYSIA.
LIAQAT, Mr. Bakhtiar, ACA *1981;* Flat 33, Pierhead Wharf, 69 Wapping High Street, LONDON, E1W 2YF.
LIAQAT, Mr. Omar, FCA *1986;* C/o Abu Dhabi Investment Council, PO Box 61999, ABU DHABI, UNITED ARAB EMIRATES.
LIARDET, Mr. Edward Mark, BSc ACA *1998;* No.03-02 Pebble Bay, 134 Tanjung Rhu Road, SINGAPORE, SINGAPORE.
•LIASIDES, Mr. Andreas, BA ACA *2008;* Alathea Audit Limited, PO Box 53590, CY 3303 LIMASSOL, CYPRUS.
LIASSIDES, Mr. Marios, MSc BA ACA *2010;* Odyssea Androutsou 7, Makedonitissa, 2413 NICOSIA, CYPRUS.
•LIASSIDES, Mr. Petrakis Liassis, BA ACA *1995;* Ernst & Young Cyprus Limited, Nicosia Tower Centre, 36 Byron Avenue, P O Box 21656, 1511 NICOSIA, CYPRUS.
LIAU, Miss. Chui Kien Josephine, BSc ACA *1984;* P O Box 314, SANDAKAN, SABAH, MALAYSIA.
LIAU, Miss. Jacqueline, BSc ACA *2001;* 373 Onan Road, #05-14 Malvern Springs, SINGAPORE 424775, SINGAPORE.
LIAW, Miss. Mabel Moy Hong, ACA *2010;* 25 Lorong Samarinda 35A, Taman Mesra, 41000 KLANG, SELANGOR, MALAYSIA.
LIBELL, Mr. Christopher John, BA ACA *2006;* 83 Elm Drive, HARROW, HA2 7BY.
LIBMAN, Miss. Simone Deborah, BSc ACA *2007;* Ground Floor Flat, 15 Taybridge Road, LONDON, SW11 5PR.
LIBOYI, Miss. Jackie, LLB ACA *2004;* Pennine Foods Drake House Crescent, Waterthorpe, SHEFFIELD, S20 7JG.
LIBSON, Mr. John Leslie, MA FCA *1964;* 41 Hollycroft Avenue, LONDON, NW3 7JQ.
LICHFIELD, Mr. Ian, ACA *1997;* Flat 9 Castle Hill, Baslow Road, BAKEWELL, DERBYSHIRE, DE45 1AA.
LICHMAN, Mr. Laurence, FCA *1973;* 10 Penman Close, ST. ALBANS, HERTFORDSHIRE, AL2 3DJ.
•LICHTEN, Mr. Michael Gary, FCA *1975;* NONE, NONE.
LICHTEN, Mr. Roger Stephen, BSc FCA *1976;* 222 Preston Hill, HARROW, HA3 9UJ.
LICKESS, Mr. Tom, BA ACA *2003;* 6/502 New Southhead Road, Double Bay, SYDNEY, NSW 2028, AUSTRALIA.
LICKISS, Sir Michael Gillam, Kt BSc(Econ) FCA CA(SA) *1959;* (President 1990 - 1991) (Member of Council 1971 - 1981 1983 - 1994), 5 Highcroft Court, EXETER, EX4 4RW. (Life Member)
•LICKISS, Mr. Peter Anthony John, BSc FCA CTA *1985;* Peter Lickiss Chartered Tax Adviser Limited, 35 Honiton Way, Aldridge, WALSALL, WS9 0JS.
LICKLEY, Mrs. Britta Emma Rebecca, BA FCA *1982;* 22 Abercorn Close, SOUTH CROYDON, Surrey, CR2 8TG.
LICKORISH, Mrs. Angela Susan, FCA *1987;* with Keens Shay Keens MK, Sovereign Court, 230 Upper Fifth Street, MILTON KEYNES, MK9 2HR.
LICKORISH, Mr. Eric Alfred, FCA *1957;* 51 Oakdene Crescent, Portslade, BRIGHTON, BN41 2RP. (Life Member)
•LICKORISH, Mr. Keith Andrew, FCA DChA *1975;* Baker Tilly Tax & Advisory Services LLP, 3rd Floor Preece House, Davigdor Road, HOVE, EAST SUSSEX, BN3 1RE. See also Baker Tilly UK Audit LLP
•LIDDELL, Mr. David George, BSc ACA *1990;* PKF (UK) LLP, New Guild House, 45 Great Charles Street, BIRMINGHAM, B3 2LX.
LIDDELL, Mr. David Lyon, BA ACA *1987;* Panmurg Gorden & Co, 155 Moorgate, LONDON, EC2M 6XB.
LIDDELL, Mr. Graeme Ian, BA FCA *1980;* 19 Lucastes Road, HAYWARDS HEATH, WEST SUSSEX, RH16 1JN.
LIDDELL, Mr. Graham George, MA ACA *1992;* Audit Commission Bicentennial Buildin, 1 Southern Gate Terminus Road, CHICHESTER, WEST SUSSEX, PO19 8EZ.
LIDDELL, Mr. Martin David, BA ACA *1996;* 480 Chartwell Road, OAKVILLE L6J 4A5, ON, CANADA.
LIDDELL, Miss. Nancy Jane, BA ACA *2007;* 144 Victoria Avenue, Bloxwich, WALSALL, WS3 3EH.
•LIDDELL, Mr. Nigel John, FCA *1982;* (Tax Fac), N.J. Liddell & Co, Moor Farm, Kings Lane, Sotherton, BECCLES, NR34 8AF.
LIDDELL, Mr. Paul, BA ACA *1992;* 5 Stonehaugh Way Ponteland, NEWCASTLE UPON TYNE, NORTHUMBERLAND, NE20 9LX.
•LIDDELL, Mr. Robert Stable, FCA FFA *1963;* MEMBER OF COUNCIL, RS Liddell Consulting Ltd, Treyarnon, Lonning Foot, Rockcliffe, CARLISLE, CA6 4AB.
•LIDDELL, Mr. Stephen Alexander, BSc FCA *1988;* K P M G Salisbury Square House, 8 Salisbury Square, LONDON, EC4Y 8BB. See also KPMG Europe LLP and KPMG LLP
LIDDELL, Mr. Stewart Kieran, MA ACA *2010;* 52 Pentland Avenue, CHELMSFORD, CM1 4AZ.
LIDDELL, Mrs. Zareen Alexander, FCA *1976;* 30a Lawley Street, NORTH BEACH, WA 6020, AUSTRALIA.
LIDDELOW, Mr. Keith Brian, FCA *1956;* 4 Medlows, HARPENDEN, HERTFORDSHIRE, AL5 3AY. (Life Member)
LIDDIARD, Mrs. Carolyn Jane, BA ACA *1999;* 88 Agamemnon Road, LONDON, NW6 1EH.
LIDDIARD, Mr. Geoffrey, FCA *1961;* 1 Glebe Way, Sanderstead, SOUTH CROYDON, SURREY, CR2 9JT. (Life Member)
LIDDIARD, Mr. John Michael, BSc FCA *1974;* The Dairy House, High Street, Porton, SALISBURY, SP4 0LH.
LIDDIARD, Mr. Jonathan William, BSc ACA *1999;* 88 Agamemnon Road, LONDON, NW6 1EH.
•LIDDIARD, Mr. Stephen Paul, FCA *1967;* Liddiard & Co, Arcturus, The Vallance, Lynsted, SITTINGBOURNE, KENT ME9 0RP.
LIDDICOAT, Mr. David, ACA *2009;* 93 Northstand Apartments, Highbury Stadium Square, LONDON, N5 1FL.
LIDDICOAT, Mr. Michael John, ACA *1978;* Units A-d Downsview House, Marlborough Road, LANCING, BN15 8SU.
LIDDINGTON, Mr. Andrew Arthur, FCA *1974;* Barn 3, Andrews Farm House Creampot Lane, Cropredy, BANBURY, OXFORDSHIRE, OX17 1NT.
LIDDLE, Mr. Andrew Peter, BA ACA *1987;* 4 Clayton Mews, Hyde Vale Greenwich, LONDON, SE10 8HZ.
•LIDDLE, Mr. Clive Alfred, MA FCA *1978;* 50 Divinity Road, OXFORD, OX4 1LJ.
•LIDDLE, Mr. David Andrew, BA ACA *1996;* Saint & Co., 4 Mason Court, Gillan Way, Penrith 40 Business Park, PENRITH, CUMBRIA CA11 9GR.
LIDDLE, Mr. James, BSc ACA *2010;* 76 Pasture Lane, Clayton, BRADFORD, WEST YORKSHIRE, BD14 6LN.
LIDDLE, Miss. Joyce Rosanne, FCA *1978;* (Tax Fac), with Thomas Coombs & Son, Century House, 29 Clarendon Road, LEEDS, LS2 9PG.
LIDDLE, Miss. Karen, BA ACA *1992;* 12 Carlton Terrace, NEWCASTLE UPON TYNE, NE2 4PD.
LIDDLE, Mr. Peter Geoffrey, FCA *1955;* 5 Windermere Drive, ALDERLEY EDGE, CHESHIRE, SK9 7UP. (Life Member)
•LIDDY, Mr. Desmond Paul, BA FCA *1989;* The Hall Liddy Partnership, 12 St. John Street, MANCHESTER, M3 4DY. See also Hall Liddy
LIDDY, Mrs. Janette Clare, BA ACA *1998;* Close Bank Guernsey Ltd, PO Box 116, Trafalgar Court, Admiral Park, St Peter Port, GUERNSEY GY1 3EZ.
LIDDY, Mr. Jason, ACA ACCA *2009;* Rose Villa, Rue Au Page, St. Saviour, GUERNSEY, GY7 9UB.
LIDGARD, Mrs. Sara Margaret, ACA *1997;* Unit 4, Chapman Street Ind Est, HULL, HU8 9DW.

LINCOLN, Mrs. Catherine Jane, BA ACA *1996;* Montpelier Tax Consultants (Northampton) Limited, 20 Market Place, Long Buckby, NORTHAMPTON, NN6 7RR.
LINCOLN, Mr. David Charles, FCA *1973;* 111 Fred Varley Drive, UNIONVILLE L3R 1T1, ON, CANADA.
LINCOLN, Miss. Jane, ACA *2011;* Lincoln, Sandy Way, Ingoldisthorpe, KING'S LYNN, NORFOLK, PE31 6NJ.
•**LINCOLN, Mrs. Joanne Mary, BSc ACA** *1995;* 2 Welldale Mews, SALE, CHESHIRE, M33 2NS.
LINCOLN, Mrs. Laura Jane, FCA *1985;* Gary Sargeant & Co, Unit 5, White Oak Square, London Road, SWANLEY, KENT BR8 7AG.
LINCOLN, Mr. Louis Albert, FCA *1958;* c/o MB Page, 17 Charterhouse Street, LONDON, EC1N 6RA. (Life Member)
LINCOLN, Miss. Natalie, BCom ACA *2000;* 1 Meadow Approach, Copthorne, CRAWLEY, RH10 3RF.
LINCOLN, Mr. Oliver William John, BA BSocSc ACA *1997;* Granary House Greenway Road, Blockley, MORETON-IN-MARSH, GL56 9BQ.
LINCOLN, Mr. Paul Gerald, BSc ACA *1993;* Ernst & Young, 9th Floor, Tower 1, NextTeracom, Cybercity, EBENE MAURITIUS.
LINCOLN, Mr. Paul Lawrence, BA ACA *1994;* Syngenta Crop Protection, Finance, Via Gallarate 139, 20151 MILAN, ITALY.
LINCOLN, Miss. Sandra Helene, ACA *2010;* Maurice Martin Street, FOREST SIDE, MAURITIUS.
•**LINCOLN, Mr. Timothy James Walter, BA ACA** *1996;* Grant Thornton UK LLP, Waters Edge, Clarendon Dock, BELFAST, COUNTY ANTRIM, BT1 3BH. See also Grant Thornton LLP
LINCOLN, Ms. Wendy Elizabeth, BSc ACA *1991;* 28 Pine Hill, Woodcote, EPSOM, KT18 7BG.
LINCOLN-WILLIAMS, Mr. Alexander John, BSc ACA *2006;* Flat C, 190 Ashmore Road, LONDON, W9 3DE.
•**LINCROFT, Dr. Christopher David, DPhil MSc FCA** *1978;* (Tax Fac), Lincroft & Company Limited, Langsyght, 160 Burntwood Lane, CATERHAM, SURREY, CR3 6TB.
LINDARS, Mr. Peter John, FCA *1973;* Tatton, Farnham Lane, HASLEMERE, SURREY, GU27 1HD.
LINDBERG-FINCH, Miss. Nina Angelia, LLB ACA *1998;* Unit 28, 6 Paul Street, Bondi Junction, SYDNEY, NSW 2022, AUSTRALIA.
LINDBLOM, Miss. Emma, ACA *2010;* Apartment 166, 51 Sherborne Street, BIRMINGHAM, B16 8FP.
LINDBLOM, Mr. John Eric, FCA *1954;* Cramond, 1 Elton Road, PURLEY, CR8 3NP. (Life Member)
LINDECK, Mr. John Michael, FCA *1955;* 9 Orchard Rise, LEDBURY, HEREFORDSHIRE, HR8 2GB. (Life Member)
LINDELL, Mr. Niko Kai Mikael, ACA *2008;* Itaranta 11 D 32, 02110 ESPOO, FINLAND.
LINDEN, Mr. Brian Andrew, BA ACA *1983;* Cinven, Warwick Court, 5 Paternoster Square, LONDON, EC4M 7AG.
LINDEN, Mrs. Gillian Lindsey, BSc ACA *1997;* VP Properties Limited, 11 Hawthorne Road, RADLETT, HERTFORDSHIRE, WD7 7BJ.
•**LINDEN, Mr. Michael John, FCA** *1972;* Nyman Linden, 105 Baker Street, LONDON, W1U 6NY.
LINDEYER, Mr. Ralph Jan Walter, FCA *1970;* Kelsall Cottage, Humboldt Court, TUNBRIDGE WELLS, TN2 3PE.
LINDFIELD, Mr. David James, BSc ACA *1984;* 32 Lynton Avenue, ROMFORD, RM7 8NR.
•**LINDFIELD, Mr. Timothy Paul, BAcc ACA** *2006;* Simpson Wreford & Partners, Suffolk House, George Street, CROYDON, CR0 0YN.
•**LINDFORD, Mr. Terence John, MA FCA** *1974;* (Tax Fac), HH Accounting & Tax Solutions Limited, 32 Duke Street, LONDON, SW1Y 6DF.
LINDH, Mr. Einar, FCA *1969;* Coombe End Cottage, Golf Club Drive, KINGSTON UPON THAMES, SURREY, KT2 7DF.
LINDH, Mr. Einar Auguste Barwick, ACA *2011;* Coombe End Cottage, Golf Club Drive, KINGSTON UPON THAMES, SURREY, KT2 7DF.
LINDILL, Mr. David Vaughan, ACA *1980;* 12/19 Victoria Street, FITZROY, VIC 3065, AUSTRALIA.
LINDLEY, Mr. Alvin Mark, BSc ACA *1981;* Clearwater Plc, First Floor Offices, Wimberley Park, Knapp Lane, Brimscombe, STROUD GLOUCESTERSHIRE GL5 2TH.
LINDLEY, Mr. Brian, FCA *1953;* Benn-Arvon, 11 Parkside Lane, Mellor, STOCKPORT, SK6 5PQ. (Life Member)
LINDLEY, Miss. Claire Marie, BA ACA *2010;* 25 Hornsby Road, Armthorpe, DONCASTER, SOUTH YORKSHIRE, DN3 3JJ.
LINDLEY, Mr. David Nigel, FCA *1983;* 38 Normanby Road, Wollaton, NOTTINGHAM, NG8 2TB.
LINDLEY, Mr. Duncan William Burns, FCA *1956;* The Priory, Abbey Road, KNARESBOROUGH, HG5 8HX. (Life Member)
LINDLEY, Mrs. Francesca Louise, BSc ACA *1990;* Anschutz Film Group, 1888 Century Park East, 14th Floor, LOS ANGELES, CA 90068, UNITED STATES.
LINDLEY, Mr. Jeremy Charles, BSocSc ACA *1992;* University of Exeter, Northcote House, The Queens Drive, EXETER, DEVON, EX4 4QJ.
LINDLEY, Miss. Lindsey Mary, BSc ACA *1979;* Fair View, East Portlemouth, SALCOMBE, TQ8 8PJ.
LINDLEY, Mr. Mark, BSc FCA *2001;* KPMG Qatar, Arab Bank Building, 25 C Ring Road, PO Box 4473, DOHA, QATAR.
•**LINDLEY, Mr. Michael Denis, BA FCA** *1982;* (Tax Fac), Guy Walmsley & Co, 3 Grove Road, WREXHAM, LL11 1DY.
LINDLEY, Mr. Patrick John, BA ACA *1995;* Apartment 3, 5 Hanway Place, LONDON, W1T 1HF.
LINDLEY, Mr. Peter Alan, FCA *1991;* with Hawsons, Pegasus House, 463a Glossop Road, SHEFFIELD, S10 2QD.
LINDLEY, Mr. Peter Malcolm, FCA *1964;* 46 Everard Avenue, SHEFFIELD, S17 4LZ.
LINDLEY, Mr. Philip Douglas, FCA *1962;* Paddock House, High Street, Yardley Hastings, NORTHAMPTON, NN7 1ER.
LINDLEY, Mr. Philip Richard, BA ACA *1992;* 52 Waterloo Road, BEDFORD, MK40 3PG.
LINDLEY, Mr. Richard Philip, BSc FCA *1996;* The Manor House, Brearton, HARROGATE, NORTH YORKSHIRE, HG3 3BX.
•**LINDLEY, Mrs. Sandra Kay, FCA** *1988;* Lindley & Co, 17 Millbrook Drive, Shenstone, LICHFIELD, WS14 0JL.
LINDLEY, Mr. Simon Richard, CEng FCA MBA *1991;* 2 Peterborough Road, Farcet, PETERBOROUGH, PE7 3BH.
LINDLEY, Miss. Sophie Helen, ACA *2008;* with BDO LLP, 2 City Place, Beehive Ring Road, GATWICK, WEST SUSSEX, RH6 0PA.
LINDLEY, Mr. Stephen Paul, BA ACA *2004;* 16 Colwick Close, LONDON, N6 5NU.
•**LINDLEY, Mr. Steven, ACA** *1985;* (Tax Fac), Gibson Booth, New Court, Abbey Road North, Shepley, HUDDERSFIELD, HD8 8BJ.
LINDLEY, Mr. Stuart, BA ACA *1983;* IFM Consulting (Beijing) Ltd, 22D Office Building Oriental Kenzo, No. 48 Dongzhimenwai Ave, Dongcheng District, BEIJING 100027, CHINA.
•**LINDLEY-ADSETT, Mrs. Alison Jane, FCA** *1990;* 33 Bridleway, Colehill, WIMBORNE, BH21 2HP.
LINDNER, Mr. Christopher John, ACA *1984;* 105 Friern Road, LONDON, SE22 0AZ.
•**LINDNER, Mr. Michael Max, FCA** *1972;* Michael Lindner, The Gallery Room, The Old Police Station, High Street, CHIPPING CAMPDEN, GLOUCESTERSHIRE GL55 6HB.
LINDO, Mr. Malcolm Leslie, FCA *1974;* 6 Birch Road, Northchurch, BERKHAMSTED, HERTFORDSHIRE, HP4 3SQ.
LINDOP, Mr. Anthony Charles, FCA *1960;* 73 Tamworth Road, LICHFIELD, STAFFORDSHIRE, WS14 9HG. (Life Member)
LINDOP, Mr. Colin Crockett, FCA *1957;* 20 Fairview Avenue, Weston, CREWE, CW2 5LX. (Life Member)
LINDOP, Mr. David Andrew, BSc ACA *2002;* 110 Bloomsbury Lane Timperley, ALTRINCHAM, CHESHIRE, WA15 6NT.
LINDOP, Mr. David John, BA ACA *1986;* 81 Sandy Lane, Cheam, SUTTON, SM2 7EP.
LINDOP, Mr. Gareth, ACA *2009;* 6 Cecil Close, BISHOP'S STORTFORD, HERTFORDSHIRE, CM23 5RD.
LINDOP, Mr. Gerard William Neale, BA(Hons) ACA *2010;* 10 Manor Road, BISHOP'S STORTFORD, HERTFORDSHIRE, CM23 5HU.
LINDOP, Mr. John David, MA FCA *1973;* Cherry Garth, 11 Bishop Burton Road, Cherry Burton, BEVERLEY, NORTH HUMBERSIDE, HU17 7RW.
LINDOP, Mrs. Karen Elizabeth, BSc ACA *2005;* 32 Mount Pleasant, WILMSLOW, CHESHIRE, SK9 4AP.
LINDOP, Mr. Tom Christian, BSc ACA *1998;* 14 King Frederick Ninth Tower, LONDON, SE16 7TH.
LINDORES, Mr. Michael Irwin, BA ACA *1988;* 32 Welbeck Rise, HARPENDEN, AL5 1SN.
LINDRIDGE, Mrs. Claire Louise, MA ACA *1999;* with Audit Inspection Unit, Financial Reporting Council, 5th Floor, Aldwych House, 71-91 Aldwych, LONDON WC2B 4HN.
LINDSAY, Mr. Alastair James, BSc ACA *1989;* Alta Seefeldstrasse 72a, 8616 RIEDIKON, SWITZERLAND.
LINDSAY, Mr. Alistair Gregory, BA ACA *2000;* 57 Gordon Avenue, TWICKENHAM, TW1 1NH.
LINDSAY, Mr. Allan Scott, MA ACA *1996;* 10 Sugden Road, LONDON, SW11 5EF.
LINDSAY, Mrs. Ann Elizabeth, BA ACA *1986;* 2 The Courtyard, Bishopthorpe, YORK, YO23 2RD.
LINDSAY, Mr. Bryce, MA ACA *2007;* Flat A, 32 Iverson Road, LONDON, NW6 2HE.
LINDSAY, Mrs. Caryl, FCA *1960;* 5 Fircliff Park, Portishead, BRISTOL, BS20 7HQ. (Life Member)
LINDSAY, Mrs. Catriona Mary, BSc ACA *1993;* 17 Cowper Road, Acton, LONDON, W3 6PZ.
LINDSAY, Mr. Courtenay Traice Thomas, BSc ACA *1989;* Trafford House, Dingleden, Benenden, CRANBROOK, TN17 4JU.
LINDSAY, Mr. Craig Stewart, LLB ACA *2000;* 73 Topstreet Way, HARPENDEN, HERTFORDSHIRE, AL5 5TY.
LINDSAY, Mr. David, BSc ACA *2009;* 101 Twilley Street, LONDON, SW18 4NW.
LINDSAY, Mr. David, BSc ACA MCT *1985;* Flat 47 Clifton Court, Northwick Terrace, LONDON, NW8 8HU.
LINDSAY, Mr. David, JP BA(Hons) FCA *1955;* (Member of Council 1977 - 1995), Mewslade, Bakers Lane, Pinkneys Green, MAIDENHEAD, SL6 6QQ. (Life Member)
LINDSAY, Mr. David Charles, BSc ACA *1990;* 26 Avondale Park Gardens, LONDON, W11 4PR.
LINDSAY, Mr. David Elliott, BSc FCA *1995;* St. Martins Farm, Thickwood Lane, Tickwood, CHIPPENHAM, WILTSHIRE, SN14 8BN.
•**LINDSAY, Mr. David Robert Hamish, FCA** *1968;* (Tax Fac), Lindsay & Co, 119 Boundary Road, WALLINGTON, SURREY, SM6 0TE.
LINDSAY, Miss. Elizabeth Marguerite Joy, MA ACA *2002;* 6 Toberdowney Manor, Ballynure, BALLYCLARE, COUNTY ANTRIM, BT39 9YX.
LINDSAY, Mr. Graham James, ACA *2007;* 70 Erithway Road, COVENTRY, CV3 6JR.
•**LINDSAY, Mr. Grahame Duncan Gordon, BSc FCA** *1971;* (Tax Fac), McKenzie Lindsay, 5 Dodds Court, Preston Street, FAVERSHAM, ME13 8PE.
LINDSAY, Mrs. Heather Jayne, BA ACA *1992;* Alte Seefeldstrasse 72a, 8616 RIEDIKON, SWITZERLAND.
LINDSAY, Mrs. Hilary Frances, MSc FCA FMAAT MBA *1974;* MEMBER OF COUNCIL, 23 Stourhead Drive, NORTHAMPTON, NN4 0UH.
LINDSAY, Mr. Hugh, FCA *1964;* 2831 West 19th Ave, VANCOUVER V6L 1E4, BC, CANADA.
LINDSAY, Mr. Hugh John Alexander, BA FCA *1961;* 4 Shadrack Street, BEAMINSTER, DORSET, DT8 3BE. (Life Member)
LINDSAY, Mr. Ian James, FCA *1968;* 14 Old Hall Park, Guilden Sutton, CHESTER, CH3 7ER.
LINDSAY, Mr. James Trevor Anthony, MEng ACA *2000;* 43 Ashley Road, WALTON-ON-THAMES, SURREY, KT12 1HG.
LINDSAY, Mr. John McGlashan, BA FCA *1984;* (Tax Fac), 6 Briton Crescent, Sanderstead, SOUTH CROYDON, Surrey, CR2 0JE.
•**LINDSAY, Mr. John Robert, ACA** *1980;* Evolution Audit LLP, 10 Evolution, Wynyard Park, BILLINGHAM, CLEVELAND, TS22 5TB.
LINDSAY, Mr. Jonathan Paul, BA ACA *1994;* Hawthorns, Station Road, Otford, SEVENOAKS, KENT, TN14 5QU.
•**LINDSAY, Mr. Keith, FCA** *1975;* (Tax Fac), 11 Asthill Grove, COVENTRY, CV3 6HN.
LINDSAY, Mr. Michael, BA ACA *1981;* 21 San Pietro, NEWPORT COAST, CA 92657, UNITED STATES.
•**LINDSAY, Mr. Noel Jon Jordan, BSc FCA** *1990;* Ballamy Woodhouse, Albert Buildings, 49 Queen Victoria Street, LONDON, EC4N 4SA.
LINDSAY, Mr. Norman, FCA *1971;* Pitfold Chase Lodge Hammer Lane, Bramshott Chase, HINDHEAD, GU26 6DD.
•**LINDSAY, Mrs. Patricia May, BA FCA** *1984;* (Tax Fac), Edzell Lindsay Limited, 8 Ashgrove Road, Redland, BRISTOL, BS6 6LY.
LINDSAY, Mr. Peter Albert, FCA *1966;* 2 Hope Cottage, Chapel Lane, Bucklow Hill, KNUTSFORD, CHESHIRE, WA16 6RF.
•**LINDSAY, Mr. Peter John, FCA** *1974;* (Tax Fac), P.J. Lindsay, 13 Beech Rd, REIGATE, RH2 9LS.
•**LINDSAY, Mr. Roger Guthrie, BA FCA** *1981;* Mason Law LLP, 9 Frederick Road, Edgbaston, BIRMINGHAM, B15 1TW.
LINDSAY, Mr. Rowan, ACA FCCA *2011;* 26 Wargrave Road, HARROW, MIDDLESEX, HA2 8LN.
LINDSAY, Mr. Scott, BSc ACA *2006;* 44 Walsingham Drive, Taverham, NORWICH, NR8 6FZ.
LINDSAY, Mrs. Sophie Clare, BA(Hons) ACA *2003;* with PricewaterhouseCoopers LLP, 1 Embankment Place, LONDON, WC2N 6RH.
LINDSAY, Mr. Stuart Robert, FCA *1976;* Castle Keep, 19 Peninsula Square, WINCHESTER, SO23 8GJ.
LINDSELL, Mr. David Clive, MA FCA *1972;* 20 Verona Court, LONDON, W4 2JD.
•**LINDSELL, Miss. Denise Rebecca, ACA** *2001;* (Tax Fac), Hardcastle Burton LLP, Lake House, Market Hill, ROYSTON, HERTFORDSHIRE, SG8 9JN.
•**LINDSELL, Mr. Philip Edmund, MA FCA** *1979;* Lindsell Business Solutions Ltd, 2 Crabtree Cottages, Savernake, MARLBOROUGH, WILTSHIRE, SN8 3HP.
•**LINDSEY, Mr. Alan Michael, BSc(Econ) FCA** *1963;* (Member of Council 1988 - 2007), (Tax Fac), Alan Lindsey & Co, 23 Gresham Gardens, LONDON, NW11 8NX.
LINDSEY, Mr. Andrew Ian, BEng ACA *2003;* Flat 4 Silvester House, 192 Joel Street Eastcote, PINNER, HA5 2RB.
•**LINDSEY, Mr. Brian, BSc FCA ATII** *1981;* (Tax Fac), Lindsey & Co, 9 Chapel Mews, WOODFORD GREEN, ESSEX, IG8 8GP. See also H.W. Fisher & Company and H W Fisher & Company Limited
LINDSEY, Mr. Craig, BSc ACA *2009;* Flat 4, 208 Kingsland Road, LONDON, E2 8AJ.
•**LINDSEY, Mrs. Elaine Vivienne, BSc ACA** *1994;* Tye Limited, The Red Barn, Thornend, Christian Malford, CHIPPENHAM, WILTSHIRE SN15 4BX.
LINDSEY, Miss. Helen Claire, MSc ACA *2002;* 23 Common Road, Claygate, ESHER, KT10 0HG.
LINDSEY, Mr. John Walter Reginald, FCA *1950;* The Manse, Old Bristol Road, Nailsworth, STROUD, GLOUCESTERSHIRE, GL6 0JE. (Life Member)
LINDSEY, Mr. Keith Kirby, FCA *1971;* Old Hall Cottage, 3 Holland Road, FRINTON-ON-SEA, CO13 9DH. (Life Member)
•**LINDSEY, Mr. Simon Nicholas Merry, BSc ACA** *1992;* (Tax Fac), LindseyTye Limited, The Stables, Manor Farm Drive, Sutton Benger, CHIPPENHAM, WILTSHIRE SN15 4RW. See also LindseyTye
•**LINDSEY-RENTON, Mr. Angus Peter, FCA** *1968;* Lindsey-Renton & Co, 43 Waterlow Road, REIGATE, SURREY, RH2 7EY.
LINDSTROM, Mr. Carl, MSc ACA *2006;* 2 Smyrna Road, LONDON, NW6 4LY.
LINDSTROM, Miss. Victoria Ann, MA ACA CFA *1996;* 32 College Cross, LONDON, N1 1PR.
LINDUP, Mr. Paul Geoffrey, BA ACA *1992;* Weobley High School Burton Wood, Weobley, HEREFORD, HR4 8ST.
LINE, Mr. Alan Stanley, BA FCA *1985;* 33 Old Broad Street, LONDON, EC2N 1HW.
LINE, Mr. Clive Malcolm, BA ACA *1985;* 9 Rosebery Avenue, NEW MALDEN, SURREY, KT3 4JR.
LINE, Mr. James Andrew David, BSc ACA *2007;* 5 Winford Drive, BROXBOURNE, EN10 6PL.
LINE, Mr. Leslie Albert, FCA *1960;* 4 St. Vincents Place, EASTBOURNE, BN20 7QW. (Life Member)
LINE, Mr. Stephen Philip, ACA *1980;* Hayeswood Cottage, 139 Ecton Lane, Sywell, NORTHAMPTON, NN6 0BB.
LINE, Mr. Timothy Robert Maxim, FCA *1972;* La Haute Bulardiere, 72150 ST VINCENT DU LOROUER, FRANCE.
LINE, Mr. Vivian William, FCA *1951;* 26 Guinevere Way, EXETER, EX4 8LQ. (Life Member)
LINEEN, Mr. David - Benjamin John, BA(Hons) ACA *2010;* 32 Lazar Walk, LONDON, N7 7RR.
LINEEN, Mr. Patrick James, BA FCA *1982;* 2 Kennelwood Road, Comberbach, NORTHWICH, CW9 6QQ.
LINEHAM, Mr. Ian Charles, BSc ACA *1989;* 4 Gander Hill, HAYWARDS HEATH, RH16 1QX.
LINEHAN, Mr. Christopher Alexander, BA(Hons) ACA *2009;* 20 Frederick Road, Edgbaston, BIRMINGHAM, B15 1JN.
LINEHAN, Miss. Ciara, BA ACA *2011;* 35 Farmhill Park, Douglas, ISLE OF MAN, IM2 2ED.
LINEHAN, Mr. Daniel Joseph Donal, BCom ACA *1991;* 95 Greenham Road, Stroud Green, NEWBURY, RG14 7JE.
LINEHAN, Mr. Sean Michael, BA ACA *1994;* Petty Wood & Co Ltd, PO Box 66, ANDOVER, HAMPSHIRE, SP10 5LA.
LINEKER, Mr. Jonathan Guy, BSc ACA *1994;* 23 Hunter Seal, Leigh, TONBRIDGE, TN11 9AW.
•**LINELL, Mr. David Michael, FCA** *1983;* D. M. Linell & Co, Design House, 27 Chesterfield Road, DRONFIELD, DERBYSHIRE, S18 2WZ.

LINES, Miss. Alexandra Marie, BA ACA *1996;* Flat 10, Mount Lodge, 53a Shepherds Hill, LONDON, N6 5QR.

LINES, Mr. Douglas John, BSc ACA *1991;* Berners Allsopp Estate Management Co Ltd, Manor Farm, Little Coxwell, FARINGDON, OXFORDSHIRE, SN7 7LW.

LINES, Mr. George Richard, MA FCA *1965;* Davies Tuner Worldwide Movers Ltd, 49 Wates Way, MITCHAM, CR4 4HR.

LINES, Mr. Gregory John, BA ACA *1995;* Heatley Farm Cottages, 43 Wet Gate Lane, LYMM, WA13 9SL.

LINES, Mr. Philip Ronald, BCom ACA *1989;* 18 Blackwood Road, SUTTON COLDFIELD, WEST MIDLANDS, B74 3PH.

LINES, Mr. Raymond Leslie, FCA *1951;* Hengistbury Halt, 15 Common Wood Rise, CROWBOROUGH, TN6 2UR. (Life Member)

LINES, Mr. Richard Anthony James, BSc ACA *1997;* First Floor Right, 2 Warriston Road, Canonmills, EDINBURGH, EH3 5LG.

LINES, Mr. Roger Thomas, FCA *1973;* 17 Foxland Close, Shirley, SOLIHULL, B90 4HS.

LINES, Mrs. Sheila Alison Mary, LLB ACA *1993;* Suite 502 12 Church Street, HAMILTON HM11, BERMUDA.

LINEY, Mr. Robert Michael, BSc FCA *1996;* 19 St Davids Road, HABERFIELD, NSW 2045, AUSTRALIA.

LINFIELD, Mr. Malcolm David, BSc FCA *1976;* 58B Queen St, Weedon, NORTHAMPTON, NN7 4RA.

LINFIELD, Ms. Melza Helen, BSc ACA *1993;* Danestone, 28 Beaufort Road, INVERNESS, IV2 3NP.

LINFIELD, Miss. Verity, BSc(Hons) ACA *2004;* 29 Crane Road, TWICKENHAM, TW2 6RX.

LINFOOT, Mr. Godfrey Atkinson, FCA *1955;* Hill View, Faceby, MIDDLESBROUGH, CLEVELAND, TS9 7BW. (Life Member)

LINFORD, Mr. Andrew William, BSc ACA CFA *1993;* Barclays Capital, 5 North Colonnade, LONDON, E14 4BB.

LINFORD, Mr. Robert Charles, BSc ACA *1981;* 51 Marland Fold, ROCHDALE, OL11 4RF.

LINFORD, Mr. Simon John Louis, BEng ACA *1993;* Caretakers Flat Grosvenor House, 14 Bennetts Hill, BIRMINGHAM, B2 5RS.

LINFORD, Mr. Stephen Geoffrey, BCom ACA *1986;* W H Brady Co Ltd, Wildmere Road, BANBURY, OXFORDSHIRE, OX16 3JU.

LING, Mr. Andrew John, BSc FCA *1978;* Ireton, Packhorse Road, Bessels Green, SEVENOAKS, TN13 2QR.

LING, Mrs. Ann Elizabeth, BSc ACA *2005;* Apartment 307, 1 Baltimore Wharf, LONDON, E14 9FS.

•**LING, Mrs. Cheryl Jayne, BA FCA** *1995;* PO Box 7081, PORT VILA, VANUATU. See also Hawkes Law

LING, Mr. Christopher Adam, FCA MInstP ACIM AMCT *2000;* 28 The Murreys, ASHTEAD, KT21 2LU.

LING, Mr. Chun Kwok, ACA *2006;* D2 1/F, Fung Yue Mansion No. 47-53, Kowloon City Road, KOWLOON CITY, HONG KONG SAR.

LING, Mr. David Robert, FCA *1966;* 36A Chaldon Common Road, Chaldon, CATERHAM, CR3 5DB. (Life Member)

LING, Mrs. Elizabeth Ann, BA ACA MBA *1998;* 5 Lime Grove, Bottesford, NOTTINGHAM, NG13 0BH.

LING, Miss. Ellie Ee Chai, BSc ACA *1989;* 139 Albert Street, LONDON, NW1 7NB.

LING, Miss. Emily Ee Sing, BSc ACA *1992;* 40 Bridport Ave, SINGAPORE 559330, SINGAPORE.

LING, Mr. Geoffrey, FCA *1952;* Hillcrest, 7 Apple Grove, Ashfield Road, STOWMARKET, IP14 3RB. (Life Member)

LING, Mr. Geoffrey John, BA ACA *2006;* 23 Dorville Crescent, LONDON, W6 0HH.

LING, Mr. Jamie Fou-Tsong, BA ACA *1993;* 12th Floor, 168 Dun Hwa North Road, TAIPEI, TAIWAN.

LING, Mr. Jonathan Richard Wentworth, FCA *1973;* 3 The Glebe, Blackheath, LONDON, SE3 9TL.

LING, Miss. June Su-Lyn, LLB ACA *2005;* Ubierstrasse 42, 59173 BONN, GERMANY.

LING, Mr. Kwok Fai Anthony, BA ACA *1983;* 86 Cholmley Gardens, Fortune Green Rd, LONDON, NW6 1UN.

LING, Miss. Lee Kiong, BA ACA *1985;* Block 1007, Apt 10-03, TeresavilleLower Delta Road, SINGAPORE 099310, SINGAPORE.

•**LING, Mr. Mark Richard, FCA** *1980;* Littlejohn LLP, 1 Westferry Circus, Canary Wharf, LONDON, E14 4HD.

LING, Mr. Nigel Richard, BEng ACA *2003;* 106 Bennett Way, Darenth, DARTFORD, DA2 7JU.

LING, Mr. Philip Bryan, BSc ACA *1993;* 39 Queens Road, KINGSTON UPON THAMES, KT2 7SL.

LING, Ms. Polly Pui Ying, BA ACA *1993;* 4/F Hospital Authority Building, 147B Argyle Street, KOWLOON CITY, KOWLOON, HONG KONG SAR.

LING, Mrs. Samantha Jane Steward, BA ACA *1991;* Jones Avens, 53 Kent Road, SOUTHSEA, PO5 3HU.

•**LING, Mr. Simon James, MA FCA** *1971;* Simon Ling & Co Ltd, Woodstock House, 29a Agates Lane, ASHTEAD, SURREY, KT21 2ND.

LING, Mr. Simon Jonathan, BSc(Hons) ACA *2002;* with BDO LLP, 125 Colmore Row, BIRMINGHAM, B3 3SD.

LING, Mr. Tung-Man, MA ACA *1991;* 51 Conduit Road E2, Skyline Mansion, CENTRAL, HONG KONG ISLAND, HONG KONG SAR.

LING, Mr. William Oswald, FCA *1963;* with Lings, Provident House, 51 Wardwick, DERBY, DE1 1HN.

LING, Mr. Yong Wah, ACA *1992;* 1F Shelford Road, #04-43 The Shelford, SINGAPORE 286891, SINGAPORE.

LINGABAVAN, Miss. Vithya, BSc ACA *2011;* 18 Warwick Road, COULSDON, SURREY, CR5 2EE.

LINGAM, Mr. Pradeep, BA ACA *2003;* The London Stock Exchange Plc, The London Stock Exchange, 10 Paternoster Square, LONDON, EC4M 7LS.

LINGARD, Mr. Mark Leonard, ACA CA(AUS) *2011;* 44 Nella Road, LONDON, W6 9PB.

LINGARD, Mrs. Meryl Louise, BA ACA *1989;* 5 Rosefield, Kippington Road, SEVENOAKS, KENT, TN13 2LP.

LINGE, Mrs. Pamela, BA ACA *1983;* Drystones, Heugh House Lane, Haydon Bridge, HEXHAM, NE47 6ND.

•**LINGER, Mr. Anthony Clive, FCA** *1971;* Linger & Co, Barrycliffe House, 2 Park View Road, Four Oaks, SUTTON COLDFIELD, B74 4PP. See also Linger Associates Limited

•**LINGHAM, Mr. Nagalingam Thiyaga, FCA** *1970;* (Tax Fac), Lingham & Co, 65 Higher Drive, PURLEY, SURREY, CR8 2HR.

•**LINGHAM, Mr. Peter, FCA** *1982;* (Tax Fac), The Lingham Consultancy Ltd, 7 Raleigh Walk, Brigantine Place, CARDIFF, CF10 4LN. See also No Nonsense Limited

LINGLEY, Mr. Gary James, MSc BSc ACA *2009;* 23 Newstead Road, Urmston, MANCHESTER, M41 0QQ.

LINGWOOD, Mr. Nigel Peter, BSc FCA *1986;* 18 Park Avenue South, Crouch End, LONDON, N8 8LT.

LINIGHAN, Mr. Patrick Thomas, BSc ACA *1991;* An Bhanrach, 86 Sherburn Street, Cawood, SELBY, NORTH YORKSHIRE, YO8 3SS.

•**LINK, Mr. Charles Richard Stephen, FCA** *1966;* (Tax Fac), C.R.S. Link, 4 Brunswick Gardens, LONDON, W8 4AJ.

•**LINK, Mr. Trevor John, MA ACA CTA MCIArb** *1985;* Ernst & Young, 19A Khreschatyk Street, 01001 KYIV, UKRAINE. See also Ernst & Young Europe LLP

LINKLETER, Mr. Neil Arthur, FCA *1968;* 12 Brampton Chase, Lower Shiplake, HENLEY-ON-THAMES, OXFORDSHIRE, RG9 3BX.

LINKOVA, Miss. Natasha, ACA *2005;* c/o Allan PELVANG, 30 Val Fleuri, L-1526 LUXEMBOURG, LUXEMBOURG.

LINKS, Mr. Mark Edward, LLB ACA *1998;* 547 Haviland Road, STAMFORD, CT 06903, UNITED STATES.

LINLEY, Mr. Craig, BA ACA *2010;* Apt 5 1302 Red Bay Yacht Club, South Sound, GEORGETOWN, GRAND CAYMAN, PO Box 510, CAYMAN ISLANDS.

LINLEY, Mr. Michael Robert, BCom FCA *1976;* 33 Kinross Road, Greylees, SLEAFORD, LINCOLNSHIRE, NG34 8GB.

•**LINLEY, Mr. Simon Timothy, BSc FCA** *1982;* (Tax Fac), Reeves & Co LLP, Third Floor, 24 Chiswell Street, LONDON, EC1Y 4YX. See also F W Stephens Taxation Limited

LINLEY-HILL, Mr. Angus, BSc ACA *1992;* Millstream Cottage, 8-10 High Street, Clophill, BEDFORD, MK45 4AB.

LINN, Mr. John Russell, FCA *1969;* Aspley Wharf Marina, St. Andrews Road, HUDDERSFIELD, HD1 6SD.

LINNARD, Mrs. Sharon Evelyn Lesley, BA FCA *1988;* 2 Fields Park Crescent, NEWPORT, NP20 5BN.

LINNECAR, Mr. Robin John Douglas, MA FCA *1974;* 81 Alric Avenue, NEW MALDEN, KT3 4JP.

LINNECOR, Mr. Barrie George, MBA BSc FCA TEP *1983;* Springfield, Route De Cobo, Castel, GUERNSEY, GY5 7UR.

LINNEGAR, Mr. Steven Charles, ACA *2008;* Flat 65 Stretton Mansions, Glaisher Street, LONDON, SE8 3JP.

LINNELL, Mr. Christopher, FCA *1961;* Flat 12, Orchard Court, 55 Sutton Road, BIRMINGHAM, B23 6QJ.

•**LINNELL, Miss. Kay Catherine Sheila Hilary, FCA** *1979;* (Tax Fac), Kay Linnell, Brick Kiln Cottage, The Avenue, Herriard, BASINGSTOKE, RG25 2PR. See also Linnell Kay & Co

LINNELL, Mr. Peter John, ACA *1985;* Rivers Reach, Hamm Court, WEYBRIDGE, KT13 8YA.

LINNELL, Mr. Peter Robert, FCA *1972;* 14 Orchard Gardens, HOVE, BN3 7BJ. (Life Member)

LINNETT, Mrs. Helen Siobhan, BA ACA *1992;* Astek Innovations Ltd Astek House, Atlantic Street Broadheath, ALTRINCHAM, CHESHIRE, WA14 5DH.

LINNETT, Mr. Michael John, FCA *1965;* Park House, Park Hill, Gaddesby, LEICESTER, LE7 4WH.

•**LINNEY, Miss. Anne Margaret, BSc FCA** *1990;* with Stafford Thursz, Cavendish House, Clarke Street, POULTON-LE-FYLDE, LANCASHIRE, FY6 8JW.

LINNEY, Mr. James William, BA ACA *2007;* 47 Simmons Field, THATCHAM, BERKSHIRE, RG18 4ET.

LINNEY, Mr. Michael David, BSc ACA *2010;* 31 Cote Lane, Farsley, PUDSEY, WEST YORKSHIRE, LS28 5ED.

LINNEY, Mr. Michael William James, FCA *1969;* 38 Downs Road, EPSOM, SURREY, KT18 5JD.

LINNEY, Mrs. Shelley Marie, BA ACA *2008;* 34 Chapel Street, THATCHAM, RG18 4QL.

LINNEY, Mr. Stephen Philip, BA FCA *1976;* Le Petit Touessrok, La Vielle Charriere, St. Martin, JERSEY, JE3 6DL.

LINSCOTT, Mr. Geoffrey Arnold, FCA *1958;* 95 St. Thomas Avenue, HAYLING ISLAND, HAMPSHIRE, PO11 0EU. (Life Member)

LINSELL, Mr. Peter Charles, FCA *1971;* Frank Crossley & Son, Orbital House, 85 Croydon Road, CATERHAM, SURREY, CR3 6PD.

LINSKILL, Miss. Claire Louise, BA ACA *1992;* Flat 30, Mackenzie House, Chadwick Street, LEEDS, LS10 1PJ.

LINSLEY, Mr. Philip Mark, BA ACA *1986;* Shippon Cottage, Cawton, YORK, YO62 4LW.

LINSLEY, Mrs. Susan Elizabeth, BSc ACA *1992;* 52 Sayesbury Road, SAWBRIDGEWORTH, HERTFORDSHIRE, CM21 0EB.

LINSTEAD, Miss. Rosemary Catherine, ACA CTA *2001;* Carter Backer Winter, Enterprise House, 21 Buckle Street, LONDON, E1 8NN.

LINSTONE, Mr. Simon Paul, BSc ACA *1989;* Progressive Enterprises, Private Bag 93306, Otahuhu, AUCKLAND 1133, NEW ZEALAND.

LINTHWAITE, Mrs. Amanda Kay, BEd ACA *1995;* 102 Broadway, DERBY, DE22 1BP.

LINTHWAITE, Mr. John Alfred, FCA *1956;* 1172 Haywood Avenue, WEST VANCOUVER V7T IT9, BC, CANADA. (Life Member)

LINTIN, Mr. Gareth James, BA FCA *2001;* 11 Sandygate Park Crescent, Sandygate, SHEFFIELD, S10 5TW.

LINTON, Mrs. Amanda Jane, BSc ACA *2001;* 2 South View Cottages, High Road, Cookham, MAIDENHEAD, BERKSHIRE, SL6 9JW.

•**LINTON, Mr. Anthony Peter, BSc FCA** *1978;* Anthony P. Linton, 8 Croome Drive, West Kirby, WIRRAL, CH48 8AH.

LINTON, Mrs. Evelyn Anne, BSc ACA *1988;* 6 Clarel Close, Penistone, SHEFFIELD, S36 6FZ.

LINTON, Mr. Kip Alonzo, ACA *2010;* Flat G, 78 Carleton Road, LONDON, N7 0ES.

•①**LINTON, Mr. Martin Henry, FCA** *1974;* Leigh Adams LLP, Brentmead House, Britannia Road, LONDON, N12 9RU.

LINTON, Mr. Nigel Robert, BSc ACA *1998;* 69 Summerlee Avenue, LONDON, N2 9QJ.

•**LINTON, Mr. Perry Iain, BA ACA** *1999;* with Baker Tilly UK Audit LLP, The Clock House, 140 London Road, GUILDFORD, SURREY, GU1 1UW.

LINTON, Mr. Ronald George, BA ACA *1982;* 17 Park View Road, Chapeltown, SHEFFIELD, S35 1WL.

LINTON, Ms. Suzanne Claire, BA ACA *1991;* Freestyle Interactive Ltd, Harwoods House Banbury Road, Ashorne, WARWICK, CV35 0AA.

LINTONBON, Mr. Robert James, FCA *1983;* with Phoebus Software Ltd, Radcliffe House, Blenheim Court, SOLIHULL, WEST MIDLANDS, B91 2AA.

LINTOTT, Miss. Amy Sarah Hamilton, BSc ACA *2007;* Brockway Bennetts Lane, Burley, RINGWOOD, HAMPSHIRE, BH24 4AT.

LINTOTT, Mr. Andrew Douglas, BA ACA *1987;* (Tax Fac), 10 Richmond Place, EASTBOURNE, EAST SUSSEX, BN21 2NQ.

LINTOTT, Mr. Christopher Guy, ACA *1982;* Shroton Brake, Iwerne Courtney, BLANDFORD FORUM, DORSET, DT11 8QR.

LINTOTT, Mr. Graham Gordon, FCA *1967;* The Magnus (Vauxhall) Co, 59 Brook Street, BRENTWOOD, ESSEX, CM14 5NB. (Life Member)

LINTOTT, Mr. James Richard David, BCom FCA *1977;* 16 Chinthurst Park, Shalford, GUILDFORD, GU4 8JH.

LINTOTT, Mr. Martin Stephen David, BSc FCA *1976;* (Tax Fac), Lastminute Networks Ltd Victoria Gate, Chobham Road, WOKING, GU21 6JD.

LINTOTT, Mr. Timothy Mark, BA ACA *1989;* 8 Seaview Road, Woodingdean, BRIGHTON, BN2 6DF.

LION, Miss. Jessica, BSc ACA *2005;* 41 Hospital Road, BURY ST. EDMUNDS, SUFFOLK, IP33 3JU.

LION, Mr. Rupert James Elphinstone, ACA *2005;* 53 Kendall Road, BECKENHAM, KENT, BR3 4PY.

LIOTA, Miss. Panagiota, MSc BA ACA *2006;* 56 Acharnon Street, GR10433 ATHENS, GREECE.

LIOUTYI, Mrs. Zeynep, BSc ACA *2005;* 8 Henrietta Place, Diageo Plc Henrietta House, 8 Henrietta Place, LONDON, W1G 0NB.

LIOW, Miss. Natasha, BA ACA *2006;* 15 Brookdale Road, BEXLEY, KENT, DA5 1RB.

LIOW, Mrs. Sharon, MEng ACA *2002;* 3 Lynwood Terrace, Henfield Road, LONDON, SW19 3LY.

LIOW, Mrs. Susan Phaik Suan, BSc(Hons) ACA *1992;* 2 Cambridge Road, UXBRIDGE, MIDDLESEX, UB8 1BG.

LIOW-YUNE-LOY, Mr. Joseph Jerry, BA ACA *1995;* 41 rue du Trabli, 1236 CARTIGNY, SWITZERLAND.

LIPINSKI, Mr. Andrew Alexander, BSc FCA *1974;* AAL Corporate Services Ltd, Old Brook House Pertenhall Road, Keysoe, BEDFORD, MK44 2HR.

LIPINSKI, Mr. Marek Antoni, BSc ACA *1979;* Albermarle Investments Limited, South Lawns, Wigton Lane, LEEDS, LS17 8SJ.

•**LIPKIN, Mr. Edward Barry, LLB FCA ATII TEP** *1963;* (Tax Fac), E Barry Lipkin, Manor Lawn, 15 Normans Place, ALTRINCHAM, CHESHIRE, WA14 2AB.

•**LIPMAN, Mr. Brian Geoffrey, FCA** *1968;* 18 Church Cresent, Whetstone, LONDON, N20 0JP.

LIPMAN, Mr. Hyman, MSc BA FCA *1964;* 4 Oakhill Avenue, PINNER, MIDDLESEX, HA5 3DN.

LIPMAN, Mr. Joshua, BSc ACA *2011;* Flat 76 Raffles House, 67 Brampton Grove, LONDON, NW4 4BX.

LIPMAN, Mr. Richard Marc, BA ACA *2001;* 9 Anthony Road, BOREHAMWOOD, HERTFORDSHIRE, WD6 4NF.

LIPMAN, Mr. Robert Alan, FCA *1971;* Flat 21, 6 Yohanatan Fridan Street, 78475 ASHKELON, ISRAEL.

•**LIPOP, Mr. David, FCA** *1976;* 3 Darleys Close, Grendon Underwood, AYLESBURY, HP18 0SE.

•**LIPOWICZ, Mr. Leslie Michael, FCA** *1977;* (Tax Fac), Leslie Michael Lipowicz & Co, Accounts House, 16 Dalling Road, Hammersmith, LONDON, W6 0JB.

LIPPETT, Mr. Paul Albert Edmond, FCA *1975;* 8 Spencer Close, Eaton Ford, ST. NEOTS, CAMBRIDGESHIRE, PE19 7LQ.

LIPPITT, Mr. Jonathan Peter, FCA *1982;* 2142 Continental Street, SAINT CLOUD, FL 34769-7068, UNITED STATES.

LIPPITT, Mr. Paul Anthony, BA ACA *1991;* 29 Great Grove, Abbeymead, GLOUCESTER, GL4 4QT.

LIPPITT, Mr. Steven, MA ACA *1991;* 31a Matheson Road, West Kensington, LONDON, W14 8SN.

LIPPMANN, Dr. Lore, PhD ACA *2010;* Pricewaterhousecoopers Abacus House, Castle Park, CAMBRIDGE, CB3 0AN.

LIPPOLD, Mr. David Michael, BSc ACA *1994;* Rose Cottage, School Road, Bursledon, SOUTHAMPTON, SO31 8BU.

LIPSCOMB, Mr. Edwin Paul, FCA FIMgt *1962;* Crane House, Rowanhurst Drive, FARNHAM COMMON, BUCKINGHAMSHIRE, SL2 3HG. (Life Member)

LIPSCOMBE, Mrs. Jennifer Kirsti, BA(Hons) ACA *2002;* 28 Highfield Road, LONDON, W3 0AL.

LIPSITH, Mr. Harvey Brian, BA FCA *1974;* Flat 7 Corfu, 14 Chaddesley Glen, POOLE, DORSET, BH13 7PG.

LIPSON, Mr. Colin Gordon, MA FCA *1976;* 35 Burnhamthorpe Park Blvd, ETOBICOKE M9A 1H8, ON, CANADA.

•**LIPTON, Mr. David Michael, BSc FCA** *1974;* Rue de la Levure 22, B-1050 BRUSSELS, BELGIUM.

LIPTON, Mr. Stephen Charles, MA ACA *1984;* Bellmannstrasse 12, 22607 HAMBURG, GERMANY.

LIPTROTT, Mr. James, BSc ACA *2005;* 16 Linden Place, NOTTINGHAM, NG3 5RB.

LIQUORISH, Mr. John Stephen, MA FCA 1975; Flat 249, Waterman Building, 14 Westferry Road, LONDON, E14 8NG.

LIRON, Mr. Geoffrey David, ACA 1985; Rosscot Ltd, Thomas Edge House, Tunnell Street, St. Helier, JERSEY, JE2 4LU.

LIS, Mr. Andrew Richard, FCA 1972; 72 Admiralty Way, TEDDINGTON, TW11 0NN.

LISBURN, Mr. Peter James, FCA 1960; 8 Alder Grove, HALESOWEN, B62 9TL. (Life Member)

LISBY, Mr. Jonathan Edward, FCA FIIA 1975; Thorn Knoll Salterns Lane, Old Bursledon, SOUTHAMPTON, SO31 8DH.

•**LISHAK, Mr. Jeffrey, FCA** 1979; (Tax Fac), Jones & Partners, Fifth Floor, 26-28 Great Portland Street, LONDON, W1W 8AS.

•**LISHAK, Mr. Jon Philip, BSc FCA** 1989; JPL Accountancy Services Limited, 110 Chandos Avenue, LONDON, N20 9DZ. See also JPL

LISHMAN, Mr. Brian Scott, BA ACA 2005; Green Bank Wilsons Road, Headley Down, BORDON, GU35 8JG.

LISHMAN, Mr. David John, ACA 1989; 226A Gloucester Terrace, LONDON, W2 6HU.

LISHMAN, Miss. Eleanor Breeze Rhiannon, BA ACA 2009; Pricewaterhousecoopers, 12 Plumtree Court, LONDON, EC4A 4HT.

LISHMAN, Miss. Emma Victoria, BSc(Hons) ACA 2003; Andy Bounds Ltd, 403-415 The Corn Exchange, Fenwick Street, LIVERPOOL, L2 7QL.

•**LISHMAN, Mr. John Vincent, BSc FCA** 1975; 14 Rosecroft, East Keswick, LEEDS, LS17 9HR.

LISING, Mr. Georges Michael David, BSc ACA 1997; 7 Asterix Road, BEAU BASSIN, MAURITIUS.

LISINSKI, Mr. George Wojciech, BA FCA 1979; Russets, Onslow Road, ASCOT, SL5 0HW.

LISK, Mrs. Georgiana, BSc ACA 2002; 62 Bellevue Road, LONDON, W13 8DE.

LISKIEWICZ, Mrs. Monika, ACA 2011; 7 Kingsmill Close, Morley, LEEDS, LS27 9RZ.

LISLE, Mr. David, FCA 1970; 15066 SW 155 TERRACE, MIAMI, FL 33187, UNITED STATES.

LISLE, Mr. George, MC FCA 1939; 31 St. Edmunds Court, Devonshire Lane, LEEDS, LS8 1EZ. (Life Member)

LISLE, Ms. Jocelyn Felicity, BSc FCA 1979; 18 Darlow Drive, Biddenham, BEDFORD, MK40 4AY.

LISLE, Mr. John Charles Teasdale, BA ACA 1993; L E C G Ltd, Davidson Building, 5 Southampton Street, LONDON, WC2E 7HA.

LISLE, Miss. Nicola Claire, ACA 2010; 79 St Heliers Bay Road, St Heliers, AUCKLAND 1071, NEW ZEALAND.

•**LISLE, Mr. Stuart Roger, BSc ACA** 1993; (Tax Fac), BDO LLP, Arcadia House, Maritime Walk, Ocean Village, SOUTHAMPTON, SO14 3TL. See also BDO Stoy Hayward LLP

LISMER, Mr. Peter Anthony, MSc BEng ACA 1980; Buchan House 7 Bridge Street, WITNEY, OXFORDSHIRE, OX28 1BY.

LISSAMAN, Mr. Anthony Andrew, BSc ACA 1998; Bramble Acre, 17 Beckett Avenue, KENLEY, CR8 5LT.

LISSAMAN, Mr. Paul, ACA 2006; Fox Evans, 7 Manor Road, COVENTRY, CV1 2FW.

LISSER, Mrs. Deborah Zoe, ACA 1983; 62 Russell Bank Road, Four Oaks, SUTTON COLDFIELD, B74 4RQ.

LISSIMORE, Mr. Adrian, ACA 2010; 22 Packington Lane, Coleshill, BIRMINGHAM, B46 3EL.

LISSOW, Mrs. Youmna Alexandra, ACA 2000; 24 Luelanden, 22880 WEDEL, GERMANY.

•**LIST, Mr. Matthew Jason, BSc ACA CF DChA** 1997; Baker Tilly Corporate Finance LLP, 1st Floor, 46 Clarendon Road, WATFORD, WD17 1JJ. See also Baker Tilly Tax and Advisory Services LLP

•**LIST, Mr. Philip William, ACA** 1993; 4 Highcroft, North Common, BRISTOL, BS30 5NP.

•**LISTER, Mr. Andrew, LLB FCA** 1998; (Tax Fac), KPMG LLP, 15 Canada Square, LONDON, E14 5GL.

LISTER, Mr. Andrew Thomas, BA ACA 2005; 311 Lumiere Apartments, 58 St. John's Hill, LONDON, SW11 1AD.

LISTER, Mr. Anthony Francis, BSc FCA 1991; (Tax Fac), 36a Broadway, Bramhall, STOCKPORT, SK7 3BU.

LISTER, Mr. Ben, MChem ACA CTA 2011; 4 Keppel Row, LONDON, SE1 0FB.

LISTER, Mr. Benedict John, ACA 2008; Rothschild Trust Guernsey Ltd, PO Box 472, GUERNSEY, GY1 6AX.

LISTER, Mrs. Claire Louise, BSc ACA 1991; Howe Hill Farm, North Deighton, WETHERBY, LS22 4EL.

LISTER, Mr. David, MA ACA 2000; Ernst & Young Llp, 10 George Street, EDINBURGH, EH2 2DZ.

LISTER, Miss. Deborah, BA ACA 2006; (Tax Fac), K P M G Quayside House, 110 Quayside, NEWCASTLE UPON TYNE, NE1 3DX.

LISTER, Mr. Edward Stuart Hardill, FCA 1960; Greenacres, 94 Hightown Road, LIVERSEDGE, WF15 8BZ. (Life Member)

LISTER, Mrs. Fiona Clare, BA ACA 1991; Lord Wandsworth College, Long Sutton, HOOK, HAMPSHIRE, RG29 1TB.

LISTER, Mr. Geoffrey Richard, CBE FCA 1960; Harbeck House, Harbeck Drive, Harden, BINGLEY, BD16 1JG. (Life Member)

LISTER, Mr. George Herbert, FCA 1957; 63 Vernon Road, Edgbaston, BIRMINGHAM, B16 9SQ. (Life Member)

LISTER, Miss. Gwyneth Margaret, BSc ACA 1994; Severn Trent Centre, General S T W Post, PO Box 5309, COVENTRY, CV3 9FH.

LISTER, Mrs. Jane Nicola, BSc ACA 1990; Woolley Cottage, Woolley Hall Gardens, Woolley, WAKEFIELD, WF4 2TA.

LISTER, Mr. Jeremy Guy, BA ACA 1982; 22 rue Soufflet, 91290 ARPAJON, FRANCE.

LISTER, Mr. John Henry Pack, FCA 1963; 43 Grange Drive, SPALDING, PE11 2DX.

LISTER, Mr. John Leonard, FCA 1974; Property Holdings (Pennine) Ltd, Trinity House, Harrison Road, HALIFAX, HX1 2JG. (Life Member)

•**LISTER, Mr. John Mark, BA ACA CF** 1985; PKF (UK) LLP, Pannell House, 6 Queen Street, LEEDS, LS1 2TW.

•**LISTER, Mr. John Prentice, FCA** 1969; (Tax Fac), John P Lister, Bay Tree House, 8 Oak Lawn, NEWTON ABBOT, DEVON, TQ12 1QP.

LISTER, Mr. John Thomas, FCA 1964; Rosilian Limited, 239 Tatham Road, Llanishen, CARDIFF, CF14 5FF.

LISTER, Mr. Joseph Julian, BSc ACA 1998; Unite Group Plc The Core, 40 St. Thomas Street, BRISTOL, BS1 6JX.

LISTER, Mr. Joseph Kenneth, FCA 1956; Southway, 1 Foxhill Green, LEEDS, LS16 5PQ. (Life Member)

LISTER, Mr. Martin Claude Charles, FCA 1972; 538 South End Road, Elm Park, HORNCHURCH, ESSEX, RM12 5UB.

LISTER, Mr. Martin Walton, BSc FCA 1975; 124 Percy Road, HAMPTON, TW12 2JW.

LISTER, Mr. Matthew John, BSocSc ACA 2002; 62 Tilehouse Green Lane, Knowle, SOLIHULL, B93 9EY.

LISTER, Mr. Michael Timothy, ACA 1988; Toppit Croft, Toppit Farm, Bagden Lane, Clayton West, HUDDERSFIELD, HD8 9LQ.

LISTER, Mrs. Nicola Louise, BA ACA 1997; 4 Woodlea, Boston Spa, WETHERBY, WEST YORKSHIRE, LS23 6SB.

•**LISTER, Mr. Richard Alan, FCA** 1975; R.A. Lister, Suite 2, 14 Rishworth Street, WAKEFIELD, WEST YORKSHIRE, WF1 3BY.

LISTER, Mr. Robert Campbell, ACA 1979; 40 Jameson Drive, CORBRIDGE, NE45 5EX.

LISTER, Mr. Robert Stephen, BSc FCA 1982; Briery Wood, Hebers Ghyll Drive, ILKLEY, LS29 9QQ.

LISTER, Mr. Roger Jeffrey, PhD MA FCA 1963; 25 Charlton Court, Prestwich, MANCHESTER, M25 0BE.

LISTER, Mr. Thomas James, BA ACA FCMA ACIS 1980; Pressure Technologies Plc, Meadowhall Road, SHEFFIELD, S9 1BT.

•**LISTER, Mr. Timothy Norman Bramham, FCA** 1992; Stephen Hill Mid Kent, 44 High Street, NEW ROMNEY, KENT, TN28 8BZ.

LISTER, Mr. Vaughan Paul Belding, BA ACA CTA 1984; Fallowfield, 250 Hillbury Road, WARLINGHAM, CR6 9TP.

•**LISTER, Mr. Victor Charles Michael, FCA** 1954; Michael Lister Associates, Buttons Barn, Magpie Street, Charsfield, WOODBRIDGE, SUFFOLK IP13 7QE.

LISTER, Miss. Victoria Charlotte, BA(Hons) ACA 2011; Wipperweg 6, (SAALE), 06122 HALLE, GERMANY.

LITCHFIELD, Mr. Andrew James, BA ACA 1992; Beaufort, Hunters Ride, STOURBRIDGE, DY7 5QN.

LITCHFIELD, Mr. Edward Stewart, MEng ACA 2009; Deloitte & Touche, 2 New Street Square, LONDON, EC4A 3BZ.

LITCHFIELD, Mrs. Julia Anne, BSc(Hons) ACA 2000; (Tax Fac), 4 Ballards Way, SOUTH CROYDON, SURREY, CR2 7JL.

LITCHFIELD, Mr. Royston David, FCA 1973; Sherwood, Pembley Green, Copthorne Common, CRAWLEY, RH10 3LF.

LITHERLAND, Mr. Bryan Anthony, FCA 1973; 7 Blurton Priory, STOKE-ON-TRENT, ST3 3PG.

•**LITHERLAND, Mr. Guy, FCA** 1971; (Tax Fac), J W Scrivens & Co Limited, Grays Court, 5 Nursery Road, Edgbaston, BIRMINGHAM, B15 3JX.

LITHERLAND, Miss. Laura Alice, BA ACA 2007; 46 Carminia Road, LONDON, SW17 8AH.

LITHERLAND, Mr. Robert Frank, BSc FCA 1978; 150a High Street, TEDDINGTON, MIDDLESEX, TW11 8HZ.

LITHGO, Mr. Stuart John, FCA 1968; 39 Goose Pasture, YARM, CLEVELAND, TS15 9EP.

LITHGOW, Mr. Patrick James, FCA 1966; Hawthorn Cottage, Coltshill Drive, Newton, SWANSEA, SA3 4SN. (Life Member)

LITJENS, Mr. Pieter Johannes Jacobus, BA ACA 1986; Fishers Oak, Saunders Lane, WOKING, SURREY, GU22 0NU.

LITLER, Mr. Robert Michael, BSc ACA 1987; 44 Gaston Avenue, Keynsham, BRISTOL, BS31 1LT.

LITSTER, Mr. Peter Thomas, BA ACA 2005; 8 Halifax Road, BICESTER, OXFORDSHIRE, OX26 4TG.

LITTEN, Mr. Mathew Francis, BSc ACA 1998; (Tax Fac), Mulberry House, 7 Mount Row St. Peter Port, GUERNSEY, GY1 1NS.

•**LITTING, Mr. Michael Bernard, BA FCA** 1978; Litting Associates Ltd, 74 Abbotsford Road, LICHFIELD, STAFFORDSHIRE, WS14 9XL.

LITTLE, Mr. Alan Patrick, BSc ACA 1987; 5 Sackville Avenue, Hayes, BROMLEY, BR2 7JS.

•**LITTLE, Mrs. Alison Margaret, BSc ACA** 1990; Church House, Woodford Road, Great Addington, KETTERING, NORTHAMPTONSHIRE, NN14 4BS.

①**LITTLE, Mr. Andrew, BA FCA** 1994; R Tait Walker & Co, Bulman House, Regent Centre Gosforth, NEWCASTLE UPON TYNE, NE3 3LS.

LITTLE, Mr. Andrew James, BSc ACA 2004; 24 Dowling Street, FRESHWATER, NSW 2096, AUSTRALIA.

•**LITTLE, Mr. Anthony, FCA** 1974; (Tax Fac), O'Reilly, Ullswater House, Duke Street, PENRITH, CUMBRIA, CA11 7LY. See also O'Reilly N.T. & Partners

LITTLE, Mrs. Baljeet, BSc ACA 2001; 4 Mount Barns, Poplar Hall Lane Chorlton-by-Backford, CHESTER, CH2 4DD.

LITTLE, Mrs. Carla Michelle, BSc(Hons) ACA 2007; with CLB Coopers, Fleet House, New Road, LANCASTER, LA1 1EZ.

LITTLE, Mrs. Catharine Jane, BSc ACA 1991; Collingwood Buildings, 38 Collingwood Street, NEWCASTLE UPON TYNE, NE1 1JF.

LITTLE, Mr. Charles Andrew, FCA 1960; 8 The Avenue, Hipperholme, HALIFAX, HX3 8NP. (Life Member)

•**LITTLE, Mr. Charles William, FCA** 1980; (Tax Fac), Keens Shay Keens Limited, 2nd Floor, Exchange Building, 16 St. Cuthberts Street, BEDFORD, MK40 3JG.

LITTLE, Mr. Christopher William, BA ACA 1985; 7 Jermyn Road, KING'S LYNN, NORFOLK, PE30 4AD.

LITTLE, Miss. Corinna, ACA 2009; 8 Eastcote Place, Fernbank Road, ASCOT, BERKSHIRE, SL5 8JD.

LITTLE, Mr. Darren Paul, BA ACA 2007; 27 Bluebell Close, KENDAL, CUMBRIA, LA9 7SH.

•**LITTLE, Mr. David, BSc FCA** 1969; D. Little, 1 Orchard Road, Burnham Green Tewin, WELWYN, AL6 0HE.

LITTLE, Mr. David Cameron, FCA 1968; 20 Woodham Gate, Woodham Village, NEWTON AYCLIFFE, COUNTY DURHAM, DL5 4UB.

LITTLE, Miss. Deborah Jane, ACA 1989; 18 Nathan Road, #04-08, Nathan Place, SINGAPORE 248747, SINGAPORE.

LITTLE, Mr. Dominic Vincent John, BSc ACA 1990; 61 Hopefield Avenue, PORTRUSH, COUNTY ANTRIM, BT56 8HE.

LITTLE, Mr. Duncan, BA(Hons) ACA 2011; 59 Sylvan Road North, WESTPORT, CT 06880, UNITED STATES.

•**LITTLE, Mrs. Eileen Ann, BSc FCA** 1973; E.A.LITTLE, Larkmount, Walmersley, BURY, BL9 6TD.

•**LITTLE, Mrs. Ellen Mary, BSc(Hons) ACA AMCT** 2002; JL Advisory LLP, 48 Chester Road, Poynton, STOCKPORT, CHESHIRE, SK12 1HA.

LITTLE, Mrs. Fiona Marie, BA ACA 1990; Welbeck, Green Lane, Crosby on Eden, CARLISLE, CA6 4QN.

LITTLE, Mr. Gary, FCA 1988; Avonmore Southdown Road, Shawford, WINCHESTER, HAMPSHIRE, SO21 2BY.

•**LITTLE, Mr. Geoffrey, BA FCA** 1989; Bell Anderson Ltd, 264-266 Durham Road, GATESHEAD, NE8 4JR. See also BLA Consulting LLP

•**LITTLE, Mr. Geoffrey Michael, FCA** 1969; (Tax Fac), Geoffrey Little & Co., 22 Orford Road, LONDON, E18 1PY.

LITTLE, Mr. Graham Stewart, BA FCA 1991; Boundary Court, Gatwick Road, CRAWLEY, WEST SUSSEX, RH10 9AX.

LITTLE, Mr. Gregory Marc, MMath ACA 2006; 49 Hatch Lane, Old Basing, BASINGSTOKE, RG24 7EB.

LITTLE, Mr. Ian Christopher, BA ACA 1991; 42 Dobbs Drift, Kesgrave, IPSWICH, IP5 2QG.

•**LITTLE, Mr. James, ACA ATII** 1979; (Tax Fac), James Little & Co, Leaside, Whittingham, ALNWICK, NORTHUMBERLAND, NE66 4UP.

LITTLE, Mr. James Robert, BA ACA 1991; 148 Dora Road, LONDON, SW19 7HJ.

LITTLE, Mrs. Jayne Ann, BSc ACA 1992; Avonmore Southdown Road, Shawford, WINCHESTER, HAMPSHIRE, SO21 2BY.

LITTLE, Mr. Jeremy Christopher Addison, FCA 1976; Parsonage Farm, Swallowcliffe, SALISBURY, SP3 5NU.

LITTLE, Mr. John, LLB DipLP ACA 1993; 2870 Peachtree Road NW, PMB # 846, ATLANTA, GA 30305-2918, UNITED STATES.

•**LITTLE, Mr. John, FCA** 1976; Saint & Co., Sterling House, Wavell Drive, Rosehill, CARLISLE, CA1 2SA.

LITTLE, Mr. John, BA ACA 1993; Turkovice 59, Ondrejov, Praha Vychod, 25165 PRAGUE, CZECH REPUBLIC.

•**LITTLE, Mrs. Linda Margaret, BSc FCA** 1976; 12 Beverley Rise, ILKLEY, WEST YORKSHIRE, LS29 9DB.

LITTLE, Mr. Mark Simon, MA ACA 1996; 4 First Avenue, LONDON, SW14 8SR.

LITTLE, Mr. Mark Stephen, BA ACA 1981; HSBC Bank PLC, 8 Canada Square, Canary Wharf, LONDON, E14 5HQ.

LITTLE, Mr. Michael Simon James, BSc ACA 1993; 14 Cade Hill Road, STOCKSFIELD, NORTHUMBERLAND, NE43 7PS.

•**LITTLE, Ms. Michele Marie, MA ACA** 1995; My Bean Counter Limited, 1 Rusthall Avenue, LONDON, W4 1BW. See also My Bean Counter

•**LITTLE, Mr. Peter Robert, FCA** 1970; P R Little, 16 Kenwyn Close, West End, SOUTHAMPTON, SO18 3PJ.

LITTLE, Mr. Richard Anthony, ACA 1979; 57 Charnhill Drive, Mangotsfield, BRISTOL, BS16 9JS.

•**LITTLE, Mr. Richard Anthony, BA ACA ATII** 1997; (Tax Fac), KPMG LLP, 1 The Embankment, Neville Street, LEEDS, LS1 4DW. See also KPMG Europe LLP

LITTLE, Mr. Robert Eric, BSc ACA 1979; 20 Flavian Close, ST. ALBANS, AL3 4JX.

LITTLE, Mr. Robin, BA(Oxon) ACA 2010; Flat 11, Mordell Court, High Street, Chesterton, CAMBRIDGE, CB4 1NJ.

LITTLE, Mr. Robin Andrew, BA FCA 1983; 1 Harrison Court, Rainsford Road, CHELMSFORD, CM1 2UY.

LITTLE, Mrs. Sally Victoria, BSc ACA 2003; 27 Kingsway, Penwortham, PRESTON, PR1 0BJ.

LITTLE, Mrs. Sarah, ACA MAAT 2004; with KPMG LLP, 15 Canada Square, LONDON, E14 5GL.

LITTLE, Miss. Sarah Jayne, MA FCA 1998; One Front Street, Suite 925, SAN FRANCISCO, CA 94111, UNITED STATES.

LITTLE, Miss. Sarayna Rose, ACA 2010; 71a Stroud Green Road, Islington, LONDON, N4 3EG.

LITTLE, Mr. Scott Andrew, BA ACA 2006; 19 Hessel Road, LONDON, W13 9ER.

LITTLE, Mr. Stephen, BSc FCA 2000; 48 Chester Road, Poynton, STOCKPORT, CHESHIRE, SK12 1HA.

LITTLE, Mr. Stephen John, ACA CA(SA) 2008; Level 18, Darling Park 1, 201 Sussex Street, SYDNEY, NSW 2000, AUSTRALIA.

LITTLE, Mr. Steven Antony, ACA 1986; Nigella, Upper Churchfields, MARLBOROUGH, WILTSHIRE, SN8 4AT.

LITTLE, Mr. Steven David, ACA 2009; 12th Floor, K P M G Llp, 15 Canada Square, LONDON, E14 5GL.

LITTLE, Mr. Steven Peter, MA FCA 1986; Winchester College, College Street, WINCHESTER, HAMPSHIRE, SO23 9NA.

•**LITTLE, Miss. Tracy, ACA** 2003; Little Accounting Solutions, Tewthwaite House, Tewthwaite Green, Blackford, CARLISLE, CA6 4EZ.

LITTLEBURY, Mr. John David Baron, FCA 1960; 44 The Avenue, RADLETT, WD7 7DW. (Life Member)

LITTLECHILD, Mr. Laurence Paul, BA ACA 2004; H S B C, 8-16 Canada Square, LONDON, E14 5HQ.

•**LITTLECHILD, Mr. Robert John, FCA** 1978; (Tax Fac), R.J. Littlechild, 5 Tintagel Court, St. Neots, ST. NEOTS, PE19 2RZ.

LITTLECOTT, Mrs. Katherine Ruth, BSc ACA 1990; with Atkinson Saul Fairholm Limited, 21a Newland, LINCOLN, LN1 1XP.

LITTLEDYKE, Mr. Graeme Thomas, ACA 1995; 8 Springwell Avenue, North End, DURHAM, DH1 4LY.

LITTLEFAIR, Mr. David, FCA 1972; Global Aerospace Underwriting Managers Limited, Fitzwilliam House, 10 St. Mary Axe, LONDON, EC3A 8EQ. (Life Member)

LITTLEFAIR, Mr. David John, FCA 1974; Manna Place, West Melton, RD5, CHRISTCHURCH 7675, NEW ZEALAND.

LITTLEFAIR, Mr. Kenneth Robert, BA FCA 1973; Shepherd Neame Ltd, 17 Court Street, FAVERSHAM, KENT, ME13 7AX.

LITTLEFAIR, Ms. Linda Frances, BA ACA *1987;* (Tax Fac), 25 Lawrance Lea, Harston, CAMBRIDGE, CB22 7QR.

•LITTLEFORD, Mr. David John, BA FCA *1993;* KPMG LLP, 15 Canada Square, LONDON, E14 5GL. See also KPMG Europe LLP

LITTLEHALES, Mr. Richard, BA FCA *1989;* Two World Option Limited, Adel Lodge, Long Causeway, Adel, LEEDS, LS16 8EF.

LITTLEJOHN, Mr. Anthony David Findon, FCA FCT *1966;* Lythe Farm, Steep, PETERSFIELD, GU32 1AU.

LITTLEJOHN, Mr. David Philip, BA ACA *1979;* 56N Warwick Square, LONDON, SW1V 2AJ.

LITTLEJOHN, Mr. George Hodge, MA FCA *1977;* 46 Battledean Road, LONDON, N5 1UZ.

LITTLEJOHN, Mr. Ian James, FCA *1966;* 13 St. Marys Avenue, MIRFIELD, WEST YORKSHIRE, WF14 0PX. (Life Member)

LITTLEJOHNS, Mr. Michael, BSc FCA *1989;* 11 Birch Grove, POTTERS BAR, EN6 1SY.

•LITTLEJOHNS, Mr. Simon, BSc FCA ATII *1983;* (Tax Fac), Burgis & Bullock, 2 Chapel Court, Holly Walk, LEAMINGTON SPA, CV32 4YS.

LITTLER, Mrs. Janette, BSc ACA *1991;* 12 York Avenue, LONDON, SW14 7LG.

LITTLER, Miss. Jennifer Angela, MSc BSc ACA *2009;* 5 Woodacre, MANCHESTER, M16 8QQ.

LITTLER, Mr. John Clive, FCA *1968;* 21 Kings Road, TEDDINGTON, TW11 0QB. (Life Member)

LITTLER, Mrs. Lee Sybil Grace, BA ACA *1988;* 89 Stock Road, BILLERICAY, CM12 0RN.

LITTLER, Mrs. Nancy Christobel, FCA *1967;* 21 Frederick Road, Edgbaston, BIRMINGHAM, B15 1JN. (Life Member)

LITTLER, Mr. Peter James, BA ACA *1993;* 15 Parkgate Gardens, LONDON, SW14 8BQ.

•LITTLER, Mr. Philip John, FCA *1978;* (Tax Fac), Maxwells, 4 King Square, BRIDGWATER, SOMERSET, TA6 3YF.

LITTLER, Dr. Stephen John, PhD BSc ACA *2009;* Pricewaterhousecoopers, 101 Barbirolli Square, MANCHESTER, M2 3PW.

•LITTLER, Mr. Stuart David, BA(Hons) ACA *2001;* Bennett Brooks & Co Ltd., St. Georges Court, Winnington Avenue, NORTHWICH, CHESHIRE, CW8 4EE.

LITTLETON, Mr. Andrew John, BA ACA *2005;* 5 Seymour Gardens, SURBITON, KT5 8QE.

LITTLETON, Mr. Richard Reginald, FCA *1975;* Essential Sales Products Ltd, Unit 39, Wimbledon Stadium Business Centre, Riverside Road, LONDON, SW17 0BA.

LITTLEWOOD, Mr. Brian, FCA *1965;* Tar-Vyn, Pike Law Lane, Scapegoat Hill, HUDDERSFIELD, HD7 4PL.

LITTLEWOOD, Miss. Elizabeth Ann, ACA *2009;* with PricewaterhouseCoopers, Darling Park Tower 2, 201 Sussex Street, GPO Box 2650, SYDNEY, NSW 1171 AUSTRALIA.

LITTLEWOOD, Mr. Graham, FCA *1966;* 6 Lakeside Crescent, BRENTWOOD, ESSEX, CM14 4JB.

LITTLEWOOD, Mrs. Jenny Louise, MMath ACA *2007;* Berg Kaprow Lewis, 35 Ballards Lane, LONDON, N3 1XW.

LITTLEWOOD, Mr. John, FCA *1964;* Scarna, 55 Mallinson Oval, HARROGATE, HG2 9HJ.

LITTLEWOOD, Mr. John, LLB(Hons) FCA *1958;* Ingleside, Durham Road, Birtley, CHESTER-LE-STREET, DH3 1LU. (Life Member)

LITTLEWOOD, Miss. Louise Alexandra, BA ACA *1993;* 27 Brewery Lane, STANSTED, ESSEX, CM24 8LB.

LITTLEWOOD, Miss. Rachel, MSc BSc ACA *2006;* with Deloitte LLP, Hill House, 1 Little New Street, LONDON, EC4A 3TR.

LITTLEWOOD, Mr. Richard, ACA *2009;* 30 Glastonbury Drive, Poynton, STOCKPORT, CHESHIRE, SK12 1EN.

LITTLEWOOD, Mr. Robert, ACA *2009;* 63 Malia Road, CHESTERFIELD, DERBYSHIRE, S41 0UF.

LITTLEWOOD, Mr. Robert David, FCA *1961;* 11 Moorcroft Drive, SHEFFIELD, S10 4GW.

LITTLEY, Miss. Amanda, BSc(Hons) ACA *2004;* 52 Whitley Court Road, Quinton, BIRMINGHAM, B32 1EY.

LITTLEY, Mr. Andrew Jonathan, FCA *1973;* Bell Tower, 14 Foley Street, Kinver, STOURBRIDGE, WEST MIDLANDS, DY7 6EP.

LITTLEY, Mr. Eugene Frederick, FCA *1959;* Beaumont, 34 Durley Road, SEATON, EX12 2HW.

LITTMAN, Mr. Anthony Frank, FCA CTA *1955;* C/O Flat 3, 1 Holly Terrace, LONDON, N6 6LX. (Life Member)

LITTMODEN, Mr. Christopher, CBE FCA *1966;* Apartment 9, Riverside Tower, The Boulevard, Imperial Wharf, LONDON, SW6 2SW.

LITTON, Mr. Patrick Mark Silvester, MA FCA *1989;* 75 Rannoch Road, LONDON, W6 9SX.

LITUMBE, Mr. Njoh, FCA *1957;* Membea House, Bokwaongo, P O Box 124, BUEA, CAMEROON. (Life Member)

LITVINTSEVA, Ms. Evgeniya, ACA *2007;* Myron Street 4 Flat 7, Zenon, 6041 LARNACA, CYPRUS.

LITWINOWICZ, Mr. Leslie Richard, BCom ACA *1985;* The Corner House, 131 Canwell Drive, Canwell, SUTTON COLDFIELD, B75 5SG.

LIU, Ms. Bertha Fung Yi, ACA *2006;* with RSM Nelson Wheeler, 29th Floor Caroline Centre, Lee Gardens Two, 28 Yun Ping Road, CAUSEWAY BAY, HONG KONG ISLAND HONG KONG SAR.

LIU, Miss. Candy Wai Yee, BA ACA *1990;* F1 5/F Block F, Villa Monte Rosa, 41a Stubbs Road, MID LEVELS, HONG KONG ISLAND, HONG KONG SAR.

LIU, Miss. Chang, MPhil ACA *2011;* Flat 5, Cotterell Court, Hop Street, LONDON, SE10 0QR.

LIU, Mr. Chi Lai, ACA *2007;* C. K. Liu & Company, 13th Floor, Wah Kit Commercial Centre, 302 Des Voeux Road, CENTRAL, HONG KONG ISLAND HONG KONG SAR.

LIU, Mr. Chi Chuen, ACA *2005;* Room 4 - 24/ F, 2 Fung Shek Street, SHA TIN, NEW TERRITORIES, HONG KONG SAR.

LIU, Mr. Chi Kin, ACA *2007;* C. K. Liu & Company, 13th Floor, Wah Kit Commercial Centre, 302 Des Voeux Road, CENTRAL, HONG KONG ISLAND HONG KONG SAR.

LIU, Miss. Choi-Fun, BA ACA *1992;* Flat E 38/ F. Tower 1, Island Harbourview, 11 Hoi Fai Road, TAI KOK TSUI, KOWLOON, HONG KONG SAR.

LIU, Mr. Chun Kit Jackie, ACA *2009;* 5 Allee David-Morse, Case Postale, 1211 GENEVA, SWITZERLAND.

LIU, Mr. Chun Ming Robin, ACA *2007;* Unique Shipping (HK) Ltd, Room 1802, Harbour Centre, 25 Harbour Road, WAN CHAI, HONG KONG ISLAND HONG KONG SAR.

LIU, Mr. Danny Man Fai, BSc ACA MBA *1994;* Flat E 28/Flr Block 1, Pokfulam Gardens, POK FU LAM, HONG KONG ISLAND, HONG KONG SAR.

LIU, Mr. David Man Kit, BSc ACA *1997;* 1 Cherrywood Close, KINGSTON UPON THAMES, SURREY, KT2 6SF.

LIU, Mr. David Wai Chang, BA ACA *1993;* Level 46, International Commerce Centre, 1 Austin Road West, TSIM SHA TSUI, KOWLOON, HONG KONG SAR.

LIU, Mr. Don Tit Shing, MA ACA *1990;* Chong Hing Bank Ltd, 18/F Chong Hing Bank Centre, 24 Des Voeux Road, CENTRAL, HONG KONG ISLAND, HONG KONG SAR.

LIU, Ms. Fang, BComm ACA *2009;* 190 West Barnes Lane, NEW MALDEN, KT3 6LS.

•LIU, Mr. Fei, MSc BA ACA *2009;* Flanton & Co, Second Floor, Berkeley Square House, Berkeley Square, LONDON, W1J 6BD.

LIU, Mr. Gar Lon, BA ACA *1993;* 25E Ning On Mansion, 28 Taikoo Shing Road, TAIKOO SHING, HONG KONG SAR.

LIU, Miss. Haibo, MA ACA *2011;* Flat 7, Pinnacle House, 15 Heritage Avenue, LONDON, NW9 5FY.

LIU, Mr. Hei Wan, BA ACA *1982;* World Trade Centre, Av. Da Amizade No. 918, 9 andar C-D, MACAU, MACAO.

•LIU, Mr. Herman Man Herman, BSc FCA *1989;* Liu Ward & Associates, Trafalgar House, 1 Grenville Place, Mill Hill, LONDON, NW7 3SA. See also Liu H.M & Co

LIU, Mr. Hing Hung, ACA *2005;* H. H. Liu & Co., 3/F Yue on Commercial Centre, 387 Lockhart Road, WAN CHAI, HONG KONG SAR.

LIU, Mr. Huaiyu, ACA *2008;* G. P. O. Box 9219, CENTRAL, HONG KONG SAR.

LIU, Mrs. Hui Min, MBA ACA *2009;* 1-5-501# Yuhuayuan Yili, Beixing Road Daxing District, BEIJING 102627, CHINA.

LIU, Mr. James, MEng ACA *2011;* Flat 91 Marathon House, 200 Marylebone Road, LONDON, NW1 5PL.

LIU, Miss. Jennifer Yun, BSc ACA *2009;* Real Estate Department, Abu Dhabi Investment Authority, 211 Corniche P.O. Box 3600, ABU DHABI, UNITED ARAB EMIRATES.

LIU, Mr. Jia-Hui, BSc ACA *2010;* 224 Jalan Seragam, Taman United, 58200 KUALA LUMPUR, FEDERAL TERRITORY, MALAYSIA.

LIU, Miss. Jiashu, MPhil ACA *2010;* Room 602 Flat 7 No 138 Chengshousi RdChaoyang District, BEIJING 100000, CHINA.

LIU, Mrs. Jing, ACA *2011;* 27 Brackley Avenue, Fair Oak, EASTLEIGH, SO50 8FJ.

LIU, Miss. Jingru, MBA ACA *2006;* 47 Hillsborough Court, Mortimer Crescent, LONDON, NW6 5NS.

LIU, Mr. Kam Wing, ACA *2005;* Flat 901 Block 7, Heng Fa Chuen, CHAI WAN, HONG KONG ISLAND, HONG KONG SAR.

LIU, Miss. Khieu Khim Katherine, ACA *1993;* Flat C 17th Floor, Li Chit Garden, 1 Li Chit Street, WAN CHAI, HONG KONG ISLAND, HONG KONG SAR.

LIU, Mr. Kwong Sang, ACA *2005;* K.S. Liu & Company CPA Limited, Unit 1003 10/F, Rightful Centre, 12 Tak Hing Street, TSIM SHA TSIU, KOWLOON HONG KONG SAR.

LIU, Mrs. Man Yee, BSc ACA *1991;* 11B Block 2, Maritime Bay, TSEUNG KWAN O, NEW TERRITORIES, HONG KONG SAR.

•LIU, Mr. Nicholas Ying Shan, BA FCA *1986;* (Tax Fac), Team Audit LLP, Kingham House, 161 College Street, ST. HELENS, MERSEYSIDE, WA10 1TY. See also Kingham Accountancy Ltd

LIU, Mr. Ning, ACA *2011;* 37 Telegraph Place, LONDON, E14 9XA.

LIU, Mrs. Priscilla Shun Yoon, BA ACA *1993;* 21 The Chine, Grange Park, LONDON, N21 6EA.

LIU, Mrs. Qi, ACA *2010;* 6 Cowper Way, READING, RG30 3EA.

LIU, Mr. Sai Hong Stephen, ACA *2005;* 90 Cecil Street, 10-02, SINGAPORE 069531, SINGAPORE.

LIU, Ms. San San, ACA *2008;* Siemens Ltd, 22/ F Two Landmark East, Kwun Tong, KWUN TONG, KOWLOON, HONG KONG SAR.

LIU, Ms. Shui, ACA *2010;* 145 Grove Green Road, LONDON, E11 4ED.

LIU, Ms. Shuk Mei, ACA *2009;* Flat A 18/F Wah Fai House, 26-34 Smithfield Road, KENNEDY TOWN, HONG KONG SAR.

LIU, Miss. Sijin, MSc BSc ACA *2010;* 58 New Road, MITCHAM, SURREY, CR4 4LT.

LIU, Mr. Stephen Chak Pong, BSc ACA *1990;* 21 The Chine, LONDON, N21 2EA.

LIU, Miss. Suet Ping, BSc ACA *2002;* Flat D 25/F, Jupiter Terrace, Tower 1, 18 Jupiter Street, CAUSEWAY BAY, HONG KONG ISLAND HONG KONG SAR.

LIU, Miss. Sui Yuk, BA ACA *1989;* 7/F Central Tower, Central Tower, Cathay Pacific City, 8 Scenic Road, HONG KONG SAR International Airport, LANTAU ISLAND NEW TERRITORIES HONG KONG SAR.

LIU, Mr. Tai Shin, FCA *1979;* 43 Jalan Limau Purut, Bangsar Park, 59000 KUALA LUMPUR, FEDERAL TERRITORY, MALAYSIA.

LIU, Mr. Timothy Wey Ming, MA FCA *1981;* 38 Greenaway Lane, Warsash, SOUTHAMPTON, SO31 9HS.

LIU, Mr. Tommy Woon Fai, BCom FCA *1982;* Flat A 21/F, The Colonnade, 152 Tai Hang Road, JARDINE'S LOOKOUT, HONG KONG ISLAND, HONG KONG SAR.

LIU, Mr. Tsz Bun, BSc ACA *1989;* KPMG, 8/F Prince's Building, 10 Chater Road, CENTRAL, HONG KONG ISLAND, HONG KONG SAR.

LIU, Mr. Vincent, BSc ACA *2011;* 76 Lawrence Drive, UXBRIDGE, MIDDLESEX, UB10 8RW.

LIU, Mr. Vincent Hoi Wah, BSc ACA *1994;* Flat 47B Tower I Central Park, 18 Hoi Ting Road, TAI KOK TSUI, KOWLOON, HONG KONG SAR.

LIU, Ms. Wai Lan, ACA *2005;* 601-1330 Clyde Avenue, WEST VANCOUVER V7T 1E7, BC, CANADA.

LIU, Mr. Wang Kit Alan, ACA *2004;* Bank of Communications, 2/F Pedder House, 20 Pedder Street, CENTRAL, HONG KONG ISLAND, HONG KONG SAR.

LIU, Ms. Wei Jung Lilian, ACA *2008;* Flat 2C Clarence Court, Clarence Terrace, WESTERN DISTRICT, HONG KONG SAR.

LIU, Miss. Xiaoqian, BA ACA *2010;* Flat 506, The Galley, 3 Basin Approach, LONDON, E16 2QW.

LIU, Mr. Xuong Dieu, BSc ACA *2002;* with KPMG, 50th Floor Plaza 66, 1266 Nanjing West Road, SHANGHAI 200040, CHINA.

LIU, Miss. Yan, MSc ACA *2010;* Flat 2, 15 Yonge Park, LONDON, N4 3NU.

LIU, Mrs. YinMin, ACA *2011;* 12th/ F 7th building, No.16 Xi Si Huan Zhong Road, Hai Dian District, BEIJING 100039, CHINA.

LIU, Mr. Yu Keung Patrick, ACA *2007;* Flat D5/FBlock 5, Fu Ho Yuen, Chi Fu Fa Yuen, POK FU LAM, HONG KONG ISLAND, HONG KONG SAR.

LIU, Mr. Yuk Tung Thomas, ACA *2004;* Room 1910-12A, Tower 3, China Hong Kong City, 33 Canton Road, TSIM SHA TSUI, KOWLOON HONG KONG SAR.

•LIU, Mr. Yun-Bonn, BCom FCA *1993;* KPMG, 8/F Prince's Building, 10 Chater Road, CENTRAL, HONG KONG ISLAND, HONG KONG SAR.

LIU, Mr. Yung Yin, ACA *2008;* Flat 6B 6/F, Tower 1, Tivoli Garden, 75 Tsing King Road, TSING YI, NEW TERRITORIES HONG KONG SAR.

LIU, Ms. Zhuoqin, ACA *2010;* 15-262BeijingqingnianchengHongjunying East RoadChaoyang District, BEIJING 100012, CHINA.

LIVADIOTOU, Miss. Eliza, MA ACA *1999;* 7 Iolis street, Strovolos, 2029 NICOSIA, CYPRUS.

•LIVER, Mr. John Robert, MA ACA *1991;* Ernst & Young LLP, 1 More London Place, LONDON, SE1 2AF. See also Ernst & Young Europe LLP

LIVERA, Miss. Evita, BSc ACA *2004;* Amfitritis 33, Flat 503, Akropoli, NICOSIA, CYPRUS.

LIVERMORE, Mrs. Janet May, BA ACA *1979;* 601 First Street South, Unit 6F, JACKSONVILLE BEACH, FL 32250, UNITED STATES.

LIVERMORE, Mr. Michael Raymond, BA ACA *1991;* 13 Colyers Lane, ERITH, KENT, DA8 3NG.

LIVERSEDGE, Mr. John Paul Miller, BSc ACA *1992;* Wine Cellars International AG, Im Junker 8, CH-8143 STALLIKON, SWITZERLAND.

LIVESEY, Mr. Anthony, FCA *1963;* 7 St Benets Close, Walton-le-Dale, PRESTON, PR5 4UT.

LIVESEY, Mr. Brian Thomas Edward, BSc FCA *1972;* Les Reveaux, Route Des Sages, St. Pierre Du Bois, GUERNSEY, GY7 9DG. (Life Member)

•①LIVESEY, Mr. Craig Anthony, BA FCA *1992;* The Beech Glade, 11 Hallside Park, KNUTSFORD, WA16 8NQ.

LIVESEY, Mr. Edward Michael, FCA *1970;* 1 Calluna Drive, Copthorne, CRAWLEY, WEST SUSSEX, RH10 3XE. (Life Member)

LIVESEY, Miss. Gwendoline Ann, BSc ACA *1987;* (Tax Fac), with Grant Thornton UK LLP, 3140 Rowan Place, John Smith Drive, Oxford Business Park South, OXFORD, OX4 2WB.

LIVESEY, Mr. James Edward, BA ACA *2005;* Theodorenstrasse 15, 65189 WIESBADEN, GERMANY.

LIVESEY, Mr. John Richard Bottomley, BA FCA CA(SA) *1970;* David Brown Gear Industries, (Pty) Ltd, P.O. Box 540, BENONI, GAUTENG, 1500 SOUTH AFRICA.

LIVESEY, Miss. Julie, ACA *2011;* 2 Sunningdale Place, Inskip, PRESTON, PR4 0UB.

LIVESEY, Mr. Kevin Francis, MA FCA *1960;* 6 Blackhouse Farm, Coldharbour Lane, EGHAM, SURREY, TW20 8TG. (Life Member)

LIVESEY, Mr. Nicholas Andrew John, BA(Hons) FCA *2000;* Sydney Airport Corporation Limited, Locked Bag 5000, Sydney International Airport, SYDNEY, NSW 2020, AUSTRALIA.

LIVESEY, Mrs. Raffaella Maria, BSc FCA *1991;* Beech Holme, 49 Wellington Road, Timperley, ALTRINCHAM, WA15 7RQ.

LIVESEY, Mr. Stephen Alan, MA ACA *1989;* (Member of Council 2005 - 2011), D.A.T.A. Services Limited, 1 Coates Place, EDINBURGH, EH3 7AA.

•LIVESLEY, Mr. Robert, BCom FCA *1962;* R. Livesley BCom FCA, 25 Groveland Road, WALLASEY, MERSEYSIDE, CH45 8JY.

•LIVETT, Mr. David George, FCA *1976;* 36 Grosvenor Road, Petts Wood, ORPINGTON, BR5 1QU.

LIVETT, Mr. John Adam, BSc ACA *1993;* Adventurize.com, 181 Rea Avenue, EL CAJON, CA 92020, UNITED STATES.

LIVETT, Mr. Leonard George, FCA *1954;* 87 Riverside Court, Victoria Road, Saltaire, SHIPLEY, BD18 3LZ. (Life Member)

LIVINGS, Mr. Simon, BA ACA *2002;* The Corn Mill, 19 Mill Court, Alvechurch, BIRMINGHAM, WEST MIDLANDS, B48 7JY.

•LIVINGSTON, Mr. Brian Keith, LLB ACA CF *1986;* Smith & Williamson Ltd, 25 Moorgate, LONDON, EC2R 6AY.

LIVINGSTON, Mr. Christopher, BSc ACA *2006;* Coventry Bldg Soc Godiva House, Binley Business Park Harry Weston Road, COVENTRY, CV3 2TB.

LIVINGSTON, Mr. Ian Paul, BA ACA *1987;* 35 Barham Avenue, Elstree, BOREHAMWOOD, HERTFORDSHIRE, WD6 3PW.

LIVINGSTON, Mr. John, FCA *1966;* 92 Tiddington Road, STRATFORD-UPON-AVON, CV37 7BA.

LIVINGSTON, Mr. Jonathan Richard, FCA *1976;* P.O.Box 583, LONEHILL, 2062, SOUTH AFRICA.

•LIVINGSTON, Mr. Steven Charles, LLB ACA *2001;* (Tax Fac), Crowe Clark Whitehill LLP, Arkwright House, Parsonage Gardens, MANCHESTER, M3 2HP. See also Horwath Clark Whitehill LLP and Crowe Clark Whitehill

LIVINGSTON-BOOTH, Mr. Julian Ashley, BSc ACA *1998;* Goldman Sachs, Peterborough Court, 133 Fleet Street, LONDON, EC4A 2BB.

LO, Mr. Wai Chung, ACA *2007;* 39C Block 5, Beverly Garden, TSEUNG KWAN O, NEW TERRITORIES, HONG KONG SAR.

LO, Mr. Wai Ho, ACA *2005;* Flat 3 Block C, 21/F Imperial Court, 62G Conduit Road, MID LEVELS, HONG KONG ISLAND, HONG KONG SAR.

LO, Ms. Wai Mei, ACA *2008;* 4th Floor, Flat E, Block 11, Tsuen King Garden, TSUEN WAN, NEW TERRITORIES HONG KONG SAR.

LO, Mr. Wai On, ACA *2007;* W.O. Lo & Co, Room 1901-2, Park-In Commercial Centre, 56 Dundas Street, MONG KOK, KOWLOON HONG KONG SAR.

LO, Mr. Wing Hung, ACA *2004;* Room 2601 26th Floor, China Insurance Group Building, 141 Des Voeux Road, CENTRAL, HONG KONG ISLAND, HONG KONG SAR.

LO, Mr. Wing Sang, ACA *2008;* Room 1709, Hong Ying Court, LAM TIN, KOWLOON, HONG KONG SAR.

LO, Miss. Ying Kwan, ACA *2011;* 4th Floor, 304 Prince Edward Road West, KOWLOON CITY, KOWLOON, HONG KONG SAR.

LO CASCIO, Mrs. Mary, BSc ACA *1985;* 13 Chain O Ponds Circuit, The Cascades, MT ANNAN, NSW 2567, AUSTRALIA.

•LO NENG FONG, Mr. Lo Kee Than, FCA *1975;* Chris Lo, 23 Rowsley Avenue, LONDON, NW4 1AP.

LO SEEN CHONG, Mr. Deans Tommy, BSc FCA *1986;* (Tax Fac), Baker Tilly Mauritius, Level 3, Alexander House, 35 Cybercity, EBENE, MAURITIUS. See also Alliance Associates

LO SEEN CHONG, Mr. Teddy, ACA *1992;* level 3 Alexander House, 35 Cybercity, EBENE, MAURITIUS.

LO TIAP KONG, Mr. Voon Tat, BSc ACA *2010;* #01-03 Tower 3, Seasons Park, 495 Yio Chu Kang Road, SINGAPORE 787080, SINGAPORE.

LOACH, Dr. Simon Charles, ACA *1991;* 37b Cannon Street, Little Downham, ELY, CAMBRIDGESHIRE, CB6 2SS.

LOADER, Mr. Francis Roy, FCA JDipMA *1952;* (Member of Council 1979 - 1985), 1 Beechnut Lane, SOLIHULL, B91 2NN. (Life Member)

LOADER, Mrs. Jane Morag, MA ACIB FCA CTA *1996;* 57 Chiltern Road, SUTTON, SM2 5QU.

•LOADER, Mrs. Linda Marion, BSc ACA *1995;* LML Accounting Solutions, Copse Cottage, Pondcopse Lane, Loxwood, BILLINGSHURST, WEST SUSSEX RH14 0XF.

LOADER, Mr. Nicholas Paul, BSc ACA *1987;* Galloway, 43 Castle Lane, Chandler's Ford, EASTLEIGH, SO53 4AH.

LOADER, Mr. Richard Edwin, BSc FCA *1984;* 4 The Drive, Amenbury Lane, HARPENDEN, AL5 2EL.

LOADER, Mr. Robert James, BSc ACA *1993;* 11 Monmouth Way, HONITON, EX14 2GY.

LOADER, Mrs. Suzanne Carol, BA ACA *1995;* 129 Hitchings Way, REIGATE, RH2 8EP.

LOADMAN, Mrs. Cindy-Ann Michelle, MA BA ACA *2005;* 10616 Rutledge Street, PARKER, CO 80134, UNITED STATES.

•LOAKE, Mr. Richard Ashwell, FCA *1975;* (Tax Fac), 20 Vaillant Road, Oatlands Drive, WEYBRIDGE, SURREY, KT13 9EP.

LOAN, Mrs. Nicola Karen, MA ACA *1997;* 151 Gurney Court Road, ST. ALBANS, HERTFORDSHIRE, AL1 4QY.

LOARING, Miss. Rachel Victoria, BSc ACA *1999;* 63 Sheepfold Road, GUILDFORD, SURREY, GU2 9TT.

LOAT, Mr. Clarence Horatio, FCA *1941;* Flat 2, Leyton Conyers, 3 Martello Park, Canford Cliffs, POOLE, DORSET BH13 7BA. (Life Member)

LOAT, Mrs. Isabel Emma, BA ACA *1979;* 65 Bourne Street, LONDON, SW1W 8JW.

LOBATTO, Mr. Ralph, FCA *1954;* 9 Manor Court, Common Lane, RADLETT, HERTFORDSHIRE, WD7 8PU. (Life Member)

LOBB, Miss. Alison Margaret Jane, BA ACA *1998;* with Deloitte LLP, 2 New Street Square, LONDON, EC4A 3BZ.

LOBB, Mr. Damian James, BA ACA *2007;* 35 Wallace Road, LONDON, N1 2PQ.

LOBB, Mr. Gareth Warwick, ACA CA(NZ) *2010;* Flat 2, 124 Sutherland Avenue, Maida Vale, LONDON, W9 2QP.

LOBB, Mrs. Laura Katharine, BEng ACA *1995;* 112 Stevedore St, WILLIAMSTOWN, VIC 3016, AUSTRALIA.

LOBB, Mr. Martin James, BSc ACA *1995;* Australia Post, Level 12, 111 Bourke Street, MELBOURNE, VIC 3000, AUSTRALIA.

•LOBB, Mr. Philip Mark, BA FCA *1984;* Deloitte LLP, Athene Place, 66 Shoe Lane, LONDON, EC4A 3BQ. See also Deloitte & Touche LLP

LOBB, Mrs. Rosemary Esther, BA ACA *2007;* 35 Wallace Road, LONDON, N1 2PQ.

LOBB, Mr. Stuart James, ACA CA(NZ) *2010;* The Lodge, 45 Inner Park Road, Wimbledon, LONDON, SW19 6DF.

LOBBAN, Mr. James Mark, BA ACA *2000;* 149 Elborough Street, LONDON, SW18 5DS.

•LOBBENBERG, Mr. Peter, MA FCA *1966;* (Tax Fac), Peter Lobbenberg & Co, 74 Chancery Lane, LONDON, WC2A 1AD.

LOBLEY, Mr. David Paul, BEng ACA *1994;* Group 4 Securicor, The Manor, Manor Royal, CRAWLEY, WEST SUSSEX, RH10 9UN.

LOBLEY, Mr. John Francis, ACA *1980;* 41st Floor Tower 42, 25 Old Broad Street, LONDON, EC2N 1HQ.

LOBLEY, Mrs. Julie Alison, BSc ACA *1990;* 10 Turners Gardens, SEVENOAKS, KENT, TN13 1QE.

LOBLEY, Mr. Samuel David, BA(Hons) ACA *2003;* with PricewaterhouseCoopers, 2 Southbank Boulevard, Southbank, MELBOURNE, VIC 3006, AUSTRALIA.

•LOBO, Mr. Anthony, BSc ACA *1996;* KPMG LLP, 15 Canada Square, LONDON, E14 5GL. See also KPMG Europe LLP

LOBO, Ms. Lydia Mary Isis, PhD MA MSci DIC ACA *2010;* 96a Greyhound Road, LONDON, W6 8NT.

•LOBO, Mrs. Margaret Dawn, BA ACA *1988;* M D Lobo Limited, 118 Radford Road, LEAMINGTON SPA, WARWICKSHIRE, CV31 1LF.

LOBO, Mr. Mark, BSc ACA *2011;* 34 Coppice Road, Woodley, READING, RG5 3QX.

LOBO, Mr. Sunil Mario, MEng ACA *1992;* 1 Foresters Close, WALLINGTON, SURREY, SM6 9DH.

LOBUE, Mr. Roberto, BSc ACA *2003;* Flat 7 St. Clements House, 33-45 Church Street, WALTON-ON-THAMES, KT12 2QN.

•LOCAL, Miss. Colleen, BSc ACA *2002;* with PricewaterhouseCoopers LLP, 7 More London Riverside, LONDON, SE1 2RT.

LOCH, Mr. James Hugh Gordon, FCA *1965;* Tallow Chandlers Company, 4 Dowgate Hill, LONDON, EC4R 2SH.

LOCHAN, Mr. Frank Neville Charrington, MSc MTax FCA *1967;* 228 Lakewood Drive, OAKVILLE L6K 1B2, ON, CANADA.

•LOCHEAD, Mr. Brian Gerard, BA FCA *1990;* PricewaterhouseCoopers LLP, Pricewaterhousecoopers, 12 Plumtree Court, LONDON, EC4A 4HT. See also PricewaterhouseCoopers

•LOCK, Mr. Andrew David, ACA *1993;* A Lock & Co Limited, Elmwood House, York Road, Kirk Hammerton, YORK, YO26 8DH. See also Positive Accountants

LOCK, Mr. Anthony John, BA FCA *1974;* East Malling Research, New Road, East Malling, WEST MALLING, KENT, ME19 6BJ.

LOCK, Mr. Christopher John, FCA *1955;* 8 The Oarchard, 12 Balcombe Road, POOLE, DORSET, BH13 6DY. (Life Member)

•LOCK, Mr. Cyril John, BA FCA *1962;* (Tax Fac), Lock & Co, Silverwood, Withyham Rd, Groombridge, TUNBRIDGE WELLS, TN3 9QR.

LOCK, Mr. David James, BA ACA *1991;* 83 Onslow Road, RICHMOND, SURREY, TW10 6QA.

•LOCK, Mr. David Paul, BSc ACA *1999;* HW Corporate Finance LLP, 7-11 Station Road, READING, BERKSHIRE, RG1 1LG.

LOCK, Mr. Ian Russell, BEng FCA *1990;* Sheahan Lock Partners, Level 8, 26 Flinders Street, ADELAIDE, SA 5000, AUSTRALIA.

LOCK, Mr. Jason David, BSc ACA *1996;* Affinity Healthcare Middleton St. George Hospital, Durham Tees Valley Airport, DARLINGTON, COUNTY DURHAM, DL2 1TS.

LOCK, Mrs. Joanna Sin Chuen, BSc(Hons) ACA *2001;* 14 South Dene, BRISTOL, BS9 2BW.

LOCK, Mr. John Frederick, FCA *1957;* 1 Grove Croft Hampton-on-the-Hill, WARWICK, CV35 8RJ. (Life Member)

LOCK, Mr. John Michael, FCA *1959;* Little Lypiatt Farm, Neston, CORSHAM, SN13 9TR. (Life Member)

LOCK, Mr. John William, FCA *1960;* Four Seasons, Littlewick Road, Knaphill, WOKING, GU21 2JX. (Life Member)

LOCK, Mrs. Margaret, ACA *2004;* 9 Somerset Road, NEWPORT, NP19 7FZ.

•LOCK, Mr. Martin Peter, BSc FCA *1990;* Francis Clark, 9 The Crescent, TAUNTON, SOMERSET, TA1 4EA. See also Francis Clark LLP

•LOCK, Mr. Michael Derrick, FCA *1964;* (Tax Fac), The Garth, Wood Lane, STANMORE, HA7 4JZ.

LOCK, Miss. Naomi Melissa, ACA *2008;* Experian 6th Floor Cardinal Place, 80 Victoria Street, LONDON, SW1E 5JL.

LOCK, Mr. Paul Robert Henry, FCA *1960;* 7 Albion Street, LONDON, W2 2AS.

LOCK, Mr. Peter Jeremy, FCA *1979;* First Equity Ltd Salisbury House, London Wall, LONDON, EC2M 5QQ.

•LOCK, Mr. Richard Alan, FCA *1968;* (Tax Fac), R A Lock & Co, 256 Old Church Road, Chingford, LONDON, E4 8BT.

LOCK, Mr. Richard Anthony, ACA *1980;* 69 Hollywoods, Courtwood Lane, CROYDON, CR0 9JJ.

•LOCK, Mr. Richard Sinclair, BSc FCA *1985;* Unit 1 333 Ernest Street, NEUTRAL BAY, NSW 2089, AUSTRALIA.

LOCK, Mr. Richard Stephen, MSc FCA DChA *1990;* YMCA England, 45 Beech Street, LONDON, EC2Y 8AD.

•LOCK, Mr. Robert Adrian, FCA *1974;* Wise & Co, Wey Court West, Union Road, FARNHAM, SURREY, GU9 7PT. See also Firmvalue Payrolls Ltd

LOCK, Mr. Roger Brian, FCA *1963;* 40 Linden Park, SHAFTESBURY, DORSET, SP7 8QZ.

LOCK, Mr. Stephen John, BA FCA *1973;* 28 Froghall Drive, WOKINGHAM, RG40 2LF.

LOCK, Mr. Thomas William, FCA *1967;* 8 River View, Stainburn, WORKINGTON, CUMBRIA, CA14 1SR. (Life Member)

LOCK, Mr. Timothy Stuart, BSc ACA *2000;* 25 Rylestone Grove, BRISTOL, BS9 3UT.

•LOCK, Mrs. Toni Marie, ACA *2008;* 2 Westfield Drive, Woodley, STOCKPORT, CHESHIRE, SK6 1LD.

LOCKE, Mr. Anthony Edward, ACA *1981;* 12 Station Road, Helmdon, BRACKLEY, NN13 5QT.

LOCKE, Mr. Anthony Paul, FCA *1962;* Apartamento 6A Edificio, Palm Beach, Pasao Maritimo, Los Bolches, Fuengirola, 29640 MALAGA SPAIN.

LOCKE, Mr. Charles Henry, FCA *1939;* 318 Hill Lane, SOUTHAMPTON, SO15 7NW. (Life Member)

•LOCKE, Mr. Christopher Baden, BA FCA *1977;* Locke Williams Associates LLP, Blackthorn House, St Paul's Square, BIRMINGHAM, B3 1RL.

LOCKE, Mr. Christopher John, BEng BCom ACA *2001;* with Ernst & Young LLP, 1 More London Place, LONDON, SE1 2AF.

LOCKE, Ms. Claire Rosemary, ACA *1989;* 49 Pittwater Road, HUNTERS HILL, NSW 2110, AUSTRALIA.

LOCKE, Mr. Daron Martin, BSc ACA *1990;* The Hawthorns, Naseby, NORTHAMPTON, NN6 6DA.

LOCKE, Mr. David, MA(Hons) MSt ACA *2009;* 38 Jubilee Road, NEWBURY, BERKSHIRE, RG14 7NN.

•LOCKE, Mr. David Alexander, BA FCA *1983;* DA Locke & Co, 3 Flaxen Field, Weston Turville, AYLESBURY, BUCKINGHAMSHIRE, HP22 5GJ.

LOCKE, Mr. David James, ACA *2008;* 25 Chichele Road, OXTED, RH8 0AE.

LOCKE, Mr. David James, BA FCA CISA *1991;* BMS World Mission, PO Box 49, 129 Broadway, DIDCOT, OXFORDSHIRE, OX11 8XA.

LOCKE, Ms. Elizabeth Theresa, ACA *2010;* 31 Wincrofts Drive, LONDON, SE9 2RG.

LOCKE, Mrs. Heather Louise, BSc ACA *1999;* 2 Gardners Drive, Hullavington, CHIPPENHAM, SN14 6EL.

LOCKE, Mr. Jonathan Charles, BA ACA *1990;* Privredna Banka Zagreb, Radnicka 44, 10000 ZAGREB, CROATIA.

•LOCKE, Mrs. Mary Elizabeth, ACA *1983;* (Tax Fac), Mary E. Locke, 3 Flaxen Field, Weston Turville, AYLESBURY, BUCKINGHAMSHIRE, HP22 5GJ.

LOCKE, Mr. Peter Nigel, MA FCA *1972;* Flat 36, Sirius Building, Atlantic Wharf, 3 Jardine Road, LONDON, E1W 3WE. (Life Member)

LOCKE, Mrs. Petra Briony, BA ACA *1991;* 5 Lawn Road, STAFFORD, STAFFORDSHIRE, ST17 9AJ.

LOCKE, Mr. Philip Christopher, FCA *1962;* Eastlands, Idsworth, WATERLOOVILLE, PO8 0AL. (Life Member)

LOCKE, Mr. Steven David, ACA *2010;* 21 Devon Road, Stowupland, STOWMARKET, SUFFOLK, IP14 4BZ.

LOCKEN, Miss. Emma Louise, BSc ACA *2003;* 69 Muggeridge Close, SOUTH CROYDON, SURREY, CR2 7LB.

LOCKER, Miss. Hazel Marie, BA ACA *2006;* 38 Sandstone Drive, Whiston, PRESCOT, MERSEYSIDE, L35 7NJ.

LOCKERBIE, Mr. Charles Brydon David, BA ACA *1990;* 9 St Heliers Avenue, HOVE, BN3 5RE. (Life Member)

•LOCKETT, Mr. Derek Ian, BSc FCA *1985;* Business Support Matters Limited, 1 Pottery Yard, Liverton, NEWTON ABBOT, DEVON, TQ12 6LR.

•LOCKETT, Mr. Peter Graham Francis, MA FCA *1972;* 8 Park Road, Thornbury, BRISTOL, BS35 1HN.

LOCKEY, Mr. Anthony David, BA ACA *1985;* 3 Cherry Orchard, Epworth, DONCASTER, DN9 1TR.

•LOCKEY, Mr. Eric, FCA *1980;* (Tax Fac), Henn & Westwood, Rumbow House, Rumbow, HALESOWEN, B63 3HU.

LOCKEY, Mrs. Julie, BSc ACA *1996;* 9 Beswick Brook Close, STOKE-ON-TRENT, ST2 7QE.

LOCKEY, Mr. Keith, BSc ACA *1983;* with KPMG, 147 Collins Street, MELBOURNE, VIC 3000, AUSTRALIA.

LOCKEY, Miss. Valerie Kay, BA ACA *2003;* 12 Lavender Row, Darley Abbey, DERBY, DE22 1DF.

LOCKHART, Mrs. Beth Suzanne, BA ACA *2003;* 2 Calderpark Court, Uddingston, GLASGOW, G71 7RL.

LOCKHART, Miss. Christina Helen, MSc ACA *1989;* 38 Chestnut Drive, Kingswood, MAIDSTONE, KENT, ME17 3PP.

LOCKHART, Mr. Dean Lee, BA ACA *2004;* 3 Aurelia Court, MOTHERWELL, LANARKSHIRE, ML1 1EH.

LOCKHART, Mr. Geoffrey John Charles, FCA *1951;* (Member of Council 1977 - 1989), Chandlers, Nayland, COLCHESTER, CO6 4LA. (Life Member)

LOCKHART, Miss. Laura, ACA *2007;* 40 Plumtree Avenue, Wear View Estate, SUNDERLAND, SR5 5TX.

LOCKHART, Mr. Mark Robert, BSc FCA DChA *1984;* Westway Development Trust, 1 Thorpe Close, LONDON, W10 5XL.

LOCKHART-WHITE, Mrs. Sarah Louise, BA ACA CTA *1990;* The Hawthorns, Church Road, Beyton, BURY ST. EDMUNDS, IP30 9AL.

LOCKIE, Miss. Jillian, BA ACA *1999;* Scottishpower, 1 Atlantic Quay Robertson Street, GLASGOW, G2 8SP.

LOCKIE, Mr. Malcolm Thomas, BSc ACA *1993;* 463 Crown Street, SURRY HILLS, NSW 2010, AUSTRALIA.

LOCKING, Mr. James, BA ACA *1998;* A4e Ltd, 105 Queen Street, SHEFFIELD, S1 1GN.

LOCKING, Mr. Jason Paul, LLB ACA *2001;* 11 Flint Way, Eynesbury, ST. NEOTS, CAMBRIDGESHIRE, PE19 2RU.

LOCKLEY, Mr. Donald Osborne, FCA *1951;* 89 Whitchurch Road, CHESTER, CH3 5QD. (Life Member)

LOCKLEY, Mrs. Emily Kate, BSc ACA *2003;* 22 Lakewood Road, BRISTOL, BS10 5HH.

LOCKLEY, Mr. Mark Alexander, BCom ACA *1991;* Rose Cottage, Walcote, ALCESTER, WARWICKSHIRE, B49 6LZ.

LOCKLEY, Mr. Oliver James, BSc ACA *2004;* with Deloitte LLP, Horton House, Exchange Flags, LIVERPOOL, L2 3PG.

LOCKLEY, Mr. Stephen John, BSc FCA *1983;* Hilltrees, 30 Albion Park, LOUGHTON, ESSEX, IG10 4RB.

LOCKLEY, Mr. Stuart, BSc ACA *1986;* 8 Cranmere Avenue, Tettenhall, WOLVERHAMPTON, WV6 8TS.

LOCKLEY, Miss. Tinha, ACA *1984;* West Kent Primary Care Trust Wharf House, Medway Wharf Road, TONBRIDGE, TN9 1RE.

•LOCKS, Mr. John George Melbourne, FCA *1971;* (Tax Fac), J Locks Limited, 18 Willowmead, HERTFORD, SG14 2AT.

LOCKTON, Mr. Geoffrey Charles, FCA *1975;* Ashcombe, 11 Wych Lane, Adlington, MACCLESFIELD, SK10 4NB.

LOCKWOOD, Mrs. Alison Rae, BSc ACA *1996;* Santander Capital House, 2 Bruntcliffe Way Morley, LEEDS, LS27 0JG.

LOCKWOOD, Mr. Benjamin, BA ACA *2003;* 15 Nichols Road, Portishead, BRISTOL, BS20 8DT.

LOCKWOOD, Mrs. Carolina Anna Pablietta, BA ACA *1988;* West of England Ship Owners Mutual Ins Association, 33 Boulevard Prince Henri, L1724 LUXEMBOURG, LUXEMBOURG.

LOCKWOOD, Mr. David Charles, OBE BA ACA FRSA *1988;* Temple Belwood, 12 Bayards, WARLINGHAM, SURREY, CR6 9BP.

LOCKWOOD, Mr. David William, FCA *1962;* 21 Hazelwood Grove, WORKSOP, S80 3EW. (Life Member)

•LOCKWOOD, Mrs. Diane Jeanette, ACA FCCA ATT *2008;* Ling Phipp, Cliffe Hill House, 22-26 Nottingham Road, Stapleford, NOTTINGHAM, NG9 8AA.

•LOCKWOOD, Mr. Geoffrey Alexander, BA ACA *1990;* Ashgroves, 14 Albert Street, Douglas, ISLE OF MAN, IM1 2QA.

LOCKWOOD, Mrs. Gillian Ai Lian, LLM FCA CTA *1975;* Flat 48, Angel House, 20-32 Pentonville Road, LONDON, N1 9HJ.

LOCKWOOD, Mrs. Juliette Simone Jane, BA ACA *1995;* 30 Walker Road, MAIDENHEAD, SL6 2QT.

LOCKWOOD, Mr. Justin Ashley, BSc ACA *1996;* Beech House, Station Road, Church Fenton, LEEDS, LS24 9RA.

LOCKWOOD, Mr. Lee Van, ACA *2008;* Begbies Traynor, 9 Bond Court, LEEDS, LS1 2JZ.

LOCKWOOD, Mr. Mark, BSc(Hons) ACA *2011;* 14 Muirfield Avenue, DONCASTER, SOUTH YORKSHIRE, DN4 6UP.

LOCKWOOD, Mr. Mark Howard, BA ACA *1985;* 45 Valentines Meadow, Cottam, PRESTON, PR4 0LF.

LOCKWOOD, Mr. Martin, FCA *1974;* 4 Bank Terrace, Terrace Road, Tideswell, BUXTON, DERBYSHIRE, SK17 8LY.

LOCKWOOD, Miss. Michelle, BSc ACA *1991;* 15 Prospect Close, Bramley, ROTHERHAM, S66 1TX.
LOCKWOOD, Miss. Natalie Elizabeth, BA(Hons) ACA *2010;* K P M G Edward VII Quay, Navigation Way Ashton-on-Ribble, PRESTON, PR2 2YF.
•LOCKWOOD, Miss. Rachel Mary, BSc(Hons) ACA *2002;* Oury Clark, PO Box 150, Herschel House, 58 Herschel Street, SLOUGH, SL1 1HD.
LOCKWOOD, Mr. Richard David, FCA *1970;* 4 Hermitage Park, Fenay Bridge, HUDDERSFIELD, HD8 0JU.
LOCKWOOD, Mr. Robert, MEng ACA *2010;* Flat 25, 22 St. James's Road, LONDON, SE16 4QJ.
LOCKWOOD, Mr. Robert David, MA FCA *1978;* Dynex Semiconducter Ltd, Doddington Road, LINCOLN, LN6 3LF.
LOCKWOOD, Mr. Robert Michael, BA ACA *1998;* 6 Milner Road, Sherwood, NOTTINGHAM, NG5 2ES.
LOCKWOOD, Mrs. Sarah Elizabeth, BAcc ACA *1999;* 6 Milner Road, NOTTINGHAM, NG5 2ES.
•LOCKWOOD, Mr. Stephen, FCA *1973;* Stephen Lockwood, Swallow Barn, Manor Road, Stutton, TADCASTER, NORTH YORKSHIRE LS24 9BR.
LOCKWOOD, Mr. Stephen John, BSc ACA *1990;* Red Roofs, 77 Putnoe Lane, Putnoe, BEDFORD, MK41 9AE.
LOCKWOOD, Miss. Victoria, BA ACA *2009;* The Old Rectory, St. Marys Street, AXBRIDGE, SOMERSET, BS26 2BN.
LOCKWOOD, Mr. William John, FCA *1975;* Micklethorn, Broughton, SKIPTON, BD23 3JA.
LOCKYEAR, Mr. Graham William, BSc FCA *1995;* Clere Futures Ltd, Harts Lane, Burghclere, NEWBURY, BERKSHIRE, RG20 9HF.
•LOCKYEAR, Mr. John Malcolm Weldon, BA ACA *1984;* 6 Normanby Chase, ALTRINCHAM, CHESHIRE, WA14 4QP.
LOCKYER, Mr. Brian Frederick, FCA *1961;* 24 Convent CLose, Little Haywood, STAFFORD, ST18 0QU.
LOCKYER, Mr. David Graham, BA FCA *1989;* with Albert Goodman LLP, Mary Street House, Mary Street, TAUNTON, TA1 3NW.
LOCKYER, Mr. James Edmund Braithwaite, BSc ACA *1989;* Brookhampton Farm, Brookhampton, Kineton, WARWICK, CV35 0NR.
LOCKYER, Ms. Karen Marie, BA(Hons) ACA *2001;* 76 Hazelwood Drive, VERWOOD, DORSET, BH31 6YQ.
LOCKYER, Mr. Kevin, ACA *1991;* 360 Hope Hollow Road, LOGANVILLE, GA 30052, UNITED STATES.
•LOCKYER, Mr. Peter, FCA *1969;* Trood Pratt & Co, GPO Box 3437, SYDNEY, NSW 1043, AUSTRALIA.
LOCKYER, Mr. Richard James Robert, BA ACA *1988;* Oberdorfstr 38, CH 6340 BAAR, SWITZERLAND.
LOCKYER, Mr. Stephen Charles, BEng ACA *1992;* 14 Bryn Rhosyn Radyr, CARDIFF, CF15 8RN.
LOCKYER, Mr. Stephen John, ACA *1986;* 87 Queens Road, HINCKLEY, LE10 1ED.
•LODDER, Mr. Richard Stuart Degge, LLB ACA *2001;* Springwood, Warwick Road, Chadwick End, SOLIHULL, WEST MIDLANDS, B93 0BP.
LODER, Miss. Jean Alice, FCA *1959;* Apartment 137 Westfield, 15 Kidderpore Avenue, LONDON, NW3 7SJ. (Life Member)
LODGE, Miss. Angela, BSc ACA *2011;* 24 Casterbridge Road, Blackheath, LONDON, SE3 9AH.
LODGE, Mrs. Angela Janet, BCom ACA *1987;* 107 Dorridge Road, Dorridge, SOLIHULL, B93 8BP.
LODGE, Mrs. Carmel, BA ACA *1993;* 7 Juniper Close, Penwortham, PRESTON, PR1 0PH.
LODGE, Mrs. Catherine Mary, BSc ACA *1996;* c/o jumeirah English Speaking School, PO Box 24942, DUBAI, UNITED ARAB EMIRATES.
LODGE, Mr. David John, FCA *1986;* Weald Cottage, Mill Lane, Sissinghurst, CRANBROOK, TN17 2HX.
LODGE, Mr. David Robert, BSc FCA *1989;* Brakes Enterprise House, Nicholas Road Eureka Science Park, ASHFORD, TN25 4AG.
LODGE, Mr. David William, FCA *1965;* 19 Windermere Drive, Great Notley, BRAINTREE, ESSEX, CM77 7UB.
LODGE, Mr. Eric Arnold, MSc BSocSc ACA *1990;* The Old Manse, 31 Bilston Street, Sedgley, DUDLEY, DY3 1JA.
•LODGE, Mr. Graham John, FCA *1968;* (Tax Fac), Graham J. Lodge & Co, 12 Main Road, Brookville, THETFORD, IP26 4RB.
LODGE, Mrs. Helen Claire, BA(Hons) ACA *2001;* Inhealth Group Beechwood Hall, Kingsmead Road, HIGH WYCOMBE, BUCKINGHAMSHIRE, HP11 1JL.
•LODGE, Ms. Jane Ann, BSc FCA *1979;* Crossbrook House Dusthouse Lane, Finstall, BROMSGROVE, WORCESTERSHIRE, B60 3AE.
LODGE, Mrs. Karen Louise, BSc ACA *1993;* 30 Hillcrest Road, PURLEY, CR8 2JE.
LODGE, Mrs. Katherine Ann, BSc ACA *1992;* Old Schoolhouse, Duns Road, Gifford, HADDINGTON, EH41 4QW.
LODGE, Mr. Martyn Joseph, BA(Hons) ACA *2002;* Lodge Tyre Co Ltd, 25-29 Lord Street, BIRMINGHAM, B7 4DE.
LODGE, Mr. Michael James, BSc ACA *1993;* Lodge Bros (Funerals) Ltd, Ludlow House, Ludlow Road, FELTHAM, TW13 7JF.
LODGE, Mr. Oliver James, MEng ACA *2004;* with National Audit Office, 157-197 Buckingham Palace Road, Victoria, LONDON, SW1W 9SP.
LODGE, Mr. Peter John, FCA *1964;* Reedmere House, Redmire, LEYBURN, NORTH YORKSHIRE, DL8 4ES.
LODGE, Mr. Philip Charles, FCA *1945;* Harwood, The Green, Goathland, WHITBY, YO22 5LX.
•LODGE, Mr. Richard Stanley, FCA *1961;* 1720 Hunters Run, OTTAWA K1C 6V9, ON, CANADA. See also Andrews & Associe CA SENC
LODGE, Mr. Simon Blakey, BA ACA *1991;* 30 Hillcrest Road, PURLEY, CR8 2JE.
•LODGE, Mr. Stuart Bernard, FCA *1967;* Stuart B. Lodge & Co, 44 Bradford Road, Idle, BRADFORD, BD10 9PE.
LODGE, Mr. Toby Daniel, BSc(Hons) ACA *2001;* (Tax Fac), 64 Queens Road, WHITSTABLE, CT5 2JG.
•LODGE, Mr. Trevor Drabes, FCA *1971;* (Tax Fac), Robertshaw Myers, Number 3, Acorn Business Park, Keighley Road, SKIPTON, NORTH YORKSHIRE BD23 2UE. See also Robertshaw & Myers
LODHI, Mr. Imran, BSc ACA *2011;* 11061 Oakridge Drive, FISHERS, IN 46038, UNITED STATES.
•LODHIA, Mr. Virendra Dhirajlal, BA FCA *1996;* PricewaterhouseCoopers LLP, Donington Court, Pegasus Business Park, Castle Donington, DERBY, DE74 2UZ. See also PricewaterhouseCoopers
•LODI-FE, Mr. Michele, FCA *1986;* KPMG Slovensko, Dvorakovo nabrezie 10, P. O. Box 7, 811 02 BRATISLAVA, SLOVAK REPUBLIC.
LODY, Mrs. Philippa Jane Goddard, BSc ACA *1997;* 24 Weyhill Gardens, Weyhill, ANDOVER, SP11 0QT.
•LOE, Mrs. Penelope Sara, BA ACA *1991;* (Tax Fac), P.S. Loe & Co., Edgecombe, Amberley, STROUD, GLOUCESTERSHIRE, GL5 5AB.
LOEB, Mr. Jeremy Ian, BSc ACA *1982;* 11 Hoober Road, Ecclesfield, SHEFFIELD, S11 9SF.
LOEBELL, Miss. Claire Marie, BA ACA *2006;* with Ernst & Young, Genesis Building, P.O. Box 510, GEORGE TOWN, GRAND CAYMAN, KY1 -1106 CAYMAN ISLANDS.
•LOEBL, Mr. John Charles, BA ACA CTA *1987;* (Tax Fac), Grant Thornton UK LLP, 4 Hardman Square, Spinningfields, MANCHESTER, M3 3EB. See also Grant Thornton LLP
•LOESCHER, Mr. Jonathan Andrew, BSc FCA *1989;* (Tax Fac), Jonathan Loescher & Co Ltd, Cherry Trees, 17 Flats Lane, Weeford, LICHFIELD, WS14 9QQ.
LOESCHER, Mrs. Julia Dianne, BSc ACA *1993;* Rosebank, Rudd Lane, Upper Timsbury, ROMSEY, SO51 0NU.
LOEWE, Mr. H Eric, MBA BA FCA *1978;* 905 S. Walter Reed Drive Apt. 104, ARLINGTON, VA 22204, UNITED STATES.
LOFFLER, Mr. Ian, BSc ACA *2009;* 16 Ryder Seed Mews, Pageant Road, ST. ALBANS, HERTFORDSHIRE, AL1 1NL.
LOFT, Mr. Owain, ACA *2011;* 33 Parolles Road, LONDON, N19 3RE.
LOFTHOUSE, Mr. Benjamin Joseph, BA ACA *2002;* Henderson Global Investors, 201 Bishopsgate, LONDON, EC2M 3AE.
LOFTHOUSE, Mrs. Jenifer Anne, BA ACA *1989;* with Nylon Capital LLP, Ingeni Building, 17 Broadwick Street, LONDON, W1F 0DJ.
LOFTHOUSE, Mr. John, BA ACA *1987;* 37 Embleton Road, WATFORD, HERTFORDSHIRE, WD19 7PJ.
•LOFTHOUSE, Mr. John Stephen, FCA *1968;* (Tax Fac), Lofthouse & Co, 36 Ropergate, PONTEFRACT, WF8 1LY.
LOFTHOUSE, Mr. Jonathan Mark, BSc ACA *1997;* 23 Old Mill Close, Burley in Wharfedale, ILKLEY, WEST YORKSHIRE, LS29 7RU.
LOFTHOUSE, Mr. Mark Peter, BSc ACA *1998;* 23 Hermitage Green, Hermitage, THATCHAM, BERKSHIRE, RG18 9SL.
LOFTHOUSE, Mr. Martin John, FCA *1973;* Homecroft, Beech Street, BINGLEY, WEST YORKSHIRE, BD16 1EX.
LOFTHOUSE, Mrs. Nicola Jane, BSc ACA *1996;* 23 Hermitage Green, HERMITAGE, BERKSHIRE, RG18 9SL.
•LOFTHOUSE, Mr. Philip John, FCA *1984;* (Tax Fac), Stead Robinson Limited, Whitby Court, Abbey Road, Shepley, HUDDERSFIELD, HD8 8ER.
LOFTHOUSE, Mr. Stephen David, BA ACA *1991;* 5 New Laithe Close, SKIPTON, NORTH YORKSHIRE, BD23 6AZ.
•LOFTING, Mr. Peter, FCA *1971;* Stephenson Smart, 22-26 King Street, KING'S LYNN, NORFOLK, PE30 1HJ.
LOFTING, Mr. Simon Hugh, BSc FCA *1996;* 24A Woodside, Wimbledon, LONDON, SW19 7AR.
LOFTS, Mr. Duncan Richard, FCA *1975;* Balcary Tower, Auchencairn, CASTLE DOUGLAS, KIRKCUDBRIGHTSHIRE, DG7 1QZ.
•LOFTS, Mr. Malcolm Charles, FCA *1978;* (Tax Fac), Lofts & Co., 6 South Terrace, South Street, DORCHESTER, DORSET, DT1 1DE.
LOFTUS, Mr. Christopher John, FCA *1973;* Grammont, Parsonage Road, NEWTON FERRERS, PLYMOUTH, PL8 1AT.
LOFTUS, Mr. David John, MBA BA FCA *1987;* 48 Oakdale Road, Downend, BRISTOL, BS16 6EA.
LOFTUS, Mr. Desmond Martin Peter, FCA *1969;* Rectory House, Tew Lane, Wootton, WOODSTOCK, OX20 1HA.
•LOFTUS, Mr. Gerard Christopher, BSc ACA *1984;* Deloitte LLP, Athene Place, 66 Shoe Lane, LONDON, EC4A 3BQ. See also Deloitte & Touche LLP
LOFTUS, Mr. John Vincent, BA ACA *1996;* 41 Whernside, Hough Green, WIDNES, WA8 4YW.
LOFTUS, Mr. Nicholas Mark Ashley, MA FCA *1973;* Boyton Hall, Finchingfield, BRAINTREE, CM7 4NZ.
•LOFTUS, Mr. Patrick Joseph, BSc ACA *1983;* Deloitte LLP, PO Box 500, 2 Hardman Street, MANCHESTER, M60 2AT. See also Deloitte & Touche LLP
LOGAN, Mr. Christopher, BA ACA *1999;* 43 Douglas Road, BEDFORD, MK41 7YF.
•LOGAN, Mr. Dean Russell, BA FCA *1981;* (Tax Fac), Hanley & Co Ltd, 18 Church Street, ASHTON-UNDER-LYNE, LANCASHIRE, OL6 6XE.
LOGAN, Mr. Douglas Roy, BSc ACA *1980;* Fermandy House, Fermandy Lane, Crawley Down, CRAWLEY, RH10 4UB.
LOGAN, Mrs. Heather Macdonald, MA ACA *1988;* 4 Montrose Gardens, Milngavie, GLASGOW, G62 8NQ.
LOGAN, The Revd. Joanne, MA ACA *1992;* 65 Riches Street, WOLVERHAMPTON, WEST MIDLANDS, WV6 0EA.
LOGAN, Mr. Jonathan David, BSc ACA AMCT *2000;* 4 Copmans Wick, Chorleywood, RICKMANSWORTH, WD3 5JW.
LOGAN, Mrs. Katy, BEng ACA *2002;* 36 Victoria Road, NEWTON-LE-WILLOWS, MERSEYSIDE, WA12 9RL.
LOGAN, Miss. Lisa, LLB ACA *1993;* 6, Webb Crescent, CHIPPING NORTON, OXFORDSHIRE, OX7 5HU.
LOGAN, Mr. Mark Derek, BSc ACA MIoD MBA *1995;* (Tax Fac), 61 Southcote Way, Tylers Green, Penn, HIGH WYCOMBE, HP10 8JS.
LOGAN, Mr. Paul Anthony, FCA *1950;* La Pinede, 28 Bury Road, Branksome Park, POOLE, BH13 7DF. (Life Member)
LOGAN, Mr. Peter Anthony, LLB FCA *1980;* 10 Pyrton Lane, WATLINGTON, OX49 5LX.
LOGAN, Mr. Peter James, FCA *1953;* 2 Hayes Close, BROMLEY, BR2 7BZ. (Life Member)
LOGAN, Mr. Richard, MSc BEng ACA CFA *1999;* Glencoe House, 9 Clarence Road, HARPENDEN, HERTFORDSHIRE, AL5 4AJ.
LOGAN, Mr. Ross, BA ACA *2003;* (Tax Fac), Miniclip Ltd, Diamond House, 36-38 Hatton Garden, LONDON, EC1N 8EB.
LOGAN, Mrs. Ruth Emma, MA MEng ACA *2004;* with Ernst & Young LLP, 100 Barbirolli Square, MANCHESTER, M2 3EY.
LOGAN, Miss. Sharon, LLB ACA *2003;* 4 Kessington Drive, Bearsden, GLASGOW, G61 2HG.
LOGAN, Mrs. Susan Elizabeth, BA ACA *1986;* 36 Lambolle Road, LONDON, NW3 4HR.
•LOGAN, Mrs. Victoria Jayne Frances, FCA CTA TEP *1995;* 10 Meon Close, Stone Cross, PEVENSEY, BN24 5PZ.
LOGAN WOOD, Mr. David, FCA *1956;* The Half Moon, Snitter, MORPETH, NE65 7EH. (Life Member)
LOGGIN, Mr. Mark Cole, BEd ACA *1986;* 2nd Vinnitskaya Ulitsa No 5, 23234 LUKA MALESHKIVKSA, UKRAINE.
LOGIE, Mr. Paul Christopher George, FCA *1973;* 61 Danemoor Lane, Hardingham, NORWICH, NR9 4EF.
LOGIE, Mr. Simon Joshua, BCom ACA *2001;* 13 Upper Heath Road, ST. ALBANS, HERTFORDSHIRE, AL1 4DN.
LOGIN, Miss. Susan Elizabeth Campbell, BA ACA *1991;* PO Box 468, MILSON'S POINT, NSW 1565, AUSTRALIA.
LOGSDAIL, Miss. Claire, ACA *2011;* 24b Green End, Granborough, BUCKINGHAM, MK18 3NT.
LOGSDON, Mr. Michael John, BA ACA *1986;* Lorica Consulting Ltd Lorica House, Fleet Mill Minley Road, FLEET, GU51 2RD.
LOGSDON, Mr. Peter Nicholas Lancashire, BSc ACA *1989;* Muntjak House, 74 High Street, Meldreth, ROYSTON, SG8 6LA.
LOGSDON, Mr. Philip Neil, BA ACA *1991;* Aviva Plc Nuos/hr Finance Carrara o, Surrey Street, NORWICH, NORFOLK, NR1 3NS.
LOGUE, Mr. Cathal Gerald, BSc ACA *2009;* 24 Cashelmore Park, LONDONDERRY, BT48 0RU.
LOGUE, Ms. Elaine, BSc ACA *1992;* 178 Loch Lomond Way, DANVILLE, CA 94526, UNITED STATES.
LOH, Miss. Aifeng, ACA *2008;* with PricewaterhouseCoopers LLP, 8 Cross Street, PWC Building No 17-00, SINGAPORE 048424, SINGAPORE.
LOH, Ms. Amy, ACA *2000;* 60 Cite Am Wenkel, L-8086 BERTRANGE, LUXEMBOURG.
LOH, Mr. Boon Beng, BA ACA *1990;* 15 Villiers Avenue, SURBITON, KT5 8BB.
LOH, Mr. David Chin Leong, FCA *1976;* 2 Greenridge Crescent, SINGAPORE 598890, SINGAPORE.
LOH, Mr. Eric Kgai Mun, ACA *1993;* 137 Lentor Street, Lentor Villas, SINGAPORE 786836, SINGAPORE.
LOH, Miss. Jia Hui, ACA *2008;* Blk 140 Bukit Batok St 11, #02-47, SINGAPORE 650140, SINGAPORE.
LOH, Mrs. Lai Pheng, ACA *1981;* 42 Blackburn Place, SUMMIT, NJ 07901, UNITED STATES.
LOH, Miss. Lay Hong, BA ACA *2007;* Agfa Healthcare Malaysia, Unit 704 Block B 7th Fl, Kelana Bus Centre, 97 Jalan SS 7/2, Kelana Jaya, 47301 PETALING JAYA SELANGOR MALAYSIA.
LOH, Miss. Leanne, BSc ACA *2010;* Flat 1, 173a Ladbroke Grove, LONDON, W10 6HJ.
LOH, Mr. Lee Soon, ACA *1981;* 42 Jalan SS20/ 26, 47400 PETALING JAYA, SELANGOR, MALAYSIA.
LOH, Miss. Mee Choo, ACA *1980;* 30 Jalan Bukit Maluri 10, Taman Bukit Maluri, 52100 KUALA LUMPUR, FEDERAL TERRITORY, MALAYSIA.
LOH, Mr. Niap Juan, ACA *1996;* 18 Springleaf Lane, SINGAPORE 788063, SINGAPORE.
LOH, Mr. Terence Sze Ti, LLB ACA *1979;* 371 Holland Road, The Serenade @ Holland, 17-01, SINGAPORE 278698, SINGAPORE.
LOH, Ms. Veronica Chiew Gwek, BCom ACA CFA *1999;* 9 Colony Road, LEXINGTON, MA 02420, UNITED STATES.
LOH, Mr. Vincent Charles, FCA *1975;* Vincent Loh, 30-16-3, Jamnah View Condominium, Jalan Buluh Perindu, Taman SA, 59000 KUALA LUMPUR MALAYSIA.
LOH, Miss. Wai Yee, BSc ACA *1995;* 156 Lorong Maarof, Bukit Bandaraya, 59000 KUALA LUMPUR, FEDERAL TERRITORY, MALAYSIA.
LOH, Mrs. Wei Lin, MSc ACA *1979;* 371 Holland Road, The Serenade @ Holland, 17-01, SINGAPORE 278698, SINGAPORE.
LOH, Ms. Wei Yuen, BEng ACA *1991;* 27 Jalan Batu Laut 2, Taman Bukit Seputeh, 58000 KUALA LUMPUR, FEDERAL TERRITORY, MALAYSIA.
LOH, Mr. Yoke Seng, BSc(Econ) ACA *2003;* with PricewaterhouseCoopers, 33/F Cheung Kong Center, 2 Queen's Road, CENTRAL, HONG KONG ISLAND, HONG KONG SAR.
LOH, Mr. Yoon Min, ACA *1983;* 56 Tanah Merah Kechil Avenue, #01-15 Casa Merah, SINGAPORE 465527, SINGAPORE.
LOH, Mr. Yoong Fook, FCA *1974;* Flat E 12th Floor, Ko Shing Building, 48 - 66 Ko Shing Street, SAI YING PUN, HONG KONG ISLAND, HONG KONG SAR.
LOHAN, Mr. Michael Peter, BSc(Eng) ACA *1998;* 116 Grove Avenue, Hanwell, LONDON, W7 3ES.
LOHIA, Mr. Aditya, BA ACA *2006;* 16 Tudor Close, LONDON, NW3 4AB.
LOHMANN, Miss. Alison Jane, BSc ACA *1995;* PO Box 1990, WELLINGTON 6001, NEW ZEALAND.
•LOIZIDES, Mr. Christis, ACA *1992;* POBOX 182456, DUBAI, UNITED ARAB EMIRATES.
LOIZIDES, Mr. Dimis, MA BSc(Econ) ACA *1996;* 17 Kapodistria street, Engomi, 2414 NICOSIA, CYPRUS.
LOIZIDES, Miss. Jacqueline, BA ACA *1994;* P.O. Box 21646, NICOSIA, CYPRUS.

•LOIZIDES, Mr. Michael A, BA FCA *1994;* KPMG, 11 16th June 1943 Street, 3022 LIMASSOL, CYPRUS. See also KPMG Metaxas Loizides Syrimis
LOIZIDES, Miss. Sylvia A, BA ACA *1994;* (Tax Fac), KPMG, 11 16th June 1943 Street, 3022 LIMASSOL, CYPRUS.
LOIZIDOU, Miss. Christina, ACA *2011;* 23 Epias Avenue, Engomi, 2411 NICOSIA, CYPRUS.
LOIZIDOU, Miss. Irene, ACA *2004;* 4 Appollonos Street, Politico, 2651 NICOSIA, CYPRUS.
•LOIZOU, Mrs. Amanda Louise, ACA *1994;* Amanda Loizou, 44 Penwortham Road, SOUTH CROYDON, SURREY, CR2 0QS.
LOIZOU, Mr. Andreas George, BSc FCA FFA *1991;* 15 Chr Karides Str, P O Box 54882, 3728 LIMASSOL, CYPRUS.
•LOIZOU, Mr. Angelos Michael, FCA *1984;* PricewaterhouseCoopers Limited, Julia House, 3 Themistocles Dervis Street, CY-1066 NICOSIA, CYPRUS.
LOIZOU, Miss. Anna, BA ACA *2002;* 15 Stadiou Street, Episkopi, CY-4620 LIMASSOL, CYPRUS.
LOIZOU, Miss. Carolina, BSc ACA *2003;* 19 Loukis-Akritas Street, 1100 NICOSIA, CYPRUS.
LOIZOU, Miss. Christina, MSc BA ACA *2007;* 8 Ayias Paraskevis Street, Makedonitissa, 2412 NICOSIA, CYPRUS.
LOIZOU, Mr. Christopher George, BA(Hons) ACA *2003;* 13a Ridgeview Road, LONDON, N20 0HH.
•LOIZOU, Mr. Constantinos, BA ACA *1995;* Joannides & Co Ltd, 13 Agiou Prokopiou Street, PO Box 25411, CY-1309 NICOSIA, CYPRUS. See also AGN Joannides & Co Ltd
LOIZOU, Mr. George, BSc ACA FCCA *2009;* Thalias 3, Rodopoli, 145-74 ATHENS, GREECE.
LOIZOU, Mr. George Antoniou, FCA *1961;* PO Box 40147, 6301 LARNACA, CYPRUS.
•LOIZOU, Mrs. Jenny Siew Ngo, FCA *1982;* Loizou & Loizou, P. Valdaseride 33, PO Box 42501, 6500 LARNACA, CYPRUS.
LOIZOU, Mr. Loizos Christoforou, BSc ACA *2003;* Pano Lefkara, 7700 LARNACA, CYPRUS.
•LOIZOU, Mr. Panayiotis George, BSc FCA *1980;* (Tax Fac), KPMG, 11 16th June 1943 Street, 3022 LIMASSOL, CYPRUS. See also KPMG Metaxas Loizides Syrimis
LOIZOU, Ms. Yianna Maria, BSc ACA *2011;* Julia House, 3rd floor, 3 Themistocles Dervis Street, CY-1066 NICOSIA, CYPRUS.
LOK, Mr. Hau Fuk Patrick, ACA *2008;* 4th Floor, Hang Shing Building, 25F Poplar Street, SHAM SHUI PO, KOWLOON, HONG KONG SAR.
LOK, Mr. Kam Chong, ACA *2008;* Suites 1303-1306A 13/F., Asian House, 1 Hennessy Road, WAN CHAI, HONG KONG SAR.
LOK, Mr. Tak Ming, ACA *2008;* No. 10-41, Block 404, Serangoon Avenue 1, SINGAPORE 550404, SINGAPORE.
LOK, Mr. Ying Kei Rocky, ACA *2008;* 32A Block 17, South Horizons, AP LEI CHAU, HONG KONG SAR.
LOKE, Miss. Christine Kay See, ACA *2009;* 61 Maplefield, Park Street, ST. ALBANS, HERTFORDSHIRE, AL2 2BE.
LOKE, Mr. Hoi Lam, FCA *1976;* MHL Consulting Ltd, 7/F Allied Kajima Building, 138 Gloucester Road, SAR, HONG KONG SAR.
LOKE, Dr. Hsin, BA ACA *2002;* with GlaxoSmithKline plc, Building 111, Stockley Park West, UXBRIDGE, MIDDLESEX, UB11 1BT.
LOKE, Mr. Wah Soon, ACA *1984;* 68 Kempe Road, Queens Park, LONDON, NW6 6SL.
LOKKERBOL, Mr. Ian, BA ACA *1996;* 25 Beaufort Close, REIGATE, RH2 9DG.
•LOLE, Mr. James Peter, BSc FCA *1990;* with RSM Tenon Audit Limited, 66 Chiltern Street, LONDON, W1U 4JT.
LOLLEY, Mrs. Carolyn Mary, ACA *1987;* West End, Church Street, Great Comberton, PERSHORE, WORCESTERSHIRE, WR10 3DS.
LOMAS, Mr. Alan John, MA FCA *1983;* 32 Greenhill Road, Timperley, ALTRINCHAM, CHESHIRE, WA15 7BG.
LOMAS, Mr. Alastair Mark, BA ACA *1996;* PO Box 3908, MOSMAN, NSW 2088, AUSTRALIA.
LOMAS, Mr. Andrew Martin, BA ACA *2003;* 83 Buckthorn Row, CORSHAM, SN13 9WE.
•LOMAS, Mr. Anthony, FCA *1964;* with Lomas & Co., 28a Hardwick Street, BUXTON, DERBYSHIRE, SK17 6DH.
•①LOMAS, Mr. Anthony Victor, BA FCA *1982;* (Member of Council 2003 - 2010), PricewaterhouseCoopers LLP, Pricewaterhousecoopers, 12 Plumtree Court, LONDON, EC4A 4HT. See also PricewaterhouseCoopers
LOMAS, Mrs. Barbara Jane, BA FCA *1984;* Penistone Reinforcements Ltd Stanley Mills, Talbot Road Penistone, SHEFFIELD, S36 9ED.
LOMAS, Mr. Barry John Young, FCA *1976;* 14 Offchurch Lane, Radford Semele, LEAMINGTON SPA, CV31 1TN.
LOMAS, Mr. Bernard, FCA *1953;* Flat 45, Healey Court, Coten End, WARWICK, CV34 4XP. (Life Member)
LOMAS, Mr. Colin Andrew, FCA *1966;* 4 Holcroft House, Fairlawn Road, LYTHAM ST. ANNES, LANCASHIRE, FY8 5QW.
LOMAS, Mr. Daniel James, BA ACA *2001;* 70 Thames Street, WALTON-ON-THAMES, KT12 2PS.
LOMAS, Mr. David Anthony, BSc ACA MCT *1988;* 2 Regency Place, 8 The Drive, LONDON, SW20 8TG.
•LOMAS, Mr. Garry Neil, FCA *1978;* Crossley Lomas LLP, 25 Ryecroft, Manor Park Road, GLOSSOP, DERBYSHIRE, SK13 7SQ.
LOMAS, Mr. Ian, BSc ACA *1993;* PO Box 10311, GEORGETOWN, GRAND CAYMAN, KY1-1003, CAYMAN ISLANDS.
LOMAS, Miss. Jennifer Rita, BSc FCA *1988;* 26 The Mount, GUILDFORD, GU2 4JA.
LOMAS, Ms. Jillian, BSc ACA *1992;* 110 The Mill, Castle Street, STALYBRIDGE, CHESHIRE, SK15 1AS.
LOMAS, Mr. John Proctor, BSc ACA *1990;* Flat 8, 2 Colville Square, LONDON, W11 2BD.
LOMAS, Mr. Keith James, MBA BA FCA *1964;* Stable Cottage, 5 Durlings Orchard, Ightham, SEVENOAKS, KENT, TN15 9HW.
LOMAS, Mr. Michael Joseph, BA(Hons) ACA *2004;* 46 Lomond Road, MANCHESTER, M22 5JD.
•LOMAS, Mr. Paul James, BA FCA ATII *1990;* (Tax Fac), Lomas & Company Accountants Limited, Bridge House, 12 Market Street, GLOSSOP, DERBYSHIRE, SK13 8AR.
LOMAS, Mr. Peter Francis, FCA *1962;* Westways, 14A Breary Lane, Bramhope, LEEDS, LS16 9AE.
•LOMAS, Mr. Philip Guy, FCA *1982;* (Tax Fac), Hawsons, Jubilee House, 32 Duncan Close, Moulton Park, NORTHAMPTON, NN3 6WL.
LOMAS, Mr. Phillip Andrew, BSc FCA *1977;* 5 Old Smithy Lane, LYMM, CHESHIRE, WA13 0NW.
LOMAS, Mr. Stephen Richard, BA ACA *1987;* Ernst & Young, Ernst & Young Building, 8 Exhibition Street, MELBOURNE, VIC 3000, AUSTRALIA.
LOMAX, Mr. Clifford Kenneth, FCA *1976;* (Tax Fac), 185 Worlds End Lane, ORPINGTON, KENT, BR6 6AT.
LOMAX, Mr. Clive, BSc ACA *2007;* 89 Mallard Drive, Horwich, BOLTON, BL6 5RN.
LOMAX, Mr. David Brian, BA ACA *2006;* 21A Barry Street, SOUTH YARRA, VIC 3141, AUSTRALIA.
LOMAX, Mr. Eric, FCA *1957;* 8 Kings Rd, PENZANCE, TR18 4LG. (Life Member)
LOMAX, Mr. George Alan Riley, BA FCA *1958;* 68 Starling Road, Radcliffe, MANCHESTER, M26 4LN. (Life Member)
LOMAX, Mr. Graham, BA(Hons) ACA *2002;* 43 Chiltern View, LETCHWORTH GARDEN CITY, HERTFORDSHIRE, SG6 3RJ.
LOMAX, Miss. Joanna Michelle, BA ACA *2007;* 43A Abberville Road, Clapham, LONDON, SW4 9JX.
LOMAX, Mr. Jordan, ACA *2008;* Level 16 PricewaterhouseCoopers, 2 Southbank Blvd, Southbank, MELBOURNE, VIC 3006, AUSTRALIA.
•LOMAX, Mr. Mark, ACA *1988;* Mark Lomax, 496 Darwen Road, Bromley Cross, BOLTON, BL7 9DX.
•LOMAX, Mr. Peter Gordon, BSc(Hons) ACA *2000;* with KPMG LLP, 100 Temple Street, BRISTOL, BS1 6AG.
LOMAX, Mr. Raymond, FCA *1977;* 21 Montgomery Way, Radcliffe, MANCHESTER, M26 3TG.
LOMAX, Mr. Richard Stephen, BSc ACA *2009;* KPMG LLP, 3 Assembly Square, CARDIFF, CF10 4AX.
LOMAX, Mr. Roger Harry, FCA *1967;* 5 Carson Road, LONDON, SE21 8HT.
LOMAX, Mr. Stephen Anthony, BSc FCA *1986;* Dunluce, 128 Ely Road, Llandaff, CARDIFF, CF5 2DA.
•LOMAX, Mrs. Suzanne Louise, BA FCA *1991;* Beever and Struthers, Central Buildings, Richmond Terrace, BLACKBURN, BB1 7AP.
•LOMBARD, Miss. Cheryl Ann, BA ACA *1999;* Lombard, 20 Pine Drive, INGATESTONE, ESSEX, CM4 9EF.
LOMBARD, Mr. Wilfred, BSc FCA *1962;* 57 The Cedars, Whickham, NEWCASTLE UPON TYNE, NE16 5TL. (Life Member)
•LOMBARDO, Mr. Marco Frans Thomas, BA ACA *1999;* 21 Culver Road, WINCHESTER, HAMPSHIRE, SO23 9JF.
LOMER, Mr. Graham Charles, BA ACA *1982;* Paddocks Croft, 3 Church View, Colne Engaine, COLCHESTER, CO6 2EP.
LOMER, Ms. Rosemary Ann, MA ACA DChA *1986;* with Menzies LLP, 3rd Floor Kings House, 12-42 Wood Street, KINGSTON UPON THAMES, SURREY, KT1 1TG.
LONCASTER, Mrs. Jenny Nancy, BSc FCA *1992;* Arco Ltd, PO Box 21, HULL, HU1 2SJ.
LONDEIX, Mr. Julien Pierre Joseph, ACA *2006;* 18 Moselle Avenue, LONDON, N22 6ES.
LONDON, Mr. Adrian Quentin, FCA *1966;* 21 Kemp Court, BAGSHOT, SURREY, GU19 5QG.
LONDON, Miss. Katy Jane, ACA *2005;* 90 Jewsbury Way, Thorpe Astley Braunstone, LEICESTER, LE3 3RR.
LONDON, Mr. Malcolm John, BSc(Econ) FCA *1964;* 42 Falcon Point, Hopton Street, LONDON, SE1 9JW.
LONDON, Mr. Steven Bruce, BSc ACA ACT *1991;* 505 Route 9D, GARRISON, NY 10524, UNITED STATES.
LONE, Mr. Adeel, BSc ACA *2005;* 33 Carrington Road, SLOUGH, SL1 3RH.
•LONERGAN, Mr. David Paul, FCA *1967;* Lonergan & Co., 107A London Road, LEICESTER, LE2 0PF.
LONERGAN, Mr. Ian Martin, BA ACA *1995;* 42 Porthill Gardens, SHREWSBURY, SY3 8SQ.
LONERGAN, Mr. Matthew James, MEng ACA *1992;* 10 Castle Way, ASHBY-DE-LA-ZOUCH, LEICESTERSHIRE, LE65 2RY.
LONERGAN, Mr. Michael John, BSc ACA *1985;* Overlook Investments Ltd, 1702 Dina House, 11 Duddell Street, CENTRAL, HONG KONG ISLAND, HONG KONG SAR.
LONERGAN, Miss. Michele Catherine, BSc ACA *1995;* 119a Chevening Road, LONDON, NW6 6DU.
LONERGAN, Mr. Roy John, BSc ACA CTA *1993;* (Tax Fac), Pricewaterhousecoopers Llp, 1 Hays Lane, LONDON, SE1 2RD.
LONERGAN, Mrs. Sheila Margaret, FCA *1982;* Rivington, Saunders Lane, Hutton, PRESTON, PR4 5SA.
LONERGAN, Mr. William Brendan, BA FCA *1980;* 393 Hawthorne Avenue, LOS ALTOS, CA 94022, UNITED STATES.
•LONEY, Mr. David Samuel, MSc BA FCA *1973;* Loney & Co, 13 Berrishill Grove, Red House Farm, WHITLEY BAY, NE25 9XU.
LONEY, Mr. Keith Edward, LLM FCA *1962;* 4 Lyle Park, SEVENOAKS, TN13 3JX. (Life Member)
LONEY, Mrs. Suzanne Christina Rosemarie, BSc FCA *1983;* Normanie Friars, JEDBURGH, ROXBURGHSHIRE, TD8 6BN.
•LONG, Mr. Alan Edward, BSc FCA CTA *1982;* (Tax Fac), The Long Partnership, 1 Castle Street, KIRKWALL, ORKNEY, KW15 1HD.
LONG, Mr. Alun Richard Kean, BA FCA *1983;* 5 Chester Street, Caversham, READING, RG4 8JH.
LONG, Mr. Andrew, BSc ACA *2009;* 71 Camborne Close, EASTLEIGH, SO50 6HA.
LONG, Mrs. Anna, BA(Hons) ACA *2001;* c/o Jon Long, International Cricket Council, Street 69, Dubai Sports City, DUBAI, 500 070 UNITED ARAB EMIRATES.
LONG, Ms. Anna, ACA *2008;* Flat 2 The Point, 5 Wemyss Road, Blackheath, LONDON, SE3 0TG.
LONG, Mr. Ashley James Snowden, BA ACA *1991;* 5 Castle Grove, The Park, NOTTINGHAM, NG7 1DN.
LONG, Miss. Beverley Ann, BSc ACA *1990;* 43 Ferndown Road, SOLIHULL, B91 2AU.
LONG, Mr. Blakeney David, LLB FCA *1965;* Oakleigh, Lower Faircox, HENFIELD, WEST SUSSEX, BN5 9UT.
LONG, Mr. Brian, FCA *1970;* 35 Camden Hurst, Pless Road, Milford on Sea, LYMINGTON, HAMPSHIRE, SO41 0WL. (Life Member)
LONG, Miss. Cheryl Sabrina, BSc ACA *2011;* 19 Galileo Close Duston, NORTHAMPTON, NN5 6GR.
LONG, Mr. Christian Julius George, BA ACA *1998;* 49 High Street, Great Wilbraham, CAMBRIDGE, CB1 5JD.
LONG, Mr. Christopher John, MA FCA *1969;* (Tax Fac), C J Long & Co, 11 Clipped Hedge, Hatfield Heath, BISHOP'S STORTFORD, HERTFORDSHIRE, CM22 7EG.
LONG, Mr. Christopher John, ACA *1981;* Old House Farm, Weald, SEVENOAKS, TN14 6ND.
LONG, Mr. Christopher Peter, BSc ACA *2006;* 37 Ifield Road, LONDON, SW10 9AX.
LONG, Mr. Christopher Thomas, FCA *1971;* C / La Garrotxa 11, 43820 CALAFELL, TARRAGONA, SPAIN.
LONG, Mr. Colin James, FCA *1959;* 29 Church Road, HAYES, MIDDLESEX, UB3 2LB. (Life Member)
LONG, Mr. David, FCA *1976;* Cirenna, Hobbs Wall, Farmborough, BATH, BA2 0BJ.
LONG, Mr. David Guy, BSc ACA *1990;* Pond Cottage, Newton Valence, ALTON, HAMPSHIRE, GU34 3RB.
LONG, Mr. David Vernon, BA ACA *1979;* Samsung Total Petrochemicals Ltd, Jung - gu, SEOUL, 100-716, KOREA REPUBLIC OF.
LONG, Mr. David William, BA ACA *1989;* 7 Hindhead Close, Hillingdon, UXBRIDGE, UB8 3UE.
LONG, Mr. Desmond Michael, BA FCA *1969;* 24 Greystoke Road, Caversham, READING, RG4 5EL.
LONG, Miss. Eleanor, MPhil BMus ACA *2011;* 6 Church Close, Church Road, CALDICOT, GWENT, NP26 4GW.
LONG, Miss. Elizabeth Jane, BSc ACA *1997;* 74 Ivygreen Road, MANCHESTER, M21 9EX.
LONG, Mr. Geoffrey Hirst, FCA *1950;* 25 Hummersknott Avenue, DARLINGTON, DL3 8LQ. (Life Member)
•LONG, Mr. Geoffrey Richard, BSc FCA *1987;* Long & Co Limited, 65a High Street, STEVENAGE, HERTFORDSHIRE, SG1 3AQ.
•LONG, Mr. Gordon Andrew, FCA *1980;* (Tax Fac), Martin & Company, 158 Richmond Park Road, BOURNEMOUTH, BH8 8TW.
•LONG, Mr. Graham, BSc ACA *1987;* Graham Long, 107 The Broadway, LEIGH-ON-SEA, SS9 1PG.
LONG, Mr. Heng Kuan, BCom ACA *1982;* 1-3-8 Kiara View, Jalan Datuk Sulaiman 6, Taman Tun Dr Ismail, 60000 KUALA LUMPUR, FEDERAL TERRITORY, MALAYSIA.
•LONG, Mr. Howard John, FCA *1973;* Howard Long, 41 St Peters Road, CROYDON, CR0 1HN.
LONG, Mr. James, BA(Hons) ACA *2009;* Ground Floor Flat, 60 Disraeli Road, LONDON, SW15 2DS.
LONG, Mrs. Janine Marie, MA ACA *1988;* Woodland Lodge, Woodland Way, Kingswood, TADWORTH, KT20 6NW.
LONG, Mr. Jeremy Paul Warwick, MA FCA *1977;* MTR Corporation, Finland House, 56 Haymarket, LONDON, SW1Y 4RN.
LONG, Miss. Jessica Elizabeth, BSc ACA *2009;* Level 31, 60 Margaret Street, SYDNEY, NSW 2011, AUSTRALIA.
LONG, Mrs. Jill, BSc ACA *1993;* Wheatley, 12 School Lane, Chalfont St. Peter, GERRARDS CROSS, SL9 9AU.
LONG, Mr. John Graham, FCA *1968;* 40 Boxgrove Avenue, GUILDFORD, GU1 1XQ.
LONG, Mr. John Malcolm, FCA *1960;* 13 Grove Park, KNUTSFORD, WA16 8QA. (Life Member)
LONG, Mr. Jonathan David, ACA *1982;* Bramley Heights, Snowdenham Links Road, Bramley, GUILDFORD, SURREY, GU5 0BX.
LONG, Mr. Jonathan James, BSc ACA *1992;* 89 Shakespeare Avenue, BATH, BA2 4RQ.
LONG, Mr. Joseph David, ACA *2009;* 6 Thorpe Lodge, Cotham Side, BRISTOL, BS6 5TJ.
LONG, Miss. Judith Ann, BSc FCA *1989;* GO North West Piccadilly Gate, Store Street, MANCHESTER, M1 2WD.
LONG, Mrs. Julie Marie, BA ACA *1995;* with Audit Inspection Unit, Financial Reporting Council, 5th Floor, Aldwych House, 71-91 Aldwych, LONDON WC2B 4HN.
LONG, Mrs. Kathryn Lisa, BSc ACA *1989;* Pond Cottage, Newton Valence, ALTON, GU34 3RB.
LONG, Mr. Kevin, BA ACA *1991;* 2 Reeves Court, East Malling, WEST MALLING, ME19 6XL.
LONG, Mr. Kevin Geoffrey, BA FCA *1992;* 16 Walhouse Drive, Penkridge, STAFFORD, ST19 5SP.
LONG, Miss. Laura, ACA *2011;* 65a Drury Avenue, Horsforth, LEEDS, LS18 4BR.
LONG, Mr. Mark Henry, BSc ACA *1992;* 11 Central Avenue, BEVERLEY, NORTH HUMBERSIDE, HU17 8LH.
LONG, Mr. Mark Vincent, BA ACA *1987;* Woodland Lodge, Woodland Way, Kingswood, TADWORTH, KT20 6NW.
•LONG, Mr. Martin Richard, LLB(Hons) BA(Hons) FCA *1989;* Begbies Traynor Group Forensic, 10th Floor Temple Point, 1 Temple Row, BIRMINGHAM, B2 5LG.
LONG, Mr. Martin William, BSc ACA *1982;* 71 Woodside Avenue, CHISLEHURST, BR7 6BT.
LONG, Mr. Matthew, BA(Econ) ACA *1999;* 12 Ninnings Road, Chalfont St. Peter, GERRARDS CROSS, BUCKINGHAMSHIRE, SL9 0EF.
LONG, Mr. Matthew William, ACA *2009;* Simpson Print Ltd Rutherford Road, Stephenson Industrial Estate, WASHINGTON, TYNE AND WEAR, NE37 3HX.
LONG, Miss. May Lin, BSc ACA *1992;* 144 Burns Avenue, FELTHAM, TW14 9HZ.

LONG, Mr. Michael Joseph, BCom FCA *1974;* 12 Bishopscourt Hill, Wilton, CORK, COUNTY CORK, IRELAND.

•LONG, Mr. Nicholas George, FCA *1974;* 208 Marshall Lake Road, Shirley, SOLIHULL, B90 4RH.

LONG, Mr. Nicholas John, FCA *1974;* Dunkirks Stable, Dunkirks Mews, Queens Road, HERTFORD, SG13 8BA.

LONG, Miss. Nicola, BSc(Hons) ACA *2011;* 573 Wimborne Road East, FERNDOWN, DORSET, BH22 9NL.

LONG, Mr. Oliver George, MA FCA *1963;* 75 NORDEN CRESCENT, TORONTO M3B 1B7, ON, CANADA. (Life Member)

LONG, Mr. Patrick, FCA *1969;* Twenty Winks, Mill Lane, Aslockton, NOTTINGHAM, NG13 9AS. (Life Member)

•LONG, Mr. Paul, BSc ACA *1986;* (Tax Fac), KPMG LLP, 15 Canada Square, LONDON, E14 5GL. See also KPMG Europe LLP, KPMG Audit plc, KPMG Holding plc

LONG, Mr. Peter Alan, BA FCA *1978;* Bracebridge House, 25 High Green, Severn Stoke, WORCESTER, WR8 9JS.

LONG, Mr. Philip, BSc ACA ATII *1987;* (Tax Fac), ROUTE DES GRAND-CHAMPS 13, 1278 LA RIPPE, VAUD, SWITZERLAND.

LONG, Mr. Philip David, FCA *1961;* 12/36 Osborne Road, MANLY, NSW 2095, AUSTRALIA. (Life Member)

•①LONG, Mr. Philip James, BSc FCA *1976;* Groby, 11 Groby Place, ALTRINCHAM, CHESHIRE, WA14 4AL.

•LONG, Mr. Raymond John Ian, FCA FCCA *1982;* (Tax Fac), Munday Long & Co Limited, Alton House, 66 High Street, NORTHWOOD, HA6 1BL. See also Munday Long Accounting Services Ltd

LONG, Dr. Richard, MSc ACA *2011;* Flat 2, 10 Albert Square, Stockwell, LONDON, SW8 1BT.

LONG, Mr. Richard, FCA *1976;* 206 Kerr Street, OAKVILLE L6K 3A8, ON, CANADA.

LONG, Mr. Richard Charles, BSc FCA *1976;* 15 Downs Road, EPSOM, KT18 5JF.

LONG, Mr. Richard Douglas, FCA *1970;* 2 Hanbury Road, Dorridge, SOLIHULL, B93 8DW.

LONG, Mr. Richard Frederick, FCA *1960;* 1a Bishops Walk, LOWESTOFT, SUFFOLK, NR32 4JN. (Life Member)

•LONG, Mr. Robert Edward, FCA *1981;* (Tax Fac), Dunbar & Co (Corporate Services) Limited, 70 South Lambeth Road, LONDON, SW8 1RL. See also Robert E. Long

LONG, Mr. Robin, FCA *1957;* 73 Pilgrims Way, Kemsing, SEVENOAKS, KENT, TN15 6TD. (Life Member)

LONG, Miss. Sarah Elizabeth, ACA *2008;* 12 Pennine Crescent, REDCAR, CLEVELAND, TS10 4AE.

LONG, Mrs. Sarah Marie, ACA *2008;* Flat 1 Seymour Court, Eversley Park Road, LONDON, N21 1JG.

LONG, Mrs. Sharon Joan, BSc ACA *1985;* 5 Sandridgebury Lane, ST. ALBANS, AL3 6DD.

LONG, Mr. Simon Michael, ACA *2009;* 13 Wintney Street, FLEET, GU51 1AL.

LONG, Mr. Simon Stewart, BA ACA *2000;* 25 Lanesborough Court, Gosforth, NEWCASTLE UPON TYNE, NE3 3BZ.

LONG, Mr. Stephen, ACA *2011;* 7 Hardy Close, Brantham, MANNINGTREE, CO11 1RQ.

LONG, Mr. Stephen James, BSc ACA *2003;* 26 Belmont Avenue, WOLLSTONECRAFT, NSW 2065, AUSTRALIA.

LONG, Mr. Stewart, FCA *1966;* 1 Whooff House, Aglionby, CARLISLE, CA4 8AQ. (Life Member)

LONG, Miss. Susan Elizabeth, BSc ACA *1994;* 130 Marshalswick Lane, ST. ALBANS, HERTFORDSHIRE, AL1 4XB.

•LONG, Mrs. Violet Anna, FCA *1970;* Anna Long, 58 Crescent Lane, LONDON, SW4 9PU.

LONG, Miss. Vivienne Carole, ACA *2008;* Flat D, 93 Hambalt Road, LONDON, SW4 9EQ.

LONG-LEATHER, Mr. Christopher, FCA *1966;* Home Farm, Stretton on Fosse, MORETON-IN-MARSH, GLOUCESTERSHIRE, GL56 9SA.

LONGAN, Mr. Daniel John David, ACA *2004;* 7 Egret Avenue, BURLEIGH WATERS, QLD 4220, AUSTRALIA.

LONGBON, Mr. Ian Graham, MBA BSc ACA *1987;* House H, Billows Villa, Hang Hung Wing Lung Road, Clear Water Bay, SAI KUNG, NEW TERRITORIES HONG KONG SAR.

•LONGBOTTOM, Mr. Charles Marcus Sykes, FCA *1992;* The Moore Scarrott Partnership LLP, Calyx House, South Road, TAUNTON, SOMERSET, TA1 3DY. See also Moore Scarrott Audit Limited

LONGBOTTOM, Mr. Kenneth Ronald, BSc ACA *1980;* 3 Church Lane, Gaddesby, LEICESTER, LE7 4WE.

LONGCAKE, Mr. Matthew James, BSc ACA *2005;* 1 Severn Grove, Pontcanna, CARDIFF, CF11 9EN.

LONGCROFT, Mr. Christopher Charles Stoddart, BSc ACA *1997;* Moaps Farm, Church Lane, Danehill, HAYWARDS HEATH, WEST SUSSEX, RH17 7EY.

LONGCROFT, Mr. Peter Martin Stoddart, FCA *1960;* 1-9939 Third Street, SIDNEY V8l 3B1, BC, CANADA. (Life Member)

LONGDEN, Mr. Alan, BSc FCA *1981;* The Barn at Firs Farm, Baxter Lane, Sibthorpe, NEWARK, NOTTINGHAMSHIRE, NG23 5PN.

LONGDEN, Miss. Carla, ACA *2011;* 60 Northbrook Street, LEEDS, LS7 4QH.

LONGDEN, Mr. Christopher William, ACA *2008;* 1a Northbrook Road, Hither Green, LONDON, SE13 5QT.

•LONGDEN, Mr. Derek, FCA *1973;* Derek Longden, 47 West Parade, WORTHING, BN11 5EF.

LONGDEN, Miss. Diane, ACA ACII ATII *1985;* Reinet Fund Manager, 35 Boulevard Prince Henri, L-1724 LUXEMBOURG, LUXEMBOURG.

LONGDEN, Mr. Edward, BSc FCA *1957;* Pond House, Village Road, Dorney, WINDSOR, SL4 6QJ. (Life Member)

LONGDEN, Mr. James Alan, BSc ACA *2001;* BPM Analytical Empowerment, Level 4 210 George Street, SYDNEY, NSW 2000, AUSTRALIA.

LONGDEN, Mrs. Karen Anne, BA ACA *1996;* 47 Dransfield Road, Crosspool, SHEFFIELD, S10 5RL.

•LONGDEN, Mr. Michael, FCA *1979;* Wall and Partners, 3 & 5 Commercial Gate, MANSFIELD, NG18 1EJ.

LONGDEN, Mr. William, FCA *1950;* 8 Cromwell Close, ASHBY-DE-LA-ZOUCH, LE65 1LU. (Life Member)

LONGDON, Mr. Jack, FCA *1965;* 2 Hatching Green Close, HARPENDEN, AL5 2LB.

•LONGE, Mr. Laurence Peter, ACA *1987;* Baker Tilly Tax and Advisory Services LLP, 25 Farringdon Street, LONDON, EC4A 4AB.

•①LONGFIELD, Mr. Simon John, BA FCA *1992;* Zolfo Cooper LLP, 10 Fleet Place, LONDON, EC4M 7RB.

LONGFIELD, Mr. Simon John Griffin, BSc FCA *1992;* B M I Mermaid House, 2 Puddle Dock, LONDON, EC4V 3DS.

LONGFORD, Mr. Peter, FCA *1968;* 45 Chesapeake Rd, Chaddesden, DERBY, DE21 6RD.

•LONGHILL, Mrs. Sarah Ann, FCA *1973;* (Tax Fac), Ireland & Longhill, 10 Station Street, Kibworth Beauchamp, LEICESTER, LE8 0LN.

LONGHORN, Mr. James Grahame, BSc FCA *1982;* 20 Nightingale Close, HARTLEPOOL, TS26 0HL.

LONGHORN, Mr. Mark, BSc FCA *1986;* 12 Branscombe Road, Stoke Bishop, BRISTOL, BS9 1SN.

LONGHURST, Mr. Colin Douglas, MA FCA *1975;* Iepenlaan 47, 2061 GJ BLOEMENDAAL, NETHERLANDS. (Life Member)

LONGHURST, Mr. Damien, ACA *2010;* 48 Bodmin Street, LONDON, SW18 4PT.

LONGHURST, Miss. Gemma Claire, BA ACA *2010;* 12 Reventlow Road, LONDON, SE9 2DJ.

LONGHURST, Mrs. Glynis Susan, FCA *1975;* The Burma Star Association, 34 Grosvenor Gardens, LONDON, SW1W 0DH.

LONGHURST, Mrs. Judy Helen, FCA *1975;* Panyagua, El Puntal 8, Almeria, 04270 SORBAS, SPAIN.

LONGHURST, Mr. Nicholas James, BA FCA *1991;* Driving Standards Agency The Axis Building, 112 Upper Parliament Street, NOTTINGHAM, NG1 6LP.

LONGHURST, Mr. Richard Anthony, MSc BA FCA *1974;* 14 Shaughnessy Boulevard, WILLOWDALE M2J 1H5, ON, CANADA.

LONGHURST, Mr. Scott Robert James, BCom FCA *1991;* Waters Meadows, Huntingdon Road, Brampton, HUNTINGDON, CAMBRIDGESHIRE, PE28 4PA.

LONGHURST, Mr. Stephen Paul, BSc ACA *2005;* LG29, 6 Carlton Gardens, LONDON, SW1Y 5AD.

LONGINOTTI, Mr. Peter Andrew, BSc FCA *1982;* Yew Tree Farm, Holmes Chapel Road, Lach Dennis, NORTHWICH, CW9 7SY.

LONGLAND, Mr. John Charles, FCA *1957;* 14 Raglan Road, REIGATE, RH2 0DP. (Life Member)

LONGLAND, Mr. John James, FCA *1948;* 157C Park Avenue, Purbrook, WATERLOOVILLE, PO7 5EY. (Life Member)

LONGLAND, Mr. Peter William, FCA *1952;* St. Bride Foundation, St. Bride Institute, Bride Lane, Fleet Street, LONDON, EC4Y 8EQ. (Life Member)

LONGLAND, Mr. Thomas, BSc ACA *2006;* 2 Roundway, CAMBERLEY, SURREY, GU15 1NS.

LONGLEY, Mr. Charles Robert, BSc FCA *1977;* 30 Huntly Road, Talbot Woods, BOURNEMOUTH, BH3 7HH.

•LONGLEY, Mr. Darren Scott, BCom FCA *1991;* Deloitte LLP, Mountbatten House, 1 Grosvenor Square, SOUTHAMPTON, SO15 2BZ. See also Deloitte & Touche LLP

LONGLEY, Mr. Dominic James, BSc ACA *2010;* 23 Burnside Grove, Tollerton, NOTTINGHAM, NG12 4ET.

LONGLEY, Mr. James Timothy Chapman, BA FCA *1983;* 59 Principal Rise, Dringhouses, YORK, YO24 1UF.

LONGLEY, Mr. John, BA ACA *2011;* 160 Murray Road, SHEFFIELD, S11 7GH.

LONGLEY, Mr. Jonathan Richard Thomas, BA ACA *1990;* Cookley Lodge, Swyncombe, HENLEY-ON-THAMES, RG9 6EJ.

•LONGLEY, Mr. Michael David, FCA *1983;* Moore Thompson, Monica House, St. Augustines Road, WISBECH, CAMBRIDGESHIRE, PE13 3AD.

•LONGLEY, Mr. Michael Richard, FCA FCCA *1979;* (Tax Fac), Longleys, 81 Melton Road, West Bridgford, NOTTINGHAM, NG2 6EN. See also Longley & Co

LONGLEY, Mr. Nicholas, BSc ACA *1995;* 3 Middle Park Close, Selly Oak, BIRMINGHAM, B29 4BT.

LONGLEY, Mr. Nicholas James, BSc ACA *2007;* One Snowhill, Snow Hill Queensway, BIRMINGHAM, B4 6GH.

•LONGLEY, Mrs. Pauline Mary, BSc FCA *1978;* 30 Huntly Road, Talbot Woods, BOURNEMOUTH, BH3 7HH.

LONGLEY, Mr. Richard, MSci ACA *2011;* 24 Coppy Lane, Bramley, LEEDS, LS13 2AT.

•LONGLEY, Mrs. Vanessa Grace Teresa, BEng ACA ATII *1994;* Longley Consulting Limited, 16 Highfield Drive, KINGSBRIDGE, DEVON, TQ7 1JR.

•LONGMAN, Mrs. Bridget, BSc FCA *1997;* Longman Accountancy Services Limited, Waterloo House, 141 Albion Road, New Mills, HIGH PEAK, DERBYSHIRE SK22 3JP.

LONGMAN, Mr. Christopher John, BSc FCA *1983;* 33 New Pond Rd, Holmer Green, HIGH WYCOMBE, HP15 6SU.

LONGMAN, Mr. Eric Iain, FCA *1965;* (Member of Council 1974 - 1989), The Cottage, 3 Courtfield Drive, Simpson Cross, HAVERFORDWEST, DYFED, SA62 6EQ.

LONGMAN, Mr. John Henry Howard, FCA *1962;* 6 Sandringham Close, HOVE, BN3 6XE. (Life Member)

LONGMAN, Mr. Michael Guy, BSc ACA *1990;* Tunder utca 18/C, H-1125 BUDAPEST, HUNGARY.

LONGMAN, Mr. Michael John, BA FCA *1983;* (Tax Fac), Old Barn, 1 Davenport Mews, Davenport, CONGLETON, CHESHIRE, CW12 4ST.

LONGMAN, Mr. Nicholas John, BSc FCA *1991;* The Farthings, Westmorland Road, MAIDENHEAD, SL6 4HB.

LONGMAN, Mr. Nicholas Winston, BA ACA *1993;* Roseland, Salisbury Road, HORSHAM, WEST SUSSEX, RH13 0AL.

LONGMAN, Mr. Roger Leslie, FCA *1974;* The Old Barn, Orchard Road, BEACONSFIELD, BUCKINGHAMSHIRE, HP9 2DZ.

LONGMAN-JONES, Mrs. Catherine, ACA *2011;* 76 Derwent Road, LONDON, N13 4PX.

LONGMIRE, Mr. Mark, BA FCA *1995;* 25 Daneswood Close, WEYBRIDGE, SURREY, KT13 9AY.

LONGMORE, Mrs. Judith, BSc ACA *1989;* 33 Broadlands, Cleadon Village, SUNDERLAND, SR6 7RD.

•LONGMORE, Mr. Martin John, BA FCA *1994;* Monahans, Lennox House, 3 Pierrepont Street, BATH, BA1 1LB. See also Monahans Limited

LONGMORE, Mr. Peter, BA ACA *1988;* Kaplan Financial, 2nd Floor Provincial House, 148-152 Northumberland Street, NEWCASTLE UPON TYNE, TYNE AND WEAR, NE1 7DQ.

LONGMUIR, Mr. John Grant, FCA *1970;* Middle Webbs, Littleham, BIDEFORD, DEVON, EX39 5HN.

LONGMUIR, Ms. Sara Wendy, BA ACA *1985;* 27 Grange Gardens, PINNER, MIDDLESEX, HA5 5QD.

LONGRIDGE, Mr. David John Ernle, FCA *1963;* Fosse Farm, Brokenborough, MALMESBURY, WILTSHIRE, SN16 0QZ.

LONGRIDGE, Dr. Elinor, MA ACA *2002;* 22 Sonning Meadows, Sonning, READING, RG4 6XB.

LONGSDON, Mr. Robert James, BA ACA *1999;* Fimalac, 30 North Colonnade, LONDON, E14 5GN.

LONGSON, Mr. Duncan Edward, ACA *2008;* SIGnet House, 17 Europa View, Sheffield Business Park, SHEFFIELD, SOUTH YORKSHIRE, S9 1XH.

LONGSON, Mr. Nicholas, MA ACA ACII ACILA *1986;* 5 Thornfield Hey, WILMSLOW, SK9 2NF.

LONGSTAFF, Mrs. Christine Ann, LLB ACA *1989;* 7 Green Curve, BANSTEAD, SM7 1NS.

LONGSTAFF, Mr. James, BA ACA *1998;* 17 Mallard Close, New Barnet, BARNET, HERTFORDSHIRE, EN5 1DH.

LONGSTAFF, Mr. John, BA(Hons) FCA CF *2000;* with Ingram Forrest Corporate Finance LLP, 2 Rutland Park, SHEFFIELD, S10 2PD.

LONGSTAFF, Mrs. Katharine Fiona, MA ACA *1992;* 17 Boroughbridge Road, KNARESBOROUGH, NORTH YORKSHIRE, HG5 0LX.

•LONGSTAFF, Mr. Philip David, FCA *1989;* Ellis Atkins, 1 Paper Mews, 330 High Street, DORKING, SURREY, RH4 2TU. See also Bray Management Services Limited

LONGSTAFF, Mrs. Rachael, BA(Hons) ACA *2009;* Home Farm House, 20 Home Farm Court, Ingestre, STAFFORD, ST18 0PZ.

LONGSTAFF-TYRRELL, Miss. Zoe, BSc(Hons) ACA DChA *2001;* The Acorns, Slaugham, HAYWARDS HEATH, WEST SUSSEX, RH17 6AL.

LONGSTAFFE, Mr. Andrew David, ACA *1983;* 320 Drub Lane, CLECKHEATON, WEST YORKSHIRE, BD19 4BX.

LONGSTER, Ms. Alison Jane, MA FCA *1994;* Credit Suisse, Endenstrasse 20, 8057 ZURICH, SWITZERLAND.

LONGSTER, Mr. John Mark, MA ACA *1992;* Zurich Financial Services, Mythenquai 2, ZURICH, 8022, SWITZERLAND.

LONGTHORN, Mr. Gary Austin, BCom ACA *1979;* 3 Pine Avenue, ORMSKIRK, L39 2YP.

•LONGTON, Mr. David Russell, FCA *1976;* (Tax Fac), Melville & Co, Unit 17/18, Trinity Enterprise Centre, Furness Business Park, Ironworks Road, BARROW-IN-FURNESS CUMBRIA LA14 2PN.

LONGWORTH, Mr. John Francis, FCA *1951;* 16A Harrod Drive, SOUTHPORT, PR8 2HA. (Life Member)

•LONGWORTH, Mr. Mark Andrew, MA ACA *1996;* KPMG LLP, 15 Canada Square, LONDON, E14 5GL. See also KPMG Europe LLP

LONGWORTH, Mr. Richard Stanley Roland, FCA *1978;* Cheadle, 36 Rydon Lane, EXETER, EX2 7AW.

LONGWORTH, Mr. Robert John, BSc FCA *1974;* 5 Heald Road, Bowdon, ALTRINCHAM, WA14 2JE.

•LONGWORTH, Ms. Sally Louise, BA ACA *1990;* Grant Thornton UK LLP, 4 Hardman Square, Spinningfields, MANCHESTER, M3 3EB. See also Grant Thornton LLP

•LONGWORTH, Mr. Simon Andrew, BSc(Hons) ACA PGCE *2004;* Cyfri Cyfrifwyr Cyfyngedig, Unit I, 8 The Science Park, ABERYSTWYTH, DYFED, SY23 3AH.

LONMON-DAVIS, Mr. Anthony Michael David, FCA *1959;* PO Box 78510, SANDTON, 2146, SOUTH AFRICA. (Life Member)

•LONNEN, Miss. Deborah Susan Margaret, BSc ACA *1992;* DSL Accountancy Ltd, 3 Ridgeview, Long Ashton, BRISTOL, BS41 9EQ.

LONNEN, Mr. John Victor, FCA *1962;* 1 Cleveland Road, ISLEWORTH, TW7 7EY. (Life Member)

LONSDALE, Miss. Alexandra Emma Rose, BA ACA *2008;* 73 Peveril Bank, Dawley Bank, TELFORD, SHROPSHIRE, TF4 2BZ.

LONSDALE, Mrs. Charlotte Jane, BMus ACA *2003;* 7 Turner Close, STEVENAGE, HERTFORDSHIRE, SG1 4AF.

LONSDALE, Ms. Karen, BA ACA *1984;* Castanea, Castle Road, WOKING, GU21 4EU.

•LONSDALE, Mrs. Mary, BA ACA *2002;* Nutshell Accountants Limited, 153 Cavendish Road, Clapham, LONDON, SW12 0BW.

LONSDALE, Mr. Michael David, BSc ACA *1999;* 83 Eskdale Avenue, CHESHAM, BUCKINGHAMSHIRE, HP5 3AY.

•LONSDALE, Mrs. Pauline Ann, BA FCA TEP *1983;* (Tax Fac), Pauline Lonsdale, 26 Elmfield Road, BROMLEY, BR1 1WA.

LONSDALE, Miss. Penelope Marion, BA ACA *1990;* 38 Fitzroy Road, FLEET, GU51 4JW.

•LONSDALE, Mr. Roger David, FCA *1961;* John A. Edgar & Company, 7 Merefield, Astley Village, CHORLEY, PR7 1UP.

LONSDALE, Mr. Simon Mark, BA ACA *1988;* 2 Water Lane Woolley, WAKEFIELD, WEST YORKSHIRE, WF4 2JQ.

LONSDALE, Mr. Stephen Philip, BA FCA *1981;* Arriva Plc, 1 Admiral Way, Doxford International Business Park, SUNDERLAND, SR3 3XP.

LONSDALE-ECCLES, Mr. Michael, ACA *2008;* 2221-938 Smithe Street, VANCOUVER V6Z 3H8, BC, CANADA.

LONSTEIN, Mr. Trevor Rael, BCom ACA *1989;* 73 Pound Avenue, FRENCHS FOREST, NSW 2086, AUSTRALIA.

LOO, Mr. Chiew Leong, BSc ACA *1987;* 54 Eagle Gardens, BEDFORD, MK41 7FE.

LOO, Mr. Christopher Craig, ACA CA(SA) *2010;* 13 Perkins Avenue, Newington, SYDNEY, NSW 2127, AUSTRALIA.
LOO, Mr. Hong Shing Vincent, ACA *2008;* Flat G, 9/F, Han Kung Mansion, TAIKOO SHING, HONG KONG SAR.
LOO, Mr. Jonathan Lip Pin, ACA *2008;* Credit Suisse, 1 Cabot Square, LONDON, E14 4QJ.
LOO, Mr. Kiah Fatt, ACA *1982;* 62 Santa Rosa Boulevard, DONCASTER EAST, VIC 3109, AUSTRALIA.
LOO, Miss. Lilin, BA ACA *1983;* TH-3A, 12-22 Dora Street, HURSTVILLE, NSW 2220, AUSTRALIA.
LOO, Mr. Pak Hong, MSc FCA *1974;* A-6-2 Vila Banyan, 49 Jalan Awan Jawa, Taman Yarl, 58200 KUALA LUMPUR, FEDERAL TERRITORY, MALAYSIA.
LOO, Ms. Wynn Keng, BSc ACA *2003;* Flat 80 Stretton Mansions, Glaisher Street, LONDON, SE8 3JP.
LOOCHIN, Mr. Ivor Bernard, FCA *1959;* (Tax Fac), 12 Fairgreen East, BARNET, EN4 0QR. (Life Member)
LOODMER, Mr. Roger Samuel, FCA *1980;* Maisemore Lodge, Maisemore, GLOUCESTER, GLOUCESTERSHIRE, GL2 8HX.
LOOI, Mr. Kem Loong, BA ACA *1999;* 48 Jalan Hujan Bubuk3, O.U.G, 5th Mile Old Klang Road, 58200 KUALA LUMPUR, FEDERAL TERRITORY, MALAYSIA.
LOOI, Miss. Lai Keun, BSc ACA *1991;* 26 Cheylesmore Drive, Frimley, CAMBERLEY, GU16 9BN.
LOOK, Mr. Guy, BCom ACA *1983;* Sa Sa International Holdings Ltd, 14/F Block B Mp Industrial Centre, 18 Ka Yip Street, CHAI WAN, HONG KONG ISLAND, HONG KONG SAR.
•LOOKER, Mr. Ian Mark, BA FCA *1993;* PricewaterhouseCoopers LLP, Benson House, 33 Wellington Street, LEEDS, LS1 4JP. See also PricewaterhouseCoopers
•LOOKER, Mr. Philip Trevor, BA FCA *1979;* P.T. Looker & Co, 3 Stonards Hill, EPPING, CM16 4QE. See also PTL Accountancy Services Limited
LOOKER, Mrs. Tracey, BSc ACA *1996;* The Old College, 273 High Street, Boston Spa, WETHERBY, WEST YORKSHIRE, LS23 6AL.
LOOMBA, Mrs. Katharine Margaret, FCA *1986;* Geraint Humphreys & Co, 5-7 Beatrice Street, OSWESTRY, SHROPSHIRE, SY11 1QE.
LOOMBA, Mr. Nalin, MCom BCom(Hons) ACA *2005;* 34 Hazelwood Close, HARROW, MIDDLESEX, HA2 6HD.
LOOMBE, Mr. Matthew David, ACA *2004;* 4 Station Road, Southwater, HORSHAM, WEST SUSSEX, RH13 9HQ.
LOON, Miss. Joanne Mary, BSc ACA *2005;* with KPMG LLP, Saltire Court, 20 Castle Terrace, EDINBURGH, EH1 2EG.
LOONEY, Mr. Peter John, FCA *1977;* 19 Beech Way, Wheathampstead, ST.ALBANS, AL4 8LY.
LOONG, Mr. Anthony Sie Hock, FCA *1963;* A.S.H. Loong & Co, 48 Meyer Road, Apt. 08-50, SINGAPORE 437872, SINGAPORE. (Life Member)
LOONG, Mr. Choe-Yuen, BA(Econ) ACA *1980;* 18 Hillview Drive, SINGAPORE 669380, SINGAPORE.
LOOPUIT, Mr. Simon Peter, LLB ACA *1987;* 34 Champion Hill, LONDON, SE5 8AP.
•LOOSELEY, Mr. Neil Francis, BSc ACA CTA *2005;* BSR Bespoke, Linden House, Linden Close, TUNBRIDGE WELLS, KENT, TN4 8HH. See also BSR Bespoke Limited
LOOSEMORE, Mr. David, MPhil BSc ACA *2002;* Ealing Dean, 20 Plas Treoda, CARDIFF, CF14 1PT.
LOOSEMORE, Mrs. Janet Zillah, BSc(Hons) ACA *2004;* with Thomas Westcott, Queens House, New Street, HONITON, DEVON, EX14 1BJ.
LOOSEMORE, Mrs. Melanie Annabel, BA ACA *2000;* Cornerstones Lisvane Road, Llanishen, CARDIFF, CF14 0SD.
LOOSER, Miss. Annys Sarah Jane, BEng FCA *2001;* National Physical Laboratory, Hampton Road, TEDDINGTON, MIDDLESEX, TW11 0LW.
LOOSLEY, Mrs. Christine, BSc ACA ATII *1991;* Innisfree, 26 Belle Meade Close, Woodgate, CHICHESTER, PO20 6YD.
LOPES, Mr. Harry Marcus George, MA ACA *2006;* 86 Faroe Road, LONDON, W14 0EP.
LOPES, Mr. Jose Eurico Da Piedade, ACA *2011;* 324 Kennington Road, LONDON, SE11 4LD.
LOPEZ, Mr. Jose Robert, ACA *1998;* 18 Hurst Street, OXFORD, OX4 1HB.
•LOPEZ, Mr. Stuart Rylan, ACA ACCA *2009;* WBV Limited, 33 Heathfield, SWANSEA, SA1 6HD. See also Lopez & Evans Limited and Heathfield Tax Consultancy Ltd
LOPEZ-CACICEDO, Miss. Catherine Jane Elizabeth, MA ACA *2001;* 1 Pembridge Place, LONDON, SW15 2QE.
LOPEZ-CACICEDO, Mr. Christopher James, MA MEng CEng ACA *2000;* 35 Gadd Close, WOKINGHAM, BERKSHIRE, RG40 5PQ.
LOPEZ JUAREZ, Mr. Oscar Lopez, ACA *2003;* Flat 7, Raymond Court, Raymond Road, LONDON, SW19 4AR.
•LOPIAN, Mr. David Zvi, BSc FCA *1974;* (Tax Fac), Lopian Gross Barnett & Co, 6th Floor, Cardinal House, 20 St. Marys Parsonage, MANCHESTER, M3 2LG. See also Harvester Consultants Limited
•LOPIAN, Mr. Simon Abner, FCA ATII *1979;* (Tax Fac), Lopian Gross Barnett & Co, 6th Floor, Cardinal House, 20 St. Marys Parsonage, MANCHESTER, M3 2LG.
LOPOKOIYIT, Mr. Philip Ruto, FCA *1995;* PO Box 35204-0200, NAIROBI, KENYA.
•LORAINE, Mr. George Sharon, FCA *1969;* Loraine & Boleat, First Floor, 7 Bond Street, St. Helier, JERSEY, JE2 3NP.
LORAM, Mr. Jonathan Jeffrey, MChem ACA *2003;* (Tax Fac), Home Decor Beighton Road East, Waterthorpe, SHEFFIELD, S20 7JZ.
LORAN, Mr. Matthew David, BSc(Hons) ACA *2001;* Honeysuckle Cottage, 1 Church Street, Norton St. Philip, BATH, BA2 7LU.
LORCA-VALVERDE, Mr. Julian, BA ACA CTA *2001;* 45 Fulmar Drive, SALE, CHESHIRE, M33 4WH.
LORD, Mr. Alistair Richard Leonard, BSc ACA *1994;* 4 Park View, Upper Bristol Road, BATH, BA1 3AW.
LORD, Mrs. Amanda, ACA CTA *1989;* Latchford Cottage, Broad Gate, TODMORDEN, LANCASHIRE, OL14 8DE.
LORD, Mr. Andrew Stephen, BSc(Econ) ACA *1998;* 31 Long Croft, Brimsham Park, Yate, BRISTOL, BS37 7YN.
LORD, Mr. Calvin, BSocSc ACA *1990;* 21 New Court Drive, Egerton, BOLTON, BL7 9XA.
LORD, Mr. Charles Alan Penn, BSc FCA *1977;* 6 Shepherd Close, Long Itchington, SOUTHAM, CV47 9RE.
LORD, Mrs. Claire Louise, BA ACA *1999;* 2 Maplewood, Ashurst, SKELMERSDALE, LANCASHIRE, WN8 6RJ.
LORD, Mr. Colin Ian, BA FCA *1990;* 150 Eastham Village Road, Eastham, WIRRAL, MERSEYSIDE, CH62 0AE.
LORD, Mr. David, FCA *1954;* The Burgage, Croydon Road, WESTERHAM, TN16 1TX. (Life Member)
LORD, Mr. Eric, FCA CTA TEP *1970;* 59 Crosland Road, Oakes, HUDDERSFIELD, HD3 3PB. (Life Member)
•LORD, Miss. Gillian Sara, BA ACA *1999;* PricewaterhouseCoopers, 7 More London Riverside, LONDON, SE1 2RT. See also PricewaterhouseCoopers LLP
LORD, Mr. Ian Burnham, FCA *1974;* 2 Highfield Road, Edenfield, Ramsbottom, BURY, BL0 0LB.
LORD, Mr. Ian Frank, ACA *2005;* 11 Hillpark Avenue, Fulwood, PRESTON, PR2 3QQ.
LORD, Mr. James, DFC FCA *1950;* 16 Wyndale Road, LEICESTER, LE2 3WR. (Life Member)
LORD, Mrs. Jeanette Catherine, BA ACA *1991;* 7 Lidgard Street, THORNLANDS, QLD 4164, AUSTRALIA.
•LORD, Miss. Joanna Lindsey, BA ACA *2001;* with KPMG LLP, Aquis Court, 31 Fishpool Street, ST. ALBANS, HERTFORDSHIRE, AL3 4RF.
LORD, Mrs. Joanne Valerie, BA ACA *1995;* 66 Clarence Road, TEDDINGTON, MIDDLESEX, TW11 0BW.
LORD, Mr. John William, FCA *1953;* Lark Rise, Pondfield Lane, Shorne, GRAVESEND, DA12 3LD. (Life Member)
•LORD, Mrs. Linda Jane, BSc FCA *1995;* Streets LLP, Tower House, Lucy Tower Street, LINCOLN, LINCOLNSHIRE, LN1 1XW.
LORD, Mrs. Lisa Catherine, BSc(Hons) ACA *2002;* with PKF (Isle of Man) LLC, PO Box 16, Analyst House, Douglas, ISLE OF MAN, IM99 1AP.
LORD, Mr. Mark Thomas, BSc ACA CF *1990;* with Smith & Williamson (Bristol) LLP, Portwall Place, Portwall Lane, BRISTOL, BS1 6NA.
LORD, Mrs. Mary Ann, BSc ACA *1991;* 63 Ridgeway Road, Long Ashton, BRISTOL, BS41 9EZ.
LORD, Mr. Nicholas John, BA ACA *2003;* 2, Alliance Boots, 2 The Heights Brooklands, WEYBRIDGE, KT13 0NY.
•LORD, Mr. Philip John, FCA *1972;* White Willows, Copthorn Road, COLWYN BAY, LL28 5YP.
LORD, Miss. Rachel, BA ACA *1991;* (Tax Fac), Morgan Stanley, 20 Bank Street, LONDON, E14 4AD.
•LORD, Miss. Rebecca Marie, ACA MAAT *2005;* Rebecca Marie Lord ACA MAAT, 52 Sparrowmire Lane, KENDAL, CUMBRIA, LA9 5PX.
LORD, Mrs. Sarah, PhD BA ACA *2002;* with Deloitte LLP, 2 New Street Square, LONDON, EC4A 3BZ.
LORD, Mrs. Sarah Lucy, BA ACA *2002;* 26 Primet Heights, COLNE, BB8 8EF.
LORD, Dr. Simon Durning, PhD BSc ACA *2002;* 11 Jersey Lane, ST. ALBANS, HERTFORDSHIRE, AL4 9AD.
LORD, Mr. Simon Martin, BA FCA *1999;* Pelham House, Ashcombe Place, Turton, BOLTON, BL7 0QN.
LORD, Dr. Stacey Marie, PhD MChem ACA *2010;* 118 Fairfield Hill, LEEDS, LS13 3DJ.
LORD, Miss. Stephanie Monica, BSc ACA *2007;* Apartment 4 Gateway, 216 Cambridge Road, Great Shelford, CAMBRIDGE, CB22 5JU.
LORD, Mr. Stephen John, BSc ACA *1993;* (Tax Fac), 22 Scotts Way, Riverhead, SEVENOAKS, TN13 2DG.
LORD, Mr. Steven Thomas, MA ACA *1994;* 66 Cyril Street West, TAUNTON, SOMERSET, TA2 6JD.
LORD, Mr. Timothy, MSc ACA *1990;* Gamekeepers Lodge Farm Hawkridge Hill, Frilsham Hermitage, THATCHAM, RG18 9XA.
LORD, Mr. Vernon James, BA ACA *1992;* 79 Stamford Road, Bowdon, ALTRINCHAM, CHESHIRE, WA14 2JJ.
•LORDING, Mr. Trevor Anthony, BSc FCA *1975;* Westfield House, Church Road, CROWBOROUGH, EAST SUSSEX, TN6 1EE.
LORENZ, Mr. Kanagaraj, FCA *1982;* 27 Moody Street, North Balwyn, MELBOURNE, VIC 3104, AUSTRALIA.
LORENZI, Mr. Peter Rudiger, BSc ACA *2000;* GlaxoSmithKline R&D, 709 Swedeland Road, KING OF PRUSSIA, PA 19406-0939, UNITED STATES.
LORENZO PEREZ, Mr. Ronan, ACA CA(SA) *2009;* 11 Shepherds Bush Place, LONDON, W12 8LX.
LORIMER, Mr. Andrew Charles, BA FCA *1982;* (Tax Fac), 87 Churchgate, SOUTHPORT, MERSEYSIDE, PR9 7JF.
LORIMER, Mrs. Helena, MA ACA *2007;* 33 Polwarth Crescent, NEWCASTLE UPON TYNE, NE3 2EE.
LORIMER, Mr. Paul Maurice, BSc ACA *1992;* Whiteways, Hatherden, ANDOVER, SP11 0HT.
LORING, Mr. Christopher Thomas, FCA *1968;* 9 Greystones Drive, REIGATE, RH2 0HA.
LORING, Mr. Stephen Charles William, BCom ACA *1993;* 6 Heathfield Square, LONDON, SW18 3HY.
LORKIN, Mr. Anthony Chatterton, FCA *1959;* Linacre, 33 Bulstrode Way, GERRARDS CROSS, SL9 7QT.
LORKIN, Mr. William James, BCom ACA *2001;* 20 Talbot Road, RICKMANSWORTH, HERTFORDSHIRE, WD3 1HE.
LORMOR, Miss. Helen, ACA *2008;* Oak Lea Moss Lane, Mobberley, KNUTSFORD, CHESHIRE, WA16 7BU.
LORRAINE, Mrs. Lesley, BA ACA *1992;* 17 The Boulevard, WOODFORD GREEN, ESSEX, IG8 8GW.
LORRIMAN, Mr. Malcolm Eric, MA BCom FCA *1972;* 15 Foster Walk, Sherburn in Elmet, LEEDS, NORTH YORKSHIRE, LS25 6EU.
LORRIMER, Mr. Anthony Peter, FCA *1969;* William Davis Ltd Forest Field, Forest Road, LOUGHBOROUGH, LEICESTERSHIRE, LE11 3NS.
•LORYMAN, Mr. Jason, BSc ACA *2000;* M J Bushell Ltd, 8 High Street, BRENTWOOD, ESSEX, CM14 4AB.
LOS, Mr. Pantelis George, BSc(Hons) ACA *2010;* Flat 114, 20 Abbey Road, LONDON, NW8 9BW.
LOSEBY, Mrs. Aimi Jane, BSc ACA *1995;* 7 Clifton Drive, Oundle, PETERBOROUGH, PE8 4EP.
LOSS, Mr. Andrew Stephan, BA ACA *2010;* Flat 9, Cloverley, 108 Brooklands Road, SALE, CHESHIRE, M33 3QE.
LOTAY, Mr. Sukhbinder Singh, BA FCA FCCA *1990;* The Courtyard, 4 Belvoir Close, Oadby, LEICESTER, LE2 4SG.
•LOTE, Mr. Alfred Roy, FCA *1975;* Roy Lote, Exchequer House, 117 Lea Street, KIDDERMINSTER, WORCESTERSHIRE, DY10 1SN.
LOTEN, Mr. David Ian, BA ACA *1994;* Tamarisk, North Street, Westbourne, EMSWORTH, HAMPSHIRE, PO10 8SR.
LOTHIAN, Mrs. Alison Jane, BSc ACA *1986;* 67 Rosebushes, Epsom Downs, EPSOM, KT17 3NT.
LOTHIAN, Mr. Stuart Laird, FCA *1975;* Lothian Associates Ltd, 7 MacFarlane Close, Impington, CAMBRIDGE, CB24 9LZ.
LOTHIAN, Mr. Thomas William, FCA *1948;* Esmond Cottage, 28 Newtown, SIDMOUTH, DEVON, EX10 8QG. (Life Member)
LOTT, Dr. David, ACA *2006;* 24 Park Avenue, Histon, CAMBRIDGE, CB24 9JU.
LOTT, Mr. Norman Alec Charles, BSc ACA *1981;* St. Anns Lodge, Ruxbury Road, CHERTSEY, SURREY, KT16 9NH.
LOTT, Mr. Richard, BSc ACA *1991;* 35 Takutai Avenue, Bucklands Beach, AUCKLAND 2012, NEW ZEALAND.
LOUCA, Mr. George, BSc ACA *2003;* KALLIPOLEOS 19A, 2325 LAKATAMIA, CYPRUS.
LOUDEN, Mr. Nicholas William, BSc ACA *1995;* 4 Coed Ceirios, Rhiwbina, CARDIFF, CF14 6HN.
LOUDON, Mr. Keith, FCA *1958;* Redmayne Bentley, 84 Albion Street, LEEDS, LS1 6AG.
LOUDON, Mr. Stephen John, BSc ACA *1992;* TNT Express, Trinity Park, BIRMINGHAM, B37 7ES.
LOUDOUN, Mr. Robin Alexander, FCA *1979;* Via di San Ginese 80, San Ginese Di Compito, 55012 CAPANNORI, ITALY.
LOUGEE, Mr. Robert Malcolm, FCA *1974;* Salesian College, Reading Road, FARNBOROUGH, HAMPSHIRE, GU14 6PA.
LOUGEE, Mr. Rupert Grafton, BA ACA *2000;* 126 Osier Crescent, Muswell Hill, LONDON, N10 1RF.
LOUGH, Mr. Francis Baxter, FCA *1949;* Tweedsyde, 15 Castle Terrace, BERWICK-UPON-TWEED, TD15 1NR. (Life Member)
LOUGHLIN, Mrs. Deborah, BA ACA *1995;* 48 Arran Drive, FRODSHAM, WA6 6AL.
LOUGHLIN, Mr. Timothy Patrick, BA ACA *1991;* 54 Wrenbeck Drive, OTLEY, LS21 2BR.
LOUGHNANE, Mr. Simon Paul, MEng ACA *2002;* Kemp House, 56-58 High Street, Stoke Goldington, NEWPORT PAGNELL, BUCKINGHAMSHIRE, MK16 8NR.
LOUGHNANE, Miss. Susan Monica, BA ACA *1997;* 15 Elmhurst Avenue, LONDON, N2 0LT.
•LOUGHNANE, Mr. Terence John, FCA *1973;* (Tax Fac), T J Loughnane Limited, The Studio, Broad Street Walk, WOKINGHAM, BERKSHIRE, RG40 1BW.
LOUGHNANE, Mr. William Patrick, MA ACA *1997;* M B N A International Bank Ltd, Chester Business Park, CHESTER, CH4 9FB.
LOUGHNEY, Mr. Daniel, ACA *2011;* Pricewaterhousecoopers, 101 Barbirolli Square, MANCHESTER, M2 3PW.
LOUGHRAN, Mr. Ian Gerard, BSc ACA *1996;* 87 Navan Fort Road, ARMAGH, BT60 4PR.
LOUGHRAN, Mrs. Joanne Marie, LLB ACA *2002;* Air Liquide UK Ltd, Station Road, Coleshill, BIRMINGHAM, B46 1JY.
LOUGHRAN, Miss. Sarah Janice, BSc ACA *1992;* 257 New Ridley Road, STOCKSFIELD, NORTHUMBERLAND, NE43 7RB.
LOUGHREY, Mr. Adrian Nial, BA ACA *1993;* Co-operative Financial Services, Miller Street, MANCHESTER, M60 0AL.
LOUGHREY, Mr. Gavin, ACA *1996; (ACA Ireland* 34 Elthiron Road, LONDON, SW6 4BW.
LOUGHREY, Mr. John Gerard, MSc ACA *1997;* 9 The Courtyard, Victoria Road, MARLOW, BUCKINGHAMSHIRE, SL7 1GR.
•LOUGHREY, Mr. Mark John, BA FCA *1990;* (Tax Fac), Loughrey & Co Ltd, 38 Market Street, Hoylake, WIRRAL, MERSEYSIDE, CH47 2AF.
LOUGHREY, Mr. Noel Peter, BA FCA *1976;* 7 Amberley Drive, Hale Barns, ALTRINCHAM, WA15 0DT.
LOUIE, Mr. Chung Wai Alfred, ACA *2007;* Flat E, 7/F Block 5, Sceneway Garden, LAM TIN, KOWLOON, HONG KONG SAR.
LOUIE, Mr. Siu Keung Chris, ACA *2005;* Flat 2505 Lim Kit House Lei Cheng Uk Estate Sham Shui Po, SHAM SHUI PO, KOWLOON, HONG KONG SAR.
LOUIS, Mr. Jaspal Singh, BA ACA *1999;* 35 Reynolds Road, BEACONSFIELD, BUCKINGHAMSHIRE, HP9 2NJ.
LOUIS, Mr. Leung Wing On, ACA *2005;* 4/F Parklane Building, 235 Queen's Road, CENTRAL, HONG KONG SAR.
LOUIS, Mr. Paul William Francis, LLB ACA *1994;* 14 The Anchorage, GIBRALTAR, GIBRALTAR.
LOUISY, Mr. Byford, BSc FCA *1988;* 313 Cardington Road, BEDFORD, MK42 0DA.
•LOUKA, Mrs. Marlen, ACA CA(AUS) *2010;* ML CA Complete Business Solutions Ltd, 16 Olympou Street, PO Box 12193, Lakatamia, 2322 NICOSIA, CYPRUS.
LOUKES, Mr. John Richard, FCA *1973;* 13 Dalewood Road, SHEFFIELD, S8 0EB.
LOUKES, Miss. Vivienne Fee, BA(Hons) ACA *2001;* 17 Beech Road, Hale, ALTRINCHAM, CHESHIRE, WA15 9HX.
LOULLOUPIS, Mr. Andreas Ioannis, BA(Hons) ACA MBA FSI *2001;* 33 Downside Crescent, LONDON, NW3 2AN.
•LOULLOUPIS, Mr. Christodoulos, BSc FCA *1993;* Baker Tilly Klitou and Partners Limassol Limited, 163 Leontiou Street, 3022 LIMASSOL, CYPRUS.

LOUNDES, Mr. Kevin Michael, BSc ACA *2005;* 2 Gorsecroft, Abbeyfields, Douglas, ISLE OF MAN, IM2 7DZ.
LOUNDS, Mr. Paul David, BSc(Econ) ACA *1995;* 3 Sutton Hall Gardens, Little Sutton, ELLESMERE PORT, CH66 4QT.
LOUNT, Mrs. Caroline Anne, BSc ACA *2004;* 11 Spruce Crescent, Branston, LINCOLN, LN4 1TG.
LOUP, Mrs. Caroline Amanda, BA ACA ATII *1990;* Coney Field House, Polhampton, Overton, BASINGSTOKE, HAMPSHIRE, RG25 3ED.
LOUPIS, Mr. Kyriacos Antonios, BSc ACA *1997;* 190 East 7th Street, Apartment 702, NEW YORK, NY 10009, UNITED STATES.
LOURENSZ, Mr. James Peter, BA ACA *2003;* Greenpark Capital, Cassini House, 57-59 St. James's Street, LONDON, SW1A 1LD.
LOURIE, Mr. Alexander Serge, MA FCA *1971;* 59 Burlington Avenue, Kew Gardens, RICHMOND, SURREY, TW9 4DG.
•**LOURIE, Mr. Nicholas Leonard, MA ACA** *1982;* 5 Kennedy Close, ASHBOURNE, DERBYSHIRE, DE6 1GR.
•**LOUTH, Mr. Peter, FCA** *1973;* Peter Louth and Company, 18 Westdown Road, Catford, LONDON, SE6 4RL.
LOUTIT, Mr. Paul Morris, BA ACA *1993;* (Tax Fac), Cadogan Estates Ltd, 18 Cadogan Gardens, LONDON, SW3 2RP.
LOUTSIOS, Mr. Christophoros, ACA *2006;* 30 Kritis Street, 2401 NICOSIA, CYPRUS.
LOUTTIT, Mr. Thomas Sinclair, BSc ACA *1989;* 11 New Road, BOURNEMOUTH, BH10 7DN.
LOUW, Mrs. Alison Elspeth, BSc ACA *2003;* 14 Heights Close, LONDON, SW20 0TH.
LOUW, Mrs. Joan Eileen, ACA CA(SA) *2009;* 26 Apperley Road, STOCKSFIELD, NORTHUMBERLAND, NE43 7PG.
•**LOUW, Mr. Rudolph Heinrich, ACA CA(SA)** *2009;* Clifton Financial Solutions Limited, 110 Coombe Lane, LONDON, SW20 0TH.
LOVAS, Mr. Peter, ACA *1995;* Silkroute financial Group 4th Floor, 43 London Wall, LONDON, EC2M 5TF.
LOVAT, Mrs. Linda Suzanne, BMus ACA *1991;* 26 Ashley Lane, Hendon, LONDON, NW4 1HG.
LOVATT, Mr. Adrian Michael, ACA *1990;* 7 Townsend Close, Humberston, GRIMSBY, DN36 4ER.
LOVATT, Dr. Clive Martin, ACA *1988;* Applegate, Southam Lane, Southam, CHELTENHAM, GL52 3NY.
LOVATT, Mr. Douglas John, FCA *1967;* Northbrook House, Lighthorne, WARWICK, CV35 0AR. (Life Member)
LOVATT, Mrs. Gillian, BAcc ACA *2003;* 100 Riverside Boulevard, Apartment 22A, NEW YORK, NY 10069, UNITED STATES.
LOVATT, Mrs. Joanna, BA(Hons) ACA *2000;* 16 Lapwing Way, ABBOTS LANGLEY, HERTFORDSHIRE, WD5 0GG.
LOVATT, Mr. Mark Andrew, BA ACA *2000;* 16 Lapwing Way, ABBOTS LANGLEY, HERTFORDSHIRE, WD5 0GG.
LOVATT, Mr. Peter Stanley, FCA *1969;* Margaritaville, 21 Kildonan Avenue, BLACKPOOL, FY4 5NL.
LOVATT, Mr. Richard James, LLB ACA *2001;* 100 Riverside Boulevard, Apt 22A, NEW YORK, NY 10019, UNITED STATES.
LOVATT, Mr. Simon David, BSc ACA *1983;* DIPT LTD, Unit 2 Riverside Road Pride Park, DERBY, DE24 8HY.
LOVATT, Mr. Warwick Godfrey, FCA *1960;* Gullholmen, Curly Hill, Middleton, ILKLEY, LS29 0DT. (Life Member)
LOVATT-SMITH, Mr. Neil Murray, FCA *1979;* 18 High Street, Tetsworth, THAME, OXFORDSHIRE, OX9 7AS.
•**LOVE, Miss. Amanda Jane, BA ACA** *1994;* Ernst & Young LLP, 1 More London Place, LONDON, SE1 2AF. See also Ernst & Young Europe LLP
LOVE, Mr. Andrew Michael, FCA *1966;* The Ritz Hotel, Casino Ltd, 86 Jermyn Street, LONDON, SW1Y 6JD.
LOVE, Mr. Benjamin William, BSc(Hons) ACA *2003;* SSP Food Travel Experts, 1 The Heights, Brooklands, WEYBRIDGE, SURREY, KT13 0NY.
LOVE, Mr. David John, ACA *2008;* Wyeth, 32 New Lane, HAVANT, PO9 2NG.
LOVE, Mr. Graham Carvell, MA FCA *1979;* 39 Smith Street, LONDON, SW3 4EP.
LOVE, Mr. Jason, BA(Hons) ACA *2001;* Monkswood 167 Spital Road, WIRRAL, MERSEYSIDE, CH62 2AE.
LOVE, Miss. Joanne Marie, LLB ACA *2006;* with Grant Thornton UK LLP, 4 Hardman Square, Spinningfields, MANCHESTER, M3 3EB.
LOVE, Mr. Mark Jonathan, BA FCA *1990;* Chemin de Grange Canal 18-20, PO Box 3941, 1211 Genev GENEVA, SWITZERLAND.
LOVE, Ms. Martha, BA ACA *1988;* Beech Tree Cottage, Cotswold Close, STAINES, TW18 2DD.
LOVE, Mrs. Melanie, BSc ACA *1997;* Old Oak Barn, Sinton Green, Hallow, WORCESTER, WORCESTERSHIRE, WR2 6NP.
LOVE, Mr. Michael Frank, BA ACA *1980;* Plowden, Cross Lane Head, BRIDGNORTH, SHROPSHIRE, WV16 4SJ.
LOVE, Mrs. Nadine Susannah, BA ACA *1998;* 167 Spital Road, WIRRAL, MERSEYSIDE, CH62 2AE.
LOVE, Dr. Nia Elizabeth, MSc BSc FCA PGCE FHEA *1992;* The East Chalet Groves Avenue, Langland, SWANSEA, SA3 4QF.
•**LOVE, Mr. Nicholas John, ACA FCCA** *2008;* Princecroft Willis LLP, Towngate House, 2-8 Parkstone Road, POOLE, DORSET, BH15 2PW. See also PW Business Solutions
LOVE, Mr. Nicholas John, BSc FCA *1976;* Moorfields, Ford Lane, Henton, WELLS, SOMERSET, BA5 1PD.
LOVE, Miss. Rachel Mary, BA ACA *2004;* 245 Roman Road, Mountnessing, BRENTWOOD, ESSEX, CM15 0UH.
LOVE, Mr. Robert David, BA ACA *2003;* 77 Warkworth Woods, NEWCASTLE UPON TYNE, NE3 5RB.
LOVE, Mr. Robert William, BSc(Econ) FCA *1962;* Portsea House, 3 Sea Lane Close, East Preston, LITTLEHAMPTON, WEST SUSSEX, BN16 1NQ.
•**LOVE, Mr. Royston Frederick, FCA** *1976;* R F Love and Company, 23 Chudleigh Road, EXETER, EX2 8TS.
LOVE, Miss. Sarah, BSc ACA CTA *2005;* 13 Beaumont Road, LONDON, W4 5AL.
LOVE, Mr. Steven John, BSc ACA *1998;* Level 21 H S B C 8-16 Canada Square, LONDON, E14 5HQ.
LOVEARD, Mr. Mark Andrew, MBA BA ACA *1990;* Arc Innovations Limited, c/o PO Box 19114, Courtney Place, WELLINGTON, NEW ZEALAND.
LOVEDAY, Miss. Emma Mary, MA ACA *2005;* Evans Randall International Limited (RAKFTZ branch), PO Box 16111, RAS AL-KHAIMAH, UNITED ARAB EMIRATES.
LOVEDAY, Mrs. Gillian Clare, BAcc ACA *1997;* Fairfield, 22a St. Catherines, ELY, CAMBRIDGESHIRE, CB6 1AP.
LOVEDAY, Mr. Glyn, BSc ACA *1996;* Fairfields, 22a St. Catherines, ELY, CAMBRIDGESHIRE, CB6 1AP.
•**LOVEDAY, Mr. Graham James, MA FCA** *1986;* Counterpoint Limited, Harberts Cottage, 1 Back Street, Ashton Keynes, SWINDON, WILTSHIRE SN6 6PD.
LOVEDAY, Mr. Guy Francis, BSc FCA *1983;* with The Professional Training Partnership, Cherwell Innovation Centre, 77 Heyford Park, Camp Road, Upper Heyford, BICESTER OXFORDSHIRE OX25 5HD.
LOVEDAY, Mr. Paul Henry, FCA *1986;* 11 Rochester Close, Kibworth Harcourt, LEICESTER, LE8 0JS.
LOVEDAY, Mr. Thomas Martin, FCA *1975;* Loveson, Belgrade Centre, Denington Raod, WELLINGBOROUGH, NN8 2QH.
LOVEGROVE, Mr. Andrew, FCA *1991;* Church House, The Square, Epwell, BANBURY, OX15 6LA.
LOVEGROVE, Miss. Deborah, BSc FCA *1998;* 11 Gloucester Crescent, LONDON, NW1 7DS.
LOVEGROVE, Mr. James Alfred Charles, ACA *2009;* 7 New Row, Woodhall Hills Calverley, PUDSEY, WEST YORKSHIRE, LS28 5QY.
LOVEGROVE, Mrs. Margaret, FCA *1968;* 1264 Lakeshore Road, SARNIA N7S 2L4, ON, CANADA.
LOVEGROVE, Mr. Terence John, FCA *1960;* 1b Mortimer Road, ROYSTON, HERTFORDSHIRE, SG8 7HS. (Life Member)
LOVEGROVE, Mr. Tristan Charles, BA ACA *1999;* Credit Suisse, 1 Cabot Square, LONDON, E14 4QJ.
LOVEJOY, Miss. Alicia, BA(Hons) ACA *2004;* 94 Brookmill Road, LONDON, SE8 4JJ.
LOVEJOY, Mr. Christopher John, FCA *1969;* 2 Willow Grove, BEVERLEY, NORTH HUMBERSIDE, HU17 8DS.
•**LOVEJOY, Ms. Nicola, BSc ACA** *1995;* Deloitte LLP, Hill House, 1 Little New Street, LONDON, EC4A 3TR. See also Deloitte & Touche LLP
LOVEJOY, Mr. Peter James, BSc ACA *1999;* 9 Hedges Way, Croxley Green, RICKMANSWORTH, HERTFORDSHIRE, WD3 3FA.
LOVEL, Mr. Digby Richard Isherwood, FCA *1976;* Ivy House, Orchard Lane, Hutton, DRIFFIELD, YO25 9PZ.
LOVELACE, Mr. Craig Barry, BSc FCA *1999;* General Healthcare Group, 4 Thameside Centre Kew Bridge Road, BRENTFORD, MIDDLESEX, TW8 0HF.
•**LOVELADY, Mr. Andrew Robert, FCA** *1980;* (Member of Council 2007 - 2011), (Tax Fac), Andrew R Lovelady, 50 Tollemache Road, PRENTON, MERSEYSIDE, CH43 8SZ.
LOVELADY, Mr. Gordon James, FCA *1954;* 2 Field Way, Corfe Mullen, WIMBORNE, DORSET, BH21 3XH. (Life Member)
LOVELAND, Mr. David, BSocSc ACA *1996;* 8 Warburton Way, Timperley, ALTRINCHAM, CHESHIRE, WA15 7XX.
LOVELAND, Mr. John Charles, BA ACA *1997;* 32 Parkwood Avenue, ESHER, KT10 8DG.
LOVELAND, Mrs. Samantha Juliette, BSc ACA *1996;* with PricewaterhouseCoopers LLP, 1 Embankment Place, LONDON, WC2N 6RH.
LOVELAND, Mr. Simon John, BSocSc FCA *1996;* 35 Sheriffs Close, LICHFIELD, WS14 9RZ.
LOVELESS, Mrs. Andrea Claire, MPhil BSc ACA *1998;* 3 Blenheim Road, ST. ALBANS, HERTFORDSHIRE, AL1 4NS.
LOVELESS, Mr. Brian Charles, FCA *1961;* Les Roses Marines B3, 153 boulevard Pierre Delmas, 06600 ANTIBES, FRANCE. (Life Member)
LOVELESS, Mr. David Charles, BA FCA *1990;* Baker Watkin, Suite 3, Middlesex House, Rutherford Close, STEVENAGE, HERTFORDSHIRE SG1 2EF.
•**LOVELESS, Miss. Jill Anita, FCA** *1983;* Strategy Engineering Associated Limited, The Lilacs, 25 Church Road, LEATHERHEAD, SURREY, KT22 8AT.
LOVELL, Mr. Alan Charles, MA FCA *1979;* The Palace House, Bishops Lane, Bishops Waltham, SOUTHAMPTON, SO32 1DP.
LOVELL, Mr. Alan James, FCA *1957;* Lockers End, Overton Road, Ibstock, LEICESTER, LE67 6PD. (Life Member)
LOVELL, Mr. Alexander Damien, LLB ACA *1999;* 118 Beech Hall Road, LONDON, E4 9NX.
LOVELL, Miss. Anna Katharine, BSc ACA *1996;* 78 Bartholomew Road, LONDON, NW5 2AL.
LOVELL, Mr. David Richard, BSc ACA *1988;* 29 Westpole Avenue, Cockfosters, BARNET, EN4 0AX.
LOVELL, Mrs. Deborah Zena, BA FCA *1994;* The Hollow, Pitt Farm, Exmouth Road, Lympstone, EXMOUTH, DEVON EX8 5AF.
LOVELL, Mrs. Fiona, BA ACA *1992;* Glaxo Smithkline plc, 980 Great West Road, BRENTFORD, MIDDLESEX, TW8 9GS.
•**LOVELL, Mr. George, BSc(Econ) ACA CTA** *1998;* Inspired Tax Solutions, Bobs Old House, Hatton Lane, Hatton, WARRINGTON, WA4 4DB.
LOVELL, Mr. Jack, FCA *1940;* 23 Penlee Manor Drive, PENZANCE, TR18 4HW. (Life Member)
LOVELL, Mr. James Anthony, BEng ACA *1992;* Bryn Glas Hawley Lane, Hale Barns, ALTRINCHAM, CHESHIRE, WA15 0DJ.
LOVELL, Mr. James David, BSocSc ACA *1999;* 22 Beech Lea, Blunsdon, SWINDON, SN26 7DE.
LOVELL, Mr. John Phillip, FCA *1982;* C/o Sheffield Forgemasters International Limited, PO Box 286 Brightside Lane, SHEFFIELD, SOUTH YORKSHIRE, S9 2RW.
•**LOVELL, Mr. Jonathan Andrew, BA FCA** *1991;* KPMG LLP, One Snowhill, Snow Hill Queensway, BIRMINGHAM, B4 6GN. See also KPMG Europe LLP
LOVELL, Mr. Jonathan Oliver, BA ACA *1999;* 9 Chilton Ridge Hatch Warren, BASINGSTOKE, HAMPSHIRE, RG22 4RG.
LOVELL, Mrs. Julia Susan, BSc ACA *1988;* (Tax Fac), 29 Westpole Avenue, Cockfosters, BARNET, HERTFORDSHIRE, EN4 0AX.
LOVELL, Mr. Keith, BSc ACA *1987;* The Barn, Taplow Vineyard, Hill Farm Road, Taplow, MAIDENHEAD, BERKSHIRE SL6 0HA.
LOVELL, Miss. Kirsty Louise, ACA *2009;* 89 High Street, KIDLINGTON, OXFORDSHIRE, OX5 2DR.
LOVELL, Mrs. Nerys Lynwen, BA(Hons) ACA *2004;* 22 Beech Lea, Blunsdon, SWINDON, SN26 7DE.
LOVELL, Mr. Paul, BSc ACA *1981;* Pounsrough Lodge, Dundle Road, TUNBRIDGE WELLS, TN3 9AG.
•**LOVELL, Mr. Paul Joseph, BSc FCA** *1988;* Lovells, 44 Elthorne Park Road, Hanwell, LONDON, W7 2JA. See also C P Lovells Ltd
LOVELL, Mrs. Philippa Jane, BA(Hons) ACA *2000;* Bobs Old House Hatton Lane, Hatton, WARRINGTON, WA4 4DB.
LOVELL, Mrs. Rachael Claire, BSc ACA *1999;* Cadbury Plc Cadbury House, Sanderson Road, UXBRIDGE, MIDDLESEX, UB8 1DH.
LOVELL, Mr. Richard Douglas Egerton, FCA *1971;* Barclay House, Beeches Hill, Bishops Waltham, SOUTHAMPTON, HAMPSHIRE, SO32 1FD.
LOVELL, Mr. Simon Peter, BSc ACA *1992;* Unipart Rail, Gresty Road, CREWE, CW2 6EH.
LOVELL, Dr. Stephen, PhD MMath ACA *2011;* 11 Roundhay Court, Sutherland Avenue, LEEDS, LS8 1BL.
LOVELL, Mr. Thomas Scott, BSc(Hons) ACA *2006;* Flat 5, 68 Upper Richmond Road, LONDON, SW15 2RP.
LOVELL, Mr. Timothy James Carey, BA ACA *1981;* 42 Stradella Road, LONDON, SE24 9HA.
LOVELL, Mr. Trevor Roy, FCA *1960;* 19 Cotham Park, BRISTOL, BS6 6BZ.
LOVELL, Mrs. Victoria Hannah Louise, BA ACA *2005;* with Armstrong Watson, Fairview House, Victoria Place, CARLISLE, CA1 1HP.
LOVELL-DAVIS, Mr. Jeremy Stuart, BSc ACA *2004;* 1 Maritime Square, #11-01 HarbourFront Centre, SINGAPORE 099253, SINGAPORE.
LOVELL MANSBRIDGE, Mr. Brian Geoffrey, FCA *1959;* 216 The Fairway, RUISLIP, HA4 0SL.
LOVELOCK, Miss. Susan Marie, BA ACA *1992;* Philip Morris Ltd, 5 Thameside Centre Kew Bridge Road, BRENTFORD, TW8 0HF.
•**LOVELUCK, Mr. Christopher Paul, FCA** *1981;* A.C. Mole & Sons, Stafford House, Blackbrook Park Avenue, TAUNTON, SOMERSET, TA1 2PX.
LOVELY, Mr. Ronald, FCA *1947;* 9 Rectory Green, West Boldon, EAST BOLDON, NE36 0QD. (Life Member)
LOVERIDGE, Ms. Anne Joan, BA ACA *1988;* PricewaterhouseCoopers, Darling Park Tower 2, 201 Sussex Street, GPO Box 2650, SYDNEY, NSW 1171 AUSTRALIA.
LOVERIDGE, Dr. David Graham, PhD FCA *1976;* 11 Admiral Place, Rotherhithe, LONDON, SE16 5NY.
LOVERIDGE, Mr. Thomas, BSc ACA *2011;* All Saints Vicarage, Churchfields, HERTFORD, SG13 8AE.
LOVERING, Mr. Brian Sinclair, BSc FCA *1977;* Over Court Cottage, Over, Almondsbury, BRISTOL, BS32 4DG.
LOVERING, Dr. Jonathan Roy, FCA *1990;* 2 Woodbury Close, CROYDON, CR0 5PR.
LOVERING, Mr. Nicholas John, BA ACA *2000;* 32 Carmalt Gardens, LONDON, SW15 6NE.
LOVERING, Mr. Roger Vincent, BSc ACA CTA *1985;* (Tax Fac), 2 Foxhanger Gardens, WOKING, GU22 7BQ.
LOVESEY, Ms. Jane Hannah, BA ACA *1992;* 61 Latimer Road, Wimbledon, LONDON, SW19 1EW.
LOVESEY, Mr. Robert John, BA FCA *1985;* 35 Chichester Court, Chessington Road, EPSOM, KT17 1TP.
LOVESY, Mr. James, BA ACA *2007;* Varvsgatan 1B 4tr, 117 29 STOCKHOLM, SWEDEN.
•①**LOVETT, Mr. Alan, BSc FCA** *1978;* Baker Tilly Restructuring And Recovery LLP, 25 Farringdon Street, LONDON, EC4A 4AB. See also Baker Tilly Tax and Advisory Services LLP
•**LOVETT, Mr. Andrew Barrington, FCA** *1977;* (Tax Fac), The Taxation Compliance Company Limited, 9 Manor Road, Wheathampstead, ST. ALBANS, AL4 8JG. See also FBL Services Limited
•**LOVETT, Mr. Andrew George, FCA** *1975;* Gilberts, Pendragon House, 65 London Road, ST. ALBANS, AL1 1LJ.
LOVETT, Mr. Brian Anthony, MSc FCA *1976;* The Platt, Great Woodford Drive, Plympton, PLYMOUTH, PL7 4RP.
LOVETT, Mr. Brian Ernest, FCA *1958;* PO Box 388, Rye, NEW YORK, NY 10580-0388, UNITED STATES. (Life Member)
LOVETT, Mr. Clive Jonathan, BSc ACA *1989;* S P Group, 9 Hedera Road, REDDITCH, WORCESTERSHIRE, B98 9EY.
•**LOVETT, Mr. David Charles, BA FCA** *1977;* AlixPartners Ltd, 20 North Audley Street, LONDON, W1K 6WE. See also AlixPartners UK LLP
LOVETT, Mr. David Ian, BSc ACA *1985;* 1 Broadbent Close, Rownhams, SOUTHAMPTON, SO16 8LQ.
LOVETT, Mr. David John, ACA *2009;* Chiltern Cottage, Chalkhouse Green, READING, RG4 9AH.
LOVETT, Mrs. Emily Jane, ACA *1989;* 31A Hall Park Hill, BERKHAMSTED, HERTFORDSHIRE, HP4 2NH.
LOVETT, Mr. Grahame Philip, FCA *1987;* 5 Rievaulx Close, KNARESBOROUGH, HG5 8NG.
•**LOVETT, Mr. Greg James, BA(Hons) ACA** *2001;* Fizz Accounting Limited, Meteor House, Eastern Bypass, THAME, OXFORDSHIRE, OX9 3RL.
•**LOVETT, Mr. Hugh Richard, BA ACA** *1984;* Thornalley & Co Limited, 143 Burton Road, LINCOLN, LN1 3LN. See also Thornalley & Co
LOVETT, Mr. Mark Alexander, BCom ACA *1999;* 33 Galanos, Long Itchington, SOUTHAM, WARWICKSHIRE, CV47 9NZ.
•**LOVETT, Mr. Richard Anthony, FCA** *1973;* 10 Homewood Road, ST. ALBANS, HERTFORDSHIRE, AL1 4BH.
•**LOVETT, Miss. Sharon Margaret, BSc ACA** *1994;* 9 Jacksons Lane, Highgate, LONDON, N6 5SR.
•**LOVETT, Mr. Stephen Peter, ACA** *1990;* Hill Barn Management, Hill Barn, Gore Lane, Uplyme, LYME REGIS, DORSET DT7 3RJ.

LOVETT, Mr. William Neil, ACA *1979;* 11 Mount Close, Poundhill, CRAWLEY, RH10 7EF.
•**LOVETT, Mrs. Yvonne, BA FCA DChA** *1987;* Barnett & Turner LLP, Cromwell House, 68 West Gate, MANSFIELD, NOTTINGHAMSHIRE, NG18 1RR. See also Barnett & Turner
LOVETT-TURNER, Mr. Ewan, ACA *2008;* 17 Ormonde Road, GODALMING, GU7 2EU.
LOVETT-TURNER, Mrs. Joanne Sarah, MSc ACA *1998;* 2 Holroyd Road, Putney, LONDON, SW15 6LN.
•**LOVIBOND, Mrs. Caroline Rosemary, BSc FCA CTA** *1990;* landtax LLP, Mitre House, Lodge Road, Long Hanborough, Business Park, WITNEY OXFORDSHIRE OX29 8SS.
LOVICK, Mr. John Graham, FCA *1975;* Church Farm Cottage, Reynalton, KILGETTY, DYFED, SA68 0PG. (Life Member)
LOVICK, Mr. Michael Trevor David, FCA *1975;* Pillar Barn, 8 Higher Hendham Barns, Woodleigh, KINGSBRIDGE, DEVON, TQ7 4DP.
LOVIS, Mr. Eric Walter, FCA *1959;* 195 Fire Dance Lane, QUALICUM BEACH V9K 2L6, BC, CANADA. (Life Member)
•**LOVITT, Mr. Robert John Clarke, BA FCA** *1990;* (Tax Fac), Greenaway, 150 High Street, SEVENOAKS, TN13 1XE.
LOW, Mr. Alan Frederick, FCA *1977;* PO Box 766, WELLINGTON, 7654, SOUTH AFRICA.
LOW, Mr. Allan Christopher Michael, BA ACA *1986;* PO Box 95, SAFAT, 13001, KUWAIT.
LOW, Miss. Amanda Frances, BA ACA *2009;* 79 Birkbeck Road, SIDCUP, DA14 4DJ.
LOW, Mr. Andrew Richard, BSc ACA *1979;* 1601 7th Street N.W., CALGARY T2M 3H7, AB, CANADA.
LOW, Mr. Check Kwang, BA ACA *1979;* 46 Meyer Road, #21-02 The View@Meyer, SINGAPORE 437871, SINGAPORE.
LOW, Ms. Cheng Ee, FCA *1974;* Thornymoor, Mogador, TADWORTH, SURREY, KT20 7HL.
LOW, Ms. Cheryl Li Choo, BA ACA *2008;* Millray, Slines Oak Road, Woldingham, CATERHAM, SURREY, CR3 7HL.
LOW, Mr. Ching Kam Michael, BA ACA *1991;* 34 Shamrock Way, Southgate, LONDON, N14 5RY.
•**LOW, Mr. Chong Han, FCA** *1979;* Chong & Co, Flat 4, 55 Lancaster Gate, LONDON, W2 3NA.
LOW, Mr. Duncan Forbes, MA ACA *2000;* KPMG S.A., 1 Cours Valmy, 92923 PARIS LA DÉFENSE, FRANCE.
LOW, Mr. Geoffrey Hadden, FCA *1959;* 7 Baldwin Avenue, Childwall, LIVERPOOL, L16 3GD. (Life Member)
LOW, Ms. Geok Beng, FCA *1975;* Flat 12, Ashbourne Lodge, 18a Hazelwood Lane, Palmers Green, LONDON, N13 5EP. (Life Member)
LOW, Mr. Hamish Ewen Scott, BSc ACA *2001;* 43 Ockendon Road, Islington, LONDON, N1 3NL.
LOW, Mr. Han Hing, FCA *1973;* Rockwills International Sdn.Bhd, Wisma Rockwills No 62 Jalan 2/131A, Off Jalan Klang Lama, 58200 KUALA LUMPUR, FEDERAL TERRITORY, MALAYSIA. (Life Member)
LOW, Mr. Ian Robert, BSc FCA *1987;* 60 Grove Park Road, Chiswick, LONDON, W4 3SD.
LOW, Mr. James Tze Fatt, FCA *1974;* P O Box 958, Pejabat Pos MPC, BB 3577, Old Airport Berekas, BANDAR SERI BEGAWAN, BB 3577 BRUNEI DARUSSALAM.
LOW, Miss. Jean Su-Im, BSc ACA *1995;* Mapletree Investments Pte Ltd, 1 Maritime Square Apt 13-01, Harbourfront Centre, SINGAPORE 099253, SINGAPORE.
LOW, Ms. Jennifer Elizabeth, BSc FCA *1988;* Level 6, 40 St Georges Terrace, PERTH, WA 6000, AUSTRALIA.
LOW, Miss. Jo-Lyn, BA ACA *2007;* 91 Jalan ss 22/32, Damansara Jaya, 47400 PETALING JAYA, SELANGOR, MALAYSIA.
LOW, Mr. John, FCA *1958;* 21 Fraser Avenue, Horsforth, LEEDS, LS18 5EA. (Life Member)
LOW, Mrs. Juliet Carole, BA ACA *1998;* Juliet C Low, KPMG, 10 Shelley Street, SYDNEY, NSW 2000, AUSTRALIA.
LOW, Mr. Khim Wah, BSc ACA *1991;* 23 Hume Avenue, #04-01 Hume Park 2, SINGAPORE 598729, SINGAPORE.
LOW, Mr. Kian Huat, PhD ACA *2009;* 27 Melrose Gardens, NEW MALDEN, KT3 3HQ.
LOW, Mr. Kok Boon, ACA *1984;* 51 Jalan Jalil Perkasa 18, Taman Esplana, Bukit Jalil, 57000 KUALA LUMPUR, FEDERAL TERRITORY, MALAYSIA.
LOW, Mr. Kok Heng, BA ACA *2001;* 7215-C Jalan Datuk Palembang, Bukit Baru, 75150 MALACCA CITY, MALACCA STATE, MALAYSIA.
LOW, Mr. Kok Teck, BA ACA *1988;* K.T. Low Management Services, 86 Lorong Tamarino, 41500 KLANG, SELANGOR, MALAYSIA.
LOW, Miss. Mairi Alison, BA ACA *1993;* c/o J E Bergasse & Co Ltd, PO Box 102, CASTRIES, SAINT LUCIA.
LOW, Ms. May-Lin, BA ACA *2004;* 24 Dublin Road, SINGAPORE 239811, SINGAPORE.
LOW, Mr. Nicholas, BA ACA *2006;* 52 Rostrevor Avenue, LONDON, N15 6LP.
LOW, Mr. Peter Boon Hock, LLB ACA *1989;* Flat 5, 186 St. John Street, LONDON, EC1V 4JZ.
LOW, Mr. Peter Michael Stuart, ACA *1986;* 385 Glen Arden Place, ATLANTA, GA 30305, UNITED STATES.
LOW, Miss. Sally Wing Sze, BA(Econ) ACA *2004;* 10 Casher Road, Maidenbower, CRAWLEY, RH10 7JG.
LOW, Miss. Shir-Ly, ACA *2009;* 90 Jalan Sepat, 1 Kaw 7 Tmnteluk Pulai, Klang, 4110 KLANG, SELANGOR, MALAYSIA.
LOW, Miss. Soh Liew, FCA *1974;* 70 Greenleaf Drive, SINGAPORE 279567, SINGAPORE.
LOW, Mr. Stephen James Clayton, BSc ACA *1982;* 21 Haglis Drive, Wendover, AYLESBURY, HP22 6LY.
LOW, Mr. Thong Meng, ACA *1979;* 25 Erlestoke Place, CASTLE HILL, NSW 2154, AUSTRALIA.
LOW, Mr. Weng Keong, FCA *1977;* 59 Sommerville Estate Road, Sommerville Park, SINGAPORE 258044, SINGAPORE.
LOW, Miss. Wye Meng, BSc ACA *1997;* 3rd Floor CBBC Portland House, Bressenden Place, LONDON, SW1E 5BH.
LOW, Miss. Yee Wai, ACA *2008;* Norges Bank Investment Management, Bankplassen 2, P.O. Box 1179 Sentrum, NO-0107 OSLO, NORWAY.
LOW ENG HUAT, Mr. Peter, ACA *1992;* PricewaterhouseCoopers LLP, 17-00 PWC Building, 8 Cross Street, SINGAPORE 048424, SINGAPORE.
LOW YOKE, Miss. Anne, ACA *1984;* 19D Rome Court, Realty Gardens, 41 Conduit Road, MID LEVELS, HONG KONG ISLAND, HONG KONG SAR.
LOWBRIDGE, Mr. Stuart, BA ACA *1994;* Bleak House, Crowle, WORCESTER, WR7 4AZ.
LOWCOCK, Miss. Margaret, BSc ACA *1979;* 18 Valley Road, Bramley, LEEDS, LS13 1EZ.
LOWCOCK, Mr. Rodney William, FCA *1966;* 3 Hempstead Road, Hempstead, GILLINGHAM, Kent, ME7 3SA.
LOWDE, Mr. Geoffrey William, BA ACA *1985;* Ardencom Ltd Unit 1 Elm Court, Meriden Business Park Copse Drive, COVENTRY, CV5 9RG.
LOWDE, Mr. James Ernest, FCA *1978;* 1 The Woodlands, Hedon, HULL, HU12 8PT.
LOWDE, Mr. Keith Roy Donald, FCA *1968;* Minoru, Pharaohs Island, SHEPPERTON, MIDDLESEX, TW17 9LN.
LOWDE, Mr. Leslie John, FCA *1979;* 62 Beverley Road, DRIFFIELD, NORTH HUMBERSIDE, YO25 6RZ.
LOWDEN, Mr. Andrew Michael, FCA *1978;* 15 Queens Road, SALE, M33 6QA.
LOWDEN, Mr. David Gibbon, FCA *1957;* Flat 401, Mountjoy House, Barbican, LONDON, EC2Y 8BP. (Life Member)
LOWDEN, Miss. Jane Louise, BSc ACA *2005;* F. W. Smith Riches & Co., 15 Whitehall, LONDON, SW1A 2DD.
LOWDEN, Mr. Peter Richard, FCA *1966;* 44 Cedar Road, FARNBOROUGH, Hampshire, GU14 7AX.
LOWDON, Mr. Lennox, FCA *1964;* Durnovaria, Barnfield Road, EXETER, EX1 1RX.
LOWDON, Mr. Martin Robert, MA *1990;* 22 Bitteswell Road, LUTTERWORTH, LEICESTERSHIRE, LE17 4EZ.
LOWDON, Ms. Sarah, BA ACA *1992;* 208 Grosvenor Drive, Wyndham, RALEIGH, NC 27615, UNITED STATES.
LOWDON, Mr. Thomas James, BSc ACA *2010;* Upper flat, 4 West Road, PRUDHOE, NORTHUMBERLAND, NE42 6HP.
LOWE, Miss. Aimee Elizabeth, ACA *2010;* 60 Borough Hill, CROYDON, CR0 4LN.
LOWE, Mr. Alan Edward, BAcc FCA *1992;* Avalon, 77 Long Lane, ICKENHAM, MIDDLESEX, UB10 8QS.
LOWE, Mr. Alexander Harvey, FCA *1974;* 21 Summer Avenue, EAST MOLESEY, KT8 9LU.
LOWE, Mrs. Alison Margaret, BA FCA *1989;* 14 Winsford Close, Balsall Common, COVENTRY, CV7 7UB.
•**LOWE, Mr. Andrew Alexander Eaton, BSc FCA** *1984;* with PricewaterhouseCoopers LLP, 1 Embankment Place, LONDON, WC2N 6RH.
LOWE, Mrs. Angela Theresa, BA FCA *1997;* 50 Milton Avenue, Eaton Ford, ST. NEOTS, CAMBRIDGESHIRE, PE19 7LE.
LOWE, Mr. Anthony Desmond, FCA *1959;* 20 Buxton Lane, CATERHAM, CR3 5HD. (Life Member)
LOWE, Mr. Basil John Assheton, MA FCA *1946;* Longcroft, 25 Sandown Road, ESHER, KT10 9TT. (Life Member)
LOWE, Miss. Bethany Jane, ACA *2007;* Abu Dhabi Basic Industries Corporation, 13th Floor Al Khazna Building, Al Najda Street, ABU DHABI, 7063, UNITED ARAB EMIRATES.
LOWE, Mr. Charles, BSc ACA *2009;* Flat 1 Heathfield Court, Heathfield Road, LONDON, SW18 3HU.
LOWE, Mr. Charles Richard, BSc ACA *2010;* Delamere, 14 Heyes Lane, ALDERLEY EDGE, CHESHIRE, SK9 7JY.
LOWE, Mr. Chris John, BSc ACA *1989;* 10 Devonshire Place, LONDON, W1G 6HS.
LOWE, Mr. Christopher, BSc ACA *2005;* with Beever and Struthers, St George's House, 215-219 Chester Road, MANCHESTER, M15 4JE.
•**LOWE, Mr. Christopher David, BSc ACA** *1985;* Camfield Chapman Lowe Limited, 9 High Street, Woburn Sands, MILTON KEYNES, MK17 8RF.
LOWE, Mr. Christopher Dennis, BSc ACA *1979;* 6 Rushett Road, THAMES DITTON, KT7 0UX.
LOWE, Mr. Christopher James, MA FCA *1963;* Hill House, Norwood Hill, HORLEY, RH6 0HP. (Life Member)
LOWE, Mr. David, FCA *1980;* (Tax Fac), 92 Regent Road, Lostock, BOLTON, BL6 4DE.
LOWE, Mr. David, FCA *1975;* Pear Tree House, Tholthorpe, YORK, YO61 1SN.
LOWE, Mr. David Alan, BCom ACA *1998;* 280 Jockey Road, SUTTON COLDFIELD, WEST MIDLANDS, B73 5XL.
LOWE, Mr. David Andrew, FCA *1977;* Elder Street, 32 Bedford Row, LONDON, WC1R 4HE.
LOWE, Mrs. Elizabeth Ann, BA(Hons) ACA *2002;* 36 Admiral Way, GODALMING, GU7 1QN.
LOWE, Mrs. Emma, BSc(Hons) ACA *2009;* PO Box 15012, NAIROBI, 00509, KENYA.
LOWE, Prof. Ernest Anthony, BSc(Econ) FCA *1953;* Southcroft, Flat 8, 33 Psalter Lane, SHEFFIELD, S11 8YL. (Life Member)
LOWE, Mr. Gareth Arnold, BSc ACA *1991;* with David Gamblin, 71 The Hundred, ROMSEY, HAMPSHIRE, SO51 8BZ.
•**LOWE, Mr. Gareth Lloyd, BSc ACA** *2004;* (Tax Fac), Aston Hughes & Co, Livingstone House, Llewelyn Avenue, LLANDUDNO, CONWY, LL30 2ER.
LOWE, Mr. George, FCA *1955;* Flat 2, 45 Park Road, New Barnet, BARNET, EN4 9QD. (Life Member)
LOWE, Ms. Helen, ACA *2008;* 11 Maple Close, CONGLETON, CHESHIRE, CW12 4TZ.
LOWE, Ms. Helen, BSc ACA *2003;* Brookes Farm, Lordship Lane, Wistow, SELBY, NORTH YORKSHIRE, YO8 3XE.
LOWE, Mrs. Hilary Ann, BSc ACA *1991;* Hall Liddy, 12 St. John Street, MANCHESTER, M3 4DY.
LOWE, Mr. Hong Check, BAcc ACA *2005;* Block 309 #26-345, Ang Mo Kio Street 31, SINGAPORE 562309, SINGAPORE.
LOWE, Mr. James, BA(Com) FCA *1955;* 70 Evans Lookout Road, BLACKHEATH, NSW 2785, AUSTRALIA. (Life Member)
LOWE, Mr. James Macdonald, BA FCA *1965;* 10 Denewood Court, Queens Road, WILMSLOW, CHESHIRE, SK9 5HP.
LOWE, Mr. James Russell, FCA *1950;* 10 Richmond Street, Worsley Mesnes, WIGAN, LANCASHIRE, WN3 5EB. (Life Member)
LOWE, Mr. James Stuart, BSc ACA *2009;* 68 Greyfriars Road, EXETER, EX4 7BS.
LOWE, Miss. Jennifer Anne, BA ACA *1994;* 41 Mount Row, St. Peter Port, GUERNSEY, GY1 1NU.
LOWE, Mr. Jeremy Clement, BSc(Hons) ACA MABRP *2001;* 7 St. Josephs Vale, LONDON, SE3 0XF.
LOWE, Mr. John, BA ACA *1998;* 26 Wilton Road, Balsall Common, COVENTRY, CV7 7QW.
LOWE, Mr. John Malcolm, FCA *1960;* 1 Barkers Well Lawn, New Farnley, LEEDS, LS12 5TS. (Life Member)
LOWE, Mr. Jonathan David, FCA *1992;* Pricewaterhousecoopers, PO Box 321, GUERNSEY, GY1 4ND.
LOWE, Mr. Jonathan William Comrie, ACA *2008;* Baker Tilly, 25 Farringdon Street, LONDON, EC4A 4AB.
LOWE, Mr. Joseph, BSc ACA *2008;* 21 Harefield Road, RICKMANSWORTH, HERTFORDSHIRE, WD3 1LZ.
•**LOWE, Miss. Julia Ellen, BA(Hons) ACA** *2002;* with Rouse Audit LLP, 55 Station Road, BEACONSFIELD, BUCKINGHAMSHIRE, HP9 1QL.
LOWE, Miss. Karen, BA ACA *1995;* 17 Coombe Road, WIRRAL, CH61 4UN.
•**LOWE, Mrs. Karen Victoria, BSc FCA** *1998;* Geens, 68 Liverpool Road, STOKE-ON-TRENT, ST4 1BG.
LOWE, Mrs. Karin, BSc ACA *1992;* 52 East Street, Long Buckby, NORTHAMPTON, NORTHAMPTONSHIRE, NN6 7RA.
LOWE, Miss. Kathryn, ACA *2010;* 34 Oval View, MIDDLESBROUGH, CLEVELAND, TS4 3SW.
LOWE, Miss. Katy Emily, BSc(Hons) ACA *2011;* 48 Crown Street, Redbourn, ST. ALBANS, HERTFORDSHIRE, AL3 7PF.
•**LOWE, Mr. Kevin Paul, BA ACA** *2000;* with PricewaterhouseCoopers LLP, 7 More London Riverside, LONDON, SE1 2RT.
•**LOWE, Mrs. Lee Lee, FCA** *1975;* Chua Lowe (JB) Limited, 5 Crookhill Road, Conisbrough, DONCASTER, SOUTH YORKSHIRE, DN12 2AD.
LOWE, Mrs. Lisa, BA ACA *2000;* 20 Long Lodge Drive, WALTON-ON-THAMES, SURREY, KT12 3BY.
•**LOWE, Mrs. Lisa Rose, ACA** *1993;* Lowe Henwood Limited, The Lodge, 149 Mannamead Road, PLYMOUTH, PL3 5NU.
LOWE, Miss. Louise Anne, BCom ACA *2000;* 63 Orchard Road West, MANCHESTER, M22 4FD.
LOWE, Mr. Martin James, BSc(Hons) ACA *2001;* 7 Brushwood Road, HORSHAM, WEST SUSSEX, RH12 4PE.
•**LOWE, Mr. Merryck Brandon, MA ACA** *1996;* (Tax Fac), B D O Stoy Hayward, 55 Baker Street, LONDON, W1U 7EU. See also BDO Stoy Hayward LLP
LOWE, Mr. Michael Anthony, FCA *1963;* 45 Manor Road, Keynsham, BRISTOL, BS31 1RB.
LOWE, Mr. Michael Bernard, BSc ACA *2005;* Brookhouse Green Farm, Smallwood, SANDBACH, CW11 2XF.
•**LOWE, Mr. Michael John, CBE FCA** *1960;* Tranter Lowe (D&W) LLP, Bank House, 66 High Street, Dawley, TELFORD, SHROPSHIRE TF4 2HD.
•**LOWE, Mr. Michael John, ACA** *1979;* Hollows Davies Crane, Hoghton Chambers, Hoghton Street, SOUTHPORT, PR9 0TB.
LOWE, Mr. Michael John Richard, BA FCA *1972;* Jasmine, Rambledown Lane, West Chiltington, PULBOROUGH, WEST SUSSEX, RH20 2NW.
•**LOWE, Mr. Michael Malcolm, FCA** *1974;* Mike Lowe, Lydford, Level Mare Lane, Eastergate, CHICHESTER, WEST SUSSEX PO20 3SA.
LOWE, Mr. Michael Peter, ACA *2011;* 16 Crowhurst Drive, WIGAN, LANCASHIRE, WN1 2QH.
LOWE, Mr. Morgan Wallace, ACA *2010;* 4 Stirling Close, LEYLAND, PR25 4UU.
LOWE, Mr. Nicholas William, BSc(Hons) ACA *2003;* 88 Abbey Road, West Bridgford, NOTTINGHAM, NG2 5NB.
LOWE, Mr. Peter Henry, MA ACA *1983;* 11 Woburn Avenue, Firwood Fold, BOLTON, BL2 3AY.
LOWE, Mr. Peter Norman Murray, FCA *1948;* 3 Easton Way, Grendon, NORTHAMPTON, NN7 1JQ. (Life Member)
LOWE, Mr. Richard, ACA *1992;* 47 Fairview Road, Danestone, ABERDEEN, AB22 8ZG.
LOWE, Mr. Richard John, ACA *2009;* Pricewaterhousecoopers Llp, 1 Hays Lane, LONDON, SE1 2RD.
LOWE, Mr. Robert Edward Assheton, FCA *1974;* Leith Ridge, 11 Milton Avenue, Westcott, DORKING, RH4 3QA.
•**LOWE, Mr. Robert James, FCA** *1975;* Ernst & Young LLP, 1 More London Place, LONDON, SE1 2AF. See also Ernst & Young Europe LLP
LOWE, Mr. Robert John, MBA FCA *1971;* 26 Castle Road, KENILWORTH, CV8 1NG.
LOWE, Mr. Robert William, FCA *1980;* 312 Ifield Drive, Ifield, CRAWLEY, RH11 0EW.
LOWE, Mr. Robin Neil, MA FCA *1992;* Citibank Korea Inc., 39 Da-dong Jung-gu, SEOUL, 100-180, KOREA REPUBLIC OF.
LOWE, Mr. Ronald Spencer, FCA *1968;* 527 Cavendish Road, COORPAROO, QLD 4151, AUSTRALIA.
LOWE, Mrs. Sarah Jane, ACA *2005;* 36 Chambersbury Lane, HEMEL HEMPSTEAD, HERTFORDSHIRE, HP3 8AZ.
LOWE, Mr. Scott Nathan, BA(Hons) ACA *2004;* 1d Hebron Street, Royton, OLDHAM, OL2 6LU.
LOWE, Mrs. Sheila Nicol Lindsay, BSc ACA *1993;* 1st Floor, St Georges Court, Upper Church Street, Douglas, ISLE OF MAN, IM1 1EE.
LOWE, Mr. Simon Charles, BSc ACA *1992;* Royal Bank of Scotland, 250 Bishopsgate, LONDON, EC2M 4AA.
LOWE, Mr. Simon David, FCA *1972;* Edale, 1 Oak Drive, Seisdon, WOLVERHAMPTON, WV5 7ET.
•**LOWE, Mr. Simon James, FCA** *1980;* Grant Thornton UK LLP, 30 Finsbury Square, LONDON, EC2P 2YU. See also Grant Thornton LLP
LOWE, Mr. Simon Mark, BSc ACA *1988;* 75 Waddicor Avenue, ASHTON-UNDER-LYNE, OL6 9HF.

LOWE, Mr. Stuart Jonathan, BSc FCA *1983;* Noble Foods Ltd., Bridgeway House, Icknield Way Industrial Estate, Icknield Way, TRING, HERTFORDSHIRE HP23 4JX.
LOWE, Mrs. Susan Nichola, BSc ACA *1984;* 235 St Heliers Bay Road, ST HELIERS 1071, NEW ZEALAND.
LOWE, Miss. Suzanne Louise, BA(Hons) ACA *2004;* 23 Corbet Avenue, NORWICH, NR7 8HS.
LOWE, Mr. Thomas Philip, FCA *1967;* 24 Ashby Road, BURTON-ON-TRENT, DE15 0LG.
LOWE, Mr. Timothy Alun, BSc ACA *1989;* 107 Heol Y Coed, Rhiwbina, CARDIFF, CF14 6HS.
LOWE, Miss. Valerie Margaret, BCom ACA *1986;* 17 Chepstow Road, LONDON, W2 5BP.
LOWE, Miss. Victoria Jane, BCom ACA *2007;* 12 Mountfield Road, TUNBRIDGE WELLS, KENT, TN1 1SG.
LOWE, Mr. William Geoffrey, BSc ACA *1988;* 9 Monument Green, WEYBRIDGE, KT13 8QS.
LOWE, Mr. William Herbert, FCA *1953;* 69 Barlaston Old Road, Trentham, STOKE-ON-TRENT, ST4 8HD. (Life Member)
•LOWE, Mr. William Robert, MA FCA *1958;* W R Lowe MA FCA, 48 Copperfields, Kemsing, SEVENOAKS, TN15 6QG.
LOWELL, Mr. Wesley William, FCA *1951;* 67 Harefield, Hinchley Wood, ESHER, KT10 9TG. (Life Member)
LOWEN, Mr. Christopher Derek, BA(Hons) ACA *2010;* 31 Nicholas Gardens, YORK, YO10 3EX.
LOWEN, Mrs. Frances Ann, BA ACA *1996;* 2 Mulberry Place, Silk Mill Road, Redbourn, ST. ALBANS, AL3 7GF.
LOWEN, Mr. James Alexander, BA ACA *1998;* 2 Mulberry Place, Redbourn, ST. ALBANS, AL3 7GF.
LOWEN, Mrs. Priscilla, FCA *1947;* 12 Aldwick Place, Aldwick, BOGNOR REGIS, PO21 4AB. (Life Member)
LOWER, Miss. Hilary Ruth, ACA DChA *1990;* Meersbrook, 9 Elsee Road, RUGBY, CV21 3BA.
LOWER, Mr. John Arthur, BSc FCA *1976;* 91 Chesterton Avenue, HARPENDEN, AL5 5ST.
LOWER, Mr. Paul Richard, BA FCA *1974;* (Tax Fac), Northend Manor, Little Dassett, SOUTHAM, CV47 2TX.
LOWER, Mr. Richard Gilbert, FCA *1966;* 50Allée de Lérins, Domaine de Seguret, 83600 LES ADRETS DE L'ESTEREL, FRANCE. (Life Member)
LOWERY, Mrs. Nicola Jane, BSc ACA *1999;* 37 Alexandra Road, Hataitai, WELLINGTON 6021, NEW ZEALAND.
LOWERY, Mr. Richard John Dent, BSc FCA *1992;* 22 Windsor Crescent, WHITLEY BAY, TYNE AND WEAR, NE26 2NT.
LOWES, Mr. Andrew Ian, ACA *2008;* Flat 11, 16 Percy Circus, LONDON, WC1X 9EE.
LOWES, Mr. David John, FCA *1977;* Mill Barton, Witheridge, TIVERTON, DEVON, EX16 8NU.
•LOWES, Mrs. Juliette Louise, BSc ACA *1995;* KPMG LLP, 15 Canada Square, LONDON, E14 5GL. See also KPMG Europe LLP
LOWES, Mr. Robert Emerson, BSc FCA *1977;* 6 The Beeches, Holly Lane East, BANSTEAD, SM7 2AZ.
LOWETH, Mrs. Catherine Joanna, BSc ACA *1995;* 115 Ember Lane, ESHER, KT10 8EQ.
LOWETH, Mr. James Paul, BA ACA *1994;* 115 Ember Lane, ESHER, SURREY, KT10 8EQ.
LOWETH, Mrs. Samantha Ellen, BA(Hons) ACA *2001;* Dogwood Cottage, Brede, RYE, EAST SUSSEX, TN31 6DY.
LOWEY, Mr. Francis Corlett, BA FCA *1968;* Orchard End, 2 The Downings, Harthill, SHEFFIELD, S26 7WD.
LOWEY, Mr. John Francis, BEng ACA *1998;* Paper Rose Ltd, Mabel Street, NOTTINGHAM, NG2 3ED.
LOWI, Mr. Jonathan Michael, BSc FCA *1975;* 29 Anderson Close, LONDON, N21 1TH.
LOWIS, Mr. Robert Alexander, FCA *1952;* P.O. Box 15180, NAIROBI, KENYA. (Life Member)
LOWIS, Mr. Robin Peter Currie, BSc FCA *1975;* with Smith & Williamson (Bristol) LLP, Portwall Place, Portwall Lane, BRISTOL, BS1 6NA.
LOWIS, Mr. Stephen John, BEng ACA *1996;* 2 Osprey Close, Collingham, WETHERBY, WEST YORKSHIRE, LS22 5LZ.
LOWLES, Mrs. Deborah Ann, LLB ACA *2000;* Berry BMW, 6 Shield Drive, BRENTFORD, MIDDLESEX, TW8 9EX.
LOWLES, Mr. Geoffrey Gordon, FCA *1967;* 1 Chyngton Lane, SEAFORD, BN25 4BP. (Life Member)
LOWMAN, Mr. James Pollock, FCA *1956;* P O Box 69, WHITE RIVER, MPUMULANGA PROVINCE, 1240, SOUTH AFRICA. (Life Member)
LOWNDES, Mr. Christopher Charles, BAcc ACA *1997;* 19 Millais Park, Mont Millais, St Helier, JERSEY, JE2 4RU.
LOWNDES, Mrs. Heather, BA ACA *1996;* Booth Ainsworth, Alpha House, 4 Greek Street, STOCKPORT, CHESHIRE, SK3 8AB.
•LOWNDES, Mr. John Peter, BSc ACA *1996;* 3 Wellington Place, ALTRINCHAM, CHESHIRE, WA14 2QH.
LOWNDES, Ms. Rachael Helen, BA ACA *1992;* 24 Ennismore Avenue, GUILDFORD, GU1 1SR.
•LOWNDES, Mr. Timothy Gilmour, BA FCA *1977;* Lowndes & Co, The Blackberry Patch, Parkstone Road, Ropley, ALRESFORD, HAMPSHIRE SO24 0EP. See also Lowndes & Co Limited
LOWNE, Mr. Jon Richard, BA ACA *1991;* 10 Wilton Hunt Road, WILTON, CT 06897, UNITED STATES.
•LOWNES, Mr. Iain James, BA FCA CF *1997;* BTG Financial Consulting LLP, 10th Floor, Temple Point, 1 Temple Row, BIRMINGHAM, B2 5LG. See also BTG McInnes Corporate Finance LLP
LOWREY, Mr. David Henry Tyson, BA ACA *1999;* 152 Ambassador Drive, RED BANK, NJ 07701, UNITED STATES.
LOWREY, Mr. Thomas Walker, FCA *1969;* 45 The Crofts, ST. BEES, CA27 0BH.
LOWRIE, Mr. David, BSc ACA *1991;* Conifer House, Grove Lane, Hinton, CHIPPENHAM, WILTSHIRE, SN14 8HF.
•LOWRY, Mr. Christopher James, FCA CF *1982;* UHY Hacker Young LLP, Quadrant House, 4 Thomas More Square, LONDON, E1W 1YW. See also UHY Corporate Finance Limited
LOWRY, Mr. Daniel, ACA *2011;* with Deloitte & Touche, P.O.Box 1787 GT, One Capital Place, GEORGE TOWN, GRAND CAYMAN, KY1 1109 CAYMAN ISLANDS.
LOWRY, Mr. Donald Fitzgerald, FCA *1974;* 94 Leicester Road, BARNET, EN5 5DB.
LOWRY, Mr. Eric Hamilton, BA FCA *1969;* Highway House Rectory Road Great Haseley, OXFORD, OX44 7JG.
LOWRY, Mr. Jeremy Malbon, MA ACA *1983;* 1 Hamilton Terrace, WHITEHAVEN, CUMBRIA, CA28 7TT.
LOWRY, Mr. Malcolm James, BCom ACA *1993;* 126 South Park Road, LONDON, SW19 8TA.
LOWRY, Mr. Nicholas Wilson, BA ACA *2005;* PO Box 1503, Station M, CALGARY T2P 2L6, AB, CANADA.
LOWRY, Mr. Nigel Mark, BSc ACA *1991;* 2 Park Drive, The Park, NOTTINGHAM, NG7 1DA.
LOWRY, Mr. Richard Anthony Johnson, BSc ACA *1998;* 10 Kilnshaw Place, Melton Place, NEWCASTLE UPON TYNE, NE3 5QQ.
LOWRY, Mrs. Ruth Ellen, BSc FCA *1993;* 28 Kingsway, Penwortham, PRESTON, PR1 0BJ.
LOWRY, Mr. Simon Grant, MA ACA *1993;* Top Floor Flat, 26 Mattock Lane, Ealing, LONDON, W5 5BH.
•LOWSON, Mr. Douglas Iain Crichton, BA FCA *1985;* BDO LLP, 55 Baker Street, LONDON, W1U 7EU. See also BDO Stoy Hayward LLP
LOWSON, Mr. Peter Harvey, FCA *1973;* 29 Thorn Park, Mannamead, PLYMOUTH, PL3 4TE.
LOWTEN, Mr. John Benjamin, BA FCA *1975;* PostNet Suite #42, Private Bag X31, KNYSNA, 6570, SOUTH AFRICA.
LOWTH, Mr. Alexis John, BA ACA *1997;* 19 Brabourne Rise, BECKENHAM, KENT, BR3 6SQ.
LOWTH, Mr. Simon, BSc ACA *2009;* with PricewaterhouseCoopers, Rua da Candelaria 65, 20091-020 RIO DE JANEIRO, BRAZIL.
LOWTHER, Mr. David John, BSc ACA CTA *1979;* Horwich House Eccles Road, Whaley Bridge, HIGH PEAK, DERBYSHIRE, SK23 7EW.
LOWTHER, Ms. Deborah, MA ACA *1985;* Girton College, CAMBRIDGE, CB3 0JG.
LOWTHER, Mrs. Jane Elizabeth, BA ACA *1986;* Kilmallock, Highfield Road, Osbaston, MONMOUTH, GWENT, NP25 3HR.
LOWTHER, Mr. Neil Illingworth, FCA *1952;* 7 Sculthorpe Close, OAKHAM, RUTLAND, LE15 6FJ. (Life Member)
•LOWTHER, Mr. Paul James Innes, BA ACA *1981;* P.J.I. Lowther, 15 Duncan Road, RICHMOND, TW9 2JD.
LOWTHER, Mr. Sean William, BA ACA *1986;* Plantation Place South, 60 Great Tower Street, LONDON, EC3R 5AD.
LOWTHIAN, Mr. Benjamin James, BSc ACA *1999;* 63 Wedmore Gardens, Archway, LONDON, N19 4SY.
LOWTHIAN, Mr. John Bardgett, FCA *1962;* Fox Cottage, Brisco, CARLISLE, CA4 0QS.
LOWTHIAN, Mr. Joseph Edward, FCA *1959;* Broomhill, Stainton, PENRITH, CA11 0EH. (Life Member)
LOWTHORPE, Mrs. Julie, BSc FCA *1985;* Davies Gimber Brown, Ryebrook Studios, Woodcote Side, EPSOM, SURREY, KT18 7HD.
LOWTHORPE, Mr. Michael, FCA *1974;* (Tax Fac), 7 Bawtree Close, SUTTON, SURREY, SM2 5LQ.
LOWTON, Mr. Mark, ACA *2008;* Ekeby, Bayleys Hill, SEVENOAKS, KENT, TN14 6HS.
LOWTON, Mr. Philip David, BA ACA *1991;* 14 Forest Drive, Shevington Moor, Standish, WIGAN, WN6 0SG.
LOXTON, Mr. Keith George, ACA *1980;* European International Reinsurance Co Ltd, Carleton Court, High Street, BRIDGETOWN, BB11128, BARBADOS.
LOXTON, Mr. Robert Brian, ACA *1979;* Park Farm, Drayton, BANBURY, OX15 6EG.
LOY, Mrs. Patricia Anne, BA ACA *1984;* 23 Beverley Rise, ILKLEY, LS29 9DB.
LOY, Mr. Peter, BSc FCA *1985;* 23 Beverley Rise, ILKLEY, LS29 9DB.
LOY, Mr. Timothy John, BA ACA *1990;* Age Partnership Ltd, 4305 Park Approach, LEEDS, LS15 8GB.
LOYD, Mr. David William Arnold, FCA *1974;* Mildenhall House, Mildenhall, MARLBOROUGH, SN8 2LP.
LOYD, Mr. John Perrin, BA FCA *1967;* 65 Calton Avenue, LONDON, SE21 7DF.
LOYD, Mr. John Stewart, ACA *2008;* 7 Rue Du Tresor, 75004 PARIS, FRANCE.
LOYDEN, Mr. Peter Nicholas, BA ACA *2000;* 38 Lloyd Road, PRESCOT, MERSEYSIDE, L34 6LG.
LOYDEN, Mrs. Suzanne Elizabeth, BA ACA *1998;* 38 Lloyd Road, PRESCOT, L34 6LG.
LOYDON, Mr. Michael Edwin, BA ACA *2009;* Pricewaterhousecoopers, 12 Plumtree Court, LONDON, EC4A 4HT.
LOYEUNG, Miss. Lew Hon Yune, BSc ACA *2003;* 181 Fencepiece Road, ILFORD, ESSEX, IG6 2TG.
LOYIDES, Mr. Antonis, BA(Hons) ACA *2002;* Filikis Etairias 7, Nea Lidra, 2549 NICOSIA, CYPRUS.
LOYLA, Mr. Rajdeep, BSc ACA *2007;* 2 Arden Close, DERBY, DE23 6LG.
LOYNES, Mr. David Guy William, BSc FCA *1976;* 5 Elm Grove, Eggbuckland, PLYMOUTH, PL6 5RS.
LOYNES, Mr. Matthew Newton, MEng ACA *2006;* 647 Wells Road, BRISTOL, BS14 9BE.
LOYNTON, Mr. Matthew James, ACA *2010;* 18 Dobell Road, LONDON, SE9 1HE.
LU, Miss. Annie, ACA *2009;* 93 Acorn Walk, LONDON, SE16 5DX.
LU, Mr. Tian, ACA *2008;* Flat 3 Fonda Court, 3 Premiere Place, LONDON, E14 8SD.
LU, Mr. Tin Yuen, ACA *2005;* 18/FFlat DBlock 7, City Garden, 233 Electric Road, NORTH POINT, HONG KONG ISLAND, HONG KONG SAR.
LU BOON HENG, Miss. April, BSc ACA *2002;* Flat 16 Lansdowne Court, Lansdowne Rise, LONDON, W11 2NR.
LUBBOCK, The Hon. Emma Rachel, MA FCA ATII MCT *1977;* 81 Lansdowne Road, LONDON, W11 2LE.
LUBBOCK, Ms. Heather, ACA *2009;* Ground Floor, 8 Kepler Road, LONDON, SW4 7NR.
LUBIENIECKI, Mr. Martin Victor, BA ACA *1989;* 25 Abinger Road, LONDON, W4 1EU.
LUBIENSKI, Mr. Mark Casimir, BSc ACA *1991;* 97 Elsenham Street, LONDON, SW18 5NY.
LUBOFF, Mr. Mark Edward, BA FCA MCT *1983;* Rathbone Brothers Plc, Rathbone Unit Trust Management Ltd, 159 New Bond Street, LONDON, W1S 2UD.
LUBOFF, Mrs. Susan Patricia, BA ACA *1984;* 6 Bolingbroke Grove, LONDON, SW11 6ES.
•LUC, Miss. Helen Bui Hoa, BA FCA *1994;* HLM Accountancy Limited, 108 Parsonage Manorway, BELVEDERE, KENT, DA17 6LY.
LUCAS, Mr. Alan, FCA *1960;* 11 Parkfields, Arden Drive, Dorridge, SOLIHULL, WEST MIDLANDS, B93 8LL. (Life Member)
LUCAS, Mr. Andrew, BA ACA *1991;* 38 Hill Rise, Chalfont St. Peter, GERRARDS CROSS, SL9 9BH.
LUCAS, Mr. Andrew Raymond, ACA *2008;* 48 Breedon Avenue, Littleover, DERBY, DE23 1LR.
LUCAS, Miss. Anita Jane, BEng FCA *1991;* Gaunts, Catthorpe Road, Shawell, LUTTERWORTH, LE17 6AQ.
LUCAS, Dr. Anthony Kenvyn, ACA *1991;* Ystrad House, 41 Pen-y-Cae, Troedyrhiw, Ystrad Mynach, HENGOED, MID GLAMORGAN CF82 7FA.
•LUCAS, Mr. Antony David, FCA *1962;* Lucas & Co., 1 Mint Street, GODALMING, GU7 1HE.
LUCAS, Mr. Barry Edward, FCA *1964;* Windyridge Cottage, Burleigh, STROUD, GLOUCESTERSHIRE, GL5 2PJ. (Life Member)
LUCAS, Mr. Bernard, FCA *1957;* 99 Moseley Wood Drive, Cookridge, LEEDS, LS16 7HD. (Life Member)
LUCAS, Mr. Brian Campbell, BSc FCA *1957;* West Dormers, Egypt Hill, COWES, PO31 8BP. (Life Member)
•LUCAS, Mr. Charles Eric, FCA *1976;* Charles E Lucas, 9 Holly Dene Drive, Lostock, BOLTON, BL6 4NP. See also Broadthunder Accounting Limited
LUCAS, Mr. Christopher George, BSc ACA *1986;* Barclays Bank Plc, 1 Churchill Place, LONDON, E14 5HP.
LUCAS, Mrs. Claire Mairead, BA ACA *2007;* Harwood Hutton, 22 Wycombe End, BEACONSFIELD, BUCKINGHAMSHIRE, HP9 1NB.
LUCAS, Mr. Craig, BSc ACA PGCE *1999;* Flat 14, Westfield Hall, Hagley Road, BIRMINGHAM, B16 9LG.
LUCAS, Mr. David Jonathan, ACA *2009;* Macquarie Bank, 1 Martin Place, SYDNEY, NSW 2000, AUSTRALIA.
•LUCAS, Mr. David Paul, FCA DChA *1976;* TLL Accountants Limited, 7-9 Station Road, Hesketh Bank, PRESTON, PR4 6SN.
LUCAS, Mr. David William Frederick, BSc ACA *2009;* 86 Inverine Road, LONDON, SE7 7NL.
LUCAS, Mrs. Denise Mary, BCom FCA *1980;* Pearl Group, 1 Wythall Green Way Wythall, BIRMINGHAM, B47 6WG.
LUCAS, Mr. Dudley Guy Dunbar, FCA *1969;* PO Box 1074 - 80108, KILIFI, KENYA. (Life Member)
LUCAS, Mr. Eric Raymond, BA FCA *1983;* PricewaterhouseCoopers, Level 21, PWC Tower, 188 Quay Street, Private Bag 92162, AUCKLAND 1142 NEW ZEALAND.
LUCAS, Mr. Gerard Anthony, BA FCA CF *1999;* 11 Rylance Road, Winstanley, WIGAN, LANCASHIRE, WN3 6LH.
LUCAS, Mr. Giles David, ACA *1979;* (Tax Fac), The Gate House, The Green, Adderbury, BANBURY, OX17 3NB.
LUCAS, Mr. Graham Stuart, FCA *1971;* Gefinor Center - Block (D), First Floor Suite 101, Clemenceau Street, PO Box 113-5144, BEIRUT, LEBANON.
LUCAS, Mr. Harold Alan, FCA *1957;* 80 Ash Lane, Hale, ALTRINCHAM, WA15 8PB. (Life Member)
LUCAS, Miss. Helen Clare Denise, BSc(Hons) ACA *2002;* W Gadsby & Son Ltd, Huntworth Business Park, BRIDGWATER, SOMERSET, TA6 6TS.
LUCAS, Mrs. Helen Patricia, BA ACA *1995;* with Spain Brothers & Co, 29 Manor Road, FOLKESTONE, KENT, CT20 2SE.
LUCAS, Mr. Ian David, BA ACA *1998;* Travelex UK Ltd, 65 Kingsway, LONDON, WC2B 6TD.
LUCAS, Mrs. Jenny Lesley, BA ACA *2005;* 74 Cardross Street, LONDON, W6 0DR.
LUCAS, Mr. Joel Matthew, ACA *2008;* 85 Blean Common, Blean, CANTERBURY, KENT, CT2 9JH.
LUCAS, Mr. John David, BEng ACA CF *2006;* 45 Tivoli Road, CHELTENHAM, GLOUCESTERSHIRE, GL50 2TD.
LUCAS, Mr. John Francis, FCA *1971;* 1 Dennis Close, Clapham, BEDFORD, MK41 6GG.
LUCAS, Mr. John Michael, FCA *1959;* 1 Cedar Close, Sudbrooke, LINCOLN, LN2 2RF. (Life Member)
LUCAS, Mr. Jonathan, BSc ACA *2006;* Apartment 321, 2 Malta Street, MANCHESTER, M4 7BL.
LUCAS, Mr. Jonathan Alan, BA ACA *1988;* Woodhouse Farm, Anson Road, Poynton, STOCKPORT, CHESHIRE, SK12 1TD.
LUCAS, Mrs. Julia Catherine, BA ACA *1990;* Baracot, Wellesbourne Road, Alveston, STRATFORD-UPON-AVON, WARWICKSHIRE, CV37 7RQ.
•LUCAS, Mrs. Julie Patricia, BA ACA *1988;* Julie Lucas, Woodhouse Farm, Anson Road, Poynton, STOCKPORT, SK12 1TD.
•LUCAS, Mrs. Kerri Jane, ACA *1996;* Lucas Accountancy Ltd, The Dell, 4 Ingleby Paddocks, Enslow, KIDLINGTON, OXFORDSHIRE OX5 3ET.
•ⓘLUCAS, Mr. Kevin, FCA *2001;* Barringtons Corporate Recovery (NW) LLP, Imperial Court, 2 Exchange Quay, MANCHESTER, M5 3EB. See also Barringtons Corporate Recovery Limited
LUCAS, Mr. Kevin Neil, ACA *1979;* 165 Princes Road, BUCKHURST HILL, IG9 5DW.
LUCAS, Mrs. Lesley Margaret, BSc ACA *1990;* University of Birmingham, Edgbaston, BIRMINGHAM, B15 2TT.
LUCAS, Mrs. Linda Jane, BA ACA *1981;* Hilbre, Arden Road, Dorridge, SOLIHULL, WEST MIDLANDS, B93 8LJ.
•LUCAS, Mr. Malcolm Ian, BSc FCA DChA *1982;* Menzies LLP, Heathrow Business Centre, 65 High Street, EGHAM, SURREY, TW20 9EY.
LUCAS, Mr. Mark, ACA *2009;* Reads & Co, PO Box 179, JERSEY, JE4 9RJ.

•LUCAS, Mr. Mark William, FCA *1989;* with RSM Tenon Audit Limited, Clive House, Clive Street, BOLTON, BL1 1ET.
LUCAS, Mr. Martin George Sydney, BA ACA *1988;* 12 Stavordale Road, Highbury, LONDON, N5 1NE.
LUCAS, Mr. Martin John, BA ACA *1990;* 16 Dene Walk, West Parley, FERNDOWN, BH22 8PQ.
•LUCAS, Mrs. Mavis, FCA *1953;* Mavis Lucas, Bolgoed Isaf, Bolgoed Road, Pontardulais, SWANSEA, SA4 8JP.
LUCAS, Mr. Michael Charles, FCA CTA *1984;* 2 Le Court Clos, La Rue Longue, St. Martin, Channel Islands, JERSEY, JE3 6ED.
LUCAS, Mr. Michael John Stilwell, FCA *1972;* Nuthatch, 19 Warren View, Shorne, GRAVESEND, DA12 3EJ. (Life Member)
LUCAS, Mr. Michael Kevin, BSc ACA *1978;* Beechfield House, Beechfield Lane, Frilsham, THATCHAM, RG18 9XD.
LUCAS, Mr. Michael Robert, BSc ACA *1985;* (Tax Fac), with RSM Tenon Limited, Sumner House, St Thomas's Rd, CHORLEY, PR7 1HP.
LUCAS, Mr. Neil Fraser, BSc FCA *1978;* Lucas Executive Ltd, 430 Hatfield Road, ST. ALBANS, HERTFORDSHIRE, AL4 0XS.
•LUCAS, Mr. Neil Stephen, ACA *1980;* N.S. Lucas & Co, The Courtyard, 80 High Street, AMERSHAM, BUCKINGHAMSHIRE, HP7 0DS.
LUCAS, Mr. Nigel Ashley, BSc ACA *1995;* 3 Glenroyd Street, MOUNT LAWLEY, WA 6050, AUSTRALIA.
LUCAS, Mr. Paul Anthony, BA ACA *1981;* 224 Jesmond Dene Road, Jesmond, NEWCASTLE UPON TYNE, NE2 2JU.
•LUCAS, Mr. Paul Martin, BSc ACA *1983;* Mazars LLP, 45 Church Street, BIRMINGHAM, B3 2RT.
•LUCAS, Mr. Peter Reginald, FCA *1973;* (Tax Fac), Peter Lucas & Co, 54 Pilsdon Drive, Canford Heath, POOLE, BH17 9HS.
LUCAS, Mr. Piers Hugh, ACA *2004;* with Deloitte LLP, Athene Place, 66 Shoe Lane, LONDON, EC4A 3BQ.
LUCAS, Mr. Richard William, BA ACA *2005;* 16a Ainsley Road, NOTTINGHAM, NG8 3PP.
LUCAS, Mr. Robert, ACA *2009;* 24 Rowleys Mill, Uttoxeter New Road, DERBY, DE22 3TJ.
LUCAS, Mr. Robert James, BA(Hons) ACA *2002;* International Fund Managers (Jersey) Ltd, PO Box 381, JERSEY, JE4 9ZF.
LUCAS, Mr. Robert Kenneth, BA ACA *1980;* 17 Parkway, WILMSLOW, CHESHIRE, SK9 1LS.
LUCAS, Mr. Roger Frank, FCA *1959;* Clevedown Winford Road, Chew Magna, BRISTOL, BS40 8QQ. (Life Member)
•LUCAS, Miss. Rosemary Carol, BSc FCA *1989;* (Tax Fac), with McShare Wright, 2 College Street, Higham Ferrers, RUSHDEN, NORTHAMPTONSHIRE, NN10 8DZ.
LUCAS, Mr. Simon, ACA *2001;* 46 Lindsey Drive, Holton-le-Clay, GRIMSBY, SOUTH HUMBERSIDE, DN36 5HE.
LUCAS, Mr. Stephen, BSc ACA *1981;* 120 Dewfalls Drive, Bradley Stoke, BRISTOL, BS32 9BT.
•LUCAS, Mr. Stephen Alexander, BA ACA *1999;* Deloitte LLP, Hill House, 1 Little New Street, LONDON, EC4A 3TR. See also Deloitte & Touche LLP
LUCAS, Mr. Stephen John, BSc ACA *1988;* 1 Heath Close, POTTERS BAR, HERTFORDSHIRE, EN6 1LT.
LUCAS, Mr. Stephen Leonard, BSc FCA *1986;* 15 Heatherdene Avenue, CROWTHORNE, RG45 6AA.
•LUCAS, Mrs. Sue, ACA *1997;* Moore Stephens (South) LLP, 9 St. Johns Place, NEWPORT, ISLE OF WIGHT, PO30 1LH. See also Moore Secretaries Limited
LUCAS, Mr. Timothy John, BSc ACA *1987;* 10 Presburg Road, NEW MALDEN, KT3 5AH.
LUCAS, Prof. Ursula Clare, BA FCA *1979;* 46 Downs Park East, Westbury Park, BRISTOL, BS6 7QE.
LUCAS-LUCAS, Mr. Jonathan Woolmer, BSc ACA *2006;* 7 Timbrell Place, LONDON, SE16 5HU.
LUCCOCK, Mrs. Anna Louise, BA ACA *2005;* Auchtubhmore House, Auchtubh, LOCHEARNHEAD, PERTHSHIRE, FK19 8NZ.
LUCE, Mr. Christoph Andreas, BSc ACA *1992;* 16 Tunley Road, LONDON, SW17 7QJ.
LUCE, Mr. Robert Andrew, MA FCA *1975;* Associating Solutions Limited, Edgerly Farm Calcroft lane, Clanfield, BAMPTON, OXFORDSHIRE, OX18 2SB.
LUCEY, Mr. Donal Finbarr, BCom ACA *1990; (ACA Ireland 1985);* with Donal Lucey Lawlor, 43 Highfield Road, DARTFORD, DA1 2JS.
LUCEY, Mr. Gareth Anthony, BSc ACA *2006;* 5 Y Dolydd, CAERPHILLY, MID GLAMORGAN, CF83 1NT.
LUCEY, Mr. Joseph Cornelius, ACA *1999;* 248 Bogert Avenue, RIDGEWOOD, NJ 07450, UNITED STATES.
•LUCEY, Dr. Shaun Peter, MA ACA *2001;* Ernst & Young LLP, 1 Colmore Square, BIRMINGHAM, B4 6HQ. See also Ernst & Young Europe LLP
LUCIA, Mr. Adrian Philip, BA ACA *2011;* 183 Parkside Avenue, BEXLEYHEATH, DA7 6NP.
LUCIA, Mr. Alan Patrick, BSc ACA *1981;* 9 Lesney Park Road, ERITH, DA8 3DQ.
LUCIANI, Ms. Patrizia, ACA CA(SA) *2008;* 74 Oxlease, WITNEY, OXFORDSHIRE, OX28 3QU.
LUCIE-SMITH, Mr. Derek Anthony, FCA *1972;* Gresham House PLC, 5th Floor, 17 Grosvenor Gardens, LONDON, SW1W 0BD.
LUCK, Mr. Allan Yardley, FCA *1963;* Kaiteur, 2 Burntwood Grove, SEVENOAKS, TN13 1PZ. (Life Member)
LUCK, Mr. Colin Frank, FCA *1966;* 105 Baldwin Avenue, EASTBOURNE, EAST SUSSEX, BN21 1UL.
LUCK, Mr. David Michael, BEng ACA *1998;* Man Group Plc Sugar Quay, Lower Thames Street, LONDON, EC3R 6DU.
LUCK, Miss. Deborah Janet, BA ACA *1994;* 182 Dyke Road, BRIGHTON, BN1 5AA.
•LUCK, Mr. George Anton, BSc FCA *1981;* (Tax Fac), Moore Stephens LLP, 150 Aldersgate Street, LONDON, EC1A 4AB. See also Moore Stephens & Co
•LUCK, Mr. Keith Michael, BA ACA *2001;* Gibbons Mannington & Phipps, 24 Landgate, RYE, EAST SUSSEX, TN31 7LJ.
LUCK, Mrs. Maureen Ann, BA ACA *1986;* 9 Wykeham Way, Haddenham, AYLESBURY, HP17 8BL.
LUCK, Mr. Richard Alistair, BSc ACA *1993;* Townhouse #14, Earl's Court Chateau, 24 Earl's Court, KINGSTON 8, JAMAICA.
LUCK, Mr. Richard Nigel, MA ACA *1986;* Mouse House, North Street, Winkfield, WINDSOR, BERKSHIRE, SL4 4TE.
LUCK, Mr. Stuart Richard, BSc ACA *1984;* 1 Kingsley Gardens, Ottershaw, CHERTSEY, KT16 0GE.
LUCK, Mrs. Susan Elizabeth, BA BSc ACA *1995;* 4 Doddington Place, NEWCASTLE, STAFFORDSHIRE, ST5 3RX.
LUCKAS, Mr. Alistair Rawson, BSc ACA *1991;* 36 Weinholt Street, SHERWOOD, QLD 4075, AUSTRALIA.
LUCKE, Mrs. Janet Ann, MMath ACA *2002;* with Deloitte LLP, Global House, High Street, CRAWLEY, RH10 1DL.
LUCKEN, Mr. Glen, BSc ARCS FCA AMCT *1985;* 18 The Cloisters, Ampthill, BEDFORD, MK45 2UJ.
LUCKEN, Mr. William George O'Sullivan, BSc ACA *2006;* 45 Southdean Gardens, LONDON, SW19 6NT.
LUCKETT, Mr. Andrew Alexander, BSc FCA *1989;* 9 The Avenue, SUTTON COLDFIELD, WEST MIDLANDS, B76 1TP.
•LUCKETT, Mr. Antony William, BCom FCA DChA *1985;* Clive Owen & Co LLP, 140 Coniscliffe Road, DARLINGTON, DL3 7RT.
LUCKETT, Mrs. Carolyn Anne, BSc ACA *1986;* 10 Carmel Grove Carmel Road South, DARLINGTON, DL3 8EQ.
LUCKETT, Miss. Christine Rosemary, BSc ACA *1994;* 12 Roding View, BUCKHURST HILL, IG9 6AQ.
LUCKETT, Miss. Julia Caroline, BMus ACA *1992;* 75 Kiln Ride, Finchampstead, WOKINGHAM, RG40 3PJ.
LUCKETT, Mr. Nigel Frederick, FCA *1964;* 108 White Hill, Kinver, STOURBRIDGE, DY7 6AU.
LUCKETT, Mr. Philip Jeffery, FCA *1976;* (Tax Fac), 6 Craig Walk, BRIDGNORTH, SHROPSHIRE, WV15 6BZ.
LUCKETT, Mr. Richard Stephen, BSc ACA *2009;* Telford Farm MachinerY & Superstore Ltd, Stableford, BRIDGNORTH, SHROPSHIRE, WV15 5LS.
LUCKHAM, Mr. Anthony Arthur, FCA *1968;* Cherry Tree Cottage, Knowle Lane, CRANLEIGH, GU6 8JW.
LUCKHURST, Mr. Barrington Henry, FCA *1974;* Oaklands, Moor Lane, Appledore, ASHFORD, KENT, TN26 2BH.
LUCKHURST, Mr. David Charles Sinclair, BA ACA MBA *1984;* First Acre, 5 Courtenay Road, Keynsham, BRISTOL, BS31 1JN.
LUCKHURST, Mr. Jonathan David, BSc(Hons) ACA *2007;* 45 Riverview Avenue, NORTH FERRIBY, NORTH HUMBERSIDE, HU14 3DT.
LUCKHURST, Mr. Stanley Thomas, FCA *1960;* 8 Ridgeway, Wargrave, READING, RG10 8AS. (Life Member)
LUCKHURST, Mrs. Susan Jane, BSc ACA *1992;* 17 Lancet Lane, Loose, MAIDSTONE, ME15 9RY.
LUCKIN, Mr. Roger Alfred Geoffrey, FCA *1974;* Rookery House, Norton, BURY ST. EDMUNDS, SUFFOLK, IP31 3NA.
•LUCKIN, Mr. Terence John, FCA *1973;* with Whitehouse Ridsdale, 26 Birmingham Road, WALSALL, WS1 2LZ.
•LUCKING, Mr. Michael James, BA ACA *1981;* C.J. Lucking & Co, 34 Cross Street, Long Eaton, NOTTINGHAM, NG10 1HD.
•LUCKING, Mr. William Raymond, FCA *1973;* (Tax Fac), Lucking Accountancy Ltd, The Lodge, Beacon End Farmhouse, London Road, Stanway, COLCHESTER CO3 0NQ.
LUCKINS, Miss. Vivien Ann, BSc ACA *1983;* Great Luckins Barn Higher Chisworth, Chisworth, GLOSSOP, DERBYSHIRE, SK13 5SA.
•LUCKMAN, Mrs. Ann Christine, ACA *1980;* A.C. Luckman & Co, 5 Hollybank Road, BIRMINGHAM, B13 0RF.
LUCKMAN, Ms. Anne Louise, BSc ACA *1992;* 101 Abbeville Road, LONDON, SW4 9JL.
•LUCKMAN, Mr. Gary Neil, FCA *1989;* 3 Leaside, BENFLEET, ESSEX, SS7 4DQ.
LUCRAFT, Mr. Paul, BSc ACA *1984;* 4 Portsmouth Wood Close, Lindfield, HAYWARDS HEATH, RH16 2DQ.
LUCUS, Mr. Richard, BSc ACA *2003;* Flat 59, Campbell Gordon Way, LONDON, NW2 6RW.
LUDDEN, Mr. Patrick Joseph, ACA *1994;* 24 Westwood Park, LONDON, SE23 3QF.
LUDDINGTON, Mr. Ben Simon, BSc(Hons) ACA *2000;* 129 Dudley Street, BEDFORD, MK40 3SY.
LUDDINGTON, Mrs. Elizabeth Anne, BA ACA *2005;* 287 Dialstone Lane, STOCKPORT, CHESHIRE, SK2 7NA.
LUDDINGTON, Mr. Michael, BSc ACA *2001;* Halewood International Ltd The Sovereign Distillery, Wilson Road, LIVERPOOL, L36 6AD.
•LUDDINGTON, Mr. Timothy Stephen, FCA CTA *1971;* West Minster, Manaccan, HELSTON, CORNWALL, TR12 6HR.
LUDER, Mr. Ian David, BSc(Econ) FCA FTII *1974;* Flat 25, Andrewes House, Barbican, LONDON, EC2Y 8AX.
LUDFORD, Mr. Daniel Charles, BA ACA *2001;* The Old Orchard, 25 Patrick's Orchard, Uffington, FARINGDON, OXFORDSHIRE, SN7 7RL.
•LUDFORD, Mr. Keith Ernest, FCA *1976;* K.E. Ludford, 17 Stibbs Way, Bransgore, CHRISTCHURCH, BH23 8HG.
LUDGATE, Mr. Stefan Rigby, MA ACA MBA *2000;* 4 Lax Terrace, Wolviston, BILLINGHAM, CLEVELAND, TS22 5LE.
•LUDLAM, Mr. Adrian Clark, BA ACA *1983;* Ludlam Accountancy, 2 Church Walk, Little Driffield, DRIFFIELD, NORTH HUMBERSIDE, YO25 5XP.
LUDLAM, Mrs. Barbara Sarah, BSc ACA *1989;* 5 Elmhurst Gardens, The Mains Giggleswick, SETTLE, NORTH YORKSHIRE, BD24 0AX.
LUDLAM, Mr. Kenneth John, FCA *1969;* Longwood House, 12a Mavelstone Close, BROMLEY, BR1 2PJ.
LUDLAM, Mr. Simon, BSc ACA *1991;* Star Capital Partners, 33 Cavendish Square, LONDON, W1G 0PW.
LUDLEY, Mr. David, FCA *1960;* Grange House, 57 Front Street, Sowerby, THIRSK, YO7 1JQ. (Life Member)
LUDLOW, Mrs. Angela Clare, ACA *1983;* The Lodge, Lympne Castle, Lympne, HYTHE, KENT, CT21 4NY.
LUDLOW, Miss. Claire Jane, BSc ACA *2011;* 45a Alexandra Road, CROYDON, CR0 6EY.
LUDLOW, Mr. Graeme, BA ACA *2007;* 133 WILMOT STREET, LONDON, E2 0BU.
LUDLOW, Mr. James Edward Paul, BSc ACA *2005;* Sungrove Farm, East End, NEWBURY, RG20 0AF.
LUDLOW, Mr. Wilfrid Norman, FCA *1940;* 19 Bramley Close, WILMSLOW, SK9 6EP. (Life Member)
LUDWIG, Mr. Richard Nathan, BA(Hons) ACA *2011;* 21 Bolbury Crescent, Swinton, Salford, MANCHESTER, M27 8AJ.
LUDWIG, Mr. Stefan Krzysztof, ACA *2008;* 23 Chaucer Road, LONDON, W3 6DR.
LUE, Mr. Mylton Vehi, BA ACA *1992;* 103 Beechcroft Road, LONDON, SW17 7BP.
LUEDER, Mr. John Edward Coltman, LLB FCA *1962;* 142 Rue de Courcelles, 75017 PARIS, FRANCE.
LUEN, Mr. Martin Alexander, BA ACA *2004;* Flat 94 Lauderdale Mansions, Lauderdale Road, LONDON, W9 1NF.
LUEN, Mr. Philip Gordon John, ACA *2008;* 9 Barnard Mews, LONDON, SW11 1QU.
LUETCHFORD, Mr. John Anthony Trevor, FCA *1966;* 22 Waterden Road, GUILDFORD, GU1 2AY. (Life Member)
•LUFF, Mr. John Peter, BA ACA *2000;* La Maison Du Puits, Rue Poudreuse, St. Martin, GUERNSEY, GY4 6NL.
LUFF, Mr. Nicholas Lawrence, BA ACA *1991;* 6 Silver Lane, PURLEY, SURREY, CR8 3HG.
LUFFMAN, Mr. David Eric, ACA *1981;* 46 Bockland Close, CULLOMPTON, DEVON, EX15 1JQ.
LUGG, Mr. Geoffrey John, BA ACA *1990;* 75A Meadowside, Tretherras View, NEWQUAY, TR7 2TW.
LUGG, Ms. Karon, BSc ACA *1992;* Hope Bowdler Hall, CHURCH STRETTON, SY6 7DD.
•LUGG, Mr. Peter Edward, BSc FCA CF *1984;* Monahans, Lennox House, 3 Pierrepont Street, BATH, BA1 1LB.
LUGG, Mr. Richard William, FCA *1963;* Islerenweg 2, 8708 MANNEDORF, SWITZERLAND.
•LUGG, Mr. Roger Bruce, FCA *1966;* (Tax Fac), Roger Lugg & Co, 12/14 High Street, CATERHAM, CR3 5UA. See also Roger Lugg & Co Limited, Lee, Dicketts & Co
LUGGAR, Mrs. Elizabeth Jane, BSc ACA *2005;* Generali Worldwide Insurance Company Limited, Generali House, Hirzel Street, St. Peter Port, GUERNSEY, GY1 4PA.
•LUGGER, Mrs. Linda, BSc FCA *1987;* Peplows, Sterling House, Wavell Drive, Rosehill, CARLISLE, CA1 2SA.
LUGO, Miss. Catherine Eleanor, BSc ACA *1994;* 40 Belmont Court, 93-107 Highbury New Park, LONDON, N5 2HA.
LUHRS, Mrs. Nicola Katharine, BSc ACA *2003;* (Tax Fac), 11 Newton Road, Little Shelford, CAMBRIDGE, CB22 5HL.
LUI, Mr. Anthony Chi Shing, FCA *1971;* 502 Golden Gate Commercial Building, 136-138 Austin Road, TSIM SHA TSUI, KOWLOON, HONG KONG SAR.
LUI, Mr. Chi Hung, ACA *2007;* 4C, Walton Mansion, 306 - 308 Prince Edward Road, MONG KOK, KOWLOON, HONG KONG SAR.
LUI, Mr. Chi Yung, ACA *2008;* Flat 808 Block P, Kornhill, 10 Hong On Street, QUARRY BAY, HONG KONG SAR.
LUI, Mr. Edwin Yiu Fun, BSc FCA *1977;* 39 Bronte Road, THORNHILL L3T 7H9, ON, CANADA.
LUI, Mr. Gary Chun Kin, ACA *2007;* c/o New Territories Investments Pty Ltd, P.O. Box 1149, Civic Square, CANBERRA, ACT 2608, AUSTRALIA.
LUI, Mr. Hung Kwong, ACA *2007;* Flat D 8/F, Scenery Mansion, 108-110 Waterloo Road, MONG KOK, KOWLOON, HONG KONG SAR.
LUI, Mr. Kevin, BSc ACA *2002;* 10/11 Varna Street, CLOVELLY, NSW 2031, AUSTRALIA.
LUI, Mr. King Wai Ray, ACA *2008;* Ray K.W Lui & Co, Room 701, 7/F Fourseas Building, 208-212 Nathan Road, TSIM SHA TSUI, KOWLOON HONG KONG SAR.
LUI, Mr. Lai Hang Kennic, ACA *2008;* KLC Kennic Lui & Co, 5/F, Ho Lee Commercial Building, 38 - 44 D' Aguilar Street, CENTRAL, HONG KONG SAR. See also Kennic L H Lui & Co Ltd
LUI, Ms. Lai Wah Olivia, ACA *2007;* 5D Block One, New Jade Gardens, CHAI WAN, HONG KONG ISLAND, HONG KONG SAR.
LUI, Mr. Man Wai, ACA *2007;* WKL & Partners C.P.A Limited, 20/F, Ka Wah Bank Centre, 232 Des Voeux Road Central, CENTRAL, HONG KONG SAR.
LUI, Mr. Man Sang, ACA *2008;* Room C 27/F, Tower 2, The Pacifica, 9 Sham Shing Road, LAI CHI KOK, KOWLOON HONG KONG SAR.
LUI, Miss. Paddy Wai-Yu, ACA *1980;* Stanford Hotels International, 29/F K. Wah International Ctr, 191 Java Road, NORTH POINT, Hong Kong Island, HONG KONG SAR.
LUI, Mr. Simon, ACA *2006;* Simon S W Lui & Co, Bank Centre 1013, Nathan Road 636, MONG KOK, KOWLOON, HONG KONG SAR.
LUI, Mr. Siu Tsuen Richard, ACA *2007;* Flat 2A Block 1, Staff Quarters, Ruttonjee Hospital, 266 Queens Road East, WAN CHAI, HONG KONG ISLAND HONG KONG SAR.
LUI, Miss. Soek Kuen, BSc(Econ) ACA *1999;* 337 Taman Fatimah, 72000 KUALA PILAH, NEGERI SEMBILAN, MALAYSIA.
LUI, Mr. Tak Yan, ACA *2008;* Flat B 21/F, Po Shan Mansion, TAIKOO SHING, HONG KONG SAR.
LUI, Mr. Tim Leung, MSc ACA *1982;* PricewaterhouseCoopers, 33/F Cheung Kong Center, 2 Queen's Road, CENTRAL, HONG KONG ISLAND, HONG KONG SAR.
LUI, Mr. Tin Nang, BSc FCA *1991;* Flat C 13/F Tower 1, The Waterfront, 1 Austin Road West, TSIM SHA TSUI, KOWLOON, HONG KONG SAR.
LUI, Mr. Tsz Pan, ACA *2006;* Flat 9, 26/F Po Yiu House, Po Pui Court, KWUN TONG, KOWLOON, HONG KONG SAR.
LUI, Mr. Wah Shing, ACA *2007;* WS Lui & Co, Unit B, 12/F, Ka Nin Wah Commercial Building, 423 - 425 Hennessy Road, WAN CHAI HONG KONG SAR.
LUI, Mr. Weng Chiew, BSc FCA *1964;* 341 Upper Bukit Timah Road, 08-15 The Hillside, SINGAPORE 588195, SINGAPORE.

LUI, Mr. Yuen Lun Peter, ACA *2005;* Unit 8B Tower 2, Parc Palais, 18 Wylie Road, Kings Park, HO MAN TIN, KOWLOON HONG KONG SAR.

LUI, Ms. Yung Yung Rachel, ACA *2007;* Flat C 26/F Blk 4, Sceneway Garden, LAM TIN, KOWLOON, HONG KONG SAR.

LUIZ, Mr. Darryck Emanuel, ACA CA(SA) *2008;* 10 Sarum Green, WEYBRIDGE, KT13 9RX.

LUK, Mr. Chi Chung Boris, ACA *2008;* 27/F Peninsula Tower, 538 Castle Peak Road, Cheung Sha Wan, SHAM SHUI PO, KOWLOON, HONG KONG SAR.

LUK, Mrs. Connie, BSc ACA *2005;* 142 Queen Ediths Way, CAMBRIDGE, CB1 8NL.

LUK, Mr. Henry Ka-Pui, BA ACA *1991;* A12 Cypresswaver Villas, 32 Cape Road, CHUNG HOM KOK, Hong Kong Island, HONG KONG SAR.

LUK, Mr. Ivor Kwok-Wang, BEng ACA *2001;* with Deloitte & Touche LLP, P.O.Box 49279, Bentall Cntr., 1055 Dunsmuir Street, VANCOUVER V7X 1P4, BC CANADA.

LUK, Ms. Kit Ying, ACA *2007;* K Y Luk & Co, Room 910, 9/F, 655 Nathan Road, HUNG HOM, KOWLOON HONG KONG SAR.

LUK, Mr. Kwok Kong Julian, ACA *2006;* Flat C, 43/F Tower 7, Tseung Kwan O Plaza, TSEUNG KWAN O, NEW TERRITORIES, HONG KONG SAR.

LUK, Mr. Peter Chi Chung, ACA *2006;* Flat E, 28/F Tower 8The Belchers, 89 Pokfulam Road, POK FU LAM, HONG KONG ISLAND, HONG KONG SAR.

LUK, Mr. Sai Yan, ACA *2007;* Chang Leung Hiu & Li CPA Limited, 12th Floor, No 3, Lockhart Road, WAN CHAI, HONG KONG ISLAND HONG KONG SAR.

LUK, Mr. Sai Wai Simon, ACA *2008;* Flat B 18/F Graces Court, 298 Un Chau Street, SHAM SHUI PO, KOWLOON, HONG KONG SAR.

LUK, Mr. Shu Kuen, ACA *2005;* S. K. Luk & Co., Rooms 502-503 5th Floor, Wanchai Commercial Centre, 194-204 Johnston Road, WAN CHAI, HONG KONG ISLAND HONG KONG SAR.

LUK, Mr. Thau Min, FCA *1959;* 39 Eden Avenue, TURRAMURRA, NSW 2074, AUSTRALIA. (Life Member)

LUK, Ms. Wai Wah Regine, ACA *2005;* JCK Shum Leung Luk & Co., 2nd Floor, Jonsim Place, 228 Queen's Road East, WAN CHAI, HONG KONG ISLAND HONG KONG SAR.

•LUK, Mr. Yui Chow, FCA *1977;* (Tax Fac), Alliotts, Imperial House, 15 Kingsway, LONDON, WC2B 6UN.

LUK TAM, Mrs. Mei Nor Mina, ACA *2008;* 20/F Princes Building, CENTRAL, HONG KONG ISLAND, HONG KONG SAR.

•LUKE, Mrs. Ann, FCA *1969;* (Tax Fac), Ann Luke, 15 Richard Hind Walk, STOCKTON-ON-TEES, TS18 3LU.

LUKE, Mr. Christopher, BA ACA *2003;* 81 Hastings Crescent, CARDIFF, CF3 5DJ.

•LUKE, Mr. Colin Douglas, FCA *1976;* (Tax Fac), Colin D Luke & Co, 79 Northumberland Road, New Barnet, BARNET, HERTFORDSHIRE, EN5 1EB.

LUKE, Mr. David Anthony, BSc ACA *1986;* 10 Nant Y Drope, Ely, CARDIFF, CF5 4UF.

LUKE, Mrs. Elizabeth Ann, BSc(Hons) ACA *2004;* with PricewaterhouseCoopers LLP, 1 Embankment Place, LONDON, WC2N 6RH.

LUKE, Mr. Gareth Edward, BSc FCA *1972;* Ty Hafan, St. Hilary Court, Copthorne Way, Culverhouse Cross, CARDIFF, CF5 6ES.

•LUKE, Mr. Gary, BA ACA *2008;* Learchild Limited, 4 Lansdowne Terrace, Gosforth, NEWCASTLE UPON TYNE, NE3 1HN.

LUKE, Mr. Harley Rochfort, ACA *2009;* 46 Regents Park Road, LONDON, NW1 7SX.

LUKE, Miss. Jacqueline Wai Ying, ACA *1983;* 3 Circus Lodge, Circus Road, LONDON, NW8 9JL.

LUKE, Mr. Jason Howard, BA ACA CTA *1997;* (Tax Fac), 5 Mantelcroft Drive, Burton on the Wolds, LOUGHBOROUGH, LEICESTERSHIRE, LE12 5AY.

•LUKE, Mr. John Kerr, BSc FCA *1993;* KPMG LLP, 15 Canada Square, LONDON, E14 5GL. See also KPMG Europe LLP

LUKE, Miss. Kirsty, ACA *2011;* 9 Harbutts Court, MIDDLEWICH, CHESHIRE, CW10 9PU.

LUKE, Ms. Sandra Mary, ACA *1990;* Pickwick House, Pickwick, CORSHAM, SN13 0HZ.

LUKE, Mrs. Susan, BSc ACA *1987;* 10 Nant-Y-Drope, St Fagans, CARDIFF, CF5 4UF.

LUKE, Mr. William Ross, FCA *1969;* 105 Palewell Park, LONDON, SW14 8JJ.

•LUKER, Mrs. Judith Ann, FCA *1974;* Nash & Co, 77 Fore Street, BODMIN, CORNWALL, PL31 2JB.

•LUKES, Mr. David Ronald Mark, FCA *1975;* (Tax Fac), De La Wyche Travis & Co, Crown House, Trafford Park Road, Trafford Park, MANCHESTER, M17 1HG.

•LUKES, Mr. Jonathan Charles, FCA *1973;* (Tax Fac), Aston Hughes & Co, Selby Towers, 29 Princes Drive, COLWYN BAY, LL29 8PE.

LUKES, Mr. Neil Thomas, FCA *1969;* 17 Birkett Way, CHALFONT ST.GILES, HP8 4BH.

LUKES, Miss. Rebekka, ACA *2009;* 10 Wroxham Road, POOLE, DORSET, BH12 1HA.

•①LUKIC, Mr. Tomislav, BSc ACA *1997;* Ernst & Young LLP, 1 Colmore Square, BIRMINGHAM, B4 6HQ. See also Ernst & Young Europe LLP

LULE, Mr. Frederick Kironde, BSc FCA *1976;* P O Box 2798, KAMPALA, UGANDA.

•LULHAM, Mr. Joseph Robert Ferris, FCA *1961;* with Slater Maidment, Baker Tilly Services Ltd, 65 Kingsway, LONDON, WC2B 6TD.

LUM, Mr. Andrew Christopher, MA ACA *1994;* with Stanley Wilkinson & Co, 139 Red Bank Road, Bispham, BLACKPOOL, LANCASHIRE, FY2 9HZ.

LUM, Mr. Chiew Mun, ACA *2008;* 11 Jalan BK 3/10 Bandar Kinrara, 47100 PUCHONG, MALAYSIA.

LUM, Mrs. Christine Janet, BA ACA *1981;* 57 Whiteoaks Drive, Bishopswood, STAFFORD, ST19 9AH.

LUM, Mr. Soong Jye, BA ACA *2002;* Room 725 Lane, 138 Chengzhong Road, Jiading District, SHANGHAI 201800, CHINA.

LUMB, Mr. Alastair John, BA ACA *1988;* 63 Stockley Crescent, Shirley, SOLIHULL, B90 3SW.

LUMB, Mr. Dacre John, BA FCA *1972;* 49 Vickery Street, MCKINNON, VIC 3204, AUSTRALIA.

LUMB, Mr. Frank Gerard, FCA *1961;* 16 Chevet La, Sandal, WAKEFIELD, WF2 6HL. (Life Member)

LUMB, Mr. Garrie, BA ACA *1987;* Springhead, 32 Smithwell Lane, Heptonstall, HEBDEN BRIDGE, HX7 7NX.

•LUMB, Mrs. Helen, BSc FCA *1993;* Insignia Finance Solutions Ltd, Barnside House, 9 Rookery Close, Alwyn Road Yoxall, BURTON-ON-TRENT, STAFFORDSHIRE DE13 8QH.

LUMB, Mr. James Ronald Alexander, BA ACA *2004;* with KPMG LLP, 1 The Embankment, Neville Street, LEEDS, LS1 4DW.

LUMB, Miss. Katherine Poppy, BSc ACA *2006;* FT Publications Inc, 14th Floor, 1330 Avenue of the Americas, NEW YORK, NY 10019, UNITED STATES.

LUMB, Mr. Michael Anthony Garnett, ACA *1986;* 26 Grange Avenue, Spofforth, HARROGATE, HG3 1AH.

LUMB, Mr. Neil Roderic, BA ACA *1982;* Postnet Suite 41, Private Bag x 23, GALLO MANOR, 2052, SOUTH AFRICA.

LUMB, Mr. Neville George Kenyon, FCA *1957;* Barn Hey, Storeton Lane, Barnston, WIRRAL, CH61 1DA. (Life Member)

LUMB, Mr. Richard Peter, ACA *1979;* 15 Brook View Drive, Keyworth, NOTTINGHAM, NG12 5JN.

LUMB, Mr. Robert Ashbel, BA(Econ) FCA *1974;* 9 Chemin du Port a L'Auguille, 77870 VULAINES SUR SEINE, FRANCE. (Life Member)

LUMB, Mr. Stephen William, FCA *1980;* 42 Riverdale Rd, SHEFFIELD, S10 3FB.

LUMB, Mr. Timothy, FCA *1968;* Birchcroft Main Street, Appleton Roebuck, YORK, YO23 7DN.

•LUMB, Mr. Tony, BSc FCA *1989;* Vincere Partners LLP, 1The Corner House, Aimson Road West, Timperley, ALTRINCHAM, CHESHIRE WA15 7XP.

LUMBORG, Mrs. Karen Ann, BSc ACA *1989;* Les Pignons, Le Mont de la Rosiere, St. Saviour, JERSEY, JE2 7WD.

LUMBY, Mr. Andrew John, BA ACA *2002;* Nottingham Bldg Soc, Nottingham House, 5-13 Upper Parliament Street, NOTTINGHAM, NG1 2BX.

•LUMBY, Mr. George Peter, BCom FCA *1972;* Insolvency Services in Spain, Sl Galeon 4, Portal A Bajoa, 28042 MADRID, SPAIN.

LUMBY, Mrs. Helen Louise, BSc(Hons) ACA *2004;* 50 Darwin Crescent, LOUGHBOROUGH, LEICESTERSHIRE, LE11 5SB.

LUMBY, Mrs. Natalie Hedda, BA ACA *1996;* The Manor House, High Street, Meonstoke, SOUTHAMPTON, SO32 3NH.

LUMBY, Mr. William Henry David, FCA *1962;* Apartado 506, 5901 - 908 VIANA DO CASTELO, PORTUGAL. (Life Member)

LUMLEY, Mrs. Alice Maureen Clare, BSc ACA *1992;* Gore Mutual Insurance Company, 252 Dundas Street North, CAMBRIDGE N1R 5T3, ON, CANADA.

LUMLEY, Mr. David Patrick, BSc ACA *1985;* Arena Wealth Chiswick Gate, 598-608 Chiswick High Road, LONDON, W4 5RT.

LUMLEY, Mr. Derek Arthur, FCA *1950;* Gwyn, South Road, WOKING, SURREY, GU21 4JN. (Life Member)

LUMLEY, Mr. Eric, MSc FCA *1979;* 29 Elmscroft Gardens, POTTERS BAR, EN6 2JP.

LUMLEY, Mrs. Margaret Sarah, BCom ACA *1987;* 31 Queen Marys Drive, Port Sunlight, WIRRAL, CH62 5DT.

LUMLEY, Mr. Richard Nicholas, BSc ACA *1994;* 3 Bavant Road, BRIGHTON, BN1 6RD.

LUMLEY, Mr. Richard Peter, MBA BA ACA *1992;* 5a Station Road, TADCASTER, NORTH YORKSHIRE, LS24 9JE.

LUMLEY-SMITH, Mrs. Sallie Louise, BCom ACA *1993;* Ayres Barn, Ayres End Lane, HARPENDEN, HERTFORDSHIRE, AL5 1AL.

LUMLEY-WOOD, Mr. David John, ACA *2002;* 9 Mowmead, OLNEY, MK46 5EF.

LUMSDEN, Mr. Charles John, ACA *1982;* 9 Curwen Road, LONDON, W12 9AF.

LUMSDEN, Mr. Christopher, BA ACA *1995;* Cayman National Fund Services Ltd., 62 Forum Lane, SEVEN MILE BEACH, GRAND CAYMAN, KY1-1201, CAYMAN ISLANDS.

LUMSDEN, Mrs. Clare, BA ACA *1996;* The National Trust for the Cayman Islands, 558 South Church Street, PO Box 31116, SEVEN MILE BEACH, GRAND CAYMAN, KY1-1205 CAYMAN ISLANDS.

LUMSDEN, Mr. Jonathan James, BA(Hons) ACA *2004;* 1 Teale Court, Chapel Allerton, LEEDS, LS7 4AY.

LUMSDEN, Mr. Mark Richard, BA ACA *2002;* 2 White Hills Croft, SKIPTON, NORTH YORKSHIRE, BD23 1LW.

•LUMSDEN, Mr. Michael Edward, BSc ACA *1990;* Moore Stephens, Rutland House, Minerva Business Park, Lynch Wood, PETERBOROUGH, PE2 6PZ.

LUMSDEN, Mr. Neil Alexander McLean, BA ACA *1996;* Little Becketts Duddenhoe End Road, Arkesden, SAFFRON WALDEN, CB11 4HG.

LUMSDEN, Peter James Scott, Esq CBE MA FCA *1956;* West Studdal Farm, West Studdal, DOVER, CT15 5BJ. (Life Member)

LUMSDEN, Mr. Richard, FCA *1975;* Croft House, White Hills Croft, SKIPTON, BD23 1LW.

LUMSDEN, Mr. Stuart John, BA ACA *2000;* 103 Clifton Street, SWINDON, SN1 3QA.

LUMSDEN, Mr. William Alexander, MBA BA FCA *1986;* 4 Albion Court, Little Harrowden, WELLINGBOROUGH, NN9 5XY.

LUMSDON, Mr. Gary John, BSc ACA *1999;* Davies Group Ltd, 2 St. Giles Court, Southampton Street, READING, RG1 2QL.

LUMSDON-TAYLOR, Mr. Mark James, BA ACA *2006;* Kate Barret Flat, Hadlow College of Agriculture & Horticl, Tonbridge Road, Hadlow, TONBRIDGE, KENT TN11 0AL.

LUN, Miss. Karen Yuen Kwan, BSc ACA *1993;* Flat 901 Block 30, Heng Fa Chuen, CHAI WAN, HONG KONG SAR.

•LUN LEUNG, Miss. Jane, FCA *1992;* Three Sixty, #02-A8 Cybertower1, EBENE, MAURITIUS.

LUNCH, Mr. John, CBE VRD FCA *1946;* (Member of Council 1970 - 1977), Martins, East Ashling, CHICHESTER, PO18 9AX. (Life Member)

LUND, Mr. Angus John, BA ACA *1998;* Morgan Stanley, 20 Bank Street, LONDON, E14 4AD.

LUND, Mr. Bryan, FCA JDipMA *1960;* Maddox, 37a Nightingale Road, RICKMANSWORTH, HERTFORDSHIRE, WD3 7DA. (Life Member)

•LUND, Mr. Derek, FCA *1969;* Lund Consulting Ltd, Silverdale Suite, Clawthorpe Hall Business Centre, Burton in Kendal, CARNFORTH, LANCASHIRE LA6 1NU.

LUND, Mrs. Judith Lynn, BSc ACA *1990;* Manor Farm, 155 Tollerton Lane, Tollerton, NOTTINGHAM, NG12 4FT.

LUND, Mr. Mark Jonathan, BA ACA *1995;* 18 St Marys Avenue, Bramley, TADLEY, RG26 5UU.

LUND, Mr. Morten Peder, BSc ACA *1983;* Olav Aukrusts Vei 2A, 0785 OSLO, NORWAY.

LUND, Mrs. Pamela Anne, BA ACA *1986;* Owlett House, Grassington Road, Stirton, SKIPTON, NORTH YORKSHIRE, BD23 3LB.

LUND, Mr. Richard Nicholas, ACA *1989;* 5 Evelyn Mansions, Carlisle Place, LONDON, SW1P 1NH.

LUND, Mr. Simon Ingemann, MA ACA *1995;* HarbourVest Partners (Asia) Limited, Citibank Tower Suite 1207, 3 Garden Road, CENTRAL, HONG KONG SAR.

LUND, Mr. Stuart Malcolm, ACA CA(AUS) *2011;* Top Floor Flat, 60 Radipole Road, LONDON, SW6 5DL.

LUND, Mr. Thomas, FCA *1953;* Hillcrest, 24 George Lane, Read, BURNLEY, BB12 7RH. (Life Member)

LUNDBERG, Mr. Ian, BSc ACA *1991;* The Firs Beresford Lane, Plumpton Green, LEWES, EAST SUSSEX, BN8 4EN.

LUNDEEN, Miss. Maria, BSc ACA *2007;* Flat 21 Manor Court, Leigham Avenue, LONDON, SW16 2DS.

LUNDERVOLD, Mr. Chris Alexander, BSc(Hons) ACA *2002;* (Tax Fac), 1440 N State Pkwy, Apt 4C, CHICAGO, IL 60610, UNITED STATES.

LUNDIE, Mr. Martin, BSc ACA *1992;* 35 Mariner Terrace, Appartment 3309, TORONTO M5V 3V9, ON, CANADA.

LUNDIE, Miss. Rachel Juliette, BSc ACA *2008;* Ogilvy & Mather Direct, 10 Cabot Square, LONDON, E14 4QB.

LUNDIE, Mr. Thomas, FCA *1973;* The Old Vicarage, 2 Bury Lane, Codicote, HITCHIN, HERTFORDSHIRE, SG4 8XT.

LUNDIN, Miss. Malin, BSc(Hons) ACA *2011;* Follys End, Warren Road, CROWBOROUGH, EAST SUSSEX, TN6 1QN.

•①LUNDY, Mr. Simon John, FCA *1974;* Begbies Traynor (Central) LLP, Ground Floor, 2 Collingwood Street, NEWCASTLE UPON TYNE, NE1 1JF.

LUNG, Mr. Chun Tak Junius, ACA *2008;* Junius C T Lung & Co, 16th Floor, Kailey Tower, 16 Stanley Street, CENTRAL, HONG KONG SAR.

LUNG, Mr. Hiu Man, ACA *2009;* Flat F, 25/F Block 2, Metro Harbour View, 8 Fuk Lee Street, TAI KOK TSUI, KOWLOON HONG KONG SAR.

•LUNG, Mrs. Phillis Wing Yi, MBA ACA *1990;* 37G Tower 1, The Belcher's, 89 Pokfulam Road, POK FU LAM, HONG KONG ISLAND, HONG KONG SAR.

•LUNG, Mr. Raymond Ka-Hon, MSc FCA *1994;* (Tax Fac), Goodbridge Ltd, 17 Hemingford Close, LONDON, N12 9HF.

LUNG, Mr. Wai Kee, ACA *2005;* Brilliant International Development Limited, Room 408, Summit Insurance Building, 789 Nathan Road, MONG KOK, KOWLOON HONG KONG SAR.

LUNN, Mr. Andrew Peter, BSc ACA CTA *1996;* B Z W, 10 South Colonnade, LONDON, E14 4PU.

LUNN, Mr. Anthony John Mcgregor, BSc FCA *1973;* Abbottsleigh, Main Street, Leire, LUTTERWORTH, LE17 5EU.

LUNN, Mr. Brian William, FCA *1953;* Chegwyn, Main Road, Lacey Green, PRINCES RISBOROUGH, BUCKINGHAMSHIRE, HP27 0PL. (Life Member)

LUNN, Mr. Colin Arthur, FCA *1957;* 58 The Chine, Grange Park, LONDON, N21 2ED. (Life Member)

LUNN, Miss. Gillian, FCA *1975;* 20 Onslow Way, WOKING, GU22 8QX.

LUNN, Mr. Graham Ian, MEng ACA *2003;* 12 William Gardens, Smallfield, HORLEY, SURREY, RH6 9EN.

LUNN, Miss. Jacqueline, BA ACA *2003;* 1st Floor Flat, 64 Venner Road, LONDON, SE26 5EL.

LUNN, Mr. Keith Michael, BSc FCA CTA *1980;* 2 Hawthorn Croft, Lofthouse, WAKEFIELD, WF3 3ST.

LUNN, Mr. Kenneth, FCA *1982;* 14 Stockbridge Park, Elloughton, BROUGH, NORTH HUMBERSIDE, HU15 1JQ.

LUNN, Mr. Marc David John, BSc ACA *1994;* 44 Windmill Lane, BELPER, DERBYSHIRE, DE56 1GP.

LUNN, Mrs. Mary, BA ACA *1980;* 140 Moorside North, Fenham, NEWCASTLE UPON TYNE, NE4 9DY.

•LUNN, Mr. Melvyn, FCA *1973;* (Tax Fac), Melvyn Lunn, 49 Church Street, Darton, BARNSLEY, S75 5HF.

LUNN, Mr. Michael Antony William, BSc ACA *2009;* Flat 7, 80-86 St. John's Road, LONDON, SW11 1PX.

•LUNN, Mr. Steven Anthony, ACA *1997;* with Ernst & Young LLP, 1 More London Place, LONDON, SE1 2AF.

•LUNNON, Mrs. Lesley Mary, FCA *1977;* Lesley M. Lunnon, The Pightle, Alscot Lane, Princes Risborough, PRINCES RISBOROUGH, HP27 9RU.

LUNSON, Mr. Andrew John, BA FCA *1973;* Bourne House Cottage, Weeford, LICHFIELD, WS14 0PJ.

LUNT, Mr. Christopher Randle, FCA *1960;* 6 Old Torrington Road, Sticklepath, BARNSTAPLE, DEVON, EX31 2DD. (Life Member)

LUNT, Miss. Diane Margaret, BA ACA *2005;* (Tax Fac), 4 Rydal Avenue, WHITCHURCH, SHROPSHIRE, SY13 1ET.

•LUNT, Mr. George Nicholas David, FCA DChA *1971;* Moor Farm House, Moor Lane, Hardington Moor, YEOVIL, BA22 9NW.

•LUNT, Mr. Gordon, BA FCA *1981;* G Lunt, 9 Gordon Road, CHELMSFORD, CM2 9LL.

LUNT, Miss. Helen, BA(Hons) ACA *2010;* Wilson Henry Partnership, 145 Edge Lane Edge Hill, LIVERPOOL, L7 2PF.

LUNT, Miss. Josephine Sarah, BSc ACA *2001;* with Deloitte LLP, PO Box 500, 2 Hardman Street, MANCHESTER, M60 2AT.

•LUNT, Mr. Martin Henry Charles, MCom BCom FCA 1973; (Tax Fac), Henry Lunt, Ashburn, Woodhart Lane, Eccleston, CHORLEY, PR7 5TB. See also Lunt M.H.C.
•LUNT, Mr. Martin Keith, FCA 1979; (Tax Fac), Creasey Son & Wickenden, Hearts of Oak House, 4 Pembroke Road, SEVENOAKS, TN13 1XR.
LUNT, Mr. Michael John Winstanley, MA FCA 1959; Boyers, Summer Lane, Combe Down, BATH, BA2 7EU. (Life Member)
LUNT, Mr. Peter Cowley Winstanley, FCA 1959; 18 Wolfe Close, CHICHESTER, PO19 6BY. (Life Member)
LUNT, The Revd. Raymond, FCA 1965; 4 Bradmoor Grove, Chellaston, DERBY, DE73 6QS.
LUNT, Mr. William Thomas, BSc FCA 1951; September Barn 5 Elmsbury Court, Netherton, PERSHORE, WORCESTERSHIRE, WR10 3JG. (Life Member)
LUO, Mr. Xi, ACA 2008; 13B Bella Vista, Ying Fai Terrace, Peel Street, CENTRAL, HONG KONG ISLAND, HONG KONG SAR.
LUO, Miss. Xiangying, MSc BA ACA 2004; with KPMG, 8th Floor, Tower E2, Oriental Plaza, 1 East Chang An Avenue, BEIJING 100738 CHINA.
LUO, Ms. Yan, ACA 2009; Audit Department 9, RSM China, 8F Block A Corporate Sq, 35 Finance Street, Xicheng District, BEIJING 100140 CHINA.
LUO, Miss. Yujun, MA ACA 2009; 1 Millennium Apartments, Browns Hill, PENRYN, CORNWALL, TR10 8GL.
LUPONDWANA, Mr. Zola, BCom ACA 1997; P.O. Box 72517, Parkview, JOHANNESBURG, 2122, SOUTH AFRICA.
LUPSON, Mr. Graham Edward John, BSc ACA 1988; 91C London Road, TONBRIDGE, TN10 3AJ.
LUPTON, Mrs. Helen Clare, BSc ACA 1999; 16519 Cabarrus Rd, CHARLOTTE, NC 28227, UNITED STATES.
LUPTON, Miss. Helen Clare, BEng ACA 1993; 36 Sudbrooke Road, LONDON, SW12 8TQ.
LUPTON, Mr. John Holden, BSc FCA 1969; 104 Hurley Road, Little Corby, CARLISLE, CA4 8QF.
•LUPTON, Mr. Paul Nigel Carus, BSc FCA CF 1989; Deloitte LLP, PO Box 500, 2 Hardman Street, MANCHESTER, M60 2AT. See also Deloitte & Touche LLP
LUSBY, Mr. James, BSocSc CA ACA 2000; with PricewaterhouseCoopers, Royal Trust Tower, Suite 3000 TD Centre, Box 82, 77 King Street West, TORONTO M5K 1G8 ON CANADA.
LUSCOMBE, Mr. Barry Gordon, FCA 1971; Moor View, 17 Humber Lane, Kingsteignton, NEWTON ABBOT, DEVON, TQ12 3DJ.
LUSCOMBE, Mr. Christopher Daniel, BA ACA 1998; 6 Wooldridge Place, Wickham Bishops, WITHAM, ESSEX, CM8 3LW.
•LUSCOMBE, Mr. Gerald Arthur, FCA 1983; (Tax Fac), Bullimores, 50 South Street, SOUTH MOLTON, DEVON, EX36 4AG.
LUSCOMBE, Miss. Nicki, BSc(Hons) ACA 2010; 1 Maison le Marchant, Grandes Maisons Road, St. Sampson, GUERNSEY, GY2 4JP.
•LUSCOMBE, Mr. Peter, FCA 1975; with Carter Backer Winter LLP, Enterprise House, 21 Buckle Street, LONDON, E1 8NN.
LUSCOMBE, Mr. Peter David, BA ACA 1999; 3rd Floor, K P M G Llp, 15 Canada Square, LONDON, E14 5GL.
LUSCOMBE, Mr. Rodney William, BA FCA 1967; Whitegates, Hempstead, SAFFRON WALDEN, CB10 2PD. (Life Member)
LUSCOMBE, Mr. Simon, BSc ACA 2007; Hobbs Limited, 72 Welbeck Street, LONDON, WC1G 0AY.
LUSH, Mr. Dennis, FCA CTA 1961; 16 Farringdon Court, Northlands Drive, WINCHESTER, SO23 7AJ. (Life Member)
LUSH, Mr. Peter Victor, FCA 1963; Scarebridge House, Woodham Walter, MALDON, CM9 6RP.
LUSH, Ms. Rachel Elizabeth, BSc ACA 2002; with Rawlinson & Hunter, Eighth Floor, 6 New Street Square, New Fetter Lane, LONDON, EC4A 3AQ.
LUSH, Mr. Robert Henry, BA FCA 1967; 125 Maplewell Road, Woodhouse Eaves, LOUGHBOROUGH, LE12 8QY.
LUSK, Mr. Brian Hugh, FCA 1953; Little Gables, Somerswey, Shalford, GUILDFORD, SURREY, GU4 8EQ. (Life Member)
•LUSMAN, Mr. Anthony Howard, FCA 1975; Anthony H Lusman & Co, 20 John Keats Lodge, Chase Side Crescent, ENFIELD, EN2 0JZ.
•LUSTIG, Mr. Roger Hugh, BD FCA MAE 1975; Lustig & Co, PO Box 59842, LONDON, SW14 9BF.
•LUSTIGMAN, Mr. Anthony Robert, FCA 1973; Lustigman & Company Limited, 27 Manor Park Crescent, EDGWARE, MIDDLESEX, HA8 7NH.
LUSTY, Mrs. Alison Joan, MA FCA 1985; 4 Wilkins Close, Barford, WARWICK, CV35 8EX.
LUSTY, Mr. Christopher Andrew, BSc ACA 1991; with Wellers, 8 King Edward Street, OXFORD, OX1 4HL.
LUSTY, Mr. Christopher Henry, ACA 1984; 115 Tarrant Road, Upper Moutere, RD1, NELSON 7173, NEW ZEALAND.
LUSTY, Mr. Justin William, MBA BSc ACA ATT 1990; 12 Colehill Lane, LONDON, SW6 5EG.
LUSTY, Mr. Peter Alan, FCA 1971; Loriners Company, Hampton House, High Street, EAST GRINSTEAD, WEST SUSSEX, RH19 3AW.
LUSTY, Mr. Robert James Greville, FCA 1965; Beke Place, Marringdean, BILLINGSHURST, RH14 9HF.
LUSTY, Mr. Stephen Anthony Michael, MSc ACA 1993; 6 Lilyville Road, LONDON, SW6 5DW.
LUTFI, Mr. Madhat Izzat, BCom FCA 1962; 15 Spencer Road, Canford Cliffs, POOLE, BH13 7ET. (Life Member)
•LUTFULLAH, Mr. Sm Tariq Jalal, ACA 1982; Husain Bulman & Co, 258 Merton Road, LONDON, SW18 5JL.
LUTHER, Mr. David Joseph, BSc ACA 1992; 11 Sells Close, GUILDFORD, GU1 3JY.
LUTHER, Mr. Stephen Peter, MSc BA FCA 1987; 13 St. Peters Way, Chorleywood, RICKMANSWORTH, HERTFORDSHIRE, WD3 5QF.
LUTHMAN, Mr. Malcolm Thomas, BSc FCA 1979; Grafton Lodge, Upper Harlestone, NORTHAMPTON, NN7 4EH.
LUTHRA, Mr. Deepak, FCA 1975; Oudshoornseweg 112, 2401LC ALPHEN AAN DEN RIJN, NETHERLANDS. (Life Member)
•LUTHRA, Miss. Shelley, BA(Hons) ACA 2001; Economical Accountant & Bookkeeper Limited, 2 Ross Close, HAYES, MIDDLESEX, UB3 1TS.
•LUTHRA, Mr. Vishwa Nath, FCA 1972; (Tax Fac), Nath Luthra & Co, Minavil House, 1st Floor, Ealing Road, WEMBLEY, HA0 4EL.
LUTLEY, Mr. Edward Jonathan, FCA 1967; Bryneglur, Beulah Road, NEWCASTLE EMLYN, SA38 9QA. (Life Member)
LUTON, Miss. Anna-Maria, MA ACA 2007; with PricewaterhouseCoopers LLP, Donington Court, Pegasus Business Park, Castle Donington, DERBY, DE74 2UZ.
LUTTON, Mr. Andrew, BCom ACA 2005; 38 Grasmere Road, LIGHTWATER, SURREY, GU18 5TJ.
LUU, Mr. Khang Ngoc, MA BA ACA 1993; 12800 Camellia Drive, SILVER SPRING, MD 20906, UNITED STATES.
LUU, Mrs. Thi Thanh Binh, MPhil ACA 2010; 59 Spencer Road, READING, RG2 8TP.
•LUXFORD, Mr. Brian Mervyn, FCA 1969; Raymond Benn & Co, 1 Sheffield Road, Southborough, TUNBRIDGE WELLS, KENT, TN4 0PD.
•LUXFORD, Mr. Keith, FCA 1976; (Tax Fac), Levicks, West Hill, 61 London Road, MAIDSTONE, ME16 8TX. See also Somerfield Consultants Limited
LUXFORD, Ms. Nicola Jane, BA ACA 1987; Threadneedle, St. Mary Axe House, 60 St. Mary Axe, LONDON, EC3A 8JQ.
LUXFORD, Miss. Victoria Jane, BA(Hons) ACA 2001; WMT LLP, Torrington House 47 Holywell Hill, ST ALBANS, HERTFORDSHIRE, AL1 1HD.
LUXMORE, Mr. Richard Martin, BA ACA 1989; 5 Glendale Close, WOKINGHAM, RG41 4EY.
LUXTON, Mrs. Clare Ann, BA ACA 1992; 6 Littledown Road, CHELTENHAM, GL53 9LP.
•LUXTON, Mr. Howard Jeffrey, ACA 1982; 22 Garden Suburbs, Pontywaun, Cross Keys, NEWPORT, GWENT, NP11 7GB.
LUXTON, Mr. Ian John, MA ACA 1979; 5 Sheridan Grange, ASCOT, SL5 0BX.
LUXTON, Mr. Jack Reginald Wynne, FCA 1978; 43 Temple Mill Island, MARLOW, BUCKINGHAMSHIRE, SL7 1SQ.
LUXTON, Miss. Julie Anne, ACA 1999; with Thomas Westcott, 26-28 Southernhay East, EXETER, DEVON, EX1 1NS.
LUXTON, Miss. Stephanie Ann, ACA 2008; 5th Fl, Bermuda House, Dr Roy's Drive, PO BOX 1044, GEORGETOWN, GRAND CAYMAN KY1 1102 CAYMAN ISLANDS.
LWIN, Mr. Kevin Timothy David, BA(Hons) ACA 2000; (Tax Fac), Barlow Andrews, 78 Chorley New Road, BOLTON, BL1 4BY.
LY, Ms. Mai, MA ACA 1993; 324 Whittington Street, MANCHESTER, NH 03104, UNITED STATES.
LYALL, Miss. Helen Kate, BSc ACA 1998; Nyn Ashlish, Baldhoon Road, Baldhoon, ISLE OF MAN, IM4 7QG.
LYALL, Miss. Jaspreet, ACA 2010; with Menzies LLP, Heathrow Business Centre, 65 High Street, EGHAM, SURREY, TW20 9EY.
LYALL, Mr. Kurt Jonathan, MEng ACA 1999; Marlings, Orchard Dell, West Chiltington, PULBOROUGH, WEST SUSSEX, RH20 2LB.
LYALL, Mr. Nicholas Mark Edward, BA ACA 1986; Citibank Tower, 3 Garden Road, CENTRAL, HONG KONG ISLAND, HONG KONG SAR.
LYALL, Mr. Robert, BSc ACA 1996; Mole Valley Farmers Ltd, Station Road, SOUTH MOLTON, DEVON, EX36 3BH.
LYALL, Mr. Scott Cameron, ACA CA(AUS) 2011; Brada Group, 6th Floor, International House, 223 Regent Street, LONDON, W1B 2QD.
LYALL, Mr. Thomas, ACA 2011; 20 Horn Lane, WOODFORD GREEN, ESSEX, IG8 9AA.
LYALL, Mr. Victor, FCA 1952; 5 Williams Way, RADLETT, WD7 7EZ. (Life Member)
LYALL-COTTLE, Mr. Hugh Maurice, BCom FCA 1971; Beech Trees Cottage, Well Lane, Mollington, CHESTER, CH1 6LD.
LYALL-COTTLE, Mr. Neil, BSc ACA 2004; Mailbox 231, Royal Automobile Club, 89-91 Pall Mall, LONDON, SW1Y 5HS.
LYCETT, Mr. Andrew, FCA 1975; 31 Hazel Road, Bradmore, WOLVERHAMPTON, WV3 7HB.
LYCETT, Mr. Andrew Richard, BSc FCA 1992; Tall Trees, Colwinston, COWBRIDGE, SOUTH GLAMORGAN, CF71 7NJ.
LYCETT, Mr. Kevin Harry John, BA FCA 1975; Anneville Manor, Anneville Road, Vale, GUERNSEY, GY6 8LY.
•LYDALL, Mr. Ian Samuel, BSc(Econ) FCA ATII 1979; PricewaterhouseCoopers (Vietnam) Ltd, 4th Floor Saigon Tower, 29 Le Duan Boulevard, District 1, HO CHI MINH CITY, VIETNAM.
LYDDON, Mr. Christopher, MEng ACA 1995; 4 Rue De La Chapelle, Gournay, 62560 VERCHOCA, FRANCE.
•LYDDON, Mr. John William, BSc FCA 1970; (Tax Fac), John Lyddon Limited, Uplands, Manor Estate, Horrabridge, YELVERTON, DEVON PL20 7RS.
LYDDON, Mr. Michael Charles, BSc ACA 2006; McCormack House, Unit 1 Axis Centre, Hogarth Business Park Burlington Lane, LONDON, W4 2TH.
LYDDON, Miss. Rachel Clare, BSc ACA 2004; Dovedale, Trevellance Lane, PERRANPORTH, CORNWALL, TR6 0AX.
LYDDON, Mr. Stephen Timothy, ACA 2008; 11 Venn Crescent, PLYMOUTH, PL3 5PJ.
LYDE, Miss. Melanie Victoria, BSc ACA 1984; 20046 T Ave, DALLAS CENTER, IA 50063, UNITED STATES.
LYDIARD, Mrs. Ann Marion, BA(Hons) FCA ATII 1998; 24 Rosedale Gardens, TROWBRIDGE, WILTSHIRE, BA14 9TL.
LYDIARD-WILSON, Mr. John Humphrey, FCA 1951; Hollowell Manor, NORTHAMPTON, NN6 8RN. (Life Member)
LYDON, Mr. Charles, MEng ACA 2011; 11a Ogden Road, Bramhall, STOCKPORT, CHESHIRE, SK7 1HJ.
•LYDON, Mr. Christopher Paul, ACA FCCA 2007; Farrar Smith Limited, 2 Woodside Mews, Clayton Wood Close, LEEDS, LS16 6QE.
LYDON, Miss. Elaine Valerie, BSc ACA 1992; 19 The Grove, RADLETT, WD7 7NF.
•LYDON, Mr. Patrick Anthony, FCA 1978; Warings, Bedford House, 60 Chorley New Road, BOLTON, BL1 4DA. See also Warings Business Advisers LLP
LYDON, Mr. Paul Brian, BSc ACA 1999; 6 Neeham Road, St. Newlyn East, NEWQUAY, CORNWALL, TR8 5LE.
LYDON, Mr. Peter Richard, BA FCA MBIM 1974; Atlantic Alpacas UK Ltd, Amberley House, Yaffle Road, WEYBRIDGE, KT13 0QF.
LYE, Mr. James Edward, BA(Hons) ACA 2002; with RSM Tenon Limited, Cedar House, Sandbrook Business Park Sandbrook Way, ROCHDALE, LANCASHIRE, OL11 1LQ.
LYE, Mr. Raymond John, FCA 1958; Flighthill Cottage, Flight Hill, Sandford St. Martin, CHIPPING NORTON, OX7 7AW. (Life Member)
LYELL, Mr. Alexander, ACA 2008; 6/1 Learmonth Terrace, EDINBURGH, EH4 1PQ.
•LYFORD, Mr. Timothy John, LLB ACA 1994; (Tax Fac), Smith & Williamson Ltd, 25 Moorgate, LONDON, EC2R 6AY.
LYKHMAN, Mr. Kostyantyn Oleksandrovych, MA ACA 2006; Barclays Capital, 5 North Colonnade, LONDON, E14 4BB.
LYKO-EDWARDS, Mr. Darren, BCom ACA 1998; 113 Wake Green Road, BIRMINGHAM, B13 9US.
LYLE, Mr. Anthony Steohen, MMath ACA 2007; 38B Palmerston Road, Birkenhead Point, AUCKLAND 0626, NEW ZEALAND.
LYLE, Mr. Anthony Welsh, FCA 1973; P O Box 109, Cehegin, 30430 MURCIA, SPAIN.
•LYLE, Mrs. Christina Marion, BSc ACA 1984; Christina Lyle BSc Hons ACA, 26 St. James Avenue, West Ealing, LONDON, W13 9DJ.
LYLE, Miss. Christine, BA ACA 1993; 8 Broadstone Close, Barnwood, GLOUCESTER, GL4 3TX.
LYLE, Mr. Colin Andrew, FCA 1972; 144 Avenue Vauban, 34110 FRONTIGNAN, FRANCE. (Life Member)
LYLE, Mrs. Emily, BA ACA 2005; Old Barn Cottage, Woodcote Park, EPSOM, KT18 7EN.
LYLE, Miss. Kim, BSc ACA 1988; Sutton Winson Ltd, St. James House, Grosvenor Road, TWICKENHAM, MIDDLESEX, TW1 4AJ.
LYLE, Mr. Nicholas Roger, FCA 1965; Manor Farm, The Street, Bessingham, NORWICH, NR11 7JR. (Life Member)
LYLE, Mr. Timothy Harold Garnett, MA FCA 1978; Salisbury House, 29 Finsbury Circus, LONDON, EC2M 5QQ.
LYLE, Mr. Timothy John Abram, ACA 1985; 66 Castelnau, Barnes, LONDON, SW13 9EX.
LYMAN, Mr. Michael Leslie, FCA 1962; The Cottage, 5 Lower Park, BEWDLEY, WORCESTERSHIRE, DY12 2DP. (Life Member)
•LYMN, Mr. Anthony John, ACA CF 1988; (Tax Fac), Ashgates, 5 Prospect Place, Millennium Way, Pride Park, DERBY, DE24 8HG. See also Ashgates Corporate Services Limited
LYMN, Miss. Carolyn Jane, LLB ACA 1988; (Tax Fac), Flat 79, Victoria Court, Royal Earlswood Park, REDHILL, RH1 6TF.
LYN, Mr. Frank Yee-Chon, BA ACA 1988; PricewaterhouseCoopers, Prince's Building, 22/F, 10 Chater Road, CENTRAL, HONG KONG ISLAND HONG KONG SAR.
LYNAGH, Ms. Catherine Elizabeth, BSc ACA 1993; Regenda Ltd., Regenda House Northgate Close, Horwich, BOLTON, BL6 6PQ.
LYNAM, Mr. David, BA ACA 1999; 213 Newland Gardens, HERTFORD, SG13 7WZ.
•LYNAM, Mrs. Gemma, ACA 2009; (Tax Fac), Lynam Tax Limited, Embankment House, 35 Edwalton Lodge Close, Edwalton, NOTTINGHAM, NG12 4DT.
LYNAM, Mr. Robert Edward, FCA 1947; Whitewalls, 174 Worlds End Lane, ORPINGTON, BR6 6AS. (Life Member)
LYNAM, Mr. Robert Iain, FCA 1975; The Aaronite Partnership LLP, 107-111 Fleet Street, LONDON, EC4A 2AB.
LYNAM, Mrs. Sylvia Joy, FCA 1972; 10 Rowan Close, WOKINGHAM, BERKSHIRE, RG41 4BH.
LYNAS, Mr. Brian Kenneth, BSc FCA 1973; Erinvale, 4 Old Chestnut Avenue, Claremont Park, ESHER, SURREY, KT10 9LS. (Life Member)
LYNAS, Mr. Jeremy David, BSc ACA 2009; 13 Burnt Hill Way, Wrecclesham, FARNHAM, GU10 4RN.
•LYNAS, Mr. Stephen James, BA ACA 1999; 13 Trinder Road, BARNET, HERTFORDSHIRE, EN5 3EE.
LYNAUGH, Mrs. Dorothy Suzanne, FCA 1964; 50 Eastfield Road, Messingham, SCUNTHORPE, SOUTH HUMBERSIDE, DN17 3PG.
LYNCH, Mr. Adam Jordan, ACA 2009; Butterfield Fulcrum, Rosebank Centre, 11 Bermudiana Road, PEMBROKE HM08, BERMUDA.
LYNCH, Mrs. Amanda, BSc ACA 1993; 11 Fretter Close Broughton Astley, LEICESTER, LEICESTERSHIRE, LE9 6TT.
LYNCH, Mrs. Amy, BA ACA 1999; 86 Topstreet Way, HARPENDEN, HERTFORDSHIRE, AL5 5TS.
LYNCH, Mr. Andrew Patrick, FCA 1980; SSP Group Ltd, 1 The Heights, Brooklands, WEYBRIDGE, SURREY, KT13 0NY.
LYNCH, Mrs. Angela, BA(Hons) ACA 2002; 37 Cold Blow Lane, LONDON, SE14 5RB.
•LYNCH, Mr. Barry Michael, LLB FCA 1975; (Tax Fac), Rothman Pantall LLP, Avebury House, 6 St. Peter Street, WINCHESTER, HAMPSHIRE, SO23 8BN.
LYNCH, Mr. Bryan Anthony, BA(Econ) ACA 1997; 11a Mandalay Road, LONDON, SW4 9ED.
LYNCH, Mr. Calum Alan, BA ACA 2002; Pike House Farm Cottage Blackburn Road, Turton, BOLTON, BL7 0QH.
LYNCH, Miss. Catherine Anne, BSc(Hons) ACA 2004; 98 Leigh Hunt Drive, Southgate, LONDON, N14 6DF.
•LYNCH, Ms. Catherine Mary, MA FCA 1982; 42 Wilton Crescent, Wimbledon, LONDON, SW19 3QS.
LYNCH, Mrs. Christine Marie, BSc(Hons) ACA 2002; 135 Tadcaster Road, Dringhouses, YORK, YO24 1QJ.
LYNCH, Mrs. Clare Elizabeth, ACA 1986; (Tax Fac), Alanmore Church Lane Doddinghurst, BRENTWOOD, ESSEX, CM15 0NJ.
LYNCH, Miss. Dara Francis, BSS ACA 1993; 14 Littleheath, Charlton, LONDON, SE7 8HU.

•**LYNCH, Mr. David John, FCA** *1974;* (Tax Fac), Lynch & Co, 194 Lonsdale Avenue, Newham, LONDON, E6 3PP.

LYNCH, Mr. Dominic Gerard, FCA *2010; (FCA Ireland 1986);* 21 Mount Nebo, TAUNTON, SOMERSET, TA1 4HG.

LYNCH, Mr. Edward John, BSc(Hons) ACA *2011;* 3 Gullet Lane, Kirby Muxloe, LEICESTER, LE9 2BL.

LYNCH, Mrs. Elizabeth Anne, BSc ACA *1993;* 15 St. Josephs Close, OLNEY, BUCKINGHAMSHIRE, MK46 5HD.

LYNCH, Mr. Gerard Sean, BA FCA *1988;* 48 Overstone Road, HARPENDEN, AL5 5PJ.

LYNCH, Mr. James Lawrence Francis, ACA *2011;* Flat 17, Cade Tyler House, Blackheath Hill, LONDON, SE10 8TG.

LYNCH, Mr. John Anthony, BCom ACA *1992;* (Tax Fac), Aram Vicarage Lane, Send, WOKING, GU23 7JN.

•**LYNCH, Mr. John David, BSc FCA** *1971;* (Tax Fac), with Towers & Gornall, Suites 5 & 6, The Printworks, Hey Road, Barrow, CLITHEROE LANCASHIRE BB7 9WB.

LYNCH, Mrs. Lorna Susan, BSc(Econ) ACA *1999;* 78 Crest View Drive, Petts Wood, ORPINGTON, KENT, BR5 1BY.

LYNCH, Mr. Mark John, ACA *2010;* 9 Oaklands Court, Aldcliffe, LANCASTER, LA1 5AT.

LYNCH, Mr. Neil, BA ACA *1999;* 70 Elm Walk, LONDON, SW20 9EE.

LYNCH, Mr. Nicholas, BSc(Hons) ACA *2011;* 25 Keep Hill Road, HIGH WYCOMBE, BUCKINGHAMSHIRE, HP11 1DW.

LYNCH, Mrs. Patricia Chantal, BSc ACA *1990;* Janus House, Earning Street, Godmanchester, HUNTINGDON, PE29 2JD.

LYNCH, Mr. Paul Anthony, BA(Hons) ACA *2010;* 35 Brooklyn Drive, Emmer Green, READING, RG4 8SR.

LYNCH, Mr. Paul Michael, BSc ACA *2005;* Deloitte & Touche Llp, 66 Shoe Lane, LONDON, EC4A 3BQ.

•**LYNCH, Mr. Peter Daniel, BA FCA** *1976;* Peter Lynch & Co, Regus House, Malthouse Avenue, Cardiff Gate Business Park, CARDIFF, CF23 8RU.

•**LYNCH, Mr. Roger John Christopher, BA FCA** *1968;* (Tax Fac), Perera Lynch, Hornhatch Hatch Farm, Rices Corner, New Road, Shalford, GUILDFORD SURREY GU4 8HS.

LYNCH, Mr. Stephen Patrick, BSc ACA *2011;* Flat 2, 21B Alderbrook Road, Balham, LONDON, SW12 8AF.

LYNCH, Mrs. Susan Paula, FCA *1991;* PO Box 18, Hanmer Springs, CANTERBURY, NEW ZEALAND.

LYNCH, Mr. Thomas Michael, MA ACA *1989;* Beechwood, 5 Marlborough Avenue, BROMSGROVE, B60 2PG.

LYNCH, Mrs. Tracy Anne, ACA CA(NZ) *2010;* 5 Kings Road, LONDON, SW14 8PF.

LYNCH, Mr. Vincent Paul, BSc ACA *1991;* Janus House, Earning Street, Godmanchester, HUNTINGDON, PE29 2JD.

•**LYNCH-BELL, Mr. Michael David, BA FCA** *1977;* Ernst & Young LLP, 1 More London Place, LONDON, SE1 2AF. See also Ernst & Young Europe LLP

LYND, Mrs. Anoushka, LLB ACA *2007;* (Tax Fac), with Sully & Co, Sully House, 7 Clovelly Road Industrial Estate, BIDEFORD, DEVON, EX39 3HN.

LYNDON, Mr. Andrew, BCom ACA FSI *1995;* 134a Norton Lane, Tidbury Green, SOLIHULL, B90 1QT.

LYNDON, Mrs. Brenda Anne, FCA *1975;* 8 Albemarle Avenue, TORONTO M4K 1H7, ON, CANADA.

LYNDON, Mr. Ross Paul William, FCA *1975;* 8 Albermarle Avenue, TORONTO M4K 1H7, ON, CANADA.

LYNDON, Mr. Simon Dennis, BA ACA *1988;* 4 Guinea Close, BRAINTREE, CM7 9DP.

•**LYNDS, Mr. Montague Randall, FCA** *1974;* Clifford Towers (Accountants) Limited, 9 High Street, Stony Stratford, MILTON KEYNES, MK11 1AA.

LYNE, Ms. Carla, BSc ACA MCIPD *1992;* 2 Heol Aer, Rhiwbina, CARDIFF, CF14 6NJ.

LYNE, Mr. Eliot, BA ACA *1998;* 2 Clarence Villas, Manningtree Road, East Bergholt, COLCHESTER, CO7 6UA.

LYNE, Mr. Jeffrey Alan, MA ACA *1996;* Deloitte & Touche Hill House, 1 Little New Street, LONDON, EC4A 3TR.

LYNE, Mr. Jonathan Mark, BA ACA *1999;* 20 Brackley Drive, SHREWSBURY, SY3 8BX.

LYNE, Mr. Joseph, LLB ACA *2011;* 5 Glenlyn Avenue, ST. ALBANS, HERTFORDSHIRE, AL1 5PF.

LYNE, Mr. Martin Francis, FCA *1970;* Pond Tail Farmhouse, Slaugham Lane, Warninglid, HAYWARDS HEATH, WEST SUSSEX, RH17 5TJ.

LYNE, Mr. Martin John, BA ACA *1990;* 1 Cranhill Road, BATH, BA1 2YF.

LYNE, Dr. Stephen Richard, ACA *1980;* 460 Church Road, Frampton Cotterell, BRISTOL, BS36 2AH.

•**LYNES, Mr. Benjamin James, BSc ACA** *2002;* Cunninghams, 61 Alexandra Road, LOWESTOFT, SUFFOLK, NR32 1PL.

LYNESS, Mr. Gary David, BA ACA *1994;* 7 Saxon Way, ASHBY-DE-LA-ZOUCH, LE65 2JR.

LYNHAM, Mr. David Paul, BA ACA *2004;* with PKF (UK) LLP, 4th Floor, 3 Hardman Street, MANCHESTER, M3 3HF.

•**LYNHAM, Mr. Philip John, FCA** *1982;* Lynham & Co, 9 Hampton Lane, Blackfield, SOUTHAMPTON, SO45 1ZA.

LYNN, Mr. Andrew Peter, BA ACA *1996;* Clear Channel UK Ltd Phillips Court, 32 Goldsworth Road, WOKING, GU21 6JT.

LYNN, Miss. Catherine Ann, BCom ACA CTA *2005;* (Tax Fac), with Bishop Fleming, 16 Queen Square, BRISTOL, BS1 4NT.

LYNN, Mr. Geoffrey John, FCA *1966;* Tiggers Pond, Church Road, Newtown, FAREHAM, PO17 6LE. (Life Member)

LYNN, Mr. George, BSc FCA *1979;* Angel Trains Ltd Portland House, Bressenden Place, LONDON, SW1E 5BH.

LYNN, Miss. Joanna, ACA *2011;* Apartment 25 Dukes Wharf, Wharf Road, NOTTINGHAM, NG7 1GD.

•**LYNN, Mr. Jonathan David, MA FCA** *1980;* AIMS - Jonathan Lynn, Coach House, Warren House, Eridge Green, TUNBRIDGE WELLS, KENT TN3 9JR.

LYNN, Mr. Jonathan Patrick, FCA *1971;* Les Clos d'Arthenay, 12 Rue de la Juridiction, 14400 BAYEUX, FRANCE.

LYNN, Mrs. Louise Emma Elizabeth, BA(Hons) ACA *2010;* 35 Stevens Lane, Breaston, DERBY, DE72 3BU.

LYNN, Mr. Michael John, FCA *1971;* Corner House, 1A Ranulf Road, LONDON, NW2 2BT.

LYNN, Mrs. Nicola Louise, BA ACA *2005;* with Deloitte LLP, Athene Place, 66 Shoe Lane, LONDON, EC4A 3BQ.

•**LYNN, Mr. Robert, FCA** *1974;* Robert Lynn FCA, 1 Pitt Court, Nymet Rowland, CREDITON, DEVON, EX17 6AN.

LYNN, Mr. Roger, FCA *1975;* 3 Mapperton Close, Westcroft, MILTON KEYNES, BUCKINGHAMSHIRE, MK4 4FF.

•**LYNN, Mr. Stephen Robert, BCom FCA** *1974;* S.R. Lynn & Co, 11 Warren Yard, Wolverton Mill, MILTON KEYNES, MK12 5NW.

LYNOTT, Mr. Mark, BA ACA *2006;* B D O Stoy Hayward, 3 Hardman Street, MANCHESTER, M3 3AT.

LYNSKEY, Mrs. Helen, BA ACA *1983;* 7 Reed Mace Drive, BROMSGROVE, WORCESTERSHIRE, B61 0UJ.

LYNSKEY, Mr. Paul Michael, BA FCA *1980;* 7 Reed Mace Drive, BROMSGROVE, WORCESTERSHIRE, B61 0UJ.

LYNSKEY, Mr. Sean Michael, BA ACA *1986;* Flat 1, 15 St. Laurence Way, SLOUGH, SL1 2BN.

LYNTON, Mr. John Michael, FCA *1966;* 103 Nottingham Terrace, LONDON, NW1 4QE.

•**LYNTON, Mr. Paul Ross, BSc ACA** *1983;* Paul Lynton ACA, 36 Mutrix Road, LONDON, NW6 4QG.

•**LYON, Mr. Alastair Ross, BSc FCA DChA** *1991;* Crowe Clark Whitehill LLP, Aquis House, 49-51 Blagrave Street, READING, RG1 1PL. See also Horwath Clark Whitehill LLP and Crowe Clark Whitehill

•**LYON, Mr. Andrew John, BSc FCA** *1990;* PricewaterhouseCoopers LLP, Donington Court, Pegasus Business Park, Castle Donington, DERBY, DE74 2UZ. See also PricewaterhouseCoopers

LYON, Mr. Andrew Michael, BA ACA *1989;* 41 Rievaulx Avenue, KNARESBOROUGH, HG5 8LD.

•**LYON, Mrs. Anita Kathleen, ACA FCCA** *2010;* Jamesons Ltd, Jamesons House, Compton Way, WITNEY, OXFORDSHIRE, OX28 3AB.

LYON, Mrs. Caroline Pamela, BA ACA *1993;* 23 Ballagyr Park, Ramsey Road, Peel, ISLE OF MAN, IM5 1UN.

LYON, Mr. Christopher James Westbrook, BA ACA *1994;* Av Providencia 1760 Piso 8, Providencia, SANTIAGO, CHILE.

LYON, Mr. Craig Finlay, MA ACA *1994;* Upperstack, Newmachar, ABERDEEN, AB21 0UT.

•**LYON, Mr. David John, BA FCA** *1987;* Calder & Co, 1 Regent Street, LONDON, SW1Y 4NW.

LYON, Mr. David Oliver, BA FCA *1986;* 41 Park Avenue North, HARPENDEN, AL5 2EE.

LYON, Mr. Donald Malcolm, FCA *1982;* (Tax Fac), 41 Marlborough Close, Broadhey, Ramsbottom, BURY, BL0 9YU.

LYON, Mr. Duncan James, BSc ACA *1988;* 51 Bowman Street, DRUMMOYNE, NSW 2047, AUSTRALIA.

LYON, Mr. Francis George, FCA *1951;* 47 Priory Street, KIDWELLY, DYFED, SA17 4TY. (Life Member)

LYON, Mr. Henry, FCA *1957;* 9 Wokingham Grove, LIVERPOOL, L36 5YX. (Life Member)

•**LYON, Mr. Howard Frank, FCA** *1975;* Howard Lyon FCA, 18 Laneside Drive, Bramhall, STOCKPORT, CHESHIRE, SK7 3AR.

LYON, Mrs. Jacqueline Anne, MSc ACA *2002;* 23 Dennis Park Crescent, LONDON, SW20 8QH.

LYON, Mr. John Frederick, FCA *1954;* Gorley Firs, North Gorley, FORDINGBRIDGE, SP6 2PS. (Life Member)

LYON, Miss. Karen Marie, ACA *2008;* 1 Seddon Road, LIVERPOOL, L19 2LJ.

LYON, Mrs. Kathleen Michelle, ACA *1996;* Albury House, Lodge Road, Hurst, READING, RG10 0SG.

LYON, Mr. Matthew Morrell, BA ACA *2004;* 8 Ashville Terrace, Cross Hills, KEIGHLEY, BD20 7LQ.

•**LYON, Mr. Michael Gordon, FCA** *1959;* Heybridge House, Mudhouse Lane, Burton, NESTON, CH64 5TN.

•**LYON, Mrs. Nicolena Ella, FCA** *1985;* (Tax Fac), Chartwells, Knightlands, North Benfleet, WICKFORD, SS12 9JR.

LYON, Mr. Nigel, BSc FCA *1985;* Lindum House, 48 Anchorage Road, SUTTON COLDFIELD, WEST MIDLANDS, B74 2PL.

LYON, Mr. Paul John, BA ACA *2003;* 8 Mersey Avenue, UPMINSTER, ESSEX, RM14 1RA.

LYON, Miss. Rachael, BSc ACA *1999;* 2 Orient Close, ST. ALBANS, HERTFORDSHIRE, AL1 1AJ.

LYON, Mr. Robert John Kevin, ACA *1987;* The Prae, Warren Lane, WOKING, SURREY, GU22 8XQ.

LYON, Mrs. Sarah Ann, BA ACA *1998;* with Ernst & Young LLP, 1 More London Place, LONDON, SE1 2AF.

LYON, Mrs. Stephanie Mary, BA FCA *1977;* Bât B, 2 rue Winston Churchill, 91300 MASSY, FRANCE.

LYON, Mr. Stephen John, MSc FCA CF FSI *1989;* (Tax Fac), The Lodge, York Road, KNARESBOROUGH, HG5 0SW.

LYON, Miss. Victoria Anne, ACA *2009;* 1 Chivalry Road, LONDON, SW11 1HT.

LYON-MARIS, Mr. Peter David, FCA *1958;* The Hydeaway, Hyde Street, Upper Beeding, STEYNING, BN44 3TT. (Life Member)

LYON-MERCADO, Mr. Peter, BEng ACA *2000;* Crescent Capital Partners, Level 7, 75 Elizabeth Street, SYDNEY, NSW 2000, AUSTRALIA.

LYONETTE, Mr. Michael Francis, FCA *1973;* Van Lennepweg 38, 2597 LK THE HAGUE, NETHERLANDS.

LYONS, Mr. Alastair David, BA FCA ATII MCT *1978;* Hencliffe Cottage Farm, Winksley, RIPON, NORTH YORKSHIRE, HG4 3PQ.

LYONS, Mr. Alistair Inglis, LLB ACA *1991;* 13 Rue De La Douzaine, Fort George St. Peter Port, GUERNSEY, GY1 2TA.

LYONS, Mrs. Amanda Carol, BSc ACA *1999;* 82 Wayside Green, Woodcote, READING, RG8 0QJ.

LYONS, Mrs. Amanda Helen, BSc FCA *1999;* 67 Cromwell Road, LONDON, SW19 8LF.

LYONS, Mr. Andrew James, BA ACA *2004;* 32 Axbridge Avenue, Sutton Leach, ST. HELENS, MERSEYSIDE, WA9 4NT.

LYONS, Mr. Barry Desmond, BA ACA *1988;* Unison, 1 Mabledon Place, LONDON, WC1H 9AJ.

LYONS, Mr. Barry Hugh, FCA *1959;* Apartment 17, 8C Nitza Boulevard, 42262 NETANYA, ISRAEL. (Life Member)

LYONS, Miss. Caroline, ACA *2011;* Flat A, 101 Talbot Road, LONDON, N6 4QX.

LYONS, Mrs. Cheryl Anne, BSc ACA ATII *1992;* (Tax Fac), with PricewaterhouseCoopers LLP, Abacus Court, 6 Minshull Street, MANCHESTER, M1 3ED.

•**LYONS, Mr. Christopher John, FCA** *1976;* (Tax Fac), Lyons & Co, 18 Barn Owl Way, Stoke Gifford, BRISTOL, BS34 8RZ.

•**LYONS, Mr. David Albert, BSc FCA** *1984;* (Tax Fac), Leonard Jones & Co, 1 Printing House Yard, LONDON, E2 7PR.

LYONS, Mr. Duncan James Anton, BA ACA *1983;* 5th Floor, Say Communications The Courtyard, 7 Francis Grove, LONDON, SW19 4DW.

LYONS, Mrs. Ellen, BSc(Hons) ACA *2000;* 18 Dukes Walk, Hale, ALTRINCHAM, CHESHIRE, WA15 8WB.

LYONS, Mr. Garrath, BSc ACA *2006;* 11 Brownley Road, Shirley, SOLIHULL, WEST MIDLANDS, B90 4QP.

LYONS, Mr. Gregory Howard, BSc ACA *1998;* 8 Drysdale Close, NORTHWOOD, MIDDLESEX, HA6 2YT.

LYONS, Mrs. Helen Margaret, BSc ACA *2003;* with PricewaterhouseCoopers LLP, 18 Northland Row, DUNGANNON, COUNTY TYRONE, BT71 6AP.

LYONS, Miss. Jacqueline Michelle, MMath ACA *2009;* 72 Arundel Crescent, SOLIHULL, B92 8RG.

LYONS, Miss. Jane Marie, ACA *2009;* Pricewaterhousecoopers, 8 Princes Parade, LIVERPOOL, L3 1QJ.

LYONS, Mr. Jeffrey Alfred, FCA *1970;* 26 The Priory, St Catherine's Terrace, HOVE, BN3 2RQ.

•**LYONS, Mr. John Gerard, BA ACA** *1999;* John Lyons & Co, Unit 44B, Capital Court, Ffordd William Morgan, St. Asaph Business Park, ST. ASAPH CLWYD LL17 0JG.

•**LYONS, Mr. John Robert, BSc ACA** *1985;* (Tax Fac), Lyons & Co Limited, 23 Yarm Road, STOCKTON-ON-TEES, CLEVELAND, TS18 3NJ.

•**LYONS, Mr. Julian Neil, ACA** *1990;* J.N. Lyons, 13 Woodbury Park Road, Ealing, LONDON, W13 8DD.

•**LYONS, Mr. Keith Francis, FCA** *1969;* The Old Woolcombers Mill, 12/14 Union street South, HALIFAX, HX1 2LE.

LYONS, Mr. Kenneth Joseph, ACA *1986;* 1 Oak Close, Oakley, BASINGSTOKE, RG23 7DD.

LYONS, Mr. Mark Simon, BA ACA *2005;* 16 Albert Road, Hale, ALTRINCHAM, CHESHIRE, WA15 9AN.

LYONS, Mr. Michael Anthony, JP BA ACA *1979;* 20 Darley Avenue, West Didsbury, MANCHESTER, M20 2YD.

LYONS, Mr. Michael Brendan, BA ACA *1981;* Mira Atlantico, Rua Quinta do Alto, Casas Novas, 2705-177 COLARES, PORTUGAL.

LYONS, Mr. Michael Robert, BSc ACA CTA *1990;* 4 Holmepark Gardens, Worsley, MANCHESTER, M28 1UQ.

LYONS, Miss. Nicola Anne, BSc(Hons) ACA *2002;* with BDO LLP, 55 Baker Street, LONDON, W1U 7EU.

LYONS, Mr. Paul Andrew, BA ACA *1983;* Ambition Group, 5/55 Clarence St, SYDNEY, NSW 2000, AUSTRALIA.

LYONS, Mr. Richard Anthony, FCA *1975;* (Tax Fac), 49 Plover Way, LONDON, SE16 7TS.

•**LYONS, Mr. Robert Eric, MA FCA** *1965;* Robert Lyons & Co, Flat 1, 42 Marryat Road, Wimbledon, LONDON, SW19 5BD.

LYONS, Mr. Robert Joseph, FCA *1970;* Gryon House, 5 avenue St Laurent, MC98000 MONACO, MONACO.

LYONS, Mr. Russell James John, BCom FCA *1985;* 12 Shouldham Street, LONDON, W1H 5FH.

LYONS, Mr. Russell John Stewart, FCA MBA *1973;* Innovation Software Ltd Innovation House, 9 New Road, ROCHESTER, ME1 1BG.

LYONS, Mrs. Simone Leah, BSc ACA *2002;* 6 Marsh Lane, LONDON, NW7 4QP.

LYONS, Mrs. Susan Joy, BA ACA *1986;* 43 Derwent Road, HARPENDEN, AL5 3NY.

LYONS, Mrs. Teresa Maureen, BSc ACA *1990;* 22 Woodburn Road, MANCHESTER, M22 4BZ.

LYONS, Mr. Timothy James, BA(Hons) ACA *2002;* 49 Northbrook Street, LEEDS, LS7 4QH.

•**LYONS, Mr. Timothy Rayner, BA ACA** *1985;* (Tax Fac), 1 Lingwood Walk, SOUTHAMPTON, SO16 7GL.

•**LYSAGHT, Mr. Mark Wickham Royse, BA FCA** *1977;* M W R Lysaght, Hazlewood House, MALLOW, COUNTY CORK, IRELAND.

LYSENKO, Mr. Karol, ACA *2010;* Flat 7, 25 Barge Walk, LONDON, SE10 0NB.

LYSSIOTIS, Mr. George, BA FCA *1996;* 10 Othonos Street, 2414 NICOSIA, CYPRUS.

LYSTER, Mr. Anthony Lyttelton, BA FCA *1955;* 13 Lyndhurst Court, Grange Road, SUTTON, SM2 6SR. (Life Member)

LYTE, Miss. Marie Denise, BA ACA *1999;* 70 Jalan Mat Jambol, SPRINGWOOD 119543, SINGAPORE.

LYTHE, Mrs. Rebecca, BA ACA *1997;* 234 High Street, Boston Spa, WETHERBY, WEST YORKSHIRE, LS23 6AD.

LYTHGOE, Mr. John Stephen, BA ACA *1984;* (Tax Fac), McMullen & Sons Ltd, The Hertford Brewery, HERTFORD, SG14 1RD.

LYTHGOE, Mrs. Kathleen Antoinette, BA ACA *1990;* Trafford College Talbot Road, Stretford, MANCHESTER, M32 0XH.

LYTHGOE, Mr. Matthew Christopher Robert, BSc ACA *1997;* Krauthofera 18d/12, 60-203, POZNAN, POLAND.

LYTHGOE, Mr. Stephen Lewis, BA ACA *1989;* with Grant Thornton UK LLP, 30 Finsbury Square, LONDON, EC2P 2YU.

LYTHGOE, Mr. Warren, FCA *1972;* 129 Wellfield Street, WARRINGTON, WA5 1NR.

LYTRAS, Mr. Andreas, BA ACA *2008;* 45 Dasoupoleos Str., Flat 303, Strovolos, 2015 NICOSIA, CYPRUS.

LYTRAS, Mr. Antonis, BA ACA *2011;* 2 Griva Digeni Street, Athienou, 7600 LARNACA, CYPRUS.

LYTTLE, Mr. Declan John, MA FCA MBA *2000;* New Syde, The Green, Urchfont, DEVIZES, WILTSHIRE, SN10 4RB.
•**LYTTLE, Mr. Victor Michael Clements, FCA** *1965;* 203 Lordswood Road, Harborne, BIRMINGHAM, B17 8QP.
•**LYTTON-BERNARD, Miss. Rosina Maria Lucy, BA ACA** *1992;* 22 Sea View Road, HAYLING ISLAND, HAMPSHIRE, PO11 9PE.
LYWOOD, Mr. Rupert Charles Gifford, ACA *1984;* Heath House The Heath, Clungunford, CRAVEN ARMS, SHROPSHIRE, SY7 0QB.
M'CARDELL, Mr. Robert Graham, FCA *1958;* 12 Gorse Bank Road, Hale Barns, ALTRINCHAM, WA15 0AL. (Life Member)
M'CAW, Mr. Philip Hepton, MA ACA *1991;* Rivendell, 87 Crabtree Lane, HARPENDEN, AL5 5PX.
MA, Mr. Andrew Chiu Cheung, BSc FCA *1970;* No. 6 Price Road, JARDINE'S LOOKOUT, HONG KONG ISLAND, HONG KONG SAR.
MA, Mr. Chi Chiu, BCom FCA *1975;* Flat A, 8th Floor, Lung Man Building, 8 Homantin Street, HO MAN TIN, KOWLOON HONG KONG SAR.
MA, Mr. Chi Shing, ACA *2008;* Flat F 55/F, Tower 9, Island Resort, 28 Siu Sai Wan Road, CHAI WAN, HONG KONG ISLAND HONG KONG SAR.
MA, Mr. Ching Lam, BA FCA *1977;* Flat 15B Century Tower 1, 1 Tregunter Path, MID LEVELS, Hong Kong Island, HONG KONG SAR.
MA, Ms. Chor Kiu Josephine, ACA *2005;* Flat D 18/F Block 11, Sea Crest Villa Phase 4, SHAM TSENG, NEW TERRITORIES, HONG KONG SAR.
MA, Mr. Chu Kin, ACA *1986;* 46G Tower 5 Caribean Coast, 2 Kin Tung Road, Tung Chung, LANTAU ISLAND, NEW TERRITORIES, HONG KONG SAR.
MA, Miss. Chuan Yun, ACA *2010;* Rm 2102 No.8, Building of Jingtongyuan Xiaoqu, Guanzhuang of Chaoyang District, BEIJING 100024, CHINA.
MA, Ms. Chui Fong, ACA *2005;* Flat B 7/F Block 31, Grand Dynasty View, 9 Ma Wo Road, TAI PO, NEW TERRITORIES, HONG KONG SAR.
MA, Mr. Chun Nam, ACA *2009;* Flat B, 13/ FMing Fai Building, 56 Yen Chow Street, SHAM SHUI PO, KOWLOON, HONG KONG SAR.
•**MA, Mr. Henry Wilson Wing Hin, MSc ACA** *2004;* with KPMG, 8/F Prince's Building, 10 Chater Road, CENTRAL, HONG KONG ISLAND, HONG KONG SAR.
MA, Ms. Jintao, BA ACA *2005;* 22 Braemar Gardens, LONDON, NW9 5LA.
MA, Mr. Kah Woh, FCA *1972;* 18 Sunset Place, SINGAPORE 597366, SINGAPORE.
MA, Mr. Kwai Yuen Terence, ACA *2007;* Wellon Consultants Ltd, Room 1902, Yue Shing Commercial Bldg15, Queen Victoria Street, CENTRAL, HONG KONG ISLAND HONG KONG SAR.
MA, Ms. Lai Shuen Diana, ACA *2008;* Diana L Ma & Co, Room 1708 17/F Hart Avenue Plaza, 5-9 Hart Avenue, TSIM SHA TSUI, KOWLOON, HONG KONG SAR.
MA, Miss. Lilian Pui Chi, ACA *2009;* 44 South Hill Park, LONDON, NW3 2ST.
MA, Miss. Ling, ACA *2009;* Flat 2503 Tower 2, 519 Macau Road, SHANGHAI 200060, CHINA.
MA, Miss. Nan, ACA *2009;* Flat A-b, 32 Lavender Sweep, LONDON, SW11 1HA.
MA, Miss. Ning, ACA *2009;* 18 Woodvale Way, Golders Green, LONDON, NW11 8SF.
MA, Mr. Patrick Yee Ming, BSc ACA *1984;* Flat B 10/F Block 1, Scenic Garden, 9 Kotewall Road, MID LEVELS, HONG KONG ISLAND, HONG KONG SAR.
MA, Miss. Peining, BSc ACA *2003;* 103 Stormont Road, LONDON, SW11 5EJ.
MA, Ms. Pui Shan, ACA *2007;* Flat 4 8/F, Yu Chiu Court, SHA TIN, NEW TERRITORIES, HONG KONG SAR.
MA, Mr. Robert Kam-Fook, FCA *1980;* 8A Swiss Towers, 113 Tai Hang Road, TAI HANG, HONG KONG ISLAND, HONG KONG SAR.
MA, Mr. Sai Ho Simon, ACA *2008;* Flat 6, 18/ F, Block B, Hamden Court, 149 Hong Ning Road, KWUN TONG KOWLOON HONG KONG SAR.
MA, Ms. Sau Wai, ACA *2007;* Flat 804, Yin King House, King Shing Court, FANLING, NEW TERRITORIES, HONG KONG SAR.
MA, Ms. Sau Wing, ACA *2008;* Flat B 49/F, Block 2, Seaview Crescent, 8 Tung CHung Waterfront Road, TUNG CHUNG, HONG KONG SAR.
MA, Miss. Vivien Man Wai, MSci ACA DChA *2004;* with Sayer Vincent, 8 Angel Gate, City Road, LONDON, EC1V 2SJ.
MA, Mr. Warren Kwok Hung, ACA *2007;* Flat 1 8/F Block C, Wisdom Court, 5 Hatton Road, MID LEVELS, HONG KONG SAR.
MA, Mr. Wing-Hong Vincent, BSc ACA *1988;* Flat 27A Casa Bella, 117 Caine Road, MID LEVELS, HONG KONG ISLAND, HONG KONG SAR.
MA, Mr. Wu Kin, BA FCA *1984;* Level 10 Tower B 821 Pacific Highway, CHATSWOOD, NSW 2067, AUSTRALIA.
MA, Mr. Yat Ming, ACA *2008;* Flat 1311, 13/F. Block K, Telford Gardens, 33 Wai Yip Street, KOWLOON BAY, KOWLOON HONG KONG SAR.
MA, Miss. Yin Fan, ACA *2007;* Flat C, 4/F Fu Wai Court, Fortress Garden, 32 Fortress Hill Road, NORTH POINT, HONG KONG ISLAND HONG KONG SAR.
MA, Miss. Yuan, ACA *2009;* 1818 China World Office 2, 1 Jianwai Dajie, BEIJING 100004, CHINA.
MA CHO SHING, Mr. Olivier, BA(Hons) ACA *2003;* 64b Haydon Park Road, LONDON, SW19 8JY.
MA-POON, Miss. Marie Irene Yok Wan, BSc ACA *2007;* 10 Lorraine Road, Timperley, ALTRINCHAM, CHESHIRE, WA15 7NA.
MAAL, Miss. Talbinder, BSc ACA *2001;* 55 Aylesbury Crescent, SLOUGH, SL1 3ER.
MAALOUF, Mr. Karim, ACA *2011;* Apt 15 D, 301 W 53rd Street, NEW YORK, NY 10019, UNITED STATES.
•**MAAS, Mr. Robert William, FCA** *1965;* (Tax Fac), Blackstone Franks LLP, Barbican House, 26-34 Old Street, LONDON, EC1V 9QR.
•**MAASS, Mrs. Jane Clare, BSc ACA** *1990;* Maass & Co, 20 Queens Road, Hoylake, WIRRAL, MERSEYSIDE, CH47 2AH.
MAASTUE, Mr. Lookman Mohmed, MA ACA *2000;* 26 Stanleyfield Road, PRESTON, PR1 1QL.
MABBETT, Miss. Catherine Elizabeth Jane, BSc ACA *1990;* 11 Ironbridge Crescent, Park Gate, SOUTHAMPTON, SO31 7FX.
MABE, Mr. Philip, MA ACA *1984;* Ramsdean House, Ramsdean, PETERSFIELD, HAMPSHIRE, GU32 1RS.
•**MABERLY, Mr. Paul Alan, FCA** *1988;* Mercer & Hole, Silbury Court, 420 Silbury Boulevard, MILTON KEYNES, BUCKINGHAMSHIRE, MK9 2AF.
•**MABEY, Mr. John Colin, BSc ACA** *1990;* (Tax Fac), Coveney Nicholls, The Old Wheel House, 31/37 Church Street, REIGATE, RH2 0AD. See also Coveney Nicholls Limited
•**MABEY, Mr. Simon John, MA FCA** *1976;* Smith & Williamson Ltd, 25 Moorgate, LONDON, EC2R 6AY.
MABLIN, Mr. Ian David, FCA *1972;* Torwoodlee, Royston Grove, Hatch End, PINNER, HA5 4HF.
MABY, Mr. Alex, BSc ACA *2000;* 134 Tranmere Road, LONDON, SW18 3QU.
MAC OSCAR, Mr. Conor Joseph, BSc ACA *1997;* The Grove, 6 Preston Park, NORTH SHIELDS, TYNE AND WEAR, NE29 9JL.
MACADIE, Mr. Christopher Eric, FCA *1971;* 26 rue de Paris, 27620 GASNY, FRANCE.
MACADIE, Mr. William Edward, MEng ACA *2010;* Rose Cottage, Buckland Hill, Cousley Wood, WADHURST, EAST SUSSEX, TN5 6QT.
MACALISTER-SMITH, Mr. Sam Henry, BSc ACA *2009;* 24 Porthamal Road, CARDIFF, CF14 6AR.
MACALLAN, Mr. Alexander Thomas, BSc ACA *1980;* Macallan Brader Associates Ltd., 7 Camden Close, CHISLEHURST, BR7 5PH.
MACALLISTER, Mrs. Christine Victoria, BA ACA *1996;* 18 Woodville Road, LONDON, W5 2SF.
MACAN MARKAR, Mr. Mohamed Hamza, FCA *1971;* O.L.M. Macan Markar, 26 Galle Face Court 2, 2 COLOMBO, SRI LANKA.
MACAN-MARKAR, Mr. Yaseen Mohamed Malik, BA ACA *2005;* Flat 2, 42 Altenburg Gardens, LONDON, SW11 1JL.
MACANDA, Ms. Zoli, ACA CA(SA) *2011;* 15 Blackwell Close, LONDON, N21 1UL.
MACANDREW, Mr. Nicholas Rupert, FCA *1971;* The Old Chapel, Deptford Lane, Greywell, HOOK, RG29 1BS.
MACANDREWS, Mr. Timothy John Joseph, FCA *1980;* Snappy Snaps Franchise Ltd, 12 Glenthorne Road, Hammersmith, LONDON, W6 0LJ.
MACARA, Mr. Iain Cameron, BA ACA *2005;* 78 Sandmere Road, LONDON, SW4 7QH.
•**MACAREE, Mr. Duncan, FCA** *1974;* 153 Cornwall Road, RUISLIP, MIDDLESEX, HA4 6AG.
MACAREE, Mrs. Kathryn Eluned John, BSc FCA *1981;* (Tax Fac), THP Limited, 34-40 High Street Wanstead, LONDON, E11 2RJ.
•**MACARIO, Mr. Martin Wayne, FCA CTA FMAAT** *1997;* Macario Lewin Ltd, Bellarmine House, 14 Upper Church Street, CHEPSTOW, GWENT, NP16 5EX.
MACARIO, Mr. Michael Anthony, FCA *1962;* Deep Purple, Hangersley Hill, Hangersley, RINGWOOD, HAMPSHIRE, BH24 3JS.
MACARTHUR, Mr. Andrew William, BSc ACA *1990;* 91 Wanstead Park Avenue, LONDON, E12 5EE.
MACARTHUR, Mr. Dougall Neile, MA ACA *2002;* 49 Jollemanhof, 1019GW AMSTERDAM, NETHERLANDS.
•**MACARTHUR, Miss. Jane Linda, BSc ACA** *2003;* (Tax Fac), Amati UK Ltd, 25A Plover Way, LONDON, SE16 7TS. See also Amati Ltd
MACARTHUR, Miss. Sonia Catherine, BSc ACA *1989;* 9 Burydell Lane, Park Street, ST. ALBANS, AL2 2PQ.
MACARTNEY, Mr. Thomas Kevin, MA ACA *1991;* The Store Barn, Theobald Street, BOREHAMWOOD, WD6 4SH.
MACASKILL, Mrs. Caroline Elaine, MChem ACA CTA AMCT *2003;* (Tax Fac), 2 Russett Gardens, Ruscombe, READING, RG10 9HB.
•**MACASKILL, Mr. Duncan, BCom FCA** *1985;* KPMG LLP, 37 Albyn Place, ABERDEEN, AB10 1JB. See also KPMG Europe LLP
MACASKILL, Mr. Ryan Stuart, BSocSc FCA *2001;* 2 Russett Gardens, Ruscombe, READING, RG10 9HB.
MACAULAY, Mr. Damien James, ACA *1997;* c/o Technicolor EDS, 2255 N. Ontario Street, Suite 350, BURBANK, CA 91504, UNITED STATES.
•**MACAULAY, Mr. David John, BSc FCA** *1974;* (Tax Fac), D J Macaulay Accountancy Ltd, Morcroft, Ellington Road, Taplow, MAIDENHEAD, SL6 0BA.
MACAULAY, Mr. George Franklin, FCA *1962;* 16 York Court, Albany Park Road, KINGSTON UPON THAMES, KT2 5ST.
MACAULAY, Mr. James Edward, ACA *2009;* 26 Rissington Drive, WITNEY, OXFORDSHIRE, OX28 5FG.
MACAULAY, Mr. John Alexander, FCA *1968;* Ullenwood, Bereweeke Close, WINCHESTER, SO22 6AR.
MACAULAY, Mr. John Arnold, BSc ACA *1983;* 51 Dove Park, Chorleywood, RICKMANSWORTH, WD3 5NY.
MACAULAY, Mr. Kenneth William, BSc ACA *1988;* Green Mantle, Ox Drove, Burghclere, NEWBURY, BERKSHIRE, RG20 9JS.
•**MACAULAY, Mrs. Louise Helen, BA ACA** *1992;* 31 Priory Close, Pilgrims Hatch, BRENTWOOD, ESSEX, CM15 9PZ.
MACAULAY, Miss. Mojisola, BSc(Hons) ACA *2003;* 31 Dunchurch Crescent, SUTTON COLDFIELD, WEST MIDLANDS, B73 6QW.
MACAULAY, Mr. Neil John, FCA *1952;* 8 Farmhill Park, Douglas, ISLE OF MAN, IM2 2EE. (Life Member)
•**MACAULAY, Mr. Robert James, BA ACA** *1989;* Pinnacle Ltd, Tyn y Mynydd, Llanddona, BEAUMARIS, GWYNEDD, LL58 8TR.
MACAULAY, Mr. Roderick Bruce, MA ACA *1984;* Langland, Huby, LEEDS, LS17 0EG.
MACAULAY, Mr. Samuel James Martin, BBS ACA CIOT *1991;* 95 Dicksons Hill Road, Ballyroney, BANBRIDGE, COUNTY DOWN, BT32 5AN.
MACAULAY JORDAN, Mrs. Sheila Anne, BSc ACA *1983;* 2b Whitegates Lane, Earley, READING, RG6 1ED.
MACAULEY, Mrs. Andrea Jane, BSc ACA *1989;* 17 Cheldon Close, WHITLEY BAY, NE25 9XS.
•**MACAULEY, Mr. Kevin Patrick, BA ACA** *1992;* Ernst & Young LLP, 1 More London Place, LONDON, SE1 2AF. See also Ernst & Young Europe LLP
MACAULEY BETT, Ms. Belinda Patricia, MA ACA *1989;* 24 Ward Close, Great Sankey, WARRINGTON, WA5 8XY.
MACBAIN, Mr. Alister Andrew, BCom ACA *1992;* 5 Holm Dell Park, INVERNESS, IV2 4GZ.
MACBEAN, Mr. David, BSc FCA *1993;* 1 Rajdoot Marg, Chanakyapuri, NEW DELHI 110021, INDIA.
MACBETH, Mr. Ian James Henderson, BA FCA *1976;* PO Box 10224, City Square, NAIROBI, 00200, KENYA.
MACBETH, Mrs. Monique Lucile, BA ACA *1994;* 59 Cloncurry Street, LONDON, SW6 6DT.
MACBETH, Mr. Stewart, BSc ACA *1994;* 59 Cloncurry Street, LONDON, SW6 6DT.
MACCABE, Mr. Aidan Laurence Niall, BSc ACA *1987;* 56 Chemin des Brulees, 1093 LA CONVERSION, SWITZERLAND.
MACCABE, Mrs. Carol Ann, BA ACA *1981;* AIB House, 25 Esplanade, ST HELIER, JE3 2AB.
MACCALLAN, Mr. James Michael Ferguson, BA FCA *1974;* Flat 2, 15 Queens Gate Gardens, LONDON, SW7 5LY.
MACCALLUM, Ms. Heather Jane, CA *2004;* Scotland KPMG Channel Islands Limited, 5 St. Andrew's Place, Charing Cross, St. Helier, JERSEY, JE4 8WQ.
MACCALLUM, Mr. Michael, ACA CA(AUS) *2008;* KPMG AB, Stockholm Office, P.O.Box 16106, SE-103 23 STOCKHOLM, SWEDEN.
•**MACCALLUM, Mr. Neil Herbertson, BSc ACA** *1980;* (Tax Fac), Maccallum & Co, 127 Atherstone Avenue, PETERBOROUGH, PE3 9UJ.
•**MACCALLUM, Mrs. Rona Kerine, BA ACA** *1980;* Rona Maccallum, 127 Atherstone Avenue, PETERBOROUGH, PE3 9UJ.
MACCARTHY, Mr. Joseph Paul, BA ACA *2005;* with Octopus Private Equity, 20 Old Bailey, LONDON, EC4M 7AN.
MACCAW, Mr. Robin Guy, FCA *1969;* Tudor Cottage, High Street, Whitchurch-on-Thames, READING, RG8 7EP.
MACCLANCY, Mrs. Mary Elizabeth Ainley, BSc ACA *1991;* Herzel House Talisman Close, CROWTHORNE, BERKSHIRE, RG45 6JE.
MACCOLL, Mr. Douglas John, BSc ACA *1997;* 49 Wisteria Crescent, CHERRYBROOK, NSW 2126, AUSTRALIA.
•**MACCORKINDALE, Mr. Peter Duncan, FCA** *1978;* (Tax Fac), MacCorkindale International Partners, 2 South Barn, Chrishall Grange, Heydon, ROYSTON, HERTFORDSHIRE SG8 7NT.
MACDIARMID, Mr. James David, BA ACA *1998;* 74 Hervey Road, Blackheath, LONDON, SE3 8BU.
MACDONALD, Mr. Alistair Donald, FCA *1969;* Thomas Meikle Stores, 90 Speke Avenue, P O Box 642, HARARE, ZIMBABWE.
•**MACDONALD, Mr. Alistair John, BSc ACA CTA TEP** *2002;* (Tax Fac), Amcan, 31 Heol Cefn Onn, Lisvane, CARDIFF, CF14 0TP.
MACDONALD, Mr. Andrew James Alexander, BSc FCA *1980;* Financial Risk Management The Adelphi, 1-11 John Adam Street, LONDON, WC2N 6HT.
MACDONALD, Mrs. Belinda Claire, BA ACA *1992;* 32 Mintaro Parade, Quinns Beach, PERTH, WA 6030, AUSTRALIA.
MACDONALD, Mr. Brian Roger, BSc FCA *1992;* North Yorkshire Police, Headquarters, Newby Wiske Hall, Newby Wiske, NORTHALLERTON, NORTH YORKSHIRE DL7 9HA.
MACDONALD, Ms. Carol Kimberley, ACA *2009;* Flat 28, 71c Drayton Park, LONDON, N5 1DA.
MACDONALD, Mrs. Cassandra Louise, MA ACA *2006;* 44 Ada Street, SHIPLEY, WEST YORKSHIRE, BD18 4PJ.
MACDONALD, Mr. Christopher Ross, BA ACA *1996;* The Old Stables, 106a Church Lane, Backwell, BRISTOL, BS48 3JW.
MACDONALD, Mr. Colin Alick, FCA *1957;* Maldon, Tranby Lane, Swanland, NORTH FERRIBY, HU14 3NB.
•**MACDONALD, Mr. David Charles, BA ACA** *1986;* (Tax Fac), The Martlet Partnership LLP, Martlet House, E1 Yeoman Gate, Yeoman Way, WORTHING, WEST SUSSEX BN13 3QZ. See also Martlet Audit Limited
MACDONALD, Mrs. Dimple Deena Sham, BA ACA *2005;* Cqs (Gobal Services) Ltd, 2 Hill Street St. Helier, JERSEY, JE2 4UA.
MACDONALD, Mr. Donald Reginald Franklin, MA FCA *1949;* 37 Pink Lane, Burnham, SLOUGH, SL1 8JP. (Life Member)
•①**MACDONALD, Mr. Douglas Colquhoun, BCom CA FCA** *1995;* The MacDonald Partnership plc, Level 25, Tower 42, 25 Old Broad Street, LONDON, EC2N 1HQ.
MACDONALD, Mr. Duncan John Tuson, BA FCA *1975;* 12 Abbotswood Road, LONDON, SW16 1AP.
MACDONALD, Mrs. Eleanor, BSc ACA *2010;* Flat 11 Loreburn House, Holloway Road, LONDON, N7 9SP.
MACDONALD, Mrs. Elisabeth, BSc ACA *2009;* 58 Tasman Road, LONDON, SW9 9LX.
MACDONALD, Mrs. Emma Louise Rintoul, BA ACA *1993;* Strome House Garthends Lane, Hemingbrough, SELBY, NORTH YORKSHIRE, YO8 6QW.
MACDONALD, Miss. Gayle, BA ACA *2003;* 30 Bigstone Meadow, Tutshill, CHEPSTOW, GWENT, NP16 7JU.
MACDONALD, Mr. Gordon Joseph Daniel, FCA *1970;* Les Reines, Rue Des Reines, St. Peters, GUERNSEY, GY7 9AE.
MACDONALD, Mr. Ian Robert, BA ACA *1998;* Les Reines Rue Des Reines, St. Pierre Du Bois, GUERNSEY, GY7 9AE.
•**MACDONALD, Mr. Jack Martin, BSc ACA** *1993;* Jack MacDonald & Co, 1 Aldersyde, TAYNUILT, ARGYLL, PA35 1AG.
MACDONALD, Dr. James Charles Alexander, FCA *1976;* Level 11, No 1 Martin Place, SYDNEY, NSW 2000, AUSTRALIA.
MACDONALD, Mr. James Douglas, FCA *1951;* The Old Laundry, Keswick, NORWICH, NR4 6TZ. (Life Member)
MACDONALD, Mr. James William Stuart, MA FCA *1964;* Harlequin House, Ickleton, SAFFRON WALDEN, CB10 1SS.
MACDONALD, Mrs. Jenny Kay, BA(Hons) ACA *2000;* with PricewaterhouseCoopers, 1 Embankment Place, LONDON, WC2N 6RH.

MACDONALD, Miss. Joanne Kirsty, BSc(Hons) ACA *2004;* with Ernst & Young LLP, 1 More London Place, LONDON, SE1 2AF.
MACDONALD, Mr. John Douglas, MA ACA *1978;* 2 Canal Road, Thrupp, KIDLINGTON, OXFORDSHIRE, OX5 1LD.
MACDONALD, Ms. Julia Lucy, ACA CA(AUS) *2009;* with AlixPartners Ltd, 20 North Audley Street, LONDON, W1K 6WE.
MACDONALD, Mrs. Katherine Penelope, BSc ACA *1992;* 10 Grand Crescent, Rottingdean, BRIGHTON, BN2 7FL.
MACDONALD, Mr. Keith Duncan, FCA *1970;* 13 Buttercup Lane, BLANDFORD FORUM, DORSET, DT11 7LQ.
MACDONALD, Dr. Keith Moray, PhD BA FCA *1953;* Cheshunt, Blackheath, GUILDFORD, GU4 8QT. (Life Member)
MACDONALD, Mr. Kevin Neil, ACA *2008;* Highstanding Farmhouse, Selham Road, West Lavington, MIDHURST, WEST SUSSEX, GU29 0EG.
•MACDONALD, Mrs. Kim Elaine, BA FCA *1987;* EDF Tax LLP, 7 Regan Way, Chetwynd Business Park, Chilwell, NOTTINGHAM, NG9 6RZ.
•MACDONALD, Mr. Lawson Ranald, FCA *1974;* (Tax Fac), Macdonald & Co., 209 Barnwood Road, GLOUCESTER, GL4 3HS.
MACDONALD, Miss. Lee-Anne, BCom ACA DChA *2007;* Unit 51, 8 Water Street, BIRCHGROVE, NSW 2041, AUSTRALIA.
MACDONALD, Mr. Malcolm Cameron, BSc ACA MBA *1998;* 3 Ogles Grove, Culcavy Road, HILLSBOROUGH, BT26 6RS.
MACDONALD, Mr. Malcolm Michael, BSc ACA *2000;* 40 Brantwood Road, LONDON, SE24 0DJ.
MACDONALD, Mr. Malcolm William, BEng FCA *1993;* PricewaterhouseCoopers, 26/F Office Tower A, Beijing Fortune Plaza, 7 Dongsanhuan Zhong Road, Chaoyang District, BEIJING 100020 CHINA.
MACDONALD, Ms. Margaret, BSc ACA *1984;* 72 The Avenue, LONDON, NW6 7NN.
•MACDONALD, Mr. Martin John, FCA *1975;* Wilkins Kennedy, 1-5 Nelson St, SOUTHEND-ON-SEA, SS1 1EG.
MACDONALD, Mr. Martin Stanley Harrison, BSc FCA *1976;* Broad Head End, Cragg Vale, HEBDEN BRIDGE, WEST YORKSHIRE, HX7 5RT.
•MACDONALD, Mr. Mervyn John, FCA CTA *1981;* (Tax Fac), Mushroom House, Edenfield, BURY, BL0 0JG.
MACDONALD, Mr. Michael George, FCA *1968;* 38 Borstal Street, ROCHESTER, ME1 3HL. (Life Member)
MACDONALD, Miss. Morag, BSc FCA *1991;* 4/2 Robertson Gait, EDINBURGH, EH11 1HJ.
MACDONALD, Mr. Neil, FCA *1975;* 13 Norfolk Road, HARROGATE, HG2 8DA.
MACDONALD, Mr. Neil Andrew, BA FCA *1981;* 21 Clarendon Road, SHEFFIELD, S10 3TQ.
MACDONALD, Mr. Peter, FCA FCMA *1966;* 5 Vanity Close, Oulton, STONE, ST15 8TZ.
MACDONALD, Mr. Peter Alexander, BA(Hons) ACA *2004;* 44 Ada Street, SHIPLEY, BD18 4PJ.
MACDONALD, Mr. Philip Iain, BSc(Hons) ACA *2001;* 2 Racecourse Crescent, SHREWSBURY, SY2 5BP.
•MACDONALD, Mr. Philip John, BA ACA *1992;* (Tax Fac), PJMA, PO Box 58218, LONDON, N1 4XN.
MACDONALD, Mr. Robert Fraser, BA ACA *1998;* 2 Station View Itchington Road Tytherington, WOTTON-UNDER-EDGE, GLOUCESTERSHIRE, GL12 8QE.
MACDONALD, Mr. Roderick Alan, FCA *1967;* Dorpsstraat 21, 2445 AJ AARLANDERVEEN, NETHERLANDS. (Life Member)
MACDONALD, Mr. Rory Charles, MA ACA *2006;* Eden Lodge, 57 Old Edinburgh Road, INVERNESS, IV2 3PG.
MACDONALD, Mr. Ross Nicholas, BSc ACA FRSA *1982;* 2762 Portomaso, ST JULIANS PTM01, MALTA.
MACDONALD, Mrs. Samantha Mary, BA HND ACA *1997;* The Homestead, Ayton Road, Stokesley, MIDDLESBROUGH, CLEVELAND, TS9 5JN.
•MACDONALD, Mr. Simon, BA(Hons) ACA *2003;* with Target Accountants Limited, 29 Ludgate Hill, LONDON, EC4M 7JE.
MACDONALD, Mr. Stuart, BSc ACA *1992;* 32 Mintaro Pardade, Quinns Rocks, PERTH, WA 6030, AUSTRALIA.
MACDONALD, Mr. Stuart Randolph, BA ACA *1985;* 125 Andrew Lane, High Lane, STOCKPORT, CHESHIRE, SK6 8JD.
•MACDONALD, Mr. Thomas James, BSocSc ACA *1992;* Deloitte LLP, Athene Place, 66 Shoe Lane, LONDON, EC4A 3BQ. See also Deloitte & Touche LLP
MACDONALD, Mrs. Zin Thin, ACA *2005;* 99 Sixth Avenue, LONDON, W10 4HH.
MACDONALD DUDLEY, Mrs. Fiona, MA ACA *1993;* University of Leeds, Woodhouse Lane, LEEDS, LS2 9JT.
MACDONALD-TAYLOR, Mr. David John, MA MBA FCA *1977;* PO Box 3600, ABU DHABI, UNITED ARAB EMIRATES.
MACDOOMBE, Mr. Jason Neil, LLB ACA *2009;* Flat 6 Westgrove Court, 31 Grove Road, SUTTON, SM1 2AB.
MACDOUGALL, Mr. Alasdair William Lorn, BA ACA *1996;* 14 Church Lane, LONDON, SW19 3PD.
MACDOUGALL, Dr. Audrey, ACA *1992;* Scottish Government, 5 Atlantic Quay, 150 Broomielaw, GLASGOW, G2 8LU.
MACDOUGALL, Mr. Craig Alasdair James, BSc(Hons) ACA *2009;* Flat 33 Tennyson Court, 50 Winn Road, SOUTHAMPTON, SO17 1ER.
•MACDOUGALL, Mr. Diarmuid Joseph Declan, BA ACA *1992;* (Tax Fac), PricewaterhouseCoopers LLP, The Atrium, 1 Harefield Road, UXBRIDGE, UB8 1EX. See also PricewaterhouseCoopers
MACDOUGALL, Mr. Forbes Duncan Rogers, BSc ACA *1988;* (Tax Fac), Girbau House Trust Industrial Estate, Wilbury Way, HITCHIN, HERTFORDSHIRE, SG4 0UZ.
MACDOUGALL, Mrs. Jennifer Marie, BA ACA *1995;* 14 Church Lane, LONDON, SW19 3PD.
MACDOUGALL, Mr. Patrick Lorn, MA FCA *1966;* 110 Rivermead Court, Ranelagh Gardens, LONDON, SW6 3SB.
MACDOWELL, Miss. Nikki, BA ACA *2008;* 31a Greenland Road, LONDON, NW1 0AX.
MACDUFF, Mrs. Diana Caroline, BSc ACA *1999;* The Old School, School Lane, Barrowden, Rutland, OAKHAM, LEICESTERSHIRE LE15 8EL.
MACDUFF, Mr. Donald Peter, BA ACA *1982;* with PKF (UK) LLP, Regent House, Clinton Avenue, NOTTINGHAM, NG5 1AZ.
MACE, Mrs. Amber Jane, BSc ACA ATII *2001;* with Ernst & Young LLP, 1 More London Place, LONDON, SE1 2AF.
MACE, Mr. David James, BA ACA *1988;* 29 Pittfields, Langdon Hills, BASILDON, ESSEX, SS16 6RD.
MACE, Mr. Gerald Alan, FCA *1972;* 10 Northfield Road, Gosforth, NEWCASTLE UPON TYNE, NE3 3UL.
MACE, Mrs. Helen Elizabeth, BSc ACA *1997;* Rutland House, Wothorpe Park, Wothorpe, STAMFORD, LINCOLNSHIRE, PE9 3LA.
MACE, Mr. Ian Robert, BSc ACA *1994;* The Silver Spoon Company, British Sugar Plc, Oundle Road, PETERBOROUGH, PE2 9QU.
•MACE, Mr. John Albert, BCom FCA *1974;* AIMS - John Mace, 54 King Edwards Road, MALVERN, WORCESTERSHIRE, WR14 4AJ.
MACE, Mr. John Roger, MSc BA FCA *1969;* Downderry, Halton Road, Nether Kellet, CARNFORTH, LA6 1EU. (Life Member)
MACE, Mr. Peter Leslie, FCA *1970;* 17 Bellevue Road, Sheldon, BIRMINGHAM, B26 2PY.
MACE, Mr. Simon John, BSc ACA *2005;* Orchard Parksuites, 11 Orchard Turn, SINGAPORE 238800, SINGAPORE.
MACE, Mr. Stuart James, ACA *2008;* with Deloitte LLP, 4 Brindley Place, BIRMINGHAM, B1 2HZ.
•MACE, Mrs. Susan Jane, FCA *1992;* Su Mace, 140 Old Norwich Road, Horsham St. Faith, NORWICH, NR10 3JF.
MACEACHARN, Mr. Miles Colin Magub, BSc FCA *1990;* Whidley House, Dunsford, EXETER, DEVON, EX6 7EA.
MACEACHERN, Mr. Ian James Alan, BSc ACA *2005;* Flat 3, 51 Leathwaite Road, LONDON, SW11 1XG.
MACEDO, Mr. David East, FCA *1975;* 9 The Coaches, HOLYWOOD, COUNTY DOWN, BT18 0LE.
•MACEFIELD, Mr. Michael James, BSc ACA *1989;* Humphrey & Co, 7-9 The Avenue, EASTBOURNE, EAST SUSSEX, BN21 3YA.
MACEWEN, Mr. Robin, BA ACA *2001;* 6 Berkhampstead Road, BELVEDERE, DA17 5EA.
MACEY, Mr. Barrie Stuart, BSc FCA *1974;* Morgan Stanley, 25 Cabot Square, Canary Wharf, LONDON, E14 4QA.
•MACEY, Mr. Charles William David, FCA *1977;* Saffery Champness, Midland House, 2 Poole Road, BOURNEMOUTH, DORSET, BH2 5QY.
MACEY, Miss. Charlotte Julia, ACA *2009;* Apt 1507, 193 Aquarius Mews, VANCOUVER V6Z 2Z2, BC, CANADA.
•MACEY, Mr. Christopher Eric, BA FCA *1969;* (Tax Fac), 33 Montague Road, West Harnham, SALISBURY, SP2 8NL.
•MACEY, Miss. Hazel, BSc ACA *1986;* (Tax Fac), HBD Accountancy Services LLP, Gladstone House, 2 Church Road, Wavertree, LIVERPOOL, L15 9EG.
MACEY, Mr. Hugo Jonathan Verner, BA ACA *1988;* 18 Cavendish Avenue, CAMBRIDGE, CAMBRIDGESHIRE, CB1 7US.
MACEY, Mr. Jeremy, MA BCom ACA *1990;* 24 Myrtle Street, Crows Nest, SYDNEY, NSW 2065, AUSTRALIA.
MACEY, Mr. Martin, ACA *2008;* Deloitte & Touche Llp, 3 Rivergate, BRISTOL, BS1 6GD.
MACEY, Mr. Michael Frank, FCA *1968;* 55 Baring Road, Cockfosters, BARNET, EN4 9BU.
MACEY, Mr. Paul Richard, FCA *1976;* 30 Wellington Square, Bowerhill, MELKSHAM, SN12 6QX.
MACFARLAND, Mr. Hugo Adrian Jonathan, FCA *1969;* 176 Sanderling Close N.W., CALGARY T3K 2Z4, AB, CANADA.
•MACFARLANE, Mr. Alistair Tom Robert, BA FCA *1974;* BW Macfarlane LLP, 3 Temple Square, LIVERPOOL, L2 5BA.
MACFARLANE, Mr. Andrew Elliott, MA FCA *1980;* Aer Lingus PLC, Head Office, Dublin Airport, DUBLIN, COUNTY DUBLIN, IRELAND.
MACFARLANE, Mrs. Anne, BA ACA *1989;* 30 Niger Street, VINCENTIA, NSW 2540, AUSTRALIA.
MACFARLANE, Miss. Emma, BA(Hons) ACA *2011;* Churchfield Cottage, Margery Lane, Tewin, WELWYN, HERTFORDSHIRE, AL6 0JP.
MACFARLANE, Mr. Ian, FCA *1956;* The Thirteenth House, Heathside Park Road, WOKING, SURREY, GU22 7JF. (Life Member)
MACFARLANE, Mr. James, BSc ACA *2009;* 22 Adams House, Rustat Avenue, CAMBRIDGE, CB1 3RE.
MACFARLANE, Mr. Murray Alexander, FCA *1968;* Pen-y-Clawdd House, Pen-y-Clawdd, MONMOUTH, NP25 4BW. (Life Member)
MACFARLANE, Mr. Norman Barclay, MA FCA *1973;* (Tax Fac), Oakleigh, 31 Queens Road, KINGSTON UPON THAMES, SURREY, KT2 7SF.
•MACFARLANE, Mr. Roy, FCA *1972;* Roy Macfarlane, Saville Court, Saville Place, Clifton, BRISTOL, BS8 4EJ.
MACFARLANE, Mrs. Wendy Anne, BSc ACA *1991;* 3 Kilrymont Road, ST. ANDREWS, FIFE, KY16 8DE.
MACFARLANE, Mr. William Selwyn, FCA *1959;* PO Box 78923, SANDTON, GAUTENG, 2146, SOUTH AFRICA. (Life Member)
MACFEE, Mr. Mark Roderick, BA FCA *1982;* Global Directories, P.O.Box 688, GEORGE TOWN, GRAND CAYMAN, KY1-1107, CAYMAN ISLANDS.
MACGIBBON, Mr. Thomas Alexander John, FCA *1965;* Appledore Cottage, 19 Broadwater Down, TUNBRIDGE WELLS, KENT, TN2 5NJ. (Life Member)
•MACGILLIVRAY, Mr. Alasdair Duncan, FCA *1982;* (Tax Fac), MacGillivray & Co, 1 Coniston Road, CAMBRIDGE, CB1 7BZ.
MACGILLIVRAY, Dr. Colin William, BSc ACA *1997;* 207 East Ohio Street, Unit 404, CHICAGO, IL 60611, UNITED STATES.
MACGILLIVRAY, Mr. David Alexander, ACA *1980;* 13 Kingswood Ave, High West Jesmond, NEWCASTLE UPON TYNE, NE2 3NS.
MACGILLIVRAY, Mr. Ian Alistair, FCA CTA MBA *1977;* (Tax Fac), 65 Longcroft Avenue, Halton, AYLESBURY, BUCKINGHAMSHIRE, HP22 5PT.
MACGOVERN, Mr. Simon Charles, BSc ACA *1998;* 22 Roman Avenue, Angmering, LITTLEHAMPTON, WEST SUSSEX, BN16 4GH.
MACGOWAN, Mr. Alastair Francis Douglas, MA ACA MCT *1983;* 3 Cedar Court, 40 Oval Way, GERRARDS CROSS, BUCKINGHAMSHIRE, SL9 8PD.
MACGOWAN, Mrs. Bridget Ellen, BA ACA *1987;* 3247 West 3rd Avenue, VANCOUVER V6K 1N5, BC, CANADA.
MACGOWAN, Mrs. Judith Dzung Ngoc, ACA CA(AUS) *2008;* 97d Comeragh Road, LONDON, W14 9HS.
MACGRAY, Mrs. Kathryn Margaret, BA ACA *2003;* with PricewaterhouseCoopers LLP, 1 Embankment Place, LONDON, WC2N 6RH.
MACGREGOR, Mr. Alexander Ian, FCA *1960;* 35 The Grange, Holloway Drive, VIRGINIA WATER, SURREY, GU25 4ST.
MACGREGOR, Mr. Anthony John, BSc FCA *1978;* Hayne Lodge, Hayne Hill, Tipton St. John, SIDMOUTH, DEVON, EX10 0AL.
MACGREGOR, Mr. David, BA FCA *1983;* 26 Wilson Street, CAMMERAY, NSW 2062, AUSTRALIA.
•MACGREGOR, Mr. Gervase, BSc FCA *1986;* BDO LLP, 55 Baker Street, LONDON, W1U 7EU. See also BDO Stoy Hayward LLP
MACGREGOR, Miss. Helen Louise, BSc ACA *1993;* 18 Moore Way, SUTTON, SM2 5BZ.
MACGREGOR, Mr. Ian David, BA FCA *1975;* (Tax Fac), 96 Aldcliffe Road, LANCASTER, LA1 5BE.
MACGREGOR, Mr. Mark Robert, BSc ACA *2006;* Willow House La Rue A Don, Grouville, JERSEY, JE3 9GA.
•MACGREGOR, Mr. Neil Holden, BA ACA ATII *1989;* (Tax Fac), Neil H MacGregor, 177-4 Craigmillar Castle Ave, EDINBURGH, EH16 4DN.
MACGREGOR, Mr. Stuart Alastair, MA ACA *1999;* Valeriusplein 3a, 1075 BG AMSTERDAM, NETHERLANDS.
MACGREGOR, Mrs. Susan Elizabeth, BSc ACA *1981;* 15 Warwick Square, CARLISLE, CA1 1LA.
MACHALE, Mr. Joseph Patrick, MA FCA *1977;* The Old House, Wonston, WINCHESTER, SO21 3LS.
MACHARG, Miss. Elisabeth Heather, BAcc ACA *2003;* Stenham Trustees Ltd, Kingsway House, Havilland Street, St. Peter Port, GUERNSEY, GY1 2QE.
MACHARG, Mr. Walter Maitland, BA FCA *1988;* (Tax Fac), 51 Palace Gates Road, LONDON, N22 7BW.
MACHARIA, Mr. James, BCom ACA *1988;* c/o NIC Bank Limited, NIC House, Masaba Road, PO Box 44599, NAIROBI, 00100 GPO KENYA.
MACHE, Miss. Eveline Helen, MSc FCA *1982;* 45 West Heath Drive, LONDON, NW11 7QG.
MACHELL, Mr. Andrew, ACA *2010;* 1a Primrose Lane, ARLESEY, BEDFORDSHIRE, SG15 6RD.
MACHELL, Ms. Carole, BA ACA *1992;* Barclays Capital, 5 North Colonnade, LONDON, E14 4BB.
MACHELL, Mr. Christopher Anthony, BA ACA *2005;* with Deloitte LLP, City House, 126-130 Hills Road, CAMBRIDGE, CB2 1RY.
•MACHELL, Mr. Ronald, FCA CTA *1965;* (Tax Fac), Ron Machell, 204 Northfield Avenue, Ealing, LONDON, W13 9SJ.
MACHELL, Mr. Simon Christopher John, BA FCA *1989;* Grove Farm, Monk Soham, WOODBRIDGE, SUFFOLK, IP13 7EL.
MACHEN, Mr. Robert Alwyn, ACA *1993;* Orchard House, Canon Square, MELKSHAM, WILTSHIRE, SN12 6LX.
MACHEN, Mrs. Sally Ann, LLB ACA *2000;* Orchard House, Canon Square, MELKSHAM, WILTSHIRE, SN12 6LX.
MACHIN, Mrs. Alexandra Beverley, BSc ACA *1989;* 2 Kingsmill Cottages, Wherwell, ANDOVER, SP11 7JH.
MACHIN, Mr. Colin, FCA *1971;* City & Guilds, 1 Giltspur Street, LONDON, EC1A 9DD.
MACHIN, Mr. Gareth Peter, BSc ACA *1986;* 2 Taliesin Drive, Rogerstone, NEWPORT, NP10 0DB.
MACHIN, Mr. Harold Norman, MA FCA *1977;* HNM Associates, 27 Riverside Gardens, PETERBOROUGH, PE3 6GE.
•MACHIN, Mr. Howard Neil, FCA *1980;* (Tax Fac), Machin & Co, 19 Seer Mead, Seer Green, BEACONSFIELD, BUCKINGHAMSHIRE, HP9 2QL.
•MACHIN, Mrs. Irene Ann, FCA *1978;* I.A. Machin, 19 Seer Mead, Seer Green, BEACONSFIELD, HP9 2QL.
MACHIN, Mrs. Jane Ann, ACA *1983;* Dexter & Sharpe, Old Fire Station, 19 Watergate, SLEAFORD, LINCOLNSHIRE, NG34 7PG.
•MACHIN, Mr. John, BSc FCA CISA *1984;* KPMG Europe LLP, 15 Canada Square, LONDON, E14 5GL. See also KPMG LLP
•MACHIN, Mr. John Wilfrid, FCA *1975;* JWP Creers, Foss Place, Foss Islands Road, YORK, YO31 7UJ. See also JWPCreers LLP
MACHIN, Mr. Robert Leigh, FCA *1967;* Pepperstitch Lodge, Kingscourt Close, GILLINGHAM, DORSET, SP8 4LF.
•MACHIN, Mr. Ronald Thomas, FCA *1960;* (Tax Fac), Douglas Fairless Partnership Ltd, 92 London Road, LIVERPOOL, L3 5NW.
MACHO, Mr. Ian James, MA MPhil ACA *2009;* Saumackerstrasse 48, 8048 ZURICH, SWITZERLAND.
•MACHON, Mr. Peter, FCA *1981;* Ivy Farm, La Rue du Grand Mourier, St John, JERSEY, JE3 4AB.
•MACHOVA, Mrs. Teresa Ann, BSc ACA *1997;* T M Accountancy, 42 Edendale Road, BEXLEYHEATH, KENT, DA7 6RW.
MACHRAY, Mrs. Lisa Ann, ACA *2001;* 64 Shenfield Road, Shenfield, BRENTWOOD, ESSEX, CM15 8EJ.
MACHRAY, Mr. Philip James, BA ACA *1996;* 64 Shenfield Road, Shenfield, BRENTWOOD, ESSEX, CM15 8EJ.
MACIEL, Mr. Kenan, BSc ACA *1992;* 40 Whitton Drive, GREENFORD, UB6 0QZ.
MACINNES, Mr. Alex Edward, BA(Hons) ACA *2000;* 16 Chancellor Grove, LONDON, SE21 8EG.
MACINNES, Mr. Andrew, ACA *2011;* 7 The Edge Apartments, Glenville Grove, LONDON, SE8 4AJ.
MACINNES, Mr. Ewen Angus, BA ACA *1984;* 78, St Albans Road, Codicote, HITCHIN, SG4 8UU.

MACINNES, Mr. Michael Richard, FCA *1968;* Glenlyn, Lower Green Road, St. Helens, RYDE, ISLE OF WIGHT, PO33 1UF.
MACINNIS, Mr. Ian Wallace, FCA *1964;* 20 Broxbourne Road, ORPINGTON, BR6 0AY.
MACINTOSH, Mr. Alasdair Iain, MBA BSocSc FCA *1981;* 6 Queens Gate, Stoke Bishop, BRISTOL, BS9 1TZ.
MACINTOSH, Mr. Andrew George, BCom FCA *1989;* Roslyn, 44 Jesson Road, WALSALL, WS1 3AX.
MACINTOSH, Mr. Andrew Ian, BSc FCA *1980;* Shelley's Cottage, Whitehill, Dane End, WARE, SG12 0JT.
MACINTOSH, Mr. John Patrick, ACA CA(AUS) *2010;* 1 Cannon Court, 5 Brewhouse Yard, LONDON, EC1V 4JQ.
MACINTOSH, Mr. Kenneth, FCA *1969;* Woodpecker Cottage, Keysworth, WAREHAM, BH20 7BH.
MACINTOSH, Mr. Paul Jevon, ACA CA(AUS) *2009;* 214 East 83rd Street, Apartment 3D, NEW YORK, NY 10028, UNITED STATES.
MACINTOSH, Mr. Roderick Graham, FCA *1951;* P.O. Box 781064, SANDTON, GAUTENG, 2146, SOUTH AFRICA. (Life Member)
MACINTOSH, Miss. Ruth Deidre, ACA *2007;* SG Hambros Bank Trust (Jersey) Ltd, PO Box 78, JERSEY, JE4 8PR.
•MACINTOSH, Mrs. Tracey Anne, BA FCA *1988;* (Tax Fac), BDO LLP, 125 Colmore Row, BIRMINGHAM, B3 3SD. See also BDO Stoy Hayward LLP
MACINTYRE, Mr. David, BA ACA *2003;* with Barber Harrison & Platt, 2 Rutland Park, SHEFFIELD, S10 2PD.
MACINTYRE, Mr. Graham Jack, BSc ACA *1992;* 132 Scott Road, NORWICH, NR1 1YR.
MACINTYRE, Mr. Ian Stewart, BSc ACA *1989;* Hallidays Accountants LLP, Riverside House, Kings Reach Business Park, Yew Street, STOCKPORT, CHESHIRE SK4 2HD.
MACINTYRE, Mrs. Leanne Jane, ACA *2007;* Barclays Bank Plc, 1 Churchill Place, LONDON, E14 5HP.
MACIVER, Mr. Alasdair, FCA *1973;* 9 Skipton Close, Willen Park, MILTON KEYNES, MK15 9DJ.
MACIVER, Mr. Donald, FCA *1967;* 2 Auchmore, KILLIN, FK21 8ST. (Life Member)
MACIVER, Mr. Roderick Donald, LLB ACA *1991;* Ernst & Young, Ernst & Young Building, Harcourt Centre, Harcourt Street, DUBLIN, COUNTY DUBLIN IRELAND.
MACIVER, Mrs. Sarah, FCA *1980;* 24 Portland Place, BRIGHTON, BN2 1DH.
MACK, Mr. Andrew Hugh Dalziel, MSc BA FCA *1977;* 76 Daleside, Cotgrave, NOTTINGHAM, NG12 3QN.
MACK, Mr. Andrew Lawrence, ACA CPFA *2010;* 69 The Drive, BECKENHAM, KENT, BR3 1EE.
MACK, Mr. Christopher James Ashworth, BA ACA *1997;* 4 Overhill Lane, WILMSLOW, CHESHIRE, SK9 2BG.
MACK, Mrs. Hannah, BA ACA *2008;* with PricewaterhouseCoopers LLP, 1 Embankment Place, LONDON, WC2N 6RH.
MACK, Mrs. Jacqueline Holt, BSc ACA CTA *1992;* (Tax Fac), The Lee, Heptonstall, HEBDEN BRIDGE, HX7 7EP.
MACK, Mrs. Karen Margaret, BA ACA *1994;* The Firs, Station Road, MAYFIELD, EAST SUSSEX, TN20 6BW.
MACK, Mr. Lewis Bernard, FCA *1969;* 116/2 Mitzpe Nevo, 98411 MA'ALAH ADUMIM, ISRAEL.
MACK, Mr. Paul, BCom FCA *1990;* The Firs, Station Road, MAYFIELD, TN20 6BW.
MACK, Mrs. Pauline Dorothy, BSc ACA *1991;* Glebelands, Witchwell Lane, Little Wenlock, TELFORD, SHROPSHIRE, TF6 5BD.
MACK, Mr. Sau Hang, ACA *2008;* 17G Han Kung Mansion, TAIKOO SHING, HONG KONG SAR.
MACK-SMITH, Miss. Rachel, BSc FCA *1989;* Kennett House2 Stores Hill, Dalham NEWMARKET, Suffolk, CB8 8TQ.
MACKANESS, Mr. James Hugh, BA ACA *1991;* 7062 Webb Canyon Drive, SAN JOSE, CA 95120, UNITED STATES.
MACKANESS, Mr. Oliver James, BSc(Hons) ACA *2002;* Billing Finance Ltd, Billing House, The Causeway, Great Billing, NORTHAMPTON, NN3 9EX.
MACKANESS, Mr. Simon Peter, FCA *1972;* Rudding Park Limited, Rudding Park, HARROGATE, HG3 1JH.
MACKAREL, Miss. Joanne, ACA *2011;* 43 Bryning Way, Buckshaw Village, CHORLEY, LANCASHIRE, PR7 7DQ.
MACKAY, Mr. Alasdair Iain, MA ACA *2006;* 10 Montagu Mansions, LONDON, W1U 6LB.
MACKAY, Mr. Alastair James, FCA *1967;* Elisalei 37, B2930 BRASSCHAAT, BELGIUM.
MACKAY, Mr. Alexander Edward, MA(Hons) MSc ACA *2009;* 24 Corbyn Street, LONDON, N4 3BZ.
MACKAY, Mr. Andrew, FCA *1974;* 39 Hillbrow Road, BROMLEY, KENT, BR1 4JL.
MACKAY, Mr. Andrew Brian, BA ACA *1987;* 20 Lakeside Gardens, Rainford, ST HELENS, MERSEYSIDE, WA11 8HH.
MACKAY, Mr. Andrew Francis, BSc ACA *1994;* 347 Norbreck Road, THORNTON-CLEVELEYS, FY5 1PB.
MACKAY, Mr. Andrew Humphrey, FCA *1973;* 26 Hinton Road, Kingsthorpe, NORTHAMPTON, NN2 8NX.
MACKAY, Mrs. Antonia Jane, BA ACA *1997;* (Tax Fac), with Grant Thornton UK LLP, 3140 Rowan Place, John Smith Drive, Oxford Business Park South, OXFORD, OX4 2WB.
MACKAY, Ms. Barbara Ross, MA ACA *1990;* Landfall, High Street, Hamble, SOUTHAMPTON, SO31 4JF.
MACKAY, Mr. Christopher Tom, FCA *1961;* Pelynt, 43 Park Road, Smallfield, HORLEY, RH6 9RZ.
MACKAY, Mr. Clive Donald Alexander, BSc ACA *1986;* 22 Awatea Road, ST IVES CHASE, NSW 2075, AUSTRALIA.
MACKAY, Mr. Craig Richard, BSocSc ACA *1995;* 16 Park Cliffe Road, BRADFORD, WEST YORKSHIRE, BD2 4NS.
MACKAY, Mr. Donald Barret, MA FCA *1962;* Rhodes Cottage, Little Budworth, TARPORLEY, CW6 9DB. (Life Member)
MACKAY, Mr. Gavin John, BSc ACA CTA *1996;* 12 Grange Drive, CHISLEHURST, KENT, BR7 5ES.
MACKAY, Mr. Ian, FCA *1973; (CA Scotland* RMT, Gosforth Park Avenue, NEWCASTLE UPON TYNE, NE12 8EG.
MACKAY, Mr. Ian George, MA FCA *1966;* The Joint Post Ltd, t/a The Joint, Hollywood Cottage, Peters Lane, Holyport, MAIDENHEAD SL6 2HW.
MACKAY, Mr. James Richard, FCA *1967;* 21 Court Road, LEE-ON-THE-SOLENT, PO13 9JN. (Life Member)
•MACKAY, Miss. Kirsty, BSc ACA *1994;* with Ernst & Young LLP, Liberation House, Castle Street, St Helier, JERSEY, JE1 1EY.
MACKAY, Mr. Neil, FCA *1976;* 1 Broad Oak Cottages, Main Street, Strelley, NOTTINGHAM, NG8 6PD.
MACKAY, Mr. Neil Donald, BSc FCA *1982;* Ann Richards Accountancy Services Unit 8-9, Borough Court Grammar School Lane, HALESOWEN, B63 3SW.
MACKAY, Mr. Neil Harrison, BA ACA *1986;* 42 Arkaringa Crescent, BLACK ROCK, VIC 3193, AUSTRALIA.
MACKAY, Mr. Paul Henry, FCA *1969;* 7 Windermere Drive, West Derby, LIVERPOOL, L12 0HU. (Life Member)
MACKAY, Ms. Penelope Clare, BSc ACA DChA *1991;* The Kings School, Wrexham Road, CHESTER, CH4 7QL.
MACKAY, Mr. Peter Robert Le, BSc ACA *1980;* P.O. Box 1363, GEORGE TOWN, GRAND CAYMAN, KY1-1108, CAYMAN ISLANDS.
MACKAY, Mr. Ronald John, BCom FCA *1967;* C/o Peter Mackay Esq, 34 Maryland Drive, GLASGOW, G52 1SN. (Life Member)
MACKAY, Mr. Rupert Gordon, BA ACA *1996;* Terra Firma Capital Partners Ltd, 2 More London Riverside, LONDON, SE1 2AP.
MACKAY, Mr. Thomas Owen, MEng ACA *2000;* Logica, 250 Brook Drive, READING, RG26UA.
•MACKAY MILLER, Mr. Alistair, FCA *1974;* 39 Court Street, FAVERSHAM, KENT, ME13 7AL.
MACKEE, Mr. Gordon Andrew, MSc ACA *1980;* 37 Priory Road, Kew, RICHMOND, TW9 3DQ.
MACKEITH, Mr. Malcolm James, BA FCA DChA *1990;* Taunton School, Staplegrove Road, TAUNTON, TA2 6AD.
MACKELLAR, Mrs. Judith Claire, BA FCA *1987;* 4 Castleton Close, NEWCASTLE UPON TYNE, NE2 2HF.
MACKELLAR, Mr. Stuart Kenneth, BSc ACA *1995;* Amlin Bermuda Ltd., Suite 604, 12 Church Street, HAMILTON HM 12, BERMUDA.
MACKEN, Mr. Simon Peter, BA ACA *1986;* Internal Audit Department, East Dunbartonshire Council Tom Johnston House, Civic Way Kirkintilloch, GLASGOW, G66 4TJ.
MACKENZIE, Mr. Adrian James Thomas Dorman, FCA *1972;* Rua Jose Felix De Oliveira 1612, Granja Viana, Cotia, SAO PAULO, 06708-645, BRAZIL.
MACKENZIE, Mr. Alan Alastair, FCA *1957;* 7 Camargue Court, 24 Downview Road, WORTHING, WEST SUSSEX, BN11 4QH. (Life Member)
MACKENZIE, Mr. Alan Kenneth, MA FCA *1969;* 16 Penrhyn Crescent, East Sheen, LONDON, SW14 7PF. (Life Member)
MACKENZIE, Mr. Alasdair Duncan, MA ACA *1983;* 6 Groveway, LONDON, SW9 0AR.
•①MACKENZIE, Mr. Alasdair Duncan, BA FCA *1980;* AD Mackenzie & Co, 75 Middle Drive, Darras Hall, Ponteland, NEWCASTLE UPON TYNE, NE20 9DN.
MACKENZIE, Mr. Alastair Alexander, FCA *1973;* 10 Lytham Court, Cardwell Crescent, Sunninghill, ASCOT, SL5 9BU.
MACKENZIE, Mr. Alistair William, BA ACA *1990;* 5 Clifford Street, LONDON, W1S 2LG.
MACKENZIE, Mr. Andrew, MLitt BA ACA *2011;* 38 Eswyn Road, LONDON, SW17 8TP.
MACKENZIE, Mr. Andrew MacGregor, MA FCA *1983;* 60 Harley Street, LONDON, W1G 7HA.
MACKENZIE, Mr. Angus John, BSc ACA *2005;* Flat 13 Constable House, Casillis Road, LONDON, E14 9LH.
•MACKENZIE, Mr. Anthony Thomas Dorman Buist, FCA *1969;* (Tax Fac), AIMS - Anthony Mackenzie FCA, 77 St. Helens Park Road, HASTINGS, EAST SUSSEX, TN34 2JW.
•MACKENZIE, Mr. Barry Martin, FCA *1969;* with BSG Valentine, Lynton House, 7/12 Tavistock Square, LONDON, WC1H 9BQ.
MACKENZIE, Mrs. Danielle, BSc(Hons) ACA *2002;* 13 Monkhams Drive, WOODFORD GREEN, IG8 0LG.
MACKENZIE, Mr. Donald James, BSc ACA *1994;* 119 North Street, Newtonville, NEWTON, MA 02460, UNITED STATES.
MACKENZIE, Hamish John, Esq OBE MA FCA *1961;* Firthview, Main Street, Portmahomack, TAIN, ROSS-SHIRE, IV20 1YS. (Life Member)
MACKENZIE, Mr. Hamish Macphail Massie, BSc ACA *1996;* 94 Bishops Road, Fulham, LONDON, SW6 7AR.
•MACKENZIE, Mr. Iain Stuart, FCA *1993;* (Tax Fac), Mackenzie & Co, 34 Hazelmoor, Hebburn Village, HEBBURN, TYNE AND WEAR, NE31 1DH.
MACKENZIE, Mr. Ian, FCA *1972;* 16a Beaufort Road, REIGATE, RH2 9DJ.
MACKENZIE, Mr. Ian, FCA *1966;* Dorma View, Clayton Road, FRESHWATER, PO40 9EL. (Life Member)
MACKENZIE, Mr. Ian Alastair, FCA *1975;* 138 Alder Road, POOLE, DORSET, BH12 4AB.
MACKENZIE, Mr. Ian Bruce, BA ACA *1990;* 14 Heathfield Close, GODALMING, SURREY, GU7 1SL.
MACKENZIE, Mr. Ian Jonathan, ACA *1989;* 18 Columbia Cres, Beachlands, AUCKLAND 2018, NEW ZEALAND.
MACKENZIE, Mr. James Malcolm, BCom ACA *1997;* 8116 Dayton Ave North, SEATTLE, WA 98103, UNITED STATES.
MACKENZIE, Mr. James Stewart, BA ACA *1995;* Mackenzie Executive Search Ltd, P O Box 38401, DUBAI, UNITED ARAB EMIRATES.
MACKENZIE, Mrs. Jane Elizabeth, BSc ACA *1978;* The Old Recotory, Ashow, KENILWORTH, CV8 2LE.
•MACKENZIE, Mrs. Jennifer Mary, FCA *1976;* J.M. MacKenzie, 119 Coverside Road, Great Glen, LEICESTER, LE8 9EB.
MACKENZIE, Mr. John David Hay, FCA *1955;* Baldromma House, Jalloo, Ramsey, Maughold, ISLE OF MAN, IM7 1AT.
MACKENZIE, Mr. John Duncan, FCA *1959;* 15 Deans Drive, BEXHILL-ON-SEA, EAST SUSSEX, TN39 4DE. (Life Member)
MACKENZIE, Mrs. Julie Elizabeth, BEng ACA *1998;* Regional Action West Midlands, Waterlinks House, Richard Street, BIRMINGHAM, B7 4AA.
•MACKENZIE, Mrs. Karen Tracey, BSc ACA *1992;* with KPMG LLP, One Snowhill, Snow Hill Queensway, BIRMINGHAM, B4 6GN.
MACKENZIE, Miss. Kirsty, BSc(Hons) ACA *2003;* 383 Hurst Road, WEST MOLESEY, SURREY, KT8 1QW.
•MACKENZIE, Mrs. Laura Michelle, ACA *2007;* Karrek Accountants Limited, 9 Hilgrove Road, NEWQUAY, CORNWALL, TR7 2QY.
MACKENZIE, Miss. Moyra Lorne, BA FCA *1969;* Spinney Lodge, Brent Hall Road, Finchingfield, BRAINTREE, CM7 4LA. (Life Member)
MACKENZIE, Miss. Natalie Anne, BA ACA *1997;* 4 Mimram Place, High Street, WELWYN, AL6 9HQ.
MACKENZIE, Mr. Neil Alexander, BA ACA *1987;* H S B C Bank Plc, Level 40, 8 Canada Square, LONDON, E14 5HQ.
MACKENZIE, Mrs. Orysia, BA(Econ) FCA *1980;* University of Huddersfield, Queensgate, HUDDERSFIELD, HD1 3DH.
MACKENZIE, Mrs. Paula Jane, BA(Hons) ACA *2002;* 3 Thorold Road, FARNHAM, SURREY, GU9 7JY.
MACKENZIE, Mrs. Rachel Louise, BSc(Hons) ACA *2002;* (Tax Fac), Pricewaterhousecoopers, 1 Embankment Place, LONDON, WC2N 6RH.
MACKENZIE, Mr. Richard John, MSci ACA *2007;* Sinodun 4 The Gardens, Church Walk Bilton, RUGBY, CV22 7LX.
MACKENZIE, Mr. Robert Chase, FCA *1973;* 9 Rock Gardens, Europa, GIBRALTAR, GIBRALTAR.
MACKENZIE, Mr. Robert David, BA ACA *1979;* The Old Rectory, Ashow, KENILWORTH, CV8 2LE.
MACKENZIE, Mr. Robert Moir, FCA *1968;* Flat 9, Dryburgh Mansions, 84 Erpingham Road, LONDON, SW15 1BG.
MACKENZIE, Mr. Roger Anthony, FCA *1968;* 14 Buccaneer Drive, WESTMOORINGS, TRINIDAD AND TOBAGO.
MACKENZIE, Mr. Ronald Alastair, BA FCA *1975;* 6 West Park Place, LEEDS, LS8 2EY.
MACKENZIE, Mrs. Rosanne Jane, MA BA ACA *2002;* Croyland House, Wicken Bonhunt, SAFFRON WALDEN, ESSEX, CB11 3UG.
MACKENZIE, Mr. Ross, MA MLitt ACA *2006;* Pricewaterhousecoopers Llp, 1 Hays Lane, LONDON, SE1 2RD.
MACKENZIE, Mr. Roy, FCA *1962;* Info.com Ltd, 170-172 Victoria Street, LONDON, SW1E 5LB.
MACKENZIE, Mr. Roy Alex, BSc ACA CTA *1991;* Lime Cottage, St Johns Hill Road, WOKING, SURREY, GU21 7RE.
MACKENZIE, Mr. Roy Michael, FCA *1968;* Parc Vince, 15 Elm Drive, BUDE, CORNWALL, EX23 8EZ.
MACKENZIE, Mr. Ruairidh Iain, BSc FCA *1982;* (Tax Fac), Apogee, 19 Neil's Plantation, ST MICHAEL, BB, BARBADOS.
MACKENZIE, Mrs. Sarah, LLB ACA *2003;* 11 Waterloo Rise, STRATFORD-UPON-AVON, WARWICKSHIRE, CV37 7HL.
MACKENZIE, Mr. Steven, BSc ACA *1992;* 23 Warren Rise, Frimley, CAMBERLEY, GU16 8SJ.
MACKENZIE, Mr. Stuart Gardner, FCA *1977;* 6 Freeman Drive, KANGAROO FLAT, VIC 3555, AUSTRALIA.
MACKENZIE, Mr. William Quentin Cook, FCA *1967;* Purification Products Ltd, Reliance Works, Saltaire Road, SHIPLEY, BD18 3HL.
MACKENZIE-PARKS, Mr. David, FCA *1975;* 30 Hillside Close, BANSTEAD, SURREY, SM7 1ET. (Life Member)
MACKENZIE-SMITH, Mr. Simon, BSc ACA *1986;* Mountains, Mountains Road, Great Totham, MALDON, CM9 8BY.
MACKENZIE-SMITH, Dr. Sydney, FCA CTA *1958;* The Pines, Broadmoor Road, Carbrooke, THETFORD, NORFOLK, IP25 6SZ. (Life Member)
MACKENZIE-THORPE, Mr. Christopher, FCA *1976;* 1 Kingston Cottages, Kingswear, DARTMOUTH, DEVON, TQ6 0EG.
MACKERELL, Mrs. Victoria Ann, ACA *2007;* 5b Malpas Drive, NORTHALLERTON, NORTH YORKSHIRE, DL7 8TU.
MACKERRELL, Mr. David Kingsley Donald, FCA *1972;* The Gatehouse, Sissinghurst, CRANBROOK, TN17 2JA. (Life Member)
MACKERVOY, Mr. Ian John, FCA *1959;* 55 Oakover Drive, Allestree, DERBY, DE22 2PR. (Life Member)
MACKESSY, Mr. Patrick Stephen, BSc FCA *1976;* Victorian Auditor-General's Office, Level 24, 35 Collins Street, MELBOURNE, VIC 3051, AUSTRALIA.
MACKETT, Miss. Jane, LLB ACA *2000;* Merrill Lynch Financial Centre, 2 King Edward Street, LONDON, EC1A 1HQ.
MACKEVOY, Mr. James Anthony, FCA *1970;* 3 Church Road, Dunton, BRENTWOOD, ESSEX, CM13 3SR.
•MACKEY, Mr. John Vinycomb, BCom FCA *1975;* Ernst & Young Audit & Associados SROC S.A, Avenida da Republica 90-6, 1600-206 LISBON, PORTUGAL.
MACKEY, Mr. Milburn Ralph Simon James, FCA *1951;* 65 Park Walk, Chelsea, LONDON, SW10 0AZ. (Life Member)
MACKEY, Mr. Peter Charles, BA ACA *1986;* 4 Joan Lane, Bamford, HOPE VALLEY, S33 0AW.
MACKEY, Mr. Robert William, FCA *1973;* 20 High Garth, ESHER, KT10 9DN.
MACKEY, Mrs. Rosalind Elizabeth, BSc ACA *1996;* 122 East Trillium Road, Mequon, THIENSVILLE, WI 53092, UNITED STATES.
MACKEY, Mr. Stephen James, BAcc ACA *1998;* 122 East Trillium Road, MEQUON, WI 53092, UNITED STATES.
MACKEY, Mrs. Tracey Jane, BA ACA *1991;* 7 Coppins Close, BERKHAMSTED, HP4 3NZ.
MACKEY, Mr. William Gawen, FCA *1949;* Sunrise Senior Living, Copsem Lane, ESHER, SURREY, KT10 9HJ. (Life Member)
MACKFALL, Mr. Nigel Stuart, ACA *1993;* 53 Bowden Grove, Dodworth, BARNSLEY, S75 3TB.
•MACKICHAN, Mr. Graham Alexander, MA FCA *1983;* Woodcote, Buckhurst Lane, WADHURST, TN5 6JY.
MACKIE, Mr. Alan Graham, MA MLitt FCA *1983;* (Tax Fac), Braeside, Frankscroft, PEEBLES, EH45 9DX.

MACKIE, Mrs. Andrea, BA ACA *1997;* (Tax Fac), Caterpillar Stockton, 2 Handley Close, Preston Farm Industrial Estate, STOCKTON-ON-TEES, CLEVELAND, TS18 3SD.
MACKIE, Mr. Brian Leslie, BCom ACA *1990;* 31 Hampton Avenue, TORONTO M4K 2Y5, ON, CANADA.
MACKIE, Mr. Clive David Andrew, FCA *1956;* Ashes Lodge, Netherfield, BATTLE, TN33 9PP. (Life Member)
MACKIE, Mr. David, LLB ACA *2007;* Deloitte & Touche, 2 New Street Square, LONDON, EC4A 3BZ.
MACKIE, Miss. Dawn Patricia, BSc ACA *1987;* 10 Via Firenze, 12 Florence Avenue, BEDFORDVIEW, GAUTENG, 2007, SOUTH AFRICA.
MACKIE, Mr. Ian Fraser, BSc ACA *1988;* 4 Village Road, Cockayne Hatley, SANDY, BEDFORDSHIRE, SG19 2EE.
MACKIE, Mr. John Angus Kinmond, BSc FCA *1989;* The Barn, Old Back Lane, Wiswell, CLITHEROE, LANCASHIRE, BB7 9BS.
MACKIE, Mr. John Taylor, TD BSc(Econ) FCA *1974;* (Tax Fac), 33 rue de la Rhode, 11500 QUILLAN, FRANCE.
MACKIE, Mr. Jonathan Lindsay, BA(Hons) ACA *2000;* 38 Stapleton Road, Headington, OXFORD, OX3 7LU.
MACKIE, Mrs. Juliet, FCA *1987;* with Sheppard Rockey & Williams Ltd, Sannerville Chase, Exminster, EXETER, EX6 8AT.
MACKIE, Mr. Raymond John, FCA *1969;* The Rosery, Mile Path, Hook Heath, WOKING, GU22 0DY.
MACKIE, Mr. Robert James, ACA *2008;* Flat 104 Garand Court, Eden Grove, LONDON, N7 8EW.
MACKIE, Miss. Susan Elizabeth, BSc ACA *1982;* 36 Nightingales, CRANLEIGH, SURREY, GU6 8DE.
MACKIN, Mrs. Janita Louise, BSc FCA *1999;* with Moore Stephens, Oakley House, Headway Business Park, 3 Saxon Way West, CORBY, NORTHAMPTONSHIRE NN18 9EZ.
MACKIN, Miss. Katherine Jane, ACA *2008;* Flat 4, 37 Woodside, LONDON, SW19 7AG.
•**MACKINLAY, Mr. Craig, BSc FCA ATII** *1992;* (Tax Fac), Beak Kemmenoe, 1-3 Manor Road, CHATHAM, ME4 6AE. See also Mackinlay
MACKINLAY, Mr. Jack Lindsay, FCA *1959;* The Cottage, Main Street, Stillington, YORK, YO61 1JU. (Life Member)
MACKINNEY, Mr. David Edward, FCA *1969;* Crowle House, Crowle Road, Lambourn, HUNGERFORD, RG17 8NR.
MACKINNON, Mr. Alan Barclay, ACA *1982;* C/O Frame Investments Limited, 4th Floor, 20-22 Berkeley Square, LONDON, W1J 6LH.
MACKINNON, Mr. Alexander Gordon, BA ACA *2006;* 106 Swaby Road, LONDON, SW18 3QZ.
MACKINNON, Mr. Andrew John, BSc ACA *2006;* 28 Archdale Road, LONDON, SE22 9HJ.
MACKINNON, Mr. Andrew Peter, BSc FCA *2000;* 6 Woodlea, ALTRINCHAM, CHESHIRE, WA15 8WH.
•**MACKINNON, Ms. Carol Dawn, ACA** *1998;* Scotland Deloitte LLP, Abbots House, Abbey Street, READING, RG1 3BD. See also Deloitte & Touche LLP
MACKINNON, Miss. Caroline Jane, MA BCom ACA *2000;* 4 Jupiter Way, WOKINGHAM, BERKSHIRE, RG41 3GE.
MACKINNON, Miss. Christina, BA ACA *1990;* Flat 3, 5-6 Bramham Gardens, LONDON, SW5 0JQ.
MACKINNON, Mrs. Emma Rosemary, MA ACA *1984;* 7 School Close, HIGH WYCOMBE, BUCKINGHAMSHIRE, HP11 1PH.
MACKINNON, Mr. Iain Francis, LLB ACA ATII *1983;* (Tax Fac), Barclays Plc, 1 Churchill Place, LONDON, E14 5HP.
MACKINNON, Mr. Ian Andrew, BSc FCA *1991;* Hindleppe, 26 Haw Street, WOTTON-UNDER-EDGE, GL12 7AQ.
MACKINNON, Mrs. Janet Sarah, BSc FCA *1983;* 4 Woodlands Drive, South Godstone, GODSTONE, SURREY, RH9 8HU.
MACKINNON, Miss. Mandy, BSc ACA *1988;* 34 Tinwell Road, STAMFORD, PE9 2SD.
MACKINNON, Mr. Michael Lars, BA ACA *1996;* 31 Applegarth Road, LONDON, W14 0HY.
MACKINNON, Mrs. Monica Ellen, BSc FCA CTA *1996;* Tangmere Cottage, Tangmere Road, Tangmere, CHICHESTER, WEST SUSSEX, PO20 2HW.
MACKINNON, Mr. Ross, LLB ACA *2009;* 29 Alderley Close, Woodley, READING, RG5 4TG.
MACKINNON, Mr. William Roderick, BSc ACA *2000;* 13 Cohen Street, FAIRLIGHT, NSW 2094, AUSTRALIA.
MACKINTOSH, Mr. Alistair Julian, BA ACA *1995;* Fulham Football Club Training Ground, Motspur Park, NEW MALDEN, KT3 6PT.
MACKINTOSH, Ms. Christina Anne, BSc FCA *1978;* 1930 Iron Court, NORTH VANCOUVER V7G 2P2, BC, CANADA.
MACKINTOSH, Miss. Jemma Caroline, ACA *2009;* with James Cowper LLP, Mill House, Overbridge Square, Hambridge Lane, NEWBURY, BERKSHIRE RG14 5UX.
•**MACKINTOSH, Viscount John Clive, MA FCA** *1984;* PricewaterhouseCoopers LLP, 1 Embankment Place, LONDON, WC2N 6RH. See also PricewaterhouseCoopers
MACKINTOSH, Mr. Lachlan Stewart, BA FCA *1968;* 36 Drummond Place, EDINBURGH, EH3 6PW. (Life Member)
MACKINTOSH, Mr. Seumas, BSc ACA *2011;* 14 Shaftesbury Road, Maidenbower, CRAWLEY, WEST SUSSEX, RH10 7HD.
MACKINTOSH, Mr. Stewart John, LLB ACA *2003;* 3/1 14 Falkland Street, GLASGOW, G12 9PR.
MACKIRDY, Mr. Calliss James, FCA *1951;* 11a Poplar Avenue, Heacham, KING'S LYNN, NORFOLK, PE31 7EB. (Life Member)
MACKISON, Mr. Neil Robert, BSc ACA *1993;* The Mill Cottage, 8 Wraylands Drive, REIGATE, RH2 0LG.
MACKLEY, Mr. Joel, MDes ACA *2011;* 14 Middlefield Court, East Morton, KEIGHLEY, WEST YORKSHIRE, BD20 5RN.
MACKLEY, Mr. Nicholas Andrew, MEng ACA *1990;* 32 Byng Road, BARNET, HERTFORDSHIRE, EN5 4NR.
MACKLIN, Mrs. Celia Margaret, BA ACA *2001;* 52 Gurney Court Road, ST. ALBANS, HERTFORDSHIRE, AL1 4RL.
MACKLIN, Mrs. Claire Rosemary, BSc ACA *1991;* Unit 28, The Metro Centre, Dwight Road, WATFORD, WD18 9SB.
MACKLIN, Mr. Joseph David, BA ACA *2007;* (Tax Fac), with Deloitte LLP, Athene Place, 66 Shoe Lane, LONDON, EC4A 3BQ.
MACKLIN, Mrs. Liene Kazocina, ACA *2009;* Apartment 25 Metro Central Heights, 119 Newington Causeway, LONDON, SE1 6BA.
MACKLIN, Mr. Peter Douglas, MA FCA *1982;* 10 Teignmouth Road, DAWLISH, EX7 0LA.
MACKMAN, Mr. Paul Keith, BSc ACA *2003;* 22 Hengrave Road, LONDON, SE23 3NW.
MACKNEY, Mr. David, BSc ACA *1996;* 61 Derwent Road, HARPENDEN, HERTFORDSHIRE, AL5 3NY.
•**MACKNEY, Mr. Owen, BSc ACA** *1994;* PricewaterhouseCoopers LLP, Marlborough Court, 10 Bricket Road, ST. ALBANS, HERTFORDSHIRE, AL1 3JX. See also PricewaterhouseCoopers
MACKO, Mr. Tony, BA ACA *1987;* 42 Greenhaven Drive, Pennant Hills, SYDNEY, NSW 2120, AUSTRALIA.
MACKOWSKA, Mrs. Katarzyna Urszula, ACA *2009;* ul. Egejska 17b m.36, 02-764 WARSAW, POLAND.
MACKOWSKI, Mrs. Gillian Anne, BSc ACA *1990;* Inland Revenue, North Yorkshire A, Hilary House, 16 St Saviour's Place, YORK, YO1 9PG.
MACKOWSKI, Mr. Przemyslaw Arkadiusz, ACA *2009;* ul. Egejska 17b m.36, 02-764 WARSAW, POLAND.
MACKRAEL, Mr. John Alan, FCA *1954;* Lancslass, Langley Road, Claverdon, WARWICK, CV35 8QA. (Life Member)
MACKRELL, Mr. Simon, BA FCA *1996;* 1 park chase, GUILDFORD, Gu1 1es.
•**MACKRIDGE, Mr. Geoffrey Roy, FCA** *1972;* Milner Boardman Limited, MBL House, 16 Edward Court, Altrincham Business Park, George Richards Way, ALTRINCHAM CHESHIRE WA14 5GL.
•**MACKRILL, Mr. Leonard John, FCA** *1986;* Weller Mackrill Ltd, South Building, Upper Farm, Wootton St. Lawrence, BASINGSTOKE, HAMPSHIRE RG23 8PE.
MACKSEY, Mr. Frederick Charles, FCA *1954;* Vine Lodge, Northend, HENLEY-ON-THAMES, RG9 6LF. (Life Member)
MACKWORTH-PRAED, Mr. Richard Edmund, MA ACA *1993;* Latchmore House, Ash Lane, Silchester, READING, RG7 2NH.
MACLACHLAN, Mrs. Caroline Joanne, BSc ACA *2000;* 23 Dunkeld Close, Ascot Park, Wardley, GATESHEAD, TYNE AND WEAR, NE10 8WH.
MACLACHLAN, Mr. Ian Robert, BA ACA *2002;* ACCA, PO Box 10640, CHELMSFORD, CM1 9PH.
MACLACHLAN, Mr. James Robert Bennett, FCA *1966;* Southfields, Milbourne, MALMESBURY, SN16 9JB. (Life Member)
MACLACHLAN, Mr. John, FCA *1972;* Greystones West, Levens, KENDAL, CUMBRIA, LA8 8ND.
MACLACHLAN, Mrs. Susan, BA ACA *2005;* 29 Tell Grove, LONDON, SE22 8RH.
MACLAREN, Mr. Patrick Alastair, BA FCA *1973;* School House, Dog Lane, Nether Whitacre, Coleshill, BIRMINGHAM, B46 2DU.
•**MACLAREN, Mr. Robert Peter Michael, MBA FCA** *1973;* Robert Maclaren Ltd, 16 Ainslie Place, EDINBURGH, EH3 6AU.
•**MACLAVERTY, Mr. Ross Graeme, FCA** *1980;* Baker Tilly Restructuring & Recovery LLP, 2 Whitehall Quay, LEEDS, LS1 4HG. See also Baker Tilly Tax and Advisory Services LLP
MACLAY, Mr. Andrew Strang, MA FCA *1984;* Acorns, 27 South Road, Chesham Bois, AMERSHAM, HP6 5LU.
MACLEAN, Mr. Andrew Ronald Macgavin, BCom FCA *1965;* Just Fish Ltd, Glan Wysc, Sennybridge, BRECON, POWYS, LD3 8PS.
MACLEAN, Mr. Corin Stephen, BA ACA *2000;* 35 Southdown Road, Portslade, BRIGHTON, BN41 2HL.
MACLEAN, Mr. Eric Iain, BSc ACA *1990;* 3544 Meadowlands Lane, SAN JOSE, CA 95135, UNITED STATES.
•**MACLEAN, Mr. Ewan John, FCA** *1995;* Eura Audit UK, St Paul's Offices, 1 Park View Court, St Paul's Road, SHIPLEY, BD18 3DZ. See also Lishman Sidwell Campbell & Price LLP
MACLEAN, Miss. Fiona Jane, BSc ACA *1992;* 10 Queensmill Road, LONDON, SW6 6JS.
MACLEAN, Mr. Francis John Hued, MA ACA *2003;* Deutsche Bank AG, 75 London Wall, LONDON, EC2M 5NG.
MACLEAN, Miss. Gillian Beryl, BSc ACA *1995;* 15 Elan Close, WYMONDHAM, NORFOLK, NR18 9LW.
MACLEAN, Mr. Graeme William, BSc ACA *1998;* George Sharkey & Sons Ltd, Newhailes Industrial Estate, Newhailes Road, MUSSELBURGH, MIDLOTHIAN, EH21 6SY.
MACLEAN, Mr. James Coll Futvoye, MA ACA *2007;* 49a Primrose Gardens, LONDON, NW3 4UL.
MACLEAN, Mr. John Rupert, BSc ACA *2001;* 9 Pitters Piece, Long Crendon, AYLESBURY, BUCKINGHAMSHIRE, HP18 9PP.
MACLEAN, Miss. Sally Victoria, MChem ACA *2008;* with Hazlewoods LLP, Windsor House, Barnett Way, Barnwood, GLOUCESTER, GL4 3RT.
MACLEAN, Mr. Simon James, ACA *2009;* 1B Annette Road, LONDON, N7 6PE.
MACLEAN, Mr. Stewart Neil Miller, BSc ACA *2000;* F N Z (UK) Ltd, 23 Silvermills Court Henderson Place Lane, EDINBURGH, EH3 5DG.
MACLEAN, Mr. Stuart Kenneth, FCA *1980;* Precision Technologies International Ltd, Mariner, TAMWORTH, STAFFORDSHIRE, B79 7UL.
MACLEAN BRISTOL, Mrs. Charlotte Chloe, MA BSc ACA *2003;* Fourward Properties Limited, Gate House Farm, Jane Lane, Midge Hall, LEYLAND, PR26 6TQ.
MACLEHOSE, Mr. Benjamin Donald Robert, BA ACA *2011;* Clantire House, Little Heath Road, Fontwell, ARUNDEL, WEST SUSSEX, BN18 0SR.
MACLELLAN, Mr. Craig, BSc ACA *2006;* 7 Audley Road, RICHMOND, SURREY, TW10 6EY.
MACLELLAN, Mr. Henry, MA(Hons) ACA *2011;* Flat 4, 54 Winchester Street, LONDON, SW1V 4NH.
MACLELLAN, Mr. Ian David, FCA *1970;* Wormleighton Grange, Wormleighton, SOUTHAM, WARWICKSHIRE, CV47 2XJ.
•**MACLELLAN, Mr. Timothy Ian, ACA FCCA** *2010;* Mitchams Accountants Limited, 1 Cornhill, ILMINSTER, SOMERSET, TA19 0AD.
MACLENNAN, Mr. Bruce John Stuart, FCA *1977;* St. Clears Farm, Clapwater, Fletching, UCKFIELD, EAST SUSSEX, TN22 3YA.
•**MACLENNAN, Mr. Roderick Euan, BSc FCA** *1972;* Holland MacLennan & Co., 115 Crockhamwell Road, Woodley, READING, RG5 3JP.
MACLEOD, Dr. Alasdair Breac, BEng ACA *2002;* 10 Catherine Place, LONDON, SW1E 6HF.
MACLEOD, Miss. Alexandra Margaret, MSc LLB ACA *2002;* Ashdene Vicarage Lane, Bowdon, ALTRINCHAM, CHESHIRE, WA14 3AS.
MACLEOD, Mr. Alisdair Duthie, BA(Hons) ACA *2002;* 3 Les Bidons, La Ruette de la Ville Es Gaudin St. Martin, JERSEY, JE3 6XG.
MACLEOD, Mr. Andrew Lewis, BSc ACA *2004;* EMAC, Gerald Edelman, 25 Harley Street, LONDON, W1G 9BR.
MACLEOD, Mr. Donald Farquhar, FCA *1962;* 3 Merton Rise, LONDON, NW3 3EN.
•**MACLEOD, Mr. Donald Iain, FCA** *1975;* (Tax Fac), Portlock & Company, Ash House, Ash Road, New Ash Green, LONGFIELD, KENT DA3 8JD.
MACLEOD, Mr. Douglas Roderick, BA ACA *1979;* 29 Cleaver Square, LONDON, SE11 4EA.
•**MACLEOD, Mr. Douglas Scott, BA ACA ATII** *2000;* Donald Scott Associates Limited, PO Box 7785, HUNGERFORD, RG17 1DB.
MACLEOD, Mrs. Emma Suzanne, BSc ACA *2000;* 69 Ranelagh Grove, Wollaton, NOTTINGHAM, NG8 1HS.
MACLEOD, Mr. Gordon Donald, BA(Hons) ACA *2001;* Firebrand Training Ltd, Langham House 308 Regent St, LONDON, W1B 3AT.
MACLEOD, Mr. Gordon Roger, BA ACA *1994;* 7 Cromwell Road, LONDON, SW19 8LE.
MACLEOD, Miss. Isobel Margaret, MA ACA *1994;* 4 St. Andrews Close, Evelyn Road, Wimbledon, LONDON, SW19 8NJ.
MACLEOD, Mr. James Alexander Kenneth, LLB ACA *2001;* 1 Brighouse Park Gardens, EDINBURGH, MIDLOTHIAN, EH4 6GY.
MACLEOD, Mr. John Cabot Reid, ACA *2008;* 22 Eaton Mews North, LONDON, SW1X 8AR.
MACLEOD, Mr. John James, BSc ACA *1996;* Independence Homes, 1 Harestone Drive, CATERHAM, SURREY, CR3 6HX.
MACLEOD, Mr. Kenneth, FCA *1960;* 46 South Street, DURHAM, DH1 4QP. (Life Member)
MACLEOD, Mr. Mark Bradley, BA(Hons) ACA *2001;* Technicolor Limited, Pinewood Studios, Pinewood Road, IVER, BUCKINGHAMSHIRE, SL0 0NH.
MACLEOD, Mr. Mark Ian, BSc FCA *1992;* Climate Change Capital, 3 More London Riverside, LONDON, SE1 2AQ.
MACLEOD, Mr. Neil Alexander, BSc ACA ATII *1992;* Talisman Energy (UK) Ltd, Talisman House, 163 Holburn Street, ABERDEEN, AB10 6BZ.
MACLEOD, Mrs. Nicola Patricia, BCom ACA *1991;* Group Treasury, The Royal Bank of Scotland Plc, 280 Bishopsgate, LONDON, EC2M 4RB.
•**MACLEOD, Mrs. Rachel Ann, BA ACA** *1996;* with KPMG LLP, Management Services Centre, 58 Clarendon Road, WATFORD, WD17 1DE.
MACLEOD, Mr. Robert James, MA ACA *1990;* Johnson Matthey Plc, PO Box 277, LONDON, EC1N 8EE.
MACLEOD, Mr. Roderick, FCA *1974;* 18 Hawthorn Gardens, Kenton Gosforth, NEWCASTLE UPON TYNE, NE3 3DE.
MACLEOD, Mr. Roderick Ferguson, BA FCA *1977;* 11 Whitehall Gardens, Undy, CALDICOT, NP26 3EW.
MACLEOD, Mr. Steven, ACA *2008;* 52 Sugden Road, LONDON, SW11 5EF.
MACLNTYRE, Mrs. Sharon, BSc ACA *2004;* with Ernst & Young LLP, 1 Bridgewater Place, Water Lane, LEEDS, LS11 5QR.
•**MACLUCAS, Mr. Ian David, BSc FCA** *1979;* (Tax Fac), I D MacLucas & Co, 104b Malthouse Yard, West Street, FARNHAM, SURREY, GU9 7EN.
MACMAHON, Miss. Michelle Louise, BSc ACA *1997;* 6th Floor Brettenham House, Lancaster Place, LONDON, WC2e7en.
MACMAHON, Mr. Paul, ACA *2008;* Flat 161 Victoria Mill, Houldsworth Street Reddish, STOCKPORT, CHESHIRE, SK5 6AX.
MACMAHON, Mr. Robert James, BA FCA ATII *1986;* 7 Marlborough Grove, YORK, YO10 4AY.
MACMANUS, Mr. Patrick Christopher Francis, BCom FCA *1971;* 28 Flower Grove, Glenageary, DUN LAOGHAIRE, COUNTY DUBLIN, IRELAND.
•ⓘ**MACMILLAN, Mr. Charles Christopher Stewart, FCA** *1979;* Beever and Struthers, St George's House, 215-219 Chester Road, MANCHESTER, M15 4JE.
MACMILLAN, Mr. Douglas Charles, FCA *1957;* Rondo Cottage, Linstock, CARLISLE, CA6 4PZ. (Life Member)
MACMILLAN, Mrs. Helen Elizabeth, FCA *1991;* Lemans, 29 Arboretum Street, NOTTINGHAM, NG1 4JA.
•**MACMILLAN, Mr. Iain Andrew, BSc ACA** *1992;* Deloitte LLP, Athene Place, 66 Shoe Lane, LONDON, EC4A 3BQ. See also Deloitte & Touche LLP
MACMILLAN, Mr. Iain Stuart, BA(Hons) ACA AKC *2001;* Foxley House, Clare Avenue, WOKINGHAM, RG40 1EB.
MACMILLAN, Mr. John Eric, FCA DChA *1966;* 3 Broadwater Rise, GUILDFORD, SURREY, GU1 2LA.
MACMILLAN, Ms. Karen, BA ACA *1989;* 95 Goldstone Road, HOVE, EAST SUSSEX, BN3 3RG.
MACMILLAN, Mr. Phillip, BA ACA *2005;* Dolphins Vicarage Close, Stoke Gabriel, TOTNES, DEVON, TQ9 6QT.
MACMILLAN, Mr. Wallace, FCA *1982;* Chemin Henri-Schmitt 1, CH-1218 LE GRAND-SACONNEX, SWITZERLAND.
MACNAB, Mr. Andrew James, BA ACA *1988;* College Farm, Main Street, Wighill, TADCASTER, NORTH YORKSHIRE, LS24 8BQ.
MACNAB, Mr. Bovain Alasdair James, ACA *1996;* 44 Cranko Road, 7925 Observatory, CAPE TOWN, WESTERN CAPE PROVINCE, SOUTH AFRICA.

MACNAB, Mrs. Jane, BA(Hons) FCA *1988;* College Farm Main Street, Wighill, TADCASTER, NORTH YORKSHIRE, LS24 8BQ.

MACNAB, Mr. Kevin John, BA ACA *1986;* 105 Luba Avenue, RICHMOND HILL L4S 1G7, ON, CANADA.

MACNAB, Ms. Sarah Jane, BSc ACA *1995;* Northlands, 22 Sandpit Lane, ST. ALBANS, HERTFORDSHIRE, AL1 4HL.

MACNABB, Mr. Ian, FCA *1974;* Copse Hill Farm, Lower Froyle, ALTON, GU34 4LW. (Life Member)

MACNAGHTEN, Dr. Alexander Hugh, MA ACA *1997;* 3 Balland Field, Willingham, CAMBRIDGE, CB24 5JT.

MACNAIR, Mr. Hubert Scipio Alison, FCA *1950;* 64 Churchbury Lane, ENFIELD, EN1 3TY. (Life Member)

•①MACNAMARA, Mr. Edward John, MEng ACA *2000;* with PricewaterhouseCoopers, 101 Barbirolli Square, Lower Mosley Street, MANCHESTER, M2 3PW.

•MACNAMARA, Mrs. Hazel June, BSc ACA *2000;* with PricewaterhouseCoopers LLP, 101 Barbirolli Square, Lower Mosley Street, MANCHESTER, M2 3PW.

MACNAMARA, Mr. James Justin, TD MA FCA *1983;* Heyford Manor, Church Lane, Lower Heyford, BICESTER, OX25 5NZ.

MACNAMARA, Mr. Rory Patrick, MA ACA *1979;* 8 Castello Avenue, LONDON, SW15 6EA.

•MACNAUGHTON, Mrs. Helen, BA ACA *1985;* 46 Westerfield Road, IPSWICH, IP4 2UT.

MACNAUGHTON, Mrs. Jenan, BA ACA *1987;* 2A West Hill Road, LONDON, SW18 1LN.

MACNAUGHTON, Mr. Kenneth Andrew, BA ACA *1990;* 2A West Hill Road, LONDON, SW18 1LN.

MACNAUGHTON, Mr. Robert Ian, MPhys ACA *2007;* 26 Notton Way, Lower Earley, READING, RG6 4AJ.

MACNAUGHTON, Mr. Robert Magnus, BSc ACA *1989;* 53 Cross Street, LONDON, N1 2BB.

MACNAUGHTON, Mrs. Tara, BSc(Hons) ACA *2004;* 26 Notton Way, Lower Earley, READING, RG6 4AJ.

•MACNAY, Mr. Bruce William, MA FCA *1977;* (Tax Fac), T W Tax Services Limited, 3 Clanricarde Gardens, TUNBRIDGE WELLS, TN1 1HQ. See also MacNay B.W.

•MACNEIL, Miss. Ishbel Janice, BSc ACA *1993;* 33 Corbiehill Crescent, Davidsons Mains, EDINBURGH, EH4 5BE.

MACNEILL, Mr. Alexander David, ACA *2008;* 28 Kingspark Court, South Woodford, LONDON, E18 2DD.

MACNEILL, Mrs. Helen, BA ACA *2000;* with BDO LLP, 55 Baker Street, LONDON, W1U 7EU.

MACNEILL, Mr. Stewart, MA ACA *2000;* Highfield House, Marton cum Grafton, YORK, YO51 9QJ.

MACNISH PORTER, Mrs. Nancy Kathryn, LLB ACA *1989;* Hillcrest, 10 Coombe Rise, Shenfield, BRENTWOOD, CM15 8JJ.

MACONACHIE, Mr. Mark Robert, BSc(Econ) ACA *2003;* Royal Bank of Scotland, 30th Floor, AIG Tower, 1 Carraught Road, CENTRAL, HONG KONG ISLAND HONG KONG SAR.

MACONICK, Mr. Adrian Nicholas Varley, MA ACA *1985;* 70 Ramsden Road, LONDON, SW12 8QZ.

•MACORISON, Mr. Philip Ian, FCA *1977;* Philip I. Macorison, 1 Abingdon Way, ORPINGTON, BR6 9WA. See also Cavernham LLP

MACORISON, Mrs. Valerie Susan, BSc ACA *1978;* (Tax Fac), 1 Abingdon Way, ORPINGTON, BR6 9WA.

MACPHAIL, Mr. Alexander James, MA ACA *2000;* 6 Sutherland Road, CHELTENHAM, NSW 2119, AUSTRALIA.

MACPHAIL, Sir Bruce Dugald, MA FCA *1965;* Thorpe Lubenham Hall, MARKET HARBOROUGH, LE16 9TR.

•MACPHAIL, Mr. Donald Barrow, MA FCA *1969;* MacPhail & Co, 12 rue Pierre-Fatio, P.O. Box 3453, 1211 GENEVA, SWITZERLAND.

MACPHAIL, Mr. Hamish Malcolm, BSc ACA *1992;* 41 West Oak Knoll Drive, SAN ANSELMO, CA 94960, UNITED STATES.

MACPHAIL, Mr. Iain, MA FCA *1974;* 50 Inner Park Road, Wimbledon Common, LONDON, SW19 6DA. (Life Member)

MACPHAIL, Mr. Nigel Bruce, MA ACA *1997;* Baker Tilly (BVI) Limited, P.O. Box 650, Tropic Isle Building, Nibbs Street, Road Town, TORTOLA VIRGIN ISLANDS (BRITISH).

MACPHEE, Mr. Alexander Arnold, BSc ACA *1986;* Yatesbury, Oval Way, GERRARDS CROSS, SL9 8PY.

MACPHEE, Mrs. Helen Margaret, BSc ACA *1989;* 58 Erpingham Road, Putney, LONDON, SW15 1BG.

MACPHEE, Mr. James Mitchell, BSc ACA *1986;* Hiflex House, Telford Road, SALISBURY, WILTSHIRE, SP2 7PH.

•MACPHERSON, Mr. Alexander James, BA ACA *2003;* Rees Pollock, 35 New Bridge Street, LONDON, EC4V 6BW.

MACPHERSON, Mr. Allan Alasdair, BA ACA *1981;* 53 Culmstock Road, LONDON, SW11 6LY.

MACPHERSON, Mr. Andrew Reid, BSc ACA *1998;* 125 Howard Road Westbury Park, BRISTOL, BS6 7UZ.

MACPHERSON, Mr. Angus John Tilney, BA FCA *1980;* 24 Kensington Gardens, KINGSTON UPON THAMES, SURREY, KT1 2JU.

MACPHERSON, Mr. Angus Stuart, BA ACA *1980;* 1 Green Lane, Wroughton, SWINDON, SN4 0RJ.

MACPHERSON, Miss. Ayesha Abbas, BA ACA *1991;* KPMG, 8/F Prince's Building, 10 Chater Road, CENTRAL, HONG KONG ISLAND, HONG KONG SAR.

MACPHERSON, Mr. Ewen Niall, MA ACA *1998;* Telereal Bastion House, 140 London Wall, LONDON, EC2Y 5DN.

MACPHERSON, Mrs. Gillian Anne, BSc FCA *1988;* 19 Mill Road, MARLOW, BUCKINGHAMSHIRE, SL7 1PX.

MACPHERSON, Mr. James Robert Brisbane, MA MSc ACA *2007;* Flat 47, 22-28 Penkivil Street, BONDI, NSW 2026, AUSTRALIA.

MACPHERSON, Mr. Neil, BSc ACA *1991;* Premier Asset Management Plc, 1 Eastgate Court High Street, GUILDFORD, GU1 3DE.

MACPHERSON, Mrs. Nisha, BA ACA *2002;* Enbloc Ltd Unit 2 Pale Lane Farm, Pale Lane Hartley Wintney, HOOK, HAMPSHIRE, RG27 8DH.

MACQUEEN, Miss. Sarah, ACA *2006;* with PKF (UK) LLP, Farringdon Place, 20 Farringdon Road, LONDON, EC1M 3AP.

MACQUIRE, Mr. Derek Owen, FCA *1952;* Bridge Farm, Melbury Osmond, DORCHESTER, DT2 0LT. (Life Member)

MACRAE, Mr. Andrew James, BA(Hons) ACA *2000;* 33 Holmesdale Avenue, REDHILL, RH1 2PB.

MACRAE, Mr. Colin Philip Robert, FCA *1975;* Ridley Hall, Ridley Hall Road, CAMBRIDGE, CB3 9HG.

MACRAE, Mr. Duncan, FCA *1966;* 1 Canberra MewsBeacon CovePort Melbourne, MELBOURNE, VIC 3207, AUSTRALIA.

•MACRAE, Mr. Gregor Charles William, LLB ACA *1991;* (Tax Fac), Vistra UK Limited, Suite 12, 55 Park Lane, Mayfair, LONDON, W1K 1NA.

MACRAE, Mrs. Leigh Alison, BA ACA *1996;* 2 Beulah Road, EPPING, CM16 6RH.

MACRAE, Mrs. Linsay S, MA FCA ACA *1993;* Rue des Bourgeois 4, 1805 JONGNY, SWITZERLAND.

MACRAE, Mr. Roderick Harris, BSc ACA *1978;* 1 Erica Drive, WOKINGHAM, RG40 2DU.

•MACRAE, Mrs. Susan Joanna, FCA *1984;* (Tax Fac), Network 4M Limited, Suite 1, Park Farm Barn, Brabourne, ASHFORD, KENT TN25 6RG.

MACRAE, Mrs. Victoria Elizabeth, MA(Hons) ACA *2000;* 2 Barnton Park, EDINBURGH, EH4 6JF.

MACRO, Miss. Samantha Jane, BSc ACA *1999;* 69 Burwell Road, Exning, NEWMARKET, SUFFOLK, CB8 7DU.

MACRORY, Ms. Terenia Veronica, BSc ACA *1997;* 12 Eskdale Avenue, HALIFAX, HX3 7NH.

•MACROW, Mr. Mark Roy, BSc ACA *2002;* WMM Consulting Limited, 70 Briggate, KNARESBOROUGH, NORTH YORKSHIRE, HG5 8BH.

MACROW-WOOD, The Revd. Antony Charles, MA ACA *1986;* The Rectory, 99 Darbys Lane, Oakdale, POOLE, DORSET, BH15 3EU.

MACTAGGART, Mrs. Claire, MA FCA *1994;* 2 Redhall House Avenue Colinton Dell, EDINBURGH, MIDLOTHIAN, EH14 1JJ.

MACTAGGART, Mr. Neil Ros, FCA *1977;* The Haven, Five Lanes Road, Marldon, PAIGNTON, DEVON, TQ3 1NQ.

MACTAVISH, Mr. Clive Robert, MA ACA MBA *1997;* 11 Gresham Road, OXTED, SURREY, RH8 0BS.

MACTAVISH, Mrs. Sophie Marieke, BA ACA *1999;* 11 Gresham Road, OXTED, RH8 0BS.

•MACVE, Prof. Richard Henry, MA FIA FCA *1972;* (Member of Council 1986 - 1993), Prof. R.H. Macve FCA, Bronwydd, 3 Trefor Road, ABERYSTWYTH, SY23 2EH.

MACVIE, Mr. Michael Frank, BA FCA *1978;* Fiddlers Green, Blackford Hill, HENLEY-IN-ARDEN, B95 5DQ.

MACWHINNIE, Mr. Antony Philip, MA ACA *1982;* 14 Lytton Park, Sandy Lane, COBHAM, KT11 2HB.

MACWHIRTER, Mrs. Leanne, BSc(Hons) ACA *2009;* 1/103 King William Road, Unley, ADELAIDE, SA 5061, AUSTRALIA.

•MACWHIRTER, Mr. Stuart B, FCA *1967;* The Hay Group, Berkeley House, Dix's Field, EXETER, EX1 1PZ. See also Hay Tax Limited

MADAHAR, Miss. Priya, ACA *2011;* 19 Endsleigh Gardens, Edwalton, NOTTINGHAM, NG12 4BQ.

MADAMS, Mr. James Richard, BA ACA *1989;* (Tax Fac), 2 High House Mews, Stoke Newington Church Street, LONDON, N16 0EN.

MADAN, Mr. Meherji Kaikaus, BSc FCA *1969;* 4515 Willard Avenue, Suite South 2309, CHEVY CHASE, MD 20815, UNITED STATES.

MADAN, Mrs. Ranjana, ACA *1980;* with Buzzacott LLP, 130 Wood Street, LONDON, EC2V 6DL.

MADAN, Ms. Sona, BSc ACA *2004;* with Ernst & Young LLP, 1 More London Place, LONDON, SE1 2AF.

MADANI, Mr. Jignesh Shashikant Amilal, BSc ACA *2003;* (Tax Fac), 48A Bowrons Avenue, WEMBLEY, MIDDLESEX, HA0 4QP.

MADARIAGA, Miss. Lisa Margaret, LLB ACA *1998;* 19 Beckenham Avenue, Mossley Hill, LIVERPOOL, L18 1JH.

MADDALENA, Mr. Bernard Dunstan, FCA *1979;* Marble Mosaic Co Ltd, Winterstoke Road, WESTON-SUPER-MARE, AVON, BS23 3YE.

MADDAMS, Mr. David, BA ACA *2006;* 3 Beech Close, Sproughton, IPSWICH, IP8 3BL.

MADDAMS, Mr. John Anthony, FCA *1952;* 38 Westland Drive, Hayes, BROMLEY, BR2 7HF. (Life Member)

MADDAMS, Mr. Nicholas Leslie, ACA MBA *1998;* 6 Waterfront Mews, Apperley Bridge, BRADFORD, WEST YORKSHIRE, BD10 0UR.

MADDAMS, Mr. Roger Jonathan, BA FCA *1987;* 22 Qwysson Avenue, BURY ST. EDMUNDS, SUFFOLK, IP33 1AH.

MADDAN, Mr. Peter, ACA *2011;* Nansenstrasse 3, 8050 ZURICH, SWITZERLAND.

•MADDEN, Mrs. Anna, FCA *1999;* Curo Professional Services Limited, Curo House, Greenbox, Westonhall Road, Stoke Prior, BROMSGROVE WORCESTERSHIRE B60 4AL.

MADDEN, Mr. Daniel, BSocSc ACA *2001;* 14, 1 Simper Street, Wembley, PERTH, WA 6018, AUSTRALIA.

MADDEN, Mr. Edward Timothy, BA ACA *1982;* (Tax Fac), 9 Poplar Piece, Inkberrow, WORCESTER, WR7 4JD.

MADDEN, Mr. James John, BSc FCA *1986;* Strawberry Fields, Blackhall Lane, SEVENOAKS, TN15 0HS.

MADDEN, Miss. Margaret Louise, BA FCA *1997;* Voyager, Fairfield Group Level, 7 Chicago Avenue Manchester Airport, MANCHESTER, M90 3DQ.

MADDEN, Miss. Mary Louise, BAcc ACA *2001;* S.B Adieu, 50 St Katharine Way, LONDON, E1W 1LA.

MADDEN, Dr. Neil Andrew, BSc DIC ACA *1997;* Worldmark International, 6 Redwood Crescent, East Kilbride, GLASGOW, G74 5PA.

•MADDEN, Mr. Rory Edward, FCA *1979;* Arthur Daniels & Company, 227a West Street, FAREHAM, PO16 0HZ.

MADDERS, Miss. Helen, BSc(Hons) ARCS ACA *2002;* 18 Franklin Street, Leederville, PERTH, WA 6007, AUSTRALIA.

MADDERS, Miss. Rosemary Margaret, BA FCA *1966;* (Tax Fac), 8 Rosemary Mews, Copse Lane, FRESHWATER, ISLE OF WIGHT, PO40 9DA.

MADDICK, Mr. Niall William, MA ACA *2004;* 2 Moorland Road, HARROGATE, NORTH YORKSHIRE, HG2 7HD.

MADDICKS, Mr. David George, BA ACA *1995;* Flat 12 Orchard Court, Knoll Hill, BRISTOL, BS9 1NT.

MADDISON, Mr. Derek John, MA FCA *1986;* Marsh Management Services Guernsey Ltd, PO Box 34, St Martins House, GUERNSEY, GY1 4AU.

MADDISON, Mr. Edward John, ACA *1990;* (Tax Fac), A S L, Bury House, 31 Bury Street, LONDON, EC3A 5AG.

MADDISON, Mr. George Michael Alexander, BA ACA *1987;* 5 Kidbrooke Grove, LONDON, SE3 0PG.

•MADDISON, Mr. Ian Errington, BSc FCA *1978;* Lordship Cottage, 1 Fardells Lane, Elsworth, CAMBRIDGE, CB23 4JE.

MADDISON, Mr. Ian William, MBA FCA CTA *1989;* 6 Lapwing Court, Burnopfield, NEWCASTLE UPON TYNE, NE16 6LP.

MADDISON, Mr. Keith, FCA *1968;* 7 Long Perry, Capel St.Mary, IPSWICH, IP9 2XD.

MADDISON, Mr. Kevin Raymond, BSc ACA *1981;* 10 Moorhill Court, SUNDERLAND, SR2 9DE.

MADDISON, Mrs. Laura Leonie, BA ACA *2007;* Ingenious Media Plc, 15 Golden Square, LONDON, W1F 9JG.

MADDISON, Mr. Nigel George, BA ACA *1991;* Flat A, 40 Ravenslea Road, LONDON, SW12 8RX.

MADDISON, Mr. Patrick James Robson, BSc ACA *1985;* Oak Tree Cottage, Maddox Lane, Bookham, LEATHERHEAD, KT23 3BT.

MADDISON, Mr. Paul, BA ACA *2003;* 25 Heatherways, LIVERPOOL, L37 7HL.

MADDISON, Mr. Philip James, BA FCA *1991;* Guntsfield, 32 Beacon Road, Ditchling, HASSOCKS, BN6 8UL.

MADDISON, Mr. Roger, FCA *1967;* Greenhills, Grasmere, AMBLESIDE, LA22 9QA.

•①MADDISON, Mr. Stuart David, BSc ACA *1989;* PricewaterhouseCoopers LLP, 9 Greyfriars Road, READING, RG1 1JG. See also PricewaterhouseCoopers

MADDOCK, Mr. David Stephen, BSc FCA *1982;* 25 Dyffryn Woods, NEATH, WEST GLAMORGAN, SA10 7QA.

MADDOCK, Mr. Frederick Ralph, FCA *1952;* 30 Ashcroft Place, Epsom Road, LEATHERHEAD, KT22 8RJ. (Life Member)

•MADDOCK, Mr. Gareth Roy, BA FCA DChA *2000;* Whitehead & Howarth, 327 Clifton Drive South, LYTHAM ST. ANNES, FY8 1HN.

MADDOCK, Mr. Nicholas William, MA ACA *1994;* Four Springs Langport Road, Long Sutton, LANGPORT, SOMERSET, TA10 9ND.

MADDOCK, Mr. Peter, FCA *1971;* 15 Nuttall Court, Locking Stumps, Birchwood, WARRINGTON, WA3 7NQ.

MADDOCK, Mr. Roger Charles, FCA *1975;* La Renaissance, Rue Louis Favez, 1854 LEYSIN, VAUD, SWITZERLAND.

MADDOCKS, Mr. Alex Charles Richard, BA FCA *1993;* Penrhos, Rock End Avenue, TORQUAY, TQ1 2DR.

MADDOCKS, Mr. Andrew John, BSc ACA *1989;* Flat 7 Ashdown, 1 Chine Crescent Road, BOURNEMOUTH, BH2 5LJ.

MADDOCKS, Mr. Andrew Philip, BA(Hons) ACA *2004;* 9 Crouchley Lane, LYMM, CHESHIRE, WA13 0AS.

MADDOCKS, Miss. Caroline Mary, ACA *2009;* 112 Meadow Way, Caversham, READING, RG4 5LY.

MADDOCKS, Mr. Nigel John, BCom ACA *1986;* The Grange, Church Lane, Thrumpton, NOTTINGHAM, NG11 0AX.

MADDOCKS, Mr. Peter Edwin, BA ACA *1981;* 12 College Road, The Historic Dockyard, CHATHAM, ME4 4QX.

MADDOCKS, Mr. Richard James, ACA *1985;* Holly Lodge, Mustow Green, KIDDERMINSTER, WORCESTERSHIRE, DY10 4LE.

MADDOWS, Mr. Robert, BA ACA *2005;* with Ernst & Young LLP, 1 More London Place, LONDON, SE1 2AF.

•MADDOX, Mr. Geoffrey, BTh FCA *1982;* (Tax Fac), Page Maddox Limited, 21 Honeysuckle Gardens, Everton, LYMINGTON, HAMPSHIRE, SO41 0EH. See also Maddox G.

MADDOX, Mr. Paul Anthony, MSc BSc ACA *2007;* 18 Blackmires Way, SUTTON-IN-ASHFIELD, NOTTINGHAMSHIRE, NG17 4JQ.

MADDOX, Mr. Paul Geoffrey, MA FCA *1985;* Runfold Manor, Hogs Back, Seale, FARNHAM, SURREY, GU10 1JX.

MADDOX, Mr. Richard William, BA ACA *1984;* Meadow View, Gittisham, HONITON, DEVON, EX14 3AW.

MADDOX, Mr. William Robert Worthington, FCA *1953;* Ross Cottage, Heath Lane, Great Barrow, CHESTER, CH3 7LL. (Life Member)

MADDRELL, Mrs. Caroline Annette, ACA *2009;* 3 Larch Hill, Douglas, ISLE OF MAN, IM2 5NQ.

MADDRELL, Mr. David, ACA *2010;* 3 Larch Hill, Douglas, ISLE OF MAN, IM2 5NQ.

•MADDRELL, Mr. Joe Hankin, ACA *1986;* (Tax Fac), JH Maddrell ACA, 1 Meadowfield, Port Erin, ISLE OF MAN, IM9 6PH.

MADDRELL, Dr. Samuel James, BSc ACA *1999;* 107a York Street, CAMBRIDGE, CB1 2PZ.

MADDY, Mr. James Edward, BSocSc ACA *2001;* 21 Huntsmans Way, Badsworth, PONTEFRACT, WEST YORKSHIRE, WF9 1BE.

MADEJ, Miss. Jolanta, ACA *2003;* 303-1450 Burnaby Street, VANCOUVER V6G 1W7, BC, CANADA.

MADELEY, Mr. David Phillip, BA ACA *1984;* 1 Castle Mill, Mill Lane, Ashley, ALTRINCHAM, WA15 0RD.

MADELEY, Mrs. Jane Elisabeth, BA ACA *1993;* Squires Cottage, 102 Leeds Road, Bramhope, LEEDS, LS16 9AN.

MADELEY, Miss. Laura Frances, BSc ACA *2006;* 24 Kaye Don Way, WEYBRIDGE, SURREY, KT13 0UX.

•MADEN, Ms. Catherine, BSc FCA *1980;* Brinsmead Maden, The Loft House, Meadow Lane, Hamble, SOUTHAMPTON, SO31 4RB.

MADEN, Mr. Clifford James, FCA *1957;* 15 Westcliffe, Great Harwood, BLACKBURN, BB6 7PH. (Life Member)
MADEN, Mrs. Nicola Ruzenka, BSc ACA *2001;* with PricewaterhouseCoopers, BusinessCommunityCenter, Katerinska 40/ 466, 120 00 PRAGUE, CZECH REPUBLIC.
MADEN, Mr. Peter, BSc FCA *1988;* 70 Raymar Place, OAKVILLE L6J 6M1, ON, CANADA.
•MADEN-WILKINSON, Mr. Mark, ACA *1989;* Pierce C A Ltd, Mentor House, Ainsworth Street, BLACKBURN, BB1 6AY. See also Pierce Group Limited
MADEWELL, Mr. William Guy, BSc FCA MCT *1974;* (Tax Fac), 43 Wickham Way, Park Langley, BECKENHAM, KENT, BR3 3AE.
•MADGE, Mr. Christopher Bartholomew, FCA *1975;* (Tax Fac), Chris Madge & Co, The Stables, Clevedon Hall, CLEVEDON, BS21 7SJ.
MADGE, Mr. Christopher William John, BSc FCA *1979;* Seasons, 62 Broadway, Duffield, BELPER, DE56 4BU.
MADGE, Mr. James, BSc(Hons) ACA *2011;* 20 Roughley Farm Road, Four Oaks, SUTTON COLDFIELD, WEST MIDLANDS, B75 5RT.
•MADGE, Mr. Thomas Alexander, BSc ACA *1990;* Tom Madge, 18 Chilcot Close, LONDON, E14 6AN.
•MADGIN, Mrs. Catharine Jane, BSc FCA *1979;* (Tax Fac), Catharine Madgin, 33 Murray Road, Wimbledon, LONDON, SW19 4PD.
MADGIN, Mr. Michael Guy, FCA *1972;* 33 Murray Road, LONDON, SW19 4PD.
MADGWICK, Mr. Derrick Lionel Edward Raymond, BSc FCA *1993;* 7 School Road, Hythe, SOUTHAMPTON, SO45 6BJ.
MADHANI, Mr. Bahadur Jafferali Lila, FCA *1974;* 424 Weldrick Road East, RICHMOND HILL L4B 2M5, ON, CANADA.
MADHANI, Mr. Sunil, BSc ACA *1993;* 5 Heron Place, Harefield, UXBRIDGE, UB9 6TA.
MADHOK, Mr. Aditya, MA BA ACA *2008;* Flat 110, Marlyn Lodge, Portsoken Street, LONDON, E1 8RB.
MADHOK, Mr. Sameer, ACA *1992;* 25 Woodthrush Court, TORONTO M2K 2A9, ON, CANADA.
MADHVANI, Miss. Chatu, MSc ACA *2003;* 1 Wades Grove, LONDON, N21 1BH.
MADHVANI, Miss. Nisha, BSc ACA *2009;* 10 Thistlecroft Gardens, STANMORE, MIDDLESEX, HA7 1PN.
MADIGAN, Mr. Alexander, BA ACA *2003;* 45 Whitethorn Road, STOURBRIDGE, WEST MIDLANDS, DY8 5XF.
MADIGAN, Mr. Philip, MMath ACA *2007;* 11 Poppy Field Drive, Penyffordd, CHESTER, CH4 0GE.
MADILL, Mr. Simon Hugh, BSc ACA ATII *1990;* Birch House, Carr Lane, Much Hoole, PRESTON, PR4 4TH.
•MADIN, Mrs. Margot Jane, BA FCA FRSA *1993;* with UHY Hacker Young, 22 The Ropewalk, NOTTINGHAM, NG1 5DT.
MADLANI, Miss. Anita Jayendra, ACA *2008;* 65 Meridian Place, LONDON, E14 9FF.
MADLANI, Mr. Rupesh Shirish, BSc(Hons) ACA *2002;* 35 Darenth Park Avenue, Dareth Village, DARTFORD, DA2 6JN.
MADLE, Mr. Alistair, BSc FCA *1992;* 221 Estado Way N.E, ST PETERSBURG, FL 33704, UNITED STATES.
•MADLEY, Mrs. Nicola, BSc ACA *1992;* Accountancy Help, 6 Kelston Place, Whitchurch, CARDIFF, CF14 2AP.
•MADON, Miss. Hutokshi Russy, BA ACA *1986;* Hutokshi Madon, 1 Bellamy Close, KNEBWORTH, SG3 6EH.
•MADON, Mr. Khurshed Russy, FCA *1977;* (Tax Fac), Madon & Co., 8th Floor, Tolworth Tower, Ewell Road, SURBITON, SURREY KT6 7EL.
MADON, Mr. Shavak Russy, FCA *1960;* 375 Poplar Drive, OAKVILLE L6J 4E3, ON, CANADA. (Life Member)
MADURAIVEERAN, Mr. Dhinesh, MEng ACA *2010;* Barclays Capital, 5 North Colonnade, LONDON, E14 4BB.
MADYIWA, Mr. Lawrence, ACA *2010;* with KPMG Channel Islands Limited, 20 New Street, St Peter Port, GUERNSEY, GY1 4AN.
MAEER, Mr. Geoffrey, FCA *1954;* Langhale Cottage, The Street, Seething, NORWICH, NR15 1AL. (Life Member)
MAEER, Mrs. Jane Elizabeth, BA FCA CTA *1989;* (Tax Fac), Appleby Mall, 86 Tettenhall Road, WOLVERHAMPTON, WV1 4TF.
•MAEER, Miss. Tracey Jane, BA ACA *1994;* (Tax Fac), Townends, 7-9 Cornmarket, PONTEFRACT, WF8 1AN.
MAER, Mr. Stephen Anthony, BA(Hons) ACA *2001;* 52 Eastern Road, SUTTON COLDFIELD, WEST MIDLANDS, B73 5NU.
MAERTENS, Mr. Henri Johannes, MSc FCA *1973;* Rue du Stand 18, CH-1898 ST-GINGOLPH, SWITZERLAND. (Life Member)
MAETING, Miss. Corina, BA ACA *2004;* 11 Swithland, Broughton, MILTON KEYNES, MK10 7BA.
MAFFEI, Mr. Paul Anthony, BSc ACA *1978;* 9 Walnut Close, WILMSLOW, SK9 2SA.
MAFFEY, Mr. Jonathan, MA ACA *2011;* The Ridings, East Cowton, NORTHALLERTON, NORTH YORKSHIRE, DL7 0DH.
MAFFI, Mr. Fabrizio Armando Vincenzo, BSc ACA *2000;* 4 Belvedere Close, WEYBRIDGE, SURREY, KT13 8XQ.
MAFFI, Mrs. Jean Helen Louise, BSc ACA *1999;* 4 Belvedere Close, WEYBRIDGE, SURREY, KT13 8XQ.
MAFFIN, Mr. Andrew Mark, LLB ACA *1986;* PO BOX 4046, LANE COVE, NSW 2066, AUSTRALIA.
MAFFIOLI, Mrs. Laura, BSc ACA *2007;* 29 Becket Gardens, WELWYN, HERTFORDSHIRE, AL6 9JE.
•MAGAGNIN, Miss. Amanda Louise, BA FCA ATII *1992;* (Tax Fac), Wilkins Kennedy, Bridge House, London Bridge, LONDON, SE1 9QR.
MAGAN, The Lord Magan of Castletown George Morgan, FCA *1969;* 9 Cambridge Place, Kensington, LONDON, W8 5PB.
MAGATTI, Miss. Teresa Veronica Anne, FCA *1984;* 89 Paynesfield Road, Tatsfield, WESTERHAM, TN16 2BQ.
MAGAURAN, Mr. Anthony Francis, MA FCA *1973;* Flat A, 7 Gloucester Street, LONDON, SW1V 2DB.
MAGDANI, Mr. Tirath, LLB FCA *2001;* 32 Adlington Road, Oadby, LEICESTER, LE2 4NA.
MAGECHA, Mr. Rishi, BSc ACA *2006;* 94 Malvern Avenue, HARROW, MIDDLESEX, HA2 9EX.
•MAGECHA, Mr. Sanjay Harilal, BA ACA *1999;* Maple Accounting & Taxation Services Limited, 10 Lulworth Close, HARROW, MIDDLESEX, HA2 9NR.
•MAGEE, Mr. Brendan Patrick Michael, MA FCA *1983;* James Magee, 34 Bower Mount Road, MAIDSTONE, ME16 8AU.
MAGEE, Mr. Dermot, BCom ACA *2004;* McAfee Ireland Ltd, Building 2000, City Gate, Mahon, CORK, COUNTY CORK IRELAND.
MAGEE, Mr. Donal James Hugh, BSc FCA *1980;* Kings Orchard, York Hill, LOUGHTON, IG10 1JA.
MAGEE, Mr. Edward, FCA *1965;* Brown Rigg, Sandy Bank, RIDING MILL, NE44 6HT. (Life Member)
MAGEE, Miss. Jacinta Catherine, MA(Hons) ACA *2002;* Andrew Brownsword Hotels Limited, 4 Queen Square, BATH, BA1 2HA.
MAGEE, Mrs. Katrina, BSc ACA *2006;* 79 Westfield Lane, South Milford, LEEDS, LS25 5AW.
•MAGEE, Mr. Laurence Frederick, FCA *1958;* Northwood Management Services, 40 Kewferry Road, NORTHWOOD, HA6 2PB.
MAGEE, Mr. Matthew, ACA *2009;* 1 Demesne Close, HOLYWOOD, COUNTY DOWN, BT18 9SF.
•MAGEE, Mr. Michael John, BA(Econ) ACA *2000;* PricewaterhouseCoopers LLP, Pricewaterhousecoopers, 12 Plumtree Court, LONDON, EC4A 4HT. See also PricewaterhouseCoopers
MAGEE, Mrs. Nathalie Lilian, BEng ACA *1996;* 254 Watford Road, ST. ALBANS, HERTFORDSHIRE, AL2 3DL.
MAGEE, Mr. Neil Joseph, FCA *1966;* 28 St. James Drive, Harrow Gate, HARROGATE, HG2 8HT.
MAGEE, Mr. Patrick Gerard, BA ACA *1989;* 68b Manse Road, Carryduff, BELFAST, BT8 8AE.
MAGEE, Mr. Sean Patrick Boyd, MA FCA *1969;* Byams House, Willesley, TETBURY, GLOUCESTERSHIRE, GL8 8QU.
MAGELL, Mr. Alexander Jonathan, BSc ACA *1996;* Dixcart Management Ltd, Le Grand Dixcart, Sark, GUERNSEY, GY9 0SD.
MAGER, Miss. Charlotte Barbara, BA ACA *1998;* 4 Deepdale Close, Friern Barnet, LONDON, N11 3FH.
MAGESVARAN, Mr. Mailvaganam, FCA *1972;* 47 Milton Avenue, BARNET, HERTFORDSHIRE, EN5 2EY.
MAGGS, Mr. Andrew Philip, BSc ACA *1997;* 8 Hill View, Spencers Wood, READING, RG7 1QB.
MAGGS, Mr. Brian Lawrence Philip, FCA *1972;* Unit 3, Northway Trading Estate Ashchurch, TEWKESBURY, GL20 8JP.
MAGGS, Mr. Erik Thomas, FCA *1969;* 45 Lyndhurst Drive, SEVENOAKS, TN13 2HG.
MAGGS, Miss. Juliet, BSc ACA *1988;* 15 Knaresborough Drive, Earlsfield, LONDON, SW18 4UT.
•MAGGS, Mr. Kenneth James, BA FCA *1995;* Moore Thompson, Bank House, Broad Street, SPALDING, LINCOLNSHIRE, PE11 1TB.
MAGGS, Mr. Peter William, BA ACA *1982;* Byeways, Blackheath, GUILDFORD, SURREY, GU4 8RD.
•MAGGS, Mr. Roger Philip, MA FCA *1974;* (Tax Fac), ST Hampden Limited, 85 Gracechurch Street, LONDON, EC3V 0AA.
MAGGS, Mr. Steven John, ACA *1995;* 2 Ford Lane, Emersons Green, BRISTOL, BS16 7DD.
MAGHDOORI, Mr. Ataollah Saeed, BSc ACA *1983;* 2 Grace Avenue, Shenley, RADLETT, HERTFORDSHIRE, WD7 9DN.
MAGILL, Mr. John Walter, FCA *1968;* Villa Chantoiseaux, 9 Chemin du Moulin, 06650 OPIO, FRANCE. (Life Member)
MAGILL, Mr. Michael Peter, FCA *1995;* 46 Falcon Drive, Hartford, HUNTINGDON, PE29 1LP.
MAGILTON, Miss. Helen, BSc ACA *1997;* 75 Lonsdale Road, BIRMINGHAM, B17 9QX.
•MAGINNIS, Mr. Robert, BA FCA *1978;* (Tax Fac), 24 Broad Street, SALFORD, M6 5BY.
MAGNAY, Mr. Michael John, BA ACA *2005;* 18 Knutsford Road, ALDERLEY EDGE, CHESHIRE, SK9 7SD.
MAGNER, Mr. Kevin Gerard, MBA FCA *1992;* with Deloitte LLP, Athene Place, 66 Shoe Lane, LONDON, EC4A 3BQ.
MAGNESS, Mr. David James, BA ACA *1997;* 2 Aubrey Road, LONDON, N8 9HH.
MAGNESS, Miss. Ella Victoria, ACA *2008;* 'Eatons', 43 Muster Green, HAYWARDS HEATH, WEST SUSSEX, RH16 4AJ.
MAGNESS, Mr. George Eric, FCA *1939;* Albury House, 4 Albury Road, GUILDFORD, GU1 2BT. (Life Member)
MAGNESS, Mr. James, BSc ACA *2004;* Flat 3 Burrage Court, Worgan Street, LONDON, SE16 7WA.
MAGNESS, Mr. Peter Richard, FCA *1973;* Eatons, 43 Muster Green, HAYWARDS HEATH, RH16 4AJ.
MAGNIEN, Mr. Jean-Philippe, ACA *2010;* 39 rue Maréchal Foch, 71200 LE CREUSOT, FRANCE.
MAGNOTTA, Mr. Gino, ACA CA(AUS) *2010;* Ground Floor Flat, 2 Miranda Road, LONDON, N19 3RB.
•MAGNUS, Mr. Stuart Irving, FCA *1974;* Newton Magnus Ltd, Arrowsmith Court, Station Approach, BROADSTONE, BH18 8AT. See also Newton Magnus & Co
MAGNUSON, Mr. David Albert Johan, BSc ACA *1997;* 30 Fairborne Way, GUILDFORD, GU2 9GB.
MAGO, Miss. Aakriti, ACA *2011;* PO Box 61035, Jebel Ali, DUBAI, UNITED ARAB EMIRATES.
MAGOOKIN, Miss. Cheryl, BA ACA *2003;* Caterpillar, Old Glenarm Road, LARNE, COUNTY ANTRIM, BT40 1EJ.
MAGOR, Miss. Bruna Harumi, BA ACA *2006;* Flat 9, 14 Manor Road, LONDON, N16 5SA.
MAGOR, Mr. Philip, BSc ACA *1982;* Stype Grange, HUNGERFORD, RG17 0RQ.
MAGOWAN, Mr. Andrew Ian, BA ACA *2006;* Flat 219 Goulden House, Bullen Street, LONDON, SW11 3HQ.
MAGRATH, Mr. Duncan Jonathan, MA FCA *1990;* Balfour Beatty Ltd, 130 Wilton Road, LONDON, SW1V 1LQ.
MAGRATH, Mr. James Michael Gason, MA ACA CTA *1997;* with Ernst & Young LLP, 1 More London Place, LONDON, SE1 2AF.
•MAGRATH, Mr. Mark Robert George, LLB FCA *1984;* (Tax Fac), Harrisons, 4 Brackley Close, South East Sector, Bournemouth International Airport, CHRISTCHURCH, DORSET BH23 6SE. See also Dorset Business Services Ltd
MAGRATH, Miss. Tina, BA ACA *2005;* 62 Cerne Road, GRAVESEND, DA12 4BP.
MAGRAW, Mr. James Edmund Grenville, MA ACA *1988;* Dudley House, Abbey Hill, KENILWORTH, WARWICKSHIRE, CV8 1LU.
MAGRI, Miss. Anna, ACA *2008;* Maersk Company Limited, Stockbridge House, Trinity Gardens, NEWCASTLE UPON TYNE, NE1 2HJ.
MAGRIS, Miss. Sonia, BA ACA *1993;* 20 Summerlands Avenue, Acton, LONDON, W3 6ER.
MAGSON, Mr. Andrew, BSc FCA *1992;* The Alumasc Group Plc, Station Road, Burton Latimer, KETTERING, NORTHAMPTONSHIRE, NN15 5JP.
•MAGSON, Mrs. Julie Yvonne, BSc ACA *1993;* Sutton Bassett House, 22 Main Street, Sutton Bassett, MARKET HARBOROUGH, LEICESTERSHIRE, LE16 8HP.
MAGSON, Mr. Nicholas John, FCA *1962;* Poplar House, Claxton, YORK, YO60 7SD.
MAGSON, Mr. Robert Thomas, MA FCA *1973;* 15 West Way, CLEVEDON, BS21 7XN.
•MAGUIRE, Mrs. Alison, BSc ACA *2003;* Alison Maquire, 10 Clovelly Avenue, WARLINGHAM, SURREY, CR6 9HZ.
MAGUIRE, Mrs. Cecilia Yuen Han, BSc FCA *1993;* Flat 9, Peak Gardens, 18 Mount Austin Road, THE PEAK, HONG KONG SAR.
MAGUIRE, Mr. David Frank, FCA *1974;* Sunny Bank, Sibford Ferris, BANBURY, OXFORDSHIRE, OX15 5RG.
MAGUIRE, Mrs. Deborah, BSc ACA *1992;* 3 Grays Lane, HITCHIN, HERTFORDSHIRE, SG5 2HD.
MAGUIRE, Mr. Geoffrey, BA(Econ) ACA *1999;* 15 Chevening Road, LONDON, SE10 0LB.
MAGUIRE, Ms. Harriet Rose, BSc(Hons) ACA *2010;* 125 Cotham Brow, BRISTOL, BS6 6AS.
•MAGUIRE, Mrs. Hilary Grace, FCA *1981;* Hilary Maguire Ltd, Sunny Bank, Sibford Ferris, BANBURY, OXFORDSHIRE, OX15 5RG.
MAGUIRE, Mr. John Kevin, BSc ACA *1982;* Flat 4, 24 Carlisle Road, EASTBOURNE, BN20 7EN.
MAGUIRE, Mr. John Michael, BA ACA *1984;* Europe Steel Ltd, 4 Curzon Square, LONDON, W1J 7FW.
MAGUIRE, Mr. John Noel, BSc ACA *1991;* Silver Birch Sandy Lane, Ivy Hatch, SEVENOAKS, TN15 0PB.
•MAGUIRE, Mrs. Josephine Patricia, BA ACA *1991;* with PricewaterhouseCoopers LLP, Benson House, 33 Wellington Street, LEEDS, LS1 4JP.
MAGUIRE, Mr. Joshua, MEng ACA *2011;* Flat 1, 88 Greencroft Gardens, South Hampstead, LONDON, NW6 3JQ.
•MAGUIRE, Mrs. Karen Anne, LLB ACA *1995;* with KPMG LLP, 3 Assembly Square, Britannia Quay, CARDIFF, CF10 4AX.
MAGUIRE, Mr. Kieran Matthieu James, BA ACA *1988;* 44 Abingdon Road, Bramhall, STOCKPORT, SK7 3HA.
•MAGUIRE, Mr. Martin Patrick, FCA *1980;* (Tax Fac), HWS, 1st Floor St Giles Hse, 15-21 Victoria Road, Bletchley, MILTON KEYNES, BUCKINGHAMSHIRE MK2 2NG.
MAGUIRE, Mr. Peter Damian, BSc(Hons) ACA *2001;* 9a Kings Road, Bramhope, LEEDS, LS16 9JW.
MAGUIRE, Mr. Peter Dominic, ACA *1979;* 9 Seafield Road, LYTHAM ST.ANNES, FY8 5PY.
MAGUIRE, Mr. Terence John, ACA *1981;* Flat 2, 17 Cambridge Park, TWICKENHAM, TW1 2JE.
MAGUIRE, Mr. Vivian James, BA FCA *1976;* North Ridge, South Bank, WESTERHAM, TN16 1EN.
MAGUIRE, Mr. William Paul, MA ACA *1984;* National Trust, Kemble Drive, SWINDON, SN2 2NA.
MAH, Mr. Kim, FCA *1974;* 2 Jln. Burhanuddin Helmi, Taman Tun Dr Ismail, 60000 KUALA LUMPUR, FEDERAL TERRITORY, MALAYSIA.
MAH, Mr. Leslie Kim Loong, FCA *1970;* 5 Jalan Senandong, SINGAPORE 288757, SINGAPORE.
MAH, Mr. Siew Khoon, BSc ACA *1995;* 33-10-7 Sri Penaga, Jalan Medang Serai, Bukit Bandaraya Bangsar, 59100 KUALA LUMPUR, FEDERAL TERRITORY, MALAYSIA.
MAH, Mr. Siew Whye David, BSc ACA *1988;* 8 Lorong Taman Pantai 1, Off Jalan Taman Pantai, 59100 KUALA LUMPUR, FEDERAL TERRITORY, MALAYSIA.
MAHABEER, Mr. Rajesh, ACA FCCA FCMA CIA *2010;* 1 The Reeds, 55 Glen Road, Bramley Park, SANDTON, 2090, SOUTH AFRICA.
•MAHABIR-SINGH, Mr. Mohan, BSc FCA *1991;* (Tax Fac), MMS, 11 Lower Hillside Street, SAN FERNANDO, TRINIDAD AND TOBAGO.
MAHACHI, Miss. Norah, ACA *2010;* 71 Rochester Avenue, BROMLEY, BR1 3DN.
•MAHADEA, Mr. Ganeshan, BSc(Hons) ACA *2004;* with Jacksons Accountants (Midlands) Limited, Deansfield House, 98 Lancaster Road, NEWCASTLE, STAFFORDSHIRE, ST5 1DS.
•MAHADEO, Mr. Hemraj, BA FCA *1985;* (Tax Fac), Hem Mahadeo Limited, 47 Hazelgrove Road, HAYWARDS HEATH, WEST SUSSEX, RH16 3PH.
MAHADEVA, Mr. Danesh, ACA *2008;* 109 Blenheim Park Road, SOUTH CROYDON, SURREY, CR2 6BL.
MAHADEVA, Mr. Muttiah, BSc FCA *1963;* 39 Baltic Avenue, TORONTO M4J 1S1, ON, CANADA. (Life Member)
MAHADZIR, Miss. Ezrina, BSc ACA *2005;* 10-3 Seri Duta 2 Condominiums, Jalan Langgak Duta, Taman Duta, 50480 KUALA LUMPUR, FEDERAL TERRITORY, MALAYSIA.
MAHAJAN, Mr. Manmohan Krishan, BSc FCA *1975;* Mahajan & Aibara, 1 Chawla House, 62 Wodehouse Road Colaba, MUMBAI 400 005, INDIA. See also Mahajan & Aibara Associates
MAHAJAN, Mr. Sandip, LLB ACA *1999;* 1 Bullers Wood Drive, CHISLEHURST, BR7 5LS.

MAHAJAN, Mr. Yash Paul, FCA *1963;* SML ISUZU LIMITED, 204-205 SECTOR 34-A, CHANDIGARH 160135, INDIA.
MAHAL, Mr. Amandeep, ACA *2008;* Henderson Global Investors, 201 Bishopsgate, LONDON, EC2M 3AE.
MAHAL, Ms. Kiranjit, BSc ACA *2001;* 16 The Spinney, BEACONSFIELD, BUCKINGHAMSHIRE, HP9 1SB.
MAHAL, Mr. Manjit Singh, BA ACA *1999;* 22 Blaydon Avenue, SUTTON COLDFIELD, WEST MIDLANDS, B75 5TE.
MAHALINGAM, Mr. Janardhan, MSc BA ACA *1992;* 78 Sheaveshill Avenue, LONDON, NW9 6RX.
•**MAHALINGHAM, Mr. Sivahar, BSc(Econ) ACA CTA** *2002;* with Alvarez & Marsal - London Office, First Floor, One Finsbury Circus, LONDON, EC2M 7EB.
•**MAHALLATI-KAZEMEINI, Mr. Abdol-Majid, FCA** *1978;* (Tax Fac), A.M. Mahallati & Co, 15 Second Street, Miremad Ave, Motahari, TEHRAN, IRAN.
•**MAHAMADI, Mr. Ali Adil, FCA** *1978;* Sarmad Global Accountancy Services Ltd, 115 London Road, MORDEN, SURREY, SM4 5HP.
MAHANTY, Miss. Lisa, ACA *2008;* Flat B, 62 Leswin Road, LONDON, N16 7NH.
MAHAPATRA, Mr. Diptimay, FCA MBCS MBA FCMC *1972;* Flat 28 Furnace House, Walton Well Road, OXFORD, OX2 6GF.
MAHAPATRA, Mr. Piyush Kumar, BSc ACA *1999;* Gloucester Park 3rd Floor, 95 Cromwell Road, LONDON, SW7 4DL.
•**MAHAPATRA, Mr. Timothy Martin, BCom FCA** *1990;* Deloitte LLP, Athene Place, 66 Shoe Lane, LONDON, EC4A 3BQ. See also Deloitte & Touche LLP
MAHARAHAJE, Mr. Novan Panday, ACA *2008;* PricewaterhouseCoopers, 3rd Floor, 18 Cybercity, EBENE, MAURITIUS.
MAHARAJ, Miss. Shivana, MSc BSc DIC ACA *2011;* 43 Park Steps, St. Georges Fields, LONDON, W2 2YQ.
MAHDI, Mr. Hasan, FCA *1975;* 8 Arundel Road, KINGSTON-UPON-THAMES, KT1 3RZ. (Life Member)
MAHDY, Mr. Habibollah, BSc FCA *1977;* 33 Sir Williams Lane, ETOBICOKE M9A 1T9, ON, CANADA.
•**MAHE, Mr. Martyn, FCA FCCA** *1980;* Chandler Backer & Co., PO Box 63, Unit 3, Houmet House, Rue Des Houmets, Castel GUERNSEY GY1 4BH.
MAHENDRA, Mr. Murugendra, BSc ACA *1992;* 9 Wellesley Road, LONDON, W4 4BS.
MAHENDRAN, Miss. Janani, BSc ACA *1994;* 28a Dene Road, NORTHWOOD, MIDDLESEX, HA6 2BT.
MAHENDRAN, Miss. Roopa, ACA ACCA *2000;* 55b Saltram Crescent, Maida Hill, LONDON, W9 3JS.
MAHENTHIRAN, Mr. Manoj Chandra, BSc ACA *1999;* PricewaterhouseCoopers, 1 North Wacker Drive, CHICAGO, IL 60606, UNITED STATES.
MAHER, Miss. Bernadette Mary, BSc ACA *2007;* 88 Hailsham Avenue, LONDON, SW2 3AH.
MAHER, Mr. Brian Gerrard, BA ACA *1994;* 12 Tasman Drive, SHELL COVE, NSW 2529, AUSTRALIA.
MAHER, Mr. Damian, BSc ACA *1992;* 55 Southwood Park, Southwood Lawn Road, LONDON, N6 5SQ.
MAHER, Ms. Deirdre Anne, BBS ACA *2002;* 32 Ivy Wood, Ballinderry Big, KILBEGGAN, COUNTY WESTMEATH, IRELAND.
MAHER, Mrs. Diana Barbara, BSc ACA *2005;* BP plc, Chertsey Road, SUNBURY-ON-THAMES, TW16 7LN.
MAHER, Mr. Ehsanullah, FCA *1977;* 3 Biton Close, Harborne, BIRMINGHAM, B17 0AL.
MAHER, Mr. James Paul, BSc ACA *2006;* with Anglo American plc, Anglo American House, 20 Carlton House Terrace, LONDON, SW1Y 5AN.
MAHER, Miss. Janina, BA FCA *1985;* 5 Hampden Road, Caversham, READING, RG4 5ED.
MAHER, Miss. Jaya, BA ACA *1990;* 27 Mickleton Drive, LEICESTER, LE5 6GE.
MAHER, Ms. Martina, BCL ACA *1992;* 21 Ramleh Park, Milltown, DUBLIN 6, COUNTY DUBLIN, IRELAND.
MAHER, Mrs. Maureen, BA ACA *1993;* The Old Barn, Hartswood Farm Barns, Slipshatch Road, REIGATE, SURREY, RH2 8HD.
MAHER, Mr. Michael John, BSc ACA *1995;* Cae Mynydd, Pentre, Minera, WREXHAM, CLWYD, LL11 3DP.
MAHER, Mr. Patrick Joseph, LLB ACA *2004;* 8 Warelands, BURGESS HILL, WEST SUSSEX, RH15 9QD.
MAHER, Mr. Patrick Joseph, ACA *1995; (ACA Ireland 1990);* Deloitte LLP, Athene Place, 66 Shoe Lane, LONDON, EC4A 3BQ. See also Deloitte & Touche LLP
•**MAHER, Mr. Paul William, FCA** *1974;* Paul W. Maher & Co., Oakley House, 46 Old Pound Close, Lytchett Matravers, POOLE, DORSET BH16 6BW.
MAHER, Mr. Peter Francis, FCA *1963;* 5 Frinton Close, SALE, M33 4ES.
•**MAHER, Mr. Peter Francis, BSc ACA** *1989;* Deloitte LLP, Athene Place, 66 Shoe Lane, LONDON, EC4A 3BQ. See also Deloitte & Touche LLP
MAHER, Mr. Raymond Vincent, BA ACA *1992;* The Olde Oak, Maurys Lane, West Wellow, ROMSEY, HAMPSHIRE, SO51 6DB.
MAHER, Mr. Stephen Peter, MEng ACA CFA *2002;* La Falaise Le Hameau Des Ecorvees, La Ruette Des Ecorvees St. Saviour, JERSEY, JE2 7BR.
•**MAHER, Mr. Timothy Vincent, BA(Hons) FCA** *1989;* 38 Jenny Lane, Woodford, STOCKPORT, CHESHIRE, SK7 1PE.
MAHERALI, Mr. Mohamed Gulamhusein, FCA *1974;* P.O. Box 52635, RIYADH, 11573, SAUDI ARABIA.
MAHESH, Mr. Krishnadat, FCA *1974;* 22 Dunvegan Drive, RICHMOND HILL L4C 6K1, ON, CANADA.
MAHI, Miss. Sangeeta, ACA *2008;* Sark Ridge, 17 Howards Thicket, GERRARDS CROSS, BUCKINGHAMSHIRE, SL9 7NT.
MAHIDHARIA, Mrs. Bhakti, ACA *2008;* 21 Manor Way, CHESHAM, BUCKINGHAMSHIRE, HP5 3BH.
MAHINDRA, Mr. Ashok Kumar, MA FCA *1968;* B-65 Greater Kailash I, NEW DELHI 110048, DELHI, INDIA.
•**MAHINDROO, Mr. Yura, ACA CA(AUS)** *2011;* 21c Eckstein Road, Battersea, LONDON, sw11 1qe.
MAHLOW, Miss. Jana, ACA *2010;* 26 Lindsay Road, MANCHESTER, M19 2JG.
MAHMOOD, Mr. Ansar, BA(Hons) ACA *2002;* with Harold Sharp, Holland House, 1-5 Oakfield, SALE, M33 6TT.
•**MAHMOOD, Mr. Babar, BA(Hons) ACA** *2001;* Bay Accountants Ltd, 215 Bacchus Road, BIRMINGHAM, B18 4RE. See also Yasbar Services Limited
MAHMOOD, Miss. Farrah, BSc ACA *2009;* Flat 7, 2a Mulgrave Road, CROYDON, CR0 1BL.
MAHMOOD, Mr. Fazal, FCA *1984;* Fazal Mahmood & Company, 147 Shadman Colony 1, LAHORE 54000, PAKISTAN.
MAHMOOD, Mr. Haroon, BSc ACA *2010;* 22 Twyford Road, BIRMINGHAM, B8 2NJ.
MAHMOOD, Miss. Mariam Syed, ACA *2008;* 2nd Floor, Thomson Reuters Ltd Aldgate House, 33 Aldgate High Street, LONDON, EC3N 1DL.
MAHMOOD, Mr. Mazhar, ACA *2010;* 5 Grantham Place, BRADFORD, WEST YORKSHIRE, BD7 1RJ.
MAHMOOD, Mrs. Muznah Iffet, MEng ACA *2001;* 58 Ditton Road, SURBITON, SURREY, KT6 6RB.
MAHMOOD, Mr. Nasir, MSc FCA *1979;* C/O Chairman's Office, Al Futtaim Private LLC, P.O.Box 152, DUBAI, UNITED ARAB EMIRATES.
•**MAHMOOD, Mr. Omar, EMBA BSc(Hons) ACA** *2003;* KPMG Fakhro, 5th Floor, Chamber of Commerce Building, P O Box 710, MANAMA, BAHRAIN.
MAHMOOD, Mr. Rehan, ACA *2009;* Flat 4 Heron Court, 53 Alexandra Road, EPSOM, KT17 4HU.
MAHMOOD, Mr. Syed Shahid, FCA *1978;* 43a Kenton Road, Kenton, HARROW, HA3 0AD.
MAHMOOD MUSTAFA, Mr. Saqib, ACA FCCA *2010;* c/o Ithmaar Bank, 4th floor Seef Tower, Al Seef District, P.O. Box 2820, MANAMA, BAHRAIN.
MAHMUD, Mr. Arshad, ACA *1981;* Restharrow, 27 Adlington Road, WILMSLOW, SK9 2BJ.
MAHMUD, Mr. Arshad, FCA *1965;* House 15A1, Street 30, F811, ISLAMABAD, PAKISTAN. (Life Member)
MAHMUD, Mr. Khalid, FCA *1974;* C-159, Clifton Block 2, KARACHI 75300, PAKISTAN.
•**MAHMUD, Mr. Nasir, FCA** *1973;* (Tax Fac), Nasir Mahmud, Falcon House, 257 Burlington Road, NEW MALDEN, KT3 4NE.
MAHOMED, Mr. Ashraf, BSc ACA *1994;* 373 Humberstone Road, LEICESTER, LE5 3DF.
MAHOMED, Mr. Ebrahim, BSc ACA *1994;* PO Box 66246, Kopje, HARARE, ZIMBABWE.
MAHOMED, Miss. Fathima, ACA *2008;* 5 Ditton Road, SURBITON, KT6 6RE.
MAHOMED, Mr. Hassam Habib, ACA *1995;* P.O. Box BE613, Belvedere, HARARE, ZIMBABWE.
MAHOMED, Mr. Shabbir Salim, FCA *1975;* Polypropylene Products Limited, 7th Floor Trade Centre, II Chundrigar Road, KARACHI 74200, PAKISTAN.
•**MAHOMED, Mrs. Shamim, BA ACA** *1990;* (Tax Fac), SKM Accountants (North West) Ltd, Pegasus House, 5 Winckley Court, Mount Street, PRESTON, PR1 8BU.
•**MAHON, Mr. Andrew Philip, BSc ACA** *1983;* (Tax Fac), A. Phillips & Co., Wilsons Park, Monsall Road, Newton Heath, MANCHESTER, M40 8WN.
MAHON, Miss. Fiona, BCom ACA *1997;* 8 Caldragh Crescent, CARRICK-ON-SHANNON, COUNTY LEITRIM, IRELAND.
•**MAHON, Mr. John Macmahon, FCA** *1966;* (Tax Fac), Mahon & Co Ltd, Marston House, Priors Marston, SOUTHAM, WARWICKSHIRE, CV47 7RP. See also Mahon & Co
MAHON, Miss. Michaela Louise, ACA *1996;* 60 Lansdowne Road, Sundridge Park, BROMLEY, BR1 3PQ.
MAHON, Mr. Sean Patrick Lauritson, FCA *1969;* 41 Stumperlowe Crescent Road, Fulwood, SHEFFIELD, S10 3PR.
MAHONEY, Mrs. Alice Sarah, LLB ACA *2003;* 26-28 Southernhay East, EXETER, EX1 1NS.
MAHONEY, Ms. Amanda Jane, BSc(Hons) ACA *2002;* PO Box 1093, Boundary Hall, Cricket Square, GEORGETOWN, KY1-1102, CAYMAN ISLANDS.
MAHONEY, Mr. Anthony Alan, BSc FCA *1973;* 21a Ashfield Road, CHEADLE, CHESHIRE, SK8 1BB. (Life Member)
•**MAHONEY, Mr. Anthony Gerard, BA ACA CTA** *1982;* (Tax Fac), Sayers Butterworth LLP, 3rd Floor, 12 Gough Square, LONDON, EC4A 3DW.
MAHONEY, Mr. Barry Joseph, BA ACA *1981;* 10 Wentworth Way, Stoke Bruerne, TOWCESTER, NN12 7SA.
MAHONEY, Mr. Colin Gordon, FCA *1963;* 41 Glebelands Avenue, Newbury Park, ILFORD, IG2 7DL. (Life Member)
MAHONEY, Mrs. Fiona Claire Needham, BSc ACA *2005;* 8 Wellfield, Lewes Road, EAST GRINSTEAD, RH19 3SX.
MAHONEY, Ms. Francesca Maria, ACA DChA *1982;* Museum of London, 150 London Wall, LONDON, EC2Y 5HN.
MAHONEY, Mr. James Robert, BA ACA *2004;* with Ernst & Young, 680 George Street, SYDNEY, NSW 2000, AUSTRALIA.
MAHONEY, Mr. John Francis, FCA *1969;* 6 Apple Grove, ReynoldstonGower, SWANSEA, SA3 1BZ.
MAHONEY, Miss. Lisa Jane, BCom ACA *1996;* 26a Beech Hill Road, SUTTON COLDFIELD, B72 1DT.
MAHONEY, Mr. Mark Albert, ACA *1985;* Keepers Cottage, Forest Farm, Pembury Road, TONBRIDGE, KENT, TN11 0ND.
MAHONEY, Mr. Michael Peter, ACA *1983;* 56 Woodland St, Balgowlah Heights, SYDNEY, NSW 2093, AUSTRALIA.
•**MAHONEY, Mr. Nicholas Paul, ACA FCCA** *2010;* Sullivans Associates Limited, 14 Gelliwastad Road, PONTYPRIDD, MID GLAMORGAN, CF37 2BW.
MAHONEY, Mr. Paul, BSc ACA *2009;* Flat A, 12 Ulverstone Road, LONDON, SE27 0AJ.
MAHONEY, Mr. Paul Benedict, BSc ACA *1992;* Lanna III Condo, 57/1 Huay Kaew Road, CHIANG MAI 50300, THAILAND.
MAHONEY, Mr. Peter James, BSc ACA *1991;* Yew Tree House, 78 Norwich Road, Stoke Holy Cross, NORWICH, NR14 8NZ.
MAHONEY, Mr. Ryan, BSc ACA *2007;* 1 Durban Road, BECKENHAM, BR3 4EY.
MAHONEY, Mr. Steve Alexander, BSc ACA *1996;* 118 Acorn Avenue, Giltbrook, NOTTINGHAM, NG16 2WJ.
MAHONEY, Mr. Tristan, BA ACA *2005;* Flat 216, Compass House, Riverside West, Smugglers Way, Wandsworth, LONDON SW18 1DQ.
MAHONEY, Mr. Vincent Joseph, BA FCA *1976;* 121 Glennbrook Court, CHALFONT, PA 18914, UNITED STATES.
MAHONY, Mr. Michael David, BCom FCA *1969;* Box 2-10 Seawright, HORNBY ISLAND V0R 1Z0, BC, CANADA. (Life Member)
MAHONY, Mr. Michael Shaun, MA ACA *1979;* Jacobi Carbons Croft Court E12, Walter Leigh Way Moss Industrial Estate, LEIGH, WN7 3PT.
MAHOOD, Mrs. Clare, ACA ACCA CTA *2007;* K P M G, PO Box 93, Douglas, ISLE OF MAN, IM99 1HN.
MAHROOF, Miss. Fathima, MSc BSc ACA *2005;* 16 Dale Avenue, HOUNSLOW, TW4 7ER.
MAHRRA, Miss. Susanna Devi, BSc ACA *1998;* Flat B, 3 Albert Terrace, LONDON, NW1 7SU.
MAIDEN, Mr. Clive Peter, BA ACA *1990;* 35 Townsend Drive, ST. ALBANS, HERTFORDSHIRE, AL3 5RF.
MAIDEN, Mr. Nicholas Anthony, BSc(Hons) ACA *2001;* 12 David Street, CONCORD, NSW 2137, AUSTRALIA.
•**MAIDEN, Mr. Steven, ACA** *1996;* Maiden Accountancy Services, 22A Cornfield Road, EASTBOURNE, EAST SUSSEX, BN21 4QE.
MAIDENS, Mrs. Sarah-Jane, LLB ACA *1990;* Meteora Partners Llp, Mutual House, 70 Conduit Street, LONDON, W1S 2GF.
MAIDENS, Mr. William Henry John, BSc ACA *1986;* Magham Down Farm, Magham Down, HAILSHAM, BN27 1PR.
MAIDMENT, Mr. Alan Tom, FCA *1964;* The Old Granary, Water Stratford Road, Finmere, BUCKINGHAM, MK18 4AT.
MAIDMENT, Miss. Alice, BA ACA *1997;* 8 Ludlow Way, LONDON, N2 0LA.
MAIDMENT, Mr. Bruce William, MA ACA *1984;* (Tax Fac), 15 Eastview Road, Wargrave, READING, RG10 8BH.
•**MAIDMENT, Mr. Christopher John, BA ACA** *1981;* PricewaterhouseCoopers LLP, First Point, Buckingham Gate, London Gatwick Airport, GATWICK, WEST SUSSEX RH6 0NT. See also PricewaterhouseCoopers
MAIDMENT, Miss. Kirsty, BSc ACA *2007;* Flat 5 Newhaven Court, 189 Willesden Lane, LONDON, NW6 7YN.
MAIDMENT, Mrs. Mary Elizabeth, BSc ACA *1992;* Witts End, Westport, LANGPORT, TA10 0BN.
•**MAIDMENT, Mr. Stephen Robert, BA ACA** *1998;* ACM Accounting Services, 12 Ashbarn Crescent, WINCHESTER, HAMPSHIRE, SO22 4LW.
MAIDSTONE, Mr. Andrew John, BA FCA *1990;* (Tax Fac), Charnwood Accountants & Business Advisors The Point, Granite Way Mountsorrel, LOUGHBOROUGH, LE12 7TZ.
MAIER, Mr. Michael, BA ACA *1982;* 4a Granville Road, Birkdale, SOUTHPORT, MERSEYSIDE, PR8 2HU.
MAILE, Mr. Geoffrey Austin, FCA *1969;* G.A. Maile, 7333 L & A Road, VERNON V1B 3S6, BC, CANADA.
MAILE, Mr. Jonathan Brian, BSc(Hons) ACA *2002;* with Grant Thornton UK LLP, The Explorer Building, Fleming Way, Manor Royal, CRAWLEY, WEST SUSSEX RH10 9GT.
MAILE, Mrs. Nicola, BSocSc ACA *2001;* 18 Saracen Drive, Balsall Common, COVENTRY, CV7 7UA.
MAILE, Mr. Nigel Kingsley, ACA *1982;* Greenacres, 59 Links Lane, ROWLAND'S CASTLE, PO9 6AF.
MAILE, Mrs. Wan Tina, BA ACA *1986;* Silver Leys, 20 The Willows, Chesham Bois, AMERSHAM, HP6 5NT.
•**MAILER, Mr. Andrew George, BA FCA** *1992;* Meadowbank, 93 Bryn Twr, ABERGELE, LL22 8DD.
•**MAILICH, Mr. Dion Perry, ACA CA(SA)** *2009;* Dion Mailich & Co, 2 Tynedale, London Colney, ST. ALBANS, HERTFORDSHIRE, AL2 1TF.
MAIN, Mr. Alistair William, ACA *2008;* 16 Avignon Road, SPALDING, LINCOLNSHIRE, PE11 1HW.
MAIN, Mr. Anthony Brian Anidjar, BA ACA *1994;* 23 Calverley Park, TUNBRIDGE WELLS, KENT, TN1 2SL.
MAIN, Mr. Anthony Frederick, FCA *1966;* Sanderson Financial Consultancy, Soane Point 6 Market Place, READING, RG1 2EG.
MAIN, Mr. Anthony Hervey, FCA *1966;* Lion Rock, Broad Haven, HAVERFORDWEST, SA62 3JP. (Life Member)
•**MAIN, Mr. Brian, MA ACA** *1990;* Johnston Carmichael, Bishops Court, 29 Albyn Place, ABERDEEN, AB10 1YL.
MAIN, Ms. Charity Eva Mary, BA ACA *1997;* 35 Brookfield Road, Sawston, CAMBRIDGE, CB22 3EH.
•**MAIN, Mr. David Gordon, ACA FCCA CF** *2008;* Hazlewoods LLP, Windsor House, Barnett Way, Barnwood, GLOUCESTER, GL4 3RT.
MAIN, Mr. David Robert, BSc(Hons) ACA *2001;* 56 Airedale Avenue, LONDON, W4 2NW.
MAIN, Mrs. Devlina, BSc ACA ATII *1993;* Lanteglos House, St. Thomas Street, WELLS, SOMERSET, BA5 2UZ.
MAIN, Mrs. Glynis Ceridwen, BA ACA *1981;* Flat 49 Faraday House, 30 Blandford Street, LONDON, W1U 4BY.
MAIN, Mr. Kenneth Michael Anidjar, BEng ACA *2001;* 92 Pinewood Avenue, CROWTHORNE, BERKSHIRE, RG45 6RG.
•**MAIN, Mrs. Linda Jane, BSc ACA** *1988;* KPMG LLP, 15 Canada Square, LONDON, E14 5GL. See also KPMG Europe LLP
MAIN, Miss. Louise, ACA FCCA *2011;* 11 Mill Road, Mile End, COLCHESTER, CO4 5LD.
MAIN, Mr. Michael Forbes, FCA *1970;* Hill House, Northfield Place, WEYBRIDGE, SURREY, KT13 0RF. (Life Member)
MAIN, Mr. Michael John, FCA *1966;* 16 Fishery Rd, Boxmoor, HEMEL HEMPSTEAD, HP1 1NB.
•**MAIN, Mr. Nicholas Frederick, BSc FCA** *1979;* with Deloitte LLP, 2 New Street Square, LONDON, EC4A 3BZ.
MAIN, Mr. Peter Robert, FCA *1956;* 35 Woodlands Park, LEIGH-ON-SEA, SS9 3TP. (Life Member)

•MAIN, Mr. Thomas Alan, BSc ACA *2004;* Tom Main, Mill Cottage, Upper Neatham Mill Lane, Holybourne, ALTON, HAMPSHIRE GU34 4EP.
MAIN, Mr. Timothy Alexander Morgan, ACA *2010;* 13 Islington Park Mews, LONDON, N1 1QL.
MAIN, Mrs. Valerie Marina, ACA *2000;* 40 Camberwell Circuit, ROBINA, QLD 4226, AUSTRALIA.
MAINE, Mr. Andrew Steven, BSc ACA *2006;* British Sky Broadcasting Ltd, 7 Centaurs Business Centre Grant Way, ISLEWORTH, MIDDLESEX, TW7 5QD.
MAINE, Mr. Iain Russell, BA ACA *1986;* 5/252 Willoughby Road, NAREMBURN, NSW 2065, AUSTRALIA.
MAINEE, Mr. Shivaji Tony, BSc ACA *1988;* 1 Winterhill Way, GUILDFORD, GU4 7JX.
MAINEY, Mrs. Julie Elizabeth, BSc ACA *1993;* Chellaston School Swarkestone Road, Chellaston, DERBY, DE73 5UB.
MAINGOT, Mr. Richard Stephen, MA(Cantab) FCA MBA CIA *1995;* Brookfield Brasil Ltda., Rua Lauro Muller 116/21 Andar, Botafogo, RIO DE JANEIRO, 22.290-160, BRAZIL.
MAINI, Mr. Baway, BSocSc ACA *1993;* 19 Astor Road, SUTTON COLDFIELD, B74 3EX.
•MAINI, Mr. Bhooshan, BA FCA *1985;* Goldwyns Limited, Rutland House, 90-92 Baxter Avenue, SOUTHEND-ON-SEA, SS2 6HZ.
MAINI, Mr. Dhanush Vir, BA ACA *1994;* Flat 1, 22 Cliveden Place, Belgravia, LONDON, SW1W 8HD.
MAINPRIZE, Mr. Patrick James, BSc FCA *1989;* Kingfisher House, Amethyst Lane, Eastrington, GOOLE, NORTH HUMBERSIDE, DN14 7PS.
MAINS, Mr. Christopher Robert, FCA *1968;* 22 Southport Street, Apartment 335, TORONTO M6S 4Y9, ON, CANADA.
MAINSTONE, Mr. Timothy Paul, BA ACA *1999;* Insisys Ltd, The Aztec Centre, Aztec West, BRISTOL, BS32 4TD.
MAINWARING, Dr. Gary, FCA ATII *1988;* 13 Townsend Drive, ST. ALBANS, AL3 5RB.
MAINWARING, Mrs. Joanna Mary Mary, BSc ACA *2006;* 10 Southville Place, Southville, BRISTOL, BS3 1AW.
MAINWARING, Mr. Jonathan James, ACA *1992;* 36 Malvern Road, HAMPTON, TW12 2LN.
•MAINWARING, Mr. Mark Robert, BA ACA *1987;* with Mazars LLP, Sixth Floor, Times House, Throwley Way, SUTTON, SURREY SM1 4JQ.
MAINWARING, Mr. Neil Kynaston, BSc(Hons) ACA *2002;* Hardwick Farms, Hardwick, ELLESMERE, SHROPSHIRE, SY12 9HG.
MAINWARING, Mr. Paul, BA ACA *2001;* 160 Dovershire Road, CHARLOTTE, NC 28270, UNITED STATES.
MAINWARING, Mr. Paul Richard, BA ACA *1988;* Tullett Prebon Group Ltd, Level 3, 155 Bishopsgate, LONDON, EC2M 3TQ.
•MAINWARING, Mr. Richard Eldon Kynaston, FCA *1972;* Mainwaring Dean Associates, Millfield House, Eaton Bishop, HEREFORD, HR2 9QS.
MAINWARING, Mr. Simon Harry, MA FCA *1968;* Water Hall, Great Canfield, DUNMOW, CM6 1JR. (Life Member)
•MAINWOOD, Mr. John Henry, FCA *1981;* Wilson Sandford Ltd, 85 Church Road, HOVE, EAST SUSSEX, BN3 2BB.
•MAINZ, Mr. Andrew Abraham Jeremy, MA FCA *1976;* with FTI Forensic Accounting Limited, 322 High Holborn, LONDON, WC1V 7PB.
MAIO, Mr. Robert, BCom ACA *2000;* 25 Broomhurst Way, Muxton, TELFORD, SHROPSHIRE, TF2 8RG.
•MAIR, Mr. Andrew John, ACA *1989;* with PricewaterhouseCoopers LLP, Donington Court, Pegasus Business Park, Castle Donington, DERBY, DE74 2UZ.
MAIR, Mr. Andrew Stuart, ACA *1996;* 25 Churchward Close, Grove, WANTAGE, OX12 0QZ.
MAIR, Mr. Graeme Martin Anderson, BA FCA *1983;* Oracle France Sa, 15 Boulevard Charles De Gaulle, 92715 NANTERRE, FRANCE.
MAIR, Mr. James Percival, ACA *1982;* 73 Rowlands Avenue, Hatch End, PINNER, MIDDLESEX, HA5 4BX.
MAIR, Mrs. Julie Ann, ACA *1992;* La Cabane, Collings Road, St. Peter Port, GUERNSEY, GY1 1FL.
MAIR, Mr. Lindsay Keith Anderson, BCom ACA *1987;* 51-55 Gresham Street, LONDON, EC2V 7HQ.
MAIR, Mr. Stephen, BA FCA *1972;* Berry House, Newman Street, Doulting, SHEPTON MALLET, BA4 4JZ.
MAIRS, Mr. William, ACA *2011;* Flat 13 Plymouth House, Devonshire Drive, LONDON, SE10 8LE.
MAIS, Miss. Stephanie, ACA *2011;* Rocklands, Heol Pant-y-Gored, Creigiau, CARDIFF, CF15 9NF.
MAISEL, Mr. Steven David, FCA *1978;* Science Business Publishing Limited, rue Belliard 197, 1040 BRUSSELS, BELGIUM.
MAISEY, Mr. John Anthony, BSc ACA *1988;* Potters Hall Toppesfield Road, Great Yeldham, HALSTEAD, ESSEX, CO9 4HE.
MAISEY, Mrs. Susan Dorothy, BSc ACA *1982;* Huntsman Tioxide, Haverton Hill Road, BILLINGHAM, CLEVELAND, TS23 1PS.
MAISONNEUVE, Miss. Christele, MSc ACA *1998;* 12 quai Saint Vincent, 69001 LYON, FRANCE.
MAITI, Mr. Tapas, BA ACA *1997;* Flat 14, The Belvedere, Homerton Street, CAMBRIDGE, CB2 0NT.
MAITLAND, Miss. Alice, ACA *2008;* Flat 4 City Lights Court, 6 Bowden Street, LONDON, SE11 4DX.
•MAITLAND, Mr. Andrew Reginald Campbell, ACA *1988;* (Tax Fac), Maitland Limited, Office C, Maple Barn, Buckham Hill, UCKFIELD, EAST SUSSEX TN22 5XZ.
MAITLAND, Mr. Christopher John, BSc(Hons) ACA *2001;* with Nyman Libson Paul, Regina House, 124 Finchley Road, LONDON, NW3 5JS.
MAITLAND, Mr. David Graham, BSc FCA *1981;* 158 Malvern Crescent, ASHBY-DE-LA-ZOUCH, LEICESTERSHIRE, LE65 2HW.
MAITLAND, Mr. David Henry, CVO FCA *1951;* 4 High Street, Odiham, HOOK, RG29 1LG. (Life Member)
MAITLAND, Miss. Emma, MA(Oxon) ACA *2011;* Baronsmead Partners LLP, International House 3rd Floor 4 Maddox Street, LONDON, W1S 1QP.
MAITLAND, Mr. James Tyler, MA ACA *1985;* Kellwood Engineering Ltd, 9 Catherinefield, DUMFRIES, DG1 3PQ.
•MAITLAND, Mr. John Benjamin Gladwin, BSc ACA *1987;* PricewaterhouseCoopers LLP, 9 Greyfriars Road, READING, RG1 1JG. See also PricewaterhouseCoopers
MAITLAND, Miss. Kate Margaret, BSc ACA *2004;* 16a Beauchamp Road, LONDON, SW11 1PQ.
MAITLAND, Miss. Marianne Jean, BSc ACA *1992;* Glencairn, Gowkhouse Road, KILMACOLM, PA13 4DH.
MAITLAND, Mr. Matthew Scott, BA(Hons) ACA *2002;* 103 Codenham Green, BASILDON, SS16 5DR.
MAITLAND, Mr. Paul, ACA *1983;* 36 Grange Road, LEIGH-ON-SEA, SS9 2HS.
MAITLAND, Ms. Rebecca Emma, MA BA ACA *2007;* 5 Old Court, ASHTEAD, SURREY, KT21 2TS.
MAITLAND, Mr. Thomas Cameron, BSc ACA *2006;* 30 Romani Close, WARWICK, CV34 4TY.
MAITLAND, Mrs. Victoria, BA ACA *2001;* 39 Grove Coach Road, RETFORD, NOTTINGHAMSHIRE, DN22 7HB.
MAITLAND SMITH, Mr. Geoffrey, FCA *1956;* Manor Barn, Church Street, Fifield, CHIPPING NORTON, OXFORDSHIRE, OX7 6HF. (Life Member)
MAITYARD, Mr. Christopher John, ACA MBA *1993;* 8 Glebe Road, Cheam, SUTTON, SURREY, SM2 7NT.
•MAJAINAH, Mr. Nowzer, FCA *1972;* (Tax Fac), Majainah Sadra Limited, 2 Martin House, 179/181 North End Road, LONDON, W14 9NL.
MAJANGE, Mr. Charles Shanyurai Calvin, BA ACA *1986;* Zvakanaka Stores, P.O. Box 467, MASVINGO, ZIMBABWE.
MAJANGE, Mr. Masiyandaita, ACA *2011;* 33 Lansdowne Court, Brighton Road, PURLEY, SURREY, CR8 2BE.
MAJARO, Ms. Nadine Beatrice, MA FCA *1982;* 55 Redington Road, Hampstead, LONDON, NW3 7RP.
MAJDALANY, Mrs. Karin, BA ACA *1997;* 12 Logan Place, LONDON, W8 6QN.
MAJDALANY, Mr. Robin Joachim Eadie, MA FCA *1963;* 18 Edith Grove, Chelsea, LONDON, SW10 0NL. (Life Member)
MAJEED, Dr. Irfan, FCA *1984;* 85-A Street No.3 Phase 1 DHA, LAHORE, PAKISTAN.
•MAJEED, Mr. Numan, BSc ACA *2006;* CBS Accountants Ltd, 27 Stratford Way, WATFORD, WD17 3DL.
MAJEED, Mr. Sohail, BSc(Hons) ACA *2003;* 6 Gloucestershire Lea, Warfield, BRACKNELL, BERKSHIRE, RG42 3XQ.
MAJENDIE, Mrs. Christabel Mary Ann, BSc ACA *2005;* with Deloitte LLP, 3 Rivergate, Temple Quay, BRISTOL, BS1 6GD.
MAJER, Mrs. Jean, FCA *1970;* 20 Whitburn Bents Road, South Bents, SUNDERLAND, SR6 8AE.
MAJEWICZ, Mrs. Sarah Jane, BSc ACA *1997;* 6 Shalstone Road, LONDON, SW14 7HR.
MAJEWSKI, Mr. Nigel Richard, BA ACA *1984;* Little Cote Lower Common, East Runton, CROMER, NORFOLK, NR27 9PG.
MAJID, Mr. Hassaan Mustapha, ACA *1994;* EDF Energy, 5th Floor, Cardinal Place, 80 Victoria Street, LONDON, SW1E 5JL.
•MAJID, Mr. Khalid, FCA *1967;* Khalid Majid Rehman, 3rd Floor Al-Malik Centre, 70 West, G-7/F7 Jinnah Avenue, ISLAMABAD 44000, PAKISTAN.
MAJITHIA, Mr. Dineshchandra Raghavji, FCA *1970;* 277 Church Road, HAYES, MIDDLESEX, UB3 2LQ.
MAJITHIA, Mr. Kishor, FCA *1976;* 132 Ducks Hill Road, NORTHWOOD, HA6 2SR.
MAJITHIA, Mr. Paresh, BSc ACA *1992;* 6 Linden Road, MANCHESTER, M20 2QJ.
•MAJITHIA, Mr. Rohit, BA ACA *1991;* Lubbock Fine, Russell Bedford House, City Forum, 250 City Road, LONDON, EC1V 2QQ.
MAJLATH, Mr. Andrew, BEng ACA *1992;* Ordogarok U 130, 1029 BUDAPEST, HUNGARY.
MAJLINDER, Mr. Richard Jan, BSc(Econ) ACA *1999;* with PricewaterhouseCoopers, Riverside Centre, 123 Eagle Street, GPO Box 150, BRISBANE, QLD 4001 AUSTRALIA.
MAJOR, Mr. Aled Stephen, BSc ACA *2010;* 21 Trem-y-Dyffryn, BRIDGEND, MID GLAMORGAN, CF31 5AP.
•MAJOR, Mrs. Cheryl Jane, BA(Hons) ACA *2004;* Cheryl Major BA(Hons) ACA, 7 Phipps Close, Whetstone, LEICESTER, LE8 6YN.
MAJOR, Mr. David Stephen, BA ACA *1986;* 51 Churchill Close, Flackwell Heath, HIGH WYCOMBE, BUCKINGHAMSHIRE, HP10 9LA.
MAJOR, Mr. Gary, BSc ACA *2005;* 66 Highland Drive, Buckshaw Village, CHORLEY, LANCASHIRE, PR7 7AD.
MAJOR, Mr. Guy Alexander, BSc(Hons) ACA *2001;* (Tax Fac), PO Box 30512, 243 Conch Pointe Road, WEST BAY, GRAND CAYMAN, KY1-1203, CAYMAN ISLANDS.
•MAJOR, Mr. Jeremy Charles Bryant, FCA *1975;* Smith & Williamson Ltd, Old Library Chambers, 21 Chipper Lane, SALISBURY, SP1 1BG.
MAJOR, Mr. John Edward, FCA *1977;* 2 Broxholm Road, LONDON, SE27 0LZ.
MAJOR, Mr. John Hildred, FCA *1969;* 48 Rendells Meadow, Bovey Tracey, NEWTON ABBOT, DEVON, TQ13 9QW.
MAJOR, Mr. John Roderick, BSc FCA *1975;* Studleigh Dunns Lane, Iwerne Minster, BLANDFORD FORUM, DORSET, DT11 8NG.
MAJOR, Miss. Lucy, BA ACA *2002;* RBS, Natwest, 1 Princes Street, LONDON, EC2R 8BP.
•MAJOR, Mr. Malcolm, FCA *1975;* Majors Limited, 8 King Street, Trinity Square, HULL, HU1 2JJ.
MAJOR, Mrs. Neeta, BSc ACA *1993;* 6 Redwell Grove, Kings Hill, WEST MALLING, KENT, ME19 4BU.
MAJOR, Mr. Paul, FCA *1960;* 36 Hammerwood Road, Ashurst Wood, EAST GRINSTEAD, RH19 3TG. (Life Member)
MAJOR, Mr. Richard Edward John, BSc FCA *1972;* 9 Rothesay Avenue, RICHMOND, TW10 5EB.
MAJOR, Mr. Richard John, BA(Hons) ACA *2002;* 7 Oxford Road, Putney, LONDON, SW15 2LG.
•MAJOR, Mr. Ronald George, FCA *1959;* R.G. Major, The Burrows, Windmill Hill, Ashill, ILMINSTER, TA19 9NT.
MAJOR, Miss. Sarah Alice, BSc ACA *2009;* 216 North End Road, LONDON, W14 9NX.
•MAJOR, Mrs. Sarah Dawn, BA FCA *1992;* (Tax Fac), Thomas May & Co, Allen House, Newarke Street, LEICESTER, LE1 5SG.
MAJUMDAR, Mr. Kalyan, FCA *1970;* Brook Cottage, 18 Laurel View, LONDON, N12 7DT.
MAJUMDAR, Mr. Samit Kumar, FCA *1966;* J-1876, Chittaranjan Park, NEW DELHI 110019, INDIA. (Life Member)
MAJUMDAR, Miss. Shuchismita Mitun, BSc ACA *2007;* Corporate Citizenship, 5th Floor Holborn Gate, 330 High Holborn, LONDON, WC1V 7QG.
MAJUMDAR, Mr. Tejen Kumar, FCA *1975;* Flat 1-3 Top Flat, Adwalpalkar Valley Darshan, Bellavista, SANGOLDA BARDEZ 403511, GOA, INDIA.
MAK, Mr. Chew Tatt, MSc FCA *1991;* 24 Jalan 2/3, Taman Tun Abdul Razak, 68000 AMPANG, SELANGOR, MALAYSIA.
MAK, Mr. Chi Wing Henry, ACA *2005;* Flat F 8th Floor, Maple Mansion, TAIKOO SHING, HONG KONG SAR.
MAK, Mr. David Wing Kwong, MA ACA *1990;* 74 Aberfeldy Crescent, THORNHILL L3T 4C4, ON, CANADA.
•MAK, Mr. George Man-Cheung, BA FCA *1987;* George M.C. Mak & Company, Office 907, 9/F, Kai Wong Commercial Building, 222-226 Queen's Road Central, SHEUNG WAN HONG KONG ISLAND HONG KONG SAR.
MAK, Mr. Hing Kwai, FCA *1975;* 108 Pasir Panjang Road, 06-00 Golden Agri Plaza, SINGAPORE 118535, SINGAPORE.
MAK, Mr. Joseph Hoi To, BSc ACA *1986;* #02-15 The Trevose, 58 Trevose Crescent, SINGAPORE 298089, SINGAPORE.
MAK, Mr. Kay Lung Dantes, ACA *2007;* D K Mak & Co, Rooms 2101-3, China Insurance Group Building, 141 Des Voeux Road Central, CENTRAL, HONG KONG SAR.
MAK, Mr. Kin Kwong, ACA *2007;* Venfund Investment Management Ltd., Suite 2808, International Chamber, Of Commercial Tower, SHENZHEN 518048, CHINA.
MAK, Mr. Leung Hei, ACA *2008;* Mak Cheung & Co, Unit 1105, Hua Qin International Building, 340 Queen's Road, CENTRAL, HONG KONG ISLAND HONG KONG SAR.
•MAK, Miss. Mai Lai Chun, BSc FCA *1984;* Kinnair & Company, Aston House, Redburn Road, NEWCASTLE UPON TYNE, NE5 1NB.
MAK, Mr. Pak-Ying Francis, BA ACA *1986;* Palm Springs, 152 Pinaceae Drive, YUEN LONG, NEW TERRITORIES, HONG KONG SAR.
MAK, Mr. Peter, MA ACA *2004;* 401/3f Tai Wo Lau, Wai Yan Street, TAI PO, HONG KONG SAR.
MAK, Mr. Peter Wing Fai, ACA *2006;* Room 1014, 25A Kung Ngam Road, SHAU KEI WAN, HONG KONG ISLAND, HONG KONG SAR.
MAK, Dr. Po-Lung Lung, PhD ACA *2007;* 35/F One Pacific Place, 88 Queensway, CENTRAL, HONG KONG ISLAND, HONG KONG SAR.
MAK, Mr. Robinson Kok Yuen, BSc ACA *1994;* 10th Floor, 34 Leighton Road, CAUSEWAY BAY, HONG KONG ISLAND, HONG KONG SAR.
MAK, Mr. Russell Kai-Lert, BA FCA *1983;* Flat G 26th Floor, Block 17 Chi Fu Fa Yuen, POK FU LAM, HONG KONG ISLAND, HONG KONG SAR.
MAK, Ms. Sau Mun Gorette, BA FCA *1990;* Flat B 10/F, Dragonview Court, 5 Kotewall Road, MID LEVELS, HONG KONG ISLAND, HONG KONG SAR.
MAK, Ms. Shirley Ying King, ACA *2008;* Flat C, 21/F, Block 5, City One, SHA TIN, NEW TERRITORIES HONG KONG SAR.
MAK, Mr. Siu Hong, ACA *2008;* Flat F 13/F Tower 4, Metro City Phase 1, 1 Wan Hang Road, TSEUNG KWAN O, NEW TERRITORIES, HONG KONG SAR.
MAK, Mr. Tak Kwong Marco, ACA *2007;* Haitong International Research Ltd., 25/F New World Tower, 16-18 Queen's Road, CENTRAL, HONG KONG ISLAND, HONG KONG SAR.
MAK, Miss. Teresa Siu Yun, BSc ACA *1994;* 50 Raffles Place #09-01, Singapore Land Tower, SINGAPORE 048623, SINGAPORE.
MAK, Mr. Vincent Yu Cheung, BA ACA *1983;* Basement Kwong Loong Tai Bldg, 1016-1018 Tai Nan West Street, LAI CHI KOK, KOWLOON, HONG KONG SAR.
MAK, Mr. Wai Chung Stanley, ACA *2008;* Flat C 22/F, Hang Sing Mansion, Tai Wing Avenue, TAIKOO SHING, HONG KONG SAR.
MAK, Mr. William Tze Leng, ACA *2008;* PricewaterhouseCoopers, Prince's Building, 22/F, 10 Chater Road, CENTRAL, HONG KONG ISLAND HONG KONG SAR.
MAK, Ms. Yee Mei, ACA *2005;* Room 3416 Lai Nga House, Hong Nga Court, LAM TIN, KOWLOON, HONG KONG SAR.
MAK, Miss. Yuet Meng, ACA *1980;* 10 N Braddell Hill, Apt. 02-62, SINGAPORE 579732, SINGAPORE.
MAKA, Mr. Yusuf Yakub, BEng ACA *2002;* 257 Thorold Road, ILFORD, IG1 4HE.
•MAKALANDA, Mr. Hegoda Amarapala, FCA *1975;* H. Amara Makalanda, 11 Drapers Road, ENFIELD, EN2 8LT.
MAKAMURE, Mr. Simbarashe, ACA CA(SA) *2010;* 23 Kingsbridge Road, READING, RG2 7RF.
MAKAMURE, Miss. Tendai Jennifer, ACA *2007;* 41 Woodhouse Road, SWINDON, SN3 2GU.
•MAKAN, Mr. Dhirajlal, FCA *1974;* (Tax Fac), Makan & Makan, Dukes Court, 91 Wellington Street, LUTON, LU1 5AF.
MAKANDA, Miss. Anna Tendai, ACA *2010;* 21 Woodberry Crescent, LONDON, N10 1PJ.
MAKANJI, Mr. Ashok Kumar Chimanlal, BA ACA *1992;* 5 Wheatley Drive, WATFORD, WD25 9LH.
MAKAR, Ms. Mira, MA FCA *1988;* 218 Ben Jonson House, LONDON, EC2Y 8DL.
MAKARIOU, Mr. George, BA FCA *1990;* P.O. Box 24332, 1703 NICOSIA, CYPRUS.
MAKAROVA, Ms. Maria, ACA *2008;* 10 Gevgelis Street, Apartment 201, 1071 NICOSIA, CYPRUS.
MAKEPEACE, Mrs. Diane Elizabeth, BA ACA *2000;* 40 Shaftesbury Way, Strawberry Hill, TWICKENHAM, TW2 5RP.

MAKEPEACE, Mr. Kevin Ian, BSc ACA *1999;* 41 Orchard Way, North Bradley, TROWBRIDGE, BA14 0SU.
MAKEPEACE, Mr. Peter James, BSc ACA *2002;* 40 Willowbank Road, Knowle, SOLIHULL, WEST MIDLANDS, B93 9QX.
MAKEPEACE, Mr. Philip Adrian, BSc ACA *1989;* 34 Priory Road, LOUGHBOROUGH, LE11 3PP.
MAKEPEACE, Mr. Richard William, MA ACA *1979;* 48 Greenway, CHESHAM, HP5 2BX.
MAKEPEACE, Mrs. Sarah Catherine, LLB ACA *2002;* 40 Willowbank Road, Knowle, SOLIHULL, WEST MIDLANDS, B93 9QX.
MAKEPEACE, Mr. Stephen Joseph, BCom ACA *1985;* 14 Stapylton Street, WINMALEE, NSW 2777, AUSTRALIA.
MAKEY, Miss. Lindsay Jayne, BSc ACA *2010;* 40 Smith Street, New Balderton, NEWARK, NOTTINGHAMSHIRE, NG24 3BA.
MAKEY, Mr. Martin, BSc ACA *1979;* Parsonage Farmhouse, Kelvedon Road, Messing, COLCHESTER, CO5 9TA.
MAKH, Mr. Satnam Singh, BA FCA *1991;* 33 Gaviots Way, GERRARDS CROSS, BUCKINGHAMSHIRE, SL9 7DU.
MAKHECHA, Mr. Bhavesh Ashokkumar, BSc(Hons) ACA *2001;* 400 Foxborough Blvd, Apartment 9112, FOXBORO, MA 02035, UNITED STATES.
MAKHIJA, Mr. Rajiv, BSc FCA *1979;* Flat 2A Tregunter Tower 1, 14 Tregunter Path, Central Mid Levels, MID LEVELS, HONG KONG ISLAND, HONG KONG SAR.
•MAKHOUL, Ms. Christina Mary Ann, ACA FCCA *2011;* M2 Tax and Accountancy Limited, The Counting House, High Street, TRING, HERTFORDSHIRE, HP23 5TE.
MAKIN, Mrs. Amy Jane, BA FCA *1999;* HMRC LBS Leeds, 1 Munroe Court White Rose Office Park Millshaw Park, LEEDS, LS11 0EA.
MAKIN, Mr. Andrew David, BA(Hons) ACA *2009;* Flat 13 Field Court, 77 Fitzjohns Avenue, LONDON, NW3 6NY.
•MAKIN, Mr. Andrew Jonathan, BA ACA CTA *1991;* Whitehead & Aldrich, 5 Ribblesdale Place, PRESTON, PR1 8BZ.
MAKIN, Mr. Brian Peter, FCA *1968;* 150 Centrium, Station Approach, WOKING, SURREY, GU22 7PE. (Life Member)
•MAKIN, Mr. Chris, FCA FCMI FAE QDR MCIArb *1968;* Chris Makin Mediator Limited, Well Cottage, 39 Water Royd Lane, MIRFIELD, WEST YORKSHIRE, WF14 9SF. See also Makin Chris
MAKIN, Miss. Elizabeth, MA FCA *1986;* 20 St. Marys Street, STAMFORD, LINCOLNSHIRE, PE9 2DG.
MAKIN, Mr. Howard John, ACA *1980;* 1 Villa Gloria Close, LIVERPOOL, L19 9EY.
MAKIN, Miss. Jennifer Susan, BSc ACA *1993;* 105 Albany Road, STRATFORD-UPON-AVON, WARWICKSHIRE, CV37 6PQ.
MAKIN, Mr. John, BA ACA MBA *1998;* 1 The Drive, West Lodge, Burley In Wharfedale, ILKLEY, LS29 7AQ.
MAKIN, Mr. Michael Ian, FCA *1951;* 21 Windhill, BISHOP'S STORTFORD, CM23 2NE. (Life Member)
•MAKIN, Mr. Paul Darren, BSc ACA *1992;* Dales Evans & Co Limited, 88/90 Baker Street, LONDON, W1U 6TQ.
MAKIN, Mr. Stephen William, BSc ACA *2005;* 81a Church Street, Orrell, WIGAN, WN5 8TQ.
MAKIN, Mrs. Susan, BA ACA *1990;* Blackshaws Ltd Lionheart Enterprise Park, Birch Close Lionheart Enterprise Park, ALNWICK, NORTHUMBERLAND, NE66 2EP.
MAKINGS, Ms. Angela Jeanette, BSc ACA *1991;* Pippin House, 7 Cox Lane, Rossett, WREXHAM, LL12 0BH.
MAKINGS, Mr. Peter William, FCA *1954;* 69 Beech Hill, Hadley Wood, BARNET, HERTFORDSHIRE, EN4 0JW. (Life Member)
MAKINS, Mr. David Harry Francis, BA ACA *1981;* Qube Global Software Westgate House, 25 Westgate, SLEAFORD, LINCOLNSHIRE, NG34 7RJ.
•MAKINSON, Mrs. Bridget Anne, MA ACA *1981;* Peter Mitchell & Co, 95 High Street, GREAT MISSENDEN, HP16 0AL.
MAKINSON, Mr. Gary Lee, ACA *2011;* 31 Birch Drive, Bottlesford, SCUNTHORPE, SOUTH HUMBERSIDE, DN16 3GU.
MAKORI, Mrs. Shannon, ACA *2002;* Goldman Sachs, Petershill, 1 Carter Lane, LONDON, EC4V 5ER.
MAKOSZ, Mr. Paul Grant, MA ACA *1979;* 1915 ESTATES PLACE, PENTICTON V2A 8Y9, BC, CANADA.
MAKRAKIS, Mrs. Jane, BSc ACA *2004;* 59 Woodstock Close Hedge End, SOUTHAMPTON, SO30 0NG.
MAKRIDOU, Miss. Emilia, BSc ACA *2011;* 14 Europes Street, Flat 203, 1087 NICOSIA, CYPRUS.
MAKRIS, Mr. Andreas, MSc BSc ACA *2006;* 10 Skopa Street, Iris Court, 2035 NICOSIA, CYPRUS.
MAKRIS, Mr. Angelo, BA ACA *2002;* 48 Sunningdale Avenue, KENILWORTH, CV8 2BZ.
•MAKRIS, Mr. George, BA ACA *1990;* Freemans Partnership LLP, Solar House, 282 Chase Road, LONDON, N14 6NZ.
MAKRIS, Mr. Petros Hadjitofi, FCA *1964;* 6 Village Farm, Bonvilston, CARDIFF, CF5 6TY.
MAKUSZENKO, Mr. Bohdan, BSc(Hons) ACA *2000;* 6 Hamilton Close, Arnold, NOTTINGHAM, NG5 8RP.
•MALACRIDA, Mr. Christopher Norman, FCA *1974;* Chantrey Vellacott DFK LLP, Russell Square House, 10-12 Russell Square, LONDON, WC1B 5LF.
MALACRIDA, Mr. Richard George, ACA *2011;* 178 Broomwood Road, LONDON, SW11 6JY.
MALADWALA, Mr. Mohamed Salim, MSc BA FCA *1990;* 6 Grimwade Avenue, CROYDON, CR0 5DG.
MALADWALA, Mr. Rafik Badrudin, FCA *1972;* 2 Stanhope Road, CROYDON, CR0 5NS. (Life Member)
MALAGUTI, Mr. Paolo, ACA *2009;* Flat 1, 154 Kensington Church Street, LONDON, W8 4BN.
MALAK, Mr. Kamal Mohammad, FCA *1974;* 13 Fernhurst Gardens, EDGWARE, HA8 7PQ.
MALANGA, Mrs. Caroline Ann, BA ACA *1995;* 3114 Crestmoor Court, PROSPECT, KY 40059, UNITED STATES.
MALARKEY, Mr. Andrew, MA ACA *1999;* KordaMentha, Level 24, 333 Collins Street, MELBOURNE, VIC 3000, AUSTRALIA.
MALASPINA, Mr. Francis Daniel, MSc BEng ACA *2009;* 4a Flat 1 Basement, Woodside, LONDON, SW19 7AR.
MALBON, Mr. Jim, ACA *2007;* 51 Cambray Road, LONDON, SW12 0DX.
MALBON, Mrs. Julie Anne, BSc ACA *1993;* 3 Badgers Hollow, Checkley, STOKE-ON-TRENT, ST10 4NW.
MALBONE, Mrs. Clare Catherine, BEng ACA *1999;* 6328 Copeland Lakes Lane, INDIANAPOLIS, IN 46221, UNITED STATES.
MALCOLM, Mr. Alastair David, FCA *1972;* Park Farm, Throwley, FAVERSHAM, ME13 0PG.
MALCOLM, Mr. Andrew David, ACA *2008;* Flat 2 Prince Arthur Court, Prince Arthur Mews, LONDON, NW3 1RD.
•MALCOLM, Mr. Andrew James, MA ACA *1989;* (Tax Fac), Mill Wynd, EAST LINTON, EAST LOTHIAN, EH40 3AE.
MALCOLM, Mr. Anthony, FCA *1964;* 175 Hunters Park Ave, Clayton, BRADFORD, BD14 6EN. (Life Member)
MALCOLM, Mr. Anthony James, FCA *1981;* Hill Farm, Hill Farm Lane, Winslow Road, Little Horwood, MILTON KEYNES, MK17 0PD.
•MALCOLM, Mr. Clive Leslie, BA FCA *1976;* Crowe Clark Whitehill LLP, St Bride's House, 10 Salisbury Square, LONDON, EC4Y 8EH. See also Horwath Clark Whitehill LLP and Crowe Clark Whitehill
MALCOLM, Mrs. Deborah Gail, BA ACA CTA *1999;* 1333 North Lake Ct, APPLETON, WI 54913, UNITED STATES.
•MALCOLM, Mr. Gary Neil, MA FCA *1979;* (Tax Fac), Gary Malcolm & Co Ltd, 9 Chandlers Court, Eaton, NORWICH, NR4 6EY.
MALCOLM, Mr. Ian, BSc FCA *1990;* Elring Klinger (GB) Ltd, Troisdorf Way, Kirkleatham Business Park, REDCAR, CLEVELAND, TS10 5RX.
MALCOLM, Mr. Neil, BA ACA *1994;* 69 Middlewood Close, SOLIHULL, WEST MIDLANDS, B91 2TZ.
MALCOLM, Mr. Neil Duncan, FCA *1972;* Oakway, Benty Heath Lane, Willaston, NESTON, CH64 1RZ.
MALCOLM, Mr. Stephen, BA ACA *1998;* Pond House, Peppard Common, HENLEY-ON-THAMES, OXFORDSHIRE, RG9 5LB.
MALCOMSON, Mr. Ian, MA ACA *2010;* 23 Burford Road, WORCESTER PARK, KT4 7SU.
MALCOMSON, Mr. Nicholas Christopher, BA(Hons) ACA *2002;* 32 Summerfield, ASHTEAD, SURREY, KT21 2LF.
•MALCOURONNE, Mr. Keith Robert, MA FCA CF *1983;* Financial Professional Support Services LLP, The Old Church, Quicks Road, Wimbledon, LONDON, SW19 1EX. See also FPSS Ltd
MALCZEWSKA, Miss. Urszula, ACA CMA *2011;* Flat 160a, Lauderdale Mansions, Lauderdale Road, LONDON, W9 1NG.
•MALDE, Mr. Anilkumar Virchand, FCA *1972;* Appleday Associates Limited, Premier House, 112-114 Station Road, EDGWARE, MIDDLESEX, HA8 7BJ. See also Appleday Associates
MALDE, Mr. Atul Shashikant, BSc ACA *1994;* 8 Hansen Drive, Highland Village, LONDON, N21 1SB.
MALDE, Mr. Binoy, BA ACA *1995;* 9 Nicholas Way, NORTHWOOD, MIDDLESEX, HA6 2TR.
MALDE, Mr. Dhiren Vaghji, BSc ACA *1982;* Platinum Financial Services, 74 Pangbourne Drive, STANMORE, MIDDLESEX, HA7 4RB.
MALDE, Mr. Dipesh, BSc FCA *1998;* 129 Grasmere Avenue, WEMBLEY, HA9 8TN.
•MALDE, Miss. Divya, BSc FCA ATII *1983;* (Tax Fac), Godley & Co., Congress House, 14 Lyon Road, HARROW, MIDDLESEX, HA1 2EN.
MALDE, Mrs. Jayshree Samir, BA ACA *1998;* Timbers, St. Nicholas Close, Elstree, BOREHAMWOOD, HERTFORDSHIRE, WD6 3EW.
MALDE, Mr. Jiten Surendra, LLB ACA *2000;* 29 Golf Close, STANMORE, MIDDLESEX, HA7 2PP.
•MALDE, Mr. Kirankumar Vaghji, BSc FCA *1976;* (Tax Fac), Chapman Associates (CA) Limited, 31 Northwick Circle, HARROW, MIDDLESEX, HA3 0EE.
MALDE, Miss. Nehal, ACA *2008;* 112a Elgin Avenue, LONDON, W9 2HD.
MALDE, Mr. Nishith, BSc FCA *1985;* (Tax Fac), Tudor House, 69 Camlet Way, Hadley Wood, BARNET, HERTFORDSHIRE, EN4 0NL.
•MALDE, Mr. Pravinchandra Laxman, BSc FCA *1967;* MMa Partnership Llp, 6 Bruce Grove, LONDON, N17 6RA.
MALDE, Mr. Rajiv Pravinlal, BSc ACA *2005;* (Tax Fac), 43 Alveston Avenue, HARROW, HA3 8TG.
MALDE, Miss. Reena, ACA *2003;* with Deloitte LLP, 2 New Street Square, LONDON, EC4A 3BZ.
MALDE, Mr. Saggar Sharad, ACA *2009;* 76 Potter Street, PINNER, MIDDLESEX, HA5 3XE.
MALDE, Mr. Samir, BA ACA *2000;* Timbers, St. Nicholas Close, Elstree, BOREHAMWOOD, HERTFORDSHIRE, WD6 3EW.
MALDE, Mr. Shishir, BSc ACA *1992;* 19 Braefell Close, West Bridgford, NOTTINGHAM, NG2 6SS.
MALDE, Mrs. Sonal, BSc ACA *1996;* Logica UK Ltd, 45 Grosvenor Road, ST ALBANS, HERTFORDSHIRE, AL1 3AW.
MALDE, Mr. Vijay Chhotalal, FCA *1979;* Grant Thornton, P O Box 410, Sarit Centre, NAIROBI, 00606, KENYA.
MALDE, Mr. Vijaykumar Mulchand, FCA *1974;* 23 Lancaster Court, 100 Lancaster Gate, LONDON, W2 3NY.
MALDE, Mr. Vipul Vaghji, BA ACA *1978;* 1 Greystone Gardens, HARROW, HA3 0EF.
MALE, Mr. David Roger, BSc ACA *1984;* Management Revisions Ltd, New Zealand House, 9th Floor, 80 Haymarket, LONDON, SW1Y 4TQ.
MALE, Mr. Henry Edward Chancellor, ACA *1993;* 4 Arminger Road, LONDON, W12 7BB.
MALE, Dr. Lucinda Helen, MA ACA *2004;* 46a Crockerton Road, LONDON, SW17 7HG.
MALE, Mr. Matthew Toby, BSc ACA *1999;* 9 Nevill Road, Bramhall, STOCKPORT, CHESHIRE, SK7 3ET.
MALE, Mr. Nicholas Leeroy, BSc ACA *1986;* 11 Broom Lane Dickens Heath, Shirley, SOLIHULL, B90 1SJ.
MALE, Mr. Oliver Samuel, BA(Hons) ACA *2009;* 33 Wilman Way, SALISBURY, SP2 8QS.
MALEGAM, Mr. Yezdi Hirji, FCA *1957;* Goolestan, 37 Cuffe Parade, MUMBAI 400005, INDIA. (Life Member)
MALEK, Mr. Haris, BA(Hons) ACA *2010;* 19 A Rodou Street, Aglantzia, 2103 NICOSIA, CYPRUS.
MALEK, Mr. Tahir Mahmood, FCA *1978;* Messila House Ltd, 51 South Audley Street, LONDON, W1K 2AA.
MALEKOS, Mr. Panayiotis Andreas, BSc ACA CF *1988;* 11 Zalongou, Strovolos, 2027 NICOSIA, CYPRUS.
MALENCZUK, Miss. Madeleine Suzanne, ACA *2008;* 69 Woodstock Road, WITNEY, OXFORDSHIRE, OX28 1EB.
•MALES, Mr. Craig John, ACA FCCA MAAT *2008;* SJ Males & Co Limited, Basepoint Business & Innovation Centre, 110 Butterfield, Great Marlings, LUTON, BEDFORDSHIRE LU2 8DL.
•MALES, Mr. John Charles, BA ACA *1999;* Watson Associates, 30-34 North Street, HAILSHAM, EAST SUSSEX, BN27 1DW.
MALET DE CARTERET, Mr. Charles Guy, MA ACA *1986;* La Caumiethe, La Ruette de la Ville A L'Eveque, Trinity, JERSEY, JE3 5DH.
•MALEWICZ, Mr. David John, BSc FCA *1986;* (Tax Fac), George Arthur, 4 Wigmores South, WELWYN GARDEN CITY, HERTFORDSHIRE, AL8 6PL.
MALEWSKI, Mr. Peter Stanislaw, BSc ACA *1994;* (Tax Fac), 20 Copes Drive, TAMWORTH, STAFFORDSHIRE, B79 8HH.
MALEY, Mrs. Caroline Denise, ACA *1995;* The National College for School Leadership Lime House, Mere Way Ruddington Fields Business Park Ruddington, NOTTINGHAM, NG11 6JS.
MALGET, Mr. Michael John Albert, FCA *1973;* 78 The Glebe, Lavendon, OLNEY, MK46 4HG.
MALGHAM, Mr. Hoshie Hirji, FCA *1963;* 309 Cumballa Crest, 42 Pedder Road, MUMBAI 400026, INDIA.
MALHI, Mr. Jaswinder Singh, BA ACA *1992;* 71 Edgbaston Road, SMETHWICK, B66 4LF.
MALHI, Mrs. Rajwant Kaur, BSc ACA *2002;* 24 Featherston Road, Streetly, SUTTON COLDFIELD, WEST MIDLANDS, B74 3JN.
MALHOTRA, Miss. Aditi, BSc ACA *2007;* 42 Southover, LONDON, N12 7ES.
MALHOTRA, Mr. Arun, FCA *1973;* 1569 Bathurst Street, TORONTO M5P 3H8, ON, CANADA.
MALHOTRA, Mr. Ashok Kumar, FCA *1979;* 92 Brondesbury Park, LONDON, NW2 5JU.
MALHOTRA, Mr. Bharat, FCA *1975;* Bharat Malhotra & Co, 20-6 Bangur Avenue, Block C, KOLKATA 700 055, INDIA.
MALHOTRA, Mr. Deepak, BSc ACA *2001;* 93 Plater Drive, OXFORD, OX2 6QU.
MALHOTRA, Mr. Deepak Prakash, BA(Hons) ACA *2004;* 29 Tennyson Road, ASHFORD, MIDDLESEX, TW15 2LN.
•MALHOTRA, Mr. Manendra Kumar, FCA *1968;* Accounting Professionals Limited, 18 West Mead, MAIDENHEAD, BERKSHIRE, SL6 7HQ.
MALHOTRA, Mr. Manish, BA ACA *1996;* London Evening Standard, Northcliffe House, 2 Derry Street, LONDON, W8 5EE.
MALHOTRA, Mrs. Manju, BSc ACA *1998;* 9 Monkville Avenue, Golders Green, LONDON, NW11 0AH.
•MALHOTRA, Mr. Rajiv, BA FCA *1993;* Smith Malhotra Limited, 40-42 High Street, Newington, SITTINGBOURNE, KENT, ME9 7JL.
MALHOTRA, Mr. Rohit, ACA *1992;* 104 Sagamore Road, MILLBURN, NJ 07041, UNITED STATES.
MALHOTRA, Miss. Sangeeta, BSc ACA *1988;* 15 Seagry Road, Wanstead, LONDON, E11 2NG.
MALHOTRA, Mr. Sanjiv, ACA *1980;* 6 Motabhoy Mansion, 104 M. Karve Road, Back Bay Reclamation, Churchgate, MUMBAI 400020, INDIA.
MALHOTRA, Mr. Shailendra, FCA *1980;* 7895 Pearl Fog Way, DUNN LORING, VA 22027, UNITED STATES.
MALHOTRA, Mr. Sunil, FCA *1972;* M-72, Greater Kailash Part 2, NEW DELHI 110 048, INDIA.
•MALHOTRA, Mr. Vijendra Nath, FCA *1974;* KPMG, P O Box 3800, Level 32, Emirates Towers, Sheikh Zayed Road, DUBAI UNITED ARAB EMIRATES.
MALHOTRA, Mr. Vikas, ACA *2000;* 404 Chertsey Road, TWICKENHAM, TW2 6LP.
MALIA, Miss. Philippa Jane, BSc ACA *2009;* 23b Queen Street, NEWCASTLE UPON TYNE, NE1 3UG.
•MALIDA, Mr. Arif, FCA *1977;* Arif Malida, 66 Moyser Road, LONDON, SW16 6SQ.
•MALIDA, Mr. Mubeen, ACA *2005;* with Arif Malida, 66 Moyser Road, LONDON, SW16 6SQ.
MALIK, Mr. Abdul, FCA *1969;* 84/50, 169 Street, Suite 605, Jamaica, NEW YORK, NY 11432-2016 UNITED STATES. (Life Member)
MALIK, Mr. Abdul Fatir, BA ACA *1985;* Via G Garibaldi, 6/M, 27010 VELLEZZO BELLINI, ITALY.
MALIK, Mr. Adnan Shakoor, BA FCA *1999;* Kuwait Finance House, PO Box 2066, MANAMA, BAHRAIN.
•MALIK, Mr. Amir Ahmed, FCA *1981;* Booth Ainsworth LLP, Alpha House, 4 Greek Street, STOCKPORT, CHESHIRE, SK3 8AB.
MALIK, Mr. Amir Ashfaq, MBA BSc(Hons) ACA *2001;* Flat 13, 10 Langland Gardens, LONDON, NW3 6PR.
MALIK, Mr. Amir Mahmud, FCA *1988;* #05-00 Juniper @ Ardmore, 6 Ardmore Park, SINGAPORE 259953, SINGAPORE.
MALIK, Mr. Ashfaque Ahmed, BSc ACA AMCT *1995;* Net Quad Center, 31st Street, Corner 4th Avenue, E-Square Zone, Crescent Park West, Bonifacio Global City TAGUIG CITY 1634 METRO PHILIPPINES.
•MALIK, Mr. Asim Naveed, ACA *2010;* 82 Manor Square, DAGENHAM, ESSEX, RM8 3SA.
MALIK, Mr. Ehsan Ali, FCA *1979;* Unilever Pakistan Care Post Room, Unilever Plc, PO Box 68, LONDON, EC4P 4BQ.
MALIK, Mr. Faisal Imran Hussain, ACA *2009;* 25 Meadow Court, Rosebank, EPSOM, KT18 7RY.
MALIK, Miss. Fakiha, MSc BSc ACA *2009;* 14 Barton Meadows, ILFORD, IG6 1JQ.

MALIK, Mr. Feroze Khan, FCA *1961;* House 516, Street No 9, Sector F 10/2, ISLAMABAD, PAKISTAN. (Life Member)
MALIK, Mr. Humayon Zaheer, ACA *1998;* Flat 5/F Hyde Park Mansions, Transept Street, LONDON, NW1 5ES.
MALIK, Mr. Imran Saeed, BEng ACA *1992;* 15 Spencer Road, SOUTH CROYDON, SURREY, CR2 7EL.
•**MALIK, Mr. Irfan Rehman, FCA** *1982;* Rahman Sarfaraz Rahim Iqbal Rafiq, 4-B, 90 Canal Park, Gulberg-II, LAHORE, PAKISTAN.
MALIK, Mr. Jamshed, MA MSc ACA CTA *2000;* (Tax Fac), 7 Roman Road, ILFORD, IG1 2NY.
•**MALIK, Mr. Kaleem, FCA** *1973;* Kaleem Malik & Co, House No. 9, A-Street, Off Khayaban-e-Shaheen, Defence Hsing Auth, Phase V KARACHI PAKISTAN.
MALIK, Miss. Kashaf, ACA *2011;* 50 Dene Avenue, HOUNSLOW, TW3 3AH.
MALIK, Mr. Kiran Bir Singh, FCA *1975;* Kenmore The Highlands, East Horsley, LEATHERHEAD, KT24 5BQ.
MALIK, Miss. Mehr, BSc ACA *2006;* 37 Woodlands Park, GUILDFORD, GU1 2TJ.
•**MALIK, Mr. Mohammed Azeem, ACA** *2006;* Rehman Michael(Accountants) Limited, 277 Roundhay Road, LEEDS, WEST YORKSHIRE, LS8 4HS.
MALIK, Mr. Mohammed Sadeek, FCA *1973;* 1 Fortnums Acre, STANMORE, HA7 3NU.
MALIK, Mr. Mujahid Asghar, FCA *1997;* Dexia Public Finance Bank Shackleton House, 4 Battle Bridge Lane, LONDON, SE1 2RB.
•**MALIK, Mr. Neal, BSc(Hons) ACA** *2002;* Sigma CA Ltd, J O Hunter House, 409 Bradford Road, HUDDERSFIELD, HD2 2RB.
•**MALIK, Mr. Omar Hayat, FCA** *1971;* Mian & Malik, 28 Sarum, Roman Wood, BRACKNELL, BERKSHIRE, RG12 8XZ.
MALIK, Mr. Pawan, BSc ACA *1991;* Flat 1, 40 Onslow Gardens, LONDON, SW7 3PY.
MALIK, Mr. Pradeep, FCA *1986;* 7th Floor Building 10 Tower B, DLF Cyber City Complex DLF City Phase II, GURGAON 122002, HARYANA, INDIA.
MALIK, Mr. Prem Kumar, CA FCA *1978;* Queensbury Strategies, 69 Yonge Street Suite 200, TORONTO M5E 1K3, ON, CANADA.
MALIK, Mr. Razi Ahmed, FCA *1972;* National Petrochemical Industrial Company, PO Box 4459, JEDDAH, 21491, SAUDI ARABIA.
MALIK, Mr. Rikki, BA ACA CFA *1997;* PO Box 9142, General Post Office, Connaught Road, CENTRAL, HONG KONG ISLAND, HONG KONG SAR.
MALIK, Mr. Rizwan Latif, BSc ACA *1997;* Ropemaker Place, Ropemaker Street, LONDON.
MALIK, Mrs. Saaiqa Saleem, MMath ACA *2011;* 21 Roundhill Road, LEICESTER, LE5 5RJ.
MALIK, Miss. Saima Sofeen, ACA *2010;* The Poplars, Ivetsey Road, Wheaton Aston, STAFFORD, ST19 9QP.
MALIK, Mr. Sarfraz Ahmad, FCA *1973;* 20-B Zafar Road Lahore Cantt., LAHORE 54000, PAKISTAN.
•**MALIK, Mr. Sarfraz Sikander, BSc ACA** *2008;* with RSM Tenon Audit Limited, 66 Chiltern Street, LONDON, W1U 4JT.
MALIK, Mrs. Sonia, BSc ACA *1999;* Maple House, 28 Eglise Road, WARLINGHAM, SURREY, CR6 9SE.
MALIK, Mr. Tariq Shafiq, FCA *1981;* 12 Edgevalley Way NW, CALGARY T3A 4X6, AB, CANADA.
MALIK, Miss. Ulya, ACA *2009;* 50 Dene Avenue, HOUNSLOW, TW3 3AH.
MALIK, Mr. Usman Bashir, BA ACA CF *2006;* with Grant Thornton UK LLP, Grant Thornton House, 22 Melton Street, Euston Square, LONDON, NW1 2EP.
MALIK, Mr. Waqar Ahmad, FCA *1983;* ICI Pakistan Limited, ICI House, 5 West Wharf, KARACHI 74000, SINDH, PAKISTAN.
MALIK, Mr. Waseem Ullah, BSc(Hons) ACA *2001;* 4 North Close, BEACONSFIELD, BUCKINGHAMSHIRE, HP9 1SW.
MALIN, Mr. Andrew Charles, BA FCA *1976;* 2 Purbeck Street, CARDIFF, CF5 1FR.
MALIN, Mr. Geoffrey Walter, FCA *1954;* 43 Lower Green, Tewin, WELWYN, AL6 0LA. (Life Member)
MALIN, Mr. John Edwin, FCA *1975;* 4 Tudor Close, Page StreetMill Hill, LONDON, NW7 2BG.
MALIN, Mr. Jonathan Adam, MA ACA MCT *1993;* Rouse & Co Intl Ltd 11th Floor, Exchange Tower 1 Harbour Exchange Square, LONDON, E14 9GE.
•**MALIN, Mr. Paul John, FCA** *1986;* HW Tax Compliance LLP, Sterling House, 71 Francis Road, Edgbaston, BIRMINGHAM, B16 8SP.
MALIN, Mr. Raymond Michael, FCA *1959;* Windermere, 11 Latchmoor Way, GERRARDS CROSS, SL9 8LW. (Life Member)
•**MALIN, Mrs. Susan Elaine, ACA CTA** *1989;* Latimers, 6 Shaw Street, WORCESTER, WR1 3QQ. See also Latimer Advisory Services LLP
MALINS, Miss. Melissa, BSc ACA *2003;* 15 Denehurst Gardens, LONDON, NW4 3QS.
MALITSKIE, Mr. Mark, ACA *1981;* Umeco Plc Concorde House, 24 Warwick New Road, LEAMINGTON SPA, CV32 5JG.
MALIZIA, Mr. Barry Edward, FCA *1969;* Bartley Grange, Bartley Grange Eadens Lane, Bartley, SOUTHAMPTON, SO40 2LB.
MALKIN, Mr. Anthony Richard, BSc ACA *1992;* 2 Peel Avenue, Bowdon, ALTRINCHAM, CHESHIRE, WA14 2UG.
MALKIN, Mr. Brian Andrew, BA ACA *2008;* 18 Gainsmore Avenue, Norton Park, STOKE-ON-TRENT, STAFFORDSHIRE, ST6 8GE.
MALKIN, Mrs. Joanne, BA ACA *1984;* Treetops, Winghouse Lane, Tittensor, STOKE-ON-TRENT, ST12 9HN.
•**MALKIN, Mr. John Michael, FCA** *1969;* Bissell & Brown Ltd, Charter House, 56 High Street, SUTTON COLDFIELD, WEST MIDLANDS, B72 1UJ.
MALKIN, Mr. Keith James, BA ACA *1983;* National Australian Bank, 33 Gracechurch Street, LONDON, EC3V 0BT.
•**MALKIN, Mrs. Lesley Margaret, BA FCA** *1983;* BW Macfarlane LLP, 3 Temple Square, LIVERPOOL, L2 5BA.
MALKIN, Mr. Peter Frederick, BCom FCA *1975;* The Grange, Wincle, MACCLESFIELD, SK11 0QE.
•**MALKIN, Mr. Roland Leo, MSc ACA** *2003;* Crowe Clark Whitehill LLP, St Bride's House, 10 Salisbury Square, LONDON, EC4Y 8EH. See also Horwath Clark Whitehill LLP
•**MALKIN, Mr. Roland Spencer Norman, BSc FCA** *1989;* (Tax Fac), Harwood & Ball, 23 Rectory Road, West Bridgford, NOTTINGHAM, NG2 6BE.
MALKINSON, Mr. Jeffrey Leon, FCA CPA *1962;* p.o.box 157, BNEI BRAQ, 51001, ISRAEL. (Life Member)
MALKINSON, Mr. Keith Norman, BBS ACA *1986;* 100 Fenchurch Street, LONDON, EC3M 5JD.
•**MALL, Mr. Lekh Raj, BSc FCA** *1990;* (Tax Fac), Appleby Mall, 86 Tettenhall Road, WOLVERHAMPTON, WV1 4TF. See also Appleby Mall Limited
MALLABON, Mr. Roger John, FCA *1969;* 47 Highfield Drive, Littleport, ELY, CAMBRIDGESHIRE, CB6 1GA.
MALLAC, Mr. David Philippe, BCom ACA *1981;* 6 Larkspur Close, WOKINGHAM, BERKSHIRE, RG41 3NA.
•**MALLAGHAN, Mr. Gerard John, FCA** *1976;* (Tax Fac), Moore Stephens, Oakley House, Headway Business Park, 3 Saxon Way West, CORBY, NORTHAMPTONSHIRE NN18 9EZ.
MALLALIEU, Miss. Helen, MSc ACA *2007;* 59 Millfields, OSSETT, WEST YORKSHIRE, WF5 8HE.
MALLARD, Mr. Jonas Dylan, BSc ACA *1998;* Stargime, Centre d'Affaires La Boursidière, 92357 LE PLESSIS-ROBINSON, FRANCE.
MALLARD, Mr. Roderick Freeman, FCA *1967;* 2/38 Freeman Avenue, TRANMERE, SA 5073, AUSTRALIA. (Life Member)
MALLATRATT, Mrs. Sarah Emily, BSc ACA *2006;* 6 New Street, SHEFFORD, BEDFORDSHIRE, SG17 5BW.
MALLEN, Mr. Paul Kevin, BSc FCA *1978;* 81 Belwell Lane, Four Oaks, SUTTON COLDFIELD, B74 4TS.
MALLEN-BEADLE, Mrs. Amanda Louise, BCom ACA *1998;* 7 Embleton Grove, Wynyard, BILLINGHAM, CLEVELAND, TS22 5SY.
MALLEN-BEADLE, Mr. Jonathan Stuart, BSc ACA *1994;* 7 Embleton Grove, Wynyard, BILLINGHAM, CLEVELAND, TS22 5SY.
MALLET, Mr. Keith Conrad, MSc BA ACA *1997;* Westwinds, Le Mont Vibert, St. Ouen, JERSEY, JE3 2EX.
MALLETT, Mr. Andrew Howard, BSc FCA *1978;* Wilton House Peers Drive, Aspley Guise, MILTON KEYNES, MK17 8JP.
MALLETT, Mr. Andrew Simon, BSc FCA CTA *1991;* Ludlow Street Healthcare, 5th Floor Harlech Court, West Bute Terrace, CARDIFF, CF10 2FE.
MALLETT, Mr. Anthony Neil, FCA *1973;* 5 South Rise, Llanishen, CARDIFF, CF14 0RF.
MALLETT, Mr. Brian, FCA *1963;* 16A Pages Lane, Great Barr, BIRMINGHAM, B43 6LL. (Life Member)
MALLETT, Mrs. Caroline Frances, MA ACA *1988;* 21 St George's Place, YORK, YO24 1DT.
MALLETT, Mr. David John, BA FCA *1968;* (Member of Council 1987 - 1993), Owengate, 12c Denbridge Road, BICKLEY, KENT, BR1 2AG.
MALLETT, Mr. Graham John, ACA *1979;* 28 Henley Way, West Hallam, ILKESTON, DERBYSHIRE, DE7 6LU.
MALLETT, Mr. John Frederick, ACA *1987;* 285 West Point Avenue, TORONTO M1C 2R9, ON, CANADA.
•**MALLETT, Mr. Kevin Anthony, FCA** *1981;* (Tax Fac), 52 Rutherwyke Close, EPSOM, SURREY, KT17 2NB.
MALLETT, Mr. Kevin James, BA FCA *1992;* Heriot Watt University, Finance Department, Edinburgh Campus, CURRIE, MIDLOTHIAN, EH14 4AS.
MALLETT, Miss. Louise, BSc ACA *2006;* 3 Jeffries Close, Rownhams, SOUTHAMPTON, SO16 8DS.
MALLETT, Mr. Michael John, FCA *1957;* (Member of Council 1995 - 2001), 106 Ivy Park Road, SHEFFIELD, S10 3LD. (Life Member)
MALLETT, Mr. Nicholas John, BA FCA *1988;* 241a High Lane East, West Hallam, ILKESTON, DE7 6HZ.
•**MALLETT, Mr. Paul Charles Quartly, FCA** *1973;* PriceWaterhouseCoopers LDA, Palacio Sottomayor, Rue Sousa Martins, No 1 - 2 Esq, 1050-217 LISBON, PORTUGAL.
MALLETT, Mrs. Penelope Jane, BSc ACA *1993;* 138 South Park Road, Wimbledon, LONDON, SW19 8TA.
MALLETT, Mr. Peter James, BSc(Econ) ACA *1996;* 29 High Park Road, FARNHAM, GU9 7JJ.
MALLETT, Mr. Richard Brian, BSc ACA *1992;* 138 South Park Road, LONDON, SW19 8TA.
MALLETT, Mr. Robert Michael, BA FCA *1975;* Rose Cottage, Ulverley Crescent, Olton, SOLIHULL, WEST MIDLANDS, B92 8BJ.
MALLETT, Mr. Stephen William, BA FCA MCIT *1977;* Cartref, Cartref Guildford Road, Fetcham, LEATHERHEAD, KT22 9DY.
MALLEY, Mr. Christopher Robert, MA MEng ACA ACCA *1999;* 85 Parkwood Boulevard, PARKWOOD, QLD 4214, AUSTRALIA.
MALLEY, Mrs. Judith Marie, BA ACA ATII *1990;* 28 High Elm Road, Hale Barns, ALTRINCHAM, CHESHIRE, WA15 0HS.
MALLEY, Mr. Nicholas Vivian, BA(Hons) ACA *1995;* 38 Hillcroft Crescent, LONDON, W5 2SQ.
•**MALLEY, Mr. Paul Mathew, BA ACA** *1990;* (Tax Fac), Paystream Accounting Services Ltd, Mansion House, Manchester Road, ALTRINCHAM, CHESHIRE, WA14 4RW.
MALLICK, Mr. Ananda Moy, FCA *1973;* Flat 402E, 11 Hindusthan Road, CALCUTTA 700029, INDIA.
MALLIN, Prof. Christine Anne, PhD BSc FCA *1986;* Pendown, 33 Lillington Road, LEAMINGTON SPA, CV32 5YS.
MALLIN-JONES, Mr. Peter John, BA(Hons) ACA *2000;* Goldman Sachs, Peterborough Court, 133 Fleet Street, LONDON, EC4A 2BB.
MALLINDER, Mr. Edward James Leslie, FCA *1962;* 33 Ledborough Lane, BEACONSFIELD, HP9 2DB.
MALLINDER, Mr. James Edward, LLB ACA *2001;* Flat A, 7 Carleton Gardens, Brecknock Road, LONDON, N19 5AQ.
MALLINSON, Mr. Andrew William, BSc ACA *1981;* 5 East Hill Drive, JACKSON, MS 39216, UNITED STATES.
MALLINSON, Mrs. Ann Louise, BA ACA *1999;* 1 Aldwych Close, Maidenbower, CRAWLEY, RH10 7HE.
MALLINSON, Mr. Anthony John, FCA *1962;* 11 Saxon Croft, Repton, DERBY, DERBYSHIRE, DE65 6FY.
MALLINSON, Mr. Ben Nicholas, MSc BA ACA *2010;* Flat 7, Holmdale Mansions, Holmdale Road, LONDON, NW6 1BG.
MALLINSON, Mr. Derek Ainley, FCA *1949;* Fairways, 56 Pashley Road, EASTBOURNE, BN20 8EA. (Life Member)
MALLINSON, Mr. Douglas Laurence, BA FCA *1980;* 16 Cheviot Way, MIRFIELD, WEST YORKSHIRE, WF14 8HW.
MALLINSON, Mr. James Rex, FCA *1963;* 29 Cecily Hill, CIRENCESTER, GLOUCESTERSHIRE, GL7 2EF. (Life Member)
MALLINSON, Mr. John Graham, BA FCA *1989;* 1 Deal Crescent, Berkeley Pendesham, WORCESTER, WR4 0LJ.
MALLINSON, Mr. John Steven, BA ACA *1981;* 56 Sunderlands Road, Bucklands Beach, AUCKLAND, NEW ZEALAND.
MALLINSON, Mr. Lawrence Stuart, MA ACA *1982;* 1a Hillgate Place, LONDON, SW12 9ER.
MALLINSON, Mr. Michael Arnold, BCom FCA *1968;* 4 Forest Hill Gardens, Stainland Road Outlane, HUDDERSFIELD, HD3 3GA.
MALLINSON, Mr. Richard John, FCA *1979;* 7 Drew Close, Bradpole, BRIDPORT, DORSET, DT6 3JG.
MALLINSON, Mr. Robin John Charteris, MA FCA *1956;* Lychgate Cottage, Well Road, Crondall, FARNHAM, GU10 5PW. (Life Member)
MALLINSON, Dr. Sarah Anne, BSc ACA *2010;* 15 Fairfax Street, OTLEY, WEST YORKSHIRE, LS21 1JX.
MALLION, Mrs. Fiona Louise, ACA *2001;* 47 Hillary Road, Penenden Heath, MAIDSTONE, ME14 2JT.
MALLION, Mr. Steven John Leigh, FCA *1996;* 47 Hillary Road, Penenden Heath, MAIDSTONE, ME14 2JT.
MALLIOTIS, Mr. Achilleas Georghiou, BSc ACA *1993;* Flat 22, 7 Georgiou Dimosthenous Street, 2008 STROVOLOS, CYPRUS.
MALLON, Mr. Andrew, MSc ACA *2007;* with KPMG LLP, Arlington Business Park, Theale, READING, RG7 4SD.
MALLON, Mr. Cormac John, ACA *2009;* 18 Wesley Apartments, 202 Wandsworth Road, LONDON, SW8 2JU.
MALLON, Mrs. Elizabeth Anne, BSc ACA *1989;* The Willows, Northside, Birtley, CHESTER LE STREET, COUNTY DURHAM, DH3 1RD.
MALLON, Mrs. Elizabeth Esther, ACA *2008;* K P M G Arlington Business Park, Theale, READING, RG7 4SD.
MALLON, Mr. Gordon Keith, BSc ACA MCSE *1991;* 6 Norfolk Road, CARLISLE, CA2 5PQ.
MALLON, Mr. Philip Stephen, BA ACA *2009;* 9 Ashberry Avenue, Douglas, ISLE OF MAN, IM2 1PY.
MALLON, Mr. Ronald Jeffrey, FCA *1974;* C/O Mercury Middle East, PO BOX 10739, MANAMA, BAHRAIN.
•**MALLON, Mr. Timothy John, BSc FCA CTA** *1987;* (Tax Fac), Ryecroft Glenton, 32 Portland Terrace, Jesmond, NEWCASTLE UPON TYNE, NE2 1QP.
MALLONEY, Mr. Thomas, BA(Hons) ACA *2011;* Appartement 202, 6 Rue Aufrèry, 31500 TOULOUSE, FRANCE.
MALLORY, Mr. Ian Wodehouse, FCA *1963;* Marshall House, 76 The Street, Kennington, ASHFORD, KENT, TN24 9HS. (Life Member)
MALLOWAH, Miss. Esther, ACA *2011;* 27 Aveley House, Iliffe Close, READING, RG1 2QF.
•**MALLOY, Ms. Josephine Michelle, BSc FCA** *1988;* JM Accountants Limited, 137 Cherry Crescent, ROSSENDALE, LANCASHIRE, BB4 6DS.
•**MALME, Mr. Stephen Edward Charles, BA FCA** *1979;* Stephen Malme, 51 Mornington Road, North Chingford, LONDON, E4 7DT.
MALMGREN, Mrs. Virginia Sara, BA ACA *1985;* 8 Springfields, AMERSHAM, HP6 5JU.
MALONE, Miss. Christine Rachel, BSc ACA *1998;* 75 Ramsden Square, CAMBRIDGE, CB4 2BN.
MALONE, Mr. Christopher Kevin, FCA FCMA FCIS *1971;* 8 Netley Court, Hayling Close, Priddy's Hard, GOSPORT, HAMPSHIRE, PO12 4LX.
•**MALONE, Mr. Richard John, ACA** *1987;* Hillier Hopkins LLP, Charter Court, Midland Road, HEMEL HEMPSTEAD, HERTFORDSHIRE, HP2 5GE. See also HH Accounting & Tax Solutions Limited and Richard Malone Associates Ltd
MALONE, Miss. Sarah Catherine, BSc ACA *2001;* 40c Edge Lane, MANCHESTER, M21 9JW.
MALONE, Mr. Sean Kevin, BSc ACA *1990;* 8 Kinnaird Avenue, BROMLEY, BR1 4HG.
MALONE, Mr. Terence Patrick, MA MTh BA FCA *1959;* 7 Hillside Gardens, BARNET, EN5 2NG. (Life Member)
MALONE, Mr. Travis Steven, BSc ACA *2009;* 25 Firtree Close, SANDHURST, BERKSHIRE, GU47 8HU.
MALONEY, Mr. Christopher George, BSc(Hons) ACA FCCA ACCA CTA *2007;* (Tax Fac), with Harris Lipman LLP, 2 Mountview Court, 310 Friern Barnet Lane, LONDON, N20 0YZ.
MALONEY, Mr. David Robert, FCA *1972;* Brendan Chase, 1 College Road, WINDERMERE, CUMBRIA, LA23 1BU.
MALONEY, Mr. Gareth George, BA ACA DChA *1980;* IBVM-Loreto Sisters, Loreto Provincial Centre, 30 Maher Gardens, MANCHESTER, M15 5PW.
MALONEY, Mr. Leslie Kristoffer, ACA *2006;* 16 Lime Grove, Hoole, CHESTER, CH2 3HW.
MALONEY, Mr. Martin, BSc ACA *1992;* 7, Old Park Lane, LONDON, W1K1QR.
MALONEY, Mr. Matthew John, BA ACA *2001;* 30 Amherst Road, SEVENOAKS, KENT, TN13 3LS.
•**MALONEY, Mr. Michael Vincent, BA FCA** *1991;* KPMG LLP, 15 Canada Square, LONDON, E14 5GL. See also KPMG Europe LLP
MALONEY, Mrs. Samantha Jayne, ACA *2003;* 1 Forest Close, Crawley Down, CRAWLEY, WEST SUSSEX, RH10 4LT.
MALONEY, Miss. Sarah, ACA *2011;* 63 Wadbrough Road, SHEFFIELD, S11 8RF.
MALONEY, Mr. Spencer Joseph Patrick, BA FCA *1988;* 203 Leigh Hunt Drive, LONDON, N14 6DS.

MALONEY, Mr. Stephen, MA ACA *2010;* Flat 7 Jessop Court, Ferry Street, BRISTOL, BS1 6HW.
MALPAS, Mr. Richard Anthony, BSc ACA *1994;* 47 Tynedale Road, LOUGHBOROUGH, LEICESTERSHIRE, LE11 3TA.
MALPAS, Mr. Robert Daniel, FCA *1959;* 16 Moss Meadow, Westhoughton, BOLTON, BL5 3NX. (Life Member)
•**MALPASS, Mr. Andrew Mark, BA FCA** *1992;* Whittingham Riddell LLP, Belmont House, Shrewsbury Business Park, SHREWSBURY, SY2 6LG.
MALPASS, Mrs. Joanne Marie, ACA *2001;* The Bay Trust, The Pines Gardens, DOVER, KENT, CT15 6DZ.
MALPASS, Mr. John Stuart, ACA *1965;* 46 Mornington Terrace, LONDON, NW1 7RT. (Life Member)
MALPASS, Mr. Mark David, ACA MAAT *2004;* 15 Wansfell Terrace, BARNSLEY, SOUTH YORKSHIRE, S71 1EW.
MALSBURY, Miss. Sarah Louise, ACA *2011;* 17 Wells Avenue, WEDNESBURY, WEST MIDLANDS, WS10 8QN.
MALTARP, Mr. Damien Patrick Scott, ACA *2001;* PP A4K, British Telecom BT Centre, 81 Newgate Street, LONDON, EC1A 7AJ.
MALTBY, Mr. Brian John, FCA *1974;* 33 Gills Road, Howick, AUCKLAND, NEW ZEALAND.
MALTBY, Mr. Daniel Philip, MA ACA *2010;* Flat 7, 152 Peckham Rye, LONDON, SE22 9QH.
MALTBY, Miss. Joanna Lindsey, ACA *2009;* 42 Rycroft Meadow, Beggarwood, BASINGSTOKE, HAMPSHIRE, RG22 4QF.
MALTBY, Prof. Josephine Anne, MA ACA *1980;* York Management School, University of York, Heslington, YORK, YO10 5DD.
MALTBY, Miss. Maria Therese, BSc ACA DChA *2003;* with Wilkins Kennedy, Bridge House, London Bridge, LONDON, SE1 9QR.
MALTBY, Mr. Michael Arthur, BA ACA *1993;* DRAMM Limited, 35, 62/1 Karamisheskaya, NAB, MOSCOW, RUSSIAN FEDERATION.
•**MALTBY, Mr. Richard, FCA** *1982;* 83 Durleigh Road, BRIDGWATER, TA6 7JD.
MALTBY, Mr. William Henry Martyn, BA ACA *1987;* Xansa, 2300 The Crescent, Birmingham Business Park, BIRMINGHAM, B37 7YE.
MALTBY, Mr. William John, BA ACA *1985;* Maltby Associates Ltd, Haughurst House Inhurst Lane, Baughurst, TADLEY, RG26 5JS.
MALTHOUSE, Mr. Christopher Laurie, BA ACA *1995;* 3 Montagu Mews North, LONDON, W1H 2JR.
MALTHOUSE, Mr. Christopher Robin, FCA *1965;* 7a South Downs Road, Hale, ALTRINCHAM, WA14 3HU. (Life Member)
MALTHOUSE, Mr. Christopher Simon, BEng ACA MBA *1994;* 7 Heald Close, Bowdon, ALTRINCHAM, CHESHIRE, WA14 2JB.
MALTHOUSE, Mr. Iain Peter, BSc ACA *2003;* 11 Warwick Gardens, Thrapston, KETTERING, NORTHAMPTONSHIRE, NN14 4XB.
MALTHOUSE, Mr. James Leonard, BA FCA *1972;* Proteome Sciences PLC, Coveham House, Downside Bridge Road, COBHAM, KT11 3EP.
•**MALTHOUSE, Mr. John Christopher, BA FCA** *1967;* (Member of Council 1998 - 2004), (Tax Fac), Malthouse & Company Ltd, America House, Rumford Court, Rumford Place, LIVERPOOL, L3 9DD.
MALTON, Mr. Gerald Anthony, MA FCA *1986;* Foxtons, 23 The Street, Little Waltham, CHELMSFORD, CM3 3NS.
MALTON, Mr. Paul Reginald, FCA *1961;* Metron Technology Ltd, Osborne House, Trull Road, TAUNTON, SOMERSET, TA1 4PX.
MALTZ, Mr. Stephen Michael, FCA *1965;* 8 Shalom Aleichem, 47265 RAMAT HASHARON, ISRAEL.
MALU, Mrs. Margaret Mbithe, ACA *1986;* The United Nations World Food Programme, Office of Internal Audit, Via Cesare Giulio Viola, 68/70 Parco De'Medici, 00148 ROME, ITALY.
MALUSTE, Mr. Raghunandan Dattatray, MBA FCA *1976;* 6A IL Palazzo, Little Gibbs Road, MUMBAI 400 006, MAHARASHTRA, INDIA.
MALUZA, Mr. Ijoma Patrick, MA ACA *2006;* 19 Muswell Avenue, LONDON, N10 2EB.
MALVERN, Mr. David Anthony, BSc ACA *1998;* Apt 15J, 55 West 26th Street, NEW YORK, NY 10010, UNITED STATES.
MALYN, Mr. Keith Leonard, FCA *1979;* 37 Sunnybank Close, Aldridge, WALSALL, WS9 0YR.
•**MALYON, Mr. David Howard, ACA** *1980;* Pawley & Malyon, 15 Bedford Square, LONDON, WC1B 3JA.
MALYON, Miss. Elizabeth Verity, BSc(Hons) ACA *2009;* 9 Staites Orchard, Upton St. Leonards, GLOUCESTER, GL4 8BG.
MALYON, Mr. Jeffrey Joseph, BSc FCA *1976;* 26 Gilderdale Way, Oakwood, DERBY, DE21 2SY.
MALYON, Mr. Richard Charles, FCA *1958;* Old Quarry House, Seale Lane, Seale, FARNHAM, GU10 1LD. (Life Member)
MALZER, Mr. Nicholas James, BSc ACA *1992;* 18 Bell Road, Warnham, HORSHAM, WEST SUSSEX, RH12 3QL.
MAMA, Mr. Sorab Gustasp, FCA *1947;* 8918 Railton, HOUSTON, TX 77080, UNITED STATES. (Life Member)
MAMAS, Mr. Kleanthis Andrea, FCA *1972;* 14 Bracken Avenue, LONDON, SW12 8BH.
•**MAMDANI, Mr. Shabir Roshanali, FCA FCCA** *1984;* (Tax Fac), Adams Moorhouse, 4 Churchill Court, 58 Station Road, North Harrow, HARROW, HA2 7ST.
MAMELOK, Mr. Andrew Adam, BSc ACA *1992;* 31 Grafton Avenue, Naremburn, SYDNEY, NSW 2065, AUSTRALIA.
MAMELOK, Mrs. Lesley, BA ACA *1992;* 31 Grafton Avenue, Naremburn, SYDNEY, NSW 2065, AUSTRALIA.
MAMELOK, Mr. Peter John, FCA *1968;* Hall Farm House, Hall Lane, INGATESTONE, CM4 9NP.
MAMET, Mr. Evenor Jean-Sebastien, BA ACA *2001;* Harel Freres, 18 Edith Cavell Street, P O Box 317, PORT LOUIS, MAURITIUS.
MAMET, Mr. Jean Evenor Damien, ACA *2003;* 4 Morcellement Bagatelle, MOKA, MAURITIUS.
MAMMATT, Miss. Jayne Carol, BA ACA *1996;* 2 Vickers Avenue, Rivonia, SANDTON, 2191, SOUTH AFRICA.
MAMTORA, Mr. Ajay, BSc ACA *2011;* 24 Fullwell Avenue, ILFORD, ESSEX, IG6 2HJ.
MAMTORA, Mr. Prashik Prabhudas, BSc ACA *1995;* 26 Ross Way, NORTHWOOD, MIDDLESEX, HA6 3HU.
•**MAMUJEE, Mr. Azam Najmudin, MA FCA** *1997;* (Tax Fac), M Cubed Limited, 186 London Road, LEICESTER, LE2 1ND. See also M Cubed
•**MAMUJEE, Mr. Kaaeed Najmudin Adamjee, BSc FCA** *1990;* M Cubed Limited, 186 London Road, LEICESTER, LE2 1ND. See also M Cubed
MAN, Mr. Benjamin Yun Fung, MSc BSc ACA *2011;* Apartment 7, Pinnacle House, 15 Heritage Avenue, LONDON, NW9 5FY.
MAN, Mr. Bernard, MA ACA *1991;* 14 Hillfield Road, West Hampstead, LONDON, NW6 1PZ.
MAN, Mr. Chiu Ming, BSc ACA *1999;* (Tax Fac), 28 Poplar Drive, Hutton, BRENTWOOD, CM13 1YU.
MAN, Ms. Chung Yan, ACA *2007;* Flat 618, Ka Lei Lau, 8 Station Lane, HUNG HOM, KOWLOON, HONG KONG SAR.
MAN, Mr. David Kin Wai, BA ACA *1998;* AIA Building, 18th Floor, 1 Stubbs Rd, WAN CHAI, HONG KONG SAR.
MAN, Mr. David Wai Cheun, BSc ACA *1993;* 16 Pinkworthy, Furzton, MILTON KEYNES, MK4 1JR.
MAN, Mr. Eddie King Chi, BSc FCA *1992;* T. C. Ng & Co. CPA Ltd., Amber Commercial Building, 13th Floor, 70-74 Morrison Hill Road, WAN CHAI, HONG KONG ISLAND HONG KONG SAR.
MAN, Miss. Elizabeth, ACA *2011;* Flat 16 Hewer House, Worsopp Drive, LONDON, SW4 9QR.
MAN, Mr. George Kai Bung, MSc BSc ACA *1999;* 85 Rusthall Avenue, LONDON, W4 1BN.
MAN, Miss. Helen Shu Yen, BA ACA *1992;* Flat E2, 21/F Blk E Beverley Hills, 6 Broadwood Road, HAPPY VALLEY, HONG KONG ISLAND, HONG KONG SAR.
MAN, Miss. Josephine Wing-Yan, BA ACA *2001;* 204 Boardwalk Place, LONDON, E14 5SQ.
MAN, Miss. Ka-Lai, BSc ACA *1996;* with Deloitte Touche Tohmatsu, 35/F One Pacific Place, 88 Queensway, CENTRAL, HONG KONG ISLAND, HONG KONG SAR.
•**MAN, Mr. Kai Wai Malcolm, ACA FCCA CTA CPA** *2005;* KHMM, Lison House, 173 Wardour Street, LONDON, W1F 8WT. See also Malcolm Man Accountancy Limited
MAN, Miss. Kitty, ACA *2009;* 23 Albatross Close, LONDON, E6 5NX.
MAN, Mr. Kwok Wai, BA ACA *1993;* Fairfax Engineering Ltd, 1 Regency Parade Finchley Road, LONDON, NW3 5EQ.
MAN, Mr. Kwok Leung, ACA *2005;* Chan & Man, 1603 16/F Island Place Tower, 510 King's Road North Point, WAN CHAI, HONG KONG SAR.
MAN, Ms. Lee Chin, BSc ACA *2003;* 23 Beryl Avenue, LONDON, E6 5JT.
MAN, Mr. Mang Wo Derek, ACA *2005;* Flat C 26/F, Wisteria Mansion, 4 Taikoo Wan Road, TAIKOO SHING, HONG KONG ISLAND, HONG KONG SAR.
MAN, Ms. Miu Sheung, ACA *2005;* 6/F KMB Building 9 Po Lun Street, LAI CHI KOK, HONG KONG SAR.
•**MAN, Mr. Mo Leung, BSc FCA** *1978;* Mazars CPA Ltd, 42F Central Plaza, 18 Harbour Road, WAN CHAI, HONG KONG ISLAND, HONG KONG SAR.
MAN, Ms. Oi Yuk Yvonne, ACA *2008;* Flat D 11/F Block 8, 1 Sceneway Garden, 8 Sceneway Road, LAM TIN, KOWLOON, HONG KONG SAR.
MAN, Miss. Sau Kuen, BA(Hons) ACA *2003;* 2 Blossom Drive, ORPINGTON, BR6 0AS.
MAN, Mr. Shing Chun, ACA *2010;* (Tax Fac), Flat 01 8th Floor, Block 16, Heng Fa Chuen, CHAI WAN, HONG KONG ISLAND, HONG KONG SAR.
•**MAN, Mrs. Siew Yoke, BA FCA** *1985;* Man & Co (UK) Ltd, 3 Garrick House, 63 St Martin's Lane, LONDON, WC2N 4JS.
MAN, Mr. Sik Wing, ACA *2008;* Flat F, 19/F, Block 1, Dragon View, 83 Chung Hau Street, HO MAN TIN HONG KONG SAR.
MAN, Mr. Simon Sai Moon, BA ACA *1983;* Flat B 15/F Block 15, Pacific Palisades, 1 Braemar Hill Road, NORTH POINT, HONG KONG ISLAND, HONG KONG SAR.
MAN, Mr. Stephen, BSc ACA *2002;* 51 Jerome Drive, ST. ALBANS, AL3 4LT.
•**MAN, Mr. Victor Tsinkeung, BSc FCA** *1985;* (Tax Fac), Man & Co, 114 Hamlet Court Road, WESTCLIFF-ON-SEA, ESSEX, SS0 7LP.
MAN, Miss. Yee Cheong, BSc ACA *2007;* Jellicoe House, Flat 747, 4 St. George Wharf, LONDON, SW8 2JF.
MANAGE, Mr. Don, ACA *2010;* ATB Financial, Enterprise Risk Management (Transit 426), 7th Floor, 9888 Jasper Avenue, EDMONTON T5J 1P1, AB CANADA.
•**MANAKTALA, Mr. Pradeep, FCA** *1980;* (Tax Fac), Manaktala & Co Limited, 17 Leeland Mansions, Leeland Road West Ealing, LONDON, W13 9HE.
MANAKTALA, Mr. Praveen, ACA *1982;* Praveen K Manaktala, PO Box 603, BROOKVALE, NSW 2100, AUSTRALIA.
MANALO, Mr. Paul Andrew, BA ACA *2010;* 20 Kimberley Road, Tottenham, LONDON, N17 9BD.
MANAMLEY, Mr. Christopher Paul, BSc ACA *1999;* 100 Linden Road, BIRMINGHAM, B30 1LA.
MANAWADU, Miss. Dilum Manori, MA(Cantab) ACA *2002;* 93 Ivydale Road, LONDON, SE15 3DS.
MANAZIR, Mr. Naveed, ACA *1984;* PO Box 125448, Suite 2411, Grosvenor House Tower, Sheikh Zayed Road, DUBAI, UNITED ARAB EMIRATES.
MANCHANDA, Mr. Harvinder Pal Singh, FCA *1977;* 501 Washington Avenue, CARLSTADT, NJ 07072, UNITED STATES.
•**MANCHANDA, Mr. Rajiv, FCA** *1977;* (Tax Fac), Manchanda And Co, 22 Doneraile Street, Fulham, LONDON, SW6 6EN.
•**MANCHELLI, Mr. Andrea, ACA** *2008;* with PricewaterhouseCoopers S.P.A., Via Monte Rosa 91, 20149 MILAN, ITALY.
MANCHESTER, Miss. Cara Louise, BA ACA *1993;* 12 Cornfield Way, Burton Latimer, KETTERING, NORTHAMPTONSHIRE, NN15 5YH.
MANCHESTER, Mr. Graham John, FCA *1977;* P.O. Box 1051, GEORGE TOWN, GRAND CAYMAN, KY1-1102, CAYMAN ISLANDS.
MANCHESTER, Mr. Paul Gerard, BA FCA *1992;* 2a Moorfield Lane, Scarisbrick, ORMSKIRK, LANCASHIRE, L40 8JD.
MANCHHARAM, Mr. Kirti Kumar, FCA *1972;* Pristine Properties Private Ltd, 77 High Street, No. 02-11 High Street Plaza, SINGAPORE 179433, SINGAPORE.
MANDAIR, Miss. Baldish Kaur, BA(Hons) ACA *2001;* (Tax Fac), 45 Donnington Drive, Chandler's Ford, EASTLEIGH, HAMPSHIRE, SO53 3PE.
MANDAIR, Mr. Rabinder Singh, ACA *1987;* Pine Tree Cottage, Oak Way, REIGATE, RH2 7ES.
•**MANDAIR, Mr. Rajinder, ACA** *2008;* Basra & Basra Ltd, 9 London Road, SOUTHAMPTON, SO15 2AE.
MANDAIR, Mr. Sandeep, BSc ACA *2010;* 10 Ardnave Crescent, SOUTHAMPTON, SO16 7FJ.
MANDAIR, Miss. Satvir Kaur, BA ACA *2008;* Redprairie Ltd Beacon House, Ibstone Road Stokenchurch, HIGH WYCOMBE, BUCKINGHAMSHIRE, HP14 3AQ.
•**MANDAIR, Mr. Tarlochen Singh, BSc ACA** *1996;* Mandair Ltd, Partnership House, 84 Lodge Road, Portswood, SOUTHAMPTON, SO14 6RG.
MANDAIR, Mr. Tarlok Singh, FCA *1971;* 21 Colbert Avenue, SOUTHEND-ON-SEA, SS1 3BH.
MANDALE, Mr. Christopher John Richard, BA ACA *1984;* Chateau de L''Oseraie, Lieu-dit L'Oseraie, 49640 CHEMRIE SUR SARTHE, FRANCE.
MANDALE, Miss. Nicola, ACA *2001;* (Tax Fac), 2 Chestnut Glen, HORNCHURCH, ESSEX, RM12 4HL.
•**MANDALIA, Mr. Ajay Mansukh, BSc ACA** *1995;* Teamwork Financial Services Limited, 31 Cheyneys Avenue, EDGWARE, MIDDLESEX, HA8 6SA.
MANDALIA, Mr. Jetan, BCom ACA *2000;* 13 Heath Road, HARROW, MIDDLESEX, HA1 4DA.
•**MANDALIA, Mr. Mukesh Ravji, BSc FCA** *1992;* Nielsens, 453 Cranbrook Road, ILFORD, ESSEX, IG2 6EW.
MANDALIA, Mr. Rahil Laxman, BSc(Hons) ACA *2001;* 42 Brook Meadow, Holden Road, LONDON, N12 7DB.
MANDALIA, Mrs. Sapna, BSc ACA *2003;* Flat 3 Sherriff Court, Sherriff Road, LONDON, NW6 2AT.
MANDANIA, Mr. Mehul, BSc ACA *2010;* 316 Mitcham Road, CROYDON, CR0 3JN.
MANDAVIA, Mr. Manish, BSc ACA *1998;* 32 The Avenue, WEMBLEY, MIDDLESEX, HA9 9QJ.
MANDEL, Mr. Paul Benjamin, BA ACA *1991;* Eldnam Ltd, 1st Floor, 269 Green Lanes, LONDON, N13 4XE.
•**MANDEL, Mr. Philip Warner Barry, FCA** *1973;* Daly Mandel, 105 Southlands Road, BROMLEY, BR2 9QT.
MANDER, Mr. Charles Wilhelm, MA ACA *2000;* Aegonplein 50, 2591 Tv Den Haag, DEN HAAG, NETHERLANDS.
MANDER, Mr. Clive William, BSc FCA *1977;* 808 Oakbrook Drive, NORMAN, OK 73072, UNITED STATES.
•①**MANDER, Mr. Guy Edward Brooke, LLB ACA** *1991;* Baker Tilly Restructuring & Recovery LLP, St Philips Point, Temple Row, BIRMINGHAM, B2 5AF. See also Baker Tilly Tax and Advisory Services LLP, and Debt Lifeboat Limited
MANDER, Mr. Nigel Carl, FCA *1987;* Birch House, Daisy Lane, Alrewas, BURTON-ON-TRENT, STAFFORDSHIRE, DE13 7EW.
MANDER, Mr. Richard, BSc ACA *2011;* Flat 17, Taymount Grange, Taymount Rise, LONDON, SE23 3UH.
MANDER, Mr. Richard Charles, BA ACA *1993;* Grosvenor, 70 Grosvenor Street, LONDON, W1K 3JP.
•**MANDER, Mr. Richard Luke, FCA** *1992;* Carter Dutton Limited, 65-66 St. Mary Street, CHIPPENHAM, WILTSHIRE, SN15 3JF.
MANDER, Mr. Robert Brian, BA ACA *1988;* RSM Bird Cameron, GPO Box 5138, SYDNEY, NSW 2001, AUSTRALIA.
MANDER, Mr. Simon Vivian, ACA *1979;* Apartment 126 Oyster Wharf, 18 Lombard Road, LONDON, SW11 3RT.
•**MANDERFIELD, Mr. Andrew Robert, FCA** *1991;* Streets Audit LLP, Halifax House, 30-34 George Street, HULL, HU1 3AJ. See also Streets ISA Ltd
MANDERS, Mr. Andrew Craig, ACA *1989;* Langleys, Butterton, NEWCASTLE, STAFFORDSHIRE, ST5 4DU.
•**MANDEVILLE, Mr. James Geoffrey, FCA** *1981;* James Mandeville, 6 Ridgeway, WELLINGBOROUGH, NORTHAMPTONSHIRE, NN8 4RX.
MANDIZHA, Mrs. Megan Clement, BA ACA *1983;* Cardiff Council, County Hall, Atlantic Wharf, CARDIFF, CF10 4UW.
MANDLA, Mrs. Seema, BSc ACA *2004;* Johnson & Johnson Ltd, Foundation Park, Roxborough Way, MAIDENHEAD, BERKSHIRE, SL6 3UG.
MANDLEBERG, Miss. Helena Jane, BSc ACA *2003;* The Carphone Warehouse, 1 Portal Way, LONDON, W3 6RS.
MANDLIK, Miss. Sinead, ACA DChA *2009;* 10 Lochaber Road, Lewisham, LONDON, SE13 5QU.
MANDON, Miss. Valerie, MSc BEng ACA *1999;* Chemin de la Maraiche 20, CH 1802 CORSEAUX, SWITZERLAND.
MANDVIWALLA, Mr. Iqbal Husein Ismail, FCA *1980;* Flat 1, Elm House, 97 Ducks Hill Road, NORTHWOOD, MIDDLESEX, HA6 2WG.
MANDY, Mr. Colin Alan, BSc ACA *2006;* 28 Linley Road, SALE, CHESHIRE, M33 7EJ.
MANDY, Mr. Philip Lawrence, FCA *1975;* University of Ghana, P.O.Box LG 50, 19 Little Legon, Legon, ACCRA, GHANA.
MANEK, Mr. Nikhil, BA(Hons) ACA *2010;* 11 Highfield, WATFORD, WD19 5DY.
MANEKSHA, Mr. Cyrus Dorab, BA ACA *1997;* 112 Jeddo Road, Shepherds Bush, LONDON, W12 9EG.
MANFIELD, Mr. William Rae, BSc ACA *1992;* 48 Bramfield Road, LONDON, SW11 6RB.
MANFORD, Mr. John, FCA *1961;* 5 Bowbrook Grange, Mytton Oak Road, SHREWSBURY, SY3 8XT. (Life Member)
MANFORD, Mr. Scott, ACA *2008;* 15 Beal Way, NEWCASTLE UPON TYNE, NE3 3EY.
MANFREDI, Mr. Cosimo, BSc ACA *1992;* with National Audit Office, 157-197 Buckingham Palace Road, Victoria, LONDON, SW1W 9SP.

MANFREDI, Mrs. Tracy, BA ACA *1997;* (Tax Fac), 52 Marlowe Road, Rudheath, NORTHWICH, CW9 7GA.
•**MANGAL, Mr. Andeep Kumar, BA(Hons) ACA** *2001;* Thapers, 14 Holyhead Road, Handsworth, BIRMINGHAM, B21 0LT.
MANGAN, Mr. Gregory, BBS ACA *1990;* Coras Iompair Eireann, Aras Eanna, 60 Gardiner Street Lower, DUBLIN 1, COUNTY DUBLIN, IRELAND.
MANGAN, Mrs. Lucy Victoria, LLB ACA CTA *2000;* (Tax Fac), with Moore Stephens LLP, 150 Aldersgate Street, LONDON, EC1A 4AB.
MANGAT, Mr. Balbeer Singh, BA ACA *1983;* B.S. Mangat & Company, 20 Cecil Street, 15-08 Equity Plaza, SINGAPORE 049705, SINGAPORE.
MANGAT, Mr. Harminder Singh, BA ACA *1988;* (Tax Fac), with KPMG LLP, 15 Canada Square, LONDON, E14 5GL.
MANGAT, Mrs. Mandeep Kaur, BSc ACA *2007;* 35 Felipe Road, Chafford Hundred, GRAYS, RM16 6NE.
MANGAT, Mr. Sachinder, BA(Hons) ACA *2009;* 35 Felipe Road, Chafford Hundred, GRAYS, RM16 6NE.
MANGAT, Mrs. Satbinder, BA ACA *2004;* Gearbulk UK Ltd, 5 The Heights, Brooklands, WEYBRIDGE, SURREY, KT13 0NY.
•**MANGER, Mr. Surjit, BA ACA** *1998;* The Small Accounts Company, 3 Nutmead Close, BEXLEY, KENT, DA5 2DT.
MANGERAH, Mr. Cassim, BEng ACA *1997;* 19 Queens Road, WINDSOR, BERKSHIRE, SL4 3BQ.
MANGHAM, Mr. Grant Arthur, BSc FCA *1964;* 43 Rowan Crescent, WORKSOP, S80 1BA.
MANGHAM, Mrs. Heather Margaret, BA ACA *1992;* with Powrie Appleby LLP, Queen Anne House, 4 6 & 8 New Street, LEICESTER, LE1 5NR.
MANGHI, Mr. Azam Alessandro Ragionevoli, ACA *1990;* Business Bay Executive Tower D, Room 1401, DUBAI, UNITED ARAB EMIRATES.
MANGHNANI, Miss. Vandana, LLB ACA *1991;* A1 9/F Wilshire Towers, 200 Tin Hau Temple Road, CAUSEWAY BAY, HONG KONG ISLAND, HONG KONG SAR.
MANGION, Mr. Joseph Bernard, FCA *1980;* 6 The Drive, ESHER, SURREY, KT10 8DQ.
•**MANGLES, Mr. David Kenneth Pasley, FCA** *1970;* Heather Lea Business Services, 49 Heather Lea Avenue, SHEFFIELD, S17 3DL.
MANGNALL, Mrs. Helen, BSc ACA *2002;* 37 Fossgill Avenue, BOLTON, BL2 3FR.
•**MANI, Mr. Ehsan, FCA** *1970;* Apartment 1913, Grosvenor House, West Marina Beach, PO Box 118500, DUBAI, UNITED ARAB EMIRATES.
MANI, Mrs. Frances Ann, FCA *1975;* 43 Queen's Grove, LONDON, NW8 6HH.
•**MANIAR, Mr. Dipak Babulal, ACA** *1994;* Virtual Finance Limited, Devonshire House, 582 Honeypot Lane, STANMORE, HA7 1JS.
MANIAR, Mrs. Tejal, BSc ACA *2011;* 70a Hindes Road, HARROW, MIDDLESEX, HA1 1SL.
•**MANIAR, Mr. Zayd, BA ACA** *2005;* Horwath Mak, P.O. Box 6747, DUBAI, UNITED ARAB EMIRATES. See also AGN MAK
MANIATAKIS, Mr. Nicholas, BA ACA *1999;* Falck Renewables Plc, 7-10 Beaumont Mews, LONDON, W1G 6EB.
MANIC, Mr. Kevin, ACA *2008;* 1a Tavistock Road, LONDON, E15 4ER.
MANICKAM, Mr. Narayanan, ACA *1980;* 26 Highbridge Road, RICHMOND HILL L4B 1Y3, ON, CANADA.
MANICKARAJAH, Miss. Mythrayi, LLB ACA *2002;* Rue de Albert Gos 5, Apartment 43A, 1206 GENEVA, SWITZERLAND.
MANIFOLD, Mr. Christopher Joseph, MSc ACA *1990;* 98 Torlesse Road, RD1, CHRISTCHURCH 7671, NEW ZEALAND.
MANIKKAVASAGAN, Mr. Muthukrishnar Thambyappah, FCA *1975;* 7 Manning Gardens, HARROW, MIDDLESEX, HA3 0PF.
MANIQUE, Mrs. Jocelyn Claire, ACA *1994;* 91A James Street, NEW FARM, QLD 4005, AUSTRALIA.
MANISTY, Mr. Alexander, BA ACA *1994;* D S Smith Packaging Beech House, Whitebrook Park 68 Lower Cookham Road, MAIDENHEAD, SL6 8JZ.
MANISTY, Mr. Harry, BSc ACA *2007;* Flat 10, 146 Lavender Hill, LONDON, SW11 5RA.
MANJANATH, Mrs. Priya, BSc ACA *2003;* Flat 1, 43 Belsize Park Gardens, LONDON, NW3 4JJ.
MANJI, Mr. Al-Noor Suleman, MA ACA *1984;* Quality Commodities Ltd, 397 A Kafue Road, P O Box 32908, LUSAKA, ZAMBIA.
MANJI, Mr. Mahmood Pyarali, FCA *1978;* P.O.Box 74445, NAIROBI, 0200, KENYA.
MANJI, Miss. Salima Mohammed Fazal, BSc ACA *1996;* 42 Mendora Road, LONDON, SW6 7NB.
•**MANJOO, Mr. Juneid Ahmad, FCA** *1976;* Andertons, Hytec House, 27 Burgess Wood Road South, BEACONSFIELD, BUCKINGHAMSHIRE, HP9 1EX.
•**MANJRA, Mr. Mohamed Yacoob, FCA** *1964;* (Tax Fac), Vallance Lodge & Co, Units 082 - 086, 555 White Hart Lane, LONDON, N17 7RN.
•**MANKELOW, Mr. Peter Kenneth, FCA** *1970;* (Tax Fac), P.K. Mankelow & Co, P.O.Box 45, CRAWLEY, RH10 3YP. See also PKM Admin Services Limited
MANKIEWITZ, Mr. Robert Werner, BA ACA *1982;* 39 St Botolph's Road, SEVENOAKS, TN13 3AG.
•**MANKIN, Mr. Paul, BSc ACA CF** *1986;* PricewaterhouseCoopers LLP, 89 Sandyford Road, NEWCASTLE UPON TYNE, NE1 8HW. See also PricewaterhouseCoopers
MANKIN, Mr. Robert Michael, FCA *1959;* 6 Atwood, Bookham, LEATHERHEAD, KT23 3BH. (Life Member)
MANKOO, Ms. Ravinderjit Kaur, MA BA ACA *1997;* Birch House, 8 Woodland Glade, Farnham Common, SLOUGH, BUCKINGHAMSHIRE, SL2 3RG.
MANKS, Mrs. Hazel Ruth, BSc ACA *1996;* 8 Torcaill Court, Portmarnock, DUBLIN 16, COUNTY DUBLIN, IRELAND.
MANKTELOW, Mr. John, BA FCA *1972;* Lower House Farm, Westburton, PULBOROUGH, RH20 1HD.
MANKU, Miss. Gurpreet Kaur, BSc ACA *2006;* 7 Munster Avenue, HOUNSLOW, TW4 5BG.
MANLEY, Mr. David Charles, BA ACA *2004;* 74 Main Street, Great Bowden, MARKET HARBOROUGH, LE16 7HD.
MANLEY, Miss. Donna Dawn, BSc ACA *2007;* 60 Andrews House, Tadros Court, Windsor Gate, HIGH WYCOMBE, BUCKINGHAMSHIRE, HP13 7GF.
MANLEY, Miss. Helen Louise, BA ACA *1996;* Optomen Television, 102 St Pancras Way, LONDON, NW1 9ND.
MANLEY, Mr. Iain Austen, BSc ACA *1997;* Flat 1, 9 Orchard Lane, EAST MOLESEY, SURREY, KT8 0BN.
MANLEY, Mr. Jonathan Brinley, FCA *1984;* with Day Smith & Hunter, Globe House, Eclipse Park, Sittingbourne Road, MAIDSTONE, KENT ME14 3EN.
MANLEY, Mrs. Julia Anne, BA ACA *1990;* (Tax Fac), 5 Bryanstone Mews, COLCHESTER, CO3 9XZ.
MANLEY, Mr. Keith Anil, FCA *1976;* 25 Hamilton Avenue, Harborne, BIRMINGHAM, B17 8AH.
MANLEY, Mr. Keith Leslie George, FCA JDipMA *1957;* 1 Crane Close, WOODBRIDGE, SUFFOLK, IP12 4TF. (Life Member)
MANLEY, Miss. Laraine Margaret, BSc ACA *1986;* Sheffield City Council, Po Box 1283, Town Hall, SHEFFIELD, S1 1UJ.
MANLEY, Mr. Michael Thomas, FCA *1974;* Elmdene, 106 Shutt Lane, Earlswood, SOLIHULL, WEST MIDLANDS, B94 6DA.
MANLEY, Mr. Nicholas Mark, BSc ACA *1994;* 7 Mortens Wood, AMERSHAM, HP7 9EQ.
MANLEY, Mr. Peter, FCA *1953;* 2 Marlow House, Institute Road, MARLOW, BUCKINGHAMSHIRE, SL7 1BB.
MANLEY, Mr. Richard Edward, BSc ACA *2005;* 2 Lindsell Road, West Timperley, ALTRINCHAM, CHESHIRE, WA14 5NX.
MANN, Mr. Alan Norman Innes, FCA *1950;* 57 Princes Road, WEYBRIDGE, SURREY, KT13 9BT. (Life Member)
•**MANN, Mrs. Aleathia Margaret, FCA** *1979;* Aleathia Mann Ltd, Springwood, Church Lane, Sparham, NORWICH, NR9 5PP. See also Aleathia Mann
MANN, Mr. Alexander Sidney Thomas, FCA *1961;* 65 Cambridge Drive, Lee, LONDON, SE12 8AG. (Life Member)
MANN, Mr. Andrew Jonathan, BSc FCA *1988;* National Australia Bank Ltd, 88 Wood Street, LONDON, EC2V 7QQ.
MANN, Mr. Andrew Steven, BSc ACA *2005;* 39 Velmead Road, FLEET, GU52 7LJ.
MANN, Miss. Anita Paula, BA ACA *1985;* 28 Leydon Croft, Kings Norton, BIRMINGHAM, B38 0AH.
MANN, Ms. Annette Christine, BA ACA *1996;* 20 Eastwood Road, Bramley, GUILDFORD, SURREY, GU5 0DS.
MANN, Mr. Charanpal Singh, FCA *1970;* 56 Friends Colony East Unit One, NEW DELHI 110065, INDIA. (Life Member)
MANN, Mr. Christopher John, MA BA(Econ) ACA *1979;* 14 High Street, Molesworth Village, HUNTINGDON, CAMBRIDGESHIRE, PE28 0QF.
MANN, Mr. Christopher John, ACA *1995;* HGP Architects Ltd, Furzehall Farm 110 Wickham Road, FAREHAM, HAMPSHIRE, PO16 7JH.
MANN, Mr. Christopher Richard, BA FCA *1991;* 5 Old Town Close, BEACONSFIELD, HP9 1LF.
MANN, Mrs. Clare Emma, BSc ACA *2006;* 37a Fairholme Road, LONDON, W14 9JZ.
MANN, Mr. David, BA ACA *1992;* Rose Bowl Plc, Botley Road, West End, SOUTHAMPTON, SO30 3XH.
MANN, Mr. David Bernard, FCA *1973;* Fairview, Odiham Rd, Riseley, READING, RG7 1SD.
•**MANN, Mr. David Jonathan, FCA** *1987;* (Tax Fac), Berry & Warren Ltd, 54 Thorpe Road, NORWICH, NR1 1RY.
MANN, Mr. Gary Stephen, BSc ACA *2005;* 235 Croxted Road, LONDON, SE21 8NL.
MANN, Miss. Gemma Carolyn, BSc ACA *2006;* Redevco UK, 1 James Street, LONDON, W1U 1DR.
MANN, Mr. George Stephen, BA FCA *1966;* Silver Howe, 12 Levens Way, Silverdale, CARNFORTH, LA5 0TG. (Life Member)
MANN, Mr. Gerald Frank, FCA *1956;* Kilmore, Shrubbs Hill, Chobham, WOKING, GU24 8ST. (Life Member)
MANN, Miss. Helen Fraser, BA(Hons) ACA *2003;* 12200 Academy Road NE, Apartment 1133, ALBUQUERQUE, NM 87111, UNITED STATES.
MANN, Mr. Ian Richard, BSc FCA *1986;* with PricewaterhouseCoopers AG, Avenue Giuseppe-Motta 50, 1211 GENEVA, SWITZERLAND.
MANN, Ms. Janette Debra, BA FCA *2000;* 39 Velmead Road, FLEET, HAMPSHIRE, GU52 7LJ.
MANN, Mrs. Jennifer Virginia, FCA *1975;* The Old Vicarage, St. James Road, Goffs Oak, WALTHAM CROSS, HERTFORDSHIRE, EN7 6TP.
MANN, Miss. Joanna C Y, ACA *2008;* 5 Priory Gardens, HAMPTON, MIDDLESEX, TW12 2PZ.
•**MANN, Mr. John Michael, FCA** *1959;* Michael Mann & Co, 71 White Horse Road, WINDSOR, BERKSHIRE, SL4 4PG.
•**MANN, Mr. Jonathan Howard, BA FCA** *1989;* Baker Tilly Tax & Advisory Services LLP, 1st Floor, 46 Clarendon Road, WATFORD, WD17 1JJ. See also Baker Tilly UK Audit LLP
MANN, Miss. Julie, MSc BA(Hons) ACA *2003;* 16 The Hawthorns Cabus, PRESTON, LANCASHIRE, PR3 1NF.
MANN, Mr. Justyn, BSc(Hons) ACA *2001;* 23 The Causeway, Burwell, CAMBRIDGE, CB25 0DU.
MANN, Mrs. Karenjit, ACA *2010;* 80 Broomfield, SMETHWICK, B67 7DR.
•**MANN, Miss. Kathryn Patricia Frances, BSc FCA** *1983;* Lambert Mann Limited, 33 Corfe Way, BROADSTONE, BH18 9ND. See also Lambert Mann
MANN, Miss. Kirstie Susan, BA ACA *2002;* 2b Grove Lane, KINGSTON UPON THAMES, SURREY, KT1 2SU.
MANN, Mrs. Lynda Janet, BA ACA *1991;* 9 Lavender Gate, Oxshott, LEATHERHEAD, KT22 0RE.
MANN, Miss. Michelle Loraine, ACA *2000;* 34 Honey Hill Road, Kingswood, BRISTOL, BS15 4HJ.
MANN, Mr. Naveen Singh, BSc ACA *1992;* 4 Browett Road, COVENTRY, CV6 1AZ.
MANN, Mr. Oliver, BSc ACA *2009;* 15 Hampden Gardens, CAMBRIDGE, CB1 3EL.
MANN, Mr. Oliver David, BSc ACA *2005;* 61 St. Mawes Avenue, NOTTINGHAM, NG11 7BX.
MANN, Mr. Paul, BA ACA *1988;* 380 Fallow Field Road, FAIRFIELD, CT 06824, UNITED STATES.
MANN, Mr. Paul Richard, BSc ACA *2002;* 28b Harewood Avenue, NEWARK, NOTTINGHAMSHIRE, NG24 4AN.
MANN, Mr. Philip David, BA ACA *2005;* 1 Chatsworth Fold, WIGAN, WN3 4LT.
MANN, Mr. Richard Alexander James, BA ACA *1998;* 10 Cromwell Avenue, Highgate, LONDON, N6 5HL.
MANN, Mr. Richard Charles, BSc FCA *1977;* 93 Grange Road, Stobhill Grange, MORPETH, NE61 2TS.
MANN, Mr. Richard Jeffrey, FCA *1975;* 76 Meadow Road, Wolston, COVENTRY, CV8 3JJ.
MANN, Mr. Richard John, BA ACA *1997;* (Tax Fac), Woodside, The Plantation, Curdridge, SOUTHAMPTON, HAMPSHIRE, SO32 2DT.
MANN, Mr. Richard John, BA ACA *2006;* 272 Pickhurst Lane, WEST WICKHAM, KENT, BR4 0HT.
•**MANN, Mr. Richard William, ACA ATII** *1982;* (Tax Fac), Sterling Tax, 84 Smugglers Lane North, Highcliffe, CHRISTCHURCH, DORSET, BH23 4NL.
MANN, Mr. Robert Charles, ACA *2008;* 58 Chantry Road, East Ayton, SCARBOROUGH, NORTH YORKSHIRE, YO13 9ER.
MANN, Mr. Roger, FCA *1963;* 12 North Court, The Ridges, Finchampstead, WOKINGHAM, BERKSHIRE, RG40 3SJ. (Life Member)
MANN, Mr. Ross, BSc ACA *2010;* Sainsburys Supermarkets Ltd, 33 Holborn, LONDON, EC1N 2HT.
MANN, Mr. Rupinder Singh, ACA *1999;* Dumgoyne, Templewood Lane, Stoke Poges, SLOUGH, SL2 4BG.
MANN, Miss. Samantha, BA ACA *2004;* 22 The Lawns, Lee Terrace, LONDON, SE3 9TB.
MANN, Mrs. Sarah, BSc ACA *1995;* Dovehayes Mill Lane, Bourton, GILLINGHAM, DORSET, SP8 5DA.
MANN, Miss. Sharon, ACA *2009;* 21 Cheryls Close, LONDON, SW6 2AX.
•**MANN, Mr. Sidney Arthur, FCA** *1957;* S.A. Mann, 4 Canons Close, EDGWARE, MIDDLESEX, HA8 7QR.
MANN, Mr. Simon Edward, BA ACA *2002;* JX Nippon, 4th Floor, 1 Finsbury Square, LONDON, EC2A 1AE.
MANN, Mr. Stephen David, BSc ACA *1999;* Elysium Fund Management Ltd, PO Box 650, GUERNSEY, GY1 3JX.
MANN, Mr. Stephen John, BSc ACA *1990;* 154 Greenvale Road, Eltham, LONDON, SE4 1PQ.
MANN, The Revd. Stephen Timothy, MA ACA *1991;* 98 Culverden Down, TUNBRIDGE WELLS, KENT, TN4 9TA.
MANN, Mr. Sukhminder, MSc ACA *2006;* 12 Claydon Drive, CROYDON, CR0 4QX.
MANN, Mrs. Susan Jill, BSc ACA *1988;* Leigh Rise, 7 Leigh Court Close, COBHAM, KT11 2HT.
MANN, Mr. Timothy David, BSc ACA *1992;* 30/F Block 28, Baguio Villa, 550 Victoria Road, POK FU LAM, HONG KONG ISLAND, HONG KONG SAR.
MANN, Mr. Timothy Philip, BSc(Hons) ACA *2002;* 21 Spring Lane, Whittington, LICHFIELD, STAFFORDSHIRE, WS14 9LX.
MANN, Mrs. Zoie Louise, BSc(Hons) ACA *2002;* 5 Cursley Way, Beeston, NOTTINGHAM, NG9 6NT.
MANNALL, Mr. Robin Gordon, MA ACA *1996;* Unit 3 Fusion Point, Ash Lane, Garforth, LEEDS, LS25 2GA.
MANNALL, Mrs. Samantha Jane, BA ACA CTA *2007;* with Deloitte LLP, 2 New Street Square, LONDON, EC4A 3BZ.
•**MANNAN, Mr. Abdul, FCA** *1971;* A. Mannan & Co, 14 Norman Road, Leytonstone, LONDON, E11 4PX.
MANNAN, Mr. Miyan Mansur, BA FCA *1979;* 4 Salisbury Road, WORCESTER PARK, KT4 7DG.
MANNAN, Mr. Rohit, BSc(Econ) ACA *1998;* Watts Building, 10 Independents Road, LONDON, SE3 9LF.
MANNAN, Mr. Salman Ahmad, MSc ACA *1991;* (Tax Fac), 1260 Greenford Road, GREENFORD, MIDDLESEX, UB6 0HH.
MANNANI, Miss. Zohra, BA ACA *2005;* (Tax Fac), 54 Glenester Close, HODDESDON, HERTFORDSHIRE, EN11 9LR.
MANNERING, Mr. Clive Trevor, TD FCA *1960;* New Biddenden Green Farm, Lewd Lane, Smarden, ASHFORD, KENT, TN27 8NP. (Life Member)
MANNERING, Mr. James Paul, ACA *2009;* Flat 118 Scotney Gardens, St. Peters Street, MAIDSTONE, ME16 0GT.
MANNERING, Mr. Jeffrey, BA ACA *1986;* 6 The Beeches, Chester Road, Helsby, FRODSHAM, WA6 0QL.
MANNERING, Mr. Karl, ACA *2008;* 67 Chillington Way, STOKE-ON-TRENT, ST6 8GJ.
MANNERING, Mr. Michael Paul, BSc ACA *1992;* New Biddenden Green Farm, Lewd LaneSmarden, ASHFORDKent, TN27 8NP.
MANNERS, Mr. Arthur, FCA *1971;* 1 Turnpole Close, STAMFORD, LINCOLNSHIRE, PE9 1DT.
MANNERS, Mr. Arthur Roger, ACA *1986;* Wardens Lodge, Knowle Hill, Kingclere, NEWBURY, RG20 4PA.
MANNERS, Mr. Brian Bishop, FCA *1948;* 20 Vicarage Farm Close, Escomb, BISHOP AUCKLAND, DL14 7UT. (Life Member)
MANNERS, Mr. Brian Edward, FCA *1965;* Wensleydale, Forest Road, East Horsley, LEATHERHEAD, SURREY, KT24 5DH. (Life Member)
MANNERS, Miss. Caroline, BA(Hons) ACA *2010;* Nissan Motor Manufacturing (UK) Ltd, Washington Road, SUNDERLAND, SR5 3NS.
MANNERS, Mr. Christopher Robert, MSc ACA *2005;* 32a Providence Square, LONDON, SE1 2EA.
•**MANNERS, Mr. John Michael, FCA** *1970;* John Manners, 3 Field Hurst, Scholes Lane Scholes, CLECKHEATON, BD19 6NG.
MANNERS, Mr. Kevin James, ACA *2008;* 11 Nascot Street, WATFORD, WD17 4YB.
MANNERS, Mr. Norman, FCA *1961;* 17 Whitworth Close, ST. AGNES, CORNWALL, TR5 0UW. (Life Member)

•MANNERS, Mr. Patrick James, FCA *1977;* Patrick J. Manners, Oak House, Tetchill Moor, ELLESMERE, SHROPSHIRE, SY12 9AL.
MANNIA, Miss. Charlotte Madeleine, BA(Hons) ACA *2004;* 6 Priory Road, WILMSLOW, CHESHIRE, SK9 5PS.
MANNING, Mrs. Alison Celia, BA ACA *1988;* Brook House, Blenheim Hill, Harwell, DIDCOT, OXFORDSHIRE, OX11 0DS.
MANNING, Mrs. Amy Louise, MA BSc ACA *2004;* with National Audit Office, 157-197 Buckingham Palace Road, Victoria, LONDON, SW1W 9SP.
MANNING, Mr. Anthony Joseph David Richard, BSc FCA *1975;* Almasa Holdings FZCO, PO Box 30166, DUBAI, UNITED ARAB EMIRATES.
MANNING, Mr. Arthur Edward, FCA *1966;* Willow Lodge, Lower Clopton, Quinton, STRATFORD-UPON-AVON, CV37 8LQ.
MANNING, Mr. Christopher, FCA *1970;* Steptime Limited, Peter Brooks Honda, 918-920 Chesterfield Road, SHEFFIELD, S8 0SH.
MANNING, Mr. Christopher Richard, BSc(Hons) ACA *2009;* Landau Forte College, Fox Street, DERBY, DE1 2LF.
MANNING, Mr. Daniel, BSc(Hons) ACA *2002;* 9 Bromar Road, LONDON, SE5 8DL.
MANNING, Mr. David Bryan, BA FCA *1979;* Denmaur Papers Bourncrete House, Bonham Drive Eurolink Business Park, SITTINGBOURNE, ME10 3RY.
•MANNING, Mr. David John, FCA *1977;* Summers Morgan, Sheraton House, Lower Road, Chorleywood, RICKMANSWORTH, WD3 5LH.
MANNING, Mr. David Robert, ACA *1992;* 2 Poors Lane, BENFLEET, SS7 2LN.
MANNING, Mr. Denis Bertie, FCA *1960;* Braddon, 12 Fenton Road, REDHILL, RH1 4BN. (Life Member)
MANNING, Mr. Edward, FCA *1973;* Rose Cottage, Ball Lane, Kennington, ASHFORD, KENT, TN25 4EQ.
MANNING, Miss. Elizabeth Jane, BSc ACA *1990;* 3 Rose Terrace, Gordon Road Clifton, BRISTOL, BS8 1AW.
MANNING, Mr. Gareth, BA ACA *2006;* 11 Tenbury Road, Cleobury Mortimer, KIDDERMINSTER, WORCESTERSHIRE, DY14 8RB.
MANNING, Mr. George, BA ACA *2011;* 4 Greenhill Gardens, GUILDFORD, GU4 7HH.
MANNING, Mr. Jan, FCA *1965;* Lakeland Thatch, Monkmead Lane, West Chiltington, PULBOROUGH, WEST SUSSEX, RH20 2PG.
•MANNING, Mrs. Janet, BA FCA *1975;* 89 Jesmond Park West, NEWCASTLE UPON TYNE, NE7 7BY.
MANNING, Mr. John Peter, BA ACA *2001;* B G Group Plc, 100 Thames Valley Park Drive, READING, RG6 1PT.
MANNING, Mr. John Richard, BA FCA *1978;* 3 Grove Leys, Grove Road, TRING, HP23 5PB.
MANNING, Mr. Jolyon William Michael Seton, BSc ACA *1999;* Flat 12, Star & Garter Mansions, Lower Richmond Road, LONDON, SW15 1JW.
MANNING, Mr. Keith Nicholas, MBA FCA DipPropInv *1979;* 3 Hursley Drive, FLEET, HAMPSHIRE, GU51 1AS.
•①MANNING, Mr. Lee Antony, BA FCA *1983;* Deloitte LLP, Athene Place, 66 Shoe Lane, LONDON, EC4A 3BQ. See also Deloitte & Touche LLP
MANNING, Mrs. Margaret Ann, BSc ACA *1987;* Flat 3, 69 Berwick Street, LONDON, W1F 8SZ.
MANNING, Mrs. Maria Elizabeth, BA(Hons) ACA *2003;* 82 White Lady Road, Plymstock, PLYMOUTH, PL9 9GB.
MANNING, Mr. Mark Richard, BSc ACA *1995;* Broadgate Estates Ltd, Exchange House, 12 Primrose Street, LONDON, EC2A 2BQ.
MANNING, Mr. Michael Atkinson, BSc FCA *1973;* 67 Postern Close, YORK, YO23 1JF.
MANNING, Mr. Michael Leon, FCA *1958;* 12 Highwood, Sunset Avenue, WOODFORD GREEN, IG8 0SZ. (Life Member)
MANNING, Mrs. Michaela Jane, BA ACA *1990;* Old Hall Church Road, Colaton Raleigh, SIDMOUTH, EX10 0LW.
MANNING, Mrs. Moira June, BA ACA *1989;* 24 Avon, Hockley, TAMWORTH, B77 5QA.
MANNING, Mr. Neil George, LLB ACA *2000;* 54 Eden Street, CAMBRIDGE, CB1 1EL.
MANNING, Mr. Paul Hurton, FCA *1984;* 4 Fawns Keep, Mottram Rise, STALYBRIDGE, SK15 2UL.
MANNING, Mr. Paul Sinclair, BSc ACA *1995;* 14 Leinster Street, MELBOURNE, VIC 3204, AUSTRALIA.
MANNING, Mr. Paul Williams, BA FCA *1995;* Department for International Development, 1 Palace Street, LONDON, SW1E 5HE.
•MANNING, Mrs. Pauline Rose, FCA *1974;* (Tax Fac), Wilkins Kennedy, Bridge House, London Bridge, LONDON, SE1 9QR.
MANNING, Mr. Richard John, FCA *1966;* 76 Magenta Crescent, NEWCASTLE UPON TYNE, NE5 1YH.
MANNING, Mr. Robert Francis, MA ACA *1998;* Close Private Asset Management, 8th Floor, 10 Exchange Square, Primrose Street, LONDON, EC2A 2BY.
MANNING, Ms. Ruth Vanessa Margaret, BSc FCA CTA *1986;* 53 Long Meadows, Bramhope, LEEDS, LS16 9DU.
•MANNING, Mr. Simon Paul, BA ACA *1996;* Deloitte LLP, 1 City Square, LEEDS, WEST YORKSHIRE, LS1 2AL. See also Deloitte & Touche LLP
•MANNING, Mr. Stuart John, FCA *1983;* MacIntyre Hudson LLP, 8-12 Priestgate, PETERBOROUGH, PE1 1JA.
•MANNING, Miss. Tracey Mary, BSc ACA *2005;* TM Accounting Limited, 120 Allington Close, TAUNTON, SOMERSET, TA1 2NF.
MANNINGS, Mr. Simon Anthony Edmund, BA ACA *1992;* 31 Downs Road, Langley, SLOUGH, BERKSHIRE, SL3 7BZ.
MANNION, Mr. Desmond James, MBA BSc FCA MCIPD *1991;* with Grant Thornton UK LLP, Bradenham Manor, Bradenham, HIGH WYCOMBE, BUCKINGHAMSHIRE, HP14 4HF.
•MANNION, Miss. Kathleen Mary, FCA *1971;* Kathleen M Mannion, 221 Chamber Road, OLDHAM, OL8 4DJ.
MANNION, Mr. Martin, BA ACA *1992;* 35, Hilltop Road, Caversham, READING, RG4 7HR.
•MANNION, Mr. Paul John, ACA ACCA *2010;* Eden Currie Limited, Pegasus House, Solihull Business Park, SOLIHULL, WEST MIDLANDS, B90 4GT.
•MANNION, Mr. Richard Francis, FCA FTII *1980;* (Tax Fac), Smith & Williamson (Bristol) LLP, Portwall Place, Portwall Lane, BRISTOL, BS1 6NA. See also Smith & Williamson Ltd
•MANNOOCH, Mr. David James, FCA *1973;* (Tax Fac), Mannooch & Co, 5 Briton Hill Road, Sanderstead, SOUTH CROYDON, Surrey, CR2 0JG.
MANNOUCH, Mrs. Gillian Beryl, BA ACA *1988;* 247 New Road, FERNDOWN, DORSET, BH22 8EQ.
MANNOUCH, Mr. Richard Paul, BSc ACA *1988;* 247 New Road, FERNDOWN, DORSET, BH22 8EQ.
MANNS, Mr. Colin Paul, BA FCA *1979;* 12 Cransley Grove, SOLIHULL, WEST MIDLANDS, B91 3ZA.
•MANOLAKI, Mrs. Fotini, MSc ACA *2004;* with PricewaterhouseCoopers, 268-270 Kifissias Avenue, Halandri, 15232 ATHENS, GREECE.
•MANOLESCUE, Mr. George Victor, FCA *1976;* (Tax Fac), Dental Business Solutions, Network House, Station Yard, THAME, OXFORDSHIRE, OX9 3UH.
MANOLIS, Dr. Konstantinos, PhD BSc ACA *2004;* 2 Old Malt Way, WOKING, SURREY, GU21 4QD.
•MANOTA, Mr. Ashok, BSc ACA *2005;* AKM, 10 Deyncourt Road, Wednesfield, WOLVERHAMPTON, WV10 0SQ.
•MANSBRIDGE, Mr. Adrian Charles, BA FCA FCCA MCIM CTA *1982;* (Tax Fac), Adrian C. Mansbridge & Company, Half Oak House, 28 Watford Road, NORTHWOOD, HA6 3NT.
MANSBRIDGE, Mr. Hamish Alaric Campbell, BA ACA *1996;* 89 Mexfield Road, Putney, LONDON, SW15 2RG.
MANSBRIDGE, Mr. Paul Robert, BSc ACA *2004;* Cable & Wireless Communications 3rd Floor 26 Red Lion Square, LONDON, WC1R 4HQ.
MANSEL, Mr. Hugh Clavell, FCA *1973;* Thornmoor House, South Middlebere, WAREHAM, BH20 5DN.
MANSELL, Mrs. Amanda Jayne, BA ACA *1998;* 69 Holdenby Close, RETFORD, NOTTINGHAMSHIRE, DN22 6UA.
MANSELL, Mr. Andrew Bruce Blakemore, BSc ACA *2006;* 63 Frimley Grove Gardens, Frimley, CAMBERLEY, SURREY, GU16 7JY.
•MANSELL, Mr. David, MA ACA *1996;* Mercer & Hole, Silbury Court, 420 Silbury Boulevard, MILTON KEYNES, BUCKINGHAMSHIRE, MK9 2AF.
•MANSELL, Mr. David Francis, BA ACA *1993;* East Ayton Accountancy Limited, 4 Castlegate, East Ayton, SCARBOROUGH, NORTH YORKSHIRE, YO13 9EJ.
•MANSELL, Mr. Godfrey, FCA *1969;* Godfrey Mansell & Co LLP, Hales Court, Stourbridge Road, HALESOWEN, WEST MIDLANDS, B63 3TT. See also Godfrey Mansell & Co Ltd
MANSELL, Mr. John Bradbury, BSc FCA *1990;* Constant Spring, Lumley Road, EMSWORTH, HAMPSHIRE, PO10 8AQ.
MANSELL, Ms. Katharine Judith, BA ACA *2006;* 123 Speakman Road, Dentons Green, ST. HELENS, MERSEYSIDE, WA10 6TF.
MANSELL, Mr. Keith Robert, MBE FCA *1957;* The Manor House, Ratlinghope, SHREWSBURY, SY5 0SR. (Life Member)
MANSELL, Mr. Peter George, FCA *1954;* 10 Station Road, Foxton, CAMBRIDGE, CB22 6SA. (Life Member)
MANSELL, Mr. Robert John, BSc ACA *1981;* Marshall Hall Marshall Estate, Hammers Lane, LONDON, NW7 4DQ.
MANSELL-JONES, Mr. Richard Mansell, MA FCA MSI *1967;* 66 Rose Square, Fulham Road, LONDON, SW3 6RS.
•MANSER, Mr. Anthony Graham, FCA *1973;* M. Wasley Chapman & Co, 3 Victoria Square, WHITBY, NORTH YORKSHIRE, YO21 1EA.
MANSER, Mr. Craig John, ACA *2008;* 64 Rockhurst Drive, EASTBOURNE, EAST SUSSEX, BN20 8XD.
MANSER, Mr. David Anthony, BA FCA *1984;* SMP Partners Ltd, Clinch's House, Lord Street, Douglas, ISLE OF MAN, IM99 1RZ.
MANSER, Mr. Jeremy Paul, FCA *1972;* with Wilder Coe, Gloucester House, Church Walk, BURGESS HILL, RH15 9AS.
MANSER, Mr. Neil David, BSc ACA *2001;* Pine House School Lane, Pirbright, WOKING, GU24 0JN.
•MANSER, Mr. Peter Andrew Ronald, FCA DChA *1985;* (Tax Fac), Reeves & Co LLP, 37 St. Margarets Street, CANTERBURY, KENT, CT1 2TU.
MANSER, Peter John, Esq CBE FCA *1965;* Chisenbury Priory, East Chisenbury, PEWSEY, SN9 6AQ.
MANSERGH, Mr. Mark, ACA *1979;* 2 Bronte Close, Kallaroo, PERTH, WA 6025, AUSTRALIA.
MANSFIELD, Mr. Brian, FCA *1953;* 58 Hucklow Road, SHEFFIELD, S5 6TF. (Life Member)
MANSFIELD, Mr. Brian Donald Frederick, FCA *1958;* Monks Way, 10 Shelley Close, ABINGDON, OX14 1PP. (Life Member)
MANSFIELD, Mr. Bryce, FCA *1966;* 5 De Lucy Avenue, ALRESFORD, SO24 9EU. (Life Member)
MANSFIELD, Miss. Caroline, MA ACA *1990;* Howe Cottage, Summerseat Lane, Ramsbottom, BURY, BL0 9UL.
MANSFIELD, Mr. Christopher James, MA BSc ACA *2005;* 122 Roslyn Road, BELMONT, VIC 3216, AUSTRALIA.
MANSFIELD, Mrs. Clare Mary, MA ACA *1989;* 97 Ashcombe Road, DORKING, SURREY, RH4 1LW.
•MANSFIELD, Mr. David Frederic Litt, FCA *1983;* Mansfield & Co, 55 Kentish Town Road, Camden Town, LONDON, NW1 8NX.
MANSFIELD, Mr. Duncan Edwin, MA ACA *2002;* Flat B2 20/F Block B, Fortune Gardens, 11 Seymour Road, MID LEVELS, HONG KONG ISLAND, HONG KONG SAR.
MANSFIELD, Dr. Felicity Louise, BSc FCA CTA *1995;* 7 Davids Garden, Pitton, SALISBURY, SP5 1ER.
MANSFIELD, Mr. George Peter, MA FCA *1984;* 4 Ridgeway, Weston Favell, NORTHAMPTON, NN3 3AN.
MANSFIELD, Mr. Gerald Edward, FCA *1961;* 2 Hannams Farm, Itchel Lane, Crondall, FARNHAM, GU10 5PR. (Life Member)
MANSFIELD, Mr. Guy Nicholas, MA ACA *1998;* Grannesveien 20, 4020 STAVANGER, NORWAY.
MANSFIELD, Mr. Iain Alexander, LLB ACA *2004;* 30 Plasturton Avenue, Pontcanna, CARDIFF, CF11 9HH.
MANSFIELD, Mr. Ian David, MA ACA *1993;* 10 Arlington Avenue, LONDON, N1 7AX.
•MANSFIELD, Mrs. Janine Verity, ACA *2003;* 19 Woolmers Mead, Pleshey, CHELMSFORD, CM3 1HH.
MANSFIELD, Miss. Jemma Lindsay, ACA *2009;* 11 Swain Court, Middleton St. George, DARLINGTON, COUNTY DURHAM, DL2 1DQ.
•MANSFIELD, Mr. Keith John, BSc ACA ATII *1990;* PricewaterhouseCoopers LLP, 1 Embankment Place, LONDON, WC2N 6RH. See also PricewaterhouseCoopers
MANSFIELD, Mr. Keith Patrick, FCA *1970;* 12 Firethorn Close, FLEET, GU52 7TY.
MANSFIELD, Mr. Michael Charles, MA FCA *1972;* The Beeches, 49 St. Nicholas Street, BODMIN, CORNWALL, PL31 1AF. (Life Member)
MANSFIELD, Mr. Robert George, FCA *1973;* The White House, Sandy Way, COBHAM, KT11 2EY.
MANSFIELD, Mr. Robert Jack, BSc FCA *1978;* 11 Tair Gwaun, PENARTH, CF64 3RG.
MANSFIELD, Miss. Sarah, BA ACA *2007;* Flat 24 Bel Air Apartments, La Rue de Trachy St. Helier, JERSEY, JE2 3BA.
MANSFIELD, Mr. Stephen Michael Rendall, BA FCA *1978;* Redcott, New Road, Prestwood, GREAT MISSENDEN, HP16 0PX.
•MANSFIELD, Mrs. Teresa Bernadette, BA(Hons) ACA *1992;* 29 Cranesbill Drive, BICESTER, OX26 3WQ.
MANSFIELD, Mr. William Scott, MA ACA *1992;* Rolls-Royce plc, PO Box 31, DERBY, DERBYSHIRE, DE24 8BJ.
•MANSFORD, Mrs. Helen Louise, BA FCA *1992;* Stevens & Willey, Grenville House, 9 Boutport Street, BARNSTAPLE, EX31 1TZ. See also Stevens & Willey Ltd
MANSHIP, Mrs. Emma Jane, BA ACA *2004;* Westview, 3 Ely Road, Littleport, ELY, CAMBRIDGESHIRE, CB6 1HG.
MANSI, Mr. Mark, MSc BA ACA *2003;* Herndale, Lingfield Road, EDENBRIDGE, TN8 5DX.
MANSIGANI, Mr. Mohan, BA FCA *1983;* 36 Copthall Drive, Mill Hill, LONDON, NW7 2NB.
MANSLEY, Mr. John Joseph, ACA *2008;* 22 Gorseburn Road, LIVERPOOL, L13 8BS.
MANSLEY, Mr. John Richard, FCA *1963;* 33 Carlaw Road, Prenton, BIRKENHEAD, CH42 8PZ. (Life Member)
•MANSLEY, Mr. Nigel Stephen, BSc FCA *1982;* Jeris Associates Ltd, 33 Ballyholme Road, BANGOR, COUNTY DOWN, BT20 5JL.
•MANSON, Mr. Alastair James, BA(Hons) ACA *2002;* Ascent Accountancy Limited, 13 Park Road, GODALMING, SURREY, GU7 1SQ.
MANSON, Mr. Christopher John, MA ACA *1993;* 348 Woodstock Road, OXFORD, OX2 8BZ.
•MANSON, Mr. Craig Stuart, BA FCA *1994;* Garbutt & Elliott LLP, Arabesque House, Monks Cross Drive, Huntington, YORK, YO32 9GW.
MANSON, Mr. David Lindsay, BA ACA *1993;* DAISY COTTAGE, 111 Lodge Road, Knowle, SOLIHULL, B93 0HG.
•MANSON, Mrs. Jayne Elizabeth, ACA *2001;* Lloyd Dowson Limited, Medina House, 2 Station Avenue, BRIDLINGTON, YO16 4LZ.
•MANSON, Mr. Jeremy, ACA *1978;* (Tax Fac), Manson Boxa Limited, 8 Kings Road, Clifton, BRISTOL, BS8 4AB.
MANSON, Mrs. Kathryn Sarah, BCom ACA *1996;* 4 Bay Willow Drive, Redland, BRISTOL, BS6 6TU.
MANSON, Miss. Lindsay Claire, ACA *2005;* 1 Bury Meadows, RICKMANSWORTH, HERTFORDSHIRE, WD3 1DR.
MANSON, Mr. Neil James, BEng ACA *2011;* Beavis Morgan Llp, 82 St. John Street, LONDON, EC1M 4JN.
MANSON, Mr. Paul Francis, BSc ACA *1986;* Hypertac GmbH, Ulrichsberger Strasse 17, 94469 DEGGENDORF, GERMANY.
MANSON, Mr. Richard, BSc ACA *1987;* Brambles Ltd, L40 Gateway, 1 Macquarie Place, SYDNEY, NSW 2070, AUSTRALIA.
MANSON-BAHR, Mr. James Gordon, BA(Hons) ACA *2004;* 32 Crediton Road, LONDON, NW10 3DU.
•MANSON-SMITH, Mrs. Laura Jean, BSc(Hons) ACA *2001;* PricewaterhouseCoopers LLP, 7 More London Riverside, LONDON, SE1 2RT. See also PricewaterhouseCoopers
MANSOOR, Mr. Bilal Mohammed, ACA *2008;* 65 Blacklands Road, LONDON, SE6 3AE.
MANSOUR, Mr. Farid Sabry, BCom FCA *1960;* 46 Raod 83, Maadi, CAIRO, 11435, EGYPT. (Life Member)
MANSOUR, Mr. Michael Rafik, BA ACA *2008;* Amattikoulunkat 6-D-35, PO Box 30100, SEINAJOKI, FINLAND.
MANSOUR EDWARDS, Mrs. Shahrazade, BA ACA *2004;* 4 The Chestnuts, Summerhill Drive Lindfield, HAYWARDS HEATH, WEST SUSSEX, RH16 2AS.
MANSURI, Mr. Feroze Amin, BSc ACA *1997;* 211 Davidson Road, CROYDON, CR0 6DP.
•MANT, Mr. David John, BA ACA *1983;* Abraham and Dobell, 230 Shirley Road, SOUTHAMPTON, SO15 3HR.
MANT, Mr. Donald Francis, BCom FCA *1952;* 3327 Erva St #201, LAS VEGAS, NV 89117, UNITED STATES. (Life Member)
MANT, Miss. Helen Victoria, LLB ACA *2001;* 107 Gorsty Lane, HEREFORD, HR1 1UN.
MANT, Mr. Julian Frazer, BSc FCA *1979;* 6 Cloncurry Street, Fulham, LONDON, SW6 6DS.
MANT, Mr. Steven James, BCom FCA *2000;* Castings Plc, Lichfield Road, Brownhills, WALSALL, WS8 6JZ.
MANTEL, Mr. Christopher John, BSc ACA *1998;* 10 Lark Hill, OXFORD, OX2 7DR.
•MANTEL, Mr. Christopher Leslie, BA ACA *1992;* with RSM Tenon Audit Limited, Vantage, Victoria Street, BASINGSTOKE, HAMPSHIRE, RG21 3BT.
MANTELL, Mr. Simon David, BEng FCA *1995;* Martin House, Compton Road, Hilmarton, CALNE, SN11 8SG.

MANTERFIELD, Mr. Charles Robert, FCA *1975;* 19 Allee De La Gare, 78110 LE VESINET, FRANCE.
MANTERFIELD, Mr. Kenneth Charles, FCA *1951;* (Member of Council 1975 - 1981 1985 - 1991), 3 The Drive, BUCKHURST HILL, IG9 5RB. (Life Member)
•**MANTERFIELD, Mrs. Linda Mary, MBA BA FCA** *1975;* Cabinet Galley Manterfield, Anatoth, 19 Allee de la Gare, Le Vesinet, 78110 PARIS, FRANCE.
MANTERFIELD, Mr. Roger David, FCA *1960;* 5 Cortworth Road, SHEFFIELD, S11 9LN.
MANTI, Miss. Eleni, BSc ACA *2009;* 4 Tefkrou Str, Geri, NICOSIA, CYPRUS.
MANTIS, Mr. Nicolas, MSc ACA *2003;* 2 Michael Kailis Street, Apt 303, Strovolos, 2008 NICOSIA, CYPRUS.
MANTLE, Mrs. Jean Mary, FCA *1971;* The Woodlands, 6 Barnetts Grove, Barnetts Lane, KIDDERMINSTER, DY10 3HG. (Life Member)
MANTLE, Mr. Robert Ian, BA(Hons) ACA *1990;* 64 Tudor Drive, LOUTH, LINCOLNSHIRE, LN11 9EE.
MANTLE, Mr. Simon Phillip, ACA *2008;* Deloitte, 1 City Square, LEEDS, LS1 2AL.
MANTON, Mr. Gary Stephen, BA ACA *1987;* 77 Ashberry Drive, Appleton Thorn, WARRINGTON, WA4 4QS.
MANTON, Mr. Leigh Andrew, BEng ACA *1999;* 51 Chadwick Crescent, DEWSBURY, WF13 2JF.
MANTON, Mr. Simon Paul, BA ACA *1994;* (Tax Fac), Tax Department AOF3, Halifax Equitable Life, Walton Street, AYLESBURY, BUCKINGHAMSHIRE, HP21 7QW.
MANTRI, Mr. Milan, ACA *1995;* Applied Strategies Consulting, 951 Mariners Island Blvd, Suite 400, SAN MATEO, CA 94404, UNITED STATES.
MANTRIPP, Miss. Lyndsey, ACA MAAT *2010;* 26 Swallow Close, EASTBOURNE, EAST SUSSEX, BN23 7RP.
MANTZ, Mr. John Martin, FCA *1977;* 11 Iris Road, Bisley, WOKING, SURREY, GU24 9HG.
•**MANTZ, Mr. William Stewart, BSc ACA** *1985;* (Tax Fac), W S Mantz & Co, 90 Brixton Hill, LONDON, SW2 1QN.
MANUEL, Mr. David, ACA CA(SA) *2010;* Apartment 109, Eustace Building, 372 Queenstown Road, LONDON, SW8 4PP.
MANUEL, Mr. David Colin, BA ACA MBA *1995;* 6b Arterberry Road, Wimbledon, LONDON, SW20 8AA.
MANUEL, Mr. David John, BSc ACA *1991;* 50 Fremont St Suite 3900, Mellon Capital Management, SAN FRANCISCO, CA 94105, UNITED STATES.
MANUEL, Mr. Jonathan Roy, BA FCA *1990;* 8 Hayward Road, THAMES DITTON, KT7 0BE.
•**MANUEL, Mr. Mohan Yrjo, MA FCA ATII** *1992;* Deloitte LLP, 2 New Street Square, LONDON, EC4A 3BZ. See also Deloitte & Touche LLP
MANUEL, Mr. Neal Saul, ACA *1985;* 7 Allée du Haut Treizan, Résidence du Golfe, 83580 GASSIN, FRANCE.
MANUEL, Mr. Philip James, BA ACA *1990;* 17 Tudor Drive, Otford, SEVENOAKS, TN14 5QP.
MANUEL, Mr. Stephen Douglas Reinier, ACA *1989;* 88 The Malthouse, Marrowbone Lane, DUBLIN 8, COUNTY DUBLIN, IRELAND.
MANUEL, Mr. Tristan, MSc ACA *2010;* Flat 6 Reflection House, 112a Cheshire Street, LONDON, E2 6HE.
MANVILLE, Mr. Christopher James, BA ACA *1987;* Lloyds TSB Bank Plc Canons House, Canons Way, BRISTOL, BS1 5LL.
MANWARING, Mr. Thomas Patrick, BSc ACA *2001;* Ingenious Media Plc, 15 Golden Square, LONDON, W1F 9JG.
MANWARING-WHITE, Mr. Edmund Roger, FCA *1948;* April Cottage, 8 Durlston Road, Parkstone, POOLE, BH14 8PQ. (Life Member)
MANYUKHIN, Mr. Vladislav, BSc ACA *2010;* Flat 12 Building 36a, Cadogan Road, LONDON, SE18 6LA.
MANZOOR, Mr. Adil, ACA MBA *2010;* Flat 2, 6 Princes Avenue, Princes Park, LIVERPOOL, L8 2TA.
•**MANZOOR, Mr. Asim, ACA** *2008;* AM & Associates, 201 Manor Road, Grange Hill, CHIGWELL, ESSEX, IG7 4JY.
MANZOOR, Miss. Fareha Nazish, ACA *2005;* 32 Tanner Street, BARKING, IG11 8QJ.
MANZOOR, Mr. Mazhar, BSc FCA MCIM ASIP CEFA *1984;* Spurs Stratford Road, Ash Vale, ALDERSHOT, GU12 5PX.
MAO, Ms. Dan, ACA MBA *1998;* Nokia China Campus, Building 2 No 5 DonghuanZhonglu?, Economic and Technology Development Area, BEIJING 100176, CHINA.
MAO, Miss. Jiali, ACA *2010;* with Deloitte Touche Tohmatsu, 8-F Tower W2, The Towers, Oriental Plaza, 1 East Chang An Avenue, BEIJING 100738 CHINA.
MAO, Mr. Wing Keung, ACA *2006;* 9H Block 10, Serenity Park, TAI PO, NEW TERRITORIES, HONG KONG SAR.
•**MAPARA, Mr. Dinesh Girdharlal, FCA** *1978;* 325 Torbay Road, Rayners Lane, HARROW, MIDDLESEX, HA2 9QD.
MAPES, Miss. Emma Claire, BSc ACA *1999;* Via Santa Lucia 30C, 25062 CONCESIO, ITALY.
MAPES, Mr. Michael James, FCA *1976;* 19 Aurora Sands, St. George Street, Prince George Drive, MUIZENBERG, 7945, SOUTH AFRICA.
MAPES, Mr. Paul, FCA *1976;* 2408 NE 27 Avenue, FORT LAUDERDALE, FL 33305, UNITED STATES.
MAPLES, Mr. Peter Howard, FCA *1972;* 11 Sycamore Avenue, SEDBERGH, CUMBRIA, LA10 5EZ.
•**MAPLES, Mr. Robert George, BA ACA** *1985;* Begbies Chettle Agar Ltd, Epworth House, 25 City Road, LONDON, EC1Y 1AR. See also Begbies Everett Chettle
MAPLESDEN, Mrs. Marian Elizabeth Claire, BA FCA *2000;* 23 Reynolds Lane, TUNBRIDGE WELLS, KENT, TN4 9XJ.
•**MAPLESTON, Mr. Paul John, BEng FCA** *1995;* Ernst & Young LLP, The Paragon, Counterslip, BRISTOL, BS1 6BX. See also Ernst & Young Europe LLP
MAPLEY, Mr. Owen Neville, BA ACA *1999;* 45 Fordwich Road, WELWYN GARDEN CITY, HERTFORDSHIRE, AL8 6EY.
MAPP, Mr. Matthew Robert, BSc ACA *1993;* 22 Green Bower Drive, BROMSGROVE, B61 0UN.
MAPPLEBECK, Mr. Philip Hugh, BCom ACA *1990;* 5 Boomerang Road, COLLAROY, NSW 2097, AUSTRALIA.
MAPUS-SMITH, Mr. John, FCA *1962;* 10 Ryston Road, Denver, DOWNHAM MARKET, PE38 0DP.
MAQBOOL, Mr. Daanish, BSc ACA *2011;* 55 Merrion Avenue, STANMORE, MIDDLESEX, HA7 4RY.
•**MAQBOOL, Mr. Mohammad, FCA** *1985;* A Maqbool & Co Limited, 192 Haydons Road, Wimbledon, LONDON, SW19 8TR.
•**MAQBOOL, Mr. Salman, BSc ACA** *2006;* Adam Accounting Services Ltd, 8 Lanercost Crescent, Monkston, MILTON KEYNES, MK10 9EB.
MAQBOOL, Mr. Zeeshan, BSc ACA *2006;* Afren Plc Kinnaird House, 1 Pall Mall East, LONDON, SW1Y 5AU.
MAQSOOD, Mr. Mohammad, BA(Hons) ACA *2001;* 60 Brantwood Drive, BRADFORD, WEST YORKSHIRE, BD9 6QS.
MAQSOOD, Mr. Nasir, ACA *2003;* HSBC Bank Canada, 885 West Georgia Street, Suite 500, VANCOUVER V6C 3E9, BC, CANADA.
MAR, Mr. Selwyn, BSc FCA *1965;* Nexia Charles Mar Fan & Co, 11/F Fortis Tower, 77-79 Gloucester Road, WAN CHAI, HONG KONG ISLAND, HONG KONG SAR.
MARA, Mr. Keith Edwin, FCA *1975;* 308 Chadwell Heath Lane, ROMFORD, RM6 4YH.
MARAIA, Mr. Antonio, FCA CTA *1991;* (Tax Fac), Cole & Son (Wallpapers) Ltd Lifford House, 199 Eade Road, LONDON, N4 1DN.
•**MARAJ, Mr. Dwight Simon, BA ACA** *1991;* Marriotts, 32 Westfield Road, Ealing, LONDON, W13 9JL.
MARAJ, Mr. Sanjay, ACA *2009;* 5th Floor Jackson House, 18 Savile Row, LONDON, W1S 3PW.
MARANDIAN, Mr. Javad, BSc ACA *1992;* 13 Grange Park Place, Wimbledon, LONDON, SW20 0EE.
•**MARANZANA, Mr. Paolo Michele, MA ACA** *1997;* 105 Bulwer Road, BARNET, HERTFORDSHIRE, EN5 5EX.
MARATHEFTI, Miss. Maria, BSc ACA *2005;* Apostolou Andrea 9 Appartment 202, 2049 STROVOLOS, CYPRUS.
MARATHOVOUNIOTIS, Mr. Tassos, BSc ACA *2001;* 12 Pindou Str Engomi, PO Box 21112, CY 1502 NICOSIA, CYPRUS.
MARAZZI, Mr. John Paul, BA FCA *1993;* Jardine Motors Group, 770 The Crescent, Colchester Business Park, COLCHESTER, CO4 9YQ.
MARBAIX, Mr. Paul Anthony, ACA *1980;* Claremont, Crendon Road, Shabbington, AYLESBURY, BUCKINGHAMSHIRE, HP18 9HE.
MARCER, Miss. Victoria Helen, BSc(Hons) ACA *2000;* The Old Bakery, 31 High Street, Barrow upon Soar, LOUGHBOROUGH, LEICESTERSHIRE, LE12 8PY.
MARCH, Mr. Ian Robert, ACA *1984;* 16 Stourport Drive, Chellaston, DERBY, DE73 6PX.
MARCH, Mr. James, FCA *1980;* 4264 West Club Lane, ATLANTA, GA 30319, UNITED STATES.
MARCH, Mr. James George, BSc ACA *2002;* 9 The Carpenters, BISHOP'S STORTFORD, HERTFORDSHIRE, CM23 4BP.
MARCH, Mrs. Katrina Elizabeth, BSc ACA *1989;* 30 Seaview Road, Redcliffe Bay Portishead, BRISTOL, BS20 8HL.
•**MARCH, Mr. Kenneth Brian, BSc FCA** *1992;* Gort & March, 308 London Road, Hazel Grove, STOCKPORT, CHESHIRE, SK7 4RF. See also GM Accountancy Services Ltd
MARCH, Mr. Kevin Andrew, BA ACA *1990;* Flat 1, 31 Berwick Street, LONDON, W1F 8RJ.
MARCHAM, Mr. Paul Robert, FCA *1974;* 93 Waverley Road, READING, RG30 2QB.
MARCHANT, Mr. Andrew Graham, ACA *2007;* Morrison Supermarkets Plc, Hilmore House, Gain Lane, BRADFORD, WEST YORKSHIRE, BD3 7DL.
MARCHANT, Mr. Andrew William, BA ACA *1980;* Dunsfold Ryse, High Street Green, Chiddingfold, GODALMING, SURREY, GU8 4YA.
MARCHANT, Miss. Betty, LLB ACA *1991;* 2404 13 Ave NW, CALGARY T2N 1L6, AB, CANADA.
•**MARCHANT, Mr. David George, FCA** *1966;* Marchant & Co, 2 Court Farm Road, NEWHAVEN, BN9 9DH.
MARCHANT, Mr. David Kevin, BA ACA *1988;* 31 Beaconsfield Parade, LINDFIELD, NSW 2070, AUSTRALIA.
MARCHANT, Mr. Edward Timothy, BA ACA *2004;* 26 Highland Avenue, BANKSTOWN, NSW 2200, AUSTRALIA.
•**MARCHANT, Mr. Geoffrey Keith, FCA** *1969;* (Tax Fac), Geoffrey Marchant & Co, Rathbond House, High Street, Staplehurst, TONBRIDGE, TN12 0AD.
MARCHANT, Mrs. Gillian Patricia, BA ACA *1983;* Hillside Farm House Upper Rodmersham, Rodmersham, SITTINGBOURNE, ME9 0QL.
MARCHANT, Mr. Guy Stephen, BSc ACA *2003;* 3 Snowshill Close, Barnwood, GLOUCESTER, GL4 3GE.
MARCHANT, Mr. Ian Derek, BA ACA *1987;* 45 Craigcrook Road, EDINBURGH, EH4 3PH.
MARCHANT, Mr. Jonathan, BA(Hons) ACA *2001;* 2 Mulberry Drive, Upton-upon-Severn, WORCESTER, WR8 0ET.
MARCHANT, Mr. Keith Michael, BA ACA *1983;* 1 Beechwood, Bowdon, ALTRINCHAM, WA14 3DW.
MARCHANT, Mr. Neil Norman, BSc ACA *1999;* 28545 Oakhaven Court, LAKE BLUFF, IL 60044-3001, UNITED STATES.
MARCHANT, Mrs. Patricia Mary, BSc ACA *1984;* Newlands, 15, Deenethorpe, CORBY, NN17 3EP.
MARCHANT, Mr. Paul Victor, FCA *1977;* 10 Astoria Close, Thornhill, CARDIFF, CF14 9DQ.
MARCHANT, Mr. Richard Norman, FCA *1972;* Brew House, 6 Main Street, Wardley, Oakham, RUTLAND, LE15 9AZ.
MARCHANT, Mr. Robert Paul, BSc FCA *1972;* The Old Vicarage, Church Lane, Stoulton, WORCESTER, WR7 4RE.
•**MARCHANT, Mr. Roger, FCA** *1968;* (Tax Fac), R. Marchant & Co, 42 Oakleigh Park South, LONDON, N20 9JN.
MARCHANT, Mrs. Susan Carol, BSc ACA *1983;* Holly House, 66 Shortheath Road, FARNHAM, GU9 8SQ.
MARCHANT, Mr. William, BEng ACA *1992;* 118 Lumley Street, Hightown, CASTLEFORD, WF10 5LU.
MARCHANT-JONES, Mr. Simon John, BA ACA *1980;* 6 Coleswood Road, HARPENDEN, HERTFORDSHIRE, AL5 1EQ.
MARCHINI, Mr. Marco, BSc ACA *2011;* 8 Gaitskell Road, New Eltham, LONDON, SE9 2DL.
MARCIANDI, Mr. Paul Julian, BSc ACA *1981;* The Hub Co Ltd St. Martins House, 1 Lyric Square, LONDON, W6 0NB.
MARCINIAK, Mrs. Dominique Manuela, BA ACA *1994;* 100 South Park Drive, Papworth Everard, CAMBRIDGE, CB23 3LF.
MARCINKIEWICZ, Ms. Kirsty Jayne, BA(Hons) ACA *2004;* Woodland House, Alfreton Road, Coxbench, DERBY, DE21 5BA.
•**MARCO, Mr. Jeffrey Stephen, FCA** *1975;* Montpelier Audit Limited, Montpelier House, 62-66 Deansgate, MANCHESTER, M3 2EN. See also Montpelier Professional (West End) Ltd
MARCO, Mrs. Pamela Louise, BSc ACA *2000;* 6 Burrsholt, Cople, BEDFORD, MK44 3UJ.
MARCO, Mrs. Susan Claire, BA ACA *1997;* 1 E Ltd, C P House, 97-107 Uxbridge Road, LONDON, W5 5TL.
•**MARCOU, Mr. Aristides, BSc FCA** *1984;* (Tax Fac), Russell Marks Limited, 21 Aylmer Parade, Aylmer Road, LONDON, N2 0AT. See also AMK Russell Marks Limited
MARCOU, Miss. Efi, BA ACA *2009;* 6 Socratous Str., Aglandjia, 2123 NICOSIA, CYPRUS.
MARCOU, Mrs. Helen, BSc ACA *2001;* 151 Victoria Road, LONDON, N22 7XH.
•**MARCOVITCH, Mr. Andrew Paul, BSc ACA** *1996;* 11 The Dell, WOODFORD GREEN, ESSEX, IG8 0QL.
MARCROFT, Mr. Adam Nicholas, BSc ACA *2005;* 35 McArthur Avenue, St Heliers, AUCKLAND 1071, NEW ZEALAND.
MARCUS, Mrs. Catherine, BSc ACA *2002;* 32 Bowes Road, WALTON-ON-THAMES, KT12 3HX.
MARCUS, Mr. Derrick Isaac, FCA *1963;* Rua Pirandello 525, Brooklin, 04623000 SAO PAULO, BRAZIL. (Life Member)
•**MARCUS, Mr. Michael David, BSc FCA FRSA** *1979;* (Tax Fac), Bond Group LLP, The Grange, 100 High Street, LONDON, N14 6TB. See also Core Resolutions LLP
MARCUS, Mr. Philip Carlyle, FCA *1935;* 24A King Albert Park, SINGAPORE 2159, SINGAPORE. (Life Member)
MARCUS, Mr. Robert John, BA(Hons) ACA *2002;* 32 Bowes Road, WALTON-ON-THAMES, SURREY, KT12 3HX.
MARCUS, Mr. Stanton Harvey, FCA *1950;* 32 Hall Park Avenue, WESTCLIFF-ON-SEA, SS0 8NR.
•**MARCUSFIELD, Mr. John Howard, FCA** *1970;* Marcusfield Dodia & Co, 19 Cumberland Road, STANMORE, HA7 1EL.
•**MARCUSON, Mr. Trevor David, FCA** *1975;* T.D Marcuson, 15 West Hill Road, Foxton, CAMBRIDGE, CB22 6SZ.
MARDALL, Mrs. Alsu, ACA *1998;* Lower Clevedale, 24 Christchurch Road, WINCHESTER, HAMPSHIRE, SO23 9SS.
MARDELL, Mrs. Diana Elizabeth, ACA *1989;* Ventham Ltd, Millhouse, 32-38 East Street, ROCHFORD, ESSEX, SS4 1DB.
MARDEN, Mr. John Bernard, BA ACA *1992;* 66 Portland Road, KINGSTON UPON THAMES, SURREY, KT1 2SH.
MARDIA, Mr. Pritesh, ACA *2011;* Mardia & Co, 26 Muker Nalla Muthu Street, CHENNAI 600001, TAMIL NADU, INDIA.
•**MARDLE, Mr. Alain Richard, BSc FCA** *1990;* (Tax Fac), Goodale Mardle Limited, Greens Court, West Street, MIDHURST, WEST SUSSEX, GU29 9NQ.
MARDLE, Miss. Jacqueline, ACA *2009;* 24 Morland Road, SUTTON, SM1 4RP.
MARDON, Mr. Crispin Paul, BA ACA *1984;* 14 St. Stephens Avenue, ST. ALBANS, HERTFORDSHIRE, AL3 4AD.
MAREK-MURRAY, Mrs. Jenny Louise, BSc ACA *2002;* 5 Le Campagne, Rue Des Buttes, St. Marys, JERSEY, JE3 3DE.
MARENINA, Mrs. Natalya, ACA MBA *2004;* 62 Raglan Street, MANLY, NSW 2095, AUSTRALIA.
•**MARETT, Mr. David William, BEng FCA** *2001;* Maretts Limited, Tall Trees House, Westwood Road, Tilehurst, READING, RG31 5PX.
MARETT, Mr. Francis Charles, FCA *1953;* 30 Windermere Crescent, Goring-by-Sea, WORTHING, BN12 6JY. (Life Member)
MARETT, Mr. Tom, BA(Hons) ACA *2010;* La Mouette, Le Mont Gras D'Eau, St. Brelade, JERSEY, JE3 8ED.
•**MARFELL, Mr. Richard Ian Wyatt, FCA** *1967;* Ian Marfell FCA, 2 Knightley Road, EXETER, EX2 4SR.
MARFFY, Mr. Joseph, BA ACA *1985;* 6 Chestnut Grove, Purley on Thames, READING, RG8 8BU.
MARFLEET, Mr. David, BSc ACA *1980;* 15 Magnolia Dene, Hazlemere, HIGH WYCOMBE, HP15 7QE.
MARFLEET, Mr. Thomas, BA ACA *2003;* GECC (Funding) Limited, The Ark 201 Talgarth Road, LONDON, W6 8BJ.
MARGARITELLI, Mr. Massimiliano, FCA *1974;* 185A Chelmsford Road, Shenfield, BRENTWOOD, Essex, CM15 8SA.
MARGARSON, Mr. John David Rhodes, FCA *1973;* 27 Maplin Way, Thorpe Bay, SOUTHEND-ON-SEA, SS1 3NN.
MARGEOT, Mr. Marie Joseph Paul Guy, BSc FCA *1964;* PO Box 21019, PORT SHEPSTONE, 4240, SOUTH AFRICA.
MARGESSON, Mr. Charles Philip, FCA *1963;* Monks Cottage Kenton Road, Monk Soham, WOODBRIDGE, SUFFOLK, IP13 7HA.
MARGETSON, Mr. Damien Paul, BA ACA *1997;* Mill View, 16 Quarry Court, Off Long Wood Gate, HUDDERSFIELD, HD3 4UQ.
MARGETSON, Mrs. Elyse Kathryn, BSc ACA *1996;* 16 Quarry Court, Longwood, HUDDERSFIELD, HD3 4UQ.
MARGETSON, Mrs. Mary Elizabeth, BSc ACA *1997;* Firbank Cottage 1 Guildown Road, GUILDFORD, SURREY, GU2 4EW.
MARGETSON-RUSHMORE, Mr. Patrick Joseph George, BA FCA *1984;* London Executive Aviation Stapleford Aerodrome, Stapleford Tawney, ROMFORD, RM4 1SJ.
MARGETTS, Mr. Andrew Neil, MA ACA *1988;* Amethyst Corporate Finance Plc, 25 Southampton Buildings, LONDON, WC2A 1AL.

MARGETTS, Mr. Brian Henry, FCA *1959;* Isichia, Grove Lane, Chalfont St. Peter, GERRARDS CROSS, BUCKINGHAMSHIRE, SL9 9LB. (Life Member)
MARGETTS, Mr. Bryan William, FCA *1953;* 32 Beadon Rd, BROMLEY, BR2 9AT. (Life Member)
MARGETTS, Mrs. Elaine, BA ACA *1989;* APT 1709, 1835 Arch Street, PHILADELPHIA, PA 19103, UNITED STATES.
•MARGETTS, Mr. Peter, FCA *1966;* (Tax Fac), Roy Sandey, 31 High Cross Street, ST AUSTELL, CORNWALL, PL25 4AN.
MARGETTS, Mr. Peter John, ACA ATII *1991;* Vesey Farm, Little Clacton Road, Great Holland, FRINTON-ON-SEA, ESSEX, CO13 0EX.
•MARGETTS, Mr. Roger Gareth, FCA *1973;* Cross & Bowen, 11 Calvert Terrace, SWANSEA, SA1 6AT.
MARGETTS, Miss. Sarah Nicole, BA ACA *1998;* Lynton, St. Leonards Road, Nazeing, WALTHAM ABBEY, EN9 2HJ.
MARGINSON, Mr. Steven John, FCA *1975;* 33 Central Avenue, BEVERLEY, NORTH HUMBERSIDE, HU17 8LL.
MARGOLIS, Mr. Benjamin, BA ACA *1994;* 7A Bolton Road, LONDON, NW8 0RJ.
MARGOLIS, Mr. Gerald Eleazer, MA FCA *1960;* 12 Cholmeley Park, Highgate, LONDON, N6 5EU. (Life Member)
MARGOSSIAN, Mr. Guy, BSc ACA *1994;* Flat 31 Gilbey House, 38 Jamestown Road, LONDON, NW1 7BY.
MARIANI, Mr. Antony James, MA ACA *1998;* Centre for Ecology and Hydiology, Lancaster Environment Centre, Library Avenue, Bailrigg, LANCASTER, LA1 4AP.
•MARIE, Mr. Adrian Cedric, FCA *1983;* Cole Marie Partners Ltd, Priory House, 45-51 High Street, REIGATE, SURREY, RH2 9AE.
MARIES, Mrs. Alexandra Fiona, BSc ACA *1994;* 55 Goldsmith Way, ST. ALBANS, AL3 5LH.
MARIES, Mr. Scott Laurence, BA ACA *1998;* 199 Water Street, 9th Floor, NEW YORK, NY 10038, UNITED STATES.
•MARIKAR, Mr. Qadir, ACA *2008;* PricewaterhouseCoopers LLP, 1 Embankment Place, LONDON, WC2N 6RH. See also PricewaterhouseCoopers
MARIN, Mr. Harry George, MA ACA *2007;* 27 Clarendon Gardens, ILFORD, IG1 3JN.
MARINER, Mr. Stuart Charles, FCA *1969;* Martin & Co, 25 St. Thomas Street, WINCHESTER, HAMPSHIRE, SO23 9HJ.
MARINHO, Mr. Festus Rotimi Adebayo, BEng FCA *1993;* 13 Wardo Avenue, Fulham, LONDON, SW6 6RA.
MARINI, Mr. Pietro, ACA *2010;* 54 Eccleston Square Mews, LONDON, SW1V 1QN.
MARINOS, Miss. Stephanie Elizabeth, BSc ACA *1987;* G.Papandreou 57b, Kastri, 14671 ATHENS, GREECE.
MARINOU, Mr. Marinos, BA ACA *2005;* 5 Kleitou Mandriti, 6043 LARNACA, CYPRUS.
MARION, Mr. Robert John, BSc FCA *1974;* 9 Villa du Golf, 91450 ETIOLLES, FRANCE.
MARIS, Mrs. Suzanne Jayne, BA ACA *2007;* Ernst and Young, Ernst and Young Centre, 680 George Street, SYDNEY, NSW 2000, AUSTRALIA.
•MARIS, Mr. Tim Ross, BSc FCA *1992;* WKH, 22/24 Kneesworth Street, ROYSTON, SG8 5AA. See also Virtual Business Source Limited
MARISCOTTI, Mr. Michael Gordon, ACA *1983;* Arrewig Farm, Arrewig Lane, Chartridge, CHESHAM, BUCKINGHAMSHIRE, HP5 2UA.
MARJASON, Mr. Reginald Allin, ACA *1984;* 11 Finches End, Walkern, STEVENAGE, SG2 7RG.
MARJORAM, Mr. Gordon Edward, BCom FCA *1967;* Glan Aber, The Square, Marchington, UTTOXETER, STAFFORDSHIRE, ST14 8LF.
•MARJORAM, Mr. John Charles, FCA *1979;* (Tax Fac), J.C. Marjoram & Co, 486 London Road South, LOWESTOFT, NR33 0LB.
MARJORAM, Mr. Philip John, BSc ACA *2000;* 1 Oak Ridge, WETHERBY, WEST YORKSHIRE, LS22 6GT.
MARJORAM, Mrs. Sarah, BA(Hons) ACA CTA *2002;* (Tax Fac), 75 Davies Road West Bridgford, NOTTINGHAM, NG2 5JB.
•MARJORAM, Mr. Stephen John, BA ACA *2003;* with RSM Tenon Audit Limited, Vantage, Victoria Street, BASINGSTOKE, HAMPSHIRE, RG21 3BT.
MARJORIBANKS, Mr. Richard John Bradley, ACA *1981;* 8 Tewit Well Avenue, HARROGATE, NORTH YORKSHIRE, HG2 8AP.
MARK, Miss. Charlie Lauren, BA(Hons) ACA *2011;* 36 Long Rowden, Peverell, PLYMOUTH, PL3 4PN.
MARK, Mr. Daniel Charles, BA ACA *2003;* 44 Sunnyfield, Mill Hill, LONDON, NW7 4RG.
MARK, Mr. John Stuart, FCA *1966;* 64 Otho Court, Augustus Close, BRENTFORD, Middlesex, TW8 8PY. (Life Member)
•MARK, Mrs. Lesley Carolyn, FCA DChA *1986;* (Tax Fac), Douglas Home & Co Limited, 47-49 The Square, KELSO, ROXBURGHSHIRE, TD5 7HW.
MARK, Mr. Peter Hinton, MA FCA *1956;* Southlands Nursing Home, 9 Ripon Road, HARROGATE, NORTH YORKSHIRE, HG1 2JA. (Life Member)
MARK, Mr. Ronald William, FCA *1956;* 29 The Open, Leazes Square, NEWCASTLE UPON TYNE, NE1 4DB. (Life Member)
MARK, Mrs. Ruth Frances, BSc ACA *1993;* Coopers Cottage, 30 Church Lane, Charnock Richard, CHORLEY, PR7 3RB.
MARKANDU, Mr. Ravindran, FCA *1976;* 25 Jalan Setiajaya, Damansara Heights, 50490 KUALA LUMPUR, FEDERAL TERRITORY, MALAYSIA. (Life Member)
MARKE, Mrs. Catherine Ann Lesley, MA(Oxon) ACA *2004;* 90 Park Rise, HARPENDEN, HERTFORDSHIRE, AL5 3AN.
MARKE, Mr. Christopher Philip Levelis, FCA *1973;* 7 Elmtree Avenue, ESHER, KT10 8JG.
•MARKE, Mr. Neil Temlett, ACA ATII *1986;* R T Marke & Co Limited, 69 High Street, BIDEFORD, DEVON, EX39 2AT.
MARKE, Mr. Richard Valentine Stuckey, BA FCA *1967;* The Bath House, 29 Van Diemens Lane, Lansdown, BATH, BA1 5TW.
MARKE, Mr. Vincent Stuckey, MSc ACA *2001;* with BDO LLP, Emerald House, East Street, EPSOM, SURREY, KT17 1HS.
MARKER, Mr. Paul Gordon, BSc FCA *1987;* Torrington Chambers, 58 North Road East, PLYMOUTH, PL4 6AJ.
MARKESON, Mr. Brian Jack, BA FCA *1974;* Coller Capital, 33 Cavendish Square, LONDON, W1G 0TT.
MARKESON, Mr. Kenny, BSc ACA *2006;* 1 Beechpark Way, WATFORD, WD17 3TY.
MARKEY, Mr. Paul Francis, BA FCA *1985;* Rosebank, Sandhurst Lane, Sandhurst, GLOUCESTER, GL2 9NP.
•MARKHAM, Mr. Alan, FCA *1974;* J.R. Watson & Co, Eastgate House, 11 Cheyne Walk, NORTHAMPTON, NN1 5PT. See also Eastgate Accounts Office Limited
MARKHAM, Miss. Anna Victoria, MA ACA *1995;* Chambers of George Bompas Q C, 4 Stone Buildings, LONDON, WC2A 3XT.
MARKHAM, Mr. David Philip, BSc ACA *1994;* Curlieu Farm House Norton Curlieu Lane Lower Norton, WARWICK, WARWICKSHIRE, CV35 8RD.
•MARKHAM, Mr. Howard Saul, FCA *1974;* (Tax Fac), Markhams Accountants Limited, 10 Perrins Lane, LONDON, NW3 1QY.
MARKHAM, Mr. James Edward, BA(Hons) ACA *2001;* 44 Belleville Road, LONDON, SW11 6QT.
MARKHAM, Mrs. Joanna Frances, BSc ACA *1993;* 10 Leigh Road, West Kirby, WIRRAL, MERSEYSIDE, CH48 5DY.
•MARKHAM, Mr. John, FCA *1978;* Landin Wilcock & Co, Queen St Chmbrs, 68 Queen St, SHEFFIELD, S1 4BD.
MARKHAM, Mr. John Michael Gervase, FCA *1964;* (Tax Fac), with Begbies Chettle Agar, Epworth House, 25 City Road, LONDON, EC1Y 1AR.
•MARKHAM, Mr. Michael Anthony, ACA *2006;* (Tax Fac), A.M. Accountants Limited, 63 Highgate High Street, LONDON, N6 5JX.
MARKHAM, Mrs. Natalie, LLB ACA *2001;* 44 Belleville Road, LONDON, SW11 6QT.
MARKHAM, Mr. Paul, FCA *1974;* Freudenberg Nonwovens L P, Lowfields Close, Lowfields Business Park, ELLAND, WEST YORKSHIRE, HX5 9DX.
MARKHAM, Mr. Paul David, BSc ACA *2004;* with Deloitte LLP, 3 Rivergate, Temple Quay, BRISTOL, BS1 6GD.
MARKHAM, Mr. Philip Andrew, BSc ACA *1993;* 1a Cloncurry Street, LONDON, SW6 6DR.
MARKHAM, Mrs. Ruth Ann, BA FCA *1965;* 22 Roslin Hall, 6 Manor Road, BOURNEMOUTH, BH1 3ES.
MARKHAM, Mr. Stephen, BA ACA *2007;* 5a Mersham Gardens, Goring-by-Sea, WORTHING, WEST SUSSEX, BN12 4TG.
•MARKIDES, Mr. Loizos Andrea, BA(Hons) FCA *2001;* PricewaterhouseCoopers Limited, Julia House, 3 Themistocles Dervis Street, CY-1066 NICOSIA, CYPRUS.
MARKIDES, Mr. Soteris, MSc BA(Hons) ACA *1998;* Flat 002, 14 Filimonds Str, 1071 NICOSIA, CYPRUS.
MARKIDES, Mr. Theodossios, BSc ACA *2004;* 4 Agias Irinis Street Nefeli House Flat 102, 3095 LIMASSOL, CYPRUS.
MARKILLIE, Mr. Howard Christopher, BSc FCA *1992;* Charter Central Services Ltd, 322 High Holborn, LONDON, WC1V 7PB.
MARKIN, Mr. Adam Dean, BSc ACA *1991;* 14827 resolves ln, CHARLOTTE, NC 28277, UNITED STATES.
MARKIN, Mr. Alexander, ACA *2009;* with Ernst & Young Moscow LLC, Sadovnieskaya Nab 77, Building 1, 115035 MOSCOW, RUSSIAN FEDERATION.
MARKINSON, Mr. Mendel, FCA *1969;* 30 Whitney Avenue, ILFORD, IG4 5PN.
MARKITSI, Miss. Maria, BA ACA *2002;* 23 Prodromos Street, Strovolos, 2063 NICOSIA, CYPRUS.
MARKLAND, Mr. Rupert James, BA ACA *1993;* Flat 12A, 34 Bromells Road, LONDON, SW4 0BG.
MARKLEW, Miss. Jenny, ACA *2000;* 40 Bahamas Key, PAPAMOA 3118, NEW ZEALAND.
MARKLEW, Mr. Stanley Gordon, FCA *1958;* Taymark, 3 Meadow View, Dunvant, SWANSEA, SA2 7UZ. (Life Member)
•MARKLEY, Mr. Stuart James, FCA *1983;* (Tax Fac), Moore Stephens LLP, 150 Aldersgate Street, LONDON, EC1A 4AB. See also Moore Stephens & Co
•MARKOU, Mr. Demetrios, MBE FCA *1972;* (Tax Fac), Marcus & Co, Bank House, 36-38 Bristol Street, BIRMINGHAM, B5 7AA. See also Taxcare Ltd
MARKOU, Mr. Marcos, BA ACA *2003;* 54 Freston Gardens, Cockfosters, BARNET, EN4 9LY.
•MARKOU, Mr. Pieris, BA FCA *1990;* (Tax Fac), Deloitte Limited, 24 Spyrou Kyprianou Avenue, P.O.Box 21675 CY-1512, 1075 NICOSIA, CYPRUS.
MARKS, Mr. Andrew William, BSc(Econ) ACA *1998;* with Simmons Gainsford LLP, 5th Floor, 7-10 Chandos Street, Cavendish Square, LONDON, W1G 9DQ.
•MARKS, Mrs. Anna Louise, BSc ACA *1996;* Deloitte LLP, Abbots House, Abbey Street, READING, RG1 3BD. See also Deloitte & Touche LLP
MARKS, Mrs. Anne Marie, BA ACA *1983;* 7 Sheffield Place, HILLARYS, WA 6025, AUSTRALIA.
MARKS, Mr. Anthony David, BA FCA *1970;* 4 Vine Lodge Court, Holly Bush Lane, SEVENOAKS, TN13 3XY.
MARKS, Mr. Anthony James, BA ACA ATII AIIT *1987;* 9 Flint Drive, NESTON, CH64 9XU.
MARKS, Mr. Arnold, FCA *1951;* 19 Woodmere Gardens, Shirley Oaks, CROYDON, CR0 7PL. (Life Member)
MARKS, Mr. Ashley Hardy, BSc ACA *2005;* 35 Heton Gardens, Hendon, LONDON, NW4 4XS.
MARKS, Mr. Augustus Rhys, FCA *1971;* Tivoli, Langbar Road, Middleton, ILKLEY, LS29 0EE. (Life Member)
MARKS, Mr. Benjamin James, MA ACA *2002;* 50 Milson Road, LONDON, W14 0LD.
MARKS, Brian John, Esq OBE FCA *1956;* 1 Pethers Piece, BURFORD, OX18 4NH. (Life Member)
MARKS, Miss. Catherine, BA ACA *2007;* Flat 7 Citadel Court, 1-9 Ronalds Road, LONDON, N5 1XH.
MARKS, Mr. Christopher Alan, BEng ACA *1998;* 116 Turney Road, LONDON, SE21 7JJ.
MARKS, Mr. Clive Maurice, OBE FCA *1955;* 39 Farm Avenue, LONDON, NW2 2BJ. (Life Member)
•MARKS, Mr. David, BA FCA *1991;* (Tax Fac), Citroen Wells, Devonshire House, 1 Devonshire Street, LONDON, W1W 5DR.
MARKS, Mr. David Bernard, BA FCA *1982;* 3 Impasse de la Haute Pierre, 78290 CROISSY SUR SEINE, FRANCE.
MARKS, Mr. David Irving, MSc FCA *1958;* Au Jane, 31230 PUYMAURIN, FRANCE. (Life Member)
•MARKS, Mr. David Jeffrey, FCA *1985;* Virginia Lodge, Royston Grove, Hatch End, PINNER, MIDDLESEX, HA5 4HE.
MARKS, Mr. David Norman, BSc FCA CTA *1978;* (Tax Fac), Apax Partners LLP, 33 Jermyn Street, LONDON, SW1Y 6DN.
MARKS, Mr. David Poole, FCA *1968;* 3 Misty Ridge Circle, KINNELON, NJ 07405, UNITED STATES.
MARKS, Miss. Hannah, BSc ACA *2006;* Basement Flat, 35 Disraeli Road, LONDON, SW15 2DR.
MARKS, Mr. Harold Harris, BSc FCA *1966;* House A Rowney, Mount Park Road, HARROW, HA1 3JP. (Life Member)
•MARKS, Mr. Howard John, FCA *1958;* Howard Marks & Co, 21 Bodley Road, NEW MALDEN, KT3 5QD.
MARKS, Mr. James Robert, ACA *2008;* Flat 14 West One House, 47 Wells Street, LONDON, W1T 3PN.
MARKS, Miss. Jane Kathryn, BSc ACA *1988;* 19 KERR AVENUE, BUNDEENA, NSW 2230, AUSTRALIA.
•MARKS, Mrs. Jennifer Helen, BSc FCA ATII *1995;* (Tax Fac), Muras Baker Jones, Regent House, Bath Avenue, WOLVERHAMPTON, WV1 4EG.
MARKS, Mr. Joel Hanoch, BA ACA *1994;* 21/1 Clarendon Crescent, EDINBURGH, EH4 1PU.
•MARKS, Mr. John Gilbert, FCA *1965;* JGM Accounting Services, 71 Church Road, HAYLING ISLAND, PO11 0NR.
•MARKS, Mr. Jonathan, BA FCA *1992;* Fisher Sassoon & Marks, 43-45 Dorset Street, LONDON, W1U 7NA.
MARKS, Mr. Laurence, BSc ACA *1991;* PO BOX 157, KANGAROO GROUND, VIC 3097, AUSTRALIA.
MARKS, Mr. Lawrence, FCA *1953;* 15 Bentley Lodge, 182 High Road, Bushey Heath, BUSHEY, WD23 1NS. (Life Member)
MARKS, Mr. Leonard Geoffrey, FCA *1960;* 1 Albert Terrace Mews, Regents Park, LONDON, NW1 7TA.
MARKS, Mr. Martin, FCA *1955;* 19/44 Haprachim Street, 43399 RA'ANANA, ISRAEL. (Life Member)
MARKS, Mr. Michael, BSc ACA *2007;* 209 Willesden Lane, LONDON, NW6 7YR.
•MARKS, Mr. Michael, BSc FCA *1981;* (Tax Fac), Nyman Linden, 105 Baker Street, LONDON, W1U 6NY. See also ITS International Limited
•MARKS, Mr. Michael John, FCA *1973;* (Tax Fac), Marks & Co, 100 Church St, BRIGHTON, BN1 1UJ.
•MARKS, Mr. Michael Laurence, FCA *1977;* The KBSP Partnership, Harben House, Harben Parade, Finchley Road, LONDON, NW3 6LH. See also Stardata Business Services Limited
MARKS, Mr. Milton Maurice, FCA *1959;* Fisher Sassoon & Marks, Farley Court, Allsop Place, LONDON, NW1 5LG. (Life Member)
MARKS, Mr. Neil Owen, BSc(Hons) ACA *2000;* 38 Hawthorn Drive, TOWCESTER, NORTHAMPTONSHIRE, NN12 7AE.
•MARKS, Mr. Philip Conrad, FCA *1970;* (Tax Fac), P.C Marks & Co, 10 Carlton Close, West Heath Road, LONDON, NW3 7UA.
MARKS, Mr. Ralph, BCom FCA *1946;* 42 Dennis Lane, STANMORE, HA7 4JW. (Life Member)
MARKS, Mrs. Rhona Claire, FCA *1971;* 3 Misty Ridge Circle, KINNELON, NJ 07405, UNITED STATES.
MARKS, Mr. Robert Frazer, BSc ACA *2005;* 118 Valley Road, LONDON, SW16 2XR.
MARKS, Mr. Robert Lewin, FCA *1970;* 27 Cliveden Gages, Taplow, MAIDENHEAD, BERKSHIRE, SL6 0GA.
MARKS, Mr. Stanley, BSc FCA *1957;* 1 M.Beilis St, JERUSALEM, 97280, ISRAEL. (Life Member)
•MARKS, Mr. Stephen, FCA *1986;* SRLV, 89 New Bond Street, LONDON, W1S 1DA.
MARKS, Mr. Stephen John William, BA ACA *1991;* 33 Kelsey Lane, Balsall Common, COVENTRY, CV7 7GR.
MARKS, Mr. Vadym, ACA *2009;* 186 Montrose Avenue, EDGWARE, MIDDLESEX, HA8 0EA.
MARKS, Mr. Warwick John, BA ACA *1992;* 15 Ivanhoe Road, LICHFIELD, STAFFORDSHIRE, WS14 9AY.
MARKS DE CHABRIS, Ms. Gloriana Ursula Chantal, MA ACA *1985;* Parsons Farm, Warren Corner, Froxfield, PETERSFIELD, HAMPSHIRE, GU32 1BJ.
MARKSON, Mr. Adam Peter, MBA BSc FCA *1994;* 134 Hemingford Road, Islington, LONDON, N1 1DE.
MARKUS, Mr. Richard Martin, BA ACA *1991;* Hawkpoint Partners Ltd, Opeontum Bockenheimer Landtsrasse 2-4, 60323 FRANKFURT AM MAIN, GERMANY.
MARKWELL, Mrs. Dawn, ACA *2003;* 53 Cruickshank Grove, Crownhill, MILTON KEYNES, MK8 0EW.
MARKWELL, Mr. John Edward, FCA *1976;* 28 Meadowvale Close, IPSWICH, IP4 4HF.
MARKWELL, Miss. Lynda Diane, BA ACA *2001;* Unit 1706, 1088 Quebec Street, VANCOUVER V6A 4H2, BC, CANADA.
MARKWICK, Mr. David Thomas, BSc FCA *1975;* 2 Rue Max Roujou, 78400 CHATOU, FRANCE.
MARKWICK, Mr. Edward Charles, FCA *1956;* 612-16 Rosedale Road, TORONTO M4W 2P4, ON, CANADA. (Life Member)
MARKWICK, Miss. Hilary, BA ACA *1992;* 4 Ladythorn Road, Bramhall, STOCKPORT, CHESHIRE, SK7 2ER.
MARKWICK, Miss. Selena Beverley, ACA *2009;* Flat 5, 98 Rope Street, LONDON, SE16 7TQ.
MARLAND, Mr. John, BCom ACA *1999;* 4 Euxton Hall Gardens, Euxton, CHORLEY, LANCASHIRE, PR7 6PB.
MARLAND, Mrs. Marie Teresa, BA ACA *1997;* 4 Euxton Hall Gardens, Euxton, CHORLEY, LANCASHIRE, PR7 6PB.
MARLAND, Mr. Richard Philip, BA ACA *2005;* Man Group Plc Riverbank House, 2 Swan Lane, LONDON, EC4R 3AD.

MARLBOROUGH, Mr. David, BSc ACA *1987;* Villa 197 Phase 1, Palm Meadows, Airport Varthur Road, BANGALORE 560066, INDIA.

MARLE, Mr. James Ilsley Baxter, FCA *1955;* Pamlico Plantation, 105 Osprey Bay, WASHINGTON, NC 27889, UNITED STATES. (Life Member)

MARLER, Mr. Richard Louis, BSc FCA *1979;* 9 Painters Close, Bloxham, BANBURY, OXFORDSHIRE, OX15 4QX.

MARLES, Mr. Ben Andrew, BSc(Hons) ACA *2002;* 16 New Barnes Avenue, ST. ALBANS, HERTFORDSHIRE, AL1 1TG.

MARLES, Mrs. Claire Elizabeth, BEng ACA *2001;* 16 New Barnes Avenue, ST. ALBANS, HERTFORDSHIRE, AL1 1TG.

MARLES, Miss. Laura Jayne, ACA *2010;* Flat 5 Ashgrove Apartments, 27-28 Cowick Street, EXETER, EX4 1AL.

MARLEY, Miss. Caroline Laura, BSc ACA *2010;* Rose Cottage, West Drive, CHELTENHAM, GLOUCESTERSHIRE, GL50 4LB.

MARLEY, Mr. Guy John, BA ACA *1983;* 17 Montpelier Road, BRIGHTON, BN1 2LQ.

MARLEY, Mr. Nicholas James, BSc ARCS FCA *1994;* 6 The Brambles Woodside, LONDON, SW19 7AY.

MARLEY, Mr. Simon Paul, BA ACA *1993;* 16 Leyfield Close, BLACKPOOL, FY3 7RQ.

MARLEY, Mr. Spencer Keith, MSci ARCS ACA *2009;* Flat 24 Ross Apartments, 23 Seagull Lane, LONDON, E16 1DE.

MARLEY, Mr. William Keith, FCA *1960;* Wychwood, 91 Merrybent, DARLINGTON, COUNTY DURHAM, DL2 2LF.

MARLOR, Mr. Alan Richard, FCA *1976;* 1 Oaklands Court Darras Hall, Ponteland, NEWCASTLE UPON TYNE, NE20 9QY.

MARLOR, Mr. John Stanley, BA FCA *1975;* 8 Beechwood Avenue, Hartford, NORTHWICH, CHESHIRE, CW8 3AR.

MARLOW, Mr. David Ellis, FCA *1958;* The Platt, Elsted, MIDHURST, GU29 0LA. (Life Member)

MARLOW, Mr. David Eric, FCA *1972;* 111 Main Road, HOCKLEY, SS5 4RN.

MARLOW, Mr. David Stuart, BA ACA *1998;* 47 Brampton Road, ST. ALBANS, HERTFORDSHIRE, AL1 4PU.

•MARLOW, Mrs. Doreen Vivienne, BSc FCA *1981;* (Tax Fac), DV Marlow & Co Limited, 72 West Street, Portchester, FAREHAM, HAMPSHIRE, PO16 9UN.

MARLOW, Mrs. Elaine Mary, ACA *1988;* 58 Spinney Road, Burton Latimer, KETTERING, NN15 5ND.

MARLOW, Mrs. Jeannine Kathy, BSc ACA *1997;* 5 High Drive, Oxshott, LEATHERHEAD, KT22 0NG.

MARLOW, Dr. Jonathan Peter, BSc ACA *1996;* Greenbanks, 5 High Drive, Oxshott, LEATHERHEAD, KT22 0NG.

MARLOW, Mrs. Nicola Louise, BA ACA *1996;* 16 Osborne Road, POTTERS BAR, HERTFORDSHIRE, EN6 1SD.

MARLOW, Mr. Reginald John, FCA *1955;* 24 Milan Street, MENTONE, VIC 3194, AUSTRALIA. (Life Member)

MARLOW, Mr. Richard James, BA(Hons) ACA *2000;* 14 Arthurs Avenue, HARROGATE, NORTH YORKSHIRE, HG2 0DX.

MARLOW, Mr. Stephen, FCA *1977;* Wall of Death Beeston Ltd, 19 Imperial Road, Beeston, NOTTINGHAM, NG9 1ET.

MARLOW, Mr. Timothy John, BA ACA *2007;* 19 Field Road, SALE, CHESHIRE, M33 5PQ.

MARMENT, Mr. Alan, FCA *1954;* 10 Lacemakers Road, MALMESBURY, WILTSHIRE, SN16 9XS. (Life Member)

MARNEROU, Miss. Constantina, BSc ACA *2001;* 11 Patron Germanou, 3095 LIMASSOL, CYPRUS.

MARNHAM, Miss. Charlotte Victoria, ACA *2010;* with PricewaterhouseCoopers LLP, 1 Embankment Place, LONDON, WC2N 6RH.

MARNHAM, Mr. John David, BSc FCA *1973;* Pollards House, Limpsfield, OXTED, RH8 0QX. (Life Member)

MARNHAM, Mr. Stephen Ralph, MA FCA *1970;* Church Cottage, Church Enstone, CHIPPING NORTON, OX7 4NN. (Life Member)

MAROO, Miss. Chetna, BSc ACA *1998;* with Ernst & Young LLP, 1 More London Place, LONDON, SE1 2AF.

MAROO, Mr. Jayesh, BSc ACA *1994;* Atos Origin, Regents Place, 4 Triton Square, LONDON, NW1 3HG.

MAROO, Mr. Mitesh, BA ACA *1988;* 10 Hillcroft Avenue, PINNER, HA5 5AW.

MAROO, Mr. Nihar Mulchand, BSc ACA *1991;* 16 Nicholas Road, Elstree, BOREHAMWOOD, HERTFORDSHIRE, WD6 3JY.

MAROO JAIN, Mrs. Aparna, BSc ACA *2005;* Jain House, 14 Alipur Road, Civil Lines, 110054, DELHI, INDIA.

•MAROUDIAS, Mr. Petros, MA ACA *2000;* PricewaterhouseCoopers Limited, Julia House, 3 Themistocles Dervis Street, CY-1066 NICOSIA, CYPRUS.

MAROUFI-BOZORGI, Mr. Mehrdad, MCom FCA *1972;* Suite 13, 25 Second Street Farnaz Ave., Mohseni, TEHRAN, IRAN.

MARPER, Mr. William John, FCA *1972;* Manderley, 34 Prestbury Road, WILMSLOW, SK9 2LL.

MARPLES, Mr. Lee Anthony, ACA MAAT *2011;* 25 Sweetbriar Close, Alvaston, DERBY, DE24 0TF.

MARPLES, Mr. Rodney Brian, BSc FCA *1970;* 11 Cranesfield, Sherborne St John, BASINGSTOKE, RG24 9LN.

MARQUES, Mr. Richard Ian, BSc ACA *2003;* Level 34 The Chifley Tower 2 Chifley Square, SYDNEY, NSW 2000, AUSTRALIA.

MARQUIS, Mr. Edward, FCA *1954;* 129 Guisborough Road, Nunthorpe, MIDDLESBROUGH, CLEVELAND, TS7 0JE. (Life Member)

MARR, Mr. Alastair Stuart Munro, FCA *1969;* Highfield House, 12 Highfield Drive, KINGSBRIDGE, DEVON, TQ7 1JR. (Life Member)

MARR, Mr. Andrew Blakey, MA ACA CFA *2000;* 13 Duke Street, ALDERLEY EDGE, CHESHIRE, SK9 7HX.

MARR, Mr. Anthony Waide, BSc FCA *1980;* 907A 9/F, China Merchants Tower, Shun Tak Centre, 168-200 Connaught Road, CENTRAL, HONG KONG ISLAND HONG KONG SAR.

MARR, Mrs. Caroline Mary, BDS ACA *1989;* 59 Westbourne Road, PENARTH, CF64 3HB.

MARR, Mr. Charles Elliott, BA FCA *1983;* Hollybank, Blackness Road, CROWBOROUGH, TN6 2NA.

MARR, Mr. Derek Lawrence, BEng ACA *1996;* 170 Dursley Road, LONDON, SE3 8PH.

MARR, Mr. Derek Percy, FCA *1957;* 6 Fisher Close, KINGS LANGLEY, WD4 8EU.

MARR, Mr. Graham Peter Wilson, BSc ACA *1984;* 15 Harebell Hill, COBHAM, SURREY, KT11 2RS.

MARR, Mr. Graham Stuart, BSc ACA *1987;* 59 Westbourne Road, PENARTH, CF64 3HB.

MARR, Mrs. Lorraine Yvonne, BA ACA *1993;* 9 Fewston Close, BOLTON, BL1 7BJ.

MARR, Mr. Richard Donald, BA ACA *1999;* Crag View, Rothbury, MORPETH, NORTHUMBERLAND, NE65 7YR.

MARR, Mr. Robert Andrew, BSc ACA MBA *1990;* (Tax Fac), William Reed Holdings Ltd, Broadfield Park, Brighton Road, Pease Pottage, CRAWLEY, WEST SUSSEX RH11 9RT.

MARR, Mr. Robert Brian, FCA *1966;* 3 Grant Walk, ASCOT, SL5 9TT. (Life Member)

MARR, Mr. William Thomas, BA ACA *1994;* 35 Park Road, BANBURY, OXFORDSHIRE, OX16 0DN.

•MARRAY, Mr. Michael John, FCA *1977;* Marray & McIntyre, Hawthorn House, 1 Medlicott Close, CORBY, NORTHAMPTONSHIRE, NN18 9NF.

MARREN, Mr. David, MA MBA FCA *1983;* Unit 6 Gateway Business Park, Pipers Road, COULSDON, CR5 2AR.

MARREN, Mr. Jonathan Anthony Frank, BSc(Hons) ACA *2000;* The Old Post Office The Street Long Sutton, HOOK, HAMPSHIRE, RG29 1SS.

MARREN, Mr. Kevin John, BA ACA *1988;* Summerfield, Bobby's Lane, Eccleston, ST.HELENS, MERSEYSIDE, WA10 5AL.

MARRET, Mrs. Cecile, BSc ACA *2000;* 1 Pembridge Mews, LONDON, W11 3EQ.

•MARRETT, Mr. Glenn John, FCA *1977;* Lever Bros & Co, The Station Masters House, 168 Thornbury Road, ISLEWORTH, MIDDLESEX, TW7 4QE.

MARRIAGE, Mr. David Jack, BEng ACA *2003;* 23 The Haydens, TONBRIDGE, TN9 1NS.

•MARRIAGE, Mr. Paul, BSc ACA *1985;* 5 Brentwood Close, Thorpe Audlin, PONTEFRACT, WEST YORKSHIRE, WF8 3ES.

•MARRIAGE, Mr. Simon Charles, BSc(Econ) FCA *1981;* Ballams, Crane Court, 302 London Road, IPSWICH, IP2 0AJ.

MARRINAN, Mr. Patrick, ACA *2009;* 19 Ravenshurst Avenue, Hendon, LONDON, NW4 4EE.

MARRINER, Mr. Kevin Michael, BA ACA *1992;* 72 Dawson Drive, Skene Westhill, ABERDEEN, AB32 6NS.

MARRINER, Mr. Nicholas Henry, FCA *1966;* Warwick Hall, 1, Warwick-On-Eden, CARLISLE, CA4 8PG.

MARRION, Mrs. Amanda Jane, BSc ACA *1998;* 64 The Shearers, BISHOP'S STORTFORD, HERTFORDSHIRE, CM23 4AZ.

MARRIOTT, Mrs. Alison Jane, BA ACA *1993;* The Pantiles, 12 Clive Road, ESHER, SURREY, KT10 8PS.

MARRIOTT, Mr. Andrew Richard, BSc FCA *1982;* Southways, Little Green Lane, FARNHAM, GU9 8TF.

MARRIOTT, Mr. Anthony John, BSS FCA *1991;* 121 Ruskin Avenue, Long Eaton, NOTTINGHAM, NG10 3HX.

MARRIOTT, Mr. Austen, LLB ACA *1992;* 5 Figaro Gardens, SINGAPORE 454980, SINGAPORE.

MARRIOTT, Miss. Catherine Dorothy, BSc ACA *2003;* Macquarie Bank Ltd, 1 Martin Place, SYDNEY, NSW 2000, AUSTRALIA.

•MARRIOTT, Mr. David, FCA *1963;* 6/10b Nitze Boulevard, 42262 NETANYA, ISRAEL.

•MARRIOTT, Mr. David Paul, ACA *2003;* (Tax Fac), DPM Accounting Services Ltd, Suite 2B Ribble Court, 1 Mead Way, Padiham, BURNLEY, LANCASHIRE BB12 7NG.

MARRIOTT, Mr. Geoffrey Michael, BA ACA *2003;* White Young Green Consulting Group Arndale Court, Arndale Centre Otley Road, LEEDS, LS6 2UJ.

MARRIOTT, Mr. Henry Elwell, FCA *1965;* Unit 20, 108-112 Stapleton Street, PENDLE HILL, NSW 2145, AUSTRALIA. (Life Member)

MARRIOTT, Mr. Ian David, BSc ACA *1995;* The Pantiles, 12 Clive Road, ESHER, SURREY, KT10 8PS.

MARRIOTT, Miss. Jill, BA ACA *1992;* 42 Wainbody Avenue North, COVENTRY, CV3 6DB.

MARRIOTT, Mr. John Richard, FCA *1978;* with The Boots Company plc, Thane Road, NOTTINGHAM, NG90 1BS.

MARRIOTT, Mr. Keith, FCA *1975;* 60 Cherry Orton Road, PETERBOROUGH, PE2 5EH.

MARRIOTT, Mr. Lee Jefferson, BSc(Econ) ACA *1997;* 20 Daleside Gardens, CHIGWELL, ESSEX, IG7 6PR.

•MARRIOTT, Mr. Martin John, FCA *1983;* (Tax Fac), W R Frost & Co Limited, Riversdale, Ashburton Road, TOTNES, DEVON, TQ9 5JU.

MARRIOTT, Mr. Paul, BA(Hons) ACA *2000;* 702/8 Cooper Street, SURRY HILLS, NSW 2010, AUSTRALIA.

•MARRIOTT, Mr. Paul, FCA *1975;* Fearns Marriott Ltd, Ford House, Market Street, LEEK, STAFFORDSHIRE, ST13 6JA.

MARRIOTT, Mr. Peter Richard, MA BA BSc FCA DChA *1976;* 1 Sandileigh Avenue, MANCHESTER, M20 3LN.

MARRIOTT, Mr. Simon Granville, FCA *1960;* 16 Church Street, Isham, KETTERING, NORTHAMPTONSHIRE, NN14 1HD. (Life Member)

MARRIOTT, Miss. Stephanie, BA(Hons) ACA *2011;* 144, Birchwood Road, BRISTOL, BS4 4RD.

MARRIOTT, Miss. Stephanie Rose, ACA *2011;* Kookaburra, 10 Oakland Vineries, La Rue Du Presbytere, St. Clement, JERSEY, JE2 6RB.

MARRIS, Mr. Anthony Hamilton, FCA *1962;* 36 Brunel Quays, Great Western Village, LOSTWITHIEL, CORNWALL, PL22 0JB.

MARRIS, Mr. Antony Kenneth, FCA *1973;* Marisco, Westmere, Hanley Swan, WORCESTER, WR8 0DG.

•MARRIS, Mr. Robert Frederick, BA FCA *1982;* (Tax Fac), RNS, 50-54 Oswald Road, SCUNTHORPE, NORTH LINCOLNSHIRE, DN15 7PQ.

MARRISON, Mr. Andrew James, BSc ACA *1999;* (Tax Fac), Urenco Ltd, 18 Oxford Road, MARLOW, BUCKINGHAMSHIRE, SL7 2NL.

MARRISON, Mr. Duncan Peter, BSc ACA *2007;* 2 Storth Avenue, SHEFFIELD, S10 3HL.

MARRISON, Mr. Michael Anthony, BSc ACA *1987;* 10 Armistead Way, Cranage, Holmes Chapel, CREWE, CW4 8FE.

MARROCCO, Mr. Adrian Robert, MA ACA *1995;* 49 Annett Road, WALTON-ON-THAMES, SURREY, KT12 2JS.

MARRS, Mrs. Lindsay Anne, ACA *2004;* with Armstrong Watson, Bute House, Montgomery Way, Rosehill, CARLISLE, CA1 2RW.

MARRUFO, Mrs. Anna Jean, BSc(Hons) ACA *2002;* Dionex UK Ltd Unit 4, Albany Court Albany Park, CAMBERLEY, GU16 7QL.

•MARSDEN, Mr. Alexander David, BA FCA CFE *1991;* BDO LLP, 6th Floor, 3 Hardman Street, Spinningfields, MANCHESTER, M3 3AT. See also BDO Stoy Hayward LLP

MARSDEN, Mr. Alistair William, BA ACA *1992;* Valley View, 208 Stanmore Lane, WINCHESTER, SO22 4BL.

MARSDEN, Mr. Andrew, MMath ACA *2004;* with Ernst & Young LLP, 1 More London Place, LONDON, SE1 2AF.

MARSDEN, Mr. Andrew Neil, ACA *1978;* 302 London Road, Appleton, WARRINGTON, WA4 5DR.

MARSDEN, Mr. Andrew Peter, BSc FCA *1983;* The Cottage, Middle Street, Galhampton, YEOVIL, BA22 7AP.

•MARSDEN, Miss. Caroline, ACA *1990;* (Tax Fac), Mount View, 3 Wigan Lane, Heath Charnock, CHORLEY, LANCASHIRE, PR7 4DD.

•①MARSDEN, Mr. Christopher, BSc ACA *1997;* Ernst & Young LLP, The Paragon, Counterslip, BRISTOL, BS1 6BX. See also Ernst & Young Europe LLP

MARSDEN, Mr. David Andrew, BSc ACA *1982;* Membury Investments Ltd, Chapelcroft Road, Membury, AXMINSTER, DEVON, EX13 7JR.

MARSDEN, Mrs. Emma Mary Alice, BA(Hons) ACA *2002;* 19 Aldersyde Way, Guiseley, LEEDS, LS20 8QS.

MARSDEN, Miss. Faye Jemifer, MA BA ACA *2010;* 6 Salisbury Court, Thornton Avenue, LONDON, W4 1QH.

MARSDEN, Mr. Gavin Edward, BSc(Hons) *2003;* 31 South View Road, Hoyland, BARNSLEY, SOUTH YORKSHIRE, S74 9EB.

MARSDEN, Mr. Guy Norman, BSc ACA *1986;* Highbridge Developments Ltd Berger House, 36-38 Berkeley Square, LONDON, W1J 5AE.

•MARSDEN, Mr. Ian Clifford, BSc FCA *1989;* PricewaterhouseCoopers LLP, 101 Barbirolli Square, Lower Mosley Street, MANCHESTER, M2 3PW. See also PricewaterhouseCoopers

MARSDEN, Mr. John Douglas, BA FCA *1977;* South View, Park Estate, La Route Des Genets, St. Brelade, JERSEY, JE3 8EQ.

MARSDEN, Mr. Johnathan David, ACA *2009;* 15 Silver Ridge, Barlaston, STOKE-ON-TRENT, ST12 9DR.

MARSDEN, Miss. Kathryn, BA ACA *2002;* 41 West Way, HARPENDEN, HERTFORDSHIRE, AL5 4QX.

MARSDEN, Mr. Keith, FCA *1947;* Rose Cottage, 80 Laycock Lane, Laycock, KEIGHLEY, BD22 0PJ. (Life Member)

MARSDEN, Mrs. Kirsty, FCA *1993;* 15 St Michaels Close, Skidby, COTTINGHAM, HU16 5TY.

MARSDEN, Ms. Lara Chantal, ACA CA(SA) *2010;* The Beeches, Ascot Gate, Sunninghill Road, ASCOT, BERKSHIRE, SL5 7RJ.

•MARSDEN, Mrs. Louise Clare, BSc ACA *2004;* Louise Marsden Ltd, 20 Poppyfields, Horsford, NORWICH, NR10 3SR.

MARSDEN, Mrs. Louise Margaret, BA ACA *1999;* 58 Wakefords Park, Church Crookham, FLEET, GU52 8EY.

•MARSDEN, Mr. Malcolm Walter, FCA *1980;* Grays, 1 Parliament Street, HULL, HU1 2AS. See also Fawley Judge & Easton

•MARSDEN, Mr. Michael Frank, FCA *1975;* (Tax Fac), Apartment Lacaille, Les Palmiers, 2 Bis Monte Fleurie, 06310 BEAULIEU SUR MER, FRANCE.

MARSDEN, Mrs. Michelle, BSc ACA *2003;* 2 Cloughlands Court, 31 South View Road, Hoyland, BARNSLEY, SOUTH YORKSHIRE, S74 9EB.

MARSDEN, Mr. Nicholas Charles Peter, FCA *1970;* Marks Cottage, 19 North Street, DRIFFIELD, NORTH HUMBERSIDE, YO25 6AS.

•MARSDEN, Mr. Nicholas Hamish Alexander, MSc BA ACA ATII *2000;* Deloitte LLP, 1 City Square, LEEDS, WEST YORKSHIRE, LS1 2AL. See also Deloitte & Touche LLP

MARSDEN, Mr. Owen Lee, ACA *2004;* Walton Dodge Forensic, Dencora Court, 2 Meridian Way, NORWICH, NR7 0TA.

MARSDEN, Mr. Paul Graham, FCA *1960;* 70 Kechill Gardens, Hayes, BROMLEY, BR2 7NG. (Life Member)

•MARSDEN, Mr. Peter Charles, FCA *1974;* (Tax Fac), Spring Court, 3 Spring Road, Hale, ALTRINCHAM, CHESHIRE, WA14 2UQ.

MARSDEN, Mr. Peter Ian Walker, FCA *1976;* Moor Farm, Ashton Road, Minety, MALMESBURY, WILTSHIRE, SN16 9QP. (Life Member)

MARSDEN, Mr. Peter Thomas, BSc FCA *1978;* 18 Sovereign Close, BRAINTREE, ESSEX, CM7 9DL. (Life Member)

MARSDEN, Mr. Philip William Frederick, FCA *1973;* with RSM Tenon Audit Limited, 66 Chiltern Street, LONDON, W1U 4JT.

MARSDEN, Mr. Phillip James, BA(Hons) ACA *2009;* Tenon The Poynt Building, 45 Wollaton Street, NOTTINGHAM, NG1 5FW.

MARSDEN, Mrs. Rachel Jane, BA ACA *2005;* 3 Phelps Street, SURRY HILLS, NSW 2010, AUSTRALIA.

•MARSDEN, Mr. Robert Greig, FCA *1981;* (Tax Fac), Myers Clark Limited, Iveco House, Station Road, WATFORD, WD17 1DL. See also Bluedome Finance Limited

•MARSDEN, Mr. Robert John, FCA *1970;* RJ Marsden, Park House, 9 Park Town, OXFORD, OX2 6SN.

MARSDEN, Mr. Robert William, BSc ACA *1999;* 28 Cairn Avenue, LONDON, W5 5HX.

MARSDEN, Mr. Sam Andrew, BSc ACA *2002;* PricewaterhouseCoopers, Darling Park Tower 2, 201 Sussex Street, SYDNEY, NSW 2000, AUSTRALIA.
MARSDEN, Mr. Simon John, BSc ACA *1998;* 30 Denison Way, CARDIFF, CF5 4SF.
MARSDEN, Mr. Simon Roger, BSc ACA *1998;* The Medeival Barn Hallgarth Manor Farm, High Pittington, DURHAM, DH6 1RE.
MARSDEN, Mr. Torsten Paul, BSc ACA *1990;* 34 Brighton Mews, HILLARYS, WA 6025, AUSTRALIA.
MARSDEN, Mr. Vernon George, FCA *1953;* 7921 Suntree Glen, Lakewood Ranch, Bradenton, BRADENTON, FL 34202, UNITED STATES. (Life Member)
•**MARSDEN, Miss. Yvonne Patricia, BSc FCA** *1986;* Cambus Consulting Ltd, 24 Lodge Close, COBHAM, SURREY, KT11 2SQ.
MARSDEN-JONES, Mr. Andrew John, BSc ACA *1980;* 35 Cuckoo Hill Road, PINNER, MIDDLESEX, HA5 1AS.
MARSH, Mr. Adrian Howard, BSc ACA *1996;* 4 The Pyghtell, Luckington, CHIPPENHAM, SN14 6QR.
MARSH, Mr. Alan, MSc FCA *1967;* 46 Kestrel Drive, Loggerheads, MARKET DRAYTON, SHROPSHIRE, TF9 2QT.
MARSH, Mr. Alan Francis, BA FCA *1982;* Rosetree Cottage, Lower Church Street, Cuddington, AYLESBURY, BUCKINGHAMSHIRE, HP18 0AS.
•**MARSH, Mr. Andrew Charles, FCA** *1973;* glm Ghest Lloyd Limited, 103-105 Brighton Road, COULSDON, SURREY, CR5 2NG.
MARSH, Mr. Andrew Colin, BSc ACA *2010;* K P M G, Salisbury Square House, 8 Salisbury Square, LONDON, EC4Y 8BB.
MARSH, Mr. Anthony William, BA ACA *1985;* with KPMG LLP, Management Services Centre, 58 Clarendon Road, WATFORD, WD17 1DE.
MARSH, Mr. Antony, BSc(Hons) ACA *2004;* Flat 5, St. Leonards Mews, 251 Hoxton Street, LONDON, N1 5LG.
•①**MARSH, Miss. Beverley Jayne, BCom ACA** *1990;* RSM Tenon Limited, 6th Floor, The White House, 111 New Street, BIRMINGHAM, B2 4EU.
•**MARSH, Mr. Brian Colin, FCA** *1983;* (Tax Fac), 17 Godre'r Mynydd, Gwernymynydd, MOLD, CLWYD, CH7 4AD.
MARSH, Mr. Bruce, BSc ACA *1993;* 2 Ash Close, ABBOTS LANGLEY, WD5 0DN.
MARSH, Mr. Bryan, BCom FCA *1965;* Wild Rose House, Llancarfan, BARRY, CF62 3AD. (Life Member)
MARSH, Mr. Byron Philip, ACA *2009;* 135 Deanery Road, BRISTOL, BS1 5QH.
•**MARSH, Ms. Charlotte Kate, ACA FCCA** *2008;* Breeze & Associates Ltd, 5 Cornfield Terrace, EASTBOURNE, EAST SUSSEX, BN21 4NN.
•**MARSH, Mr. Christopher David, BSc ACA** *1998;* 7 Kensington Close, ST. ALBANS, HERTFORDSHIRE, AL1 1JT.
MARSH, Mr. Christopher Howard, ACA *1981;* Marsh Business Services Ltd, 10 Florence Avenue, DROITWICH, WORCESTERSHIRE, WR9 8NJ.
•**MARSH, Mr. Christopher John, BSc ACA** *1980;* (Tax Fac), Chris Marsh, 3 Sherringham Court, 13 The Ridgeway, ENFIELD, MIDDLESEX, EN2 8NS.
MARSH, Mr. Christopher Richard Roff, BA ACA *1996;* Darenth Hulme Shacklands Road, Shoreham, SEVENOAKS, TN14 7TU.
MARSH, Miss. Clare Janet, BSc FCA *1998;* Red Cedars, Smithy Lane, Pensnett, BRIERLEY HILL, DY5 4UE.
MARSH, Mr. Colin Alan, ACA *1996;* About Thyme Hollicarrs Close, Escrick, YORK, YO19 6EF.
MARSH, Mr. Daniel, ACA *2008;* Flat 21 Benedictine Place, 1 Marlborough Road, ST. ALBANS, HERTFORDSHIRE, AL1 3WA.
MARSH, Mr. David, BSc ACA *1987;* 50 Sanderstead Hill, SOUTH CROYDON, SURREY, CR2 0HA.
MARSH, Mr. David Brian, MSc FCA *1970;* 39 Bedford Road, East Finchley, LONDON, N2 9DB.
MARSH, Mr. David Howard, BA ACA *1980;* 8 Harlech Fold, Lodge Moor, SHEFFIELD, S10 4NS.
MARSH, Mr. David Richard, BA ACA *1992;* Glaxo Smithkline Plc, G S K House, 980 Great West Road, BRENTFORD, MIDDLESEX, TW8 9GS.
MARSH, Miss. Deborah Louise, BSc ACA *1994;* 10 Angletarn Close, West Bridgford, NOTTINGHAM, NG2 6TB.
MARSH, Mr. Edmund Nicholas, FCA *1967;* Apartment 12, 2 Romana Square, ALTRINCHAM, CHESHIRE, WA14 5QB.
MARSH, Mr. Edward Alexander, BSc ACA *2011;* 18 High Street, Ravensthorpe, NORTHAMPTON, NN6 8EH.
•**MARSH, Mr. Edward James, BSc ACA DChA** *2006;* with Burton Sweet, Pembroke House, 15 Pembroke Road, Clifton, BRISTOL, BS8 3BA.
MARSH, Mrs. Elizabeth Fiona, MA ACA *1984;* 4 Bowers Way, HARPENDEN, AL5 4EW.
MARSH, Miss. Gail Alison Louise, BA(Hons) ACA *2002;* 40 Park Hill, LONDON, SW4 9PB.
MARSH, Mr. Gary John, BA ACA *1984;* Thales Training & Simulation, Gatwick Road, CRAWLEY, WEST SUSSEX, RH10 9RL.
MARSH, Mrs. Gaynor, BA ACA *1992;* (Tax Fac), 22 Claremont Field, OTTERY ST. MARY, EX11 1NP.
•**MARSH, Mr. Howard, FCA** *1987;* (Tax Fac), Metcalfes, 1-3 St. Marys Place, BURY, LANCASHIRE, BL9 0DZ.
MARSH, Mr. Howard Alexander David, BCom ACA *1999;* 33 Rogers Way, WARWICK, CV34 6PY.
MARSH, Mr. Ian Edward, FCA *1958;* 208 Uxbridge Road, Harrow Weald, HARROW, HA3 6SW. (Life Member)
MARSH, Mr. Ian John, BSc FCA *1980;* 4 Mayfield Road, WEYBRIDGE, KT13 8XE.
MARSH, Mr. James, BSc ACA *1996;* 75 Selwyn Avenue, Mission Bay, AUCKLAND 1071, NEW ZEALAND.
MARSH, Mr. James Webster, BSc FCA *1991;* 42 Bell View, ST. ALBANS, AL4 0SQ.
•**MARSH, Mr. Jason David, MA ACA** *1995;* Deloitte LLP, 2 New Street Square, LONDON, EC4A 3BZ. See also Deloitte & Touche LLP
MARSH, Ms. Jill Katharine, BA ACA *1990;* 36 Peppercombe Road, EASTBOURNE, EAST SUSSEX, BN20 8JH.
•**MARSH, Mrs. Joanne, BA ACA** *1990;* Joanne Marsh & Co, 24 Amaroo Avenue, ELANORA HEIGHTS, NSW 2101, AUSTRALIA.
MARSH, Mr. John, BA ACA *2006;* 4th floor, Berger House, 36-38 Berkeley Square, LONDON, W1J 5AJ.
MARSH, Mr. Jonathan James, BA ACA *1994;* Holly Mark, 27 Hollymead Road, Chipstead, COULSDON, SURREY, CR5 3LQ.
MARSH, Mr. Jonathan Patrick Justyn, BA ACA *1982;* The Old Malthouse North Street, Sheldwich, FAVERSHAM, ME13 0LN.
MARSH, Mr. Jonathan Paul, MMath ACA *2003;* 108 Strathville Road, LONDON, SW18 4RE.
MARSH, Mr. Joseph William, MCMI FCA *1974;* Tibia Villa, Lilian Avenue, WALLSEND, TYNE AND WEAR, NE28 8QJ.
MARSH, Mrs. Kristin Lee Groethe, FCA *1994;* 302 Wildwood, ANN ARBOR, MI 48103, UNITED STATES.
MARSH, Miss. Lisa Catherine, LLB ACA *2004;* 74 The Platters, GILLINGHAM, ME8 0DJ.
•**MARSH, Mr. Malcolm Robert, FCA** *1974;* Malcolm Marsh & Co. Ltd, 13 Burnieboozle Crescent, ABERDEEN, AB15 8NN.
MARSH, Mr. Mark, BA ACA *1997;* 3 Mill Court, Primrose Hill Bournemoor, HOUGHTON LE SPRING, DH4 6DJ.
MARSH, Ms. Mary Teresa, BSc ACA *1993;* 42 Alexandra Road, MALVERN, WORCESTERSHIRE, WR14 1HF.
MARSH, Mrs. Maura Catherine, BSc(Hons) ACA *2000;* Swallow House, 17 Northall Road, Eaton Bray, DUNSTABLE, BEDFORDSHIRE, LU6 2DQ.
•**MARSH, Mr. Michael John, BA ACA** *1989;* (Tax Fac), Thomas Westcott, 26-28 Southernhay East, EXETER, DEVON, EX1 1NS.
MARSH, Mr. Paul Colin, BA FCA *1981;* 1 Cranmer House, Maybush Lane, FELIXSTOWE, SUFFOLK, IP11 7NA.
MARSH, Mr. Paul Richard, BA FCA *1987;* 10 Crawford Lane, Kesgrave, IPSWICH, IP5 2GY.
MARSH, Mr. Peter, FCA *1959;* 6 Tollgate Drive, LONDON, SE21 7LS. (Life Member)
MARSH, Mr. Peter Edward, ACA CA(SA) *2008;* PO Box 2927, BEDFORDVIEW, 2008, SOUTH AFRICA.
MARSH, Ms. Rachel, BA(Hons)Oxon ACA *2011;* Orchard House, 10a Burntwood Road, SEVENOAKS, KENT, TN13 1PT.
MARSH, Mr. Richard Laurence, BSc FCA *1980;* 69 Erpingham Road, Putney, LONDON, SW15 1BH.
•**MARSH, Mr. Richard Webster, BA FCA** *1984;* Hawsons, 5 Sidings Court, White Rose Way, DONCASTER, SOUTH YORKSHIRE, DN4 5NU.
MARSH, Mr. Robert Richmond, BSc ACA *2000;* 8 Nursery Lane, LEEDS, LS17 7HN.
•①**MARSH, Mr. Roger, BSc FCA** *1980;* PricewaterhouseCoopers LLP, Benson House, 33 Wellington Street, LEEDS, LS1 4JP. See also PricewaterhouseCoopers
MARSH, Mr. Roger Gareth, BA FCA *1978;* 36 Tyning End, BATH, BA2 6AP.
•**MARSH, Mrs. Rowena Mary, FCA** *1972;* (Tax Fac), Rowena M Marsh FCA MAE, 9 St. Ives Park, Ashley Heath, RINGWOOD, HAMPSHIRE, BH24 2JX.
MARSH, Miss. Sarah Elizabeth, BA(Hons) ACA *2002;* #2206 120 Milross Avenue, VANCOUVER V6A 4K7, BC, CANADA.
•**MARSH, Mr. Simon Charles Caldwell, BA ACA** *1987;* WSM Partners LLP, Pinnacle House, 17/25 Hartfield Road, Wimbledon, LONDON, SW19 3SE. See also Windsor Stebbing Marsh
MARSH, Mr. Simon Robert, BSc ACA *1985;* 1 Adams Road, WOLVERHAMPTON, WV3 8EQ.
MARSH, Mr. Stephen George, BSc ACA *1991;* West Bromwich Building Society, 374 High Street, WEST BROMWICH, B70 8LR.
MARSH, Mr. Stephen Nicholas Bowyer, BA ACA *1992;* Dovehouse Shott, Smiths End Lane, Barley, ROYSTON, SG8 8LL.
•**MARSH, Mr. Stephen Robert, FCA** *1976;* Stephen R Marsh, 7 Worths Way, STRATFORD-UPON-AVON, WARWICKSHIRE, CV37 0RR.
•**MARSH, Mr. Steven Ian, FCA** *1980;* Marsdens Limited, Tudor House, High Road, Thornwood, EPPING, ESSEX CM16 6LT.
•**MARSH, Mrs. Susan Elizabeth, BEd FCA** *1982;* SM & Co, 1 Cranmer House, Maybush Lane, FELIXSTOWE, SUFFOLK, IP11 7NA.
MARSH, Miss. Suzanne, ACA *2009;* Flat 4, 63 Alexandra Road, READING, RG1 5PS.
•**MARSH, Mr. Terence George, FCA** *1972;* (Tax Fac), Terry Marsh, Barley Mow House, Woods Lane, Cliddesden, BASINGSTOKE, RG25 2JG.
MARSH, Mr. Timothy, BSc FCA *1976;* Orchard House, 10a Burntwood Road, SEVENOAKS, TN13 1PT.
MARSH, Ms. Tracey Clare, MSc BSc ACA *2002;* 9 Porthamal Road, Rhiwbina, CARDIFF, CF14 6AQ.
MARSH, Mr. William John, FCA *1965;* 11 Whittingtons Way, HASTINGS, TN34 2AS. (Life Member)
MARSHALL, Miss. Abigail Serena June, ACA *2009;* 60 Dolphin Road, NORWICH, NR5 0UR.
MARSHALL, Mr. Alan Paul, MA ACA *1989;* Shotover House Shotover Corner, Uffington, FARINGDON, OXFORDSHIRE, SN7 7RH.
MARSHALL, Mr. Alan Stanley, FCA *1957;* 2 Penrice Close, WESTON-SUPER-MARE, BS22 9AH. (Life Member)
MARSHALL, Mr. Alasdair Keith, MA ACA *1995;* Pricewaterhousecoopers Cornwall Court, 19 Cornwall Street, BIRMINGHAM, B3 2DT.
MARSHALL, Mr. Alastair James Bruce, MA ACA *2004;* Flat 28, Churchfield Mansions, 321-345 New Kings Road, Parsons Green, LONDON, SW6 4RA.
MARSHALL, Mr. Alexander James McInnes, BA(Hons) ACA *2011;* Widdrims, Lodge Road, Turnberry, GIRVAN, AYRSHIRE, KA26 9LX.
MARSHALL, Mr. Alexander Robert Lea, BA FCA *1967;* 400 High Street, KEW, VIC 3101, AUSTRALIA.
MARSHALL, Mrs. Alison, BSc ACA *1989;* Java, Tilford Road, HINDHEAD, GU26 6SF.
MARSHALL, Mrs. Alison Clare, MA ACA *1992;* M & MR Ltd, 5 Manor Farm Offices, Northend Road, Fenny Compton, SOUTHAM, WARWICKSHIRE CV47 2YY.
MARSHALL, Mr. Andrew, FCA *1965;* Ballyragget Barn, Tosside, SKIPTON, BD23 4SX.
•**MARSHALL, Mr. Andrew Gerard, BSc FCA** *1991;* KPMG LLP, 15 Canada Square, LONDON, E14 5GL. See also KPMG Europe LLP
MARSHALL, Mr. Andrew James, BEng ACA *2000;* Geldards LLP, Dumfries House, Dumfries Place, CARDIFF, CF10 3ZF.
MARSHALL, Mr. Andrew Jonathan, ACA *2011;* 4 Charmouth Road, BATH, BA1 3LJ.
MARSHALL, Mr. Andrew Neil, BA FCA *1990;* Java, Tilford Road, HINDHEAD, GU26 6SF.
MARSHALL, Mr. Andrew Paul, BSc ACA *2007;* 103 Spectrum Apartments, Central Promenade Douglas, ISLE OF MAN, IM2 4JL.
MARSHALL, Mr. Andrew Robert, BSc ACA *1997;* 81 Wattleton Road, BEACONSFIELD, BUCKINGHAMSHIRE, HP9 1RS.
MARSHALL, Mr. Andrew Simon, BA ACA *1998;* 32 Tai Maes, MOLD, CLWYD, CH7 1RW.
MARSHALL, Miss. Angela Elizabeth, BSc ACA *1996;* 1 Queens Close, NORWICH, NR4 7PE.
•**MARSHALL, Mr. Angus Alexander, BSc FCA** *1987;* RSM Tenon Audit Limited, 2 Wellington Place, LEEDS, LS1 4AP.
MARSHALL, Miss. Anna, BSc ACA *1988;* 16 Marden Avenue, CHICHESTER, PO19 2RB.
•**MARSHALL, Mr. Anthony, BA FCA ATII** *1989;* Anthony Marshall Ltd, 70 Market Street, Tottington, BURY, BL8 3LJ.
•**MARSHALL, Mr. Anthony John, BSc FCA** *1981;* (Tax Fac), Marshall Roche Limited, 1 Portland Buildings, Stoke Road, GOSPORT, HAMPSHIRE, PO12 1JH.
MARSHALL, Mr. Anthony John, FCA *1966;* 13 Tideswell Road, LONDON, SW15 6LJ. (Life Member)
MARSHALL, Mr. Anthony John, BSc ACA *1986;* Priory Woodfield Engineering Ltd, Millbrook Works, Lower Horseley Fields, WOLVERHAMPTON, WV1 3DZ.
MARSHALL, Mrs. Antonia Larla, ACA *2006;* 29 Station Road, LEIGH-ON-SEA, ESSEX, SS9 1ST.
MARSHALL, Mr. Augustus Ralph, ACA *1975;* Unit17, Impian Bukit Tunku, No 8 Jalan Tunku, KUALA LUMPUR, FEDERAL TERRITORY, MALAYSIA.
•**MARSHALL, Mr. Barry John, BA FCA** *1986;* PricewaterhouseCoopers LLP, 1 Embankment Place, LONDON, WC2N 6RH. See also PricewaterhouseCoopers
•**MARSHALL, Mr. Brian Arthur, FCA** *1971;* Berkeley Hall Marshall Limited, 6 Charlotte Street, BATH, BA1 2NE.
•**MARSHALL, Mr. Brian Edward, FCA** *1982;* Knox Cropper, 24 Petworth Road, HASLEMERE, GU27 2HR.
MARSHALL, Mr. Cameron, ACA CA(AUS) *2008;* 91 Herkomer Road, BUSHEY, WD23 3LS.
MARSHALL, Mr. Charles Howe, MA FCA *1975;* Liberty Living Plc, 30 St. Mary Axe, LONDON, EC3A 8BF.
MARSHALL, Mr. Christopher, BA ACA *2006;* State Street Global Services, 18 King William Street, LONDON, EC4N 7BP.
MARSHALL, Mr. Christopher John, BA ACA *1991;* 20 Dryburgh Road, LONDON, SW15 1BL.
MARSHALL, Mrs. Claire Estelle, BSc ACA *1988;* Cherry Tree Lodge, 9 Northall Road, Eaton Bray, DUNSTABLE, LU6 2DQ.
MARSHALL, Mr. Colin John, BA ACA *1985;* 219 Evergreen Court, SIMI VALLEY, CA 93065, UNITED STATES.
MARSHALL, Mr. Craig Thomas, MSc ACA *2001;* 71 Findhorn Place, EDINBURGH, EH9 2PD.
MARSHALL, Mr. Daniel, BA(Hons) ACA *2000;* 53 Haliburton Road, TWICKENHAM, TW1 1PD.
MARSHALL, Mr. David, BSc ACA *1979;* 14 Wilmot Road, LONDON, N17 6LH.
•**MARSHALL, Mr. David, FCA** *1980;* Lemans, 29 Arboretum Street, NOTTINGHAM, NG1 4JA.
MARSHALL, Mr. David, ACA *1988;* Edward Billington & Son Ltd, Cunard Building, LIVERPOOL, L3 1EL.
MARSHALL, Mr. David Andrew, BSc ACA *1995;* Lloyds, 10 Gresham Street, LONDON, EC2V 7AE.
MARSHALL, Mr. David Bruce, MA FCA FCT *1985;* Brackens, Heathdown Road, Pyrford, WOKING, SURREY, GU22 8LX.
•**MARSHALL, Mr. David Clifford, FCA** *1975;* (Tax Fac), D.C. Marshall & Co, Giles Croft, 1a Ferriby High Road, NORTH FERRIBY, NORTH HUMBERSIDE, HU14 3LD.
•**MARSHALL, Mr. David Frederick William, BSc ACA** *1991;* with Ernst & Young LLP, Wessex House, 19 Threefield Lane, SOUTHAMPTON, SO14 3QB.
MARSHALL, Mr. David John, ACA MAAT *2009;* Morris Owen, 43-45 Devizes Road, SWINDON, SN1 4BG.
MARSHALL, Mr. David John, BA ACA *1988;* Flat 10 Elder Court, 83 Heaton Moor Road, STOCKPORT, CHESHIRE, SK4 4FX.
MARSHALL, Mr. David Nicholas, FCA *1980;* Nampara, 16 Bennett Way, West Clandon, GUILDFORD, GU4 7TN.
MARSHALL, Mr. David Peter, BEng FCA AMCT *1992;* The Beeches, 18 Hallen Road, Henbury, BRISTOL, BS10 7QX.
•**MARSHALL, Mr. David William, BSc ACA** *2007;* Marshall & Co (Hull) Limited, The Jenko Building, 21 Hessle Road, Clive Sullivan Way, HULL, HU3 2AA.
MARSHALL, Mrs. Dawn Marie, LLB ACA *1997;* 39 Deerfold Crescent, BURNTWOOD, WS7 9AX.
•**MARSHALL, Mrs. Deirdre Patricia, BSc FCA** *1974;* (Tax Fac), D.P. Marshall, 25 Highfield Road, Bickley, BROMLEY, BR1 2JN.
MARSHALL, Mrs. Diana Sheridan, BA ACA *1983;* Holy Cross Hospital, Hindhead Road, HASLEMERE, GU27 1NQ.
MARSHALL, Miss. Donna Charmaine, BA ACA *1985;* 4 Lindsay Close, Stanwell Village, STAINES, TW19 7LF.
MARSHALL, Mr. Duncan Richard, BA ACA *1992;* (Tax Fac), 15 Stratheden Road, WAKEFIELD, WEST YORKSHIRE, WF2 0DD.
•**MARSHALL, Mr. Edward, FCA** *1957;* (Tax Fac), 39 Ebbage Court, Mount Hermon Road, WOKING, SURREY, GU22 7SX.
MARSHALL, Mr. Edward Kenneth, BA ACA *1992;* 2 Brick House Villas, Chelmsford Road Good Easter, CHELMSFORD, CM1 4PX.
MARSHALL, Mrs. Emily Kate, BSc ACA *2007;* with Deloitte LLP, 3 Rivergate, Temple Quay, BRISTOL, BS1 6GD.
MARSHALL, Mr. Gareth Robertson, ACA *2008;* 34 Treherne Road, NEWCASTLE UPON TYNE, NE2 3NP.

•**MARSHALL, Mr. Garrath James, BSc ACA** *1999;* 46 Hazlemere Road, Penn, HIGH WYCOMBE, BUCKINGHAMSHIRE, HP10 8AD.
MARSHALL, Mr. Gary Stewart, BA ACA *1985;* Miller Freeman Asia Ltd, 17/F China Resources Bldg, 26 Harbour Road, WAN CHAI, HONG KONG ISLAND, HONG KONG SAR.
MARSHALL, Mr. Gavin Thomas, BSc ACA *2004;* Computershare, The Pavilions, Bridgwater Road, BRISTOL, BS13 8AE.
MARSHALL, Mrs. Georgina Anne, BA ACA *1989;* Spindlehyrst, School Lane, Brantham, MANNINGTREE, ESSEX, CO11 1QE.
•**MARSHALL, Mr. Glen, BA FCA** *1992;* Landin Wilcock & Co, Queen St Chmbrs, 68 Queen St, SHEFFIELD, S17 4BD.
MARSHALL, Mr. Graeme Andrew, BA FCA *1994;* 174 Mount Street, COOGEE, NSW 2034, AUSTRALIA.
MARSHALL, Mr. Graeme Calder Walker, BA FCA *1977;* Black Knoll House, Rhinefield Road, BROCKENHURST, SO42 7QE.
MARSHALL, Mr. Graham, BA ACA *1982;* British Petroleum Co Plc, 20 Canada Square, LONDON, E14 5NJ.
MARSHALL, Mr. Graham Neil, FCA *1974;* 69 Spring View, Gildersome, LEEDS, LS27 7HG.
MARSHALL, Mr. Guy William, BSc ACA *1992;* Little Sallings, Middle Common, Bockleton, TENBURY WELLS, WORCESTERSHIRE, WR15 8PX.
MARSHALL, Miss. Helen Claire, BSc ACA *2006;* 7 Marsh Lane, SOLIHULL, B91 2PG.
MARSHALL, Mr. Henry, ACA *2010;* 18 Nicholson Court, Pocklington, YORK, YO42 2PF.
MARSHALL, Mr. Henry John Francis, BA FCA *1964;* 15 Bd Victor Hugo, 78100 ST. GERMAIN-EN-LAYE, FRANCE. (Life Member)
MARSHALL, Mr. Hugh Charles, BSc ACA *1988;* 2 Fish Street Farm High Street, Redbourn, ST. ALBANS, AL3 7NS.
MARSHALL, Mr. Ian, MA FCA *1974;* 1 Whitecliff Road, POOLE, DORSET, BH14 8DU.
MARSHALL, Mr. Ian Bruce, BA FCA *1974;* Hungershall Lodge, Hungershall Park, TUNBRIDGE WELLS, TN4 8ND.
MARSHALL, Mr. Ian Edward, BSc FCA *1978;* Chiltington International Ltd, Holland House, 1-4 Bury Street, LONDON, EC3A 5AW.
MARSHALL, Mr. Ian Stephen, BA ACA *2006;* Nieuwe Looiersstraat 120c, 1017 VE AMSTERDAM, NETHERLANDS.
MARSHALL, Mr. Ian Thompson, FCA *1980;* P.O. Box 2004, RIVONIA, GAUTENG, 2128, SOUTH AFRICA.
MARSHALL, Mr. Ivan, FCA *1964;* 2 Brownfield Way, Blackmore End, Wheathampstead, ST. ALBANS, AL4 8LL.
MARSHALL, Mr. James, MA FCA *1980;* 13 Sydney Buildings, BATH, BA2 6BZ.
MARSHALL, Mr. James, ACA *2008;* 19 Marescroft Road, SLOUGH, SL2 2LN.
MARSHALL, Mr. James Ernest, BSc ACA *2006;* 2 Inglewood Avenue, HUDDERSFIELD, HD2 2DS.
MARSHALL, Mr. James Patrick, MSc FCA *1999;* Newton Heath, Lodge Lane, Salfords, REDHILL, RH1 5DH.
MARSHALL, Mr. James William, FCA *1967;* 2 (B) Lonsdale Drive, ENFIELD, MIDDLESEX, EN2 7LH. (Life Member)
•**MARSHALL, Mrs. Jane Elizabeth, BA FCA DChA** *1987;* Barber Harrison & Platt, 2 Rutland Park, SHEFFIELD, S10 2PD.
MARSHALL, Mrs. Janet Allison, ACA *1999;* 6 Bembridge Close, Great Sankey, WARRINGTON, WA5 3RH.
MARSHALL, Mr. Jason, BA FCA *1996;* Vicarage Fell, Ibstone, HIGH WYCOMBE, BUCKINGHAMSHIRE, HP14 3XZ.
MARSHALL, Mrs. Jennifer Ann, BSc ACA *1997;* (Tax Fac), with PricewaterhouseCoopers LLP, 1 Embankment Place, LONDON, WC2N 6RH.
MARSHALL, Mr. Jeremy, BSc ACA *1996;* 5 Egret Close, St. Marys Island, CHATHAM, KENT, ME4 3EG.
MARSHALL, Mrs. Jessica, ACA *2011;* 5 Littlefield, Quedgeley, GLOUCESTER, GL2 4GZ.
MARSHALL, Ms. Joanne, BA ACA *1995;* 19 Strawberry How, COCKERMOUTH, CUMBRIA, CA13 9XZ.
•**MARSHALL, Mr. John, BA FCA** *1991;* (Tax Fac), Cowgill Holloway LLP, Regency House, 45-51 Chorley New Road, BOLTON, BL1 4QR. See also Cowgill Holloway Liverpool LLP and Cowgill Holloway Care 1 Limited
MARSHALL, Mr. John Cornelius Christopher, BA ACA *1983;* 9 Wish Valley Mews, Talbot Road Hawkhurst, CRANBROOK, TN18 4EQ.
MARSHALL, Mr. John Francis, FCA *1963;* 36 Manvers Road, EASTBOURNE, BN20 8HJ.
MARSHALL, Mr. John Fretwell, FCA *1959;* 7 High Street, Ixworth, BURY ST. EDMUNDS, SUFFOLK, IP31 2HH. (Life Member)
MARSHALL, Mr. John James, BA(Hons) FCA *2000;* Bp Group, Chertsey Road, SUNBURY-ON-THAMES, MIDDLESEX, TW16 7BP.
MARSHALL, Mr. John James, MSc BA(Econ) FCA *1999;* 58 Napier Road, Eccles, MANCHESTER, M30 8AG.
MARSHALL, Mr. John Matthew, MA ACA *1994;* 62 Haldon Road, LONDON, SW18 1QG.
MARSHALL, Mr. John Nicholas, BA FCA *1978;* 37 St. Vincent Road, WALTON-ON-THAMES, SURREY, KT12 1PA.
MARSHALL, Mr. Jonathan, BEng ACA *2001;* 37 Craiglee Drive, CARDIFF, CF10 4BN.
MARSHALL, Mr. Jonathan Gareth, ACA *2008;* 1 Ffordd yr Ysgol, FLINT, CLWYD, CH6 5ET.
•**MARSHALL, Mr. Jonathan Marcus, FCA** *1973;* (Tax Fac), J.M. Associates, 21A Craven Terrace, LONDON, W2 3QH.
MARSHALL, Mr. Jonathan Paul Kershaw, LLB ACA *1989;* 93 Alexandra Rd, Ascot, BRISBANE, QLD 4007, AUSTRALIA.
MARSHALL, Mr. Keith, MA ACA *1990;* St. Mawgan House Newquay Airport, Carloggas St. Mawgan, NEWQUAY, CORNWALL, TR8 4RQ.
•①**MARSHALL, Mr. Keith Allan, BSc(Hons) ACA** *2001;* with RSM Tenon Audit Limited, 2 Wellington Place, LEEDS, LS1 4AP.
MARSHALL, Mr. Keith Cecil Lote, FCA *1969;* 1 Kenwood Gardens, Copthorne, SHREWSBURY, SY3 8AG.
MARSHALL, Mr. Kenneth Richard Paul, FCA *1958;* Yew Tree Cottage, 84 East End Lane, Ditchling, HASSOCKS, BN6 8UR. (Life Member)
MARSHALL, Mr. Lee, BA(Hons) ACA *2002;* Prospect House, Madam Lane, Barnby Dun, DONCASTER, SOUTH YORKSHIRE, DN3 1EW.
•**MARSHALL, Mrs. Lesley Elizabeth, BSc ACA** *1982;* L E Marshall & Co, Unit C3, Fairoaks Airport, Chobham, WOKING, SURREY GU24 8HU.
MARSHALL, Mr. Matthew Anthony, BSc(Hons) ACA *2002;* Rosebank Common Hill, West Chiltington, PULBOROUGH, WEST SUSSEX, RH20 2NL.
MARSHALL, Mr. Michael Alfred, FCA *1964;* 19 Wykeham Road, Netley Abbey, SOUTHAMPTON, SO31 5DY. (Life Member)
MARSHALL, Mr. Michael Andrew, BSc FCA *1976;* 35 Jubilee Place, LONDON, SW3 3TD.
MARSHALL, Miss. Natalie Anne, ACA *2000;* 4 Longmore Crescent, SOUTHAMPTON, SO19 9FY.
MARSHALL, Mr. Neil, BSc ACA *1992;* Trimworth, Model Farm, Main Road, Crockham Hill, EDENBRIDGE, KENT TN8 6SR.
MARSHALL, Mr. Neil Christopher, BA FCA *1993;* with Smith Craven, Kelham House, Kelham Street, DONCASTER, DN1 3RE.
MARSHALL, Mr. Neil Francis, FCA *1961;* 21 Bereweeke Way, WINCHESTER, SO22 6BJ. (Life Member)
MARSHALL, Mr. Neil Roger, FCA *1970;* Flat 4 Kimber Court, Sea View Road, FALMOUTH, CORNWALL, TR11 4ER.
MARSHALL, Mr. Nicholas Charles Gilmour, FCA *1974;* Glanhonddu House, Llandefaelog Fach, BRECON, LD3 9PP.
MARSHALL, Mr. Nicholas James, MA ACA *1979;* Arderyth, 3 Forbes Park, Bramhall, STOCKPORT, SK7 2RE. (Life Member)
MARSHALL, Mr. Nicholas John, BA ACA *1985;* Spring House, Fieldgate Lawn, KENILWORTH, CV8 1RR.
MARSHALL, Miss. Nicola Elizabeth, BA(Hons) ACA *2001;* 33a Waldron Road, LONDON, SW18 3TB.
MARSHALL, Mrs. Nicola Ruth, BEng ACA *2002;* Whispering Chimneys, Walton Street, Walton-in-Gordano, CLEVEDON, AVON, BS21 7AP.
MARSHALL, Mr. Nigel John, BA ACA *1983;* Balfour Beatty Capital Projects Ltd, 6th Floor 350 Euston Road, Regents Place, LONDON, NW1 3AX.
MARSHALL, Miss. Patricia Joyce, BSc FCA *1976;* 255 Langley Way, WEST WICKHAM, BR4 0DW.
MARSHALL, Mr. Paul, MA ACA *1996;* 12 Moorland House, Ordnance Wharf, Queensway Quay, GIBRALTAR, GIBRALTAR.
MARSHALL, Mr. Paul, BA ACA *2011;* Flat 8, 72-74 Bridport Place, LONDON, N1 5DS.
MARSHALL, Mr. Paul, ACA *1985;* Cherry Tree Lodge, 9 Northall Road, Eaton Bray, DUNSTABLE, LU6 2DQ.
MARSHALL, Mr. Paul, BSc LLB(Hons) ACA *1992;* (Tax Fac), 17 Holywell Cottages, Thornton Road, Nash, MILTON KEYNES, MK17 0EY.
MARSHALL, Mr. Paul David, FCA *1986;* Old Mutual Plc Millennium Bridge House, 2 Lambeth Hill, LONDON, EC4V 4GG.
MARSHALL, Mr. Paul Douglas, ACA *1990;* PO Box 255, MUNDARING, WA 6073, AUSTRALIA.
•**MARSHALL, Mr. Paul Edwin, BSc ACA** *1980;* Paul E Marshall ACA BSc, 28 Ryder Crescent, SOUTHPORT, MERSEYSIDE, PR8 3AE.
•**MARSHALL, Mr. Paul Ernest Francis, FCA** *1969;* (Tax Fac), Southwell Tyrrell & Co, 9 Newbury Street, LONDON, EC1A 7HU.
•**MARSHALL, Mr. Paul Francis, FCA** *1974;* (Tax Fac), Paul Marshall & Co, 138 George V Avenue, WORTHING, BN11 5RX.
MARSHALL, Paul Raymond, Esq OBE FCA *1965;* 4 Coed Briwnant, Rhiwbina, CARDIFF, CF14 6QU.
•**MARSHALL, Mr. Paul Simon, ACA CTA** *2006;* PSM, 32 Worsley Road, NEWPORT, ISLE OF WIGHT, PO30 5JD.
MARSHALL, Mr. Peter Eric, FCA *1954;* 43 Howards Thicket, GERRARDS CROSS, SL9 7NU. (Life Member)
MARSHALL, Mr. Peter Hellyer, BSc ACA *1993;* Houlihan Lokey Howard & Zukin (UK) Ltd, 83 Pall Mall, LONDON, SW1Y 5ES.
•**MARSHALL, Mr. Peter Ian, MA FCA** *1969;* Peter Marshall, 38 Oakley Street, LONDON, SW3 5HA.
•**MARSHALL, Mr. Peter William, BA ACA** *1982;* Peter Marshall, 20 Highfield Road, Keyworth, NOTTINGHAM, NG12 5JE.
MARSHALL, Mr. Philip, FCA *1982;* PricewaterhouseCoopers GmbH, Olof-Palme-Strasse 35, 60439 FRANKFURT AM MAIN, GERMANY.
MARSHALL, Mr. Philip Arthur Frederick, FCA *1969;* 3 Poui Hill Road, Lady Chancellor Road, St. Anns, Newtown PO, PORT OF SPAIN, TRINIDAD AND TOBAGO.
MARSHALL, Mr. Philip Gale, FCA *1971;* Lewis Marshall Holdings Ltd, Harlescott Lane, SHREWSBURY, SY1 3AG.
MARSHALL, Mr. Philip Norman, FCA *1975;* (Tax Fac), Burns Cottage, Sivils Yard, Burgh le Marsh, SKEGNESS, LINCOLNSHIRE, PE24 5LH.
•**MARSHALL, Mr. Philip Robert, BSc FCA** *1975;* Philip Marshall Limited, Gatwick Farm House, Stantway Lane, WESTBURY-ON-SEVERN, GLOUCESTERSHIRE, GL14 1QG.
MARSHALL, Mrs. Philippa Mary, BSc ACA *1981;* Scullsgate Oast House Coldharbour Road, Benenden, CRANBROOK, TN17 4LD.
MARSHALL, Mrs. Phyllis Heather, FCA *1967;* 71 St. Martin's Road, CAERPHILLY, CF83 1EG. (Life Member)
MARSHALL, Mr. Ralph Fredrick, FCA *1970;* 93 Bath Hill Court, Bath Road, BOURNEMOUTH, BH1 2HU.
MARSHALL, Mr. Richard Cecil, MA FCA *1966;* 12 Churchfields Avenue, WEYBRIDGE, KT13 9YA.
•**MARSHALL, Mr. Richard Leslie Barnett, FCA** *1966;* (Tax Fac), R.L.B. Marshall, 51 Clare Crescent, LEATHERHEAD, SURREY, KT22 7RA.
MARSHALL, Mr. Robert, BA ACA *2007;* 4 Honey Pot Fold, Baildon, SHIPLEY, BD17 5TW.
MARSHALL, Mr. Robert, BSc ACA *2004;* with Deloitte LLP, Athene Place, 66 Shoe Lane, LONDON, EC4A 3BQ.
MARSHALL, Mr. Robert Charles, FCA *1968;* 257 Stapleford Lane, Beeston, NOTTINGHAM, NG9 6JG. (Life Member)
MARSHALL, Mr. Robert Gavin, MEng FCA AMCT *1998;* B M B Group, The Granary Building, 1 Canal Wharf, Holbeck, LEEDS, LS11 5BB.
MARSHALL, Mr. Robert James, MA ACA FCIE *1990;* 26 Kingsway, Chalfont St. Peter, GERRARDS CROSS, SL9 8NT.
MARSHALL, Mr. Robert Sydney, FCA *1965;* 46 Longfield Drive, AMERSHAM, HP6 5HE.
MARSHALL, Mr. Roger Michael James, BSc FCA *1973;* The Snipe Lock Lane, Birdham, CHICHESTER, WEST SUSSEX, PO20 7BB.
MARSHALL, Mr. Roger Toward, FCA *1977;* Persimmon Capital Ltd, 12/F On Lan Centre, On Lan Streeet, CENTRAL, HONG KONG ISLAND, HONG KONG SAR.
MARSHALL, Mr. Ronald Edward, BSc FCA *1971;* 2 Gorsty Hill Close, Balterley, CREWE, CW2 5QS.
MARSHALL, Mr. Ross Alexander, BSc(Hons) ACA *2001;* 11 Aylwards Way, Nether Wallop, STOCKBRIDGE, HAMPSHIRE, SO20 8HB.
MARSHALL, Mrs. Sandra Diane, BA ACA *2005;* 3 Pine Tree Avenue, Scotter, GAINSBOROUGH, LINCOLNSHIRE, DN21 3TY.
MARSHALL, Mr. Simon David, MA ACA *1992;* 41 Thirlmere Road, Muswell Road, LONDON, N10 2DL.
•**MARSHALL, Mr. Simon Edmund, BSc FCA** *1975;* Thomas May & Co, Allen House, Newarke Street, LEICESTER, LE1 5SG.
MARSHALL, Mr. Stephen Daniel Mark, BA ACA *1996;* 3 Brecon Road, BRISTOL, BS9 4DT.
MARSHALL, Mr. Stephen David, MA ACA *1992;* 9 Swan Ridge, EDENBRIDGE, TN8 6AS.
•**MARSHALL, Mr. Stephen Denithorne, BSc ACA** *1982;* 2 Woodland Way, BRIGHTON, BN1 8BA.
MARSHALL, Mr. Stephen Douglas John, FCA *1978;* 87 Grove Park, TRING, HERTFORDSHIRE, HP23 5JR.
MARSHALL, Mr. Stephen Patrick, FCA *1974;* 31 Hill Lane, Bassetts Pole, SUTTON COLDFIELD, B75 6LE.
MARSHALL, Mr. Stephen Peter, MSc BA ACA *2010;* 25 High Beeches, BANSTEAD, SURREY, SM7 1NB.
MARSHALL, Mr. Steven Charles, BSc FCA *1978;* Colemans Cottage, May Hill, LONGHOPE, GL17 0NP.
MARSHALL, Mr. Stuart McAdam, MA ACA *1997;* Rannoch, Allendale Road, HEXHAM, NORTHUMBERLAND, NE46 2NB.
MARSHALL, Mrs. Susan Elizabeth, BA ACA *1980;* 8 Wentworth Drive, LICHFIELD, WS14 9HN.
•**MARSHALL, Mr. Terence Ashley, FCA** *1971;* TAM & Sons Limited, 12 Market Street, HEBDEN BRIDGE, WEST YORKSHIRE, HX7 6AD.
MARSHALL, Mr. Thomas Ian, FCA *1968;* 2 The Court, Hoo Gardens, EASTBOURNE, EAST SUSSEX, BN20 9AX.
MARSHALL, Mrs. Tracey Anne, BA ACA *1989;* 27 Kings Road, WINDSOR, SL4 2AD.
MARSHALL, Ms. Tracey Jayne, BA ACA *1989;* 160 Regents Park Road, LONDON, NW1 8XN.
MARSHALL, Mrs. Tracy Anne, MSc BA ACA *2001;* 7 Windmill Way, REIGATE, RH2 0JB.
MARSHALL, Mr. Warren Charles, BAcc ACA *2001;* 7 Windmill Way, REIGATE, RH2 0JB.
MARSHALL, Mrs. Wendy Anne, BA ACA *1983;* 44 The Mount, Curdworth, SUTTON COLDFIELD, B76 9HR.
MARSHALL, Mr. William, FCA *1950;* with ICAEW, Metropolitan House, 321 Avebury Boulevard, MILTON KEYNES, MK9 2FZ. (Life Member)
MARSHALL, Mr. William George, BA ACA *1984;* Field Barn, Far Sawrey, AMBLESIDE, CUMBRIA, LA22 0LL.
MARSHALL, Mr. William Michael, FCA *1970;* Intertek Group Plc, 25 Savile Row, LONDON, W1S 2ES.
•**MARSHALL, Mr. William Robert David, BA FCA** *1978;* Ash House, Ardleigh Road, Little Bromley, MANNINGTREE, CO11 2QA.
MARSHALL, Mr. William Stuart Henderson, LLB ACA *2005;* 6 Ryland Road, LONDON, NW5 3EA.
•**MARSHALL-BIRKS, Mrs. Emma Elizabeth, BA FCA MBA** *1993;* Marshall & Co, St. Mary's House, Crewe Road, Alsager, STOKE-ON-TRENT, ST7 2EW. See also Marshall & Co Accountants LLP
MARSHALL-BROOM, Mr. Campbell, MA FCA *1974;* 124 East 79th Street, NEW YORK, NY 10021, UNITED STATES. (Life Member)
MARSHALL-LEE, Mr. Robert James, BSc ACA *1999;* Redover Coldharbour Road, WEST BYFLEET, SURREY, KT14 6JL.
MARSHALL-SMITH, Mrs. Angela, BSc ACA CPFA *1993;* 70 Cadman Road, BRIDLINGTON, NORTH HUMBERSIDE, YO16 6YZ.
MARSHALSEA, Mrs. Alison Marie, BA ACA *2004;* 60 Moorlands Drive Stainburn, WORKINGTON, CUMBRIA, CA14 4UJ.
MARSHALSEA, Mr. John William Andrew, ACA *2010;* Alcan Packaging, Salterbeck Trading Estate, Salterbeck, WORKINGTON, CUMBRIA, CA14 5DX.
•**MARSHAM, Mr. Nicholas Laurence, ACA** *2003;* Barnard Sampson LLP, 3a Quay View Business Park, Barnards Way, LOWESTOFT, SUFFOLK, NR32 2HD.
MARSHMAN, Miss. Jacqueline Ann, BSc ACA *1988;* 46 Barnfield Wood Road, Park Langley, BECKENHAM, KENT, BR3 6SU.
MARSHMAN, Mr. Paul Hardy, ACA *2006;* with PricewaterhouseCoopers LLP, 1 Embankment Place, LONDON, WC2N 6RH.
MARSHMAN, Mr. Roger, FCA *1981;* Thistledown, Spy Lane, Loxwood, BILLINGSHURST, RH14 0SS.
MARSHMAN, Mrs. Sophie Caroline, BSocSc ACA *2006;* 2 Pound Lane, Knockholt, SEVENOAKS, KENT, TN14 7NE.
MARSLAND, Mr. Craig Richard, BEng ACA *1997;* 4 White House Lane, Wooburn Green, HIGH WYCOMBE, BUCKINGHAMSHIRE, HP10 0NR.

MARSLAND, Mr. Michael Peter, FCA *1970;* Lime Tree Farm Lime Tree Lane, High Legh, KNUTSFORD, CHESHIRE, WA16 6NU.
MARSLIN, Mr. Michael George, BA(Hons) ACA *2010;* 44 Morris Way, London Colney, ST. ALBANS, HERTFORDSHIRE, AL2 1JL.
MARSON, Mr. Anthony Charles, BA FCA *1976;* Top Farm, Admington, SHIPSTON-ON-STOUR, WARWICKSHIRE, CV36 4JL.
•**MARSON, Mr. Francis John, FCA** *1973;* (Tax Fac), Lings, Provident House, 51 Wardwick, DERBY, DE1 1HN.
MARSON, Mr. James, BA ACA *2003;* with KPMG LLP, 1 The Embankment, Neville Street, LEEDS, LS1 4DW.
MARSON-SMITH, Mr. Paul Christopher, BA ACA *1987;* Saints Hill House, Saints Hill, Penshurst, TONBRIDGE, KENT, TN11 8EN.
MARSTON, Mr. Allan Stewart, FCA *1970;* 4 Rosemary Drive, LITTLEBOROUGH, OL15 8RZ. (Life Member)
MARSTON, Mr. Andrew, BSc ACA *2010;* Apartment 8, La Colline House, Royal Garden, Bosq Lane, St. Peter Port, GUERNSEY GY1 2JE.
•**MARSTON, Mr. Brian, FCA** *1959;* 2 Chapel Close, Little Thetford, ELY, CAMBRIDGESHIRE, CB6 3HS.
MARSTON, Mr. Brian Edward, FCA *1968;* Blagrave Lodge, Blagrave Farm Lane, Mapledurham, READING, RG4 7JX. (Life Member)
MARSTON, Prof. Claire Lesley, BSc FCA *1978;* 54 Newbattle Terrace, EDINBURGH, EH10 4RX.
MARSTON, Mr. David Charles, BA FCA *1979;* 65 Turle Road, Norbury, LONDON, SW16 5QW.
•**MARSTON, Mr. David Laurence, FCA** *1977;* David Marston & Co., Suite A8 Kebbell House, Delta Gain, Carpenders Park, WATFORD, WD19 5BE.
MARSTON, Mrs. Debra Louise, BSc ACA *1997;* 108 Bremner Crescent, FORT SASKATCHEWAN T8L 0E2, AB, CANADA.
MARSTON, Mr. Derek Clive, BA ACA *1997;* 22 Beaumaris Close, ANDOVER, HAMPSHIRE, SP10 2UB.
MARSTON, Mr. Frank Roger, FCA *1959;* 39 Hanger Way, PETERSFIELD, HAMPSHIRE, GU31 4QE. (Life Member)
MARSTON, Mr. Jonathan Charles, BA(Hons) ACA *2003;* Cedar House, Endican Lane, Thornton le Moor, NORTHALLERTON, NORTH YORKSHIRE, DL7 9FB.
•**MARSTON, Mr. Jonathan Thomas, BA FCA** *1986;* Kendall Wadley LLP, Merevale House, 27 Sansome Walk, WORCESTER, WR1 1NU.
MARSTON, Mrs. Rachel, ACA *2008;* 191 Aldershot Road, Church Crookham, FLEET, HAMPSHIRE, GU52 8JS.
MARSTON, Miss. Sian Alexandra, ACA *2009;* 30 Lower Village, HAYWARDS HEATH, WEST SUSSEX, RH16 4GS.
MARSTON, Mr. Stuart Adrian, BSc ACA *1999;* 6 Goodwood Rise, MARLOW, SL7 3QE.
•**MARSTON-WESTON, Miss. Linda, LLB FCA** *1991;* Ernst & Young LLP, 1 Colmore Square, BIRMINGHAM, B4 6HQ. See also Ernst & Young Europe LLP
MARTEL, Mr. Andrew Mark, MA FCA CTA *1994;* 46 Sussex Street, LONDON, SW1V 4RH.
MARTEL, Mr. George Frederick, FCA *1948;* Flat 6, 12 Clarence Road South, WESTON-SUPER-MARE, SOMERSET, BS23 4BN. (Life Member)
MARTEL, Mr. Timothy John, MA BA ACA *2001;* Mulberry Cottage Pollards Moor Road, Copythorne, SOUTHAMPTON, SO40 2NZ.
MARTEL, Mr. Wayne David, BA(Hons) ACA *2001;* Arganchy, Sous Les Courtils, Albecq, Castel, GUERNSEY, GY5 7EZ.
•**MARTELL, Mr. John Peter, BSc FCA** *1979;* (Tax Fac), J P Martell & Co Limited, 22 Bushby Avenue, Rustington, LITTLEHAMPTON, BN16 2BY.
MARTEN, Mr. Harry, MA(Hons) ACA *2011;* The Pump House, Newton Valence, ALTON, HAMPSHIRE, GU34 3RB.
MARTEN, Mr. Lee, FCA *1974;* 30 The Round Meade, Green Park, Maghull, LIVERPOOL, L31 8DZ.
MARTEN, Mr. Richard Charles, BCom ACA *2002;* 8 Fairfields Drive, Ravenshead, NOTTINGHAM, NG15 9HR.
MARTENS, Mr. Christopher Thomas, BSc ACA *1999;* 8-17-7 Danau Permai Condo, 3/109F Taman Danau Desa, 58100 KUALA LUMPUR, FEDERAL TERRITORY, MALAYSIA.
MARTIDES, Mrs. Liana Soteriou, BA ACA *1998;* HELLENIC BANK, CORPORATE DIVISION, 131 ARCH. MAKARIOS AVENUE, P.O. BOX 51791, 3508 LIMASSOL, CYPRUS.
MARTIN, Miss. Abigail, BA ACA *2006;* 36 High Street, Wingham, CANTERBURY, CT3 1AB.
MARTIN, Mr. Adrian, MSc BSc ACA *2011;* 10 Westfield, REIGATE, SURREY, RH2 0DZ.
MARTIN, Mr. Adrian Howard, FCA *1975;* Flat 73, 69 Hopton Street, LONDON, SE1 9LF.
MARTIN, Mr. Adrian Spencer, BSc ACA *1996;* 25 Green Lane, Chesham Bois, AMERSHAM, BUCKINGHAMSHIRE, HP6 5LN.
MARTIN, Mr. Adrian William, FCA *1967;* 17 St Vincents Way, SOUTHPORT, PR8 2AH.
MARTIN, Mr. Alan, BA(Hons) ACA *2004;* 9 Waveney Road, HARPENDEN, HERTFORDSHIRE, AL5 4QY.
MARTIN, Mr. Alan Christopher, BSc ACA *1990;* 68 Upper Grosvenor Road, TUNBRIDGE WELLS, KENT, TN1 2ET.
MARTIN, Mr. Alan Paul, BSc ACA *1995;* East Winds, 11 Park Lawn Road, WEYBRIDGE, KT13 9EU.
MARTIN, Mr. Alan Renwick, BA FCA *1968;* 11 Harrison Lane, Balls Park, HERTFORD, SG13 8FE.
MARTIN, Mr. Alexander Giles Howard, BA ACA *1995;* Martin Howard Associates S.L., Calle Aribau, 177 Ent 1A, Barcelona, 08036 BARCELONA, SPAIN.
MARTIN, Mr. Alexander James, BA ACA *2007;* Flat 2, 97 Palace Road, LONDON, SW2 3LB.
MARTIN, Mrs. Alison, ACA *2009;* 7 St. Pauls Terrace, YORK, YO24 4BL.
•**MARTIN, Mrs. Alison Marie, FCA** *1987;* (Tax Fac), Hunters, 9 New Square, LONDON, WC2A 3QN.
MARTIN, Mrs. Alwyn Mary, BSc FCA *1993;* 21 Lothian Drive, Clarkston, GLASGOW, G76 7NA.
MARTIN, Mr. Andrew, BSc ACA *2006;* Flat 5 Ladywood Grange, Lady Margaret Road, ASCOT, SL5 9QG.
MARTIN, Mr. Andrew David, FCA *1972;* Langmans West, West Buckland, KINGSBRIDGE, DEVON, TQ7 3AQ.
•**MARTIN, Mr. Andrew David, BA ACA ATII** *1985;* 5 Dalkeith Road, HARPENDEN, AL5 5PP.
MARTIN, Mr. Andrew James, BSc ACA *1999;* Flat 1 Fernhill Place, 21-23 Chartfield Avenue, LONDON, SW15 6DX.
•**MARTIN, Mr. Andrew James, BSc ACA** *2005;* AJM Accountancy & Taxation, 20 Kensington Drive, WOODFORD GREEN, ESSEX, IG8 8LR.
MARTIN, Mr. Andrew James, BEng ACA *1990;* 23 Falcons Court, MUCH WENLOCK, SHROPSHIRE, TF13 6BF.
•**MARTIN, Mr. Andrew Paul, FCA** *1982;* Andrew Martin & Co, Unit 35, Timothys Bridge Road, STRATFORD-UPON-AVON, WARWICKSHIRE, CV37 9NQ.
MARTIN, Mr. Andrew Thomas, FCA *1974;* (Tax Fac), Royal Holloway University Of London, Egham Hill, EGHAM, TW20 0EX.
MARTIN, Mr. Andrew Warren, BA ACA *1998;* 55 Meadow Way, Old Windsor, WINDSOR, BERKSHIRE, SL4 2NY.
MARTIN, Mr. Andrew William, BA ACA *1985;* Zenith Bank (UK) Ltd, 39 Cornhill, LONDON, EC3V 3NU.
•①**MARTIN, Mr. Angus Matthew, MA FCA** *1984;* Deloitte LLP, Athene Place, 66 Shoe Lane, LONDON, EC4A 3BQ. See also Deloitte & Touche LLP
MARTIN, Miss. Anita Joanne, BA ACA *1996;* 20 High Street, Ditchling, HASSOCKS, WEST SUSSEX, BN6 8TA.
MARTIN, Mrs. Anne, FCA *1946;* 45 Colts Bay, Craigwell, BOGNOR REGIS, PO21 4EH. (Life Member)
MARTIN, Mr. Anthony, BSc ACA *1990;* 89 Church Hill Road, SUTTON, SM3 8LL.
MARTIN, Mr. Anthony David, FCA *1975;* The Great Barn, 6 The Barns, Shackleford, GODALMING, SURREY, GU8 6BU.
•**MARTIN, Mr. Anthony Graham, BA FCA** *1989;* (Tax Fac), Hammond McNulty, 3 Mallard Court, Mallard Way, Crewe Buisness Park, CREWE, CW1 6ZQ.
MARTIN, Mr. Anthony Ian, BA FCA *1973;* Stonecroft, Quarry Close, OXTED, RH8 9HG.
MARTIN, Mr. Anthony James, FCA *1971;* 7 Hazeldene Drive, PINNER, MIDDLESEX, HA5 3NJ.
MARTIN, Mr. Anthony James, BA ACA *1993;* 33 Devonshire Buildings, BATH, BA2 4SU.
MARTIN, Mr. Anthony John, FCA *1965;* Whitestone House, Whitestone, EXETER, EX4 2JY.
MARTIN, Mr. Anthony Patrick, BSc ACA *1989;* (Tax Fac), 143 Graham Road, Ranmoor, SHEFFIELD, S10 3GP.
MARTIN, Mr. Ashley Graham, FCA *1981;* Hope House, Darrs Lane, Northchurch, Berkhampstead, HERTFORD, HERTFORDSHIRE HP4 3TT.
•**MARTIN, Mrs. Barbara Elizabeth, ACA** *1990;* (Tax Fac), Cooks Accountancy Services Limited, 28 Clappers Meadow, Alfold, CRANLEIGH, SURREY, GU6 8HH.
MARTIN, Mr. Barrie Scott, BA ACA *2002;* Barratt House City West Business Park, Scotswood Road, NEWCASTLE UPON TYNE, NE4 7DF.
MARTIN, Mr. Benjamin Wade, BA ACA *2000;* Ledcor Industries Inc, 1200 1067 West Cordova Street, VANCOUVER V6C 1C7, BC, CANADA.
MARTIN, Miss. Brenda Janice, ACA *1992;* 3 Pembroke Road, CHIPPENHAM, WILTSHIRE, SN15 3UE.
MARTIN, Mr. Brian James, FCA *1970;* Jordan Reflectors Ltd, 9-10 Seax Way, BASILDON, ESSEX, SS15 6SW.
•**MARTIN, Mr. Brian Lawrence, FCA** *1973;* Suite 1, 7-13 Melior Street, London Bridge, LONDON, SE1 3QP.
MARTIN, Mr. Bryan Robert, BSc ACA *1990;* 36 Oakhill Road, SEVENOAKS, KENT, TN13 1NS.
MARTIN, Mr. Carl Paul, BA ACA *1993;* 39 Southleigh, BRADFORD-ON-AVON, BA15 2EQ.
MARTIN, Mrs. Carol Susan, FCA *1988;* 145 The Broadway, DUDLEY, DY1 3EB.
MARTIN, Mrs. Caroline, BSc ACA *1993;* 38 Exeter Gardens, STAMFORD, LINCOLNSHIRE, PE9 2RN.
MARTIN, Mrs. Caroline Denise, BA ACA *1995;* 110 Station Road, HARPENDEN, HERTFORDSHIRE, AL5 4TT.
•**MARTIN, Miss. Caroline Jayne, BSc ACA** *2004;* CJ Accountancy and Bookkeeping Services, 31 Crescent Drive North, BRIGHTON, BN2 6SP.
MARTIN, Mrs. Catherine Alethea, BSc ACA *1999;* 15 Matlock Road, Caversham, READING, RG4 7BP.
MARTIN, Miss. Catherine Lindsay, BA ACA *1992;* 36 Blythsford Road, Hall Green, BIRMINGHAM, B28 0UR.
MARTIN, Mr. Christian John, FCA *1979;* Rath House, Q A Xpertise, 55-65 Uxbridge Road, SLOUGH, SL1 1SG.
MARTIN, Miss. Christina Louise, BSc ACA *1996;* 5 Fernleigh Close, Tallentire, COCKERMOUTH, CA13 0NS
MARTIN, Mrs. Christine Joan, BSc ACA *1984;* with PricewaterhouseCoopers LLP, Erskine House, 68-73 Queen Street, EDINBURGH, EH2 4NH.
MARTIN, Mr. Christoper Luke, BSc ACA *2003;* 12 Francis Street, READING, BERKSHIRE, RG1 2QB.
MARTIN, Mr. Christopher David, FCA *1967;* Sandpipers Glen, Coastguard Lane, FRESHWATER, ISLE OF WIGHT, PO40 9QX.
MARTIN, Mr. Christopher Francis, BSc ACA *2000;* 34 Finchley Road, Hale, ALTRINCHAM, CHESHIRE, WA15 9RD.
MARTIN, Mr. Christopher Giles, BSc ACA *1993;* Honeycroft, 1 Worley Place, Seer Green, BEACONSFIELD, BUCKINGHAMSHIRE, HP9 2QF.
MARTIN, Mr. Christopher Jan, BA FCA *1974;* 11 Carlton Gardens, Warwick Avenue, Earlsdon, COVENTRY, CV5 6DH.
MARTIN, Mr. Christopher John, BSc ACA *1992;* 37 Blackberry Way, Pontprennau, CARDIFF, CF23 8FE.
MARTIN, Mr. Christopher Keith, BA ACA *1993;* Factory Road West, Sandycroft, DEESIDE, FLINTSHIRE, CH5 2QJ.
MARTIN, Mr. Christopher Nicholas, BA ACA FRSA *1984;* Musgrave Group Plc, Airport Road, Ballycurreen, CORK, COUNTY CORK, IRELAND.
•**MARTIN, Mr. Christopher Robert, BSc FCA** *1992;* Profit Plus (UK) Limited, Queens Chambers, Eleanors Cross, DUNSTABLE, BEDFORDSHIRE, LU6 1SU.
MARTIN, Mr. Christopher Vandeleur, BA FCA MBA *1988;* Unit 16 Rufus Business Centre, Ravensbury Terrace, LONDON, SW18 4RL.
MARTIN, Mrs. Claire, BCom ACA *1997;* Valewood Grange, Fernden Lane, HASLEMERE, SURREY, GU27 3LB.
MARTIN, Miss. Clare Elizabeth, ACA *2008;* Rosemanowas Farm, Stithians, TRURO, CORNWALL, TR3 7BZ.
MARTIN, Mrs. Clare Louise, BSc ACA *1995;* 11 Park Lawn Road, WEYBRIDGE, SURREY, KT13 9EU.
MARTIN, Mrs. Clare Louise, BA(Hons) ACA *2001;* (Tax Fac), 14 Lodge Lane, Prestwood, GREAT MISSENDEN, HP16 0SU.
MARTIN, Mr. Clifford John, FCA *1973;* 8 Trilley Fields, Maulden, BEDFORD, MK45 2US. (Life Member)
MARTIN, Mr. Colan Paul, BA ACA *1992;* Flat 1, 42 Eardley Road, SEVENOAKS, KENT, TN13 1XT.
MARTIN, Mr. Colin Bruce, FCA *1984;* 61-63 The Green, Stotfold, HITCHIN, HERTFORDSHIRE, SG5 4AN.
•**MARTIN, Mr. Colin Stuart, BEng ACA** *1997;* KPMG LLP, 15 Canada Square, LONDON, E14 5GL. See also KPMG Europe LLP
MARTIN, Mr. Craig, MEng ACA *1998;* (Tax Fac), Novartis Pharmaceuticals Ltd, 200 Frimley Business Park Frimley, CAMBERLEY, GU16 7SR.
MARTIN, Mr. Craig Stewart, LLB ACA *2002;* P K F, Pannell House, 6 Queen Street, LEEDS, LS1 2TW.
MARTIN, Mr. Daniel, ACA *2011;* 17 Millbrook Grove, Milton, STOKE-ON-TRENT, ST2 7DY.
MARTIN, Mr. David, BA(Hons) ACA *2010;* 16C Caxton Road, LONDON, W12 8AJ.
MARTIN, Mr. David, ACA *2009;* Pricewaterhousecoopers, 1 Embankment Place, LONDON, WC2N 6RH.
MARTIN, Mr. David, FCA *1976;* 7893 Valencia Court, NAPLES, FL 34113-3186, UNITED STATES.
MARTIN, Mr. David Charles, BA ACA *1982;* Prudential PLC, 12 Arthur Street, LONDON, EC4R9AE.
MARTIN, Mr. David Francis, FCA *1959;* Saxon Farm, Oake, TAUNTON, TA4 1JA. (Life Member)
MARTIN, Mr. David Harry, FCA *1973;* West House, Commonmoor, LISKEARD, CORNWALL, PL14 6EP.
MARTIN, Mr. David John, BA ACA *1998;* with Ernst & Young LLP, 1 Bridgewater Place, Water Lane, LEEDS, LS11 5QR.
MARTIN, Mr. David Keith, BA ACA *1991;* Flat 8, Matcham Court, 30 Clevedon Road, TWICKENHAM, TW1 2TF.
•**MARTIN, Mr. David Laurence, MA FCA** *1977;* Streets, Charter House, 62-64 Hills Road, CAMBRIDGE, CB2 1LA. See also Streets Whitmarsh Sterland
•**MARTIN, Mr. David Lawrence, FCA** *1984;* Thomas Nock Martin Ltd, 5 Hagley Court South, The Waterfront, Level Street, BRIERLEY HILL, WEST MIDLANDS DY5 1XE.
MARTIN, Mr. David Richard, MEng ACA CIOT *1992;* 1Sheridan Place, EAST GRINSTEAD, WEST SUSSEX, RH19 1SU.
MARTIN, Mr. David Robert, BA(Hons) FCA *1989;* High View, Scackleton, YORK, YO62 4NB.
•**MARTIN, Mr. David Wedgwood, BSc FCA** *1989;* Knill James, One Bell Lane, LEWES, EAST SUSSEX, BN7 1JU.
MARTIN, Mr. David William, FCA *1975;* (Tax Fac), Harris Systems Ltd, Eskdale Road, Winnersh Triangle, WOKINGHAM, BERKSHIRE, RG41 5TS.
MARTIN, Mr. David William, FCA *1987;* 43 Whipton Lane, Heavitree, EXETER, EX1 3DJ.
MARTIN, Mrs. Dawn Heather, ACA *1989;* 127 Western Road, BILLERICAY, CM12 9JH.
MARTIN, Mr. Derek Adrian, BSc ACA *1985;* Sherwoods The Street, Plaistow, BILLINGSHURST, RH14 0PT.
MARTIN, Mrs. Diane Elizabeth, FCA *1976;* 11 Heathfield Road, PETERSFIELD, HAMPSHIRE, GU31 4DG.
MARTIN, Mr. Dominic James, MEng ACA *2002;* UBS Securities LLC, 1285 Avenue of Americas (11th floor), NEW YORK, NY 10019, UNITED STATES.
MARTIN, Mr. Douglas, FCA *1963;* 5 Middle Crescent, Denham, UXBRIDGE, UB9 5EF.
MARTIN, Mr. Duncan Conrad, BSc ACA MBA CISA CIA *1987;* 22 Stirling Drive, ROCKYVIEW, QLD 4701, AUSTRALIA.
MARTIN, Mr. Edward John, BSc ACA *2008;* BDO, 55 Baker Street, LONDON, W1U 7EU.
MARTIN, Mrs. Elizabeth Louise, BSc ACA *1992;* Waterhales, Horseman Side, BRENTWOOD, ESSEX, CM14 5ST.
MARTIN, Mrs. Elizabeth Mary, BSc FCA *1978;* Higher Croft, City, Bledlow Ridge, HIGH WYCOMBE, BUCKINGHAMSHIRE, HP14 4AB. (Life Member)
MARTIN, Mrs. Emily Ruth Mary, BA ACA *2004;* Jackel International Ltd, Northumberland Business Park, CRAMLINGTON, NORTHUMBERLAND, NE23 7RH.
MARTIN, Mrs. Emma Louise, BA ACA *2000;* Ogilvy House, Level 2, 72 Christie Street, ST LEONARDS, NSW 2065, AUSTRALIA.
MARTIN, Mr. Eric Arthur, FCA *1957;* 20 Oban Road, Browns Bay, AUCKLAND 0630, NEW ZEALAND. (Life Member)
MARTIN, Mrs. Eve Kelly, BA ACA *1998;* Orchard House, Hartwell Road, Ashton, NORTHAMPTON, NN7 2JR.
MARTIN, Mr. Francis James, BSc ACA *1992;* 1 Laurel Close, YORK, YO32 9FW.
•**MARTIN, Mr. Frank, FCA FCCA** *1977;* (Tax Fac), Martin + Heller, 5 North End Road, LONDON, NW11 7RJ.
MARTIN, Mr. Frank Tyson, FCA *1952;* Cherry Cottage, The Square High Street, Hadlow, TONBRIDGE, TN11 0DD. (Life Member)
MARTIN, Mr. Gareth David, BSc ACA *1999;* Kimberly Clark Europe, Douglas House, 40 London Road, REIGATE, SURREY, RH2 9QP.

MARTIN, Mr. Gavin Paul, BSc(Hons) ACA *2001;* 17 Wagtail Walk, BECKENHAM, KENT, BR3 3XH.

MARTIN, Mrs. Gemma, BA(Hons) ACA *2011;* 5 Rossendale Close, CHESTERFIELD, DERBYSHIRE, S40 3EL.

MARTIN, Mr. Geoffrey Charles, FCA *1968;* Yew Tree House, Cliff Road, Sherston, MALMESBURY, SN16 0LN.

MARTIN, Mr. Geoffrey Gransden, MA FCA *1967;* Copperfields, Weydown Road, HASLEMERE, GU27 1DT.

MARTIN, Mr. Geoffrey Peter, BA ACA *1995;* 20 Castleford Drive, Prestbury, MACCLESFIELD, CHESHIRE, SK10 4BG.

MARTIN, Mr. Geoffrey William, FCA *1966;* 20 Birch Way, HAYWARDS HEATH, WEST SUSSEX, RH17 7SG.

MARTIN, Mr. George Jeremy, BA ACA *1999;* 73 Shirland Road, LONDON, W9 2EL.

MARTIN, Mr. George William, FCA *1951;* April Cottage, 8 Palmerston Street, Westwood, NOTTINGHAM, NG16 5JA. (Life Member)

•MARTIN, Mrs. Gillian, MBA BA FCA *1989;* New Prospect, Horsham Road, Cowfold, HORSHAM, WEST SUSSEX, RH13 8BX.

MARTIN, Mr. Godfrey James, FCA JDipMA *1955;* 2701 EPICA, 9 Railway Street, CHATSWOOD, NSW 2067, AUSTRALIA. (Life Member)

MARTIN, Mr. Graham Paul Moss, BSc ACA *2001;* Aviva International Insurance Ltd St. Helens, 1 Undershaft, LONDON, EC3P 3DQ.

•MARTIN, Mr. Graham Peter, FCA *1972;* Eastleigh Accountants Limited, 89 Leigh Road, EASTLEIGH, HAMPSHIRE, SO50 9DQ.

MARTIN, Mr. Grant Charles, ACA *2011;* Apartment 16, Somerville Point, 305 Rotherhithe Street, LONDON, SE16 5EQ.

MARTIN, Mrs. Helen, BSc ACA *1996;* 90 Albert Road, Grappenhall, WARRINGTON, WA4 2PG.

MARTIN, Miss. Helen Mary Claire, BSc ACA *1990;* The Hawthorns, Barton Road, Welford On Avon, STRATFORD-UPON-AVON, CV37 8EY.

•MARTIN, Mr. Howard David, BA FCA *1984;* Ernst & Young LLP, 1 More London Place, LONDON, SE1 2AF. See also Ernst & Young Europe LLP

MARTIN, Mr. Ian, BSc FCA *1978;* 11 Carleton Avenue, SKIPTON, BD23 2TE.

MARTIN, Mr. Ian Donald, FCA *1958;* 11 The Oaks, BROADSTAIRS, KENT, CT10 3BT.

MARTIN, Mr. Ian Dunlop, JP BSc FCA *1958;* 5 Hogarth Drive, Barton Seagrave, KETTERING, NORTHAMPTONSHIRE, NN15 5UQ. (Life Member)

•MARTIN, Mr. Ian Frederick, BSc FCA *1972;* (Tax Fac), First Floor, The Well House, Market Street, BROMSGROVE, B61 8DA.

MARTIN, Mr. Ian Herbert, BA ACA *1983;* 10 Westfield, Raglan Road, REIGATE, SURREY, RH2 0DZ.

MARTIN, Mr. Ian James, BEng ACA *1991;* 19 The Grove, RADLETT, WD7 7NF.

MARTIN, Mr. Ian James, BA FCA *1976;* Edif el Traves, Piso 2 Porta 6, Carrera El Traves, LA MASSANA, ANDORRA.

MARTIN, Mr. Ian Richard, BA FCA *1979;* Frenches Farm, Tower Hill, Chipperfield, KINGS LANGLEY, WD4 9LN.

MARTIN, Mr. Ian Wesley, BSc FCA *1976;* 'Forsythia', 26 Almond Way, LUTTERWORTH, LEICESTERSHIRE, LE17 4XJ.

MARTIN, Mrs. Ira Lynette, ACA *2009;* 57 Prospect Street, ALFRETON, DERBYSHIRE, DE55 7GY.

MARTIN, Mr. James, BA FCA *1973;* J. Martin, P O Box 695, KENMORE, QLD 4069, AUSTRALIA.

MARTIN, Mr. James Alexander Hunter, BA ACA *1996;* TTP Group plc, Melbourn Science Park, Cambridge Road, Melbourn, ROYSTON, HERTFORDSHIRE SG8 6EE.

MARTIN, Mr. James Hugh, BA ACA MCT *1988;* 6 Badger Way, Ewshot, FARNHAM, SURREY, GU10 5TE.

MARTIN, Mr. James Michael, BSc ACA *1989;* Garlands, Priory Wood, Clifford, HEREFORD, HR3 5HF.

•①MARTIN, Mr. James Patrick Nicholas, BA FCA *1988;* 3 Shakespeare Meadows, Main Street, Repton, DERBY, DE65 6SB.

MARTIN, Mr. James Wallace, BCom FCA *1960;* 6 Foxdell Way, Chalfont St.Peter, GERRARDS CROSS, SL9 0PN. (Life Member)

•MARTIN, Mr. James William Herbert, FCA *1961;* J W H Martin, 1 Cherry Tree Walk, BECKENHAM, BR3 3PF.

MARTIN, Mrs. Jane Anna Louise, BSc ACA *2001;* 15 Prestbury Avenue, NEWCASTLE, STAFFORDSHIRE, ST5 4QY.

MARTIN, Mrs. Jeanette Ann, BA ACA *1986;* 5 Dalkeith Road, HARPENDEN, AL5 5PP.

MARTIN, Mr. John, FCA *1957;* 56 Jenner Court, Stavordale Road, Westham, WEYMOUTH, DT4 0AF. (Life Member)

MARTIN, Mr. John Anthony Wyard, FCA *1969;* Gatehouse, Mashbury, CHELMSFORD, CM1 4TG. (Life Member)

MARTIN, Mr. John Bannerman Christopher, FCA *1963;* 11 Idlewild Road, Knightsbridge Cascade, PORT OF SPAIN, TRINIDAD AND TOBAGO. (Life Member)

MARTIN, Mr. John Edgar, FCA *1967;* Eton House, Sedgeford Road, Docking, KING'S LYNN, NORFOLK, PE31 8PN.

•MARTIN, Mr. John Errol Thomas, BSc ACA *1982;* Errol Martin, 2nd Floor, 272 London Road, WALLINGTON, SURREY, SM6 7DJ.

MARTIN, Mr. John Hampden, BA FCA *1987;* Holwell Farm House, Mells, FROME, BA11 3RH.

MARTIN, Mr. John Joseph, MA FCA *1976;* 89 Gartmoor Gardens, Wimbledon Park, LONDON, SW19 6NX.

MARTIN, Mr. John Philip Baynes, TD FCA ATII *1953;* The Old Rectory, Stoke Charity, WINCHESTER, SO21 3PG. (Life Member)

MARTIN, Mr. John Richard Gardiner, FCA *1962;* The Link House, 53 Mornington Road, WOODFORD GREEN, IG8 0TL.

MARTIN, Mr. John Stuart, MA FCA *1972;* 495 Bolton Road West, Holcombe Brooke, BURY, LANCASHIRE, BL0 9RN.

MARTIN, Mr. John Walley, BSc ACA *1991;* Valewood Grange, Fernden Lane, HASLEMERE, SURREY, GU27 3LB.

MARTIN, Mr. John William Rolfe, MA FCA *1978;* (Tax Fac), Christopher House, Station Road, SIDCUP, KENT, DA15 7BS.

MARTIN, Mr. Jonathan Colin, BSc ACA *1986;* Meadow View Meadow View Drive, Colkirk, FAKENHAM, NORFOLK, NR21 7JU.

MARTIN, Mr. Jonathan James, BA(Hons) ACA *2011;* 5 Eggbridge Lane, Waverton, CHESTER, CH3 7PE.

•MARTIN, Mr. Jonathan Michael, BSc(Hons) ACA *2001;* with KPMG Audit plc, 15 Canada Square, LONDON, E14 5GL.

MARTIN, Mr. Joshua Benjamin, BA FCA MBA *2000;* with KPMG AG, Badenerstrasse 172, CH 8004 ZURICH, SWITZERLAND.

MARTIN, Mr. Joward Paul, BA(Hons) ACA AMCT *2004;* Northern Rock (Asset Managment) Prudhoe Building Floor 2, Regent Centre Gosforth, NEWCASTLE UPON TYNE, NE3 4PL.

•①MARTIN, Mrs. Julia Anne, BA FCA *1986;* 17 Eborne Croft, Off Station Road, Balsall Common, COVENTRY, CV7 7RF.

•MARTIN, Mr. Justin Frank, LLB FCA *2001;* PricewaterhouseCoopers LLP, 80 Strand, LONDON, WC2R 0AF. See also PricewaterhouseCoopers

MARTIN, Mrs. Karen Judith, BSc ACA *1989;* LF BEAUTY UK LTD, AINTREE AVENUE WHITE HORSE BUSINESS PARK, TROWBRIDGE, BA14 OXB.

MARTIN, Mrs. Karen Louise, BSc ACA *1989;* 144 Moreton Road, BUCKINGHAM, MK18 1PW.

MARTIN, Miss. Katherine Jane, BA(Hons) ACA *2009;* 207 Ashburton Road, Hugglescote, COALVILLE, LEICESTERSHIRE, LE67 2HE.

MARTIN, Mr. Keith Andrew Grierson, FCA *1959;* 148 Friern Park, LONDON, N12 9LU. (Life Member)

MARTIN, Mr. Keith Christopher, FCA *1964;* 18 Homefield Road, BUSHEY, WD23 3FA.

MARTIN, Mr. Keith Joseph, BSc FCA *1968;* Westover Group Ltd, 382 Charminster Road, BOURNEMOUTH, BH8 9SA.

MARTIN, Mr. Keith William, BSc FCA *1991;* 2 Drovers Walk, KIDDERMINSTER, WORCESTERSHIRE, DY10 1NZ.

MARTIN, Mr. Kenneth Alexander, FCA *1956;* 13 Chestnut Grove, Hawarden, DEESIDE, CH5 3HD. (Life Member)

MARTIN, Mr. Kevin, BA(Hons) ACA *2001;* 5 Bottrells Lane, CHALFONT ST. GILES, BUCKINGHAMSHIRE, HP8 4EX.

MARTIN, Mr. Kim Ian, FCA *1981;* Little Dene, 13 Manor Rise, Bearsted, MAIDSTONE, ME14 4DB.

MARTIN, Miss. Laura, BSc ACA *2010;* 2 Clinton Close, Grange Park, SWINDON, SN5 6BP.

MARTIN, Mrs. Layla, BSc ACA *2006;* 25 Orsett Heath Crescent, GRAYS, ESSEX, RM16 4UZ.

MARTIN, Mr. Linburgh Rae Rolando, BA ACA *1994;* PO Box 31125 SMB, SEVEN MILE BEACH, GRAND CAYMAN, KY1-1205, CAYMAN ISLANDS.

MARTIN, Mr. Lionel, FCA *1973;* 17 Windsor Road, Finchley, LONDON, N3 3SN.

MARTIN, Miss. Lisa Anne, ACA *2005;* 10 West Road, SOUTHAMPTON, SO19 9AJ.

MARTIN, Mr. Malcolm, FCA *1970;* (Tax Fac), Flat 3, 233 Nithsdale Road, GLASGOW, G41 5PY.

MARTIN, Mr. Marc Joseph, BA ACA *1993;* 5 Dunure Drive, Newton Mearns, GLASGOW, G77 5TH.

•MARTIN, Mrs. Marguerita Teresa, BSc FCA *1994;* PricewaterhouseCoopers LLP, 9 Greyfriars Road, READING, RG1 1JG.

MARTIN, Mrs. Marianne, BSc ACA *1998;* 21 Guest Lane, Silkstone, BARNSLEY, SOUTH YORKSHIRE, S75 4LF.

•MARTIN, Mrs. Marilyn, BSc FCA *1979;* (Tax Fac), PKF (UK) LLP, 16 The Havens, Ransomes Europark, IPSWICH, IP3 9SJ.

•MARTIN, Mr. Mark John, FCA CTA *1990;* (Tax Fac), Caldwell Penn, 1 Bramley Business Centre, Station Road, Bramley, GUILDFORD, SURREY GU5 0AZ.

•MARTIN, Mr. Mark Richard, ACA *1991;* MRM Accounting, 90 Albert Road, Grappenhall, WARRINGTON, WA4 2PG.

MARTIN, Mrs. Mary Julia, MA FCA *1977;* Flat 8, 194 Harborne Road, BIRMINGHAM, B15 3JJ.

MARTIN, Mr. Michael Alexander Hugh, BA FCA *1973;* 3 Northanger, Hascombe Road, Munstead, GODALMING, SURREY, GU8 4AA.

MARTIN, Mr. Michael Anthony Holmes, FCA *1965;* 30 NAMUTONI, 9 Maiden Street, ROBINDALE EXT.1, JOHANNESBURG, 2194, SOUTH AFRICA.

MARTIN, Mr. Michael Christopher, BA FCA *1977;* 2423 Bennie Place, PORT COQUITLAM V2B 7M6, BC, CANADA.

MARTIN, Mr. Michael John, FCA *1979;* 20 Wilby Road, #03-08, The Tessarina, SINGAPORE 276305, SINGAPORE.

•MARTIN, Mr. Michael Leigh, FCA *1981;* (Tax Fac), Lloyd & Co, 103-105 Brighton Road, COULSDON, SURREY, CR5 2NG.

MARTIN, Mr. Michael Stephen Luke, BSc FCA *1986;* 329 Hurst Road, BEXLEY, KENT, DA5 3DZ.

MARTIN, Mr. Michael William, MEng ACA *1997;* 15 Alders Brook Hilton, DERBY, DE65 5HF.

MARTIN, Mr. Nathan, BEng ACA *2010;* Flat 17 Dollar Bay Court, 4 Lawn House Close, LONDON, E14 9YJ.

MARTIN, Mr. Neil, BSc FCA *1999;* 16 Blakeman Way, LICHFIELD, STAFFORDSHIRE, WS13 8FH.

MARTIN, Mr. Neil Ashley, BSc(Hons) ACA *2003;* C T C London Ltd John Stow House, 18 Bevis Marks, LONDON, EC3A 7JB.

MARTIN, Mr. Neil Brett, ACA *1983;* Sefton Hotel Ltd Harris Promenade, Douglas, ISLE OF MAN, IM1 2RW.

MARTIN, Mr. Nicholas, BA ACA *2011;* 47 Dalberg Road, LONDON, SW2 1AJ.

MARTIN, Mr. Nicholas, BSc ACA *1997;* Bank of America, 5 Canada Square, LONDON, E14 5AQ.

MARTIN, Mr. Nicholas Andrew James, LLB ACA *2005;* 6a King Street, Wilton, SALISBURY, SP2 0AX.

MARTIN, Mr. Nicholas David, MBA BA ACA *1990;* Yew Tree Cottage Old Hill, Christchurch, NEWPORT, GWENT, NP18 1JZ.

MARTIN, Mr. Nicholas Edwin John, BSc ACA *1983;* 4700 KAUST, Nicholas martin, Box 1112, THUWAL, 23955, SAUDI ARABIA.

•MARTIN, Mr. Nicholas Ford, FCA *1970;* (Tax Fac), Nicholas Ford Martin, 61 Temple Road, Kew, RICHMOND, SURREY, TW9 2EB.

MARTIN, Mr. Nicholas Graeme, BA ACA *1992;* H & B Foods Ltd, 44-54 Stewarts Road, LONDON, SW8 4DF.

MARTIN, Mr. Nicholas James, BSc ACA *2001;* 54 Heathfield Road, BROMLEY, BR1 3RN.

MARTIN, Mr. Nicholas James, ACA FCCA *2009;* 1 Rue Neuf Ville, 54730 GORCY, FRANCE.

MARTIN, Mr. Nicholas Rupert Zelenka, MA ACA *1989;* 33 Dents Road, LONDON, SW11 6JA.

MARTIN, Mr. Nicholas Simon, BSc ACA *1990;* 149 Carshalton Park Road, CARSHALTON, SM5 3SF.

MARTIN, Dr. Nicola Catherine, PhD BSc ACA MRSC *2000;* 12 Old Sun Wharf, 40 Narrow Street, Limehouse, LONDON, E14 8DG.

•MARTIN, Mrs. Nicole Louise, BA ACA *1996;* with KPMG LLP, Arlington Business Park, Theale, READING, RG7 4SD.

MARTIN, Mr. Nigel George, BA ACA *1995;* 110 Station Road, HARPENDEN, HERTFORDSHIRE, AL5 4TT.

MARTIN, Mr. Nigel John, FCA *1977;* 849 Almar Avenue, Suite C, Box 184, SANTA CRUZ, CA 95060, UNITED STATES.

•MARTIN, Mr. Nigel John, FCA *1983;* Scott & Wilkinson, Dalton House, 9 Dalton Square, LANCASTER, LA1 1WD. See also Scott & Wilkinson LLP

MARTIN, Mr. Nigel Peter, BSc FCA *1988;* 19 Holmefield, Farndon, NEWARK, NOTTINGHAMSHIRE, NG24 3TZ.

MARTIN, Mr. Nigel Thomas, BA FCA *1981;* 174 Court Lane, Dulwich, LONDON, SE21 7ED.

MARTIN, Mr. Nigel Timothy Devlin, BSc FCA *1991;* Owen Harris Building, Floor 4, Queen Alexandra Road, HIGH WYCOMBE, BUCKINGHAMSHIRE, HP11 2JZ.

MARTIN, Mr. Norman Thomas David, FCA *1960;* 282 Wallace Terrace, TE AWAMUTU 3800, NEW ZEALAND. (Life Member)

MARTIN, Mr. Oliver Day, BA ACA *2006;* 103a St. Georges Square, LONDON, SW1V 3QP.

MARTIN, Mr. Owen Neil, FCA *1953;* Broome, 17 Waterlow Road, REIGATE, RH2 7EY. (Life Member)

MARTIN, Mr. Patrick Noel, FCA *1963;* 11 Church Road, Shenstone, LICHFIELD, WS14 0NG. (Life Member)

MARTIN, Mr. Patrick William, BSc(Econ) ACA *2010;* 16 Starbuck Road, MILFORD HAVEN, DYFED, SA73 2BA.

•MARTIN, Mr. Paul, BA ACA *1982;* CMB Partnership, Chapel House, 1 Chapel Street, GUILDFORD, SURREY, GU1 3UH.

MARTIN, Mr. Paul, ACA *2002;* 15 Galingale View, NEWCASTLE, STAFFORDSHIRE, ST5 2GQ.

MARTIN, Mr. Paul Arthur, FCA *1967;* 4 Carisbrook Road, ST. ALBANS, AL2 3HR. (Life Member)

•MARTIN, Mr. Paul Grant, BA FCA *1990;* Price Bailey LLP, Causeway House, 1 Dane Street, BISHOP'S STORTFORD, HERTFORDSHIRE, CM23 3BT. See also Price Bailey Private Client LLP

•MARTIN, Mr. Paul Henry, BSc ACA *1995;* Ernst & Young LLP, 1 More London Place, LONDON, SE1 2AF. See also Ernst & Young Europe LLP

MARTIN, Mr. Paul James, MSc ACA *2003;* Myrtle Cottage Reading Road, Burghfield Common, READING, RG7 3BT.

MARTIN, Mr. Paul John Charles, BSc FCA *1975;* Lucksvillebob, 65a Pinchbeck Road, SPALDING, LINCOLNSHIRE, PE11 1QF.

MARTIN, Mr. Paul Robert, BSc ACA *1992;* 103 Valley Road, KENLEY, CR8 5BY.

MARTIN, Mr. Paul Santo, BSc ACA *1996;* 3 Hogarth Road, STRATFORD-UPON-AVON, CV37 9YU.

MARTIN, Mr. Paul Stewart, FCA *1974;* DGS Group plc, Sycamore Road, Castle Donington, DERBY, DERBYSHIRE, DE74 2NP.

MARTIN, Mr. Paul William, BSc ACA *1994;* 413 SW 11 Court, FORT LAUDERDALE, FL 33315, UNITED STATES.

MARTIN, Miss. Penelope Jane, BA ACA *2001;* 53a Abbey Road West Bridgford, NOTTINGHAM, NG2 5NE.

MARTIN, Mr. Peter, FCA *1966;* Linkside, 17 Corry Road, Beacon Hill, HINDHEAD, GU26 6PB.

MARTIN, Mr. Peter Donald, BSc FCA *1983;* Thompson & Bryan Ltd, Thompson House, Bull Street, Harborne, BIRMINGHAM, B17 0HH.

MARTIN, Mr. Peter Gordon, FCA *1963;* 1 Maxwell Drive, WEST BYFLEET, KT14 6PZ. (Life Member)

MARTIN, Mr. Peter Harold, BA FCA *1964;* 17 Oak Tree Lane, EASTBOURNE, EAST SUSSEX, BN23 8BB.

MARTIN, Mr. Peter James, DL FCA *1967;* Longwood Chase, The Ridge, Little Baddow, CHELMSFORD, CM3 4RZ.

MARTIN, Mr. Peter Leonard, FCA JDipMA *1963;* 6 Gadley Close, BUXTON, DERBYSHIRE, SK17 6YQ. (Life Member)

MARTIN, Mr. Peter Nicholas, MA FCA *1977;* Chartered Insurance Institute, 20 Aldermanbury, LONDON, EC2V 7HY.

MARTIN, Mr. Peter Patrick, BA ACA *1983;* Finance department, Mid Staffordshire General Hospitals NHS Trust, Staffordshire General Hospital Weston Road, STAFFORD, ST16 3SA.

MARTIN, Mr. Peter Phillip, BSc FCA *1988;* Meggitt Plc, Atlantic House, 3 Aviation Park West, Bournemouth International Airport, Hur, CHRISTCHURCH DORSET BH23 6EW.

MARTIN, Mr. Peter Reginald, FCA *1959;* 3 Filkins Hall, Filkins, LECHLADE, GL7 3JJ. (Life Member)

MARTIN, Mr. Peter Robert Strudwyck, FCA *1968;* 550 West 12th Avenue, Apt 807, VANCOUVER V5Z 1M3, BC, CANADA.

MARTIN, Mr. Philip David, BA ACA *1995;* Zeltweg 13, CH-8032 ZURICH, SWITZERLAND.

MARTIN, Mr. Philip Jeremy, BSc FCA *1988;* (Tax Fac), Nomura International plc, 1 St Martins-le-Grand, LONDON, EC1A 4AS.

MARTIN, Mr. Philip John, BSc ACA *1982;* Runwick Hill, Runwick Lane, Dippenhall, Runwick, FARNHAM, SURREY GU10 5EE.

•MARTIN, Mr. Philip John, BSc ACA *1992;* Philip Martin Limited, Crown House, 4 High Street, Tyldesley, MANCHESTER, M29 8AL.

MARTIN, Mr. Phillip, BSc ACA *1991;* Enstar (Eu) Ltd Avaya House, Cathedral Hill, GUILDFORD, GU2 7YL.

MARTIN, Mrs. Rachel, BSc ACA *2006;* 296 Teignmouth Road, TORQUAY, TQ1 4RW.
MARTIN, Mrs. Rachel Anne, LLB ACA *2002;* 55 Bonnyrigg Road, Eskbank, Dalkeith, MIDLOTHIAN, EH22 3HQ.
MARTIN, Mr. Ralph Kim, BSc FCA *1977;* Higher Croft The City, Chinnor Road Bledlow Ridge, HIGH WYCOMBE, BUCKINGHAMSHIRE, HP14 4AB.
MARTIN, Mr. Ralph Richard, BA(Hons) ACA *2004;* 74/9 Herbert Street, ST LEONARDS, NSW 2065, AUSTRALIA.
•**MARTIN, Mr. Raymond David, FCA** *1970;* R D Martin & Co, 28 Church Road, STANMORE, MIDDLESEX, HA7 4XR.
MARTIN, Mr. Rex Francis, FCA *1970;* High Beeches, WYCH CROSS, EAST SUSSEX, RH18 5JP.
MARTIN, Mr. Richard Brownlow, FCA *1978;* Little Stoke House, Best Beech Hill, WADHURST, EAST SUSSEX, TN5 6JH.
MARTIN, Mr. Richard David, BSc(Hons) ACA *2001;* 14 Lodge Lane, Prestwood, GREAT MISSENDEN, HP16 0SU.
MARTIN, Mr. Richard David, BSc ACA *1991;* 3rd Floor Building A004, Al Sufouh 2, Knowledge Village, DUBAI, 500321, UNITED ARAB EMIRATES.
MARTIN, Mr. Richard Douglas, BSc ACA *1996;* T-Mobile (UK) Ltd Unit 1, Mosquito Way, HATFIELD, AL10 9BW.
MARTIN, Mr. Richard Joseph Fitzgerald, MA FCA *1983;* Brook Farm Drinkstone Road, Beyton, BURY ST. EDMUNDS, SUFFOLK, IP30 9AQ.
MARTIN, Mr. Richard Tod, MA ACA *1980;* 18 Druce Road, LONDON, SE21 7DW.
MARTIN, Mr. Richard Vincent Robert, FCA *1977;* Freshlands, Sway Road, BROCKENHURST, HAMPSHIRE, SO42 7SG.
MARTIN, Mr. Richard Vincent William, BEng ACA *1992;* 2 Defford Close, REDDITCH, B97 5WR.
MARTIN, Mr. Robert Charles, BA ACA *2003;* 2 Highcroft Avenue, Douglas, ISLE OF MAN, IM2 5BP.
MARTIN, The Revd. Robert David Markland, MA FCA *1974;* 33 Kennedy Gardens, SEVENOAKS, KENT, TN13 3UG.
MARTIN, Mr. Robert Edward, BSc FCA *1976;* 25 Syddal Road, Bramhall, STOCKPORT, SK7 1AB.
MARTIN, Mr. Robert James, BSc(Hons) FCA FCII FIRM *1977;* 38a Hauxton Road, Little Shelford, CAMBRIDGE, CB22 5HJ.
MARTIN, Mr. Robert William, FCA *1972;* Flat 16 Bridgewalk Heights, 80 Weston Street, LONDON, SE1 3QZ.
MARTIN, Mr. Robin Sweeting, BSc FCA *1971;* 2a Sheen Gate Gardens, LONDON, SW14 7NY. (Life Member)
•**MARTIN, Mr. Roger, FCA** *1973;* Centre For Education & Finance Management Limited, Red Lion House, 9-10 High Street, HIGH WYCOMBE, BUCKINGHAMSHIRE, HP11 2AZ.
MARTIN, Mr. Roger John, BA FCA *1970;* 68 Sir Harrys Road, Edgbaston, BIRMINGHAM, B15 2UX.
MARTIN, Mr. Roger William, FCA *1970;* 49 Arcadian Place, LONDON, SW18 5JF. (Life Member)
MARTIN, Mr. Roland Augustus, BSc ACA *2008;* 3 The Moorings, BRAUNTON, DEVON, EX33 1AN.
•**MARTIN, Mr. Ross, ACA** *2007;* Kelsall Steele Limited, Woodlands Court, Truro Business Park, TRURO, CORNWALL, TR4 9NH.
MARTIN, Mr. Ross David, BSc ACA *2011;* Marchmead, Shottery Village, Shottery, STRATFORD-UPON-AVON, WARWICKSHIRE, CV37 9HA.
•**MARTIN, Mr. Roy Christopher, BSc FCA** *1984;* (Tax Fac), Roy C. Martin, 7 Hawkridge, Shoeburyness, SOUTHEND-ON-SEA, SS3 8AU.
MARTIN, Miss. Sabine Sharmini, BA ACA *2003;* with Baker Tilly Tax and Advisory Services LLP, 25 Farringdon Street, LONDON, EC4A 4AB.
MARTIN, Miss. Sarah, ACA *1983;* 1 Ellington Road, LONDON, N10 3DD.
MARTIN, Mrs. Sarah Emma Rebecca, BSc ACA *1995;* Austens Farm, Twitchells Lane, Jordans, BEACONSFIELD, BUCKINGHAMSHIRE, HP9 2RA.
MARTIN, Miss. Sarah Joanne, BSc(Hons) ACA *2010;* 46 Stonecrop Close, Birchwood, WARRINGTON, WA3 7PD.
MARTIN, Miss. Sarah Louise, BA ACA *2003;* 12 Bambrook Close, Desford, LEICESTER, LE9 9FY.
•**MARTIN, Mrs. Sheila Isabel, BSc ACA** *1991;* (Tax Fac), Sumit (UK) Limited, 17 Cosgrove Road, Old Stratford, MILTON KEYNES, MK19 6AG.
MARTIN, Miss. Sheila Jacqueline Alice, BA ACA MCT *1979;* 41 Pembroke Square, LONDON, W8 6PE.
MARTIN, Mrs. Shirley Anne, BSc ACA *1982;* (Tax Fac), 5 Eton Road, FRINTON-ON-SEA, CO13 9JA.
MARTIN, Mr. Simon, BSc ACA *2000;* 4 Belvedere Close, FAVERSHAM, KENT, ME13 7GQ.
MARTIN, Mr. Simon, ACA *2009;* 6 Jessop Fold, Honley, HOLMFIRTH, HD9 6AJ.
MARTIN, Mr. Simon Anthony, BSc FCA CISA *1992;* KPMG, 10 Shelley Street, SYDNEY, NSW 2000, AUSTRALIA.
MARTIN, Mr. Simon John, BSc FCA *1985;* 10 The Readings, Chorleywood, RICKMANSWORTH, WD3 5SY.
MARTIN, Mr. Simon Lee Stuart, BSc ACA *1999;* Woodlea Farm, Station Approach, Medstead, ALTON, HAMPSHIRE, GU34 5EN.
MARTIN, Mr. Simon Nicholas, RD FCA *1970;* The Lodge, Robin Hood Lane, Sutton Green, GUILDFORD, GU4 7QG.
MARTIN, Mr. Spencer Andrew Charles, BA ACA *2011;* Basement Flat, 129 Shirland Road, LONDON, W9 2EP.
MARTIN, Mrs. Stephanie Ruth, BSc ACA *1999;* Effective Brands, 28-30 Little Russell Street, LONDON, WC1A 2HN.
MARTIN, Mr. Stephen, DL MA FCA *1964;* Hotham Hall, Hotham, YORK, YO43 4UA.
MARTIN, Mr. Stephen, BA ACA *1994;* 1 Highridge Place, Oak Avenue, ENFIELD, EN2 8LE.
MARTIN, Mr. Stephen James, BA ACA *2009;* 50 Grove Road, LONDON, E3 5AX.
MARTIN, Mr. Stephen James, ACA *2010;* Royal Institute of International Affairs Chatham House, 10 St. James's Square, LONDON, SW1Y 4LE.
MARTIN, Mr. Stephen Victor, BA ACA *1992;* 4 Barnard Hill, LONDON, N10 2HB.
MARTIN, Mr. Steve, ACA *2010;* 10 Garfield Road, LONDON, SW11 5PN.
MARTIN, Mr. Steven Andrew, BA ACA *1992;* 76 Garricks House, Wadbrook Street, KINGSTON UPON THAMES, KT1 1HS.
MARTIN, Mr. Steven Edward, ACA *1999;* 2 Holly Blue Road, WYMONDHAM, NORFOLK, NR18 0XJ.
MARTIN, Mr. Steven James, BSc ACA *1986;* 53 Garraways, Wootton Bassett, SWINDON, SN4 8NQ.
•**MARTIN, Mr. Stewart Paul, FCA** *1988;* Edmund Carr LLP, 146 New London Road, CHELMSFORD, CM2 0AW. See also EC (Management Services) Ltd
MARTIN, Mrs. Susan, FCA *1976;* 6 Glebe Corner, Wickham, FAREHAM, PO17 6HL.
MARTIN, Mr. Terence John, BA FCA *1974;* 525 Holcombe Road, Greenmount, BURY, BL8 4EL. (Life Member)
MARTIN, Mrs. Teresa Mary, BSc ACA *1993;* Queens Acre, 37 Prince Consort Drive, ASCOT, BERKSHIRE, SL5 8AW.
MARTIN, Mrs. Theresa Sylvia, BA ACA *1985;* 188, Wendover Road, Weston Turville, AYLESBURY, HP22 5TG.
MARTIN, Miss. Therese Florise Jocelyne, BSc ACA *1995;* c/o Promotion and Development Ltd, 8th Floor Dias Pier, Le Caudan Waterfront, PORT LOUIS, MAURITIUS.
MARTIN, Mr. Thomas, BSc(Hons) ACA *2004;* 15 Albert Road, RICHMOND, TW10 6DJ.
MARTIN, Mr. Timothy, FCA *1964;* 42 Elizabeth Road, HENLEY-ON-THAMES, RG9 1RA.
•**MARTIN, Mr. Timothy Allen, MA ACA** *2005;* Allen Martin & Company Limited, 9 Ravenhill Park Gardens, BELFAST, BT6 0DH.
•**MARTIN, Mr. Timothy Ian, FCA** *1981;* (Tax Fac), Moore Thompson, Bank House, Broad Street, SPALDING, LINCOLNSHIRE, PE11 1TB.
MARTIN, Mr. Timothy Peter, BSc ACA *2004;* 21 Mirfield Drive, Eccles, MANCHESTER, M30 9LH.
MARTIN, Mr. Tony James Cathcart, FCA *1960;* 156 Connaught Road, FLEET, GU51 3QX. (Life Member)
MARTIN, Mr. Trevor Caleb, BA FCA CTA *1985;* (Tax Fac), 2 Little Green, RICHMOND, SURREY, TW9 1QH.
Ⓓ**MARTIN, Mrs. Vanessa Dawn, BSc FCA** *1982;* Ladymede, Grimms Hill, GREAT MISSENDEN, BUCKINGHAMSHIRE, HP16 9BG.
MARTIN, Mrs. Victoria Jane, BA ACA *1996;* 25 Green Lane, Chesham Bois, AMERSHAM, BUCKINGHAMSHIRE, HP6 5LN.
MARTIN, Miss. Victoria Louise, ACA *2008;* 11 Tenbury Drive, Middleton, MANCHESTER, M24 1ST.
MARTIN, Mrs. Wendy, BSc ACA ATII *1995;* The State of Jersey, Chief Ministers Department, Cyril Le Marquand House, PO Box 140, St Helier, JERSEY JE4 8QT.
•**MARTIN, Mr. William Scott, FCA** *1976;* Langdale Restructuring LLP, Langdale, Legh Road, KNUTSFORD, CHESHIRE, WA16 8NT.
MARTIN-FISHER, Miss. Henrietta Kate, MA ACA *2007;* with PKF (UK) LLP, Farringdon Place, 20 Farringdon Road, LONDON, EC1M 3AP.
MARTIN-JONES, Mrs. Judith Elizabeth, BSc ACA *1996;* 90 South Road, Oundle, PETERBOROUGH, PE8 4BP.
•**MARTIN-LONG, Mrs. Valerie Anne, BA FCA** *1980;* (Tax Fac), PKF (UK) LLP, Pannell House, Park Street, GUILDFORD, SURREY, GU1 4HN.
MARTIN PEREIRA, Mrs. Clare, BSc ACA *1994;* 17 Oakhurst Drive, Gosforth, NEWCASTLE UPON TYNE, NE3 4JS.
•Ⓓ**MARTIN-SKLAN, Mr. Alexander, FCA** *1981;* (Tax Fac), Martin Sklan & Co, 133 Golders Green Road, LONDON, NW11 8HJ.
MARTIN SMITH, Mr. David, BA(Hons) ACA *2011;* 99d Cambridge Street, LONDON, SW1V 4PY.
MARTINDALE, Mr. Alan Shane, BEng ACA *1996;* 3 Oak Grove, ROCHESTER, IL 62563, UNITED STATES.
MARTINDALE, Ms. Ann Elizabeth, BA ACA *1987;* Erin Holme, Broad Oak Avenue, Garstang, PRESTON, PR3 1QQ.
MARTINDALE, Mr. Deryk, LLB FCA *1962;* 6 Marbury Grove, Standish, WIGAN, WN6 0UF.
MARTINDALE, Mr. Ian James, FCA *1981;* Tailored Roofing Systems Ltd, Unit A2, Lecturers Close, BOLTON, BL3 6DG.
MARTINDALE, Mr. James David, BA ACA *2004;* 14 Quinton Street, LONDON, SW18 3QS.
MARTINDALE, Mr. Kenneth Horace Ralph, FCA *1965;* Kevington, Montgomery Hill, Caldy, WIRRAL, MERSEYSIDE, CH48 1NE. (Life Member)
•**MARTINDALE, Mr. William George, FCA** *1964;* JurisPublications Limited, Southbank House, Black Prince Road, LONDON, SE1 7SJ.
MARTINDALE, Mr. William Kenneth, FCA *1955;* Rock Cottage, Finsthwaite, ULVERSTON, CUMBRIA, LA12 8BH. (Life Member)
MARTINE, Mrs. Charlotte Emma, ACA *2007;* 11 Northolt Way, HORNCHURCH, ESSEX, RM12 5RR.
•**MARTINE, Mr. Daniel Trevor, ACA** *2001;* Kingston Smith LLP, Orbital House, 20 Eastern Road, ROMFORD, RM1 3PJ. See also Kingston Smith Limited Liability Partnership, Devonshire Corporate Services LLP and Kingston Smith Consulting LLP
MARTINELLI, Mr. Franco, BSc ACA *1986;* Babcock International Group Plc, 33 Wigmore Street, LONDON, W1U 1QX.
MARTINELLI, Mrs. Tracey Jean, BA ACA *1986;* Honeyfields Overstream, Loudwater, RICKMANSWORTH, HERTFORDSHIRE, WD3 4LD.
MARTINEZ, Mr. Andrew, BSc ACA *1995;* 8103 Skye Loch Drive, WAXHAW, NC 28173, UNITED STATES.
MARTINEZ, Miss. Antonia, ACA *2009;* 23 Grigor Avenue, EDINBURGH, EH4 2PQ.
MARTINEZ, Mr. Liam, ACA *2010;* Flat 355, Neutron Tower, 6 Blackwall Way, LONDON, E14 9GT.
MARTINEZ-ATKINSON, Mr. Daniel, MA BSc ACA *2010;* 41 Pinfold Pond, WOBURN, BEDFORDSHIRE, MK17 9PW.
MARTINGELL, Mr. Paul, ACA *2002;* Flat 8 Littleacre, Hermitage Lane, WINDSOR, SL4 4AZ.
MARTINI, Ms. Catherine Anne, BSc ACA *1989;* 16 Garden Close, Briston, MELTON CONSTABLE, NORFOLK, NR24 2SF.
MARTINI, Mr. Thomas, MA BA FCA *1983;* Heidrehmen 37, D-22589 HAMBURG, GERMANY.
MARTINI, Ms. Victoria Louise, ACA *2008;* Inglenook, Milton Avenue, Chalfont St. Peter, GERRARDS CROSS, BUCKINGHAMSHIRE, SL9 8QW.
MARTINIELLO, Ms. Alessandra, ACA *2011;* 23C Hornsey Lane Gardens, LONDON, N6 5NX.
MARTINO, Miss. Sarah Jane, BA(Hons) ACA *2002;* Flat 3, 19 St Alphonsus Road, LONDON, SW4 7AW.
MARTINOS, Mr. Philip George, BA ACA *2002;* with PricewaterhouseCoopers LLP, 1 Embankment Place, LONDON, WC2N 6RH.
MARTINOVIC, Mrs. Anita Kathryn, BSc ACA *1980;* 1 Somerville Close, Saltford, BRISTOL, BS31 3HT.
MARTINS, Mrs. Gabriel Ursula, BA ACA *1986;* 37 Birling Road, TUNBRIDGE WELLS, TN2 5LY.
•**MARTINS, Mr. Graham, BSc FCA** *1984;* Villa A-81, Cedre Villa Complex, Dubai Silicon Oasis, DUBAI, UNITED ARAB EMIRATES.
MARTINS, Mr. Karl Michael, BSc ACA *1993;* 29 Hadley Road, ENFIELD, MIDDLESEX, EN2 8JT.
MARTINS, Mr. Mervyn Ronaldo, BSc ACA *1987;* 3 rue de Capellen, L 8393 OLM LUXEMBOURG, LUXEMBOURG.
MARTINS, Mr. Steven Mark, ACA *2007;* (Tax Fac), Pricewaterhousecoopers, 12 Plumtree Court, LONDON, EC4A 4HT.
MARTIROSSIAN, Mr. Ara, ACA *1993;* MEMBER OF COUNCIL, 3 Ashburnham Gardens, EASTBOURNE, EAST SUSSEX, BN21 2NA.
MARTLAND, Mr. David John, ACA *2007;* Holmes House, Blundell Lane, Blackrod, BOLTON, BL6 5LP.
MARTLAND, Mrs. Lisa, BSc(Hons) ACA MCT *2001;* 25 Greystones Close, Aberford, LEEDS, LS25 3AR.
MARTLE, Mr. David Henry James, FCA *1960;* The Cedars, 9 Caroon Drive, Sarratt, RICKMANSWORTH, HERTFORDSHIRE, WD3 6DD. (Life Member)
MARTLE, Mr. Simon David, BSc FCA *1996;* Church Farm, Main Street, Harborough Magna, RUGBY, WARWICKSHIRE, CV23 0HS.
MARTON, Mrs. Janet, BA(Hons) CA *2008;* Scotland 2003); 14 Woodlands Park, Lower Swainswick, BATH, BA1 7BQ.
MARTYN, Mr. Andrew Richard Wentworth, BA ACA *1995;* 74 Spencer Road, Killara, SYDNEY, NSW 2071, AUSTRALIA.
•**MARTYN, Mr. Brian Frederick, BA FCA** *1974;* D'Arcy Howard Castleford Limited, 7A Pontefract Road, CASTLEFORD, WF10 4JE.
•**MARTYN, Mr. John Hocken, BA ACA** *1990;* John Martyn Limited, Cages Farm, Tuffields Road, Whepstead, BURY ST. EDMUNDS, SUFFOLK IP29 4TL.
MARTYN, Miss. Olivia Jane, BA(Hons) ACA *2010;* 22 Royal Chase, TUNBRIDGE WELLS, TN4 8AY.
MARTYN-JOHNS, Mr. Richard Andrew, BSc FCA *1981;* The Rookery, East Dundry Lane, Dundry, BRISTOL, BS41 8NJ.
MARU, Miss. Archana, ACA *1990;* Flat 211, Quadrangle Tower, Cambridge Square, LONDON, W2 2PJ.
MARU, Mr. Vimlesh, BSc(Econ) ACA *1997;* 86 The Quadrangle, LONDON, W2 2RR.
MARUKUTIRA, Mrs. Priscilla Simbisayi, ACA *2009;* PO Box 26313, Game City, GABORONE, BOTSWANA.
MARUTHIAH, Mr. Devaraj Pillai, BA ACA *1982;* 49 Lorong Burung Sintar 1, Taman Bukit Maluri, Kepong, 52100 KUALA LUMPUR, FEDERAL TERRITORY, MALAYSIA.
MARVANOVA, Miss. Lenka, BA(Hons) ACA *2011;* 17 Briar Court, Guardian Road, NORWICH, NR5 8PR.
MARVEL, Mr. Christopher, BSc ACA *2010;* 10 The Ladysmith, ASHTON-UNDER-LYNE, OL6 9AR.
MARVELL, Mr. Barry, FCA *1956;* 13 Bridgefield, FARNHAM, GU9 8AN. (Life Member)
MARVELL, Mr. Timothy Lloyd, BA ACA *1989;* 44 Bloomfield Park, BATH, BA2 2BX.
MARVEN, Mr. Gary, BA ACA *1984;* 41 Waine Close, BUCKINGHAM, MK18 1FF.
MARVI, Mr. Junaid, BA ACA *1995;* 2C / 14 Seacliff Apartments, Clifton Block 2, KARACHI, PAKISTAN.
MARVIN, Mr. Anthony Lloyd, MA ACA *1988;* 4 Penarth Road, Northenden, MANCHESTER, M22 4AR.
•**MARVIN, Mr. Joseph Anthony, FCA** *1964;* J.A. Marvin, 378 Thurmaston Boulevard, LEICESTER, LE4 9LE.
MARWICK, Mr. James Francis, TD JP FCA *1968;* 85 Herba Street, BIRKIRKARA BKR2325, MALTA.
MARWOOD, Mr. Francis, BSc ACA *1997;* 14 St Peters Grove, Clifton, YORK, YO30 6AQ.
MARWOOD, Mrs. Helen, BSc ACA *1989;* The Laithe Barn, Old Mount Farm, Woolley, WAKEFIELD, WEST YORKSHIRE, WF4 2LD.
•**MARWOOD, Mr. Ian Ralph, BSc ACA CF** *1987;* Grant Thornton UK LLP, 1 Whitehall Riverside, Whitehall Road, LEEDS, WEST YORKSHIRE, LS1 4BN. See also Grant Thornton LLP
MARWOOD, Mr. Michael Harold, FCA *1953;* 4 Woodthorpe Avenue, Woodthorpe, NOTTINGHAM, NG5 4FD. (Life Member)
•**MARWOOD, Mr. Philip David La Borde, MA FCA** *1980;* (Tax Fac), with KPMG LLP, 15 Canada Square, LONDON, E14 5GL.
MARX, Mr. Howard Michael, BSc ACA *1980;* The Old Vicarage, Rectory Hill, West Dean, SALISBURY, WILTSHIRE, SP5 1JL.
MARX, Mr. Michael Henry, FCA *1969;* The Orchard, California Lane, Bushey Heath, BUSHEY, WD23 1ES.
•**MARY, Mr. Shaun Carlton, ACA FCCA** *2008;* Banham Graham, Windsor Terrace, 76-80 Thorpe Road, NORWICH, NR1 1BA. See also Banham Graham Corporate Limited
MASASSO, Mrs. Dawn Louise, BCom ACA *2000;* 83 - 85 Petersen Street, FRESHWATER, QLD 4870, AUSTRALIA.
MASCARENHAS, Mr. Amyas Luis Xavier, BSc FCA *1976;* 63 Knoll Road, BEXLEY, DA5 1AY.
•**MASCARENHAS, Miss. Claire Lisa, BA ACA** *2005;* Kinetic Partners LLP, One London Wall, Level 10, LONDON, EC2Y 5HB.

MASCARENHAS, Mrs. Emma Isobel Rachael, MA ACA *2003;* 14 Burcott Road, PURLEY, SURREY, CR8 4AA.
MASCARENHAS, Mr. Eric Vincent, FCA *1973;* P.O. Box 68043, Crowfoot RPO, CALGARY T3G 3N8, AB, CANADA. (Life Member)
MASCARENHAS, Mr. Ovid Luis Xavier, FCA *1978;* Mascarenhas Consultancy Ltd, 6 Hollywell Road, Knowle, SOLIHULL, WEST MIDLANDS, B93 9JY.
MASCARENHAS, The Revd. Peter Adrian Richard, FCA *1962;* 26 Delamere Road, NANTWICH, CHESHIRE, CW5 7DL.
MASCORD, Mr. David Anthony, BA FCA *1978;* 11 Underwood Drive, Stoney Stanton, LEICESTER, LE9 4TD.
MASCOTT, Mr. William Thomas David, BSc FCA *1975;* 20922 4th Avenue, LANGLEY V2Z 1T6, BC, CANADA.
MASDING, Mr. Nigel Richard, MA FCA MBA *1997;* Longview Partners, Thames Court, 1 Queenhithe, LONDON, EC4V 3RL.
MASEFIELD, Mr. Dean Anthony, FCA *1995;* 6 Clos de L'Ecole, La Rue de la Mare Ballam, St. John, JERSEY, JE3 4EL.
MASERA, Mr. Riccardo, BA BSc FCA *2000;* Kimberly Clark Ltd Mocatta House, Trafalgar Place, BRIGHTON, BN1 4BG.
MASHEDER, Mr. Stefan Lawerence Francois, ACA *2009;* with KPMG LLP, 15 Canada Square, LONDON, E14 5GL.
•**MASHEN, Mr. Jonathan Scott, BSc FCA** *1991;* Lang Bennetts, The Old Carriage Works, Moresk Road, TRURO, CORNWALL, TR1 1DG. See also Lang Bennetts (Falmouth) Limited
MASHI, Mr. Mashendra Kumar, CA ACA *2011;* 103A M.P.Regency, R.K. Bhattacharya Road, PATNA 800001, INDIA.
MASHITER, Mr. Peter David, BSc FCA *1978;* Aiglemont, 60270 GOUVIEUX, FRANCE.
MASHKOOR, Mr. Asar, BEng ACA *1996;* PO Box 214138, Villa No. 3 Street 18a, Jumeirah 1, DUBAI, UNITED ARAB EMIRATES.
•**MASHOOD, Mr. Farid, FCA** *1980;* 42 Temple Avenue, Whetstone, LONDON, N20 9EH.
MASHRU, Mr. Paresh, BSc FCA *1983;* 11 Albion Street, LONDON, W2 2AS.
MASKALL, Mr. Michael Edwin, FCA *1961;* Alverstoke, Brockwell Lane, Wooton Courtenay, MINEHEAD, TA24 8RN. (Life Member)
MASKELL, Mr. Alexis Robert, BEng ACA *2001;* Flat 6, 44 Beaufort Gardens, LONDON, SW3 1PN.
MASKELL, Mr. James David, BA ACA *1999;* Pargue Empresarial Cristalia Edificio 2 - Planta 5, C/Via De Los Poblados, 28042 MADRID, SPAIN.
MASKELL, Mr. John Jeffrey, BA FCA *1969;* Cherrywood, 78 West End Lane, ESHER, KT10 8LF.
MASKELL, Mr. Philip John, BSc ACA *1983;* Aspex Semiconductor Ltd, Aspex House, 44-45 Oxford Street, HIGH WYCOMBE, BUCKINGHAMSHIRE, HP11 2DJ.
MASKERY, Mr. Andrew John, BSc ACA *1996;* Firth Rixson, 111 Founders Plaza, Suite 1802, EAST HARTFORD, CT 06108, UNITED STATES.
MASLEN, Mr. Benjamin Gulliver, BSc ACA *1998;* 100, Strathville Road, LONDON, SW18 4RB.
•**MASLEN, Mr. Christopher John, FCA** *1972;* (Tax Fac), Christopher Maslen, Old Tan House, Cottingley Bridge, BINGLEY, BD16 1NB.
•**MASLEN, Mr. David John, MA ACA** *1995;* Old Mill Audit LLP, The Old Rectory, South Walks Road, DORCHESTER, DORSET, DT1 1DT.
MASLEN, Mrs. Susan Elaine, BSc ACA *1989;* (Tax Fac), 28 Ravenhurst Road, Harborne, BIRMINGHAM, B17 9SE.
MASLIANIA, Miss. Anna, BSc(Hons) ACA *2004;* PricewaterhouseCoopers, Darling Park Tower 2, 201 Sussex Street, SYDNEY, NSW 1171, AUSTRALIA.
MASLIN, Mrs. Ann Margaret, MA ACA *1983;* 31 Cullerne Close, Ewell, EPSOM, KT17 1XY.
•**MASLIN, Mr. Christopher James, ACA CTA** *2008;* Maslins Accountants LLP, 140 Camden Road, TUNBRIDGE WELLS, KENT, TN1 2QZ.
MASLIN, Miss. Kelly, BSc ACA *2010;* Flat 1, 11 Northcote Road, LONDON, SW11 1NG.
MASLIN, Mr. Roger Michael, BA ACA *1986;* Juniper Cottage, 90 Hill Farm Road, MARLOW, BUCKINGHAMSHIRE, SL7 3LU.
•**MASLIN, Mr. Stephen, BSc FCA** *1983;* Grant Thornton UK LLP, Grant Thornton House, 22 Melton Street, Euston Square, LONDON, NW1 2EP. See also Grant Thornton LLP
MASLINSKI, Mr. Robert Martin, FCA *1974;* Forsley Limited, Flat 11 Rossetti Garden Mansions, Flood Street, LONDON, SW3 5QY.
MASLO, Mr. Abraham, BCom FCA *1953;* 23 Gloucester Gardens, LONDON, NW11 9AB. (Life Member)
MASNARI, Miss. Maryteresa, BSc ACA *2005;* Trafalgar Travel Ltd Picquet House The Albany, South Esplanade St. Peter Port, GUERNSEY, GY1 1AF.
MASON, Mr. Adam George, BSc ACA *2010;* 57 Britannia Gardens, Hedge End, SOUTHAMPTON, SO30 2RN.
MASON, Mr. Alan Michael, BSc FCA *1989;* 8 South View, BARROW-IN-FURNESS, CUMBRIA, LA14 5NN.
MASON, Ms. Alexandra Melissa, ACA *2011;* 104 Perry Hill Road, OLDBURY, WEST MIDLANDS, B68 0BJ.
MASON, Mrs. Alison Louise, BA ACA *2006;* 3 Amberley Way, Wickwar, WOTTON-UNDER-EDGE, GLOUCESTERSHIRE, GL12 8LW.
MASON, Mr. Alister Kenneth, PhD FCA *1963;* 115 St Clements Ave, TORONTO M4R 1H1, ON, CANADA.
MASON, Mr. Alvin Alastair, FCA *1952;* 11 Heath Drive, Gidea Park, ROMFORD, RM2 5QB. (Life Member)
MASON, Mr. Andrew Charles, BSc ACA *2006;* 24 Maxwell Street, Breaston, DERBY, DE72 3AH.
MASON, Mr. Andrew John Cleland, BA ACA *1990;* 16 Griffiths Street, FAIRLIGHT, NSW 2094, AUSTRALIA.
MASON, Mr. Andrew Owen, ACA CTA *2004;* Flat 6, Queens Court, 64 Greencroft Gardens, LONDON, NW6 3JH.
MASON, Mr. Andrew Philip, BA FCA *1998;* 53a Thornton Close, Girton, CAMBRIDGE, CB3 0NF.
MASON, Miss. Anita Caroline, BA(Hons) ACA *2010;* Woodside, 33 The Farthings, Astley Park, CHORLEY, PR7 1TP.
MASON, Miss. Annabel Jane, ACA *2010;* Pricewaterhousecoopers Cornwall Court, 19 Cornwall Street, BIRMINGHAM, B3 2DT.
MASON, Mr. Archie, ACA *2011;* 4B Aliwal Road, LONDON, SW11 1RD.
MASON, Mr. Brian Roy, MA FCA *1973;* Millstones, South Bush Lane, GILLINGHAM, Kent, ME8 8PS. (Life Member)
MASON, Mr. Bryan, FCA *1968;* Alexandra House, High Street, Goudhurst, CRANBROOK, KENT, TN17 1AL. (Life Member)
MASON, Miss. Caroline Anne, BSc ACA *2007;* Deloitte & Touche, 3 New Street Square, LONDON, EC4A 3BT.
MASON, Mr. Charles Edward Aiden, ACA *1985;* 27 Cedar Mount, Mottingham Lane, Mottingham, LONDON, SE9 4RU.
MASON, Miss. Cheryl Anne, BA ACA *2007;* 63 Cumberland Road, Chafford Hundred, GRAYS, ESSEX, RM16 6EU.
MASON, Miss. Christina Penelope, BA ACA *1987;* with Ernst & Young LLP, 1 More London Place, LONDON, SE1 2AF.
MASON, Mrs. Christine Ann, BSc ACA *1988;* Euroclydon, Beckenham Place Park, BECKENHAM, BR3 5BN.
MASON, Mr. Christopher, ACA *1981;* 9 Stone Road, Rough Close, STOKE-ON-TRENT, ST3 7PT.
MASON, Mr. Christopher Adam, BSc(Hons) ACA *2009;* 19 Victoria Road, South Woodham Ferrers, CHELMSFORD, CM3 5LR.
MASON, Mr. Christopher Alan, BA ACA *1993;* 93a Fairfield Road, MARKET HARBOROUGH, LEICESTERSHIRE, LE16 9QH.
MASON, Mr. Christopher Patrick Charles, FCA *1969;* Karwendel, 5 Orchardleigh, LEATHERHEAD, KT22 8NF.
•**MASON, Mr. Christopher Peter, FCA** *1979;* Nabarro, 3/4 Great Marlborough Street, LONDON, W1F 7HH.
MASON, Mr. Christopher Rhea, FCA *1960;* 5 Nursery Close, TRURO, CORNWALL, TR1 1TZ. (Life Member)
MASON, Mr. Christopher Stanley, BA ACA *1991;* 1 North Wall Quay, DUBLIN, COUNTY DUBLIN, IRELAND.
MASON, Mr. Clive, MA ACA *1983;* 16 Pavillion Close, Aldridge, WALSALL, WS9 8LS.
MASON, Mr. Colin Andrew, BA FCA *1985;* (Tax Fac), 2 Kings Gardens, Gonerby Hill Foot, GRANTHAM, LINCOLNSHIRE, NG31 8TY.
•**MASON, Mr. Colin John Stewart, FCA** *1971;* (Tax Fac), Mason Dharsi Limited, 29 Cuthbert Road, CROYDON, CR0 3RB.
MASON, Mr. Darren Clifford, ACA *1995;* 4 Polperro Close, NORMANTON, WEST YORKSHIRE, WF6 2SA.
•**MASON, Mr. Darren Michael, ACA MAAT** *2001;* Grant Thornton UK LLP, 30 Finsbury Square, LONDON, EC2P 2YU. See also Grant Thornton LLP
MASON, Mr. David Graham, BA ACA *1990;* 130 Tanjong Rhu Road, #11-05 Pebble Bay, SINGAPORE 436918, SINGAPORE.
MASON, Mr. David Kenneth Adlington, BSc FCA *1981;* Applecote, 5 Coolers Farm, Broughton, STOCKBRIDGE, SO20 8BN.
MASON, Mr. David Llewellyn, BA ACA *1980;* Glebe Farm, Helmdon, BRACKLEY, NN13 5QG.
•**MASON, Mr. David Michael, FCA** *1972;* Mallett Jones & Co, Lee House, 6a Highfield Road, Edgbaston, BIRMINGHAM, B15 3ED. See also Secretarial Administration Ltd
MASON, Mr. David Patrick Ellis, BA FCA *1959;* Berkswell, Rewlands Drive, WINCHESTER, SO22 6PA. (Life Member)
MASON, Mr. David Robert, BSc(Hons) ACA *2001;* 31 Moorlands Avenue, KENILWORTH, WARWICKSHIRE, CV8 1RZ.
MASON, Mr. David Stuart, FCA *1976;* Ballindarroch Cottage, Scaniport, INVERNESS, IV2 6DL.
MASON, Mr. David William, MA ACA *1979;* Aker Business Services Ltd, 1 Port Way, Port Solent, PORTSMOUTH, PO6 4TZ.
MASON, Mrs. Debra, BA ACA *1992;* with PricewaterhouseCoopers LLP, 1 Embankment Place, LONDON, WC2N 6RH.
MASON, Mr. Dennis William, FCA *1961;* 13 Exeter Road, CHICHESTER, PO19 5EF.
MASON, Miss. Emma Louise, MMath ACA *2006;* with PricewaterhouseCoopers, Princess Court, 23 Princess Street, PLYMOUTH, PL1 2EX.
MASON, Mr. Francis John, FCA *1958;* 7 Greenbanks, Llandogo, MONMOUTH, GWENT, NP25 4TG. (Life Member)
MASON, Frank Charles, Esq OBE FCA *1970;* (Tax Fac), 4 The Leys, Normanton on the Wolds, Keyworth, NOTTINGHAM, NG12 5NU.
MASON, Mr. Geoffrey, FCA *1960;* Apartment 38, Gorselands Court, Aigburth Vale, LIVERPOOL, L17 0DG.
MASON, Mr. Geoffrey Stuart, BSc ACA *1980;* 142 Higham Lane, TONBRIDGE, TN10 4BW.
•**MASON, Mr. George, FCA** *1959;* Mason + Co, Somerville House, 20-22 Harborne Road, Edgbaston, BIRMINGHAM, B15 3AA.
MASON, Miss. Georgina Marie, BSc ACA *2005;* 39 Shrubbery Avenue, WORCESTER, WR1 1QP.
MASON, Mr. Graham Ian, BSc ACA MBA *1991;* 20 Franklyn Gardens, Biddenham, BEDFORD, MK40 4QE.
MASON, Mr. Graham Vincent, BA ACA *2006;* 7 Dorrigo Avenue, NORTH BALGOWLAH, NSW 2093, AUSTRALIA.
MASON, Miss. Hannah Louise, ACA *2010;* 32 Chelkar Way, YORK, YO30 5ZH.
MASON, Mrs. Helen Mary, BSc ACA *2002;* 3 Hides Close, Winchester Road, WHITCHURCH, HAMPSHIRE, RG28 7HW.
MASON, Mr. Henry, BA ACA *2010;* Swan House, Wick Road, Langham, COLCHESTER, CO4 5PG.
MASON, Mr. Howard Brent, MA ACA *1981;* 5 Harbourside 1, PARADISE ISLAND, BAHAMAS.
•**MASON, Mr. Ian, BA FCA** *1983;* Ian Mason, 17 Glebe Park, Balderton, NEWARK, NG24 3GN.
MASON, Mr. Ian David, BSc ACA *1989;* PricewaterhouseCoopers AG, 50 Avenue Giuseppe-Motta, CH-1202 GENEVA, SWITZERLAND.
MASON, Mr. Ian James, BA(Hons) ACA *2009;* B301/55 Bay Street, PORT MELBOURNE, VIC 3207, AUSTRALIA.
MASON, Mr. Ian John, FCA *1977;* 29 Morningtons, HARLOW, CM19 4QH.
MASON, Mrs. Janet Cecilia, FCA *1986;* with W. Osborne & Co, Harwood House, Park Road, MELTON MOWBRAY, LE13 1TX.
MASON, Miss. Joanne Marie, BSc ACA *2005;* 57 Harpenden Rise, HARPENDEN, HERTFORDSHIRE, AL5 3BG.
MASON, Mr. John Avery, FCA *1970;* Cwm Rhondda, Park Road, BARRY, C562 6NU.
•**MASON, Mr. John Barry, FCA** *1970;* P.O Box 32269, Chichiri, BLANTYRE, 3, MALAWI.
MASON, Mr. John Francis Julian, FCA *1963;* 18 Dr. Brown's Close, Minchinhampton, STROUD, GL6 9DW. (Life Member)
MASON, Mr. John Hugh Montague, FCA *1966;* 3168 Deer Ridge Drive, WEST VANCOUVER V7S 4W1, BC, CANADA. (Life Member)
MASON, Mr. John Irsay, FCA *1955;* 3 Chapel Cottages, Hartfield Road, FOREST ROW, EAST SUSSEX, RH18 5BF. (Life Member)
MASON, Mr. John Michael, BA ACA *1982;* 21 Holly Grove, Paddington, WARRINGTON, WA1 3HB.
MASON, Mr. John Owen, MBA BA FCA *1987;* 39 Woodpark Drive, KNARESBOROUGH, HG5 9DN.
MASON, Mr. John Philip Fairfax, FCA *1966;* Duranton Services SA, 14 Rue Etienne-Dumont, PO Box 3145, 1211 GENEVA, SWITZERLAND.
MASON, Mr. Julian John Ramsay, MA FCA *1975;* 58 Belswains Lane, HEMEL HEMPSTEAD, HERTFORDSHIRE, HP3 9PP.
MASON, Mrs. Karen, BA ACA *1992;* 9 Townsend Close, Wyton, HUNTINGDON, PE28 2AR.
MASON, Miss. Karen, BSc ACA *1995;* 21 Cowper Road, HARPENDEN, HERTFORDSHIRE, AL5 5NF.
MASON, Mr. Keith John, BSc ACA *1986;* O F W A T, Centre City House, 7 Hill Street, BIRMINGHAM, B5 4UA.
•**MASON, Mr. Keith Jonathan, BSc FCA ATII** *1993;* Barnes Roffe LLP, 16-19 Copperfields, Spital Street, DARTFORD, DA1 2DE.
MASON, Mr. Keith William, BA ACA *1999;* with ICAEW, Metropolitan House, 321 Avebury Boulevard, MILTON KEYNES, MK9 2FZ.
MASON, Mr. Lee David, BSc ACA DipFDA *2003;* 34 Clifford Road, DROITWICH, WR9 8UR.
MASON, Mr. Leo Clifford, BA ACA *1986;* 124 Rugby Drive, Tytherington, MACCLESFIELD, SK10 2JF.
•**MASON, Mr. Michael Edward, FCA** *1975;* Michael E Mason FCA, PO Box 268, UCKFIELD, TN22 9DE.
MASON, Mr. Neil Laurence, BSc ACA *1995;* 27 Willow Way, Ponteland, NEWCASTLE UPON TYNE, NORTHUMBERLAND, NE20 9RF.
MASON, Mr. Nicholas, BA ACA *1983;* 145 Parkside, Wollaton, NOTTINGHAM, NG8 2NL.
MASON, Mr. Nicholas, BSc ACA *2006;* Hanson Aggregates The Ridge, Chipping Sodbury, BRISTOL, BS37 6AY.
MASON, Mr. Nicholas Erskine Home, FCA *1971;* C. Czarnikow Sugar Ltd, 24 Chiswell Street, LONDON, EC1Y 4SG.
MASON, Mr. Nicholas James, BA FCA *1999;* 171 Crescent Road, OXFORD, OX4 2NX.
MASON, Mrs. Nicola, MA(Cantab) ACA DChA *1999;* 14 Longcroft, Barton, PRESTON, PR3 5AL.
MASON, Miss. Nicola Sarah, ACA *2010;* 151 Wilsthorpe Road, Breaston, DERBY, DE72 3AF.
MASON, Mr. Nigel, BA ACA *1984;* 25 Bancroft Close, Hilton, DERBY, DE65 5WB.
MASON, Mr. Oliver, LLM ACA *2010;* 11 St. Ann Street, SALISBURY, SP1 2DP.
MASON, Mrs. Patricia Mary, ACA *1980;* (Tax Fac), with Mitchell Charlesworth, 24 Nicholas Street, CHESTER, CH1 2AU.
MASON, Mr. Paul Ashley, ACA *1993;* 28 Harvest Road, NORTH FREMANTLE, WA 6159, AUSTRALIA.
MASON, Mr. Paul Colin, BSc ACA *1995;* Fidelity Investment Management Ltd, Oakhill House, 130 Tonbridge Road, Hildenborough, TONBRIDGE, KENT TN11 9DZ.
MASON, Mr. Paul Lindsay, MA FCA *1976;* Manor Barn, Aldsworth, CHELTENHAM, GLOUCESTERSHIRE, GL54 3QZ.
MASON, Mr. Paul Trevor, FCA *1971;* Edif. Millenium Apt. 9A, 54th Street, PO Box 0843-00342, PANAMA CITY, PANAMA.
MASON, Mrs. Paula, BSc ACA *1994;* 27 Willow Way, Ponteland, NEWCASTLE UPON TYNE, NORTHUMBERLAND, NE20 9RF.
•**MASON, Mr. Peter David, FCA** *1973;* Peter Mason, 35 New Road, Great Kingshill, HIGH WYCOMBE, BUCKINGHAMSHIRE, HP15 6DR.
MASON, Mr. Peter Dennington, BSc FCA *1976;* The Gate House, Langley Road, Claverdon, WARWICK, CV35 8PJ.
MASON, Mr. Peter Jonathan, ACA *2009;* Church Cottage, Winterbourne, NEWBURY, BERKSHIRE, RG20 8AU.
MASON, Mr. Peter Robert, BSc(Hons) ACA ATII MCT *1988;* (Tax Fac), 48 Deacons Hill Road, Elstree, BOREHAMWOOD, HERTFORDSHIRE, WD6 3LH.
•**MASON, Mr. Peter William, FCA** *1972;* (Tax Fac), Armstrong Chase, Suite 1, Winwood Court, Norton Road, STOURBRIDGE, WEST MIDLANDS DY8 2AE.
MASON, Mr. Philip, FCA *1972;* Cross Lanes Farm House, Ashton Lane, Bishops Waltham, SOUTHAMPTON, SO32 1FR.
MASON, Mr. Philip Hugh, BSc ACA *1979;* Castell Management Ltd, 78 Widney Lane, SOLIHULL, B91 3LR.
MASON, Mr. Philip James, ACA *2002;* 37b Popes Lane, LONDON, W5 4NU.
•**MASON, Mrs. Rachel Anne, BMus ACA** *2003;* Rachel Mason, 31 Harefield Road, COVENTRY, CV2 4BX.
MASON, Dr. Rachel Elizabeth, ACA *1981;* 83 Durleigh Road, BRIDGWATER, TA6 7JD.
MASON, Miss. Rachel Emma, ACA *2005;* 9 Cams Hill, FAREHAM, HAMPSHIRE, PO16 8QY.
•**MASON, Mr. Richard David, FCA** *1980;* (Tax Fac), Percy Pemberton & Co, 11 Sandal Cliff, Sandal, WAKEFIELD, WF2 6AU.
•**MASON, Mr. Richard John Spencer, FCA** *1974;* (Tax Fac), Moore Stephens LLP, 150 Aldersgate Street, LONDON, EC1A 4AB. See also Moore Stephens & Co

MASON, Mr. Richard Michael, BA ACA CTA *1988;* (Tax Fac), 46 High Street, BRIGHOUSE, WEST YORKSHIRE, HD6 1DE.
MASON, Mr. Robert, BA ACA *1988;* with PricewaterhouseCoopers LLP, Donington Court, Pegasus Business Park, Castle Donington, DERBY, DE74 2UZ.
MASON, Mr. Roderick Stewart, BA(Econ) ACA CTA *2001;* 90 Parsonage Road, STOCKPORT, CHESHIRE, SK4 4JL.
MASON, Mr. Roger Stewart, FCA *1969;* 11 Hill Park, Ballakillowey, Colby, ISLE OF MAN, IM9 4BF.
MASON, Mr. Roy, FCA *1964;* 37 Summercourt Square, KINGSWINFORD, DY6 9QJ.
•**MASON, Mr. Russell, FCA CTA** *1993;* 9ine Accounting Limited, 76 Bridgford Road, West Bridgford, NOTTINGHAM, NG2 6AX.
MASON, Mr. Russell Bradley, BSc ACA *1990;* 17 Lister Street, ILKLEY, WEST YORKSHIRE, LS29 9ET.
•**MASON, Miss. Sarah Elizabeth, MEng FCA DChA** *1994;* Baker Tilly Tax & Advisory Services LLP, 1st Floor, 46 Clarendon Road, WATFORD, WD17 1JJ. See also Baker Tilly UK Audit LLP
MASON, Miss. Sarah Jane, BA ACA *1997;* Deutsche Bank, PO Box 135, LONDON, EC2A 2HE.
MASON, Mrs. Sarah Louise, BA ACA *1998;* The Dingle, Hazeley Heath, HOOK, RG27 8LZ.
MASON, Mr. Simon, BA(Hons) ACA *2011;* 20 Grove Road, SOUTHAMPTON, SO15 3GG.
MASON, Mr. Simon Christopher, LLB ACA *2003;* Flat 2, 10 Thornton Hill, LONDON, SW19 4HS.
MASON, Mr. Simon Richard, BSc ACA *2004;* with Bulley Davey, 6 North Street, Oundle, PETERBOROUGH, PE8 4AL.
MASON, Mr. Soren Graham, BA ACA *1981;* Vejlemosevej 7A, 2840 HOLTE, DENMARK.
MASON, Mrs. Stephanie, MA FCA DChA *1988;* with Baker Tilly Tax and Accounting Limited, St. Philips Point, Temple Row, BIRMINGHAM, B2 5AF.
MASON, Mr. Stephen James, BEng ACA *2005;* 43 Moorfields Road, Nailsea, BRISTOL, BS48 2AP.
•**MASON, Mr. Stephen John, BA ACA** *1993;* Baker Tilly Corporate Finance LLP, 25 Farringdon Street, LONDON, EC4A 4AB. See also Baker Tilly Tax and Advisory Services LLP
•**MASON, Mr. Stephen Robert, BSc ACA** *1992;* FKCA Limited, Prospero House, 46-48 Rothesay Road, LUTON, LU1 1QZ. See also Foxley Kingham Medical LLP
MASON, Mr. Steven John, BSc FCA *1986;* 123 Leicester Road, NEW BARNET, HERTFORDSHIRE, EN5 5EA.
MASON, Mr. Stuart Paul, BA ACA *2003;* 248 Spahr Street, PITTSBURGH, PA 15232, UNITED STATES.
MASON, Mr. Stuart Paul, BSc(Hons) ACA *2003;* 23a Finchcroft Lane, Prestbury, CHELTENHAM, GLOUCESTERSHIRE, GL52 5BD.
MASON, Mr. Swithun Joseph Kolbe, BSc FCA *1999;* 4 Beachside Cottages, La Rue Du Pont Grouville, JERSEY, JE3 9BT.
MASON, Mr. Terence Harold, FCA *1964;* Stratton Court, Long Common, Claverley, WOLVERHAMPTON, WV5 7AX. (Life Member)
MASON, Mr. Terence Victor, FCA *1980;* Alba Marlbrook Lane, Pattingham, WOLVERHAMPTON, WV6 7BS.
MASON, Mr. Theodore Islay Richard, BEng ACA *2000;* 85 Sommerville Road, BRISTOL, BS7 9AE.
MASON, Mr. Thomas, ACA *2009;* 38 Wellington Hill, BRISTOL, BS7 8SR.
MASON, Mr. Thomas Edward, LLB(Hons) ACA *2010;* 86b Victoria Road, ALTON, HAMPSHIRE, GU34 2DD.
MASON, Mrs. Tina Luisa Elisabeth, ACA *2002;* 26 Fennel Road, Portishead, BRISTOL, BS20 7FB.
MASON, Miss. Wendy, BSc ACA *2003;* 40 Park View, Wideopen, NEWCASTLE UPON TYNE, NE13 6LH.
MASON, Mrs. Wendy Frances, BSc ACA *2000;* 154 Moss Lane, Bramhall, STOCKPORT, SK7 1BG.
•**MASON, Mr. Wesley Stuart Leonard, ACA** *2002;* 22 Ames Way, Kings Hill, WEST MALLING, KENT, ME19 4HU.
MASON, Mr. William Peter, BA ACA *1990;* Flat 9 Denewood, 62 Worple Road, LONDON, SW19 4HB.
MASON-WILLIAMS, Mr. Michael David, BA FCA *1986;* K P M G Llp, 15 Canada Square, LONDON, E14 5GL.
MASOOD, Mr. Itrat, CA *2003; (CA Scotland* 309-1525 Pendrell Street, VANCOUVER V6G 1S6, BC, CANADA.
MASOOD, Mr. Salman, FCA *1975;* F11 4Th Gizri Street, Defence Housing Society, KARACHI, PAKISTAN.
MASOOD, Mr. Usman, BSc ACA *2010;* Tenon Ltd, 1 Bede Island Road, LEICESTER, LE2 7EA.
MASRI, Mr. Frederick Naji, MA DPhil FCA *1975;* 30 Horwood Close, OXFORD, OX3 7RF.
MASRI, Mr. Sammy Naji, MA FCA *1974;* Post Box 220126, Great Neck, NEW YORK, NY 11022, UNITED STATES.
MASROOR, Mr. Farooq, FCA *1993;* 696/4 Block Z Phase III, Defense Housing Authority, LAHORE 54792, PUNJAB, PAKISTAN.
•**MASSARELLA, Mr. Anthony Michael, BA FCA** *1974;* Business Focus & Systems Limited, 4 Chevin Mill, Leeds Road, OTLEY, WEST YORKSHIRE, LS21 1BT.
MASSER, Mr. Kenneth, BSc ACA *2011;* 10 Rifle Street, Haslingden, ROSSENDALE, LANCASHIRE, BB4 6NR.
MASSEY, Mr. Alan Joseph, BSc FCA *1964;* 10 Timberley Gardens, UCKFIELD, TN22 5SZ.
MASSEY, Mr. Alex James, ACA *2009;* 20 Elwill Way, BECKENHAM, KENT, BR3 3AD.
MASSEY, Mr. Alexander Russell, BA(Hons) ACA *2002;* Flat 21 Overstrand Mansions, Prince of Wales Drive, LONDON, SW11 4EZ.
MASSEY, Miss. Alison, BSc ACA *1993;* 15 Serin Close, NEWTON-LE-WILLOWS, WA12 9XL.
MASSEY, Mrs. Alison Eve, BA ACA *1992;* (Tax Fac), Merck Services UK, 1301 Hedon Road, HULL, HU9 5NJ.
MASSEY, Mr. Andrew Richard, FCA *1981;* 2230 Stratford Road, Hockley Heath, SOLIHULL, B94 6NU.
•**MASSEY, Mrs. Ann, FCA** *1973;* Ann Massey, 229 Ombersley Road, WORCESTER, WR3 7BY.
MASSEY, Mrs. Anne Gilian, BSc ACA *1980;* Ringmerit Limited, LCP House, Then Pensnett Estate, KINGSWINFORD, WEST MIDLANDS DY6 7NA.
MASSEY, Mr. Anthony Stephen, MA ACA *2009;* (Tax Fac), 143a Fawe Park Road, LONDON, SW15 2EG.
MASSEY, Mr. Christopher John, BSc ACA *2003;* 17 Chiltern Close, Ampthill, BEDFORD, MK45 2QA.
MASSEY, Mrs. Doreen Elizabeth, BSc ACA *1993;* 56 Shottery Road, STRATFORD-UPON-AVON, CV37 9QB.
•**MASSEY, Mrs. Jacqueline Susan, FCA** *1978;* Massey & Massey, Au Castillon, 32340 PLIEUX, FRANCE.
MASSEY, Mr. James Alan, BSc ACA *2001;* 8 Trefoil Close, WOKINGHAM, BERKSHIRE, RG40 5YQ.
MASSEY, Mrs. Jill Elizabeth Ann, FCA *1968;* 15 Hatch Close, Chapel Row, READING, RG7 6NZ. (Life Member)
MASSEY, Mr. John Michael, FCA *1960;* Penderlee, 3a Burntwood Road, SEVENOAKS, KENT, TN13 1PS.
MASSEY, Mr. Jonathan Hugh, FCA *1971;* Roseleigh House, North Moor Road, Walkeringham, DONCASTER, DN10 4LW.
MASSEY, Mrs. Kirsty Anne, MSc ACA *1997;* 61 Holt Road, North Elmham, DEREHAM, NORFOLK, NR20 5JS.
MASSEY, Miss. Leanne Charlotte, BSc ACA *2001;* 10 Laneside Hollow, NORTHAMPTON, NN4 0SR.
MASSEY, Miss. Pamela Anne, BSc ACA *1988;* 46 Market Street, Stoneclough, Radcliffe, MANCHESTER, M26 1HB.
MASSEY, Mr. Paul Andrew, ACA *1985;* (Tax Fac), 7 Harefield Grove, CHELTENHAM, GL50 2SJ.
MASSEY, Mr. Paul Ashley, MSc FCA *1978;* Summerford Oast The Green, Matfield, TONBRIDGE, TN12 7JU.
MASSEY, Mr. Paul Jonathan, BSc FCA *1998;* 34 Treadwell Road, EPSOM, KT18 5JX.
MASSEY, Mr. Peter James, FCA *1963;* Cymla Cottage, Gretton, CHELTENHAM, GL54 5EP.
MASSEY, Mr. Peter Kenneth, FCA FCCA *1973;* 7 Tabors Avenue, Great Baddow, CHELMSFORD, CM2 7ES.
MASSEY, Mr. Richard Antony, BSc ACA *1998;* 1 The Terrace, Church Street Shoreham, SEVENOAKS, TN14 7SN.
•**MASSEY, Mr. Richard John, BSc ACA** *2004;* Christian Douglass LLP, 2 Jordan Street, Knott Mill, MANCHESTER, M15 4PY.
MASSEY, Mr. Roger David, BA ACA *1986;* 2 Whitley Cottages, Nuffield Lane, Benson, WALLINGFORD, OX10 6QQ.
•**MASSEY, Mr. Simon James, FCA ATII** *1990;* (Tax Fac), Menzies LLP, Woking Office, Midas House, 62 Goldsworth Road, WOKING, SURREY GU21 6LQ.
MASSEY, Mr. Thomas Reid Edmonds, FCA *1975;* 28 Greencroft Gardens, LONDON, NW6 3LS.
MASSIAH, Mr. Christopher David, MA FCA *1963;* 76 Argyle Road, HARROW, HA2 7AJ.
MASSIE, Miss. Brenda Mary, LLB ACA *2001;* 3/2 37 Edgemont Street, GLASGOW, G41 3EJ.
MASSIE, Mr. Graham John, BSc FCA *1982;* Centre for Effective Dispute Resolution, 70 Fleet Street, LONDON, EC4Y 1EU.
MASSIE, Mr. Ian, FCA *1954;* 62 Woodland Drive, Anlaby, HULL, HU10 7HX. (Life Member)
MASSIE, Mrs. Naomi, BA(Hons) ACA *2001;* 33 Great Percy Street, LONDON, WC1X 9RD.
MASSING, Mr. Alan Harvey, FCA *1956;* 6 Bentley Lodge, 182 High Road, Bushey Heath, BUSHEY, WD23 1NS. (Life Member)
•**MASSING, Mr. Jonathan Fraser, BSc** *1984;* Kingswood, 3 Coldbath Square, LONDON, EC1R 5HL. See also Kingswood Corporate Finance Limited
•**MASSINGALE, Mrs. Moira, FCA** *1974;* (Tax Fac), Gant Massingale, Fairlight, Meadway, BERKHAMSTED, HP4 2PN.
•**MASSINGBERD-MUNDY, Mrs. Janet, FCA** *1980;* (Tax Fac), W.R. Kewley & Co, The Old Post Office, The Street, West Raynham, FAKENHAM, NORFOLK NR21 7AD.
MASSINGHAM, Ms. Janice Ann, BSc ACA *1988;* 183 Fallsbrook Road, LONDON, SW16 6DY.
MASSINGHAM, Mr. Keith John, FCA *1965;* 7 Larkshall Road, North Chingford, LONDON, E4 7HS. (Life Member)
MASSON, Mr. Bruce Edward, BA(Hons) ACA *2003;* 66 Wardo Avenue, LONDON, SW6 6RE.
MASSON, Miss. Helene Michelle, BA(Hons) ACA *2009;* 1 Sunhill Cottages, Croit-E-Quill Road, Laxey, ISLE OF MAN, IM4 7JJ.
MASSON, Mr. Ian Hamilton Maclean, BCom ACA CA(SA) *1981;* 2 Soetvlei Avenue, Constantia Hills, CAPE TOWN, 7806, SOUTH AFRICA.
MASSON, Mr. Kenneth Ely Brooke, FCA *1957;* (Tax Fac), Fleet House, Bosham Hoe, Bosham, CHICHESTER, WEST SUSSEX, PO18 8ES. (Life Member)
MASSON, Mrs. Michelle Suzanne, BSc ACA *2006;* 66 Wardo Avenue, LONDON, SW6 6RE.
MASSON, Mr. Stephen Clark, BSc FCA *1990;* The Sanger Centre, Wellcome Trust Genome Campus, Hinxton, Cambridge, SAFFRON WALDEN, ESSEX CB10 1SA.
MAST, Dr. Isabelle Veronica, MA MSt ACA *2001;* Fidelity Investments Ltd, 25 Cannon Street, LONDON, EC4M 5TA.
•**MASTERMAN-SMITH, Mrs. Fiona, BA FCA** *1982;* (Tax Fac), Harper Broom, Aston House, York Road, Maidenhead, MAIDENHEAD, BERKSHIRE SL6 1SF.
MASTERS, Mr. Alexis David, MA ACA *1998;* Rothschild (Singapore) Limited, One Raffles Quay, North Tower, 1 Raffles Quay 10-02, SINGAPORE 048583, SINGAPORE.
•**MASTERS, Mr. Benjamin John, BSc(Hons) ACA** *2004;* HSJ Accountants Limited, Severn House, Hazell Drive, NEWPORT, GWENT, NP10 8FY.
MASTERS, Mrs. Carol Susan, MSc BSc FCA *1988;* 40 Mousehole Lane, Midanbury, SOUTHAMPTON, SO18 4EY.
MASTERS, Mr. Christopher Paul, FCA *1965;* 32 Arun Vale, Coldwaltham, PULBOROUGH, WEST SUSSEX, RH20 1LP. (Life Member)
MASTERS, Mr. Craig Douglas, BA ACA *2002;* 52 Orchard Drive, WATFORD, WD17 3DY.
MASTERS, Mr. Daniel James, BSc ACA *1991;* 37 Azalea Close, Napsbury Park, London Colney, ST. ALBANS, HERTFORDSHIRE, AL2 1UA.
MASTERS, Mr. Darren Raymond, ACA *1992;* 13 Monkhams Avenue, WOODFORD GREEN, ESSEX, IG8 0HB.
MASTERS, Mr. David, BSc ACA *1996;* 122 The Lakes, Larkfield, AYLESFORD, KENT, ME20 6FY.
MASTERS, Mr. David, BSc ACA *2005;* 30 The Paddock, GODALMING, GU7 1XD.
MASTERS, Mr. David, FCA *1964;* 74 Kechill Gardens, Hayes, BROMLEY, BR2 7NG.
MASTERS, Mr. Dudley Redway, FCA *1966;* 17 Penrhos, Radyr, CARDIFF, CF15 8RJ.
MASTERS, Mr. Graham John, FCA *1978;* South House, 5a Maltings Road, Gretton, CORBY, NN17 3BZ.
MASTERS, Mr. Henry John, FCA *1962;* 37b County Gate, New Barnet, BARNET, HERTFORDSHIRE, EN5 1EH. (Life Member)
MASTERS, Mr. Ian, ACA *2009;* 2 Long Sutton Drive, FLEET, HAMPSHIRE, GU51 1EA.
MASTERS, Mr. John Paul James, BSc ACA *1994;* 48 Heath Court, LEIGHTON BUZZARD, BEDFORDSHIRE, LU7 3JR.
MASTERS, Mr. Jonathan Ian, BA ACA *1988;* 8th Floor, 55 Bryanston Street, LONDON, W1H 7AA.
MASTERS, Mr. Jonathan Patrick, BSc ACA *1984;* A-Gas Intl Holdings Ltd, Clifton Heights, Triangle West, BRISTOL, BS8 1EJ.
MASTERS, Mr. Julian James, BSocSc ACA *1999;* Bowmark Capital Llp, 3 St. James's Square, LONDON, SW1Y 4JU.
MASTERS, Miss. Katharine, BSc ACA *1990;* Covance Laboratories Ltd, Otley Road, HARROGATE, NORTH YORKSHIRE, HG3 1PY.
MASTERS, Miss. Lee, BSc ACA *1991;* Garden Cottage, Nettleden Road, Little Gaddesden, BERKHAMSTED, HERTFORDSHIRE, HP4 1PN.
MASTERS, Mrs. Lucilla Marie-Madeleine Lascelles, BA ACA *1996;* 3 Fassett Road, KINGSTON UPON THAMES, SURREY, KT1 2TD.
MASTERS, Mrs. Mary Julia Caroline, LLB ACA *1993;* 37 Azalea Close, Napsbury Park, London Colney, ST. ALBANS, HERTFORDSHIRE, AL2 1UA.
MASTERS, Miss. Nicola, BSc ACA *2009;* Metlife, 1 Canada Square, LONDON, E14 5AA.
MASTERS, Miss. Nicola Louise, BA ACA *2005;* 8 Plattes Close, Shaw, SWINDON, SN5 5SA.
MASTERS, Mr. Paul, BSc(Hons) ACA MBA *1992;* 14 Stroud Close, WINDSOR, SL4 4YR.
MASTERS, Mr. Paul, BA FCA *1979;* Kingsmead, 14 Westview Road, WARLINGHAM, CR6 9JD.
•①**MASTERS, Mr. Paul David, BSc FCA FSPI** *1988;* Leonard Curtis, 85-89 Colmore Row, BIRMINGHAM, B3 2BB. See also DTE Leonard Curtis Limited
MASTERS, Mr. Paul Stanton, FCA *1975;* Corney & Barrow Group Limited, 1 Thomas More Street, LONDON, E1W 1YZ.
•**MASTERS, Mr. Robert, FCA** *1976;* (Tax Fac), RMCA Ltd, The Counting House, 9 High Street, TRING, HERTFORDSHIRE, HP23 5TE. See also Pulse Accountants Limited
•**MASTERS, Mr. Roger Gerald, FCA** *1972;* (Tax Fac), Masters, Knoll Cottage, 15 Gills Hill, RADLETT, WD7 8DA.
MASTERS, Baroness Sheila Valerie, DBE LLB FCA *1973;* (President 1999 - 2000) (Member of Council 1987 - 2002), Church House, High Street, GOUDHURST, TN17 1AJ.
•**MASTERS, Mr. Stephen Charles Alexander, BA ACA** *1992;* KPMG LLP, 15 Canada Square, LONDON, E14 5GL. See also KPMG Europe LLP, KPMG Audit plc
MASTERS, Mr. Steven, ACA *2007;* Flat 166 Ruskin Park House, Champion Hill, LONDON, SE5 8TL.
MASTERS, Mr. Timothy Adrian, BSc FCA *1989;* 75 Highbank, HAYWARDS HEATH, WEST SUSSEX, RH16 4TT.
MASTERS, Mr. Timothy Peter, BA ACA *1998;* 31 Firecrest Road, BASINGSTOKE, HAMPSHIRE, RG22 5UL.
MASTERS, William Frederick, Esq MBE FCA *1938;* David Gresham House, 226 Pollards Oak Road, Hurst Green, OXTED, RH8 0JP. (Life Member)
MASTERS-THOMAS, Mr. Peter Geoffrey, FCA *1952;* 76 Main Road, Wilby, WELLINGBOROUGH, NN8 2UE. (Life Member)
MASTERSON, Mr. Colin Raymond Wellings, FCA *1969;* The Meridian, 8 Penarth Portway, PENARTH, SOUTH GLAMORGAN, CF64 1SQ.
MASTERSON, Mr. Michael John, BA ACA *1990;* The Old Vicarage, High Street, Hardingstone, NORTHAMPTON, NN4 6BZ.
MASTERSON, Mr. Neil Thomas, BA ACA *1995;* 411 East 53rd Street, Apartment 10H, NEW YORK, NY 10022, UNITED STATES.
MASTERSON, Mr. Peter Thomas, FCA *1959;* 10 Tudor Mansions, Beach Road Birkdale, SOUTHPORT, PR8 2BP. (Life Member)
MASTERTON, Miss. Deborah Mary, BSc ACA *2007;* The Crocks, Naisby Drive, Great Brickhill, BUCKINGHAM, MK17 9BL.
MASTERTON, Mr. Graham Bruce, BAcc ACA *2002;* 29 Leverton Gate, SWINDON, SN3 1ND.
MASTERTON, Mr. Noel John, FCA *1956;* 59 Manor Road, Dorridge, SOLIHULL, B93 8DZ. (Life Member)
MASTERTON, Miss. Rachel Anna-Marie, BA ACA *2002;* Flat 3, 22 Sheen Gate Gardens, LONDON, SW14 7NY.
MASTERTON, Mrs. Sally Beresford, ACA *1987;* Kinniny Braes Crombie Point, Crombie, DUNFERMLINE, FIFE, KY12 8LQ.
MASTORIS, Mrs. Carol Lynne, BA ACA *1992;* 4701 Hedgemore Drive, CHARLOTTE, NC 28209, UNITED STATES.
MASTOROUDES, Miss. Virginia Nicholas, BCom ACA *2004;* 3a Chaironias Street, 3055 LIMASSOL, CYPRUS.
MASTROGIOVANNI, Miss. Mariana, BSc ACA *2010;* Flat 3, 54 Kingswood Road, LONDON, SW2 4JJ.
MATA, Mrs. Gabrielle Louise, ACA CA(SA) *2009;* Bishop Challoner Catholic Collegiate School, Hardinge Street, LONDON, E1 0EB.
MATAR, Mr. Mohamed, BSC ACA *2011;* Spencer Heights, Flat 16, 28 Bartholomew Close, LONDON, EC1A 7ES.

MATCHAM, Mrs. Janet, MA ACA *1998;* Welfare Road, LODI, ST. EUSTATIUS, NETHERLANDS ANTILLES.
MATCHAM, Mr. Keith, BSc ACA *1989;* 2043 Malbrook Road, OAKVILLE L6J 1YB, ON, CANADA.
MATCHETT, Mrs. Geraldine, MPhil BSc ACA *2001;* La Daille, Route des Arénys, 1261 LE VAUD, SWITZERLAND.
•**MATE, Mr. Andrew Paul, FCA** *1985;* (Tax Fac), Platt Rushton LLP, Sutherland House, 1759 London Road, LEIGH-ON-SEA, ESSEX, SS9 2RZ. See also Sutherland Corporate Services Ltd
MATE, Miss. Matambira Judy, MBA ACA *1988;* 10125 Turnberry Place, OAKTON, VA 22124, UNITED STATES.
MATEER, Mr. Ian William, FCA *1973;* Summerhill, 18 Russell Avenue, SWANAGE, DORSET, BH19 2ED.
MATEER, Mr. Roy Steele, BSc FCA *1973;* 47 Oatlands Road, Shinfield, READING, RG2 9DN.
•**MATEJTSCHUK, Mrs. Susan Carol, FCA** *1984;* (Tax Fac), S.C. M. Accountancy Services Ltd, 28 Witter Avenue, Ickleford, HITCHIN, SG5 3UF.
MATEMERA, Ms. Lucille Kudakwashe, ACA *2011;* KPMG Channel Islands Limited, 20 New Street, ST PETER PORT, GY1 4AN.
MATHARU, Mrs. Baljit Kaur, BA(Hons) ACA *2002;* Lloyds Pharamacy Ltd, Sapphire Court, Coventry Walsgrave Triangle, COVENTRY, CV2 2TX.
MATHARU, Mr. Balraj Singh, MA(Hons) ACA *2010;* 34 Kingswood Gardens, LEEDS, LS8 2BH.
•**MATHARU, Mrs. Davinder Kaur, BSc FCA** *1989;* LSD Accountants Ltd, 21 Stockwood Business Centre, REDDITCH, WORCESTERSHIRE, B96 6SX.
MATHARU, Miss. Evie, BSc ACA *2007;* 59 Benton Road, ILFORD, IG1 4AS.
MATHARU, Mr. Harvinder-Pal, BA ACA *1997;* Hillview, Goatacre Road, Medstead, ALTON, GU34 5PU.
MATHARU, Mr. Narinder Singh, BA ACA *1994;* 9 Oakington Avenue, Little Chalfont, AMERSHAM, BUCKINGHAMSHIRE, HP6 6SY.
MATHARU, Mrs. Rominda, ACA *1996;* (Tax Fac), Kirrik, 24 Brook Road, LOUGHTON, ESSEX, IG10 1BW.
MATHER, Miss. Angela Denise, BSc(Econ) ACA *1998;* Garden Flat, 6 Randall Road, Clifton, BRISTOL, BS8 4TP.
MATHER, Mr. Christopher Macqueen, BA ACA *2005;* Basement Flat, 19 Leathwaite Road, LONDON, SW11 1XG.
MATHER, Mr. Colin Stuart, FCA *1960;* 46 Davenport Avenue, HESSLE, HU13 0RP. (Life Member)
•**MATHER, Mr. David, FCA** *1973;* AIMS - David Mather, 19 St Christophers Close, Upton, CHESTER, CH2 1EJ.
MATHER, Mr. Denys Raymond Alexander, FCA *1954;* South Barn, Manor Farm, Laddingford, MAIDSTONE, ME18 6BX. (Life Member)
MATHER, Mr. Derek, LLB FCA *1952;* 16 Thorp Arch Park, Thorp Arch, WETHERBY, LS23 7AN. (Life Member)
MATHER, Mrs. Georgina Margaret, BSc ACA *1991;* Barton House, Church Street, TETBURY, GL8 8JG.
MATHER, Mr. James Selvanathan, BSc FCA *1959;* Apartment No. 9/4, Queen's Court, 22 Queen's Road, 3 COLOMBO, SRI LANKA.
MATHER, Mrs. Jane Pamela, BA FCA *1988;* 18 Marlborough Avenue, HESSLE, HU13 0PN.
MATHER, Miss. Jennifer Mary, BSc(Hons) ACA *2003;* with KPMG LLP, 757 Third Avenue, NEW YORK, NY 10017, UNITED STATES.
MATHER, Mr. John, LLB FCA *1953;* C01, 39 Springfield Av, CHESTERFIELD, S40 1HL. (Life Member)
MATHER, Mr. John Frederick, FCA *1977;* 7 Thorneycroft, LEIGH, WN7 2TH.
MATHER, Mr. Jonathan Paul, BA ACA *1995;* 38 Derbyshire Road, SALE, M33 3EE.
•①**MATHER, Mr. Neil John, BSc FCA MABRP** *1990;* Begbies Traynor, 32 Cornhill, LONDON, EC3V 3BT. See also Begbies Traynor(Central) LLP and Begbies Traynor Limited
MATHER, Mr. Nicholas Charles Holt, ACA *1983;* Newells House, Newells Lane, Cutmill Bosham, CHICHESTER, PO18 8PS.
MATHER, Mr. Nicholas Richard, BA ACA *1986;* Lambda House, Christopher Martin Road, BASILDON, SS14 3EL.
MATHER, Dr. Paul Julian, BSc ACA *2000;* 79 Verulam Road, ST. ALBANS, HERTFORDSHIRE, AL3 4DJ.
MATHER, Dr. Paul Rohan, PhD MA FCA FCPA *1980;* School of Accounting, La Trobe University, BUNDOORA, VIC 3086, AUSTRALIA.
MATHER, Mr. Philip John, BSc ACA *1999;* 1 The Kingsway, TORONTO M8X 2S9, ON, CANADA.
MATHER, Mr. Roger Thomas, BA FCA *1991;* Mulberry Co (Design) Ltd The Rookery, Chilcompton, RADSTOCK, BA3 4EH.
MATHER, Mr. Simon, ACA *2008;* Apartment 203, Lanai 1177, Uehara, Shibuya-ku 2-11-10, TOKYO, 151-0064 JAPAN.
MATHER, Mrs. Teleri Wyn, BA ACA *2001;* The Exchange Tower, 130 King Street West, TORONTO M5X 1J2, ON, CANADA.
•**MATHER, Mr. Vincent Francis, FCA** *1979;* V F Mather & Co, 4 Houldsworth Square, Reddish, STOCKPORT, SK5 7AF.
•**MATHERS, Mr. Adrian, FCA** *1992;* Venthams Limited, Millhouse, 32-38 East Street, ROCHFORD, SS4 1DB.
•**MATHERS, Mr. Alastair McLeod, BSc FCA** *1992;* (Tax Fac), Stiddard Mathers Limited, Kent CCC, Worsley Bridge Road, BECKENHAM, KENT, BR3 1RL.
MATHERS, Mrs. Alison, BA ACA *1980;* Deira, Station Road South, PETERCULTER, AB14 0LL.
MATHERS, Mr. Alistair Henry, FCA *1969;* AHM Finincial Consultancy, 4 Golf Course Road, Stanton-on-the-Wolds, Keyworth, NOTTINGHAM, NG12 5BH.
MATHERS, Mr. David Stuart, BSc ACA CF *1984;* Appletreewick, Three Households, CHALFONT ST. GILES, BUCKINGHAMSHIRE, HP8 4LL.
MATHERS, Mrs. Gillian Elisabeth, BA ACA *1991;* 17 The Hermitage, RICHMOND, TW10 6SH.
MATHERS, Miss. Katriona, MSc ACA *2003;* with National Audit Office, 157-197 Buckingham Palace Road, Victoria, LONDON, SW1W 9SP.
•**MATHERS, Mr. Kenneth Edgar, FCA** *1968;* K.E. Mathers & Co, Nethercroft, Upper Batley Lane, BATLEY, WF17 0AR.
MATHERS, Mr. Peter John, BA ACA CTA *1992;* 2 Hornbeam Close, Elizabeth Park Barkham, WOKINGHAM, RG41 4UR.
MATHESON, Mr. Andrew James, BA ACA *1992;* 11706 Glenhurst Street, MAPLE RIDGE V2X 2K6, BC, CANADA.
MATHESON, Miss. Beth Verity, BSc ACA *2005;* 85 Grove Lane, LONDON, SE5 8SN.
MATHESON, Miss. Eleanor Ruth, BSc ACA *2005;* 105 Wakehurst Road, LONDON, SW11 6BZ.
MATHESON, Mr. James, FCA *1966;* Magnolia House, Shirwell, BARNSTAPLE, EX31 4JU.
MATHESON, Mrs. Louisa Eelin, MA MSc ACA *2005;* 15 Henslow Mews, CAMBRIDGE, CB2 8BX.
MATHESON, Mr. Neil John, BSc FCA *1977;* 12 Grace Close, WHITFIELD, QLD 4870, AUSTRALIA.
•**MATHESON, Mrs. Tania, ACA CTA** *1998;* 7 Clover Close, BIGGLESWADE, BEDFORDSHIRE, SG18 8SS.
MATHESON, Mr. Trevor Ernest Graham, FCA *1972;* No. 609, 1415 St Georges Avenue, NORTH VANCOUVER V7L 4R9, BC, CANADA.
MATHEW, Mr. Bivin Thomas, MSc ACA *2010;* 277 Albany Road, CARDIFF, CF24 3NX.
MATHEW, Mr. Charles Christopher Bruce, MA FCA *1971;* Parsonage House, Main Road, Stanton Harcourt, WITNEY, OX29 5RP.
MATHEW, Mr. Vergis, FCA *1975;* 2 Jalan Perwira 2, Taman Titiwangsa, 86000 KLUANG, Johor, MALAYSIA.
•**MATHEW-JONES, Mr. Hugh Robert, BA FCA** *1986;* PKF (UK) LLP, Farringdon Place, 20 Farringdon Road, LONDON, EC1M 3AP.
•**MATHEW-JONES, Mr. Trevor John, LLB ACA** *1982;* Trevor J Mathew-Jones, 30 Bertram Drive, Hoylake, WIRRAL, MERSEYSIDE, CH47 0LQ.
MATHEWS, Mr. Andrew John, LLB ACA *2001;* Conferma Ltd, 4 Lapwing Lane, MANCHESTER, M20 2WS.
MATHEWS, Mrs. Benita Alice Rolt, BA FCA *1976;* 44 Alwyne Road, Wimbledon, LONDON, SW19 7AE.
MATHEWS, Mr. Damian Gregory, BSc ACA *2001;* Commonwealth Bank of Australia, 599 Lexington Avenue (Level 17), NEW YORK, NY 10022, UNITED STATES.
MATHEWS, Miss. Joanne Kate, ACA *2010;* Flat 4, 55 Buckley Road, LONDON, NW6 7LX.
MATHEWS, Mrs. Margaret Jane, BSc FCA *1980;* 48 Byng Drive, POTTERS BAR, HERTFORDSHIRE, EN6 1UF.
MATHEWS, Mrs. Rebecca Jane, BSc(Hons) ACA *2004;* 24 Green Lane, Radnage, HIGH WYCOMBE, BUCKINGHAMSHIRE, HP14 4DN.
•**MATHEWS, Mr. Roger Gordon, FCA** *1962;* (Tax Fac), Roger Mathews, 10 Durrington Park Road, Wimbledon, LONDON, SW20 8NX.
•**MATHEWS, Mr. Stephen Henry, MA FCA** *1982;* Stephen Matthews, 5 Detillens Lane, OXTED, SURREY, RH8 0DH.
MATHEWS, Mr. Wayne Brinley, BSc ACA *1983;* 24 Glendale Drive, LONDON, SW19 7BG.
MATHEWSON, Mr. David Eric Mark, FCA *1976;* The Coach House, Carclew Street, TRURO, CORNWALL, TR1 2DZ.
•**MATHIAS, Ms. Ann Sarah, BA ACA** *1986;* Fulling Ridge, 30 Oakhill Drive, WELWYN, HERTFORDSHIRE, AL6 9NW.
MATHIAS, Mr. Anthony Robert, MBA BEng ACA *1994;* 7 Maryland Place, South West, CALGARY T2S 4EV, AB, CANADA.
MATHIAS, Mr. Charles Frederick Wynn, BSc ACA *1987;* 11 Glentham Road, Barnes, LONDON, SW13 9JB.
MATHIAS, Mr. Derek Peter, FCA *1968;* Millgarth Back Road, Lindale, GRANGE-OVER-SANDS, CUMBRIA, LA11 6LQ.
•**MATHIAS, Mr. Dermot Colin Anthony, BSc FCA** *1976;* The Old Mill, Berry Lane, Blewbury, DIDCOT, OX11 9QJ.
MATHIAS, Mr. Edgar George, FCA *1934;* Penrith, Down Road, TAVISTOCK, PL19 9AG. (Life Member)
MATHIAS, Miss. Emma Louise, BSc ACA *2005;* 7 St. Helens Road, CARDIFF, CF14 4AR.
•**MATHIAS, Mr. Jon Ashwoode, FCA FCCA MAE** *1969;* Golborne Old Hall, Tattenhall, CHESTER, CH3 9DR.
MATHIAS, Mr. Jonathan Cushman, BSc FCA *1977;* Starborough Manor Moor Lane, Marsh Green, EDENBRIDGE, KENT, TN8 5QY.
MATHIAS, Mr. Michael Charles Egerton, FCA *1971;* C S L Business Machines Ltd, 28-34 Hinckley Road, LEICESTER, LE3 0RA.
MATHIAS, Mr. Nicholas Jeremy, FCA *1973;* Nine Acres, Chesham Road, Wiggington, TRING, HP23 6JE.
MATHIAS, Mr. Paul John, FCA *1972;* Lias Cottage, 120 Station Road, Clutton, BRISTOL, BS39 5PD. (Life Member)
MATHIAS, Mrs. Sarah Louise, BSc ACA *1989;* 11 Glentham Road, LONDON, SW13 9JB.
MATHIESON, Mr. Alistair David, MA ACA *2000;* Hillsborough, Hollocombe, CHULMLEIGH, DEVON, EX18 7QE.
MATHIESON, Ms. Elinor Cecelia, MA ACA *1998;* with PKF (UK) LLP, New Guild House, 45 Great Charles Street, BIRMINGHAM, B3 2LX.
•**MATHIESON, Mrs. Elizabeth Anne, BA FCA** *1976;* (Tax Fac), E A Mathieson Associates Ltd, 97 Broomleaf Road, FARNHAM, SURREY, GU9 8DH.
•**MATHIESON, Mr. Ian Forsyth, BSc FCA** *1994;* PKF (UK) LLP, Farringdon Place, 20 Farringdon Road, LONDON, EC1M 3AP.
MATHIESON, Mrs. Joanna Frances, BSc ACA *2000;* The Lagger, Lagger Lane, South Woodchester, STROUD, GLOUCESTERSHIRE, GL5 5EJ.
•**MATHIESON, Mr. Kenneth Norman, BSc ACA** *1990;* ETM Consulting Limited, The Old Stables, Hendal Farm, Groombridge, TUNBRIDGE WELLS, KENT TN3 9NU.
MATHIESON, Mrs. Kristina Annette, FCA *1995;* (Tax Fac), Thomson Snell & Passmore, 3 Lonsdale Gardens, TUNBRIDGE WELLS, KENT, TN1 1NX.
MATHIESON, Mr. Muir James, BSc ACA *1999;* The Lagger Lagger Lane, South Woodchester, STROUD, GLOUCESTERSHIRE, GL5 5EJ.
MATHIESON, Mr. Shane Vincent Norman, ACA CA(NZ) *2009;* E D & F Man Holdings Ltd, Cottons Centre, Hays Lane, LONDON, SE1 2QE.
MATHIESON, Mr. Stuart David, FCA *1971;* Springfield Lodge, Colchester Road, CHELMSFORD, CM2 5PW.
MATHIESON, Mr. Stuart Ian, MA ACA *2002;* Babson Capital, 61 Aldwych, LONDON, WC2B 4AE.
MATHISON, Mr. John Arthur, BSc(Econ) FCA *1958;* Via Zandonai 75, 00135 ROME, ITALY. (Life Member)
MATHON, Mr. Dominic James Alexander, MA ACA *1997;* 238 Caledonian Road, LONDON, N1 0NG.
MATHUR, Mr. Anil Kumar, FCA *1980;* Linton Park Plc, Linton, MAIDSTONE, KENT, ME17 4AB.
MATHUR, Miss. Anita, BSc(Hons) ACA *2000;* 8 Knottocks End, BEACONSFIELD, BUCKINGHAMSHIRE, HP9 2AN.
MATHUR, Mr. Ashok Jang Bahadur, FCA *1980;* PED-ADIA, PO Box 3600, ABU DHABI, UNITED ARAB EMIRATES.
MATHUR, Mr. Satish, BA FCA *1979;* 55 Caswell Road, Caswell, SWANSEA, SA3 4RH.
MATHYS, Miss. Claire, BA ACA *2011;* 1 Beresford Road, SUTTON, SURREY, SM2 6EW.
MATIK, Mr. Miloslav, BA ACA *1999;* 33 The Fairway, RUISLIP, HA4 0SP.
MATISCHOK, Mr. Paul Jason, ACA MAAT *2010;* Linton, Ffordd Gwynach, RUTHIN, CLWYD, LL15 1DE.
MATKIN, Miss. Lucinda, MSc BSc ACA *2007;* 10 Malthouse Close, Wirksworth, MATLOCK, DE4 4FT.
MATKIN, Mrs. Melodie Lucia, ACA CTA *2001;* 42 Windmill Lane, BELPER, DERBYSHIRE, DE56 1GN.
•**MATKINS, Mr. David Brian, MA FCA** *1986;* Bourner Bullock, Sovereign House, 212-224 Shaftesbury Avenue, LONDON, WC2H 8HQ.
•**MATLEY, Mr. David Nuttall, FCA** *1974;* (Tax Fac), D. Matley & Co, 500 Hartshill Road, Hartshill, STOKE-ON-TRENT, ST4 6AD.
MATLEY, Mr. Edward John, BSc ACA *1999;* PO Box 5550, SQUAMISH V8B 0C2, BC, CANADA.
MATLEY, Mr. Mark, ACA *2011;* 24 Portland Drive, HINCKLEY, LEICESTERSHIRE, LE10 1SE.
MATON, Mr. Andrew Mark, ACA MCT *1991;* 10 Lucastes Road, HAYWARDS HEATH, WEST SUSSEX, RH16 1JL.
MATON, Mr. John Charles, FCA *1965;* Stour View House, 39a Wick Lane, CHRISTCHURCH, BH23 1HU. (Life Member)
•**MATON, Mr. Michael Grant, FCA** *1961;* Tudor House, Westmancote, TEWKESBURY, GL20 7ES.
MATON, Mr. Richard, BA(Hons) ACA *2011;* Willow House, 11 The Pastures, LONDON, N20 8AN.
MATON, Mr. Steven Roger, BA FCA *1982;* Legal & General Investment Management, 1 Coleman Street, LONDON, EC2R 5AA.
•**MATON, Mr. Timothy, BSc ACA** *1989;* Armida Limited, Bell Walk House, High Street, UCKFIELD, TN22 5DQ. See also Armida Business Recovery LLP
MATRANGA, Mr. Matthew John, BA ACA *2005;* Flat 8 Trafalgar Court, Waterloo Road, STOKE-ON-TRENT, ST6 3JS.
•**MATRAVERS, Mr. Malcolm David, BA FCA CTA** *1977;* Matravers, Bridgewater House, Caspian Road, Atlantic Street, Broadheath, ALTRINCHAM CHESHIRE WA14 5HH. See also Matravers & Co
MATSON, Mr. David Howard, FCA *1972;* 7 Knoll Croft, Shirley, SOLIHULL, B90 4JL.
MATSON, Mr. Paul Dominic, ACA *1992;* Lower Nappers Farm Vann Road, Fernhurst, HASLEMERE, GU27 3JN.
MATSON, Mr. Robert William Nelson, BA ACA *1996;* 45 Cahard Road, BALLYNAHINCH, COUNTY DOWN, BT24 8YD.
MATTAR, Mr. Antoine Naim, BA FCA *1960;* CCC House, 11a West Halkin Street, LONDON, SW1X 8JL.
MATTAR, Miss. Deena Elizabeth, BSc FCA *1990;* 71a West Common, HARPENDEN, HERTFORDSHIRE, AL5 2LD.
MATTAR, Mr. Timothy Antoine, BA ACA *1989;* Investcorp Bank EC, P.O. Box 5340, MANAMA, BAHRAIN.
MATTEN, Mr. Christopher Paul, BA FCA *1985;* with PricewaterhouseCoopers LLP, 17-00 PWC Building, 8 Cross Street, SINGAPORE 048424, SINGAPORE.
MATTEY, Mr. David Gary, BA ACA *1986;* Ultratown Ltd, Lawrence House, Goodwyn Avenue, LONDON, NW7 3RH.
MATTEY, Mr. David Gordon, FCA *1967;* Greenlands House, Foots Hill, Cann, SHAFTESBURY, DORSET, SP7 0BW. (Life Member)
MATTEY, Mr. Rob, BA(Hons) ACA *2003;* Flat 45GH Tower 2, The Pacifica, 9 Sham Shing Road, LAI CHI KOK, KOWLOON, HONG KONG SAR.
MATTHAI, Mr. Arjun Yohanan, BA FCA *1978;* 31 Cranbourne Gdns, LONDON, NW11 0HS.
MATTHAMS, Mr. William James, BA FCA *1976;* (Tax Fac), 15 Cloudesley Place, Islington, LONDON, N1 0JA.
MATTHEW, Mr. Malcolm Gordon, BCom FCA *1973;* 32 rue Huron, Dollard-des-Ormeaux, MONTREAL H9G 2C3, QUE, CANADA.
MATTHEW, Mr. Philip Gregory, FCA *1964;* 19 Prince of Wales Road, Upton, NORWICH, NR13 6BW. (Life Member)
MATTHEW, Miss. Susan Anne, BA(Hons) ACA *1994;* Flat 264 Jefferson Building, 12 Westferry Road, LONDON, E14 8LR.
MATTHEW, Mr. Walter John, FCA *1965;* The Laurels, 1 Priory Close, Boxgrove, CHICHESTER, WEST SUSSEX, PO18 0EA. (Life Member)
•**MATTHEWMAN, Mr. Colin, FCA** *1969;* Callow Matthewman & Co., Atholl House, 29-31 Hope Street, Douglas, ISLE OF MAN, IM1 1AR.
MATTHEWMAN, Mr. John Stuart, FCA *1957;* Flat 12, Pegasus Court, 55 Hill Village Road, SUTTON COLDFIELD, WEST MIDLANDS, B75 5BH. (Life Member)
•**MATTHEWMAN, Mr. Mark Vincent, BA ACA** *1990;* KPMG LLP, Aquis Court, 31 Fishpool Street, ST. ALBANS, HERTFORDSHIRE, AL3 4RF. See also KPMG Europe LLP
•**MATTHEWMAN, Mr. Philip, BA FCA** *1993;* Trinity South Limited, The Joiners Shop, The Historic Dockyard, CHATHAM, KENT, ME4 4TZ.

MATTHEWS, Mr. Alan, FCA *1951;* 4 Pineways Drive, Newbridge, WOLVERHAMPTON, WV6 0LL. (Life Member)
MATTHEWS, Mr. Alan John, FCA *1967;* 165 Musters Road, NOTTINGHAM, NG2 7AF.
MATTHEWS, Mr. Alan Roy, MA ACA *1987;* Malmesbury, 14 Southborough Close, SURBITON, KT6 6PU.
MATTHEWS, Mr. Alastair Sean, BSc FCA *1988;* 15 Coy Pond Road, Branksome, POOLE, BH12 1JT.
MATTHEWS, Mrs. Andrea Jacqueline, BSc ACA *1995;* 70 Green Street, Chorleywood, RICKMANSWORTH, WD3 5QR.
MATTHEWS, Mr. Andrew James Evenden, ACA AMCT *1998;* 44 Gordon Road, Claygate, ESHER, SURREY, KT10 0PQ.
MATTHEWS, Miss. Anna Kate, BA ACA *1993;* Jigsaw, 159Mortlake Road, RICHMOND, TW9 4AW.
•**MATTHEWS, Mr. Anthony John, BSc FCA** *1977;* (Tax Fac), D.R.E. & Co (Audit) Limited, 7 Lower Brook Street, OSWESTRY, SHROPSHIRE, SY11 2HG. See also DRE & Co (Knighton) Limited and DRE & Co
•**MATTHEWS, Mr. Anthony Richard, MA FCA** *1987;* Williamson West, 10 Langdale Gate, WITNEY, OX28 6EX.
MATTHEWS, Mr. Anthony William, BA ACA *2003;* 18 White House Way, Epworth, DONCASTER, SOUTH YORKSHIRE, DN9 1GS.
MATTHEWS, Mrs. Barbara Joan, FCA *1971;* 40 Grebe Close, ALTON, GU34 2LR.
•**MATTHEWS, Mr. Barry John, BSc FCA** *1971;* MEMBER OF COUNCIL, (Tax Fac), Bissell & Brown Ltd, Charter House, 56 High Street, SUTTON COLDFIELD, WEST MIDLANDS, B72 1UJ. See also Bissell & Brown Birmingham Ltd
MATTHEWS, Mr. Brian Peter, BSc FCA *1976;* Redburn Partners, 75 King William Street, LONDON, EC4N 7BE.
MATTHEWS, Mr. Bruce John, ACA CA(SA) *2010;* The Granary, Guileshill Lane, Ockham, WOKING, SURREY, GU23 6NG.
•**MATTHEWS, Mr. Bryan, FCA** *1973;* Shelvoke Pickering Janney & Co, 57-61 Market Place, CANNOCK, WS11 1BP.
MATTHEWS, Mrs. Catherine Elisabeth, BA ACA *1992;* 18 Becket Wood, Newdigate, DORKING, RH5 5AQ.
MATTHEWS, Mr. Chris Richard, BA ACA *2007;* 1/49 Spenser Street, St Kilda, MELBOURNE, VIC 3182, AUSTRALIA.
MATTHEWS, Mr. Christopher Ian James, FCA *1978;* 30 Paxton Crescent, Shenley Lodge, MILTON KEYNES, MK5 7PY.
•**MATTHEWS, Mr. Christopher James, BSc FCA** *1995;* Ernst & Young LLP, Liberation House, Castle Street, St Helier, JERSEY, JE1 1EY. See also Ernst & Young Europe LLP
•**MATTHEWS, Mr. Christopher John, FCA** *1970;* Matthews Mist & Co, Westbury House, 14 Bellevue Road, SOUTHAMPTON, SO15 2AY.
MATTHEWS, Mrs. Claire Hilary, BSc ACA *2010;* 7 Allerdean Walk, STOCKPORT, CHESHIRE, SK4 3RP.
MATTHEWS, Mr. Darren Kenneth, ACA MAAT *1999;* Northfields, 3 Gables Court, LEICESTER, LE17 5EG.
MATTHEWS, Mr. David, BA ACA *1999;* 13 East Avenue, NEWCASTLE UPON TYNE, NE12 9PH.
•**MATTHEWS, Mr. David, BA FCA** *1991;* Linwood, St. Peters Road, Arnesby, LEICESTER, LE8 5WJ.
MATTHEWS, Mr. David Egon, FCA *1973;* c/o BNH Group, P.O. Box 843, MANAMA, BAHRAIN.
•**MATTHEWS, Mr. David Geoffrey, FCA** *1961;* Matthews & Co., 40 Ferrers Road, Yoxall, BURTON-ON-TRENT, DE13 8PS.
MATTHEWS, Mr. David John, BSc ACA *1989;* Oakley House, 2 Oakley Road, Caversham Heights, READING, RG4 7RL.
MATTHEWS, Mr. David Paul, BSc FCA *1975;* 19 Riverbank, Laleham Road, STAINES, TW18 2QE. (Life Member)
MATTHEWS, Mr. David Peter, ACA *1992;* 174 Cumnor Hill, OXFORD, OX2 9PJ.
MATTHEWS, Mr. David Victor, BSc CA *1997; (CA Scotland 1985);* MEMBER OF COUNCIL, KPMG LLP, 15 Canada Square, LONDON, E14 5GL. See also KPMG Europe LLP
MATTHEWS, Mrs. Dawn Patricia, BSc ACA *1992;* 101 Grange Road, SOLIHULL, B91 1BZ.
MATTHEWS, Mr. Donald Ivor, LLB FCA *1958;* 2 Clifton Cottages, Bromyard RoadCotheridge, WORCESTER, WR6 5LX. (Life Member)
MATTHEWS, Mr. Duncan, BSc ACA *1999;* 67 Gains Road, SOUTHSEA, PO4 0PJ.
MATTHEWS, Mr. Edward, BA FCA *1993;* Nomura International Plc, 1 Angel Lane, LONDON, EC4R 3AB.
MATTHEWS, Mr. Edward Graham, BSc ACA *1986;* FWP Matthews Ltd., Station Road, Shipton-Under-Wychwood, CHIPPING NORTON, OX7 6BH.
•**MATTHEWS, Miss. Elizabeth Anne, FCA** *1979;* (Tax Fac), Elizabeth A. Matthews & Co, Parklands, Barton Road, WISBECH, PE13 1LE.
MATTHEWS, Mrs. Elizabeth Anne, MSc ACA CTA *2000;* 25 Farringdon Street, LONDON, EC4A 4AB.
MATTHEWS, Mrs. Elizabeth Anne Enid, BA FCA *1977;* 25 Sandpiper Close, Bishopton, STRATFORD-UPON-AVON, WARWICKSHIRE, CV37 9EY.
MATTHEWS, Miss. Emily, ACA *2008;* with PricewaterhouseCoopers LLP, Benson House, 33 Wellington Street, LEEDS, LS1 4JP.
•**MATTHEWS, Mrs. Francoise, BA FCA** *1992;* Age Concern Enterprises Ltd, Linhay House, ASHBURTON, DEVON, TQ13 7UP.
MATTHEWS, Mrs. Gillian Elizabeth, BSc ACA *1999;* 44 Gordon Road, Claygate, ESHER, KT10 0PQ.
MATTHEWS, Mr. Graeme, BSc ACA *1995;* 11 Moor Allerton Crescent, Moortown, LEEDS, LS17 6SH.
MATTHEWS, Mr. Graham Charles, BA ACA *1996;* with PricewaterhouseCoopers, 11//F, PricewaterhouseCoopers Center, 2 Corporate Avenue, 202 Hu Bin Road, SHANGHAI 200021 CHINA.
MATTHEWS, Mr. Graham David, BSc ACA *1994;* Sunnyside Cottage, Cox Hill, Chacewater, TRURO, TR4 8LY.
•**MATTHEWS, Mr. Graham John, MSc FCA** *1979;* Greenaway, 150 High Street, SEVENOAKS, TN13 1XE.
MATTHEWS, Mr. Guy Vincent, ACA *1991;* Sarasin & Partners LLP, Juxon House 100 St Pauls Churchyard, LONDON, EC4M 8BU.
MATTHEWS, Miss. Hannah, ACA *2011;* Flat 26, Kingswood Court, 48 West End Lane, West Hampstead, LONDON, NW6 4SX.
MATTHEWS, Mrs. Helen, BSc FCA *1979;* Ridgewood House, Ridgemead Road, Englefield Green, EGHAM, TW20 0YD.
MATTHEWS, Mrs. Hilary Jane, MPhil ACA *1986;* 79 Hillfield Avenue, LONDON, N8 7DS.
•**MATTHEWS, Mr. Howard John, BA FCA** *1981;* Howard Matthews Partnership, Queensgate House, 23 North Park Road, HARROGATE, HG1 5PD.
MATTHEWS, Mr. Hugh Napier, FCA *1966;* Haslenstrasse 8, 8903 BIRMENSDORF, SWITZERLAND.
MATTHEWS, Mr. Ian, FCA *1972;* Avery Healthcare Ltd, 1b Basset Court, Loake Close, Grange Park, NORTHAMPTON, NN4 5EZ.
•**MATTHEWS, Mr. Ian Charles, FCA** *1976;* I.C. Matthews, Ivor House, 200 London Road North, Merstham, REDHILL, RH1 3BG.
MATTHEWS, Mr. Ian David, BSc ACA *1988;* 125 Cranbrook Road, Redland, BRISTOL, BS6 7DE.
MATTHEWS, Mr. Ian Rhys, BSc(Hons) ACA *2009;* 179 Albury Road, Merstham, REDHILL, RH1 3LW.
MATTHEWS, Mr. Iestyn Lloyd, BA ACA *2005;* Ernst & Young Llp, 1 More London Place, LONDON, SE1 2AF.
MATTHEWS, Miss. Jade, BA ACA *2010;* 35 Firbank Road, DAWLISH, DEVON, EX7 0NW.
MATTHEWS, Mr. James Arnold Mccalmont, FCA *1951;* 12 Charlesbye Close, ORMSKIRK, L39 2XZ. (Life Member)
MATTHEWS, Mr. James Palliser, FCA *1956;* Dove House, 9 Chase Avenue, Walton Park, MILTON KEYNES, MK7 7HG. (Life Member)
MATTHEWS, Mr. Janek Paul, MA FCA *1969;* (Tax Fac), Pump Court Tax Chambers, 16 Bedford Row, LONDON, WC1R 4EF.
MATTHEWS, Miss. Janice Elizabeth, BA FCA *1999;* 8 Bramley Grove, ASHTEAD, SURREY, KT21 2EA.
MATTHEWS, Mrs. Joanne Maree, BSc ACA *2002;* 25 Eldon Road, CHELTENHAM, GL52 6TX.
MATTHEWS, Mr. John, FCA *1970;* 13 Gladys Road, HOVE, BN3 7GL.
MATTHEWS, Mr. John Graham, FCA *1958;* 7 Watermans Way, Wargrave-on-Thames, READING, BERKSHIRE, RG10 8HR. (Life Member)
•**MATTHEWS, Mr. John Otto, FCA** *1983;* Ensors, Cardinal House, 46 St Nicholas Street, IPSWICH, IP1 1TT.
MATTHEWS, Mr. John Stephen, BA ACA *1986;* Standard House, 12 - 13 Essex Street, LONDON, WC2R 3AA.
MATTHEWS, Mr. John Waylett, FCA *1967;* S D L International Globe House, Clivemont Road, MAIDENHEAD, SL6 7DY.
MATTHEWS, Mr. Jonathan William, BA ACA *2007;* 9 Dozmere Feock, TRURO, CORNWALL, TR3 6RJ.
MATTHEWS, Mr. Joseph Byron, FCA *1971;* Meadowbank, 79 White House Lane, BOSTON, LINCOLNSHIRE, PE21 0BE. (Life Member)
MATTHEWS, Mrs. Juliet Sian, BSc ACA *1996;* 9 Castle Road, WEYBRIDGE, SURREY, KT13 9QP.
MATTHEWS, Mr. Justin Neil, BA ACA *2007;* 2 Surrenden Cottage, High Street, Staplehurst, TONBRIDGE, KENT, TN12 0BJ.
MATTHEWS, Mrs. Katharine, BA ACA *2004;* 13 East Avenue, Benton, NEWCASTLE UPON TYNE, NE12 9PH.
MATTHEWS, Mrs. Katherine, BA ACA *1987;* 1 Blenheim Place, Teddington Park, TEDDINGTON, TW11 8NZ.
•**MATTHEWS, Mr. Keith Anthony, FCA** *1974;* 9 Bowring Park, Moretonhampstead, NEWTON ABBOT, DEVON, TQ13 8GB.
MATTHEWS, Mr. Kenneth, BA FCA *1986;* 1006/229 Masterview Condo, Between Soi 34 and Soi 36, Charoen Nakhon Road, Banglum Phulang Klongsan, BANGKOK 10600, THAILAND.
MATTHEWS, Mr. Kenneth John, FCA *1972;* West Orchard, 20 Back Lane, Leadenham, LINCOLN, LN5 0PW.
MATTHEWS, Mr. Kenneth John, FCA *1948;* Avening, West Hill Road, West Hill, OTTERY ST.MARY, EX11 1UZ. (Life Member)
MATTHEWS, Mr. Kevin John, BSc FCA *1982;* 8 Salmon Close, Bloxham, BANBURY, OX15 4PJ.
MATTHEWS, Mr. Kurt, ACA *2011;* 15 Peake Avenue, Kirby Cross, FRINTON-ON-SEA, ESSEX, CO13 0SQ.
MATTHEWS, Mr. Lester, FCA *1964;* 13 Lon Coed Parc, Sketty, SWANSEA, SA2 0TT. (Life Member)
MATTHEWS, Mrs. Lianne Lesley, BSc(Hons) ACA *2001;* Flat 1 78 Goldhurst Terrace, LONDON, NW6 3HT.
MATTHEWS, Miss. Lindsay Michelle, ACA *2011;* 5 The Hatch, ENFIELD, MIDDLESEX, EN3 5NH.
•**MATTHEWS, Miss. Lucia Mary Caitriona, FCA** *1974;* (Tax Fac), Mary Matthews, 140 Clifton, YORK, YO30 6BH.
MATTHEWS, Miss. Lucy Cathryn Nagy, ACA *2011;* 6 Sandringham Mount, Moortown, LEEDS, LS17 8DN.
MATTHEWS, Mrs. Lydia, ACA *2008;* Pembroke House, Reading Road, WALLINGFORD, OXFORDSHIRE, OX10 9DT.
•**MATTHEWS, Mr. Martin John, BA ACA** *2003;* with Landers Accountants Ltd, Church View Chambers, 38 Market Square, Toddington, DUNSTABLE, BEDFORDSHIRE LU5 6BS.
MATTHEWS, Mr. Mervyn Douglas, FCA *1965;* 12 Rectory Close, Ashington, PULBOROUGH, RH20 3LP. (Life Member)
•**MATTHEWS, Mr. Michael James, BA ACA** *2000;* Dexter Matthews Ltd, 99 Walter Road, SWANSEA, SA1 5QE.
MATTHEWS, Mr. Michael Keith, BSc ACA *1999;* Customer Services Centre Alliance & Leicester Plc, Carlton Park Narborough, LEICESTER, LE19 0AL.
MATTHEWS, Mr. Michael Ralph Eastwood, MA FCA *1967;* Lake House, Avington, WINCHESTER, HAMPSHIRE, SO21 1DE. (Life Member)
MATTHEWS, Miss. Natalie, BA ACA *1993;* Heath Farm Ponsongath, Coverack, HELSTON, CORNWALL, TR12 6SQ.
•ⒹMATTHEWS, Mr. Neil, BSc FCA** *1985;* with Deloitte LLP, One Trinity Gardens, Broad Chare, NEWCASTLE UPON TYNE, NE1 2HF.
•**MATTHEWS, Mr. Nicholas George, FCA** *1982;* (Tax Fac), Matthews & Company, 52 Killigrew Street, FALMOUTH, CORNWALL, TR11 3PP. See also Matthews Cooper Limited, The Tax Shop(Falmouth) Ltd
MATTHEWS, Mr. Nicholas John, FCA *1974;* 5 Searson Close Tallington, STAMFORD, LINCOLNSHIRE, PE9 4RF.
•**MATTHEWS, Mr. Nicolas Paul, BSc FCA** *1993;* Kinetic Partners LLP, One London Wall, Level 10, LONDON, EC2Y 5HB. See also Kinetic Partners (Cayman) Limited
MATTHEWS, Mr. Noel David, BSc ACA *2003;* 49 Broomleaf Road, FARNHAM, GU9 8DQ.
MATTHEWS, Mrs. Patricia Margaret, BSc ACA *1983;* Four Winds, Court Road, Newton Ferrers, PLYMOUTH, PL8 1DD.
•**MATTHEWS, Mr. Paul Keith, BSc ACA** *2002;* BSR Bespoke Limited, Hilden Park House, 79 Tonbridge Road, Hildenborough, TONBRIDGE, KENT TN11 9BH.
MATTHEWS, Mr. Paul Kennedy, FCA *1960;* Mill House, Bridgetown, DULVERTON, SOMERSET, TA22 9JR. (Life Member)
MATTHEWS, Mr. Paul William, LLB ACA *2003;* 320 Bull Lane, Eccles, AYLESFORD, KENT, ME20 7HE.
MATTHEWS, Mr. Philip Geoffrey, FCILT FCA *1972;* 55 Pantain Road, LOUGHBOROUGH, LE11 3LZ.
MATTHEWS, Miss. Philippa Anne, BA FCA ATII *1990;* (Tax Fac), The Old Chapel, Galphay, RIPON, NORTH YORKSHIRE, HG4 3NJ.
MATTHEWS, Mrs. Rebecca, BA(Hons) ACA *2003;* Heatherlea, Godshill, FORDINGBRIDGE, SP6 2LG.
MATTHEWS, Mr. Richard, ACA CA(NZ) *2010;* 82 Hardy Road, Surrey, LONDON, SW19 1HZ.
MATTHEWS, Mr. Richard, BA(Econ) ACA *1998;* J Rothschild Capital Management, 29 St. James's Place, LONDON, SW1A 1NR.
MATTHEWS, Mr. Richard Ian, BA ACA *1993;* J & J L Brown Ltd, Whitestone Park, HEREFORD, HR1 3SE.
•**MATTHEWS, Mr. Richard John, BA ACA** *1994;* with BDO LLP, 2 City Place, Beehive Ring Road, GATWICK, WEST SUSSEX, RH6 0PA.
•**MATTHEWS, Mr. Richard John, FCA** *1986;* (Tax Fac), Parkinson Matthews LLP, Cedar House, 35 Ashbourne Road, DERBY, DE22 3FS.
MATTHEWS, Mr. Richard Thomas, BSc ACA *2009;* 17 Brook Road, Fair Oak, EASTLEIGH, HAMPSHIRE, SO50 7AZ.
•**MATTHEWS, Mr. Robert Anthony, BSc FCA** *1979;* Deloitte LLP, 2 New Street Square, LONDON, EC4A 3BZ. See also Deloitte & Touche LLP
•**MATTHEWS, Mr. Robert Curtis, BA FCA** *1985;* The Highgrove Practice, 6 Highgrove Gardens, WORTHING, BN11 4SN.
•**MATTHEWS, Mr. Robert Edmund, MSc FCA** *1980;* (Tax Fac), R.E. Matthews, Garn Hebogydd, Gwbert on Sea, CARDIGAN, SA43 1PR.
MATTHEWS, Mr. Robert Michael, FCA *1971;* 62 Barholm Road, SHEFFIELD, S10 5RS.
MATTHEWS, Mr. Robert Neil, FCA *1968;* P O Box 26256, Game City, GABORONE, BOTSWANA.
MATTHEWS, Mr. Roderic John, BA ACA *1992;* Warren Farm, Toddington, CHELTENHAM, GL54 5BN.
MATTHEWS, Mr. Rodney Gordon, FCA *1970;* The Forge, Manor Farm Court, Lower Pennington Lane, Pennington, LYMINGTON, HAMPSHIRE SO41 8AN.
MATTHEWS, Mr. Roger Ian, FCA *1971;* 8 Heston Close, Portskewett, CALDICOT, GWENT, NP26 5RU.
MATTHEWS, Mr. Roger John, BSc ACA *1979;* Ridgewood House, Ridgemead Road, Englefield Green, EGHAM, TW20 0YD.
MATTHEWS, Mr. Ronald George, FCA *1959;* 21 Woodside Crescent, Smallfield, HORLEY, RH6 9NA. (Life Member)
•**MATTHEWS, Mr. Ross, ACA FCCA** *2011;* The Haggart, Lilley Green Road, Alvechurch, BIRMINGHAM, B48 7HD.
MATTHEWS, Mr. Rupert, ACA *2008;* Simmons Bakery Ltd, 2 The Parade St. Albans Road East, HATFIELD, HERTFORDSHIRE, AL10 0EY.
•**MATTHEWS, Mr. Rupert Nicholas Charles, BA ACA** *2006;* (Tax Fac), Fourways 4 Business Ltd, 1a Melbourn Street, ROYSTON, HERTFORDSHIRE, SG8 7BP.
MATTHEWS, Ms. Ruth Elizabeth, BA ACA *1996;* 6 Falkirk Avenue, WIDNES, CHESHIRE, WA8 9DX.
MATTHEWS, Mrs. Sally, BSc ACA *2004;* 49 Broomleaf Road, FARNHAM, GU9 8DQ.
MATTHEWS, Mrs. Sandra Maire, BA ACA *1985;* 46 Awaba Street, MOSMAN, NSW 2088, AUSTRALIA.
MATTHEWS, Miss. Sarah Angela, BSc ACA *2004;* 34 Reeves Close, Staplehurst, TONBRIDGE, TN12 0NN.
MATTHEWS, Miss. Sarah Louise, BA(Hons) FCA *2001;* 1 St. Annes Drive, Wick, BRISTOL, BS30 5PN.
MATTHEWS, Mr. Shaun Kenneth, BSc FCA *1994;* with PricewaterhouseCoopers LLP, 350 South Grand Avenue, LOS ANGELES, CA 90071, UNITED STATES.
MATTHEWS, Mrs. Shenola, BEng ACA *2002;* 7 Marlborough Avenue, High Harrington, WORKINGTON, CUMBRIA, CA14 4NW.
MATTHEWS, Mr. Simon, ACA *1995;* Cherry Tree Cottage, 34 High Street, Long Wittenham, ABINGDON, OX14 4QJ.
MATTHEWS, Mr. Simon David, BEng ACA *2002;* 185 Highbury Hill, LONDON, N5 1TB.
MATTHEWS, Mr. Simon John, BSc ACA *1987;* National Express Group Plc, 60 Charlotte Street, LONDON, W1T 2NU.
MATTHEWS, Mr. Simon Romer, MA ACA *1985;* 74 Highbury New Park, LONDON, N5 2DJ.
MATTHEWS, Mrs. Sophie Ellen, BSc ACA *2005;* 83 Queens Road, East Sheen, LONDON, SW14 8PH.
MATTHEWS, Mr. Stephen James, BSc ACA FFin *1981;* GPO Box 4578, SYDNEY, NSW 2001, AUSTRALIA.
MATTHEWS, Mr. Stephen John, FCA *1975;* 2 Marjory Street, FAWKNER, VIC 3060, AUSTRALIA.

MATTHEWS, Mr. Steven Roy, BSc ACA *1992;* 24 Stevens Lane, COHASSET, MA 02025, UNITED STATES.
•MATTHEWS, Mrs. Susan Amanda, BSc ACA *1988;* Matthews Accounting, 125 Cranbrook Road, Redland, BRISTOL, BS6 7DE.
•MATTHEWS, Mrs. Susan Mary, BA FCA *1981;* Matthews Sutton & Co Ltd, 48-52 Penny Lane, LIVERPOOL, L18 1DG. See also The Company Specialists (Accounting Services) Ltd
MATTHEWS, Ms. Susan Rosemary, BCom ACA *2005;* The Leadership Foundation for Higher Education, 88 Kingsway, LONDON, WC2B 6AA.
MATTHEWS, Mrs. Suzanne Jane, BSc ACA FHEA *1986;* Applehay, Moorledge Lane, Chew Magna, BRISTOL, BS40 8TL.
MATTHEWS, Mr. Thomas, FCA FCMA *1951;* Flat 16, Richmond House, Street Lane, LEEDS, LS8 1BW. (Life Member)
MATTHEWS, Mr. Thomas, FCA *1928;* Nowra, Rua Da Bela Vista 356, Vale Do Lobo, ALMANCIL, PORTUGAL. (Life Member)
MATTHEWS, Mr. Thomas Glenmore, FCA *1970;* Beaulah House, Mill Lane, Welwick, HULL, HU12 0SG. (Life Member)
MATTHEWS, Mr. Timothy Brian, ACA *2007;* First Floor Flat, 46 Tivoli Crescent, BRIGHTON, BN1 5ND.
MATTHEWS, Ms. Tineke Jane, ACA *2002;* with PricewaterhouseCoopers LLP, Benson House, 33 Wellington Street, LEEDS, LS1 4JP.
MATTHEWS, Mr. William John, BA FCA *1963;* 217 Hills Road, CAMBRIDGE, CB2 2RN.
MATTHEWS, Mr. William Paul, FCA *1965;* 2 Twentyman Close, WOODFORD GREEN, ESSEX, IG8 0EW. (Life Member)
MATTHEWS, Mr. Wolfgang Peter, FCA *1984;* Strutt & Parker, 13 Hill Street, LONDON, W1J 5LQ.
•MATTHEWSON, Mrs. Julie Ann, BSc ACA FCCA *1991;* Hull Matthewson Ltd, 33 Boston Road, Holbeach, SPALDING, LINCOLNSHIRE, PE12 7LR.
•MATTHIAE, Ms. Judith, BA ACA *1990;* (Tax Fac), J Matthiae & Co Limited, The Tythings, The Plantation, West Winterslow, SALISBURY, SP5 1RE.
•MATTHISSEN, Mr. Colin Ainslee, BSc ACA CF *1982;* Sheen Stickland LLP, 4 High Street, ALTON, HAMPSHIRE, GU34 1BU.
MATTINGLEY, Ms. Katy-Jane, BSc ACA *2001;* Dairy Lodge, 6 Dundas Home Farm, SOUTH QUEENSFERRY, WEST LOTHIAN, EH30 9SS.
MATTINGLY, Mr. Gordon Charles, BSc ACA *1997;* 29 Limeworth, Carriganara, BALLINCOLLIG, COUNTY CORK, IRELAND.
•MATTINGLY, Mr. Laurence Colin, BA ACA *1992;* 45 Chivalry Road, LONDON, SW11 1HX.
•MATTINGLY, Mr. Robert Colin, LLB ACA *1991;* 9/57 Garling Street, LANE COVE, NSW 2066, AUSTRALIA.
MATTINSON, Mrs. Amanda Dawn, BA ACA *1998;* 39 Hurley Road, Little Corby, CARLISLE, CA4 8QY.
MATTINSON, Mr. David Leigh, BA FCA *1976;* 36 Blakesley Road, The Meadows, Wigston Magna, WIGSTON, LE18 3WD.
MATTINSON, Mrs. Marie Louise, BA ACA *1992;* Beesley House Farm, Inglewhite Road, Goosnargh, PRESTON, PR3 2EL.
MATTINSON, Mr. Nigel James, BA(Hons) ACA *2002;* Flat 2 Juniper House, 2 Edge Hill, LONDON, SW19 4LP.
MATTIOLI, Mr. Paul Robert, BSc ACA *1979;* 68 Main Street, Swithland, LOUGHBOROUGH, LE12 8TH.
MATTISON, Mr. David Harris, FCA *1971;* 6 Eastcote View, PINNER, HA5 1AT.
•MATTISON, Miss. Deidre Anne Helen, BA ACA *1986;* 22 April Croft, BIRMINGHAM, B13 9HP.
•MATTISON, Mr. John, FCA *1957;* Mattison & Co., 10A Royal Parade, CHISLEHURST, BR7 6NR.
MATTLEY, Mrs. Jane Kathryn, ACA *2002;* McGregors Business Services, Prince William House, 10 Lower Church Street, ASHBY-DE-LA-ZOUCH, LEICESTERSHIRE, LE65 1AB.
MATTOCK, Mr. David Holmes, FCA *1975;* 50 Moor Park Drive, Addingham, ILKLEY, LS29 0PT.
MATTOCK, Mr. John Clive, FCA *1967;* Beacon Platt, Dormansland, LINGFIELD, RH7 6RB.
MATTOCKS, Mr. David Edmund, MBA ACA *1986;* Keeble Hawson Moorhouse Old Cathedral Vicarage, 7-15 St. James Row, SHEFFIELD, S1 1XA.
•MATTOCKS, Mr. Giles, BEng ACA *2002;* Mattocks Grindley Limited, Unit 25, Enterprise Greenhouse, Salisbury Street, ST. HELENS, MERSEYSIDE WA10 1FY.
MATTOK, Mr. Michael James, BA ACA CTA MABRP *1983;* Norwood House, 8 Green Hall Park, Shelf, HALIFAX, WEST YORKSHIRE, HX3 7PZ.
MATTU, Mr. David Rugbinder Singh, BA ACA *1985;* 9 Bourne Avenue, Fenham, NEWCASTLE UPON TYNE, NE4 9XL.
MATTU, Miss. Ninderpal, ACA *2002;* with Ernst & Young, P.O Box 251, Ernst & Young Tower, TORONTO M5K 1J7, ON, CANADA.
MATU, Mrs. Susan Constance, BSc ACA *1987;* Hillview House, 110a Bates Lane, Helsby, FRODSHAM, WA6 9LJ.
MATUK, Miss. Thelma, BSc FCA *1988;* 6 Betteridge Drive, Manor Park, SUTTON COLDFIELD, B76 1FN.
MATURI, Mr. Brian David, MBA BA FCA *1977;* 22356 Chase Drive, NOVI, MI 48375-4784, UNITED STATES.
•MATUSIEWICZ, Mr. Robert Francis, ACA *1982;* Quantico, Nottingham Castle Marina, Marina Road, NOTTINGHAM, NG7 1TN.
MATVEEV, Mr. Vladimir, BA ACA MBA *2006;* Presnenski Val 16/2, Flat 40, 123557 MOSCOW, RUSSIAN FEDERATION.
MATVEIEFF, Mr. Nicholas, FCA *1965;* Kronospan Ltd, Chirk, WREXHAM, CLWYD, LL14 5NT.
MATYSZCZYK, Mr. Romek Jeremi, BSc ACA *1981;* Woolgate Exchange, 5th Floor, 25 Basinghall Street, LONDON, EC2V 5HA.
MAU, Mr. Chi Fat, ACA *2008;* Room 826, Tin Ming House, Tin Ping Estate, SHEUNG SHUI, NEW TERRITORIES, HONG KONG SAR.
MAU, Mr. Chung Yin, ACA *2006;* 13E Brilliance Court, Hillgrove Court, DISCOVERY BAY, NEW TERRITORIES, HONG KONG SAR.
MAU, Mr. Joseph Shing, ACA *2007;* Hong Kong Exchanges & Clearing Limited, 12/F One International Finance Centre, 1 Harbour View Street, CENTRAL, HONG KONG SAR.
MAU, Miss. Marianne, BA FCA *1987;* with ICAEW, Chartered Accountants' Hall, Moorgate Place, LONDON, EC2P 2BJ.
•MAUDARBOCUS, Mr. Mohammad Ali Ashraf, ACA *2009;* A & S Accountants, 135 Belgrave Road, Walthamstow, LONDON, E17 8QF.
MAUDE, Mr. Albert James, MA ACA *1989;* 32 Vernon Street, BROOKLINE, MA 02446, UNITED STATES.
MAUDE, Mr. Christopher Simon, MA FCA *1977;* RWC Partners Limited, 60 Petty France, LONDON, SW1H 9EU.
MAUDE, Mr. Nicholas John Eustace, BSc ACA *1980;* Covington House, Upton Grey, BASINGSTOKE, RG25 2RH.
MAUDSLEY, Ms. Alison Diana, BSc ACA *1984;* 68 High Street, Stokesley, MIDDLESBROUGH, CLEVELAND, TS9 5BA.
•MAUDSLEY, Mr. Clive Stewart, BSc FCA *1992;* Flat B 12-3, 1 Watson Street, MANCHESTER, M3 4EH.
MAUDSLEY, Mr. Douglas Garson, MA BA(Hons) ACA *2009;* 14 Parkwood Close, Shelley, HUDDERSFIELD, HD8 8JP.
MAUGER, Mr. Brian Andrew, BA ACA *1989;* Legis Group Ltd, PO Box 91, GUERNSEY, GY1 3EG.
MAUGER, Mrs. Katharine Sarah, BA(Hons) ACA *2002;* 4A Patna Street, Ngaio, WELLINGTON 6035, NEW ZEALAND.
MAUGER, Mr. Nicholas Paul, BSc ACA MBA *1995;* 8 Dunmow Walk, Popham Street, LONDON, N1 8QX.
•MAUGHAM, Mr. Alan Bryan, FCA *1968;* (Tax Fac), Hope Jones, Dunlop House, 23a Spencer Road, NEW MILTON, BH25 6BZ.
•MAUGHAM, Mr. Colin Roy, FCA *1974;* UHY Hacker Young LLP, Quadrant House, 4 Thomas More Square, LONDON, E1W 1YW.
MAUGHAM, Mr. Stewart Colin, MA FCA *1976;* 34 Southwood Park, Southwood Lawn Road, LONDON, N6 5SG.
MAUGHAN, Mr. Christopher John Spibey, FCA *1964;* The Gabled House, Aisby, GRANTHAM, NG32 3NF. (Life Member)
MAUGHAN, Mr. Colin, FCA *1960;* 2 Hawkesley Court, Watford Road, RADLETT, HERTFORDSHIRE, WD7 8HH. (Life Member)
MAUGHAN, Mr. David John, BA FCA *1988;* Lower Reach, 4 Water Lane, Eastwell, MELTON MOWBRAY, LE14 4ER.
MAUGHAN, Mr. Edward Peter, FCA *1969;* Meadow Bank, Great Urswick, ULVERSTON, LA12 0ST.
•MAUGHAN, Mr. Gordon, ACA *1983;* Gordon Maughan, 15 Bellister Park, PETERLEE, COUNTY DURHAM, SR8 1PH.
•MAUGHAN, Mr. Grahame Martin, BA FCA CF *1991;* Ryecroft Glenton, 32 Portland Terrace, Jesmond, NEWCASTLE UPON TYNE, NE2 1QP.
MAUGHAN, Mrs. Jane Alexandra Helen, BA ACA *1988;* Vodafone Plc, Vodafone House, The Connection, NEWBURY, BERKSHIRE, RG14 2FN.
MAUGHAN, Mrs. Jenny Elizabeth, BSc ACA *2003;* 56 Riverside Park, OTLEY, LS21 2RW.
MAUGHAN, Miss. Joanne Claire, BSc FCA *1996;* Manor Cottage, Sandy Lane, GUILDFORD, SURREY, GU3 1HB.
MAUGHAN, Mr. Lee Foster, BSc ACA *2005;* with Deloitte LLP, City House, 126-130 Hills Road, CAMBRIDGE, CB2 1RY.
•MAUGHAN, Mr. Nicholas John, FCA *1989;* Maughans Limited, Norfolk House, 75 Bartholomew Street, NEWBURY, BERKSHIRE, RG14 5DU.
MAUGHAN, Mrs. Suzanne Davina, BSc ARCS ACA *1999;* with Financial Services Authority, 25 The North Colonnade, Canary Wharf, LONDON, E14 5HS.
MAUGHFLING, Mr. Bruce Rosewarne, FCA *1953;* 4 Grafton Road, The Park, CHELTENHAM, GL50 2ES. (Life Member)
MAUGHFLING, Mr. David John, FCA *1963;* 181 Leckhampton Road, CHELTENHAM, GL53 0AD.
MAUGHFLING, Mr. William Guy, BA ACA *1989;* with PricewaterhouseCoopers, Rahimtulla Tower, Upper Hill Road, PO Box 43963, NAIROBI, 00100 KENYA.
MAUKONEN, Mrs. Kathryn Anne, BA ACA *2006;* 2 Stephenson Close, Twyford, READING, RG10 9FG.
MAULDRIDGE, Mr. Kevin Paul, MA ACA *1992;* Affinion International Ltd, Charter Court, 50 Windsor Road, SLOUGH, SL1 2EJ.
MAULDRIDGE, Mrs. Kirsty Anne, BA ACA *1996;* 52 Midway, ST. ALBANS, HERTFORDSHIRE, AL3 4BQ.
MAULDRIDGE, Mr. Oliver, BSc ACA *2010;* 27 Goldsworthy Road, Urmston, MANCHESTER, M41 8TY.
MAULE, Mr. Eric Edwin, FCA *1961;* Salix House, Falkenham, IPSWICH, IP10 0QY. (Life Member)
MAULE, Mr. Peter Allen, BA LLB FCA *1969;* 47 Kestrel Close, STOCKTON-ON-TEES, CLEVELAND, TS20 1SF. (Life Member)
•MAULE, Mr. Richard John Ramsay, BA FCA *1982;* Dick Maule, Little Bosullow Cottage, Little Bosullow, PENZANCE, CORNWALL, TR20 8NS.
MAULE, Mrs. Sally Louise, BSc ACA *1998;* Langford House, Providence Lane, Long Ashton, BRISTOL, BS41 9DJ.
MAULER, Mr. Harold Ernest William, FCA *1959;* Dene Weg, Squires Close, Bussage, STROUD, GL6 8BB. (Life Member)
•MAULTBY, Mr. David Herbert, MSc ACA *1986;* (Tax Fac), HW, Sterling House, 22 St. Cuthberts Way, DARLINGTON, COUNTY DURHAM, DL1 1GB. See also Haines Watts
MAULTBY, Mrs. Ella Joy, ACA *2009;* (Tax Fac), 48 Holmesdale Road, LONDON, N6 5TQ.
MAUND, Mr. David Giles, BA ACA *1997;* No. 1803-788 Richards Street, VANCOUVER V6B 0C7, BC, CANADA.
MAUNDER, Mr. Adrian, BSc ACA *1993;* 10 Aviary Close, Hambrook, CHICHESTER, WEST SUSSEX, PO18 8UN.
MAUNDER, Mr. Andrew Haydn, LLB ACA *2008;* 18 Blacktown Gardens, Marshfield, CARDIFF, CF3 2SF.
MAUNDER, Mr. John William, BSc FCA *1971;* Chantry Rise, Washington Road, Storrington, PULBOROUGH, RH20 4BZ.
MAUNDER, Mr. Michael David, MBA FCA *1972;* The Old Vicarage, Edlingham, ALNWICK, NE66 2BL.
MAUNDER, Miss. Penelope Elizabeth, BA ACA *1993;* 60, Great Portland Street, LONDON, W1W 7RT.
MAUNDER, Mr. Peter Lloyd, BSc ACA *1991;* Bradford Farm, Uplowman Road, Tiverton, Devon, EX16 7DQ, TIVERTON DEVON EX16 7DQ.
MAUNDER, Mr. Sam, ACA *2009;* 41 Croft Gardens, Charlton Kings, CHELTENHAM, GL53 8LG.
MAUNDER, Mr. Timothy John, BA ACA *1982;* Dragons The City, Chinnor Road Bledlow Ridge, HIGH WYCOMBE, BUCKINGHAMSHIRE, HP14 4AB.
•MAUNDRELL, Mr. Colin Neil, FCA *1982;* (Tax Fac), Paul & Maundrell, The Athenaeum, Kimberley Place, FALMOUTH, TR11 3QL.
MAUNDRELL, Mr. Peter Douglas, FCA *1987;* Peter Maundrell & Company, P.O. Box 1824, EMERALD, QLD 4720, AUSTRALIA.
MAUNG, Mr. Hla, FCA *1966;* 9 South Court, Kersfield Road, LONDON, SW15 3HQ. (Life Member)
•MAUNSELL, Mr. Robin Guy Debonnaire, FCA *1975;* (Tax Fac), R.G.D. Maunsell & Co, Pear Tree Cottage, 27 Rasen Road, Tealby, MARKET RASEN, LINCOLNSHIRE LN8 3XL.
MAURER, Mr. Benjamin Michael, BSc ACA *2004;* 45 Goldsmith Way, ST. ALBANS, HERTFORDSHIRE, AL3 5LH.
MAURICE, Mr. Derek John, FCA *1963;* 33 Brook View, South Street, Letcombe Regis, WANTAGE, OXFORDSHIRE, OX12 9JY.
MAURICE, Mr. Neil, ACA *2008;* 8 Tenterden Drive, LONDON, NW4 1ED.
•MAURICE, Mr. Paul Gary, FCA *1980;* (Tax Fac), with FSPG, 21 Bedford Square, LONDON, WC1B 3HH.
MAURICE-WILLIAMS, Mr. Julian Robert Cecil, ACA *2008;* 29 Fairland Road, LONDON, E15 4AF.
•MAVAHEBI, Mr. Bahram, BSc ACA *1984;* Bahrams Ltd, 46 Bushey Way, Park Langley, BECKENHAM, KENT, BR3 6TB.
MAVANI, Miss. Avni, BA ACA *1993;* 4 Arnold Grove, Shirley, SOLIHULL, B90 3JR.
MAVANI, Mr. Mohamedraza Yusufali, BA(Hons) ACA *2002;* 3 Sudbury Court, PETERBOROUGH, PE2 8UW.
MAVANI, Mr. Rajesh Anantray, FCA *1983;* (Tax Fac), 7 Heathside Road, NORTHWOOD, HERTFORDSHIRE, HA6 2EE.
MAVANI, Ms. Sneha, LLB ACA *2001;* 4 Arnold Grove, Shirley, SOLIHULL, B90 3JR.
MAVIMBA, Mr. Jabulani, MSc ACA *1984;* Ernst & Young, Cnr Julius Nyerere Way, Kwame Nkrumah Avenue, HARARE, ZIMBABWE.
MAVOR, Mr. Alexander Charles Gerald, BA FCA *1979;* 1 Cochrane Drive, Dundonald, KILMARNOCK, KA2 9ED.
•MAVROCORDATOS, Mr. Costakis Lucas, FCA *1984;* PricewaterhouseCoopers Limited, Julia House, 3 Themistocles Dervis Street, CY-1066 NICOSIA, CYPRUS.
MAVROMICHALIS, Mr. Marinos, BSc ACA *2011;* Flat 104, 9 Spetson Street, Engomi, 2416 NICOSIA, CYPRUS.
MAVROMMATIS, Mr. Demetris, BSc ACA *2002;* Flat 203 6 Tripoleos Street Aglantzia, 2107 NICOSIA, CYPRUS.
MAVROMMATIS, Mr. Ioannis John Phokas, MSc BA ACA *1992;* with PricewaterhouseCoopers LLP, 1 Embankment Place, LONDON, WC2N 6RH.
MAVROMMATIS, Mr. Marios, MSc BA ACA *2003;* 6 Charalambou Mouskou, Engomi Street, 2406 NICOSIA, CYPRUS.
•MAVRON, Mr. Panycos Chris, BSc FCA *1979;* (Tax Fac), Union Partners Limited, 38 South Molton Street, Mayfair, LONDON, W1K 5RL.
MAVROS, Mr. Kyriacos, ACA *2009;* 90 B April 1st Avenue, LARNACA, CYPRUS.
MAVROU, Miss. Eleftheria, MA ACA *2006;* Nausikas 8, 17672 ATHENS, GREECE.
MAVROU, Miss. Elena, ACA *2010;* 25 Ant Christou Photi, Engomi, 2416 NICOSIA, CYPRUS.
MAW, Mr. Antony Cedric, FCA *1973;* 17 Calle La India, 03730 JAVEA, ALICANTE, SPAIN. (Life Member)
•MAW, Mr. Christopher, BSc ACA *1986;* PricewaterhouseCoopers LLP, The Atrium, St. Georges Street, NORWICH, NR3 1AG. See also PricewaterhouseCoopers
MAW, Mr. David John, MA FCA ATII *1980;* (Tax Fac), with KPMG LLP, One Snowhill, Snow Hill Queensway, BIRMINGHAM, B4 6GN.
•MAW, Mr. Peter Loseby Trentham, FCA *1965;* (Tax Fac), P.L.T. Maw & Co., 192 Harestone Valley Road, CATERHAM, CR3 6BT.
MAW, Mr. Richard Jonathon Crompton, MBA BSc ACA *1981;* Ashley Croft, Two Dells Lane, Ashley Green, CHESHAM, HP5 3RB.
MAW, Mrs. Sarah Katherine, BA ACA *1991;* 11 Thorngate Place, BARNARD CASTLE, COUNTY DURHAM, DL12 8GP.
MAW, Mr. Trevor Gareth, BA FCA *1987;* 16 Overcroft Rise, SHEFFIELD, S17 4AX.
•MAW, Mr. William Louis, FCA *1982;* 4 Pell Farm Road, SADDLE RIVER, NJ 07458, UNITED STATES.
MAWANI, Mr. Adil, BSc ACA *2009;* 6 The Mount, RICKMANSWORTH, HERTFORDSHIRE, WD3 4DW.
MAWANI, Mr. Aladin Walji, MBA FCA *1976;* 19 Pining Road, THORNHILL L3T 5N5, ON, CANADA.
MAWBEY, Mr. Nigel William, BSc ACA *1999;* 33 Pendrell Road, Brockley, LONDON, SE4 2PB.
MAWBY, Mr. Allen, BA FCA *1973;* Priors Court, Aylton, LEDBURY, HR8 2QE.
MAWBY, Mr. Colin Arthur, FCA *1951;* Coppers, 9 Farr Hall Drive, Heswall, WIRRAL, CH60 4SF. (Life Member)
MAWBY, Mr. Colin George, FCA *1969;* 1 Pembury Avenue, Longford, COVENTRY, CV6 6JT.
MAWBY, Mr. Cornelius Leonard, MA FCA *1996;* 1 St Andrew's Place, Charing Cross, ST HELIER, JE2 3RP.
MAWBY, Mr. Jack Edward, FCA *1964;* 5 Hawthorn Rise, Peterchurch, HEREFORD, HR2 0RQ. (Life Member)
MAWBY, Mr. John David, FCA *1969;* The Homestead, Main Street, Lyddington, Oakham, RUTLAND, LE15 9LS.
MAWBY, Mr. Jonathan, BA(Hons) ACA *2011;* 115a Highbury New Park, LONDON, N5 2HG.

MAWBY, Mr. Robin Gareth, LLB ACA *1999;* LCP Management LTD, Lcp House, Building 36, First Avenue, Pensnett Trading Estate, KINGSWINFORD WEST MIDLANDS DY6 7NA.
MAWBY, Mrs. Susan Patricia, FCA *1971;* Allithwaite House, 34 Station Road, Stow-cum-Quy, CAMBRIDGE, CB25 9AJ.
MAWBY, Mr. Timothy Joseph, BA ACA *2000;* (Tax Fac), Deltec House, NASSAU, N-7549, BAHAMAS.
MAWBY, Mr. Timothy Stephen Sprigg, BSc FCA *1979;* Saba Software (UK) Limited, Circa The Ring, BRACKNELL, RG12 1AA.
MAWBY, Mr. Trevor John Charles, FCA *1971;* Allithwaite House, 34 Station Road, Stow-cum-Quy, CAMBRIDGE, CB25 9AJ.
MAWDSLEY, Mr. Arundel James Basil, FCA *1953;* Flat 104 Valiant House Vicarage Crescent, LONDON, SW11 3LX. (Life Member)
MAWDSLEY, Mr. Byron, BSc(Hons) ACA *2004;* 30 Langborough Road, WOKINGHAM, RG40 2BT.
MAWDSLEY, Miss. Helen Margaret, BSc ACA *1983;* 14 Farlers End, Nailsea, BRISTOL, BS48 4PG.
MAWDSLEY, Mr. Ian, BA ACA *1984;* Gloucestershire County Council Environment Department, Shire Hall Westgate Street, GLOUCESTER, GL1 2TH.
MAWDSLEY, Mr. John Colin, BSc FCA CTA *1994;* 60 King Edward Avenue, AYLESBURY, BUCKINGHAMSHIRE, HP21 7JE.
MAWDSLEY, Mrs. Lynn Christine, BA ACA *1987;* Claremont House Stony Lane Little Kingshill, GREAT MISSENDEN, BUCKINGHAMSHIRE, HP16 0DS.
MAWDSLEY, Mrs. Theresa Mary, BSc ACA *1994;* 60 King Edward Avenue, AYLESBURY, BUCKINGHAMSHIRE, HP21 7JE.
MAWE, Mr. Christopher, BEng FCA *1991;* Heimatstrasse 21b, 6340 BAAR, SWITZERLAND.
•①**MAWER, Mr. Kevin Roy, BA FCA** *1986;* with KPMG LLP, 1 The Embankment, Neville Street, LEEDS, LS1 4DW.
MAWHOOD, Mr. Andrew Christopher, BA ACA *2002;* 15 Townley Manor, Tullyallen, DROGHEDA, COUNTY LOUTH, IRELAND.
•**MAWHOOD, Mr. Richard, ACA** *1982;* (Tax Fac), Richard Mawhood, 9 Far Lane, Wadsley, SHEFFIELD, S6 4FA.
•**MAWJI, Mr. Amin Mohamed, BSc FCA** *1982;* Ernst & Young LLP, 1 More London Place, LONDON, SE1 2AF. See also Ernst & Young Europe LLP
MAWJI, Mr. Haider, BA(Hons) ACA *2000;* iCX Europe, 120 Moorgate, LONDON, EC2m6UR.
•**MAWJI, Mr. Iqbal Ebrahim, FCA FCCA** *1974;* Fairman Law, Fairman Law House, 1-3 Park Terrace, WORCESTER PARK, SURREY, KT4 7JZ. See also Fairman Davis
MAWSON, Mr. Alastair David, FCA *1975;* 1 Park Mews Cottages, Vicarage Lane, Little Budworth, TARPORLEY, CW6 9BP.
•**MAWSON, Mr. Charles Iain Hayton, FCA** *1982;* MA Partners LLP, 7 The Close, NORWICH, NORFOLK, NR1 4DJ. See also M + A Partners (North Norfolk) Limited
MAWSON, Miss. Rebecca Jane, BA ACA *1994;* 39 Colyford Road, SEATON, DEVON, EX12 2DG.
MAWSON, Mr. Simon John, MA ACA *1996;* Jardine Lloyd Thompson Ltd Jardine House, 6 Crutched Friars, LONDON, EC3N 2PH.
MAX, Mr. Peter, BA ACA *2000;* Integra Community Living Options Ltd The Maltings, East Tyndall Street, CARDIFF, CF24 5EA.
•**MAXEY, Mr. John Fredric, BSc ACA ATII** *1990;* Deloitte LLP, Athene Place, 66 Shoe Lane, LONDON, EC4A 3BQ. See also Deloitte & Touche LLP
MAXFIELD, Mr. Andrew Michael, BSc(Hons) FCA CTA *1992;* (Tax Fac), with Grant Thornton UK LLP, 1 Whitehall Riverside, Whitehall Road, LEEDS, WEST YORKSHIRE, LS1 4BN.
MAXFIELD, Ms. Anne, MA ACA *1992;* 151 Windmill Road, Headington, OXFORD, OX3 7DW.
MAXFIELD, Mr. Jeremy David, ACA *1987;* Bride Hall, 49 Hays Mews, Mayfair, LONDON, W1J 5QQ.
MAXFIELD, Mr. John Frederick, ACA *1982;* North Lodge, Myskyns, Stonegate, WADHURST, TN5 7DS.
•**MAXFIELD, Mrs. Maree June, ACA CA(NZ)** *2011;* Maxama, Kirkland, Longdown Road, FARNHAM, SURREY, GU10 3JS.
MAXTED, Mr. Benjamin John, ACA *2008;* 15 Mayfield Road, Gosforth, NEWCASTLE UPON TYNE, NE3 4HE.
MAXTED, Mr. Jonathan Ian, BA(Hons) ACA *2002;* 41 Houstead Road, SHEFFIELD, S9 4BX.
MAXWELL, Mr. Adam Alexander, BSc ACA *1995;* Woodlands Cottage Burchetts Green Road, Burchetts Green, MAIDENHEAD, SL6 6QZ.
MAXWELL, Mr. Andrew James, BA(Hons) ACA MBA *2000;* Standard Bank Plc, 20 Gresham Street, LONDON, EC2V 7JE.
MAXWELL, Mr. Bryce Good, BA ACA *1992;* 12 Manor House Drive, NORTHWOOD, HA6 2UJ.
MAXWELL, Mr. Cameron Anderson, FCA *1964;* (Member of Council 1999 - 2011), Albury, 3 Myln Meadow, Stock, INGATESTONE, CM4 9NE.
MAXWELL, Mr. Charles Joseph Patrick, FCA *1960;* 6 Elmsleigh Road, WESTON-SUPER-MARE, BS23 4JN.
•**MAXWELL, Mr. David Alfred, BA FCA** *1965;* Beechams LLP, 3rd Floor, 167 Fleet Street, LONDON, EC4A 2EA.
•**MAXWELL, Mr. David Anthony Stuart, BSc FCA** *1983;* Grant Thornton UK LLP, Grant Thornton House, 22 Melton Street, Euston Square, LONDON, NW1 2EP. See also Grant Thornton LLP
MAXWELL, Mr. David William, MA FCA *1980;* 96 Guibal Road, Lee, LONDON, SE12 9LZ.
MAXWELL, Mr. David Wynne, BA ACA *1991;* 22 Guessens Road, WELWYN GARDEN CITY, HERTFORDSHIRE, AL8 6RA.
MAXWELL, Miss. Emma Rachel, BA ACA *2005;* 95 Moorcroft, New Brighton, MOLD, CLWYD, CH7 6RX.
MAXWELL, Mr. George Charles Durant, BA ACA *2008;* William Grant & Sons Ltd, 84 Lower Mortlake Road, RICHMOND, SURREY, TW9 2HS.
MAXWELL, Mr. Gerald Anthony, FCA *1962;* Piper's Croft, 41 Barton Hey Drive, Caldy, WIRRAL, MERSEYSIDE, CH48 1PZ.
MAXWELL, Mrs. Helen Mary, MA FCA CTA *1982;* (Tax Fac), Resolution Plc, Juxon House, 100 St. Paul's Churchyard, LONDON, EC4M 8BU.
MAXWELL, Mr. Herbert Henry, MA FCA *1974;* 24 Gunterstone Road, LONDON, W14 9BU.
•**MAXWELL, Mr. Hugh William George, FCA** *1972;* Maxwell & Co Limited, 10 St. Georges Yard, FARNHAM, SURREY, GU9 7LW.
MAXWELL, Mr. James Robert Iain, BSc ACA *1998;* 4 Temple Sheen, LONDON, SW14 7RP.
MAXWELL, Miss. Jennifer Anne, BA(Hons) ACA *2011;* 10 Falcon Drive, GRETNA, DUMFRIESSHIRE, DG16 5JU.
MAXWELL, Mr. John David, BA FCA *1963;* Braestones, Hob Lane, Turton, BOLTON, BL7 0PT.
MAXWELL, Miss. Katherine Jane, BSc ACA *2010;* 17 Heathfield Road, Penenden Heath, MAIDSTONE, KENT, ME14 2AD.
MAXWELL, Miss. Lorraine Erin, ACA *2011;* 18 Athol Street, Douglas, ISLE OF MAN, IM1 1JA.
MAXWELL, Mr. Nicholas, BSc FCA *1978;* Mount Jessop, Roborough, PLYMOUTH, DEVON, PL6 7BZ.
MAXWELL, Mr. Patrick Ronald Vernon, BA ACA *1990;* Sutton Plack Managers LLp, 6th Floor, 6 Chesterfield Gardens, LONDON, W1J 5BQ.
MAXWELL, Mr. Peter Willis, BSc ACA *1990;* 41 Banbury Road, STRATFORD-UPON-AVON, WARWICKSHIRE, CV37 7HW.
MAXWELL, Mr. Richard William, MBA BSc FCA *1990;* 69 Foley Road Claygate, ESHER, SURREY, KT10 0LY.
•①**MAXWELL, Mr. Robert Alexander Henry, BSc ACA** *1991;* Begbies Traynor, 9th Floor, Bond Court, LEEDS, LS1 2JZ. See also Begbies Traynor(Central) LLP and Begbies Traynor Limited
MAXWELL, Mr. Robert James Anthony, BSc ACA MBA *1991;* 59 Lorne Ave. East Unit 4, STRATFORD N5A 6S4, ON, CANADA.
MAXWELL, Mr. Rowan Paul, BSc ACA *2007;* 13 Kenwood Road, LEICESTER, LE2 3PL.
MAXWELL, Mrs. Sheila Frances, BSc ACA *1991;* The Old Dairy, Hascombe Road, GODALMING, SURREY, GU8 4AE.
MAXWELL, Mr. Stephen Alexander, BA(Hons) ACA *2002;* Princess Grace Hospital, 42-52 Nottingham Place, LONDON, W1U 5NY.
MAXWELL, Mr. Thomas Leslie, ACA *2011;* 2 Villa Court Apartments, Castlemona Avenue, Douglas, ISLE OF MAN, IM2 4EA.
•**MAXWELL-GUMBLETON, Mr. Richard Vaney, FCA** *1973;* Maxwell-Gumbleton & Co, 1 West St, LEWES, BN7 2NZ. See also Keymer Haslam & Co
MAXWELL-HOLROYD, Miss. Victoria Ellen, BA ACA *1996;* 31 Gladwyn Road, LONDON, SW15 1JY.
MAXWELL-SCOTT, Mr. Andrew Nicholas Hugh, BA FCA *1992;* with KPMG LLP, 15 Canada Square, LONDON, E14 5GL.
MAXWELL-SCOTT, Mrs. Sarah-Jane, BA(Hons) ACA *2003;* Flat 10 Willow Lodge, 195 Cedars Road, LONDON, SW4 0PU.
MAXWELL-SCOTT, Mr. Simon Magnus, ACA *1987;* Flat 10, Willow Lodge, 195 Cedars Road, LONDON, SW4 0PU.
MAXWELL-TIMMINS, Miss. Zoe, ACA *2011;* K P M G Llp, 15 Canada Square, LONDON, E14 5GL.
MAY, Mr. Alan Walton, FCA *1962;* 1 Furzefield Road, BEACONSFIELD, HP9 1PQ.
MAY, Mr. Alan Wotton, FCA *1967;* 20 Tregaric, Bowood Park, CAMELFORD, CORNWALL, PL32 9RF.
MAY, Mr. Alastair, MA BSc ACA *2004;* 1 Moore Close, Appleby Magna, SWADLINCOTE, DERBYSHIRE, DE12 7AT.
MAY, Mr. Andrew Colin, ACA *1997;* Stonecroft, Les Mourants Road, St. Andrew, GUERNSEY, GY6 8RA.
MAY, Mr. Andrew John, JP MA FCA *1976;* Buckshaw House, Holwell, SHERBORNE, DT9 5LD.
MAY, Mr. Barry, BSc FCA *1982;* 8 Barnfield Way, Copmanthorpe, YORK, YO23 3RT.
MAY, Mr. Benjamin Dominic, BA ACA *2006;* with PricewaterhouseCoopers LLP, 1 Embankment Place, LONDON, WC2N 6RH.
•**MAY, Mr. Bertram Michael, FCA** *1971;* B.M. May & Co, 41 Salisbury Road, CARSHALTON, SM5 3HA.
MAY, Mr. Brian Michael, BSc ACA *1988;* 8 Hartsbourne Avenue, Bushey Heath, BUSHEY, WD23 1JL.
MAY, Miss. Carolyn Anne Louise, BA ACA *2001;* C/O Monitor, Independent Regulator of NHS Foundation Trust, 4 Matthew Parker Street, LONDON, SW1H 9NP.
MAY, Mr. Christopher Gooding, FCA *1956;* 9 The Glebe, Lavendon, OLNEY, MK46 4HY. (Life Member)
MAY, Mr. Christopher John Rutton, MA FCA *1967;* Froghole Oast House, Crockham Hill, EDENBRIDGE, TN8 6TD.
MAY, Mr. Clifford Paul, BA FCA *1978;* 22 Lynton Avenue, Whitecraigs, GLASGOW, G46 7JP.
MAY, Mr. Darren Alexander, LLB ACA *2006;* 6 Chelsea Gardens, BOURNEMOUTH, BH8 8EL.
•**MAY, Mr. David Anthony James, BA ACA CF** *1980;* 46 Gloucester Mews, LONDON, W2 3HE.
MAY, Mr. David John, BSc ACA *2010;* 17 Woodcombe Close, BRIERLEY HILL, DY5 3PQ.
•**MAY, Mr. Gayling Richard, FCA** *1965;* The Eastern Africa Association, Room 512, Jubilee Place - 5th Floor, Mama Ngina/ General Kago Street, P O Box 41272, NAIROBI 00100 KENYA.
MAY, Mr. Geoffrey Francis, BA FCA *1970;* 5 Eton Villas, LONDON, NW3 4SX.
MAY, Mrs. Gillian, BSc ACA *1993;* 11 Islet Park Drive, MAIDENHEAD, BERKSHIRE, SL6 8LF.
MAY, Mrs. Gillian Ann, FCA *1971;* M G M Motor Co Brookside Garage, Hatchet Lane Winkfield, WINDSOR, BERKSHIRE, SL4 2EE.
MAY, Mr. Graham Seymour, MA MPhil ACA *1986;* 21 Abingdon Road, Cumnor, OXFORD, OX2 9QN.
MAY, Mrs. Helen, BSc ACA *1999;* Hewlett Packard Ltd, Cain Road, BRACKNELL, BERKSHIRE, RG12 1HN.
MAY, Miss. Jacqueline Karen, BA ACA *2005;* CME, 52 Charles Street, LONDON, W1J 5EU.
MAY, Mrs. Jacqueline Louise, BSc ACA *1990;* Harvest Cottage, Petersfield Road, Ropley, ALRESFORD, SO24 0EQ.
MAY, Mr. James Robert, BA(Hons) ACA *2004;* 19 Blessington Street, ST KILDA, VIC 3182, AUSTRALIA.
MAY, Mr. John, BA FCA *1959;* 40 Dalmahoy Crescent, BALERNO, EH14 7BZ. (Life Member)
MAY, Mr. John Howard, FCA *1980;* Pytches Rise, 8a Pytches Road, WOODBRIDGE, SUFFOLK, IP12 1ET.
•**MAY, Mr. John Joseph, BA FCA** *1974;* John J May, 2 Belmont Mews, CAMBERLEY, GU15 2PH.
MAY, Mr. John Stephen, BSc FCA *1975;* 12 Hall Hill, Bollington, MACCLESFIELD, CHESHIRE, SK10 5ED.
MAY, Mr. Justin Paul Hine, LLB ACA *2001;* Holme Cottage, Church Lane, Ruscombe, READING, RG10 9UA.
MAY, Ms. Katharine Jane, BA(Hons) ACA *2002;* 31a Hawes Street, LONDON, N1 2DT.
MAY, Mr. Keith Robert, BSc FCA *1974;* 94 Knowle Wood Road, Dorridge, SOLIHULL, WEST MIDLANDS, B93 8JP.
MAY, Mr. Kenneth Stanley, FCA *1960;* 50 Hillbourne Close, WARMINSTER, BA12 0BL. (Life Member)
•**MAY, Mr. Kenton Charles, BSc FCA CTA MAE** *1992;* (Tax Fac), Burgess Hodgson, Camburgh House, 27 New Dover Road, CANTERBURY, CT1 3DN.
MAY, Mrs. Laura Louise, BCom ACA *2002;* Broxholme, 5 Old Church Green, Kirk Hammerton, YORK, YO26 8DL.
MAY, Mr. Lee Patrick, BSc ACA *2005;* Rackitt Benckiser, Wellcroft House, Wellcroft Road, SLOUGH, SL1 4AQ.
•**MAY, Mr. Martin Irvin, BA FCA** *1980;* (Tax Fac), MMAS Limited, 399 Hendon Way, LONDON, NW4 3LH.
MAY, Miss. Mary Cecilia, ACA *2009;* 7 York Place, Clifton, BRISTOL, BS8 1AH.
•**MAY, Mr. Michael Anthony, FCA** *1968;* Michael May, 47 Algitha Road, SKEGNESS, PE25 2AJ.
MAY, Mr. Michael David Arthur, BA ACA *1979;* 4 George Court, George Street, CHELMSFORD, CM2 0JU.
MAY, Mr. Michael Hans, FCA *1974;* 225 Hook Rise South, SURBITON, KT6 7LD.
MAY, Mr. Michael Robert, MA BA ACA *1990;* (Tax Fac), with Lawrence Grant, 2nd Floor, Hygeia House, 66 College Road, HARROW, MIDDLESEX HA1 1BE.
MAY, Ms. Nerys Ann, BSc(Hons) ACA *2001;* Electrocomponents Plc, 8050 Alec Issigonis Way Oxford Business Park North, OXFORD, OX4 2HW.
MAY, Mr. Nicholas Guy, MBA BA ACA *1986;* Bath & Wells Diocesan, The Old Deanery, WELLS, SOMERSET, BA5 2UG.
•**MAY, Mrs. Nicola Marie, MA(Cantab) ACA** *2000;* with KPMG LLP, 1 Forest Gate, Brighton Road, CRAWLEY, WEST SUSSEX, RH11 9PT.
MAY, Mr. Nigel John, BA FCA ATII *1984;* 36 Oak Crescent, ASHBY-DE-LA-ZOUCH, LEICESTERSHIRE, LE65 1FX.
MAY, Mr. Peter James, BSc ACA *1980;* with Ernst & Young LLP, 1 More London Place, LONDON, SE1 2AF.
MAY, Mr. Peter Norman James, MA ACA *1980;* Lawn Farm, GILLINGHAM, DORSET, SP8 5QP.
MAY, Mr. Philip Henry, FCA *1952;* 15 Bedford Gardens, WOKINGHAM, RG41 3HZ. (Life Member)
MAY, Miss. Rachel Barbara, ACA *2008;* Apartment 18, 19 Dock Street, HULL, HU1 3AH.
MAY, Mrs. Rachel Emma, MMath ACA *2003;* 41 Lakeview Drive, Tamerton Foliot, PLYMOUTH, PL5 4LW.
MAY, Mr. Rupert Nigel, BA ACA CPA *1998;* 1438 Strathmore Mews, VANCOUVER V6Z 3B1, BC, CANADA.
MAY, Mr. Simon James, ACA *2008;* 53 Clarence Road, LONDON, SW19 8QF.
MAY, Mr. Stephen John, BSc ACA *1988;* I P C Media Blue Fin Building, 110 Southwark Street, LONDON, SE1 0SU.
MAY, Mr. Steven, ACA *2011;* 69c Holly Hill, SOUTHAMPTON, SO16 7ES.
MAY, Mrs. Susan, MA ACA *2001;* Ashbury House, 8a Herons Way, ST. ALBANS, HERTFORDSHIRE, AL1 1UX.
MAY, Mr. Thomas Willaim Maynard, MA ACA *2011;* Buckshaw House, Holwell, SHERBORNE, DORSET, DT9 5LD.
MAY, Mr. Timothy Simon, BSc ACA *1992;* 40 Garden Road, Fendalton, CHRISTCHURCH 8001, NEW ZEALAND.
MAY, Mr. Timothy William, BSc ACA *1987;* 16 Dukes Walk, Hale, ALTRINCHAM, CHESHIRE, WA15 8WB.
MAY-BOWLES, Mr. David Marshall, FCA *1953;* 21 Edinburgh Gardens, Kings Road, WINDSOR, SL4 2AN. (Life Member)
MAY-HILL, Mrs. Hilary Vera, FCA *1966;* 5 Westbourne Crescent, Whitchurch, CARDIFF, CF14 2BL. (Life Member)
MAY-HILL, Mr. Richard Clive, FCA *1968;* 5 Westbourne Crescent, Whitchurch, CARDIFF, CF14 2BL. (Life Member)
MAY-HILL, Mr. Rupert Richard Andrew, BA(Hons) ACA CISA *2001;* 14 Millbrook Park, Lisvane, CARDIFF, CF14 0UH.
MAYALL, Mr. David Anthony, BA ACA *1991;* 14 Forest View, ROCHDALE, OL12 6HF. (Life Member)
MAYALL, Mrs. Lynn Margaret, BA FCA *1975;* Green Farm, Green Lane, Cutthorpe, CHESTERFIELD, DERBYSHIRE, S42 7AR.
MAYALL, Mr. Richard James, BA ACA *2000;* 117 Dorset Road, LONDON, SW19 3EQ.
MAYANJA, Mr. Uthman, BA ACA *2001;* PricewaterhouseCoopers, PO Box 882, 10th Floor Communications House, 1 Colville Street, KAMPALA, UGANDA.
MAYATT, Mr. Peter Humphrey, FCA *1966;* 8 rue de la Mouliere, 62380 REMILLY-WIRQUIN, FRANCE.
MAYBANK, Mr. John, FCA *1971;* The Gate House, Home Farm Grove, Arthingworth, MARKET HARBOROUGH, LEICESTERSHIRE, LE16 8NJ.
•①**MAYBERY, Mr. Andrew Johnson, FCA** *1975;* Hart Shaw LLP, Europa Link, Sheffield Business Park, SHEFFIELD, S9 1XU.
MAYBIN, Mr. Robert Alexander, FCA *1971;* 26a Morland Avenue, CROYDON, CR0 6EA.

•**MAYBREY, Mr. Peter Charles, BSc ACA** *1993;* PricewaterhouseCoopers LLP, Hays Galleria, 1 Hays Lane, LONDON, SE1 2RD. See also PricewaterhouseCoopers
MAYBURY, Mrs. Stella Tracey, ACA *1990;* 33 DOUBLING ROAD, GREENWICH, CT 06830, UNITED STATES.
MAYCOCK, Mr. Alan John, FCA *1982;* 2 Old Mead, Broadmead Village, FOLKESTONE, CT19 5UR.
MAYCOCK, Mr. Alexander Edward, BSc ACA *2003;* with KPMG, 10 Shelley Street, SYDNEY, NSW 2000, AUSTRALIA.
MAYCOCK, Mr. Brian Charles, BA FCA *1959;* 33 Netherfield Road, CHESTERFIELD, S40 3LS. (Life Member)
MAYCOCK, Mr. Ian Charles, BA ACA *1990;* 40 Wilby Street, NORTHAMPTON, NN1 5JX.
MAYCOCK, Mr. James Edward D'Auvergne, MA ACA *2001;* Rosaria, 31 Court Road, TUNBRIDGE WELLS, KENT, TN4 8EB.
MAYCOCK, Mrs. Jane Caroline Margaret, BSc ACA *1978;* Old Chimneys, 6 Rocky Bay Lane, DEVONSHIRE DV07, BERMUDA.
MAYCOCK, Mrs. Sonia Margaret, BSc ACA *1991;* Hunters Moon, Sherborne Street, LECHLADE, GLOUCESTERSHIRE, GL7 3AH.
MAYCOCK, Mr. Stephen Robert, BA FCA *1984;* Aeronautical & General Instruments Ltd Unit A-b, Fleetspoint Business Centre Willis Way, POOLE, DORSET, BH15 3SS.
•**MAYCOX, Mr. Paul, BA ACA** *1996;* Ambry Cottage, The Street, West Clandon, GUILDFORD, SURREY, GU4 7ST.
•**MAYCROFT, Miss. Melanie Alysia, ACA CTA MAAT** *2002;* landtax LLP, Mitre House, Lodge Road, Long Hanborough, Business Park, WITNEY OXFORDSHIRE OX29 8SS.
MAYE, Miss. Christine Ann, BA ACA *1992;* Citigroup, 33 Canada Square, Canary Wharf, LONDON, E14 5LB.
MAYE, Miss. Jawahir, BA(Hons) ACA *2004;* Convention tower office, P.O. Box 7497, DUBAI, UNITED ARAB EMIRATES.
MAYE, Mr. Roger, BA FCA CTA MSI *1998;* 19 St. Pauls Way, Finchley, LONDON, N3 2PP.
MAYELL, Mr. Charles Timothy, BSc FCA *1987;* Cherry Tree Cottage, Hawkswood Grove, Fulmer, SLOUGH, SL3 6JF.
MAYER, Mr. Allen, ACA *2007;* 25 Barnsbury Square, LONDON, N1 1JP.
MAYER, Mr. Charles Henry, BA ACA *2005;* 68 Brookwood Road, LONDON, SW18 5BY.
MAYER, Miss. Claire Rebecca, ACA *2009;* 6 Scobell Close, Shinfield, READING, RG2 9HH.
•**MAYER, Mr. David Anthony, ACA FCCA** *2007;* Jacksons Accountants (Midlands) Limited, Deansfield House, 98 Lancaster Road, NEWCASTLE, STAFFORDSHIRE, ST5 1DS. See also Jacksons Contables S.L
MAYER, Mr. Dean Scott, BSc CA ACA MCT *1997;* Apt. 213 Munkenbeck, 5 Hermitage Street, LONDON, W2 1PW.
MAYER, Mrs. Emma Michelle, BSc ACA *2004;* with KPMG LLP, St. Nicholas House, 31 Park Row, NOTTINGHAM, NG1 6FQ.
MAYER, Miss. Gina, ACA MAAT *2002;* Apartado de Correos 207, 30320 FUENTE ALAMO, MURCIA, SPAIN.
MAYER, Mr. Jeremy, ACA *2009;* The Basement, 50 Doughty Street, LONDON, WC1N 2JS.
MAYER, Mr. John Gilbert, FCA *1973;* with Downham Mayer Clarke Limited, 41 Greek Street, STOCKPORT, CHESHIRE, SK3 8AX. (Life Member)
MAYERS, Mr. Adam James, BSc(Hons) ACA *2000;* 3 Field Close, Bramhall, STOCKPORT, CHESHIRE, SK7 1HZ.
MAYERS, Mr. John Alfred Dugard, FCA *1971;* Gannaway Farm House, Henley Road, Norton Lindsey, WARWICK, CV35 8JT.
•**MAYERS, Mr. Nicholas John, BA FCA** *1983;* Davies Mayers Barnett LLP, Pillar House, 113-115 Bath Road, CHELTENHAM, GLOUCESTERSHIRE, GL53 7LS. See also Barnett DM Limited
•**MAYERS, Mr. Patrick Guy, FCA** *1959;* (Tax Fac), GMAK, 5-7 Vernon Yard, Portobello Road, LONDON, W11 2DX. See also GMAK Services Limited
MAYERS, Mr. Peter David, FCA *1974;* 3 Collins Close, CAVES BEACH, NSW 2281, AUSTRALIA.
MAYERS, Mr. Richard Daniel, BA(Hons) ACA *2002;* 14 Allfarthing Lane, LONDON, SW18 2PQ.
MAYES, Mr. Anthony, BA ACA *2001;* 71 Lower Road, Fetcham, LEATHERHEAD, KT22 9HG.
•**MAYES, Mrs. Brenda Wiseman, FCA** *1975;* William J Mayes, Vansittart Estate, Arthur Road, WINDSOR, SL4 1SE.
MAYES, Mr. Colin Anthony Horsley, FCA *1965;* 73 Castelau, LONDON, SW13 9RT.
MAYES, Mr. Derrick Alan, FCA *1962;* Riseley Farm, Swallowfield, READING, RG7 1TB.
•**MAYES, Mr. Edward Graham, FCA** *1958;* Twitten End, The Street, Aylmerton, NORWICH, NR11 8AA. (Life Member)
MAYES, Mr. Frank Arthur, FCA *1976;* 2 Lowlands Cottages, Rue Des Vignes St Peter, JERSEY, JE3 7BE.
MAYES, Mr. Gregory Ian, BSc ACA *1995;* High Pines, Ismays Road, Ivy Hatch, SEVENOAKS, KENT, TN15 0NZ.
MAYES, Mrs. Hannah Catherine, BSc(Hons) ACA *2000;* 117 Gwydir Street, CAMBRIDGE, CB1 2LG.
MAYES, Mrs. Kay, BSc FCA *1989;* 1a Orton Lane, Norton juxta Twycross, ATHERSTONE, CV9 3PU.
MAYES, Mr. Maurice Gerard Peter, FCA *1963;* 72 Beach Road, Selsey, CHICHESTER, WEST SUSSEX, PO20 0TA.
MAYES, Mr. Peter George, BCom FCA *1974;* 2a Bournside Road, CHELTENHAM, GLOUCESTERSHIRE, GL51 3AH.
MAYES, Mr. Raymond John, BA FCA *1970;* (Tax Fac), The Bee Garden, Norley Wood, LYMINGTON, SO41 5RX.
MAYES, Mr. Robert Jack, FCA *1970;* 73 Wolfs Corner Road, NEWTON, NJ 07860, UNITED STATES.
MAYES, Mr. Robin John, BA FCA *1967;* 495 Victoria Avenue, WESTMOUNT H3Y 2R3, QUE, CANADA.
•**MAYES, Mr. William John, FCA** *1976;* William J Mayes, Vansittart Estate, Arthur Road, WINDSOR, SL4 1SE.
MAYFIELD, Mr. Antony Miles Westlake, FCA *1959;* 43 Aldenham Avenue, RADLETT, WD7 8HZ. (Life Member)
•**MAYFIELD, Mr. David Thomas, FCA** *1983;* (Tax Fac), Mayfield & Company, 2nd Floor, 27 The Crescent, King Street, LEICESTER, LE1 6RX. See also Mayfield & Co (Accountants) Ltd
•**MAYFIELD, Mr. Kim, ACA** *1983;* (Tax Fac), RHP Partnership, Lancaster House, 87 Yarmouth Road, NORWICH, NORFOLK, NR7 0HF.
MAYFIELD, Mr. Oliver Alan, FCA *1963;* Bank House, Market Place, COLYTON, DEVON, EX24 6JS.
MAYFIELD, Mr. Philip John, FCA *1969;* Greengates, Gypsy Lane, Bleasby, NOTTINGHAM, NG14 7GG.
MAYFIELD, Mr. Richard Andrew, MA ACA *1994;* Pangbourne Lodge, Tidmarsh Road, Pangbourne, READING, RG8 7AZ.
MAYGER, Mr. Ian Barclay, FCA *1962;* Woodgate Orchard Cottage, Howe Road, WATLINGTON, OXFORDSHIRE, OX49 5EL.
MAYHEAD, Mrs. Anna Ilse Agneta, ACA *2008;* 11 Rannoch Court, 26 Adelaide Road, SURBITON, SURREY, KT6 4TE.
MAYHEW, Miss. Gemma Jean, BSc(Hons) ACA *2010;* 51 Danforth Close, Framlingham, WOODBRIDGE, SUFFOLK, IP13 9HP.
MAYHEW, Mr. James Robert, MEng ACA *1998;* 126 Purley Oaks Road, SOUTH CROYDON, SURREY, CR2 0NS.
MAYHEW, Mrs. Julie, BSc FCA *1995;* 18 Melbury Gardens, LONDON, SW20 0DJ.
•**MAYHEW, Mr. Nicholas, BA ACA** *1994;* Price Bailey Private Client LLP, The Quorum, Barnwell Road, CAMBRIDGE, CB5 8RE. See also Price Bailey LLP
•**MAYHEW, Mrs. Nicola Louise, BA(Hons) ACA** *2002;* Kingsley Accountancy, 18 Kingsley Way, Whiteley, FAREHAM, HAMPSHIRE, PO15 7NL.
MAYHEW, Mr. Nigel Marsden, FCA *1971;* 3 Oakdene, Kirton, IPSWICH, IP10 0NS.
MAYHEW, Mr. Peter, FCA *1960;* P O Box 5040, GREENWICH, NSW 2065, AUSTRALIA. (Life Member)
MAYHEW, Mr. Richard James, BSc ACA *1992;* Barford House, 40 Ditton Road, SURBITON, SURREY, KT6 6QZ.
MAYHEW, Mr. Robert, LLB ACA *2001;* 13 Windermere Avenue, LONDON, NW6 6LP.
MAYHEW, Miss. Sara Arlene, BA ACA *1989;* 21 Wilderness Road, Earley, READING, RG6 7RU.
MAYHEW, Mr. Steven John, BA FCA *1982;* Old Stables, Alchester Road, Chesterton, BICESTER, OXFORDSHIRE, OX26 1UN.
MAYHEW, Mr. Thomas Oswald, FCA *1960;* 55 Frances Road, WINDSOR, SL4 3AQ. (Life Member)
MAYHEW-SANDERS, Sir John Reynolds, Kt MA FCA *1958;* Great Deptford House, High Bickington, UMBERLEIGH, EX37 9BP. (Life Member)
MAYHO, Mr. Paul Stewart, BSc ACA *1990;* Ballinttrae 6th Floor, 125 Old Broad street, LONDON, EC2N 1AR.
MAYHO, Mr. Peter, FCA *1960;* Cobbers, Ridgeway Close, Horsell, WOKING, GU21 4RD. (Life Member)
MAYHOOK, Mr. Paul Richard, BA ACA *1990;* 5 Foxdown Close, KIDLINGTON, OX5 2YE.
MAYLAND, Mr. David John, ACA *2010;* 42B Sistova Road, Balham, LONDON, SW12 9QS.
MAYLE, Mr. Edward Anthony, BA ACA *1994;* Pernod Ricard Sweden, Årstaängsvägen 19 A, SE- 117 97 STOCKHOLM, SWEDEN.
•**MAYLED, Mr. Stephen John, FCA** *1972;* (Tax Fac), Stephen Mayled & Associates Ltd, Cottage Farm, Michaelston-le-Pit, DINAS POWYS, SOUTH GLAMORGAN, CF64 4HE.
MAYLED, Mr. William Victor, FCA *1961;* High Marryats Limited, 19 High Marryats, Grove Road, Barton On Sea, NEW MILTON, BH25 7DW. (Life Member)
•**MAYLIN, Mr. Christopher David, BSc FCA** *1993;* WKH, PO Box 501, The Nexus Building, Broadway, LETCHWORTH GARDEN CITY, HERTFORDSHIRE SG6 9BL. See also Virtual Business Source Limited
MAYLOR, Mr. Clifford Gary, ACA *1987;* The Maltings, 98-100 Wilderspool Causeway, WARRINGTON, WA4 6PU.
MAYMAN, Mr. David, BSc ACA *2005;* 10 Dotterel Glen, Morley, LEEDS, LS27 8GR.
MAYMAN, Mr. Frank Alexander, BA FCA *1973;* Fine Foods International (Manufacturing) Ltd Unit B, Chiltern Park Industrial Estate Boscombe Road, DUNSTABLE, BEDFORDSHIRE, LU5 4LT.
•**MAYMAN, Mr. Michael, FCA** *1975;* Kenneth Easby LLP, Oak House, Market Place, 35 North End, BEDALE, NORTH YORKSHIRE DL8 1AQ.
MAYMAN, Miss. Wendy Melinda, FCA *1987;* 13 Westgate Grove, Lofthouse, WAKEFIELD, WEST YORKSHIRE, WF3 3NP.
MAYNARD, Mr. Alan David, BA ACA *1990;* Foxcote House, Templewood Lane, Farnham Common, SLOUGH, SL2 3HJ.
MAYNARD, Mrs. Alison Ruth, BSc FCA *1986;* 54 Station Road, Ashwell, BALDOCK, SG7 5LS.
•**MAYNARD, Mr. Alistair Stephen, ACA CTA** *1998;* Jane Maynard Limited, 37 Mill Street, BIDEFORD, DEVON, EX39 2JJ.
MAYNARD, Mr. Andrew Michael, BSc ACA *1997;* Church House Church Path, Ipplepen, NEWTON ABBOT, DEVON, TQ12 5RZ.
MAYNARD, Mr. Brian Stuart, ACA *1983;* 4 Wentworth Drive, PINNER, MIDDLESEX, HA5 2PS.
MAYNARD, Mr. Brian William, BSc ACA *1999;* 6 Rushmoor Close, SUTTON COLDFIELD, B74 2PW.
MAYNARD, Mr. Derek Charles, FCA *1977;* 9 Bouvel Drive, BURNHAM-ON-CROUCH, CM0 8TW.
MAYNARD, Mr. Henry Charles Edward, BSc FCA *1967;* 56 Settrington Road, LONDON, SW6 3BA. (Life Member)
•**MAYNARD, Mrs. Jane Carter, FCA** *1996;* (Tax Fac), Jane Maynard Limited, 37 Mill Street, BIDEFORD, DEVON, EX39 2JJ.
MAYNARD, Mrs. Jennifer Ann, BSc ACA *1988;* The White House, Hill, Leamington Hastings, RUGBY, CV23 8DX.
MAYNARD, Mr. John Charles, BSc FCA *1973;* Fox Hollow, Heathway, CAMBERLEY, GU15 2EL.
MAYNARD, Mr. Lars-Olaf, BSc FCA *1985;* White House, Hill, RUGBY, CV23 8DX.
MAYNARD, Ms. Lisa Corrine, BSc ACA AMCT *1997;* ESV Hassan & Co, PO Box 230, 9/4 ICC, Casemates, GIBRALTAR, GIBRALTAR.
MAYNARD, Mr. Michael-Sven, BA FCA *1982;* Sint Hendrikstraat 87, 1200 BRUSSELS, BELGIUM.
MAYNARD, Mr. Neil, BA(Hons) ACA *2002;* Baker Tilly (Cayman) Ltd, P.O. Box 1782, GEORGE TOWN, GRAND CAYMAN, KY1-1109, CAYMAN ISLANDS.
MAYNARD, Mr. Neil John, BSc ACA *1991;* Stanaway Farm Charity Lane, Otley, IPSWICH, IP6 9NA.
MAYNARD, Mr. Nicholas John, BA(Hons) ACA *2010;* Basement Flat, 467 Kingsland Road, LONDON, E8 4AU.
MAYNARD, Ms. Nicola Jane, BSc ACA ATII *1987;* Gilderdale, 23 North Park, GERRARDS CROSS, SL9 8JS.
MAYNARD, Mr. Paul William, BA ACA *1990;* Winterthur Life, Winterthur Way, BASINGSTOKE, RG21 6SZ.
•**MAYNARD, Mr. Piers Graham Boutflower, FCA** *1979;* 19 Campden Hill Road, LONDON, W8 7DX.
MAYNARD, Mr. Richard Alan Robert, BA ACA *2005;* Flat 10, Victoria Mansions, Queen's Club Gardens, LONDON, W14 9TG.
MAYNARD, Mr. Robert James, BSc(Econ) ACA *1999;* 8 Beech Avenue, SOUTH CROYDON, CR2 0NL.
MAYNARD, Mr. Stephen John, MBA BA FCA *1987;* Brightleigh Farm House, Millers Lane, Outwood, REDHILL, RH1 5PZ.
MAYNARD, Mr. Timothy Sven, ACA *1986;* Cressford, Waterend Lane, Redbourn, ST. ALBANS, AL3 7JZ.
MAYNE, Mr. Christopher Simon, BA(Hons) ACA *2001;* 3 Courtfields, HARPENDEN, HERTFORDSHIRE, AL5 5RX.
•**MAYNE, Mr. Kevin Richard, FCA** *1975;* Mayne & Company, Beach House, Petit Port, St. Brelade, JERSEY, JE3 8HL.
MAYNE, Ms. Margaret, BA ACA *1990;* Pond Cottage, Selling Road, Old Wives Lees, CANTERBURY, KENT, CT4 8BD.
MAYNELL, Mr. James Harold Alexander, MA BA(Hons) ACA *2003;* with Ernst & Young LLP, 1 More London Place, LONDON, SE1 2AF.
MAYNELL, Mrs. Sophia Charlotte, BSc(Hons) ACA *2003;* 11 Whittall Street, Kings Sutton, BANBURY, OXFORDSHIRE, OX17 3RD.
MAYNES, Mr. Jeremy John, MA FCA *1973;* (Tax Fac), Dean House, 35 Deanfield Avenue, HENLEY-ON-THAMES, OXFORDSHIRE, RG9 1UE.
MAYO, Mr. Alan Philip, BSc FCA *1986;* L'Abri, Alexander Lane, Hutton, BRENTWOOD, CM13 1AG.
MAYO, Miss. Catherine Margaret, BSc ACA *1993;* 24 Manville Road, LONDON, SW17 8JN.
•**MAYO, Mr. Christian, BA ACA CF** *1996;* KPMG LLP, St. James's Square, MANCHESTER, M2 6DS. See also KPMG Europe LLP
MAYO, Mr. Christopher, BSc(Hons) ACA *2004;* 43 St. Albans Road, KINGSTON UPON THAMES, SURREY, KT2 5HH.
MAYO, Mr. Daniel Roderick, ACA *2008;* 33 Sefton Street, LONDON, SW15 1NA.
MAYO, The Revd. Inglis John, FCA *1969;* 49b St. Catherines Road, BOURNEMOUTH, BH6 4AQ.
①**MAYO, Mrs. Janet Frances Mary, BSc ACA** *1991;* 9 Woodlands Road, Pownall Park, WILMSLOW, CHESHIRE, SK9 5QB.
MAYO, Mr. John Charles, FCA *1959;* Spring Hill, Kineton, WARWICK, CV35 0JH. (Life Member)
MAYO, Mr. John Charles, CBE ACA *1981;* Celtic Pharma, Leverton House, 13 Bedford Square, LONDON, WC1B 3RA.
MAYO, Mrs. Mary Patricia, FCA *1974;* 26 Sunset Lane RR2, NAPANEE K7R 3K7, ON, CANADA.
MAYO-SMITH, Mr. Brian, BA FCA *1978;* BDO Spicers, PO Box 2219, AUCKLAND, NEW ZEALAND. See also BDO International
MAYOH, Mr. John Derek, FCA *1951;* Old Orchard, Prendergast, Solva, HAVERFORDWEST, SA62 6XA. (Life Member)
MAYOR, Miss. Catherine Anne, BSc ACA *1995;* 19b Montpelier Road, eALING, LONDON, W5 2QT.
MAYOR, Ms. Diane Elizabeth, ACA CA(SA) *2011;* 13D Aldridge Road Villas, LONDON, W11 1BL.
MAYOR, Mr. Hedley John, BSc ACA *1992;* with Octopus Private Equity, 20 Old Bailey, LONDON, EC4M 7AN.
•**MAYOR, Mr. John Richard, FCA** *1973;* J.R. Mayor, 39 Pear Tree Park, Holme, CARNFORTH, LANCASHIRE, LA6 1SD.
MAYOR, Mr. Norman Ogden, FCA *1947;* 1 Norwood Drive, Torrisholme, MORECAMBE, LA4 6LT. (Life Member)
MAYOR, Mr. Roger, LLB ACA *2006;* 12/5 Hermand Crescent, EDINBURGH, EH11 1LP.
MAYOR, Mr. Sandeep, BA FCA ATII *1994;* (Tax Fac), 93 Shaftesbury Avenue, Kenton, HARROW, HA3 0RB.
MAYOR, Mr. Sukesh Chander, BSc ACA *1989;* 55 Moorgate, LONDON, EC2R 6PA.
MAYRS, Mr. Peter Robert, ACA *2011;* 15 East Street, TONBRIDGE, KENT, TN9 1HP.
•**MAYS, Mr. John Philip, FCA** *1975;* J Mays, 10 Kirkdale Crescent, LEEDS, LS12 6AS.
•**MAYSTON, Mr. Albert Peter, FCA** *1963;* (Tax Fac), Peter Mayston, Jacobs Farm, Wiggens Green, Helions Bumpstead, HAVERHILL, SUFFOLK CB9 7AD.
MAYSTON, Mr. Peter James, ACA *2008;* Ebookers.Com, 140 Aldersgate Street, LONDON, EC1A 4HY.
•**MAYSTON, Mr. Simon James, BSc ACA** *1995;* Blick Rothenberg, 12 York Gate, Regent's Park, LONDON, NW1 4QS.
MAYURAN, Mr. Shanmuganathan, ACA *2009;* 20 Latimer Drive, Calcot, READING, RG31 7AP.
MAZABA, Mr. Mwendamo Isaac, ACA *2007;* PO Box 33595, LUSAKA, ZAMBIA.
MAZAHERI, Mr. Amir, BA(Hons) ACA ACMA *2007;* Septopont Ltd Unit R-s Orchard Business Centre, St. Barnabas Close Allington, MAIDSTONE, ME16 0JZ.
MAZARS, Mrs. Vanessa, ACA *2002;* 3 Avenue Le Notre, 92420 VAUCRESSON, FRANCE.
MAZHAR, Mr. Mohammad, FCA *1972;* 23 Sector A-1, Township, LAHORE 54770, PAKISTAN. (Life Member)
•**MAZLOOMIAN, Mr. Farid, BSc ACA** *1983;* F. Mazloomian & Co, 73/75 Princess Street, MANCHESTER, M2 4EG.
MAZURKIEWICZ, Mr. Stephen Julian, MA FCA *1985;* rue de la Vignette 96, 1160 BRUSSELS, BELGIUM.

MAZZEO, Mr. John, BA FCA *1989;* Via Stresa 92, Int 6, 00135 ROME, ITALY.
MAZZOTTI, Mr. Gary Wheatley, BA ACA *1987;* (Tax Fac), Zelena 365, 25262 STATENICE, PRAHOVA, CZECH REPUBLIC.
MBA, Mr. Chukwudelu Udemezue, MBA BSc FCA *1985;* MBA & Co, B19 Admirality Towers, 8 Gerrard Road, P O Box 51847, Ikoyi, LAGOS NIGERIA.
MBAE, Mr. John K Murithi, ACA *1988;* Schlehenweg 32, 53177 BONN, GERMANY.
MBANEFO, Mr. Arthur Christopher Izuegbunam, FCA *1962;* 27N Glover Road, Ikoyi, PO Box 70668, Victoria, LAGOS, NIGERIA. (Life Member)
MBANEFO, Mr. Arthur Ubaka, FCA *1991;* 85 Lovell Road, New Rochelle, NEW YORK, NY 10804, UNITED STATES.
MBANEFO, Miss. Cynthia Obianuju, BA ACA *1997;* 28 Braxted Park, LONDON, SW16 3DU.
MBUGUA, Miss. Jeanne Caroline, LLB ACA *2002;* Flat A, 64 Marlborough Road, LONDON, N19 4NJ.
MC EVOY, Mrs. Samantha Jane, BSc ACA CTA *1994;* 137 Sabine Road, LONDON, SW11 5LU.
MCADAM, Mrs. Catherine Emma, BSc ACA *1994;* 5 Corraback, BELTURBET, COUNTY CAVAN, IRELAND.
MCADAM, Mr. Darren William, BSc(Hons) ACA *2000;* 1 Beck Close, Emersons Green, BRISTOL, BS16 7HD.
MCADAM, Mr. David Philip Laurence, BSc ACA *1996;* Ist Floor Warwick House, B A E Systems, PO Box 87, FARNBOROUGH, HAMPSHIRE, GU14 6YU.
•**MCADAM, Mr. Derek, BA ACA** *1991;* McAdam And Company, 7 Chalmers Road, AYR, KA7 2RQ.
MCADAM, Mrs. Helen Mott, BA ACA *1992;* (Tax Fac), 7 Chalmers Road, AYR, KA7 2RQ.
MCADAM, Mr. Kevin Dermott, FCA *1969;* 11 Birchley Avenue, Billinge, WIGAN, WN5 7QW.
MCADAM, Miss. Lyndsay Joanna, BSc ACA *2005;* with PKF (Isle of Man) LLC, PO Box 16, Analyst House, 20-26 Peel Road, Douglas, ISLE OF MAN IM1 4LZ.
MCADAM, Mr. Stephen Frederick, BA FCA *1979;* Storrington, 13 Ledborough Wood, BEACONSFIELD, HP9 2DJ.
MCADAMS, Mr. Joseph, BBS ACA *1996;* ING Capital LLC, 1325 Avenue Of The Americas, NEW YORK, NY 10019, UNITED STATES.
MCADOO, Mr. John Richard, BA ACA *1991;* 580 Channing Avenue, PALO ALTO, CA 94301, UNITED STATES.
MCALEAR, Mr. Duncan John Howard, BA ACA *1996;* Tall Trees Oxford Road, Tilehurst, READING, RG31 6UT.
•**MCALEAVY, Mr. Francis, FCA** *1972;* (Tax Fac), M D Coxey & Co Limited, 25 Grosvenor Road, WREXHAM, CLWYD, LL11 1BT.
MCALEELY, Mr. Christopher Simon, BSc ACA *2002;* with KPMG LLP, 15 Canada Square, LONDON, E14 5GL.
MCALEENAN, Mrs. Jill Patricia, BSc FCA *1975;* 78 Hazlewell Rd, LONDON, SW15 6UR.
MCALEENAN, Mr. Michael Creagh, FCA *1973;* Treasury Office, The Honourable Society of Gray's Inn, 8 South Square, LONDON, WC1R 5ET.
MCALEENAN, Mr. Patrick David, FCA *1973;* UBM Medica Limited, LONDON, SE1 9UY.
MCALEESE, Mr. Hugh Lyle, BSc ACA *1996;* The Limes Bates Hill, Ightham, SEVENOAKS, KENT, TN15 9HB.
MCALEESE, Mrs. Jenny Louise, MA ACA *1990;* The Retreat, Heslington Road, YORK, YO10 5BN.
MCALINDEN, Mr. Barry Patrick, BA ACA *2000;* 11C Panorama Gardens, 103 Robinson Road, MID LEVELS, HONG KONG ISLAND, HONG KONG SAR.
MCALINDON, Ms. Caroline Elizabeth, BA ACA *1993;* with Salt Union Ltd, Astbury House, Bradford Road, WINSFORD, CHESHIRE, CW7 2PA.
MCALINDON, Mr. Roman William, BSc FCA *1974;* McAlindon Associates Limited, The Sharrow, 34 Lickey Square, Barnt Green, BIRMINGHAM, B45 8HB.
MCALISTER, Miss. Lynne, BSc ACA *1982;* 74 Brockman Rise, BROMLEY, BR1 5RF.
MCALISTER, Mrs. Samantha, BSc(Hons) ACA CTA *2004;* 3 Bishopslea Close, WELLS, SOMERSET, BA5 1TG.
•**MCALLAN, Mr. Derek Ian, BSc ACA** *1992;* KPMG LLP, Arlington Business Park, Theale, READING, RG7 4SD. See also KPMG Europe LLP
MCALLEN, Miss. Nikoletta Polli, MA ACA *1998;* 101A The Eyrie, EAGLEMONT, VIC 3084, AUSTRALIA.
MCALLESTER, Mr. Ian Charles, FCA *1954;* 8 The Elms, Leek Wootton, WARWICK, CV35 7RR. (Life Member)
•**MCALLISTER, Mr. Daniel James, BSc FCA** *2000;* Simpson Wood, Bank Chambers, Market Street, HUDDERSFIELD, HD1 2EW.
MCALLISTER, Mr. Gavin Alan, ACA CA(SA) *2009;* PO BOX 781377, SANDTON, 2146, SOUTH AFRICA.
MCALLISTER, Mr. James Adam, BA(Hons) ACA *2003;* The Old Chapel Cottage, Sheepcote Lane, Darley, HARROGATE, NORTH YORKSHIRE, HG3 2RP.
MCALLISTER, Mr. Jonathan David, MA ACA *2002;* 8 Vicars Lane, NEWCASTLE UPON TYNE, NE7 7NS.
•**MCALLISTER, Mr. Michael James, BSc ACA** *1997;* with Target Consulting Limited, 6th Floor, Reading Bridge House, Reading Bridge, READING, RG1 8LS.
MCALLISTER, Mr. Michael John, FCA *1963;* 34 Tideswell Close, NORTHAMPTON, NN4 9XY.
MCALLISTER, Mr. Timothy John, BA ACA *2001;* with PricewaterhouseCoopers, 34 Al - Farabi Ave, Building A, 4th Floor, ALMATY 050059, KAZAKHSTAN.
MCALLISTER, Miss. Vicki, BA ACA *2006;* 11a Burnley Road, SOUTHPORT, MERSEYSIDE, PR8 3LR.
MCALOON, Mr. John Rowland, BA FCA *1981;* 24 Bertram Drive, WIRRAL, MERSEYSIDE, CH47 0LQ.
MCALPINE, Mr. Douglas, BSc ACA *2010;* Flat 8, Aspect House, 521 Manchester Road, LONDON, E14 3NX.
MCALPINE, Mrs. Louise Ann, ACA *1993;* 1018 Ridgewood Drive, NORTH VANCOUVER V7R 1H8, BC, CANADA.
•**MCALPINE, Mrs. Pauline Blair, BA FCA** *1982;* (Tax Fac), SBM & Co, 117 Fentiman Road, LONDON, SW8 1JZ.
•**MCALPINE, Mr. Stephen Blair, BA(Econ) FCA** *1983;* SBM & Co, 117 Fentiman Road, LONDON, SW8 1JZ.
MCANDREW, Mr. Douglas Allister, BSc ACA *2001;* Capital Values UK Ltd, 13 Albemarle Street, LONDON, W1S 4HJ.
MCANDREW, Mr. Ian Christopher, MA FCA *1978;* Flat B, 27 Nevern Square, LONDON, SW5 9PD.
MCANDREW, Mr. Paul Richard, MA(Hons) ACA *2004;* 106F Constitution Street, ABERDEEN, AB24 5DZ.
MCANDREW, Mrs. Rachael, BSc(Hons) ACA *2004;* 106F Constitution Street, ABERDEEN, AB24 5DZ.
•**MCANOY, Mr. Gordon Ashley, FCA** *1971;* (Tax Fac), Cleeve Accounting and Taxation Services Limited, Hunters End, Southam Lane, Southam, CHELTENHAM, GLOUCESTERSHIRE GL52 3NY.
MCARA, Mr. Dominic Robert, BA ACA CF *1992;* 49 High Street, Kegworth, DERBY, DE74 2DA.
•**MCARA, Mrs. Susannah Jane, BSc ACA** *1993;* Soar Valley Accountancy Services Limited, 49 High Street, Kegworth, DERBY, DE74 2DA.
MCARDLE, Mr. Andrew Barry, MA BSc ACA *1993;* Y Felin, Windmill Lane, WELSHPOOL, POWYS, SY21 9HX.
MCARDLE, Mr. Anthony James, BSc ACA *1993;* Fa Yuen, Melton Road, Melton, WOODBRIDGE, SUFFOLK, IP12 1NY.
•**MCARDLE, Mr. Eamonn Michael, BA FCA** *1974;* (Tax Fac), BMS (Silchester) Limited, Whistlers Barn, Whistlers Lane, Silchester, READING, RG7 2NE.
MCARDLE, Mrs. Gabrielle, LLB ACA *1993;* Bank of Ireland, 11 Market Street, MAGHERAFELT, COUNTY LONDONDERRY, BT45 6EE.
MCARDLE, Mr. Gary Charles, BSc ACA *1986;* 28 Shelley Road, BATH, BA2 4RJ.
MCARDLE, Mr. Ian James, MEng ACA *2006;* Auto T X T Ltd Unit 15, Sugarswell Business Park Shenington, BANBURY, OXFORDSHIRE, OX15 6HW.
•**MCARDLE, Mr. Patrick John, FCA** *1979;* Brambletye Ridgeway, Horsell, WOKING, GU21 4QP.
•**MCAREAVEY, Mr. Paul George, BComm FCA** *1991;* (Tax Fac), PGM, 405 Lisburn Road, BELFAST, COUNTY ANTRIM, BT9 7EW.
•**MCAREE, Mr. Craig Ernest, BSc ACA** *1994;* Ernst & Young LLP, 1 More London Place, LONDON, SE1 2AF. See also Ernst & Young Europe LLP
MCAREE, Mr. John Richard, BSc(Hons) ACA *2010;* with Mazars LLP, The Atrium, Park Street West, LUTON, LU1 3BE.
MCAREE, Mr. Neil Martin, BSc ACA FSI *1998;* 11a Woodside, ORPINGTON, KENT, BR6 6JR.
MCARTHUR, Mr. Alexander Nigel, FCA *1970;* 138 King Charles Road, SURBITON, KT5 8QN.
MCARTHUR, Mr. John Fraser, FCA *1958;* The Wainhouse, 3 The foldyard, Hay-On-Wye, HEREFORD, HR3 5PP. (Life Member)
MCARTHUR, Mr. Jonathan Hugh George, ACA *1988;* 55 Lordship Road, LONDON, N16 0QJ.
MCARTHUR, Mr. Malcolm James, BA(Hons) ACA *2002;* 12 Hazelmere Road, ST. ALBANS, HERTFORDSHIRE, AL4 9RW.
MCARTHUR, Miss. Mary Elizabeth, BSc ACA DChA *2005;* with Clive Owen & Co LLP, 140 Coniscliffe Road, DARLINGTON, COUNTY DURHAM, DL3 7RT.
MCARTHUR, Mrs. Natasha, BSc ACA *2002;* with Deloitte LLP, Hill House, 1 Little New Street, LONDON, EC4A 3TR.
MCARTHUR, Mr. Robert Geoffrey, FCA *1966;* 5/2 Tranquil Place, ALEXANDRA HEADLAND, QLD 4572, AUSTRALIA. (Life Member)
MCARTNEY, Mr. David James, BA ACA *1985;* 1 Tolmers Park, Newgate Street, HERTFORD, SG13 8RG.
MCATEE, Mr. Christopher, ACA *2011;* 33 Selkirk Road, Chadderton, OLDHAM, OL9 8AD.
MCATEER, Mr. Peter Joseph, ACA *1981;* Well House, Holywell Lane, Braithwell, ROTHERHAM, S66 7AF.
MCATEER, Mrs. Ruth, MA ACA *2011;* 173 Howlands, WELWYN GARDEN CITY, HERTFORDSHIRE, AL7 4RL.
MCATEER, Mr. William James, BA ACA *1984;* 146 Tomswood Hill, ILFORD, IG6 2QP.
•**MCAUGHEY, Mr. Peter John, BA ACA** *1993;* (Tax Fac), PJM Accounting, Trevean, Yeolmbridge, LAUNCESTON, CORNWALL, PL15 8NJ. See also PJM Accounting Direct
MCAULAY, Mr. Damien Crawford, ACA *2008;* J T International Ltd The Alexandra, 200-220 The Quays, SALFORD, M50 3SP.
•**MCAULAY, Mr. Kenneth William, FCA** *1974;* Josolyne & Co, Silk House, Park Green, MACCLESFIELD, CHESHIRE, SK11 7QW. See also Josolyne Medical Services Ltd
MCAULEY, Mr. David Charles, BSc FCA *1960;* 15 High Drive, NEW MALDEN, KT3 3UJ. (Life Member)
MCAULEY, Mr. Gerard Anthony, BA ACA *1993;* 3 Ferndale Road, HOVE, BN3 6EU.
MCAULEY, Mrs. Janet Elizabeth, BA ACA *1990;* 21 Cicada Road, LONDON, SW18 2NN.
MCAULEY, Mr. Peter Andrew Edward, FCA *1986;* 38 Fairview Place, HAVELOCK NORTH 4130, NEW ZEALAND.
MCAULIFFE, Mr. Andrew, BA(Hons) ACA *2001;* L'Oreal UK Ltd, 255 Hammersmith Road, LONDON, W6 8AZ.
MCAULIFFE, Mr. Anthony David, BCom ACA *1996;* Meelaghans, TULLAMORE, COUNTY OFFALY, IRELAND.
MCAULIFFE, Mr. Conor, BA FCA *1997;* Christies, 8 King Street, LONDON, SW1Y 6QT.
MCAULIFFE, Mrs. Elizabeth Clare, BA ACA *1988;* Monahans Financial Services Ltd Clarks Mill, Stallard Street, TROWBRIDGE, BA14 8HH.
MCAULIFFE, Mr. James, BSc ACA *1988;* 17 High Street, Rode, FROME, BA11 6NZ.
MCAULIFFE, Mr. John Edward, BA ACA *2000;* Highland Capital Management Europe Ltd, 130 Jermyn Street, LONDON, SW1Y 4UR.
MCAULIFFE, Mrs. Kim, ACA *2004;* Bagshot Manor, Green Lane, BAGSHOT, SURREY, GU19 5NL.
MCAULIFFE, Mr. Niall Richard, BSc ACA *2010;* PO Box 905, Strathvale House, GEORGETOWN, GRAND CAYMAN, KY1-1103, CAYMAN ISLANDS.
MCAULIFFE, Mr. Paul Christopher, BA ACA *1990;* 8 Manor Avenue, HORNCHURCH, ESSEX, RM11 2EB.
MCAULIFFE, Mr. Terence Michael, FCA *1959;* Bury House, Clifton Lawns, Chesham Bois, AMERSHAM, HP6 5PT. (Life Member)
MCAVAN, Mrs. Katherine, BA ACA *1998;* O2, 260 Bath Road, SLOUGH, SL1 4DX.
MCAVOY, Mr. David Warren, BSc(Hons) ACA *2009;* 89 Southcote Road, BOURNEMOUTH, BH1 3SH.
MCAVOY, Miss. Jennifer Jane Elaine, ACA *2011;* 3 Ravensdene Mews, BELFAST, BT6 0BG.
MCAVOY, Ms. Kellie, BA ACA *2006;* 19 Little London Court, Mill Street, LONDON, SE1 2BF.
MCAVOY, Ms. Lesley Jean, BA ACA *1990;* 11 St Georges Road, Chiswick, LONDON, W4 1AU.
MCAWEANEY, Mr. Francis Joseph, MA FCA *1984;* 41 Dovercourt Road, LONDON, SE22 8SS.
MCBAIN, Ms. Fiona Catherine, MA ACA *1985;* Scottish Friendly Assurance Society Ltd, Scottish Friendly House 16 Blythswood Square, GLASGOW, G2 4HJ.
MCBAIN, Mr. Robert James, BA ACA *1999;* with Clifford Chance LLP, 40th Floor, Bund Centre, 222 Yan An Road East, SHANGHAI 200002, CHINA.
MCBARRON, Mr. Paul Kevin, ACA *1987;* 12 Hallowhill, ST. ANDREWS, FIFE, KY16 8SF.
MCBAY, Mrs. Patricia Lilian, BA FCA *1980;* Lawnmuir View, Glenalmond Road, Methven, PERTH, PH1 3SZ.
•**MCBOYLE, Mr. Colin Finlayson, FCA** *1970;* C F McBoyle Ltd, Omega Court, 370 Cemetery Road, SHEFFIELD, S11 8FT.
MCBRATNEY, Miss. Anne-Louise, BA ACA *2008;* 74 Holmsley Field Lane Oulton, LEEDS, LS26 8TN.
MCBREARTY, Mrs. Karolina Magdalena, BA ACA *2010;* 68 Rawlinson Road, CRAWLEY, WEST SUSSEX, RH10 7DP.
MCBREARTY, Mr. Richard James, BSc ACA *2007;* 68 Rawlinson Road, CRAWLEY, WEST SUSSEX, RH10 7DP.
MCBREEN, Mr. Robert Anthony, BA ACA *2006;* 33 Elm Road, WINDSOR, SL4 3NB.
MCBRIDE, Mrs. Angela Caroline, BA ACA *1991;* 6 Crofts Close, Chiddingfold, GODALMING, GU8 4SG.
MCBRIDE, Mr. Christopher Ian, FCA *1966;* Kymestones, 277 High Street, Boston Spa, WETHERBY, WEST YORKSHIRE, LS23 6AL.
•**MCBRIDE, Mr. Craig Thomas, MSc FCA** *1988;* Gilchrist Tash, Cleveland Bldgs., Queen's Square, MIDDLESBROUGH, TS2 1PA.
MCBRIDE, Mr. David Ian, BA FCA *1987;* MEMBER OF COUNCIL, 105 Riverview Gardens, LONDON, SW13 8RA.
MCBRIDE, Mr. Denis, FCA *1958;* Stoneleigh New Road, Llanddulas, ABERGELE, CLWYD, LL22 8EL. (Life Member)
MCBRIDE, Mr. John Kristian Lars, MA MSc ACA *1982;* 61 Arthur Road, LONDON, SW19 7DN.
MCBRIDE, Mr. John Paul, FCA CF *1970;* Cedar Lodge, Norman Street, Ide Hill, SEVENOAKS, KENT, TN14 6BJ.
MCBRIDE, Mr. John Sidney, FCA *1974;* Thomas Horton Llp, Strand House 70 The Strand, BROMSGROVE, WORCESTERSHIRE, B61 8DQ.
MCBRIDE, Miss. Katherine, BSc ACA *2010;* Ground floor flat, 39 Leathwaite Road, LONDON, SW11 1XG.
MCBRIDE, Mrs. Katherine Lisa, MA MSc ACA *2005;* 36 Circus Street, LONDON, SE10 8SN.
MCBRIDE, Mr. Mark Edward, BSc ACA *1992;* 34 Abbeystead Road, LIVERPOOL, L15 7JF.
•**MCBRIDE, Mr. Peter, FCA** *1973;* (Tax Fac), Welbeck Associates Limited, 31 Harley Street, LONDON, W1G 9QS. See also McBrides
MCBRIDE, Mr. Richard Anthony, BA ACA *1992;* Inspicio Group Ltd, 10 Buckingham Street, LONDON, WC2N 6DF.
MCBRIDE, Mr. Richard Thomas John, BSc ACA *1990;* (Tax Fac), PO Box 9304, DUBAI, UNITED ARAB EMIRATES.
MCBRIDE, Mr. Robert Peter, ACA *2010;* 9 Chandley Close, SOUTHPORT, MERSEYSIDE, PR8 2SJ.
MCBRIDE, Mrs. Stephanie Jane, BA ACA *1994;* 28 St. Georges Road, TWICKENHAM, TW1 1QR.
MCBRIDE, Mr. William Struan, BA ACA *1988;* 18 Coldharbour Lane, Hildenborough, TONBRIDGE, TN11 9JT.
MCBRIEN, Mr. Michael David, BSocSc ACA *1989;* Global Tea & Commodities, United House, Mayflower Court, Mayflower Street, LONDON, SE16 4JL.
MCBRINN, Mr. Ian Patrick David, BSc ACA *1993;* 33 Claremont Road, TEDDINGTON, MIDDLESEX, TW11 8DH.
•**MCBROOM, Mr. Archibald Ian, FCA** *1957;* McBroom & Co, Unit 12, South West Centre, Troutbeck Road, SHEFFIELD, S7 2QA.
MCBURNEY, Mr. James, BCom ACA *1989;* (Tax Fac), Backwood Hall West, Boathouse Lane, Parkgate, NESTON, CH64 3SZ.
•**MCBURNIE, Mr. Russell Sinclair, MA ACA** *1999;* Premier Strategies Limited, The Poynt, 45 Wollaton Street, NOTTINGHAM, NG1 5FW.
MCCABE, Mr. Alexander, BA(Hons) ACA *2011;* Apartment 69, Aqua Building, Lifeboat Quay, POOLE, DORSET, BH15 1LS.
MCCABE, Miss. Anne Marie, FCA *1984;* with BDO LLP, 55 Baker Street, LONDON, W1U 7EU.
MCCABE, Mr. Anthony, FCA *1976;* 57 Frankholmes Drive, Monkspath Shirley, SOLIHULL, B90 4YB.
MCCABE, Mrs. Carolyn Teresa, BA ACA *1990;* 32 First Avenue, ROSSMOYNE, WA 6148, AUSTRALIA.
MCCABE, Mr. David, ACA *1990;* 6 Charwelton Drive, Strawberry Fields, RUGBY, CV21 1TU.
MCCABE, Mr. David Owen, BA ACA *1992;* Flat 3 Cliff Bank Hamlet, Burnley Road East, ROSSENDALE, LANCASHIRE, BB4 9QR.
MCCABE, Ms. Helen, MA ACA *1995;* 46 Gold Hill Avenue, Hills Apartment #05-46, SINGAPORE 309029, SINGAPORE.
MCCABE, Miss. Jane Victoria, MA(Hons) ACA *2010;* 5 Page Court, Halsall Lane, LIVERPOOL, L37 3PY.

MCCABE, Mr. John Edward, JP FCA *1961;* 4 Preston Close, Eccles, MANCHESTER, M30 0DJ.
MCCABE, Mr. Michael Lindsay, BA ACA *1998;* Elsevier Ltd, The Boulevard, KIDLINGTON, OXFORDSHIRE, OX5 1GB.
MCCABE, Miss. Nicola Jane, BA ACA *2006;* Apartment 439 Block 9 Spectrum, Blackfriars Road, SALFORD, M3 7DZ.
•MCCABE, Mr. Robert Stuart, BA ACA *1990;* 2 The Paddocks, Blackmore Way, Wheathampstead, ST. ALBANS, HERTFORDSHIRE, AL4 8HE.
MCCABE, Miss. Ruth Dilys, BSc ACA *2004;* Imperial College Administration, Imperial College, LONDON, SW7 2AZ.
MCCABE, Miss. Sara-Jane, BSc ACA *2000;* 100b Lowden Road, LONDON, SE24 0BQ.
MCCABE, Mrs. Susan Kim, BSc ACA *1991;* 2 The Paddocks, Blackmore Way Wheathampstead, ST. ALBANS, HERTFORDSHIRE, AL4 8HE.
•MCCAFFERTY, Mr. Mark John, BA ACA *1993;* Alchemy Business Solutions Limited, The Axis Building, Maingate, Team Valley, GATESHEAD, TYNE AND WEAR NE11 0NQ. See also Alchemy Business Solutions
MCCAFFERY, Mr. John James, LLB ACA *2001;* with Grant Thornton UK LLP, Royal Liver Building, Pier Head, LIVERPOOL, L3 1PS.
MCCAFFERY, Miss. Julia, ACA *2008;* 2nd Floor Flat, 47 Redcliffe Square, LONDON, SW10 9HG.
MCCAFFERY, Mr. Stephen Ainsley, ACA *2009;* 16 Stoneborough Lane, BUDLEIGH SALTERTON, DEVON, EX9 6HL.
•MCCAFFREY, Mrs. Katrina Anne, BSc FCA *1997;* Chantrey Vellacott DFK LLP, Russell Square House, 10-12 Russell Square, LONDON, WC1B 5LF.
MCCAFFREY, Mrs. Patricia Ann, BSc FCA *1994;* 161 Lack Road, DP1 Tedd, Irvinestown, ENNISKILLEN, COUNTY FERMANAGH, BT94 1BU.
MCCAGNEY, Mr. John Gerard, FCA *1966;* Cranmere Sandy Lane, Kingswood, TADWORTH, KT20 6NQ.
MCCAHILL, Mr. Dennis Ronald, FCA DChA *1968;* Meads Cottage, Farthingstone Road, Weedon, NORTHAMPTON, NN7 4RP.
MCCALE, Mr. Jeffrey William, FCA *1969;* Oakfield, Wild Oak Lane, Trull, TAUNTON, TA3 7JS.
•MCCALL, Mr. Andrew John, BA FCA CF *1993;* Langtons, The Plaza, 100 Old Hall Street, LIVERPOOL, L3 9QJ.
MCCALL, Mrs. Catherine Emma, BA ACA *2000;* 17 Farr Hall Drive, WIRRAL, MERSEYSIDE, CH60 4SF.
MCCALL, Mr. Michael David, MA ACA *1990;* 15 Carnie Close, Elrick, WEST HILL, ABERDEENSHIRE, AB32 6HX.
MCCALL, Mrs. Nicola Mary, BSc(Hons) ACA *2002;* Hillcroft, Berry Close, RICKMANSWORTH, HERTFORDSHIRE, WD3 7EZ.
MCCALL, Mr. Richard James, MEng ACA *2001;* 9 Tudor Park, AMERSHAM, BUCKINGHAMSHIRE, HP6 5JS.
MCCALL, Mr. Stephen Philip, BSc ACA *1992;* Breeze (Lancashire) Ltd Ben Terra, Lower Fold Off Belmont Road, BOLTON, BL7 9QS.
MCCALL, Mrs. Susan Amanda, LLM ACA *1992;* 160A Old South Lambeth Road, LONDON, SW8 1XX.
MCCALL, Mr. William Harry Home, BA ACA *1998;* Cunningham Lindsey, Apex Plaza, Forbury Road, READING, BERKSHIRE, RG1 1AX.
MCCALL, Mr. William Stuart David, FCA *1974;* Birchwood House, Ashfields Lane, East Hanney, WANTAGE, OX12 0HN.
MCCALLIN, Mrs. Susan Caroline, ACA *1985;* Private Bag X06, 71 Berg'n See, HERMANUS, 7200, SOUTH AFRICA.
MCCALLION, Mr. Damian Thomas, ACA *1984;* Jobsite UK & Worldwide Ltd Langstone Technology Park 2b, Langstone Road, HAVANT, HAMPSHIRE, PO9 1SA.
MCCALLION, Mrs. Helen Mary, BA ACA *1996;* 6 Hillier Road, GUILDFORD, GU1 2JQ.
MCCALLION, Mr. Michael Gerald, BSc FCA *1997;* 27 Salisbury Road, Garston, LIVERPOOL, L19 0PH.
MCCALLION, Mr. Robert Alexander, BA ACA *1984;* Potash House, Drayton Parslow, MILTON KEYNES, BUCKINGHAMSHIRE, MK17 0JE.
MCCALLION, Mrs. Ruth Anne, BA ACA *1985;* Potash House, Drayton Parslow, MILTON KEYNES, MK17 0JE.
•MCCALLION, Mr. Sean John Martin, BA ACA *1997;* KPMG Europe LLP, 15 Canada Square, LONDON, E14 5GL. See also KPMG LLP
MCCALLUM, Mr. Alexander James, MA FCA *1987;* 28 Ouseley Road, LONDON, SW12 8EF.
MCCALLUM, Mr. Angus William, BA FCA *1980;* Seafield High Street Aberlady, LONGNIDDRY, EAST LOTHIAN, EH32 0RB.
MCCALLUM, Dr. Donald George, BSc ACA *2005;* 9 Kingswood Close, NORWICH, NR4 6JF.
MCCALLUM, Mr. Douglas George, MA ACA *2009;* 1 Merefield, SAWBRIDGEWORTH, HERTFORDSHIRE, CM21 9HN.
MCCALLUM, Mrs. Felicity Clare, BCom ACA *1994;* 10 Loxley Road, LONDON, SW18 3LJ.
MCCALLUM, Mr. Graeme Reid, BSc FCA *1971;* The Poplars, Whinfield Road, Dodford, BROMSGROVE, B61 9BG.
MCCALLUM, Mr. Hamish Alexander, BA ACA MCIBS *1999;* PO BOX FL402, FLATTS FL BX, BERMUDA.
MCCALLUM, Ms. Katharine Mary, LLB ACA *1979;* St Andrew, 18 West Common, Lindfield, HAYWARDS HEATH, RH16 2AH.
MCCALLUM, Mr. Neil, BA ACA *1987;* 8 Birch Vale, COBHAM, SURREY, KT11 2PX.
MCCALLUM, Mrs. Nicola, BSc ACA *1993;* 17 Hillside Way, Withdean, BRIGHTON, BN1 5FE.
MCCALLUM, Mrs. Sally, BA ACA *1988;* 34 High Street, Sutton, SANDY, BEDFORDSHIRE, SG19 2NE.
•MCCALLUM, Mr. Stuart, ACA ACCA *2008;* Taylor Viney & Marlow, 46-54 High Street, INGATESTONE, CM4 9DW.
MCCALLUM, Mr. Thomas Jack, BA ACA *2007;* PricewaterhouseCoopers, 119 The Terrace, WELLINGTON, NEW ZEALAND.
MCCALVEY, Miss. Clare, BA ACA *2006;* 8d Clarence Avenue, LONDON, SW4 8HU.
MCCAMBRIDGE, Mr. Alastair Shaun, BSc ACA *1993;* Avenue Maxime Van Praag 2, 1180 BRUSSELS, BELGIUM.
MCCAMBRIDGE, Mr. David Patrick, BSc ACA *1989;* 38 Gardenside Drive, Apt 14, SAN FRANCISCO, CA 94131, UNITED STATES.
MCCANCE, Mr. Mark James, BA ACA *1994;* Croft House, Cross Haw Lane, Clapham, LANCASTER, LA2 8DZ.
MCCANDLESS, Mr. Christopher Paul, BA ACA *2003;* (Tax Fac), 36 Ravenscroft Road, BECKENHAM, KENT, BR3 4TR.
MCCANN, Mr. Alistair John, FCA *1976;* 9 Montserrat Road, LEE-ON-THE-SOLENT, PO13 9LT.
MCCANN, Miss. Angela Agnes, BA ACA *1987;* 8 am Daerchen, Moutfort, L-5336 LUXEMBOURG, LUXEMBOURG.
•MCCANN, Mr. Barry John, FCA *1972;* Barry McCann, Westfield, 10 Westfield Gardens, Westcott Road, DORKING, SURREY RH4 3DX.
•MCCANN, Mr. Brian Francis, BA ACA CF *1984;* with Vanguard Corporate Finance, Liverpool Science Park, 131 Mount Pleasant, LIVERPOOL, L3 5TF.
MCCANN, Mr. Christopher Conor, BA FCA *1972;* 10 Lonsdale Square, LONDON, N1 1EN.
MCCANN, Ms. Corrie Lyndis, BSc ACA *1985;* Elmcroft, 23 Portsmouth Road, THAMES DITTON, KT7 0SY.
MCCANN, Mr. David Thomas, BA ACA *1981;* 11F Kennedy Apartments, 34A Kennedy Road, MID LEVELS, HONG KONG SAR.
MCCANN, Mr. Desmond Brian, BA FCA *1973;* Cricketshill House, Potters Lane, Send, WOKING, GU23 7JH. (Life Member)
•MCCANN, Mr. Eugene Colin, BSc FCA *1982;* PricewaterhouseCoopers LLP, Princess Court, 23 Princess Street, PLYMOUTH, PL1 2EX. See also PricewaterhouseCoopers
MCCANN, Miss. Fiona, BA ACA *2003;* 7 Cravens Heath, BLACKBURN, BB2 4JB.
MCCANN, Mrs. Helen Elizabeth, BSc ACA *1986;* 16 Salmon Close, Spencers Wood, READING, RG7 1EG.
•MCCANN, Mr. Ian, FCA *1971;* (Tax Fac), Ian McCann & Co, 4 Rowan Close, The Paddocks, PENARTH, CF64 5BU.
MCCANN, Mr. Ian, ACA *2007;* 24 Clarkes Lane, Beeston, NOTTINGHAM, NG9 5BL.
MCCANN, Mrs. Jane Ellen, BA ACA *1986;* 1 Pagefield Crescent, CLITHEROE, LANCASHIRE, BB7 1LH.
MCCANN, Mrs. Kathryn Claire, BA FCA *1995;* Greggs Plc Fernwood House, Clayton Road, NEWCASTLE UPON TYNE, NE2 1TL.
MCCANN, Mr. Kieran Paul, MA ACA *1984;* Basement Flat, 32 Sillwood Road, BRIGHTON, BN1 2LE.
MCCANN, Mrs. Louisa Claire, FCA *1990;* Coniscliffe Beckspool Road, Frenchay, BRISTOL, BS16 1NU.
MCCANN, Mrs. Louise Michelle, ACA *2010;* 37 Woodlands Green, Middleton St. George, DARLINGTON, COUNTY DURHAM, DL2 1EE.
MCCANN, Mr. Neil Stephen, BA ACA *1987;* 25 Rectory Road, LONDON, SW13 0DU.
MCCANN, Mr. Peter John, FCA *1976;* Randall & Quilter, 9-13 Fenchurch Buildings Fenchurch Street, LONDON, EC3M 5HR.
MCCANN, Mrs. Preetha, MA FCA *1999;* 27 West Lodge Avenue, LONDON, W3 9SE.
MCCANN, Mr. Richard Philip, BA(Hons) ACA *2004;* BPP Professional Education O T C Hilary House 19 Hilary Street St. Helier, JERSEY, JE2 4SX.
MCCANN, Mr. Ronald Anthony, FCA *1970;* 45 May Road, Swinton, MANCHESTER, M27 5FS.
MCCANN, Mr. Stephen, ACA *1981;* 45 Wakerfield Close, HORNCHURCH, RM11 2TH.
MCCANN, Mr. Stephen John, BA ACA *1986;* Razanac PO Box 20, 23248 RAZANAC, CROATIA.
MCCANN, Mr. Terence Michael Paul, BSc FCA *1987;* Messerschmittstrasse 49, 93049 REGENSBURG, GERMANY.
MCCANN, Mr. Timothy Joseph Mary, BA(Hons) ACA *2000;* (Tax Fac), 42 Latimer Gardens, PINNER, HA5 3RA.
MCCANN, Mr. Trevor William, FCA *1959;* Field House, 125 Bridge End, WARWICK, CV34 6PD. (Life Member)
MCCARRICK, Miss. Ailsa, MA(Hons) ACA *2010;* 46 Mackenzie Road, BIRMINGHAM, B11 4EL.
MCCARRICK, Mrs. Kathryn Hannah, ACA *2008;* 21 Berry Woods Avenue, Douglas, ISLE OF MAN, IM2 7DA.
MCCARROLL, Miss. Helen Anne, BCom ACA *2004;* 21 Pittlesden, TENTERDEN, TN30 6HJ.
MCCARTHY, Miss. Alison, ACA *2008;* 21 Theobalds Avenue, LONDON, N12 8QG.
•MCCARTHY, Mr. Andrew James, ACA *1994;* Connelly & Co Limited, Permanent House, 1 Dundas Street, HUDDERSFIELD, HD1 2EX.
MCCARTHY, Mr. Andrew John, BSc ACA *1994;* G M W Partnership, PO Box 1613, LONDON, W8 6SL.
MCCARTHY, Mr. Andrew Thomas, MA ACA *1999;* Highfield House, Woodhead, Burley in Wharfedale, ILKLEY, WEST YORKSHIRE, LS29 7AS.
MCCARTHY, Mr. Aodhan James Garrett, LLB ACA *2001;* 5 Wavendon Avenue, LONDON, W4 4NP.
MCCARTHY, Mr. Brian Patrick, FCA *1974;* 22 Cavendish Avenue, WELLING, KENT, DA16 2EP.
MCCARTHY, Mr. Brian Robert, ACA FCCA *2009;* La Vallette, 5 Melbourne Park Estate, St. John, JERSEY, JE3 4EQ.
MCCARTHY, Mr. Charlie, MBS BA ACA *2004;* RBS 6th Floor, A B N Amro Bank NV, 250 Bishopsgate, LONDON, EC2M 4AA.
MCCARTHY, Mr. Christopher Denis, FCA *1972;* 30C Surrey Street, EPPING, NSW 2121, AUSTRALIA.
MCCARTHY, Mr. Colin Michael, BA FCA *1961;* Badgers Glory, Herons Close, Copthorne, CRAWLEY, RH10 3HF. (Life Member)
MCCARTHY, Mr. Daniel Charles, MBA FCA *1980;* 16 De Vere Close, Hatfield Peverel, CHELMSFORD, ESSEX, CM3 2LS.
MCCARTHY, Mr. Darren Lee, BA ACA *1999;* 233 Monroe Street, Apt 2S, HOBOKEN, NJ 07030, UNITED STATES.
MCCARTHY, Mr. David, FCA *1973;* 89 Hertford Road, STEVENAGE, SG2 8SE.
MCCARTHY, Mr. David James, BSc ACA *1991;* Knapp House, Far End, Sheepscombe, STROUD, GLOUCESTERSHIRE, GL6 7RL.
MCCARTHY, Mr. Denis Fighin Knox, FCA *1977;* (Tax Fac), 25 Langleys Road, Selly Oak, BIRMINGHAM, B29 6HR.
MCCARTHY, Mrs. Diane, ACA *1992;* 70 Overbury Avenue, BECKENHAM, BR3 6PY.
MCCARTHY, Mr. Guy Jonathan, MBA BSc ACA *1988;* Everglades Cambridge Road, Foxton, CAMBRIDGE, CB22 6SH.
MCCARTHY, Miss. Helen Elizabeth, BA ACA *1987;* 12 Meadow Green, HUDDERSFIELD, WEST YORKSHIRE, HD7 5TL.
MCCARTHY, Miss. Helen Josephine, BA ACA *1993;* 2 Johnsons Drive, HAMPTON, TW12 2EQ.
MCCARTHY, Mr. James Bernard, BSc FCA *1976;* Houndsfield, Rouncil Lane, KENILWORTH, CV8 1NL. (Life Member)
MCCARTHY, Mr. James Richard, BA ACA *2006;* Waverley House, 10 The Spinnakers, LIVERPOOL, L19 3RZ.
MCCARTHY, Mr. James William, BA(Hons) ACA *2002;* 9 Midnight Court, Prestbury, CHELTENHAM, GLOUCESTERSHIRE, GL52 5FE.
MCCARTHY, Ms. Joanne Louise, BA ACA *1990;* 1 Brierholme Avenue, Egerton, BOLTON, BL7 9XL.
MCCARTHY, Mr. John, BSc FCA *1974;* 8 HAMBLY AVENUE, TORONTO M4E 2R6, ON, CANADA.
MCCARTHY, Mr. John Denis, BSc(Econ) ACA *1998;* Torr Nan Caorach, Blackwaterfoot, ISLE OF ARRAN, KA27 8EX.
MCCARTHY, Mr. John Gerard Martin, FCA AITI *2011;* Ireland John McCarthy Consulting Limited, 53 Watson Drive, KILLINEY, COUNTY DUBLIN, IRELAND.
MCCARTHY, Mr. Kevin Roy, FCA *1977;* Flat 8, Block B, Maison Victor Hugo, Greve D'Azette, St. Clement, JERSEY JE2 6PW.
MCCARTHY, Miss. Kyrstyan Louise, MSc ACA *2002;* Apartment 91 Berkeley Tower, 48 Westferry Circus, LONDON, E14 8RP.
MCCARTHY, Miss. Lynsey, BSc ACA *2006;* 65 Ajax Drive, BURY, BL9 8EF.
MCCARTHY, Mrs. Marisa Elena, BSc(Hons) ACA *2000;* 71 Bis Rue Principale, 62560 VERCHOCQ, FRANCE.
MCCARTHY, Mr. Michael Anthony, FCA *1972;* Europa House, Chiltern Park Chiltern Hill, CHALFONT ST. PETER, BUCKINGHAMSHIRE, SL9 9FG.
MCCARTHY, Mr. Myles Bryan Challenor, BSc FCA *1998;* 29 The Windings, SOUTH CROYDON, CR2 0HW.
MCCARTHY, Mrs. Nicola Jane, BSc ACA ATII *1986;* Rempstone House Grange Drive, Wooburn Green, HIGH WYCOMBE, BUCKINGHAMSHIRE, HP10 0QD.
•MCCARTHY, Mr. Patrick Paul, BEng FCA *1995;* McCarthy & Co, 17 The Village, Knockboy, WATERFORD, COUNTY WATERFORD, IRELAND.
MCCARTHY, Mr. Paul, BA ACA *1990;* 1 Brierholme Avenue, Egerton, BOLTON, BL7 9XL.
MCCARTHY, Mr. Paul Stephen, BBS ACA *1992;* 24 Monkstown Road, Blackrock, DUBLIN, COUNTY DUBLIN, IRELAND.
MCCARTHY, Mr. Peter, ACA *1981;* 22 The Drive, WALLINGTON, SM6 9LX.
MCCARTHY, Mr. Peter, BSc ACA *1987;* Northgate Plc Norflex House, 20 Allington Way, DARLINGTON, DL1 4DY.
MCCARTHY, Mr. Peter Graham, FCA *1973;* 13 Queensway, WELLINGBOROUGH, NN8 3RA.
MCCARTHY, Mr. Philip Sean, LLB(Hons) ACA ACIS *2009;* 3 Ashfield Avenue, Union Mills, ISLE OF MAN, IM4 4LN.
MCCARTHY, Mr. Philip Stephen, FCA *1973;* Fidrex, 14 Rue De La Pepiniere, 75008 PARIS, FRANCE.
MCCARTHY, Miss. Rachel Catherine, BSc ACA *2005;* Flat 2, 2a Queenstown Road, LONDON, SW8 3RX.
•MCCARTHY, Mr. Richard George, BA FCA *1992;* KPMG LLP, 15 Canada Square, LONDON, E14 5GL. See also KPMG Europe LLP
MCCARTHY, Mr. Robert James, BSc ACA *1999;* Alvarez & Marsal, 600 Lexington Avenue, 6th Floor, NEW YORK, NY 10022, UNITED STATES.
MCCARTHY, Mrs. Ruth, ACA *1993;* Oak House, Hatherton Road, Hunsterson, NANTWICH, CHESHIRE, CW5 7RB.
MCCARTHY, Mr. Sean William, ACA *1987;* 57 Saffron Close, Chineham, BASINGSTOKE, HAMPSHIRE, RG24 8XQ.
MCCARTHY, Mr. Terence Michael, BSc ACA *1991;* 23 Spring Meadows, Great Shefford, HUNGERFORD, RG17 7EN.
MCCARTHY, Mrs. Tracy Margaret, BA ACA *1994;* Knapp House, Far End, Sheepscombe, STROUD, GLOUCESTERSHIRE, GL6 7RL.
MCCARTHY, Mr. William James, BA ACA *1987;* 22 Kensington Avenue, Victoria Park, CARDIFF, CF5 1BU.
MCCARTHY-WINTERBOTTOM, Mrs. Amanda Louise, BA ACA *2005;* 129 Cairnwell Road, Chadderton, OLDHAM, OL9 0NF.
•MCCARTNEY, Mr. Alan Leonard, MA FCA *1977;* (Tax Fac), Flinthams, 277-279 Chiswick High Road, Chiswick, LONDON, W4 4PU.
•MCCARTNEY, Mr. Andrew Mitchelburne, BSc FCA *1975;* McCartney & Co, Grove House, 27 Hawkin Street, LONDONDERRY, BT48 6RE. See also North West Office Services
•MCCARTNEY, Mr. Danny, ACA *2003;* MWS, Kingsridge House, 601 London Road, WESTCLIFF-ON-SEA, ESSEX, SS0 9PE.
MCCARTNEY, Miss. Elizabeth Helen, ACA *2009;* Flat 2, 61 Madeley Road, LONDON, W5 2LT.
MCCARTNEY, Mrs. Emma Katharine, BA ACA *1996;* 31 Grays Lane, ASHTEAD, KT21 1BZ.
MCCARTNEY, Ms. Haley Jeanette, BA ACA *1996;* 16 Heyworth Ride, HAYWARDS HEATH, WEST SUSSEX, RH16 4TN. (Life Member)
MCCARTNEY, Mr. Ian Richard, BCom ACA *2001;* 2 Meadow Park North, Crawfordsburn, BANGOR, COUNTY DOWN, BT19 1HR.
MCCARTNEY, Mrs. Janet Elizabeth, ACA *1993;* 14 Waterside View, Droylsden, MANCHESTER, M43 6EN.
MCCARTNEY, Mrs. Lisa Jane, BA ACA *1992;* 10 The Greenacres, LYMM, CHESHIRE, WA13 9NT.
MCCARTNEY, Dr. Paul Bernard, PhD BA FCA *1982;* 17 Cranwell Grove, Kesgrave, IPSWICH, IP5 2YN.
MCCARTNEY, Mr. Paul Stephen, BSc ACA *2001;* K P M G Salisbury Square House, 8 Salisbury Square, LONDON, EC4Y 8BB.

MCCARTNEY, Mr. Philip Edward, BSc ACA *2000;* Flat 31, Reed Place, Clapham, LONDON, SW4 7LD.
MCCARTNEY, Mr. Robert Denis, BSc ACA *1998;* 13 clos Saint Martin, 31530 LASSERRE, FRANCE.
MCCARTNEY, Mrs. Sandra Elizabeth, BSc ACA *1999;* 115 Shaftesbury Way, TWICKENHAM, TW2 5RW.
MCCARTNEY, Mr. Sean, MA FCA *1982;* School of Business and Management, Queen Mary University of London, 327 Mile End Road, LONDON, E1 4NS.
MCCARTNEY, Mr. Steven, ACA CA(AUS) *2010;* 10 Murray Street, CROYDON, NSW 2132, AUSTRALIA.
•MCCARTNEY, Mr. Tony Brian, BA ACA *1995;* Ernst & Young LLP, Compass House, 80 Newmarket Road, CAMBRIDGE, CB5 8DZ. See also Ernst & Young Europe LLP
MCCARVILLE, Miss. Geraldine Theresa, BCom ACA *1992;* 84 Weavers Meadow, CRUMLIN, BT29 4YH.
MCCASKILL, Mr. Malcolm Gordon, BA FCA *1980;* Mintflower Place, 8 Par-la-Ville Road, P.O. Box HM 2983, HAMILTON HM MX, BERMUDA.
MCCASKILL, Mr. Ross Hillier, BA ACA *2007;* 26 Yeatman Road, Highgate, LONDON, N6 4DT.
MCCAUGHAN, Miss. Alana Majella, BSc(Hons) ACA *2010;* Yn Fea Alexander Drive, Douglas, ISLE OF MAN, IM2 3QU.
MCCAULEY, Mr. Graham John, FCA *1974;* 66 Harvest Loop, Edgewater, PERTH, WA 6027, AUSTRALIA.
MCCAUSLAND, Mr. Martin Patrick, BA ACA *1986;* 9 Garland Crescent, DORCHESTER, DORSET, DT1 2SX.
MCCAVENY, Miss. Leigh, BSc(Hons) ACA CTA *2001;* 13 Merestone Road, CORBY, NORTHAMPTONSHIRE, NN18 8DH.
MCCAW, Mr. Thomas, ACA *2009;* 94 Edenbane Road, Garvagh, COLERAINE, COUNTY LONDONDERRY, BT51 5XE.
•MCCAY, Mr. James Brendan, FCA *1986;* (Tax Fac), The McCay Partnership, Financial House, 14 Barclay Road, CROYDON, CR0 1JN.
•MCCAY, Mr. Kevin Paul, BA FCA *1976;* De La Wyche Baker Limited, 7 St. Petersgate, STOCKPORT, CHESHIRE, SK1 1EB.
MCCAY, Mr. Michael John, BA ACA *1987;* 26 Appleby Road, Gatley, CHEADLE, SK8 4QD.
MCCHESNEY, Mr. Justin Samuel Jackson, BA ACA *1998;* Springfield Barn, Haworth Road, Cullingworth, BRADFORD, BD13 5EE.
•MCCHESNEY, Mr. Nicholas Robb, BAcc ACA *1987;* McChesney LLP, 22 Lonsdale Road, LONDON, SW13 9EB.
MCCLAFFERTY, Mrs. Victoria Jane, BSc(Hons) ACA *2001;* with Baker Tilly Tax & Advisory Services LLP, 1 Old Hall Street, LIVERPOOL, L3 9SX.
MCCLARTY, Mr. Alexander Jonathan, ACA *1996;* 12 Manor Crescent, SURBITON, SURREY, KT5 8LQ.
MCCLARTY, Mrs. Janet Elizabeth, FCA *1975;* 3 Sunningdale Road, Kenilworth, CAPE TOWN, C.P., 7700, SOUTH AFRICA.
MCCLEA, Mr. James, ACA *2008;* 19 Equity Square, LONDON, E2 7EQ.
MCCLEA, Mr. Richard Noel, FCA *1970;* 4 Marksmead, Drimpton, BEAMINSTER, DORSET, DT8 3RZ.
•MCCLEAN, Mrs. Alison Anastasia, LLB ACA *2003;* AAM Accountants, 118 Rodeheath, LUTON, LU4 9XA.
MCCLEAN, Mr. Andrew Damian, BA ACA *1989;* 9 Longborough Court, Castledene, NEWCASTLE UPON TYNE, NE3 4PL.
•MCCLEAN, Miss. Anna Maria, FCA *1984;* Lee & Company, Crown House, Armley Road, LEEDS, LS12 2EJ.
MCCLEAN, Mr. Eric William, BSc ACA *1981;* 153 Sheen Road, RICHMOND, SURREY, TW9 1YS.
MCCLEAN, Mr. James Constantine Stuart, ACA *1983;* Waterfield Petworth Road, Chiddingfold, GODALMING, GU8 4UF.
MCCLEARNS, Mr. Peter, FCA *1975;* 16 Rue des Vignerons, 85470 BRETIGNOLLES SUR MER, FRANCE.
MCCLEERY, Mr. Alasdair Valentine, BSc ACA *1992;* 27 Queensbury Street, BUNBURY, WA 6230, AUSTRALIA.
MCCLEERY, Mr. Nicholas Ian, BSc FCA *1988;* 4 Hill Gardens, Streatley, READING, RG8 9QF.
MCCLEERY, Mrs. Samantha Jane, BSc FCA *1992;* 1 Cornerways, Kelly, LIFTON, DEVON, PL16 0HJ.
MCCLELLAN, Mr. James Edward, BSc ACA MCIM *1991;* Eden House, Weavering Street, MAIDSTONE, ME14 5JQ.
MCCLELLAN, Mrs. Karen Jane, ACA *1992;* Megeth, Grove Green Lane, Weavering, MAIDSTONE, KENT, ME14 5JW.
MCCLELLAN, Ms. Kate Elizabeth, BSc ACA *1998;* 48 Hazlewell Road, LONDON, SW15 6LR.
MCCLELLAND, Mr. Martin Stephen, FCA *1975;* Welford House, 94 Gregories Road, BEACONSFIELD, HP9 1HL.
MCCLELLAND, Mr. Michael Thompson Frank, FCA *1958;* 8H Kate Sheppard Apts, 42 Molesworth St, Thorndon, WELLINGTON, NEW ZEALAND. (Life Member)
MCCLEMENTS, Mrs. Rachel, BSc ACA *1988;* Day Group Ltd, Transport Avenue, BRENTFORD, MIDDLESEX, TW8 9HF.
MCCLENAGHAN, Mr. Samuel Mark, BSocSc ACA *1995;* 51 Westbourne Road, Olton, SOLIHULL, B92 8AT.
•MCCLETCHIE, Mr. Stuart Donald, BA ACA *1994;* Pollorosso, Flat 2, Redcliffe House, 33 Cavendish Road East, NOTTINGHAM, NG7 1BB.
MCCLEVERTY, Mr. Ian, FCA *1976;* Chelston, 39 The Mere, ASHTON-UNDER-LYNE, LANCASHIRE, OL6 9NH.
MCCLIMONDS, Mr. Robert John, BA FCA *1974;* 49 Ryfold Road, LONDON, SW19 8DF.
MCCLINTOCK, Mr. Henry Richard Oliver, LLB ACA *2005;* 36 Abbott Street, Ngaio, WELLINGTON 6035, NEW ZEALAND.
MCCLOSKEY, Miss. Frances, BSc ACA *1999;* 66 Lorn Road, Dunbeg, OBAN, ARGYLL, PA37 1QQ.
MCCLOSKEY, Mr. Hugh Vincent, BCom FCA *1975;* 44 York Road, Rathgar, DUBLIN 6, COUNTY DUBLIN, IRELAND.
MCCLOSKEY, Mr. Samuel Allan, BSc ACA *2010;* 35 Orchard Grove, Chalfont St. Peter, GERRARDS CROSS, BUCKINGHAMSHIRE, SL9 9ET.
MCCLOUD, Miss. Karen Elizabeth, BSc ACA *1992;* 24 Castle Gardens, BATH, BA2 2AN.
MCCLOY, Mr. Thomas Joseph, FCA *1981;* April Rise, 3 Conchar Road, SUTTON COLDFIELD, B72 1LW.
MCCLUGGAGE, Mr. Jonathan David Campbell, BA ACA *2006;* 100 Ballybarnes Road, NEWTOWNARDS, COUNTY DOWN, BT23 4TD.
MCCLURE, Mr. Andrew Charles Alister, MA ACA *1987;* Fair View, 31 Corner Lane, Horsford, NORWICH, NR10 3DG.
MCCLURE, Ms. Charlotte Rose, ACA *2009;* 23a Conewood Street, LONDON, N5 1BZ.
MCCLURE, Mrs. Dawn Alison, BA ACA *1998;* Cedar Lodge, Ellesmere Road, WEYBRIDGE, SURREY, KT13 0HZ.
MCCLURE, Mr. Gary, BA ACA *1994;* cedar lodge, ellesmere road, WEYBRIDGE, ky13 0hz.
MCCLURE, Mr. James Gordon, LLB FCA *1976;* 11 Hurle Crescent, Clifton, BRISTOL, BS8 2SX.
MCCLURE, Mrs. Jayne Claire, ACA MAAT *2002;* Farm & Cottage Holidays, 5 The Quay, BIDEFORD, DEVON, EX39 2XX.
MCCLURE, Mr. Neil James, BA FCA *1978;* Flat 903 Grenville House, Dolphin Square, LONDON, SW1V 3LR.
MCCLURE, Mr. Richard James, BSc ACA *1992;* 5 Wendover Close, Jersey Farm, ST. ALBANS, AL4 9JW.
MCCLURE, Mr. Scott David John, BA ACA *1994;* 13 Trainer's Brae, NORTH BERWICK, EAST LOTHIAN, EH39 4NR.
•MCCLURE, Mrs. Teresa Ann, FCA *1984;* (Tax Fac), Wakelin & Day, 9 Pound Lane, GODALMING, GU7 1BX.
MCCLUSKEY, Mr. Colmog Michael, MBA LLB ACA *2001;* British Telecom, pp. RT11.18, Riverside Tower, 5 Lanyon Place, BELFAST, BT1 3BT.
MCCLUSKEY, Dr. Karen, BSc ACA *1992;* 83 Hove Park Road, HOVE, BN3 6LN.
MCCLUSKEY, Mr. Paul, BA FCA *1989;* White House Farm, Wetherby Road, Rufforth, YORK, YO23 3QB.
MCCLUSKEY, Mr. Simon Keith, BA ACA *2000;* 7 Wicks Close, Haydon Wick, SWINDON, SN2 3QH.
•MCCLUSKY, Mr. Andrew, BA FCA *1989;* (Tax Fac), Moors Andrew McClusky & Co, Halton View Villas, 3-5 Wilson Patten Street, WARRINGTON, WA1 1PG.
MCCLYMONT, Mr. Malcolm James, BA FCA *1988;* Genavco Insurance Ltd, Michaels House, 10-12 Alie Street, LONDON, E1 8DE.
•MCCOLE, Mrs. Lisa-Marie, ACA *2006;* Ashleys (Hitchin) Limited, Invision House, Wilbury Way, HITCHIN, HERTFORDSHIRE, SG4 0TY.
MCCOLGAN, Mr. Mark Anthony, BA ACA *1994;* E Q Chartered Accountants, 64 West High Street, FORFAR, ANGUS, DD8 1BJ.
MCCOLL, Mr. Angus Robert, BA ACA *1989;* Presbytere, Lyeway Lane, Ropley, ALRESFORD, SO24 0DW.
MCCOLL, Ms. Caroline Susan, BSc ACA *1989;* Presbytere, Lyeway Lane, Ropley, ALRESFORD, SO24 0DW.
MCCOLL, Mrs. Fiona Ann, BSc ACA *1989;* 4 Coombe Road, Irby, WIRRAL, CH61 4UR.
MCCOLL, Mr. Mark John, BA FCA *1988;* The Old School, Stoke St. Milborough, LUDLOW, SHROPSHIRE, SY8 2EJ.
MCCOLL, Miss. Morna Jean, BA ACA *2003;* 57 Mantilla Road, LONDON, SW17 8DY.
MCCOLLUM-OLDROYD, Dr. David Andrew, BA ACA *1983;* 87 Grange Road, MORPETH, NORTHUMBERLAND, NE61 2TS.
MCCOLM, Mrs. Marion Elizabeth, BSc ACA *2006;* T-Mobile (UK) Ltd, Unit 1, Hatfield Business Park, Mosquito Way, HATFIELD, HERTFORDSHIRE AL10 9BW.
MCCOMB, Mr. Andrew, BSc ACA *1983;* Burnaby Building, 16 Burnaby Street, HAMILTON HM 11, BERMUDA.
MCCOMBE, Mr. Gary Stephen, BA ACA *2005;* (Tax Fac), 11 Burrator Drive, EXETER, EX4 2EN.
MCCOMBE, Mrs. Sarah Louise, BA ACA *2005;* 11 Burrator Drive, EXETER, EX4 2EN.
MCCOMBE, Mr. Stephen, BA ACA *1991;* 8 Oakdene Crescent, Marple, STOCKPORT, CHESHIRE, SK6 6NZ.
MCCOMBIE, Mr. James Michael, BSc FCA *1974;* Wayside, Stapleford Road, Stapleford Abbotts, ROMFORD, RM4 1EJ.
MCCONACHIE, Mr. Ben Andrew, MMath ACA *2009;* Kanalstr. 9, 80538, MUNICH, GERMANY.
MCCONAGHIE, Miss. Nicola Anne, BA ACA *1993;* Flat 21 Novello Court, 39 Dibden Street, LONDON, N1 8RH.
MCCONALOGUE, Miss. Helen Maeve, BA ACA *2007;* 14 Oak Avenue, UPMINSTER, RM14 2LB.
MCCONCHIE, Mrs. Sally Linda, ACA *2008;* 125 Bernard Street, SOUTHAMPTON, HAMPSHIRE, SO14 3DY.
MCCONKEY, Mr. Roy David, FCA *1965;* Chy-cara, Golberdon, CALLINGTON, PL17 7NG.
MCCONNELL, Mr. Andrew, BSc FCA *1978;* 5 Churchfield Close, LIVERSEDGE, WF15 6JW.
MCCONNELL, Mr. Anthony Sudlow, FCA *1965;* 3b Connaught House, Clifton Gardens, LONDON, W9 1AL.
MCCONNELL, Mr. David John, BA ACA *2007;* 7 Quartly Drive, Bishops Hull, TAUNTON, TA1 5BF.
MCCONNELL, Mrs. Denise, BA FCA *1984;* Newfields, Gatebridge, Galphay, RIPON, NORTH YORKSHIRE, HG4 3NT.
MCCONNELL, Mr. Frank Howard, FCA *1951;* 41 St. Winifreds Road, HARROGATE, NORTH YORKSHIRE, HG2 8LW.
MCCONNELL, Mr. Graham Anthony, BA FCA *1985;* Sycamore House, 1 New Shaw Lane, Blackshawhead, HEBDEN BRIDGE, HX7 7HZ.
MCCONNELL, Mr. Howard Arthur, BBS FCA AITI *1977;* 3 Hainault Grove, Foxrock, DUBLIN 18, COUNTY DUBLIN, IRELAND.
MCCONNELL, Mr. Joseph, BSc ACA *2004;* First Floor East, H B O S Tower House, Charterhall Drive, CHESTER, CH88 3AN.
MCCONNELL, Mrs. Mandakini, BSc ACA *1993;* Red Deer Park Lodge, Briestfield Road, Briestfield, DEWSBURY, WEST YORKSHIRE, WF12 0NR.
MCCONNELL, Mr. Neil Gerard, ACA *1980;* General Guarantee Collection Ltd, Trident One, Styal Road, MANCHESTER, M22 5XB.
•MCCONNELL, Mr. Richard, BSc FCA *1986;* 163c Southend Road, WICKFORD, SS11 8EE.
MCCONNELL, Mr. Shaun Patrick, FCA *1984;* 17 Evelyn Crescent, Upper Shirley, SOUTHAMPTON, SO15 5JF.
MCCONNELL, Mr. Tim, BSc ACA *2010;* 2 Wordsworth Avenue, Eaton Ford, ST. NEOTS, CAMBRIDGESHIRE, PE19 7RB.
MCCONNELL, Mrs. Vanessa Kate, ACA *2009;* Duncan & Toplis, 26 Park Road, MELTON MOWBRAY, LEICESTERSHIRE, LE13 1TT.
MCCONVILLE, Mrs. Fiona Elizabeth, LLB ACA *1979;* Appleton House, Church Road, Snitterfield, STRATFORD-UPON-AVON, CV37 0LE.
MCCONVILLE, Ms. Tracey Margaret, BSc ACA *2001;* 31/11 Addison Road, MANLY, NSW 2095, AUSTRALIA.
MCCONWAY, Mr. James Christopher, PhD MSc FCA *1980;* Kinvara, 23 Fairyhill, Newtown Park Avenue, BLACKROCK, COUNTY DUBLIN, IRELAND.
MCCOOEY, Mrs. Aemilia Ruth Gaussen, BSc ACA *1989;* Catlands Cottage, Catlands Foot, Mealsgate, WIGTON, CUMBRIA, CA7 1DF.
MCCORD, Mr. Richard Matthew, MEng ACA *2001;* Centrica Plc Millstream, Maidenhead Road, WINDSOR, SL4 5GD.
MCCORKELL, Mr. Henry Nigel Pakenham, FCA *1973;* The Hatch, Gaunts Common, WIMBORNE, BH21 4JP.
MCCORMACK, Mr. Alan Frank, BA ACA *1996;* K P M G Llp, 15 Canada Square, LONDON, E14 5GL.
MCCORMACK, Mr. Alan Paul, BA ACA *1998;* Narrow Water, Knipp Hill, COBHAM, SURREY, KT11 2PE.
MCCORMACK, Mrs. Angela Joanna, BEng ACA *2002;* 2 Glencross Avenue, Chorlton, MANCHESTER, M21 9NF.
MCCORMACK, Miss. Caren Ann, BSc ACA *1990;* 71 Springfield Road, WINDSOR, SL4 3PR.
MCCORMACK, Mrs. Jill, BA ACA *1988;* 221 Hazeltine Circle, BLUE BELL, PA 19422, UNITED STATES.
MCCORMACK, Mrs. Joanne Rachael, BSc FCA *1989;* Skip2bfit Ltd, 100 Pierremont Avenue, BROADSTAIRS, KENT, CT10 1NT.
MCCORMACK, Mr. Michael Price, BSc ACA *1995;* 4 Laurelgrove Park, BELFAST, BT8 6ZH.
MCCORMACK, Mr. Paul Michael, BA ACA *1995;* Hoo Corner, Christchurch Road, TRING, HP23 4EF.
MCCORMACK, Mr. Peter Douglas, BA ACA *2007;* 26 Ferndale Drive, Appley Bridge, WIGAN, WN6 9BB.
MCCORMACK, Mrs. Rebecca Anne, BA ACA *1999;* Narrow Water, Knipp Hill, COBHAM, SURREY, KT11 2PE.
MCCORMACK, Mr. Robert George, ACA *2008;* with KPMG LLP, 15 Canada Square, LONDON, E14 5GL.
MCCORMACK, Mr. Stephen, BSc BSc(Hons) ACA *2010;* 59 Springbank Crescent, WINSFORD, CHESHIRE, CW7 1HT.
MCCORMICK, Mrs. Alison Sarah, BSc ACA *2007;* 8 Charlotte Street, PLYMOUTH, PL2 1RH.
•MCCORMICK, Mrs. Andrea Elizabeth, BA ACA *2000;* (Tax Fac), Fast Accounting Services Limited, PO Box 803, Ampthill, BEDFORD, MK45 9AJ.
MCCORMICK, Mrs. Caroline Selina, BSc ACA *1989;* Hobbs Farmhouse, Hawk Street, Bromham, CHIPPENHAM, WILTSHIRE, SN15 2HU.
MCCORMICK, Mr. David Anthony, BSc ACA *1989;* Hobbs Farmhouse, Hawk Street, Bromham, CHIPPENHAM, WILTSHIRE, SN15 2HU.
MCCORMICK, Mrs. Elizabeth Anne, ACA *1991;* 1 Pine Tree Close, WIMBORNE, DORSET, BH21 1BP.
MCCORMICK, Dr. Helena Claire, BA ACA ATII *1997;* 16 Christchurch Road, NORWICH, NR2 2AE.
•MCCORMICK, Mr. John Kenneth, BSc FCA *1979;* Alexander Myerson & Co, 32 Derby Street, ORMSKIRK, L39 2BY.
MCCORMICK, Mrs. Kelly Lesley, BA ACA *2001;* Brierfield, 66 Manchester Road, WILMSLOW, CHESHIRE, SK9 2JY.
MCCORMICK, Mr. Kenneth, BSc ACA *1991;* Cobham plc, Brook Road, WIMBORNE, DORSET, BH21 2BJ.
MCCORMICK, Mr. Kenneth Hugh, FCA *1953;* 1 Naseby Road, SOLIHULL, B91 2DR. (Life Member)
MCCORMICK, Mr. Kevin, FCA CTA(Fellow) *1970;* Forest Dene, 26 Little Forest Road, BOURNEMOUTH, BH4 9NW. (Life Member)
•MCCORMICK, Mr. Maurice David Alexander, BA ACA *2001;* Ernst & Young LLP, 1 More London Place, LONDON, SE1 2AF. See also Ernst & Young Europe LLP
MCCORMICK, Miss. Melissa Christina, BSc(Hons) ACA *2002;* 2 Florence Road, LONDON, SW19 8TJ.
MCCORMICK, Ms. Nora, ACA *1994;* (Tax Fac), National Grid Plc Grand Buildings, 1-3 Strand, LONDON, WC2N 5EH.
MCCORMICK, Mr. Ronald Joseph, FCA *1972;* Ghaistrills Wharfeside Avenue, Threshfield, SKIPTON, NORTH YORKSHIRE, BD23 5BS.
MCCORMICK, Mrs. Susan Barbara, BA ACA *1991;* 25 Dunstanburgh Court, Woodstone Village, HOUGHTON LE SPRING, TYNE AND WEAR, DH4 6TU.
MCCORMICK, Mr. Timothy Brian, BA FCA *1971;* 24 Dartmouth Walk, DUBLIN 6, COUNTY DUBLIN, IRELAND.
MCCORQUODALE, Mr. Hamish Norman, FCA *1969;* The Old Rectory, Main Street, Hethe, BICESTER, OX27 8ES.
MCCOSH, Mr. Roger James, BSc ACA *1983;* Hilltown of Mause, BLAIRGOWRIE, PH10 6TD.
MCCOTTER, Miss. Catherine Ann, LLB ACA *2007;* 18 Viceroys Wood, BANGOR, COUNTY DOWN, BT19 1WF.
MCCOTTER, Mr. Richard Andrew, FCA *1964;* 9 Oldnall Road, KIDDERMINSTER, DY10 3HW.
MCCOUBREY, Miss. Anne Elizabeth, MA ACA *1988;* (Tax Fac), 4 Copley Glen, Copley, HALIFAX, HX3 0UB.
MCCOUBREY, Miss. Karin Anne, BA ACA *2010;* 27 Carr Road, LISBURN, COUNTY ANTRIM, BT27 6YD.
MCCOURT, Mr. Christopher, BSc(Hons) ACA *2003;* with BTG Financial Consulting LLP, 2 Collingwood Street, NEWCASTLE UPON TYNE, NE1 1JF.
MCCOURT, Mrs. Helen, BSc ACA *1996;* K P M G, St. James's Square, MANCHESTER, M2 6DS.
MCCOURT, Mr. Owen Columba, FCA *1956;* 1 Dennett Close, Woolston, WARRINGTON, WA1 4EF. (Life Member)

MCCOURT, Mr. Robert Fitzgerald, BSc ACA *1996;* 31 Manor Way, BECKENHAM, BR3 3LH.
MCCOURT, Mrs. Sarah Elizabeth, BA ACA *1993;* 31 Manor Way, BECKENHAM, BR3 3LH.
MCCOURT, Ms. Victoria Margaret, BCom FCA *1988;* Hillside House, 14 Hurworth Road, Hurworth Place, DARLINGTON, DL2 2DA.
•**MCCOWIE, Mr. George, FCA** *1964;* (Tax Fac), McCowie & Co, 52-54 Leazes Park Rd, NEWCASTLE UPON TYNE, NE1 4PG.
•**MCCOY, Mr. Colin Edward, BA ACA** *1993;* (Tax Fac), McKenzies, 14-16 Station Road West, OXTED, SURREY, RH8 9EP.
•**MCCOY, Mrs. Dympna Geraldine, BSc ACA** *1993;* 34 Long Park, Chesham Bois, AMERSHAM, BUCKINGHAMSHIRE, HP6 5LA.
MCCOY, Mrs. Jayne Louise, BA ACA *1994;* 27 Bandon Rise, WALLINGTON, SM6 8PT.
MCCOY, Mr. John, BA FCA *1974;* 37 Pennington Place, Southborough, TUNBRIDGE WELLS, TN4 0AQ.
MCCOY, Mr. Peter Aidan, FCA *1972;* Flat 1, 16 Woodside Grove, LONDON, N12 8QU. (Life Member)
MCCOY, Mr. Robin Edward, BSc ACA *1992;* 5th Floor Fountain House, 130 Fenchurch Street, LONDON, EC3M 5DJ.
MCCOY, Mr. Simon Brian, BA ACA *1989;* 34 Long Park, Chesham Bois, AMERSHAM, HP6 5LA.
MCCOY, Mr. Stephen Gerard David, ACA *1983;* Brook House, Millbrook, BEDFORD, MK45 2JB.
•**MCCOY, Miss. Toni Ann, BSc(Hons) ACA MAAT** *2006;* 1 Lockwood Street, SHIPLEY, BD18 3JY.
MCCRACKEN, Mr. Robert Ralston, CA *1988; (CA Scotland 1983);* Ernst & Young Europe LLP, 1 More London Place, LONDON, SE1 2AF. See also Ernst & Young LLP
•**MCCRAE, Mr. Alan Hugh, LLB FCA** *1991;* PricewaterhouseCoopers LLP, 1 Embankment Place, LONDON, WC2N 6RH. See also PricewaterhouseCoopers
MCCRANOR, Mr. David James, FCA *1988;* Beechwood, Gortroe, LEAP, COUNTY CORK, IRELAND.
MCCRANOR, Mr. Henry James, FCA *1951;* Merevale, 89 Brinklow Road, COVENTRY, CV3 2JB. (Life Member)
MCCREA, Mrs. Nicola Jane Victoria, ACA *1994;* 22 Cadogan Park, BELFAST, BT9 6HG.
•**MCCREA, Mr. Nigel Robert, BA ACA** *1991;* Deloitte LLP, Hill House, 1 Little New Street, LONDON, EC4A 3TR. See also Deloitte & Touche LLP
MCCREA, Mr. Paul Anthony, BA ACA *1993;* Saint-Gobain Formula, 34 Avenue Franklin-Roosevelt, 92282 SURESNES, FRANCE.
MCCREADIE, Mr. Paul, MEng ACA *2006;* with E C I Partners, Brettenham House, Lancaster Place, LONDON, WC2E 7EN.
MCCREADY, Mr. Andrew Ian, BA ACA *1999;* 143/83 Whiteman Street, SOUTHBANK, VIC 3006, AUSTRALIA.
MCCREADY, Mr. Damian John, LLB ACA *1999;* 16 ATALANTA RISE, OCEAN REEF, WA 6027, AUSTRALIA.
MCCREADY, Mr. John Francis, ACA *1983;* Eastbury House, Eastbury, HUNGERFORD, RG17 7JJ.
MCCREANOR, Mrs. Leah, BSc ACA *2004;* 23 Nicosia Road, LONDON, SW18 3RN.
MCCREARY, Mr. Paul, BA(Hons) ACA *2010;* 15 Vernon Close, SOUTH SHIELDS, TYNE AND WEAR, NE33 5DF.
MCCREATH, Ms. Alice Elizabeth, BA ACA *1994;* 19 rue des petits carreaux, 75002 PARIS, FRANCE.
MCCREATH, Mr. Nicholas James Stewart, BSc ACA *1991;* 21 Wentworth Grange, WINCHESTER, HAMPSHIRE, SO22 4HZ.
MCCREERY, Mr. Stuart Alexander, BA ACA *1992;* 3 Aldous Court, Fowlmere, ROYSTON, HERTFORDSHIRE, SG8 7WA.
MCCREESH, Mr. Gerrard Anthony, BSc FCA *1988;* 19 Gorse Farm Road, NUNEATON, WARWICKSHIRE, CV11 6TH.
MCCREESH, Mr. Kevan Anthony, BA ACA *1994;* 14 Walsingham Close, LUTON, LU2 7AP.
MCCRIMMON, Mr. Robert, BSc(Econ) ACA *2011;* Wilson Henry Llp, 145 Edge Lane, Edge Hill, LIVERPOOL, L7 2PF.
MCCRINDELL, Mr. Michael Ian, LLB ACA *1988;* PO Box 2191, ACCRA, GHANA.
MCCRINDLE, Mr. Alastair David, FCA *1954;* 4 Old School Mews, Uppingham, OAKHAM, LE15 9TF. (Life Member)
MCCRINDLE, Mr. David James, BA ACA *2006;* 18 Elm Court, Whickham, NEWCASTLE UPON TYNE, NE16 4PS.
•**MCCRINK, Mr. Eugene Michael, BEng FCA** *1994;* Accountax Plus Limited, Throstle Nest, Whinney Brow Lane, Forton, PRESTON, PR3 0AE. See also Fraser Campbell LLP
MCCRINK, Mr. Robin John, BA(Hons) ACA *2003;* 43 Acacia Avenue, Hale, ALTRINCHAM, CHESHIRE, WA15 8QY.
MCCRISTALL, Miss. Vanessa, BA ACA *1991;* Randlestone House Monyash Road, Over Haddon, BAKEWELL, DERBYSHIRE, DE45 1HZ.
MCCRONE, Mr. Derek Scott, MEng ACA *2001;* Greenmount Chevening Road, Chipstead, SEVENOAKS, TN13 2SA.
MCCRORY, Mrs. Norma, BA ACA *1984;* 14 St Leonards Road, HORSHAM, RH13 6EJ.
•**MCCROSSON, Mr. Andrew James, BSc ACA** *1990;* PricewaterhouseCoopers LLP, 7 More London Riverside, LONDON, SE1 2RT. See also PricewaterhouseCoopers
MCCROSSON, Mr. Robert George, ACA *2010;* Flat 25, 17 Keats Mews, MANCHESTER, M23 9SG.
MCCRUM, Miss. Carrie, BA ACA *2004;* 37 Hillgate Place, LONDON, SW12 9ES.
MCCUBBIN, Miss. Kirsty, ACA *2009;* 30 Austenway, Chalfont St. Peter, GERRARDS CROSS, BUCKINGHAMSHIRE, SL9 8NW.
MCCUBBIN, Mr. Thomas Paul, DPhil BA ACA *1997;* 5 Church Close, Farmoor, OXFORD, OX2 9NP.
MCCUDDEN, Miss. Fiona Margaret, LLB ACA *1999;* 8 Eden View, Markethill, ARMAGH, BT60 1LB.
MCCUE, Mr. Darren, ACA *2008;* 2nd Floor, 2 Hill Street, ST HELIER, JE2 4UA.
MCCUE, Ms. Lindsay, BA ACA *2007;* 1 Digpal Road, Churwell Morley, LEEDS, LS27 7GE.
MCCUE, Miss. Louise Claire, BA ACA *2005;* 60 Pine Ridge, CARSHALTON, SM5 4QH.
•**MCCUIN, Mr. John Spencer, BSc FCA** *1975;* John S McCuin Bsc FCA, 21 Repton Gardens, ROMFORD, RM2 5LS.
MCCULLAGH, Mrs. Clare Elizabeth, MA ACA *2003;* 4 Sumner Close, Fetcham, LEATHERHEAD, KT22 9XF.
MCCULLAGH, Mr. John Coltman, FCA *1959;* Bramleys, Alleyns Lane, Cookham, MAIDENHEAD, SL6 9AE. (Life Member)
MCCULLAGH, Miss. Julia Emma, BA ACA *1999;* 221 Cavendish Road, LONDON, SW12 0BP.
•**MCCULLAGH, Mr. Martin Joseph, BSc ACA** *1993;* MMC Accountancy Services, 6 Linenhall Street, LIMAVADY, COUNTY LONDONDERRY, BT49 0HQ.
MCCULLAGH, Mr. Toby John, BA ACA *2000;* Flat 4, 4-6 Islington Green, LONDON, N1 2XA.
MCCULLAGH, Miss. Una, BSc(Hons) ACA *2000;* 17 Ballsbridge Avenue, DUBLIN 4, CO. DUBLIN, IRELAND.
MCCULLOCH, Mr. Alan, FCA *1969;* 9 Adare Dr, Asthill Gr, COVENTRY, CV3 6AD.
MCCULLOCH, Mr. Bruce Martin, BSc ACA *1994;* 72 Melody Road, Wandsworth, LONDON, SW18 2QF.
•**MCCULLOCH, Mr. David Godwin, BSc ACA** *1998;* Baker Tilly Tax & Advisory Services LLP, 12 Gleneagles Court, Brighton Road, CRAWLEY, WEST SUSSEX, RH10 6AD. See also Baker Tilly Corporate Finance LLP
MCCULLOCH, Mrs. Emma Jane, ACA *2004;* 9 Edkins Close, LUTON, LU2 7SS.
MCCULLOCH, Ms. Fiona Jill, BA ACA *1991;* Central Herts YMCA, 2 Tewin Court Tewin Rd, WELWYN GARDEN CITY, HERTFORDSHIRE, AL7 1AU.
MCCULLOCH, Mr. Gordon Robert, MA ACA *1990;* B/75, Albion Riverside Building, 8 Hester Road, LONDON, SW11 4AP.
MCCULLOCH, Mr. Graham Steven, MSc FCA *1993;* 19 Furness Drive, Wrenthorpe, WAKEFIELD, WEST YORKSHIRE, WF2 0NH.
MCCULLOCH, Miss. Jane, ACA *1982;* 6 Hardwicke Mews, Lloyd Baker Street, LONDON, WC1X 9AE.
•**MCCULLOCH, Mrs. Karen Emma, BA ACA** *1996;* with KPMG LLP, 15 Canada Square, LONDON, E14 5GL.
MCCULLOCH, Miss. Kathleen Jane, MA(Hons) ACA CTA *2002;* Flat 133 Elmhurst Mansions, Edgeley Road, LONDON, SW4 6EX.
MCCULLOCH, Mr. Keith Murray, BA FCA *1971;* 87-171 Wireless Road, All Seasons Mansion, Pathumwan, BANGKOK, 10330, THAILAND.
MCCULLOCH, Ms. Maureen Geraldine, BA ACA *1984;* 19 Cowleigh Road, MALVERN, WORCESTERSHIRE, WR14 1QF.
MCCULLOCH, Miss. Morag Joy, BSc ACA *2009;* 69 Abbott Avenue, LONDON, SW20 8SG.
MCCULLOCH, Miss. Nicola, BA ACA *2010;* First Floor Flat, 10 Oakland Road, Redland, BRISTOL, BS6 6ND.
MCCULLOCH, Mr. Niels Michael, ACA *2011;* Craigdene, Lochwinnoch Road, KILMACOLM, RENFREWSHIRE, PA13 4DZ.
MCCULLOCH, Mrs. Penelope Jane Margaret, BSc ACA *1988;* 285 Bayside Drive, CLEARWATER BEACH, FL 33767, UNITED STATES.
MCCULLOCH, Mrs. Penny, ACA ATII *1989;* Fleur De Lys, High Cross Road, Ivy Hatch, SEVENOAKS, KENT, TN15 0NR.
MCCULLOCH, Mr. Peter David, MEng ACA *2004;* Kennels New Farm, Two Acre Lane, Strinesdale, OLDHAM, OL4 3RD.
•**MCCULLOCH, Mr. Robert, BA FCA** *1980;* (Tax Fac), Rob McCulloch Limited, 18 Barn Close, Cumnor Hill, OXFORD, OX2 9JP. See also Aries Accountants Limited
MCCULLOCH, Mr. Steven Alan, BSc ACA *1998;* 13 Osterley Avenue, ISLEWORTH, MIDDLESEX, TW7 4QF.
MCCULLOCH, Mr. Stewart William Robert, BSc ACA *1988;* 7 Turners Crescent, BISHOP'S STORTFORD, HERTFORDSHIRE, CM23 4FZ.
MCCULLOCH, Mr. Wayne, BA FCA *1992;* 44 Clare Drive, Highfields Caldecote, CAMBRIDGE, CB23 7GA.
MCCULLOUGH, Mr. John Patrick, FCA *1980;* (Tax Fac), 2 Highcroft Road, Felden, HEMEL HEMPSTEAD, HP3 0BU.
MCCULLOUGH, Mr. Neil, BA FCA *1995;* 5 Gale Close, LUTTERWORTH, LE17 4LL.
•**MCCURDY, Mr. Kieran Laughlin, ACA CTA** *2002;* Plummer Parsons, 4 Frederick Terrace, Frederick Place, BRIGHTON, BN1 1AX. See also Plummer Parsons Accountants Ltd
MCCURRACH, Mr. Ian Henderson, ACA *1980;* Avenue De L'Horizon 5, B-1380 OHAIN, BELGIUM.
MCCURRICH, Mr. John Martin, MA FCA *1959;* Unit 116 Bougainvillea, 260-270 Military Road, NEUTRAL BAY, NSW 2089, AUSTRALIA. (Life Member)
•**MCCUSKER, Mr. David Anthony, FCA** *1992;* Stewart & Co, Knoll House, Knoll Road, CAMBERLEY, GU15 3SY. See also Stewart & Co Accountancy Services Ltd
•**MCCUSKER, Mr. Declan Edward, ACA FCCA** *2009;* Perrys, 32-34 St. Johns Road, TUNBRIDGE WELLS, KENT, TN4 9NT.
MCCUSKER, Miss. Jennifer Claire, MSc BA ACA *2009;* Pricewaterhousecoopers Llp, 1 Hays Lane, LONDON, SE1 2RD.
MCCUTCHEON, Mrs. Kathryn, ACA *1995;* 704 228th NE PMB 184, SAMMAMISH, DC 98074, UNITED STATES.
MCCUTCHEON, Miss. Linda Ann, BA(Hons) ACA *2003;* BPP Professional Education Ltd, Marcello House, 236-240 Pentonville Road, LONDON, N1 9JY.
MCCUTCHEON, Miss. Nicola Clare, BA BSc ACA *1999;* 73 Rue du Chateau, 01630 CHALLEX, FRANCE.
•**MCDADE, Mr. Alastair James Knighton, ACA** *2001;* James Knighton, 2 Copythorne Road, BRIXHAM, DEVON, TQ5 8QQ.
MCDAID, Mr. Andrew, ACA FCCA *2010;* Mitchells Chartered Accountants & Business Advisers, 91-97 Saltergate, CHESTERFIELD, DERBYSHIRE, S40 1LA.
MCDAID, Mr. Andrew Hugh, ACA *2003;* Redbus Outdoor Holdings Ltd Orwell House, 16-18 Berners Street, LONDON, W1T 3LN.
MCDANELL, Mr. Philip Neil, FCA *1976;* 86 Ladbroke Grove, LONDON, W11 2HE.
MCDERMOTT, Mrs. Allison Nicola, BA(Hons) ACA *2004;* JT International Business Services Ltd, The Alexandra, 200-220 The Quays, SALFORD, M50 3SP.
MCDERMOTT, Mr. Anthony, BSc(Hons) ACA *2000;* 22 Raddlebarn Road, Selly Oak, BIRMINGHAM, B29 6HA.
MCDERMOTT, Mr. Brendan John, BSc ACA *1990;* 20 Broadfields, Norton, RUNCORN, CHESHIRE, WA7 6UE.
•**MCDERMOTT, Mr. Brian Patrick, BSc ACA** *1987;* (Tax Fac), McDermott & Co, 1 Hardwick's Square, LONDON, SW18 4AW.
MCDERMOTT, Miss. Caroline, ACA *2008;* 689 Wandsworth Road, LONDON, SW8 3JE.
MCDERMOTT, Mr. Gregory Desmond, BA ACA *1987;* 5 Burnside Avenue, Kirkintilloch, GLASGOW, G66 1ES.
MCDERMOTT, Mr. James Richard, FCA *1963;* 15 Belle Vue Road, WARE, HERTFORDSHIRE, SG12 7BD. (Life Member)
•**MCDERMOTT, Miss. Jannine Sandra, FCA** *2000;* (Tax Fac), Jan McDermott & Co Limited, Third Floor, 51 Hamilton Square, BIRKENHEAD, MERSEYSIDE, CH41 5BN. See also Jan McDermott & Associates Limited
MCDERMOTT, Mr. John Patrick, BA ACA *2001;* 20 Ambleside Road, Urmston, MANCHESTER, M41 6PH.
MCDERMOTT, Mr. Kevin, BSc ACA *2000;* 2 Tilside Grove, Lostock, BOLTON, BL6 4BX.
MCDERMOTT, Mr. Marc Keith, BA ACA *2002;* 29 Oaklands, NEWCASTLE UPON TYNE, NE3 4YQ.
MCDERMOTT, Mr. Peter James, ACA *2008;* with Deloitte LLP, 2 New Street Square, LONDON, EC4A 3BZ.
MCDERMOTT, Mr. Robert, BA(Hons) ACA *2003;* with BDO LLP, 1 Bridgewater Place, Water Lane, LEEDS, LS11 5RU.
MCDERMOTT, Mr. Sean-Pierre, BA FCA *1997;* 16 Quain Mansions, Queen's Club Gardens, LONDON, W14 9TW.
•**MCDERMOTT, Mrs. Shirley Sandra, BA FCA** *1988;* S.S. McDermott, 15 Childwall Crescent, Childwall, LIVERPOOL, L16 7PG.
MCDERMOTT, Miss. Sian, BSc ACA MBA *1999;* 52 Lavender Way, Rogerstone, NEWPORT, GWENT, NP10 9BA.
MCDEVITT, Mr. Matthew Richard Arden, MChem ACA *2010;* Flat 3, 15 Acol Road, LONDON, NW6 3AA.
MCDIARMID, Mrs. Adriana Danielle, ACA *2007;* with PricewaterhouseCoopers LLP, Cornwall Court, 19 Cornwall Street, BIRMINGHAM, B3 2DT.
MCDIARMID, Mr. Duncan James, BA FCA *1990;* The Old Post Office Cottage, High Street, Childrey, WANTAGE, OX12 9UE.
MCDIARMID, Mr. Neil, BSc FCA *1991;* John Nixon Limited, 1, Water Street, NEWCASTLE UPON TYNE, NE4 7AX.
MCDIARMID, Mr. Ross, BSc ACA *2011;* 67 Coed y Wenallt, Rhiwbina, CARDIFF, CF14 6TN.
MCDONAGH, Mrs. Alison Jane, BA ACA *1984;* 15 Rue des Vieux Chênes, 86350 ST MARTIN L'ARS, FRANCE.
MCDONAGH, Miss. Ann Christine, BSc ACA *1994;* Flat 212, Skyline Central 1, 50 Goulden Street, MANCHESTER, M4 5EH.
MCDONAGH, Mr. David Adam, FCA *1993;* 9 Branksea Street, Fulham, LONDON, SW6 6TT.
MCDONAGH, Mr. James Patrick, BA ACA *1987;* 3 Greenacres, Walmley, SUTTON COLDFIELD, B76 1DN.
•**MCDONAGH, Mr. Martin, FCA** *1987;* Hart Shaw LLP, Europa Link, Sheffield Business Park, SHEFFIELD, S9 1XU.
•**MCDONAGH, Miss. Mary Ann, ACA** *1987;* Kilsby & Williams LLP, Cedar House, Hazell Drive, NEWPORT, GWENT, NP10 8FY.
•**MCDONAGH, Mr. Michael Joseph, BA FCA CF** *1992;* KPMG LLP, 15 Canada Square, LONDON, E14 5GL. See also KPMG Europe LLP
•**MCDONAGH, Mr. Raymond Thomas, FCA** *1973;* (Tax Fac), Crane & Partners, Leonard House, 5-7 Newman Road, BROMLEY, BR1 1RJ. See also Armada Computer Accounting Ltd and Quanast Services
MCDONAGH, Miss. Sarah Kate, BSc(Hons) ACA *2004;* Oakdene, 38 Crescent Road, SIDCUP, DA15 7HW.
MCDONAGH, Mr. Stuart, BA ACA *1992;* 19 Greek Thomson Road, Balfron, GLASGOW, G63 0RE.
MCDONAGH, Mrs. Valentyna, ACA *2008;* 39 Glenton Road, LONDON, SE13 5RS.
MCDONALD, Mr. Alastair, MSci ACA *2006;* Flat 508, Omega Building, Smugglers Way, Wandsworth Town, LONDON, SW18 1AZ.
MCDONALD, Mr. Alastair John, FCA *1968;* The Lagg House, Culmer Lane, Wormley, GODALMING, SURREY, GU8 5SP.
•**MCDONALD, Mr. Andrew James Baird, MA ACA** *1985;* Ashley House, Whittingham Lane, Haighton, PRESTON, PR2 5SL.
MCDONALD, Mr. Andrew Michael, BA(Hons) ACA *2010;* 45 Waldeck Street, READING, RG1 2RF.
MCDONALD, Mr. Columcille Francis, BCom FCA ACIS *1972;* 9 Kincora Road, Clontarf, DUBLIN 3, COUNTY DUBLIN, IRELAND.
MCDONALD, Mr. Damien Patrick, BSc ACA *1999;* Driver Group Ltd, Driver House, 4 St. Crispin Way, Haslingden, ROSSENDALE, LANCASHIRE BB4 4PW.
•**MCDONALD, Mr. David, ACA** *1992;* Jacksons Accountants (Midlands) Limited, Deansfield House, 98 Lancaster Road, NEWCASTLE, STAFFORDSHIRE, ST5 1DS.
MCDONALD, Miss. Fiona Elizabeth, MA ACA *2007;* 29 Laneside Drive, Bramhall, STOCKPORT, CHESHIRE, SK7 3AR.
MCDONALD, Mr. Geoffrey William Stewart, BSc(Hons) ACA *1983;* 3 Cortayne Road, LONDON, SW6 3QA.
MCDONALD, Mr. Graham Keith, JP BSc FCA *1973;* Steeton Lodge, 21 East Street, Leven, BEVERLEY, HU17 5NG.
MCDONALD, Mr. Grahame Robert, FCA *1972;* 60 Mount Road, SUNDERLAND, SR4 7NS. (Life Member)
MCDONALD, Mr. Ian Alexander, FCA *1970;* Pheasants Nest Farm, Weston Underwood, OLNEY, MK46 5LA.
•**MCDONALD, Mr. Ian Malcolm, BA FCA** *1963;* C. McDonald & Co, Ditton Lodge, 16 Southborough Road, SURBITON, SURREY, KT6 6JN.
MCDONALD, Mrs. Jacqueline Ann, BA ACA *1997;* HIgh Tilt Farmhouse, Golford, CRANBROOK, TN173PB.
MCDONALD, Mr. James, MChem ACA *2011;* Flat 4, 41 Coley Avenue, READING, RG1 6LL.
MCDONALD, Mr. James Andrew, LLB ACA *2007;* 66 Shelsley Way, SOLIHULL, WEST MIDLANDS, B91 3UZ.

MCDONALD, Mr. James Damian, BSc ACA *1989;* 14 Gorse Lane, West Kirby, WIRRAL, CH48 8BH.
•**MCDONALD, Mr. James Keith, MA LLB FCA** *1965;* Creaction Limited, 27 Meads Road, GUILDFORD, SURREY, GU1 2NB. See also McDonald Keith
MCDONALD, Miss. Jennifer, BA ACA *2007;* #06-03, 46 Meyer Road, The View @ meyer, SINGAPORE 437871, SINGAPORE.
MCDONALD, Mr. John Stewart, FCA *1972;* Prime Raftery, Marlborough House, Warwick Road, SOLIHULL, WEST MIDLANDS, B91 3DA. See also Prime Pilleys and Raftery & Co
MCDONALD, Miss. Kate Emma, ACA *2009;* Flat 403 Fennel Apartments, 3 Cayenne Court, LONDON, SE1 2PJ.
MCDONALD, Mr. Keith Lyle, FCA *1979;* CliniSys, Administrative Centre, Two Bridges, Guildford Street, CHERTSEY, SURREY KT16 9AU.
MCDONALD, Mr. Keith Scott, FCA *1964;* Croft House, Beal Bank, Warkworth, MORPETH, NE65 0TA.
MCDONALD, Mr. Ken Richard, FCA *1970;* 2 Greenfields, STANSTED, CM24 8AH.
MCDONALD, Mr. Lars Tarquin, EMBA BA ACA *2004;* 6 Station Road, HAMPTON, MIDDLESEX, TW12 2BX.
MCDONALD, Miss. Lisa, ACA *2008;* 13 Matfield Crescent, MAIDSTONE, ME14 5NH.
MCDONALD, Ms. Mhairi Crawford, BSc ACA *1991;* 61 Titwood Road, GLASGOW, G41 2DG.
MCDONALD, Mr. Michael, FCA *1969;* 162 Route De Luxembourg, L4973 DIPPACH, LUXEMBOURG.
MCDONALD, Mr. Newton Alexander, BSc ACA *1981;* bss, 163 Eversholt Street, LONDON, NW1 1BU.
•**MCDONALD, Miss. Nicola Jayne, MA ACA** *1998;* Argentica Limited, 356 Broadway, Horsforth, LEEDS, LS18 4RE.
MCDONALD, Mr. Norman Osmond, FCA *1954;* Flat No 70, 111 Piccadilly, MANCHESTER, M1 2HX. (Life Member)
MCDONALD, Mr. Peter Anthony, ACA *2008;* 43 Heathfield Park, WIDNES, CHESHIRE, WA8 9WY.
MCDONALD, Mrs. Rachel Jean, MA(Hons) ACA *2001;* 7 Crofts Drive, Grimsargh, PRESTON, PR2 5LW.
MCDONALD, Mr. Richard Henry, LLB ACA *1995;* 34 Rodway Road, BROMLEY, BR1 3JL.
•**MCDONALD, Mr. Robert, FCA** *1979;* Robert McDonald, 15 Vicarage Gate, LONDON, W8 4AA.
MCDONALD, Mr. Robert Francis, BA(Hons) ACA *2002;* 3 Standrick Hill Rise, STALYBRIDGE, CHESHIRE, SK15 3RT.
MCDONALD, Mr. Robert John, BSc ACA *1991;* 1 Oxford Square, MALVERN, WR14 2LD.
MCDONALD, Mr. Robert Stewart, FCA *1963;* 1 Syerscote Lane, Haunton, TAMWORTH, STAFFORDSHIRE, B79 9HD.
MCDONALD, Mr. Ross, BA ACA *2006;* 28A Highbury Hill, LONDON, N5 1AL.
MCDONALD, Mrs. Sandra Louise, BA ACA *1989;* 145 Hammersmith Avenue, TORONTO M4E 2W7, ON, CANADA.
MCDONALD, Mrs. Sheena Mary, MA FCA CTA TEP *1985;* Milne Craig, Abercorn House, 79 Renfrew Road, PAISLEY, RENFREWSHIRE, PA3 4DA.
MCDONALD, Mr. Stuart Alexander Baird, MA ACA *1986;* 47 Barrow Road, Burton-On-The-Wolds, LOUGHBOROUGH, LE12 5TB.
•**MCDONALD, Mrs. Susan, BSc FCA DChA** *1983;* Montpelier Professional (Lancashire) Limited, Charter House, Pittman Way, Fulwood, PRESTON, PR2 9ZD. See also Montpelier Audit Limited
MCDONALD, Mrs. Susan Elaine, BA(Hons) ACA *2003;* 13 Highbury Crescent, CAMBERLEY, GU15 1JZ.
MCDONALD, Mrs. Victoria, ACA *2006;* with Morris Owen, 43-45 Devizes Road, SWINDON, SN1 4BG.
MCDONALD, Mrs. Victoria Alyson, BA ACA *2006;* 12 Foxley Close, NEWCASTLE UPON TYNE, NE12 6FX.
MCDONALD WOOD, Mr. Ian Leslie, MBA FCA *1970;* The Forge, Cheriton, ALRESFORD, SO24 0QA.
MCDONNELL, Mr. Adam James, BA ACA *2002;* 10 Tanners Row, WOKINGHAM, BERKSHIRE, RG41 4EL.
MCDONNELL, Mr. Alexander, MSc BA ACA *2011;* Flat 1, 54a Penton Street, Islington, LONDON, N1 9QA.
MCDONNELL, Mrs. Catherine, BA ACA *2000;* 21 Dean Gardens, SHILDON, DL4 1EX.
MCDONNELL, Mr. David Croft, CBE FCA *1965;* Burn Lea, 18 The Serpentine, Grassendale, LIVERPOOL, L19 9DT.
MCDONNELL, Mr. Francis Kevin, BA ACA *1999;* with PricewaterhouseCoopers LLP, 80 Strand, LONDON, WC2R 0AF.
MCDONNELL, Mr. James, BBA ACA *2011;* 18 Bayswater Terrace, HALIFAX, WEST YORKSHIRE, HX3 0NB.
MCDONNELL, Mr. James Edward, BSc ACA *1979;* 19 Woodlands, WOKING, SURREY, GU22 7RU.
MCDONNELL, Mrs. Jane Clare, FCA *1977;* 39 Park Avenue, GILLINGHAM, KENT, ME7 4AQ.
MCDONNELL, Ms. Joanne Elizabeth, BA ACA *1998;* 22 Fairfax Avenue, Didsbury, MANCHESTER, M20 6AJ.
MCDONNELL, Mr. Michael Patrick, MA BBS FCA *1989; (ACA Ireland 1985);* 21 Vanessa Close, Celbridge, KILDARE, COUNTY KILDARE, IRELAND.
MCDONNELL, Mr. Philip Anthony, ACA *2004;* with Wilkins Kennedy, 1-5 Nelson St, SOUTHEND-ON-SEA, SS1 1EG.
MCDONNELL, Mr. Stephen Charles, BA FCA *1988;* 4a Lower Street, Thriplow, ROYSTON, SG8 7RJ.
MCDONNELL, Mr. Stephen Gerard, BSc ACA *1992;* BMW Canada Inc, 50 Ultimate Drive, Richmond Hill, ONTARIO L4S 0C8, ON, CANADA.
MCDONNELL, Mr. Terence Paul Edmund, MSc FCA *1959;* Woodlands, Oxford Road, GERRARDS CROSS, SL9 7DL. (Life Member)
MCDONNELL, Mr. William Rufus Benjamin, BA ACA *1999;* 8 Elmstone Road, LONDON, SW6 5TN.
MCDONOUGH, Mrs. Amanda Theresa, BA ACA ATII *1991;* Carrer L'Ametlla de Mar 1, Esc 3 1B, Salou, 43840 TARRAGONA, CATALONIA, SPAIN.
MCDONOUGH, Mrs. Charlotte Louise, ACA *2005;* 59 MacDonald Road, LIGHTWATER, GU18 5XY.
MCDONOUGH, Mrs. Emma Victoria, BSc(Hons) ACA *2003;* 47 Whinlatter Drive, West Bridgford, NOTTINGHAM, NG2 6QS.
MCDONOUGH, Mr. George, BSc FCA *2000;* 59 MacDonald Road, LIGHTWATER, GU18 5XY.
MCDONOUGH, Ms. Julia, BA ACA *2010;* 4 Russell Close, LONDON, W4 2NU.
•**MCDOUGAL, Mr. Alastair John, BA FCA** *1982;* Underwood Barron LLP, Monks Brook House, 13-17 Hursley Road, Chandler's Ford, EASTLEIGH, HAMPSHIRE SO53 2FW. See also Underwood Barron Associates Limited
MCDOUGALL, Mr. Alisdair, BSc ACA *1991;* Glen Lodge Megg Lane, Chipperfield, KINGS LANGLEY, HERTFORDSHIRE, WD4 9JW.
MCDOUGALL, Mr. Brian, FCA *1958;* 3 Minge Lane, Upton-upon-Severn, WORCESTER, WR8 0NN. (Life Member)
MCDOUGALL, Mr. Brian James, MA ACA *1986;* 80 Braywick Road, MAIDENHEAD, SL6 1DE.
MCDOUGALL, Mr. Gordon Euan, MSc BSc ACA *2007;* 60 Cranley Gardens, LONDON, N13 4LS.
MCDOUGALL, Mr. Gordon Park, FCA *1972;* Park House, Top Road, Calow, CHESTERFIELD, S44 5AF.
MCDOUGALL, Mr. Henry John Arundel, MA FCA *1966;* Sustead Old Hall, Sustead, NORWICH, NR11 8RU.
MCDOUGALL, Mr. Ian Philip, MBA BA(Hons) ACA *2001;* WESCO Dubai, Nr Roundabout 10, PO Box 11419, Jebel Ali Free Zone, DUBAI, 11419 UNITED ARAB EMIRATES.
MCDOUGALL, Mr. Ian Robert, ACA *1983;* 34 New Road, North Runcton, KING'S LYNN, PE33 0QR.
MCDOUGALL, Mrs. Julie Mary, BA ACA *1993;* 23 St. Johns Road, DRIFFIELD, NORTH HUMBERSIDE, YO25 6RS.
MCDOUGALL, Miss. Kimberly, BSc ACA *2006;* 27 Wickham Avenue, Boston Spa, WETHERBY, LS23 6NJ.
MCDOUGALL, Mr. Neil, ACA *1984;* 3 Copperfields, TARPORLEY, CW6 0UP.
MCDOUGALL, Mr. Neil Morton, BA FCA *1988;* Naldrett House, Naldretts Lane, Rudgwick, HORSHAM, WEST SUSSEX, RH12 3BU.
MCDOUGALL, Mr. Robert Lorn, FCA *1970;* Coombe Hill Farm, Lower Road, Hinton Blewett, BRISTOL, BS39 5AT.
MCDOUGALL, Mr. Simon, BA(Hons) ACA *2001;* Promontory, 14 Devonshire Square, LONDON, EC2M 4YT.
MCDOUGALL, Mrs. Victoria Charlotte, BSc ACA *2009;* 60 Cranley Gardens, LONDON, N13 4LS.
MCDOWALL, Mr. Alan Neil, BSc FCA *1983;* 12 Sharon Close, Bookham, LEATHERHEAD, KT23 3LB.
MCDOWALL, Mr. Charles Philip, BA FCA *1981;* 34 Grange Court Road, BRISTOL, BS9 4DR.
MCDOWALL, Mr. Christopher John, MBA FCA *1971;* 1 Alcot Close, CROWTHORNE, BERKSHIRE, RG45 7NE.
MCDOWALL, Mr. Colin James McCutcheon, BA ACA *1993;* 5 Elliot Place, EDINBURGH, EH14 1DR.
MCDOWALL, Mr. David Martin, MEng ACA ACGI AMCT *1999;* 8 Nevinson close, LONDON, SW18 2TF.
MCDOWALL, Mrs. Tanaquil Jane, BSc ACA MBA *1994;* J P Morgan Fleming Asset Management Finsbury Dials, 20 Finsbury Street, LONDON, EC2Y 9AQ.
MCDOWELL, Mr. Alexander Paul, BA(Econ) ACA *2002;* P K F (UK) Llp New Guild House, 45 Great Charles Street Queensway, BIRMINGHAM, B3 2LX.
MCDOWELL, Mr. Andrew Ian, BA ACA *1987;* 6 Silver Lane, Needingworth, ST.IVES, CAMBRIDGESHIRE, PE27 4SL.
•**MCDOWELL, Mr. Angus, FCA** *1969;* McDowell CPA PC, 410 Park Avenue, 15th Floor, NEW YORK, NY 10022, UNITED STATES.
MCDOWELL, Mr. Horace John, FCA *1937;* c/o Mr H McDowell, 1 Tudor Close, LICHFIELD, STAFFORDSHIRE, WS14 9RX. (Life Member)
MCDOWELL, Mr. John Alexander, FCA *1954;* Goldammerweg 6, 54550 NEUNKIRCHEN AM SAND, GERMANY. (Life Member)
MCDOWELL, Mr. Mark Andrew Charles, BSc ACA *1980;* 30 Churchfield Road, WELLING, KENT, DA16 2AA.
MCDOWELL, Mr. Robert Edward, FCA *1964;* 33 Gatesmead, HAYWARDS HEATH, WEST SUSSEX, RH16 1SN.
MCDOWELL, Mr. Shaun, FCA *1967;* Rozel, The Common, Penn, HIGH WYCOMBE, BUCKINGHAMSHIRE, HP10 8LJ.
MCDOWELL, Mr. Simon James, BA ACA *1999;* B G Group Plc 100 Thames Valley Park Drive, READING, RG6 1PT.
MCDOWELL-HOOK, Mr. Christopher Paul, BSc ACA *1987;* 2 Hamana Street, Devonport, AUCKLAND 1309, NEW ZEALAND.
MCDUFF, Mr. David, FCA *1984;* Private Bag x6, GALLO MANOR, 2052, SOUTH AFRICA.
•**MCDWYER, Mr. Michael Raymond, FCA AITI** *1973;* McDwyer Lennon & Co, Esker Place, Cathedral Road, CAVAN, COUNTY CAVAN, IRELAND.
MCEACHRANE, Mr. Howard Noel, FCA *1970;* PO Box 792, Basseterre, ST KITTS, SAINT KITTS AND NEVIS.
MCELDON, Mr. Paul John, BA ACA *1991;* 31 The Croft, Thornholme Road, SUNDERLAND, SR2 7NR.
MCELHATTON, Mr. Michael Edward, BA FCA *1990;* Media Planning Ltd, 11 Great Newport Street, LONDON, WC2H 7JA.
•**MCELHINNEY, Mr. James Brian, ACA** *1979;* Scrutton Bland, Sanderson House, Museum Street, IPSWICH, IP1 1HE.
MCELHINNEY, Ms. Lynsey Erica, BAcc ACA *2010;* Grant Thornton UK Llp Grant Thornton House, 22 Melton Street, LONDON, NW1 2EP.
MCELHINNEY, Mr. Mark, MSc LLB ACA *2000;* 5 Whitethorn, Greenisland, CARRICKFERGUS, COUNTY ANTRIM, BT38 8FH.
•**MCELHOLM, Mr. John Alexander, FCA** *1973;* J.A. McElholm, 71 Beech Avenue, Newton Mearns, GLASGOW, G77 5QR.
•**MCELLIGOTT, Mr. Iain David, FCA** *1993;* MLC 105-153 Miller Street, NORTH SYDNEY, NSW 2060, AUSTRALIA.
MCELLIN, Ms. Ann, MA ACA *1993;* McEllin Kelly Abacus House, 35 Cumberland Street, MACCLESFIELD, CHESHIRE, SK10 1DD.
MCELROY, Mr. Colin Joseph, BSc FCA *1975;* 11 Surrey Close, Burbage, HINCKLEY, LE10 2NY.
•**MCELROY, Miss. Elaine Frances, BA FCA** *1991;* Lonsdale & Marsh, Orleans House, Edmund Street, LIVERPOOL, L3 9NG.
MCELROY, Mr. John Anthony Martin, BSc ACA *1987;* OPUS CORPORATE FINANCE, 1 Bell Yard, LONDON, WC2A 2JR.
MCELROY, Mr. Thomas, ACA *2011;* 37 Danforth Drive, Framlingham, WOODBRIDGE, SUFFOLK, IP13 9HH.
MCELWAINE, Mr. Timothy James, BA ACA *1993;* U N W Llp, Citygate, St. James Boulevard, NEWCASTLE UPON TYNE, NE1 4JE.
MCELWAINE, Miss. Yvonne Marie, MA ACA *1993;* 2 Lonsdale Road, LONDON, SW13 9EB.
MCERLAIN, Mr. Andrew Robert, FCA *1974;* K C S Group, Capella Court, Brighton Road, PURLEY, SURREY, CR8 2PG.
MCERLEAN, Mr. Thaddeus Mary, BCom FCA *1972;* Rixons, Lewes Road, Horsted Keynes, HAYWARDS HEATH, WEST SUSSEX, RH17 7DP.
MCEVILLY, Mr. Robin Angelo, ACA CA(SA) *2011;* (Tax Fac), Top Floor Flat, 37 Honeybrook Road, LONDON, SW12 0DP.
MCEVILLY, Mrs. Susan Carol, BSc ACA *1987;* 29 Bingara Road, BEECROFT, NSW 2119, AUSTRALIA.
•**MCEVOY, Mr. Andrew John, BA ACA** *1989;* AJM Business Services, Holmleigh, Eastham Street, CLITHEROE, LANCASHIRE, BB7 2HY.
MCEVOY, Mrs. Claire Michelle, ACA *2008;* 67 Collins Drive, RUISLIP, MIDDLESEX, HA4 9EG.
MCEVOY, Mrs. Deborah, ACA *1990;* Holmleigh, Eastham Street, CLITHEROE, LANCASHIRE, BB7 2HY.
MCEVOY, Mr. John Clark, BSc ACA *1987;* 9 Gunbower Road, Mt Pleasant, PERTH, WA 6153, AUSTRALIA.
MCEVOY, Mr. Kieran Augustine, FCA *1974;* 7 The Cloisters, North Circular Road, LIMERICK, CO. LIMERICK, IRELAND.
MCEVOY, Mrs. Michele, ACA CA(SA) *2011;* 21 Bushy End, Warwick Gates, WARWICK, CV34 6GJ.
MCEVOY, Mr. Peter Brian, ACA MAAT *1996;* 54 East Street, GUILDFORD, WA 6055, AUSTRALIA.
MCEWAN, Mr. Christopher William, BA ACA *2010;* 28 Victoria Street, Quorn, LOUGHBOROUGH, LEICESTERSHIRE, LE12 8BZ.
MCEWAN, Mr. Desmond William James, MA(Cantab) ACA *2005;* with Deloitte LLP, Hill House, 1 Little New Street, LONDON, EC4A 3TR.
MCEWAN, Mr. Donald, JP FCA *1964;* 17 Broxholm Road, Heaton, NEWCASTLE UPON TYNE, NE6 5RL.
MCEWAN, Mrs. Emily Bell, ACA *2009;* 12 Odette Gardens, TADLEY, HAMPSHIRE, RG26 3PS.
MCEWAN, Mrs. Emma Margaret Jeanne, BA ACA CTA *2006;* (Tax Fac), 36 Windermere Road, LONDON, W5 4TD.
MCEWAN, Miss. Kayleigh, BA ACA *2011;* 7 Smithys Close, ST. LEONARDS-ON-SEA, EAST SUSSEX, TN37 7SU.
MCEWAN, Miss. Lyndsay Anne, ACA *2004;* 1 Wentworth Drive, HARROGATE, NORTH YORKSHIRE, HG2 7LA.
MCEWAN, Miss. Mary Victoria, BA ACA AMCT *1992;* 80 Southwood Gardens, NEWCASTLE UPON TYNE, NE3 3BX.
MCEWAN, Mr. Neil Tom, MSc ACA *2004;* Flat 40 The Piper Building, Peterborough Road, LONDON, SW6 3EF.
MCEWAN, Mr. Ross, BA ACA *1993;* Furzehill Farm Runnon Moor Lane, Hatherleigh, OKEHAMPTON, DEVON, EX20 3PL.
MCEWEN, Mr. Benedict Patrick, ACA *2009;* 45 Cubitt Terrace, Clapham, LONDON, SW4 6AU.
MCEWEN, Miss. Claire Louise, ACA *2010;* 34 Piggotts Road, Caversham, READING, RG4 8EN.
MCEWEN, Mr. Colin Trevor, BA ACA *1993;* Caparo Hotels Ltd, Osborne Hotel, Hesketh Crescent, Meadfoot, TORQUAY, TQ1 2LL.
•**MCEWEN, Mr. Luke Merlin Jasper, BA ACA** *1993;* McEwen & Co Ltd, Forum House, Stirling Road, CHICHESTER, WEST SUSSEX, PO19 7DN.
MCEWEN, Mrs. Samantha Ann, BSocSc ACA *2002;* 24 Lollards Close, AMERSHAM, BUCKINGHAMSHIRE, HP6 5JL.
MCEWEN MASON, Mr. David Johnston, LLB FCA *1974;* Mill Farm, Manaton, NEWTON ABBOT, TQ13 9UN.
MCEWING, Mr. John Gerard, BA ACA *1992;* 77 Haldon Road, LONDON, SW18 1QF.
MCFADDEN, Mr. Peter Alistair, BSc ACA *1997;* Murray International Holdings, 9 Charlotte Square, EDINBURGH, EH2 4DR.
•**MCFADYEN, Mr. Christopher Alec, FCA** *1973;* (Tax Fac), La Fosse Farm, Rue du Caen, St Martin, JERSEY, JE3 6AL.
MCFADYEN, Miss. Jenny Marie, ACA *2010;* Apartment 3, Highfield Court, Eastwick Road, Bookham, LEATHERHEAD, SURREY KT23 4BJ.
MCFADYEN, Miss. Joanna Mary, BA(Hons) ACA *2000;* 223 Tennal Road, BIRMINGHAM, B32 2HH.
MCFADYEN, Mr. Mark Joseph, BSc ACA *2003;* 7 Rozelle Place, Newton Mearns, GLASGOW, G77 6YT.
MCFADZEAN, The Hon. Gordon Barry, MA FCA MSI *1964;* La Roseraie Du Cap, 134 Boulevard Francis Meilland, Cap d' Antibes, 06160 ANTIBES, FRANCE.
MCFADZEAN, Mrs. Louise Kerr, BA ACA *1993;* Patshull Hall, Burnhill Green, WOLVERHAMPTON, WV6 7HY.
MCFARLAND, Mr. Anthony Basil Scott, BA ACA *1988;* Kingston Lodge, Hays, NAVAN, COUNTY MEATH, IRELAND.
MCFARLAND, Mr. Robert Gordon, FCA *1962;* 99 Gunterstone Road, West Kensington, LONDON, W14 9BT. (Life Member)
MCFARLAND, Mr. Robert Stanley, FCA *1971;* Flat 57 Harvard Court, Honeybourne Road, LONDON, NW6 1HN.
MCFARLANE, Mr. Andrew Neil, BA ACA *2004;* BDO, Level 19, 2 Market Street, SYDNEY, NSW 2000, AUSTRALIA.

MCFARLANE, Mrs. Clare Louise, BSc ACA *1993;* Hilarion, Yew Tree Way, Prestbury, MACCLESFIELD, SK10 4EX.
MCFARLANE, Miss. Emma Louise, BA(Hons) ACA *2004;* 2 Kelmscott Place, ASHTEAD, KT21 2HD.
MCFARLANE, Mr. Iain Alexander, BSc ACA *1995;* (Tax Fac), A E A Technology Plc Fermi Avenue, Harwell Science & Innovation Campus, DIDCOT, OXFORDSHIRE, OX11 0QJ.
•MCFARLANE, Mr. Kenneth Irvine, BA FCA *1985;* Deloitte LLP, Athene Place, 66 Shoe Lane, LONDON, EC4A 3BQ. See also Deloitte & Touche LLP
MCFARLANE, Mr. Peter Hugh, BA CA ACA CFE *1987;* 70 University Avenue, Suite 200, TORONTO M5J 2M4, ON, CANADA.
•MCFARLANE, Miss. Roslyn Grace, BSc FCA *2000;* (Tax Fac), HW, 30 Camp Road, FARNBOROUGH, HAMPSHIRE, GU14 6EW. See also Haines Watts
MCFARLANE, Mrs. Stephanie Jane, BA ACA *1994;* The Old Post Office, Priston, BATH, BA2 9EE.
MCFARLANE, Mrs. Tabitha Jane, BA ACA *1993;* 14 Clyde Road, HAWTHORNDENE, SA 5051, AUSTRALIA.
MCFARLANE, Mrs. Terresa Leah, BSc(Hons) ACA *2001;* The Conifers Les Amarreurs Road, Vale, GUERNSEY, GY3 5SH.
MCFARLANE, Mr. William John, MA ACA *1999;* Apartment 12 Carrington House, 1a Montague Road, LONDON, SW19 1TZ.
MCFARTHING, Mrs. Melanie, BSc ACA *1999;* 1 Glover Close, WARWICK, CV34 6RU.
MCFEELEY, Miss. Michelle, BSc ACA *1993;* Mulberry, 70 Kenley Lane, KENLEY, CR8 5DD.
MCFERRAN, Mr. Peter Robert, MA FCA *1968;* P O Box 58555, CY 3735 LIMASSOL, CYPRUS.
MCFETRICH, Mr. Daniel R, MA ACA CFA *2000;* Bahati, Beaconsfield Road, Farnham Royal, SLOUGH, SL2 3BW.
MCFETRICH, Mrs. Joanna Louise, BSc ACA *1999;* Deepend Cottage, 93 Eastwood Road, Bramley, GUILDFORD, SURREY, GU5 0DX.
MCFIE, Mrs. Emma Laetitia, BA(Hons) ACA *2000;* 10 Bywater Street, LONDON, SW3 4XD.
MCFIE, Mr. Peter Andrew Charles, BSc ACA *1991;* (Tax Fac), 10 Bywater Street, LONDON, SW3 4XD.
MCGAFFNEY, Miss. Victoria, BA ACA *2007;* 12 Harcourt Road, Wimbledon, LONDON, SW19 1LS.
•MCGAIN, Mr. Andrew Ian, BSc ACA *2003;* Moore Stephens (North West) LLP, 6th Floor, Blackfriars House, Parsonage, MANCHESTER, M3 2JA.
•MCGAIN, Mr. Brian, FCA *1970;* Moore Stephens (North West) LLP, 110-114 Duke Street, LIVERPOOL, L1 5AG.
•MCGAIN, Mr. Simon Timothy, BSc ACA *2006;* Moore Stephens (North West) LLP, 110-114 Duke Street, LIVERPOOL, L1 5AG.
MCGAIN-HARDING, Mr. Daniel Edward, BA ACA *2007;* 3 Ashdene Gardens, Wordsley, STOURBRIDGE, DY8 5JQ.
MCGALE, Ms. Caroline, BSc ACA *1998;* 52 New Street, Randalstown, ANTRIM, BT41 3AF.
MCGANN, Mrs. Alexandra Jane, BA ACA *1986;* 36 Westcombe Park Road, LONDON, SE3 7RB.
MCGANN, Miss. Davinia Louise, ACA *2009;* B P P Holdings Plc Aldine House, 142-144 Uxbridge Road, LONDON, W12 8AA.
MCGANN, Mr. Martin Francis, BSc ACA *1989;* L S I Management Llp, 21 St. James's Square, LONDON, SW1Y 4JZ.
MCGAREL, Miss. Sarah Frances, BSc ACA *2009;* with PricewaterhouseCoopers LLP, 125 High Street, BOSTON, MA 02110, UNITED STATES.
MCGAREL GROVES, Mr. Anthony Robin, BSc ACA *1981;* Clapton Revel, Falcons Croft, Wooburn Moor, HIGH WYCOMBE, BUCKINGHAMSHIRE, HP10 0NH.
MCGAREL GROVES, Mr. Hugh Macmilan Julian, MA FCA *1978;* Home Farm, Salters Lane, Ludgershall, AYLESBURY, HP18 9NY.
MCGARRAGHY, Mrs. Janette Catherine, BA(Econ) ACA *2002;* 41 Leigh Close, Tottington, BURY, LANCASHIRE, BL8 4HL.
MCGARRAGHY, Mr. Neil, ACA *2003;* 41 Leigh Close Tottington, BURY, LANCASHIRE, BL8 4HL.
•MCGARRY, Mr. David, ACA *1980;* Dutton Moore, 6 Silver Street, HULL, HU1 1JA.
•MCGARRY, Mr. David Keith, BBS FCA *1987; (FCA Ireland 1979);* KPMG LLC, Heritage Court, 41 Athol Street, Douglas, ISLE OF MAN, IM99 1HN. See also KPMG Audit LLC
•MCGARRY, Mr. Mark Dominic, FCA *1984;* (Tax Fac), Saffery Champness, Lion House, Red Lion Street, LONDON, WC1R 4GB.
MCGARRY, Mrs. Martha Elizabeth, ACA *1982;* 26 Gilling Road, RICHMOND, DL10 5AA.
MCGARRY, Mr. Stephen, BA ACA *1990;* U F I Ltd, Dearing House, 1 Young Street, SHEFFIELD, S1 4UP.
MCGAUGHEY, Miss. Laura Elisabeth, MA ACA *2003;* 186 Canbury Park Road, KINGSTON UPON THAMES, KT2 6LF.
MCGAVIGAN, Miss. Katharine, BSc ACA *2000;* 28 Lynwood, GUILDFORD, SURREY, GU2 7NY.
MCGAW, Mr. George William, FCA *1962;* 4 Cecil Court, Ponteland, NEWCASTLE UPON TYNE, NE20 9EE. (Life Member)
MCGAW, Mrs. Helen, BA ACA *2007;* AXA Wealth Marlborough House, Marlborough Street, BRISTOL, BS1 3NX.
MCGEACHIN, Miss. Elizabeth Anne, BA ACA *1989;* 2 Chapel Close, Chapel of Garioch, INVERURIE, ABERDEENSHIRE, AB51 5HG.
MCGEE, Miss. Jenna, BSc ACA *2011;* 59 High Street, AMERSHAM, BUCKINGHAMSHIRE, HP7 0DT.
MCGEE, Mr. Matthew James, BSc ACA *1999;* 258 Canbury Park Road, KINGSTON UPON THAMES, SURREY, KT2 6LG.
MCGEE, Ms. Pauline Martina, BA(Hons) FCA *2008; (ACA Ireland* with BDO LLP, 55 Baker Street, LONDON, W1U 7EU.
MCGEE, Mr. Stephen Robert, BSc ACA *1995;* 50 Woodcrest Road, BOXFORD, MA 01921, UNITED STATES.
MCGEEHAN, Ms. Rhona Ann, BA(Hons) ACA *2001;* 49a Danehurst Street, LONDON, SW6 6SA.
MCGEEVER, Mr. Terence, ACA *1984;* 3 Whitburn Road, Cleadon, SUNDERLAND, SR6 7QL.
MCGEORGE, Mrs. Caroline Anne Elizabeth, BSc ACA *1988;* 23b Torkington Road, WILMSLOW, CHESHIRE, SK9 2AE.
MCGEOWN, Mr. Ciaran, BSc(Hons) ACA *2001;* Appt 415, 438 Richmond St W, TORONTO M5V 3S6, ON, CANADA.
MCGEOWN, Mr. Steven Ross, BA(Hons) ACA *2011;* 19 Bosville, EASTLEIGH, HAMPSHIRE, SO50 4QA.
•MCGEOWN, Mr. Timothy George, FCA *1973;* 19 Bosville, EASTLEIGH, HAMPSHIRE, SO50 4QA.
•MCGERTY, Mr. Paul Frederick, BSc(Hons) ACA *2002;* McLintocks Ltd, 56 Hamilton Street, BIRKENHEAD, MERSEYSIDE, CH41 5HZ. See also McLintocks
MCGERTY, Miss. Rebecca Louise, BA ACA *2005;* 41 Warwick Avenue, LONDON, W9 2PR.
MCGETTIGAN, Miss. Nuala Marie, BSc ACA *2005;* 8 Holly Road, NORTHAMPTON, NN1 4QR.
•MCGHEE, Mr. Alexander Freeburn, ACA *1994;* (Tax Fac), A. F. McGhee & Co, First Floor Offices, 54 Main Road, WINDERMERE, CUMBRIA, LA23 1DX.
MCGHEE, Miss. Alexandra, BA(Hons) ACA *2002;* 8 Telferscot Road, LONDON, SW12 0QD.
MCGHEE, Miss. Charlotte Fleur, BSc FCA *1997;* 22 The Coppice, ENFIELD, MIDDLESEX, EN2 7BY.
MCGHEE, Miss. Margaret Jane, LLB ACA *2001;* with National Audit Office, 157-197 Buckingham Palace Road, Victoria, LONDON, SW1W 9SP.
MCGHIE, Mr. Graham Thomas, MA CA *2001; (CA Scotland 1983);* (Tax Fac), The Mudd Partnership, Lakeview House, 4 Woodbrook Crescent, BILLERICAY, ESSEX, CM12 0EQ.
MCGIBBON, Mr. Alan, BA FCA *1983;* 2 Kenton Close, Formby, LIVERPOOL, L37 7EA.
MCGIBBON, Mr. John Downie, FCA *1972;* Laurel Cottage, Southdown Road, Shawford, WINCHESTER, HAMPSHIRE, SO21 2BX.
MCGIBBON, Mr. Lewis, FCA *1959;* May Trees, Golf Lane, Church Brampton, NORTHAMPTON, NN6 8AY. (Life Member)
MCGIBBON, Mrs. Marion Lorraine, BA ACA *1993;* Belfast Education & Library Board, 40 Academy Street, BELFAST, BT1 2NQ.
MCGIBBON, Miss. Michelle Louise, ACA *2005;* 15 Duntshill Road, LONDON, SW18 4QN.
•MCGIBBON, Mrs. Sarah Elizabeth, BA ACA *1997;* Target Chartered Accountants Reading Bridge House, Reading Bridge, READING, RG1 8LS.
•MCGILL, Mr. Alan David, BSc FCA *1995;* PricewaterhouseCoopers LLP, 7 More London Riverside, LONDON, SE1 2RT. See also PricewaterhouseCoopers
•①MCGILL, Mr. Andrew Stephen, BSc ACA *1990;* with KPMG LLP, One Snowhill, Snow Hill Queensway, BIRMINGHAM, B4 6GN.
MCGILL, Ms. Caroline, MA ACA *2006;* 180 Brunswick Quay, LONDON, SE16 7PT.
MCGILL, Mr. Edward Alexander, ACA CA(NZ) *2010;* 8 Spencer Mansions, Queen's Club Gardens, LONDON, W14 9TL.
MCGILL, Mr. Ian David, BA ACA *1978;* Greenheys Management Ltd, 3 Bell Mews, WHITCHURCH, HAMPSHIRE, RG28 7BG.
MCGILL, Mr. Roger Andrew Stuart, BA ACA *2006;* McGill Electrical Ltd, Harrison Road, DUNDEE, DD2 3SN.
MCGILL, Miss. Sally Elizabeth, MA BA ACA *1989;* 22 Whitehaven Gardens, MANCHESTER, M20 2SY.
MCGILLIAN, Mrs. Faye Louise, BSc ACA *2001;* K P M G Management Services Centre, 58 Clarendon Road, WATFORD, WD17 1DE.
MCGILLICUDDY, Mr. Mark Howard, BSc ACA *1987;* 12 Manor Road, Dorridge, SOLIHULL, B93 8DX.
MCGILVRAY, Mr. Richard Howard, FCA *1958;* 8 Ardyne Terrace, Innellan, DUNOON, PA23 7TL. (Life Member)
MCGING, Mr. Thomas Patrick, MA FCA *1977;* West End House 26a West End, WITNEY, OXFORDSHIRE, OX28 1NE.
MCGING, Mr. Tony Michael, BSc ACA *1991;* 144 Pollards Hill North, Norbury, LONDON, SW16 4PA.
•MCGINLEY, Mr. James Benedict, BCom FCA *1975;* (Tax Fac), Helmores UK LLP, Grosvenor Gardens House, 35-37 Grosvenor Gardens, LONDON, SW1W 0BY.
MCGINN, Mrs. Alison, BSc(Hons) ACA *2002;* Flat 22, 9th Floor, Block B, Repulse Bay Apartments, 101 Repulse Bay Road, REPULSE BAY HONG KONG SAR.
MCGINN, Mr. Hugh Somerville, FCA *1973;* 12 Allerton Close, Westhoughton, BOLTON, BL5 3UG.
MCGINN, Miss. Vicki Louise, BA ACA *2001;* 6 Homestead, Broomfield, CHELMSFORD, ESSEX, CM1 7WT.
MCGINNIS, Mr. Paul James, BSc ACA *1993;* 22 Ross Avenue, Whitefield, MANCHESTER, M45 7FH.
MCGINTY, Mr. Francis Patrick, FCA *1973;* 9 Crocus Field, Leyland, PRESTON, PR25 3DY.
MCGINTY, Miss. Helen Jane, BA(Hons) ACA *2003;* 5 Woodeson Lea, Rodley, LEEDS, LS13 1RJ.
MCGINTY, Miss. Joanne, BA(Hons) ACA *2001;* 29 Trehern Close, Knowle, SOLIHULL, WEST MIDLANDS, B93 9HA.
•MCGINTY, Mr. Robert Gerard Anton, FCA *1969;* (Tax Fac), Cintra, 4 Coley Avenue, WOKING, GU22 7BT.
MCGIVERN, Mr. Arthur Joseph, BSc ACA *1989;* 5 Howard Place, REIGATE, RH2 9NP.
MCGIVERN, Mr. James Patrick, BA ACA *2000;* 3 The Ridge, WIRRAL, MERSEYSIDE, CH60 6SP.
MCGIVERN, Mr. Paul, FCA *1976;* 9 Albany Avenue, NEWCASTLE UPON TYNE, NE12 8AS.
MCGIVERN, Miss. Polly Clare, BSc ACA *2002;* Prince of Wales Office, Clarence House, St. James's, LONDON, SW1A 1BA.
MCGLADDERY, Miss. Sharon Jane, BA FCA *1992;* 7 Fairford Mount, LEEDS, LS6 4QY.
MCGLADE, Mrs. Marie-Claire, BSc ACA *2004;* (Tax Fac), Flat 16, Roberts Court, 23 Essex Road, LONDON, N1 2SA.
•MCGLASHAN, Mr. John Braithwaite, FCA *1963;* R.F. Frazer & Co, 112a Wallasey Road, WALLASEY, MERSEYSIDE, CH44 2AE.
MCGLASHAN, Mr. Kenneth Michael John, MA FCA *1973;* 134 Hempstead Road, WATFORD, WD17 4LG.
MCGLAUGHLIN, Miss. Anna Rose, ACA *2009;* 59 Repton Way, Croxley Green, RICKMANSWORTH, HERTFORDSHIRE, WD3 3PN.
MCGLAULIN, Miss. Rachel Bethan, ACA *2008;* Bank of America, 5 Canada Square, LONDON, E14 5AQ.
MCGLENNON, Mrs. Kirsten Fay, MA ACA *2001;* 26 Broomfield Lane, Hale, ALTRINCHAM, CHESHIRE, WA15 9AU.
•MCGLINCHEY, Mr. John Frederick, FCA *1963;* John F. McGlinchey, 1st Floor, Champleys Mews, Market Place, PICKERING, YO18 7AE.
MCGLOGAN, Mr. John, LLB FCA *1966;* Mill Barn, Elsted, MIDHURST, GU29 0LA.
MCGLONE, Mr. Roy Vickers, MA ACA *1978;* Walnut Cottage, Binfield Heath, HENLEY-ON-THAMES, RG9 4DP.
MCGLYNE, Mrs. Sarah Louise, BA ACA *1996;* Jasmine Cottage, High Street, Whitchurch on Thames, READING, RG8 7ET.
MCGLYNN, Miss. Catherine Amanda, LLB ACA *2004;* Flat 2, 29 Wolsey Road, LONDON, N1 4QG.
MCGLYNN, Mrs. Jane Ann, BA ACA *1995;* 33 Arrol Drive, AYR, KA7 4AG.
MCGOAY, Mrs. Anita, BEng ACA *2002;* 9 Gleneagles Drive, Brockhall Village, Old Langho, BLACKBURN, BB6 8BF.
MCGOLDRICK, Mrs. Margaret Josephine, BSc ACA *1979;* 77 Stonor Road, Hall Green, BIRMINGHAM, B28 0QP.
MCGOLPIN, Mr. Daniel Scott, MA ACA *2000;* BBC, Room 6239, BBC Television Centre, LONDON, W12 7RJ.
MCGONAGLE, Mr. Donald Victor, BSc ACA *1992;* 68 Bloxham Road, BANBURY, OXFORDSHIRE, OX16 9JR.
MCGONIGAL, Miss. Claire Elizabeth, ACA *2010;* 11 Lapwing Court, LIVERPOOL, L26 7WH.
MCGONIGLE, Mrs. Alison Jane, BA ACA *1992;* 11 Ferrands Close, Harden, BINGLEY, BD16 1JA.
•MCGONIGLE, Mr. David Joseph, ACA *1989;* Paragon Financial Management Limited, 11 Ferrands Close, Harden, BINGLEY, WEST YORKSHIRE, BD16 1JA.
MCGONIGLE, Miss. Emily Jane, BSc ACA *2006;* Thicketts, Copt Hall Road, Ightham, SEVENOAKS, TN15 9DU.
MCGOOHAN, Mr. Stephen James, BA(Hons) ACA *2004;* Flat 9 Carrington Court, 104 Green Dragon Lane, LONDON, N21 2LY.
MCGORRIGAN, Mr. John, BA ACA *1987;* 7 Dolphinholme Mill, Dolphinholme, LANCASTER, LA2 9AU.
MCGOUGH, Mr. Michael Jack, BSc(Eng) MCIJ FCA *1976;* 24 Wellfields, LOUGHTON, IG10 1NX.
MCGOUGH, Mr. Simon Robert, ACA *2010;* Flat 14, 102 Great Titchfield Street, LONDON, W1W 6SL.
MCGOURTY, Miss. Paula Kim, BSc ACA *1997;* 105 Elborough Street, Southfields, LONDON, SW18 5DS.
•MCGOVERN, Mr. Anthony Gerard, BA ACA *1982;* (Tax Fac), McGoverns, 24 Westpole Avenue, Cockfosters, BARNET, EN4 0AY.
MCGOVERN, Mr. Anton Francis, BBS FCA *1989;* Hammercot, Grouse Road, Colgate, HORSHAM, WEST SUSSEX, RH13 6HT.
MCGOVERN, Mrs. Katie Sarah, BSc ACA *2001;* Calle Doce 15, 08860 CASTELLDEFELS, CATALONIA, SPAIN.
MCGOVERN, Mr. Kevin Allan, BSc FCA *1999;* Calle 12 No.15, Castedellfels, 08860 BARCELONA, SPAIN.
MCGOVERN, Mrs. Michelle, BSc ACA *1990;* Thirlmere, Tattenham Crescent, Epsom Downs, EPSOM, KT18 5NR.
MCGOWAN, Mr. Adam, ACA *2006;* 11 Elmsley Road, LIVERPOOL, L18 8AY.
MCGOWAN, Miss. Anne Kostka, BSc FCA *1979;* 10 Dudley Court, 24 Lethington Avenue, GLASGOW, G41 3HY.
MCGOWAN, Mr. Barry Keith, FCA *1971;* 31 Redruth Road, WALSALL, WS5 3EJ.
MCGOWAN, Mr. Brian Dennis, FCA *1967;* Catalyst Corporate Finance LLP, 9th Floor, Bank House, 8 Cherry Street, BIRMINGHAM, B2 5AL.
•MCGOWAN, Mr. Derek, FCA *1971;* 1674 Bucksglen Court, WESTLAKE VILLAGE, CA 91361, UNITED STATES.
MCGOWAN, Mr. Desmond Andrew, BCom FCA *1975;* 2-4 Merville Road, Stillorgan, DUBLIN 19, COUNTY DUBLIN, IRELAND.
MCGOWAN, Mr. Iain William, LLB(Hons) DipLP ACA CISA FSI *1990;* 351 Birchanger Lane, Birchanger, BISHOP'S STORTFORD, HERTFORDSHIRE, CM23 5QR.
MCGOWAN, Mrs. Janis Rosemary Adelaide, MA FCA *1976;* 6 Dower Close, Knotty Green, BEACONSFIELD, BUCKINGHAMSHIRE, HP9 1XZ. (Life Member)
MCGOWAN, Miss. Laura Joanne, BSc ACA *2007;* 110 Willow Road, ENFIELD, MIDDLESEX, EN1 3AY.
MCGOWAN, Mrs. Lorraine, BA ACA *1988;* Urban Space Holdings Ltd, Trinity Buoy Wharf, 64 Orchard Place, LONDON, E14 0JW.
•MCGOWAN, Mr. Michael Joseph, BSc FCA *1981;* Easting House, Piltdown, UCKFIELD, EAST SUSSEX, TN22 3XN.
MCGOWAN, Mr. Neil Alexander, ACA *2009;* Apartment 19, Kings Hall, 53 Wake Green Road, BIRMINGHAM, B13 9HW.
MCGOWAN, Mr. Nigel Hampton, BSc ACA *1991;* Hampton Services Limited, 14 - 16 Peel Road, Douglas, ISLE OF MAN, IM1 4LR.
MCGOWAN, Mr. Peter Frederick, FCA *1965;* Nethergreen House, 9 The Green, Ruddington, NOTTINGHAM, NG11 6DY.
MCGOWAN, Mr. Philip, MA(Oxon) ACA *2011;* 19 Maryland Court, Stapleford, NOTTINGHAM, NG9 8LP.
MCGOWAN, Mr. Robert Graeme, MA FCA FCT *1975;* 6 Dower Close, BEACONSFIELD, HP9 1XZ.
MCGOWAN, Mr. Stephen Mark, BSc ACA *1990;* 4 Silverdale Close, Weston, CREWE, CW2 5GW.
MCGOWAN, Mr. Steven, ACA *2008;* 7 Bush Hill Road, LONDON, N21 2DR.
MCGOWAN, Mr. Terence Francis, FCA *1969;* Wincroft, Easton, WINCHESTER, SO21 1ER.
MCGOWAN, Mr. Thomas Andrew, BA ACA *1988;* 1 Yuthet, La Rue Du Becq Trinity, JERSEY, JE3 5FR.
•MCGOWAN, Dr. Victoria Anne, PhD BSc FCA *1995;* (Tax Fac), V A McGowan, 5 Hartington Road, Bramhall, STOCKPORT, SK7 2DZ.

MCGRADY, Mr. George, BSc ACA *1996;* 188 Finedon Road, Irthlingborough, WELLINGBOROUGH, NORTHAMPTONSHIRE, NN9 5UB.
MCGRADY, Mr. Matthew Robert, LLB ACA *1999;* Merit Merrell Technology, 3 Silverton Court Northumberland Business Park, CRAMLINGTON, NORTHUMBERLAND, NE23 7RY.
MCGRAHAN, Miss. Ailsa, BA(Hons) ACA *2011;* Flat 204, Dryden Building, 37 Commercial Road, LONDON, E1 1LF.
MCGRAIL, Mr. Garry John, BA(Hons) ACA *2010;* 3 Le Borowe, Church Crookham, FLEET, GU52 6ZA.
MCGRAIL, Mr. John Joseph Anthony, BA ACA *1994;* 25 Brook Road, LYMM, CHESHIRE, WA13 9AH.
MCGRAIL, Mr. Patrick Thomas, LLB ACA *1991;* 64 Woodburn Street, DALKEITH, MIDLOTHIAN, EH22 2EW.
MCGRANAGHAN, Mr. Martin Anthony Patrick, BSc FCA *1972;* 22 Goodwood Close, Cowplain, WATERLOOVILLE, PO8 8BG.
MCGRATH, Mr. Andrew, MMath ACA *2007;* 9 The Royal, Wilton Place, SALFORD, M3 6WP.
MCGRATH, Mr. Anthony Charles Ormond, BA BSc FCA *1974;* Town Place, Freshfield, Nr Scaynes Hill, HAYWARDS HEATH, RH17 7NR.
MCGRATH, Mr. Dennis, BA ACA *1983;* White Young Green Plc, Arndale House, Headingley, LEEDS, LS6 2UJ.
•MCGRATH, Mr. Eamonn John, BA FCA *1980;* Ernst & Young LLP, 1 More London Place, LONDON, SE1 2AF. See also Ernst & Young Europe LLP
MCGRATH, Mrs. Emma Wendy, BCom ACA *1990;* 1A Azalea Gardens, WAHROONGA, NSW 2076, AUSTRALIA.
MCGRATH, Mr. Gary Christopher, BSc ACA *1994;* Avenue Louise 391, 1050 BRUSSELS, BELGIUM.
MCGRATH, Mr. Gerald James, BEng ACA *1993;* 19 Garners Road, Chalfont St. Peter, GERRARDS CROSS, BUCKINGHAMSHIRE, SL9 0HA.
MCGRATH, Mr. Gregory William, BA ACA *1991;* 25 Chequers Hill, AMERSHAM, BUCKINGHAMSHIRE, HP7 9DQ.
MCGRATH, Mrs. Helen Elizabeth, BA(Hons) ACA *2003;* 86 Cirrus Drive, Shinfield, READING, RG2 9FL.
MCGRATH, Mr. Hugh Brendan, FCA *1969;* Penrose Glebe, Henley Road, Stubbings, MAIDENHEAD, BERKSHIRE, SL6 6QW.
MCGRATH, Miss. Jennifer Helen, MA FCA *1985;* Kummrutistrasse 62, CH - 8810, HORGEN, SWITZERLAND.
MCGRATH, Mr. John Paul, BCom ACA *2001;* Hiestand International AG, Ifangstrasse 11, 8952 SCHLIEREN, SWITZERLAND.
MCGRATH, Mr. Liam, BA ACA *2005;* SC10R031081, B Z W, 10 South Colonnade, LONDON, E14 4PU.
MCGRATH, Mrs. Lucinda Margaret, BA ACA *1991;* 46, 46 Mill Road, Higher Bebington, WIRRAL, MERSEYSIDE, CH63 5PB.
MCGRATH, Mr. Michael Augustine, BCom FCA *1969;* 7 Killegland Rise, ASHBOURNE, COUNTY MEATH, IRELAND.
MCGRATH, Mrs. Paula Margaret, BSc ACA *2002;* 55 Long John Hill, NORWICH, NR1 2JW.
MCGRATH, Miss. Sonia Helen, BSc ACA *1991;* 29 Inchcolm Drive, North Queensferry, INVERKEITHING, FIFE, KY11 1LD.
MCGRATH, Mr. William Brendan, BA ACA *1984;* Aga Rangemaster Group Plc, 4 Arleston Way, Shirley, SOLIHULL, WEST MIDLANDS, B90 4LH.
MCGRAW, Mr. Anthony, BSc(Hons) ACA *2011;* 25 Moorholme, WOKING, SURREY, GU22 7QZ.
MCGRAW, Mr. James, PhD BSc ACA *2010;* Flat 42, Twyford Court, Fortis Green, LONDON, N10 3ET.
MCGRAW, Mrs. Tracey Jane, BA ACA *1998;* 70 Pilots Way, HULL, HU9 1PS.
MCGREADY, Mrs. Kristina Frances, BA(Hons) ACA *2002;* 32 Gainsborough Road, IPSWICH, IP4 2XG.
•MCGREADY, Mr. Malcolm Robert, BSc FCA *1999;* Ensors, Cardinal House, 46 St Nicholas Street, IPSWICH, IP1 1TT.
MCGREEVY, Mr. Andrew Francis, BA ACA *1991;* 17 St. Stephens Road, Prenton, BIRKENHEAD, MERSEYSIDE, CH42 8PP.
MCGREEVY, Miss. Elise, BSc ACA *1992;* Yew Court Riverview Road, Pangbourne, READING, RG8 7AU.
MCGREEVY, Miss. Jacqueline Ann, BA ACA *1991;* 35 Byron Road Twyford, READING, RG10 0AE.
MCGREEVY, Mr. Julian Mark, LLB ACA *1996;* 950 N. Kings Road, Unit 216, WEST HOLLYWOOD, CA 90069, UNITED STATES.
MCGREEVY, Mrs. Paula Christine, MA ACA *1992;* 17 St. Stephens Road, Prenton, BIRKENHEAD, CH42 8PP.
MCGREEVY, Mr. Stefan, BA(Hons) ACA *2002;* Heath Mount, Le Mont Des Corvees, St. Ouen, JERSEY, JE3 2ES.
MCGREEVY, Mrs. Susanne, ACA *1995;* 27 Prideaux Road, EASTBOURNE, EAST SUSSEX, BN21 2ND.
•MCGREGOR, Mrs. Anne Maxwell, FCA *1980;* (Tax Fac), DNG Dove Naish, Eagle House, 28 Billing Road, NORTHAMPTON, NN1 5AJ.
MCGREGOR, Mr. Daniel James, BA ACA *1999;* 724 4th Street NE, WASHINGTON, DC 20002, UNITED STATES.
MCGREGOR, Mr. Douglas Currie, BA ACA *1991;* 19 Eglinton Crescent, EDINBURGH, EH12 5BY.
MCGREGOR, Miss. Fiona Skasenniio, BA ACA CTA *1989;* 27 Manor Close, Buckden, ST. NEOTS, PE19 5XR.
MCGREGOR, Mr. Gerald Alexander Richard, BA FCA *1975;* 44 Abinger Road, Bedford ParkChiswick, LONDON, W4 1EX.
MCGREGOR, Miss. Gillian Margaret, BSc ACA *1994;* 16 Seething Wells Lane, SURBITON, KT6 5NR.
MCGREGOR, Mr. Glenn Frederick, BSc FCA *1981;* Countrywide Plc Countrywide House, 88-103 Caldecotte Lake Drive Caldecotte, MILTON KEYNES, MK7 8JT.
MCGREGOR, Mr. Graeme Leddie, ACA CA(SA) *2010;* 14 Mountstewart, Wynyard, BILLINGHAM, CLEVELAND, TS22 5QN.
MCGREGOR, Miss. Hiroka, ACA *2008;* Flat 2, 8 Heath Drive, LONDON, NW3 7SN.
MCGREGOR, Mr. Ian Alistair, BSc ACA *1983;* Greenlooms House, Homington, SALISBURY, SP5 4NL.
MCGREGOR, Mr. Ian Donald, BA ACA *1988;* The Royal Household, Buckingham Palace, LONDON, SW1A 1AA.
MCGREGOR, Miss. Julie Lynne, BA ACA *1991;* Carpe Diem, Ash Lane, Down Hatherley, GLOUCESTER, GL2 9PS.
•MCGREGOR, Mr. Keith, BSc ARCS ACA *1991;* Ernst & Young LLP, 1 More London Place, LONDON, SE1 2AF. See also Ernst & Young Europe LLP
MCGREGOR, Mrs. Lindsey, ACA *2002;* The Cottage, 26 Old Gloucester Street, LONDON, WC1N 3AN.
MCGREGOR, Miss. Maree Leah, ACA *2009;* 11/10-12 Clement Street, Rushcutters Bay, SYDNEY, NSW 2011, AUSTRALIA.
•MCGREGOR, Mr. Michael Stewart, ACA *1991;* Inverearn, St. Fillans, CRIEFF, PH6 2NF.
MCGREGOR, Mr. Richard Robert, FCA *1963;* Garth Cottage, Ascot Road, Holyport, MAIDENHEAD, SL6 2HY. (Life Member)
MCGREGOR, Mr. Robert Ian, FCA *1957;* 105 Grange Cres, CHIGWELL, IG7 5JD. (Life Member)
MCGREGOR, Mr. Roger Keith, FCA *1970;* Ridgewood, Uvedale Road, OXTED, SURREY, RH8 0EN.
MCGREGOR, Miss. Samantha, BSc ACA *2011;* 9 Kirkly Close, SOUTH CROYDON, SURREY, CR2 0ET.
MCGREGOR-SMITH, Mr. Graham David, BA ACA *1988;* Forest Ridge, Bagshot Road, ASCOT, BERKSHIRE, SL5 9JL.
MCGREGOR SMITH, Mr. Iain Murdoch, BSc ACA *1991;* 8 West Way, PINNER, HA5 3NX.
MCGREGOR-SMITH, Mrs. Ruby, BA ACA *1991;* Forest Ridge, Bagshot Road, ASCOT, BERKSHIRE, SL5 9JL.
MCGREGOR-VINEY, Mr. Bruce, MA ACA MSI *1988;* International Centre for Financial Regulation, 41 Moorgate, LONDON, EC2R 6PP.
MCGRIGOR, Mr. Robert Angus Buchanan, BSc FCA *1991;* Holly Tree House, Radford, CHIPPING NORTON, OXFORDSHIRE, OX7 4EB.
•MCGRORY, Mr. Colm Andrew, BA FCA *1992;* Ormerod Rutter Limited, The Oakley, Kidderminster Road, DROITWICH, WORCESTERSHIRE, WR9 9AY. See also Ormerod Rutter Solutions Ltd
MCGRORY, Mrs. Gillian, ACA *1983;* The Paddock, 66 High Street, Hook, GOOLE, DN14 5NY.
•MCGRORY, Mr. Iain Robert Charles, FCA *1967;* Iain McGrory, Le Bourg, 24610 ST MEARD DE GURCON, FRANCE.
MCGRORY, Mr. Michael Thomas, BA ACA *1986;* 12 Brook Road, TWICKENHAM, TW1 1JE.
MCGRORY, Ms. Susan Margaret, BSc ACA *1995;* Demica Plc Crowne House, 56-58 Southwark Street, LONDON, SE1 1UN.
MCGROTHER, Mr. John, BA FCA *1975;* 1 Westview Terrace, Eaglescliffe, STOCKTON-ON-TEES, TS16 0EE.
MCGUCKIN, Miss. Kirsty, ACA MAAT *2011;* 19 The Limes, HITCHIN, HERTFORDSHIRE, SG5 2AY.
MCGUCKIN, Mrs. Tracey Anne, ACA *2009;* 10 Inglewood Close, BLYTH, NORTHUMBERLAND, NE24 4LT.
MCGUIGAN, Miss. Alison, BA ACA *1992;* 8 Grantham Street, BLYTH, NORTHUMBERLAND, NE24 3EA.
MCGUIGAN, Mr. Ciaran Francis, BA ACA *2003;* 23 Claremont Road, EDINBURGH, EH6 7NH.
MCGUIGAN, Mr. Thomas Stephen, BA ACA *2009;* 117 Mount Pleasant Road, LONDON, E17 5RU.
•MCGUINNESS, Miss. Cristy-Ann, BSc ACA *2002;* MAC Consulting Limited, 38 Rosemoor Gardens, Appleton, WARRINGTON, WA4 5RG.
MCGUINNESS, Mr. Ian, FCA *1972;* 25 Dewhurst Clough Road, Egerton, BOLTON, BL7 9TY.
MCGUINNESS, Miss. Julie Kay, BA ACA *1995;* National Audit Office, 157-197 Buckingham Palace Road, LONDON, SW1W 9SP.
MCGUINNESS, Mr. Kevin Francis, BA ACA *1979;* 3 Linden Grove, DUMFRIES, DG1 2QL.
MCGUINNESS, Miss. Madeleine Rose, BSc ACA *1993;* 24 Channel Reach, Channel Road, Blundellsands, LIVERPOOL, L23 6TA.
MCGUINNESS, Mr. Peter Timothy, BSc ACA *1996;* 19 Winkurra St, Kensington, SYDNEY, NSW 2033, AUSTRALIA.
MCGUINNESS, Ms. Sarah, BSc ACA *2001;* 17 Pine Valley Grove, RATHFARNHAM 16, COUNTY DUBLIN, IRELAND.
MCGUINNESS, Miss. Sheena Caroline, BA ACA CTA *2000;* 9 Southwood Avenue, Highgate, LONDON, N6 5RY.
MCGUINNESS, Mr. Simon, ACA *2011;* 29 West View Grove, Whitefield, MANCHESTER, M45 7NQ.
MCGUINNESS, Mr. Stephen James, BA ACA *1990;* Hedgesupport, 6 Duke Street, St James, LONDON, SW1Y 6BN.
•MCGUINNESS, Mr. Stephen John, FCA *1980;* (Tax Fac), Spencer Hyde Limited, 272 Regents Park Road, LONDON, N3 3HN.
MCGUINNESS-SMITH, Mr. Mark Rowley, BA ACA *1996;* 43 Bennerley Road, LONDON, SW11 6DR.
MCGUIRE, Miss. Aileen Marshall, BSc ACA *1988;* Richemont International Ltd, 175 Piccadilly, LONDON, W1J 9DJ.
MCGUIRE, Mr. Damian Gerald, MBA BA(Hons) ACA *1992;* 89 Moss Lane, Bramhall, STOCKPORT, CHESHIRE, SK7 1EG.
MCGUIRE, Mr. Dominic James, MA ACA *1993;* 19 Tuckton Road, BOURNEMOUTH, BH6 3HP.
MCGUIRE, Mr. Gordon Ian, BA ACA *2004;* 29 6-12 Pacific Street, MANLY, NSW 2095, AUSTRALIA.
MCGUIRE, Mrs. Helena Kirsten, BA ACA *2005;* 10 Parklands Gate, Bramhope, LEEDS, LS16 9AG.
MCGUIRE, Miss. Leesa Sandra, BA ACA *2004;* Glengairn, Mill Lane, Felbridge, EAST GRINSTEAD, WEST SUSSEX, RH19 2PF.
MCGUIRE, Mr. Mark John, BA ACA *1999;* 18 Gibsons Road, STOCKPORT, CHESHIRE, SK4 4JX.
MCGUIRE, Mr. Neil, FCA *1987;* 25 Beech Avenue, UPMINSTER, RM14 2HW.
MCGUIRE, Mr. Paul Kenneth, BA FCA *1980;* Rte de la Genevrausaz 14, 1822 CHERNEX, SWITZERLAND.
MCGUIRE, Mr. Phil, ACA *2010;* 101b-101g Torriano Avenue, LONDON, NW5 2RX.
MCGUIRE, Mr. Shaun James, BA ACA *1992;* Flat 39 Studley Court, 4 Jamestown Way, LONDON, E14 2DA.
•MCGUIRE, Mr. Stephen William, FCA *1974;* H.M.C. Associates Limited, 9 Guipavas Road, CALLINGTON, CORNWALL, PL17 7PL.
MCGUIRK, Miss. Helen Brigid, BA ACA *2003;* 3/53 Esplanade Park Parade, FAIRLIGHT, NSW 2094, AUSTRALIA.
•MCGURGAN, Mr. Dennis Anthony, FCA *1984;* (Tax Fac), Grant Thornton, PO Box 307, 3rd Floor, Exchange House, 54-58 Athor Street, Douglas ISLE OF MAN IM99 2BE.
MCGURK, Mr. David, BSc FCA *1987;* Crown House, 191 Silver Street, Mountfitchet, STANSTED, CM24 8HB.
MCGURK, Mr. Peter John, LLB ACA *1991;* 65 Henwick Lane, THATCHAM, BERKSHIRE, RG18 3BX.
MCGURK, Mr. Sean Patrick, BA ACA *1992;* Crowe Horwath, Level 6, 256 St Georges Terrace, PERTH, WA 6000, AUSTRALIA.
MCGURN, Mr. Christopher Paul, BSc ACA *1998;* 15 Corinthian Way, HULL, HU9 1UF.
MCHALE, Miss. Amy, ACA *2009;* 6/78 O'Brien Street, Bondi Beach, SYDNEY, NSW 2026, AUSTRALIA.
MCHALE, Mr. Christopher Andrew, FCA *1972;* Penthouse, Ocean Reef Apartments, WORTHING, BB15000, BARBADOS.
MCHALE, Mr. Henry, MA FCA *1968;* 10 Sloane Gardens, LONDON, SW1W 8DL. (Life Member)
•MCHALE, Mr. James Joseph, FCA *1974;* (Tax Fac), Higgisons, Higgison House, 381/383 City Road, LONDON, EC1V 1NW.
MCHALE, Mr. John, BA(Hons) ACA *2004;* 12 Umpire Close, WAKEFIELD, WEST YORKSHIRE, WF1 3QR.
MCHARRIE, Mr. Bruce Fielding, ACA *1989;* Inst for Child Health Research, PO Box 855, PERTH, WA 6872, AUSTRALIA.
MCHATTIE, Mr. Frederick, ACA CA(SA) *2010;* (Tax Fac), Beggars Bush, Buckhurst Lane, WADHURST, EAST SUSSEX, TN5 6JU.
MCHOUL, Mr. Ian Philip, BSc ACA *1985;* 42 Bowerdean Street, LONDON, SW6 3TW.
MCHUGH, Mrs. Alison Jane, BA ACA *1992;* BPP Learning Media Ltd, BPP House, Aldine Place, 142-144 Uxbridge Road, Shepherds Bush, LONDON W12 8AA.
MCHUGH, Mr. David Edward, ACA *2009;* 8 Horton Close, CONSETT, COUNTY DURHAM, DH8 7EN.
MCHUGH, Mrs. Diane Louise, BSc(Hons) ACA *2002;* Pirelli Tyres Ltd, Derby Road, Stretton, BURTON-ON-TRENT, STAFFORDSHIRE, DE13 0BH.
MCHUGH, Miss. Kelly Ann, BA ACA *2010;* 16 Barn Croft, Helsby, FRODSHAM, WA6 0PJ.
MCHUGH, Miss. Laura, BSc(Hons) ACA *2004;* 25a Stromness Road, SOUTHEND-ON-SEA, SS2 4JG.
•MCHUGH, Mr. Liam Michael, ACA *2006;* McCabe Ford Williams, Bank Chambers, 1 Central Ave., SITTINGBOURNE, ME10 4AE.
MCHUGH, Miss. Lorraine Tracey, BA(Hons) ACA *2003;* 104 Geary Road, Willesden, LONDON, NW10 1HR.
MCHUGH, Mrs. Lynne Diane, LLB ACA *2000;* (Tax Fac), Killernan, KILMAINE, COUNTY MAYO, IRELAND.
MCHUGH, Miss. Maureen Angela, BA FCA *1986;* 92 Purnells Way, Knowle, SOLIHULL, B93 9ED.
MCHUGH, Mr. Michael Harry, BA FCA *1973;* The Old Chapel, Netherton Fold, HUDDERSFIELD, HD4 7HB.
MCHUGH, Mr. Michael Robin Henry, FCA *1957;* 9 Kingsfield Close, BRADFORD-ON-AVON, BA15 1AW. (Life Member)
MCHUGH, Mrs. Nichola Michelle, BA ACA BBusSci *2000;* 211 Khalidiya Village, Khalidiya, ABU DHABI, UNITED ARAB EMIRATES.
MCHUGH, Mrs. Orla Mary, BEng ACA *2006;* Merrill Lynch Financial Centre, 2 King Edward Street, LONDON, EC1A 1HQ.
MCHUGH, Mr. Peter, BA ACA *1989;* 10 Stead Lane, HUDDERSFIELD, HD5 0JP.
MCHUGH, Mr. Philip, ACA *1985;* Sellafield Ltd, SEASCALE, CUMBRIA, CA20 1PG.
MCHUGH, Mr. Samuel, ACA *2011;* 23 Lumiere Court, 209 Balham High Road, LONDON, SW17 7BQ.
MCHUGH, Mr. Shaun Christopher, MA ACA *1991;* 21 Glena Mount, Benhill Wood Road, SUTTON, SM1 4HW.
MCHUGH, Mrs. Susan Mary, BA ACA *1986;* 21 Glendor Road, HOVE, EAST SUSSEX, BN3 4LP.
MCHUGO, Mr. Christopher Benedict, MA FCA *1974;* 31 Fairdene Road, COULSDON, CR5 1RD.
•MCILQUHAM, Mr. Mark, BSc ACA *2000;* Deloitte LLP, Hill House, 1 Little New Street, LONDON, EC4A 3TR. See also Deloitte & Touche LLP
MCILRATH, Mr. Ian David Caldwell, BEng ACA *1995;* Royal Caribbean Cruise, Building 2, Aviator Park, Station Road, ADDLESTONE, SURREY KT15 2PG.
•MCILRATH, Ms. Lisa Jayne, BEng ACA *1993;* (Tax Fac), Lisa McIlrath ACA, 116 Offington Avenue, WORTHING, WEST SUSSEX, BN14 9PR.
MCILRATH, Miss. Sherry Eileen, BA FCA ACIS *1986;* 2 Badgers Close, ASHFORD, MIDDLESEX, TW15 2SB.
MCILROY, Mrs. Catherine Margaret, BSc ACA *1994;* 3 The Badgers, Langdon Hills, BASILDON, SS16 6AU.
MCILROY, Mr. David Thomas Charles, BSc(Hons) ACA *2001;* 48 Catmint Close, Chandler's Ford, EASTLEIGH, HAMPSHIRE, SO53 4NT.
•MCILROY, Mr. Jeremy Malise, BA ACA *1980;* The Old Dairy, 30 The Street, Puttenham, GUILDFORD, SURREY, GU3 1AR.
MCILROY, Mrs. Rachel Jane, BSc(Hons) ACA *2002;* The Brendoncare Foundation, The Old Malthouse, Victoria Road, WINCHESTER, HAMPSHIRE, SO23 7DU.
MCILVENNY, Mr. Patrick Paul, BA(Hons) ACA *2004;* Elan Corporation plc, Treasury Building, Lower Grand Canal Street, DUBLIN 2, COUNTY DUBLIN, IRELAND.
MCILWAINE, Mr. Paul Thomas, BCom ACA FPC *1998;* 15 Norwood Gardens, BELFAST, BT4 2DX.

•MCILWEE, Mr. Frank Edward, BA FCA *1979;* Wolstenholme McIlwee Limited, Marlet House, E1 Yeoman Gate, Yeoman Way, WORTHING, WEST SUSSEX BN13 1QZ.
MCILWRAITH, Mr. Alastair Sutherl Herd, MSc FCA *1974;* 24 Linden Close, THAMES DITTON, SURREY, KT7 0DG.
MCILWRAITH, Mr. Peter, FCA *1971;* The Old Mill, Stanton Drew, BRISTOL, BS39 4HF.
•MCILWRAITH, Mrs. Rachel, MA(Cantab) ACA *1997;* with PricewaterhouseCoopers LLP, 101 Barbirolli Square, Lower Mosley Street, MANCHESTER, M2 3PW.
MCINALLY, Mr. Simon Antony, BA ACA *2004;* 53 The Meadows, Burnopfield, NEWCASTLE UPON TYNE, NE16 6QW.
MCINDOE, Mr. Iain George, BAcc ACA *1987;* 16 Broadmoor street, Kenmore Hills, KENMORE, QLD 4069, AUSTRALIA.
MCINERNEY, Mrs. Karen Linda, BA ACA *1991;* Computacenter UK Ltd Administration Centre, Hatfield Avenue, HATFIELD, HERTFORDSHIRE, AL10 9TW.
MCINERNEY, Mr. Paul Anthony, BA ACA *1986;* c/- Credit Agricole Egypt, 4 Hassan Sabry Street, Zamalek, CAIRO, EGYPT.
•MCINERNEY, Mr. Robert Andrew, FCA *1975;* (Tax Fac), 165 Botley Road, Burridge, SOUTHAMPTON, SO31 1BJ.
MCINNES, Mr. Charles Malcolm, ACA *1979;* 20 Willoughby Close, Alveston, BRISTOL, BS35 3RW.
MCINNES, Mr. Donald King, BA FCA *1956;* 7 King Edward Road, BRAY, COUNTY WICKLOW, IRELAND. (Life Member)
MCINNES, Mr. James Alexander, ACA *2008;* Pepsi Cola International Ltd, 63 Kew Road, RICHMOND, TW9 2QL.
MCINNES, Miss. Samantha Angela, ACA *2009;* 19 Dean Close, Rossington, DONCASTER, SOUTH YORKSHIRE, DN11 0XH.
MCINNES, Miss. Shelly, LLB ACA *2006;* Level 13, 10 Shelley Street, SYDNEY, NSW 2000, AUSTRALIA.
•MCINNES, Mr. Timothy Ian, BSc ACA *1988;* (Tax Fac), Hightrees Executive Services Ltd, 34 Cumberland Drive, Bowdon, ALTRINCHAM, CHESHIRE, WA14 3QP.
MCINTEE, Miss. Caroline, BA ACA *2007;* Flat 26, Taffrail House, Burrells Wharf Square, LONDON, E14 3TG.
MCINTOSH, Mr. Alistair Gordon, BSc ACA *2004;* Corner Cottage, 1 The Strand, Quainton, AYLESBURY, BUCKINGHAMSHIRE, HP22 4AS.
MCINTOSH, Mrs. Christine Anne, MA ACA *1985;* 8 Great Notley Avenue, Great Notley, BRAINTREE, CM77 7UW.
MCINTOSH, Mr. Clive Allan, FCA *1974;* 2 Flawforth Avenue, Ruddington, NOTTINGHAM, NG11 6LH.
MCINTOSH, Mr. David Neil, ACA *2004;* 116 Grosvenor Avenue, CARSHALTON, SURREY, SM5 3EP.
MCINTOSH, Mr. Donald Andrew, BSc ACA *1990;* 1a Moss Lane, Timperley, ALTRINCHAM, WA15 6TA.
MCINTOSH, Miss. Gillian, BA ACA *1991;* Ciena Ltd Ciena House, 43-51 Worship Street, LONDON, EC2A 2DX.
•MCINTOSH, Mrs. Gillian, BSc FCA *1988;* MMO Limited, Wellesley House, 204 London Road, WATERLOOVILLE, PO7 7AN. See also Murray McIntosh O'Brien
MCINTOSH, Mrs. Gillian Elizabeth, BSc ACA *1992;* 2 Chase Side Court, Dringhouses, YORK, YO24 2NN.
MCINTOSH, Mr. Gordon Martin, FCA *1952;* 12 Robinson Drive, HARROGATE, NORTH YORKSHIRE, HG2 9DJ. (Life Member)
MCINTOSH, Mrs. Helen Jane, BA ACA *1992;* The Coach House, Avenue Elmers, SURBITON, SURREY, KT6 4SL.
•MCINTOSH, Mr. Iain Alexander, FCA *1987;* McIntosh (Ilkeston) Limited, 20 Burns Street, ILKESTON, DERBYSHIRE, DE7 8AA. See also Wynniatt-Husey Ltd
MCINTOSH, Mr. Iain Peter, MA FCA *1989;* 8 Heatherfield Lane, WEYBRIDGE, KT13 0AS.
MCINTOSH, Mr. Ian Alexander Neville, MA FCA *1964;* Charingworth Chase, CHIPPING CAMPDEN, GLOUCESTERSHIRE, GL55 6NU.
•MCINTOSH, Mrs. Jane, BSc ACA *1991;* 1a Moss Lane Timperley, ALTRINCHAM, CHESHIRE, WA15 6TA.
MCINTOSH, Mr. Jeffrey Alder, MA FCA *1978;* Silanchia, Norham, BERWICK-UPON-TWEED, TD15 2JZ.
MCINTOSH, Miss. Joanna Elizabeth Mary, BSc ACA *1998;* Universal Music Publishing International, 347-353 Chiswick High Road, LONDON, W4 4HS.
MCINTOSH, Mrs. Julie Angela, BSc ACA AMCT *1996;* Spandex Ltd, 1600 Park Avenue, Aztec West, Almondsbury, BRISTOL, BS32 4UA.
MCINTOSH, Mrs. Karen Lesley, BSc ACA *2002;* 14 Fiennes Road, Dussindale, NORWICH, NR7 0YP.
MCINTOSH, Mrs. Paula, MSc ACA *1995;* 7 Cottonwood, HOUGHTON LE SPRING, DH4 7TA.
MCINTOSH, Mr. Philip Ian, BSc ACA *1987;* (Tax Fac), with Reeves & Co LLP, 37 St. Margarets Street, CANTERBURY, KENT, CT1 2TU.
MCINTOSH, Mr. Richard Charles, ACA *2007;* 95/4 Constitution Street, EDINBURGH, EH6 7AE.
MCINTOSH, Mr. Richard George, MA ACA *1985;* 8 Great Notley Avenue Great Notley, BRAINTREE, ESSEX, CM77 7UW.
MCINTOSH, Ms. Ruth Joanne, LLB ACA *1988;* 18 Connaught Square, LONDON, W2 2HJ.
•MCINTOSH, Mr. Simon Alexander, BSc FCA *1989;* with Grant Thornton UK LLP, Earl Grey House, 75-85 Grey Street, NEWCASTLE UPON TYNE, NE1 6EF.
MCINTOSH, Mr. Simon Daniel, BA ACA *1991;* Vivid Imaginations Ltd, Ashbourne House, The Guildway, Old Portsmouth Road, GUILDFORD, SURREY GU3 1LS.
MCINTOSH, Mr. Stephen Peter, BA ACA *1982;* 43 Willowside, Woodley, READING, RG5 4HJ.
MCINTOSH, Mr. Steven, BA ACA *2007;* Po Box 1569 GT, Ground Floor Harbour Centre, GEORGE TOWN, GRAND CAYMAN, KY1-1110, CAYMAN ISLANDS.
MCINTOSH, Mrs. Susan, MA ACA *1993;* PO Box 417, CREMONA T0M 0R0, AB, CANADA.
•MCINTYRE, Mr. Andrew James, MA ACA *1982;* Ernst & Young LLP, 1 More London Place, LONDON, SE1 2AF. See also Ernst & Young Europe LLP
MCINTYRE, Mr. Angus Richard Kennedy, MA ACA *1986;* 15 Mill Lane, Bentley Heath, SOLIHULL, B93 8PA.
MCINTYRE, Mr. David William, BSc ACA *2002;* with PKF (UK) LLP, 4th Floor, 3 Hardman Street, MANCHESTER, M3 3HF.
MCINTYRE, Mrs. Deborah Chloe Elizabeth, BA ACA *1989;* 15 Mill Lane, Dorridge, SOLIHULL, B93 8PA.
MCINTYRE, Ms. Diane Josephine, MA ACA *1999;* 16 Blackwater Rise, Calcot, READING, RG31 7BB.
MCINTYRE, Mr. Duncan James, BA ACA *1985;* Warnford Court, 29 Throgmorton Street, LONDON, EC2N2AT.
MCINTYRE, Mr. Gordon, FCA *1963;* Hunters Quay, Timms Lane, Waddington, LINCOLN, LN5 9RQ. (Life Member)
MCINTYRE, Mr. Ian, FCA *1980;* Longmead, Nailsbourne, TAUNTON, SOMERSET, TA2 8AF.
MCINTYRE, Mr. James, BA ACA *2004;* 20 Balham New Road, LONDON, SW12 9PG.
MCINTYRE, Mr. James Gordon, FCA *1963;* 34 High Street, KIRKCUDBRIGHT, DG6 4JX. (Life Member)
MCINTYRE, Mrs. Jayne, BSc ACA *1983;* 3 Glebe Crescent, Kings Park, STIRLING, FK8 2JB.
•MCINTYRE, Mr. John Francis, MA FCA *1971;* 7 Mulgrave Road, CROYDON, CR0 1BL.
•MCINTYRE, Mr. John Matthew, FCA *1987;* Wilkins Kennedy FKC Limited, Stourside Place, 35-41 Station Road, ASHFORD, KENT, TN23 1PP. See also W K Finn-Kelcey & Chapman Limited
MCINTYRE, Ms. Katharine Sarah, BA ACA *1989;* Lammas House, Ling Lane, Scarcroft, LEEDS, LS14 3HX.
MCINTYRE, Miss. Lucy Fiona, BSc ACA *2000;* 59 Hayes Grove, LONDON, SE22 8DF.
MCINTYRE, Ms. Mary-Anne Bridgett, BA ACA *1991;* Coombe House, High Street, Chieveley, NEWBURY, BERKSHIRE, RG20 8UX.
MCINTYRE, Mr. Simon, LLB ACA *2000;* 3 Glebe Grove, EDINBURGH, EH12 7SH.
MCINTYRE, Mr. Stanley George, FCA *1951;* 11 Old Mill Close, Eynsford, DARTFORD, DA4 0BN. (Life Member)
MCINTYRE, Mr. Trevor Alan, ACA CA(SA) *2010;* 3 All Hallows Square, Drumcondra, DUBLIN 9, COUNTY DUBLIN, IRELAND.
MCINTYRE-BROWN, Mr. Roger David, BA FCA *1965;* Glebe House, Garth Road, LETCHWORTH GARDEN CITY, HERTFORDSHIRE, SG6 3NG. (Life Member)
MCINTYRE-BROWN, Mrs. Sally Victoria, BA ACA *2003;* 56 Pulborough Road, Southfields, LONDON, SW18 5UH.
MCISAAC, Miss. Catherine, MA(Oxon) ACA *2011;* 76a Edith Road, LONDON, W14 9AR.
MCISAAC, Mr. Ian, FCA *1969;* 28 Hereford Square, LONDON, SW7 4NB. (Life Member)
MCIVER, Mr. Andrew Ross, BSc ACA *1990;* Beechcroft, Beech Lawn, GUILDFORD, SURREY, GU1 3PE.
MCIVER, Mr. David, ACA *2011;* 2 Grosvenor Road, WIDNES, CHESHIRE, WA8 9RT.
MCIVER, Mr. David Kenneth Fraser, FCA *1961;* Fincharn House, Broadstone Lane, Hardington, Mandeville, YEOVIL, SOMERSET BA22 9PR. (Life Member)
MCIVER, Mrs. Jillian, BSc ACA *1993;* Calle Sancho Rosa, 47 Fuenze Del Fresno, 28708 MADRID, SPAIN.
MCIVER, Mr. Jonathan David, BA ACA *1991;* 11 Floris Place, LONDON, SW4 0HH.
MCIVOR, Mr. Alan James, MA ACA *1990;* 2 Talbot Road, OXFORD, OX2 8LL.
MCIVOR, Mr. Joseph Gerard, ACA *2008;* Flat 4, 5 Kingsland Passage, LONDON, E8 2BA.
MCIVOR, Ms. Sara Anne, BA ACA *1992;* 83 Kooyong Road, ARMADALE, VIC 3143, AUSTRALIA.
MCIVOR, Mrs. Suzanne Phryne, BSc ACA *1990;* 2 Talbot Road, OXFORD, OX2 8LL.
MCIVOR-OAKLEY, Ms. Stephanie Anne, MSc ACA *2002;* with McIvor-Oakley Ltd, 8 Belleville Road, Battersea, LONDON, SW11 6QT.
MCJANNET, Mr. Robert Bryan, FCA *1966;* 25 Chisholm Street, OAKVILLE L6K 3W2, ON, CANADA. (Life Member)
MCKAIL, Mr. Callum Howden, MSc BSc ACA CTA *2005;* 66 Beacon Way, RICKMANSWORTH, HERTFORDSHIRE, WD3 7PD.
MCKAIN, Mr. Christopher, BSc ACA *2011;* 33 Carnegie Crescent, MELTON MOWBRAY, LEICESTERSHIRE, LE13 1RP.
MCKAY, Mr. Anthony Frank, ACA CA(SA) *2010;* 6 Hazel Close, EPSOM, KT19 8FW.
MCKAY, Mr. Charles Richard Harvey, BCom FCA *1991;* 50 Stewart Road, HARPENDEN, HERTFORDSHIRE, AL5 4QB.
•①MCKAY, Mr. Christopher Nigel, BA FCA *1995;* McTear Williams & Wood, 90 St Faiths Lane, NORWICH, NR1 1NE.
•MCKAY, Mr. Colin John, MA ACA *1983;* 19 Winding Lane, DARIEN, CT 06820, UNITED STATES.
MCKAY, Mr. David, ACA *2011;* 4a Little Shardeloes, High Street, AMERSHAM, BUCKINGHAMSHIRE, HP7 0EF.
MCKAY, Mr. David Alan, BSc FCA *1977;* 70 Cannon Hill Road, COVENTRY, CV4 7BS.
•MCKAY, Miss. Fiona Jean, BSc FCA CF *1995;* (Tax Fac), Price Pearson Ltd, Finch House, 28-30 Wolverhampton Street, DUDLEY, DY1 1DB. See also Finch House Properties Limited
•MCKAY, Ms. Gillian Jamieson, MA BSc(Hons) ACA DChA *2001;* (Tax Fac), Gillian McKay Accountancy Services, 13 Pasquier Road, Walthamstow, LONDON, E17 6HB.
MCKAY, Mr. Gordon Malcolm, ACA *2008;* 10 Thoresby Court, NOTTINGHAM, NG3 5EH.
MCKAY, Miss. Janette Kathleen, FCA *1973;* Janette McKay, Glassocks, Rye Road, Sandhurst, CRANBROOK, KENT TN18 5PH.
MCKAY, Mr. Jonathan, BA ACA *1988;* Shepley Old Hall, Station Road Shepley, HUDDERSFIELD, WEST YORKSHIRE, HD8 8DG.
MCKAY, Miss. Julia Kathleen, BA ACA *2004;* 14 Leighton Road, CHELTENHAM, GLOUCESTERSHIRE, GL52 6BD.
•MCKAY, Mr. Kenneth Murdo, LLB ACA *1997;* KPMG LLP, 1 The Embankment, Neville Street, LEEDS, LS1 4DW. See also KPMG Europe LLP
MCKAY, Mrs. Lesley, BA ACA *2007;* 122 Chester Avenue, POULTON-LE-FYLDE, LANCASHIRE, FY6 7RY.
MCKAY, Ms. Lesley Anne, MA ACA *1991;* 1 Kirkstyle Gardens, KIRKLISTON, WEST LOTHIAN, EH29 9HD.
MCKAY, Miss. Lisa, ACA *2008;* 13 Canopus Close, St. Mellons, CARDIFF, CF3 1NR.
•MCKAY, Mr. Martin James, BSc ACA *1987;* Toscafund Asset Management LLP, 7th Floor, 90 Long Acre, LONDON, WC2E 9RA. See also Daverns Audit Services Limited
MCKAY, Mr. Michael William Hoy, FCA *1967;* Hoy McKay Associates Ltd, 20 Occupation Road, Orton-on-the-Hill, ATHERSTONE, CV9 3NE.
MCKAY, Mr. Nicholas John, BA ACA *2004;* 146 Clarence Road, LONDON, SW19 8QD.
MCKAY, Ms. Oonagh, ACA CTA *1997;* with Ernst & Young LLP, Bedford House, 16-22 Bedford Street, BELFAST, COUNTY ANTRIM, BT2 7DT.
•MCKAY, Mr. Peter Holtby, BA FCA *1968;* Peter McKay, 73 High Street, Yardley Hastings, NORTHAMPTON, NN7 1ER.
•MCKAY, Mr. Peter Joseph, BSc ACA *1985;* Nicholsons, Watermead House, 2 Codicote Road, WELWYN, AL6 9NB.
MCKAY, Mr. Simon Richard, LLB ACA *2003;* 22 Squirrel Close, Grange Park, NORTHAMPTON, NN4 5DL.
MCKAY, Mr. Stuart Donald, BSc ACA *2009;* Flat 1, 148 Dyke Road, BRIGHTON, BN1 5PA.
MCKAY, Mr. Stuart Sinclair, FCA *1968;* Mousley Hill Cottage, Mousley End, Hatton, WARWICK, CV35 7JE.
MCKAY, Mrs. Susannah Elizabeth, BSc ACA *2005;* 22 Squirrel Close, Grange Park, NORTHAMPTON, NN4 5DL.
MCKAY, Mr. Timothy, BSc FCA *1984;* 3/7 East Suffolk Park, EDINBURGH, EH16 5PL.
MCKAY, Mr. William Trevor, BBS FCA *1974;* 1 West Court, WEMBLEY, HA0 3QQ. (Life Member)
MCKAY FORBES, Mr. Alistair James Bruce, FCA *1977;* Blanketmill Farm House, Goose Rye Road, Worplesdon, GUILDFORD, SURREY, GU3 3RQ.
MCKEAN, Mr. Andrew Joseph, BAcc ACA *1997;* 42 Knightley Road, EXETER, EX2 4SR.
MCKEAN, Mr. Andrew William John, BSc ACA *1989;* 39 Denmark Street, BEDFORD, MK40 3TG.
MCKEAN, Mr. John Roger, BA FCA *1971;* Buscot, Bradfield, READING, BERKSHIRE, RG7 6JB.
MCKEAN, Mr. Kenneth, FCA *1954;* Road Ends, Armathwaite, CARLISLE, CA4 9SL. (Life Member)
MCKEAN, Miss. Stacey, ACA *2010;* 15 Chatton Avenue, SOUTH SHIELDS, TYNE AND WEAR, NE34 7TU.
MCKECHNIE, Mr. Dermot Robert Lyndon, BSc ACA *1988;* 22 Sisters Avenue, LONDON, SW11 5SQ.
MCKECHNIE, Mr. Duncan Alexander James, BA FCA *1984;* Cogent Resources Ltd, 50 Fenchurch Street, LONDON, EC3M 3JY.
•MCKECHNIE, Mr. Ian, MA(Cantab) FCA FCCA *1989;* Ian McKechnie and Company Ltd, 21 Birchwood Drive, Rushmere St. Andrew, IPSWICH, IP5 1EB.
MCKEE, Mr. Alan Lindsay Graham, BSc FCA *1963;* Loubejac, St Laurent, 46800 LOLMIE, FRANCE.
MCKEE, Mr. Colin, BSc ACA *2002;* 2 Avoca Road, LONDON, SW17 8SQ.
MCKEE, Mr. David John Innes, BSc ACA *1998;* 55c Talbot Road, LONDON, N6 4QX.
MCKEE, Miss. Emma Jane, BSc ACA *1994;* Moy Park Ltd Unit 39, Seagoe Industrial Area Portadown, CRAIGAVON, COUNTY ARMAGH, BT63 5QE.
•MCKEE, Mr. John Hugh, FCA *1971;* J.V. Banks, Banks House, Paradise Street, RHYL, LL18 3LW.
MCKEE, Mr. Michael Alan, LLB FCA *2000;* 45c Oakhurst Grove, LONDON, SE22 9AH.
MCKEE, Mr. Peter Verney, BSc(Hons) ACA *2001;* 38 Cambray Road, LONDON, SW12 0DY.
MCKEE, Miss. Tammy, BA ACA *2011;* 5 Maltkiln Cottages, Lincoln Road, Goltho, MARKET RASEN, LINCOLNSHIRE, LN8 5NF.
MCKEEVE, Miss. Clare Julie, LLB ACA *2003;* Aletheia Partners Simon House, 2 Eaton Gate, LONDON, SW1W 9BJ.
MCKEEVER, Mr. Liam Michael, BA ACA *1989;* G F Holding Contractors Ltd, St Andrews Court, Lees Lane, Mottram St Andrew, MACCLESFIELD, SK10 4LJ.
MCKEEVOR, Mr. Liam James, BSc ACA *2010;* Buzzacott & Co, 12 New Fetter Lane, LONDON, EC4A 1AG.
MCKEITH, Mr. David William, MA FCA *1982;* Copper Beeches, 27 Carrwood Avenue, Bramhall, STOCKPORT, SK7 2PY.
MCKELVEY, Mr. David Neal, BA FCA *1985;* 10 Murch Street, Everton Park, BRISBANE, QLD 4053, AUSTRALIA.
MCKELVEY, Mrs. Hayley, BA ACA *2007;* with Deloitte LLP, 2 New Street Square, LONDON, EC4A 3BZ.
MCKELVEY, Miss. Laura Helen, BSc ACA *2009;* 8 Jordans Road, Penn Heights, RICKMANSWORTH, WD3 8GN.
•MCKELVIE, Mr. Allan William, FCA *1978;* (Tax Fac), McKelvie & Company, 82 Wandsworth Bridge Road, Fulham, LONDON, SW6 2TF.
MCKELVIE, Mr. Andrew James, BSc ACA *1986;* 9 Admirals Court, 30 Horsleydown Lane, LONDON, SE1 2LJ.
MCKELVIE, Mr. Andrew John, BSc ACA *1997;* AIG/Lincoln, ul Grzybowska 5a, 00-132 WARSAW, POLAND.
•MCKELVIE, Mr. Kenneth Erle, FCA *1974;* Deloitte Touche Tohmatsu, 35/F One Pacific Place, 88 Queensway, CENTRAL, HONG KONG ISLAND, HONG KONG SAR. See also Deloitte & Touche
MCKENDRY, Mr. Brian John, FCA *1974;* Orchard House, Mile Path, WOKING, GU22 0JX.
MCKENDRY, Miss. Fiona Theresa, ACA *2008;* Flat 2, West Kensington Mansions, Beaumont Crescent, LONDON, W14 9PE.
MCKENDRY, Mr. Francis James, BA FCA *1982;* 26/28 Avenue Raymond Poincare, 75016 PARIS, FRANCE.
MCKENNA, Mrs. Annette, BA ACA *1997;* 6 Radnor Road, BRACKNELL, RG12 9FD.
MCKENNA, Mr. Anthony William, ACA *1984;* 37 Farmlands Close, ST LEONARDS-ON-SEA, EAST SUSSEX, TN37 7UE.
MCKENNA, Mr. Bryan John, BSc ACA *1983;* 47 Druid Hill, Stoke Bishop, BRISTOL, BS9 1EH.
MCKENNA, Miss. Catherine, MSc ACA *2005;* Mersey Internal Audit Agency, Regatta Place, Brunswick Business Park, LIVERPOOL, L3 4BL.

•**MCKENNA, Mrs. Dawn Elaine, BSc** *1991;* with Dawn McKenna Bsc ACA, The Kings Arms, Bourne Lane, Brimscombe, STROUD, GLOUCESTERSHIRE GL5 2RP.
MCKENNA, Mr. Donal Philip, FCA *1976;* Beck House, Water End, Wrestlingworth, SANDY, SG19 2HA.
MCKENNA, Mr. Henry Peter, BA(Hons) ACA *2001;* Level 31, 60 Margaret Street, SYDNEY, NSW 2000, AUSTRALIA.
MCKENNA, Mrs. Janet Joy, ACA *1981;* Chase Manor Farm, Lickfold Road, Fernhurst, HASLEMERE, GU27 3JA.
MCKENNA, Mr. John, FCA *1978;* 12 Streamside Close, Timperley, ALTRINCHAM, WA15 7PE.
MCKENNA, Mr. John Bernard, ACA *1979;* 21 Beaumont Close, COLCHESTER, CO4 5XE.
MCKENNA, Mr. John Gerard, BSc ACA *1992;* Flat 9, Claremont, 16 St. John's Avenue, Putney, LONDON, SW15 2AB.
•**MCKENNA, Mr. John James, FCA** *1973;* John J McKenna, 16 Wilder Grove, HARTLEPOOL, CLEVELAND, TS25 4PB.
MCKENNA, Mr. John Patrick, BA CA ACA *1991;* with PricewaterhouseCoopers, Royal Trust Tower, Suite 3000 TD Centre, Box 82, 77 King Street West, TORONTO M5K 1G8 ON CANADA.
MCKENNA, Mrs. Judith Ann, ACA *2002;* 2 Luis Court, Baildon, SHIPLEY, WEST YORKSHIRE, BD17 5LJ.
MCKENNA, Mrs. Louisa Margaret, BA ACA *1991;* 116 Station Road, Greenisland, CARRICKFERGUS, COUNTY ANTRIM, BT38 8UW.
MCKENNA, Miss. Louise, BA ACA *1994;* 42 Furry Park Road, Killester, DUBLIN 5, COUNTY DUBLIN, IRELAND.
MCKENNA, Mr. Mark, ACA *2008;* (Tax Fac), Cobham Murphy, 116 Duke Street, LIVERPOOL, L1 5JW.
MCKENNA, Mr. Mark Patrick, ACA *2010;* Deloitte & Touche, 2 New Street Square, LONDON, EC4A 3BZ.
•**MCKENNA, Mr. Michael David, ACA** *1990;* (Tax Fac), Inspire Your Business Limited, 20 Kingsway House, Team Valley, GATESHEAD, TYNE AND WEAR, NE11 0HW. See also Inspire Compliance Limited
MCKENNA, Mr. Paul John, MA ACA *1983;* Carillion, 3rd Floor, 25 Maddox Street, LONDON, W1S 2QN.
MCKENNA, Mrs. Philippa Jane, BA ACA *1984;* 4 Collins Street, BRIGHTON, VIC 3186, AUSTRALIA.
MCKENNA GOGA, Mrs. Carolyn Siobhan, BA ACA *1997;* PO Box 10488, BAINBRIDGE ISLAND, WA 98110, UNITED STATES.
MCKENZIE, Mr. Alexander Arthur, BA FCA *1975;* Flat 4, 33 Queens Road, HERTFORD, SG13 8AZ.
MCKENZIE, Mr. Andrew, ACA *2007;* 53 Parkview Road, LONDON, SE9 3QP.
MCKENZIE, Mr. Barry, FCA *1966;* 2 Merlewood, 17 Langham Road, Bowdon, ALTRINCHAM, CHESHIRE, WA14 2HT. (Life Member)
•**MCKENZIE, Mr. Bernard John, FCA** *1971;* McKenzies, 14-16 Station Road West, OXTED, SURREY, RH8 9EP. See also Professional Financial Consultants(Purley)Limited
MCKENZIE, Mr. Brian Godfrey, BA ACA *1990;* Archway House Fairfield Road, Goring, READING, RG8 0EX.
MCKENZIE, Miss. Brittany Jane, ACA *2008;* 35 The Bury, Pavenham, BEDFORD, MK43 7PY.
MCKENZIE, Mr. Christopher John, BSc ACA *1993;* Atlantic Container Line UK Ltd, 8 Princes Parade, St Nicholas Place, Pier Head, LIVERPOOL, L3 1DL.
MCKENZIE, Mr. David Robertson, BSc ACA *1986;* 20 Falconers Field, HARPENDEN, HERTFORDSHIRE, AL5 3ES.
MCKENZIE, Mr. Derek, BSc ACA *1982;* 68 Goodhart Place, LONDON, E14 8EQ.
MCKENZIE, Mr. Douglas, BSc ACA *2003;* with Moore Stephens LLP, 150 Aldersgate Street, LONDON, EC1A 4AB.
MCKENZIE, Mrs. Fiona Jane, MA ACA *1996;* 4 Dixon Close, STONE, ST15 8GN.
•**MCKENZIE, Mrs. Fiona Joan Keess, BSc ACA** *1986;* Blue Note Solutions, 4 St. Annes Road, Headington, OXFORD, OX3 8NL.
MCKENZIE, Miss. Hannah Lynn, BSc(Hons) ACA *2010;* 20 Kirby Drive, Bramley, TADLEY, RG26 5FN.
MCKENZIE, The Revd. Ian Colin, FCA *1956;* 21 Crafts Way, SOUTHWELL, NG25 0BL. (Life Member)
MCKENZIE, Miss. Joanne Gail, BA(Hons) ACA *2009;* 23 Bakehurst Close, New Mills, HIGH PEAK, DERBYSHIRE, SK22 4PT.
MCKENZIE, Mr. John Alexander, BA ACA *1999;* 90 Stanbrook Road, Shirley, SOLIHULL, WEST MIDLANDS, B90 4US.
MCKENZIE, Mr. John Nicholson, BCom FCA *1953;* The Gables, 105 High Street, HENLEY-IN-ARDEN, B95 5AU. (Life Member)
MCKENZIE, Miss. Laura, BA ACA *2002;* c/o Starfish Ventures, Level 1, 120 Soliment Road, EAST MELBOURNE, VIC 3002, AUSTRALIA.
MCKENZIE, Mr. Peter, BCom ACA *1992;* Mac Lench, 32 Village Street, Harvington, EVESHAM, WR11 5NQ.
MCKENZIE, Mrs. Sheila Patricia, BA ACA DChA *1987;* 5 Ferne Close, Goring, READING, RG8 0AR.
MCKENZIE, Mr. Thomas Dale, BSc ACA *1989;* Holly Cottage, Lymden Lane, Stonegate, WADHURST, EAST SUSSEX, TN5 7EF.
MCKENZIE, Miss. Tracy Erin, ACA *2010;* 16 Bemerton Street, LONDON, N1 0BS.
MCKENZIE, Lord William David, BA FCA *1971;* (Tax Fac), 6 Sunset Drive, LUTON, LU2 7TN.
MCKENZIE, Mr. William Ernest, FCA *1974;* (Tax Fac), Ofgem, 9 Millbank, LONDON, SW1P 3GE.
MCKENZIE-BOYLE, Mr. Edward Charles Albert, BSc ACA *2007;* Flat 6, 3 Downside Crescent, LONDON, NW3 2AN.
MCKENZIE GREEN, Mrs. Marianne, BA ACA *1981;* 19 Eagle Brow, LYMM, CHESHIRE, WA13 0PY.
MCKENZIE-WILSON, Miss. Lauren Alexandra, LLB ACA *2004;* 1 Goldfinch House, Gilbert White Close Perivale, GREENFORD, MIDDLESEX, UB6 7FJ.
MCKENZIE-WYNNE, Mrs. Elizabeth Jane, MA ACA *1985;* Fosse Farm, Beech Pike, Elkstone, CHELTENHAM, GLOUCESTERSHIRE, GL53 9PL.
MCKEON, Miss. Katherine Helen, ACA *2009;* 34 South Park Road, Gatley, CHEADLE, CHESHIRE, SK8 4AN.
MCKEON, Mr. Mark Robin, BSc ACA *1980;* 9 Inwood Place, The Gap, BRISBANE, QLD 4061, AUSTRALIA.
•**MCKEOWN, Mr. Adrian James Peter, FCA** *1992;* Trevor Jones & Co., Old Bank Chambers, 582-586 Kingsbury Road, Erdington, BIRMINGHAM, B24 9ND.
MCKEOWN, Miss. Claire Roberta, BAcc ACA *2006;* 24 Coolagh Road, MAGHERA, COUNTY LONDONDERRY, BT46 5JR.
MCKEOWN, Mr. Craig Ashley, ACA CA(AUS) *2010;* 21 Bemish Road, LONDON, SW15 1DG.
MCKEOWN, Mr. David Thomas, BA ACA *1999;* 20 Willow Park, Willow Bank, Fallowfield, MANCHESTER, M14 6XT.
MCKEOWN, Mrs. Jane, BA ACA *1989;* 103 Richmond Park Road, KINGSTON-UPON-THAMES, KT2 6AF.
MCKEOWN, Mr. John Michael, BSc ACA *1990;* 32 Aarons court, RIDGEFIELD, CT 06877, UNITED STATES.
MCKEOWN, Mrs. Lisa Michelle, BSc(Eng) ACA *1991;* 27 Rugeley Road, BURNTWOOD, STAFFORDSHIRE, WS7 9BE.
MCKEOWN, Mr. Mark, ACA *2008;* 308 Lumiere Apartments, 58 St. John's Hill, LONDON, SW11 1AD.
MCKEOWN, Mr. Matthew Robin, MA ACA *2004;* Smiths Group Plc, 80 Victoria Street, LONDON, SW1E 5JL.
MCKEOWN, Mr. Michael Christopher, BSc ACA *2010;* Flat 2 Sanders Court, Bridge Street, WARWICK, CV34 5PQ.
MCKEOWN, Mrs. Sunita, BA(Hons) ACA *2003;* with PricewaterhouseCoopers LLP, 1 Embankment Place, LONDON, WC2N 6RH.
MCKERAN, Mr. Alexander Charles, MA FCA CTA AMCT *2000;* (Tax Fac), Flat 11, Bramis House, 135-137 Main Road, Biggin Hill, WESTERHAM, KENT TN16 3DX.
MCKERCHAR, Mr. John Stewart, FCA *1950;* Tylers, Berry Barn Lane, West Wittering, CHICHESTER, PO20 8AX. (Life Member)
MCKERCHAR, Mr. Max James Andrew, MA BA(Econ) ACA *2006;* 71 Lyric Road, LONDON, SW13 9QA.
MCKERGAN, Miss. Diane, BSc ACA *1990;* 25 Clay Pit Way, Barlborough, CHESTERFIELD, DERBYSHIRE, S43 4WN.
MCKERNAN, Ms. Bernadette Mary, BA ACA *1992;* 17 Radnor Mews, LONDON, W2 2SA.
MCKERSIE, Mrs. Angela, BSc ACA *1990;* Fleet Lodge, 65a Pinkneys Road, MAIDENHEAD, SL6 5DT.
MCKEW, Mr. John Paul, MSc BA FCA AMCT *1993;* 9 Sweet Briar Avenue, BENFLEET, SS7 1JU.
•**MCKEY, Mr. Gerard Francis John, FCA** *1996;* Arthur G Mead Limited, Adam House, 1 Fitzroy Square, LONDON, W1T 5HE.
MCKIBBIN, Mr. Alexander John, MSc ACA *1991;* Mill Farm, East Buckland, BARNSTAPLE, DEVON, EX32 0TD.
MCKIBBIN, Mr. Anthony Desmond, BA(Hons) ACA *2010;* 2 Coolsara Park, LISBURN, COUNTY ANTRIM, BT28 3BG.
MCKIE, Ms. Alison Jayne, LLB ACA *1999;* 7 Telfords Yard, LONDON, E1W 2BQ.
•**MCKIE, Mr. David Alister, BA FCA** *1993;* Reighton Hall, FILEY, NORTH YORKSHIRE, YO14 9RX.
MCKIE, Mrs. Denise, BA ACA *1987;* Fulbrook Cottage, Farnham Road, Holt Pound, FARNHAM, SURREY, GU10 4JZ.
MCKIE, Mr. Gordon Robert, BA ACA *1998;* 13 Mayfield Grange, Little Trodgers Lane, MAYFIELD, EAST SUSSEX, TN20 6BF.
MCKIE, Miss. Nicola Emma, MA ACA *2009;* Hurst View, Hurst Lane, EGHAM, SURREY, TW20 8QJ.
MCKIE, Mr. Robert Alastair, FCA *1965;* Jura, Station Road, Tarbolton, MAUCHLINE, AYRSHIRE, KA5 5NT.
•**MCKIE, Mr. Simon Peter, MA FCA CTA(Fellow)** *1983;* (Member of Council 1998 - 1999 2000 - 2001), (Tax Fac), McKie & Co (Advisory Services) LLP, Rudge Hill House, Rudge, FROME, SOMERSET, BA11 2QG. See also McKie & Co Limited
MCKIERNAN, Miss. Elizabeth, BA ACA *2005;* 3rd Floor, 66 Hanover Street, EDINBURGH, EH2 1HH.
MCKIERNAN, Mr. John Gerard, BSc ACA *1993;* 39 Simpkins Drive, Barton-le-Clay, BEDFORD, MK45 4RX.
MCKIERNAN, Miss. Sophie Jane, BSc ACA *1996;* 38 Ashcroft Park, COBHAM, KT11 2DN.
MCKILLOP, Miss. Catherine, ACA *2011;* 77 Leigh Road, Worsley, MANCHESTER, M28 1LG.
MCKILLOP, Mr. Raymond Michael, BSc FCA *1983;* 115 East Acton Lane, LONDON, W3 7HB.
MCKINLAY, Mr. Andrew John Robert, BSc ACA *1983;* The White Cottage, Main Road, Plumtree, NOTTINGHAM, NOTTINGHAMSHIRE, NG12 5NB.
MCKINLAY, Mr. Andrew Robert, MSc ACA *2001;* 101 Gateland Lane, LEEDS, LS17 8LW.
MCKINLAY, Mr. Christopher Ian, MA ACA *1998;* 7 Rue de Rouvray, 92200 NEUILLY-SUR-SEINE, FRANCE.
MCKINLAY, Mr. Colin Grant, BA ACA *1995;* 8 Skye Close, Alwalton, PETERBOROUGH, PE2 6DT.
MCKINLAY, Mr. Crawford, DBA FCA *1965;* High Barn, 11 Courtenay Road, WINCHESTER, HAMPSHIRE, SO23 7ER.
MCKINLAY, Mr. David Thomas, BA ACA *1982;* Via Primo Levi 12, 20060 BUSSERO, ITALY.
MCKINLAY, Mr. Scott, BSc ACA *2010;* 11 rue de Bettborn, Reichlange, L-8558 LUXEMBOURG, LUXEMBOURG.
MCKINLEY, Miss. Claire, ACA *2011;* Browhill, Mill Lane, Codsall, WOLVERHAMPTON, WV8 1EG.
MCKINLEY, Mr. Colin, BSc ACA *1981;* 7 Downland Road, Woodhall Park, SWINDON, SN2 2RD.
MCKINLEY, Mr. James Alexander Robert, BCom ACA *2002;* M J McKinley, 35 Market Street, WIRRAL, MERSEYSIDE, CH47 2BG.
MCKINLEY, Mr. James David, BSc FCA *1973;* 16 Southway, Hampstead Garden Suburb, LONDON, NW11 6RU.
MCKINLEY, Mr. Martin John, BSc ACA *1990;* 14 Henry Street, PICTON, NSW 2571, AUSTRALIA.
MCKINNELL, Mrs. Anne Hale, MA ACA *1989;* The Chase, Round Oak Road, WEYBRIDGE, KT13 8HT.
MCKINNELL, Mr. Duncan James, BSc FCA *1975;* Friars Croft, Sidegate, HADDINGTON, EH41 4BU.
•**MCKINNELL, Mr. Malcolm William, BSc ACA** *1988;* (Tax Fac), Ward Williams Group Limited, Park House, 25-27 Monument Hill, WEYBRIDGE, SURREY, KT13 8RT. See also Ward Williams Limited
MCKINNEY, Mr. David Alexander, ACA *2008;* Flat 6 Metropolis Apartments, Shipka Road, LONDON, SW12 9QU.
MCKINNEY, Ms. Rachael, BA ACA MBA *1999;* 1/35-37 Ashburn Place, GLADESVILLE, NSW 2111, AUSTRALIA.
MCKINNEY, Mr. William John, BSc ACA *1989;* PepsiCo, 20th Floor Caroline Centre, 28 Yun Ping Road, CAUSEWAY BAY, HONG KONG ISLAND, HONG KONG SAR.
MCKINNON, Mr. Andrew Stuart, BEng ACA *1994;* 90 Warwick Way, LONDON, SW1V 1SB.
MCKINNON, Miss. Rebecca Sarah Elizabeth, ACA *2008;* Lodge Naseby Hall, Naseby, NORTHAMPTON, NN6 6DP.
MCKINNON, Mrs. Sarah-Jane, BSc ACA *1993;* 90 Warwick Way, LONDON, SW1V 1SB.
•**MCKINVEN, Mr. James Donald, BA ACA** *1984;* 4 Hawcroft, Longdon, RUGELEY, WS15 4QT. See also KPMG Europe LLP and Firm created for CD only - see SJB
MCKITTRICK, Mrs. Clare, MA ACA *1999;* 9 Cricket Lane, LOUGHBOROUGH, LE11 3PD.
MCKNESPIEY, Mr. Paul Neil, PhD BSc ACA *2000;* Sandoe House, 4 Carlton Gardens, Stanwix, CARLISLE, CA3 9NP.
MCKNIGHT, Mr. Kevin John, BA ACA *1985;* Cobbett Hill Cottage, Cobbett Hill Road, Normandy, GUILDFORD, SURREY, GU3 2AA.
MCKNIGHT, Mr. Robert Andrew, ACA *2008;* 10 Greenwood Park, CARRICKFERGUS, COUNTY ANTRIM, BT38 7UW.
MCKNIGHT, Miss. Tanya Michelle, BSc ACA *2007;* 101 Robert Street, LONDON, NW1 3QT.
MCKOWN, Mr. Brian, FCA *1959;* 164 Green Lane, OLDHAM, OL8 3BB.
MCKRELL, Mr. Mark Nigel, BSc FCA *1992;* Avnet EMG Ltd, Avnet House, STEVENAGE, HERTFORDSHIRE, SG1 2EF.
MCLACHLAN, Mrs. Carol, BA FCA *1990;* 26 Alton Road, PRENTON, CH43 1XA.
MCLACHLAN, Mr. David George, BA FCA *1972;* 4 Clement Road, Wimbledon, LONDON, SW19 7RJ. (Life Member)
MCLACHLAN, Mrs. Eliza Catherine, BA ACA *1981;* East Castle Mount, 32 North Castle Street, ST. ANDREWS, FIFE, KY16 9BG.
MCLACHLAN, Miss. Eve Nicola, BSc ACA CTA *2010;* Top Floor Flat, 32 Caledonia Place, Clifton, BRISTOL, BS8 4DN.
MCLACHLAN, Mr. Gordon, CBE LLD BCom FCA *1947;* 95 Ravenscourt Road, LONDON, W6 0UJ. (Life Member)
MCLACHLAN, Mr. John James, FCA *1966;* Amberwood, Woodland Rise, SEVENOAKS, KENT, TN15 0HZ.
MCLACHLAN, Mr. Keith Ian, FCA *1967;* 26 Newbury Hill Extn., Glencoe, PORT OF SPAIN, TRINIDAD AND TOBAGO. (Life Member)
MCLACHLAN, Mr. Neil Andrew, BA FCA *1988;* Deise, Langhurstwood Road, HORSHAM, WEST SUSSEX, RH12 4QD.
MCLACHLAN, Mr. Roy Jackson, PhD BSc ACA *1979;* East Castle Mount, 32 North Castle Street, ST. ANDREWS, FIFE, KY16 9BG.
MCLACHLAN, Miss. Sarah Jane, BA(Hons) ACA *2001;* 12 Sawrey Court, BROUGHTON-IN-FURNESS, CUMBRIA, LA20 6JQ.
MCLANEY, Miss. Caroline Ann, BSc ACA *1992;* The Garden Flat, 3 West Mall, Clifton, BRISTOL, BS8 4BH.
MCLANEY, Mr. Darren, BA ACA *1995;* Dromonby Grange Busby Lane, Kirkby-in-Cleveland, MIDDLESBROUGH, CLEVELAND, TS9 7AP.
MCLANEY, Mr. Edward John, MA FCA *1969;* 22 Scotts Close, Churchstow, KINGSBRIDGE, TQ7 3RB.
MCLANEY, Mrs. Navjeet Kaur, BSc ACA *1995;* 46 Bielby Avenue, BILLINGHAM, TS23 3YG.
MCLANNAHAN, Mrs. Caroline Suzanne, MA ACA *2003;* Ground Floor, Flat A, 4 Coastline Villas, Discovery Bay City, LANTAU ISLAND, NEW TERRITORIES HONG KONG SAR.
MCLANNAHAN, Ms. Dinah Jean, ACA *2006;* Mental Health Management Trafalgar House, 47-49 King Street, DUDLEY, DY2 8PS.
MCLAREN, Mr. Alan John, BSc ACA *1980;* with Landsbanki, Old Change House, 128 Queen Victoria Street, LONDON, EC4V 4BJ.
MCLAREN, Miss. Alison, BSc(Hons) ACA CTA *2004;* (Tax Fac), 70 Albert Road, BEXLEY, DA5 1NW.
MCLAREN, Ms. Andrea Louise, BSc ACA *1994;* 27 Fairmead Avenue, HARPENDEN, HERTFORDSHIRE, AL5 5UD.
•**MCLAREN, Mr. Andrew John, BSc FCA** *1995;* Beever and Struthers, St George's House, 215-219 Chester Road, MANCHESTER, M15 4JE.
MCLAREN, Ms. Diana Jacqueline, MA ACA *1988;* 28 Bis, Rue Gabriel Luneau, 44000 NANTES, FRANCE.
MCLAREN, Mrs. Felicity Ann, FCA *1966;* 9 Fordington Gardens, Kings Road, DORCHESTER, DT1 1AN.
MCLAREN, Mr. Ian, BA ACA CDir *1993;* Oaklands, Marley Lane, HASLEMERE, SURREY, GU27 3PZ.
MCLAREN, Mr. Julian David, BSc ACA *1991;* 12 Highfields, Westoning, BEDFORD, MK45 5EN.
MCLAREN, Mrs. Julie Elizabeth, BA ACA *1983;* with Bright Grahame Murray, 131 Edgware Road, LONDON, W2 2AP.
MCLAREN, Mr. Matthew, BSc(Hons) ACA *2001;* 61 Longacres, ST. ALBANS, AL4 0SL.
MCLAREN, Ms. Melanie Elizabeth, MA ACA *1990;* Westwold, Norrels Drive, East Horsley, LEATHERHEAD, SURREY, KT24 5DL.
MCLAREN, Mr. Michael Gerald, BSc FCA *1987;* October House, The Mount Drive, REIGATE, RH2 0EZ.

MCLAREN, Mr. Michael Lawrence, FCA *1973;* 57 Russell Drive, Ampthill, BEDFORD, MK45 2TU. (Life Member)
MCLAREN, Mr. Samuel Paterson, FCA *1964;* 60 Greenfield Gardens, LONDON, NW2 1HY. (Life Member)
MCLAREN, Miss. Sandra Margaret, BSc FCA *1981;* A 2 Housing Spelthorne House, Thames Street, STAINES, TW18 4TA.
MCLARNEY, Mr. Justin James, LLB ACA *2000;* 19 Seymour Road, Ladybay, West Bridgford, NOTTINGHAM, NG2 5EE.
MCLARNON, Miss. Esme Jane, BSc(Hons) ACA *2009;* 15 Bishops Close, RICHMOND, TW10 7DF.
•MCLARTY, Mr. Malcolm Charles, BSc ACA *1979;* KPMG S.A., 1 Cours Valmy, Paris La Défense Cedex, 92923 PARIS LA DÉFENSE, FRANCE.
MCLAUCHLAN, Mr. Alex, BA ACA *2004;* 43 Central Drive, ST. ALBANS, HERTFORDSHIRE, AL4 0UN.
MCLAUCHLAN, Mr. James, BA ACA *1981;* 6 The Coach House, Lawton Hall Drive, Church Lawton, STOKE-ON-TRENT, ST7 3BG.
MCLAUCHLAN, Mr. Michael, BA FCA *1978;* Flat 2, 62 Frith Street, LONDON, W1D3JN.
MCLAUGHLAN, Mrs. Helen Clare, BA ACA *1990;* The Coach House, 84 Ranelagh Road, Ealing, LONDON, W5 5RP.
MCLAUGHLAN, Mr. Stuart James, BA FCA *1990;* 67 Queen Annes Grove, LONDON, W5 3XP.
•MCLAUGHLIN, Mr. Andrew Bernard, FCA *1980;* McMillan & Co LLP, 28 Eaton Avenue, Buckshaw Village, CHORLEY, LANCASHIRE, PR7 7NA.
MCLAUGHLIN, Mrs. Catherine Michelle, ACA *2005;* 25 Badgers Rise, Woodley, READING, RG5 3AJ.
MCLAUGHLIN, Mr. David Patrick Crofton, BA ACA *1985;* Simmons & Simmons, Citypoint, 1 Ropemaker Street, LONDON, EC2Y 9SS.
MCLAUGHLIN, Mr. Iain, BA(Hons) ACA *2004;* 25 Badgers Rise, Woodley, READING, RG5 3AJ.
•MCLAUGHLIN, Mr. Ian Stuart, FCA *1967;* (Tax Fac), 23 West Farm Avenue, ASHTEAD, SURREY, KT21 2LD.
MCLAUGHLIN, Mr. James, BA ACA *1981;* Snow Meadow Barn, Middle Stoughton, WEDMORE, SOMERSET, BS28 4PT.
•MCLAUGHLIN, Mr. James Henry Philip, BA ACA *1988;* (Tax Fac), James H.P. McLaughlin, 34 Ludlow Close, Willsbridge, BRISTOL, BS30 6EB.
MCLAUGHLIN, Mrs. Joy Felicity, BA ACA *1986;* 5 Crescent Road, KINGSTON UPON THAMES, KT2 7RD.
•MCLAUGHLIN, Mr. Neil, BCom FCA *1996;* Crana Trading Limited, 133 Bath Road, STROUD, GLOUCESTERSHIRE, GL5 3LL.
MCLAUGHLIN, Mr. Noel Andrew, ACA *2006;* KPMG, 1 Harbourmaster Place, IFSC, DUBLIN 1, COUNTY DUBLIN, IRELAND.
MCLAUGHLIN, Mr. Paul Joseph, BA FCA *1986;* with Grant Thornton UK LLP, Grant Thornton House, Kettering Parkway, Kettering Venture Park, KETTERING, NORTHAMPTONSHIRE NN15 6XR.
•MCLAUGHLIN, Mr. Seamus Peter, BSc FCA *1993;* Martin and Company, 25 St Thomas Street, WINCHESTER, SO23 9HJ. See also Martin and Company Accountants Limited
MCLAUGHLIN, Mr. Sean Patrick, BA FCA *1987;* The Access Bank UK Limited, 1 Cornhill, LONDON, EC3v 3ND.
MCLAUGHLIN, Mr. Sean Patrick, BCom ACA *1989;* 455 St James Lane, COVENTRY, CV3 3FG.
MCLAUGHLIN, Mrs. Victoria Louise, BSc(Hons) ACA AMCT *2003;* John Lewis Plc, Partnership House, Carlisle Place, LONDON, SW1P 1BX.
MCLAUGHLIN, Mr. William, CA *1974; (CA Scotland 1957);* 23 Lostock Hall Road, Poynton, STOCKPORT, SK12 1DP. (Life Member)
MCLEAN, Mr. Alan Daniel, BA FCA *1992;* (Tax Fac), Royal Dutch Shell plc, Carel van Bylandtlaan 16, PO Box 162, 2501 AN THE HAGUE, NETHERLANDS.
MCLEAN, Mr. Alan James, LLB ACA *1988;* (Tax Fac), BP plc, Chertsey Road, SUNBURY-ON-THAMES, MIDDLESEX, TW16 7LN.
MCLEAN, Mr. Alisdair John, BSc ACA *1987;* Hawthorn House, Cranfield Road, Moulsoe, NEWPORT PAGNELL, MK16 0HL.
MCLEAN, Mr. Andrew Stuart, BSc ACA *1999;* 57 Linden Park, Burnage, MANCHESTER, M19 2PG.
•MCLEAN, Mr. Christopher Harry, FCA *1976;* Moss & Williamson, 3 Mellor Road, Cheadle Hulme, CHEADLE, SK8 5AT. See also Moss & Williamson Ltd
MCLEAN, Mr. David Alan, MA ACA *1983;* Flat 43, The Pryors, East Heath Road, LONDON, NW3 1BP.
MCLEAN, Mr. Donald Frederick, FCA *1954;* 30 Brampton Road, BEXLEYHEATH, DA7 4HD. (Life Member)
MCLEAN, Ms. Fiona, ACA *2009;* 6A, John Smeaton Court, MANCHESTER, M1 2NR.
MCLEAN, Mr. James Stewart, BA ACA *1986;* Allied Glass Containers Ltd, South Accommodation Road, LEEDS, LS10 1NQ.
MCLEAN, Mrs. Janet Elizabeth, BA FCA *1997;* 11 Castle Rising Road, South Wootton, KING'S LYNN, PE30 3HP.
MCLEAN, Mr. John, FCA *1954;* 6 Briercliffe Road, BRISTOL, BS9 2DB. (Life Member)
MCLEAN, Mr. John Nigel Major, FCA *1977;* Atholl House, Church Lane, Worplesdon, GUILDFORD, GU3 3RU.
MCLEAN, Mr. Kaber Andrew, BSc(Econ) ACA *1996;* HSBC Main Building, Level 15 GBM Management Office, 1 Queen's Road, CENTRAL, HONG KONG ISLAND, HONG KONG SAR.
MCLEAN, Miss. Mairi Cerian, LLB ACA *2006;* Cararra Floor 3, Norwich Union Insurance Group, PO Box 6, NORWICH, NR1 3NS.
•MCLEAN, Mr. Mark Richard, FCA *1994;* Fox Evans Limited, Abbey House, 7 Manor Road, COVENTRY, CV1 2FW.
MCLEAN, Mr. Nicholas David, ACA MP *2002;* 33 Fairholme Road, MANCHESTER, M20 4SA.
MCLEAN, Mr. Nicholas James, BA ACA *2001;* 25 Crown Street, Redbourn, ST. ALBANS, AL3 7JX.
MCLEAN, Mr. Robin Adrian, BA ACA *1992;* 12 Liphook Crescent, LONDON, SE23 3BW.
MCLEAN, Mr. Ryan Danny, ACA *2010;* 42 Kent Avenue, CANTERBURY, KENT, CT1 1RN.
MCLEAN, Mrs. Sandra Vivienne, PhD BSc FCA *1986;* (Tax Fac), 1 Carr Road, Hale, ALTRINCHAM, CHESHIRE, WA15 8DX.
•MCLEAN, Mr. Simon Andrew, BSc FCA *1991;* (Tax Fac), AGP, Sycamore House, Sutton Quays Business Park, Sutton Weaver, RUNCORN, CHESHIRE WA7 3EH.
•MCLEAN, Mr. Trevor David, FCA *1981;* McLean Business Solutions Limited, 4 Poise Brook Drive, Offerton, STOCKPORT, CHESHIRE, SK2 5JG.
MCLEAY, Prof. Stuart James, MSc FCA *1969;* Bangor Business School Hen Goleg, University of Wales Bangor, College Road, BANGOR, GWYNEDD, LL57 2DG.
MCLEEN, Mr. Gregory David, MA ACA *1986;* 2 The Avenue, Roundhay, LEEDS, LS8 1DW.
MCLEISH, Mr. Jonathon Richard, ACA *2008;* 20 River Court Apt 3112, JERSEY CITY, NJ 07310, UNITED STATES.
MCLELLAN, Mr. Andrew, BA ACA *1988;* (Tax Fac), Crown Eyeglass Plc, Unit 403, Glenfield Park Two, Blakewater Road, BLACKBURN, BB1 5QH.
MCLELLAN, Mr. Brian, BA ACA *1983;* 5 The Pastures, Calverton, NOTTINGHAM, NG14 6GB.
MCLELLAN, Mr. Duncan, BA ACA *1982;* 19 Fairways, FRODSHAM, WA6 7RU.
•MCLELLAN, Miss. Jeannette, BA ACA *1983;* (Tax Fac), 17 Grosvenor Road, Sketty, SWANSEA, SA2 0SP.
MCLELLAN, Mrs. Jessica May, ACA *2009;* Pricewaterhousecoopers, 101 Barbirolli Square, MANCHESTER, M2 3PW.
•MCLELLAN, Mrs. Karen Christine, FCA *1997;* HW Hereford Ltd, Charlton House, St. Nicholas Street, HEREFORD, HR4 0BG.
•MCLELLAN, Mr. Richard Martin Stuart, MSc FCA *1974;* (Tax Fac), 14 Woodfield Avenue, NORTHWOOD, MIDDLESEX, HA6 3EA.
•MCLELLAND, Mr. Charles John Adam, BA ACA *1997;* Alvarez & Marsal Transaction Advisory Group Europe LLP, 1 Finsbury Circus, LONDON, EC2M 7EB.
MCLELLAND, Miss. Keth Jane Goergina, ACA *2009;* PricewaterhouseCoopers Australia, Darling Park Tower 2, 201 Sussex Street, SYDNEY, NSW 2000, AUSTRALIA.
MCLENNAN, Mr. Robert Gordon, FCA *1971;* 24 Whin Hill Rd, Bessacar, DONCASTER, DN4 7AF.
MCLEOD, Mr. Alasdair Simpson, BA FCA *1990;* 47 Salisbury Road, Redland, BRISTOL, BS6 7AR.
MCLEOD, Mr. Andrew, ACA *2011;* 64 Avondale Road, RAYLEIGH, ESSEX, SS6 8NL.
•MCLEOD, Mr. Donald Bremner, JP BCom FCA MBA *1979;* PO Box 7228, St Kilda Road, MELBOURNE, VIC 8004, AUSTRALIA.
MCLEOD, Mr. Euan David, BSc ACA *1998;* HSBC Bank Plc, Canary Wharf, LONDON, E14 5HQ.
MCLEOD, Mr. Gary Robert, ACA *1995;* 17 New Road, Impington, CAMBRIDGE, CB24 9LU.
MCLEOD, Mr. Gerald John Moreton, FCA *1959;* Porthview, 9 The Lugger, Portscatho, TRURO, TR2 5HE. (Life Member)
MCLEOD, Mr. Ian Daniel, BSc ACA *1992;* Lowood House, 5 Apperley Road, STOCKSFIELD, NORTHUMBERLAND, NE43 7PD.
MCLEOD, Miss. Isobel, MSc ACA *2009;* 26 Perigee, Shinfield Park, READING, RG2 9FT.
MCLEOD, Mr. John, MBA BSc FCA *1975;* Children North East, 89 Denhill Park, NEWCASTLE UPON TYNE, NE15 6QE.
•MCLEOD, Mr. John Comline, BA FCA *1977;* 11 Overstone Road, Hammersmith, LONDON, W6 0AA.
MCLEOD, Mr. Keith George, BSc ACA *1989;* European Islamic Investment Bank Plc, 131 Finsbury Pavement, LONDON, EC2A 1NT.
MCLEOD, Miss. Kirsty Ann, BA FCA *1995;* with RSM Tenon Audit Limited, 2 Wellington Place, LEEDS, LS1 4AP.
MCLEOD, Mr. Neil, BA FCA *1989;* The Seafood Restaurant, Riverside, PADSTOW, CORNWALL, PL28 8BY.
MCLEOD, Mr. Philip Thornton, FCA *1972;* Philip T. McLeod, 582 St. Andrews Place, WEST VANCOUVER V7S 1V8, BC, CANADA.
•MCLEOD, Mr. Robert Alexander, FCA *1977;* (Tax Fac), R A McLeod (Financial Services) Limited, 10 Portland Business Centre, Manor House Lane, Datchet, SLOUGH, SL3 9EG. See also R A McLeod & Co
MCLEOD, Mr. Stuart, BSc ACA *1991;* Abbey House, 25 Clarendon Road, REDHILL, RH1 1QF.
MCLEOD- JONES, Mrs. Helen Claire, BA ACA *2003;* 7th floor, Ernst & Young, 1 Colmore Square, BIRMINGHAM, B4 6HQ.
MCLEOD-MORE, Miss. Victoria Abigail, BA(Hons) ACA *2003;* 44 Burntwood Lane, LONDON, SW17 0JZ.
MCLERNON, Dr. Conor, ACA *2011;* 51 Hanbury Street, LONDON, E1 5JP.
MCLERNON, Mrs. Eva Maria Barbara, BSc ACA CTA *1995;* Neuhofstrasse 38, 6345 NEUHEIM, SWITZERLAND.
MCLERNON, Mr. Malachy, BSc ACA *1995;* Neuhofstrasse 38, 6345 NEUHEIM, SWITZERLAND.
•MCLERNON, Mr. Sean Anthony, FCA *1989;* with RSM Tenon Limited, Cedar House, Sandbrook Business Park, Sandbrook Way, ROCHDALE, LANCASHIRE OL11 1LQ.
•MCLINTOCK, Mr. John Alexander, FCA FCCA *1972;* (Tax Fac), McLintocks, 2 Hilliards Court, Chester Business Park, CHESTER, CH4 9PX. See also McLintocks Ltd and McLintocks Partnership
MCLISTER, Mr. Colm, BSc ACA *1987;* Facet Industrial UK Ltd, G1-G4, Unit, Treforest Industrial Estate, PONTYPRIDD, MID GLAMORGAN CF37 5YL.
MCLORIE, Mr. Don Paul, BSc(Hons) ACA *2009;* with PricewaterhouseCoopers LLP, 8 Princes Parade, St Nicholas Place, LIVERPOOL, L3 1QJ.
MCLOUGHLIN, Mr. Anthony Francis, FCA *1958;* Telford House, 1 Claremont Bank, SHREWSBURY, SY1 1RW. (Life Member)
MCLOUGHLIN, Mr. Bryan Alexander, ACA *2009;* 25 Castle Row, CANTERBURY, KENT, CT1 2QY.
MCLOUGHLIN, Miss. Claire, BA ACA *2005;* 17 Thistle Bank, East Leake, LOUGHBOROUGH, LE12 6RS.
MCLOUGHLIN, Mrs. Helen Bridget, FCA *1973;* 28 Kenton Park Rd, Kenton, HARROW, HA3 8TY.
•MCLOUGHLIN, Mrs. Jennifer Claire, BSc(Hons) ACA *2001;* J McLoughlin Ltd, Signpost Cottage, The Camp, STROUD, GLOUCESTERSHIRE, GL6 7HN.
MCLOUGHLIN, Miss. Johanna, MSc ACA *2004;* Flat 3, 107 Church Road, RICHMOND, TW10 6LS.
MCLOUGHLIN, Mr. Martin Eamon, BA ACA *1993;* 15 Yiremba Place, FORESTVILLE, NSW 2087, AUSTRALIA.
MCLOUGHLIN, Mr. Matthew, ACA *2008;* Deloitte & Touche Llp, 2 Hardman Street, MANCHESTER, M3 3HF.
MCLOUGHLIN, Mr. Maurice Julian, BSc(Hons) ACA *2003;* Dales Brow Farm Dales Brow, Swinton, MANCHESTER, M27 0YN.
MCLOUGHLIN, Mr. Michael, ACA *1980;* 6 Brookside Close, Atherton, MANCHESTER, M46 9RL.
•①MCLOUGHLIN, Mr. Michael Vincent, BA FCA *1983;* Spinney Lodge, Old Road, Ruddington, NOTTINGHAM, NG11 6NF.
MCLOUGHLIN, Mr. Stephen James, BSc ACA *2006;* 47 Frenches Road, REDHILL, RH1 2HR.
MCLOUGHLIN, Mrs. Suzanne Elizabeth, BA ACA *1996;* Byland House, Seaton Ross, YORK, YO42 4LT.
•MCLOUGHNEY, Mrs. Lorraine Theresa, FCA *1978;* The Beckett Partnership LLP, Beckett House, Sovereign Court, Wyrefields, Poulton Industrial Estate, POULTON-LE-FYLDE LANCASHIRE FY6 8JX.
MCLUCAS, Mr. Ashley Trevor, BEng ACA *1993;* Willow Lodge, Manor Way, Oxshott, LEATHERHEAD, SURREY, KT22 0HU.
MCLUCKIE, Miss. Jan, BA ACA *1995;* 5 Pinewood Avenue, Northburn Chase, CRAMLINGTON, NE23 3TX.
MCLURE, Mr. Nicholas David, MSc ACA *2002;* 9 Golf Links Avenue, TADCASTER, NORTH YORKSHIRE, LS24 9HF.
MCMAHON, Mr. Anthony James, BSc FCA *1978;* Gurdons House, Gurdons Lane, Wormley, GODALMING, SURREY, GU8 5UE.
MCMAHON, Mr. Bernard John, BA ACA *1980;* 8 Clockhouse Mews, Chorleywood House Drive, Chorleywood, RICKMANSWORTH, HERTFORDSHIRE, WD3 5GN.
MCMAHON, Mr. Christopher Patrick, MA ACA *1991;* 73 Horn Book, SAFFRON WALDEN, ESSEX, CB11 3JW.
MCMAHON, Mr. David, FCA *1976;* Hurleston Grange, Chester Road, Hurleston, NANTWICH, CHESHIRE, CW5 6BU.
MCMAHON, Mr. Gavin Morgan, BSc(Econ) ACA *2003;* Sun Life Assurance Company of Canada, 150 King Street West, TORONTO M5H 1J9, ON, CANADA.
MCMAHON, Mr. John Paul, BA ACA *1999;* 27 Summercroft Close, Golborne, WARRINGTON, WA3 3WL.
MCMAHON, Mrs. Katie Louise, BA(Hons) ACA *2002;* 23 The Drive, Henleaze, BRISTOL, BS9 4LD.
MCMAHON, Miss. Keda Louise, BA(Hons) ACA *2010;* 14 Heather Close, New Haw, ADDLESTONE, SURREY, KT15 3PF.
MCMAHON, Mr. Michael Christopher, FCA *1969;* 151 Riverview Circle, FAIRFIELD, CT 06824, UNITED STATES.
MCMAHON, Mr. Michael James, ACA *2003;* 10a North Street, Charminster, DORCHESTER, DORSET, DT2 9QS.
MCMAHON, Mrs. Orla O'Connell, MA BA ACA *1999;* 77 Avenue Road, INGATESTONE, CM4 9HB.
MCMAHON, Mr. Patrick, MA FCA *1979;* Beagle Asset Management Ltd, 15 Frederick Place, Clifton, BRISTOL, BS8 1AS.
MCMAHON, Mr. Paul Anthony, BA ACA *1991;* 10 Sutcliffe Close, LONDON, NW11 6NT.
•MCMAHON, Mr. Paul Kenneth, ACA *2005;* UHY Torgersens, Somerford Buildings, Norfolk Street, SUNDERLAND, SR1 1EE.
MCMAHON, Mr. Philip Richard John, BSc(Econ) ACA *2004;* Flat 8 Ashfield House, Bayshill Lane Bayshill Road, CHELTENHAM, GLOUCESTERSHIRE, GL50 3AX.
MCMAHON, Mr. Rodney Kington, BA FCA *1982;* Moons Mill, Mill Lane, Ramsbury, MARLBOROUGH, WILTSHIRE, SN8 2RE.
MCMAHON, Mr. Stephen, BA ACA *2006;* 1 Les Parcqs, La Rue de la Vallee St. Helier, JERSEY, JE2 3FA.
MCMAHON, Mrs. Tracey Ann, ACA *2008;* 16 Cronk Ny Greiney, Douglas, ISLE OF MAN, IM2 5LW.
•MCMANNERS, Mr. Thomas William, BSc ACA ACMI *1991;* (Tax Fac), TTCA Ltd, 269 Farnborough Road, FARNBOROUGH, HAMPSHIRE, GU14 7LY.
MCMANUS, Miss. Alison Joanne, BSc ACA *2006;* Flat 7 Henry Harrison Court, North Side Wandsworth Common, LONDON, SW18 2SR.
MCMANUS, Mr. Andrew Craig, BSc ACA *1989;* SMC Mobile Crushers and Screeners Limited, Hearthcote Road, SWADLINCOTE, DERBYSHIRE, de11 9du.
•MCMANUS, Mr. Andrew John, BSc FCA *1983;* (Tax Fac), The Shepherd Partnership Limited, Albion House, Rope Walk, Otley Street, SKIPTON, NORTH YORKSHIRE BD23 1ED.
MCMANUS, Miss. Anna, FCA *1953;* 47 Oxford Road, Waterloo, LIVERPOOL, L22 8QE. (Life Member)
MCMANUS, Mr. Anthony, FCA *1963;* 47 Parklands, Great Linford, MILTON KEYNES, MK14 5DZ.
MCMANUS, Mr. Charles Ashley, BA ACA *1987;* Thames Court, 1 Queenhithe, LONDON, EC4V 4DE.
MCMANUS, Mr. Christopher Charles, MSc FCA *1977;* Barnsfield, Norwood Lane, Meopham, GRAVESEND, DA13 0YF.
•MCMANUS, Mrs. Elizabeth Margaret, FCA *1981;* E.M. McManus, 2 Heatherlands Thakeham Road, Storrington, PULBOROUGH, RH20 3NE.
MCMANUS, Ms. Finola Josephine, FCA *1992;* 18 Dubrae Close, ST. ALBANS, AL3 4JT.
MCMANUS, Mrs. Frances Theresa, BA ACA *1984;* The Mid Ocean Club, 1 Mid Ocean Drive, TUCKERS TOWN HS01, BERMUDA.
MCMANUS, Mr. Grant, ACA *2009;* Flat 3, 4-6 Oxford Road, LONDON, SW15 2LF.
•MCMANUS, Mr. Iain Christopher, BA ACA CTA *1989;* Sanders, 1 Bickenhall Mansions, Bickenhall Street, LONDON, W1U 6BP.

MCMANUS, Mr. John Robert George, BSc ACA *1994;* 3 Clyde Road, MANCHESTER, M20 2NJ.
MCMANUS, Mr. Kieran, BSc BEng FCA CPA *1993;* Av. Francisco Matarazzo 1400, Torre Torino 14° andar, Água Branca, SAO PAULO, 05001-903, BRAZIL.
•**MCMANUS, Mrs. Marian Jane, BA ACA** *1993;* McManus Hall, Office 8, Consett Innovation Centre, Ponds Court Business Park, Genesis Way, CONSETT COUNTY DURHAM DH8 5XP.
MCMANUS, Mr. Michael, BA FCA *1963;* 45 Shirley Avenue, SOUTHAMPTON, SO15 5NH. (Life Member)
MCMANUS, Mr. Michael Anthony, FCA *1959;* 18 Hartington Road, Dentons Green, ST.HELENS, MERSEYSIDE, WA10 6AQ. (Life Member)
MCMANUS, Mr. Michael Stewart, FCA *1972;* Wildfell, 49 Apperley Rd, STOCKSFIELD, NE43 7PQ.
MCMANUS, Mr. Neil Alexander, BA ACA *2007;* 10 Oakwell Oval, Roundhay, LEEDS, LS8 4AL.
MCMANUS, Mr. Paul, BA ACA *1992;* Display Led Screens Limited, Unit 20, The Coda Centre, 189 Munster Road, LONDON, SW6 6AW.
MCMANUS, Mr. Paul, BA ACA *1990;* The Hamlet, Hornbeam Park, HARROGATE, NORTH YORKSHIRE, HG2 8RE.
MCMANUS, Mr. Paul Christopher, MSc FCA *1968;* 12 Mayfield Drive, KENILWORTH, CV8 2SW.
MCMANUS, Mr. Paul Robert John, BA FCA *1999;* Serious Fraud Office, Elm House, 10-16 Elm Street, LONDON, WC1X 0BJ.
•**MCMANUS, Mrs. Sarah Penelope, BSc ACA** *2007;* D A Clark & Co Limited, 4 Peel House, Barttelot Road, HORSHAM, WEST SUSSEX, RH12 1DE.
MCMANUS, Mr. Thomas Geoffrey, FCA *1976;* B A S F Plc PO Box 4, Cheadle Hulme, CHEADLE, CHESHIRE, SK8 6QG.
MCMANUS, Mr. Timothy, ACA *2009;* with PricewaterhouseCoopers, One Spencer Dock, North Wall Quay, DUBLIN 1, COUNTY DUBLIN, IRELAND.
MCMARTIN, Mr. Ian Douglas, BSc FCA *1986;* Lawers Conseil SARL, 75 rue du Faubourg St.-Antoine, 75011 PARIS, FRANCE.
MCMARTIN, Mr. Stuart Andrew, BSc ACA *1996;* Ballechroisk Belton, MUNLOCHY, ROSS-SHIRE, IV8 8PF.
MCMASTER, Miss. Helen Louise, MSc ACA *2000;* 3 Field Close, Bramhall, STOCKPORT, CHESHIRE, SK7 1HZ.
MCMASTER, Mrs. Janet Deborah, ACA *1986;* 29 Grayling Road, Rosewood Park, Lobley Hill, GATESHEAD, NE11 9ND.
MCMASTER, Mrs. Katerina, BSc(Hons) ACA *2002;* Yew Tree Cottage, Bookhurst Road, CRANLEIGH, SURREY, GU6 7DN.
MCMASTER, Mr. Robert Fredwin James, MA ACA *1986;* 18 College Road, READING, RG6 1QB.
MCMASTER, Mr. William, FCA *1965;* 17 Grassholme Close, CONSETT, COUNTY DURHAM, DH8 7UL.
MCMATH, Ms. Clare Mary Astrid, BA ACA ATII *1998;* Little Firs, The Avenue, ASCOT, SL5 7LY.
MCMATH, Miss. Judith Helen, BSc FCA *1988;* 146 Chatsworth Road, Worsley, MANCHESTER, M28 2NT.
MCMEEKIN, Mrs. Delia Denise, BA ACA CTA *2005;* G E Healthcare, Amersham Place, AP05, Little Chalfont, AMERSHAM, BUCKINGHAMSHIRE HP7 9NA.
MCMEEKIN, Mrs. Susan Michele, BA ACA *1991;* 2 Rues des Charrons, Tnac-Lautrait, 16200 COGNAC, FRANCE.
MCMEEKING, Mr. Robert John, BA ACA *1992;* Lavendon Access Services (UK) Ltd, 15 Midland Court Central Park, LUTTERWORTH, LE17 4PN.
MCMEEKING, Mr. Ross, ACA *2008;* 32 Tyle'r Hendy, Miskin, PONTYCLUN, MID GLAMORGAN, CF72 8QU.
MCMENAMIN, Mr. Eamon Michael, BSc ACA *1995;* The Pines, 1a The Spinney, BERKHAMSTED, HERTFORDSHIRE, HP4 3YS.
MCMENEMY, Mr. Philip James, MA ACA *1997;* 3 Temple House, Hoop Lane, LONDON, NW11 7NG.
MCMICHAEL, Mr. Peter John James, BA ACA *1996;* Atkins Limited, The Barbican, East Street, FARNHAM, SURREY, GU9 7TB.
MCMICHAEL, Mrs. Sarah Louise, BA ACA *1999;* 3 Micheldever Road, LONDON, SE12 8LX.
MCMICKING DAVIES, Mrs. Miranda May, BSc(Hons) ACA *2001;* 2003 Chisholm Trail, FRISCO, TX 75034, UNITED STATES.
MCMILLAN, Mr. Adrian David Graeme, MA FCA *1988;* 50 Haldon Road, LONDON, SW18 1QG.
•**MCMILLAN, Mr. Alistair James, LLB ACA** *1984;* (Tax Fac), AM Tax Services Ltd, 24a Priory Lane, WEST MOLESEY, SURREY, KT8 2PS.
MCMILLAN, Mr. Andrew James, BA ACA *2010;* 53 Chevening Road, LONDON, SE19 3TD.
MCMILLAN, Mrs. Anne Mary, BSc FCA *1991;* 2/173 Bateman Road, BRENTWOOD, WA 6153, AUSTRALIA.
MCMILLAN, Mrs. Bozena Irene Collette, MA ACA *1989;* 131 Weald Way, CATERHAM, CR3 6EP.
MCMILLAN, Mr. Craig David, BA(Hons) ACA *2002;* PricewaterhouseCoopers LLP, 250 Howe Street, VANCOUVER V6C3S7, BC, CANADA.
MCMILLAN, Miss. Debra Natasha, MBA BSc ACA *1990;* Windrush, 27 Braybrooke Road, Wargrave, READING, BERKSHIRE, RG10 8DU.
MCMILLAN, Mr. Ian Marshall, BSc FCA *1989;* 131 Weald Way, CATERHAM, CR3 6EP.
•**MCMILLAN, Mr. John Frederick Douglas, FCA** *1971;* McMillan & Co LLP, 28 Eaton Avenue, Buckshaw Village, CHORLEY, LANCASHIRE, PR7 7NA. See also McMillan & Co Accounting Services Ltd
MCMILLAN, Mr. John Robert, FCA *1980;* Primavera, 2 Badger's Close, Manton, OAKHAM, LE15 8SQ.
MCMILLAN, Mrs. Katherine Anne, BSc ACA *1995;* 22 Essenden Road, SOUTH CROYDON, CR2 0BU.
•**MCMILLAN, Mrs. Natasha, MA(Hons) ACA** *2001;* with PricewaterhouseCoopers, 7 More London Riverside, LONDON, SE1 2RT.
•**MCMILLAN, Mr. Neil Robert Douglas, BA ACA** *2003;* McMillan & Co LLP, 28 Eaton Avenue, Buckshaw Village, CHORLEY, LANCASHIRE, PR7 7NA.
MCMILLAN, Mr. Richard John, BSc FCA *1982;* 3 Rushmere Gate, Green Lane Hambledon, WATERLOOVILLE, PO7 4SS.
MCMILLAN, Mr. Ronald Scorgie, BSc FCA *1972;* 30 Seymour Walk, LONDON, SW10 9NF.
•**MCMILLAN, Mr. Ronald Thomas, BSc FCA** *1978;* Pricewaterhousecoopers, 1 Embankment Place, LONDON, WC2N 6RH.
MCMILLAN, Mr. Scott, ACA *2007;* 24b Mount View Road, LONDON, N4 4HX.
MCMILLAN, Mr. Sean David, BSc ACA *1996;* 33 Hathaway Green Lane, STRATFORD-UPON-AVON, CV37 9HX.
MCMILLAN, Mrs. Susan Margaret, BSc ACA *1989;* 5 First Avenue, Netherlee, GLASGOW, G44 3UA.
MCMILLAN, Mrs. Victoria Jane, BA ACA *2006;* 3323 West 2nd Avenue, VANCOUVER V6R1H9, BC, CANADA.
MCMILLAN-BROWSE, Miss. Caroline Mary, BCom ACA *1998;* ETI, Holywell Building, Holywell Way, LOUGHBOROUGH, LEICESTERSHIRE, LE11 3UZ.
MCMILLAN-PURI, Mrs. Alison Claire, LLB FCA *1984;* 9 Norfolk Road, BRIGHTON, BN1 3AA.
•**MCMILLIN, Mrs. Judith De Quincey, BSc FCA CTA** *1977;* Judith McMillin BSc FCA CTA, Stoneleigh, Ferncliffe Drive, KEIGHLEY, WEST YORKSHIRE, BD20 6HN.
MCMINN, Mr. Alan James, FCA *1966;* 6 Chestnut Court, Middle Lane, LONDON, N8 8NU.
MCMINN, Mr. Andrew Scott, ACA *1990;* 18 Poulton Road, SOUTHPORT, PR9 7BE.
MCMINN, Mr. Clive, FCA *1977;* Frances House, Sir William Place, St Peter Port, GUERNSEY, GY1 4EA.
MCMINN, Mr. Nigel John, BA ACA *1995;* 26 North Avenue, Gosforth, NEWCASTLE UPON TYNE, NE3 4DQ.
MCMINN MITCHELL, Mr. Philip James, BA FCA CPA *1994;* Technical Assistance to PEPFAR's New Partner Initiative, Nakawa House, PO Box 4290, KAMPALA, UGANDA.
MCMINNIES, Mr. Stuart Russell, BEng ACA *1993;* 30 Herondale Avenue, LONDON, SW18 3JL.
MCMONEAGLE, Mrs. Carolyn Mary, BA ACA *1993;* 12 Holtspur Top Lane, BEACONSFIELD, BUCKINGHAMSHIRE, HP9 1DR.
MCMONEAGLE, Mr. Grant Findlay, BSc ACA *1994;* The Laurels, 12 Holtspur Top Lane, BEACONSFIELD, BUCKINGHAMSHIRE, HP9 1DR.
•**MCMORRAN, Mr. Frederick Keith, FCA** *1963;* Keighwood Limited, 12 The Range, Langham, OAKHAM, LEICESTERSHIRE, LE15 7EB.
MCMORRIS, Miss. Catherine, BSc ACA *1993;* 57 Bloemfontein Avenue, LONDON, W12 7BJ.
MCMORROW, Mr. Jason, BA ACA *2011;* Cough Bright King, 91 Gower Street, LONDON, WC1E 6AB.
MCMULLAN, Mrs. Dinah, FCA *1969;* Brierley, Ramsden Road, GODALMING, GU7 1QE.
MCMULLAN, Mr. Edward Brownlow, ACA *1986;* 16 Acfold Road, LONDON, SW6 2AL.
MCMULLAN, Mrs. Hannah Susan, BSc ACA *2005;* 15 East Towers, PINNER, MIDDLESEX, HA5 1TN.
MCMULLAN, Mr. Ian Stuart, BSc ACA *1994;* Canada Life Ltd, 3 Rivergate, Temple Quay, BRISTOL, BS1 6ER.
MCMULLAN, Mr. James, MA ACA *2011;* Brierley, Ramsden Road, GODALMING, SURREY, GU7 1QE.
MCMULLAN, Mr. John Hugh, BSc ACA *1987;* Summerhill, 86 Hopton Lane, Upper Hopton, MIRFIELD, WF14 8JS.
MCMULLAN, Mr. Jonathan, ACA *2009;* 118 Gaskarth Road, LONDON, SW12 9NW.
MCMULLAN, Mr. Paul, BEng ACA *1992;* The Montague, 2 Montague lane, ALBERT PARK, VIC 3206, AUSTRALIA.
MCMULLAN, Mr. Peter James, BSc(Hons) ACA *2004;* 15 East Towers, PINNER, MIDDLESEX, HA5 1TN.
MCMULLAN, Mr. Stephen, BSc FCA CF *2000;* Temple Point, 1 Temple Row, BIRMINGHAM, B2 5LG.
MCMULLAN, Mr. William David, BA ACA *2010;* Brierley, Ramsden Road, GODALMING, SURREY, GU7 1QE.
MCMULLEN, Mr. Alexander Brodie, ACA *2008;* Top Flat, 40 Stanhope Gardens, LONDON, SW7 5QY.
MCMULLEN, Miss. Angela, BA ACA *1992;* Chello Broadband Ltd Michelin House, 81 Fulham Road, LONDON, SW3 6RD.
•**MCMULLEN, Mr. Mark Kerry, MA FCA** *1989;* (Tax Fac), Smith & Williamson Ltd, 25 Moorgate, LONDON, EC2R 6AY.
MCMULLEN, Mr. Simon Ross Harden, BEng ACA *1997;* 7 Priory Road, Chalfont St. Peter, GERRARDS CROSS, BUCKINGHAMSHIRE, SL9 8SB.
MCMULLEN, Mrs. Susan Lynn, BA ACA *1992;* 54 Broadway, Bebington, WIRRAL, CH63 5NL.
•**MCMULLEN, Mr. Toni Michael, FCA** *1961;* T.M. McMullen FCA, 5 Milnthorpe Lane, Bramham, WETHERBY, WEST YORKSHIRE, LS23 6SW.
MCMURDO, Mr. Andrew, BA FCA *1979;* Midgill House, Radley Road, Halam, NEWARK, NG22 8AQ.
MCMURRAY, Mr. Andrew, LLB ACA *1985;* 53 The Ridgeway, LONDON, NW11 8QL.
MCMURRAY, Mrs. Helen Elizabeth, BA ACA *1999;* 57 Stevens Lane, Claygate, ESHER, SURREY, KT10 0TJ.
MCMURRAY, Mr. Steven Roy, BA ACA *1999;* 57 Stevens Lane, Claygate, ESHER, SURREY, KT10 0TJ.
MCMURRAY, Mr. Stuart, ACA *2009;* 1 Kings Acre, Bowdon, ALTRINCHAM, CHESHIRE, WA14 3SE.
MCMURTRIE, Mr. Robert St John, ACA *1980;* 44 Waterbridge Way, TORONTO M1C 5B9, ON, CANADA.
•**MCMURTRY, Mr. Ian James, FCA** *1983;* Thomas Westcott, Timberly, South Street, AXMINSTER, DEVON, EX13 5AD.
MCMURTRY, Mr. James Hugh, BA ACA *1991;* Libra Drinks Wholesale Ltd, 9 Ashville Close, Queens Drive Industrial Estate, NOTTINGHAM, NG2 1LL.
MCMUTRIE, Mrs. Lucy, BSc ACA *1998;* Woodend Corner, Grassendale Lane, LIVERPOOL, L19 0NH.
MCMYN, Mr. James Alexander, MA FCA *1965;* 151 Rose Park Drive, TORONTO M4T 1R6, ON, CANADA.
MCNAB, Miss. Alison Jane, BA ACA *2004;* Wateraid, 2nd Floor, 47-49 Durham Street, LONDON, SE11 5JD.
MCNAB, Miss. Catherine Mary, BA ACA *1989;* Via delle Cerchia 5, 53100 SIENA, ITALY.
MCNAB, Miss. Claire Lucy, BSc ACA *2007;* 9 Bucklands Lane, Nailsea, BRISTOL, BS48 4PJ.
•**MCNAB, Mr. Duncan Arthur, BA FCA** *1980;* Clement Keys, 39/40 Calthorpe Road, Edgbaston, BIRMINGHAM, B15 1TS.
•**MCNAB, Mr. Duncan James, BSc FCA** *1993;* PricewaterhouseCoopers LLP, Hays Galleria, 1 Hays Lane, LONDON, SE1 2RD. See also PricewaterhouseCoopers
MCNAB, Mrs. Tracey Hannah, BSc ACA *1999;* 17 Amberleigh Close, Appleton Thorn, WARRINGTON, WA4 4TD.
MCNAB, Miss. Victoria Juliana, ACA *2008;* 25 Sneinton Hermitage, NOTTINGHAM, NG2 4BT.
MCNABB, Miss. Fiona Anne, BA FCA *1985;* Grove House, 37 Lodge Hill Road, Lower Bourne, FARNHAM, GU10 3RE.
MCNAIR, Mr. Duncan Robert, BEng ACA *1990;* 2b Mostyn Road Merton Park, Wimbledon, LONDON, SW19 3LH.
MCNAIR, Dr. Fiona Isobel, BSc ACA *2000;* 12 Hawthorn Grove, STOCKPORT, SK4 4HZ.
MCNAIR, Mr. Graham Hugh, BA ACA *1996;* 1 Alcester Avenue, Cheadle Heath, STOCKPORT, SK3 0QP.
•**MCNAIR, Mr. Iain Peter, FCA** *1977;* (Tax Fac), Moore Scott & Co, Aden Chambers, South Crescent, LLANDRINDOD WELLS, LD1 5DH.
MCNAIR, Mr. Ian Charles, BCom FCA *1985;* Marley Extrusions Ltd, Dickley Lane, Lenham, MAIDSTONE, KENT, ME17 2DE.
MCNAIR, Mr. John, FCA *1958;* Wern Newydd, Painscastle, BUILTH WELLS, POWYS, LD2 3JW. (Life Member)
MCNAIR, Mr. Neill Ellman, FCA *1968;* 6 Downs Hill, BECKENHAM, KENT, BR3 5HB.
MCNAIR SCOTT, Mr. Nigel Guthrie Mcnair, MA FCA *1970;* Huish House, Huish Lane, Old Basing, BASINGSTOKE, RG24 7AA.
MCNALLY, Mr. Anthony John, ACA *1993;* 78 Halfmoon Lane, DUNSTABLE, BEDFORDSHIRE, LU5 4AD.
MCNALLY, Miss. Eleanor Jane, ACA *2008;* 3 Llanarth Villas, Cheltenham Road, BRISTOL, BS6 5RQ.
MCNALLY, Mr. Emond John, BA ACA *1993;* (Tax Fac), 77 Kings Road, WINDSOR, SL4 2AD.
•**MCNALLY, Mr. James Martin, BA ACA** *1979;* 15 High Garth, ESHER, SURREY, KT10 9DN.
MCNALLY, Mr. Peter Joseph, FCA *1955;* Flat 3, 16 Bolton Gardens, LONDON, SW5 0AJ. (Life Member)
MCNALLY, Miss. Rachael, MSc BA ACA *2010;* Flat 7, 91 Worple Road, LONDON, SW19 4JG.
MCNALLY, Mr. Rob, ACA *2007;* Woodlands Mount, ALNWICK, NORTHUMBERLAND, NE66 2PW.
MCNALLY, Mr. Ronald Thomas, FCA *1954;* Trelawne, 114 Lovibonds Avenue, ORPINGTON, BR6 8EN. (Life Member)
MCNALLY, Miss. Sarah, BSc ACA *2011;* 16 Planetree Court, Dene Park, Marton, MIDDLESBROUGH, CLEVELAND, TS7 8QT.
MCNAMARA, Mrs. Anna Jane, MA ACA *2004;* R J Kiln & Co Ltd, Furness House, 106 Fenchurch Street, LONDON, EC3M 5NR.
MCNAMARA, Mrs. Catherine Mary, ACA *2009;* 50 Shaw Park, CROWTHORNE, BERKSHIRE, RG45 7QL.
MCNAMARA, Mr. Edward, BSc(Hons) ACA *2004;* 32 Dault Road, LONDON, SW18 2NQ.
MCNAMARA, Miss. Jane Louise, BSc ACA *1988;* 38 Brynmaer Road, LONDON, SW11 4EW.
•**MCNAMARA, Mr. John Michael, BSc(Econ) FCA CF** *1969;* Windy Haugh, 143 Manchester Road, Chapel-en-le-Frith, HIGH PEAK, SK23 9TN.
MCNAMARA, Miss. Katherine Jane, MA(Hons) ACA *2004;* 70 Manvers Road, West Bridgford, NOTTINGHAM, NG2 6DH.
MCNAMARA, Miss. Kathryn Lorna, MOcean ACA *2011;* 2 The Park, Alkington, WHITCHURCH, SHROPSHIRE, SY13 3NX.
MCNAMARA, Mr. Kevin Paul, MA FCA *1973;* The White House, Pyrton, WATLINGTON, OXFORDSHIRE, OX49 5AN.
MCNAMARA, Mr. Peter Jeremy, BSc ACA *1990;* 6 Stockgrove Park House, Stockgrove, LEIGHTON BUZZARD, BEDFORDSHIRE, LU7 0BB.
MCNAMARA, Mr. Richard Patrick, BA ACA *1993;* Henderson Global Investors, 201 Bishopsgate, LONDON, EC2M 3AE.
•**MCNAMARA, Miss. Sandra Mary, BCom ACA** *1995;* Sandra McNamara & Co, 9 Vernon Grove, Rathgar, DUBLIN 6, COUNTY DUBLIN, IRELAND.
MCNAMARA, Mr. Stuart, BSc ACA *2009;* Harvey Nichols Head Office, 67 Brompton Road, LONDON, SW3 1DB.
MCNAMEE, Mrs. Angela, FCA *1984;* National Space Centre, Exploration Drive, LEICESTER, LE4 5NS.
MCNAMEE, Ms. Gwendolen, BSc ACA *1993;* Maltrostveien 38D, 0786 OSLO, NORWAY.
MCNAMEE, Mr. John Peter, MBA BA ACA *1989;* 8 Cyprus Gardens, BELFAST, BT5 6FB.
MCNAMEE, Mr. Peter Nicholas, MA(Oxon) ACA *2001;* Swedish Chamber of Commerce, 5 Upper Montagu Street, LONDON, W1H 2AG.
•**MCNAUGHT, Mr. Andrew John, FCA** *1970;* McNaught & Co, 189 Wokingham Road, Earley, READING, RG6 1LT.
MCNAUGHT, Mr. Bruce David, BA(Hons) FCA TEP *1987;* Granary House, The Grange Road, St. Peter Port, GUERNSEY, GY1 2QG.
MCNAUGHT, Miss. Katie, ACA *2011;* 1a Balfour Road, LONDON, SW19 1JU.
MCNAUGHT, Mr. Roger Sanderson, MA FCA *1972;* Dame Johane Bradbury School, Ashdon Road, SAFFRON WALDEN, ESSEX, CB10 2AL.
•**MCNAUGHT, Miss. Sarah Kate Gilchrist, BSc ACA** *1992;* KPMG LLP, 15 Canada Square, LONDON, E14 5GL. See also KPMG Europe LLP

•**MCNAUGHTAN, Mr. Anthony Hugh, BSc ACA** *1986;* PricewaterhouseCoopers, 9th Floor East Tower, Abu Dhabi Trade Centre, PO Box 45263, ABU DHABI, UNITED ARAB EMIRATES.
MCNAUGHTON, Mr. Justin Niall, BA ACA *1999;* 106 Abbotsbury Gardens, PINNER, MIDDLESEX, HA5 1SU.
•**MCNAUGHTON, Mr. Robert Frederick, BSc FCA** *1978;* PKF (UK) LLP, Pannell House, 6 Queen Street, LEEDS, LS1 2TW.
•**MCNAUGHTON, Mr. Scott Roberton Goodwin, BSc FCA** *1999;* BDO LLP, 55 Baker Street, LONDON, W1U 7EU. See also BDO Stoy Hayward LLP
MCNAUGHTON, Mr. Stewart Cameron, BA ACA *1998;* 32 Corstorphine Hill Crescent, EDINBURGH, EH12 6LL.
MCNAY, Mr. Ross, BSc(Hons) ACA *2009;* Haregills Farm, Ecclefechan, LOCKERBIE, DUMFRIESSHIRE, DG11 3JJ.
•**MCNEAL, Mr. Timothy Robin, ACA** *1982;* Hardings, 6 Marsh Parade, NEWCASTLE, ST5 1DU.
MCNEE, Mr. Christopher John Forbes, FCA *1969;* Pentera Trust Co Ltd, PO Box 79, JERSEY, JE4 8PS.
MCNEE, Mrs. Wendy Margaret, LLB ACA *1998;* 56 Riber View Close, Tansley, MATLOCK, DERBYSHIRE, DE4 5HB.
MCNEECE, Mr. Paul Antony, BSc FCA *1986;* 141 Sheoak Road, BELAIR, SA 5052, AUSTRALIA.
MCNEELY, Mr. Gerard Martin, LLB ACA *2003;* Flat A, 42 Aberdeen Road, LONDON, N5 2XD.
MCNEIL, Mr. Andrew, ACA *1985;* 16 Lindale Avenue, Urmston, MANCHESTER, M41 5SB.
MCNEIL, Mrs. Catherine Jane, BSc ACA CTA *1986;* (Tax Fac), 13 Oakhill Road, ORPINGTON, BR6 0AE.
MCNEIL, Mr. Colin David, BSc ACA *2005;* with Ernst & Young LLP, 100 Barbirolli Square, MANCHESTER, M2 3EY.
MCNEIL, Mr. David, FCA *1971;* Route d'Hermance 127B, CH-1245 COLLONGE BELLERIVE, SWITZERLAND.
MCNEIL, Mr. David Keith, FCA *1968;* Littlethwaite, Low Lorton, COCKERMOUTH, CUMBRIA, CA13 0RW. (Life Member)
•**MCNEIL, Mr. David Kerr, BSc ACA CTA** *2000;* Deloitte LLP, 20 route de Pre-Bois, ICC Building H, 1215 GENEVA, SWITZERLAND. See also Deloitte & Touche LLP
MCNEIL, Miss. Hilary Claire, BA ACA *1999;* Sidings, 3 Dukes Ride, GERRARDS CROSS, BUCKINGHAMSHIRE, SL9 7LD.
MCNEIL, Mr. Ian Laurence Clark, BA FCA *1966;* La Fleur de Lys, 81140 ROUSSAYROLLES, FRANCE.
MCNEIL, Mr. Ian Robert, MBE JP FCA *1955;* (President 1991 - 1992) (Member of Council 1981 - 1996), 6 The Daisycroft, HENFIELD, WEST SUSSEX, BN5 9LH. (Life Member)
MCNEIL, Miss. Lois, BA ACA *2005;* 35 Stirling Crescent, Hedge End, SOUTHAMPTON, SO30 2SA.
•**MCNEIL, Miss. Lorna, BSc(Hons) ACA** *2000;* with Ernst & Young LLP, 1 Colmore Square, BIRMINGHAM, B4 6HQ.
MCNEILE, Mr. Robert John, BA FCA *1955;* Nonsuch Cottage, Bromham, CHIPPENHAM, SN15 2ED. (Life Member)
MCNEILL, Mrs. Alison Margaret, BA ACA *1994;* 14 Peppard Road, Maidenbower, CRAWLEY, RH10 7QS.
MCNEILL, Mr. Charles, BSc FCA *1985;* Level 10, 114 Albert Road, SOUTH MELBOURNE, VIC 3205, AUSTRALIA.
MCNEILL, Mr. Christopher James, BSc(Hons) ACA *2001;* 14/56 Harbour Street, MOSMAN, NSW 2088, AUSTRALIA.
MCNEILL, Mr. David Alan, MA FCA *1985;* 14 Thornwood Close, Thornhill, CARDIFF, CF14 9FE.
•**MCNEILL, Mr. Hugh, BSc FCA** *1986;* (Tax Fac), MN Accountants Limited, The Lilacs, West Hill Road North, South Wonston, WINCHESTER, HAMPSHIRE SO21 3HJ. See also MN Tax Consulltants Limited
•**MCNEILL, Mr. John, BA FCA** *1990;* 1 Grayling Road, Rosewood Park, GATESHEAD, NE11 9ND.
MCNEILL, Mr. John Christopher, BSc ACA *1987;* Department for Regional Development, Road Service, Clarence Court, 12-18 Adelaide Street, BELFAST, BT2 8GB.
MCNEILL, Mr. Jonathan Edwin, BSc ACA *1997;* Montana House, 63 Derby Square, Douglas, ISLE OF MAN, IM1 3LR.
MCNEILL, Mrs. Jovita Shirani, ACA *1988;* 10 Balcombe Court, DONVALE, VIC 3111, AUSTRALIA.
•**MCNEILL, Mr. Malcolm Gordon, FCA** *1974;* Court House, Hooe, BATTLE, EAST SUSSEX, TN33 9HJ.
MCNEILL, Mr. Philip, MA FCA CTA *1987;* (Tax Fac), Silverhill, ACHARACLE, ARGYLL, PH36 4JG.
MCNEILL, Mr. Sean Patrick, BA ACA *1997;* 5 Redwood Street, UPPER COOMERA, QLD 4209, AUSTRALIA.
MCNEILL, Mrs. Sheena Diane, MA ACA *1990;* Bottle House, Carringtons Road, Great Bromley, COLCHESTER, CO7 7XA.
MCNEILL, Mr. Stuart Graeme, BA ACA *1981;* 9 Hilberry Court, School Lane, BUSHEY, WD23 1BS.
MCNELLY, Mr. Nigel Peter, MA ACA *1983;* 71 Highbury New Park, LONDON, N5 2EU.
MCNELLY, Mr. Peter, FCA *1956;* 70 Ashley Gardens, Ambrosden Avenue, LONDON, SW1P 1QG. (Life Member)
MCNERNEY, Mrs. Gill, BSc ACA *2005;* 15 Tir Wat, Mynydd Isa, MOLD, CLWYD, CH7 6SD.
MCNICHOL, Mr. Adam Peter John, ACA *2009;* The Fruit Farm, Hawk Street, Bromham, CHIPPENHAM, WILTSHIRE, SN15 2HU.
MCNICHOL, George Alexander, Esq OBE FCA *1952;* 11 Edgewood, Ponteland, NEWCASTLE UPON TYNE, NE20 9RY. (Life Member)
MCNICHOLAS, Mr. David Anthony, BA ACA CF *1999;* APE Uplift 2nd Floor, West Wing, Diamond House, Thornes Moor Road, WAKEFIELD, WEST YORKSHIRE WF2 8PT.
MCNICHOLAS, Ms. Maria, ACA *1991;* 3 Salisbury Close, POTTERS BAR, EN6 5AX.
MCNICHOLAS, Mrs. Nicola Anne, BCom ACA *1996;* 101 Clybaun Heights, Knocknacarra, GALWAY, COUNTY GALWAY, IRELAND.
MCNICHOLL, Mr. Graham, BA(Hons) ACA *2010;* Flat 51, Flaxman Court, Flaxman Terrace, LONDON, WC1H 9AP.
•**MCNICHOLLS, Miss. Karen, BA(Econ) ACA** *1999;* Deloitte LLP, 2 New Street Square, LONDON, EC4A 3BZ. See also Deloitte & Touche LLP
MCNICOL, Mr. Ian Cairns, BSc FCA *1975;* 1 Oakhill Court, Oakhill Road, SURBITON, KT6 6EL.
MCNICOL, Miss. Jayne Susan, BA ACA *1991;* with Ernst & Young, Suite 200, Building 1, 1001 Page Mill Road, PALO ALTO, CA 94304 UNITED STATES.
•**MCNICOLL, Mr. Peter John, ACA** *1985;* Riverside Accountancy, 52 Ray Park Avenue, MAIDENHEAD, BERKSHIRE, SL6 8DX.
MCNIFF, Mr. Anthony John, LLB ACA *1992;* The Rectory Market Place, Colerne, CHIPPENHAM, SN14 8DF.
MCNIFF, Mr. John Joseph, FCA *1967;* The Cottage, 1 Carlisle Close, KINGSTON UPON THAMES, KT2 7AU.
MCNIFFE, Mr. John, LLB ACA *2001;* 23 Alanby Drive, BRADFORD, WEST YORKSHIRE, BD10 9JF.
MCNISH, Mr. Ivor, FCA *1959;* Harlaxton, 11 Lincoln Rd, Skellingthorpe, LINCOLN, LN6 5UT. (Life Member)
MCNISH, Mr. Michael Robin, BA ACA *1985;* 65 Chelsham Road, LONDON, SW4 6NN.
MCNULTY, Mr. Andrew James, BSc(Hons) ACA *2001;* 52 Kendal Avenue, MAPLEWOOD, NJ 07040-1143, UNITED STATES.
MCNULTY, Mr. Francis Joseph, MSc ACA CTA AITI *2002;* (Tax Fac), Bellkelly, Ogonnelloe, SCARRIFF, COUNTY CLARE, IRELAND.
MCNULTY, Miss. Kate Mary, ACA *2008;* 49 Dalewood, WELWYN GARDEN CITY, HERTFORDSHIRE, AL7 2JP.
MCNULTY, Mr. Nicholas Colin, BSc ACA *2006;* with Deloitte LLP, 2 New Street Square, LONDON, EC4A 3BZ.
MCNULTY, Mr. Paul Howard, BAcc ACA *1995;* 4 Dalesway, Guiseley, LEEDS, WEST YORKSHIRE, LS20 8JN.
•**MCNULTY, Mr. Peter, BSc ACA** *1994;* Hammond McNulty, Bank House, Market Square, CONGLETON, CW12 1ET.
MCNULTY, Mr. Peter Stephen Joseph, BA(Hons) ACA *2010;* Flat 8, St Catherines Church Apartments, Bridgefoot Street, DUBLIN 8, COUNTY DUBLIN, IRELAND.
MCNULTY, Mrs. Sarah Jane, BSc(Hons) ACA *2003;* 42 Park Parade, WHITLEY BAY, TYNE AND WEAR, NE26 1DX.
•**MCNULTY, Mrs. Wendy Jacqueline, BA FCA** *1991;* SB&P LLP, Oriel House, 2-8 Oriel Road, BOOTLE, MERSEYSIDE, L20 7EP. See also Satterthwaite Brooks & Pomfret LLP and SB&P Corporate Finance Ltd
MCNUTT, Mr. James John Robert, BA ACA *2003;* 16 Warley Dene, HALIFAX, WEST YORKSHIRE, HX2 7RS.
•**MCOWAT, Miss. Elizabeth, BA ACA** *1989;* LMAC LTD, Lower Ground Floor, 5 Brunswick Place, HOVE, EAST SUSSEX, BN3 1EA.
•**MCOWAT, Mr. Thomas Robin Hardy, FCA** *1965;* T.R.H. McOwat, 8 Armley Grange Drive, LEEDS, LS12 3QH.
MCOWEN, Miss. Anna Louise, BSc(Econ) FCA *1990;* 30 Hopton Crofts, LEAMINGTON SPA, WARWICKSHIRE, CV32 6NT.
MCPARLAND, Mr. Daniel John, ACA *2008;* Flat 3 Dane House, 8 Kinnaird Road, MANCHESTER, M20 4QL.
MCPARLAND, Mrs. Susanna Claire, BA(Hons) ACA *2007;* 49 Claudian Place, ST. ALBANS, HERTFORDSHIRE, AL3 4JG.
MCPARLIN, Ms. Gabrielle Joan, BSc ACA *1996;* with Deloitte LLP, PO Box 500, 2 Hardman Street, MANCHESTER, M60 2AT.
MCPARTLAN, Mr. Terence David, BSc ACA *1980;* 2 The Hornbeams, Hatherop, CIRENCESTER, GLOUCESTERSHIRE, GL7 3NA.
MCPARTLIN, Mr. Gregory John, LLB ACA *1998;* Petkovskovo Nabrezje 47, 1000 LJUBLJANA, SLOVENIA.
MCPARTLIN, Mr. Guy Christopher, BSc ACA *1998;* Bank of Bermuda, 6 Front Street, HAMILTON, BERMUDA.
MCPARTLIN, Mr. Paul Anthony, FCA *1967;* The Dene, 11 Cadehill Road, STOCKSFIELD, NE43 7PB.
MCPARTLIN, Mr. Robert, BSc ACA *2002;* Legal & General Assurance Society Ltd, Legal & General House, St. Monicas Road, Kingswood, TADWORTH, SURREY KT20 6EU.
MCPEAKE, Mrs. Amanda, BA ACA *1993;* Greenways, Elmgrove Road West, Hardwicke, GLOUCESTER, GL2 4PU.
MCPHAIL, Mr. Archie, FCA *1953;* 65 Stamford Road, Bowdon, ALTRINCHAM, WA14 2JJ. (Life Member)
MCPHAIL, Mr. Matthew Douglas, FCA *1962;* Farmton, AUCHTERARDER, PERTHSHIRE, PH3 1HZ.
•**MCPHAIL, Mr. Philip Anthony, ACA** *2002;* (Tax Fac), PMC Limited, 124 Main Street, Burley in Wharfedale, ILKLEY, WEST YORKSHIRE, LS29 7JP.
MCPHEE, Mrs. Clare Bridget, BSc ACA *1990;* 14 Kettlewell Close, Horsell, WOKING, GU21 4HZ.
MCPHEE, Mrs. Vanessa Lyndsay, BSc(Hons) ACA *2001;* 6 Arleston Drive, Wollaton, NOTTINGHAM, NG8 2FS.
MCPHEELY, Mr. Robert Craig, BSc ACA *1989;* PO Box 5309, COVENTRY, CV3 9FH.
MCPHERSON, Mrs. Annette Ruth, BSc ACA *1989;* nutleigh, Hervines Road, AMERSHAM, BUCKINGHAMSHIRE, HP6 5HS.
MCPHERSON, Mr. Duncan James, BA ACA *1994;* Mountmill Farm Stratford Road, Wicken, MILTON KEYNES, MK19 6DG.
MCPHERSON, Mr. Grant Alan, MSc ACA *1999;* 51 Waldron Road, LONDON, SW18 3TA.
MCPHERSON, Mr. Julian Andrew, BA ACA *1999;* 15 Curban Street, Balgowlah Heights, SYDNEY, NSW 2093, AUSTRALIA.
MCPHERSON, Mr. Keith, FCA *1968;* Southrise, 172 Hastings Road, BATTLE, TN33 0TW.
•**MCPHERSON, Mr. Keith Robert, FCA** *1967;* (Tax Fac), McPherson Accountancy Limited, 60 Chertsey Street, GUILDFORD, GU1 4HL.
MCPHERSON, Mr. Kemp Murray, ACA CA(SA) *2011;* 20 Wolseley Avenue, LONDON, SW19 8BQ.
MCPHERSON, Mrs. Lenka Claire, ACA *1999;* 15 Curban Street, BALGOWLAH HEIGHTS, NSW 2093, AUSTRALIA.
MCPHERSON, Mr. Neil Jonathan, ACA MAAT *1998;* Lilac Cottage, School Lane, Danehill, HAYWARDS HEATH, RH17 7JQ.
MCPHIE, Mr. Andrew Cameron, BA ACA *1999;* Flat 7 Wilton House, 6 Nottingham Road, SOUTH CROYDON, Surrey, CR2 6LN.
MCPHIE, Mr. Angus James, BEng ACA PGCE *1999;* 5 Lillian Road, LONDON, SW13 9JG.
MCPHIE, Mr. Iain Allan Hamish, FCA *1968;* Uppercot, Devon Road, SALCOMBE, TQ8 8HJ.
MCPHILLIPS, Mr. Stephen Robert, BA ACA *1992;* Gardrum, Greenhithe Terrace, Rumford, FALKIRK, FK2 0SR.
MCQUADE, Mrs. Alison Jane, BA ACA *1992;* 48 Velsheda Road, Shirley, SOLIHULL, B90 2JN.
MCQUADE, Mr. James Pascal, BSc ACA *1998;* European Court of Auditors, 12 Alcide de Gasperi, L1615 LUXEMBOURG, LUXEMBOURG.
MCQUAID, Mrs. Catherine, BSc ACA *1999;* The Coign, Bury Lane, Horsell, WOKING, SURREY, GU21 4RP.
MCQUAID, Mr. Joseph, BA ACA *1994;* with Ernst & Young LLP, Apex Plaza, Forbury Road, READING, RG1 1YE.
MCQUAID, Mrs. Nicola Helen, BA ACA *2006;* Apartment 601 The Gateway North, Crown Point Road, LEEDS, LS9 8BX.
•**MCQUATER, Mr. Alastair, BA FCA ATII** *1993;* (Tax Fac), Buzzacott LLP, 130 Wood Street, LONDON, EC2V 6DL.
MCQUATER, Mr. Andrew, FCA *1961;* Barnside, Milton, Dunscore, DUMFRIES, DG2 0UP. (Life Member)
MCQUATER, Mrs. Elizabeth Mary, BSc ACA *1989;* 22 Victor Road, WINDSOR, SL4 3JU.
MCQUATER, Mrs. Elizabeth Sarah, BA(Hons) ACA *2001;* 1 Horsell Grange, Kettlewell Hill, WOKING, GU21 4JA.
MCQUATTIE, Mr. Ian Frederick, BSc FCA *1973;* 49 The Avenue, Kew Gardens, RICHMOND, TW9 2AL. (Life Member)
MCQUEEN, Mr. Anthony Brian, FCA *1981;* Spinneybrook, 21 Huntley Drive, SOLIHULL, B91 3FL.
MCQUEEN, Mr. Colin John, BA ACA *1988;* 58 Abbots Green, Willington, CROOK, COUNTY DURHAM, DL15 0QZ.
MCQUEEN, Mr. James Fraser, BSc ACA CTA *1994;* Next Retail Ltd Desford Road, Enderby, LEICESTER, LE19 4AT.
•**MCQUEEN, Mr. Mark Philip, BSc ACA** *1997;* Deloitte LLP, Hill House, 1 Little New Street, LONDON, EC4A 3TR. See also Deloitte & Touche LLP
MCQUEEN, Miss. Sally Ann, LLB ACA ACCA *2002;* 4 Lastingham Road, LEEDS, LS13 1JU.
MCQUISTON, Mr. David Read, BA FCA *1985;* La Freziere, Route de Villefranche du Perigord, 47500 SAUVETERRE LA LEMANCE, FRANCE.
•**MCRAE, Mrs. Alison Margueretta, MA ACA** *1993;* A.M. Accounting Limited, 191A Finchampstead Road, WOKINGHAM, RG40 3HE.
MCRAE, Mr. Andrew James, BSc ACA *1985;* H C L Plc Greener House, 66-68 Haymarket, LONDON, SW1Y 4RF.
MCRAE, Mrs. Karen Susan, MA ACA *1989;* 5 Fallow Road, Crombie Meadow, Skene Westhill, ABERDEEN, AB32 6PT.
MCRITCHIE, Mr. Andrew Lloyd Anderson, BSc ACA *2007;* 84 Purves Road, LONDON, NW10 5TB.
MCRITCHIE, Mrs. Ruth Elizabeth, ACA *1990;* 9 Churchfarm Close, Yate, BRISTOL, BS37 5BZ.
MCROBERTS, Mr. Andrew James, BA ACA *1990;* 20 Barlow Fold Road, Romiley, STOCKPORT, CHESHIRE, SK6 4LH.
MCSHANE, Mrs. Leigh Janet, BA ACA *2008;* Downview, Princes Crescent, BRIGHTON, BN2 3RA.
MCSHANE, Mrs. Susan Jane, FCA *1976;* Finance Office, Leicester University, University Road, LEICESTER, LE1 7RH.
MCSHEAFFREY, Mr. Paul Kevin, BSc FCA *2000;* KPMG, 8/F Prince's Building, 10 Chater Road, CENTRAL, HONG KONG ISLAND, HONG KONG SAR.
MCSHEE, Mr. Ian, BA FCA *1996;* 33 Bray Road, GUILDFORD, GU2 7LH.
MCSHERA, Mr. Liam, ACA *2009;* Gostling Ltd, Unit 6, Acorn Business Park, Keighley Road, SKIPTON, NORTH YORKSHIRE BD23 2UE.
MCSHERRY, Mrs. Sarah Elaine, LLB ACA *2001;* 20 Digg Lane, WIRRAL, MERSEYSIDE, CH46 6AQ.
MCSORLEY, Mr. John, BSc ACA *2011;* 505 W 37th Street, Apartment 4003, NEW YORK, NY 10018, UNITED STATES.
MCSPARRON-EDWARDS, Ms. Allison Jane, BSc ACA *1982;* Consultrix, Bennath, Back Lane, Blunsdon, SWINDON, WILTSHIRE SN26 7BJ.
MCSWEENEY, Mr. David Keith, FCA *1983;* 42 Links Road, ASHTEAD, KT21 2HJ.
MCSWEENEY, Mr. James Noel, BA ACA *2001;* Glencree Heath Road, Woolpit, BURY ST. EDMUNDS, IP30 9QU.
MCSWEENEY, Mrs. Laura Claire, BSc ACA *2009;* Flat 2, 76 Osborne Road, WINDSOR, SL4 3EN.
MCSWEENEY, Miss. Louise Catherine Clare, BA ACA *1999;* Barclays Capital, 5 North Colonnade, Canary Wharf, LONDON, E14 4BB.
MCSWEENEY, Mr. Michael Joseph, BA ACA *1989;* Priory House, 12 Belle Vue Road, STROUD, GL5 1JT.
MCSWEENEY, Mrs. Ruth Mary Elizabeth, BA ACA *1992;* 49 Pewterspear Green Road, Appleton, WARRINGTON, WA4 5FE.
•**MCSWEENY, Mr. Alan John, FCA** *1982;* Nigel Webster & Co Ltd, 129 North Hill, PLYMOUTH, PL4 8JY.
MCTAGGART, Mr. John, FCA *1969;* 61 Lanercost Road, LONDON, SW2 3DR.
MCTAVISH, Mr. Alexander William John, MA ACA *2002;* 7 The Avenue, Old Windsor, WINDSOR, SL4 2RS.
•①**MCTEAR, Mr. Andrew Ian, FCA** *1986;* McTear Williams & Wood, 90 St Faiths Lane, NORWICH, NR1 1NE.
MCTEAR, Miss. Helen Elizabeth, BA ACA *2004;* balderton capital, 20 balderton street, LONDON, w1k 6tl.
•**MCTEAR, Mr. Robert James Fraser, FCA** *1976;* Humphrey & Co, 7-9 The Avenue, EASTBOURNE, EAST SUSSEX, BN21 3YA.
MCTERNAN, Mrs. Ann, BA ACA *1991;* Manor Farm House, Moor Road, North Owersby, MARKET RASEN, LINCOLNSHIRE, LN8 3PR.
MCTIERNAN, Dr. Michelle Maria, BSc ACA *2001;* 196 Sutherland Avenue, Maida Vale, LONDON, W9 1RX.

MCTURK, Mr. James Douglas, BA FCA *1977;* 44 Earswick Chase, Earswick, YORK, YO32 9FY.

MCVAY, Miss. Deborah Jane, BSc ACA *1999;* Kenneth Easby Llp Trinity House, Northallerton Business Park Thurston Road, NORTHALLERTON, NORTH YORKSHIRE, DL6 2NA.

MCVEIGH, Mr. Michael Patrick, ACA *1982;* 1 Temple Close, BUCKINGHAM, MK18 1JB.

•MCVEIGH, Mr. Peter William, BSc FCA *1980;* (Tax Fac), M D Coxey & Co Limited, 25 Grosvenor Road, WREXHAM, CLWYD, LL11 1BT.

MCVEIGH, Miss. Wendy Margaret, BSc ACA *2006;* with KPMG, Stokes House, 17-25 College Square East, BELFAST, BT1 6DH.

•MCVIETY, Mr. Alan, FCA *1979;* Dodd & Co., Clint Mill, Cornmarket, PENRITH, CA11 7HW.

MCVITTIE, Mr. David, BSc FCA *1978;* 15 Lauderdale Mansions, Lauderdale Road Maida Vale, LONDON, W9 1LX.

MCWALTER, Miss. Alison, BSc ACA *1995;* 6th Floor Hammer House, 113-117 Wardour Street, LONDON, W1F 0UN.

MCWHINNIE, Mr. Andrew Colin, MA ACA *1984;* 34 Bishops Avenue, RANDWICK, NSW 2031, AUSTRALIA.

MCWHINNIE, Mr. Colin David, FCA *1962;* Unit 3, 18-30, Sir Leslie Thiess Drive, TOWNSVILLE, QLD 4810, AUSTRALIA. (Life Member)

MCWHIRTER, Mr. Colin Andrew, BSc FCA *1980;* Andrew McWhirter Associates, 51 Riverdale, Wrecclesham, FARNHAM, SURREY, GU10 4PJ.

MCWHIRTER, Mrs. Katherine Juliet, BA ACA *1992;* Stonehaven, Petworth Road, Wormley, GODALMING, SURREY, GU8 5TR.

•MCWHIRTER, Mr. Paul Richard, FCA *1986;* The McWhirter Partnership Limited, 1 Foley Place, Common Road, Claygate, ESHER, SURREY KT10 0HU.

MCWHIRTER, Mr. Simon Andrew Platt, BSc ACA *1992;* U B S AG, 100 Liverpool Street, LONDON, EC2M 2RH.

MCWILLIAM, Miss. Denise, BA ACA *1997;* 27 Ashen Grove, LONDON, SW19 8BW.

MCWILLIAMS, Mrs. Beverley Rachel, ACA *2001;* 12 Thiele Crescent, WEST LAKES SHORE, SA 5020, AUSTRALIA.

MCWILLIAMS, Ms. Deborah Jane, BSc ACA CTA *1996;* 12 Daneshill, REDHILL, RH1 2DN.

MCWILLIAMS, Mr. Derek John, FCA *1977;* 2 Tudor Rose Close, COLCHESTER, CO3 5SD.

MCWILLIAMS, Mrs. Joanne Kathleen, RD BA ACA *2005;* 19 Princess Avenue, WARRINGTON, WA1 3PE.

MCWILLIAMS, Mrs. Karen Samantha, BA(Hons) ACA *2003;* 18 Hillside Circuit, CRANEBROOK, NSW 2749, AUSTRALIA.

MCWILLIAMS, Mr. Owen Anthony, BA(Hons) ACA CTA *2001;* G E Commercial Finance Ltd, Enterprise House, Bancroft Road, REIGATE, SURREY, RH2 7RT.

MCWILLIAMS, Mr. Terence, FCA *1972;* 39 Lynch Road, FARNHAM, GU9 8BT.

MD SALLEH, Mr. Ahmad Zakri, ACA CFA CA(AUS) *2008;* Level 81 Tower 1, Petronas Twin Towers, Kuala Lumpur City Centre, 50088 KUALA LUMPUR, FEDERAL TERRITORY, MALAYSIA.

MDLALOSE, Mr. Selusiwe, ACA *2006;* 6 Cooil Farrane, Douglas, ISLE OF MAN, IM2 1NX.

MEACHAM, Mr. Maxwell Brian, FCA *1953;* 13 Reading Close, Washingborough, LINCOLN, LN4 1SL. (Life Member)

MEACHEN, Mr. Mark, BA(Hons) ACA *2000;* with Deutsche Bank AG, CIB Global Markets, Winchester House, 1 Great Winchester Street, LONDON, EC2N 2DB.

•MEACHER, Mr. Paul Frederick, FCA *1986;* Fiander Tovell LLP, Stag Gates House, 63/64 The Avenue, SOUTHAMPTON, SO17 1XS.

•MEACHER-JONES, Mr. David Richard, BA FCA *1996;* Meacher-Jones & Company Limited, 6 St. Johns Court, Vicars Lane, CHESTER, CH1 1QE.

MEACOCK, Mr. Donald Henry Harold, FCA *1950;* 2 Persfield Close, Ewell, EPSOM, SURREY, KT17 1PQ. (Life Member)

MEACOCK, Mr. Henry James, BSc ACA *2005;* 105 Chestnut Drive, SALE, CHESHIRE, M33 4HS.

MEACOCK, Mr. Matthew William, ACA *2009;* 95 Ham Green, Pill, BRISTOL, BS20 0HF.

•MEAD, Mr. Andrew David, MBA BSc FCA *1993;* with KPMG LLP, Aquis Court, 31 Fishpool Street, ST. ALBANS, HERTFORDSHIRE, AL3 4RF.

MEAD, Mrs. Anne Elizabeth, BSc ACA *1985;* with Coulsons, 2 Belgrave Crescent, SCARBOROUGH, NORTH YORKSHIRE, YO11 1UB.

MEAD, Mr. Anthony Frederick John, BSc FCA *1967;* Wykeham Cottage, Southdown Road, Woldingham, CATERHAM, CR3 7DP.

MEAD, Mr. Anthony John, RD BA FCA DipRS *1965;* 10 Castle Street, TOTNES, DEVON, TQ9 5NU. (Life Member)

MEAD, Mr. Brian Leonard, FCA *1967;* The Haven, 5 Sylvan Lane, Hamble, SOUTHAMPTON, SO31 4QG.

•MEAD, Mrs. Carol Anne, FCA *1975;* (Tax Fac), Tittensor & Co LLP, Fourwinds, Wengeo Lane, WARE, HERTFORDSHIRE, SG12 0EH.

MEAD, Mr. Colin, FCA *1951;* Bwthyn Yr Abad, Tyddyn Mawr, TALYBONT, GWYNEDD, LL43 2BZ. (Life Member)

•MEAD, Mr. Damien Joseph, ACA *1983;* 62 Birtles Road, MACCLESFIELD, CHESHIRE, SK10 3JQ.

MEAD, Mr. David Harry, BA ACA *1989;* Willowbank, Pirton, WORCESTER, WR8 9ED.

•MEAD, Mr. David Henry, BSc FCA *1984;* (Tax Fac), PKF (UK) LLP, Anstey Park House, Anstey Road, ALTON, HAMPSHIRE, GU34 2RL.

•MEAD, Mr. David John, ACA *1991;* Goodier Smith and Watts Limited, Devonshire House, Manor Way, BOREHAMWOOD, HERTFORDSHIRE, WD6 1QQ.

MEAD, Mr. Derrick Frank, LVO FCA *1955;* Pinhaye, Nottingham Road South, Heronsgate, RICKMANSWORTH, WD3 5DL. (Life Member)

MEAD, Mrs. Diana Herietta Irene, BA ACA DChA *1985;* All Souls College, High Street, OXFORD, OX1 4AL.

MEAD, Mr. Howard Ioan, BSc ACA *2010;* 65 Watkins Drive, Prestwich, MANCHESTER, M25 0DR.

MEAD, Mr. John Richard, BA ACA *1991;* 10 Fosseway, Clandown, RADSTOCK, BA3 3BL.

MEAD, Mr. Jonathan Richard, BA ACA *1989;* The Capital Markets Company, Broadgate West, 9 Appold Street, LONDON, EC2A 2AP.

MEAD, Mr. Jonathan William, FCA *1974;* 18 Lister Drive, NORTHAMPTON, NN4 9XE.

MEAD, Mr. Julian James, MA ACA *1985;* South West Water Limited, Peninsula House, Rydon Lane, EXETER, EX2 7HR.

MEAD, Miss. Lindsay Kirk, BSc ACA *1986;* 83 Canon Street, WINCHESTER, SO23 9JQ.

MEAD, Mr. Matthew, BA ACA *1989;* Woodlands Lodge, 75 Kiln Ride, Finchampstead, WOKINGHAM, BERKSHIRE, RG40 3PJ.

•MEAD, Mr. Michael John, FCA *1985;* Jervis Limited, 20 Harborough Road, Kingsthorpe, NORTHAMPTON, NN2 7AZ.

•MEAD, Mrs. Pearl Lesley, FCA *1985;* (Tax Fac), Metherell Gard Ltd, Burn View, BUDE, CORNWALL, EX23 8BX. See also M G Trustees Ltd

MEAD, Mr. Peter Frederic, FCA *1963;* 5 Rossendale Close, Worle, WESTON-SUPER-MARE, BS22 9HA. (Life Member)

MEAD, Mr. Philip Charles, ACA *1990;* 8 Woodside Way, Linslade, LEIGHTON BUZZARD, LU7 2PN.

MEAD, Mr. Richard, BA(Hons) ACA *2001;* 35 Woodsland Road, HASSOCKS, WEST SUSSEX, BN6 8HG.

MEAD, Mr. Richard Barwick, MA FCA CF *1972;* Clayfurlong House, Kemble, CIRENCESTER, GL7 6BS.

MEAD, Mr. Richard David William, MSc BA FCA *1970;* 294 Erskine Road, STAMFORD, CT 06903, UNITED STATES.

MEAD, Miss. Sally Anne, BSc ACA *1988;* Genworth Financial, Building 11, Chiswick Park, 566 Chiswick High Road, LONDON, W4 5XR.

MEAD, Mr. Stefan James, BA(Hons) ACA *1993;* 82a Aslett Street, LONDON, SW18 2BQ.

MEAD, Mr. Stephen, BSc ACA *1991;* Eden Glen 224 Eden Way, BECKENHAM, KENT, BR3 3DT.

•MEAD, Mr. Warren William, BA ACA *1998;* KPMG LLP, 15 Canada Square, LONDON, E14 5GL.

MEADE, Mr. Eric Cubitt, FCA *1957;* (Member of Council 1969 - 1979), 56 Hurlingham Court, Ranelagh Gardens, LONDON, SW6 3UP. (Life Member)

MEADE, Mr. Peter, FCA *1954;* Oak Lawn, 18 Sandown Road, ESHER, KT10 9TU. (Life Member)

MEADE, Miss. Sarah, ACA *2010;* 9 Hipley Court, Warren Road, GUILDFORD, SURREY, GU1 2HT.

•MEADER, Mr. James Edmund, ACA *1998;* Ernst & Young LLP, 1 More London Place, LONDON, SE1 2AF. See also Ernst & Young Europe LLP

•MEADES, Mrs. Karen Lesley, ACA *1983;* Karen Meades, The Old Rectory, Chipping Warden, BANBURY, OX17 1LR.

•MEADES, Mr. Patrick Andrew, BSc ACA *1993;* with PricewaterhouseCoopers LLP, 101 Barbirolli Square, Lower Mosley Street, MANCHESTER, M2 3PW.

MEADOWCROFT, Mr. James Robert, ACA *2009;* 25 Avon Road, Hale, ALTRINCHAM, CHESHIRE, WA15 0LB.

MEADOWCROFT, Mr. John, FCA *1964;* 1 Park Terrace, Burrows Road Melton, WOODBRIDGE, SUFFOLK, IP12 1GP.

MEADOWCROFT, Mr. John Boyne, BA ACA *1998;* Fuller Smith & Turner Plc, Griffin Brewery, Chiswick Lane South, LONDON, W4 2QB.

MEADOWCROFT, Mr. Robin, FCA *1970;* 9 Cedar Drive, Urmston, MANCHESTER, M41 9HY.

MEADOWS, Mr. Andrew Christopher Ainsworth, BSc FCA *1980;* 5 Highcroft Court, Bookham, LEATHERHEAD, KT23 3QU.

•MEADOWS, Mr. Anthony Kenneth, FCA *1976;* AKM Consulting, PO Box 84, LEWES, EAST SUSSEX, BN8 4XB.

MEADOWS, Mr. Arnold Stephen, BA FCA *1976;* 76 Brighton Road, ATLANTA, GA 30309, UNITED STATES.

MEADOWS, Mr. Christopher John, BSc ACA *1992;* 5 Mary's Close, Wymeswold, LOUGHBOROUGH, LE12 6TH.

•MEADOWS, Mr. David, BA FCA *1999;* Bourne & Co, 6 Lichfield Street, BURTON-ON-TRENT, DE14 3RD.

MEADOWS, Mrs. Emma, BSc ACA *2006;* 9 Red Robin Close, Tharston, NORWICH, NR15 2ZD.

MEADOWS, Mrs. Fiona Alison, BA ACA *1993;* 5 Mary's Close, Wymeswold, LOUGHBOROUGH, LE12 6TH.

MEADOWS, Mr. Graham John, ACA *1982;* Farramere, Woodwards Close, BURGESS HILL, WEST SUSSEX, RH15 0DS.

MEADOWS, Mr. Haydn Clive, BA ACA *1991;* PO Box 107, HUA HIN 77110, THAILAND.

MEADOWS, Mr. Jeremy Philip William, ACA *1991;* Royal Bank of Scotland, 2nd Floor, 125 Colmore Row, BIRMINGHAM, B3 3AE.

MEADOWS, Mrs. Julie Marie, BSc ACA *1996;* Camm View, Sheep Hill Lane, Clayton-Le-Woods, CHORLEY, PR6 7ER.

MEADOWS, Mrs. Louise Kay, ACA *2008;* 14 London Road, BUNTINGFORD, HERTFORDSHIRE, SG9 9JN.

•MEADOWS, Mr. Matthew James, BSc(Hons) ACA *2002;* Kingston Smith LLP, Devonshire House, 60 Goswell Road, LONDON, EC1M 7AD. See also Kingston Smith Limited Liability Partnership, Devonshire Corporate Services LLP, Kingston Smith Consulting LLP and Devonshire Corporate Finance Limited

MEADOWS, Mrs. Michelle, BA ACA *1998;* 25 Cambridge Park, TWICKENHAM, TW1 2JH.

•①MEADOWS, Mr. Paul James, BA(Hons) ACA *2001;* with Deloitte LLP, 4 Brindley Place, BIRMINGHAM, B1 2HZ.

MEADOWS, Miss. Radhika Yasmin, BA ACA *1999;* 4 Larchvale Court, Westmoreland Drive, SUTTON, SURREY, SM2 6AN.

•MEADOWS, Mr. Richard Carl, BA FCA *1988;* Whiting & Partners, 12/13 The Crescent, WISBECH, PE13 1EP.

MEADOWS, Miss. Sarah, BSc(Econ) ACA *2010;* Flat 6, 105 Kingston Road, TAUNTON, SOMERSET, TA2 7SP.

MEADOWS, Mrs. Sarah Claudine, BA ACA *1991;* 39 Quaker Road, Princeton Junction, PRINCETON, NJ 08550, UNITED STATES.

MEADOWS, Mrs. Sarah Sian, BA ACA CTA *2001;* G K N Group Services Ltd, PO Box 55, REDDITCH, B98 0TL.

MEADOWS, Mr. Simon Nicholas, MEng ACA *1999;* G K N Automotive Ltd, PO Box 4128, REDDITCH, WORCESTERSHIRE, B98 0WR.

•MEADOWS, Mr. Thomas Rory St John, BSc ACA *1990;* (Tax Fac), Steele Robertson Goddard, 28 Ely Place, LONDON, EC1N 6AA.

MEADOWS, Mr. William John, FCA *1973;* 29 Mount Close, Pound Hill, CRAWLEY, RH10 7EF. (Life Member)

MEADOWS, Mr. Zek, BSc ACA *2005;* 9 Red Robin Close, Tharston, NORWICH, NR15 2ZD.

MEADS, Mrs. Alison Jane, MA ACA *1995;* 631 South Lincoln Street, HINSDALE, IL 60521, UNITED STATES.

MEADS, Mr. Colin, BA ACA *1988;* 16 Pond Lane, Chalfont St Peter, GERRARDS CROSS, SL9 9HZ.

MEADS, Mr. Ivan Peter, BSc FCA *1995;* 631 S Lincoln St, HINSDALE, IL 60521, UNITED STATES.

MEADS, Mr. Paul Simon, BSc(Hons) ACA *2004;* 6211 Rosebriar Lane, CHARLOTTE, NC 28277, UNITED STATES.

MEADS, Mr. Warren Dennis, FCA *1993;* 270 High Street, Boston Spa, WETHERBY, LS23 6AJ.

•MEAGER, Mr. Colin Grant, BSc FCA *1975;* Colin Meager & Co Limited, 32-35 Hall Street, BIRMINGHAM, B18 6BS.

•MEAGER, Mr. Graham Stephen, FCA *1985;* Graham Meager, 12 Wendover Close, ST. ALBANS, HERTFORDSHIRE, AL4 9JW.

•MEAGHER, Mrs. Hayley Ann, ACA *2009;* Butlers Financial Limited, 10 Dobsons Close, RAYLEIGH, ESSEX, SS6 7NZ.

MEAGHER, Mr. John-Paul, ACA *2010;* 10 Havre Des Pas Gardens, St. Helier, JERSEY, JE2 4PU.

MEAKIN, Mr. Alan Mark, ACA *1988;* 4 Crescent Close, STOCKPORT, CHESHIRE, SK3 8SH.

MEAKIN, Mr. Alexander James, ACA *2007;* 43 Westcliff Gardens, Appleton, WARRINGTON, WA4 5FQ.

MEAKIN, Miss. Annabel Daisy, ACA *2008;* 9 Dorlcote Road, LONDON, SW18 3RT.

•MEAKIN, Mr. Brian, FCA *1962;* Brian Meakin, Ward Cottage, 83 Main Street, Papplewick, NOTTINGHAM, NG15 8FE.

•MEAKIN, Mr. George Robert, FCA *1975;* Hextall Meakin Limited, Argon House, Argon Mews, LONDON, SW6 1BJ.

MEAKIN, Mr. Glenn, FCA *1973;* with Walkers Accountants Limited, 16-18 Devonshire Street, KEIGHLEY, WEST YORKSHIRE, BD21 2DG.

MEAKIN, Mr. John David, MA FCA *1964;* 7 Park Avenue, East Sheen, LONDON, SW14 8AT.

•MEAKIN, Mr. Michael Tony, FCA *1974;* Clement Keys, 39/40 Calthorpe Road, Edgbaston, BIRMINGHAM, B15 1TS.

MEAKIN, Mr. Nigel Dominic, BSc FCA *1992;* TD Waterhouse Tower, 79 Wellington Street, Suite 2010, TORONTO M5K 1G8, ON, CANADA.

MEAKIN, Mr. Richard John, BA(Hons) ACA *2004;* 142 Argyle Street, CAMBRIDGE, CB1 3LS.

•MEAKIN, Mr. Rolf Erik, MA FCA *1988;* PricewaterhouseCoopers LLP, 7 More London Riverside, LONDON, SE1 2RT. See also PricewaterhouseCoopers

MEAKIN, Mr. Simon Alexander, BA ACA *1991;* 52 Barrow Road, Burton-on-the-Wolds, LOUGHBOROUGH, LEICESTERSHIRE, LE12 5TB.

MEAKIN, Mr. Simon Andrew, BA(Econ) ACA *1997;* 7 Penrith Road, NEW MALDEN, SURREY, KT3 3QR.

MEAKIN, Mr. William John, BSc ACA *1982;* 39 Kings Road, Long Ditton, SURBITON, SURREY, KT6 5JE.

MEAKING, Mrs. Fiona Baden, BA ACA *1997;* Stoke Hill House, 10 Warminster Road, Limpley Stoke, BATH, BA2 7GL.

MEAKINGS, Mr. Kevin John, ACA *1981;* 4876 Northwood Place, WEST VANCOUVER V7S 3C4, BC, CANADA.

•MEALEY, Mr. Matthew Cornelius, BA ACA *1996;* Ernst & Young LLP, 1 More London Place, LONDON, SE1 2AF. See also Ernst & Young Europe LLP

MEALOR, Dr. Simon Evan, ACA *2003;* 15 Westridge Avenue, Purley On Thames, READING, RG8 8DE.

MEANLEY, Mr. Martin Peter, BSc ACA *1988;* Highlands, 7 Ridgegate Close, REIGATE, RH2 0HT.

MEANOCK, Mr. Tim Ian, BA ACA *2006;* Caird Capital, Pegasus House, 37-43 Sackville Street, LONDON, W1S 3DL.

MEANWELL, Mr. David Robert, BSc ACA *1982;* Xerox Limited, Riverview House, Oxford Road, UXBRIDGE, UB8 1HS.

MEAR, Mr. Donald Robert, BA FCA *1962;* Long Acre, Hookwood Park, OXTED, RH8 0SQ. (Life Member)

MEARA, Mrs. Sarah Rebecca Denman, BA ACA *1996;* 1 Pell Court, Wooldale Road, HOLMFIRTH, HD9 1QZ.

•MEARDON, Mr. Edward Roy, ACA *2000;* R T Marke & Co Limited, 69 High Street, BIDEFORD, DEVON, EX39 2AT.

MEARDON, Miss. Fiona Jean, ACA *2006;* R T Marke & Co, 69 High Street, BIDEFORD, DEVON, EX39 2AT.

MEARING-SMITH, Mr. Nicholas Paul, BSc FCA *1974;* 9 Clonmore Street, LONDON, SW18 5EU.

MEARNS, Mr. Alastair Richard, MA FCA *1985;* Howes Percival Oxford House, Cliftonville, NORTHAMPTON, NN1 5PN.

MEARNS, Mr. Mark Justin, BSc ACA *2004;* 60 Mayfair Gardens, SOUTHAMPTON, SO15 2TW.

MEARS, Mr. Alan Vincent, FCA *1983;* 31 Chigwell Rise, CHIGWELL, IG7 6AQ.

MEARS, Mr. Alex Benjamin Albert, FCA *1953;* 10 Old Brewery Lane, HENLEY-ON-THAMES, OXFORDSHIRE, RG9 2DE. (Life Member)

MEARS, Mr. Andrew Simon, BSc ARCS FCA *1990;* 901 Banbury Ct, MCLEAN, VA 22102-1301, UNITED STATES.

MEARS, Mr. Clive Stephen, FCA *1950;* 46 High View Road, South Woodford, LONDON, E18 2HJ. (Life Member)

MEARS, Mr. David, BA ACA *1988;* Spillers of Chard Ltd, The Aga Cooker Centre, Leach Road, Chard Business Park, CHARD, SOMERSET TA20 1FA.

MEARS, Mr. Gary Edward, ACA *2008;* Flat 32 St. Asaphs Court, St. Asaph Road, LONDON, SE4 2EE.
MEARS, Mr. Geoffrey Robert, FCA *1975;* Venon Educational Trust, Danes Hill School, Leatherhead Road, Oxshott, LEATHERHEAD, SURREY KT22 0JG.
•**MEARS, Mr. Harry Edward, MA ACA** *1991;* with KPMG LLP, Dukes Keep, Marsh Lane, SOUTHAMPTON, HAMPSHIRE, SO14 3EX.
MEARS, Mr. John William Andrew, FCA *1965;* Fairfield, Woodpecker Lane, Newdigate, DORKING, SURREY, RH5 5DT.
MEARS, Mrs. Julie Anne, ACA *1993;* 87 Junction Road, ANDOVER, SP10 3JB.
MEARS, Mrs. Kristin Astrid, BCom ACA *1993;* 901 Banbury Court, MCLEAN, VA 22102-1301, UNITED STATES.
MEARS, Miss. Lucy Anne, BA(Hons) ACA *2009;* 11 Hildenfields, TONBRIDGE, TN10 3DQ.
•**MEARS, Mr. Martin Edward, FCA** *1978;* Peyton Tyler Mears, Middleborough House, 16 Middleborough, COLCHESTER, CO1 1QT.
MEARS, Mr. Paul Anthony, BSc ACA *1993;* 16A Tower 1 Bel Air on The Peak 8 Bel Air Peak Avenue, POK FU LAM, HONG KONG SAR.
MEARS, Mr. Peter, ACA *2011;* Baker Tilly, 1210 Centre Park Square, WARRINGTON, WA1 1RU.
MEARS, Mr. Richard Paul, BA FCA AMCT *1986;* T3 Enterprises Ltd, 7 Hillier Road, GUILDFORD, SURREY, GU1 2JG.
MEARS, Mr. Robert John, BSc ACA *1992;* 36 Lambert Road, Finchley, LONDON, N12 9ES.
MEARS, Mr. Roger William, BSc FCA *1975;* 25 Fairwood Court, Fairlop Road, Leytonstone, LONDON, E11 1BJ.
MEARS, Mr. Russell Andrew John, BA ACA *1992;* Freightliner Ltd, 1 Eversholt Street, LONDON, NW1 2FL.
MEARZA, Mr. Abdul Wahid Shearzad, FCA *1977;* PO Box 102928, DUBAI, UNITED ARAB EMIRATES.
•**MEASURES, Mrs. Amanda Jane, BSc FCA** *1991;* A J Measures, 157-197 Buckingham Palace Road, LONDON, SW1W 9SP.
MEASURES, Mr. Michael Geoffrey, FCA *1974;* Hideaway House, Headley Hill Road, Headley, BORDON, GU35 8DS.
MEASURES, Ms. Nicola Ann, BA ACA *1996;* 63 Rances Lane, WOKINGHAM, BERKSHIRE, RG40 2LG.
MEASURES, Mr. Paul Steven, BSc ACA *2002;* Punch Taverns Ltd Jubilee House, Second Avenue Centrum One Hundred, BURTON-ON-TRENT, DE14 2WF.
MEATYARD, Mr. George Anthony, FCA *1963;* Ivy House Farm, Chapel Lane, Rolleston on Dove, BURTON-ON-TRENT, DE13 9AG.
MECKLENBURGH, Mr. Malcolm Leslie Gover, FCA *1964;* Seaward Cottage, 25 Seaward Avenue, NEW MILTON, HAMPSHIRE, BH25 7HL.
MECKLENBURGH, Mr. Richard Niall, BA ACA *1996;* Vordere Dorfstrasse 3, 8803 RUSCHLIKON, SWITZERLAND.
MECREDY, Mr. Mark Richard, MA ACA *1982;* 9 Little Parks, Holt, TROWBRIDGE, BA14 6QR.
•**MEDAK, Mr. Timothy Michael, BSc FCA** *1990;* Ernst & Young LLP, 1 More London Place, LONDON, SE1 2AF. See also Ernst & Young Europe LLP
MEDANY, Ms. Jane Susan, BSc ACA *1997;* B A C S Drake House, Homestead Road, RICKMANSWORTH, HERTFORDSHIRE, WD3 1FX.
MEDANY, Mrs. Rita Harpreet Kaur, ACA *1993;* 4 Evesham Green, AYLESBURY, BUCKINGHAMSHIRE, HP19 9RX.
•**MEDAYIL, Mr. Roy Joseph, BSc FCA** *1991;* Roy Joseph & Company Limited, 19 Bradmore Green, Brookmans Park, HATFIELD, HERTFORDSHIRE, AL9 7QR.
MEDAZOUMIAN, Mr. Garabed Shant, BA FCA *1988;* Grove End Housing, Grove End Gardens, 33 Grove End Road, LONDON, NW8 9LN.
MEDCALF, Mr. Jonathan Russell, MA ACA *1998;* Citigroup, BL09-08, 33 Canada Square, Canary Wharf, LONDON, E14 5LB.
MEDCALF, Mr. Kevin John, BSc ACA *1986;* Cheshire Building Society, Head Office, Castle Street, MACCLESFIELD, CHESHIRE, SK11 6AF.
MEDCALF, Mr. Richard John, FCA *1974;* 26 Wansfell Gardens, Thorpe Bay, SOUTHEND-ON-SEA, SS1 3SW.
•**MEDCALF, Mr. Tony, BSc ACA** *1995;* Moore and Smalley LLP, Richard House, 9 Winckley Square, PRESTON, PR1 3HP.
MEDDICK, Mr. Neil Leighton, ACA *1993;* Hilltop, 5a Roundabout Lane, WELWYN, AL6 0TH.
MEDDINGS, Mr. Brian John, FCA *1974;* Well Garden Cottage, Bell Green Lane, Kings Norton, BIRMINGHAM, B38 0EN.
MEDDINGS, Mr. David William, FCA *1969;* Niton Partners Llp, 20 Eastcheap, LONDON, EC3M 1EB.
MEDDINGS, Mr. Peter Mckenzie, BCom FCA *1973;* WJ Meddings (Holdings) Ltd, Kingsley Close, East Way, Lee Mill Industrial Estate, IVYBRIDGE, DEVON PL21 9LL.
MEDDINGS, Mr. Richard Henry, MA ACA *1984;* Downgate, Silverden Lane, Sandhurst, CRANBROOK, KENT, TN18 5NU.
MEDDINGS, Mr. William Andrew John, BA ACA *2007;* 11 Bear Hill, Alvechurch, BIRMINGHAM, B48 7JX.
MEDHURST, Mr. Nigel Brian Stephens, MA FCA *1993;* Buckleswood East Grinstead Road, North Chailey, LEWES, EAST SUSSEX, BN8 4JA.
MEDHURST, Mr. Paul Ronald, BA ACA *1989;* 7 Hethersett Close, REIGATE, RH2 0HQ.
MEDHURST, Mr. Rex Gordon, FCA *1953;* Holly Cottage, Smithy Lane, NEW MILTON, HAMPSHIRE, BH25 5TF. (Life Member)
MEDHURST, Mrs. Sarah Elizabeth, BSc ACA *2002;* 6 Butler Road, BAGSHOT, SURREY, GU19 5QF.
MEDHURST, Mr. Scott, ACA *2010;* 115 Bradbourne Vale Road, SEVENOAKS, KENT, TN13 3DJ.
MEDICI, Mr. Noel, BSc ACA *1986;* 38 Longdown Lane North, EPSOM, KT17 3JQ.
MEDINE, Mr. Michael Sinclair, ACA *2008;* 1 Clare Court, NORTH BERWICK, EAST LOTHIAN, EH39 4BZ.
MEDLAM, Miss. Florence Livia, BA ACA *2007;* Moore Stephens, 150 Aldersgate Street, LONDON, EC1A 4AB.
MEDLAM, Mr. Jonathan Robert, MA ACA MCT *1986;* 20 Ashchurch Park Villas, LONDON, W12 9SP.
MEDLAND, Mr. Anthony Edwin, MA FCA *1970;* Rodney House, 133 Farleigh Road, Backwell, BRISTOL, BS48 3PN.
•**MEDLAND, Mr. David Arthur, FCA** *1971;* 2 Castleton Court, 4/5 Cleveland Gardens, LONDON, W2 6HA.
MEDLEY, Dr. Alice Jane, ACA *2010;* 4 Graftons, The Avenue, Christs Hospital, HORSHAM, WEST SUSSEX, RH13 0LU.
MEDLEY, Mr. Guy Blake, ACA *1993;* Lovell Partnership Ltd, 15-17 The Crescent, LEATHERHEAD, KT22 8DY.
MEDLEY, Miss. Jane Louise, ACA *2010;* 28 South Edge, SHIPLEY, WEST YORKSHIRE, BD18 4RA.
MEDLEY, Mrs. Lucy Emma, BSc ACA *2007;* with Muras Baker Jones, Regent House, Bath Avenue, WOLVERHAMPTON, WV1 4EG.
MEDLEY, Mr. Richard James, BSc FCA *1992;* International Power plc, Senator House, 85 Queen Victoria Street, LONDON, EC4V 4DP.
MEDLEY, Mrs. Sally Michelle, BA ACA *2008;* 16 Gaddesden Crescent, Wavendon Gate, MILTON KEYNES, MK7 7SG.
MEDLICOTT, Mr. Mark Keith, BA(Hons) ACA *2001;* 41 Westwood Drive, Rubery Rednal, BIRMINGHAM, B45 9WF.
MEDLICOTT, Mrs. Sandra Kay, BSc ACA *1987;* 43 Norwood Drive, BELFAST, BT4 2EB.
MEDLICOTT, Mr. Steven, BA ACA *1992;* 8 Frenchay Road, OXFORD, OX2 6TG.
MEDLICOTT, Mr. William Jonathan, MA ACA *1985;* I T V Plc, 200 Gray's Inn Road, LONDON, WC1X 8HF.
MEDLOCK, Mr. Charles Richard Kenneth, BA FCA *1985;* Littlebrook House Earleydene, ASCOT, BERKSHIRE, SL5 9JY.
MEDLOCK, Mr. Daniel, BSc(Hons) ACA *2011;* Flat 17, Eagle Works West, 56 Quaker Street, LONDON, E1 6ST.
•**MEDLYN, Mrs. Claire Francoise, FCA** *1981;* Resource Revision S.A.R.L, 36 Rue Gabriel Lippmann, L-1943 LUXEMBOURG, LUXEMBOURG.
MEDORA, Mr. Cyrus Keki, BA ACA *1982;* 147 Duchess Avenue, SINGAPORE 269169, SINGAPORE.
MEDORA, Mr. Sammy Phiroze, FCA *1978;* KPMG, Lodha Excelus, Apollo Mills Compound, NM Joshi Marg, Mahalaxmi, MUMBAI 400011 INDIA.
MEDORA, Mr. Xerxes Jamshid, BA(Hons) ACA *2003;* JK Medora & Co 22 Malacca Street Royal Brothers Building #03-02, SINGAPORE 048980, SINGAPORE.
MEDORI, Mr. Cristiano, ACA *2001;* Ernst & Young Llp, 1 More London Place, LONDON, SE1 2AF.
MEDWAY, Mrs. Djhoanna, BA ACA *2001;* 144 Kings Road, CARDIFF, CF11 9DG.
MEE, Mr. Darren, BSc FCA *1990;* (Tax Fac), 64 Dorling Drive, Ewell, EPSOM, KT17 3BH.
•**MEE, Mr. Howard Robert, BSc FCA** *1994;* Smith Craven, Unit 4, 12 O'Clock Court, 21 Attercliffe Road, SHEFFIELD, S4 7WW.
MEE, Mr. James, ACA *2011;* Flat 393, Anchor House, Smugglers Way, LONDON, SW18 1EN.
MEE, Mr. Michael John Robert, BSc ACA *1997;* (Tax Fac), Flat 92 South Block, 1b Belvedere Road, LONDON, SE1 7GD.
•**MEE, Mr. Ross Stephen, ACA** *1983;* Nixon Mee Ltd, Unit 9, Whitwick Business Centre, Stenson Road, COALVILLE, LEICESTERSHIRE LE67 4JP.
MEE, Miss. Victoria Elizabeth, BA ACA *2000;* 123 Worthington Road, Fradley, LICHFIELD, STAFFORDSHIRE, WS13 8PG.
MEECH, Mr. Christopher Michael, FCA *1973;* Gemella, 110 Haslemere Road, LIPHOOK, GU30 7BU.
MEECH, Mr. Nicholas Adrian, BSc ACA *1998;* Flat 45 Chandlery House, 40 Gowers Walk, LONDON, E1 8BH.
MEECH, Mrs. Susan Margaret, MA FCA *1992;* The Forge, Swinbrook, BURFORD, OXFORDSHIRE, OX18 4ED.
MEECHAN, Mrs. Kathryn Ruth, BA(Hons) ACA *2002;* Duncan Lawrie Offshore Services, 13 Mount Havelock Douglas, ISLE OF MAN, IM1 2QG.
MEECHAN, Mr. Lawrence, MA ACA *1987;* 14 Melbury Gardens, LONDON, SW20 0DJ.
MEECHAN, Miss. Margaret Mary, ACA *1991;* (Tax Fac), Foxhole, Foxhole Lane, Bolney, HAYWARDS HEATH, WEST SUSSEX, RH17 5NB.
MEEHAN, Mr. Andrew David, MA ACA *1979;* Southview, Church Lane, Lighthorne, WARWICK, CV35 0AT.
MEEHAN, Miss. Clare, BSc ACA *2009;* Flat 5 Fairlawns, Putney Hill, LONDON, SW15 6BD.
•**MEEHAN, Mr. Clinton John, BSc FCA** *1988;* Manex Accountants Limited, 9 Castle Court, 2 Castlegate Way, DUDLEY, WEST MIDLANDS, DY1 4RD.
MEEHAN, Mr. Michael Patrick, BSc ACA *1999;* 55 Cranley Gardens, LONDON, N10 3AB.
MEEHAN, Mr. Michael Richard, BA ACA *1987;* Vi-Spring Ltd, Ernesettle Lane, Ernesettle, PLYMOUTH, PL5 2TT.
•**MEEHAN, Mr. Peter Noel, BCom FCA** *1987;* KPMG LLP, One Snowhill, Snow Hill Queensway, BIRMINGHAM, B4 6GN. See also KPMG Europe LLP
MEEHAN, Mr. Richard John, BA(Hons) ACA *2001;* 19 Hollowgate, Barnburgh, DONCASTER, SOUTH YORKSHIRE, DN5 7HB.
MEEK, Mr. Andrew James, ACA *2009;* 60 Breck Road, POULTON-LE-FYLDE, FY6 7AQ.
MEEK, Mr. Andrew James, BSc ACA *1991;* Norfolk Line Shipping, Eastern Docks, DOVER, CT16 1JA.
MEEK, Mr. Andrew Leslie, BSc ACA *1999;* with Audit Inspection Unit, Financial Reporting Council, 5th Floor, Aldwych House, 71-91 Aldwych, LONDON WC2B 4HN.
MEEK, Mr. Brian, BA FCA *1974;* Mole End, Long Compton, SHIPSTON-ON-STOUR, CV36 5LE.
MEEK, Mrs. Clare Louise, BA ACA *2006;* with Ernst & Young LLP, 1 Bridgewater Place, Water Lane, LEEDS, LS11 5QR.
MEEK, Mrs. Colette, BA ACA *1992;* Provident Insurance Plc, Blackwall, HALIFAX, HX1 2PZ.
•**MEEK, Mr. Darren Lindsay, LLB FCA** *1993;* PricewaterhouseCoopers LLP, Hays Galleria, 1 Hays Lane, LONDON, SE1 2RD. See also PricewaterhouseCoopers
MEEK, Mr. David John, BSocSc ACA *1984;* Hazelwood, Mill Lane, Calcot, READING, RG31 7RS.
MEEK, Mr. Derek Colin, FCA *1963;* Woodland Rise, Ventnor Road, Niton Undercliff, VENTNOR, ISLE OF WIGHT, PO38 2LY.
MEEK, Mr. Henry, ACA *1998;* Flat 5, 8 Montague Road, LONDON, SW19 1SY.
MEEK, Mr. Ian, BA ACA *1992;* Brenntag UK Ltd, Unit 1, Albion House, Rawdon Park, Yeadon, LEEDS LS19 7XX.
MEEK, Mrs. Janet, BSc ACA *1987;* Hazelwood, Mill Lane, Calcot, READING, RG31 7RS.
MEEK, Mrs. Lucinda Carol, BSc ACA *1992;* IAMM, Basepoint Business Centre, Oakfield Close, Tewkesbury Business Park, TEWKESBURY, GLOUCESTERSHIRE GL20 8SD.
MEEK, Mr. Nigel Kingsley, BA ACA *1982;* 55 Eaton Terrace, LONDON, SW1W 8TR.
MEEK, Mr. Richard Stephen, BSc FCA *1991;* 156-158 Buckingham Palace Road, LONDON, Sw1W 9TR.
MEEK, Mr. Robert, BA ACA *1990;* 45 Grange View, LINLITHGOW, EH49 7HY.
•**MEEK, Mr. Robert Charles, FCA CTA** *1975;* (Tax Fac), Rob Meek FCA CTA, Woodland Lodge, White House Drive, Barnt Green, BIRMINGHAM, B45 8HF.
MEEK, Mr. Stephen Charles, BSc FCA *1984;* YWAM PO Box 926, WORCESTER, 6849, SOUTH AFRICA.
MEEK, Mr. Stephen John, ACA *1980;* Connaught House, 5 Bearmains, South Hanningfield, CHELMSFORD, CM3 8GY.
•**MEEKE, Mr. Anthony Gordon Richard, ACA** *1982;* PricewaterhouseCoopers LLP, 1 Embankment Place, LONDON, WC2N 6RH. See also PricewaterhouseCoopers
MEEKE, Mr. Harold Gordon, FCA *1951;* 21 Low Field Lane, Staveley, KNARESBOROUGH, NORTH YORKSHIRE, HG5 9LB. (Life Member)
MEEKE, Miss. Susannah, ACA *2008;* 3 The Quadrant, EXETER, EX2 4LE.
MEEKING, Miss. Eleanor Ruth, BSc ACA *2002;* Flat 38, Falconwood Court, 24 Montpelier Row, LONDON, SE3 0RS.
MEEKINS, Mr. Douglas Edward, FCA *1965;* 6 Springwood Hall, Springwood Park, TONBRIDGE, TN11 9LZ.
•**MEEKS, Ms. Anna Jane, BSc ACA** *1989;* Robinson Udale Limited, The Old Bank, 41 King Street, PENRITH, CUMBRIA, CA11 7AY.
MEEKS, Miss. Polly, BA ACA *2011;* 11 Clarkson Road, CAMBRIDGE, CB3 0EH.
MEEKS, Mr. Timothy David, BA ACA *2002;* 30 Massingberd Way, Tooting Bec, LONDON, SW17 6AB.
MEELBOOM, Mr. Anthony Crispin, BSc ACA *1979;* 28 Meadow Close, NOTTINGHAM, NG2 3HZ.
MEENAN, Mr. Declan Joseph, BA(Hons) ACA *2002;* Hermes GPE LLP, Hermes Pensions Management Ltd Lloyds Chambers, 1 Portsoken Street, LONDON, E1 8HZ.
•**MEENAN, Miss. Niamh Bernadette, BCom FCA** *1989;* Grant Thornton, 24-26 City Quay, DUBLIN 2, COUNTY DUBLIN, IRELAND.
MEERE, Mrs. Julia Claire, MA ACA CTA *2000;* (Tax Fac), The Granary, Mill Lane, Askham Richard, YORK, YO23 3NW.
MEERS, Mrs. Elise, BMus ACA *1999;* STALLAND HOUSE, Stalland Cottage The Stalland, Deopham, WYMONDHAM, NORFOLK, NR18 9ED.
MEERS, Mr. William, ACA *2011;* 4 Navy Street, LONDON, SW4 6EZ.
MEERTS, Mr. Frank Daniel Theodoor, ACA *2002;* Waltherlaan 32, 1402 BUSSUM, NETHERLANDS.
MEES, Mr. Alexander Clive, MA ACA *1998;* 14 Smith Street, ROZELLE, NSW 2039, AUSTRALIA.
MEESON, Mr. Anthony, JP FCA FCCA *1952;* Woodlands, 11 Milner Drive, COBHAM, SURREY, KT11 2EZ. (Life Member)
MEESON, Mr. Martin Edward, BA ACA *1997;* 16 East Green, Heighington Village, NEWTON AYCLIFFE, COUNTY DURHAM, DL5 6PP.
MEESON, Mr. Roger William, BSc FCA *1972;* 5 Regency Lodge, Oatlands Chase, WEYBRIDGE, KT13 9RZ. (Life Member)
MEESON, Miss. Sophie Anne, BA ACA *2009;* Broadfields, Argos Hill, Rotherfield, CROWBOROUGH, EAST SUSSEX, TN6 3QH.
•**MEESON-SMITH, Mrs. Kerstin Pamela, FCA** *1978;* with Tyrrell & Company, Unit D, South Cambridge Business Park, Babraham Road, Sawston, CAMBRIDGE CB22 3JH.
•**MEETEN, Mr. Jonathan Philip, BA ACA ATII** *1995;* (Tax Fac), KPMG LLP, Saltire Court, 20 Castle Terrace, EDINBURGH, EH1 2EG. See also KPMG Europe LLP
MEGARRY, Mr. Kevin Arthur, BSc FCA *1974;* 41 Mount Albany, Newtownpark Avenue, BLACKROCK, COUNTY DUBLIN, IRELAND.
MEGAW, Mr. Ian David, ACA *1980;* 27 Euclid Street, SWINDON, SN1 2JW.
MEGAW, Mr. Robert Chapman, FCA *1967;* Apartado 1352, P-8400, CARVOEIRO, PORTUGAL.
MEGCHIANI, Mr. Rajesh Surendra, ACA *2003;* 1A/16 Chapman Street, AUCKLAND, NEW ZEALAND.
MEGEARY, Mrs. Fiona Alexandra, ACA *1987;* La Durandiere, 61210, 61210 STE. HONORINE LA GUILLAUME, NORMANDIE, FRANCE.
MEGGINSON, Mr. David, BA ACA *1988;* 8 Beverley Road, LONDON, SW13 0LX.
•**MEGGITT, Mr. David Keith, FCA** *1962;* David K Meggitt, 5 Parkside, 172 Kew Road, RICHMOND, TW9 2AS.
MEGGY, Miss. Alexandra Clare, ACA *2008;* 2 Old Rowfant Cottages, Rowfant, CRAWLEY, WEST SUSSEX, RH10 4TB.
MEGHANI, Mr. Cyril Dhanji, BSc(Econ) FCA *1998;* 11 Bedford Road, NORTHWOOD, MIDDLESEX, HA6 2BA.
•**MEGHANI, Mrs. Fahreen, BA ACA** *2005;* Fairman Law, Fairman Law House, 1-3 Park Terrace, WORCESTER PARK, SURREY, KT4 7JZ. See also Fairman Davis
MEGHANI, Mr. Muhammad Asif, ACA *2009;* Flat A, 356 Brockley Road, LONDON, SE4 2BY.
MEGHJEE, Miss. Fatima, ACA *2011;* 99 Marsh Lane, STANMORE, MIDDLESEX, HA7 4TH.
•**MEGHJEE, Mr. Muntazir, FCA** *1992;* 95 Valley Road, RICKMANSWORTH, HERTFORDSHIRE, WD3 4BL.

•**MEGHJEE-CAINE, Mrs. Shama, FCA CTA** *1997;* (Tax Fac), Cooper Dawn Jerrom Limited, Units SCF 1 & 2, Western International Market, Hayes Road, SOUTHALL, MIDDLESEX UB2 5XJ.

MEGHJI, Mr. Amirali Gulamhussein, FCA *1975;* P.O. Box 22705, NAIROBI, 00400, KENYA.

MEGHJI, Mr. Mohamedraza Amirali, BA ACA *1999;* with Grant Thornton, PO Box 1620, Warba Centre, Deira, Abu Baker Al Siddique Road, DUBAI UNITED ARAB EMIRATES.

MEGHJI, Mrs. Sofia Hussain, BSc ACA *2006;* 7 Furham Feild, PINNER, HA5 4DX.

MEGSON, Mrs. Claire Marie, BA ACA *2001;* 49 Buckingham Road, STOCKPORT, SK4 4RB.

•**MEGSON, Mr. Paul Anthony, FCA** *1975;* 1.2.1 Accountancy Services, 4 Railway Cottages, Low Row, BRAMPTON, CA8 2LG.

•**MEHAN, Mrs. Anshu, FCA CTA** *1998;* HSKS Limited, 18 St. Christophers Way, Pride Park, DERBY, DE24 8JY.

MEHAN, Mr. Vivek Kumar, BA ACA *2002;* Oakleigh, The Avenue, WEST WICKHAM, KENT, BR4 0DY.

MEHANNA, Mr. Omar, BSc ACA *2000;* HSBC Bank, 8 Canada Square, LONDON, E14 5HQ.

MEHARG, Mr. Brian, BSc FCA *1977;* Greengarth, Winhill, LIVERPOOL, L25 6JR.

MEHBOOB, Mr. Khalid, FCA *1969;* Via Guerrieri 15, 00153 ROME, ITALY.

MEHDI, Mr. Syed Ali, BSc(Hons) ACA *2003;* Pan Peninsula, Flat 2605, 1 Pan Peninsula Square, LONDON, E14 9HJ.

MEHDWAN, Mr. Juggu Harjinder Singh, BSc ACA *1993;* 4 Applegate Court, CRANBURY, NJ 08512, UNITED STATES.

•**MEHDYOUN, Mr. Hamid Abdol, BSc(Econ) FCA** *1981;* GMG Roberts, 47 Queen Anne Street, LONDON, W1G 9JG.

MEHEW, Mr. Anthony John, BSc FCA *1970;* Moretons, Meadway, BERKHAMSTED, HERTFORDSHIRE, HP4 2PL.

MEHEW, Ms. Natalie, BA ACA *2000;* with Deloitte LLP, Athene Place, 66 Shoe Lane, LONDON, EC4A 3BQ.

•**MEHEW, Mr. Paul David, BCom ACA** *2000;* 7 Maldale, Wilnecote, TAMWORTH, STAFFORDSHIRE, B77 4PH.

•**MEHIGAN, Mr. John Anthony, LLB FCA CTA** *1984;* (Tax Fac), N T Advisors LLP, First Floor, 10 Charles II Street, LONDON, SW1Y 4AA.

MEHIGAN, Mr. Paul James, BA ACA *1984;* Amerada Hess The Adelphi, 1-11 John Adam Street, LONDON, WC2N 6AG.

MEHMOOD, Mr. Ahsan, ACA *2009;* Pricewaterhousecoopers Abacus House, Castle Park, CAMBRIDGE, CB3 0AN.

•**MEHMOOD, Mr. Khalid, ACA FCCA ACCA CTA MSI** *2007;* Hadleys & Co, 5 Malvern House, 199 Marsh Wall, Meridan Gate, LONDON, E14 9YT.

MEHMOOD, Mr. Nasir, FCA *1975;* Arundel, Cloweswood Lane, Earlswood, SOLIHULL, B94 5SE. (Life Member)

MEHMOOD, Mr. Tariq, FCA *1971;* PAK Kuwait Textiles Ltd, 29 Shadman II, LAHORE 54000, PUNJAB, PAKISTAN.

MEHMOOD, Mr. Tariq Jamal, MA ACA *2000;* 3rd Floor, The Royal Bank of Scotland Plc, 280 Bishopsgate, LONDON, EC2M 4RB.

MEHMOOD, Mrs. Tehseen, ACA *2008;* 12 Crosier Close, LONDON, SE3 8NT.

MEHRA, Mr. Anil, FCA *1971;* 14 Marrowells, Oatlands Chase, WEYBRIDGE, SURREY, KT13 9RN. (Life Member)

MEHRA, Mr. Anil Kumar, FCA *1969;* B-223-B Greater Kailash, NEW DELHI 110048, INDIA.

MEHRA, Mr. Arun, FCA *1974;* 203 Prestige Benson Court, 26 Benson Road, Benson Town, BANGALORE 560046, INDIA.

•**MEHRA, Mr. Arun, BEng FCA** *1999;* Samera Ltd, Samera House, 138 High Street, ESHER, SURREY, KT10 9QJ.

MEHRA, Mr. Pradeep, FCA *1978;* Villa No. E 2 Mansoor Gardens 5, P.O. Box 10826, MANAMA, BAHRAIN.

MEHRA, Mr. Rahul, BA FCA *1988;* 501 - 9330 University Crescent, BURNABY V5A 4X9, BC, CANADA.

MEHRA, Mr. Vidhur, BSc ACA *2000;* 42 Royston Park Road, PINNER, HA5 4AF.

MEHRA, Mr. Vinod Kumar, FCA *1974;* VAVA Accountants Ltd, 42 Royston Park Road, Hatch End, PINNER, MIDDLESEX, HA5 4AF.

MEHRA, Miss. Vrinda, MSc BA ACA *2010;* Villa No 84 Ground FloorBlock I, Charmswood Eros Garden Surajkund, FARIDABAD 121009, HARYANA, INDIA.

MEHRABANI-ZARDOSHTI, Mr. Kourosh, FCA CF *1990;* The Willows, 14 Willow Way, Prestbury, MACCLESFIELD, CHESHIRE, SK10 4XB.

MEHRALI, Mr. Naushad Mohamedali Hajee, BA ACA *1980;* Quest Vitamins Ltd., 8 Venture Way, Aston Science Park, BIRMINGHAM, B7 4AP.

MEHROTRA, Miss. Pretta Latha, ACA *1992;* No 3 Jalan 10/14A, 46000 PETALING JAYA, SELANGOR, MALAYSIA.

MEHTA, Mr. Abhaykant Sukhlal, FCA *1961;* 1 Drummond Drive, STANMORE, MIDDLESEX, HA7 3PF. (Life Member)

•**MEHTA, Mr. Alkesh, BSc ACA ATII MBA** *1990;* Prestons & Jacksons Partnership LLP, 364-368 Cranbrook Road, ILFORD, ESSEX, IG2 6HY. See also Prestons

MEHTA, Mr. Amit, BSc ACA *1996;* 8 Solutions, C4-C12, Unit, Intake Road, Bolsover Business Park, Bolsover CHESTERFIELD DERBYSHIRE S44 6BB.

MEHTA, Mr. Amit Kishor, BSc ACA *1998;* 2 Graces Mews, 20 Abbey Road, LONDON, NW8 9AZ.

MEHTA, Mr. Anand Swarup, FCA *1974;* Post Box No 211628, Villa No 135, Street No 71A, Jummerah Beach Road, DUBAI, UNITED ARAB EMIRATES.

MEHTA, Mr. Anish, ACA *2010;* Deloitte & Touche, 1001 City Tower 2, Sheikh Zayed Road, PO Box 4254, DUBAI, 4254 UNITED ARAB EMIRATES.

MEHTA, Mr. Anouj, BSc ACA *1996;* Asian Development Bank, 6 ADB Avenue, Mandaluyong City, MANILA 1550, METRO MANILA, PHILIPPINES.

MEHTA, Ms. Archna, BSc ACA *2003;* 21 Regal Close, LONDON, W5 2SB.

MEHTA, Mr. Arjun, ACA *2000;* A3 / 801 Uniworld City, Sector 30, GURGAON 122001, HARYANA, INDIA.

MEHTA, Mr. Arun, FCA *1973;* 7 Sheldon Avenue, LONDON, N6 4JS. (Life Member)

MEHTA, Mr. Ashesh Jawahar, ACA *1991;* 2521 Condor Drive, AUDUBON, PA 19403, UNITED STATES.

MEHTA, Mr. Ashoni Kumar, BPharm ACA *1993;* 12 Manor Road, TWICKENHAM, TW2 5DF.

•**MEHTA, Mr. Asvinkumar Nathalal Bhagwanji, FCA** *1975;* Walters Associates Ltd, Suite 21, Third Floor, Barkat House, 116-118 Finchley Road, LONDON NW3 5HT.

•**MEHTA, Mr. Bipinchandra Babulal, FCA** *1975;* (Tax Fac), B.B. Mehta & Co, 28 Lindsay Drive, Kenton, HARROW, HA3 0TD.

MEHTA, Mr. Brijesh, ACA *2009;* 105 Highfield Way, RICKMANSWORTH, HERTFORDSHIRE, WD3 7PL.

MEHTA, Mr. Darius Russa, FCA *1965;* Honeysuckle Cottage, 95 The Common, Broughton Gifford, MELKSHAM, WILTSHIRE, SN12 8ND.

MEHTA, Mr. Daxesh, BSc ACA *1992;* Omkara, Crofters Road, NORTHWOOD, MIDDLESEX, HA6 3EB.

MEHTA, Mr. Dev, ACA *2008;* 52 Dagmar Avenue, WEMBLEY, MIDDLESEX, HA9 8DF.

MEHTA, Mr. Dhiren Gajsukumar, BA ACA *1992;* Unicore Holdings (PTY) Ltd, Office 1, 4 Dundee Street, Blue Valley Gold Estate, MIDRAND, SOUTH AFRICA.

MEHTA, Mr. Dimple Shashikant, ACA *1990;* P.O. Box 81249, MOMBASA, KENYA.

MEHTA, Mr. Dineshkumar Ishwerlal Khushalbhai, BSc ACA *1980;* 20 Rydal Gardens, ASHBY-DE-LA-ZOUCH, LE65 1FJ.

MEHTA, Miss. Grupti, BA ACA *1996;* Flat 6 Carlton Court, 277-279 Nether Street, LONDON, N3 1PD.

MEHTA, Mr. Hiten, BCom ACA *1985;* 23 Nagle Grove, Rusheymead, LEICESTER, LE4 7RU.

MEHTA, Mr. Hitesh Manherlal, BSc FCA *1993;* 6435 Cypress Street, VANCOUVER V6M 3S4, BC, CANADA.

•**MEHTA, Mr. Homiar Erach, FCA** *1981;* Silver Levene LLP, 37 Warren Street, LONDON, W1T 6AD.

MEHTA, Mr. Jagan Nath, FCA *1966;* Apt 204, 32700 Coastsite Drive, RANCHO PALOS VERDES, CA 90275, UNITED STATES. (Life Member)

MEHTA, Mr. Jagdish Amritlal, FCA *1974;* (Tax Fac), 81 Grimsdyke Road, Hatch End, PINNER, HA5 4PZ.

•**MEHTA, Mr. Jal, FCA** *1978;* Aytons, 32 Bathurst Road, ILFORD, IG1 4LA.

MEHTA, Mr. Jal Maneckshaw, BA LLB FCA *1955;* Chheda Sadan, 115 Churchgate Reclamation, MUMBAI 400 020, MAHARASHTRA, INDIA. (Life Member)

•**MEHTA, Mr. Jayantkumar Dasubhai, ACA** *1979;* (Tax Fac), 16 Brancaster Road, Newbury Park, ILFORD, IG2 7ER.

•**MEHTA, Mr. Jayesh Chandrakant, BSc FCA** *1992;* SMS Abacus & Co Ltd, Rowlandson House, 289-293 Ballards Lane, LONDON, N12 8NP.

•**MEHTA, Mr. Jehangir Jamshed, ACA** *1981;* (Tax Fac), Mehta & Tengra, 24 Bedford Row, LONDON, WC1R 4TQ.

MEHTA, Mr. Jitendra Gajanand, FCA *1982;* 52 Robin Hood Way, Kingston Vale, LONDON, SW15 3PH.

MEHTA, Mr. Kalpesh Kantilal, BA(Econ) FCA *1997;* P O Box 2073, DAR ES SALAAM, TANZANIA.

MEHTA, Mrs. Kamini Bina, BSc FCA *1993;* 6435 Cypress Street, VANCOUVER V6M 3S4, BC, CANADA.

MEHTA, Mr. Khurshed Nariman, ACA *1983;* 5 Bridge Close, WALTON-ON-THAMES, KT12 1DX.

MEHTA, Mrs. Lalita Nandkishore, FCA *1978;* 5 Greenhill Crescent, ST. IVES, NSW 2075, AUSTRALIA.

MEHTA, Mr. Mahesh Kumar, FCA *1976;* 145 Ceylon Road, SINGAPORE 1542, SINGAPORE.

MEHTA, Mr. Manish Ashok, BSc ACA *1995;* 19 York Close, Chandler's Ford, EASTLEIGH, HAMPSHIRE, SO53 4LF.

MEHTA, Mr. Nandkishore Champaklal, FCA *1977;* 5 Greenhill Crescent, ST. IVES, NSW 2075, AUSTRALIA.

MEHTA, Mr. Navinchandra Virji, FCA *1973;* Apt 441 - 2096 Blackmud Creek Drive SW, EDMONTON T6W 0G1, AB, CANADA.

MEHTA, Mr. Nitesh, BSc ACA *2009;* 10 The Paddocks, WEMBLEY, MIDDLESEX, HA9 9HE.

MEHTA, Mr. Paresh Lalchand, BA FCA *1989;* (Tax Fac), 22 Chestnut Avenue, RICKMANSWORTH, HERTFORDSHIRE, WD3 4HB.

MEHTA, Mr. Pinesh, ACA *2008;* 70 Glastonbury Drive, Poynton, STOCKPORT, CHESHIRE, SK12 1EN.

MEHTA, Miss. Puja, BSc ACA *2009;* 33 Bromefield, STANMORE, MIDDLESEX, HA7 1AA.

MEHTA, Miss. Radha, MA BSc ACA *1998;* Connaught House, Flat 3, Mount Row, LONDON, W1K 3RA.

MEHTA, Mr. Rajan Baboolal, FCA *1976;* 2 Edgeland Close NW, CALGARY T3A 3B1, AB, CANADA.

MEHTA, Mr. Rajeev, BSc ACA *2005;* with Deloitte Middle East, Currency House, Building 1 Level 5, DIFC, PO Box 282056, DUBAI UNITED ARAB EMIRATES.

MEHTA, Mr. Rajeev Satish, BA(Hons) ACA *2004;* 35 Swallow Close, Chafford Hundred, GRAYS, RM16 6RH.

MEHTA, Mr. Rajendrakumar Jamnadas, FCA *1977;* 23 Ainsdale Road, Western Park, LEICESTER, LE3 0UD.

MEHTA, Mr. Rajiv, ACA *2010;* 1 Willow End, NORTHWOOD, MIDDLESEX, HA6 3QA.

•**MEHTA, Mr. Ramesh Harilal Lalchand, FCA** *1975;* Mehta and Company, 221 Cranbrook Road, ILFORD, ESSEX, IG1 4TD.

•**MEHTA, Mrs. Reshma Paresh, FCA** *1991;* RPM Associates, 22 Chestnut Avenue, RICKMANSWORTH, HERTFORDSHIRE, WD3 4HB.

MEHTA, Miss. Rupal, ACA *2010;* 76 Church Hill Road, BARNET, HERTFORDSHIRE, EN4 8XA.

•**MEHTA, Mr. Sailesh Pushkar, BSc ACA** *1981;* H W Fisher & Company, Acre House, 11-15 William Road, LONDON, NW1 3ER. See also H W Fisher & Company Limited

MEHTA, Miss. Sapna, BSc ACA *2007;* Sai Kanchan Nivas, Northgate, NORTHWOOD, MIDDLESEX, HA6 2TH.

MEHTA, Mrs. Shefalika Raj, MA ACA *1993;* 48 Lulworth Drive, PINNER, HA5 1NE.

MEHTA, Mr. Sohrab Boman, FCA *1973;* 1 Belvedere Court, Pinner Road, Oxhey, WATFORD, WD19 4FB. (Life Member)

MEHTA, Mr. Sunil, FCA *1973;* 2 Deerhill Drive, HO HO KUS, NJ 07423, UNITED STATES.

MEHTA, Mr. Surendra Dipchand, BSc FCA *1975;* 21 Waltham Avenue, Kingsbury, LONDON, NW9 9SH.

•**MEHTA, Mr. Vinaychandra Kantilal, BCom FCA FCCA** *1969;* (Tax Fac), VKM Accountants Limited, 25 Balham High Road, LONDON, SW12 9AL.

MEHTA, Mr. Vinesh Kirtikumar, ACA *1998;* 19 Oakleigh Gardens, EDGWARE, MIDDLESEX, HA8 8EA.

MEHTA, Mr. Vipul Manharlal, BSc ACA *1995;* 37 Howberry Road, EDGWARE, HA8 6SS.

MEHTA, Mr. Vishal Paresh, BSc(Econ) ACA *1996;* 22 Cedar Close, IVER, BUCKINGHAMSHIRE, SL0 0QX.

MEHTA, Mr. Zarin Mehli, FCA *1962;* 255 West 84th Street, Apartment 4E, NEW YORK, NY 10024, UNITED STATES.

MEIER, Mr. Ian, FCA *1967;* Brunger Cottage, Appledore Road, TENTERDEN, KENT, TN30 7DD.

MEIER, Mrs. Kirsten Elizabeth, MA(Oxon) ACA *2006;* Ground Floor Flat, 375 Fulham Palace Road, Fulham, LONDON, SW6 6TA.

MEIER, Mr. Robert William, BA ACA *1999;* The Malthouse, St. Clement, TRURO, CORNWALL, TR1 1SZ.

MEIGH, Miss. Helen Rebecca Alexandra, BSc(Hons) ACA *2001;* 17 Percival Drive, Stockton Brook, STOKE-ON-TRENT, STAFFORDSHIRE, ST9 9PE.

MEIGHAN, Mr. Kevin Eric Francis, BSc ACA *1995;* Bell Cottage, 72 Chapel Road, TADWORTH, SURREY, KT20 5SE.

•**MEIJS, Miss. Fleur, PhD ACA** *2000;* PricewaterhouseCoopers LLP, Hays Galleria, 1 Hays Lane, LONDON, SE1 2RD. See also PricewaterhouseCoopers

•**MEIKLE, Mr. Alan John, BSc FCA** *1987;* Barbara M Thompson FCCA, Summerdale, Head Dyke Lane, Pilling, PRESTON, PR3 6SJ.

MEIKLE, Mr. Andrew David, BSc ACA *1996;* Woodlands, 43 Charlwood Drive, Oxshott, LEATHERHEAD, SURREY, KT22 0HB.

MEIN, Mr. Alastair William, CA *1985; (CA Scotland 1972);* (Tax Fac), Shipleys LLP, Market House, 10 Market Walk, SAFFRON WALDEN, ESSEX, CB10 1JZ.

MEIN, Mr. David Michael, FCA *1973;* John Cotton Group Plc, Nunbrook Mills, MIRFIELD, WEST YORKSHIRE, WF14 0EH.

MEIN, Mr. Kenneth Andrew, FCA *1973;* Water Falls, Whitebrook, MONMOUTH, GWENT, NP25 4TU.

MEINS, Mr. John Charles, FCA *1963;* 31 Butlers Court Road, BEACONSFIELD, BUCKINGHAMSHIRE, HP9 1SQ. (Life Member)

MEINTJES, Mr. Charles Christiaan, ACA CA(SA) *2010;* 21C Grosvenor Road, Chiswick, LONDON, W4 4EQ.

MEINTJES, Mr. Leon Hammersley, ACA CA(SA) *2010;* 500 W 56th Street, Apt 2208, NEW YORK, NY 10019, UNITED STATES.

MEISSNER, Mr. Nicholas, PhD BSc FCA *1977;* Reikemstraat 12, 3020 HERENT, BELGIUM.

MEISTER, Mrs. Jennifer Wendy, ACA CA(SA) *2009;* 7 Parkside Drive, EDGWARE, MIDDLESEX, HA8 8JU.

•①**MEITNER, Mr. Paul, MA ACA** *1986;* 17 Montpelier Walk, LONDON, SW7 1JL.

MEIVATZIS, Mr. Charalambos, BSc ACA *2005;* 53 Kyrenia Avenue, Plati, 2114 NICOSIA, CYPRUS.

MEIVATZIS, Mr. Constantinos, BSc(Hons) ACA *2002;* Charalambou Ioannou 28, 2224 LATSIA, CYPRUS.

•**MEIZOSO, Ms. Regina, LLB ACA** *1998;* Aria Personal Tax Consultancy Ltd, 4 Penyston Road, MAIDENHEAD, BERKSHIRE, SL6 6EH.

MEKIE, Mr. Duncan John Cameron, FCA *1968;* 47 Park Road, TEDDINGTON, TW11 0AU.

MELBOURNE, Mr. David Charles, FCA *1974;* Daleside Bedale Road, Burneston, BEDALE, NORTH YORKSHIRE, DL8 2HS.

MELBOURNE, Ms. Hanife, BSc ACA *1992;* 50 Ringwood Way, Winchmore Hill, LONDON, N21 2QX.

MELBOURNE, Mr. John William, BSc FCA *1991;* 136 Woodland Way, LONDON, N21 3PU.

MELBOURNE, Mr. Malcolm, FCA *1958;* 11 Bradfield House, The Boulevard, WOODFORD GREEN, IG8 8GR. (Life Member)

MELBOURNE WEBB, Mr. Barry, MA FCA *1974;* St Anthony, 32 Birling Road, TUNBRIDGE WELLS, TN2 5LY. (Life Member)

MELDRUM, Mr. Alan Craig, BA ACA *1996;* 29 Alderwood Avenue, Valley Park, Chandler's Ford, EASTLEIGH, HAMPSHIRE, SO53 4TH.

MELDRUM, Mr. Grant Macalistair, MEng ACA *2004;* 37 Braybrooke Gardens, LONDON, SE19 2UN.

MELDRUM, Mr. Neil, BA ACA *1997;* 14 Depleach Road, CHEADLE, CHESHIRE, SK8 1DZ.

MELE, Ms. Romina Sandra, ACA *2010;* 69 Stillingfleet Road, LONDON, SW13 9AF.

MELECH, Mr. Nehemia, BA FCA *1958;* 3 Even Sapir Street, 69546 TEL AVIV, ISRAEL. (Life Member)

MELEKKI, Ms. Anna, BSc ACA *2010;* 12 Monemvasias Street, 4152 LIMASSOL, CYPRUS.

MELETIOU, Miss. Josephina, BA ACA *2004;* 23 Kyriakou Matsi Avenue, Flat 501, Nicosia 1082, Cyprus, 1082 NICOSIA, CYPRUS.

MELETIOU, Mr. Pavlos Nicou, ACA *1981;* PO BOX 28584, 2080 NICOSIA, CYPRUS.

MELHUISH, Mr. Anthony John, FCA *1968;* 20 Ridgeway Road, Osterley, ISLEWORTH, TW7 5LA.

MELHUISH, Mr. Edward Charles, BSc ACA *2002;* Arqiva Ltd Crawley Court, Crawley, WINCHESTER, SO21 2QA.

MELHUISH, Mrs. Jane Marie, BSc ACA *2000;* 50 Mosside Terrace, BATHGATE, WEST LOTHIAN, EH48 2UJ.

MELHUISH, Mr. Jeremy Piers, FCA *1973;* M H J Land & Water Services Weston Yard, Albury, GUILDFORD, SURREY, GU5 9AF.

MELHUISH, Mrs. Marian Catherine, FCA *1977;* 63 Pavilion Way, RUISLIP, HA4 9JR.

•**MELHUISH, Mr. Robert John, BEng ACA** *2001;* Accountwise Limited, 19 Woosehill Lane, WOKINGHAM, BERKSHIRE, RG41 2TR.
•**MELHUISH-HANCOCK, Mr. Douglas Charles, FCA** *1957;* Flat 22, Nightingale House, 50 Thomas More Street, LONDON, E1W 1UA.
MELIA, Miss. Clara Alexis Ellen, BA(Hons) ACA *2011;* Flat 10/A, Lanark Mansions, 12 Lanark Road, LONDON, W9 1DB.
•**MELIA, Mr. Gerard Thomas, BA ACA** *1989;* Darwen Management Services Ltd, 27 Bolton Road, DARWEN, LANCASHIRE, BB3 1DF.
MELIA, Mr. Graham Peter, BSc FCA *1985;* Oscar Mayer Limited, Ash Road South, Wrexham Industrial Estate, WREXHAM, CLWYD, LL13 9UG.
MELIA, Mr. Ian Charles, MA FCA *1976;* St Giles House, 32A Storey's Way, CAMBRIDGE, CB3 0DT.
MELIA, Mrs. Lynsey, BA ACA *2006;* 14 Tavington Road Halewood, LIVERPOOL, L26 6BA.
MELIA, Mr. Philip James, MEng ACA *2004;* (Tax Fac), 155 Broomhill, DOWNHAM MARKET, NORFOLK, PE38 9QU.
•**MELINEK, Mr. Aryeh Yehudah, BSc ACA** *2003;* Melinek Fine LLP, Ground Floor, Forframe House, 35-37 Brent Street, LONDON, NW4 2EF.
MELL, Mr. Richard John, BA ACA *1994;* 66 Oakwood Avenue, PURLEY, SURREY, CR8 1AQ.
•**MELL, Mr. Scott Paul, BA FCA** *1994;* Gibson Booth, 12 Victoria Road, BARNSLEY, SOUTH YORKSHIRE, S70 2BB. See also Salary Solutions Limited
•**MELLALIEU, Mr. Christopher Fred, FCA** *1969;* Powell & Powell Limited, 107 Wellington Road, STOCKPORT, CHESHIRE, SK1 3TL. See also Lacy, Watson
MELLALIEU, Mr. John Turton, FCA *1955;* 41 Round Hill Meadow, Great Boughton, CHESTER, CH3 5XR. (Life Member)
MELLAR, Mrs. Susan, FCA *1987;* (Tax Fac), 143 Walsall Wood Road, Aldridge, WALSALL, WS9 8RD.
MELLER, Mr. Clive Howard, ACA *1979;* No 270 Via della Scrofa 16, 00186 ROME, ITALY.
MELLER, Mr. David Brian, MA(Oxon) MBA ACA *1990;* Milton Park, Stroude Road, EGHAM, TW20 9EL.
MELLER, Mr. John Patrick, FCA *1967;* Les Fauxquets De Haut, Rue Des Fauxquets, Castel, GUERNSEY, GY5 7QA. (Life Member)
MELLER, Mr. Richard James, BA(Hons) ACA CTA *2005;* (Tax Fac), 6 Holm Oak Close, VERWOOD, DORSET, BH31 7PP.
MELLER, Mrs. Susan Jane, ACA *1980;* 48 Moore Street, LANE COVE, NSW 2066, AUSTRALIA.
MELLETT, Prof. Howard James, MSc FCA *1973;* 6 Tyla Teg, CARDIFF, CF14 7TL.
MELLETT, Mr. John Hilton, BSc ACA *1989;* (Tax Fac), Mid-Market Team Level 26, H S B C, 8-16 Canada Square, LONDON, E14 5HQ.
MELLETT, Miss. Tara Louise, ACA *2009;* with Oury Clark, PO Box 150, Herschel House, 58 Herschel Street, SLOUGH, SL1 1HD.
MELLETT, Mr. Thomas Francis, BCom ACA *1993;* 407 W51st Street, Apt 1B, NEW YORK, NY 10019, UNITED STATES.
MELLING, Mr. Andrew, BA ACA *2011;* 21 Merchants Quay, East Street, LEEDS, LS9 8BA.
MELLING, Mrs. Christine Elizabeth, BA FCA *1992;* 3 The Heys, Parbold, WIGAN, WN8 7DU.
MELLING, Mr. Frederick Walter, FCA *1970;* Le Bourg, 50430 LAULNE, NORMANDY, FRANCE. (Life Member)
MELLING, Mr. Ian Clifford, MSc ACA *2005;* Smith & Nephew Inc, 4721 Emperor Blvd Ste 100, DURHAM, NC 27703, UNITED STATES.
MELLING, Mrs. Jane Lisa, BAcc ACA *2006;* with Moore and Smalley LLP, Richard House, 9 Winckley Square, PRESTON, PR1 3HP.
MELLING, Mr. John, FCA *1977;* with Greenbank Partnership Limited, Greenbank House, 152 Wigan Lane, WIGAN, LANCASHIRE, WN1 2LA.
MELLING, Mr. John Kennedy, FCA *1949;* 44a Tranquil Vale, Blackheath, LONDON, SE3 0BD. (Life Member)
MELLING, Mr. Michael Johan, FCA *1973;* Broadbank, Wark, HEXHAM, NE48 3HE.
MELLING, Mr. Paul Fletcher, BA ACA *1995;* 899/199 The Star Estate@Narathiwas, Thanon Narathiwas, Yannawa, BANGKOK 10120, THAILAND.
•**MELLING, Mr. Rupert Benedict, MA FCA** *1987;* Rawlinson & Hunter, Eighth Floor, 6 New Street Square, New Fetter Lane, LONDON, EC4A 3AQ.
MELLING, Mrs. Sarah Elizabeth, BA FCA *1992;* 24 Mereworth, Caldy, WIRRAL, MERSEYSIDE, CH48 1QT.
MELLING, Miss. Sarah Louise, BCom FCA *2001;* (Tax Fac), 26 Canadian Way, BASINGSTOKE, RG24 9RE.
MELLING, Mr. Simon Charles, MSc BA ACA *1989;* 5 St. Peter's Avenue, Upper Walthamstow, LONDON, E17 3PU.
MELLING, Mr. Stephen James, BSc ACA *1991;* St. Peters Hospice, Charlton Road, Brentry, BRISTOL, BS10 6NL.
MELLIS, Mr. Darren Lee, BSc ACA *1999;* 249 Manford Way, CHIGWELL, IG7 4DQ.
MELLIS, Mr. Kevin Lloyd, BSc(Hons) ACA *2001;* 19 The Badgers, Langdon Hills, BASILDON, SS16 6AU.
MELLIS, Mr. Stuart Colin, BA(Econ) ACA *2001;* Unit 10, Easter Court, Woodward Avenue, Yate, BRISTOL, BS37 5YS.
MELLISH, Mr. Joseph John, LLB ACA *2003;* 39 Bishopsthorpe Road, LONDON, SE26 4PA.
MELLISH, Mr. Richard Paul, ACA *1985;* 3rd Floor, 2 Babmaes Street, LONDON, SW1Y 6HD.
MELLISH, Miss. Vicky, LLB ACA *2009;* 7 Maple Lodge, Riversmeet, HERTFORD, SG14 1LW.
MELLISS, Mr. Oliver Simon, ACA *2008;* Primary Capital Limited, Augustine House, 6a Austin Friars, LONDON, EC2N 2HA.
MELLISS, Mr. Simon Richard, BA FCA *1978;* Hammerson Plc, 10 Grosvenor Street, LONDON, W1K 4BJ.
MELLMAN, Mr. Laurence Adrian, BCom ACA *1991;* Buckfield, Theobald Street, RADLETT, HERTFORDSHIRE, WD7 7LR.
MELLONS, Mrs. Claire, ACA *2008;* 15 Buddle Street, CONSETT, COUNTY DURHAM, DH8 7JX.
MELLOR, Mr. Andrew James, BA(Hons) ACA *2004;* 36 Pentney Road, LONDON, SW12 0NX.
MELLOR, Mrs. Ann Jennifer, BA FCA *1975;* 6 Bramalea Close, Highgate, LONDON, N6 4QD.
•**MELLOR, Mr. Anthony David Gordon, FCA** *1984;* (Tax Fac), Mellor & Co, 1st Floor, 31 Sandiway, KNUTSFORD, WA16 8BU.
MELLOR, Mr. Carl Victor, BA ACA *1983;* Skelton Hall, The Village, Skelton, YORK, YO30 1XX.
MELLOR, Mrs. Caroline Mary, BA ACA *1993;* The Hawthorns, Warren Carr, Darley Dale, MATLOCK, DE4 2LN.
MELLOR, Mr. Charles, FCA *1970;* 13 Greenbanks Drive, Horsforth, LEEDS, LS18 5BH.
MELLOR, Mr. Christopher David, BSc FCA *1982;* NVM Private Equity Limited, Northumberland House, Princess Square, NEWCASTLE UPON TYNE, NE1 8ER.
MELLOR, Mr. Darren Michael, LLB ACA *2006;* Flat 33, 4 New Crane Place, Wapping, LONDON, E1W 3TS.
•**MELLOR, Mr. David Charles, BEng ACA** *1995;* (Tax Fac), Dixon Wilson, 22 Chancery Lane, LONDON, WC2A 1LS.
•**MELLOR, Mr. David Craig, MA ACA ATII** *1994;* (Tax Fac), Crowe Clark Whitehill LLP, St Bride's House, 10 Salisbury Square, LONDON, EC4Y 8EH. See also Horwath Clark Whitehill LLP and Crowe Clark Whitehill
•**MELLOR, Mr. David John, FCA** *1984;* (Tax Fac), Johnson Tidsall, 81 Burton Road, DERBY, DE1 1TJ. See also Derby Payroll Services Limited
MELLOR, Mr. David Lloyd, FCA *1966;* 3 Frederick Road, SUTTON COLDFIELD, B73 5QW.
MELLOR, Mrs. Fiona Elizabeth, BCom ACA *2003;* 18 Groves Way, CHESHAM, BUCKINGHAMSHIRE, HP5 2WL.
MELLOR, Mr. Harry Michael, BA ACA *1990;* Flat 201, 72 Great Titchfield Street, LONDON, W1W 7QW.
MELLOR, Mrs. Helen Louise, BA ACA *1996;* 145 East Park Farm Drive, Charvil, Twyford, READING, BERKSHIRE, RG10 9UQ.
MELLOR, Mr. James David, BSc ACA *1996;* Straight Plc, 1 Whitehall Riverside, LEEDS, LS1 4BN.
MELLOR, Mr. James Peter, FCA *1951;* 12 Orchard Rise, Gee Cross, HYDE, SK14 5SB. (Life Member)
•**MELLOR, Mrs. Jane Sarah, BA(Hons) ACA FCCA** *2008;* Glover & Co, 13/15 Netherhall Road, DONCASTER, DN1 2PH.
MELLOR, Mr. John Charles Hugh, BA FCA *1971;* 23 Ralph Swingler Place, LETCHWORTH GARDEN CITY, HERTFORDSHIRE, SG6 3GZ. (Life Member)
MELLOR, Mr. John Frederick, FCA *1953;* 132 Grove Road, WALLASEY, CH45 0JF. (Life Member)
MELLOR, Mrs. Julie, BA ACA *1987;* 11 Tower Close, Bassingbourn, ROYSTON, HERTFORDSHIRE, SG8 5JX.
MELLOR, Mrs. Louisa Marie, ACA *2009;* 31 White Hart Lane, Barnes, LONDON, SW13 0PU.
MELLOR, Mrs. Louise Emma, BA(Hons) ACA *2003;* 8 Close Oard, Clifton Park, Ramsey, ISLE OF MAN, IM8 3PY.
•**MELLOR, Mr. Malcolm Robert, FCA** *1970;* MR Mellor & Co Ltd, Panton House, Panton Place, High Street, HOLYWELL, CH8 7LD.
•**MELLOR, Mr. Martin Paul, FCA** *1973;* Page Kirk LLP, Sherwood House, 7 Gregory Boulevard, NOTTINGHAM, NG7 6LB.
MELLOR, Mrs. Mary Louise, BA FCA *1992;* 69 Nore Road, Portishead, BRISTOL, BS20 6JZ.
MELLOR, Mr. Michael George, BA FCA *1975;* 37 Avondale Road, FLEET, GU51 3BS.
MELLOR, Mr. Neil Barry, BCom ACA *2003;* 18 Groves Way, CHESHAM, BUCKINGHAMSHIRE, HP5 2WL.
MELLOR, Mr. Nicholas Peter, ACA *1993;* Capital House, 39 Anchorage Road, SUTTON COLDFIELD, B74 2PJ.
•**MELLOR, Mr. Paul Brian, BA ACA** *2003;* Clarke Nicklin LLP, Clarke Nicklin House, Brooks Drive, Cheadle Royal Business Park, CHEADLE, CHESHIRE SK8 3TD.
MELLOR, Mrs. Penny Kate, ACA *2011;* 39 Kent Road, STOCKPORT, CHESHIRE, SK3 0JD.
MELLOR, Mr. Peter Gordon, FCA *1958;* 8 Albion Park, LOUGHTON, IG10 4RB. (Life Member)
MELLOR, Mr. Peter Matthew, BA(Hons) ACA *2003;* 4 Arley Walk, Ettiley Heath, SANDBACH, CHESHIRE, CW11 3ZN.
•**MELLOR, Mr. Peter Stuart, BA FCA** *1986;* (Tax Fac), Glover & Co, 13/15 Netherhall Road, DONCASTER, DN1 2PH.
MELLOR, Miss. Sally-Anne, ACA *2006;* 91 Urban Road, SALE, CHESHIRE, M33 7TS.
MELLOR, Mr. Simon John, ACA *2009;* 32 Stock Lane, Shavington, CREWE, CW2 5ED.
MELLOR, Miss. Susan Jane, BA(Hons) ACA *2003;* 12 Ansdell Avenue, MANCHESTER, M21 8TP.
MELLOR, Mrs. Yvette Anne, ACA *1985;* Isle of Man Government Department of Social Care, Hillary House Prospect Hill Douglas, ISLE OF MAN, IM1 1EQ.
•**MELLOR-JONES, Mrs. Jacqueline, BSc ACA** *1993;* Atkinson & Co Ltd, Victoria House, 87 High Street, TILLICOULTRY, CLACKMANNANSHIRE, FK13 6AA.
MELLORS, Mr. Brian, BSc ACA *1978;* Ashmead, 5 Buckingham Drive, Radcliffe-on-Trent, NOTTINGHAM, NG12 2NE.
MELLORS, Mr. David Antony, MA ACA *1995;* 14 Lower Sand Hills, SURBITON, KT6 6RP.
MELLORS, Mr. Ernest, FCA *1953;* 12 Middlebeck Drive, Arnold, NOTTINGHAM, NG5 8AL. (Life Member)
MELLORS, Miss. Katy, BA ACA *2010;* 28 Lower Keyford, FROME, SOMERSET, BA11 4AS.
MELLORS, Mr. Keith Michael, MA ACA *1980;* York Trust Llp, Smithfield House 92 North Street, LEEDS, LS2 7PN.
MELLORS, Mrs. Louise Jane, BSc ACA *1994;* 14 Lower Sand Hills, SURBITON, KT6 6RP.
MELLORS, Mr. Niall Fraser, MA ACA *1988;* 21 Beechwood Crescent, Chandler's Ford, EASTLEIGH, SO53 5PE.
MELLORS, Mr. Peter, FCA *1975;* 29 Cumberland Avenue Chilwell, Beeston, NOTTINGHAM, NG9 4DH.
MELLORS, Mr. Robert Frank, BSc FCA *1975;* The Warrener, Warren Row, READING, BERKSHIRE, RG10 8QS.
MELLOW, Mrs. Anne Hilary, BA FCA *1985;* 42 Hale Road, FARNHAM, GU9 9QH.
MELLOWES, Mr. Stephen James, MEng ACA *2011;* 88 Heol Trecastell, CAERPHILLY, MID GLAMORGAN, CF83 1AF.
•**MELLOWS, Mr. John Stanley, FCA** *1971;* 133 Cecil Street, #15-02 Keck Seng Tower, Singapore 069535, SINGAPORE 069535, SINGAPORE.
MELLOWS, Mr. Peter James, FCA *1952;* 22 Beaumont Place, Hadley Highstone, BARNET, HERTFORDSHIRE, EN5 4PR. (Life Member)
MELLS, Mr. Robert Arthur, FCA *1961;* 81 Kent Rd, HALESOWEN, B62 8PE. (Life Member)
MELLSTROM, Mr. Graham Frederick Charles, FCA *1954;* Colesfield House, Woolmer Farm Woolmer Lane, Bramshott, LIPHOOK, HAMPSHIRE, GU30 7RD. (Life Member)
MELLSTROM, Miss. Karen Frances, BA ACA *1990;* Somerdale, Pennymead Drive, East Horsley, LEATHERHEAD, KT24 5AH.
MELLUISH, Mr. David Hector, BSc ACA *1990;* 16 Malvern Avenue, Shepshed, LOUGHBOROUGH, LE12 9ES.
MELLY, Mrs. Susan Coryn, BSc ACA *1993;* 109 Highview Road, West Ealing, LONDON, W13 0HL.
MELMAN, Mr. David Martin, FCA *1959;* 10 North View, Wimbledon Common, LONDON, SW19 4UJ.
MELMANE, Mr. Arun Arvind, ACA *2009;* 38 Abercorn Road, LONDON, NW7 1JL.
MELMOTH, Ms. Kay Lesley, LLB ACA *2001;* Teachers Provident Society, Tringham House, Deansleigh Road, BOURNEMOUTH, BH7 7DT.
MELODY, Mr. Robert Joseph, BA ACA ADIT *2003;* Barclays Capital, 5 The North Colonnade, Canary Wharf, LONDON, E14 4BB.
MELROSE, Mr. Ian David, BA ACA *1979;* 2 Dingleton Drive, MELROSE, ROXBURGHSHIRE, TD6 9JL.
MELROSE, Mr. Jason John, ACA *1994;* 5 School Croft, Riddings, ALFRETON, DE55 4EA.
MELROSE, Mr. John Samuel, BCom FCA *1988;* Deloitte, PO Box 187, First Floor, Indebank House, Kaohsiung Road, BLANTYRE MALAWI.
MELSOM, Mr. Stuart Campbell, FCA *1965;* Chiltern Lea, 12 North Approach, Moor Park, NORTHWOOD, HA6 2JG.
MELSON, Miss. Janet Elizabeth, MA BSc(Hons) ACA *2004;* 26 Blade Road, COLCHESTER, CO4 5ZU.
MELTHAM, Mr. John David, ACA *1983;* Willow Garth, Howden Croft Hill, Ellerker, BROUGH, HU15 2DE.
MELTON, Mr. Clive, FCA *1982;* 14 Istiklal Sokak, LAPTA MERSIN 10, TURKEY.
MELTON, Mrs. Kay Letitia, BA ACA *1999;* 3 Orchard Ridge, Longdon, TEWKESBURY, GL20 6AY.
MELTON, Mr. Paul John Denis, BSc ACA *1989;* Midtown, Flat 1, 322 High Holborn, LONDON, WC1V 7PB.
MELTON, Mr. Peter Stanley, BSc FCA *1978;* 47 Penlon Place, ABINGDON, OXFORDSHIRE, OX14 3QN.
MELTZER, Mrs. Naomi Joan, FCA *1972;* 8 Penn Road, Park Street, ST. ALBANS, AL2 2QS.
MELUNSKY, Mr. David Joseph, ACA *1984;* 56 Temple Sheen Road, East Sheen, LONDON, SW14 7QG.
MELVILLE, Mr. Alan John, FCA *1972;* 7 Sanderson Drive, NOTTINGHAM, NG3 5PB.
MELVILLE, Mr. Andrew Robert, BCom ACA *1993;* JP Morgan Chase Bank, 60 Victoria Embankment, LONDON, EC4Y 0JP.
MELVILLE, Mr. Colin David, MA ACA *1986;* 3 Hartwell Drive, BEACONSFIELD, BUCKINGHAMSHIRE, HP9 1JA.
MELVILLE, Mr. Mark Christopher, MChem ACA *2005;* 8 Mickleby Close, Nunthorpe, MIDDLESBROUGH, CLEVELAND, TS7 0QX.
MELVILLE, Mrs. Martina, ACA *2011;* 84 Wyndham Road, SALISBURY, SP1 3AQ.
MELVILLE, Mr. Nigel Edward, MA MSc FCA *1970;* Braehead House, Longstock, STOCKBRIDGE, SO20 6DJ.
MELVILLE, Mr. Simon Alistair, LLB ACA *1986;* 2 Dibbinview Grove, Spital, WIRRAL, CH63 9FW.
MELVILLE, Mr. Stephen, ACA *2008;* Cuplahills Farm, Balmullo, ST. ANDREWS, FIFE, KY16 0AL.
MELVILLE, Mr. Timothy John, FCA CTA(Fellow) *1972;* (Member of Council 1973 - 1974), Bramble Cottage, 1 Daltongate Court, ULVERSTON, CUMBRIA, LA12 7UA.
•**MELVIN, Mr. Alan Valentine, FCA** *1970;* Meadow House, Two Dells Lane, Ashley Green, CHESHAM, HP5 3RB.
MELVIN, Mr. David Logan, BA ACA *1987;* Merrill Lynch Int'l & Co, 2 King Edward Street, LONDON, EC1A 1HQ.
MELVIN, Mr. James, BA ACA *2011;* 3 Oxford Street, RUGBY, CV21 3NF.
MELVIN, Mr. James, MA ACA *1990;* 2 Mentone Avenue, Portobello, EDINBURGH, EH15 1HZ.
MELVIN, Mr. Jan Donat Patrick, BSc FCA *1979;* R G C Jenkins & Co, 26 Caxton Street, LONDON, SW1H 0RJ.
MELVIN, Mr. Lindsay Vyvyan, BSc ACA *1982;* 23 Park Avenue, SOLIHULL, B91 3EJ.
MELVIN, Mr. Mark Joseph, FCA CFA *1979;* PO Box 2802, HAMILTON HM LX, BERMUDA.
MELVIN, Mrs. Nicola Jane, BSc ACA *1991;* AdEPT Telecom plc 1st Floor, 77 Mount Ephraim, TUNBRIDGE WELLS, TN4 8BS.
MEMMOTT, Mr. Robert William, BSc ACA *1998;* Glenholme Drury Lane, Pannal, HARROGATE, NORTH YORKSHIRE, HG3 1ET.
MEMON, Mr. Ali, BSc FCA *1978;* 2111 Holly Hall St, Apt 4202, HOUSTON, TX 77054, UNITED STATES.
MEMON, Mr. Anwar Hussain, FCA *1977;* Office # 4 & 5, Mezannine Floor, Zulfiqar Centre, Opposite Saint Mary's School, Foujdari Road, HYDERABAD 71000 PAKISTAN.
MEMON, Mr. Mohammad Shoaib Jan, ACA *2009;* 10 Gaynes Hill Road, WOODFORD GREEN, ESSEX, IG8 8HY.
MEMON, Mr. Mohsin, ACA *2011;* 50 Windermere Gardens, Redbridge, ILFORD, ESSEX, IG4 5BZ.
MEMON, Miss. Saima Mohamed Haroon, ACA *2002;* 15-B, 12 Central Street, Phase II, DHA, KARACHI 75500, PAKISTAN.

MEMON, Mr. Shakir Nabeel, FCA *1971;* 8 Benhilton Court, 87 Benhill Wood Road, SUTTON, SURREY, SM1 3ST.

•**MEMON, Mr. Umar Adam, BSc FCA** *1995;* Jack Ross, Barnfield House, The Approach, MANCHESTER, M3 7BX.

MEMORY, Mr. David William, BCom ACA *1983;* Maxima Holdings Plc, Cotswold Court, Lansdown Road, CHELTENHAM, GLOUCESTERSHIRE, GL50 2JA.

•**MENA, Mr. Albert Anthony, BA FCA** *1992;* 11 Naval Hospital Hill, GIBRALTAR, GIBRALTAR.

MENARRY, Mr. David John, PhD MA ACA *2005;* with Lyon Griffiths Limited, 17 Alvaston Business Park, Middlewich Road, NANTWICH, CHESHIRE, CW5 6PF.

MENARRY, Mr. David Michael, BSc FCA *1990;* 4 Griffin Crescent, MANNING, WA 6152, AUSTRALIA.

MENCE, Mr. Joseph Alan, JP FCA *1947;* Peelers, High Street, YARMOUTH, PO41 0PL. (Life Member)

MENDAHUN, Miss. Yemisrach Abebe, BSc ACA *2009;* Apt 44, La Charroterie Mills, St. Peter Port, GUERNSEY, GY1 1DR.

MENDEL, Mr. Philip Baron, FCA *1959;* 127 Chiltern Avenue, BUSHEY, WD23 4QE. (Life Member)

MENDELSOHN, Mr. Alan, BSc ACA *1988;* 34 St. Georges Road, LONDON, NW11 0LR.

MENDELSOHN, Mr. Fredric William, BA ACA *1990;* 57G Randolph Avenue, LONDON, W9 1BQ.

•**MENDELSON, Mr. Philip Mark, BA FCA** *1989;* (Tax Fac), Marsden & Co, 41 Knowsley Street, BURY, LANCASHIRE, BL9 0ST.

MENDELSSOHN, Mr. Peter, FCA *1956;* The Coach House, Uckfield Lane, Hever, EDENBRIDGE, TN8 7LQ. (Life Member)

•**MENDELSSOHN, Mr. Ronald Guy, FCA** *1959;* (Tax Fac), R.G. Mendelssohn, 31 Bromsgrove Road, STUDLEY, B80 7PH.

MENDENHALL-BYRNE, Mr. Bryon, BSc(Econ) ACA *2002;* Hewlett Packard Ltd, Cain Road, BRACKNELL, BERKSHIRE, RG12 1HN.

•**MENDES, Mr. Antonio Francisco Remedio, FCA** *1975;* (Tax Fac), A Mendes & Co Limited, 55A London Road, LEICESTER, LE2 0PE. See also Gray Carpendale Ltd, Witherington & Co Ltd

MENDES, Miss. Maria Fanny Camila, ACA *1987;* 203 Church Road, BEXLEYHEATH, DA7 4DT.

MENDES, Mr. Ronald Aloysius, BSc FCA *1976;* Abbotts Inn, 88 High Street, Hillmorton, RUGBY, CV21 4EE.

MENDES DA COSTA, Ms. Caroline, MSc ACA *2010;* Blue 4, National Audit Office, 157-197 Buckingham Palace Road, LONDON, SW1W 9SP.

MENDIS, Mr. Daniel, MEng ACA *2010;* 122 Limes Road, Hardwick, CAMBRIDGE, CB23 7XU.

•**MENDLESOHN, Mr. Jeffrey Howard, FCA** *1978;* DJM Accountants LLP, Fourth Floor, Brook Point, 1412 High Road, LONDON, N20 9BH.

MENDONCA, Mr. Basil Christopher, BSc ACA *1996;* National Express Ltd Spencer House, Digbeth, BIRMINGHAM, B5 6DD.

MENDONCA, Mr. Derek Sinclair, FCA MBA *1978;* Flat 9, 1-3 Little Titchfield Street, LONDON, W1W 7BU.

MENDONCA, Mr. Philip Joseph, BA FCA *1985;* Peal House Keffolds, Bunch Lane, HASLEMERE, GU27 1AJ.

MENDOZA, Mr. Malcolm Berkeley, FCA *1961;* 3 Angel Mews, Rochampton, LONDON, SW15 4HU.

MENDOZA, Miss. Margot Eraine, MA ACA *1990;* 26 St. Stephens Avenue, Ealing, LONDON, W13 8ES.

MENDS, Mr. Daniel David, BA ACA *2006;* 39 Bellwood Road, LONDON, SE15 3DE.

MENDS, Mr. David Graham, FCA *1973;* 28 Pilkington Avenue, SUTTON COLDFIELD, B72 1LA.

MENELAOU, Mr. Menelaos, BSc ACA *1992;* Omilos Group, 39-41 Academiei Street, 4th Floor, 1st District, 010013 BUCHAREST, ROMANIA.

MENELAOU, Mrs. Olga, BA ACA *2003;* 9 Aristogitonos Street, Saint John, CY 3016 LIMASSOL, CYPRUS.

MENELAOU, Miss. Polyxeni, ACA *2007;* 3 Alamanas street, Flat 201, 2415 NICOSIA, CYPRUS.

MENELAOU, Ms. Rebecca, BA ACA *1991;* Markou Mbotsari 4, Strovolos, 2054 NICOSIA, CYPRUS.

MENELL, Mr. Jeremy Jacob, BEng ACA *1997;* 95 Burnham Green Road, WELWYN, HERTFORDSHIRE, AL6 0NH.

•**MENESES, Mrs. Donna Louise, BSc ACA** *2002;* DLM Accountancy Services, 19 Warren Road, BANSTEAD, SURREY, SM7 1LG.

•**MENEZ, Mr. Kristian Charles, BSc ACA** *2004;* PricewaterhouseCoopers, Intnl Commercial Centre, Casemates Square, GIBRALTAR, GIBRALTAR.

MENEZES, Mr. Gerald Stany, FCA *1973;* 11-1 Seaplace, Juhu Tara Road Juhu, MUMBAI 400049, INDIA. (Life Member)

MENEZES, Mr. Irvin George Luis, ACA *1993;* 8 Jalan Bukit Desa 2, Taman Bukit Desa, 58100 KUALA LUMPUR, FEDERAL TERRITORY, MALAYSIA.

•**MENEZES, Mr. Michael Patrick, FCA** *1963;* Menezes & Co, 16 Kings Avenue, BROMLEY, BR1 4HW. See also Michael Patrick Menezes

MENG, Mr. Hua, ACA *2009;* Room 602 Unit 1 Building 8, No.100 Gong Ye Nan Road, Lixia District, JINAN 250100, SHANDONG PROVINCE, CHINA.

MENHENITT, Mr. James Saunders Neal, BSc ACA *2000;* Terre Norgiot Cottage, Rue De La Terre Norgiot, St Saviour, GUERNSEY, GY7 9JW.

MENMUIR, Mr. Paul Richard, FCA *1971;* Flat 7, 22 Down Street, LONDON, W1J 7AR.

MENNELL, Mr. John Richard, FCA *1973;* 4 Dale View, ILKLEY, LS29 9BP.

MENNELL, Miss. Laura Marie, BA ACA *2005;* 74, Flat 74 The Circle, Queen Elizabeth Street, LONDON, SE1 2JG.

MENNELL, Mrs. Sarah Louise, BA ACA *1999;* Volker Rail Ltd, Carolina Court, DONCASTER, SOUTH YORKSHIRE, DN4 5RA.

MENNIE, Mr. Iain Malcolm David, BSc ACA *1988;* SCA Packaging Limited, 10-12 Cloberfield, Milngavie, GLASGOW, G62 7LN.

MENNIE, Mrs. Sarah Louise, ACA *2002;* 17 Harlech Drive, Hazel Grove, STOCKPORT, SK7 5NA.

MENON, Mr. Gopakumar, BSc ACA *1998;* Thomson Reuters, PO Box 1426, DUBAI, UNITED ARAB EMIRATES.

MENON, Mr. Kelvin Suresh, BSc ACA *1991;* Surrey Heath Borough Council Surrey Heath House, Knoll Road, CAMBERLEY, SURREY, GU15 3HD.

MENON, Mr. Kondath Praveen Kumar, BCom ACA CTA *2002;* Flat 12 Repton House, 20 Scott Avenue, LONDON, SW15 3PB.

MENON, Mr. Krishnan, FCA *1975;* 17 Jalan Tijani 4, Tijani 2 South, off Jalan Langgak Tunku, 50480 KUALA LUMPUR, FEDERAL TERRITORY, MALAYSIA.

MENON, Mr. Mohan Parmeshwar, FCA *1986;* 98 HOLLAND GROVE VIEW, SINGAPORE 276255, SINGAPORE.

MENON, Mr. Preman, BA(Hons) ACA *2002;* Unit B-12-4, Menara Bangsar, 297 Jalan Maarof, 59100 KUALA LUMPUR, FEDERAL TERRITORY, MALAYSIA.

MENON, Mrs. Sophie, BA ACA *1999;* 30 Sandford Road, BROMLEY, BR2 9AW.

•**MENON, Mr. Vikram, BEng FCA** *1995;* 9 Heyford Avenue, LONDON, SW8 1EA.

MENON, Ms. Vimala, ACA *1980;* No 11 Jalan SS19/4E, 47500 SUBANG, SELANGOR, MALAYSIA.

MENSAH, Mr. Bernard, BSocSc ACA *1992;* Merrill Lynch Financial Centre, 2 King Edward Street, LONDON, EC1A 1HQ.

MENSAH, Mr. Daniel, MSc BA ACA *2010;* 3 Dering Road, CROYDON, CR0 1DS.

MENSFORTH, Mr. Stephen, BSc ACA *1982;* 1A Cloister Way, LEAMINGTON SPA, CV32 6QE.

•**MENSFORTH, Ms. Susan, FCA** *1967;* Susan Baron, The Old School, Over Haddon, BAKEWELL, DERBYSHIRE, DE45 1JE.

•**MENTON, Mr. Mark, BA(Hons) ACA** *2002;* with PricewaterhouseCoopers, 89 Sandyford Road, NEWCASTLE UPON TYNE, NE1 8HW.

MENTZ, Mrs. Susan Elizabeth, BSc ACA *1979;* 34 Barley Farm Road, Redhills, EXETER, EX4 1NN.

MENZIES, Mr. Alan Brown, FCA *1955;* 4 Moor Park Mount, Headingley, LEEDS, LS6 4BU. (Life Member)

MENZIES, Mr. Alexander, BSc ACA *2007;* Flat 6, 19 Colville Terrace, LONDON, W11 2BU.

MENZIES, Mr. Euan Hector, MA ACA *1995;* 24 Balcombe Road, HAYWARDS HEATH, RH16 1PF.

MENZIES, Mr. Gary Neil, BSc ACA *1991;* First/Keolis Transpennine Limited, 7th Floor, Bridgewater House, 60 Whitworth Street, MANCHESTER, M1 6LT.

MENZIES, Mr. Ian Barnes, BA FCA *1975;* 16 The Drive, Horton, NORTHAMPTON, NN7 2AY.

MENZIES, Mrs. Nicola, BSc ACA *1995;* The Shieling, 4 Raglan Road, REIGATE, SURREY, RH2 0DP.

•**MENZIES, Mr. Stewart George Cameron, ACA** *1978;* Menzies Cameron Limited, Rowden House, 25 Rowden Hill, CHIPPENHAM, SN15 2AQ.

MENZIES-CONACHER, Mr. Ian Duncan, JP BSc(Econ) ACIB FCA ATII *1974;* (Tax Fac), 9 St. Peter's Close, PRINCES RISBOROUGH, HP27 0SS.

MENZIES-WILSON, Mr. James Ralph, BSc ACA *1983;* Mill House, Tredington, TEWKESBURY, GLOUCESTERSHIRE, GL20 7BW.

MEPHAM, Mr. Brian William, FCA *1961;* Millstones, Portmore Park Road, WEYBRIDGE, KT13 8HA. (Life Member)

MEPHAM, Mr. Neil, BA ACA *1988;* New Haven, Oldhill Wood, Studham, DUNSTABLE, BEDFORDSHIRE, LU6 2NE.

MEPHAM, Mr. Wayne, BA FCA *1999;* 67 Gibbon Road, KINGSTON UPON THAMES, KT2 6AD.

MERALI, Mr. Abbasali Mohamed, BSc ACA *2001;* 19 Mountview, NORTHWOOD, HA6 3NZ.

MERALI, Mr. Allaudin Shivji, FCA *1975;* 12808-66 Avenue, EDMONTON T6H 1Y7, AB, CANADA.

MERALI, Mr. Alnoor Gulamhussein Abdulrasul, ACA *1984;* 2 Shelley Close, NORTHWOOD, HA6 3HX.

MERALI, Mr. Hasnain Mohamedtaki, ACA *1993;* 12 The Fairway, NORTHWOOD, HA6 3DY.

MERALI, Mr. Jawad, ACA *2008;* 21 Bedford Road, Moor Park, NORTHWOOD, MIDDLESEX, HA6 2BA.

•**MERALI, Mr. Mahmud Pyarali Kassamali, FCA** *1976;* (Tax Fac), Meralis, First Floor, Scottish Provident House, 76-80 College Road, HARROW, MIDDLESEX HA1 1BQ.

•**MERALI, Mr. Mohammed Azeem Mohamed, BEng ACA** *1997;* Grant Thornton UK LLP, 30 Finsbury Square, LONDON, EC2P 2YU. See also Grant Thornton LLP

MERALI, Mr. Salim, FCA CISA CFP *1981;* 1807 -109 Street, EDMONTON T6J 6K3, AB, CANADA.

MERALI, Mr. Shabbir Hassanali Walimohamed, FCA *1982;* 21 Leigh Rodd, Carpenters Park, WATFORD, WD19 5BJ.

MERATH, Mrs. Kirsty Ann, BA ACA *2007;* with PricewaterhouseCoopers, Royal Trust Tower, Suite 3000 TD Centre, Box 82, 77 King Street West, TORONTO M5K 1G8 ON CANADA.

•**MERATI, Mr. Abolghassem, BSc FCA** *1970;* KPMG Bayat Rayan, 3rd Floor, 239 Motahari Ave, TEHRAN, 15876, IRAN.

MERATI, Mr. Bruce, BSc FCA *1985;* 12648 Caminito Radiante, SAN DIEGO, CA 92130, UNITED STATES.

MERCADO, Mr. David Simon, BA(Hons) ACA *2002;* 15 Newmans Way, BARNET, HERTFORDSHIRE, EN4 0LP.

MERCER, Mr. Adam, ACA *2009;* Flat 2, 154 Goswell Road, LONDON, EC1V 7DX.

•**MERCER, Mr. Anthony Brian, FCA** *1969;* A.B. Mercer, Broad Dale, Pennington Lane, ULVERSTON, LA12 7SE.

•**MERCER, Mr. Brian Philip, FCA** *1981;* Pepperings, Coast Road, Normans Bay, PEVENSEY, EAST SUSSEX, BN24 6PR.

MERCER, Miss. Claire Susan, MMath ACA DChA *2004;* 75 Upper George Street, HIGHAM FERRERS, NORTHAMPTONSHIRE, NN10 8JN.

MERCER, Mr. David Edward, FCA *1967;* 19 Bridgewater Drive, Great Glen, LEICESTER, LE8 9DX. (Life Member)

MERCER, Mr. Francis Charles, FCA *1969;* 20 Ramleh Park, Blundellsands, LIVERPOOL, L23 6YD.

MERCER, Mr. Henry, FCA *1962;* 8 Fairleigh Rise, Kington Langley, CHIPPENHAM, SN15 5QF. (Life Member)

MERCER, Mr. James Frank Eric, MA BA ACA *2007;* Victoria University of Wellington, 18 Kelburn Parade, PO Box 600, WELLINGTON 6140, NEW ZEALAND.

MERCER, Mrs. Jane, BA ACA *1999;* Deep Secure, 1 Nimrod House, Sandys Road, MALVERN, WORCESTERSHIRE, WR14 1JJ.

MERCER, Mrs. Jane Renee, BA FCA *1976;* 188 Eglinton Avenue East, Unit # 313, TORONTO M4P 2X7, ON, CANADA.

MERCER, Mr. John Alexander, FCA *1964;* Apartment 27 H Q, 11 Nuns Road, CHESTER, CH1 2LH.

•**MERCER, Mr. John Duncan, FCA** *1973;* J.D. Mercer & Co Ltd, 9 Chapel Street, POULTON-LE-FYLDE, FY6 7BQ.

MERCER, Mr. John Michael, ACA *1982;* The Law Society Ipsley Court, Berrington Close, REDDITCH, WORCESTERSHIRE, B98 0TD.

•**MERCER, Mr. John Vaughan, BA ACA** *1994;* with BDO LLP, Fourth Floor, One Victoria Street, BRISTOL, BS1 6AA.

•**MERCER, Mr. Jonathan Francis, BA ACA** *2000;* Leonard Curtis Recovery Limited, Hollins Lane, BURY, LANCASHIRE, BL9 8DG. See also DTE Leonard Curtis Limited

MERCER, Miss. Kathryn Hilary, BSc ACA *1987;* 35 Dean Close, Pyrford, WOKING, GU22 8NX.

MERCER, Mr. Lindsay Cordell Johnstone, FCA FIIA CITP MBCS *1973;* LCM Solutions Ltd, 19 Fallowfield Drive, Barton under Needwood, BURTON-ON-TRENT, STAFFORDSHIRE, DE13 8DH.

•**MERCER, Mr. Nigel John, BA ACA** *1986;* Deloitte LLP, 2 New Street Square, LONDON, EC4A 3BZ. See also Deloitte & Touche LLP

•**MERCER, Mr. Peter Martin, FCA** *1970;* Mercer Lewin Ltd, 41 Cornmarket Street, OXFORD, OX1 3HA.

•**MERCER, Mr. Roger William, FCA** *1956;* R.W.Mercer & Co, Welford House, Matlock Street, BAKEWELL, DE45 1EE.

MERCER, Mrs. Ruth Elaine, BA ACA *1995;* 5 Burnt Stones Grove, Sandygate, SHEFFIELD, S10 5TU.

MERCER, Mrs. Sandra, ACA *1982;* 14 Airmyn Road, GOOLE, DN14 6XE.

MERCER, Mr. Terence Andrew, BSc FCA *1983;* 4 Rambler Close, Thornhill, CARDIFF, CF14 9FH.

MERCHANT, Mr. Abdul Khalick, FCA *1975;* 81 Devonshire Road, LONDON, NW7 1DR.

MERCHANT, Mr. Aqueel Ebrahim, FCA *1992;* C/O Ernst & Young Ford Rhodes Sidat Hyder., 6th Floor Progressive Plaza, Beaumont Road, PO Box 15541, KARACHI 75530, PAKISTAN.

MERCHANT, Mrs. Bridget Jean, BA ACA *1991;* 28 Denham Road, EPSOM, KT17 3AA.

MERCHANT, Mr. David Timothy, BSc(Econ) ACA *2001;* 2 St. Dunstans Close, Monks Risborough, PRINCES RISBOROUGH, BUCKINGHAMSHIRE, HP27 9BN.

•**MERCHANT, Mr. Jamal, FCA** *1976;* 3 Gordondale Road, Wimbledon Park, LONDON, SW19 8EN.

MERCHANT, Mrs. Joanne, BSc ACA *1992;* Glengairn House, 85 Castledine Street, LOUGHBOROUGH, LEICESTERSHIRE, LE11 2DX.

MERCHANT, Mr. Mahboob Ali, ACA *1981;* (Tax Fac), 28 Denham Road, EPSOM, KT17 3AA.

MERCHANT, Mr. Mahmood Hasan, BSc FCA *1995;* PO Box 131185, ABU DHABI, UNITED ARAB EMIRATES.

MERCHANT, Mr. Mohammed Abbas, BSc ACA *2005;* 572 Rayners Lane, Harrow, PINNER, MIDDLESEX, HA5 5HY.

MERCHANT, Mr. Paul Geoffrey, BSc ACA *1995;* Man & Machine Ltd, Unit 8, Thame Forty, Jane Morbey Road, THAME, OXFORDSHIRE OX9 3RR.

MERCHANT, Mrs. Rebecca Louise, BSc ACA *2003;* 34 Albert Road North, REIGATE, SURREY, RH2 9EG.

•**MERCHANT, Mr. Roger Leonard, BSc FCA** *1983;* (Member of Council 2009 - 2011), PKF (UK) LLP, Regent House, Clinton Avenue, NOTTINGHAM, NG5 1AZ.

•**MERCHANT, Mr. Sadruddin Ashraf, FCA** *1973;* (Tax Fac), Sam Merchant, 73 Gorsewood Road, St. John's, WOKING, GU21 8XG.

MERCHANT, Mr. Simon John, MA FCA ATII *1975;* 4 Shepherds Way, RICKMANSWORTH, WD3 7NJ.

MERCHANT, Mr. Vijay, BSc ACA *2009;* 8 Brook Way, BIRMINGHAM, B16 0QR.

MERCIECA, Mr. Andrew Paul, BA ACA *1991;* 2 Hunter Road, LONDON, SW20 8NZ.

MERCOURI, Mr. Andreas, BSc ACA *2008;* Flat 204, Zachariou Court 2, Nikolaou Mantzarou 17, 6042 LARNACA, CYPRUS.

MERDIS, Mr. Christos, BSc ACA *2010;* 6 Feidiou Street, Pano Lakatamia, 2314 NICOSIA, CYPRUS.

MEREDITH, Mr. Alan, FCA *1961;* A4 Harewood Court, Marsland Road, SALE, M33 3WW.

MEREDITH, Mr. Andrew William, MA ACA *1990;* 62 Charlock Way, Southwater, HORSHAM, RH13 9GZ.

•**MEREDITH, Mr. Ashley John Burton, FCA** *1970;* Ashley J. B. Meredith, 22 Riverside Road, West Moors, FERNDOWN, BH22 0LQ.

MEREDITH, Mr. Carl Anthony, MEng ACA *2003;* 31 Cannon Street, ST. ALBANS, HERTFORDSHIRE, AL3 5JR.

•**MEREDITH, Mrs. Caroline Louise, FCA CTA FMAAT** *1999;* Caroline Meredith, 9 Bowling Green Lane, Purley on Thames, READING, RG8 8EJ.

•**MEREDITH, Mr. Christopher Thomas Arthur, FCA** *1964;* (Tax Fac), Meredith Thomas, Suite No 1, Royal Arcade, PERSHORE, WR10 1AG. See also Pershore Management Services Ltd

MEREDITH, Mr. Darren Craig William, BA(Hons) ACA *2001;* (Tax Fac), North Bakers Barn, Kingsley, BORDON, HAMPSHIRE, GU35 9NJ.

MEREDITH, Mr. David, ACA *2010;* 2 Eleanor Street, BOLTON, BL1 8RZ.

•**MEREDITH, Mr. David John Rouse, MA FCA** *1986;* Busbys, Unit 7, Pickhill Business Centre, Smallhythe Road, TENTERDEN, KENT TN30 7LZ. See also Busby C R & Co
•**MEREDITH, Mr. Duncan Gabriel, BSc FCA** *1985;* (Tax Fac), Meredith Tax LLP, Unit 16, Clifton Moor Business Village, Clifton Moor, YORK, YO30 4XG.
MEREDITH, Mr. Edward John, BEng ACA *2001;* c/o KPMG, 18 Viaduct Harbour Ave, AUCKLAND 1011, NEW ZEALAND.
MEREDITH, Mr. Edward Thornton, FCA *1949;* 66 Millfield Lane, Nether Poppleton, YORK, YO26 6LZ. (Life Member)
MEREDITH, Mrs. Eleanor Heather, BA FCA *1992;* 95 Cranbrook Road, BRISTOL, BS6 7DA.
MEREDITH, Ms. Gillian Carol, BA ACA *1989;* Coats Plc, 1 The Square, Stockley Park, UXBRIDGE, MIDDLESEX, UB11 1TD.
MEREDITH, Mrs. Gillian Doreen, BSc FCA *1981;* 14 High View Road, Endon, STOKE-ON-TRENT, ST9 9HT.
MEREDITH, Mr. Gordon, FCA *1954;* 8 Seaton Drive, ASHFORD, Middlesex, TW15 3ET. (Life Member)
MEREDITH, Mrs. Helen, LLB ACA *2002;* A S L, Bury House, 31 Bury Street, LONDON, EC3A 5AG.
MEREDITH, Mr. James, BSc ACA *2000;* 190 Mincinglake Road, Stoke Hill, EXETER, EX4 7DS.
•**MEREDITH, Mr. Jonathan Charles, FCA** *1971;* Orchard Cottage, Lower Wardington, BANBURY, OX17 1SL.
•**MEREDITH, Mr. Neil David, BA ACA** *1994;* KPMG LLP, One Snowhill, Snow Hill Queensway, BIRMINGHAM, B4 6GN. See also KPMG Europe LLP
•**MEREDITH, Mr. Nigel Headley, FCA** *1976;* (Tax Fac), Folkes Worton LLP, 15-17 Church Street, STOURBRIDGE, WEST MIDLANDS, DY8 1LU.
•**MEREDITH, Mr. Nigel John, BA FCA** *1987;* Ernst & Young LLP, 1 Colmore Square, BIRMINGHAM, B4 6HQ. See also Ernst & Young Europe LLP
MEREDITH, Mr. Oliver Duplan, BSc FCA *1995;* Linfold, Franks Hollow Road, Bidborough, TUNBRIDGE WELLS, KENT, TN3 0UD.
MEREDITH, Mr. Paul Vanstan, FCA *1975;* The Croft, Tamworth Road, Cliff Nr Kingsbury, TAMWORTH, B78 2DL.
MEREDITH, Mr. Peter George, MA FCA *1967;* Leylands, St. Wilfrids St, Calverley, PUDSEY, LS28 5RQ.
MEREDITH, Mr. Philip, FCA *1963;* Snape Clock House, Snape Lane, WADHURST, TN5 6NS. (Life Member)
MEREDITH, Mr. Philip James, BSc(Hons) ACA *2000;* 7 Plassey Square, PENARTH, SOUTH GLAMORGAN, CF64 1HB.
•**MEREDITH, Mr. Robert William, FCA** *1962;* R.W.Meredith, 256 Higham Lane, NUNEATON, CV11 6AR.
MEREDITH, Mr. Simon Paul, BSc ACA *1981;* 208 Kennedy Street West, AURORA L4G 2L7, ON, CANADA.
•**MEREDITH, Mr. Stephen John, BA FCA DChA** *1993;* Alliotts, Friary Court, 13-21 High Street, GUILDFORD, SURREY, GU1 3DL.
•**MEREDITH, Mr. William Rufus Charles, BA ACA** *1992;* KPMG LLP, 15 Canada Square, LONDON, E14 5GL. See also KPMG Europe LLP
MERFYN, Mrs. Lisa Jane, BSc ACA *2007;* 11 Drysgol Road, Radyr, CARDIFF, CF15 8BT.
MERFYN, Mr. Ynyr, BSc ACA *2006;* 11 Drysgol Road, Radyr, CARDIFF, CF15 8BT.
MERIC, Mr. Mustafa, BSc(Hons) ACA *2002;* 10 Emerson Road, ILFORD, ESSEX, IG1 4XA.
MERICAN, Mr. Johan Mahmood, BA ACA *1999;* 9 Lorong Jarak Kanan, Bukit Damansara, 50490 KUALA LUMPUR, FEDERAL TERRITORY, MALAYSIA.
MERICAN, Mr. Mohamed Khadar, ACA *1982;* A17-8 Mutiara Upper East Ampang 39 Jalan 1/76, Desa Pandan, 55100 KUALA LUMPUR, FEDERAL TERRITORY, MALAYSIA.
MERICAN, Mr. Mohd Hassan Bin, FCA *1978;* Petroliam Nasional Berhad, Level 81 Tower 1, Petronas Twin Towers, Kuala Lumpur City Centre, 50088 KUALA LUMPUR, FEDERAL TERRITORY MALAYSIA.
MERIFIELD, Mr. David Anthony, FCA *1963;* 12 Tewkesbury Av, PINNER, HA5 5LH.
MERIFIELD, Mr. Robert Keith, BA(Hons) ACA *2003;* Town Hall, New Forest District Council Town Hall, Avenue Road, LYMINGTON, HAMPSHIRE, SO41 9ZG.
MERIFIELD, Mrs. Victoria, BA ACA *2000;* 66 Doe Copse Way, NEW MILTON, HAMPSHIRE, BH25 5GN.
MERISON, Mr. Paul Owen, BA ACA *1996;* 20 Leonie Hill, #12-20, SINGAPORE 239222, SINGAPORE.
MERKENS, Mrs. Marion Georgina, BA FCA *1975;* Jasmine House, Hollington, ASHBOURNE, DE6 3GD.
MERKIN, Mr. Howard Sidney, FCA *1952;* 3 Harolds Close, Walsoken, WISBECH, PE14 7BS. (Life Member)
MERKLER, Mr. Andrew, FCA *1959;* 7A Sheridan Road, LONDON, SW19 3HW. (Life Member)
MERLE, Mr. Gerard Daniel, FCA *1964;* 13 Rue Ste. Marie, 97400, ST. DENIS, REUNION. (Life Member)
MERMAGEN, Mr. Matthew Robert Pellow, MSc BA ACA *2000;* 4900 S Monaco Street, DENVER, CO 80210, UNITED STATES.
MERONE, Mr. Paul Stephen, BSc ACA CF *1993;* Bobbin Mill Gate, Caldbeck, WIGTON, CUMBRIA, CA7 8EW.
MERRELL, Mr. Alan Stuart, ACA *1984;* 21 Fryer Avenue, LEAMINGTON SPA, CV32 6HY.
MERRELL, Mr. Paul David, BSc ACA CTA *1998;* (Tax Fac), with EDF Tax LLP, 7 Regan Way, Chetwynd Business Park, Chilwell, NOTTINGHAM, NG9 6RZ.
MERRETT, Mr. Adam Michael, ACA *2009;* 201 Vauxhall Bridge Road, LONDON, SW1V 1ER.
MERRETT, Mr. Andrew Gregory Glyn, BSocSc ACA *1996;* Weavers Cottage Bristol Road, Cambridge, GLOUCESTER, GL2 7BG.
MERRETT, Mr. Colin Andrew, MA ACA *1998;* Flat 12, 9-11 Belsize Grove, LONDON, NW3 4UU.
MERRETT, Mr. Keith James, FCA *1962;* 10 Riverside Court, Dee Banks, Great Boughton, CHESTER, CH3 5UX.
MERRETT, Mr. Paul Steven, BA FCA *1986;* British American Tobacco Plc, 4 Temple Place, LONDON, WC2R 2PG.
MERRETT, Mr. Simon John, FCA *1975;* 1 Kyrle Gardens Batheaston, BATH, BA1 7RE.
MERREY, Mr. Paul Richard, MA ACA MBA *1999;* with KPMG LLP, 15 Canada Square, LONDON, E14 5GL.
MERRIAM, Mr. Andrew William Kennedy, FCA *1972;* Oak Lawn House, EYE, IP23 7NN.
•**MERRICK, Mr. Andrew David, BSc ACA** *1989;* Reinsbrook Sambourne Park, Sambourne Lane, Sambourne, REDDITCH, B96 6PE.
MERRICK, Mrs. Caragh, MA FCA *1982;* 28 Battenhall Road, WORCESTER, WR5 2BL.
MERRICK, Mrs. Ceridwen Mary, FCA *1959;* 15637 South 26th Court, PHOENIX, AZ 85048, UNITED STATES. (Life Member)
MERRICK, Mrs. Claire, ACA *2008;* Infinis Ltd, 500 Pavilion Drive, NORTHAMPTON, NN4 7YJ.
MERRICK, Ms. Elizabeth, BSc ACA *1986;* 21 Wayneflete Tower Avenue, ESHER, KT10 8QQ.
MERRICK, Mr. Ian Aveling Claude, FCA *1975;* Kenilworth Heneage Lane, Falfield, WOTTON-UNDER-EDGE, GL12 8DN. (Life Member)
MERRICK, Mr. Mark Peter, BA ACA *1995;* A M Seafoods Ltd, Siding Road, FLEETWOOD, LANCASHIRE, FY7 6NS.
MERRICK, Mr. Matthew David, BSc ACA *2007;* 21 St. Michaels Road, ALDERSHOT, GU12 4JH.
MERRICK, Mr. Matthew Graham, BA ACA *2004;* The Garden House, 28 High Street, Haversham, MILTON KEYNES, MK19 7DX.
MERRICK, Mr. Nigel Alexander Shaun, FCA *1976;* Home Farm House, Somerby, BARNETBY, DN38 6EX.
•**MERRICKS, Mr. Graham Wyatt, FCA** *1960;* Winters Grace, Nags Head Lane, Avening, TETBURY, GLOUCESTERSHIRE, GL8 8NZ.
MERRICKS, Ms. Zara Louise, BSc(Hons) ACA *2002;* 50 Quarry Street, GUILDFORD, GU1 3UA.
MERRIEN, Mr. John Francis, MSc ACA ACIS *2004;* Ashlyn, Les Hautes Landes, Vale, GUERNSEY, GY3 5DA.
MERRIFIELD, Mr. Christopher, FCA *1964;* Willow Bank, 6 The Fairway, DEVIZES, SN10 5DX.
MERRIFIELD, Miss. Susan, BSc ACA *1990;* 25 Canadian Bay Road, MOUNT ELIZA, VIC 3930, AUSTRALIA.
•**MERRILL, Mr. Mark, MSc LLB FCA DChA** *1974;* Mark Merrill, PO Box 2164, 142 The Borough, Downton, SALISBURY, WILTSHIRE SP2 2ES.
MERRILL, Mr. Stephen, BSc ACA *1985;* 11 Trent Avenue, Ealing, LONDON, W5 4TL.
MERRIMAN, Mr. Andrew John, BA FCA *1992;* Florance House Withyham Road, Groombridge, TUNBRIDGE WELLS, TN3 9QR.
MERRIMAN, Mr. Anthony Malcolm, BA FCA *1960;* Danby, The Causeway, Congresbury, BRISTOL, BS49 5DJ. (Life Member)
MERRIMAN, Mr. Brendan Richard, FCA *1983;* The Fairway, 17 Kestrel Close, Ewshot, FARNHAM, GU10 5TW.
MERRIMAN, Mr. Sebastian Philip, LLM LLB ACA CTA *2002;* Pricewaterhousecoopers Audit LLC, Central Tower, 6th Floor, Suite 601, ULAANBAATAR 14200, MONGOLIA.
•**MERRIMAN, Mr. Steven Willis, FCA** *1980;* Pells, 17 Newstead Grove, NOTTINGHAM, NG1 4GZ. See also T Wilford Pell & Company
MERRIN, Mr. Duncan Samuel Rothwell, FCA *1964;* 42 Pasir Panjang Hill, #04-01, SINGAPORE 118894, SINGAPORE.
MERRINGTON, Mr. Brian George, FCA *1970;* 61 Yorkshire Place, Warfield, BRACKNELL, RG42 3XF.
MERRINGTON, Mr. Matthew Peter Anthony, BA(Hons) ACA *2009;* 1 Bunning Way, LONDON, N7 9UN.
MERRIS, Mr. Paul Trevor, BSc ACA *1998;* with BDO LLP, 125 Colmore Row, BIRMINGHAM, B3 3SD.
MERRISON, Mr. Peter Andrew, BSc ACA *1979;* The Chalfonts Community College Narcot Lane, Chalfont St. Peter, GERRARDS CROSS, BUCKINGHAMSHIRE, SL9 8TP.
MERRITT, Mrs. Annetta Mary, ACA *1994;* 7 La Rue de la Forge, Grouville, JERSEY, JE3 9BH.
MERRITT, Mrs. Caroline Joy, BA ACA *1992;* 21 Grove Park Gardens, Chiswick, LONDON, W4 3RY.
MERRITT, Mr. David James, MA ACA *2010;* Flat 14 The Junxion, Station Approach, LEEDS, LS5 3HR.
MERRITT, Mr. David John, FCA *1963;* 4 St. Edmunds Apartments, Lower Baxter Street, BURY ST. EDMUNDS, SUFFOLK, IP33 1EF.
•**MERRITT, Mr. Dean Edward John, BA ACA** *1992;* Talbot Hughes McKillop LLP, 6 Snow Hill, LONDON, EC1A 2AY.
MERRITT, Miss. Louise Karen, MEng ACA *2000;* Flat 2, Escote Court, 16 Park Hill Road, BROMLEY, BR2 0LE.
•**MERRITT, Mr. Michael William, MA FCA** *1983;* (Tax Fac), Lewis Brownlee, Avenue House, Southgate, CHICHESTER, WEST SUSSEX, PO19 1ES. See also Lewis Brownlee Sherlock
MERRIWEATHER, Mr. Simon Martin, BSc ACA *1990;* Hadley West Monkton, TAUNTON, SOMERSET, TA2 8QZ.
•**MERRON, Ms. Amanda, BSc ACA** *1988;* Kingston Smith LLP, 141 Wardour Street, LONDON, W1F 0UT. See also Kingston Smith Limited Liability Partnership, Devonshire Corporate Services LLP and Kingston Smith Consulting LLP
MERRY, Miss. Barbara Jane, BA ACA *1984;* 1st Floor, Fitzwilliam House, 10 St Mary Axe, LONDON, EC3A 8NA.
MERRY, Mr. Christopher James, BA FCA *1986;* 5 The Drive, KINGSTON UPON THAMES, SURREY, KT2 7NY.
MERRY, Mrs. Claire, BSc ACA *1996;* Longueville House, Hardwick Close, Oxshott, LEATHERHEAD, SURREY, KT22 0HZ.
MERRY, Mr. John Eric, FCA *1960;* 102 Clearwater Road, WINNIPEG R2J 2T5, MB, CANADA. (Life Member)
MERRY, Mrs. Julie Carina, BSc ACA *1988;* Zircadian Ltd Tuition House, 27-37 St. Georges Road, LONDON, SW19 4EU.
MERRY, Mr. Leigh, BSc FCA *1989;* (Tax Fac), with Stephenson Smart, 22-26 King Street, KING'S LYNN, NORFOLK, PE30 1HJ.
MERRY, Mrs. Rosemary Vivienne, MA ACA *1981;* Monks Down, 12 Warwicks Bench Road, GUILDFORD, GU1 3TL.
MERRY, Mr. Scott Iain, BSc FCA *1992;* Morgan Stanley, 20 Bank Street, LONDON, E14 4AD.
•**MERRY, Mr. Stewart Scott, BSc ACA** *1989;* (Tax Fac), Robertson Craig, 3 Clairmont Gardens, GLASGOW, G3 7LW. See also Robertson Craig & co
MERRYMAN, Mr. Dean, BA ACA *1996;* Dairy Crest Ltd Claygate House, Littleworth Road, ESHER, KT10 9PN.
MERRYWEATHER, Mrs. Heather, BA ACA *1996;* Broadlands, 13 Preston Crowmarsh, WALLINGFORD, OXFORDSHIRE, OX10 6SL.
MERRYWEATHER, Mr. Mark Ian, BA ACA *1988;* Pheasant Cottage, Frensham, FARNHAM, SURREY, GU10 3DH.
MERSON, Mrs. Anne Louise, BSc ACA *1999;* PO Box 8428, RANCHO SANTA FE, CA 92067, UNITED STATES.
MERSON, Miss. Hannah Margaret, BSc ACA *2001;* 1 Levens Close, West Bridgford, NOTTINGHAM, NG2 6SN.
•**MERSON, Mrs. Joanna Katharine, MA ACA** *1991;* Rupert Merson LLP, 24 Ribblesdale Road, LONDON, SW16 6SE.
MERSON, Mr. Mark Simon, MA ACA *1993;* Barclays Capital, 5 North Colonnade, LONDON, E14 4BB.
MERSON, Mrs. Nicola, BSc ACA *1997;* 43 Barham Avenue, Elstree, BOREHAMWOOD, HERTFORDSHIRE, WD6 3PW.
MERSON, Mr. Richard David, MA ACA *1980;* Fern Lea, 14 Beach Road, NORTHWICH, CW8 4BB.
MERSON, Mr. Robert Anthony, FCA *1974;* Tanyard House, 13a Bridge Square, FARNHAM, GU9 7QR.
•**MERSON, Mr. Rupert James, MA ACA** *1988;* Rupert Merson LLP, 24 Ribblesdale Road, LONDON, SW16 6SE.
MERSON, Mrs. Ruth Paula, ACA *1993;* High Briars, Grassy Lane, SEVENOAKS, TN13 1PW.
MERSON, Ms. Valerie, BA ACA *1984;* 26 Lattimer Place, LONDON, W4 2UB.
MERTENS, Mrs. Sinah, BA(Hons) ACA *2000;* Emmastr. 25, 50937 COLOGNE, GERMANY.
MERTON, Mr. Jeremy Louis, BSc ACA *1992;* 19 Brayburne Avenue, Clapham, LONDON, SW4 6AD.
MERTON, Mr. Michael Ralph, FCA *1975;* Shottesbrooke Cottage Smewins Road, White Waltham, MAIDENHEAD, SL6 3SR.
MERVART, Mr. Roland, BA ACA *2005;* Flat D, 38 Sherriff Road, LONDON, NW6 2AU.
MERVIS, Mrs. Vivienne, BA ACA *1987;* 52 Fitzalan Road, LONDON, N3 3PE.
MESECK, Mrs. Fiona Jane, BSc ACA *1990;* 105 Bucklow Gardens, LYMM, CHESHIRE, WA13 9RN.
•**MESHER, Mr. Geoffrey Lee, BA FCA** *1997;* Grant Thornton UK LLP, 11-13 Penhill Road, CARDIFF, CF11 9UP. See also Grant Thornton LLP
•**MESHER, Mr. Stephen Charles, FCA** *1977;* S Charles Mesher & Co, 4 Newnham Park, HOOK, RG27 9QL.
MESRIE, Mr. Michael Edward, BCom ACA *1989;* with Amazon House Properties Limited, Amazon House, 3 Brazil Street, MANCHESTER, M1 3PJ.
MESRIE, Mr. Robert Alan Edward, BCom ACA *1997;* Flat 8, 80-82 Gloucester Avenue, LONDON, NW1 8JD.
MESSAGE, Mr. Daniel Charles, BA ACA *2010;* 12 Rydal Avenue, RAMSGATE, KENT, CT11 0PT.
MESSAGE, Mr. John Eric, BA ACA *1988;* 29 Vincent Road, Stoke D'Abernon, COBHAM, KT11 3JA.
MESSENGER, Mrs. Carol, BA ACA *2001;* Oakwood, 119A Bourne Vale, BROMLEY, BR2 7NY.
MESSENGER, Mr. Daniel James, ACA *2009;* B/2/B/008, Halifax Bank of Scotland, 10 Canons Way, BRISTOL, BS1 5LF.
MESSENGER, Mr. Iain Ernest Bradley, BSc ACA *1991;* 12a The Harrage, ROMSEY, SO51 8AE.
MESSENGER, Mr. Michael Anthony, FCA *1955;* 58A Myrtle Avenue, RUISLIP, HA4 8RZ. (Life Member)
MESSENGER, Mr. Rodney Clive, BCom FCA *1971;* Alga Lodge, 3 Alga Terrace, SCARBOROUGH, NORTH YORKSHIRE, YO11 2DF.
MESSENGER, Mr. Shaun Jack Graham, BA ACA *2010;* with PricewaterhouseCoopers LLP, Marlborough Court, 10 Bricket Road, ST. ALBANS, HERTFORDSHIRE, AL1 3JX.
MESSER, Mrs. Susan Sinead, BSc(Hons) ACA *2003;* Ringstraße 8, 55283 NIERSTEIN, GERMANY.
MESSIAS, Mr. David, MA BA(Hons) FCA *1958;* Sandalwood, Pinner Hill, PINNER, HA5 3XT. (Life Member)
MESSIAS, Mr. Jeffrey Jacob, FCA *1972;* 18 Wavendon House Drive, Wavendon, MILTON KEYNES, MK17 8AJ.
•**MESSIK, Mr. Richard Frederick, FCA** *1974;* RFM Associates, 10 Carew Way, WATFORD, WD19 5BG.
•**MESSOM, Mr. William Ernest, FCA** *1979;* Higson & Co, White House, Wollaton St, NOTTINGHAM, NG1 5GF.
•**MESSORE, Mr. John Salvadore, MA ACA ATII ACT** *1990;* (Tax Fac), Innovation Professional Services LLP, Merlin House, Priory Drive, Langstone, NEWPORT, GWENT NP18 2HJ.
MESTON, Mrs. Anna, BSc(Hons) ACA *2004;* STASCO, Shell Mex House, 80 Strand, LONDON, WC2R 0ZA.
MESTON, Mr. John William, FCA *1966;* 1 Rue Des Jardins, 34320 NIZAS, FRANCE. (Life Member)
MESTON, Mr. Thomas James Dougall, BSc(Hons) ACA *2004;* 39 Worfield Street, LONDON, SW11 4RB.
MESTRAUD, Mr. Stephen Lee, FCA *1981;* 13205 Johnny Moore Lane, CLIFTON, VA 20124, UNITED STATES.
METAXAS, Mr. Socrates, MBA FCA *1992;* 45 Kostis Palamas Street, 4001 LIMASSOL, CYPRUS.
METCALF, Mrs. Anne Marguerite, FCA DChA *1982;* 1 Yewlands Avenue, Fulwood, PRESTON, PR2 9QR.

•METCALF, Mr. Anthony Charles, FCA CTA 1982; Anthony Russel Ltd, Winghams House, 9 Freeport Office Village, Century Drive, BRAINTREE, ESSEX CM77 8YG. See also Kaizen Projects LLP
METCALF, Ms. Catherine Jane, BA ACA 2002; 119 Ravensbury Road, LONDON, SW18 4RY.
METCALF, Mr. David Felton James, BSc ACA 1994; Apartment 48 Warnes, Steyne Gardens, WORTHING, WEST SUSSEX, BN11 3DW.
METCALF, Mr. David Richard, FCA 1961; 14 Frome Court, Longmead Way, TONBRIDGE, KENT, TN10 3TS. (Life Member)
METCALF, Mrs. Deborah Jane, LLB FCA 1984; 22 Trowlock Avenue, TEDDINGTON, TW11 9QT.
METCALF, Mr. Geoffrey Vaughan, FCA 1974; Lower Stream Farm, Stogumber, TAUNTON, SOMERSET, TA4 3TR.
METCALF, Mr. Graham Steven, BA FCA 1994; 24 Earlspark Crescent, Bieldside, ABERDEEN, AB15 9AY.
METCALF, Miss. Helen, BA(Hons) ACA 2011; Apartment 7, 6 The Waterfront, MANCHESTER, M11 4AY.
METCALF, Mr. Julian Robert, BSc ACA 1992; 1 Aldridge Park, Winkfield Row, BRACKNELL, BERKSHIRE, RG42 7NU.
METCALF, Mr. Matthew Alan, ACA 2007; 24 Ella Road, NORWICH, NR1 4BS.
•METCALF, Mr. Michael John, BSc FCA 1990; KPMG LLP, 15 Canada Square, LONDON, E14 5GL. See also KPMG Europe LLP
METCALF, Mr. Nigel James, BSc ACA 1992; 6 Green Lane, LONDON, W7 2PB.
METCALF, Mr. Paul Jon, BA ACA 2001; Hydratight Pty Unit 5 7 Marchesi street Kewdale, PERTH, WA 6105, AUSTRALIA.
METCALF, Mr. Peter Gilbert Herbert, FCA 1950; Leasow Farm, Highfield Lane, Muggington, ASHBOURNE, DE6 4PQ. (Life Member)
METCALF, Mr. Peter Robert, MBE FCA DChA 1973; with Moore and Smalley LLP, Richard House, 9 Winckley Square, PRESTON, PR1 3HP.
METCALF, Mr. Richard Brian, BA FCA 1991; Whitewoods Lye Lane, Bricket Wood, ST. ALBANS, HERTFORDSHIRE, AL2 3TF.
METCALF, Mr. Robert David George, LLB ACA CISA 2000; with PricewaterhouseCoopers LLP, Cornwall Court, 19 Cornwall Street, BIRMINGHAM, B3 2DT.
METCALF, Mr. Roger, FCA 1965; 33 Somerset Road, WALSALL, WS4 2DW.
METCALFE, Mr. Alan William, BA ACA CF 1988; 29 Churchill Avenue, COTTINGHAM, HU16 5NJ.
METCALFE, Miss. Anne Kathleen, FCA 1971; 44 Fuchsia Grove, Ballasalla, ISLE OF MAN, IM9 2DT. (Life Member)
METCALFE, Mr. Anthony, FCA 1970; 14 Horncop Lane, KENDAL, CUMBRIA, LA9 4SR.
METCALFE, Mr. Antony Dennis, BSc ACA 1989; with Lloyds TSB Corporate Markets, 4th Floor, 25 Gresham Street, LONDON, EC2V 7HN.
•METCALFE, Mrs. Catherine Hilary, FCA 1968; Catherine Metcalfe, October House, Jonas Lane, WADHURST, TN5 6UJ.
METCALFE, Mr. Charles George, BSocSc FCA 1979; Hillgate, Silvington, Cleobury Mortimer, KIDDERMINSTER, WORCESTERSHIRE, DY14 0RL.
METCALFE, Mr. David Frank, BSc ACA 1980; British Gas Plc, 30 The Causeway, STAINES, MIDDLESEX, TW18 3BY.
METCALFE, Mr. David John, BCom FCA 1985; ID Support Services, Unit B2, Brookside Business Park, Greengate, Middleton, MANCHESTER M24 1GS.
METCALFE, Mr. Ian James, BSc FCA 1984; 122 Oxford Road, Cumnor, OXFORD, OX2 9PQ.
METCALFE, Mr. James Stevan, MA(Hons) ACA 2004; 62 Rosamond Avenue, SHEFFIELD, S17 4LT.
METCALFE, Mrs. Jennifer Anne, ACA 2001; Wm Morrison, Supermarkets Plc, Hilmore House, 71 Gain Lane, BRADFORD, WEST YORKSHIRE BD3 7DL.
METCALFE, Mr. Jeremy Paul, BSc ACA 1989; 128 Fonda Road, Rockville Centre, NEW YORK, NY 11570, UNITED STATES.
METCALFE, Mr. Jonathan Paul, BA ACA 2003; 6 Albert Street, KNUTSFORD, CHESHIRE, WA16 6JA.
METCALFE, Mr. Kenneth Charles, FCA 1969; 201 74th Ave North, MYRTLE BEACH, SC 29572, UNITED STATES.
METCALFE, Miss. Kerry, ACA 2002; Scarborough Borough Council Town Hall, St. Nicholas Street, SCARBOROUGH, NORTH YORKSHIRE, YO11 2HG.
METCALFE, Mr. Malcolm, FCA 1965; Walldub, Brunstock, CARLISLE, CA6 4QQ.
METCALFE, Mr. Michael, BSc ACA 1993; The Old Manor House, 25 Station Road, THAMES DITTON, KT7 0NU.
•METCALFE, Mr. Michael, BSc ACA 1984; Novae Group Plc, 71 Fenchurch Street, LONDON, EC3M 4HH.
METCALFE, Mr. Michael Graham, FCA 1971; 1 Bay Tree Cottage, Back Lane, Duddon, TARPORLEY, CHESHIRE, CW6 0EZ.
METCALFE, Ms. Nancy Claire, BSc ACA 2005; Wehrenbachhalde 47, 8053 ZURICH, SWITZERLAND.
METCALFE, Mr. Peter, FCA 1969; Plants Farm, Greenside, Ainsworth, BOLTON, BL2 5SF. (Life Member)
METCALFE, Mr. Peter James Christopher, FCA 1966; Peter J C Metcalfe, Hildersley Cottage, ROSS-ON-WYE, HEREFORDSHIRE, HR9 7NJ.
METCALFE, Mr. Richard, FCA 1961; 54 Greenacre Park, Rawdon, LEEDS, LS19 6AR.
•METCALFE, Mr. Richard William, BA ACA 1992; Mazars LLP, Tower Bridge House, St. Katharines Way, LONDON, E1W 1DD.
METCALFE, Mrs. Sally Elizabeth, BA FCA 1988; 10 The Grangeway, Grange Park, LONDON, N21 2HA.
METCALFE, Miss. Susan Elizabeth, MA BA(Hons) FCA 1988; 23 Caedmon Crescent, DARLINGTON, DL3 8LF.
METCALFE, Mr. Thomas Rodger, FCA 1970; 17 Houndtrail Drive, WATERDOWN L0R 2H3, ON, CANADA.
METCALFE, Mr. Timothy Charles, BA ACA 1995; Holly Bank Farm Scropton Road, Scropton, DERBY, DE65 5PS.
METCALFE, Mr. Timothy James, BA ACA 1999; 18/3 Lynedoch Place, EDINBURGH, EH3 7PY.
•METHARAM, Mr. Paul, BSc ACA 1989; (Tax Fac), B & M Accountancy Limited, 52 Dale View Avenue, Chingford, LONDON, E4 6PL.
•METHERELL, Mr. John, FCA ACCA 1963; (Tax Fac), Palmer Riley & Co, First Floor, Wallington Court, Fareham Heights, Standard Way, FAREHAM HAMPSHIRE PO16 8XT.
METHLEY, Mr. Christopher John, BA ACA 1983; Flat 352, Lauderdale Tower, Barbican, LONDON, EC2Y 8NA.
METHVEN, Mr. Ian, BA FCA 1969; 1 Parrish Place, MOUNT COLAH, NSW 2079, AUSTRALIA.
METIVIER, Miss. Nicole, BA ACA 1994; London Borough of Newham Newham Dockside, 1000 Dockside Road, LONDON, E16 2QU.
METLISS, Mr. Cyril, FCA 1947; 25 Foscote Road, Hendon, LONDON, NW4 3SE. (Life Member)
•METSON, Mr. Adrian William, BA(Hons) FCA 2000; (Tax Fac), Metsons Accountants Limited, 13a The Parade, Wrotham Road, Meopham, GRAVESEND, KENT DA13 0JL. See also Metsons
METSON, Mr. Denis Alwyn, FCA 1958; 12 Orchardmede, Winchmore Hill, LONDON, N21 2DL. (Life Member)
METT, Mr. Ian, ACA 2007; (Tax Fac), 36 Ambrose Avenue, LONDON, NW11 9AN.
METTERS, Mr. Christopher John, BA FCA 1996; Lindor, Tudor Close, PULBOROUGH, WEST SUSSEX, RH20 2EF.
METTERS, Mr. Derek George, BA FCA 1972; 14 St. Tudors View, BLACKWOOD, GWENT, NP12 1AQ.
METTERS, Mr. John Edmund De Vahl, MA FCA 1968; Court House, The Street, Hullavington, CHIPPENHAM, SN14 6DU. (Life Member)
METUKU, Mr. Adithya, ACA BEng(Hons) 2010; Flat 40, Settlers Court, 17 Newport Avenue, LONDON, E14 2DG.
METZGEN, Mr. Nicholas David, MEng ACA 2011; 37 Raphael Drive, THAMES DITTON, SURREY, KT7 0BL.
METZGER, Mr. Ronald, FCA 1955; Trewan, 16 Valencia Road, STANMORE, MIDDLESEX, HA7 4JH. (Life Member)
METZGER, Miss. Sarah Anne, BSc ACA 2003; 21 Telegraph Lane, Claygate, ESHER, KT10 0DT.
MEUNIER, Mr. Peter Christopher, FCA 1982; 29 Bush Grove, STANMORE, MIDDLESEX, HA7 2DY.
MEVILLOT, Mrs. Louise Marie, BA ACA 2004; Rue des Vollandes 38, 1207 GENEVA, SWITZERLAND.
•MEW, Mr. John David, MA FCA 1977; Grant Thornton UK LLP, Grant Thornton House, 22 Melton Street, Euston Square, LONDON, NW1 2EP. See also Grant Thornton LLP
MEW, Mr. Nicholas Stephen Proctor, ACA 1982; P.O. Box 1378, CRAMERVIEW, GAUTENG, 2060, SOUTH AFRICA.
MEW, Mr. Simon, BSc ACA 2002; 78 St. Margarets Grove, TWICKENHAM, TW1 1JG.
MEW, Mr. Simon John, BA FCA 1979; The Stables, Rectory Lane, Kingston Bagpuize, ABINGDON, OXFORDSHIRE, OX13 5DS.
MEWAWALLA, Mr. Cyrus Homi, MA FCA 1993; Amaris, Hill Close, HARROW, MIDDLESEX, HA1 3PQ.
MEWIS, Mr. David George, FCA 1962; Old Tiles, Old Barn Close, EASTBOURNE, EAST SUSSEX, BN20 9HJ.
MEWS, Mr. Ashley John, ACA 1987; Lavender House, 49 Beeleigh Link, CHELMSFORD, CM2 6PH.
MEWSE, Mr. Darren, ACA 2006; JFW Robinson & Co:, Oxford Chambers, New Oxford Street, WORKINGTON, CUMBRIA, CA14 2LR.
MEYAPPAN, Mr. Sithambaram, BSc ACA 1982; LMS Timur Holdings Sdn Bhd, B-2626 First Floor, Jalan Beserah, 25300 KUANTAN, MALAYSIA.
MEYER, Mrs. Amanda Jane, BSc ACA 1997; Aberdeen Business School, The Robert Gordon University Faculty of Management, Garthdee Road, ABERDEEN, AB10 7QE.
MEYER, Mr. Christian Ingo Albert, MSc ACA 2001; Flat 24, Wymering Mansions, Wymering Road, LONDON, W9 2NB.
•MEYER, Mr. Emanuel, BSc FCA 1990; 30 Holmfield Avenue, LONDON, NW4 2LN.
•MEYER, Mr. John Leonard, FCA 1966; Meyer Williams, Queen Alexandra House, 2 Bluecoats Avenue, HERTFORD, HERTFORDSHIRE, SG14 1PB.
MEYER, Mr. Lars Oliver, MSc ACA 2003; with KPMG LLP, 15 Canada Square, LONDON, E14 5GL.
MEYER, Mr. Nigel Sinclair, BA ACA 1992; 6 Mill Pightle, Aylsham, NORWICH, NR11 6LX.
MEYER, Mr. Peter Anthony Roger, BA FCA 1977; 165 Sussex Gardens, LONDON, W2 2RH.
•MEYER, Mr. Peter John Herman, BA FCA 1961; Brian Bell Meyer & Co Limited, Plymouth Chambers, 23 Bartlett Street, CAERPHILLY, MID GLAMORGAN, CF83 1JS.
MEYER, Mr. Richard Edward, FCA 1956; 41 Kenley Road, Merton Park, LONDON, SW19 3JJ. (Life Member)
•MEYER, Mr. Roger Douglas, FCA FCCA 1969; 1 Rotten Row, LEWES, EAST SUSSEX, BN7 1TN.
MEYER, Miss. Sallyanne Louise, MA ACA 1996; 15 Ganghill, GUILDFORD, SURREY, GU1 1XE.
MEYER, Ms. Tina, BA ACA 2002; The White House Bickers Hill, Laxfield, WOODBRIDGE, SUFFOLK, IP13 8DP.
MEYERHOFF, Mr. David, FCA 1978; Brinkwater, Glen Auldyn, Ramsey, ISLE OF MAN, IM7 2AQ.
•MEYERS, Mr. Martin Leigh, FCA CTA 1976; (Tax Fac), 7 South Court Avenue, DORCHESTER, DORSET, DT1 2BY.
MEYERS, Mr. Richard John, MA FCA 1973; Minit Group, Suite 1a, Princes House, 38 Jermyn Street, LONDON, SW1Y 6DN.
MEYERS, Mr. Spencer S, BSc ACA 1993; 107 Bridge Lane, LONDON, NW11 0EU.
MEYNELL, Mr. Thomas Roy, BSc ACA 2007; 27 Mandarin Drive, NEWBURY, BERKSHIRE, RG14 7WE.
MEYRICK, Mr. Andrew, FCA 1974; 23 John Archer Way, LONDON, SW18 2TQ.
MEYRICK, Mr. Andrew Peter Stewart, MA ACA 1986; 9 Richmond Road, OXFORD, OX1 2JJ.
MEYRICK, Mr. Christopher John, BSc(Econ) ACA 2004; 153 Churchill Drive, GLASGOW, G11 7EY.
MEYRICK, Mr. Phillip John, BSc ACA 1984; Bank of America, 5 Canada Square, LONDON, E14 5AQ.
MEYRICK, Mrs. Rachel Ann, BA ACA 1991; 9 Richmond Road, OXFORD, OX1 2JJ.
MEYRICK, Mrs. Shona M, MA ACA 2005; 84 Mt Pleasant Rd, Aro Valley, WELLINGTON 6012, NEW ZEALAND.
MEZHER, Mr. David Richard, ACA CA(SA) 2011; 10 Twickenham Road, TEDDINGTON, MIDDLESEX, TW11 8AG.
MEZULANIK, Mr. J Francis Charles, ACA 1979; PO Box N-7816, NASSAU, BAHAMAS.
MI, Ms. Lisa Man See, MAcc MBA ACA FCCA 2006; Anova, Unit 505 5/F Tower II, Cheung Sha Wan Plaza, 833 Cheung Sha Wan Road, KOWLOON TONG, KOWLOON HONG KONG SAR.
•MIAH, Mr. Ali Ahmed Thoskir, BSc(Hons) ACA FCCA ACCA 2007; (Tax Fac), Taylor Edward Limited, 3 Broadway Court, High Street, CHESHAM, BUCKINGHAMSHIRE, HP5 1EG. See also Francis and Howe Ltd
MIAH, Mr. Gumayel, BA(Hons) ACA 2010; 17 Corona Road, Langdon Hills, BASILDON, SS16 6HH.
MIAH, Mr. Mohammed Koyas, BSc BSc(Hons) ACA 2011; 65 St. Benedicts Road, BIRMINGHAM, B10 9DR.
•MIAH, Mr. Moshin, LLB(Hons) ACA FCCA 2011; MSCO, Suda House, 100a Mile End Road, LONDON, E1 4UN.
MIAH, Mr. Sadik, BSc ACA 1994; Rua Santo Isidro, Vivenda, Santa Maria, Paradas, A-Dos-Cunhados, 2560-053 LISBON PORTUGAL.
MIAH, Mr. Shanoor, BSc ACA 2009; 18 Rectory Road, LONDON, E12 6JA.
MIALL, Mr. Geoffrey, BSc FCA 1976; Box 1001, JUKSKEI PARK, 2153, SOUTH AFRICA.
MIAN, Mr. Abdul Waheed, FCA 1972; Abdul Waheed Mian, 178-M Defence Housing Auth., LAHORE 54792, PAKISTAN.
MIAN, Mr. Asif Ahmad, FCA 1975; GF1 Block 41, Sea View Township, Phase V Extension DHA, KARACHI 75500, PAKISTAN.
MIAN, Mrs. Helen Ann, BA ACA 1995; 11 West Parade, NORWICH, NR2 3DN.
MIAN, Mr. Imran Farooq, BSc ACA 1987; 76 C TECH SOCIETY, LAHORE, PAKISTAN.
MIAN, Mr. Kamran Ajmal, ACA 1993; 1-A/1 North Avenue, Phase I, Defence Society, KARACHI 73600, PAKISTAN.
MIAN, Mr. Karim-Ud-Din, BSc ACA 1991; 1 Prince of Wales Terrace, Kensington, LONDON, W8 5PG.
MIAN, Mr. Khurram Ajmal, ACA 1996; PO Box 9267, 28 Floor Al Attar Business Tower, Sheikh Zayed Road, DUBAI, UNITED ARAB EMIRATES. See also Ernst & Young
MIAN, Mr. Mohammad Abdul Jalil, FCA 1968; 3/12 Block E, Flat No D1, Lalmatia, DHAKA 7, BANGLADESH.
MIAN, Mr. Muhammad Arif Ali, FCA 1978; 5530 Glen Erin Drive Unit 96, MISSISSAUGA L5M 6E8, ON, CANADA.
MIAN, Mr. Muhammad Khalil, FCA 1959; 188 Shah Jamal, LAHORE, PUNJAB, PAKISTAN. (Life Member)
MIAN, Mr. Muneer Ud Din, ACA 1982; Mian Muneer ud din, Beaufort Associates FZ-LLC, P O Box 500329, DUBAI, UNITED ARAB EMIRATES.
MIAN, Mr. Najam, BA ACA 2000; 4 Southlands Avenue, LEEDS, LS17 5NU.
MIAN, Mr. Qaisar, FCA 1962; 94/B Bathisland, KARACHI 75530, SINDH, PAKISTAN. (Life Member)
MIAN, Mr. Shahid Anwar Ali, MBA ACA 1993; 11 West Parade, NORWICH, NR2 3DN.
MIAO, Miss. Florence Wen Yuan, BA ACA 1994; 12 Manor House Drive, NORTHWOOD, MIDDLESEX, HA6 2UJ.
MIAO, Mr. Philip Yin-Wei, BSc ACA 2000; 28 Scotts Road, #14-01, SINGAPORE 228223, SINGAPORE.
MICALLEF, Mr. Richard David, FCA 1969; 3 Beech Lane, Prestwood, GREAT MISSENDEN, HP16 9DP.
MICHAEL, Mr. Adrian John, BA ACA 1992; (Tax Fac), with KPMG LLP, Arlington Business Park, Theale, READING, RG7 4SD.
MICHAEL, Miss. Alexia Theodosiou, ACA 2009; 5 Peloponnisou Street, Dali, 2540 NICOSIA, CYPRUS.
MICHAEL, Mr. Andreas, BSc ACA 2009; 49 Kretes street, Petevinos Court 8, Appartment 301, Kapsalos, 3087 LIMASSOL, CYPRUS.
MICHAEL, Mrs. Bethan, BSc(Hons) ACA 2011; 76 Coed Celynen Drive, Abercarn, NEWPORT, GWENT, NP11 5AT.
•MICHAEL, Mr. Bill, ACA 2004; KPMG Europe LLP, 15 Canada Square, LONDON, E14 5GL. See also KPMG Audit plc and KPMG LLP
MICHAEL, Mr. Charalambos, BSc ACA 2006; Ayias Elenis 5, Aplantzia, 2102 NICOSIA, CYPRUS.
MICHAEL, Miss. Erma, MSc ACA 2011; Alkinoou 8 Kapsalos, 3087 LIMASSOL, CYPRUS.
MICHAEL, Mr. Frixos, BSc ACA 1999; with PricewaterhouseCoopers LLP, 488 Almaden Boulevard, SAN JOSE, CA 95110, UNITED STATES.
MICHAEL, Miss. Georgia, BA ACA 2006; 6 TYMFRISTOU STREET, 3011 LIMASSOL, CYPRUS.
MICHAEL, Mr. Georgios, BA(Hons) ACA 2010; 4 Eolou, Ay Andreas, 1101 NICOSIA, CYPRUS.
MICHAEL, Mr. Gregory Morris, BSc ACA 1979; Lucknow, Elizabeth Road, HENLEY-ON-THAMES, RG9 1RA.
MICHAEL, Miss. Irene, ACA 2010; 20 Ilia Venezi, Mesa Yitonia, 4001 LIMASSOL, CYPRUS.
•MICHAEL, Mr. Jerry, ACA 2010; Baginsky Cohen, 930 High Road, North Finchley, LONDON, N12 9RT.
•MICHAEL, Mr. John, FCA 1977; (Tax Fac), J Michael & Co Ltd, 274 Northdown Road, Cliftonville, MARGATE, CT9 2PT.
MICHAEL, Mr. Jonathan Martin, BSc ACA 1990; The Old Stables, Altrincham Road, Styal, WILMSLOW, CHESHIRE, SK9 4LH.
•MICHAEL, Mr. Leonidas, BA ACA 2005; J Michael & Co Ltd, 274 Northdown Road, Cliftonville, MARGATE, CT9 2PT.
MICHAEL, Miss. Maria, BSc ACA 2007; 8A Likavitou Street, Nea Ekali, 3111 LIMASSOL, CYPRUS.

MICHAEL, Mr. Mark, MSc BBA ACA *2010;* with BDO Alto Limited, Windward House, La Route de la Liberation, St Helier, JERSEY, JE1 1BG.
MICHAEL, Mr. Michael, BSc FCA *2000;* 31A RIK Avenue, Platy, 2122 AGLANTZIA, CYPRUS.
•**MICHAEL, Mr. Michael Cosmas, BSc FCA** *1991;* (Tax Fac), M C Michael, 32 Avondale Road, Hoylake, WIRRAL, CH47 3AS.
•**MICHAEL, Mr. Michael Yiannis, BA BA(Hons)Oxon ACA** *1997;* Odyssey Advisers Limited, Baskerville House, Centenary Square, BIRMINGHAM, B1 2ND.
•**MICHAEL, Mr. Michalakis, BSc ACA** *1996;* (Tax Fac), KPMG LLP, 15 Canada Square, LONDON, E14 5GL. See also KPMG Europe LLP
MICHAEL, Mr. Michalis, BA(Hons) ACA *2010;* 8 GLADSTONOS STREET, 2021 NICOSIA, CYPRUS.
MICHAEL, Mr. Michalis A, BA ACA *2008;* 80 Tseriou Street, Lakatamia, 2314 NICOSIA, CYPRUS.
MICHAEL, Mr. Nicholas, MSc BA ACA *2006;* 240 Colney Hatch Lane, LONDON, N10 1BD.
•**MICHAEL, Mr. Nicolas, BA FCA** *1996;* Elliott Bunker Ltd, 3-8 Redcliffe Parade West, BRISTOL, BS1 6SP.
MICHAEL, Mr. Panayiotis, BA ACA *2005;* Etolias 6, 3048 LIMASSOL, CYPRUS.
MICHAEL, Mrs. Rosalind, ACA *2008;* Flat 1/2, 52 Fortrose Street, GLASGOW, G11 5LP.
MICHAEL, Mr. Stavros, BSc ACA *2011;* 5 Kazantzaki Street, Strovolos, 2007, NICOSIA, CYPRUS.
MICHAEL, Mr. Stephen Andrew, BA ACA *1989;* 257 Hillbury Road, WARLINGHAM, CR6 9TL.
MICHAELIDES, Mr. Andreas, FCA *1970;* P.O.Box 25193, 1307 NICOSIA, CYPRUS.
MICHAELIDES, Mr. Andrew, MA FCA *1989;* 2 Copse Bank, Seal, SEVENOAKS, TN15 0DE.
MICHAELIDES, Mr. Angelos, BSc ACA *2011;* Photiou 9 Street, Agioi Omoloyetes, 1095 NICOSIA, CYPRUS.
MICHAELIDES, Mr. Charalambos Nicolaou, FCA TEP *1983;* 21 Archangelou Michael, Ayios Dometios, 2369 NICOSIA, CYPRUS.
MICHAELIDES, Mr. Konstantinos, BEng ACA MBA *2005;* Sofokleous 40, Strovolos, 2008 NICOSIA, CYPRUS.
MICHAELIDES, Mr. Leonidas, ACA *2010;* 4 Evripidou Street, Kato Lakatamia, 2323 NICOSIA, CYPRUS.
MICHAELIDES, Mr. Marios Christou, BEng ACA *1990;* Quendon Cottage, Cambridge Road, Quendon, SAFFRON WALDEN, ESSEX, CB11 3XJ.
•**MICHAELIDES, Mr. Michael, ACA FCCA** *2010;* EA (UK) LLP, 869 High Road, LONDON, N12 8QA.
MICHAELIDES, Mr. Michalis, ACA *2008;* 4A Peloponnisou street, Strovolos, 2027 NICOSIA, CYPRUS.
MICHAELIDES, Ms. Monica, BSc ACA *1989;* P.O.Box 54246, 70 Mikinon, 4045 YERMASOYIA, CYPRUS.
MICHAELIDES, Mr. Panos George, BA(Hons) ACA *2011;* 19 Great North Road, Brookmans Park, HATFIELD, HERTFORDSHIRE, AL9 6LB.
•**MICHAELIDES, Mr. Paul Damien, BA(Hons) ACA** *2003;* Michaelides Warner & Co Ltd, 102 Fulham Palace Road, LONDON, W6 9PL.
MICHAELIDES, Mr. Petros, BSc ACA *2009;* FLAT 101KAFKASOU 5AGLATZIA, 2112 NICOSIA, CYPRUS.
MICHAELIDES, Mr. Polydoros Andrea, FCA *1984;* Andrea Pavlides 1, Engomi, 2411 NICOSIA, CYPRUS.
MICHAELIDES, Mrs. Sonia Louise Estelle, BSc ACA *1992;* Quendon Cottage, Cambridge Road, Quendon, SAFFRON WALDEN, ESSEX, CB11 3XJ.
•**MICHAELIDES, Mr. Stephen, BSc FCA** *1990;* Grant Thornton, P.O. Box 23907, 1687 NICOSIA, CYPRUS.
MICHAELIDES KYPRAGORAS, Mrs. Efthymia, BSc(Econ) ACA *1995;* HELLENIC BANK PUBLIC COMPANY LTD, GROUP CORPORATE BANKING, 173 Athalassa Ave POBOX 24747, 1394 NICOSIA, CYPRUS.
MICHAELIDOU, Mrs. Maria, BA(Hons) ACA *2001;* 15 Lycourgiou Street, Flat 301, Acropolis, 2001 NICOSIA, CYPRUS.
MICHAELIDOU, Ms. Maria, BSc ACA *2003;* Polymnias 14A, 2102 Aglantzia, NICOSIA, CYPRUS.
MICHAELIDOU, Miss. Penelope, BSc ACA *2008;* 170 Carronade Court, Eden Grove, LONDON, N7 8GP.
MICHAELIDOU, Miss. Tatiana, BSc ACA *2007;* 10A Michalaki Karaoli, Mesa Gitonia, 4000 LIMASSOL, CYPRUS.
MICHAELOUDIS, Mr. Neil Savvas, BA ACA *1994;* 51 Bellamy Drive, STANMORE, HA7 2DD.
MICHAELS, Mr. Alan Paul, FCA *1960;* 20 Oakleigh Gardens, EDGWARE, HA8 8EA. (Life Member)
MICHAELS, Mr. Leslie David, MBA FCA *1966;* Time Products Luxury Ltd Dover House, 34 Dover Street, LONDON, W1S 4NG.
•**MICHAELS, Mr. Nicholas Peter, FCA** *1982;* Jeffreys Henry LLP, Finsgate, 5-7 Cranwood Street, LONDON, EC1V 9EE. See also Alfred Henry Corporate Finance Limited
MICHAELS, Mr. Sam, BA ACA *2011;* 71 Spencer Close, LONDON, N3 3TY.
•**MICHAELS, Mr. Simon Harvey, BSc ACA** *1996;* S2 Solutions Limited, 34 Hillview Road, PINNER, MIDDLESEX, HA5 4PA.
MICHAELSON, Mr. Joseph Martin, FCA *1969;* 58 Cheyne Walk, LONDON, N21 1DE. (Life Member)
•**MICHAELSON, Mr. Simon Paul, BA(Econ) ACA** *1997;* Ernst & Young LLP, 1 More London Place, LONDON, SE1 2AF. See also Ernst & Young Europe LLP
•**MICHAIL, Mr. Savvas Costa, FCA** *1978;* PricewaterhouseCoopers Limited, City House, 58 Grivas Dighenis Avenue, CY-8047 PAPHOS, CYPRUS.
MICHALIAS, Mr. George Gabriel, ACA *1982;* 3rd Floor, 1 Torrington Park, LONDON, N12 9SU.
•**MICHALOPOULOS, Mr. Michael, FCA** *1981;* Michael Michalopoulos FCA, 70 Kennedy Avenue, Papavasilou Building, 3rd Floor, Office 304, PO Box 28783 CY2082 NICOSIA CYPRUS.
MICHALOS, Mr. Kyriacos Andrea Nicolaou, BSc ACA *1997;* 10 MORFOU STREET, NEA LEDRA, DALI, 2540 NICOSIA, CYPRUS.
MICHALOWICZ, Miss. Annette Ewa, BSc(Hons) ACA *2001;* 301/30 Warayama Place, Balmain Shores, ROZELLE, NSW 2039, AUSTRALIA.
MICHEL, Mr. James Edward, BA FCA *1993;* BKS Family Office Limited, 22 Colomberie, ST HELIER, JE1 4XA.
MICHEL, Mrs. Jane Margaret Grant, BSc ACA *1986;* 1 Hill Farm Cross Cottages, Sutton Scotney, WINCHESTER, SO21 3NS.
MICHEL, Mrs. Michaela Jane, BA ACA *1993;* MJM Accounting Services, Fremont House, La Rue de Fremont, St John, JERSEY, JE3 4DA.
MICHEL, Mr. Russel Andrew Peter, ACA *1986;* Avalon, Les Huriaux, St. Andrew, GUERNSEY, GY6 8RF.
•**MICHELI, Mr. Fabrizio, ACA** *2007;* FSCA Limited, Regency House, 2 Wood Street, Queen Square, BATH, BA1 2JQ.
MICHELL, Mr. Andrew Penry, FCA *1970;* 4 Beaumont Avenue, ST. ALBANS, HERTFORDSHIRE, AL1 4TJ.
MICHELL, Mr. Antony Peter, BSc ACA *1990;* The Henley Group Limited, Suite 2004-08, 20/F St Georges Building, 2 Ice House Street, CENTRAL, HONG KONG SAR.
MICHELL, Mr. Darren Gregson, BA ACA *2001;* 24 Kewstoke Road, Kewstoke, WESTON-SUPER-MARE, AVON, BS22 9YD.
MICHELL, Miss. Joan Millicent, FCA *1975;* (Tax Fac), 33 London Road, HARROW, HA1 3JJ.
•**MICHELL, Mr. Peter Howard, FCA** *1966;* P.H. Michell & Co Ltd, Providence Cottage, Bracken Lane, Storrington, PULBOROUGH, WEST SUSSEX RH20 3HS.
MICHELL, Mr. Richard, FCA *1972;* Comax UK Ltd, 11 Witney Road, POOLE, BH17 0GJ.
MICHELL, Mr. Simon Toby, BA ACA *1991;* TALLY WEIJL Trading AG, Service and Support Center, Viaduktstrasse 42, CH-4051 BASEL, SWITZERLAND.
•**MICHELMORE, Miss. Jennifer Mary, BSc ACA** *1983;* (Tax Fac), Francis Clark LLP, Sigma House, Oak View Close, Edginswell Park, TORQUAY, TQ2 7FF.
•**MICHELSON, Mr. Allan Denis, FCA** *1971;* A.D. Michelson, 33 North Avenue, Gosforth, NEWCASTLE UPON TYNE, NE3 4DQ.
MICHELSON, Mrs. Debi Mary, LLB FCA *1987;* The Children's Centre, 94 Woodbourne Road, Douglas, ISLE OF MAN, IM2 3AS.
MICHIE, Mr. Andrew John, BA ACA *1998;* Cuna Mutual, 5910 Mineral Point Road, MADISON, WI 53701, UNITED STATES.
MICHIE, Mr. Brian, FCA *1964;* 16 Alveston Close, Ipsley, REDDITCH, WORCESTERSHIRE, B98 0TF.
MICHIE, Mrs. Charlotte Elizabeth, BSc(Hons) ACA *2004;* 119 Tranmere Road, LONDON, SW18 3QP.
MICHIE, Mr. Hamish, ACA *1991;* 16, Eagle Close, ALTON, GU34 2LJ.
MICKLE, Mr. Joshua James, BA ACA *2003;* 12 Swan Court, Agnes Street, Westferry, LONDON, E14 7DG.
MICKLEBOROUGH, Mrs. Leah Ann, ACA *2008;* 8 Briar Gardens, ATTLEBOROUGH, NORFOLK, NR17 2GY.
MICKLEBURGH, Mr. Andrew Robert, FCA *1982;* Dennor, 16 Long Lane, Mulbarton, NORWICH, NR14 8AW.
MICKLEBURGH, Mr. Brinsley Peter, FCA *1975;* Apartment 6 Elmfield House, 63 South Street, COTTINGHAM, NORTH HUMBERSIDE, HU16 4AP.
MICKLEM, Mr. James Richard Fenwick, BA ACA *1988;* Home Farm House, Henton, CHINNOR, OX39 4AH.
MICKLER, Mr. Peter Allan, BA FCA *1969;* 13 Wilson Gardens, NEWCASTLE UPON TYNE, NE3 4JA.
MICKLETHWAITE, Mrs. Judith Ann, LLB FCA *1975;* 14 The Crescent, LEEDS, LS17 7LX.
MICKLEWRIGHT, Mr. Ashley James, BSc ACA *1985;* Bluebell (Asia) Limited, 21/F Dorset House, QUARRY BAY, HONG KONG ISLAND, HONG KONG SAR.
•**MICKLEWRIGHT, Mr. Colin Malcolm, FCA** *1965;* C Micklewright & Co, High Sheriff's House, Trenowth, Grampound Road, TRURO, TR2 4EH.
MICROMATIS, Mr. Alvinos Christos, BEng ACA *2001;* 18/F HSBC Centre Tower 1, 1 Sham Mong Road, KOWLOON CITY, KOWLOON, HONG KONG SAR.
MIDDLE, Mr. John Roderick, BA FCA *1962;* Minsterley House, Hackmans Gate, Clent, STOURBRIDGE, DY9 0EW. (Life Member)
MIDDLEBROOK, Miss. Claire Elizabeth, BA ACA *2008;* Wood Farm, Ecclerigg, WINDERMERE, CUMBRIA, LA23 1LG.
•①**MIDDLEBROOK, Mrs. Claire Louise, BA ACA** *2005;* Henderson Loggie, 34 Melville Street, EDINBURGH, EH3 7HA.
MIDDLEDITCH, Mr. Adam Edward, BSc ACA *2000;* 87 Middleton Place, LOUGHBOROUGH, LEICESTERSHIRE, LE11 2BY.
MIDDLEHURST, Mr. Martin John, MA FCA *1977;* 10 Spencer Road, LONDON, SW20 0QP.
MIDDLEMAS, Mr. Paul, BSc ACA *1982;* 10 The Terrace, LONDON, SW13 0NP.
MIDDLEMASS, Mr. Graham Weston, BSc FCA *1986;* Chiene & Tait Ca, Cairn House, 61 Dublin Street, EDINBURGH, EH3 6NL.
MIDDLEMASS, Mrs. Margaret, BSc FCA *1979;* Gresham House, 5-7 St. Pauls Street, LEEDS, LS1 2JG.
MIDDLEMAST, Mr. Philip, FCA *1980;* 7 Heyford Grove, SOLIHULL, B91 3XX.
MIDDLEMISS, Mr. Giles William, FCA *1973;* Moorfield Farm, 55 Main Street, Thorner, LEEDS, LS14 3BU.
MIDDLEMISS, Mr. Stuart Alan, FCA *1968;* 71 Pierrefondes Avenue, FARNBOROUGH, Hampshire, GU14 8PA.
MIDDLETON, Mr. Andrew Michael, BSc ACA *1992;* 10 Studland Road, KINGSTON-UPON-THAMES, KT2 5HJ.
MIDDLETON, Mr. Anthony, FCA *1960;* Bronhaul, Knockin Heath, OSWESTRY, SHROPSHIRE, SY10 8DT. (Life Member)
MIDDLETON, Mr. Anthony John, ACA *1979;* Shrublands, 10 St. Nicholas Grove, Wrea Green, PRESTON, LANCASHIRE, PR4 2WB.
MIDDLETON, Mr. Anthony John, BA ACA *1989;* 107 Riddlesdown Road, PURLEY, CR8 1DH.
MIDDLETON, Mr. Chris Louis, BA(Hons) ACA *2010;* 129 Hales Road, CHELTENHAM, GLOUCESTERSHIRE, GL52 6ST.
MIDDLETON, Miss. Christine, BSc ACA *1986;* 21 Fawnbrake Avenue, LONDON, SE24 0BE.
MIDDLETON, Mr. Christopher, BSc ACA *2003;* Av Alfonso XIII 139 4C Esc Izq, 28016 MADRID, SPAIN.
MIDDLETON, Mr. Colin James, FCA *1962;* Liams Orchard, 1 Michel Grove, EASTBOURNE, BN21 1JU.
MIDDLETON, Mr. David Ewan, FCA *1968;* 4 Sole Farm Road, Grreat Bookham, LEATHERHEAD, SURREY, KT23 3DR.
MIDDLETON, Mr. David George, FCA *1968;* 38 Richmond Court Gardens, Colne Road, CROMER, NORFOLK, NR27 9AQ. (Life Member)
MIDDLETON, Mr. David Gordon Souter, FCA *1961;* David Middleton, 8 Marton Moor Road, Nunthorpe, MIDDLESBROUGH, CLEVELAND, TS7 0BH. (Life Member)
MIDDLETON, David Miles, Esq CBE FCA *1962;* Stanegate, St. Helens Lane, CORBRIDGE, NORTHUMBERLAND, NE45 5JD.
•**MIDDLETON, Mr. David Robert, BA ACA FCCA CF** *2008;* Cole Associates Corporate Finance, 19 Spring Gardens, MANCHESTER, M2 1FB.
MIDDLETON, Mr. David Roy, BA(Hons) ACA *2001;* with PricewaterhouseCoopers LLP, 1 Embankment Place, LONDON, WC2N 6RH.
MIDDLETON, Miss. Deborah Clare, BA(Hons) ACA *2001;* with Deloitte LLP, Athene Place, 66 Shoe Lane, LONDON, EC4A 3BQ.
MIDDLETON, Mr. Derek Edward Thomas, FCA *1975;* 2 Malcolm Drive, Southborough, SURBITON, KT6 6QS.
MIDDLETON, Mr. Derek James, FCA *1960;* 11 Bankfold, Barrowford, NELSON, BB9 6JW. (Life Member)
MIDDLETON, Mr. Edward Bernard, FCA *1971;* Barrans, Bury Green, Little Hadham, WARE, SG11 2ES.
MIDDLETON, Ms. Elaine, BA FCA *1982;* 26 Sandhill Mount, LEEDS, LS17 8EQ.
MIDDLETON, Mrs. Elizabeth Kim, BSc ACA *1981;* 15 Pannal Ash Drive, HARROGATE, NORTH YORKSHIRE, HG2 0JA.
MIDDLETON, Miss. Fiona Alexandra, ACA *2011;* 36b Northenden Road, Gatley, CHEADLE, CHESHIRE, SK8 4DN.
MIDDLETON, Mr. Frank John, BSc FCA *1978;* 8 Aylesby Close, KNUTSFORD, CHESHIRE, WA16 8AE.
MIDDLETON, Mr. Giles Christopher, FCA *1987;* The Hole Farm, Aston Pigott, SHREWSBURY, SY5 9HH.
MIDDLETON, Mr. Graham Peter, FCA *1978;* Gepp & Sons, 58 New London Road, CHELMSFORD, CM2 0PA.
MIDDLETON, Mr. Howard John, FCA *1966;* Pindelfin, 32 Adlington Road, WILMSLOW, SK9 2BJ.
MIDDLETON, Mr. Hugh Neil, BA FCA *1982;* Funkwerk Information Technologies York Ltd Jervaulx House, 6 St. Marys Court, YORK, YO24 1AH.
MIDDLETON, Mr. Ian George Alexander, BA ACA *1981;* 24 Crescent East, Hadley Wood, BARNET, HERTFORDSHIRE, EN4 0EN.
MIDDLETON, Mr. Ian Richard, ACA *1987;* with Hargreaves Brown & Benson, 1 Bond Street, COLNE, LANCASHIRE, BB8 9DG.
•**MIDDLETON, Mr. James Christopher, BA(Hons) ACA** *2003;* One Zone Tax Solutions Ltd, 5 Chelsea Close, Biddulph, STOKE-ON-TRENT, ST8 6UA.
MIDDLETON, Mr. John James, FCA *1975;* 1639 Route 104, CAMBRIDGE, VT 05444, UNITED STATES. (Life Member)
MIDDLETON, Mrs. Julie Louise, BA ACA *2004;* (Tax Fac), W S P Group Ltd, 3 White Rose Office Park Millshaw Park Lane, LEEDS, LS11 0DL.
MIDDLETON, Miss. June Elizabeth, BSc FCA *1983;* 33 Ridgway Place, LONDON, SW19 4EW.
•**MIDDLETON, Mr. Keith, FCA** *1977;* Wenn Townsend, 30 St Giles', OXFORD, OX1 3LE. See also Wenn Townsend Accountants Limited
MIDDLETON, Miss. Laura, MA MPhil ACA *2010;* Apartment 149, The Quadrangle, 1 Lower Ormond Street, MANCHESTER, M1 5QD.
•**MIDDLETON, Mr. Mark, BSc FCA** *2001;* LB Group Limited, 1 Vicarage Lane, Stratford, LONDON, E15 4HF.
•**MIDDLETON, Mr. Martin John, FCA** *1964;* with Price & Company, 30/32 Gildredge Road, EASTBOURNE, BN21 4SH.
MIDDLETON, Mr. Martin Ross, BA(Hons) ACA *2004;* 19 Rushford Close, Headcorn, ASHFORD, KENT, TN27 9QE.
MIDDLETON, Mr. Michael James, FCA *1954;* 6 Hall Close, KETTERING, NN15 7LQ. (Life Member)
•**MIDDLETON, Mr. Michael Paul, BSc(Hons) ACA CTA** *2001;* Blue Spire South LLP, Unit E1, Cumberland Business Centre, Northumberland Road, SOUTHSEA, HAMPSHIRE PO5 1DS.
MIDDLETON, Mr. Neil Gordon, BSc FCA *1981;* Westfold, Redbourn Lane, HARPENDEN, AL5 2LN.
MIDDLETON, Mr. Neil Stuart, FCA *1953;* 6 St. Giles Close, Chideock, BRIDPORT, DORSET, DT6 6LQ. (Life Member)
MIDDLETON, Mrs. Nicola Jane, BA ACA *1988;* 107 Riddlesdown Road, PURLEY, CR8 1DH.
MIDDLETON, Mr. Paul David, BA MSt ACA *2001;* 211 Kings Hall Road, BECKENHAM, KENT, BR3 1LL.
MIDDLETON, Mr. Peter John Howe, FCA *1969;* c/o Canadian Public Accountability Board, 150 York Street Suite 200, P.O. Box 90, TORONTO M5H 3S5, ON, CANADA.
MIDDLETON, Dr. Richard David, MA ACA *1996;* 119 Sandy Lane, CHEAM, SURREY, SM2 7ER.
•**MIDDLETON, Mr. Richard Stephenson, BA FCA** *1972;* (Tax Fac), High Close House, WYLAM, NORTHUMBERLAND, NE41 8BL.
MIDDLETON, Mr. Robert George, BSc(Econ) FCA *1985;* 20 Hemingford Gardens, YARM, TS15 9ST.
MIDDLETON, Mr. Ronald Alfred Wilson, FCA *1977;* 24 Kelmscott Road, Harborne, BIRMINGHAM, B17 8QN.
MIDDLETON, Mr. Rosslyn Paul, FCA *1972;* 25 Whitworth Drive, Radcliffe on Trent, NOTTINGHAM, NG12 2DE.
MIDDLETON, Mrs. Sarah Joy, BA ACA *1989;* The Haybarn, Whitlenge Lane, Hartlebury, KIDDERMINSTER, DY10 4HD.
MIDDLETON, Mr. Stanley Alan, FCA *1948;* (Member of Council 1966 - 1982), 40 Montagu Avenue, Gosforth, NEWCASTLE UPON TYNE, NE3 4JN. (Life Member)

MIDDLETON, Mr. Stephen John, BA ACA *1990;* 20 Marriott Grove, Sandal, WAKEFIELD, WEST YORKSHIRE, WF2 6RP.
MIDDLETON, Mr. Stuart John, BSc ACA *1984;* Holchem Laboratories Ltd, Premier House, 175 Grane Road, Haslingden, ROSSENDALE, LANCASHIRE BB4 5ER.
MIDDLETON, Mr. Trevor Carrick, FCA *1953;* Lambert Hill, Longhorsley, MORPETH, NE65 8QW. (Life Member)
MIDDLETON, Mrs. Victoria, BSc ACA *2006;* 34 College Cross, LONDON, N1 1PR.
MIDDLETON-DARBY, Mrs. Penelope Ann, BA FCA *1976;* 67 Trinity Road, Limbury, LUTON, LU3 2LN.
MIDDLETON-JONES, Mr. Robert Charles, BSc ACA *1985;* 28 White Street, Balgowlah, SYDNEY, NSW 2093, AUSTRALIA.
MIDDLETON SCARR, Mrs. Lindsay Joy, BA ACA *1996;* 11 Hartington Close, REIGATE, SURREY, RH2 9NL.
MIDDLETON-WALKER, Mr. John David, FCA *1976;* St. Edward's Lodge, 64 High Street, Clifford, WETHERBY, LS23 6HJ.
MIDDLEWICK, Mr. Peter Hugh, BA ACA *1978;* Lombard Asset Finance Group, 3 Princess Way, REDHILL, RH1 1NP.
•**MIDDUP, Mr. Jonathan William, BSc ACA** *1997;* Ernst & Young LLP, 1 Colmore Square, BIRMINGHAM, B4 6HQ. See also Ernst & Young Europe LLP
MIDGLEY, Mr. Andrew John, BA FCA *1988;* Mead Cottage, 9 Lock Mead, MAIDENHEAD, BERKSHIRE, SL6 8HF.
MIDGLEY, Mrs. Anne Lorraine, ACA *1978;* 7 Spade Oak Farm, Coldmoorholme Lane, BOURNE END, BUCKINGHAMSHIRE, SL8 5PS.
MIDGLEY, Ms. Cheryl Elizabeth, ACA *2002;* Foss Place, Foss Islands Road, YORK, YO31 7UJ.
MIDGLEY, Mr. David Clark, BA ACA *1987;* 6 Cliffe Crest, Hallcliffe Road, Horbury, WAKEFIELD, WF4 6NL.
MIDGLEY, Mr. Donald Edward, BA FCA *1960;* Pellinore, Sleepers Hill, WINCHESTER, SO22 4ND. (Life Member)
•**MIDGLEY, Mr. Gordon William, FCA** *1982;* Hall Robinson Limited, 25 Teak Drive, Kearsley, BOLTON, BL4 8RR.
MIDGLEY, Mr. Harry, FCA *1968;* Lightermans Barn, 7 Spade Oak Farm, Coldmoorholme Lane, BOURNE END, SL8 5PS.
MIDGLEY, Mr. James Keith, BCom ACA *1981;* 7025 Willingdon Avenue, BURNABY V5J 3R4, BC, CANADA.
•**MIDGLEY, Mr. Joe Anthony, FCA** *1971;* Haywood & Co., 24-26 Mansfield Road, ROTHERHAM, S60 2DR.
MIDGLEY, Mr. John Antony, BA ACA *1992;* R S L Steeper Unit 7 Hunslet Trading Estate, Severn Road Hunslet, LEEDS, LS10 1BL.
MIDGLEY, Mr. John Edward Berry, BA(Hons) ACA *2003;* 6 Grange Close, Outlane, HUDDERSFIELD, HD3 3FU.
MIDGLEY, Mrs. Pamela Louise, BSc ACA *1987;* 38 Braywick Road, MAIDENHEAD, SL6 1DA.
MIDGLEY, Mr. Peter, FCA MCT *1974;* 12 Meadowcroft, Chalfont St. Peter, GERRARDS CROSS, BUCKINGHAMSHIRE, SL9 9DH.
MIDGLEY, Mr. Richard James, BSc ACA *1990;* 12 Deer Leap, LIGHTWATER, GU18 5PF.
•**MIDGLEY, Mr. Richard James, FCA** *1966;* (Tax Fac), 1 Ceylon Road, LONDON, W14 0PY.
MIDGLEY, Mr. Ross, BA FCA *1983;* Unit A Blois Meadow Business Centre, Blois Road Steeple Bumpstead, HAVERHILL, SUFFOLK, CB9 7BN.
MIDGLEY, Mr. Roy Edward, FCA *1956;* 189 Shay Lane, Walton, WAKEFIELD, WEST YORKSHIRE, WF2 6NW. (Life Member)
MIDGLEY-CARVER, Mr. Philip David, BSc(Hons) ACA *2004;* (Tax Fac), A B S Europe Ltd ABS House, 1 Frying Pan Alley, LONDON, E1 7HR.
•**MIDWINTER, Mr. Henry Errol, FCA** *1962;* H.E. Midwinter FCA, 13 St. Peters Road, ABINGDON, OX14 3SJ.
MIDWINTER, Mr. Howard Guy, FCA *1971;* Channel View, Sennen, PENZANCE, TR19 7AD.
MIDWOOD, Mr. Simon James, BSc(Hons) ACA *2010;* 3 Pasture Grove, LEEDS, LS7 4QP.
MIDWORTH, Mr. Timothy Samuel, BA ACA *2004;* St Barts, Byron Road, Twyford, READING, RG10 0AE.
MIEBS, Mr. Roderick James, FCA *1968;* 20 Farm Drive, Shirley, CROYDON, CR0 8HR.
MIELCZAREK, Mr. Andrew Ray, BSc(Econ) ACA *1997;* Sunnycroft, Middle Lane, Cold Hatton, TELFORD, TF6 6QA.
MIELKE, Mr. Erik, MPA BSc ACA *2010;* 25 Church Street, Aptartment 1, BOSTON, MA 02116, UNITED STATES.
MIESEGAES, Mr. Simon James Victor, BA ACA *1991;* St. Dennis Farm, Honington, SHIPSTON-ON-STOUR, WARWICKSHIRE, CV36 5EN.
MIESNER, Mr. John James, BSc ACA *2006;* with KPMG LLP, 15 Canada Square, LONDON, E14 5GL.
MIFFLIN, Mr. Andrew, BSc ACA *2006;* M H L, Brunswick Court, NEWCASTLE, STAFFORDSHIRE, ST5 1HH.
MIFFLIN, Mr. Ian Fredrick, BSc ACA *2005;* I M G, McCormack House, Burlington Lane, LONDON, W4 2TH.
•**MIFSUD BONNICI, Mr. Frederick Joseph, FCA** *1975;* PricewaterhouseCoopers, 167 Merchants Street, VALLETTA VLT 1174, MALTA.
MIGDALE, Mr. Philip Roger, FCA *1960;* Meadow Lea, Stream Lane, Nutbourne, PULBOROUGH, RH20 2HG. (Life Member)
MIGHELL, Mr. Howard Stanley, BA ACA *1987;* 25 Goldings Close, Kings Hill, WEST MALLING, ME19 4BE.
MIGNANO, Mr. Alfred Alexander, FCA *1952;* 10 Oaklands, LONDON, N21 3DD. (Life Member)
MIGNANO, Mr. David Jeffery, BA ACA *1984;* 7 Glebe Avenue, ENFIELD, MIDDLESEX, EN2 8NZ.
MIHILL, Mr. Dennis George, FCA *1954;* 7 Bourchier Close, SEVENOAKS, KENT, TN13 1PD. (Life Member)
MIHILL, Mr. Ian Nicholas, BSc ACA *1987;* The Lodge, 191 Barrowby Road, GRANTHAM, LINCOLNSHIRE, NG31 8NN.
MIHILL, Mrs. Jane, BSc ACA *1986;* The Lodge, 191, Barrowby Road, GRANTHAM, NG31 8NN.
MIK, Mr. Oliver James, ACA *2009;* Brockwood House, Stroxton, GRANTHAM, LINCOLNSHIRE, NG33 5DA.
MIKA, Mr. Daniel Geoffrey, ACA *2008;* Flat 82 Denman House, Lordship Terrace, LONDON, N16 0JH.
MIKE, Mr. Hamlyn Roy, BA FCA *1969;* Hamlyn Mike and Co, 13 Mayfield Road, VALSAYN, TRINIDAD AND TOBAGO.
MIKHAIL, Miss. Suzanne Yacoub, BSc ACA *2007;* 3/36 Buckland Street, CHIPPENDALE, NSW 2008, AUSTRALIA.
MIKHMANOV, Mr. Dilshod, ACA *2011;* 6 Patey Street, MANCHESTER, M12 5RP.
MILBANK, Mr. Nigel Paul, MA ACA ACT *1988;* 6 Wildacres, Sandy Lane, NORTHWOOD, HA6 3JD.
MILBANK, Mr. Raymond Charles, FCA *1973;* The Institute of Materials Minerals & Mining, 1 Carlton House Terrace, LONDON, SW1Y 5AF.
MILBANK, Mr. Richard Henry John, BSc ACA *1991;* 13 Oldfield Wood, WOKING, GU22 8AN.
MILBANK, Mrs. Valerie Jane, LLB ACA *1980;* The Old School House, Great Henny, SUDBURY, CO10 7NW.
•**MILBANKE, Mrs. Catherine Fyfe, BSc FCA** *1995;* 3S Accountancy Services, 12 The Greenhouse, Greencroft Industrial Park, STANLEY, COUNTY DURHAM, DH9 7XN. See also Third Sector Accountancy Services Limited
MILBORROW, Mr. David Clifford, FCA *1969;* 12 Popham Close, Blundells Road, TIVERTON, EX16 4GA. (Life Member)
MILBOURN, Mr. Ian Leathley, BA(Hons) ACA *2001;* Notion Capital Partners, Suite 101, Montpellier Drive, CHELTENHAM, GLOUCESTERSHIRE, GL50 1TA.
MILBOURN, Mr. John Geoffrey, FCA *1966;* 8 Seawalls, Sea Walls Road, Sneyd Park, BRISTOL, BS9 1PG. (Life Member)
MILBURN, Mr. Andrew John, LLB ACA *2001;* 10 Lostrigg Close, Little Clifton, WORKINGTON, CUMBRIA, CA14 1WD.
MILBURN, Mr. David John, FCA *1972;* Napley House, Napley, MARKET DRAYTON, TF9 4DS.
MILBURN, Mr. Leonard, FCA *1969;* Rolf C Hagen (UK) Ltd, California Drive, CASTLEFORD, WEST YORKSHIRE, WF10 5QH.
MILBURN, Miss. Lindsay Lita, ACA *2009;* 7 Kidgate Mews, LOUTH, LINCOLNSHIRE, LN11 9HA.
MILBURN, Mr. Paul Brian, BSc ACA *1981;* 22 Warwick Farm Road, OLINDA, VIC 3788, AUSTRALIA.
MILBURN, Mr. Peter Charles Richard, BSc ACA DChA *1989;* The Harpur Trust, Princeton Court, The Pilgrim Centre, Brickhill Drive, BEDFORD, MK41 7PZ.
•**MILBURN, Mr. Robert John, BA FCA** *1984;* PricewaterhouseCoopers LLP, 1 Embankment Place, LONDON, WC2N 6RH. See also PricewaterhouseCoopers
MILBURN, Mr. Ross Paul, BA ACA *1994;* 34 Hollingbourne Road, Herne Hill, LONDON, SE24 9ND.
•**MILBURN, Mr. Simon Alan Nicholas, MA FCA** *1976;* H & E Johnson, Sandall House, 230 High Street, HERNE BAY, KENT, CT6 5AX. See also Mumford & Co Ltd
MILBURN SMITH, Mr. Adam Henry, BA(Hons) ACA *2001;* Ernst & Young Llp Compass House, 80 Newmarket Road, CAMBRIDGE, CB5 8DZ.
•**MILDENER, Mr. Damian Spencer, LLB ACA** *2001;* Clayman & Co, 189 Bickenhall Mansions, Bickenhall StreetBaker Street, LONDON, W1U 6BX.
•**MILDENER, Mr. Irving, FCA** *1967;* Clayman & Co, 189 Bickenhall Mansions, Bickenhall StreetBaker Street, LONDON, W1U 6BX.
MILDNER, Miss. Katja, BA ACA *2003;* 25 Leigh Road, COBHAM, KT11 2LF.
•**MILDREN, Mr. Malcolm Keith, FCA** *1963;* Malcolm Mildren, 1 Tanfield Lane, NORTHAMPTON, NN1 5RN.
MILEHAM, Mr. Christopher Charles, ACA *1979;* 38 Brookmead, Hildenborough, TONBRIDGE, KENT, TN11 9DW.
MILEHAM, Mr. Ronald Charles, FCA *1975;* Manningtons, 39 High Street, BATTLE, EAST SUSSEX, TN33 0EE.
MILES, Mr. Adam Philip Braddock, BSc ACA *2009;* Crostover Hawksdown, Walmer, DEAL, CT14 7PL.
MILES, Ms. Alison Frances, BA ACA *1992;* 3 Wilmot Close, Binfield, BRACKNELL, BERKSHIRE, RG42 4LR.
MILES, Miss. Amanda Claire, BSc(Hons) ACA *2004;* 38 Chestnut Close Rushmere St. Andrew, IPSWICH, IP5 1ED.
MILES, Mr. Andrew David, BA ACA *1990;* The Beeches, 1 Swallow Drive, STOWMARKET, IP14 5BY.
MILES, Mr. Andrew Gruszewicz, FCA *1968;* Luppa Vidor utca 8, 2013 POMAZ, HUNGARY.
•**MILES, Mr. Andrew Ronald, FCA** *1987;* (Tax Fac), Burgess Hodgson, Camburgh House, 27 New Dover Road, CANTERBURY, CT1 3DN.
MILES, Mr. Anthony Charles, BA ACA *1986;* 8 Orchard Terrace, Boroughbridge, YORK, YO51 9AF.
MILES, Mr. Anthony Llewellyn, FCA *1960;* 12 Heritage Way, Raunds, WELLINGBOROUGH, NN9 6RX. (Life Member)
MILES, Mr. Anthony Neil, BA FCA *1986;* 10 Trowlock Avenue, TEDDINGTON, TW11 9QT.
MILES, Mr. Barry Hugh, FCA *1959;* 3 Sandown Avenue, Goring-By-Sea, WORTHING, BN12 4PX. (Life Member)
MILES, Mrs. Ceri Louise, BA ACA *2004;* (Tax Fac), Enterprise Rent A Car, Enterprise House, Delta Way, EGHAM, SURREY, TW20 8RX.
MILES, Mr. Charles Kenneth Zachary, MA FCA *1976;* Flat 4, Cornwall Mansions, 33 Kensington Court, LONDON, W8 5BG.
MILES, Mr. Christopher Andrew, BA FCA *1973;* 2 Greenslate Avenue, Appley Bridge, WIGAN, WN6 9LG.
•**MILES, Mr. Christopher John, FCA** *1979;* (Tax Fac), MILES cmc, Stanley House, 33-35 West Hill, Portishead, BRISTOL, BS20 6LG.
MILES, Mr. Christopher Paul, BA ACA *2006;* 11 Appledore Drive, Oakwood, DERBY, DE21 2LN.
MILES, Mrs. Clare Elisabeth, BA ACA *1984;* The Hospice of St. Francis, Spring Garden Lane, BERKHAMSTED, HERTFORDSHIRE, HP4 3GW.
MILES, Mr. Darren John, BSc(Econ) ACA *1998;* The Woodlands, Condover, SHREWSBURY, SY5 7BH.
MILES, Mr. David Glyn, FCA *1969;* 3 Meadow Park, Burton, MILFORD HAVEN, DYFED, SA73 1NZ. (Life Member)
MILES, Mr. David James, BSc ACA *1988;* 13 Sorrel Garth, HITCHIN, SG4 9PS.
•**MILES, Mr. David John, FCA** *1988;* Miles & Partners Consulting LLP, Harella House, 90-98 Goswell Road, LONDON, EC1V 7RD.
MILES, Mr. David John, BSc FCA *1992;* (Tax Fac), Intel Corp (UK) Ltd, Pipers Way, SWINDON, SN3 1RJ.
MILES, Mr. David Randel, BSc FCA *1978;* 22 Redland Grove, BRISTOL, BS6 6PT.
MILES, Mr. David Ronald, FCA *1972;* The Old Dairy, Main Street, Turweston, BRACKLEY, NN13 5JU.
MILES, Mr. Dennis Brian, BSc FCA *1981;* (Tax Fac), 120 Claverham Road, Claverham, BRISTOL, BS49 4LQ.
•**MILES, Mr. Derek William, FCA** *1961;* Derek W Miles, 6 Wybourne Rise, TUNBRIDGE WELLS, TN2 5JG.
•**MILES, Mr. Geoffrey William, FCA** *1971;* (Tax Fac), Hammonds, Burnhill Business Centre, Provident House, Burrell Row, BECKENHAM, BR3 1AT.
MILES, Mr. Gerwyn John, BSc FCA *1980;* 98 Rhydypenau Road, CARDIFF, CF23 6PW.
MILES, Mr. Glenn, BSc ACA *1989;* The World Bank, (MSN MC8-801), 1818 H Street NW, WASHINGTON, DC 20433, UNITED STATES.
•**MILES, Mr. Ian David, BSc FCA TEP** *1984;* (Tax Fac), James Cowper LLP, North Lea House, 66 Northfield End, HENLEY-ON-THAMES, OXFORDSHIRE, RG9 2BE.
MILES, Mr. Ian George, BA ACA *1989;* Via Barra 3, Pecetto Torinese, 10020 TORINO, ITALY.
MILES, Miss. Jane Helena Louise, ACA *2008;* 12 Luxborough House, Luxborough Street, LONDON, W1U 5BJ.
•**MILES, Mr. Jonathan Marcus, BSc ACA CTA** *1995;* Orchard Cottage, Mackley Lane, Norton St. Philip, BATH, BA2 7NL.
MILES, Mrs. Kate Louise, BSc ACA *1992;* 18 Royal Oak Drive, CROWTHORNE, RG45 6LU.
MILES, Miss. Kathryn Charlotte Helen, MMath ACA *2005;* Mills & Boon (Publishers) Ltd Eton House, 18-24 Paradise Road, RICHMOND, TW9 1SR.
MILES, Mr. Keith Charles, OBE FCA *1964;* 19 Elmtree Green, GREAT MISSENDEN, BUCKINGHAMSHIRE, HP16 9AF. (Life Member)
MILES, Mr. Keith Walter, FCA *1969;* Four Winds, 16 Oxlea Road, TORQUAY, DEVON, TQ1 2HF. (Life Member)
MILES, Mr. Laurence Ralph, BA FCA *1967;* Broad Oaks, Ockley Lane, BURGESS HILL, RH15 0BJ.
MILES, Mr. Leslie Collins, FCA *1958;* 16 The Glebelands, Bowring Mead, Moretonhampstead, NEWTON ABBOT, DEVON, TQ13 8LE. (Life Member)
MILES, Mr. Mark Andrew Simon, BSc ACA *1991;* SBM Offshore NV, 24 Av de Fontvieille, PO Box 199, MONTE CARLO, MC 98007, MONACO.
MILES, Mr. Martin, BA ACA *1999;* 26 Albany Mews, KINGSTON-UPON-THAMES, KT2 5SL.
MILES, Mr. Martin Terence, BSc ACA *1993;* HMV Group plc, Shelley House, 2-4 York Road, MAIDENHEAD, SL6 1SR.
MILES, Mr. Matthew Charles, BA ACA *2002;* EFG Offshore Ltd, PO Box 641, No. 1 Seaton Place, St. Helier, JERSEY, JE4 8YJ.
MILES, Mr. Michael Gruszewicz, FCA *1971;* 1 Durham Lodge, Durham Road, LONDON, SW20 0TN.
MILES, Mr. Michael Robert, BSc FCA *1976;* Rockwood Specialities Ltd, Moorfield Road, WIDNES, CHESHIRE, WA8 3AA.
•**MILES, Mr. Michael Robert Frank, FCA** *1958;* M.R.F.Miles, 191a High Street, STREET, SOMERSET, BA16 0NE.
MILES, Mr. Neil Rowland, BSc ACA *1994;* 27 Bradgate Drive, Four Oaks, SUTTON COLDFIELD, WEST MIDLANDS, B74 4XG.
•**MILES, Mr. Nicholas Christopher Francis, BSc ACA** *1987;* (Tax Fac), Peregrine Accountants & Business Advisors Ltd, The Old Bank, The Triangle, Paulton, BRISTOL, BS39 7LE.
MILES, Mr. Nicholas Edward, MA ACA *2003;* 1 Calton Road, BATH, BA2 4PP.
MILES, Mr. Nigel Timothy Grenfell, FCA *1969;* J T Group Ltd, 70 Prince Street, BRISTOL, BS1 4HU.
MILES, Mr. Paul Lewis, BA ACA ATII *1996;* Juxon House, 100 St Paul's Churchyard, LONDON, EC4M 8BU.
MILES, Mr. Paul Michael, MA ACA *1990;* Elsevier BV, Radarweg 29, 1043 NX AMSTERDAM, NETHERLANDS.
•**MILES, Mr. Peter John Perry, BA ACA** *1983;* West and Foster Limited, 2 Broomgrove Road, SHEFFIELD, SOUTH YORKSHIRE, S10 2LR.
MILES, Mr. Peter Thomas, FCA *1962;* The Old Barn, Cakebole, Chaddesley Corbett, KIDDERMINSTER, DY10 4RF. (Life Member)
MILES, Miss. Rachel Lora, BSc ACA *2006;* with PricewaterhouseCoopers LLP, 101 Barbirolli Square, Lower Mosley Street, MANCHESTER, M2 3PW.
MILES, Mrs. Raina Margaret, MA ACA *1987;* (Tax Fac), Signet Group Limited, 15 Golden Square, LONDON, W1F 9JG.
•**MILES, Mr. Richard David, ACA** *1987;* 3 Glenair Avenue, POOLE, DORSET, BH14 8AD.
•**MILES, Mr. Richard Michael, BSc FCA** *1978;* Jackson Robson Licence Limited, 33/35 Exchange Street, DRIFFIELD, NORTH HUMBERSIDE, YO25 6LL. See also Jackson Robson Licence
MILES, Mr. Robert, BA(Hons) ACA *2011;* 4/13 Kangaroo Street, MANLY, NSW 2095, AUSTRALIA.
MILES, Mr. Robert Gerard, MA ACA *1990;* 5 Penyston Road, MAIDENHEAD, SL6 6EJ.
MILES, Mrs. Roberta Caroline, MA FCA *1989;* 11 The Woodlands, Chesterton, BICESTER, OXFORDSHIRE, OX26 1TN.
MILES, Mr. Roger Frank, BSc FCA *1975;* 66 Albany Road, FLEET, GU51 3PT.
MILES, Mr. Roger Malcolm, BA FCA *1982;* 1 Elm Bank Gardens, LONDON, SW13 0NU.
MILES, Mrs. Ruth Alison, BSc ACA *1992;* 28 Magellan Crescent, SIPPY DOWNS, QLD 4556, AUSTRALIA.
MILES, Ms. Sarah Jane, BA ACA *2002;* 11 Skye Crescent, MILTON KEYNES, MK3 5AY.
MILES, Mr. Sean Richard, BA ACA *2000;* 15 Millington Gate, Willen, MILTON KEYNES, MK15 9HT.
MILES, Mr. Simon David, FCA *1983;* 3 Winchester Grove, SEVENOAKS, TN13 3BL.

•MILES, Mr. Steven William, FCA *1986;* (Tax Fac), Berry & Partners, West Walk House, 99 Princess Road East, LEICESTER, LE1 7LF.
MILES, Ms. Susan Elizabeth, BA ACA *1992;* 42 Durleston Park Drive, Great Bookham, LEATHERHEAD, KT23 4AJ.
MILES, Mr. Toby Matthew Adam, ACA *2006;* 76 Great Mead, CHIPPENHAM, WILTSHIRE, SN15 3QJ.
MILES, Miss. Tracey Anne, BSc ACA *1998;* Court House Nore Marsh Road, Wootton Bassett, SWINDON, SN4 8BQ.
•MILES, Mr. Victor Alfred, FCA *1977;* (Tax Fac), J.P.B. Harris & Co, 54 St. Marys Lane, UPMINSTER, ESSEX, RM14 2QT. See also JPB Harris & Co Ltd
MILES, Mr. Vivian, FCA *1970;* 10 Fairview Road, DARTMOUTH, DEVON, TQ6 9EN.
MILES-KINGSTON, Mrs. Charlotte Ann, BA(Hons) ACA *2001;* Harpsden Way House, Harpsden Way, HENLEY-ON-THAMES, OXFORDSHIRE, RG9 1NL.
MILEWSKI, Mr. Adrian Charles, ACA MAAT *2004;* 33 Rodyard Way, COVENTRY, CV1 2UD.
MILEY, Mr. Lee Graham, BA ACA *1998;* 16 Priory Gardens, STAMFORD, LINCOLNSHIRE, PE9 2EG.
MILFORD, Miss. Nicola, BSc ACA *1999;* 190 Newchurch Road, Stacksteads, BACUP, OL13 0EE.
MILFORD, Mr. Peter Henry, BSc ACA *1987;* 131 Clifton Road, PAIGNTON, DEVON, TQ3 3JY.
MILFORD, Miss. Sian Marie Catherine, BA ACA *2000;* K P M G Llp, 15 Canada Square, LONDON, E14 5GL.
MILHAM, Mr. Mark Anthony, BSc ACA *1993;* Elsenheimerstrasse 33, 80687 MUNICH, GERMANY.
MILHENCH, Mrs. Helen Danuta, BSc ACA *1993;* 26 Dulwich Village, LONDON, SE21 7AL.
MILHOFER, Mr. Peter John, MA ACA *1994;* PO Box 162, 2501 DEN HAAG, NETHERLANDS.
MILI, Mr. Demetris Kyriakou, MSc BEng ACA *2003;* 40 Narkissou Street, Paleo Psychiko, 15452 ATHENS, GREECE.
MILIA, Ms. Apostolia, MSc ACA *2004;* Salaminos 65, Vrilissia, 15235 ATHENS, GREECE.
MILIOTIS, Mr. Marios, BCom ACA CFA *1998;* 43 Armenias Street, Akropolis, 2003 NICOSIA, CYPRUS.
MILIOTOU, Miss. Andria, BSc ACA *2009;* 6 Pente Pigadia, Flat 501, Agious Omologites, NICOSIA, CYPRUS.
MILL, Mr. Douglas, BA ACA *1989;* Sirus Russell House, Littleburn Industrial Estate Langley Moor, DURHAM, DH7 8HJ.
MILLAR, Mr. Alan John, BSc ACA *1994;* 8 Shandon Street, EDINBURGH, EH11 1QH.
•MILLAR, Mr. Allan, MA BSocSc FCA CTA *1992;* AM Accountancy Services Limited, 6 Brunel Court, TRURO, TR1 3AE.
•MILLAR, Mr. Angus James, MA FCA *1996;* Ernst & Young LLP, 1 More London Place, LONDON, SE1 2AF. See also Ernst & Young Europe LLP
MILLAR, Mr. Anthony Bruce, FCA *1964;* Frensham Vale House, Gardeners Hill Road, Lower Bourne, FARNHAM, GU10 3JB. (Life Member)
•MILLAR, Mrs. Ceri, BA FCA *1984;* (Tax Fac), Ceri Millar Ltd, 39 John Street, PORTHCAWL, MID GLAMORGAN, CF36 3AP.
MILLAR, Mr. Dale, BSc ACA ATII *1999;* Flat 4B, 70 Electric Road, TIN HAU, HONG KONG SAR.
•MILLAR, Ms. Frances Catherine, BSc ACA *1999;* with RSM Tenon Limited, Vantage, Victoria Street, BASINGSTOKE, RG21 3BT.
MILLAR, Mrs. Georgina Mary, BA ACA *1985;* The Red House, STRATHPEFFER, IV14 9DH.
MILLAR, Mr. Graham, FCA *1968;* The White House, 28 Water End, Clifton, YORK, YO30 6LP. (Life Member)
•MILLAR, Mr. Ian Duncan George, FCA *1985;* Millar & Co, 17 Farm View, Tupton, CHESTERFIELD, DERBYSHIRE, S42 6BD.
MILLAR, Mr. Jamie, BSc ACA *1993;* 30 Oakley Road, Caversham, READING, RG4 7RL.
MILLAR, Mr. John, BA FCA *1995;* Boendlerstrasse 52, 8802 KILCHBERG, SWITZERLAND.
MILLAR, Mr. Jonathan Robert, BSc ACA *1993;* 12 Sheringham Close, Woodthorpe View, Arnold, NOTTINGHAM, NG5 6PY.
MILLAR, The Revd. Julie Ann, BA BTh FCA *1992;* 6 Brunel Court, TRURO, CORNWALL, TR1 3AE.
MILLAR, Mr. Keith Malcolm Hedley, DL MA FCA *1960;* Beaumans Farmhouse, WADHURST, TN5 6HL. (Life Member)
MILLAR, Mr. Kieran Thomas, BSc ACA *1993;* Du Pre Plc, The Vo-Tec Centre, Hambridge Lane, NEWBURY, BERKSHIRE, RG14 5TN.
MILLAR, Mrs. Kim, BA ACA *1993;* 30 Oakley Road, Caversham, READING, RG4 7RL.
MILLAR, Mr. Malcolm James Ewan, BA(Hons) ACA *2001;* 4 Quarry Road, LONDON, SW18 2QJ.
MILLAR, Mr. Martin George, BSc ACA *2011;* Crestwood House, BROCKENHURST, HAMPSHIRE, SO42 7PB.
MILLAR, Mr. Matthew Charles, BA ACA *1998;* Greys Mead, Thame Park Road, THAME, OX9 3PL.
MILLAR, Miss. Michelle Jane, MSc BSc ACA *2010;* 23 Shortheath Road, FARNHAM, SURREY, GU9 8SN.
MILLAR, Ms. Niamh, MSc ACA *2010;* 14 Cottimore Lane, WALTON-ON-THAMES, SURREY, KT12 2BT.
•ⓘMILLAR, Mr. Nigel, FCA *1978;* Baker Tilly Restructuring & Recovery LLP, Abbotsgate House, Hollow Road, BURY ST. EDMUNDS, SUFFOLK, IP32 7FA. See also Baker Tilly Tax and Advisory Services LLP
MILLAR, Mr. Peter Christopher Bamford, BA ACA *1988;* Beccott, Broadway Road, Charlton Adam, SOMERTON, TA11 7AU.
•MILLAR, Mr. Peter Milford, FCA *1983;* Taylor Rowlands, 8 High Street, YARM, TS15 9AE. See also Rowlands
MILLAR, Mr. Piers Malcolm Charles, MA ACA *1998;* Intermediate Capital Group Plc, 20 Old Broad Street, LONDON, EC2N 1DP.
MILLAR, Mr. Richard Alexander, FCA *1971;* Flint Cottage, 12 Top Road, Belaugh, NORWICH, NR12 8XB.
MILLAR, Mr. Roderick Lythall Mcdougal, BA ACA *1981;* 4459 West Coast Highway, NEWPORT BEACH, CA 92663, UNITED STATES.
MILLAR, Mr. Roland Ralph William, BA ACA *1986;* Minstrels, 46 Frant Road, TUNBRIDGE WELLS, KENT, TN2 5LJ.
MILLAR, Mr. Ronald Miller, MA ACA *1985;* 9 Forth Park, Dalmeny, SOUTH QUEENSFERRY, WEST LOTHIAN, EH30 9HB.
MILLAR, Mr. Ronald Norman, FCA *1960;* Honiton Lodge, 4 The Avenue, SALISBURY, SP1 1NF. (Life Member)
MILLAR, Miss. Sarah Ann, BSc ACA *1994;* 5 Gatcombe Crescent, ASCOT, SL5 7HA.
MILLAR, Mr. Tom, BA ACA MSI *2003;* 63 Linnell Road, LONDON, SE5 8NJ.
MILLARD, Mr. Adrian, BSc ACA *1985;* Kinyo UK Ltd, 1 Scala Court, Leathley Road, LEEDS, LS10 1JD.
MILLARD, Mr. Andrew Clive, BSocSc FCA *1986;* Barton Barn, Kittisford, WELLINGTON, SOMERSET, TA21 0RZ.
MILLARD, Mr. Andrew David, BA ACA *1993;* Kingswood Hampton Lovett, DROITWICH, WORCESTERSHIRE, WR9 0LX.
•MILLARD, Mr. Anthony John, FCA *1979;* (Tax Fac), BDWM Limited, Ground Floor, Hallow Park, Hallow, WORCESTER, WR2 6PG.
MILLARD, Mr. Bernard Albert, FCA *1960;* Peasridge Oast, Frittenden, CRANBROOK, TN17 2BD. (Life Member)
MILLARD, Mrs. Catherine Rachel, BSc ARCS ACA ATII *1994;* (Tax Fac), 5 Lower Road, Stuntney, ELY, CAMBRIDGESHIRE, CB7 5TN.
MILLARD, Mr. Christopher Alan, BSc FCA *1969;* Foxton, School Lane, Burghfield Common, READING, RG7 3ES.
MILLARD, Mr. Colin Trevor, BA ACA *1980;* with Co-Operative Financial Services Ltd, 18th Floor CIS Building, Miller Street, MANCHESTER, M60 0AL.
MILLARD, Mr. Craig Gordon, ACA *1997;* 3 Paddock Close, Bidford-on-Avon, ALCESTER, WARWICKSHIRE, B50 4PJ.
MILLARD, Mr. Daniel George, BSc ACA *2004;* Financial Management NH A1, Nationwide Bldg Soc Nationwide House, Pipers Way, SWINDON, SN3 1TA.
MILLARD, Mr. David Antony, BSc ACA *1993;* 8 Charles Street, REDFERN, NSW 2016, AUSTRALIA.
MILLARD, Mr. David John, MEng ACA *1996;* 5 Lower Road, Stuntney, ELY, CAMBRIDGESHIRE, CB7 5TN.
MILLARD, Mrs. Deborah Helen, BA ACA *1997;* 6 Lawrence Close, PERTH, DARLINGTON, WA 6070, AUSTRALIA.
MILLARD, Mrs. Diane Elizabeth, BSc ACA *1980;* 55 Lyme Road, Hazel Grove, STOCKPORT, SK7 6LH.
MILLARD, Mr. Hugh, FCA *1956;* 22/38 Kings Park Road, West Perth, PERTH, WA 6005, AUSTRALIA. (Life Member)
MILLARD, Mr. James Edward, BSc ACA CFA *1998;* 23 Bath Road, EMSWORTH, HAMPSHIRE, PO10 7EP.
MILLARD, Mr. John Leslie, BSc FCA *1976;* 6 Waverley Gardens, STAMFORD, PE9 1BH.
MILLARD, Mr. John Stuart, MA ACA *1979;* Winston, Perry Long Lane, Broadway, DERBY, DE22 1AX.
MILLARD, Mr. Jon Matthew, BA(Hons) ACA *2002;* 52 Goulden Road, MANCHESTER, M20 4YF.
MILLARD, Mr. Jonathan Richard, BSocSc ACA *2004;* HTSE IT Planning & Finance, H S B C, Griffin House, Silver Street Head, SHEFFIELD, S1 3GG.
MILLARD, Mr. Mark, BA ACA *2010;* 3 Colchester Avenue, Penylan, CARDIFF, CF23 9BN.
•MILLARD, Mr. Michael Alan, FCA *1982;* Lewis Rowell, 20 Springfield Road, CRAWLEY, WEST SUSSEX, RH11 8AD.
MILLARD, Mr. Nicholas Robert, MA FCA *1978;* Foxhole Farm, Croftland Lane, Drayton, LANGPORT, SOMERSET, TA10 0LP.
MILLARD, Mr. Nick, BSc ACA *2010;* 53 Lorne Road, BATH, BA2 3BZ.
MILLARD, Mr. Peter, BSc ACA *1981;* 2 Westwood Cottages, Westwood Lane Normandy, GUILDFORD, GU3 2JD.
MILLARD, Mr. Robert Anderton, BSc FCA *1978;* Anderton House, Church Str., Oughtibridge, SHEFFIELD, S35 0FU.
MILLATT, Miss. Katherine Mary, MA ACA *1998;* 4 Newton Road Knowle, SOLIHULL, WEST MIDLANDS, B93 9HL.
MILLBERY, Mr. Richard William, FCA *1976;* Little Beck, New Valley Road, Milford-on-Sea, LYMINGTON, SO41 0SA.
MILLEA, Miss. Kathryn Anne Victoria, ACA *2010;* Flat 7, 46 Charles Street, IPSWICH, IP1 3JG.
MILLEA, Mr. Robert Ian, FCA *1980;* MEMBER OF COUNCIL, 17 Rivish Lane, Long Melford, SUDBURY, CO10 9TH.
MILLEDGE, Mr. Paul Joseph, BA ACA *1994;* Odos Boinobitz 23, TK84600 AGIA YPAKOI, GREECE.
MILLEN, Mrs. Helen, BA ACA *2006;* 14 Tudor Walk, Honington, BURY ST. EDMUNDS, SUFFOLK, IP31 1LS.
MILLEN, Mrs. Nyuk Woon, BA ACA *1982;* 14A Tutus Street, BALGOWLAH HEIGHTS, NSW 2093, AUSTRALIA.
MILLEN, Mr. Peter Stephen, BSc ACA *2004;* with Hazlewoods LLP, Windsor House, Barnett Way, Barnwood, GLOUCESTER, GL4 3RT.
MILLEN, Mr. Richard John, BA ACA *1983;* PricewaterhouseCoopers, Darling Park Tower 2, 201 Sussex Street, GPO Box 2650, SYDNEY, NSW 1171 AUSTRALIA.
MILLEN, Mr. Roger James, FCA *1969;* Thornley, 20 Victoria Avenue, ILKLEY, LS29 9BL. (Life Member)
MILLEN, Miss. Sally Ann, ACA *2009;* ELG Recycling Processors, 170 Northbourne Road, CAMPBELLFIELD, VIC 3061, AUSTRALIA.
MILLEN, Mrs. Susan Elizabeth, BA ACA *2002;* 58 Priors Road, CHELTENHAM, GLOUCESTERSHIRE, GL52 5AA.
MILLEN, Mrs. Veronica Anne, MA ACA *1985;* 38 Highfield Road, PURLEY, CR8 2JG.
•MILLENER, Mr. Paul Anthony, BSc FCA *1979;* (Tax Fac), Millener Davies, Southfield House, Southfield Road, Westbury On Trym, BRISTOL, BS9 3BH.
•MILLER, Mr. Alan, FCA *1963;* Alan Miller & Co, 5 Ranelagh Drive, EDGWARE, MIDDLESEX, HA8 8HJ.
MILLER, Mr. Alan, FCA *1960;* September Cottage, 3 Bridge Lane, Greetham, OAKHAM, LE15 7NE. (Life Member)
MILLER, Mr. Alan Grant, BA ACA *1989;* 78 Weoley Hill, Selly Oak, BIRMINGHAM, B29 4BL.
MILLER, Mr. Alan John, FCA *1961;* 67 Newbury Lane, Silsoe, BEDFORD, MK45 4EX.
MILLER, Mr. Alastair, BSc FCA *1982;* New Look New Look House, Mercery Road, WEYMOUTH, DORSET, DT3 5HJ.
MILLER, Miss. Alison Eva, BA ACA *1979;* 33 Braemar Avenue, LONDON, N22 7BY.
MILLER, Mr. Alistair McKenzie, BA ACA *1993;* Liberata UK Ltd, 1 London Bridge, LONDON, SE1 9AJ.
MILLER, Mrs. Amanda Jane, BA ACA *1993;* 4 Windward Loop, OCEAN REEF, WA 6027, AUSTRALIA.
MILLER, Mr. Andrew Blake, BCom FCA *1995;* (Tax Fac), 19 Hartfield Avenue, Elstree, BOREHAMWOOD, WD6 3JB.
MILLER, Mr. Andrew Charles, BSc ACA CF *1998;* with BTG Financial Consulting LLP, 9th Floor, Bond Court, LEEDS, LS1 2JZ.
•MILLER, Mr. Andrew David, BSc FCA *1991;* Rothman Pantall LLP, 2nd floor, Old Inn House, 2 Carshalton Road, SUTTON, SURREY SM1 4RA.
MILLER, Mr. Andrew Gideon, BA(Hons) ACA *2000;* 1 North Wacker, PricewaterhouseCoopers, CHICAGO, IL 60606, UNITED STATES.
•MILLER, Mr. Andrew Gordon, BCom ACA *1987;* (Tax Fac), Andrew Miller & Co, The Mews, Stratton Cleeve, Cheltenham Road, CIRENCESTER, GL7 2JD.
•MILLER, Mr. Andrew Horne, FCA *1971;* (Tax Fac), Reeves & Co LLP, Third Floor, 24 Chiswell Street, LONDON, EC1Y 4YX.
MILLER, Mr. Andrew Ian, BA ACA *1992;* 10 Horotutu Road, Greenlane, AUCKLAND 1061, NEW ZEALAND.
MILLER, Mr. Andrew James, BSc(Hons) ACA CTA *2004;* 30 St Mary Axe, LONDON, EC3A 8EP.
MILLER, Mr. Andrew John, BCom ACA *1996;* 11 The Swift, Tassagard Greens, Saggart, DUBLIN, COUNTY DUBLIN, IRELAND.
MILLER, Mr. Andrew Jonathon, BSc ACA *1996;* A19, Discovery Bay Marina Club, DISCOVERY BAY, HONG KONG SAR.
MILLER, Mr. Andrew Lloyd, BSc ACA *2007;* with BPU Limited, Radnor House, Greenwood Close, Cardiff Gate Business Park, CARDIFF, CF23 8AA.
MILLER, Mr. Andrew Michael, BSc ACA *1979;* with Harris & Sheldon Group Ltd, North Court, Packington Park, Meriden, COVENTRY, CV7 7HF.
MILLER, Miss. Angela Gaynor, BA ACA *1992;* Bay Tree Cottage, 38 New Road, Shenley, RADLETT, HERTFORDSHIRE, WD7 9EA.
MILLER, Mrs. Angharad Mary, BA FCA *1983;* 53 Ashurst Road, West Moors, FERNDOWN, BH22 0LR.
MILLER, Miss. Ann, BA ACA *1992;* 3 James Street, Arnold, NOTTINGHAM, NG5 7BE.
MILLER, Miss. Ann Christine, BA ACA *1981;* PO BOX 2076, BORONIA PARK, NSW 2111, AUSTRALIA.
MILLER, Mrs. Anne, MA BSc ACA *2009;* Pricewaterhousecoopers, 33 Wellington Street, LEEDS, LS1 4JP.
•MILLER, Mrs. Anne, BSc FCA *1975;* e-practice, The Studio, Drift Road, BORDON, HAMPSHIRE, GU35 9DZ.
•MILLER, Mr. Anthony, ACA *1978;* A Miller & Co, Evans House, 107 Marsh Road, PINNER, MIDDLESEX, HA5 5PA.
MILLER, Mr. Anthony Charles, ACA *1990;* 18 Audrey Gardens, WEMBLEY, HA0 3TG.
•ⓘMILLER, Mr. Asher David, BSc FCA *1997;* David Rubin & Partners LLP, Pearl Assurance House, 319 Ballards Lane, North Finchley, LONDON, N12 8LY. See also David Rubin & Partners
MILLER, Mr. Ashley Rupert James Patrick, BA ACA *1996;* 24 Farmcombe Road, TUNBRIDGE WELLS, TN2 5DF.
MILLER, Mr. Ben James Alexander, BA FCA *1998;* 6, Graylands, Theydon Bois, EPPING, ESSEX, CM16 7LB.
MILLER, Mr. Bernard Thomas, FCA *1952;* 9 Bayfield Road, HORLEY, SURREY, RH6 8ET. (Life Member)
MILLER, Mr. Bernard Victor, FCA *1964;* 11 Grandborough Drive, SOLIHULL, B91 3TS.
MILLER, Mrs. Beverley Alexandra, BA ACA *2006;* 14 The Oaks, Bloxwich, WALSALL, WS3 2NY.
MILLER, Mrs. Bonita Jane, BSc ACA *1994;* Priors Hall, Church End, Stebbing, DUNMOW, CM6 3SW.
MILLER, Mr. Bruce Summers, BSc FCA *1977;* 28 Dacre Road, Fulwell, SUNDERLAND, SR6 8EL.
MILLER, Mrs. Carolyn Margaret, BA ACA *1984;* 6 Penrhyn Crescent, East Sheen, LONDON, SW14 7PF.
MILLER, Miss. Catherine Alison, BA ACA *1996;* 29 Oriental Road, Sunninghill, ASCOT, BERKSHIRE, SL5 7AZ.
MILLER, Mrs. Catherine Margaret, BSc ACA *1991;* Harman International SNC, 2 Route de Tours, 72500 CHATEAU DU LOIR, FRANCE.
MILLER, Mr. Charles Raymond, FCA *1937;* 5 Mercia Court, Larkhill, BEXHILL-ON-SEA, EAST SUSSEX, TN40 1TY. (Life Member)
MILLER, Ms. Cheryl, BSc ACA *2006;* 8/123 Beaconsfield Parade, ALBERT PARK, VIC 3206, AUSTRALIA.
MILLER, Mrs. Christine Ellenor, BA FCA *1984;* 22591 Avenida Empresa, RANCHO SANTA MARGARITA, CA 92688, UNITED STATES.
MILLER, Mr. Christopher John, BA FCA *1969;* Park House, 123 Church Street, Shirley, SOUTHAMPTON, SO15 5LW. (Life Member)
MILLER, Mrs. Claire Elizabeth, BA FCA *1993;* with RSM Tenon Limited, Ferryboat Lane, SUNDERLAND, SR5 3JN.
MILLER, Mrs. Claire Marion, BSc ACA *2000;* Claverley House, Queens Road, St. Peter Port, GUERNSEY, GY1 1PT.
MILLER, Mrs. Clare, MA ACA *1988;* Affinity Sutton Group Ltd, 6 More London Place, LONDON, SE1 2DA.
MILLER, Mr. Clifford Leroy, FCA *1965;* The Beacons, Cadmore End, HIGH WYCOMBE, HP14 3PL.
MILLER, Mr. Craig, ACA CA(AUS) *2011;* Supercrease Limited, Unit 5 The Moorings, Waterside Road, LEEDS, LS10 1DG.
MILLER, Mr. Darren Roy, BSc ACA *1991;* Tenon Recovery, Highfield Court, Tollgate, Chandler's Ford, EASTLEIGH, HAMPSHIRE SO53 3TY.

MILLER, Mr. David, BSc FCA ACIS *1983;* Commercial Management Ltd, Chelsea House, 8-14 The Broadway, HAYWARDS HEATH, WEST SUSSEX, RH16 3AP.
MILLER, Mr. David, BA ACA *1987;* International Hotel Group, 1 First Avenue, Centrum One Hundred, BURTON-ON-TRENT, STAFFORDSHIRE, DE14 2WB.
MILLER, Mr. David Ford, BA CA *2003; (CA Scotland 1981);* Grant Thornton UK LLP, Grant Thornton House, 22 Melton Street, Euston Square, LONDON, NW1 2EP. See also Grant Thornton LLP
MILLER, Mr. David Frederick Peter, BSc FCA *1977;* Sunnyhouse, 208 Grindley Lane, Blythe Bridge, STOKE-ON-TRENT, ST11 9JS.
MILLER, Mr. David John, BSc ACA *1987;* 1 Asmara Road, LONDON, NW2 3SS.
MILLER, Mr. David John, FCA *1958;* 39 Maidenhead Court Park, MAIDENHEAD, SL6 8HN. (Life Member)
•MILLER, Mr. David John, BA ACA *1978;* David J Miller & Co, 8 Savoy Grove, Blackwater, CAMBERLEY, SURREY, GU17 9JW.
•MILLER, Mr. David Paul, BA FCA *1991;* (Tax Fac), S 9 Limited, 18 Merlin Way, Mickleover, DERBY, DE3 0SL.
•MILLER, Mr. David Philip, BSc FCA *1986;* Bartfields (UK) Limited, Burley House, 12 Clarendon Road, LEEDS, LS2 9NF. See also Bartfields Business Services LLP
MILLER, Mr. David Robert, BSc FCA *1986;* Elmwood House, 27A The Ridgeway, STANMORE, HA7 4BE.
MILLER, Mrs. Dawn Elizabeth, BA ACA *2004;* 66 Radnor Road, WEYBRIDGE, KT13 8JU.
•MILLER, Mrs. Deborah, FCA *1978;* David J Miller & Co, 8 Savoy Grove, Blackwater, CAMBERLEY, SURREY, GU17 9JW.
MILLER, Mr. Derek, FCA *1959;* 3 Park Gate Close, Horsforth, LEEDS, LS18 5SS. (Life Member)
•MILLER, Ms. Diana Hilary, BSc FCA *1992;* Robinson Miller, 68 West Street, WARMINSTER, WILTSHIRE, BA12 8JW.
MILLER, Mrs. Elizabeth Anne, BSc ACA *1998;* 5 Foxley Close, LYMM, CHESHIRE, WA13 0BS.
MILLER, Mr. Fenwick Neil, BSc ACA *2001;* 18 Water Street, Lynfrae, CLAREMONT, WESTERN CAPE PROVINCE, 7700, SOUTH AFRICA.
MILLER, Mr. Gary, BA ACA *2002;* 12 Lingwell Park, WIDNES, CHESHIRE, WA8 9YP.
•MILLER, Mr. Gary Andrew, ACA *1990;* H W Fisher & Company, Acre House, 11-15 William Road, LONDON, NW1 3ER. See also Fisher Corporate Plc and H W Fisher & Company Limited
MILLER, Mr. Gary Thomas, BSc FCA *1984;* H S B C Private Bank (C.I.) Ltd Park Place, Park Street St. Peter Port, GUERNSEY, GY1 1EE.
•MILLER, Mr. Gary William, FCA *1978;* Price Bailey LLP, Causeway House, 1 Dane Street, BISHOP'S STORTFORD, HERTFORDSHIRE, CM23 3BT. See also Price Bailey Private Client LLP
•MILLER, Mr. Geoffery John, FCA *1983;* RHK Business Advisers LLP, Coburg House, 1 Coburg Street, GATESHEAD, TYNE AND WEAR, NE8 1NS. See also RHK Corporate Finance LLP
•MILLER, Mr. Grahame, FCA *1978;* Argents, 15 Palace Street, NORWICH, NR3 1RT.
MILLER, Miss. Hannah Jane, BA ACA DChA *2006;* Flat 79 Belvedere Court, 372-374 Upper Richmond Road, LONDON, SW15 6HZ.
MILLER, Mr. Harold, BSc ACA *1995;* 14 Flower Lane, Mill Hill, LONDON, NW7 2JB.
MILLER, Ms. Heather, BA(Hons) ACA *2003;* Business Innovation & Skills, 1 Victoria Street, LONDON, SW1H 0ET.
MILLER, Miss. Helen Jane, BSc ACA *1990;* Apartment 47 Viva, 10 Commercial Street, BIRMINGHAM, B1 1RH.
•MILLER, Mrs. Helen Louise, BSc ACA *1991;* Helen Miller Accountancy Services, 5 Bincleaves Road, WEYMOUTH, DORSET, DT4 8RL.
MILLER, Miss. Helen Louise, LLB ACA *2002;* 2/16 Carr Street, WAVERTON, NSW 2060, AUSTRALIA.
MILLER, Mr. Humphrey John, FCA *1968;* Keystone Wood Ltd, 29 The Crescent, Hampton-in-Arden, SOLIHULL, WEST MIDLANDS, B92 0BN.
MILLER, Mr. Ian Alexander, FCA *1956;* 31 West Gate, Plumpton Green, LEWES, BN7 3BQ. (Life Member)
MILLER, Mr. Ian Robert, BA(Hons) ACA FABRP *1993;* (Tax Fac), 9 Ludlow Road, LONDON, W5 1NX.
MILLER, Mr. James Christopher, MA FCA *1977;* 27 Fife Road, LONDON, SW14 7EJ.
MILLER, Mrs. Jane, BSc ACA *1992;* Hillside Barn, Turweston Hill Farm, Turweston, BRACKLEY, NORTHAMPTONSHIRE, NN13 5JB.
MILLER, Mrs. Janet Lesley, BA ACA *1989;* Applecross, School Road, Hightown, LIVERPOOL, L38 0BN.
MILLER, Mr. Jeremy, BSc ACA *2010;* with KPMG LLP, 15 Canada Square, LONDON, E14 5GL.
MILLER, Mr. Jeremy Ronald St John, BA ACA *1984;* 9 Denmark Avenue, LONDON, SW19 4HF.
•MILLER, Miss. Jessica Laura, LLB ACA *2005;* 3 Lang Rigg, SOUTH QUEENSFERRY, WEST LOTHIAN, EH30 9WN.
MILLER, Mrs. Joanne Marie, BSc(Hons) ACA *2004;* 8 West View, ORMSKIRK, LANCASHIRE, L39 2DJ.
MILLER, Mr. John, FCA *1965;* 87 Lodge Road, Writtle, CHELMSFORD, CM1 3HZ. (Life Member)
MILLER, Air Commodore John, CBE DFC AFC FCA *1947;* Orchard Close, Pitchcombe, STROUD, GL6 6LJ. (Life Member)
MILLER, Mr. John Axel, FCA *1960;* 2 King's House Studios, Lamont Road Passage, Chelsea, LONDON, SW10 0HN. (Life Member)
MILLER, Mr. John David, BA FCA *1985;* Apple Orchard, Windmill Road, Weald, SEVENOAKS, TN14 6PH.
MILLER, Mr. John David, BA ACA *1993;* 53 The Ridgeway, Kenton, HARROW, HA3 0LW.
MILLER, The Revd. John Douglas, FCA *1948;* 35 Branscombe Close, Colyford, COLYTON, EX24 6RF. (Life Member)
MILLER, Mr. John Graham Rex, BA FCA *1983;* Turners (Soham) Limited, Fordham Road, NEWMARKET, SUFFOLK, CB8 7NR.
•MILLER, Mr. John Henry, FCA *1977;* John H. Miller & Co, 21 Elm Road, ORPINGTON, KENT, BR6 6BA.
MILLER, Mr. John James, FCA *1966;* with Moore Stephens (North West) LLP, 110-114 Duke Street, LIVERPOOL, L1 5AG.
MILLER, Mr. John Lorimer, FCA *1964;* Cherry Tree Cottage, Horsham Road, Holmbury St. Mary, DORKING, SURREY RH5 6PD.
MILLER, Mr. John Michael, FCA *1972;* Old Bell Cottage, Church Hill, Bisley, STROUD, GLOUCESTERSHIRE, GL6 7AB. (Life Member)
MILLER, Mr. John Ritson, BSc ACA *1981;* 2767 Dublin Street, HALIFAX B3L 3K1, NS, CANADA.
MILLER, Mr. Jonathan Mark, LLB ACA *1989;* 48 Wykeham Road, LONDON, NW4 2SU.
•MILLER, Mr. Jonathan Mark Bramwell, BA FCA DChA *1992;* Full Circle Accountancy Limited, 29-30 Cornmarket, PENRITH, CUMBRIA, CA11 7HS.
•MILLER, Mr. Jonathan Richard Paul, BA ACA *1986;* Evolve Legal Business Solutions Limited, 20 Bonville Chase, ALTRINCHAM, CHESHIRE, WA14 4QA.
MILLER, Mr. Jonathan Theodore, MA ACA *1998;* 41 Dale Street, LONDON, W4 2BY.
•MILLER, Mrs. Judith Alison, BA FCA DChA *1993;* Sayer Vincent, 8 Angel Gate, City Road, LONDON, EC1V 2SJ.
•MILLER, Mrs. Karen Anne, BA ACA *1984;* (Tax Fac), Miller & Co, 2 The Pavilions End, CAMBERLEY, GU15 2LD.
MILLER, Mrs. Kathleen Anne, BSc ACA *1981;* Atlas Works, College Road, STOKE-ON-TRENT, ST1 4DQ.
MILLER, Miss. Katrina Catherine, BA ACA *2005;* 2 Hiliary Gardens, STANMORE, HA7 2NQ.
MILLER, Miss. Kay, BSc ACA *1998;* Cheddar Post Office, Bath Street, CHEDDAR, SOMERSET, BS27 3AA.
•MILLER, Mr. Keith James, FCA *1988;* Moore Stephens (North West) LLP, 110-114 Duke Street, LIVERPOOL, L1 5AG.
•MILLER, Mr. Keith John, BSc FCA *1988;* Albert Goodman LLP, Hendford Manor, YEOVIL, BA20 1UN.
MILLER, Mr. Keith John, BSc FCA CTA *1982;* (Tax Fac), Flat 2, Kent Lodge, 43 Chalkwell Avenue, WESTCLIFF-ON-SEA, ESSEX, SS0 8NA.
MILLER, Mr. Keith Stuart, BA ACA *2001;* Harb Levy & Weiland LLP, One Market Suite 620, SAN FRANCISCO, CA 94105, UNITED STATES.
MILLER, Mr. Kenneth Gordon, FCA *1976;* 2 Coltsfoot Close, CAMBRIDGE, CB1 9YH.
MILLER, Mr. Kenneth William, FCA *1961;* South Cottage, The Street, Compton, GUILDFORD, GU3 1EB.
•MILLER, Mr. Kevin George, MA FCA *1974;* (Tax Fac), with Ernst & Young LLP, 1 More London Place, LONDON, SE1 2AF.
MILLER, Mr. Kevin Richard, BA FCA *1985;* 20 De Beauvoir Square, LONDON, N1 4LD.
MILLER, Mr. Lawrence Raymond Reginald, FCA *1953;* Vieni, 14 Worrin Close, Shenfield, BRENTWOOD, ESSEX, CM15 8DG. (Life Member)
•MILLER, Mr. Leslie Douglas, FCA *1982;* Miller & Company, 17 Grove Place, BEDFORD, MK40 3JJ.
MILLER, Mrs. Lindsay, BSS ACA *1994;* 23 Whitefield Close, Rufford, ORMSKIRK, L40 1US.
MILLER, Mr. Lloyd, FCA *1965;* 11 Warwick Road, Worsley, MANCHESTER, M28 7BW. (Life Member)
MILLER, Mrs. Louisa, BA ACA *1999;* Harrods Ltd, Brompton Road, Knightsbridge, LONDON, SW1X 7XL.
MILLER, Miss. Lyn Susan, BSc(Hons) ACA *2001;* The Jude Partnership Ltd, 18 Chester Road, Poynton, STOCKPORT, CHESHIRE, SK12 1EU.
MILLER, Mrs. Lynn, ACA *2009;* 16 Bede Avenue, BERWICK-UPON-TWEED, TD15 1PY.
MILLER, Mr. Malcolm John, ACA *1986;* NHS Northamptonshire Francis Crick House, 6 Summerhouse Road Moulton Park Industrial Estate, NORTHAMPTON, NN3 6BF.
MILLER, Mrs. Marie Claire, ACA *2003;* 168 Warwick Road, RAYLEIGH, ESSEX, SS6 8UL.
MILLER, Mr. Mark Johnstone, BSc ACA *1998;* 22 East Stratton, WINCHESTER, SO21 3DU.
MILLER, Mr. Martin Alan, BSc ACA *1990;* I N G Bank, 60 London Wall, LONDON, EC2M 5TQ.
MILLER, Dr. Martin Neil, FCA *1992;* 64 Pine County Place, BELLBOWRIE, QLD 4070, AUSTRALIA.
MILLER, Mr. Matthew Kerr, BSc ACA *1981;* 106 Hollins Lane, Marple Bridge, STOCKPORT, SK6 5DA.
MILLER, Mr. Maurice, BCom FCA *1972;* Maurice Miller, 111 Dean Clough Office Park, HALIFAX, WEST YORKSHIRE, HX3 5AX.
MILLER, Mr. Maxwell Ian, BSc ACA *2000;* 8 Seaview Street, CAULFIELD SOUTH, VIC 3162, AUSTRALIA.
MILLER, Mr. Mendel, BSc FCA *1969;* 1 Barnwood Close, Pine Grove, LONDON, N20 8DF.
MILLER, Mr. Michael Bradbury, FCA *1984;* F M C B, Hathaway House, Popes Drive, Finchley, LONDON, N3 1QF.
MILLER, Mr. Michael David, BSc ACA *1985;* Flat 67, Clifton Court, Northwick Terrace, LONDON, NW8 8HU.
MILLER, Mr. Michael John, FCA *1979;* Crown House, 11 Regent Hill, BRIGHTON, BN1 3ER.
MILLER, Mrs. Michelle Louise, BSc ACA *2001;* 21 Angus Close, Ramleaze, SWINDON, SN5 5PS.
MILLER, Mrs. Morag Elizabeth, BAcc ACA *1999;* with Grant Thornton UK LLP, 1 Whitehall Riverside, Whitehall Road, LEEDS, WEST YORKSHIRE, LS1 4BN.
MILLER, Mr. Neil Eldridge, BA ACA *1992;* 10 Great Leys Court, Beningfield Drive, London Colney, ST. ALBANS, HERTFORDSHIRE, AL2 1GJ.
MILLER, Mr. Nicholas Anthony, BA FCA *1971;* Quarry House Cottage, Springbottom Lane, Bletchingley, REDHILL, RH1 4QZ. (Life Member)
MILLER, Mr. Nicholas Henry James, BSc ACA *1984;* 6 Penrhyn Crescent, East Sheen, LONDON, SW14 7PF.
MILLER, Mr. Nicholas John, MSc BSc ACA CTA *2002;* 6 Scalpcliffe Close, BURTON-ON-TRENT, STAFFORDSHIRE, DE15 9AX.
MILLER, Miss. Nicola Marie, BSc ACA *1994;* 16 Newlands Avenue, RADLETT, HERTFORDSHIRE, WD7 8EL.
•MILLER, Mrs. Nicola Ruth, MA FCA *1979;* (Tax Fac), Hughes Waddell Limited, Hughes Waddell, 2 Meadrow, GODALMING, SURREY, GU7 3HN.
MILLER, Mr. Nigel, BA ACA *1997;* Beech End, 10 Woodlands Glade, BEACONSFIELD, BUCKINGHAMSHIRE, HP9 1JZ.
MILLER, Ms. Pamela May, FCA *1980;* 65 Haven Village, Promenade Way, Brightlingsea, COLCHESTER, CO7 0LW.
•MILLER, Mr. Paul Anthony, BSc FCA *1987;* (Tax Fac), Cornish Accounting Solutions, 20 Crockwell Street, BODMIN, PL31 2DS. See also Miller P.A. & Co
MILLER, Mr. Paul Sydney, BSc FCA *1982;* 6 Clickers Road, NORWICH, NR3 2DD.
MILLER, Mr. Paul Timothy, BSc ACA *1992;* Millhead House, 10 Gurnard Heights, COWES, PO31 8EF.
•MILLER, Mr. Peter, MA(Hons) ACA *2002;* with Ernst & Young LLP, PO Box 9, Royal Chambers, St Julian's Avenue, St Peter Port, GUERNSEY GY1 4AF.
MILLER, Mr. Peter Douglas, BSc FCA *1982;* 12 Clements Gate, Diseworth, DERBY, DE74 2QE.
MILLER, Mr. Peter Duncan, FCA *1966;* Tethers End, ABINGDON, OX13 6RW.
MILLER, Mr. Peter John, FCA *1968;* Flat 4, 78 Wickham Road, BECKENHAM, KENT, BR3 6QH. (Life Member)
MILLER, Mrs. Preeta, BA ACA *2005;* 15 The Moorings, DONAGHADEE, COUNTY DOWN, BT21 0EQ.
MILLER, Ms. Rebecca Jane, BA ACA *2004;* 17 Meridian Place, BRISTOL, BS8 1JG.
MILLER, Mr. Richard, BSc ACA *1991;* with PricewaterhouseCoopers LLP, 1 Embankment Place, LONDON, WC2N 6RH.
MILLER, Mr. Richard James, FCA *1970;* 19 Green Gardens, POOLE, BH15 1XX.
•MILLER, Mr. Richard Julian, BA ACA *1990;* Dafferns LLP, 1 Eastwood, Harry Weston Road, Binley Business Park, COVENTRY, CV3 2UB. See also Richard J Miller Limited
MILLER, Mr. Robert, MA FCA *1974;* Flat 16, Old Vicarage Court, 273 Clifton Drive South, LYTHAM ST. ANNES, LANCASHIRE, FY8 1HW.
•MILLER, Mr. Robert, BSc(Hons) ACA *2005;* R M A, 86 Park Lane, Whitefield, MANCHESTER, M45 7PL.
•MILLER, Mr. Robert Leslie, BSc ACA *1986;* (Tax Fac), BDO LLP, Emerald House, East Street, EPSOM, SURREY, KT17 1HS. See also BDO Stoy Hayward LLP
•MILLER, Mr. Robert Stephen, FCA *1978;* Bowcock & Pursaill, 54 St Edward Street, LEEK, STAFFORDSHIRE, ST13 5DJ.
MILLER, Mr. Robin, FCA *1959;* (Tax Fac), 32 Summerdown Lane, East Dean, EASTBOURNE, BN20 0LE. (Life Member)
MILLER, Mrs. Rochelle Leana, BA ACA *1997;* 14 Blattner Close, Elstree, BOREHAMWOOD, HERTFORDSHIRE, WD6 3PD.
MILLER, Mr. Roger George, FCA *1967;* Calle Panama 14, 03737 JAVEA, SPAIN. (Life Member)
MILLER, Mr. Ronald Albert, FCA *1951;* 4 Fleming Walk, Church Village, PONTYPRIDD, MID GLAMORGAN, CF38 1GF. (Life Member)
MILLER, Mrs. Rowena Gillian, BA ACA *2003;* 7 Manor Drive, AMERSHAM, BUCKINGHAMSHIRE, HP6 5NH.
MILLER, Miss. Ruth Jasmine, BSc ACA *2006;* 536 Kenilworth Road, Balsall Common, COVENTRY, CV7 7DQ.
MILLER, Ms. Samantha Jane, BEng ACA CFA *1992;* House 122, Mau Po, CLEARWATER BAY, NEW TERRITORIES, HONG KONG SAR.
MILLER, Miss. Sarah Ann, ACA MAAT *2005;* Lime Court, Pathfields Business Park, SOUTH MOLTON, DEVON, EX36 3LH.
MILLER, Mrs. Sarah Jane, BSc ACA *2007;* 192 Baddow Road, CHELMSFORD, CM2 9QW.
MILLER, Mrs. Sarah Louise, BSc ACA *1992;* 15 Elgin Gardens, STRATFORD-UPON-AVON, WARWICKSHIRE, CV37 7BG.
MILLER, Mrs. Sheryl Andrea, ACA *1999;* Tarmac Ltd Millfields Road, Ettingshall, WOLVERHAMPTON, WV4 6JP.
MILLER, Mr. Simon Jonathan, BSc FCA *1988;* Martin McColl House, Ashwells Road, BRENTWOOD, ESSEX, CM15 9ST.
MILLER, Mr. Simon Rupert, LLB ACA *1986;* Trident, Royce Way, West Wittering, CHICHESTER, WEST SUSSEX, PO20 8LN.
MILLER, Mr. Spencer Martyn Lewis, BA ACA *1997;* Optrust, 15th Floor, 33 Cavendish Square, LONDON, W1G 0PW.
•MILLER, Mr. Stephen, BSc ACA CTA *1990;* Bridge Accounting Limited, 1 The Old Brushworks, 56 Pickwick Road, CORSHAM, WILTSHIRE, SN13 9BX.
•MILLER, Mr. Stephen Charles, FCA *1982;* (Tax Fac), S C Miller Ltd, Clock Offices, High Street, Bishops Waltham, SOUTHAMPTON, SO32 1AA.
•MILLER, Mr. Stephen David, FCA *1973;* Stephen Miller, 117 George Lane, South Woodford, LONDON, E18 1AN.
MILLER, Mr. Stephen James, BA FCA *1978;* Mountfield, 103a Walton Road, Stockton Heath, WARRINGTON, WA4 6NR.
•MILLER, Mr. Stephen Peter, FCA *1984;* Fithlers Hall, Highwood, CHELMSFORD, ESSEX, CM1.
MILLER, Mr. Steven David, ACA *2001;* 24 Pelham Road, COWES, ISLE OF WIGHT, PO31 7DS.
MILLER, Mr. Steven John, BSc ACA *1993;* 94 Westbourne Road, PENARTH, SOUTH GLAMORGAN, CF64 3HG.
MILLER, Mr. Stewart Keith, BA ACA *1987;* 15 Havelins, Stourpaine, BLANDFORD FORUM, DORSET, DT11 8TH.
MILLER, Mr. Stuart Neilege, BCom ACA *1995;* 16 Little Lane, Great Gransden, SANDY, BEDFORDSHIRE, SG19 3AE.
MILLER, Mrs. Susan Margaret, FCA ATII *1989;* Briarwood, 15 Premier Avenue, ASHBOURNE, DERBYSHIRE, DE6 1LH.
MILLER, Mr. Terry John, FCA *1962;* Apartado 3593, 8035 ALMANCIL, ALGARVE, PORTUGAL. (Life Member)
MILLER, Mr. Thomas Patrick, FCA CPA *1961;* 726 Avenue L West, CALIMESA, CA 92320, UNITED STATES. (Life Member)
MILLER, Miss. Victoria, ACA *2000;* Park Lodge, Ugley Green, BISHOP'S STORTFORD, HERTFORDSHIRE, CM22 6HL.

MILLER, Mrs. Victoria Louise, BSc ACA *1993;* 19 Lyonsdown Avenue, New Barnet, BARNET, HERTFORDSHIRE, EN5 1DU.
MILLER, Mr. William Derek Roy, FCA *1970;* 49 Blenheim Way, MORETON-IN-MARSH, GLOUCESTERSHIRE, GL56 9NA. (Life Member)
MILLER, Mr. William Gordon, FCA *1952;* 28 Millfield Grove, Tynemouth, NORTH SHIELDS, NE30 2PZ. (Life Member)
MILLER, Mr. William Scott, BA ACA *1989;* 10C Ravenna Road, Putney, LONDON, SW15 6AW.
MILLER-JONES, Mr. Donald, FCA *1968;* School Farm House, Birchgrove, Horsted Keynes, HAYWARDS HEATH, RH17 7DQ.
MILLER-JONES, Mr. Thomas Charles Simon Gawain, BSc ACA *1986;* GPO Box 4144, CENTRAL, HONG KONG ISLAND, HONG KONG SAR.
MILLERCHIP, Mr. Mark, ACA *1991;* 30 Lee Crescent, BIRMINGHAM, B15 2BJ.
MILLERCHIP, Mr. Simon John, BA ACA *1998;* Twemlow Lodge, Twemlow Green, Holmes Chapel, CREWE, CW4 8BL.
MILLERCHIP, Mr. Steven John, ACA *2011;* 10 Abbey Farm View, Cudworth, BARNSLEY, SOUTH YORKSHIRE, S72 8SJ.
MILLES, Mr. William David, BA ACA *1996;* Eli Lilly & Co Ltd, Lilly House, Priestley Road, BASINGSTOKE, HAMPSHIRE, RG24 9NL.
MILLEST, Miss. Rachel Lucy, BSc ACA *2007;* Flat 48 Avon Court, Keswick Road, LONDON, SW15 2JU.
•MILLET, Mr. Andrew, BA FCA *1995;* Wisteria Limited, Cavendish House, 369 Burnt Oak Broadway, EDGWARE, MIDDLESEX, HA8 5AW. See also Wisteria Consulting Limited
MILLETT, Mrs. Ann Elizabeth, MSc ACA *1989;* Jones Avens, 53 Kent Road, SOUTHSEA, PO5 3HU.
MILLETT, Miss. Elizabeth Ruth, BSc ACA *1986;* Crossgreen Farmhouse, 26 Ecclesmachan Road, Uphall, BROXBURN, EH52 6DB.
MILLETT, Mr. Hugh Iain, FCA *1969;* 46 Church Street, WHITSTABLE, CT5 1PG.
MILLETT, Mr. James Michael Ian, BSc ACA *2000;* Rustlings, The Street, Plaxtol, SEVENOAKS, KENT, TN15 0QQ.
MILLETT, Mr. Noel Dennis, FCA *1950;* 3 Bridge End, Ockham Lane, WOKING, GU23 6NR. (Life Member)
MILLETT, Mr. Richard, BA ACA *1997;* The Moat Penshurst Road, Penshurst, TONBRIDGE, KENT, TN11 8DD.
•MILLETT, Mr. Roger Frank, FCA *1976;* G M Agencies, Orchard Cottage, Old Apley, MARKET RASEN, LINCOLNSHIRE, LN8 5JQ.
•MILLETT, Mr. Timothy Peter, ACA *1985;* (Tax Fac), Jones Avens Limited, 53 Kent Road, SOUTHSEA, HAMPSHIRE, PO5 3HU.
MILLETT, Mr. William James, MSc BSc ACA *2010;* Barclays Capital, 10 South Colonnade, Canary Wharf, LONDON, E14 4PU.
MILLGATE, Mr. Brian, FCA *1963;* 5 Chiltern Close, Garforth, LEEDS, LS25 2HS.
MILLGATE, Mr. Sean, ACA *1987;* Beech Tree, 49 Kings Barn Lane, STEYNING, WEST SUSSEX, BN44 3YR.
MILLICHAMP, Miss. Donna Marie, ACA *2004;* 1 Filby Lane, Ormesby, GREAT YARMOUTH, NORFOLK, NR29 3JR.
MILLICHAMP, Mr. Guy, BSc ACA *1988;* Y M H A, 161 Briggate, LEEDS, LS1 6LY.
MILLICHAP, Mr. Kenneth Andrews, FCA *1950;* The Croft, Wrigleys Lane, Formby, LIVERPOOL, L37 7DR. (Life Member)
MILLICHIP, Miss. Joanne Louise, BSc(Econ) ACA *1997;* 31 Celestial Gardens, Lewisham, LONDON, SE13 5RP.
MILLIGAN, Mr. Brendan John, FCA *1976;* 43 High Bangor Road, DONAGHADEE, COUNTY DOWN, BT21 0PB.
•MILLIGAN, Mr. David, FCA *1969;* Ryecroft Glenton, 32 Portland Terrace, Jesmond, NEWCASTLE UPON TYNE, NE2 1QP.
MILLIGAN, Ms. Janet, BSc ACA *1993;* Embankment Place, Pricewaterhousecoopers, 1 Embankment Place, LONDON, WC2N 6RH.
MILLIGAN, Mrs. Jessica Elizabeth, MSci BA ACA *2005;* Intermediate Capital Group, 3rd Floor 100 St Paul's Churchyard, LONDON, EC4M 8BU.
MILLIGAN, Mr. Neil, BA ACA *1998;* 22 Ellerton Way, Hartford Green, CRAMLINGTON, NE23 3HX.
MILLIGAN, Mr. Norman Alan, FCA *1967;* 10 Oaklands Park, Grasscroft, OLDHAM, OL4 4JY. (Life Member)
MILLIGAN, Mr. Simon David, BSc ACA *1991;* Davies Wood House, Kingston Hospital N H S Trust Kingston Hospital, Galsworthy Road, KINGSTON UPON THAMES, KT2 7QB.
MILLIGAN, Mr. Simon Gibson, BA FCA *1981;* 19 Tino Terrace, Warners Park, CHRISTCHURCH, BARBADOS.
MILLIGAN, Mrs. Susan Joan, BSc ACA *1998;* 369 Manchester Road, Birch, HEYWOOD, LANCASHIRE, OL10 2QD.
MILLIGAN, Mrs. Victoria Louise, BA ACA *1998;* Pound House, Midhurst Road, PETWORTH, WEST SUSSEX, GU28 0ET.
•MILLIKEN, Mr. Terence John, FCA *1984;* (Tax Fac), Milliken & Co, 9 Vennel Street, Stewarton, KILMARNOCK, KA3 5HL.
MILLIKEN-SMITH, Mr. Peter Richard, FCA *1959;* The Cider House, Manor Farm, Motcombe, SHAFTESBURY, DORSET, SP7 9PL.
MILLINCHAMP, Mr. Julian William, BA ACA *1980;* Stables, Lulsley, Knightwick, WORCESTER, WR6 5QN.
MILLINCHAMP, Mrs. Linda Jane, BCom ACA *1980;* The Stables, Lulsley Court, Lulsley, Knightwick, WORCESTER, WR6 5QN.
MILLING, Mr. Alexander Michael, FCA *1959;* Forest House, Old Frensham Road, FARNHAM, GU10 3HD. (Life Member)
•MILLINGS, Mr. Alan Stephen, BSc(Hons) ACA *2001;* Ernst & Young LLP, 1 More London Place, LONDON, SE1 2AF. See also Ernst & Young Europe LLP
MILLINGTON, Mr. Andrew, ACA *2005;* 20 Malvern Street, BURTON-ON-TRENT, STAFFORDSHIRE, DE15 9DY.
•MILLINGTON, Mr. Andrew John, BEng FCA CF *1987;* Mazars LLP, 45 Church Street, BIRMINGHAM, B3 2RT. See also Mazars Corporate Finance Limited
MILLINGTON, Mr. Andrew John, FCA *1972;* 19 Hillway, Woburn Sands, MILTON KEYNES, MK17 8UL.
MILLINGTON, Mr. Anthony Geoffrey, BSc ACA *1990;* 26 Marlborough Road, Woodthorpe, NOTTINGHAM, NOTTINGHAMSHIRE, NG5 4FG.
MILLINGTON, Mr. Brian John, FCA *1955;* 4 The Manor House, Upper Green, Tettenhall, WOLVERHAMPTON, WV6 8QJ. (Life Member)
MILLINGTON, Mr. John, BSc ACA *1984;* 5 Lingfield Avenue, Hazel Grove, STOCKPORT, CHESHIRE, SK7 4SL.
MILLINGTON, Mr. John Peter, BA FCA *1982;* (Tax Fac), 27 Newborough Close, Austrey, ATHERSTONE, CV9 3EX.
MILLINGTON, Mr. John Robert, ACA *1979;* (Tax Fac), 16 Hallam Grange Crescent, Fulwood, SHEFFIELD, S10 4BA.
MILLINGTON, Mrs. Judith Ann, BSc ACA *1990;* Pricewaterhousecoopers Cornwall Court, 19 Cornwall Street, BIRMINGHAM, B3 2DT.
MILLINGTON, Mrs. Kirsty Helen, BSc ACA *1995;* 91 Penmere Drive, Pentire, NEWQUAY, TR7 1NS.
MILLINGTON, Ms. Laura, BSc(Hons) ACA *2001;* Grosvenor Estate, Eaton Estate Office, Eaton Park, Eccleston, CHESTER, CH4 9ET.
MILLINGTON, Miss. Pamela Kathryn, BSc ACA *1999;* Fil Limited, Pembroke Hall, 42 Crow Lane, PEMBROKE HM19, BERMUDA.
MILLINGTON, Mr. Paul Leonard, FCA *1972;* White Light Group, 20 Merton Industrial Park Jubilee Way, LONDON, SW19 3WL.
MILLINGTON, Mr. Paul Terence, BA FCA *1989;* Evans Management Ltd, Millshaw, LEEDS, LS11 8EG.
MILLINGTON, Mr. Peter Andre, BA ACA *1986;* Flat 2 New Caledonian Wharf, 6 Odessa Street, LONDON, SE16 7TN.
MILLINGTON, Mr. Robert John, FCA *1975;* 2 Leddington Court, Ross Road, LEDBURY, HEREFORDSHIRE, HR8 2LP.
MILLINGTON, Mr. Stephen Martin, BA(Hons) ACA *2002;* Kroll, Office 701, Liberty House, PO Box 506829, DUBAI, UNITED ARAB EMIRATES.
MILLINGTON-HORE, Mr. Alex Lee, BEng ACA *2006;* 15 Christian Court, Willen, MILTON KEYNES, MK15 9HX.
•MILLINGTON-HORE, Mr. Christopher David Bevis, FCA *1974;* Millington Hore, 9 Arlesey Road, Ickleford, HITCHIN, SG5 3UN.
•MILLINGTON-HORE, Mrs. Rosemary Susan, FCA *1976;* Millington Hore, 9 Arlesey Road, Ickleford, HITCHIN, SG5 3UN.
MILLION, Mrs. Clare Josephine, BA ACA DChA *1983;* 38 Galveston Road, LONDON, SW15 2SA.
•MILLION, Mr. David Paul, FCA *1975;* (Tax Fac), Royce Peeling Green Limited, 15 Buckingham Gate, LONDON, SW1E 6LB.
MILLIS, Mr. Derek Maunsell, FCA *1953;* Chaldon, Oval Way, GERRARDS CROSS, SL9 8PZ. (Life Member)
•MILLMAN, Mr. Arthur Ronald, FCA *1978;* Goldwyns Limited, Rutland House, 90-92 Baxter Avenue, SOUTHEND-ON-SEA, SS2 6HZ.
•MILLMAN, Mr. Eric, FCA *1974;* (Tax Fac), 1 Harewood Gardens, Littledown, BOURNEMOUTH, DORSET, BH7 7RH.
MILLMAN, Mr. Frank Joseph, FCA *1973;* PO Box 386, RIVONIA, 2128, SOUTH AFRICA.
MILLMAN, Ms. Sonya Lesley, BSc ACA *1985;* 53 Maidenhead Road, STRATFORD-UPON-AVON, CV37 6XU.
MILLMAN, Mr. Stuart Paul, BSc ACA *2008;* 1c Gibbon Road, KINGSTON UPON THAMES, KT2 6AD.
•MILLNER, Mr. Anthony Edward, BSc ACA *1987;* TM Accountancy Ltd, 54 Milverton Road, Knowle, SOLIHULL, B93 0HY.
MILLNER, Mr. David Stephen, FCA *1975;* Apdo 379, Garrucha, 04630 ALMERIA, SPAIN.
MILLOY, Mr. Raymond Albert, MA FCA *1940;* 23 Heslop Road, Lesmurdie, PERTH, WA 6076, AUSTRALIA. (Life Member)
•MILLRINE, Mr. Brian, BA ACA *2001;* with Brookson Limited, Brunel House, 340 Firecrest Court, Centre Park, WARRINGTON, WA1 1RG.
MILLS, Mr. Adam Francis, FCA *1966;* Otterwood Gate Exbury Road, Beaulieu, BROCKENHURST, SO42 7YS.
MILLS, Mr. Adrian Paul, BSc ACA *1991;* Sourdioux, 87400 MOISSANNES, FRANCE.
MILLS, Mr. Allen John, BA FCA *1963;* 11 Divinity Road, OXFORD, OX4 1LH.
MILLS, Mr. Andrew George Dickson, BSc ACA *1988;* Xyratex Langstone Technology Park, Langstone Road, HAVANT, PO9 1SA.
MILLS, Mr. Andrew John, BA ACA *1999;* 240 Bath Road, SLOUGH, SL1 4DX.
MILLS, Mr. Andrew John Worster, MA ACA *2000;* 16 Carpenders Close, HARPENDEN, HERTFORDSHIRE, AL5 3HN.
MILLS, Mrs. Angela Marie, BA ACA *2003;* School of Tropical Medicine Anson House, 25 Anson Street, LIVERPOOL, L3 5NY.
MILLS, Ms. Anne Maureen, ACA *1989;* 5 Swithland Lane, Rothley, LEICESTER, LE7 7SG.
•MILLS, Mr. Anthony, ACA *1992;* (Tax Fac), ma2, 5 Crescent East, THORNTON-CLEVELEYS, LANCASHIRE, FY5 3LJ.
•MILLS, Mr. Anthony James, BSc ACA MBA *1998;* (Tax Fac), PO Box 642, Thurston, BURY ST. EDMUNDS, SUFFOLK, IP31 3WY. See also Anthony Mills
MILLS, Mr. Anthony Warwick, FCA *1962;* 9 Gazelle Glade, GRAVESEND, DA12 4PU.
MILLS, Mr. Anthony William, ACA *2004;* 6 Lazy Hill, Stonnall, WALSALL, WS9 9DT.
MILLS, Mr. Arthur Patrick, FCA *1955;* 29 Oakleigh Court, Station Road West, OXTED, RH8 9EY. (Life Member)
MILLS, Mr. Ben Samuel, BSc ACA *2006;* Flat 6, Coombe Lodge, 6 Manorgate Road, KINGSTON UPON THAMES, SURREY, KT2 7AL.
MILLS, Mr. Brian Peter, BSc ACA *1984;* A & L Chapman Ltd, Headley Road East, Woodley, READING, RG5 4SL.
MILLS, Mr. Charles Alexander, BSc ACA *1982;* 23 Queens Crescent, Putnoe, BEDFORD, MK41 9BN.
MILLS, Mr. Christopher, BA ACA *2011;* 1 Heritage Drive, Marl Pits, Rawtenstall, ROSSENDALE, LANCASHIRE, BB4 7SJ.
MILLS, Mr. Christopher Andrew, BSc(Hons) ACA *2002;* 10 The Score, Blagdon, BRISTOL, BS40 7SH.
MILLS, Mr. Christopher David, BA(Hons) ACA *2002;* 12 Wissey Way, ELY, CB6 2WW.
MILLS, Mr. Christopher Douglas Francis, MA ACA *1990;* Orchard View, Forge Hill, Hampstead Norreys, THATCHAM, BERKSHIRE, RG18 0TE.
MILLS, Mr. Christopher John, BA ACA *1998;* 25 Old Hall Close, Calverton, NOTTINGHAM, NG14 6PU.
•MILLS, Mr. Clifford John, FCA *1984;* (Tax Fac), Amlbenson Limited, AML Maybrook House, 97 Godstone Road, CATERHAM, CR3 6RE.
•MILLS, Mr. Colin George, ACA DChA *1978;* Larkings Ltd, 180 Upper Pemberton, Eureka Business Park, ASHFORD, KENT, TN25 4AZ. See also Larkings (S.E) LLP
MILLS, Mr. Colin Nigel, BA FCA *1996;* with Critchleys LLP, Greyfriars Court, Paradise Square, OXFORD, OX1 1BE.
MILLS, Mr. Darren Edward, MA(Hons) ACA *2002;* DMGT Risk and Assurance, 2 Derry Street, LONDON, W8 5TT.
MILLS, Mr. David, BA ACA *1991;* 17 Bryants Hill, BRISTOL, BS5 8QY.
MILLS, Mr. David Gareth Howard, BSc ACA *1991;* North Star, 19 North End, Ditchling, HASSOCKS, BN6 8TD.
MILLS, Mr. David James, BSc ACA *1987;* The Rise, Stow Road, Purleigh, CHELMSFORD, CM3 6RR.
MILLS, Mr. David Nicholas, BA ACA *1996;* Flat 2, 5 Crouch Hall Road, LONDON, N8 8HT.
MILLS, Mr. Derek Peter, FCA *1970;* 23 Merrybent, DARLINGTON, COUNTY DURHAM, DL2 2LB.
MILLS, Miss. Diane, ACA *2005;* with Mazars LLP, The Lexicon, Mount Street, MANCHESTER, M2 5NT.
•MILLS, Mr. Dominic, BSc ACA *1993;* (Tax Fac), Dominic Mills, 66b High Street, Black Swan Yard, ANDOVER, SP10 1NG.
MILLS, Mr. Donald George, FCA *1961;* 13 Rydal Drive, WEST WICKHAM, KENT, BR4 9QH. (Life Member)
MILLS, Mr. Duncan Richard, BSc ACA *1994;* Chillies East, Chillies Lane, CROWBOROUGH, EAST SUSSEX, TN6 3TB.
MILLS, Mr. Edward Richard, BA FCA *1999;* (Tax Fac), Hogan Lovells International LLP, Atlantic House, 50 Holborn Viaduct, LONDON, EC1A 2FG.
MILLS, Mrs. Emily, MA ACA *2005;* 33 Alexandra Gardens, LONDON, N10 3RN.
MILLS, Mr. Eric Charles, MSc ACA *2000;* Garden Flat, 1 Cotham Grove, BRISTOL, BS6 6AL.
MILLS, Mr. Ernest Alfred William, FCA *1954;* 15 Heathcliffe Court, Redhills Road, Arnside, CARNFORTH, LA5 0AT. (Life Member)
MILLS, Mrs. Francesca Rose Gravely, MA ACA *1991;* Tow Acres, Tidmarsh Lane, Tidmarsh, READING, RG8 8HG.
•MILLS, Mr. Geoffrey John, FCA *1982;* Mills Pyatt Limited, Unit 11, Kingfisher Business Park, Arthur Street, REDDITCH, WORCESTERSHIRE B98 8LG.
MILLS, Mr. George Robert, ACA *2008;* 18 Colestown Street, LONDON, SW11 3EH.
MILLS, Mrs. Georgina Cheryl, BA ACA CTA *1999;* with Rickard Keen LLP, 7 Nelson Street, SOUTHEND-ON-SEA, SS1 1EH.
MILLS, Mrs. Georgina Elizabeth, BSc ACA *2000;* 5 Crag Gardens, Bramham, WETHERBY, WEST YORKSHIRE, LS23 6RP.
MILLS, Mr. Gerald Keith, FCA *1969;* 9 Scots Lane, COVENTRY, CV6 2DQ.
MILLS, Miss. Gina Elisabeth, MA(Hons) ACA *2003;* with Ernst & Young, 41 Shortland Street, PO Box2146, AUCKLAND 1140, NEW ZEALAND.
MILLS, Mr. Granville Walker, FCA *1956;* The Barn, Lark Hill Lane, Delph, OLDHAM, OL3 5QQ. (Life Member)
MILLS, Mrs. Helen Catherine, BA(Hons) ACA *2010;* with Mazars LLP, The Lexicon, Mount Street, MANCHESTER, M2 5NT.
MILLS, Mr. Hugo Christopher Adam, BA ACA *1998;* 13 The Hummicks, Dock Lane, Beaulieu, BROCKENHURST, HAMPSHIRE, SO42 7YU.
MILLS, Sir Ian, FCA *1960;* 60 Belmont Hill, LONDON, SE13 5DN. (Life Member)
•MILLS, Mr. Ian Edward, BA FCA *1981;* 15 Hendham Drive, ALTRINCHAM, WA14 4LY.
MILLS, Mr. Ian Ralph Arthur, AE MBA BFA FCA CA(SA) *1955;* PO Box 442, HERIOT BAY V0P 1H0, BC, CANADA. (Life Member)
MILLS, Mr. Ian Richard, FCA *1971;* 132 Oakside Close S.W., CALGARY T2V 4T9, AB, CANADA.
MILLS, Mr. Ian William, BA FCA *1982;* Lane End, Blackheath Lane, Wonersh, GUILDFORD, SURREY, GU5 0PN.
•MILLS, Mrs. Jacquelyn Anne, BA FCA *1993;* Team 4 Accounting Ltd, Cressfield House, School Lane, Headbourne Worthy, WINCHESTER, SO23 7JX.
MILLS, Mr. James Alan, BA ACA *2005;* 12 The Drive, Southwick, BRIGHTON, BN42 4RR.
MILLS, Mr. James Leonard, FCA *1975;* 316 Brownhill Road, Hither Green, LONDON, SE6 1AX. (Life Member)
MILLS, Ms. Jane, BCom ACA *1992;* 67 Brownlow Drive, NOTTINGHAM, NG5 5AA.
MILLS, Mrs. Jane Rosamond, BSc ACA *2000;* with KPMG, 10 Customhouse Quay, WELLINGTON, NEW ZEALAND.
MILLS, Mrs. Jean Blamey, BCom ACA *1981;* Contree Moulins, Prince Albert's Road, St Peter Port, GUERNSEY, GY1 1EZ.
MILLS, Mr. John, FCA *1974;* 43 Glebe Crescent, Broomfield, CHELMSFORD, CM1 7BH.
•MILLS, Mr. John Charles Harvey, LLB FCA *1965;* (Tax Fac), Allen Mills Howard & Co, 23 Stockport Road, ASHTON-UNDER-LYNE, OL7 0LA.
MILLS, Mr. John David, BSc ACA *1982;* Minster Cleaning, Rosehill Business Centre, Normanton Road, DERBY, DE23 6RH.
MILLS, Mr. John David, MBA BSc FCA *1989;* Exova (UK) Ltd, Westerton House, Westerton Road, East Mains Industrial Estate, BROXBURN, WEST LOTHIAN EH52 5AU.
MILLS, Mr. John David, FCA *1969;* with J S Bethell & Co, 70 Clarkehouse Road, SHEFFIELD, S10 2LJ.
MILLS, Mr. John Harold, FCA *1969;* 37 Badgers, Thorley Park, BISHOP'S STORTFORD, CM23 4ET.
MILLS, Mr. John James, BA ACA *1986;* A B N Amro Bank NV, 250 Bishopsgate, LONDON, EC2M 4AA.
MILLS, Mr. John Kevin, BA ACA *1979;* Contree Moullins Prince Albert Road, St. Peter Port, GUERNSEY, GY1 1EZ.

MILLS, Mr. John Nicholas, BSc ACA *1981;* 145 The Green, Worsley, MANCHESTER, M28 2PA.
•**MILLS, Mr. John William, FCA** *1975;* (Tax Fac), Robert Whowell & Partners, 78 Loughborough Road, Quorn, LOUGHBOROUGH, LEICESTERSHIRE, LE12 8DX.
MILLS, Mr. Jonathan, BSc ACA *2010;* 135 Queens Road, LONDON, SW19 8NS.
•**MILLS, Mr. Jonathan Charles, BSc FCA** *1977;* Jon Mills FCA, The Old School House, Church Lane, Easton, WINCHESTER, HAMPSHIRE SO21 1EH. See also Fiander Tovell LLP
•**MILLS, Mr. Jonathan Magnus, BSc FCA** *1995;* KPMG LLP, 15 Canada Square, LONDON, E14 5GL. See also KPMG Europe LLP
•**MILLS, Mr. Jonathan Patrick Kearns, BA ACA** *1992;* J P Mills & Co, 6 Suffolk Street, DUBLIN 2, COUNTY DUBLIN, IRELAND.
MILLS, Mrs. Katherine Jane, BA ACA *1987;* 5 Tankerville Terrace, NEWCASTLE UPON TYNE, NE2 3AH.
MILLS, Mr. Keith Charles, FCA *1962;* Chelshams, 14A Bromley Grove, Shortlands, BROMLEY, BR2 0LN. (Life Member)
MILLS, Mrs. Kerry Lorraine, ACA *2010;* 467 Redditch Road, Kings Norton, BIRMINGHAM, B38 8NB.
MILLS, Mrs. Laura Frances, BA ACA *2002;* 22 Winchester Road, WALTON-ON-THAMES, KT12 2RG.
MILLS, Mr. Laurence Jan, BA ACA *2000;* with BDO LLP, 125 Colmore Row, BIRMINGHAM, B3 3SD.
MILLS, Mr. Laurence John, BCom ACA *1997;* 171 Upper Grosvenor Road, TUNBRIDGE WELLS, KENT, TN1 2EF.
MILLS, Mr. Lee James, MA ACA *1983;* 7 Ffordd Dylan, WREXHAM, LL12 7LT.
MILLS, Mrs. Lesley Ann, BSc ACA *1995;* Avonholme Blidworth Waye Papplewick, NOTTINGHAM, NG15 8GB.
MILLS, Miss. Lisa, ACA *2008;* 110 Draperfield, CHORLEY, LANCASHIRE, PR7 3PN.
MILLS, Miss. Louise Jayne, BA(Hons) ACA *2004;* 22 Gayville Road, LONDON, SW11 6JP.
MILLS, Miss. Lucy Elspeth, BA ACA *2005;* Warner Bros, 98 Theobalds Road, LONDON, WC1X 8WB.
•**MILLS, Mr. Lyndon John, BSc FCA** *1975;* LJ Mills FCA, Lower Church Farm, Church Lane, Cockfield, BURY ST. EDMUNDS, SUFFOLK IP30 0LA.
MILLS, Mr. Marcus Lee, BA ACA *2000;* 5 Crag Gardens, Bramham, WETHERBY, WEST YORKSHIRE, LS23 6RP.
•①**MILLS, Miss. Margaret Elizabeth, BSc FCA** *1980;* Ernst & Young LLP, 1 More London Place, LONDON, SE1 2AF. See also Ernst & Young Europe LLP
MILLS, Mr. Michael Barry Millar, MA ACA *2007;* Ernst & Young Building, Level 26, 8 Exhibition Street, MELBOURNE, VIC 3000, AUSTRALIA.
MILLS, Mr. Michael John, BSc FCA *1971;* Pentavia Limited, Maple Heath, Parsonage Lane, Farnham Common, SLOUGH, BUCKINGHAMSHIRE SL2 3NZ.
MILLS, Mr. Michael John Machell, FCA *1966;* Barbary Barn, Milbrook Hill, Nutley, UCKFIELD, TN22 3HP. (Life Member)
MILLS, Mrs. Nicola Jane, LLB ACA *2003;* Selborne, Plichons Lane, St. Sampson, GUERNSEY, GY2 4XL.
MILLS, Mr. Nigel John, BA ACA *1984;* Mills Group Ltd, 7-11 Earsdon Road, WHITLEY BAY, TYNE AND WEAR, NE25 9SX.
MILLS, Mr. Nigel John, BA(Hons) ACA *2000;* with Deloitte LLP, 1 Woodborough Road, NOTTINGHAM, NG1 3FG.
MILLS, Mr. Nigel Jonathan Scott, MA ACA *1984;* MM&K Ltd, 1 Bengal Court, Birchin Lane, LONDON, EC3V 9DD.
MILLS, Mr. Paul Andrew, BSc ACA *1984;* 8 Hall Orchard, Bramshall, UTTOXETER, STAFFORDSHIRE, ST14 5DF.
MILLS, Mr. Paul Martin, BA ACA *1992;* 1131 Mayfair Road, OAKVILLE L6M 1G6, ON, CANADA.
MILLS, Mr. Paul Richard, BA ACA *2004;* 15 Turners Mill Road, HAYWARDS HEATH, WEST SUSSEX, RH16 1NW.
MILLS, Mr. Peter Anthony, FCA *1973;* 26 Leamside House, Lucas Court, LEAMINGTON SPA, WARWICKSHIRE, CV32 5JL.
MILLS, Mr. Peter David, BCom ACA *1997;* Coromandel, La Planque Lane, Forest, GUERNSEY, GY8 0DU.
MILLS, Mr. Peter Derek, FCA *1954;* 5 Chescombe Road, Yatton, BRISTOL, BS49 4EJ. (Life Member)
•**MILLS, Mr. Peter Francis, BA FCA JDipMA** *1970;* 1st Consult Ltd, Rowley Stables, Combe Hay, BATH, BA2 7EF.
MILLS, Mr. Peter George, BSc FCA *1988;* 66 Brookmans Avenue, Brookmans Park, HATFIELD, HERTFORDSHIRE, AL9 7QQ.
•**MILLS, Mr. Peter John, FCA** *1973;* 305 Rosevears Drive, ROSEVEARS, TAS 7277, AUSTRALIA.
MILLS, Mr. Peter William, BSc ACA *1990;* The Thatchers, High Street, Wanborough, SWINDON, SN4 0AD.
MILLS, Mr. Peter William Joseph, FCA *1975;* Lafarge UK Services, Regent House, Station Approach, DORKING, SURREY, RH4 1TH.
•**MILLS, Mr. Philip David, BSc ACA ATII** *1993;* Deloitte LLP, 2 New Street Square, LONDON, EC4A 3BZ. See also Deloitte & Touche LLP
•**MILLS, Mr. Raymond, BSc ACA** *1988;* PricewaterhouseCoopers LLP, 80 Strand, LONDON, WC2R 0AF. See also PricewaterhouseCoopers
MILLS, Mr. Reginald Brian, FCA *1961;* Bank House, Stanford Bridge, WORCESTER, WR6 6RU.
MILLS, Mr. Richard, BSc FCA *1979;* 156 Dale Valley Road, Shirley, SOUTHAMPTON, SO16 6QW.
MILLS, Mr. Richard John, BA FCA *1980;* Delvyns Farm, Church Street, Gestingthorpe, HALSTEAD, ESSEX, CO9 3AX.
MILLS, Mr. Richard Kevin, BA ACA *1997;* Bramblewood Coulsdon Lane, Chipstead, COULSDON, SURREY, CR5 3QH.
MILLS, Mr. Richard Michael Cameron, BSc ACA *2005;* 65 Beryl Road, LONDON, W6 8JS.
MILLS, Mr. Robert Andrew Nathan, BSc ACA *2002;* The Old Court Lees Hill, Upton Grey, BASINGSTOKE, HAMPSHIRE, RG25 2EX.
MILLS, Mr. Robert James, BSc ACA *2010;* Flat 21 The Lion Brewery, St. Thomas Street, OXFORD, OX1 1JE.
MILLS, Mr. Robert Peter, BMus ACA *2002;* Mountgrange Investment Management LLP, 6 Cork Street, LONDON, W1S 3NX.
MILLS, Mr. Roger James, FCA *1966;* 4 Willis Avenue, SUTTON, SM2 5HS. (Life Member)
MILLS, Mr. Ronald Kingsley, FCA *1960;* 7 Snowberry Gardens, 609 Warwick Road, SOLIHULL, WEST MIDLANDS, B91 1AP. (Life Member)
MILLS, Mr. Russell James, BSc ACA *2010;* 1 Ashford Road, FELTHAM, TW13 4QR.
MILLS, Mr. Rye James, BSc ACA *2001;* 31 Oaklands Road, BEXLEYHEATH, DA6 7AN.
MILLS, Miss. Sarah Jayne, BSc ACA *1992;* 55b Riddell Rd, GLENDOWIE 1071, AUCKLAND, NEW ZEALAND.
MILLS, Miss. Sarah Louise, BSc ACA *2000;* 30 Green Lane, Formby, LIVERPOOL, L37 7DL.
MILLS, Mr. Shaun Michael, BSc FCA *1983;* Angel Trains International Ltd Eggington House, 25-28 Buckingham Gate, LONDON, SW1E 6LD.
MILLS, Mr. Simon John, BSc ACA *2005;* 303 Rossetti Place, 2 Lower Byrom Street, MANCHESTER, M3 4AN.
MILLS, Miss. Stephanie Louise, BA(Hons) ACA *2001;* Channel Four Television, 124-126 Horseferry Road, LONDON, SW1P 2TX.
MILLS, Mr. Stephen Geoffrey, FCA *1968;* Directing Success Ltd, Park House, 59 Pittville Lawn, CHELTENHAM, GLOUCESTERSHIRE, GL52 2BJ.
MILLS, Mr. Stephen James, BA ACA CCSA CIA *1989;* 75 Poplar Street, APT 5A, BROOKLYN, NY 11201, UNITED STATES.
•**MILLS, Mr. Stephen John, BA FCA** *1995;* Grant Thornton UK LLP, 1 Dorset Street, SOUTHAMPTON, SO15 2DP. See also Grant Thornton LLP
MILLS, Mr. Stephen John, BSc ACA ACIS *1988;* 33 Wigmore Street, LONDON, W1U 1AU.
MILLS, Mr. Stephen Macnaughton, MA FCA *1963;* 47 Bluehouse Lane, OXTED, RH8 0AJ. (Life Member)
•**MILLS, Mr. Terence Edward, FCA** *1974;* Reeves & Co LLP, 37 St. Margarets Street, CANTERBURY, KENT, CT1 2TU.
MILLS, Mr. Thomas William, BSc(Hons) ACA *2004;* with Hilton Sharp & Clarke, Atlantic House, Jengers Mead, BILLINGSHURST, WEST SUSSEX, RH14 9PB.
MILLS, Mr. Timothy David, FCA *1993;* 419 Burns Boulevard, KING CITY L7B 1E1, ON, CANADA.
MILLS, Mr. Timothy Seton, FCA *1974;* 22 Anchorage Road, SUTTON COLDFIELD, WEST MIDLANDS, B74 2PL.
•**MILLS, Mr. Trevor James, FCA** *1973;* AIMS - Trevor Mills, High Dyke, Church Lane, Bury, PULBOROUGH, WEST SUSSEX RH20 1PB.
MILLS, Miss. Victoria Louise, BA(Hons) ACA *2010;* 7 Claybrick Avenue, HOCKLEY, ESSEX, SS5 4PS.
MILLS, Mrs. Yvonne Patricia, FCA *1982;* Pennyfarthing, Chapel Lane, Wanborough, SWINDON, SN4 0AJ.
MILLS-BAKER, Mr. Andrew James, BA FCA *1974;* 8 The Warren, HARPENDEN, AL5 2NH.
MILLS-HICKS, Mr. Nicolas Paul, BEng ACA *1996;* Flat 54, Circus Lodge, Circus Road, LONDON, NW8 9JN.
MILLS-HICKS, Mr. Roger James, MSc FCA CDir *1976;* 16 Silver Birches Way, Elstead, GODALMING, SURREY, GU8 6JA.
MILLS-WEBB, Mr. Thomas James, ACA *2008;* 4 Calvert Road, LONDON, SE10 0DF.
MILLSON, Mr. Timothy, BA ACA *1999;* Cartus, Frankland Road, Blagrove, SWINDON, WILTSHIRE, SN5 8RS.
MILLWARD, Mrs. Catherine Elizabeth, MSci ACA *2003;* 25 Allingham Street, LONDON, N1 8NX.
MILLWARD, Mr. David Stephen, BSc ACA *2004;* Holiday Break Plc, Hartford Manor, Greenbank Lane, NORTHWICH, CHESHIRE, CW8 1HW.
MILLWARD, Mr. Guy Leighton, BA ACA *1990;* 15 Basing Close, THAMES DITTON, SURREY, KT7 0NY.
MILLWARD, Mr. John, FCA *1971;* 2 Kite Close, Broughton Astley, LEICESTER, LE9 6RY.
MILLWARD, Mr. John Andrew James, BA ACA *2004;* 4 Nevis Road, LONDON, SW17 7QX.
•**MILLWARD, Mrs. Judith, FCA** *1977;* (Tax Fac), Judith Millward, 31 Augustus Road, Edgbaston, BIRMINGHAM, B15 3PQ.
MILLWARD, Mr. Keith Roger, BCom ACA *1978;* Commercial First Mortgages Ltd Lutea House, Warley Hill Business Park, The Drive, Great Warley, BRENTWOOD, ESSEX CM13 3BE.
MILLWARD, Mr. Kevin John, FCA *1974;* Eveson Fuels Ltd, Eveson House, Birmingham Road, KENILWORTH, WARWICKSHIRE, CV8 1PT.
•**MILLWARD, Mr. Peter John, BSc FCA** *1976;* 31 Augustus Road, BIRMINGHAM, B15 3PQ.
MILLWARD, Mr. Piers Dominic, BSc ACA *2000;* 25 Allingham Street, LONDON, N1 8NX.
MILLWARD, Mr. Simon Philip, BA ACA *1995;* 12 Frankley Avenue, HALESOWEN, WEST MIDLANDS, B62 0EH.
MILLWARD, Mr. Stewart John, BSc ACA *2011;* 24 Gower Road, HALESOWEN, WEST MIDLANDS, B62 9BZ.
•**MILLWARD, Mr. Timothy John, FCA** *1974;* Cheyne Consulting Limited, 3 Cheyne Close, AMERSHAM, BUCKINGHAMSHIRE, HP6 5LT.
MILLWARD, Mr. Timothy John, BA ACA *1982;* 5 Clover Hill, WALSALL, WS5 3DF.
MILLWARD, Mr. William Nicholas Grant, FCA *1969;* Baronsfield, Lilley Bottom, Lilley, LUTON, LU2 8NH.
MILLWOOD, Mr. Christopher, BA(Hons) ACA *2010;* 35 Roxwell Road, CHELMSFORD, CM1 2LY.
MILN, Mr. John Kingsley, MA FCA *1961;* Rushtons, Grove Hill, Mawnan Smith, FALMOUTH, TR11 5ER. (Life Member)
MILNE, Mr. Adrian Leslie James, BSc ACA *1986;* 27-32 Old Jewry, LONDON, EC2R 8DQ.
•**MILNE, Mr. Alan Martin, FCA** *1969;* (Tax Fac), Milne Thomas & Co, 27 Seller Street, CHESTER, CH1 3NA.
MILNE, Mr. Alan Meldrum, MA ACA AIIT *1989;* (Tax Fac), with MS&Co, Suite 124, Grosvenor Gardens House, 35-37 Grosvenor Gardens, LONDON, SW1W 0BS.
MILNE, Mr. Alastair James Williamson, MEng ACA *2005;* Henderson Global Investors, 201 Bishopsgate, LONDON, EC2M 3AE.
MILNE, Mrs. Amy Olivia, BSc ACA *2004;* 28a Woodrow Drive, WOKINGHAM, BERKSHIRE, RG40 1RS.
MILNE, Mr. Anthony Howard, FCA *1973;* 140 Alwoodley Lane, LEEDS, LS17 7PP.
MILNE, Mr. Ashley, ACA *2010;* 19 Medway Drive, Chandler's Ford, EASTLEIGH, HAMPSHIRE, SO53 4SR.
MILNE, Ms. Christine, BA ACA *2000;* M E P C Ltd Rosewood Crockford Lane, Chineham Business Park Chineham, BASINGSTOKE, HAMPSHIRE, RG24 8UT.
MILNE, Mr. Christopher David, MA ACA *2005;* Scottish Hydro Electric Plc Inveralmond House, 200 Dunkeld Road, PERTH, PH1 3AQ.
MILNE, Mr. Christopher Richard Edward, BSc ACA *2005;* 128 Common View, LETCHWORTH GARDEN CITY, HERTFORDSHIRE, SG6 1DQ.
MILNE, Miss. Ciara, ACA *2008;* 6 Tennyson Street, Morley, LEEDS, LS27 8QN.
MILNE, Mr. Darren James Ivor, BSc FCA *1997;* Daffodil House, Chedworth Road, Withington, CHELTENHAM, GL54 4BN.
MILNE, Mr. David Geoffrey, MSc ACA *1990;* (Tax Fac), 45 Old Palace Road, GUILDFORD, SURREY, GU2 7TX.
MILNE, Mr. David Gordon, MA FCA *1985;* 22 Church Row, Hampstead, LONDON, NW3 6UP.
MILNE, Mr. Douglas John Williamson, FCA *1965;* Castle Godwyn, Painswick, STROUD, GL6 6TN.
MILNE, Mr. Duncan Robert, LLM LLB(Hons) ACA CTA *1998;* 24 Marjorys Avenue, Chapel, KIRKCALDY, FIFE, KY2 6ZJ.
MILNE, Miss. Fiona Louise, BA ACA *2007;* 6 Ashlar Grove, LIVERPOOL, L17 0DX.
MILNE, Mrs. Helen Jane, MA ACA *1995;* with PricewaterhouseCoopers LLP, 31 Great George Street, BRISTOL, BS1 5QD.
MILNE, Mr. Henry Bruce, FCA *1956;* Dowerfield House, Long Bredy, DORCHESTER, DT2 9AA. (Life Member)
MILNE, Ms. Hilary Martha, LLB ACA *2005;* Sport England Victoria House, Southampton Row, LONDON, WC1B 4SE.
MILNE, The Hon. Iaian Charles Luis, FCA *1974;* Casilla 533 Talca, Villa Esmeralda Lote D Sur, V11 Region, TALCA, CHILE. (Life Member)
MILNE, Mr. Ian Alasdair Ross, MA ACA *1981;* 35 Bonython Street, Windsor, BRISBANE, QLD 4030, AUSTRALIA.
MILNE, Mr. Ian Richard, ACA *1986;* 103 Woodlands Road, Bookham, LEATHERHEAD, KT23 4HN.
MILNE, Mrs. Ingrid Margarethe, BSc ACA *1992;* 21 Old Mill Road, WESTON, CT 06883, UNITED STATES.
MILNE, Mr. James Nicholas Lynch, BSc FCA *2000;* 2 Briar Lea Road, Mortimer Common, READING, RG7 3SA.
MILNE, Mr. John Duncan, FCA *1961;* 35 Woodside Park Avenue, Horsforth, LEEDS, LS18 4TF. (Life Member)
MILNE, Mr. John Phineas, BSc FCA *1954;* 3 Highfield Court, Southgate, LONDON, N14 4DX. (Life Member)
•**MILNE, Miss. Katherine Mary, BSc ACA** *1992;* Milne & Co, 1 Highlever Road, LONDON, W10 6PP.
MILNE, Mr. Leigh Sterling, FCA *1967;* Barncot Place, Hare Lane, Blindley Heath, LINGFIELD, RH7 6JB.
MILNE, Mrs. Linda Jane, BA FCA *1983;* Beck Cottage, Flexford Road, Normandy, GUILDFORD, SURREY, GU3 2EE.
MILNE, Mr. Peter Bruce, FCA *1956;* Westfield, Oakcroft Road, WEST BYFLEET, KT14 6JH. (Life Member)
MILNE, Mr. Richard John, BA(Hons) ACA *2004;* 11a King Street, Morley, LEEDS, LS27 9ES.
MILNE, Mr. Robert John Coutts, BA ACA *1992;* 47 September Lane, WESTON, CT 06883, UNITED STATES.
MILNE, Mr. Roderick Bruce, FCA *1962;* 4 Fairways, Inchmarlo, BANCHORY, KINCARDINESHIRE, AB31 4GA.
MILNE, Miss. Sandra Ann, LLB ACA *1993;* 6 Salisbury Court, St Leonards Crag, EDINBURGH, EH8 9SP.
MILNE, Mr. Warwick Simon, ACA *1984;* Flat 9 Cherry Gardens, Oakwood Drive, Heaton, BOLTON, BL1 5WD.
MILNE, Mrs. Wendy Karen Erika, BSc ACA *1982;* Postern House, Church Lane, Worplesdon, GUILDFORD, GU3 3RU.
MILNE, Mr. William Douglas, ACA *1990;* 204 Glasgow Road, PAISLEY, PA1 3LS.
MILNE-REDHEAD, Mrs. Yvonne, BSc FCA *1993;* 12 Warwick Drive, CLITHEROE, LANCASHIRE, BB7 2BG.
•**MILNER, Mr. Andrew Colin, BSc FCA** *1992;* KPMG LLP, 15 Canada Square, LONDON, E14 5GL. See also KPMG Europe LLP
MILNER, Mr. Andrew Thomas Henry, BA ACA *2006;* 10 Mandarin Drive, NEWBURY, RG14 7WE.
MILNER, Miss. Bernadette, BSc ACA *2005;* Flat 21 Grove Court, Drayton Gardens, LONDON, SW10 9QY.
•**MILNER, Mr. Charles John Henry, BSc(Econ) FCA CISI** *1985;* KPMG Safi Al-Mutawa & Partners, P O Box 24, SAFAT, 13001, KUWAIT.
MILNER, Mr. David Allan, FCA *1972;* 5 St Georges Crescent, RHYL, LL18 3NN.
MILNER, Miss. Elaine Janet, BSc ACA *1987;* Federal-Mogul Limited Manchester International Office Centre, Styal Road, MANCHESTER, M22 5TN.
MILNER, Mrs. Haydee Ann, BA ACA *2004;* (Tax Fac), with KPMG LLP, Arlington Business Park, Theale, READING, RG7 4SD.
MILNER, Mrs. Helen Louise, MA ACA *2000;* Heath Cottage, Donibristle, COWDENBEATH, FIFE, KY4 8ET.
•**MILNER, Mr. Ian, FCA** *1986;* (Tax Fac), Ian Milner, 2 Langthorne Court, Morley, LEEDS, LS27 9DR.
MILNER, Mr. James Wilson, BSc FCA *1969;* Stonyford, Bagshaw, Chapel-en-le-Frith, HIGH PEAK, SK23 0QU.
•①**MILNER, Miss. Joanne Elizabeth, BA ACA** *1990;* W H Cork & Co LLP, 52 Brook Street, LONDON, W1K 5DS.
MILNER, Miss. Louise Amanda, BA BSc ACA *1996;* 1 Hillfield Gardens, NANTWICH, CHESHIRE, CW5 7BU.
•**MILNER, Mr. Martin Peter, FCA** *1980;* Martin Milner & Co, Riverdale, 89 Graham Road, SHEFFIELD, S10 3GP.

MILNER, Mr. Michael, BA FCA *1972;* 7 Springfield, Oakley, BASINGSTOKE, RG23 7DR.
MILNER, Mrs. Nicola Jane, MA ACA *2000;* 44 Wilton Avenue, LONDON, W4 2HY.
MILNER, Mr. Paul John, BA ACA *1990;* North Acre, Southwell Road, Thurgarton, NOTTINGHAM, NG14 7GP.
MILNER, Mr. Peter Benjamin, BSc ACA *1987;* BG, Mergers Aquistions & Disposals, Thames Valley Park Drive, READING, RG6 1PT.
MILNER, Mr. Peter Nicholson, FCA *1966;* York House Great Barugh, MALTON, NORTH YORKSHIRE, YO17 6UZ. (Life Member)
MILNER, Mr. Rene Eric William, BSc ACA *1991;* 31 Hare Hill Close, WOKING, SURREY, GU22 8UH.
MILNER, Mr. Richard John, FCA *1995;* 12 Royal Meadow Way, SUTTON COLDFIELD, B74 2FE.
MILNER, Mrs. Sheila Paula Lucy, BSc ACA *1978;* Vertec Scientific Ltd, Unit 44, Easter Park, Benyon Road, Silchester, READING RG7 2PQ.
MILNER, Mr. Stephen Eric Leslie, BSc FCA *1982;* 1 High Street, Eydon, DAVENTRY, NORTHAMPTONSHIRE, NN11 3PP.
MILNER, Mr. Stephen Frederick, BA ACA *1997;* Shell International Ltd, Shell Centre, York Road, LONDON, SE1 7NA.
MILNER, Mr. Trevor Winston, FCA *1963;* 3 Brownroyd Walk, BRADFORD, BD6 1SB.
MILNER, Mr. William Noel Woodville, BA(Hons) ACA *2000;* 44 Wilton Avenue, LONDON, W4 2HY.
MILNER-MOORE, Miss. Sharon Christine, BA ACA *1998;* 128 Hartfield Road, Wimbledon, LONDON, SW19 3TG.
•MILNES, Mr. Andrew, BA FCA *1988;* Hurst & Company Accountants LLP, Lancashire Gate, 21 Tiviot Dale, STOCKPORT, CHESHIRE, SK1 1TD.
MILNES, Mr. Andrew, BA ACA *2006;* 44 Laithe Hall Avenue, CLECKHEATON, WEST YORKSHIRE, BD19 6UB.
•MILNES, Mr. David James, FCA *1974;* David Milnes Limited, Premier House, Bradford Road, CLECKHEATON, WEST YORKSHIRE, BD19 3TT.
MILNES, Mr. David Sides, FCA *1962;* Horseshoe Cottage, North Farm Ramper Road, Letwell, WORKSOP, S81 8DR.
MILNES, Mrs. Farrah Jade, ACA *2009;* 44 Laithe Hall Avenue, CLECKHEATON, WEST YORKSHIRE, BD19 6UB.
MILNES, Mrs. Hazell Mary, BA ACA *1996;* 150 Desborough Avenue, HIGH WYCOMBE, HP11 2SU.
MILNES, Mrs. Helen Elizabeth, ACA *2008;* 8 Oaken Royd Croft, BARNSLEY, SOUTH YORKSHIRE, S74 8AX.
MILNES, Miss. Lucy Francesca, BA ACA *2001;* 29 Ray Lea Close, MAIDENHEAD, SL6 8QW.
MILNES, Ms. Marianne, ACA *2008;* Flat 36 Dover Court, 201 St. John Street, LONDON, EC1V 4LZ.
MILNES, Mr. Matthew John, ACA *2009;* 8 Oaken Royd Croft, Elsecar, BARNSLEY, S74 8AX.
MILNES, Mr. Richard John, MA ACA *1998;* 18 Southwood Gardens, Hinchley Wood, ESHER, SURREY, KT10 0DE.
MILNES-JAMES, Mr. Richard Llewelyn, BA ACA *1999;* 2a Fitzroy Road, FLEET, HAMPSHIRE, GU51 4JH.
MILNOR, Miss. Lisa Rachael, BSc ACA *1992;* Shaping Clarity, Goal Farm, Hellifield, SKIPTON, BD23 4JR.
•MILNS, Miss. Lisa Anne, ACA MAAT *2004;* with Hailwood Accountants Ltd, 392-394 Hoylake Road, WIRRAL, MERSEYSIDE, CH46 6DF.
•MILONE, Mr. Libero Emidio, FCA *1975;* Vocabolo Petrarca 22, Ponte Naia, 06059 TODI, ITALY.
MILROY, Mr. Alasdair, ACA CA(AUS) *2010;* (Tax Fac), with Rawlinson & Hunter Limited, Trafalgar Court, 3rd Floor, West Wing, St Peter Port, GUERNSEY GY1 2JA.
MILROY, Mr. Herbert David, FCA *1948;* 2 Holly Close, WOKING, SURREY, GU21 7QZ. (Life Member)
MILROY, Mr. John Peter, BA FCA *1979;* Farthing Hall, The Street, Cressing, BRAINTREE, ESSEX, CM77 8DG.
MILROY, Mr. Peter Douglas, MA FCA *1975;* 14 Trevor Road, LONDON, SW19 3PW.
MILROY, Mr. Stephen, FCA *1981;* 6 Sandwick Close, Fulwood, PRESTON, PR2 9RZ.
MILSOM, Mr. Andrew, ACA *2010;* Flat 6, Compass Court, 39 Shad Thames, LONDON, SE1 2NJ.
•MILSOM, Mrs. Anne Carmel, BSc ACA *1990;* Francis J Woods & Company Limited, Balbriggan Business Campus, BALBRIGGAN, COUNTY DUBLIN, IRELAND.
MILSOM, Miss. Donna Louise, BSc ACA CTA *1986;* (Tax Fac), 2 Itchen Close, West Wellow, ROMSEY, SO51 6GX.
•①MILSOM, Mr. John David Thomas, BA ACA *1988;* KPMG LLP, 15 Canada Square, LONDON, E14 5GL. See also KPMG Europe LLP
MILSOM, Mr. John Francis Sidney, BTech FCA *1980;* 41 Harbour Reach, La Rue de Carteret, St. Helier, JERSEY, JE2 4HR.
•MILSOM, Mr. Mathew Craig, ACA *2001;* MM Accountancy Services, Lychgate House, Tyr Winch Road, Old St Mellons, CARDIFF, CF3 5UW.
MILSOM, Mr. Neal Andrew, BA ACA *1989;* Orange, St. James Court, Great Park Road, Almondsbury, Bradley Stoke, BRISTOL BS32 4QJ.
MILSOM, Mr. Stephen Charles, FCA *1973;* with Moore Stephens, P O Box 236, First Island House, Peter Street, St. Helier, JERSEY JE4 8SG.
MILSOM, Mrs. Terrina Jayne, BA ACA *1992;* 25a Temple Road, Dorridge, SOLIHULL, WEST MIDLANDS, B93 8LE.
MILSOM, Mrs. Valerie, ACA *1996;* 23 St Austell Close, Stainton Manor, Hemlington, MIDDLESBROUGH, TS8 9NQ.
MILSON, Mr. Arthur David, BSc ACA *2000;* 20 South Oswald Road, EDINBURGH, EH9 2HG.
MILSTED, Mr. Laurence James, BA FCA *1986;* Freshfields Bruckhaus Deringer, 65 Fleet Street, LONDON, EC4Y 1HS.
MILSTED, Miss. Louise Mary Anne, ACA *2009;* 74 Clarke Crescent, Kennington, ASHFORD, TN24 9SA.
MILSTED, Mrs. Rosemary Anne, FCA *1978;* Alsted Properties Ltd, 332 Cheriton Road, FOLKESTONE, KENT, CT19 4DP.
MILSTED, Mr. Simon John, BSc FCA *1982;* 2 Brock Terrace, Grange Road, St. Peter Port, GUERNSEY, GY1 1RQ.
•MILSTON, Mr. Jeffrey, FCA *1962;* Milston & Co, 57 Wolmer Gardens, EDGWARE, MIDDLESEX, HA8 8QB.
MILSTONE, Mr. Dennis Michael, FCA *1948;* 31 Trinity Close, Dene Road, NORTHWOOD, HA6 2AF. (Life Member)
MILTIADOU, Mr. Marios Elia, BSc ACA *1980;* PO Box 51865, 21 Marathovounou Street, Ayios Georgios Havousas, 3509 LIMASSOL, CYPRUS.
MILTIADOUS, Miss. Elina Karayianni, BA(Hons) ACA *2000;* Grigori Afxentiou 8a, 3021 LIMASSOL, CYPRUS.
•MILTIADOUS, Mr. Miltiades, BA FCA FCCA *1996;* Bramil Associates, Rex House, 354 Ballards Lane, North Finchley, LONDON, N12 0DD.
MILTON, Mr. Andrew, MSc BA ACA *1997;* 921 40th Street, BROOKLYN, NY 11219, UNITED STATES.
MILTON, Mr. Arthur, MA FCA *1977;* 29 Hurlingham Square, Fulham, LONDON, SW6 3DZ.
MILTON, Mr. Ashley Giles, BA ACA *1995;* 5b Bramley Close, Mill Hill, LONDON, NW7 4BR.
•MILTON, Mr. Derek John, FCA *1955;* Milton & Co., Cranford, Wheal Venture Road, ST. IVES, TR26 2PQ.
MILTON, Mr. Ian Robert, BSc ACA *1981;* 141 Vernon Road, Poynton, STOCKPORT, SK12 1YS.
MILTON, Mr. Jonathan Paul, BA ACA *2002;* with KPMG LLP, 15 Canada Square, LONDON, E14 5GL.
MILTON, Miss. Karen Jane, BSc ACA *1995;* UK Payments Administration Ltd, 2 Thomas More Square, LONDON, E1W 1YN.
MILTON, Mr. Keith Bertram, ACA *1993;* 74 Moor Road North, NEWCASTLE UPON TYNE, NE3 1AB.
MILTON, Mr. Michael, ACA CA(SA) *2009;* with Creaseys LLP, 12 Lonsdale Gardens, TUNBRIDGE WELLS, KENT, TN1 1PA.
MILTON, Mr. Peter David, BSc ACA *1991;* William Clowes Ltd, Copland Way, Ellough, BECCLES, SUFFOLK, NR34 7TL.
•MILTON, Mr. Philip David, ACA *2004;* Milton Financial Management Limited, 16 Berkshire Green, Shenley Brook End, MILTON KEYNES, MK5 7FL.
MILTON, Mr. Philip William Arthur, BA FCA *1977;* 16 Rutherford Close, ABINGDON, OXFORDSHIRE, OX14 2AT.
MILTON, Mr. Richard David, ACA *1982;* 1 Culvers Croft, Seer Green, BEACONSFIELD, BUCKINGHAMSHIRE, HP9 2YU.
MILTON, Mr. Robert John, BA(Hons) ACA *2001;* 3 Updown Hill, HAYWARDS HEATH, WEST SUSSEX, RH16 4GD.
MILWARD, Mrs. Kate Louise, BA(Hons) ACA *2003;* 8 Lambourne Avenue, ASHBOURNE, DERBYSHIRE, DE6 1BP.
MILWARD-OLIVER, Mr. Kim Alston, BA ACA FRSA *2009;* 44 Barnsbury Road, LONDON, N1 0HD.
MILWAY, Mr. Daniel, BSc ACA *2011;* 10 Shelley Street, SYDNEY, NSW 2000, AUSTRALIA.
MIMMACK, Mr. Geoffrey Alan, BSc ACA *1986;* 3 Annandale Road, Kirk Ella, HULL, HU10 7UT.
MIN, Mr. Didier, BSc ACA *2006;* 9 Tiverton Road, RUISLIP, MIDDLESEX, HA4 0BW.
MIN, Miss. Jie, ACA *2010;* Flat 7 Cotterell Court, Hop Street, LONDON, SE10 0QR.
MINA, Ms. Elena, BA ACA *2004;* 5a Akropoleos Street, Kaimakli, 1021 NICOSIA, CYPRUS.
•MINA, Mr. Paolo, MSc BEng ACA *2002;* (Tax Fac), AccounTrust Ltd, Royalty House, 32 Sackville Street, Mayfair, LONDON, W1S 3EA. See also ITP Business Advisers Limited
•MINAEIAN, Mr. Faramarz, BSc FCA *1982;* Minayan & Co Limited, 8B Accomodation Road, LONDON, NW11 8ED.
•MINAEIAN, Mr. Fariborz, BSc FCA *1985;* Hanleys Limited, Spring Court, Spring Road, Hale, ALTRINCHAM, CHESHIRE WA14 2UQ. See also Hale Financial Limited
MINALL, Mrs. Angela Gillian, BSc ACA *1989;* Lloyds TSB Plc, Private Banking, 25-27 Perrymount Road, HAYWARDS HEATH, WEST SUSSEX, RH16 3SP.
MINALL, Mr. Stephen Follett, BSc ACA *1991;* pp 2.0E, British Telecom Telephone Exchange, Freshfield Road, BRIGHTON, BN2 0BJ.
MINARDS, Mr. Bruce Elgin, FCA *1952;* 7 Neale Close, Weston Favell, NORTHAMPTON, NN3 3DB. (Life Member)
MINARDS, Mrs. Elaine Mary, BCom ACA *1989;* The Conifers, Cheverells Green, Markyate, ST ALBANS, AL3 8RN.
•MINARDS, Mr. John Edwin Beaton, BA ACA *1988;* PricewaterhouseCoopers LLP, Marlborough Court, 10 Bricket Road, ST. ALBANS, HERTFORDSHIRE, AL1 3JX. See also PricewaterhouseCoopers
MINAS, Mr. Andreas Savva, BEng ACA *1993;* c/o SMC (Dr Gillies), RAF Akrotiri, BFPO, 57.
MINAS, Mr. Andrew George, BA ACA *1990;* DunnHumby, 71-75 Uxbridge Road, LONDON, W5 5SL.
MINAS, Mr. Christos, BSc ACA *2011;* Albert Swaitzer 13A, 3015 LIMASSOL, CYPRUS.
MINAS, Miss. Katerina, BA ACA *2006;* 6 GRAVIAS AVENUE, PLATY, AGLANTZIAS, 2114 NICOSIA, CYPRUS.
MINASHI, Mr. Mark Anthony, BA ACA *1997;* Gema Services Ltd, 21 Nightingale Road, RICKMANSWORTH, WD3 7DE.
MINAY, Mrs. Francesca, FCA *1996;* Isle of Man Insurance and Pensions Authority, Government Insurance Fourth Floor HSBC House, Ridgeway Street Douglas, ISLE OF MAN, IM1 1ER.
•MINCHELL, Mr. Peter Taylor, BSc FCA *1977;* Clarkson Hyde LLP, 3rd Floor, Chancery House, St. Nicholas Way, SUTTON, SURREY SM1 1JB. See also Business Matters (UK) Ltd
•MINCHELLA, Mr. Mark Andrew, FCA *1998;* Davies Mayers Barnett LLP, Pillar House, 113-115 Bath Road, CHELTENHAM, GLOUCESTERSHIRE, GL53 7LS. See also Barnett DM Limited
MINCHER, Mr. Aidan, BA FCA *1997;* 23 Marsh Rise, PUDSEY, LS28 7QD.
MINCHEW, Miss. Sarah Elizabeth, BSc ACA *1999;* 83 Barnwood Avenue, GLOUCESTER, GL4 3AG.
MINCHIN, Mr. Francis George, BA ACA CTA *1981;* with Spofforths LLP, 2nd Floor, Comewell House, North Street, HORSHAM, WEST SUSSEX RH12 1RD.
MINCHIN, Mrs. Kathryn Elizabeth, BA(Hons) ACA *2002;* 21 Longcroft, STANSTED, ESSEX, CM24 8JD.
MINCHINGTON, Miss. Clare, MA FCA FCCA *1992;* ACCA, 29 Lincoln's Inn Fields, LONDON, WC2A 3EE.
MINDEL, Mr. Dan, LLB ACA *2000;* with Ernst & Young LLP, 1 More London Place, LONDON, SE1 2AF.
MINDEL, Mrs. Hannah Katherine, BSc(Hons) ACA *2002;* with BDO LLP, 55 Baker Street, LONDON, W1U 7EU.
MINDELL, Mrs. Belinda, BSc ACA *1992;* Fred Olsen Ltd, 64-65 Vincent Square, LONDON, SW1P 2NU.
•MINDHAM, Mr. Anthony John, BSc FCA *1974;* (Tax Fac), A.J. Mindham & Co, 1 Westleigh Hall, Wakefield Road, Denby Dale, HUDDERSFIELD, HD8 8QJ.
MINDHAM, Mr. Anthony John, FCA *1987;* with Ernst & Young LLP, 1 More London Place, LONDON, SE1 2AF.
MINDHAM, Miss. Patricia Mary, BSc ACA *1993;* 4 The Terrace, Lauradale Road, East Finchley, LONDON, N2 9LX.
MINDHAM, Mr. Simon John, BA ACA *1991;* 24 Kings Avenue, Muswell Hill, LONDON, N10 1PB.
MINEARD, Mr. Craig, ACA *1992;* 520 Madison Ave, NEW YORK, NY 10022, UNITED STATES.
•MINER, Mr. Richard John, ACA FCCA *2008;* Weatherer Bailey Bragg LLP, Victoria Chambers, 100 Boldmere Road, SUTTON COLDFIELD, WEST MIDLANDS, B73 5UB.
•MINERS, Miss. Dawn Kathleen, FCA *1981;* (Tax Fac), Dawn Miners, 34 Fairfield Avenue, BATH, BA1 6NH.
•MINERS, Ms. Jane, BA ACA *1983;* Jane Miners, 2 Turlake Mews, Cowley, EXETER, EX5 5ER.
MINES, Mr. Anthony James, BSc ACA *2001;* 32 Ravensbury Road, LONDON, SW18 4RZ.
MINES, Mr. James Alexander, BA ACA *2006;* with Hurst Morrison Thomson, The Hub, 14 Station Road, HENLEY-ON-THAMES, OXFORDSHIRE, RG9 1AY.
MINES, Mrs. Nicola Michelle, BSc ACA *2002;* 32 Ravensbury Road, LONDON, SW18 4RZ.
•MINES, Mr. Thomas John, FCA *1964;* (Tax Fac), Thomas David, Orchard House, 5 The Orchard, HERTFORD, SG14 3HQ.
MINES, Mr. William John, BA FCA *1987;* 31 Rolling Hill Road, RIDGEFIELD, CT 06877, UNITED STATES.
•MINETT, Mr. David Charles, ACA FCCA *2010;* Harben Barker Limited, Drayton Court, Drayton Road, SOLIHULL, WEST MIDLANDS, B90 4NG.
•MINETT, Mr. Keith, FCA *1970;* (Tax Fac), Pinner Darlington, 25 Church Street, KIDDERMINSTER, DY10 2AW.
•MINETT, Mr. Martin Clifford, FCA *1980;* 60 Crouchfield, Boxmoor, HEMEL HEMPSTEAD, HP1 1PD.
MINFORD, Mr. Alexander Patrick, BA FCA *1987;* Reed Elsevier Grand Buildings, 1-3 Strand, LONDON, WC2N 5JR.
•MINFORD, Mr. Allen John, BSc FCA *1987;* (Tax Fac), Minford, Moyola House, 31 Hawthorn Grove, YORK, YO31 7UA. See also John Minford Associates
MINFORD, Mrs. Ann Louise, BA ACA *1989;* Ambac Assurance UK Ltd, Level 7, 6 Broadgate, LONDON, EC2M 2QS.
MINFORD, Mrs. Hilary Elise, LLB ACA *1985;* Minford, Moyola House 31 Hawthorne Grove, YORK, YO31 7YA.
MINGARD, Mrs. Carol Ann, FCA *1976;* The Langley Academy, Langley Road, SLOUGH, SL3 7EF.
MINHAS, Miss. Kiran, MSc ACA *2010;* 9 The Lindens, LOUGHTON, ESSEX, IG10 3HS.
MINHAS, Miss. Nazish, BA ACA *2005;* 209 Willesden Lane, LONDON, NW6 7YR.
MINHAT, Dr. Marizah, ACA CA(NZ) *2011;* 31 Chandlers Court, STIRLING, FK8 1NR.
MINHINNICK, Mrs. Jenny Ann, BA ACA *1990;* Compass Group Plc Compass House, Guildford Street, CHERTSEY, KT16 9BQ.
MINICHIELLO, Mr. Giuseppe Marcello, BA ACA *1996;* Edgefield London Road, Stanford Rivers, ONGAR, CM5 9PH.
•MINIFIE, Mr. Andrew Stephen, BCom FCA *1984;* HW, Sterling House, 97 Lichfield Street, TAMWORTH, STAFFORDSHIRE, B79 7QF. See also Haines Watts (East Midlands) Limited, Haines Watts Glasgow Limited, HW Prescott Gendy Limited, HW (Leeds) LLP, HW Transaction Services LLP, Wilkinson & Company, Haines Watts, HW Edinburgh, Walker, Smyth & Marshall and HW Forensic
MINIFIE, Mr. Charles Frederick, FCA *1968;* 8 True Lovers Court, Rickmansworth Road, NORTHWOOD, MIDDLESEX, HA6 2QN.
MINIHANE, Mr. Mark Richard, LLB ACA *2000;* 18 Harrington Heath, TELFORD, SHROPSHIRE, TF5 0LE.
MINIKIN, Mrs. Claire Louise, BA ACA *1993;* Dunholme, Manor close, East Horsley, LEATHERHEAD, KT24 6SA.
MINIKIN, Mr. Garth, BA FCA *1978;* 42A Burkes Road, BEACONSFIELD, HP9 1PN.
MINKIN, Mr. Dean Mark, BA(Econ) ACA *1998;* 8 Douglas Close, ILFORD, IG6 2DB.
MINKNER, Ms. Elisabeth, MA ACA *1997;* Molenstraat 8, 2071AH SANTPORT NOORD, NETHERLANDS.
MINKOFF, Mr. Paul Jason, BSc ACA *1993;* 7 Little Potters, BUSHEY, WD23 4QT.
MINNAAR, Mr. Benjamin, ACA CA(SA) *2009;* 1 Vernon Avenue, Raynes Park, LONDON, SW20 8BN.
MINNESS, Mr. Paul Stephen, BSc ACA *1998;* with Ernst & Young LLP, 1 Colmore Square, BIRMINGHAM, B4 6HQ.
•MINNEY, Mr. Leslie, FCA *1980;* Minney & Co, 59 Union Street, DUNSTABLE, LU6 1EX.
MINNS, Mr. Andrew George, FCA *1974;* 20 Charlotte Close, POOLE, DORSET, BH12 5HR.
•MINNS, Mr. Gavin Brent, BA FCA *1992;* (Tax Fac), Clenshaw Minns Ltd, 30 Market Place, SWAFFHAM, PE37 7QH.
MINNS, Mr. Gregory Leslie John, BA ACA *1990;* 113 Paddick Drive, Lower Earley, READING, RG6 4HF.

MINNS, Mr. Nicholas James, MChem ACA *2010;* Flat 9, 81 St. Georges Drive, LONDON, SW1V 4DB.
MINNS, Mr. Phillip Ashley, BSc ACA *1988;* 32 Stag Leys, ASHTEAD, KT21 2TF.
•MINNS, Mr. Richard Edward, FCA *1989;* Johnson Tidsall, 81 Burton Road, DERBY, DE1 1TJ. See also Derby Payroll Services Limited
MINOPRIO, Miss. Alice, BA ACA *2007;* 85a Campden Hill Court, Campden Hill Road, LONDON, W8 7HW.
MINOPRIO, Ms. Fiona Annette, LLB ACA *1983;* with PricewaterhouseCoopers LLP, 1 Embankment Place, LONDON, WC2N 6RH.
MINOR, Mr. Jonathan Charles, ACA MCT *1982;* Investcorp Bank BSC, Diplomatic Area, PO Box 5340, MANAMA, BAHRAIN.
•MINSHALL, Mr. Alan Anthony, BSc FCA *1978;* (Tax Fac), Alan Minshall Accountants Ltd, 222 Woodlands Road, Woodlands, SOUTHAMPTON, SO40 7GL.
MINSHALL, Mr. John Graham, BSc FCA *1972;* 19 Chestnut Grove, Barnton, NORTHWICH, CW8 4ST.
•MINSHALL, Mr. Mark Richard, BA FCA *1979;* Minshalls Ltd, 370-374 Nottingham Road, Newthorpe, NOTTINGHAM, NG16 2ED.
MINSHALL, Mrs. Natalie Michelle, BA ACA *2008;* 18 Yorkville Avenue, Apt.1105, TORONTO M4W 3Y8, ON, CANADA.
MINSHALL, Mr. Rehman John, BSc ACA *2008;* 19 Chestnut Grove, Barnton, NORTHWICH, CHESHIRE, CW8 4ST.
MINSHALL, Mr. Simon, LLB ACA *1993;* Half Moon House, Jevington Place, Knotty Green, BEACONSFIELD, BUCKINGHAMSHIRE, HP9 2TN.
MINSHALL, Mr. Simon Clifford, BSc FCA *1978;* 9A Parkvale Drive, Discovery Bay, DISCOVERY BAY, NEW TERRITORIES, HONG KONG SAR.
•MINSHAW, Mr. David Charles, FCA *1972;* David C. Minshaw, 3501 Parkside, 88 Queensway, ADMIRALTY, HONG KONG ISLAND, HONG KONG SAR.
MINSHULL, Mrs. Andrea, BA ACA *1993;* (Tax Fac), Finlay Robertson, 5th Floor Brook House, 77 Fountain Street, MANCHESTER, M2 2EE.
MINSHULL, Mr. William Travers Gordon, MA FCA *1970;* 52 Archers Court, Castle Street, SALISBURY, SP1 3WE. (Life Member)
MINSKY, Mr. Andrew, BSc ACA *2010;* 19 Deacons Hill Road, Elstree, BOREHAMWOOD, HERTFORDSHIRE, WD6 3HY.
MINSON, Ms. Ann Louise, MA ACA *1995;* (Tax Fac), 6 Gorse Road, Reydon, SOUTHWOLD, SUFFOLK, IP18 6NQ.
MINTER, Mr. Andrew James, BA ACA *1992;* 12 Trafalgar Avenue, BROXBOURNE, EN10 7DX.
MINTER, Mr. Christopher John, MA FCA *1994;* Purkis House, Lower Farm Road, Borley Green, SUDBURY, SUFFOLK, CO10 7AG.
MINTER, Mr. Ivan William, FCA *1968;* 3 Bulls Cross, ENFIELD, MIDDLESEX, EN2 9HE.
MINTERN, Mr. Andrew Haydn, BA ACA *1985;* 63 Trinity Church Square, LONDON, SE1 4HT.
MINTO, Mr. Dylan Paul, BA ACA *2007;* Flat 37 New Atlas Wharf, 3 Arnhem Place, LONDON, E14 3SS.
MINTOFT, Mrs. Gillian Mary, ACA *1991;* 11 Topstreet Way, HARPENDEN, HERTFORDSHIRE, AL5 5TU.
•MINTON, Mr. Brian Arthur, BSc(Econ) FCA *1976;* (Tax Fac), Davies Williams, 21 St. Andrews Crescent, CARDIFF, CF10 3DB. See also DW Consultancy Services Ltd
MINTON, Mr. Howard Mark, BA FCA *1980;* 5 Bayford Lodge, Wellington Road, PINNER, HA5 4NJ.
•MINTON, Mr. James William, ACA *1981;* J.W. Minton & Co., 103a High Street, Lees, OLDHAM, OL4 4LY.
MINTON, Mr. Paul Andrew, BA ACA *1993;* 107 Raymond Street, DARIEN, CT 06820, UNITED STATES.
MINTY, Mr. Damian Alan, BSc ACA *1999;* Flat 3, The Choirs, 249 Marsland Road, SALE, CHESHIRE, M33 7UJ.
MINTY, Mr. Robert Donald, BA ACA *2006;* 26 Clos de L'Abri, La Grande Route de la Cote, St. Clement, JERSEY, JE2 6GW.
•MINTY, Mr. Robert Francis, FCA *1974;* 24 Old London Road, Wheatley, OXFORD, OX33 1YW.
MINTZ, Mr. Jonathan, BSc ACA *1995;* McBains Cooper Consulting Ltd, 120 Old Broad Street, LONDON, EC2N 1AR.
MINTZ, Mr. Norman, FCA *1977;* 125 Dollis Road, Mill Hill, LONDON, NW7 1JX.
•MINUS, Mr. Mark Ernest James, BA FCA *1990;* Spain Brothers & Co, 29 Manor Road, FOLKESTONE, KENT, CT20 2SE.
MIOTLA, Mr. Jacek Antoni, BSc FCA *1992;* 29 Wimbledon Road, BRISTOL, BS6 7YA.
MIR, Mr. Nouman Aziz, BCom ACA FCCA *2006;* PO Box 213311, Dubai Group (Dubai Holding), DUBAI, UNITED ARAB EMIRATES.
MIR, Mr. Syed Ahmed Tariq, FCA *1970;* 8 Park Way, Burnt Oak, EDGWARE, MIDDLESEX, HA8 5EZ. (Life Member)
MIRABAUD, Mrs. Susan Jane, BA FCA *1977;* 100 High Street, LEWES, BN7 1XH.
•MIRAJ, Mr. Ahsan, FCA *1999;* Bright Grahame Murray, 131 Edgware Road, LONDON, W2 2AP.
MIRAJ, Mr. Mohammad Ali, BSc ACA *2000;* I N G Syndicated Finance, 60 London Wall, LONDON, EC2M 5TQ.
MIRANDA, Mrs. Jaymini, BCom ACA *1993;* 2 The Mount, WEYBRIDGE, SURREY, KT13 9LT.
MIRCHANDANI, Mr. Dayal Ramchand, FCA *1966;* 401 Lamour Apartments, Turner Road Bandra West, MUMBAI 400050, MAHARASHTRA, INDIA. (Life Member)
MIRCHANDANI, Mr. Kishore Hiranand, BSc FCA *1976;* 845 UN Plaza, NEW YORK, NY 10017, UNITED STATES.
MIRCHANDANI, Miss. Shobha Vasdev, BA ACA *1999;* 114 King Henrys Road, LONDON, NW3 3SN.
MIRFIELD, Mr. Thomas, ACA *2007;* 4 Priory Road, LONDON, W4 5JB.
MIRFIN, Mr. Alexander Robert, ACA *2008;* Phipps Henson McAllister, 4 South Bar Street, BANBURY, OXFORDSHIRE, OX16 9AA.
MIRFIN, Mr. Stephen Darren, ACA *1993;* 17 Scholes Moor Road, Scholes, HOLMFIRTH, HD9 1SR.
MIRIYALA, Mr. Ramalingam, FCA *1972;* PO Box 28237, DUBAI, UNITED ARAB EMIRATES. (Life Member)
MIRLACH, Mr. Michael, BA(Hons) ACA *2010;* Flat 520, Baltic Quay, 1 Sweden Gate, LONDON, SE16 7TG.
MIRO, Mr. Pierre Abdulkarim, FCA *1976;* Al Bakri Building Maadi Street, PO Box 3757, JEDDAH, 21481, SAUDI ARABIA.
MIRON, Mr. Neil, BSc ACA *1992;* 9 Beech Drive, BOREHAMWOOD, WD6 4QU.
MIROW, Mr. John Charles Henry, FCA *1982;* (Tax Fac), 13 Kingsley Avenue, Banstead Village, BANSTEAD, SM7 2JH.
MIRRINGTON, Mr. Charles Richard John, BA ACA *2002;* 16 West Way, Petts Wood, ORPINGTON, KENT, BR5 1LW.
MIRRINGTON, Mrs. Natasha Louise, BA(Econ) ACA *2002;* Stephenson Harwood, One, St. Paul's Churchyard, LONDON, EC4M 8SH.
MIRRINGTON, Mr. Stephen Andrew, BSc FCA *1976;* 52 Oak Lodge Tye, Springfield, CHELMSFORD, CM1 6GZ.
MIRZA, Mr. Ahsan, BSc ACA *2002;* with Fisher Corporate plc, Acre House, 11/15 William Road, LONDON, NW1 3ER.
MIRZA, Mrs. Andrea, BSc ACA *1998;* 74 Sunny Gardens Road, LONDON, NW4 1RY.
MIRZA, Mr. Boman Maneckji, FCA *1955;* Darayus 8-2-697-14/A, Road No12, Banjara Hills, HYDERABAD 500034, INDIA. (Life Member)
MIRZA, Mr. Farrukh Mahmud, ACA *1996;* 91-94 Saffron Hill, LONDON, EC1N 8QP.
MIRZA, Mr. Fayyaz Sarwar, ACA *1983;* Arabian Trading Supplies Ltd, P.O.Box 15694, JEDDAH, 21454, SAUDI ARABIA.
•①MIRZA, Mr. Hasan Imam, BA ACA *1991;* AG Associates, Cantium House, Railway Approach, WALLINGTON, SURREY, SM6 0DZ. See also CMB Partners LLP
•MIRZA, Mr. Hussain, FCA CPA *1966;* Hussain Mirza, 78 Crawford Terrace, New Rochelle, NEW YORK, NY 10804, UNITED STATES.
MIRZA, Mr. Kamran, FCA *1969;* PAKISTAN BUSINESS COUNCIL, M-02 Mezzanine Floor, Beaumont Plaza, 10 Beaumont Road, KARACHI 75520, PAKISTAN.
MIRZA, Mr. Kokab Raza, FCA *1972;* Almana & Partners, POBox 49, DOHA, QATAR.
MIRZA, Mr. Mohammed Anwer, BA ACA *2004;* Flat 1, 8 Blackdown Close, East Finchley, LONDON, N2 8JF.
MIRZA, Mr. Omar, MEng ACA *2005;* 256 Franklin Road, Bournville, BIRMINGHAM, B30 2EJ.
MIRZA, Mr. Rizwan-ul-Haque, MA(Oxon) ACA ATT IMC *2009;* 5 Baldry Gardens, LONDON, SW16 3DL.
MIRZA, Mrs. Romana, BA ACA *1992;* 309 Bramhall Lane South, Bramhall, STOCKPORT, CHESHIRE, SK7 3DW.
MIRZA, Mr. Safeer-Ur-Rehman, MBA ACA FCMA CFA *1992;* Corporate Treasury (MS 3), Cargill Inc, 15407 McGinty Road West, WAYZATA, MN 55391, UNITED STATES.
MISCAMPBELL, Mr. Alexander James, BA ACA *1991;* Level 2, H S B C, 8-16 Canada Square, LONDON, E14 5HQ.
MISCAMPBELL, Mrs. Catherine Elizabeth, BSc ACA *1992;* 40 Princedale Road, LONDON, W11 4NL.
MISCAMPBELL, Mr. Ian Alexander Francis, BA FCA *1988;* Long Meadow, 22 Mill Road, Slapton, LEIGHTON BUZZARD, BEDFORDSHIRE, LU7 9BT.
MISCHEL, Miss. Nicola Sara, BSc ACA *1998;* Gates Engineering Co Ltd, Sway Road Garage, Sway Road, BROCKENHURST, HAMPSHIRE, SO42 7SH.
MISKIMMIN, Mr. Stewart, FCA *1969;* 54 Minster Road, GODALMING, GU7 1SR.
MISKIN, Mr. Andrew Edward, BSc ACA *2001;* 41 Alford Close, SANDHURST, GU47 8DX.
MISKIN, Mr. Edgar, FCA *1952;* 412 South Willaman DR#402, LOS ANGELES, CA 90048, UNITED STATES. (Life Member)
•MISKIN, Mr. Warren David, BSc FCA *1977;* Warren D Miskin, 2 Forest Close, Snaresbrook, LONDON, E11 1PY.
MISRA, Mr. Ashutosh, BSc ACA *1989;* 62 Borough Road, LONDON, SE1 1DZ.
MISRA, Mr. Madhav, FCA *1975;* 233 Eldridge Avenue, MILL VALLEY, CA 94941, UNITED STATES.
MISSELBROOK, Mr. John, FCA *1973;* Flat 41 Burghley House, Somerset Road, LONDON, SW19 5JB.
•MISSEN, Mr. David Christopher, BA FCA CTA TEP *1983;* (Tax Fac), Larking Gowen, Summerhill House, 1 Sculthorpe Road, FAKENHAM, NORFOLK, NR21 9HA.
MISSON, Mrs. Rachel Lorna, BMus ACA *1982;* Spring Farm, Warwick Road, STRATFORD-UPON-AVON, CV37 0PZ.
•MIST, Mr. John William James, FCA *1971;* Matthews Mist & Co, Westbury House, 14 Bellevue Road, SOUTHAMPTON, SO15 2AY.
MISTREE, Mr. Khojeste Pudam, MA(Oxon) FCA *1973;* K. R. Cama Oriental Institute Bldg., Ground Floor, 136 Bombay Samachar Marg, MUMBAI 400 023, MAHARASHTRA, INDIA.
MISTRI, Mr. Jehangir D, MA ACA *1982;* J.D. Mistri, 701 Sharda Chambers, 15 New Marine Lines, MUMBAI 400 020, MAHARASHTRA, INDIA.
MISTRY, Mr. Amit, BSc ACA *2009;* 52 Romway Road, LEICESTER, LE5 5SA.
MISTRY, Miss. Aneetaben, BSc ACA *2006;* 10 Repton Road, Kenton, HARROW, HA3 9QD.
MISTRY, Mr. Anil Gopal, BA FCA *1989;* Windrush Gullet Lane, Kirby Muxloe, LEICESTER, LE9 2BL.
MISTRY, Ms. Anjna, BA(Econ) ACA *2001;* 77 Dacre Park, LONDON, SE13 5BX.
MISTRY, Mr. Anup Ramniklal, MChem ACA CTA *2007;* 46 Byewaters, WATFORD, WD18 8WJ.
MISTRY, Mr. Binoy Shashikant, BA ACA *2005;* 16 Lulworth Gardens, HARROW, MIDDLESEX, HA2 9NP.
•MISTRY, Mr. Burjor Jehangir, FCA *1977;* B J Mistry & Co, Flat 7, Hanover Court, 112-116 Bessborough Road, HARROW, MIDDLESEX HA1 3DU.
MISTRY, Mr. Chetan, ACA *2008;* 12 Ozonia Avenue, WICKFORD, SS12 0PF.
MISTRY, Mr. Chetan Champaklal, BA ACA *1995;* 8 Furlong Lane, POULTON-LE-FYLDE, LANCASHIRE, FY6 7HQ.
MISTRY, Mr. Dara, LLM FCA *1964;* C P 154, 19, CH-1211 GENEVA, SWITZERLAND. (Life Member)
MISTRY, Mr. Dev, ACA *2011;* Flat 3, 40 Mapesbury Road, LONDON, NW2 4JD.
MISTRY, Mr. Dharmendra Jamiyatlal, MEng ACA *1994;* 41 Mount Drive, HARROW, HA2 7RW.
MISTRY, Mr. Dharmesh, ACA *2008;* 2 Medway Crescent, ALTRINCHAM, CHESHIRE, WA14 4UB.
MISTRY, Mr. Dinshaw Maneck, FCA *1952;* Sethna Building, Nowroji Seth Street, Thakurd War, MUMBAI 400002, MAHARASHTRA, INDIA. (Life Member)
MISTRY, Mr. Diwyang Champaklal, BSc FCA *1990;* 18 Shenley Hill, RADLETT, HERTFORDSHIRE, WD7 7BB.
MISTRY, Mr. Garry, MEng ACA *2003;* 30 Highfield Grove, BRISTOL, BS7 8QH.
•MISTRY, Mr. Gulabrai, BSc FCA *1978;* (Tax Fac), Mistry Accountants Ltd, 89 B & C Far Gosford Street, Gosford Green, COVENTRY, CV1 5EA.
•MISTRY, Mr. Harish Bhagwanji, ACA *1978;* (Tax Fac), H B Mistry & Co Limited, Tudor House, Mill Lane, Calcot, READING, RG31 7RS.
•MISTRY, Mr. Harishkumar, BSc FCA *1991;* 8 Sandringham Gardens, Barkingside, ILFORD, ESSEX, IG6 1NY.
MISTRY, Miss. Janita Jayantilal, BA ACA *2010;* Delancey Group Plc, 6th Floor, Lansdowne House, 57 Berkeley Square, LONDON, W1J 6ER.
MISTRY, Mr. Jason, ACA *2009;* Harper Collins Publishers Elsinore House, 77 Fulham Palace Road, LONDON, W6 8JB.
MISTRY, Mr. Jay, BCom ACA *2000;* 242 Walstead Road, Delves, WALSALL, WEST MIDLANDS, WS5 4DP.
MISTRY, Mr. Jayesh, BSc ACA *1998;* with PricewaterhouseCoopers LLP, Cornwall Court, 19 Cornwall Street, BIRMINGHAM, B3 2DT.
MISTRY, Mr. Jaykumar Vijay, BSc ACA *2007;* Flat 5 Stafford House, 9 Scott Avenue, Putney, LONDON, SW15 3PA.
MISTRY, Miss. Jyoti, BA FCA *1990;* (Tax Fac), PricewaterhouseCoopers Place, Stand No 2374, Thabo Mbeki Road, P O Box 30942, LUSAKA, ZAMBIA.
MISTRY, Mr. Kaikobad Behram, FCA *1986;* Bayer Cropscience Ltd, Bayer House, Central Avenue, Hiranandani Gardens, MUMBAI 400 076, MAHARASHTRA INDIA.
MISTRY, Mr. Kamleshkumar, BSc ACA *1993;* 4 Kettlebrook Road, Shirley, SOLIHULL, WEST MIDLANDS, B90 4YL.
•MISTRY, Mr. Kantilal Dhanjibhai, FCA *1980;* K.D. Mistry & Co, 70 Station Road, NORTH HARROW, MIDDLESEX, HA2 7SJ.
•MISTRY, Mr. Kirit Ratanji, BSc ACA *1988;* PKF (UK) LLP, Farringdon Place, 20 Farringdon Road, LONDON, EC1M 3AP.
MISTRY, Mrs. Mala, BSc ACA *2005;* 13 Bedford Road, HARROW, MIDDLESEX, HA1 4LY.
•MISTRY, Mr. Narendrakumar Narendrakumar, BA FCA *1985;* (Tax Fac), 45 Exeter Road, HARROW, MIDDLESEX, HA2 9PW. See also Daniel Auerbach & Company LLP
MISTRY, Mr. Nareshkumar, BA ACA *1991;* 51 Winton Crescent, Croxley Green, RICKMANSWORTH, HERTFORDSHIRE, WD3 3QX.
MISTRY, Mrs. Neela, ACA *1994;* 67 Ferncroft Avenue, RUISLIP, MIDDLESEX, HA4 9JE.
MISTRY, Mrs. Nimita, BSc ACA *2007;* Flat 5, Stafford House, 9 Scott Avenue, LONDON, SW15 3PA.
MISTRY, Mr. Nitesh, BSc ACA *1998;* 8 Kingswood Park, LONDON, N3 1UG.
MISTRY, Mr. Phenil, BSc(Econ) ACA *2002;* 36 Fauna Close, STANMORE, MIDDLESEX, HA7 4PX.
MISTRY, Miss. Poonam, ACA *2009;* 3 Thornton Drive, Narborough, LEICESTER, LE19 2GX.
MISTRY, Mr. Pramod, BSc ACA *2009;* 1 Undine Road, LONDON, E14 9UW.
MISTRY, Mrs. Purvi, BSc ACA *1998;* 9F Villa Elegance, 1 Robinson Road, MID LEVELS, HONG KONG SAR.
MISTRY, Mrs. Raheela, ACA *2009;* Walker Morris Solicitors Kings Court, 12 King Street, LEEDS, LS1 2HL.
MISTRY, Mr. Rajesh, BA FCA *1994;* 93 Leamington Road, COVENTRY, CV3 6GQ.
MISTRY, Mr. Ritesh, BSc(Hons) ACA *2001;* with KPMG, 10 Shelley Street, SYDNEY, NSW 2000, AUSTRALIA.
MISTRY, Mrs. Sangita, BA ACA *1997;* 8 Kingswood Park, LONDON, N3 1UG.
MISTRY, Mr. Sanjay Yashvantlal, BSc ACA *2002;* 23 Bramley Avenue, COULSDON, CR5 2DS.
MISTRY, Mr. Sharad Gopalji, BSc FCA *1979;* 1750 801-6th Avenue SW, CALGARY T2P 3W2, AB, CANADA.
MISTRY, Mr. Sunil Anilkumar, ACA *2008;* Laxmi Ltd, 43 Brisbane Road, ILFORD, ESSEX, IG1 4SP.
MISTRY, Mr. Tarunkumar Vallabhbhai, BSc ACA AMCT *1994;* Grant Thornton UK LLP, 30 Finsbury Square, LONDON, EC2P 2YU.
MISTRY, Miss. Trishna, BSc(Hons) ACA *2010;* 172 Cairnfield Avenue, LONDON, NW2 7PJ.
MISTRY, Mr. Umesh, BSc ACA *2004;* 2 Walsgrave Avenue, LEICESTER, LE5 6PU.
MISTRY, Mr. Umesh, BSc ACA *2003;* 213 The Parkway, IVER, BUCKINGHAMSHIRE, SL0 0RQ.
MISTRY, Miss. Vanisha, BA ACA *2004;* 235 Sternhold Avenue, LONDON, SW2 4PG.
•MISTRY, Mrs. Varsa, BSc FCA *1986;* Premier House, 112 Station Road, EDGWARE, HA8 7BJ. See also Mistry V. & Co
MISTRY, Mr. Vasant, ACA *1985;* Flat 15 Aura House, 39 Melliss Avenue, RICHMOND, SURREY, TW9 4BX.
MISTRY, Mr. Vijay, ACA *2011;* 2 Beadlow Road, LUTON, LU4 0QY.
MISTRY, Mr. Vikash Kumar Trikamdass, BSc ACA *1998;* 9 Floor, Villa Elegance, 1 Robinson Road, MID LEVELS, HONG KONG SAR.
MISTRY, Mr. Vinod Parbhubhai, MBA ACA ACMA *1994;* 184 Carlton Avenue East, WEMBLEY, HA9 8PT.
MITCALFE, Mr. Thornton Percival, FCA *1956;* Riverslea, 99 Merrybent, DARLINGTON, COUNTY DURHAM, DL2 2LF. (Life Member)
MITCHAM, Mr. Arthur David, FCA *1958;* (Tax Fac), The Old Schoolhouse, Cudworth, ILMINSTER, TA19 0PS. (Life Member)
MITCHAM, Mrs. Nicola Jayne, BA ACA *2005;* 22 Winsford Road, BURY ST. EDMUNDS, SUFFOLK, IP32 7JJ.

•**MITCHARD, Mrs. Shirley Anne, BA ACA** *1979;* 40 Cavalry Square, LONDON, SW3 4RB.
MITCHARD, Mr. St John Edward James, MA FCA *1984;* Little Orchard, 197 The Slade, Headington, OXFORD, OX3 7HR.
MITCHEL, Ms. Eithne Catherine, LLB BL ACA *2001;* (Tax Fac), 7 Stradbroke Road, LONDON, N5 2PZ.
MITCHEL, Mr. John Oliver, BEng ACA *1992;* 42 Cloudesley Road, LONDON, N1 0EB.
MITCHELL, Mr. Adrian Clifford, BSocSc ACA *1996;* The Granary, Mill Street, Packington, ASHBY-DE-LA-ZOUCH, LEICESTERSHIRE, LE65 1WN.
•**MITCHELL, Mr. Alan, FCA** *1970;* Clayton Stark & Co, 5th Floor Charles House, 108-110 Finchley Road, LONDON, NW3 5JJ.
MITCHELL, Mr. Alan Christopher, FCA *1981;* Apt 04-01 Beaverton Court, 45 Mount Sinai Rise, SINGAPORE 276958, SINGAPORE.
MITCHELL, Mr. Alan Patrick, BA ACA *1998;* 2 Sparkes Close, BROMLEY, BR2 9GE.
MITCHELL, Mr. Alan Robert, ACA *1981;* Hampsfell, 4 South Downs Road, Hale, ALTRINCHAM, WA14 3HU.
MITCHELL, Mr. Alan Shaun, BA FCA *1991;* Supacat Ltd, The Airfield, Dunkeswell, HONITON, DEVON, EX14 4LF.
MITCHELL, Mr. Alastair John, BSc ACA *1986;* Denley House, 2 Heath Hill, Heddon-on-the-Wall, NEWCASTLE UPON TYNE, NE15 0DQ.
MITCHELL, Mr. Alastair John, FCA *1988;* Linklaters, 1 Silk Street, LONDON, EC2Y 8HQ.
MITCHELL, Miss. Alison Marie, BSc ACA *1995;* 5 Cooba Street, CANTERBURY, VIC 3126, AUSTRALIA.
MITCHELL, Mrs. Andrea Michelle, BSc(Econ) ACA *1998;* Hewett Villa 16 Erpingham Road, LONDON, SW15 1BG.
MITCHELL, Mr. Andrew Buchanan, MA ACA *1994;* 30 Station Road, Scalby, SCARBOROUGH, YO13 0QA.
•**MITCHELL, Mr. Andrew Duncan, BA FCA** *1991;* with Dyke Yaxley Limited, 1 Brassey Road, Old Potts Way, SHREWSBURY, SY3 7FA.
MITCHELL, Mr. Andrew Fraser John, FCA *1977;* Felons Oak, 12 Redacre, Poynton, STOCKPORT, SK12 1DB.
MITCHELL, Mr. Andrew Geoffrey, BSc ACA *1992;* Powell Tolner & Associates, 29 Red Lion Street, CHESHAM, BUCKINGHAMSHIRE, HP5 1EJ.
•**MITCHELL, Mr. Andrew Ian, BSc FCA** *1996;* Walter Dawson & Son, Revenue Chambers, St. Peters Street, HUDDERSFIELD, HD1 1DL.
MITCHELL, Mr. Andrew Michael, MA ACA *1985;* 214 Croxted Road, LONDON, SE24 9DG.
•**MITCHELL, Mr. Andrew Robert, BA ACA** *1979;* Mitchell & Co, 13 Verran Road, Watchetts Lake, CAMBERLEY, GU15 2ND. See also Adams Mitchell
MITCHELL, Ms. Angela Maria, BA ACA *1984;* 1 West Road, SURREY HILLS, VIC 3127, AUSTRALIA.
MITCHELL, Ms. Angela Marie, ACA FCCA *2011;* Square Oast, Gatehouse Farm, Hunton Road, Marden, TONBRIDGE, KENT TN12 9SG.
MITCHELL, Miss. Anita Mary, BSocSc ACA *1998;* 22 Broom Lane, Chobham, WOKING, SURREY, GU24 8RQ.
MITCHELL, Miss. Ann Sarah, BA ACA *2007;* with KPMG LLP, St. James's Square, MANCHESTER, M2 6DS.
MITCHELL, Mrs. Anne, BA ACA *1984;* The Old Barn, 42 Church Street, Fordham, ELY, CB7 5NJ.
MITCHELL, Miss. Anne, ACA *1987;* 8 Douglas Close, Jacob's Well, GUILDFORD, SURREY, GU4 7PB.
•**MITCHELL, Mr. Anthony Eamonn, MA ACA** *1991;* (Tax Fac), A.E. Mitchell & Co, The Coach House, Fields Road, Chedworth, CHELTENHAM, GL54 4NQ.
MITCHELL, Mr. Arthur Edward, FCA *1953;* The Hallowes, 92 Hallowes Lane, DRONFIELD, S18 1UA. (Life Member)
MITCHELL, Mr. Arthur Siddle, FCA *1953;* Victoria Cottage, Weetwood Mill Lane, LEEDS, LS16 5NY. (Life Member)
•①**MITCHELL, Mr. Barry Gibson, BA FCA** *1969;* Barry Mitchell & Company, Pentre Farm House, Mamhilad, PONTYPOOL, NP4 0JH.
MITCHELL, Mr. Benjamin, ACA *2011;* 20 Ditchling Rise, BRIGHTON, BN1 4QL.
MITCHELL, Mr. Benjamin Henry John, BSc(Hons) ACA *2002;* 4 Kelman Close, LONDON, SW4 6JE.
MITCHELL, Miss. Beverley Ann, BSc ACA *1994;* 4 Station Road, Ebrington, CHIPPING CAMPDEN, GLOUCESTERSHIRE, GL55 6LG.
MITCHELL, Mr. Brian, FCA *1965;* Flat 88, Keverstone Court, 97 Manor Road, BOURNEMOUTH, BH1 3BZ. (Life Member)
MITCHELL, Mr. Brian Jack, FCA *1960;* Round Oak, Old Station Road, WADHURST, TN5 6TZ. (Life Member)
MITCHELL, Mrs. Carla Esther, BSc ACA *1992;* 67 Sandpit Lane, ST. ALBANS, HERTFORDSHIRE, AL1 4EY.
MITCHELL, Miss. Catherine, BSc ACA *2011;* 35 Kingfisher Drive, MARKET RASEN, LINCOLNSHIRE, LN8 3TH.
MITCHELL, Mr. Charles Basil, FCA *1961;* Maple House, Cann Lane North, Appleton, WARRINGTON, CHESHIRE, WA4 5NF. (Life Member)
•**MITCHELL, Mr. Christopher David, BA ACA** *1984;* (Tax Fac), C. Mitchell & Co, Deremar, 33 Faesten Way, BEXLEY, DA5 2JB.
•**MITCHELL, Mr. Christopher John, FCA** *1971;* Mitchells (UK) Ltd, St Michaels Mews, 18-22 St. Michaels Road, LEEDS, LS6 3AW.
MITCHELL, Mr. Christopher Moray, FCA *1972;* Esk Bank, Stile Road, TODMORDEN, OL14 5NU.
MITCHELL, Mrs. Claire, BSc(Hons) ACA *2001;* 942 Leeds Road, DEWSBURY, WF12 7QP.
MITCHELL, Mrs. Claire Helen, BA ACA *1999;* 17 Bishops Avenue, BROMLEY, BR1 3ET.
•**MITCHELL, Mrs. Clare Marion, BSc ACA** *1982;* C.M. Mitchell, 111 Wolsey Drive, KINGSTON UPON THAMES, KT2 5DR.
•**MITCHELL, Mr. Colin Stuart, BSc(Econ) FCA CTA** *1976;* (Tax Fac), C M Tax Consultants Limited, 95 Wellington Road North, STOCKPORT, CHESHIRE, SK4 2LP.
•**MITCHELL, Mr. Craig, ACA FCCA** *2009;* Browne Craine Associates Limited, Burleigh Manor, Peel Road, Douglas, ISLE OF MAN, IM1 5EP.
MITCHELL, Mr. David, BCom FCA *1973;* 66 Williams Way, RADLETT, WD7 7HB.
MITCHELL, Mr. David Bruce, FCA *1960;* 32 Mulberry Hill, Shenfield, BRENTWOOD, CM15 8JS. (Life Member)
•**MITCHELL, Mr. David Christopher, BA(Hons) ACA** *2003;* Mitchells (UK) Ltd, St Michaels Mews, 18-22 St. Michaels Road, LEEDS, LS6 3AW. See also Mitchells (Knaresborough) Limited and Barber Harrison & Platt
•**MITCHELL, Mr. David Edward, FCA** *1963;* Cherry Orchard, Hithercroft, South Moreton, DIDCOT, OXFORDSHIRE, OX11 9AL.
MITCHELL, Mr. David John, ACA *2009;* 9 Valley Gardens, Darrington, PONTEFRACT, WEST YORKSHIRE, WF8 3SL.
MITCHELL, Mr. David Kenneth, ACA *2008;* 2 Goodwood Close, Sadberge, DARLINGTON, COUNTY DURHAM, DL2 1WA.
•**MITCHELL, Mr. David Neil, BA FCA** *1987;* Entigy Ltd, Imperial Chambers, Prince Albert Street, CREWE, CW1 2DX.
•**MITCHELL, Mr. David Nigel, BA FCA** *1983;* (Tax Fac), Mitchells, St Johns House, Castle Street, TAUNTON, SOMERSET, TA1 4AY.
MITCHELL, Mr. David Stuart, BSocSc ACA *1998;* 24 Bright Street, Brighton East, MELBOURNE, VIC 3187, AUSTRALIA.
MITCHELL, Mr. David William, FCA *1974;* Room No 102 33/5 Visunee Mansion, Soi Nai Lert, Wittayu Road, Lumpini Patumwan, BANGKOK, 10330 THAILAND.
MITCHELL, Mr. Dean, BA ACA *1987;* Hunting Plc, 3 Cockspur Street, LONDON, SW1Y 5BQ.
MITCHELL, Mrs. Demelza Elizabeth, ACA *1982;* 19 Little Fryth, Hollybush Ride Finchampstead, WOKINGHAM, RG40 3RN.
•**MITCHELL, Mr. Derek James, FCA** *1971;* (Tax Fac), The Kings Mill Partnership, 75 Park Lane, CROYDON, CR9 1XS. See also Kingsmill Ltd
MITCHELL, Mr. Derek William, MSc BA FCA *1975;* Kiltoorish, Manor Avenue, Greystones, BRAY, COUNTY WICKLOW, IRELAND.
MITCHELL, Mr. Desmond Gerrard, BSc ACA *1984;* AI Global Investments sarl, 2-4 rue Beck, L-1222 LUXEMBOURG, LUXEMBOURG.
MITCHELL, Mr. Dominic Lopez, BA ACA *2002;* Le Vivier La Rue de la Viltole, Torteval, GUERNSEY, GY8 0PR.
MITCHELL, Mr. Douglas Esplin, ACA *1979;* 171-173 Edinburgh Road, Castlecrag, SYDNEY, NSW 2068, AUSTRALIA.
•**MITCHELL, Mr. Duncan James Edwin, ACA** *1995;* with CED Accountancy Services Limited, Unit 1, Lucas Bridge Business Park, 1 Old Greens Norton Road, TOWCESTER, NORTHAMPTONSHIRE NN12 8AX.
MITCHELL, Mr. Edward Allen, FCA *1962;* 49 The Park, Bookham, LEATHERHEAD, KT23 3LN. (Life Member)
•**MITCHELL, Mrs. Elizabeth, BA ACA** *2002;* Jackson Mitchell Limited, 5 Bell Lane, Syresham, BRACKLEY, NORTHAMPTONSHIRE, NN13 5HP.
MITCHELL, Mrs. Elizabeth Mary, BSc ACA *2004;* 8 Hatfield Drive, BILLERICAY, CM11 2NQ.
MITCHELL, Dr. Emily Victoria, MSc ACA *2005;* 11 Paddock Way, Laverstock, SALISBURY, SP1 1SJ.
MITCHELL, Mrs. Emma Louise, ACA *2005;* with Walker Moyle, Alverton Pavilion, Trewithen Road, PENZANCE, CORNWALL, TR18 4LS.
MITCHELL, Mr. Eric Edward, FCA *1969;* The Penthouse, 1st May Court, Triq il-Porzjunkula, QAWRA SPB1254, MALTA.
MITCHELL, Miss. Fiona Helen Louise, BA ACA *1991;* New Castle House, Castle Boulevard, NOTTINGHAM, NG7 1FT.
MITCHELL, Mr. Fred Debney, FCA *1952;* 60 Hall Lane, HARROGATE, HG1 3DZ. (Life Member)
MITCHELL, Miss. Gabrielle Sarah, BSc(Hons) ACA *2010;* 44 Belvedere Court, Alwoodley, LEEDS, LS17 8NF.
MITCHELL, Mr. Gareth Chamberlain, BSc(Hons) ACA *2001;* Challenger Limited, Level 15, 255 Pitt Street, SYDNEY, NSW 2000, AUSTRALIA.
MITCHELL, Mr. Gary James, BA ACA *1992;* The Old Vicarage, Church End, Haynes, BEDFORD, MK45 3QP.
MITCHELL, Mr. Gary Martin, BSc ACA *1986;* 35 Ledgate Lane, Burton Salmon, LEEDS, LS25 5JY.
•**MITCHELL, Mr. Geoffrey, FCA** *1976;* Geoff Mitchell, 40 Eastgate Street, BURY ST. EDMUNDS, SUFFOLK, IP33 1YW.
MITCHELL, Mr. Geoffrey Bentley, OBE FCA *1982;* (Member of Council 2001 - 2004), Flat 20, Swaylands, Penshurst Road, Penshurst, TONBRIDGE, KENT TN11 8DZ.
MITCHELL, Mr. George Anthony John, BA ACA *1980;* Diana Lodge, Thibet Road, SANDHURST, BERKSHIRE, GU47 9AR.
MITCHELL, Mr. George Benjamin, ACA *2011;* 10 Stag Hill, GUILDFORD, GU2 7TW.
MITCHELL, Mr. George Elder, BSc FCA *1975;* 3 Gandish Close, East Bergholt, COLCHESTER, CO7 6SZ.
MITCHELL, Mr. George Watt, BSc ACA *1986;* 51 Langdon Park, TEDDINGTON, MIDDLESEX, TW11 9PR.
MITCHELL, Mrs. Gillian L, BA ACA *1985;* The Old Hatchgate, Cockpole Green, Wargrave, READING, RG10 8NT.
MITCHELL, Mr. Gordon Philip, FCA *1970;* Charles Kendall Freight Ltd, Spur Road, FELTHAM, MIDDLESEX, TW14 0SL.
MITCHELL, Mr. Graham John, BA ACA *1992;* Henderson Industries Ltd, Teddington Controls, Daniels Lane, ST. AUSTELL, CORNWALL, PL25 3HG.
MITCHELL, Mr. Gregory Hayden, FCA *1970;* Rua Morgado De Mateus 290, Apartamento 71, Vila Mariana, SAO PAULO, 04015-050, BRAZIL. (Life Member)
MITCHELL, Miss. Hannah Rachel, ACA *2006;* with Deloitte LLP, 2 New Street Square, LONDON, EC4A 3BZ.
MITCHELL, Mrs. Helen Mary, BSc ACA *2003;* 1 Glenfield Cottages, Clyst St. Mary, EXETER, EX5 1BR.
MITCHELL, Mrs. Helen Rosemary, BSc ACA *1991;* 21 The Maltings, LIPHOOK, GU30 7DG.
MITCHELL, Ms. Hilary Jane, BA ACA *1992;* West House, 30 Southlands Mount, Riddlesden, KEIGHLEY, BD20 5HH.
MITCHELL, Miss. Hollie, ACA *2009;* 26a, Ballater Road, LONDON, SW2 5QR.
•**MITCHELL, Mr. Hugh Ralph, BA ACA CTA** *1991;* High Path VAT Consultancy, 14 High Path, WELLINGTON, SOMERSET, TA21 8NH.
MITCHELL, Mr. Ian Alexander, BSc ACA *2009;* with WSM Partners LLP, Pinnacle House, 17/25 Hartfield Road, Wimbledon, LONDON, SW19 3SE.
MITCHELL, Mr. Ian Bruce, BSc ACA *1991;* (Tax Fac), British Telecom, Bt Centre, 81 Newgate Street, LONDON, EC1A 7AJ.
MITCHELL, Mr. Ian Christopher, BA ACA *1993;* 10 Arrunden, HOLMFIRTH, HD9 2RN.
MITCHELL, Mr. Ian Christopher, FCA *1973;* The Norville Group Ltd Service House, Magdala Road, GLOUCESTER, GLOUCESTERSHIRE, GL1 4DG.
•**MITCHELL, Mr. Ian Douglas, BA FCA** *1976;* with Old Mill Accountancy LLP, The Old Mill, Park Road, SHEPTON MALLET, SOMERSET, BA4 5BS.
MITCHELL, Mr. Ian James, BSc FCA *1992;* The Royal Bank of Scotland plc, 280 Bishopsgate, LONDON, EC2M 4RB.
•**MITCHELL, Mr. Ian Randall, FCA** *1974;* (Tax Fac), Mitchell Meredith Limited, 34 High Street, BRECON, POWYS, LD3 7AN.
•**MITCHELL, Mrs. Jacqueline Lorraine, FCA** *1996;* Crowe Clark Whitehill LLP, Aquis House, 49-51 Blagrave Street, READING, RG1 1PL. See also Horwath Clark Whitehill LLP and Crowe Clark Whitehill
MITCHELL, Mr. James Ernest, FCA *1951;* Cantire, 2A Vale Street, Henstridge, TEMPLECOMBE, BA8 0SQ. (Life Member)
•**MITCHELL, Mr. James Russell Ian, FCA** *1972;* (Tax Fac), J R I Mitchell FCA, 44 Lucastes Road, HAYWARDS HEATH, WEST SUSSEX, RH16 1JP.
MITCHELL, Mrs. Jane, ACA *1989;* 15 Haslingden Close, HARPENDEN, HERTFORDSHIRE, AL5 3EW.
•**MITCHELL, Mr. Jason Michel, MBA BSc FCA** *1990;* HMT Assurance LLP, 5 Fairmile, HENLEY-ON-THAMES, OXFORDSHIRE, RG9 2JR.
MITCHELL, Mr. Jeremy Clyde, BSc ACA *1990;* 12 Malting Lane, Aldbury, TRING, HERTFORDSHIRE, HP23 5RH.
MITCHELL, Mr. Jeremy David Barraclough, FCA *1960;* Mariners, Maple Lane, Wimbish, SAFFRON WALDEN, ESSEX, CB10 2XG. (Life Member)
MITCHELL, Miss. Jo-Anne, BSc ACA *2006;* 15 Evergreen Lane, Silverglade, Fish Hoek, CAPE TOWN, WESTERN CAPE PROVINCE, 7975 SOUTH AFRICA.
MITCHELL, Mr. John, ACA *1980;* c/o 22nd Floor, Princes Building, CENTRAL, HONG KONG ISLAND, HONG KONG SAR.
MITCHELL, Mr. John Forbes, FCA *1969;* 3 Ennerdale Road, Stubbington, FAREHAM, PO14 2DS.
MITCHELL, Mr. John Gordon, FCA *1971;* Heather Hills, Crosswater Lane, Churt, FARNHAM, GU10 2JN. (Life Member)
•**MITCHELL, Mr. John Peter, FCA** *1982;* Winter Rule LLP, Lowin House, Tregolls Road, TRURO, CORNWALL, TR1 2NA. See also Francis Clark LLP
MITCHELL, Mr. John Stephen, BA ACA *1989;* Hawthorne Cottage, Winterbourne, NEWBURY, RG20 8BB.
MITCHELL, Mr. John Stuart, BSc ACA *1999;* Flat 5, 6 Millennium Drive, LONDON, E14 3GF.
MITCHELL, Mr. John Wallace, FCA *1957;* Whetherly House, 52 Shirley Drive, HOVE, BN3 6UF. (Life Member)
•**MITCHELL, Mr. Jonathan, BSc FCA** *1986;* Red Pillars, 183 Ashford Road, Bearsted, MAIDSTONE, ME14 4NE.
MITCHELL, Mr. Jonathan Lingley, BA ACA *1987;* 3 Fallowfield, Beyton, BURY ST. EDMUNDS, SUFFOLK, IP30 9BN.
MITCHELL, Mr. Jonathan Michael, BSc ACA *1997;* Flat 1 Flat 75 York Street, LONDON, W1H 1QF.
MITCHELL, Mr. Jonathan Niall, BSc ACA *1992;* 76 Chase Way, Southgate, LONDON, N14 5DG.
MITCHELL, Mr. Jonathan William, BSc ACA *1990;* 120 Addison Road, GUILDFORD, GU1 3QF.
MITCHELL, Mr. Joseph Gordon, FCA *1957;* 1 Sycamore Drive, Addingham, ILKLEY, LS29 0NY.
MITCHELL, Miss. Kandy Elizabeth, BSc ACA *1999;* British Monomarks Ltd Monomark House, 27 Old Gloucester Street, LONDON, WC1N 3AX.
MITCHELL, Mrs. Kate, BA(Hons) ACA *2000;* with PricewaterhouseCoopers LLP, Benson House, 33 Wellington Street, LEEDS, LS1 4JP.
MITCHELL, Miss. Katharine Ann, BA ACA *2002;* Chapel Cottage, Whelpley Hill, CHESHAM, BUCKINGHAMSHIRE, HP5 3RL.
MITCHELL, Mr. Keith Ian David, ACA *1984;* 76 Goldieslie Road, SUTTON COLDFIELD, B73 5PG.
MITCHELL, Mr. Keith Malcolm, BSc ACA *1984;* 27 Rossiter Road, LONDON, SW12 9RY.
MITCHELL, Mr. Keith Ronald, CBE FCA *1967;* Leaders Office, County Hall, OXFORD, OX1 1ND.
MITCHELL, Mr. Kenneth Rabey, BSc CEng ACA *1998;* 19 Davids Close, Alveston, BRISTOL, BS35 3LR.
•**MITCHELL, Mr. Kerr John, BA FCA** *1991;* Deloitte LLP, 3 Victoria Square, Victoria Street, ST. ALBANS, HERTFORDSHIRE, AL1 3TF. See also Deloitte & Touche LLP
•**MITCHELL, Mrs. Kerry Anne, ACA** *1993;* 61 Cecil Avenue, HORNCHURCH, ESSEX, RM11 2NA.
•**MITCHELL, Mrs. Lesley Joy, BA(Hons) ACA** *2001;* with PricewaterhouseCoopers LLP, Benson House, 33 Wellington Street, LEEDS, LS1 4JP.
MITCHELL, Miss. Lisa, BSc ACA *1994;* 328 Ormskirk Road, Rainford, ST.HELENS, WA11 7SP.
MITCHELL, Mrs. Lisa Jayne, BSc ACA *1996;* 3 Mill Close, Wolston, COVENTRY, CV8 3PA.
MITCHELL, Mrs. Louise Ann, BA ACA *1993;* 12 Johnston Green, GUILDFORD, GU2 9XS.
MITCHELL, Mr. Malcolm, FCA *1956;* 22 Morewood Crescent, WESTVILLE, KWAZULU NATAL, 3629, SOUTH AFRICA. (Life Member)
MITCHELL, Mr. Mark Ian Parry, FCA *1982;* INEOS AG, Avenue des Uttins 3, 1180 ROLLE, SWITZERLAND.
MITCHELL, Mr. Mark Kenneth, BSc ACA *1990;* 7 Bodmin Road, Springfield, CHELMSFORD, CM1 6LH.

MITCHELL, Mr. Martin, MSc FCA *1952;* 28 Orchard Avenue, Finchley, LONDON, N3 3NL. (Life Member)
MITCHELL, Mr. Martin Keith, FCA *1979;* J. H. Trease & Co, 26 Wilford Lane, West Bridgford, NOTTINGHAM, NG2 7QX.
MITCHELL, Mr. Martin Robert, BSc ACA MSI *1985;* 22 Tenison Avenue, CAMBRIDGE, CB1 2DY.
MITCHELL, Mr. Martyn John, BSc ACA *1982;* PO Box 4155, BALGOWLAH, SYDNEY, NSW 2093, AUSTRALIA.
MITCHELL, Mr. Matthew James, ACA *2008;* 1 Grand Stand, Scapegoat Hill Golcar, HUDDERSFIELD, HD7 4NQ.
MITCHELL, Mr. Max Anthony, LLB ACA *2000;* 56A Larkhall Rise, Clapham, LONDON, SW4 6JY.
MITCHELL, Mr. Michael, FCA *1969;* 99 Barnsley Road, Upper Cumberworth, HUDDERSFIELD, HD8 8NN. (Life Member)
MITCHELL, Mr. Michael Anthony Gammons, FCA *1967;* Hartside, Back Lane, Bucks Horn Oak, FARNHAM, SURREY, GU10 4LW.
MITCHELL, Mr. Michael Bruce, FCA *1970;* 586 Tena Place, VICTORIA V9C 1M7, BC, CANADA.
MITCHELL, Mr. Michael Horsfield, BA FCA *1974;* 7 The Laurels, Potten End, BERKHAMSTED, HP4 2SP.
MITCHELL, Mr. Michael John, BA FCA *1962;* 11 Chestnut Terrace, Charlton Kings, CHELTENHAM, GLOUCESTERSHIRE, GL53 8JQ.
MITCHELL, Miss. Michelle, BSc ACA MCT *2003;* with Deloitte Touche Tohmatsu, 550 Bourke Street, MELBOURNE, VIC 3000, AUSTRALIA.
MITCHELL, Mrs. Natasha Michelle, ACA *2009;* 17 Ringtail Close, Irthlingborough, WELLINGBOROUGH, NORTHAMPTONSHIRE, NN9 5GG.
MITCHELL, Mr. Neil Andrew, BSc ACA *2004;* 34 Calverley Lane, Horsforth, LEEDS, LS18 4EB.
MITCHELL, Mr. Neil Gordon, BSc FCA *1984;* Aszalvölgyi út 9-11, 8000 SZEKESFEHERVAR, HUNGARY.
•MITCHELL, Mr. Nicholas James, FCA *1981;* (Tax Fac), Mitchell Glanville Limited, 41 Rodney Road, CHELTENHAM, GL50 1HX.
MITCHELL, Mr. Nicholas John, BSc FCA *1987;* Middleton Hall, Old Hall Farm Main Road, Stoney Middleton, HOPE VALLEY, DERBYSHIRE, S32 4TN.
MITCHELL, Ms. Nicola Cecilia, BEng ACA *1994;* 13 Linkfield Lane, REDHILL, SURREY, RH1 1JF.
MITCHELL, Miss. Nicola Kate Mackay, BA ACA *2004;* 181b Leathwaite Road, LONDON, SW11 6RW.
•MITCHELL, Mrs. Nicola Marie, BA FCA *1992;* Deloitte LLP, 2 New Street Square, LONDON, EC4A 3BZ. See also Deloitte & Touche LLP
MITCHELL, Mr. Norman Frederick, FCA *1962;* 10 Broadstrand, Rustington, LITTLEHAMPTON, WEST SUSSEX, BN16 2EP.
•MITCHELL, Mrs. Patricia M.D, ACA CA(AUS) *2009;* (Tax Fac), The Counting House, Flat 64, Exeter House, Putney Heath, LONDON, SW15 3SX.
•MITCHELL, Mr. Paul, ACA *2008;* PM&G Limited, Mainwood Farm, Kneesall, NEWARK, NOTTINGHAMSHIRE, NG22 0AH.
MITCHELL, Mr. Paul, BSc FCA *1975;* Long Meadow, Snelson Lane, Marthall, KNUTSFORD, WA16 8SR.
MITCHELL, Mr. Paul, BSc(Hons) ACA *2002;* 53 Brierley Green, Buxworth, HIGH PEAK, DERBYSHIRE, SK23 7NL.
MITCHELL, Mr. Paul David, BA(Hons) ACA CTA *2000;* 43 Park Drive, HARROGATE, NORTH YORKSHIRE, HG2 9AX.
MITCHELL, Mr. Paul James, BSc FCA *1999;* 50 Mere Close, Bracklesham Bay, CHICHESTER, WEST SUSSEX, PO20 8AG.
•MITCHELL, Mr. Paul Kurt, FCA *1990;* 3 Glenwood, Nutshell Lane, Upper Hale, FARNHAM, SURREY, GU9 0FE.
MITCHELL, Mr. Paul Simon, BA ACA *2001;* 121 Rusthall Avenue, LONDON, W4 1BN.
MITCHELL, Mr. Paul Thomas, BA ACA *1978;* 127 Woking Road, GUILDFORD, SURREY, GU1 1QS.
MITCHELL, Mr. Peter Andrew, BSc ACA *1992;* 208 Cockayne Rd Ngaio, WELLINGTON, NEW ZEALAND.
MITCHELL, Mr. Peter James, MSc BSc(Econ) ACA *1998;* 39 Heol Pearetree Rhoose, BARRY, CF62 3LB.
•MITCHELL, Mr. Peter John David, FCA *1966;* MEMBER OF COUNCIL, (Tax Fac), Peter Mitchell & Co, 95 High Street, GREAT MISSENDEN, HP16 0AL.
MITCHELL, Mr. Peter Thomas, BSc FCA *1993;* 3 South View Road, Carlton, NOTTINGHAM, NG4 3QN.
MITCHELL, Mr. Peter William, FCA *1972;* Number 9, 2121-98 Avenue S.W., CALGARY T2V 456, AB, CANADA. (Life Member)
•MITCHELL, Mr. Philip, BSc ACA *1996;* Alvarez & Marsal Tax, First Floor, One Finsbury Circus, LONDON, EC2M 7EB. See also Alvarez & Marsal Transaction Advisory Group Europe LLP
MITCHELL, Mr. Philip John, FCA *1972;* 16 Hilltop Road, REIGATE, RH2 7HL.
MITCHELL, Mr. Philip John, MA FCA *1968;* Upper Flat, 13 Rectory Road, Barnes, LONDON, SW13 0DU.
•MITCHELL, Mr. Philip Ross, BSc FCA *1981;* Finers Stephens Innocent LLP, 179 Great Portland Street, LONDON, W1W 5LS.
MITCHELL, Mr. Philip William Lewin, FCA *1940;* 6 Phoenix Green, Norfolk ParkEdgbaston, BIRMINGHAM, B15 3NR. (Life Member)
•MITCHELL, Mrs. Prudence Gaynor, BCom ACA *1990;* Prue Mitchell, 130 Canford Cliffs Road, POOLE, DORSET, BH13 7ER.
MITCHELL, Mrs. Rachel Ann, BSc ACA *1988;* GP Batteries (UK) Ltd, Monument View Chelston Buisness Park, WELLINGTON, SOMERSET, TA21 9ND.
MITCHELL, Mr. Richard Bruce, BSc ACA *2000;* Small Dean, Chorleywood Road, RICKMANSWORTH, HERTFORDSHIRE, WD3 4EL.
•MITCHELL, Mr. Richard Paul, BCom FCA *1968;* R.P.Mitchell & Co, 81 Rochestown Avenue, Dun Laoire, DUBLIN, COUNTY DUBLIN, IRELAND.
MITCHELL, Mr. Robert George, BSc ACA *2011;* 17 The Spinney, LANCASTER, LA1 4JQ.
MITCHELL, Mr. Robert James, BA ACA *2001;* 7 Kodiak Springs Cove, COCHRANE T4C 0B6, AB, CANADA.
MITCHELL, Mr. Robert James, LLB ACA ATII *1986; (CA Scotland* 9 Sherwood Drive, HAYWARDS HEATH, RH16 1EW.
MITCHELL, Mr. Robert Stephen, ACA *2010;* 173 Lane Top, Linthwaite, HUDDERSFIELD, HD7 5SG.
MITCHELL, Mr. Robert Walter, FCA FCCA CTA *1976;* 54 Somerset Road, Edgbaston, BIRMINGHAM, B15 2PD.
MITCHELL, Mr. Roderic Wallace, FCA FCCA *1965;* Fairlands, Jack Haye Lane, Light Oaks, STOKE-ON-TRENT, ST2 7NG. (Life Member)
MITCHELL, Mr. Rory Matthew, MA ACA *1991;* Morledge House, Marston Montgomery, ASHBOURNE, DE6 2FF.
MITCHELL, Mr. Ross, MA ACA *2006;* 14 Brancaster Road, ILFORD, ESSEX, IG2 7ER.
MITCHELL, Mrs. S Jane, BSc FCA *1987;* 5 Laurel Way, AYLESBURY, HP21 7TW.
MITCHELL, Mr. Sampson Ross, MA ACA *1985;* Wood Mitchell Printers Ltd, Festival Way, STOKE-ON-TRENT, ST1 5TH.
•MITCHELL, Mr. Samuel William Ellis, ACA *2006;* Lambert Roper & Horsfield Limited, The Old Woolcombers Mill, 12-14 Union Street South, HALIFAX, WEST YORKSHIRE, HX1 2LE.
MITCHELL, Mrs. Sandra, BSc ACA *1987;* Denley House, 2 Heath Hill, Station Road, Heddon-on-the-Wall, NEWCASTLE UPON TYNE, NE15 0DQ.
MITCHELL, Ms. Sara Kwan, BEd ACA *1993;* Bishop Flemming, Stratus House, 1 Emperor Way, Exeter Business Park, EXETER, EX1 3QS.
MITCHELL, Miss. Sarah Ann, BA ACA *1987;* Kensey Foods, A Division of Samworth Brothers Limited, Pennygillam Way, Pennygillam Industrial Estate, LAUNCESTON, CORNWALL PL15 7AF.
MITCHELL, Mrs. Sarah Elizabeth, ACA *2008;* 24 Denholme Road, NOTTINGHAM, NG8 4GQ.
MITCHELL, Mrs. Sarah Elizabeth, BSc(Hons) ACA *2002;* Walnut Tree House, 3 Little Close, Stroud Road Bisley, STROUD, GLOUCESTERSHIRE, GL6 7BH.
MITCHELL, Mr. Sean Damian, BA ACA CTA *1998;* (Tax Fac), 2 Bentgate Close, Newhey, ROCHDALE, LANCASHIRE, OL16 4NB.
MITCHELL, Mr. Sean David, ACA *2008;* Flat C, 7 Middleton Grove, LONDON, N7 9LU.
MITCHELL, Mrs. Selina, BCom ACA *1994;* Kirkstalls, Perry Green, MUCH HADHAM, HERTFORDSHIRE, SG10 6DU.
MITCHELL, Mr. Simon John, BA FCA *1981;* Bunge London Limited, 38 Threadneedle Street, LONDON, EC2R 8AY.
MITCHELL, Miss. Stephanie Louise, ACA *2009;* 30 Yukon Road, LONDON, SW12 9PU.
MITCHELL, Mr. Stephen David, ACA *1981;* Vision Asset Management 5th Floor Devon House, 171 - 177 Great Portland Street, LONDON, W1W 5PQ.
•MITCHELL, Mr. Stephen Paul, FCA *1982;* Foot & Ellis-Smith, Abacus House, 68A North Street, ROMFORD, RM1 1DA. See also Foot & Ellis-Smith Ltd
MITCHELL, Mr. Steven Keith, BA(Hons) ACA *2001;* 1 Green End, WELWYN, HERTFORDSHIRE, AL6 9QF.
•MITCHELL, Mr. Stuart Ernest, FCA *1975;* (Tax Fac), Mitchell & Co, 143/147 High Street, NEWTON-LE-WILLOWS, WA12 9SQ.
MITCHELL, Miss. Susan, ACA *2011;* Lightfoot Farm, Lightfoot Lane, Higher Bartle, Fulwood, PRESTON, PR4 0AJ.
MITCHELL, Mrs. Susan Lynne, BSc ACA *1990;* (Tax Fac), 41 Deanhill Road, East Sheen, LONDON, SW14 7DQ.
•MITCHELL, Mr. Terence John, FCA *1964;* Terrence J. Mitchell & Co, PO Box 15025, HURLYVALE, 1611, SOUTH AFRICA.
MITCHELL, Mr. Thomas Andrew, BSc ACA *2007;* TDR Capital LLP, 1 Stanhope Gate, LONDON, W1K 1AF.
MITCHELL, Mr. Thomas James, ACA *2009;* 127 Woking Road, GUILDFORD, SURREY, GU1 1QS.
MITCHELL, Mr. Thomas Luke, ACA *2010;* 45A Station Road Ashley Down, BRISTOL, BS7 9LA.
•MITCHELL, Mr. Timothy John, BSc FCA *2000;* McLintocks, 2 Hilliards Court, Chester Business Park, CHESTER, CH4 9PX. See also McLintocks Ltd and McLintocks Partnership
MITCHELL, Mrs. Tracey Julia, ACA MAAT *1995;* The Granary, Mill Street, Packington, ASHBY-DE-LA-ZOUCH, LEICESTERSHIRE, LE65 1WN.
•MITCHELL, Mr. Trevor John, BSc ACA *1985;* Its Purely Financial Limited, Laurel Cottage, The Batch, Butcombe, BRISTOL, BS40 7UY.
MITCHELL, Mrs. Valerie Anne Maureen, ACA MAAT *2004;* Bracken House, Brookroyd Avenue, BRIGHOUSE, HD6 4BX.
MITCHELL, Mrs. Veronica Anne, FCA *1980;* 18 Cedarwood Avenue, INVERNESS, IV2 6GW.
MITCHELL, Mr. Victor James, FCA *1962;* 32 St. Johns Drive, WINDSOR, BERKSHIRE, SL4 3RA. (Life Member)
MITCHELL, Mr. Warren James, BSc FCA *1992;* Hooigaardestraat 26, 1800 VILVOORDE, BELGIUM.
MITCHELL, Mr. William George, BA FCA *1985;* 1 Holroyd Road, LONDON, SW15 6LN.
MITCHELL, Mr. William John, FCA *1951;* Toad Hole, Preston New Road, BLACKBURN, BB2 7AJ. (Life Member)
MITCHELL, Mr. William Thomas, FCA *1959;* 3 thornbury crescent, ETOBICOKE M9A 2M1, ON, CANADA. (Life Member)
MITCHELL, Mrs. Zoe Suzanne, BSc ACA *2002;* PMP Limited, Level 12 67 Albert Avenue, Chatswood, SYDNEY, NSW 2067, AUSTRALIA.
•MITCHELL-CLARK, Mr. Neil Antony, FCA *1983;* 3 Best Road, DURAL, NSW 2158, AUSTRALIA.
MITCHELL-INNES, Mrs. Constance Maureen, BSc ACA *1982;* Pinnacle Regeneration Group Ltd, Pinnacle House, 6 Hoffmans Way, CHELMSFORD, ESSEX, CM1 1GU.
MITCHELL-INNES, Mr. David Ian, MA *1963;* Woods Farm, Sutton-On-The-Forest, YORK, YO61 1DW. (Life Member)
MITCHELL-KNIGHT, Mrs. Fiona Candida, BA FCA *1992;* 15 Moorfoot Gardens, Lindsay View, East Kilbride, GLASGOW, G75 9GD.
•MITCHELL-ROSS, Mr. John Mark, BA FCA *1990;* PO Box 3600, ABU DHABI, UNITED ARAB EMIRATES.
MITCHELMORE, Mr. Daniel, BA(Hons) ACA *2001;* 2 Malham Close, Maidenbower, CRAWLEY, WEST SUSSEX, RH10 7JD.
MITCHELMORE, Mr. John Robin James, FCA *1964;* May-Rana, Rosemary Lane, Thorpe, EGHAM, TW20 8QF. (Life Member)
MITCHENER, Mr. Brian Edward, FCA *1970;* 15 Olivers Battery Crescent, WINCHESTER, SO22 4EU.
MITCHEV, Mr. Peter, BSc ACA *2011;* 18 Rope Street, LONDON, SE16 7TE.
MITCHINSON, Mr. John Howard, BA ACA *1983;* 3 Bronwen Terrace, HARLECH, GWYNEDD, LL46 2YS.
MITCHINSON, Ms. Laura Jane, MA ACA DChA *1998;* 7 Bramble Court, Pool in Wharfedale, OTLEY, WEST YORKSHIRE, LS21 1QW.
MITCHINSON, Mrs. Michelle Sandra, BSc ACA *1993;* 58 Langley Road, DURHAM, DH1 5LR.
•MITCHISON, Mr. Ralph Michael, FCA CF *1990;* Menzies LLP, Lynton House, 7-12 Tavistock Square, LONDON, WC1H 9LT.
•MITCHISON, Mr. Stephen, FCA *1981;* Menzies LLP, Ashcombe House, 5 The Crescent, LEATHERHEAD, KT22 8DY.
•MITCHLEY, Mr. John Anthony, FCA *1951;* J.A. Mitchley, 17 Frogs Hall, Bluntisham, HUNTINGDON, PE28 3XD.
MITCHLEY, Miss. Margaret Sybil, BA FCA *1980;* 14 Fenners Lawn, CAMBRIDGE, CB1 2EH. (Life Member)
MITFORD, Mr. Peter Vernon, FCA *1953;* 22 Merrybent, DARLINGTON, DL2 2LE. (Life Member)
MITHA, Miss. Aniskhatun Badruddin Ali, ACA *1980;* 225 Maweni Streeet, Upanga, PO Box 20598, DAR ES SALAAM, TANZANIA.
MITHANI, Mr. Ashit Dinesh, BSc(Econ) ACA *2002;* The William Pears Group, Haskel House 152 West End Lane, LONDON, NW6 1SD.
MITHANI, Miss. Priti Chimanlal, BA ACA *1993;* (Tax Fac), Doughty Hanson & Co, 45 Pall Mall, LONDON, SW1Y 5JG.
MITHANI, Mrs. Vinita, BSc(Econ) ACA *2001;* with Arram Berlyn Gardner, 30 City Road, LONDON, EC1Y 2AB.
MITILINEOS, Mr. Antonis, BA ACA AMCT *1997;* Ellinas House, 6 Theotoki Street, 1055 NICOSIA, CYPRUS.
MITILINEOS, Mr. Ioannis Andrea, BSc ACA FSI *1995;* U B S, 1 Finsbury Avenue, LONDON, EC2M 2PP.
MITKUTE, Miss. Grazina, ACA *2010;* Grosvenor Place, Level 8, 225 George Street, SYDNEY, NSW 2000, AUSTRALIA.
•MITRA, Mr. Alok Kumar, FCA *1978;* A Mitra & Co, 137 Cassiobury Drive, WATFORD, WD17 3AH.
MITRA, Mr. Gautam, MEng ACA *1995;* 30 North Colonnade, LONDON, E14 5GN.
•MITRA, Mrs. Jennifer Gwendoline, MA ACA *1981;* A Mitra & Co, 137 Cassiobury Drive, WATFORD, WD17 3AH.
MITRA, Mr. Monojit, BSc FCA *1989;* 2 Ladycroft Walk, STANMORE, MIDDLESEX, HA7 1PE.
MITRA, Mr. Partha, FCA *1978;* Lovelock & Lewes, Plot No Y-14 Block EP, Sector V Salt Lake Electronic Complex, Bidhan Nagar, CALCUTTA 700091, INDIA. See also Partha Mitra and PricewaterhouseCoopers Ltd
MITRA, Mr. Saurav, MPhil ACA *2003;* 2 Wilton Court, Sheen Road, RICHMOND, TW9 1AH.
MITRA, Mr. Tarit, ACA *1994;* 380 Jodhpur Park, CALCUTTA 700 068, INDIA.
MITSON, Mr. Alan Henry, BSc FCA *1975;* 9 Cheriton Field, Fulwood, PRESTON, PR2 3WH.
MITSON, Ms. Jane Victoria, BSc ACA *2000;* 88 Ashton Fitchett Drive, Brooklyn, WELLINGTON 6021, NEW ZEALAND.
MITTAL, Mr. Harsh, ACA *2011;* Flat 198 Ability Place, 37 Millharbour, LONDON, E14 9DF.
MITTAL, Mr. Manish, MSc ACA CTA *2000;* 36 Rosemary Drive, London Colney, ST. ALBANS, HERTFORDSHIRE, AL2 1UD.
MITTAL, Mr. Rajnesh Kumar, MSc BEng ACA *2005;* 60a Birmingham Road, WALSALL, WS1 2NH.
MITTEL, Mr. Ashish, MSci ACA *2006;* 48 Lulworth Avenue, HOUNSLOW, TW5 0TZ.
•MITTEN, Mrs. Mandy, FCA *1986;* Mitten Clarke Limited, Festival Way, Festival Park, STOKE-ON-TRENT, ST1 5TQ.
MITTEN, Mr. Patrick Anthony, BSc FCA *1982;* Ridings, New York Lane, Rawdon, LEEDS, LS19 6JJ.
MITTEN, Mr. Thomas, ACA *2010;* 33 Woodsend Road, Urmston, MANCHESTER, M41 8QY.
MITTER, Mr. Biswadev, FCA *1971;* Flat 2A Avani Residency, 21 Meghnad Saha Sarani, Southern Avenue, KOLKATA 700026, WEST BENGAL, INDIA. (Life Member)
MITTER, Mr. Joyshil, FCA *1973;* C9 Epsilon Yemlur Main Road, Off Old Airport Road, BENGALURU 560037, INDIA.
MITTIAS, Mr. Armia, FCA *1961;* 2105 Teeside Court, MISSISSAUGA L5M 3E7, ON, CANADA. (Life Member)
MITTON, Mr. Antony Edward, MA ACA *1993;* 33 Kemsing Road, LONDON, SE10 0LL.
MITTON, Mr. Benjamin John Guy, BSc ACA *2010;* 7 Lumiere Court, 209 Balham High Road, LONDON, SW17 7BQ.
MITTON, Mr. Charles Donald, BSocSc ACA *1985;* 3 Buttacre Lane, Askham Richard, YORK, YO23 3PE.
MITTON, Mr. Paul Robert, MBA BA ACA *1987;* The Manor House, 10 The Green, Freethorpe, NORWICH, NR13 3NY.
MITTON, Miss. Susan, LLB ACA *1996;* Hudson Clough Farm, Kebcote, TODMORDEN, OL14 8SA.
MIU, Mr. Hon Kit Thomas, ACA *2004;* Level 28 One Pacific Place, 88 Queensway, ADMIRALTY, HONG KONG SAR.
MIYAKE, Mr. Jun, MEng ACA *2000;* Ryan Tax Services UK Limited, Brettenham House Lancaster Place, LONDON, WC2E 7EN.
MIZEN, Mr. Jonathan Eric, LLB FCA *2001;* Mizen Consultancy Limited, 77 South Road, West Bridgford, NOTTINGHAM, NG2 7AH.
MIZIOS, Mr. Panagiotis, MSc ACA *2001;* Apartment 24, 12 Pond Street, LONDON, NW3 2PS.
MIZLER, Mr. Gary, BSc ACA *2010;* 11 Birley Spa Close, Hackenthorpe, SHEFFIELD, S12 4BY.
MIZON, Mr. Neil Richard, ACA *2009;* 72 Knowsley Road, NORWICH, NR3 4PS.
MIZZI, Mr. Alan Alfred, ACA *1986;* 2 Triq Il Fjorin, Victoria Gardens, SLIEMA, MALTA.

MIZZI, Mr. Kenneth Christopher, FCA *1970;* 11 Museum Esplanade, RABAT, MALTA.
MIZZI, Mr. Matthew James, LLB ACA *2002;* Via Monte Della Farina 50, INT. 3, 00186 ROME, ITALY.
MIZZI, Miss. Stephanie Ann, BA FCA *1990;* Square Enix Europe, Wimbledon Bridge House, 1 Hartfield Road, LONDON, SW19 3RU.
MO, Miss. Jenny Chun Lei, BA ACA *2006;* 25 Nassau Street Flat A 18th Floor, MEI FOO SUN CHUEN, KOWLOON, HONG KONG SAR.
MO, Mr. Jerry Yiu Leung, BSc FCA *1984;* 33 Ho Chung New Village, SAI KUNG, HONG KONG SAR.
MO, Mr. Tai Ling, ACA *2004;* Wing Hang Bank Limited, Internal Audit Division, Unit 1002, 10/F Eastern Central Plaza, 3 Yiu Hing Road, Shau Kei Wan CENTRAL HONG KONG ISLAND HONG KONG SAR.
MO, Mr. Wai Bun, ACA *2005;* Flat 2D Block 3, Academic Terrace, 101 Pok Fu Lam Road, POK FU LAM, HONG KONG ISLAND, HONG KONG SAR.
MOADDEL, Mr. Massoud, BSc ACA *1991;* Flat 3, 5 Lawson Close, LONDON, SW19 5EL.
MOAKES, Mr. Christopher John, FCA *1970;* Low Green, Loughrigg Meadow, AMBLESIDE, LA22 0DZ. (Life Member)
MOAKLER, Miss. Colette Josephine, BSc ACA *1992;* Barclays Bank Plc, 1st Floor Block 12, Radbroke Hall, KNUTSFORD, CHESHIRE, WA16 9EU.
MOAN, Mr. Liam Daniel Anthony, BSc FCA *1973;* 50 Baldwins Lane, Croxley Green, RICKMANSWORTH, WD3 3LR.
•MOATE, Mr. John Frank, FCA *1973;* D.B. Lye & Co, 34 Cheriton Gardens, FOLKESTONE, CT20 2AX.
MOATE, Mr. Keith Alan, FCA *1961;* Coltsfoot, Itchenor Road, Itchenor, CHICHESTER, PO20 7DD. (Life Member)
MOATE, Mr. Martin George, FCA *1991;* MacIntyre Hudson Llp, 30-34 New Bridge Street, LONDON, EC4V 6BJ.
MOATE, Mr. Roger Nicholas Martin, BA FCA *1972;* Hillcrest, Orchard Vale, Flushing, FALMOUTH, CORNWALL, TR11 5TT.
MOBBERLEY, Mr. Andrew George, BSc ACA *1988;* 111 Middle Harbour Road, LINDFIELD, NSW 2070, AUSTRALIA.
MOBBERLEY, Mr. Paul, FCA *1966;* 26 Leaholme Gardens, Pedmore, STOURBRIDGE, DY9 0XX.
MOBBS, Mr. Edgar Richard, FCA *1965;* Newnham Fields, Church Street, Newnham, DAVENTRY, NORTHAMPTONSHIRE, NN11 3ET. (Life Member)
MOBBS, Mr. Julian John Austin, FCA *1965;* Marlbrek, Barford Road, Marlingford, NORWICH, NR9 5HU.
MOBERLEY, Mr. Stuart Greville, FCA *1968;* Old Berrow Hill Farm, Berrow Hill Lane, Feckenham, REDDITCH, B96 6QL. (Life Member)
MOBERLY, Mrs. Angela, FCA *1961;* Old Tiles, Leigh Place, COBHAM, SURREY, KT11 2HL. (Life Member)
MOBERLY, Mr. William James Dorward, MA FCA *1963;* Old Tiles, Leigh Place, COBHAM, SURREY, KT11 2HL.
MOBIN, Mr. Muhammad Umar, ACA *2010;* Deloitte Corporate Finance Limited, Currency house Building 1 Level 5 DIFC, P.O. Box 282056, DUBAI, UNITED ARAB EMIRATES.
MOBLEY, Mr. Anthony John, FCA *1984;* 23 Sandy Lane, Charlton Kings, CHELTENHAM, GLOUCESTERSHIRE, GL53 9DF.
MOBLEY, Mr. Timothy Richard, MSc BA(Hons) ACA *2001;* Drey Coppice, College Road, BATH, BA1 5RR.
MOBSBY, Mr. Peter Michael Quinn, FCA MIMC DipPT IIST *1963;* Downs End, 113 Wodeland Avenue, GUILDFORD, SURREY, GU2 4LD.
MOCATTA, Mr. David William, BSc ACA *1988;* 15 Crestway, Roehampton, LONDON, SW15 5BX.
MOCATTA, Mr. John Edward Abraham, MA FCA *1962;* Bridgewater Lodge, Golf Club Road, Little Gaddesden, BERKHAMSTED, HP4 1LY.
MOCATTA, Mr. William Elkin, FCA *1976;* Sir Elly Kadoorie & Sons Ltd, St. George's Building, CENTRAL, HONG KONG ISLAND, HONG KONG SAR.
MOCHRIE, Mr. Ewan Campbell, BEng ACA *1991;* 51 Laburnum Park, BOLTON, BL2 3BX.
MOCK, Mr. Anthony William Sanders, BSc FCA *1975;* 21 Emlyn Road, LONDON, W12 9TF.
MOCK, Mrs. Patricia Mary, BSc ACA *1978;* 21 Emlyn Road, LONDON, W12 9TF.
MOCKERIDGE, Mr. Michael Peter, FCA *1964;* Amberley, Tilehurst Lane, Binfield, BRACKNELL, RG42 5JS.
•MOCKETT, Mr. Hugh Norman, FCA *1970;* Percy Gore & Co, 39 Hawley Square, MARGATE, KENT, CT9 1NZ.
MOCKFORD, Mr. Alan, BA ACA *2006;* 14 Crofton Close, WATERLOOVILLE, PO7 5LP.
MOCKRIDGE, Miss. Harriet Petherick, BA ACA *1990;* H M P Dartmoor, Dartmoor, Princetown, YELVERTON, DEVON, PL20 6RR.
MOCTON, Mr. Jonathan Joseph, BA ACA *1997;* 24 Cavendish Road, SALFORD, M7 4WW.
MODASIA, Mr. Bhaven Chandrakant, BSc ACA *2007;* 18 Lawson Gardens, Northwood Hills, PINNER, HA5 2EB.
MODASIA, Mr. Chandrakant Jivraj, FCA *1971;* Aval Jeev, 18 Lawson Gardens, PINNER, MIDDLESEX, HA5 2EB. (Life Member)
MODE, Mrs. Lorna Katherine, BSc(Hons) ACA *2001;* Pemby Oldlands Avenue, Balcombe, HAYWARDS HEATH, WEST SUSSEX, RH17 6LS.
MODHA, Miss. Alpa, BSc ACA *2007;* 15 Bradford Drive, EPSOM, SURREY, KT19 0AQ.
MODHA, Miss. Falguni, BSc ACA *2010;* 203 Whitton Avenue East, GREENFORD, MIDDLESEX, UB6 0QG.
MODHA, Mrs. Vanisha, BSc ACA *2005;* 104 Elms Crescent, LONDON, SW4 8QT.
MODI, Mr. Amanpreetsingh Harmindersingh, ACA *2008;* First Floor Flat, 32 Woodlands Road, HARROW, HA1 2RS.
MODI, Miss. Amira, MSc BSc ACA *2007;* 11 Charles Court, Larden Road, LONDON, W3 7DR.
MODI, Mr. Anant, BSc ACA *1994;* Flat 18, 9 Devonhurst Place Heathfield Terrace, LONDON, W4 4JB.
MODI, Mr. Anurag Kishore, BA ACA *2003;* 130 Britten Close, LONDON, NW11 7HW.
•MODI, Mr. Ashok Kumar GordhandasTulsidas, FCA *1974;* Andrew Murray & Co, 144-146 Kings Cross Road, LONDON, WC1X 9DU.
•MODI, Mr. Bharat Vallabhdas, BSc FCA CTA *1984;* Modi & Co Ltd, 27 High View Close, Hamilton Office Park, LEICESTER, LE4 9LJ.
MODI, Mr. Hiren Shirish, BA ACA *1992;* The Pines, Links Road, Kirby Muxloe, LEICESTER, LE9 2BP.
MODI, Mr. Jamshed Rustom, FCA *1958;* 28 Glenora Crescent, BRAMPTON L6S 1E2, ON, CANADA. (Life Member)
MODI, Miss. Meera, BSc ACA *2011;* 28 Mostyn Avenue, DERBY, DE23 6HW.
MODI, Mr. Mitesh, BSc ACA *1986;* Flat 5 Dasuki Liberty Court, 16 Briardale Gardens, LONDON, NW3 7PP.
MODI, Mr. Montu Dashrathlal, MA(Oxon) ACA *2002;* P & O Ferries Ltd Channel House, Channel View Road, DOVER, CT17 9TJ.
MODI, Mr. Phiroze Jal, BSc FCA *1962;* The Imperial Jute Press Pvt Ltd, 12 Dalhousie Square, CALCUTTA 700 001, INDIA. (Life Member)
MODI, Mr. Rahul, MEng ACA *2002;* 3rd Floor Marketing, RasGas Company Limited, PO Box 24200, DOHA, QATAR.
MODI, Mr. Rajul Kishore, BA FCA *1993;* 26 Spencer Walk, Chorleywood, RICKMANSWORTH, HERTFORDSHIRE, WD3 4EE.
MODI, Mr. Sailesh, BA ACA ATII *1990;* 19 Coppice Walk, Totteridge, LONDON, N20 8BZ.
MODI, Mr. Soli Ardershir, LLB FCA *1959;* Flat No 5, Jami Lodge, 618 Jam-E-Jamshed Road, Parsi Colony, Dadar, MUMBAI 400014 MAHARASHTRA INDIA. (Life Member)
MODI, Mr. Sudhir Gordhandas, FCA *1973;* PO Box 3603, ST JOHNS, ANTIGUA AND BARBUDA.
•MODI, Mr. Suresh Dahyalal, FCA *1979;* S.D. Modi & Co, Windsor Chambers, 367a Bearwood Road, SMETHWICK, WEST MIDLANDS, B66 4DL.
•MODI, Mr. Umesh Jamnadas, BA ACA *1987;* (Tax Fac), Silver Levene LLP, 37 Warren Street, LONDON, W1T 6AD.
MODI, Mr. Vinodchandra Dahyalal, FCA *1970;* 38 Fairlawn Court, ANCASTER L9G 3S6, ON, CANADA.
•MODIRI HAMEDAN, Mr. Mehrdad, FCA *1982;* (Tax Fac), Modiri & Co, Tapton Park Innovation Centre, Brimington Road, Tapton, CHESTERFIELD, DERBYSHIRE S41 0TZ.
MODLE, Mr. Andrew Colin, BA ACA *1993;* Devonshire House School, 2 Arkwright Road, LONDON, NW3 6AE.
MODLEN, Miss. Alison Jane, BSc ACA *1992;* 65 Swithland Lane, Rothley, LEICESTER, LE7 7SG.
MODY, Mr. Cyrus, MA ACA MMus *2005;* Flat 58 Abbott's Wharf, 93 Stainsby Road, LONDON, E14 6JL.
MODY, Mr. Kiran, BA(Hons) ACA *2003;* 4 Kings Place, LOUGHTON, ESSEX, IG10 4PW.
MODY, Mr. Pheroze Rustam, FCA *1975;* 10W Navroze apts, 35 Bhulabhai Desai Road, MUMBAI 400026, INDIA.
•MOED, Mr. David Daniel, BSc FCA *1980;* David Moed, 8 Hart Grove, LONDON, W5 3NB.
MOEDER, Mrs. Dawn, MSc ACA *1999;* Lane Gorman Trubitt LLP, 2626 Howell 7th Floor, DALLAS, TX 75204, UNITED STATES.
MOEHLE, Mr. David, BEng ACA *2011;* 10 Les Jardins de la Chapelle, La Rue Au Blancq Grouville, JERSEY, JE3 9HR.
MOELWYN-WILLIAMS, Mrs. Clair Louise, BSc FCA *2001;* 6 Bracewell Drive, SHREWSBURY, SY3 6BU.
MOELWYN-WILLIAMS, Mr. Edward James, BCom ACA *2002;* 6 Bracewell Drive, SHREWSBURY, SY3 6BU.
MOFFAT, Mr. Anthony David, BSc ACA *1990;* Po Box 113156, DUBAI, UNITED ARAB EMIRATES.
MOFFAT, Sir Brian Scott, Kt OBE FCA *1962;* Springfield Farm, Earlswood, CHEPSTOW, NP16 6AT.
MOFFAT, Mr. David Cunningham, FCA *1966;* 17 Newbold Terrace, LEAMINGTON SPA, CV32 4EG.
MOFFAT, Mr. Ian Logan, BA FCA *1985;* 8 Morham Lea, EDINBURGH, EH10 5GL.
MOFFAT, Miss. Jennifer Elizabeth, BA ACA *2005;* 60 Old Gorse Way, Mawsley, KETTERING, NORTHAMPTONSHIRE, NN14 1GJ.
•MOFFAT, Mr. John Eskdale, BA ACA *2000;* Mann Judd Gordon, 24-26 Lewis Street, STORNOWAY, ISLE OF LEWIS, HS1 2JF.
MOFFAT, Miss. Lindsey Anne, BSc(Hons) ACA *2001;* 104 Rouncil Lane, KENILWORTH, WARWICKSHIRE, CV8 1FQ.
•MOFFAT, Mr. Mark William, BA(Hons) ACA *2001;* PricewaterhouseCoopers LLP, 1 Embankment Place, LONDON, WC2N 6RH. See also PricewaterhouseCoopers
MOFFAT, Mr. Richard John Crawford, BA ACA *1992;* Pullingers Barn Pullingers Farm, Hattingley Road Medstead, ALTON, GU34 5NQ.
MOFFAT, Mr. Robert Malcolm Unwin, BSc(Hons) ACA *2001;* 24 Lockharton Avenue, EDINBURGH, EH14 1AZ.
MOFFAT, Miss. Ruth, BSc ACA *1997;* 28 Racecourse Lane, NORTHALLERTON, DL7 8RD.
•MOFFAT, Mrs. Sheilagh, FCA *1970;* MEMBER OF COUNCIL, (Tax Fac), Moffat Gilbert, 5 Clarendon Place, LEAMINGTON SPA, CV32 5QL.
•MOFFAT, Mr. William, ACA CTA *1979;* (Tax Fac), Reid Moffat & Co Limited, 15 Niffany Gardens, SKIPTON, NORTH YORKSHIRE, BD23 1SZ.
MOFFAT, Mr. William Rae, BSc FCA *1984;* 3 Mossdale Road, Sherwood, NOTTINGHAM, NG5 3GX.
MOFFATT, Mr. Alastair James, MA ACA *1994;* Rose Cottage, Church Hill, Plaxtol, SEVENOAKS, KENT, TN15 0QB.
MOFFATT, Mrs. Alexandra Mary, BA ACA *2006;* 11 Golf Road, Hale, ALTRINCHAM, CHESHIRE, WA15 8AJ.
MOFFATT, Mr. Anthony Joseph, FCA *1959;* 10 Priory Court, BRIDGWATER, SOMERSET, TA6 3NR. (Life Member)
MOFFATT, Mr. James Murray, BA ACA *2005;* 1 Appold Street, Deutsche Bank, PO Box 135, LONDON, EC2A 2HE.
MOFFATT, Miss. Katharine Emma, BSc(Hons) ACA *2010;* 8 Morlais, Emmer Green, READING, RG4 8PQ.
MOFFATT, Mr. Melvyn John, ACA *1981;* 38 Lucknow Drive, NOTTINGHAM, NG3 5EU.
•MOFFATT, Mr. Michael David, BA ACA *1984;* David Moffatt, Windy Ridge, Station Hill, WIGTON, CA7 9BJ.
•MOFFATT, Mr. Robert Iain, BA FCA *1986;* KPMG LLP, 1 The Embankment, Neville Street, LEEDS, LS1 4DW. See also KPMG Europe LLP
MOFFATT, Mr. Simon Timothy, BSc ACA *1987;* 5 Great Auclum Place, Burghfield Common, READING, RG7 3ED.
•MOFFATT, Mr. Stuart, BSc ARCS FCA ATII *1979;* Stuart Moffatt, 53 Crestway, LONDON, SW15 5DB.
•MOFFATT, The Revd. Thomas, FCA *1975;* Thomas Moffatt & Co Ltd, 3rd Floor, The Sion, Crown Glass Place, BRISTOL, BS48 1RB.
MOFFET, Mr. David John, FCA *1973;* 58 Manton Drive, LUTON, LU2 7DJ.
MOFFETT, Mr. Carl William, BSocSc ACA *1999;* Ringtons Holdings Ltd, Algernon Road, Heaton, NEWCASTLE UPON TYNE, NE6 2YN.
MOFFITT, Ms. Katie Ann, ACA CA(AUS) *2009;* Cork Gully LLP, 52 Brook Street, LONDON, W1K 5DS.
MOFFITT, Mr. Peter, ACA CA(AUS) *2009;* Deutsche Bank, Winchester House, 1 Great Winchester Street, LONDON, EC2N 2DB.
MOGAN, Mr. Thomas, ACA *1990;* 108 Berkeley Road South, COVENTRY, CV5 6EE.
MOGANO, Mr. Stephen Carlo, BSc ACA *1985;* 95 West End Drive, CLECKHEATON, BD19 6JD.
MOGFORD, Mr. Robert Daniel, BEng ACA *1994;* 38 Forest Ridge, KESTON, KENT, BR2 6EQ.
MOGFORD, Mr. Stephen John, FCA *1970;* Oaklands, The Ridgeway, Sheets Heath Brookwood, WOKING, GU24 0EP.
MOGG, Miss. Catherine Rachel, BSc ACA *2006;* with PricewaterhouseCoopers LLP, 101 Barbirolli Square, Lower Mosley Street, MANCHESTER, M2 3PW.
MOGG, Mr. Jonathan, BA(Hons) ACA *2001;* 24 Brossa Street, 53134 WARSAW, POLAND.
MOGGERIDGE, Mr. James, ACA MAAT *2010;* 44 Leslie Road, RAYLEIGH, ESSEX, SS6 8PB.
MOGGRIDGE, Mr. Brian Roger, FCA *1976;* 2 Nymans Close, LUTON, LU2 8RP.
MOGHAL, Mr. Abdulmajid Ali Mohammad, FCA *1974;* 87 Ellison Road, LONDON, SW16 5DB.
•MOGILNER, Mr. Leonard, FCA *1969;* (Tax Fac), Leonard Mogilner & Co, 30 Leys Gardens, Cockfosters, BARNET, EN4 9NA.
MOGLIA, Mr. Geoffrey Graham, FCA *1955;* 3 Ringley Close, Whitefield, MANCHESTER, M45 7HR. (Life Member)
MOGLIA, Mr. Nicholas Julian, BA ACA *1985;* Zycko, Inda House, The Mallards, South Cerney, CIRENCESTER, GL7 5TQ.
MOGRIDGE, Mr. Christopher, MSc ACA *1995;* 9 Victoria Terrace, LONDON, N4 4DA.
MOHAMAD, Mr. Megat Iskandar Shah, BSc ACA *2005;* 5-2 Jalan Tunku, Bukit Tunku, 50480 KUALA LUMPUR, FEDERAL TERRITORY, MALAYSIA.
MOHAMAD, Mr. Mohamad Nor, FCA *1959;* 5-2 Jalan Tunku, 50480 KUALA LUMPUR, FEDERAL TERRITORY, MALAYSIA. (Life Member)
MOHAMAD, Mr. Mustamir, BSc(Econ) FCA *1999;* No 9 Jalan Ara SD 7/1B, Bandar Sri Damansara, 52200 KUALA LUMPUR, FEDERAL TERRITORY, MALAYSIA.
MOHAMED, Mr. Azman, BSc ACA *2004;* 72 Jalan Terasek 3, Bangsar Baru, 59100 KUALA LUMPUR, FEDERAL TERRITORY, MALAYSIA.
MOHAMED, Mr. Hamid Rizmy, ACA *1983;* Robert Walters, 55 Strand, LONDON, WC2N 5WR.
MOHAMED, Mr. Hussein, BSc ACA CF *2000;* with KPMG, Falcon Tower, 16th Floor, Al Nasr Street, PO Box 7613, ABU DHABI UNITED ARAB EMIRATES.
MOHAMED, Mr. Iqbal Shamsudin, BSc ACA *1979;* (Tax Fac), United Gulf Management Inc., 176 Federal Street, BOSTON, MA 02110, UNITED STATES.
•MOHAMED, Mr. Mohamed Abdel Halim, BA FCA *1955;* Mohamed Abdel Halim & Co, PO Box 1595, KHARTOUM, 11111, SUDAN.
MOHAMED, Mr. Mohamed Farah, BA FCA CISA *1982;* OryxGTL Finance, Dolphin Tower 708, DOHA, 22533, QATAR.
MOHAMED, Mr. Naveed, BSc ACA *1999;* 18 Bryngwyn Road, Cycnoed, CARDIFF, CF23 6PQ.
MOHAMED, Mr. Nurain, BSc ACA *2010;* 59 Cole Valley Road, BIRMINGHAM, B28 0DE.
MOHAMED, Mr. Rafique, ACA *2008;* Associated Newspapers Ltd Northcliffe House, 2 Derry Street, LONDON, W8 5TT.
MOHAMED, Mr. Ramli, ACA CA(NZ) *2009;* 4806 Jalan Bayam, 15200 KOTA BAHRU, KELANTAN, MALAYSIA.
MOHAMED, Miss. Sanaa, BSc ACA *2011;* 27 Church Road, LONDON, W7 3BD.
•MOHAMED, Mr. Sultanali Kassamali, FCA *1977;* (Tax Fac), Eskays & Co, 34 Bellfield Avenue, HARROW, MIDDLESEX, HA3 6SX.
MOHAMED ABD SALAM, Mr. Abdul Kadir, ACA *2011;* 22, Jalan 19/144 A, Taman Bukit Cheras, 56000 KUALA LUMPUR, MALAYSIA.
MOHAMED ALI, Mr. Afendy, BA ACA *2001;* Level 25, Tower 1, PETRONAS Twin Towers, 50088 KUALA LUMPUR, FEDERAL TERRITORY, MALAYSIA.
MOHAMED IBRAHIM, Mr. Abdul Samad, ACA *2008;* 11 Jalan BU 2/7, Bandar Utama Damansara, 47800 PETALING JAYA, MALAYSIA.
MOHAMED-YUSOFF, Mr. Izzuddin, BSc ACA *1999;* Flat 4, 1-6 Bateman's Row, LONDON, EC2A 3HH.
MOHAMED YUSOFF, Dato' Yusli, BA ACA *1988;* Bursa Malaysia Berhad, 14th Floor Exchange Square, Bukit Kewangan, 50200 KUALA LUMPUR, FEDERAL TERRITORY, MALAYSIA.
MOHAMMAD, Miss. Fazrina, BA(Hons) ACA *2004;* 12 Ashwell Place, WATFORD, WD24 5JX.

MOHAMMAD, Mr. Shah, FCA *1973;* (Tax Fac), 10 Dirdene Close, EPSOM, KT17 4AY.
MOHAMMAD, Mr. Syed, FCA *1961;* 6/1 A Street, Phase VI DHA, KARACHI, PAKISTAN. (Life Member)
MOHAMMAD NOR, Miss. Karina, BCom ACA *2003;* 202 3 9, Sri Suajaya Condominium, Jalan Sentul, 51100 KUALA LUMPUR, FEDERAL TERRITORY, MALAYSIA.
•MOHAMMADI, Mr. Majid, FCA *1980;* Benjamin Kay & Brummer, York House, Empire Way, WEMBLEY, HA9 0QL.
MOHAMMADPOUR, Mr. Masoud, BA ACA *2006;* Flat 3 West Point, Putney Hill, LONDON, SW15 6RU.
MOHAMMED, Mr. Ashfaq Ahmed, BSc ACA *1993;* 18 Bluebell Court, Ty Canol, CWMBRAN, GWENT, NP44 6JN.
MOHAMMED, Miss. Asma Batool, BA ACA *2007;* with PricewaterhouseCoopers LLP, 101 Barbirolli Square, Lower Mosley Street, MANCHESTER, M2 3PW.
MOHAMMED, Mr. Faris Mehdi Kadhim, BA FCA *1988;* 2 Brook Farm Road, COBHAM, KT11 3AX.
•MOHAMMED, Mr. Farouq, BA(Hons) ACA *2002;* Avicenna Consulting Ltd, 124 Yardley Road, Acocks Green, BIRMINGHAM, B27 6LG.
MOHAMMED, Miss. Ferhet Naseem, LLB ACA *2003;* 8 Roman Road, LONDON, N10 2NH.
MOHAMMED, Mr. Kaleem, ACA *2008;* 16 Torvill Drive, NOTTINGHAM, NG8 2BU.
MOHAMMED, Mr. Khalil, BA(Hons) ACA *2006;* 6 Welbeck Road, HYDE, CHESHIRE, SK14 5PN.
MOHAMMED, Mr. Muzamal, BSc(Hons) ACA *2004;* 29 Forest Edge, BUCKHURST HILL, ESSEX, IG9 5AD.
MOHAMMED, Mr. Shahid Anwar, ACA *2008;* 247 Kings Road, Chorlton cum Hardy, MANCHESTER, M21 0XG.
MOHAMMED, Mrs. Shamira, BA ACA *1992;* 3 The Broadway, Oadby, LEICESTER, LE2 2HD.
MOHAMMED, Mr. Sohail, BA ACA *2005;* with Deloitte LLP, 2 New Street Square, LONDON, EC4A 3BZ.
MOHAMMED, Miss. Tarwa, BA ACA *2006;* COUCH BRIGHT KING & CO, LONDON, WC1E 6AB.
MOHAMMED SHARIFF, Mr. Zahar Bin, FCA *1970;* 33 Persiaran, Burhanuddin Helmi, Taman Tun Dr Ismail, 60000 KUALA LUMPUR, FEDERAL TERRITORY, MALAYSIA.
MOHAN, Mr. Aditya, FCA *1974;* State Street Global Markets 6th floor, State Street Financial Center, One Lincoln Center Box 5501, BOSTON, MA 02206, UNITED STATES.
MOHAN, Mr. Ajay Kumar, FCA *1974;* SwitzGroup, PO Box 29321, DUBAI, UNITED ARAB EMIRATES.
MOHAN, Miss. Binthu, ACA *2009;* 38 Wydehurst Road, CROYDON, CR0 6NG.
MOHAN, Mrs. Kalpana, BSc ACA *1998;* 3 Southcote Road, Sanderstead, SOUTH CROYDON, Surrey, CR2 0EQ.
MOHAN, Mr. Sreenivas, ACA *2011;* 801 Lemonade Building, 3 Arboretum Place, BARKING, IG11 7PX.
MOHAN, Mr. Sugrim, FCA JDipMA *1967;* 18 McPhillips Ave, MARKHAM L3P 1C3, ON, CANADA.
•MOHAN-DENNIS, Mrs. Sashikala, BSc ACA *2007;* with Crouch Chapman, 62 Wilson Street, LONDON, EC2A 2BU.
MOHAN RAJ, Mr. Prem Anand, BSc ACA *1997;* Brockton Capital Llp, 89-91 Wardour Street, LONDON, W1F 0UB.
MOHANKUMAR, Ms. Vijayalakshmi, ACA *2010;* 81 Grange Way, IVER, BUCKINGHAMSHIRE, SL0 9NT.
•MOHANLAL, Mr. Anil Amratlal, FCA *1983;* Kumar Strategic Consultants Ltd, 255-261 Horn Lane, Acton, LONDON, W3 9EH.
MOHANLAL, Mr. Hitesh Amratlal, BA ACA *1996;* 50 Balmoral Street, KURABY, QLD 4112, AUSTRALIA.
MOHANTY, Miss. Lucyann, BSc PgDL ACA *2010;* Flat 8 The Clock House, 83 Tweedy Road, BROMLEY, BR1 1RP.
MOHAZAB, Mr. Amir Abbas, BSc ACA *1995;* Marshaw, Boyn Hill Avenue, MAIDENHEAD, SL6 4ER.
MOHD HAIRI, Miss. Eznurein Suraya, BA ACA *2002;* 2 Lorong Masjid 3/69b, 46000 PETALING JAYA, Selangor, MALAYSIA.
MOHD HATTA, Miss. Noraida Maria, BA(Hons) ACA *2003;* 14 Jalan 1/5, Taman Tun Abdul Razak, 68000 AMPANG, SELANGOR, MALAYSIA.
MOHD HUSSIN, Mr. Khairuddin, BA ACA *2004;* B-28-6 The Plaza Condominium, Jalan Wan Kadir 3, Taman Tun Dr Ismail, 60000 KUALA LUMPUR, FEDERAL TERRITORY, MALAYSIA.
MOHD HUSSIN, Miss. Nadia, BSc ACA *2010;* B-28-6 The Plaza Condominium, Jalan Wan Kadir 3, Taman Tun Dr Ismail, 60000 KUALA LUMPUR, FEDERAL TERRITORY, MALAYSIA.
MOHD ILHAN, Miss. Fazlin Hanoum Binti, BSc ACA *2004;* 31 Jalan ss2/47, Selangor Darul Ehsan, 47300 PETALING JAYA, SELANGOR, MALAYSIA.
MOHD KAMALUDDIN, Ms. Diyana, BSc ACA *2011;* 77 Apollo Building, 1 Newton Place, LONDON, E14 3TS.
MOHD PERAI, Miss. Narimah, ACA *1981;* No 4 Jalan SS 19/3B, Subang Jaya47500, PETALING JAYASelangor, MALAYSIA.
MOHD ROHANI, Mr. Mohd Fadley, ACA *2010;* 32 Jalan SS19/1J, 47500 SUBANG, SELANGOR, MALAYSIA.
MOHD SHARIF, Mr. Mohd Adam, ACA *2010;* Flat 119 Quadrangle Tower, Cambridge Square, LONDON, W2 2PL.
MOHD TAHIR, Mr. Tajul Rahim, BCom ACA *1991;* No 21 Jalan BU 3/5, Bandar Utama, 47800 PETALING JAYA, MALAYSIA.
MOHD YUSOF, Mr. Nor Hisham, BA CA ACA *1997;* 1 Jalan Adda 1/9, Adda Heights, 81100 JOHOR BAHRU, JOHOR, MALAYSIA.
MOHD YUSOF, Miss. Shariza Sharis, BSc ACA *2000;* 19 Jalan 15/1, Taman Tun Abdul Razak, 68000 AMPANG, MALAYSIA.
MOHIDIN, Mr. Reza Jerome, ACA *2011;* Flat 7, Tower Court, 232-234 Ballards Lane, LONDON, N3 2LY.
MOHINDRA, Mr. Ashavani Kumar, BSc ACA *1984;* 12 Beaumont Road, Upper Norwood, LONDON, SE19 3QZ.
MOHINDRA, Mr. Chander Bhushan, FCA *1969;* 1214 Riverhaven Place, HOOVER, AL 35244-2557, UNITED STATES.
MOHINDRA, Ms. Lindsay Jane, MA ACA *1985;* 12 Beaumont Road, LONDON, SE19 3QZ.
•MOHINDRA, Mr. Manoj, FCA *1992;* (Tax Fac), Mohindra & Co, Finance Place, 9 Widecombe Gardens, ILFORD, IG4 5LR.
MOHINDRA, Mr. Neraj, MSc ACA *1998;* Crescent Lodge, Woodcote Park Avenue, PURLEY, SURREY, CR8 3NH.
MOHINDRA, Miss. Tesula, BA ACA *1991;* 1 Moncorvo Close, LONDON, SW7 1NQ.
MOHIT, Mr. Khiran Prakash, ACA *2011;* Flat 246 Bromyard House, Bromyard Avenue, LONDON, W3 7BN.
MOHIUDDIN, Mr. Aamir, BSc ACA *2006;* 4 Berrystead, Caldecotte, MILTON KEYNES, MK7 8LT.
•MOHIUDDIN, Mr. Mohamed Afzal, BSc FCA *1975;* Dean & Co, 48 Norbury Hill, LONDON, SW16 3LB.
•MOHMED, Mr. Esfak, BSc ACA *2004;* Aquarius Tax Consultancy Ltd, Atria Building, Spa Road, BOLTON, BL1 4AG.
•MOHYUDDIN, Mr. Asaf, FCA *1972;* c/o Arab Banking Corp, PO Box 5698, MANAMA, BAHRAIN.
MOHYUDDIN, Mr. Faiz, ACA CPA *2011;* 91 Quince Crescent, MARKHAM L35 3T2, ON, CANADA.
MOILLIET, Mr. James Andrew Keir, FCA *1966;* 25 Meadway, Bramhall, STOCKPORT, CHESHIRE, SK7 1JZ. (Life Member)
MOINI, Mr. Syed Abdul Rashid, BSc FCA *1963;* PO Box 41, DUBAI, Dubai, UNITED ARAB EMIRATES.
MOIR, Mr. Alistair David, ACA *1989;* Basingstoke College of Technology, Worting Road, BASINGSTOKE, HAMPSHIRE, RG21 8TN.
MOIR, Mr. Anthony George, BA FCA *1974;* 118 Grange Road, Olton, SOLIHULL, B91 1DA.
MOIR, Mr. Christopher Ernest, FCA *1976;* Clear House, 173a Kingston Road, NEW MALDEN, KT3 3SS.
MOIR, Mrs. Colleen Jane, FCA *1967;* Alwyne, Bulkington Road, Wolvey, HINCKLEY, LEICESTERSHIRE, LE10 3LA.
MOIR, Mr. David Lindsay, BSc FCA *1975;* 10218 Cedar Pond Drive, VIENNA, VA 22182, UNITED STATES.
MOIR, Mrs. Elizabeth Claire, ACA *1990;* 15 Cibbons Road, Chineham, BASINGSTOKE, HAMPSHIRE, RG24 8TD.
MOIR, Mr. Geoffrey William, BA ACA *1978;* 16 Eldon Road, MACCLESFIELD, CHESHIRE, SK10 3SA.
MOIR, Miss. Gillian, ACA *1982;* 6 Abingdon Gardens, Odd Down, BATH, BA2 2UY.
MOIR, Mr. Ian James, FCA *1960;* Minton House, Minton, CHURCH STRETTON, SHROPSHIRE, SY6 6PS. (Life Member)
MOIR, Mr. Leslie George Stephen, FCA *1961;* Alwyne, Bulkington Road, Wolvey, HINCKLEY, LEICESTERSHIRE, LE10 3LA.
MOIR, Mr. Malcolm Joseph Peckston, ACA *1985;* Ferrises, Upper Woolhampton, READING, RG7 5TG.
MOISAN, Mr. John Arthur, FCA *1972;* 52 Eagleswell Road, Boverton, LLANTWIT MAJOR, CF61 2UG.
MOISAN-HILL, Ms. Carol Patricia, FCA *1971;* 16 Andover Close, BARRY, SOUTH GLAMORGAN, CF62 8AG.
MOISEY, Mr. Richard Dennis, FCA *1972;* 12 Allens Farm Road, BIRMINGHAM, B31 5RG.
MOISSI, Ms. Kakia, MSc BA ACA *2000;* SKOUFA 2 YERMASOYIA, 4044 LIMASSOL, CYPRUS.
MOIST, Mr. Richard Colin, BCom ACA *2005;* with Grant Thornton UK LLP, Enterprise House, 115 Edmund Street, BIRMINGHAM, B3 2HJ.
MOIZER, Prof. Peter, PhD FCA *1977;* (Member of Council 2000 - 2004), Maurice Keyworth Building, University of Leeds, Woodhouse Lane, LEEDS, LS2 9JT.
MOJAB, Mr. Rahmat, BA ACA *1979;* D M H Stallard Gainsborough House, Pegler Way, CRAWLEY, WEST SUSSEX, RH11 7FZ.
•MOJABI, Mr. Mir Majid, BSc ACA *1990;* Mojabi & Co, 205 Crescent Road, BARNET, HERTFORDSHIRE, EN4 8SB.
MOK, Mr. Chadwick Cham Hung, MA FCA *1991;* House C6, St Andrews Place, 38 Kam Chui Road, SHEUNG SHUI, HONG KONG SAR.
MOK, Mr. Chew Yin, ACA CF *1981;* with BDO, 12th Floor Menara Uni. Asia, Jalan sultan Ismail, 50250 KUALA LUMPUR, FEDERAL TERRITORY, MALAYSIA.
•MOK, Mr. David Hung Heng, FCA *1982;* (Tax Fac), David Mok, 10 Queensberry Mews West, South Kensington, LONDON, SW7 2DU.
MOK, Mr. King Tong Eric, ACA *2005;* Mok & Fong CPA Limited, Unit 2706, 113 Argyle Street, MONG KOK, KOWLOON, HONG KONG SAR.
MOK, Miss. Kitty Kit Ting, BSc ACA *1994;* Pacific Basin Shipping (HK) Ltd, 7th Floor, Hutchinson House, 10 Harcourt Road, CENTRAL, HONG KONG ISLAND HONG KONG SAR.
MOK, Ms. Kwok Fong, ACA *2006;* Flat A 20/F Block 5, Mountain Shore, 8 Yuk Tai Street, Ma On Shan, SHA TIN, NEW TERRITORIES HONG KONG SAR.
MOK, Mr. Peter Chi Wai, ACA *2009;* 13 Garford Street, LONDON, E14 8JG.
MOK, Mr. Pui Keung, ACA *2008;* Flat B 27/F Tower 1, Residence Oasis, TSEUNG KWAN O, NEW TERRITORIES, HONG KONG SAR.
MOK, Mr. Richard Joe Kuen, BSc ACA CPA *1989;* c/o Ulmus Investment Limited, 11th Floor, Vogue Building, 67 Wyndham Street, CENTRAL, HONG KONG SAR.
MOK, Miss. Suk Man, ACA *2011;* Flat 7 Walbrook Court, 2 Hemsworth Street, LONDON, N1 5LF.
MOK, Mr. Ting San, ACA *2008;* Flat D 12/F Block 10, Villa Rhapsody, Symphony Bay, No 533 Sai Sha Road, SAI KUNG, NEW TERRITORIES HONG KONG SAR.
MOK, Mr. Wing Kai Henry, ACA *2008;* Flat 11D, 11th Floor Continental Mansion, 294 King's Road, NORTH POINT, HONG KONG ISLAND, HONG KONG SAR.
MOK, Mrs. Yvonne Yee Fong, MBA ACA *1984;* Flat 1A Cliffview Mansions, 17/19 Conduit Road, PUN SHAN KUI, Hong Kong Island, HONG KONG SAR.
MOKHA, Mr. Prabh, ACA *2003;* 162 Wicksteed Street, PO Box 185, WANGANUI 4500, NEW ZEALAND.
MOKHTAR, Miss. Azlin Maria, BSc(Econ) ACA *2003;* Level 56, Tower 1 PETRONAS Twin Towers, KLCC, 50088 KUALA LUMPUR, FEDERAL TERRITORY, MALAYSIA.
•MOKHTAR, Mr. Iraj Nasrollah, FCA CPA *1968;* I.N. Mokhtar & Co, 7 Chartfield, HOVE, EAST SUSSEX, BN3 7RD. See also Mokhtar Edwards & Co
MOKHTAR, Miss. Maznida, BSc ACA *1993;* 22 Jalan Daun Inai 2, Sunway SPK Damansara, 52200 KUALA LUMPUR, FEDERAL TERRITORY, MALAYSIA.
MOKHTAR, Miss. Maznita, BSc ACA *1995;* 60 Jalan Setiakasih 9, Damansara Heights, 50490 KUALA LUMPUR, FEDERAL TERRITORY, MALAYSIA.
MOLD, Mr. Graham Nigel, BA FCA *1989;* Malt House 12-13 Narborough Wood Park, Desford Road Enderby, LEICESTER, LE19 4XT.
MOLD, Mr. John Kenneth, JP FCA *1953;* (Tax Fac), 36 Linden Drive, Evington, LEICESTER, LE5 6AH. (Life Member)
MOLD, Mrs. Nina, BA ACA MBA *1999;* The Doveloft, 1 Whitethorns Close, Swinford, LUTTERWORTH, LEICESTERSHIRE, LE17 6BF.
MOLD, Mr. Richard Charles, BA ACA *1989;* Groitscherstrasse 31, 04179, 04179 LEIPZIG, GERMANY.
•MOLE, Mr. Adrian Nicholas, FCA ATII *1993;* (Tax Fac), Quove Accounting Ltd, Talpa Hall, Station Road, Old Newton, STOWMARKET, SUFFOLK IP14 4HQ.
MOLE, Mr. Alexander Andrew, BEng ACA *1992;* DJO UK Ltd, 7 The Pines Business Park, Broad Street, GUILDFORD, SURREY, GU3 3BH.
MOLE, Mrs. Andrea, BA ACA *1988;* T E S Garage Services Ltd Unit 170, Wellworthy Road, LYMINGTON, SO41 8JY.
MOLE, Mr. Andrew Ashley, FCA *1985;* Bow Cottage, Smarden Road, Pluckley, ASHFORD, KENT, TN27 0RE.
MOLE, Mr. Andrew Bains, BSc ACA *2005;* 23 Lindley Street, NORWICH, NR1 2HF.
MOLE, Mr. Christian Russell, LLB ACA *1994;* 3 Davema Close, CHISLEHURST, BR7 5QZ.
MOLE, Mr. Colin David, BA ACA *1994;* 9 Grange Road, Bromley Cross, BOLTON, BL7 9AU.
MOLE, Mr. Davin Richard, BSc ACA *2000;* Alte Landstrasse 73, 8700 KUESNACHT, SWITZERLAND.
MOLE, Mrs. Helen Louise, BA(Hons) ACA *2003;* 26 The Broadway, NORTH SHIELDS, TYNE AND WEAR, NE30 2LG.
MOLE, Mr. James Edward Richard, FCA *1975;* 26 Cherry Grove, HUNGERFORD, RG17 0HP.
MOLE, Mr. Mitchell, BSc ACA *2010;* Dept Smith 8th Floor, K P M G One Snowhill, Snow Hill Queensway, BIRMINGHAM, B4 6GH.
MOLEDINA, Mr. Inayat, ACA *2011;* 23 Danzey Grove, Kings Heath, BIRMINGHAM, B14 6JY.
•MOLESHEAD, Mr. Brian Leonard, CA FCA *1984; (CA Scotland 1976);* McBrides Accountants LLP, Nexus House, 2 Cray Road, SIDCUP, KENT, DA14 5DA. See also McBrides Corporate Finance Limited
MOLESKIS, Ms. Stella, BA(Econ) ACA *2002;* Flat 203 6 Tripoleos street Aglantzia, 2107 NICOSIA, CYPRUS.
MOLESWORTH, Mr. Allen Henry Neville, MA FCA *1963;* 31 Norland Square, LONDON, W11 4PU. (Life Member)
MOLHO, Mr. Alexis Robert Raphael, BSc ACA *2010;* 6 Rue Caulaincourt, 75018 Paris, PARIS, FRANCE.
MOLINEUX, Mr. Keith Leslie, ACA *1981;* Hillcrest Care Ltd Langstone Gate, Solent Road, HAVANT, PO9 1TR.
MOLKENTHIN, Mr. Robert Anthony, BA ACA *1982;* 98 Clement Drive, KARRINYUP, WA 6018, AUSTRALIA.
•MOLL, Dr. Adrian Thomas James, BSc FCA *1997;* Moore Stephens, P O Box 236, First Island House, Peter Street, St. Helier, JERSEY JE4 8SG. See also Moore Stephens Limited
MOLL, Ms. Emily Bridget, BSc(Hons) ACA *2001;* 6 Approach Road, ST. ALBANS, HERTFORDSHIRE, AL1 1SR.
MOLL, Mr. Simon Andrew, BA FCA *1980;* 172 Seaside Drive, ATLANTIC SHORES, CHRIST CHURCH, BB17135, BARBADOS.
MOLL, Mr. Steven David, MEng ACA *2002;* 6 Approach Road, ST. ALBANS, HERTFORDSHIRE, AL1 1SR.
•MOLLART, Mr. Jonathan Robert, FCA *1977;* 6 Fulmere Court, Swinton, MANCHESTER, M27 0FD.
MOLLER, Mr. David James, FCA *1970;* 15 Mayfair Court, GUELPH N1G 2S2, ON, CANADA.
•MOLLER, Mr. Peter Kristen, BA ACA *1988;* Deloitte LLP, Stonecutter Court, 1 Stonecutter Street, LONDON, EC4A 4TR. See also Deloitte & Touche LLP
MOLLER, Mr. Thomas, BSc ACA *2011;* Bauersvej 6, 3250 GILLELEJE, DENMARK.
MOLLET, Mr. Peter Neville Ellis, FCA *1965;* Quinta do Alto da Bonita, Ranholas, S. Pedro de Sintra, 2710 SINTRA, PORTUGAL. (Life Member)
MOLLETT, Mr. Andrew John, BA ACA *1986;* 19 Crieff Road, Wandsworth, LONDON, SW18 2EB.
MOLLETT, Mr. Charles Sylvester, FCA *1953;* Half Acre, Les Huriaux, St. Andrew, GUERNSEY, GY6 8RF. (Life Member)
•MOLLETT, Mr. Simon, PhD ACA *1979;* Lingfield Partners LLP, The Barn, Park Farm, Felbridge, EAST GRINSTEAD, WEST SUSSEX RH19 2RB. See also Beechcroft Associates Limited
MOLLISON, Mr. Neil Arthur, BSc ACA *1992;* Salamander Energy (E&P) Limited, 17-02 Q House Lumpini Building, 1 South Sathorn Road, Kwaeng Tungmahamek, Khet Sathorn, BANGKOK 10120 THAILAND.
MOLLITT, Miss. Jacqueline Anne, BA(Hons) ACA *2003;* 6 Newlands Grove, HALIFAX, HX3 7HZ.
MOLLITT, Mr. Simon Wesley, BSc ACA *2005;* Pearson Driving Assessment Ltd, The Lighthouse, 14 The Quays, SALFORD, M50 3BF.
MOLLON, Mr. John Richard, BA FCA *1980;* 10 Avonborne Way, Chandler's Ford, EASTLEIGH, HAMPSHIRE, SO53 1TF.
MOLLOY, Miss. Angela, ACA *2011;* Navigant Consulting, 5th Floor Woolgate Exchange, 25 Basinghall Street, LONDON, EC2V 5HA.

MOLLOY, Miss. Felicity Helene, ACA *2010;* Princess Court, Pricewaterhousecoopers, 23 Princess Street, PLYMOUTH, PL1 2EX.
MOLLOY, Miss. Joanne Marie, BA ACA *1997;* 12 Aintree Drive, ROCHDALE, OL11 5SH.
•MOLLOY, Mr. John, BA ACA *1997;* 39 Willow Lane, Milton, ABINGDON, OXFORDSHIRE, OX14 4EG.
MOLLOY, Mr. Michael James, BA FCA *1997;* Nolan Transport, Oaklands, NEW ROSS, COUNTY WEXFORD, IRELAND.
MOLLOY, Mrs. Rachel Jane, ACA *2009;* Swandec Ltd, 550 Valley Road, NOTTINGHAM, NG5 1JJ.
MOLODOVA, Ms. Ekaterina, ACA *2004;* 2 Harford Close, Coombe Dingle, BRISTOL, BS9 2QD.
MOLONEY, Mr. Barry William, LLB ACA *1987;* Little Chantry, Bull Lane, Chalfont St. Peter, GERRARDS CROSS, SL9 8RH.
MOLONEY, Mr. William Francis, BA FCA *1969;* 5 Chatter End, Farnham Green, BISHOP'S STORTFORD, CM23 1HL.
MOLONY, Miss. Clare Anne, ACA MAAT *2001;* 42 Somerford Road Broughton, CHESTER, CH4 0SZ.
MOLONY, Mr. David John, BSc ACA *1992;* 4 Palmerston Crescent, Palmers Green, LONDON, N13 4UA.
MOLONY, Mrs. Joanne Marguerite, FCA *1993;* 27 Evesham Road, Bishops Cleeve, CHELTENHAM, GLOUCESTERSHIRE, GL52 8SA.
MOLONY, Mr. John Benjamin, BA ACA *1992;* 98 Fairfax Road, TEDDINGTON, MIDDLESEX, TW11 9BX.
MOLONY, Mr. Peter John, MA FCA *1963;* Mill House, Great Elm, FROME, SOMERSET, BA11 3NY. (Life Member)
MOLOZIAN, Mr. Garo Garbis, BSc FCA *1984;* The Cedars, 141 French Street, Lower Sunbury, SUNBURY-ON-THAMES, TW16 5JY.
MOLTON, Mr. Matthew Leonard, MA ACA *2009;* 4 Devon Mansions, Tooley Street, LONDON, SE1 2UD.
MOLTON, Miss. Maxine Joy, ACA *1995;* 164 Longmead Avenue, BRISTOL, BS7 8QQ.
MOLTU, Mr. Norman Russell, BSc(Hons) ACA *1997;* 12 East Street, Coggeshall, COLCHESTER, CO6 1SH.
MOLYNEAUX, Mr. David Stewart, BSc FCA *1974;* 12 Ryecroft Lane, Belmont Village, BOLTON, BL7 8AH.
MOLYNEUX, Mrs. Alison Jane, BSc ACA *1991;* 24 Park Lane, Allestree, DERBY, DE22 2DT.
MOLYNEUX, Mrs. Anne Beth, BSc ACA MBA *1997;* 7 Bowers Way, HARPENDEN, HERTFORDSHIRE, AL5 4EP.
MOLYNEUX, Mrs. Anne Eugenie, ACA CA(AUS) *2008;* Reinacherstrasse 9, 8032 ZURICH, SWITZERLAND.
MOLYNEUX, Mr. Austin David, FCA *1960;* 67 Windle Grove, Windle, ST.HELENS, MERSEYSIDE, WA10 6HP.
MOLYNEUX, Mr. Brian, BA ACA *2003;* Janes Field, Duddenhoe End, SAFFRON WALDEN, CB11 4UU.
MOLYNEUX, Mr. Graham John, BSc ACA *1988;* Cragside House, 9 Queen Ethelburga's Park, HARROGATE, HG3 2GE.
MOLYNEUX, Mr. John Frank, FCA *1977;* Nabarro LLP, Lacon House, 84 Theobalds Road, LONDON, WC1X 8RW.
MOLYNEUX, Mr. Mark Thomas John, BSc FCA *1981;* Rockfield Park, Rockfield, MONMOUTH, NP25 5QB.
MOLYNEUX, Mr. Matthew, BA ACA *2009;* Apartment 1/5, 1 Rice Street, MANCHESTER, M3 4JL.
MOLYNEUX, Mr. Matthew Ian, BA ACA *1988;* Curzon & Co, 10 Shepherd Market, LONDON, W1J 7QF.
MOLYNEUX, Mr. Nicholas John, BEng ACA *1997;* 168 Kenrick Road, NOTTINGHAM, NG3 6EX.
MOLYNEUX, Mr. Philip, BSc ACA *1982;* 12 Jumelles Drive, Calverton, NOTTINGHAM, NG14 6QD.
•MOLYNEUX, Mr. Reginald Stuart, FCA *1975;* Kelly Molyneux & Co, Security House, 1 Queen Street, Burslem, STOKE-ON-TRENT, ST6 3EL.
MOLYNEUX, Mr. Robert Allan, FCA *1971;* 20 Thornton Close, Rufford, ORMSKIRK, L40 1UW.
MOLYNEUX, Mrs. Shona Jane, BA ACA *2002;* Janes Field, Duddenhoe End, SAFFRON WALDEN, CB11 4UU.
MOLYNEUX-WEBB, Mr. Steven Alexander, BA ACA *2010;* with PricewaterhouseCoopers LLP, 1 Embankment Place, LONDON, WC2N 6RH.
MOMNANI, Mr. Farhan, ACA *2008;* Canary Central, Flat 56 Lowry House, Cassilis Road, LONDON, E14 9LL.
•MON, Mr. James, MA FCA *1978;* The McCay Partnership, Financial House, 14 Barclay Road, CROYDON, CR0 1JN.
MONAGHAN, Miss. Alexandra Charlotte Louise, BEng ACA *2003;* 9 Clarkson Avenue, WISBECH, CAMBRIDGESHIRE, PE13 2EF.
MONAGHAN, Mr. Brian Charles, BCom FCA *1960;* 20 Caiystane Hill, EDINBURGH, EH10 6TE. (Life Member)
•MONAGHAN, Ms. Catherine, BCom ACA *1996;* Catherine Monaghan, South View, Clairemorris Road, BALLA, COUNTY MAYO, IRELAND.
MONAGHAN, Mrs. Eleanor Ann, FCA *1980;* The Copse, Old Beaumont Hill, ST. PETER, JERSEY, JE3 7EA.
•MONAGHAN, Mr. John Patrick, BSc FCA *1992;* Child & Co, 20 Kirkgate, Sherburn In Elmet, LEEDS, LS25 6BL.
MONAGHAN, Miss. Laura, MSc BSc ACA *2010;* Group Taxation, 7 Floor, Standard Chartered, 1 Basinghall Avenue, LONDON, EC2V 5DD.
MONAGHAN, Mr. Mark, BSc ACA *1981;* Champion Sports Ireland, Westgate Business Park, Ballymount, DUBLIN 24, COUNTY DUBLIN, IRELAND.
•MONAGHAN, Mr. Paul, BSc ACA *1983;* Paul Monaghan, 18 Hartshill Close, Hillingdon, UXBRIDGE, MIDDLESEX, UB10 9LH.
MONAGHAN, Mr. Richard Leslie, BSc FCA *1981;* Culduthel, Links Road, WINCHESTER, HAMPSHIRE, SO22 5HP.
MONAGHAN, Mr. Stephen John, BSc ACA *1998;* Flat 1-4, 57 Cator Road, LONDON, SE26 5DT.
MONAGHAN, Mrs. Yvonne May, BSc FCA *1982;* 26 Utkinton Road, TARPORLEY, CHESHIRE, CW6 0HS.
•MONAHAN, Mr. Peter John, FCA *1969;* Peter J. Monahan & Co, 16 Farmhill Park, Douglas, ISLE OF MAN, IM2 2EE.
MONCKTON, Mrs. Margaret Jane Pierce, BSc ACA *1996;* 102 Main Street, Willoughby on the Wolds, LOUGHBOROUGH, LEICESTERSHIRE, LE12 6SZ.
MONCRIEFF, Mr. Robert David, LLB FCA *1992;* Ernst & Young, 5 Times Square, NEW YORK, NY 10036, UNITED STATES.
•MONCRIEFF, Mr. Ronald Mcculloch, FCA *1973;* (Tax Fac), Moncrieff & Co, 13 Freda Avenue, Gedling, NOTTINGHAM, NG4 4FY.
MONCUR, Miss. Juliette Chisholm, BA(Hons) ACA *2001;* 37 Thorpe Lane, HUDDERSFIELD, HD5 8TA.
•MOND, Mr. David Emanuel Merton, FCA *1971;* Hodgsons, Nelson House, Park Road, Timperley, ALTRINCHAM, CHESHIRE WA14 5BZ.
MOND, Mr. Gary Stephen, MA FCA CF *1985;* 1 Abbey View, LONDON, NW7 4PB.
MONDIN, Mr. Brian Leslie, FCA *1966;* 14 Knyvett Green, Ashwellthorpe, NORWICH, NR16 1HA.
MONDON, Mr. Andrew Paul, ACA *1992;* 3 Adel Park Gardens, LEEDS, LS16 8BN.
•MONDON-BALLANTYNE, Mr. Herve Jean-Marie, ACA *1987;* Deloitte & Touche Bakr Abulkhair & Co, PO Box 442, 12 Floor, Saudi Business Center, Madinah Road, JEDDAH 21411 SAUDI ARABIA.
•MONDY, Mr. Steven Derek, ACA *1983;* (Tax Fac), Crossley & Davis, 348-350 Lytham Road, BLACKPOOL, FY4 1DW. See also Campbell Crossley & Davis
MONEDERO, Miss. Clementa, BSc ACA *1984;* 33 Palace View, SHIRLEY, CROYDON, CR0 8QW.
MONEEB, Mr. Sharif, BSc ACA *2008;* 24 Windsor Gardens, WHITLEY BAY, TYNE AND WEAR, NE26 3BG.
MONEMI, Mr. Ali, BSc ACA *2004;* 96 Whitton Avenue East, GREENFORD, UB6 0PX.
MONERAWELA, Ms. Suchinta Lankuei Manashree, BA ACA *1993;* 1011 Moorfield Hill Grove, VIENNA, VA 22180, UNITED STATES.
MONEY, Mr. Daniel Edward, BSc ACA *1993;* 29 Fennfields Road, South Woodham Ferrers, CHELMSFORD, CM3 5RZ.
•ⓘMONEY, Mr. James Douglas Ernle, ACA *1986;* PKF (UK) LLP, Farringdon Place, 20 Farringdon Road, LONDON, EC1M 3AP.
MONEY, Mrs. Julia Wynne, MA ACA ATII *1992;* The Shropshire Group, Barway, ELY, CAMBRIDGESHIRE, CB7 5TZ.
MONEY, Mrs. Karen Louise, LLB ACA *1993;* 39 Wold View, South Cave, BROUGH, HU15 2EF.
MONEY, Mr. Timothy John, BA FCA *1992;* Riverdale, 148 Peperharow Road, GODALMING, SURREY, GU7 2PW.
MONEY-COUTTS, Mr. Benjamin Burdett, ACA *1986;* Overbury Court, Old Odiham Road, ALTON, HAMPSHIRE, GU34 4BX.
MONEY-COUTTS, Mr. Giles Thomas Nevill, BA ACA *1983;* 10 Kensington Mansions, Trebovir Road, LONDON, SW5 9TF.
•MONFRIES, Mrs. Mary Cicely Florence, BA ACA *1992;* (Tax Fac), PricewaterhouseCoopers LLP, 1 Embankment Place, LONDON, WC2N 6RH. See also PricewaterhouseCoopers
MONFRIES, Mr. Thomas Wallace, BA ACA *1992;* Oakfield House, Charter Alley, TADLEY, HAMPSHIRE, RG26 5PY.
•MONGAN, Mr. John Gerard, BSc ACA *1987;* PricewaterhouseCoopers LLP, 1 Embankment Place, LONDON, WC2N 6RH. See also PricewaterhouseCoopers
MONGELARD, Mr. Joseph Claude, BA FCA *1970;* 7310 rue de Chambois, MONTREAL H3R 3E5, QUE, CANADA. (Life Member)
MONGER, Mr. Christopher James, BSc ACA *2002;* 27 Kenilworth Road, Winklebury, BASINGSTOKE, HAMPSHIRE, RG23 8JA.
•MONGER, Mr. Edwin George, FCA *1968;* Isle of Wight County Press Group Ltd, Brannon House, 123 Pyle Street, NEWPORT, ISLE OF WIGHT, PO30 1ST. See also Edwin G. Monger
MONGER, Mr. Stephen John, BSc ACA *1993;* 10 St. Ediths Road, Kemsing, SEVENOAKS, TN15 6PT.
MONGIELLO, Dr. Marco, ACA *2009;* 1st Floor, 20 Parsifal Road, LONDON, NW6 1UH.
•MONICO, Mr. Stephen Neil, BSc FCA DChA *1983;* Steve Monico Limited, 19 Goldington Road, BEDFORD, MK40 3JY.
MONIER-WILLIAMS, Mr. Ian Lawrence Mackay, FCA *1980;* with PricewaterhouseCoopers LLP, 1 Embankment Place, LONDON, WC2N 6RH.
MONIS, Ms. Elizabeth Helen, BSc ACA *1992;* Magnolia House, 24 West Way, RICKMANSWORTH, HERTFORDSHIRE, WD3 7EN.
MONJACK, Mr. Philip, FCA *1965;* Whytes Cottage, 14 The Warren, RADLETT, WD7 7DX.
MONK, Mrs. Anne, BSc FCA *1988;* 2nd Floor Quadrant House, Riverside Drive, DUNDEE, DD1 4NY.
•MONK, Mrs. Caroline Ruth, BA FCA *1993;* Beever and Struthers, St George's House, 215-219 Chester Road, MANCHESTER, M15 4JE.
MONK, Mr. David John, MA BSc FCA *1977;* 25 South Drive, CHEAM, SURREY, SM2 7PH.
•MONK, Miss. Elizabeth Ann, BSc FCA CTA *1988;* (Tax Fac), Place Campbell, Wilmington House, High Street, EAST GRINSTEAD, RH19 3AU.
MONK, Mr. Gary Andrew, MSc ACA *1997;* Ellerman Investments Ltd, 3rd Floor, 20 St. James's Street, LONDON, SW1A 1ES.
MONK, Mr. George Martin, BSc FCA *1978;* 800 Saratoga Avenue, Apt A-209, SAN JOSE, CA 95129-2507, UNITED STATES.
•MONK, Mrs. Helen Christine, BSc ACA *1982;* H.C. Monk, 49 Barrow Road, Burton-on-the-Wolds, LOUGHBOROUGH, LEICESTERSHIRE, LE12 5TB.
•MONK, Mr. Ian Leonard, BSc FCA MCIArb *1980;* with RSM Tenon Audit Limited, Stoughton House, Harborough Road, Oadby, LEICESTER, LE2 4LP.
•MONK, Mrs. Kia-Mui, FCA *1975;* Monk & Co, 114 Stock Road, BILLERICAY, ESSEX, CM12 0RT.
MONK, Mr. Michael, FCA *1977;* 114 Stock Road, BILLERICAY, CM12 0RT.
MONK, Mr. Michael Jon, BA ACA *2006;* 20 Folds Crescent, SHEFFIELD, S8 0EQ.
MONK, Mr. Paul Edward, BSc(Hons) ACA *2001;* 81 Manor Road, Streetly, SUTTON COLDFIELD, WEST MIDLANDS, B74 3NF.
MONK, Mr. Peter John, BA ACA MBA *1998;* 34 Woodside Avenue, CHISLEHURST, BR7 6BU.
MONK, Mr. Peter Loftus, FCA *1965;* Longfield House, Hamsterley, BISHOP AUCKLAND, DL13 3PP. (Life Member)
MONK, Miss. Rebecca Jean, ACA *2009;* 6 Talbot Road, LONDON, SE22 8EH.
MONK, Mr. Robert Geoffrey, FCA *1964;* 40 Park House Gdns, TWICKENHAM, TW1 2DE.
MONK, Mr. Roger David, BCom FCA *1969;* 65 Lockwood Road, BIRMINGHAM, B31 1QE.
MONK, Miss. Sara Kathleen Elizabeth, BA ACA *1993;* 17 Plum Tree Road, Lower Stondon, HENLOW, BEDFORDSHIRE, SG16 6NE.
•MONK, Mr. Stephen Guy, FCA *1974;* Parker Business Services Ltd, Cornelius House, 178-180 Church Road, HOVE, EAST SUSSEX, BN3 2DJ.
MONK, Mrs. Vanessa Jayne, BSc ACA *2000;* with Ernst & Young LLP, City Gate West, Toll House Hill, NOTTINGHAM, NG1 5FY.
MONKCOM, Mr. Jonathan David, BA ACA *1985;* Wessex Group, Jewry House, Jewry Street, WINCHESTER, HAMPSHIRE, SO23 8RZ.
MONKHOUSE, Mr. Andrew Laurence, BA ACA MCT *1992;* 2 Blair Drive, SEVENOAKS, TN13 3JR.
MONKHOUSE, Mr. John Graham, BSc FCA *1978;* 109 Fairfield Road, STOCKTON-ON-TEES, TS19 7BS.
MONKHOUSE, Mr. Richard Eric, BSc ACA *1999;* 20/242 Exhibition Street, MELBOURNE, VIC 3000, AUSTRALIA.
MONKHOUSE, Mrs. Sarah Margaret, BA ACA *1992;* 2 Blair Drive, SEVENOAKS, TN13 3JR.
MONKS, Mr. Anthony James, FCA *1975;* 73 Common Road, Kensworth, DUNSTABLE, BEDFORDSHIRE, LU6 3RH.
MONKS, Mr. Christopher Robert, ACA *2002;* Reilly McMordie, Richmond House, Mersey Road, SALE, CHESHIRE, M33 6BB.
MONKS, Ms. Patricia Anne, BEng ACA *2001;* 11 Green Lane, Blackwater, CAMBERLEY, SURREY, GU17 9DG.
•MONKS, Mr. Richard Julian, MA ACA *1981;* Crossley & Davis, 52 Chorley New Road, BOLTON, BL1 4AP.
MONKS, Mr. Stanton Mangnall, FCA *1965;* Rocqueberg View, Rue De Samares, St Clement, JERSEY, JE2 6LS. (Life Member)
MONKS, Miss. Susannah Elizabeth, ACA *2008;* 163 Jago Court, NEWBURY, BERKSHIRE, RG14 7EZ.
MONKS, Mr. Terence John, BA FCA MCT *1974;* Cusgarne House, Cusgarne, TRURO, CORNWALL, TR4 8RL.
MONNEY, Miss. Katherine Emma, BA(Hons) ACA *2001;* Chorion Ltd, Aldwych House, 71-91 Aldwych, LONDON, WC2B 4HN.
MONNICKENDAM, Mrs. Vanessa Gail, BSc FCA *1986;* 14 Weetwood Crescent, LEEDS, LS16 5NS.
MONNIER, Mr. Paul David John, FCA *1974;* 3 Pintail Close, BASINGSTOKE, HAMPSHIRE, RG22 5UG.
•MONNINGTON, Mr. Christopher John, FCA *1983;* LMW Limited, Riverside View, Basing Road, Basing, BASINGSTOKE, HAMPSHIRE RG24 7AL.
MONNINGTON, Mrs. Emily Rachel, BSc ACA *1998;* 151 Wyndora Avenue, Freshwater, SYDNEY, NSW 2096, AUSTRALIA.
MONNINGTON, Mr. Frank William, FCA *1975;* 17 Hilmay Drive, Boxmoor, HEMEL HEMPSTEAD, HP1 1TZ.
MONNINGTON, Mr. Stephen Anthony, ACA *1980;* Mayfield Media Strategies Ltd, 28E Wellesley Road, LONDON, W4 4BN.
MONRO, Mrs. Claire Louise, BA ACA *1987;* 36 East Street, Chickerell, WEYMOUTH, DT3 4DT.
MONRO, Dr. Duncan, BSc ACA *1994;* 10 Parry Street, Claremont, PERTH, WA 6010, AUSTRALIA.
MONRO, Miss. Joanna Louise, BCom ACA *2010;* 63 Katherine Road, SMETHWICK, WEST MIDLANDS, B67 5QZ.
MONRO HIGGS, Mr. David, MSc BA ACA *1997;* Mincombe Posts Farm, Mincombe Posts, Sidbury, SIDMOUTH, DEVON, EX10 0QW.
MONRO HIGGS, Ms. Helen Frances, BSc ACA *1996;* Mincombe Post Farm Mincombe Post, Sidbury, SIDMOUTH, DEVON, EX10 0QW.
MONROE, Mr. William Kenneth Godfrey, FCA *1967;* 40 Ashburn Place, LONDON, SW7 4JR.
MONSELL, Ms. Susan, BSc FCA *1984;* 24 Nightjar Close, POOLE, DORSET, BH17 7YN.
•ⓘMONSON, Mrs. Fiona Elizabeth, BSc ACA *1990;* Armida Business Recovery LLP, Bell Walk House, High Street, UCKFIELD, EAST SUSSEX, TN22 5DQ.
•MONSON, Mr. Kevin, BSc ACA *2007;* (Tax Fac), Kevin Monson ACA, 72 Commonside West, MITCHAM, SURREY, CR4 4HB. See also Monson Accountants
MONSON, Mr. Timothy James, ACA *1987;* Froghollow, Town Littleworth, Cooksbridge, LEWES, BN8 4TB.
MONSURATE, Miss. Charlotte Margaret, BA FCA *1987;* 2c Bycullah Road, ENFIELD, EN2 8EE.
MONTAGNA, Mr. Giulio Cesare Benito, FCA *1953;* Ben Montagna, 26 Park Street East, Apartment 308, MISSISSAUGA L5G 1L6, ON, CANADA. (Life Member)
MONTAGU, Mr. Howard Alan, BSc ACA *1995;* Forest Hall Beaconsfield Road, Chelwood Gate, HAYWARDS HEATH, WEST SUSSEX, RH17 7LE.
MONTAGUE, Mrs. Emily Catherine, BSc ACA *1991;* 9 Rollscourt Avenue, Herne Hill, LONDON, SE24 0EA.
MONTAGUE, Mr. Eric David, FCA *1975;* 3 Grafton Close, CHRISTCHURCH, DORSET, BH23 3LQ. (Life Member)
MONTAGUE, Mr. Hugh Clifford, FCA *1962;* 63 Covert Road, Northchurch, BERKHAMSTED, HP4 3SS. (Life Member)
MONTAGUE, Mr. John Anthony Victor, FCA *1967;* Greyber, 20 Berceau Walk, WATFORD, HERTFORDSHIRE, WD17 3BL.
MONTAGUE, Mr. Leonard James, FCA *1968;* 23 King Edward Place, Wheathampstead, ST. ALBANS, HERTFORDSHIRE, AL4 8FJ.
•MONTAGUE, Mr. Nicholas Peter, FCA *1984;* 35 Clover Drive, Pickmere, KNUTSFORD, CHESHIRE, WA16 0WF.

•**MONTAGUE, Mrs. Nyuk Ken, MSc BA ACA** *1996;* GKM Associates Limited, 8 Caspian Close, PURFLEET, ESSEX, RM19 1LH.
MONTAGUE, Mr. Robert John, BA ACA *1992;* 9 Rollscourt Avenue, LONDON, SE24 0EA.
MONTAGUE, Mr. William Edward Henry, BA ACA *1999;* 8 West Ley, Honley, HOLMFIRTH, HD9 6RY.
MONTAGUE-FULLER, Mr. Peter Malcolm, MA ACA *1996;* (Tax Fac), Cosworth Electronics Ltd Brookfield Technology Centre, Twentypence Road Cottenham, CAMBRIDGE, CB24 8PS.
MONTAGUE-JOHNSTONE, Mr. Torquil James, FCA *1978;* Nine Elms Farm House, Bucklebury, READING, RG7 9NS.
MONTANA, Mrs. Ioanna Savvidou, ACA *2010;* Flat 6, Courtlands, Castlebar Hill, LONDON, W5 1TF.
MONTANARI, Mrs. Susan Caroline, BSc ACA *1989;* 705 Claremont Residence, 1 St Quentin Avenue, CLAREMONT, WA 6010, AUSTRALIA.
MONTANES, Mrs. Ann Margaret, BA ACA *1990;* 67 Rue Francois Charles Ostyn, 927000 COLOMBES, FRANCE.
•**MONTEIRO, Mr. Michael Joseph, FCA** *1965;* Baker Tilly Monteiro Heng, Monteiro & Heng Chambers, No. 22-1 Jalan Tun Sambanthan 3, 50470 KUALA LUMPUR, FEDERAL TERRITORY, MALAYSIA. See also Monteiro & Heng
•**MONTEITH, Mr. Andrew Craig, BSc ACA** *1998;* Baker Tilly Tax & Advisory Services LLP, 1st Floor, 46 Clarendon Road, WATFORD, WD17 1JJ. See also Baker Tilly UK Audit LLP
MONTEITH, Mrs. Anita, BSc FCA CTA *1982;* (Member of Council 1997 - 2001), (Tax Fac), with ICAEW, Chartered Accountants' Hall, Moorgate Place, LONDON, EC2P 2BJ.
MONTEITH, Mr. James Henry George Cameron, BA FCA *1981;* Dogs Trust Bolton House, 17-26 Wakley Street, LONDON, EC1V 7RQ.
MONTEITH, Mrs. Sharon Maria, BSc ACA *2004;* 16 The Maltings, Hunton Bridge, KINGS LANGLEY, HERTFORDSHIRE, WD4 8QL.
MONTENERO, Miss. Lucy, BA ACA *2004;* 55 Draper Close, ISLEWORTH, MIDDLESEX, TW7 4SX.
MONTFORD, Mr. Neil Macgregor, BSc ACA *1994;* 14 First Avenue, WILLOUGHBY, NSW 206, AUSTRALIA.
MONTFORD, Mrs. Teresa Anne, BSc ACA *1995;* 14 First Avenue, WILLOUGHBY, NSW 2068, AUSTRALIA.
MONTGOMERIE, Mr. Charles, MEng ACA *1998;* 42 Orlando Road, LONDON, SW4 0LF.
MONTGOMERY, Mr. Alexander Stafford, BA ACA *1999;* 25 Haffenden Road, TENTERDEN, TN30 6QE.
•**MONTGOMERY, Mr. Bruce James, BA FCA** *1992;* Smith Cooper, St John's House, 54 St John Street, ASHBOURNE, DE6 1GH. See also Smith Cooper LLP
•**MONTGOMERY, Mr. David George, FCA** *1971;* D. Montgomery & Co, P O Box 119, 118 Abercromby Street, PORT OF SPAIN, TRINIDAD AND TOBAGO.
•**MONTGOMERY, Mr. David John, FCA DChA** *1980;* Kingston Smith LLP, Surrey House, 36-44 High Street, REDHILL, RH1 1RH. See also Kingston Smith Limited Liability Partnership, Devonshire Corporate Services LLP and Kingston Smith Consulting LLP
MONTGOMERY, Mr. Edward, BA FCA *1979;* 333 Durham Drive, REGINA S4S 4Z6, SK, CANADA.
MONTGOMERY, Mr. Fraser Stewart, MSc BA ACA *1996;* Merlin Entertainments Group Ltd Unit 5-6, Silverglade Business Park Leatherhead Road, CHESSINGTON, KT9 2QL.
•**MONTGOMERY, Mr. Gordon Scott Alexander, FCA** *1983;* The Onboard Partnership LLP, Chilton House, Charnham Lane, HUNGERFORD, BERKSHIRE, RG17 0EY.
MONTGOMERY, Mr. Hugh, MA FCA *1975;* 44 Arundel Lodge, 2 Shelley Road, WORTHING, WEST SUSSEX, BN11 1XN. (Life Member)
MONTGOMERY, Mr. Ian, FCA *1967;* (Tax Fac), 5 Heather Close, Cleadon, SUNDERLAND, SR6 7PW.
MONTGOMERY, Dr. Ian David, LLB FCA *1969;* Av Santa Cruz 1012, DPTO 803, Miraflores, LIMA, 18, PERU.
MONTGOMERY, Mr. Ian James, FCA *1961;* Highcroft, Hanbury, BURTON-ON-TRENT, DE13 8TF. (Life Member)
MONTGOMERY, Mr. James Dobbin Keith, FCA *1976;* Burnfield, Old Epperstone Road, Lowdham, NOTTINGHAM, NG14 7BS.
MONTGOMERY, Mr. John Alexander, FCA *1968;* 9 Orchard Close, East Hanney, WANTAGE, OX12 0JD.
MONTGOMERY, Mr. Miles Scott, ACA *2005;* Flat 10, 176 High Street, TONBRIDGE, TN9 1AF.
MONTGOMERY, Mr. Nicholas Palmer Kyle, FCA *1975;* Adams Farm, Graffham, PETWORTH, WEST SUSSEX, GU28 0NZ.
MONTGOMERY, Mr. Nigel John, FCA *1973;* South View, Reading Road, Heckfield, HOOK, HAMPSHIRE, RG27 0JY.
MONTGOMERY, Mr. Peter James, BA FCA *1974;* Flat 21, The Towers, Lower Mortlake Road, RICHMOND, SURREY, TW9 2JR.
MONTGOMERY, Dr. Susan, ACA *1991;* with David Taylor, 15 Hill Rise, WOODSTOCK, OXFORDSHIRE, OX20 1AA.
MONTGOMERY, Mr. Tom Richard, BSc ACA *2005;* Grosvenor, 70 Grosvenor Street, LONDON, W1K 3JP.
•**MONTI, Ms. Angela Helen, BA ACA** *1996;* Angela Monti Accountancy Services Limited, 84 Elmhurst Road, READING, RG1 5HY.
MONTIER, Mr. David John, FCA *1958;* Eyebrook, Oldfield Road, Bickley, BROMLEY, BR1 2LF. (Life Member)
MONTIS, Mr. Constantinos, BSc ACA *2011;* 29 Agiou Andronikou Street, Strovolos, 2054 NICOSIA, CYPRUS.
MONTSERRAT, Mr. Stuart David, BSc(Hons) ACA *2009;* 5a Tattershall Drive, The Park, NOTTINGHAM, NG7 1BX.
MONTY, Mr. Harry Michael, FCA *1963;* 38 Fourth Avenue, WILLOUGHBY EAST, NSW 2068, AUSTRALIA.
MONUMENT, Mr. Laurence John, FCA *1963;* La Ferme, Les Grands Vaux, St Helier, JERSEY, JE2 4GF. (Life Member)
MONUMENT, Miss. Sarah Victoria, BSc ACA *2002;* 102 Shrubland Road, LONDON, E8 4NH.
MOO, Mr. Hean Chong, ACA *1978;* 30 Jln SS 22/32, Damansara Jaya, 47400 PETALING JAYA, SELANGOR, MALAYSIA.
MOOCHHALA, Mr. Hasnain, ACA *1986;* 47 Chuan Drive, SINGAPORE 554848, SINGAPORE.
MOOD, Dr. Jonathan, PhD MA BA ACA *2010;* 3 Poplar Crescent, Bensham, GATESHEAD, TYNE AND WEAR, NE8 1QD.
MOODIE, Miss. Catherine Elizabeth, ACA *2010;* Flat 4, Flat 3-7, 141 Highbury New Park, LONDON, N5 2LJ.
MOODIE, Mr. David Ian Park, FCA *1966;* The Elms, Olveston, BRISTOL, BS35 4DR. (Life Member)
MOODIE, Mr. Steven Andrew, ACA *1991;* Honeysuckle Cottage Sunset Lane, West Chiltington, PULBOROUGH, WEST SUSSEX, RH20 2PB.
MOODY, Mr. Alistair, BSc ACA *1992;* Apartment 17, The Convent, 4 College Street, NOTTINGHAM, NG1 5AU.
•**MOODY, Mr. Christopher John, BSc FCA CTA** *1977;* (Tax Fac), CJM Consultancy Limited, Oriel House, Thames Road, Goring, READING, RG8 9AH.
MOODY, Mr. Christopher Martin, ACA *2006;* 30 Stranding Street, EASTLEIGH, SO50 5GQ.
MOODY, Mr. Colin Ian, BA ACA *1992;* The Grove, Beechwood Avenue, WEYBRIDGE, SURREY, KT13 9TF.
•**MOODY, Mr. David Frank, BCom FCA** *1978;* with ICAEW, Metropolitan House, 321 Avebury Boulevard, MILTON KEYNES, MK9 2FZ.
MOODY, Mr. David John, BSc ACA *1992;* 7 Hitherfield Road, LONDON, SW16 2LW.
MOODY, Mr. Edward George, BSc ACA *2005;* Zurich Financial Services, UK Life Centre, Station Road, SWINDON, WILTSHIRE, SN1 1EL.
MOODY, Mr. Edward Philip, BA ACA *2002;* Manor Hey, The Lee, GREAT MISSENDEN, BUCKINGHAMSHIRE, HP16 9NA.
MOODY, Mrs. Elizabeth Ann May, ACA *2008;* Second Floor Flat, 160 Westbury Road, Westbury-on-Trym, BRISTOL, BS9 3AH.
MOODY, Miss. Fiona Miranda Chineme, BSc(Hons) ACA *2001;* 7 Wilson Street, BENTLEY, VIC 3204, AUSTRALIA.
MOODY, Mr. Frederick Anthony, FCA *1969;* Acorn Cottage, Ringshall Road, Little Gaddesden, BERKHAMSTED, HP4 1PE.
MOODY, Mr. Graham Andrew, BSc ACA *2006;* 7 Wigton Place, LONDON, SE11 4AN.
MOODY, Ms. Helen Jayne, BA ACA *1990;* 12 Holdenby Close, MARKET HARBOROUGH, LE16 8JE.
MOODY, Mr. Iain Alexander, BSc(Hons) ACA *2002;* C/Recreo N°6, 30366 ALMERIA, MURCIA, SPAIN.
MOODY, Mr. Ian Grant, BA(Hons) ACA *2002;* with PricewaterhouseCoopers, Riverside Centre, 123 Eagle Street, GPO Box 150, BRISBANE, QLD 4001 AUSTRALIA.
MOODY, Mr. James, BA ACA *2005;* 138 Turney Road, Dulwich, LONDON, SE21 7JJ.
MOODY, Mr. James Richard, BEng ACA *2008;* 3 Mount Road, LONDON, SW19 8ES.
MOODY, Mr. John, BSc ACA *2003;* 14 Melltowns Green, Pickhill, THIRSK, NORTH YORKSHIRE, YO7 4LL.
MOODY, Mr. John, BA ACA *1990;* 5 Banstead Court, Southlands Grove, BROMLEY, BR1 2DF.
MOODY, Mr. John Nigel Drury, FCA *1967;* 23 West Branch Road, WESTPORT, CT 06880-1249, UNITED STATES. (Life Member)
MOODY, Mrs. Karen Jane, BSc(Hons) ACA *2004;* 14 Melltowns Green, Pickhill, THIRSK, NORTH YORKSHIRE, YO7 4LL.
•**MOODY, Mr. Lee Stephen, ACA** *2004;* 9 Sandown Close, Blackwater, CAMBERLEY, GU17 0EL.
MOODY, Mr. Michael John, FCA *1974;* 7 Birch Grove, Elm, WISBECH, CAMBRIDGESHIRE, PE14 0AP.
MOODY, Miss. Nicola, ACA *2011;* 10 Brudenell Close, AMERSHAM, BUCKINGHAMSHIRE, HP6 6FH.
MOODY, Mrs. Patricia Rita, BSc FCA *1980;* Longridge, Golden Orb Wood, Binfield, BRACKNELL, RG42 4BW.
MOODY, Mr. Philip, BA FCA *1978;* Manor Hay, The Lee, GREAT MISSENDEN, BUCKINGHAMSHIRE, HP16 9NA.
•**MOODY, Mr. Philip Edward, FCA ATII CF** *1980;* Smith & Williamson Ltd, Portwall Place, Portwall Lane, BRISTOL, BS1 6NA.
•**MOODY, Mr. Robert John, BA(Hons) FCA** *2001;* Ernst & Young LLP, 1 More London Place, LONDON, SE1 2AF. See also Ernst & Young Europe LLP
MOODY, Mr. Roy, FCA *1954;* 44 Dorrington Road, SALE, M33 5EB. (Life Member)
MOODY, Mr. Steven John, ACA *2011;* 3 Sydenham Court, 52 Sydenham Road, CROYDON, CR0 2EF.
MOODY, Mr. Stuart James, BSc(Hons) ACA *2000;* 23 Morwick Road, Warkworth, MORPETH, NORTHUMBERLAND, NE65 0TG.
MOODY-STUART, Mr. Alexander, MA ACA ATII *1996;* 215 Chao Chang Di Village, Cui Ge Zhuang Town, Chao Yang District, BEIJING 100015, CHINA.
MOOIJ, Mr. Adam, ACA *2009;* 15 Wayfarers Drive, NEWTON-LE-WILLOWS, MERSEYSIDE, WA12 8DF.
MOOKERJEE, Mr. Sagnik, FCA *1975;* PO Box 2051, DANDENONG, VIC 3175, AUSTRALIA.
MOOKERJI, Mr. Bimanbihari, FCA *1970;* 19/20 Mantri Memories Co-op Hsg. Society, Off South Main Road Koregaon Park, PUNE 411001, INDIA. (Life Member)
MOON, Mr. Alexander Gordon, FCA *1951;* Woolton House, Maltmans Lane, GERRARDS CROSS, SL9 8RS. (Life Member)
MOON, Ms. Alison Arabella, BSc ACA *1993;* 84 Turney Road, LONDON, SE21 7JH.
MOON, Mrs. Amy Elizabeth, BSc(Hons) ACA *2010;* 18 Vindomis Close, Holybourne, ALTON, GU34 4HL.
MOON, Mrs. Catriona Susan, ACA *2002;* 2 Balmoral Close, North Millers Dale, CHANDLER'S FORD, HAMPSHIRE, SO53 1TG.
MOON, Mrs. Cheryl Lynn, ACA *2010;* 7 Holly Close, Purdis Farm, IPSWICH, IP3 8GB.
MOON, Mr. Christopher Herbert, FCA *1974;* 14 Camm Lane, MIRFIELD, WEST YORKSHIRE, WF14 9JQ.
MOON, Mr. Derek James, MEng ACA *1998;* 245 Leamore Court, 1 Meath Crescent, LONDON, E2 0QA.
MOON, Mr. Frank Albert, FCA *1951;* 9 Varlian Close, Westhead, ORMSKIRK, L40 6HJ. (Life Member)
MOON, Mr. Frank Michael Shane, ACA *1988;* Le Camelie, Avenue Vivier, Ville Au Roi, St. Peter Port, GUERNSEY, GY1 1PG.
•**MOON, Mr. Gerald, FCA** *1960;* (Tax Fac), G. Moon & Co, 74 Duke Street, BARROW-IN-FURNESS, CUMBRIA, LA14 1RX.
MOON, Ms. Hee Kyung Claire, ACA CA(NZ) *2010;* 65 Aland Court, Finland Street, LONDON, SE16 7LA.
MOON, Mr. Ian Robert, BA FCA *1980;* Mutual Clothing & Supply Ltd, 39-43 Bedford Street South, LEICESTER, LE1 3JN.
MOON, Mrs. Jayne Louise, BSc ACA *2006;* 4 The Meads, EAST GRINSTEAD, WEST SUSSEX, RH19 4DF.
MOON, Mr. Jeremy Guy, BA ACA *1985;* Medway Hospital, Windmill Road, GILLINGHAM, ME7 5NY.
MOON, Mr. Jonathan Godfrey, MBA BA ACA *1987;* 129 The Grove, LONDON, W5 3SL.
MOON, Mr. Julian, BA ACA *1991;* 16 Hartswood Road, LONDON, W12 9NQ.
MOON, Mrs. Karen, BA ACA *1992;* Reeves & Co, 37 St. Margarets Street, CANTERBURY, CT1 2TU.
MOON, Miss. Lesley, BSc ACA *1993;* 29 Avenue de Dauphine, 06000 NICE, FRANCE.
MOON, Mr. Nigel William George, FCA *1980;* (Tax Fac), Reeves & Neylan, 37 St. Margarets Street, CANTERBURY, CT1 2TU.
•**MOON, Mr. Paul Simon, BA ACA** *1985;* P.S. Moon and Company, 22 The Piece, Churchdown, GLOUCESTER, GL3 2EX.
MOON, Mrs. Pauline, BSc ACA *1991;* 16 Hartswood Road, LONDON, W12 9NQ.
MOON, Mr. Philip Brian, BSc ACA *1989;* GE Real Estate Europe, 2-4 Rue Pillet Will, 75009 PARIS, FRANCE.
MOON, Mr. Richard David, BA ACA *1981;* Tempest Hilary Ltd, Eversley Chase, Eversley, HOOK, HAMPSHIRE, RG27 0LU.
MOON, Mr. Stephen, BA(Hons) ACA *2006;* 4 The Meads, EAST GRINSTEAD, WEST SUSSEX, RH19 4DF.
MOON, Miss. Susan Anne, BA ACA *1986;* 1 Knole Paddock, Seal Hollow Road, SEVENOAKS, TN13 3RX.
MOON, Mrs. Suzanne, BSc ACA *1989;* New House Farm, Hanney Road, Southmoor, ABINGDON, OXFORDSHIRE, OX13 5HR.
MOONAN, Mrs. Mary Kit May, FCA *1976;* 7 Elm Avenue, Bayshore, PORT OF SPAIN, TRINIDAD AND TOBAGO.
MOONEY, Mrs. Alexandra Helen, ACA *2008;* 157 Redlands Road, PENARTH, SOUTH GLAMORGAN, CF64 2QP.
MOONEY, Mr. Andrew John, BA ACA *1987;* Rydes Hill Lodge, Aldershot Road, GUILDFORD, GU3 3AG.
•**MOONEY, Mrs. Brenda Teresa, BA ACA** *1978;* Brenda Mooney, The Oast House, The Street, Brook, ASHFORD, KENT TN25 5PG.
MOONEY, Miss. Colette Elizabeth, BSc ACA *2002;* 35a Hopton Road, LONDON, SW16 2EH.
MOONEY, Miss. Emma Clare, ACA *2010;* 39 Trent Avenue, Flitwick, BEDFORD, MK45 1SH.
MOONEY, Mr. George James, ACA *2008;* 4 Highview Avenue, Langdon Hills, BASILDON, ESSEX, SS16 6ET.
MOONEY, Mr. Giles Edward, BSc ACA *2000;* (Tax Fac), 9 Samwell Way, NORTHAMPTON, NN4 9QJ.
MOONEY, Mrs. Iona, BSc ACA CTA *2003;* 64 Gunner Lane, Rubery, Rednal, BIRMINGHAM, B45 9EX.
•**MOONEY, Miss. Marie Therese, BSc FCA MBA** *1991;* (Tax Fac), MWM, 11 Great George Street, BRISTOL, BS1 5RR. See also Mooney Williams May Limited
MOONEY, Mr. Michael Peter, BSc ACA *1978;* The Oast House, The Street, Brook, ASHFORD, KENT, TN25 5PG.
MOONEY, Ms. Olivia Susan, BCom ACA *1998;* 1 Hanley Terrace, Maugheraboy Road, SLIGO, COUNTY SLIGO, IRELAND.
MOONEY, Mr. Patrick Kieran, BSc FCA *1990;* 27 Morley Square, Bishopston, BRISTOL, BS7 9DW.
MOONEY, Mr. Patrick Michael Thomas, BSc ACA *2007;* 7/98 Walcott Street, MOUNT LAWLEY, WA 6050, AUSTRALIA.
MOONEY, Mr. Paul Robert, BSc ACA *2009;* 10 Mutrix Road, LONDON, NW6 4QG.
MOONEY, Miss. Rebecca, ACA MAAT *2011;* 31 Lysander Way, Cottingley, BINGLEY, WEST YORKSHIRE, BD16 1WF.
MOONEY, Mr. Ronald David, FCA *1953;* 3 Baytree Close, CHICHESTER, WEST SUSSEX, PO19 5UF. (Life Member)
MOONEY, Mrs. Tracey Rose, BA FCA *1999;* Health & Safety Executive, 6.4 Redgrave Court, Merton Road, BOOTLE, MERSEYSIDE, L20 7HS.
MOONG, Miss. Pooi Funn, ACA *2011;* Flat 33, Boswell House, Boswell Street, LONDON, WC1N 3PR.
MOONIE, Mr. Roderick James, FCA *1968;* Kelpie, Deadhearn Lane, CHALFONT ST. GILES, BUCKINGHAMSHIRE, HP8 4HG.
MOONSTONE, Ms. Alison Jane, BSc ACA *1994;* 24 Sweyn Place, LONDON, SE3 0EZ.
MOOR, Mr. Jonathan Edward, CBE BA FCA *1990;* 8 Mynchen End, BEACONSFIELD, BUCKINGHAMSHIRE, HP9 2AT.
MOOR, Mr. Richard John, BA ACA *1996;* 10 Bishop Close, Pateley Bridge, HARROGATE, HG3 5LJ.
MOOR, Mr. Richard Michael, ACA *2002;* 99 Clay Street, Soham, ELY, CAMBRIDGESHIRE, CB7 5HL.
MOOR, Miss. Ruth Elizabeth, BSc FCA *1992;* 20 Cheshire Avenue, Shirley, SOLIHULL, B90 2LJ.
•**MOORBY, Mr. Andrew John, FCA** *1990;* (Tax Fac), Tait Walker LLP, Bulman House, Regent Centre, Gosforth, NEWCASTLE UPON TYNE, NE3 3LS. See also Tait Walker Management Limited
MOORBY, Mr. Andrew Mark, BSc ACA *2000;* with Ernst & Young, Ernst & Young House, 34 - 36 Cranmer Square, CHRISTCHURCH, NEW ZEALAND.
•**MOORBY, Mr. Charles Roy, BA ACA** *1984;* B M Howarth Limited, West House, Kings Cross Road, HALIFAX, WEST YORKSHIRE, HX1 1EB.
•**MOORBY, Mr. Timothy John, FCA** *1961;* T.J. Moorby, 8 Melton Grange Road, Melton, WOODBRIDGE, SUFFOLK, IP12 1SA.

•**MOORCRAFT, Mr. John David, FCA** *1979;* Gordon Wood Scott & Partners, Dean House, 94 Whiteladies Road, Clifton, BRISTOL, BS8 2QX. See also Moorcraft J.D.
MOORCRAFT, Mr. Ronald Gordon, FCA *1956;* 9 Cuton Grove, Springfield, CHELMSFORD, CM2 6TA. (Life Member)
MOORCROFT, Mr. David Alexander Lee, MA ACA *1999;* Silvestria, 84 Bridge Lane, Bramhall, STOCKPORT, SK7 3AW.
•**MOORCROFT, Mr. James Langford, BSc FCA ATII** *1985;* (Tax Fac), Cannon Moorcroft Limited, 3 Manor Courtyard, Hughenden Avenue, HIGH WYCOMBE, HP13 5RE.
MOORCROFT, Miss. Marguerita, FCA *1964;* Flat 17 Stokes Court, Diploma Avenue, East Finchley, LONDON, N2 8NX. (Life Member)
MOORE, Mr. Adrian Paul, BSc ACA *1993;* 8 Ashfurlong Close, Dore, SHEFFIELD, S17 3NN.
MOORE, Mr. Adrian Richard, BSc ACA *1992;* The Childcare Corporation St. Pancras House, Jacobs Yard, BASINGSTOKE, RG21 7PE.
MOORE, Mr. Adrian Stanley, FCA *1970;* Dormers, 2 Inchbrook Road, KENILWORTH, WARWICKSHIRE, CV8 2EX.
MOORE, Mr. Alexander, MChem ACA *2006;* 59 Kings Road, CHALFONT ST. GILES, HP8 4HP.
MOORE, Mr. Alexander James, MA BA ACA *2001;* 27 Ennerdale Drive, WATFORD, WD25 0NG.
MOORE, Mrs. Alexandra Sharon, BSc(Hons) ACA *2001;* 7 Sherbourne Drive, LEEDS, LS6 4QX.
MOORE, Miss. Alisa, ACA *2000;* 29 Ridgeway Weston Favell, NORTHAMPTON, NN3 3AP.
MOORE, Ms. Alison Jane, BSc FCA *1993;* 25 Green Lane, Paddock Wood, TONBRIDGE, TN12 6BF.
MOORE, Mr. Alistair John, BEng FCA *1993;* Woodside Cottage, Bluey's Farm, Frieth Road, MARLOW, BUCKINGHAMSHIRE, SL7 2HT.
MOORE, Miss. Amy, ACA *2011;* Ty Canol, Old Lane, Tatsfield, WESTERHAM, KENT, TN16 2LH.
MOORE, Mrs. Andrea, BA ACA *1991;* 51 Bleakhouse Road, Mellons Bay, AUCKLAND 2014, NEW ZEALAND.
•**MOORE, Mr. Andrew, BSc ACA** *2000;* PricewaterhouseCoopers, 7 More London Riverside, LONDON, SE1 2RT. See also PricewaterhouseCoopers LLP
•**MOORE, Mr. Andrew David, BA ACA CF** *1989;* Clearwater Corporate Finance LLP, 6th Floor, 9 Colmore Row, BIRMINGHAM, B3 2BJ.
MOORE, Mr. Andrew Dominic, BA ACA *1995;* 22 Kings Road, WILMSLOW, SK9 5PZ.
•**MOORE, Mr. Andrew Duncan, BA FCA** *1990;* Old Mill Accountancy LLP, The Old Mill, Park Road, SHEPTON MALLET, SOMERSET, BA4 5BS. See also Old Mill Audit LLP
MOORE, Mr. Andrew Gareth, BA FCA *1980;* Pearmain House, The Manors of Shelsley, Clifton-on-Teme, WORCESTER, WR6 6ED.
MOORE, Mr. Andrew Michael, BSc ACA *1992;* 28 Hill View, Henleaze, BRISTOL, BS9 4PY.
MOORE, Mr. Andrew Peter, BSc FCA ATII *1982;* Allmendstrasse 24, CH-8142 UITIKON WALDEGG, SWITZERLAND.
MOORE, Mr. Andrew Quentin Scott, MA FCA *1977;* 69 Long Fallow, Chiswell Green, ST. ALBANS, AL2 3ED.
MOORE, Mr. Andrew Richard, MA LLB ACA *2001;* Old Beams Northwood Lane, High Legh, KNUTSFORD, CHESHIRE, WA16 0QX.
MOORE, Mr. Andrew Roy, BSc FCA *1970;* 15 Ryhall Road, STAMFORD, PE9 1UB.
MOORE, Mr. Andrew Stephen, BSc ACA CISA CISSP *1999;* 3 Cheltenham Close, MACCLESFIELD, CHESHIRE, SK10 2WD.
MOORE, Mrs. Ann Elizabeth, BA ACA *1987;* Vincent Cottage Acton Reynald, SHREWSBURY, SY4 4DS.
MOORE, Mr. Anthony Denis, BSc ACA *1979;* 17 Warwick Close, MAIDENHEAD, SL6 3AL.
MOORE, Mr. Anthony Edward, MEd BSc FCA *1982;* with PricewaterhouseCoopers LLP, 17-00 PWC Building, 8 Cross Street, SINGAPORE 048424, SINGAPORE.
MOORE, Mr. Anthony George, BSc ACA *1992;* 1/39 Nungerner Street, BALWYN, VIC 3103, AUSTRALIA.
MOORE, Mr. Anthony John, MSc BSc ACA *1984;* 2 The Glade, WOODFORD GREEN, IG8 0QA.
MOORE, Mr. Anthony John, BSc ACA *1989;* MAM Funds Plc, 10-14 Duke Street, READING, RG1 4RU.
MOORE, Mr. Anthony John, FCA *1969;* 214 Norton Lane, Earlswood, SOLIHULL, WEST MIDLANDS, B94 5LT. (Life Member)
MOORE, Mr. Anthony Pethick, FCA *1966;* Coryton Villa, Trematon Terrace, PLYMOUTH, PL4 6QS.
•**MOORE, Mr. Anthony Russell, FCA** *1971;* (Member of Council 1983 - 1989), The Yews Farm, Perkins Lane, Grimston, MELTON MOWBRAY, LE14 3DB.
MOORE, Mr. Antony David, BCom ACA *1980;* 66 Gemini Court, BURLEIGH HEADS, QLD QLD 4220, AUSTRALIA.
MOORE, Ms. Barbara Alice, ACA MAAT *2003;* with Mazars LLP, Cartwright House, Tottle Road, NOTTINGHAM, NG2 1RT.
MOORE, Miss. Barbara Joyce, FCA *1973;* 2 Wychwood Rise, GREAT MISSENDEN, BUCKINGHAMSHIRE, HP16 0HB.
MOORE, Mr. Barrie Nicholson, FCA *1965;* 39 Tadcaster Road, Copmanthorpe, YORK, YO23 3UN.
MOORE, Mr. Barry Vincent, FCA *1974;* Dayman International Ltd, Merryhills Enterprise Park, Park Lane, WOLVERHAMPTON, WV10 9TJ.
MOORE, Mr. Ben Patrick, ACA *2010;* Medlock Electric Ltd, 109-115 Eleanor Cross Road, WALTHAM CROSS, HERTFORDSHIRE, EN8 7NT.
MOORE, Mr. Benjamin, BSc ACA *2010;* Flat A, 307a Gray's Inn Road, LONDON, WC1X 8QS.
MOORE, Mr. Benjamin James, ACA *2009;* London Mining Plc, 39 Sloane Street, LONDON, SW1X 9LP.
MOORE, Mr. Benjamin John Christopher, BA ACA *1997;* with Deloitte Middle East, Currency House, Building 1 Level 5, DIFC, PO Box 282056, DUBAI UNITED ARAB EMIRATES.
•**MOORE, Mrs. Bethan Alison, BSc FCA** *1983;* (Tax Fac), Dowsett Moore, 17 Station Road, HINCKLEY, LE10 1AW. See also Dowett A J & Co
MOORE, Mr. Brian Robert, BSc FCA *1978;* 218 Rolleston Road, BURTON-ON-TRENT, DE13 0AY.
MOORE, Mr. Carl Robert, ACA *2008;* Flat 18 Chesil Court, Bonner Road, LONDON, E2 9JZ.
MOORE, Miss. Caroline Elizabeth, MA ACA *2007;* with PricewaterhouseCoopers, Strathvale House, PO Box 258, GEORGE TOWN, GRAND CAYMAN, KY1-1104 CAYMAN ISLANDS.
MOORE, Mrs. Caroline Louise, BA ACA *1991;* Yarlington Housing Group, Lupin Way, YEOVIL, SOMERSET, BA22 8WN.
MOORE, Mr. Casey Daniel, ACA *1997;* 1/32 Brittain Street, COMO, WA 6152, AUSTRALIA.
MOORE, Miss. Catherine Fiona Isobel, ACA *2011;* Throstle Nest, Hollins Lane, Hampsthwaite, HARROGATE, NORTH YORKSHIRE, HG3 2HW.
MOORE, Mr. Charles Anthony Laughton, ACA *1986;* Openlot Systems Asia, 7500A Beach Road #07-320, The Plaza, SINGAPORE 199591, SINGAPORE.
MOORE, Mr. Chris, BSc ACA *2007;* Flat 9, 2 Henfield Road, LONDON, SW19 3HU.
MOORE, Mrs. Christine Jean, BSc ACA *1992;* Jasmine Cottage, Feltham Road, Pucklechurch, BRISTOL, BS16 9SH.
MOORE, Mrs. Christine Margaret, FCA *1980;* Flat 6, 14 Grange Park, LONDON, W5 3PL.
MOORE, Mr. Christopher Alan, FCA *1962;* Boxtree Cottage, 4 Great Pasture, Burley-in-Wharfedale, ILKLEY, LS29 7DD.
•**MOORE, Mr. Christopher Hedworth, MA ACA** *1983;* Hedworth Moore, Hollybank Cottage, Mill Lane, Audlem, CREWE, CW3 0AY.
MOORE, Mr. Christopher James, BA ACA *1991;* Elta Group Ltd, Unit 46 Third Avenue, Pensnett Trading Estate, KINGSWINFORD, WEST MIDLANDS, DY6 7US.
•**MOORE, Mr. Christopher James Dowsland, ACA FCCA** *2008;* Dutton Moore, 6 Silver Street, HULL, HU1 1JA.
MOORE, Mr. Christopher John, MEng ACA *2005;* Flat E, 195 Munster Road, LONDON, SW6 6BY.
MOORE, Mr. Christopher Mark, MA FCA *1969;* Thornborough Grounds, BUCKINGHAM, MK18 2AB.
MOORE, Mrs. Claire Annette, BSc ACA *1990;* 7 Waldegrave Road, BROMLEY, BR1 2JP.
MOORE, Mrs. Claire Lesley, BSc ACA *1989;* 23 Lowndes Avenue, CHESHAM, BUCKINGHAMSHIRE, HP5 2HH.
•**MOORE, Mr. Colin Richard, ACA** *1979;* Moore Stephens LLP, 150 Aldersgate Street, LONDON, EC1A 4AB. See also Moore Stephens & Co
MOORE, Mr. Daniel Jonathan, BA(Hons) ACA *2001;* 26 Sutherland Road, Heaton, BOLTON, BL1 5LR.
MOORE, Mr. David Bruce, BCom FCA *1976;* Badger House, Riverview Road, Pangbourne, READING, BERKSHIRE, RG8 7AU.
MOORE, Mr. David Gwyn, BA ACA *1981;* 27 The Chase, Great Glen, LEICESTER, LE8 9EQ.
MOORE, Mr. David James, BSc ACA *2003;* 30 Forge Croft, EDENBRIDGE, KENT, TN8 5BW.
MOORE, Mr. David James, FCA *1978;* Tara, College Road, CAMELFORD, CORNWALL, PL32 9TL.
MOORE, Mr. David John, FCA *1968;* 24 Maitland Court, Lancaster Terrace, LONDON, W2 3PA.
MOORE, Mr. David John, BA FCA *1963;* 432 St. Clements Avenue, TORONTO M5N 1M1, ON, CANADA.
MOORE, Mr. David John, FCA *1972;* 10 Howlett Road, CLEETHORPES, SOUTH HUMBERSIDE, DN35 0EF.
MOORE, Mr. David John, BA ACA *1982;* 438 Bradgate Road, Newtown Linford, LEICESTER, LE6 0HA.
MOORE, Mr. David John, LLB ACA *1992;* 16 Marquis Lane, HARPENDEN, AL5 5AA.
•**MOORE, Mr. David Robert John, MA ACA** *1996;* Ernst & Young LLP, Liberation House, Castle Street, St Helier, JERSEY, JE1 1EY. See also Ernst & Young Europe LLP
•**MOORE, Mr. David Rodney, FCA** *1969;* Lister Gilleard & Co, Standard House, George Street, HUDDERSFIELD, HD1 2JF.
MOORE, Mr. Dean Roderick, BSc FCA *1985;* The Willows Appleby Lane, Snarestone, SWADLINCOTE, DERBYSHIRE, DE12 7BZ.
MOORE, Mrs. Deborah Jane, BSc ACA *1978;* The Lodge, 52 Milvil Road, LEE-ON-THE-SOLENT, HAMPSHIRE, PO13 9LX.
MOORE, Mr. Denis Shane, FCA *1972;* 908 Edificio Regal, Carrer del Sol 13, 07184 CALA VINAS, MALLORCA, SPAIN.
MOORE, Mr. Derrick, FCA *1979;* Add Value Solutions Ltd, 2 Westfield Road, HARPENDEN, HERTFORDSHIRE, AL5 4HL.
MOORE, Mr. Desmond, BA(Hons) ACA *2004;* Flat 2, 184 Upper Richmond Road West, LONDON, SW14 8AN.
MOORE, Miss. Dianne Helen, MA ACA *1992;* 5 Chantry Road, Moseley, BIRMINGHAM, B13 8DL.
MOORE, Miss. Donna Anne, ACA *2008;* 5 Park Court, Sheen Gate Gardens, LONDON, SW14 7PB.
MOORE, Mr. Dudley, FCA *1961;* 26 The Butts, Little Weighton, HULL, HU20 3XD.
MOORE, Mr. Dudley Charles Dowsland, FCA *1965;* Freshfield, Elloughton, BROUGH, NORTH HUMBERSIDE, HU15 1HP.
MOORE, Mr. Duncan James, BA ACA *1992;* River House, Atherstone on Stour, STRATFORD-UPON-AVON, CV37 8NE.
MOORE, Mr. Edward James, BSc ACA *2003;* 1 Willowbrook Close, Sharnford, HINCKLEY, LE10 3PZ.
•**MOORE, Mrs. Eira Monica Elisabeth, BSc ACA** *1994;* (Tax Fac), Eira Moore, 1 Church Meadow, SHIFNAL, SHROPSHIRE, TF11 9AD.
MOORE, Mrs. Eleanor Jessica, BA ACA *2004;* 9 Castelnau Mansions, Castelnau, Barnes, LONDON, SW13 9QX.
MOORE, Ms. Elizabeth Janet, BSc ACA *1995;* 16 Elmfield Road, LONDON, SW17 8AL.
MOORE, Mr. Eric Stanley, FCA *1959;* 18 Grove Vale Avenue, Great Barr, BIRMINGHAM, B43 6BZ. (Life Member)
•**MOORE, Mr. Ernest Anthony, FCA** *1973;* Dorrell Oliver Ltd, 26 Monk Street, ABERGAVENNY, GWENT, NP7 5NF.
MOORE, Mr. Ewan, BA ACA *1999;* 8 Chesham Road, WILMSLOW, CHESHIRE, SK9 6HA.
MOORE, Ms. Fiona Lynn, ACA *1988;* 28 Montague Avenue, Sanderstead, SOUTH CROYDON, SURREY, CR2 9NH.
MOORE, Mr. Fionn Patrick, BA ACA *1992;* University of Otago Christchurch, 2 Riccarton Avenue, CHRISTCHURCH 8011, NEW ZEALAND.
MOORE, Mr. Francis, ACA *2011;* 11 Chelsea Park Gardens, LONDON, SW3 6AF.
MOORE, Mr. Frederic, ACA *2008;* Thornborough Grounds, Bourton, BUCKINGHAM, BUCKINGHAMSHIRE, MK18 2AB.
MOORE, Mr. Gavin Robert John, BSc ACA *1993;* 63 Beulah Road, Rhiwbiba, CARDIFF, CF14 6LW.
MOORE, Mr. Geoffrey, FCA *1971;* 77 Horsendale Avenue, Nuthall, NOTTINGHAM, NG16 1AQ.
MOORE, Mr. Geoffrey George, FCA *1964;* 4 Lonsdale Road, Cyncoed, CARDIFF, CF23 9JF. (Life Member)
MOORE, Mr. Geoffrey Watson, OBE FCA *1960;* 4626 SW 97th Terrace, GAINESVILLE, FL 32608, UNITED STATES. (Life Member)
•**MOORE, Mr. George Edward, FCA** *1960;* Edward Moore & Partners, Le Pont De Vaux, 86150 MILLAC, FRANCE.
•**MOORE, Mr. George Frank, BA FCA** *1972;* (Tax Fac), Montpelier Professional (Galloway) Limited, 1 Dashwood Square, NEWTON STEWART, WIGTOWNSHIRE, DG8 6EQ.
MOORE, Mr. Gerald, FCA *1968;* 12 Shingle Bank Drive, Milford-on-Sea, LYMINGTON, SO41 0WQ.
•**MOORE, Mrs. Gillian Barbara, FCA** *1972;* Bell & Company, 64 Harpur Street, BEDFORD, MK40 2ST.
MOORE, Mr. Glenn, BSc ACA *2001;* Holly Cottage, Morley Road, CHISLEHURST, KENT, BR7 5PP.
MOORE, Mrs. Glynis Leslie, MA FCA *1988;* Lavender House, Fishery Road, Bray, MAIDENHEAD, SL6 1UP.
MOORE, Mr. Gordon Benjamin, FCA *1976;* 17 highview drive, SEWICKLEY, PA 15143, UNITED STATES.
MOORE, Mr. Graham Bernard, BSc FCA *1984;* 5B Dor Fook Mansion, 126 Pokfulam Road, POK FU LAM, HONG KONG ISLAND, HONG KONG SAR.
•**MOORE, Mr. Graham John, FCA** *1981;* 7 King Orry Road, Glen Vine, Douglas, ISLE OF MAN, IM4 4ER.
•**MOORE, Mr. Graham John, FCA** *1975;* Tait Walker LLP, Bulman House, Regent Centre, Gosforth, NEWCASTLE UPON TYNE, NE3 3LS. See also Tait Walker Management Limited
MOORE, Mr. Graham Robert, BA FCA *1990;* 11 Elger Close, Biddenham, BEDFORD, MK40 4AL.
MOORE, Mrs. Hannah Marianne, BA ACA *2000;* 43 Osier Crescent, LONDON, N10 1QS.
MOORE, Mr. Harold Jonathan, FCA *1972;* Addison House, Addison Road, Wimblington, MARCH, PE15 0QT.
•**MOORE, Mr. Harry Charles, FCA** *1970;* (Tax Fac), Harry Moore, 2 Limekiln Close, Claydon, IPSWICH, IP6 0AW.
MOORE, Mrs. Hayley Clare, BA(Hons) ACA *2001;* 2 Horton Crescent, Livingstone park, EPSOM, SURREY, KT19 8AA.
MOORE, Miss. Helen Lucy, BSc(Hons) ACA *2003;* 22 Rossington Drive, Littleover, DERBY, DE23 3UP.
MOORE, Mrs. Helen Margaret, BSc ACA *1991;* 1 Princes Avenue, Carshalton Beeches, CARSHALTON, SM5 4NZ.
MOORE, Mr. Henry George, FCA *1954;* 20 Beverley Close, Ewell East, EPSOM, KT17 3HB. (Life Member)
•**MOORE, Mr. Herbert John, FCA** *1958;* (Tax Fac), Herbert J. Moore, 35 Edgcumbe Park Drive, CROWTHORNE, RG45 6HU.
MOORE, Mr. Iain Dominic, BSc FCA *1993;* I M I Kynoch Plc Lakeside Unit 4040, Solihull Parkway Birmingham Business Park, BIRMINGHAM, B37 7XZ.
MOORE, Mrs. Jade Louise, MA ACA *2000;* Malmsmead, Bayleys Hill, SEVENOAKS, TN14 6HS.
MOORE, Mr. James Christopher, ACA *1998;* 9 Forge Leys, Wombourne, WOLVERHAMPTON, WV5 8JX.
MOORE, Mr. James Edward, ACA *2010;* 70 Craster Road, LONDON, SW2 2AX.
•**MOORE, Mr. James Robert, BA FCA ATII ASFA** *1980;* (Tax Fac), Chapman Robinson & Moore Limited, 30 Bankside Court, Stationfields, KIDLINGTON, OX5 1JE.
•**MOORE, Mrs. Jane Elizabeth, BSc ACA** *1991;* Jane Moore, 3 John Morgan Close, HOOK, HAMPSHIRE, RG27 9RP.
MOORE, Miss. Jane Maureen, MA FCA CTA *1983;* (Tax Fac), 32 Woodside Road, SEVENOAKS, KENT, TN13 3HF.
•**MOORE, Mr. Jason Derek, BSc ACA** *1994;* Deloitte LLP, 2 New Street Square, LONDON, EC4A 3BZ. See also Deloitte & Touche LLP
•**MOORE, Mr. Jeffrey Roy, ACA FCCA** *2009;* Ashdown Hurrey LLP, 20 Havelock Road, HASTINGS, EAST SUSSEX, TN34 1BP.
MOORE, Mrs. Jennifer, BA(Hons) ACA *2004;* with PKF (UK) LLP, Regent House, Clinton Avenue, NOTTINGHAM, NG5 1AZ.
MOORE, Mrs. Jillian, BA ACA *1993;* The Little Barn, Charity Farm, Skipwith, SELBY, YO8 5SL.
MOORE, Mr. Jj, ACA *2008;* Phildraw House Phildraw Road, Ballasalla, ISLE OF MAN, IM9 3EG.
MOORE, Mr. Joel Daniel, BA ACA *1997;* Luth House Petworth Road, Wisborough Green, BILLINGSHURST, WEST SUSSEX, RH14 0BJ.
MOORE, Mr. John, FCA *1968;* 23 Oldfield Road, MAIDENHEAD, SL6 1TX.
MOORE, Mr. John, FCA *1958;* Highview, 3 Little Meadow Close, Prestbury, MACCLESFIELD, SK10 4HA. (Life Member)
•**MOORE, Mr. John Edward, BSc FCA** *1988;* (Tax Fac), Kingly Brookes LLP, 415 Linen Hall, 162-168 Regent Street, LONDON, W1B 5TE.
MOORE, Mr. John Edward, FCA *1961;* 1 Mylnhurst Road, SHEFFIELD, S11 9HU.

MOORE, Mr. John Francis, BA ACA *1981;* Moat Cottage, The Bridge, Water Lane, KINGS LANGLEY, HERTFORDSHIRE, WD4 8HJ.
MOORE, Mr. John Francis, FCA *1971;* (Tax Fac), 10 Ember Gardens, THAMES DITTON, SURREY, KT7 0LN. (Life Member)
MOORE, Mr. John Gary, BA ACA *1998;* 20 Phillpotts Avenue, BEDFORD, MK40 3UH.
•**MOORE, Mr. John George, BA FCA** *1987;* Day Smith & Hunter, Globe House, Eclipse Park, Sittingbourne Road, MAIDSTONE, KENT ME14 3EN.
MOORE, Mr. John Gordon Donald, FCA *1969;* 3 Birchmount Road, SCARBOROUGH M1N 3J3, ON, CANADA.
•**MOORE, Mr. John Gordon Ison, FCA** *1972;* 1 Linton Avenue, SOLIHULL, WEST MIDLANDS, B91 3NN.
MOORE, Mr. John Howard, MA FCA *1975;* Chelford, 8 Havercroft Park, BOLTON, BL1 5AB.
MOORE, Mr. John Mitchell, FCA *1967;* 80 Bristol Road, CHIPPENHAM, SN15 1NS. (Life Member)
MOORE, Mr. John Paul, BA ACA *1993;* Lloyds TSB Bank Plc, The Pentagon, 48 Chiswell Street, LONDON, EC1Y 4XX.
•**MOORE, Mr. John Richard, BA FCA** *1978;* Alexander Moore & Co., 2nd Floor, Monument House, 215 Marsh Road, PINNER, MIDDLESEX HA5 5NE.
MOORE, Mr. Jonathan, ACA *2005;* Mecom Group Plc, 70 Jermyn Street, LONDON, SW1Y 6NY.
MOORE, Mr. Jonathan Dennis, ACA *2008;* C/ Mateo Inurria 15, MADRID, SPAIN.
MOORE, Mr. Jonathan Paul, BA ACA *1991;* 79 Southam Road, Hall Green, BIRMINGHAM, B28 0AA.
MOORE, Mr. Jonathan Paul, BA(Hons) ACA *2001;* 23 Riddings Hill, Balsall Common, COVENTRY, CV7 7RA.
MOORE, Mr. Julian William Sewell, BSc ACA *1993;* 36 Kirkstall Road, LONDON, SW2 4HF.
MOORE, Miss. Julie Agnes, BSc ACA *2000;* Flat 4, 113 Graham Road, LONDON, SW19 3SP.
•**MOORE, Mr. Justin Michael, BSc ACA** *1997;* (Tax Fac), Arnold Hill & Co LLP, Craven House, 16 Northumberland Avenue, LONDON, WC2N 5AP. See also Arnold Hill & Co
MOORE, Mrs. Karen Louise, BSc ACA *1993;* 27 Rowland Burn Way, ROWLANDS GILL, TYNE AND WEAR, NE39 2PU.
MOORE, Mr. Karl, BA(Hons) ACA *2001;* 17 Milliners Way, BISHOP'S STORTFORD, HERTFORDSHIRE, CM23 4GG.
MOORE, Miss. Katherine Margaret, ACA *2009;* 11 Kingsend, RUISLIP, MIDDLESEX, HA4 7DD.
MOORE, Mr. Keith, ACA *2007;* Siamo, 1 New Forge Court, Towthorpe Road, Haxby, YORK, YO32 3YA.
MOORE, Mr. Keith Charles, FCA *1960;* 62 Roman Reach, Caerleon, NEWPORT, GWENT, NP18 3SQ. (Life Member)
MOORE, Mrs. Kelly, BA ACA *2004;* Lower Flat, 2 Angerstein Road, PORTSMOUTH, PO2 8HL.
MOORE, Mr. Kenneth Douglas, FCA *1950;* Appledene, 1 Balcarras Retreat, Charlton Kings, CHELTENHAM, GL53 8QU. (Life Member)
MOORE, Mr. Kenneth Joseph, FCA *1962;* Moores Jewellers Ltd, 7a High Street, CHELMSFORD, CB1 1BE.
•**MOORE, Mr. Kevin Peter, BSc FCA** *1982;* KPMG LLP, 15 Canada Square, LONDON, E14 5GL. See also KPMG Europe LLP
MOORE, Mrs. Kim, BSc ACA *1999;* 72 Suffolk Avenue, COLLAROY, NSW 2097, AUSTRALIA.
MOORE, Mrs. Kirsty Victoria, BSc(Econ) CA ACA *2002;* 109 Melbourne Road, WILLIAMSTOWN, VIC 3016, AUSTRALIA.
•**MOORE, Mr. Laurence Philip, BA FCA** *1983;* (Tax Fac), Prime Accountants and Business Advisors Ltd, 5 Argosy Court, Scimitar Way, Whitley Business Park, COVENTRY, CV3 4GA. See also Prime Pilleys, Prime Accountants Group Limited and Prime Coventry Ltd
MOORE, Mr. Leonard Albert, BCom FCA *1956;* Little Oaks, 127 Carr Lane, Dronfield Woodhouse, DRONFIELD, DERBYSHIRE, S18 8XF. (Life Member)
MOORE, Mrs. Linda Jane, MA ACA *2010;* 3 Llys y Ddraenog, Margam, PORT TALBOT, WEST GLAMORGAN, SA13 2TQ.
①**MOORE, Mrs. Lindsey, BSc ACA** *1995;* 19 Fenemore Road, KENLEY, SURREY, CR8 5GJ.
MOORE, Mrs. Loretta Alison, BA ACA *1994;* 8 Court Close, MAIDENHEAD, BERKSHIRE, SL6 2DL.
MOORE, Mrs. Louise, LLB ACA *1999;* 8 Chesham Road, WILMSLOW, CHESHIRE, SK9 6HA.
MOORE, Miss. Lucie, BA ACA *2011;* Flat D, 156 Blackstock Road, LONDON, N4 2DY.
MOORE, Miss. Lucy Anne, MSc ACA *2007;* 41 Green Lanes, Wylde Green, SUTTON COLDFIELD, WEST MIDLANDS, B73 5JJ.
MOORE, Mrs. Lynn, BA ACA *2005;* 37 Leonard Ropner Drive, Fairfield, STOCKTON-ON-TEES, CLEVELAND, TS19 7QG.
MOORE, Mr. Malcolm, FCA *1969;* Bloxham House, Sidmouth Road, LYME REGIS, DORSET, DT7 3ES. (Life Member)
MOORE, Mrs. Marion Gwyneth, MA ACA DChA *1992;* Cloudlands A2, 35-37 Plantation Road, THE PEAK, HONG KONG SAR.
MOORE, Mr. Mark John, BSc(Hons) ACA *2000;* 2 Tomlinson Drive, BARTON-UPON-HUMBER, SOUTH HUMBERSIDE, DN18 5GZ.
MOORE, Mr. Mark Robin Westwood, BA ACA *1992;* 51 Bleakhouse Road, Mellons Bay, Howick, AUCKLAND 2014, NEW ZEALAND.
MOORE, Mr. Martyn William, BSc ACA *1981;* 23 Mountway, POTTERS BAR, HERTFORDSHIRE, EN6 1ER.
MOORE, Miss. Mary, BSc ACA *1989;* Keelogues, BARNTOWN, COUNTY WEXFORD, IRELAND.
MOORE, Mr. Matthew Charles, BSc ACA *2006;* Close Asset Management Holdings Ltd, 10 Exchange Square Primrose Street, LONDON, EC2A 2BY.
MOORE, Mr. Matthew Christopher, BSc ACA *2006;* 49 Canonbury Road, Islington, LONDON, N1 2DG.
MOORE, Mr. Matthew James, ACA *1993;* Audit Commission, 3 Leeds City Office Business Park Holbeck, LEEDS, WEST YORKSHIRE, LS11 5BD.
MOORE, Mr. Matthew James, BSc ACA *2009;* 16 Kiln Croft, Etwall, DERBY, DE65 6HW.
MOORE, Mr. Matthew John, BSc ACA *2000;* 15 Winfrith Road, LONDON, SW18 3BE.
MOORE, Mr. Matthew John, BSc ACA *2002;* 1106 Skyline Plaza, BASINGSTOKE, RG21 7AZ.
MOORE, Mr. Matthew Jon, BSc ACA *2005;* 39 Homeway, ROMFORD, RM3 0HD.
MOORE, Mrs. Maureen Anne, FCA *1956;* Apartment 2, Boughton Hall, Filkins Lane, CHESTER, CH3 5BG. (Life Member)
MOORE, Mr. Michael, BA(Hons) ACA *2001;* 1 Northway, ALTRINCHAM, CHESHIRE, WA14 1NN.
•**MOORE, Mr. Michael, FCA** *1968;* Buckleys, Marshall House, 124 Middleton Road, MORDEN, SURREY, SM4 6RW.
MOORE, Mr. Michael David, ACA *1989;* Catholic Archdiocese of Sydney, Level 16/ 133 Liverpool St, SYDNEY, NSW 2000, AUSTRALIA.
MOORE, Mr. Michael Houghton, FCA *1962;* 836 B-Southampton Rd. #291, BENICIA, CA 94510, UNITED STATES. (Life Member)
•**MOORE, Mr. Michael John, FCA** *1977;* (Tax Fac), Larkings, 31 St. Georges Place, CANTERBURY, KENT, CT1 1XD. See also Larkings Ltd
MOORE, Mr. Michael Joseph, BA FCA *1966;* Throstle Nest, Hollins Lane, Hampsthwaite, HARROGATE, HG3 2HW. (Life Member)
MOORE, Mr. Michael Roger, FCA *1962;* 39 Springfield Park, Twyford, READING, RG10 9JG. (Life Member)
MOORE, Miss. Michaela Jane, BSc ACA *1996;* Wisteria Cottage Bowood Lane, Wendover, AYLESBURY, BUCKINGHAMSHIRE, HP22 6PY.
MOORE, Miss. Michelle, BA(Hons) ACA *2009;* 9/370 Barker Road, Subiaco, PERTH, WA 6008, AUSTRALIA.
•**MOORE, Mr. Munro Yuon, FCA** *1968;* Munro Moore, Glynsk, Liscarney, WESTPORT, COUNTY MAYO, IRELAND.
MOORE, Mr. Nathan Lewis, BA(Hons) ACA *2002;* Hawkslease, Chapel Lane, LYNDHURST, HAMPSHIRE, SO43 7FG.
MOORE, Mr. Neill Lewis McDonald, BSc ACA *1992;* 1 Donald Aldred Drive Burley in Wharfedale, ILKLEY, WEST YORKSHIRE, LS29 7SG.
MOORE, Mr. Nicholas Anthony Charles, FCA *1972;* Stonefield, Linchmere, HASLEMERE, GU27 3NE.
MOORE, Mrs. Nicola, BA ACA *2002;* 4 Summer Hill, ST. LEONARDS-ON-SEA, EAST SUSSEX, TN38 0GP.
MOORE, Mrs. Nicola Dorothy, BA ACA CTA *1986;* PTP Group Limited, Sleechwood, Talbot Road, LYME REGIS, DORSET, DT7 3BB.
MOORE, Ms. Nicola Jane, ACA *1995;* Forrester Research Inc, 400 Technology Square, CAMBRIDGE, MA 02139, UNITED STATES.
MOORE, Mr. Nigel Sandford Johnson, FCA *1968;* Vines Gate, Brasted Chart, WESTERHAM, KENT, TN16 1LR.
MOORE, Mrs. Pamela May, BSc FCA *1982;* 3 Mereside Avenue, CONGLETON, CW12 4JZ.
•**MOORE, Mrs. Patricia, FCA CF** *1975;* Crowe Clark Whitehill LLP, Hatherton House, Hatherton Street, WALSALL, WS1 1YB. See also Horwath Clark Whitehill LLP and Crowe Clark Whitehill
•**MOORE, Mr. Patrick Vincent, BSc FCA** *1997;* Moore Accounting & Tax Solutions, 28 Good Road, Parkstone, POOLE, DORSET, BH12 3PJ.
•**MOORE, Mr. Paul, FCA** *1974;* Young & Associates Ltd, St. Georges House, Bay View Road, Port St. Mary, ISLE OF MAN, IM9 5AE.
MOORE, Mr. Paul Anthony, BSc FCA *1997;* 24 Poundfield Way, Twyford, READING, RG10 0XR.
MOORE, Mr. Paul Anthony, BA ACA *1982;* 5/ F Gulestan, 125 Repulse Bay Road, REPULSE BAY, HONG KONG ISLAND, HONG KONG SAR.
•**MOORE, Mr. Paul Leslie, FCA** *1971;* (Tax Fac), Moore & Co., Unit 22, Mountbatten Business Centre, Millbrook Road East, SOUTHAMPTON, SO15 1HY.
MOORE, Mr. Paul Steven, BSc ACA *2002;* 2 Horton Crescent, Livingstone Park, EPSOM, SURREY, KT19 8AA.
MOORE, Mrs. Paula Marion, BSc ACA *1988;* The Barn Beacon Lane, Staplecross, ROBERTSBRIDGE, EAST SUSSEX, TN32 5QP.
MOORE, Mr. Peter David, FCA *1969;* Richmond Vikings Ltd, The Athletic Ground, Kew Foot Road, RICHMOND, SURREY, TW9 2SS. (Life Member)
MOORE, Mr. Peter George John, FCA *1956;* Apartment 2, Boughton Hall, Filkins Lane, CHESTER, CH3 5BG. (Life Member)
•**MOORE, Mr. Peter John, BA ACA** *1981;* Peter Moore, 5 Sillwood Hall, Montpelier Road, BRIGHTON, BN1 2LQ.
MOORE, Mr. Peter Murray, FCA *1964;* Old Timbers, High Beech Lane, Handcross, HAYWARDS HEATH, RH17 6HQ. (Life Member)
MOORE, Mr. Peter Oliver Stace, BSc ACA *1995;* 71 Miskin Road, DARTFORD, DA1 2LX.
MOORE, Mr. Peter Robert, FCA *1968;* The Woodlands, 36 Longwood Road, Aldridge, WALSALL, WS9 0TA.
•**MOORE, Mr. Peter Russell, FCA** *1967;* Peter R. Moore, 20 Carisbrooke Drive, Napperley Park, NOTTINGHAM, NG3 5DS.
MOORE, Mr. Peter Seward, BSc ACA *1992;* 10 Hopedene Mews, BELFAST, BT4 3DS.
MOORE, Mr. Peter Stallard, FCA *1956;* Somerton, Church Street, Great Shefford, HUNGERFORD, BERKSHIRE, RG17 7DZ. (Life Member)
MOORE, Mr. Peter Stanley, FCA *1955;* 50 Calder Avenue, Brookmans Park, HATFIELD, AL9 7AG. (Life Member)
MOORE, Mr. Philip Andrew, MA ACA *1995;* with PricewaterhouseCoopers LLP, 31 Great George Street, BRISTOL, BS1 5QD.
•**MOORE, Mr. Philip George, FCA** *1961;* Philip Moore, Torridon, Wood Road, HINDHEAD, SURREY, GU26 6PX.
MOORE, Mr. Philip Steven, BSc ACA *1987;* 8D Portman Mansions, Porter Street, LONDON, W1H 3LA.
MOORE, Mrs. Rachel Elizabeth, BA(Hons) ACA CTA *2003;* with PricewaterhouseCoopers, Abacus House, Castle Park, CAMBRIDGE, CB3 0AN.
MOORE, Mrs. Rebecca Isobel, MA BSc ACA *2001;* 16 Marquis Lane, HARPENDEN, HERTFORDSHIRE, AL5 5AA.
MOORE, Mr. Reginald Stanley, FCA *1958;* 8 The Damsells, TETBURY, GL8 8JA. (Life Member)
MOORE, Mr. Richard, BSc ACA *1992;* with Ernst & Young LLP, 1 More London Place, LONDON, SE1 2AF.
•**MOORE, Mr. Richard Alan, FCA** *1966;* Richard Moore & Co, 6 Bridge End, Dorchester on Thames, WALLINGFORD, OX10 7JP.
MOORE, Mr. Richard David, FCA *1960;* High Leys, 126 Burnmill Road, MARKET HARBOROUGH, LEICESTERSHIRE, LE16 7JG. (Life Member)
MOORE, Mr. Richard Derek, FCA *1950;* Tamaki, The Cliff, BORTH, SY24 5NN. (Life Member)
•**MOORE, Mr. Richard Hobart John De Courcy, FCA** *1972;* Moore Stephens LLP, 150 Aldersgate Street, LONDON, EC1A 4AB. See also Moore Stephens & Co
MOORE, Mr. Richard John, FCA *1953;* 26 Hallams Lane, Chilwell, NOTTINGHAM, NG9 5FH. (Life Member)
MOORE, Mr. Richard Joseph, BSocSc ACA *2003;* 2 Purley Close, Maidenbower, CRAWLEY, WEST SUSSEX, RH10 7QR.
MOORE, Mr. Richard Lawrence Hamilton, BA ACA *1999;* 96 Taybridge Road, Battersea, LONDON, SW11 5PZ.
MOORE, Mr. Richard Martin, MA ACA *1984;* 27 Old Bath Road, Sonning, READING, RG4 6SY.
MOORE, Mr. Richard Michael, BSc ACA *1993;* 62 Soar Road, Quorn, LOUGHBOROUGH, LEICESTERSHIRE, LE12 8BW.
MOORE, Mr. Richard William, BSc FCA *1975;* Roslon, Illogan Downs, REDRUTH, CORNWALL, TR15 3UZ.
MOORE, Mr. Richard William, BSc ACA *2006;* with Deloitte LLP, 4 Brindley Place, BIRMINGHAM, B1 2HZ.
MOORE, Mr. Robert, MChem ACA *2005;* 68 Bradford Road, Guiseley, LEEDS, LS20 8NH.
•**MOORE, Mr. Robert Anthony, FCA** *1977;* R.A. Moore, 421 Middleton Rd, Middleton, MANCHESTER, M24 4QZ.
MOORE, Mr. Robert Henry, BA FCA *1968;* Park Cottage, Reading Road North, FLEET, GU51 4AD.
MOORE, Mr. Robert James, ACA *2009;* 28 Freshwater Road, LONDON, SW17 9TH.
MOORE, Mr. Robert John, MA FCA *1987;* Tree Tops, 22 Heatherdene Avenue, CROWTHORNE, BERKSHIRE, RG45 6AA.
•**MOORE, Mr. Robert Keith, BA ACA** *1989;* (Tax Fac), Bright Grahame Murray, 131 Edgware Road, LONDON, W2 2AP.
MOORE, Mr. Rodney Ivor, FCA *1961;* Unit 4, 18 - 22 Gilroy Road, TURRAMURRA, NSW 2074, AUSTRALIA. (Life Member)
•**MOORE, Mr. Roger Earl, BA(Hons) ACA** *2003;* Beaufort Chancery, 27a High Street, ESHER, SURREY, KT10 9RL.
•**MOORE, Mr. Roger Kevin, FCA** *1985;* (Tax Fac), Hilton Sharp & Clarke, 30 New Road, BRIGHTON, BN1 1BN.
MOORE, Mr. Roger Patrick Jonas, BCom FCA *1975;* 6 Cherwell Road, Emmer Green, READING, RG4 8QH.
MOORE, Mrs. Rosaleen Anne, BCom ACA *2003;* (Tax Fac), 14 Whitstone Lane, BECKENHAM, KENT, BR3 3FZ.
MOORE, Miss. Sally Catherine, BA ACA *1991;* Brookmead House, The Warren, East Horsley, LEATHERHEAD, SURREY, KT24 5RH.
MOORE, Mrs. Sarah Alison, BA FCA *1989;* Market Street Practice Ton-y-Felin Surgery, Bedwas Road, CAERPHILLY, MID GLAMORGAN, CF83 1XP.
MOORE, Mrs. Sarah Ann, BA(Hons) ACA *2004;* 188 War Lane, BIRMINGHAM, B17 9RU.
MOORE, Mrs. Sarah Louise, BA(Hons) ACA *2001;* 23 Riddings Hill, Balsall Common, COVENTRY, CV7 7RA.
MOORE, Mrs. Sarah Rosemary, BA ACA *1984;* Old Seven Stars, Sandpit Lane, Bledlow, PRINCES RISBOROUGH, HP27 9QQ.
MOORE, Mrs. Shirley Helen, LLB FCA *1988;* Beechings Way, Thorverton, EXETER, EX5 5LX.
MOORE, Mr. Simon Andrew, BA(Hons) ACA *2002;* 66 Berwick Avenue, CHELMSFORD, CM1 4BD.
MOORE, Mr. Simon Charles, ACA *2009;* The Manse, Brayford, BARNSTAPLE, DEVON, EX32 7QF.
MOORE, Mr. Simon Ian, BSc ACA *2003;* 13 Jasmine Gardens, HARROW, HA2 9DE.
MOORE, Mr. Simon James, BSc ACA *1999;* with KPMG LLP, St. James's Square, MANCHESTER, M2 6DS.
MOORE, Mr. Simon Paul, BSc ACA CISA CISM *1991;* 14 Leconfield Walk, HORNCHURCH, RM12 6NZ.
MOORE, Mr. Stephen, ACA *2011;* 4 Mosford Close, HORLEY, SURREY, RH6 8JS.
MOORE, Mr. Stephen Craig, FCA *1982;* Lavender House, Fishery Road, Bray, MAIDENHEAD, SL6 1UP.
MOORE, Mr. Stephen Jeremy, BA ACA *1988;* (Tax Fac), Grosvenor Group Limited, The Grosvenor Office, 70 Grosvenor Street, LONDON, W1K 3JP.
MOORE, Mr. Stephen Michael, BA ACA *1988;* Partnership Assurance, Sackville House, 143-149 Fenchurch Street, LONDON, EC3M 6BN.
MOORE, Mr. Stephen Norman, BSc ACA *1997;* Doosan House, Crawley Business Quarter, Manor Royal, CRAWLEY, WEST SUSSEX, RH10 9AD.
MOORE, Mr. Stephen Robert, BSc ACA *2004;* Alvarez & Marsal Canada ULC, Royal Bank Plaza, South Tower, 200 Bay Street, Suite 2900, PO Box 22 TORONTO M5J 2J1 ON CANADA.
•**MOORE, Mr. Steven, BA ACA** *1988;* MacIntyre Hudson LLP, Peterbridge House, The Lakes, NORTHAMPTON, NN4 7HB.
•**MOORE, Mrs. Sudipta Shima, BSc ACA** *2000;* Moore Accountancy Limited, 1 Northway, ALTRINCHAM, CHESHIRE, WA14 1NN.
MOORE, Mrs. Susan Anne, BA ACA *1992;* The Old Rectory, Shrawley, WORCESTER, WR6 6TN.

•MOORE, Mrs. Susan Elizabeth, BSc FCA CTA TEP *1979;* (Tax Fac), Sue Moore, Orchard House, Main Street, Countesthorpe, LEICESTER, LE8 5QX.
MOORE, Mrs. Susan Jane, BSc ACA *1992;* 40 Moodys Road, Clarkville, Kaiapoi RD2, CHRISTCHURCH 7692, NEW ZEALAND.
MOORE, Ms. Susan Jennifer, BSc ACA AMCT *1992;* (Tax Fac), Peartree Cottage, Sleaford Road, Beckingham, LINCOLN, LN5 0RF.
•MOORE, Miss. Susan Linda, BSc ACA *1993;* Coolbell Limited, Wigley Manor, Romsey Road, Ower, ROMSEY, HAMPSHIRE SO51 6AF.
MOORE, Mrs. Susan Mary, MA ACA *1989;* Noble Tree House, Noble Tree Road, Hildenborough, TONBRIDGE, KENT, TN11 8NB.
MOORE, Mr. Tercel Roderick, BA ACA *2002;* 33 Westwick Gardens, LONDON, W14 0BU.
MOORE, Mr. Thomas, BSc ACA *2011;* 21a Wycliffe Road, LONDON, SW19 1ES.
MOORE, Mr. Thomas, ACA *2011;* 5 Beech Close, MARKFIELD, LEICESTERSHIRE, LE67 9RT.
MOORE, Mr. Thomas, BSc ACA MCT *1997;* 23 Caroline Road, Wimbledon, LONDON, SW19 3QL.
•MOORE, Mr. Thomas Joseph, BCom ACA *2001;* Kingston Smith LLP, Devonshire House, 60 Goswell Road, LONDON, EC1M 7AD. See also Kingston Smith Limited Liability Partnership, Devonshire Corporate Services LLP and Kingston Smith Consulting LLP
MOORE, Mr. Thomas Stephen, BA ACA *1999;* N M Rothschild & Sons, 1 Park Row, LEEDS, LS1 5NR.
MOORE, Mr. Timothy, MA FCA *1973;* 19 Filton Court, Farrow Lane, LONDON, SE14 5DL.
•MOORE, Mr. Vernon Francis, FCA *1969;* GPO Box 7516, CENTRAL, HONG KONG ISLAND, HONG KONG SAR.
MOORE, Miss. Vicky Emma, ACA *2003;* 190 Cubbington Road, LEAMINGTON SPA, CV32 7AJ.
MOORE, Mr. Victor Michael, FCA *1970;* 13E Woodstock Avenue, Golders Green, LONDON, NW11 9RG.
•MOORE, Mr. William George Park, BA ACA *2003;* Saint & Co., Barclays Bank Chambers, Market Square, KESWICK, CUMBRIA, CA12 5BE.
MOORE, Mr. William John, FCA *1958;* 375 High Street, London Colney, ST ALBANS, AL2 1EA. (Life Member)
MOORE, Mrs. Yolande, BSc ACA *1987;* The Willows, 1 Willis Close, CHIPPENHAM, SN15 3GJ.
MOORE-SHUPICK, Miss. Sasha Louise, BA ACA *2002;* 17 Audrey Street, BALGOWLAH, NSW 2093, AUSTRALIA.
MOOREHEAD, Mr. Richard Michael John, BSc ACA *2007;* 29 Campbell Park Avenue, BELFAST, BT4 3FL.
MOOREHEAD, Mr. Simon Charles Wheeler, ACA *1987;* Croft Cottage, Kings Lane, Byley, MIDDLEWICH, CHESHIRE, CW10 9NB.
MOORES, Mr. Adrian Paul, ACA *1998;* 48 Rose Avenue, ABINGDON, OXFORDSHIRE, OX14 1XX.
MOORES, Miss. Alison Jane, BSc ACA *2001;* 46 Natal Road, LONDON, SW16 6HZ.
MOORES, Mrs. Amanda Susan, BA ACA *1991;* Hillside, 52 Vineyards Road, Northaw, POTTERS BAR, HERTFORDSHIRE, EN6 4PE.
MOORES, Mrs. Catherine Annette, BSc ACA *1996;* 30 Aldershot Road, Church Crookham, FLEET, HAMPSHIRE, GU52 8LG.
MOORES, Mrs. Claire Amanda, BSc(Hons) ACA *2003;* Quintain Estates, 16 Grosvenor Street, LONDON, W1K 4QF.
•MOORES, Mr. Geoffrey, FCA *1969;* 5 Dovedale Close, High Lane, STOCKPORT, CHESHIRE, SK6 8DU.
MOORES, Mrs. Gillian Ann, FCA *1964;* 143 Beaumont Road, Petts Wood, ORPINGTON, KENT, BR5 1JG.
•MOORES, Mr. Ian David, FCA *1979;* (Tax Fac), Lang Bennetts, The Old Carriage Works, Moresk Road, TRURO, CORNWALL, TR1 1DG.
MOORES, Mrs. Joanne Louise, BSc ACA *1999;* 2 College Gardens, NEW MALDEN, KT3 6NT.
MOORES, Mr. Mark David, BSc ACA *1999;* 147 Hoole Lane, CHESTER, CH2 3EQ.
MOORES, Mr. Martin John, BSc ACA *1980;* The Garden Cottage, Tokenbury, Pensilva, LISKEARD, PL14 5PJ.
MOORES, Mr. Michael John, BA ACA *1981;* 94 The Avenue, SUNBURY-ON-THAMES, TW16 5EX.
MOORES, Mr. Patrick Appleton, MA ACA *1983;* 4 Canning Place, LONDON, W8 5AD.
MOORES, Mr. Robert Patrick, BSc ACA *1987;* South Lodge, Sandy Lane, GUILDFORD, SURREY, GU3 1HF.
MOORES, Mr. Robert Paul, BA(Hons) ACA *2002;* SABMiller House, S A B Miller S A B Miller House, Church Street West, WOKING, GU21 6HS.
MOORES, Mr. Timothy Scott, FCA *1972;* 7 Holland Avenue, Knowle, SOLIHULL, WEST MIDLANDS, B93 9DW.
MOORES, Mr. William Richard, BSc ACA *1990;* Hillside, Vineyards Road, Northaw, POTTERS BAR, HERTFORDSHIRE, EN6 4PE.
MOOREY, Mr. Anthony John, FCA *1965;* 8 Mark Way, GODALMING, GU7 2BE. (Life Member)
•MOOREY, Mr. Philip Ian, FCA *1983;* (Tax Fac), Swindells LLP, 20-21 Clinton Place, SEAFORD, EAST SUSSEX, BN25 1NP.
MOORHEAD, Mr. Dominic Peter, BSc FCA *1988;* Therwilerstrasse 92, BL 4153 REINACH, SWITZERLAND.
MOORHEAD, Mrs. Erica Lucy, BSc ACA *1991;* Kinnersley House, Hollington Lane, Highclere, NEWBURY, BERKSHIRE, RG20 9SB.
MOORHEAD, Mr. Patrick Denton, FCA *1951;* North Hall, Staplefield, HAYWARDS HEATH, RH17 6AS. (Life Member)
MOORHEAD, Mr. Robert James, MA ACA *1991;* Kinnersley House, Hollington Lane, Highclere, NEWBURY, BERKSHIRE, RG20 9SB.
MOORHEAD, Ms. Sandra, BA ACA *1997;* 4 / 22 Speight Road, Kohimarama, AUCKLAND 1071, NEW ZEALAND.
MOORHOUSE, Mr. David, FCA *1964;* West Lea, Dalby, ISLE OF MAN, IM5 3BP. (Life Member)
MOORHOUSE, Mr. David Philip, MA ACA *1980;* International Coffee Organization, 22 Berners Street, LONDON, W1T 3DD.
MOORHOUSE, Mrs. Dolores Anne, MA ACA *1990;* 33 Fernhurst Road, LONDON, SW6 7JN.
MOORHOUSE, Mrs. Heather Susan, BA ACA *1993;* 8 Ferry Villas, Park Avenue, Barbourne, WORCESTER, WR3 7AQ.
MOORHOUSE, Mr. John, ACA *1982;* Arrow Commercial Centre Ltd, Grove Garage, Guy Edge, Linthwaite, HUDDERSFIELD, HD7 5TQ.
•MOORHOUSE, Mr. Kevin Peter, FCA *1993;* Kevin P Moorhouse ACA, 6 Royston Avenue, MANCHESTER, M16 8AL.
MOORHOUSE, Mr. Martin James, BA FCA *1982;* polkomtez 8a, ul posrepu 3, 02-676 WARSAW, POLAND.
MOORHOUSE, Mr. Nigel James, BSc ACA *1987;* Roman Lodge Holdings Limited, Dane Mill, Broadhurst Lane, CONGLETON, CHESHIRE, CW12 1LA.
MOORHOUSE, Mr. Paul Eon, BA FCA *1975;* Irwins Ltd, Woodbottom Mills, Low Hall Road, Horsforth, LEEDS, LS18 4EF.
MOORHOUSE, Mr. Peter, BSc(Econ) FCA *1961;* 42 Somerset Grove, ROCHDALE, OL11 5YS.
MOORHOUSE, Mr. Peter, BA ACA *2006;* (Tax Fac), Rue Marignac 3, 1206 GENEVA, SWITZERLAND.
MOORHOUSE, Mr. Richard David, ACA *2010;* 131 Riversdale Road, LONDON, N5 2SU.
MOORHOUSE, Mr. Simon, BA ACA *2001;* 255 Loughborough Road, West Bridgford, NOTTINGHAM, NG2 7EG.
•MOORHOUSE, Mr. Stephen Thomas, FCA *1975;* Sixty Circular Road, Circular Road, Douglas, ISLE OF MAN, IM1 1SA.
MOORIN, Mr. Richard Neil, BA ACA *1996;* 20 Sheldon Grove, Gosforth, NEWCASTLE UPON TYNE, NE3 4JP.
MOORJANI, Mr. Dilip Lachmandas, ACA *2010;* 148 Grasmere Avenue, WEMBLEY, MIDDLESEX, HA9 8TH.
•MOORS, Mr. Gareth Shone, BSc ACA *1995;* (Tax Fac), Moors Gibson Limited, 31 Holland Road, Kensal Rise, LONDON, NW10 5AH.
MOORS, Mr. Michael Eric, FCA *1970;* Eaton Cottage, Eaton, CONGLETON, CW12 2NA.
MOORSE, Mr. Laurence, BSc ACA *1998;* 57 Pine Road, Chandler's Ford, EASTLEIGH, HAMPSHIRE, SO53 1JU.
MOORSE, Mr. Peter Geoffrey Williams, LLB FCA *1972;* Ingon Cottage, Ingon Lane, STRATFORD-UPON-AVON, CV37 0QE.
MOORSE, Mr. Terence Wilfred, FCA *1959;* 13 North St, Nazeing, WALTHAM ABBEY, EN9 2NH.
MOORSE, Mrs. Valerie Suzanne, BCom ACA *1990;* 38 Church Avenue, Clent, STOURBRIDGE, DY9 9QT.
MOORSOM, Mr. Patrick William Pierre, MA FCA *1968;* 37 Sterndale Road, LONDON, W14 0HT.
MOORTHY, Mr. Kunal, ACA *2010;* 21 Church Meadow, Long Ditton, SURBITON, SURREY, KT6 5EP.
MOORWOOD, Mrs. Alison Louise, BSc ACA *1998;* 155 Parsonage Lane, ENFIELD, EN1 3UJ.
MOOSAJEE, Mr. Huzaifa Abdullah, MEng BA ACA *2001;* 36 Caledonian Court, 2 Taywood Road, NORTHOLT, MIDDLESEX, UB5 6GA.
MOOSAJEE, Mr. Shiraz Asker, BSc ACA *1990;* 815 St Paul Street, DENVER, CO 80206, UNITED STATES.
MOPPETT, Mr. John Stanley, FCA *1959;* Quantock, Southview Road, Findon, WORTHING, BN14 0UA. (Life Member)
MORAES, Mr. Adriano Santiago Alexander, BSc ACA *2005;* Flat 6, Arc Court, 1 Friern Barnet Road, LONDON, N11 1PT.
MORAES, Mr. John, ACA CA(AUS) *2009;* PO Box 18130, DOHA, QATAR.
MORALEE, Mr. Benjamin Stuart, BSc ACA *2003;* Serena Software Europe Ltd, Abbey View, Everard Close, ST. ALBANS, HERTFORDSHIRE, AL1 2PS.
MORALEE, Mr. Peter Lindsay, BA FCA *1975;* Leuvensestraat 64, 2587 GJ THE HAGUE, NETHERLANDS.
MORALLEE, Mr. Brian, BSc ACA *1984;* 11 Earldom Road, Putney, LONDON, SW15 1AF.
MORALLEE, Mrs. Karen Jane, BA ACA *1985;* 11 Earldom Road, Putney, LONDON, SW15 1AF.
MORAN, Mrs. Alison Patricia, BA ACA *1993;* Thames Valley Police, Meadow House, Spires Business Park, OXFORD, OX1 1SZ.
•MORAN, Mrs. Amanda Jane, BSc FCA *1984;* (Tax Fac), Amanda J Moran, 7 Goosebrook Close, Comberbach, NORTHWICH, CHESHIRE, CW9 6BX.
MORAN, Mrs. Angela Joy, BA ACA *1992;* R & B Ltd, Meteor House, Whittle Road, SALISBURY, SP2 7YW.
MORAN, Miss. Anita, BA ACA *1993;* Lombardy, Promenade de Verdun, PURLEY, SURREY, CR8 3LN.
MORAN, Mr. Carl Patrick, BSc ACA *1991;* (Tax Fac), 97 Harlington Road West, FELTHAM, TW14 0JG.
MORAN, Miss. Caroline, BA ACA *2002;* 26 Cresswell Grove, West Didsbury, MANCHESTER, M20 2NH.
MORAN, Miss. Caroline Anna, ACA *2009;* 110 Woodhouse Lane, SALE, CHESHIRE, M33 4LH.
MORAN, Ms. Claire Bernadette, BSc ACA *1989;* Garden House, Garden House Lane, Rickinghall, DISS, NORFOLK, IP22 1EA.
MORAN, Mr. Damian John, ACA *2008;* 191 Willow Avenue, BIRMINGHAM, B17 8HJ.
MORAN, Mr. David Charles, BSc ACA *1993;* West Springs, North Side, Steeple Aston, BICESTER, OX25 4SE.
MORAN, Mr. David John, BSc ACA *1991;* 46 Barclay Road, LONDON, SW6 1EH.
MORAN, Mrs. Deborah, ACA *1982;* The White House, 35 Arthog Road, Hale, ALTRINCHAM, CHESHIRE, WA15 0LY.
MORAN, Mrs. Elizabeth Ann, BSc FCA *1988;* Lane Croft, Back Lane, Airton, SKIPTON, BD23 4AL.
MORAN, Mr. Graham James, BSc ACA *1992;* 10 Norfolk Court, Victoria Point, BRISBANE, QLD 4165, AUSTRALIA.
MORAN, Mrs. Jacqueline Ruth, BA ACA *1993;* 24 Douglas Avenue, Gosforth, NEWCASTLE UPON TYNE, NE3 4XD.
MORAN, Miss. Julie Anne, BA ACA *2002;* 29 Druids Cross Gardens, LIVERPOOL, L18 3EB.
•MORAN, Miss. Kathryn Louise, BSc FCA *1993;* Wingrave Yeats Partnership LLP, 101 Wigmore Street, LONDON, W1U 1QU. See also Wingrave Yeats Limited
MORAN, Mr. Mark, BA ACA *1989;* 11 Elbe Street, LONDON, SW6 2QP.
MORAN, Mr. Michael George, FCA *1960;* Nailbourne Oast, Boughton-under-Blean, FAVERSHAM, KENT, ME13 9NB. (Life Member)
MORAN, Mr. Michael John, ACA *2006;* Deloitte, Level 19 Uptown 1 Damansara Uptown, 1 Jalan SS 21/58, 47400 PETALING JAYA, MALAYSIA.
MORAN, Mr. Michael Joseph, BCom FCA *1976;* Maraussan, Gorsewood Road, Hartley, LONGFIELD, KENT, DA3 7DH.
•MORAN, Mr. Michael Thomas, BA FCA *1997;* RL Moran Limited, Fernwood House, Fernwood Road, Jesmond, NEWCASTLE UPON TYNE, NE2 1TJ.
MORAN, Mr. Nicholas, BSc ACA *1986;* New Finance Capital Partners, 20 North Audley Street, LONDON, W1K 6WE.
•MORAN, Mr. Paul Burnett, BSc FCA *1989;* with KPMG LLP, Quayside House, 110 Quayside, NEWCASTLE UPON TYNE, NE1 3DX.
MORAN, Ms. Ruth, BSc ACA *1991;* 502 Broad Lane, Bramley, LEEDS, LS13 3HB.
MORAN, Mr. Sean, BA ACA *1992;* 15 Waun Y Felin, Penclawdd, SWANSEA, SA4 3RD.
MORAN, Mr. Stephen George, BA ACA *1997;* Newcastle Marriott Gosforth Park Hotel, High Gosforth Park, NEWCASTLE UPON TYNE, NE3 5HN.
MORAN, Mrs. Susan Elizabeth, BA ACA *2006;* 8 Broomlee Close, NEWCASTLE UPON TYNE, NE7 7GF.
MORAN, Mr. Timothy Neil, MA ACA *2003;* 32 Coronet Avenue, NORTHWICH, CW9 8FW.
MORAN, Mr. William, FCA *1972;* (Tax Fac), 57a Lisson Street, LONDON, NW1 5DA.
MORANA, Mr. Stephen Gavin, BA ACA *1998;* Betfair Ltd, Hammersmith Embankment, Winslow Road, Hammersmith, LONDON, W6 9HP.
MORANDI, Mr. Fabio, BSc(Econ) ACA CFA *2001;* Flat 1, 55 Greencroft Gardens, LONDON, NW6 3LL.
MORANDI, Mr. Marco, BA ACA *2010;* Flat 1, 55 Greencroft Gardens, LONDON, NW6 3LL.
MORANT, Mr. Leslie Guy Mark, FCA *1969;* 20 Seeleys Road, BEACONSFIELD, HP9 1SZ.
MORANT, Mr. Mark, BA FCA *1982;* 8 Beaver Ridge Court, ELGIN, SC 29045, UNITED STATES.
MORANT, Mr. Stephen Peter, FCA *1973;* The Old Rectory, West Knoyle, WARMINSTER, BA12 6AF.
MORAR, Mrs. Sandhya, BA ACA CTA *1995;* with KPMG LLP, 15 Canada Square, LONDON, E14 5GL.
MORARBHAI, Mr. Naresh Harilal, BSc ACA *1994;* (Tax Fac), 22 Severn Road, Oadby, LEICESTER, LE2 4FY.
MORARI, Mrs. Clare Louise, BA ACA *1985;* Flat 103, Sterea Court No. 6, Pinelopis Street Neapolis, 3101 LIMASSOL, CYPRUS.
MORAWIECKA, Mrs. Elizabeth Diana, BCom ACA *1990;* Warham Farmhouse, Breinton, HEREFORD, HR4 7PE.
MORBEY, Mr. John David, BA ACA *1981;* 49 The Oaks, WEST BYFLEET, KT14 6RN.
MORBEY, Mr. Mark Geoffrey, MA ACA *1985;* Prudential Plc, Governors House, Laurence Pountney Hill, LONDON, EC4R 0HH.
MORCELLA, Mrs. Clare Alexandra, LLB ACA *2000;* 96 Christopher Street, MONTCLAIR, NJ 07042, UNITED STATES.
MORCELLA, Mr. Richard, BSc(Hons) ACA *2002;* Flat 4, 213 Putney Bridge Road, LONDON, SW15 2NY.
MORCH, Mrs. Shirley Wigham, BSc FCA *1987;* Peach Tree Barn, Back Lane, Kirkby Lonsdale, CARNFORTH, LA6 2AP.
MORCHER, Mr. David John, ACA *2010;* Flat 4, 80 Aberdeen Road, LONDON, N5 2XA.
MORCOM, Mr. Geoffrey Colin, FCA *1953;* hawkswick, Horsebridge Road, Broughton, STOCKBRIDGE, HAMPSHIRE, SO20 8BD. (Life Member)
MORCOS, Mr. Jean-Louis Magdi-Louis, MSc BSc ACA *2008;* Flat 1507 East Tower, 3 Pan Peninsula Square, LONDON, E149HP.
•MORCOS, Mr. Magdi Louis, BA FCA *1971;* 88 Abdul Salaam Aref, Glym, ALEXANDRIA, EGYPT.
MORCOS, Mr. Raafat Saad, FCA *1990;* Paradiesweg 14, 8645 JONA, SWITZERLAND.
•MORDAN, Mrs. Keren Elizabeth, FCA *1991;* (Tax Fac), Metherell Gard, Old Memorial Hall, Morval, LOOE, CORNWALL, PL13 1PN.
MORDANT, Mr. Simon David, ACA *1983;* 1/ 101 Darling Point Road, DARLING POINT, NSW 2027, AUSTRALIA.
MORDECAI, Mr. David Jonathan, ACA *1985;* Three Chimneys, Tylers Green, Cuckfield, HAYWARDS HEATH, RH17 5EA.
MORDY, Mr. William Henry John, MBE FCA *1964;* (Member of Council 1980 - 1995), 14 Manor Close, Bramhope, LEEDS, LS16 9HQ. (Life Member)
MORE, Mrs. Caroline Susan, BSc ACA *1989;* Scott Brownrigg Ltd, St Catherines Court, 46-48 Portsmouth Road, GUILDFORD, GU2 4DU.
MORE, Mr. James Leighton, BA(Hons) ACA *2001;* 11 Holder Close, Shinfield, READING, RG2 9HQ.
MORE, Miss. Julie Ann, ACA *1993;* 2nd FLoor, 10i Hing Keng Shek, SAI KUNG, HONG KONG SAR.
MORE-KING, Mr. William Sharp, BSc ACA *1998;* 15 Cotton Lane, BIRMINGHAM, B13 9SA.
MORE O'FERRALL, Mr. Brian Denis, LLB ACA *1995;* 62 Inglethorpe Street, LONDON, SW6 6NX.
MOREA, Mr. Victor Rudolph, FCA *1952;* 42 Buccaneer Close, Woodley, READING, RG5 4XP. (Life Member)
MOREAR, Mr. Daniel John, BA(Hons) ACA *2002;* 3 Barrymore Crescent, Comberbach, NORTHWICH, CHESHIRE, CW9 6PA.
MORECOMBE, Mr. Richard Henry Whitman, ACA *1988;* Numis Securities, Cheapside House, 138 Cheapside, LONDON, EC2V 6LH.
MOREIN, Mr. David Mendel, FCA *1956;* 10 Blandford Close, LONDON, N2 0DH. (Life Member)

MOREL, Mr. William John, FCA *1968;* Laburnham Cottage, 16 Wappenham Road, Abthorpe, TOWCESTER, NN12 8QU. (Life Member)
MORELAND, Mr. Dominic Michael, BSc(Econ) ACA *1993;* 39 The Crescent, MAIDENHEAD, SL6 6AG.
MORELAND, Mrs. Pamela Ann, BA FCA *1982;* (Tax Fac), Lime Cottage, Kiln Lane, Brambridge, EASTLEIGH, SO50 6HT.
MORELL, Mr. David Charles, BA FCA *1985;* 10 Fernbank, Finchampstead, WOKINGHAM, RG40 4XB.
MORELLI, Mr. Antonio Carlo, BA FCA *1984;* Corner Farm, Huntingfield, HALESWORTH, IP19 0LL.
MORELLI, Mr. Charles Timothy, BA ACA *2005;* Chess Rooks, Mayfield Lane, WADHURST, TN5 6JE.
MOREMAN, Mrs. Susan Ann, BSc ACA *1992;* Eglantine House, Sand Road, WEDMORE, SOMERSET, BS28 4BY.
MORETON, Mr. Alastair John, BSc ACA *1987;* 8 Grove Way, ESHER, KT10 8HL.
MORETON, Mr. Christopher John, FCA *1967;* 505 Water Shadow Lane, ALPHARETTA, GA 30022, UNITED STATES.
MORETON, Mr. Christopher Quinton, BA FCA *1975;* 7 Fuller Close, WADHURST, EAST SUSSEX, TN5 6HY.
MORETON, Mrs. Elisabeth Claire, BSc ACA *1990;* Moreton & Co, Armscote House, Dowdeswell, CHELTENHAM, GLOUCESTERSHIRE, GL54 4LU.
•MORETON, Mr. Gary Kevin, BA FCA DChA *1984;* Baker Tilly UK Audit LLP, St Philips Point, Temple Row, BIRMINGHAM, B2 5AF. See also Baker Tilly Tax and Advisory Services LLP
MORETON, Mr. James Edward, BSc ACA *2010;* Flat 3, 3-11 Marshall Street, SURRY HILLS, NSW 2010, AUSTRALIA.
•MORETON, Mr. James Walter Edward, BA FCA *1987;* Moreton & Co, Armscote House, Upper Dowdeswell, Andoversford, CHELTENHAM, GLOUCESTERSHIRE GL54 4LU.
MORETON, Mrs. Julie Kay, ACA *1986;* D H Jones (Hardware) Ltd, T/AS International Door Controls, Unit 23 Timmis Road, Lye, STOURBRIDGE, WEST MIDLANDS DY9 7BQ.
MORETON, Mr. Nigel Keef, BSc ACA *1986;* Garrick House, 2 Queen Street, LICHFIELD, STAFFORDSHIRE, WS13 6QD.
MORETON, Mr. Richard, MPhys ACA *2009;* 1 Malmesbury Road, LONDON, E3 2EB.
MORETTA, Miss. Louise Joanne, BSc ACA *2001;* 475 48th Avenue, Apartment 409, LONG ISLAND CITY, NY 11109, UNITED STATES.
MORETTI, Mr. Philip Edward, BA ACA *1990;* Casey Lester, Equity House, 57 Hill Avenue, AMERSHAM, BUCKINGHAMSHIRE, HP6 5UN.
MOREY, Mr. Alexandre Du Hautbourg, BSc ACA *1992;* Lambriggan Court Lambriggan, Penhallow, TRURO, CORNWALL, TR4 9LU.
MOREY, Mrs. Anne, BSc FCA *1983;* Mannin Veen, Roundwood Avenue, Hutton, BRENTWOOD, ESSEX, CM13 2ND.
MOREY, Mr. Christopher John, BA(Hons) ACA *2003;* with Kaplan Financial, Woodhall Duckham House, 11 The Boulevard, CRAWLEY, WEST SUSSEX, RH10 1UX.
MOREY, Mrs. Clare Helen, BA ACA *1992;* 3 Quarry Gardens, Waterloo Road, TONBRIDGE, TN9 2SG.
•MOREY, Mr. Colin, BSc FCA *1980;* (Tax Fac), Colin Morey, 22 Charlock Way, Burpham, GUILDFORD, SURREY, GU1 1YB.
MOREY, Mr. David Lawrence, BSc ACA *1986;* The Old Barn, Lower Street, Hildenborough, TONBRIDGE, KENT, TN11 8PT.
MOREY, Mr. Ian Malcolm, BSc FCA *1982;* Visteon Eng Serv Ltd, 1 Springfield Lyons Approach, Springfield, CHELMSFORD, CM2 5LB.
MOREY, Miss. Lyn Rosalie, BSc FCA CTA *1986;* with Hazlewoods LLP, Staverton Court, Staverton, CHELTENHAM, GLOUCESTERSHIRE, GL51 0UX.
MOREY, Mr. Neil, BA ACA *1992;* 3 Quarry Gardens, Waterloo Road, TONBRIDGE, TN9 2SG.
MOREY, Mr. Paul John, BSc ACA *1998;* Cherry Cottage, Stoke Hamlet Back Stoke Lane, Westbury on Trym, BRISTOL, BS9 3QT.
•MORFAKIS, Mr. Costas, BA FCA FCCA FCMA *1992;* Bond Partners LLP, The Grange, 100 High Street, LONDON, N14 6TB. See also Bond Group LLP
MORFETT, Mr. Thomas, ACA *2008;* 29 Marathon Avenue, Douglas, ISLE OF MAN, IM2 4JB.
MORGAN, Mr. Adrian Lyn, BSc ACA *1990;* 22 Grange Gardens, LONDON, N14 6QP.
MORGAN, Mr. Alan, FCA *1954;* 22 Jesmond Park West, NEWCASTLE UPON TYNE, NE7 7BY. (Life Member)
MORGAN, Mr. Alan John, MA FCA ATII *1984;* Chilcomb Manor, Chilcomb, WINCHESTER, SO21 1HR.
MORGAN, Mr. Alan Martin, BA ACA CTA *1997;* (Tax Fac), 32 Windmill Gardens, ENFIELD, EN2 7DU.
MORGAN, Mr. Alexander John, MEng ACA *2004;* Flat 3, 17 Woodville Gardens, LONDON, W5 2LL.
MORGAN, Mr. Alexander Leslie, MBA FCA *1973;* 11 Millers Way, NORTHAMPTON, NN4 5AL.
MORGAN, Miss. Alison, ACA *2011;* 139 Willersley Avenue, SIDCUP, KENT, DA15 9EP.
MORGAN, Miss. Alison Goldie, BA ACA *1981;* 2 Heath Common, Heath, CHESTERFIELD, S44 5SR.
MORGAN, Mr. Alistair, BA ACA *2006;* 1 Rissington Avenue, BIRMINGHAM, B29 7SX.
•MORGAN, Mr. Alistair David Miles, MA FCA CTA *2000;* Rawlinson & Hunter Limited, Trafalgar Court, 3rd Floor, West Wing, St Peter Port, GUERNSEY GY1 2JA.
MORGAN, Mr. Andre Sylvain, FCA *1970;* 45 Kimberley Drive, LYDNEY, GL15 5AF.
MORGAN, Mr. Andrew Keith, BSc(Econ) ACA *1999;* 64 Elm Grove Road, LONDON, SW13 0BS.
•MORGAN, Mr. Andrew Raymond John, BSc FCA CTA *1991;* (Tax Fac), KPMG LLP, Arlington Business Park, Theale, READING, RG7 4SD. See also KPMG Europe LLP
•MORGAN, Mr. Andrew Rees, BA FCA *1991;* PricewaterhouseCoopers, 7 More London Riverside, LONDON, SE1 2RT. See also PricewaterhouseCoopers LLP
MORGAN, Mr. Andrew Richard, BSc FCA *1991;* 72 Risca Road, NEWPORT, NP20 4JA.
•MORGAN, Mr. Andrew Robert Quayle, FCA *1972;* (Tax Fac), Andrew R Q Morgan Ltd, Oaklea, LLANSANTFFRAID, SY22 6TE.
MORGAN, Mr. Andrew Thomas Bainbridge, BA ACA *2005;* Flat 1, 19 Upper Brighton Road, SURBITON, SURREY, KT6 6QX.
MORGAN, Mr. Andrew Timothy, MA MEng ACA *2006;* 5 Brassey Road, WINCHESTER, SO22 6RZ.
MORGAN, Mrs. Anna Marie, BSc ACA *1999;* 70 Clarence Road, LONDON, SW19 8QE.
MORGAN, Mr. Anthony David, BSc FCA *1978;* Mewslade, St Andrews Road, DINAS POWYS, CF64 4AT.
MORGAN, Mr. Anthony Gerald, BSc FCA *1973;* Kimber Cottage, Woodstock Road, Charlbury, CHIPPING NORTON, OXFORDSHIRE, OX7 3ET.
•MORGAN, Mr. Anthony Paul, BSc FCA *1970;* A.P. Morgan, 17 Friths Drive, REIGATE, RH2 0DS.
MORGAN, Mr. Anthony Tregerthen, BA ACA *1982;* Abbotswood, Abbotswood Drive, WEYBRIDGE, kt13 0lt.
MORGAN, Mr. Arwel Brynmor, FCA *1978;* 2 Havergal Close, Caswell, SWANSEA, SA3 4RL.
MORGAN, Dr. Barry Ronald, FCA *1976;* 33 Tongdean Avenue, HOVE, BN3 6TL.
•MORGAN, Mrs. Belinda Jane, ACA *1986;* CK, No 4 Castle Court 2, Castlegate Way, DUDLEY, WEST MIDLANDS, DY1 4RH.
MORGAN, Mr. Bernard Thomas, FCA *1971;* Ty-Haf, School Lane, Llantrisent, USK, NP15 1LG.
MORGAN, Mrs. Beverley Jayne, FCA *1990;* 242 Cooden Drive, Cooden, BEXHILL-ON-SEA, TN39 3AG.
•MORGAN, Mr. Brian Anthony, FCA *1960;* Morgan Revill Accountants, 73 Sheepwalk Lane, Ravenshead, NOTTINGHAM, NG15 9FD.
MORGAN, Mrs. Caroline Mary, ACA *1989;* La Verna Bagatelle Lane, St. Saviour, JERSEY, JE2 7TD.
MORGAN, Mrs. Catherine Susan, ACA *1986;* Mill Farm, Moor Lee Lane, Great Heck, GOOLE, NORTH YORKSHIRE, DN14 0BP.
MORGAN, Mrs. Catrin Sarah Louise, MChem ACA *2010;* 6 The Village, Brancepeth, DURHAM, DH7 8DG.
MORGAN, Miss. Cerys Louise, BA ACA *2006;* 573a, 573 Garratt Lane, LONDON, SW18 4ST.
MORGAN, Mr. Charles Edward John, FCA *1960;* Old School House, 1 Church Street, USK, NP15 1AG. (Life Member)
MORGAN, Mr. Charles William Thomas, MA ACA MCT *1988;* 1025 Smith Ridge Road, NEW CANAAN, CT 06840, UNITED STATES.
MORGAN, Miss. Charlotte Elisabeth Diana, MA FCA AMCT *1980;* (Tax Fac), 72 Richmond Ave, LONDON, N1 0NA.
MORGAN, Mrs. Charlotte Maria, BA ACA *1996;* 4th Floor, 60 Sloane Avenue, LONDON, SW3 3XB.
MORGAN, Mr. Christopher, BSc ACA *2005;* 28 Cordingley Road, RUISLIP, MIDDLESEX, HA4 7HQ.
MORGAN, Mr. Christopher David, BA FCA *1995;* 20 Tynedale Avenue, WHITLEY BAY, NE26 3BA.
MORGAN, Mr. Christopher Hugh, MA ACA *1988;* 9 York Mansions, Prince of Wales Drive, LONDON, SW11 4DN.
MORGAN, Mr. Christopher James, MA(Oxon) ACA *2009;* Flat 11 Woolcombes Court, Princes Riverside Road, LONDON, SE16 5RQ.
MORGAN, Mr. Christopher Paul, BSc ACA *1987;* Carnoustie, La Rue Des Buttes, St. Mary, JERSEY, JE3 3DE.
MORGAN, Mrs. Claire Elizabeth, BA ACA *1999;* 68 Theynes Croft, Long Ashton, BRISTOL, BS41 9NA.
MORGAN, Mrs. Claire Meredith, BSc ACA *1993;* 30 Woodmere Way, BECKENHAM, BR3 6SL.
MORGAN, Mr. Colin Graham, ACA *1995;* 30 Cardy Road, HEMEL HEMPSTEAD, HERTFORDSHIRE, HP1 1SQ.
MORGAN, Mr. Cyril Gerald, FCA *1974;* 59 Woodstock Road, LONDON, NW11 8QD.
MORGAN, Mr. Cyril Herbert, FCA *1960;* 12 Acorn Drive, WOKINGHAM, BERKSHIRE, RG40 1EQ. (Life Member)
MORGAN, Mr. Daniel John, BSc ACA *1994;* 30 Woodmere Way, BECKENHAM, KENT, BR3 6SL.
•MORGAN, Mr. Daniel William, ACA *2007;* Haines Watts, 2nd Floor, Argyll House, 23 Brook Street, KINGSTON UPON THAMES, SURREY KT1 2BN.
MORGAN, Mr. David, FCA *1960;* Golden Grove, Red Bank, WELSHPOOL, SY21 7PT. (Life Member)
MORGAN, Dr. David Andrew, BSc FCA *1996;* (Tax Fac), with PricewaterhouseCoopers LLP, Pricewaterhousecoopers, 12 Plumtree Court, LONDON, EC4A 4HT.
MORGAN, Mr. David Clement, FCA *1961;* Somersby, Oatlands Avenue, WEYBRIDGE, KT13 9TN.
MORGAN, Mr. David Edward, ACA *1989;* 3105 El Portal, ALAMEDA, CA 94502, UNITED STATES.
MORGAN, Mr. David Eric, MA FCA *1968;* Ness Hall, Station Road, Ravenscar, SCARBOROUGH, NORTH YORKSHIRE, YO13 0LX. (Life Member)
MORGAN, Mr. David Euan, BSc ACA *1987;* 4 Penrith Way, AYLESBURY, HP21 7JZ.
MORGAN, Mr. David James, BSc(Hons) ACA *2010;* Apartment 22, 4 The Waterfront, MANCHESTER, M11 4AU.
MORGAN, Mr. David James, MA ACA *1979;* Driver and Vehicle Licensing Agency, Longview Road, SWANSEA, SA6 7JL.
MORGAN, Mr. David John, ACA *2009;* 150 WRAYSBURY DRIVE, WEST DRAYTON, MIDDLESEX, UB7 7FR.
•MORGAN, Mr. David John, FCA *1976;* Crowe Morgan, 8 St. George's Street, Douglas, ISLE OF MAN, IM1 1AH.
MORGAN, Mr. David John, ACA *1992;* Flat 20 Rowan Court, Ely Road, CARDIFF, CF5 2JB.
•MORGAN, Mr. David Leonard, FCA *1960;* Campion Accountancy, St. Marys House, Clifton Road, WINCHESTER, HAMPSHIRE, SO22 5BP.
MORGAN, Mr. David Llewellyn, FCA *1960;* Chudleigh, The Close, RUSTINGTON, WEST SUSSEX, BN16 2DW. (Life Member)
•MORGAN, Mr. David Llewellyn Thomas, FCA *1969;* David Morgan & Co, 52 High Street, Harrow-on-the-Hill, HARROW, HA1 3LL.
MORGAN, Mr. David Robert, FCA *1967;* 28 Highfield Way, RICKMANSWORTH, HERTFORDSHIRE, WD3 7PR. (Life Member)
MORGAN, Mr. David Wayne, BSc FCA *1979;* 21 Duchess Drive, SEAFORD, BN25 2XL.
MORGAN, Mr. David William, MA ACA *1983;* The Old Parsonage, Rolvenden, CRANBROOK, TN17 4LS.
•MORGAN, Mr. David William, FCA *1968;* David W. Morgan, 32 Llanforda Rise, OSWESTRY, SY11 1SY.
MORGAN, Mrs. Dawn Caroline, FCA *1988;* Seaview St. Clair Hill, St. Sampson, GUERNSEY, GY2 4DS.
MORGAN, Mr. Dennis Gerald, FCA *1974;* ACORN HOUSE, 7a Station New Road, Brundall, NORWICH, NR13 5PQ.
MORGAN, Mrs. Diana, BA ACA *2006;* Flat 1, St Bernards, 19 Upper Brighton Road, SURBITON, SURREY, KT6 6QX.
MORGAN, Mr. Dominic Albert Daniel, BA(Hons) ACA CTA *2003;* Emerson Process Management, Blegistrasse 23, 6341 BAAR, SWITZERLAND.
MORGAN, Mr. Donald Edward, FCA *1961;* 3 Richmond Road, SOLIHULL, B92 7RN. (Life Member)
MORGAN, Mr. Douglas Guy Richard, BA FCA *1985;* Associated Newspapers Ltd, Room 345, Northcliffe House, 2 Derry Street, LONDON, W8 5TT.
MORGAN, Mr. Douglas James William, FCA *1952;* 61 Exeter Road, HARROW, HA2 9PQ. (Life Member)
MORGAN, Mr. Eiddig Sion, ACA *2009;* Sarnau, Bwlchllan, LAMPETER, DYFED, SA48 8QH.
MORGAN, Miss. Felicity Amy, MA ACA *2000;* 2 Old Park, Norwood Lane, Graffham, PETWORTH, WEST SUSSEX, GU28 0QQ.
MORGAN, Mr. Gareth, BA ACA *2007;* with Deloitte LLP, 5 Callaghan Square, CARDIFF, CF10 5BT.
MORGAN, Mr. Gareth, MSc BSc ACA *2004;* with HSBC Bank plc, 62-76 Park Street, LONDON, SE1 9DZ.
MORGAN, Mr. Gareth Huw, BA ACA *1988;* 27 Brandywine Road, SKILLMAN, NJ 08558, UNITED STATES.
MORGAN, Mr. Gareth Peter, BA ACA *1995;* Flat 31 Grierson House, Aldrington Road, LONDON, SW16 1TN.
MORGAN, Mr. Gavin, MA ACA *1999;* Micross IT Ltd, The Maltings, East Tyndall Street, CARDIFF, CF24 5EA.
MORGAN, Mr. Gavin Haydn, BSc(Hons) ACA *2003;* 40 Lakeside Drive, CARDIFF, CF23 6DG.
MORGAN, Mr. Geoffrey Damien, MA ACA *2001;* Flat 1, 31 Greencroft Gardens, LONDON, NW6 3LN.
MORGAN, Mr. Geoffrey William, PhD BA ACA *1980;* 26 Highworth Road, FARINGDON, SN7 7EE.
•MORGAN, Mr. Gerald Charles, BSc FCA *1987;* (Tax Fac), G C Morgan Limited, Clive House, Severn Road, WELSHPOOL, POWYS, SY21 7AL.
MORGAN, Mr. Glyn James, ACA *2008;* 3 St. Ethelberts Close, Sutton St. Nicholas, HEREFORD, HR1 3BF.
•MORGAN, Mr. Graham Anthony, FCA *1975;* (Tax Fac), Kingston Smith LLP, Devonshire House, 60 Goswell Road, LONDON, EC1M 7AD. See also Kingston Smith Limited Liability Partnership, Devonshire Corporate Services LLP and Kingston Smith Consulting LLP
•MORGAN, Mr. Guy Johnathan, BSc(Econ) FCA *1995;* Crowe Clark Whitehill LLP, Hatherton House, Hatherton Street, WALSALL, WS1 1YB. See also Horwath Clark Whitehill LLP and Crowe Clark Whitehill
MORGAN, Mr. Guy Kenneth, BSc ACA *1989;* Craglee, Leny Road, CALLANDER, FK17 8AL.
•MORGAN, Mr. Gwilym Rees, FCA *1977;* Gwilym R Morgan, 25 Seafield Close, East Wittering, CHICHESTER, WEST SUSSEX, PO20 8DP.
MORGAN, Mr. Harry Robert, ACA *2008;* Flat 17, 43-44 Nevern Square, LONDON, SW5 9PF.
MORGAN, Mrs. Helen Margaret Lilian, MA(Cantab) ACA *2000;* 17 Seer Mead, Seer Green, BEACONSFIELD, BUCKINGHAMSHIRE, HP9 2QL.
MORGAN, Mrs. Hilary Mary, BSc ACA *1980;* Llandaff Diocesan Office, The Court, Coychurch, BRIDGEND, MID GLAMORGAN, CF35 5EH.
MORGAN, Miss. Holly, BSc ACA *2011;* 14 Dragon Lane, Newbold Verdon, LEICESTER, LE9 9NG.
MORGAN, Mr. Hugh Owen, BSc ACA *1992;* 19 Penmaes, Pentyrch, CARDIFF, CF15 9QS.
•MORGAN, Mr. Hugh William, BSc FCA *1990;* with Baker Tilly UK Audit LLP, The Clock House, 140 London Road, GUILDFORD, SURREY, GU1 1UW.
MORGAN, Mr. Huw Jonathan, MSc BA ACA *1992;* 300 Rochdale Road, TODMORDEN, OL14 7PT.
MORGAN, Mr. Iain Kenneth, MA ACA *1988;* 11 Eastwick Drive, Bookham, LEATHERHEAD, KT23 3PY.
•MORGAN, Mr. Ian David, FCA *1966;* (Tax Fac), Hendraws Limited, 23 Blatchington Road, TUNBRIDGE WELLS, KENT, TN2 5EG.
MORGAN, Mr. Ian Hugh, BSc FCA *1992;* 13 Draper Street, ORMOND, VIC 3204, AUSTRALIA.
MORGAN, Mr. Ioan Christopher, BA FCA *1970;* P O Box 3804, MBABANE, SWAZILAND.
MORGAN, Mr. James Anthony Edward, BSc ACA *2000;* 61 Robert Street, BENTLEIGH, VIC 3204, AUSTRALIA.
MORGAN, Mr. James Robert, BA(Hons) ACA *2003;* PricewaterhouseCoopers, Dorchester House, 7Church Street, HAMILTON HM11, BERMUDA.
•MORGAN, Mrs. Janet, BSc FCA *1984;* Smith Cooper, Wilmot House, St James Court, Friar Gate, DERBY, DE1 1BT. See also Smith Cooper LLP
MORGAN, Miss. Janet, BSc FCA *1981;* Oakfield, 3 Maescelyn, BRECON, POWYS, LD3 7NL. (Life Member)

MORGAN, Mr. Jeffrey Woosnam, BSc FCA *1982;* Yr Hen Felin, Blaenffos, BONCATH, SIR BENFRO, SA37 0JA.
MORGAN, Miss. Jennifer, BSc ACA *2005;* FTSE International, Floor 12, 10 Upper Bank Street, LONDON, E14 5NP.
MORGAN, Miss. Jennifer Anne, LLB ACA *1994;* Flat 2, 6 Greenlaw Avenue, PAISLEY, PA1 3RA.
•MORGAN, Mrs. Jennifer Jane, BSc ACA *1990;* KPMG LLP, One Snowhill, Snow Hill Queensway, BIRMINGHAM, B4 6GN. See also KPMG Europe LLP
MORGAN, Mr. Jeremy Paul David, BSc FCA *1974;* New York Air Brake Corporation, 748 Starbuck Avenue, WATERTOWN, NY 13601, UNITED STATES.
MORGAN, Mrs. Joanne, ACA *2008;* Rogers Spencer, Newstead House, Pelham Road, NOTTINGHAM, NG5 1AP.
MORGAN, Mrs. Joanne, LLB FCA *1999;* 1 Corfe Close, ALRESFORD, HAMPSHIRE, SO24 9PH.
MORGAN, Mrs. Joanne Elizabeth, BA ACA *1990;* The White Horse Medical Practice, The Faringdon Medical Centre Volunteer Way, FARINGDON, OXFORDSHIRE, SN7 7YU.
•MORGAN, Mr. John, FCA *1977;* J Morgan & Co, 3 Woodford Way, Wombourne, WOLVERHAMPTON, WV5 8HD.
MORGAN, Mr. John Anthony, BA ACA *1982;* 69 Nassau Road, Barnes, LONDON, SW13 9QG.
•MORGAN, Mr. John Dennis, BSc FCA *1977;* PricewaterhouseCoopers LLP, 1 Embankment Place, LONDON, WC2N 6RH. See also PricewaterhouseCoopers
MORGAN, Mr. John Edwin, FCA *1994;* 14 Marlborough View, Cove, FARNBOROUGH, HAMPSHIRE, GU14 9YA.
MORGAN, Mr. John Gareth, BA FCA *1955;* Parc Llettis, Penpergwm, ABERGAVENNY, NP7 9AE. (Life Member)
MORGAN, Mr. John Henry, FCA *1962;* Sparrows Farm, Henham Road, Debden Green, SAFFRON WALDEN, ESSEX, CB11 3LZ.
MORGAN, Mr. John Howell, FCA *1960;* 64 Wyvern Villas, Falcondale Road, Westbury On Trym, BRISTOL, BS9 3JH. (Life Member)
•MORGAN, Mr. John Jeffrey, BSc FCA *1975;* (Tax Fac), John Morgan (Accountancy) Ltd, Ivy Cottage, Sennybridge, BRECON, LD3 8PG.
MORGAN, Mr. John Kenneth Seymour, MA ACA *1981;* Flat 1, 1 Strathmore Gardens, LONDON, W8 4RZ.
MORGAN, Mr. John Peter William, MSc FCA *1970;* Maes-y-Mor, 14 Forrest Road, PENARTH, SOUTH GLAMORGAN, CF64 5BT.
MORGAN, Mr. John Richard, FCA *1951;* Shadrack Barn, Burton Bradstock, BRIDPORT, DT6 4QG. (Life Member)
MORGAN, Mr. John James Grubb, MPhys ACA *2010;* 6 The Village, Brancepeth, DURHAM, DH7 8DG.
MORGAN, Mr. Jonathan Michael, BSc FCA *1999;* 15702 Hinkle Avenue, BELTON, MO 64012, UNITED STATES.
MORGAN, Mr. Jonathan William, MA ACA *1999;* The Flat, 62 Highgate High Street, LONDON, N6 5HX.
MORGAN, Mr. Julian Timothy, BSc ACA *1989;* Little Leadon, Fromes Hill, LEDBURY, HR8 1HT.
MORGAN, Miss. Julie Meryl Joan, BSc FCA *1984;* 62 Eastbury Grove, Chiswick, LONDON, W4 2JU.
•MORGAN, Mrs. June Elizabeth, FCA *1971;* (Tax Fac), Morgan & Morgan, 9 Lakeside Gardens, MERTHYR TYDFIL, MID GLAMORGAN, CF48 1EN.
MORGAN, Miss. Karen Anne, BA ACA *2002;* 10 Whitegate Road, WINSFORD, CHESHIRE, CW7 2NL.
MORGAN, Miss. Kate Louise, BSc ACA *2009;* 21 Foxboro Road, REDHILL, RH1 1TD.
MORGAN, Miss. Katie Victoria, BA ACA *2005;* 9 Blackbird Close, Burghfield Common, READING, RG7 3PQ.
•ⓘMORGAN, Mr. Keith Roger, FCA *1982;* 54 Dan-y-Graig, Pantmawr, CARDIFF, CF14 7HL.
MORGAN, Mr. Kenneth, FCA *1968;* with Summers Morgan, Sheraton House, Lower Road, Chorleywood, RICKMANSWORTH, WD3 5LH.
MORGAN, Mr. Kenneth Frank, FCA *1970;* The Dell, Hurst Lane, EGHAM, SURREY, TW20 8QJ.
MORGAN, Mrs. Kerry Leanne, BA ACA *2005;* Estate House, 26 High Street, HOLYWELL, FLINTSHIRE, CH8 7LH.
MORGAN, Mr. Kevin Michael, BSc ACA *1999;* 92 Lakeside Gardens, MERTHYR TYDFIL, CF48 1EW.
MORGAN, Mr. Laurence Andrew Thomas, BSc ACA *2007;* 40 Salford Road, LONDON, SW2 4BQ.
MORGAN, Mr. Lee, BSc FCA *1992;* Lancashire County Cricket Club Limited, Old Trafford, MANCHESTER, M16 0PX.
MORGAN, Mr. Lee Stuart, BSc ACA *2006;* 43 Woodhouse Gardens, Hilperton, TROWBRIDGE, WILTSHIRE, BA14 7QX.
MORGAN, Mrs. Lindsay Nicola, ACA *2008;* The Hoolets, Hopgarden Lane, SEVENOAKS, TN13 1PX.
MORGAN, Mrs. Lisa, ACA *1996;* 1 Mallory Road, NORWICH, NR6 6DJ.
MORGAN, Mr. Lloyd Trevor, BA FCA *1978;* 49 Pine Road, Bramhall, STOCKPORT, SK7 2JN.
MORGAN, Mrs. Lucy Anne, BSc ACA *1992;* 146 Malmesbury Road, Shirley, SOUTHAMPTON, SO15 5EY.
•MORGAN, Mrs. Margaret Elizabeth, BA FCA *1974;* (Tax Fac), Margaret Morgan, Barnspiece, 60A Church Lane, North Bradley, TROWBRIDGE, BA14 0TA.
•MORGAN, Mrs. Margaret Mary, BSc ACA *1979;* (Tax Fac), M M Morgan & Co, 34 Wolverton Road, NEWPORT PAGNELL, BUCKINGHAMSHIRE, MK16 8HU.
MORGAN, Mrs. Maria Louise, BSc ACA *1990;* 31 Bedarra Street, REDLAND BAY, QLD 4165, AUSTRALIA.
MORGAN, Mr. Mark, MA ACA *1990;* 49 Prowse Avenue, Bushey Heath, BUSHEY, WD23 1LB.
MORGAN, Mr. Mark John, BSc ACA *1991;* Pipestyle House, Uphampton, Ombersley, DROITWICH, WORCESTERSHIRE, WR9 0JP.
MORGAN, Mr. Maurice Brian, BCom ACA *1998;* 70, Clarence Road, LONDON, SW19 8QE.
MORGAN, Mr. Meirion, FCA *1961;* 4 Morgans Hill Close, Nailsea, BRISTOL, BS48 4NZ. (Life Member)
MORGAN, Mr. Michael Bartlett, BSc FCA *1990;* Devonhurst, Mayfield Lane, WADHURST, EAST SUSSEX, TN5 6JE.
MORGAN, Mr. Michael John, BSc ACA *1980;* Euro Disney Associates SCA, F-77777 MARNE LA VALLEE, FRANCE.
MORGAN, Miss. Natalie, BA(Hons) ACA *2002;* with KPMG LLP, 3 Assembly Square, Britannia Quay, CARDIFF, CF10 4AX.
MORGAN, Mr. Nathan David, ACA *2009;* with PricewaterhouseCoopers LLP, 31 Great George Street, BRISTOL, BS1 5QD.
MORGAN, Mrs. Naveeda, BSc(Econ) ACA *2003;* 40 Lakeside Drive, CARDIFF, CF23 6DG.
MORGAN, Mr. Neil, BSc ACA *1992;* 4 York Court, Cowper Road, BERKHAMSTED, HERTFORDSHIRE, HP4 3FW.
MORGAN, Mrs. Nia Eleri, BSc FCA *2000;* 1 Ger y Nant, Birchgrove, SWANSEA, SA7 0HD.
•MORGAN, Mr. Nicholas David, FCA *1971;* Nicholas D Morgan, 5 Walnut Paddock, Harby, MELTON MOWBRAY, LEICESTERSHIRE, LE14 4BD.
•MORGAN, Mr. Nicholas David, BSc FCA *1987;* Warrener Stewart Limited, Harwood House, 43 Harwood Road, LONDON, SW6 4QP.
MORGAN, Mr. Nicholas Henry, FCA *1975;* 8 Coldicott Leys, Ebrington, CHIPPING CAMPDEN, GLOUCESTERSHIRE, GL55 6NZ.
MORGAN, Mr. Nicholas Mark, BA ACA *1985;* Dukes House, 53 Dukes Wood Drive, GERRARDS CROSS, SL9 7LJ.
MORGAN, Mr. Nicholas Talbot, BA(Hons) ACA *2000;* 2 Greswell Street, LONDON, SW6 6PP.
MORGAN, Miss. Nicola Jane, BA ACA *1999;* 7 Pilgrims Way, GUILDFORD, SURREY, GU4 8AB.
MORGAN, Mrs. Nicola Louise, BA(Hons) ACA *2001;* with KPMG LLP, 303 East Wacker Drive, CHICAGO, IL 60601-5255, UNITED STATES.
•MORGAN, Mr. Nigel, MA FCA *1971;* (Tax Fac), 4 Anne Greenwood Close, Iffley, OXFORD, OX4 4DN.
MORGAN, Mr. Nigel Denis, FCA *1970;* 137 East 36th Street, Apt 21G, NEW YORK, NY 10016-3568, UNITED STATES.
MORGAN, Mr. Nigel Henry, ACA *1980;* St John's Vicarage, 2 St. Johns Avenue, Churchdown, GLOUCESTER, GL3 2DB.
MORGAN, Mr. Norman Raymond, MSc BSc FCA MCT *1976;* 19 Chesterton Park, CIRENCESTER, GL7 1XU.
•MORGAN, Mrs. Olwen Mary, BA FCA *1982;* O M Morgan & Co, 153 Verulam Road, ST. ALBANS, AL3 4DN.
MORGAN, Mr. Owen Edward, ACA *2009;* Avalon Management Group Ltd, 4a Exmoor Street, LONDON, W10 6BD.
MORGAN, Mr. Patrick Neil, BSc ACA *1989;* Plateau de Frontenex 9D, 1223 COLOGNY, SWITZERLAND.
MORGAN, Mr. Paul Nicholas, MSc BSc(Hons) ACA *2001;* 20 Goldney Avenue, Warmley, BRISTOL, BS30 5JG.
MORGAN, Mr. Peter, FCA *1953;* 22 Norfolk Road, Edgbaston, BIRMINGHAM, B15 3PZ. (Life Member)
MORGAN, Mr. Peter Charles John, BSc FCA *1990;* 31 Bedarra Street, Redland Bay, BRISBANE, QLD 4165, AUSTRALIA.
MORGAN, Mr. Peter Clark, FCA *1961;* 17 Irwin Drive, HORSHAM, WEST SUSSEX, RH12 1NL. (Life Member)
•MORGAN, Mr. Peter Hellings, BSc(Hons) ACA *1992;* (Tax Fac), Kingscott Dix Limited, 60 Kings Walk, GLOUCESTER, GL1 1LA.
MORGAN, Mr. Peter James, BA FCA *1973;* Longacre, Horseshoe Lane, ALDERLEY EDGE, CHESHIRE, SK9 7QP.
MORGAN, Mr. Peter John, FCA *1972;* L'Abri Des Hougues, Cotes du Nord, Trinity, JERSEY, JE3 5BJ.
MORGAN, Mr. Peter John, FCA *1968;* Sherborne, Effingham Common Road, Effingham, LEATHERHEAD, SURREY, KT24 5JG.
•MORGAN, Mr. Peter Joseph, BSocSc ACA *1996;* Talbot Hughes McKillop LLP, 6 Snow Hill, LONDON, EC1A 2AY.
•MORGAN, Mr. Peter Martin, FCA *1985;* Morgan & Co, Cockshott Farmhouse, Highgate Hill, Hawkhurst, CRANBROOK, KENT TN18 4LS.
MORGAN, Mr. Peter Nigel Charles, BSc FCA *1982;* 19 St. Peters Grove, Hammersmith, LONDON, W6 9AY.
MORGAN, Mr. Peter Richard, BA FCA *1972;* Avenida Rufo Garcia Rendueles 11, Escalera A 9 Izq., 33203 GIJON, SPAIN.
MORGAN, Mr. Peter William John, MSc ACA *1981;* 5 Nantlais, Corntown, BRIDGEND, MID GLAMORGAN, CF35 5SA.
•MORGAN, Mr. Philip, FCA *1967;* Philip Morgan, 9 Lakeside Gardens, MERTHYR TYDFIL, CF48 1EN.
MORGAN, Mr. Philip David, BSc ACA *1997;* Gocompare.com Limited, Unit 6, The Courtyard, Imperial Park, NEWPORT, GWENT NP10 8UL.
MORGAN, Mr. Philip Richard, BSc FCA *1971;* 20 Nightingale Road, HAMPTON, TW12 3HX.
MORGAN, Mr. Philip Robert, LLB ACA *2000;* Kings Mill House Kings Cross Lane, South Nutfield, REDHILL, RH1 5NG.
MORGAN, Mrs. Phillipa Jane, BSc ACA *1995;* 242 Hanworth Road, HAMPTON, MIDDLESEX, TW12 3EP.
MORGAN, Mr. Piers John, MA ACA *1992;* AMT, PO Box 22506, 1100DA AMSTERDAM, NETHERLANDS.
MORGAN, Mr. Richard, BA ACA *2004;* 17 Spring Vale Road, Hayfield, HIGH PEAK, DERBYSHIRE, SK22 2LD.
MORGAN, Mr. Richard Ashley, FCA *1969;* 16 Churchwood Way, ST. LEONARDS-ON-SEA, EAST SUSSEX, TN38 9JW.
•MORGAN, Mr. Richard Douglas, MBE MA FCA *1974;* Richard Morgan and Company, 59 Victoria Road, SURBITON, SURREY, KT6 4NQ. See also Morgan AVN Limited
MORGAN, Mr. Richard Gareth Huw, BSc ACA *1998;* 14 Eversley Road, Charlton, LONDON, SE7 7LD.
MORGAN, Mr. Richard Glyn, BSc FCA CF *1989;* Richard Morgan Advisory, 72 rue du Faubourg Saint-Honoré, 75008 PARIS, FRANCE.
•MORGAN, Mr. Richard John Craig, BMus FCA *1991;* (Tax Fac), Iterix Limited, 86 High Street, CARSHALTON, SURREY, SM5 3AE.
MORGAN, Mr. Robert, BA ACA *2011;* 65 Bankhead Lane, Hoghton, PRESTON, PR5 0AB.
MORGAN, Mr. Robert, FCA *1958;* 29 Moorlands Drive, Wybunbury, NANTWICH, CHESHIRE, CW5 7PA. (Life Member)
MORGAN, Mr. Robert Andrew, BA ACA *1997;* 1 Riding Way, Woosehill, WOKINGHAM, RG41 3AH.
MORGAN, Mr. Robert John, MEng ACA *2007;* 1 Pond Road, LONDON, E15 3BD.
MORGAN, Mr. Robert John, ACA *2008;* 105 Aveling Close, PURLEY, SURREY, CR8 4DY.
MORGAN, Mr. Robert John, BA ACA *1998;* 17 Seer Mead, Seer Green, BEACONSFIELD, BUCKINGHAMSHIRE, HP9 2QL.
MORGAN, Mr. Robert Lloyd, MA ACA *1999;* with PricewaterhouseCoopers LLP, 9 Greyfriars Road, READING, RG1 1JG.
MORGAN, Mr. Robert Peter, BA ACA *2003;* 41 Marler Road, LONDON, SE23 2AE.
MORGAN, Mr. Rodney Price, BA ACA *1983;* Shalesbrook Coach House, Shalesbrook Lane, FOREST ROW, EAST SUSSEX, RH18 5LS.
MORGAN, Mr. Roger, BA ACA *1986;* (Tax Fac), 7 Westfield, New Ash Green, LONGFIELD, DA3 8QN.
MORGAN, Mr. Roger James, BEng ACA *1991;* The Old Coach House, 146a Wakefield Road, Lightcliffe, HALIFAX, HX3 8TH.
MORGAN, Mrs. Sarah Ann, BSc ACA *2003;* 20 Goldney Avenue, Warmley, BRISTOL, BS30 5JG.
MORGAN, Mrs. Sarah Bennett, ACA *1985;* 119 Florence Road, LONDON, N4 4DL.
MORGAN, Miss. Sarah Louise, BA ACA *2005;* 6 Glen Road, Whatstandwell, MATLOCK, DERBYSHIRE, DE4 5EH.
MORGAN, Mrs. Sharon Elizabeth, BSc ACA *2000;* 9 The Fennings, AMERSHAM, BUCKINGHAMSHIRE, HP6 5LE.
MORGAN, Ms. Sian Elizabeth, LLB ACA ATII *1992;* 67 Warwick Way, Pimlico, LONDON, SW1V 1QR.
MORGAN, Miss. Sian Frances, LLB ACA *2001;* Flat 29, Spriggs House, Canonbury Road, LONDON, N1 2AJ.
MORGAN, Mr. Simon Peter Campbell, BEng ACA *1999;* Cobham plc, Flight Refuelling Ltd, Brook Road, WIMBORNE, DORSET, BH21 2BJ.
MORGAN, Mr. Simon Philip, MA ACA *2002;* 13 Kingsdown Road, SUTTON, SM3 8NZ.
•MORGAN, Mr. Stephen Gareth, BSc(Econ) FCA *1999;* Wise & Co, Wey Court West, Union Road, FARNHAM, SURREY, GU9 7PT.
MORGAN, Mr. Stephen Huw Perrott, BA ACA *1986;* 40 Ridgeway, NEWPORT, GWENT, NP20 5AG.
MORGAN, Mr. Stephen John, BA FCA *1981;* Flat 116 Centrium, Station Approach, WOKING, SURREY, GU22 7PD.
MORGAN, Mr. Stephen John, MA ACA *1982;* 55 Parklands, WOTTON-UNDER-EDGE, GL12 7NR.
MORGAN, Mr. Stephen John, BSc ACA *1985;* 47 Sandhills Road, Barnt Green, BIRMINGHAM, B45 8NP.
MORGAN, Mr. Stephen Paul, BA ACA *1996;* 4 Hollyoak Road, SUTTON COLDFIELD, B74 2FG.
MORGAN, Mr. Stephen Richard, BA ACA *1993;* Dare, 101 New Cavendish Street, LONDON, W1W 6XH.
•MORGAN, Mr. Steven Charles, BSc FCA *1991;* AGL Accountants Limited, 89 Fore Street, KINGSBRIDGE, TQ7 1AB. See also AGL
MORGAN, Mr. Stuart De Warrenne, ACA *2001;* 11 Middle Street, Kilsby, RUGBY, CV23 8XT.
MORGAN, Mrs. Susan Caroline, BSc ACA *1987;* The Old Parsonage, Rolvenden, CRANBROOK, TN17 4LS.
MORGAN, Mrs. Susan Mary, BSc ACA *1992;* Devonshurst, Mayfield Lane, WADHURST, EAST SUSSEX, TN5 6SG.
MORGAN, Miss. Susan Rosalind, BSc FCA *1990;* 25 Maraval Road, St Clair, PORT OF SPAIN, TRINIDAD AND TOBAGO.
•MORGAN, Mr. Terence Alfred Rhys, FCA *1972;* Warren Lodge, 34 Mayfield Road, SUTTON, SURREY, SM2 5DT.
MORGAN, Mrs. Tessa Jane, ACA *2000;* M & A Partners, 7 The Close, NORWICH, NR1 4DJ.
MORGAN, Mr. Thomas Brinley, BSc ACA *2000;* Parsons Brinckerhoff Ltd, Westbrook Mills, Borough Road, GODALMING, SURREY, GU7 2AZ.
MORGAN, Mr. Thomas Christopher, BSc FCA *1992;* 10 Albert Road, WILMSLOW, CHESHIRE, SK9 5HT.
MORGAN, Mr. Thomas Christopher, BSc ACA *1998;* Bus Eireann, Finance Office, Broadstone, DUBLIN 7, COUNTY DUBLIN, IRELAND.
MORGAN, Mr. Thomas David, ACA *2010;* Flat 268 Bromyard House, Bromyard Avenue, LONDON, W3 7BS.
•MORGAN, Mr. Thomas Robert, BSc ACA *2002;* Baker Tilly UK Audit LLP, Elgar House, Holmer Road, HEREFORD, HR4 9SF. See also Baker Tilly Tax and Advisory Services LLP
•MORGAN, Mr. Timothy David, BSc ACA *1991;* Tim Morgan, 7 Fowberry Crescent, Fenham, NEWCASTLE UPON TYNE, NE4 9XH.
MORGAN, Mr. Timothy Edward, ACA *2009;* Franklins Farm, Ickford Road, Shabbington, AYLESBURY, BUCKINGHAMSHIRE, HP18 9HN.
MORGAN, Mr. Timothy Frank Gerald, MA ACA *1998;* 33 Enfield Cloisters, Fanshaw Street, LONDON, N1 6LD.
MORGAN, Mr. Timothy James, BSc ACA *2001;* Mint Digital Limited, 125-127 Westminster Business Square, Durham Street, Vauxhall, LONDON, SE11 5JH.
MORGAN, Mrs. Tina, BA(Hons) ACA *2003;* 68 Nutbrook Street, LONDON, SE15 4LE.
MORGAN, Mr. Trevor David, FCA *1968;* Coombe House, Sotwell Street, Brightwell-Cum-Sotwell, WALLINGFORD, OX10 0RG.
MORGAN, Mrs. Wendy Marion, FCA *1991;* 14 Marlborough View, FARNBOROUGH, Hampshire, GU14 9YA.
MORGAN, Mr. William, FCA *1955;* Kilbirnie, Queensway, Newton, CHESTER, CH2 1PF. (Life Member)

MORGAN, Mr. William Alexander, BA(Hons) ACA *2003;* Inchcape Latin America, Av. Las Condes 12907, Las Condes, SANTIAGO, CHILE.
MORGAN, Mr. William Eric Keith, FCA *1964;* 24 Sanderstead Court, Addington Road, SOUTH CROYDON, Surrey, CR2 8RA. (Life Member)
•**MORGAN, Mr. William John, MA FCA** *1979;* PricewaterhouseCoopers LLP, 1 Embankment Place, LONDON, WC2N 6RH. See also PricewaterhouseCoopers
MORGAN, Mr. William Roy, BSc ACA *1980;* Flat C 1st floor Block 3 Grandeur Villa, 21 Tat Chee Avenue, YAU YAT TSUEN, KOWLOON, HONG KONG SAR.
•**MORGAN-JONES, Mr. Digby, FCA** *1955;* Morgan-Jones & Co, Wychwood Cottage, 38 High Street, Riseley, BEDFORD, MK44 1DX.
MORGAN-JONES, Mrs. Julie Marie, ACA *2001;* Clock Tower House, East Foxdale Road, Foxdale, ISLE OF MAN, IM4 3HQ.
MORGAN-JONES, Mr. Rhydian James, FCA *1968;* Woolley Park, Woolley, WANTAGE, OXFORDSHIRE, OX12 8NJ.
MORGAN-JONES, Mr. Richard, BMus ACA *1992;* 78 Ringway, Waverton, CHESTER, CH3 7NR.
MORGAN-OWEN, Miss. Sally Jane, BA ACA *1990;* (Tax Fac), Coppice Cottage, Grenville Road, Shackleford, GODALMING, SURREY, GU8 6AX.
MORGAN-THOMAS, Mrs. Ruth Yvonne, FCA *1981;* Flat 80 Hermitage Court, Woodford Road, LONDON, E18 2EP.
MORGAN-WYNNE, Mr. Timothy Mark, BA ACA *1994;* 24 Dartmouth Road, LONDON, NW2 4EX.
MORGANS, Miss. Alison Cynthia Wendy, BA ACA *1990;* Holly Cottage, High Street, WATLINGTON, OX49 5PY.
MORGANS, Miss. Amanda Jane, ACA *1994;* Oak Cottage, Greenway Lane, Gretton, CHELTENHAM, GL54 5ER.
•**MORGANS, Mr. Christopher, BA ACA** *1995;* 58 Whinney Moor Way, RETFORD, NOTTINGHAMSHIRE, DN22 7BL.
MORGANS, Mrs. Rachel Alison Louise, MA ACA *1998;* PO Box 82110, BUDAIYA, BAHRAIN.
MORGANS, Miss. Rhiannon Victoria, BSc ACA *2003;* 10 Acer Way, Rogerstone, NEWPORT, GWENT, NP10 9LB.
MORGANS, Miss. Sophie, BA ACA *2007;* 20 Wynton Grove, WALTON-ON-THAMES, KT12 1LW.
MORGANTI, Mr. Alberto, MA ACA *2001;* 61 Old Park Avenue, ENFIELD, EN2 6PN.
MORGENROTH, Mr. Alan Martin, ACA *1981;* Deepway Farmhouse, Deepway, Sidbury, SIDMOUTH, DEVON, EX10 0SA.
MORI, Ms. Ruth, ACA CA(NZ) *2010;* Flat 24, Millbrooke Court, Keswick Road, LONDON, SW15 2RA.
MORIARTY, Mr. Daniel, ACA *2011;* 2 Wren Street, Haworth, KEIGHLEY, WEST YORKSHIRE, BD22 8JQ.
MORIARTY, Mr. David John, BSc ACA PGCE *2001;* 45 Elmbridge Road, GLOUCESTER, GL2 0NX.
MORIARTY, Mr. Edward Thomas, BA FCA *1962;* Medway, Longsight Road, Copster Green, BLACKBURN, BB1 9EU.
MORIARTY, Mr. Paul Patrick, BSc ACA *1996;* 12 Hilltop Road, Pittville, CHELTENHAM, GL50 4NN.
•**MORIARTY, Mr. Sean Thomas, ACA** *1994;* Haines Watts Corporate Finance (NW), 1st Floor, Northern Assurance Buildings, Albert Square, 9-21 Princess Street, MANCHESTER M2 4DN.
MORIARTY, Mr. Shaun Patrick Desmond, FCA *1970;* 4 Fernwood Close, St. Ives, RINGWOOD, BH24 2NQ.
•**MORIARTY, Mr. Timothy Michael, FCA** *1981;* Whittle & Partners LLP, Century House South, North Station Road, COLCHESTER, CO1 1RE.
MORIATY, Mrs. Anne Patricia, FCA *1978;* with ICAEW, Metropolitan House, 321 Avebury Boulevard, MILTON KEYNES, MK9 2FZ.
MORING, Miss. Kate Elizabeth, ACA *2009;* Apartment 77 Springfield Court, 2 Dean Road, SALFORD, M3 7EH.
MORISON, Mr. Kenneth Dreyer, ACA CA(SA) *2009;* 601 West Knightsbridge, CENTURY CITY, 7441, SOUTH AFRICA.
MORISON, Mr. Norman Denis Bedlington, BSc FCA *1973;* The Old Vicarage, Vicarage Rd, Gailey, STAFFORD, ST19 5PU.
MORISON, Mrs. Suzanne Sharn, BSc FCA *1975;* The Old Vicarage, Vicarage Road, Gailey, STAFFORD, ST19 5PU.
MORITZ, Mr. Brian Michael, FCA *1961;* Waterden Lodge, 27 Waterden Road, GUILDFORD, GU1 2AZ.
MORITZ, Mr. Jonathan Michael, BSc ACA *1993;* Pattonair International Ltd, Unit A2, Kingswey Business Park, Forsyth Road, WOKING, GU21 5SA.
MORITZ, Mr. Nicholas John, BSc ACA *1989;* 93 Farnham Road, GUILDFORD, SURREY, GU2 7PF.
MORIYAMA, Mr. Susumu, FCA *1996;* PricewaterhouseCoopers, Woluwe Garden, Woluwedal 18, 1932 SINT STEVENS WOLUWE, BELGIUM.
MORJARIA, Mr. Arun, FCA *1971;* 6 Howard Gardens, Boxgrove Park, GUILDFORD, SURREY, GU1 2NX. (Life Member)
MORJARIA, Mr. Asvin, BAcc ACA FCCA *2010;* 5 Rothersthorpe, Giffard Park, MILTON KEYNES, MK14 5JL.
MORJARIA, Mr. Atul Narandas, BSc FCA *1974;* John Cumming Ross Ltd, 1st Floor, Kirkland House, 11-15 Peterborough Road, HARROW, MIDDLESEX HA1 2AX.
MORJARIA, Mr. Bijesh, BA(Hons) ACA *2002;* (Tax Fac), 23 Whitebeam Road, Oadby, LEICESTER, LE2 4EA.
•**MORJARIA, Mr. Dinesh Mohanlal, BSc FCA** *1973;* D Morjaria & Co Ltd, 69 Lynwood Road, Ealing, LONDON, W5 1JG.
MORJARIA, Mrs. Kalpa, BSc(Hons) ACA *2002;* Westwick House, 208 Lye Green Road, CHESHAM, BUCKINGHAMSHIRE, HP5 3NH.
MORJARIA, Mrs. Kalpa Prabhudas, BA ACA *1999;* 14 Orchard Drive, EDGWARE, MIDDLESEX, HA8 7SD.
MORJARIA, Mr. Kalpesh, BSc ACA *2005;* 119 Carshalton Park Road, CARSHALTON, SURREY, SM5 3SJ.
•**MORJARIA, Mr. Ketan Devram, ACA** *1982;* P.O. Box 3072, KAMPALA, UGANDA.
MORJARIA, Mr. Nishad Dinesh, LLB ACA *2001;* 69 Lynwood Road, Ealing, LONDON, W5 1JG.
MORJARIA, Mr. Ram, ACA *1982;* Dunkeld, Llanbadoc, USK, NP15 1TG.
•**MORJARIA, Mr. Rohit Narottam, FCA** *1985;* Carringtons, Carrington House, 170 Greenford Road, HARROW, HA1 3QX.
MORJARIA, Mr. Shilen Surendra, BSc ACA *2002;* 20b Pinner Hill Road, PINNER, HA5 3SB.
MORLAND, Mrs. Angela Mary, ACA *1985;* The Malt House, Tilford Road, Tilford, FARNHAM, GU10 2BZ.
MORLAND, Mr. Christopher Ross, BCom FCA *1967;* 23 Quoitings Drive, MARLOW, BUCKINGHAMSHIRE, SL7 2PD. (Life Member)
MORLAND, Mrs. Claire Celia, BA FCA *1989;* (Tax Fac), 16 Elmcroft Avenue, LONDON, NW11 0RR.
•**MORLAND, Mr. Derek, BSc FCA** *1978;* (Tax Fac), Evans & Partners, 9 Bank Road, Kingswood, BRISTOL, BS15 8LS.
MORLAND, Mr. Giles Philip Maxwell, ACA *1991;* Mirabaud Pereire Holdings Ltd, 21 St James Square, LONDON, SW1Y 4JP.
MORLAND, Mr. Nicholas Charles, BA ACA *1997;* Chipley Park House, Langford Budville, WELLINGTON, SOMERSET, TA21 0QU.
MORLAND, Mr. Nigel Antony, FCA *1984;* Ashurst, 5 Appold Street, LONDON, EC2A 2HA.
MORLAND, Mr. Paul Gilmer, BSc FCA *1986;* Canford, Ashcott, BRIDGWATER, SOMERSET, TA7 9QN.
MORLAND, Mr. Peter, BSc ACA *2004;* 55 Meadow Vale Shiremoor, NEWCASTLE UPON TYNE, NE27 0BD.
MORLAND, Mr. Peter Daniel, MSc ACA *2002;* 9 Clayfield, Yate, BRISTOL, BS37 7PE.
MORLAND, Mrs. Sarah Jane, MA ACA *2004;* 55 Meadow Vale, Shiremoor, NEWCASTLE UPON TYNE, NE27 0BD.
MORLEY, Mr. Adrian Richard, BSc ACA *1993;* 8 Morrison Park Road, West Haddon, NORTHAMPTON, NN6 7BJ.
MORLEY, Mr. Alastair James, BA ACA MSI *2006;* Flat 2, 13 Ashburn Gardens, LONDON, SW7 4DG.
MORLEY, Mr. Andrew, FCA *1972;* 4 Appleton Court, Bishopthorpe, YORK, YO23 2RY.
MORLEY, Miss. Angela Hazel, BSc ACA *1986;* 22 Claremont Road, Bickley, BROMLEY, BR1 2JL.
MORLEY, Dr. Barbara Jane, PhD BSc ACA *1979;* 11 Tylney Avenue, LONDON, SE19 1LN.
•**MORLEY, Mr. Bruce Kelvin, FCA** *1970;* TWP Accounting LLP, The Old Rectory, Church Street, WEYBRIDGE, SURREY, KT13 8DE. See also Bruce Morley Limited
•**MORLEY, Mrs. Catherine Susanna, BA ACA** *1991;* with KPMG, 8/F Prince's Building, 10 Chater Road, CENTRAL, HONG KONG ISLAND, HONG KONG SAR.
MORLEY, Mr. Christopher John, BSc ACA *1989;* 9 Foster Park Grove, Denholme, BRADFORD, WEST YORKSHIRE, BD13 4BQ.
MORLEY, Mr. Colin James, BA(Hons) ACA *2000;* 8 Dawnay Close, ASCOT, BERKSHIRE, SL5 7PQ.
MORLEY, Mr. Colin Richard, BA ACA *1990;* 17A Frederick Road, Edgbaston, Birmingham, BIRMINGHAM, b15 1jn.
MORLEY, Mr. Darren Jason, BA ACA *1997;* 171 Mount Pleasant Lane, Bricket Wood, ST. ALBANS, AL2 3XW.
MORLEY, Mr. David Denis Cecil, BA FCA *1963;* Copper Lodge, Church Lane, Northney, HAYLING ISLAND, HAMPSHIRE, PO11 0SB. (Life Member)
MORLEY, Mr. David George, FCA MBA *1976;* 5 Charlesworth Park, HAYWARDS HEATH, WEST SUSSEX, RH16 3JG.
MORLEY, Mr. David John, ACA *1993;* The Retreat, High Street, Pavenham, BEDFORD, BEDFORDSHIRE, MK43 7NU.
•**MORLEY, Mr. Gary Cornwell, FCA** *1981;* MacIntyre Hudson LLP, New Bridge Street House, 30-34 New Bridge Street, LONDON, EC4V 6BJ.
MORLEY, Mr. Gerald Desmond, FCA *1973;* Apek UK Ltd Unit 1, Beech Court Crystal Drive, SMETHWICK, B66 1RD.
MORLEY, Mr. Harry Michael Charles, BA ACA *1992;* Blackland Farm, Blackland, CALNE, WILTSHIRE, SN11 8PS.
MORLEY, Mrs. Helen Morag, BSc ACA *1989;* 9 Whitchurch Road, Audlem, CREWE, CW3 0EE.
MORLEY, Mr. James, BSc FCA *1973;* Virginia House, St. Marys Road, ASCOT, BERKSHIRE, SL5 9JE.
MORLEY, Mr. James Brennan, FCA *1967;* Curbar, Doctors Road, Blofield, NORWICH, NR13 4LF.
MORLEY, Mr. James William, FCA *1960;* Hazelwood, 8 Fisher Lane, Bingham, NOTTINGHAM, NG13 8BQ. (Life Member)
MORLEY, Ms. Jayne, BSc ACA *2002;* 32 Netherfield, BENFLEET, SS7 1TY.
MORLEY, Mr. John, FCA *1974;* Rothwell Lodge, Casthorpe Road, Denton, GRANTHAM, LINCOLNSHIRE, NG32 1JT.
MORLEY, Mr. John Arthur, FCA *1961;* 20 Tithebarn Drive, Parkgate, NESTON, CH64 6RQ. (Life Member)
MORLEY, Mr. John Robert, MA FCA *1968;* 7 Middle Furlong, SEAFORD, BN25 1SR.
MORLEY, Mr. John Streatfeild, FCA *1958;* 29 Hurst Lane, Cumnor, OXFORD, OX2 9PR. (Life Member)
•**MORLEY, Mr. Jonathan, FCA** *1985;* (Tax Fac), J W Smith & Co Ltd, 17a Yorkersgate, MALTON, NORTH YORKSHIRE, YO17 7AA.
MORLEY, Mr. Joseph, BA FCA *1957;* 7 Brunstead Road, Westbourne, POOLE, BH12 1EJ. (Life Member)
MORLEY, Mrs. Julia Eva, MA MSc FCA *1991;* 68 Doneraile Street, LONDON, SW6 6EP.
MORLEY, The Revd. Keith Russell, BSc ACA *1983;* 243 Wingrove Road, Fenham, NEWCASTLE UPON TYNE, NE4 9DD.
MORLEY, Miss. Kerry Louise, BSc ACA *2003;* 1 Gourham Drive, Cheadle Hulme, CHEADLE, CHESHIRE, SK8 6AD.
MORLEY, Mr. Lee, BSc(Hons) ACA *2000;* 3 Chantry Close, ILKLEY, LS29 9JA.
•**MORLEY, Mrs. Lisa Julie, ACA** *2004;* Dimbleby & Dale, Junction House, 58 High Street, Beighton, SHEFFIELD, S20 1ED.
MORLEY, Mrs. Margaret Ann, FCA *1960;* 15 Alstone Road, TIVERTON, DEVON, EX16 4LH. (Life Member)
MORLEY, Mrs. Marisa Belinda, BSc ACA *2007;* 67 Friday Street, Warnham, HORSHAM, WEST SUSSEX, RH12 3QY.
•**MORLEY, Mr. Mark Christopher James, BA** *1983;* (Tax Fac), Morleys, Kings House Business Centre, Station Road, KINGS LANGLEY, HERTFORDSHIRE, WD4 8DH.
MORLEY, Mr. Michael Francis, BA FCA *1966;* 8 The Ridings, SEAFORD, BN25 3HW. (Life Member)
MORLEY, Mr. Michael Guy, FCA *1969;* Tides, 2 Malam Court, Warren Drive, Deganwy, CONWY, GWYNEDD LL31 9ST.
•**MORLEY, Mr. Neil, FCA** *1976;* Morley & Co (UK) LLP, 2 Cricklade Court, Cricklade Street, Old Town, SWINDON, SN1 3EY. See also MPS Associates Ltd
MORLEY, Mr. Neil Roy, BSc ACA *2007;* 73 Newhall Road, Kirk Sandall, DONCASTER, DN3 1QQ.
MORLEY, Mrs. Nicola Jayne, ACA *2007;* International Hotel Group, 1 First Avenue Centrum One Hundred, BURTON-ON-TRENT, STAFFORDSHIRE, DE14 2WB.
•**MORLEY, Mr. Nigel, BA ACA** *2004;* Morley & Co, 83 Marathon House, 200 Marylebone Road, LONDON, NW1 5PL.
MORLEY, Mr. Raymond Victor, FCA *1974;* 11a Church Street, Needingworth, ST. IVES, CAMBRIDGESHIRE, PE27 4TB.
MORLEY, Miss. Rebecca, BA(Hons) ACA *2002;* Upper Flat, 5 Riverside Road, Alnmouth, ALNWICK, NORTHUMBERLAND, NE66 2RY.
•**MORLEY, Mr. Richard Anthony, BSc FCA** *1982;* The Lodge, Main Street, Fiskerton, SOUTHWELL, NG25 0UL.
MORLEY, Mr. Robert James, BA ACA *1993;* Kingstownworks Ltd, Connaught Road, Kingswood, HULL, HU7 3AP.
MORLEY, Mr. Roger Herbert, FCA *1970;* 12 Under Ffrydd Wood, KNIGHTON, POWYS, LD7 1EF.
•**MORLEY, Mr. Simon James, BA ACA** *2001;* with PricewaterhouseCoopers LLP, 1 Embankment Place, LONDON, WC2N 6RH.
MORLEY, Mr. Stephen Douglas, FCA *1975;* 10 St. Bartholomews, NEWENT, GLOUCESTERSHIRE, GL18 1BX.
•**MORLEY, Mr. Stephen Robert, FCA** *1973;* (Tax Fac), Morley Haswell, 4 St James Court, Bridgnorth Road, Wollaston, STOURBRIDGE, DY8 3QG. See also Morley Haswell Consultants Limited
MORLEY, Mr. Timothy John, BSc ACA *1992;* Church House, Church Place, PULBOROUGH, WEST SUSSEX, RH20 1AE.
MORLEY-DAVIES, Miss. Jane, BSc ACA *2003;* Aon Insurance Managers Ltd., Aon House, 30 Woodbourne Avenue, PEMBROKE HM08, BERMUDA.
MORLEY-FLETCHER, Mr. Michael Francis, BA ACA *1992;* Ernst & Young Llp, 1 More London Place, LONDON, SE1 2AF.
MORLEY GRIFFITHS, Mr. Jeremy Robin, FCA *1967;* 11 The Poplars, Yapton, ARUNDEL, WEST SUSSEX, BN18 0EQ. (Life Member)
MORLEY-JACOB, Mr. Richard Charles, BSc ACA *1995;* South House, South Street, Great Waltham, CHELMSFORD, CM3 1DP.
MORLEY-KIRK, Mr. Jonathan Charles Rowell, FCA FCSI TEP *1986;* Pigneaux Farm House, Princes Tower Road, St. Saviour, JERSEY, JE2 7UD.
MORLEY-SMITH, Mr. Jorge, BA ACA *2002;* Ground Floor Flat, 26 Ritherdon Road, LONDON, SW17 8QD.
MORLING, Dr. Susan Evelyn Mary, PhD MSc BSc ACA *2007;* with PricewaterhouseCoopers LLP, 31 Great George Street, BRISTOL, BS1 5QD.
MORONEY, Mr. Thomas Joseph, ACA *2010;* 1A Vaucrossons Crescent, PEMBROKE HM13, BERMUDA.
MOROSS, Mrs. Julia Dorothy, BA ACA *1986;* 27 The Crescent, Barnes, LONDON, SW13 0NN.
•**MOROZ, Mr. Peter Johannes, FCA ATII** *1989;* Innovation Professional Services LLP, The Arena, Stockley Park, UXBRIDGE, MIDDLESEX, UB11 1AA.
MORPETH, Mr. Andrew Graham, FCA *1990;* 16 Rowfant Road, Balham, LONDON, SW17 7AS.
MORPETH, Sir Douglas, Kt TD BCom FCA *1952;* (President 1972 - 1973) (Member of Council 1964 - 1984), Winterden House, Shamley Green, GUILDFORD, GU5 0UD. (Life Member)
MORPETH, Mr. Michael, FCA *1972;* Strawberry Bank, Skelghyll Lane, AMBLESIDE, LA22 0HF.
•**MORPHAKIS, Mr. Stelios, BA ACA** *1985;* (Tax Fac), Morphakis Stelios & Co, 22 Parkway, Southgate, LONDON, N14 6QU.
MORPHET, Mr. Andrew Richard, BEng ACA *1992;* 43 St. Oswalds Crescent, Brereton, SANDBACH, CW11 1RW.
MORPHEW, Mr. John Bernard, FCA *1959;* (Tax Fac), 6 The Charter, Maze Green Road, BISHOPS STORTFORD, HERTFORDSHIRE, CM23 2PF.
MORPHI, Ms. Nayia, BSc(Hons) ACA *2001;* 18 Alexandros Papadiamandis street, 2123 NICOSIA, CYPRUS.
•**MORPHITIS, Mr. Geoffrey Christopher Antony, BA FCA** *1976;* Cape and Dalgleish, 22 Melton Street, Euston Square, LONDON, NW1 2BT.
MORRALL, Mrs. Fiona Louise, ACA *1995;* 14 Larkfield, Eccleston, CHORLEY, PR7 5RN.
MORRALL, Mrs. Karen Marie, BA ACA *1995;* 47 Avenue Road, Dorridge, SOLIHULL, B93 8JZ.
MORRAN, Mr. Colin Neil, BA ACA *1997;* 26 Merestones Drive, CHELTENHAM, GLOUCESTERSHIRE, GL50 2SS.
MORREALE, Mr. Tony, BA ACA *1995;* (Tax Fac), 20 Crichton Road, CARSHALTON, SURREY, SM5 3LS.
MORRELL, Mr. Colin, FCA *1975;* Village Farm, 15 Main Street, Kinoulton, NOTTINGHAM, NG12 3EA.
MORRELL, Miss. Gillian Laura, BSc ACA *2006;* Flat B, 141 Tranmere Road, LONDON, SW18 3QP.
MORRELL, Mrs. Joanne, BSc(Hons) ACA *2003;* Whitbread Plc Whitbread Court Porz Avenue, Houghton Hall Park Houghton Regis, DUNSTABLE, BEDFORDSHIRE, LU5 5XE.
MORRELL, Mr. John, FCA *1950;* W J James & Co Limited, Bishop House, 10 Wheat Street, BRECON, LD3 7DG. (Life Member)
MORRELL, Mr. John Charles, FCA *1964;* 77 Hatherley Road, CHELTENHAM, GL51 6EG.

MORRELL, Mr. Michael Christopher Estcourt, BA FCA *1962;* Karibu, 3 Miz Maze, Leigh, SHERBORNE, DT9 6JJ.
•MORRELL, Mr. Nicholas John, BCom FCA *1976;* W J James & Co Limited, Bishop House, 10 Wheat Street, BRECON, LD3 7DG.
MORRELL, Mr. Nick, MA BSc ACA *2007;* Chemin de Buffard 7, Apartment 24, 1254 JUSSY, SWITZERLAND.
MORRELL, Mr. Philip Henry, ACA *1981;* 175 Rutland Road, SHEFFIELD, S3 9PT.
MORRELL, Mrs. Rachael, BSc ACA *1999;* Hill Farm, Brodsworth, DONCASTER, DN5 7XH.
•MORRELL, Mrs. Sheila Jayne, FCA *1980;* (Tax Fac), SJ Morrell, The Triangle, Grafton Villas, Crossgates, LEEDS, LS15 8SH.
MORRELL, Mr. Simon Philip, BA ACA *1987;* 47 Charles Street, LONDON, W1J 5EL.
MORRELL, Mr. Stephen James, ACA CA(SA) *2011;* Impala Lodge, The Slype, Wheathampstead, ST. ALBANS, HERTFORDSHIRE, AL4 8SA.
•MORREY, Mr. Kenneth Henry, FCA *1969;* Brookside, New Road, Wrenbury, NANTWICH, CHESHIRE, CW5 8HF.
•MORRICE, Mr. Michael James, FCA *1968;* Michael Morrice FCA, 14B Kennington Oval, LONDON, SE11 5SG.
MORRILL, Miss. Rebecca Elizabeth, BA ACA *2000;* Flat 16 Holst Mansions, 96 Wyatt Drive, LONDON, SW13 8AJ.
MORRILL, Mrs. Rosalind Emily, BA ACA *1983;* 27 Strawberry Hill Road, Strawberry Hill, TWICKENHAM, TW1 4PZ.
MORRILL, Mr. Shaun Michael, ACA MAAT *2011;* 30 Bellfield Drive, Willerby, HULL, HU10 6HQ.
MORRIN, Mr. Damian John, BSc FCA *1994;* 17 Hilltop Avenue, GLEN IRIS, VIC 3146, AUSTRALIA.
MORRIN, Mrs. Sarah Elizabeth, MEng ACA *2010;* Pricewaterhousecoopers, 1 Embankment Place, LONDON, WC2N 6RH.
MORRIS, Mr. Adrian Gareth, FCA *1971;* 5 Greystokes, Aughton, ORMSKIRK, LANCASHIRE, L39 5HE.
MORRIS, Mr. Adrian Robert, BSc FCA *1971;* Advance Housing & Support Ltd, 2 Witan Way, WITNEY, OXFORDSHIRE, OX28 6FH.
•MORRIS, Mr. Adrian William, ACA *1988;* (Tax Fac), The Old Bakery, Lower Street, Leeds, MAIDSTONE, ME17 1RL.
MORRIS, Mr. Alan, FCA *1949;* Rievaulx, Westfield Road, Oakley, BEDFORD, MK43 7SU. (Life Member)
•MORRIS, Mr. Alan Farmer, MA FCA *1993;* 21 St. Alban's Park, Sandymount, DUBLIN, COUNTY DUBLIN, IRELAND.
MORRIS, Mr. Alan Harold, FCA *1957;* 1 Elizabeth Avenue, HOVE, BN3 6WA. (Life Member)
•MORRIS, Mr. Alan Richard, FCA *1976;* 20 Flag Walk, PINNER, MIDDLESEX, HA5 2EP.
MORRIS, Mr. Albert Gerard, FCA *1964;* 11 Orchard Gardens, CRANLEIGH, SURREY, GU6 7LG.
MORRIS, Mr. Alexander James, BA ACA *1986;* Falkirk, Long Barn Road, SEVENOAKS, KENT, TN14 6NJ.
MORRIS, Mr. Alfred, CBE DL MA FSS FCA *1963;* (Member of Council 2007 - 2011), 81a Fore Street, SALCOMBE, DEVON, TQ8 8BY. (Life Member)
•MORRIS, Mrs. Alison Clare Munro, MA FCA *1986;* PricewaterhouseCoopers LLP, 7 More London Riverside, LONDON, SE1 2RT. See also PricewaterhouseCoopers
MORRIS, Mr. Alistair Robert, BSc(Hons) FCA *1994;* 3 Chase Close, Coleshill, AMERSHAM, BUCKINGHAMSHIRE, HP7 0LX.
MORRIS, Mrs. Allyson Jayne, BSc ACA *1996;* 1 Alltmawr Road, CARDIFF, CF23 6NQ.
MORRIS, Mrs. Amanda Jane, BSocSc ACA *1992;* 8 Needwood Park, Barton-under-Needwood, BURTON-ON-TRENT, DE13 8PA.
MORRIS, Miss. Amee, BSc(Econ) ACA *2011;* Bennett Brooks & Co Ltd, St. Georges Court, Winnington Avenue, NORTHWICH, CHESHIRE, CW8 4EE.
•MORRIS, Mr. Andrew, ACA FCCA CTA *2010;* (Tax Fac), with Pritchett & Co Limited, 16 Wynnstay Road, COLWYN BAY, CLWYD, LL29 8NB.
•MORRIS, Mr. Andrew Charles, BSc ACA *1981;* Ashbrook House, 21 Ladywood Road, SUTTON COLDFIELD, WEST MIDLANDS, B74 2QN.
•MORRIS, Mr. Andrew David, FCA DChA *1985;* (Tax Fac), Bramwell Morris, 133 Albert Road, WIDNES, CHESHIRE, WA8 6LB.
•MORRIS, Mr. Andrew David, BA ACA *1998;* Deloitte LLP, 2 New Street Square, LONDON, EC4A 3BZ. See also Deloitte & Touche LLP
MORRIS, Mr. Andrew James, BSc ACA *1993;* 247 West 87th Street, Apt 14D, NEW YORK, NY 10024, UNITED STATES.
MORRIS, Mr. Andrew James, MPhil BA ACA MBA MSI *1998;* RBS, Khalid Bin Waleed Road, PO Box 2567, DUBAI, UNITED ARAB EMIRATES.
MORRIS, Mr. Andrew John, MBA ACA *1996;* Integrated Dental Holdings, Sunset Business Centre, Manchester Road, Kearsley, BOLTON, LANCASHIRE BL4 8RH.
MORRIS, Mr. Andrew Jonathan, BSc ACA *1992;* 6 Ospringe Place, Sandown Park, TUNBRIDGE WELLS, KENT, TN2 4QD.
MORRIS, Mr. Andrew Kingsley, BEng ACA CF *1997;* Mount Croft, Malkins Bank, SANDBACH, CHESHIRE, CW11 4XP.
MORRIS, Mr. Andrew Montague, ACA *2002;* Deutsche Asset Management, 1 Appold Street, LONDON, EC2A 2UU.
•MORRIS, Mr. Andrew Paul, FCA DChA *1993;* Dains LLP, Unit 306, Third Floor, Fort Dunlop, Fort Parkway, BIRMINGHAM B24 9FD.
MORRIS, Mr. Andrew Paul, BEng ACA *1999;* The Spinney, 2 Bramcote Drive, Beeston, NOTTINGHAM, NG9 1AW.
MORRIS, Mr. Andrew Robert, BA FCA *1975;* (Tax Fac), 11 Rodman Close, Augustus RoadEdgbaston, BIRMINGHAM, B15 3PE.
MORRIS, Mr. Andrew Russell, ACA *1981;* 24 Greville Street, LONDON, EC1N 8SS.
•MORRIS, Mrs. Ann Herta, ACA *1980;* Morris Hartdene Limited, 1 Hartdene House, Bridge Road, BAGSHOT, SURREY, GU19 5AT.
•MORRIS, Miss. Anne Pamela, FCA *1979;* BW Macfarlane LLP, 3 Temple Square, LIVERPOOL, L2 5BA.
MORRIS, Miss. Anthea, MA BSc(Hons) ACA MCIPD DChA *2001;* 63 Primrose Hill Road, LONDON, NW3 3DE.
•MORRIS, Mr. Anthony Charles, FCA *1971;* 62 Cunningham Drive, LUTTERWORTH, LEICESTERSHIRE, LE17 4YR.
•MORRIS, Mr. Anthony Harry, FCA *1963;* Chappell Cole & Co Ltd, Heritage House, 34 North Cray Road, BEXLEY, DA5 3LZ. See also Morris & Associates
MORRIS, Mr. Anthony John, FCA *1961;* 1 Chaffinch Walk, Ridgewood, UCKFIELD, EAST SUSSEX, TN22 5YQ. (Life Member)
•MORRIS, Mr. Anthony John, BSc ACA *1986;* Deloitte LLP, 2 New Street Square, LONDON, EC4A 3BZ. See also Deloitte & Touche LLP
MORRIS, Mr. Antony Charles, BA ACA *1990;* Monitise, 8th Floor, Nexxus Building, 41 Connaught Road, CENTRAL, HONG KONG ISLAND HONG KONG SAR.
MORRIS, Mr. Antony John Gravell, MA ACA *1993;* No 5 Siglap Road, 12-45 Mandarin Gardens, SINGAPORE, SINGAPORE.
MORRIS, Mr. Arthur Cyril, FCA *1954;* 2 Livingston Drive, CANNING VALE, WA 6155, AUSTRALIA. (Life Member)
MORRIS, Mr. Barry, FCA *1977;* 35 Bennett Road, Crumpsall, MANCHESTER, M8 5ED.
•MORRIS, Mr. Benjamin Harry, FCA *1973;* Benjamin Morris & Co, Brook House, 18a Brook Street, NESTON, CHESHIRE, CH64 9XL.
MORRIS, Mr. Benjamin James, BA ACA *1984;* Pilgrim's View, 67 Park Road, OXTED, SURREY, RH8 0AN.
•MORRIS, Mr. Benjamin James, BA ACA *2005;* Wellers, Stuart House, 55 Catherine Place, LONDON, SW1E 6DY.
MORRIS, Miss. Bethan Kay, BA ACA *1999;* South View Cooks Hill, Clutton, BRISTOL, BS39 5RB.
MORRIS, Mr. Brian, FCA *1959;* Cranged Farm, St. Nicholas, GOODWICK, PEMBROKESHIRE, SA64 0LX. (Life Member)
MORRIS, Mr. Brian Edward, FCA *1972;* 6 Wood Ride, Petts Wood, ORPINGTON, BR5 1PX.
•MORRIS, Mr. Brian Edward, FCA *1972;* Holly House, Wenlock Road, BRIDGNORTH, WV16 4QB.
•MORRIS, Mr. Brian Hamilton, BA FCA *1979;* Les Quatres Regnes, La Route Du Francfief, St. Brelade, JERSEY, JE3 8BG.
MORRIS, Mr. Brian Valentine, FCA *1952;* Flat A, 27 Bramham Gardens, Earls Court, LONDON, SW5 0JE. (Life Member)
MORRIS, Mr. Bruce James, BA ACA *1989;* 4 Brackenhill, BERKHAMSTED, HERTFORDSHIRE, HP4 2PU.
MORRIS, Mr. Cecil George, FCA *1950;* Vue de la Normandie, Calais Road, St. Martin, GUERNSEY, GY4 6AR. (Life Member)
MORRIS, Mrs. Charlotte Anna, BSc ACA *2006;* 199 Burntwood Lane, LONDON, SW17 0AL.
MORRIS, Miss. Charlotte Louise Stafford, ACA *2009;* Flat 11, Flat 8-11, 47 Bennett Park, LONDON, SE3 9RA.
MORRIS, Ms. Cheryl Amanda, BA FCA *1986;* Via Melchiorre Gioia 8, 20124 MILAN, MI, ITALY.
•MORRIS, Mr. Christian Philip James, BSc ACA *2000;* Wyatt Morris Golland & Co, Park House, 200 Drake Street, ROCHDALE, OL16 1PJ.
•①MORRIS, Mr. Christopher, FCA *1967;* Begbies Traynor (Central) LLP, 32 Cornhill, LONDON, EC3V 3LJ. See also Begbies Traynor Limited
•MORRIS, Mr. Christopher Alan, BSc FCA *1988;* Muras Baker Jones, Regent House, Bath Avenue, WOLVERHAMPTON, WV1 4EG. See also Muras Management Services Ltd
MORRIS, Mr. Christopher Frederick, FCA *1968;* 22 Furnace Farm Road, CRAWLEY, WEST SUSSEX, RH10 6QA. (Life Member)
•MORRIS, Mr. Christopher Glyn, BA ACA *1982;* (Tax Fac), Newman Morris Ltd, Wellington House, 273-275 High Street, London Colney, ST. ALBANS, HERTFORDSHIRE AL2 1HA.
MORRIS, Mr. Christopher Paul, BSc ACA *1996;* Late Rooms Ltd, 2 Cheetham Hill Road, MANCHESTER, M4 4EW.
•MORRIS, Miss. Clare Louise, BA(Hons) ACA *2002;* Absolute Accounts (UK) Limited, 8 Vale Road, Parkstone, POOLE, DORSET, BH14 9AU.
MORRIS, Mr. Colin John, BA FCA *1986;* 52 Court Road, BARRY, SOUTH GLAMORGAN, CF63 4EU.
MORRIS, Mr. Conrad Friedrich, BSc ACA *1989;* Scisys Ltd, Methuen Park, CHIPPENHAM, SN14 0GB.
MORRIS, Mr. Daren, MA ACA *1997;* 38 Ashcroft Park, COBHAM, KT11 2DN.
MORRIS, Mr. David, BA ACA *1996;* 4 Woodland Drive, WATFORD, WD17 3BX.
MORRIS, Mr. David, FCA *1974;* 2 Rookwood, Eccleston, CHORLEY, LANCASHIRE, PR7 5RG.
•MORRIS, Mr. David, BSc FCA *1998;* with Whittingham Riddell LLP, Hafren House, 5 St Giles Business Park, NEWTOWN, POWYS, SY16 3AJ.
MORRIS, Mr. David, FCA *1969;* One Highfield Hall, Barrows Green, KENDAL, CUMBRIA, LA8 0AA. (Life Member)
MORRIS, Mr. David Anthony, ACA *2009;* 16 Hurstfold Avenue, MANCHESTER, M19 1RE.
MORRIS, Mr. David Brian, BEng ACA *1993;* 176 Paseo Del Rio, MORAGA, CA 94556, UNITED STATES.
MORRIS, Mr. David Charles, MA FCA *1970;* 5 Rokeby Place, Wimbledon, LONDON, SW20 0HU.
•MORRIS, Mr. David Edward, FCA *1969;* Quick House, Quick Road, Mossley, ASHTON-UNDER-LYNE, OL5 0RN.
MORRIS, Mr. David Edward Alban, MA FCA FCT *1962;* 3 Spencer Hill, LONDON, SW19 4PA. (Life Member)
MORRIS, Mr. David Eric, FCA *1948;* 7 Pinsley View, Wrenbury, NANTWICH, CHESHIRE, CW5 8HP. (Life Member)
MORRIS, Mr. David Gordon, BSc ACA *1993;* Red Architectural Ltd Monaghan House, Clarendon Street, HYDE, CHESHIRE, SK14 2EP.
MORRIS, Mr. David Gwyn, BSc ACA *1990;* The Barn Bondend Road, Upton St. Leonards, GLOUCESTER, GL4 8ED.
MORRIS, Mr. David James, ACA *2000;* 25 Mercers Road, LONDON, N19 4PW.
MORRIS, Mr. David Richard, BA FCA *1975;* 9 Heath Park, ILKLEY, WEST YORKSHIRE, LS29 9PX.
MORRIS, Mr. David Stanley, FCA *1950;* 6 Lansdown Place West, BATH, BA1 5EZ. (Life Member)
MORRIS, Mr. David Thomas Martin, BA ACA *1981;* 41 Middle Patent Road, Armonk, NEW YORK, NY 10504, UNITED STATES.
MORRIS, Mr. David Thomas Winn, ACA CA(AUS) *2009;* 398 Kallang Road, #16-01, SINGAPORE 339098, SINGAPORE.
•MORRIS, Ms. Debra Lisa, BA ACA *1990;* Debra Morris ACA, 9 Grosvenor Road, LONDON, N3 1EY.
MORRIS, Mrs. Della Joy, ACA *1989;* Peter Clarke & Co, 53 Henley Street, STRATFORD-UPON-AVON, WARWICKSHIRE, CV37 6PT.
MORRIS, Mrs. Diane Christine, OAM JP FCA *1963;* 40A Blyth Street, PARKSIDE, SA 5063, AUSTRALIA.
•MORRIS, Mr. Donald William, MSc BSc FCA *1982;* 14 Henderland Road, EDINBURGH, EH12 6BB.
MORRIS, Mr. Douglas Edward, FCA *1975;* Pear Tree Cottage, Penllyn, COWBRIDGE, SOUTH GLAMORGAN, CF71 7RQ. (Life Member)
•①MORRIS, Mr. Duncan Roderick, BA FCA MABRP *1990;* The Redfern Partnership, Redfern House, 29 Jury Street, WARWICK, CV34 4EH.
MORRIS, Mr. Edward Antony, FCA *1951;* 87 Banners Lane, HALESOWEN, WEST MIDLANDS, B63 2AU. (Life Member)
MORRIS, Mr. Edward Peter, BA FCA *1975;* E.P Morris & Company Ltd, 20 Harris Business Park, Hanbury Road, Stoke Prior, BROMSGROVE, WORCESTERSHIRE B60 4DJ.
MORRIS, Mrs. Elayne Margaret, MSc ACA *1988;* 8 Charborough Road, BROADSTONE, BH18 8NE.
MORRIS, Miss. Eleanor, BA ACA *1996;* Warford Hall Farm, Merrimans Lane, Great Warford, ALDERLEY EDGE, SK9 7TN.
MORRIS, Mrs. Elena, BA FCA *1978;* 87 Rehov Hagefen, 76858 ASSERET, ISRAEL.
MORRIS, Miss. Elizabeth Ann, BSc ACA *2011;* 12 Latium Close, Holywell Hill, ST. ALBANS, HERTFORDSHIRE, AL1 1XU.
MORRIS, Ms. Ella, ACA *2008;* 25 Eastbrook Road, Portslade, BRIGHTON, BN41 1LN.
MORRIS, Miss. Emma, ACA *2010;* Flat 165, Watermans Place, 3 Wharf Approach, LEEDS, LS1 4GN.
MORRIS, Mr. Ernest Stephen, FCA *1960;* Rose Cottage, Pontneathvaughan, Glynneath, NEATH, SA11 5NB. (Life Member)
•MORRIS, Mrs. Fiona Jane, BSc ACA *1992;* JFM Growing Business Solutions Limited, 38 Triscombe Drive, CARDIFF, SOUTH GLAMORGAN, CF5 2PN. See also Morris White Limited
MORRIS, Mr. Francis Simon Thomas, MBA FCA *1976;* Yellow 1., School of Law and Business, Charles Darwin University, Ellengowan Drive, CASUARINA, NT 0909 AUSTRALIA.
MORRIS, Mr. Gareth Andrew, BSc(Hons) ACA *2003;* 4 Welby Road, CARDIFF, CF5 1PA.
MORRIS, Mr. Gareth David, BSc ACA *1983;* 5 Palmerston House, 66A St Paul Street, Islington, LONDON, N1 7EE.
•MORRIS, Mr. Gareth Rutt, BA FCA *1995;* FRP Advisory LLP, 10 Furnival Street, LONDON, EC4A 1YH.
•MORRIS, Mr. Gary Alan, FCA *1974;* Morris Hartdene Limited, 1 Hartdene House, Bridge Road, BAGSHOT, SURREY, GU19 5AT.
MORRIS, Mr. Gavin Peter, BA ACA *1994;* 93 Reedley Road, BRISTOL, BS9 3TB.
MORRIS, Mrs. Gaynor, ACA *1987;* Curtis House, Stoke Dry, Oakham, RUTLAND, LEICESTERSHIRE, LE15 9JG.
MORRIS, Mr. Geoffrey Robert, FCA *1970;* Harewelle, 56a Norman Avenue, ABINGDON, OX14 2HL. (Life Member)
MORRIS, Mr. George, ACA *2010;* 6The Coppins, Dawnay Close, ASCOT, BERKSHIRE, SL5 7PQ.
MORRIS, Mr. George Eryl, BSc FCA *1968;* Broad Oak, Devonshire Avenue, AMERSHAM, HP6 5JE.
MORRIS, Mr. Gerald Furnival, BCom FCA *1956;* 22 Cramond Vale, EDINBURGH, EH4 6RB. (Life Member)
MORRIS, Mr. Gilbert Stanley, FCA *1953;* Woodhey, 47 Foxgrove Road, BECKENHAM, BR3 5AR. (Life Member)
MORRIS, Miss. Gillian Pauline, BSc ACA *1990;* 39 Salisbury Road, IPSWICH, IP3 0NP.
MORRIS, Mrs. Gillian Yvonne, BSc ACA *1989;* Specsavers Optical Group Ltd, La Villiaze Road, St. Andrew, GUERNSEY, GY6 8YP.
MORRIS, Mr. Glyn, BA ACA *1984;* 12 Derby Road, Urmston, MANCHESTER, M41 0UE.
•MORRIS, Mrs. Glynis Dawn, BA FCA *1979;* (Tax Fac), Glynis D. Morris, Cae Ceffylau, Drefach, LLANYBYDDER, DYFED, SA40 9SX.
MORRIS, Mrs. Gordana, ACA *1982;* St. Peters Church, Longtown, HEREFORD, HR2 0LD.
•MORRIS, Mr. Graham, FCA *1965;* Wyatt Morris Golland & Co, Park House, 200 Drake Street, ROCHDALE, OL16 1PJ.
MORRIS, Mr. Graham Charles, BSc FCA *1968;* Mulberry Tree House, Devonshire Avenue, AMERSHAM, BUCKINGHAMSHIRE, HP6 5JF. (Life Member)
•MORRIS, Mr. Gregory David, BA FCA *1985;* (Tax Fac), Gregory Morris, 160 Tamworth Road, SUTTON COLDFIELD, WEST MIDLANDS, B75 6DJ.
MORRIS, Mrs. Hannah Louise Vann, BA FCA *1989;* 66 South Court Avenue, DORCHESTER, DORSET, DT1 2BZ.
MORRIS, Mr. Harold Burgess, FCA *1954;* Smithills, 4 Wincote Drive, Tettenhall, WOLVERHAMPTON, WV6 8LR. (Life Member)
MORRIS, Miss. Helen, BSc ACA *1982;* 12 Harlech Grove, Lodge Moor, SHEFFIELD, S10 4NP.
MORRIS, Miss. Helen Elizabeth, BEd ACA *1993;* Berwin Leighton Paisner Adelaide House, London Bridge, LONDON, EC4R 9HA.
MORRIS, Mrs. Helen Elizabeth, MBA BA ACA *1993;* 10514 Madrone Ct, CUPERTINO, CA, 95014, UNITED STATES.
MORRIS, Mrs. Helen Elizabeth, BA FCA *1986;* South Acres Lodge, The Park, CHELTENHAM, GLOUCESTERSHIRE, GL50 2SD.
MORRIS, Mrs. Helen Louise, BA ACA *1998;* with PricewaterhouseCoopers LLP, 31 Great George Street, BRISTOL, BS1 5QD.

MORRIS, Mrs. Helen Mary, BA FCA CIA MIIA *1989;* 69 Basils Road, STEVENAGE, SG1 3PU.
MORRIS, Mr. Howard, FCA *1975;* P O Box 395, Richmond, MELBOURNE, VIC 3121, AUSTRALIA.
MORRIS, Mr. Howard Bleddyn, FCA *1968;* Lumley Castle Hotel Ltd, CHESTER LE STREET, DH3 4NX.
•**MORRIS, Mr. Howard Lionel, FCA** *1974;* Accountancy Experts Ltd., 6 Shirehall Park, Hendon, LONDON, NW4 2QL. See also H Moris & Co
•**MORRIS, Mr. Iain David, BSc ACA** *2002;* Chavereys, Mall House, The Mall, FAVERSHAM, KENT, ME13 8JL.
MORRIS, Mr. Ian David, BA ACA *1995;* 4 Acland Road, BRIDGEND, MID GLAMORGAN, CF31 1TF.
MORRIS, Mr. Ivor David, MA ACA *2002;* KPMG, 15th Floor Oxford House, Taikoo Place, 979 Kings Road, QUARRY BAY, HONG KONG ISLAND HONG KONG SAR.
MORRIS, Mr. James Edward, MA ACA *1992;* (Tax Fac), 1 Barrington Road, LONDON, N8 8QR.
MORRIS, Mr. James Hurst, FCA *1949;* 18 Thurlwood Croft, Westhoughton, BOLTON, BL5 3RF. (Life Member)
•**MORRIS, Mr. James Ian, OBE FCA** *1960;* (President 2005 - 2006) (Member of Council 1984 - 2009), Turner Peachey, Column House, London Road, SHREWSBURY, SY2 6NN.
MORRIS, Mr. James William, BA ACA *1990;* (Tax Fac), 83 Selborne Road, LONDON, N14 7DE.
MORRIS, Mr. Jamie, BA FCA *2000;* 11 Pullman Lane, GODALMING, SURREY, GU7 1XY.
MORRIS, Mrs. Jane, BA(Hons) ACA *2001;* 2 Bourne Place Meadows, Nizels Lane Hildenborough, TONBRIDGE, TN11 8NW.
MORRIS, Mrs. Jayne Bridie, BCom ACA *1986;* The Old Barn, 12 Aston Court Mews, SHIFNAL, SHROPSHIRE, TF11 8TP.
MORRIS, Mr. Jeffrey, BSc ACA *1991;* Long Marston Manor, Angram Road, Long Marston, YORK, YO26 7LR.
MORRIS, Mr. Jeffrey Owen, FCA *1963;* 8 Hutchwns Close, PORTHCAWL, MID GLAMORGAN, CF36 3LD. (Life Member)
MORRIS, Miss. Jennie, ACA *2008;* 110 Bryn Coch, Beaufort, EBBW VALE, GWENT, NP23 5DU.
•**MORRIS, Mr. Jeremy Rich, BSc ACA** *1992;* (Tax Fac), JFM Growing Business Solutions Limited, 38 Triscombe Drive, CARDIFF, SOUTH GLAMORGAN, CF5 2PN. See also Morris White Limited
MORRIS, Mrs. Jill Anna, ACA *2004;* with CLB Coopers, Laurel House, 173 Chorley New Road, BOLTON, BL1 4QZ.
MORRIS, Ms. Joan Elizabeth, BA ACA *1995;* Flat 28 Forest House, 1 Russell Cotes Road, BOURNEMOUTH, BH1 3UA.
MORRIS, Miss. Joanna Lucy, ACA *2009;* Garbutt & Elliott 2 Stable Court, Beechwoods Estate Elmete Lane, LEEDS, LS8 2LQ.
MORRIS, Mr. John, BA FCA *1984;* 2 Coachgates, Flockton, WAKEFIELD, WEST YORKSHIRE, WF4 4TT.
MORRIS, Mr. John, FCA *1976;* 48 St. Marys Avenue Central, SOUTHALL, MIDDLESEX, UB2 4LT.
•**MORRIS, Mr. John Andrew, BSc ACA** *1988;* KPMG LLP, 15 Canada Square, LONDON, E14 5GL. See also KPMG Europe LLP
MORRIS, Mr. John Brian Roper, BCom FCA *1955;* 27 Marine Parade, LEIGH-ON-SEA, SS9 2NA. (Life Member)
MORRIS, Mr. John Edward, BA ACA *1996;* Somerby House, Fenwick Lane, Fenwick, DONCASTER, SOUTH YORKSHIRE, DN6 0HA.
MORRIS, Mr. John Maxwell Tuke, FCA *1947;* 14 Lone Pine Drive West Parley, FERNDOWN, DORSET, BH22 8LL. (Life Member)
MORRIS, Mr. John Peter Mervyn, FCA *1949;* 8 Foxhollow Close, MOUNTAIN GREEN VILLAGE, 7945, SOUTH AFRICA. (Life Member)
MORRIS, Mr. John Richard, BSc FCA *1994;* (Tax Fac), 1000 North Randolph Street, Apt 808, ARLINGTON, VA 22201-5629, UNITED STATES.
MORRIS, Mr. John Simon Thrale, BA FCA *1972;* Potterfields, Potter Row, GREAT MISSENDEN, HP16 9LU.
•**MORRIS, Mr. John Stanley, FCA** *1962;* (Tax Fac), John S. Morris, Rowan House, New Lane Hill, Tilehurst, READING, RG30 4JJ.
MORRIS, Mr. John Thomson, BSc FCA *1991;* Fisherman's Cottages, Route de la Lague, St. Pierre Du Bois, GUERNSEY, GY7 9BU.
MORRIS, Mr. John Vaux, FCA *1954;* 42 Stocks Moor Road, Stocksmoor, HUDDERSFIELD, HD4 6XQ. (Life Member)
MORRIS, Mr. Jon, ACA *2011;* 15 Lincoln Close, GREENFORD, UB6 8NR.
•**MORRIS, Mr. Jon Edward William, BA ACA** *1995;* Ernst & Young LLP, 1 More London Place, LONDON, SE1 2AF. See also Ernst & Young Europe LLP
MORRIS, Mr. Jonathan Barrie, BEng ACA *2002;* 15 Hilden Avenue, Hildenborough, TONBRIDGE, TN11 9BY.
MORRIS, Mr. Jonathan Roger, BSc FCA *1993;* Little Crouches Farm, Flitterbrook Lane, Rushlake Green, HEATHFIELD, EAST SUSSEX, TN21 9PL.
MORRIS, Mr. Jonathan Wesley, BSc ACA *1987;* 1 Davis Street, BRISTOL, BS11 9JN.
MORRIS, Miss. Joyce Caroline, BSc ACA *1990;* 14 Bradley Gardens, Ealing, LONDON, W13 8HF.
MORRIS, Mrs. Julia, BSc ACA *2000;* 247 West 87th ST, Apt. 14 D, NEW YORK, NY 10024, UNITED STATES.
MORRIS, Mr. Julian Maitland, ACA *1987;* Oxfield Farm, Low Lane, Howsham, YORK, YO60 7PL.
MORRIS, Mr. Julien Michael William Rainfray, MA FCA *1991;* Jefferies International Ltd Vintners Place, 68 Upper Thames Street, LONDON, EC4V 3BJ.
•**MORRIS, Mrs. Juliet Sarah Ann, BA FCA** *1993;* Redshield Business Solutions Limited, Unit 2, Birchden Farm, Broadwater Forest Lane, Groombridge, TUNBRIDGE WELLS KENT TN3 9NR.
MORRIS, Mr. Justin Henry, BA ACA *1988;* E M I Group Plc Kensley House, 27 Wrights Lane, LONDON, W8 5SW.
MORRIS, Mrs. Justine Nicola, BSc ACA *1993;* 31 Agatha Gardens, Fernhill Heath, WORCESTER, WR3 8PB.
MORRIS, Mrs. Karen Simone, BA ACA *1998;* Lismore, 21 Regent Road St. Helier, JERSEY, JE2 4XP.
MORRIS, Mrs. Kate, BA(Hons) ACA *2003;* 20 Spinney Green, Eccleston, ST. HELENS, MERSEYSIDE, WA10 5AH.
MORRIS, Mrs. Katherine Emma, MA ACA *1998;* Wheelwrights, High Street, Urchfont, DEVIZES, SN10 4QL.
MORRIS, Mrs. Kathryn Beryl, BSc FCA *1986;* 83 Ely Road, Llandaf, CARDIFF, CF5 2BY.
MORRIS, Mrs. Kaye, BSc ACA *1990;* (Tax Fac), 80 Timothy Rees Close, Danescourt, CARDIFF, CF5 2AU.
MORRIS, Mr. Keith Douglas, ACA *1985;* 86-100 Victoria Drive, JIMBOOBA, QLD 4280, AUSTRALIA.
MORRIS, Mr. Keith Ian, BA ACA *1987;* Coopers Hill House, Coopers Hill, GLOUCESTER, GL3 4SB.
MORRIS, Mr. Keith Norton, FCA *1973;* Wood Mill Farm, Platt Lane Ellerdine, TELFORD, SHROPSHIRE, TF6 6RT.
MORRIS, Mrs. Kerry, BSc ACA *1999;* The Spinney, 2 Bramcote Drive, Beeston, NOTTINGHAM, NG9 1AW.
•**MORRIS, Mr. Kevin David, MA ACA** *1992;* PricewaterhouseCoopers LLP, 7 More London Riverside, LONDON, SE1 2RT. See also PricewaterhouseCoopers
MORRIS, Miss. Laura Elizabeth, ACA *2010;* 141 Atlantic Road, BIRMINGHAM, B44 8LN.
MORRIS, Ms. Lesley, BSc ACA *1993;* Coleman & Co Ltd, Shady Lane, Great Barr, BIRMINGHAM, B44 9ER.
•**MORRIS, Miss. Lisa Naomi, BA(Hons) ACA** *2001;* The 41GP Partnership, 41 Great Portland Street, LONDON, W1W 7LA. See also The 41GP Partnership LLP
MORRIS, Mrs. Loraine Mary, BSc ACA *1995;* 41 Pembridge Road, Bovingdon, HEMEL HEMPSTEAD, HP3 0QN.
MORRIS, Mr. Luke George, MSci BA ACA *2004;* Ernst & Young LLP, 2700 Commodity Exchange Tower, 360 Main Street, WINNIPEG R3C 4G9, MB, CANADA.
MORRIS, Miss. Lyn Annette, BA FCA *1995;* G PO Box 961, General Post Office, CENTRAL, HONG KONG ISLAND, HONG KONG SAR.
MORRIS, Mrs. Lynda Jane, ACA *1988;* (Tax Fac), 7 Dovey Drive, Walmley, SUTTON COLDFIELD, B76 1YW.
•**MORRIS, Mrs. Lynn, FCA** *1974;* (Tax Fac), L Morris FCA, 5 Greystokes, Aughton, ORMSKIRK, L39 5HE.
MORRIS, Mr. Marcus Card, BA ACA *1987;* Golden Grove Capital Solutions Inc, Golden Grove Great House, ST PHILIP, BARBADOS.
MORRIS, Mrs. Marion Elizabeth, ACA *1981;* Les Quatres Regnes, La Route Du Francfief, St. Brelade, JERSEY, JE3 8BG.
MORRIS, Mr. Mark Christopher, BSc FCA *1986;* Curtis House Main Street, Stoke Dry, OAKHAM, LE15 9JG.
MORRIS, Mr. Martin Robert, BA ACA *1982;* Learning Skills Council Kent & Medway, 26 Kings Hill Avenue, Kings Hill, WEST MALLING, KENT, ME19 4AE.
MORRIS, Mr. Matthew Edward, BA(Hons) ACA *2002;* (Tax Fac), with Farmiloes LLP, Winston Churchill House, 8 Ethel Street, BIRMINGHAM, B2 4BG.
•**MORRIS, Mr. Melville, FCA** *1949;* Melville Morris, 3rd Floor, Trident House, 31-33 Dale Street, LIVERPOOL, L2 2HF.
MORRIS, Mr. Michael, LLB FCA *1961;* 19 Geariesville Gardens, ILFORD, IG6 1JH.
MORRIS, Mr. Michael Dale, BSc ACA *1980;* 916 Wendover Court, RANDOLPH, NJ 07869, UNITED STATES.
•**MORRIS, Mr. Michael James, ACA FCCA** *2010;* UNW LLP, Citygate, St. James Boulevard, NEWCASTLE UPON TYNE, NE1 4JE.
MORRIS, Mr. Michael John, BSc FCA *1985;* Plas Glyndwr, Welsh Assembly, Kingsway, CARDIFF, CF10 3AH.
•**MORRIS, Mr. Michael John, FCA** *1961;* 83 Little Bushey Lane, BUSHEY, HERTFORDSHIRE, WD23 4SD.
MORRIS, Mr. Michael Leonard, BSc FCA *1977;* 10 Cheveley Road, Saxon Street, NEWMARKET, SUFFOLK, CB8 9RN.
MORRIS, Mr. Michael Solomon, FCA *1958;* Tnuat Hameri 6/2, Kiryat Ono, 52286 TEL AVIV, ISRAEL. (Life Member)
•①**MORRIS, Mr. Morgan Lawn, BSc FCA** *1996;* 4 East Park Road, HARROGATE, NORTH YORKSHIRE, HG1 5QT.
MORRIS, Mr. Neil Thomas, MBA *2000;* 164 Walton Park, Pannal, HARROGATE, NORTH YORKSHIRE, HG3 1RJ.
MORRIS, Mr. Nicholas, BA(Hons) ACA *2011;* Martinshaw Farm, Markfield Road, Ratby, LEICESTER, LE6 0LU.
MORRIS, Mr. Nicholas James, MA ACA *1997;* 53 Masbro Road, LONDON, W14 0LU.
MORRIS, Mr. Nicholas John, MSc ACA *2000;* Ofcom, Riverside House, 2a Southwark Bridge Road, LONDON, SE1 9HA.
MORRIS, Miss. Nicola, ACA *2011;* 19 Clayton Croft Road, Wilmington, DARTFORD, DA2 7AU.
MORRIS, Miss. Nicola Jane, BSc ACA *1999;* 31 Buckley Road, Kilburn, LONDON, NW6 7LY.
MORRIS, Mr. Nigel John Grant, FCA *1971;* 28 St. Margarets View, EXMOUTH, DEVON, EX8 5BJ.
•**MORRIS, Mr. Nigel John Vivian, BSc FCA** *1977;* Hayvenhursts, Lermon Court Fairway House, Links Business Park, St. Mellons, CARDIFF, CF3 0LT.
•**MORRIS, Mr. Nigel Roy, BA FCA** *1993;* Matthew Edwards & Co, Clinches House, Lord Street, Douglas, ISLE OF MAN, IM1 4LN.
MORRIS, Mr. Noel Patrick, MSc BA FCA *1980;* APT Finance, Post Office, 22 Reading Road, HENLEY-ON-THAMES, OXFORDSHIRE, RG9 1AG.
MORRIS, Mr. Olaf Philip, BEng ACA *1995;* 20 Morley Square, Bishopston, BRISTOL, BS7 9DW.
MORRIS, Mr. Oliver Piers Alexander Gwyn, BA ACA *2007;* 4 Clearview Mews, Clearview Street, St. Helier, JERSEY, JE2 3YY.
•**MORRIS, Mr. Patrick James, MSc BSc ACA CTA** *1995;* (Tax Fac), Fairhurst, Douglas Bank House, Wigan Lane, WIGAN, WN1 2TB.
MORRIS, Mr. Paul, BSc ACA *2004;* with PricewaterhouseCoopers LLP, Benson House, 33 Wellington Street, LEEDS, LS1 4JP.
MORRIS, Mr. Paul Andre, BEng ACA *2006;* Flat 312 Cardamom Building, 31 Shad Thames, LONDON, SE1 2YR.
•**MORRIS, Mr. Paul Andrew, BA ACA CTA** *1998;* (Tax Fac), with Target Consulting Limited, Lawrence House, Lower Bristol Road, BATH, BA2 9ET.
MORRIS, Mr. Paul David, BSc ACA *1982;* (Tax Fac), 6 Yew Tree Close, Hatfield Peverel, CHELMSFORD, CM3 2SG.
MORRIS, Mr. Paul David, BA(Hons) ACA *2002;* with PricewaterhouseCoopers LLP, 9 Greyfriars Road, READING, RG1 1JG.
•**MORRIS, Mr. Paul Gareth Stephen, BSc ACA** *1994;* Arram Berlyn Gardner, 30 City Road, LONDON, EC1Y 2AB. See also ABG Business Support Services Ltd
MORRIS, Mr. Paul Simon, BA ACA *1998;* 243 Spixworth Road, NORWICH, NR6 7DZ.
•**MORRIS, Mr. Paul Stephen, FCA** *1968;* Haines Watts, 69/73 Theobalds Road, LONDON, WC1X 8TA.
MORRIS, Mr. Paul William, BEng ACA *2005;* 53 Severus Avenue, Acomb, YORK, YO24 4LX.
MORRIS, Mr. Peter, FCA *1963;* 1 Restharrow Road, Weavering, MAIDSTONE, ME14 5UH. (Life Member)
•**MORRIS, Mr. Peter Christopher, FCA ATII** *1988;* (Tax Fac), Morris Wheeler & Co Limited, 26 Church Street, BISHOP'S STORTFORD, HERTFORDSHIRE, CM23 2LY.
MORRIS, Mr. Peter George, FCA *1968;* Flat 29 Veric, 16-18 Eaton Gardens, HOVE, EAST SUSSEX, BN3 3UB.
•**MORRIS, Mr. Peter John, BA FCA** *1993;* Hayles & Partners Limited, 39 Castle Street, LEICESTER, LE1 5WN.
•**MORRIS, Mr. Peter John Richard, BA ACA** *1986;* South Acres Lodge, The Park, CHELTENHAM, GLOUCESTERSHIRE, GL50 2SD.
MORRIS, Mr. Peter Vaughan, BA FCA *1972;* Bonaventure, Hamm Court, WEYBRIDGE, SURREY, KT13 8YB.
MORRIS, Mr. Philip Charles, BSc ACA *1979;* 49 Benaroon Avenue, St Ives, SYDNEY, NSW 2075, AUSTRALIA.
MORRIS, Mr. Philip John Garton, BA FCA *1990;* Vane House, Horcott Road, FAIRFORD, GLOUCESTERSHIRE, GL7 4BX.
MORRIS, Mr. Philip William, BSc ACA *2010;* 19 Woodthorne Road, WOLVERHAMPTON, WV6 8TU.
MORRIS, Mr. Phillip James, ACA *2005;* Lynwood House Tostock Road, Beyton, BURY ST. EDMUNDS, SUFFOLK, IP30 9AG.
MORRIS, Mr. Raymond Charles, FCA *1971;* 36 Northiam, Woodside Park, LONDON, N12 7HA.
•**MORRIS, Mr. Raymond John, FCA** *1965;* 8 Hameyasdim Street, 43217 RA'ANANA, ISRAEL.
MORRIS, Mr. Raymond Robert, FCA *1960;* 293 Church Road, St Annes, LYTHAM ST.ANNES, FY8 3NP.
MORRIS, Mrs. Rebecca Jane, BA ACA DChA *1999;* Oxford Diocesan Church House North Hinksey Lane, Botley, OXFORD, OX2 0NB.
MORRIS, Mr. Richard, BSc ACA *1993;* 36 Fairfield Rise, BILLERICAY, CM12 9NP.
MORRIS, Mr. Richard Charles, BSc(Econ) FCILT FCA *1977;* The Ancre Hill, MONMOUTH, NP25 5HS.
MORRIS, Mr. Richard Colin, MSc BA FCA *1964;* 1 Waterside Court, Skip's LaneChristleton, CHESTER, CH3 7BU.
MORRIS, Mr. Richard Crosbie, BA FCA *1978;* 208 de Guyenne Apt. 203, ST LAMBERT J4S 1G9, QC, CANADA.
MORRIS, Mr. Richard Geoffrey, BA ACA *1987;* 8 Holt Close, LONDON, N10 3HW.
MORRIS, Mr. Richard John, BSocSc ACA MIIA *1999;* 78 Lyon Road, VIEWBANK, VIC 3084, AUSTRALIA.
•**MORRIS, Mr. Richard Leonard, FCA** *1979;* Lovewell Blake LLP, Sixty Six, North Quay, GREAT YARMOUTH, NORFOLK, NR30 1HE.
MORRIS, Mr. Richard Peter, BSc ACA *1990;* Federal-Mogul Friction Prod, Hayfield Road, Chapel-En-Le-Frith, HIGH PEAK, SK23 0JP.
MORRIS, Mr. Richard Roderick, ACA *1992;* Owl's Cliff, 105 Harrington Sound Road, SMITHS HS02, BERMUDA.
MORRIS, Mr. Richard Stewart, ACA *2008;* 85 Hillview Gardens, LONDON, NW4 2JP.
•**MORRIS, Mr. Robert, FCA** *1985;* Lyon Griffiths Limited, 17 Alvaston Business Park, Middlewich Road, NANTWICH, CHESHIRE, CW5 6PF.
MORRIS, Mr. Robert Armor, BSc ACA *1982;* with KLC Kennic Lui & Co, 5/F, Ho Lee Commercial Building, 38 - 44 D' Aguilar Street, CENTRAL, HONG KONG SAR.
MORRIS, Mr. Robert Christopher, BSc ACA *1980;* Border Cottage, Shire Lane, Cholesbury, TRING, HP23 6NA.
MORRIS, Mr. Robert Edward, FCA *1969;* Blue Star Holdings Pty Ltd, 8th Floor, 2 Long Street, CAPE TOWN, C.P., 8001 SOUTH AFRICA.
MORRIS, Mr. Robert James, BA ACA *1993;* 44 Gilmore Crescent, THORNHILL L4J 3A1, ON, CANADA.
MORRIS, Mr. Robert John, BSc ACA *1989;* Northrop Grumman Information Technology Ltd, Stratford Road, SOLIHULL, WEST MIDLANDS, B90 4ZS.
MORRIS, Mr. Roderick Gruffydd, BA ACA *1985;* Raphael Health Care Ltd, Briar Hey, Mill Lane, Rainhill, PRESCOT, MERSEYSIDE L35 6NE.
•**MORRIS, Mr. Roger, BA FCA** *1996;* (Tax Fac), HAT Group of Accountants, 12 Cock Lane, LONDON, EC1A 9BU. See also Holborn Accountancy Tuition Limited
MORRIS, Mr. Roger, FCA *1947;* Langlaithes, Askham, PENRITH, CUMBRIA, CA10 2PG. (Life Member)
MORRIS, Mr. Roger Macdonald, MA FCA *1974;* 24 Brook Farm Road, COBHAM, SURREY, KT11 3AX.
•**MORRIS, Mr. Roger Paul, ACA** *1981;* (Tax Fac), Morris Lane, 31/33 Commercial Road, POOLE, DORSET, BH14 0HU. See also Morris Lane & Co.
MORRIS, Mr. Roger Philip, FCA *1968;* 69 Elgin Crescent, LONDON, W11 2JE. (Life Member)

MORRIS, Miss. Rosemary Margaret, BSc FCA *1970;* 16 Somerdale Road, Northfield, BIRMINGHAM, B31 2EG. (Life Member)
MORRIS, Miss. Rowena Ann, BSc(Hons) ACA PGCE *2002;* B P P Professional Education, Mallard Complex, La Villiaze Road, Forest, GUERNSEY, GY8 0HG.
MORRIS, Miss. Sally Anne, BSc ACA *1989;* Trust Head Office The Lodge, Runwell Hospital Runwell Chase, Runwell, WICKFORD, ESSEX, SS11 7XX.
•**MORRIS, Mrs. Sally Elizabeth, BSc ACA** *1993;* Sally Morris Accountancy, 15 Broadway Road, Bishopston, BRISTOL, BS7 8ES.
MORRIS, Miss. Samantha, ACA *2011;* 15 Model Terrace, Cockfield, BISHOP AUCKLAND, COUNTY DURHAM, DL13 5DX.
MORRIS, Miss. Sarah, BSc ACA *2006;* 25 Malin Close, Hale Village, LIVERPOOL, L24 5RU.
MORRIS, Mr. Shaun Anthony, BSocSc FCA *1990;* 76 Church Lane, Hanford, STOKE-ON-TRENT, ST4 4QD.
MORRIS, Mr. Sidney, FCA *1948;* Flat 8, 15 Hyde Park Gardens, LONDON, W2 2LU. (Life Member)
•**MORRIS, Mr. Simon Charles, BA FCA** *1980;* Grant Thornton UK LLP, Grant Thornton House, 22 Melton Street, Euston Square, LONDON, NW1 2EP. See also Grant Thornton LLP
MORRIS, Mr. Simon John, BSc ACA *1993;* 21a Longsight Road, Ramsbottom, BURY, BL0 9SL.
MORRIS, Mr. Simon Paul, MA ACA *1989;* Analysys Mason FZ-LLC, PO Box 502064, Al Shatha Tower 3110, Dubai Internet City, DUBAI, UNITED ARAB EMIRATES.
MORRIS, Ms. Sonia Isobel, BA ACA *1993;* MLC Limited, 105-153 Miller Street, NORTH SYDNEY, NSW 2060, AUSTRALIA.
MORRIS, Mr. Stephen Anthony, BSc FCA *1979;* (Tax Fac), Pennaf Limited, 72 Ffordd William Morgan, St. Asaph Business Park, ST. ASAPH, CLWYD, LL17 0JD.
MORRIS, Dr. Stephen James, PhD MEng ACA *2009;* 79 Ballabrooie Avenue, Douglas, ISLE OF MAN, IM1 4EZ.
MORRIS, Mr. Stephen Michael, BSc ACA *1998;* 14 Stewart Close, Moulton, NORTHAMPTON, NN3 7WU.
MORRIS, Mr. Stephen Paul, MSc(Econ) ACA *1999;* 31 West Way, BOURNEMOUTH, BH9 3DT.
•**MORRIS, Mr. Steven, BA FCA** *2000;* Steve Morris Accountants Limited, 84 Robertson Drive, St. Annes Park, BRISTOL, BS4 4RG.
MORRIS, Mr. Steven Andrew, ACA *2007;* 147 Sileby Road, Barrow upon Soar, LOUGHBOROUGH, LE12 8LW.
MORRIS, Mr. Steven John, BA FCA *1993;* 5 Woodhall Lane, Balsham, CAMBRIDGE, CB21 4DT.
MORRIS, Mr. Stewart, MA(Cantab) ACA *2006;* Pricewaterhousecoopers Llp, 1 Hays Lane, LONDON, SE1 2RD.
MORRIS, Mr. Stuart Michael, FCA *1963;* 18 The Lane, Alwoodley, LEEDS, LS17 7BS.
MORRIS, Mrs. Susan Caroline, BA ACA *1990;* Jonathan Morris Construction Limited, 12 Bosley Way, CHRISTCHURCH, DORSET, BH23 2HF.
MORRIS, Mr. Sydney, MA FCA *1963;* Rainbow Road Lyford Cay, P.O. Box N-4802, NASSAU, BAHAMAS.
MORRIS, Mr. Terrance Colin, FCA *1972;* Lansbury International Ltd, 1 Cloth Court, LONDON, EC1A 7LS.
MORRIS, Miss. Tessa Mary, BA(Econ) ACA *2002;* with PricewaterhouseCoopers LLP, 1 Embankment Place, LONDON, WC2N 6RH.
MORRIS, Mr. Tim, BA(Hons) ACA *2003;* 20 Spinney Green, Eccleston, ST. HELENS, MERSEYSIDE, WA10 5AH.
MORRIS, Mr. Timothy, FCA *1977;* 18 allee du Saut du Loup, Parc du Chateau, 95000 NEUVILLE SUR OISE, FRANCE.
MORRIS, Mr. Timothy Bruce, FCA *1972;* Westholme, Underton, BRIDGNORTH, SHROPSHIRE, WV16 6TY.
•**MORRIS, Mr. Timothy John, BA ACA** *1997;* Ernst & Young LLP, 1 More London Place, LONDON, SE1 2AF. See also Ernst & Young Europe LLP
MORRIS, Mr. Timothy John, BSc ACA *1986;* Flat 1, 18 Dufferin Street, LONDON, EC1Y 8PD.
•**MORRIS, Mr. Timothy Richard Thomas, BA FCA** *1972;* (Tax Fac), Liles Morris Limited, Park House, 233 Roehampton Lane, LONDON, SW15 4LB.
MORRIS, Mr. Wayman Stewart, BA FCA *1977;* Shadowbrook, Shadowbrook Lane, Hampton In Arden, SOLIHULL, B92 0DQ.
MORRIS-JONES, Mr. David Trevorr, FCA *1959;* 21 Pineways, Appleton, WARRINGTON, WA4 5EJ.
MORRIS-RICHARDSON, Mr. Andrew John, FCA *1980;* Windsor House, 30 Old Coach Road, Wollaton, NOTTINGHAM, NG8 1GT.
MORRIS-SLOANE, Mrs. Harriet Louise, ACA *2008;* 85 Hillview Gardens, LONDON, NW4 2JP.
MORRIS SMITH, Mr. Timothy Justin, BA ACA *1992;* PO Box 25, Harbord Post Office, FRESHWATER, NSW 2096, AUSTRALIA.
MORRISEY, Miss. Julie Anne, BA ACA *1992;* Asp House Farm, Stainsacre, WHITBY, NORTH YORKSHIRE, YO22 4LR.
MORRISH, Mr. Anthony John, FCA *1963;* 178 Kimbolton Road, BEDFORD, MK41 8DW. (Life Member)
MORRISH, Mr. Eric Andrew, BA ACA *1982;* 4 Sudley Road, BOGNOR REGIS, WEST SUSSEX, PO21 1EU.
MORRISH, Mr. John Sutherland Cavers, MA LLB FCA *1973;* Redlands, 23 Thorn Road, Bearsden, GLASGOW, G61 4BS. (Life Member)
MORRISH, Mrs. Karen Dawn, BA ACA *1985;* Spanish Place, Coastal Road, East Preston, LITTLEHAMPTON, BN16 1SJ.
MORRISH, Mr. Lancelot Peter, BSc ACA *1985;* Cacketts Farmhouse, Horsmonden, TONBRIDGE, TN12 8BX.
•**MORRISH, Mr. Phillip Anthony, FCA** *1982;* (Tax Fac), Apsleys, 21 Bampton St, TIVERTON, EX16 6AA. See also A + B Bookkeeping Ltd
MORRISH, Mrs. Rebecca Karen, BSc ACA *2003;* 72 Pewley Way, GUILDFORD, SURREY, GU1 3QA.
MORRISH, Mr. Richard John, ACA *2008;* 24 Mill Way, Totton, SOUTHAMPTON, SO40 7JF.
MORRISH, Mr. Robert Nicholas Lutwyche, BA FCA *1974;* Shafts Farm, West Meon, PETERSFIELD, GU32 1LU.
•**MORRISON, Mr. Alan Eric, LLB FCA** *1991;* DMS Partners, 31 Rutland Square, EDINBURGH, EH1 2BW.
•**MORRISON, Mrs. Alison Thorpe, BA FCA** *1995;* Alison Morrison Limited, Austens, Chestnut Walk, Tangmere, CHICHESTER, WEST SUSSEX PO20 2HH.
•**MORRISON, Mrs. Amanda Joanne, BCom ACA** *1992;* KPMG LLP, 15 Canada Square, LONDON, E14 5GL. See also KPMG Europe LLP
MORRISON, Mr. Andrew David, BA ACA *2005;* 27a Holdenby Road, LONDON, SE4 2DA.
MORRISON, Mr. Anthony Kenneth, FCA *1972;* Goldman Sachs, Peterborough Court, 133 Fleet Street, LONDON, EC4A 2PP.
MORRISON, Mr. Benjamin Samuel, MEng ACA *2003;* 30 Park Lane, BISHOP'S STORTFORD, HERTFORDSHIRE, CM23 3NH.
MORRISON, Mr. Bruce Anthony, ACA *1988;* 3 Chapel Row Maidstone Road, Matfield, TONBRIDGE, TN12 7LD.
MORRISON, Miss. Caroline Anne, MA ACA *2004;* 122 Glasgow Road, PAISLEY, RENFREWSHIRE, PA1 3LX.
•**MORRISON, Mr. Charles Bruce, BA ACA CF** *1983;* Hurst Morrison Thomson Corporate Finance LLP, The Hub, 14 Station Road, HENLEY-ON-THAMES, OXFORDSHIRE, RG9 1AY. See also Hurst Morrison Thomson
MORRISON, Mr. Christopher Robert, BSc ACA *1990;* with Kitchen & Brown, Alpha House, 40 Coinagehall Street, HELSTON, TR13 8EQ.
MORRISON, Mr. David, MA ACA *2010;* 24 Woodland Road, Sawston, CAMBRIDGE, CB22 3DU.
•**MORRISON, Mr. David, ACA FCCA** *2009;* Nyman Libson Paul, Regina House, 124 Finchley Road, LONDON, NW3 5JS.
MORRISON, Mr. David Michael Allen, BA ACA *1990;* Northern Rock (Asset Management) Plc, Prudhoe Building, Regent Centre, Gosforth, NEWCASTLE UPON TYNE, NE3 4AW.
MORRISON, Mr. David Neil, BSc ACA *2004;* 105 Ballabrooie Avenue, Douglas, ISLE OF MAN, IM1 4HA.
•**MORRISON, Mr. David Nicholas, MA FCA MBA** *1975;* Morrison Forensic, 97 Camden Road, LONDON, NW1 9HA.
•**MORRISON, Mr. David Peter, MA FCA** *1973;* Morrison & Co, The Tile House, Bagshot Road, Worplesdon Hill, WOKING, SURREY GU22 0QY.
MORRISON, Miss. Deborah Mary, BSc ACA *1989;* 9 The Close, SALISBURY, SP1 2EB.
MORRISON, Mr. Ernest Albert, FCA *1948;* 93 Gilbert Scott Court, Whielden Street, AMERSHAM, BUCKINGHAMSHIRE, HP7 0AR. (Life Member)
MORRISON, Mrs. Gabriella Mary Bethan, LLB ACA *1996;* Moorlands, Whitegate, East Keswick, LEEDS, LS17 9HB.
MORRISON, Mrs. Gioia Rosemary Antonia, MA ACA *2001;* 22 Mentone Road, Heaton Moor, STOCKPORT, CHESHIRE, SK4 4HF.
•**MORRISON, Mr. Gordon Anderson, FCA** *1981;* Ardhurst Accountants Limited, 200 Brook Drive, Green Park, READING, RG2 6UB.
MORRISON, Mr. Graham, BA ACA *1998;* 24 White Eagle Road, SWINDON, SN25 1TN.
•**MORRISON, Mr. Hamish Moir, MA(Hons) ACA** *2000;* Baker Tilly Tax & Advisory Services LLP, 2 Whitehall Quay, LEEDS, LS1 4HG. See also Baker Tilly Corporate Finance LLP
•**MORRISON, Mr. Ian Jonathan, BA ACA** *1996;* PricewaterhouseCoopers LLP, Benson House, 33 Wellington Street, LEEDS, LS1 4JP. See also PricewaterhouseCoopers
MORRISON, Mrs. Jennifer, BSc ACA *2007;* Bupa House, B U P A BUPA House, 15-19 Bloomsbury Way, LONDON, WC1A 2BA.
MORRISON, Mrs. Kathryn Muir, BSc FCA CTA *1991;* Alan Steel Asset Management Ltd Noble House, Regent Centre Blackness Road, LINLITHGOW, WEST LOTHIAN, EH49 7HU.
MORRISON, Mr. Keith, LLB ACA *1990;* 22 Ernle Road, Wimbledon, LONDON, SW20 0HJ.
MORRISON, Mr. Kenneth John, BSc FCA *1986;* 62A Whartons Lane, Ashurst, SOUTHAMPTON, SO40 7EF.
•**MORRISON, Mr. Kenneth Stephen, FCA** *1980;* (Tax Fac), Morrisons, 7 Grove Place, BEDFORD, MK40 3JJ. See also Morrisons Business Advisers
MORRISON, Mrs. Lucy Clare, BA ACA *1992;* Brick House, Braxted Road, Kelvedon, COLCHESTER, CO5 9BS.
•**MORRISON, Mrs. Lynsey Marie, BA ACA** *2007;* 168 Mather Avenue, LIVERPOOL, L18 7HD.
MORRISON, Miss. Mairi Elizabeth, ACA *2008;* 3 Bramber Mews, Caversham, READING, RG4 6NN.
MORRISON, Mrs. Margaret Jane, MA ACA *1992;* 14 Kingsburgh Road, EDINBURGH, EH12 6DZ.
MORRISON, Mr. Michael Charles, ACA *1982;* Morgan Stanley, 25 Cabot Square, Canary Wharf, LONDON, E14 4QA.
•**MORRISON, Mr. Nicholas Jon, BSocSc ACA** *2002;* with PricewaterhouseCoopers LLP, 7 More London Riverside, LONDON, SE1 2RT.
•**MORRISON, Mr. Nigel, BA FCA** *1989;* Grant Thornton UK LLP, Hartwell House, 55-61 Victoria Street, BRISTOL, BS1 6FT. See also Grant Thornton LLP
MORRISON, Mr. Patrick Connor, ACA *1994;* Armstrong Medical Ltd, Wattstown Business Park, Newbridge Road, COLERAINE, COUNTY LONDONDERRY, BT52 1BS.
MORRISON, Mr. Paul Stephen Marshall, BA ACA *1984;* Starpoint, Wykham Lane, Bodicote, BANBURY, OXFORDSHIRE, OX15 4BW.
MORRISON, Mr. Peter George, FCA *1957;* 4 Bennett Way, West Clandon, GUILDFORD, GU4 7TN. (Life Member)
MORRISON, Miss. Rachel, BSc ACA *2011;* 19 South Park Crescent, GERRARDS CROSS, BUCKINGHAMSHIRE, SL9 8HJ.
MORRISON, Mrs. Rachel Jane, BA ACA *1995;* (Tax Fac), White House Main Street, Allexton, OAKHAM, LE15 9AB.
•**MORRISON, Ms. Sarah, BA FCA** *1989;* Littlejohn LLP, 1 Westferry Circus, Canary Wharf, LONDON, E14 4HD.
•**MORRISON, Mr. Simon James, BSc(Hons) ACA** *2003;* with Target Consulting Limited, Lawrence House, Lower Bristol Road, BATH, BA2 9ET.
MORRISON, Mr. Stephen, BCom FCA *1975;* Apartment 9, 6 Ibbotsons Lane, LIVERPOOL, L17 1AL.
MORRISON, Mr. Stephen, BCom FCA CTA *1986;* 53 Bury Road, Edenfield Ramsbottom, BURY, BL0 0EN.
MORRISON, Mrs. Susan Juliet, BA ACA *2001;* Nissan Motor Manufacturing (UK) Ltd, Washington Road, SUNDERLAND, SR5 3NS.
MORRISON-SMITH, Mr. Robin, FCA CTA *1991;* Cambridge Silicon Radio Churchill House, Cambridge Business Park Cowley Road, CAMBRIDGE, CB4 0WZ.
MORRISROE, Dr. James Martin, ACA *1985;* Linden House, 4 Fulmer Drive, GERRARDS CROSS, BUCKINGHAMSHIRE, SL9 7HJ.
MORRISS, Mr. Alexander James, BSc(Hons) ACA *2004;* 15 Ravenscroft Park, BARNET, HERTFORDSHIRE, EN5 4ND.
MORRISS, Mr. Andrew Jonathan, BSc(Econ) ACA *1998;* Robinson Road Post Office, PO Box 278, SINGAPORE, SINGAPORE.
MORRISS, Mrs. Elizabeth Ann Saxby, BSc(Hons) ACA *2004;* 15 Ravenscroft Park, BARNET, HERTFORDSHIRE, EN5 4ND.
MORRISS, Mr. John Richard, FCA *1961;* Spindle Wood, 2 Doddshill Road, Dersingham, KING'S LYNN, NORFOLK, PE31 6LW. (Life Member)
MORRISS, Miss. Katie Jayne, MSc ACA *2007;* 3 Blyth Road, WIRRAL, MERSEYSIDE, CH63 0HP.
MORRISS, Mr. Nigel Robert, FCA *1967;* 6 New Farm Avenue, BROMLEY, BR2 0TX.
MORRISS, Mrs. Susanna Elizabeth, MA BA ACA *1990;* 4 Orestes Mews, LONDON, NW6 1AP.
MORRISSEY, Mr. Ian Patrick, ACA *1985;* 9 Tasso Road, LONDON, W6 8LY.
MORRISSEY, Mr. James Arthur, FCA *1968;* 2 Perrywood Lane, Watton At Stone, HERTFORD, SG14 3RB.
•**MORRISSEY, Miss. Margaret Mary Louise, BSc ACA** *1991;* KPMG LLP, 15 Canada Square, LONDON, E14 5GL. See also KPMG Europe LLP
MORRISSEY, Mr. Neil Michael Declan, BA ACA *2000;* 12 Cromwell Close, Harvard Road, LONDON, W4 4EB.
MORRISSEY, Mr. Paul Simon, FCA *1975;* 2 Shottendane Road, LONDON, SW6 5TJ.
MORRISSEY, Mr. Peter Joseph, FCA *1974;* 23 Trafalgar Place, LYMINGTON, SO41 9BN.
MORRISSEY, Mrs. Rachel Jane, BA ACA *1993;* Child Maintenance and Enforcement Commission, Benton Park View, NEWCASTLE UPON TYNE, NE98 1YX.
MORRISSY, Mrs. Clare Elizabeth, BSc ACA *1994;* 238 Strines Road, Strines, STOCKPORT, SK6 7GA.
•**MORRITT, Mr. David, BSc ACA** *1993;* KPMG LLP, 1 The Embankment, Neville Street, LEEDS, LS1 4DW. See also KPMG Europe LLP
MORRITT, Mr. Robert Matthew, FCA *1960;* Farlands, 44 The Street, Brooke, NORWICH, NR15 1JT. (Life Member)
MORROD, Miss. Deborah Yvonne, ACA *1984;* 54 Balcaskie Road, Eltham, LONDON, SE9 1HQ.
MORROW, Mr. Andrew Martin, BSc(Econ) ACA CTA *1995;* (Tax Fac), Holmwood, 30 Church Way, Whetstone, LONDON, N20 0LA.
•**MORROW, Mr. David Peter Stewart, BA ACA DChA** *2000;* with Beever and Struthers, 3rd Floor, Alperton House, Bridgewater Road, WEMBLEY, MIDDLESEX HA0 1EH.
•**MORROW, Mr. John Anthony, FCA** *1969;* P O Box 653204, BENMORE, GAUTENG, 2010, SOUTH AFRICA.
MORROW, Mrs. Katherine, BA(Hons) ACA *2001;* High Trees Court, Chart Lane, REIGATE, RH2 7EF.
•**MORROW, Miss. Kay Juliana, BSc ACA** *1997;* with Buzzacott LLP, 130 Wood Street, LONDON, EC2V 6DL.
MORROW, Mr. Michael Charles Stewart, MA FCA *1969;* 19 Charlwood Drive, 6 Strand Drive, RICHMOND, SURREY, TW9 4DP.
•**MORROW, Mrs. Pamela, LLB ACA CTA** *2000;* (Tax Fac), Pamela Morrow, 30 Church Way, LONDON, N20 0LA.
MORROW, Mr. Timothy Edward, BA(Hons) ACA *2001;* High Trees Court, Chart Lane, REIGATE, RH2 7EF.
•**MORSE, Mr. Andrew Paul, BA ACA** *1991;* Priory Practice Limited, 3 Hunter Street, CHESTER, CH1 2AR.
MORSE, Mr. Barry, BSc FCA *1982;* The Gables, High Street, Swineshead, BEDFORD, MK44 2AA.
MORSE, Mr. Jonathan Richard, BSc ACA *1981;* 79 Porlock Drive, Sully, PENARTH, CF64 5QB.
MORSE, Mrs. Nichola Lorraine, BSc ACA *2003;* 33 Tower Close, Bassingbourn, ROYSTON, HERTFORDSHIRE, SG8 5JX.
MORSE, Mr. Philip, ACA *2009;* 12 Ffordd Daniel Lewis, St. Mellons, CARDIFF, CF3 0RQ.
MORSE, Mr. Richard Barry, MA FCA FCCA *1974;* Upper Mill, 4 Chepstow Road, USK, NP15 1BL.
MORSE, Ms. Stella Helen, BSc ACA *1992;* Achnacarry, Trochry, DUNKELD, PERTHSHIRE, PH8 0DY.
MORSE, Mrs. Susan Elizabeth, BSc ACA *1993;* 62 Barkers Mead, Yate, BRISTOL, BS37 7LF.
MORSHEAD, The Revd. Ivo Francis Trelawny, FCA *1952;* 28 Edge Street, Kensington, LONDON, W8 7PN. (Life Member)
MORSHEAD, Mr. Piers Nigel, MA FCA *1955;* 2 Mill Lane, Abbots Worthy, WINCHESTER, HAMPSHIRE, SO21 1DS. (Life Member)
MORSHED, Mr. Ali Amer Saleh, ACA *1980;* Saudi Industrail Projects Co (Pepsi Cola), PO Box 301, JEDDAH, 21411, SAUDI ARABIA.
MORSHED, Mr. Ali Omer Golam, ACA *1983;* Sidat Hyder Morshed Ass Ltd, Room 601-605, Beaumont Plaza, Beaumont Road, P O Box 15541, KARACHI 75530 PAKISTAN.
MORSON, Mr. Richard James, BSc(Hons) FCA *2001;* 4 Edge Green, Ellenbrook, Worsley, MANCHESTER, M28 7XP.
MORT, Mr. Andrew David, BA ACA *1996;* 111 Five Ashes Road, CHESTER, CHESHIRE, CH4 7QA.

MORT, Mr. David Lawrence, FCA *1963;* 29 Shelly Crescent, Shirley, SOLIHULL, B90 4YW.
MORT, Miss. Gail Christina, BA ACA *1995;* 52 Riverton Road, East Didsbury, MANCHESTER, M20 5GH.
MORT, Mr. Richard Brian, PhD BEng ACA *1992;* 59 Ennerdale Drive, CONGLETON, CW12 4FJ.
MORT, Mrs. Ruth, BA ACA *1992;* 25 Saxon Rise, Molescroft, BEVERLEY, NORTH HUMBERSIDE, HU17 7SN.
MORT, Mr. Simon Anthony Miller, MEng ACA *2002;* NBC Universal, 6th Floor, Oxford House, 76 Oxford Street, LONDON, W1D 1BS.
MORTALI, Mr. Stefano Massimo Paolo, BSc ACA *2002;* 14 Battledean Road, Highbury, LONDON, N5 1UZ.
MORTELL, Mr. David James, BA ACA *1996;* (Tax Fac), 2 Greenleas, HOVE, BN3 8AD.
MORTELL, Mr. Kevin Edward, BSc FCA *1979;* The Coach House, Brookhill, HORSHAM, RH13 8AH.
MORTEN, Mrs. Amanda Lorraine Mary, BA ACA *1999;* 93 Gravel Lane, WILMSLOW, CHESHIRE, SK9 6LZ.
MORTEN, Mr. Stuart Norman, BA ACA *1998;* 93 Gravel Lane, WILMSLOW, CHESHIRE, SK9 6LZ.
MORTENSEN, Mr. James S McC, BSc ACA *2006;* Smith & Nephew Plc, 15 Adam Street, LONDON, WC2N 6LA.
•**MORTER, Mr. Gerald Raymond, FCA** *1968;* (Tax Fac), King Morter Proud & Co, Kings Arms Vaults, The Watton, BRECON, LD3 7EF.
•**MORTER, Mr. James Raymond, BA ACA** *2000;* Grant Thornton UK LLP, 30 Finsbury Square, LONDON, EC2P 2YU. See also Grant Thornton LLP
MORTER, Mr. Nicholas, BA ACA *1979;* 1 Rue Des Jardins, 92600 ASNIERES SUR SEINE, FRANCE.
MORTIBOYS, Mr. Gary, BSc FCA *1988;* 41 Willoughby Drive, Hillfield, SOLIHULL, B91 3GB.
MORTIMER, Mr. Arthur Hugh Wyness, FCA *1970;* P.O.Box 22424, WINDHOEK, 9100, NAMIBIA.
MORTIMER, Mr. Barry, FCA *1964;* 15 Greenmount, SIDMOUTH, EX10 9DB. (Life Member)
MORTIMER, Mr. David Douglas, ACA *2010;* Riverslea, Tarholm, Annbank, AYR, KA6 5HX.
MORTIMER, Mr. David John, FCA *1968;* 85a Lauderdale Avenue, FAIRLIGHT, NSW 2093, AUSTRALIA.
MORTIMER, Mrs. Denise Norma, BSc ACA *1996;* 7 Waterside View, Droylsden, MANCHESTER, M43 6EN.
MORTIMER, Mrs. Gillian, BA ACA *1985;* 38 Pelham Road, Wimbledon, LONDON, SW19 1NP.
MORTIMER, Mrs. Irene, MA ACA *2001;* 18 Birchwood Avenue, Dordon, TAMWORTH, STAFFORDSHIRE, B78 1QU.
•**MORTIMER, Mr. Ivan Lee, FCA** *1968;* Mortimer & Co, Ashfield Hse., 304 High St., Boston Spa, WETHERBY, LS23 6AJ.
MORTIMER, Mr. James Neil, BA ACA *2005;* with Deloitte LLP, Athene Place, 66 Shoe Lane, LONDON, EC4A 3BQ.
MORTIMER, Mr. John, BA ACA *1987;* 38 Pelham Road, LONDON, SW19 1NP.
MORTIMER, Mr. Jonathan Charles, BA FCA *1996;* Na Vyspe 40 Hodkovicky Praha 4, 140 00 PRAGUE, CZECH REPUBLIC.
MORTIMER, Mrs. Julie Ann, BA ACA *1998;* Volvo Group UK Ltd, Wedgnock Industrial Estate, WARWICK, CV34 5YA.
MORTIMER, Mr. Keith Anthony, BA ACA *1999;* Yellow Stones Pie Corner, Flamstead, ST. ALBANS, HERTFORDSHIRE, AL3 8BW.
MORTIMER, Mr. Kevin James Michael, BA ACA *1988;* 31 Home Close, Renhold, BEDFORD, MK41 0LB.
MORTIMER, Miss. Louise Carolyn Brooke, BA ACA *2002;* 53 All Saints Close, WOKINGHAM, RG40 1WE.
•**MORTIMER, Mr. Martin Howard, FCA** *1977;* MH Mortimer Ltd, 27 Beaumont Road, Petts Wood, ORPINGTON, KENT, BR5 1JL.
MORTIMER, Mr. Neil Austin, ACA *1982;* West End, Walkers Lane, Shorwell, NEWPORT, ISLE OF WIGHT, PO30 3JZ.
MORTIMER, Miss. Nicola Jan, BSc ACA *2004;* 47 Shelley Road, CHELMSFORD, CM2 6ER.
•**MORTIMER, Mr. Stephen, BCom FCA** *1982;* Mortimer S, 1 Chilwell Close, SOLIHULL, B91 3YL.
MORTIMER, Mr. Stuart Herbert, FCA *1963;* 5 Harley Bank, Low Bentham Road Lower Bentham, LANCASTER, LA2 7BU. (Life Member)
MORTIMER, Mrs. Susan Mary, MA(Oxon) CA FCA *1997;* 3 Heneage Drive, West Cross, SWANSEA, SA3 5BR.
MORTIMER, Mr. Timothy Spencer, MBA FCA *1970;* 6 Carmel Grove, DARLINGTON, DL3 8EQ.
MORTIMER-ROBERTS, Mr. Emyr, BA ACA *2009;* 14 Y Ddol, Bethel, CAERNARFON, GWYNEDD, LL55 1RE.
MORTIMORE, Mr. David Robert, BA ACA *1987;* with KPMG LLP, St. James's Square, MANCHESTER, M2 6DS.
MORTLEMAN, Ms. Lynette Kay, ACA CA(NZ) *2009;* 7a Cotton Street, HAMILTON, NEW ZEALAND.
MORTLOCK, Mrs. Clare, BSc ACA *2000;* Transport for London, Group Financial Accounting, 18th Floor, Windsor House, 42-50 Victoria Street, LONDON SW1H 0TL.
MORTLOCK, Mr. David James, BA ACA *1993;* 4 Langcliffe Avenue, HARROGATE, NORTH YORKSHIRE, HG2 8JQ.
MORTLOCK, Mr. Paul Edmund, BA ACA *1993;* 4 Borley Way, Teversham, CAMBRIDGE, CB1 9BT.
MORTLOCK, Mr. Philip John, MA FCA *1963;* Gwynfryn, Llangybi, LAMPETER, SA48 8NB.
MORTON, Mr. Alan Denis, BSc ACA *2000;* Prudential Vietnam Fund Management Company, 23F Saigon Trade Center, 37 Ton Thang Street, District 1, HO CHI MINH CITY, VIETNAM.
MORTON, Mr. Alan Harold, FCA *1963;* Hill Brow, Bragmans Lane, Sarratt, RICKMANSWORTH, WD3 4NR. (Life Member)
MORTON, Mr. Alan James, FCA *1969;* 9 Gateland Drive, Shadwell, LEEDS, LS17 8HU.
MORTON, Mr. Andrew, ACA MSI *1996;* 3 The Hollies, Bailiffs Cross Road, St. Andrew, GUERNSEY, GY6 8RY.
MORTON, Mr. Andrew David, MA FCA *1995;* Flat 5, 75 Philbeach Gardens, Earls Court, LONDON, SW5 9EY.
MORTON, Mr. Andrew Neil, BSc ACA *1994;* 3 Burneham Close, East Bridgford, NOTTINGHAM, NG13 8NT.
•**MORTON, Mr. Arthur Leonard Robert, FCA** *1964;* Hawk House, Park Estate, La Route Des Genets, JERSEY, JE3 6EQ.
•**MORTON, Miss. Barbara Jeanne Eunice, ACA** *2008;* Nobot Limited, 30 Woolpack Lane, The Lace Market, NOTTINGHAM, NG1 1GA.
•**MORTON, Mr. Bruce, BSc FCA** *1979;* 83 Marsh Lane, SOLIHULL, B91 2PE.
MORTON, Mrs. Carole Ann, BSc ACA *1986;* Longwood House, Mile Path (West), Hook Heath, WOKING, GU22 0JX.
MORTON, Mr. Christopher John, BA ACA *1980;* 9 Beverley Crescent, BEDFORD, MK40 4BX.
MORTON, Mr. Clive, FCA *1974;* Covent Garden Market Authority Covent House, New Covent Garden Market, LONDON, SW8 5NX.
MORTON, Mr. Craig Euan, BSc ACA *1995;* Group Chief Accountants Business House F, The Royal Bank of Scotland Plc, PO Box 1000, EDINBURGH, EH12 1HQ.
MORTON, Mr. Daniel John, BA(Hons) ACA *2010;* 15 Elson Road, LIVERPOOL, L37 2EG.
MORTON, Mrs. Daphne Pauline, FCA *1973;* United Reformed Church, 86 Tavistock Place, LONDON, WC1H 9RT.
MORTON, Mr. David John, BA *1985;* Longwood House, Mile Path (West), Hook Heath, WOKING, GU22 0JX.
MORTON, Mrs. Deborah Ann, BSc ACA *2005;* with McGills, Oakley House, Tetbury Road, CIRENCESTER, GL7 1US.
MORTON, Mr. Denis, BSc FCA *1953;* 42 East End, Walkington, BEVERLEY, HU17 8RY. (Life Member)
MORTON, Mr. Drew Stewart, BSc ACA *2008;* Flat 2, 4 The Drive, LONDON, SW20 8TG.
MORTON, Miss. Emma Elizabeth, BSc(Hons) ACA *2003;* The Tack House, Chapel Lane, Shipton-under-Wychwood, CHIPPING NORTON, OXFORDSHIRE, OX7 6DJ.
MORTON, Mrs. Fiona Ruth, LLB ACA *2004;* Oyster Rock Les Godaines Avenue, George Road St. Peter Port, GUERNSEY, GY1 1BE.
MORTON, Mr. Fred Stephen, BSc ACA *1986;* The Old Post Office, 20 Main Road, Etton, PETERBOROUGH, PE6 7DA.
MORTON, Miss. Geraldine Ann, BA ACA *1980;* 11 Grove End Road, FARNHAM, SURREY, GU9 8RD.
MORTON, Mr. Howard George, BSc ACA *1980;* Addax Petroleum NZE Inc., Z.I. OPRAG (B.P. 452), Nouveau Port, PORT GENTIL, GABON.
MORTON, Mr. Ian John, BSc ACA *2006;* 19 Centre Way, GLENROY, VIC 3046, AUSTRALIA.
MORTON, Mr. James, LLB ACA *2002;* 45 Garthorne Road, LONDON, SE23 1EP.
MORTON, Mr. Jamie Christopher, BA(Hons) ACA *2001;* Vodafone Group Plc, Edison House, The Connection, NEWBURY, BERKSHIRE, RG14 2FN.
MORTON, Ms. Janette, BSc ACA *1994;* 11 Trevor Road, LONDON, SW19 3PW.
MORTON, Mr. John, FCA *1959;* 65 Farringdon Road, NORTH SHIELDS, TYNE AND WEAR, NE30 3EX. (Life Member)
MORTON, Mr. John David, FCA *1967;* 39 Sark Close, Lowry Hill, CARLISLE, CA3 0DY.
•**MORTON, Mr. Keith, BA ACA** *1982;* Milford & Co, Duke Street, SETTLE, BD24 9DJ.
MORTON, Mrs. Kristin Bohne, BA ACA *1993;* 81 Linfit Lane, Kirkburton, HUDDERSFIELD, HD8 0UA.
MORTON, Mr. Lee Alex, FCA *1983;* with Newby Castleman, West Walk Building, 110 Regent Road, LEICESTER, LE1 7LT.
MORTON, Mrs. Lorna, BA(Hons) ACA *2001;* Orchard End, Sulhamstead Hill, Sulhamstead, READING, RG7 4DE.
MORTON, Mr. Mark David, ACA *1984;* P O BOX 2110, PORT MORESBY, PAPUA NEW GUINEA.
MORTON, Mr. Matthew Thomas, BA ACA *2005;* 3225 Gallows Road, FAIRFAX, VA 22037, UNITED STATES.
MORTON, Mr. Michael, FCA *1962;* 67 Rodney Court, 6-8 Maida Vale, LONDON, W9 1TJ. (Life Member)
MORTON, Mr. Michael, FCA *1964;* 18 The Green, Allestree, DERBY, DE22 2RH. (Life Member)
MORTON, Mr. Michael Francis, FCA *1971;* 13 Albert Road, Cheadle Hulme, CHEADLE, SK8 5DB.
•**MORTON, Mr. Michael Thomas, FCA** *1972;* Michael Morton & Co, Strathmore, The Nap, KINGS LANGLEY, WD4 8ES.
MORTON, Mr. Neil, BA(Hons) ACA *2002;* Flat 13, Nairn Court, 7 Trinity Road, LONDON, SW19 8QT.
MORTON, Mr. Neville Hugh, FCA ATII *1971;* 53 Dobbins Lane, Wendover, AYLESBURY, HP22 6DL.
MORTON, Mrs. Nicola Caroline, BSc ACA *1994;* Church Farm House, Church Road, Barningham, BURY ST. EDMUNDS, IP31 1DD.
MORTON, Mr. Oliver Hugh Craig, LLB ACA *2005;* Flat 6, 1 The Park, Highgate, LONDON, N6 4EU.
MORTON, Mr. Owen Thomas, MA FCA *1975;* The Old Masons, Piper Lane, Bradford Road, OTLEY, WEST YORKSHIRE, LS21 3EQ.
MORTON, Mr. Patrick Devenish, FCA *1983;* 91 Edgar Road, WINCHESTER, SO23 9TW.
MORTON, Mr. Paul, BA ACA *2005;* Perform Group, Sussex House, 2 Plane Tree Crescent, FELTHAM, MIDDLESEX, TW13 7HE.
MORTON, Mr. Paul, BSc ACA CF *1999;* Tower House, Kirklees Hall, Kirklees, BRIGHOUSE, WEST YORKSHIRE, HD6 4HD.
MORTON, Mr. Paul Scott, BA ACA *1990;* Brookfield, Chain House Lane, Whitestake, PRESTON, PR4 4LD.
MORTON, Mr. Richard Simon, BSc ACA *1993;* 20 Henfordh Grange, LISKEARD, PL14 6DP.
•**MORTON, Mr. Robert Dryden, FCA** *1973;* 15 Meadowfield, Red House Farm, WHITLEY BAY, NE25 9YD.
MORTON, Mr. Robert George, BA FCA *1976;* Hazlebank, Chelsfield Lane, ORPINGTON, BR6 7RS.
•**MORTON, Mr. Rodney Robert, BSc FCA** *1977;* 203 Rosendale Road, LONDON, SE21 8LW.
MORTON, Mr. Rupert William, ACA *2009;* 91 Edgar Road, WINCHESTER, HAMPSHIRE, SO23 9TW.
MORTON, Mrs. Sarah Anne, BSc ACA *1994;* Sytner Group Limited, 2 Penman Way, Grove Park, Enderby, LEICESTER, LE19 1ST.
MORTON, Mr. Shaun, ACA *2008;* 68 Dragon Avenue, HARROGATE, NORTH YORKSHIRE, HG1 5DT.
MORTON, Mr. Simon David, BEng ACA *1993;* 1 Sundial Close, Brailsford, ASHBOURNE, DERBYSHIRE, DE6 3DP.
MORTON, Mr. Stephen John, FCA *1975;* 38 Little Roke Avenue, KENLEY, SURREY, CR8 5NG.
MORTON, Mrs. Tessa, BSc ACA *2002;* 37 Thornhill Park, SUTTON COLDFIELD, B74 2LQ.
•**MORTON, Mr. Tom Martyn, BTech FCA** *1977;* (Tax Fac), Tom Morton, Carcosa, 2 Forbes Park, Bramhall, STOCKPORT, SK7 2RE.
MORTON, Mrs. Victoria Louise Winchester, BA ACA *1999;* Tower House, Kirklees Hall, Kirklees, BRIGHOUSE, WEST YORKSHIRE, HD6 4HD.
MORTON-AIKEN, Mr. Anthony William, MSc BSc ACA *2010;* 48 Eustis Street, Unit 6, CAMBRIDGE, MA 02140, UNITED STATES.
MORTON-DARE, Ms. Deborah Anne, BSc ACA *1985;* 70 Ramsden Road, LONDON, SW12 8QZ.
•**MORWOOD-LEYLAND, Mr. Antony Michael, FCA ACII** *1972;* (Member of Council 2003 - 2003 2004 - 2005), (Tax Fac), Morwood-Leyland & Co, Suite 48, 88-90 Hatton Garden, LONDON, EC1N 8PN. See also Integrated Mailing Limited
MORYSON, Mr. Michael Christopher, FCA *1969;* 11 Saltergate Drive, HARROGATE, HG3 2YE. (Life Member)
MOSAFI, Mr. Eliot, BA(Hons) ACA *2002;* Cable Finance Ltd, Fo Frame House 35-37 Brent Street, LONDON, NW4 2EF.
MOSBERGER, Miss. Alexandra, ACA *2009;* 36 Petley Road, LONDON, W6 9ST.
•**MOSBY, Mr. Andrew, BSc ACA** *2001;* with Menzies LLP, 3rd Floor Kings House, 12-42 Wood Street, KINGSTON UPON THAMES, SURREY, KT1 1TG.
•**MOSCA, Mr. Lorenzo Giuseppe, BSc ACA** *1992;* Saffery Champness, Lion House, Red Lion Street, LONDON, WC1R 4GB.
•**MOSCROP, Mr. Gerald Ian, FCA** *1971;* (Tax Fac), GM Associates, 7 Viga Road, Grange Park, LONDON, N21 1HH.
MOSE, Miss. Margaret Louise, LLB ACA *1981;* 4 Compton Crescent, Chiswick, LONDON, W4 3JA.
MOSEBY, Ms. Lana Jane, ACA CA(NZ) *2009;* P O Box 61136, LONDON, E3 9BG.
MOSEDALE, Mr. John Harry, FCA *1965;* Fitz House Cottage, 47a Station Road, KESWICK, CUMBRIA, CA12 4NB.
•**MOSELEY, Mr. Benjamin, BA ACA CTA** *2003;* Deloitte LLP, PO Box 500, 2 Hardman Street, MANCHESTER, M60 2AT. See also Deloitte & Touche LLP
MOSELEY, Mr. James David Simon, BSc ACA *1988;* 20 Ryecroft Road, LONDON, SW16 3EG.
MOSELEY, Miss. Kelly, ACA *2011;* 11 Kestrel Close, Bishops Waltham, SOUTHAMPTON, SO32 1RN.
MOSELEY, Mr. Neil Christopher, ACA *1985;* 378 Oldfield Road, ALTRINCHAM, CHESHIRE, WA14 4QT.
MOSELEY, Miss. Rhian, ACA *1994;* Quintain Estates & Development Ltd, 16 Grosvenor Street, LONDON, W1K 4QF.
MOSELEY, Mr. Richard John, BSc(Hons) ACA *2002;* Vodafone Group Plc Vodafone House, The Connection, NEWBURY, RG14 2FN.
MOSELEY, Mr. Saxon, BSc(Hons) ACA *2010;* 238 Ivydale Road, LONDON, SE15 3BU.
MOSELEY, Mr. Stephen, BSc ACA *2010;* 8 Autumn Walk, Wargrave, READING, BERKSHIRE, RG10 8BS.
MOSELING, Mr. Michael, BA FCA *1972;* 15 Flanchford Road, Reigate Heath, REIGATE, RH2 8AB.
MOSENTHAL, Mr. Max Balfour, BSc ACA *1981;* 22 Gartmoor Gardens, Southfields, LONDON, SW19 6NY.
MOSER, Mr. George Matthew Branthwaite, FCA *1958;* The Lilacs, Main Street, Badby, DAVENTRY, NN11 3AN. (Life Member)
MOSER, Mr. Robin Allan Shedden, FCA *1971;* Mallows Green Farm, Mallows Green, Manuden, BISHOP'S STORTFORD, HERTFORDSHIRE, CM23 1BS.
•**MOSES, Mrs. Amanda Ann, BA FCA** *1979;* with KPMG LLP, Arlington Business Park, Theale, READING, RG7 4SD.
MOSES, Mrs. Diana Maria, BSc FCA *1974;* 198 Cookham Road, MAIDENHEAD, BERKSHIRE, SL6 7HN.
MOSES, Mrs. Diane Marie, BSc FCA *1992;* Haste Hill House, Haste Hill, HASLEMERE, GU27 2NW.
MOSES, Mrs. Emma Jayne, ACA MAAT *2008;* 73 Lodge Farm Drive, NORWICH, NR6 7LP.
•**MOSES, Mr. Geoffrey Ian, BA FCA** *1977;* Williams Ross Ltd, 4 Ynys Bridge Court, Gwaelod Y Garth, CARDIFF, CF15 9SS. See also Epiphany Business Solutions Limited
•**MOSES, Mr. Hugh Frederick, FCA** *1970;* (Tax Fac), Hugo & Co, 198 Cookham Road, MAIDENHEAD, BERKSHIRE, SL6 7HN.
MOSES, Mr. Kelly, BSc(Econ) FCA *1992;* 90 Alveston Drive, WILMSLOW, CHESHIRE, SK9 2GA.
•**MOSES, Mr. Maurice, BA FCA** *1982;* Ernst & Young LLP, 1 More London Place, LONDON, SE1 2AF. See also Ernst & Young Europe LLP
MOSES, Mr. Menasey Marc, ACA *1992;* H S B C Bank Plc, Level 21, 8 Canada Square, LONDON, E14 5HQ.
MOSES, Mr. Nicholas Hayward, BA ACA *1992;* Haste Hill House, Haste Hill, HASLEMERE, GU27 2NW.
•**MOSEY, Mrs. Claire Amanda, BA(Hons) ACA** *2000;* Claire Mosey ACA, Woodstock, Bigby Road, BRIGG, SOUTH HUMBERSIDE, DN20 8HN.
MOSHA, Mr. James, MSc ACA *2001;* Bnp Paribas, 10 Harewood Avenue, LONDON, NW1 6AA.
MOSHIRFATEMI, Miss. Shirin, BSc FCA *1985;* 27 Fajr Street, TEHRAN, IRAN.

MOSKWA, Mrs. Rachael Clair-Anne, ACA MAAT *2002;* Nottingham NHS Treatment Centre, Lister Road, NOTTINGHAM, NG7 2FT.
MOSLEY, Mrs. Alison Claire, BSc ACA *1990;* 30 Horsley Drive, KINGSTON UPON THAMES, SURREY, KT2 5GG.
MOSLEY, Mr. Darren John, BSc ACA *1989;* Perry Bishop & Chambers Ltd, 2 Silver Street, CIRENCESTER, GLOUCESTERSHIRE, GL7 2BL.
MOSLEY, Mr. David, FCA *1961;* 60 Whitby Crescent, Woodthorpe, NOTTINGHAM, NG5 4LY.
•MOSLEY, Mr. Geoffrey, BA FCA *1977;* Heymoor Cottage, 21 Abbey road, Shepley, HUDDERSFIELD, WEST YORKSHIRE, HD8 8EP.
MOSLEY, Mr. Ian Christopher, FCA *1965;* Middlewood House, Jordans Way, Jordans, BEACONSFIELD, HP9 2SP. (Life Member)
MOSLEY, Mr. Matthew David, BSc ACA *1998;* Telent Technology Service Ltd Point, 3 Haywood Road, WARWICK, CV34 5AH.
•MOSLEY, Mrs. Maureen Elizabeth, BA ACA *1987;* 57 Droxford Crescent, TADLEY, HAMPSHIRE, RG26 3BA.
MOSLEY, Mrs. Nicola Amanda, BA ACA *1992;* 5 Pickering Road, Leckhampton, CHELTENHAM, GLOUCESTERSHIRE, GL53 0LF.
MOSLEY, Mr. Philip Graham, ACA *1982;* Chimneys, Stretton On Fosse, MORETON-IN-MARSH, GL56 9QU.
MOSS, Mr. Adrian John, BA ACA *1991;* 12 Picklers Hill, ABINGDON, OXFORDSHIRE, OX14 2BA.
MOSS, Mr. Adrian Martyn, BA ACA *1997;* Unit 1501 twr 1, 506 Huangpi Nan Road, Luwan, SHANGHAI 200021, CHINA.
MOSS, Mr. Andrew, BSc ACA *1992;* Blue Crest Capital Management Ltd, 40 Grosvenor Place, LONDON, SW1X 7AW.
•MOSS, Mr. Andrew Derek, BA FCA *1992;* Duncan Sheard Glass, Castle Chambers, 43 Castle St, LIVERPOOL, L2 9TL. See also DSG Accountancy and Taxation Services Limited
•MOSS, Mr. Andrew Gary, FCA *1981;* (Tax Fac), AGM, Rockware Business Centre, Rockware Avenue, GREENFORD, MIDDLESEX, UB6 0AA.
MOSS, Mr. Andrew Gomez, BA(Hons) ACA *2003;* 10 Tompkins Pl, BROOKLYN, NY 11231, UNITED STATES.
•MOSS, Mr. Andrew Graham, FCA *1987;* Lewis Golden & Co, 40 Queen Anne Street, LONDON, W1G 9EL.
MOSS, Mr. Andrew John, BA ACA *1984;* Aviva Plc, St Helens, 1 Undershaft, LONDON, EC3P 3DQ.
MOSS, Mr. Andrew John, BSc ACA *1991;* The Paddocks, Station Road, Alvescot, BAMPTON, OXFORDSHIRE, OX18 2PS.
MOSS, Mr. Andrew John, BA ACA *2006;* 13 Roses Cottages, West Street, DORKING, RH4 1QL.
MOSS, Mr. Andrew John, BSc ACA *1993;* Select Appointments plc, Select Education Plc Regent Court, Laporte Way, LUTON, LU4 8SB.
MOSS, Mr. Andrew Simon John, BA ACA *1999;* Briar Clough, Cross Oak Road, BERKHAMSTED, HERTFORDSHIRE, HP4 3NA.
MOSS, Mrs. Angela Clair, BA ACA *1991;* 1902 Block 82, Bamboo Grove, 82 Kennedy Road, MID LEVELS, HONG KONG ISLAND, HONG KONG SAR.
MOSS, Mrs. Anthea Francesca, BA ACA *1988;* 21 Ashlyns Road, BERKHAMSTED, HP4 3BN.
MOSS, Mr. Anthony Edward, BA FCA *1971;* School House, Strait Lane, Huby, LEEDS, LS17 0EA.
MOSS, Mr. Anthony James, MEng ACA *2001;* 15 Wallacebrae Walk, Danestone, ABERDEEN, AB22 8YL.
MOSS, Mrs. Barley Abigail, BSc(Hons) ACA *2003;* Dartford Cottage, 54 Dertford, Corsley, WARMINSTER, BA12 7NP.
MOSS, Mr. Brian, FCA *1963;* Apartment P5, Admirals Place, 24-27 The Leas, WESTCLIFF-ON-SEA, ESSEX, SS0 7BF. (Life Member)
MOSS, Mrs. Caroline Jane, BSc ACA *1983;* Papula La Ruette Du Petit Cocq, Le Coudre St. Pierre Du Bois, GUERNSEY, GY7 9HX.
MOSS, Mrs. Caroline Ruth, BSc ACA *2002;* The Limes, Priory Road, ASCOT, BERKSHIRE, SL5 8EB.
MOSS, Mrs. Carolyn Joan, MSci ACA *2009;* 51 Tredegar Road, Emmer Green, READING, RG4 8PF.
MOSS, Miss. Chloe Louise, ACA *2009;* 10 Moorcroft House, Archdale Close, CHESTERFIELD, DERBYSHIRE, S40 2GB.
•MOSS, Mr. Christopher John, BSc ACA *1992;* with RSM Tenon Audit Limited, Sumner House, St. Thomas's Road, CHORLEY, LANCASHIRE, PR7 1HP.
MOSS, Mr. Christopher Roger, OBE BA FCA *1967;* Swaw Back, Paley Green Lane, Giggleswick, SETTLE, NORTH YORKSHIRE, BD24 0DZ.
MOSS, Mr. Christopher Stephen, BA ACA *1995;* 4 Jasmine Close, BIGGLESWADE, SG18 8SW.
MOSS, Mr. Christopher William Symon, MSc FCA *1976;* 43 Gurdon Road, Grundisburgh, WOODBRIDGE, SUFFOLK, IP13 6XA.
MOSS, Mrs. Claudia Odette, BA ACA *1992;* 29 Ossulton Way, Hampstead Garden Suburb, LONDON, N2 0DT.
MOSS, Mr. Clive Maurice, FCA *1954;* 43 Circus Road, LONDON, NW8 9JH. (Life Member)
MOSS, Mr. David, FCA *1977;* Tall Pines, Cross Lanes, Pentrecoed, ELLESMERE, SHROPSHIRE, SY12 9EB.
•MOSS, Mr. David George Wood, MA FCA *1957;* Denes Place, Eaton Bank, Duffield, BELPER, DERBYSHIRE, DE56 4BH.
MOSS, Mr. David John, FCA *1977;* Maytime, High Street, Little Chesterford, SAFFRON WALDEN, ESSEX, CB10 1TS.
MOSS, Mr. David Michael, ACA *2007;* 46 Princes Road, FELIXSTOWE, SUFFOLK, IP11 7QZ.
MOSS, Mrs. Denise Lynn, BSc ACA *1995;* Investec Asset Management, P.O Box 1655, CAPE TOWN, C.P., 8000, SOUTH AFRICA.
MOSS, Mr. Derek John Keith, FCA *1972;* The Knap, Mildenhall, MARLBOROUGH, SN8 2LY.
MOSS, Mrs. Dominique Jehanne, BSc ACA *1994;* 12 Picklers Hill, ABINGDON, OXFORDSHIRE, OX14 2BA.
MOSS, Mr. Duncan James Christopher, BA ACA *1994;* J Sainsbury Plc, 33 Holborn, LONDON, EC1N 2HT.
MOSS, Dr. Edward Thomas, PhD BSc ACA *2002;* with PricewaterhouseCoopers LLP, 101 Barbirolli Square, Lower Mosley Street, MANCHESTER, M2 3PW.
•MOSS, Mrs. Elizabeth Ann, BA ACA CTA *1998;* Amicustax Limited, 16 Dover Street, Mayfair, LONDON, W1S 4LR. See also Steven Friend & Co Ltd
MOSS, Mrs. Emma Frances, BA ACA *2000;* Brunel House, 340 Firecrest Court Centre Park, WARRINGTON, WA1 1RG.
MOSS, Miss. Gail, MA FCA *1977;* 44a Dryden Road, LONDON, SW19 8SG.
•MOSS, Mr. Gary Jonathan, BA(Hons) ACA FCCA *2006;* (Tax Fac), Sterlings Ltd, Lawford House, Albert Place, LONDON, N3 1QA.
•MOSS, Mr. Gordon Leslie, FCA *1970;* Gordon Moss, 159 Pencisely Road, Llandaff, CARDIFF, CF5 1DN.
MOSS, Mr. Graham Howard, BSc FCA *1972;* 46 Stradella Road, LONDON, SE24 9HA.
MOSS, Mr. Graham John, BA FCA *1977;* 104 Folders Lane, BURGESS HILL, RH15 0DX.
MOSS, Mrs. Helen Mackay, MA FCA *1980;* 1 Lynton Gardens, HARROGATE, HG1 4TE.
•MOSS, Mr. Howard Simon, BCom FCA *1980;* (Tax Fac), Kingswood, 3 Coldbath Square, LONDON, EC1R 5HL. See also Kingswood Corporate Finance Limited
MOSS, Mr. Ian Donald, BSc FCA *1986;* Hannsfield Cottage, Stourton Caundle, STURMINSTER NEWTON, DORSET, DT10 2JN.
MOSS, Mr. James Richard, MChem ACA *2006;* with Grant Thornton UK LLP, Grant Thornton House, 22 Melton Street, Euston Square, LONDON, NW1 2EP.
MOSS, Mrs. Jane, BA FCA *1984;* Saddle Bow Cottage, Saddle Bow Lane, Claverdon, WARWICK, CV35 8PQ.
•MOSS, Mrs. Jane Dummott, BA FCA ATII *1981;* (Tax Fac), Business Tax Services Ltd, 58 Vineyard Hill Road, Wimbledon, LONDON, SW19 7JH.
MOSS, Mrs. Jane Elizabeth, BSc ACA *1997;* Peter Carring Farnham Road, Odiham, HOOK, RG29 1AB.
MOSS, Mr. John Newton, FCA *1962;* 50 Blacketts Wood Drive, Chorleywood, RICKMANSWORTH, HERTFORDSHIRE, WD3 5QH.
•MOSS, Mr. John Webster, FCA *1961;* (Tax Fac), John W. Hirst & Co, 62 Wellington Road South, STOCKPORT, SK1 3SU.
MOSS, Mr. Karl Alan, BSc ACA *1998;* 8 Barrington Close, Winstanley, WIGAN, LANCASHIRE, WN3 6JU.
•MOSS, Mrs. Katharine Mary, BSc FCA DChA *1990;* Katharine Moss Consulting Limited, Greyfriars Court, Paradise Square, OXFORD, OX1 1BE.
MOSS, Mr. Keith Charles, FCA *1963;* 11 Sandlea Park, West Kirby, WIRRAL, CH48 0QE.
MOSS, Mr. Keith Richard, BSc ACA *1992;* 7 Mitchell Road, WEST MALLING, ME19 4RF.
MOSS, Mr. Kenneth Grant, BSc FCA *1972;* 23 Downs Wood, Epsom Downs, EPSOM, KT18 5UJ.
MOSS, Mr. Kevin Michael, BA ACA *1991;* Ash Cottage, Main Road, Lacey Green, PRINCES RISBOROUGH, BUCKINGHAMSHIRE, HP27 0QT.
MOSS, Mrs. Kimberley Gordon, BSc ACA *1991;* Bank House, High Street, Chipstead, SEVENOAKS, TN13 2RR.
MOSS, Mrs. Laura Therese, ACA *1993;* 85 Cottage Lane, ORMSKIRK, LANCASHIRE, L39 3NF.
MOSS, Mrs. Lauren Emily, ACA *2007;* 16 Arcot Street, PENARTH, SOUTH GLAMORGAN, CF64 1ET.
MOSS, Mr. Lionel David, BSc FCA *1970;* 46 Henley Street, OXFORD, OX4 1ES.
MOSS, Mr. Malcolm, FCA *1958;* Ravensmead, 4 Temple Gardens, RICKMANSWORTH, WD3 1QJ. (Life Member)
MOSS, Mr. Martin Hartley, BSc ACA *1994;* C/O Harney Westwood & Riegels, PO Box 71, ROAD TOWN, PO Box 71, VIRGIN ISLANDS (BRITISH).
MOSS, Mr. Michael David, FCA *1963;* 10 Cecil Court, 2 Acol Road, LONDON, NW6 3AP. (Life Member)
MOSS, Mr. Michael Eric, FCA *1955;* High Halden, Wilmslow Park North, WILMSLOW, CHESHIRE, SK9 2BD. (Life Member)
MOSS, Mr. Nicholas David, BA ACA *1987;* Bordeaux Court, Virtus Trust Ltd, PO Box 634, GUERNSEY, GY1 3DR.
MOSS, Mr. Nicholas James, BA ACA *1991;* 11 Hunting Close, ESHER, KT10 8PB.
MOSS, Miss. Nicola Janet, BA ACA *2000;* 2 Marden Way, PETERSFIELD, HAMPSHIRE, GU31 4PW.
MOSS, Mr. Nigel Adam, MA ACA *1987;* Cunard House, 15 Regent Street, LONDON, SW1Y 4LR.
•MOSS, Mrs. Patricia Jill, FCA *1984;* (Tax Fac), Patricia Moss FCA, Maytime, High Street, Little Chesterford, SAFFRON WALDEN, ESSEX CB10 1TS.
MOSS, Mr. Paul Andrew, MA ACA *1993;* 126 Station Road, Rolleston-on-Dove, BURTON-ON-TRENT, STAFFORDSHIRE, DE13 9AB.
MOSS, Mr. Paul Nigel, BA ACA CF *1993;* 9 Holmwood Road, Didsbury, MANCHESTER, M20 3JY.
•MOSS, Mr. Peter Richard, FCA *1972;* P.R. Moss, 12 Hawkshaw Bank Road, BLACKBURN, BB1 8JS.
•MOSS, Mr. Philip George Richard, BA FCA *1977;* Accountants for Small Business, Pattinson House, Beresford Road, Bowness-on-Windermere, WINDERMERE, CUMBRIA LA23 2JG. See also TaxAssist Direct
MOSS, Mr. Philip Wallace, FCA *1952;* 79 Hormare Crescent, Storrington, PULBOROUGH, WEST SUSSEX, RH20 4QW. (Life Member)
•MOSS, Mr. Phillip John, BSc FCA *1996;* (Tax Fac), 59 St. Albans Road, KINGSTON UPON THAMES, SURREY, KT2 5HH.
MOSS, Mr. Ralph, FCA *1962;* Flat 20, Chessington Lodge, Regents Park Road, LONDON, N3 3AA.
MOSS, Mr. Ralph Harold, FCA *1953;* Apartment 5, 15 Gordon Avenue, STANMORE, MIDDLESEX, HA7 3QE. (Life Member)
MOSS, Mr. Richard George Aidan, BA ACA *2002;* 2 Shires Walk, EDENBRIDGE, KENT, TN8 6GE.
MOSS, Mr. Richard Henry, FCA *1965;* 27 Greenfields, Holbeach, SPALDING, PE12 7BJ.
•MOSS, Mr. Robert Harold, BSc FCA *1995;* (Tax Fac), Robert Moss, 94 Malthouse Lane, Earlswood, SOLIHULL, WEST MIDLANDS, B94 5SA.
•MOSS, Mr. Robert James, FCA *1990;* Moss James Limited, Titsey Estate Office, Pilgrims Lane, OXTED, SURREY, RH8 0SE. See also Moss James
MOSS, Mr. Roderick Adam, BSc ACA *1988;* 5 Toressian Place, CASHMERE, QLD 4500, AUSTRALIA.
MOSS, Mr. Roger Clive, BSc FCA *1974;* Pine Hill, Stowting, ASHFORD, KENT, TN25 6BD.
MOSS, Ms. Rosalind Helen, ACA *1999;* 31 Pewley Way, GUILDFORD, GU1 3SB.
MOSS, Mr. Samuel David James, BA ACA *1995;* Unit 6093, 99 Erinvale Avenue, Erinvale Golf Estate, SOMERSET WEST, WESTERN CAPE PROVINCE, 7129 SOUTH AFRICA.
MOSS, Mr. Samuel Gerald, FCA *1956;* 77 Blandford Street, LONDON, W1U 8AD. (Life Member)
MOSS, Mrs. Sarah Mary, BSc ACA *1987;* Hannsfield Cottage, Stourton Caundle, STURMINSTER NEWTON, DORSET, DT10 2JN.
MOSS, Mrs. Sasha Elizabeth, BA ACA *1997;* 11 Hunting Close, ESHER, KT10 8PB.
MOSS, Mr. Sidney Norman, FCA *1951;* 32 Waylands Mead, The Knoll, BECKENHAM, BR3 5XT. (Life Member)
MOSS, Mr. Stephen Alan, BA ACA *1998;* 45 Hove Park Road, HOVE, EAST SUSSEX, BN3 6LH.
MOSS, Mr. Stephen Andrew, ACA *1978;* 42 Bridgewater Road, RUISLIP, HA4 0EB.
MOSS, Mr. Stephen Colin, BA ACA *1991;* 1902 Block 82, Bamboo Grove, 82 Kennedy Road, MID LEVELS, HONG KONG ISLAND, HONG KONG SAR.
MOSS, Mr. Thomas James, BSc ACA *2004;* 9 Florence Street, HITCHIN, HERTFORDSHIRE, SG5 1QZ.
MOSS, Mr. Timothy, BSc ACA *1991;* 30 Dovedale Road, STOCKPORT, CHESHIRE, SK2 5DY.
MOSS, Mr. Timothy Campbell, FCA *1959;* 6 Rushmead Close, CROYDON, CR0 5JG. (Life Member)
MOSS, Mr. Timothy Gerard, BA(Hons) ACA *2006;* WRU, Millennium Stadium, Westgate Street, CARDIFF, CF10 1NS.
MOSS, Mr. Trevor David, BSc ACA *1990;* Bank House, High Street, Chipstead, SEVENOAKS, TN13 2RR.
MOSS, Mr. Victor Robert, FCA *1951;* P O Box 438, CHISIPITE, HARARE, ZIMBABWE. (Life Member)
MOSS, Mr. William Keith, FCA *1970;* 4a Lyndhurst Gardens, LONDON, NW3 5NR.
MOSSFORD, Mr. Anthony Clive Errol, BA FCA *1964;* Driftwood, 14 The Paddocks, PENARTH, CF64 5BW.
MOSSLEY, Mrs. Amelia Jean, BSc ACA *1993;* 3 Nursery Close, HOOK, HAMPSHIRE, RG27 9QX.
•MOSSMAN, Mr. Peter Lawrence, FCA *1970;* (Tax Fac), Peter Mossman Consultants Ltd, Cushy Dingle, Watery Lane, Llanishen, CHEPSTOW, GWENT NP16 6QT.
MOSSOP, Mr. David Stanley, BSc FCA *1977;* La Faraz, 46 Chemin des Vignes, 1814 LA TOUR-DE-PEILZ, SWITZERLAND. (Life Member)
MOSSOP, Mrs. Gemma Suzanne, BSc ACA *2007;* 72 Malmesbury Road, Cheadle Hulme, CHEADLE, CHESHIRE, SK8 7QL.
MOSSOP, Ms. Harriet Mary, BA ACA *2000;* A5-902, World Spa East, Sector 41, GURGAON 122001, HARYANA, INDIA.
MOSTAFA, Miss. Shahina, BSc ACA *2007;* 87 Green Lane, ST. ALBANS, AL3 6HF.
MOSTARI, Mr. Andrew, LLB ACA *2002;* Raytheon Systems Ltd, Barrows Road, HARLOW, CM19 5BB.
•MOSTON, Mr. Paul John, FCA *1989;* Mostons, 29 The Green, Winchmore Hill, LONDON, N21 1HS.
MOSTYN, Mr. Gareth, BA ACA *1997;* Anglo American Plc, Anglo American House, 20 Carlton House Terrace, LONDON, SW1Y 5AN.
MOSTYN, Miss. Tracey, BSc ACA *2004;* 24 Rosemount Buildings, EDINBURGH, EH3 8DB.
MOTABAR, Mr. Mohammad, BSc ACA *1986;* KERKEBOSLAAN 15, WASSENAAR, NETHERLANDS.
MOTABAR, Mr. Nezam, MSc FCA *1973;* P O Box 3111, GAITHERSBURG, MD 20885-3111, UNITED STATES.
MOTALA, Mr. Shakil, BSc ACA *2011;* 56 Thomas Jacomb Place, LONDON, E17 6GR.
•MOTASHAW, Mehernosh Murzban, Esq FCA *1977;* (Tax Fac), Motashaw's, 110 Ward Avenue, GRAYS, RM17 5RL.
•MOTAZEDI, Mr. Ahmad Reza, BA FCA DChA *1986;* with Deloitte LLP, 2 New Street Square, LONDON, EC4A 3BZ.
MOTE, Mr. John Hurden, BSc ACA *2005;* Flat 13, 47 Brunswick Court, LONDON, SE1 3LH.
MOTH, Mr. John, BA ACA *2006;* 709 Rossetti Place, 2 Lower Byrom Street, MANCHESTER, M3 4AN.
MOTHA, Mrs. Angela, BA ACA *1995;* 20 Somerset Gardens, TEDDINGTON, TW11 8TA.
MOTIKAT, Mr. Frank, ACA *2008;* with KPMG, 10 Shelley Street, SYDNEY, NSW 2000, AUSTRALIA.
MOTLEY, Mr. Peter John Frank, BA ACA *1991;* 27 Village Du Bocage, ST. PETER, JERSEY, JE3 7AT.
MOTSON, Dr. Kathleen Maria, PhD BSc ACA *2007;* 10 Orchard Field Road, GODALMING, SURREY, GU7 3PB.
•MOTT, Mr. Alan Roger, FCA *1962;* A.R.Mott, 4 Beaumont Road, ORPINGTON, BR5 1JN.
MOTT, Mrs. Charlotte, BSc ACA *2004;* 3 Russell Way, Winnersh, WOKINGHAM, RG41 5SN.
•MOTT, Mr. Dennis Phillip, FCA *1971;* (Tax Fac), Dennis Mott & Co, 6a The Pavement, ST. IVES, PE27 5AD.
MOTT, Mr. Gregory Fred, BA ACA *1995;* 59 Roman Road, BROADSTONE, DORSET, BH18 9DH.
MOTT, Mr. Julian Martin Harding, BSc ACA *1992;* Mapeley Estates Ltd, Blue Fin Building, 110 Southwark Street, LONDON, SE1 0TA.

MOTT, Mr. Malcolm Robert, MBA BSc FCA *1978;* Court Farmhouse, Huddington, DROITWICH, WR9 7LJ.
•MOTT, Mr. Michael Charles, ACA *1985;* 10 Worcester Close, LICHFIELD, STAFFORDSHIRE, WS13 7SP.
MOTT, Mr. Richard James Patrick, ACA *2009;* with PricewaterhouseCoopers LLP, 7 More London Riverside, LONDON, SE1 2RT.
MOTT, Mr. Simon Courtenay, BA ACA CF *1998;* 17 Laburnum Grove, Chiswell Green, ST. ALBANS, HERTFORDSHIRE, AL2 3HQ.
MOTT, Mr. Toby, ACA *2009;* 152b Ramsden Road, LONDON, SW12 8RE.
•MOTT-COWAN, Mr. Simon Maurice, BCom ACA *2002;* H W Fisher & Company Limited, Acre House, 11/15 William Road, LONDON, NW1 3ER. See also H.W. Fisher & Company
MOTTERAM, Mr. Jeremy Clive, MA ACA *1989;* Home Retail Group, 489-499 Avebury Boulevard, Saxon Gates West, MILTON KEYNES, MK9 2NW.
MOTTERSHAW, Mr. Stuart Roger, FCA *1967;* La Vielle Guilleaumerie, La Rue De La Guilleaumerie, St. Saviour, JERSEY, JE2 7HQ.
MOTTERSHEAD, Mr. Arthur Anthony, FCA *1952;* West House, 115 Prestbury Road, MACCLESFIELD, CHESHIRE, SK10 3BU. (Life Member)
MOTTERSHEAD, Mrs. Claire Elizabeth, LLB ACA *1999;* 47 Barnmead Road, BECKENHAM, KENT, BR3 1JF.
MOTTERSHEAD, Mr. David Brian, MEng ACA *1998;* 6 Stapleton Avenue, BOLTON, BL1 5ES.
MOTTERSHEAD, Mr. Geoffrey George, FCA *1957;* 3 Gerddi Victoria, Upper Colwyn Bay, COLWYN BAY, Clwyd, LL29 6DQ. (Life Member)
MOTTERSHEAD, Mr. Nicholas John Leigh, BSc FCA *1992;* 47 Barnmead Road, BECKENHAM, KENT, BR3 1JF.
MOTTERSHEAD, Mrs. Victoria, ACA *1985;* The Rowans Hospice, Purbrook Heath Road, Purbrook, WATERLOOVILLE, HAMPSHIRE, PO7 5RU.
MOTTERSHEAD-NEEDS, Mr. Jonathan Cary, ACA *1993;* (Tax Fac), 59 Upper Grotto Road, Strawbery Hill, TWICKENHAM, TW1 4NG.
MOTTON, Mrs. Natasha Louise, BA ACA *1999;* with PricewaterhouseCoopers LLP, Marlborough Court, 10 Bricket Road, ST. ALBANS, HERTFORDSHIRE, AL1 3JX.
MOTTON, Mr. Stephen James, ACA *2008;* 5 Savoy Road, DARTFORD, DA1 5AN.
MOTTRAM, Mr. Anthony John, BSc ACA *1992;* Cornerways Beggars Lane, Longworth, ABINGDON, OXFORDSHIRE, OX13 5BL.
MOTTRAM, Mr. Christopher John, BSc ACA *1990;* F6, Green Villas 700, Biyun Road Pudong, SHANGHAI 201206, CHINA.
MOTTRAM, Mr. Darrell Frederick, FCA *1962;* 83 Shrewley Common, Shrewley, WARWICK, CV35 7AN. (Life Member)
MOTTRAM, Mr. Derek William, FCA *1975;* 19 Millers Croft, Copmanthorpe, YORK, YO23 3TW.
MOTTRAM, Mr. Harold Eric, FCA *1961;* 16 Shaws Lane SS1, NIAGARA-ON-THE-LAKE L0S 1J0, ON, CANADA.
MOTTRAM, Mr. John Michael, FCA *1965;* Willand Cottage, Broom Way, WEYBRIDGE, KT13 9TG.
MOTTRAM, Miss. Katherine, ACA *2011;* 37c Grosvenor Avenue, Highbury, LONDON, N5 2NP.
MOTTRAM, Mr. Kenneth Charles, FCA *1953;* 2 Vaughan Close, Formby, LIVERPOOL, L37 1XZ. (Life Member)
MOTTRAM, Mr. Mark Charles, BA ACA *1998;* Mitchells & Butlers Plc, 27 Fleetstreet, BIRMINGHAM, B3 1JP.
MOTTRAM, Mr. Nicholas David, BSc ACA *1993;* 17 Kew Gardens, Nuthall, NOTTINGHAM, NG16 1RG.
MOTTRAM, Mr. Nicholas James, BA ACA *1989;* 35 Acacia Way, SIDCUP, DA15 8WW.
MOTTRAM, Mr. Robin John Nicholas, FCA *1979;* 9 Revel Garth, Denby Dale, HUDDERSFIELD, HD8 8TG.
MOTTRAM, Mr. Timothy John, BSc ACA *1992;* Halifax House, Provident Insurance Plc, Blackwall, HALIFAX, HX1 2PZ.
MOTTRAM, Ms. Zoe Jane, BSc ACA *1998;* Nomura Singapore Ltd., 6 Battery Road #34-01 Singapore, 049909 Singapore, Tel: 65 6420 1811, Fax: 65 6420 1888, SINGAPORE SINGAPORE.
MOTYCZAK, Mr. Roman Paul, BEng ACA *1991;* 3 Aldwickbury Crescent, HARPENDEN, HERTFORDSHIRE, AL5 5RS.
•MOTYER, Mr. Mark Timothy, FCA *1977;* Goldwyns, 13 David Mews, Porter Street, LONDON, W1U 6EQ. See also Goldwyns (London) Limited
•MOUAT, Miss. Carolyn Emma, BSc(Hons) ACA *2001;* (Tax Fac), Mouat Accountancy Limited, Newton Red House, Mitford, MORPETH, NORTHUMBERLAND, NE61 3QW.
MOUGHTON, Mr. Christopher, ACA *2010;* 43 Bull Road, IPSWICH, IP3 8GN.
•MOUGHTON, Mr. Jonathan Robert Parr, BA FCA *1988;* Haines Watts, Sterling House, 177-181 Farnham Road, SLOUGH, BERKSHIRE, SL1 4XP. See also Haines Watts London LLP, Haines Watts Slough LLP
•MOUKTARIS, Mr. George Anastasiou, FCA *1976;* (Tax Fac), Mouktaris & Co, 156A Burnt Oak Broadway, EDGWARE, HA8 0AX.
MOULAND, Mr. Ian James, BSc ACA *1989;* Mouland Bloom, Sicilian House, 7 Sicilian Avenue, LONDON, WC1A 2QH.
•MOULD, Mr. Andrew, BSc FCA *1982;* Baker Tilly Tax & Advisory Services LLP, 2 Humber Quays, Wellington Street West, HULL, HU1 2BN.
MOULD, Brian Piercy, Esq MBE FCA *1953;* Hawtrey, 28 New Road, ESHER, KT10 9PG. (Life Member)
MOULD, Mr. Christopher James, ACA *2005;* 4 Beech Road, Barton under Needwood, BURTON-ON-TRENT, STAFFORDSHIRE, DE13 8LG.
MOULD, Mrs. Clare, BSc ACA *1991;* Dower House, Cranleigh Road, Wonersh, GUILDFORD, SURREY, GU5 0PB.
MOULD, Mr. David Barry Allan, FCA *1974;* Tudor Lea, Minstrel Walk, POULTON-LE-FYLDE, FY6 7EF.
MOULD, Miss. Jayne, ACA *2011;* Fields Farm, The Pinfold, Newton Burgoland, COALVILLE, LEICESTERSHIRE, LE67 2SQ.
MOULD, Mr. John Charles, BEng FCA *1991;* Dower House, Cranleigh Road, Wonersh, GUILDFORD, SURREY, GU5 0PB.
MOULD, Mr. John Frederick, FCA *1980;* Fields Farm, The Pinfold, Newton Burgoland, COALVILLE, LEICESTERSHIRE, LE67 2SQ. (Life Member)
MOULD, Mr. John Gray, FCA *1953;* 33 Thickthorn Close, KENILWORTH, CV8 2AF. (Life Member)
MOULD, Mr. John Spencer, FCA *1957;* 25 Charnock Close, The Orchards, Hordle, LYMINGTON, SO41 0GU. (Life Member)
MOULD, Ms. Patricia, MSc BA FCA *1983;* University of Hull, Cottingham Road, HULL, HU6 7RX.
MOULD, Mr. Simon John, BSc ACA *1986;* The Maples, 99 Tattenham Crescent, EPSOM, SURREY, KT18 5NY.
•MOULDER, Mr. Christopher John, BSc FCA *1990;* Reads & Co Limited, PO Box 179, 40 Esplanade, St Helier, JERSEY, JE4 9RJ. See also Reads & Co. Group Limited and Reads (Audit) Limited
•MOULDER, Mr. Christopher John George, MA FCA *1989;* KPMG LLP, 15 Canada Square, LONDON, E14 5GL. See also KPMG Europe LLP
MOULDER, Mrs. Nella Rita, FCA *1947;* 23 Old Mill Drive, Storrington, PULBOROUGH, RH20 4NH. (Life Member)
MOULDER, Mr. William Charles Robert, ACA *2008;* Floor 8, The Prudential Assurance Co Ltd Minster House, 12 Arthur Street, LONDON, EC4R 9AQ.
•MOULDING, Mr. David James, FCA *1965;* (Tax Fac), 131 Swifts Green Road, Stopsley, LUTON, BEDFORDSHIRE, LU2 8BP. See also David Moulding
MOULDING, Mr. Matthew John, BA ACA *1997;* 4 The Woodlands, The Grange Hartford, NORTHWICH, CHESHIRE, CW8 1GJ.
MOULDING, Mr. Neil, BA FCA *1995;* 3 Mascotte Road, Putney, LONDON, SW15 1NN.
•MOULDING, Mr. Paul, BSc FCA *1986;* Pierce C A Ltd Mentor House, Ainsworth Street, BLACKBURN, BB1 6AY.
MOULDS, Mr. Adrian Paul, MA FCA *1978;* Adrisu Consultants Ltd, Ferris House, Newbarn Lane, Seer Green, BEACONSFIELD, BUCKINGHAMSHIRE HP9 2QZ.
MOULE, Miss. Elizabeth Ellen, FCA *1969;* 6 Church Lane, Milton, CAMBRIDGE, CB24 6AB.
•MOULSDALE, Mr. Jonathan Mark, MA FCA *1980;* Rees Pollock, 35 New Bridge Street, LONDON, EC4V 6BW.
•MOULSDALE, Mr. Nicholas Geoffrey, FCA *1975;* Moulsdale & Co, Ivy Cottage, Castley, OTLEY, WEST YORKSHIRE, LS21 2PY.
•MOULSDALE, Mr. Robert Alan, BA ACA *1990;* (Tax Fac), Alan Moulsdale Limited, Dale House, Tewitfield, CARNFORTH, LANCASHIRE, LA6 1JH.
MOULSON, Mr. John David, MBA BA FCA *1988;* 10 Tayben Avenue, TWICKENHAM, TW2 7RA.
MOULSON, Mr. Richard Anthony, BSc FCA *1986;* Betton Hall Farm, Betton, MARKET DRAYTON, TF9 4AE.
MOULSON, Mr. Robin Wayne, BA FCA CMC *1976;* 28 Tory, BRADFORD-ON-AVON, BA15 1NN.
MOULSON, Miss. Sarah Louise, ACA *2009;* Tower Cottage Garrison, St. Mary's, ISLES OF SCILLY, TR21 0LS.
MOULT, Mr. Andrew David, BSc ACA *1989;* 10 Harrow Road, FLEET, HAMPSHIRE, GU51 1JD.
MOULT, Mr. Patrick Henry, BSc ACA *1990;* 103/45 Bowman Street, PYRMONT, NSW 2009, AUSTRALIA.
MOULT, Mrs. Susan, BA ACA *1985;* Hillhead House, Countsswells Road, Cults, ABERDEEN, AB15 9QA.
MOULTON, Mr. Andrew John, BA ACA *1992;* The Garden House, St Nicholas Avenue, Bookham, LEATHERHEAD, SURREY, KT23 4AY.
•MOULTON, Miss. Angela, BA FCA *1988;* (Tax Fac), Bennett Brooks & Co Ltd, 2 Maple Court, Davenport Street, MACCLESFIELD, CHESHIRE, SK10 1JE.
MOULTON, Mrs. Angela Jane, BSc ACA *1984;* Roseland, 5 Church Lane, Holybourne, ALTON, HAMPSHIRE, GU34 4HD.
MOULTON, Mrs. Angela Mary, BA ACA *1993;* 28 East 35th Street, BAYONNE, NJ 07002, UNITED STATES.
MOULTON, Mr. David William, FCA *1971;* Old School House, Boldre Lane, Boldre, LYMINGTON, HAMPSHIRE, SO41 8PD.
MOULTON, Mr. John Christopher, MA FCA *1971;* Cribbs Farm, Laurel Court Cribbs Causeway, BRISTOL, BS10 7TU.
MOULTON, Mr. Jonathan Paul, BA FCA CF *1977;* Better Capital LLP, 39-41 Charing Cross Road, LONDON, WC2H 0AR.
•MOULTON, Mr. Peter Stuart, FCA *1973;* Moulton Johnson, Bank Chambers, 15 High Road, Byfleet, WEST BYFLEET, SURREY KT14 7QH. See also MJ Results Ltd, Moulton Johnson Limited
MOULTON, Mr. Richard Paul, BA ACA *2001;* 199 Barclay Road, SMETHWICK, WEST MIDLANDS, B67 5LA.
•MOUNCEY, Mr. David John, BSc FCA ATII *1985;* Smith & Williamson (Bristol) LLP, Portwall Place, Portwall Lane, BRISTOL, BS1 6NA. See also Smith & Williamson Ltd
MOUND, Mr. Bernard William, FCA *1955;* Flat 24, Lowen Court, Quay Street, TRURO, CORNWALL, TR1 2GA. (Life Member)
MOUNFIELD, Mr. Stephen Geoffrey, FCA *1969;* 89 Curzon Avenue, Birstall, LEICESTER, LE4 4AG.
MOUNGER, Mr. Victor Frederick Clayton, FCA *1967;* 3 Ascot Park, Kam Hang Road, Tam Tsin, SHEUNG SHUI, NEW TERRITORIES, HONG KONG SAR. (Life Member)
MOUNSEY, Mr. Andrew John, BSocSc ACA *2002;* Ernst & Young Llp, 1 More London Place, LONDON, SE1 2AF.
MOUNSEY, Mr. Barry, BSc FCA *1989;* 63 Lowercroft Road, Lowercroft, BURY, BL8 2EX.
MOUNSEY, Mr. John Edmund, BSc(Hons) ACA *2002;* 91 Barnacre Close, Fulwood, PRESTON, PR2 9WP.
•MOUNSEY, Mr. Jonathan Howard Henry, FCA *1973;* JHH Mounsey FCA, Owl Cote, 12 Park West, Heswall, WIRRAL, CH60 9JF.
MOUNSEY, Dr. Jonathan Robert, BSc ACA *2007;* 5 Newton Close, HARPENDEN, HERTFORDSHIRE, AL5 1SP.
MOUNSEY, Dr. Julia Kate, PhD BSc ACA *2005;* 24 Butterfield Road, Wheathampstead, ST. ALBANS, HERTFORDSHIRE, AL4 8QH.
MOUNSEY, Mr. Paul James, ACA *2003;* 6 Smalley Croft, Penwortham, PRESTON, PR1 9TZ.
MOUNSEY, Mr. Richard, ACA *2009;* 21 Beacon Avenue, Fulwood, PRESTON, PR2 3QY.
MOUNSEY, Miss. Sarah Anne, BA ACA *2005;* (Tax Fac), 128 Plymouth Road, SCUNTHORPE, SOUTH HUMBERSIDE, DN17 1TS.
MOUNT, Mrs. Jacqueline Ann, BSc ACA *1992;* Quaives Cottage, Wickham Lane, Ickham, CANTERBURY, CT3 1RD.
MOUNT, Mrs. Karen Julie, BSc FCA CTA *1990;* 60A Jubilee Road, Littlebourne, CANTERBURY, CT3 1TP.
•MOUNT, Mr. Stephen George, MBA BSc FCA *1982;* PricewaterhouseCoopers LLP, 9 Greyfriars Road, READING, RG1 1JG. See also PricewaterhouseCoopers
MOUNT, Mr. William James, FCA *1970;* 15 Loosen Drive, MAIDENHEAD, BERKSHIRE, SL6 3UR.
MOUNTAIN, Mr. Darren James, BA ACA *1999;* 53 Henniker Gate, CHELMSFORD, CM2 6SD.
MOUNTAIN, Miss. Diana Claire, BA ACA *1992;* 40 Hart Road, DORKING, RH4 1LA.
MOUNTAIN, Mrs. Donna Victoria, BA ACA *2001;* 16 Hilltop Walk, HARPENDEN, HERTFORDSHIRE, AL5 1AU.
•MOUNTAIN, Mr. Geoffrey Robert, FCA *1987;* Jackson Robson Licence Limited, 33/35 Exchange Street, DRIFFIELD, NORTH HUMBERSIDE, YO25 6LL. See also Jackson Robson Licence
MOUNTAIN, Mr. Gordon Thomas, FCA *1962;* with Jackson Robson Licence Limited, 33/35 Exchange Street, DRIFFIELD, NORTH HUMBERSIDE, YO25 6LL. (Life Member)
MOUNTAIN, Miss. Helen Ruth, ACA *2008;* 8 Elim Estate, Weston Street, LONDON, SE1 4BY.
MOUNTAIN, Mr. John Raymond, FCA *1969;* Pascali, 50 The Common, Parbold, WIGAN, WN8 7EA. (Life Member)
•MOUNTAIN, Mrs. Karen Janet, FCA *1985;* Karen Mountain, 4/6 Royd View, Windy Bank Lane, Amblerthorn Queensbury, BRADFORD, BD13 2NW.
•MOUNTAIN, Mrs. Karin Ann, ACA CTA *1995;* EDF Tax LLP, 7 Regan Way, Chetwynd Business Park, Chilwell, NOTTINGHAM, NG9 6RZ.
MOUNTAIN, Miss. Mary Catherine, BSc FCA *1982;* 4 Lower Merton Rise, Primrose Hill, LONDON, NW3 3SP.
•MOUNTER, Mr. Robert Neil, FCA *1972;* (Tax Fac), Agincourt Practice Limited, 6 Agincourt Street, MONMOUTH, GWENT, NP25 3DZ.
MOUNTFORD, Mr. Clive, ACA CTA *1983;* 21 Byfleet Ave, Old Basing, BASINGSTOKE, RG24 7HD.
MOUNTFORD, Mr. John Toby, BA ACA *1980;* 67 Hendham Road, LONDON, SW17 7DH.
MOUNTFORD, Mr. Mark Anthony, BA ACA *1990;* 38 Glenorchil Crescent, AUCHTERARDER, PERTHSHIRE, PH3 1PY.
MOUNTFORD, Mr. Michael John, FCA *1973;* 65 Farrington Road, Ettingshall Park, WOLVERHAMPTON, WV4 6QJ.
MOUNTFORD, Mr. Peter, FCA *1982;* 19 Woodside Avenue, BEACONSFIELD, BUCKINGHAMSHIRE, HP9 1JL.
•MOUNTFORD, Mr. Stephen Neil, ACA *1984;* Beaumonts, 29-31 Moorland Road, Burslem, STOKE-ON-TRENT, ST6 1DS.
MOURANT, Mr. Michael Rupert John, BSc ACA *1993;* Pytchley Barn, Stanford Road, Swinford, LUTTERWORTH, LE17 6BJ.
MOURANT, Mr. Nicholas Claud Le Quesne, BA FCA *1984;* 68 Roundwood Lane, HARPENDEN, AL5 3EP.
MOURGUE, Mr. Anthony John, ACA *1984;* U G C Ltd, Unipart House, Garsington Road, OXFORD, OX4 2PG.
MOURLA, Miss. Georgia, BSc ACA *1991;* 6 Anaxagora Road, 16675 ATHENS, GREECE.
MOUROUZIDES, Mr. Charalambos, BSc ACA *2002;* Kasou 16, Apt. H34, Agioi Omoloyites, 1086 NICOSIA, CYPRUS.
MOUROUZIDES, Mr. Constantinos, BSc ACA MBA *2000;* 17 Ayios Efstratios street, 2055 STROVOLOS, CYPRUS.
MOUSER, Mr. George Henry William, FCA *1964;* Wyley Cottage, Rectory Road, Weeley Heath, CLACTON-ON-SEA, ESSEX, CO16 9BH.
MOUSKOS, Mr. Stavros, ACA *2009;* Flat 4 The Westbourne, 1 Artesian Road, LONDON, W2 5DL.
•MOUSLEY, Ms. Christine Kay, PhD BSc FCA *1986;* Senergy Ternan House, North Deeside Road, BANCHORY, KINCARDINESHIRE, AB31 5SD.
MOUSLEY, Miss. Elizabeth Ruth, BSc ACA *2004;* 304 Maritime House, Oldtown Clapham, LONDON, SW4 0JW.
MOUSLEY, Mr. John Rieve, BSc ACA *1994;* 12 New Barn Close, ROSSENDALE, BB4 4LN.
MOUSLEY, Mr. Martin Leif, MA ACA *1999;* 21 Hollinwood Drive, Rawtenstall, ROSSENDALE, LANCASHIRE, BB4 8DE.
MOUSLEY, Mr. Michael John, BSc ACA *1978;* The Quarto Group Inc., 226 City Road, LONDON, EC1V 2TT.
MOUSLEY, Miss. Sandra, MSc FCA *1977;* Castlebalfour, 36 Thorny Road, ISLE OF MAN, IM2 5EG.
MOUSSA, Mr. Maurice Wahba, FCA *1963;* Maurice W. Moussa, Suite 51 Bourg El Zamalek, 18 Shargarret El Dorr Street, Zamalek, CAIRO, 11211 EGYPT. (Life Member)
MOUSSA, Ms. Sarah Anne, ACA CA(SA) *2010;* (Tax Fac), Flat 1, 15a Grove Vale, LONDON, SE22 8ET.
•MOUSTAFA, Mr. Shenol Mustafa, BA FCA *1992;* Hurshens Limited, 14 Theobald Street, BOREHAMWOOD, HERTFORDSHIRE, WD6 4SE.
MOUTSOURI, Mrs. Chryso, BA ACA *2008;* 1 Galileou Street, Derynia, 5380 FAMAGUSTA, CYPRUS.
•MOUZOURIS, Mr. Nicos Melios, BA FCA *1992;* N Mouzouris Ltd, 12 Navarinou Str, 3041 LIMASSOL, CYPRUS. See also Mouzouris & Polyviou Limited
MOUZOUROS, Mr. Kypros, BSc ACA *2001;* NP LANITIS LTD, P.O. BOX 50203, 3602 LIMASSOL, CYPRUS.

MOVERLEY, Mrs. Jane Victoria, BA ACA *1999;* Route de Bonmont 13, 1275 CHESEREX, SWITZERLAND.
MOVERLEY, Mr. Roger David, BA ACA *1995;* Route de Bonmont 13, 1275 CHESEREX, SWITZERLAND.
MOWAT, Mr. David John, BSc ACA *1981;* Willowdene, 42 Hough Lane, WILMSLOW, SK9 2LH.
MOWAT, Mr. Magnus Charles, FCA *1964;* Westcott farm, Brompton Ralph, TAUNTON, TA4 2SF.
MOWAT, Mr. Steven Andrew, BSc FCA *1977;* 3 Langford Close, Burley-in-Wharfedale, ILKLEY, LS29 7NP.
MOWBRAY, Mrs. Alayne Margaret Cooper, ACA *1998;* Avanade Europe Services Limited, Abbey Business Centres Abbey House, 18-24 Stoke Road, SLOUGH, SL2 5AG.
MOWBRAY, Mr. Ian Robert, BSc FCA *1984;* 26 Victoria Road, KINGSTON UPON THAMES, KT1 3DW.
•MOWBRAY, Mrs. Katherine Vanessa, BA(Hons) ACA *2002;* Katherine Mowbray, 17 High Street, Wainfleet, SKEGNESS, LINCOLNSHIRE, PE24 4BP.
MOWER, Mr. Paul, BSc FCA *1974;* Holly House, 2B Keiths Wood, KNEBWORTH, SG3 6PU.
MOWER, Mr. Paul Fenton, BSc FCA *1981;* Electric Motors Limited, Unit C, Lyttleton Road, NORTHAMPTON, NN5 7ET.
MOWJEE, Miss. Farhana, BA ACA *1989;* Razaque Steels (PVT) Ltd, B(30)B Estate Avenue, Shershah SITE, KARACHI 75700, SINDH, PAKISTAN.
MOWLE, Mr. Lee Christian, BSc FCA *1992;* 8 Chapman Square, Parkside Wimbledon, LONDON, SW19 5QQ.
MOWLES, Mrs. Margaret Helen, BA ACA *1988;* 28 Squires Way, Heatherton, Littleover, DERBY, DE23 3XB.
MOWLL, Mr. James, MSc BA ACA *2004;* 4a Fulton Mews, LONDON, W2 3TY.
MOXEY, Mr. Paul Pitt, MBA BSc ACA *1983;* 1 Hale Avenue, NEW MILTON, HAMPSHIRE, BH25 6EZ.
MOXHAM, Mr. David John, MSc BEng ACA *1999;* 154 Brook Drive, CORSHAM, WILTSHIRE, SN13 9AZ.
MOXHAM, Mr. Donald Sidney, FCA *1952;* 3 Millhams Close, Kinson, BOURNEMOUTH, BH10 7LW. (Life Member)
MOXHAM, Mr. Simon John, ACA *1981;* Aerosystems International, Alvington, YEOVIL, SOMERSET, BA22 8UZ.
MOXON, Mr. Colin Frederick Thomas, FCA *1956;* Colburn House, The Platt, Dormansland, LINGFIELD, RH7 6RA. (Life Member)
MOXON, Mr. David Richard, BA ACA *1983;* Aviva UK General Insurance, 8 Surrey Street, NORWICH, NR1 3NG.
MOXON, Mr. Graham Ernest, FCA *1980;* Westbridge International Group, Westbridge House, Holland Street, Hyson Green, NOTTINGHAM, NG7 5DS.
MOXON, Mr. Jeremy George, FCA *1973;* 10 Brockhurst Lane, Dickens Heath, Shirley, SOLIHULL, B90 1RG.
MOXON, Mrs. Joanne, BSc ACA *1990;* 3 Ecton Leys, Hillside, RUGBY, CV22 5SL.
MOXON, Mr. John, ACA *2009;* 17 Caldey Road, DRONFIELD, DERBYSHIRE, S18 1RS.
MOXON, Mr. John Ralph Thomas, FCA *1967;* Coolbay Investments (Pty) Limited, Suite No 1, Steenberg House, Steenberg Office Park, 8 Silverwood Close, TOKAI 7945 SOUTH AFRICA.
MOXON, Mr. Jonathan David, BSc ACA *1992;* Sandy Burrows, Seven Hills Road, COBHAM, SURREY, KT11 1ER.
MOXON, Mr. Paul Keith, BA ACA *1997;* A A C Capital Partners Ltd, 1 Carey Lane, LONDON, EC2V 8AE.
•MOY, Mr. Philip James, BSc FCA *1987;* (Tax Fac), Larking Gowen, 43 Bull Street, HOLT, NR25 6HP.
MOY, Mr. Pun Ki, ACA *2008;* with PricewaterhouseCoopers, 33/F Cheung Kong Center, 2 Queen's Road, CENTRAL, HONG KONG ISLAND, HONG KONG SAR.
MOY, Mr. Roger Mervyn, FCA *1968;* 42 Dibbinsdale Road, WIRRAL, CH63 0HH.
MOYCE, Mr. Stuart John, BA ACA *1988;* U B S Warburg, 1-2 Finsbury Avenue, LONDON, EC2M 2PP.
MOYE, Mr. Andrew Dennis, BSc ACA *1988;* A A C Capital Partners Ltd, 1 Carey Lane, LONDON, EC2V 8AE.
MOYE, Mr. John Graham, BCom FCA *1963;* Avenida Santa Lucia 1967, Condominio Fazendinha, Granja VianaCarapicuiba, SAO PAULO, 06355-450 SP, BRAZIL. (Life Member)
MOYE, Mrs. Susan Elizabeth, BSc ACA ATII *1988;* 39 Cator Road, LONDON, SE26 5DT.
MOYES, Mr. Michael Paul, BA(Hons) ACA *2007;* 12 Northumberland Street, South West Lane, EDINBURGH, EH3 6JD.
MOYES, Miss. Sarah, MSci ACA *2010;* 23 Farrington Road, BIRMINGHAM, B23 7HT.
MOYLE, Mr. Andrew Leigh, ACA CA(AUS) *2011;* 41 Lynda Meadows, NEWTOWNABBEY, COUNTY ANTRIM, BT37 0AT.
•MOYLE, Mr. Christopher Anthony, FCA *1978;* (Tax Fac), Walker Moyle, Alverton Pavilion, Trewithen Road, PENZANCE, CORNWALL, TR18 4LS.
MOYLE, Mr. David Barrie, BSc FCA *1989;* with Grant Thornton UK LLP, Grant Thornton House, 202 Silbury Boulevard, MILTON KEYNES, BUCKINGHAMSHIRE, MK9 1LW.
MOYLE, Mr. Geoffrey Harcourt, FCA *1974;* The Gatehouse, Queens Drive, Oxshott, LEATHERHEAD, KT22 0PB.
MOYLE, Mr. Peter Hillyer, BA FCA *1966;* 4 Murrells Walk, Bookham, LEATHERHEAD, KT23 3LP. (Life Member)
MOYLES, Mr. David Henry, BA ACA *1993;* Premier Foods Plc, Centrium Business Park, Griffiths Way, ST. ALBANS, HERTFORDSHIRE, AL1 2RE.
MOYNIHAN, Mr. Benjamin James, BSc FCA *1998;* Boehringer Ingelheim Ltd, Ellesfield Avenue, BRACKNELL, BERKSHIRE, RG12 8YS.
•MOYNIHAN, Mr. Edward James, BA ACA *1989;* (Tax Fac), Moynihan & Co, Suite 7, Claremont House, 22-24 Claremont Road, SURBITON, SURREY KT6 4QU.
MOYNIHAN, Ms. Sarah Jane, BSc FCA *1995;* Marshall of Cambridge Ltd, The Airport, Newmarket Road, CAMBRIDGE, CB5 8RX.
MOYNIHAN, Miss. Siobhan Djihan, BSc ACA *2004;* London Capital Group, 12 Appold Street, LONDON, EC2A 2AW.
MOYO-MAJWABU, Miss. Nozipho, LLB ACA *2007;* Bank of New Zealand, 80 Queen Street, AUCKLAND 1010, NEW ZEALAND.
MOYS, Mr. John Ernest, FCA *1955;* 2 Paynes Close, LETCHWORTH GARDEN CITY, HERTFORDSHIRE, SG6 1AT. (Life Member)
MOYS, Mr. Peter Herbert Challen, FCA *1958;* 4 Nicholas Way, NORTHWOOD, HA6 2TS. (Life Member)
MOYS, Mr. Peter John, BA ACA *1987;* 63 Harestone Valley Road, CATERHAM, SURREY, CR3 6HP.
•MOYSE, Mr. Alan Richard, FCA *1973;* Alan R. Moyse, 12 Shepherds Croft, Withdean, BRIGHTON, BN1 5JF.
MOYSE, Mr. Eric, FCA *1978;* 8 Caversham Wharf, Waterman Place, READING, RG1 8DS. (Life Member)
MOYSE, Mr. Ernest John, FCA *1963;* 4 St. Carantoc Way, Crantock, NEWQUAY, CORNWALL, TR8 5SB. (Life Member)
MOYSE, Mr. Geoffrey Stuart, FCA *1958;* 18 Chichester Avenue, RUISLIP, HA4 7EH. (Life Member)
MOYSEOS, Mr. Andreas, MSc ACA *2000;* 14 Perikleous Street, 2020 STROVOLOS, CYPRUS.
•MOYSER, Mr. Ian Robin, BSc ACA *1997;* KPMG, 10 Shelley Street, SYDNEY, NSW 2000, AUSTRALIA.
MOYSER-CARR, Miss. Laura, BSc ACA *2010;* 702-2001 Beach Avenue, VANCOUVER V6G1Z3, BC, CANADA.
•MOYSEY, Mr. Nigel Peter, ACA *1980;* (Tax Fac), Milsted Langdon LLP, Motivo House, Alvington, YEOVIL, SOMERSET, BA20 2FG.
MOYSI, Mr. Demetris, ACA *2010;* 14 Azaleon, 4043 LIMASSOL, CYPRUS.
•MOZLEY, Mr. John Charles, MA FCA *1982;* PricewaterhouseCoopers KFT, Wesselenyi u 16, BUDAPEST, H-1077, HUNGARY.
MPANDE, Mr. Freedom, BSc ACA *1992;* 3 Clayfield Road, Pocklington, YORK, YO42 2RG.
MPOFU, Mr. Selby Zwelithini, ACA *2009;* P O Box 2206, HILLCREST, KWAZULU NATAL, 3650, SOUTH AFRICA.
MROTZEK, Mrs. Peggy, BA ACA *2006;* 97 Exeter Road, LONDON, N14 5JU.
MSWABUKI, Mr. Mduduzi, ACA CA(SA) *2009;* with Ernst & Young LLP, 1 More London Place, LONDON, SE1 2AF.
MTETWA, Miss. Thandiwe Tanisha, BSc(Hons) ACA DChA *2009;* 204 Haselbury Road, LONDON, N9 9TS.
MTWANA, Miss. Shani, ACA MAAT *2009;* 31 Retford Road, ROMFORD, RM3 9LX.
MUCHALL, Ms. Karin Judith, BSc ACA *1995;* 563 Hillsdale Avenue East, TORONTO M4S 1V1, ON, CANADA.
MUCHENJE, Mr. Lazarus, ACA CA(SA) *2009;* 1 Pyrian Close, WOKING, SURREY, GU22 8LD.
MUCK, Mrs. Ka Yin, BEng ACA *1993;* Flat F, 21/F Phase 1, Blessings Garden, 95 Robinson Road, MID LEVELS, HONG KONG ISLAND HONG KONG SAR.
MUCK, Dr. Kin Ling, ACA *1993;* 21\F Flat F Blessings Garden, 95 Robinson Road, MID LEVELS, HONG KONG ISLAND, HONG KONG SAR.
MUCKLE, Mr. Adam, ACA *2011;* 68 Dalyell Road, LONDON, SW9 9UP.
MUCKLOW, Mr. Andrew William, BSc ACA *2001;* with Nyman Libson Paul, Regina House, 124 Finchley Road, LONDON, NW3 5JS.
MUDD, Mrs. Sarah Catherine, MA(Oxon) ACA *2006;* 40A Brighton Street, FRESHWATER, NSW 2096, AUSTRALIA.
MUDD, Mr. William Kirton, MA(Oxon) ACA *2006;* 40A Brighton Street, FRESHWATER, NSW 2096, AUSTRALIA.
•MUDDASSIR, Mrs. Fozia Anjum, ACA ACCA *2008;* Reddy Siddiqui & Kabani, Park View, 183-189 The Vale, LONDON, W3 7RW. See also Reddy Siddiqui
MUDDIMAN, Mr. James Reginald, FCA *1973;* Greeninch, Cookstown Road, ENNISKERRY, COUNTY WICKLOW, IRELAND. (Life Member)
MUDDIMAN, Miss. Sally-Anne, BA ACA *1987;* Room 621, Associated Newspapers Ltd Northcliffe House, 2 Derry Street, LONDON, W8 5TT.
MUDGE, Mr. Dominic, BSc FCA *2000;* 72 Printshop Road, Nutts Corner, CRUMLIN, COUNTY ANTRIM, BT29 4YN.
MUDGE, Mr. Kieron John, BSc ACA *1998;* Apartment 608, 12 Bankmore Street, BELFAST, BT7 1AQ.
MUDHAR, Mr. Narinder Singh, BSc(Hons) ACA *2001;* 28 Denham Drive, Gants Hill, ILFORD, IG2 6QU.
MUDHAR, Mr. Sandeep, BA ACA *1997;* 55 Manor Vale, Boston Manor Road, BRENTFORD, TW8 9JN.
MUDIE, Mr. Ian Douglas, FCA *1994;* West Corporation Limited, PO Box 16 Analyst House, 20-26 Peel Road, Douglas, ISLE OF MAN, IM2 1PD.
MUDUNKOTUWE, Mr. Rajasinghe, FCA *1974;* 1 Hadley Close, Winchmore Hill, LONDON, N21 1HG.
MUEFFKE, Mrs. Adina, ACA *2006;* Avenue des Rogations 49, 1200 BRUSSELS, BELGIUM.
MUELLER, Mr. Simon, BA ACA *1997;* SUITE 205, 8210 N.W. 27TH STREET, MIAMI, FL 33122, UNITED STATES.
MUELLER, Mr. Zachary, BSc ACA *2011;* 8 Bardon Hall Mews, Weetwood Lane, LEEDS, LS16 5TY.
MUESING, Mr. George Wilhelm Hans, BSc FCA *1983;* Geschwister-Scholl-Str. 45, 14471 POTSDAM, GERMANY.
MUFFITT, Mr. Brian Travers, FCA *1958;* Pear Tree Cottage, 1 Sadler Way Church Lane, Adel, LEEDS, LS16 8NL. (Life Member)
MUFFITT, Mr. Neil Geoffrey, BSc FCA *1984;* 1 Crag Vale, Crag Lane, LEEDS, LS17 0BS.
MUFTI, Mr. Humayaun Sultan, FCA *1960;* C/o Venture Pharmaceuticals (PVT) Ltd, D-90, Block-2, Clifton, KARACHI, PAKISTAN. (Life Member)
MUFTI, Mr. Shahryar, BSc ACA *2002;* Peace Haven, Shinfield Rise, READING, RG2 8EA.
•MUFTIZADE, Mr. Hakki Tamer, BA FCA *1977;* Tatar & Co, 11 Hasene Ilgaz Str, P.O. Box 768, LEFKOSA MERSIN 10, TURKEY.
MUGFORD, Mr. Denis William, BSc FCA *1977;* 312 Langer Lane, Wingerworth, CHESTERFIELD, S42 6UB.
MUGFORD, Mrs. Gail, BSc ACA *1989;* 5 Lime Avenue, Westergate, CHICHESTER, PO20 3UF.
MUGFORD, Mr. Stephen Ronald, MA ACA *1992;* 5 Lime Avenue, Westergate, CHICHESTER, WEST SUSSEX, PO20 3UF.
MUGFORD, Mrs. Suzy, BSc ACA *2002;* IBM United Kingdom Ltd, PO Box 41, North Harbour, Cosham, PORTSMOUTH, PO6 3AU.
MUGGERIDGE, Mr. Stephen John, ACA *1986;* 2 Daws Place, REDHILL, SURREY, RH1 2NZ.
•MUGGLESTON, Mr. John, MA BA FCA *1974;* Muggleston & Co, 50 Southway, Eldwick, BINGLEY, BD16 3DT.
•MUGGLESTONE, Mr. Steven Robert, BA FCA *1990;* McGregors Corporate, 13-15 Regent Street, NOTTINGHAM, NG1 5BS. See also McGregors Corporate (Nottingham) Ltd
MUGGLETON, Mrs. Kate, BSc ACA *2006;* CPM Retail, Thames House, Thames Road, Crayford, DARTFORD, DA1 4QP.
MUGGRIDGE, Mr. Alan Paul, BA FCA *1987;* 21 Clayton Way, Chantry Park, MALDON, CM9 6WB.
MUGGRIDGE, Miss. Caroline Michelle, ACA *1997;* 14c Mill Street, HOLT, NORFOLK, NR25 6JB.
MUGHAL, Mr. Amir Mohammed, MSci ACA *2005;* Balfour Beatty Ltd, 350 Euston Road, LONDON, NW1 3AX.
MUGHAL, Mr. Mohamed Sarwar, BSc FCA *1990;* 6 Audley Road, Hendon, LONDON, NW4 3EY.
MUGHAL, Mr. Mohammad Irfan, BSc ACA *1996;* 15 Darville Road, LONDON, N16 7PT.
MUGHAL, Mr. Mohammed Sabir, BA ACA *2000;* Independent Regulator of NHS Foundation Trust, 4 Matthew Parker Street, LONDON, SW1H 9NP.
MUGHAL, Mr. Muhammad Ismail, FCA *1970;* Union Securities, c/o P O Box 76102, DUBAI, UNITED ARAB EMIRATES.
MUGHAL, Mr. Saqib, ACA *2009;* 36 Stanley Green East, SLOUGH, SL3 7RF.
MUGRIDGE, Mrs. Claire Joan, BSc ACA *1991;* 88 Durham Road, East Finchley, LONDON, N2 9DS.
MUGRIDGE, Mr. Nicholas John, BSc ACA *1989;* Fishpools Ltd, 115 High Street, WALTHAM CROSS, HERTFORDSHIRE, EN8 7AL.
MUHAMMAD, Mr. Eqhwan Mokhzanee, MA BA ACA *2001;* 2 Jalan 5/2A, Taman Tun Abdul Razak, Ampang Jaya, 68000 AMPANG, SELANGOR, MALAYSIA.
MUHAMMAD ALAM CHAUDHARY, Mr. Usman, ACA *2011;* PricewaterhouseCoopers, Level 40, Emirates Tower, Sheikh Zayad Road, DUBAI, 11987 UNITED ARAB EMIRATES.
MUHAMMAD RADZI, Mr. Ahmad Hakimi, BA(Hons) ACA *2000;* 2e Wolseley Road, LONDON, N8 8RP.
•MUHITH, Mr. Abdul, ACA *1984;* Mohammad Shah & Co, 209 Merton Road, South Wimbledon, LONDON, SW19 1EE. See also Abdul Mubith
MUIR, Mr. Alastair, BA(Hons) ACA *2011;* 20 Wheeler Road, Maidenbower, CRAWLEY, WEST SUSSEX, RH10 7UF.
MUIR, Mr. Alexander Douglas, BSc FCA *1985;* Chestnut House, 3 The Grange, Enborne, NEWBURY, BERKSHIRE, RG14 6RJ.
MUIR, Mr. Alexander John, BSc ACA *2009;* 26 Pepper Wood Drive, Northfield, BIRMINGHAM, B31 5HX.
MUIR, Mr. Andrew John, BA ACA *2005;* 13c Church Terrace, LONDON, SE13 5BT.
MUIR, Mr. Arthur William, FCA *1938;* 162 Benfieldside Road, Blackhill, CONSETT, DH8 0RW. (Life Member)
MUIR, Mr. Christopher James Russell, BA ACA *2001;* Northgate Plc, Norflex House, 20 Allington Way, DARLINGTON, COUNTY DURHAM, DL1 4DY.
MUIR, Mr. David John, ACA *2008;* 28E, 8 Kennedy Street, WAN CHAI, HONG KONG SAR.
MUIR, Miss. Fiona Elizabeth, BA ACA *1997;* 17 Branscombe Gardens, LONDON, N21 3BP.
MUIR, Mr. Iain Robertson, FCA *1954;* 5 Old Hall Farm, Pakenham, BURY ST. EDMUNDS, SUFFOLK, IP31 2NG. (Life Member)
MUIR, Mr. Ian Andrew, BCom FCA *1963;* Flat 2, Islet Park House, Islet Park, MAIDENHEAD, BERKSHIRE, SL6 8LE.
MUIR, Mr. Ian Stuart, BA ACA *1986;* 3 Ernle Road, Wimbledon, LONDON, SW20 0HH.
•MUIR, Mr. John Isherwood, BA FCA *1973;* F & CO, Room 1/101 Old Admiralty Building, LONDON, SW1A 2PA.
•MUIR, Mr. Jonathan William, BSc ACA *1990;* C/O IPS, PO Box 296, Suite 2 F9, 9 Arkwright Road, Colnbrook, SLOUGH SL3 0HJ.
•MUIR, Mrs. Judith Anne Elizabeth, ACA *1983;* (Tax Fac), Holmcott Ltd, 82 High Street, TENTERDEN, KENT, TN30 6JG.
MUIR, Miss. Karen, BA ACA *1990;* 74 Ravenswood Road, Heaton, NEWCASTLE UPON TYNE, NE6 5TX.
MUIR, Miss. Kirsty Campbell, BSc ACA *1998;* Flat A, 92 Narbonne Avenue, LONDON, SW4 9LG.
MUIR, Mr. Mark Lee, BA ACA ATII *1993;* 28 Lane End Drive, Knaphill, WOKING, GU21 2QG.
•MUIR, Mr. Nicholas Hamish, BA(Econ) FCA *1998;* 2 The Wayside, HEMEL HEMPSTEAD, HERTFORDSHIRE, HP3 8NR. See also Martin Greene Ravden LLP
•MUIR, Mr. Peter Richard, BA ACA *1993;* Deloitte LLP, Hill House, 1 Little New Street, LONDON, EC4A 3TR. See also Deloitte & Touche LLP
MUIR, Miss. Philippa Victoria, BA FCA *1996;* c/o KPMG Azsa Center Building 12/f, 1-2 Tsukudo-cho, Shinjuku-ku, TOKYO, 162-8551 JAPAN.
MUIR, Miss. Sarah Ann, BA ACA *2007;* Flat 9 Tyseley House, Swanwick Lane Broughton, MILTON KEYNES, MK10 9NS.
MUIR, Mrs. Sarah Jane, MSc BA ACA *2007;* 23 Marston Road, THAME, OXFORDSHIRE, OX9 3YG.
MUIR, Mr. Simon Ritchie, BSc ACA *1989;* 7 Spindle Glade, Woodlands, Vintners Park, MAIDSTONE, ME14 5RQ.
•MUIR, Mr. Stephen Menzies, BA ACA *2002;* Whale Rock Accounting Limited, 4th Floor, 15 Basinghall Street, LONDON, EC2V 5BR. See also Whale Rock Limited
MUIRHEAD, Mr. Alastair William, BA ACA *1980;* Phoenix Equity Partners, 33 Glasshouse Street, LONDON, W1B 5DG.
MUIRHEAD, Mrs. Cheryl Jean, BSc FCA *1975;* Fieldfares, 4 Warwick Close, Aston Clinton, AYLESBURY, HP22 5JF.

MUIRHEAD, Mr. James Cameron, BEng ACA *1999;* Obika, via della Scrofa14, 00198 ROME, LAZIO, ITALY.
•MUIRHEAD, Mr. Martin Andrew, FCA *1979;* (Tax Fac), Kingston Smith LLP, Devonshire House, 60 Goswell Road, LONDON, EC1M 7AD. See also Kingston Smith Limited Liability Partnership, Devonshire Corporate Services LLP and Kingston Smith Consulting LLP
MUK, Mr. Chung Wing, ACA *2008;* KPMG, 8/F Prince's Building, 10 Chater Road, CENTRAL, HONG KONG ISLAND, HONG KONG SAR.
MUK, Miss. Sook Yee, BSc ACA *2001;* Flat 28 Riceyman House, Lloyd Baker Street, LONDON, WC1X 9BH.
MUKERJI, Mr. Arijit, BSc ACA *2000;* Flat 1, 22 Hatherley Grove, LONDON, W2 5RB.
MUKERJI, Mr. Debashis, ACA *1993;* 1478 Rhine Crescent, PORT COQUITLAM V3B 7V9, BC, CANADA.
MUKERJI, Mr. Swagatam, BCom ACA MBA *1987;* 3 Drews Park, Knotty Green, BEACONSFIELD, BUCKINGHAMSHIRE, HP9 2TT.
MUKHAWALA, Mr. Vijay, BSc ACA *1994;* 72 Beechcroft Gardens, WEMBLEY, MIDDLESEX, HA9 8EP.
MUKHERJEE, Mr. Debojit, BSc ACA *2008;* 18 Rycluff Square, LONDON, SE3 0SN.
MUKHERJEE, Mr. Nigel, BA ACA *1992;* 12B London Court, Realty Gardens, 41 Conduit Road, CENTRAL, HONG KONG ISLAND, HONG KONG SAR.
MUKHERJEE, Miss. Priya, MSc BA ACA *2011;* Flat 209, Utah Building, Deals Gateway, LONDON, SE13 7RP.
MUKHERJEE, Mr. Robin Nath, LLB FCA *1999;* Flat 16 Landseer House, Cureton Street, LONDON, SW1P 4EB.
•MUKHERJEE, Mr. Suman, BSc(Econ) ACA *2001;* 77 Granville Close, Park Hill, CROYDON, CR0 5PY.
MUKHERJI, Mr. Prasanta Kumar, BA BSc FCA *1957;* 3A Suman Apartments, 60/2 Lake Road, CALCUTTA 700 029, INDIA. (Life Member)
MUKHI, Miss. Manisha Sham, BSc(Econ) ACA *2010;* Claremont Court Lodge, Le Mont Millais, St. Helier, JERSEY, JE2 4RA.
MUKHTAR, Mr. Naveed, MSc ACA *2004;* 139 Woodlands, North Harrow, HARROW, HA2 6EN.
MUKHTAR, Mr. Saeedul, FCA *1974;* 139 Woodlands, North Harrow, HARROW, MIDDLESEX, HA2 6EN.
MUKONDE, Mr. Yagan, BSc ACA *1995;* Botswana Housing Corporation, P.O. Box 412, GABORONE, BOTSWANA.
MULCAHY, Mr. Vincent Valentine, BSc FCA *1971;* Apt 610, 197 8th Street, Charlestown, BOSTON, MA 02129, UNITED STATES.
MULCAHY, Mr. William John, MA ACA *1981;* Phu Tara, 210/11 Moo 1, Khiang Doi Road, T. Chang Phuak, CHIANG MAI 50300, THAILAND.
MULCAIRE, Mr. George Thomas, FCA *1966;* PO Box 737, RANDBURG, GAUTENG, 2125, SOUTH AFRICA.
MULCHANDANI, Mr. Girdhar Devidas, BSc ACA *1984;* 8 Hodford Road, LONDON, NW11 8NP.
MULCHINOCK, Mrs. Charlotte, BA(Hons) ACA *2002;* 79 High Street, Ridgmont, BEDFORD, MK43 0TY.
•MULDERRIG, Mr. Brian David, BSc ACA *1986;* (Tax Fac), Gittins Mulderrig, 6 High Street, NORTHWOOD, MIDDLESEX, HA6 1BN.
MULDOON, Miss. Brenda Margaret, MA BBS ACA *1992;* 38 Silchester Road, Glenageary, DUBLIN, COUNTY DUBLIN, IRELAND.
MULDOON, Mr. David Richard, FCA *1963;* 315 Perry Street, BILLERICAY, CM12 0RF.
MULDOON, Mr. Stephen David, BA ACA *1998;* 25 Charmouth Road, ST. ALBANS, HERTFORDSHIRE, AL1 4RS.
MULDOON, Mr. Thomas Anthony, FCA *1970;* 15 South Avenue, Darley Abbey, DERBY, DE22 1FB.
•MULEA, Mr. Adrian, BA ACA *1992;* with Ernst & Young LLP, 1 More London Place, LONDON, SE1 2AF.
MULES, Mr. William Richard Roy, BA FCA *1969;* Hedgehope, Dunmow Rd, Great Bardfield, BRAINTREE, CM7 4SF.
MULFORD, Miss. Laura, ACA *2010;* 47 Tenth Street, Greymont, JOHANNESBURG, GAUTENG, 2195, SOUTH AFRICA.
MULFORD, Mr. Michael Timothy, BSc ACA *1990;* St James House, Oldbury, BRACKNELL, RG12 8TH.
MULGREW, Mr. Mark, BA ACA *2006;* 47 Highmeadow, Outwood, MANCHESTER, M26 1YN.
MULGROVE, Miss. Sophie Alexandra, ACA *2008;* 10 All Hallows Road, Walkington, BEVERLEY, NORTH HUMBERSIDE, HU17 8SJ.
•MULHALL, Miss. Hazel Mary, BSc FCA DChA *2000;* Tudor John Ltd, Nightingale House, 46-48 East Street, EPSOM, SURREY, KT17 1HQ. See also John Tudor
•MULHALL, Mr. James Bernard, FCA *1964;* Mulhall & Company, 2 Langdon Av, AYLESBURY, HP21 9UX.
MULHALL, Mr. Jonathan Thomas Kenneth, BEng ACA MBA *2003;* Apt 5a, 60 Elm Street, MORRISTOWN, NJ 07960, UNITED STATES.
MULHEARN, Ms. Kathryn Louise, BA(Hons) ACA *2001;* 11 Sturdy Lane, Woburn Sands, MILTON KEYNES, MK17 8GD.
•MULHOLLAND, Mr. David, FCA *1975;* Cambridge-Lee (UK) Ltd, 1 Camphill Industrial Estate, WEST BYFLEET, SURREY, KT14 6EW.
MULHOLLAND, Mr. Ian Michael, MA ACA *1987;* 2 Southgate Mews, 24 St. Cross Road, WINCHESTER, SO23 9HX.
MULHOLLAND, Mrs. Jane Lesley, BA ACA *1989;* 2 Southgate Mews, 24 St. Cross Road, WINCHESTER, SO23 9HX.
MULHOLLAND, Mr. Jeffrey, FCA *1963;* Pemberley, 9 St. Philips Drive, Burley-in-Wharfedale, ILKLEY, LS29 7EN.
•MULHOLLAND, Mrs. Jennifer Margaret, BSc FCA *1991;* Smethurst & Buckton Ltd, 12 Abbey Road, GRIMSBY, SOUTH HUMBERSIDE, DN32 0HL. See also Smethurst & Buckton
MULHOLLAND, Mr. Richard Peter, BEng ACA *2001;* Service Solutions Group, Solutions House, Fairways Office Park, Fulwood, PRESTON, PR2 9WT.
MULHOLLAND, Mrs. Roxaan, BSc ACA *1985;* 20 Berkeley Drive, HORNCHURCH, RM11 3PY.
MULLA, Mr. Ebrahim Tayabali, FCA *1960;* Ebrahim Mulla & Co, P.O. Box 81518, MOMBASA, KENYA.
MULLA, Miss. Miryam, BSc ACA *2002;* 238 East Park Road, LEICESTER, LE5 5FD.
MULLAHY, Miss. Maureen Elizabeth, FCA *1976;* 27 Glengate, South Wigston, WIGSTON, LEICESTERSHIRE, LE18 4SQ.
MULLAN, Mr. Denis Gerald Wilson, BSc FCA *1978;* Zytronic Displays, Whiteley Road, BLAYDON-ON-TYNE, TYNE AND WEAR, NE21 5NJ.
MULLAN, Mr. George Timothy, ACA *2009;* (Tax Fac), 92 Boulevard de la Pertreuse, 2320 Luxembourg, 2320 LUXEMBOURG, LUXEMBOURG.
MULLAN, Mr. Homi Phiroz Rustom, MBA FCA *1972;* PO Box 283087, DUBAI, UNITED ARAB EMIRATES.
MULLAN, Mr. James Boyd, MA MSc ACA *2002;* with PricewaterhouseCoopers LLP, Erskine House, 68-73 Queen Street, EDINBURGH, EH2 4NH.
MULLAN, Mr. Mansoor Ul-Haq, BEng ACA *1999;* 10 Limedene Close, PINNER, HA5 3PX.
•MULLAN, Mr. Nigel Joseph Richard, MSc LLB FCA *1977;* Bridge Renewables Ltd, 19 St Gabriels Manor, 25 Cormont Road, LONDON, SE5 9RH.
MULLANE, Mrs. Gaynor Louise, BA ACA *1992;* 39 Kings Hall Road, BECKENHAM, KENT, BR3 1LT.
MULLANE, Mr. Grant, MEng ACA *2003;* Morgan Stanley UK Ltd, 20 Cabot Square, Canary Wharf, LONDON, E14 4QW.
MULLARD, Miss. Carol Susan, BSc ACA *1993;* 15 Redwood Close, LONDON, SE16 5NJ.
MULLARD, Mr. Thomas Edward, ACA *2009;* Flat 1, 263 Magdalen Road, LONDON, SW18 3NZ.
MULLARKEY, Mr. Stephen Patrick, BSc FCA *1981;* 1 Lightfoot Court, Walton Park, MILTON KEYNES, MK7 7HZ.
MULLEN, Mr. Anthony, FCA *1975;* 2 Rolfe Close, BEACONSFIELD, HP9 1RU.
MULLEN, Mr. Ian Nicholas, BA ACA *1994;* 198 Bridle Path Lane, NEW CANAAN, CT 06840, UNITED STATES.
MULLEN, Mr. James Alexander, BCom ACA *1997;* 12 Georges River Cresent, OYSTER BAY, NSW 2225, AUSTRALIA.
MULLEN, Mr. Joseph, BSc ACA *2006;* with PricewaterhouseCoopers LLP, 9 Greyfriars Road, READING, RG1 1JG.
MULLEN, Mrs. Julie Elizabeth, BA ACA *1999;* Allotts Chartered Accountants, Sidings Court, Lakeside, DONCASTER, SOUTH YORKSHIRE, DN4 5NU.
MULLEN, Mr. Marc Charles, BSc ACA *1995;* 9 Eaton Park Road, LONDON, N13 4ED.
•MULLEN, Mr. Neil, ACA FCCA *2008;* (Tax Fac), Mullen Stoker, Mullen Stoker House, Mandale Business Park, Belmont Industrial Estate, DURHAM, DH1 1TH.
MULLEN, Ms. Sarah Claire, BSc ACA *2007;* with PricewaterhouseCoopers LLP, 9 Greyfriars Road, READING, RG1 1JG.
MULLEN, Mrs. Sarah Elizabeth, BSc ACA *1995;* Mays Farmhouse, Romford Road, Pembury, TUNBRIDGE WELLS, KENT, TN2 4BA.
MULLEN, Mr. Shaun Robert, ACA *2008;* 17B Midland Court 58-62 Caine Road, MID LEVELS, HONG KONG SAR.
MULLEN, Mr. William Thomas, BA ACA *1986;* Birchwood, 75a Coggeshall Road, Marks Tey, COLCHESTER, CO6 1LS.
MULLENS, Mr. Brian John, BSc ACA *1997;* McDonalds Restaurants Ltd, 11-59 High Road, East Finchley, LONDON, N2 8AW.
•MULLENS, Mr. Henry Arthur, BSc FCA *1993;* Chavereys, 1Penn Farm, Harston Road, Haslingfield, CAMBRIDGE, CB23 1JZ.
MULLENS, Mrs. Jacqueline, BEng ACA *1991;* Rock Villa, Wood End Off Woburn Road, Marston Moretaine, BEDFORD, MK43 0NJ.
MULLENS, Mrs. Mary Katherine, FCA *1974;* Parkers Farm Bungalow, Biddestone, CHIPPENHAM, SN14 7DF. (Life Member)
MULLENS, Mr. Stephen Bryan, MSc FCA *1993;* Cereform Ltd Barn Way, Lodge Farm Industrial Estate, NORTHAMPTON, NN5 7UW.
MULLER, Mr. Colin Sidney, FCA *1959;* 29 Gordon Lane, New Aberdour, FRASERBURGH, AB43 6LF. (Life Member)
MULLER, Mr. Kersten Joachim, BSc ACA *2003;* with Deloitte LLP, Hill House, 1 Little New Street, LONDON, EC4A 3TR.
MULLER, Mr. Mark Francis, BSc ACA *1992;* Boots the Chemists Ltd D90 Head Office, Thane Road, NOTTINGHAM, NG90 1BS.
MULLER, Mrs. Michelle Caroline, BSc ACA *1983;* 7a Knutsford Road, ALDERLEY EDGE, SK9 7SD.
MULLER, Miss. Rene, BA ACA *2007;* 9/20 Princes Street, ST KILDA, VIC 3182, AUSTRALIA.
•MULLER, Mr. Robert, FCA *1969;* Ballards Newman (Finchley) Limited, Apex House, Grand Arcade, Tally Ho Corner, LONDON, N12 0EH.
•MULLETT, Mr. Andrew Keith, FCA *1978;* Andrew Mullett FCA, 10 Highbury Place, Camden, BATH, BA1 2JW.
MULLETT, Mr. Christopher Daniel, BA ACA *1999;* 16 Macdonald Road, LIGHTWATER, SURREY, GU18 5TN.
MULLETT, Mr. Clifford Charles, FCA *1961;* 17 Lilford Road, BILLERICAY, ESSEX, CM11 1BS. (Life Member)
MULLETT, Mr. Geoffrey Peter, BSc(Econ) FCA *1974;* Woodmeade, 46 School Road, Charlton Kings, CHELTENHAM, GLOUCESTERSHIRE, GL53 8BD.
MULLETT, Mr. John Darlington, BA FCA *1973;* Merrycroft, 209 Rushmere Road, IPSWICH, IP4 3LN.
MULLETT, Mr. Michael Andrew, BSc ACA *1987;* 9 Stafford Place, Park Street, SHIFNAL, SHROPSHIRE, TF11 9BH.
MULLETT, Mr. Simon Richard, ACA *1990;* Acacia House, Back Lane, Kenninghall, NORWICH, NORFOLK, NR16 2EE.
•MULLEY, Miss. Caroline Jean, MA ACA ATII *1996;* with Ernst & Young LLP, Citygate, St James' Boulevard, NEWCASTLE UPON TYNE, NE1 4JD.
•MULLEY, Mr. Paul, BA ACA *1983;* Paul Mulley, 13 Newmans Drive, Hutton, BRENTWOOD, ESSEX, CM13 2PZ.
MULLEY, Mrs. Sharon Virginia, BSc ACA *1985;* (Tax Fac), 43-45 High Street, Little Wilbraham, CAMBRIDGE, CB21 5JY.
MULLEY-SMITH, Mrs. Sandra, BSc ACA *1994;* 8 St. Andrews Croft, LEEDS, LS17 7TP.
MULLICK, Mr. Asim, BSc ACA *1994;* 3 Lyncroft Gardens, LONDON, NW6 1LB.
•MULLICK, Mr. Rupendro, FCA *1985;* R. Mullick, 10 Chatteris Way, Lower Earley, READING, RG6 4JA.
MULLIGAN, Mr. Andrew Kyle, BSc FCA *1990;* 186 Cockburn Crescent, BALERNO, MIDLOTHIAN, EH14 7LU.
MULLIGAN, Miss. Clare Louise, MSci ACA *2002;* 98 Whistler Street, MANLY, NSW 2095, AUSTRALIA.
MULLIGAN, Mr. Colin Derek, BSc FCA *1988;* 11A Willoughbys Walk, Downley, HIGH WYCOMBE, HP13 5UB.
MULLIGAN, Mr. David Kevin, BA FCA *1995;* Danehurst, 34 Kingsway, Chalfont St. Peter, GERRARDS CROSS, SL9 8NU.
MULLIGAN, Mr. David Ross, ACA *1996;* 7 Marvell Green, NORWICH, NR7 0WX.
MULLIGAN, Mr. Ian Arthur, BA(Hons) ACA *2001;* 84A, Newington Green Road, LONDON, N1 4RN.
•MULLIGAN, Mr. Luke Thomas, BA(Hons) ACA *2001;* (Tax Fac), Mulligan Williams, 4 Long Street, Stoney Stanton, LEICESTER, LE9 4DQ.
MULLIGAN, Mr. Martin John, BSc FCA *1996;* 10 Gloucester Row, BRISTOL, BS8 4AW.
MULLIGAN, Miss. Mary-anne Catherine, BSc(Econ) ACA *2010;* Basement Flat, 5 Bellevue, BRISTOL, BS8 1DA.
MULLIGAN, Miss. Michelle McNeil, BA ACA *1993;* Flat 5, 6 Greenlaw Avenue, PAISLEY, RENFREWSHIRE, PA1 3RA.
MULLIGAN, Mrs. Sian Elizabeth, BSc ACA *1988;* 182 Wood Lane, Handsworth Wood, BIRMINGHAM, B20 2AA.
•MULLIGAN, Mr. Thomas Francis, FCA *1975;* Mulligan Williams, 4 Long Street, Stoney Stanton, LEICESTER, LE9 4DQ.
MULLIN, Mrs. Helen, MA ACA *1996;* Aegon Asset Management UK Plc, Aegon House, 3 Lochside Avenue, Edinburgh Park, EDINBURGH, EH12 9SA.
•MULLIN, Mr. Martin Thomas, FCA *1975;* (Tax Fac), Martin T. Mullin FCA, 120 Bloomsbury Lane, Timperley, ALTRINCHAM, WA15 6NT.
MULLIN, Mr. Stuart David, BSc ACA *1994;* Leopard Films, 1-3 St. Peter's Street, LONDON, N1 8JD.
MULLIN, Mr. Thomas Anthony, FCA *1972;* 8 Croft Park Grove, BARROW-IN-FURNESS, LA13 9NJ.
MULLINEAUX, Mr. Anthony Philip, BA ACA *1993;* House B51, Regalia Bay, 88 Wong Ma Kok Road, STANLEY, HONG KONG SAR.
•MULLINEAUX, Mr. Richard John David, FCA *1969;* Whitehead & Aldrich, 5 Ribblesdale Place, PRESTON, PR1 8BZ.
MULLINEAUX, Miss. Sarah, ACA *2008;* 219 Liverpool Road, Hutton, PRESTON, PR4 5FE.
MULLINEUX GARDNER, Mrs. Kate Elisabeth, BA ACA *2002;* 39/9 Comely Bank Street, EDINBURGH, EH4 1AR.
MULLINEUX-JONES, Mr. Paul Maxwell, BSc ACA *1993;* 14 Macefin Avenue, Chorlton-cum-hardy, MANCHESTER, M21 7QQ.
MULLINEX, Mr. Gareth, MA ACA *2002;* 1 Arretine Close, ST. ALBANS, HERTFORDSHIRE, AL3 4JL.
•MULLINGER, Mr. Louis Neville Clarke, FCA *1972;* Edward Jones, 12324 Hampton Way Drive, Ste 102, WAKE FOREST, NC 27587, UNITED STATES.
MULLINGTON, Mrs. Tina Jane, BA(Hons) ACA ATII *2000;* with Baker Tilly Tax & Advisory Services LLP, Festival Way, Festival Park, STOKE-ON-TRENT, ST1 5BB.
MULLINS, Mr. Andrew Dale, BSc FCA *1985;* Courtways, Box Ridge Avenue, PURLEY, CR8 3AQ.
MULLINS, Mrs. Carol, BA ACA *2004;* 63 Kitsbury Road, BERKHAMSTED, HERTFORDSHIRE, HP4 3EG.
MULLINS, Ms. Claire Louise, BA ACA *1995;* 20 Dane Road, SALE, CHESHIRE, M33 7AR.
MULLINS, Mr. Derek, FCA *1960;* Orchard House, 3 The Maltings, CREDITON, EX17 1HT. (Life Member)
MULLINS, Mrs. Fiona Margaret, BSc ACA *2002;* 14 Besbury Close, Dorridge, SOLIHULL, B93 8NT.
•MULLINS, Mr. Giles Martin, ACA *2005;* 17 Cooper Close, TOWCESTER, NORTHAMPTONSHIRE, NN12 7AN.
MULLINS, Mrs. Helen Louisa, BA ACA *2004;* Brook House, 30 Ensign Way, DISS, NORFOLK, IP22 4GP.
MULLINS, Mr. James Anthony, BA(Hons) ACA JIEB *2003;* 63 Kitsbury Road, BERKHAMSTED, HERTFORDSHIRE, HP4 3EG.
MULLINS, Mr. John Dominic, BA FCA *1975;* 19 Stone Hall Road, Winchmore Hill, LONDON, N21 1LR.
•MULLINS, Mr. Mark Antony Michael, BA ACA *1989;* Deloitte LLP, Abbots House, Abbey Street, READING, RG1 3BD. See also Deloitte & Touche LLP
•MULLINS, Mr. Matthew Robert, BA ACA *1995;* PricewaterhouseCoopers LLP, Cornwall Court, 19 Cornwall Street, BIRMINGHAM, B3 2DT. See also PricewaterhouseCoopers
MULLINS, Mr. Michael Eric, FCA *1952;* 42A Batchworth Lane, NORTHWOOD, HA6 3DT. (Life Member)
MULLINS, Mr. Roger John, LLB ACA *2002;* 85 Redgrove Park, CHELTENHAM, GL51 6QZ.
MULLINS, Mr. Rupert D'almada, TD FCA *1937;* Mare Barn Cottage, Lynchmere, HASLEMERE, GU27 3NE. (Life Member)
•MULLINS, Mr. Shaun, ACA *1996;* Baker Tilly UK Audit LLP, 2 Whitehall Quay, LEEDS, LS1 4HG. See also Baker Tilly Tax and Advisory Services LLP
MULLIS, Mr. James, BSc(Hons) ACA *2011;* Flat 30, Gainsborough House, Erasmus Street, LONDON, SW1P 4HX.
MULLIS, Mr. Paul Stephen, BA FCA *1994;* Durham Aged Mineworkers Homes Association, PO Box 31, CHESTER LE STREET, COUNTY DURHAM, DH3 3YH.
MULLIS, Mr. Philip Peter, BA FCA *1984;* with Grant Thornton UK LLP, 300 Pavilion Drive, Northampton Business Park, NORTHAMPTON, NN4 7YE.
MULLOCK, Mr. Keith Howard, BA ACA *1987;* Harper Collins Publishers, Elsinore House, 77-85 Fulham Palace Road, LONDON, W6 8JB.
MULLOCK, Mr. Philip, DPhil FCA *1948;* Little Meadow, Upper Wyke, St. Mary Bourne, ANDOVER, HAMPSHIRE, SP11 6EA. (Life Member)

MULLOCK, Mr. Richard Alan, BSc ACA *1994;* 37441 Wineberry Lane, PURCELLVILLE, VA 20132, UNITED STATES.
MULLOY, Mrs. Vanessa Jayne, BA ACA *1992;* 7 Coxs Road, Shrivenham, SWINDON, SN6 8EL.
MULROY, Miss. Isabelle Ann, BA ACA *1989;* 74 Esmond Road, Chiswick, LONDON, W4 1JF.
MULROY, Miss. June Patricia, BSc FCA *1976;* 50 Shafesbury Way, Strawberry Hill, TWICKENHAM, TW2 5RP.
MULROY, Mr. Peter, BA(Hons) ACA *2003;* H B O S Plc, PO Box 93, LEEDS, LS1 1NS.
MULRYAN, Miss. Annemarie Clare, MA LLB ACA *2002;* 29 Cranes Park Avenue, SURBITON, SURREY, KT5 8BS.
MULRYAN, Mr. John Denis, FCA *1974;* with Mulryan & Co Ltd, 15 Queen Street, HENLEY-ON-THAMES, OXFORDSHIRE, RG9 1AR.
MULVEE, Mr. Patrick Joseph, FCA *1974;* 33 Foxrock Avenue, Foxrock, DUBLIN 18, COUNTY DUBLIN, IRELAND.
MULVEY, Mr. John Philip, BSocSc ACA *1999;* 16 Hathaway Close, Balsall Common, COVENTRY, CV7 7EP.
MULVEY, Mr. Patrick Brendan, BSc FCA *1975;* 21 Grange Grove, LONDON, N1 2NP.
MULVEY, Mr. Peter Robert, FCA *1971;* 6 Barnsbury Square, LONDON, N1 1JL.
MULVIHILL, Miss. Martina, BSc ACA *2000;* Hillcrest, Templeathea, ATHEA, COUNTY LIMERICK, IRELAND.
MUMBI, Mr. Stanley Chiluba, BSc ACA *1991;* 6 Sherwood Road, Forest Town, JOHANNESBURG, 2193, SOUTH AFRICA.
MUMBY, Mr. David Kris, BA ACA *1988;* 126 Dean Street, STRATHFIELD, NSW 2136, AUSTRALIA.
•MUMBY, Mr. Jeremy Andrew D'arcy, FCA *1977;* (Tax Fac), Mumby Heppenstall, Wellingore Hall, Wellingore, LINCOLN, LN5 0HX.
•MUMFORD, Mr. Andrew Michael, FCA *1977;* Upper Cross Farm, Thornton Lane, Eastry, SANDWICH, KENT, CT13 0EU.
•MUMFORD, Mr. Brian Frederick, FCA *1973;* Mumford & Co, The Old Rectory, Church Street, WEYBRIDGE, SURREY, KT13 8DE.
MUMFORD, Miss. Emily Anne, BSc ACA *2006;* 154 St. Davids Square, LONDON, E14 3WD.
MUMFORD, Mr. Frederick Augustus, FCA *1980;* 17 Ludgate Avenue, KIDDERMINSTER, DY11 6JP.
MUMFORD, Mrs. Heather, BSc ACA *1995;* 34 Pimms Grove, HIGH WYCOMBE, HP13 7EF.
MUMFORD, Mr. Hugh Antony Lewis Holland, MA FCA *1971;* Amwell House, 6 Millington Road, CAMBRIDGE, CB3 9HP.
MUMFORD, Mr. Laurence John, BSc FCA *1990;* 18 Cavendish Avenue, WOODFORD GREEN, IG8 9DA.
MUMFORD, Mr. Peter John, BSc ACA *1997;* 47 Cranbrook Road, BRISTOL, BS6 7BP.
MUMME, Miss. Susan Annalouise, BA ACA *1983;* Ashton Manor, Lower Ashton, EXETER, DEVON, EX6 7QW.
MUMMERY, Mr. Gavin Thomas, PhD ACA *2010;* 35 Milverton Road, MANCHESTER, M14 5PJ.
MUMMERY, Mr. Peter, LLB(Hons) ACA *2004;* 31 Stainburn Crescent, Moortown, LEEDS, LS17 6NE.
MUMMERY, Mr. Tony Jack, FCA *1975;* London & Quadrant Housing Trust Osborn House, Osborn Terrace, LONDON, SE3 9DR.
MUN, Mr. Cheong Fai, ACA *1980;* 2D Hong San Walk, #04-04 Palm Gardens, SINGAPORE 689050, SINGAPORE.
MUNASINGHE, Miss. Subhashini, ACA *2010;* No:15A Rotherfield Place, 7 COLOMBO, SRI LANKA.
MUNBODH, Miss. Roshni Sangeeta, BSc ACA *2005;* Coombes Lane, VACOAS, MAURITIUS.
MUNCASTER, Mrs. Josephine, BA(Hons) ACA *2011;* 22 Brookfield Avenue, Bredbury, STOCKPORT, CHESHIRE, SK6 1DF.
MUNCASTER, Mrs. Luna Malabika, BSc ACA *1995;* 96 Broomfield Avenue, Palmers Green, LONDON, N13 4JP.
MUNCASTER, Mr. Simon Vernon, BSc ACA *1982;* United Westminster Schools Alexandra House, 55a Catherine Place, LONDON, SW1E 6DY.
•MUNCASTER, Mr. Stephen, ACA ACMA MBA *2008;* IFRS 2009 Ltd, Heron House, 45 Riversdale Grove, EDINBURGH, EH12 5QS.
MUNCER, Mr. Stuart Douglas, MA ACA *2003;* Domestic & General Group Limited, Swan Court, 11 Worple Road, LONDON, SW19 4JS.
MUNCEY, Mr. Andrew Dalrymple, BSc ACA *1993;* Mandeville House, Borough Lane, SAFFRON WALDEN, ESSEX, CB11 4AG.
MUNCEY, Mr. John Culverhouse, BA ACA *1988;* Sumner House, Preston Candover, BASINGSTOKE, HAMPSHIRE, RG25 2EE.
•MUNCEY, Mr. Stephen John Scott, MSc BSc FCA *1987;* KPMG LLP, 37 Hills Road, CAMBRIDGE, CB2 1XL. See also KPMG Europe LLP
MUNCH, Miss. Susan Alison, BSc ACA *2005;* with Deloitte LLP, Athene Place, 66 Shoe Lane, LONDON, EC4A 3BQ.
MUNDAIR, Miss. Narinderjit, ACA *2010;* 110 Hardy Road, LONDON, SW19 1HZ.
MUNDAY, Mrs. Carolyn Eleanor, BSc FCA *1985;* Unisto Ltd, Postford Mill, Mill Lane, Chilworth, GUILDFORD, SURREY GU4 8RT.
MUNDAY, Mrs. Christina Mary Theresa, MA ACA *1986;* 30 Alderney Street, LONDON, SW1V 4EV.
MUNDAY, Mr. Christopher Lloyd Digby, MSc FCA *1975;* 60 Riplingham Road, Kirk Ella, HULL, HU10 7TR.
MUNDAY, Mr. Colin Peter, FCA *1972;* Hops, Lyewood Common, Withyham, HARTFIELD, TN7 4DD.
•MUNDAY, Colin Roy, Esq FCA *1971;* CRM, 33 New Road, BROXBOURNE, HERTFORDSHIRE, EN10 7LN.
MUNDAY, Mr. David, FCA *1972;* Springfield, 52 Links Lane, ROWLANDS CASTLE, PO9 6AF. (Life Member)
MUNDAY, Mr. Eric Alec, FCA *1955;* 25 Pettits Lane, ROMFORD, RM1 4HL. (Life Member)
MUNDAY, Mr. Jasmeet, BSc ACA *2011;* 20 Blossom Waye, HOUNSLOW, TW5 9HD.
MUNDAY, Mr. Jeremy David Lewis, BA ACA *1988;* 17 Rue de Seine, 78360 MONTESSON, FRANCE.
MUNDAY, Mr. John, FCA *1962;* 2 Highwaymans Ridge, Snows Ride, WINDLESHAM, GU20 6JY. (Life Member)
•MUNDAY, Mr. Jonathan Martin, FCA ATII *1991;* (Tax Fac), Rees Pollock, 35 New Bridge Street, LONDON, EC4V 6BW.
MUNDAY, Mrs. Katherine Anne, ACA *2001;* 56 Back Hill, ELY, CAMBRIDGESHIRE, CB7 4BZ.
•MUNDAY, Miss. Lynn Elizabeth, BSc ACA *1989;* Forecast Flow, 107 New Road, CHATTERIS, CAMBRIDGESHIRE, PE16 6BT.
MUNDAY, Mr. Neil John, MA ACA *1997;* 1 Bothar na Scoile, Aghyohill, ENNISKEAN, COUNTY CORK, IRELAND.
MUNDAY, Mr. Paul Jonathan, FCA *1973;* AVENUE DE MAI 181, 1200 BRUSSELS, BELGIUM.
MUNDAY, Mr. Philip James, BSc FCA *1975;* 21 Hauptville Circle, Constantia, CAPE TOWN, 7806, SOUTH AFRICA.
•MUNDAY, Mr. Roger Derek, FCA *1971;* Josolyne Rogers, The Acorn, 10 Little Lane, Clophill, BEDFORD, MK45 4BG.
MUNDAY, Mrs. Shona Claire, BA ACA *2003;* 68 Brockswood Lane, WELWYN GARDEN CITY, HERTFORDSHIRE, AL8 7BQ.
MUNDE, Mrs. Janis Claire, FCA *1985;* 79 Harestone Valley Road, CATERHAM, SURREY, CR3 6HQ.
MUNDE, Mr. Kuljit Raj Singh, BA ACA *1984;* 79 Harestone Valley Road, CATERHAM, CR3 6HQ.
MUNDELL, Miss. Helen Louise, BSc(Hons) ACA *2002;* 4 Walton Street, ST. ALBANS, HERTFORDSHIRE, AL1 4DQ.
MUNDEN, Mr. William, BA(Hons) ACA *2011;* Hayleigh Lodge, Streat Lane, Streat, HASSOCKS, WEST SUSSEX, BN6 8RU.
MUNDY, Mr. Adrian Howard, BA ACA CF *1989;* Bulldog Corporate Finance Ltd, Flat 3, 36 Elm Park Road, LONDON, SW3 6AX.
MUNDY, Mrs. Alison Jane, ACA *2007;* 27 Watergate, Methley, LEEDS, LS26 9BX.
•MUNDY, Mr. Andrew Stephen, FCA *1981;* (Tax Fac), A S Mundy, 73 High Street, Shoreham, SEVENOAKS, TN14 7TB.
MUNDY, Mr. Anthony David, FCA FCMA *1957;* (Member of Council 1983 - 1988), 41 Foxdown, Egloshayle, WADEBRIDGE, PL27 6BD. (Life Member)
•MUNDY, Mr. Christopher Michael, BMus FCA *1991;* (Tax Fac), Grant Thornton UK LLP, 3140 Rowan Place, John Smith Drive, Oxford Business Park South, OXFORD, OX4 2WB. See also Grant Thornton LLP
MUNDY, Mr. Dennis Victor, FCA *1950;* The Chase, Harescombe, GLOUCESTER, GL4 0XD. (Life Member)
MUNDY, Mr. Edward, BA ACA *2006;* 61 Lower Richmond Road, LONDON, SW15 1ET.
MUNDY, Mrs. Elizabeth Margaret, BSc(Hons) ACA *2002;* 44 Barley Lane, EXETER, EX4 1TD.
•MUNDY, Mrs. Margaret Mary, BA ACA *1979;* (Tax Fac), Margaret Mundy Limited, 5 Beauley Road, BRISTOL, BS3 1PX.
•MUNDY, Mr. Nigel Hayward Waring, ACA *1980;* Mundy & Co, 15 Williams Mead, Bartestree, HEREFORD, HR1 4BT.
MUNDY, Mr. Nigel Rodney, FCA *1960;* (Tax Fac), Meadow Cottage, 21 Cygnet Close, NORTHWOOD, HA6 2SY.
•MUNDY, Mr. Peter Francis, FCA *1973;* Moffatt & Co, 396 Wilmslow Road, Withington, MANCHESTER, M20 3BN.
MUNDY, Mr. Stephen Jolyon, BSc ACA *1998;* 42 Matthews Avenue, LANE COVE, NSW 2066, AUSTRALIA.
MUNDZIC, Mr. Michael, BSc ACA *2006;* with Deloitte LLP, Athene Place, 66 Shoe Lane, LONDON, EC4A 3BQ.
MUNEER, Mr. Mohammad Sohaib, BSc ACA *2004;* #9972 116th Street, SURREY V3V 7Y4, BC, CANADA.
MUNEER, Mr. Zahid, BSc FCA *1992;* 16 Ethorpe Close, GERRARDS CROSS, BUCKINGHAMSHIRE, SL9 8PL.
MUNFORD, Mr. Roy Mervyn, ACA *1979;* H.M.L., 3 Grooms Court, Parbrook, BILLINGSHURST, RH14 9EU.
•MUNGLY, Mr. Abdool Kader, FCA MIPA CA(SA) *1975;* 43 Dr Lesur Street, Cascadelle, BEAU BASSIN, MAURITIUS.
MUNIF, Mr. Mohammed Seim, MA ACA *2004;* with PricewaterhouseCoopers LLP, 1 Embankment Place, LONDON, WC2N 6RH.
MUNIR, Mr. Ali, FCA *1975;* MCB Bank Ltd. SPIG 6th Floor 15 Main Gulberg, LAHORE 54660, PAKISTAN.
MUNIR, Mr. Anseb, ACA *2011;* Flat 11, Queen of the Isle Apartments, 1 East Ferry Road, LONDON, E14 3NY.
•MUNIR, Mr. Cemal Teki, BA FCA *1984;* (Tax Fac), CTM Partnership Limited, 838 Wickham Road, CROYDON, CR0 8ED.
MUNIR, Mr. Kamran, MA ACA *1999;* 155 Coombe Park Road, COVENTRY, CV3 2PD.
MUNIR, Mr. Mohammad, FCA *1962;* 37L Gulberg II, LAHORE 54660, PAKISTAN. (Life Member)
MUNIR, Mr. Mohammed, BCom ACA *2002;* 24 Birchfield Close, WORCESTER, WR3 8LQ.
MUNIR AHMED, Mr. Munsoor, FCA *1972;* P O Box 15877, JEDDAH, 21454, SAUDI ARABIA.
•MUNK, Mr. Philip John, ACA FCCA *2008;* TWP Accounting LLP, The Old Rectory, Church Street, WEYBRIDGE, SURREY, KT13 8DE. See also Philip Munk Limited
MUNN, Mr. Andrew Kevin, BA ACA *1987;* with Whyatt Pakeman Partners, Colkin House, 16 Oakfield Rd, Clifton, BRISTOL, BS8 2AP.
MUNN, Mrs. Claudia Jane, BA ACA *1995;* Tesla Motors Ltd, Kings Chase107 King Street, MAIDENHEAD, SL6 1DP.
MUNN, Mr. David Leslie, BSc FCA *1976;* Daisy Cottage, Upper Hill Street, Elmsted, ASHFORD, KENT, TN25 5JT.
MUNN, Mrs. Katie, BA(Hons) ACA *2003;* 5 Lambert Drive, NEWBURY, RG14 2RS.
•MUNN, Mr. Kenneth MacGregor, BSc FCA *1985;* Carston & Co Limited, First Floor, Tudor House, 16 Cathedral Road, CARDIFF, CF11 9LJ. See also Sullivans Associate Limited and Carston & Co (Cardiff) Limited
MUNN, Mr. Neil Andrew, BSc ACA *1991;* Clarke Willmott, 1 Georges Square, Bath Street, BRISTOL, BS1 6BA.
MUNNINGS, Mr. Alan David, FCA *1972;* 1 The Drive, Waltham, GRIMSBY, DN37 0FB.
MUNNINGS, Miss. Elizabeth Audrey, BSc ACA *2000;* with KPMG, 10 Shelley Street, SYDNEY, NSW 2000, AUSTRALIA.
MUNNINGS, Mrs. Karen Jane, BSc ACA CTA *1988;* Shrub House, Castle Combe, CHIPPENHAM, SN14 7JA.
MUNNINGS, Mr. Roger Llewelyn, CBE MA(Oxon) FCA *1977;* Shrub House, Castle Combe, CHIPPENHAM, WILTSHIRE, SN14 7JA.
MUNNS, Mr. David Charles John, FCA *1971;* 31 The Street, Bawdsey, WOODBRIDGE, IP12 3AH.
MUNNS, Mr. David Howard, LLB FCA *1990;* Kaplan, 52 Grosvenor Gardens, LONDON, SW1W 0AU.
MUNNS, Mr. David William, FCA *1968;* 12 Whytewell Road, WELLINGBOROUGH, NN8 5BE.
MUNNS, Mr. Karl Sean, ACA *1995;* Everest Ltd Everest House, Sopers Road Cuffley, POTTERS BAR, HERTFORDSHIRE, EN6 4SG.
MUNOZ, Mrs. Elena, BA ACA *2009;* 30 Greenbank Road, LIVERPOOL, L18 1HN.
MUNOZ ALVAREZ-NET, Mr. Enrique Caesar, BSc ACA *1988;* with PricewaterhouseCoopers, Almagro 40, 28010 MADRID, SPAIN.
MUNRO, Mr. Alan Peter, ACA CA(SA) *2010;* 32 The Copse, Rowledge, FARNHAM, SURREY, GU10 4BH.
MUNRO, Mr. Alexander Stewart, BA ACA *2003;* 9 Ulysses Road, West Hampstead, LONDON, NW6 1ED.
MUNRO, Mr. Andrew Charles, BCom FCA *1985;* 16 Granary Way, Wick, LITTLEHAMPTON, WEST SUSSEX, BN17 7QY.
MUNRO, Mr. Andrew Graham, BA ACA *2005;* 92 Judge Street, WATFORD, WD24 5AW.
MUNRO, Mrs. Anna Louise, BA(Hons) ACA *2010;* 3 Tiverton Close, HOUGHTON LE SPRING, TYNE AND WEAR, DH4 4XR.
MUNRO, Mrs. Beverley Kay, BA ACA *1994;* Devro (Scotland) Ltd, Gartferry Road, Moodiesburn, GLASGOW, G69 0JD.
MUNRO, Mr. Charles George, BEng ACA *2003;* Kirkmichael House, Kirkmichael, BALLINDALLOCH, BANFFSHIRE, AB37 9AR.
MUNRO, Mr. Charles John, BA FCA *1971;* Kirkmichael House, Ballindalloch, BALLINDALLOCH, AB37 9AR.
•MUNRO, Ms. Clare, LLB FCA *1986;* Haslers, Old Station Road, LOUGHTON, ESSEX, IG10 4PL.
MUNRO, Mr. Fergus Stephen John, BA ACA *1998;* 179 Gloucester Avenue, LONDON, NW1 8LA.
•MUNRO, Mrs. Heike Christa Helene, ACA *1997;* AlixPartners UK LLP, 20 North Audley Street, LONDON, W1K 6WE.
•MUNRO, Mr. Henry Martin, FCA *1983;* KPMG LLP, 15 Canada Square, LONDON, E14 5GL. See also KPMG Europe LLP
MUNRO, Mr. Ian James, BA FCA *1982;* 16b Castle Street, FLEET, HAMPSHIRE, GU52 7ST.
MUNRO, Mr. James Alexander, ACA ACCA ACMA *2007;* 113 Cradlehall Park, Westhill, INVERNESS, IV2 5DB.
MUNRO, Miss. Julie Louise, BA ACA CTA *1995;* 43 St. James Court, ALTRINCHAM, CHESHIRE, WA15 8FG.
MUNRO, Mr. Mark Andrew, BA ACA *2007;* 10 Springfield Road, WANTAGE, OX12 8ES.
MUNRO, Mr. Neil John Tarry, FCA *1964;* 17 Paxton Close, Kew Road, RICHMOND, SURREY, TW9 2AW.
MUNRO, Mr. Peter John, FCA *1985;* PO BOX 4624, CAIRNS, QLD 4870, AUSTRALIA.
MUNRO, Mr. Richard David Harrison, BA ACA *1989;* P M I Ltd, The Courtyard, Hall Lane, Wincham, NORTHWICH, CW9 6DG.
MUNRO, Mr. Robert George, BSc ACA *1992;* BG Group plc, 100 Thames Valley Park Drive, READING, RG6 1PT.
MUNRO, Mr. Robert Kenneth Campbell, BSc ACA *1991;* (Tax Fac), Packway, Hosey Hill, WESTERHAM, KENT, TN16 1TA.
MUNRO, Mr. Steven John, MA ACA *1998;* 37 Warwick Drive, BEVERLEY, NORTH HUMBERSIDE, HU17 9TB.
MUNRO, Mr. Stuart Ian, BSc FCA *1993;* 80 The Thatchers, BISHOP'S STORTFORD, CM23 4FN.
•MUNRO, Mrs. Yvonne Marion, ACA *1996;* with PricewaterhouseCoopers LLP, 1 Embankment Place, LONDON, WC2N 6RH.
MUNRO-COWGILL, Mrs. Victoria Harriet Louise, MA ACA *1996;* Fernleigh, 10 Hobbiton Road, WESTON-SUPER-MARE, BS22 7HP.
MUNRO-FAURE, Mr. Charles Napier, BA(Hons) ACA *2009;* 68 Kings Road, Caversham, READING, RG4 8DT.
MUNRO-FAURE, Mr. Malcolm Douglas, BSc ACA *1985;* Fox Barn, 225 Thame Road, Warborough, WALLINGFORD, OXFORDSHIRE, OX10 7DH.
MUNRO-MORRIS, Mr. Scott, BSc ACA *1998;* 76 Cog Road, Sully, PENARTH, SOUTH GLAMORGAN, CF64 5TE.
MUNROE, Mr. Philip Mark, BSc ACA *1995;* Pelham House, Great Austins, FARNHAM, SURREY, GU9 8JG.
MUNSIE, Mr. Michael Charles, FCA *1954;* PO Box 1433, Saxonwold, JOHANNESBURG, 2132, SOUTH AFRICA. (Life Member)
MUNSIFF, Mr. Shahrook Cyrus, FCA *1974;* 7 Saker Apartments, Pochkhanawala Road, Worli, MUMBAI 400030, INDIA.
MUNSLOW, Mr. Peter Conway, BSc ACA *1990;* 68 Langdale Way, EAST BOLDON, TYNE AND WEAR, NE36 0UF.
•MUNSON, Mr. Alma Russell, FCA *1962;* (Tax Fac), A.R. Munson, 8 Devonshire Mews West, LONDON, W1G 6QE.
MUNSON, Mr. Anthony Robert, FCA *1962;* 8864 Huntington Pointe Drive, SARASOTA, FL 34238, UNITED STATES. (Life Member)
MUNSON, Mr. David Geoffrey, TD BSc ACA *1983;* 12 Cilgant y Meillion, Rhoose, BARRY, SOUTH GLAMORGAN, CF62 3LH.
MUNSON, Mr. Douglas Kevin, BSc ACA *1985;* 22 Hamilton Avenue, WOKING, SURREY, GU22 8RS.
MUNSON, Ms. Elizabeth Anne, BA ACA *1989;* The Ferns, The Avenue, GRAYSHOTT, GU26 6JY.
MUNSON, Mrs. Gayle Nicole, BSc ACA *2003;* Macquarie Group, Level 6, 1 Martin Place, SYDNEY, NSW 2000, AUSTRALIA.
MUNSON, Mr. James Derek, BSc ACA *1997;* Hidcote House, 14 Grove Road, Sherston, MALMESBURY, WILTSHIRE, SN16 0NF.

MURRAY, Mr. Neil Alexander, BSc ACA *1992;* Taunton & Somerset N H S Trust, Musgrove Park Hospital, TAUNTON, SOMERSET, TA1 5DA.
MURRAY, Mr. Niall John, FCA *1984;* Bay View, Le Mont Cambrai, St. Lawrence, JERSEY, JE3 1JN.
MURRAY, Mr. Nigel Stuart, FCA *1962;* The Dolls House, Rookery Lane, Ettington, STRATFORD-UPON-AVON, WARWICKSHIRE, CV37 7TN.
MURRAY, Mr. Norman Wood, FCA *1953;* 6 Monkhams Drive, WOODFORD GREEN, IG8 0LQ. (Life Member)
MURRAY, Mr. Patrick James, MBA BSc ACA *1996;* Berncroft, Top Street, Bolney, HAYWARDS HEATH, WEST SUSSEX, RH17 5PP.
MURRAY, Mr. Paul, BSc ACA *2003;* KH Capital Ltd, A200 Graceway House, Leeward Highway, PROVIDENCIALES, TURKS AND CAICOS ISLANDS.
•MURRAY, Mr. Paul Ian, FCA *1976;* Law & Co, Pool House, Arran Close, 106 Birmingham Road, Great Barr, BIRMINGHAM B43 7AD.
MURRAY, Mr. Peter, BSc FCA *1986;* 1 Gillard Place, Ringwood North, MELBOURNE, VIC 3134, AUSTRALIA.
MURRAY, Mr. Philip John, BA ACA *1997;* 44 Hauxley Drive, Waldridge Park, CHESTER LE STREET, DH2 3TE.
•MURRAY, Mr. Richard John, BBS FCA *1975;* Belhaven Guildford Road, East Horsley, LEATHERHEAD, SURREY, KT24 5RX.
MURRAY, Mr. Richard Paul, BA ACA *1993;* 14 Tidmington Close, Hatton Park, WARWICK, CV35 7TE.
MURRAY, Mr. Robert, BSc ACA *1984;* 17 Lime Walk, Acton, SUDBURY, CO10 0UU.
MURRAY, Mr. Robert, BA ACA *1979;* Quarries, 9 Windywood, Bargate Wood, GODALMING, GU7 1XX.
MURRAY, Mr. Robert Jack, MA FCA *1993;* 3rd Floor Eastbrook, Shaftesbury Road, CAMBRIDGE, CB2 8BF.
MURRAY, Mr. Robin Paul, BSc ACA MBA *1992;* 2500 Sand Hill Road, Ste. 100, MENLO PARK, CA 94402, UNITED STATES.
MURRAY, Ms. Ruth Alison, ACA MAAT *2011;* 48 Scholars Road, LONDON, SW12 0PG.
MURRAY, Mrs. Sarah Louise, ACA *2008;* 28 St. Michaels Way, Burley in Wharfedale, ILKLEY, WEST YORKSHIRE, LS29 7PP.
MURRAY, Mr. Sean Stephen, ACA *2009;* 134a Manor Way, RUISLIP, MIDDLESEX, HA4 8HR.
•MURRAY, Mr. Simon Alexander, FCA *1981;* Simon Murray & Co, Woburn House, YELVERTON, PL20 6BS.
•MURRAY, Mr. Simon Nicolas, BA FCA *1988;* (Tax Fac), MurraYoung Limited, 15 Home Farm, Luton Hoo Estate, LUTON, LU1 3TD.
MURRAY, Miss. Sophie Elizabeth, ACA *2010;* 47 Cresswell Road, WALLSEND, TYNE AND WEAR, NE28 8QE.
MURRAY, Mr. Stephen, BCom ACA *2003;* Apartment 3, 19 Moor Green Lane, BIRMINGHAM, B13 8NE.
•MURRAY, Mr. Stephen Paul, FCA *1976;* MMO Limited, Wellesley House, 204 London Road, WATERLOOVILLE, PO7 7AN. See also Murray McIntosh O'Brien
MURRAY, Mr. Stephen Young, FCA *1983;* 26 Alfreda Avenue, Hullbridge, HOCKLEY, ESSEX, SS5 6LT.
MURRAY, Mr. Steven Michael, MMath ACA *2006;* 9 Addiscombe Court Road, CROYDON, CR0 6TT.
MURRAY, Mr. Thomas Anthony, ACA *1993;* 42 Albany Road West Bergholt, COLCHESTER, CO6 3LD.
MURRAY, Mr. Thomas Hugh, BSc ACA *2010;* 21 Playsteds Lane, Great Cambourne, CAMBRIDGE, CB23 6GA.
MURRAY, Miss. Victoria Ann, ACA *2008;* 8 Greenhey, LYTHAM ST. ANNES, FY8 4HL.
MURRAY, Mrs. Victoria Jane, ACA *2009;* 121 Upper Weybourne Lane, FARNHAM, GU9 9DD.
MURRAY, Mr. Wayne Roger, FCA *1976;* Todden Coath Farm, Paul, PENZANCE, CORNWALL, TR19 6UQ.
MURRAY, Mrs. Zowie Louise, ACA *2009;* 15 Holly Place, The Oaks, RANGIORA 7400, CANTERBURY REGION, NEW ZEALAND.
MURRAY-BROWN, Mr. James Ian, BSc FCA *1992;* Blair Hullichan Cottage, Aberfoyle, STIRLING, FK8 3TN.
MURRAY-BROWN, Mr. Timothy David, BSc ACA *1994;* 40 Glenavon Park, BRISTOL, BS9 1RP.
•MURRAY-WILLIAMS, Mr. Simon, BA FCA *1986;* (Tax Fac), Harold Smith, Unit 32, Llys Edmund Prys, St. Asaph Business Park, ST. ASAPH, LL17 0JA.
MURRELL, Mr. Andrew John, BA ACA CF *1994;* 5 Wood Ride, Petts Wood, ORPINGTON, KENT, BR5 1PZ.
MURRELL, Mr. David Brian, FCA *1968;* Ashley Court, 20a Ashley Rise, WALTON-ON-THAMES, SURREY, KT12 1ND.
•MURRELL, Mr. John, FCA *1974;* John Murrell FCA, 8 Lawn Crescent, Thorpe End, NORWICH, NR13 5BP.
MURRELL, Mr. Mark John, BA ACA *2000;* 42 Garthwaite Crescent, Shenley Brook End, MILTON KEYNES, MK5 7AX.
MURRELL, Miss. Pamela Kathleen, BSc FCA *1980;* 19 Dovedale Road, LONDON, SE22 0NF.
MURRELL, Mr. Paul Thomas, BSc ACA *2010;* 105 Hatherley Court, Hatherley Grove, LONDON, W2 5RF.
MURRELL, Mr. Peter, MPhys ACA *2010;* 24 Stanley Avenue, BECKENHAM, KENT, BR3 6PX.
MURRELL, Mrs. Victoria Jane, MBA BSc FCA *1991;* 21 Eghams Wood Road, BEACONSFIELD, HP9 1JU.
MURRELLS, Mrs. Taryn Louise, BSc ACA *2008;* 5 Tall Trees, COLCHESTER, CO4 5DU.
MURREY, Mr. Ben, ACA *2008;* 17 Bellard Drive, Hoole, CHESTER, CH2 3JP.
MURRILL, Mr. Alex Joseph, ACA *2008;* 20 Mantilla Road, LONDON, SW17 8DT.
•MURRILLS, Mr. Stephen Andrew, FCA *1977;* Royce Peeling Green Limited, The Copper Room, Deva Centre, Trinity Way, MANCHESTER, M3 7BG.
MURRIN, Mr. Jonathan Charles, BA ACA *1995;* Land Securities Trillium Bastion House, 140 London Wall, LONDON, EC2Y 5DN.
•MURRIN, Mr. Patrick Joseph, FCA *1979;* Le Douit Farm, Rue Du Douit, Castel, GUERNSEY, GY5 7JX.
•MURRIN, Mr. Richard John, FCA *1975;* (Tax Fac), John Murrin FCA MIoD, 6 Church Street, PADSTOW, CORNWALL, PL28 8BG.
•MURSALEEN, Mr. Zia, BSc FCA *1981;* Zia Mursaleen, 53 Leatherhead Road, ASHTEAD, KT21 2TP.
MURSELL, Mr. Haydn Jonathan, BA ACA *1997;* 62 Fowlmere Road, Heydon, ROYSTON, HERTFORDSHIRE, SG8 8PU.
MURSELL, Mr. William Geoffrey, FCA *1968;* 1 Leuty Avenue, TORONTO M4E 2R2, ON, CANADA. (Life Member)
MURTAGH, Mr. David James, BA ACA *1990;* 11 Glebe Court, Melsonby, RICHMOND, DL10 5NU.
MURTAGH, Mr. Denis Michael, BA FCA *1976;* The Corner House, Winston Avenue, TADLEY, RG26 3SR.
•MURTAGH, Mrs. Lesley Ann Katie, BSc(Hons) ACA *2003;* (Tax Fac), John P. Murtagh & Co, 36 Arden Close, Balsall Common, COVENTRY, CV7 7NY.
•MURTAGH, Mr. Rory Damian, BSc(Hons) ACA *2003;* John P. Murtagh & Co, 36 Arden Close, Balsall Common, COVENTRY, CV7 7NY.
MURTAGH, Mr. Stephen Paul, ACA *1983;* 66 Robin Road, BURY, BL9 5QP.
MURTAZA, Mr. Javed, ACA CA(AUS) *2008;* 44 X Phase 3, Defence Housing Authority, LAHORE, PAKISTAN.
MURTHI, Mr. Satish Dakshina, BSc(Econ) ACA *1998;* 7 West Cedar Place SW, CALGARY T3H 5T9, AB, CANADA.
MURTLAND, Mr. James Campbell, BA ACA *2002;* D S Smith Plc Whitebrook Park, Lower Cookham Road, MAIDENHEAD, SL6 8XY.
•MURTLAND, Mr. John Campbell, FCA *1969;* Thomas Coombs & Son, Century House, 29 Clarendon Road, LEEDS, LS2 9PG.
MURTLAND, Mr. Matthew John, BA ACA *2002;* 1 Sandlewood Crescent, Meanwood Park, LEEDS, LS6 4RT.
MURTON, Mr. Andrew Charles, BA ACA *1982;* PO Box 5484, CHATSWOOD WEST, NSW 1515, AUSTRALIA.
•MURTON, Mr. Derek Brian, FCA *1964;* Derek Brian Murton, Baden-croft, Falmouth Avenue, NEWMARKET, SUFFOLK, CB8 0NB.
MURTON, Miss. Sophie Elizabeth, ACA *2007;* 6 Oysell Gardens, FAREHAM, HAMPSHIRE, PO16 8GB.
MURTY, Mr. Anthony Leslie, FCA *1957;* (Tax Fac), Finchampstead, Porters Hill, ST JAMES, BB24023, BARBADOS.
MURTY, Mr. William Peter, BA FCA *1977;* Burford, Heathside Park Road, WOKING, GU22 7JE.
MURUGASU, Mr. Kesvaran, BSc FCA *1985;* 10 Jalan 22/38, 46300 PETALING JAYA, Selangor, MALAYSIA.
MURUGASU, Ms. Leelawathy Dharmapalan, BA ACA CTA *1996;* 60 Glenthorne Road, Friern Barnet, LONDON, N11 3HJ.
•MURUGESAN, Mr. Ganesh Babu, ACA *2010;* GBM Accounting Services, 8 Bulstrode Avenue, HOUNSLOW, MIDDLESEX, TW3 3AB.
MURUGIAH, Mr. Arumugan Vairamuttu, FCA *1965;* Aaran Murray & Co, 22 Hazelwood Road, P.O. Box 1211, MORWELL, VIC 3840, AUSTRALIA. (Life Member)
MUSA, Mr. Muhammad Lukman, BA(Hons) ACA *2003;* No 16 Jalan Putra Mahkota 7/2H, Putra Heights, 47650 SUBANG, SELANGOR, MALAYSIA.
•MUSAAMIL, Mr. Ahmed Mohideen, ACA *2007;* Anderson Musaamil & Co, 101 Epsom Road, SUTTON, SURREY, SM3 9EY. See also Musaamil & Co
MUSAJI, Mrs. Aarwa, BSc ACA *2009;* with BAE Systems plc, B A E Systems, Farnborough Aerospace Centre, PO Box 87, York House, FARNBOROUGH HAMPSHIRE GU14 6YU.
MUSAJI, Mr. Salim Adamali, FCA *1974;* 410-215 Wynford Drive, TORONTO M3C 3P5, ON, CANADA.
•MUSANNIF, Mr. Djemal Yenal, BA FCA *1973;* 15 Sht. Fevzi Ozturk Sokak, Ortakoy, LEFKOSA MERSIN 10, TURKEY.
MUSARAVAKKAM, Mr. Sriram, ACA *2010;* PO Box 8597, Ghusais Area, Behind Grand Hotel, DUBAI, DXB, UNITED ARAB EMIRATES.
MUSCAT, Mr. Andrew, ACA *2005;* 13 Flock Mill Place, LONDON, SW18 4QJ.
MUSCAT, Mr. Bernard David, BSc ACA *2009;* National Audit Office, 157-197 Buckingham Palace Road, LONDON, SW1W 9SP.
•MUSCAT, Mr. Joseph Samuel, FCA *1983;* Muscat & Co, Kingswood Lodge, Kingswood Lane, WARLINGHAM, CR6 9AB.
MUSCATT, Mr. James, ACA *2008;* 5 Ennismore Court, NEWCASTLE UPON TYNE, NE12 9PF.
•MUSCHAMP, Mr. Michael, FCA *1975;* (Tax Fac), Titus Thorp & Ainsworth Limited, 132 Highfield Road, BLACKPOOL, FY4 2HH.
•MUSCHAMP, Mr. Richard Robert James, MA ACA *1997;* Deloitte LLP, 2 New Street Square, LONDON, EC4A 3BZ. See also Deloitte & Touche LLP
MUSCROFT, Mr. Brian David McArthur, LLB FCA *1990;* Carfield Castle, 119 Hadham Road, BISHOP'S STORTFORD, HERTFORDSHIRE, CM23 2QG.
MUSCROFT, Miss. Kathryn Louise Anderson, BA ACA *2007;* Flat 302 The Circle, Queen Elizabeth Street, LONDON, SE1 2JW.
MUSENDO, Mr. Brice, ACA *2008;* Flat7, Aspen Court, Norfolk Close, DARTFORD, DA1 5PD.
•MUSGRAVE, Mr. Christopher Francis, FCA *1965;* Eden Consultants Limited, 24 Cloth Fair, LONDON, EC1A 7JQ.
MUSGRAVE, Ms. Claire Jayne, BSocSc FCA *1998;* Marshall Wace Asset Management The Adelphi, 1-11 John Adam Street, LONDON, WC2N 6HT.
MUSGRAVE, Mr. Ian Crossley, FCA *1969;* Flat 89 Majestic Apartments, King Edward Road Onchan, ISLE OF MAN, IM3 2BE.
MUSGRAVE, Mr. John Paul, BSc ACA *1981;* 63 Manor Road, Dorridge, SOLIHULL, B93 8TT.
MUSGRAVE, Miss. Karen Denise, BA ACA *2000;* 29 Chichester Avenue, Atherton, MANCHESTER, M46 0QF.
MUSGRAVE, Miss. Kathryn Lorraine, BA ACA *2000;* 2 April Glen, Mayow Road, LONDON, SE23 2XP.
•MUSGRAVE, Mr. Peter Alan, FCA *1977;* with RSM Tenon Audit Limited, 66 Chiltern Street, LONDON, W1U 4JT.
MUSGRAVE, Mr. Robert, ACA *2008;* Flat 9 Ambassador Court, 30 Inglewood Road, LONDON, NW6 1RY.
MUSGRAVE, Mrs. Sally Ann, FCA *1973;* Church Place, Church Street, Hadlow, TONBRIDGE, KENT, TN11 0DB.
MUSGROVE, Miss. Marie Elizabeth, BA FCA *1995;* (Tax Fac), 10 Balmoral Close, Westleigh Avenue, LONDON, SW15 6RP.
MUSGROVE, Mr. Neil Robert, BSc ACA *2004;* 65 Southcliffe Road, Carlton, NOTTINGHAM, NG4 1ES.
MUSHENS, Mr. Jeffrey Stephen Peter, BA ACA *1979;* Lorien, 18 Seven Ash Green, CHELMSFORD, CM1 7SE.
MUSHLIN, Mr. David Raphael, FCA *1963;* 18 Grove Road, PINNER, HA5 5HW. (Life Member)
MUSIKANT, Mr. Daniel, BSc FCA *1999;* Flat 6 Cranbourne Court, Briar Close, Finchley, LONDON, N2 0SD.
MUSK, Mr. Jeffrey Trevor, BA ACA *1988;* Eilert Sundts Gate 36, 0259 OSLO, NORWAY.
MUSK, Mr. John, BA(Hons) ACA *2002;* Nomura International Plc, 1 Angel Lane, LONDON, EC4R 3AB.
MUSK, Mr. Martin Sinclair, BA ACA *1998;* with PricewaterhouseCoopers LLP, 1 Embankment Place, LONDON, WC2N 6RH.
•MUSKER, Mr. David James, FCA *1971;* David J Musker, Tullich, Forest Lane, Hightown Hill, RINGWOOD, HAMPSHIRE BH24 3HF.
MUSKER, Miss. Gwen Angela, BSc ACA *2010;* 2 The Shrublands, Horsford, NORWICH, NR10 3EJ.
MUSKER, Mr. Ian Mark, BSc ACA *1995;* 14 Kings Hey Drive, Churchtown, SOUTHPORT, PR9 7JB.
•MUSKER, Mr. Raymond, FCA *1991;* Musker & Garrett Limited, Edward House, North Mersey Business Centre, Woodward Road, Knowsley Industrial Park, LIVERPOOL L33 7UY.
MUSKETT, Mr. Brian David, FCA *1959;* 11 The Meadway, Cuffley, POTTERS BAR, EN6 4ET. (Life Member)
•MUSKETT, Mr. Michael James, FCA *1977;* (Tax Fac), PKF (UK) LLP, East Coast House, Galahad Road, Beacon Park, Gorleston, GREAT YARMOUTH NORFOLK NR31 7RU.
MUSKETT, Mr. Rodney Charles, BSc FCA *1994;* Golitha, Station Hill, Chudleigh, NEWTON ABBOT, DEVON, TQ13 0EE.
•MUSKETT, Mr. Stuart, BA ACA *1996;* Grant Thornton UK LLP, 4 Hardman Square, Spinningfields, MANCHESTER, M3 3EB. See also Grant Thornton LLP
MUSKIN, Miss. Julie, BSc ACA *2004;* W Brindley Garages Ltd, 55 Penn Road, WOLVERHAMPTON, WV2 4WW.
MUSOKE, Mrs. Samantha, MA BA(Hons) ACA *2001;* 14 York Terrace, Kololo, PO Box 7681, KAMPALA, UGANDA.
MUSPRATT, Mr. Graham Edmund, FCA *1965;* 62 Quai Boissy D'Anglais, 78380 BOUGIVAL, FRANCE. (Life Member)
•MUSPRATT, Mr. Iain David, FCA *1966;* Iain D. Muspratt, Backwater House, 50 Common Lane, Hemingford Abbots, HUNTINGDON, PE28 9AW.
MUSPRATT, Miss. Lynn, BA ACA *2002;* Flat 10, Rathnew Court, 5 Meath Crescent, LONDON, E2 0QG.
MUSRY, Mr. Alan Philip David, BSc ACA *1989;* M & N Textiles Ltd, Wrengate House, 221 Palatine Road, MANCHESTER, M20 2EE.
MUSSELLE, Mr. Christopher Paul, ACA *1981;* Artisan (UK) Plc, Vantage House, Vantage Park, Washingley Road, HUNTINGDON, CAMBRIDGESHIRE PE29 6SR.
MUSSELLWHITE, Mr. Jonathan, BSc ACA *1994;* 29 Christchurch Hill, LONDON, NW3 1LA.
MUSSELWHITE, Mrs. Madeleine Suzanne, BA(Hons) ACA *2001;* 2 Richards Way, SALISBURY, SP2 8NT.
MUSSELWHITE, Miss. Sarajayne, BSc FCA *1999;* Perry Farm, La Rue Du Maistre, St. Mary, JERSEY, JE3 3EL.
MUSSEN, Mrs. Helen, BA ACA *2004;* 1 Dukes Place, 19 Watford Road Croxley Green, RICKMANSWORTH, HERTFORDSHIRE, WD3 3DP.
MUSSEN, Mr. Rupert James, MEng ACA *1999;* 1 Dukes Place, 19 Watford Road, Croxley Green, RICKMANSWORTH, HERTFORDSHIRE, WD3 3DP.
MUSSENDEN, Mrs. Sarah Elizabeth, BSc ACA *1995;* British Airways Plc, Waterside, PO Box 365, Harmondsworth, WEST DRAYTON, MIDDLESEX UB7 0GB.
MUSSETT, Miss. Polly Joanna, BA ACA *2009;* Flat 11 Austen House, 81 North Walls, WINCHESTER, SO23 8DA.
MUSSON, Mr. Alexander Hugh, BA ACA *1999;* Riverhill Partners LLP Amadeus House, Floral Street, LONDON, WC2e 9DP.
MUSSON, Mr. Christopher William, FCA *1969;* 2 Hill View, STRATFORD-UPON-AVON, CV37 9AY.
MUSSON, Mr. Dean Andrew, MPhil BSc FCA *1996;* 24 Bradford Road, CORSHAM, WILTSHIRE, SN13 0QR.
MUSSON, Mr. Glenn Konrad, BSc FCA *1991;* 18 Evelegh Road, PORTSMOUTH, PO6 1DL.
MUSSON, Mr. Richard William, MA FCA *1978;* 1 The Borough, Yealmpton, PLYMOUTH, PL8 2LR.
MUSSON, Mr. Roger Dixon, MA FCA *1967;* Hollowfield, Littleton, GUILDFORD, SURREY, GU3 1HN.
MUSSON, Mr. Roger Geoffrey, BCom FCA *1973;* 5 The Dentons, EASTBOURNE, EAST SUSSEX, BN20 7SW.
MUSSON, Mr. William, ACA *2011;* Flat 5, Salisbury House, Kersteman Road, BRISTOL, BS6 7BY.
•MUSTAFA, Mr. Erol, MA ACA *1994;* Ernst & Young LLP, 1 More London Place, LONDON, SE1 2AF. See also Ernst & Young Europe LLP
•MUSTAFA, Mr. Guner, BA FCA *1985;* Guner Associates Ltd, 9 Beaumont Gate, Shenley Hill, RADLETT, HERTFORDSHIRE, WD7 7AR. See also Guner Wolfson Ltd
•MUSTAFA, Mr. Rashed, BCom ACA *1991;* RM Accountants, 1 Slowmans Close, Park Street, ST. ALBANS, HERTFORDSHIRE, AL2 2DJ.
MUSTAFA, Miss. Sarita, BSc ACA *2011;* Second Floor Flat, 46 Belsize Square, LONDON, NW3 4HN.
MUSTAFA, Mr. Tasnim, ACA *2010;* 35 Ashburton Road, RUISLIP, HA4 6AA.

MUSTAFFA, Mr. Muhammad Ramizu, BSc ACA *2004;* KLCC Property Holdings Berhad, Level 4 & City Point, Kompleks Dayabumi, Jalan Sultan Hishamuddin, 50050 KUALA LUMPUR, FEDERAL TERRITORY MALAYSIA.
MUSTOE, Mrs. Stephanie Maria, BSc(Hons) ACA DChA *2001;* with PricewaterhouseCoopers LLP, 31 Great George Street, BRISTOL, BS1 5QD.
MUSTOE, Mr. Stephen Thomas, BSc FCA *1974;* 18 Daylesford Avenue, Putney, LONDON, SW15 5QR.
MUSTON, Mr. Michael Edward, FCA *1974;* UNITEX, 23 Blvd Albert 1er, MC98000 MONACO, MONACO.
MUTANGADURA, Ms. Gillian, ACA *2010;* B D O Novus Ltd, PO Box 180, GUERNSEY, GY1 3LL.
MUTCH, Mr. Alastair James Fletcher, FCA *1963;* Draw Well, Lyth, KENDAL, CUMBRIA, LA8 8DF.
MUTCH, Mr. Brian Noel, FCA *1959;* P.O. Box 40717, CLEVELAND, 2022, SOUTH AFRICA. (Life Member)
MUTCH, Mr. Chris, BA(Hons) ACA *2001;* Pricewaterhousecoopers, 1 Embankment Place, LONDON, WC2N 6RH.
MUTCH, Miss. Susan Jane, MA(Hons) ACA ARe *2002;* 2 Far Meadow Lane, WIRRAL, MERSEYSIDE, CH61 4YU.
MUTETE, Mr. Tichaona Cleopas, ACA *2007;* Flat 1, 7 Nelson Street St. Helier, JERSEY, JE2 4TL.
MUTHALAGAPPAN, Mrs. Kannahi Soundaram, BSc FCA *1995;* 22 Stoneleigh Road, COVENTRY, CV4 7AD.
•MUTHALAGAPPAN, Mr. Kumar Periakaruppan, OBE BSc FCA *1987;* 22 Stoneleigh Road, COVENTRY, CV4 7AD. See also KM Business Advisors Limited
MUTHU, Mr. Joseph, FCA *1988;* rue Philippe-Plantamour 42, 1201 GENEVA, SWITZERLAND.
MUTHUMALA, Miss. Aruni Varusha, MSc ACA *2004;* House of Commons, 7 Millbank, LONDON, SW1P 3JA.
MUTI, Mrs. Clare, BA ACA *1989;* 25 Woburn Drive, Hale, ALTRINCHAM, WA15 8NA.
MUTKIN, Mr. Henry Gerald, MA FCA *1961;* 89 Platts Lane, LONDON, NW3 7NH. (Life Member)
•MUTKIN, Mr. Malcolm, FCA *1972;* (Tax Fac), 13 The Grove, RADLETT, WD7 7NF.
•MUTLOW, Mr. Roy Wilton, FCA *1969;* (Tax Fac), Wilton Mutlow & Co, 3 College Yard, Lower Dagnall Street, ST. ALBANS, HERTFORDSHIRE, AL3 4PA.
MUTONGO, Mr. Rusunungukо, ACA CA(SA) *2011;* 4 Bordeaux Court, Rocques Barrees Road, Vale, GUERNSEY, GY3 5LU.
MUTTER, Mr. Christopher George, BA ACA *1987;* (Tax Fac), Hill Top, Hempstead Road, Bovingdon, HEMEL HEMPSTEAD, HERTFORDSHIRE, HP3 0DS.
MUTTITT, Mr. Paul, FCA *1971;* Piccolo, Dunburgh Road, Geldeston, BECCLES, SUFFOLK, NR34 0LL. (Life Member)
MUTTON, Mr. Colin Frank, ACA *1979;* 2118 Wilshire Blvd. #920, SANTA MONICA, CA 90403-5784, UNITED STATES.
•MUTTON, Mrs. Julie Amanda, MA FCA *1992;* Smith & Williamson Ltd, Imperial House, 18-21 Kings Park Road, SOUTHAMPTON, HAMPSHIRE, SO15 2AT. See also Nexia Audit Limited
MUTTON, Mr. Philip Alexander, BA FCA *1973;* 5 Braybon Avenue, BRIGHTON, BN1 8EA.
MUTUCUMARANA, Mr. Robert, BA ACA *2007;* 46 Aland Court, Finland Street, LONDON, SE16 7LA.
MUTVALLI, Mrs. Zainab, ACA *2011;* Mazars LLP London, Tower Bridge House, St. Katharines Way, LONDON, E1W 1DD.
MUXWORTHY, Mr. David John, BA ACA *1992;* 24 Robinswood Close, PENARTH, SOUTH GLAMORGAN, CF64 3JG.
•MUXWORTHY, Mr. Peter Rice, FCA *1963;* (Tax Fac), with Bevan & Buckland, Langdon House, Langdon Road, SA1 Swansea Waterfront, SWANSEA, SA1 8QY.
MUYAMBO, Mr. Bray Tawanda, ACA *2004;* 150 The Keep, KINGSTON UPON THAMES, KT2 5UF.
MUYEED, Mr. Suleman Abdul, LLB(Hons) ACA *2011;* 203 New Century House, 8 Jude Street, LONDON, E16 1FG.
MUZANENHAMO, Mr. Alan Tonderai, ACA CA(SA) *2009;* 5 Radstone Court, WOKING, GU22 7NB.
MUZIKA, Mr. Francis Charles, ACA *1982;* 2 Beeches Park, BEACONSFIELD, HP9 1PH.
MUZONZINI, Mr. Christopher, ACA CA(SA) *2011;* 8 Trinity Court, Kingswood, BRISTOL, BS15 4FG.
MUZZLEWHITE, Mr. David John, FCA *1968;* 6 Cumberland Road, Heatherside, CAMBERLEY, GU15 1AG.
MUZZLEWHITE, Mr. Nicholas Peter, BA ACA *2005;* with PricewaterhouseCoopers LLP, 31 Great George Street, BRISTOL, BS1 5QD.
MWANZA, Mr. Cephas, BEng ACA *2005;* 109 Kingshill Avenue, WORCESTER PARK, SURREY, KT4 8BZ.
MWENYA, Mr. Makungu, BSc ACA *2003;* 126 Greenhaven Drive, Woolwich Thamesmead, LONDON, SE28 8FT.
MYALL, Mr. Jonathan, BA ACA *1982;* 35 Jacksons Lane, BILLERICAY, CM11 1AH.
•MYALL-SCHOFIELD, Miss. Emma Louise, BSc ACA *1998;* PricewaterhouseCoopers LLP, 300 Madison Avenue, NEW YORK, NY 10017, UNITED STATES. See also PricewaterhouseCoopers
MYANGAR, Mr. Sanjay, BSc(Hons) ACA *2001;* 32 Shirley Road, COVENTRY, CV2 2EN.
MYANGER, Mr. Yogesh Dalsukh, ACA *1992;* Flat B2 Skyline Apartments, 43 Romain Rolland Street, PONDICHERRY 605001, INDIA.
MYATT, Mrs. Amanda Louise, BA ACA DipM *2001;* 8 Northam Close, Lower Earley, READING, RG6 3AJ.
MYATT, Mr. Michael David, FCA *1971;* 2 Bishops Walk, Cricklade Street, CIRENCESTER, GLOUCESTERSHIRE, GL7 1JH.
•MYATT, Miss. Nicola Dora, BSc FCA *1985;* (Tax Fac), N D Myatt & Co, 194 Coombe Lane, LONDON, SW20 0QT.
MYATT, Mr. Richard Geoffrey, BSc ACA *1997;* 473 Streetsbrook Road, SOLIHULL, B91 1LA.
MYCHAJLUK, Mrs. Clare Louise, BCom ACA *1993;* 5 Montsford Close, Knowle, SOLIHULL, B93 9QT.
MYCHAJLUK, Mr. Michael, BA ACA *1993;* 5 Montsford Close, Knowle, SOLIHULL, B93 9QT.
MYCHALKIW, Mr. Petro, BA ACA *1994;* 6 Haddon Close, WEYBRIDGE, KT13 9ND.
•MYCOCK, Mr. Peter David, FCA *1980;* Mycock Associates Limited, 129 Middleton Boulvard, Wollaton Park, NOTTINGHAM, NG8 1FW.
MYDDELTON, Mr. Alexander James, BSc FCA *1974;* 2 South Close, LONDON, N6 5UQ. (Life Member)
MYDDELTON, Mr. David Roderic, FCA *1961;* 20 Nightingale Lodge, Admiral Walk, LONDON, W9 3TW. (Life Member)
MYDDLETON, Mr. Roger John, BCom ACA *2003;* 28 Anstey Road, LONDON, SE15 4JY.
•MYEARS, Mr. Laurence Charnock, FCA *1975;* Laurence Myears, 6 Beechcroft Road, Longlevens, GLOUCESTER, GL2 9HF.
MYERS, Mr. Alan, BA ACA *1978;* 19 German Mills Road, THORNHILL L3T 4H4, ON, CANADA.
•MYERS, Mr. Allan Paul Michael, FCA *1971;* Maurice Apple, 3rd Floor, Marlborough House, 179-189 Finchley Road, LONDON, NW3 6LB. See also Maco Administration Ltd
•MYERS, Mr. Andrew Barry, BSc(Hons) *2001;* A B M Ventures Ltd, 175 High Street, TONBRIDGE, KENT, TN9 1BX. See also Abacus Accountancy Partners Ltd
MYERS, Mr. Andrew Leon, BA(Econ) ACA *1999;* 12 Haslemere Gardens, LONDON, N3 3EA.
MYERS, Mr. Andrew William, BEng ACA *1991;* McLaren Racing Ltd, McLaren Technology Centre, Chertsey Road, WOKING, SURREY, GU21 4YH.
MYERS, Mr. Anthony Charles Arthur, FCA *1960;* 11 Forest Park, Maresfield, UCKFIELD, EAST SUSSEX, TN22 2NA. (Life Member)
•MYERS, Mr. Anthony Michael, FCA *1953;* Anthony M. Myers & Co, 28 West End Avenue, PINNER, MIDDLESEX, HA5 1BJ.
MYERS, Mr. Bernard Ian, BSc FCA *1968;* Rothschilds Continuation Ltd, New Court, St Swithin's Lane, LONDON, EC4P 4DU.
MYERS, Mr. Brian, FCA *1955;* 7 Cotterdale Holt, Collingham, WETHERBY, LS22 5LS. (Life Member)
MYERS, Mr. Christopher Colin, BSc ACA *1999;* Maison le Coin, Le Jardin de la Fontaine, La Grande Route de St. Martin, St. Saviour, JERSEY, JE2 7JD.
MYERS, Miss. Collette Margaret, BSc ACA *1998;* 28 Vickery Street, Bentleigh, MELBOURNE, VIC 3204, AUSTRALIA.
•MYERS, Mr. Daniel Barry, FCA *1984;* (Tax Fac), Cohen Arnold, New Burlington House, 1075 Finchley Road, Temple Fortune, LONDON, NW11 0PU. See also Cohen Arnold & Co
MYERS, Mr. David John, FCA *1971;* 1 Henry Lewis Close, Whimple, EXETER, EX5 2UU. (Life Member)
MYERS, Miss. Emma, ACA *2011;* 13 Kenmore Road, MANCHESTER, M22 4AE.
MYERS, Mr. Frank Hanson William, FCA *1950;* P.O. Box 72473, LYNNWOOD RIDGE, 0040, SOUTH AFRICA. (Life Member)
MYERS, Mr. Gary Evan, BA ACA *1990;* Comet Group Plc, George Street, HULL, HU1 3AU.
•MYERS, Mr. Gerald Joseph, FCA *1955;* G J Myers FCA, 22 Bracknell Gardens, LONDON, NW3 7ED.
MYERS, Miss. Gordaine Elizabeth, BSc ACA *1992;* 13201 Edmonton Drive, MIDLOTHIAN, VA 23113, UNITED STATES.
MYERS, Mr. Graham Lloyd, LLB ACA *1990;* (Tax Fac), 7 Swan Close, Deighton, YORK, YO19 6HY.
MYERS, Miss. Helen Louise, BA(Hons) ACA *2009;* 13 Boston Road, HENLEY-ON-THAMES, OXFORDSHIRE, RG9 1DY.
MYERS, Mr. Howard Laurie Platt, BSc FCA *1991;* 47 Brynland Avenue, BRISTOL, BS7 9DX.
MYERS, Mr. Ian Geoffrey, BSc ACA *1996;* 14 Langbaurgh Road, Hutton Rudby, YARM, CLEVELAND, TS15 0HL.
MYERS, Mr. John Alan, FCA *1971;* 8 Princess Street, Rawdon, LEEDS, LS19 6BS. (Life Member)
MYERS, Mr. John Robert, BSc ACA *1993;* Building G, BP International Ltd, Chertsey Road, SUNBURY-ON-THAMES, MIDDLESEX, TW16 7LN.
MYERS, Mrs. Judith Sandra, BSc FCA *1990;* 32 Firs Road, Over Hulton, BOLTON, BL5 1EZ.
MYERS, Mr. Karl, BA ACA *2002;* 303 Stockport Road, Timperley, ALTRINCHAM, CHESHIRE, WA15 7SP.
MYERS, Miss. Katie, BA ACA *2007;* 60 The Royal, Wilton Place, SALFORD, M3 6WP.
MYERS, Mr. Kenneth, FCA *1960;* Gwendraeth, 33 Hillcrest Drive, GATESHEAD, NE11 9QS. (Life Member)
•MYERS, Mr. Kevin, BSc ACA *1993;* (Tax Fac), Hardcastle Burton (Redbourn) Limited, Old School, The Common, Redbourn, ST. ALBANS, HERTFORDSHIRE AL3 7NG.
MYERS, Mr. Laurence, FCA *1960;* 31 Devonshire Place Mews, LONDON, W1G 6DB. (Life Member)
MYERS, Mr. Lawrence Alan, FCA *1970;* 12 Springfield Gardens, LONDON, NW9 0RS.
MYERS, Mr. Leigh, BA ACA *2006;* 3 Howe Close, Shenley, RADLETT, HERTFORDSHIRE, WD7 9JF.
•MYERS, Mr. Martin Andrew, FCA *1978;* (Tax Fac), Goldwyns (London) Limited, 13 David Mews, Porter Street, LONDON, W1U 6EQ. See also Goldwyns
MYERS, Mr. Neal Tracey, BA(Hons) ACA *2001;* 5 Burneham Close, East Bridgford, NOTTINGHAM, NG13 8NT.
MYERS, Mr. Neville Keith, FCA *1976;* 81 Orchard Road, LYTHAM ST.ANNES, FY8 1PG.
MYERS, Mr. Nigel, MEng ACA *1992;* 2 St. James Grove, Hart, HARTLEPOOL, CLEVELAND, TS27 3BA.
MYERS, Mr. Peter Joseph, BCom ACA *1982;* PO Box 2936, KNYSNA, WESTERN CAPE PROVINCE, 6570, SOUTH AFRICA.
MYERS, Mr. Philip Charles, BA ACA *1999;* JP Morgan Chase, 168 Robinson Road, 18th Floor, Capital Tower, SINGAPORE 068912, SINGAPORE.
MYERS, Mr. Philip David, BSc ACA *1991;* 46A Park Road, Prestwich, MANCHESTER, M25 0FA.
MYERS, Mr. Richard John Herbert, BA FCA *1974;* 38 Kiln Lane, Lower Bourne, FARNHAM, GU10 3LU.
MYERS, Mr. Robert Arthur, MA FCA *1958;* The Old Rectory, Upton Lane, Seavington, St.Michael, ILMINSTER, SOMERSET TA19 0PZ. (Life Member)
MYERS, Mr. Robert Nathaniel, BSc FCA *1973;* 19 Hampstead Way, LONDON, NW11 7JE.
MYERS, Mr. Robert William Clement, ACA *2008;* 19 Langton Drive, HORNCASTLE, LINCOLNSHIRE, LN9 5AJ.
MYERS, Mr. Robin David, BA(Hons) ACA *2010;* 7 Duxbury Gardens, CHORLEY, LANCASHIRE, PR7 3JZ.
•MYERS, Mr. Rodney Saul, FCA *1983;* (Tax Fac), M. Epstein & Co, 250 Middleton Road, Crumpsall, MANCHESTER, M8 4WA.
MYERS, Mr. Roger, FCA *1971;* GR 5112, Grande Riviere, GROS ISLET, SAINT LUCIA.
MYERS, Mrs. Sharon, BSc ACA *1992;* RL Davison & Co LTD, 99 Sunnyfield, Mill Hill, LONDON, NW7 4RE.
MYERS, Mr. Simon, MSc ACA *1978;* West London Synagogue of British Jews, 33 Seymour Place, LONDON, W1H 5AU.
MYERS, Mr. Val John, FCA *1971;* 33 Ennerdale Avenue, STANMORE, HA7 2LB.
MYERS, Mr. Wayne Hilton, BA ACA *1989;* 26 Milford Gardens, EDGWARE, MIDDLESEX, HA8 6EY.
•MYERS, Mr. William Berwyn, FCA *1985;* Accware Limited, 32 Firs Road, BOLTON, BL5 1EZ.
MYERSCOUGH, Mrs. Alison Mary, BSc FCA *1977;* 38 Southway, Carshalton Beeches, CARSHALTON, SM5 4HW.
MYERSCOUGH, Mrs. Helen Jane, BSc ACA *1990;* (Tax Fac), Crosstrees, Broom Heath, WOODBRIDGE, IP12 4DL.
MYERSCOUGH, Miss. Laura Ann, MChem ACA *2005;* Toll Holdings Ltd, Level 7 380 Kilda Road, MELBOURNE, VIC 3004, AUSTRALIA.
MYERSCOUGH, Mr. Martin William, BSc ACA ATII *1991;* Cross Trees, Broomheath, WOODBRIDGE, IP12 4DL.
MYERSCOUGH, Mr. Tony Alexander, BA ACA *1993;* TDP Textiles Ltd, TDP House, Rawdon Road, Moira, SWADLINCOTE, DE12 6DT.
MYERSON, Mr. David James, BSocSc ACA *2002;* 9 The Crest, LONDON, NW4 2HN.
•MYERSON, Mr. Richard Godfrey, FCA *1970;* Alexander Myerson & Co, Alexander House, 61 Rodney Street, LIVERPOOL, L1 9ER.
MYHILL, Mr. David Frank, FCA *1970;* 1150 S. Peak View Drive, CASTLE ROCK, CO 80109-9525, UNITED STATES.
MYLAND, Mr. Ronald Edward Clayton, FCA *1972;* Wold Aston, Willingham Road, MARKET RASEN, LINCOLNSHIRE, LN8 3RE.
MYLCHREEST, Ms. Graihagh, MSc ACA *1989;* Narradale, Ballamenagh Road, Baldrine, ISLE OF MAN, IM4 6AL.
MYLCHREEST, Mr. Simon, BSc ACA *1998;* 141 Fishguard Way, LONDON, E16 2RU.
MYLES, Mrs. Catherine, BA ACA *1997;* 152 Pannal Ash Road, HARROGATE, NORTH YORKSHIRE, HG2 9AJ.
MYLES, Miss. Helen Elizabeth, BSc ACA *2004;* 12 Windermere Avenue, ASHBY-DE-LA-ZOUCH, LEICESTERSHIRE, LE65 1FA.
MYLES, Mr. Howard Vivian Peter, BA FCA *1978;* Chalet Carline, Residence Les Tremplins du Praz, 73120 LE PRAZ DE ST BON, FRANCE.
MYLES, Mr. Keith Alexander Frederick Newton, FCA *1968;* Mere End Farmhouse, Tootle Lane, Rufford, ORMSKIRK, LANCASHIRE, L40 1TJ.
MYLONAS, Mr. Michael Andrea, BSc(Econ) FCA *1996;* Nomura International Plc, 1 Angel Lane, LONDON, EC4R 3AB.
MYLONAS, Mr. Michalis, BA ACA *2006;* 6 Gregori Afxentiou, Pera Chorio Nisou, 2572 NICOSIA, CYPRUS.
MYLROI, Miss. Janice Elizabeth, BA ACA *1982;* 1 Moor Place, Gosforth, NEWCASTLE UPON TYNE, NE3 4AL.
MYLVAGANAM, Mr. Niranjan, BSc ACA *2010;* Plot 60038/10, Block 7, GABORONE, BOTSWANA.
MYLVAGANAM, Mr. Sasitharan, ACA *1983;* 9 Ashwell Avenue, CAMBERLEY, GU15 2AR.
MYNARD, Mr. Ryan James, BSc ACA *2006;* 13 Cook Close, Walton Park, MILTON KEYNES, MK7 7JA.
MYNORS, Mr. Robert David Baskerville, MA FCA *1966;* Parsley Cottage, Little Bognor, Fittleworth, PULBOROUGH, WEST SUSSEX, RH20 1JT.
MYNOTT, Mrs. Carol, BSc ACA *1999;* with PricewaterhouseCoopers LLP, Pricewaterhousecoopers, 12 Plumtree Court, LONDON, EC4A 4HT.
MYNOTT, Mr. Sean, BSc ACA *2003;* Ground Floor Flat, 28 Forthbridge Road, LONDON, SW11 5NY.
•MYNOTT, Mr. Timothy James, MA FCA *1980;* Mynotts Ltd, Long Cottage, Homington Road, Coombe Bissett, SALISBURY, SP5 4LR.
MYRING, Miss. Catherine Helen, BA ACA *1997;* 417 South 13th Street, PHILADELPHIA, PA 19147-1142, UNITED STATES.
MYRING, Mr. Henry William, BA(Hons) ACA *2003;* 5 Staunton Road, Headington, OXFORD, OX3 7TJ.
MYRONAKI-LAZET, Ms. Stella, MSc BSc ACA *2002;* Biesboschstraat 5 - II, 1078 MK AMSTERDAM, NETHERLANDS.
MYSLIWIEC, Ms. Magdalena Anna, ACA *2011;* Flat 2, 75 Hindes Road, HARROW, MIDDLESEX, HA1 1SQ.
MYSON, Mr. Ian Derek, MA MCMI ACA PGCE CMgr *1987;* Chartered Management Institute, Management House, Cottingham Road, CORBY, NORTHAMPTONSHIRE, NN17 1TT.
MYSZKA, Miss. Catherine Helena, BA(Hons) ACA *2006;* Travelex Worldwide House, Thorpe Wood, PETERBOROUGH, PE3 6SB.
MYTTON, Miss. Abigail, BA ACA *2006;* 18 Sunderland Grove, Leavesden, WATFORD, WD25 7GL.
•NABARRO, Mr. Anthony Keith, FCA *1976;* (Tax Fac), Nabarro Poole, 31 Church Road, Northenden, MANCHESTER, M22 4NN. See also Nabarro & Co
NABARRO, Mrs. Linda Susan, FCA *1974;* 29 Cumberland Road, Brooklands, SALE, CHESHIRE, M33 3EW.
•NABARRO, Mr. Ralph, FCA *1972;* Newhaven Corporate Services L.imited, PO Box 362, ROAD TOWN, TORTOLA ISLAND, VG1110, VIRGIN ISLANDS (BRITISH).
NABAVI, Mr. Paul Iraj, BA ACA *1986;* New House Farm, Cottenden Road, Stonegate, WADHURST, TN5 7DX.

NABI, Mr. Abdul Majid, BA FCA *1987;* 24 Calton Road, New Barnet, BARNET, EN5 1BY.
NABI, Mr. Shamshad, FCA MBA *1966;* 30 B4th South Street, Phase-2, Defence Housing Authority, KARACHI, PAKISTAN. (Life Member)
NABULSI, Mr. Karim, BSc ACA *1994;* Jabal Amman 5th Circle, Zahran Street, Building No 190, P.O.Box 248, AMMAN, 11118 JORDAN.
NACOUZI, Mr. Pavlos, BSc ACA *1993;* 2 Romanou Street, Tlais Tower, 1st Floor, CY1070 NICOSIA, CYPRUS.
NACOUZI, Mr. Petros, LLB ACA *1996;* CORNER OF 69 MAKARIOA AVE & 2 ROMANOS STR TLAIS TOWER FIRST FLOOR, CY 1070 NICOSIA, CYPRUS.
NADARAJAH, Mrs. Anju, BSc ACA *2005;* 3 Walton Avenue, SUTTON, SURREY, SM3 9UA.
NADARAJAH, Mr. Sivasathiasilan, FCA *1978;* 9A CREEWOOD STREET, CONCORD, NSW 2137, AUSTRALIA.
NADEEM, Mr. Kashif, ACA FCCA *2010;* Regional Finance & Control, Gulf Countries & South Africa, 3rd Floor Harbour Tower (West), Bahrain Financial Harbour Bahrain, P. O. Box 5253., MANAMA BAHRAIN.
NADEN, Mr. Garrie Charles, BA ACA *1988;* 105 Clifton Road, Ruddington, NOTTINGHAM, NG11 6DA.
NADESAN, Mr. Visva, MPhil ACA *1990;* Evergreens, 15 Hall Road, WALLINGTON, SM6 0RT.
NADIN, Mr. John, BA FCA *2000;* 3 Quantock Mews, LONDON, SE15 4RG.
NADIN, Mr. Peter William Ralph, BCom FCA *1954;* Berry Ring House, Billington, STAFFORD, ST18 9DH. (Life Member)
NADIN, Mr. Richard Embrey, FCA *1968;* Beech House, Bowers, Standon, STAFFORD, ST21 6RD.
NADJM-TEHRANI, Miss. Soussan, BSc ACA *1984;* 8617 Aqueduct Road, POTOMAC, MD 20854, UNITED STATES.
NAECK, Mr. Bhavish, BSc FCA *1996;* 3A Telfair Avenue, QUATRE-BORNES, MAURITIUS.
NAEEM, Miss. Amna, BSc(Econ) ACA *2001;* 14 Deans Close, CROYDON, CR0 5PU.
NAEEM, Mr. Mian Muhammad Farooq, ACA FCCA *2011;* 15k Hannards Way, ILFORD, ESSEX, IG6 3TB.
•**NAFTALIN, Miss. Ruth Marion, BSc FCA DChA** *1973;* Ruth Naftalin, 14 Park Crescent, LONDON, N3 2NJ.
NAGAR, Miss. Mala, BSc ACA *2009;* 25 Asquith Boulevard, LEICESTER, LE2 6FD.
NAGARAJ, Mr. Karthikaya Nirvana Mallikarjun, BA(Hons) ACA *2010;* 309 The Mill, South Hall Street, SALFORD, M5 4JH.
NAGARAJAH, Mr. Chandra Nivasa, BSc FCA *1983;* 14-15 Columbus Circle, WESTMOORINGS, TRINIDAD AND TOBAGO.
NAGARAJAH, Mr. Parthiban, BSc(Hons) ACA *2011;* 102 Bramley Road, Southgate, LONDON, N14 4HS.
•**NAGARAJAH, Mr. Ponnampalam Sinniah, BSc FCA** *1975;* P.S. Nagarajah, 64 Oakington Avenue, WEMBLEY, MIDDLESEX, HA9 8HZ.
NAGARETNAM, Mr. Selvarajah, FCA *1983;* 16Lynden Street, CAMBERWELL, VIC 3124, AUSTRALIA.
•**NAGARI, Mr. Francesco, ACA** *2011;* Deloitte LLP, Hill House, 1 Little New Street, LONDON, EC4A 3TR. See also Deloitte & Touche LLP
•**NAGEL, Mr. Frank Uwe, BA ACA** *1998;* KPMG Deutsche Treuhand-Gesellschaft, Wirtschaftsprüfungsgesellschaft, Ganghoferstrasse 29, 80339 MUNICH, GERMANY.
NAGELE, Mr. Christian Edward, BA ACA *1999;* Christmas Cottage, Chapel Hill, Speen, PRINCES RISBOROUGH, HP27 0SP.
•**NAGELE, Mrs. Melanie Joy Emma, BA ACA** *2003;* (Tax Fac), Melanie Nagele ACA, Christmas Cottage, Chapel Hill, Speen, PRINCES RISBOROUGH, BUCKINGHAMSHIRE HP27 0SP.
NAGI, Mr. Mohammad Asim, BSc ACA *2008;* 259 M Model Town Extension, LAHORE, PAKISTAN.
NAGJI, Mr. Dhiran, MSc BSc(Hons) ACA *2011;* 9 Linden Way, PURLEY, SURREY, CR8 3PH.
NAGJI, Mr. Vipul, MSc BSc ACA *2002;* Deepa & Vipul, End of 12th Main Shubh Enclave, Haralur Road, BANGALORE 560102, INDIA.
NAGLE, Mr. Alasdair Gordon, MA ACA *1990;* 1301, AIA Central, 1 Connaught Road Central, CENTRAL, HONG KONG SAR.
NAGLE, Mr. John, BA ACA *1979;* Lower Grange, Newington, WALLINGFORD, OXFORDSHIRE, OX10 7AA.
NAGLE, Mr. John Bernard, BSc ACA *1988;* 14 Downview Park West, BELFAST, BT15 5HN.
NAGLE, Mr. Michael, FCA ATII *1967;* L'Etac, 2 Upland Road, St. Peter Port, GUERNSEY, GY1 1UJ. (Life Member)
NAGLE, Mr. Richard James, FCA *1966;* Derrybrook, 4 Greenfields, STANSTED, ESSEX, CM24 8AH. (Life Member)
•**NAGLER, Mr. Stuart Martin, FCA** *1968;* with Nagler Simmons, 5 Beaumont Gate, Shenley Hill, RADLETT, HERTFORDSHIRE, WD7 7AR.
NAGLER, Mr. Tristan Howard, BA(Hons) ACA *2001;* 19 Egerton Gardens, LONDON, NW4 4BB.
NAGLIK, Mr. Adam Stanislaw, BA ACA *1992;* 12 Elitis Maya, Valencia, Sungai Buloh, 47000 KUALA LUMPUR, FEDERAL TERRITORY, MALAYSIA.
NAGPAL, Miss. Kamaljit Kaur, MPhil(Cantab) BSc(Hons) ACA *2011;* 45 Avenue Road, SOUTHALL, MIDDLESEX, UB1 3BW.
NAGRA, Mr. Harinderjit Singh, BSc FCA *1984;* 32 Ashridge Gardens, LONDON, N13 4LA.
NAGRA, Miss. Kiranjit, ACA *2011;* 25 Manor Road, Thurmaston, LEICESTER, LE4 8AH.
•**NAGRA, Mr. Kulwarn Singh, BSc FCA** *1987;* Rawlinson & Hunter, Lower Mill, Kingston Road, Ewell, EPSOM, KT17 2AE.
NAGRA, Mrs. Maninderjit, BSc ACA *2005;* 22 Gallys Road, WINDSOR, SL4 5QY.
NAGRA, Mr. Satinder Singh, LLB ACA GradDipMgmt *1997;* 5 Popov Avenue, Newington, SYDNEY, NSW 2127, AUSTRALIA.
•**NAGUS, Mr. Clive Lawrence, FCA** *1974;* King Nagus Bakerman, KNB House, 7 Rodney Street, LIVERPOOL, L1 9HZ.
NAGY, Mr. Timothy John, BSc ACA *1992;* 33 Narcissus Road, West Hampstead, LONDON, NW6 1TL.
NAHAL, Mr. Jatinder Singh, ACA *2010;* 90 Empress Avenue, ILFORD, ESSEX, IG1 3DF.
NAHAL, Miss. Rubinder, BA(Hons) ACA *2011;* 2 Bainbridge Road, SMETHWICK, WEST MIDLANDS, B66 4SY.
NAHON, Mr. Leon Rodolfo, FCA *1961;* Garden Cottage, Garden Road, LONDON, NW8 9PR.
NAHOUM, Mr. Isaac Elias, FCA *1962;* Rehov Haarazim 114, 99553 BET SHEMESH, ISRAEL. (Life Member)
NAHOUM, Mr. Moses Elias, FCA *1961;* 33 Woodlands, LONDON, NW11 9QJ. (Life Member)
NAI, Mr. Sebastian, ACA *2008;* 12 Ashlake Road, LONDON, SW16 2BB.
NAIDOO, Mr. Sasha, ACA *2010;* 71 Pursers Cross Road, LONDON, SW6 4QZ.
•**NAIDOO, Mr. Vassi, ACA CA(SA)** *2008;* Deloitte LLP, 2 New Street Square, LONDON, EC4A 3BZ. See also Deloitte & Touche LLP
•**NAIK, Mr. Hitendra Ramanlal, BA FCA** *1989;* (Tax Fac), Naik & Co, 66 Montpelier Rise, WEMBLEY, MIDDLESEX, HA9 8RQ.
NAIK, Mr. Nirav, BSc ACA *2010;* 40 Montpelier Rise, WEMBLEY, MIDDLESEX, HA9 8RQ.
NAIK, Mr. Ragesh, BA ACA *1992;* P O Box 33299, LUSAKA, ZAMBIA.
NAIK, Mr. Shaileshkumar Dhirubhai, BA ACA *1991;* 40 Montpelier Rise, WEMBLEY, HA9 8RQ.
•**NAIK, Mr. Suresh, BA ACA** *1987;* Thomas Neilson, 108 Catlins Lane, PINNER, MIDDLESEX, HA5 2BX.
NAILOR, Mr. Hans Peter, BCom FCA *1978;* 104 South Lane, Ash, ALDERSHOT, HAMPSHIRE, GU12 6NJ.
NAIMIAN, Miss. Leila, BA ACA *2005;* 57 Barnfield, Urmston, MANCHESTER, M41 9EW.
•**NAIR, Mr. Hari, FCA** *1976;* H Nair & Co, Flat 3 Cuckoos Nest, 60 Crawley Green Road, LUTON, LU2 0QW. See also H Nair FCA
•**NAIR, Mr. Raj, FCA** *1976;* Raj Nair, CRC Cabinet de Revision & Conseil SA, Pl. des Eaux-Vives 6, P O Box 3444, 1211 GENEVA, SWITZERLAND.
NAIR, Mr. Rajendran, FCA *1974;* 191 Cooriengah Heights Road, ENGADINE, NSW 2233, AUSTRALIA.
NAIR, Mrs. Suchitra, MSc ACA *2005;* Deloitte & Touche Hill House, 1 Little New Street, LONDON, EC4A 3TR.
NAIRN, Mr. Christopher Frank Spencer, MA FCA *1974;* Culligran, Struy, BEAULY, INVERNESS-SHIRE, IV4 7JX.
•**NAIRN, Mr. David Albert, FCA** *1978;* (Tax Fac), Rowlands, Rowlands House, Portobello Road, Birtley, CHESTER LE STREET, COUNTY DURHAM DH3 2RY. See also Rowlands Limited
NAIRN, Mr. John Michael, MA FCA *1979;* 5 Kayes Close, WEYMOUTH, DT4 9LX.
NAISH, Mr. Andrew William, FCA *1965;* 1 Beechcroft Close, Chandler's Ford, EASTLEIGH, SO53 2HU. (Life Member)
NAISH, Miss. Claudia Martha, BSc ACA *2006;* 15 Collins Street, LONDON, SE3 0UG.
NAISH, Mrs. Katharine Elizabeth, BEng ACA ATII *1995;* with PricewaterhouseCoopers LLP, 1 Embankment Place, LONDON, WC2N 6RH.
NAISH, Mr. Paul Gordon James, FCA *1974;* Orchard House, Avenue Road, STRATFORD-UPON-AVON, CV37 6UN.
NAISH, Mr. Richard, MSc FCA *1991;* Qi Concepts Limited, 77 Parkside, Wollaton, NOTTINGHAM, NG8 2NQ.
NAISH, Miss. Sarah Jane, BSc ACA *1992;* 8 The Saffrons, BURGESS HILL, WEST SUSSEX, RH15 8TB.
NAISMITH, Mrs. Josephine Isabel, BA ACA *1982;* Crockham Hill Farm, Kent Hatch Road, Crockham Hill, EDENBRIDGE, KENT, TN8 6SU.
NAISMITH, Mr. Keith, BA BSc FCA *1956;* 14 Lees Road, Bramhall, STOCKPORT, SK7 1BT. (Life Member)
NAJAK, Mr. Bahadurali Dhalla, MSc FCA *1975;* Bazat, Peel Avenue, Gilesgate Moor, DURHAM, DH1 2HU.
•**NAJEFY, Mr. Shiraz, FCA** *1982;* (Tax Fac), Najefy & Co, 46 Victoria Road, WORTHING, WEST SUSSEX, BN11 1XE.
NAJIB, Mrs. Homera, ACA *2008;* 4 Daffodil Court, Allerton, BRADFORD, BD15 7DW.
NAJIB, Mr. Nizar, BA ACA *2009;* 38 Jalan 4M, 68000 AMPANG, SELANGOR, MALAYSIA.
NAJJARI-FARIZHENDI, Mr. Hossein, FCA *1976;* No. 4 Bon Bast Taleghani, Shariati Road, Eastgah Darb Dovom, Opp British Embassy, TEHRAN, 1914744931 IRAN.
NAJJINGO, Miss. Zaharah, BA(Hons) ACA *2009;* with PricewaterhouseCoopers, Communications House, 10th Floor, 1 Colville Street, KAMPALA, UGANDA.
NAKHODA, Mr. Abbasbhoy Haider, BSc FCA *1965;* 22 Dalvey Estate, SINGAPORE 259545, SINGAPORE. (Life Member)
•**NAKHODA, Mr. Shahnawaz, BSc ACA** *2002;* with KPMG, P O Box 3800, Level 32, Emirates Towers, Sheikh Zayed Road, DUBAI UNITED ARAB EMIRATES.
NAKHOODA, Mrs. Sophia, ACA *2009;* 65 Vardon Way, BIRMINGHAM, B38 8YA.
NAKHWA, Mr. Rayhaan Latefe, BSc ACA *2000;* Kessler Financial Services, 102 Jermyn Street, LONDON, SW1Y 6EE.
NAKUM, Miss. Heena, ACA *2009;* 58 Ashurst Drive, ILFORD, ESSEX, IG2 6SB.
NALKIN, Mr. Daniel Stanley, FCA *1959;* 2 Palmach Street, NETANYA, 42249, ISRAEL. (Life Member)
NALL, Mr. Charles William Joseph, BA ACA *1992;* 144 Highlever Road, LONDON, W10 6PJ.
NALLA, Mrs. Harisha, BSc(Hons) ACA *2001;* 172 Stewart Drive, SUDBURY P3E 2R5, ON, CANADA.
NALLIAH, Mr. Andrew James, BA ACA *2010;* 4 Seaton Close, Yaxley, PETERBOROUGH, PE7 3WZ.
NALLIAH, Mr. Ravi, BSc(Hons) ACA *2003;* 47 Phoenix Way, CARDIFF, CF14 4PR.
•**NALLY, Mr. Eamon Philip Peter, BSc ACA** *1987;* (Tax Fac), InTax Libya Ltd, Cutlers Farm House, Marlow Road, Lane End, HIGH WYCOMBE, BUCKINGHAMSHIRE HP14 3JW.
NALSON, Mr. Philip Dean, BSc ACA *1993;* Vossemberg 15A, Vossem, 3080 TERVUREN, BELGIUM.
NAM, Mr. Cheung Ching Adrian, MSc MPA CA ACA CISA *2005;* 11 Cheung Sha Wan Road, 5th Floor, SHAM SHUI PO, KOWLOON, HONG KONG SAR.
NAMASIVAYAM, Mr. Sivagurunathan, ACA *1984;* 7 Beckway Road, LONDON, SW16 4HB.
NAMBIAR, Miss. Shobha, BSc ACA *2010;* 18 Torrent Lodge, 11 Merryweather Place Greenwich High Road, LONDON, SE10 8EQ.
NAMERUA, Mrs. Christine, BA ACA *1988;* PO Box 18128, SUVA, FIJI.
NAMEY, Mr. Ian, BA ACA *2002;* 59 Lincoln Road, LONDON, N2 9DJ.
NAMEY, Mr. Robert Anselm, FCA *1969;* 7 St. Georges Road, WALLINGTON, SM6 0AS.
•**NAMVARI, Mr. Hamid, BA FCA** *1982;* Agahan & Co, PO Box 11365-4731, 32/1 Shadab Street, Gharani Avenue, TEHRAN, 15989 IRAN.
•**NANAVATI, Mr. Pankaj Govindji, FCA** *1977;* Nanavati & Co, 34 Burwell Avenue, GREENFORD, UB6 0NU.
NANAVATI, Ms. Shilpa Jayant, BA(Hons) ACA *2002;* Flat 1, 314 Upper Richmond Road West, LONDON, SW14 7JN.
NANAYAKKARA, Mr. Godakande Aratchige Kishantha, ACA ACMA *2011;* 176/3 Stanley Tillekerathne Mawatha, NUGEGODA, SRI LANKA.
NANCARROW, Mr. Charles Edward, MA BSc ACA *1996;* with National Audit Office, 157-197 Buckingham Palace Road, Victoria, LONDON, SW1W 9SP.
NANCARROW, Miss. Emma Catherine, BSc ACA *1995;* 6 Midway, South Crosland, HUDDERSFIELD, HD4 7DA.
•**NANCE, Mr. Martin, BA FCA** *1978;* Martin Nance, P.O. Box 223, CORNWALL, CT 06796, UNITED STATES.
NAND, Mr. Ambika, FCA *1970;* 45 Beulah Drive, MARKHAM L3S 3N2, ON, CANADA.
NAND-LAL, Mr. Andrew Paul, BA ACA *1991;* PO Box 508, MAYLANDS, WA 6931, AUSTRALIA.
NANDA, Mr. Dave Kumar, BCom ACA *1994;* 56 Whitemoor Drive, Shirley, SOLIHULL, B90 4UL.
NANDA, Mr. Rajan Parkash, FCA *1970;* Full Circle Technologies, 25 Garden Street, BOSTON, MA 02114, UNITED STATES.
NANDA, Mr. Shiv Parkash, FCA *1964;* Assarain Group, PO Box 1475, Ruwi, 112 MUSCAT, OMAN.
NANDA, Mr. Vinay, BSc ACA *2010;* 56 Argyle Avenue, HOUNSLOW, TW3 2LF.
NANDHA, Mrs. Susannah Margaret, BSc(Hons) ACA *2005;* 2 Gainsborough Crescent, Ramsey, ISLE OF MAN, IM8 3NH.
NANDHRA, Mr. Kulwant, ACA *2009;* Flat 30 Prichard House, 214a Kennington Road, LONDON, SE11 6AU.
NANDHRA, Mrs. Sukhwant Kaur, BSc ACA *2000;* 96 Sand Hill, FARNBOROUGH, HAMPSHIRE, GU14 8JS.
•**NANDLAL, Mrs. Linda Rosemary, FCA** *1973;* Archer Hayes, Castle House, 39 Nork Way, BANSTEAD, SURREY, SM7 1PB.
NANDLAL, Miss. Zoe Christina, BSc ACA *2005;* Rapid 3360, Luggate-Cromwell Road, RD3, CROMWELL 9383, OTAGO, NEW ZEALAND.
NANDRA, Mr. Ankush, MA ACA *1998;* 5 Foxdell, NORTHWOOD, MIDDLESEX, HA6 2BU.
NANDRA, Mr. Manjit Singh, BSc FCA *1989;* Beeches 24hour Rescue & Recovery, Paper Mill End Industrial Estate, BIRMINGHAM, B44 8NH.
NANDRA, Miss. Valdip, ACA *2008;* 11a York Crescent, WEST BROMWICH, B70 0JT.
NANGPAL, Mr. Rajnish, BSc FCA *1999;* U B S AG, 100 Liverpool Street, LONDON, EC2M 2RH.
NANIA, Mr. Viraf Kali, ACA *1994;* 17 Brassbell Millway, TORONTO M2L 1P8, ON, CANADA.
NANIK, Mr. Sunil Daryanani, BA ACA *1991;* 20 St Edmunds Court, St. Edmunds Terrace, St Johns Wood, LONDON, NW8 7QL.
NANJI, Mr. Ali Madatali, ACA *1980;* Apt 1304, 3970 Carrigan Court, BURNABY V3N 4S5, BC, CANADA.
NANJI, Mr. David, BSc ACA *1992;* 43 Forge End, Chiswell Green, ST. ALBANS, AL2 3EQ.
NANJI, Mrs. Ranee, BSc ACA *2002;* 5 Sunningdale, 40 London Road, HARROW, MIDDLESEX, HA1 3LY.
•**NANKIVELL, Mr. Fernley, FCA** *1950;* Fernley Nankivell, 1 St. Pauls Road, NEWTON ABBOT, DEVON, TQ12 2HP.
•**NANKIVELL, Mr. Guy Dunell, FCA** *1975;* Nankivells, 45 Green Drift, ROYSTON, SG8 5BX.
NANOVICH, Mr. Mark, ACA CA(AUS) *2008;* Tilbrook, Tilthams Green, GODALMING, SURREY, GU7 3BT.
NANSON, Mr. Grahame Ross, BA ACA *1998;* with PricewaterhouseCoopers, Darling Park Tower 2, 201 Sussex Street, GPO Box 2650, SYDNEY, NSW 1171 AUSTRALIA.
NANTALE, Ms. Immaculate, ACA *2009;* Flat 15, Hathersley House, Tulse Hill, LONDON, SW2 2EN.
NANWANI, Mr. Vinod Arjan, BA ACA *1983;* Gerad Ltd, 61 Hallmark Trading Centre, Fourth Way, WEMBLEY, HA9 0LB.
NAPIER, Miss. Caroline, ACA *2011;* 2a Banyard Close, The Quadrangle, CHELTENHAM, GLOUCESTERSHIRE, GL51 7SX.
NAPIER, Miss. Carolyn Elizabeth, BSc ACA *1990;* 18 Elm Quay Court, Nine Elms Lane, LONDON, SW8 5DE.
NAPIER, Ms. Catherine Jane, BSc ACA *1989;* JCW Enterprises Ltd, c/o Freeroberts, Howe Lane, Great Sampford, SAFFRON WALDEN, ESSEX CB10 2NY.
NAPIER, Prof. Christopher John, PhD MA MSc FCA *1978;* (Member of Council 1997 - 2000), Royal Holloway University of London, Egham Hill, EGHAM, TW20 0EX.
•**NAPIER, Mr. Stephen, BSc ACA** *1984;* (Tax Fac), Stephen Napier & Company, First Floor, Hodges Chambers, Crane Street, PONTYPOOL, NP4 6LY.
NAPIER-FENNING, Mr. William, BSc ACA *2005;* 33 Woodside, Dunkirk, FAVERSHAM, ME13 9NY.
NAPPER, Mr. Edward Charles, BSc ACA *2005;* 12 Martingale Close, CAMBRIDGE, CB4 3TA.
NAPPER, Mr. Grahame, FCA *1975;* 24 David Hockney Drive, DIAMOND CREEK, VIC 3089, AUSTRALIA.
NAPPER, Mr. James Benjamin, ACA *2009;* 86 Clayton Road, CHESSINGTON, KT9 1NJ.

NAPPER, Mr. John Derek, FCA *1973;* Woodview, Holly Close, Eversley, HOOK, RG27 0PH.
•**NAPPER, Mr. Robert Francis, FCA** *1980;* Grant Thornton UK LLP, 1-4 Atholl Crescent, EDINBURGH, EH3 8LQ. See also Grant Thornton LLP
NAQI, Mr. Mansoor, ACA *1981;* 3601 Highway # 7, West Tower, Suite 509, MARKHAM L3R 0M3, ON, CANADA.
NAQIB, Mr. Tareq Isam, BEng ACA *2000;* Flat 1 Chestnut Court, Abbots Walk, LONDON, W8 5UN.
NAQVI, Mr. Shariq Hussain, BSc(Econ) ACA *2001;* Noor Investment Group, 8th Floor, Emmar Business Square, DUBAI, 8822, UNITED ARAB EMIRATES.
NAQVI, Mr. Syed Asad Ahmad, FCA *1998;* Riyad Bank, Head Office Room 606, King Abdul Aziz Road, PO Box 22609, RIYADH, 11416 SAUDI ARABIA.
NAQVI, Mr. Syed Mahboob Ahmad, FCA *1970;* 38 Alexandra Road, Wimbledon, LONDON, SW19 7JZ.
•**NAQVI, Mr. Syed Zakir Hussain Haider, MA FCA FCCA FCIS** *1973;* Haider Naqvi & Co, Concept House, 225 Hale Lane, EDGWARE, MIDDLESEX, HA8 9QF.
NARAGHI, Mr. Ali Reza Faghihi, BSc ACA *1995;* with DTE Business Advisory Services Limited, Park House, 26 North End Road, LONDON, NW11 7PT.
NARAGHI-SHAH, Miss. Lida, BSc ACA *1984;* (Tax Fac), T U I UK, Wigmore House, Wigmore Place, Wigmore Lane, LUTON, LU2 9TN.
NARAIN, Mr. Ajit Kumar, FCA *1973;* 720 Sindh Society, Aundh, Pune, PUNE 411007, INDIA.
•**NARAIN, Mr. Kapil, FCA** *1979;* K. Narain & Co, 6A Belsize Square, LONDON, NW3 4HT.
NARAIN, Mr. Kevin Dhruva, FCA *1982;* 13 Riverside Close, WALLINGTON, SM6 7DH.
NARAIN, Mr. Lakshmi, MSc BTech FCA *1977;* (Tax Fac), with Baker Tilly Tax and Advisory Services LLP, 25 Farringdon Street, LONDON, EC4A 4AB.
NARANG, Miss. Gunjan, ACA *2011;* 123 Elm Bark, READING, RG30 2HU.
NARANG, Mr. Vipan, BCom ACA *1996;* Institution of Structural Engineers 11 Upper Belgrave Street, LONDON, SW1X 8BH.
•**NARAYAN, Miss. Sonia Jayne Elizabeth, BSc(Hons) ACA** *2002;* 44 Priory Road, ARUNDEL, WEST SUSSEX, BN18 9EW.
NARAYANAN, Miss. Karunya, ACA *2011;* 44 Briar Crescent, NORTHOLT, MIDDLESEX, UB5 4ND.
NARAYANAN, Miss. Thulasibrinda, ACA *1985;* SS Holdings Sdn Bhd, 1 Lorong 11/ 4c, Section 11, 46200 PETALING JAYA, SELANGOR, MALAYSIA.
NARBETH, Mr. Christopher Nicolas, BSc ACA *1989;* Little Buckland Farm, Buckland Lane, MAIDSTONE, ME16 0BH.
NARBOROUGH, Mr. Leonard, FCA *1954;* 32 Scullin Place, WAHROONGA, NSW 2076, AUSTRALIA. (Life Member)
NARDECCHIA, Mr. Simon Allister, MA FCA *1984;* Syngenta LTD, Surrey Research Park, 30 Priestley Road, GUILDFORD, SURREY GU2 7YH.
NARDELL, Mr. George Philip, FCA *1972;* 25 Chemin du Paradis, 46800 MONTCUQ, FRANCE.
NARES, Mr. Anthony James Brewis, FCA *1981;* Forest House, Hatfield Oak Hotel, Roehyde Way, HATFIELD, HERTFORDSHIRE, AL10 9AF.
NARGOLWALA, Mr. Kaikhushru Shiavax, FCA *1975;* 1 Raffles Link, #03/#04-01 South Lobby, SINGAPORE 039393, SINGAPORE.
NAROD, Mr. Mohammad Ebrahim, ACA FCCA *2010;* 85 Salt Hill Way, SLOUGH, BERKSHIRE, SL1 3TT.
NARRACOTT, Mr. Simon Graham, BA FCA *1995;* 27 Kechill Gardens, BROMLEY, BR2 7NG.
NARRAINEN, Mr. Terence Jason, BA ACA *1999;* 276 Ocean Drive, Unit 03-29 The Coast, Sentosa Cove, SENTOSA 098449, SINGAPORE.
•**NARRAMORE, Mr. Peter John, FCA** *1975;* P.J. Narramore, 3 Williams Way, Higham Ferrers, RUSHDEN, NN10 8AJ.
NARRAWAY, Mr. Robert James, BA ACA *2005;* 12 Bank Place Apartments, Green Lane, WILMSLOW, CHESHIRE, SK9 1LL.
NARULA, Mr. Gurvinder Singh, BPharm ACA *2003;* 82 Farm Road, EDGWARE, MIDDLESEX, HA8 9LT.
•**NARULA, Mr. Sam, BSc FCA** *1987;* (Member of Council 2001 - 2005), (Tax Fac), Samuels LLP, 3 Locks Yard, High Street, SEVENOAKS, KENT, TN13 1LT. See also Samuels & Co
•**NASEEM, Mr. Khurram, ACA** *2002;* with PricewaterhouseCoopers, Emirates Towers Offices, PO Box 11987, Level 40, Sheikh Zayed Road, PO Box 11987 DUBAI UNITED ARAB EMIRATES.
NASEEM, Mr. Muhammad, FCA *1968;* c/o A.F. Ferguson & Co, State Life Bldg No 1-C, I I Chundrigar Road, PO Box 4716, KARACHI 74000, PAKISTAN. (Life Member)
NASEER, Mr. Muhammad Usman, ACA *2011;* 26 Archery Close, HARROW, MIDDLESEX, HA3 7RT.
NASER, Miss. Clare Victoria, BA ACA *2007;* Flat 3 Chestnut House, 32 York Road, GUILDFORD, GU1 4DF.
NASH, Mr. Alan Spencer, BSc FCA *1989;* 54 Mallards Reach, SOLIHULL, B92 7BX.
NASH, Mr. Alexander Henry, BA ACA *2004;* Abbey National Plc, Internal Audit, 2 Triton Square, Regents Place, LONDON, NW1 3AN.
NASH, Mr. Alistair Dennis, FCA *1984;* (Tax Fac), HBOS PLC, Walton Street, AYLESBURY, HP21 7QW.
NASH, Mr. Andrew Charles, MBA ACA *1981;* 3 Chemin Paul Sieppel, 1231 CONCHES, SWITZERLAND.
NASH, Mr. Andrew Lee, BSc(Econ) ACA *1995;* 4 Neatscourt Road, LONDON, E6 5ST.
NASH, Mr. Andrew Meyrick, ACA CTA BSAC *1997;* (Tax Fac), with Baker Tilly Tax and Advisory Services LLP, 25 Farringdon Street, LONDON, EC4A 4AB.
NASH, Mr. Anthony Roy, FCA *1960;* P O Box 110, MALENY, QLD 4552, AUSTRALIA. (Life Member)
NASH, Mrs. Barbara Anne, BEng ACA *1999;* 3 Vanderbilt Road, LONDON, SW18 3BG.
NASH, Mr. Brian Patrick, FCA *1969;* 77 Bramstead Avenue, Compton, WOLVERHAMPTON, WV6 8AT.
NASH, Mr. Brian Paul, BSc(Hons) ACA *2003;* Allied Bakeries, 1 Kindgsmill Place, Vanwall Road, Vanwall Business Park, MAIDENHEAD, BERKSHIRE SL6 4UF.
•**NASH, Mrs. Catherine Nora Bruce, BA ACA** *1983;* Lethenty Accounts, Burnside, Lethenty, INVERURIE, ABERDEENSHIRE, AB51 0HQ.
NASH, Mr. Charles John, MA ACA *1981;* (Tax Fac), 31 High Meadows, Compton, WOLVERHAMPTON, WV6 8PH.
•**NASH, Mr. Christopher Douglas, ACA** *1981;* C D Nash Limited, 1st Floor, 15a Hill Avenue, AMERSHAM, BUCKINGHAMSHIRE, HP6 5BD.
NASH, Miss. Claire Emma, ACA *2003;* Marston & Langinger, 13 George Edwards Road, FAKENHAM, NORFOLK, NR21 8NL.
NASH, Mr. Colin Charles, FCA *1958;* Blue Pines, Boxhill Road, TADWORTH, SURREY, KT20 7JN. (Life Member)
NASH, Mr. Craig, BSc(Hons) ACA *2006;* 17 Beresford Drive, SUTTON COLDFIELD, B73 5QZ.
NASH, Mr. Daniel Marc, MA ACA *2004;* Flat 9 Thornton House, Cambridge Park, LONDON, E11 2PZ.
•**NASH, Mr. David Harwood, FCA** *1963;* (Tax Fac), Nash & Co, Highclose Farm, Bath Road, HUNGERFORD, BERKSHIRE, RG17 0SP.
NASH, Mr. David Percy, FCA *1962;* 17 Shoreacres, 141 Banks Road, Sandbanks, POOLE, DORSET, BH13 7QH. (Life Member)
NASH, Mr. Desmond John, BSc ACA *1987;* 10 Morer Estate Road, Smith's Parish, HAMILTON FL05, BERMUDA.
NASH, Miss. Eloise Anna, BSc ACA *1998;* 42 Albert Road, EPSOM, KT17 4EH.
•**NASH, Ms. Emma, BSc FCA** *1990;* Chapman Nash LLP, Unit 4, Barford Exchange, Wellesbourne Road, Barford, WARWICK CV35 8AQ.
NASH, Mrs. Fiona Christine, BA ACA *1989;* 6 Cottingvale, MORPETH, NORTHUMBERLAND, NE61 1DW.
NASH, Mr. Graham Paul, BA ACA *1980;* 33 Westbury Lodge Close, PINNER, HA5 3FG.
NASH, Mr. Grant, BSc(Hons) ACA *2003;* 92 Reading Road, HENLEY-ON-THAMES, OXFORDSHIRE, RG9 1DN.
NASH, Mr. Harold Christopher, BCom ACA *1985;* 15 Rue de la Gare, L-5540 REMICH, LUXEMBOURG.
•**NASH, Mr. Harry, FCA** *1962;* 1 Saddlescombe Way, LONDON, N12 7LS.
NASH, Henry John, Esq OBE FCA *1952;* 80 Clarence Road, Four Oaks, SUTTON COLDFIELD, B74 4AR. (Life Member)
NASH, Mr. Hilary Gordon, FCA *1969;* 75 Manor Road, KEYNSHAM, BRISTOL, BS31 1RE. (Life Member)
NASH, Mr. Hugh Raymond Spencer, FCA *1968;* 89 Brindwood Road, LONDON, E4 8BA. (Life Member)
NASH, Mr. Ian Victor, BSc ACA *1981;* Lower Farm, Effingham Common Road, Effingham, LEATHERHEAD, KT24 5JG.
NASH, Mr. James Frederick, BA ACA *1995;* 21 Arlington Drive, RUISLIP, MIDDLESEX, HA4 7RJ.
NASH, Mrs. Janette Lynn, BSc ACA *1984;* Turner & Co, 4 Bridle Ways, East Bridgford, NOTTINGHAM, NG13 8PT.
NASH, Mr. Jeffery Frederick, BSc ACA *1991;* (Tax Fac), The Coach House, St. Matthews Road, Ealing, LONDON, W5 3JT.
NASH, Mr. Jonathan, BSc ACA *2005;* 14 Twineham Gardens, Alderbury, SALISBURY, SP5 3TF.
NASH, Mr. Jonathan, BSc ACA *1993;* Close Brothers Group Plc, 10 Crown Place, LONDON, EC2A 4FT.
NASH, Mr. Lloyd Spencer, BSc ACA *1998;* 3 Vanderbilt Road, LONDON, SW18 3BG.
NASH, Mr. Malcolm Thomas, FCA *1974;* 'Shepherds', 4 Redcroft Walk, CRANLEIGH, GU6 8DS.
NASH, Mr. Matthew James, BSocSc ACA *1999;* 1 Parc Plas Aney, MOLD, CLWYD, CH7 1NN.
NASH, Mrs. Michele, BSc ACA *1992;* 21 Porson Road, CAMBRIDGE, CB2 2ET.
NASH, Mr. Norman Charles Russell, FCA *1952;* The Vine House, Burdrop, Sibford Gower, BANBURY, OXFORDSHIRE, OX15 5RW. (Life Member)
NASH, Mrs. Patricia Le May, BSc ACA *1996;* Volkswagen Group UK Ltd Yeomans Drive, Blakelands, MILTON KEYNES, MK14 5AN.
•**NASH, Mr. Paul Harold, BSc FCA** *1988;* PricewaterhouseCoopers LLP, Hays Galleria, 1 Hays Lane, LONDON, SE1 2RD. See also PricewaterhouseCoopers
NASH, Mrs. Paula Jayne, ACA *1992;* 19 Church Road, Lytham, LYTHAM ST. ANNES, LANCASHIRE, FY8 5LH.
NASH, Mr. Peter Thomas, BSc ACA *1990;* with Deloitte LLP, City House, 126-130 Hills Road, CAMBRIDGE, CB2 1RY.
•**NASH, Mr. Philip Jonathan, ACA** *1979;* (Tax Fac), Johnson Murkett & Hurst, Rawdon House, Rawdon Terrace, ASHBY-DE-LA-ZOUCH, LE65 2GN. See also Johnson, Murkett & Hurst (Computer Services) Ltd
NASH, Mr. Philip Tudor, BSc ACA *1998;* The Briars, 26 Vyner Road South, PRENTON, MERSEYSIDE, CH43 7PR.
NASH, Mr. Phillip Anthony, BSc ACA *1998;* 64 Butler Lane, NEW CANAAN, CT 06840, UNITED STATES.
NASH, Mrs. Rachelle, BSc ACA *1988;* Rayfield, 39 Oakleigh Park South, Whetstone, LONDON, N20 9JR.
NASH, Mr. Robert Leslie, BSc ACA *1986;* 12 Manor Fields Drive, ILKESTON, DE7 5FA.
NASH, Miss. Sarah Anne, BA ACA *1991;* 25 College Fields, MARLBOROUGH, WILTSHIRE, SN8 1UA.
NASH, Mrs. Sarah Jane, ACA CTA *1993;* (Tax Fac), Ipeco Europe Ltd, Building 4, Aviation Way, Southend Airport, SOUTHEND-ON-SEA, SS2 6UN.
NASH, Mrs. Shirley Theresa, BSc ACA *1990;* 4 Beccles Road, SALE, CHESHIRE, M33 3RP.
•**NASH, Mr. Stephen Alan, BA ACA** *1992;* Ernst & Young LLP, 1 More London Place, LONDON, SE1 2AF. See also Ernst & Young Europe LLP
NASH, Mr. Stephen David, ACA *2008;* 27 Grovelands Road, READING, RG30 2PN.
NASH, Mr. Stuart William, BSc FCA *1997;* 19 Ivo Street, Nundah, BRISBANE, QLD 4012, AUSTRALIA.
NASH, Mrs. Tracy Louise, BSc ACA *2003;* 19 Lundy Drive, West Cross, SWANSEA, SA3 5QL.
NASH, Mr. Wayne Gary, BA ACA *1991;* Sherborne, Manor Close, Penn, HIGH WYCOMBE, HP10 8HZ.
NASIM, Ms. Shahida, ACA CPFA *2010;* Audit Commission Millbank Tower, 21-24 Millbank, LONDON, SW1P 4HQ.
NASIM, Ms. Shareen Huma, LLB ACA *2002;* 24 Prior Avenue, SUTTON, SM2 5HX.
NASIR, Mr. Abid, BSc ACA *2001;* Flat 16 Eyre Court 3-21 Finchley Road, LONDON, NW8 9TT.
NASIR, Mr. Asad, BA BSc ACA *2005;* 14 Robincroft Mews, Greenwich, LONDON, SE10 8DN.
NASIR, Mr. Hasan, BSc ACA *1982;* 3670 Autumnleaf Crescent, MISSISSAUGA L5L IK8, ON, CANADA.
NASIR, Mr. Imran Mohammad, BSc ACA *2003;* 242 Wanstead Park Road, ILFORD, IG1 3TT.
NASIR, Mr. Osman, BSc(Hons) ACA *2002;* 93 Heythorp Street, Southfields, LONDON, SW18 5BT.
NASIR, Mr. Tahir Ahmed, BSc CA *1993; (CA Scotland 1993);* 1 Blake House, Waterside, Admirals Way, LONDON, E14 9UJ.
NASIRUDDIN, Miss. Sofia Meriam, BSc ACA *2005;* flat 2, 71a Salcott Road, LONDON, SW11 6DF.
•**NASON, The Revd Canon Thomas David, BA FCA** *1968;* (Tax Fac), David Nason, 1 St Richards Walk, Canon Lane, CHICHESTER, PO19 1QA.
NASR, Mr. Kamal Shukri, FCA *1971;* Apartment 47 Charlesworth House, 48 Stanhope Gardens, LONDON, SW7 5RD.
NASR, Mr. Nael Ramzi, ACA *2000;* 905 Juniper Street, Unit 802, ATLANTA, GA 30309, UNITED STATES.
NASRULLAH, Mr. Imran Jehangir, FCA MBA *1997;* Cargill Asia Pacific Pte Ltd, 23-01 Concourse, 300 Beach Road, SINGAPORE 199555, SINGAPORE.
•**NASS, Mr. Harold David, FCA** *1977;* Harold D. Nass, 20 Heath View, LONDON, N2 0QA.
NASSER, Miss. Sahinaz, BA FCA *1985;* 3 Wonford Close, KINGSTON UPON THAMES, KT2 7XA.
NATH, Ms. Felicity Harriet, BSc ACA *2003;* 51 Church Hill, LOUGHTON, IG10 1QP.
NATH, Mr. Virendra, FCA *1975;* 11 Palace Gardens Terrace, LONDON, W8 4SA.
NATHA, Miss. Shaheda Ismail, ACA CTA MAAT *2003;* 6 Wellwood Road, Goodmayes, ILFORD, IG3 8TR.
NATHAN, Mr. Brian Hugh, FCA *1960;* The White House, 2 Halsbury Close, STANMORE, MIDDLESEX, HA7 3DY. (Life Member)
NATHAN, Mr. Christopher David John, BSc ACA *1983;* (Tax Fac), 36 Shawpark Crescent, SELKIRK, TD7 4EX. (Life Member)
NATHAN, Mr. David, ACA *2011;* Ernst & Young Llp, 1 More London Place, LONDON, SE1 2AF.
NATHAN, Ms. Deborah Judith, BSc ACA *1995;* 15 Meadow Drive, Hendon, LONDON, NW4 1SD.
NATHAN, Mr. Geoffrey, FCA *1956;* Geoffrey Nathan International Limited, Le Roccabella, 24 Avenue Princess Grace, 98000 MONTE CARLO, MONACO. (Life Member)
NATHAN, Mr. James Adam, ACA *1997;* 100 Elvendon Road, Goring, READING, RG8 0DR.
NATHAN, Mrs. Josephine, LLB ACA *2004;* 42 Bromefield, STANMORE, MIDDLESEX, HA7 1AE.
NATHAN, Mr. Marie Ambrose, BA CA FCA *1984;* c/o G4S Security Services Sdn Bhd, LB 127 Simpang 164, Jalan Tutong, BANDAR SERI BEGAWAN, BA2112, BRUNEI DARUSSALAM.
NATHAN, Mr. Michael Ronald, FCA *1951;* 1 Martlett Lodge, Oak Hill Park, LONDON, NW3 7LE. (Life Member)
NATHAN, Mr. Ravi Paul, MA ACA *1996;* 13 Wyatt Road, LONDON, N5 2JU.
NATHAN, Mr. Raymond, FCA *1955;* 17 Forest Heights, Epping New Road, BUCKHURST HILL, IG9 5TE. (Life Member)
NATHAN, Mr. Robert Mark, BA(Hons) ACA *2004;* Deloitte & Touche, 2 New Street Square, LONDON, EC4A 3BZ.
•**NATHAN, Mr. Russell, BA FCA** *1990;* H W Fisher & Company, Acre House, 11-15 William Road, LONDON, NW1 3ER. See also H W Fisher & Company Limited
NATHAN, Mr. Sacha, BSc ACA *2006;* 99 Waverley Road, Stoneleigh, EPSOM, KT17 2LL.
NATHAN, Mr. Stuart Michael, FCA *1974;* Aero Inventory (UK), 30 Lancaster Road, BARNET, HERTFORDSHIRE, EN4 8AP.
NATHAN, Mr. Tharma, ACA *1983;* 19 Jalan SS22A/1, Damansara Jaya, 47400 PETALING JAYA, SELANGOR, MALAYSIA.
NATHANAEL, Miss. Chryso Costa, MA ACA *2002;* 11 Kimonos Street, Building Kimon 2, Flat 302, 3095 LIMASSOL, CYPRUS.
NATHANI, Mrs. Nashina, MPhil ACA *2003;* P.O.Box 66695-00800, NAIROBI, KENYA.
NATHANI, Mr. Talib Bahadurali, BEng ACA *2004;* P O Box 66695-00800, NAIROBI, KENYA.
NATHOO, Mr. El Nasir, BSc ACA *1995;* 45A Blomfield Road, LONDON, W9 2PF.
NATHOO, Mr. Gavarali Mohamed, FCA *1969;* 21 Downalong, Bushey Heath, BUSHEY, WD23 1HZ. (Life Member)
NATHOO, Mr. Maheboob, FCA *1976;* Soyaworld Inc, Unit 200, 4190 Lougheed Highway, BURNABY V5C 6A8, BC, CANADA.
NATHWANI, Mr. Amar Harilal, BEng ACA *1993;* 34A Ramsdale Street., Doubleview, PERTH, WA 6018, AUSTRALIA.
NATHWANI, Mr. Amish, BA ACA *1986;* 74 Copse Wood Way, NORTHWOOD, MIDDLESEX, HA6 2UA.
NATHWANI, Mr. Amool Jivraj Keshavji, FCA *1977;* Vista Management, Consultant Ltd, P.O. Box 11, NAIROBI, 00606, KENYA.
NATHWANI, Mr. Harilal Jivraj Keshavji, BSc FCA *1964;* P O 47844 - 00100, NAIROBI, KENYA.
•**NATHWANI, Mr. Kaushik Chunilal, ACA** *1980;* (Tax Fac), Nagle James Associates Limited, 51/53 Station Road, HARROW, HA1 2TY. See also Nagle James Financial Planning Ltd
•**NATHWANI, Mr. Meeten, ACA ATT CTA** *2005;* (Tax Fac), 4 Elmhurst Close, BUSHEY, WD23 2QB.
NATHWANI, Mr. Nirav Amool, ACA *2009;* Nirav A Nathwani, P.O Box 11 - 00606, Sarit Centre, NAIROBI, KENYA.
NATHWANI, Miss. Nisha, ACA *2009;* 2 Woodridge Way, NORTHWOOD, MIDDLESEX, HA6 2BE.

NATHWANI, Mr. Punit Rameshchandra, BA ACA *2006;* 21 Gray Court, 73 Marsh Road, PINNER, MIDDLESEX, HA5 5PD.

•**NATHWANI, Mr. Vijay Mukundlal, BA ACA** *1988;* (Tax Fac), Ashtons, 79 Ashness Gardens, GREENFORD, MIDDLESEX, UB6 0RW.

NATION, Mr. Oliver Grant, BSc(Hons) ACA *2003;* 117 Royal Worcester Crescent, BROMSGROVE, WORCESTERSHIRE, B60 2TN.

NATOFF, Miss. Hilary, BA ACA *1998;* Fidelity Investments Ltd, 25 Cannon Street, LONDON, EC4M 5TA.

•**NATT, Mr. Jagdish Singh, BSc FCA** *1985;* Leigh Carr, 72 New Cavendish Street, LONDON, W1G 8AU.

•**NATT, Mr. John Robert, ACA** *1981;* Wilkins Kennedy, 3-4 Eastwood Court, Broadwater Road, ROMSEY, HAMPSHIRE, SO51 8JJ.

NATT, Mr. Mohamed Bin Mohamed, FCA *1974;* 33 Jalan SS 21/38, 47400 PETALING JAYA, SELANGOR, MALAYSIA. (Life Member)

NATTRASS, Mrs. Alison Jennet, BA(Hons) ACA *2004;* 31 Hollins Walk, READING, RG30 2BU.

•**NATTRASS, Mr. Graham Leslie, BSc ACA** *1994;* Ernst & Young LLP, Apex Plaza, Forbury Road, READING, RG1 1YE. See also Ernst & Young Europe LLP

NATTRASS, Mr. John Crosthwaite, BA FCA *1968;* 29 Ollerbarrow Road, Hale, ALTRINCHAM, CHESHIRE, WA15 9PP. (Life Member)

NATTRASS, Miss. Sandra Olive, BA FCA *1982;* Whickham House, 4 The Causeway, Glanton, ALNWICK, NORTHUMBERLAND, NE66 4AY.

NATU, Mr. Sameer, ACA *2010;* 7 West Towers, PINNER, MIDDLESEX, HA5 1TZ.

•**NAUDI, Mr. Christopher Joseph, FCA** *1990;* (Tax Fac), Ernst & Young, Fourth Floor, Regional Business Centre, Achille Ferris Street, MSIDA MSD1751, MALTA. See also Ernst & Young Europe LLP

NAUGHER, Miss. Teresa Marie, LLB ACA *1999;* 11 Druridge Avenue, Seaburn, SUNDERLAND, SR6 8DU.

NAUGHTEN, Mr. Duncan Grant, FCA *1968;* 2 Carlton Bank, Station Road, HARPENDEN, AL5 4SU.

•**NAUGHTEN, Mrs. Elaine Avril, FCA** *1967;* Naughten & Co, 2 Carlton Bank, Station Road, HARPENDEN, AL5 4SU.

NAUGHTON, Mr. Liam Brendan George, BA ACA *1992;* with PricewaterhouseCoopers, Marie-Curie-Strasse 24-28, D-60439 FRANKFURT AM MAIN, GERMANY.

NAUGHTON, Mr. Mark Christopher Crichton, BA ACA CF *1994;* 5 Fernbank Road, BRISTOL, BS6 6QA.

NAUGHTON-RUMBO, Mr. Mark Howard, BSc ACA *1985;* Creation House, Lemon Street, DUBLIN 2, COUNTY DUBLIN, IRELAND.

NAULLS, Mr. Michael, FCA *1965;* 69 Eastgate, LOUTH, LINCOLNSHIRE, LN11 9PL.

NAVARATNAM, Miss. Gowrie, FCA *1982;* 11 Jalan Oh Cheng Keat, Off Lorong Rani, 30350 IPOH, PERAK, MALAYSIA.

NAVARATNAM, Mr. Jayendran, ACA *2011;* 12a Bulstrode Court, GERRARDS CROSS, BUCKINGHAMSHIRE, SL9 7RR.

NAVARATNE, Miss. Geraldine Rochelle, BSc ACA *2007;* 86 Plover Way, LONDON, SE16 7TT.

NAVARATNE, Mr. Leroy Jerome Ronan, BA(Hons) ACA *2004;* 34 Bywater Place, LONDON, SE16 5ND.

NAVAREDNAM, Miss. Rebecca Annapillai, FCA *1975;* Flat 26, Foster Court, Royal College Street, LONDON, NW1 9NL.

NAVATO, Miss. Gina Rebecca, BA ACA *1999;* Flat 29 Marlborough Mansions, Cannon Hill, LONDON, NW6 1JR.

•**NAVESEY, Mr. Michael Anthony, FCA** *1962;* (Tax Fac), Aldington Navesey & Co Ltd, 19 Billericay Road, Herongate, BRENTWOOD, Essex, CM13 3PS. See also Aldington Navesey & Co

NAVEY, Mr. Julian John, BA ACA *1991;* 31 Swanmore Road, Boscombe East, BOURNEMOUTH, BH7 6PB.

NAVSARIA, Mr. Ravindra Ambaram, BSc ACA *1986;* Calyon Broadwalk House, 5 Appold Street, LONDON, EC2A 2DA.

NAWAB, Mr. Ather Asgher, ACA *1991;* 69 B-II, Q Street Phase 7, Defence Housing Society, KARACHI, PAKISTAN.

NAWAB, Mr. Muhammad Tayyab, ACA FCCA *2009;* Flat 12 Consero Court, 120 Ladbroke Road, REDHILL, RH1 1PU.

NAWAB, Mr. Nasar Ali, ACA ACCA *1994;* 4 Stoneyfields Gardens, EDGWARE, MIDDLESEX, HA8 9SP.

NAWALRAI, Mr. Vinod, BEng ACA *1991;* CHIPANA 2040, DEPT. 402 TORRE 1, IQUIQUE, CHILE.

NAWAZ, Miss. Halima, ACA *2011;* Overdale, Eccup Lane, LEEDS, LS16 8AJ.

NAWAZ, Mr. Khalid, BSc ACA *1999;* with Deloitte LLP, 4 Brindley Place, BIRMINGHAM, B1 2HZ.

•**NAWAZ, Mr. Taher, FCA MBA** *1974;* T Nawaz & Co Ltd, Cambridge House, 66 Little Horton Lane, BRADFORD, WEST YORKSHIRE, BD5 0HU. See also T Nawaz & Co Ltd

NAYAK, Mr. Krisna Christopher, BA(Econ) ACA *2001;* 21 Ivygreen Road, MANCHESTER, M21 9FF.

NAYAR, Mr. Arrikath Kumaran, FCA *1970;* 57 Willesden Lane, LONDON, NW6 7RL.

NAYAR, Mr. Arun, FCA *1976;* 9 Roszel Road, PRINCETON, NJ 08540, UNITED STATES.

NAYAR, Mr. Paul, BSc ACA *1999;* Abbey International, PO Box 545, JERSEY, JE4 8XG.

NAYEEM, Mr. Abu Sayed Mohammed, MSc ACA *1980;* ACNABIN Chartered Accountants 13th Floor BSRS Bhaban 12 Kawran Bazar, DHAKA 1215, BANGLADESH.

•**NAYLER, Mrs. Alison Lucinda, BSc FCA** *1996;* Wilkins Kennedy, Cecil House, 52 St Andrew Street, HERTFORD, SG14 1JA.

NAYLER, Mr. James St John, BSc FCA *1999;* with BDO LLP, 55 Baker Street, LONDON, W1U 7EU.

NAYLER, Mrs. Jennifer Clare, BSc ACA *1990;* Carpenter Box Llp Grafton Lodge, 15 Grafton Road, WORTHING, WEST SUSSEX, BN11 1QR.

NAYLER, Mr. Jonathan Mark, BA ACA CTA *1985;* (Tax Fac), 1 Penfold Close, LIVERPOOL, L18 3NQ.

NAYLER, Miss. Kirsten Emma, LLB ACA *2004;* 6/32 Coogee Street, RANDWICK, NSW 2031, AUSTRALIA.

NAYLOR, Mr. Andrew, BA ACA *2007;* 2nd Floor, 117 Jermyn Street, LONDON, SW1W 6HH.

NAYLOR, Mr. Andrew, ACA *2010;* 6 Burford Gardens, LONDON, N13 4LP.

•**NAYLOR, Mr. Andrew Craig, BSc ACA** *1989;* Andrew Naylor & Co, 51 Glastonbury Drive, MIDDLEWICH, CW10 9HR.

NAYLOR, Mr. Andrew Gary, BEng ACA *1993;* Hill Top, Bridge End Lane, Prestbury, MACCLESFIELD, CHESHIRE, SK10 4DJ.

NAYLOR, Mr. Andrew John, LLB ACA *1990;* I M Group Ltd, I M House, South Drive, Coleshill, BIRMINGHAM, B46 1DF.

NAYLOR, Mr. Andrew Mark, BSc ACA *1981;* Henry Colbeck Limited, Seventh Avenue, Team Valley Trading Estate, GATESHEAD, NE11 0HG.

NAYLOR, Mrs. Anne Margaret, ACA *1979;* 21 Kilnhouse Bank, Holmbridge, HOLMFIRTH, HD9 2QW.

•**NAYLOR, Mrs. Anne-Marie, BSc FCA** *1992;* (Tax Fac), Harts LLP, Westminster House, 10 Westminster Road, MACCLESFIELD, CHESHIRE, SK10 1BX. See also Hart Shaw Macclesfield LLP

NAYLOR, Mr. Anthony Richard, FCA *1960;* 66 Sheen Park, RICHMOND, TW9 1UP. (Life Member)

NAYLOR, Mr. Bruce, ACA CA(AUS) *2009;* 14c Greenwich South Street, LONDON, SE10 8TY.

NAYLOR, Mr. Charles Guy, FCA ATII *1975;* 31 Wildcroft Road, Henleaze, BRISTOL, BS9 4HZ.

NAYLOR, Mr. Christopher Bruce, FCA *1974;* The Briars, Briardene, Oulton, LEEDS, LS26 8LE.

NAYLOR, Mr. Christopher David, MA ACA *2000;* 58 Avondale Avenue, LONDON, N12 8EN.

NAYLOR, Miss. Claire Adel, BA ACA *2009;* 17 Orchard Grove, BRADFORD, WEST YORKSHIRE, BD10 9BX.

NAYLOR, Mr. Clive, BSc FCA *1973;* St. James's Place Partnership, Sunlight House, Quay Street, MANCHESTER, M3 3LF.

NAYLOR, Mr. David Arthur, FCA *1970;* Kipling Cottage, Greenhow Hill, HARROGATE, NORTH YORKSHIRE, HG3 5JQ.

NAYLOR, Mr. David Jonathan, ACA *1984;* The Grammar School at Leeds, Harrogate Road, LEEDS, WEST YORKSHIRE, LS17 8GS.

NAYLOR, Mr. David Malcolm Broadley, FCA *1966;* 1 Abrams View, Holbeck Hill, SCARBOROUGH, NORTH YORKSHIRE, YO11 3YE.

•**NAYLOR, Mrs. Dawn Michelle, BSc ACA** *2005;* Eura Audit UK, 370 Heysham Road, Heysham, MORECAMBE, LANCASHIRE, LA3 2BJ. See also Lishman Sidwell Campbell & Price LLP

NAYLOR, Mrs. Delia, BA ACA *1989;* 17 Heyhouses Lane, LYTHAM ST. ANNES, LANCASHIRE, FY8 3RT.

NAYLOR, Mrs. Denise Joy, BSc FCA *1979;* 236 St. Helier Avenue, MORDEN, SURREY, SM4 6JZ.

•**NAYLOR, Mr. Derek Arthur, FCA** *1955;* Derek A Naylor FCA, Woodthorpe House, Packington Lane, Hopwas, TAMWORTH, B78 3AY.

NAYLOR, Mr. Edward George, MA BA FCA *1989;* 31 Great Percy Street, LONDON, WC1X 9RD.

NAYLOR, Miss. Elizabeth Ann, ACA *2009;* Flat 4, 80-86 St Johns Road, LONDON, SW11 1PX.

NAYLOR, Mrs. Fiona Evelyn, MA ACA *2005;* 14c Greenwich South Street, Greenwich, LONDON, SE10 8TY.

NAYLOR, Miss. Jacquelyn, BA(Hons) ACA *2010;* Flat 3, 34 Long Lane, LONDON, SE1 4NN.

NAYLOR, Mr. James Frederick, MSc BSc ACA *1992;* 36 Lavengro Road, LONDON, SE27 9EG.

NAYLOR, Ms. Jean Margaret, BA FCA *1980;* 95 Richmond Park Road, LONDON, SW14 8JY.

NAYLOR, Mr. Jeffrey Robert, BA FCA *1994;* with Zolfo Cooper Ltd, Toronto Square, Toronto Street, LEEDS, LS1 2HJ.

•**NAYLOR, Mrs. Katharine, BA FCA CTA** *1996;* (Tax Fac), Sagars LLP, Gresham House, 5-7 St. Pauls Street, LEEDS, LS1 2JG.

NAYLOR, Mrs. Kathryn Louise, MBA BSc ACA *1996;* Ganders Oak, Broomfield Park, ASCOT, BERKSHIRE, SL5 0JT.

NAYLOR, Mr. Kenneth Peter, FCA *1966;* The Old Joinery, Hall Park Road, Walton, WETHERBY, WEST YORKSHIRE, LS23 7DQ.

NAYLOR, Miss. Linda, BSc FCA *1987;* Greeway, East Meon, PETERSFIELD, HAMPSHIRE, GU32 1QJ.

NAYLOR, Mrs. Louise, ACA *2011;* 11c Gladys Road, West Hampstead, LONDON, NW6 2PU.

NAYLOR, Mr. Matthew James, BA FCA *2001;* Finning (UK) Limited, Watling Street, CANNOCK, STAFFORDSHIRE, WS11 8LL.

NAYLOR, Mr. Michael Thomas Arthur, BA ACA *1986;* 4 Speedwell Close, Oakwood, DERBY, DE21 2XR.

NAYLOR, Mr. Nicholas John, BA ACA *1993;* Claridge House, 32 Davies Street, LONDON, W1K 4ND.

•**NAYLOR, Mr. Paul, FCA** *1974;* Naylor Wintersgill Ltd, Carlton House, Grammar School Street, BRADFORD, WEST YORKSHIRE, BD1 4NS.

NAYLOR, Mr. Paul Michael, BA(Hons) ACA *2004;* 39 Wilsthorpe Road, Breaston, DERBY, DE72 3EA.

•**NAYLOR, Mr. Paul Phillip, BA ACA** *2000;* Grant Thornton UK LLP, 101 Cambridge Science Park, Milton Road, CAMBRIDGE, CB4 0FY. See also Grant Thornton LLP

NAYLOR, Mr. Peter Charles Illsley, FCA *1973;* 11 Barford Drive, Lowton, WARRINGTON, CHESHIRE, WA3 1DD.

NAYLOR, Mr. Peter Leonard, FCA *1973;* 41 Romany Way, Norton, STOURBRIDGE, DY8 3JR.

NAYLOR, Mr. Philip Arthur, BA FCA *1977;* Spent Oak, Owler Park Road, ILKLEY, LS29 0BG.

NAYLOR, Mr. Philip David, BA ACA *1985;* Apt 39, 106 Shahsi Badalbeyli Kucesi, BAKU AZ 1010, AZERBAIJAN.

NAYLOR, Mr. Robert Graham, BA(Hons) ACA ASI *2000;* 21 Staveley Road, LONDON, W4 3HU.

NAYLOR, Mr. Sam Edward James, ACA *2008;* 14 Hugon Road, LONDON, SW6 3EN.

NAYLOR, Miss. Sarah Jane, BA ACA *1995;* 19 Upper Welland Terrace, SPALDING, LINCOLNSHIRE, PE11 2TA.

NAYLOR, Ms. Stephanie Jane, FCA FCCA *2000;* Badgers Rest, 9 Ffordd Cae Llwyn, Connah's Quay, DEESIDE, CH5 4ZB.

NAYLOR, Mr. Stephen, BSc ACA *1983;* 2 Grange Cliffe Close, SHEFFIELD, S11 9JE.

NAYLOR, Mrs. Suzanne, BSc ACA *1992;* 64 Winster Avenue, Dorridge, SOLIHULL, WEST MIDLANDS, B93 8ST.

NAYLOR, Mr. Thomas Peter, FCA *1950;* The Clock House, Far Sawrey, AMBLESIDE, LA22 0LJ. (Life Member)

NAYLOR-SMITH, Mr. John, FCA *1960;* Hollycroft, Sycamore Close, AMERSHAM, BUCKINGHAMSHIRE, HP6 6BW. (Life Member)

NAZAR, Mr. Nasser, BSc ACA *2002;* Laroze Industrials Ltd, Hoppingwood Farm, Robin Hood Way, LONDON, SW20 0AB.

NAZARIAN, Mr. Daniel Miran, MA(Cantab) BA(Hons) ACA *2011;* 40 Fillebrook Road, Leytonstone, LONDON, E11 4AT.

NAZERALI, Mr. Shirazali Janmohamed, FCA *1975;* 12323 17 Street SW, CALGARY T2W 4A1, AB, CANADA.

NAZEYROLLAS, Miss. Pascale Marie-France, BA ACA *1992;* Doumazac, 19120 SIONIAC, FRANCE.

•**NAZIM-UD-DIN, Mr. Mohammad, ACA** *1980;* Nazim & Co, Suite 1C, Cranbrook House, 61 Cranbrook Road, ILFORD, ESSEX IG1 4PG.

NAZIR, Mr. Mohammad Majid, BSc ACA *2004;* 44 Brompton Park Crescent, Seagrave Road, Fulham, LONDON, SW6 1SW.

NAZIRUD DIN, Mr. Mohammed, FCA *1969;* 250 WEBB DRIVE SUITE 502, MISSISSAUGA L5B 3Z4, ON, CANADA.

NAZRI, Miss. Nazlin Mohd, BSc ACA *2006;* 13 Millicent Grove, Enfield, LONDON, N13 6HF.

NDAWULA, Mr. Bobby, BSc(Hons) ACA *2002;* 7 Chelwood Mount, Roundhay, LEEDS, LS8 2AY.

NDEGWA, Mr. Peter Ciera, ACA *1993;* British American Tobacco Kenya Ltd, PO Box 30000-0100 GPO, NAIROBI, KENYA.

NDIWENI, Mr. Timothy Bubby, ACA *2007;* 201 Talgarth Road, LONDON, W6 8BJ.

NDLOVU, Mr. Alaster Nunn, ACA *2007;* 11 Gainsborough Drive, WOLVERHAMPTON, WV6 7NR.

NDONYE, Mr. Daniel Mutisya, FCA *1977;* Deloitte & Touche, Deloitte Place, Waiyaki Way, Muthangari, P O Box 40092, GPO 00100 NAIROBI KENYA.

NDU, Mr. Ikechukwu Chukwukeluo, MSc BSc ACA *2000;* 12/14 Lobito Crescent, Independence Layout, ENUGU, NIGERIA.

NDUNGU, Mr. Martin Kariuki, BCom ACA *1997;* Martin Ndungu, P O Box 43651 00100, Nairobi, NAIROBI, 00100 GPO, KENYA.

NEADES, Mrs. Cara, BSc(Hons) ACA *2003;* Baare y Tonne, 3 Parsonage Glebe, St. Johns, ISLE OF MAN, IM4 3LT.

NEADS, Mrs. Alison Hilary, BSc ACA *1993;* Cell Telecom Ltd Lees House, 21-23 Dyke Road, BRIGHTON, BN1 3FE.

•**NEAL, Mr. Adrian Charles, BA FCA** *1989;* (Tax Fac), Berry Accountants, Bowden House, 36 Northampton Road, MARKET HARBOROUGH, LEICESTERSHIRE, LE16 9HE.

NEAL, Miss. Anna, BSc ACA *2003;* 40 Trusley Brook, Hilton, DERBY, DE65 5LA.

NEAL, Mr. Barry James, BSc ACA *1995;* 6 Astley Hall Drive, Ramsbottom, BURY, BL0 9DF.

NEAL, Mr. Charles Roger, BA FCA *1978;* The Neal Consultancy Ltd, Vale Cottage, 39 Casterton Road, STAMFORD, LINCOLNSHIRE, PE9 2UA.

NEAL, Mr. David James, ACA *2009;* 120 Vaughan Road, HARROW, HA1 4ED.

NEAL, Mr. David John, BA ACA *1986;* 7 Nant-y-Glyn Road, COLWYN BAY, CLWYD, LL29 7PU.

NEAL, Mr. David William, FCA *1977;* Minett Group Ltd, 1-2 Raymond Close, Industrial Estate, Wollaston, WELLINGBOROUGH, NORTHAMPTONSHIRE NN29 7RG.

NEAL, Mr. Edward England, FCA *1965;* 3 Redhouse Drive, Sonning Common, READING, RG4 9NT.

NEAL, Mr. Geoffrey Michael, FCA *1975;* Afford Rent A Car, Royal Oak Garage, Fenton, STOKE-ON-TRENT, STAFFORDSHIRE, ST4 2PX.

•**NEAL, Mr. Ian Keith, FCA CTA** *1980;* (Tax Fac), Bates Weston Audit Limited, The Mill, Canal Street, DERBY, DE1 2RJ. See also BW Business Services Limited

NEAL, Ms. Jane Caroline, BSc ACA *1993;* Barclays Capital, 5 North Colonnade, LONDON, E14 4BB.

NEAL, Mr. John Gersham, BSc FCA *1980;* P.O.HM 2129, HAMILTON HM JX, BERMUDA.

NEAL, Mr. John Raymond, BSc ACA *1984;* Secure One Ltd Unit 14, Warren Park Way Enderby, LEICESTER, LE19 4SA.

NEAL, Mr. Jonathan, BSc ACA *2006;* 164 Eastcombe Avenue, LONDON, SE7 7LW.

NEAL, Mr. Jonathon Sinclair, BEng ACA *2003;* 10705 SE 29th Street, BEAUX ARTS, WA 98004, UNITED STATES.

NEAL, Mr. Keith, FCA *1968;* 8 Raley Road, Locks Heath, SOUTHAMPTON, SO31 6PD.

NEAL, Miss. Lucy Jane, BA ACA *2010;* 2 Medway Crescent, ALTRINCHAM, CHESHIRE, WA14 4UB.

NEAL, Mr. Matthew, LLB ACA *2005;* 29 Frederica Road, LONDON, E4 7AL.

NEAL, Mr. Matthew James, ACA *2008;* with PricewaterhouseCoopers LLP, 1 Embankment Place, LONDON, WC2N 6RH.

NEAL, Mr. Nicholas John, BSc(Hons) ACA *2000;* 17 Denewood Court, Victoria Road, WILMSLOW, CHESHIRE, SK9 5HP.

NEAL, Mrs. Nicola, BA ACA *1997;* Saffron House La Route de Sausmarez, St. Martin, GUERNSEY, GY4 6SG.

NEAL, Mr. Paul Brian, BA FCA *1990;* 5 Dunslade Close, MARKET HARBOROUGH, LE16 8AF.

NEAL, Mr. Richard John, BSc ACA *2001;* Ellerman Investments Ltd, 20 St. James's Street, LONDON, SW1A 1ES.

•**NEAL, Mr. Roger, FCA** *1974;* Turner & Smith, Westgate House, Royland Road, LOUGHBOROUGH, LE11 2EH. See also APBS Limited

Members - Alphabetical NEAL - NEIL

•NEAL, Mr. Sidney Roger, BCom FCA *1965;* Neal & Co, Shakespeare Building, 26 Cradley Road, CRADLEY HEATH, WEST MIDLANDS, B64 6AG.
NEAL, Mr. Simon John, FCA *1995;* Linden House, Bagatelle Road, St. Saviour, JERSEY, JE2 7TY.
NEAL, Mr. Simon Nicholas, BA(Hons) ACA *2001;* 24 Patterdale Road, Woodthorpe, NOTTINGHAM, NG5 4LQ.
•NEAL, Mr. Stephen Howard, BA ACA FCCA *2009;* Shaw Gibbs LLP, 264 Banbury Road, OXFORD, OX2 7DY.
•NEAL, Mr. Steven, FCA *1975;* Kingston Smith LLP, Devonshire House, 60 Goswell Road, LONDON, EC1M 7AD. See also Kingston Smith Limited Liability Partnership, Devonshire Corporate Services LLP, Kingston Smith Consulting LLP, Kingston Smith Services Limited and Devonshire Corporate Finance Limited
NEAL, Mr. Trevor James, FCA *1960;* 23 Ridgewood Close, Porthpean, ST AUSTELL, CORNWALL, PL26 6AT. (Life Member)
•NEALE, Mr. Brian George, FCA *1961;* Brian G. Neale, Was-Thatched, Hambleton, OAKHAM, LE15 8TH.
NEALE, Mr. Brook, ACA *2009;* 2 Foskett Road, LONDON, SW6 3LZ.
NEALE, Mr. Christopher Charles Anthony, BA ACA MBA *1986;* 11 Chipstead Street, LONDON, SW6 3SR.
NEALE, Mr. Christopher James, BA(Hons) ACA *2001;* 143 Bradbourne Park Road, SEVENOAKS, TN13 3LB.
NEALE, Mr. David Anthony, FCA *1957;* Espace Mirabeau, Avenue Jean Giono, 04100 MANOSQUE, FRANCE. (Life Member)
NEALE, Mr. David Roy, FCA *1972;* Hollybrook House, Theale, WEDMORE, SOMERSET, BS28 4SL.
NEALE, Mr. Duncan John, BA ACA *1997;* 18 Fielding Road, LONDON, W14 0LL.
•NEALE, Mr. Graham, BA FCA *1987;* KPMG LLP, One Snowhill, Snow Hill Queensway, BIRMINGHAM, B4 6GN. See also KPMG Europe LLP
NEALE, Mr. Guy Duncan, BEng ACA *1993;* 17 The Mount, LONDON, NW3 6SZ.
NEALE, Mrs. Katharine, ACA *2008;* 10 Warren Avenue, CHEADLE, CHESHIRE, SK8 1ND.
•NEALE, Mr. Keith George, FCA *1969;* 44 Larch Walk, Kennington, ASHFORD, TN24 9BW.
NEALE, Mrs. Linda Susan, ACA *1986;* Barrule, Maudlyn Parkway, STEYNING, BN44 3PT.
•NEALE, Mr. Matthew, ACA ACCA *2008;* HWEA Ltd, 8 Hopper Way, Diss Business Park, DISS, NORFOLK, IP22 4GT. See also Haines Watts, Haines Watts, Haines Watts, Haines Watts Colchester Ltd
NEALE, Mr. Matthew, ACA *2010;* 11 Spring Vale Garden Village, DARWEN, LANCASHIRE, BB3 2HJ.
•NEALE, Mr. Michael John, FCA *1979;* Nexia Smith & Williamson Audit Limited, Portwall Place, Portwall Lane, BRISTOL, BS1 6NA. See also Smith & Williamson Ltd and Nexia Audit Limited
NEALE, Mr. Mike, BSc ACA *2009;* 18 Stonybeck Close, Westlea, SWINDON, SN5 7AQ.
NEALE, Mr. Paul Andrew, BSc FCA *1993;* 3B Coastline Villa, DISCOVERY BAY, HONG KONG SAR.
NEALE, Mr. Paul John, BSc ACA *1993;* 10 Highfields, SAFFRON WALDEN, ESSEX, CB10 2AD.
NEALE, Mrs. Philippa Jayne, BSc ACA *1981;* Merston Cottage, Holcombe Rogus, WELLINGTON, TA21 0PE.
NEALE, Mr. Richard William, FCA *1974;* 3 Les Marchandises, Sainte Pience, 50870 MANCHE, FRANCE.
NEALE, Mr. Robert James, BSc ACA *2003;* 14 Lakeside Approach, Barkston Ash, TADCASTER, NORTH YORKSHIRE, LS24 9PH.
NEALE, Mr. Thomas Carman, BA FCA *1984;* Avenue Parmentier 80, Woluwe Saint Pierre, B-1150 BRUSSELS, BELGIUM.
NEALE, Mr. Timothy David, BSc(Hons) ACA *2001;* Kirk Rice, The Courtyard, 69 High Street, ASCOT, BERKSHIRE, SL5 7HP.
NEALE, Mr. Timothy Peter Graham, FCA *1963;* 20 Raglan Rd, REIGATE, RH2 0DP. (Life Member)
NEALEY, Mr. Duncan Patrick, MA(Oxon) FCA *2000;* 3 Summers Place, off Sunderland Avenue, OXFORD, OX2 8FA.
NEALON, Mr. Michael, BSc FCA *1971;* Flat 1, 24 Bromley Grove, BROMLEY, BR2 0LN.
•NEAME, Mrs. Jane Claire, ACA ATII *1989;* J C Neame, The Elders, 52 Ham Shades Lane, Tankerton, WHITSTABLE, CT5 1NX.
•NEARS, Mrs. Lesley Eryl, BA ACA *1983;* Lesley Nears, 8 St Johns Road, Hazel Grove, STOCKPORT, SK7 5HG.
NEARY, Mr. Daniel Richard, BA(Hons)Oxon ACA *2001;* 169 Neville Street, MIDDLE PARK, VIC 3206, AUSTRALIA.
NEARY, Mrs. Melanie, BSc ACA *2001;* 35a St Annes Road, SOUTHAMPTON SN01, BERMUDA.
NEARY, Mr. Paul James, BA ACA *2004;* Lower Apartment, 35a St Annes Road, Southampton, HAMILTON SN0 1, BERMUDA.
NEARY, Mr. Rory Patrick, BSc ACA *2000;* 24 Hithercroft Road, Downley, HIGH WYCOMBE, BUCKINGHAMSHIRE, HP13 5LS.
NEASHAM, Mr. Christopher, BSc ACA *1996;* Gilchrist Tash, Cleveland Buildings, Queens Square, MIDDLESBROUGH, TS2 1PA.
•NEASHAM, Mr. Paul, FCA FMAAT *1999;* Paul Neasham Accountancy Limited, 6 Oak Tree Road, BEDALE, NORTH YORKSHIRE, DL8 1UE.
NEAT, Mr. Phillip Gary, BSc ACA *1984;* 2 Brendon Drive, ESHER, KT10 9EQ.
•NEATE, Miss. Cherry Margaret, ACA *1986;* C. Neate, 15 Mill Road, STEYNING, WEST SUSSEX, BN44 3LN.
•NEATE, Mr. David Robert Charles, BSc ACA *1998;* Springboard Corporate Finance Limited, Baskerville House, Centenary Square, BIRMINGHAM, B1 2ND.
•NEATE, Mr. Francis Vincent Hugh, BA ACA *1995;* KPMG LLP, 15 Canada Square, LONDON, E14 5GL. See also KPMG Europe LLP
NEATE, Mr. Hugh Greville, FCA *1968;* 8 Elm Cl, Chipping Sodbury, BRISTOL, BS37 6HE.
NEATE, Mr. Jonathan Charles, BA ACA *1994;* 50 Melbourne Avenue, Dronfield Woodhouse, DRONFIELD, DERBYSHIRE, S18 8YW.
NEATE, Mr. Keith Antony, BA ACA *1987;* St Johns, 39 White Cedar Road, PULLENVALE, QLD 4069, AUSTRALIA.
•NEATE, Mr. Paul, ACA FCCA *2009;* Old Mill Accountancy LLP, The Old Mill, Park Road, SHEPTON MALLET, SOMERSET, BA4 5BS. See also Old Mill Audit LLP
•NEATE, Mr. Robert Henry, BSc ACA *1990;* Mazars LLP, Tower Bridge House, St. Katharines Way, LONDON, E1W 1DD.
NEATE, Mrs. Sarah Louise, ACA *1994;* 29 St. Pauls Road, STAINES, MIDDLESEX, TW18 3HQ.
NEATH, Mrs. Emma Jane, LLB ACA CTA *1994;* 26 Curlew Close, OKEHAMPTON, DEVON, EX20 1SE.
NEATH, Mr. Mark John, BA ACA CF *1999;* Old Mill Group, Tenon Recovery, Berkeley House, Dix's Field, EXETER, EX1 1PZ.
NEATHERCOAT, Mr. Simon John, FCA *1973;* Knole Field, Blackhall Lane, SEVENOAKS, TN15 0HS.
NEATHERCOAT, Mr. Timothy William, BA ACA *2005;* with BDO LLP, 55 Baker Street, LONDON, W1U 7EU.
NEAVE, Mrs. Diane Elizabeth, BSc ACA *1989;* 20 The Steils, EDINBURGH, EH10 5XD.
NEAVE, Mrs. Jayne, BA ACA *1994;* 50 Dean Brook Road, Netherthong, HOLMFIRTH, HD9 3UF.
NEAVE, Mr. Jonathan Antony, BSc ACA *1996;* 22 Saugatuck River Road, WESTON, CT 06883, UNITED STATES.
NEAVE, Mr. Michael William Smith, BSc ACA *1979;* Actia UK Ltd, Unit 81, Mochdre Industrial Estate, Mochdre, NEWTOWN, POWYS SY16 4LE.
NEAVE, Mr. Richard John William, BSc ACA *1991;* with PricewaterhouseCoopers LLP, Erskine House, 68-73 Queen Street, EDINBURGH, EH2 4NH.
•ⓘNEAVE, Mrs. Valerie Laura, BA ACA *1991;* Benedict Mackenzie, The Grange, Aston-on-Carrant, TEWKESBURY, GLOUCESTERSHIRE, GL20 8HL. See also Benedict Mackenzie LLP
NEAVERSON, Mrs. Hazel Margaret, ACA *1980;* 122 Windermere Road, Ealing, LONDON, W5 4TH.
NEAVES, Mr. Dean Christopher, BSc(Hons) FCA *1999;* with PricewaterhouseCoopers, Abacus House, Castle Park, CAMBRIDGE, CB3 0AN.
NEBBETT, Mrs. Christine Wendy, BSc ACA *1992;* Faraway Farm, Gittisham, HONITON, EX14 3TZ.
NEBHRAJANI, Ms. Sharmila, MA ACA *1992;* 8 Chesham Street, BRIGHTON, BN2 1NA.
NECCHI, Mr. Peter Luigi, FCA *1977;* Three Farthings, Terminus Road, Blackboys, UCKFIELD, TN22 5LX.
•NEDAS, Mr. Jeffrey Lawrence, MA FCA *1972;* Jeffrey Nedas & Co, 24 Upper Brook Street, LONDON, W1K 7QB.
NEDDERMAN, Mr. Anthony, MBA FCA *1963;* 327 Coughlan Street, VALLEJO, CA 94590, UNITED STATES.
•NEDELEC, Mr. Bruno Pascal Raymond, ACA *2011;* Outre-Manche Expertise Limited, 17 Trinity House, Station Road, BOREHAMWOOD, HERTFORDSHIRE, WD6 1DA.
•NEDEN, Mr. Andrew Frederick John, MA FCA *1987;* KPMG LLP, 15 Canada Square, LONDON, E14 5GL. See also KPMG Europe LLP
NEECH, Mr. Brian Sanders, FCA *1965;* Eastholme, Tunstead Road, Hoveton, NORWICH, NR12 8QN.
NEEDHAM, Mr. Andrew, ACA *2011;* 25 Worthington Road, SALE, CHESHIRE, M33 2JJ.
•NEEDHAM, Mr. Andrew, BSc ACA *1988;* The Johnson Walker Partnership Limited, Horizon House, 2 Whiting Street, SHEFFIELD, S8 9QR. See also Franchise Logistics Ltd
NEEDHAM, Mr. Andrew, ACA *1994;* 25 Cutlers Close, BISHOP'S STORTFORD, HERTFORDSHIRE, CM23 4FW.
NEEDHAM, Mr. Andrew Craig, ACA *1983;* 13 Prospect Avenue, FARNBOROUGH, HAMPSHIRE, GU14 8JT.
NEEDHAM, Mr. Ben, ACA *2009;* 7b Thirsk Road, LONDON, SW11 5SU.
NEEDHAM, Mrs. Beverley, BSocSc ACA *1993;* Winterfold House School Winterfold, Chaddesley Corbett, KIDDERMINSTER, WORCESTERSHIRE, DY10 4PW.
NEEDHAM, Mrs. Christelle Katherine, BA(Hons) ACA *2000;* 34 Greenway Road, Timperley, ALTRINCHAM, WA15 6BJ.
NEEDHAM, Mr. Christopher William, BSc FCA *1983;* 57 Avenue de Auderghem, Boite 11, Etterbeek, 1040 BRUSSELS, BELGIUM.
NEEDHAM, Miss. Claire, BSc ACA *1999;* 9 Crawshay Drive, Emmer Green, READING, RG4 8SX.
NEEDHAM, Miss. Claire Louise, BSc ACA *2005;* Flat 7, 10/12 Clyde Road, West Didsbury, MANCHESTER, M20 2WH.
NEEDHAM, Mrs. Clare, BA ACA *2003;* 64 Middle Meadow, Shireoaks, WORKSOP, NOTTINGHAMSHIRE, S81 8PX.
NEEDHAM, Mr. Clive John, BSc ACA *1993;* 20 Westfield Road, Bengeo, HERTFORD, SG14 3DJ.
•NEEDHAM, Mr. Clive Ronald, BA FCA *1993;* C.R. Needham, Watersmeet, Westfield Drive, Ramsey, ISLE OF MAN, IM8 3ER.
NEEDHAM, Mr. David Kevin, ACA *1978;* (Tax Fac), 6 Firsway, Wightwick, WOLVERHAMPTON, WV6 8BJ.
NEEDHAM, Mr. David Michael, BA FCA *1985;* 6 Priory Close, Walton, CHESTERFIELD, S42 7HQ.
•NEEDHAM, Miss. Deborah, BA(Hons) ACA *1999;* D N Accounting Solutions, Brynawel, Velindre, LLANDYSUL, DYFED, SA44 5UU.
•NEEDHAM, Mrs. Dianne Christine Augusta, ACA *1984;* with The Johnson Walker Partnership Limited, Horizon House, 2 Whiting Street, SHEFFIELD, S8 9QR.
•NEEDHAM, Mrs. Elizabeth Dawn, ACA *1992;* Kendall Wadley LLP, Granta Lodge, 71 Graham Road, MALVERN, WORCESTERSHIRE, WR14 2JS.
NEEDHAM, Mr. Graham Raymond, MA FCA *1993;* The Lodge, Welton Cliff, LINCOLN, LN2 3PX.
NEEDHAM, Miss. Helen Anne, BA(Hons) ACA *2002;* (Tax Fac), 2 High View Gardens, Kirkby-in-Ashfield, NOTTINGHAM, NG17 9DQ.
NEEDHAM, Mrs. Jane Elizabeth, BSc ACA AIRM *1995;* 18 Rue de Gervily, 22490 TRIGAVOU, BRITTANY, FRANCE.
•NEEDHAM, Mr. John Charles, MEng ACA *2003;* Littlejohn LLP, 1 Westferry Circus, Canary Wharf, LONDON, E14 4HD.
NEEDHAM, Mr. John Gerard, BA ACA *1989;* 131 Homefield Park, SUTTON, SM1 2DY.
•NEEDHAM, Mr. John Kenyon, FCA *1974;* John Needham & Co., Shefford Business Centre, 71 Hitchin Road, SHEFFORD, SG17 5JB.
NEEDHAM, Mr. Jonathan Stuart, BA FCA *1979;* 13 Rosedale Way, Kempston, BEDFORD, MK42 8JE.
NEEDHAM, Mr. Keith Michael William, BSc ACA *2010;* 14 Allerton Grange Crescent, LEEDS, LS17 6LN.
•NEEDHAM, Ms. Laura, BSc ACA *2003;* with PricewaterhouseCoopers, 7 More London Riverside, LONDON, SE1 2RT.
•NEEDHAM, Mr. Malcolm Edward, FCA *1962;* Needham Chipchase Manners & Co, 30b Market Place, RICHMOND, DL10 4QG.
NEEDHAM, Mr. Mark Richard, BA ACA *2002;* 75 meyer Road, 15-01 Hawaii Towers, SINGAPORE 437901, SINGAPORE.
NEEDHAM, Mr. Michael Barry, FCA *1965;* 5285 Aspen Drive, WEST VANCOUVER V7W 2Z7, BC, CANADA. (Life Member)
NEEDHAM, Mr. Peter, BA ACA *1989;* 7 Juniper Place, WESTON-SUPER-MARE, AVON, BS22 9XD.
•NEEDHAM, Mr. Philip, BA FCA *1984;* Hornbeam Accountancy Services Ltd, Hornbeam House, Bidwell Road, Rackheath, NORWICH, NR13 6PT.
NEEDHAM, Mr. Philip Christopher, FCA *1970;* 71 Marstone Crescent, Totley, SHEFFIELD, S17 4DG.
NEEDHAM, Mrs. Shelagh, BA ACA *1989;* 21 Eastlands Lane, Church Warsop, MANSFIELD, NG20 0SD.
NEEDLE, Mr. Raymond, FCA *1963;* 47 Lentune Way, LYMINGTON, HAMPSHIRE, SO41 3PE. (Life Member)
NEEDLEMAN, Mr. John Elliot, FCA *1974;* Glacial Properties Ltd, 7a Hampstead High Street, LONDON, NW3 1PR.
NEEDLEMAN, Mr. Michael Paul, BA ACA *1987;* house, 60 Lyndhurst Gardens, LONDON, N3 1TD.
NEEDLER, Mr. George Henry Christopher, MA FCA *1968;* L'Espadon, Apt 31, 41 Ave des Papalins, MC 98000 MONACO, MONACO.
•NEEDS, Mr. Cary John, FCA *1963;* 18 Foxe Road, Frampton Cotterell, BRISTOL, BS36 2AE.
NEEDS, Dr. Richard Leslie, PhD ACA ATII *2001;* (Tax Fac), The Wolery, Forest Road, ASCOT, BERKSHIRE, SL5 8QG.
•NEEDS, Mr. Robert Edward, FCA *1975;* (Tax Fac), R.E. Needs Ltd, 42 Huddersfield Road, BARNSLEY, S75 1DW. See also R E Needs
NEEL, Mr. David Clive, FCA *1978;* E C Delegation, 25 Main Regent Road, Leicester Square, P O Box 1399, FREETOWN, SIERRA LEONE.
NEELY, Mr. Guy David, MA FCA *1956;* Staplecross, 2 Bromley Lane, CHISLEHURST, BR7 6LE. (Life Member)
NEELY, Mr. Sean Alexander, BSc FCA *1990;* 13 Coombe Rise, KINGSTON UPON THAMES, SURREY, KT2 7EX.
NEEN, Mr. William Thomas, FCA *1972;* West Lodge, Old Wokingham Road, WOKINGHAM, BERKSHIRE, RG40 3BT.
NEEP, Mr. Craig, BA ACA *2010;* 35 Hazel Close, Taverham, NORWICH, NR8 6YE.
NEER, Miss. Mandeep Kaur, BSc ACA *2003;* 55a Graceville Avenue, Graceville, BRISBANE, QLD 4075, AUSTRALIA.
NEESHAM, Mrs. Rachel Louise, BA(Hons) ACA *2001;* Sweet Briars, 14 Oak Tree Road, Milford, GODALMING, SURREY, GU8 5JN.
NEETHLING, Mrs. Elisha, ACA *2011;* Flat 4, Sterling House, 3 Burston Road, LONDON, SW15 6AR.
NEETHLING, Mr. Johan Deetlefs, BSc(Hons) ACA CTA *2011;* Flat 4, Sterling House, 3 Burston Road, Putney, LONDON, SW15 6AR.
NEEVE, Miss. Maria Louise, BSc ACA *2000;* 43 Pepys Road, LONDON, SW20 8NL.
NEEVE, Mr. Philip James, BA ACA *1999;* Ligsalzstr. 13, 80339 MUENCHEN, GERMANY.
•NEEVE, Mr. Robert, FCA *1979;* (Tax Fac), 4 Rowland Burn Way, Sherburn Towers, ROWLANDS GILL, NE39 2PU.
NEFEDOV, Mr. Ilya, ACA *2010;* Azovskaya St, 24/1Apt 399, MOSCOW, MOSCOW REGION, RUSSIAN FEDERATION.
NEGANDHI, Mr. Jayraj, FCA *1983;* 45 Highland Road, AMERSHAM, HP7 9AX.
NEGUS, Miss. Caroline Hannah, BA ACA *1999;* 84 Sistova Road, LONDON, SW12 9QS.
NEGUS, Mr. Matthew, ACA *2008;* 50 High Street, Landbeach, CAMBRIDGE, CB25 9FT.
NEGUS, Mr. Terence James, FCA *1976;* The Old Nursery, Lunghurst Road, Woldingham, CATERHAM, SURREY, CR3 7HF.
•NEICHO, Mrs. Fiona Gordon, FCA *1988;* (Tax Fac), J M H Financials Limited, Cumbrae, Brittains Lane, SEVENOAKS, KENT, TN13 2NF.
•NEIGHBOUR, Mr. John Frederick Thomas, FCA *1968;* HBAS Limited, Amwell House, 19 Amwell Street, HODDESDON, HERTFORDSHIRE, EN11 8TS. See also Hardcastles Limited
NEIGHBOUR, Mr. Peter, FCA *1975;* Ark House, 15 Exchange Road, WATFORD, WD18 0JD.
NEIGHBOURS, Mr. Martin Edwin, BSc ACA *1993;* 49 Aubreys, LETCHWORTH GARDEN CITY, HERTFORDSHIRE, SG6 3TU.
NEIL, Mr. Alrick Albert, BA ACA *1992;* 18 York Road, Ealing, LONDON, W5 4SG.
NEIL, Mrs. Amanda, MA ACA *1993;* c/o Andrew Neil (045643), BFPO 5546, RUISLIP, MIDDLESEX, HA4 6EP.
NEIL, Mr. Andrew Craig, ACA *2011;* Greystoke Hill Drive, Failand, BRISTOL, BS8 3UX.
NEIL, Mr. Christopher, BA ACA *2011;* 52 Regents Park Road, SOUTHAMPTON, SO15 8PG.
NEIL, Mr. Derek Richard, BA FCA *1999;* with BDO LLP, 55 Baker Street, LONDON, W1U 7EU.
NEIL, Miss. Jennifer Jean, BA(Hons) ACA *2002;* 76 Childwall Park Avenue, LIVERPOOL, L16 0JQ.
NEIL, Mr. Mark Robert, BA FCA *1994;* 4a Bourne Way, Mayford, WOKING, SURREY, GU22 9QU.
•NEIL, Mr. Ronald George, MA FCA *1969;* Neil & Co, 30 Cedar Avenue, BARNET, HERTFORDSHIRE, EN4 8DX.

NEIL - NEOPTOLEMOU Members - Alphabetical

NEIL, Mr. Simon Duncan, BSc FCA ATII *2000;* (Tax Fac), 1 Upper Stroud Close, Chineham, BASINGSTOKE, HAMPSHIRE, RG24 8EG.
NEIL, Miss. Victoria Joan, BSc ACA *2004;* 30 Cedar Avenue, East Barnet, BARNET, EN4 8DX.
NEILAN, Mrs. Anne Marie, MA ACA *1985;* 17 Castle Oak, USK, GWENT, NP15 1SG.
•**NEILAN, Mr. Michael Joseph, BSc ACA CTA** *1997;* Price & Company, 30/32 Gildredge Road, EASTBOURNE, BN21 4SH.
NEILD, Mr. Christopher David, BA ACA *1990;* P P D Development Granta Park, Great Abington, CAMBRIDGE, CB21 6GQ.
NEILD, Mr. Frederick John, FCA *1966;* 5 Laurier Road, Dartmouth Park, LONDON, NW5 1SD.
NEILD, Mrs. Jennifer Susanne, BSc ACA *1993;* Pavilion End, Rectory Lane, Fowlmere, ROYSTON, HERTFORDSHIRE, SG8 7TL.
NEILL, Mr. Andrew, MA ACA *1993;* 13 Malting Lane, Aldbury, TRING, HERTFORDSHIRE, HP23 5RH.
NEILL, Mr. Andrew Denis Guy, BSc ACA *1993;* 20 Cordwell Close, Castle Donington, DERBY, DE74 2JL.
NEILL, Mr. David John Clarke, FCA *1963;* 4 Fowlmere Road, Foxton, CAMBRIDGE, CB22 6RS.
NEILL, Mr. David Laurence, FCA *1963;* 3 Cove Avenue, Groomsport, BANGOR, COUNTY DOWN, BT19 6HX. (Life Member)
NEILL, Miss. Emma Elizabeth Mary, BSc ACA *1995;* 5 Garratts Lane, BANSTEAD, SM7 2DZ.
NEILL, Mr. James Isambard, BSc ACA *2003;* with KPMG LLP, Dukes Keep, Marsh Lane, SOUTHAMPTON, HAMPSHIRE, SO14 3EX.
NEILL, Miss. Jennifer Anne, ACA *2008;* Apartment 33 Century Building, Esplanade St. Helier, JERSEY, JE2 3AD.
NEILL, Mrs. Joanna Maria, ACA *1983;* Holly House, 46a Victoria Drive, LONDON, SW19 6BG.
NEILL, Mr. John Whitley, FCA *1961;* The Sycamores, Elmhurst Walk, Goring on Thames, READING, RG8 9DE. (Life Member)
NEILL, Mrs. Karina Else, ACA *1992;* 56 Glenhill Drive, COCHRANE T4C 1H1, AB, CANADA.
NEILL, Mr. Matthew James, MA BA(Hons) ACA *2010;* 1 Highlands, Wiltshire Way, TUNBRIDGE WELLS, TN2 3UF.
NEILL, Ms. Melanie Jane, LLB ACA *1988;* 41 Holmesdale Road, TEDDINGTON, TW11 9LJ.
•**NEILL, Mr. Peter, ACA** *1988;* Jones Harris Limited, 17 St. Peters Place, FLEETWOOD, LANCASHIRE, FY7 6EB.
NEILL, Mr. Roderick Charles, ACA *1995;* 56 Glenhill Drive, COCHRANE T4C 1H1, AB, CANADA.
NEILL, Mr. Timothy Piers Patrick, MA ACA *1982;* 41 Holmesdale Road, TEDDINGTON, TW11 9LJ.
•**NEILON, Mr. Marc James, BA FCA** *1990;* Jamesons Ltd, Jamesons House, Compton Way, WITNEY, OXFORDSHIRE, OX28 3AB.
NEILSON, Mrs. Alison Christine, BA ACA *1981;* 5 Rostrevor Road, Wimbledon, LONDON, SW19 7AP.
NEILSON, Mr. Barrie Douglas, BCom ACA *2003;* Flat 4 Kelvinside House, 2 Beaconsfield Road, GLASGOW, G12 0PW.
NEILSON, Mr. Christopher, BA ACA *1979;* 3 The Orchards, Off Frewland Avenue Davenport, STOCKPORT, SK3 8UH.
NEILSON, Miss. Emily Jane Easton, MA ACA *2001;* 3 York Cottages, 20 York Road, MAIDENHEAD, BERKSHIRE, SL6 1SS.
NEILSON, Mr. George, FCA *1976;* P.O. Box 364, WARWICK PARISH WK BX, BERMUDA.
•**NEILSON, Mr. George Strain, BA ACA** *1990;* Neilson Renton & Co Ltd, 101 Main Street, Uddingston, GLASGOW, G71 7EW. See also Neilson Renton & Co
NEILSON, Miss. Laura Elizabeth, BA ACA *2005;* with KPMG LLP, 15 Canada Square, LONDON, E14 5GL.
NEILSON, Mr. Paul Gregory Tyler, BA FCA *1989;* Shutebridge Farm, Marwood Road, Aylesbeare, EXETER, EX5 2BW.
NEISH, Mr. Barry, FCA *1968;* 18 King Edwards Grove, TEDDINGTON, MIDDLESEX, TW11 9LU. (Life Member)
NEIVENS, Mr. Andrew Charles, BSc ACA *1980;* rue du Grand-Pré 70c, 1202 GENEVA, SWITZERLAND.
NEIWERT, Mr. Richard Stephen, BSc ACA *1980;* Eidelstedter Weg 290, 25469 HALSTENBEK, GERMANY.
•**NELDER, Miss. Jennifer Anne, BA FCA** *1981;* Bruce Sutherland & Co, Moreton House, MORETON-IN-MARSH, GL56 0LH.
NELIGAN, Mrs. Katherine Jane, BA ACA *1990;* Air Products, Carburos Metalicos, C Aragon 300, BARCELONA, SPAIN.
NELKIN, Mr. Peter Simon, FCA *1970;* Laurel Farmhouse, Totteridge Green, LONDON, N20 8PH.
NELKON, Mr. Alan Philip, FCA *1961;* 23 Saddlescombe Way, LONDON, N12 7LS.
•**NELKON, Mr. Nigel Clifford Alastair, BSc FCA CTA** *1995;* (Tax Fac), Ernst & Young LLP, 1 More London Place, LONDON, SE1 2AF. See also Ernst & Young Europe LLP
NELL, Mr. Nicholas Sherwood, BSc FCA *1978;* Round Hill House, Brook, LYNDHURST, HAMPSHIRE, SO43 7HG.
•**NELLEMOSE, Mr. Peter Michael, FCA** *1976;* Averillo & Associates, 16 South End, CROYDON, CR0 1DN. See also Averillo Taxation Services Limited
NELLIGAN, Mr. Mark, BA ACA *1990;* Pershing Securities Singapore Pte Ltd, One Temasek Avenue, #02-01 Millenia Tower, SINGAPORE 039192, SINGAPORE.
NELLIGAN, Mr. Mark Jonathan Philip, ACA *2009;* 21C, 21 Haldon Road, LONDON, SW18 1QD.
NELLIGAN, Miss. Mary Therese, BA ACA *1994;* 15 Wood Ride, Petts Wood, ORPINGTON, KENT, BR5 1PZ.
NELLIS, Mrs. Julie Ann, MSc ACA *1996;* Lloyds TSB Bank Plc, Canons House, Canons Way, BRISTOL, BS1 5LL.
NELLIST, Mr. Ian Andrew, BA ACA *1980;* 24 Thomas Street, CAERNARFON, GWYNEDD, LL55 1PB.
NELLIST, Mr. Robert Henry Harger, MA FCA JDipMA *1964;* 5 The Old School, Church Street, Shillington, HITCHIN, HERTFORDSHIRE, SG5 3LJ. (Life Member)
NELMES, Mr. Ronald Thomas, BSc ACA *1990;* 122 Tippendell Lane, Park Street, ST. ALBANS, HERTFORDSHIRE, AL2 2HE.
NELMS, Mr. Axel Albert, MA CPM MAPM FCA CITP MBCS *1974;* 9 Clifton Close, BRISTOL, BS8 3LR.
NELMS, Mr. Christopher Anthony, MSc BSc FCA CISA CISM *1982;* Financial Services Authority, 25 North Colonnade, LONDON, E14 5HS.
NELSON, Miss. Ailis, ACA *2009;* 49 Cavendish Road, Heaton Mersey, STOCKPORT, CHESHIRE, SK4 3DP.
NELSON, Miss. Alexandra, MMath ACA *2005;* 5 Beaulieu Place, Rothschild Road, LONDON, W4 5SY.
NELSON, Miss. Alicia Newall, BSc ACA *1990;* 41 Langholm Crescent, DARLINGTON, DL3 7ST.
NELSON, Mrs. Amanda Jane, BA ACA *1998;* Koninginneweg 195HS, 1075 CR AMSTERDAM, NETHERLANDS.
NELSON, Mr. Andrew, BA(Hons) ACA *2001;* C B P E Capital, 2 George Yard, LONDON, EC3V 9DH.
NELSON, Mr. Andrew Christopher, BA ACA *2000;* with KPMG LLP, St. James's Square, MANCHESTER, M2 6DS.
NELSON, Mr. Andrew Latham, BSc ACA *1983;* Amey plc, 1 Waterhouse Square 138-142 Holborn, LONDON, EC1N 2ST.
NELSON, Mrs. Angela Helen, BA ACA *2000;* 8 Newall Road, ANDOVER, SP11 8HP.
NELSON, Mrs. Annabel Margaret, BA ACA *1999;* Wardsdown Coppice, Union Street, Flimwell, WADHURST, EAST SUSSEX, TN5 7NX.
NELSON, Mr. Brendan Robert, CA *1984; (CA Scotland 1973);* 22 Blanford Road, REIGATE, SURREY, RH2 7DR.
NELSON, Mr. Bruce Stephen, BSc FCA *1974;* Richmond House, Back Lane, Caythorpe, GRANTHAM, NG32 3EE. (Life Member)
NELSON, Byron Bernard, Esq OBE FCA *1962;* 1 La Genetiere, La Route Orange, St. Brelade, JERSEY, JE3 8GP. (Life Member)
NELSON, Mr. Carlton Anthony Gordon, ACA *2008;* Old Vicarage Easebourne Street, Easebourne, MIDHURST, WEST SUSSEX, GU29 0AL.
•**NELSON, Mr. Chris John, BSc FCA** *1981;* The Oil & Pipelines Agency, York House, 23 Kingsway, LONDON, WC2B 6UJ.
NELSON, Mr. David Charles, BSc FCA *1980;* 4 Farm Lane, Tetchill, ELLESMERE, SHROPSHIRE, SY12 9AT.
•**NELSON, Mr. David Howard, BSc ACA** *1988;* (Tax Fac), Dixon Wilson, 22 Chancery Lane, LONDON, WC2A 1LS.
•**NELSON, Mr. David William, ACA** *1979;* (Tax Fac), Lowe & Whitwell, 134 Highgate, KENDAL, LA9 4HL.
•**NELSON, Mr. Donald Charles Scott, FCA** *1988;* Tudor John, Nightingale House, 46/48 East Street, EPSOM, KT17 1HQ.
NELSON, Mr. Edward Bertram, BCom ACA *1981;* 11 Deepdale, Wimbledon, LONDON, SW19 5EZ.
NELSON, Mr. Frank Thornton, FCA *1959;* 1 Mayfield, BARNARD CASTLE, COUNTY DURHAM, DL12 8EA. (Life Member)
NELSON, Mrs. Gayle Charmaine, BSc ACA *2010;* 14 Romans Close, GUILDFORD, GU1 2ST.
•**NELSON, Mr. Gregory Carlisle, BSc FCA** *1975;* Greg Nelson Limited, The Anchorage, Malpas Village, TRURO, TR1 1SN.
NELSON, Mrs. Helen Elizabeth, BSc ACA *1998;* 52 Lady Acre Close, Lymm, WARRINGTON, CHESHIRE, WA13 0SR.
NELSON, Mr. Howard, BSc FCA *1972;* Saville Products Ltd, Millstream Lane, MANCHESTER, M40 1QT.
NELSON, Mr. Ian James, FCA *1985;* Karinya, Bungay Road, Hempnall, NORWICH, NR15 2NG.
NELSON, Mr. Ian Roy, FCA *1975;* 4 Willian Way, LETCHWORTH GARDEN CITY, SG6 2HG.
NELSON, Mr. Ian Stewart, BA FCA CF *1979;* 9 Vincent Road, Stoke D'Abernon, COBHAM, KT11 3JA.
NELSON, Mr. James Adam, BSc ACA *1999;* 41 Herbert Road, SMETHWICK, WEST MIDLANDS, B67 5DD.
NELSON, Mr. James Philip, MSc BA ACA *2005;* 45 Waters Reach, Mossley, ASHTON-UNDER-LYNE, OL5 9FG.
NELSON, Mrs. Jane Elizabeth, MA ACA *1987;* 3333 Allen Parkway, Apt 1705, HOUSTON, TX 77019, UNITED STATES.
NELSON, Mr. John Frederick, FCA *1970;* 66 Lyford Road, LONDON, SW18 3JW.
NELSON, Miss. Julia, MSc BA ACA *2006;* 4 Camberwell Grove, LONDON, SE5 8RE.
NELSON, Dr. Julie Kate, ACA *2002;* University of Stirling, Finance Office, STIRLING, FK9 4LA.
NELSON, Mr. Keith David, BSc FCA *1992;* 43 Park Avenue, Cheadle Hulme, CHEADLE, CHESHIRE, SK8 6EU.
NELSON, Mr. Keith John, BSc FCA *1978;* 51 Sandy Vale, HAYWARDS HEATH, WEST SUSSEX, RH16 4JH.
NELSON, Mr. Keith Reginald, BA FCA *1992;* 20 Picktree Terrace, CHESTER-LE-STREET, DH3 3ST.
NELSON, Mrs. Lisa Jayne, BA ACA *1998;* 11 Cronkbourne Avenue, Douglas, ISLE OF MAN, IM2 3LA.
NELSON, Mrs. Lisa Suzanne, BSc FCA *1997;* Ruhpolding, Mill Lane, Hemingford Grey, HUNTINGDON, CAMBRIDGESHIRE, PE28 9DQ.
NELSON, Mrs. Lorraine, BA ACA *1990;* N B M Timber Products Ltd, Sitwell Street, HULL, HU8 7BG.
NELSON, Mr. Mark Richard, BA ACA *1992;* Field View Barn, Tanners Lane, Chalkhouse Green, READING, RG4 9AB.
NELSON, Mrs. Meridel Lenore, ACA CITP MBCS *1995;* 20 rue des Deux Foirails, 19410 PERPEZAC LE NOIR, FRANCE.
•**NELSON, Mr. Michael Edward John, BA FCA** *1982;* Third Floor 101, Wigmore Street, LONDON, W1U 1QU.
NELSON, Mr. Michael John, BSc ACA *1979;* 14 Parkside Avenue, LONDON, SW19 5ES.
NELSON, Mr. Michael Paul, BSc ACA *2009;* 12 Holme Close, Scotby, CARLISLE, CA4 8BN.
NELSON, Ms. Nicolette, ACA *2011;* 43 Dryburgh Road, LONDON, SW15 1BN.
NELSON, Mr. Paul Edward, MSc BEng DIC ACA *1998;* Ruhpolding, Mill Lane, Hemingford Grey, HUNTINGDON, CAMBRIDGESHIRE, PE28 9DQ.
NELSON, Mr. Paul Gerard, BSc ACA *2006;* Middlebriars, Priorsfield Road, GODALMING, GU7 2RG.
NELSON, Mr. Peter Andrew, MBA FCA *1969;* Rua Doctor Peireira do Nascimento Nº 19, LUANDA, 939, ANGOLA.
NELSON, Mrs. Rachel Anne, BSc ACA *2003;* 3 Darraway Gardens, Chellaston, DERBY, DE73 5AA.
NELSON, Mr. Richard, BSc ACA *1990;* Company Television LTD, New London House, 172 Drury Lane, LONDON, WC2B 5QR.
NELSON, Mr. Richard Campbell, MSc FCA *1966;* 8 Pembridge Place, LONDON, W2 4XB. (Life Member)
•**NELSON, Mr. Robert Anthony, BA FCA DChA** *1990;* (Tax Fac), MacIntyre Hudson LLP, Lyndale House, Ervington Court, Harcourt Way, Meridian Business Park, LEICESTER LE19 1WL.
NELSON, Mr. Robert Geoffrey Horatio, FCA JDipMA *1937;* 27 Beechwood, FORDINGBRIDGE, HAMPSHIRE, SP6 1DB. (Life Member)
•**NELSON, Mr. Robert Haig, FCA** *1958;* Robert H. Nelson, 15 South Drive, WOKINGHAM, RG40 2DH.
NELSON, Mr. Robert Ian, FCA CIOT *1980;* Foxcroft Projects Limited, Foxcroft, 3 Spinney Lane, KNUTSFORD, WA16 0NQ.
NELSON, Miss. Shirley Anne, BSc ACA *2002;* Gordian Knot Lansdowne House, 57 Berkeley Square, LONDON, W1J 6AB.
NELSON, Mr. Stephen Harry, BA ACA *1983;* 30 Templand Park, Allithwaite, GRANGE-OVER-SANDS, CUMBRIA, LA11 7QS.
NELSON, Mr. Stephen Peter, BA(Hons) ACIB ACA *2001;* 1 Carnoustie Drive, Ramsbottom, BURY, BL0 9QL.
NELSON, Mr. Steven, BSc ACA *1992;* 45 Hermitage Gardens, CHESTER LE STREET, DH2 3UD.
NELSON, Mr. Stuart Thomas, BA ACA AMCT *1999;* Centrica Plc, Millstream, Maidenhead Road, WINDSOR, BERKSHIRE, SL4 5GD.
NELSON, Mr. Walter John, FCA *1964;* White Moss Farm, Moss Lane, SKELMERSDALE, WN8 9TJ.
NELSON, Mr. William Lawrence, FCA *1958;* 35 Locust Way, BATTLEMENT MESA, CO 81635, UNITED STATES. (Life Member)
NELSON-GIRTCHEN, Mr. Stephen, ACA *2008;* Asda Stores Ltd, Asda House, Great Wilson Street, LEEDS, LS11 5AD.
NELSON-SMITH, Mr. Richard John, FCA *1982;* Imperial Tobacco Group Plc, PO Box 244, Southville, BRISTOL, BS99 7UJ.
NEMATADZIRA, Mr. Paradzai, ACA *2009;* 11331 - 22 Avenue NW, EDMONTON T6J 4V8, AB, CANADA.
NEMAZEE, Mr. Mahmood, FCA *1973;* 388 Upper Richmond Road West, East Sheen, LONDON, SW14 7JU.
NEMBHARD, Miss. Anthea Marie, BSc ACA *1989;* Flat 4, 38 Ladbroke Grove, LONDON, W11 2PA.
NEMKO, Mr. Michael Terence, FCA *1968;* Quadrant Partnership Ltd, The Georgian House, Park Lane, STANMORE, MIDDLESEX, HA7 3DY.
NENDICK, Mr. Andrew John, MSc(Eng) BSc(Hons) ACA MCIM MBA DipM *1998;* 6 The Crest, SURBITON, KT5 8JZ.
NENDICK, Mr. Jonathan, BSc ACA *2009;* 38 St. Lukes Court, HATFIELD, HERTFORDSHIRE, AL10 0FD.
NENDICK, Mr. Nicholas Arthur Challoner, FCA *1957;* 2 Oakwell Close, STEVENAGE, SG2 8UG. (Life Member)
NENDICK, Miss. Sarah Elizabeth, BA FCA *1997;* 6 The Crest, SURBITON, SURREY, KT5 8JZ.
NENER, Mr. John, MSc ACA *1997;* 1 Steeple Court, Coventry Road, LONDON, E1 5QZ.
NEO, Miss. Li Ping, ACA *2010;* No 17, Jalan Seksyen 1/13, Taman Kajang Utama, 43000 KAJANG, SELANGOR, MALAYSIA.
NEOCLEOUS, Mr. Costas, BSc ACA *2003;* Flat 2, 3 Philokyprou Street, Strovolos, 2049 NICOSIA, CYPRUS.
NEOCLEOUS, Ms. Katerina, BSc(Econ) FCA *1999;* 59 Carpenter Gardens, Winchmore Hill, LONDON, N21 3HH.
NEOCLEOUS, Mr. Nicolas, BSc ACA *2004;* Aipias 45engomi, NICOSIA, CYPRUS.
NEOCLEOUS, Mr. Nicos, BSc(Econ) ACA *2000;* Local PArtnershio LLP Layden House, 76-78 Turnmill Street, LONDON, EC1M 5LG.
NEOCLEOUS, Mr. Petros, BSc ACA *2002;* 42 The Avenue, Muswell Hill, LONDON, N10 2QL.
NEOFITOU, Miss. Marianna, BA ACA *2000;* with Clear Channel Outdoor, 33 Golden Square, LONDON, W1F 9JT.
NEOGY, Mr. Abhijit, FCA *1967;* (Tax Fac), 15 Dale View Avenue, LONDON, E4 6PJ.
NEOH, Miss. Emma Yee Cheng, BSc ACA *2011;* 25 Torrington Place, LONDON, E1W 2UY.
NEOH, Mr. Patrick Hooi Leang, ACA *1984;* 3/96 Tunstall Road, DONVALE, VIC 3111, AUSTRALIA.
NEOH, Miss. Sheau Xian, BSc ACA *2011;* Flat 156, Centrillion Point, 2 Masons Avenue, CROYDON, CR0 9WY.
•**NEOPHYTOU, Mr. Christopher, MEng ACA** *2005;* Xhi Accounting Limited, United House, North Road, LONDON, N7 9DP. See also XHI Consulting Limited
NEOPHYTOU, Mr. Costas, BSc ACA *2007;* 3 Lapithou Street, Egkomi, CY 2410 NICOSIA, CYPRUS.
NEOPHYTOU, Miss. Elena, BSc ACA *2003;* 1 Ioanni Metaxa, 1057 NICOSIA, CYPRUS.
NEOPHYTOU, Mr. George, BA ACA *2005;* 2A Pindou Street, Engomi, 2409 NICOSIA, CYPRUS.
NEOPHYTOU, Mr. Herodotos, ACA *2011;* 8Alexandrou Rangavistr, 1020 NICOSIA, CYPRUS.
NEOPHYTOU, Mr. Ioannis, BA ACA *2000;* 20 Dalias Str, Ekali Area, 3110 LIMASSOL, CYPRUS.
•**NEOPHYTOU, Mr. Neophytos, FCA** *1976;* Ernst & Young Cyprus Limited, Nicosia Tower Centre, 36 Byron Avenue, P.O Box 21656, 1511 NICOSIA, CYPRUS. See also Ernst & Young Europe LLP
NEOPHYTOU, Mrs. Stella, BA ACA *2005;* The Wellcome Trust, 215 Euston Road, LONDON, NW1 2BE.
NEOPTOLEMOU, Mr. Haris, BA ACA *2008;* P.O. Box 57455, 32 Terpsihoris Street, Petrou & Pavlou, 3086 LIMASSOL, CYPRUS.
NEOPTOLEMOU, Mr. Marios Leandrou, BSc ACA CFA *1992;* Olympias 14, Apt 403, 1070 NICOSIA, CYPRUS.

NEPALI, Ms. Geeta Ganesh, ACA *2003;* with PKF (Channel Islands) Ltd, PO Box 296, Sarnia House, Le Truchot, St Peter Port, GUERNSEY GY1 4NA.

NEPOGODIEV, Mr. Mikhail, BA ACA *2007;* Apartment 63 Centenary Plaza, 18 Holliday Street, BIRMINGHAM, B1 1TB.

NEPPL, Mr. Brent Allen, BA ACA *2000;* 19 Tye Common Road, BILLERICAY, ESSEX, CM12 9NR.

NERDEN, Mr. Marc Justin, LLB ACA *2000;* 13 The Grove, Golders Green, LONDON, NW11 9SJ.

NERURKER, Mr. Vijoy Ganpat, FCA *1964;* 6 Kayemoor Road, SUTTON, SURREY, SM2 5HT.

NESBIT, Mr. Alexander Daniel, MA ACA *2006;* Deutsche Bank, 6 Bishopsgate, LONDON, EC2N 4DA.

NESBIT, Mr. David Norman, FCA *1962;* 3 Park Hall, Crooms Hill, Greenwich, LONDON, SE10 8HQ. (Life Member)

NESBIT, Mr. David William, BSc FCA *1978;* 17 Tewkesbury Close, Poynton, STOCKPORT, CHESHIRE, SK12 1QJ.

NESBIT, Mr. Gary, BSc(Hons) ACA *2003;* Lucite International UK Ltd, PO Box 34, DARWEN, LANCASHIRE, BB3 1QB.

NESBIT, Mrs. Naomi Diana Yvonne, ACA *2006;* 8 Tavistock Close, ROMSEY, HAMPSHIRE, SO51 7TQ.

•NESBIT, Mr. Simon, FCA *1987;* (Tax Fac), Nesbits, Robertsfield, Holland Road, Hurst Green, OXTED, SURREY RH8 9BQ.

•NESBITT, Mr. Alan Graeme, BA FCA *1995;* Forrester Boyd, Waynflete House, 139 Eastgate, LOUTH, LN11 9QQ.

NESBITT, Mrs. Bhavika, LLB ACA *2005;* 9 Parsley Way, MAIDSTONE, KENT, ME16 0FS.

NESBITT, Mr. Derek Latimer, MMath ACA MIMA *2004;* 9 Parsley Way, MAIDSTONE, KENT, ME16 0FS.

NESBITT, Mr. Robert Nelson, FCA *1970;* 2 Ling Drive, LIGHTWATER, SURREY, GU18 5PA.

NESBITT, Mr. Timothy James, BAcc ACA *2000;* PricewaterhouseCoopers, Level 26, 2 Southbank Boulevard, SOUTHBANK, VIC 3006, AUSTRALIA.

NESER, Mr. John Eric, BSc ACA *1993;* 53 Aristride Avenue, KALLAROO, PERTH, WA 6025, AUSTRALIA.

NESS, Mr. James Stein, FCA *1953;* 11 Priestden Park, ST ANDREWS, FIFE, KY16 8DL. (Life Member)

NESS, Mr. Michael David Henry, FCA *1967;* 6 Tresillian Gardens, Topsham, EXETER, EX3 0BA. (Life Member)

•NESTEL, Mr. Lewis Alfred Leslie, FCA *1951;* Lewis Nestel & Co, 17 Woodside Avenue, LONDON, N12 8AN.

NESTEL, Mr. Myles, BSc ACA *1993;* 8391 Beverly Blvd, #436, LOS ANGELES, CA 90048, UNITED STATES.

NESTOR-SHERMAN, Mr. Peter Edward, ACA *2009;* Flat 28 Candlemakers Apartments, 112 York Road, LONDON, SW11 3RS.

NESTOUR, Mr. Michel, MA ACA *2000;* 33 Ryland Road, LONDON, NW5 3EH.

NETHERCLIFT, Miss. Rosemary Clare, BSc ACA *2007;* 192 Newcome Road, PORTSMOUTH, PO1 5DX.

NETHERTON, Mr. George, ACA *2011;* 29 Lakeside Road, LONDON, W14 0DX.

NETHERWAY, Mr. Robert William, FCA *1971;* 6 Nathan Close, SUTTON COLDFIELD, WEST MIDLANDS, B75 6SR.

NETLEY, Mr. Brian Malcolm, FCA *1958;* Owls Hoot, 11 St Margarets Place, BRADFORD-ON-AVON, BA15 1DT. (Life Member)

NETLEY, Miss. Kristina Kathleen, ACA *2006;* 17 Tilney Road, DAGENHAM, ESSEX, RM9 6HL.

NETSCHER, Mr. Francis Edward, FCA *1952;* 7 Rolinsden Way, KESTON, BR2 6HY. (Life Member)

NETTELL, Mr. John Patten, FCA *1974;* Patchways, The Street, Dockenfield, FARNHAM, GU10 4JH.

NETTLESHIP, Mr. John Stewart Richard, BA FCA *1992;* 11 Elmores Meadow, Bleasby, NOTTINGHAM, NG14 7HF.

NETTLETON, Mr. Andrew Paul, BA ACA *1995;* 21 Loeman Street, STRATHMORE, VIC 3041, AUSTRALIA.

•NETTLETON, Mr. Jeffrey Peter, BA FCA *1987;* Jackson Feldman & Co, Alexander House, 3 Shakespeare Road, Finchley, LONDON, N3 1XE.

NETTLETON, Mr. John James Dering, ACA *2008;* Newington House, Newington, WALLINGFORD, OXFORDSHIRE, OX10 7AG.

NETTLETON, Mr. John Oldfield, FCA *1951;* Troedrhiwchwarel, LLANGAMMARCH WELLS, LD4 4EN. (Life Member)

•NETTLETON, Mr. Malcolm Leslie, MBA MSc BSc(Econ) FCA FCMA *1967;* Azur Consultancy, Gouvia Lodge, Chollacott Lane, Whitchurch, TAVISTOCK, DEVON PL19 9DD.

NETTLETON, Mrs. Paula, BA ACA *1994;* 10 Guernsey Drive, Ancells Farm, FLEET, GU51 2TG.

NETTLETON, Mr. Philip, BA ACA *1993;* 10 Guernsey Drive, Ancells Farm, FLEET, HAMPSHIRE, GU51 2TG.

NETTLETON, Mr. Richard Edward D'Arcy, FCA *1967;* 3 Claude Avenue, CREMORNE, NSW 2090, AUSTRALIA.

NETTLETON, Mr. Stephen Michael, BSc ACA *1981;* 11 Church Lane, Garforth, LEEDS, LS25 1NW.

NETTO, Mr. Anil Noel, FCA *1985;* 10-10-4 Sri Saujana, Lorong Sungai Dua, Gelugor, 11700 PENANG, MALAYSIA.

NETTRE, Miss. Nathalie, ACA *2008;* 405-5805 Balsam Street, VANCOUVER V6M 4B8, BC, CANADA.

NEUBERGER, Mr. Rafael Max, FCA *1979;* 35 Golders Gardens, LONDON, NW11 9BP.

NEUDEGG, Mr. Jeremy Paul, BA ACA *1985;* 11 Pirbright Road, FARNBOROUGH, HAMPSHIRE, GU14 7AB.

NEUDEGG, Mr. Stephen, BSc ACA *2010;* PricewaterhouseCoopers, Royal Trust Tower, Suite 3000, 77 King Street West, TORONTO M5K 1G8, ON CANADA.

NEUDEGG, Mr. Timothy Stephen, BSc ACA *1981;* TRW Steering Systems, Resolven Plant, Resolven, NEATH, WEST GLAMORGAN, SA11 4HN.

NEUFELD, Mrs. Cynthia, FCA *1972;* 6 Hawker Close, WIMBORNE, BH21 1XW.

NEUFFER, Mrs. Lindsay, BSc ACA *1989;* PO Box 5424, Gold Coast Mail Centre, GOLD COAST, QLD 9726, AUSTRALIA.

•NEUHOFF, Mrs. Marianne Elisabeth, FCA *1970;* (Tax Fac), Neuhoff & Co, Claydons Barns, 11 Towcester Road, Whittlebury, TOWCESTER, NN12 8XU.

NEULING, Mr. Alexander James, BSc ACA *2002;* PO Box 556, COTTESLOE, WA 6011, AUSTRALIA.

NEUMANN, Mr. Benny William, FCA *1958;* 2 Aylmer Close, STANMORE, HA7 3EQ. (Life Member)

NEUMANN, Mr. Charles Anthony, BSc ACA *1995;* Drosselstrasse 15, 8038 ZURICH, SWITZERLAND.

NEUMANN, Mr. Jonathan Charles, BSc ACA *1993;* 49 Lincoln Avenue, TWICKENHAM, TW2 6NH.

•NEUMANN, Mr. Joshua Aaron, FCA *1989;* Cohen Arnold, New Burlington House, 1075 Finchley Road, Temple Fortune, LONDON, NW11 0PU.

NEUMANN, Mr. Klaus Jurgen, ACA *2004;* with KPMG Deutsche Treuhand Group, Ganghoferstrasse 29, 80339 MUNICH, GERMANY.

NEVARD, Mr. Christopher John, BA FCA *1979;* 15 The Pastures, Edlesborough, DUNSTABLE, LU6 2HL.

NEVE, Mr. David George, FCA *1974;* 1 Robins Close, Wootton Bassett, SWINDON, SN4 8NU.

•NEVE, Mr. James Alexander, ACA *2006;* James Neve & Co Limited, 5 Wessington Court, CALNE, WILTSHIRE, SN11 0SS.

•NEVE, Mr. Martin Roy, FCA *1981;* Haines Watts Gatwick LLP, 3rd Floor, Consort House, Consort Way, HORLEY, SURREY RH6 7AF.

NEVES, Mr. Christopher John, BA CA ACA *1994;* BDO Auckland, PO Box 2219, Shortland Street, AUCKLAND 1040, NEW ZEALAND.

NEVETT, Mr. Edward Rex, BSc FCA *1973;* 16 Badgers Copse, CAMBERLEY, GU15 1HW.

NEVILE, Mr. Hugh Simon, BSc ACA *1988;* 8 Wilfred Street, LONDON, SW1E 6PL.

NEVILL, Mr. Alan Geoffrey, FCA *1977;* Finance and Planning, Head Office, Arab National Bank, PO Box 56921, RIYADH, 11564 SAUDI ARABIA.

NEVILL, Mr. Gary Charles, FCA *1978;* Matthew & Matthew, 194 Seabourne Road, BOURNEMOUTH, BH5 2JD.

NEVILL, Mr. Keith Robert, BA ACA *1999;* 27 Cedars Road, COLCHESTER, CO2 7BS.

•NEVILL, Mr. Richard Anthony Charles, FCA *1974;* (Tax Fac), Nevill Stormont & Co, 1155 A London Road, LEIGH-ON-SEA, ESSEX, SS9 3JE.

NEVILLE, Mr. Andrew James, BEng ACA *1998;* Allianz Global Investors, 155 Bishopsgate, LONDON, EC2M 3AD.

NEVILLE, Mr. Andrew John, ACA *2009;* 43 Victoria Drive, BOGNOR REGIS, WEST SUSSEX, PO21 2TQ.

NEVILLE, Mrs. Anita Margaret, BSc FCA *1991;* Neville & Co, 10-11 Lynher Building Queen Annes Battery, PLYMOUTH, PL4 0LP.

NEVILLE, Mr. Anthony, FCA *1969;* Glen Wood, 18 Sheephouse Green, Wotton, DORKING, RH5 6QW. (Life Member)

NEVILLE, Mr. Christopher Robert, BA ACA *1997;* The Hall Falcon Manor, Towcester Road Greens Norton, TOWCESTER, NORTHAMPTONSHIRE, NN12 8BN.

•NEVILLE, Mr. David Henry, FCA *1975;* Flint & Thompson Limited, 1325A Stratford Road, Hall Green, BIRMINGHAM, WEST MIDLANDS, B28 9HL.

NEVILLE, Mr. David Ian, FCA *1972;* 20 Fern Avenue, Oswaldtwistle, ACCRINGTON, BB5 3BA.

NEVILLE, Mrs. Elizabeth Jane, BA ACA *1999;* The Hall Falcon Manor, Towcester Road Greens Norton, TOWCESTER, NORTHAMPTONSHIRE, NN12 8BN.

NEVILLE, Mr. Jeremy Luke, BSc ACA *2004;* Milton House, K B R Hill Park Court, Springfield Drive, LEATHERHEAD, KT22 7NL.

NEVILLE, Miss. Katherine, BA FCA *1985;* Somerleaze House, Wookey, WELLS, SOMERSET, BA5 1JU.

NEVILLE, Miss. Marianne June, BA ACA *2005;* 35 Whites Road, Bitterne, SOUTHAMPTON, SO19 7NR.

NEVILLE, Mr. Matthew James, BSc FCA *1994;* 9 The Brickall, Long Marston, STRATFORD-UPON-AVON, WARWICKSHIRE, CV37 8QL.

•NEVILLE, Mrs. Myfanwy Margaret, BSc ACA *2005;* with Berg Kaprow Lewis LLP, 35 Ballards Lane, LONDON, N3 1XW.

NEVILLE, Mrs. Nicole Suzanne, BSc(Hons) ACA CTA *2000;* BPP Professional Education, Marcello House, 236-240 Pentonville Road, Kings Cross, LONDON, N1 9JY.

NEVILLE, Mr. Paul Howard, BSc ACA *1992;* Moonrakers Church Lane, Finchampstead, WOKINGHAM, RG40 4LN.

•NEVILLE, Mr. Paul Jonathan, FCA *1988;* Pawley & Malyon, 15 Bedford Square, LONDON, WC1B 3JA.

NEVILLE, Mr. Peter John, MA FCA *1971;* Morningside Bulwer Avenue, St. Sampson, GUERNSEY, GY2 4LB. (Life Member)

NEVILLE, Mr. Peter Michael, BA ACA *1979;* 22 Nottingham Road, Keyworth, NOTTINGHAM, NG12 5FD.

NEVILLE, Mr. Richard John, BSc ACA *1999;* 12 Sorrel Close, Wootton, NORTHAMPTON, NN4 6EY.

•ⒾNEVILLE, Mr. Richard Patrick, BSc ARCS FCA FABRP *1977;* Neville & Co, 10-11Lynher Buildings, Queen Anne Battery, PLYMOUTH, PL4 0LP.

NEVILLE, Mr. Robert Hood, FCA *1957;* 3 Headley Park, Tilley Lane, Headley, EPSOM, SURREY, KT18 6EE. (Life Member)

•NEVILLE, Mr. Roger Drummond, FCA *1970;* (Tax Fac), Vantis Group Ltd, 3rd Floor, Crown House, 151 High Road, LOUGHTON, IG10 4LG. See also Alwyns LLP and Roger D. Neville

NEVILLE, Mr. Roy Norman, FCA *1963;* 113 Queen Alexandra Road, SUNDERLAND, SR2 9HN.

•NEVILLE, Mr. William John Cecil, BSc ACA *1992;* Lewis Brownlee, Avenue House, Southgate, CHICHESTER, WEST SUSSEX, PO19 1ES. See also Lewis Brownlee Sherlock

NEVIN, Mrs. Bethan Mary, BSc ACA *1991;* 17 Roxburgh Road, Yeomans Green, Little Sutton, ELLESMERE PORT, CH66 4YU.

NEVIN, Mr. James David, BA ACA *2006;* 48 Windsor Road, TEDDINGTON, MIDDLESEX, TW11 0SF.

NEVIN, Mr. Mark, BSc ACA ATII *1992;* (Tax Fac), 110 Westmoreland Road, Urmston, MANCHESTER, M41 9HP.

NEVIN, Mr. Michael Eric, BA ACA *1987;* 19 Tyrone Road, SOUTHEND-ON-SEA, SS1 3HE.

NEVIN, Mr. Samuel David, MA FCA *1978;* 15 Whitecroft Way, BECKENHAM, BR3 3AQ.

NEVITT, Mr. Gareth Alastair, BA FCA *1986;* 3904 Wauna Vista Drive, VANCOUVER, WA 98661, UNITED STATES.

NEVITT, Mr. Philip, FCA *1969;* C.W. Ducker & associados Lda, Av. Guerra Popular, 3rd Floor, MAPUTO, 1028, MOZAMBIQUE.

NEW, Mr. Cyrus, BSc ACA *2009;* Flat 4, 14 Ivanhoe Road Aigburth, LIVERPOOL, L17 8XQ.

NEW, Mr. Edward Vincent, BA ACA *1992;* 24 Heath Drive, SUTTON, SM2 5RP.

NEW, Miss. Elaine, MA ACA *1987;* 136-144 New Kings Road, LONDON, SW6 4LZ.

NEW, Mr. James Edward, BA ACA *1994;* Flushing House, Church Road, Bookham, LEATHERHEAD, SURREY, KT23 3JT.

•NEW, Mrs. Julia Beverley, BSc FCA *1991;* Julia New Limited, Tudor House, Loxley Road, STRATFORD-UPON-AVON, WARWICKSHIRE, CV37 7DP.

NEW, Mr. Kheng Chee, BSc ACA *2009;* 126 Jalan SS22/32 Damansara Jaya, 47400 PETALING JAYA, SELANGOR, MALAYSIA.

NEW, Mr. Michael Gordon, FCA *1973;* 37 Woodland Close, BAMPTON, DEVON, EX169DN.

NEW, Mr. Nicholas Simon, FCA *1977;* 14 Park Crescent, Riverwood Frenchay, BRISTOL, BS16 1PD.

NEW, Mr. Paul Stephen, BA ACA *1994;* 1 Hollybush Lane, AMERSHAM, HP6 6EB.

NEW, Mr. Trevor David, FCA *1985;* 40 Berton Close, Blunsdon, SWINDON, SN26 7BE.

NEWALL, Mr. Brian Tennant, FCA *1975;* The Ridgeway, Wibtoft, LUTTERWORTH, LE17 5BB.

NEWALL, Mr. Frank, BSc FCA *1976;* 18 Camperdown, MAIDENHEAD, SL6 8DU.

NEWBALD, Mr. Peter Edward Francis, FCA *1969;* Chestnut Grove La Route Du Mont Mado, St. John, JERSEY, JE3 4DN.

NEWBEGIN, Mr. Timothy Philip, BSc ACA *1998;* 43 Elmwood Road, LONDON, W4 3DY.

•NEWBERRY, Mr. Alan Edward, FCA *1968;* (Tax Fac), Albert Goodman CBH Limited, The Lupins Business Centre, 1-3 Greenhill, WEYMOUTH, DORSET, DT4 7SP. See also Coyne Butterworth Hardwicke Limited

NEWBERRY, Mr. Andrew Robin, BSc ACA *1979;* Radian Group Limited Collins House, Bishopstoke Road, EASTLEIGH, HAMPSHIRE, SO50 6AD.

NEWBERRY, Mrs. Gillian, BA ACA *2006;* B P P Professional Education, 1st Floor Aquis House, 49-51 Blagrave Street, READING, RG1 1PL.

NEWBERRY, Mr. John Frederick, FCA *1961;* 16 Oldenburg Park, PAIGNTON, TQ3 2UA. (Life Member)

NEWBERRY, Miss. Lynda Mary, FCA *1976;* 10 Valley Mead, Anna Valley, ANDOVER, SP11 7SB.

•NEWBERRY, Mr. Patrick John, BSc FCA *1980;* PricewaterhouseCoopers LLP, 7 More London Riverside, LONDON, SE1 2RT. See also PricewaterhouseCoopers

NEWBERY, Mr. Andrew Jonathan George, BSc ACA *1992;* 67 St Johns Avenue, GORDON, NSW 2072, AUSTRALIA.

NEWBERY, Mr. Michael Rafe Selwyn, FCA *1971;* The Goat Farm, Oreham Common, HENFIELD, BN5 9SB.

NEWBERY, Mr. William Edward, FCA *1948;* 271 South Arm School Road, BRUSHGROVE, NSW 2460, AUSTRALIA. (Life Member)

NEWBIGGING, Mr. James, BSc ACA *2003;* 22 Derwent Close, DARTFORD, DA1 2TT.

NEWBIGIN, Mr. Michael Paul, BSc ACA *1980;* (Tax Fac), 8 Huntington Gardens, LONDON, W4 3HX.

NEWBLE, Mr. David Allan, BSc ACA *1998;* Little Chilfords, Back Road, Linton, CAMBRIDGE, CB21 4LF.

•NEWBOLD, Mr. Alan David, FCA *1974;* Jones Harris Limited, 17 St. Peters Place, FLEETWOOD, LANCASHIRE, FY7 6EB. See also The North West Business Support Centre Limited

NEWBOLD, Mr. David Robert, FCA *1972;* Shearings Ltd Victoria Mill, Miry Lane, WIGAN, LANCASHIRE, WN3 4AG.

NEWBOLD, Mr. David Ronald, BSc FCA *1974;* 28 Spinney Lane, WELWYN, HERTFORDSHIRE, AL6 9TF.

NEWBOLD, Mr. Derek, FCA *1957;* 4 Kingsway, Welton, LINCOLN, LN2 3FQ. (Life Member)

NEWBOLD, Mr. Douglas Brian, FCA *1957;* 3 Hawthorn Villas, The Green, WALLSEND, NE28 7NT. (Life Member)

NEWBOLD, Miss. Lisa Jane, ACA *2009;* 5 Chapel Bank Apartments, Walkley Bank Road, SHEFFIELD, S6 5AJ.

•NEWBOLD, Mr. Mark Antony, ACA *2004;* Eacotts Limited, Grenville Court, Britwell Road, Burnham, SLOUGH, SL1 8DF. See also Eacotts

NEWBOLD, Miss. Michele Faye, BSc ACA *1993;* 50 Bowes Hill, ROWLAND'S CASTLE, HAMPSHIRE, PO9 6BP.

NEWBOLD, Mr. Oliver Arthur, ACA MAAT *2005;* with Randall & Payne, Rodborough Court, Walkley Hill, STROUD, GLOUCESTERSHIRE, GL5 3LR.

•NEWBOLD, Mr. Paul Nicholas, BA ACA *1987;* UHY Torgersens Limited, 7 Grange Road West, JARROW, TYNE AND WEAR, NE32 3JA. See also UHY Torgersens

•NEWBOLD, Mr. Paul Robert, FCA *1972;* (Tax Fac), Old Mill Associates (BA) Ltd, 53 Old Mill Road, Broughton Astley, LEICESTER, LE9 6PQ. See also Astley Private Clients Ltd

NEWBOLD, Mr. Peter, ACA *1983;* 71 Main Street, Papplewick, NOTTINGHAM, NG15 8FE.

NEWBON, Mr. Paul James, MMath ACA *2004;* 5b Granville Park, LONDON, SE13 7DY.

•NEWBOROUGH, Mr. David Mark, BSc ACA FCCA *1999;* Ashgates, 5 Prospect Place, Millennium Way, Pride Park, DERBY, DE24 8HG. See also Ashgates Corporate Services Limited

NEWBOROUGH, Mrs. Nicola Claire, BSc ACA *1999;* 8 Brook End, The Parklands, East Leake, LOUGHBOROUGH, LE12 6HH.

NEWBOROUGH, Mr. Philip William, BA ACA *1988;* Bridges Community Ventures, 1 Craven Hill, LONDON, W2 3EN.

•NEWBOULD, Mr. Anthony Albert, BA FCA 1989; The Rickyard Woodrow, Chaddesley Corbett, KIDDERMINSTER, WORCESTERSHIRE, DY10 4QE.
NEWBOULD, Mr. Richard Robert, BEng ACA 2003; 42 Sheepfold Lane, AMERSHAM, BUCKINGHAMSHIRE, HP7 9EJ.
NEWBOULD, Mr. Robert Charles, BSc FCA 1975; Mount Villa, 11 Westfield Lane, South Milford, LEEDS, LS25 5AP.
NEWBOULD, Miss. Roseanne, BA(Hons) ACA 2011; Flat 2, The Red House, 49-53 Clerkenwell Road, LONDON, EC1M 5RS.
NEWBOULT, Mr. James Michael Scott, MA FCA 1962; Casa Lena Belinda 1, Calle Almeria, Sitio De Calahonda, 29649 MALAGA, SPAIN. (Life Member)
NEWBOULT, Mr. Richard Mark, BSc ACA 1989; Goodrich Control Systems, Stratford Road, Shirley, SOLIHULL, WEST MIDLANDS, B90 4LA.
•NEWBOUND, Mr. Cecil Patrick, FCA 1957; Newbound & Co., 578 St Mary's Road, WINNIPEG R2M 3L5, MB, CANADA.
•NEWBURY, Mr. Guy William, FCA 1972; Kemp Taylor LLP, The Oval, 14 West Walk, LEICESTER, LE1 7NA.
NEWBURY, Mr. Martin John, BA ACA 1993; 10 Priors Crescent, Dunvant, SWANSEA, SA2 7UP.
NEWBURY, Mr. Simon Philip, ACA 1980; Emporiki Bank of Greece S A, 4 London Wall Buildings, LONDON, EC2M 5NT.
NEWBY, Mr. Christopher John, FCA 1972; 178 Ashley Gardens, Emery Hill Street, LONDON, SW1P 1PD.
NEWBY, Mr. David, FCA 1966; 62 Hillsway, Littleover, DERBY, DE23 3DW. (Life Member)
NEWBY, Mr. David Stanley, FCA 1986; 3617 8A Street S.W., CALGARY T2T 3B4, AB, CANADA.
NEWBY, Mr. Donald Anthony, FCA 1958; Langdale, Phildraw Road, Ballasalla, ISLE OF MAN, IM9 3EG.
NEWBY, Mrs. Enid Agnes, FCA 1958; Langdale, Phildraw Road, Ballasalla, ISLE OF MAN, IM9 3EG. (Life Member)
NEWBY, Mr. Raymond Paul, BA ACA 1999; Prudential Plc Governors House, 5 Laurence Pountney Hill, LONDON, EC4R 0HH.
•NEWBY, Mr. Richard John, BA FCA MBA 1987; 23 Brunswick Gardens, CORBY, NORTHAMPTONSHIRE, NN18 9ER.
NEWBY-ROBSON, Mr. Jonathan Lancelot, BA ACA 1981; 15 Fairoak Close, KENLEY, CR8 5LJ.
NEWCOMB, Mr. Charles Buckle, FCA 1951; Sycamore Cottage, Main Street, Northiam, RYE, EAST SUSSEX, TN31 6NA. (Life Member)
NEWCOMB, Mr. John Walter, FCA 1958; 1 Chapel Street, Church Gresley, SWADLINCOTE, DERBYSHIRE, DE11 9LX. (Life Member)
NEWCOMB, Mr. Peter John, FCA 1979; 28 Thomas Street, NEDLANDS, WA 6009, AUSTRALIA.
NEWCOMBE, Mr. David Keith, FCA 1975; Middlecroft, Bredon's Norton, TEWKESBURY, GL20 7HB.
NEWCOMBE, Mr. David Rhodri, BA FCA 1991; 129 Repton Road, Chelsfield, ORPINGTON, BR6 9HY.
NEWCOMBE, Mr. Graham Martin, BSc ACA 1979; 73 Kinross Crescent, East Cosham, PORTSMOUTH, PO6 2NP.
NEWCOMBE, Mrs. Julie Anne, BA ACA 1985; 129 Repton Road, ORPINGTON, BR6 9HY.
NEWCOMBE, Mrs. Karen Jane, BA ACA 1987; 7 Westhorpe Hall, Westhorpe, Southwell, NOTTINGHAM, NOTTINGHAMSHIRE, NG25 0HG.
NEWCOMBE, Mr. Paul Charles, BA FCA 1989; 29a Loscombe Road, Four Lanes, REDRUTH, CORNWALL, TR16 6QA.
NEWCOMBE, Mr. Stephen Thomas, BSc FCA 1991; (Tax Fac), HSBC Group Investment Business Limited, Level 21, 8 Canada Square, LONDON, E14 5HQ.
NEWELL, Mr. Alan, FCA 1960; Grindel House, Cliffords Mesne, NEWENT, GL18 1JN. (Life Member)
NEWELL, Mr. Allan, BA FCA 1963; 9 Madgeways Close, Great Amwell, WARE, HERTFORDSHIRE, SG12 9RU.
NEWELL, Mr. Christopher David, BSc ACA 1986; 16 Pembridge Place, LONDON, W2 4XB.
NEWELL, Miss. Claire Louise, BA ACA 1999; 10 Austen Gardens, Whiteley, FAREHAM, HAMPSHIRE, PO15 7HW.
•NEWELL, Mrs. Elizabeth Jane, BA(Hons) ACA 2004; with Keens Shay Keens MK, Sovereign Court, 230 Upper Fifth Street, MILTON KEYNES, MK9 2HR.
•NEWELL, Mr. John Robert, BSc FCA 2000; 64 Cannon Hill Gardens, WIMBORNE, DORSET, BH21 2TA.
•ⓘNEWELL, Mr. Jonathan David, BSc FCA 1978; PKF (UK) LLP, 5 Temple Square, Temple Street, LIVERPOOL, L2 5RH.
NEWELL, Mrs. Kirsty Tamsin, BSc ACA 2002; Belle Vue, 34 Nations Hill, Kingsworthy, WINCHESTER, HAMPSHIRE, SO23 7QY.
NEWELL, Mrs. Lorraine, BSc ACA 2006; 1 Dickenson Road, COLCHESTER, CO4 5BL.
NEWELL, Mr. Mark Verity, BA ACA 1982; Honeysuckle Lodge, Badgers Holt, STORRINGTON, WEST SUSSEX, RH20 3ET.
•NEWELL, Mr. Paul Andrew, BSc ACA CF 1992; Clearwater Corporate Finance LLP, 21-23 Castle Gate, NOTTINGHAM, NG1 7AQ.
NEWELL, Mr. Peter Alan, ACA 1986; Goonpiper House, Feock, TRURO, TR3 6RA.
NEWELL, Mr. Philip, BSc FCA 1982; 24 Hill Rise Chalfont St. Peter, GERRARDS CROSS, BUCKINGHAMSHIRE, SL9 9BH.
NEWELL, Miss. Philippa, BSc ACA 2011; 156 Iverson Road, LONDON, NW6 2HH.
NEWELL, Mr. Robert Duncan, BSc ACA 2000; 1 Firgrove, St. Johns, WOKING, SURREY, GU21 7RD.
NEWELL, Mr. Robert Nigel, FCA 1975; Peacehaven Thornhill Road, Stalbridge, STURMINSTER NEWTON, DORSET, DT10 2PS.
NEWELL, Mrs. Rosemary Patricia, BA FCA 1982; 24 Hill Rise, Chalfont St. Peter, GERRARDS CROSS, SL9 9BH.
NEWELL, Mrs. Tina, ACA ACCA 1999; Armstrong Watson, Currer House, 34-36 Otley Street, SKIPTON, BD23 1EW.
•NEWELL, Mr. Trevor Lewis, FCA 1974; (Tax Fac), Trevor L. Newell & Co, 155 Wellingborough Road, RUSHDEN, NN10 9TB.
NEWEY, Mrs. Angela Clare, BA ACA 1987; Westmead, 29 Serpentine Road, SEVENOAKS, TN13 3XR.
NEWEY, Miss. Claire, ACA 2009; 25/27 Marshall Street, MANLY, NSW 2095, AUSTRALIA.
NEWEY, Mr. Leslie John, FCA 1955; Osterley, 54 Parkway, Gidea Park, ROMFORD, RM2 5PA. (Life Member)
NEWEY, Miss. Rachel, BA ACA 2007; Snax, 9 Boyces Avenue, BRISTOL, BS8 4AA.
NEWGROSH, Mr. Anthony, BSc ACA 1995; 6 Robin Lane, LONDON, NW4 1EU.
NEWHAM, Mr. Colin Richard, BEng ACA 1996; 15 Middle Green, Brockham, BETCHWORTH, SURREY, RH3 7JL.
NEWHOOK, Mr. Kevin, BSc FCA 1973; Ty Glyn, Unit 1, Brecon Court, William Brown Close, Llantarnam Park, CWMBRAN NP44 3AB.
NEWING, Mr. Kenneth John, ACA 1981; (Tax Fac), 167 Summerhouse Drive, Wilmington, DARTFORD, DA2 7PD.
NEWING, Miss. Mary Theresa, ACA 1988; 92/108 Elizabeth Bay Road, ELIZABETH BAY, NSW 2011, AUSTRALIA.
NEWING, Mr. Peter John Stephen, BSc ACA 1992; 256 Laurel Wood Avenue, SINGAPORE 275911, SINGAPORE.
NEWING, Mr. Rodney James, MBA FCA 1972; 11 Lord Napier Place, Upper Mall, LONDON, W6 9UB.
NEWITT, Mr. Simon, MA BA ACA 2006; 1 Geoffrey Avenue, DURHAM, DH1 4PF.
•NEWLAND, Mr. Andrew David William, MA ACA 1985; 3 Frederick Sanger Road, Surrey Research Park, GUILDFORD, SURREY, GU2 7YD.
NEWLAND, Mr. David John, BA FCA 1982; Patience House, Inkpen Road, Kintbury, HUNGERFORD, RG17 9UA.
NEWLAND, Miss. Jessica Anne, BSc ACA 2007; Flat 20 Renbold House, Blissett Street, LONDON, SE10 8UT.
NEWLAND, Miss. Kate Louise, BSc ACA 2009; 9 The Green, LEEDS, LS17 6QL.
NEWLAND, Ms. Lesley Jennifer, ACA 1996; WHK Gosling Chapman, P.O. Box 158, AUCKLAND 1140, NEW ZEALAND.
NEWLAND, Mr. Mark Daniel, ACA 2005; Cedarwood Station Road, Elsenham, BISHOP'S STORTFORD, HERTFORDSHIRE, CM22 6LG.
NEWLAND, Mr. Matthew James, ACA 2009; 10 Thompson Drive, Strensall, YORK, YO32 5ZN.
NEWLAND, Mr. Nicholas John, FCA 1971; Manor Farm, Main Road, Curbridge, WITNEY, OX29 7NT.
NEWLAND, Mr. Oliver William, FCA 1961; Badgworth Cottage, 21 Gloucester Road, Almondsbury, BRISTOL, BS32 4HD.
NEWLAND, Mr. Peter John, FCA 1966; Charlecote, 8 Badminton Gardens, BATH, BA1 2XS.
NEWLANDS, Mr. Andrew Edward, BSc(Hons) ACA 2002; 21 South End, Long Houghton, ALNWICK, NE66 3AW.
NEWLANDS, Mr. Andrew James, LLB ACA 1978; Claymore Group Ltd, Market Place, PO Box 64, PROVIDENCIALES, TURKS AND CAICOS ISLANDS.
NEWLANDS, Mr. David Baxter, FCA 1969; Lane End, Chucks Lane, Walton On The Hill, TADWORTH, KT20 7UB.
NEWLANDS, Mr. David John, MA ACA 1994; Four Seasons The Island, Steep, PETERSFIELD, GU32 1AE.
NEWLANDS, Mr. George Stewart, FCA 1970; Maison Gruchy, La Route du Sud, St Brelade, JERSEY, JE3 8HT. (Life Member)
NEWLANDS, Mr. Gordon John, BSc ACA 1997; 37 Kings Road, WALTON-ON-THAMES, SURREY, KT12 2RB.
NEWLANDS, Miss. Melanie Victoria, BA ACA 1998; 111 Wilberforce Road, LONDON, N4 2SP.
NEWLANDS, Mrs. Monique, MSc BSc ACA 1994; Four Seasons, The Island, Steep, PETERSFIELD, HAMPSHIRE, GU32 1AE.
NEWLING, Mr. Timothy John, FCA 1968; 12 Brookway, LONDON, SE3 9BJ. (Life Member)
NEWLYN, Mr. Nigel Charles, FCA 1975; Argent Personal Finance Managers Ltd, 60 Lombard Street, LONDON, EC3V 9EA.
NEWLYN, Mr. Philip Peter, ACA 1986; Toadshole Cottage, Old Road, Feering, COLCHESTER, CO5 9RN.
NEWLYN, Mr. Simon Clement Charles, BA ACA 1988; 12 Holdenby Close, MARKET HARBOROUGH, LE16 8JE.
NEWMAN, Mr. Adrian Barry Nathan, BA ACA 1978; 1644 Funston Avenue, SAN FRANCISCO, CA 94122, UNITED STATES.
NEWMAN, Mr. Alan, FCA 1971; Chy L'An Gwedh, Wells Road, Rodney Stoke, CHEDDAR, BS27 3XB.
•NEWMAN, Mr. Alan Philip Stephen, MA FCA 1982; Yougov, 50 Featherstone Street, LONDON, EC1Y 8RT.
NEWMAN, Mrs. Alison Cara, BSc ACA 1992; M S Instruments Plc Unit 4, Ravensquay Business Centre Cray Avenue, ORPINGTON, BR5 4BQ.
NEWMAN, Mr. Andrew Gwyn, FCA 1960; 3 Gliddon Avenue, ST THOMAS N5R 1G3, ON, CANADA. (Life Member)
NEWMAN, Mr. Andrew Jonathan Charles, BA ACA 1999; The Walnuts, Walnuts Lane, Wickham Market, WOODBRIDGE, SUFFOLK, IP13 0RZ.
NEWMAN, Mr. Andrew Paul, BSc ACA 2006; 118 William Street, Petone, LOWER HUTT 5012, NEW ZEALAND.
NEWMAN, Ms. Angela Deborah, BSc ACA 1992; 13 Adelong Road, SHAILER PARK, QLD 4128, AUSTRALIA.
NEWMAN, Mrs. Annalie Jane, BSc ACA 2001; 2 Spey Close, Quedgeley, GLOUCESTER, GL2 4NW.
NEWMAN, Ms. Anne Penelope, BA ACA 1987; 118 Babington Road, LONDON, SW16 6AH.
NEWMAN, Mr. Anthony Charles, MA FCA 1963; Avenis Farm, Bournes Green, Oakridge, STROUD, GL6 7NL.
NEWMAN, Mr. Anthony Julian, MA FCA 1977; TY ISAF, LLANYMAWDDWY, MACHYNLLETH, SY20 9AQ.
•NEWMAN, Mr. Antony Paul, ACA FCCA 2009; George Hay, Brigham House, 93 High Street, BIGGLESWADE, BEDFORDSHIRE, SG18 0LD. See also GH Online Accounting Ltd
NEWMAN, Mr. Barry Victor, FCA 1981; P.O. Box N 1019, NASSAU, BAHAMAS.
NEWMAN, Mr. Brendan Anthony, FCA 1972; 4 Kingston Close, Long Buckby, NORTHAMPTON, NN6 7RZ.
NEWMAN, Mr. Bryan Alfred, FCA 1959; 20 Mount Grace Road, POTTERS BAR, EN6 1RE. (Life Member)
NEWMAN, Ms. Catherine Lucy, BA(Hons) ACA 2002; Fairways Dene Close, Chilworth, SOUTHAMPTON, SO16 7HL.
NEWMAN, Mr. Chris, BSc ACA 2009; The Pines, Beechway, Merrow, GUILDFORD, SURREY, GU1 2TA.
NEWMAN, Mr. Christopher Alexander, BA ACA 2004; 1 Gleneagles Close, WILMSLOW, CHESHIRE, SK9 2RD.
NEWMAN, Mr. Christopher James, FCA 1971; (Tax Fac), The Old Nursery, Baltonsborough Road, Butleigh, GLASTONBURY, BA6 8SN.
NEWMAN, Mr. Christopher James, MA ACA 1997; 93 Salisbury Road, Moseley, BIRMINGHAM, B13 8LB.
NEWMAN, Mr. Clive William, BSocSc ACA 1992; Coolmation, Unit 7, Millstream Trading Estate, Christchurch Road, RINGWOOD, HAMPSHIRE BH24 3SD.
•NEWMAN, Mr. Colin Maurice, FCA 1971; Newman & Co, Regent House, 1 Pratt Mews, LONDON, NW1 0AD.
•NEWMAN, Mr. David Alan, FCA 1974; Newman Brown, Kinetic Centre, Theobald Street, BOREHAMWOOD, WD6 4BA.
NEWMAN, Mr. David Angus Winkworth, FCA 1958; 30G La Vina De Calpe, La Merced, 03710 Calpe, ALICANTE, SPAIN. (Life Member)
NEWMAN, Mr. David Anthony, BA FCA 1980; with PricewaterhouseCoopers LLP, 101 Barbirolli Square, Lower Mosley Street, MANCHESTER, M2 3PW.
NEWMAN, Mr. David Charles, FCA 1958; 26a Kivernell Road, Milford on Sea, LYMINGTON, HAMPSHIRE, SO41 0PQ. (Life Member)
NEWMAN, Mr. David Foster, MSc ACA 2004; with Deloitte Touche Tohmatsu, Woodside Plaza Level 14, 240 St Georges Terrace, PERTH, WA 6000, AUSTRALIA.
NEWMAN, Mr. David Francis, BA FCA 1971; 44 Hartington Road, Chiswick, LONDON, W4 3TX.
NEWMAN, Mr. David Frederick, BSc ACA 1984; 10 Kempster Road, Scarsdale, NEW YORK, NY 10583, UNITED STATES.
NEWMAN, Mr. David Robert, FCA 1965; 72 Starbold Crescent, Knowle, SOLIHULL, B93 9JX.
NEWMAN, Mr. David Trevor, FCA 1994; 70 Framfield Road, LONDON, W7 1NH.
NEWMAN, Mr. Donald Stanley, FCA 1953; 3 Maple Drive, Lower Road, Bookham, LEATHERHEAD, SURREY, KT23 4AX. (Life Member)
NEWMAN, Mrs. Donna-Marie, LLB ACA 2004; 46 Maple Drive, Taverham, NORWICH, NR8 6TF.
NEWMAN, Mrs. Elizabeth, BA ACA 1988; 39 Alderminster Road, SOLIHULL, B91 3YT.
NEWMAN, Miss. Elizabeth Helen, BSc ACA 2004; Flat 1 Villa Menorca, 15 Burton Road, POOLE, DORSET, BH13 6DT.
•NEWMAN, Mr. Frank Richard, FCA 1957; Frank Newman & Co, Flat 3, Elderberry Court, 39b Bycullah Road, ENFIELD, MIDDLESEX EN2 8FF. See also Newman Raphael Limited
•NEWMAN, Mr. Giles Robert, BSc FCA 1994; 12 Springhead Lane, ELY, CAMBRIDGESHIRE, CB7 4QY.
NEWMAN, Mr. Graham Anthony, BCom FCA 1970; Newman Wright Financial Advisors Buckingham House West, Buckingham Parade The Broadway, STANMORE, MIDDLESEX, HA7 4EB.
NEWMAN, Mr. Harold Eric, FCA 1952; 22 Winsu Avenue, Preston, PAIGNTON, TQ3 1QF. (Life Member)
NEWMAN, Mr. Harold Maurice, FCA 1959; Brookside, 7 Green Lane, STANMORE, MIDDLESEX, HA7 3AH.
NEWMAN, Mr. Henry George, FCA 1962; 9 Large Acres, Selsey, CHICHESTER, PO20 9BA. (Life Member)
•NEWMAN, Mr. Ian Roy, BSc 1993; 5 Lammas Gate, Abbey Street, FAVERSHAM, KENT, ME13 7ND.
NEWMAN, Mr. James, ACA 1993; Rowans, 137 Shelford Road, CAMBRIDGE, CAMBRIDGESHIRE, CB2 2ND.
NEWMAN, Mr. James Alexander, ACA 2007; 16 Greens Meade, Woodfalls, SALISBURY, SP5 2NL.
NEWMAN, Mr. James Allen, BSc ACA 1989; Ely House, Ely Grange, Frant, TUNBRIDGE WELLS, KENT, TN3 9DY.
NEWMAN, Mr. James Henry, FCA 1972; West Wood House, Main Street, Sutton on Derwent, YORK, YO41 4BT.
NEWMAN, Mr. James Peter, BSc FCA 1976; 863 Bright Meadow Drive, LAKE MARY, FL 32746-4863, UNITED STATES.
NEWMAN, Mr. Jason John, BSc ACA 2006; British Petroleum Co Plc, 20 Canada Square, LONDON, E14 5NJ.
•NEWMAN, Mr. Jeremy Steven, FCA 1982; BDO LLP, 55 Baker Street, LONDON, W1U 7EU. See also BDO Stoy Hayward LLP
•NEWMAN, Mr. Jeremy William Gare, BSc(Econ) FCA CTA MAE MEWI 1988; (Tax Fac), 5 Hasting Close, Bray, MAIDENHEAD, SL6 2DA.
NEWMAN, Mrs. Joan Ann, FCA 1963; 20 Mount Grace Road, POTTERS BAR, HERTFORDSHIRE, EN6 1RE. (Life Member)
NEWMAN, Mr. Joe James, BSocSc ACA 2002; Flat 59, 1 Tarves Way, LONDON, SE10 9JE.
•NEWMAN, Mr. Joel, BSc FCA 1978; (Tax Fac), Nyman Libson Paul, Regina House, 124 Finchley Road, LONDON, NW3 5JS.
•NEWMAN, Mr. John Antony, BA FCA 1973; Blick Rothenberg, 12 York Gate, Regent's Park, LONDON, NW1 4QS.
•NEWMAN, Mr. John Arthur, MA FCA MAAT 1970; (Member of Council 1987 - 1993 1995 - 1997), John A Newman MA FCA MAAT, Thornford House, Church Road, Thornford, SHERBORNE, DORSET DT9 6QE.
NEWMAN, Mr. John Watson, FCA 1968; TTelectronics plc, Fernside Place, 179 Queens Road, WEYBRIDGE, SURREY, KT13 0AH.
NEWMAN, Mr. Jonathan David, ACA 2009; with Page Kirk LLP, Sherwood House, 7 Gregory Boulevard, NOTTINGHAM, NG7 6LB.
NEWMAN, Mr. Jonathan Mark, ACA 2009; Flat 8 Raffles House, 67 Brampton Grove, LONDON, NW4 4BU.
NEWMAN, Mr. Jonathan Rupert, MA ACA 2004; 12 Ossian Road, LONDON, N4 4EA.

NEWMAN, Mrs. Judith, BA ACA *1987;* 26 Allandale Avenue, LONDON, N3 3PJ.

NEWMAN, Mr. Julian Daniel, FCA *1978;* J Newman Textiles, Unit 1H, Highgate Business Centre, 33 Greenwood Place, LONDON, NW5 1LB.

NEWMAN, Mrs. Kathryn Jane, BA ACA *1992;* Trigonos, N Power Communication Ltd Windmill Hill Business Park, Whitehill Way, SWINDON, SN5 6PB.

•NEWMAN, Mr. Keith Andrew, BSc ACA *1980;* Crowe Clark Whitehill LLP, 10 Palace Avenue, MAIDSTONE, KENT, ME15 6NF. See also Horwath Clark Whitehill LLP and Crowe Clark Whitehill

•NEWMAN, Mrs. Kirsty Louise, ACA CTA *1993;* Northacre Well Road, Northaw, POTTERS BAR, HERTFORDSHIRE, EN6 4BP. See also Deloitte & Touche LLP

•NEWMAN, Mr. Laurence David, FCA *1984;* Lubbock Fine, Russell Bedford House, City Forum, 250 City Road, LONDON, EC1V 2QQ.

•NEWMAN, Mr. Lawrence Howard, MA LLB FCA *1962;* L.H. Newman & Co, 148 Walton Street, LONDON, SW3 2JJ.

•NEWMAN, Mr. Leslie Robert, FCA *1979;* (Tax Fac), Waveney Accountants Limited, 4b Church Street, DISS, NORFOLK, IP22 4DD.

NEWMAN, Miss. Louise Rachel, BA(Hons) ACA *2011;* 21 Meadowdown, Weavering, MAIDSTONE, KENT, ME14 5TN.

NEWMAN, Mr. Malcolm Charles, BSc FCA *1984;* SCOR, 10 Lime Street, LONDON, EC3M 7AA.

NEWMAN, Mr. Malcolm James Gare, FCA *1961;* 13 Hall Place Drive, WEYBRIDGE, SURREY, KT13 0AJ.

NEWMAN, Mr. Marc Alexander Michael, BA ACA *2010;* 6 The Oaze, WHITSTABLE, KENT, CT5 4TQ.

NEWMAN, Mrs. Maria, ACA *1993;* with Lakin Clark Limited, Delandale House, 37 Old Dover Road, CANTERBURY, KENT, CT1 3JF.

NEWMAN, Mr. Mark, BA(Hons) ACA *2002;* 15 South Croft, BRISTOL, BS9 4PS.

NEWMAN, Mr. Mark, MMath ACA *2005;* 6th Floor, A B N Amro Bank NV, 250 Bishopsgate, LONDON, EC2M 4AA.

NEWMAN, Mr. Mark Andrew, BSc FCA *1978;* 12 Forsells End, Houghton On The Hill, LEICESTER, LE7 9HQ.

NEWMAN, Mr. Mark David, BSc ACA *1986;* 9 Lacebark Close, The Hollies, SIDCUP, DA15 8WD.

NEWMAN, Mr. Mark Gavin, ACA *2011;* 27 Barker Lane, Mellor, BLACKBURN, BB2 7ED.

NEWMAN, Mr. Martin Ernest St John, BSc ACA MCT *1983;* 15 Dale Close, Long Itchington, SOUTHAM, CV47 9SE.

NEWMAN, Mr. Martin Peter, BA ACA DChA *1984;* Francis Clark, Vantage Point, Pynes Hill, EXETER, EX2 5FD.

NEWMAN, Mr. Michael Henry, FCA *1968;* 37 Wool Road, LONDON, SW20 0HN. (Life Member)

•NEWMAN, Mr. Michael Peter, BA FCA *1986;* PricewaterhouseCoopers LLP, Hays Galleria, 1 Hays Lane, LONDON, SE1 2RD. See also PricewaterhouseCoopers

NEWMAN, Mr. Michael Robert Frank, LLB FCA *1974;* Boxford House, Eaton Park, COBHAM, KT11 2JF.

NEWMAN, Mrs. Nanette, FCA *1948;* Taormina, Nashdom Lane, Burnham, SLOUGH, SL1 8NJ. (Life Member)

•NEWMAN, Mr. Neville Jonathan, FCA *1984;* Harris & Trotter LLP, 65 New Cavendish Street, LONDON, W1G 7LS.

•NEWMAN, Mr. Nigel Peter Courtney, MA ACA *1984;* AIMS - Nigel Newman ACA, 4 Monmouth Close, CHARD, SOMERSET, TA20 1HQ.

NEWMAN, Mr. Paul, BA ACA *1986;* Afkap, 10 The Heathers, EVESHAM, WORCESTERSHIRE, WR11 2PF.

NEWMAN, Mr. Paul David, ACA *2011;* 10 Austen Close, BILLINGHAM, CLEVELAND, TS23 3GT.

NEWMAN, Mr. Paul Mark, BEng ACA *1996;* Lerins White-Ladies-Aston, WORCESTER, WR7 4QH.

NEWMAN, Mr. Paul Michael, BSc ACA *1986;* BT Global Services, 1 Sovereign Street, LEEDS, LS1 4BT.

NEWMAN, Mr. Paul Richard, ACA *1996;* 56 Churchway, Haddenham, AYLESBURY, BUCKINGHAMSHIRE, HP17 8HA.

•NEWMAN, Mr. Paul Spencer, BSc ACA *1991;* Baker Tilly Tax and Advisory Services LLP, 25 Farringdon Street, LONDON, EC4A 4AB. See also Baker Tilly UK Audit LLP

NEWMAN, Mr. Peter Herbert Heinz, BSc FCA *1955;* (Tax Fac), 16 Widecombe Way, LONDON, N2 0HL. (Life Member)

NEWMAN, Mr. Peter John, MA FCA *1979;* 5 Caenshill Place, WEYBRIDGE, SURREY, KT13 0SQ.

NEWMAN, Mr. Peter Thomas Lydston, MA FCA *1970;* The Manor House, Coryton, OKEHAMPTON, EX20 4PG.

NEWMAN, Mr. Philip, FCA *1954;* 11 Hawkesley Court, Watford Road, RADLETT, HERTFORDSHIRE, WD7 8HH. (Life Member)

NEWMAN, Mr. Philip John, BSc ACA *1993;* 31 Gainsborough Drive, Lawford, MANNINGTREE, CO11 2LF.

NEWMAN, Mrs. Rani, BCom ACA ATII *2002;* (Tax Fac), 54 Gladstone Grove, Heaton Moor, STOCKPORT, CHESHIRE, SK4 4DA.

NEWMAN, Mr. Richard, BA ACA *2005;* 16 Ednall Lane, BROMSGROVE, WORCESTERSHIRE, B60 2BZ.

•NEWMAN, Mr. Richard Henry, BA FCA *1978;* Newman Peters, 19 Fitzroy Square, LONDON, W1T 6EQ.

NEWMAN, Mr. Richard Hugh, BSc ACA *1993;* 142 Station Road, Knowle, SOLIHULL, B93 0EP.

•NEWMAN, Mr. Robert, FCA *1980;* Moore Stephens (South) LLP, 33 The Clarendon Centre, Salisbury Business Park, Dairy Meadow Lane, SALISBURY, SP1 2TJ. See also Moore Secretaries Limited

NEWMAN, Mr. Robert Neil, FCA *1967;* Flat 9 Clarence Apartments, 2/3 Clarence Terrace, St Helier, JERSEY, JE2 4QT. (Life Member)

NEWMAN, Mr. Robin Alfred, FCA *1960;* Linden Lea, Stratton Chase Drive, CHALFONT ST. GILES, BUCKINGHAMSHIRE, HP8 4PZ. (Life Member)

NEWMAN, Mrs. Robin Clare, BA ACA *1998;* Nine Wells House Granhams Road, Great Shelford, CAMBRIDGE, CB22 5JY.

NEWMAN, Mr. Robin Dallas Max, FCA *1969;* 21 Kings Paddock, Park Close, HAMPTON, MIDDLESEX, TW12 2EF.

NEWMAN, Mr. Ronald William, FCA *1952;* High & Over, 21 Westview Road, WARLINGHAM, CR6 9JD. (Life Member)

NEWMAN, Mrs. Sarah Caroline, BSc FCA *1989;* Chethams School of Music, Long Millgate, MANCHESTER, M3 1SB.

NEWMAN, Mr. Simon Julian, BSc ACA *1991;* 44a Audley Way, ASCOT, SL5 8EF.

NEWMAN, Miss. Stacey Marie, ACA *2010;* 51 Ravensdale, BASILDON, ESSEX, SS16 5HU.

•NEWMAN, Mr. Stephen Alexander, BSc ACA *1993;* with RSM Tenon Audit Limited, Charterhouse, Legge Street, BIRMINGHAM, B4 7EU.

NEWMAN, Mr. Stephen Paul, BA FCA *1986;* Ardbraccan, Cross Oak Road, BERKHAMSTED, HP4 3NA.

NEWMAN, Mr. Steven James, MEng ACA *2002;* #07-06 Claremont, 161 Killiney Road, SINGAPORE 239569, SINGAPORE.

NEWMAN, Mr. Steven Lee, LLB ACA *2004;* 1 Plantin Road, Carrington Point, NOTTINGHAM, NG5 1QT.

•NEWMAN, Mr. Stuart Bruce, BA ACA *1993;* PricewaterhouseCoopers LLP, Abacus House, Castle Park, CAMBRIDGE, CB3 0AN. See also PricewaterhouseCoopers

NEWMAN, Mrs. Susan Jane, BA ACA *1992;* 18 Festing Road, SOUTHSEA, HAMPSHIRE, PO4 0NG.

NEWMAN, Mrs. Susan Jean Louise, ACA *1986;* Torus Insurance, 88 Leadenhall Street, LONDON, EC3A 3BP.

NEWMAN, Mrs. Talitha Margaret, BA ACA *1997;* 19 Rees Street, LONDON, N1 7AR.

NEWMAN, Mrs. Tamsin Amber, BSc ACA *2006;* Flat 2 Elton Lodge, Florence Road, LONDON, W5 3TX.

•NEWMAN, Mr. Terence James, FCA *1971;* 44 Eagles View, Deer Park Heights, LIVINGSTON, WEST LOTHIAN, EH54 8AE.

NEWMAN, Mr. Theodore Jay, FCA *1953;* 4 Hilary Court, 1 Lichfield Grove, Finchley, LONDON, N3 2JG. (Life Member)

NEWMAN, Mr. Theron Anthony, LLB ACA *1992;* Lambeth Council, Adults & Community Services, Phoenix House, 8 Wandsworth Road, Vauxhall, LONDON SW8 2LL.

NEWMAN, Mr. Timothy Carlo, LLB ACA MCT *1987;* Fitness First Clubs Ltd, 58 Fleets Lane, POOLE, DORSET, BH153BT.

•NEWMAN, Ms. Tracy Lorraine, MBA BA FCA *1993;* (Tax Fac), Tracy Newman & Co Ltd, 14 High Street, Wilburton, ELY, CAMBRIDGESHIRE, CB6 3RB.

NEWMAN, Mr. Trevor Malcolm, FCA *1970;* 26 The Glade, WOODFORD GREEN, IG8 0QA. (Life Member)

•NEWMAN, Mrs. Yvonne Carol, BA ACA *1986;* Newman James Limited, 43 St. Francis Avenue, SOLIHULL, WEST MIDLANDS, B91 1EB. See also Newman Stevens Limited

NEWMARCH, Mr. Patrick, BA ACA *1991;* 5 Priory Road, HASTINGS, TN34 3JL.

NEWMARK, Mr. John Lindsey Graham, MA FCA *1974;* 7 Scarth Road, LONDON, SW13 0ND.

NEWMARK, Mr. Steve, ACA *2011;* 9 Rush Common Mews, LONDON, SW2 3RN.

NEWNES, Mrs. Rebecca, BA ACA *2006;* 2C St James Road, GRAVESEND, KENT, DA11 0HE.

NEWNES, Mrs. Sally Jane, ACA *1989;* 212 Earlham Road, NORWICH, NR2 3RW.

NEWNES, Mr. William George, FCA *1957;* 6 Gatcombe Gardens, OSWESTRY, SY11 2YG. (Life Member)

•NEWNES-SMITH, Mr. Roger, FCA *1964;* (Tax Fac), Roger Newnes-Smith, Woodend, Lower Moushill Lane, Milford, GODALMING, GU8 5JX.

•NEWNES-SMITH, Ms. Suzanne Gabrielle, ACA *1991;* SNS Consultancy Ltd, Woodford Lodge, Ramsden Road, GODALMING, SURREY, GU7 1QE.

•NEWNHAM, Mr. Eric Robert, FCA *1968;* (Tax Fac), Newnham & Co, 65 Morden Hill, LONDON, SE13 7NP.

NEWNHAM, Mr. Geoffrey William, FCA *1974;* Jaidah Motors & Trading Co., P.O Box 150, DOHA, QATAR.

NEWNHAM, Mr. Jack Gilchrist, MA ACA *1996;* 26 Prince George Road, LONDON, N16 8BY.

•NEWNHAM, Mr. John Roger, FCA *1972;* (Tax Fac), Lovelawn Limited, Lawn Cottage, Portsmouth Road, Milford, GODALMING, GU8 5HZ.

NEWNHAM, Mrs. Kathryn, BSc ACA *1994;* 44 Wilton Crescent, Wimbledon, LONDON, SW19 3QS.

NEWNHAM, Miss. Mary Laura, ACA *2010;* Clare House, The Street, Patching, WORTHING, WEST SUSSEX, BN13 3XF.

NEWNHAM, Mr. Michael David, BA ACA *1992;* 44 Wilton Crescent, Wimbledon, LONDON, SW19 3QS.

NEWNHAM, Miss. Rebecca Kate, MA MSc BA ACA *2005;* 9 Duncan Gardens, Upper Weston, BATH, BA1 4NQ.

NEWNHAM, Mr. Trevor Ainley, FCA *1959;* The Birches, 32 Lees Lane, NORTHALLERTON, NORTH YORKSHIRE, DL7 8DB. (Life Member)

•NEWPORT, Mr. Alan John, BA FCA *1965;* Flat 12, Allerton House, 30 Leyton Road, LONDON, SW19 1DL. (Life Member)

NEWPORT, Miss. Ann, BSc ACA *1987;* 38 Sunnyside Road, TEDDINGTON, TW11 0RT.

NEWPORT, Mrs. Ann, BA ACA *1993;* 4 Wimpole Close, The Glade, Usworth Hall, WASHINGTON, NE37 3LJ.

NEWPORT, Mr. David James, ACA *2011;* 10 Tennyson Close, Cheadle, STOKE-ON-TRENT, ST10 1XF.

NEWPORT, Mr. James, BSc ACA *2005;* Dove House The Green Leafield, WITNEY, OXFORDSHIRE, OX29 9NP.

NEWPORT, Mrs. Suzanne Elizabeth, BSc ACA *1997;* Woodgrove House Fulbrook Hill, Fulbrook, BURFORD, OXFORDSHIRE, OX18 4BH.

NEWSAM, Ms. Denise Festinia Philippa, MA FCA *1981;* 32 Garlies Road, LONDON, SE23 2RT.

•NEWSAM, Mrs. Julie Anne, BSc ACA *1996;* (Tax Fac), J Newsam & Co, 22 Broadlands Crescent, Bramley, ROTHERHAM, SOUTH YORKSHIRE, S66 1WE.

NEWSAM, Mr. Michael William, BA ACA *1981;* 32 Garlies Road, Forest Hill, LONDON, SE23 2RT.

•NEWSAM, Mr. Peter Frederick, FCA ATII ATT *1979;* (Tax Fac), UHY Wingfield Slater, 6 Broadfield Court, Broadfield Way, SHEFFIELD, S8 0XF.

NEWSHAM, Miss. Emma, BSc ACA *2011;* 162 Henry Doulton Drive, Tooting Bec, Heritage Park, LONDON, SW17 6DG.

•NEWSHAM, Mrs. Heather, FCA *1998;* (Tax Fac), Newsham & Co Ltd, 11 Allanhall Way, Kirk Ella, HULL, HU10 7QU.

NEWSHAM, Mr. John Vincent, BA FCA *1984;* 7 Woodlands Rd, WILMSLOW, SK9 5QB.

•NEWSHAM, Miss. Kay, BSc FCA CTA *1981;* (Tax Fac), Newsham Tax, 1 New Mills, Forest Road, LYDNEY, GL15 4ET.

NEWSHAM, Mr. Lee Richard, FCA *1998;* P D R Construction Ltd Salisbury House, Saxon Way Priory Park, HESSLE, NORTH HUMBERSIDE, HU13 9PB.

•NEWSHAM, Mr. Paul Charles, ACA *1990;* Haines Watts (Preston) Limited, 120-124 Towngate, LEYLAND, PR25 2LQ. See also HW Technology Limited and Miller R.F.& Co

•NEWSHOLME, Mr. Martin, BA ACA *1990;* KPMG LLP, Edward VII Quay, Navigation Way, Ashton-on-Ribble, PRESTON, PR2 2YF. See also KPMG Europe LLP

NEWSHOLME, Mr. Richard John, FCA *1983;* 2 Torre Crescent, Horton Bank Top, BRADFORD, BD6 3PE.

NEWSOM, Mrs. Virginia Cathryn, BA ACA *1989;* The Well House, South Weirs, BROCKENHURST, HAMPSHIRE, SO42 7UQ.

•NEWSOME, Mr. Andrew Jonathon, BA ACA *1987;* Deloitte LLP, Athene Place, 66 Shoe Lane, LONDON, EC4A 3BQ. See also Deloitte & Touche LLP

NEWSOME, Mr. David Christopher, FCA *1974;* 46 Robinwood Drive, Seal, SEVENOAKS, TN15 0TA.

NEWSOME, Mr. Jack, FCA *1954;* 230 Huddersfield Road, LIVERSEDGE, WF15 7QQ. (Life Member)

NEWSON, Mr. Christopher Howard, ACA *1987;* Chequers, Stock Road, Galleywood, CHELMSFORD, CM2 8JS.

NEWSON, Mr. Edwyn Graham, FCA *1956;* 17 Durleston Park Drive, Great Bookham, LEATHERHEAD, KT23 4AJ. (Life Member)

NEWSON, Mrs. Jemma Jane, BA(Hons) ACA *2002;* 5 Agnew Road, LONDON, SE23 1DH.

•NEWSTEAD, Mr. David Allen, BSc FCA *1991;* Grant Thornton UK LLP, Grant Thornton House, 202 Silbury Boulevard, MILTON KEYNES, BUCKINGHAMSHIRE, MK9 1LW. See also Grant Thornton LLP

NEWSTEAD, Mr. John Arthur William, BA ACA *1999;* Interna Ltd, 53 New Street, WORCESTER, WR1 2DL.

•NEWSTONE, Mr. Richard Eric, FCA *1975;* Newstone & Co., 2 Pepper Court, Great Chesterford, SAFFRON WALDEN, ESSEX, CB10 1NZ.

NEWSUM, Mr. Richard Nevin, FCA *1977;* (Tax Fac), 19 Stratfield Park Close, Winchmore Hill, LONDON, N21 1BU.

NEWSUM, Mr. Thomas George Harvey, FCA *1956;* Flat 3, 29a Lingfield Road, LONDON, SW19 4PU. (Life Member)

•NEWSUM-SMITH, Mr. Andrew Maltby, FCA *1972;* (Tax Fac), Newsum-Smith & Co, 17 Burleigh Road, West Bridgford, NOTTINGHAM, NG2 6FP.

NEWTH, Mr. John Thompson, FCA *1959;* 16 Ashburnham Gardens, EASTBOURNE, EAST SUSSEX, BN21 2NA. (Life Member)

NEWTH, Mr. Martin Edward James, MEng BA ACA *2006;* with Deloitte LLP, Athene Place, 66 Shoe Lane, LONDON, EC4A 3BQ.

NEWTH, Mr. Rodney Arthur Leslie, BA FCA *1960;* Pipers End, Paddock Way, Ashley Green, CHESHAM, BUCKINGHAMSHIRE, HP5 3RE. (Life Member)

NEWTH, Mr. Simon Jeremy, BA ACA *1987;* Priory Cottage Fullers Wood Lane, South Nutfield, REDHILL, RH1 4EF.

NEWTON, Mr. Adrian Stower, FCA *1968;* P.O. Box 2007, WHITE RIVER, 1240, SOUTH AFRICA.

NEWTON, Mrs. Alice Louise, BA ACA *1998;* 45 Highbury Station Road, Islington, LONDON, N1 1SY.

NEWTON, Miss. Alison Louise, MA ACA *2004;* Financial Services Authority, 25 North Colonnade, Canary Wharf, LONDON, E14 5HS.

NEWTON, Mr. Benjamin Alexander, MPhil BSc ACA *1999;* 45 Highbury Station Road, LONDON, N1 1SY.

NEWTON, Mr. Benjamin James, LLB ACA *2005;* 45 Clement Road, Marple Bridge, STOCKPORT, CHESHIRE, SK6 5AG.

NEWTON, Ms. Bernadette Angela Mary, BA ACA *1997;* Flat 26, Capital Wharf, 50 Wapping High Street, LONDON, E1W 1LY.

NEWTON, Mrs. Caroline Dolores, LLM ACA *2000;* 56 Wilding Road, WALLINGFORD, OXFORDSHIRE, OX10 8AS.

NEWTON, Mr. Christopher James, FCA *1965;* Halstow House, Wood Barton, Woodleigh, KINGSBRIDGE, DEVON, TQ7 4EH. (Life Member)

NEWTON, Mr. Christopher James, ACA *2008;* Ir. Jakoba Mulderplein 172, 1018MZ AMSTERDAM, NETHERLANDS.

NEWTON, Ms. Claire Patricia, MA ACA MCT *1981;* 245 Lonsdale Road, LONDON, SW13 9QN.

NEWTON, Mr. David Alan, FCA *1975;* Avalon, Warren Road, Hayes, BROMLEY, BR2 7AN. (Life Member)

NEWTON, Mr. David Charles, BSc ACA *1989;* 5 Knowsley Crescent, Cosham, PORTSMOUTH, PO6 2PJ.

NEWTON, Mr. David Christopher, ACA *2010;* 4 Whickham Park, Whickham, NEWCASTLE UPON TYNE, NE16 4EH.

NEWTON, Mr. David George, BSocSc ACA *1996;* 46 Castle Road East, OLDBURY, WEST MIDLANDS, B68 9BG.

NEWTON, Mr. David Iain, MA ACA *1989;* 10 St Helens Avenue, LEEDS, LS16 8LR.

NEWTON, Mr. David John, BA ACA FIS *1998;* 80 Chipperfield Road, KINGS LANGLEY, HERTFORDSHIRE, WD4 9JD.

•NEWTON, Mr. David Michael, BSc ACA *1981;* PricewaterhouseCoopers LLP, Hays Galleria, 1 Hays Lane, LONDON, SE1 2RD. See also PricewaterhouseCoopers

NEWTON, Mr. David Robert Nicholas, BA FCA *1989;* Haymarket Media Ltd, 23/F The Centrium, 60 Wyndham Street, CENTRAL, HONG KONG ISLAND, HONG KONG SAR.

•NEWTON, Mrs. Deborah, BSc FCA *1991;* Ritsons, The Tower, 103 High Street, ELGIN, MORAYSHIRE, IV30 1EB.
NEWTON, Mr. Derek Hinds, BA FCA *1960;* Number 3, 141 Old Woking Road, WOKING, GU22 8PD. (Life Member)
•NEWTON, Mr. Frederick Douglas, FCA *1974;* Douglas & Co Limited, Broadway House, 8-10 Broadway, Douglas, ISLE OF MAN, IM2 4EL.
NEWTON, Mr. Gareth John, BSc ACA *1995;* The Coach House, 128A Castelnau, Barnes, LONDON, SW13 9ET.
NEWTON, Mr. Geoffrey Harold, FCA *1949;* 8 Turnpike, Aldbourne, MARLBOROUGH, SN8 2BZ. (Life Member)
NEWTON, Mr. Geoffrey Hector, FCA *1952;* 12 Victoria Avenue, ILKLEY, LS29 9BL. (Life Member)
NEWTON, Mr. Geoffrey Richard, FCA *1969;* 19 Springbank, Bollington, MACCLESFIELD, SK10 5LQ. (Life Member)
NEWTON, Mr. Graeme John, MEng ACA *2003;* Flat 10, 1 Hornton Street, LONDON, W8 7NP.
NEWTON, Mr. Guy Glascott Marie, MA ACA *1980;* PFMS, 43 Ferry Road, KIDWELLY, CARMARTHENSHIRE, SA17 5EQ.
•NEWTON, Mrs. Heather Claire, BCom ACA *1995;* Heather Newton, Court Cottage, Little Heath Lane, Potten End, BERKHAMSTED, HP4 2RT.
NEWTON, Mr. Hugh Mcgregor, BSc FCA *1978;* 15 Tweedmouth Court, South Gosforth, NEWCASTLE UPON TYNE, NE3 1YP. (Life Member)
NEWTON, Mr. Iain David, FCA *1961;* South Meadow, Humber View, Swanland, NORTH FERRIBY, NORTH HUMBERSIDE, HU14 3ND.
NEWTON, Mr. Ian Geoffrey, FCA *1971;* Greycote, 44 Cornwall Road, CHEAM, SM2 6DS.
NEWTON, Mr. Ian Roger, BA ACA *1978;* 138 Moss Lane, Bramhall, STOCKPORT, SK7 1EE.
NEWTON, Mr. Ian Ross, MEng ACA *2001;* 46 Gloucester Road, ASHBURTON, VIC 3147, AUSTRALIA.
NEWTON, Miss. Isobel Julia, BA FCA *1988;* 8 Derriman Close, Ecclesall, SHEFFIELD, S11 9LB.
NEWTON, Mr. James Scott, BCom ACA *2003;* 87 Hither Farm Road, LONDON, SE3 9QU.
NEWTON, Mrs. Jane Mary, BA ACA *1983;* 1 West Meadows Road, Cleadon, SUNDERLAND, SR6 7TX.
NEWTON, Miss. Jennifer Anne Felicity, FCA *1966;* Misburn, Babylon Lane, Lower Kingswood, TADWORTH, KT20 6XE.
NEWTON, Mr. Jeremy, MA FCA *1979;* Hill Crofts House, Church End, Weston Colville, CAMBRIDGE, CB21 5PE.
NEWTON, Mrs. Joanna Marie, ACA *2002;* 17 King George Avenue, WALTON-ON-THAMES, SURREY, KT12 3LP.
NEWTON, Mr. John, FCA *1961;* Westmains House, Uppingham Road, Tugby, LEICESTER, LE7 9XH. (Life Member)
NEWTON, Mr. John Dean, BA ACA *2001;* 18 Worrelle Avenue, Middleton, MILTON KEYNES, MK10 9GZ.
•NEWTON, Mr. Jonathan, BSc ACA *1989;* Certax Accounting (Doncaster) Limited, 117 Wivelsfield Road, DONCASTER, SOUTH YORKSHIRE, DN4 0UY. See also Certax Accounting Ltd
NEWTON, Mr. Jonathan James, FCA *1970;* Wetherspoon Holdings, 18/20 Headfort Place, LONDON, SW1X 7DH.
NEWTON, Mr. Jonathan Mark, BSc ACA *2007;* 2 Howard Close, Wilstead, BEDFORD, MK45 3JW.
•NEWTON, Mrs. Judith, BSc FCA *1992;* Grant Thornton UK LLP, Grant Thornton House, 202 Silbury Boulevard, MILTON KEYNES, BUCKINGHAMSHIRE, MK9 1LW. See also Grant Thornton LLP
NEWTON, Miss. Judith Ann, BA ACA *1993;* Flat 8 Tivoli, Tower Gate Preston, BRIGHTON, BN1 6WT.
NEWTON, Mrs. Karen Ann, BA ACA *1999;* 51 Boundary Lane, St. Leonards, RINGWOOD, HAMPSHIRE, BH24 2SE.
NEWTON, Mr. Kevin, BA ACA *1999;* 29 Brownberrie Lane, Horsforth, LEEDS, LS18 5SD.
NEWTON, Mr. Marcus James, ACA *1992;* 8 Iddesleigh Road, BRISTOL, BS6 6YJ.
NEWTON, Mr. Mark Robert, MA(Cantab) ACA *2010;* 6 Morningside, WASHINGTON, TYNE AND WEAR, NE38 9JH.
•NEWTON, Mr. Mervyn Ian, MBA BSc FCA *1982;* Maesygroes Uchaf, Llanafanfawr, BUILTH WELLS, POWYS, LD2 3PG.
NEWTON, Mr. Michael, BA ACA *1990;* 40 Sherbourne Road, WITNEY, OXFORDSHIRE, OX28 5FH.
NEWTON, Mr. Michael, PhD BTech FCA *1985;* 45 Clement Road, Marple Bridge, STOCKPORT, CHESHIRE, SK6 5AG.
NEWTON, Mr. Michael Anthony, BA ACA *1989;* Department of Health, Room 2N09, Quarry House, Quarry Hill, LEEDS, LS2 7UE.
NEWTON, Mr. Michael Robert, MEng ACA *2002;* Wesier LLP, 135 West 50th Street, 14th Floor, NEW YORK, NY 10028, UNITED STATES.
NEWTON, Mrs. Natalie Anne, BA ACA *1993;* 10 Anderson Road, CONCORD, NSW 2137, AUSTRALIA.
NEWTON, Ms. Natalie Ruth, BA(Hons) ACA *2001;* 49 Branksome Hill Road, BOURNEMOUTH, BH4 9LF.
NEWTON, Mr. Nicholas Howard, BSc ACA *1989;* 54 Whirlow Park Road, SHEFFIELD, S11 9NP.
NEWTON, Mr. Nigel Christopher, BA ACA *1983;* 100, Vivacta Ltd, 100 Guillat Avenue Kent Science Park, SITTINGBOURNE, ME9 8GU.
NEWTON, Mr. Oliver Peter, BSc ACA *2003;* Tarchon Capital Management, 7th Floor, 16 Berkeley Street, LONDON, W1J 8DZ.
NEWTON, Mr. Paul Anthony, BEng ACA *1992;* Croda International Plc, Cowick Hall, Snaith, GOOLE, NORTH HUMBERSIDE, DN14 9AA.
NEWTON, Mr. Paul David, BSc ACA *1996;* Phoenix House, Bewick Garth, Mickley, STOCKSFIELD, NORTHUMBERLAND, NE43 7AU.
NEWTON, Mr. Paul Derek, BSc ACA *2002;* with Jacob Cavenagh & Skeet, 5 Robin Hood Lane, SUTTON, SURREY, SM1 2SW.
NEWTON, Mr. Paul Desmond George, BSc ACA *1990;* 23 Wood End Road, HARPENDEN, HERTFORDSHIRE, AL5 3EE.
NEWTON, Mr. Paul Graeme, MBA BA(Hons) ACA *1984;* Longwood House, 531 Halifax Road, Hightown, LIVERSEDGE, WEST YORKSHIRE, WF15 8HL.
NEWTON, Mr. Paul Michael, BA ACA *1989;* Over Hall, Flag Lane, Bretherton, PRESTON, PR26 9AD.
NEWTON, Mr. Peter, BSc FCA *1975;* 109 Broadway North, WALSALL, WS1 2QD.
NEWTON, Mr. Peter James, BSc(Hons) ACA *2001;* 50-28 245th Street, DOUGLASTON, NY 11362-1627, UNITED STATES.
NEWTON, Mr. Richard, MA(Hons) ACA *2001;* 33 Jermyn Street, LONDON, SW1Y 6DN.
•NEWTON, Mr. Richard, ACA *1985;* (Tax Fac), Richard Newton, 15 Manningford Close, WINCHESTER, SO23 7EU.
NEWTON, Mr. Richard, LLB ACA *2011;* Flat 60, Qube, 12 Scotland Street, BIRMINGHAM, B1 2EJ.
NEWTON, Mr. Richard Bowstead, FCA *1965;* 42 Wychwood Avenue, Knowle, SOLIHULL, WEST MIDLANDS, B93 9DG. (Life Member)
•NEWTON, Mr. Richard John Ernest, FCA *1968;* (Tax Fac), Richard Newton, Church View, 162 Main Street, Alrewas, BURTON-ON-TRENT, STAFFORDSHIRE DE13 7ED.
NEWTON, Mr. Robert Paul, LLB ACA *2006;* Whitehaven, 6 Clos de Fosse Andre, Fosse Andre St. Peter Port, GUERNSEY, GY1 1XZ.
NEWTON, Mr. Robert Paul James, FCA *1964;* 131 Springdale Road, BROADSTONE, BH18 9BW.
NEWTON, Mr. Russell Scott, BSc ACA FSI *1993;* 19 Dyers Yard, NORWICH, NR3 3QY.
NEWTON, Miss. Sandra Mary, BA FCA *1983;* Oxfam BG, Oxfam House John Smith Drive, OXFORD, OX4 2JY.
NEWTON, Mr. Simon James, BSc ACA *1991;* AMU Group Ltd, 151 Marylebone Road, LONDON, NW1 5QE.
NEWTON, Mr. Simon James, BSc ACA *1996;* 26 Trevor Road, LONDON, SW19 3PW.
NEWTON, Mr. Simon Russell, BSc ACA *1991;* Court Cottage, Little Heath Lane, Potten End, BERKHAMSTED, HP4 2RT.
NEWTON, Mr. Stanley, FCA *1950;* 2 Everard Road, SOUTHPORT, PR8 6NA. (Life Member)
NEWTON, Mr. Stewart Worth, FCA *1965;* Sussex Research limited, 6th Floor, Elizabeth House, 39 York Road, LONDON, SE1 7NQ.
NEWTON, Mr. Thomas Mackenzie, BSc ACA *1994;* 8 Devoil Close, GUILDFORD, SURREY, GU4 7FG.
NEWTON, Mr. Timothy, BSc ACA *2007;* (Tax Fac), 109 Broadway North, WALSALL, WS1 2QD.
NEWTON, Mr. Timothy James, MA ACA *1983;* Cambridge Environmental Research Consultants, 3 Kings Parade, CAMBRIDGE, CB2 1SJ.
NEWTON, Miss. Tracy Ann, BSc ACA CTA *1996;* (Tax Fac), 117 Fakenham Road, Great Ryburgh, FAKENHAM, NR21 7AQ.
•NEWTON, Mrs. Ursula Farrell, BSc ACA *1993;* PricewaterhouseCoopers LLP, 1 Embankment Place, LONDON, WC2N 6RH. See also PricewaterhouseCoopers
•NEWTON, Mr. William Justin, FCA *1978;* Lean Newton & Cary, 58 York Gardens, WALTON-ON-THAMES, SURREY, KT12 3EW.
NEWTON, Mr. William Peter, BSc ACA *1999;* 1 Old Applecroft, SANDBACH, CHESHIRE, CW11 3NR.
NEWTON WEBB, Mr. Philip Andrew, BSc FCA *1980;* Lugano, 22 Stanfield Road, FERNDOWN, BH22 9PA.
NEYLON, Miss. Bridget Mary Teresa, BA ACA *1989;* Wragge & Co, 55 Colmore Row, BIRMINGHAM, B3 2AS.
NEYLON, Mr. David, FCA *1962;* 1 Chelford Avenue, Lowton St Lukes, WARRINGTON, WA3 2RU. (Life Member)
NG, Mr. Alvin Chee Vui, ACA *1994;* 200a Dalling Road, LONDON, W6 0ER.
NG, Mr. Anas, ACA *2004;* Anas Ng, Room 1506-1508, 15/F Asia Orient Tower, 33 Lockhart Road, WAN CHAI, HONG KONG ISLAND HONG KONG SAR.
NG, Mr. Andrew Shu Bun, BA FCA *1990;* 13th Floor, Amber Commercial Building, 70 Morrison Hill Road, WAN CHAI, HONG KONG ISLAND, HONG KONG SAR.
NG, Mrs. Ann, BSc ACA *1993;* 6 Umbria Street, LONDON, SW15 5DP.
NG, Mr. Anthony, MSc MSc BSc(Hons) ACA IMC *2011;* 16 Trevor Square, Knightsbridge, LONDON, SW7 1DT.
NG, Ms. Ashley Mee, ACA *1986;* 20A Baverstock Road, Dannemora, MANUKAU CITY 2016, AUCKLAND, NEW ZEALAND.
NG, Mr. Boon Hiang, ACA *2008;* N3-03-09, Subang Perdana Court 7, Jalan USJ 14/1, Selangor De, 47630 SUBANG, SELANGOR MALAYSIA.
NG, Mr. Boon Yew, ACA *1982;* Bismac Consultant Pte Ltd, 24 Fernhill Crescent, SINGAPORE 259178, SINGAPORE.
NG, Miss. Candy, MSc BSc ACA *2006;* 42 Railway Street, CHELMSFORD, CM1 1QS.
NG, Ms. Carrie, ACA *2007;* Flat D, 7/F Hoi Shing Mansion, 10 Taikoo Shing Road, TAIKOO SHING, HONG KONG ISLAND, HONG KONG SAR.
NG, Mr. Chak Man, ACA *2007;* Flat 2B, Albron Court, 99 Caine Road, MID LEVELS, HONG KONG ISLAND, HONG KONG SAR.
•NG, Mr. Chee Khoon, FCA *1980;* (Tax Fac), Nicholas Ng and Company Ltd, 201 Lordship Lane, LONDON, SE22 8HA.
NG, Mr. Chen Kok, ACA *2004;* BLK 195C PUNGGOL ROAD, #14-524, SINGAPORE 823195, SINGAPORE.
NG, Ms. Cheng Cheng Fiona, BA(Hons) ACA *2004;* 36 Sheridan Road, BEXLEYHEATH, KENT, DA7 4AP.
NG, Mr. Cheong Seng, ACA *2008;* 46 Jalan 3/39, Taman Megah Kepong, 52100 KUALA LUMPUR, FEDERAL TERRITORY, MALAYSIA.
NG, Mr. Cheung, ACA *2006;* Ernst & Young Hua Ming, Level 16 Ernst & Young Tower, Oriental Plaza, No. 1 East Chang An Avenue, Dong Cheng District, BEIJING 100738 CHINA.
NG, Mr. Chi Keung, ACA *2008;* Fairwood Holdings Ltd, 2/F TRP Commercial Centre, 18 Tanner Road, NORTH POINT, HONG KONG SAR.
NG, Mr. Chi Keung, ACA *2008;* Flat D 28/F, Block 6, La Cite Noble, 1 Ngan O Road, TSEUNG KWAN O, NEW TERRITORIES HONG KONG SAR.
NG, Mr. Chi Kwong, ACA *2006;* c/o Citybus Ltd, 7/F 8 Chong Fu Road, CHAI WAN, HONG KONG ISLAND, HONG KONG SAR.
NG, Mr. Chi Wa Thomas, ACA *2008;* Room 1407, Choi Yeung House, Choi Ming Court, TSEUNG KWAN O, NEW TERRITORIES, HONG KONG SAR.
NG, Mr. Chi Wai, ACA *2008;* Flat B, 11/F, Block 26, Baguio Villa, 555 Victoria Road, POK FU LAM HONG KONG SAR.
NG, Mr. Chi Wai, ACA *2008;* Flat D 7th Floor, Block 8, City Garden, 233 Electric Road, NORTH POINT, HONG KONG SAR.
NG, Mr. Chi Yin, ACA *2005;* Flat B 28/F, Tower 2 Marbella, 23 On Chun Street, Ma On Shan, SHA TIN, NEW TERRITORIES HONG KONG SAR.
NG, Miss. Chi-Ing, BSc ACA *2004;* Fortress Investment Group, 5 Saville Row, LONDON, W1S 3PD.
NG, Mr. Ching Wai, ACA *2008;* Flat B 24/F, Woodland Court, 2-3 Woodlands Terrace, MID LEVELS, HONG KONG SAR.
NG, Ms. Chit Ying Lydia, ACA *2005;* Room 1801, 18/F, Public Bank Centre, 120 Des Voeux Road, CENTRAL, HONG KONG ISLAND HONG KONG SAR.
NG, Miss. Chiunga, LLB ACA CTA *2002;* with Deloitte LLP, PO Box 500, 2 Hardman Street, MANCHESTER, M60 2AT.
NG, Mr. Choo Beng, BSc ACA *1992;* 555 Hong Xu Lu, Hong Qiao Golf Villa Unit 106, Minghang District, SHANGHAI 200032, CHINA.
NG, Ms. Christine Chi Mei, BSc ACA *1989;* Flat 15B, 1 Tai Hang Road, TAI HANG, Hong Kong Island, HONG KONG SAR.
NG, Mr. Chun Fai, ACA *2008;* 4/67-69, Railway Street, Baulkham Hills, SYDNEY, NSW 2153, AUSTRALIA.
NG, Mr. Chun Lei, BSc ACA *2011;* Flat 11, 1 Yeoman Street, LONDON, SE8 5DP.
NG, Mr. Chung Wai David, ACA *2007;* TPI(Holdings) Co Ltd, c/o Chan and Man CPA, 1603 Island Place Tower, 510 Kings Road, NORTHPORT, HONG KONG ISLAND HONG KONG SAR.
NG, Mr. Derek Kwok Wai, BSc ACA *1996;* 327 OXBOW CRESCENT, MISSISSAUGA L4Z 2S4, ON, CANADA.
NG, Mr. Earn Chin, BSc ACA *1993;* Bangunan Ming Annexe 05-00, 9 Jalan Ampang, 50450 KUALA LUMPUR, FEDERAL TERRITORY, MALAYSIA.
NG, Mr. Fernando, ACA *2009;* Flat 2B Albron Court, 99 Caine Road, MID LEVELS, HONG KONG SAR.
NG, Ms. Foong Mai, ACA *1984;* Block F, Spanish Villa, 151 Nam Wai, SAI KUNG, NEW TERRITORIES, HONG KONG SAR.
NG, Mr. Frederick Kar-Yin, BA FCA MBA *1986;* Flat 3 21/F Block B, Lai Chi Kok Bay Gardens, 272 Lai King Hill Road, KWAI CHUNG, NT, HONG KONG SAR.
NG, Mr. Fuk Leung, ACA *2006;* Tommy NG & Co, Suite B, 11/F Foo Cheong Building, 82-86 Wing Lok Street, SHEUNG WAN, HONG KONG ISLAND HONG KONG SAR.
NG, Mr. Fuk Yan Samuel, ACA *2008;* Ng Fuk Yan Samuel, 2003 Wayson Commercial House, 68 Lockhart Road, WAN CHAI, HONG KONG ISLAND, HONG KONG SAR.
NG, Miss. Gek Siu, ACA *1980;* 3 Jalan SS 25/26, Taman Mayang, 47301 PETALING JAYA, Selangor, MALAYSIA.
NG, Miss. Geok-Hwoon, ACA *1979;* Angie G H NG Inc, 1133 - 56th Street, DELTA V4L 2A2, BC, CANADA.
NG, Mr. Gerry Joo Yeow, BSc ACA *1990;* Baring Asset Management (Asia) Ltd, 19/F Edingburgh Tower, 15 Queen's Road, CENTRAL, HONG KONG ISLAND, HONG KONG SAR.
NG, Miss. Guat Leng, BSc ACA *1989;* Apt 50A Tower 6 Bel-Air No. 8, 8 Bel-Air Peak Avenue, Island South, POK FU LAM, HONG KONG SAR.
NG, Mr. Henry Shu Lau, BSc ACA *1992;* Flat 15 Beechcroft House, 47-49 Park View Road, LONDON, W5 2JF.
NG, Mr. Hoi Yue Herman, ACA *2007;* Grant Thornton, 6th Floor, Sunning Plaza, 10 Hysan Avenue, CAUSEWAY BAY, HONG KONG SAR.
NG, Mr. Hon Wah, ACA *1989;* Flat A, 5/F Block 1, Golf Parkview, 83 Castle Peak Road, SHEUNG SHUI, NEW TERRITORIES HONG KONG SAR.
NG, Mr. Hon Pong Joseph, ACA *2008;* Flat 4B, Tower 2, Robinson Heights, 8 Robinson Road, MID LEVELS, HONG KONG SAR.
NG, Mr. Hon Wai Derek, ACA *2011;* Flat 1, 9th Floor Block C, Flora Garden, 50 Cloud View Road, NORTH POINT, HONG KONG ISLAND HONG KONG SAR.
•NG, Mr. Hong Kee, FCA *1974;* K Consulting(Surrey) Limited, Suite 1, Central House, Woodside Park Commerical Centre, Catteshall Lane, GODALMING SURREY GU7 1LG. See also K Consulting (Surrey) Limited
NG, Mr. Hooi Chong, LLB ACA *1996;* 47E Tower 6 The Belcher's, 89 Pokfulam Road, POK FU LAM, HONG KONG ISLAND, HONG KONG SAR.
NG, Miss. Ing Peng, ACA *1984;* 69 Jalan Sri, Hartamas 17, 50480 KUALA LUMPUR, FEDERAL TERRITORY, MALAYSIA.
NG, Mr. Jarvis Lung Wah, ACA *2008;* 6C Broadview Terrace, 40 Cloud View Road, NORTH POINT, HONG KONG SAR.
NG, Miss. Jenni Yen Li, BA ACA *2005;* RBS, 135 Bishopsgate, LONDON, EC2M 3UR.
NG, Miss. Jie Wey Grace, BSc ACA *2007;* with PricewaterhouseCoopers LLP, 1 Embankment Place, LONDON, WC2N 6RH.
NG, Mr. Jonathan Tai Sing, BA FCA ACCA CPA *1999;* with HKICPA, 37/F Wu Chung House, 213 Queen's Road East, WAN CHAI, HONG KONG ISLAND, HONG KONG SAR.
NG, Mr. Jui Sia, ACA *1981;* 39A Chiltern Drive, Braddell Height Estate, SINGAPORE 359762, SINGAPORE.
NG, Mr. Ka Kin, ACA *2010;* Flat H 39/F, Tower 3, Park Central, 9 Tong Tak Street, TSEUNG KWAN O, NEW TERRITORIES HONG KONG SAR.
NG, Mr. Ka Luen, ACA *2005;* A3 8/F Shun Lee Building Block A, 240 Ferry Street, YAU MA TEI, KOWLOON, HONG KONG SAR.
NG, Ms. Ka Wah Nancy, ACA *2008;* Flat A, 6th Floor Block 6, Villa Concerto, Symphony Bay, 530 Sai Sha Raod, SAI KUNG NEW TERRITORIES HONG KONG SAR.

NG, Miss. Kai Kai Vanessa, ACA *2008;* Room 1402, No 130, Lane 999 Xin Er Road, Bao Shan District, SHANGHAI 200439, CHINA.
NG, Mr. Kai Yeung, ACA *2007;* Room B 9th Floor, Amtel Building, 144-148 Des Vouex Road, CENTRAL, HONG KONG ISLAND, HONG KONG SAR.
NG, Mr. Kam Chiu, ACA *2006;* KC Ng & Company, Suite B, 13th Floor, Tak Lee Commercial Building, 113-117 Wanchai Road, WAN CHAI HONG KONG ISLAND HONG KONG SAR.
NG, Mr. Kam Choon, ACA *1981;* 6 Fairmont Court, NARRE WARREN NORTH, VIC 3804, AUSTRALIA.
NG, Mr. Kam Keung Derek, ACA *2008;* Derek Ng & Company, Room 702, Hollywood Plaza, 610 Nathan Road, MONG KOK, KOWLOON HONG KONG SAR.
NG, Mr. Kam Wah Webster, ACA *2005;* Webster Ng & Co., Rooms 1306-7 13/F, Park-In Commerical Centre, 56 Dundas Street, MONG KOK, KOWLOON HONG KONG SAR.
NG, Mr. Kar Ling Johnny, ACA *2005;* KPMG, 8/F Prince's Building, 10 Chater Road, CENTRAL, HONG KONG ISLAND, HONG KONG SAR.
NG, Miss. Karen Su Hiah, BA ACA MMus *1998;* 23 Caroline Road, Wimbledon, LONDON, SW19 3QL.
NG, Mr. Kay Lam, BCom ACA *1984;* Room 1106. 11th Floor, Kai Wong Commercial Building, 222-226 Queens Road Central, SHEUNG WAN, HONG KONG ISLAND, HONG KONG SAR.
NG, Mr. Kenneth Shih Yek, BSc ACA *1994;* 99/1 Soi Rajakroo, Phaholyothin Road, BANGKOK, 10400, THAILAND.
NG, Mr. Kevin, ACA *2011;* Flat 51, Gaugin Court, 3 Stubbs Drive, LONDON, SE16 3EB.
NG, Mr. Kevin Ka-Wing, MA ACA *1991;* 32 Kennedy Road, Flat 4A, MID LEVELS, HONG KONG SAR.
NG, Mr. Ki Cheung, ACA *2006;* Flat A, 20/F No. 56 Broadway, Mei Fao Sun Chuen, LAI CHI KOK, KOWLOON, HONG KONG SAR.
NG, Mr. Kian Ann, MBA FCA *1991;* 94 Jln Bu10/1, Bandar Utama, 47800 PETALING JAYA, Selangor, MALAYSIA.
NG, Mr. Kim Cheang, FCA *1984;* 5 Sunset Terrace, SINGAPORE 597262, SINGAPORE.
NG, Mr. Kim Ling, BA ACA *2004;* A-4-2 Block A, Highbank Condominium, Sri Bukit Persekutuan, 50480 KUALA LUMPUR, FEDERAL TERRITORY, MALAYSIA.
NG, Mr. Kin Fai, ACA *2011;* with Deloitte Touche Tohmatsu, 35/F One Pacific Place, 88 Queensway, CENTRAL, HONG KONG ISLAND, HONG KONG SAR.
NG, Mr. Kin Lok Eric, ACA *2010;* Rm.803-805, Workingport Comm. Building, 3 Hau Fook Street, TSIM SHA TSUI, KOWLOON, HONG KONG SAR.
NG, Mr. Kin Man Wilfred, ACA *2008;* 774 West 68th Avenue, VANCOUVER V6P 2T9, BC, CANADA.
•**NG, Mr. Kin-Chung, BA FCA** *1989;* (Tax Fac), Ng & Co, 7 Lyndhurst Avenue, LONDON, NW7 2AD.
NG, Mr. Kit Ho, LLB ACA *2001;* 125 Jalan SS 22/37, Damansara Jaya, 47400 PETALING JAYA, SELANGOR, MALAYSIA.
NG, Mr. Ko Seng, FCA *1983;* (Tax Fac), Star Cruises Ltd, 1501 Ocean Centre, 5 Canton Road, TSIM SHA TSIU, KOWLOON, HONG KONG SAR.
•**NG, Mr. Kon Thai, ACA** *1981;* KTNG, 3rd Floor, 12-13 Little Newport Street, LONDON, WC2H 7JJ.
NG, Mr. Koon Fai, ACA *2005;* Flat A, 11F, Pine Tree Garden, Ede Road, KOWLOON TONG, HONG KONG SAR.
NG, Mr. Kui Kwan, BA ACA *1987;* Flat B 10/F, Jolly Garden, 151 Reclamation Street, YAU MA TEI, KOWLOON, HONG KONG SAR.
NG, Mr. Kwai Yew, FCA *1974;* Apt Block 251 Bishan Street 22 #04-400, SINGAPORE 570251, SINGAPORE.
NG, Mr. Kwok Hung, BSc FCA *1989;* Room 413, Block B, Cofco Plaza, 8 Jiamguomennei Dajie, BEIJING 100005, CHINA.
NG, Mr. Kwok Wai, ACA *2006;* Flat D 33/F Block 3, Vision City, Tsuen Wan, TSUEN WAN, NEW TERRITORIES, HONG KONG SAR.
NG, Mr. Kwok Ho Joseph, ACA *2007;* No.2 7/F. Block D, Sunshine City, Ma On Shan, SHA TIN, NEW TERRITORIES, HONG KONG SAR.
NG, Mr. Kwok Kei Sammy, ACA *2004;* Sammy K. K. Ng, Unit 302, Kam On Building, 176a Queens Road, CENTRAL, HONG KONG ISLAND HONG KONG SAR.
NG, Mr. Kwok Yin, ACA *2008;* 12/F Fung House, 19-20 Connaught Road, CENTRAL, HONG KONG SAR.
NG, Mr. Kwong Sang, ACA *2007;* 9/F, Fortune House, 61 Connaught Road, CENTRAL, HONG KONG ISLAND, HONG KONG SAR.
NG, Ms. Lai Hung, ACA *2008;* 32H Block 3, Royal Peninsula, 8 Hung Lai Road, HUNG HOM, KOWLOON, HONG KONG SAR.
NG, Dr. Lai Man Carmen, ACA *2007;* Cosmos Certified Public Accountants Limited, 808 8th Floor, Sun Hung Kai Centre, 30 Harbour Road, WAN CHAI, HONG KONG SAR. See also Cachet
•**NG, Miss. Laura Yuet Yu, BSc FCA** *1993;* L Y Y Ng Accounting Services Limited, 65 Lower Essex Street, BIRMINGHAM, B5 6SN.
NG, Miss. Lee Cheng, BSc ACA *1987;* Robinson Road P O Box 1612, SINGAPORE 903212, SINGAPORE.
NG, Miss. Li-Fei, ACA *2009;* 31 Jalan 21/5, 46300 PETALING JAYA, SELANGOR, MALAYSIA.
•**NG, Mr. Lui Ming, BSc ACA** *1982;* Fisher Ng Limited, 2 Kings Road, London Colney, ST. ALBANS, HERTFORDSHIRE, AL2 1EN.
NG, Miss. Man Lan, BSc ACA *1991;* 10 Waterside Avenue, BECKENHAM, BR3 3GJ.
NG, Miss. Man Yi, BSc ACA *2000;* 1 Cherrywood Close, KINGSTON UPON THAMES, SURREY, KT2 6SF.
NG, Mr. Man Chung Siman, ACA *2005;* M.C. Ng & Co, Room 1502 Double Building, 22 Stanley Street, CENTRAL, HONG KONG ISLAND, HONG KONG SAR.
NG, Ms. Man Ngo Helen, ACA *2008;* Flat F 25/F, Block 7, Sceneway Garden, LAM TIN, KOWLOON, HONG KONG SAR.
NG, Ms. Man Yee Karen, ACA *2005;* Flat D 8/F Block 8, Monte Vista, Ma On Shan, SHA TIN, NEW TERRITORIES, HONG KONG SAR.
NG, Miss. Melissa Jodie, BSc ACA *1994;* PO Box 61741, Royal Mail Callers Office, 9 Howick Place, LONDON, SW1P 1AA.
NG, Mrs. Mi Li, BSc FCA *1993;* PricewaterhouseCoopers, P.O.Box 10192, Level 10 1 Sentral, Jalan Travers, 50470 KUALA LUMPUR, FEDERAL TERRITORY MALAYSIA.
NG, Mr. Michael Eng Choon, FCA *1969;* 48A Toh Tuk Road, 8th Floor Number 7, Signature Park, SINGAPORE 596740, SINGAPORE.
NG, Miss. Michelle Huey Nah, ACA *2011;* 403 Block L8, Jalan Pandan 3, Pandan Jaya, 55100 KUALA LUMPUR, MALAYSIA.
NG, Mr. Ming San, FCA *1972;* 23 Lilitan Sg. Emas, Batu Feringghi, 11100 PENANG, MALAYSIA.
NG, Mr. Ming Chu, ACA *2008;* 8G, Block 2 Site 5, Whampoa Garden, HUNG HOM, KOWLOON, HONG KONG SAR.
NG, Miss. Nadine Loon Angela, BSc ACA *1992;* Parkwood Holdings Plc Parkwood House, Berkeley Drive Bamber Bridge, PRESTON, PR5 6BY.
NG, Miss. Ngin Hooi, FCA *1984;* 99 Tudor Avenue South, RIVERTON, WA 6148, AUSTRALIA.
NG, Ms. Nyi Hong, FCA *1976;* 27 Jalan Sri Hartamas 12, Sri Hartamas (12/70A), 50480 KUALA LUMPUR, FEDERAL TERRITORY, MALAYSIA.
NG, Ms. Oi Sim Carolyn, ACA *2008;* Unit2 13 Shenfield Ave, Chelsea VIC 3196, MELBOURNE, VIC 3196, AUSTRALIA.
•**NG, Mr. Paul Hon Sun, FCA** *1982;* (Tax Fac), Paul Ng & Associates, 15 Halifax Way, WELWYN GARDEN CITY, AL7 2QH.
NG, Mr. Paul Siu Bor, ACA *2007;* Hong Kong Land, 5/F One Exchange Square, CENTRAL, HONG KONG SAR.
NG, Miss. Pearly Pei En, ACA *2009;* 131 Church Road, Erdington, BIRMINGHAM, B24 9BG.
NG, Miss. Pek Geok, ACA *1980;* 14 Delaware Street, Epping, SYDNEY, NSW 2121, AUSTRALIA.
NG, Mr. Philip Liang Jin, BSc ACA *1982;* 29 Aitken Drive, Winthrop, PERTH, WA 6150, AUSTRALIA.
NG, Mr. Ping Kit, ACA *2007;* Flat 2501, Tsui Pak House, Tsui Ping Estate, KWUN TONG, HONG KONG ISLAND, HONG KONG SAR.
NG, Mr. Po Tung, ACA *2007;* Room 1906, Empress Plaza, 17-19 Chatham Road South, TSIM SHA TSUI, KOWLOON, HONG KONG SAR.
NG, Mr. Po Wing Patrick, ACA *2005;* Flat 4A Tai Kut House, 7 Greig Road, QUARRY BAY, HONG KONG SAR.
NG, Mr. Poh Seng, BSc FCA *1993;* 16 Jalan BU 11/5, Bandar Utama Petaling Jaya, Selangor Darul Ehsan, 47800 KUALA LUMPUR, FEDERAL TERRITORY, MALAYSIA.
NG, Mr. Pyak Yeow, FCA *1971;* Ng Lee & Partners, Suite Nos. A 23-1 & 2 23rd Floor, Menara UOA Bangsar, No.5 Jalan Bangsar Utama 1, 59000 KUALA LUMPUR, FEDERAL TERRITORY MALAYSIA. See also Ng, Ho & Partners
NG, Mr. Quek Peng, BSc ACA *1980;* 30 Jalan Merlimau, SINGAPORE 308719, SINGAPORE.
NG, Ms. Sau Han Stephanie, ACA *2007;* P O Box 33939, Sheung Wan Post Office, SHEUNG WAN, HONG KONG ISLAND, HONG KONG SAR.
NG, Mr. Say Beng, BA ACA *1994;* 5 Jalan Mutiara Seputeh 3, Mutiara Seputeh, 58000 KUALA LUMPUR, FEDERAL TERRITORY, MALAYSIA.
NG, Mr. Seng Hoong, BA ACA *1990;* Briar Dene, Main Street, East Keswick, LEEDS, LS17 9EJ.
NG, Mr. Shiu Hong, BSc ACA CPA *1985;* BDO Limited, 25/F Wing On Centre, 111 Connaught Road, CENTRAL, HONG KONG ISLAND, HONG KONG SAR. See also BDO McCabe Lo & Limited
NG, Ms. Shiu Mun, ACA *2007;* with Ernst & Young, 18/F, Two International Finance Centre, 8 Finance Street, CENTRAL, HONG KONG ISLAND HONG KONG SAR.
•**NG, Mr. Sho See, ACA** *1980;* 63 JALAN 5/98 TAMAN SUPREME, 56100 KUALA LUMPUR, MALAYSIA.
NG, Ms. Shuk Ming, ACA *2007;* Flat B, 24/F Block 4, Provident Centre, Wharf Road, NORTH POINT, HONG KONG ISLAND HONG KONG SAR.
NG, Ms. Shuk Mun Rosa, ACA *2008;* Unit 3105, Block B, Kornhill, 25-27 Hong Shing Street, QUARRY BAY, HONG KONG SAR.
NG, Mr. Siek Chuan Soon Lai, FCA *1977;* 20 Jalan Setia Murni 6, Damansara Heights, 50490 KUALA LUMPUR, FEDERAL TERRITORY, MALAYSIA.
NG, Mr. Siew Ge, ACA *1986;* 4 Elite Park Avenue, South Union Park, SINGAPORE 458825, SINGAPORE.
NG, Mr. Simon Sai Lam, BSc FCA *1991;* Flat A 45th Floor, Tower 5, The Belcher's, 89 Pok Fu Lam Road, POK FU LAM, HONG KONG ISLAND HONG KONG SAR.
NG, Ms. Siu Ching, ACA *2007;* Room A, 20/F Tak Lee Commercial Building, 113-117 Wanchai Road, WAN CHAI, HONG KONG SAR.
NG, Miss. Siu Chun, BSc ACA *2009;* 33 Scott Farm Close, Sugden Road, THAMES DITTON, SURREY, KT7 0AN.
NG, Miss. Sofronie, BSc ACA *1992;* 9B Princess Margaret Road, Third Floor, MONG KOK, KOWLOON, HONG KONG SAR.
NG, Ms. Sok Yee Maria, BA(Econ) ACA *2004;* #201 Maison D'or Blanc, 15-4 Shirokane 4-Chome, Minato-Ku, TOKYO, 108-0072 JAPAN.
NG, Miss. Stephanie Wei Quan, ACA *2011;* Flat 109, Devon Mansions, Tooley Street, LONDON, SE1 2NX.
NG, Miss. Sue Ling, MSc BA(Hons) ACA *2005;* 404/19 Cadigal Avenue, PYRMONT, NSW 2009, AUSTRALIA.
NG, Mr. Sui Wa, ACA *2008;* 1/F No 221, Shalan Villas, Shuen Wan, TAI PO, NEW TERRITORIES, HONG KONG SAR.
•**NG, Mrs. Susan Hannah, FCA** *1994;* NG Accountancy Services, 36 Sutherland Place, WICKFORD, ESSEX, SS12 9HD.
NG, Miss. Susanna Shui Shan, BSc ACA *1993;* Lloyd George Management, Suite 3808, 1 Exchange Square, CENTRAL, HONG KONG ISLAND, HONG KONG SAR.
NG, Mr. Tek Swee, ACA *1983;* 38 Jalan Sri, Hartamas 18, 50480 KUALA LUMPUR, FEDERAL TERRITORY, MALAYSIA.
NG, Mr. Timothy Charles, BSc ACA *1992;* 4673 Blackcomb Way, WHISTLER V0N 1B4, BC, CANADA.
NG, Mr. Tin Ming Frank, ACA *2008;* YipNg & Company, Room A-B, 15/F, Ritz Plaza, 122 Austin Road, TSIM SHA TSUI KOWLOON HONG KONG SAR.
NG, Mr. Toh San Chris, BSc ACA *2004;* 19 Shelford Rd, #08-01, SINGAPORE 288408, SINGAPORE.
NG, Mr. Tony Kin Yung, BSc ACA *1984;* Kingston CPA Ltd, 6/F Greenwich Centre, 260 Kings Road, NORTH POINT, HONG KONG SAR.
NG, Mr. Tsz Wai Felix, ACA *2006;* Felix Ng, Dascom Technology Limited, Room 1811-12, Nan Fung Center, 298 Castle Peak Road, TSEUNG KWAN O NEW TERRITORIES HONG KONG SAR.
NG, Mr. Tze Kin David, ACA *2007;* Hong Kong Great Wall CPA Ltd, 3/F Malaysia Building, 50 Gloucester Road, WAN CHAI, 852, HONG KONG SAR.
NG, Ms. Tze Ling, ACA *2011;* 32 Jalan 19/154, Taman Bukit Anggerik, Cheras, 56000 KUALA LUMPUR, FEDERAL TERRITORY, MALAYSIA.
NG, Miss. Vern ai, ACA *2011;* 21 SS24/15, Taman Megah, 47301 PETALING JAYA, MALAYSIA.
NG, Mr. Vincent Wing-Chung, MSc BSc ACA CPA CFA *2005;* House 2, 3-4 Lot 146 Tso Tsui Ha, Kwun Yam Garden, SHA TIN, NEW TERRITORIES, HONG KONG SAR.
NG, Mr. Wai Kei, ACA *2007;* Room 2820, Hok Sam House, Lung Hang Estate, SHA TIN, NEW TERRITORIES, HONG KONG SAR.
NG, Miss. Wai Yin, BA ACA *1984;* 133 St. Matthews Gardens, CAMBRIDGE, CB1 2PS.
NG, Ms. Wai Chi Josephine, ACA *2008;* Sino Trade Services Ltd, 4007 Central Plaza, 18 Harbour Road, WAN CHAI, HONG KONG SAR.
NG, Mr. Wai Ching, ACA *2008;* Flat D, 19th Floor, Block 6, City One Shatin, SHA TIN, NEW TERRITORIES HONG KONG SAR.
NG, Mr. Wai Chiu Lewis, ACA *2008;* Flat D, 19/FBlock 8, Royal Ascot, SHA TIN, NEW TERRITORIES, HONG KONG SAR.
NG, Miss. Wai foong, ACA *2009;* Flat 4, 11-12 Lower Marsh, LONDON, SE1 7RJ.
NG, Mr. Wai Kee, ACA *2008;* WK Ng & Co, Room 2001, 20/F Grandtech Centre, 8 On Ping Road, SHA TIN, NEW TERRITORIES HONG KONG SAR.
NG, Ms. Wai Kwun, ACA *2008;* Flat 120212/F, Block A, Peninsula Heights, 63 Broadcast Drive, KOWLOON TONG, KOWLOON HONG KONG SAR.
NG, Mr. Wai Wah, ACA *2009;* 1617 Lee Ming House, Shun Lee Estate, KWUN TONG, KOWLOON, HONG KONG SAR.
NG, Miss. Wei Ann, BSc ACA *2010;* 20 Jalan Setiamurni 6, Bukit Damansara, 50490 KUALA LUMPUR, FEDERAL TERRITORY, MALAYSIA.
NG, Mr. Wei Keat, BSc(Hons) ACA *2001;* with KPMG LLP, 15 Canada Square, LONDON, E14 5GL.
NG, Mr. Wei Teck, FCA *1975;* 50 Raffles Place, #40/05, Singapore Land Tower, SINGAPORE 048623, SINGAPORE.
NG, Mr. Wei Tjia Shaun, ACA MCT MSF CFA *1999;* 6928 Girard Street, MCLEAN, VA 22101, UNITED STATES.
NG, Mr. William, ACA *2007;* C8, 16/F, 22-36 Paterson Street, CAUSEWAY BAY, HONG KONG SAR.
NG, Mr. Wilson Chin Heng, BA ACA *2007;* GKN Plc, PO Box 55, Ipsley House, Ipsley Church Lane, REDDITCH, WORCESTERSHIRE B98 0TL.
NG, Mr. Wing Fai, ACA *2005;* Room 1907 Dominion Centre, Nos 43-59 Queens Road East, WAN CHAI, HONG KONG ISLAND, HONG KONG SAR.
NG, Mr. Wing Hang Patrick, ACA *2007;* Patrick NG & Company, 20th Floor, HONG KONG SAR Trade Centre, 161-167 Des Voeux Road, CENTRAL, HONG KONG ISLAND HONG KONG SAR. See also NCN CPA Limited
NG, Ms. Winifred Shuk On, ACA *2007;* 25B Tower 8, The Palazzo, SHA TIN, NEW TERRITORIES, HONG KONG SAR.
NG, Mrs. Winnie Soue Ding, BA ACA *1988;* 10 Lakepoint Drive #04-60, SINGAPORE 648927, SINGAPORE.
NG, Mr. Yat Tung, FCA *1975;* 35 Fountains Crescent, Southgate, LONDON, N14 6BG.
NG, Ms. Yi Kum, ACA *2005;* Suite 3201, 32/F Bank of America Tower 12 Harcourt Road, CENTRAL, HONG KONG ISLAND, HONG KONG SAR.
NG, Mrs. Yoke Kian, FCA *1975;* 49 Dyson Road, SINGAPORE 1130, SINGAPORE.
NG, Miss. Yoke Ling, FCA *1975;* 9 Jalan Setiamurni 12, Bukit Damansara, 50490 KUALA LUMPUR, FEDERAL TERRITORY, MALAYSIA.
NG, Mr. Yuk Keung, ACA *2006;* 10/F Asia Pacific Building No 333 Zhaojiabang Road, SHANGHAI 200031, CHINA.
NG CHENG HIN, Mr. Yan Chong, MSc ACA *2001;* Leclezio Street, CUREPIPE, MAURITIUS.
NG CHEONG FOOK, Mr. Michel Steeve, ACA *1992;* 84 Sevington Road, Hendon, LONDON, NW4 3RS.
NG CHEONG TIN, Mr. Louis Emmanuel, FCA *1973;* De Chazal du Mée, PO Box 799, 10 Frere Felix de Valois St, PORT LOUIS, MAURITIUS. (Life Member)
NG CHEONG WONG, Miss. Cune Chue, BSc ACA *1991;* 25 Avenue des Flaments, Morcellement Sodnac, QUATRE-BORNES, MAURITIUS.
NG-CHIT-WING, Mr. Thierry Joel Shui Hing, BA ACA *2001;* 12 Andleigh Drive, MULGRAVE, VIC 3170, AUSTRALIA.
•**NG HING CHEUNG, Mr. Harold, MSc FCA** *1996;* Jar & Associates, Hillgate Place, 8 Nahaboo Solim Street, PORT LOUIS, MAURITIUS. See also King Fook Business Link Ltd
NG HOI KUONG, Miss. Natacha Deborah Niuk Fong, BA(Hons) ACA *2001;* Goldman Sachs (Singapore) Pte, 1 Raffles Link #07-01 South Lobby, SINGAPORE 039393, SINGAPORE.
•**NG MAN CHUEN, Mr. Jean-Luc, BSc FCA** *1993;* NMC, Suite 306, St James Court, St Denis Street, PORT LOUIS, MAURITIUS.

NG TAI MUI, Mrs. Vicki, MSc ACA *2003;* 8 Montagu House, 109 Whitfield Street, LONDON, W1T 4HJ.
NG TANG FUI, Mr. Jean Daniel, BA ACA *1998;* 423 Manchester Drive, NUTLEY, NJ 07110, UNITED STATES.
NG TANG FUI, Mr. Jean Noel, ACA *2009;* Flat 313, Central Apartments, 455 High Road, WEMBLEY, MIDDLESEX, HA9 7AF.
NG TANG FUI, Mrs. Rachel Anne, BA(Econ) ACA *2002;* 423 Manchester Drive, NUTLEY, NJ 07110, UNITED STATES.
NG TIM HONG, Miss. Karen, ACA *2009;* 38 Hazelbourne Road, LONDON, SW12 9NS.
NG TSEUNG, Mr. Jean Michel, BSc ACA CF *1993;* The Mauritius Commercial Bank, MCB Centre 10th Floor, Sir William Newton Street, PORT LOUIS, MAURITIUS.
NG TSEUNG, Mr. Patrick, BSc ACA *1997;* Ernst & Young, 9th Floor, Tower 1, NextTeracom, Cybercity, EBENE MAURITIUS.
NG TUNG HING, Mr. Eric Victor Linley Kwet Chen, MA(Cantab) ACA FSI *1997;* Flat 4E Venice Garden, 91-93 Blue PoolRoad, HAPPY VALLEY, HONG KONG ISLAND, HONG KONG SAR.
NG WAH, Mr. Michael Steven Chee Yeng, MSc BSc ACA *2006;* Unit 608, 10 Southgate Road, LONDON, N1 3LY.
NG WING LIT, Miss. Milly Ah Soye, ACA *2010;* 26c Coombe Lane, LONDON, SW20 8ND.
•NG WING LIT, Ms. Virginie Chow Youn, ACA CA(SA) *2004;* 44 Cite Millewee, L-8064 BERTRANGE, LUXEMBOURG.
NG YAN LUK, Mr. Louis Roger Ng Bee Voon, FCA *1976;* Apt 24 Kensington Palms, Sir Guy Forget Avenue, QUATRE-BORNES, MAURITIUS.
•NG YIM ON, Mr. Eric, ACA *1992;* Three Sixty, #02-A8 Cybertower 1, EBENE, MAURITIUS.
NGAI, Ms. Pui Ming Juni, ACA *2010;* (Tax Fac), 16C Block 12 Phase 4, Sea Crest Villa, TSING LUNG TAU, NEW TERRITORIES, HONG KONG SAR.
NGAI, Mr. Sai Hung, ACA *2007;* Flat D 49/F Block 3, Aqua Marine, 8 Sham Shing Road, LAI CHI KOK, KOWLOON, HONG KONG SAR.
NGAN, Mr. Chin Fai, MEng ACA *1992;* 30 The Avenue, Wanstead, LONDON, E11 2EF.
NGAN, Ms. Edith Manling, ACA *1992;* 4B Twin Brook, 43 Repulse Bay Road, REPULSE BAY, HONG KONG ISLAND, HONG KONG SAR.
NGAN, Ms. Wing See, ACA *2008;* Flat A 9/F, Yee Hoi Mansion, Lee King Wan, SAI WAN HO, HONG KONG SAR.
NGAN, Mr. Yu Loong, ACA *2006;* Y L Ngan & Company, Suite 1019, 10/F China Chem Golden Plaza, 77 Mody Road, TSIM SHA TSUI, KOWLOON HONG KONG SAR.
NGO, Mr. Steven Hung Tan, BA ACA *1994;* Flat D 27/F Block 2, Ronsdale Garden, 25 Tai Hang Drive, JARDINE'S LOOKOUT, HONG KONG ISLAND, HONG KONG SAR.
NGU, Dr. Jude Thaddeus Anye, PhD MSc BSc ACA *2000;* 28 Cerone Ct, WEST ORANGE, NJ 07052, UNITED STATES.
NGUI, Miss. Aileen, BSc(Econ) ACA *2001;* 7 Jervois Close, #09-15 One Jervois, SINGAPORE 249103, SINGAPORE.
NGUI, Miss. Lee Ken Connie, BSc ACA *1983;* Jet Air (UK) Ltd, 188 Hammersmith Road, LONDON, W6 7DJ.
NGUNZE, Mr. Mbuvi, ACA *1995;* PO Box 19002-00501, Embakasi, NAIROBI, KENYA.
NGUYEN, Mr. Don, BSc ACA *2004;* Flat 17, 7 New Inn Broadway, LONDON, EC2A 3PR.
NGUYEN, Mr. Duy-Quang, BSc ACA *1997;* 21 Kew Drive, SINGAPORE 466235, SINGAPORE.
NGUYEN, Miss. Giang Huong, BSc ACA *2011;* 6 Boreham Avenue, LONDON, E16 3AG.
NGUYEN, Ms. Khue Thi-Minh, BSc ACA *2006;* 651 Bach Dang Chuong Duong Ward Hoan Kiem District, HANOI, VIETNAM.
NGUYEN, Mr. Vu Anh, BSc ACA *2009;* Orbis Investments Wimbledon Bridge House, 1 Hartfield Road, LONDON, SW19 3RU.
NGWA, Mr. William Forchu, BA FCA *1991;* with PricewaterhouseCoopers, Immeuble Bel Air, Rue Du Marechal Joffre, BP 5689, DOUALA, CAMEROON.
•NI CHINNEIDE, Miss. Rioghnach, BA ACA *2000;* Ground Floor East, 59 Cadogan Square, LONDON, SW1X 0HZ.
NI DHONAILL, Ms. Una Brid, BCom ACA *1993;* 22 Bushnell Road, LONDON, SW17 8QP.
NIAZI, Mr. Mohammad Waseem, BEng ACA *1992;* 40 Clinton Close, Calabash Ridge, SYDNEY, NSW 2082, AUSTRALIA.
NIAZI, Mr. Sultan Alam Khan, FCA *1975;* 19 Kisco Park Drive, Mount Kisco, NEW YORK, NY 10549, UNITED STATES.
NIBLETT, Mr. James Richard, MA ACA DChA *2003;* Hospice of Hope Romania, 28a High Street, Otford, SEVENOAKS, KENT, TN14 5PQ.
•NIBLETT, Mr. James Vincent, BA ACA *1984;* Deloitte LLP, Abbots House, Abbey Street, READING, RG1 3BD. See also Deloitte & Touche LLP
NIBLETT, Mr. Jonathan Peter, BSc ACA *1992;* M&G Ltd, Prudential Plc Governors House, 5 Laurence Pountney Hill, LONDON, EC4R 0HH.
NIBLOCK, Mrs. Sarah, BSc ACA *1989;* 35 Rectory Road, BECKENHAM, BR3 1HL.
•NICANDROU, Miss. Eleni, MSc BA ACA *2005;* 12 Bouboulinas Street, Holargos, 15562 ATHENS, GREECE.
NICANDROU, Mr. Nicolaos Andreas, BA ACA *1991;* The Prudential Assurance Co Ltd Minster House, 12 Arthur Street, LONDON, EC4R 9AQ.
NICE, Mr. Andrew James, BA ACA *1986;* 169 Rustlings Road, SHEFFIELD, S11 7AD.
NICE, Mr. Anthony John, FCA *1975;* University of Washington, Applied Physics Laboratory, 1013 NE 40th Street, SEATTLE, WA 98105-6698, UNITED STATES.
NICE, Mrs. Clare Ann Helen, BSc ACA *1990;* 169 Rustlings Road, SHEFFIELD, S11 7AD.
•NICE, Mr. Daniel Adam, BA ACA *2002;* MWS, Kingsridge House, 601 London Road, WESTCLIFF-ON-SEA, ESSEX, SS0 9PE.
NICE, Mr. Jamie Alex, ACA *2009;* 34 Fairway Gardens, LEIGH-ON-SEA, ESSEX, SS9 4QB.
NICE, Mrs. Marguerite Elizabeth Mary, ACA *1986;* The Green Farmhouse, The Green, Barrow, BURY ST.EDMUNDS, IP29 5AA.
NICE, Mr. Richard Frederick, BSc FCA *1977;* SYLVANER, THE STREET, TESTON, MAIDSTONE, ME18 5AQ.
NICE, Mr. Richard Lingham Kinder, FCA *1972;* Well House, Common Wood, Chipperfield, KINGS LANGLEY, WD4 9BB.
NICE, Mr. Richard Michael, FCA *1983;* 147 St Lawrence Drive, MISSISSAUGA L5G 4V2, ON, CANADA.
NICE, Miss. Sarah Louise, LLB ACA *2004;* ALLIES COMPUTING LTD, Manor Farm Barns, Fox Road, Framingham Pigot, NORWICH, NR14 7PZ.
NICE, Mr. Simon Oliver, BEng ACA *1995;* Lime Cottage, 42 Woodcote Close, EPSOM, KT18 7QJ.
NICHOL, Mr. Alistair John, BA ACA *1986;* 10 Beechfield, Sandal, WAKEFIELD, WF2 6AW.
•NICHOL, Mr. Andrew John, BSc FCA *1992;* A Nichol & Co, 191 New Ridley Road, STOCKSFIELD, NORTHUMBERLAND, NE43 7QD.
•NICHOL, Mr. Anthony John, MA ACA *1986;* 7a Metalistiv Street, 03057 KIEV, UKRAINE.
NICHOL, Mr. Brian Richard, FCA *1960;* 56 Homeworld Drive, NARANGBA, QLD 4504, AUSTRALIA. (Life Member)
NICHOL, Mr. David Brett, FCA *1968;* Rossie House, Forgandenny, PERTH, PH2 9EH.
NICHOL, Mrs. Denise Concepta, BA ACA *1999;* Kilteel, NAAS, COUNTY KILDARE, IRELAND.
•NICHOL, Mr. Derek, BA ACA *1979;* (Tax Fac), Nichol Goodwill Brown Ltd, 112 Whitley Road, WHITLEY BAY, TYNE AND WEAR, NE26 2NE.
•NICHOL, Mr. Dominic Paul, BA FCA *1973;* DPN Consulting Services Ltd, 5 Gravel Hill, UXBRIDGE, UB8 1PB.
NICHOL, Mr. Glen John, BSc FCA *1973;* Allport, Allport House, 1 Cowley Business Park, High Street, Cowley, UXBRIDGE MIDDLESEX UB8 2AD.
NICHOL, Mr. Ian James, MA FCA *1980;* 22 Park Road, RUGBY, WARWICKSHIRE, CV21 2QH.
NICHOL, Ms. Katherine Deirdre, MA ACA *1991;* 42 Sudlow Road, LONDON, SW18 1HP.
NICHOL, Miss. Kimberley Jayne, BSc ACA *2010;* 2 Willsmer Close, Broughton Astley, LEICESTER, LE9 6UL.
NICHOL, Mr. Paul Davidson, BA ACA *1979;* Stonewall House, Stonewall Cottage Lane, Stamford Bridge, YORK, YO41 1DF.
NICHOL, Miss. Sarah Katherine, BA ACA *1997;* 24 Springfield Road, WINDSOR, BERKSHIRE, SL4 3PQ.
NICHOL, Mr. Simon Peter, BA ACA *1989;* 72 Brook Lane, Timperley, ALTRINCHAM, WA15 6RS.
NICHOL, Mr. Timothy James, BA ACA *1987;* Newcastle Business School, University of Northumbria, Ellison Building, Ellison Road, NEWCASTLE UPON TYNE, NE1 8ST.
NICHOLAS, Mr. Alan Paul, BSc ACA *1986;* Belton House 15a Wellands Road, LYNDHURST, HAMPSHIRE, SO43 7AB.
NICHOLAS, Mr. Andrew John, ACA *1992;* 16 Wales Avenue, CARSHALTON, SM5 3QN.
NICHOLAS, Mr. Ashley Peter, BSc ACA *1998;* 147 Devonshire Road #05-03, The Beaumont Amica Block, SINGAPORE 239894, SINGAPORE.
NICHOLAS, Mr. Cecil Alfred, FCA *1940;* 10A The Grove, MERTHYR TYDFIL, CF47 8YR. (Life Member)
NICHOLAS, Mr. David John, BSc AMIMA ACA *2006;* Apex Dental Ltd, Castle Court, 41 London Road, REIGATE, SURREY, RH2 9RJ.
•NICHOLAS, Mr. David Paul, FCA *1970;* 13 Quilp Drive, CHELMSFORD, CM1 4YA.
•NICHOLAS, Mr. Duncan James, BSc ACA *2002;* with Target Accountants Limited, Lawrence House, Lower Bristol Road, BATH, BA2 9ET.
NICHOLAS, Mr. Francis, BSc ACA *1989;* 31 Lorong Chuan, #04-01 The Chuan, SINGAPORE 556820, SINGAPORE.
NICHOLAS, Mr. Graham, BSc FCA *1977;* Highgate House, 9 Upper Belgrave Road, BRISTOL, BS8 2XH.
NICHOLAS, Mr. James Malcolm, FCA *1963;* The Jays, Bassett Hill, Upper Langwith, MANSFIELD, NG20 9RD.
NICHOLAS, Mr. John Daniel, MA FCA *1972;* Hopton Acre, Stoke Lacy, BROMYARD, HR7 4HX.
NICHOLAS, Mr. John Morgan, BSc ACA *2002;* 73 Nornabell Drive, BEVERLEY, NORTH HUMBERSIDE, HU17 9GJ.
NICHOLAS, Mr. John Roger, FCA *1967;* Craig-y-Deri, Bangor Teifi, LLANDYSUL, SA44 5BE.
NICHOLAS, Mr. John Stuart, FCA *1972;* Zurich Financial Services, Mythenquai 2, 8022 ZURICH, SWITZERLAND.
NICHOLAS, Mrs. Margaret Gillian, BSc FCA *1977;* 14 Masefield Grove, The Chelwoods Childwall, LIVERPOOL, L16 3GF.
NICHOLAS, Mr. Milton James, BA ACA *1983;* 39 Chandos Avenue, Whetstone, LONDON, N20 9ED.
NICHOLAS, Mr. Nicholas, BA ACA *1988;* 68 The Woodlands, LONDON, N14 5RX.
NICHOLAS, Mr. Paul, MA ACA *1987;* Barclays Bank International Plc, PO Box 12, POOLE, BH15 2BB.
NICHOLAS, Mr. Richard, BA ACA *2007;* Flat, 148a Clapham High Street, LONDON, SW4 7UH.
NICHOLAS, Mrs. Sally Louise, BA ACA *1990;* Group Line, 22-24 Torrington Place, LONDON, WC1E 7HJ.
NICHOLAS, Mr. Simon John, BSc ACA *2003;* 20/189 Phillip Street, WATERLOO, NSW 2017, AUSTRALIA.
•NICHOLAS, Mr. Simon Paul, BSc ACA *2002;* with KPMG LLC, Heritage Court, 41 Athol Street, Douglas, ISLE OF MAN, IM99 1HN.
NICHOLAS, Mr. Stephen Richard, BEng ACA *1991;* 9 Esther Road, Balmoral, SYDNEY, NSW 2088, AUSTRALIA.
NICHOLAS, Mr. Timothy Louis, FCA *1962;* Summerfield, 51A Brimstage Road, Heswall, WIRRAL, CH60 1XE. (Life Member)
NICHOLAS, Mr. Timothy Stephen, BSc(Hons) ACA *2001;* 8 Charles Street, BALMAIN, NSW 2041, AUSTRALIA.
•NICHOLL, Mr. Alan Charles, FCA *1977;* Appledene, Higham Lane, Hadlow, TONBRIDGE, TN11 9QR.
•NICHOLL, Mr. Andrew Alan, BSc FCA *1977;* Moore Stephens, 150 Aldersgate Street, LONDON, EC1A 4AB.
•NICHOLL, Mr. Bernard John, FCA *1976;* Keens Shay Keens Letchworth, 5 Gernon Walk, LETCHWORTH GARDEN CITY, HERTFORDSHIRE, SG6 3HW.
NICHOLL, Mr. John, BSc ACA *1996;* 21 Miller Close, Redbourn, ST. ALBANS, HERTFORDSHIRE, AL3 7BG.
NICHOLL, Mr. John Mitchell, FCA *1970;* 2 Jackson Meadows, Barkisland, HALIFAX, WEST YORKSHIRE, HX4 0DD.
NICHOLL, Mr. Michael Derek, FCA *1973;* with Spenser Wilson & Co, Equitable House, 55 Pellon Lane, HALIFAX, WEST YORKSHIRE, HX1 5SP.
•NICHOLLS, Mr. Adrian Colin, BA ACA *1995;* Ernst & Young LLP, 1 More London Place, LONDON, SE1 2AF. See also Ernst & Young Europe LLP
NICHOLLS, Mr. Alan David, FCA *1972;* 11 Medow Mead, RADLETT, WD7 8ES. (Life Member)
NICHOLLS, Miss. Amanda Jane, BA ACA *1983;* 19 Rectory Road, Walthamstow, LONDON, E17 3BG.
NICHOLLS, Mrs. Amelia Jane, BSc ACA *2007;* Flat 1, 1a Red Lion Street, RICHMOND, SURREY, TW9 1RJ.
•NICHOLLS, Mr. Andrew Mark, FCA *1988;* Hill Eckersley & Co, 62 Chorley New Road, BOLTON, BL1 4BY. See also Hill Eckersley & Co Limited
NICHOLLS, Mr. Andrew Paul, ACA *2009;* 1/56 Long Drive, St Heliers, AUCKLAND 1071, NEW ZEALAND.
NICHOLLS, Mr. Andrew Peter, BSc ACA *2001;* Taylor Hobson Ltd, PO Box 36, 2 New Star Road, LEICESTER, LE4 9JQ.
NICHOLLS, Mr. Barry, BA ACA *1999;* Nottingham High School, Waverley Mount, NOTTINGHAM, NG7 4ED.
NICHOLLS, Mr. Brian Howard, FCA *1953;* 3 Old Park Road, DUDLEY, DY1 3NA. (Life Member)
NICHOLLS, Mrs. Catherine Jane, LLB ACA *2001;* 485 Hoddle Street, Clifton Hill, MELBOURNE, VIC 3068, AUSTRALIA.
NICHOLLS, Miss. Chanelle, BA(Hons) ACA *2000;* FLAT G 1st FLOOR, 23 Warwick Square, LONDON, SW1V 2AB.
NICHOLLS, Mr. Christopher William, MA FCA *1995;* 32 Bernard Gardens, LONDON, SW19 7BE.
NICHOLLS, Mrs. Claire Helen, BA ACA *1985;* Willows End, Harwoods Lane, Rossett, WREXHAM, LL12 0EU.
NICHOLLS, Mr. Derek Evan, FCA *1972;* 9 The Dingle, WOLVERHAMPTON, WV3 9ET. (Life Member)
NICHOLLS, Mrs. Diana Margaret, MA ACA *1985;* 26 Dornden Drive, Langton Green, TUNBRIDGE WELLS, TN3 0AB.
NICHOLLS, Mr. Dudley Clive, BSocSc ACA *1988;* The Mill House, 4 Puttenham Court, Puttenham, TRING, HERTFORDSHIRE, HP23 4PY.
NICHOLLS, Mr. Duncan, FCA *1975;* Tanglin, Manor Road, Penn, HIGH WYCOMBE, BUCKINGHAMSHIRE, HP10 8HY.
NICHOLLS, Mr. Edward Tobids, BA ACA *2006;* C I T Group, 7 Curzon Street, LONDON, W1J 5HG.
NICHOLLS, Mrs. Emma Jane, BSc ACA *1993;* 11 Dalkeith Road, HARPENDEN, HERTFORDSHIRE, AL5 5PP.
NICHOLLS, Mr. George Edward, FCA *1949;* 7 Castle Close, Henbury, BRISTOL, BS10 7QU. (Life Member)
NICHOLLS, Mr. Greville Vincent, FCA *1969;* Albemarle & Bond County House, 17 Friar Street, READING, RG1 1DB.
NICHOLLS, Miss. Helena Jayne Elizabeth, BA ACA *2005;* Apartment 40 Velocity East, 4 City Walk, LEEDS, LS11 9BF.
NICHOLLS, Ms. Janine, BSc ACA *1994;* Hermes Pensions Management Ltd Lloyds Chambers, 1 Portsoken Street, LONDON, E1 8HZ.
NICHOLLS, Mrs. Jennifer Mary, BSc FCA *1982;* Brockenhurst, Heath Ride, Finchampstead, WOKINGHAM, RG40 3QN.
NICHOLLS, Mr. Jeremy, BA(Hons) ACA *2003;* Ladbrokes Ltd Imperial House, Imperial Drive, HARROW, MIDDLESEX, HA2 7JW.
NICHOLLS, Mr. Jeremy Andrew, BSc ACA *1988;* 38 Ullet Road, LIVERPOOL, L17 3BP.
NICHOLLS, Mrs. Joanna Amanda, LLB ACA *2002;* 20 The Crescent, LEATHERHEAD, SURREY, KT22 8EE.
NICHOLLS, Mr. John Thomas, FCA ACIS *1960;* 11 Hamilton Close, LONDON, NW8 8QY.
NICHOLLS, Mr. Jonathan Clive, BA ACA *1983;* Longmeadow, Prinsted Lane, Prinsted, EMSWORTH, HAMPSHIRE, PO10 8HR.
•NICHOLLS, Mrs. Julie Carol, BA ACA *1983;* 9 Addison Grove, Chiswick, LONDON, W4 1EP.
NICHOLLS, Mrs. Julie Olwyn, BSc ACA *1989;* The Mill House, 4 Puttenham Court, Puttenham, TRING, HERTFORDSHIRE, HP23 4PY.
•NICHOLLS, Mr. Kevin Wallace, FCA *1982;* Thandi Nicholls Ltd, Wolverhampton Science Park, Creative Industries Centre, Glaisher Drive, WOLVERHAMPTON, WV10 9TG.
NICHOLLS, Mr. Mark Charles, BSc ACA *1989;* Burefield House, 24 Church Lane, Wroxham, NORWICH, NR12 8SH.
NICHOLLS, Mr. Mark Christopher, ACA *1989;* Woodfolds House, Oaksey, MALMESBURY, SN16 9SD.
NICHOLLS, Mr. Michael David, BSc FCA *1992;* MN Associates Ltd, 11 Governor Street, GIBRALTAR, GIBRALTAR.
•NICHOLLS, Mr. Michael Jon, ACA FCCA *2008;* Stacey & Partners, 9 North Street Parade, SUDBURY, SUFFOLK, CO10 1GL. See also Stacey & Partners Limited
NICHOLLS, Mr. Michael Philip, BSc ACA *1986;* Linpac Plastics Ltd A1 Business Park, Knottingley Road, KNOTTINGLEY, WF11 0BL.
NICHOLLS, Mr. Michael Robert Gray, BA FCA *1962;* 159 Harestone Valley Road, CATERHAM, CR3 6HT.
NICHOLLS, Miss. Michelle, BSc(Hons) ACA *2010;* 87 Normandy Drive, TAUNTON, SOMERSET, TA1 2LE.
NICHOLLS, Miss. Pascale, BA ACA *2000;* 128 Farm Lane, LONDON, SW6 1QH.
NICHOLLS, Mr. Paul, BSc ACA *2000;* Apartment 5 Clement House, The Blundells, KENILWORTH, WARWICKSHIRE, CV8 2PE.
NICHOLLS, Mr. Peter, BA(Hons) ACA *2010;* Middlemost, Ridgeway Meads, Chinnor Road, Bledlow, PRINCES RISBOROUGH, BUCKINGHAMSHIRE HP27 9QF.
NICHOLLS, Mr. Peter Alan, BA FCA *1992;* 5 Handpost Lodge Gardens, Leverstock Green, HEMEL HEMPSTEAD, HP2 4FB.

NICHOLLS, Mr. Peter John, FCA *1984;* Rose Villa Barn, Little Polgooth, ST. AUSTELL, CORNWALL, PL26 7DD.

•NICHOLLS, Mr. Peter Robert, FCA *1987;* Bessler Hendrie, Albury Mill, Mill Lane, Chilworth, GUILDFORD, SURREY GU4 8RU.

NICHOLLS, Mr. Raymond, ACA *2008;* 5/372 Soi 18, Samakkee Road, Bangtalad, Pakkret, NONTHABURI 11120, THAILAND.

NICHOLLS, Mr. Richard Andrew, LLB ACA *2005;* Flat 1, 1a Red Lion Street, RICHMOND, SURREY, TW9 1RJ.

NICHOLLS, Mr. Robert Andrew, BA ACA *2003;* 71 Nelson Road, LONDON, SW19 1HU.

NICHOLLS, Mr. Robert Stephen, FCA *1974;* 18 Hyacinth Avenue, HOLLYWELL, QLD 4216, AUSTRALIA.

NICHOLLS, Ms. Sarah Elizabeth, BSc(Hons) ACA ACCA *2007;* 72 Cedar Terrace, RICHMOND, SURREY, TW9 2BZ.

NICHOLLS, Miss. Sarah Jayne, BSc(Hons) ACA *2004;* 34 Milton Road, LONDON, SW14 8JR.

NICHOLLS, Mr. Simon Anthony, BSc ACA *1997;* Ingenious Media Plc, 15 Golden Square, LONDON, W1F 9JG.

NICHOLLS, Mr. Simon James, BSc ACA *1989;* Windybrae The Highlands, East Horsley, LEATHERHEAD, SURREY, KT24 5BQ.

NICHOLLS, Mr. Stuart Roy, FCA *1979;* Freshwater Group of Companies Freshwater House, 158-162 Shaftesbury Avenue, LONDON, WC2H 8HR.

NICHOLLS, Miss. Tessa, ACA *2008;* Sanctuary Housing Association, Chamber Court, Castle Street, WORCESTER, WR1 3ZQ.

NICHOLLS, Miss. Tracey Anne, BSc ACA *2010;* 33 Wimslow Close, WALLSEND, TYNE AND WEAR, NE28 8TB.

NICHOLLS, Mr. Tudor Puleston, PhD MSc FCA *1980;* with PricewaterhouseCoopers LLP, Pricewaterhousecoopers, 12 Plumtree Court, LONDON, EC4A 4HT.

NICHOLLS, Mr. Vincent William, FCA *1983;* Winkhurst Farm House, Coopers Corner, Ide Hill, SEVENOAKS, KENT, TN14 6LB.

•NICHOLLS, Mrs. Wendy Elisabeth, BSc FCA CTA *1985;* (Tax Fac), Grant Thornton UK LLP, Grant Thornton House, 22 Melton Street, Euston Square, LONDON, NW1 2EP. See also Grant Thornton LLP

NICHOLLS-PRATT, Mr. Ronald Edward, FCA *1959;* Stuart Lodge, Sausmarez Road, St. Martin, GUERNSEY, GY4 6SE. (Life Member)

NICHOLS, Mr. Alan John, ACA *1979;* Credit Suisse Trust Ltd, PO Box 122, GUERNSEY, GY1 4EE.

NICHOLS, Mr. Alex Paul, BA(Hons) ACA *2002;* 12 Stretton Close, Ashwell Gardens, Tylers Green, HIGH WYCOMBE, BUCKINGHAMSHIRE, HP10 8EW.

NICHOLS, Mr. Alistair Richard, BA ACA *1987;* 46 Oakbury Road, LONDON, SW6 2NW.

•NICHOLS, Mr. Andrew James, LLB ACA MIPA MICM FABRP *1989;* Redman Nichols Butler, Maclaren House, Skerne Road, DRIFFIELD, YO25 6PN.

NICHOLS, The Revd. Barry Edward, FCA *1963;* 19 Arterberry Road, Wimbledon, LONDON, SW20 8AF.

NICHOLS, Mr. Brian Frederick, FCA *1964;* 22 Deanfield Road, HENLEY-ON-THAMES, RG9 1UG.

NICHOLS, Miss. Caroline, ACA *1996;* Holly Tree House, 10 Back Lane, Asselby, GOOLE, NORTH HUMBERSIDE, DN14 7HD.

NICHOLS, Mrs. Catherine Anne, BA ACA *1995;* 36 Waverley Lane, FARNHAM, GU9 8BJ.

NICHOLS, Mrs. Catherine Juliet, BA ACA *1990;* Eskadale Bridge of Canny, BANCHORY, KINCARDINESHIRE, AB31 4AT.

NICHOLS, Mr. Corin, BSc ACA *2005;* PartyGaming Plc, 2nd Floor Regal House, 711 Europort, GIBRALTAR, GIBRALTAR.

NICHOLS, Mr. Darren Joseph, BA ACA *1999;* First Databank Europe Ltd Swallowtail House, Grenadier Road Exeter Business Park, EXETER, EX1 3LH.

NICHOLS, Mr. David William, MSc BSc ACA *1982;* 8 Tangmere Close, Friars Cliff, CHRISTCHURCH, BH23 4LZ.

•NICHOLS, Mrs. Diane Jane, BSc FCA *1990;* Diane J Nichols BSc FCA, Little Moss Farm, Red Cat Lane, Crank, ST. HELENS, MERSEYSIDE WA11 8QZ.

NICHOLS, Miss. Elizabeth Margaret, BA ACA *1998;* 2 Delapre Drive, BANBURY, OXFORDSHIRE, OX16 3WP.

NICHOLS, Mrs. Frances Ann, BA ACA *1987;* Heath Gables, Bell Lane, Nuthampstead, ROYSTON, HERTFORDSHIRE, SG8 8ND.

NICHOLS, Mr. Gareth Michael, BEng ACA *1995;* Research in Motion Ltd, 451 Phillip Street, WATERLOO N2L 3X2, ON, CANADA.

NICHOLS, Mr. Garry, BA ACA *1980;* Holly Cottage, Salt Lane, Hydestile, GODALMING, GU8 4DH.

NICHOLS, Mr. Gerard Martin, BA ACA *1991;* 25710 Barnett Lane, STEVENSON RANCH, CA 91381, UNITED STATES.

NICHOLS, Miss. Hannah Mary, ACA *2009;* 1/1 15 Dorset Street, GLASGOW, G3 7AG.

•NICHOLS, Mr. Howard George, BSc FCA *1984;* Wright & Co, 57 High Street, South Norwood, LONDON, SE25 6EF.

NICHOLS, Mr. James Andrew, FCA *1965;* Brittenden, Waldron, HEATHFIELD, TN21 0RG. (Life Member)

NICHOLS, Mr. James Jonathan, BA(Hons) ACA *2002;* 16 Church Hill, Bramhope, LEEDS, LS16 9BA.

NICHOLS, Miss. Jennifer Louise, BA ACA *2006;* 70 Acorn Gardens, Burghfield Common, READING, RG7 3GN.

NICHOLS, Mr. John Wilfrid Lee, BA FCA *1953;* Mill House, Holton, HALESWORTH, IP19 8PW. (Life Member)

NICHOLS, Mrs. Julia, BSc ACA *2001;* 2 Oakdale Drive, Pool in Wharfedale, OTLEY, LS21 1LJ.

NICHOLS, Ms. Katherine, ACA *2010;* 2588 American River Drive, SACRAMENTO, CA 95864, UNITED STATES.

NICHOLS, Mr. Kenneth James, FCA *1976;* Tileflair Ltd, Highwood Lane, Patchway, BRISTOL, BS34 5TQ.

NICHOLS, Miss. Laura Anne, BA ACA *1999;* 5 Robin Close, BILLERICAY, ESSEX, CM12 0SJ.

NICHOLS, Mrs. Lorraine Seychelle, BSc ACA *1997;* Apple Tree House, Orchard Rise, HENLEY-IN-ARDEN, B95 5FL.

NICHOLS, Mrs. Lucy May, BA ACA *1992;* Nichols & Co (Accountancy) Ltd, Unit 7, Mulberry Place, Pinnell Road, LONDON, SE9 6AR. See also Nichols Financial LLP

•NICHOLS, Mr. Matthew Stewart, BA ACA *2001;* PricewaterhouseCoopers LLP, Hays Galleria, 1 Hays Lane, LONDON, SE1 2RD. See also PricewaterhouseCoopers

NICHOLS, Mr. Michael, BSc ACA *2011;* 4 Ledbury Road, REIGATE, SURREY, RH2 9HN.

•NICHOLS, Mr. Michael David, FCA *1964;* Michael D. Nichols, 28 Boughton Lane, Loose, MAIDSTONE, ME15 9QN.

•NICHOLS, Mr. Paul, BA(Hons) ACA *2000;* with KPMG LLP, 15 Canada Square, LONDON, E14 5GL.

NICHOLS, Mr. Paul Raymond Lowrie, BA ACA *1985;* Paices House Church Road, Mortimer West End, READING, RG7 2HY.

NICHOLS, Mr. Paul William, BA ACA *1999;* 41 Speldhurst Road, LONDON, W4 1BX.

NICHOLS, Mrs. Philippa Janice, BA ACA *1992;* 2 St. Edmunds, 86 Christchurch Road, WINCHESTER, HAMPSHIRE, SO23 9TE.

NICHOLS, Mrs. Rachael Elizabeth, BA ACA *1990;* 77 Beechcroft Avenue, NEW MALDEN, SURREY, KT3 3EE.

NICHOLS, Mr. Richard Simon, BA ACA *1995;* 46 Sunnyvale Drive, Longwell Green, BRISTOL, BS30 9YQ.

NICHOLS, Mr. Richard Stephen, MA ACA *1991;* College Hill, The Registry, Royal Mint Court, LONDON, EC3N 4QN.

NICHOLS, Mr. Simon Andrew, BA ACA *1998;* 2 Oakdale Drive, Pool in Wharfedale, OTLEY, WEST YORKSHIRE, LS21 1LJ.

NICHOLS, Mr. Simon Jeremy, BSc ACA *1996;* 8a Quick Street, LONDON, N1 8HL.

NICHOLS, Mr. Simon Paul, BSc ACA *1981;* 12 Higher Downs, ALTRINCHAM, WA14 2QL.

•NICHOLS, Mr. Steven, BA FCA CTA *1989;* Nichols & Co (Accountancy) Ltd, Unit 7, Mulberry Place, Pinnell Road, LONDON, SE9 6AR. See also Nichols Financial LLP

NICHOLS, Mr. Steven Edward, BSc ACA *1996;* The Byre, Bury Farm Bury Lane, EPPING, ESSEX, CM16 5JA.

NICHOLS, Mrs. Tabitha Jane, BSc ACA *1992;* 4a Stoney Lane, WINCHESTER, HAMPSHIRE, SO22 6DN.

NICHOLS, Mr. Thomas James, MA ACA *2003;* Ground Floor Flat, 2 Carmalt Gardens, LONDON, SW15 6NE.

NICHOLS, Mr. Timothy Charles, FCA *1974;* 32 Wenban Road, WORTHING, WEST SUSSEX, BN11 1HY.

NICHOLS, Mr. Wesley, ACA CA(AUS) *2011;* Build A Bear Workshop, St Stephens House, Arthur Road, WINDSOR, BERKSHIRE, SL4 1RU.

NICHOLS, Mr. William Pengelley, FCA *1961;* Newcourt Farmhouse, Silverton, EXETER, DEVON, EX5 4HT.

NICHOLS, Miss. Zara Marguertte, ACA *2011;* 26 The Wyvern, Grafham, HUNTINGDON, CAMBRIDGESHIRE, PE28 0GG.

NICHOLSON, Mrs. Aislean Olivene, LLB ACA *2006;* 39 Foxley Road, LONDON, SW9 6EX.

NICHOLSON, Mr. Alexander James, BA ACA *1996;* Flat 3 Beaulieu Court, 1 Park Road, HARROGATE, HG2 9AZ.

NICHOLSON, Mr. Andrew Eric, FCA *1974;* with Watersheds Ltd, 2nd Floor, The Old Granary, Cotton End, NORTHAMPTON, NN4 8HP.

•NICHOLSON, Mr. Andrew Maxwell, BSc ACA *1999;* KPMG LLP, 15 Canada Square, LONDON, E14 5GL. See also KPMG Europe LLP

•NICHOLSON, Mr. Andrew Richard, FCA *1992;* Shieling, The Orchard, Staverton, DAVENTRY, NORTHAMPTONSHIRE, NN11 6JA.

NICHOLSON, Mr. Anthony Charles, BSc ACA *1996;* 24 Chiltern Road, Wendover, AYLESBURY, BUCKINGHAMSHIRE, HP22 6DB.

NICHOLSON, Mr. Anthony Valentine, FCA *1960;* Longnor Hall Farm, Longnor, SHREWSBURY, SHROPSHIRE, SY5 7PZ.

NICHOLSON, Mr. Barry Keith, BA FCA *1977;* 1 Farne Way, Wootton Bassett, SWINDON, SN4 8LX. (Life Member)

NICHOLSON, Mr. Brett, MEng ACA *1999;* 2/5 McCarthy Grove, MONTMORENCY, VIC 3094, AUSTRALIA.

•NICHOLSON, Mr. Brian David, FCA *1971;* Lancaster & Co, Granville House, 2 Tettenhall Rd, WOLVERHAMPTON, WV1 4SB. See also Lancaster Haskins LLP

NICHOLSON, Sir Bryan, GBE FCA(Honorary) Financial Reporting Council, 5th Floor Aldwych House, 71-91 Aldwych, LONDON, WC2B 4HN.

NICHOLSON, Mrs. Carole Julia, BSc FCA *1982;* The Old Mill House, Plumpton Lane, Plumpton, LEWES, BN7 3AH.

NICHOLSON, Mr. Christopher George, ACA *1982;* 814 Chalfonte Dr, ALEXANDRIA, VA 22305, UNITED STATES.

NICHOLSON, Mr. Christopher William, ACA *1979;* Fir Trees, Bilsborrow Lane, Bilsborrow, PRESTON, PR3 0RP.

NICHOLSON, Miss. Claire Louise, BA ACA *1998;* 86 New Road, MARLOW, BUCKINGHAMSHIRE, SL7 3NW.

•NICHOLSON, Mr. Clive Anthony Holme, FCA *1969;* Saffery Champness, Lion House, Red Lion Street, LONDON, WC1R 4GB.

NICHOLSON, Mrs. Daryl Jane, BSc ACA *1993;* with Haines Watts Gatwick LLP, 3rd Floor, Consort House, Consort Way, HORLEY, SURREY RH6 7AF.

NICHOLSON, Mr. David Fletcher, BA ACA *1993;* 5 Avenue De Miremont, 1206, GENEVA, SWITZERLAND.

•NICHOLSON, Mr. David William, BA FCA *1991;* Russell Payne & Co Ltd, Landmark House, 1 Riseholme Road, LINCOLN, LN1 3SN.

NICHOLSON, Mr. David William, BSc ACA *1985;* 64 Trowbridge Road, BRADFORD-ON-AVON, BA15 1EN.

NICHOLSON, Mr. Edward Anthony Spours, FCA *1974;* Durwood Cottage The Holt, Upham, SOUTHAMPTON, SO32 1HR.

NICHOLSON, Mrs. Elizabeth Ann Louise, LLB ACA *2005;* M C G Graphics Ltd Citadel Trading Park, Citadel Way, HULL, HU9 1TQ.

NICHOLSON, Ms. Emma Louise, BA ACA *2006;* Flat 3, 2 Clement Avenue, LONDON, SW4 7TY.

NICHOLSON, Mr. Glenn, ACA *2009;* 4 Uplands, Ripponden, SOWERBY BRIDGE, HX6 4JG.

NICHOLSON, Mr. Graham Peter, FCA *1977;* 19 St. Aidans Court, Shrewsbury Road, PRENTON, CH43 8TP.

NICHOLSON, Mr. Grahame Royds Gordon, ACA *1979;* Buttermead House, Haugh, Winsley, BRADFORD-ON-AVON, BA15 2JD.

NICHOLSON, Miss. Hannah Louise, BA(Hons) ACA *2003;* McCann-Erickson Manchester Ltd Bonis Hall, Bonis Hall Lane, MACCLESFIELD, CHESHIRE, SK10 4EF.

NICHOLSON, Ms. Helen Clair, LLB ACA AMCT *2000;* 2 Mersey Meadows, Didsbury, MANCHESTER, M20 2GB.

NICHOLSON, Mrs. Helen Jane, BSc(Hons) ACA *2002;* (Tax Fac), with Blinkhorns, 27 Mortimer Street, LONDON, W1T 3BL.

NICHOLSON, Mr. Henry, PhD BSc FCA *1974;* 15 Henson Grove, Timperley, ALTRINCHAM, WA15 7QA. (Life Member)

•NICHOLSON, Mr. Henry Michael Hugh, BSc ACA *1994;* Deloitte LLP, Athene Place, 66 Shoe Lane, LONDON, EC4A 3BQ. See also Deloitte & Touche LLP

NICHOLSON, Mr. Howard Philip, BA ACA *1992;* 40 Norwood Avenue, SOUTHPORT, MERSEYSIDE, PR9 7EG.

NICHOLSON, Mr. Hugh Palmer, FCA *1965;* Welltrees, Church Hill, Hempstead, SAFFRON WALDEN, CB10 2PA.

NICHOLSON, Mr. Ian John, BA ACA *1992;* 6 Oakdene Close, Bookham, LEATHERHEAD, KT23 4PT.

NICHOLSON, Mr. James Adam, ACA *1993;* 4 High Street, Stanwick, WELLINGBOROUGH, NN9 6QA.

NICHOLSON, Mrs. Jane, ACA *2009;* 12 Academy Court, 34 Glengall Road, Kilburn, LONDON, NW6 7FB.

NICHOLSON, Miss. Jennie, LLB ACA *2010;* Flat 29, Edge Hill Court, Edge Hill, LONDON, SW19 4LL.

NICHOLSON, Mr. Jeremy Dawson, FCA *1968;* Cedar House, Bacombe Lane, Wendover, AYLESBURY, BUCKINGHAMSHIRE, HP22 6EQ. (Life Member)

NICHOLSON, Mrs. Joanna Marie, BA(Hons) ACA *2001;* 2 Lindrick Close, DAVENTRY, NORTHAMPTONSHIRE, NN11 4SN.

NICHOLSON, Mr. John, FCA *1970;* 18 Poplar Close, WIMBORNE, BH21 1TL.

NICHOLSON, Mr. John, BSc FCA *1978;* 24 Acomb Court, Hirst Head Grange, BEDLINGTON, NE22 5QP.

NICHOLSON, Mr. John Edward, BSc ACA CF *1991;* Deloitte, Makenzijeva 24, 11 000 BELGRADE, SERBIA.

•NICHOLSON, Mr. John Roger, FCA *1967;* Nicholson & Co., Monument House, 215 Marsh Road, PINNER, HA5 5NE.

NICHOLSON, Mr. John William, FCA *1950;* 15 Ferndene Court, Moor Road South, NEWCASTLE UPON TYNE, NE3 1NN. (Life Member)

•NICHOLSON, Mr. Jonathan Sydney, FCA *1981;* Financial Consulting & Accounting Ltd, Grosvenors Square, Unit 3-213, 23 Lime Tree Bay Avenue, PO Box 1976, GEORGE TOWN GRAND CAYMAN CAYMAN ISLANDS.

NICHOLSON, Mrs. Julie, BA ACA *1989;* 71 Palace Road, LONDON, SW2 3LB.

NICHOLSON, Mr. Kane, MA ACA CTA *2003;* 24/8 Jacques Avenue, BONDI BEACH, NSW 2026, AUSTRALIA.

NICHOLSON, Mrs. Kathryn Jane, BA ACA *1999;* 9 Highcroft, Horsley, NEWCASTLE UPON TYNE, NE15 0PD.

NICHOLSON, Mr. Keith, MA FCA *1974;* 71 Palace Road, LONDON, SW2 3LB.

•NICHOLSON, Mr. Kevin James, BSc FCA *1988;* (Tax Fac), The Accounts People, 25 Priory Mead, Doddinghurst, BRENTWOOD, ESSEX, CM15 0NB.

NICHOLSON, Mr. Lee, BSc ACA *2006;* 4 Cliff Road, Dovercourt, HARWICH, CO12 3PP.

NICHOLSON, Mrs. Lee-Lian, FCA *1977;* Pinetrees 26 Woodside Road, COBHAM, SURREY, KT11 2QR.

NICHOLSON, Mr. Mark, BA ACA *1984;* Yorkshire Property & Investment Company Ltd, Tudor House, Harrogate Road, Huby, LEEDS, LS17 0EF.

NICHOLSON, Mr. Mark, BA ACA *1998;* 23 Derwentdale Gardens, High Heaton, NEWCASTLE UPON TYNE, NE7 7QN.

•NICHOLSON, Mr. Mark Alan, FCA *1986;* (Tax Fac), AYP Advisory Limited, Windrush House, 15 Marshall Avenue, WORTHING, BN14 0ES.

NICHOLSON, Mr. Mark Andrew, BA ACA *1986;* 10 Rockingham Hills, Oundle, PETERBOROUGH, PE8 4QA.

NICHOLSON, Mr. Mark David Yeaman, MA ACA *2002;* 11 Fir Tree Close, LONDON, W5 2JY.

NICHOLSON, Miss. Mary Evelyn Meta, MA FCA *1998;* Macquarie Group Limited, Level 11, No. 1 Martin Place, SYDNEY, NSW 2000, AUSTRALIA.

NICHOLSON, Mr. Matthew Paul Lewis, ACA *2008;* with Deloitte LLP, 1 City Square, LEEDS, WEST YORKSHIRE, LS1 2AL.

NICHOLSON, Mr. Michael Edward, MA ACA *1978;* Upper Vobster Farm, Upper Vobster, RADSTOCK, BA3 5SA.

NICHOLSON, Mr. Michael James, BSc ACA *1994;* M&G, Governors House, 5 Laurence Pountney Hill, LONDON, EC4R 0HH.

NICHOLSON, Mr. Michael William, FCA *1966;* The Magazine Farm, Sedgeford, HUNSTANTON, PE36 5LW.

NICHOLSON, Mr. Miles Tristram, ACA *1984;* 1 Rothschild Road, LONDON, W4 5HS.

NICHOLSON, Mr. Neil, BSc FCA *1984;* 8 Sandmartin Lane, Norton, STOCKTON-ON-TEES, TS20 1LP.

NICHOLSON, Mrs. Nicola, BSc ACA *2006;* Braye Farm Cottage, Carriere Lane, Vale, GUERNSEY, GY3 5QJ.

NICHOLSON, Mrs. Nicola Jane, BSc ACA *2004;* 47 Stratford Drive, Wooburn Green, HIGH WYCOMBE, BUCKINGHAMSHIRE, HP10 0QQ.

•NICHOLSON, Mr. Nigel Anthony, BSc FCA *1977;* Nicholson & Co, Suite 21, 3 Ludgate Square, LONDON, EC4M 7AS.

NICHOLSON, Mr. Norman Fletcher, FCA *1960;* Oaktree Cottage, Cholesbury Lane, Cholesbury, TRING, HERTFORDSHIRE, HP23 6NG. (Life Member)

NICHOLSON, Miss. Patricia Anne Mary, BA FCA DChA *1977;* First Mangament Services Ltd, 20 Thayer Street, LONDON, W1U 2DD.

NICHOLSON, Mr. Paul, BA ACA *1999;* Quorum 5, Balliol Business Park East, Benton Lane, Balliol Business Park, NEWCASTLE UPON TYNE, NE12 8EZ.
•**NICHOLSON, Mr. Paul, BSc FCA** *1986;* 5 Windlehurst Hall, High Lane, STOCKPORT, CHESHIRE, SK6 8HG.
NICHOLSON, Sir Paul Douglas, Kt MA FCA *1965;* Quarry Hill, Brancepeth, DURHAM, DH7 8DW.
NICHOLSON, Mr. Paul William, BA FCA *1981;* Old Mill House Plumpton Lane, Plumpton, LEWES, EAST SUSSEX, BN7 3AH.
NICHOLSON, Mr. Peter, FCA *1964;* 2 Summerhayes Close, WOKING, GU21 4JD.
•**NICHOLSON, Mr. Phillip Michael, ACA ACCA** *2008;* Stopford Associates Limited, Synergy House, 7 Acorn Business Park, Commercial Gate, MANSFIELD, NOTTINGHAMSHIRE NG18 1EX.
NICHOLSON, Mr. Raymond Edgar, FCA *1960;* 23 Brickhill Drive, BEDFORD, MK41 7QA. (Life Member)
NICHOLSON, Mr. Robert Brian, BSc ACA *1980;* 16B Arts Mansion, 43 Wong Nai Chung Road, HAPPY VALLEY, HONG KONG SAR.
NICHOLSON, Mr. Rodney Malcolm, FCA *1957;* Postnet Suite 35, Private Bag X17, WELTEVREDEN PARK, 1715, SOUTH AFRICA. (Life Member)
NICHOLSON, Mr. Roy Knollys Ellard, FCA *1971;* Field Barn, Binham Road, Field Dalling, HOLT, NORFOLK, NR25 7LJ.
•**NICHOLSON, Miss. Sally, BSc ACA** *2002;* with PricewaterhouseCoopers LLP, 1 Embankment Place, LONDON, WC2N 6RH.
NICHOLSON, Miss. Samantha, BSc(Hons) ACA *2011;* Warren Court Farm House, West Tytherley, SALISBURY, SP5 1LU.
NICHOLSON, Miss. Sara Elizabeth, BA ACA *1995;* 4 Primrose Crescent, HYDE, SK14 5BX.
NICHOLSON, Miss. Sarah, BA(Hons) ACA *2011;* 8 The Moorings, NORTH FERRIBY, NORTH HUMBERSIDE, HU14 3ED.
NICHOLSON, Mr. Simon James, MSc ACA *2002;* 117 Northfield Road, SHEFFIELD, S10 1QP.
NICHOLSON, Mr. Simon Jon, BA ACA *1996;* 10 Lucas, Horsted Keynes, HAYWARDS HEATH, WEST SUSSEX, RH17 7BN.
•**NICHOLSON, Mr. Stephen, FCA** *1974;* Mills & Black, Derwent House, 141-143 Dale Road, MATLOCK, DE4 3LU.
NICHOLSON, Mr. Stephen John, FCA *1972;* 48 Wolseley Gardens, Chiswick, LONDON, W4 3LS. (Life Member)
NICHOLSON, Mr. Stephen John, BA ACA *1988;* Consumer Credit Counselling Services, Wade House, 52 Merrion Centre, LEEDS, LS2 8NG.
NICHOLSON, Mr. Stuart, BCom FCA *1993;* 4th Floor Citymark, Bank of Scotland, 150 Fountainbridge, EDINBURGH, EH3 9PE.
NICHOLSON, Mrs. Susan Julie, BA ACA *1989;* 5 Marlborough Villas, Menston, ILKLEY, LS29 6DB.
NICHOLSON, Mrs. Wendy, BA ACA *1996;* 9 Wharfedale Gardens, Baildon, SHIPLEY, WEST YORKSHIRE, BD17 6TN.
NICHOLSON, Mr. William Alexander, BSc ACA *2006;* with Ernst & Young LLP, 1 More London Place, LONDON, SE1 2AF.
NICHOLSON-SMITH, Mr. James Timothy, BSc ACA *1993;* 15 Murray Close, Bishops Cleeve, CHELTENHAM, GLOUCESTERSHIRE, GL52 8XE.
•**NICKALLS, Mr. Derek Gibson Sproat, FCA** *1973;* Nickalls & Co Ltd, 4 Bridge Street, Amble, MORPETH, NORTHUMBERLAND, NE65 0DR.
NICKALLS, Mr. Graham Robert, FCA *1973;* Performance Abrasives Group, 1060 Stacey Court Unit A, MISSISSAUGA L4W 2X8, ON, CANADA.
NICKALLS, Mr. Mark Robert, BSc ACA *1985;* Apartment 42 Britannic Park, 15 Yew Tree Road Moseley, BIRMINGHAM, B13 8NQ.
NICKELL, Mr. Paul Hilary, FCA *1959;* Little Ashford Barn, Steep, PETERSFIELD, HAMPSHIRE, GU32 1AA. (Life Member)
NICKELS, Mr. Terry Edouard, FCA *1970;* 1 Totnes Road, NEWTON ABBOT, DEVON, TQ12 1LY.
NICKLESS, Mr. James Hamilton, BSc ACA *2005;* 15 Lodge Lane, CHALFONT ST. GILES, BUCKINGHAMSHIRE, HP8 4AF.
NICKLIN, Mr. David Royston, FCA *1973;* Hapag-Lloyd House, 48a Cambridge Road, BARKING, IG11 8HH.
NICKLIN, Mr. George Peter, BA ACA *1988;* Baxter Healthcare SA, Postfach, 8010 ZURICH, SWITZERLAND.
NICKLIN, Mr. Jon Michael, BSc ACA *2010;* 94 Cranborne Avenue, SURBITON, KT6 7JT.
NICKLIN, Mr. Philip George, BA FCA *1966;* AHRM Limited, 24 Arlington House, Arlington Street, LONDON, SW1A 1RL.
•**NICKLIN, Mr. Philip Gerard, BSc FCA** *1983;* Deloitte LLP, Athene Place, 66 Shoe Lane, LONDON, EC4A 3BQ. See also Deloitte & Touche LLP
NICKLIN, Mr. Richard Anthony William, BA ACA *1979;* 3 Howbeck Drive, Oxton, PRENTON, CH43 6UY.
NICKLIN, Mrs. Sarah Mary Gwenllian, BSc ACA *1978;* 3 Howbeck Drive, Oxton, PRENTON, CH43 6UY.
NICKLIN, Miss. Stephanie Louise, ACA *2004;* 20 Great Elms Road, HEMEL HEMPSTEAD, HERTFORDSHIRE, HP3 9TJ.
NICKS, Mrs. Diane Margaret, FCA *1987;* (Tax Fac), 7 Sussex Place, SLOUGH, SL1 1NH.
•**NICKS, Mr. Geoffrey, BA FCA** *1978;* Tree Aid Brunswick Court, Brunswick Square, BRISTOL, BS2 8PE.
•**NICKSON, Mr. David Anthony, BSc ACA ATII** *1997;* (Tax Fac), KPMG LLP, 15 Canada Square, LONDON, E14 5GL. See also KPMG Europe LLP
NICKSON, Mr. John William, BCom FCA ACII *1988;* 76 Brookbank Close, CHELTENHAM, GLOUCESTERSHIRE, GL50 3NB.
NICKSON, Mrs. Linda Ann, BSc FCA *1988;* Crickley Cottage, 6 Gwinnett Court, Shurdington, CHELTENHAM, GL51 4GQ.
•**NICKSON, Mr. Philip, BA FCA** *1985;* with Philip Nickson & Co Ltd, 10 Lancaster Road, Kempsford, FAIRFORD, GLOUCESTERSHIRE, GL7 4DW.
NICKSON, Miss. Susannah Louise, ACA *2010;* 29a Heath Road, BEACONSFIELD, BUCKINGHAMSHIRE, HP9 1DD.
NICODEMOU, Miss. Andry, ACA *2009;* 3 Evagora, Karageorgiade Street, Tsirio, 3081 LIMASSOL, CYPRUS.
NICOL, Mr. Alex James, BA ACA *1992;* 3 Timber Lane, Woburn, MILTON KEYNES, MK17 9PL.
NICOL, Mr. Alexander William, MA ACA *2003;* 35 Showell Grove, DROITWICH, WORCESTERSHIRE, WR9 8UD.
NICOL, Mr. Andrew John Diarmid, MA ACA *1990;* (Tax Fac), 19 Burstock Road, LONDON, SW15 2PW.
•**NICOL, Mr. Anthony Richard Craig, BSc(Hons) ACA** *2002;* with PricewaterhouseCoopers LLP, 1 Embankment Place, LONDON, WC2N 6RH.
NICOL, Mr. Carl Anthony, BA ACA *1993;* T N T Post Ltd, Unit E, Orbital, 24 Oldham Street, Denton, MANCHESTER M34 3SU.
NICOL, Mr. David John, BSc ACA *1985;* Mandarin, Burtons Way, CHALFONT ST. GILES, BUCKINGHAMSHIRE, HP8 4BP.
NICOL, Mrs. Edwina Margot, BA FCA *1973;* Amethyst Green, The Holloway, DROITWICH, WR9 7AH.
NICOL, Mr. Fraser Mcleod, BA FCA *1977;* Willow End, 111 Cambridge Road, Waterbeach, CAMBRIDGE, CB5 9NJ.
•**NICOL, Mr. Glenn William, BSc(Hons) ACA** *2001;* with Francis Clark LLP, Vantage Point, Woodwater Park, Pynes Hill, EXETER, EX2 5FD.
NICOL, Miss. Helen Fiona, MA ACA MCIPD *1990;* 16 Edward Road, Hampton Hill, HAMPTON, MIDDLESEX, TW12 1LG.
•**NICOL, Mrs. Hilary Maria, BA ACA** *1986;* The Old Vicarage, Bury Lane, Withnell, CHORLEY, LANCASHIRE, PR6 8SN.
NICOL, Mr. Ian Trevor, FCA *1975;* Amethyst Green, The Holloway, DROITWICH, WR9 7AH.
NICOL, Mrs. Joanna Clare, BA(Hons) ACA *2002;* 59 Southway, Horsforth, LEEDS, LS18 5RN.
•**NICOL, Mr. John, FCA** *1982;* (Tax Fac), John Nicol & Co, 161 Park Lane, MACCLESFIELD, SK11 6UB. See also John Nicol Ltd
NICOL, Mr. John Stuart, FCA *1967;* 28 Whistlers Avenue, LONDON, SW11 3TS.
NICOL, Mrs. Karen Linda, BA ACA *1986;* Mandarin, Burtons Way, CHALFONT ST. GILES, BUCKINGHAMSHIRE, HP8 4BP.
NICOL, Miss. Laura Jane, BSc ACA *2011;* 5 Thornbury, HARPENDEN, HERTFORDSHIRE, AL5 5SN.
•**NICOL, Mr. Peter Gordon, BSc FCA** *1986;* Horsfield-Smith Limited, Tower House, 269 Walmersley Road, BURY, LANCASHIRE, BL9 6NX.
NICOL, Mr. Richard Craig, FCA *1969;* 25 Manor Road, SUTTON, SM2 7AG.
NICOL, Miss. Sarah Anne, BSc ACA *2007;* 111 Cambridge Road, Waterbeach, CAMBRIDGE, CB25 9NJ.
NICOLA, Miss. Maria, BSc ACA *1996;* 19 Lithrodonta Street, Latsia, 2221 NICOSIA, CYPRUS.
NICOLAE, Mrs. Violeta, BA ACA *2004;* Neudorfstrasse 45, 8810 HORGEN, SWITZERLAND.
NICOLAIDES, Mr. Charis, BA ACA *1996;* Evagora pallikaride 10, Mesa Chorio, 8290 PAPHOS, CYPRUS.
NICOLAIDES, Mr. Constantinos Kyprou, MA FCA CF CMC AMCT *1997;* with KPMG LLP, 15 Canada Square, LONDON, E14 5GL.
•**NICOLAIDES, Mr. Costas Michael, BA FCA** *1980;* PricewaterhouseCoopers Limited, Artemidos Tower, 7th & 8th Floors, 3 Artemidos Avenue, 6020 LARNACA, CYPRUS.
NICOLAIDES, Mr. Demetris, BSc ACA *2004;* with Deloitte Limited, Maximos Plaza, Tower 1 3rd Floor, 214 Arch Makarios III Avenue, CY 3105 LIMASSOL, CYPRUS.
NICOLAIDES, Mr. Demos, MSc BA ACA *2006;* 26 Tamassos Street, Platy Aglatzia, 2115 NICOSIA, CYPRUS.
NICOLAIDES, Mr. Marios, BA ACA *1997;* 12 Filimona Street, Strovolos, 2036 NICOSIA, CYPRUS.
NICOLAIDES, Mr. Michael, ACA *2011;* 23 Perran Road, LONDON, SW2 3DJ.
•**NICOLAIDES, Mr. Neoclis, BA FCA** *1986;* Neoserve Audit Limited, P.O Box 70585, 3800 LIMASSOL, CYPRUS.
•**NICOLAIDES, Mr. Nicos Costa, BSc FCA** *1978;* Abacus Limited, P O Box 25549, CY-1310 NICOSIA, CYPRUS.
NICOLAIDOU, Ms. Panayiota, ACA *2003;* 4 Roentgen Street, Zakaki, 3046 LIMASSOL, CYPRUS.
NICOLAOU, Mr. Alexis John, BA ACA *1997;* 26 DIKOMOU STREET, STROVOLOS, 2054 NICOSIA, CYPRUS.
NICOLAOU, Mr. Anastasis, ACA *2009;* 1 Ymittou Street, 6043 LARNACA, CYPRUS.
NICOLAOU, Mr. Angelos Yangou, BCom FCA *1957;* 25 Annis Komninis Street, 1061 NICOSIA, CYPRUS. (Life Member)
•**NICOLAOU, Mr. Antonios, FCA** *1962;* Nicolaou & Co, 25 Heath Drive, POTTERS BAR, EN6 1EN.
NICOLAOU, Miss. Christina, BSc ACA *2011;* Sfakion 14, Agios Spyridonas, 3048 LIMASSOL, CYPRUS.
NICOLAOU, Mr. Costas, FCA *1971;* 54 Brookdale, LONDON, N11 1BN.
NICOLAOU, Mr. George, BA FCA *1985;* Central Bank of Cyprus, P.O. Box 5529, NICOSIA, CYPRUS.
•**NICOLAOU, Mr. Harry, MSc FCA** *1980;* Harry Nicolaou & Co., 38b Stroud Green Road, LONDON, N4 3ES. See also Harry Nicolaou & Co Ltd
NICOLAOU, Miss. Ioanna, BA ACA *2007;* 24 Aristofanous Strovolos, 2039 NICOSIA, CYPRUS.
NICOLAOU, Mr. Marcus, BA ACA CTA *2000;* 20 Freeman Close, COLCHESTER, CO4 5FJ.
NICOLAOU, Miss. Marina, BSc ACA *2007;* 35 Stisixorou, Agia Fila, 3117 LIMASSOL, CYPRUS.
•**NICOLAOU, Mr. Modestinos John, BA FCA** *1998;* BSG Valentine, Lynton House, 7/12 Tavistock Square, LONDON, WC1H 9BQ.
•**NICOLAOU, Mr. Nicholas, FCA CF** *1994;* Kyprianides Nicolaou & Associates, 48 Themistoclis Avenue, Office 401, 1066 NICOSIA, CYPRUS. See also Kyprianides, Nicolaou & Economides
NICOLAOU, Mr. Nicolaos, ACA *2008;* 28 Eptanison street, Anthoupoli, 2302 NICOSIA, CYPRUS.
NICOLAOU, Mr. Nicolas Costa, BSc ACA *1999;* with PricewaterhouseCoopers Limited, Julia House, 3 Themistocles Dervis Street, CY-1066 NICOSIA, CYPRUS.
NICOLAOU, Miss. Niki Nicolet, BA(Hons) ACA *2003;* Deloitte Limited, Maximos Plaza, Tower 1 3rd Floor, 213 Arch Makariou 3rd Avenue, 3030 LIMASSOL, CYPRUS.
NICOLAOU, Miss. Panayiota, BA ACA *2004;* 16 Eleftherias Street, 2675 NICOSIA, CYPRUS.
NICOLAOU, Ms. Rodoulla, BA ACA *2010;* 12 Amathountos Street, Dali, 2540 NICOSIA, CYPRUS.
NICOLAOU, Miss. Stephanie, BSc(Econ) ACA *2010;* 2 Zaimis Street, Archangelos, 2334 NICOSIA, CYPRUS.
NICOLAOU, Mr. Varnavas, MEng ACA *2003;* P.o Box 21532, 1510 NICOSIA, CYPRUS.
•**NICOLAOU-TODD, Mrs. Niki Andreou, FCA** *1982;* Bertram Todd, 5 Oxford House, Oxford Road, WOKINGHAM, RG41 2YE.
•**NICOLET, Mr. Denis, FCA** *1974;* South Barn, Muzwell Farm, Moor Common, Lane End, HIGH WYCOMBE, BUCKINGHAMSHIRE HP14 3HX.
NICOLETTIS, Mr. Marios Georgiou, BSc ACA *1995;* J Patatsou Str, No 6, Acropolis, NICOSIA, CYPRUS.
•**NICOLL, Mr. Bruce Kenneth, BSc FCA** *1986;* (Tax Fac), Impact Totnes Limited, 2 Warland, TOTNES, DEVON, TQ9 5EL.
NICOLL, Mrs. Eileen Catriona Winck, BA ACA *1998;* Gladman House Petersfield Road, Ropley, ALRESFORD, SO24 0EE.
•**NICOLL, Miss. Karyn, BA ACA** *2002;* with KPMG LLP, 15 Canada Square, LONDON, E14 5GL.
NICOLL, Miss. Kirsty Reid, MA ACA *2010;* Flat 1, 111 Lavender Hill, LONDON, SW11 5QL.
NICOLL, Mrs. Lucy Josephine, ACA *2008;* 77 Hinau Road, RD 1, WAIMAUKU 0881, NEW ZEALAND.
NICOLL, Mr. Stuart David, BA ACA *1993;* 70 Browning Road, SHORT HILLS, NJ 07078, UNITED STATES.
NICOLL, Mrs. Victoria, BA ACA *2007;* with Price Bailey LLP, 260 The Quorum, Barnwell Road, CAMBRIDGE, CB5 8RE.
NICOLLE, Mr. Alan William Hubert, FCA *1958;* La Vieille Maison, Ville Amphrey, St. Martin, GUERNSEY, GY4 6DR. (Life Member)
NICOLLE, Mrs. Fiona Mary, BA(Hons) ACA *2003;* 24 Greenway, BERKHAMSTED, HERTFORDSHIRE, HP4 3JD.
NICOLLE, Mr. Jean-Pierre William Sarre, MEng ACA *1999;* (Tax Fac), Grasmere, Brock Road, St. Peter Port, GUERNSEY, GY1 1RS.
NICOLLE, Mr. Martin De Garis, BA FCA *1974;* Hanjague, Bryher, ISLES OF SCILLY, TR23 0PR.
NICOLSON, Mr. Alastair John, BSc ACA *1999;* Euro Canterbury, Broad Oak Road, CANTERBURY, KENT, CT2 7QH.
NICOLSON, Mr. Christopher Edward, ACA *2009;* 82 Birchwood Avenue, SIDCUP, KENT, DA14 4JU.
NICOLSON, Mr. Derick, BSc ACA *1994;* 51 Finland Street, LONDON, SE16 7TP.
NICOLSON, Mrs. Gail Helen, BSc ACA *1992;* 17 Styvechale Avenue, Earlsdon, COVENTRY, CV5 6DW.
NICOLSON, Ms. Jennifer Ann, BA ACA *1984;* (Tax Fac), Moore Thompson, Bank House, Broad Street, SPALDING, LINCOLNSHIRE, PE11 1TB.
NICOLSON, Mr. William Andrew Craigie, BSc ACA *1991;* Mercia Hardware Ltd, Units K & L, Cavans Close, Binley Industrial Estate, COVENTRY, CV3 2SF. (Life Member)
NICUM, Mr. Pinal Jayawantrao, BSc ACA *1996;* 16 Lynwood Road, THAMES DITTON, KT7 0DN.
NIDDRIE, Mr. Robert Charles, FCA *1958;* Morestead House, Morestead, WINCHESTER, SO21 1LZ. (Life Member)
NIE, Mr. Zhaolong, ACA *2009;* Flat 121, 25 Barge Walk, LONDON, SE10 0FN.
NIEBOER, Mrs. Fleur, BA ACA *2003;* K P M G Llp, 15 Canada Square, LONDON, E14 5GL.
•**NIELD, Mr. Alan Robert, FCA** *1954;* A.R. Nield, 114 Brookvale Road, Olton, SOLIHULL, B92 7JB.
NIELD, Mr. Alexander Nicholas, BSc ACA *1994;* 114 Carisbrooke Road, LEEDS, LS16 5RX.
NIELD, Mr. Cyril Walter, FCA *1958;* 217 Dowson Road, HYDE, CHESHIRE, SK14 5BR. (Life Member)
NIELD, Mr. Richard Ian, BA ACA *1991;* Cargill, Knowle Hill Park, Fairmile Lane, COBHAM, SURREY, KT11 2PD.
NIELD, Mr. Robert George, FCA *1976;* 22 The Riviera, 10 Pik Sha Road, CLEARWATER BAY, KOWLOON, HONG KONG SAR.
NIELD, Mrs. Sarah Kay, MMath ACA *2004;* 8 Kensington Close, Milnrow, ROCHDALE, LANCASHIRE, OL16 3HJ.
NIELSEN, Mr. Alan, FCA *1949;* 2 Parkholme, 39 Meads Road, EASTBOURNE, BN20 7PS. (Life Member)
NIELSEN, Mr. Charles Peter, FCA *1957;* Godstone House, St. Andrews Road, Littlestone, NEW ROMNEY, KENT, TN28 8RB. (Life Member)
NIELSEN, Mr. Gorm Ward, BSc ACA *1988;* (Tax Fac), N D S Ltd, 1 London Road, STAINES, MIDDLESEX, TW18 4EX.
NIELSEN, Mr. Jens Otto, MA ACA *1998;* Flat 401, Diamond 3, Dubai Marina, PO Box 215385, DUBAI, UNITED ARAB EMIRATES.
NIELSEN, Mrs. Rehanna, BSc ACA *1992;* 14 Ashcroft Park, COBHAM, KT11 2DN.
NIEM, Miss. Annette An-Liang, BSc ACA *1990;* Flat 11 B, Woodbury Court, 137 Pokfulam Road, POK FU LAM, HONG KONG ISLAND, HONG KONG SAR.
NIEM, Mr. Philip, BSc ACA *1984;* 5B Woodbury Court, 137 Pokfulam Road, POK FU LAM, HONG KONG ISLAND, HONG KONG SAR.
•**NIEMANN, Mr. Martin Karl, BA FCA** *1988;* Martin & Co, 71 Ashcroft Road, Stopsley, LUTON, LU2 9AX. See also Roberts & Partners
NIEMBRO, Mr. Joe, BSc ACA *2001;* 156 Tenison Road, CAMBRIDGE, CB1 2DP.
•**NIEWIADOMSKI, Mr. Roman Stanislaw, BSc ACA** *1992;* Petrolinvest SA, 5th floor, LIM Corporate Centre, Jerozolimakie 65/79, 00-697 WARSAW, POLAND.
NIEWOLA, Miss. Nicola Marianne, ACA *2008;* 31 Route de Malagnou, 1208 GENEVA, SWITZERLAND.

NIGAM, Mr. Ankush, ACA *1993;* 32 Pavenham Close, Lower Earley, READING, RG6 4DX.
NIGHOSKAR, Mr. Sandeep Suresh, BA ACA ACIS *1993;* Woodcote, Wannock Road, POLEGATE, EAST SUSSEX, BN26 5EA.
NIGHTALL, Mr. Timothy James, BSc ACA *2003;* 5 Gleneagles Drive, SUTTON COLDFIELD, WEST MIDLANDS, B75 6UN.
NIGHTINGALE, Mr. Andrew Mark, BSc ACA *1989;* 6 avenue des ligures 2CMS6, MC 98000 MONACO, MONACO.
NIGHTINGALE, Mr. Barry Graham Kirk, BA ACA *1986;* Bet Fred Spectrum Arena, Benson Road Birchwood, WARRINGTON, WA3 7PQ.
NIGHTINGALE, Mrs. Carron Elisabeth Louise, BA ACA *1992;* Lower Stream Farm, Mill Lane, Laughton, LEWES, EAST SUSSEX BN8 6AJ.
•NIGHTINGALE, Mr. Clifford John, FCA *1972;* Simpkins Edwards LLP, Michael House, Castle Street, EXETER, EX4 3LQ.
NIGHTINGALE, Mr. Craig James, BA ACA *2006;* Care International, P.O. Box 1157, GOROKA, PAPUA NEW GUINEA.
NIGHTINGALE, Mr. Eric Wilfred, FCA *1983;* 1 Lochrin Square, H B O S Plc, 92 Fountainbridge, EDINBURGH, EH3 9QA.
NIGHTINGALE, Miss. Fiona Elizabeth, BSc ACA *1998;* 44 Abbeydale Oval, LEEDS, LS5 3RF.
NIGHTINGALE, Mrs. Gillian Lisa, BA ACA *1995;* 94 Billington Gardens, Hedge End, SOUTHAMPTON, SO30 2RT.
NIGHTINGALE, Mr. Jonathan Robert, BA ACA *1998;* Flat 8, Copthorne Place, Forest Road, Effingham Junction, LEATHERHEAD, SURREY KT24 5HL.
NIGHTINGALE, Mrs. Karen, BA ACA *2003;* 4 Alderson Drive, Stretton, BURTON-ON-TRENT, STAFFORDSHIRE, DE13 0QQ.
NIGHTINGALE, Mrs. Pauline Yvonne, FCA *1972;* 15 Aragon Avenue, Ewell, EPSOM, KT17 2QL.
NIGHTINGALE, Mr. Robert, BSc ACA *1997;* Pear Tree Farm, Locko Lane, Pilsley, CHESTERFIELD, S45 8AW.
NIGHTINGALE, Mr. Robin Jack, FCA *1965;* 59 Larch Road, Maybush, SOUTHAMPTON, SO16 5EX. (Life Member)
NIGHTINGALE, Mr. Stephen Lee, BSc ACA *1997;* New Broad Street House, New Broad Street, LONDON, EC2M 1NH.
NIGHTINGALE, Mr. Stuart, MEng ACA *1997;* 3909 Releigh Court, MCKINNEY, TX 75070, UNITED STATES.
NIGHTINGALE, Mr. Thomas Alan, BA ACA *1998;* 14 Meadow Hill, PURLEY, SURREY, CR8 3HL.
NIGHTINGALE - NEWTON, Mrs. Jenny, BA ACA *2010;* 18 Church Lane, Calow, CHESTERFIELD, DERBYSHIRE, S44 5AH.
NIGRELLI, Mr. Salvatore, BSc ACA *1998;* with PricewaterhouseCoopers LLP, 1 Embankment Place, LONDON, WC2N 6RH.
NIHALANI, Mrs. Ahkalya, BSc ACA *1998;* 11 Grovelands Road, PURLEY, CR8 4LB.
•NIJHAWAN, Mr. Sukhbir, BA FCA *1983;* Nijhawan, The Old Queen Victoria, High Street, Rattlesden, BURY ST. EDMUNDS, SUFFOLK IP30 0RA.
NIJHAWAN, Mr. Valentine, FCA *1974;* PricewaterhouseCoopers Ltd, Building 8-B, 7th & 8th Floors, DLF Cyber City, GURGAON 122002, HARYANA INDIA.
NIJJAR, Mr. Hardip Singh, BSc ACA *2010;* 125 Salisbury Avenue, BARKING, ESSEX, IG11 9XP.
NIJJAR, Mr. Harjinder, BSc ACA *1996;* 6 Stoneyfield, GERRARDS CROSS, BUCKINGHAMSHIRE, SL9 7LU.
NIJJAR, Mrs. Kuldip Kaur, BA ACA *1994;* 1 Stoneleigh Way, Shadwell Lane, Moortown, LEEDS, LS17 8FL.
NIJJAR, Mr. Parmveer, ACA *2008;* 57 Gilbert Scott Court, Whielden Street, AMERSHAM, BUCKINGHAMSHIRE, HP7 0AR.
NIJJAR, Mrs. Sukhdeep Kaur, ACA *2010;* 6 Paddock Gardens, WALSALL, WS5 3NZ.
NIK ABDUL AZIZ, Mr. Nik Azlan, ACA *2002;* 6 Lorong Rahim Kajai 7, Taman Tun Dr Ismail, 60000 KUALA LUMPUR, FEDERAL TERRITORY, MALAYSIA.
NIK AFFANDI, Miss. Nik Faizanira, BA ACA *2000;* NO. 4 Jalan Bidai U8/22b Bukit Jelutong 470150 Shah Alam Selangor., 470150 SHAH ALAM, MALAYSIA.
NIKAIIN, Mr. Afkham, FCA *1975;* 1334 Park Avenue, LONG BEACH, CA 90804, UNITED STATES.
NIKAS, Mr. George, MBA ACA *2006;* with PricewaterhouseCoopers, 268-270 Kifissias Avenue, Halandri, 15232 ATHENS, GREECE.
NIKAS, Mrs. Sarah Louise, BA ACA *1996;* 15407 McGinty Road West MS #46, WAYZATA, MN 55391, UNITED STATES.
NIKIFOROU, Mrs. Maria, BSc ACA *2010;* 8 Themistocleous Street, Flat 303, 2060 STROVOLOS, CYPRUS.
NIKOLAEV, Mr. Denis, ACA *2008;* Flat 2, 23 Abercorn Place, LONDON, NW8 9DX.
NIKOLAIDIS, Mr. Nikolas, ACA *2009;* Paparigopoulou 22, 8046 PAPHOS, CYPRUS.
NIKOLIC, Mr. Danilo, BA ACA *2003;* Kraljice Natalie 11, 11070 BELGRADE, SERBIA.
NIKOVSKA, Ms. Ana, BA ACA *1998;* Barnett B.V, 206 Van Dismenstraat, 1013 CP AMSTERDAM, NETHERLANDS.
NIKOVSKI, Mr. Aleksandar, BA ACA *1998;* Ul Marko Cepenkov 46b, 1000 SKOPJE, MACEDONIA.
NIKZAD, Mr. Babak, BSc ACA *1991;* KPMG, 8/F Prince's Building, 10 Chater Road, CENTRAL, HONG KONG ISLAND, HONG KONG SAR.
NILAND, Mr. John James, ACA *2011;* 20 Raymond Avenue, South Woodford, LONDON, E18 2HG.
NILSEN, Mr. John Peter, ACA CA(NZ) *2009;* (Tax Fac), Flat 3, Waterford Court, Leeland Terrace, LONDON, W13 9HL.
NILSSON, Miss. Claire Elisabeth, BSc ACA *1980;* 12 Littlecote Close, LONDON, SW19 6RL.
NILSSON, Mr. Daniel Harald, ACA *2010;* Flat 1140, 19 St. George Wharf, LONDON, SW8 2FG.
NILSSON, Mr. Roger Frederick, FCA *1969;* Penny Place, Holyport Road, MAIDENHEAD, BERKSHIRE, SL6 2HA.
NIMALASURIYA, Mr. Ajit, MA FCA *1980;* 305 W 98th St Apt 7F-N, NEW YORK, NY 10025, UNITED STATES.
•NIMAN, Mr. Edmund Brian, BSc FCA *1981;* (Tax Fac), NWN Blue Squared Ltd, 7 Bourne Court, Southend Road, WOODFORD GREEN, ESSEX, IG8 8HD.
NIMAN, Mrs. Sandra Sema Rachel, BBS ACA *1979;* 9 Windsor Road, Prestwich, MANCHESTER, M25 0DZ.
NIMMO, Ms. Margaret Burnett, MBA BSc FCA *1985;* 14 Station Road, BIGGLESWADE, BEDFORDSHIRE, SG18 8AL.
NINEBERG, Mr. Dorian Grant, ACA *1982;* regent house, BOREHAMWOOD, wd6 4rs.
NINNES, Mr. Christopher Harvey, FCA *1958;* 'Cal-Enys', No.6 Moonrakers, Parc Owles, Carbis Bay, ST. IVES, CORNWALL TR26 2RE. (Life Member)
NINNIM, Mrs. Alison Gail, BA FCA *1996;* Honeysuckle Cottage, 53 Main Road, Tolpuddle, DORCHESTER, DORSET, DT2 7ES.
NINNIS, Miss. Caron Gay, BSc ACA *1991;* 50 Northbrook Road, Shirley, SOLIHULL, B90 3NP.
NINNIS, Miss. Charlotte, BSc ACA *2011;* 22 Hollyhock Close, BASINGSTOKE, HAMPSHIRE, RG22 5RF.
NIP, Mr. David, ACA *2007;* 1713, Yiu Tung House, Tung Tau Estate, KOWLOON CITY, KOWLOON, HONG KONG SAR.
NIP, Mr. Ho Chung Daniel, ACA *2005;* Flat C 30/F, Tower 2, Park Belvedere, SHA TIN, NEW TERRITORIES, HONG KONG SAR.
NIP, Mr. Oi Man, ACA *2005;* Unit 42F Block 7, Shimao Riveria Gardens, No.2 Wei Fang Xi Road, Lu Jia Zui, PUDONG 200122, CHINA.
NIRDOSH, Ms. Mamta, ACA *2011;* Flat 24 Manor Court, Aylmer Road, LONDON, N2 0BS.
•NIREN, Mr. Charles Jeffrey, FCA *1974;* (Tax Fac), Niren Blake LLP, Brook Point, 1412 High Road, LONDON, N20 9BH.
NIRMALANANTHAN, Mr. Sathijeevan, BSc ACA *2011;* 100 Wickham Lane, Abbey Wood, LONDON, SE2 0XW.
•NIRSIMLOO, Mr. Jayananda Bramadoo, BSc FCA *1983;* KPMG S.A., 1 Cours Valmy, Paris La Défense Cedex, 92923 PARIS LA DÉFENSE, FRANCE.
NIRSIMLOO, Mr. Nitish Rowin, ACA *2010;* Morcellement Hossenbux, Eau Coulee, CUREPIPE, MAURITIUS.
NISAR, Mr. Saqib, ACA ACCA *1999;* with Ernst & Young, P.O. Box 74, SAFAT, 13001, KUWAIT.
NISBET, Mr. Christopher James, BA(Hons) ACA *2011;* 46 St. Margarets Grove, Great Kingshill, HIGH WYCOMBE, BUCKINGHAMSHIRE, HP15 6HP.
NISBET, Mr. Keith George, ACA *1982;* 98 Warwick Road, SOUTH SHIELDS, NE34 0RY.
NISBET, Mr. Malcolm Alexander, ACA *2010;* Flat 1, Crown Court, Lacy Road, LONDON, SW15 1NS.
NISBET, Mr. Nicholas Anthony, MA ACA *1996;* San Julian Del Camino 3 4A, Las Tablas, MADRID, SPAIN.
NISBET, Mr. Peter Stewart, BA ACA *1988;* 57 Oban Road, CITY BEACH, WA 6015, AUSTRALIA.
NISBET, Mr. Robert Simson, BSc FCA *1976;* Arturo Soria 279, 28033 MADRID, SPAIN.
NISBET EVANS, Miss. Ann, BSc ACA *1993;* Wilhelminapark 4, 2342AG OEGSTGEEST, NETHERLANDS.
•NISBETT, Mr. Mark Peter, BA ACA *1999;* with RSM Tenon Audit Limited, 66 Chiltern Street, LONDON, W1U 4JT.
NISKIN, Mr. Richard, BA ACA *2009;* with Ensors, Anglia House, 285 Milton Road, CAMBRIDGE, CB4 1XQ.
•NISNER, Mr. Maxwell John, FCA *1974;* (Tax Fac), M J N Consulting Services LLP, Woodside, 17 Aylmer Drive, STANMORE, MIDDLESEX, HA7 3EJ.
NISSAN, Mr. Salman, BA ACA *1994;* C R A International UK, 99 Bishopsgate, LONDON, EC2M 3XD.
NISSEN, Mr. Peter Charles Maitland, MA FCA *1950;* 140 Swan Court, Chelsea Manor Street, LONDON, SW3 5RU. (Life Member)
•NISSEN, Mr. Robert Ian, BA FCA *1990;* Stein Richards Limited, 10 London Mews, LONDON, W2 1HY.
NITHIANANTHAN, Mr. Kajan, ACA *2008;* 2 Fowler Close, YARM, CLEVELAND, TS15 9SL.
NIVEN, Mr. Craig Lees Baxter, MA ACA *1983;* 2nd Floor, Arlington Group, 18 Pall Mall, LONDON, SW1Y 5LU.
•NIVEN, Mr. Euan Niall Macnaughton, FCA *1974;* (Tax Fac), Craigton Limited, 13 Greville Park Road, ASHTEAD, SURREY, KT21 2QU.
NIVEN, Miss. Frances, ACA *2011;* Flat 30, Bentham House, 7 Falmouth Road, LONDON, SE1 4JY.
NIVEN, Mr. Graham John, BSc ACA *1985;* 14 Monton Green, Eccles, MANCHESTER, M30 9LW.
NIVEN, Mr. Ian McGregor, MA ACA *1983;* 27 Joseph Banks Drive, Whitby, PORIRUA 5024, NEW ZEALAND.
NIVEN, Mr. Lawrence, LLB ACA *1980;* 36 Main Street, Great Glen, LEICESTER, LE8 9GG.
NIVEN, Mr. Paul Mark, BA ACA *1988;* Apt 2 Northland, Grey Road, ALTRINCHAM, CHESHIRE, WA14 4BT.
NIVEN, Mrs. Radhika B, ACA *2008;* 1/1 1 Battlefield Crescent, GLASGOW, G42 9JS.
NIVEN, Mr. Trevor, FCA *1970;* Mayfield House, Thelnetham, DISS, IP22 1JL.
NIVEN, Mr. Trevor Raymond, FCA *1974;* with Crown Agents, St. Nicholas House, St. Nicholas Road, SUTTON, SURREY, SM1 1EL.
NIVEN, Mrs. Veronica Mary, BSc ACA *1988;* Leigh House, 37 Leigh Road, Hale, ALTRINCHAM, CHESHIRE, WA15 9BJ.
NIX, Mr. David William, BSc ACA *2000;* Neway House, Little Oak Drive Annesley, NOTTINGHAM, NOTTINGHAMSHIRE, NG15 0PR.
NIXEY, Mrs. Victoria Louise, BSc ACA *2005;* Lobbersdown Farm, Rycote Lane, Milton Common, THAME, OXFORDSHIRE, OX9 2PB.
•NIXEY, Mr. William Albert, BSc ACA CTA *2004;* Martin and Company, The Old Farm Office, Rycote Lane Farm, Milton Common, THAME, OXFORDSHIRE OX9 2NZ. See also Martin and Company Accountants Limited
NIXON, Mr. Adrian Michael, BSc ACA *1998;* 7 Woodlands Road, Handforth, WILMSLOW, SK9 3AW.
NIXON, Mr. Alan Arthur, BA ACA *1984;* The Old House, Brown Heath, ELLESMERE, SY12 0LB.
NIXON, Mr. Anthony Felix, FCA *1966;* 10b Wester Coates Gardens, EDINBURGH, EH12 5LT.
NIXON, Mrs. Antigone, BA ACA *1992;* 59 Lakeside Road, LONDON, N13 4PS.
NIXON, Miss. Claire, ACA *2011;* 10 Haugh Lane, HEXHAM, NORTHUMBERLAND, NE46 3PR.
•NIXON, Mr. Daniel, BA ACA *2006;* Wilkins Kennedy, Bridge House, London Bridge, LONDON, SE1 9QR.
NIXON, Mr. David Henry, FCA *1959;* 3 Holywell Terrace, Holywell Street, SHREWSBURY, SY2 5DF.
•NIXON, Mr. David Michael, BA FCA *1977;* Nixon D M, 25 Castlegate, NEWARK, NG24 1AZ.
NIXON, Mr. Dominic Andrew, BSc ACA *1986;* PricewaterhouseCoopers LLP, 17-00 PWC Building, 8 Cross Street, SINGAPORE 048424, SINGAPORE.
NIXON, Mr. Ian Lindsay, FCA *1969;* (Tax Fac), Meadowside, Little Onn Road, Church Eaton, STAFFORD, ST20 0AY.
NIXON, Mr. John, FCA *1964;* Woodlands, Chapel Hill, SKIPTON, NORTH YORKSHIRE, BD23 1NL.
•NIXON, Mr. John Michael, BA FCA *1983;* (Tax Fac), John M Nixon & Company, 39 Wynford Avenue, West Park, LEEDS, LS16 6JN.
NIXON, Mrs. Josephine Laura, MA ACA *2002;* Kadant Johnson Systems International Ltd, Little Lane, ILKLEY, WEST YORKSHIRE, LS29 8HY.
NIXON, Mr. Mark Andrew, BA FCA *1979;* The Old Vicarage, Matterdale, PENRITH, CUMBRIA, CA11 0LD.
•NIXON, Mr. Neville John, FCA *1956;* John H. Nixon & Co, Athena House, 35 Greek Street, STOCKPORT, SK3 8BA.
NIXON, Mrs. Nicola Jane, BA(Hons) ACIB ACA *2000;* Orchard Cottage, Healey Green Lane, Houses Hill, HUDDERSFIELD, HD5 0PB.
•NIXON, Mr. Paul, BA ACA *1983;* PricewaterhouseCoopers LLP, Benson House, 33 Wellington Street, LEEDS, LS1 4JP. See also PricewaterhouseCoopers
•NIXON, Mr. Paul Anthony, ACA *1994;* with Wilkins Kennedy FKC Limited, Stourside Place, 35-41 Station Road, ASHFORD, KENT, TN23 1PP.
NIXON, Mr. Peter John, FCA *1965;* 15481 SW 164 Street, MIAMI, FL 33187, UNITED STATES.
NIXON, Mr. Peter Michael, BSc ACA *1986;* 6 Bradda Mount, Bramhall, STOCKPORT, CHESHIRE, SK7 3BX.
NIXON, Mr. Peter Thomas, FCA *1952;* 160 Codsall Road, Tettenhall, WOLVERHAMPTON, WV6 9QQ. (Life Member)
•NIXON, Mr. Philip John, MA FCA *1981;* (Tax Fac), Edwin Smith, 32 Queens Road, READING, RG1 4AU.
NIXON, Mr. Richard John, BSc ACA *1992;* Browning House, Wothorpe Park First Drift, Wothorpe, STAMFORD, PE9 3LA.
NIXON, Mr. Roger, BA ACA *2007;* K P M G Edward VII Quay, Navigation Way Ashton-on-Ribble, PRESTON, PR2 2YF.
NIXON, Miss. Sarah, ACA *2011;* 1 Warren Bank, MANCHESTER, M9 6FE.
NIXON, Mr. Stephen, BSc ACA *1993;* Lighterlife Cavendish House, Parkway Harlow Business Park, HARLOW, CM19 5QF.
NIXON, Mrs. Susan, BSc ACA *1979;* 63 Endeavour Street, RED HILL, ACT 2603, AUSTRALIA.
•NIXON, Mrs. Susannah Wendy, BA ACA *1992;* Lamont Pridmore, Milburn House, 3 Oxford Street, WORKINGTON, CA14 2AL. See also Lamont Pridmore Limited
NIXON, Mr. William Anthony John, FCA *1979; (ACA Ireland 1971);* Department of Accountancy, & Business Finance, University of Dundee, DUNDEE, DD1 4HL.
NIXON-CANEY, Mrs. Ann Christine, FCA *1963;* 112 Golden Drive, Eaglestone, MILTON KEYNES, MK6 5BN. (Life Member)
•NIXSEAMAN, Miss. Helen Mary, MSc FCA *1986;* PricewaterhouseCoopers LLP, Cornwall Court, 19 Cornwall Street, BIRMINGHAM, B3 2DT. See also PricewaterhouseCoopers
NIXSON, Mr. Vivian Alan, FCA *1960;* 57 Eight Acres, ROMSEY, SO51 5BP. (Life Member)
NJOROGE, Mr. Andrew Ndegwa, ACA *1999;* P O Box 16794, NAIROBI, 00620, KENYA.
NJOROGE, Mr. Joseph Thuku, ACA *1994;* Old Mutual Specialised Finance (Pty) Ltd, PO Box 66, CAPE TOWN, 8000, SOUTH AFRICA.
NJOROGE, Mr. Richard Githinji, ACA *1992;* C/O PricewaterhouseCoopers, P.O. Box 41500, NAIROBI, 00100, KENYA.
•NJUMBE, Dr. Sylvester Kome, PhD ACA *2002;* with PricewaterhouseCoopers, Immeuble Bel Air, Rue Du Marechal Joffre, BP 5689, DOUALA, CAMEROON.
NKRUMAH, Mrs. Elizabeth Jane, BA ACA *2007;* 4 Rosehill, Claygate, ESHER, SURREY, KT10 0HL.
NKRUMAH, Mr. Francis Kwamie, MSc BSc ACA *2007;* 4 Rosehill, Claygate, ESHER, KT10 0HL.
•NOAD, Mr. Stuart Ian, BA FCA *1985;* (Tax Fac), Stuart Noad BA FCA, 34 Brighton Road, SOUTHPORT, MERSEYSIDE, PR8 4DD.
NOAD, Mrs. Vida, BSc ACA *1987;* The Gables, 7 Manor Lane, Baydon, MARLBOROUGH, SN8 2JD.
NOAK, Mrs. Sarah Elizabeth, BA(Hons) ACA *2000;* 74 Craddocks Avenue, ASHTEAD, SURREY, KT21 1PG.
NOAKE, Mr. Paul William, BA ACA *1983;* 195 Linden Court, Brunswick Road Ealing, LONDON, W5 1AL.
NOAKE, Mr. Richard Geoffrey, FCA FCCA *1969;* 36 St. Marys Road, Harborne, BIRMINGHAM, B17 0HA.
NOAKES, Mrs. Carolyn Jane, ACA *1993;* 24 Holmwood Avenue, Shenfield, BRENTWOOD, CM15 8QS.
NOAKES, Miss. Jessica Amy, MSc ACA *2007;* 15 Meadow Lane, Slaithwaite, HUDDERSFIELD, HD7 5EX.
•NOAKES, Ms. Katharine Sian, BA FCA *1986;* with Kate Noakes & Co, 3 Darell Road, Caversham, READING, RG4 7AY.
NOAKES, Mr. Peter Edward, BSc FCA *1952;* Anderida Lodge, 23 Mountbatten Drive, Leverington, WISBECH, PE13 5AF. (Life Member)

NOAKES, Mr. Peter John, FCA *1963;* Lynncrest, Hempnall Road, Woodton, BUNGAY, NR35 2LR.
•**NOAKES, Mr. Simon John, FCA** *1973;* 8 Snowdenham Hall, Snowdenham Lane, Bramley, GUILDFORD, SURREY, GU5 0DB.
•**NOAKES, Mr. Stuart Robert, BSc(Hons) ACA** *1993;* (Tax Fac), Carpenter Box LLP, Amelia House, WORTHING, WEST SUSSEX, BN11 1QR.
NOBBS, Mr. David Michael, BSc ACA *2006;* Flat 11, Nightingale Court, Park Road, RADLETT, HERTFORDSHIRE, WD7 8EA.
•**NOBBS, Mr. Graham Albert, BSc ACA** *1986;* A.H.Cross & Co, 16 Quay Street, NEWPORT, ISLE OF WIGHT, PO30 5BG.
NOBBS, Mr. Stephen Spencer, FCA *1974;* 23 Prospect Lane, HARPENDEN, HERTFORDSHIRE, AL52PL.
NOBEEBUX, Mrs. Noor-E-Zaina, MEng ACA *2009;* 7 Southern Road, BASINGSTOKE, HAMPSHIRE, RG21 3DX.
NOBES, Miss. Jacqueline Elisabeth, BSc ACA *1997;* Business Systems Group, PO Box 2657, CAPE TOWN, 8000, SOUTH AFRICA.
NOBES, Mrs. Julia Kathleen, BA ACA *1990;* Summerleaze Forest Road Hale, FORDINGBRIDGE, HAMPSHIRE, SP6 2NP.
•**NOBLE, Mr. Alfred Braham, FCA** *1972;* Braham Noble Denholm & Co., York House, Empire Way, WEMBLEY, HA9 0PA. See also BND Audits Limited
NOBLE, Mr. Andrew Christopher John, BSc ACA *1987;* 25 Oaken Lane, Claygate, ESHER, KT10 0RG.
NOBLE, Mr. Andrew David, BA(Hons) ACA *2001;* 4 Eaton Road, ST. ALBANS, HERTFORDSHIRE, AL1 4UE.
NOBLE, Mr. Andrew James, ACA *2009;* Southview, Somersham Road, Pidley, HUNTINGDON, CAMBRIDGESHIRE, PE28 3DG.
•**NOBLE, Mr. Arthur Caspar Petrie, MA ACA ATII** *1999;* Ernst & Young LLP, 1 More London Place, LONDON, SE1 2AF. See also Ernst & Young Europe LLP
NOBLE, Miss. Charlotte Louise, ACA *2008;* 12 Newbold Close, Bentley Heath, SOLIHULL, WEST MIDLANDS, B93 9BS.
NOBLE, Mr. Christopher, BSc ACA *2007;* 16 Farington Close, MAIDSTONE, KENT, ME16 0WN.
NOBLE, Mr. Christopher Howard, BCom FCA *1967;* Alley Cross, 25 Corbett Avenue, DROITWICH, WR9 7BE. (Life Member)
NOBLE, Mr. Colin Henry, FCA *1962;* 11 Woodland Avenue, LYMM, CHESHIRE, WA13 0BJ.
•**NOBLE, Mr. David Andrew, FCA** *1976;* 8 Oak Dene Close, PUDSEY, WEST YORKSHIRE, LS28 9LW.
NOBLE, Mr. David Mark, MA ACA *1995;* 2 Broom Lock, TEDDINGTON, MIDDLESEX, TW11 9QP.
NOBLE, Mr. David Michael, ACA *2011;* 7 Furze Croft, Furze Hill, HOVE, EAST SUSSEX, BN3 1PB.
•**NOBLE, Mrs. Doreen, FCA** *1975;* (Tax Fac), Doreen Noble, 81 Woodcot Avenue, Baildon, SHIPLEY, BD17 6QR.
NOBLE, Mr. Edward Nelson, BSc FCA *1972;* 4 Gardenia Way, WOODFORD GREEN, ESSEX, IG8 0BL.
NOBLE, Mrs. Elisa, LLB ACA *2003;* 2 Indus Road #03-10, Emerald Park, SINGAPORE 169586, SINGAPORE.
•**NOBLE, Mrs. Elisabeth Jane, BA FCA** *1990;* (Tax Fac), Noble Accountancy Ltd, 41 Guildford Road, West End, WOKING, SURREY, GU24 9PW. See also financial Professional Support Services LLP
NOBLE, Miss. Elise, BA ACA *2007;* 126 Clive Road, West Dulwich, LONDON, SE21 8BP.
•**NOBLE, Ms. Elizabeth, BA FCA CTA** *1995;* (Tax Fac), Liz Noble FCA CTA, Westerlands, Belle Cross Road, KINGSBRIDGE, DEVON, TQ7 1NL.
NOBLE, Mr. Francis Alexander, FCA *1958;* 55 Cable Street, Formby, LIVERPOOL, L37 3LU. (Life Member)
NOBLE, Mr. Garry Grant, ACA *1980;* Invermore, High Road, Fobbing, STANFORD-LE-HOPE, SS17 9HT.
NOBLE, Miss. Gaylene Marie, BA ACA *2000;* AAR International, Joint Sentry Support Team, Royal Air Force Waddington, LINCOLN, LN5 9NB.
•**NOBLE, Mr. George Cochran, FCA** *1968;* Noble & Co, Abacus House, Mona Street, Douglas, ISLE OF MAN, IM1 3AE.
NOBLE, Mr. James Julian, MA FCA *1984;* 20 Charlbury Road, OXFORD, OX2 6UU.
NOBLE, Mr. John Arthur, BSc FCA *1958;* John Noble, Shurdington House, Main Road, Shurdington, CHELTENHAM, GLOUCESTERSHIRE GL51 4XJ. (Life Member)
•**NOBLE, Mr. John Timothy, FCA** *1980;* John T. Noble, 273 High Street, EPPING, ESSEX, CM16 4DA.
NOBLE, Dr. Kate, BSc ACA *2004;* 18 Den Bank Crescent, Crosspool, SHEFFIELD, S10 5PD.
•**NOBLE, Mr. Kenneth Lee Michael, BA FCA** *1992;* Sterling Financial Accountancy Services Limited, 27 Lincoln Croft, Shenstone, LICHFIELD, STAFFORDSHIRE, WS14 0ND. See also Thompson Prior Accountancy Services Limited
NOBLE, Mr. Laurence William, FCA *1947;* Flat 39, Richmond Court, Richmond Street, HERNE BAY, KENT, CT6 5LL. (Life Member)
•**NOBLE, Mr. Lee, BEng ACA** *1991;* (Tax Fac), Noble Accountants Ltd, Tarn Villa, Culgaith, PENRITH, CUMBRIA, CA10 1QL.
NOBLE, Mr. Mark John Whitfield, MA FCA AMCT *1973;* C F B T, 60 Queens Road, READING, RG1 4BS.
NOBLE, Mrs. Paula, MA ACA *1998;* 34 Clarence Road, Hale, ALTRINCHAM, WA15 8SF.
NOBLE, Mrs. Peta Anne Dorothy, MA FCA *1979;* 16 Lariat Lane, ROLLING HILLS ESTATES, CA 90274, UNITED STATES.
NOBLE, Mr. Peter James, BA FCA *1975;* 31 West Park, Mottingham, LONDON, SE9 4RZ.
NOBLE, Mr. Peter Robert, BSc ACA *2006;* Automobile Association Fanum House, Basing View, BASINGSTOKE, RG21 4EA.
NOBLE, Mr. Ray Christopher, FCA *1977;* Rua de S. Gabriel 3C, 2760-107 CAXIAS, PORTUGAL.
•**NOBLE, Mr. Richard Grant, BA ACA** *1986;* The Field House, Tyrrells Wood, LEATHERHEAD, KT22 8QJ.
•**NOBLE, Mr. Richard Michael, BSc ACA** *1980;* RN Consultancy Ltd, 4 Butterbur Place, CARDIFF, CF5 4QZ.
NOBLE, Mr. Robert Michael, BSc ACA *1978;* Grove House, Meanwood Grove, LEEDS, LS6 4QQ.
NOBLE, Mr. Roger Harold, FCA *1969;* 2 Hardings Reach, BURNHAM-ON-CROUCH, CM0 8LL.
NOBLE, Mrs. Sarah Jayne, BA ACA *2001;* 11 Stirrup Lane, FLEMINGTON, NJ 08822, UNITED STATES.
NOBLE, Mr. Stuart Jason, BSc ACA *1994;* (Tax Fac), The Old Forge Park Lane, Pulford, CHESTER, CH4 9HB.
NOBLE-NESBITT, Mr. Deryck, MA ACA *1997;* 33 Cannon Street, ST. ALBANS, HERTFORDSHIRE, AL3 5JR.
NOBLE SINGH, Mr. Rahul John, ACA *2011;* 12 Queen Margarets Grove, LONDON, N1 4QD.
NOBLETT, Miss. Amy Louise, ACA *2009;* 1 Avenham Colonnade, PRESTON, PR1 3LY.
NOCK, Mr. Brian Peter, FCA *1971;* 13 Granada Place, ANDOVER, SP10 1LB.
NOCK, Mr. David Timothy, BA ACA *1997;* with Mazars LLP, 45 Church Street, BIRMINGHAM, B3 2RT.
NOCK, Mr. Keith Malcolm, FCA *1965;* 14 Drew Road, STOURBRIDGE, WEST MIDLANDS, DY9 0UY.
NOCK, Mr. Kevin Barry, FCA *1967;* 136 Wentworth Road, BIRMINGHAM, B17 9SX.
NOCK, Mr. Michael Andrew, BSc ACA *1993;* 3 Malvern View, Clows Top, WORCESTER, DY14 9JE.
NOCK, Mr. Simon David, LLM LLB ACA *2003;* EFG Wealth Management (Cayman) Ltd, Strathvale House, 90 North Church Street, PO Box 10360, GEORGE TOWN, GRAND CAYMAN KY1-1103 CAYMAN ISLANDS.
NOCK, Mr. Steven Roy, BSc ACA *1998;* 87 New Road, Armitage, RUGELEY, WS15 4BH.
•**NOCKELS, Mr. Aubrey George, FCA** *1977;* (Tax Fac), Nockels Hornsey, 24 Bath Street, ABINGDON, OX14 3QH.
NOCKLES, Mr. Adrian Gerard, BSc ACA CISA *1995;* North Yorkshire County Council, 50 South Parade, NORTHALLERTON, NORTH YORKSHIRE, DL7 8SL.
NOCKOLDS, Mr. Stephen Lindsay, BA ACA *1993;* Spencers Cottage Upham Street, Upham, SOUTHAMPTON, SO32 1JD.
NODDING, Mr. John, FCA *1971;* 6 Midgley Drive, Four Oaks, SUTTON COLDFIELD, B74 2TW.
NODEN, Mr. Nicholas David James, MA ACA *2002;* 131 Casino Avenue, LONDON, SE24 9PP.
•**NOEL, Mr. Andrew Herbert, FCA** *1983;* Noel & Co., 4 Parliament Close, Prestwood, GREAT MISSENDEN, HP16 9DT.
•**NOEL, Mr. Charles William, MA FCA** *1972;* CW Noel & Co, 97 Harbord Street, LONDON, SW6 6PN.
•**NOEL, Mr. Clive, FCA FCCA** *1985;* (Tax Fac), Baker Noel Limited, Cheribourne House, 45A Station Road, Willington, BEDFORD, MK44 3QL.
•**NOEL, Mr. Edward James, BA FCA** *1989;* Two Plus Two Accounting Limited, Tous Ensamble, La Rue de Haut, St Lawrence, JERSEY, JE3 1JQ.
NOEL, Mr. Frank Joseph Anthony, FCA *1961;* 29 Ben Austins, Redbourn, ST. ALBANS, AL3 7DR. (Life Member)
NOEL, Mr. Jean Pierre Guy, BSc ACA *1981;* The Mauritius Commercial Bank, Sir William Newton Street, P O Box 52, PORT LOUIS, MAURITIUS.
•**NOEL, Ms. Linda Margaret, BSc FCA** *1977;* Noel & Co., 4 Parliament Close, Prestwood, GREAT MISSENDEN, HP16 9DT.
NOEL, Ms. Stella Kathleen, BSc ACA *1985;* Amerada Hess The Adelphi, 1-11 John Adam Street, LONDON, WC2N 6AG.
NOEL, Miss. Valerie Marie Frederique, MA ACA *2004;* C/ Calanda 6, 4 B, 28043 MADRID, SPAIN.
•**NOICE, Mrs. Karen Elizabeth, BSc ACA** *1995;* Duncan Noice Limited, 5 Cherrytree, Union Road, Nether Edge, SHEFFIELD, S11 9EF.
NOIK, Mr. Darryl Sean, FCA *1992;* 12 Foxmore Street, LONDON, SW11 4PU.
NOINTIN, Mr. Jikulin, BSc ACA *1991;* Jetama SDN BHD, Lot 8 AF11/12, 8th Floor Block A, Kompleks Karamunsing, 88300 KOTA KINABALU, MALAYSIA.
NOKE, The Revd. Christopher William, MA MSc FCA *1972;* Cedar Lodge, Church Road, Ham, RICHMOND, TW10 5HG.
NOKES, Mr. John Peter, FCA *1975;* The Old Vicarage, Little Bedwyn, MARLBOROUGH, WILTSHIRE, SN8 3JG.
NOKES, Mr. Michael John, FCA *1973;* 30 Northampton Lane, Dunchurch, RUGBY, CV22 6PS.
NOLAN, Mrs. Alexandra Clio Royde, BA(Hons) ACA *2001;* c/o MCS, PO Box 2740GT, GEORGE TOWN, GRAND CAYMAN, KY1-1111, CAYMAN ISLANDS.
NOLAN, Mr. Andrew Rigby, BA ACA *1998;* Seehaldenstrasse 17, CH 8802 KILCHBERG, SWITZERLAND.
•**NOLAN, Mrs. Anna Louise, BA ACA** *1993;* Anna Preedy, 45 Anne Boleyns Walk, Cheam, SUTTON, SURREY, SM3 8DE.
NOLAN, Mr. Antony Michael, BA ACA *1993;* Whirlpools' End, Rise Road, Skirlaugh, HULL, HU11 5BH.
NOLAN, Miss. Clare, BSc(Hons) ACA *2004;* 6 Holly Road, Aspull, WIGAN, LANCASHIRE, WN2 1RU.
NOLAN, Mr. David, BSc(Hons) ACA *2002;* RSM Tenon, Bentley Jennison Charter House, Legge Street, BIRMINGHAM, B4 7EU.
NOLAN, Mr. David John, BSc(Hons) ACA *2004;* Worldwide Clinical Trials UK Ltd Isaac Newton Centre, Nottingham Science & Technology Park, NOTTINGHAM, NG7 2RH.
NOLAN, Mr. David Rodney, FCA *1970;* 51 Backmoor Court, Backmoor Road, SHEFFIELD, S8 8LB.
NOLAN, Mr. Francis Edward Victor, MA FCA *1945;* The Aylsham Manor, Norwich Road, Aylsham, NORFOLK, NR11 6BN. (Life Member)
NOLAN, Mr. Gary James, BSc ACA *2007;* B E Aerospace (UK) Ltd Nissen House, Grovebury Road, LEIGHTON BUZZARD, BEDFORDSHIRE, LU7 4TB.
NOLAN, Mr. Henry Christopher, BSc FCA *1980;* 86 Kennylands Road, Sonning Common, READING, RG4 9JT.
NOLAN, Mr. Ian Michael, BA FCA *1988;* Mark Ash, Abinger Lane, Abinger Common, DORKING, SURREY, RH5 6JA.
NOLAN, Mr. Jeremy Grant, BA FCA *1970;* 19 Wynchgate Road, Hazel Grove, STOCKPORT, SK7 6NZ. (Life Member)
NOLAN, Mr. John Joseph, BSc ACA *1992;* Royal & Sunalliance, UK Finance, New Hall Place, PO Box 144, LIVERPOOL, L69 3EN.
NOLAN, Mr. John Mark, BA ACA *1997;* International Federation of Phonographic Industry, Swan Gardens 10 Piccadilly, LONDON, W1J 0DD.
NOLAN, Mrs. Julie Bo Ying, BA FCA *1990;* 66 Romney Close, HARROW, MIDDLESEX, HA2 7EH.
NOLAN, Mrs. Kate Rachel Elizabeth Cecilia, BSc ACA *1994;* Seehaldenstrasse 17, 8802 KILCHBERG, SWITZERLAND.
•**NOLAN, Mrs. Marion Nicola, FCA** *1984;* Saint & Co., 26 High Street, ANNAN, DG12 6AJ.
•**NOLAN, Mr. Mark John, BA(Hons) ACA CTA** *2004;* Nolan Williams Ltd, Kintyre House, 70 High Street, FAREHAM, HAMPSHIRE, PO16 7BB. See also Alliott Wingham Limited
NOLAN, Mr. Mark Peter, MSc BSc ACA *2007;* 44 Fox Chase Run, HILLSBOROUGH, NJ 08844, UNITED STATES.
NOLAN, Mr. Nicholas Robert, BA ACA *1986;* 7 Swinhoe Gardens, Woodlands Park, Wideopen, NEWCASTLE UPON TYNE, NE13 6AF.
NOLAN, Mr. Paul, BSc ACA *2005;* 881 North Bridge Road, 12-08 Southbank, SINGAPORE 198784, SINGAPORE.
NOLAN, Mr. Paul Stephen, FCA *1972;* 29 West Park Avenue, LEEDS, LS8 2EB. (Life Member)
NOLAN, Mr. Peter Leonard, MA ACA *1986;* Kelstedge Farm, Vernon Lane, Ashover, CHESTERFIELD, S45 0EA.
NOLAN, Mr. Richard, BA ACA *2010;* Flat 5, 21 Dartmouth Row, LONDON, SE10 8AW.
NOLAN, Mr. Roger Stephen, FCA *1973;* 16 Vaughan Avenue, TONBRIDGE, TN10 4EB.
NOLAN, Miss. Rosemary Anne, BA ACA *1999;* Level 14, 23 Hunter Street, SYDNEY, NSW 2000, AUSTRALIA.
NOLAN, Miss. Sally, BA FCA *1987;* 59 Ellerton Road, LONDON, SW18 3NQ.
NOLAN, Mr. Trevor Frank, PhD ACA *2001;* 19 Churchward Drive, Stretton, BURTON-ON-TRENT, DE13 0AU.
NOLAN, Mrs. Vanessa Maria, LLB FCA *1993;* (Tax Fac), South Lodge, 1 The Parade, Moor Road, FILEY, NORTH YORKSHIRE, YO14 9GA.
NOLAN, Mr. William Barrie, FCA *1957;* The Mistal, Dob Park, OTLEY, LS21 2NA. (Life Member)
NOLAND, Mr. Paul Stuart, BSc ACA *2005;* with Deloitte LLP, PO Box 500, 2 Hardman Street, MANCHESTER, M60 2AT.
•**NOLAS, Mr. Tasos Nicou, BSc FCA** *1997;* PricewaterhouseCoopers Limited, City House, 6 Karaiskakis Street, CY-3032 LIMASSOL, CYPRUS.
NOLLETH, Miss. Sarah, BA ACA *2005;* Flat 4 98 Clapham Common South Side, LONDON, SW4 9DN.
•**NOMANI, Mr. Muhammad Aslam Alam, BSc FCA MBA** *2001;* Javed & Co, 109 Hagley Road, Edgbaston, BIRMINGHAM, B16 8LA.
NOOKHWUN, Mr. Jaroong, BSc FCA *1971;* 112 Soi Areesampan 2, Paholyothin Road, BANGKOK, 10400, THAILAND.
NOON, Mrs. Beverley Denise, BA(Econ) ACA *1997;* 23 Howbeck Road, PRENTON, MERSEYSIDE, CH43 6TD.
•**NOON, Mr. David Allan, BA ACA** *1995;* Deloitte LLP, 2 New Street Square, LONDON, EC4A 3BZ. See also Deloitte & Touche LLP
NOON, Mrs. Kathryn Anne, ACA *1995;* Walton Lodge, North Kilworth, LUTTERWORTH, LEICESTERSHIRE, LE17 6JG.
NOON, Mr. Paul Victor, FCA *1968;* Bag End Cottage, Forest Lane, TADLEY, HAMPSHIRE, RG26 3NX.
•**NOON, Mrs. Teresa Anne, BSc ACA ATII CTA** *1990;* (Tax Fac), Indigo Tax & Accountancy Ltd, The Barn, Brighton Road, Lower Beeding, HORSHAM, WEST SUSSEX RH13 6PT.
NOONAN, Mr. Anthony, ACA *2008;* 30 Barbondale Close, Great Sankey, WARRINGTON, WA5 3HU.
NOONAN, Mrs. Mary Christina, BSc ACA *1987;* 49 Avenue Road, Dorridge, SOLIHULL, WEST MIDLANDS, B93 8JZ.
NOONAN, Mr. Stephen Francis, BA ACA *1986;* 49 Avenue Road, Dorridge, SOLIHULL, WEST MIDLANDS, B93 8JZ.
NOONAN, Mr. Thomas, MA ACA *1989;* 39 Clover Drive, Bartley Green, BIRMINGHAM, B32 3DJ.
NOONAN, Mr. Thomas Patrick, ACA *2009;* 44c, 44 Almeric Road, LONDON, SW11 1HL.
NOONE, Mrs. Caroline Anne, BA ACA CTA *1983;* (Tax Fac), North Lea House, 66 Northfield End, HENLEY-ON-THAMES, OXFORDSHIRE, RG9 2BE.
NOONE, Mr. Derek Andrew, ACA *1984;* Oak House Stortford Road, Hatfield Heath, BISHOP'S STORTFORD, HERTFORDSHIRE, CM22 7DL.
NOONE, Miss. Julie Ann, BA ACA *1991;* Kaplan Financial, 10-14 White Lion Street, LONDON, N1 9PD.
NOONE, Mr. Stephen Anthony, BA ACA *2001;* Apartment 8, 4 Maida Vale, LONDON, W9 1SP.
NOOR, Mr. Bashir Ahmed, BSc ACA *2010;* 49 Jellicoe Avenue, GRAVESEND, DA12 5HU.
NOOR, Mr. Qaiser, ACA ACMA *2009;* Ashcroft Long Mill Lane, Platt, SEVENOAKS, TN15 8LG.
•**NOORANI, Mr. Asad Fazal, FCA** *1976;* Tayabali-Tomlin Limited, Kenton House, Oxford Street, MORETON-IN-MARSH, GLOUCESTERSHIRE, GL56 0LA.
NOORANI, Mr. Mustafa Abassbhai, FCA *1974;* 71 Murray Avenue, BROMLEY, BR1 3DJ.
•**NOORIZADEH, Mr. Hamid, BA FCA** *1982;* Boroumand & Associates, 6th Floor, 94-96 Wigmore Street, LONDON, W1U 3RF.
NOORMOHAMED, Mr. Aly, BSc ACA *1992;* 2909 Broken Bow Way, PLANO, TX 75093, UNITED STATES.
•**NOORMOHAMED-OOSMAN, Mr. Mushtaq Mohamed Oomar, FCA** *1981;* PricewaterhouseCoopers, 18 CyberCity, EBENE, MAURITIUS.

NOORUDDIN, Mr. Riyaz, ACA *2009;* PO Box 905, GEORGE TOWN, GRAND CAYMAN, KY1-1103, CAYMAN ISLANDS.
NOR, Mr. Abu Bakar Bin Haji Mohd, BSc ACA *1981;* Peremba (Malaysia) Sdn Bhd, Level 10 Block A, Peremba Square, Saujana Resort, Seksyen U2, 40150 SHAH ALAM SELANGOR MALAYSIA.
NORAT, Mr. Adil, ACA *2008;* 27 Nigel Road, LONDON, E7 8AW.
NORBURY, Mrs. Heather Diane, BAcc ACA *2003;* Moor End Barn, 100 Moor End Road, Mellor, STOCKPORT, CHESHIRE, SK6 5NQ.
NORBURY, Mr. James Frederick, FCA *1964;* 1 Pendleton Avenue, ROSSENDALE, LANCASHIRE, BB4 8UX.
NORBURY, Mr. John Karel, BSc FCA *1968;* Station House, Station Road, MUCH WENLOCK, SHROPSHIRE, TF13 6JE. (Life Member)
•**NORBURY, Mr. Paul John, BSc ACA** *1998;* PricewaterhouseCoopers LLP, Exchange House, Central Business Exchange, Midsummer Boulevard, MILTON KEYNES, MK9 2DF. See also PricewaterhouseCoopers
NORBURY, Mr. Richard John, BSc ACA *2010;* 5 Henry Road, Beeston, NOTTINGHAM, NG9 2BE.
NORBURY, Mr. Robert Leslie, FCA *1960;* Flat 10, 29-31 Sloane Court West, LONDON, SW3 4TE. (Life Member)
NORCLIFFE, Mr. Mark Ian, BA ACA *1989;* Big Hand Ltd, 27 Union Street, LONDON, SE1 1SD.
NORCOTT, Mr. Kevin David, BEng ACA *2005;* 35 Brookfield, West Allotment, NEWCASTLE UPON TYNE, NE27 0BJ.
NORDAL, Mrs. Gillean Annabel Dean, LLB ACA *2003;* Deloitte AS, Karenslyst Alle 20, PB 347, Skoyen, 0213 OSLO, NORWAY.
NORDEN, Mr. Geoffrey Robert, FCA *1956;* 13 Redlands Road, SEVENOAKS, TN13 2JZ. (Life Member)
•**NORDEN, Mr. Mark, FCA** *1990;* Mark Norden & Co Limited, 158 Hermon Hill, South Woodford, LONDON, E18 1QH.
NORDIN, Miss. Nita, BA(Hons) ACA *2003;* NO 15 JALAN SS1/2, KAMPUNG TUNGKU, 47300 PETALING JAYA, MALAYSIA.
NORDIN, Mr. Norhazardin Shah, BSc ACA *2004;* The Bank of New York Mellon, The Bank of New York Mellon Centre, 160 Queen Victoria Street, LONDON, EC4V 4LA.
NOREY, Mr. Ronald George, FCA *1957;* Beech House, Pen-y-Lan, COWBRIDGE, CF71 7RY. (Life Member)
NORFOLK, Ms. Carol Ann, MA ACA *1986;* 46 Percival Road, Hillmorton, RUGBY, CV22 5JT.
NORFOLK, Mr. Edward Lionel Stanley, FCA *1976;* 40 Bower Mount Road, MAIDSTONE, ME16 8AU. (Life Member)
•**NORFOLK, Mr. Graham Richard, BA ACA** *1990;* Acorn Capital Partners Limited, Metropolitan House, Station Road, Cheadle Hulme, CHEADLE, CHESHIRE SK8 7AZ.
NORFOLK, Mr. Howard William, FCA *1974;* 7 Pine Crest, WELWYN, HERTFORDSHIRE, AL6 0EQ.
•**NORFOLK, Mr. James Barry, FCA** *1967;* J B Norfolk & Co, 12 Chatsworth Grove, Boroughbridge, YORK, YO51 9BB.
NORFOLK, Mrs. Julie, BSc ACA *1990;* Fawside Farm, Longnor, BUXTON, DERBYSHIRE, SK17 0RA.
NORFOLK, Miss. Lucy, ACA *2006;* 1a Barker Place, LEEDS, LS13 4BU.
NORFOLK, Mr. Malcolm David, FCA *1967;* 6 Carr Close, Rawdon, LEEDS, LS19 6PE.
•**NORFOLK, Mr. Robert Geoffrey, BSc ACA** *2008;* Bryan and Ridge, The Gatehouse, 2 Devonhurst Place, Heathfield Terrace, LONDON, W4 4JD.
NORFOLK, Mr. Stanley, FCA *1951;* Highways, Cubert, NEWQUAY, TR8 5HJ. (Life Member)
NORGATE, Ms. Lucy, BCom ACA *1994;* (Tax Fac), 9a Briarwood, Finchampstead, WOKINGHAM, BERKSHIRE, RG40 4XA.
NORGATE, Mr. Mark Kenneth, BA ACA *1995;* 15 Bickfords Green, Liverton, NEWTON ABBOT, TQ12 6GH.
NORGETT, Mr. Ian Martin, FCA *1969;* 166 London Road, BRAINTREE, CM77 7QF.
NORGROVE, Miss. Riah, BA(Hons) ACA *2011;* K P M G Llp, 15 Canada Square, LONDON, E14 5GL.
NORIEL, Mr. Nodilio Jasper, BA ACA *2006;* 46 Harbinger Road, LONDON, E14 3AA.
NORMAN, Mr. Andrew Peter Livesay, BSc ACA *1988;* 1 Wallett Court Cottages, Southernden Road Headcorn, ASHFORD, TN27 9LN.
NORMAN, Mrs. Antoinette Elizabeth, BSc FCA *1978;* 7 Priestlands Park Road, SIDCUP, DA15 7HR.
NORMAN, Mrs. Bethan, MSc ACA *1991;* 21 Malvern Close, WORTHING, BN11 2HE.
NORMAN, Miss. Charlotte Mary, BA(Hons) ACA *2002;* (Tax Fac), 35 Westwater Way, DIDCOT, OXFORDSHIRE, OX11 7SN.
•①**NORMAN, Mr. Christopher, BA ACA MIPA FABRP** *1988;* with Begbies Traynor (Central) LLP, First Floor, Balliol House, Southernhay Gardens, EXETER, EX1 1NP.
NORMAN, Mrs. Claire Helen, ACA *1988;* Timbers, Perry Hill, Worplesdon, GUILDFORD, GU3 3RB.
NORMAN, Mrs. Claire Joanne, BA(Hons) ACA *2000;* 103 Merthyrmawr Road, BRIDGEND, MID GLAMORGAN, CF31 3NS.
NORMAN, Mr. Colin Peter, BA ACA *1980;* 364 Crewe Road, Wistaston, CREWE, CW2 6QR.
NORMAN, Mr. Daryl Peter Thomas, BSc ACA *1998;* 19 Fairways, Braiswick, COLCHESTER, CO4 5TX.
NORMAN, Mr. David Charles, FCA *1973;* NGI Ltd, Norman House, La Grande Route de St. Martin, St. Saviour, JERSEY, JE2 7GR.
NORMAN, Mr. David John, FCA *1984;* (Tax Fac), Deneclough, 31 Woodlands Lane, Quarndon, DERBY, DE22 5JU.
NORMAN, Mr. Dean Anthony, BSc ACA *2001;* 2 Pobbles Close, Southgate, SWANSEA, SA3 2BW.
NORMAN, Mrs. Diane Elizabeth, BSc ACA *1990;* Laurel Cottage, Gussage St. Michael, WIMBORNE, DORSET, BH21 5HX.
NORMAN, Miss. Eilidh Elliot, BA ACA *2001;* TaxPro Sàrl, 2 Rue de la Faïencerie, 1227 CAROUGE, SWITZERLAND.
NORMAN, Ms. Emma Alexandra Elisabeth, MA ACA *2000;* 6 Netheravon Road, LONDON, W4 2NA.
•**NORMAN, Mr. Geoffrey Kenneth, BA FCA** *1974;* (Member of Council 2001 - 2005), Badgers, Buckley Green, HENLEY-IN-ARDEN, B95 5QE.
NORMAN, Mr. Harold William, FCA *1940;* 35 Fairlawn, Hall Place Drive, WEYBRIDGE, KT13 0AY. (Life Member)
NORMAN, Miss. Heather Joy, FCA *1988;* 1b Montagu Street, Eynesbury, ST. NEOTS, CAMBRIDGESHIRE, PE19 2TD.
NORMAN, Miss. Helen Louise, ACA *2008;* 43 Dawson Road, KINGSTON UPON THAMES, KT1 3AU.
NORMAN, Mr. Ian Stuart, MA ACA *1994;* Telecom New Zealand Limited, PO Box 293, WELLINGTON, NEW ZEALAND.
•**NORMAN, Mr. Jeffrey Michael, BSc FCA** *1969;* 8 Priory View, Bushey Heath, BUSHEY, WD23 4GN.
NORMAN, Mr. John, MSc BSS FCA *1971;* 65/1 Albert Road, MELBOURNE, VIC 3004, AUSTRALIA. (Life Member)
NORMAN, Mr. John Anthony George, BA FCA *1974;* Thatches, South Street, Holcombe Rogus, WELLINGTON, SOMERSET, TA21 0PD.
•**NORMAN, Ms. Kerry Louise, BA ACA** *2000;* 139 Beeleigh Link, CHELMSFORD, CM2 6PH.
NORMAN, Mr. Leslie, FCA *1971;* LGL Trustees Limited, P.O Box 167 3rd Floor Hill Street, ST HELIER, JE4 8RY.
NORMAN, Miss. Lucy Emma, BA ACA *2010;* 24 Hill Grove, BRISTOL, BS9 4RJ.
NORMAN, Mr. Mark Richard, BA ACA *1989;* 19 Burpham Lane, GUILDFORD, GU4 7LN.
NORMAN, Mr. Matthew James, BSc ACA *1998;* 31 Bloomfield Road, HARPENDEN, HERTFORDSHIRE, AL5 4DD.
•**NORMAN, Mrs. Melanie Jane, ACA** *1993;* Le Cache Accounting Limited, Le Courtil Cache Rue de la Cache, St. Andrew, GUERNSEY, GY6 8TH.
•**NORMAN, Mr. Michael Barney, FCA** *1969;* (Tax Fac), M B Norman Limited, 46-48 Nelson Road, TUNBRIDGE WELLS, KENT, TN2 5AN.
NORMAN, Mr. Michael Charles, BSc ACA FCIPD *1991;* 64 Farm Road, MAIDENHEAD, BERKSHIRE, SL6 5JD.
NORMAN, Miss. Michelle, BA ACA *2010;* 12 Campion Park, Up Hatherley, CHELTENHAM, GLOUCESTERSHIRE, GL51 3WA.
•**NORMAN, Mr. Nigel Andrew, FCA** *1977;* N.A. Norman & Co., 31 High Street, Winslow, BUCKINGHAM, MK18 3HE.
NORMAN, Mr. Paul, BEng ACA *2007;* B2 Group, Abbey Business Centres, 53 Fountain Street, MANCHESTER, M2 2AN.
NORMAN, Mr. Peter, BCom ACA *1984;* 6 Park Avenue, Crosby, LIVERPOOL, L23 2SP.
•**NORMAN, Mr. Peter John, FCA** *1974;* Peter John Norman FCA, Bosgarrack, Hellangove Farm, Gulval, PENZANCE, CORNWALL TR20 8XD.
NORMAN, Mr. Peter John, FCA *1959;* 18 Oakside Close, Evington, LEICESTER, LE5 6SN. (Life Member)
NORMAN, Mr. Philip, BSc ACA *2010;* 60 Victoria Court, New Street, CHELMSFORD, CM1 1GP.
NORMAN, Mr. Philip, BA ACA *1993;* La Grange, La Rue Des Boulees, Trinity, JERSEY, JE3 5HN.
NORMAN, Mr. Philip Alfred, FCA *1974;* 6th Floor, 155 Fenchurch Street, LONDON, EC3M 6AL.
NORMAN, Mr. Richard Francis, FCA *1963;* 5 Thames Crescent, MAIDENHEAD, BERKSHIRE, SL6 8EY.
NORMAN, Mr. Robert, BA ACA *1999;* Flybe Jack Walker House, Exeter Airport Clyst Honiton, EXETER, EX5 2HL.
•**NORMAN, Mr. Robert Andrew, BSc FCA** *1983;* Moore and Smalley LLP, Fylde House, Skyways Commercial Campus, Amy Johnson Way, BLACKPOOL, FY4 3RS.
NORMAN, Mr. Robert Michael Neville, BA ACA *1988;* Timbers, Perry Hill, Worplesdon, GUILDFORD, SURREY, GU3 3RB.
NORMAN, Mr. Rodney Hugh, BA FCA *1989;* 12 Grange Park Place, LONDON, SW20 0EE.
NORMAN, Miss. Sarah, BSc ACA *1998;* 260 Beverley Road, Anlaby, HULL, HU10 7BG.
•**NORMAN, Mr. Simon, BSc ACA** *1997;* 261 High Street, Eston, MIDDLESBROUGH, CLEVELAND, TS6 8DA.
•**NORMAN, Mr. Stewart Stanley, BSc FCA** *1976;* (Tax Fac), CW Energy LLP, 4th Floor, 40 Queen Street, LONDON, EC4R 1DD. See also CW Energy Tax Consultants Ltd
NORMAN, Mr. Thomas Matthew, BSc ACA *2010;* 21 Orchard Drive, WOKING, SURREY, GU21 4BN.
NORMAN, Mr. Tim, BSc(Econ) ACA *1995;* Kraft Foods, St. Georges House, Bayshill Road, CHELTENHAM, GLOUCESTERSHIRE, GL50 3AE.
NORMAN, Mr. Timothy John, BSc ACA *2001;* 82/8 Water Street, BIRCHGROVE, NSW 2041, AUSTRALIA.
NORMAN, Mr. Trevor Lennard, BA FCA TEP *1983;* 1 Le Jardin de L'Est, La Rue de la Rosiere St. Mary, JERSEY, JE3 3DG.
NORMAN, Mrs. Victoria Ann, BSc ACA *1995;* 50 Berkeley Street, LONDON, W1J 8HA.
NORMAN, Mrs. Victoria Jane, BA(Hons) ACA *2002;* 18 Beresford Park, Thornhill, SUNDERLAND, SR2 7JU.
NORMAND, Mrs. Clare Joanna, BA ACA *1993;* St. Johns, Bishopswood Lane, Baughurst, TADLEY, RG26 5LT.
NORMAND, Mr. James Patrick, FCA *1979;* 36 Englewood Road, LONDON, SW12 9NZ.
NORMANDALE, Mr. Christopher John, FCA *1953;* Tollgate Cottage, 57 North Trade Road, BATTLE, TN33 0HS. (Life Member)
NORMILE, Mr. Andrew Terence, BA ACA *1996;* 335 Watford Road, ST. ALBANS, HERTFORDSHIRE, AL2 3DA.
NORMINGTON, Mrs. Desiree Frances, LLB ACA *1999;* 3 Ash Grove, PUDSEY, WEST YORKSHIRE, LS28 8PA.
NORMINGTON, Mr. Duncan Macrae, BA ACA *2005;* W M Robb Ltd Unit 3, Bamfurlong Industrial Park Staverton, CHELTENHAM, GLOUCESTERSHIRE, GL51 6SX.
NORMINGTON, Mr. John Philip, BSc ACA *1999;* Sycamore House, Briggate, Nesfield, ILKLEY, LS29 0BS.
NORMINGTON, Mr. Michael Charles, BSc ACA *1981;* C/O Corporate Pensions 7th Floor, Unilever Plc Unilever House, 100 Victoria Embankment, LONDON, EC4Y 0DY.
NORONHA, Mr. Ivan Francis, FCA *1968;* Avenida Santa Lucia 1501, Fazendinha, 06355 450 Carapicuiba, SAO PAULO, BRAZIL.
•**NORONHA, Miss. Michele Bernadette, BA ACA** *1993;* M B Noronha, 15 Sandy Lane, West Kirby, WIRRAL, MERSEYSIDE, CH48 3HY.
NORONHA, Miss. Sonia, LLB ACA *2002;* 40 Wolmer Gardens, EDGWARE, MIDDLESEX, HA8 8QD.
NORRIDGE, Ms. Philippa Kate, BA ACA *2007;* Albion, 1.03 The Tea Building, 56 Shoreditch High Street, LONDON, E1 6JJ.
NORRIE, Mr. Andrew Guy, BA ACA *1998;* Olive Catering Services Ltd, Barn Farm, Sibson Road, Ratcliffe Culey, ATHERSTONE, WARWICKSHIRE CV9 3PH.
•**NORRIE, Mr. Michael Anthony, FCA CF** *1975;* Castle Corporate Finance Limited, 158 High Street, TONBRIDGE, KENT, TN9 1BB.
NORRIE, Mr. Redvers, ACA CA(AUS) *2009;* 20 Prah Road, Finsbury Park, LONDON, N4 2RB.
NORRIE, Mr. Roger Thomas, FCA *1965;* Rivers Keep, 140 Itchen Stoke, ALRESFORD, HAMPSHIRE, SO24 0QZ. (Life Member)
NORRINGTON, Mr. James, ACA MAAT *2011;* 17 Greenhill Avenue, CATERHAM, CR3 6PR.
NORRINGTON, Mrs. Nicola Dorothy, BSc ACA *1999;* Archimedes Pharma Limited, 250 South Oak Way, Green Park, READING, RG2 6UG.
NORRINGTON, Mr. Peter John Courtenay, BSc FCA *1977;* 25 Reeds Avenue, Earley, READING, RG6 5SP.
NORRINGTON, Mr. Simon Guy, BSc ACA *1998;* 40 Ditton Place, Ditton, AYLESFORD, KENT, ME20 6SX.
NORRIS, Mr. Allan William, FCA *1977;* J P Morgan Chase, 125 London Wall, LONDON, EC2Y 5AJ.
NORRIS, Mr. Andrew Michael, BA ACA *1993;* 2 Grove Hill Gardens, TUNBRIDGE WELLS, TN1 1SS.
NORRIS, Mr. Andrew Paul, MA MSci ACA *2003;* with PricewaterhouseCoopers LLP, 1 Embankment Place, LONDON, WC2N 6RH.
NORRIS, Mr. Anthony, BA ACA *1991;* with RSM Tenon Limited, Salisbury House, 31 Finsbury Circus, LONDON, EC2M 5SQ.
•**NORRIS, Mr. Antony Alfred, ACA** *1982;* Antony Norris ACA Ltd, 31 Vicarage Crescent, Grenoside, SHEFFIELD, S35 8RE.
NORRIS, Mr. Benedict James, BA ACA *1997;* 16 Stuart Road, LONDON, SW19 8DH.
NORRIS, Mr. Benjamin Charles, BA(Hons) ACA *2003;* 3 Crewdson Road, LONDON, SW9 0LH.
NORRIS, Mr. Benjamin Edward, BA ACA *1998;* Highbridge, Highbridge Lane, East Chiltington, LEWES, EAST SUSSEX, BN7 3QY.
NORRIS, Mr. Christopher, ACA *2010;* 705/610 St Kilda Road, MELBOURNE, VIC 3004, AUSTRALIA.
NORRIS, Mr. Cyril, FCA *1967;* 54 Dales Lane, Whitefield, MANCHESTER, M45 7NN. (Life Member)
NORRIS, Mr. David, BSc ACA *2011;* 10 Haywain, OXTED, SURREY, RH8 9LL.
NORRIS, Mr. David Alan, FCA *1969;* Wey Lodge, Amerden Close, Bath Road, MAIDENHEAD, SL6 0EF.
•**NORRIS, Mr. David John, MA ACA** *1978;* (Tax Fac), 20 Cattley Close, BARNET, HERTFORDSHIRE, EN5 4SN.
NORRIS, Mr. David John, BA FCA *1997;* Springdale, Combe Raleigh, HONITON, DEVON, EX14 4TN.
NORRIS, Mr. David Oliver, BSc ACA *1983;* Keble House, 7 Manorfields, Putney, LONDON, SW15 3LS.
•**NORRIS, Mr. David William Worsley, BA FCA** *1971;* AIMS - David Norris, Tidmarsh House, Tidmarsh Lane, Pangbourne, READING, RG8 8HA.
NORRIS, Miss. Deborah Joy, BA ACA *1995;* (Tax Fac), 44a Whippingham Street, BRIGHTON, BN2 3LL.
NORRIS, Mrs. Delia Mary, FCA *1966;* Maidencroft Little Frieth, Frieth, HENLEY-ON-THAMES, OXFORDSHIRE, RG9 6NU.
NORRIS, Mr. Derek John, BSc FCA *1975;* 358 Lelekepue Place, HONOLULU, HI 96821, UNITED STATES.
NORRIS, Mr. Gareth Martin, ACA *2008;* MacIntyre Hudson, Peterbridge House, 3 The Lakes, NORTHAMPTON, NN4 7HB.
NORRIS, Ms. Genevieve Margaret, BSc ACA *1991;* 40 Goodings Green, WOKINGHAM, RG40 1SB.
NORRIS, Mr. Gordon Andrew, BA ACA *1988;* MacIntyre Hudson Llp, 30-34 New Bridge Street, LONDON, EC4V 6BJ.
NORRIS, Mr. Gordon Hubert, FCA *1951;* 29 Queens Court, Alderham Close, SOLIHULL, WEST MIDLANDS, B91 2PR. (Life Member)
NORRIS, Mr. Gordon Jack, BSc FCA *1977;* Keymer Tiles Ltd, Nye Road, BURGESS HILL, WEST SUSSEX, RH15 0LZ.
NORRIS, Mrs. Helen Mair, BCom ACA *1988;* Yalham Farm, Culmhead, TAUNTON, SOMERSET, TA3 7ED.
NORRIS, Mr. Ian Philip, FCA *1952;* Cherry Tree Cottage, 43 Locks Ride, ASCOT, BERKSHIRE, SL5 8QZ. (Life Member)
NORRIS, Mr. Ian William, BSc ACA *1990;* (Tax Fac), 88 Abbeydale Park Rise, SHEFFIELD, S17 3PF.
NORRIS, Mr. John, BA FCA *1955;* 47 Moor Crescent, NEWCASTLE UPON TYNE, NE3 4AQ. (Life Member)
NORRIS, Mr. John David, BSc ACA *1983;* with PricewaterhouseCoopers LLP, 31 Great George Street, BRISTOL, BS1 5QD.
NORRIS, Mr. John David George, BSc ACA *1988;* 46b Holmesdale Road, TEDDINGTON, MIDDLESEX, TW11 9LF.
NORRIS, Mr. John Randall, FCA *1951;* 10 Willow Drive, DROITWICH, WORCESTERSHIRE, WR9 7QE. (Life Member)
NORRIS, Mr. Karl John, BA ACA *2001;* 55 Parkedge Close, LEIGH, LANCASHIRE, WN7 3UR.
NORRIS, Mr. Kenneth James, LLB FCA *1964;* 27 Highfield Drive, Standish, WIGAN, WN6 0EJ.
NORRIS, Mr. Mark Edward Michael, BA FCA *1987;* 39 Brattle Wood, SEVENOAKS, KENT, TN13 1QS.
NORRIS, Mr. Mark Graham, LLB FCA *1985;* 5 Lesnaya Street, Building B, 125047 MOSCOW, RUSSIAN FEDERATION.
NORRIS, Mrs. Mary-Anne, BSc ACA *1983;* 17 The Squirrels, PINNER, HA5 3BD.

NORRIS - NORVAL Members - Alphabetical

NORRIS, Mrs. Melanie Louise, MA ACA *1992;* 2 Grove Hill Gardens, TUNBRIDGE WELLS, TN1 1SS.
NORRIS, Mr. Michael John, BSc FCA *1977;* 16 Mount Ararat Road, RICHMOND, TW10 6PA.
NORRIS, Mr. Michael Victor, FCA *1978;* 12 Glebe Avenue, HARROGATE, HG2 0LT.
NORRIS, Miss. Nicola, BA(Hons) ACA *2011;* 107 Lucas Avenue, CHELMSFORD, CM2 9JP.
NORRIS, Mr. Paul Francis Walter, ACA MBA *1996;* Institute of Cancer Research, 123 Old Brompton Road, LONDON, SW7 3RP.
NORRIS, Mr. Peter John, BA ACA *1988;* 17 Barncroft Way, ST. ALBANS, HERTFORDSHIRE, AL1 5QZ.
NORRIS, Mr. Peter Richard, BSc ACA CFA *1993;* Imagine Group, 4th Floor, 70 Gracechurch Street, LONDON, EC3V 0XL.
NORRIS, Mr. Peter Walter, BA(Hons) FCA *1995;* 436 Thornaby Road Thornaby, STOCKTON-ON-TEES, CLEVELAND, TS17 8QH.
NORRIS, Mr. Richard Anthony, BA FCA *1969;* 66 Sheffield Terrace, MARLBOROUGH, MA 01752, UNITED STATES.
NORRIS, Mr. Richard Charles, BA ACA *1999;* 16 Lionel Court, DUNCRAIG, WA 6023, AUSTRALIA.
NORRIS, Mr. Richard George, FCA *1969;* 26 Sutton Court, Chiswick, LONDON, W4 3JE.
NORRIS, Mr. Richard Paul, FCA *1970;* 14A Taurou Street, P.O. Box 21039, CY-1500 NICOSIA, CYPRUS.
NORRIS, Mr. Robert, BA ACA CTA *1984;* (Tax Fac), 18 Cransley Grove, SOLIHULL, B91 3ZA.
NORRIS, Mr. Robert Michael, BSc FCA *1975;* 25 Browns Coppice Avenue, SOLIHULL, WEST MIDLANDS, B91 1PL.
NORRIS, Mr. Robert Stirling, BSc FCA *1990;* 70 Av. General Guisan, CH1009 PULLY, SWITZERLAND.
NORRIS, Mr. Rodwell Harvey, FCA *1959;* 7 Balfour Road, SOUTHPORT, PR8 6LE. (Life Member)
NORRIS, Mr. Steven Anthony, BEng ACA *1994;* with PricewaterhouseCoopers LLP, 31 Great George Street, BRISTOL, BS1 5QD.
NORRIS, Mr. Steven Robert, BSc ACA *2007;* Lockhart Catering Equipment Lockhart House, Brunel Road Theale, READING, RG7 4XE.
NORRIS, Mr. Trevor, FCA *1984;* Arden House, 17, Highfield Road, Edgbaston, BIRMINGHAM, B15 3DU.
NORRIS, Mr. Walter John, FCA *1972;* 38 Tiverton Drive, NUNEATON, CV11 6YL.
NORRIS CERVETTO, Mrs. Rachel Elizabeth, ACA *2010;* Expro International Group Davidson House, Forbury Square, READING, RG1 3EU.
NORRIS-SMALL, Mr. Jonathan James, BSc ACA *2010;* Flat 6 Clarke Court, 81 Clarkehouse Road, SHEFFIELD, S10 2LG.
•NORRIS-SMALL, Mr. Leslie Edward, BA FCA *1972;* Norris-Small, 2 Camino Road, Harborne, BIRMINGHAM, B32 3XE.
NORRMAN, Mr. Bjorn Gunnar, ACA *2010;* Flat P, 4 Windsock Close, LONDON, SE16 7FL.
NORTCLIFFE, Mrs. Alexandra Jane, ACA *2005;* 18 Woodlands Drive, Garforth, LEEDS, LS25 2JW.
NORTH, Mr. Andrew Christopher, BSc FCA *1993;* 8 Shelley Crescent, Oulton, LEEDS, LS26 8ER.
NORTH, Mr. Andrew Hilary Lauraine, FCA *1968;* 33 Wellesley Road, LONDON, W4 4BU.
•NORTH, Mr. Barry Edward, FCA *1962;* (Tax Fac), North & Co (Accounts & Tax) Limited, Suite 3, The Old Stables, Hillhurst Farm, Westenhanger, HYTHE KENT CT21 4HU.
NORTH, Mr. Brendan John, ACA *2008;* 2 Greenview, Seabrook Manor, Station Road, Portmarnock, DUBLIN, COUNTY DUBLIN IRELAND.
NORTH, Mr. Charles Michael, BA ACA ATII *1982;* 70 Ashley Road, WALTON-ON-THAMES, KT12 1HR.
NORTH, Mrs. Claire, BSc ACA *2011;* 18 Cartwright Way, Beeston, NOTTINGHAM, NG9 1RL.
NORTH, Mr. David, BA ACA *2006;* Flat 1, 34 Craven Street, LONDON, WC2N 5NP.
NORTH, Mr. David Ian, LLB FCA *1962;* The Briars, Barmby Moor, YORK, YO42 4HQ. (Life Member)
NORTH, Mr. David John, BA FCA *1984;* White Lodge, 4 Hill Rise, Chalfont St. Peter, GERRARDS CROSS, BUCKINGHAMSHIRE, SL9 9BH.
NORTH, Mr. David St John, LLB ACA *1999;* 1 Glenbank Road, Lenzie Kirkintilloch, GLASGOW, G66 5AG.
NORTH, Mr. Donald Henry, FCA *1953;* Jesters, The Street, BETCHWORTH, RH3 7DJ. (Life Member)
NORTH, Mr. Gavin Walter, BSc ACA *1994;* 161 Millisle Road, DONAGHADEE, COUNTY DOWN, BT21 0LA.
NORTH, Mr. Harold, FCA *1953;* Flat 3, 3 Byron Court, Beech Grove, HARROGATE, NORTH YORKSHIRE, HG2 0LL. (Life Member)
NORTH, Mrs. Helen Margaret, MEng FCA ACA *2004;* 12 Shiels Drive, Bradley Stoke, BRISTOL, BS32 8EA.
•NORTH, Mr. Ian Reginald, BSc FCA *1980;* Ian R. North, 12 Manvers House, Pioneer Close, Wath-upon-Dearne, ROTHERHAM, SOUTH YORKSHIRE S63 7JZ.
•NORTH, Mrs. Jill Margaret, FCA *1978;* Avalon Accounting, Equity House, 4-6 School Road, Tilehurst, READING, RG31 5AL. See also Lee Consulting Limited
NORTH, Mr. John Harry, FCA FSI *1959;* 14C Homefield Road, Wimbledon, LONDON, SW19 4QF.
NORTH, Mrs. Judith Anne, BEd ACA *1991;* (Tax Fac), 10 Clarence Road, TEDDINGTON, TW11 0BQ.
NORTH, Mrs. Kathryn Audrey, BSc ACA *1984;* Rough Acres, Comp Lane, Platt, SEVENOAKS, KENT, TN15 8NP.
NORTH, Mrs. Katie, BSc ACA *2001;* 23 Red Cap Lane, BOSTON, LINCOLNSHIRE, PE21 9LJ.
NORTH, Mrs. Katrina Lorraine, ACA MAAT *2004;* 15 Oaklands Grove, WATERLOOVILLE, PO8 8PR.
NORTH, Mrs. Lana, BSc ACA *1993;* Barnstones, 1 Millway, REIGATE, SURREY, RH2 0RH.
NORTH, Mr. Malcolm Richard, BA FCA *1979;* 14 Farnaby Gardens, High Green, SHEFFIELD, S35 4FZ.
NORTH, Mr. Neil Leslie, FCA *1963;* 7 The Burrows, Narborough, LEICESTER, LE19 3WS.
NORTH, Mr. Peter Watson, FCA *1948;* Linksway, May Tree Lane, STANMORE, HA7 3RZ. (Life Member)
NORTH, Mr. Rhys James, BSc ACA *1989;* Farnley Park High School Chapel Lane, New Farnley, LEEDS, LS12 5EU.
NORTH, Mr. Richard Conway, MA FCA *1976;* 8 St Simons Avenue, LONDON, SW15 6DU.
NORTH, Mr. Robert Charles, BSc ACA *1985;* Rough Acres, Comp Lane, Platt, SEVENOAKS, KENT, TN15 8NP.
NORTH, Mr. Robert John Roger, FCA *1967;* 14 Poppyfields Drive, Snettisham, KING'S LYNN, PE31 7UD.
NORTH, Mr. Rodney Cappus, VRD FCA CTA CPFA *1961;* 12 Buchanan's Wharf North, Ferry Street, BRISTOL, BS1 6HN. (Life Member)
NORTH, Mr. Russell Alan, BA ACA *1992;* National Grid Plc, 1-3 Strand, LONDON, WC2N 5EH.
NORTH, Mr. Stephen William, BA FCA *1976;* 2 Warren Close, Woodsetts, WORKSOP, NOTTINGHAMSHIRE, S81 8SL.
NORTH, Mrs. Susan Joyce, ACA *1983;* Kaplan Financial, The Blade, Abbey Street, READING, RG1 3BA.
NORTH-COOMBES, Mr. James Christopher Paul, ACA *2008;* Farthings, Brox Lane, Ottershaw, CHERTSEY, SURREY, KT16 0LL.
NORTHAGE, Mr. Derek Henry, FCA JDipMA *1955;* Al Arish, Halls Road, Mow Cop, STOKE-ON-TRENT, ST7 3NR. (Life Member)
NORTHAGE, Mr. Ross Frank, FCA *1974;* 2 Alvanley Court, Fairweather Green, BRADFORD, WEST YORKSHIRE, BD8 0NG.
NORTHALL, Mrs. Rebecca Louise, ACA *2005;* Bryn Melyn Care, 2 High Street Dawley, TELFORD, SHROPSHIRE, TF4 2ET.
NORTHALL, Mr. Ross James, ACA *2008;* 46 Causey Farm Road, Hayley Green, HALESOWEN, WEST MIDLANDS, B63 1EL.
NORTHAM, Mr. James William, MSc FCA *1967;* 5660 Southern Hills Drive, FRISCO, TX 75034, UNITED STATES.
•NORTHCOTT, Mr. Barry James, FCA *1963;* Barry J. Northcott, Langstone Manor Cottage, Brentor, TAVISTOCK, DEVON, PL19 0NE.
NORTHCOTT, Mr. Brian Edward, FCA *1972;* 41 Seymour Park, Mannamead, PLYMOUTH, PL3 5BQ. (Life Member)
NORTHCOTT, Mr. Francis Richard, FCA *1970;* 5 Seymour Walk, LONDON, SW10 9NE.
NORTHCOTT, Mr. Geoffrey, BA FCA *1965;* 10 Wren Close, Northam, BIDEFORD, DEVON, EX39 1UU.
•NORTHCOTT, Mr. Guy Ian, BSc FCA DChA *1990;* Northcott Trumfield, Devonshire Villa, 52 Stuart Road, Stoke, PLYMOUTH, PL3 4EE.
NORTHCOTT, Dr. Mark Edward, BSc ACA *1993;* Fairlea The Village, Burrington, BRISTOL, BS40 7AD.
NORTHCOTT, Mrs. Victoria Kathryne, BSc ACA *1994;* Woodbury House Yarkhill, HEREFORD, HR1 3SU.
NORTHCROFT, Mr. David, FCA *1966;* Rock Hill House, Egerton, ASHFORD, KENT, TN27 9DP. (Life Member)
NORTHEDGE, Mr. David John, FCA *1961;* 11 Gimble Walk, Harborne, BIRMINGHAM, B17 8SL.
NORTHEDGE, Mrs. Helen Margaret, BA ACA *1980;* St. Anthonys, Tuesley Lane, GODALMING, SURREY, GU7 1SG.
NORTHEDGE, Mr. Stuart Peter, BA ACA *1980;* St. Anthonys, Tuesley Lane, GODALMING, SURREY, GU7 1SG.
NORTHEN, Mr. Ian Christopher Anthony, MA FCA *2000;* 1 The Dell, ROYSTON, HERTFORDSHIRE, SG8 9BJ.
NORTHEY, Mr. David Frederick, MSc ACA *1992;* 4 Sussex Place, SOUTHSEA, HAMPSHIRE, PO5 3EZ.
NORTHEY, Mr. David Joseph, BA ACA *1980;* 67 Glenside, Appley Bridge, WIGAN, WN6 9EG.
NORTHEY, Mr. John Arthur, FCA *1969;* Ballabank, South Cape, Laxey, ISLE OF MAN, IM4 7JB.
•NORTHFIELD, Mr. David Neil, BSc ACA *1990;* David Northfield, 412 Daws Heath Road, BENFLEET, ESSEX, SS7 2UD.
NORTHFIELD, Mr. Ephraim John, FCA *1956;* 19 Lombardy Lodge, Beeston, NOTTINGHAM, NG9 6EE. (Life Member)
NORTHING, Miss. Joanne Louise, BA(Hons) ACA *2004;* R N Store & Co, The Poplars, Bridge Street, BRIGG, LINCOLNSHIRE, DN20 8NQ.
NORTHOVER, Mr. Andrew, BA ACA *2007;* 10 Inott Furze, Headington, OXFORD, OX3 7ES.
NORTHOVER, Mr. Malcolm Paul, BA FCA *1986;* with Grant Thornton UK LLP, 300 Pavilion Drive, Northampton Business Park, NORTHAMPTON, NN4 7YE.
NORTHOVER, Mr. Matthew John, BA ACA *1996;* 44 Providence Lane, Long Ashton, BRISTOL, BS41 9DJ.
•NORTHOVER, Mr. Michael Alan, FCA *1975;* (Tax Fac), Northover Bennett & Co Ltd, 130 Bournemouth Road, Chandler's Ford, EASTLEIGH, HAMPSHIRE, SO53 3AL. See also Collinson & Co (Accountants) Ltd and Northover Michael A.
NORTHOVER, Mr. Stephen John, FCA *1977;* 11 Heathfield Road, Hasbury, HALESOWEN, WEST MIDLANDS, B63 1AD.
NORTHWAY, Mr. Christopher John, BA ACA *2011;* 146 Twenty Twenty, Skinner Lane, LEEDS, LS7 1BE.
•NORTHWOOD, Mr. Christopher John, BSc FCA *1993;* Hannaways Business Support Limited, Trios House, Reform Road, MAIDENHEAD, BERKSHIRE, SL6 8BY.
NORTHWOOD, Miss. Rachel Bronwen, BA ACA *1996;* with PricewaterhouseCoopers LLP, 141 Bothwell Street, GLASGOW, G2 7EQ.
NORTON, Mr. Alan James, BA FCA *1997;* The Capita Group plc c/o, Tribal Group Plc, 87-91 Newman Street, LONDON, W1T 3EY.
NORTON, Mr. Alexander Jonathan, BEng ACA *2001;* 47 Bennerley Road, LONDON, SW11 6DR.
NORTON, Mr. Alexander Michael, BSc FCA *1975;* Harris Watson Holdings Plc, Unit 3 First Floor, Ashted Lock, Dartmouth Middleway, Aston Science Park, BIRMINGHAM B7 4AZ.
NORTON, Ms. Amanda Jane, BA ACA *1996;* SRA Second Floor, 24 Martin Lane, LONDON, EC4R 0DR.
•NORTON, Mr. Andrew Howard, FCA *1983;* Nortons Group, Highlands House, Basingstoke Road, Spencers Wood, READING, RG7 1NT. See also Nortons Recovery Limited, Nortons Group LLP
NORTON, Mr. Andrew James, BSc ACA *1997;* 9 Starlight Way, ST. ALBANS, HERTFORDSHIRE, AL4 0JH.
NORTON, Mr. Andrew Thomas Robert, ACA *1995;* 50 Langley Hall Road, Olton, SOLIHULL, B92 7HE.
NORTON, Mr. Anthony James, BA(Hons) FCA CTA *2000;* (Tax Fac), 42 Anderson Drive, Whitnash, LEAMINGTON SPA, WARWICKSHIRE, CV31 2RN.
NORTON, Mr. Brian George, BSc ACA *1980;* Willowgate 7 Frogge Lane, Gt. Hautbois Common, Coltishall, NORWICH, NR12 7JT.
NORTON, Mr. Brian Roy, BA FCA *1974;* P.O.Box 70421, BRYANSTON, GAUTENG, 2021, SOUTH AFRICA.
NORTON, Mr. Colin Stanley, BA FCA *1979;* Twincot, Winston Avenue, TADLEY, RG26 3NN.
•NORTON, Mr. David Charles, BSc ACA *1987;* Deloitte LLP, Abbots House, Abbey Street, READING, RG1 3BD. See also Deloitte & Touche LLP
•NORTON, Mr. David Edward, BA FCA *1989;* The Norton Partnership, The Croft, Park Road, Cross Hills, KEIGHLEY, WEST YORKSHIRE BD20 8BG.
NORTON, Mr. David John, MA FCA *1960;* Unit 102, 40 King Street, WAVERTON, NSW 2060, AUSTRALIA. (Life Member)
NORTON, Mr. Dean, BSc ACA *1997;* 11 Mana View Road, Paremata, PORIRUA 5026, NEW ZEALAND.
•NORTON, Mr. Geoffrey Norman, FCA *1961;* (Tax Fac), Norton Lewis & Co, 246/248 Great Portland St, LONDON, W1W 5JL.
NORTON, Mr. Geoffrey Thomas, BA ACA *1989;* 14 Hampshire Way, Yate, BRISTOL, BS37 7RS.
NORTON, Mr. Graham Howard, FCA *1983;* The Old Cottage, 199 The Street, West Horsley, LEATHERHEAD, SURREY, KT24 6HR.
NORTON, Mr. Ivor Bertram, FCA *1964;* Hillcrest, Binton Road, Welford-on-avon, STRATFORD-UPON-AVON, CV37 8PP.
NORTON, Mr. James Adam Jonathan, ACA APFS CFP FSI *1999;* Mulberry House, Oxford Street, Lee Common, GREAT MISSENDEN, BUCKINGHAMSHIRE, HP16 9JP.
NORTON, Mr. James Victor, BA ACA *2005;* Frank Key Ltd, Portland Street, Daybrook, NOTTINGHAM, NG5 6BL.
NORTON, Mr. Jeremy Scott, BSc FCA *1984;* 9 Harpenden Road, ST. ALBANS, HERTFORDSHIRE, AL3 5LL.
NORTON, Mr. John, FCA *1958;* Buena Vista, Church Lane, Waddington, LINCOLN, LN5 9RP. (Life Member)
NORTON, Mr. John Charles, MA FCA *1964;* 6 Parkside Gardens, LONDON, SW19 5EY.
NORTON, Mrs. Julia May, BSc FCA *1977;* Orchard House, 2 Tower House Lane, Wraxall, BRISTOL, BS48 1JP.
NORTON, Mr. Kenneth Anthony, FCA *1963;* 23 Sounds Lodge, Crockenhill, SWANLEY, BR8 8TD. (Life Member)
•NORTON, Mrs. Kerry, BSc FCA *1999;* with Grundy Anderson & Kershaw Limited, 123-125 Union Street, OLDHAM, OL1 1TG.
NORTON, Ms. Lisa, BA ACA *1992;* 15 Greenacres Drive, CASTLEFORD, WEST YORKSHIRE, WF10 4SW.
NORTON, Mrs. Lorraine, ACA FCCA *2000;* 14 Drovers Way, Desford, LEICESTER, LE9 9DW.
•NORTON, Mr. Mark Jonathan, ACA *1985;* Wilkins Kennedy, 1-5 Nelson St, SOUTHEND-ON-SEA, SS1 1EG.
NORTON, Mr. Michael James, BSc FCA *1977;* Atkins Plc Woodcote Grove, Ashley Road, EPSOM, KT18 5BW.
NORTON, Mr. Michael William Parkinson, BSc FCA *1998;* 147 Deganwy Road, Llanrhos, LLANDUDNO, CONWY, LL30 1NE.
NORTON, Mr. Nicholas Charles, BSc ACA *1981;* Fortis Insurance Ltd Fortis House, Tollgate Chandler's Ford, EASTLEIGH, SO53 3YA.
NORTON, Mr. Paul Emil, BA ACA *1988;* Zweiackerstr 12, CH-8053 ZURICH, SWITZERLAND.
•NORTON, Mr. Richard Jonathan, FCA *1964;* (Tax Fac), Richard Norton & Co, 342 Regents Park Road, LONDON, N3 2LJ.
NORTON, Mr. Richard Michael, FCA *1975;* Hilton House Graveley Way, Hilton, HUNTINGDON, CAMBRIDGESHIRE, PE28 9NN.
NORTON, Miss. Samantha Olivia, ACA *2008;* Corner House, Church and Parliament Streets, PO Box HM 1556, HAMILTON HM FX, BERMUDA.
NORTON, Miss. Sarah, BSc ACA *1997;* (Tax Fac), 45 Roxwell Road, CHELMSFORD, CM1 2LY.
NORTON, Ms. Shari Rachel Louise, BSc ACA *1997;* Flat 1, 17 Cambridge Park, TWICKENHAM, TW1 2JE.
NORTON, Mr. Stephen John, FCA *1974;* (Tax Fac), 9 Clematis Gardens, WOODFORD GREEN, IG8 0BU.
NORTON, Mr. Steven Robert, BSc ACA *2005;* Styles & Co, Heater House, 473 Warrington Road, Culcheth, WARRINGTON, WA3 5QU.
•NORTON, Mr. Theodore Michael John, FCA *1957;* T.M.J. Norton, 25 Beauworth Avenue, Greasby, WIRRAL, CH49 3QY.
NORTON, Miss. Tracy Lyn, MBA BSc ACA *1992;* 17B Elspeth Road, Battersea, LONDON, SW11 1DW.
NORTON, Mrs. Veronica Mary, FCA *1970;* Stonecourt Membland, Newton Ferrers, PLYMOUTH, PL8 1HP. (Life Member)
NORTON, Mr. William Richard, FCA *1976;* Chine Cottage, 4 Chine Road, Upper Woodford, SALISBURY, SP4 6NX.
NORTON-GRIFFITHS, Sir John, Bt FCA *1966;* P O Box 396, RUTLAND, VT 05702, UNITED STATES. (Life Member)
NORVAL, Mr. Christiaan Michiel, ACA CA(SA) *2011;* 15 Neville Avenue, NEW MALDEN, SURREY, KT3 4SN.
NORVAL, Mr. John Alexander, BA FCA *1980;* H M Revenue & Customs: Large Business Se, 101 Victoria Street, BRISTOL, BS1 6DQ.

NORVILL, Mrs. Sophie Ann, BA ACA *1999;* 65 Craven Road, NEWBURY, RG14 5NH.
NORVILLE, Mr. Kevin John, FCA *1981;* 7 Kingly House, Hyde Place, Middleway, OXFORD, OX2 7JD.
NORWELL, Mr. Ben, ACA *2009;* 6 Nene View, Oundle, PETERBOROUGH, PE8 4LY.
NORWOOD, Mr. Anthony Edward, BA(Hons) ACA *2001;* L D C, 1 City Square, LEEDS, LS1 2ES.
•**NORWOOD, Mrs. Claire Catherine, BSc FCA ATII** *1990;* Jones Avens Limited, Piper House, 4 Dukes Court, Bognor Road, CHICHESTER, PO19 8FX.
NORWOOD, Mr. Fraser Callum, BSc ACA *1993;* 85 Frant Road, TUNBRIDGE WELLS, KENT, TN2 5LP.
NORWOOD, Mr. John David Watson, BSc ACA *1980;* 158 Rue De Calaisis, 62370 AUDRUICQ, FRANCE.
NORWOOD, Mr. Michael Clutterbuck, FCA *1957;* 4 Dryburn Park, DURHAM, DH1 5AD. (Life Member)
NORWOOD, Mr. Trevor Peter, BA ACA *1985;* Eukleia Training, 20 Birchin Lane, LONDON, EC3V 9DU.
NOSEGBE, Mr. Michael Sunday Chukudi, FCA *1970;* PO Box 2625, Surulere, LAGOS, NIGERIA. (Life Member)
NOTARO, Ms. Donna Maria Angela, BSc ACA *1992;* American Express Europe Ltd, Belgrave House, 76 Buckingham Palace Road, LONDON, SW1W 9AX.
NOTHER, Mr. Philip, BSc ACA *1989;* 2931 Elm Hill Pike, NASHVILLE, TN 37214, UNITED STATES.
NOTHERS, Mr. John Richard, BSc ACA *2009;* 30 Park Hill, LONDON, SW4 9PB.
NOTLEY, Mr. John Shaw, FCA *1953;* Little Caerlicken Caerlicyn Lane, Langstone, NEWPORT, GWENT, NP18 2JZ. (Life Member)
NOTLEY, Mr. Martyn Anthony, FCA *1966;* 42 Chester Drive, North Harrow, HARROW, HA2 7PU.
NOTON, Mr. Andrew David, BSc(Hons) ACA *2004;* with Lubbock Fine, Russell Bedford House, City Forum, 250 City Road, LONDON, EC1V 2QQ.
NOTON, Mr. Barry Clayton, FCA *1967;* Apartado De Correos1065, 18697 LA HERRADURA, GRANADA, SPAIN. (Life Member)
NOTON, Mr. David James, BA(Hons) ACA *2001;* 6 Plane Tree Avenue, Alwoodley, LEEDS, LS17 8UB.
NOTT, Mr. Alan Richard, BA ACA MBCS *1988;* 42 Mount William Street, GORDON, NSW 2072, AUSTRALIA.
NOTT, Mr. Benjamin Edward, BSc ACA *2004;* 7 Dixon Gardens, BATH, SOMERSET, BA1 5HH.
NOTT, Miss. Catherine, BA(Hons) ACA *2011;* 33 Perrers Road, LONDON, W6 0EY.
•**NOTT, Mr. Clive Gilbert, FCA** *1971;* (Tax Fac), Notts Ltd, 38 Rothesay Road, LUTON, LU1 1QZ.
•**NOTT, Mr. Paul, BSc ACA** *1999;* with PricewaterhouseCoopers LLP, Donington Court, Pegasus Business Park, Castle Donington, DERBY, DE74 2UZ.
•**NOTT, Mr. Peter Charles, BSc FCA** *1974;* (Tax Fac), Nott & Co, 24 Chase Road, Southgate, LONDON, N14 4EU. See also Nott & Co(Accountants) Ltd
•**NOTTAGE, Mr. Brian Ian, FCA** *1968;* Melford Lodge, Orchard Avenue, Ramsden Bellhouse, BILLERICAY, ESSEX, CM11 1PH.
•**NOTTAGE, Mr. George Henry, FCA** *1971;* (Tax Fac), 25 Reed Pond Walk, Gidea Park, ROMFORD, RM2 5PH.
NOTTAGE, Mr. Jonathan Bruce, BA FCA *1977;* Dolby Laboratories Inc, Wootton Bassett, SWINDON, SN4 8QJ.
NOTTIDGE, Mr. Rupert Norman Rolfe, BA ACA *1992;* 8 Woodbury Park Gardens, TUNBRIDGE WELLS, KENT, TN4 9JT.
NOTTINGHAM, Miss. Abigail Louise, BSc ACA *2004;* Unit 425, 221-229 Sydney Park Road, ERSKINEVILLE, NSW 2043, AUSTRALIA.
NOTTINGHAM, Mr. Alan Raymond, BA FCA *1973;* 9 Manhood Cottages, Almodington Lane, Almodington, CHICHESTER, WEST SUSSEX, PO20 7JT.
NOTTINGHAM, Miss. Donna Lorelle, BA(Hons) ACA *2002;* (Tax Fac), Russell New Beeding Court, Shoreham Road Upper Beeding, STEYNING, WEST SUSSEX, BN44 3TN.
NOTTINGHAM, Mr. George Edward Dobell, MA ACA *2001;* 44 Perrers Road, Hammersmith, LONDON, W6 0EZ.
①**NOTTINGHAM, Mrs. Gillian, BA ACA** *1984;* 23 Stone Delf, SHEFFIELD, S10 3QX.
NOTTINGHAM, Mr. John Richard Anthony, FCA *1965;* Rosemerryn, Booilushag, Ballajora Hill, Ballajora, Ramsey, ISLE OF MAN IM7 1BD. (Life Member)
NOUHOV, Mrs. Eleanor Stephanie, BSc ACA *2003;* 139 Alcester Road Hollywood, BIRMINGHAM, B47 5NR.
NOURSE, Mr. William Arthur Thomas, BA ACA *1998;* 75 Cambridge Street, LONDON, SW1V 4PS.
NOUSS, Ms. Hunada, MA FCA *1984;* Flat 6, 10 Northwick Terrace, LONDON, NW8 8JE.
NOUTCH, Miss. Jemimah, BSc(Hons) ACA *2011;* Flat 1, 44 Imperial Road, Beeston, NOTTINGHAM, NG9 1FN.
NOVAK, Mr. Richard, BA ACA *1985;* Baden House, 106 Baden Powell Road, CHESTERFIELD, DERBYSHIRE, S40 2RL.
NOVAKOVIC, Mr. Novica, BA ACA *1994;* 15 Saracens Wharf, Bletchley, MILTON KEYNES, MK2 2AL.
NOVELL, Mr. David Edward, BA FCA *1968;* Unit 5 938 High Street Road, GLEN WAVERLEY, VIC 3150, AUSTRALIA.
NOVICK, Mr. Jamie, ACA *2010;* Glara Mara, The Clump, RICKMANSWORTH, HERTFORDSHIRE, WD3 4BB.
•**NOVIS, Mr. Roy William, FCA** *1973;* Roy W. Novis, Stone Lodge, Ling Lane, Scarcroft, LEEDS, LS14 3HY.
NOVIS, Mr. Terry James, ACA *2003;* 33 Blackwood Chine, South Woodham, CHELMSFORD, CM3 5FZ.
•**NOVITT, Mr. Brian, PhD FCA** *1973;* (Tax Fac), Novitt Bamford Ltd, Pennyfarthing House, 560 Brighton Road, SOUTH CROYDON, SURREY, CR2 6AW.
•**NOVITT, Mr. Mark Simon, BA ACA CTA** *1998;* (Tax Fac), Novitt Harris & Co Limited, Unit H Ver House, London Road, Markyate, ST. ALBANS, HERTFORDSHIRE AL3 8JP.
NOVOSELSKAYA, Miss. Olga, ACA *2009;* Nagorniy bulvar 24-74, MOSCOW, RUSSIAN FEDERATION.
NOVY, Mr. John Vernon, FCA *1983;* Tanglewood, 13 Waring Way, Dunchurch, RUGBY, CV22 6PH.
NOVY, Mr. Vaclav Jan, BSc(Econ) FCA *1959;* 53 Annandale Road, Kirk Ella, HULL, HU10 7UR. (Life Member)
NOWAK, Mr. Alexander Jan, BA(Hons) ACA *2003;* 20 Manor Road, LONDON, SW20 9AE.
NOWAK, Mr. Michael, ACA *2008;* Ul. Barska 7/9 m.80, 02-315 WARSAW, POLAND.
NOWELL, Mrs. Clare, BSc ACA *1991;* 22 Schoolfields Road, Shenstone, LICHFIELD, WS14 0LW.
•**NOWELL, Mrs. Gillian, FCA** *1987;* Clifton House Hill Head, Bradwell, HOPE VALLEY, DERBYSHIRE, S33 9HY. See also Nowell Gillian
NOWELL, Mr. Herbert Anthony, FCA *1957;* 57 Quickswood, Hampstead, LONDON, NW3 3SA. (Life Member)
NOWELL, Mr. John George, BSc FCA *1974;* Limedale, Bank Hill, Woodborough, NOTTINGHAM, NG14 6EF. (Life Member)
NOWELL, Mr. Peter Benjamin, BA ACA *1998;* 13 Broxash Road, Clapham, LONDON, SW11 6AD.
•**NOWELL, Mr. Richard Samuel, BA FCA** *1979;* 23 Magnolia Court, Beeston, NOTTINGHAM, NG9 3LG.
NOWELL, Mr. Stephen David, BA(Hons) ACA *2001;* J L T Management Services Ltd, 2 Seething Lane, LONDON, EC3N 4AT.
NOWELL-WITHERS, Mr. David Brian, FCA JDipMA *1959;* Wood Ash, Gatesdene Close, Little Gaddesden, BERKHAMSTED, HP4 1PB. (Life Member)
NOWICKI, Mrs. Alison Mary, BSc ACA *1988;* 39 Newcastle Drive, The Park, NOTTINGHAM, NG7 1AA.
NOWICKI, Mr. Gerald, BSc ACA *1987;* 16 Woods Lane, Dobcross Saddleworth, OLDHAM, OL3 5AN.
NOWIKOW, Mr. Mark, BSc ACA *1982;* 4th Floor The Point, Caribtours Ltd, 210 New Kings Road, LONDON, SW6 4NZ.
NOWN, Mrs. Patricia Ann, BA ACA ATT CTA *1990;* (Tax Fac), 15 Bingley Road, Littlethorpe, LEICESTER, LE19 2HY.
NOY, Mr. Colin Alan, FCA *1954;* 1 Grangemoor, Papplewick, NOTTINGHAM, NG15 8EX. (Life Member)
•**NOYCE, Mr. Peter Richard, BA FCA** *1991;* Menzies LLP, Woking Office, Midas House, 62 Goldsworth Road, WOKING, SURREY GU21 6LQ.
•**NOYE-ALLEN, Mr. Robert, BA ACA** *1989;* Moore Stephens LLP, 150 Aldersgate Street, LONDON, EC1A 4AB.
•**NOYES, Mr. Adrian Dennis, BA FCA** *1975;* (Tax Fac), A.D. Noyes, 22 Truro Road, Ashton, BRISTOL, BS3 2AE.
NOYS, Mr. Terence John, BA FCA *1987;* 50 Birkbeck Road, LONDON, NW7 4AT.
NSOFOR, Mr. Amaechi, BAcc ACA *2002;* 12 Earlsbrook Road, REDHILL, RH1 6DP.
NUBBERT, Mr. David Andrew, BSc ACA *1986;* 16 The Hydons, Hydestile, GODALMING, GU8 4DD.
•**NUCKCHADY, Mr. Mahamood, FCA** *1975;* IMN & Co, 53 Queen Annes Grove, Bush Hill Park, ENFIELD, MIDDLESEX, EN1 2JS.
•**NUDDS, Mr. Barry John, ACA** *1981;* Barry J Nudds, PO Box 667, 56 Hepworth Avenue, BURY ST. EDMUNDS, SUFFOLK, IP33 9EU.
NUDDS, Ms. Elisabeth Sarah, BA ACA *1989;* 29 Foster Road, Chiswick, LONDON, W4 4NY.
•**NUDDS, Mr. Terence Raymond, BA FCA** *1968;* Lawrence Nudds & Co, Alpha House, 176a High Street, BARNET, HERTFORDSHIRE, EN5 5SZ.
NUFRIO, Mr. Harry, MBA BA MCMI FCA CTA *1983;* (Tax Fac), 38 Temple Grange, Werrington, PETERBOROUGH, PE4 5DN.
NUGENT, Mr. David Mark Nigel, BA ACA *1987;* Grace Consulting, Orchard House, The Street, Albury, GUILDFORD, SURREY GU5 9AG.
NUGENT, Mr. John James Christoph, FCA *1974;* La Rosiere La Rue de la Corbiere, St. Brelade, JERSEY, JE3 8HN. (Life Member)
NUGENT, Mr. John McNicol, MEng FCA *1999;* 8 Rue de la Juvinière, 78350 LES LOGES EN JOSAS, FRANCE.
NUGENT, Dr. Marianne, PhD MA ACA *1994;* with Nomura International Plc, 1 Angel Lane, LONDON, EC4R 3AB.
NUGENT, Mrs. Mary Lavinia, BA ACA *1987;* Littleleys Gosden Common, Bramley, GUILDFORD, GU5 0AQ.
NUGENT, Mr. Michael, FCA *1963;* 1 Yew Tree Drive, SALE, M33 2EX.
NUGENT, Mr. Paul, BSc FCA *1992;* 43 Lakeside Drive, Chobham, WOKING, GU24 8BD.
NUGENT, Mr. Paul Anthony, BA FCA *1983;* Senator Management Services Ltd, 14 Fenchurch Avenue, LONDON, EC3M 5BS.
NUGENT, Sir Walter Richard Middleton, Bt FCA *1972;* 61-6 Yaguchi - Dai, Naka-ka, YOKOHAMA, 231-0831 JAPAN.
NUNAN, Mrs. Alison Naomi, BA ACA *1994;* 59 Dean Court Road, Rottingdean, BRIGHTON, BN2 7DL.
NUNAN, Mr. Patrick Joseph, FCA *1967;* 9 Cairnhill, Westminster Road, Foxrock, DUBLIN 18, COUNTY DUBLIN, IRELAND. (Life Member)
NUNAN, Mr. Simon Peter, BSc ACA *1995;* 59 Dean Court Road, Rottingdean, BRIGHTON, BN2 7DL.
NUNAN, Mr. Timothy Gerald, BSc(Hons) ACA *2002;* Commercial Bank, PO Box 3232, DOHA, 3232, QATAR.
•**NUNES, Mr. Edward Joseph, FCA** *1966;* Homer & Co, 27A Saddle Road, MARAVAL, TRINIDAD AND TOBAGO.
NUNN, Mr. Andrew Thomas, BSc ACA *2011;* Flat 61 Fountain House, The Boulevard, LONDON, SW6 2TQ.
NUNN, Miss. Brenda Jean, BA ACA *1993;* Leicester College, Freemens Park Campus, Aylestone Road, LEICESTER, LE2 7LW.
NUNN, Mr. Brian Raymond, FCA *1956;* 3 Church Leat, Downton, SALISBURY, SP5 3PD. (Life Member)
NUNN, Mr. Christopher John, BA ACA CTA *1999;* 23 Tintagel Crescent, LONDON, SE22 8HT.
•**NUNN, Mr. Christopher John, FCA** *1975;* (Tax Fac), BCL Accountants Ltd, 30-38 Dock Street, LEEDS, LS10 1JF.
NUNN, Mr. Christopher Leslie, BSc FCA *1968;* Trewinnard House, 1 Robins Nest Hill, Little Berkhamsted, HERTFORD, SG13 8LS. (Life Member)
NUNN, Mr. Colin Vincent Austin, BCom ACA *1989;* Blackhills, Cobbetts Hill, WEYBRIDGE, KT13 OUA.
NUNN, Mr. Craig Stuart, MA ACA ATII *1994;* 10 King Edwards Grove, TEDDINGTON, MIDDLESEX, TW11 9LU.
NUNN, Mr. David, FCA *1972;* 42 Ferncliffe Drive, Baildon, SHIPLEY, BD17 5AQ. (Life Member)
•**NUNN, Mr. Derrick James, FCA** *1975;* (Tax Fac), Derrick J. Nunn, 54 Shirley Street, HOVE, BN3 3WG.
NUNN, Mr. Ian Alan, BA FCA *1984;* Mill House, North Field Kingsclere Road, Overton, BASINGSTOKE, RG25 3JY.
•**NUNN, Mr. Ian Michael, FCA** *1981;* Nunn Hayward, Sterling House, 20 Station Road, GERRARDS CROSS, SL9 8EL.
•**NUNN, Mrs. Jacqueline Elizabeth, FCA** *1992;* (Tax Fac), Jacqueline Nunn FCA, 271 St. Albans Road, HEMEL HEMPSTEAD, HERTFORDSHIRE, HP2 4RP.
NUNN, Mr. John Stephen, FCA *1977;* Buckinghamshire Housing Association Ltd Unit 4, Stokenchurch Business Park Ibstone Road Stokenchurch, HIGH WYCOMBE, BUCKINGHAMSHIRE, HP14 3FE.
NUNN, Mr. Kelvin, BA FCA *1983;* 238 Shepherds Lane, DARTFORD, DA1 2PW.
NUNN, Mr. Malcolm Ian, FCA *1973;* 4 Brighthampton, 67 Oatlands Avenue, WEYBRIDGE, KT13 9TL.
NUNN, Mr. Martin George, BA ACA *1999;* 2/95 Michaels Avenue, ELLERSLIE 1051, NEW ZEALAND.
NUNN, Mr. Nicholas James, BA(Hons) ACA *2002;* 41 Harestone Hill, CATERHAM, CR3 6SG.
NUNN, Mrs. Ogechi Obioma Chinwe, BA(Hons) ACA *2003;* 23 Tintagel Crescent, LONDON, SE22 8HT.
NUNN, Mr. Richard Barry, BSc FCA *1993;* 2461 Capilano Crescent, OAKVILLE L6H 6L3, ON, CANADA.
•**NUNN, Mr. Simon Maxwell, BA ACA** *1991;* (Tax Fac), S Nunn & Co Limited, Unit 2, Guards Avenue, The Village, CATERHAM, SURREY CR3 5XL.
NUNN, Mrs. Susan Claire, BA ACA CTA *1996;* (Tax Fac), The Croft, 30 Red Lion Road, Chobham, WOKING, SURREY, GU24 8RE.
•**NUNN, Miss. Trina Jane, ACA MAAT** *1999;* (Tax Fac), Whiting & Partners, Garland House, Garland Street, BURY ST. EDMUNDS, SUFFOLK, IP33 1EZ.
NUNN, Miss. Victoria Louise, LLB ACA *2010;* 22 Primezone Mews, LONDON, N8 9JP.
NUNNS, Mrs. Astra Jayne, BA ACA *1989;* 28 Culverhay, ASHTEAD, SURREY, KT21 1PR.
•**NUNNS, Mr. Graham Anthony, BA ACA** *1982;* with Grant Thornton UK LLP, 1 Whitehall Riverside, Whitehall Road, LEEDS, WEST YORKSHIRE, LS1 4BN.
NUNNS, Mr. Graham Victor, BA ACA *1991;* Deloitte, 1 City Square, LEEDS, LS1 2AL.
NUNNS, Mr. Richard Owen, BA ACA *1991;* 28 Culverhay, ASHTEAD, KT21 1PR.
NUNNY, Mr. Mark Ian, BCom ACA *2003;* 38d Stanhope Road, Highgate, LONDON, N6 5NG.
NUNNY, Mr. Paul Ian, FCA *1972;* 5 Rawstorn Road, St Marys, COLCHESTER, ESSEX, CO3 4JF.
NUNWA, Mr. Raghbir Singh, BSc ACA *1991;* 46 Royal Oak Road, WOKING, SURREY, GU21 7PJ.
•**NURBHAI, Mr. Iqbal Fazleabbas, FCA** *1980;* Fordhams & Co, Second Floor, 61 Old Street, LONDON, EC1V 9HX.
NURBHAI, Miss. Maria, ACA *2010;* 13 Torbay Road, HARROW, MIDDLESEX, HA2 9QQ.
NURDEN, Mr. Christopher John, BSc FCA *1985;* 17 Kingsbridge Way, Bramcote, NOTTINGHAM, NG9 3LW.
NURDEN, Mr. Donald Broderick, FCA *1951;* 6 Cambridge Road, FRINTON-ON-SEA, CO13 9HN. (Life Member)
NURDEN, Mrs. Pauline Amy, FCA *1950;* 6 Cambridge Road, FRINTON-ON-SEA, CO13 9HN. (Life Member)
•**NURICK, Mr. Paul Elan, ACA CA(SA)** *2010;* Care Home Accounting Limited, 66 Longfield Avenue, LONDON, NW7 2EG.
NURMOHAMED, Mr. Abdulali Pyarali, FCA *1972;* 195 Albury Drive, Hatch End, PINNER, MIDDLESEX, HA5 3RH.
NURPURI, Mr. Jatinder Pal Singh, BSc ACA *1988;* 5 Wallace Court, Cheslyn Hay, WALSALL, WS6 7PG.
NURSAW, Mr. Robert Graham, FCA *1960;* 27 Wyedale Crescent, BAKEWELL, DE45 1BE. (Life Member)
NURSE, Mr. Anthony Wilfred Richard, FCA *1975;* 32 Woodford Green Road, Hall Green, BIRMINGHAM, B28 8PL. (Life Member)
NURSE, Mr. Bramwell William Henry, FCA *1948;* 2 Yare Valley Drive, Cringleford, NORWICH, NR4 7SD. (Life Member)
•**NURSE, Mr. Christopher Hart, MA FCA DChA** *1979;* (Tax Fac), Hart Nurse Limited, The Old Coach House, Southern Road, THAME, OXFORDSHIRE, OX9 2ED. See also Hart Nurse
NURSE, Mr. Gary John, BSc ACA *1991;* c/o TRO Limited, Penfold Drive, WYMONDHAM, NORFOLK, NR18 0WZ.
NURSE, Miss. Joanne Tracey Natalie, MA ACA *2002;* 17 Cherry Lane, Bearley, STRATFORD-UPON-AVON, CV37 0SX.
NURSE, Mr. Roger Denis, FCA *1952;* 12 Wootton Road, HENLEY-ON-THAMES, RG9 1QD. (Life Member)
NURSE, Mrs. Sarah Anne, BSc ACA *1986;* 21 Dauntless Road, Burghfield Common, READING, RG7 3NZ.
NURSE, Mr. Timothy Allan, JP FCA *1966;* 12 The Anchorage, Montego Freeport P.O.Box 61, MONTEGO BAY, JAMAICA.
NURSEY, Miss. Charlotte Anne, ACA *2007;* Bramble Cottage, Woodgate Lane, Swanton Morley, DEREHAM, NORFOLK, NR20 4NS.
NURTON, Mrs. Iraina Marcella Francesca, BD FCA *1992;* Elveden House Churchill Road, Bovington, WAREHAM, BH20 6JS.
•**NURUN NABI, Mr. Tajul Islam Mohammad, FCA** *1968;* N. Nabi & Co, 75 Hillside Gardens, WALLINGTON, SURREY, SM6 9NX.
•**NURUZZAMAN, Mr. Abul Khair Muhammod, FCA** *1975;* N. Zaman & Co, 35a Westbury Avenue, LONDON, N22 6BS.
NUSSBAUM, Mr. Jeremy, BSc ACA CTA *1987;* Orange Eyewear Ltd Rico House, George Street Prestwich, MANCHESTER, M25 9WS.

NUSSEY, Mr. James Peter, PhD MPhys ACA *2009;* Tribal Education Ltd, 1-4 Portland Square, BRISTOL, BS2 8RR.
NUSUM, Miss. Kelli Nicole, BA(Hons) ACA *2010;* Validus Reinsurance Ltd, Bermuda Commercial Bank Building, 19 Par-La-Ville Road, HAMILTON HM11, BERMUDA.
•**NUTBROWN, Mr. Alan, FCA** *1981;* Linden Villa, Park Estate, St Brelade, JERSEY, JE3 8EQ.
NUTBROWN, Mrs. Alison Gaynor, BSc ACA ATII *1996;* New Inn Cottage, Hampstead Norreys, THATCHAM, BERKSHIRE, RG18 0TF.
NUTBROWN, Mr. James Peter, FCA *1970;* Princess Works, Q F M Group, 10 Brightside Lane, SHEFFIELD, S9 3YE.
NUTHALL, Mr. Richard Frank, BA ACA CTA *1979;* 4 Kings Green, DAVENTRY, NN11 4UB.
NUTLEY, Mr. Steven Mark, BSc FCA *1990;* KPMG Albania Sh p k, Deshmoret e Kombit Blvd, Twin Tower Buildings, FL 13 TIRANA, ALBANIA.
NUTT, Mr. David Noel Bernard, FCA *1963;* Ravenswood, 47 Lower Herne Road, HERNE BAY, KENT, CT6 7ND. (Life Member)
NUTT, Miss. Gabrielle Elizabeth Mary, LLB(Hons) ACA *2010;* National Audit Office, 157-197 Buckingham Palace Road, LONDON, SW1W 9SP.
NUTT, Mr. John Allister, FCA *1958;* The Stone House, Church Street, Yetminster, SHERBORNE, DORSET, DT9 6LG. (Life Member)
•**NUTT, Mr. Mark Robert, FCA** *1991;* Bourne & Co, 6 Lichfield Street, BURTON-ON-TRENT, DE14 3RD.
NUTT, Mr. Michael William Robert, FCA *1966;* 25 Shipley Mill Close, Park Farm, Kingsnorth, ASHFORD, KENT, TN23 3NR.
NUTT, Mr. Paul Henry Andre, FCA *1954;* 91 Windy Arbour, KENILWORTH, CV8 2BJ. (Life Member)
•**NUTTALL, Mr. Alastair John Richard, BA ACA** *1994;* Ernst & Young LLP, 100 Barbirolli Square, MANCHESTER, M2 3EY. See also Ernst & Young Europe LLP
NUTTALL, Miss. Alison Mary, BSc ACA *1984;* Pearson Shared Services, Edinburgh Gate, HARLOW, ESSEX, CM20 2JE.
•**NUTTALL, Mr. Clive Anthony, FCA** *1975;* Horsfield-Smith Limited, Tower House, 269 Walmersley Road, BURY, LANCASHIRE, BL9 6NX.
NUTTALL, Mr. Clive Gordon, BA ACA *1989;* 90 Derriads Lane, CHIPPENHAM, WILTSHIRE, SN14 0QL.
NUTTALL, Mr. Cyril Adam, FCA *1953;* Flat 8, Grosvenor Court, Ellerbeck Road, THORNTON-CLEVELEYS, LANCASHIRE, FY5 1TD. (Life Member)
NUTTALL, Mrs. Felicity Claire, BSc(Hons) ACA *2000;* Cunliffes Barn, Colliers Row Road, BOLTON, BL1 7PH.
NUTTALL, Mr. Gary, BA(Hons) ACA *2001;* 51 Skaife Road, SALE, CHESHIRE, M33 2HA.
NUTTALL, Mr. Geoffrey Ellis, FCA *1958;* 64 Meadows Avenue, THORNTON-CLEVELEYS, FY5 2TW. (Life Member)
NUTTALL, Miss. Giorgia Maria, BSc ACA *2011;* 9 Eliza Street, Ramsbottom, BURY, LANCASHIRE, BL0 0AT.
NUTTALL, Miss. Harriet, MMath ACA *2011;* 25 Seymour Park, Mannamead, PLYMOUTH, PL3 5BQ.
NUTTALL, Mr. Ian Derek, BSc ACA *1992;* 34 Standidge Drive, HULL, HU8 0RW.
NUTTALL, Miss. Jennifer, BA(Hons) ACA *2011;* 69 Becconsall Drive, CREWE, CW1 4RP.
NUTTALL, Mr. John Michael, FCA *1953;* c/o Norman Nuthall, 90 Derriads Lane, CHIPPENHAM, WILTSHIRE, SN14 0QL. (Life Member)
NUTTALL, Mr. Jonathan Peter Thomas, LLB ACA *2002;* Pricewaterhousecoopers, 101 Barbirolli Square, MANCHESTER, M2 3PW.
•**NUTTALL, Mr. Philip, FCA CF** *1976;* Clearwater Corporate Finance LLP, 7th Floor, Chancery Place, 50 Brown Street, MANCHESTER, M2 2JT.
•①**NUTTALL, Mr. Philip Andrew, FCA** *1985;* Varden Nuttall Limited, Release House, Heap Bridge, BURY, LANCASHIRE, BL9 7JR. See also Nuttalls Insolvency Solutions Limited
•**NUTTALL, Mr. Philip Robert, FCA** *1982;* Montpelier Professional (Leeds) Limited, Sanderson House, Station Road, Horsforth, LEEDS, LS18 5NT. See also Montpelier Audit Limited
NUTTALL, Miss. Philippa Jan, BA ACA *2009;* Deloitte Llp Mountbatten House, 1 Grosvenor Square, SOUTHAMPTON, SO15 2BZ.
NUTTALL, Mr. Richard Harvey James, BSc ACA *1992;* Sheffield & Regional Properties Ltd Warth Business Centre, Warth Industrial Park Warth Road, BURY, BL9 9TB.
NUTTALL, Mr. Richard Joseph, ACA *2011;* 12 Souberie Avenue, LETCHWORTH GARDEN CITY, HERTFORDSHIRE, SG6 3JA.
NUTTALL, Mr. Roger, ACA *2007;* KPMG, Level 3, 62 Worcester Boulevard, PO Box 1739, CHRISTCHURCH 8140, NEW ZEALAND.
NUTTALL, Mrs. Sharon Marjorie, BSc ACA *1990;* Oakview House, Cann Lane South, Appleton, WARRINGTON, WA4 5NJ.
NUTTALL, Mr. Simon, BA ACA *1984;* Whitebridge, St. Georges Crescent, Port Erin, ISLE OF MAN, IM9 6HR.
•**NUTTALL, Mr. Simon George, FCA** *1992;* McGills, Oakley House, Tetbury Road, CIRENCESTER, GL7 1US.
•**NUTTALL, Mr. Simon James, ACA** *2003;* Lloyd Dowson Limited, Medina House, 2 Station Avenue, BRIDLINGTON, YO16 4LZ.
NUTTALL, Mr. Stephen, BCom ACA *1996; (CA Scotland 1992);* 24 Hartington Close, Dorridge, SOLIHULL, WEST MIDLANDS, B93 8SU.
•**NUTTALL, Mr. Stephen James, LLB ACA CTA** *2002;* Deloitte LLP, PO Box 500, 2 Hardman Street, MANCHESTER, M60 2AT. See also Deloitte & Touche LLP
NUTTALL, Mr. Timothy Mark, BSc FCA AMCT *1991;* Oakview House, Cann Lane South, Appleton, WARRINGTON, WA4 5NJ.
NUTTALL, Mr. William Eric, FCA *1972;* Tonichon, 33790 PELLEGRUE, FRANCE. (Life Member)
NUTTER, Mr. James Edward, FCA *1960;* 5 The Mere, Cheadle Hulme, CHEADLE, CHESHIRE, SK8 5LA. (Life Member)
•**NUTTER, Mr. Leslie, FCA** *1984;* Cassons, Rational House, 64 Bridge Street, MANCHESTER, M3 3BN. See also Cassons & Associates
NUTTER, Mrs. Louisa Ann, BSc(Hons) ACA *2002;* 7 Lakeside Drive, Shirley, SOLIHULL, B90 4SX.
NUTTER, Mr. Mark Timothy, BSc(Hons) ACA *2002;* 7 Lakeside Drive, Shirley, SOLIHULL, B90 4SX.
NUTTER, Mr. Paul James, BEng ACA *2003;* 128 Edenbridge Road, Hall Green, BIRMINGHAM, B28 8PN.
NUTTER, Mr. Richard Norman, BA ACA *1993;* Royal Blackburn Hospital, Haslingden Road, BLACKBURN, BB2 3HH.
•**NUTTER, Mr. Thomas Edward, BSc FCA** *1982;* Pierce C A Ltd, Mentor House, Ainsworth Street, BLACKBURN, BB1 6AY.
NUTTER, Mr. Thomas Kane, BA FCA *1977;* Spa Web Limited, Metcalf Drive, Altham, ACCRINGTON, BB5 5TU.
NUTTING, Mrs. Deborah Ann, LLB ACA *1992;* Level 11, 35 Pitt Street, SYDNEY, NSW 2000, AUSTRALIA.
NUTTING, Mr. Glyn Adrian, BSc ACA *1983;* 38 Chaldon Road, Fulham, LONDON, SW6 7NJ.
NUTTING, Mr. Jonathan William, BA ACA *1988;* Rustlewood, Parkside, BINGLEY, BD16 3DG.
NUTTING, Mrs. Lynda, FCA *1991;* (Tax Fac), Willow Tree House, 176 Old Bath Road, CHELTENHAM, GL53 7DR.
•**NUTTON, Mr. Ivor John, BSc FCA CF** *1982;* The Barn, 5 Springwell Farm, Crow Tree lane, Adwick-on-Dearne, MEXBOROUGH, S64 0NT.
NUTTON, Mr. Mark David, BSc ACA *1990;* 8 Oxbow Crescent, MARCH, CAMBRIDGESHIRE, PE15 9UJ.
•**NUTTON, Mr. Paul Adrian, FCA** *1980;* Peel Walker, 11 Victoria Rd, ELLAND, HX5 0AE.
NUTTYCOMBE, Miss. Alison Laura, BSc ACA *2009;* 19 Lichfield House, Rustat Avenue, CAMBRIDGE, CB1 3RD.
NUVOLONI, Mr. Marco, BSc ACA *1997;* 6 Blackwood Place, Ongar Chase, DUBLIN 15, COUNTY DUBLIN, IRELAND.
NWAOZUZU, Miss. Ngozi, BA ACA *2005;* 7 Lloyd Avenue, LONDON, SW16 5RA.
NWOKOLO, Mr. Ike, FCA *1965;* PO Box 965, Town Planning Way Ade, Akinsanya Street, Llupeju, LAGOS, NIGERIA. (Life Member)
NWOSU, Mr. Peter, BA FCA *1990;* Procter & Gamble Ltd The Heights, Brooklands, WEYBRIDGE, SURREY, KT13 0XP.
NYAJEKA, Mr. Lawrence Tapiwa, ACA *2010;* Flat 25, Oceanis Apartments, 19 Seagull Lane, LONDON, E16 1BY.
NYAMANE, Mr. Banele Musa, ACA CA(SA) *2010;* PO Box A615, Swazi Plaza, MBABANE, H101, SWAZILAND.
NYANDORO, Ms. Makura Evita, ACA CA(SA) *2011;* 38 Cadet Drive, Bermondsey, LONDON, SE1 5RT.
NYANDORO, Mr. Stewart Taipaneyi, ACA CA(SA) *2009;* 63 Kentlea Road, LONDON, SE28 0JY.
NYANDORO, Mr. Tendai, ACA *2009;* 7 Galahad Road, BROMLEY, BR1 5DS.
NYAUNZWI, Mr. Tafara Keith, ACA CA(SA) *2010;* Flat 34 Trinity House, Trinity Lane, WALTHAM CROSS, HERTFORDSHIRE, EN8 7EF.
•**NYE, Mr. David William, FCA** *1970;* (Tax Fac), 9 Connaught Road, HARPENDEN, HERTFORDSHIRE, AL5 4TW.
NYE, Mr. Jeffrey Raymond, BSc ACA *2003;* 47 Frankholmes Drive, Shirley, SOLIHULL, WEST MIDLANDS, B90 4YB.
•**NYE, Mr. John Elliott, FCA** *1970;* (Tax Fac), Martin Nye & Co, 186 High Street, Winslow, BUCKINGHAM, MK18 3DQ.
NYE, Mr. Paul Richard, FCA MBA *1983;* Sandford House, Lucas Road, HIGH WYCOMBE, HP13 6QG.
NYE, Mr. Philip Ernest George, BSc ACA *1979;* 6 Hawbush Rise, WELWYN, AL6 9PN.
•**NYE, Mr. Stephen John Beresford, MSc BA FCA** *1989;* KPMG Audit, 9 Allee Scheffer, 2520 LUXEMBOURG, LUXEMBOURG.
NYE, Mr. Timothy Peter John, BSc ACA *1992;* with Ernst & Young LLP, 1 More London Place, LONDON, SE1 2AF.
•①**NYGATE, Mr. Antony David, BSc ACA** *1990;* BDO LLP, 55 Baker Street, LONDON, W1U 7EU. See also BDO Stoy Hayward LLP
NYLANDER, Mrs. Elaine Florence, BA FCA *1991;* Greggs Plc, Fernwood House, Clayton Road, NEWCASTLE UPON TYNE, NE2 1TL.
•**NYMAN, Mr. Barry, BA(Hons) FCA** *2000;* MJG Accounts Ltd, Hollinwood Business Centre, Albert Street, OLDHAM, OL8 3QL.
NYMAN, Mr. Eddie Matthew, FCA *1962;* 23 Prowse Avenue, Bushey Heath, BUSHEY, WD23 1JS.
•**NYMAN, Mr. Roger, BSc FCA** *1979;* RDP Newmans LLP, Lynwood House, 373/375 Station Road, HARROW, MIDDLESEX, HA1 2AW.
NYMAN, Mr. Roger David, ACA *1982;* 4 Linksway, NORTHWOOD, HA6 2XB.
NYMAN, Mrs. Susan Annette, BSc FCA CF *1981;* with Grant Thornton UK LLP, Grant Thornton House, 22 Melton Street, Euston Square, LONDON, NW1 2EP.
NYOGERI, Mrs. Laura Anne, MA(Hons) ACA *2011;* Hall Floor Flat, 18 Montrose Avenue, BRISTOL, BS6 6EQ.
NYSINGH, Mr. Paul James, BA ACA *1997;* Lynwood Ham Manor Close, Angmering, LITTLEHAMPTON, BN16 4JD.
NYSINGH, Mr. Richard Hans, BSc ACA *1990;* 6a Hammond Close, Norton, YARMOUTH, PO41 0RP.
•**O' KEEFFE, Mrs. Deborah, BA(Hons) ACA** *2002;* Deborah O'Keefe (ACA), 23 Fairfield Avenue, Victoria Park, CARDIFF, CF5 1BR.
•**O'BEIRNE, Mr. Ralph Piaras Regis, FCA CF** *1973;* Chantrey Vellacott DFK LLP, Russell Square House, 10-12 Russell Square, LONDON, WC1B 5LF.
O'BERG, Mr. Kevin Leslie, FCA *1970;* 4 Friary Walk, Eastgate, BEVERLEY, NORTH HUMBERSIDE, HU17 0HE.
O'BOYLE, Mrs. Jayne, BA ACA *1993;* Haworths Chartered Accountants The Old Tannery, Eastgate, ACCRINGTON, BB5 6PW.
•**O'BOYLE, Mr. Kevin, FCA** *1977;* KSi House, 10 Whitefriars, Aungier Street, DUBLIN 2, COUNTY DUBLIN, IRELAND.
O'BOYLE, Mr. Paul, BA ACA *2006;* 9 Ambleside Close, Woodley, READING, RG5 4JJ.
O'BOYLE, Miss. Sarah Elizabeth, ACA *2010;* 8 Cliff Road, BRIDGNORTH, SHROPSHIRE, WV16 4EY.
O'BREE, Mr. Michael Peter, FCA *1974;* 11 Kirkwood Avenue, BEACONSFIELD H9W 5L1, QUE, CANADA. (Life Member)
O'BRIEN, Mr. Andrew Kenneth, BSocSc ACA *1999;* Aggreko UK Ltd, Jebel Ali Free Zone, DUBAI, PO 17576, UNITED ARAB EMIRATES.
O'BRIEN, Miss. Ann Fionnuala, BA ACA *1992;* 32 Templemere, WEYBRIDGE, SURREY, KT13 9PB.
O'BRIEN, Mrs. Anna Louise, BSc ACA *1996;* The Beeches France Lane Hawkesbury Upton, BADMINTON, AVON, GL9 1AS.
O'BRIEN, Mr. Anthony Denis, BCom ACA *1984;* 19 Forestville Court, KALLAROO, WA 6025, AUSTRALIA.
O'BRIEN, Mr. Anthony John, BSc ACA *1994;* 1 Mallard Place, DROITWICH, WR9 8WD.
O'BRIEN, Miss. Caroline Mary, BA ACA *1992;* Peugeot Citroen Automobiles UK Ltd Pinley House, 2 Sunbeam Way, COVENTRY, CV3 1ND.
•**O'BRIEN, Ms. Cathryn Janet, BA ACA** *1993;* (Tax Fac), C.J. O'Brien & Co, Batemill Farmhouse, Batemill Lane, Over Peover, MACCLESFIELD, CHESHIRE SK11 9BW.
O'BRIEN, Mr. Christopher, MSc ACA *1992;* Maro Developments Ltd Metropolitan House, Station Road Cheadle Hulme, CHEADLE, CHESHIRE, SK8 7AZ.
O'BRIEN, Mr. Christopher Patrick James, BA ACA *1993;* 66 Constable Road, IPSWICH, IP4 2UZ.
O'BRIEN, Ms. Ciara, BA ACA *2006;* Ballinamona, Mitchelstown, CORK, COUNTY CORK, IRELAND.
O'BRIEN, Mrs. Cora Mary, BSc ACA CTA *1992;* (Tax Fac), 32 Brighton Square, Rathgar, DUBLIN 6, COUNTY DUBLIN, IRELAND.
O'BRIEN, Mr. Crispin Martin, BSc FRGS FCA *1980;* 14 Woodlands Road, Barnes, LONDON, SW13 0JZ.
O'BRIEN, Mr. Damian Patrick, ACA CA(NZ) *2010;* 2103 Harcourt House, 39 Gloucester Road, WAN CHAI, HONG KONG SAR.
O'BRIEN, Mr. Daniel Philip, BA ACA *1992;* 26 Ellis Fields, ST. ALBANS, HERTFORDSHIRE, AL3 6BQ.
O'BRIEN, Mr. David Martin John, LLB FCA *1965;* 10 Vallance Road, HOVE, BN3 2DA.
O'BRIEN, Ms. Deirdre Anne, LLB ACA *2000;* 2 Arbutus Grove, QUIN, COUNTY CLARE, IRELAND.
•**O'BRIEN, Mr. Dermot Timothy James, BA ACA** *1985;* (Tax Fac), Tim O'Brien, The Green, Datchet, SLOUGH, SL3 9AS.
O'BRIEN, Mr. Douglas Graham, FCA *1959;* The Bank, Far Westrip, STROUD, GL6 6HE. (Life Member)
O'BRIEN, Miss. Freya Anne, BSc ACA *2003;* 56 Seventh Ave, Apt 10H, NEW YORK, NY 10011-6672, UNITED STATES.
O'BRIEN, Mr. Gary Anthony, BA ACA *1986;* 128 St. Andrews Road, HENLEY-ON-THAMES, OXFORDSHIRE, RG9 1PL.
O'BRIEN, Mr. Gary Sean, ACA MAAT *1996;* 40 Lancaster Road, RAYLEIGH, ESSEX, SS6 8UP.
O'BRIEN, Mr. George, FCA *1963;* Heathfield, 10 Carlton Road, Hale, ALTRINCHAM, WA15 8RJ. (Life Member)
•**O'BRIEN, Mr. Gerald, FCA** *1966;* G. O'Brien, Ullenwood, Manor Close, East Horsley, LEATHERHEAD, KT24 6SA.
O'BRIEN, Mr. Ian Charles, BA FCA *1990;* KPMG, 8/F Prince's Building, 10 Chater Road, CENTRAL, HONG KONG ISLAND, HONG KONG SAR.
O'BRIEN, Mr. James, BA ACA *1995;* The Beeches France Lane, Hawkesbury Upton, BADMINTON, AVON, GL9 1AS.
•**O'BRIEN, Mr. James Charles, FCA** *1986;* (Tax Fac), Reeves & Co LLP, Third Floor, 24 Chiswell Street, LONDON, EC1Y 4YX.
O'BRIEN, Mr. James Patrick, BSc ACA *2007;* 2nd Floor Flat, 12 York Place, Clifton, BRISTOL, BS8 1AH.
O'BRIEN, Mrs. Jennifer Christine, BSc ACA *1979;* Deluxe Laboratories Ltd North Orbital Road, Denham, UXBRIDGE, UB9 5HQ.
O'BRIEN, Mr. Jeremiah Stephen, FCA *1957;* 37 Durnsford Way, CRANLEIGH, SURREY, GU6 7LW. (Life Member)
O'BRIEN, Mr. Jeremiah Thomas, FCA *1973;* Danly UK Ltd Lygon Court, Hereward Rise, HALESOWEN, B62 8AN.
•**O'BRIEN, Mr. John, BCom FCA** *1985;* KPMG LLP, 8 Princes Parade, LIVERPOOL, L3 1QH. See also KPMG Europe LLP
•**O'BRIEN, Mr. John Francis, FCA** *1961;* J F O'Brien Taxation Services Ltd, 7 Abbey Court, WALTHAM ABBEY, EN9 1RF.
O'BRIEN, Mr. John James, BSc FCA *1976;* 27 Kings Road, BERKHAMSTED, HP4 3BH.
O'BRIEN, Mr. John Joseph, BA ACA *1992;* c/o Fossil East Ltd., 5F CDW Building, 388 Castle Peak Road, TSUEN WAN, NEW TERRITORIES, HONG KONG SAR.
O'BRIEN, Mr. John Paul, FCA *1973;* 47 Synge Street, DUBLIN 8, COUNTY DUBLIN, IRELAND.
O'BRIEN, Mr. John Richard, BSc ACA *1992;* Hawthorne Farmhouse Hawthorne Farm Ince Lane Wimbolds Trafford, CHESTER, CH2 4JP.
O'BRIEN, Mr. Jonathan Spencer Andrew, MA FCA *1995;* (Tax Fac), 30 Marlborough Street, BOSTON, MA 02116, UNITED STATES.
O'BRIEN, Mr. Julian Mark, ACA *2009;* 16 Wilde Avenue, KILLARNEY HEIGHTS, NSW 2087, AUSTRALIA.
O'BRIEN, Miss. Katherine Louise, ACA *2009;* Flat 4, 26 Ellison Road, LONDON, SW16 5BY.
•**O'BRIEN, Mrs. Kay, BA FCA** *1989;* (Tax Fac), Accountability GB Ltd, Portland House, 21 Narborough Road, Cosby, LEICESTER, LE9 1TA.
•**O'BRIEN, Mr. Kevin, BA FCA** *1985;* with DTE Business Advisory Services Limited, DTE House, Hollins Mount, Hollins Lane, BURY, BL9 8AT.
O'BRIEN, Mr. Kevin Christopher, FCA *1968;* PO Box 2732, RIYADH, 11461, SAUDI ARABIA.
•**O'BRIEN, Mrs. Lorna Jane, BA FCA** *1994;* L J O'Brien, Hawthorne Farmhouse, Ince Lane, Wimbolds Trafford, CHESTER, CH2 4JP.
O'BRIEN, Miss. Lucy, BSc ACA *2011;* 52 Saffron Close, Chineham, BASINGSTOKE, HAMPSHIRE, RG24 8XQ.
O'BRIEN, Mr. Mark Edward, BA ACA *1996;* 83 Melrose Avenue, LONDON, NW2 4LR.
•**O'BRIEN, Mr. Mark Thomas, FCA** *1973;* Mark O'Brien & Co, 22 New Street, CHIPPING NORTON, OX7 5LJ.

O'BRIEN, Mr. Matthew, ACA *2009;* 212 / 2 Albert Road, SOUTH MELBOURNE, VIC 3205, AUSTRALIA.
O'BRIEN, Mr. Matthew David, BA(Hons) ACA *2002;* 1 Staunton Road, KINGSTON UPON THAMES, SURREY, KT2 5TJ.
O'BRIEN, Mr. Michael, BA FCA *1973;* Nass Landscapes, P.O.Box 669, MANAMA, BAHRAIN.
•**O'BRIEN, Mr. Michael, ACA MAAT** *2004;* Reeves & Co LLP, Third Floor, 24 Chiswell Street, LONDON, EC1Y 4YX.
O'BRIEN, Mr. Michael Anthony, BA FCA *1975;* Beresford House, Beresford Lane, Plumpton Green, LEWES, BN8 4EN.
O'BRIEN, Mr. Michael John, FCA *1974;* L'Vov Cottage, Rue Des Vallees, Faldouet, St Martin, JERSEY, JE3 6BB.
O'BRIEN, Ms. Moira Jane, FCA *1969;* 68 Rathmore Terrace, CORK, COUNTY CORK, IRELAND.
O'BRIEN, Mr. Neil Christopher, BA ACA *1989;* South Gables, 7a The Crescent, HARTFORD, CHESHIRE, CW8 1QS.
•**O'BRIEN, Mr. Neil Edward, BA(Hons) ACA** *2003;* 50 Knox Road, GUILDFORD, SURREY, GU2 9AH.
•**O'BRIEN, Mr. Neil Terence, BA ACA ATII** *1995;* KPMG LLP, 15 Canada Square, LONDON, E14 5GL. See also KPMG Europe LLP
•**O'BRIEN, Mr. Nicholas David, FCA** *1978;* Kime O'Brien Limited, 1 Church Mews, Churchill Way, MACCLESFIELD, CHESHIRE, SK11 6AY.
O'BRIEN, Mr. Patrick Gerald, BSc(Hons) ACA *2004;* with Grant Thornton UK LLP, 30 Finsbury Square, LONDON, EC2P 2YU.
O'BRIEN, Mr. Patrick Matthew, FCA *1976;* 12 Edwards Grove, KENILWORTH, WARWICKSHIRE, CV8 2QY.
•**O'BRIEN, Mr. Paul Anthony, BA(Hons) FCA** *2000;* Edwards Veeder LLP, Alex House, 260-268 Chapel Street, SALFORD, M3 5JZ.
•**O'BRIEN, Mr. Paul Gerard, BA FCA** *1989;* (Tax Fac), TFD Dunhams, 11 Warwick Road, Old Trafford, MANCHESTER, M16 0QQ.
O'BRIEN, Mr. Peter Gareth, BSc ACA *2007;* Pricewaterhousecoopers Llp, 1 Hays Lane, LONDON, SE1 2RD.
O'BRIEN, Mr. Peter Michael, FCA *1971;* (Tax Fac), Sevenoaks Sound and Vision Limited, 111 London Road, SEVENOAKS, KENT, TN13 1BH.
O'BRIEN, Mr. Peter Terence, BSc ACA *1990;* Cazenove Asia Ltd, Room 2516 25th Floor, M Thai Tower, All Seasons Place, 87 Wireless Road, BANGKOK 10300 THAILAND.
O'BRIEN, Mr. Philip Charles, BSc FCA *1977;* Mulberry Cottage, 50 Braywick Road, MAIDENHEAD, BERKSHIRE, SL6 1DA.
O'BRIEN, Mr. Philip Michael, LLB ACA *1985;* Cherry Orchard, Chapel Lane, Wanborough, SWINDON, SN4 0AJ.
O'BRIEN, Miss. Rebecca, MSc ACA *2005;* 23 Uxbridge Road, SLOUGH, SL1 1SN.
O'BRIEN, Mr. Richard, BSc ACA *2011;* 3 Woodland Grove, BATH, BA2 7AT.
O'BRIEN, Mr. Richard Darius, BA ACA *2001;* 7611 Pagewood lane, HOUSTON, TX 77063, UNITED STATES.
O'BRIEN, Mr. Richard Geoffrey, BSc(Hons) FCA *2001;* 25A Rathcoole Avenue, LONDON, N8 9LY.
O'BRIEN, Mr. Richard Maurice, BSc ACA *1992;* 30 Drovers Way, Radyr, CARDIFF, CF15 8GG.
O'BRIEN, Mr. Richard Michael, MA MSci ACA *2003;* Schneckenburgerstr. 24, 81675 MUNICH, GERMANY.
O'BRIEN, Mr. Sean, ACA *2011;* 4 The Ridgeway, RUISLIP, MIDDLESEX, HA4 8QS.
O'BRIEN, Mrs. Sharon Elizabeth, BSc(Hons) ACA CTA *2002;* 57 George Street, Hurstead, ROCHDALE, LANCASHIRE, OL16 2RR.
•**O'BRIEN, Mr. Simon Anthony, BA ACA** *1997;* PricewaterhouseCoopers LLP, 1 Embankment Place, LONDON, WC2N 6RH. See also PricewaterhouseCoopers
O'BRIEN, Mr. Stephen Andrew, BSc ACA *1992;* 10 Carlton Road, Hale, ALTRINCHAM, WA15 8RJ.
O'BRIEN, Mr. Stephen Patrick, MEng ACA *1997;* with PricewaterhouseCoopers, 2 Southbank Boulevard, Southbank, MELBOURNE, VIC 3006, AUSTRALIA.
•**O'BRIEN, Mr. Stephen William, BA FCA** *1982;* O'Brien & Co, 31A Finkle Street, SELBY, YO8 4DT.
O'BRIEN, Mrs. Susan Lynn, BA ACA *1993;* Telereal Trillium Bastion House, 140 London Wall, LONDON, EC2Y 5DN.
O'BRIEN, Mr. Terence, FCA MBA *1974;* Unitech, 25 Bernard Street, EDINBURGH, EH6 6SH.
O'BRIEN, Mr. Terence Michael, FCA *1955;* Flat 32, The Pinnacle, Horder Mews, Old Town, SWINDON, WILTSHIRE SN1 3ED. (Life Member)
O'BRIEN, Mr. Terence Michael, BA ACA *1994;* 11 Calliandra Place, THORNLANDS, QLD 4164, AUSTRALIA.
O'BRIEN, Mr. Terence Patrick, BA(Hons) ACA *2001;* 20 Downs Cote Drive, BRISTOL, BS9 3TP.
O'BRIEN, Mrs. Theresa Bernadette, BA FCA *1989;* 11 Hollingford Place, KNUTSFORD, CHESHIRE, WA16 9DP.
O'BRIEN, Mr. Timothy James, MA FCA *1979;* Shell International Petroleum Co Ltd, Shell Centre, York Road, LONDON, SE1 7NA.
•**O'BRIEN, Mr. Timothy Joseph, BCom FCA** *1975;* with Optimum Support, 90 Long Acre, Covent Garden, LONDON, WC2E 9RZ.
O'BRIEN, Mr. Timothy Patrick, MA FCA *1979;* The Old Forge, 45 North Road, Highgate, LONDON, N6 4BE.
O'BRIEN, Mr. Vincent Gerald, BA ACA *1984;* Montagu Private Equity Llp, 2 More London Riverside, LONDON, SE1 2AP.
O'BRIEN THRING, Mrs. Una, BA FCA *1986;* Favray Court T6B22, Tigne Point, ST JULIANS TP01, MALTA.
O'BRYEN, Mr. Christoper Mark, BA FCA *1955;* 3 Devonport Road, LONDON, W12 8NZ. (Life Member)
O'BYRNE, Mrs. Elaine Penman, BSc ACA *1991;* 14 Rusthall Avenue, LONDON, W4 1BP.
O'BYRNE, Mr. Kevin, BBS FCA *1991;* Kingfisher Plc, 3 Sheldon Square, LONDON, W2 6PX.
•**O'CALLAGHAN, Mr. Andrew Edward, BCom FCA** *1993;* PricewaterhouseCoopers, One Spencer Dock, North Wall Quay, DUBLIN 1, COUNTY DUBLIN, IRELAND.
O'CALLAGHAN, Mrs. Ann Frances, BA ACA *1989;* 9 Mallard Walk, Mickleover, DERBY, DE3 0TF.
O'CALLAGHAN, Mr. Declan, BA(Hons) ACA *2001;* with Deloitte Touche Tohmatsu, Grosvenor Place, 225 George Street, P.O. Box N 250, SYDNEY, NSW 2000 AUSTRALIA.
O'CALLAGHAN, Mr. Gerard, MSc BA(Hons) ACA *2000;* 11 London Court, Frogmore, LONDON, SW18 1HH.
O'CALLAGHAN, Mrs. Jennifer, BSc(Hons) ACA *2003;* Isis Waterside Regeneration Canal Cottage, Vesta Street, MANCHESTER, M4 6EQ.
•**O'CALLAGHAN, Mr. John Patrick, FCA** *1972;* Dawstown, BLARNEY, COUNTY CORK, IRELAND.
O'CALLAGHAN, Mr. Joseph, BSc FCA *1989;* 9 Mallard Walk, Mickleover, DERBY, DE3 0TF.
O'CALLAGHAN, Miss. Mara, BA(Hons) ACA *2001;* 14 The Moors, REDHILL, RH1 2PE.
•**O'CALLAGHAN, Mr. Michael Henry Desmond, FCA** *1964;* (Tax Fac), M H D O'Callaghan, 36 Seymour Street, CAMBRIDGE, CB1 3DQ.
O'CALLAGHAN, Mr. Owen Michael, BA FCA *1988;* 4 Pretoria Road, HIGH WYCOMBE, BUCKINGHAMSHIRE, HP13 6QW.
O'CALLAGHAN, Mr. Richard Stephen, MBA FCA *1972;* PO Box 2889, SAXONWOLD, GAUTENG, 2132, SOUTH AFRICA.
O'CALLAGHAN, Mr. Shaun Matthew Paul, MA ACA FRSA *1995;* 15c George street, SAFFRON WALDEN, cb10 1ed.
O'CALLAGHAN, Mr. Terence Eugene, BSc ACA *1986;* Amillan Ltd, Connection House, Unit 3a, Parkway Industrial Estate, Heneage Street, BIRMINGHAM B7 4LY.
O'CALLAGHAN, Mr. Tyler Kelsey, ACA *2010;* 96 Pollards Hill North, LONDON, SW16 4NZ.
•**O'CARROLL, Mr. Rory Eamon, ACA CA(SA)** *2011;* 85 Hemingford Road, Islington, LONDON, N1 1BY.
O'CLAREY, Mr. Gerard Mark, BCom ACA *1983;* 3 Priory Crescent, LEWES, BN7 1HP.
•**O'CLEIRIGH, Mr. Barry Conor, BA ACA** *1983;* Ashworth Treasure (BOC) Limited, 17-19 Park Street, LYTHAM ST. ANNES, LANCASHIRE, FY8 5LU.
O'CLEIRIGH, Mr. Terence Paul, BA ACA *1988;* 25 Meadway, Harrold, BEDFORD, MK43 7DR.
O'CONNELL, Mrs. Ann Margaret, BA ACA *1995;* 1300 Campus Drive, Berkeley, SAN FRANCISCO, CA 94708, UNITED STATES.
O'CONNELL, Mr. Brian Michael Thomas, MSci ACA *2003;* Royal Bank of Scotland, 135 Bishopsgate, LONDON, EC2M 3UR.
O'CONNELL, Mr. Christian John, FCA *2000;* Old Bramley House, 52 Six Acres, Broughton Astley, LEICESTER, LE9 6PX.
•**O'CONNELL, Mr. Donal Peter, BA(Hons) ACA** *2001;* Shaw Gibbs LLP, 264 Banbury Road, OXFORD, OX2 7DY.
O'CONNELL, Mr. James Nicholas, BEng ACA *1993;* Talktalk Direct Ltd, Belgrave House, 1 Greyfriars, NORTHAMPTON, NN1 2TT.
O'CONNELL, Mr. Kerry Eamonn, ACA *1979;* Bank of America, 5 Canada Square, LONDON, E14 5AQ.
O'CONNELL, Mr. Martin Francis, BSc ACA *1984;* Bristan Group Ltd, Birch Coppice Business Park, Dordon, TAMWORTH, STAFFORDSHIRE, B78 1SG.
O'CONNELL, Mr. Martin Hartley, BA FCA *1977;* Abbeylands, Stackhouse, SETTLE, BD24 0DN.
O'CONNELL, Mr. Michael Brendan Anthony, FCA *1974;* 32 Snaresbrook Drive, STANMORE, HA7 4QW.
•**O'CONNELL, Mr. Michael James, BEng ACA** *1995;* Isosceles Finance Limited, PO Box 502, STAINES, MIDDLESEX, TW18 9AG.
O'CONNELL, Mr. Michael Patrick Andrew, FCA *1973;* M S International plc, Carr Hill, Balby, DONCASTER, DN4 8DH.
•**O'CONNELL, Mr. Peter, FCA** *1973;* Peter O'Connell FCA, Bickley, Westerdunes Park, NORTH BERWICK, EAST LOTHIAN, EH39 5HJ.
O'CONNELL, Mr. Peter Raymond, BA ACA *1995;* 1300 Campus Drive, Berkeley, SAN FRANCISCO, CA 94708, UNITED STATES.
O'CONNELL, Mr. Philip, BA ACA *2003;* Redwood Publishing Ltd, 7 St. Martin's Place, LONDON, WC2N 4HA.
O'CONNELL, Mr. Roly, BA ACA *2007;* 10 Seaforth Loop, Kallaroo, PERTH, WA 6025, AUSTRALIA.
O'CONNELL, Miss. Sarah, BSc ACA *2007;* Flat 45, 6 Hester Road, LONDON, SW11 4AL.
•**O'CONNELL, Mr. Sean Patrick, FCA** *1977;* O'Connell & Co, The Barn, 12a High Street, Wheathampstead, ST. ALBANS, AL4 8AA.
•**O'CONNELL, Mr. Timothy Stuart, BA ACA** *1985;* (Tax Fac), Business Wizards Limited, 12 Darley Mead Court, Hampton Lane, SOLIHULL, WEST MIDLANDS, B91 2QA.
O'CONNOR, Mrs. Andrea, BSc ACA *2005;* Speedy Hire PLC Number 1, The Parks, NEWTON-LE-WILLOWS, MERSEYSIDE, WA12 0JQ.
O'CONNOR, Ms. Aoife, BComm ACA *2003;* 6 Stockton Lawn, CASTLEKNOCK 15, COUNTY DUBLIN, IRELAND.
O'CONNOR, Mr. Austin John, FCA *1968;* 4 rue de l'Eglise, L-5481 WORMELDANGE, LUXEMBOURG.
O'CONNOR, Mr. Ben Thomas, ACA *2008;* with KPMG LLP, One Snowhill, Snow Hill Queensway, BIRMINGHAM, B4 6GN.
•**O'CONNOR, Mr. Brendan, MBA BBS ACA** *1991;* Brendan O'Connor, Rock Cottage, Kilnaclasha, SKIBBEREEN, COUNTY CORK, IRELAND.
O'CONNOR, Mr. Brendan John, BSc FCA *1994;* Apartment 2, 14 East Road, LONDON, SW19 1UY.
O'CONNOR, Mr. Charles Edward Patrick, BSc FCA *1979;* 17 Kings Oak Close, Monks Risborough, PRINCES RISBOROUGH, BUCKINGHAMSHIRE, HP27 9LB.
O'CONNOR, Mr. Christopher Patrick, BSc ACA *1984;* Psytechnics Ltd, 23 Museum Street, IPSWICH, IP1 1HN.
O'CONNOR, Miss. Claire Antonette, BSc ACA *1991;* All Saints Church, Foster Street, HARLOW, CM17 9HR.
O'CONNOR, Mr. Damian Joseph, ACA *2008;* Moss Fold, 13 Brookfield Lane, Clayton-le-Woods, CHORLEY, LANCASHIRE, PR6 7EG.
•**O'CONNOR, Mr. David, FCA** *1984;* Ernst & Young, Podsosensky Pereulok 20/12, 103062 MOSCOW, RUSSIAN FEDERATION. See also Ernst & Young Europe LLP
O'CONNOR, Mr. David Michael, BSc ACA *1994;* 10 Newlands Road, Southgate, CRAWLEY, WEST SUSSEX, RH11 8AL.
•**O'CONNOR, Ms. Dawn, BA FCA** *1985;* Yannons Limited, The Basement, 5 Orchard Gardens, TEIGNMOUTH, DEVON, TQ14 8DP.
O'CONNOR, Mrs. Deborah Anne, BSc ACA *1993;* 8 Edgell Road, STAINES, MIDDLESEX, TW18 2ES.
O'CONNOR, Mr. Denis James, FCA *1982;* 38B Crayford Road, LONDON, N7 0ND.
O'CONNOR, Mr. Edward Brendan, LLB ACA *1987;* (Tax Fac), Halifax Bank of Scotland, 10 Canons Way, BRISTOL, BS1 5LF.
O'CONNOR, Mr. Gerard Joseph, ACA *1980;* Emco Wheaton UK Ltd, Channel Road, Westwood Industrial Estate, MARGATE, CT9 4JR.
O'CONNOR, Mr. Huw, FCA *1992;* 32 Orchard Road, TWICKENHAM, TW1 1LY.
O'CONNOR, Mr. James Terence, ACA *2008;* Liebigstrasse 46, 60323 FRANKFURT AM MAIN, GERMANY.
O'CONNOR, Mrs. Joanna, BSc ACA *1998;* 1800 Pomelo, Dasmarinas Village, MAKATI CITY, PHILIPPINES.
O'CONNOR, Mr. John Peter, BSc FCA *1983;* PricewaterhouseCoopers, QVI Building, 250 St George's Terrace, GPO Box D198, PERTH, WA 6000 AUSTRALIA.
O'CONNOR, Mr. Joseph Michael, BA ACA *2005;* with Ernst & Young LLP, 1 More London Place, LONDON, SE1 2AF.
O'CONNOR, Mrs. Kate Yvonne, BA ACA *1999;* with Ernst & Young Global Ltd, Becket House, 1 Lambeth Palace Road, LONDON, SE1 7EU.
O'CONNOR, Mrs. Kay Denise, FCA *1968;* P O Box 3463, Cape Province, SOMERSET WEST, 7129, SOUTH AFRICA. (Life Member)
•**O'CONNOR, Mr. Kevin Patrick, BA FCA** *1985;* Baker Tilly Tax & Advisory Services LLP, 2 Whitehall Quay, LEEDS, LS1 4HG.
O'CONNOR, Mr. Liam Dennis Taaffe, MEng ACA *2002;* Zizzi, Floor 5, 2 Balcombe Street, LONDON, NW1 6NW.
O'CONNOR, Miss. Lisa Jane, ACA *2009;* 35 Savannah Place, Great Sankey, WARRINGTON, WA5 8GN.
O'CONNOR, Mr. Mark Skeen, BA ACA *1988;* Bollitree Lawns, Weston under Penyard, ROSS-ON-WYE, HEREFORDSHIRE, HR9 7PF.
O'CONNOR, Mr. Michael George James, BA ACA *1998;* Citigroup Centre, 33 Canada Square, LONDON, E14 5LB.
•**O'CONNOR, Mr. Michael Joseph Anselm, LLB FCA** *1985;* 3 Cresswell Park, LONDON, SE3 9RD.
O'CONNOR, Mr. Michael Peter, BCom ACA *1998;* 1800 Pomelo Street, Das Marinas Village, MAKATI CITY, PHILIPPINES.
O'CONNOR, Mrs. Michele Elizabeth, ACA MAAT *2002;* 35 Westgate, WETHERBY, WEST YORKSHIRE, LS22 6NH.
•**O'CONNOR, Mr. Neville George, BSc FCA** *1983;* O'Connor & Co, 22 Kendals Close, RADLETT, HERTFORDSHIRE, WD7 8NQ.
O'CONNOR, Mr. Patrick Anthony, BCom ACA *1996;* 23 The Glade, COULSDON, CR5 1SR.
O'CONNOR, Mr. Patrick Edward, BA ACA *2003;* 30 Tanah Merah Kechil Road, 02-06 East Meadows, SINGAPORE 465558, SINGAPORE.
O'CONNOR, Mr. Philip Andrew, BA ACA *1990;* Przy Parku, No 84, 05080 LIPKOW, POLAND.
O'CONNOR, Mrs. Sophie Jane, BA ACA *1995;* Egge 3, Fritzens, 6122 INNSBRUCK, AUSTRIA.
O'CONNOR, Mr. Stephen Anthony, BA FCA *1986;* The Business School, Sth Bank University, 103 Borough Road, LONDON, SE1 0AA.
O'CONNOR, Mr. Stephen Clifford, BSc ACA *1991;* 6 Ffordd Deg, CAERPHILLY, MID GLAMORGAN, CF83 1HZ.
O'CONNOR, Mr. Stephen Joseph Peter, BA FCA *1983;* The Homestead, Sycamore Rise, CHALFONT ST.GILES, HP8 4LD.
O'CONNOR, Mrs. Susie, ACA *2009;* 4c Southlands Grove, BROMLEY, BR1 2DQ.
O'CONNOR, Mr. Thomas Anthony, BCom ACA *1992;* Office 19, Wiejska 17, 00-480 WARSAW, POLAND.
O'CONNOR, Mr. Thomas Joseph, BA ACA *2003;* 35 Westgate, WETHERBY, LS22 6NH.
•**O'CONNOR, Mr. Timothy Edward, ACA FCCA** *2009;* Scrutton Bland, 820 The Crescent, Colchester Business Park, COLCHESTER, CO4 9YQ.
O'CONNOR, Mr. William Christopher Matthew, BA ACA *1993;* 17a Woodville Road, Harborne, BIRMINGHAM, B17 9AS.
O'CONNOR, Mr. William John, MSc BA FCA *1976;* 34 Medway Crescent, LEIGH-ON-SEA, SS9 2UY.
•**O'CONOR, Mr. Patrick Francis, BSc FCA** *1983;* (Tax Fac), Patrick O'Conor BSc FCA, 51 Downs Park West, Westbury Park, BRISTOL, BS6 7QL.
O'DEA, Mr. Bernard Philip, MA FCA *1968;* Flat 6/D Hyde Park Mansions, Cabbell Street, LONDON, NW1 5BJ.
O'DEA, Mr. John Brendan, BA ACA *1995;* Tremedda, Zennor, ST. IVES, CORNWALL, TR26 3BS.
O'DEA, Mr. Michael Patrick, BSc ACA *1989;* 24 Mount Ararat Road, RICHMOND, SURREY, TW10 6PG.
O'DOCHARTAIGH, Mr. Ruairi Eoghan, BSc(Hons) ACA *2003;* 70 Oak Road, BRISTOL, BS7 8RZ.
O'DOHERTY, Mr. Christopher Patrick, MA ACA *1988;* Valnord Cottage, Valnord Road, St. Peter Port, GUERNSEY, GY1 1DU.
O'DOHERTY, Mr. Liam, BSc ACA *1998;* 1 Welton Drive, WILMSLOW, CHESHIRE, SK9 6HF.
O'DOMHNAILL, Mr. Eamonn, BCom FCA *1994;* 16 Crichton Road, CARSHALTON, SM5 3LS.
O'DONNELL, Mrs. Angela, ACA *2003;* 73 Lindale Garth, Kirkhamgate, WAKEFIELD, WF2 0RW.
O'DONNELL, Mr. Brendan Daniel, BA FCA *1989;* (Tax Fac), George Arthur, 4 Wigmores South, WELWYN GARDEN CITY, HERTFORDSHIRE, AL8 6PL.
O'DONNELL, Miss. Claire Victoria, BSc ACA *2006;* with Deloitte LLP, 3 Rivergate, Temple Quay, BRISTOL, BS1 6GD.

•**O'DONNELL, Mr. Colin Patrick, FCA** *1973;* C.P. O'Donnell & Co., Homeland, Hempstead Road, Bovingdon, HEMEL HEMPSTEAD, HP3 0HF.
O'DONNELL, Mr. Conrad Mark, BSc ACA *1999;* 10 Ashlar Avenue, Cumbernauld, GLASGOW, G68 0GL.
O'DONNELL, Mrs. Deborah Jane, BA ACA *1989;* The Palms, 4 Cut Road, ST GEORGES GE04, BERMUDA.
O'DONNELL, Mr. Derek Michael John, MSc LLB ACA *1996;* 2 Ashley Park Crescent, WALTON-ON-THAMES, SURREY, KT12 1EX.
•**O'DONNELL, Miss. Elaine, BA ACA** *1996;* Ernst & Young LLP, 100 Barbirolli Square, MANCHESTER, M2 3EY. See also Ernst & Young Europe LLP
•**O'DONNELL, Mrs. Ellen, FCA** *1986;* Camerons Accountancy Consultants Limited, 9 Worton Park, Worton, WITNEY, OXFORDSHIRE, OX29 4SX. See also Camerons
O'DONNELL, Miss. Fidelma Ann, BA ACA *1993;* 17 Wroughton Road, Battersea, LONDON, SW11 6BE.
O'DONNELL, Miss. Fiona Alison, BA ACA *1994;* Homeland, Hempstead Road, Bovingdon, HEMEL HEMPSTEAD, HP3 0HF.
O'DONNELL, Mr. Hugh Michael, ACA CFA CPCU *1989;* Imagine Group, 4th Floor, 7 Reid Street, HAMILTON HM 11, BERMUDA.
O'DONNELL, Mr. James Christopher, BSc ACA *1991;* 13 Blind Quay Apartments, Lower Exchange Street, DUBLIN 8, COUNTY DUBLIN, IRELAND.
O'DONNELL, Miss. Jill Rosemary, BSc ACA *2004;* 83 St. Johns Road, DONCASTER, SOUTH YORKSHIRE, DN4 0QJ.
•**O'DONNELL, Mr. John Joseph Butler, BSc FCA** *1987;* with ICAEW, Metropolitan House, 321 Avebury Boulevard, MILTON KEYNES, MK9 2FZ.
•**O'DONNELL, Mr. John Patrick, BSc FCA** *1974;* Flat 3, Dartmouth House, Dartmouth Row, LONDON, SE10 8BF.
O'DONNELL, Mr. John Paul, MA BSc ACA *1994;* 10 Whitehall Road, Didsbury, MANCHESTER, M20 6RY.
O'DONNELL, Mrs. Julia Karen, BA FCA *1996;* Berkswell, Rewlands Drive, WINCHESTER, SO22 6PA.
O'DONNELL, Mrs. Kirsty Sarah, BA(Hons) ACA *2002;* Flat 14 Cavendish House, Southdowns Park, HAYWARDS HEATH, WEST SUSSEX, RH16 4SL.
O'DONNELL, Mr. Liam, MSc BSc ACA *2007;* Flat 1 Saffron Court, Saffron Close Earley, READING, RG6 7AB.
O'DONNELL, Mrs. Lisa, ACA *2011;* 25 Bridgeacre Gardens, COVENTRY, CV3 2NQ.
O'DONNELL, Miss. Majella, BSc ACA ACCA *1997;* 25 Wellington Terrace, HARROW, MIDDLESEX, HA1 3EP.
O'DONNELL, Mrs. Maria Sinead, BA ACA *2007;* with Grant Thornton UK LLP, Enterprise House, 115 Edmund Street, BIRMINGHAM, B3 2HJ.
O'DONNELL, Mr. Marshall John, BSc ACA *2003;* 16 Elm Drive, Northfield, BIRMINGHAM, B31 5JQ.
O'DONNELL, Mr. Matthew, ACA *2011;* 84 Lexicon Apartments, Mercury Gardens, ROMFORD, RM1 3HG.
•**O'DONNELL, Mr. Michael Richard, FCA** *1975;* (Tax Fac), Priory Practice Limited, 1 Abbots Quay, Monks Ferry, BIRKENHEAD, CH41 5LH.
O'DONNELL, Mr. Michael Robert Gerard, ACA *1987;* 33 The Avenue, HITCHIN, SG4 9RJ.
O'DONNELL, Mr. Owen Francis, BSc ACA *1992;* 11 Glenburn Road, Giffnock, GLASGOW, G46 6RE.
O'DONNELL, Mr. Patrick Joseph, BA ACA *2002;* 48 Melody Street, COOGEE, NSW 2034, AUSTRALIA.
O'DONNELL, Mr. Patrick Vincentt, FCA *1956;* 43 Swinburne Avenue, COVENTRY, CV2 5LH. (Life Member)
O'DONNELL, Mr. Paul Vincent, BSc ACA DChA *1989;* 7 Ullswater Road, COVENTRY, CV3 2DH.
•**O'DONNELL, Mr. Peter Nathan, FCA** *1989;* Stones Accountancy Limited, Outset House, Turkey Mill, Ashford Road, MAIDSTONE, KENT ME14 5PP.
O'DONNELL, Mrs. Philippa Jo, BA ACA ACCA *1998;* Water End, Longwater Lane, Finchampstead, WOKINGHAM, BERKSHIRE, RG40 4NX.
O'DONNELL, Mrs. Rachel Susan, BA ACA CTA *1991;* with PricewaterhouseCoopers LLP, Marlborough Court, 10 Bricket Road, ST. ALBANS, HERTFORDSHIRE, AL1 3JX.
O'DONNELL, Mr. Richard James, BSc ACA *1992;* 6 Model Cottages Vapery Lane Pirbright, WOKING, SURREY, GU24 0QB.
•**O'DONNELL, Mr. Rory Anthony, FCA** *1975;* BJ Dixon Walsh Limited, St. Marys House, Magdalene Street, TAUNTON, SOMERSET, TA1 1SB.
O'DONNELL, Mrs. Sarah Jane, MEng ACA *2001;* 16 Elm Drive, Northfield, BIRMINGHAM, B31 5JQ.
O'DONNELL, Mrs. Sarah Jane, BA ACA *1999;* 20 Saxon Road, Birkdale, SOUTHPORT, MERSEYSIDE, PR8 2AX.
O'DONNELL BOURKE, Mr. Patrick Francis John, BA ACA *1983;* Sherenden, Curtisden Green, Nr Goudhurst, CRANBROOK, KENT, TN17 1LJ.
O'DONNELL-KEENAN, Ms. Niamh, BBS *1989; (ACA Ireland 1981);* 142 Hampstead Way, LONDON, NW11 7XH.
O'DONOGHUE, Mr. Eugene Michael, FCA *1968;* 76a South Beach, TROON, KA10 6EG.
O'DONOGHUE, Miss. Lisa, ACA *2007;* 4 Waalwyk Drive, CANVEY ISLAND, SS8 8BN.
O'DONOGHUE, Miss. Maureen Teresa, MA ACA ATII *1991;* 77/1 Sadovnicheskaya Nab., 115035 MOSCOW, RUSSIAN FEDERATION.
•**O'DONOGHUE, Mr. Peter Sean James, BA FCA** *1993;* Deloitte LLP, 2 New Street Square, LONDON, EC4A 3BZ. See also Deloitte & Touche LLP
O'DONOGHUE, Mr. Rodney Charles, FCA *1961;* 30 Canonbury Park South, LONDON, N1 2FN.
O'DONOGHUE, Mr. Sean William, BCom FCA *1994;* 1748 Voorhees Ave, MANHATTAN BEACH, CA 90266, UNITED STATES.
O'DONOGHUE, Mr. Thomas Gerard, BSc FCA *1988;* IPGRI, Via dei Tre Denari, 472/a, Maccarese, 00057 ROME, ITALY.
•**O'DONOVAN, Mr. Brian, MSc ACA** *1993;* KPMG LLP, 15 Canada Square, LONDON, E14 5GL. See also KPMG Europe LLP
O'DONOVAN, Mr. James Alastair, BSc ACA *2002;* 10 Lothair Road, LONDON, W5 4TA.
•**O'DONOVAN, Miss. Kathleen Anne, BSc ACA** *1984;* Bird & Co International, 8 St. James's Place, LONDON, SW1A 1NP.
O'DONOVAN, Miss. Kelley Louise, ACA *2002;* 102 Sterling Way, Upper Cambourne, CAMBRIDGE, CB23 6AR.
O'DONOVAN, Mr. Malcolm, BA ACA *1993;* 35 Wexfenne Gardens, Pyrford, WOKING, GU22 8TX.
O'DONOVAN, Mr. Matthew Thomas, ACA *2009;* Flat 9 Wessex Court, Putney Hill, LONDON, SW15 6BG.
•**O'DONOVAN, Mr. Nicholas James, FCA** *1992;* Lonsdale & Marsh, Orleans House, Edmund Street, LIVERPOOL, L3 9NG.
O'DONOVAN, Mr. Peter Anthony, BA ACA *1992;* c/o Ms A Killingworth, 1 Pentwood Avenue, Redhill, NOTTINGHAM, NG5 8RR.
O'DOWD, Mrs. Enid Margaret, BA FCA *1973;* 34 Moyne Road, Ranelagh, DUBLIN 6, COUNTY DUBLIN, IRELAND.
O'DOWD, Mr. Lee, ACA *2009;* 35A Turnstone Drive, CARLISLE, CUMBRIA, CA2 7NU.
O'DRISCOLL, Mr. Brendan, BA(Hons) ACA *2001;* Flat 4 Highstone House, 21 Highbury Crescent, LONDON, N5 1RX.
O'DRISCOLL, Mrs. Heather Ann, FCA *2005;* Ireland 2004); Waltons Clark Whitehill LLP, Oakland House, 40 Victoria Road, HARTLEPOOL, CLEVELAND, TS26 8DD. See also Horwath Clark Whitehill (North East) LLP
O'DRISCOLL, Mr. Kevin Charles, FCA *1969;* 3 Moss Lane, PINNER, HA5 3BB. (Life Member)
O'DRISCOLL, Mr. Padraig Joseph, BCom ACA MBA *1998;* 12 Castlegate Grove, ADAMSTOWN, COUNTY DUBLIN, IRELAND.
O'DWYER, Miss. Deirdre Catherine Mary, BBS ACA *1993;* 3 Grosvenor Avenue, WIRRAL, MERSEYSIDE, CH48 7HA.
O'DWYER, Mr. Mark Joseph, BA FCA CertPFS *1992;* Close Haven, Ballaughton Meadows, Douglas, ISLE OF MAN, IM2 1JG.
•**O'DWYER, Mr. Richard, ACA** *1998;* KPMG LLP, 15 Canada Square, LONDON, E14 5GL. See also KPMG Europe LLP
O'DWYER, Mr. Stephen John, BSc ACA *1996;* M M A Insurance, Norman Place, READING, RG1 8DA.
O'EHLEY, Mrs. Jayne Michelle, MA ACA CTA *2006;* 3 Portland House, 1a St. Anns Terrace, LONDON, NW8 6PH.
O'FARRELL, Mr. Nicholas Patrick, BA FCA *1964;* Flat 3, 32 Sussex Street, LONDON, SW1V 4RL. (Life Member)
•**O'FARRELL, Mr. William, MBA BA FCA** *1971;* O'Farrell, 1 Chaucer Drive, LONDON, SE1 5TA.
O'FLAHERTY, Mr. Aidan, BSc ACA *2009;* 67 Hendale Avenue, LONDON, NW4 4LP.
O'FLAHERTY, Ms. Corrina Marie, BAcc ACA *2003;* with KPMG LLP, 15 Canada Square, LONDON, E14 5GL.
O'FLAHERTY, Dr. Emma, ACA *2009;* 26C Churchtown Road Lower, DUBLIN 14, COUNTY DUBLIN, IRELAND.
•**O'FLAHERTY, Mr. Sean Patrick, ACA FCCA** *2009;* Rosscot Limited, Thomas Edge House, Tunnell Street, St Helier, JERSEY, JE2 4LU. See also Rosscot Assurance Limited
O'GARA, Ms. Catherine Jane, BA ACA *1991;* 42 Kent Road, HARROGATE, NORTH YORKSHIRE, HG1 2ET.
O'GARA, Mrs. Sally Jane, ACA *2004;* 8 Landview Gardens, ONGAR, CM5 9EQ.
O'GOAN, Mrs. Lynn Michelle, BSc ACA *1994;* 168 Canterbury Road, HARROW, HA1 4PB.
O'GORMAN, Dr. Catriona Maria Theresa, PhD BSc ACA *2005;* 36 Maigh Dara, QUIN, COUNTY CLARE, IRELAND.
O'GORMAN, Mr. John Bernard, ACA *1996;* 1 Stafford Crescent, BRAINTREE, CM7 9PS.
O'GORMAN, Mr. Mark Christopher, BA(Hons) ACA *2002;* 8 Greencourt Road, Petts Wood, ORPINGTON, BR5 1QW.
O'GORMAN, Mr. Patrick Joseph, FCA *1975;* 48 The Grove, Little Aston, SUTTON COLDFIELD, B74 3UD.
•**O'GORMAN, Mr. Roy James, FCA** *1969;* Leigh Carr, 72 New Cavendish Street, LONDON, W1G 8AU.
O'GORMAN, Mr. Simon John, BA ACA *1990;* (Tax Fac), 7 Bridgewater Road, BERKHAMSTED, HP4 1HN.
O'GORMAN, Miss. Sinead, LLB ACA *2001;* 25 Chantrey Road, LONDON, SW9 9TD.
O'GRADY, Mr. Austin Joseph, FCA *1981;* 18 Oaklands, Robin Hood, WAKEFIELD, WF3 3UA.
O'GRADY, Mr. Brendan, ACA *2009;* Silverfleet Capital Partners LLP, One New Fetter Lane, LONDON, EC4A 1HH.
O'GRADY, Mr. Crevan Thomas, BAcc ACA *1996;* 375 Park Avenue, Suite 3001, NEW YORK, NY 10152, UNITED STATES.
O'GRADY, Mr. Martin, BA ACA *1990;* 3 Headlands Drive, BERKHAMSTED, HERTFORDSHIRE, HP4 2PG.
O'GRADY, Mr. Neil, BA ACA *1991;* 9 Clarence Road, Walthamstow, LONDON, E17 6AG.
O'GRADY, Mr. Ralph James, FCA *1960;* 5 Shadwell Park Court, Shadwell, LEEDS, LS17 8TS.
O'HAGAN, Mr. Antony Richard, TD DL FCA *1970;* 4 Chapel Close, Empingham, OAKHAM, RUTLAND, LE15 8BX.
O'HAGAN, Mr. Bernard Gerard, MA ACA *1986;* 46 Forest Grove, Eccleston Park, PRESCOT, MERSEYSIDE, L34 2RZ.
O'HAGAN, Mr. Colin, MA BAcc ACA *2004;* 8 Ormiston Avenue, GLASGOW, G14 9EZ.
O'HAGAN, Mr. Owen Richard, BA(Hons) ACA *2002;* 6 St. Marks Close, BEXHILL-ON-SEA, EAST SUSSEX, TN39 4PW.
O'HAGAN, Mr. Raymond Vincent Patrick, BA ACA *1985;* Rolls Royce, P O Box 31, DERBY, DE24 8BJ.
O'HAGAN, Mrs. Sandra Elizabeth, BA ACA *1995;* 4 Colwick Avenue, ALTRINCHAM, CHESHIRE, WA14 1LQ.
O'HAGAN, Miss. Susan Ann, BA ACA *2009;* La Fontaine Mews Les Petites Fontaines, St. Peter Port, GUERNSEY, GY1 1HX.
O'HALE, Miss. Leona, ACA *2004;* 30 Sundridge Avenue, BROMLEY, BR1 2PX.
•**O'HALLORAN, Mr. Philip Martin, FCA** *1986;* GCA, Beacon House, South Road, WEYBRIDGE, SURREY, KT13 9DZ. See also GCA (Surrey) Ltd
O'HANLON, Mr. Christopher, MA ACA *1980;* 40 Upper Park Road, KINGSTON-UPON-THAMES, KT2 5LD.
O'HANLON, Mr. David John, BA ACA *1986;* 28 Station Road, Haddenham, AYLESBURY, BUCKINGHAMSHIRE, HP17 8AN.
•**O'HANLON, Ms. Deborah Anne, BA ACA** *1991;* Ernst & Young LLP, Apex Plaza, Forbury Road, READING, RG1 1YE. See also Ernst & Young Europe LLP
O'HANLON, Miss. Gemma, ACA *2011;* Hazlewoods Windsor House, Barnett Way Barnwood, GLOUCESTER, GL4 3RT.
O'HANLON, Mr. Gerard Patrick, BSc ACA *1988;* 30 Larch Avenue, Bricket Wood, ST. ALBANS, AL2 3SN.
O'HANLON, Prof. John Francis, MA BA FCA *1978;* University of Lancaster, Department of Accounting &, Finance, LANCASTER, LA1 4YX.
O'HANLON, Mr. John Francis, MA ACA *1995;* 16 Monks Mead, Brightwell-cum-Sotwell, WALLINGFORD, OXFORDSHIRE, OX10 0RL.
O'HANRAHAN, Mrs. Joy Caroline, BA(Hons) ACA *2003;* 116 Merchants Quay, East Street, LEEDS, LS9 8BB.
O'HANRAHAN, Mr. Mark, BA ACA *2007;* 220 Wickersley Road, ROTHERHAM, SOUTH YORKSHIRE, S60 4JR.
O'HARA, Mr. Bernard Griffin, BSc FCA *2001;* K P M G Stokes House, 17-25 College Square East, BELFAST, BT1 6DH.
O'HARA, Mr. David John, BA FCA *1986;* 6 Brookfield, Oxspring, SHEFFIELD, S36 8WG.
O'HARA, Miss. Elizabeth Clare, ACA *2002;* 25 Kirkdale Road, HARPENDEN, HERTFORDSHIRE, AL5 2PT.
O'HARA, Mr. Hubert Joseph, BSc ACA *1991;* 95 Boundary Road, WOKING, GU21 5BS.
O'HARA, Mr. John Charles, BA(Hons) ACA *2002;* 13 California Close, SUTTON, SM2 6DQ.
O'HARA, Mr. Mark Stephen, BA FCA *1985;* Clarity Financial Solutions LLP, Newlands House, Goldbridge Road, Newick, LEWES, EAST SUSSEX BN8 4QP.
O'HARA, Mr. Mark Thomas Gerard, BA ACA *1990;* 3110 Richview Blvd., OAKVILLE L6M 0B8, ON, CANADA.
O'HARA, Mr. Peter Sean, MA FCA *1992;* 4 Stoneyhurst Road West, Gosforth, NEWCASTLE UPON TYNE, NE3 1PG.
O'HARA, Miss. Rachael Elizabeth, BA(Hons) ACA CTA *2000;* (Tax Fac), with BDO LLP, 55 Baker Street, LONDON, W1U 7EU.
O'HARA, Mr. Shaun David, BSc ACA *1993;* 8 Market Square, Stony Stratford, MILTON KEYNES, MK11 1BE.
O'HARA, Mr. Stephen, BTech ACA *1984;* 5a Munster Road, TEDDINGTON, TW11 9LR.
O'HARA, Mr. Steven Eric, JP MBA FCA *1976;* 1 Jubilee Gardens, Westbury, SHREWSBURY, SY5 9EQ.
O'HARE, Mr. Brendan, BBA ACA *2006;* 8 Grace Mews, BECKENHAM, BR3 1BF.
•**O'HARE, Miss. Carol, BA ACA** *1982;* PricewaterhouseCoopers LLP, 101 Barbirolli Square, Lower Mosley Street, MANCHESTER, M2 3PW. See also PricewaterhouseCoopers
O'HARE, Mrs. Catherine Grace, MEng ACA *2002;* 30 Edward Road, FARNHAM, GU9 8NP.
O'HARE, Ms. Debbie Marcia, BSc FCA *1992;* 6 Seafields, Warrenpoint, NEWRY, COUNTY DOWN, BT34 3TG.
O'HARE, Mr. James Boyd, BSc ACA *1982;* 31 Portico Road, Littleover, DERBY, DE23 3NJ.
•**O'HARE, Mr. John Daniel, FCA** *1969;* (Tax Fac), Robinson & Co, 72 Lowther Street, WHITEHAVEN, CA28 7AH. See also Robinson J.F.W. & Co
O'HARE, Miss. Natalie Jean, ACA *2008;* 45 Tremadoc Road, LONDON, SW4 7NA.
•**O'HARE, Mr. Sean Gerald Eugene, BSc ACA** *1980;* (Tax Fac), PricewaterhouseCoopers LLP, Pricewaterhousecoopers, 12 Plumtree Court, LONDON, EC4A 4HT. See also PricewaterhouseCoopers
O'HARE, Mr. Steven Jonathan, BA(Hons) ACA *2001;* Woodcote, The Circle, Mereside Road, Mere, KNUTSFORD, CHESHIRE WA16 6QY.
•**O'HEHIR, Mr. Geoffrey David, MA FCA** *1970;* G D O'Hehir & Co Ltd, 22/23 Clyde Terrace, SPENNYMOOR, DL16 7SE.
•**O'HERN, Mr. Jon Erik, FCA** *1992;* Wright Vigar Limited, 1st Floor, 13 Needham Road, LONDON, W11 2RP. See also Camamile Limited
O'KANE, Mr. Daniel Brian, FCA *1965;* 9 Narrow Lane, NORTH FERRIBY, HU14 3EN.
O'KANE, Miss. Helen Clare, MA ACA *1997;* 4 Culver Road, SOUTHSEA, HAMPSHIRE, PO4 9QP.
O'KANE, Mrs. Lindsay Clare, BA(Hons) ACA CTA *2002;* 7 Catesby Croft, Loughton, MILTON KEYNES, MK5 8FH.
O'KANE, Mr. Matthew James, MA ACA MCSI *2005;* 7 Catesby Croft, Loughton, MILTON KEYNES, MK5 8FH.
O'KANE, Mr. Terence Charles, FCA *1975;* Cromdale, 66 Sunderland Road, Forest Hill, LONDON, SE23 2PY.
•**O'KEEFE, Mrs. Anne Clare, BSc FCA** *1990;* with Zolfo Cooper Ltd, The Zenith Building, 26 Spring Gardens, MANCHESTER, M2 1AB.
O'KEEFE, Miss. Paula, BA ACA *1988;* 44 Water Lane, PURFLEET, ESSEX, RM19 1GS.
O'KEEFE, Mr. Peter Michael Mark, BA ACA *1997;* 29 Orchard Avenue, THAMES DITTON, KT7 0BB.
O'KEEFE, Dr. Stephen Christopher, ACA *2009;* 22 Alma Court, BRISTOL, BS8 2HH.
O'KEEFE, Mr. Stephen John, BA FCA *1983;* 16 Court Corner, OLNEY, MK46 5QH.
•**O'KEEFE, Mr. Timothy Eugene, FCA** *1971;* Acklands Limited, Waterloo House, Waterloo Street, Clifton, BRISTOL, BS8 4BT.
O'KEEFFE, Mrs. Anna Catherine, BA(Hons) ACA *2001;* 87 Kennel Lane, BILLERICAY, ESSEX, CM11 2SW.
•**O'KEEFFE, Mr. David John, BSc FCA ATII** *1988;* 18 Cotsford Avenue, NEW MALDEN, SURREY, KT3 5EU.
O'KEEFFE, Miss. Fiona Marian Bernadette, BA ACA *1998;* 51 Copse Hill, Wimbledon, LONDON, SW20 0NJ.
O'KEEFFE, Mrs. Jill Rowena, BSc ACA *1988;* Springfield, Legh Road, KNUTSFORD, CHESHIRE, WA16 8NT.

O'KEEFFE, Mr. John Kevin, BSc ACA *2006;* 41 Rushendon Furlong, Pitstone, LEIGHTON BUZZARD, BEDFORDSHIRE, LU7 9QX.
O'KEEFFE, Mr. Kieran Paul, BA ACA *1992;* 10 Dukes Road, Lindfield, HAYWARDS HEATH, WEST SUSSEX, RH16 2JH.
O'KEEFFE, Mr. Liam Francis, BSc ACA *1988;* Calyon Broadwalk House, 5 Appold Street, LONDON, EC2A 2DA.
O'KEEFFE, Mr. Michael Timothy, BCom FCA *1972;* Kingsleigh House, Drury Lane, Martin Hussingtree, WORCESTER, WR3 8TD.
O'KEEFFE, Mr. Neil William, BSc ACA MCT *1999;* 4 The Rose Walk, RADLETT, HERTFORDSHIRE, WD7 7JS.
O'KEEFFE, Mrs. Nicola Jayne, BSc ACA *1998;* 35 Wedgewood Gardens, ST.HELENS, MERSEYSIDE, WA9 5GA.
O'KEEFFE, Mr. Paul, BBS ACA *2001;* Flat 3 Montana Building, Deals Gateway, LONDON, SE13 7QF.
•O'KEEFFE, Mr. Timothy Michael, BA ACA *1990;* (Tax Fac), Lawrence Johns, 202 Northolt Road, HARROW, HA2 0EX.
O'KELLY, Mr. Mark Charles, BA ACA DChA *1987;* Childhood First, 150 Waterloo Road, LONDON, SE1 8SB.
•O'LEARY, Mr. Brian Michael, BSc FCA *1977;* Brian Paul Limited, Chase Green House, 42 Chase Side, ENFIELD, MIDDLESEX, EN2 6NF.
O'LEARY, Mr. Christopher John, MA FCA *1989;* 7 Angel Road, THAMES DITTON, KT7 0AU.
•O'LEARY, Mr. David, BA ACA CTA *1999;* Deloitte LLP, PO Box 500, 2 Hardman Street, MANCHESTER, M60 2AT. See also Deloitte & Touche LLP
O'LEARY, Miss. Emma Fionnuala, BA ACA *2010;* 45 Broadhurst Gardens, West Hampstead, LONDON, NW6 3QT.
O'LEARY, Mr. Gerard, FCA *1976;* Line up Communications Ltd, 6 Castle Row Horticultural Place, LONDON, W4 4JQ.
O'LEARY, Mr. John Francis, FCA *1977;* 815 Leeds Road, Chidswell, DEWSBURY, WF12 7HT.
O'LEARY, Mrs. Kelly, ACA *2008;* 11 Ravenoak Park Road, Cheadle Hulme, CHEADLE, CHESHIRE, SK8 7EH.
O'LEARY, Mrs. Kirsty Blair, BSc ACA *1990;* Disc Work Ltd, 16 Blackchapel Drive, ROCHDALE, LANCASHIRE, OL16 4QU.
O'LEARY, Mr. Mark Adrian, BA ACA *1990;* 14 Trowley Hill Road, Flamstead, ST. ALBANS, AL3 8EE.
O'LEARY, Mr. Martin Vincent, BSc ACA ACT *1990;* 14 Whitlaw Close, CHAPPAQUA, NY 10514, UNITED STATES.
O'LEARY, Mr. Michael George, FCA *1972;* 9 Ashdown Road, Hillingdon, UXBRIDGE, MIDDLESEX, UB10 0HY. See also Richings & Co
•O'LEARY, Mr. Patrick Joseph, BSc FCA CPA *1981;* SPX Corporation, 13515 Ballantyne Corp Place, CHARLOTTE, NC 28277, UNITED STATES.
O'LEARY, Mr. Paul Simon, BA ACA *1993;* The Old Croft, Bellingdon, CHESHAM, BUCKINGHAMSHIRE, HP5 2XW.
•O'LEARY, Mr. Raymond, ACA *1981;* Raymond O'Leary, 62 Ski View, SUNDERLAND, SR3 1NP.
O'LEARY, Mr. Richard Ernest, MA BSc FCA *1977;* Packard Bell, Immeuble Optima, 10 Rue Godefroy, Cedex, 92821 PUTEAUX, FRANCE.
O'LEARY, Mr. Stephen, BSc ACA *1982;* with Baker Tilly Corporate Finance LLP, 2 Whitehall Quay, LEEDS, LS1 4HG.
•O'LOUGHLIN, Miss. Fiona Margaret, BSc FCA *1993;* with DTE Business Advisory Services Limited, DTE House, Hollins Mount, Hollins Lane, BURY, BL9 8AT.
O'LOUGHLIN, Mr. Sean Edward, BA ACA *1999;* 9a Castle Road, WEYBRIDGE, KT13 9QP.
O'MAHONEY, Mr. Derek, BSc ACA ACCA *1999;* 48 The Mount, Cheylesmore, COVENTRY, CV3 5GU.
O'MAHONEY, Mr. Graham David, BA ACA *1999;* 2 Groby Road, ALTRINCHAM, CHESHIRE, WA14 1RS.
O'MAHONEY, Mr. Kevin Patrick, BSc FCA *1967;* 4 Dockacre Road, LAUNCESTON, CORNWALL, PL15 8BW. (Life Member)
O'MAHONEY, Mr. Michael, BSc ACA *1986;* 1 Giles Travers Close, Thorpe Village, EGHAM, SURREY, TW20 8UQ.
O'MAHONY, Mrs. Anne, ACA *1984;* Eddie Stobart Ltd, Solway Business Centre, Kingstown, CARLISLE, CA6 4BY.
•O'MAHONY, Mrs. Jane Sari Teresa, BCom ACA *1984;* Solutions 4 Business LLP, 5 Fairmile, HENLEY-ON-THAMES, OXFORDSHIRE, RG9 2JR.
•O'MAHONY, Dr. John, PhD ACA *1994;* Grant Thornton UK LLP, Grant Thornton House, 22 Melton Street, Euston Square, LONDON, NW1 2EP. See also Grant Thornton LLP
•O'MAHONY, Mr. John Finbarr, BSc ACA *1986;* Solutions 4 Business LLP, 5 Fairmile, HENLEY-ON-THAMES, OXFORDSHIRE, RG9 2JR.
O'MAHONY, Mrs. Lucy Caroline Eleanor, BSc ACA *2007;* (Tax Fac), 13 John Archer Way, LONDON, SW18 2TQ.
O'MAHONY, Mr. Paul Dominic, ACA *1990;* KPMG Corporate Finance, 1 Cours Valmy, 92923 PARIS LA DEFENCE CEDEX, FRANCE.
O'MAHONY, Mr. Simon Glenisterr, MA ACA *1978;* 70 Alleyn Road, Dulwich, LONDON, SE21 8AH.
O'MAHONY KSG, Mr. John Ivor, BSc(Econ) FCA *1961;* Overstrand, 20 Shirley Road, HOVE, BN3 6NN. (Life Member)
O'MALLEY, Miss. Bridget Mary, BA ACA *1990;* 5 Ingham Road, Bawtry, DONCASTER, SOUTH YORKSHIRE, DN10 6NN.
O'MALLEY, Mrs. Emily Frances, BSc ACA *2001;* Oakshaw, 25 Station Avenue, WALTON-ON-THAMES, KT12 1NF.
•O'MALLEY, Mr. Graham Robert, FCA *1975;* (Tax Fac), Gane Jackson Scott LLP, 144 High Street, EPPING, ESSEX, CM16 4AS.
•O'MALLEY, Mr. Kevin John, ACA *1980;* Brevins Ltd, 23 Porters Wood, ST. ALBANS, HERTFORDSHIRE, AL3 6PQ.
•O'MALLEY, Mr. Liam James Paul, FCA *1981;* (Tax Fac), Clifford Roberts, 63 Broad Green, WELLINGBOROUGH, NORTHAMPTONSHIRE, NN8 4LQ.
O'MALLEY, Mr. Martin James, BSc ACA *1995;* Standard Bank, Group Internal Audit, 5 Simmonds Street, JOHANNESBURG, 2000, SOUTH AFRICA.
O'MALLEY, Mr. Raymond Antony Hugh, BA ACA *1990;* Stable Cottage, 90 New Road, Haslingfield, CAMBRIDGE, CB23 1LP.
O'MARA, Dr. Jason Andrew, BSc ACA *1999;* 11 Ashcombe Road, Wimbledon, LONDON, SW19 8JP.
O'MARA, Mrs. Philippa Jane, BSc FCA *1992;* Diva Business Solutions Limited, PO Box 632, PUKEKOHE 2340, NEW ZEALAND.
O'MEARA, Mr. Michael Patrick, FCA *1974;* Flat 3, 44 Triq Il Mandragg, BIRGU, MALTA.
O'MULLOY, Miss. Gillian, MA ACA *1982;* 38 Birchgrove Road, Balmain, SYDNEY, NSW 2041, AUSTRALIA.
O'NEAL, Mr. Harvey Harry Alexander, ACA *2007;* Woodlands, 18 Shirley Church Road, CROYDON, CR0 5EE.
O'NEIL, Mr. Andrew James, ACA *2008;* 34 Oval View, MIDDLESBROUGH, NORTH YORKSHIRE, TS4 3SW.
O'NEIL, Miss. Katie, BSc(Hons) ACA *2010;* 14 Merrow Avenue, POOLE, DORSET, BH12 1PX.
O'NEIL, Mr. Martin James, BA(Hons) ACA *2002;* A G Thames Holdings Ltd Thames House, Thames Road Crayford, DARTFORD, DA1 4QP.
O'NEILL, Mr. Anthony Dennis, BSc ACA *1980;* 46 Kingswood Firs, Grayshott, HINDHEAD, GU26 6ES.
O'NEILL, Mr. Brian, ACA *2008;* Byways, Friary Road, ASCOT, SL5 9HD.
O'NEILL, Mr. Callum, BSc ACA *2011;* 6 Harbour Walk, 91 Cumberland Road, BRISTOL, BS1 6UJ.
O'NEILL, Miss. Catherine, BA ACA *2007;* 122 Crystal Palace Road, LONDON, SE22 9ER.
O'NEILL, Miss. Charlotte, ACA *2007;* 94a Mysore Road, LONDON, SW11 5SA.
O'NEILL, Mr. Chris, BSc ACA *2003;* 3 The Crescent, Stretton Road Great Glen, LEICESTER, LE8 9HD.
O'NEILL, Mr. Christopher Robert, BCom ACA *1999;* 29 Horseshoe Crescent, Burghfield Common, READING, RG7 3XW.
O'NEILL, Miss. Claire, BSc ACA *2009;* 33a Maygrove Road, LONDON, NW6 2EE.
O'NEILL, Mr. Collingwood Arthur, FCA *1956;* 1 Longlands Spinney, Charmandean, WORTHING, BN14 9NU. (Life Member)
O'NEILL, Mr. David Michael, BSc ACA *2005;* with Deloitte LLP, Athene Place, 66 Shoe Lane, LONDON, EC4A 3BQ.
O'NEILL, Mrs. Elisabeth Rhona, BA ACA *1987;* 159 Upper Grosvenor Road, TUNBRIDGE WELLS, KENT, TN1 2EB.
O'NEILL, Miss. Elizabeth Hannah, BA(Hons) ACA *2010;* 25 The Pavement, LONDON, SW4 0JA.
O'NEILL, Mrs. Elspeth Katherine, BA(Hons) ACA *2002;* Brookside Callerton Lane, Ponteland, NEWCASTLE UPON TYNE, NE20 9EG.
O'NEILL, Mr. Eugene Malcolm, FCA *1968;* 11 Biggar Bank Road, Walney Island, BARROW-IN-FURNESS, CUMBRIA, LA14 3YF. (Life Member)
O'NEILL, Mr. Garry, MA ACA *1998;* (Tax Fac), with KPMG LLP, 15 Canada Square, LONDON, E14 5GL.
O'NEILL, Miss. Hannah Katie, BA(Hons) ACA CTA *2004;* Flat 5, 46 Keswick Road, LONDON, SW15 2JE.
O'NEILL, Miss. Jane, BA ACA *2007;* 243c Queenstown Road, Battersea, LONDON, SW8 3NP.
O'NEILL, Mr. Jeffrey Paul, BA ACA *1993;* Nepia Ltd, 100 The Quayside, NEWCASTLE UPON TYNE, NE1 3DU.
O'NEILL, Mrs. Jennifer Michelle, BSc ACA *2003;* 19 Maryville Avenue, BELFAST, BT9 7HE.
O'NEILL, Mr. John Paul, MBA FCA *1972;* Coombe Langly, Kingston Hill, KINGSTON UPON THAMES, SURREY, KT2 7JZ.
O'NEILL, Mr. John Richard, BSc ACA *2005;* Unit 12 Adelaide Business Centre, Apollo Road, BELFAST, BT12 6HP.
O'NEILL, Miss. Karen Julie, BSc ACA *1997;* 52 Blandfield Road, Clapham, LONDON, SW12 8BG.
O'NEILL, Mrs. Kathryn Lynne Ryding, ACA *2008;* 32 Waldron Road, LONDON, SW18 3TE.
O'NEILL, Mrs. Kay Alexandra, BSc ACA *1999;* 71 Cotham Brow, BRISTOL, BS6 6AW.
O'NEILL, Mr. Kevin Edward, BSc ACA *1984;* 61 Cedar Road, BERKHAMSTED, HERTFORDSHIRE, HP4 2LB.
O'NEILL, Mr. Michael Robert, BA ACA *1993;* Langley Vale, 134 Chipperfield Road, KINGS LANGLEY, WD4 9JD.
O'NEILL, Mrs. Myrtle Dorothy, FCA *1972;* Hitachi Europe Ltd, Whitebrook Park, Lower Cookham Road, MAIDENHEAD, BERKSHIRE, SL6 8YA.
•O'NEILL, Mr. Nigel Anthony, FCA *1974;* Amicus Consulting LLP, 3 Gray's Inn Square, LONDON, WC1R 5AH.
•O'NEILL, Mr. Patrick Edward Francis, FCA DChA *1976;* Crowe Clark Whitehill LLP, Aquis House, 49-51 Blagrave Street, READING, RG1 1PL. See also Horwath Clark Whitehill LLP and Crowe Clark Whitehill
•O'NEILL, Mr. Peter Matthew, BSc FCA *1979;* Ernst & Young LLP, Apex Plaza, Forbury Road, READING, RG1 1YE. See also Ernst & Young Europe LLP
O'NEILL, Miss. Rachel Claire, BA(Hons) ACA *2011;* Flat 54, Brockwell Court, Effra Road, Brixton, LONDON, SW2 1NA.
O'NEILL, Mr. Robert Hugh, MA ACA *1985;* Sayga Flour Mills, Industrial Area North, KHARTOUM, SUDAN.
O'NEILL, Mrs. Rosaleen Anne, LLB ACA ATII CTA *1989;* 39 Largy Road, Carnlough, BALLYMENA, COUNTY ANTRIM, BT44 0EZ.
O'NEILL, Miss. Sally Ann, BA FCA DChA *1987;* Royal Opera House, Covent Garden, LONDON, WC2E 9DD.
O'NEILL, Mr. Samuel Luke, ACA *2009;* Flat 5, 46 Keswick Road, LONDON, SW15 2JE.
O'NEILL, Mr. Sean, BA(Hons) ACA *2011;* 51 Rockleigh Road, Bassett, SOUTHAMPTON, SO16 7AQ.
•O'NEILL, Mr. Shane Oliver Francis, BA(Hons) ACA *2001;* Shane O'Neill Esq. BA ACA, 26 Montreal Street, Levenshulme, MANCHESTER, M19 3BY.
•O'NEILL, Mr. Simon Daniel, BSc ACA *1999;* Ernst & Young LLP, 1 Colmore Square, BIRMINGHAM, B4 6HQ. See also Ernst & Young Europe LLP
O'NEILL, Mr. Simon Hugh, BA FCA *1999;* Flat 5 Newell House, Newell Street, LONDON, E14 7HQ.
•O'NEILL, Mr. Stephen Christopher, FCA *1976;* Gibsons Financial Limited, Foresters Hall, 25-27 Westow Street, LONDON, SE19 3RY. See also Gibsons
O'NEILL, Mr. Stephen John, MA ACA *1985;* 3 Hillary Close, Llanishen, CARDIFF, CF14 5AU.
O'NEILL, Miss. Susan, BA ACA *2006;* RCN, 20 Cavendish Square, LONDON, WC1X 8HL.
O'NEILL, Mrs. Susan Maria, BA ACA *1993;* Merlin Housing Society Riverside Court, Bowling Hill Chipping Sodbury, BRISTOL, BS37 6JX.
O'NEILL, Miss. Susan Stephanie, LLB ACA *1997;* 9 Haverstock Place, LONDON, N1 8BX.
O'NEILL, Mr. Thomas, ACA *2008;* Byways, Friary Road, ASCOT, BERKSHIRE, SL5 9HD.
O'NEILL, Mr. Thomas Roy Doylee, FCA *1953;* Juniper Hill, Little Lane, Wrawby, BRIGG, DN20 8RW. (Life Member)
O'NEILL, Mr. Timothy, BSc(Hons) ACA *2011;* 2 Nelson Mandela Road, LONDON, SE3 9QR.
O'NEILL, Mrs. Tracey Lorraine, BSc ACA *2003;* 1 Warstock Close, SOLIHULL, B91 1JE.
O'NEILL, Mrs. Vicki Anne, BA ACA *2006;* 2 Delville Avenue, Keyworth, NOTTINGHAM, NG12 5JA.
O'NEILL, Mr. William Michaell, FCA *1956;* Flat 2, 3 The Parks, Belfast Road, HOLYWOOD, COUNTY DOWN, BT18 9EH. (Life Member)
O'REGAN, Mr. David Joseph, MSc BA FCA *1994;* Office of Internal Oversight and Evaluation Services, Pan American Health Organization, 525 23rd Street NW, WASHINGTON, DC 20037, UNITED STATES.
O'REGAN, Mrs. Jacqueline Margaret, BA ACA *1997;* Newnham House, Ridge Lane, Newnham, HOOK, HAMPSHIRE, RG27 9AS.
O'REILLY, Mr. Anthony, FCA *1975;* 71 Buckstones Road Shaw, OLDHAM, OL2 8DW.
O'REILLY, Mr. Anthony John, BA ACA *1988;* PricewaterhouseCoopers LLP, 125 High Street, BOSTON, MA 02110, UNITED STATES. See also PricewaterhouseCoopers
O'REILLY, Mrs. Anya Marjorie, BA ACA *1999;* 4 Dunchurch Road, SALE, CHESHIRE, M33 5FD.
O'REILLY, Miss. Carmel Mary, MA FCA CTA *1982;* 30 Upwood Road, LONDON, SE12 8AD.
O'REILLY, Miss. Catherine Mary, BA ACA *1996;* 22c Acol Road, South Hampstead, LONDON, NW6 3AG.
O'REILLY, Mr. Christopher Danny, BSc ACA *1986;* 1 Lanhill View, CHIPPENHAM, SN14 6XS.
O'REILLY, Mr. Derek Michael, BA ACA *1990;* 36 St. Marys Road, LEAMINGTON SPA, CV31 1JP.
O'REILLY, Mr. Hugh John Joseph, FCA *1947;* St. Rita's Nursing Home, St. Georges Park, Ditchling Road, BURGESS HILL, WEST SUSSEX, RH15 0GT. (Life Member)
O'REILLY, Mr. John Andrew, BSc ACA *1999;* 77 Holtspur Top Lane, BEACONSFIELD, BUCKINGHAMSHIRE, HP9 1DR.
O'REILLY, Mrs. Kathryn, BA ACA *2004;* 111b Ramsden Road, Balhan, LONDON, SW12 8RD.
•O'REILLY, Mrs. Kay Francis, LLB FCA *1991;* (Tax Fac), Cube Partners Limited, 5 Giffard Court, Millbrook Close, NORTHAMPTON, NN5 5JF.
O'REILLY, Miss. Mary-Anne, BSc FCA *1991;* 112 North Road, St. Andrews, BRISTOL, BS6 5AL.
O'REILLY, Mr. Paul Levins Michael, BA FCA *1980;* 535 Woodlands Road, Harrison, NEW YORK, NY 10528, UNITED STATES.
O'REILLY, Mr. Stephen John, BSc ACA *1983;* 29 Lawson Close, Woolston, WARRINGTON, WA1 4EG.
O'REILLY, Mr. Thomas, BSc ACA *1992;* 444 Stratford Road, Shirley, SOLIHULL, B90 4AQ.
O'REILLY, Mr. Thomas Carl, BSc ACA *1994;* The Byre, Manor Farm, Holton, WINCANTON, SOMERSET, BA9 8AX.
•O'REILLY, Mr. William Patrick Joseph, BA ACA *1983;* KPMG LLP, One Snowhill, Snow Hill Queensway, BIRMINGHAM, B4 6GN. See also KPMG Europe LLP
O'RIORDAN, Mr. Brian Roy, FCA *1958;* 41 Lawn Lane, CHELMSFORD, CM1 6PR. (Life Member)
O'RIORDAN, Mr. Christopher David, BA ACA *1992;* 5 Guarlford Road, MALVERN, WR14 3QW.
O'RIORDAN, Mr. Daniel Joseph, MA ACA *1999;* Flat 12, 34A Whitechapel Street, MANCHESTER, M20 6TX.
O'RIORDAN, Mrs. Ellen Patricia, LLB ACA *1993;* 6 Hillyfields, WOODBRIDGE, SUFFOLK, IP12 4DX.
O'RIORDAN, Mr. Eugene, ACA AITI *1998;* 6 Woodbrook Drive, Bishopstown, CORK, COUNTY CORK, IRELAND.
O'RIORDAN, Mr. Robert, BSc ACA *1980;* Les Cheseaux Dessus G5, CH-1264 SAINT CERGUE, SWITZERLAND.
O'ROARKE, Mr. John Brendan, BA ACA *1984;* Overhills Northdown Road, Woldingham, CATERHAM, CR3 7BB.
O'RORKE, Mr. Timothy Mawdesley, MA FCA *1955;* Denstone, WADHURST, TN5 6SX. (Life Member)
O'ROURKE, Miss. Carmel, BA ACA *1996;* Merseyrail Electrics 2000 Ltd, Rail House, Lord Nelson Street, LIVERPOOL, L1 1JF.
O'ROURKE, Miss. Elizabeth, BSc ACA *2011;* 123 Blackburn Avenue, BROUGH, NORTH HUMBERSIDE, HU15 1EU.
O'ROURKE, Ms. Emma Ruth, BA ACA *1992;* Northstar Equity Investor Maybrook House, 27 Grainger Street, NEWCASTLE UPON TYNE, NE1 5JE.
•O'ROURKE, Mr. James, BA ACA *2002;* Blue Spire South LLP, Cawley Priory, South Pallant, CHICHESTER, WEST SUSSEX, PO19 1SY.
O'ROURKE, Mr. John Dominic, BCom FCA *1984;* 5 Overdale Grange, Knaresborough Road, SKIPTON, BD23 6AG.
•O'ROURKE, Mr. Paul Aloysius, BSc FCA *1993;* (Tax Fac), Adler Shine LLP, Aston House, Cornwall Avenue, LONDON, N3 1LF.

O'SHAUGHNESSY, Miss. Anna Frances Grace, BA ACA *2007;* Financial Services Authority, 25 North Colonnade, LONDON, E14 5HS.
O'SHAUGHNESSY, Miss. Caroline, ACA *2009;* Autobar Group Ltd, 389 Chiswick High Road, LONDON, W4 4AJ.
O'SHAUGHNESSY, Mrs. Holly Alana, BSc ACA *2000;* 23 Chalvington Drive, ST LEONARDS-ON-SEA, EAST SUSSEX, TN37 7SB.
O'SHAUGHNESSY, Ms. Isobel, BA ACA *1997;* X L Services UK Ltd, XL House, 70 Gracechurch Street, LONDON, EC3V 0XL.
O'SHAUGHNESSY, Mr. Kevin John, BSc FCA *1985;* Bromarv Limited, Unit 2211 Shell Tower, Times Square, 1 Matheson Street, CAUSEWAY BAY, HONG KONG SAR.
O'SHAUGHNESSY, Mr. Luke Christopher, ACA *2011;* 16 St Peter's Court, Horbury, WAKEFIELD, WEST YORKSHIRE, WF4 6AP.
O'SHAUGHNESSY, Mr. Michael Timothy, FCA *1974;* Kidd Rapinet, 33 Queen Street, MAIDENHEAD, SL6 1ND.
O'SHAUGHNESSY, Mr. William John, BCom ACA *1980;* 81 Marshall's Drive, ST. ALBANS, AL1 4RD.
O'SHEA, Miss. Bridget Catherine, BA ACA *1989;* 70 Los Balcones, ALAMO, CA 94507-2053, UNITED STATES.
O'SHEA, Ms. Eimear, ACA *2008;* Flat 1-3, 53 Blackheath Park, LONDON, SE3 9SQ.
O'SHEA, Mrs. Emily Joan, BSc ACA *2004;* 40 Quarry Road, Chadlington, CHIPPING NORTON, OXFORDSHIRE, OX7 3PB.
O'SHEA, Mr. Finbarr Emmett, FCA *1976;* Finbarr O'Shea, Donnellan Drive, Loughrea, GALWAY, COUNTY GALWAY, IRELAND. (Life Member)
O'SHEA, Mr. Gerald, ACA *1990;* 31 Tudor Way, Hillingdon, UXBRIDGE, UB10 9AA.
O'SHEA, Mr. Ian David, BSc ACA *1988;* (Tax Fac), Villa Claude, 5 De L'Avenue St. Michael, 98000 MONTE CARLO, MONACO.
O'SHEA, Mr. John, FCA *1964;* 6 rue de Champagne, 67450 LAMPERTHEIM, FRANCE.
O'SHEA, Mrs. Julie Patricia, ACA *1987;* 27 Chalfield Close, Keynsham, BRISTOL, BS31 1JZ.
O'SHEA, Mrs. Katharine Judith, BA ACA *1996;* BBH Ltd, 60 Kingly Street, LONDON, W1R 6DS.
O'SHEA, Mr. Maurice Joseph, MBA BA ACA *1986;* Highpoint Dorking Road Warnham, HORSHAM, WEST SUSSEX, RH12 3RZ.
•**O'SHEA, Mr. Richard Kenneth Cuan, BA ACA** *1979;* Cuan O'Shea, Langdon House, Langdon Road, SA1 Swansea Waterfront, SWANSEA, SA1 8QY.
O'SHEA, Mr. Stephen Michael, BA ACA *1986;* 65 Glasslyn Road, LONDON, N8 8RJ.
O'SHEA, Mr. William James, BSc ACA *1989;* Grevelingen 16, 1423 DN UITHOORN, NETHERLANDS.
O'SULLIVAN, Miss. Amy Dawn, ACA *2009;* 44 Victoria Street, Wall Heath, KINGSWINFORD, DY6 0JL.
O'SULLIVAN, Mr. Anthony Patrick, BA ACA *1998;* Ernst & Young, Level 28 Al Attar Bus Tower, Sheikh Zayed Road, PO Box 9267, DUBAI, UNITED ARAB EMIRATES.
O'SULLIVAN, Mr. Brian, BA FCA *1988;* Plastic Omnion Automotive Ltd Westminster Industrial Estate, Measham, SWADLINCOTE, DERBYSHIRE, DE12 7DS.
O'SULLIVAN, Mr. Brian Christopher, MA BSc FCA MCT *1983;* Thomas Miller & Co Ltd, 90 Fenchurch Street, LONDON, EC3M 4ST.
O'SULLIVAN, Miss. Claire Andrea, BSc ACA *1989;* 5 River Mead, Bocking, BRAINTREE, CM7 9AX.
O'SULLIVAN, Mr. Daniel John, FCA *1962;* 18 Shrewsbury, DUBLIN 4, COUNTY DUBLIN, IRELAND. (Life Member)
O'SULLIVAN, Mr. Eugene, BA FCA *1996;* The Atrium, Anadarko Algeria Corporation, PO Box 576, UXBRIDGE, MIDDLESEX, UB8 1YH.
O'SULLIVAN, Mrs. Evelyn Anne, BSc ACA *1992;* Huttenweg 5c, 8909 ZWILLIKON, SWITZERLAND.
O'SULLIVAN, Mrs. Hazel May, BSc ACA *1991;* 32 Woodside, Wimbledon, LONDON, SW19 7AW.
O'SULLIVAN, Mrs. Helen Ruth, BSc ACA *1986;* 10 Hadley Road, BARNET, HERTFORDSHIRE, EN5 5HH.
O'SULLIVAN, Mr. James Edward, ACA *2008;* Davisons Ltd Lime Court, Pathfields Business Park, SOUTH MOLTON, DEVON, EX36 3LH.
•①**O'SULLIVAN, Mr. Jeremiah Anthony, FCA** *1980;* Bishop Fleming, Stratus House, Emperor Way, Exeter Business Park, EXETER, EX1 3QS.
O'SULLIVAN, Mrs. Joanna Claire, BA ACA *1998;* 1 Holly Mount, LONDON, NW3 6SG.
O'SULLIVAN, Mr. John, BA ACA *1987;* 5 Owens Farm Drive, STOCKPORT, CHESHIRE, SK2 5EA.
O'SULLIVAN, Mr. John Peter, BEng ACA *1989;* 5 Marford Close, NORTHWICH, CW9 8WW.
•**O'SULLIVAN, Mr. Joseph Michael, FCA** *1977;* (Tax Fac), The JMO Practice, 631 Linen Hall, 162-168 Regent Street, LONDON, W1B 5TE.
O'SULLIVAN, Mrs. Karen, BA ACA *1997;* 5 Easter Wooden Farm Cottages, Eckford, KELSO, ROXBURGHSHIRE, TD5 8ED.
O'SULLIVAN, Miss. Katie, ACA *2009;* Flat 3 Orpington Mansions, Orpington Road, LONDON, N21 3PJ.
O'SULLIVAN, Mrs. Kerry Elizabeth, BSc(Hons) ACA *2001;* Locksley House Coxs Drove, Fulbourn, CAMBRIDGE, CB21 5HE.
O'SULLIVAN, Mr. Lee Scott, BA ACA *2000;* 1 The Mount Caversham, READING, RG4 7RU.
O'SULLIVAN, Mr. Liam, BA ACA *1997;* 113 Douglas Road, SURBITON, SURREY, KT6 7SD.
O'SULLIVAN, Mr. Luke, ACA *2011;* Flat 12, Napier Court, Ranelagh Gardens, LONDON, SW6 3UT.
O'SULLIVAN, Mr. Mark Jerome, BSc ACA *1981;* 15930 St Andrews Road, CALEDON L7C 2R8, ON, CANADA.
O'SULLIVAN, Mr. Mark Jonathan, BSc ACA *1998;* with PricewaterhouseCoopers LLP, 1 Embankment Place, LONDON, WC2N 6RH.
O'SULLIVAN, Mr. Mark Joseph, BCom ACA *2004;* with Ernst & Young LLP, 1 More London Place, LONDON, SE1 2AF.
O'SULLIVAN, Miss. Mary Theresee, BCom ACA *1981;* Tax Department, Royal Bank Of Canada, 71-71a Queen Victoria Street, LONDON, EC4V 4DE.
O'SULLIVAN, Mr. Matthew, BSc ACA *1989;* 7 Queens Crescent, RICHMOND, SURREY, TW10 6HG.
O'SULLIVAN, Mr. Michael John, FCA *1971;* 20 Leaside Avenue, LONDON, N10 3BU.
O'SULLIVAN, Mr. Michael John, BSc ACA *1990;* Canes, Hopgarden Lane, SEVENOAKS, KENT, TN13 1PX.
O'SULLIVAN, Ms. Noreen M, BCom ACA *1983; (ACA Ireland 1980);* 9 Howitt Road, LONDON, NW3 4LT.
O'SULLIVAN, Mr. Patrick Michael, BSc ACA *1993;* Meadows End, Ilfracombe Road, BRAUNTON, DEVON, EX33 2ER.
O'SULLIVAN, Mrs. Rebekah Anne, BSc ACA *1998;* 116 Clifton Road, KINGSTON UPON THAMES, SURREY, KT2 6PN.
O'SULLIVAN, Mrs. Sarah Jane, BSc ACA *2002;* Gateway House, Gargrave Road, SKIPTON, NORTH YORKSHIRE, BD23 1UD.
O'SULLIVAN, Mr. Simon Charles, BA ACA *1995;* Ty Nant, Grawen Lane, Cefn Coed, MERTHYR TYDFIL, CF48 2NN.
O'SULLIVAN, Mr. Terence Desmond, FCA *1970;* 6 Harrow View Road, Ealing, LONDON, W5 1LZ.
O'TOOLE, Mr. Colin Robert, ACA *2008;* with KPMG LLP, 15 Canada Square, LONDON, E14 5GL.
O'TOOLE, Mr. Damien Peter, BA(Hons) ACA *2002;* 17 Leigh Terrace, Douglas, ISLE OF MAN, IM1 5AN.
O'TOOLE, Mr. Gerard Augustine, MA FCA *1975;* Cedar House Park West Business Park, Nangor Road, DUBLIN 12, COUNTY DUBLIN, IRELAND.
O'TOOLE, Mr. Justin Peter, BA ACA *1996;* 7 Twyford Avenue, Adderbury, BANBURY, OX17 3JF.
O'TOOLE, Mr. Kevin Barry John, FCA *1963;* P O Box 651, HARARE, ZIMBABWE.
O'TOOLE, Ms. Lisa Marie, BSc ACA *2000;* Network Rail K X R P, 1 Battle Bridge Road, LONDON, NW1 2AH.
O'TOOLE, Miss. Lorraine Theresa, BSc FCA *1999;* with MoneyPlus Group Limited-, Lawson House, 22-26 Stockport Road, ALTRINCHAM, CHESHIRE, WA15 8EX.
O'TOOLE, Mr. Nicholas James, ACA *1982;* 74a Woodcote Grove Road, COULSDON, CR5 2AD.
O'TOOLE, Mr. Paul William, BAcc ACA *2000;* Cherry Lodge 7 Trinity Road St. Helier, JERSEY, JE2 4NH.
O'TOOLE, Mr. Phil, BA ACA *2006;* 18 Fairmead Avenue, HARPENDEN, HERTFORDSHIRE, AL5 5UE.
O'TOOLE, Mr. Stephen Joseph, MEng ACA *1995;* Endeka Ceramics Holding SLU, Calle Botiguers 3, 4G, 46980 PATERNA, VALENCIA PROVINCE, SPAIN.
O MURCHU, Mr. Caoimhin, BA ACA *1992;* with KPMG LLP, 15 Canada Square, LONDON, E14 5GL.
O MURCHU, Mrs. Helen Clare, BSocSc FCA *1992;* Mailpoint 9 Floor 0 Finance, Churchill Insurance Co Ltd Churchill Court, Westmoreland Road, BROMLEY, BR1 1DP.
O NEILL, Mr. Brian, BSc ACA *2007;* 17 Ridgewood Villas, NEWCASTLE UPON TYNE, NE3 1SH.
OAG, Mr. Alistair, FCA *1975;* 11 The Paddock, Vigo Village, GRAVESEND, DA13 0TE.
OAK, Mr. David Charlton, BSc ACA *2002;* Pricewaterhousecoopers, Cornwall Court, 19 Cornwall Street, BIRMINGHAM, B3 2DT.
•**OAKE, Mr. Stuart Noel, BSc ACA** *1988;* Stuart Oake Limited, 3 Portland Place, PENRITH, CUMBRIA, CA11 7QN.
•**OAKENSEN, Mr. David Alan, FCA** *1974;* Munro Accountants Limited, 31 Stallard Street, TROWBRIDGE, WILTSHIRE, BA14 9AA. See also Munro Harradine Ltd
OAKENSEN, Miss. Helen Jane, ACA DChA *2008;* B D O Stoy Hayward Llp, 2 City Place, Beehive Ring Road, London Gatwick Airport, GATWICK, WEST SUSSEX RH6 0PA.
OAKES, Mr. Andrew Peter, BA ACA *1984;* P W Imports Ltd, 20 Chapel Lane, Formby, LIVERPOOL, L37 4DU.
•**OAKES, Mr. Anthony Clarke, FCA** *1964;* (Tax Fac), Couch Bright King & Co, 91 Gower Street, LONDON, WC1E 6AB.
OAKES, Mr. David, FCA *1954;* Arnwood, Oldfield Way, WIRRAL, CH60 6RG. (Life Member)
OAKES, Mr. David James, BA FCA *1982;* with PKF (UK) LLP, Regent House, Clinton Avenue, NOTTINGHAM, NG5 1AZ.
OAKES, Mr. David Robin, BA FCA *1981;* 18 Parker Close, LETCHWORTH GARDEN CITY, HERTFORDSHIRE, SG6 3RT.
OAKES, Mrs. Emma, BA ACA *2005;* 25 Bowland Road, GLOSSOP, DERBYSHIRE, SK13 6PE.
OAKES, Miss. Emma Louise, BA ACA *2007;* 124 Wakefield Road, PONTEFRACT, WEST YORKSHIRE, WF8 4DZ.
OAKES, Mr. George Henry Peter, FCA *1949;* 1 Pomeroy Road, TIVERTON, DEVON, EX16 4LX. (Life Member)
OAKES, Miss. Gillian Philippa, MA BA ACA MArch *1979;* 6 Ravenna Road, Putney, LONDON, SW15 6AW.
•**OAKES, Miss. Jacqueline Mary, BA ACA** *2004;* with Nexia Smith & Williamson Audit Limited, 25 Moorgate, LONDON, EC2R 6AY.
OAKES, Mr. James Ian, BSc FCA *1983;* Mi Technology Group Ltd, Aston Way, Leyland, PRESTON, PR26 7TZ.
OAKES, The Revd Canon Jeremy Charles, FCA *1975;* Canford Cliffs Vicarage, 14 Flaghead Road, POOLE, DORSET, BH13 7JW.
OAKES, Mr. John Nigel, FCA *1972;* 1306 L. Ron Hubbard Way, LOS ANGELES, CA 90027, UNITED STATES.
OAKES, Mrs. Judith Ann, BSc FCA *1974;* NEWTON LEY, 7 Mead Road, WINCHESTER, SO23 9RF.
OAKES, Mrs. Kate Elizabeth, BSc(Hons) ACA CTA *2004;* 5 The Gateways, Pendlebury, Swinton, MANCHESTER, M27 6LA.
OAKES, Mr. Paul Harry, BA ACA *1997;* 12 Harley Road, Ecclesball, SHEFFIELD, S11 9SD.
•**OAKES, Mr. Richard James, FCA CPFA** *1974;* Oakes & Co, Bramble Hill Lodge, Main Street, Dry Doddington, NEWARK, NOTTINGHAMSHIRE NG23 5HU.
OAKES, Mr. Robin Geoffrey, BCom FCA *1971;* 102 Green End Road, HEMEL HEMPSTEAD, HERTFORDSHIRE, HP1 1RT.
OAKES, Mrs. Sandra Elizabeth, BA ACA *1982;* 18 Parker Close, LETCHWORTH GARDEN CITY, SG6 3RT.
OAKES, Mr. Steven Antony, BA(Hons) ACA *2002;* 7 Heydon Close, LEEDS, LS6 4QR.
OAKES, Mrs. Suzanne Rachel, BSc ACA *2001;* 7 Heydon Close, LEEDS, LS6 4QR.
OAKES, Mr. Thomas, FCA *1950;* 4 Ward Road, Blundellsands, LIVERPOOL, L23 8TB. (Life Member)
OAKES, Mrs. Yvonne Christina, ACA CA(SA) *2008;* 3 Seymour Road, WESTCLIFF-ON-SEA, SS0 8NJ.
OAKEY, Mrs. Bernadette Joanne, BA ACA *1992;* Shotley Cottage, Shotley, Harringworth, CORBY, NN17 3AG.
OAKEY, Mr. Jonathan Philip, ACA *2008;* 55 Harding Avenue, EASTBOURNE, EAST SUSSEX, BN22 8PL.
•**OAKEY, Mr. Norman Thomas, FCA** *1979;* Norman Oakey ACA, Cwm Islwyn, Cwm y Gaist, Llanbister Road, LLANDRINDOD WELLS, POWYS LD1 5UW.
OAKHAM, Mr. Benjamin Alexander, ACA *2009;* Radiodetection Ltd, 1 Western Drive, Whitchurch, BRISTOL, BS14 0AF.
•**OAKLAND, Mr. Gareth Simeon, MBA BA ACA** *1983;* PricewaterhouseCoopers, 80 Strand, LONDON, WC2R 0AF. See also PricewaterhouseCoopers LLP
OAKLEY, Mr. Christopher Richard, BCom FCA *1990;* 29 Long Park, Chesham Bois, AMERSHAM, BUCKINGHAMSHIRE, HP6 5LA.
OAKLEY, Mr. David John Philip, FCA *1968;* Flat 82, Candlemakers Apartments, 112 York Road, LONDON, SW11 3RS.
OAKLEY, Mr. David Stephen, BSc ACA *1995;* Cranmere House, Middleton Road, CAMBERLEY, SURREY, GU15 3TT.
•①**OAKLEY, Mr. Derek John, BSc ACA** *1990;* Debt Free Direct Limited, Fairclough House, Church Street, Adlington, CHORLEY, LANCASHIRE PR7 4EX.
OAKLEY, Mr. Edward Robert, FCA *1964;* Obeetee Ltd, P.O. Box 4, Besunderpur, Civil Lines, MIRZAPUR 231001, INDIA.
OAKLEY, Miss. Jeri Davina, BA(Hons) ACA *2010;* 1 Crescent Gardens, Crescent Road, FAREHAM, HAMPSHIRE, PO16 0HL.
OAKLEY, Mr. John Anthony, FCA *1970;* The Chestnuts, 25 Warwick Road, BISHOP'S STORTFORD, CM23 5NH.
OAKLEY, Mr. John Evan, MPhil BSc(Hons) ACA *2001;* 37 Anthony Grove, Abercanaid, MERTHYR TYDFIL, MID GLAMORGAN, CF48 1YX.
OAKLEY, Mr. John Frank, FCA *1969;* Brassworks Cottage, Simeon Way, STONE, STAFFORDSHIRE, ST15 8FJ.
•**OAKLEY, Mr. Jonathan James, BSc FCA** *1982;* Beatons Limited, York House, 2-4 York Road, FELIXSTOWE, IP11 7QG. See also BG Outsourcing Ltd and BG Audit LLP
OAKLEY, Mr. Joseph Roger, BSc FCA *1971;* 51 Gledhow Lane, LEEDS, LS8 1RT.
OAKLEY, Mr. Julian Patrick, BA ACA *1993;* 84 Sterndale Road, LONDON, W14 0HX.
OAKLEY, Mr. Kenneth John, MA ACA CTA *1988;* Thames Water, Clearwater Court, Vastern Road, READING, RG1 8DB.
OAKLEY, Mr. Mark William, BA ACA *1990;* Azlan Logistics Ltd, Lion House, 4 Pioneer Business Park, Amy Johnson Way, Clifton Moor, YORK YO30 4GH.
OAKLEY, Mr. Matthew James, BA ACA CFE *2004;* H S B C, Level 28 Canada Square, LONDON, E14 5HQ.
OAKLEY, Mr. Norris Alan, FCA *1963;* 41 Chelsworth Drive, ROMFORD, RM3 0ES.
OAKLEY, Miss. Rachel Katherine, MEng ACA *2006;* Flat 202 Albion House, 6-7 Benjamin Street, LONDON, EC1M 5QL.
OAKLEY, Mr. Richard William, FCA *1975;* 25 Hadrian Way, Sandiway, NORTHWICH, CW8 2JR.
OAKLEY, Mr. Robert James, FCA *1957;* 8 Marston Gardens, LUTON, LU2 7DU. (Life Member)
OAKLEY, Mr. Simon Ernest, BSc ACA *1987;* Oxford Aviation Academy UK Ltd, Fleming Way, CRAWLEY, WEST SUSSEX, RH10 9UH.
OAKLEY, Mr. Stephen Edward, FCA *1974;* 31 Barlings Road, Beesonend, HARPENDEN, AL5 2AW.
OAKLEY, Mr. William Morrell, BA FCA *1964;* Montagu Cottage, Purbrook Heath, WATERLOOVILLE, PO7 5RX. (Life Member)
•①**OAKLEY SMITH, Mr. Ian Christopher, BSc FCA** *1989;* with PricewaterhouseCoopers LLP, Pricewaterhousecoopers, 12 Plumtree Court, LONDON, EC4A 4HT.
OAKLEY SMITH, Mrs. Sally Jane, BSc ACA *1989;* 8A Croham Manor Road, SOUTH CROYDON, CR2 7BE.
OAKLEY-WHITE, Mr. Paul Edward, FCA *1961;* 20 Bereweeke Road, WINCHESTER, SO22 6AN.
OAKSHETT, Mr. Charles, BA ACA *2007;* BetterCapital LLP, 39-41 Charing Cross Road, LONDON, WC2H 0AR.
OASTLER, Mr. Alastair James Stratton, BSc(Hons) ACA *2002;* Helical Bar Plc, 11-15 Farm Street, LONDON, W1J 5RS.
OASTLER, Mr. Peter Harold, BSc ACA *2002;* Pricewaterhousecoopers, 1 Embankment Place, LONDON, WC2N 6RH.
•**OASTLER, Mr. William Robert Lewis, ACA** *2009;* GGS Consulting Limited, 12a Marlborough Place, BRIGHTON, BN1 1WN.
OATEN, Mr. Andrew Peter, ACA *2008;* 55 Tudor Drive, YATELEY, GU46 6DB.
OATEN, Mr. John, FCA *1971;* 11a Greenwood Court, DISCOVERY BAY, NEW TERRITORIES, HONG KONG SAR.
OATEN, Mr. Michael John, BSc FCA CF *1967;* Corporate Advisors SA, Chalet Chantauvent, Route Grande Parapis, 1874 CHAMPERY, SWITZERLAND.
•**OATEN, Mr. Roger Charles, FCA** *1968;* Roger C. Oaten, First Floor, 23 Westfield Park, Redland, BRISTOL, BS6 6LT. See also Investment Recovery Services Limited
OATEN, Mr. Simon James, BA(Hons) ACA *2004;* 42 Hill Street, ST. ALBANS, HERTFORDSHIRE, AL3 4QT.
OATES, Mr. Alan Clucas, BA ACA *1989;* Second Floor, Goldie House, 4 Goldie Terrace, Douglas, ISLE OF MAN, IM1 1EB.
OATES, Mr. Andrew Gordon, BA ACA *1999;* Woods Farm, 176 Earlswood Common, Earlswood, SOLIHULL, B94 5SQ.
OATES, Ms. Anne Barbara, BA ACA *1993;* Together Working for Wellbeing, 12 Old Street, LONDON, EC1V 9BE.

•**OATES, Mrs. Christine Ann, BA FCA** *1994;* (Tax Fac), Ernst & Young LLP, 1 Colmore Square, BIRMINGHAM, B4 6HQ. See also Ernst & Young Europe LLP
•**OATES, Mr. David John, FCA FCCA** *1975;* D.J. Oates & Co, Suite 59, 42 St Johns Road, SCARBOROUGH, NORTH YORKSHIRE, YO12 5ET. See also One Stop Business Advisers Limited and D. J. Oates & Co
OATES, Mr. David Matthew, BA ACA *1991;* 1 Holland Park, BURTON-ON-TRENT, DE13 8DU.
OATES, Mr. David Richard, BSc ACA *1994;* Kodak Limited, Hemel One, Boundary Way, HEMEL HEMPSTEAD, HERTFORDSHIRE, HP2 7YU.
OATES, Mr. Geoffrey, FCA *1949;* Thornedene Residential Home, 107 Thorne Road, DONCASTER, SOUTH YORKSHIRE, DN2 5BE. (Life Member)
OATES, Mr. Gerard Charles Holland, BSc ACA *1981;* 8 Silverlea Gardens, HORLEY, SURREY, RH6 9BB.
OATES, Miss. Helen Elizabeth, BSc ACA *1998;* 4th Floor, 14 King Street, LEEDS, LS1 2HL.
OATES, Mrs. Helen Mary, FCA *1966;* Garden Palace, 47 Rue Plati, MONTE CARLO, MC 98000, MONACO.
OATES, Mr. James, BA ACA *2009;* Freshwater Place Level 19, 2 Southbank Boulevard, Southbank, MELBOURNE, VIC 3006, AUSTRALIA.
OATES, Mrs. Jane Anne, FCA *1984;* Longacre, St Mary's Lane, Winkfield, WINDSOR, SL4 4SH.
OATES, Mr. Jonathan Peter, BSc ACA *1997;* Icera, 2520 The Quadrant, Aztec West, Almondsbury, BRISTOL, BS32 4AQ.
•**OATES, Mrs. Julie, ACA** *1988;* Julie Oates ACA, 2 Camlork Place, Union Mills, ISLE OF MAN, IM4 4NY.
•**OATES, Mr. Keith Alan, FCA** *1974;* KAO Financial Management Services, 16 Buckfast Road, SALE, M33 5QB.
•**OATES, Mr. Nigel Christopher, FCA** *1972;* Atkin Macredie & Co Ltd, Westbourne Place, 23 Westbourne Road, SHEFFIELD, S10 2QQ.
OATES, Mr. Rodger Anthony William, MSc ACA *1998;* The Capital Markets Co UK Ltd, 9 Appold Street, LONDON, EC2A 2AP.
OATES, Mr. Roger Nelson, FCA *1967;* White Cottage, Bacon Lane, West Markham, NEWARK, NOTTINGHAMSHIRE, NG22 0GU. (Life Member)
OATES, Miss. Sara, BA ACA *1997;* 193 Brooke Avenue, NORTH YORK M5M 2K7, ON, CANADA.
OATES, Mr. Warren, FCA *1964;* The Willows, Dimples Lane, East Morton, KEIGHLEY, BD20 5SU. (Life Member)
•**OATES, Mr. William, BA ACA** *2005;* Brooks Mayfield, 12 Bridgford Road, West Bridgford, NOTTINGHAM, NG2 6AB. See also Brooks Mayfield Audit Limited
•**OATES, Mr. William John, BSc FCA MBCS FCIM** *1975;* Swallowfield, Slade Lane, Mobberley, KNUTSFORD, WA16 7QN.
OATLEY, Mrs. Jane Mary, BA ACA *1994;* Pauls Farm Cottage, Ensfield Road, Leigh, TONBRIDGE, KENT, TN11 8RX.
OATLEY, Mr. Philip John Fernley, BA ACA *1981;* Chantry Business Management Ltd, The Chantry, Lacock Road, CORSHAM, WILTSHIRE, SN13 9HS.
•**OATRIDGE, Mr. William Edward Robin, FCA** *1966;* Rowes Accountants, 57 Newgate Lane, Whitestake, PRESTON, PR4 4JU.
OATWAY, Mr. Keith Mark, FCA *1975;* 38 Furze Lane, PURLEY, SURREY, CR8 3EG.
OBADA, Mr. Olorunfemi, ACA *2011;* 2 Gabby Adeosun Street, Off Admiralty Way, Lekki Scheme 1, LAGOS, LAGOS STATE, NIGERIA.
OBAIDULLAH, Mr. Arsalan, BSc ACA *2007;* 72 Flower Lane, LONDON, NW7 2JL.
•①**OBARAY, Mr. Mohamed Shaffi, FCA** *1976;* Ableman Shaw & Co, Mercury House, 1 Heather Park Drive, WEMBLEY, HA0 1SX.
OBBARD, Mrs. Laura, BSc ACA *1998;* 36 henzell street, dicky beach, CALOUNDRA, QLD 4551, AUSTRALIA.
OBBARD, Mr. Robert Stuart, BA ACA *1983;* Moorings Yachting, 82 rue Beaubourg, 75003 PARIS, FRANCE.
OBBARD, Mr. William, ACA *2008;* 41a Midmoor Road, LONDON, SW12 0ES.
OBEE, Mr. Geoffrey William, BCom FCA *1980;* 16 Hunters Park, BERKHAMSTED, HP4 2PT.
OBEROI, Mr. Rishi, ACA *2008;* 5438 Black Avenue, PLEASANTON, CA 94566, UNITED STATES.
OBERST, Mr. Simon Julian, MA ACA *1984;* MacMillan Cancer Relief Camelford House, 87-90 Albert Embankment, LONDON, SE1 7UQ.
OBERTELLI, Dr. Sandro David, BSc FCA *1996;* 11a View Road, LONDON, N6 4DJ.
OBEY, Mrs. Anne, BA FCA *1989;* Nationwide Bldg Soc, Ground Floor A, Nationwide House, SWINDON, SN38 1GN.
OBEY, Mr. Paul Anthony, BSc ACA *1994;* 1 White Hart Wood, SEVENOAKS, KENT, TN13 1RR.
OBI-EZEKPAZU, Mr. Anthony Ifeanyichukwu, BSc ACA *1992;* 49 Ulleswater Road, Southgate, LONDON, N14 7BL.
OBOLENSKAYA, Ms. Anna, ACA *2011;* Flat 123, Lauderdale Mansions, Lauderdale Road, LONDON, W9 1LY.
OBOLENSKY, Mr. Andrew, FCA *1975;* Mutual Trust SA, 24 Avenue Paul Creosole, C4 1800 VEVEY, SWITZERLAND.
OBORNE, Mr. Nicholas David, BA ACA *1988;* Low Farm, Brook Street, Elsworth, CAMBRIDGE, CB3 8HX.
OBRIEN, Mr. Thomas Francis, MA FCA *1979;* 5 Longridge View, COULSDON, CR5 3QX.
•**OCCLESTON, Mr. David, MA FCA** *1984;* Occleston & Co Limited, The Old Post Office, East Rounton, NORTHALLERTON, NORTH YORKSHIRE, DL6 2LF.
OCHIENG, Mr. Michael Omolo, BCom ACA *1992;* 3213 Decatur Avenue, KENSINGTON, MD 20895, UNITED STATES.
OCHIENG, Mrs. Sara Ann, BA ACA *1991;* The International School of Uganda, Plot 272 Lubowa Estate, P.O. Box 4200, KAMPALA, UGANDA.
OCKENDEN, Mr. Giles, BSc(Hons) ACA *2004;* 48a Thirsk Road, LONDON, SW11 5SX.
OCKHAM, Mr. Sam, ACA *2008;* Flat 2, Buckland Court, 13 Rubeck Close, REDHILL, RH1 1TH.
OCKLETON, Mrs. Nicola, BA ACA *1993;* 27 Demontfort Way, UTTOXETER, ST14 8XY.
ODAM, Mr. Simon, BA(Hons) ACA *2004;* (Tax Fac), 4 Prunus Close, West End, WOKING, GU24 9NU.
ODDIE, Mr. Christopher Peter, FCA *1973;* 22 Meadow Lane, Hamble, SOUTHAMPTON, SO31 4RD.
•**ODDIE, Ms. Elaine Anne, OBE MA FCA** *1979;* (Member of Council 1991 - 2001), (Tax Fac), NSO Associates LLP, 75 Springfield Road, CHELMSFORD, CM2 6JB.
ODDS, Mr. Ernest James, LLB ACA *1995;* Matthew Arnold & Baldwin, 21 Station Road, WATFORD, HERTFORDSHIRE, WD17 1HT.
ODDS, Mr. Richard Barry Madle, FCA *1970;* Wintergates, Pope Street, Godmersham, CANTERBURY, CT4 7DL.
ODDY, Mr. Christopher Michael, MEng ACA *2004;* 235 West 48 Street, The Ritz Plaza, Apt 30E, NEW YORK, NY 10036, UNITED STATES.
ODDY, Mr. Frederick Michael, FCA *1957;* Gledholt, 73 Station Lane, Birkenshaw, BRADFORD, BD11 2JE. (Life Member)
ODDY, Miss. Joanne, ACA *2008;* Railway Pensions Management Ltd Stooperdale Offices, Brinkburn Road, DARLINGTON, COUNTY DURHAM, DL3 6EH.
ODDY, Mr. John William Frank, FCA *1970;* 83 Spring Lane, HEMEL HEMPSTEAD, HERTFORDSHIRE, HP1 3QY. (Life Member)
ODDY, Mr. Matthew Ian, LLM LLB ACA *2005;* 2e Adamson Gardens, MANCHESTER, M20 2TQ.
•**ODDY, Mr. Philip Douglas, FCA MBA** *1975;* (Tax Fac), Philip Oddy, Albion House, 24 Roundhay Road, LEEDS, LS7 1BT.
ODDY, Mr. Richard James Robert, BSc ACA *2002;* 26 Albacore Close, LEE-ON-THE-SOLENT, HAMPSHIRE, PO13 8GG.
ODDY, Mr. Robert Lewis, FCA *1963;* The Chase, Overthorpe, BANBURY, OX17 2AH. (Life Member)
•**ODDY, Mr. Simon Patrick, BA ACA** *2001;* RGL Forensic Accountants, 5 Hanover Square 502, NEW YORK, NY 10004, UNITED STATES.
ODE, Miss. Tomoko, BA ACA *2003;* PricewaterhouseCoopers Consultants, 7th Floor PricewaterhouseCoopers Center, 202 Hu Bin Road, SHANGHAI 200021, CHINA.
ODEDIRAN, Mr. Tunde, ACA *2009;* Flat 3 Lancaster Court, 110 Ducks Hill Road, NORTHWOOD, MIDDLESEX, HA6 2XU.
ODEDRA, Mr. Sandip, BA(Hons) ACA *2011;* 173 Prestwold Road, LEICESTER, LE5 0EZ.
ODELL, Miss. Charlotte Jane, ACA *2008;* 88 Glenfield Drive, Great Doddington, WELLINGBOROUGH, NORTHAMPTONSHIRE, NN29 7TE.
ODELL, Mrs. Felicity, MEng ACA *2003;* 3 Mill Lane, Abbots Worthy, WINCHESTER, HAMPSHIRE, SO21 1DS.
ODELL, Mr. John Arthur, FCA *1970;* 28 Anglesey Drive, Poynton, STOCKPORT, SK12 1BU.
ODELL, Mr. John Richard, MEng ACA *1998;* Flat 24 Blenheim Court, King & Queen Wharf Rotherhithe Street, LONDON, SE16 5ST.
ODELL, Mr. Martin Andrew, FCA *1974;* Westbury, Grayswood Road, HASLEMERE, SURREY, GU27 2BS.
ODELL, Mr. Michael Edward, ACA *2009;* 702-2001 Beach Avenue, VANCOUVER V6G 1Z3, BC, CANADA.
ODELL, Mr. Timothy Earnleigh, ACA CA(SA) *2009;* 51 Pine Grove, Brookmans Park, HATFIELD, HERTFORDSHIRE, AL9 7BL.
ODELL, Mr. Toby, ACA *2008;* 18/18 Riverbend Place, BULIMBA, QLD 4171, AUSTRALIA.
ODENEYE, Dr. Adetunji Michael, PhD BSc ACA *2009;* 9 Cochrane Drive, DARTFORD, DA1 2GE.
ODGERS, Mr. Matthew Ian, BSc ACA *2001;* Flat 30 Paramount Building 206-212, St. John Street, LONDON, EC1V 4JY.
ODHIAMBO, Mr. Jorum Steven, ACA *1987;* P.O. Box 17774, GPO 00100, NAIROBI, NAIROBI PROVINCE, 00100, KENYA.
ODIASE, Mr. Victor Osevegie, MSc FCA *1972;* V O ODIASE & CO, GPO Box 9209, Marina, LAGOS, NIGERIA.
•**ODLIN, Mr. Graham, BSc ACA** *1989;* Grant Thornton UK LLP, 4 Hardman Square, Spinningfields, MANCHESTER, M3 3EB. See also Grant Thornton LLP
ODLIND, Mr. Lars Fredrik, BSc ACA *1999;* Garden Flat, 14 Santos Road, LONDON, SW18 1NS.
ODLUM, Mr. Philip Edwin, BBS ACA *1980;* 109 Anglesea Road, Ballsbridge, DUBLIN 4, COUNTY DUBLIN, IRELAND.
ODOM, Mr. Christopher James, MSc BSc FCA MCT *1976;* 19 Embercourt Road, THAMES DITTON, KT7 0LH.
•**ODOOM, Mr. Richard Sena, FCA** *1985;* Odoom & Co, 59 Upper Tollington Park, LONDON, N4 4DD.
ODOZI, Miss. Isioma Oluwatoyin, MSc BSc ACA *2003;* 61 Cadman Court, Chaseley Drive, LONDON, W4 4BD.
ODUAH, Mr. Philip, BA ACA *1992;* 58 Leslie Road, LONDON, N2 8BJ.
ODUNSI, Mr. Adedeji Oluwole, BA ACA *1993;* 7A Fowler Road, Ikoyi, LAGOS, NIGERIA.
ODUNSI, Mr. Bolaji Adekunle, BSc ACA *1989;* Rose Of Sharon, George Road, Coombe Hill, KINGSTON UPON THAMES, KT2 7NU.
ODUSOTE, Mrs. Abiola Olufunke, MA ACA *1989;* 24 Ingle Road, CHEADLE, SK8 2EU.
ODY, Mr. James Franklin William, FCA *1980;* 392 Hurst Road, BEXLEY, DA5 3JY.
ODY, Mr. Keith Alan, FCA *1964;* 3 Billett Avenue, WATERLOOVILLE, PO7 7SZ. (Life Member)
ODYSSEAS, Mrs. Sarah Elaine, BSc ACA *1998;* Finch House, Gammons Farm Lane, Newchurch, ROMNEY MARSH, KENT, TN29 0ED.
•**ODYSSEOS, Mr. Andreas, BA FCA** *1988;* Thomas Alexander & Company Ltd, 590 Green Lanes, LONDON, N13 5RY.
ODYSSEOS, Mr. George, BA ACA *2000;* 29 Stone Hall Road, LONDON, N21 1LR.
OEHLCKE, Mr. James Matthew, BEng ACA *2001;* 21 Tiepigs Lane, WEST WICKHAM, BR4 9BT.
OEI, Miss. Nicola, BA ACA *1996;* Flat 34 Globe Wharf, 205 Rotherhithe Street, LONDON, SE16 5XS.
OERTLI, Mr. Wilfrid, FCA *1948;* PO Box 746, OLIVEDALE, 2158, SOUTH AFRICA. (Life Member)
OESTERGAARD, Mr. Lars, BEng ACA *1999;* 4240 Bassett Creek Drive, GOLDEN VALLEY, MN 55422, UNITED STATES.
OFFEI, Mr. William Boadu, ACA *2009;* 16 Burwell Close, Lower Earley, READING, RG6 4BB.
•**OFFEN, Mr. Andrew James, FCA** *1989;* Blois, Port Soif Lane, Vale, GUERNSEY, GY6 8AG.
OFFENBERG, Miss. Suzanne Henriette Eileen, BA(Econ) ACA *1999;* 2 Beenong Close, NELSON BAY, NSW 2315, AUSTRALIA.
OFFER, Mr. Frederick Henry Paul, FCA *1956;* 41 Grove Way, ESHER, KT10 8HQ. (Life Member)
OFFER, Mr. James Aubrey Charles, FCA *1965;* 155 Prestbury Road, MACCLESFIELD, SK10 3DF. (Life Member)
•**OFFER, Mr. Kevin James, BSc FCA ATII AIIT** *1987;* (Tax Fac), Chown Dewhurst LLP, 51 Lafone Street, LONDON, SE1 2LX.
OFFER, Miss. Serena Louise, BA ACA *2005;* Lion Capital, 21 Grosvenor Place, LONDON, SW1X 7HF.
OFFER, Mr. William Thomas Charles, FCA *1965;* Farmers Green Cottage, Castle Hill, Mottram St Andrew, MACCLESFIELD, SK10 4AX. (Life Member)
OFFICER, Mr. Paul, BCom ACA *2001;* 4 / 30 - 32 Melrose Parade, CLOVELLY, NSW 2031, AUSTRALIA.
OFFLER, Ms. Rachel, BSocSc ACA *2003;* Truro School, Trennick Lane, TRURO, CORNWALL, TR1 1TH.
OFFORD, Mr. Philip Graham, BA ACA *2007;* Flat 13 Dawn Court, Bakers Close, ST. ALBANS, HERTFORDSHIRE, AL1 5FH.
OFORI, Mr. Michael Kwabena, MA ACA *1996;* 120 Dekruif Place, Apartment 30B, Bronx, NEW YORK, NY 10475, UNITED STATES.
OFOSU-ADJEI, Mr. Alexander, ACA *2011;* 11 Manton Close, HAYES, MIDDLESEX, UB3 2BA.
OGBECHIE, Mr. Anthony Emeka, MSc ACA *2007;* 308 Long Lane, LONDON, N2 8JP.
OGBU, Mr. Donald Samuel, MBA BA ACA *1990;* PO Box 1711, Morningside, SANDTON, GAUTENG, 2057, SOUTH AFRICA.
OGDEN, Mr. Alan James, BA FCA *1963;* Trevallett, Goonvrea, ST AGNES, CORNWALL, TR5 0NN.
OGDEN, Mr. Anthony John, FCA *1957;* Calle Barbastro 3, Javea, 03737 ALICANTE, SPAIN. (Life Member)
OGDEN, Mrs. Catherine Louise, BA(Hons) ACA *2000;* Higher Oaklands Barn, Pasture Lane, Barrowford, NELSON, BB9 6QZ.
OGDEN, Mr. Dennis Graham, BA ACA *1984;* 25 Braemar Avenue, Neasden, LONDON, NW10 0DU.
OGDEN, Mr. Derek William, FCA *1966;* Sugar Lodge, Water End Road, Potten End, BERKHAMSTED, HP4 2SH.
OGDEN, Mrs. Fiona May, BSc ACA *2010;* 115 Westward Deals, Kedington, HAVERHILL, SUFFOLK, CB9 7PW.
OGDEN, Mr. Gareth John, MA(Hons) ACA *2002;* 11 Crabtree Hall, Rainville Road, LONDON, W6 9HB.
OGDEN, Mr. Geoffrey, BA FCA *1965;* 15 Barn Hayes, SIDMOUTH, DEVON, EX10 9EE.
OGDEN, Mr. John, FCA *1952;* 23 Cordery Road, St Thomas, EXETER, EX2 9DH. (Life Member)
OGDEN, Mr. John Edward, FCA *1962;* 1 Ashton Street, Lytham, LYTHAM ST.ANNES, FY8 5NT. (Life Member)
OGDEN, Miss. Katharine Anne, BSc ACA *1992;* Full Moon, Mountain Road, Betws, AMMANFORD, SA18 2PN.
OGDEN, Mr. Keith, FCA *1966;* 682 Hollins Road, Hollinwood, OLDHAM, OL8 4JZ.
OGDEN, Mr. Neil Joseph, BSc ACA *1992;* The Funding Corporation, International House, Kingsfield Court, Chester Business Park, CHESTER, CH4 9RF.
OGDEN, Mr. Nicholas Anthony, BSocSc ACA *1999;* Norman Hay Plc, Godiva Place, COVENTRY, CV1 5PN.
OGDEN, Mr. Philip James, BSc FCA *1973;* The Croft, Sandy Lane, Stockton On The Forest, YORK, YO32 9UU.
OGDEN, Mr. Robert, BSc ACA *2006;* 15B Phase 2, Blessings Garden, 56 Conduit Road, MID LEVELS, HONG KONG ISLAND, HONG KONG SAR.
OGDEN, Mr. Stephen Paul, BA FCA *1993;* Flat 32 Avenue Mansions, Finchley Road, LONDON, NW3 7AX.
OGDEN, Mr. William Robert Campbell, FCA *1952;* 21 Oakridge Avenue, RADLETT, WD7 8EW. (Life Member)
•**OGG, Mr. Andrew Alexander, BSc FCA** *1992;* Andrew Ogg FCA, Holme Farm, Chapel Lane, Spalford, NEWARK, NOTTINGHAMSHIRE NG23 7HD.
OGIER, Mr. Batiste, ACA *2008;* KPMG Corporate Finance, 5th Floor Montague Sterling Centre, East Bay Street, NASSAU, N-123, BAHAMAS.
OGIER, Mr. Gerrard, MA ACA *1992;* Schroder Investment Management Ltd Garrard House, 31-45 Gresham Street, LONDON, EC2V 7QA.
OGIER, Mr. Jonathan, BA ACA *1992;* 2 Grafton Square, LONDON, SW4 0DE.
OGILVIE, Miss. Caroline Danielle, BA ACA *2006;* Forge Cottage Main Street, Bleasby, NOTTINGHAM, NG14 7GH.
OGILVIE, Mr. Charles Macaulay, MA ACA *1992;* Entertainment One UK Ltd, 120 New Cavendish Street, LONDON, W1W 6XX.
•**OGILVIE, Mr. David Charles Nasmith, MA FCA TEP** *1980;* (Tax Fac), Ogilvie & Company Limited, 25 Rutland Square, EDINBURGH, EH1 2BW.
OGILVIE, Mr. Kenneth David Buchanan, FCA *1969;* Forge Cottage, Main Street, Bleasby, NOTTINGHAM, NG14 7GH. (Life Member)
•**OGILVIE, Mr. Michael James Davidson, FCA** *1979;* (Tax Fac), OBC The Accountants Limited, 2 Upperton Gardens, EASTBOURNE, EAST SUSSEX, BN21 2AH.
•**OGILVIE, Mr. Philip John, CJC FCA** *1971;* Philip Ogilvie, PO Box 29, 1st Floor, 6 Casemates Square, GIBRALTAR, GB1 1ZZ GIBRALTAR.
OGILVIE, Miss. Tamara Isabel, ACA *2010;* 329G Eastern Valley Way, CASTLE COVE, NSW 2069, AUSTRALIA.
OGILVY, Mr. Ian Andrew, BSc ACA *2004;* 10 Cooper Gardens Ruddington, NOTTINGHAM, NG11 6AZ.
OGILVY, Miss. Katherine Elizabeth, BSc ACA *2010;* Flat K/05 Du Cane Court, Balham High Road, LONDON, SW17 7JY.
OGILVY, Mr. Peter Anthony, BSc ACA *1998;* 29 Mimosa Road, TURRAMURRA, NSW 2074, AUSTRALIA.

OGILVY WATSON, Mr. Donald Edgar, MA FCA *1965;* Ashbourne Commercial Property, PO BOX 132, GREYSTONES, COUNTY WICKLOW, IRELAND.

OGINO, Mr. Tetsuya, ACA *2011;* 11 Prince Regent Mews, LONDON, NW1 3EW.

OGLE, Mr. Christopher John Rathmell, BA ACA *1988;* Tedwood, 18 St Omer Road, GUILDFORD, GU1 2DB.

OGLE, Mrs. Elaine Charlotte, MEng BA ACA *1999;* (Tax Fac), 11 Torrington Road, Claygate, ESHER, SURREY, KT10 0SA.

OGLE, Mr. Malcolm Hugh Melvin, FCA *1967;* The Garden House, Chelwood Vachery, Nutley, UCKFIELD, TN22 3HR.

OGLE, Mr. Nicholas Craig, ACA *2006;* 13a Woodside, Wimbledon, LONDON, SW19 7AR.

•OGLE, Mr. Robert Charles, FCA *1983;* (Tax Fac), Robert Ogle, 6 The Elms, Doncaster Road, ROTHERHAM, S65 1DY. See also Cottage Properties Ltd and Ogle Robert

OGLE, Mr. Simon David, MA ACA *1996;* (Tax Fac), Kingfisher Plc, 3 Sheldon Square, LONDON, W2 6PX.

OGLE, Mr. Simon Frederick, ACA *1986;* 112 Alderbrook Road, LONDON, SW12 8AA.

OGLE, Stephen Robert, Esq OBE FCA *1967;* Cobblestones, Chelmsford Road, Felsted, DUNMOW, CM6 3EP.

OGLESBY, Mr. David Michael, MSc BSc ACA *2006;* BC Partners Limited, 40 Portman Square, LONDON, W1H 6DA.

OGLESBY, Mr. Howard, FCA *1965;* 12 Brackley House, High Street, BRACKLEY, NN13 7EN.

OGLESBY, Mr. Timothy, BA ACA *1988;* Olive House, 3 Springfield Rd, HINCKLEY, LEICESTERSHIRE, LE10 1AN.

OGLETHORPE, Mr. Charles Stuart, FCA *1975;* Elmstead Horsell Vale, WOKING, SURREY, GU21 4QU.

OGLETHORPE, Mr. David Ralph Theodore, MA ACA *1988;* Coventry Cathedral & Diocese, 1 Hill Top, COVENTRY, CV1 5AB.

OGLEY, Mr. Adrian Edward, BA FCA *1975;* (Tax Fac), 9 Lifford Street, LONDON, SW15 1NY.

OGLEY, Mrs. Ann Louise, BSc FCA CTA *1989;* Maes Ltd, Hope Street, ROTHERHAM, SOUTH YORKSHIRE, S60 1LH.

OGLEY, Mr. Thomas Alwyn, BA FCA *1954;* 1a The Grove, Totley Rise, SHEFFIELD, S17 4AR. (Life Member)

•OGRAM, Mr. Andrew, BA ACA *1998;* Ernst & Young LLP, 1 More London Place, LONDON, SE1 2AF. See also Ernst & Young Europe LLP

•OGSTON, Mr. Alan, FCA *1972;* Ogstons, 6 Norfolk Road, ST. IVES, CAMBRIDGESHIRE, PE27 3DP.

OGUN-MUYIWA, Mr. Patrick, BSc ACA *2005;* Health Care Project Unit 3, White Oak Square London Road, SWANLEY, BR8 7AG.

OGUNDIWIN, Miss. Funsho, ACA *2008;* 19 Deal Court, Hazel Close, LONDON, NW9 5FT.

•OGUNMOLA, Mr. Michael Olumide, FCA MBA *1990;* Flat 18, 1 Hodford Road, LONDON, NW11 8NL.

•OGUNSOLA, Mr. Christopher Olukayode, FCA *1995;* Gibsons Financial Limited, Foresters Hall, 25-27 Westow Street, LONDON, SE19 3RY. See also Gibsons

OGURA FREIGANG, Mrs. Mari Catherine, BA ACA *1999;* Quellenstrasse 3, 8135 LANGNAU AM ALBIS, SWITZERLAND.

OGUTUGA, Mr. Dolanimi Babafemi Olabamidele, FCA *1964;* 11 Tinubu Road, Palm Grove Estate, GPO Box 2442, LAGOS, NIGERIA. (Life Member)

OGWUAZOR, Mr. Patrick Peter Enebeli, BSc FCA *1985;* with Grant Thornton UK LLP, Grant Thornton House, 22 Melton Street, Euston Square, LONDON, NW1 2EP.

OGWUMA, Mr. Paul Ponneya Agbai, BSc FCA *1967;* 13 Diadou Street, Off Keffi St SW Ikoyi, LAGOS, NIGERIA. (Life Member)

OH, Mr. Chong Peng, FCA *1969;* 5 Laman Setiakasih Lapan, Bukit Damansara, 50490 KUALA LUMPUR, FEDERAL TERRITORY, MALAYSIA.

OH, Mr. Kevin, CA ACA *2008;* 11 Partridge House, 3 Periwood Crescent, PERIVALE, MIDDLESEX, UB6 7FL.

OH, Mr. Kim Hong, FCA *1977;* Grandville Davaro Road Section 32 Lot 5 unit 3, PO Box 5243 Boroko NCD 111, PORT MORESBY, PAPUA NEW GUINEA.

OH, Mr. Kok Chi, ACA *2005;* K.C. Oh & Company, 8th Floor New Henry House, 10 Ice House Street, CENTRAL, HONG KONG ISLAND, HONG KONG SAR.

OH, Miss. Li-Yin, LLB ACA *1998;* KPMG, 28th floor Oxford House, Taikoo Place, 979 King's Road, Island East, SAI WAN HO HONG KONG ISLAND HONG KONG SAR.

OH, Mr. Seong Lye, FCA *1974;* Terence OH & Associates, 3-6 6th Floor The Boulevard, Mid-Valley City, Lingkaran Syed Putra, P O Box 10528, 50716 KUALA LUMPUR FEDERAL TERRITORY MALAYSIA.

OH, Miss. Serene Shihhui, ACA *2005;* 221 Queensway #04-09, SINGAPORE 276750, SINGAPORE.

OH, Mr. Teik Khim, ACA *1980;* Plato Capital Ltd, c/o Plato Solutions SDN BHD, 6th Floor Wisma Genting, Jalan Sultan Ismail, 50250 KUALA LUMPUR, FEDERAL TERRITORY MALAYSIA.

OH, Mr. Teik Peng, FCA *1982;* P O Box 198, WEMBLEY, WA 6913, AUSTRALIA.

OHARE, Mrs. Kathryn Vivien, FCA *1970;* (Tax Fac), Beauparc, Grinshill, SHREWSBURY, SY4 3BP.

OHAYON, Mr. Joseph Daniel, ACA *1987;* 21C Charleson Street, MYAREE, WA 6154, AUSTRALIA.

•OHLSEN, Mr. Mark, FCA *1976;* (Tax Fac), Thomas Westcott, London House, Fore Street, HOLSWORTHY, DEVON, EX22 6EB.

•OHLY, Mr. Christopher John, FCA *1971;* Chywidn, Budock Vean, Mawnan Smith, FALMOUTH, TR11 5LG.

OHM, Mr. Marcus Richard, BA(Hons) ACA *2002;* Level 4, 130 Stirling Street, PERTH, WA 6000, AUSTRALIA.

OHNG, Mr. Kevin Kok Yeong, BSc(Econ) ACA *2000;* with PricewaterhouseCoopers LLP, 17-00 PWC Building, 8 Cross Street, SINGAPORE 048424, SINGAPORE.

OHRENSTEIN, Mr. Anthony Peter, FCA *1959;* 93 Wise Lane, Mill Hill, LONDON, NW7 2BD.

•OHRENSTEIN, Mr. Robert Ivor, BSc FCA *1993;* KPMG LLP, 15 Canada Square, LONDON, E14 5GL. See also KPMG Europe LLP

OHRI, Mr. Rajiv, FCA *1974;* Al Tayer Group LLC, Garhoud Atrium 3rd floor, Garhoud, P.O.Box 2623, DUBAI, UNITED ARAB EMIRATES.

OHTA, Mr. Naoki, BA ACA *2002;* Greenpark Capital, Cassini House, 57-59 St. James's Street, LONDON, SW1A 1LD.

OHTANI, Miss. Marika, ACA *2008;* 17 Woodforde Close Ashwell, BALDOCK, HERTFORDSHIRE, SG7 5QE.

•①OIRSCHOT, Mr. Richard Anthony, BSc FCA *1985;* 208 Pickhurst Lane, WEST WICKHAM, KENT, BR4 0HL.

OJANY, Mr. Richard Philip Otieno, ACA *1993;* Birch Rise Chilworth Road, Chilworth, SOUTHAMPTON, SO16 7JR.

•OJIKE, Chief Igwe, FCA *1970;* Ojike Okechukwu & Co, 5th Floor, 18 Oba Akran Avenue, Ikeja, GPO Box 2495, Marina LAGOS 101221 NIGERIA. See also Igwe Ojike & Co

OJLA, Miss. Kiran Jeet Kaur, BA(Hons) ACA *2002;* Agivey, Cogan Pill, Llandough, PENARTH, CF64 2NB.

OJO, Mr. Olufunmiso Adetokunbo, BA ACA *1981;* Templeton Business Consulting, 6th Floor, 27/29 King George V Road, PO Box 51217, Falomo, Ikoyi LAGOS NIGERIA.

OKE, Mrs. Claire Janine, ACA *2008;* 1 Fairview Rise, BRIGHTON, BN1 5GL.

OKE, Mr. Ebenezer Folorunso, BSc FCA *1966;* P.O. Box 2890, LAGOS, NIGERIA.

OKE, Ms. Heidi Andrea, BA ACA *1997;* 18 Thorn Street, IPSWICH, QLD 4305, AUSTRALIA.

OKEEFFE, Mr. Neil Anthony, BSc ACA *1999;* Bank of Scotland, 5 St. Pauls Square, LIVERPOOL, L3 9SJ.

OKELL, Mr. Andrew Keith, BA ACA *1985;* Chateau Lameraux, Listrac, Puisseguin, 33570 GIRONDE, FRANCE.

OKIKIADE, Miss. Kerry Louise, BA ACA *1999;* 11 Jessamine Road, LONDON, W7 3SQ.

OKIKIOLU, Ms. Jeannie Adetokunbo, MA ACA *1988;* 104 Ramillies Road, LONDON, W4 1JA.

•OKIN, Mr. Stewart Bernard, FCA *1978;* Glazers, 843 Finchley Road, LONDON, NW11 8NA. See also Glazers Ltd

OKINES, Mr. Keith Alan, FCA *1969;* York House, 22 Stanley Avenue, CHESHAM, BUCKINGHAMSHIRE, HP5 2JG.

•OKOBI, Chief Celestine Emeodibuisienu, BSc FCA *1963;* Celeste Industries Ltd, 160 Umejei Road, P O Box 500, IBUSA, NIGERIA. See also C.E. Okobi & Co (Life Member)

OKOH, Miss. Akosua Karle, BA ACA *2006;* P. O. Box 7416, No 8 Third Close, ACCRA, GHANA.

OKOH, Mr. George Victor, FCA *1966;* P O Box AN7416, Accra North, ACCRA, GHANA. (Life Member)

OKOLI, Mrs. Sanyade Daisy Julia, BA ACA *1999;* Travant Capital, 6B George Street, Ikoyi, LAGOS, NIGERIA.

OKORO, Mr. Yves Gerald, BSc ACA *2010;* Vodafone, 1 Kingdom Street, LONDON, W2 6BY.

OKOROAFOR, Mr. Kenneth, ACA *2009;* 308 Greenhaven Drive, LONDON, SE28 8FY.

OKOYE, Mr. Peter Chuma, BSc FCA *1965;* 37 Owa Street, Ogbete, P.O. Box 378, ENUGU, NIGERIA. (Life Member)

•OKOYE, Mr. Sylvanus Ifeanyi Chukwu, FCA *1975;* Sylva & Co, 105 Loampit Vale, Lewisham, LONDON, SE13 7TG.

OKUBANJO, Mrs. Abiola, BSc ACA *2005;* 58 Greenstead Avenue, WOODFORD GREEN, ESSEX, IG8 7ES.

OKUKENU, Miss. Lara, ACA *2011;* Flat 11, Edward Kennedy House, 196 Wornington Road, LONDON, W10 5FP.

OKUNOLA, Mr. Abayomi Abiodun, ACA FCCA *2011;* 86 Stanley Road, TEDDINGTON, MIDDLESEX, TW11 8TX.

OKYERE-DARKO, Mr. Antwi Barimah, ACA *2010;* 18 Greenfields Road, READING, RG2 8SE.

OLADEINDE, Mr. Joseph Olawale, FCA *1972;* 4 Kugbuyi Street, Idi-Oro Surulere, LAGOS, NIGERIA. (Life Member)

OLALEYE, Mr. Stephen, BSc ACA *1991;* 9 Delisle Road, Thamesmead West, LONDON, SE28 0JD.

OLAORE, Ms. Mhari-Jean, LLB ACA *1993;* Rebels Roost, Finches Lane, Twyford, WINCHESTER, SO21 1QF.

OLATUNDE, Pastor Olayiwola, FCA *1970;* Temitope Akantioke House, 59 Moore Street PO Box 7, ILE IFE, OSUN STATE, NIGERIA.

OLBY, Mr. Alan Musgrave, BA ACA *1997;* Sinclair Pharmaceuticals Ltd, Godalming Business Centre, Woolsack Way, GODALMING, SURREY, GU7 1XW.

OLBY, Mrs. Emma Beatrice, BA ACA *2006;* Meadowview, Pockford Road, Chiddingfold, GODALMING, SURREY, GU8 4TP.

OLBY, Mrs. Kate Emma, BSc ACA *2006;* Nightingale Lodge, Craymere Road, Briston, MELTON CONSTABLE, NORFOLK, NR24 2LS.

OLD, Mr. James George Leonard, BSc ACA *2007;* 29 Chevalier Grove, Crownhill, MILTON KEYNES, MK8 0EJ.

OLD, Mr. Shaun Peter, BSc ACA *2006;* 31 Pound Lane, POOLE, DORSET, BH15 3PS.

OLDALE, Mr. Andrew David, BA ACA *1994;* Co-Operative Group, Co-operative Retail, 3rd Floor Federation Building, Dantzic Street, MANCHESTER, M60 4ES.

OLDALE, Mr. Andrew Richard, BA ACA *1992;* Smith & Nephew Pty Ltd, PO Box 242, MOUNT WAVERLEY, VIC 3149, AUSTRALIA.

OLDALE, Mr. David Leonard, FCA *1958;* 48 Netherleigh Road, CHESTERFIELD, S40 3QJ. (Life Member)

OLDAM, Mr. Barrie Alexander, FCA *1960;* (Member of Council 1989 - 1992), 1 The Mount, Town Street, Rawdon, LEEDS, LS19 6QN. (Life Member)

OLDBURY, Mr. William David, FCA *1959;* 4 Lower House Drive, Lostock, BOLTON, BL6 4JX. (Life Member)

•OLDCORN, Mr. John Neil, BA ACA *1998;* KPMG LLP, 15 Canada Square, LONDON, E14 5GL. See also KPMG Europe LLP

OLDENZIEL, Mr. Arend, ACA *2008;* with KPMG, 8/F Prince's Building, 10 Chater Road, CENTRAL, HONG KONG ISLAND, HONG KONG SAR.

•OLDER, Mr. Keith Wilson, FCA *1974;* Keith Older & Company, 8 Barford Close, Ainsdale, SOUTHPORT, PR8 2RS.

OLDERSHAW, Mr. David, FCA *1968;* 16 Fordwater Road, Streetly, SUTTON COLDFIELD, B74 2BQ.

OLDERSHAW, Mrs. Sonia Frances, FCA *1968;* Dunkeld, Queens Drive, WIRRAL, CH60 6SH.

•OLDFIELD, Mr. Alan Geoffrey, FCA *1972;* Oldfield & Co, 2A Hutcliffe Wood Road, SHEFFIELD, S8 0EX.

OLDFIELD, Mr. David John, BSc(Hons) ACA *2011;* 33 Spring Lane, Lees, OLDHAM, OL4 5AZ.

•OLDFIELD, Mr. Derek Robert, FCA *1965;* Brampton Grange, Brampton Road, Brampton-en-le-Morthen, ROTHERHAM, SOUTH YORKSHIRE, S66 9BD.

OLDFIELD, Mr. Donald Walter, FCA *1963;* 3 St. Mary's Road, Westonzoyland, BRIDGWATER, TA7 0LF. (Life Member)

OLDFIELD, Mr. Hedley Roger, FCA *1958;* 43 Newfield Crescent, Dore, SHEFFIELD, S17 3DE. (Life Member)

OLDFIELD, Miss. Jane Marie, BSc ACA CTA *1991;* 48 Spring Bank Drive, Norristhorpe, LIVERSEDGE, WF15 7QS.

•OLDFIELD, Mr. Jesse Nicholson, FCA *1970;* JN Oldfield LLP, Broomedge Post Office, 286 Higher Lane, LYMM, CHESHIRE, WA13 0RW. See also Oldfield Jessie

①OLDFIELD, Mr. Mark Bradbury, BSc ACA *1986;* The Bothy, Nettleden Road, Little Gaddesden, BERKHAMSTED, HERTFORDSHIRE, HP4 1PL.

OLDFIELD, Mr. Michael, ACA CA(SA) *2008;* 5 Kings Court, 40 Hersham Road, WALTON-ON-THAMES, SURREY, KT12 1JE.

OLDFIELD, Mr. Nicholas Stuart Robert, BSc ACA *1998;* Computershare Limited, The Pavilions, Bridgwater Road, BRISTOL, BS99 7NH.

OLDFIELD, Mr. Philip David, MBA BA ACA *1987;* 3 Bedale Close, Skelmanthorpe, HUDDERSFIELD, HD8 9TX.

•OLDFIELD, Mr. Richard, BA FCA *1996;* PricewaterhouseCoopers LLP, 1 Embankment Place, LONDON, WC2N 6RH. See also PricewaterhouseCoopers

OLDFIELD, Mr. Richard St John Carlton, FCA *1974;* Spinney Cottage, Sicklinghall Road, WETHERBY, WEST YORKSHIRE, LS22 4AF.

OLDFIELD, Mr. Robert Graham, BSc ACA *2000;* Interpublic Ltd, 84 Eccleston Square, LONDON, SW1V 1PX.

•OLDFIELD, Mr. Roger Howard, FCA *1971;* with KPMG LLP, 15 Canada Square, LONDON, E14 5GL.

OLDFIELD, Mrs. Sarah Louise, ACA *2009;* 1 Rosewell Place, Whickham, NEWCASTLE UPON TYNE, NE16 5SY.

OLDFIELD, Mr. Simon, BA ACA *1982;* 216 Cropston Road, Anstey, LEICESTER, LE7 7BN.

OLDFIELD, Mr. Stephen John, BA ACA *1988;* Techtex, 7-8 Rhodes Business Park, Silburn Way, Middleton, MANCHESTER, M24 4NE.

OLDFIELD, Mr. Stephen Robin, MA FCA *1976;* (Tax Fac), with Dixon Wilson, 22 Chancery Lane, LONDON, WC2A 1LS.

OLDFIELD, Miss. Susanna Maria, BSc ACA *2005;* 27 Westcar Lane, Hersham, WALTON-ON-THAMES, KT12 5ER.

OLDFIELD, Mrs. Tara Samantha, BA ACA *1999;* 46 Woodbines Avenue, KINGSTON UPON THAMES, SURREY, KT1 2AY.

OLDFIELD, Mr. Timothy Simon, BSc FCA *1989;* 9 Mayfield Road, Bramhall, STOCKPORT, SK7 1JU.

OLDHAM, Mr. Andrew Martin, BA ACA *2000;* 106 Mercers Road, LONDON, N19 4PU.

OLDHAM, Mr. David John, MA(Oxon) ACA *2001;* 131 Fairview Avenue, TORONTO M6P 3A6, ON, CANADA.

OLDHAM, Mr. David John, BA FCA *1986;* 25 King Edward VII Road, NEWMARKET, SUFFOLK, CB8 0ET.

OLDHAM, Miss. Hilary Jane, BA FCA *1980;* New Creation Farm, Furnace Lane Nether Heyford, NORTHAMPTON, NN7 3LB.

OLDHAM, Mr. Hugh Scott, BA FCA *1954;* 83 Linden Way, BOSTON, LINCOLNSHIRE, PE21 9DT. (Life Member)

OLDHAM, Mr. Jason Robert, BSc(Econ) ACA *1996;* 6 Besbury Close, Dorridge, SOLIHULL, WEST MIDLANDS, B93 8NT.

OLDHAM, Mrs. Joanne Louise, BA ACA *1996;* 6 Besbury Close, Dorridge, SOLIHULL, WEST MIDLANDS, B93 8NT.

OLDHAM, Mr. John Edward, FCA *1967;* 743 Clarkson Road South, MISSISSAUGA L5J 2V1, ON, CANADA. (Life Member)

OLDHAM, Mr. Kenneth Michael, MEd MSc FCA *1957;* 1 Cellars Farm Road, Southbourne, BOURNEMOUTH, BH6 4DL. (Life Member)

OLDHAM, Mr. Martin Paul, ACA *1982;* with Wilkins Kennedy, 3-4 Eastwood Court, Broadwater Road, ROMSEY, HAMPSHIRE, SO51 8JJ.

OLDHAM, Mr. Michael Jonathan, FCA *1976;* Sheraton House, 4 Swan Road, HARROGATE, NORTH YORKSHIRE, HG1 2SS.

•①OLDHAM, Mr. Michael Jonathan Christopher, BA ACA *1982;* Tree Tops, Cherry Hill, Loudwater, RICKMANSWORTH, HERTFORDSHIRE, WD3 4JT.

OLDHAM, Mr. Nigel David Massey, BA ACA *1984;* Foxmeade Iping Road, Milland, LIPHOOK, GU30 7NA.

OLDHAM, Mr. Paul Leslie, BA ACA CF *1989;* 66 Llwyn-Y-Grant Road, Penylan, CARDIFF, CF23 9HL.

OLDHAM, Mr. Stephen, FCA MAAT *1995;* 2 Bembridge Road, Haughton Green, Denton, MANCHESTER, M34 7GU.

OLDING, Mr. Andrew William Annan, MA ACA *2002;* 15 Landford Road, LONDON, SW15 1AQ.

OLDING, Mr. Keith, FCA MBA *1993;* Flat 2, 132 Peperharow Road, GODALMING, GU7 2PW.

OLDING, Miss. Leanne, BA ACA *2000;* The Order of St John Care Trust, Wellingore Hall, Wellingore, LINCOLN, LN5 0HX.

•OLDKNOW, Mr. David, LLB FCA *1990;* Ernst & Young LLP, 1 More London Place, LONDON, SE1 2AF. See also Ernst & Young Europe LLP

OLDMAN, Dr. Alfred Maurice, FCA *1970;* Chestnut Lodge, Weston Lane, BATH, BA1 4AA.

OLDMAN, Mr. Reginald John, FCA CPFA *1972;* Old Cottage, Weobley Road, Credenhill, HEREFORD, HR4 7DN.

OLDNALL, Mr. Scott, BA(Hons) ACA *2000;* 1 Thetford Avenue, WORCESTER, WR4 0RB.

OLDNALL, Mrs. Tracey Lynne, MEng ACA *1999;* 1 Thetford Avenue, Berkeley Heywood, WORCESTER, WR4 0RB.
•**OLDONI, Mr. John Patrick, ACA** *1999;* Sajid & Sajid Limited, 26 Dover Street, Mayfair, LONDON, W1S 4LY.
OLDREIVE, Mr. Hugh Richard, BSc ACA *2006;* Flat 10 Chequer Court, 3 Chequer Street, LONDON, EC1Y 8PW.
OLDREY, Mr. Arthur David Gerald, FCA *1962;* Waterfield Farm, Cold Brayfield, OLNEY, MK46 4HS. (Life Member)
OLDROYD, Mr. Bernard Stuart, FCA *1966;* 32 Shillbank View, MIRFIELD, WF14 0QG.
OLDROYD, Mrs. Esther Fiona, BA ACA *1998;* 5 Fieldhead Court, Boston Spa, WETHERBY, LS23 6TL.
OLDROYD, Mr. George Martin, FCA *1967;* Walton Du Varclin, Le Varclin, St. Martin, GUERNSEY, GY4 6AW.
OLDROYD, Mr. Jeremy James, LLB ACA *1994;* 4 Stonehill Road, LONDON, SW14 8RW.
OLDROYD, Mr. John Robert, BSc ACA *2006;* The Cottage, Raglands, Bishopstone, SALISBURY, WILTSHIRE, SP5 4BE.
OLDROYD, Miss. Karen Elizabeth, ACA *2004;* 39 Blackmoor Foot, Linthwaite, HUDDERSFIELD, HD7 5TR.
OLDROYD, Mr. Simon John, ACA *1979;* Spa Farmhouse, Spa Lane, Lathom, ORMSKIRK, L40 6JG.
OLDROYD, Mr. Stephen Paul, BSc ACA *1995;* 5 Fieldhead Court, Boston Spa, WETHERBY, LS23 6TL.
OLDROYDE, Mr. John Derrick, FCA *1952;* 2 Highview, Upper Oldfield Park, BATH, BA2 3JT. (Life Member)
OLDS, Mr. Richard Philip, BA ACA *1995;* Tolcarne, Began Road, Old St. Mellons, CARDIFF, CF3 6XJ.
OLDS, Mr. Simon Francis, MSc BA ACA *2001;* 106 Rue Des Eaux-Vives, 1207 GENEVA, SWITZERLAND.
OLDWORTH, Mr. Richard Anthony, ACA *1981;* Standlands, River, PETWORTH, WEST SUSSEX, GU28 9AS.
OLEINIKOV, Mr. Alexandre, BA ACA *2000;* Flat 66, Lissenden Mansions, Lissenden Gardens, LONDON, NW5 1PR.
•**OLESIUK, Mr. Andrew, BSc FCA** *1981;* Andrew Olesiuk & Co, 9 Norley Drive, Sale Moor, SALE, M33 2JE.
OLFORD, Mr. William Keith, FCA *1965;* 23 Biscovey Road, Biscovey, PAR, CORNWALL, PL24 2HW. (Life Member)
OLIFF, Mrs. Gillian, BA ACA ACIS *1985;* 13 Forest House Lane, Leicester Forest East, LEICESTER, LE3 3NU.
OLIFFE, Mrs. Joanna, MSc BSc ACA *2006;* 153 Whitton Road, TWICKENHAM, TW2 7QU.
OLIFFE, Mr. Paul Mark, BSc ACA *2006;* with National Audit Office, 157-197 Buckingham Palace Road, Victoria, LONDON, SW1W 9SP.
OLIN, Ms. Emma, ACA *1997;* 1 Cristowe Road, LONDON, SW6 3QF.
OLIPHANT, Mr. Robert Joseph, MA ACA *1979;* Macquarie Bank, 1 Martin Place, SYDNEY, NSW 2000, AUSTRALIA.
OLIVA, Mr. Anthony Vincent, BA FCA *1978;* 6 The Meadway, BUCKHURST HILL, IG9 5PG.
OLIVA, Dr. Daniela, ACA *2009;* Flat 13, 87 Vincent Square, LONDON, SW1P 2PQ.
OLIVA-HAUXWELL, Mrs. Elizabeth Mary Virginia, BSc(Hons) ACA *2001;* 17 St. Marys Avenue, TEDDINGTON, MIDDLESEX, TW11 0HZ.
OLIVARI, Mr. Albert Charles, BSc ACA *1990;* 2B Sutherland Avenue, ORPINGTON, BR5 1QZ.
OLIVARI, Mrs. Clair Elizabeth, BSc ACA *1990;* 2B Sutherland Avenue, Petts Wood, ORPINGTON, BR5 1QZ.
OLIVE, Mr. Christopher David, BA ACA *2000;* 86 Grosvenor Road, LONDON, N10 2DS.
OLIVE, Mr. Daniel Peter, BSc ACA *1998;* 63 Elfort Road, Highbury, LONDON, N5 1AX.
OLIVE, Mr. Leslie William, FCA *1955;* 4 Harlands Close, HAYWARDS HEATH, WEST SUSSEX, RH16 1PS. (Life Member)
OLIVE, Mr. Paul Anthony, FCA *1968;* Flat 8, Glengarry, 32 East Beach, LYTHAM ST. ANNES, LANCASHIRE, FY8 5EX.
OLIVEIRA, Miss. Jacquelyn Emilia, ACA *2009;* with KPMG LLP, Two Financial Center, 60 South Street, BOSTON, MA 02111, UNITED STATES.
OLIVER, Mr. Adam Keith, ACA *2001;* B J Champion Contractors Ltd Champion House, Roentgen Court Roentgen Road, BASINGSTOKE, HAMPSHIRE, RG24 8NT.
OLIVER, Mr. Alan Lindsay, FCA *1963;* Yeadon, Bell Hill, Lindale, GRANGE-OVER-SANDS, LA11 6LD.
•**OLIVER, Ms. Alison, FCA** *1991;* (Tax Fac), Bishop Fleming, Chy Nyverow, Newham Road, TRURO, TR1 2DP.
OLIVER, Miss. Alison Kate, BA(Hons) ACA *2001;* Flat 22, 317 Upper Richmond Road, LONDON, SW15 6ST.
OLIVER, Mr. Antony, ACA *2010;* Houseboat Current Affairs, Cheyne Walk, LONDON, SW10 0DG.
OLIVER, Mr. Aubrey Thomas, BSc FCA *1971;* 117 Hoarwithy Road, HEREFORD, HR2 6HD.
OLIVER, Mrs. Caroline Dulcie Irene, BSc ACA *1989;* D J Reynolds & Co, 15 Alverton Street, PENZANCE, CORNWALL, TR18 2QP.
OLIVER, Mrs. Christine Anne, BSc FCA *1980;* Energy Solutions Ltd Unit B Future Court, George Summers Close Medway City Estate, ROCHESTER, ME2 4EL.
OLIVER, Mr. Christopher Charles, FCA *1973;* 135 Ardmore Lane, BUCKHURST HILL, IG9 5SB.
OLIVER, Mrs. Clare Elaine, BA ACA *2000;* 1 Copperfields, SAFFRON WALDEN, ESSEX, CB11 4FG.
OLIVER, Mr. Courtney Ambrose, FCA *1961;* 4 Riverbourne Road, Milford, SALISBURY, SP1 1NP. (Life Member)
OLIVER, Mr. David, BA ACA *1982;* East Northamptonshire Council East Northamptonshire House, Cedar Drive Thrapston, KETTERING, NORTHAMPTONSHIRE, NN14 4LZ.
OLIVER, Mr. David Henry Maxwell, BA FCA *1987;* 263 Lonsdale Road, Barnes, LONDON, SW13 9QL.
•**OLIVER, Mr. David Isaac, MBA BA FCA** *1984;* PricewaterhouseCoopers LLP, 7 More London Riverside, LONDON, SE1 2RT.
OLIVER, Mr. David John, BSc FCA *1972;* 39a Palmerston Road, BUCKHURST HILL, IG9 5PA. (Life Member)
OLIVER, Mr. David Matthew Joseph, LLB ACA *1986;* with RSM Tenon Limited, 66 Chiltern St, LONDON, W1U 4JT.
•**OLIVER, Mr. David Melvyn, ACA** *1985;* HW Forensic, Keepers Lane, The Wergs, WOLVERHAMPTON, WEST MIDLANDS, WV6 8UA.
OLIVER, Mr. David Michael, FCA *1971;* 2 Ravenscourt Park, LONDON, W6 0TH.
OLIVER, Miss. Emma Jane, BSc(Hons) ACA *2003;* 39 Hawkswood Drive, HAILSHAM, EAST SUSSEX, BN27 1UP.
OLIVER, Mrs. Emma Louise, BSc ACA *2007;* 36 Killarney Road, LONDON, SW18 2DX.
OLIVER, Mr. Gary, BA ACA *1982;* Foley Lodge, Prestwood, STOURBRIDGE, DY7 5AN.
•**OLIVER, Mr. Gary, BSc ACA** *1993;* Mazars LLP, The Atrium, Park Street West, LUTON, LU1 3BE.
OLIVER, Mr. Gary Bruce, BSc ACA *1992;* Court Farm Common Road, Dorney, WINDSOR, SL4 6QA.
OLIVER, Mr. Gordon Richard, BCom FCA *1984;* 115 Stone Pit Lane, Croft, WARRINGTON, WA3 7DX.
OLIVER, Mr. Graham, BSc ACA *1992;* 4 Stanbury Close, Thruxton, ANDOVER, HAMPSHIRE, SP11 8QD.
•**OLIVER, Miss. Hannah Jane, ACA CTA** *2002;* H2O Accounting Ltd, Ground Floor, 1000 Lakeside North Harbour, Western Road, PORTSMOUTH, PO6 3EZ.
•**OLIVER, Mr. Ian David, ACA** *1998;* 17 Sunderland Gardens, NEWBURY, BERKSHIRE, RG14 6BN.
OLIVER, Mr. Ian Richard, FCA *1968;* 8 Oakfield Drive, Sandiacre, NOTTINGHAM, NG10 5NH. (Life Member)
OLIVER, Mr. James Andrew, MA ACA *1986;* Hillside House, 40 Kenilworth Avenue, LONDON, SW19 7LW.
OLIVER, Mr. James Edward, FCA *1953;* Flat 3 Greenside View, Springfield Road, CAMBERLEY, GU15 1AB. (Life Member)
OLIVER, Mr. James Martin, BA ACA *2001;* 19 Worthington Crescent, Whitecliff, POOLE, BH14 8BW.
OLIVER, Mr. James Richard, BSc ACA *2003;* 24 Crail Close, WOKINGHAM, BERKSHIRE, RG41 2PZ.
OLIVER, Mr. James Richard, BSc ACA *2003;* with Deloitte Touche Tohmatsu, Grosvenor Place, 225 George Street, P.O. Box N 250, SYDNEY, NSW 2000 AUSTRALIA.
OLIVER, Mrs. Jane Elizabeth, BSc(Hons) ACA *2001;* 17 Sunderland Gardens, NEWBURY, BERKSHIRE, RG14 6BN.
OLIVER, Mrs. Jennifer Susan, BSc ACA *2000;* 24 Crail Close, WOKINGHAM, BERKSHIRE, RG41 2PZ.
OLIVER, Mr. John Alfred, FCA *1951;* 4 Clos Du Fond, La Rue Au Blancq, St. Clement, JERSEY, JE2 6QS. (Life Member)
OLIVER, Mr. John Charles, MA FCA *1980;* The White Cottage, Crampshaw Lane, ASHTEAD, KT21 2UD.
OLIVER, Mr. John David Bagnall, MA FCA *1960;* 7 St. Peters Street, Islington, LONDON, N1 8JD. (Life Member)
OLIVER, Mr. Jonathan Edward Frederick, MA FCA *1992;* RBS Aviation Capital, IFSC House, IFSC, DUBLIN, COUNTY DUBLIN, IRELAND.
OLIVER, Mr. Joseph Edward, OBE FCA *1964;* 4A Binnenweg, 1750 GASSBEEK, BELGIUM. (Life Member)
OLIVER, Mrs. Julie, BA ACA *1985;* 12 Moss Close, Willaston, NESTON, CH64 2XQ.
OLIVER, Ms. Julie Lilian, BSc ACA *1988;* St. Edwards School, Woodstock Road, OXFORD, OX2 7NN.
OLIVER, Mrs. Karen, BSc ACA *1996;* 38 Beaumont Avenue, RICHMOND, TW9 2HE.
OLIVER, Ms. Karen Jane, BSc ACA *1989;* 11 Puriri Street, Woburn, LOWER HUTT 5010, NEW ZEALAND.
OLIVER, Miss. Katy, BA ACA *2007;* 5 Percy Road, EXETER, EX2 8JY.
OLIVER, Mrs. Kirsty Anne, ACA *1998;* Kingfishers, 141 Main Road, Sundridge, SEVENOAKS, TN14 6EH.
OLIVER, Mrs. Lisa Ann, BCom ACA *1992;* 8 Rhoscolyn Drive, Tattenhoe, MILTON KEYNES, MK4 3AE.
OLIVER, Ms. Louisa Jane, ACA *2011;* Flat 4, Kingsley Court, 73 New Dover Road, CANTERBURY, KENT, CT1 3DZ.
OLIVER, Miss. Lucy Ann, BSc ACA *1992;* Brindwood House Millthorpe Lane, Holmesfield, DRONFIELD, DERBYSHIRE, S18 7SA.
OLIVER, Mr. Malcolm Gerard, ACA *1991;* 333 Glasgow Road, Eaglesham, GLASGOW, G76 0ER.
OLIVER, Mr. Mark Anthony, BA FCA *1982;* 44 Emmerson Avenue, STRATFORD-UPON-AVON, WARWICKSHIRE, CV37 9DX.
OLIVER, Mr. Martin, BA FCA *1989;* Breemstraat 54, 1540 HERNE, BELGIUM.
OLIVER, Mr. Martin Ian, BEng ACA *1994;* 67 Watling Street, ST. ALBANS, AL1 2QF.
OLIVER, Mr. Martin James, BA ACA *1993;* Connell Residential Cumbria House, 16-20 Hockliffe Street, LEIGHTON BUZZARD, BEDFORDSHIRE, LU7 1GN.
OLIVER, Mrs. Mary Louise, LLB ACA *2006;* 128 Oakcliffe Road, MANCHESTER, M23 1DD.
OLIVER, Mr. Matthew, BA ACA *1992;* 42 Hurst Green Road, HALESOWEN, B62 9QU.
OLIVER, Mr. Michael Anthony, FCA *1970;* 96 Elizabeth Avenue, Parkmore 2196, JOHANNESBURG, SOUTH AFRICA.
OLIVER, Mr. Michael Thomas, ACA *2011;* 22 Lakemore, PETERLEE, COUNTY DURHAM, SR8 1DZ.
OLIVER, Miss. Natasha, BA ACA *2004;* 84 Emerald Hill Road, SINGAPORE 229360, SINGAPORE.
OLIVER, Mr. Neil Paul, BA FCA *1987;* 22 Cornwall Road, Greenhill, HERNE BAY, CT6 7SY.
•**OLIVER, Mr. Nicholas Simon Anthony, FCA** *1980;* (Tax Fac), Pearson May, 37 Great Pulteney Street, BATH, BA2 4DA.
OLIVER, Mr. Nik, MA ACA *2006;* with Merrill Lynch Europe Plc, 2 King Edward Street, LONDON, EC1A 1HQ.
OLIVER, Mr. Oded, CA ACA *2008;* 175 Lichfield Court, Sheen Road, RICHMOND, SURREY, TW9 1AZ.
OLIVER, Mr. Paul Christopher, BA ACA MBA *1994;* Emirates Investment Authority, P.O. Box 3235, Building C67, Street 32, Diagonally Opposite BWM And the One, Khalidya Abu Dhabi ABU DHABI UNITED ARAB EMIRATES.
OLIVER, Mr. Paul Gregory, FCA *1968;* 4 Heatherwood Crescent, UNIONVILLE L3R 8W7, ON, CANADA.
OLIVER, Mr. Paul Lee, BSc ACA *1994;* 37 Hillside Road, BUSHEY, WD23 2HB.
OLIVER, Mr. Peter, FCA *1969;* (Tax Fac), 69 Spencer Close, Potton, SANDY, SG19 2QR.
OLIVER, Mr. Peter James, OBE FCA *1963;* The Briar Patch, Trevereux Hill, Limpsfield Chart, OXTED, RH8 0TL.
•**OLIVER, Mr. Philip, BSc FCA** *1977;* UHY Hacker Young, 22 The Ropewalk, NOTTINGHAM, NG1 5DT. See also UHY Hacker Young LLP
OLIVER, Miss. Rachel Amanda, BSc(Hons) ACA *2003;* 27 Leeds Road, Rawdon, LEEDS, LS19 6NN.
OLIVER, Mrs. Rebecca, BA(Hons) ACA *2003;* 20 Wenlock Drive, West Bridgford, NOTTINGHAM, NG2 6UD.
OLIVER, Mrs. Rebecca, BSc ACA *2009;* 27 Comets Garth, DARLINGTON, COUNTY DURHAM, DL2 2FL.
OLIVER, Mr. Richard John, BA ACA *1993;* 47 Marina Avenue, NEW MALDEN, KT3 6NE.
OLIVER, Mr. Richard John, BSc ACA *1997;* 80 Clifton Road, KINGSTON UPON THAMES, KT2 6PN.
OLIVER, Mr. Richard John, MBA BSc FCA *1990;* Murdoch House, 30 Garlic Row, CAMBRIDGE, CAMBRIDGESHIRE, CB5 8HW.
OLIVER, Mr. Robert Andrew, ACA *1979;* 41 Sand Hill Road, VERNON, NJ 07462, UNITED STATES.
OLIVER, Mr. Robert Anthony, BA ACA *1984;* 2B High Street, Eyeworth, SANDY, BEDFORDSHIRE, SG19 2HH.
OLIVER, Mr. Robert John, FCA *1976;* 9 Aragon Place, Kimbolton, HUNTINGDON, PE28 0JD.
OLIVER, Mr. Robin Alister, FCA *1973;* 9 Rosemary Close, Crundale, HAVERFORDWEST, PEMBROKESHIRE, SA62 4EF.
OLIVER, Mr. Royston Walter, FCA *1965;* Crofton, Hurstwood Lane, TUNBRIDGE WELLS, TN4 8YA.
OLIVER, Mrs. Sarah Elizabeth, FCA *1979;* Hillside House, 40 Kenilworth Avenue, Wimbledon, LONDON, SW19 7LW.
OLIVER, Mrs. Sarah Jane, BA ACA *2000;* 11 Becketts Lane, CHESTER, CHESHIRE, CH3 5RN.
•**OLIVER, Mr. Stephen John, FCA DChA** *1987;* (Tax Fac), Oliver & Co, 259 Otley Road, West Park, LEEDS, LS16 5LQ.
OLIVER, Mr. Stephen John, ACA *1992;* 23 Coleman Avenue, HOVE, BN3 5ND.
OLIVER, Ms. Susan Jennifer, BA ACA *1996;* 75 Rampton Road, Willingham, CAMBRIDGE, CB24 5JQ.
OLIVER, Mr. William Alder, BSc FCA *1980;* Westfields Court, Moreton Morrell, WARWICK, CV35 9DB.
OLIVER, Mr. William Andrew Dickinson, BEng ACA *2007;* 36 Killarney Road, LONDON, SW18 2DX.
•**OLIVERA, Mr. Johann, BA FCA** *1999;* Baker Tilly (Gibraltar) Limited, Regal House, Queensway, PO Box 191, GIBRALTAR, GIBRALTAR.
OLIVERO, Mr. Graham Joseph Gerard, BSc ACA *1996;* 2 Jasmine House, Waterport Terraces, GIBRALTAR, GIBRALTAR.
OLIVEY, Mr. Alan Keith, FCA *1970;* 48 Bucknall Way, BECKENHAM, KENT, BR3 3XN. (Life Member)
OLIVEY, Mr. Richard, MChem ACA *2007;* 270 The Avenue, WEST WICKHAM, BR4 0ED.
OLIVIER, Mr. James, BA ACA *2006;* Flat 9, Victoria Lodge, 34 Arterberry Road, Wimbledon, LONDON, SW20 8AQ.
OLIVIER, Mr. Jean-Marc William, BCom ACA *1987;* Upper Woodside, Woodside Lane, Farringdon, ALTON, HAMPSHIRE, GU34 3EX.
OLIVIER, Mr. John Eric Hordern, BA FCA *1965;* 3 Vineyard Hill Road, Wimbledon, LONDON, SW19 7JL. (Life Member)
OLIVIER, Mr. Philippus Louis, ACA CA(SA) *2010;* 80 Thistle Grove, WELWYN GARDEN CITY, HERTFORDSHIRE, AL7 4AQ.
OLIVIER, Mr. Robert David, BSc ACA *1985;* Level 9, 56 Clarence Street, SYDNEY, NSW 2000, AUSTRALIA.
OLLARD, Mr. John Deacon, BSc FCA JDipMA *1972;* 69 Pine Walk, CARSHALTON, SM5 4HA.
OLLARD, Mr. Mark Deacon, BA ACA *1998;* 58 Alexandra Road, RICHMOND, TW9 2BS.
OLLECH, Mrs. Miriam Esther, ACA *2005;* 77 Wentworth Road, LONDON, NW11 0RH.
•**OLLEY, Mrs. Anna, BSc ACA** *1992;* A H Olley BSc ACA, Thyme Cottage, The Green, Whiteparish, SALISBURY, SP5 2RP.
•**OLLEY, Mr. Charles William, FCA** *1984;* (Tax Fac), Price Bailey LLP, The Quorum, Barnwell Road, CAMBRIDGE, CB5 8RE. See also Price Bailey Private Client LLP, PB Financial Planning Ltd and Colin Pickard & Company Limited
•**OLLEY, Mrs. Joanne Nicola, ACA** *1994;* Joanne Olley, 31 Denton Crescent, Black Notley, BRAINTREE, ESSEX, CM77 8ZZ.
OLLIER, Mrs. Alison Mary, BSc(Hons) ACA *2001;* Home Farm, Sandford, West Felton, OSWESTRY, SHROPSHIRE, SY11 4EX.
OLLIER, Mr. Barrett Andrew, BA ACA *1980;* 47 Cedar Drive, Sunningdale, ASCOT, BERKSHIRE, SL5 0UA.
OLLIER, Mr. Craig Robert, ACA *2010;* Apartment 116, 21-33 Worple Road, LONDON, SW19 4BG.
•**OLLIER, Mr. Jonathan Matthew, BSc FCA** *1996;* (Tax Fac), Turner Peachey, Column House, London Road, SHREWSBURY, SY2 6NN.
•**OLLIFFE, Mr. Graham Hedley, FCA CTA** *1968;* (Tax Fac), Cooper Paul, Abacus House, 14-18 Forest Road, LOUGHTON, IG10 1DX.
OLLIFFE, Ms. Sarah, BSc ACA *2005;* Flat 2, 37 Beacon Hill, WOKING, SURREY, GU21 7NP.
OLLINGTON, Mr. Patrick John, BSc ACA *1984;* Holly Lodge, 2 Wentworth Close, Ripley, WOKING, SURREY, GU23 6DA.
OLLIVER, Mr. Daniel Guy, BEng ACA *1993;* Old Mutual Plc Millennium Bridge House, 2 Lambeth Hill, LONDON, EC4V 4GG.
•**OLLMAN, Mr. Robert Ian, FCA** *1977;* Company Contracts and Services Limited, 11 The Shrubberies, George Lane, LONDON, E18 1BD.

OLNEY, Mr. David John, BA ACA *1991;* Olney Headwear Ltd, 106 Old Bedford Road, LUTON, LU2 7PD.
OLNEY, Mr. Jeffrey, ACA CA(AUS) *2009;* 6 Poplar Road, ESHER, SURREY, KT10 0DD.
OLNEY, Mrs. Joanna Mary, BSc ACA *1992;* 98 High Street, Sandridge, ST. ALBANS, HERTFORDSHIRE, AL4 9BY.
OLNEY, Mrs. Katie Elizabeth, BSc ACA *1998;* Nutts Orchard, Woodbury Salterton, EXETER, EX5 1PG.
OLNEY, Mr. Richard Keith, BSc ACA *1992;* Blue Arrow, 800 Capability Green, LUTON, LU1 3BA.
OLNEY, Mr. Stephen John, FCA *1965;* The Lodge, Brick Kiln Lane, Horsmonden, TONBRIDGE, TN12 8EJ. (Life Member)
OLOFSSON, Miss. Catharina Erica, BSc ACA *1993;* Tegnersgatan 20, 41252 GOTHENBURG, SWEDEN.
OLOKO, Mr. Akinbiyi Olasunkanmi, BA ACA *1991;* 2A BAYO KUKU ROAD, P.O.BOX 2442 MARINA LAGOS., IKOYI, NIGERIA.
•OLOYEDE, Mr. Emmanuel Adeolu, BSc ACA *1991;* Emmanuel Stephens & Co, 62 Beechwood Road, LONDON, E8 3DY. See also East London Accountancy Services
•OLSBERG, Mr. Bernard, FCA *1973;* (Tax Fac), B Olsberg, 2nd Floor Newbury House, 401 Bury New Road, SALFORD, M7 2BT.
OLSBERG, Mr. Jonathan David, FCA *1971;* 9 Wingate Road, LONDON, W6 0UR.
OLSEN, Mr. David, FCA *1955;* 25 Royal Sands, WESTON-SUPER-MARE, BS23 4NH. (Life Member)
OLSEN, Mr. Graeme David, BSc ACA *1995;* Heritage Capital Management Limited, Broadway House, Tothill Street, LONDON, SW1H 9NQ.
OLSEN, Ms. Lise-Lotte, BCom FCA *1980;* Ferriers, Woolmongers Lane, Blackmore, INGATESTONE, ESSEX, CM4 0JX.
•OLSEN, Mr. Peter Norman, FCA *1973;* Peter N Olsen, Norse Cottage, Elwick, HARTLEPOOL, CLEVELAND, TS27 3EF.
OLSEN, Mrs. Sarah, BA ACA *1995;* Vine Cottage, Main Street, Ellerton, YORK, YO42 4PB.
OLSEN, Mr. Simon Derek, MA ACA *2003;* with Deloitte LLP, Abbots House, Abbey Street, READING, RG1 3BD.
OLSEN, Mr. Simon Viggor, BA ACA *1979;* 28 Mill Road, Buckden, ST. NEOTS, CAMBRIDGESHIRE, PE19 5SS.
OLSEN, Mr. Thomas Anthony Lewis, ACA *2008;* 38 Wontner Road, LONDON, SW17 7QT.
OLSSON SPEAK, Ms. Karin Margareta, ACA *2006;* 152 Harestone Valley Road, CATERHAM, SURREY, CR3 6HJ.
OLVER, Mr. Andrew Gilbert, FCA *1970;* Chelvey Court, Chelvey, Nr. Backwell, BRISTOL, BS48 4AA.
OLVER, Mr. David William, FCA *1968;* 13 Weld Blundell Avenue, Lydiate, LIVERPOOL, L31 4JR.
OLVER, Mr. Edward John, BA ACA *1980;* 13 Balmoral Avenue, Thornaby, STOCKTON-ON-TEES, TS17 7JP.
OLVER, Mr. Gregory James Littleton, BSc ARCS ACA *2004;* 7 Coastal Road, West Kingston, LITTLEHAMPTON, BN16 1SJ.
OLVER, Mr. Richard Nowell Linley, BSc ACA *1992;* Atlantic House, 50 Holborn Viaduct, LONDON, EC1A 2FG.
OLVER, Mr. Simon Colin James, BA ACA *2005;* Flat 8, 54 Park Lane East, REIGATE, SURREY, RH2 8HR.
OLYMBIOS, Mr. Andrew Panayiotis, BSc ACA *2004;* with Deloitte LLP, 2 New Street Square, LONDON, EC4A 3BZ.
OLYMBIOU, Mr. Andreas Sokratis, BA ACA *2009;* 28 Meadow View Road, Boughton Monchelsea, MAIDSTONE, KENT, ME17 4LJ.
OLYOTT, Mr. Jonathan Marc, BSc FCA *1986;* with Sully Partnership, 8 Unity Street, College Green, BRISTOL, BS1 5HH.
OMAN, Mrs. Sally Elizabeth, BSc ACA *1989;* 16 Dacre Street, MORPETH, NE61 1HW.
•OMAR, Mr. Abu Ahmed Ismail, FCA *1973;* A. Omar & Co, 23 Jalan Merah Saga, Apt 04-05, Mera Saga, SINGAPORE 278102, SINGAPORE.
OMAR, Mr. Ariffin, BSc(Hons) ACA MBA *2000;* 30 Craven Street, LONDON, WC2N 5NT.
OMAR, Mr. Awais, BSc(Econ) ACA *1997;* Safari, Lake View Road, Furnace Wood Felbridge, EAST GRINSTEAD, RH19 2QE.
OMAR, Mr. Ibrahim Mohamed El-Sayed, BCom FCA *1968;* 25 Devonshire Avenue, LEEDS, LS8 1AU.
OMAR, Mr. Nasir, LLB ACA *2001;* 22 St. Georges Road, ILFORD, ESSEX, IG1 3PQ.
OMER, Mr. Raif, FCA *1972;* Raif Omer & Co, P.K. 533, Atacag Ishani, 9 Ali Ruhi Sokak, LEFKOSA MERSIN 10, TURKEY.
OMID, Mr. Jafar, BSc FCA *1986;* Pentagon Capital Management Plc, 25-26 Albemarle Street, LONDON, W1S 4HX.
OMIDIORA, Mr. Adedokun Olugbenga, ACA *1987;* 20 Georgian Close, STANMORE, HA7 3QT.
OMIDIORA, Chief Johnson Olabisi Olaobaju, BSc FCA *1966;* 10 Balogun Bisi Omidara Road, APAPA, NIGERIA. (Life Member)
OMO-OSAGIE, Mr. Christopher Ehioze, BA(Hons) ACA *2003;* 701 - 942 Yonge Street, TORONTO M4W 3S8, ON, CANADA.
OMRAN, Mr. Ramzy, BSc ACA *2000;* 109 Loder Road, BRIGHTON, BN1 6PN.
ONABANJO, Mr. Vincent Olugboyega, FCA *1977;* Flat 44, Northways, College Crescent, LONDON, NW3 5DR.
ONDHIA, Mr. Yashvantrai Vallabhji, FCA *1973;* 2 Elveden Close, Off Newmarket Rd, NORWICH, NR4 6AS.
ONEILL, Miss. Colette, BA ACA *2005;* 5 Chorley Hall Lane, ALDERLEY EDGE, CHESHIRE, SK9 7EU.
ONG, Mr. Adrian Chu Jin, ACA *1994;* CIMB Investment Bank Berhad, UL Wisma Amanah Raya Berhad, Jalan Semantan, Damansara Heights, 50490 KUALA LUMPUR, FEDERAL TERRITORY MALAYSIA.
ONG, Mr. Ah Hing, FCA *1974;* 18 Hazelmere Road, Sandringham, AUCKLAND 1025, NEW ZEALAND.
ONG, Miss. Ai Lin, BA ACA *1982;* PricewaterhouseCoopers, P.O.Box 10192, Level 10 1 Sentral, Jalan Travers, 50470 KUALA LUMPUR, FEDERAL TERRITORY MALAYSIA.
ONG, Mr. Andrew, BSc ACA *2006;* 1 Martin Place, SYDNEY, NSW 2000, AUSTRALIA.
ONG, Miss. Beatrice Cheng-Bee, BA ACA *1992;* c/o Shell Eastern Petroleum (Pte) Ltd, Shell House #04-00, 83 Clemenceau Avenue, SINGAPORE 239920, SINGAPORE.
ONG, Miss. Bee Pheng, BA(Hons) ACA *2003;* 135 Sunset Way, Clementi Park, #09-07, SINGAPORE 597158, SINGAPORE.
ONG, Mr. Beng Chye, FCA *1993;* 853 Mountbatten Road, #05-03 East Mews, SINGAPORE 437838, SINGAPORE.
ONG, Mr. Boon Bah, FCA *1958;* No: 20-03 Block B Fraser Tower, Gasing Heights, No:92 Jalan 5/60, 46000 PETALING JAYA, SELANGOR, MALAYSIA. (Life Member)
ONG, Mr. Cheng Yin, FCA *1981;* 1 Old Beecroft Road, Cheltenham, SYDNEY, NSW 2119, AUSTRALIA.
ONG, Mr. Chin Lin, FCA *1977;* Blk 498G, 10-432, Tampines Street 45, SINGAPORE 525498, SINGAPORE.
ONG, Mr. Ching Han, MA LLM ACA *1980;* 3 William Street, BALMAIN, NSW 2041, AUSTRALIA.
ONG, Mr. Choa Huat, BSc FCA *1966;* C.H.Ong & Co, 110 Jalan Jurong Kechil, Apt 02-01 Sweebi House, SINGAPORE 2159, SINGAPORE. (Life Member)
ONG, Mr. Chor Wei Alan, LLB ACA *1993;* UPB International Capital Ltd, Unit 1007 10/F, Wing on Center, 111 Connaught Road Central, CENTRAL, HONG KONG ISLAND HONG KONG SAR.
ONG, Mr. Daniel Chon-Min, BA ACA MBA *1997;* 20 East Sussex lane, Republic of Singapore, SINGAPORE 279806, SINGAPORE.
ONG, Miss. Eelain, BSc FCA *1999;* 24 Lancaster Drive, Isle of Dogs, LONDON, E14 9PT.
ONG, Miss. Eily Ooi Kheng, MSc LLB ACA *2005;* Apartment 45, Wood Wharf Apartments, Horseferry Place, Greenwich, LONDON, SE10 9BB.
ONG, Miss. Elaine Yee Lynn, ACA *2011;* 50 Lorong BLM 2/5, Bandak Laguna Merbok, 08000 SUNGAI PETANI, KEDAH, MALAYSIA.
ONG, Mr. Eng Kooi, FCA *1961;* A2-15-3 BUKIT UTAMA 1, 3 CHANGKAT BANDAR UTAMA, PJU6 BANDAR UTAMA, 47800 PETALING JAYA, MALAYSIA. (Life Member)
ONG, Mr. Eng Shing, BA ACA *1985;* C/O Foodworks Melton, 413-429 High Street, MELTON, VIC 3337, AUSTRALIA.
ONG, Mr. Eng Hin, BEng FCA *1981;* 4 Clover Rise, SINGAPORE 579156, SINGAPORE.
ONG, Miss. Gaik Ee, LLB ACA *1993;* 107 Clementi Road, Apt 09-08 Block F, Kent Vale, SINGAPORE 129790, SINGAPORE.
ONG, Mr. George Eng Poh, BSc ACA *1979;* EPGO Consulting, 7 Farrer Drive #01-05, SINGAPORE 259278, SINGAPORE.
ONG, Mr. Ghee Eng, ACA *1984;* Sheldans, 47 Wadham Parade, MOUNT WAVERLEY, VIC 3149, AUSTRALIA.
ONG, Mr. Ghee Sai, BSc ACA *1988;* 13A - 04 Tara Condominium, 33 Jalan Ampang Hilir, 55000 KUALA LUMPUR, FEDERAL TERRITORY, MALAYSIA.
ONG, Miss. Hai Choo, BSc FCA *1978;* 45 Jalan Batai, Damansara Heights, KUALA LUMPUR, FEDERAL TERRITORY, MALAYSIA.
ONG, Miss. Hooi Yuen Adrine, BA ACA *2003;* 24 Jalan Serambi U8/26, Bukit Jelutong, 40150 SHAH ALAM, SELANGOR, MALAYSIA.
ONG, Mr. Hung Siong, MA ACA *1986;* F2 Henredon Court, 8 shouson Hill road, DEEP WATER BAY, HONG KONG SAR.
ONG, Mr. Ie Huat, FCA *1972;* 96 Sidney Road, ANNANDALE, NJ 08801, UNITED STATES.
ONG, Mr. James Mathew, BA ACA *2001;* Evander Glazing & Locks Lakeside, 300 Old Chapel Way Broadland Business Park, NORWICH, NR7 0WG.
ONG, Mr. Ken Yong, BSc ACA *2003;* 39 Lorong Zaaba, Taman Tun Dr Ismail, 60000 KUALA LUMPUR, FEDERAL TERRITORY, MALAYSIA.
ONG, Mr. Kok-Chiong Chris, FCA *1984;* 5 Derbyshire Road, Apt 07-07, SINGAPORE 309461, SINGAPORE.
ONG, Mrs. Li Fuen, ACA *1980;* 7 Farrer Drive, Apt 01-05 Sommerville Grandeur, SINGAPORE 259278, SINGAPORE.
ONG, Mr. Liang Beng, ACA *1983;* 6 Jalan Jujur 1/6, Taman Bakti, 68000 AMPANG, MALAYSIA.
ONG, Mr. Liang Win, BA ACA *1988;* No 16 Jalan BU 11/2, Bandar Utama, 47800 PETALING JAYA, SELANGOR, MALAYSIA.
ONG, Mr. Lu Yuan, BSc FCA *2000;* 26 Taman Sentosa, Bukit Baru, 75150 MALACCA CITY, MALACCA STATE, MALAYSIA.
ONG, Miss. May May, BA(Hons) ACA *2005;* with KPMG LLP, 16 Raffles Quay, # 22-00, Hong Leong Building, SINGAPORE 048581, SINGAPORE.
ONG, Ms. Ming Ai, LLB ACA CTA *2003;* 117 Holland Grove View, SINGAPORE 276274, SINGAPORE.
ONG, Miss. Patricia Buan Tee, FCA *1975;* 52 Jalan USJ 11/4J, 47600 SUBANG, SELANGOR, MALAYSIA.
ONG, Ms. Poh Luan, ACA *1987;* 7 Stock Farm Avenue, BAULKHAM HILLS, NSW 2153, AUSTRALIA.
ONG, Mr. Puay Seong, ACA *2009;* B-10-7 Saffron Condominium, No 1 Jalan Sentul Indah, 51100 KUALA LUMPUR, MALAYSIA.
ONG, Miss. Rui Chi, BA ACA *2002;* Glan y Gro, Llangower, BALA, GWYNEDD, LL23 7BT.
ONG, Mr. Samuel Yee Peng, BSc(Econ) FCA *2001;* with PricewaterhouseCoopers, Jl HR Rasuna Said Kav X-7 No. 6, JAKARTA, 12940, INDONESIA.
ONG, Miss. Say Leng, ACA *1983;* 21 Jln Sri Hartamas 15, 50480 KUALA LUMPUR, FEDERAL TERRITORY, MALAYSIA.
ONG, Miss. Siew Mooi, ACA *1988;* PO Box 39148, Howick, MANUKAU CITY 2145, AUCKLAND, NEW ZEALAND.
•ONG, Miss. Su Lin, BA FCA *1986;* DCDM Consulting, 10 Frere Felix De Valois, Champ de Mars, PORT LOUIS, MAURITIUS.
ONG, Miss. Suan Chin, BSc(Hons) ACA *2005;* 16A Jervois Lane, #02-06 Clydesview, SINGAPORE 159192, SINGAPORE.
ONG, Miss. Swee-Bee, BSc ACA *2004;* Level 1, 1 Martin Place, SYDNEY, NSW 2010, AUSTRALIA.
ONG, Mr. Teng Lam, FCA *1974;* 27 Jalan Istana Larut, 34000 TAIPING, PERAK, MALAYSIA.
ONG, Miss. Tin Chie, FCA *1976;* 7 Greenview Crescent, SINGAPORE 289317, SINGAPORE.
ONG, Mr. Wei Dong, BSc FCA *1986;* HKICPA, 37 Floor, Wu Chung House, 213 Queen's Road East, WAN CHAI, HONG KONG ISLAND HONG KONG SAR.
ONG, Mr. Wei Hiam, MSc FCA *1999;* Flat B 16/F, Block 2 Ronsdale Garden, 25 Tai Hang Drive, CAUSEWAY BAY, HONG KONG ISLAND, HONG KONG SAR.
ONG, Miss. Wei Shie, BSc ACA *1984;* A1 8th Floor, Nicholson Tower, 8 Wong Nai Chung Gap Road, HAPPY VALLEY, HONG KONG ISLAND, HONG KONG SAR.
ONG, Mr. Yew Huat, BA ACA *1982;* Ernst & Young, One Raffles Quay, North Tower, Level 18, SINGAPORE 048583, SINGAPORE. See also Ong Y.H.
ONG, Mr. Yu-Kee, BA ACA *1994;* Flat A Block 2, The Paragon, 9 Shan Yin Road, TAI PO, NT, HONG KONG SAR.
ONGLEY, Mr. Chris Ian, ACA *2010;* 3 Woodland Terrace, LONDON, SE7 8EW.
ONION, Mr. Allen Stanley, FCA *1969;* 1 Seal Close, SUTTON COLDFIELD, B76 1FJ. (Life Member)
ONIONS, Mrs. Victoria, BSc ACA *2006;* 99 Needlers End Lane, Balsall Common, COVENTRY, CV7 7AE.
•ONISIFOROU, Mr. Gabriel, BA(Econ) ACA *1995;* Ernst & Young Cyprus Limited, Nicosia Tower Centre, 36 Byron Avenue, P.O Box 21656, 1511 NICOSIA, CYPRUS.
ONISIFOROU, Mr. Onisiforos, MBA FCA CCSA CIA *1994;* 6 Menandrou Street, Strovolos, 2060 NICOSIA, CYPRUS.
ONLEY, Mr. Richard Myles, BA ACA *1996;* 44 Tollerton Lane, Tollerton, NOTTINGHAM, NG12 4FQ.
ONONA, Mr. Eric James, BA ACA *1996;* (Tax Fac), 42 Deansway, LONDON, N2 0JE.
ONONA, Mr. Ted, MEng ACA *1998;* 22 Vivian Way, LONDON, N2 0AE.
•ONONYE, Mr. Anthony, ACA *1978;* Anthony Ononye & Co, 2 Iya-Agan Lane, Ebute-Metta (West), P O Box 74774 Victoria Island, LAGOS, NIGERIA. See also Obiora Monu & Co.
ONOUFRIOU, Mr. Polyvios, BA ACA *1996;* 3 Kefallinias str., 16672 VARI, ATTICA, GREECE.
ONSLOW, Mr. Arthur Alan Maxwell, MA FCA *1951;* P O Box 268, ST.IVES 2075, NSW 2075, AUSTRALIA. (Life Member)
ONSLOW, Mrs. Emma Jane May Louise, ACA *2003;* 37 Union Road, MACCLESFIELD, CHESHIRE, SK11 7BN.
ONUEKWUSI, Miss. Francisca, BSc ACA *2011;* 4 Denmark Road, LONDON, N8 0DZ.
ONUKOGU, Mr. Hilary Enyimegbulam, BSc FCA *1972;* Hilary Onukogu & Co, Chartered Accountants, 20 Oweh Street, Fadeyi Yaba P.O. Box 70383, Victoria Island, LAGOS NIGERIA.
ONUORA, Mr. Chiz, BEng ACA *1993;* 11 Corfield Road, Winchmore Hill, LONDON, N21 1SF.
ONWOOD, Mr. Michael, MA FCA *1971;* 4155 Blueridge Crescent, Apt. 4C, MONTREAL H3H 1S7, QC, CANADA.
ONYANGO, Mr. Samuel Okech, FCA *1985;* Deloitte & Touche, Deloitte Place, Waiyaki Way, Muthangari, P O Box 40092, GPO 00100 NAIROBI KENYA. See also Gill & Johnson
•ONYEWUCHI, Mr. Herbert Iromuanya, FCA *1971;* 416 Bentworth Court, Granby Street, LONDON, E2 6DW.
OO, Mr. Yang Ping, BSc ACA *2000;* Ernst & Young LLP, One Raffles Quay, North Tower Level 18, SINGAPORE 048583, SINGAPORE.
OOI, Miss. Bee Wah, ACA *1981;* 32 Lintang Delima 3, Taman GembiraGelugor, 11700 PENANG, MALAYSIA.
OOI, Miss. Chee Kar, FCA *1980;* PricewaterhouseCoopers LLP, 17-00 PWC Building, 8 Cross Street, SINGAPORE 048424, SINGAPORE.
OOI, Miss. Elizabeth, ACA *2009;* Flat 6, Vandon Court, 64 Petty France, Westminster, LONDON, SW1H 9HE.
OOI, Mr. Eng Hooi, BSc FCA *1984;* C-08-11 DESA PERMAI CONDO, JLN. MORIB TMN DESA, 58100 KUALA LUMPUR, FEDERAL TERRITORY, MALAYSIA.
OOI, Mr. Lee Meng, BSc ACA *1988;* 2A Jalan PJU 1A/33A, Ara Damansara, 47301 PETALING JAYA, SELANGOR, MALAYSIA.
OOI, Ms. Pei She, BSc ACA *2003;* 3 Woodlawn Road, LONDON, SW6 6NQ.
OOI, Mr. Teng Chew, FCA *1970;* Teng Chew Ooi, 28-A Jesselton Crescent, 10450 PENANG, MALAYSIA.
OOI, Mr. Thiam Poh, ACA *2010;* BDO International, 12th Floor Menara Uni. Asia, Jalan sultan Ismail, 1008 KUALA LUMPUR, FEDERAL TERRITORY, MALAYSIA.
OOI, Miss. Yang Ming, BA ACA *1992;* 8 Allison Grove, LONDON, SE21 7ER.
•OOI, Mr. Yang Chew, BSc(Hons) FCA MSI MIRM *1990;* Xi Jiao Jia Jing Yuan - Villa 208, 50 Jin Bang Road, Changning District, SHANGHAI 200335, CHINA.
OOMER, Mr. Rashid Suleman, FCA *1974;* Al Barr F.H. Ltd, India House, No2 Kcmps Corner, MUMBAI M00036, INDIA.
OON, Miss. Ai Li, BCom ACA *1995;* Flat F 24th Floor, Panorama Gardens, 103 Robinson Road, MID LEVELS, HONG KONG ISLAND, HONG KONG SAR.
OON, Ms. Christina Wei-Li, MEng ACA *2002;* Flat 25 Edison Court, Greenroof Way, LONDON, SE10 0DQ.
OON, Mr. Patrick Jin Chye, BSc ACA *1993;* 26 Endersleigh Gardens, LONDON, NW4 4SD.
OOSTERVELD, Mr. Mettinus Margarethus, ACA *1997;* 24 Sceptre Crescent, Bloubergrant, MILNERTON, 7441, SOUTH AFRICA.
OOSTHUIZEN, Mr. Daniel Charl Stephanus, MA ACA *1987;* South Western Electricity Plc, Avonbank, Feeder Road, BRISTOL, BS2 0TB.
OOSTHUIZEN, Mr. Derek, ACA CA(SA) *2010;* 30 Surbiton Hill Park, SURBITON, SURREY, KT5 8ES.
OOSTHUIZEN, Miss. Heidi, ACA *2009;* 53d Bridge Road, EAST MOLESEY, KT8 9ER.
OOSTHUIZEN, Mr. Okker Andries, BCom FCA *1955;* P O Box 3100, Wilropark, ROODEPOORT, GAUTENG, 1731, SOUTH AFRICA. (Life Member)
OPENSHAW, Mr. Andrew Nicolas, FCA *1974;* 2 Marlow Road, LEICESTER, LE3 2BQ.

OPENSHAW, Mr. Harry Forrest, FCA *1963;* Edge Hill, 71 Lowercroft Road, BURY, BL8 2EP. (Life Member)
OPENSHAW, Mr. James Ronald, BSc ACA *1993;* 62 Quayside, ELY, CAMBRIDGESHIRE, CB7 4BA.
OPENSHAW, Mr. John Davis, FCA *1964;* 753 St. John Cove, NICEVILLE, FL 32578, UNITED STATES.
OPENSHAW, Ms. Lucy Rose, ACA *2008;* Deloitte & Touche, 2 New Street Square, LONDON, EC4A 3BZ.
OPENSHAW, Mr. Steven, BSc FCA *1999;* 67 George Street, Hadleigh, IPSWICH, IP7 5BW.
OPENSHAW, Mr. Steven John, BSc ACA *2006;* with BDO LLP, 55 Baker Street, LONDON, W1U 7EU.
OPIE, Mrs. Jennifer Anne, BA ACA DChA *2007;* with Atkins Ferrie, 1 Water-Ma-Trout, HELSTON, CORNWALL, TR13 0LW.
OPIE, Mr. Simon John, FCA *1971;* 45 Long Park, Chesham Bois, AMERSHAM, HP6 5LF.
•OPPENHEIM, Mr. Bernard Henry, ACA *1980;* Oppenheim and Company Limited, 52 Great Eastern Street, LONDON, EC2A 3EP. See also Think Map Corporation Limited
•OPPENHEIM, Mr. Martin John Marcus, FCA *1973;* (Tax Fac), Oppenheims Accountancy Limited, PO Box 2385, MAIDENHEAD, BERKSHIRE, SL6 7WQ.
•OPPENHEIM, Mr. Nicholas Stephen, FCA *1980;* (Tax Fac), Oppenheims, PO Box 3578, MAIDENHEAD, BERKSHIRE, SL6 3WH.
OPPENHEIMER, Ms. Belinda Jane, ACA *1991;* 34/44 Collins Street, ANNANDALE, SYDNEY, NSW 2038, AUSTRALIA.
OPPENHEIMER, Mr. Ronald Martin, FCA *1966;* Apartado De Correos 13, 29680 ESTEPONA, MALAGA, SPAIN.
OPPERMAN, Mr. Peter Adam Ernest, BSc ACA *1986;* Nether Doyley, Hurstbourne Tarrant, ANDOVER, HAMPSHIRE, SP11 0DW.
OPPONG, Mr. Sylvester, BA ACA *2007;* 3 Rowden Road, BECKENHAM, BR3 4NA.
OPRAVA, Mrs. Kate, MSc ACA *1999;* 53 Romilly Road, CARDIFF, CF5 1FJ.
•①OPREY, Mr. David John, FCA *1979;* Chantrey Vellacott DFK LLP, 1st Floor, 16-17 Boundary Road, HOVE, EAST SUSSEX, BN3 4AN.
OPUMINJI, Mr. Anthony Ibiosiya, BSocSc ACA *1994;* Flat 6, 337 Kennington Lane, LONDON, SE11 5QY.
OR, Miss. Patricia Siu Ngam, FCA *1991;* Gammon Construction Limited, 28/F Devon House, QUARRY BAY, HONG KONG ISLAND, HONG KONG SAR.
OR, Mr. Wai King, ACA *2006;* Flat 507, Block B, New Providence Wharf, 1Fairmount Avenue, LONDON, E14 9PB.
ORAM, Miss. Gemma, BSc ACA *2009;* 26 Wythenshawe Road, SALE, CHESHIRE, M33 2JP.
ORAM, Mr. James Roderick Talbot, FCA *1975;* Deloitte Touche Tohmatsu, Caixa Postal 1338, CEP 20001-970, RIO DE JANEIRO, BRAZIL.
•ORAM, Mr. James Stephen, LLB FCA *1971;* James Oram & Co., Cadoro, Roman Drive, Chilworth, SOUTHAMPTON, SO16 7HT.
ORAM, Mrs. Jennifer Mary, BSc ACA *2007;* 4 Conister Close, Onchan, ISLE OF MAN, IM3 4BH.
ORAM, Mr. John Leonard, FCA *1967;* P O Box 533, BEDFORD HILLS, NY 10507, UNITED STATES.
ORAM, Ms. Katy, BA ACA *2000;* 66 Brandwood Crescent, Kings Norton, BIRMINGHAM, B30 3PZ.
ORAM, Mr. Patrick, BSc ACA *1986;* Woodville House, 126 Woodside Road, AMERSHAM, BUCKINGHAMSHIRE, HP6 6NP.
ORAM, Miss. Rebecca Jane, BA ACA *1994;* Asda Stores Ltd, Asda House, Great Wilson Street, LEEDS, LS11 5AD.
ORAM, Mr. Robert James, ACA *2005;* with Bush & Co, 2 Barnfield Crescent, EXETER, EX1 1QT.
ORAM, Mr. Stephen Marcus, ACA *1990;* Shernold House, 1a Paynes Lane, MAIDSTONE, KENT, ME15 9QT.
ORANGE, Mr. Andrew Michael Ford, BA ACA *1979;* The Grove, Chute Forest, ANDOVER, HAMPSHIRE, SP11 9DG.
ORANGE, Mr. Charles William, FCA *1966;* Hascombe Place Nore Lane, Hascombe, GODALMING, GU8 4JT.
ORANGE, Mr. Hugh James, BA ACA *2006;* Flat 1 35 Dafforne Road, 35 Dafforne Road, LONDON, SW17 8TY.
ORANGE, Mr. Timothy Stuart, MA ACA *1990;* Cambridge Water Co Ltd, 90 Fulbourn Road, CAMBRIDGE, CB1 9JN.
ORBAN, Mr. Alfred, BSc ACA *1986;* 30 Sundridge Avenue, BROMLEY, BR1 2PX.
ORBAN, Mr. Stefan, BA ACA ATII *1990;* 14 Dunlin Rise, Merrow, GUILDFORD, GU4 7DX.
•ORBECK, Mr. Kenneth, BSc ACA *2002;* New Door Partnerships Limited, 12 Crow Hill, BROADSTAIRS, KENT, CT10 1HT.
ORBELL, Mrs. Lorraine Elizabeth, BSc ACA *1986;* 19 Daintrees Road, Fen Drayton, CAMBRIDGE, CB24 4TE.
ORBELL, Miss. Madeleine, BSc ACA *2002;* 38 Stanley Road, BRIGHTON, BN1 4NJ.
ORBELL, Miss. Vicki, BA ACA *2004;* 11A Orchard Estate, Little Downham, ELY, CB6 2TU.
ORCHANT, Miss. Sonia, BSc ACA *2009;* 1591 Rue Marie Claire, LASALLE H8N1R8, QC, CANADA.
ORCHARD, Mrs. Angharad Sarah, BA ACA *2003;* 2 Ash View, Randwick, STROUD, GLOUCESTERSHIRE, GL6 6JF.
ORCHARD, Mr. Christopher William, BSc FCA *1976;* 3 Manor Way, CHESHAM, BUCKINGHAMSHIRE, HP5 3BG.
•ORCHARD, Mrs. Gillian Mary, BSc ACA *1990;* Gill Orchard ACA, Warreston House, Slade Cross, Cosheston, PEMBROKE DOCK, SA72 4SX.
ORCHARD, Mr. John Ross, MA FCA *1960;* 1 The Cenacle, CAMBRIDGE, CB3 9JS. (Life Member)
•ORCHARD, Mr. Jonathan Richard, BA ACA *1999;* Jonathan Orchard Ltd, 2 Ash View, Randwick, STROUD, GLOUCESTERSHIRE, GL6 6JF.
ORCHARD, Mr. Jonny Paul, ACA *2010;* 122 Nelson Street, HYDE, CHESHIRE, SK14 1PB.
ORCHARD, Mr. Laurence Augustine, FCA *1973;* Sabien Technology Ltd, 34 Clarendon Road, WATFORD, WD17 1JJ.
ORCHARD, Mr. Matthew John Charles, BSc ACA *2002;* 13 Somersham Road, BEXLEYHEATH, DA7 4SA.
ORCHISON, Miss. Gabrielle Owen, MSc BA ACA *1995;* 20 Morley Square, Bishopston, BRISTOL, BS7 9DW.
ORD, Miss. Hazel, BSc ACA *2004;* UK Land Estates Unit 7, Queens Park Team Valley Trading Estate, GATESHEAD, TYNE AND WEAR, NE11 0QD.
ORD, Miss. Helen Ruth Campbell, BSc ACA *2006;* 87a Archel Road, LONDON, W14 9QL.
ORD, Mrs. Rebecca, ACA *2011;* 7 Machin Drive, Broughton Astley, LEICESTER, LE9 6HP.
ORD, Mr. Richard Stanley, FCA *1969;* 16a Levenside, STOKESLEY, NORTH YORKSHIRE, TS9 5BJ. (Life Member)
ORD, Mr. Stuart James, BA(Hons) ACA *2001;* 96 Park Rise, HARPENDEN, HERTFORDSHIRE, AL5 3AN.
ORDMAN, Mr. David Andrew, BEng FCA *1996;* Mulroy Talbot Road, Bowdon, ALTRINCHAM, CHESHIRE, WA14 3JD.
ORDONEZ, Miss. Beatrice, LLB ACA *1998;* 22 Mercer Street, Apt 2B, NEW YORK, NY 10013, UNITED STATES.
ORFORD, Mr. Michael Elvey, FCA *1969;* 12 Deepdene, HASLEMERE, GU27 1RE.
•ORFORD, Mr. Neil Peter, ACA FCCA CF *2009;* Lovewell Blake LLP, 102 Prince of Wales Road, NORWICH, NORFOLK, NR1 1NY.
ORFORD, Mrs. Olivia Katherine, LLB ACA *2005;* Lloyds TSB Group, Canons House, Canons Way, BRISTOL, BS1 5LL.
ORGAN, Mr. Harold Peter Murray, FCA *1948;* Rowan Cottage, Rosemary Lane, Abbotsbury, WEYMOUTH, DT3 4JN. (Life Member)
ORGAN, Mr. Keith, FCA *1968;* 37 Coward Drive, Oughtibridge, SHEFFIELD, S35 0JP.
ORGAN, Mr. Robert Charles William, BA ACA *1996;* Beechcroft, George Eyston Drive, WINCHESTER, HAMPSHIRE, SO22 4PE.
ORGAN, Mrs. Susan Mary, BA ACA ACCA *1996;* Beechcroft, George Eyston Drive, WINCHESTER, SO22 4PE.
ORGER, Mr. Christopher Charles, BA ACA *2001;* 8 Grassendale Road, Grassendale, LIVERPOOL, L19 0NA.
ORLEBAR, Mr. Edward, BA ACA *2004;* 25 Dighton Road, LONDON, SW18 1AN.
ORLEDGE, Mr. Kenneth Samuel Murray, BA(Econ) ACA *2004;* Michaelmas House, Main Street, Padbury, BUCKINGHAM, MK18 2AY.
ORLEDGE, Mr. Stephen Murray, FCA *1969;* St. Briavels House, Pystol Lane, St. Briavels, LYDNEY, GLOUCESTERSHIRE, GL15 6TE.
ORLIK, Mr. Simon George, FCA *1969;* 23 Downsview Gardens, DORKING, SURREY, RH4 2DX.
ORLOFF, Mr. Simon Mark George, BSc ACA *1991;* 2 Crofters Road, NORTHWOOD, MIDDLESEX, HA6 3ED.
ORLOVA ANDREOU, Mrs. Anna, BA ACA *2004;* Kodrou 2 Dasoupoly, 2028 NICOSIA, CYPRUS.
ORLOVSKY, Mr. Marcus, BSc ACA *1982;* 2a Kenilworth Avenue, LONDON, SW19 7LW.
ORMAN, Mr. David Henry, FCA *1958;* Turnberry Hill, 1612 Bennett Lake Road, RR#1, BALDERSON K0G 1A0, ON, CANADA. (Life Member)
ORME, Miss. Charlene Adele, BSc ACA *2005;* with Grant Thornton UK LLP, Enterprise House, 115 Edmund Street, BIRMINGHAM, B3 2HJ.
ORME, Mr. Christopher Alexander, FCA *1968;* Holts, Little Horkesley, COLCHESTER, CO6 4DR.
ORME, Mr. David John, BSocSc ACA *1990;* Tomlins, Bucklebury, READING, RG7 6TP.
•ORME, Mrs. Delia Joan, FCA *1981;* (Tax Fac), Delia Orme, Branksome House, Filmer Grove, GODALMING, SURREY, GU7 3AB.
ORME, Mr. Edward Charles Macaulay, MA ACA *2006;* 3 Shooters Paddock Layton Lane, SHAFTESBURY, DORSET, SP7 8AB.
ORME, Mr. Geoffrey Michael, FCA ATII *1982;* 8 Grange Road, LYTHAM ST. ANNES, LANCASHIRE, FY8 2BN.
ORME, Mrs. Helen Louise, BA(Hons) ACA *2004;* 6 Little Overwood, West Timperley, ALTRINCHAM, CHESHIRE, WA14 5UE.
ORME, Mr. Jeremy David, MA FCA *1969;* 38 Methley Street, LONDON, SE11 4AJ.
ORME, Miss. Nicola Margaret, MEng ACA *2003;* Flat 137, 14 New Crane Place, LONDON, E1W 3TU.
ORME, Mr. Timothy Rupert, BA FCA *1987;* 11 Dunmore Road, LONDON, SW20 8TN.
ORME, Dr. Wendy, BSc ACA *2002;* 25 St. Johns Road, HITCHIN, HERTFORDSHIRE, SG4 9JP.
ORMEROD, Mr. Anthony Keith Raymond, FCA *1971;* Flat 1, 5 The Causeway, LONDON, N2 0PR.
ORMEROD, Mrs. Carole, BA ACA *1985;* Lane End, 90 Cherry Lane, LYMM, WA13 0PD.
•ORMEROD, Mr. Howard Keith, BSc FCA *1988;* 11 Belle Vue Terrace, YORK, YO10 5AZ.
ORMEROD, Mr. John, MA FCA *1973;* 20a Broadlands Road, LONDON, N6 4AN.
ORMEROD, Mr. John, MA FCA FRSA *1977;* Flat 6, Exeter House, Putney Heath, LONDON, SW15 3SU.
ORMEROD, Mr. John Michael, FCA *1974;* Ormerod Allen & Co, 3rd Floor, 15 Devonshire Square, LONDON, EC2M 4YW.
•ORMEROD, Miss. Nicole, FCA *1990;* Ormerod Rutter Limited, The Oakley, Kidderminster Road, DROITWICH, WORCESTERSHIRE, WR9 9AY.
•ORMEROD, Mr. Peter Steven, FCA *1982;* with Ormerod Rutter Limited, The Oakley, Kidderminster Road, DROITWICH, WORCESTERSHIRE, WR9 9AY.
ORMEROD, Mr. Robert, MA ACA *2011;* 11 Raleigh Street, LONDON, N1 8NN.
ORMESHER, Mr. John Michael, BSc ACA *1988;* 14 Leadhall Crescent, HARROGATE, HG2 9NG.
ORMISHER, Mr. Stuart, BSc ACA *2011;* 24 Melling Avenue, STOCKPORT, CHESHIRE, SK4 5JG.
•ORMISTON, Mr. John Andrew, MA FCA *1980;* Morris Gregory, County End Business Centre, Jackson Street, Springhead, OLDHAM, OL4 4TZ. See also Morris Gregory Ltd
ORMISTON, Mr. Robert Wallace, BSc(Econ) ACA *1997;* 69 Fitzroy Drive, Oakwood, LEEDS, LS8 4AG.
•ORMISTON, Mr. Simon John, MA FCA *1999;* Monks, Abacus House, Castle Park, CAMBRIDGE, CB3 0AN. See also PricewaterhouseCoopers LLP
ORMISTON SMITH, Miss. Katherine Helen, BSc ACA *2009;* 560 Wandsworth Road, LONDON, SW8 3JT.
ORMOND, Miss. Charlotte Helen, BA ACA *1989;* 26303 Esperanza Drive, LOS ALTOS HILLS, CA 94022, UNITED STATES.
ORMOND, Ms. Louise, BA ACA *1997;* 54 Warwick Square, LONDON, SW1V 2AJ.
•ORMONDROYD, Mr. Andrew Derek, BA ACA *1994;* A & R Accountancy Limited, Tarn House, 77 High Street, Yeadon, LEEDS, LS19 7SP.
ORMONDROYD, Mr. James Andrew, BSc ACA *1997;* Aspley House, Chesham Road, BERKHAMSTED, HERTFORDSHIRE, HP4 3AE.
ORMROD, Mr. John Philip, BA FCA *1974;* 65 Andersey Way, ABINGDON, OX14 5NW.
ORMROD, Mr. Lewis, BA ACA *2010;* 17 Southlands, EAST GRINSTEAD, WEST SUSSEX, RH19 4DB.
ORMROD, Mr. Phillip, MA BCom ACA *1984;* 18a Waterloo Road, Birkdale, SOUTHPORT, PR8 2NE.
ORMSBY, Mr. David Edward, ACA *1985;* Dalton House, Islay Road, LYTHAM ST. ANNES, FY8 4AD.
ORMSBY, Miss. Elizabeth Ann, BA ACA *2004;* 202 - 1625 15 Ave SW, CALGARY T3C 0Y3, AB, CANADA.
ORMSBY, Mr. Geoffrey Anthony, FCA *1973;* 20 Whitby Avenue, LONDON, NW10 7SF.
ORMSHAW, Miss. Suzanne Catherine, BA ACA *2007;* 12/41-43 Spray Street, ELWOOD, VIC 3184, AUSTRALIA.
ORMSON, Mr. Andrew Forrester, BA ACA *1993;* 21 South End Avenue, #737, NEW YORK, NY 10280, UNITED STATES.
ORMSTON, Mrs. Alison Jane, BSc ACA *2005;* 9b Elland Road, Churwell, LEEDS, LS27 7SY.
ORMSTON, Mr. John Robert, FCA *1976;* H R Wallingford Group Ltd, Howbery Park, WALLINGFORD, OXFORDSHIRE, OX10 8BA.
ORMSTON, Mr. Michael Phillip, BSc FCA *1978;* 1 Constable Drive, Marple Bridge, STOCKPORT, CHESHIRE, SK6 5BH.
ORMSTON, Mr. Neil, BA ACA *2005;* 9b Elland Road, Churwell, Morley, LEEDS, LS27 7SY.
ORNADEL, Mr. Stephen Philip, BA ACA *1999;* 6 Manor Drive, LONDON, NW7 3NE.
ORNSTEIN, Mr. Anthony, ACA *2008;* 1 Flora Close, STANMORE, MIDDLESEX, HA7 4PY.
•ORNSTEIN, Mr. Gerald Richard, FCA *1972;* (Tax Fac), Fisher Phillips, Summit House, 170 Finchley Road, LONDON, NW3 6BP. See also Fisher Phillips 2010 Ltd
OROOMCHI, Mr. Massood, BSc FCA *1977;* Finex Group, 38 Deer Ridge Crescent, KITCHENER N2P 2L3, ON, CANADA.
OROVAL, Mrs. Sally Margaret, BSc ACA *2002;* Flat 17 Grosvenor Court, Grosvenor Hill, LONDON, SW19 4RX.
ORPEN, Mr. James Robert Moriarty, BSc ACA *2006;* First Drinks Brand Ltd, 17 Bartley Wood Business Park Bartley Way, HOOK, RG27 9XA.
ORPEN, Mr. John Kristian Stewart, FCA *1973;* Red Oaks, Weald Chase, Staplefield Road, Cuckfield, HAYWARDS HEATH, WEST SUSSEX RH17 5HY.
ORPEN, Mrs. Natasha Lisa, BSc ACA *2007;* 15 Dorchester Road, WEYBRIDGE, KT13 8PG.
ORPHANIDOU, Miss. Pavlina, BSc ACA *1994;* 9 SPETSON STREET, APT.001, AYIOI OMOLOYITES, 1082 NICOSIA, CYPRUS.
ORPHANOS, Mr. Marios Christou, BA(Econ) ACA *1998;* PO Box 57354, 3315 LIMASSOL, CYPRUS.
ORPHANOU, Miss. Anastasia, BA ACA *1992;* P O Box 28914, 2084 NICOSIA, CYPRUS.
ORPIN, Mr. Michael John, BA FCA *1976;* Bat Finance Ltd, 3rd Floor, 31 The Parade, St. Helier, JERSEY, JE2 3QQ.
ORR, Mrs. Alexandra Anne Pooler, BSc ACA *1997;* 78 Gayville Road, Battersea, LONDON, SW11 6JP.
ORR, Mr. Allan John, ACA *2009;* Flat 29 Medlar House, Hemlock Close, LONDON, SW16 5PS.
ORR, Mr. Cyril James, FCA *1943;* Rydal, 64 Plainwood Close, Summersdale, CHICHESTER, PO19 5YB. (Life Member)
•ORR, Mr. Derrek James, PhD BSc FCA *1978;* (Tax Fac), Belhus Limited, 14 Dublin Crescent, Henleaze, BRISTOL, BS9 4NA.
ORR, Mr. Duncan Forrest, BSc ACA *1989;* 21 Woodlands Road, ISLEWORTH, TW7 6NR.
ORR, Mrs. Eleanor Mary, MA ACA *1983;* 35 Kitto Road, LONDON, SE14 5TW.
ORR, Mr. James Montrose Ronald, MEng ACA *2004;* 25/2 Roseneath Place, EDINBURGH, EH9 1JD.
ORR, Mrs. Jane Alexandra, BA ACA *1990;* Town Head Barn, Lazonby, PENRITH, CUMBRIA, CA10 1AJ.
•ORR, Miss. Jane Suzanne, BA FCA *1980;* 60 Hastings Road, SHEFFIELD, S7 2GU.
ORR, Mr. Jonathan Rupert, BA ACA *1991;* Cox's Meadow, Lower Froyle, ALTON, GU34 4LL.
ORR, Miss. Judith Patricia, BA ACA *1985;* Argyll & Bute Council, Office Building, Witchburn Road, CAMPBELTOWN, ARGYLL, PA28 6JU.
•ORR, Mrs. Karen Tracy, BA ACA *1993;* KPMG LLP, 1 The Embankment, Neville Street, LEEDS, LS1 4DW. See also KPMG Europe LLP
ORR, Mrs. Lauren, BSc ACA *2006;* W H Smith Retail Ltd, 180 Wardour Street, LONDON, W1F 8FY.
ORR, Mr. Murray Leonard, BSc ACA *1983;* 2 Admiral Square, Chelsea Harbour, LONDON, SW10 0UU.
ORR, Mr. Nicholas Gordon, MBA BA ACA *1991;* Pinewood, 5 Barnston Road, Heswall, WIRRAL, CH60 2SN.
ORR, Mrs. Nicola Anne, LLB ACA *2002;* 49 High Street, Flore, NORTHAMPTON, NN7 4LL.
•ORR, Mr. Robert Dermot, BA ACA FCCA *2008;* Brooking Ruse & Co Limited, 3 Beaconsfield Road, WESTON-SUPER-MARE, SOMERSET, BS23 1YE.
ORR, Mr. Robert Michael, FCA *1962;* 38 Brandy Hole Lane, CHICHESTER, WEST SUSSEX, PO19 5RY. (Life Member)
ORR, Miss. Sarah Elizabeth, BSc(Hons) ACA *2010;* Second Floor Flat, 60 St. Pauls Road, Clifton, BRISTOL, BS8 1LP.

•ORR, Mr. Thorsten John, BA ACA *1993;* (Tax Fac), Thorsten Orr Limited, Flat 7, 5 Little Stanhope Street, BATH, BA1 2BH.
ORR BURNS, Mr. Colin Douglas, MBA BSc FCA CPA *1981;* B G Group Plc, 100 Thames Valley Park Drive, READING, RG6 1PT.
ORRELL, Ms. Gillian Suzanne, BA ACA ALCM *1999;* 10 Iveson Road, HEXHAM, NORTHUMBERLAND, NE46 2LX.
ORRELL, Mr. Mark David, BSc ACA *1987;* 3 Unwin Crescent, STOURBRIDGE, DY8 3UY.
ORRELL, Mr. Peter Anthony, ACA *1981;* SHADWELL HOUSE, F G F Ltd Shadwell House, Shadwell Street, BIRMINGHAM, B4 6LJ.
ORRELL, Mr. Stewart, BSc(Econ) ACA ACCA *1996;* 18 Staunton Road, KINGSTON-UPON-THAMES, KT2 5TJ.
ORRELL-JONES, Mr. Sebastian Keith, ACA *1998;* 6 Gerald Road, LONDON, SW1W 9EQ.
ORRIDGE, Mr. John Geoffrey, BA ACA *1999;* 18 Windsor Road, Waltham on the Wolds, MELTON MOWBRAY, LEICESTERSHIRE, LE14 4AS.
ORRIN, Mr. John Michael, BA FCA *1969;* 35 Rue Coquilliere, 75001 PARIS, FRANCE.
•ORRIN, Mr. Mark Andrew, BSc ACA *1997;* (Tax Fac), Orrin Accountancy Limited, 12 Tavern Street, STOWMARKET, SUFFOLK, IP14 1PH.
ORRIN, Miss. Sylvia, FCA *1952;* 542 Nell Gwynn House, Sloane Avenue, LONDON, SW3 3BD. (Life Member)
•ORRISS, Mrs. Melanie Zoe, BSc ACA ATT CTA *1999;* (Tax Fac), Baker Tilly Tax & Advisory Services LLP, 1st Floor, 46 Clarendon Road, WATFORD, WD17 1JJ.
•ORRISS, Mr. Stephen James, ACA CF *1992;* Baker Tilly Tax & Advisory Services LLP, 1st Floor, 46 Clarendon Road, WATFORD, WD17 1JJ. See also Baker Tilly Corporate Finance LLP
ORROW, Mr. Royston James, FCA *1964;* Peppers, 3 Pilgrims Place, REIGATE, SURREY, RH2 9LF.
ORSBORN, Mr. Derek Charles, FCA *1977;* 9 Moreland Road, WICKFORD, SS11 7JU.
ORTH, Mr. Lars, ACA *2007;* 28 Napier Road, OXFORD, OX4 3JA.
ORTON, Mr. Christopher David, BA FCA *1987;* 52 Highfield, LETCHWORTH GARDEN CITY, HERTFORDSHIRE, SG6 3PZ.
•ORTON, Mrs. Helen Mary Grace, BSc ACA *1996;* with PricewaterhouseCoopers LLP, Savannah House, 3 Ocean Way, Ocean Village, SOUTHAMPTON, SO14 3TJ.
ORTON, Mr. Laurence Michael, BA ACA *1998;* 76 South Georges Hill Road, SOUTHBURY, CT 06488, UNITED STATES.
ORTON, Mr. Michael Eric, BSc ACA *1989;* 49 Swithland Lane, Rothley, LEICESTER, LE7 7SG.
ORTON, Mrs. Mythili, MA ACA *2003;* Flat 4, Ascot House, Park Court, Lawrie Park Road, LONDON, SE26 6EH.
ORTON, Mr. Nick, ACA *2009;* 101 Bearton Road, HITCHIN, HERTFORDSHIRE, SG5 1UF.
ORTON, Mr. Rex Alastair, BSc ACA *1991;* Latchways Plc, Waller Road, Hopton Park Industrial Estate, DEVIZES, WILTSHIRE, SN10 2JP.
ORTON, Mrs. Sharon, BSc ACA *2006;* with PricewaterhouseCoopers LLP, Cornwall Court, 19 Cornwall Street, BIRMINGHAM, B3 2DT.
ORTTEWELL, Mr. Alexander Frank, FCA *1964;* Domaine de la Chatellerie, Le Bourg, 24240 RIBAGNAC, FRANCE. (Life Member)
•ORVES, Mr. Andrew Michael, BSc ACA *2005;* Sexty & Co., 124 Thorpe Road, NORWICH, NR1 1RS.
•ORWIG, Mrs. Eirwen, MSc FCA *1982;* (Tax Fac), J.Emyr Thomas & Co, Tegfan, 7 Deiniol Road, BANGOR, GWYNEDD, LL57 2UR.
•ORWIN, Mr. Adrian, BA ACA *1992;* Orwin Oliver Ltd, 24 King Street, ULVERSTON, CUMBRIA, LA12 7DZ.
ORWIN, Mr. Daniel Paul, MA BSc ACA *2009;* 9 Burnsdale, Allerton, BRADFORD, WEST YORKSHIRE, BD15 9DA.
ORWIN, Mr. Robert Charles, BSc ACA *1999;* 118 Royal Avenue, Onchan, ISLE OF MAN, IM3 1LF.
OSAKWE, Mr. Alphonsus Ikeme, MA ACA *1980;* GRID Consulting Ltd, 3a Eko Akete Close, PO Box 52453, Ikoyi, LAGOS, NIGERIA.
OSAKWE, Mr. Edward Ogbogu, ACA *1983;* 26 Lucina Joseph St., Surulere, LAGOS, NIGERIA.
OSATCH, Mr. Ivor, FCA *1966;* 2 Crofton Lane, ORPINGTON, BR5 1HL.
OSBALDESTON, Mr. Colin, FCA *1967;* Orchard Cottage, Grange Drive, Chartridge, CHESHAM, HP5 2TG.
•OSBALDESTON, Mr. John Arnold, FCA *1976;* Grundy Anderson & Kershaw Limited, 123-125 Union Street, OLDHAM, OL1 1TG.
OSBALDISTON, Mr. John Anthony, MSc FCA *1980;* Ashley House, Manor Road, Penn, HIGH WYCOMBE, HP10 8HY.
OSBORN, Mr. Andrew Alexander, MEng ACA *2005;* with PricewaterhouseCoopers LLP, Benson House, 33 Wellington Street, LEEDS, LS1 4JP.
OSBORN, Mr. Charles Eric, BSc ACA *1981;* (Tax Fac), Haysmacintyre Fairfax House, 15 Fulwood Place, LONDON, WC1V 6AY.
•OSBORN, Mr. Charles Robert, FCA *1970;* (Tax Fac), Farmiloes LLP, Winston Churchill House, 8 Ethel Street, BIRMINGHAM, B2 4BG.
OSBORN, Mrs. Christine, BSc ACA CTA *1993;* (Tax Fac), 5 Gore Avenue, SALFORD, M5 5LF.
OSBORN, Mr. Gerald John, BSc FCA *1956;* Weavers Hill House, Ashmore Green, THATCHAM, RG18 9HQ. (Life Member)
OSBORN, Mr. Hamish Duncan Adam, BA ACA *1999;* Q Holdings Limited, Unit 4, Orchard Business Park, Bramyard Road, LEDBURY, HEREFORDSHIRE HR8 1LE.
OSBORN, Mrs. Johanne, BEng ACA *1996;* Kuoni Travel Ltd Kuoni House, Deepdene Avenue, DORKING, RH5 4AZ.
OSBORN, Mr. John William, FCA *1976;* Fiander Tovell LLP, Stag Gates House, 63/64 The Avenue, SOUTHAMPTON, SO17 1XS.
OSBORN, Mr. Jonathan Paul, BEng ACA *2007;* Beechwood 2 Rue Maze Clos, Rue Maze, St. Martin, GUERNSEY, GY4 6LJ.
OSBORN, Miss. Kerry Ann, BA(Hons) ACA *2001;* 53 Liberty Drive, NORTHAMPTON, NN5 6TU.
OSBORN, Mr. Michael Peter, BSc ACA *1993;* 19 Penrose Way, Four Marks, ALTON, HAMPSHIRE, GU34 5BG.
OSBORN, Mr. Michael Vincent Isted, ACA *1990;* (Tax Fac), 10 Hollycroft Close, SOUTH CROYDON, SURREY, CR2 7FE.
OSBORN, Mr. Neil Ernest, BA FCA *1973;* 66 Oakwood Road, Hampstead Garden Suburb, LONDON, NW11 6RN.
OSBORN, Mr. Paul Gerard, ACA *1978;* with Chantrey Vellacott DFK LLP, Cheviot House, 53 Sheep Street, NORTHAMPTON, NN1 2NE.
OSBORN, Mr. Paul James, BA ACA *1990;* 19 Clowes Avenue, BOURNEMOUTH, BH6 4ER.
•OSBORN, Mr. Peter Andrew, MA MSc FCA *1979;* The Burns Partnership, 138 Peperharow Road, GODALMING, SURREY, GU7 2PW.
OSBORN, Mrs. Stephanie Alison, BA(Hons) ACA *2000;* The Old House, 16 Station Road, Littlethorpe, LEICESTER, LE19 2HS.
OSBORN, Mr. Stephen Mark, BA ACA *1999;* c/o BUPA International Victory House, Trafalgar Place, BRIGHTON, BN14FU.
OSBORN, Mrs. Vay, MBA BA ACA *2006;* 3/F Elizabeth House, Confiance Ltd, PO Box 191, GUERNSEY, GY1 4HW.
OSBORN, Mr. William Joseph, MBE FCA *1972;* Blackwood Hodge (Zambia) Ltd, P O Box, 22700, KITWE, ZAMBIA.
OSBORN-SMITH, Mr. Grant Erle, BSc ACA *1996;* Flurstrasse 24, 6332 HAGENDORN, SWITZERLAND.
OSBORNE, Mrs. Alison, ACA *1981;* C A S S Business School, 106 Bunhill Row, LONDON, EC1Y 8TZ.
OSBORNE, Mrs. Alison Deborah, BSc ACA *2005;* 42 Cooper Road, Westbury-on-Trym, BRISTOL, BS9 3RA.
OSBORNE, Mr. Andrew Charles, BSc ACA *1991;* 23 Mount Nebo, TAUNTON, TA1 4HG.
OSBORNE, Mr. Andrew David, BA ACA *1987;* 42 Alanthus Close, Lee, LONDON, SE12 8RE.
OSBORNE, Mr. Andrew Simon Charles, MA ACA *1993;* Geoffrey Osborne Ltd, 51 Fishbourne Road East, CHICHESTER, WEST SUSSEX, PO19 3HZ.
OSBORNE, Mr. Antony Eric, ACA *1994;* Papworth Trust, Papworth Everard, CAMBRIDGE, CB23 3RG.
OSBORNE, Mr. Benedict John, MEng ACA *2005;* 42 Cooper Road, BRISTOL, BS9 3RA.
•OSBORNE, Mr. Christopher James Moffett, BSc FCA *1986;* with FTI Consulting Limited, 322 Midtown, High Holborn, LONDON, WC1V 7PB.
•OSBORNE, Mr. Christopher John, LLB ACA *2003;* with Alvarez & Marsal Dispute Analysis & Forensic Services LLP, 1st Floor, 1 Finsbury Circus, LONDON, EC2M 7AF.
OSBORNE, Mrs. Claire, ACA *2009;* 3 Ruskin Road, CARSHALTON, SURREY, SM5 3DD.
OSBORNE, Mrs. Clare Michele, BSc ACA ATII *1989;* Arran Torfoot Steadings, Drumclog, STRATHAVEN, LANARKSHIRE, ML10 6QG.
OSBORNE, Mr. David, LLM MA(Hons) ACA CTA *2004;* La Niche La Route de Vinchelez, St. Ouen, JERSEY, JE3 2DA.
OSBORNE, Mr. David Anthony, FCA *1972;* 19 Lawnswood, SAUNDERSFOOT, DYFED, SA69 9HX.
OSBORNE, Mrs. Deborah, BSc ACA *1993;* 18 Brookfields, West Wellow, ROMSEY, HAMPSHIRE, SO51 6GS.
OSBORNE, Mr. Dennis George, FCA *1959;* Grange Cottage, Station Road, Pulham Market, DISS, NORFOLK, IP21 4TD. (Life Member)
OSBORNE, Mr. Graham, MA ACA *1992;* Old Post House Bowlhead Green, GODALMING, SURREY, GU8 6NW.
OSBORNE, Mr. Haydn, FCA *1966;* 231 Derlwyn, Dunvant, SWANSEA, SA2 7PE. (Life Member)
OSBORNE, Mr. James, ACA *2006;* with National Audit Office, 157-197 Buckingham Palace Road, Victoria, LONDON, SW1W 9SP.
OSBORNE, Mr. James, BSc(Hons) ACA *2004;* Lloyds, 10 Gresham Street, LONDON, EC2V 7AE.
OSBORNE, Mrs. Jane Rose, BSc ACA *1983;* Smithy Garth, Pickhill, THIRSK, YO7 4JG.
•OSBORNE, Mrs. Janis, BSc FCA *1990;* Bird Luckin limited, Aquila House, Waterloo Lane, CHELMSFORD, CM1 1BN.
OSBORNE, Mrs. Joanna Beatrice, BA FCA *1978;* Brook Farm Barn, Sychem Lane, Five Oak Green, TONBRIDGE, KENT, TN12 6TT.
OSBORNE, Mr. Joel Gary Livingstone, BA ACA *1998;* with PricewaterhouseCoopers LLP, 1 Embankment Place, LONDON, WC2N 6RH.
OSBORNE, Mr. John Grosvenor, FCA *1974;* Harvest Cottage, Hatton Farm, Birmingham Road, WARWICK, CV35 7EY.
OSBORNE, Mr. John Trevor, FCA *1953;* 60 Foxdown Close, KIDLINGTON, OX5 2YE. (Life Member)
OSBORNE, Mr. Jonathan, LLB ACA *1994;* 16 Marine Crescent, LIVERPOOL, L22 8QP.
OSBORNE, Mr. Julian Alastair, MA(Hons) ACA *2010;* Flat 2, 114 St. Dunstans Road, LONDON, W6 8RA.
OSBORNE, Ms. Juliet Clare, BA ACA *1997;* Tribal, 87-91 Newman Street, LONDON, W1T 3EY.
OSBORNE, Mr. Kenneth Walter, BMus ACA DChA *2000;* Royal Scottish National Orchestra, 73 Claremont Street, GLASGOW, G3 7JB.
OSBORNE, Miss. Kerrie Ann, FCA *1995;* 18 Sunray Avenue, Hutton, BRENTWOOD, CM13 1PR.
OSBORNE, Miss. Linda Vivienne, BA ACA *1981;* 2264 Glenfield Road, OAKVILLE L6M 3V1, ON, CANADA.
•OSBORNE, Mr. Martin Paul, FCA *1982;* (Tax Fac), Rothman Pantall LLP, 10 Little Park Farm Road, Segensworth, FAREHAM, HAMPSHIRE, PO15 5TD.
OSBORNE, Mr. Martyn John, FCA *1981;* Dindermead Sleight Lane, Dinder, WELLS, SOMERSET, BA5 3PP.
•OSBORNE, Mrs. Mary, FCA *1966;* Mrs Mary Osborne, 6 Russet Gardens, CAMBERLEY, SURREY, GU15 2LG.
OSBORNE, Mr. Matthew Richard, MChem ACA *2004;* 42 Brenda Gautrey Way, Cottenham, CAMBRIDGE, CB4 8XW.
OSBORNE, Mr. Michael, ACA *1982;* Unity Trust Bank Plc Nine Brindleyplace, 4, BIRMINGHAM, B1 2HB.
•OSBORNE, Mr. Michael Winston, BSc FCA *1972;* W. Osborne & Co, Harwood House, Park Road, MELTON MOWBRAY, LE13 1TX.
OSBORNE, Mr. Neil Lawrence, BSc FCA *1975;* P.O. Box 1305, LAFAYETTE, CA 94549, UNITED STATES.
OSBORNE, Mr. Neil Richard, MA FCA *1996;* Flat 106 Cascades Tower, 4 Westferry Road, LONDON, E14 8JL.
OSBORNE, Mr. Nigel Richard, MA ACA *1991;* Meadowland, 36 Bloomfield Park, BATH, BA2 2BX.
•OSBORNE, Miss. Patricia, BSc FCA *1987;* Moore Stephens & Co, L'EstorilBloc C, 31 Avenue Princesse Grace, MC 98000 MONTE CARLO, MONACO. See also Moore Stephens LLP
OSBORNE, Mr. Paul John, BSc ACA *1998;* with Deloitte LLP, Stonecutter Court, 1 Stonecutter Street, LONDON, EC4A 4TR.
•OSBORNE, Mr. Peter James, FCA *1975;* (Tax Fac), Osbornes Accountants Limited, 20 Market Place, KINGSTON UPON THAMES, SURREY, KT1 1JP.
OSBORNE, Mr. Philip Neville Wayne, BSc ACA *1983;* 22 Dairy Meadows, Holders Hill, ST JAMES, BB23001, BARBADOS.
•OSBORNE, Mr. Philip Wesley, BSc FCA *1993;* P W Osborne & Co, 29 Westbridge Road, Trewoon, ST AUSTELL, CORNWALL, PL25 5TF.
OSBORNE, Mr. Raymond John, FCA *1972;* (Tax Fac), 24 Leslie Road, RAYLEIGH, ESSEX, SS6 8PB.
OSBORNE, Mr. Richard Graham, FCA *1974;* 38 Halepit Road, Bookham, LEATHERHEAD, KT23 4BS.
OSBORNE, Mr. Richard William, BSc FCA *1974;* Bryanston Brittains Lane, SEVENOAKS, KENT, TN13 2ND.
OSBORNE, Mr. Robin Graham, FCA *1968;* Timbers, 25 Smugglers Lane South, CHRISTCHURCH, DORSET, BH23 4NG.
OSBORNE, Mr. Roland James, BA ACA *1990;* Flat 14, Pencarwick House, Louisa Place, EXMOUTH, EX8 2AL.
OSBORNE, Mr. Stephen, BEng ACA *1995;* RiverStone Management Limited, Park Gate, 161-163 Preston Road, BRIGHTON, BN1 6AU.
OSBORNE, Mr. Stephen Kingsley, ACA *2008;* Grant Thornton UK LLP, 30 Finsbury Square, LONDON, EC2P2YU.
OSBORNE, Mr. Stephen Ronald, FCA *1982;* 24 Keynsham Road, CHELTENHAM, GLOUCESTERSHIRE, GL53 7PX.
OSBORNE, Mr. Stewart Peter, ACA *1992;* Cheyne Court, 146 Weston Street, PORTLAND, DT5 2DH.
OSBORNE, Mr. Tobias Charles, BA ACA *1994;* (Tax Fac), 24 Chiswell Street, LONDON, EC1Y 4SG.
OSBORNE, Mrs. Vivien Jean, BSc ACA *1987;* with KPMG LLP, 1 The Embankment, Neville Street, LEEDS, LS1 4DW.
OSBORNE, Mr. William Leslie Frank, FCA *1964;* 154 Clasemont Road, Morriston, SWANSEA, SA6 6AJ.
•OSBORNE, Mr. Winston, BEM FCA *1955;* W. Osborne & Co, Harwood House, Park Road, MELTON MOWBRAY, LE13 1TX.
OSBOURN, Mr. Paul Keith, BA(Hons) ACA *2001;* 3 Lovelace Road, LONDON, SE21 8JY.
OSBOURN, Mr. Sidney George, FCA *1976;* Flat 7 Cubitt Wharf, Storers Quay, LONDON, E14 3BF.
OSBOURNE, Mr. James Scott, FCA *1956;* Flat 2, Lalgates Court, 119 Harlestone Road, NORTHAMPTON, NN5 7AF. (Life Member)
OSBOURNE, Miss. Jodie, ACA *2008;* 11 Redwood Drive, CLEETHORPES, SOUTH HUMBERSIDE, DN35 0RN.
OSBOURNE, Mrs. Louise Andrea, BSc ACA *2001;* The Poplars, 17 Barrow Road, Burton-on-the-Wolds, LOUGHBOROUGH, LEICESTERSHIRE, LE12 5AA.
OSELAND, Mr. Norman John, FCA *1975;* 43 Fairways Drive, Blackwell, BROMSGROVE, B60 1BB.
OSEMAN, Mr. Russell Wayne, BA ACA *1988;* 16 Cranbourne Close, Timperley, ALTRINCHAM, WA15 6LR.
OSEN, Mr. Gideon Paul, BSc ACA *1992;* 2 Lingmere Close, CHIGWELL, IG7 6LH.
OSENI, Mr. Cornelius Oladipo Sunday, BSc FCA *1963;* 54 Longfields, SWAFFHAM, NORFOLK, PE37 7RJ. (Life Member)
OSENTON, Mr. David Stephen, FCA *1966;* 24 Ross Road, DARTFORD, DA1 3NH. (Life Member)
OSER, Miss. Keren, BSc ACA *2005;* 43 Wentworth Road, LONDON, NW11 0RT.
OSGERBY, Mrs. Julia Clare, BSocSc ACA *1998;* 24 Horsell Park Close, WOKING, SURREY, GU21 4LZ.
OSGOOD, Mr. Oliver James Spencer, ACA *2008;* V G F Advisers (UK) Llp, 6 Kean Street, LONDON, WC2B 4AS.
•OSHINAIKE, Mr. Justino Adekunle, BA FCA *1975;* Kunle Oshinaike & Co, P.O. Box 8930, Marina, LAGOS, NIGERIA.
OSLER, Mr. Glenton Derek, BSc ACA *1987;* 1 Teal Close, Burton Latimer, KETTERING, NN15 5TP.
•OSLER, Mr. Nicholas Charles, MA FCA *1986;* (Tax Fac), Smith & Williamson Ltd, 25 Moorgate, LONDON, EC2R 6AY.
OSMAN, Mr. Anas Nasrun Mohd, BSc ACA *2002;* UMW Advantech Sdn. Bhd., No. 10 Jalan Utas 15/7, P.O. Box 7052, Selangor Darul Ehsan, 40915 SHAH ALAM, MALAYSIA.
•OSMAN, Mr. David Robert, FCA *1967;* David Osman Ltd, 20 Rougemont Avenue, TORQUAY, TQ2 7JP. See also David Osman
OSMAN, Mr. Dean, BSc FCA *1987;* Pine Ridge, Pinelands Road, Chilworth, SOUTHAMPTON, SO16 7HH.
•OSMAN, Mr. Imtiaz Ahmed, ACA *1980;* I A Osman & Company Ltd, 16 Leicester Road, Blaby, LEICESTER, LE8 4GQ.
OSMAN, Mrs. Julie, FCA *1989;* Pine Ridge, Pinelands Road, Chilworth, SOUTHAMPTON, SO16 7HH.
OSMAN, Mr. Leigh, ACA CA(NZ) *2009;* Room 15, 46 Norfolk Square, Paddington, LONDON, W2 1RT.
OSMAN, Mr. Mohamed Sajid, BCom ACA *2003;* KPMG Botswana, Plot 67977, Fairgrounds, P O Box 1519, GABORONE, BOTSWANA.
OSMAN, Mr. Peter Michael, FCA *1970;* 24 Walden Road, WELWYN GARDEN CITY, HERTFORDSHIRE, AL8 7PF.

OSMAN, Mr. Raymond George, FCA *1975;* Hollycroft, 5 Park Edge, HARROGATE, HG2 8JU.
OSMAN, Miss. Rebecca Louise, BSc ACA *2006;* Tui Travel House, Crawley Business Quarter, Fleming Way, CRAWLEY, WEST SUSSEX, RH10 9QL.
OSMAN, Mr. Siddique, ACA *1982;* Flat 4 The Water Gardens, Warren Road, KINGSTON UPON THAMES, KT2 7LF.
OSMAN ALI, Mr. Sohail, FCA *1973;* F-38 Feroze Nana Road, Bath Island, KARACHI, PAKISTAN.
OSMANI, Mr. Imtiaz Alam, BSc(Econ) FCA *1968;* KONGEVEJEN 229, 2830 VIRUM, DENMARK. (Life Member)
OSMANY, Mr. Maarouf Zaid, ACA *2010;* Apartment no 24 Edge Apartments, 1a Lett Road, LONDON, E15 2HP.
OSMENT, Mr. John Howard, BSc ACA *2010;* 69 Ringwood Road, FERNDOWN, DORSET, BH22 9AA.
•OSMENT, Mr. Robert John, BSc FCA *1981;* (Tax Fac), Morgan Griffiths LLP, Cross Chambers, 9 High Street, NEWTOWN, POWYS, SY16 2NY.
•OSMENT, Mr. Simon, ACA *2005;* Perrins Limited, Custom House, The Strand, BARNSTAPLE, DEVON, EX31 1EU.
•OSMER, Mr. Simon Philip, BA ACA *1996;* KPMG LLP, 15 Canada Square, LONDON, E14 5GL. See also KPMG Europe LLP
OSMON, Mr. Jonathan Michael, BSc FCA *1995;* 6 The Avenue, LONDON, N10 2QL.
OSMOND, Mr. Gerald Ian, BSc FCA *1974;* 25 Arabia Close, North Chingford, LONDON, E4 7DU.
OSMOND, Mr. Jeffrey, LLB FCA *1964;* 98/57 Tropicanaville, Bangna Trad KM 39, Bang Samak, Bangpakong, CHACHEONGSAO, 24180 THAILAND. (Life Member)
OSMOND, Mr. Mark Jonathan, BSc ACA *1991;* Medicx Group, 5 Godalming Business Centre, Woolsack Way, GODALMING, SURREY, GU7 1XW.
OSMOND, Mr. Rupert Ian, BEng FCA AMCT *1993;* 12 Medina Avenue, ESHER, SURREY, KT10 9TH.
OSOBA, Miss. Oluwatoyin Abiola, BSc ACA *1999;* 73 Little Bushey Lane, BUSHEY, WD23 4RA.
OSOBASE, Mr. Sylvester Sunday, FCA *1971;* 3 Kernel Street, Surulere, LAGOS, NIGERIA. (Life Member)
OSOLAKE, Mr. Adebayo, MA ACA *2002;* PO Box 6787, Marina, LAGOS, NIGERIA.
OSORIO, Mrs. Charlotte Lindsay, BSc ACA *1990;* Mill Farmhouse, Ravensworth, RICHMOND, NORTH YORKSHIRE, DL11 7EU.
•OSPER, Mr. Howard John, FCA *1975;* Inimex Associates Limited, 33 Anthony Road, BOREHAMWOOD, WD6 4NF. See also Osper H.J. & Co
OSSELTON, Mrs. Louise, ACA *2008;* 6 Day's Ground, Shrivenham, SWINDON, SN6 8ET.
•OSSMAN, Mr. Mohamed Hassan Lutfy, BSc FCA *1987;* (Tax Fac), Ossmans Limited, 591 London Road, North Cheam, SUTTON, SURREY, SM3 9BX. See also Sedley Richard Laurence Voulters
OST, Mr. Roger Alan Marshall, FCA *1955;* 7 Links Avenue, SOUTHPORT, PR9 9QB. (Life Member)
OSTASZEWSKI, Mr. Andrew Peter Paul, BSc FCA *1977;* 10 Ashbourne Close, LONDON, W5 3EF.
OSTASZEWSKI, Mr. Karol Andrzej, MA(Hons) ACA *2009;* 1 Warwick Place, LONDON, W5 5PS.
•OSTER, Mr. Benjamin Mark, BA ACA *2005;* (Tax Fac), Bailey Oster, Grosvenor House, St. Thomas's Place, STOCKPORT, CHESHIRE, SK1 3TZ. See also TWD Tax Services Ltd
OSTER, Mr. Richard Anthony, LLB ACA *1992;* Little Mount, Riding Lane, Hildenborough, TONBRIDGE, KENT, TN11 9LR.
OSTERMEYER, Miss. Jo-Anne, BA FCA *1999;* 25 Allen Street, MAIDSTONE, ME14 5AH.
OSTICK, Mr. Charles Drury, BA ACA *1987;* PricewaterhouseCoopers, 15/F Bangkok City Tower, 179/74-80 South Sathorn Road, BANGKOK, 10120, THAILAND.
OSTLER, Mrs. Annis Catherine, BA ACA *2005;* Sealed Air Ltd, Clifton House, 1 Marston Road, ST. NEOTS, CAMBRIDGESHIRE, PE19 2HN.
OSTLER, Mrs. Patricia Ann, BA FCA *1963;* 53 Linver Road, LONDON, SW6 3RA. (Life Member)
OSTRIDGE, Miss. Amy Louise, ACA *2010;* 56 Mounsey Road, Bamber Bridge, PRESTON, PR5 6LU.
•OSTROWSKI, Mr. Adrian Ilbert Tadeusz, BA ACA *1990;* (Tax Fac), Wells Richardson, Cannon House, Rutland Road, SHEFFIELD, S3 8DP.
OSWALD, Mr. Alexis George, ACA *2008;* Flat 9 St. Andrews Mansions, Dorset Street, LONDON, W1U 4EQ.
•OSWALD, Mr. Campbell Grant, BSc ACA *1997;* Deloitte LLP, 4 Brindley Place, BIRMINGHAM, B1 2HZ. See also Deloitte & Touche LLP
OSWALD, Miss. Eleanor Lucy, ACA *2011;* 17 Kandahar, Aldbourne, MARLBOROUGH, WILTSHIRE, SN8 2EE.
OSWALD, Miss. Fleur, BSc ACA *2003;* Brook Farm, Washbourne, TOTNES, DEVON, TQ9 7UB.
OSWALD, Miss. Jennifer, MSc ACA *2005;* 16 Beech Grove, Maltby, MIDDLESBROUGH, CLEVELAND, TS8 0BL.
•OSWALD, Mr. John Howard, BA FCA *1977;* Stephenson Coates, Asama Court, West 2, Newcastle Business Park, NEWCASTLE UPON TYNE, NE4 7YD.
OSWALD, Mrs. Josephine Anne, BSc ACA *1998;* 128 Old Station Road, Hampton-in-Arden, SOLIHULL, B92 0HF.
OSWALD, Mr. Keith Robert, ACA *1981;* Concept Group Ltd, Concept House, Fairbairn Road, LIVINGSTON, WEST LOTHIAN, EH54 6TS.
OSWALD, Mr. Michael Adrian, MA ACA *1998;* UNRWA Jordan Field Office, PO Box 143464, AMMAN, 11814, JORDAN.
•OSWALD, Mr. Robert Richard, BSc FCA *1974;* Appleby & Wood, 40 The Lock Building, 72 High Street, LONDON, E15 2QB. See also Appleby & Wood Consulting Ltd
OSWALD, Mr. Tim, BSc ACA *2005;* 25 Carlton Drive, LEIGH-ON-SEA, ESSEX, SS9 1DE.
•OSWELL, Mr. Jeremy Nicholas, FCA *1980;* (Tax Fac), Smith & Williamson Ltd, Old Library Chambers, 21 Chipper Lane, SALISBURY, SP1 1BG. See also Oswell J N
OSWELL, Mr. Nigel Douglas, BSc ACA *1989;* Greencoat Ltd, Wonastow Road Industrial Estate (West), MONMOUTH, NP25 5JA.
OSWICK, Ms. Emma Jane, BA ACA *1999;* Flat 1, 43 Regents Park Road, LONDON, NW1 7SY.
OSWIN, Mrs. Kim Allison, MBA ACA *1989;* 35 Lemonwood Place, The Gardens, Manurewa, AUCKLAND, NEW ZEALAND.
OSZYWA, Mr. Michael Nicholas, BA ACA *1995;* 15 Falcon Wood, LEATHERHEAD, SURREY, KT22 7TF.
OTAR, Miss. Janish Jyoti, BSc ACA *1998;* 16 Rushford Drive, LEICESTER, LE4 9UF.
OTFORD, Baron John, FCA FCMA *1948;* Hornchurch Hall, 7 Parkstone Avenue, HORNCHURCH, RM11 3LX. (Life Member)
OTHEN, Mr. Christopher Mark, BSc ACA *1997;* 2 Beadnell Drive, Penketh, WARRINGTON, WA5 2EG.
•OTHICK, Mr. David Michael, BEd ACA *1979;* David M. Othick, 12 Parr Fold Avenue, Worsley, MANCHESTER, M28 7HD.
OTHMAN, Miss. Lynda, BA(Hons) ACA *2002;* 13 Avenue de la Barre, 91430 IGNY, FRANCE.
OTIKO, Mr. Andrew Olatunji, MSc ACA *2009;* with RSM Tenon Audit Limited, 66 Chiltern Street, LONDON, W1U 4JT.
OTLEY, Mr. Gordon Henry Michael, FCA *1984;* 10 Stokelake, Chudleigh, NEWTON ABBOT, DEVON, TQ13 0EF.
OTLEY, Mr. Martin John, BA ACA *2005;* Pricewaterhousecoopers, 12 Plumtree Court, LONDON, EC4A 4HT.
OTLEY, Mr. Nicholas William, FCA *1966;* Cornwall Lodge, 5 Bathwick Hill, BATH, BA2 6EP. (Life Member)
OTLEY, Mr. Richard Reverdy, BSc ACA *2001;* 4 Osborne Way, Wigginton, TRING, HERTFORDSHIRE, HP23 6EN.
OTLEY, Mr. Thomas Richard, FCA *1964;* 10 Kingsbury Street, MARLBOROUGH, WILTSHIRE, SN8 1HU. (Life Member)
OTTAWAY, Mrs. Anne Patricia, BA FCA *1990;* Criminal Investigation Directorate, HMRC, PO Box 520, LEEDS, LS1 4WU.
OTTAWAY, Mr. John Edward, FCA *1963;* The Grange, 2 Mount Road, Parkstone, POOLE, BH14 0QW.
OTTAWAY, Mr. Richard John, BSc ACA *1997;* Carclo Technical Plastics Ltd, 47 Wates Way, MITCHAM, SURREY, CR4 4HR.
OTTEN, Mr. Rupert John Simon, BSc FCA *1976;* Middle Hunt House, Walterstone, HEREFORD, HR2 0DY.
•OTTER, Mr. Christopher John, FCA *1971;* Chegwidden & Co, Priestley House, Priestley Gardens, Chadwell Heath, ROMFORD, RM6 4SN.
OTTER, Mr. David John, BA ACA *1994;* TPS Rental Systems Ltd, Unit 349, Rushock Trading Estate, Rushock, DROITWICH, WORCESTERSHIRE WR9 0NR.
OTTER, Mr. David John, FCA *1957;* 19 Carlton Ave, BILLINGHAM, TS22 5HT. (Life Member)
OTTER, Ms. Karen Michelle, MA ACA *1985;* 142 Marshalswick Lane, ST. ALBANS, AL1 4XB.
OTTER, Mr. Keith Henry, FCA *1967;* 11 Green Close, CHELMSFORD, CM1 7SL. (Life Member)
OTTERBURN, Mr. Andrew Raymond, BA ACA *1978;* Otterburn Legal Consulting, 1 Holme View Park, Upperthong, Holmfirth, HUDDERSFIELD, HD9 3HS.
OTTERBURN, Mr. Stephen John, FCA *1972;* 25 Alexander Crescent, CATERHAM, SURREY, CR3 5ZG.
OTTERWELL, Miss. Sarah Kathryn, ACA *2009;* Flat 3, 5 Almorah Crescent, Lower Kings Cliff St. Helier, JERSEY, JE2 3GU.
OTTESEN, Mr. Sindre Johan, MSc ACA *2000;* Bjerkelundsveien 4, 1358 JAR, NORWAY.
OTTEWELL, Miss. Jenny, BSc ACA ATII *1990;* Manchester LBS, Inland Revenue, Albert Bridge House, 1 Bridge Street, MANCHESTER, M60 9BH.
OTTEWELL, Mrs. Laura, BSc ACA *2009;* 28 Tudor Court, Gypsy Lane, Draycott, DERBY, DE72 3YQ.
OTTEWELL, Mr. Robert Charles, ACA *2009;* Pricewaterhousecoopers Donington Court Herald Way, East Midlands Airport Castle Donington, DERBY, DE74 2UZ.
OTTEY, Mr. Charles Robert, MA FCA MCSI *1998;* 94 Weir Road, Balham, LONDON, SW12 0NB.
OTTEY, Mrs. Karen Elizabeth, BEng ACA *2000;* 94 Weir Road, Balham, LONDON, SW12 0NB.
OTTNER, Mr. Simon Paul, BSc ACA *2003;* The Dell House, 6 Charmwood Close, NEWBURY, RG14 1XA.
OTTON, Mr. Charles Edward Philip, BSc ACA *1992;* UBS, 299 Park Avenue, NEW YORK, NY 10171, UNITED STATES.
OTTY, Mr. John William Lorimer, MA ACA *1990;* 1 Harvest Place, Wargrave, READING, BERKSHIRE, RG10 8AQ.
OTTY, Miss. Kirstine Louise, BA ACA *2006;* Flat 2 18 Talbot Road, LONDON, W2 5LH.
•OTTY, Mr. Mark David, ACA CA(SA) *2008;* Ernst & Young LLP, 1 More London Place, LONDON, SE1 2AF. See also Ernst & Young Europe LLP
OTWAY, Miss. Isabelle, BSc ACA *2006;* Trimedia Communications UK Trimedia House, 29-35 Lexington Street, LONDON, W1F 9AH.
OTWAY, Mr. Timothy John, BA ACA *1992;* Chemin des Grands Champs, 1261 VAUD, SWITZERLAND.
OUARBYA, Mrs. Sarah Elizabeth, BSc FCA *2000;* with Mazars LLP, Tower Bridge House, St. Katharines Way, LONDON, E1W 1DD.
OUKO, Mr. Edward Rakwar Otieno, FCA *1983;* AFRICAN DEVELOPMENT BANK, BP 323 BELVEDERE TUNIS, TUNIS, 1002, TUNISIA.
OULD, Mr. Adrian John Brenchley, FCA *1970;* 3 St Mary's House, 6 St Mary's Close, RYDE, PO33 3HJ.
OULD, Mrs. Michele Georgina, BA ACA *1987;* Ch. de Madame de Warens7a, 1816 Chailly-Montreux, VAUD, SWITZERLAND.
OURA, Mr. Roger Antony, BSc ACA *1991;* 46 Littlehampton Road, WORTHING, BN13 1QH.
•OURY, Mr. Andrew Charles, BEng ACA *2003;* Oury Clark, PO Box 150, Herschel House, 58 Herschel Street, SLOUGH, SL1 1HD.
OURY, Mr. Gerald Vivian Libert, FCA *1962;* 5 Lingfield Road, LONDON, SW19 4QA.
•OURY, Mr. James Edward, LLB FCA *1997;* Oury Clark, 10 John Street, LONDON, WC1N 2EB.
•ⓘOURY, Mr. Richard Anthony, JP FCA FCCA *1964;* Oury Clark, PO Box 150, Herschel House, 58 Herschel Street, SLOUGH, SL1 1HD.
OUSELEY, Mr. Roger Sidney, BA FCA *1975;* 461 Cloverdale Road, OTTAWA K1M 0Y5, ON, CANADA.
OUSEY, Mr. Ian Ryder Marchant, BA ACA *1988;* Fremantle Group Ltd, 1 Stephen Street, LONDON, W1T 1AW.
OUSEY, Mr. Richard John, BA(Hons) ACA *2003;* 22 Kirklands, SALE, CHESHIRE, M33 3SQ.
•OUSTON, Mr. Michael Christopher Geeve, FCA *1962;* Ouston Sidders & Co., 9 Aplins Close, HARPENDEN, HERTFORDSHIRE, AL5 2PZ.
•OUTEN, Mr. Jeremy James, MA FCA *1992;* KPMG LLP, 15 Canada Square, LONDON, E14 5GL. See also KPMG Europe LLP
OUTHWAITE, Mr. Anthony, FCA *1970;* 6 Hawthorne Rise, Ackworth, PONTEFRACT, WF7 7DR.
OUTHWAITE, Mr. David Michael, BSc ACA *1991;* Agie Charmilles Ltd, North View, COVENTRY, CV2 2SJ.
OUTLAW, Mr. Colin Ernest, BSc ACA *1986;* Harvest Barn, Hoe Road, Bishops Waltham, SOUTHAMPTON, SO32 1DS.
OUTRAM, Mr. David Peter, BSc ACA *1991;* Rotherfield, 10 Bird Wood Court, Sonning Common, READING, RG4 9RF.
OUTRAM, Mrs. Jacqueline Ann, BA ACA *1991;* 10 Bird Wood Court, Sonning Common, READING, RG4 9RF.
•OUTRAM, Mr. Jason, FCA DChA *1987;* Hedley Dunk Limited, Trinity House, 3 Bullace Lane, DARTFORD, DA1 1BB.
OUTRAM, Mr. Vernon, BA FCA *1952;* Cranfield, Malthouse Lane Froggatt, Calver, HOPE VALLEY, S32 3ZA. (Life Member)
OUTTEN, Mr. Mark, BSc ACA *1997;* Mansell, Roman House, Grant Road, CROYDON, CR9 6BU.
OUTTERSIDE, Miss. Emma Louise, BSc ACA *2007;* 25 Hillcrest, PRUDHOE, NORTHUMBERLAND, NE42 5LE.
OUTTRIM, Mr. David John, BA ACA *1997;* Suite No. 1392, 48 Par La Ville Road, HAMILTON HM11, BERMUDA.
OVENDEN, Mr. David Michael, BSc ACA *1989;* 8 Viceroy Close, Raunds, WELLINGBOROUGH, NN9 6PJ.
OVENDEN, Miss. Diane Valerie, BSc ACA *1980;* Cornerwinds, Park View Road, Woldingham, CATERHAM, CR3 7DH.
OVENDEN, Mrs. Joanne, BSc ACA *1995;* PO Box 1783, CLEARWATER V0E1N0, BC, CANADA.
OVENDEN, Mr. Kevin Francis, BSc ACA *1988;* Acteon Group Ltd, Ferryside, Ferry Road, NORWICH, NR1 1SW.
OVENDEN, Mrs. Natalie Michele, BA ACA *1999;* 218 Priests Lane, Shenfield, BRENTWOOD, ESSEX, CM15 8LG.
OVENDEN, Mr. Philip Sydney, FCA *1965;* The Coach House, 10 Broadwater Down, TUNBRIDGE WELLS, TN2 5NG.
OVENDEN, Mr. Thomas Edward, BA ACA *1999;* 218 Priests Lane, Shenfield, BRENTWOOD, ESSEX, CM15 8LG.
OVENS, Mrs. Ashleigh Marie, BA(Hons) ACA *2011;* 6 Colebridge Avenue, GLOUCESTER, GL2 0RH.
OVENS, Mr. Christopher Steven Cooper, BA(Hons) ACA *2010;* 6 Colebridge Avenue, GLOUCESTER, GL2 0RH.
OVENS, Mr. Robert, FCA *1982;* Eversley, 4 Bradbourne Park Road, SEVENOAKS, TN13 3LJ.
OVER, Mr. Derek George, ACA *1980;* The Warren, Bramshill Road, Eversley, HOOK, RG27 0PR.
OVER, Mr. Richard John, FCA *1961;* The Stumps, 4 Wicket Hill, Off Bat & Ball Lane, FARNHAM, GU10 4RD.
OVERALL, Mr. John Richard, FCA *1975;* 1 The Grange, High Street, Puckeridge, WARE, HERTFORDSHIRE, SG11 1RH.
OVERALL, Mr. Paul James, ACA *2009;* 2 New Pond Cottages, Oxford Road, GERRARDS CROSS, BUCKINGHAMSHIRE, SL9 7RL.
OVERD, Mr. Christopher Michael, ACA *2010;* 14 Hampton Road, FARNHAM, SURREY, GU9 0DQ.
OVEREND, Mr. David Melvin, BA FCA *1984;* (Tax Fac), 44 Low Wood, Wilsden, BRADFORD, BD15 0JS.
OVEREND, Mr. Richard John, FCA *1963;* Lychcote, Shipton Lane, Burton Bradstock, BRIDPORT, DT6 4NQ. (Life Member)
•OVEREND, Mr. Robert, MA ACA *1986;* Ernst & Young LLP, 1 More London Place, LONDON, SE1 2AF. See also Ernst & Young Europe LLP
•OVERFIELD, Mr. Mark Richard, BSc FCA *1999;* with Deloitte LLP, 1 City Square, LEEDS, WEST YORKSHIRE, LS1 2AL.
•OVERFIELD, Mr. Martin, FCA *1990;* Smailes Goldie, Regents Court, Princess Street, HULL, HU2 8BA.
OVERFIELD, Mrs. Sandra, BSc(Hons) ACA *2002;* 29 Lister Street, ILKLEY, WEST YORKSHIRE, LS29 9ET.
OVERHILL, Mr. Ashley, ACA *1982;* PO Box R218, Royal Exchange, SYDNEY, NSW 1225, AUSTRALIA.
OVERS, Mr. Anthony John, MA ACA *1983;* Border Holdings UK Ltd, The Grove, CRAVEN ARMS, SHROPSHIRE, SY7 8DA.
OVERSTALL, Ms. Lorna, BSc ACA *2005;* 1 Brunswick Mews, HOVE, EAST SUSSEX, BN3 1HD.
OVERTON, Mr. Andrew, MChem ACA *2011;* 30 Milman Road, READING, RG2 0AY.
OVERTON, Miss. Emma, ACA *2001;* 10 Regent Road, Harborne, BIRMINGHAM, B17 9JU.
OVERTON, Mr. Gideon, BA ACA *1992;* 415 Watling Street, RADLETT, HERTFORDSHIRE, WD7 7JG.
OVERTON, Mr. Gregory, ACA *2011;* 614A, Flat Above, 614 Kingston Road, LONDON, SW20 8DN.
OVERTON, Miss. Jenny Marie, BSc ACA *1996;* Hurst & Co, Lancashire Gate, 21 Tiviot Dale, STOCKPORT, CHESHIRE, SK1 1TD.
OVERTON, Mr. John Leslie, FCA *1963;* Corner Cottage, Clifton, Severn Stoke, WORCESTER, WR8 9JF.
OVERTON, Mrs. Zeenat, ACA MAAT BEng(Hons) *2010;* 16 High Busy Lane, SHIPLEY, WEST YORKSHIRE, BD18 1HD.
OVERTON-SMITH, Mr. Nicholas James, BSc ACA *1999;* Wayside House, Hampers Lane, Storrington, PULBOROUGH, WEST SUSSEX, RH20 3HU.

OVERTON-SMITH, Mr. Roger Barry, BA FCA *1972;* Pine Tops, Fox Court, Storrington, PULBOROUGH, RH20 4JL.
OVERTOOM, Mr. Franciscus Johannes Carolus, BEng ACA *1992;* 63 New Bond Street, LONDON, W1A 3BS.
OVERY, Mr. Andrew Kevin, BSc ACA *1992;* Legal & General Investment Management, 1 Coleman Street, LONDON, EC2R 5AA.
OVERY, Miss. Laura Jane, ACA *2009;* 9f Thistle Grove, LONDON, SW10 9RR.
OVERY, Mrs. Tehseen Yunus, BSc ACA *1995;* Five Arrows Ltd, 32/33 St. James's Place, LONDON, SW1A 1NP.
OVINGTON, Mr. David Robert, BA ACA *1993;* Rio Tinto, 2 Eastbourne Terrace, LONDON, W2 6LG.
OVINGTON, Mr. Robert Lewis, FCA *1970;* PO Box 188, 11 Akyuz Sokak, LAPTA MERSIN 10, TURKEY.
•**OW, Mr. Fook Sheng, FCA** *1972;* Ow Fook Sheng & Co, 76 Tanjong Pagar Road, SINGAPORE 088497, SINGAPORE.
OW-YONG, Mr. Johnny Ho Kun, FCA *1975;* 30 Sembawang Drive, Apt 12-12 Syn Plaza, SINGAPORE 757713, SINGAPORE. (Life Member)
OWDEN, Mrs. Wendy Anne, BA ACA *1986;* 1 Drakes Farm, Peasemore, NEWBURY, RG20 7DF.
OWEN, Mr. Adam, ACA *1997;* (Tax Fac), 39 Lynn Grove, Gorleston, GREAT YARMOUTH, NORFOLK, NR31 8AR.
OWEN, Mr. Adam Edward, BA(Hons) ACA *2002;* with Deloitte LLP, 4 Brindley Place, BIRMINGHAM, B1 2HZ.
OWEN, Mr. Alexander, BA(Hons) ACA *1998;* 50 St. James's Road, SEVENOAKS, KENT, TN13 3NG.
OWEN, Mrs. Alexandra Rachael, BSc(Hons) ACA *2002;* Fairline Nene Valley Business Park, Oundle, PETERBOROUGH, PE8 4HN.
•**OWEN, Mr. Alistair Grant, BA ACA** *1988;* Owen & Co, 41 Ashley Terrace, EDINBURGH, EH11 1RY.
OWEN, Mr. Andrew Derek Walter, BSc FCA *1994;* British Film Institute, 21 Stephen Street, LONDON, W1T 1LN.
OWEN, Mr. Andrew Ian, BSc(Hons) ACA *2001;* 8 Saxton Close, Hasland, CHESTERFIELD, DERBYSHIRE, S41 0SL.
OWEN, Mr. Andrew John, LLB FCA *1966;* Bramcote, 3 Lancaster Avenue, FARNHAM, GU9 8JY.
OWEN, Mr. Andrew Paul, LLB ACA *1998;* 31 Riseldine Road, Honor Oak Park, LONDON, SE23 1JT.
OWEN, Dr. Aneirin Sion, PhD BA ACA *1990;* 33 East Quay, Wapping Dock, LIVERPOOL, L3 4BU.
OWEN, Miss. Anne, BSc ACA *1983;* 27 Maes Cadwgan, Creigiau, CARDIFF, CF15 9TQ.
OWEN, Mrs. Barbara Mary, BA ACA *1986;* The Shepherds House, Littleworth Road, Seale, FARNHAM, SURREY, GU10 1JN.
•**OWEN, Mr. Barry, BSc FCA** *1979;* The Carley Partnership, St. James's House, 8 Overcliffe, GRAVESEND, DA11 0HJ. See also Carleys Integrated Solutions Ltd
OWEN, Mrs. Bethan Emlyn, BSc ACA *1992;* Linden Court, The Orchards, Ilex Close, Llanishen, CARDIFF, CF14 5DZ.
OWEN, Mr. Brian Thomas, FCA *1960;* Blays Hill, 51 Southend, Garsington, OXFORD, OX44 9DJ. (Life Member)
OWEN, Mr. Bryn Eiron, BSc ACA *1986;* Wells Fargo Bank, Plantation Place, 30 Fenchurch Street, LONDON, EC3M 3BD.
OWEN, Mrs. Caroline Elizabeth, BSc ACA *1986;* Brackley House, Staplehurst Road, Staplehurst, TONBRIDGE, TN12 0RJ.
OWEN, Ms. Caroline Mary, BSc ACA *1994;* 10 Brook House, 47/48 Clapham Common Southside, Clapham, LONDON, SW4 9BX.
OWEN, Ms. Carolyn Judith, BEd ACA *1983;* 40 Mayfair Gardens, WOODFORD GREEN, IG8 9AB.
OWEN, Mr. Charles Stewart Patrick, ACA CTA *2006;* 19 Heene Way, WORTHING, BN11 4LT.
OWEN, Mr. Charles William, FCA *1975;* 116 Lichfield Road, Four Oaks, SUTTON COLDFIELD, B74 2TA.
OWEN, Dr. Chris, PhD MSc BSc ACA *2011;* 3 The Steadings, Wootton Bassett, SWINDON, SN4 8BD.
OWEN, Miss. Christine Mary, FCA *1971;* Flat 4 Beaupre, 3 Woodville Road, ALTRINCHAM, CHESHIRE, WA14 2AN. (Life Member)
OWEN, Mr. Christopher, BA(Hons) ACA *2011;* 79 Devonshire Road, DURHAM, DH1 2BJ.
OWEN, Mr. Christopher David, BSc ACA *1990;* with KPMG LLP, 1 The Embankment, Neville Street, LEEDS, LS1 4DW.
•**OWEN, Mr. Christopher Ian, FCA** *1970;* Off The Square Limited, Wheelwright Cottage, Cherington, SHIPSTON-ON-STOUR, CV36 5HS.
OWEN, Mr. Christopher Paul, BSc ACA *1992;* Wilton Lodge, 3 The Avenue, HITCHIN, SG4 9RQ.
OWEN, Mr. Christopher Simon, ACA *1985;* West Barn Church Road, Farnham Royal, SLOUGH, SL2 3AW.
OWEN, Miss. Clair Elizabeth, BSc ACA *1999;* Flat 2, 17 Claremont Gardens, SURBITON, KT6 4TL.
OWEN, Mrs. Claire, BSc ACA *1995;* Jaga Heating Products UK Ltd, Jaga House, Orchard Business Park, Bromyard Road, LEDBURY, HEREFORDSHIRE HR8 1LG.
•**OWEN, Mr. Clive Faulkner, FCA** *1970;* Clive Owen & Co LLP, 140 Coniscliffe Road, DARLINGTON, COUNTY DURHAM, DL3 7RT.
OWEN, Mr. Clive Michael, BSc ACA *1993;* 14 Russell Street, CHICHESTER, WEST SUSSEX, PO19 7EL.
OWEN, Mr. Colin Anthony, BA FCA *1959;* Southfield, Park Road, STROUD, GLOUCESTERSHIRE, GL5 2JQ. (Life Member)
OWEN, Mr. Darren Mark, FCA *1993;* with Fox Evans, Abbey House, 7 Manor Road, COVENTRY, CV1 2FW.
OWEN, Mr. David Christopher, MA ACA *1979;* 5 Clares Green Road, Spencers Wood, READING, RG7 1DY.
OWEN, Mr. David Franklin, BSc ARCS ACA *1995;* Russell Cooke Solicitors, 2 Putney Hill, LONDON, SW15 6AB.
OWEN, Mr. David Geraint Ashley, BCom FCA *1950;* West Sheepcote, Wooburn Common, HIGH WYCOMBE, HP10 0JS. (Life Member)
OWEN, Prof. David Lloyd, BA ACA *1978;* 60 Don Avenue, Wharncliffe Side, SHEFFIELD, S35 0BZ.
OWEN, Mr. David William, BSc FCA *1975;* 2 St. Marys Road, Bluntisham, HUNTINGDON, PE28 3XA.
•**OWEN, Miss. Dawn Corrinne, BA(Hons) ACA** *2001;* Turner Peachey, Column House, London Road, SHREWSBURY, SY2 6NN.
OWEN, Mr. Deian Llwyd, ACA *2010;* 10 Clos Ger y Bryn, Tircoed Forest Village, Penllergaer, SWANSEA, SA4 9JL.
OWEN, Mr. Derrick Christopher, FCA *1974;* 19 Sandford Way, Dunchurch, RUGBY, CV22 6NB.
OWEN, Mr. Deryck, FCA *1955;* The CoppiceBromley Green Road, Upper Ruckinge ASHFORD, Kent, TN26 2EF. (Life Member)
OWEN, Miss. Diana Valerie, BCom FCA *1985;* 6 Cavendish Court, 86 Waldegrave Road, TEDDINGTON, TW11 8LN.
•**OWEN, Mr. Duncan Glen, BA ACA** *1996;* G C Morgan Limited, Clive House, Severn Road, WELSHPOOL, POWYS, SY21 7AL.
•**OWEN, Mr. Edward John, FCA** *1957;* E J Owen, 1 Beech Cliffe, WARWICK, CV34 5HY.
OWEN, Mrs. Elizabeth Ann, BA ACA *1993;* 97 Dunstable Street, Ampthill, BEDFORD, MK45 2NG.
•**OWEN, Mrs. Elizabeth Jane, ACA** *1993;* Liz Owen Accounting Services, 24 Knighton Road, Woodthorpe, NOTTINGHAM, NG5 4FL.
•**OWEN, Miss. Elizabeth Wyn, FCA** *1980;* E W Owen Limited, Broyan House, Priory Street, CARDIGAN, DYFED, SA43 1BZ.
•**OWEN, Mr. Eric Thomas, FCA** *1964;* (Tax Fac), Eric T.Owen F.C.A, 25 Lynton Green, Woolton, LIVERPOOL, L25 6JB.
•**OWEN, Mr. Gary, BSc FCA** *1999;* Owen Business Solutions Limited, 1 Cobham Close, ENFIELD, MIDDLESEX, EN1 3SD.
OWEN, Mr. Gary David, ACA ATII *1988;* (Tax Fac), Flat 47 Copper Beech House, Heathside Crescent, WOKING, GU22 7BB.
•**OWEN, Mr. Gary Henry, BSc FCA** *1973;* Altman Blane & Co, Middlesex House, 29/45 High Street, EDGWARE, HA8 7LH.
OWEN, Mr. Gary John, BSc ACA *1998;* Silverdene, West Knapton, MALTON, NORTH YORKSHIRE, YO17 8JB.
OWEN, Mr. Gary John, BA ACA *1978;* 2660 Puesta Del Sol, SANTA BARBARA, CA 93105, UNITED STATES.
OWEN, Mr. Gary Martin, BEng ACA *1993;* 4 Heron Close, Harden, BINGLEY, WEST YORKSHIRE, BD16 1QN.
OWEN, Mr. Geoffrey Cooper, FCA *1968;* 45 Station Road, Dove Holes, BUXTON, DERBYSHIRE, SK17 8DH.
OWEN, Mr. Geoffrey Ivor, BSc FCA *1992;* 9 Homestead Close, Frampton Cotterell, BRISTOL, BS36 2FB.
OWEN, Mr. Giles James, BA FCA *1992;* (Tax Fac), 1 Croft Lane, Temple Grafton, ALCESTER, WARWICKSHIRE, B49 6PA.
OWEN, Mr. Glyn Philip Dovener, BCom ACA *1982;* Rue du Noyer 338, 1030, BRUSSELS, BELGIUM.
OWEN, Mr. Graham Antony, ACA *1978;* Vermont Leathercraft Manufacturers, P.O. Box 1404, FERNDALE, 2160, SOUTH AFRICA.
•**OWEN, Mr. Harvey John, FCA** *1972;* Nicklin LLP, Church Court, Stourbridge Road, HALESOWEN, WEST MIDLANDS, B63 3TT. See also Nicklin Management Services Limited and HSP Nicklin
OWEN, Mrs. Helen Elizabeth, BSc ACA *1986;* Llwyn Onn, 42 Green Pastures Road, Wraxall, BRISTOL, BS48 1ND.
OWEN, Mr. Huw, MSc LLB ACA *2010;* 9 Swan Lane, Bunbury, TARPORLEY, CHESHIRE, CW6 9RA.
OWEN, Mr. James Garfield, BA ACA *1996;* James Owen, Box 30600, SEVEN MILE BEACH, GRAND CAYMAN, KY1-1203, CAYMAN ISLANDS.
OWEN, Mr. James Martin, FCA *1969;* Westlands, Turners Hill Road, Crawley Down, CRAWLEY, WEST SUSSEX, RH10 4HG.
OWEN, Mr. James Stanhope, BSc ACA MBA *1995;* Manor Farm South Side, Steeple Aston, BICESTER, OXFORDSHIRE, OX25 4RT.
OWEN, Mrs. Jane Elizabeth Sarah, BCom ACA *1989;* Meadfields Farm, Three Gates Lane, HASLEMERE, SURREY, GU27 2LD.
OWEN, Mrs. Janine Louise, BSc ACA CTA *1993;* 62 Wear Bay Road, FOLKESTONE, KENT, CT19 6PU.
OWEN, Mr. Jeremy Martin, MA MSc ACA *1988;* Land Use Consultants, 43 Chalton Street, LONDON, NW1 1JD.
OWEN, Mr. John, BCom ACA *1982;* 13 Avenue des Papalins, MONTE CARLO, MC98000, MONACO.
OWEN, Mr. John, FCA *1956;* Flat A, 10 Park Avenue, HARROGATE, HG2 9BQ. (Life Member)
OWEN, Mr. John Arthur, FCA *1956;* Springfield Nineteen Limited, 19 Hockers Lane, Detling, MAIDSTONE, ME14 3JL.
OWEN, Mr. John David, MA ACA *1980;* Shrewsbury College, Radbrook Campus, Radbrook Road, SHREWSBURY, SY3 9BL.
OWEN, Mr. John Douglas, BSc FCA *1979;* 39 Richmond Avenue, Merton Park, LONDON, SW20 8LA.
•**OWEN, Mr. John Douglas, FCA** *1981;* John D. Owen, Commerce House, 34-38 King Street, NEWCASTLE, STAFFORDSHIRE, ST5 1HX.
OWEN, Mr. John Harold Tierney, FCA *1962;* Charnwood, 28 Hodge Lane, Hartford, NORTHWICH, CW8 3AJ. (Life Member)
•**OWEN, Mr. John Herbert, MA FCA** *1978;* (Tax Fac), Chantrey Vellacott DFK LLP, Russell Square House, 10-12 Russell Square, LONDON, WC1B 5LF.
OWEN, Mr. John Humphrey Ynyr, FCA *1940;* Flat 5, 35 Westbourne Villas, HOVE, BN3 4GF. (Life Member)
OWEN, Mr. John Martin, PhD FCA *1968;* 16 Majestic Apartments, King Edward Road, Onchan, ISLE OF MAN, IM3 2BD. (Life Member)
OWEN, Mr. John Roger, MA ACA *1979;* 4 Milford Copse, Harborne, BIRMINGHAM, B17 9TF.
OWEN, Mr. Jonathan Spencer, BA ACA *1994;* 42 Woodland Avenue, HOVE, BN3 6BL.
OWEN, Mr. Jonathan William Mark, BSc FCA *1992;* Citigroup Centre, 33 Canada Square, LONDON, E14 5LB.
OWEN, Ms. Julia Ann, BA ACA *2001;* Kabulonga, Goat Hall Lane, CHELMSFORD, CM2 8PG.
OWEN, Mrs. Karen, BSc(Hons) ACA *2000;* 33 The Serpentine, Aughton, ORMSKIRK, LANCASHIRE, L39 6RN.
OWEN, Miss. Katherine, BSc ACA *2007;* International Monetary Fund, HQ2 12A-351, 1900 Pennsylvania Avenue, WASHINGTON, DC, UNITED STATES.
OWEN, Mrs. Kelly, BA FCA *2000;* Dendy Neville, 3-4 Bower Terrace, MAIDSTONE, ME16 8RY.
OWEN, Mr. Keri Joseph Hooson, BSc ACA *1979;* The Priory Partnership, 1 Abbots Quay, Monks Ferry, BIRKENHEAD, MERSEYSIDE, CH41 5LH.
OWEN, Mr. Kevin David, BSc ACA *1990;* 2016 Picardy, VAUDREUIL-DORION J7V 8P7, QC, CANADA.
OWEN, Mr. Lawrence Searle, FCA *1960;* 6 West Winds, Langland, SWANSEA, SA3 4TA. (Life Member)
•**OWEN, Mr. Malcolm Vernon, FCA** *1970;* Gravestock & Owen Ltd, 33 Market Place, WILLENHALL, WV13 2AA.
OWEN, Mr. Marc Bryan, ACA *2008;* 22 Copeland Road, Birstall, LEICESTER, LE4 3AA.
•**OWEN, Mrs. Marcell Ann, BA ACA** *1997;* Owen Accountancy, April Cottage, Poundfield Lane, Cookham, MAIDENHEAD, BERKSHIRE SL6 9RY.
OWEN, Mr. Mark Christopher, BSc ACA *1991;* 44 Rowlands Road, BURY, LANCASHIRE, BL9 5NF.
OWEN, Mr. Mark Kevin, ACA *1993;* IS-Rayfast Ltd, 2 Westmead, SWINDON, SN5 7SY.
OWEN, Mr. Martin David Edward, BSc ACA *1990;* Wates Group, Wates House, Station Approach, LEATHERHEAD, SURREY, KT22 7SW.
OWEN, Mr. Martin Neville, MA FCA *1973;* St. Anthonys Castle Street, WINCHELSEA, EAST SUSSEX, TN36 4EL. (Life Member)
•**OWEN, Mr. Martyn, ACA** *1980;* (Tax Fac), O'Shea & Owen, 5 Willow Walk, COWBRIDGE, CF71 7EE.
OWEN, Mr. Matthew, BA ACA *2008;* 14 Mountford Close, Oakwood, DERBY, DE21 2TW.
OWEN, Mr. Matthew Alexander, BSc ACA *1999;* Lantau, Oak End Way, Woodham, ADDLESTONE, SURREY, KT15 3DY.
OWEN, Mr. Matthew James, ACA *2005;* 2/28 Cameron Street, Birchgrove, SYDNEY, NSW 2041, AUSTRALIA.
OWEN, Mr. Michael, FCA *1971;* 1 Thornfield Gardens, Sandown Park, TUNBRIDGE WELLS, TN2 4RZ.
OWEN, Mr. Michael, BA ACA *1989;* 31 Menton Road, Heaton Moor, STOCKPORT, SK4 4HF.
•**OWEN, Mr. Michael John, FCA** *1974;* Michael J Owen and Company Ltd, 2 Haygate Drive, Wellington, TELFORD, TF1 2BY.
OWEN, Mr. Michael Sydney, FCA *1948;* 6 The Hermitage, THORNTON-CLEVELEYS, FY5 2TH. (Life Member)
OWEN, Mr. Michael Wynne, ACA *2008;* 114 East 11th Street, Apt 4W, NEW YORK, NY 10003, UNITED STATES.
•**OWEN, Miss. Michelle Louise, BSc ACA** *1999;* Baker Tilly Tax & Advisory Services LLP, Festival Way, Festival Park, STOKE-ON-TRENT, ST1 5BB.
OWEN, Mr. Nathan Paul, BSc ACA *1998;* LAZ Parking Ltd LLC, 15 Lewis Street, HARTFORD, CT 06103, UNITED STATES.
OWEN, Mrs. Nia Rhian, BSc ACA *2005;* Galeri Caernarfon Cyf, Victoria Dock, CAERNARFON, GWYNEDD, LL55 1SQ.
OWEN, Mr. Nicholas Edward, FCA *1970;* The Paddocks, Lydiard Millicent, SWINDON, SN5 3LU. (Life Member)
•**OWEN, Mr. Nicholas Robson, BCom ACA** *1989;* Deloitte LLP, Stonecutter Court, 1 Stonecutter Street, LONDON, EC4A 4TR. See also Deloitte & Touche LLP
OWEN, Mr. Nicolas Daniel, BA FCA *1990;* 1 Bruce Grove, ORPINGTON, KENT, BR6 0HF.
OWEN, Mr. Patrick Guy Austen, MA ACA *1996;* 22 Cotesbach Road, LONDON, E5 9QJ.
OWEN, Mr. Paul Bryan, BA ACA *2005;* Apartment 1003, Royal Ocean Plaza, GIBRALTAR, GIBRALTAR.
OWEN, Mr. Paul David, BA(Hons) ACA *2001;* H W C A Ltd, Northern Assurance Buildings, 9-21 Princess Street, MANCHESTER, M2 4DN.
OWEN, Mr. Paul Jeffrey, BSc FCA *1980;* 14 Cumlodden Avenue, EDINBURGH, EH12 6DR.
•**OWEN, Mr. Peter, BSc ACA** *1989;* Wingrave Yeats Partnership LLP, 101 Wigmore Street, LONDON, W1U 1QU.
•**OWEN, Mr. Peter Ernest, BSc ACA** *1994;* 80 Pendle Gardens, Culcheth, WARRINGTON, WA3 4LU.
OWEN, Mr. Peter Godber, FCA *1969;* Church Cottage, Greenwood Lane, Durley, SOUTHAMPTON, SO32 2AP.
OWEN, Mr. Peter John, FCA *1954;* Whitelands Farm, Ashington, PULBOROUGH, WEST SUSSEX, RH20 3DE. (Life Member)
•**OWEN, Mr. Philip, BSc ACA** *1992;* JPO Accountancy Limited, 5th Floor, Hanover House, Hanover Street, LIVERPOOL, L1 3DZ.
OWEN, Mr. Philip Charles, BA ACA *1990;* 7 Ash Tree Close, Radyr, CARDIFF, CF15 8RX.
OWEN, Mr. Philip James Lawrence, MBA BSc FCA CTA AMCT *1992;* 6 The Green, Culham, ABINGDON, OX14 4LZ.
OWEN, Mrs. Philippa Kate, BSc(Hons) ACA *2000;* 55 Wike Ridge Avenue, LEEDS, LS17 9NN.
OWEN, Mr. Prys, BSc ACA *2005;* 3 Browns Coppice Avenue, SOLIHULL, B91 1PL.
OWEN, Mrs. Rachael, BA(Hons) ACA *2004;* 34 Tarnside Road, Orrell, WIGAN, WN5 8RN.
OWEN, Mrs. Rachel Kirsty, BA ACA *2003;* 15 Oregon Walk, Finchampstead, WOKINGHAM, RG40 4PG.
OWEN, Mrs. Rachel Louise, BA ACA *1996;* 20 Lennox Gardens, LEEDS, LS15 0PA.
OWEN, Miss. Rhiannon Mary, ACA *2009;* 76 Rochester Avenue, BROMLEY, BR1 3DW.
OWEN, Mr. Richard Alan David, BA ACA *1982;* 2 Greenways, Pembroke Road, WOKING, GU22 7DY.
OWEN, Mr. Richard Bleddyn, BCom ACA *1980;* 104 rue du Parc de Villard, 01210 ORNEX, FRANCE.

OWEN, Mr. Richard Henfryn, BCom ACA *1993;* 8 Wilton Road, COVENTRY, CV7 7QW.
OWEN, Mr. Richard Paul, ACA *1994;* 62 Wear Bay Road, FOLKESTONE, KENT, CT19 6PU.
OWEN, Mr. Richard Wilfred, FCA *1958;* Flat 25 Gainsborough House, Frognal Rise, Hampstead Village, LONDON, NW3 6PZ. (Life Member)
•OWEN, Mr. Robert Scholefield, FCA *1973;* Finrob Limited, Suite 5b, Brook House, 77 Fountain Street, MANCHESTER, M2 2EE.
OWEN, Mr. Rodger, FCA *1974;* 5 Midge Hall Drive, Bamford, ROCHDALE, OL11 4AX.
•OWEN, Mr. Roger Alan, ACA *1980;* Chancellers, 38/39 Bucklersbury, HITCHIN, SG5 1BG.
OWEN, Mr. Roger Edwardes, FCA *1971;* 41 Church Hill, LONDON, N21 1LE.
OWEN, Mr. Roger George, FCA *1971;* with O'Hara Wood Limited, 29 Gay Street, BATH, BA1 2NT.
•OWEN, Mr. Roger Thomas, BCom FCA *1980;* AIMS - Roger Owen, 69 Laurel Drive, Eccleston, ST. HELENS, WA10 5JB. See also AIMS - Roger Thomas Owen
OWEN, Mrs. Ruth, BA ACA *1993;* 2 Passford House Cottages, Mount Pleasant, LYMINGTON, SO41 8LS.
OWEN, Miss. Ruth Victoria, ACA *2008;* 20 Sunnindale Drive, Tollerton, NOTTINGHAM, NG12 4ES.
OWEN, Mrs. Samantha Jane, BSc(Hons) ACA *2002;* DB Schemker (UK) Limited, E W S, Carolina Way, DONCASTER, SOUTH YORKSHIRE, DN4 5PN.
OWEN, Mr. Simon Francis, BA FCA *1995;* 6 Wembley Lane, BURNTWOOD, STAFFORDSHIRE, WS7 1FL.
OWEN, Mr. Simon John, BSc ACA *1999;* Merrill Lynch, 2049 Century Park East, Suite 1100, CENTURY CITY, CA 90067, UNITED STATES.
OWEN, Mr. Stephen John, BA ACA CTA *1986;* Galebrook Farm Sandy Lane, Antrobus, NORTHWICH, CHESHIRE, CW9 6NU.
OWEN, Mr. Steven Jonathan, LLB FCA MCT *1982;* Flat 3 Maxwell Place, 130-136 Maxwell Road, BEACONSFIELD, BUCKINGHAMSHIRE, HP9 1AQ.
OWEN, Mr. Stuart Guy, BA(Hons) ACA *2001;* (Tax Fac), The Jam Factory, Flat 205, Block A, 27 Green Walk, LONDON, SE1 4TT.
OWEN, Mrs. Suzanne Claire, MSci ACA *2004;* 6 Weldon Road, ALTRINCHAM, CHESHIRE, WA14 4EH.
OWEN, Mr. Timothy Brian, BSc ACA *1986;* 5 Holmes Close, ASCOT, SL5 9TJ.
OWEN, Mr. Timothy John, FCA *1975;* Yew Tree House, Pedlinge, HYTHE, KENT, CT21 4JL. (Life Member)
OWEN, Mr. Toby, ACA *2009;* 21 Thornton Street, HERTFORD, SG14 1QH.
OWEN, Mrs. Tracy, ACA *1992;* 137 Priory Grove Ditton, AYLESFORD, KENT, ME20 6BD.
OWEN, Mrs. Valerie, BSc ACA *1982;* 29 West Road, Nottage, PORTHCAWL, MID GLAMORGAN, CF36 3SN.
OWEN, Mr. William, FCA *1973;* with Ian Richmond Limited, Chapel Ash House, 6 Compton Road, WOLVERHAMPTON, WV3 9PH.
•OWEN, Mr. William Beresford, FCA *1973;* Baker Tilly Tax & Advisory Services LLP, Hanover House, 18 Mount Ephraim Road, TUNBRIDGE WELLS, KENT, TN1 1ED. See also Baker Tilly UK Audit LLP
•OWEN, Mr. William Glynne, FCA *1970;* W Glynne Owen & Co Limited, 2 Caradog Villas, Glanhwfa Road, LLANGEFNI, GWYNEDD, LL77 7EN.
OWEN, Mr. William John Michael, MA ACA *1985;* 25922 Santa Susana Drive, SANTA CLARITA, CA 91321, UNITED STATES.
OWEN-CONWAY, Mr. David, BMus ACA *2008;* Apartment 108 Munkenbeck Building, 5 Hermitage Street, LONDON, W2 1PW.
OWEN-CONWAY, Mr. Gareth, ACA *1989;* H S B C Bank Plc, 8 Canada Square, Canary Wharf, LONDON, E14 5HQ.
•OWEN-JONES, Mrs. Rachel Louisa, BA(Hons) ACA *2002;* OJC Accountancy Services, 17 King Henrys Road, KINGSTON UPON THAMES, SURREY, KT1 3QA.
OWEN-RAFFERTY, Mr. Gerard, BA ACA *2010;* Flat 1, 22a Leopold Road, LONDON, SW19 7BD.
OWEN-RAFFERTY, Miss. Karina Louise, BSc ACA CTA *2004;* 43 Alexandra Mews, TAMWORTH, STAFFORDSHIRE, B79 7HT.
OWENS, Mr. Christian Geraint Edward, BSc ACA *1997;* Institute of Occupational Medicine, 49 Research Park Riccarton, CURRIE, MIDLOTHIAN, EH14 4AP.
•OWENS, Mr. Christopher John, FCA *1980;* (Tax Fac), Nortons Group LLP, Highlands House, Basingstoke Road, Spencers Wood, READING, RG7 1NT.
OWENS, Mr. Christopher Mark, MA ACA *1998;* 38 Clarina Street, CHAPEL HILL, QLD 4069, AUSTRALIA.
OWENS, Mr. Darren Paul, BSc FCA *1996;* ul na polach 15, 31 344 KRAKOW, POLAND.
OWENS, Mr. David Paul, FCA *1980;* Upper Balladhoo Mansion, Baldrine Road, Lonan, ISLE OF MAN, IM4 6EH.
•OWENS, Mr. David William, BSc FCA *1987;* KTS Owens Thomas Limited, The Counting House, Dunleavy Drive, CARDIFF, CF11 0SN.
OWENS, Miss. Elizabeth, ACA *2011;* 68 Winchester Avenue, SHEFFIELD, S10 4EB.
OWENS, Mr. Gareth Thomas, BA FCA *1981;* (Tax Fac), with J P Morgan Chase Bank, 125 London Wall, LONDON, EC2Y 5AJ.
OWENS, Mrs. Gillian Helena, BA ACA *1988;* Glenbervie, 12 Westerfield Road, IPSWICH, IP4 2UJ.
OWENS, Mr. Ifan Rion Brooke, FCA *1965;* 34 Fairholme Rd, ASHFORD, Middlesex, TW15 2LH.
OWENS, Mr. Iwan Llyr, BSc ACA *2006;* 5 Corlan y Rhos, Llanrug, CAERNARFON, GWYNEDD, LL55 4JA.
OWENS, Mr. James Joseph, BCom FCA *1977;* 9 Abberton Grove, Shirley, SOLIHULL, B90 4YQ.
OWENS, Mr. James Richard, ACA *2008;* 4/ 11A Flood Street, BONDI, NSW 2026, AUSTRALIA.
•OWENS, Mr. John, FCA *1980;* Argot Accounting and Business Services, 16 Queen Street, REDCAR, CLEVELAND, TS10 1AF. See also Owens. John
OWENS, Mr. John Patrick, BCom ACA *1993;* Whittington Insurance Markets Ltd, 33 Creechurch Lane, LONDON, EC3A 5EB.
OWENS, Mr. John Robert, FCA *1959;* 23 Nelson Court, Birkdale, SOUTHPORT, MERSEYSIDE, PR8 2SH. (Life Member)
OWENS, Mr. John Robin, MA FCA *1971;* Park Cottage Livesey Street Teston, MAIDSTONE, KENT, ME18 5AY. (Life Member)
OWENS, Mrs. Josephine Kathryn, BSc ACA *1992;* Oakbank, 24 Nightingale Road, GUILDFORD, SURREY, GU1 1ER.
•OWENS, Mr. Julian Spencer, BSc FCA *1999;* (Tax Fac), Griffith Clarke, 701 Stonehouse Business Park, Sperry Way, STONEHOUSE, GLOUCESTERSHIRE, GL10 3UT.
OWENS, Miss. Kate Louise, BSc ACA *2006;* 6 rue des Thibault, 77930 CHAILLY EN BIERE, FRANCE.
OWENS, Mr. Luke Gregory, BA FCA *2000;* with BDO LLP, 55 Baker Street, LONDON, W1U 7EU.
OWENS, Mrs. Megan Elinor, ACA *2008;* 14 Clos Henblas, Broadlands, BRIDGEND, MID GLAMORGAN, CF31 5EU.
OWENS, Mr. Nicholas Legard, MA ACA *1981;* 8 Hurst Road, HASSOCKS, WEST SUSSEX, BN6 9NJ.
OWENS, Mr. Paul Anthony, BSc ACA *1986;* Glenbervie, 12 Westerfield Road, IPSWICH, IP4 2UJ.
OWENS, Mr. Paul Justin, BSc ACA *1984;* 6 Daylesford Avenue, Roehampton, LONDON, SW15 5QR.
OWENS, Mr. Peter Keith, BA FCA *1975;* Tudor Mount, 223 Pensby Road, Heswall, WIRRAL, MERSEYSIDE, CH61 5UA.
OWENS, Miss. Rebecca Grace, ACA *2009;* 30 Queen Street, RUSHDEN, NORTHAMPTONSHIRE, NN10 0AZ.
OWENS, Mr. Richard Ian, MA ACA *1999;* 24 Peck Slip, Apt 3E, NEW YORK, NY 10038, UNITED STATES.
OWENS, Mrs. Rosalind Ellen MaCaulay, BSc ACA *1991;* 73 Park Road, Duffield, BELPER, DE56 4GR.
OWENS, Mr. Seton Jerome, FCA *1963;* 9 Deer Park Walk, Lycrome Road Lye Green, CHESHAM, HP5 3LJ.
OWENS, Mr. Steven Edward, ACA *2000;* 194 Bishopsteignton, Shoeburyness, SOUTHEND-ON-SEA, SS3 8BQ.
OWENS, Mr. Stuart Gary, BA ACA *1991;* Oakbank, 24 Nightingale Road, GUILDFORD, SURREY, GU1 1ER.
OWENS, Mr. Stuart Gordon, ACA *2004;* 29 Friars Avenue, Shenfield, BRENTWOOD, CM15 8HY.
OWENS, Mrs. Tamsin Katherine, BSc(Hons) ACA *2001;* 29 Friars Avenue, Shenfield, BRENTWOOD, ESSEX, CM15 8HY.
•OWERS, Mr. Antony Wicks, FCA *1974;* Jansofat 38, WILLEMSTAD, CURACAO, NETHERLANDS ANTILLES.
•OWERS, Mr. David John, FCA *1971;* (Tax Fac), Owers & Co, Round Maples, Edwardstone, SUDBURY, SUFFOLK, CO10 5PR.
OWERS, Mr. David Rodney, FCA *1957;* 4 Dart Grove, Auckley, DONCASTER, DN9 3JH. (Life Member)
OWERS, Mr. John Howard, MA MPhil ACA *1997;* 107 Mayfield Road, LONDON, N8 9LN.
•OWERS, Mr. Simon James, BA ACA *2000;* Simon Owers Corporate Limited, Fairfield Cottage, Warrington Road, Great Budworth, NORTHWICH, CHESHIRE CW9 6HB.
OWLES, Mr. Brian Raymond Beaumont, FCA *1967;* 66 Shadforth Street, MOSMAN, NSW 2088, AUSTRALIA. (Life Member)
OWLES, Mr. John Maxwell Harding, FCA *1972;* 51 Mickle Hill, SANDHURST, BERKSHIRE, GU47 8QP.
OWLES, Mr. Peter Alan Gallard, BSc FCA *1974;* Rental Research Ltd, 893 Plymouth Road, SLOUGH, SL1 4LP.
OWLETT, Miss. Christine Anne, ACA *1987;* Absaloms Oast Cottage, Underriver, SEVENOAKS, TN15 0SL.
OWLETT, Miss. Elizabeth, BA ACA *2006;* 102-1140 Pendrell Street, VANCOUVER V6E 1L4, BC, CANADA.
•OWRAM, Mr. Derek, FCA *1960;* Derek Owram, Meadow Bank, 2 Hall Rise, Bramhope, LEEDS, LS16 9JG.
OWTON, Mrs. Nita Caroline, ACA *1997;* 10 Bentsbrook Park, North Holmwood, DORKING, RH5 4JN.
•OWUSU-ADJEI, Ms. Teresa Sylvia, BSc ACA *2009;* PricewaterhouseCoopers LLP, Hays Galleria, 1 Hays Lane, LONDON, SE1 2RD. See also PricewaterhouseCoopers
OXBERRY, Mrs. Linda Susan, FCA *1979;* Honeywell House, Arlington Business Park, Downshire Way, BRACKNELL, RG12 1EB.
•OXBOROUGH, Mr. Christopher Joshua, BSc FCA *1995;* KPMG LLP, 15 Canada Square, LONDON, E14 5GL. See also KPMG Europe LLP
•OXBY, Mr. Martin Andrew, ACA *2009;* Nene Business Services Limited, Unit 3, Bramley Road, ST. IVES, CAMBRIDGESHIRE, PE27 3WS.
OXENFORTH, Mr. Keith Alan, FCA *1963;* Fernbank, Clay Head Road, Baldrine, ISLE OF MAN, IM4 6DR. (Life Member)
•OXENHAM, Mr. Andrew Charles John, FCA *1974;* (Tax Fac), Andrew Oxenham FCA, Pylewell House, Field Way, Compton Down, WINCHESTER, SO21 2AF. See also Andrew Oxenham
OXENHAM, Miss. Charlotte-Louise Frances Anne, ACA *2008;* Pylewell House, Field Way, Compton, WINCHESTER, HAMPSHIRE, SO21 2AF.
OXER, Mr. Timothy Stephen, BSc ACA *1990;* Suite 1, Castlethorpe Court, Castlethorpe, BRIGG, SOUTH HUMBERSIDE, DN20 9LG.
OXLADE, Dr. David Philip, ACA *2008;* 52 Harrington Close, NEWBURY, RG14 2RQ.
•OXLADE, Ms. Julia Anne, FCA *1985;* Oxlade Limited, The Old Bakehouse, Holton, OXFORD, OX33 1PZ.
OXLADE, Mr. Richard Graham, FCA *1955;* 15 Harriotts Lane, ASHTEAD, KT21 2QG. (Life Member)
•OXLAND, Mr. David Stuart, FCA *1973;* Mellor Oxland LLP, 2 King Street, NOTTINGHAM, NG1 2AS.
OXLEY, Miss. Catherine Louise, ACA *2006;* 24b Mount View Road, LONDON, N4 4HX.
OXLEY, Mr. David Stuart, FCA *1970;* 14 Paddock Wood, HARPENDEN, HERTFORDSHIRE, AL5 1JS. (Life Member)
•OXLEY, Mr. Gary William, BA ACA *1986;* (Tax Fac), Oxley Accountants and Business Advisors Limited, 17 Manor Road, EAST MOLESEY, SURREY, KT8 9JU.
OXLEY, Mr. Julian Christopher, MA FCA *1965;* Forge Cottage, Newbury Road, Shefford Woodlands, HUNGERFORD, BERKSHIRE, RG17 7AG.
•OXLEY, Mr. Leslie Thomas, BA ACA *1992;* (Tax Fac), Oxley Accountants Limited, Top Floor, The Greyhound Building, 17 Moor Street, CHEPSTOW, GWENT NP16 5DB.
OXLEY, Mr. Paul Steven, ACA *1981;* 23 Longley Road, HARROW, HA1 4TG.
OXLEY, Mr. Peter Duncan, LLB ACA *2001;* with Linklaters, 1 Silk Street, LONDON, EC2Y 8HQ.
OXLEY, Mr. Richard, MSc ACA MCT *1988;* Amcor Central Services, 83 Tower Road North Warmley, BRISTOL, BS30 8XP.
OXLEY, Mr. Roland Francis, FCA *1959;* 1 Westway, Pembury, TUNBRIDGE WELLS, TN2 4EX. (Life Member)
•OXLEY, Mr. Stephen Richard, BSc ACA *1996;* KPMG LLP, 15 Canada Square, LONDON, E14 5GL. See also KPMG Europe LLP
•OXLEY, Miss. Tania Karen Vair, BA ACA *1989;* Tania Oxley, 26 York Street, Harborne, BIRMINGHAM, B17 0HG. See also AIMS Tania Oxley
•OXLEY, Mr. William, FCA *1964;* William Oxley, 6 The Mount, Furzeham, BRIXHAM, TQ5 8QY.
OXLEY, Mr. William Henry Malcolm, MA(Hons) ACA *2002;* 13 Greenhill Way, FARNHAM, GU9 8SZ.
OXNAM, Mr. Benjamin James, BSc ACA *2001;* Mail Stop SJCH/2/3, 250 West Tasman Drive, SAN JOSE, CA 95134, UNITED STATES.
OXTOBY, Mrs. Sophie, BA ACA *1994;* Watson Wyatt Westgate, 120-130 Station Road, REDHILL, RH1 1WS.
OYEDIRAN, Mr. Cecil Oyeniyi Olurotimi, BSc FCA *1965;* PO Box 3531, GPO Marina, LAGOS, NIGERIA. (Life Member)
OYELEKE, Mr. Yunus Abioye, FCA *1961;* 1 Waziri Ibrahim Crescent, Victoria Island P.O. Box 52005, Falomo, LAGOS, NIGERIA.
•OYINZE, Mr. Edwin Ihemalolo, FCA *1974;* Edwin Oyinze & Associates, 29 Ogui Road, P.O. Box 2555, ENUGU, NIGERIA.
OYLER, Mr. Edmund John Wilfried, MA LLM MTh FCA *1961;* (Member of Council 1996 - 1999), 20 Bedford Gardens, LONDON, W8 7EH. (Life Member)
OZA, Mr. Nikhil Narendra, ACA *2010;* with Chantrey Vellacott DFK LLP, Russell Square House, 10-12 Russell Square, LONDON, WC1B 5LF.
OZANNE, Mr. Julian Victor, MA ACA *1982;* Black Charles Barn Carters Hill, Underriver, SEVENOAKS, TN15 0RY.
OZCELIK, Mrs. Fatima, BA FCA *2000;* National Audit Office, 157-197 Buckingham Palace Road, LONDON, SW1W 9SP.
•OZDAL, Mr. Ahmet, FCA *1970;* Ahmet Ozdal, 135 Sht Huseyin Amca, Caddesi, Gonyeli, PO Box 478, LEFKOSA MERSIN 10 TURKEY.
OZENBAS, Mr. Erol, BA(Hons) ACA *2010;* Greenacres Farm Billington Road, Stanbridge, LEIGHTON BUZZARD, BEDFORDSHIRE, LU7 9HL.
OZIN, Mr. Stephen Daryl, BSc ACA *1989;* (Tax Fac), Electra Partners Ltd, Paternoster House, 65 St. Paul's Churchyard, LONDON, EC4M 8AB.
OZOLINS, Ms. Zinta, MPhil BSc ACA *1991;* 47 Laurel Avenue, TWICKENHAM, TW1 4HZ.
OZTEN, Mr. Akchay, ACA *1993;* 54 Skeena Hill, LONDON, SW18 5PL.
•OZTOPRAK, Mr. Niyazi Yalchin, ACA *2008;* NYO Limited, Rowlandson House, 289-293 Ballards Lane, LONDON, N12 8NP.
PAANS, Miss. Michelle Merrill, BA ACA *2006;* 8-10 Mangrove Lane, TAREN POINT, NSW 2229, AUSTRALIA.
PABANI, Mr. Akberali Khan, BA ACA *1991;* 3 Somerset Lane, MALVERN, PA 19355, UNITED STATES.
PABANI, Mr. Sadrudin, FCA *1976;* Pabani & Co, 30 Wertheim Court, Suite 14B, RICHMOND HILL L4B 1B9, ON, CANADA.
PABANI, Mrs. Shamim Allahrakhia Jaffer, FCA *1977;* 700 University Avenue, H7J17, TORONTO M5G 1X6, ON, CANADA.
PABARI, Mr. Ajay, BA ACA *1988;* 3 Sherborne Place, NORTHWOOD, HA6 2BH.
PABARI, Mr. Martin Rajesh, BA FCA *1995;* Flat 3, 48 Millbank, LONDON, SW1P 4RL.
PABARI, Mr. Nikesh Vallabhdas, ACA *2009;* Pricewaterhousecoopers The Atrium, 1 Harefield Road, UXBRIDGE, MIDDLESEX, UB8 1EX.
PABARI, Mr. Paresh J, ACA *1983;* 46 Fursby Avenue, LONDON, N3 1PL.
PABARI, Mr. Tushar, BA ACA *2003;* 34 West Avenue, LONDON, N3 1AX.
PACE, Mrs. Jennifer Ann, MA ACA *1992;* Flat 5 Durward House, 31 Kensington Court, LONDON, W8 5BH.
PACE, Mr. John Matthew, BSc(Hons) ACA *2001;* 4 Station Road, Dunton Green, SEVENOAKS, TN13 2XA.
•PACE, Mr. Louis James Colin Gerard, BA FCA *1991;* PC Accountancy Ltd, 3 The Retreat, Glebe Lane, Abberton, COLCHESTER, CO5 7NW. See also Pace Tax Ltd and Pace Accountancy Ltd
•PACE, Mrs. Nicola Margery, FCA *1981;* Josolyne & Co, Silk House, Park Green, MACCLESFIELD, CHESHIRE, SK11 7QW. See also Josolyne Medical Services Ltd
PACE, Miss. Rachel, ACA *2009;* 39 Ayresome Avenue, LEEDS, LS8 1BB.
PACE, Mrs. Susan, BSc ACA *1980;* The Dean & Chapter of York, Church House, 10-14 Ogleforth, YORK, YO1 7JN.
PACE, Mr. Valerio, BEng ACA *1992;* Flat 5 Durward House, 31 Kensington Court, LONDON, W8 5BH.
PACE BONELLO, Mr. Alexander, FCA *1981;* Anglo American Luxembourg Sarl, Boite Postale 185, L-2011 LUXEMBOURG, LUXEMBOURG.
PACE-BONELLO, Mrs. Carole Louise, FCA *1985;* 31 Rue de La Liberte, Helmsange, L-7263 LUXEMBOURG, LUXEMBOURG.
PACEY, Mr. Alan Robert, FCA JDipMA *1971;* 75 Underwood Close, Callow Hill, REDDITCH, WORCESTERSHIRE, B97 5YS.
PACEY, Mr. Colin, PhD BSc ACA *2003;* 35 Wolseley Road, GODALMING, GU7 3EA.
PACEY, Mrs. Jamie-Leigh, ACA *2006;* 51 Boundary Road, NEWARK, NOTTINGHAMSHIRE, NG24 4AJ.
•PACHE, Mr. John Bower, BSc ACA *2003;* (Tax Fac), Barter Durgan, 10 Victoria Road South, SOUTHSEA, PO5 2DA.

PACHOL - PAGE Members - Alphabetical

PACHOL, Mrs. Mandy Louise, BA ACA *1993;* Ramblers Turners Hill Road, Crawley Down, CRAWLEY, RH10 4HA.
PACHOUMI, Ms. Myrto, ACA *2011;* 4A Madritis street, 3096 LIMASSOL, CYPRUS.
PACHTER, Mr. Selwyn Derrick, ACA CA(SA) *2010;* 64 Albury Drive, PINNER, MIDDLESEX, HA5 3RF.
PACIELLO, Ms. Jane Elizabeth, BA ACA *1989;* 6 Oakwood Close, CHISLEHURST, BR7 5DD.
PACIFICO, Mr. Jack Henry, FCA *1966;* Les Faisans, Sornard, 1997 NENDAZ, VALAIS, SWITZERLAND. (Life Member)
PACK, Miss. Anna Elizabeth, BSc ACA *1989;* (Tax Fac), InterContinetal Hotels Group, 1 First Avenue, Centrum One Hundred, BURTON-ON-TRENT, STAFFORDSHIRE, DE14 2WB.
PACK, Mr. Anthony, BSc ACA *2010;* 6a Priory Terrace, LONDON, NW6 4DH.
PACK, Miss. Arabella, BSc(Hons) ACA *2002;* Flat 50 Robin House, Newcourt Street, LONDON, NW8 7AA.
PACK, Miss. Claire Margaret, BSc ACA *2010;* Mauri Products Ltd, Stockholm Road, HULL, HU7 0XW.
PACK, Miss. Emma Jane, BSc ACA *2000;* 11 Clarence Road, HORSHAM, RH13 5SJ.
PACK, Mrs. Janet, MA ACA *1993;* 18 Quarry Hill, HAYWARDS HEATH, RH16 1NQ.
•PACK, Mr. John Walter, BA FCA ATII *1964;* John W. Pack, 3 Leydens Court, Hartfield Road, EDENBRIDGE, KENT, TN8 5NH.
PACK, Miss. Louise Joy, BSc ACA *2005;* 18 Chelwood Grove, Plympton, PLYMOUTH, PL7 2AX.
PACK, Miss. Marie, ACA *2009;* 19 Old School Close, Netley Abbey, SOUTHAMPTON, SO31 5QJ.
PACK, Mr. Michael Anthony, BSc FCA *1978;* Walnut Tree Cottage, Harwood Road, MARLOW, SL7 2AS.
PACK, Mr. Stephen Howard John, MA FCA *1975;* 64 Camlet Way, Hadley Wood, BARNET, EN4 0NX.
PACKARD, Mr. Philip John, BSc(Hons) ACA *2010;* 3B Alderbrook Road, LONDON, SW12 8AF.
PACKE, Mr. Maxwell Gordon, FCA *1967;* Jessamies Barn, Eastleach, CIRENCESTER, GLOUCESTERSHIRE, GL7 3NG.
PACKER, Mrs. Alison Claire, BSc ACA *1993;* 98 Blinco Grove, CAMBRIDGE, CB1 7TS.
•PACKER, Mr. Andrew, ACA *1988;* (Tax Fac), Anser Solutions Limited, Suite 3, Warren House, Main Road, HOCKLEY, ESSEX SS5 4QS. See also Ansers Consulting Limited
PACKER, Mr. Ian, MA FCA *1977;* Baker & Finnemore Ltd, 199 Newhall Street, BIRMINGHAM, B3 1SN.
PACKER, Mr. James Nigel Lewis, FCA CTA TEP *1961;* Green Gables, Leighton Road, Parkgate, NESTON, CH64 3SW.
PACKER, Mr. James Richard, BSc ACA *2004;* 20 Fiddlers Lane, Saughall, CHESTER, CH1 6DH.
PACKER, Mr. William Alfred, FCA *1958;* 505 Williamson Road, GLADWYNE, PA 19035, UNITED STATES. (Life Member)
PACKER, Mr. William Rees, MA FCA *1959;* (Tax Fac), Church Meadow, The Knoll, Alderton, WOODBRIDGE, SUFFOLK, IP12 3BS.
PACKHAM, Mr. Christopher Gordon, FCA *1970;* 182 Station Road, Cropston, LEICESTER, LE7 7HF.
PACKHAM, Mr. Harvey Lawrence, BA ACA *1998;* 7 Methuen Close, BRADFORD-ON-AVON, BA15 1UQ.
PACKHAM, Mrs. Helen Marion, BA ACA *1988;* Long Acre, 3 Ridgeway Road, Long Ashton, BRISTOL, BS41 9EX.
PACKHAM, Miss. Lisa Alaine, ACA *2008;* 58 Charles Knott Gardens, SOUTHAMPTON, SO15 2TG.
PACKHAM, Mr. Nicholas John, FCA *1968;* 107 Parkgate, Upper College Street, NOTTINGHAM, NG1 5AP.
PACKHAM, Mr. Stephen Michael, BSc FCA *1992;* 28 Blakeman Way, LICHFIELD, STAFFORDSHIRE, WS13 8FH.
•PACKMAN, Mr. Andrew, BA ACA *1989;* PricewaterhouseCoopers LLP, The Atrium, 1 Harefield Road, UXBRIDGE, UB8 1EX. See also PricewaterhouseCoopers
•PACKMAN, Mr. Jeremy David, BSc(Econ) FCA *1970;* (Tax Fac), Packman Leslie & Co., Gresham House, 144 High Street, EDGWARE, MIDDLESEX, HA8 7EZ.
PACKMAN, Mr. John Christopher, BSc ACA *1990;* The Hollies, Frogham, FORDINGBRIDGE, SP6 2HN.
PACKMAN, Mr. Martin John, MA FCA *1973;* 14 Fore Street, HATFIELD, HERTFORDSHIRE, AL9 5AH.
PACKWOOD, Mr. James Ralph, FCA *1971;* 7 Rimsdale Close, Gatley, CHEADLE, CHESHIRE, SK8 4LL.
PACKWOOD, Miss. Julia Florence, LLB ACA *2002;* 4a Crescent Road, BROMLEY, BR1 3PW.
PACKWOOD, Mrs. Mellissa, BA ACA *2007;* 3 Oak View, Austins Mead, Bovingdon, HEMEL HEMPSTEAD, HERTFORDSHIRE, HP3 0LH.
PACKWOOD, Miss. Samantha, BSc ACA *2011;* 81 Oak Hill, Wood Street Village, GUILDFORD, GU3 3DA.
•PACTAT, Mr. Matthew Jason, BEng ACA *1993;* AFM, Unit 4 Kernel Court, Walnut Tree Close, GUILDFORD, GU1 4UD.
•PADAMSEY, Mr. Abdulaziz Pyarali, FCA *1979;* (Tax Fac), APP & Co, 7 Merrows Close, NORTHWOOD, MIDDLESEX, HA6 2RT. See also AP & Associates Limited and Padamsey A.P. & Co
PADAYACHEE, Mr. Kevindrin, ACA CA(SA) *2010;* 38B Windermere Avenue, Queens Park, LONDON, NW6 6LN.
PADBURY, Mrs. Angela Jane, BSc(Hons) ACA *2002;* 31 Taw Road, Chivenor, BARNSTAPLE, DEVON, EX31 4BL.
PADBURY, Mr. Kenneth, FCA *1950;* Rose Croft, 11 Hollybush Green, Collingham, WETHERBY, WEST YORKSHIRE, LS22 5BE. (Life Member)
PADBURY, Mr. Nigel Stephen, BA ACA *1979;* 151 Princess Drive, SEAFORD, BN25 2QT.
PADDEN, Mr. Neil Derek, ACA *1982;* 7 Station Road, ESHER, KT10 8DY.
•PADDEN, Mrs. Nicola, BA ACA CTA *2003;* Westbury, 145/157 St John Street, LONDON, EC1V 4PY.
PADDEN, Dr. Nicole, PhD BSc ACA MBA *2011;* Basement Flat, 98 Ifield Road, LONDON, SW10 9AD.
PADDICK, Mrs. Amanda Jane, BSc ACA *2004;* 5 Load Lane, Westonzoyland, BRIDGWATER, SOMERSET, TA7 0LW.
PADDISON, Mr. Henry John, BSc ACA *2009;* 17 Paradise Lane, FLATTS FL04, BERMUDA.
PADDISON, Mr. Jonathan Christopher, FCA *1975;* Timber Cottage, 67 High Street, Wargrave, READING, RG10 8BU.
PADDOCK, Ms. Anita Claire, BA(Hons) ACA *2000;* with Deloitte Touche Tohmatsu, Grosvenor Place, 225 George Street, P.O. Box N 250, SYDNEY, NSW 2000 AUSTRALIA.
PADDOCK, Mr. Dennis James, BA FCA *1972;* 25 St. Ives Road, WALSALL, WS5 3EN. (Life Member)
PADDOCK, Mr. Jonathan Nicholas, ACA *2008;* 25 Bexmore Drive, Streethay, LICHFIELD, STAFFORDSHIRE, WS13 8LB.
PADDOCK, Mr. Keith Thomas, FCA *1970;* 29 Treforest Road, WADEBRIDGE, PL27 7HE. (Life Member)
PADDOCK, Mr. Michael Norman, BA FCA *1972;* 6 Nelson Gardens, Boxgrove, GUILDFORD, GU1 2NZ.
PADFIELD, Mr. Graeme Alan, BA ACA *1989;* Ferromatik Milacron Ltd Klockner House, Carrwood Road, CHESTERFIELD, DERBYSHIRE, S41 9QB.
PADFIELD, Mrs. Joanne, ACA MAAT *1995;* 14 Queen Victoria Road, Totley, SHEFFIELD, S17 4HT.
PADFIELD, Mr. John, BMus ACA *1992;* 28 Moorbridge Close, Netherton, BOOTLE, MERSEYSIDE, L30 7RL.
PADFIELD, Mrs. Laura Joanna, BSc ACA *2003;* Flat A 207 Gloucester Terrace, LONDON, W2 6HX.
PADGET, Mr. Ian David, BSc(Hons) ACA *2000;* Stanley House, Stanley Security Solutions Ltd Stanley House, Bramble Road Techno Trading Estate, SWINDON, SN2 8ER.
•PADGETT, Mr. Christopher Raistrick, FCA *1985;* Watson Buckle LLP, York House, Cottingley Business Park, BRADFORD, BD16 1PE.
PADGETT, Mr. Robert Alan, MA FCA *1968;* 14 Century Court, Montpellier Grove, CHELTENHAM, GLOUCESTERSHIRE, GL50 2XR.
PADGETT, Mr. Stephen John, ACA *1997;* Old Hall Wild Hill Lane, Hunton, BEDALE, NORTH YORKSHIRE, DL8 1QJ.
PADGHAM, Mrs. Michelle Eleanor, BA ACA *2002;* 18 Melbourne Way, Waddington, LINCOLN, LN5 9XJ.
PADHIAR, Mrs. Bansi, BSc ACA *2006;* 34 Donegal Road, SUTTON COLDFIELD, B74 2AA.
PADIDAR, Mr. Abbass, FCA *1974;* Apt 3 Rockhampton, La Route de St. Aubin, St. Helier, JERSEY, JE2 3RY.
PADILLA, Mrs. Renata, BA ACA *2006;* 74 Westerlands, Stapleford, NOTTINGHAM, NG9 7JG.
PADLEY, Mr. Brian Eric, BA ACA *1980;* Chemin des Oiseaux 6B, 1297 FOUNEX, VAUD, SWITZERLAND.
PADLEY, Mr. John, FCA *1969;* 3 The Paddock, Woolley, WAKEFIELD, WF4 2LZ.
PADMANATHAN, Mrs. Cheryl, BSc ACA *1993;* Societe Generale, Level 12, 3 Pacific Place, 1 Queen's Road East, MID LEVELS, HONG KONG SAR.
PADMANATHAN, Mr. Kumaresan, BSc ACA *1988;* Flat 31 Wingfield Court, 4 Newport Avenue, LONDON, E14 2DR.
PADMANATHAN, Miss. Soumitra Pathmaranie, BSc ACA CTA *1992;* 37 Fernihough Close, WEYBRIDGE, SURREY, KT13 0UY.
PADMORE, Mr. Andrew, BSc ACA *2003;* The Poplars, Grange Lane, Alvechurch, BIRMINGHAM, B48 7DJ.
PADMORE, Mrs. Gemma Louise, MEng ACA *2003;* The Poplars Grange Lane, Alvechurch, BIRMINGHAM, B48 7DJ.
PADOL, Miss. Irena Elzbieta, BSc FCA *1982;* (Tax Fac), with BDO LLP, Emerald House, East Street, EPSOM, SURREY, KT17 1HS.
PADOUVA, Miss. Stephanie, ACA *2008;* 15 Michalaki Paridi Street, 3091 LIMASSOL, CYPRUS.
PADOVAN, Mr. John Mario Faskally, LLB BCL FCA *1964;* 15 Lord North Street, LONDON, SW1P 3LD.
PADRINI, Mr. Alberto, MSc ACA *1988;* AP Capital Partners AG, P.O.Box 439, Baarerstrasse 10, 6301 ZUG, SWITZERLAND.
•PADUA, Miss. Elizabeth Ann, BSc FCA *1980;* (Tax Fac), Elizabeth Padua & Co, 21 Bangalore Street, Putney, LONDON, SW15 1QD.
PADWICK, Mr. David Charles, FCA *1975;* with Humphrey & Co, 7-9 The Avenue, EASTBOURNE, EAST SUSSEX, BN21 3YA.
PADWICK, Mr. Henry Arthur, FCA *1967;* 1436 Livingston Road, OAKVILLE L6H 3G4, ON, CANADA. (Life Member)
PAESANO, Mr. Biagio, BSc ACA *2003;* 54 Upton Court Road, SLOUGH, SL3 7LZ.
PAFFARD, Mr. Thomas Edward, ACA *2009;* Pricewaterhousecoopers Llp, 80 Strand, LONDON, WC2R 0AF.
PAGAN, Miss. Clare Noelle, BA ACA *1987;* 56 Minster Court, Hillcrest Road, LONDON, W5 1HH.
PAGAN, Mr. Michael John, MA FCA *1963;* 18143 NE 146th Way, WOODINVILLE, WA 98072, UNITED STATES. (Life Member)
•PAGDEN, Mr. Laurence, BA FCA MIPA FIPA *1990;* Benedict Mackenzie LLP, 62 Wilson Street, LONDON, EC2A 2BU. See also Crouch Chapman
PAGDIN, Mr. John Roy, ACA *2007;* 11 Kingsway Close, CHRISTCHURCH, BH23 2TP.
PAGE, Mr. Adrian Peter, BSc ACA *1990;* The Manor House, 22 Mill Street, Packington, ASHBY-DE-LA-ZOUCH, LEICESTERSHIRE, LE65 1WL.
PAGE, Mr. Alastair, ACA *1996;* 8 Anglesea Terrace, PORT MACQUARIE, NSW 2444, AUSTRALIA.
PAGE, Mrs. Alison Claire, BSc ACA *1996;* 6 Rue des chenes, 34160 BEAULIEU, FRANCE.
PAGE, Mr. Andrew, BA ACA *1982;* The Restaurant Group Plc, Leonard House, 5-7 Marshalsea Road, LONDON, SE1 1EP.
•PAGE, Mr. Andrew, BA FCA *1990;* Moore Stephens, Kings House, 40 Billing Road, NORTHAMPTON, NN1 5BA.
PAGE, Mr. Andrew Christopher, FCA *1977;* 4 Melbourne Street, Pendlebury Swinton, MANCHESTER, M27 8TE.
PAGE, Mr. Andrew Cooper, ACA CTA *1994;* 14 Stanley Gardens, SOUTH CROYDON, SURREY, CR2 9AH.
PAGE, Mr. Andrew John Edward, FCA *1966;* Scoseria 2940 Ap 601, Pocitos, MONTEVIDEO, CP11305, URUGUAY. (Life Member)
PAGE, Mrs. Ann Jane, BSc FCA CTA *1988;* 1 The Ridgeway, MARLOW, BUCKINGHAMSHIRE, SL7 3LQ.
PAGE, Mr. Anthony William, FCA *1961;* Stratford, 31 Spinners Way, MIRFIELD, WEST YORKSHIRE, WF14 8PU. (Life Member)
PAGE, Mr. Antony John, BSc FCA *1979;* A. John Page & Associates Inc., Suite 447 100 Richmond St. West, TORONTO M5H 3K6, ON, CANADA.
•PAGE, Mr. Barry Declan, FCA *1972;* Barry Page & Co, 72 Pentyla Baglan Road, PORT TALBOT, SA12 8AD.
PAGE, Mrs. Carol, BA ACA *1989;* Financial Reporting Council, Aldwych House, 71-91 Aldwych, LONDON, WC2B 4HN.
PAGE, Mrs. Carol-Anne, BA FCA *1991;* 8 Devonshire Drive, ALDERLEY EDGE, CHESHIRE, SK9 7HT.
PAGE, Mrs. Caroline Ann, BA ACA *1987;* Royal Grammar School, High Street, GUILDFORD, GU1 3BB.
PAGE, Miss. Caroline Elizabeth, ACA *2009;* Seefeldstrasse 26, 8008 ZURICH, SWITZERLAND.
PAGE, Miss. Catherine Mary, BSc FCA CTA *1989;* with Barron & Barron, Bathurst House, 86 Micklegate, YORK, YO1 6LQ.
PAGE, Mr. Christopher Hugh, BSc FCA *1978;* Whitefoord Ltd, International House, 66 Chiltern Street, LONDON, W1U 4JT.
PAGE, Mr. Christopher John, BSc FCA *1991;* 2 Fernihough Close, WEYBRIDGE, KT13 0UY.
PAGE, Mr. David Andrew, BSc ACA *1989;* 34 Hitherwood, CRANLEIGH, SURREY, GU6 8BW.
•PAGE, Mr. David Leslie, FCA *1984;* The Ollis Partnership Limited, 2 Hamilton Terrace, Holly Walk, LEAMINGTON SPA, WARWICKSHIRE, CV32 4LY.
PAGE, Mrs. Deborah Helen, MA FCA *1974;* 121 Church Street, SOUTHAMPTON, SO15 5LW.
PAGE, Mr. Dominic Martin Etienne, BSc ACA *1994;* Dixons Stores Group Plc Maylands Avenue, Hemel Hempstead Industrial Estate, HEMEL HEMPSTEAD, HERTFORDSHIRE, HP2 7TG.
PAGE, Mr. Edward Gareth, BSc ACA *1998;* Page & Page Group Limited, Unit 10B, Gothenburg Way, HULL, HU7 0YG.
PAGE, Mr. Edward Hugh, FCA *1962;* Flat 1 Borrowdale, 74 Gores Lane, Formby, LIVERPOOL, MERSEYSIDE, L37 7DF. (Life Member)
PAGE, Miss. Eleanor Charlotte, ACA *2009;* 30 Beechwood Grove, Horbury, WAKEFIELD, WEST YORKSHIRE, WF4 5JQ.
PAGE, Mrs. Emma, BA ACA *1992;* Little Badgers, Possingworth Park, Cross In Hand, HEATHFIELD, TN21 0TN.
PAGE, Mr. Everard Donald Stirling, MA FCA *1969;* 24 Elms Road, LONDON, SW4 9EX.
PAGE, Mrs. Gail Karen, BSc ACA *1995;* 23 Northampton Street, BATH, BA1 2SW.
•PAGE, Mr. Graham David, FCA *1989;* Ensors, Saxon House, Moseleys Farm, Business Centre, Fornham All Saints, BURY ST. EDMUNDS SUFFOLK IP28 6JY.
PAGE, Mr. Graham John, FCA *1971;* 18 Southernhay Road, LEICESTER, LE2 3TJ.
PAGE, Mr. Gregory Paul Richard, FCA *1971;* Excel Couriers, Unit 10, Faraday Way Idustrial Park, Faraday Way, ORPINGTON, KENT BR5 3QW.
PAGE, Miss. Holly Frances, BSc(Hons) ACA *2001;* 181 Franciscan Road, LONDON, SW17 8HP.
PAGE, Mr. James Raymond, FCA *1956;* 19 Margards Lane, VERWOOD, BH31 6JP. (Life Member)
PAGE, Mrs. Joanne Patricia, ACA *1995;* 33 Eresbie Road, LOUTH, LN11 8YG.
PAGE, Mr. John Henry, FCA *1975;* North End Cottage, Naburn, YORK, YO19 4PR.
•PAGE, Mr. John Martin, FCA *1969;* J.M. Page & Co, 14 Tudor Grove, SUTTON COLDFIELD, WEST MIDLANDS, B74 2LL.
PAGE, Mr. John Michael, FCA *1953;* Belcombe House, The Street, Saxlingham Nethergate, NORWICH, NR15 1AJ. (Life Member)
PAGE, Mr. John Richard, BSc ACA *1979;* 2755 West 31st Avenue, VANCOUVER V6L 1Z9, BC, CANADA.
PAGE, Mr. John Ross, FCA *1955;* The Old Armoury, Court Barton, CREWKERNE, TA18 7HP. (Life Member)
PAGE, Mr. John Stanley, BA FCA *1974;* Moor Cottage, East Taphouse, LISKEARD, PL14 4NJ.
PAGE, Mr. John Stewart, FCA *1956;* Langleys, 9 Long Wall, Haddenham, AYLESBURY, HP17 8DL. (Life Member)
PAGE, Mr. Jonathan, BEng ACA *1996;* 16 The Dene, Abinger Hammer, DORKING, RH5 6PX.
PAGE, Mr. Jonathan Richard, BSc ACA *1993;* Swantech Ltd, Breighton Airfield, Bubwith, SELBY, NORTH YORKSHIRE, YO8 6DJ.
•PAGE, Mr. Justin Ralph Simon, ACA *2001;* Justin Page Accountancy, Red Lodge, High Street, High Littleton, BRISTOL, BS39 6HW.
PAGE, Miss. Katherine Ellen, BCom ACA *2002;* 41 Quinton Close, Hatton Park, WARWICK, CV35 7TN.
PAGE, Miss. Kelly Tania, BA(Hons) ACA *2001;* Flat 16 Tideway Court, 238 Rotherhithe Street, LONDON, SE16 5QS.
PAGE, Miss. Kelly-Anne, BSc ACA *2009;* 334 Ipswich Road, COLCHESTER, CO4 0ET.
PAGE, Mr. Kevin William, ACA *1979;* Teknicast Sdn Bhd, Lot 2139 Jalan Enggang, Batu 9 Kebun Baru, Teluk Panglima Garang, 42500 KUALA LANGAT, MALAYSIA.
PAGE, Mr. Lindsay Dennis, MA ACA *1984;* Ted Baker plc, The Ugly Brown Building, 6 St Pancras Way, LONDON, NW1 0TB.
PAGE, Miss. Lucy, BA ACA *2000;* 41 Amesbury Road, CARDIFF, CF23 5DX.
PAGE, Mrs. Marion, BSc FCA *1990;* The Rising, 30 Torkington Road, WILMSLOW, CHESHIRE, SK9 2AE.
PAGE, Mr. Mark, BA ACA *1989;* James Grant Management, 94 Strand on the Green, LONDON, W4 3NN.

Members - Alphabetical

PAGE - PALIN

PAGE, Mr. Martin John, ACA *1983;* Okeover House, 1 Manor Court, Wymeswold, LOUGHBOROUGH, LEICESTERSHIRE, LE12 6SJ.
PAGE, Mr. Martin John, BA ACA *2004;* 19 Milton Avenue, SUTTON, SURREY, SM1 3QB.
PAGE, Miss. Mary Caroline, BA ACA *1994;* 66 Wayland Avenue, BRIGHTON, BN1 5JN.
PAGE, Mr. Matthew James, BSc ACA *1995;* Tall Trees, Ivy House Lane, BERKHAMSTED, HERTFORDSHIRE, HP4 2PP.
PAGE, Mr. Matthew Paul, BSc ACA *2001;* 21 Wynfield Gardens, BIRMINGHAM, B14 6EY.
PAGE, Mr. Michael Anthony, BSc FCA *1981;* The Rising, 30 Torkington Road, WILMSLOW, CHESHIRE, SK9 2AE.
PAGE, Mr. Michael Barrie, MA FCA *1989;* D E Beers UK Ltd, 17 Charterhouse Street, LONDON, EC1N 6RA.
PAGE, Mr. Michael Charles, BSc FCA *1976;* 81 Lansdowne Road, LONDON, W11 2LE. (Life Member)
PAGE, Prof. Michael James, FCA *1974;* Portsmouth Business School, Richmond Building, Portland Street, PORTSMOUTH, HAMPSHIRE, PO1 3DE.
PAGE, Mr. Michael Leslie, MA FCA *1974;* Dixcart Trust Corporation Ltd, Dixcart House, Sir William Place, St Peter Port, GUERNSEY, GY1 4EZ.
PAGE, Mr. Michael Robert, FCA *1965;* Boords Farm, Batcombe, SHEPTON MALLET, BA4 6HD. (Life Member)
PAGE, Mr. Nicholas Hurst, BA FCA *1977;* 7 Ravenslea Road, LONDON, SW12 8SA.
•**PAGE, Mr. Nicholas Robert, BEng FCA** *1994;* PricewaterhouseCoopers LLP, 7 More London Riverside, LONDON, SE1 2RT. See also PricewaterhouseCoopers
•**PAGE, Mr. Nicholas Scott, PhD BSc FCA** *2000;* Grant Thornton UK LLP, The Explorer Building, Fleming Way, Manor Royal, CRAWLEY, WEST SUSSEX RH10 9GT. See also Grant Thornton LLP
PAGE, Mrs. Nina Kathryn Wynne, BA(Hons) ACA *2001;* Johnson Matthey Plc, 25 Farringdon Street, LONDON, EC4A 4AB.
PAGE, Mr. Peter Howard, FCA *1962;* 4 Beck Boulevard PH-2, PENETANGUISHENE L9M 2H3, ON, CANADA. (Life Member)
PAGE, Mrs. Rachel, BSc FCA *1993;* M E P C Ltd Rosewood Crockford Lane, Chineham Business Park Chineham, BASINGSTOKE, HAMPSHIRE, RG24 8UT.
•**PAGE, Mr. Richard John, BA FCA** *1984;* 5 South Dene, Stoke Bishop, BRISTOL, BS9 2BW.
PAGE, Mr. Richard Peter, BA ACA *2002;* 17 Court Gardens, West Bridgford, NOTTINGHAM, NG2 7SN.
PAGE, Mr. Richard Rupert Waddington, BSc FCA *1974;* 20 Oakbrook Court, Graham Road, SHEFFIELD, S10 3HR.
PAGE, Mr. Robert Hoyles, MBA LLB ACA ATII ADIT *1984;* 88 Elmwood Crescent, LUTON, LU2 7HZ.
PAGE, Mr. Robert John, BSc ACA *2010;* 4 Hillside, GRAYS, ESSEX, RM17 5SX.
PAGE, Miss. Sally Jane, ACA *1984;* 58 Westminster Road, YORK, YO30 6LY.
PAGE, Mr. Simon James, BSc ACA *1993;* Little Badgers, Possingworth Park, Cross In Hand, HEATHFIELD, TN21 0TN. (Life Member)
PAGE, Mr. Simon John, BSc ACA *1998;* 69 Highbury New Park, LONDON, N5 2EU.
PAGE, Mr. Simon Terence, BA ACA *2008;* 21 Sandheys Avenue, LIVERPOOL, L22 7RP.
PAGE, Mr. Stephen David, MA FCA *1997;* 45 Jordan Road, SUTTON COLDFIELD, B75 5AD.
•**PAGE, Mr. Stephen Richard, ACA** *1993;* PricewaterhouseCoopers LLP, Cornwall Court, 19 Cornwall Street, BIRMINGHAM, B3 2DT. See also PricewaterhouseCoopers
PAGE, Ms. Suzanna Jayne, ACA *2005;* 9 Burnell Gate, CHELMSFORD, CM1 6ED.
PAGE, Mrs. Tanya Ruth, BSc ACA CTA AMCT *1997;* 24 Mile End Road, NORWICH, NR4 7QY.
PAGE, Mr. Thomas Noel, FCA *1966;* Pond House, Bishops Down Park Road, TUNBRIDGE WELLS, TN4 8XY.
PAGE, Mr. Timothy Guy, BCom FCA *1963;* Twizel, 2 Old Orchard, WILMSLOW, CHESHIRE, SK9 5DH. (Life Member)
PAGE, Colonel Walter Fountain, MC TD FCA *1937;* 29 Three Crowns House, South Quay, KING'S LYNN, PE30 5DT. (Life Member)
PAGE-WOOD, Mr. Marcus Johnn, FCA *1960;* L'Asselinais, 50520 LE MESNIL RAINFRAY, FRANCE. (Life Member)
PAGE-WOOD, Mrs. Patricia Margaret, FCA *1968;* L'Asselinais, 50520 LE MESNIL RAINFRAY, FRANCE.
PAGEL, Ms. Celia Ann, BSc ACA *1985;* Windy Ridge Ladder Hill, Wheatley, OXFORD, OX33 1HY.
PAGELLA, Mr. Maurice Vondy, MA FCA *1970;* (Tax Fac), Woodside House, Park Lane, ASHTEAD, SURREY, KT21 1DW.
PAGET, Mr. Daniel, BSc ACA *2006;* Sunnyside, Broad Street, KINGSWINFORD, WEST MIDLANDS, DY6 9LR.
•**PAGET, Mr. David James, MA FCA** *1974;* Newhaven Cottage, Wellhead Mews, Hall Lane Chapelthorpe, WAKEFIELD, WF4 3JG.
PAGET, Mr. David Vernon John, BA ACA *1986;* Chenies, Liphook Road, Headley, BORDON, GU35 8NF.
PAGET, Mr. Duncan Victor, BA ACA *1993;* Medical Research Council, North Star House, North Star Avenue, Hawksworth Trading Estate, SWINDON, SN2 1FF.
PAGET, Mr. Joseph Alexander, BSc ACA *2004;* Phones 4 U, Phones 4 U House, Ore Close, Lymedale Business Park, NEWCASTLE, STAFFORDSHIRE ST5 9QD.
PAGET, Miss. Lynne Rhonda, LLB ACA *1993;* 10 Allen Circle, BOXFORD, MA 01921, UNITED STATES.
•**PAGET, Mr. Malcolm George, MPhil BA ACA** *1989;* Malcolm Paget Limited, 117 Whitchurch Gardens, EDGWARE, HA8 6PG.
PAGET, Mrs. Susan Pamela, BA ACA *1985;* (Tax Fac), 8 Sherwood Court, Long Whatton, LOUGHBOROUGH, LEICESTERSHIRE, LE12 5DY.
PAGETT, Mr. Michael Dennis, FCA *1979;* The Heyes, Eaton-Upon-Tern, MARKET DRAYTON, TF9 2BX.
PAGLIARINI, Miss. Roberta, BSc ACA *1999;* 17 Carrholm Grove, LEEDS, LS7 2NR.
PAGNIER, Miss. Julie Elizabeth, FCA *1988;* 4 Les Camps Du Moulin, St Martins, GUERNSEY, GY4 6DX.
PAHAL, Mr. Kuljinder, MSc BSc ACA *2010;* 18 Capel Crescent, STANMORE, MIDDLESEX, HA7 4WN.
•**PAHWA, Mr. Sanjiv, BA FCA** *1991;* Citycas Limited, Fifth Floor, Linen Hall, 162-168 Regents Street, LONDON, W1B 5TF.
PAIBA, Mr. Michael David, FCA *1957;* 3 Maya Road, Heath View, LONDON, N2 0PP. (Life Member)
PAICE, Ms. Joanna Ruth Alexandra, BSc ACA *2003;* 18 Bemish Road, LONDON, SW15 1DG.
PAICE, Miss. Sarah Claire, BSc ACA *2008;* Burberry Ltd Horseferry House, Horseferry Road, LONDON, SW1P 2AW.
PAIGE, Mr. David Victor, BA FCA *1975;* Acorn House, 37 Ravenswood Avenue, CROWTHORNE, RG45 6AX.
•**PAIGE, Mr. Michael, FCA** *1982;* (Tax Fac), Michael Paige, Limeshaw, Wappingthorn, STEYNING, BN44 3AB.
•**PAIN, Mr. Guy Nickson, BA FCA CF** *1985;* Cottons Accountants LLP, 338 Stratford Road, Shirley, SOLIHULL, WEST MIDLANDS, B90 3DN.
PAIN, Mr. Ian Richard, BSc ACA *1990;* Westward House Berries Road, Cookham, MAIDENHEAD, BERKSHIRE, SL6 9SD.
PAIN, Mr. John Anthony, BSc ACA *2000;* 21 Brodrick Road, LONDON, SW17 7DX.
PAIN, Mr. John Edward, FCA *1954;* 1 Brightside., FRINTON-ON-SEA, CO13 0UB. (Life Member)
PAIN, Mr. Mark Andrew, BSc FCA *1987;* 38 Cuckoo Hill Road, PINNER, HA5 1AY.
PAIN, Mr. Richard John, MSc ACA *2001;* Hazelside, Mardens Hill, CROWBOROUGH, EAST SUSSEX, TN6 1XW.
PAIN, Mr. Richard John, LLB FCA *1976;* 2 Almeida Street, LONDON, N1 1TA.
•**PAIN, Mr. Robert William, FCA** *1975;* (Tax Fac), R.W. Pain and Co, The Old Post Office, Main Street, Burton Overy, LEICESTER, LE8 9DL.
PAIN, Mr. Simon Charles, BA ACA *1992;* 28th Floor Citibank Building, 25 Canada Square, LONDON, E14 5LQ.
PAIN, Mr. Simon Gerald, FCA *1969;* Avocets, Rock, WADEBRIDGE, CORNWALL, PL27 6LD. (Life Member)
•**PAINE, Mr. Anthony Philip, BEd ACA** *1989;* Chalmers HB Limited, 20 Chamberlain Street, WELLS, BA5 2PF.
PAINE, Miss. Christine Elizabeth, BSc ACA *2005;* 50 Anthony Close, WATFORD, WD19 4NE.
PAINE, Mr. Geoffrey Alan, JP FCA *1960;* (Member of Council 1979 - 1991), 11 Lucerne Road, OXFORD, OX2 7QB.
PAINE, Mr. Nicholas, BSc FCA *1986;* Graff Diamonds Ltd, 28-29 Albemarle Street, LONDON, W1S 4JA.
PAINE, Mr. Robert Nicholas, MA ACA *1982;* 15C Sprott Road, KOHIMARAMA 1071, NEW ZEALAND.
PAINE, Miss. Rosalind, FCA *1976;* 71 Eastern Avenue, PINNER, MIDDLESEX, HA5 1NW.
•**PAINE, Mr. Stephen John, ACA** *1982;* Ingram Micro Asia Pacific PTE. LTD., 260 Orchard Road, #09-01 The Heeren, SINGAPORE 238855, SINGAPORE.
PAINE, Mr. Thomas, BSc ACA *2006;* 37 Middle Street, Brockham, BETCHWORTH, SURREY, RH3 7JT.
PAINE, Mr. William, FCA *1975;* 3 Honeysuckle Close, IVER, BUCKINGHAMSHIRE, SL0 0LZ.
PAINTER, Miss. Claire, BSc ACA *2002;* Flat 274 Building 22, Cadogan Road, LONDON, SE18 6YR.
PAINTER, Mr. Colin John, BSc ACA *1991;* 19 Exbury Way, NUNEATON, WARWICKSHIRE, CV11 4RY.
PAINTER, Mrs. Deborah Jayne, BA ACA *1990;* 60 Kiln Road, FAREHAM, PO16 7UG.
•**PAINTER, Mr. Gordon Samuel, FCA** *1972;* Green Gables, Whitchurch Hill, READING, RG8 7PG.
PAINTER, Miss. Heather, BA ACA *2004;* 1 Scott Street, MAIDSTONE, ME14 2TA.
•**PAINTER, Mr. Howard Noel, BSc FCA** *1977;* Howard Painter & Company Ltd, 26 Sansome Walk, WORCESTER, WR1 1LX. See also Sargent Services LLP
•**PAINTER, Mr. Iain Anderson, FCA** *1980;* (Tax Fac), Caerwyn Jones, Emstrey House, Shrewsbury Business Park, SHREWSBURY, SY2 6LG.
PAINTER, Mr. John, BA(Hons) ACA *2003;* 1 Wing Close, MARLOW, BUCKINGHAMSHIRE, SL7 2RA.
•**PAINTER, Mr. John Harvey, BA FCA** *1981;* Crowther Beard LLP, Suite 1A, Shire Business Park, Wainwright Road, WORCESTER, WORCESTERSHIRE WR4 9FA.
PAINTER, Mrs. Julie Ann, ACA *1991;* The Cottage, Two Dells Lane, Ashley Green, CHESHAM, HP5 3RB.
PAINTER, Mrs. Nicola Careen, MBA BA ACA *1992;* 48b Arbor Lane, Winnersh, WOKINGHAM, BERKSHIRE, RG41 5JD.
PAINTER, Mr. Paul Anthony, BEng ACA *1995;* Zaun Ltd, Steel Drive, WOLVERHAMPTON, WV10 9ED.
PAINTER, Mr. Richard James, BA ACA *1979;* Redgate Hall, Redgate Bank, Wolsingham, BISHOP AUCKLAND, COUNTY DURHAM, DL13 3HH.
PAINTER, Mrs. Ruth, FCA *1966;* 17 Deepslade Close, Southgate, SWANSEA, SA3 2DQ.
PAINTER, Mr. William Mark David, BSc ACA *2007;* 2 Moss Rise, LEEDS, LS17 7NX.
PAINTER GANDHI, Mrs. Sakina, BSc(Econ) ACA *1999;* with Deloitte LLP, Hill House, 1 Little New Street, LONDON, EC4A 3TR.
PAINTING, Ms. Laura Lynn, ACA *2005;* 111 Archery Grove, Woolston, SOUTHAMPTON, SO19 9ET.
•**PAINTING, Mr. Robert Philip, BSc FCA** *1978;* SC2000 Limited, 5 Boultbee Road, SUTTON COLDFIELD, B72 1DW. See also RP Painting
PAINTON, Mr. Peter Henry, BSc FCA *1973;* 19 Bushwood Road, Kew, RICHMOND, TW9 3BG.
PAISH, Miss. Claire Emma, ACA *2008;* 4 Doncaster Close, CHIPPENHAM, SN14 0XT.
•**PAISLEY, Mr. Allen Gerald, BA FCA** *1976;* Deloitte LLP, Hill House, 1 Little New Street, LONDON, EC4A 3TR. See also Deloitte & Touche LLP
PAISLEY, Mr. Howard James, ACA *2008;* 1 Priory New Road, CORSHAM, WILTSHIRE, SN13 0AZ.
PAISLEY, Mrs. Ruth Mary, BSc ACA *1990;* Shard House, Old Bridge Lane, Hambleton, POULTON-LE-FYLDE, LANCASHIRE, FY6 9BT.
PAIZES, Ms. Chelane, ACA CA(SA) *2008;* 9 Sunnymead, Tyler Hill, CANTERBURY, CT2 9NW.
PAK, Mr. Chi Hoi Dick, ACA *2008;* Deloitte Touche Tohmatsu, 35/F One Pacific Place, 88 Queensway, CENTRAL, HONG KONG ISLAND, HONG KONG SAR.
PAK, Miss. Pui Man, ACA *2011;* Flat A, 21/F Block 4, Elegance Garden, TAI PO, HONG KONG SAR.
PAKEMAN, Mr. Gordon Howard, FCA *1957;* Red Roofs, 22 Druid Road, Stoke Bishop, BRISTOL, BS9 1LH. (Life Member)
PAKENHAM, Mr. Robin Thomas Cliff, BSc ACA CF *1990;* Frithsden End, Frithsden, BERKHAMSTED, HERTFORDSHIRE, HP4 1NW.
PAKENHAM-WALSH, Mr. John Elliott, BSc FCA *1987;* Hampshire Trust Plc, 69 High Street, FAREHAM, PO16 7BB.
PAKES, Mr. Philip John, BSc ACA *1992;* 3A Tower 1, Harbour Green, 8 Sham Mong Road, TAI KOK TSUI, KOWLOON, HONG KONG SAR.
PAKKALA, Mrs. Terhi, MA BA ACA *2005;* Naissaarenkuja 3 D 7, 02480 KIRKKONUMMI, FINLAND.
PAKSHONG, Mr. Michael Wong, BA FCA *1959;* 12 Swiss Club Road, SINGAPORE 288105, SINGAPORE. (Life Member)
PAL, Miss. Anindita, MSc BSc ACA *2005;* Flat 74 Wheel House, 1 Burrells Wharf Square, LONDON, E14 3TB.
PAL, Mr. Prosanto Ramon, FCA *1964;* 31 Bis Rue Guilleminot, 92370 CHAVILLE, FRANCE.
PAL, Mr. Tarun, ACA ACMA *1994;* A-18 Nizamuddin West, First Floor, NEW DELHI 110013, DELHI, INDIA.
PALA, Mrs. Hasmita, BSc ACA *2004;* 18 Heath Green Way, COVENTRY, CV4 8GU.
PALADINA, Mr. Nicholas, BA FCA *1989;* 14 Hurst Rise Road, OXFORD, OX2 9HQ.
PALAK, Mr. Andrzej Marek, BSc FCA *1976;* Apt. 733, 860 Midridge Drive, CALGARY T2X 1K1, AB, CANADA.
PALAN, Mr. Nilesh Vithaldas, BSc ACA *1986;* 48 Westwood Avenue, HARROW, MIDDLESEX, HA2 8NS.
PALAN, Mr. Nitin Ratilal, FCA *1977;* 9 Manor House Drive, LONDON, NW6 7DE.
PALAU, Mr. Giles William Maxwell, ACA *2009;* with PricewaterhouseCoopers, Avenida Francisco Matarazzo 1400, Torre Torino, Agua Branca, SAO PAULO, 05001-903 BRAZIL.
PALCHAUDHURI, Mr. Ajay Kumar, FCA *1965;* Palchaudhuri House, 1 Palchaudhuri Street, PO Ranaghat, DIST NADIA 741201, INDIA. (Life Member)
PALEJOWSKA, Mrs. Julia Clare, BA ACA *1992;* Brasenose College, Radcliffe Square, OXFORD, OX1 4AJ.
•**PALER, Mrs. Lesley Anne, BSc ACA** *1987;* (Tax Fac), Moore Stephens (Guildford) LLP, Priory House, Pilgrims Court, Sydenham Road, GUILDFORD, SURREY GU1 3RX. See also Moore Stephens LLP
PALER, Mr. Simon Edward, BA(Hons) FCA ATII AMCT *1989;* 174 Stephens Road, TUNBRIDGE WELLS, TN4 9QE.
PALESCHI, Miss. Emma Alice, BA ACA *2005;* 20D Chepstow Crescent, LONDON, W11 3EB.
PALETHORP, Mr. Ian, BA ACA *1979;* (Tax Fac), 36 St. John's Road, Hampton Wick, KINGSTON-UPON-THAMES, KT1 4AN.
•**PALETHORPE, Mrs. Elizabeth Anne, BSc FCA** *1980;* (Tax Fac), Elizabeth Palethorpe, 4 Chanters Hill, BARNSTAPLE, DEVON, EX32 8DQ.
PALETHORPE, Mrs. Fiona, BA ACA *1992;* 19a Cotterstock Road, Oundle, PETERBOROUGH, PE8 5HA.
PALETHORPE, Mr. Mark John, BA FCA *1990;* 19a Cotterstock Road, Oundle, PETERBOROUGH, PE8 5HA.
•**PALEY, Mr. Christopher Timothy Geofrey John Philip, BSc FCA** *1976;* 11a Icehouse Wood, OXTED, RH8 9DN.
PALEY, Mr. Simon Richard, LLB ACA *1995;* 128 Redditch Road, Kings Norton, BIRMINGHAM, B38 8RD.
PALFRAMAN, Mr. Keith Richard, BSc ACA *1993;* Nottingham County Council, Trent Bridge House, West Bridgford, NOTTINGHAM, NG2 7QZ.
PALFREMAN, Mrs. Karen Lindsay, ACA *1994;* Centrica SHB Ltd, South Humber Bank Power Station, South Marsh Road, Stallingborough, GRIMSBY, SOUTH HUMBERSIDE DN41 8BZ.
PALFREMAN, Mr. Stephen Hugh, BA FCA *1967;* 4 Loudhams Road, AMERSHAM, HP7 9NY. (Life Member)
PALFREY, Mr. Andrew, MChem ACA *2011;* 11 Gilstrap Road, Fornham St. Martin, BURY ST. EDMUNDS, SUFFOLK, IP31 1TD.
PALFREY, Mr. Andrew Robert, BSc ACA *1993;* 11 Lillian Road, LONDON, SW13 9JG.
PALFREY, Mr. David Gwyn, FCA *1966;* Bay Horse Cottage, 19 Main Street, Ebberston, SCARBOROUGH, YO13 9NR. (Life Member)
•ⓘ**PALFREY, Mr. Gregory Andrew, BSc ACA** *1991;* Smith & Williamson Ltd, Imperial House, 18-21 Kings Park Road, SOUTHAMPTON, HAMPSHIRE, SO15 2AT.
PALFREY, Mr. Mark Jonathan, BSc ACA *1995;* 1604 Winding Drive, NORTH WALES, PA 19454-3625, UNITED STATES.
•**PALFREYMAN, Mr. Donald Edward, FCA** *1964;* (Tax Fac), D.E. Palfreyman, 176 Leach Green Lane, Rednal, BIRMINGHAM, B45 8EH.
PALFREYMAN, Mr. Jonathan Reid, FCA *1975;* 10 Church Walk, Lubenham, MARKET HARBOROUGH, LE16 9TA.
•**PALFREYMAN, Mr. Philip Richard Arthur, FCA** *1977;* P.R.A Palfreyman, 83 Nottingham Road, Codnor, RIPLEY, DE5 9RH.
PALICICA, Mr. Victor Patrick, BSc ACA *2011;* 79 Padstow Avenue, Fishermead, MILTON KEYNES, MK6 2ER.
PALIM, Mr. Ralph Godfrey, FCA *1956;* AV.Gen. Dossin De, St Georges 3, B-1050 BRUSSELS, BELGIUM. (Life Member)
PALIN, Mr. Arthur, FCA *1961;* 2 Jericho Court, Jericho Close, LIVERPOOL, L17 5AY. (Life Member)
PALIN, Mr. Derek, FCA *1977;* 1 Bertha Road, ROCHDALE, OL16 5BE.
•**PALIN, Mr. John Huw, BA ACA** *1989;* BPU Limited, Radnor House, Greenwood Close, Cardiff Gate Business Park, CARDIFF, CF23 8AA.

PALIN, Mr. Michael John, FCA *1958;* Regal Villa, Monument Gardens, St. Peter Port, GUERNSEY, GY1 1UL.
PALIN, Mr. Nicholas John, BA FCA *1985;* Forum of Private Business, Ruskin Chambers, Drury Lane, KNUTSFORD, CHESHIRE, WA16 6H9.
PALING, Mr. Richard John, BSc ACA *1995;* The Farmhouse, 5 Riverlands Close, Gunthorpe, NOTTINGHAM, NG14 7GA.
•PALIWAL, Mr. Ajay, BEng ACA *1994;* Jiva Capital Limited, 9 Crondal Place, Edgbaston, BIRMINGHAM, B15 2LB.
PALIWAL, Miss. Sonja, BA ACA *2007;* 294 Rue St Paul Ouest, Apt. 41, MONTREAL H2Y 2A3, QC, CANADA.
PALK, Mr. Carl Steven, ACA *1987;* 64 Deanery Close, East Finchley, LONDON, N2 8NT.
PALK, Mr. Harold Rupert Lawrence, BA FCA *1951;* 16 Newtown, BEAMINSTER, DT8 3EW. (Life Member)
PALK, Mr. Kenneth Leonard, FCA *1947;* The Outlook, Eype Road, BRIDPORT, DT6 5LA. (Life Member)
•PALK, Mr. Robert John, BSc(Hons) ACA *2002;* Nero Accounting Limited, Crows Nest Business Park, Ashton Road, Billinge, WIGAN, LANCASHIRE WN5 7XX.
•PALLACE, Mrs. Janet Elizabeth, FCA *1982;* (Tax Fac), J.E. Pallace, 19 Private Road, ENFIELD, EN1 2EH.
PALLANT, Mr. Ivan Stanley, BSc ACA *1980;* D J Evans (Bury) Ltd, St. Botolphs Lane, BURY ST. EDMUNDS, SUFFOLK, IP33 2AU.
PALLATT, Mr. Thomas William, ACA *2003;* 40 Station Road, Earl Shilton, LEICESTER, LE9 7GA.
PALLATT, Mrs. Tracey Ann, ACA *2008;* 40 Station Road, Earl Shilton, LEICESTER, LE9 7GA.
PALLESCHI, Mr. Dominic, FCA *1988;* Arriva Plc, 1 Admiral Way, Doxford International Business Park, SUNDERLAND, SR3 3XP.
PALLESCHI, Mrs. Emma, FCA *1991;* (Tax Fac), 2 Holdernesse, Wynyard Woods, Wynyard, BILLINGHAM, CLEVELAND, TS22 5RY.
•PALLETT, Mr. Darren Simon, BA FCA *1991;* Highclere, 15 Wisdom Drive, HERTFORD, SG13 7RF.
PALLETT, Mr. James, BA(Hons) ACA *2011;* 26a Sandmere Road, LONDON, SW4 7QJ.
PALLETT, Miss. Josephine Alicia, BA(Hons) ACA *2001;* Trinity Cottage, Hanley Road, MALVERN, WORCESTERSHIRE, WR14 4HZ.
•PALLETT, Mr. Phillip Robinson, FCA *1975;* PKF (UK) LLP, Farringdon Place, 20 Farringdon Road, LONDON, EC1M 3AP.
PALLETT, Mr. Simon David, MA ACA *1979;* 15 Crossway, Jesmond, NEWCASTLE UPON TYNE, NE2 3QH.
PALLIKAROPOULOS, Mr. Panos, BSc ACA *2005;* Flat 2, Westside, 55 Priory Road, LONDON, NW6 3NG.
PALLIN, Farrer Jonathan Paul Lascelles, Esq OBE MBA FCA *1968;* rua dona mara 154, vila de são fernando, COTIA, 06706-901, BRAZIL.
PALLISER, Miss. Amy Elizabeth, BSc(Hons) ACA *2011;* with Hardcastle France, 30 Yorkersgate, MALTON, YO17 7AW.
PALLISTER, Mr. Benjamin Joshua, BSc ACA *2004;* 60 Wolsey Drive, KINGSTON UPON THAMES, KT2 5DN.
PALLISTER, Mr. Calum Thomas William, BA(Hons) ACA *2001;* 3 Ciss Lane, Urmston, MANCHESTER, M41 9AG.
PALLISTER, Mr. Nicholas Hugh Alexander, FCA *1968;* 25 King Edgar Close, ELY, CAMBRIDGESHIRE, CB6 1DP.
PALLISTER, Mr. Richard Lorne, BSc ACA *1995;* (Tax Fac), with PricewaterhouseCoopers LLP, 31 Great George Street, BRISTOL, BS1 5QD.
PALLOT, Mr. Ian David Glen, ACA *1979;* PO Box 4066, DURBANVILLE, 7551, SOUTH AFRICA.
PALLOT, Mr. Michael Gerard, FCA *1974;* Gatewood, Wembury, PLYMOUTH, PL9 0DZ.
PALLOT, Mrs. Sarah Karina Margaret, BA ACA *1995;* 1 Melbourne Park Estate, St. John, JERSEY, JE3 4EQ.
PALLOT, Mr. Timothy John Robert, BA(Hons) ACA *2000;* Group Finance Legal & General, One Coleman Street, LONDON, EC2R 5AA.
PALMER, Mr. Adam, ACA *2010;* 4 Birch Avenue, Beeston, NOTTINGHAM, NG9 1LL.
PALMER, Mr. Adrian Michael, MBA BEng ACA *1993;* 4 Queen Street, TRING, HERTFORDSHIRE, HP23 6BQ.
PALMER, Mr. Adrian Russell, BEng ACA CF *1997;* Fielden villa, 18 Roughdown Road, HEMEL HEMPSTEAD, HERTFORDSHIRE, HP3 9AX.
PALMER, Mr. Alan Henry, FCA *1967;* 130 Kennet Street, Wapping, LONDON, E1W 2JJ.
•PALMER, Mr. Alan William Francis, FCA *1959;* 77 Folly Road, Mildenhall, BURY ST. EDMUNDS, SUFFOLK, IP28 7BX.
PALMER, Mrs. Alison Elaine, BSc FCA *1986;* with PricewaterhouseCoopers LLP, 10-18 Union Street, LONDON, SE1 1SZ.
•PALMER, Miss. Alison Irene, FCA *1986;* McGills, Oakley House, Tetbury Road, CIRENCESTER, GL7 1US.
PALMER, Ms. Amanda Ann, BA ACA *1991;* 63 Heath Road, WIDNES, CHESHIRE, WA8 7NU.
PALMER, Mr. Andrew Douglas, BA ACA *2008;* Flat 1 Lowry House, Cassilis Road, LONDON, E14 9LL.
•PALMER, Mr. Andrew Russell, MA ACA *1983;* PricewaterhouseCoopers LLP, Pricewaterhousecoopers, 12 Plumtree Court, LONDON, EC4A 4HT. See also PricewaterhouseCoopers
PALMER, Mr. Andrew William, FCA *1977;* Fathing Street Farm, Fathing Street, Downe, ORPINGTON, BR6 7JB.
PALMER, Miss. Anne Elizabeth, BA ACA *1987;* Hall House, The Street, Crudwell, MALMESBURY, SN16 9ET.
PALMER, Mr. Anthony Noel, FCA *1953;* 1 Richmond Close, EPSOM, SURREY, KT18 5EY. (Life Member)
PALMER, Mr. Anthony Stephen, BA ACA *1984;* 10 Partridge Close, CHESHAM, BUCKINGHAMSHIRE, HP5 3LH.
PALMER, Mrs. Antje, ACA *2000;* with PricewaterhouseCoopers LLP, 1 Embankment Place, LONDON, WC2N 6RH.
•PALMER, Mrs. Balvinder, BSc ACA *1996;* Rouse Partners LLP, 55 Station Road, BEACONSFIELD, BUCKINGHAMSHIRE, HP9 1QL. See also Rouse Audit LLP
PALMER, Mr. Barrie Richard, FCA *1968;* 8 Mountnessing Lane, Doddinghurst, BRENTWOOD, Essex, CM15 0TS.
PALMER, Mr. Barry Raymond, FCA *1974;* 12 St Johns Road, Petts Wood, ORPINGTON, BR5 1HX.
PALMER, Mr. Benjamin Kirk, BSc ACA *1995;* Electronic Arts, Place du Molard8, 1204 GENEVA, SWITZERLAND.
PALMER, Mr. Christopher James, BSocSc ACA *2003;* 13 Crossfield Road, LONDON, NW3 4NS.
•PALMER, Mr. Christopher Michael John, BA ACA *1994;* (Tax Fac), Palmers, 28 Chipstead Station Parade, Chipstead, COULSDON, SURREY, CR5 3TF.
•PALMER, Miss. Claire Alison, BSc FCA CF *1999;* Littlejohn LLP, 1 Westferry Circus, Canary Wharf, LONDON, E14 4HD.
PALMER, Miss. Clare, BSc ACA *2005;* 176A Nelson Road, Crouch End, LONDON, N8 9RN.
PALMER, Mr. Colin Roderick, BSc FCA *1969;* 37 Westland Road, Kirk Ella, HULL, HU10 7PH.
PALMER, Mr. Craig, BEng ACA *2010;* 44 Cissbury Ring, PETERBOROUGH, PE4 6QJ.
PALMER, Mr. Dan, BSc ACA *2001;* 10 Berwick Grove, SWORDS, COUNTY DUBLIN, IRELAND.
PALMER, Mr. Daniel Garvey, BSc ACA *1991;* Braeside The Warren, East Horsley, LEATHERHEAD, KT24 5RH.
•PALMER, Mr. Daniel James, BA ACA *2004;* Nunn Hayward, Sterling House, 20 Station Road, GERRARDS CROSS, SL9 8EL.
PALMER, Mr. Daniel Lee, MA BSc ACA *2011;* Flat 202, Idaho Building, Deals Gateway, LONDON, SE13 7QG.
PALMER, Ms. Danielle, BA ACA *2011;* Basement Flat, 44 Oval Road, CROYDON, CR0 6BJ.
PALMER, Mrs. Danielle, BSc ACA *2007;* with John Laing plc, Allington House, 150 Victoria Street, LONDON, SW1E 5LB.
PALMER, Mr. David, MBA BSc ACA *1978;* Guggenbuehl 11, 5306 TEGERFELDEN, SWITZERLAND.
PALMER, The Revd. David Andrew Patrick, BA FCA CTA MCIPD *1979;* 20 Brooke Road, KENILWORTH, CV8 2BD.
PALMER, Mr. David Nigel, ACA *1983;* George Street Clothing Ltd, Grove House, Lanthwaite Road, Clifton, NOTTINGHAM, NG11 8LD.
PALMER, Mr. David Nigel, FCA *1977;* Pulham Maltings House, Station Road, Pulham St Mary, DISS, IP21 4QT.
PALMER, Mr. David Thor, BSc ACA *1993;* Bradfield College Enterprises, Bradfield College, Bradfield, READING, BERKSHIRE, RG7 6AU.
PALMER, Mr. Donald Angus, BA BSc FCA *1964;* 9 Summerhouse Close, GODALMING, GU7 1PZ. (Life Member)
PALMER, Mr. Douglas John, FCA *1972;* Thorpe House, Dodsley Grove, Easebourne, MIDHURST, GU29 9AB. (Life Member)
PALMER, Mr. Edward Bennet, MA FCA *1955;* 6 Silver Street, MALMESBURY, WILTSHIRE, SN16 9BU. (Life Member)
PALMER, Mrs. Elizabeth, BBA ACA *2006;* 394 Buckfield Road, LEOMINSTER, HEREFORDSHIRE, HR6 8SD.
PALMER, Mr. Emlyn Adekunle, ACA *1996;* Strathmore Capital Portland House, Bressenden Place, LONDON, SW1E 5BH.
PALMER, Mr. Gareth John, BSc ACA *2005;* 10 Crescent Gardens, LONDON, SW19 8AJ.
PALMER, Mr. Garth Mervyn, ACA CA(AUS) *2011;* 47 Charles Street, LONDON, W1J 5EL.
PALMER, Mrs. Gemma Louise, ACA *2011;* 11 St. Andrews Close, HASLEMERE, SURREY, GU27 2FE.
PALMER, Mr. George, ACA *2011;* 64 Trinity Church Square, LONDON, SE1 4HT.
PALMER, Mr. George Ivor, FCA *1968;* George Palmer, 53 Marlin Drive, WONGA BEACH, QLD 4873, AUSTRALIA.
PALMER, Mr. Giles John, BSc ACA *1996;* Brandwatch, 68 Middle Street, BRIGHTON, BN1 1AL.
PALMER, Miss. Gillian Margaret, BA FCA *1992;* 1 Post House Lane, Bookham, LEATHERHEAD, KT23 3EA.
PALMER, Mr. Glyn John, BA FCA *1983;* 48 Darnick Road, SUTTON COLDFIELD, B73 6PF.
PALMER, Mr. Graham Frederick Boyd, BA ACA *2006;* GECC (Funding) Ltd, 30 Berkeley Square, LONDON, W1J 6EX.
PALMER, Miss. Hanna, ACA *2010;* 38 Roxholme Avenue, LEEDS, LS7 4JF.
•PALMER, Mrs. Helen Elizabeth, BA ACA *1984;* AIMS Helen Palmer, 22 Croftdown Road, BIRMINGHAM, B17 8RB.
PALMER, Mr. Howard Charles, BSc FCA *1972;* Woodland, Springbank Avenue, HORNSEA, HU18 1ED.
•PALMER, Mr. Ian Richard, MEng ACA *2001;* Elman Wall Limited, 5-7 John Princes Street, LONDON, W1G 0JN.
PALMER, Mr. Ian Robert, FCA *1987;* The Malt Barn Marton Road, Birdingbury, RUGBY, CV23 8EH.
•PALMER, Mr. Ivor Patrick, FCA *1993;* Palmer, 64 Northbourne Avenue, Northbourne, BOURNEMOUTH, BH10 6DQ.
PALMER, Mr. James Hedley, BSc ACA *1994;* Hallett Retail Ltd, 26a Church Lane, LONDON, N2 8DT.
PALMER, Mr. James Richard, BSc ACA *1994;* 25 Percy Crescent, CHAPMAN, ACT 2611, AUSTRALIA.
•PALMER, Mr. James Roderick, FCA *1959;* J R Palmer, 16 The Crescent, Colwall, MALVERN, WR13 6QN.
PALMER, Mr. James William, MEng BA ACA *2000;* Flat 10, Osprey House, 5 Victory Place, LONDON, E14 8BG.
•PALMER, Mrs. Jane Ingrid, BSc FCA *1980;* Jane Palmer, 18 Exeter Drive, Haughton Grange, DARLINGTON, DL1 2SE.
PALMER, Miss. Jennifer Sara, BSc ACA *2010;* (Tax Fac), Grant Thornton Churchill House, Chalvey Road East, SLOUGH, SL1 2LS.
PALMER, Mr. Jeremy, ACA *1981;* (Tax Fac), Stowe House, Fleet Hill, Finchampstead, WOKINGHAM, RG40 4LJ.
PALMER, Mrs. Jill Susan, BSc ACA *1992;* (Tax Fac), 3 I Group, 16 Palace Street, LONDON, SW1E 5JD.
PALMER, Miss. Joanne Claire, BSc FCA *1999;* 54A Alfred Road, CLAREMONT, WA 6010, AUSTRALIA.
PALMER, Miss. Joanne Denise, BA(Hons) ACA *2002;* Kilima Farm, Main Dereham Road, Colkirk, FAKENHAM, NR21 7JG.
PALMER, Mr. John Albert, FCA *1964;* 36 Bradmore Way, Brookmans Park, HATFIELD, AL9 7QX. (Life Member)
PALMER, Mr. John Brian, FCA *1956;* Flat 4, Rustlings Mews, Catherington Lane, Horndean, WATERLOOVILLE, HAMPSHIRE PO8 9GU. (Life Member)
PALMER, Mr. John Brian, BSc(Econ)Hons ACA *1980;* 26 Chesterfield Road, Downend, BRISTOL, BS16 5RQ.
•PALMER, Mr. John Frederick, FCA *1980;* (Tax Fac), Richard Place Palmer, 52a Carfax, HORSHAM, WEST SUSSEX, RH12 1EQ.
PALMER, Mr. John Michael, BA FCA *1983;* 178 Banbury Road, STRATFORD-UPON-AVON, WARWICKSHIRE, CV37 7HX.
PALMER, Mrs. Judith, ACA *1981;* Doctors Surgery, 165-167 Woodbridge Road, IPSWICH, IP4 2PE.
PALMER, Mr. Julian Galsworthy, BA ACA *1995;* Beech Farm House, Roundstreet Common, Wisborough Green, BILLINGSHURST, WEST SUSSEX, RH14 0AN.
PALMER, Ms. Julie Marie, BSc ACA *1997;* 4 Golwg Yr Afon, Pontarddulais, SWANSEA, SA4 1XS.
PALMER, Mr. Keith, FCA *1955;* 3 St Johns Avenue, Warley, BRENTWOOD, Essex, CM14 5DF. (Life Member)
PALMER, Mr. Keith, FCA *1966;* 79 Upperwood Road, Darfield, BARNSLEY, S73 9RQ. (Life Member)
PALMER, Mr. Keith, MBA FCA CA(AUS) *1987;* Tractiv Group Ltd, Unit 316, Hartlebury Trading Estate, Hartlebury, KIDDERMINSTER, WORCESTERSHIRE DY10 4JB.
PALMER, Mrs. Kelly-Anne, BSc(Hons) ACA *2010;* 1 Bree Hill, South Woodham Ferrers, CHELMSFORD, CM3 7AD.
•PALMER, Mr. Lee Jonathan, BA(Hons) FCA CTA *2000;* (Tax Fac), Wenn Townsend, 30 St Giles', OXFORD, OX1 3LE. See also Wenn Townsend Accountants Limited
PALMER, Miss. Lisa Michelle, BSc FCA *2000;* 5 Brockway Road, Mount Claremont, PERTH, WA 6010, AUSTRALIA.
PALMER, Miss. Lorna, BSc ACA *2007;* 16c Marlborough Road, LONDON, W4 4ET.
PALMER, Mrs. Louise, BA(Hons) ACA *2001;* 12 The Pinfold, Glapwell, CHESTERFIELD, DERBYSHIRE, S44 5PU.
•PALMER, Mrs. Lynda Ann, ACA *1995;* Palmer Accounting Services, Lincoln House, 21 Dunstable Street, Ampthill, BEDFORD, BEDFORDSHIRE MK45 2NJ.
•PALMER, Mr. Malcolm Calvin, FCA *1991;* A4G LLP, Kings Lodge, London Road, West Kingsdown, SEVENOAKS, KENT TN15 6AR. See also Hill Stephen Limited
PALMER, Mr. Mark John, BSc FCA *1991;* Finance & ICT, The Moray Council Office, High Street, ELGIN, MORAYSHIRE, IV30 1BX.
•PALMER, Mr. Mark William, BSc ACA *1995;* Cottons Accountants LLP, The Stables, Church Walk, DAVENTRY, NORTHAMPTONSHIRE, NN11 4BL.
PALMER, Mr. Martin Garratt, BSc FCA *1974;* with PricewaterhouseCoopers LLP, 10-18 Union Street, LONDON, SE1 1SZ.
PALMER, Mr. Martin James, LLB ACA *2003;* 109 Maitland Street, DUNEDIN 9016, NEW ZEALAND.
PALMER, Mr. Mathew, BA ACA *2006;* OSTC Ltd, Imperial House, 21-25 North Street, BROMLEY, BR1 1SD.
PALMER, Mr. Matthew Edward, LLB ACA *2003;* Homes & Communities Agency St. Georges House, Kingsway Team Valley Trading Estate, GATESHEAD, TYNE AND WEAR, NE11 0NA.
PALMER, Mr. Max David, FCA *1963;* 7 Creskeld Garth, Bramhope, LEEDS, LS16 9EW. (Life Member)
PALMER, Mr. Michael Jeremy, FCA *1965;* 2 Fullers Wood, Shirley Woods, CROYDON, CR0 8HZ.
•PALMER, Mr. Michael John, FCA *1967;* The Gallagher Partnership LLP, PO Box 698, 2nd Floor, Titchfield House, 69/85 Tabernacle Street, LONDON EC2A 4RR.
•PALMER, Michael John, Esq MBE FCA *1960;* The Deerings, Southerns Lane, Chipstead, COULSDON, SURREY, CR5 3SN.
•PALMER, Mr. Michael John, BSc ACA *1988;* Intega Ltd, 106 Mill Studio, WARE, HERTFORDSHIRE, SG12 9PY.
PALMER, Lord Monroe Edward, OBE FCA *1963;* Lord Palmer of Childshill, House of Lords, Houses of Parliament, LONDON, SW1A 0PW. (Life Member)
•PALMER, Mr. Neil James, MA FCA *1997;* with KPMG LLP, 15 Canada Square, LONDON, E14 5GL.
PALMER, Miss. Nicola Anne, ACA *2010;* Pearson Shared Services Ltd Shell Mex House, 80 Strand, LONDON, WC2R 0RL.
PALMER, Mr. Nigel Anthony Frederick, BA FCA *1977;* Compass Group Plc Compass House, Guildford Street, CHERTSEY, KT16 9BQ.
PALMER, Mr. Patrick John, BA FCA *1979;* Advantage West Midlands, 3 Priestley Wharf, Holt Street, Aston Science Park, BIRMINGHAM, B7 4BN.
•PALMER, Mr. Peter Edward, BCom FCA *1972;* Hilltop Farm, Asenby, THIRSK, NORTH YORKSHIRE, YO7 3QN.
PALMER, Mr. Peter Frederick, FCA *1949;* Petley Lodge, Whatlington, BATTLE, TN33 0ND. (Life Member)
PALMER, Mrs. Rachael Louise, ACA *2008;* 50 Plantation Road, AMERSHAM, BUCKINGHAMSHIRE, HP6 6HL.
PALMER, Lord Ralph Matthew, BA FCA *1976;* House Of Lords, LONDON, SW1A 0PW.
PALMER, Mrs. Rebecca Elizabeth, MA BA(Hons) ACA *2008;* BDO, Governors Square, PO Box 31118, GEORGE TOWN, GRAND CAYMAN, KY1 1205 CAYMAN ISLANDS.
PALMER, Richard Augustus, Esq OBE TD DL MA FCA *1937;* Brenda Lodge, 19a The Avenue, Dallington, NORTHAMPTON, NN5 7AJ. (Life Member)
PALMER, Mr. Richard John, BSc ACA *2001;* 19 Gore Road Burnham, SLOUGH, SL1 8AB.
PALMER, Mr. Richard Keith, BSc ACA *1992;* 1000 Chrysler Drive, AUBURN HILLS, MI 48326, UNITED STATES.

PALMER, Mr. Richard Neil, BA FCA *1984;* (Tax Fac), Grant Thornton UK Llp Grant Thornton House, 22 Melton Street, LONDON, NW1 2EP.

PALMER, Mr. Robert Douglas, ACA *2010;* Merrilyns, Oakhill Avenue, PINNER, MIDDLESEX, HA5 3DN.

PALMER, Mr. Robert John Samuel, FCA *1974;* 5 Belton Close, Hockley Heath, SOLIHULL, B94 6QU.

PALMER, Mr. Robert Michael, BA ACA *1992;* 5 Millers Mead, COLCHESTER, CO5 9SS.

PALMER, Mr. Robert Michael, MA ACA *1992;* 17 Park Avenue, SOLIHULL, B91 3EJ.

•ⒹPALMER, Mr. Robert Stephen, FCA *1979;* (Tax Fac), The Gallagher Partnership LLP, PO Box 698, 2nd Floor, Titchfield House, 69/85 Tabernacle Street, LONDON EC2A 4RR.

•PALMER, Mr. Robin George, BA FCA *1983;* (Tax Fac), PricewaterhouseCoopers LLP, Hays Galleria, 1 Hays Lane, LONDON, SE1 2RD. See also PricewaterhouseCoopers

•PALMER, Mr. Rowan John, BA ACA *1984;* Chapman Davis LLP, 2 Chapel Court, LONDON, SE1 1HH.

PALMER, Mrs. Sally Victoria Louise, ACA *2008;* 1 Cooper Barns, Camel Street Marston Magna, YEOVIL, SOMERSET, BA22 8DB.

PALMER, Miss. Sarah Margaret, BSc ACA *1992;* 25C Ashley Road, LONDON, N19 3AG.

PALMER, Dr. Simon James, BSc ACA *2002;* 21 The Barton, COBHAM, KT11 2NJ.

•PALMER, Mr. Simon Ramsay, BSocSc ACA *1990;* Armstrong Watson, Central House, 47 St Pauls Street, LEEDS, LS1 2TE.

•PALMER, Mr. Simon Robin, BSc ACA *1987;* (Tax Fac), KPMG LLP, 15 Canada Square, LONDON, E14 5GL. See also KPMG Europe LLP

PALMER, Mr. Stephen Brian, BA ACA *1995;* 79a Lynmouth Crescent, Furzton, MILTON KEYNES, MK4 1JP.

PALMER, Mr. Stephen Frank, BA ACA *1984;* with Deloitte, 560 rue de Neudorf, L2220 LUXEMBOURG, LUXEMBOURG.

PALMER, Mr. Stephen John, BSc FCA *1977;* Barnstaple House, Bungay Road, Poringland, NORWICH, NR14 7NA.

PALMER, Mr. Stephen John, BSc FCA *1990;* 6 Elm Bank Mansions, The Terrace, Barnes, LONDON, SW13 0NS.

PALMER, Mr. Steven Mark, BSc FCA *1984;* Nettlecombe, Pyle Hill, Mayford, WOKING, SURREY, GU22 0SR.

PALMER, Mr. Stuart George, BSc ACA *1983;* 6 Pembroke Vale, Clifton, BRISTOL, BS8 3DN.

PALMER, Mr. Stuart Ian, BA(Hons) ACA *2002;* Milner, 78 Northshore Road, DEVONSHIRE DV 05, BERMUDA.

PALMER, Miss. Suzanne Jane, BSc(Hons) ACA *2010;* Flat 50 The Eye, Barrier Road, CHATHAM, ME4 4SD.

PALMER, Mrs. Tamsin, BSc ACA *2006;* 55 Sherland Road, TWICKENHAM, TW1 4HB.

PALMER, Miss. Tanya Jaqueline, BA ACA *1992;* Corelogic Ltd Suncourt House, 18-26 Essex Road, LONDON, N1 8LN.

PALMER, Mr. Thomas Stapleton, BSc FCA *1969;* Albury House, Berry Lane, East Hanney, WANTAGE, OX12 0JB. (Life Member)

•PALMER, Mr. Warren Julian, ACA *1981;* W.J. Palmer & Co., 21 Jesmond Way, STANMORE, MIDDLESEX, HA7 4QR. See also London Financial & Management Services Limited

PALMER, Mr. William Charles Davy, BA ACA *1986;* 74 Bobbin Head Road, TURRAMURRA, NSW 2074, AUSTRALIA.

PALMER, Miss. Yvonne Valerie, BSc FCA *1974;* 13 Lodge End, RADLETT, WD7 7EB.

PALMER-ANTUNES, Mrs. Joyce Mendes, ACA *2009;* 2 Fairlawn Wharf, East St. Helen Street, ABINGDON, OXFORDSHIRE, OX14 5ED.

PALMER-JONES, Mrs. Karen Barbara, BSc(Hons) ACA CTA *1990;* British Petroleum Co Plc, 20 Canada Square, LONDON, E14 5NJ.

PALMER-MORGAN, Miss. Tanya, BA(Hons) ACA *2007;* 37 Redwood Close, WATFORD, WD19 6HQ.

PALMIER, Mr. Alexander Percival, LLB FCA *1957;* 75 Beddington Gardens, CARSHALTON, SM5 3HL. (Life Member)

PALOTAI, Mrs. Angela Rosemary, BA ACA *1992;* 26A Trinity Road, CHELMSFORD, CM2 6HR.

PALPHRAMAND, Mrs. Julia Helen, BSc ACA *2003;* 19 Crafts Way, SOUTHWELL, NOTTINGHAMSHIRE, NG25 0BL.

PALTA, Mr. Ashwin, ACA *2009;* Flat 401, 4th Floor, Jewel Building, Reclamation, Behind Lilavati Hospital, Bandra (West) MUMBAI 400050 MAHARASHTRA INDIA.

PALTA, Mr. Mukesh, FCA *1975;* Flat 3D Belmont, 18/2 Alipore Road, KOLKATA 700027, WEST BENGAL, INDIA. (Life Member)

PALTAYIAN, Mr. Nassos, BA ACA *2009;* 1 Ezekia Papaioannou Street, Melinda Court, Flat 51, 1075 NICOSIA, CYPRUS.

PALUBICKI, Miss. Janette Eileen, LLB FCA CFE *1986;* 20 Topiary Gardens, Locks Heath, SOUTHAMPTON, SO31 6RX.

PALUCH, Mr. Timothy, ACA *2008;* 86 Apartments La Charroterie Mills, La Charroterie St. Peter Port, GUERNSEY, GY1 1DR.

PAMELY, Mr. Philip, BSc ACA *1984;* 11 Pages Croft, WOKINGHAM, RG40 2HN.

PAMMA, Mrs. Lauren, BSc(Hons) ACA *2004;* 74 Brown Street, ALTRINCHAM, CHESHIRE, WA14 2ET.

PAMMENT, Mrs. Louise Mary, BA ACA *1992;* 66 Meadowside, Tilehurst, READING, RG31 5QE.

PAMPEL, Mr. Norman Nathan, FCA *1951;* 53 Edmunds Walk, LONDON, N2 0HU. (Life Member)

PAMPHILON, Mr. Ross Alger, BSc ACA *1995;* European Credit Management, 34 Grosvenor Street, LONDON, W1K 4QU.

PAMPHLETT, Mr. David, MA FCA *1973;* Stroheckgasse 12/12, 1090 VIENNA, AUSTRIA.

PAMPHLETT, Mr. Martin, ACA *2010;* Gregor-Mendel Strasse, 12-14/Stg.4/9, 1180 VIENNA, AUSTRIA.

PAMPLIN, Mr. Neil Charles, BA ACA *1992;* (Tax Fac), 1 Coulter Mews, BILLERICAY, CM11 1LN.

PAN, Mr. Leonard Ming Yan, ACA *2009;* Apartment 28 E, 25 Conduit Road, Mid-Levels, CENTRAL, HONG KONG SAR.

PAN, Mr. Wei James, FCA CPA *1972;* 38 Liberta Ct, DANVILLE, CA 94526, UNITED STATES.

PAN, Ms. Yan, ACA *2011;* Room 309, 39F, Office Tower A, Beijing Fortune Plaza, 7 No. Dongsanhuan Zhong Road, Chaoyand District BEIJING CHINA.

PAN, Mr. Yu Lei, ACA *2007;* No. 2088, Leman Lake, Hou Sha Yu, Bai Xing Zhuang, Shunyi District, BEIJING 101300 CHINA.

PAN YAN, Miss. Christel, ACA *2010;* Flat 1 Yarra House, 33 Beaconsfield Road, ST. ALBANS, HERTFORDSHIRE, AL1 3RG.

PAN YAN, Miss. Jennifer Niat Lyn, BSc ACA *2003;* c/o FIL Limited, Pembroke Hall, 42 Crow Lane, HAMILTON HM19, BERMUDA.

PANAGI, Miss. Melina, BA ACA *2006;* 16 Rigainis Street, Flat 201, 2nd floor, 2114 NICOSIA, CYPRUS.

PANAGIDES, Miss. Thecla, BCom ACA *1997;* 27 Tycehurst Hill, LOUGHTON, IG10 1BX.

PANAITE, Mr. Vlad, ACA *2002;* Flat B64, The Ropeworks, 35 Little Peter Street, MANCHESTER, M15 4QJ.

PANAYI, Mr. Alekos, BSc ACA *1993;* 50 Roxborough Park, HARROW, MIDDLESEX, HA1 3AY.

PANAYI, Mrs. Doulla, ACA *1991;* 6 Belmont Avenue, BARNET, EN4 9LJ.

PANAYI, Mr. James Andrew, BA(Hons) ACA *2011;* 24 Elvington Close, BILLINGHAM, CLEVELAND, TS23 3YS.

PANAYI, Mr. Panayiotis, ACA *2011;* 8 Panayioti Marinou, CY5510 FAMAGUSTA, CYPRUS.

PANAYI, Miss. Silia, BSc ACA *2010;* 12 Vrisidos Street, LIMASSOL, CYPRUS.

PANAYI, Mrs. Valentina, BSc ACA *2002;* 5 Katinas Paxinou Street, Kato Polemidia, 4154 LIMASSOL, CYPRUS.

PANAYIDES, Miss. Alexandra Joanna, BA ACA *2008;* P.O. Box 54682, 3726 LIMASSOL, CYPRUS.

PANAYIDES, Mr. Constantinos, BSc(Hons) ACA *2001;* 12 Lefkonos Street, Aglantzia, 2122 NICOSIA, CYPRUS.

PANAYIDES, Mr. Efstratios Herodotos, BA ACA *1988;* POBox 25252, Lefkosia, CY-1308 NICOSIA, CYPRUS.

PANAYIDES, Mr. George, BA ACA *2004;* 17 Charalambou Mouskou Street, Kontovathkia, 4001 LIMASSOL, CYPRUS.

PANAYIDES, Mr. George Andrea, BSc ACA *1999;* 4 OTHON STR., PALLOURIOTISSA, 1040 NICOSIA, CYPRUS.

PANAYIDES, Mr. Marios, BSocSc ACA *1997;* 13 Pnytagoras Street, 2406 NICOSIA, CYPRUS.

PANAYIDES, Mr. Stavros, BSc ACA *2004;* TRITONOS 12 STROVOLOS, 2039 NICOSIA, CYPRUS.

•PANAYIDOU, Ms. Christiana, BSc(Hons) FCA *2000;* Ernst & Young, 11 klm National Road, Athens-Lamia, PC 14451 METAMORFOSIS, GREECE. See also Ernst & Young Europe LLP

PANAYIDOU, Miss. Maria Constantinou, BSc ACA *1979;* 41 Kountourioti Street, Strovolos, 2045 NICOSIA, CYPRUS. (Life Member)

PANAYIOTIDES, Mr. George, ACA *2001;* 3 Marinou Geroulanou Street, 3077 LIMASSOL, CYPRUS.

PANAYIOTIDES, Mr. Lambros, BA ACA *1984;* 26 Byron Street, PO Box 24616, 1301 NICOSIA, CYPRUS.

•PANAYIOTOU, Mr. Angelos, BSocSc ACA *2000;* A & L Audit Services Ltd, Checknet House, 153 East Barnet Road, BARNET, HERTFORDSHIRE, EN4 8QZ. See also A&L

PANAYIOTOU, Mr. Charalambos Papanicola, BSc ACA *1996;* 12A Simou Menardou Str, 8010 PAPHOS, CYPRUS.

PANAYIOTOU, Miss. Eftychia, MSc BSc ACA *2010;* 24 Natara Street, Mesa Yitonia, 4007 LIMASSOL, CYPRUS.

PANAYIOTOU, Miss. Elena, BSc ACA *2007;* 80 Makarios III Avenue, 2643 Ergates, NICOSIA, CYPRUS.

•PANAYIOTOU, Mr. George, FCA *1980;* George Panayiotou FCA, Corner 25th March Avenue, & Mystra Street, Papapetrou Building, Office 101 1st Floor, Egomi 2408 NICOSIA CYPRUS.

PANAYIOTOU, Mr. Georgios, BA ACA *1996;* 38 Cromwell Avenue, BROMLEY, BR2 9AQ.

PANAYIOTOU, Miss. Maria, MSc BSc ACA *2010;* 13 Narkissou Street, Strovolos, 2045 NICOSIA, CYPRUS.

PANAYIOTOU, Mr. Marios Yiannaki, BA(Econ) ACA *2003;* 88A Kamelias Street, Ekali, 3110 LIMASSOL, CYPRUS.

PANAYIOTOU, Mr. Panayiotis, ACA *1986;* Panayiotou Kittos Soteriou & Co, 68 Spyrou Kyprianou Av, Nicolaides Shopping City, Joanna Ct 2nd FL, PO Box 42529, 6500 LARNACA CYPRUS.

PANAYIOTOU, Mr. Panayiotis, BA FCA *1985;* 40 Ocean Drive, Sentosa Cove, SENTOSA 098360, SINGAPORE.

PANAYIOTOU, Mr. Stratos, BA BSc ACA ACCA *2005;* with KPMG, PO Box 50161, 3601 LIMASSOL, CYPRUS.

PANCHAL, Mr. Bharat Thakorbhai, ACA *1986;* Hurst Morris Associates Ltd, Enterprise House, 5 Telford Close, AYLESBURY, BUCKINGHAMSHIRE, HP19 8DZ.

PANCHAL, Mr. Mahesh, BSc ACA *1990;* E.on UK plc, Westwood Way, Westwood Business Park, COVENTRY, CV4 8LG.

PANCHAL, Mr. Neekesh, MEng ACA *2009;* 1st Floor Flat, 45 Woodlawn Road, LONDON, SW6 6NQ.

PANCHAL, Mr. Rahul, ACA BEng(Hons) *2010;* 19 Cherrycroft Gardens, Westfield Park, PINNER, MIDDLESEX, HA5 4JU.

PANCHOLI, Mr. Sandeep, BA ACA *1990;* 23 Heybridge Road, Humberstone Park, LEICESTER, LE5 OAP.

PANCHOLI-MOORE, Mrs. Smita, BSc ACA *1992;* 62 Soar Road, Quorn, LOUGHBOROUGH, LEICESTERSHIRE, LE12 8BW.

•PANCZAK, Mr. Eric John, MA ACA *1979;* Balvaird Consulting Services, Meadowview, Westbrook, Boxford, NEWBURY, BERKSHIRE RG20 8DJ.

•PANDAY, Mr. Ramiyar Jehangir, FCA *1982;* Eurorevision, Pez Volador 32, 28007 MADRID, SPAIN.

PANDE, Mr. Neil David, MA FCA *1999;* 47 Meridian Place, LONDON, E14 9FE.

PANDE, Mr. Niraj, ACA *1994;* 1003 MARATHON OMEGA 10TH FLOOR, NEXT TO PHOENIX TOWERS, SENAPATI BAPAT MARG LOWER PAREL (WEST), MUMBAI 400013, MAHARASHTRA, INDIA.

PANDELIDIS, Mr. John Rene, MA FCA *1992;* Syngrou Avenue 194, Kallithea, ATHENS, GREECE.

•PANDEY, Mr. Daleep, BSc ACA ATII *1989;* (Tax Fac), Pandey & Co Limited, Cambridge House, 32 Padwell Road, SOUTHAMPTON, SO14 6QZ. See also Accounting Innovations Limited

PANDEY, Mr. Narendra Kumar, ACA *1979;* 3 The Cygnets, STAINES, TW18 2JF.

•PANDIAN, Mr. Mohan David Koilpillai, BA FCA *1986;* 30 Woodland Rise, GREENFORD, MIDDLESEX, UB6 0RD.

PANDIT, Mr. Arvind Jivanlal, MBA FCA *1975;* 33 Oakvale, West End, SOUTHAMPTON, SO30 3SE.

PANDITHARATNA, Mr. Nugegoda Gabadage Pablis, BSc FCA *1957;* 47 Galle Face Terrace, 3 COLOMBO, SRI LANKA. (Life Member)

PANDJI, Miss. Angelika, ACA *2009;* Flat 76, Marathon House, 200 Marylebone Road, LONDON, NW1 5PL.

PANDOR, Mr. Akber, BSc ACA *1985;* 20 Stafford Court, Kensington High Street, LONDON, W8 7DJ.

PANDYA, Miss. Amee, ACA *2011;* 11 Shaftesbury Avenue, SOUTHALL, MIDDLESEX, UB2 4HQ.

PANDYA, Mr. Balram Bhagwanji, BA FCA *1960;* Flat No 606, Supath Nr Vijay Char Rasta, Navrangpura, AHMEDABAD 380 009, INDIA. (Life Member)

PANDYA, Mr. Bhavik, ACA *2009;* 324 Thorold Road, ILFORD, ESSEX, IG1 4HD.

PANDYA, Miss. Bhavini, ACA *2010;* with PricewaterhouseCoopers LLP, 1 Embankment Place, LONDON, WC2N 6RH.

•PANDYA, Mr. Dhananjay Ramanlal, FCA *1975;* (Tax Fac), D.R. Pandya, Porch House, Little Raveley, HUNTINGDON, PE28 2NQ.

PANDYA, Mr. Dipak Champaklal, ACA *1984;* 37 Lammas Drive, BRAINTREE, ESSEX, CM7 3LJ.

PANDYA, Mr. Hemal, ACA *2011;* 3 Pavilion Way, RUISLIP, MIDDLESEX, HA4 9JR.

•PANDYA, Mr. Kishor Kantilal, FCA *1982;* Clarke & Co, Acorn House, 33 Churchfield Road, Acton, LONDON, W3 6AY. See also Datacount Limited

•PANDYA, Mr. Manoj Vinayak, FCA *1981;* (Tax Fac), Newmans, Jubilee House, Merrion Avenue, STANMORE, MIDDLESEX, HA7 4RY.

•PANDYA, Mr. Milan, BSc ACA *1999;* (Tax Fac), Blick Rothenberg, 12 York Gate, Regent's Park, LONDON, NW1 4QS.

•PANDYA, Mr. Mitul Pankaj, BSc ACA *2007;* JP Money Ltd, Premier House, 112 Station Road, EDGWARE, MIDDLESEX, HA8 7BJ.

•PANDYA, Mr. Mukesh Kumar Natverlal, FCA *1977;* 309 E.Paces Ferry Rd N.E., ATLANTA, GA 30305-2377, UNITED STATES.

PANDYA, Mr. Nilesh Kundanlal, BA ACA *1996;* Seletar, Loudhams Wood Lane, CHALFONT ST. GILES, BUCKINGHAMSHIRE, HP8 4AP.

PANDYA, Miss. Priya, ACA *2008;* 9 Middle Mead Court, Standens Barn, NORTHAMPTON, NN3 9TE.

PANDYA, Mr. Rajiv Kishor, BSc(Hons) ACA *2010;* Jalian, 10 St. Marys Avenue South, Norwood Green, SOUTHALL, MIDDLESEX, UB2 4LS.

PANDYA, Miss. Rakhee, BSc ACA *2010;* 115 Beechwood Gardens, ILFORD, ESSEX, IG5 0AQ.

PANDYA, Mr. Sangiv, BSc ACA *2007;* 9 Middle Mead Court, NORTHAMPTON, NN3 9TE.

PANDYA, Miss. Seema, BA ACA *2000;* Flat 2, Queens Court, West End Lane, West Hampstead, LONDON, NW6 1UT.

PANEK, Mrs. Linda Joy, ACA *1985;* 1a Norfolk Way, Moorgate, ROTHERHAM, SOUTH YORKSHIRE, S60 3BS.

PANES, Mr. Nicholas George, FCA *1973;* The Laurels4 Hook Hill, Sanderstead SOUTH CROYDON, Surrey, CR2 0LA.

PANES, Mr. Richard Elton, BSc ACA *1992;* Airsprung Beds Ltd, Canal Road, TROWBRIDGE, BA14 8RQ.

PANES, Miss. Tracey, BSc ACA *1993;* 26 Yale Court, Honeybourne Road, West Hampstead, LONDON, NW6 1JG.

PANESAR, Mr. Balwinder Singh, BEng ACA *1991;* Hidd Power Company, PO Box 50710, HIDD, BAHRAIN.

PANESAR, Miss. Lara, ACA *2008;* 12 Station Terrace, Twyford, READING, RG10 9NE.

PANESAR, Mr. Mandeep, BSc ACA CTA *2006;* Lion Capital Ltd, 21-24 Grosvenor Place, LONDON, SW1X 7HF.

PANESAR, Mr. Raminderpal Singh, MA(Oxon) ACA *1989;* Mullions, West End Lane, Stoke Poges, SLOUGH, SL2 4ND.

PANG, Mr. Adolf Man-Yin, MSc BA FCA *1994;* 21A Smith Court, 83 Smithfield, KENNEDY TOWN, HONG KONG ISLAND, HONG KONG SAR.

PANG, Mr. Allen Yuk Leung, BA ACA FHKICPA *1984;* 22/F. Block 36, Baguio Villas, 550 Victoria Road, POK FU LAM, HONG KONG ISLAND, HONG KONG SAR.

PANG, Miss. Ann On Chee, BSc ACA *1994;* 51 Bras Basah Road, #07-03 Plaza by the Park, SINGAPORE 189554, SINGAPORE.

PANG, Miss. Hengyan, ACA *2011;* 103 Grove Road, MITCHAM, SURREY, CR4 1AE.

PANG, Mr. Henry, MA ACA *1993;* 11 Godolphin House, 76 Fellows Road, LONDON, NW3 3LG.

PANG, Mr. Ho Choi Robin, ACA *2008;* Robin Pang & Co, 2/F, Xiu Ping Comm. Bldg, 104 Jervois Street, SHEUNG WAN, HONG KONG SAR.

PANG, Mr. Hok Tung, BSc(Econ) ACA *2000;* Flat 3, 1 John Street, LONDON, WC1N 2ES.

PANG, Mr. Hon Chung, ACA *2007;* 3/F Malaysia Building, 50 Gloucester Road, WAN CHAI, HONG KONG ISLAND, HONG KONG SAR.

PANG, Mr. Joseph Cho Hung, FCA *1980;* 16A Dorset Road, Northbridge, SYDNEY, NSW 2063, AUSTRALIA.

PANG, Mr. Kan Chiu, BSc ACA *1995;* 127A, Fanling Village, FANLING, NEW TERRITORIES, HONG KONG SAR.

PANG, Ms. Lai Ping, ACA *2007;* 199 Covepark Place NE, CALGARY T3K 6A1, AB, CANADA.

PANG, Mr. Man Chung Patrick, ACA *2010;* Flat B 2/F, No.7 Caperidge Drive, Peninsula Village, Discovery Bay, LANTAU ISLAND, HONG KONG SAR.

•PANG, Mr. Michael Lik Thien, BA ACA *1993;* (Tax Fac), Panaco International Limited, First Floor, 27 Gloucester Place, LONDON, W1U 8HU. See also Accelsior Limited

PANG, Ms. Oy Yen, LLB ACA *2011;* 6 Hannah Mary Way, LONDON, SE1 5QG.
PANG, Mr. Pak Lok, FCA *1982;* Ernst & Young, 2nd FloorBangunan Sabah Bank, Jalan Utara 91000 TAWAU, Sabah, MALAYSIA.
PANG, Miss. Priscilla Wai-Man, BSc FCA *1995;* 28 Tin Hau Temple Road, c-10\F, CAUSEWAY BAY, Hong Kong Island, HONG KONG SAR.
PANG, Ms. Sau Yee, ACA *2008;* Smart Fortune Services Ltd, Room 1109 11/F, 118 Connaught Road West, SAI YING POON, HONG KONG ISLAND, HONG KONG SAR.
PANG, Ms. Sin Mei Ada, ACA *2007;* Flat F 12th Floor, Ko Fung Court Harbour Heights, 5 Fook Yum Road, NORTH POINT, HONG KONG SAR.
PANG, Mr. Siu Kai, ACA *2005;* Flat 413, 4/F, Block B, Kornhill, QUARRY BAY, HONG KONG SAR.
PANG, Mr. Stuart, ACA *2008;* 10 Osborne Road, BUCKHURST HILL, ESSEX, IG9 5RR.
PANG, Miss. Su, BSc ACA *2006;* 200 The Mall, HARROW, MIDDLESEX, HA3 9TT.
PANG, Mr. Tak Kuen, ACA *2009;* 49F The Lee Gardens, 33 Hysan Avenue, CAUSEWAY BAY, HONG KONG SAR.
PANG, Mr. Tatman Dustine, BSc FCA *1993;* 4 Halcyon Avenue, WAHROONGA, NSW 2076, AUSTRALIA.
PANG, Mr. Tze Fung, ACA *2008;* (Tax Fac), Deloitte & Touche Hill House, 1 Little New Street, LONDON, EC4A 3TR.
PANG, Mr. Tze Fai, ACA *2007;* Flat B 27/F Tower 1, Lake Silver, Ma On Shan, SHA TIN, NEW TERRITORIES, HONG KONG SAR.
PANG, Mrs. Wai Yee, ACA *1982;* 100 Andrew Circle, MEDIA, PA 19063, UNITED STATES.
PANG, Mr. Wai Hang, ACA *2008;* Flat F 9/F, Tower 7 Laguna Verde, HUNG HOM, KOWLOON, HONG KONG SAR.
PANG, Mr. Wan Kee Stephen, MA MSc ACA *2002;* with Capita Group Plc, 71 Victoria Street, LONDON, SW1H 0XA.
PANG, Mr. Wing Kuen, ACA *2005;* Flat 15 10/F, Fung Chuen Court, DIAMOND HILL, KOWLOON, HONG KONG SAR.
PANG, Ms. Yuk Fong, ACA *2007;* Y.F.Pang & Co, Unit 1801-2, 18/F Jubilee Centre, 46 Gloucester Road, WAN CHAI, HONG KONG SAR.
•PANGBOURNE, Mr. David Geoffrey, FCA *1963;* D.G. Pangbourne, High Trees, Gustard Wood, Wheathampstead, ST. ALBANS, HERTFORDSHIRE AL4 8RP.
PANGBOURNE, Mr. John Richard, FCA *1960;* Overmonnow House, St. Thomas Square, MONMOUTH, GWENT, NP25 5ES. (Life Member)
•PANGBOURNE, Mr. Rodney Bryan, FCA *1966;* (Tax Fac), Rodney Pangbourne, 33 Pennal Grove, Ingleby Barwick, STOCKTON-ON-TEES, CLEVELAND, TS17 5HP.
PANGBOURNE, Miss. Sara, LLB ACA *2004;* with Deloitte LLP, Stonecutter Court, 1 Stonecutter Street, LONDON, EC4A 4TR.
PANGBURN, Miss. Lesley Elaine, MA FCA CTA *1991;* (Tax Fac), with Kay Johnson Gee, Griffin Court, 201 Chapel Street, MANCHESTER, M3 5EQ.
PANICAN, Ms. Ioana Raluca, ACA *2011;* 36 Byng Street, LONDON, E14 8LP.
PANIKKER, Mr. Prakash, BSc ACA *2003;* 94 Parkfield Avenue, HARROW, HA2 6NP.
PANJA, Mrs. Anita, BSc ACA *1998;* 64 The Mall, LONDON, N14 6LN.
PANJA, Mr. Sayantan, MA ACA *2002;* 135 Shirley Drive, HOVE, EAST SUSSEX, BN3 6UJ.
•PANKHANIA, Miss. Alka, BA(Hons) ACA *2002;* 34 St. Thomas Drive, PINNER, MIDDLESEX, HA5 4SS.
PANKHANIA, Mr. Jayesh, BSc FCA *1995;* 20 Wilmington Avenue, Chiswick, LONDON, W4 3HA.
PANKHANIA, Mr. Jaysel Kanti, BSc ACA *2011;* 35 Great North Road, Stanborough, WELWYN GARDEN CITY, HERTFORDSHIRE, AL8 7TJ.
PANKHANIA, Mr. Pritesh Murji, BA ACA *1995;* 14 Cedar Walk, Kingswood, TADWORTH, KT20 6HW.
PANKHURST, Mrs. Andrea Elizabeth, BSc ACA *1993;* 9 Sough Lane, Wirksworth, MATLOCK, DERBYSHIRE, DE4 4FQ.
PANKHURST, Mr. David Trevor Richard, BSc FCA *1993;* 9 Sough Lane, Wirksworth, MATLOCK, DERBYSHIRE, DE4 4FQ.
PANKHURST, Miss. Margaret Jane, MA FCA *1991;* 76 Church Crescent, LONDON, N10 3NE.
PANNELL, Miss. Cara Louise, BA ACA *2007;* 44a Squirrels Heath Lane, HORNCHURCH, ESSEX, RM11 2EA.
PANNELL, Mr. Jeremy William, ACA *2009;* with Target Consulting Limited, Lawrence House, Lower Bristol Road, BATH, BA2 9ET.
PANNELL, Mrs. Karen Michelle, BSc ACA *1997;* Deerhurst, Todenham, MORETON-IN-MARSH, GL56 9NY.
PANNETT, Mrs. Jacqueline Ann, BCom ACA *2000;* 6 Limmers Mead, Great Kingshill, HIGH WYCOMBE, BUCKINGHAMSHIRE, HP15 6LT.
PANNETT, Mr. Jeremy Lewis, BSc ACA *1998;* with Deloitte LLP, Athene Place, 66 Shoe Lane, LONDON, EC4A 3BQ.
•PANNETT, Mr. John Christopher, BSc FCA *1976;* (Tax Fac), Haines Watts Gatwick LLP, 3rd Floor, Consort House, Consort Way, HORLEY, SURREY RH6 7AF.
PANNETT, Mr. Thomas Dalton John, BSc FCA *1975;* Oakland Calvert Consultants Ltd Unit 20, Greenwich Centre Business Park 53 Norman Road, LONDON, SE10 9QF.
PANNOZZO, Mr. Domenico, BA(Hons) ACA *2003;* The Little Barn, 1 Cromwell Court, Thornborough Road Nash, MILTON KEYNES, MK17 0NL.
PANNU, Mrs. Katie Ann, BA ACA *1998;* Shepherd Partnership, Albion House, Rope Walk, Otley Street, SKIPTON, NORTH YORKSHIRE BD23 1ED.
PANOVA, Miss. Maya Ognianova, BA(Hons) ACA *2003;* 24 Railway Street, CHATHAM, KENT, ME4 4JT.
PANTALEO, Mr. Gianluca, ACA *2011;* 17 Rosebery Court, Rosebery Avenue, LONDON, EC1R 5HP.
•PANTAZIS, Mr. Chris, BA ACA *1990;* CPS & Co, 10a Aldermans Hill, Palmers Green, LONDON, N13 4PJ.
PANTELI, Mr. Andreas, BSc ACA *1993;* 61 Ashley Road, EPSOM, SURREY, KT18 5BN.
PANTELI, Mrs. Angelie, ACA *2006;* (Tax Fac), 4 Hadley Close, Winchmore Hill, LONDON, N21 1HG.
PANTELI, Mr. Constantinos, BA ACA *2006;* 18 Omonia Avenue, 3052 LIMASSOL, CYPRUS.
PANTELI, Mr. John, ACA *2002;* 29 Selsdon Road, SOUTH CROYDON, SURREY, CR2 6PY.
PANTELI, Miss. Maria, BA ACA *2005;* 27 VRISIDOS STR.KAPSALOS, 3087 LIMASSOL, CYPRUS.
PANTELIDES, Mr. Elias, BSc ACA *1982;* 11A Vizantiou, Aylantzia, 2123 NICOSIA, CYPRUS.
PANTELIDES, Mr. Yiannis, ACA *2008;* 182-184 Edgware Road, LONDON, W2 2DS.
PANTELIDOU, Miss. Marianna, BA ACA *1996;* 1 Agios Dorotheos Street, Strovolos, 2054 NICOSIA, CYPRUS.
PANTELIDOU, Ms. Monica, BA(Econ) ACA *2001;* 12 Filimona Street, CY-2036 NICOSIA, CYPRUS.
PANTER, Mr. Alan James, BA ACA *1998;* E D & F Man Holdings Ltd, Cottons Centre, Hays Lane, LONDON, SE1 2QE.
PANTER, Mr. Gary, BSc ACA *1984;* Phyllis Court Club, Marlow Road, HENLEY-ON-THAMES, OXFORDSHIRE, RG9 2HT.
PANTER, Mr. Raymond Stanley, FCA *1969;* Glenmoira, Gascoigne Lane, Ropley, ALRESFORD, SO24 0BT. (Life Member)
PANTER, Mr. Richard Barry, FCA *1971;* 180 Kimbolton Road, BEDFORD, MK41 8DW.
PANTHAKEE, Mr. Dinyar Noshir, FCA *1974;* EAST MEADOWS 2B, 34 TANAH MERAH KECHIL ROAD, UNIT 07-29, SINGAPORE 465560, SINGAPORE.
•PANTHAKY, Mr. Khushroo Jamshedji, FCA *1971;* 2 King Charles Walk, LONDON, SW19 6JA.
PANTLIN, Mr. Russel James Vincent, FCA *1970;* 18 Sister Dora Avenue, St Matthews, BURNTWOOD, STAFFORDSHIRE, WS7 9QD. (Life Member)
•PANTLING, Mr. John Michael, BSc ACA *1996;* J. Humphrey Jones & Co, Suite 3C, St Christopher House, Wellington Road South, STOCKPORT, SK2 6NG.
PANTLING, Mr. Kevin Andrew, BA ACA *1988;* (Tax Fac), Lavendon Group plc, 15 Midland Court Central Park, LUTTERWORTH, LEICESTERSHIRE, LE17 4PN.
PANTON, Mr. Craig Stuart, BSc(Hons) ACA *2004;* 15 Marriner Crescent, LINCOLN, LN2 1BB.
•PANTON, Miss. Donna Marie, BSc(Econ) ACA *1998;* JP Accountancy & Taxation Solutions Ltd, 17 St. Leonards Avenue, Kenton, HARROW, MIDDLESEX, HA3 8EJ.
•PANTZARIS, Mr. Stavros, BEng FCA *1992;* Ernst & Young Cyprus Limited, Nicosia Tower Centre, 36 Byron Avenue, P.O Box 21656, 1511 NICOSIA, CYPRUS. See also Ernst & Young Europe LLP
PAPA, Mr. Andrew, BA(Hons) ACA *2004;* 24 Ryecroft Road, LONDON, SW16 3EG.
•PAPA, Mr. Carmine, BSc FCA *1981;* Littlejohn LLP, 1 Westferry Circus, Canary Wharf, LONDON, E14 4HD.
•PAPA, Mrs. Joanne Susan, BA FCA *1984;* with Withall & Co Ltd, Squires House, 205A High Street, WEST WICKHAM, BR4 0PH.
PAPACHARALAMBOUS, Mr. Elias, BSc ACA *2005;* Iolaou 3 Agios Georgios Havouzas, 3071 LIMASSOL, CYPRUS.
PAPACHARALAMBOUS, Miss. Vasiliki Anthimou, BA ACA *2010;* 36a Macedonia Street, Kato Lakatamia, 2324 NICOSIA, CYPRUS.
PAPACHRISTODOULOU, Mr. Christodoulos Kyriacoy, BA ACA *1991;* Kentavrou 24, Aglantjia, 2113 NICOSIA, CYPRUS.
•PAPACHRISTODOULOU, Mr. Demetres, BSc FCA *1982;* DKP Consultants Limited, PO Box 24856, 1304 NICOSIA, CYPRUS.
PAPACHRISTOU, Ms. Katerina, ACA *2011;* 12, Demetriou Charalambous, 3020 LIMASSOL, CYPRUS.
PAPACONSTANTINOU, Mr. Andreas Loizou, BA ACA CISA CIA *1999;* 13 Artemidos Street, 2058 STROVOLOS, CYPRUS.
PAPACONSTANTINOU, Mr. Stefan, MSc ACA *2003;* Kafkasou 51, 11363 ATHENS, GREECE.
PAPADAKIS, Mrs. Francesca, BA ACA *1990;* 26 Furlong Road, LONDON, N7 8LS.
PAPADAKIS, Mr. Konstantinos, BA ACA *2005;* 6b Athinas St, Melissia, 15127 ATHENS, GREECE.
PAPADAKIS, Mr. Marios, BA ACA *1986;* Flat 101, 7 Verenikis Street, Strovolos, 2002 NICOSIA, CYPRUS.
•PAPADAKIS, Mr. Michalakis, BSc(Eng) FCA MCIM DipM *1980;* M. Papadakis & Co, Maria House 5th Floor, 1 Avlonos Street, 1075 NICOSIA, CYPRUS.
PAPADAKIS, Mr. Panikos, FCA *1978;* Dragoumi 9, Engomi, 2412 NICOSIA, CYPRUS.
•PAPADAMOU, Mr. Adam Kosta, BSc FCA *1978;* (Tax Fac), A.K. Papadamou & Co, 573 Chester Road, SUTTON COLDFIELD, WEST MIDLANDS, B73 5HU.
PAPADATOS, Mr. Andreas, BSc ACA *2005;* 10 Grammou Street, Flat 203, STROVOLOS, CYPRUS.
•PAPADEMETRIOU, Mr. Charis Demetraki, BA ACA FCCA TEP *2009;* Papademetriou & Partners Ltd, P.O.Box 21865, 1514 NICOSIA, CYPRUS.
•PAPADEMETRIOU, Mr. Loukis Demetraki, BA(Hons) ACA FCCA *2009;* Papademetriou & Partners Ltd, P.O.Box 21865, 1514 NICOSIA, CYPRUS.
•PAPADEMETRIS, Miss. Maria, BSc ACA *1998;* MCA Papademetres LLP, Loukis Pierides Street, Lysion Court, Flat 1, 6021 LARNACA, CYPRUS. See also DM Globus Audit Services Ltd
PAPADEMETRIS, Mrs. Nicoletta, BSc(Hons) ACA *2002;* (Tax Fac), 85 Elizabeth Street, LONDON, SW1W 9PG.
PAPADOPOULOS, Mr. Alexandros, Bsc ACA *2011;* 86 Lefkosias Street, Latsia, CY 2236 NICOSIA, CYPRUS.
PAPADOPOULOS, Mr. Alkis Demetriou, BSc ACA *1998;* Herodou Attikou & Souliou 15 Maroussi, 15124 ATHENS, GREECE.
•PAPADOPOULOS, Mr. Andreas Demetriou, BSc ACA *1996;* Ernst & Young, Dunajska Cesta 111, 1000 LJUBLJANA, SLOVENIA. See also Ernst & Young Europe LLP
PAPADOPOULOS, Mr. Anthony William, BA ACA *1991;* 27 Oakdale Road, WEYBRIDGE, KT13 8EJ.
PAPADOPOULOS, Mr. Charis, BSc ACA *1998;* 32 Georgiou Michael Street, Strovolos, 2023 NICOSIA, CYPRUS.
PAPADOPOULOS, Mr. Chrysanthos Ioanni, ACA *2009;* 8A Kostaki Pantelide, 3020 LIMASSOL, CYPRUS.
PAPADOPOULOS, Mr. Constantinos Andreas, ACA *2009;* 17 Odysseos Street, Apt 103, Strovolos, 2028 NICOSIA, CYPRUS.
•PAPADOPOULOS, Mr. Constantinos Neocleous, BSc FCA *1978;* PricewaterhouseCoopers Limited, Julia House, 3 Themistocles Dervis Street, CY-1066 NICOSIA, CYPRUS.
PAPADOPOULOS, Mr. Demetrakis Taki, BA ACA *1993;* PO Box 57110, 3312 LIMASSOL, CYPRUS.
PAPADOPOULOS, Mr. George, ACA *2009;* 19 Amfissis street, Aglantzia, 2112 NICOSIA, CYPRUS.
PAPADOPOULOS, Mr. Lambros George, BA ACA *1997;* 4 Mihail Kasialou, 4044 LIMASSOL, CYPRUS.
PAPADOPOULOS, Mr. Lefkos Michael, MSc FCA *1993;* Emiliou Monia 8A, 2402 ENGOMI, CYPRUS.
PAPADOPOULOS, Mr. Marios, BSc ACA *2006;* 11 Eressos Street, 1070, NICOSIA, CYPRUS.
PAPADOPOULOS, Mr. Michael Andreas, BSc(Hons) ACA CMA *2003;* 60 Polykleitou Street, Strovolos, 2045 NICOSIA, CYPRUS.
PAPADOPOULOS, Mr. Nicholas, BSc ACA *1987;* OZCO, PO Box 18148, Jebel Ali, DUBAI, UNITED ARAB EMIRATES.
•PAPADOPOULOS, Mr. Panos, BSc FCA *1990;* Deloitte Limited, 24 Spyrou Kyprianou Avenue, P.O.Box 21675 CY-1512, 1075 NICOSIA, CYPRUS.
PAPADOPOULOU, Miss. Aliki Christou, BA(Econ) ACA *1999;* 13 Vassilis Michaelides, 2121 Aglantzia, NICOSIA, CYPRUS.
PAPADOPOULOU, Ms. Argyroula, ACA ACCA *1997;* 2 Viotias Street, 6051 LARNACA, CYPRUS.
PAPADOPOULOU, Miss. Elena, BSc ACA *2006;* 10 Nicodemos Mylonas Street, 1070 NICOSIA, CYPRUS.
PAPADOPOULOU, Miss. Eliana, BA(Hons) ACA *2001;* 96 Park Rise, HARPENDEN, HERTFORDSHIRE, AL5 3AN.
PAPADOPOULOU, Ms. Kyriaki, MA ACA *1998;* 3 Michael Kasialou, Strovolos, 2036 NICOSIA, CYPRUS.
PAPADOPOULOU, Miss. Lydia, ACA MBA *2002;* 24 Basileos Pavlou St., Voula, GR 16673 ATHENS, ATTIKI, GREECE.
PAPADOURIS, Mr. Petros Charalambos, BSc ACA *2010;* 4 Praxandrou, Flat 302, Strovolos, NICOSIA, CYPRUS.
PAPAEFSTATHIOU, Miss. Myrto, MSc BSc ACA *2010;* 5 Michael Kasialou, 1076 NICOSIA, CYPRUS.
PAPAEVRIPIDES, Mr. Alex, ACA *2011;* 17 Broad Walk, LONDON, N21 3DA.
PAPAGAPIOU, Mr. Andreas, MSc ACA *2001;* Flat 401, Mary Court, Evagora Pallkaridi & Psaron, Mesa Gitonia, 4000 LIMASSOL, CYPRUS.
PAPAGEORGIOU, Mr. Georgios, ACA *1996;* 3 Achilleos Street, Kaimakli, 1021 NICOSIA, CYPRUS.
PAPAGIANNAKI, Mrs. Loukia, MSc ACA *2004;* 28 C.Palaiologou Avenue, Kifissia, 14563 ATHENS, GREECE.
PAPAIOANNOU, Mr. George, BA ACA *2002;* 12 Omonias Ave, 3052 LIMASSOL, CYPRUS.
PAPAKYRIACOU, Mr. Christos, BSc ACA *2003;* 3 Karchidonos Street, 2413 NICOSIA, CYPRUS.
•PAPAKYRIACOU, Mr. Elias, BSc FCA *1989;* Joannides & Co Ltd, 13 Agiou Prokopiou Street, PO Box 25411, CY-1309 NICOSIA, CYPRUS. See also AGN Joannides & Co Ltd
•PAPAKYRIACOU, Mr. Georges Demetriou, FCA CF *1978;* Monday Papakyriacou DFK, 340 Kifissias Avenue, Psyhico, 15451 ATHENS, GREECE.
•PAPAKYRIACOU, Mr. Nicos Demetriou, BSc FCA *1985;* Deloitte Limited, 24 Spyrou Kyprianou Avenue, P.O.Box 21675 CY-1512, 1075 NICOSIA, CYPRUS.
PAPALAMBRIANOU, Mr. Lambros, BA ACA *1994;* 5 Medontos, 2028 NICOSIA, CYPRUS.
PAPALEONTIOU, Ms. Christiana, BSc ACA *2006;* 6 Omirou Street, Kaimakli, 1021 NICOSIA, CYPRUS.
PAPALEONTIOU, Mr. Lucas, ACA *2008;* Hermes Airports Ltd, PO Box 43027, 6650 Larnaca Airport, LARNACA, CYPRUS.
PAPALEXANDROU, Mr. Alexandros, MSc FCA *1999;* Augoustinou 36A, Kapsalos, 3086 LIMASSOL, CYPRUS.
•PAPALOIZOU, Mr. Tasos, BA ACA *1989;* Tasos Papaloizou, 260 Sussex Way, LONDON, N19 4HY.
PAPAMICHAEL, Mr. Constantinos, MSc BSc ACA *2006;* 5 Stylianou Lena Street, Marina Court, Flat 201, Pallouriotissa, 1046 NICOSIA, CYPRUS.
PAPAMICHAEL, Mr. George, BSc(Hons) ACA *2003;* 11 Stone Hall Road, LONDON, N21 1LR.
PAPAMICHAEL, Mr. George, BSc ACA *2002;* Avgoustinou 29A, 3086 LIMASSOL, CYPRUS.
•PAPAMICHAEL, Mr. Panayiotis, BSc FCA *1986;* Deloitte Limited, 24 Spyrou Kyprianou Avenue, P.O.Box 21675 CY-1512, 1075 NICOSIA, CYPRUS.
PAPAMICHAEL, Mr. Philip Demosthenes, LLB ACA *1992;* Alisbachweg 30, 6315 OBERAEGERI, SWITZERLAND.
PAPAMICHAEL, Mr. Yiannis, ACA *2011;* 4 Asias Street, 3050 LIMASSOL, CYPRUS.
PAPANASTASIOU, Miss. Anastasia, ACA *2011;* 7 Timotheou Street, Kaimakli, 1022 NICOSIA, CYPRUS.
PAPANGELOU, Mr. Markos, MA ACA *1995;* 12 Palmerston Road, LONDON, SW14 7PZ.
•PAPANICOLA, Mr. Theodoulos, FCA *1974;* Bond Partners LLP, The Grange, 100 High Street, LONDON, N14 6TB. See also Bond Group LLP
PAPANTONIOU, Mr. Pantelis Georgiou, FCA *1978;* Orfeos 5, 1070 NICOSIA, CYPRUS.
PAPAPETROPOULOS, Mr. Theodore, BSc ACA *1991;* Rodon 60, Ekali, 14578 ATHENS, GREECE.
PAPAPHILIPPOU, Mr. Yiannos, BA ACA *2006;* Pythagorou 7, Aglatzia, 2122 NICOSIA, CYPRUS.
•PAPAPRODROMOU, Mr. Demetris, MSc BA ACA *2002;* with Centaur Trust Services (Cyprus) Ltd, 2082 Strovolos, PO Box 28770, NICOSIA, CYPRUS.

PAPARIDES, Mr. Loucas, BSc ACA *2002;* 12 Vasilikou Street, Strovolos, 2060 NICOSIA, CYPRUS.

•①**PAPAS, Mr. Panos, BSc ACA** *1988;* with Smith & Williamson Ltd, 25 Moorgate, LONDON, EC2R 6AY.

PAPASOLOMONTOS, Mr. Anastasios, BSc ACA *2005;* 97 Huntingfield Road, LONDON, SW15 5EA.

PAPASOLOMONTOS, Mr. George, BA ACA FRM *1997;* 43 Sunset Square, SINGAPORE 597335, SINGAPORE.

•**PAPASOLOMONTOS, Mrs. Jane Marie, BSc ACA** *2003;* 97 Huntingfield Road, Putney, LONDON, SW15 5EA.

PAPASTAVROU, Mr. Stavros, BA(Hons) ACA *2005;* 3 Victoros Hugo Street, Aglandjia, 2107 NICOSIA, CYPRUS.

PAPATHOMAS, Mr. Antonis Andrea, BSc(Econ) ACA *1999;* Ayiou Nicolaou 12, Flat 002, Lykavitos, 1055 NICOSIA, CYPRUS.

•**PAPATHOMAS, Mr. Augoustinos, BSc FCA** *1991;* Grant Thornton, 10 Filiou Zannetou Str, 2nd Floor, PO Box 55299, 3820 LIMASSOL, CYPRUS.

PAPATHOMAS, Mr. Pantelis, BA ACA *2001;* 32 Arlington Avenue, LEAMINGTON SPA, CV32 5UD.

PAPE, Mr. Andrew John, FCA *1988;* 43 Sellers Drive, Leconfield, BEVERLEY, HU17 7NA.

PAPE, Mr. Ben, BA ACA *2007;* 9 Clover Court, CAMBRIDGE, CB1 9YN.

PAPE, Mr. Christopher Simon, BSc(Hons) ACA *2002;* with Deloitte LLP, PO Box 500, 2 Hardman Street, MANCHESTER, M60 2AT.

PAPHITIS, Mr. Costas, BSc ACA *2003;* Nikiforou Foka 8, Latsia, 2236 NICOSIA, CYPRUS.

•**PAPHITIS, Mr. Michael, ACA ACCA** *2008;* Brooking Ruse & Co Limited, 3 Beaconsfield Road, WESTON-SUPER-MARE, SOMERSET, BS23 1YE.

PAPIRI, Miss. Maria Andrea, MSc BSc ACA *2010;* 6 Samos Street, Akaki, 2720 NICOSIA, CYPRUS.

PAPOULA, Miss. Eleni, ACA *2009;* Apartment 21, Drapers Court, 59 Lurline Gardens, LONDON, SW11 4DF.

PAPOUTSAS, Mr. Kleanthis, BSc ACA *2009;* 43 1st of April Street, Athienou, 7600 LARNACA, CYPRUS.

PAPOUTSOU, Miss. Georgia, ACA *2008;* 8 Arachovas Street, Lygia Court, Block B Flat 101, Strovolos, 2021 NICOSIA, CYPRUS.

PAPPS, Mr. Christopher John Lambert, BSc ACA *1986;* 17 Margaret Street, POINT CLARE, NSW 2250, AUSTRALIA.

PAPPS, Mr. Jeffrey Clive Tannock, MA ACA *1995;* PricewaterhouseCoopers, GPO Box 2650, SYDNEY, NSW 1171, AUSTRALIA.

PAPWORTH, Mr. Christian Douglas, ACA *2008;* 18 Park Hill Court, Addiscombe Road, CROYDON, CR0 5PG.

PAPWORTH, Mr. Graham Charles, FCA *1964;* 5 West Pallant, CHICHESTER, PO19 1TD.

PAPWORTH, Mr. Graham Russell, BSc FCA *1992;* CM Group Ltd, Tortworth House, WOTTON-UNDER-EDGE, GLOUCESTERSHIRE, GL12 8HQ.

•**PAPWORTH, Mr. Henry Simon, BSc FCA** *1986;* BJCA Limited, Rumwell Hall, Rumwell, TAUNTON, SOMERSET, TA4 1EL. See also BJ Dixon Walsh Limited

•**PAPWORTH-SMITH, Mr. Paul Anthony, BSc FCA** *1986;* P.P.S., 29 Devizes Road, SWINDON, SN1 4BG.

PARACHA, Mr. Mahmud Zia, ACA *2010;* 7 Cross Road, LONDON, SW19 1PL.

PARALIMNITOU, Ms. Andia, MSc ACA *2008;* 12 Costa Soteriade, Panthea, CY-4105 LIMASSOL, CYPRUS.

PARAMANATHAN, Mrs. Vasantha Malar Sharmini, ACA *1979;* Berliozlaan 4, 2102 EE HEEMSTEDE, NETHERLANDS.

•**PARAMESWARAN, Mr. Kandaswami, FCA** *1975;* (Tax Fac), Param & Co, 18 Foxley Lane, PURLEY, CR8 3ED.

PARAMESWRAN, Mr. Krishna Georg, BA ACA *1994;* Bachforellenweg, 18, 60327, FRANKFURT AM MAIN, GERMANY.

PARAMOR, Mr. David Richard, BSc ACA *1998;* with Kingfisher plc, 3 Sheldon Square, Paddington, LONDON, W2 6PX.

PARAMOR, Mrs. Gemma Gillam, BA(Hons) ACA *2001;* Newton Investment Management Limited, The Bank of New York Mellon Financial Centre, 160 Queen Victoria Street, LONDON, EC4V 4LA.

•**PARAMOR, Mr. Ian Edward, BA FCA** *1994;* Royce Peeling Green Limited, The Copper Room, Deva Centre, Trinity Way, MANCHESTER, M3 7BG.

PARAMORE, Mr. Neil, BSc FCA *1986;* Astra Games Ltd Astra House, 1 Kingsway Bridgend Industrial Estate, BRIDGEND, MID GLAMORGAN, CF31 3RY.

PARAMOUR, Mr. John Christopher, FCA *1960;* 17 Angell's Meadow, Ashwell, BALDOCK, SG7 5QS. (Life Member)

PARANJAPE, Mr. Nitin, BEng ACA ACT *1993;* 4 Denbridge Road, BROMLEY, KENT, BR1 2AG.

PARASKEVA, Mr. Nicholas, BSc ACA *1988;* 222 Park Avenue South, Apartment 5A, NEW YORK, NY 10003, UNITED STATES.

PARASKEVA, Mr. Nikias, BA ACA *2003;* Nicosia Tower Centre, 36 Byron Avenue, P.O. Box 21656, 1511 NICOSIA, CYPRUS.

PARBHOO, Mrs. Sandhya, ACA CA(SA) *2010;* 33 Alveston Avenue, Kenton, HARROW, MIDDLESEX, HA3 8TG.

•**PARCELL, Mr. Nicholas Roch, ACA** *1987;* (Tax Fac), Parcell & Associates, Aldreth, Pearcroft Road, STONEHOUSE, GL10 2JY.

PARDEN, Mr. Matthew Barnet, BSc FCA *1993;* 77 Pendle Road, LONDON, SW16 6RX.

PARDO, Mr. Philip John, ACA *1980;* P.O Box 1214, CAMROSE T4V 1XZ, AB, CANADA.

•**PARDOE, Mr. Adrian Robert, BSc ACA** *1979;* 46 Tilstock Crescent, SHREWSBURY, SY2 6HJ.

•**PARDOE, Mr. Alan Percy, FCA** *1954;* Alan Pardoe, 52 Owen Gardens, WOODFORD GREEN, ESSEX, IG8 8DJ.

•**PARDOE, Mr. Colin, FCA** *1980;* (Tax Fac), Bird Luckin limited, Aquila House, Waterloo Lane, CHELMSFORD, CM1 1BN.

PARDOE, Mr. Edward Hyde John, BSc ACA *1991;* 18 Brooklands, Headcorn, ASHFORD, KENT, TN27 9QS.

PARDOE, Mr. Nicholas Graham Frederick, BA FCA CFA *1985;* 3586 Sharpes Meadow Lane, FAIRFAX, VA 22030, UNITED STATES.

PARDOE, Miss. Stephanie Jayne, ACA *2011;* 17 Shirley Drive, Syston, LEICESTER, LE7 1LU.

PARDON, Mr. Alan William, FCA *1980;* Hillview, Alweston, SHERBORNE, DT9 5JR.

PARDY, Mr. Justin Marc, BA ACA *1999;* 5 Harvard Close, Giffard Park, MILTON KEYNES, MK14 5PZ.

PARE, Mr. Gordon Daniel, BSc ACA *1993;* (Tax Fac), Arminel, Corilhead Road, BRAUNTON, DEVON, EX33 2EW.

PAREKH, Mrs. Darshana Ottamchand, BSc ACA *1999;* 4 Hadley Close, Elstree, BOREHAMWOOD, HERTFORDSHIRE, WD6 3LB.

PAREKH, Mr. David Hitesh, BSc(Hons) ACA *2001;* 175 Conway Drive, Fulwood, PRESTON, PR2 3ES.

PAREKH, Mr. Deepak Ramesh, BSc(Econ) ACA *2000;* 2 St. Margarets, Little Aston, SUTTON COLDFIELD, WEST MIDLANDS, B74 4HU.

PAREKH, Mr. Deepak Shantilal, FCA *1969;* Housing Dev Finance Corp Ltd, Ramon House, 5th Floor, 169 Backbay Reclamation, MUMBAI 400 020, MAHARASHTRA INDIA.

PAREKH, Miss. Deval, BA ACA *2006;* 30 Hartington Close, HARROW, MIDDLESEX, HA1 3RJ.

PAREKH, Mr. Girish, BSc ACA *1991;* GE Healthcare, 9900 W. Innovation Drive, RP 2170, WAUWATOSA, WI 53226, UNITED STATES.

•**PAREKH, Mr. Girish Ishvarlal, FCA** *1973;* (Tax Fac), 29 Hammond End, FARNHAM COMMON, BUCKINGHAMSHIRE, SL2 3LG.

•**PAREKH, Mr. Narendra Champaklal, FCA** *1979;* Parekh & Associates - Chartered Accountants, 19 The Ridgeway, LONDON, N3 2PG.

PAREKH, Mr. Premal Priyam, ACA *2011;* 47 Kendal Drive, Gatley, CHEADLE, CHESHIRE, SK8 4QJ.

•**PAREKH, Mr. Ranjit Rajnikant Dahyabhai, FCA** *1971;* Parekhs, 16 Sevington Street, Maida Hill, LONDON, W9 2QN.

•**PAREKH, Mr. Sanjay Girdharlal, FCA** *1990;* (Tax Fac), Alan Heywood & Co, 78 Mill Lane, West Hampstead, LONDON, NW6 1JZ.

PAREKH, Mr. Sanjay Pranlal, BA FCA *1989;* HT & Co (Drinks) Limited, 31-37 Park Royal Road, Park Royal, LONDON, NW10 7LQ.

PAREKH, Ms. Seema, BSc ACA *2011;* 1550 Katy Fort Bend Road, Apartment no. 3102, KATY, TX 77494, UNITED STATES.

PARELLO, Miss. Jayne Roberta, BSc ACA *2006;* 22 Azalea Gardens, Quedgeley, GLOUCESTER, GL2 4GA.

PAREMAIN, Mr. John Stuart, FCA *1972;* Maryknoll, Church Road, CROWBOROUGH, EAST SUSSEX, TN6 1BL.

PAREMAIN, Mrs. Rosemary, FCA *1972;* Maryknoll, Church Road, CROWBOROUGH, TN6 1BL.

PAREN, Mr. Keith David, BSc ACA *1990;* Cambridge Silicon Radio Churchill House, Cambridge Business Park Cowley Road, CAMBRIDGE, CB4 0WZ.

PARFECT, Mrs. Emma-Louise, LLB ACA *2002;* 1 South Bank, OXTON, MERSEYSIDE, CH43 5UP.

PARFITT, Mr. Anthony John, FCA *1976;* Chez Voix, 16130 SEGONZAC, FRANCE.

•**PARFITT, Mr. Anthony Ronald William, FCA** *1975;* H.W. Fisher & Company, Acre House, 3-5 Hyde Road, WATFORD, HERTFORDSHIRE, WD17 4WP. See also VAT Assist Limited and H W Fisher & Company Limited

PARFITT, Mr. Brian Berwyn, FCA *1974;* Flat 24 TY Wern Court, Philip Close, Rhiwbina, CARDIFF, CF14 4SD.

PARFITT, Mr. David John, BA FCA *1975;* 8 Bideford Gardens, LUTON, LU3 1UE.

PARFITT, Mr. Derek Conrad, FCA *1958;* 97 Gretton Road, Winchcombe, CHELTENHAM, GLOUCESTERSHIRE, GL54 5YS. (Life Member)

PARFITT, Mr. Geoffrey Steven, BSc FCA *1978;* Turville, Lincoln Road, CHALFONT ST. PETER, BUCKINGHAMSHIRE, SL9 9TG.

PARFITT, Mr. Gerald Francis, FCA *1970;* 38 Perpetual House, Station Road, HENLEY-ON-THAMES, OXFORDSHIRE, RG9 1AF.

•**PARFITT, Mr. Justin Michael, BA ACA** *1994;* Parfitt & Co, 22 High Street, Rowledge, FARNHAM, SURREY, GU10 4BS.

PARFITT, Mr. Michael Peter, FCA *1962;* Trees, 34B Fairdene Road, COULSDON, CR5 1RB.

PARFITT, Miss. Rebecca Elisabeth, MChem *2010;* 9 The Firs, Bath Road, READING, RG1 6HN.

PARFITT, Mr. Stuart Roger, BSc ACA *1996;* 292 Laurel Wood Avenue, The Teneriffe, SINGAPORE 275929, SINGAPORE.

PARGETER, Mr. Colin David, BA ACA *1993;* 10 Blewitt Court, Littlemore, OXFORD, OX4 4PB.

PARGETER, Mr. Ian Keith, BSc FCA *1990;* Meggitt Plc Atlantic House, 3 Aviation Park West Bournemouth International Airport Hur, CHRISTCHURCH, DORSET, BH23 6EW.

PARGETER, Mr. Mark, FCA *1975;* Ross & Craig, 12a Upper Berkeley Street, LONDON, W1H 7QE.

PARGETER, Mrs. Sandra, BSc ACA *1992;* 19 Lower Swanwick Road, Lower Swanwick, SOUTHAMPTON, SO31 7HG.

PARGETTER, Mr. Craig Peter, BSc ACA *1996;* Woodside, Chinnor Road, CHINNOR, OXFORDSHIRE, OX39 4BP.

PARGETTER, Mrs. Samantha Margaret, BSc ACA *1994;* Woodside, Chinnor Road, CHINNOR, OXFORDSHIRE, OX39 4BP.

PARHAM, Mr. Iain Michael, BA ACA *1982;* CVC Capital Partners Ltd, 5th Floor, 110-112 Strand, LONDON, WC2R 0AG.

PARHAM, Dr. Steven, ACA *2011;* Tree Tops, Burton Lane, East Coker, YEOVIL, SOMERSET, BA22 9LJ.

PARIKH, Mr. Bharat Amritlal, BSc FCA *1973;* 60 Windsor Avenue, LONDON, SW19 2RR.

PARIKH, Mrs. Gabrielle Jayne, MA ACA *1991;* 102 Beaumont Avenue, ST. ALBANS, AL1 4TP.

PARIKH, Mr. Gitakumar Balmukund Punjalal, FCA *1966;* Aundhia & Parikh, 81 Cachet Parkway, MARKHAM L6C 1C7, ON, CANADA. (Life Member)

PARIKH, Mr. Michael William, MA ACA *1991;* U B S AG, 100 Liverpool Street, LONDON, EC2M 2RH.

PARIS, Mr. Antony Edward, FCA *1960;* 10 Morlands Drive, Charlton Kings, CHELTENHAM, GLOUCESTERSHIRE, GL53 8LR.

PARIS, Mrs. Emma Jane, BCom ACA *2005;* 2 Leas Road, COLCHESTER, CO2 9PH.

PARIS, Mr. Gerard Darell, FCA *1954;* Lynedoch House, 20 Cross Road, Albrighton, WOLVERHAMPTON, WV7 3RB. (Life Member)

•**PARIS, Mr. Lee Anthony Robert, BA FCA** *1985;* The Paris Partnership LLP, Russell House, 140 High Street, EDGWARE, MIDDLESEX, HA8 7LW.

PARIS, Miss. Lia Carla, ACA *2008;* KPMG LLP, 10 Shelley Street, SYDNEY, NSW 2024, AUSTRALIA.

PARIS, Mr. Nicholas John, BSc FCA *1984;* 47 Lammas Park Road, LONDON, W5 5JD.

PARIS, Mr. Nigel John, MA FCA *1973;* 39 Pevensey Road, WORTHING, WEST SUSSEX, BN11 5NS.

•**PARIS, Mr. Robert John, FCA** *1972;* Whittingham Riddell LLP, Belmont House, Shrewsbury Business Park, SHREWSBURY, SY2 6LG.

PARISH, Mr. Brian Terence, FCA *1966;* P.O. Box 40572, SAN FRANCISCO, CA 94140, UNITED STATES.

PARISH, Mr. Daniel James Bintliff, ACA *2008;* 47 Langridge Drive, Portslade, BRIGHTON, BN41 2JB.

•**PARISH, Mr. David John, BSc ACA** *1988;* RSM Tenon Audit Limited, The Poynt, 45 Wollaton Street, NOTTINGHAM, NG1 5FW. See also Tenon Audit Limited

PARISH, Mr. David William, FCA *1967;* Michanda, Spring Road Annables Est., Kinsbourne Green, HARPENDEN, AL5 3PP. (Life Member)

PARISH, Mr. James Maxwell, BA ACA *2004;* 12 Holyoake Road, Headington, OXFORD, OX3 8AE.

PARISH, Mr. Jeffrey Richard, ACA *1983;* Peters Elworthy & Moore Salisbury House, 2-3 Salisbury Villas, CAMBRIDGE, CB1 2LA.

PARISH, Mr. Jeremy, ACA *1996;* 11 Church Street, BUCKINGHAM, BUCKINGHAMSHIRE, MK18 1BY.

PARISH, Mrs. Melanie, BA ACA *1999;* 49 London Road, Pakefield, LOWESTOFT, SUFFOLK, NR33 7AB.

PARISH, Mr. Michael Robert, FCA *1972;* St Jude, 2a Oaklands Drive, Cringleford, NORWICH, NR4 7SA.

•**PARISH, Mr. Rick, ACA** *1988;* (Tax Fac), Ellis Atkins, 1 Paper Mews, 330 High Street, DORKING, SURREY, RH4 2TU. See also Bray Management Services Limited

PARISH, Mr. Tom William, ACA *2010;* with Baker Tilly (BVI) Limited, P O Box 650, Tropic Isle Building, Nibbs Street, ROAD TOWN, TORTOLA ISLAND VIRGIN ISLANDS (BRITISH).

PARISH, Mrs. Veronica Ann, BSc ACA *1986;* 39 Irwin Street, EAST FREEMANTLE, WA 6158, AUSTRALIA.

PARISI, Miss. Angela Elizabeth, BSc ACA *2007;* 22 Alfred Gardens, KINGSTON, TAS 7050, AUSTRALIA.

PARK, Mrs. Amy, BA(Hons) ACA *2011;* 19 Cragside Gardens, BEDLINGTON, NORTHUMBERLAND, NE22 5YX.

PARK, Mr. Andrew, LLB ACA *2007;* 50 Wormholt Road, LONDON, W12 0LS.

PARK, Mr. Andrew Martin, MA FCA *2001;* (Tax Fac), 99 Annandale Road, LONDON, SE10 0JY.

PARK, Ms. Bethan Mair, BA ACA *1991;* Red Maids School, Westbury Road, Westbury-on-Trym, BRISTOL, BS9 3AW.

PARK, Mrs. Carole Florence, MA ACA *1992;* 23 Briarwood, Freckleton, PRESTON, PR4 1ZB.

PARK, Ms. Clare Mary, BA ACA *1996;* with Deloitte LLP, 2 New Street Square, LONDON, EC4A 3BZ.

PARK, Mr. Cyril Atkinson, MA FCA *1956;* Gelli Pant, Pont-Y-Pant, DOLWYDDELAN, LL25 0PJ. (Life Member)

PARK, Mr. Daniel Stephen, BSc ACA *2010;* 1 Oulton Road, RUGBY, CV21 1AE.

•**PARK, Mr. David John, BSc FCA** *1996;* Ocean Consultancy Ltd, Parliament Square, Parliament Street, CREDITON, DEVON, EX17 2AW.

PARK, Mr. Douglas, FCA *1960;* 8 Bute Close, Thornaby, STOCKTON-ON-TEES, CLEVELAND, TS17 0HL. (Life Member)

•**PARK, Mr. Eric Campbell, FCA** *1971;* Campbell Park, 54 Woods Avenue, HATFIELD, HERTFORDSHIRE, AL10 8LY.

PARK, Mr. Geoffrey, ACA *2010;* 1 Victoria Street, Calverley, PUDSEY, WEST YORKSHIRE, LS28 5PQ.

PARK, Mr. Graham Russell, BSc(Hons) ACA *2000;* 23 Morgan Close, Yaxley, PETERBOROUGH, PE7 3GE.

PARK, Miss. Hye-Jung, BSc ACA *2002;* European Bank for Reconstruction & Development, 1 Exchange Square Primrose Street, LONDON, EC2A 2JN.

•**PARK, Mr. Ian Bruce, FCA** *1975;* (Tax Fac), Hill Wooldridge & Co Limited, 107 Hindes Road, HARROW, MIDDLESEX, HA1 1RU.

PARK, Mr. Ian Watret, FCA *1958;* 10 Miles McInnes Court, CARLISLE, CA3 9AJ. (Life Member)

•**PARK, Miss. Jane Ellen, BA ACA** *2001;* Fizz Accounting Limited, Meteor House, Eastern Bypass, THAME, OXFORDSHIRE, OX9 3RL.

PARK, Mrs. Joan Elizabeth, FCA *1973;* 3 Tuns Lane, Silverton, EXETER, EX5 4HY.

PARK, Mr. John, BA(Hons) ACA *2002;* 16 Taylor Way, Great Baddow, CHELMSFORD, CM2 8ZG.

PARK, Mr. John Rory, BSc ACA *1992;* 31 Stroud Road, Wimbledon, LONDON, SW19 8DQ.

PARK, Mrs. Karen Elizabeth, BSc FCA *1977;* 7 Kirkleas Road, SURBITON, SURREY, KT6 6QJ.

PARK, Miss. Kathryn Louise, BSc ACA *2005;* 72 Gardinar Close, Standish, WIGAN, LANCASHIRE, WN1 2UN.

PARK, Mr. Kenneth Norman, BA FCA *1964;* 16 Oakfields, Middleton Tyas, RICHMOND, NORTH YORKSHIRE, DL10 6SD.

PARK, Miss. Linda Margaret, BA ACA *1986;* 18 Station Road, THAMES DITTON, KT7 0NR.

PARK, Mrs. Melanie Jane, BSc ACA *1998;* The Cottage, Chapel Lane, Aslockton, NOTTINGHAM, NG13 9AR.

PARK, Mr. Michael John, BA(Hons) ACA *2003;* Little Sarum, 9 South Park View, GERRARDS CROSS, BUCKINGHAMSHIRE, SL9 8HN.

•**PARKIN, Mr. Robert David, ACA** *2009;* (Tax Fac), 14 Yarwell Drive, Maltby, ROTHERHAM, SOUTH YORKSHIRE, S66 8HZ.
PARKIN, Mr. Robin Giles, BSc ACA *1996;* Croft Farm Main Street, Monk Fryston, LEEDS, LS25 5DU.
PARKIN, Mr. Russell, ACA *2011;* 51 Martin Close, Aughton, SHEFFIELD, S26 3RJ.
PARKIN, Mr. Simon Basil, FCA *1966;* The Warren, Warren Farm Lane, CHICHESTER, WEST SUSSEX, PO19 5RU. (Life Member)
PARKIN, Mr. Terence Rowland, BCom FCA *1964;* Allport Cottage, The Common Allport Road, Bromborough, WIRRAL, CH62 6AF.
PARKINS, Mr. David Graham, FCA *1976;* The Wells East Road East Mersea, COLCHESTER, CO5 8TA.
PARKINS-GODWIN, Mr. Paul Alexander, BA(Hons) FCA *2000;* 58 St. Marys Road, Long Ditton, SURBITON, SURREY, KT6 5EY.
PARKINSON, Mr. Adrian Nicholas, BSc ACA *1994;* UFG Asset Management, Petrovka 5, Floor 3 Berlin House, 107031, MOSCOW, RUSSIAN FEDERATION.
PARKINSON, Mr. Alec, BA ACA *2005;* Primary Capital Ltd, Augustine House, Austin Friars, LONDON, EC2N 2HA.
PARKINSON, Mr. Andrew Michael Reay, FCA *1968;* Tadlow House, Tadlow, ROYSTON, SG8 0EL.
PARKINSON, Mrs. Ann Delyth, FCA *1964;* Westside, Banchory Devenick, ABERDEEN, AB12 5XQ.
PARKINSON, Lord Cecil Edward, MA FCA *1960;* The House of Lords, LONDON, SW1A 0PW.
PARKINSON, Mr. Charles Nigel Kennedy, MA FCA *1978;* 2 Mont Bleu, Les Cotils St. Peter Port, GUERNSEY, GY1 2LY.
PARKINSON, Mrs. Charlotte Clare, ACA *2010;* 2nd Floor Flat, 15 Castletown Road, LONDON, W14 9HF.
PARKINSON, Mr. Christopher James, ACA *2004;* 2 Gumtree Park, 17 Wellington Street, Ngunnawal, CANBERRA, ACT, AUSTRALIA.
PARKINSON, Mr. David John, BSc ACA *2002;* 20 Holtermann Street, CROWS NEST, NSW 2065, AUSTRALIA.
PARKINSON, Miss. Debora Christine, BSc ACA *2006;* with Smith & Williamson Ltd, 25 Moorgate, LONDON, EC2R 6AY.
PARKINSON, Mr. Derek Henry, FCA *1951;* 9151 No 5 Road, RICHMOND V7A 4T9, BC, CANADA. (Life Member)
•**PARKINSON, Mrs. Elizabeth Anne, BSc ACA** *1981;* T.A. Parkinson, Linton Close, Trip Lane, Linton, WETHERBY, WEST YORKSHIRE LS22 4HX.
PARKINSON, Mr. Frank, LLB FCA *1962;* 18 Aldbourne Avenue, Earley, READING, RG6 7DB. (Life Member)
PARKINSON, Mr. Geoffrey Richard Lionel, FCA *1963;* 16 Sturdee Gardens, Jesmond, NEWCASTLE UPON TYNE, NE2 3QT. (Life Member)
PARKINSON, Mr. Geoffrey Silby, BSc FCA *1974;* 11 Eastglade, NORTHWOOD, HA6 3LD.
PARKINSON, Mr. George Scott, FCA *1971;* 6 Crosthwaite Gardens, KESWICK, CUMBRIA, CA12 5QF.
PARKINSON, Mrs. Heather Jane, BEng FCA FCILA *1990;* Parkinson Consulting Ltd, Old Paddock, Church Road, Stevington, BEDFORD, MK43 7QB.
•**PARKINSON, Mr. Ian David, FCA** *1982;* Brays Ltd, 23 Market Place, WETHERBY, WEST YORKSHIRE, LS22 6LQ.
PARKINSON, Mr. Ian Michael, BSc ACA *1995;* 63 Summerleys Road, PRINCES RISBOROUGH, HP27 9PZ.
•**PARKINSON, Mrs. Jacqueline Lindsay, FCA** *1971;* (Tax Fac), Grant Harrod Parkinson, 49a High Street, RUISLIP, MIDDLESEX, HA4 7BD. See also Grant Harrod Parkinson LLP
PARKINSON, Mrs. Jane Elizabeth, BA ACA *1993;* 2 St Thomas Road, Great Glen, LEICESTER, LE8 9EH.
PARKINSON, Mr. Jeremy John William, MEng ACA *2001;* 34 Boundary Road, ST. ALBANS, HERTFORDSHIRE, AL1 4DW.
PARKINSON, Mr. John, BEng ACA *2002;* 52 Holifast Road, Wylde Green, SUTTON COLDFIELD, WEST MIDLANDS, B72 1AE.
PARKINSON, Mr. John Anthony, FCA *1971;* 22 Brambling Drive, Westhoughton, BOLTON, BL5 2SW.
•**PARKINSON, Mr. John Ironside, FCA** *1979;* BDO LLP, Kings Wharf, 20-30 Kings Road, READING, RG1 3EX. See also BDO Stoy Hayward LLP
PARKINSON, Mr. John Lindsay, BA ACA *1986;* Drake Extrusion Inc, 790 Industrial Park Drive, MARTINSVILLE, VA 24148, UNITED STATES.
PARKINSON, Mr. John Murray, PhD FCA JDipMA *1971;* York University, Atkinson College, 4.700 Keele Street, NORTH YORK M3J 1P3, ON, CANADA.
•**PARKINSON, Mr. John Phillips, FCA** *1960;* Phillips Parkinson & Co, 2 Fawns Keep, WILMSLOW, SK9 2BQ. See also Personal Numbers Ltd
PARKINSON, Mr. John Whalley, FCA *1970;* Coniston, 162 St. Annes Road East, LYTHAM ST. ANNES, LANCASHIRE, FY8 3HW.
PARKINSON, Mr. Joseph, FCA *1950;* Mount Tabor, 10 Maple Court, St. Georges Park, Ditchling Road, BURGESS HILL, WEST SUSSEX RH15 0SW. (Life Member)
•**PARKINSON, Mr. Kevin, FCA** *1977;* Parkinson Matthews LLP, Cedar House, 35 Ashbourne Road, DERBY, DE22 3FS. See also KPRM Limited
PARKINSON, Mr. Malcolm Leslie, FCA *1977;* 30 Coldstream, Ouston, CHESTER-LE-STREET, DH2 1LH.
•**PARKINSON, Mr. Michael Anthony, BSc ACA** *1992;* Barnes Roffe LLP, 3 Brook Business Centre, Cowley Mill Road, Cowley, UXBRIDGE, MIDDLESEX UB8 2FX.
PARKINSON, Mr. Michael Frederick, BSc ACA *1985;* 282 Fir Tree Road, EPSOM, KT17 3NN.
PARKINSON, Mr. Michael John, BA FCA *1997;* Brewin Dolphin Time Central, 32 Gallowgate, NEWCASTLE UPON TYNE, NE1 4SR.
PARKINSON, Miss. Nicola, BSc ACA CTA *2000;* Armstrong Watson, 51 Rae Street, DUMFRIES, DG1 1JD.
PARKINSON, Mr. Philip David, FCA *1977;* Rohan Designs Ltd, 30 Maryland Road Tongwell, MILTON KEYNES, MK15 8HN.
PARKINSON, Mr. Philip Richard, MA FCA *1983;* 2 Chubb Close, Tetbury Hill, MALMESBURY, WILTSHIRE, SN16 9JW.
PARKINSON, Mr. Richard, ACA *2010;* 17 Marsh Street, CLECKHEATON, WEST YORKSHIRE, BD19 5BW.
PARKINSON, Mr. Richard Arthur, BA FCA *1981;* 12 Dukes Avenue, Muswell Hill, LONDON, N10 2PT.
PARKINSON, Mr. Richard Horrox, BSc FCA *1989;* (Tax Fac), 87 Quinta Drive, Arkley, BARNET, EN5 3DA.
PARKINSON, Mr. Richard Penrose, FCA *1971;* Old Peppering Eye Farmhouse, Peppering Eye, BATTLE, TN33 0ST.
PARKINSON, Mr. Richard Turner, FCA *1954;* The Old Rectory, Clyst St George, EXETER, DEVON, EX3 0RE. (Life Member)
PARKINSON, Mr. Robert, BSc ACA *1989;* (Tax Fac), 15 Alison Way, Orams Mount, WINCHESTER, SO22 5BT.
PARKINSON, Ms. Sally Jane, MSc ACA *2002;* 23 Chandos Road South, MANCHESTER, M21 0TH.
•**PARKINSON, Mr. Stephen John, BA ACA** *1980;* Ernst & Young LLP, 1 More London Place, LONDON, SE1 2AF. See also Ernst & Young Europe LLP
PARKINSON, Mr. Stuart Hargreaves, MA FCA DChA *1996;* Baker Tilly The Clock House, 140 London Road, GUILDFORD, GU1 1UW.
PARKINSON, Mr. Thomas, ACA *2011;* 509/133 Goulburn Street, Sydney Mansion, SURRY HILLS, NSW 2010, AUSTRALIA.
•**PARKINSON, Mr. Timothy Andrew, BA FCA** *1979;* T.A. Parkinson, Linton Close, Trip Lane, Linton, WETHERBY, WEST YORKSHIRE LS22 4HX.
PARKINSON, Mr. Timothy Charles, BA FCA *1989;* 43 West Down, Bookham, LEATHERHEAD, SURREY, KT23 4LJ.
PARKINSON, Miss. Victoria Susan, ACA *2009;* (Tax Fac), 188 Victoria Avenue, Princes Avenue, HULL, HU5 3DY.
PARKINSON, Mr. Wilfred, FCA *1968;* 3 Woodland Court, Marsh House Lane, DARWEN, BB3 3SP.
•**PARKINSON-ATHERTON, Mrs. Kathryn, BA ACA** *1985;* KPA & Co, 41 Oakfield Road, Poynton, STOCKPORT, SK12 1AS.
•**PARKS, Mr. Anthony Douglas, ACA** *1985;* A D Parks & Co, 30 High Street, Wendover, AYLESBURY, HP22 6EA.
•**PARKS, Mr. Antony Lloyd, BA FCA** *1986;* 2 Swale Road, SUTTON COLDFIELD, B76 2BH.
PARKS, Mr. David James, ACA *2009;* 8 Poplars, WELWYN GARDEN CITY, HERTFORDSHIRE, AL7 2AL.
•**PARKS, Miss. Elizabeth Anne, MA FCA** *1987;* (Tax Fac), Miss E A Parks, 68 Murray Road, Wimbledon, LONDON, SW19 4PE.
PARKS, Mr. John, FCA *1971;* 20 Laurel Road, SALTBURN-BY-THE-SEA, CLEVELAND, TS12 1HU. (Life Member)
PARKS, Mr. John Andrew, BSc ACA *1989;* PO Box 437, CASTRIES, SAINT LUCIA.
PARKS, Mrs. Nancy Alice Olivia, BSc ACA *2006;* 65 Beechwood Avenue, ST. ALBANS, HERTFORDSHIRE, AL1 4XR.
PARKS, Mr. Peter Eric, FCA *1960;* 8 Ross Road, COBHAM, SURREY, KT11 2AZ. (Life Member)
PARKS, Mr. Stanley William, FCA *1956;* Longcross House, Long Cross, SHAFTESBURY, SP7 8QP. (Life Member)
PARKS, Mr. Thomas Charles, FCA *1955;* 1 Brembridge Close, Sywell, NORTHAMPTON, NN6 0AU. (Life Member)
PARLA, Mrs. Kerry, ACA *2005;* 62 Meadway, HODDESDON, HERTFORDSHIRE, EN11 8AT.
PARLALIDOU, Mrs. Andriana, BSc ACA *2006;* 19 Pipinou Street, Mesa Yitonia, 4002 LIMASSOL, CYPRUS.
PARLANE, Mr. Andrew John, FCA *1962;* 230 Maplin Way North, Thorpe Bay, SOUTHEND-ON-SEA, SS1 3NT. (Life Member)
•**PARLANE, Mr. Ian Michael, MA ACA** *1990;* I.M. Parlane, 2 Magazine Mews, The Garrison, Shoeburyness, SOUTHEND-ON-SEA, SS3 9QB.
PARLE, Mr. Christopher, BA(Hons) FCA *2000;* Bibby Financial Services Limited, 105 Duke Street, LIVERPOOL, MERSEYSIDE, L1 5JQ.
PARLING, Mrs. Claire Laura Mary, BA ACA *2006;* 6 Danesfield Close, WALTON-ON-THAMES, KT12 3BP.
PARLONS, Miss. Alison, BSc(Hons) ACA *2001;* (Tax Fac), 1 Linnell Close, LONDON, NW11 7LN.
PARLOUR, Mr. John, ACA *1992;* 91 Laurel Crescent, Rush Green, ROMFORD, RM7 0RU.
PARMAR, Mrs. Bindu, BA(Hons) ACA *2001;* 29 Hazell Way, Stoke Poges, SLOUGH, SL2 4DD.
PARMAR, Dr. Chetan Kumar, PhD BSc ACA *2005;* 29 Hazell Way, Stoke Poges, SLOUGH, SL2 4DD.
PARMAR, Ms. Deepa Mulji, BA ACA *1999;* 1 Highland Road, NORTHWOOD, MIDDLESEX, HA6 1JP.
PARMAR, Miss. Dina Maganlal, BSc ACA *1994;* 8 Glover Drive Sandy Bay, HOBART, TAS 7005, AUSTRALIA.
PARMAR, Mr. Dipak Prabhudas, BSc ACA *1992;* C/O Oxford Taylors, PO Box 31757, LUSAKA, ZAMBIA.
•**PARMAR, Mr. Haresh, BA ACA** *1986;* (Tax Fac), 76 Colin Crescent, LONDON, NW9 6EY.
PARMAR, Mrs. Harsha, BCom ACA *1989;* Osborne Clarke, 2 Temple Back East, BRISTOL, BS1 6EG.
PARMAR, Mrs. Kalpana Pravinlal, BSc ACA *1991;* Al Futtaim Carillion, Ras Al Khor, DUBAI, PO 1811, UNITED ARAB EMIRATES.
•**PARMAR, Mr. Kiran Singh, MA FCA** *1979;* 23 High View, PINNER, HA5 3NZ.
•**PARMAR, Mr. Mahendra Amratlal, BA FCA** *1989;* (Tax Fac), M. Parmar & Co, 1st Floor, 244 Edgware Road, LONDON, W2 1DS.
PARMAR, Mr. Manoj Kumar, BA ACA *1994;* 6 Northdown Road, Chalfont St. Peter, GERRARDS CROSS, BUCKINGHAMSHIRE, SL9 0LQ.
•**PARMAR, Mrs. Meera Menon, BSc ACA** *1991;* Cowgill Holloway LLP, 4th Floor, 49 Peter Street, MANCHESTER, M2 3NG.
•**PARMAR, Ms. Penelope Jane, FCA** *1982;* Baxter Payne & Haigh Limited, Claremont House, Deans Court, BICESTER, OX26 6BW.
•**PARMAR, Mr. Pradeep, BSc ACA** *1987;* 18 The Woodlands, AMERSHAM, BUCKINGHAMSHIRE, HP6 5LD.
PARMAR, Mr. Ramesh Dayalji, BSc FCA *1997;* 30 Grange Close, Nascot Wood, WATFORD, WD17 4HQ.
•**PARMAR, Mr. Rashpal Singh, BA FCA** *1988;* (Tax Fac), Bowker Orford, 15/19 Cavendish Place, LONDON, W1G 0DD.
PARMAR, Mr. Ravi, ACA *2011;* 3 Lydney Close, Broughton, MILTON KEYNES, MK10 7AG.
•**PARMAR, Mr. Ravindra Babulal, FCA** *1977;* (Tax Fac), Beechams LLP, 3rd Floor, 167 Fleet Street, LONDON, EC4A 2EA.
PARMAR, Mr. Sanjay, MEng ACA *2010;* 19 Woolford Close, BRACKNELL, BERKSHIRE, RG42 7PR.
•**PARMAR, Mr. Sanjay Ratilal, ACA** *1990;* Jeffreys Henry LLP, Finsgate, 5-7 Cranwood Street, LONDON, EC1V 9EE.
PARMAR, Mrs. Sejal, ACA *2009;* Augentius Fund Administration LLP, 2 London Bridge, LONDON, SE1 9RA.
•**PARMAR, Mr. Udaibir Singh, FCA** *1984;* (Tax Fac), Udai Parmar & Co Ltd, 29 New Way Road, LONDON, NW9 6PL.
PARMAR, Mr. Veekash, BEng ACA *1999;* Charles Taylor Consulting Standard House, 12-13 Essex Street, LONDON, WC2R 3AA.
PARMAR-DAWES, Mrs. Pritti, BA ACA *2003;* 53 Skylark Way, Shinfield, READING, RG2 9AD.
PARMENTER, Mr. Anthony, BSc FCA *1965;* DAIRY BARN HOUSE, -, High Street, Charlton On Otmoor, KIDLINGTON, OX5 2UG. (Life Member)
PARMENTER, Miss. Charlene Emma, ACA *2010;* 3 The Ridings, BURGESS HILL, WEST SUSSEX, RH15 0LW.
PARMENTER, Mrs. Claire Louise, BA ACA *2004;* 90 Chiltern Drive, SURBITON, KT5 8LX.
PARMENTER, Mr. David Vernon, BCom FCA *1979;* 20 John Street, Titahi Bay, PORIRUA 5022, NEW ZEALAND.
•**PARMENTER, Ms. Hilary Jane, BSc ACA** *1991;* Hilary Parmenter ACA, 1 The Willows, North Warnborough, HOOK, HAMPSHIRE, RG29 1DR.
PARMENTER, Mr. Martin David, BSc FCA *1982;* 4 Keymer Gardens, BURGESS HILL, RH15 0AF.
PARMESSUR, Miss. Leena Devi, BSc ACA *2003;* Pricewaterhousecoopers, 1 Embankment Place, LONDON, WC2N 6RH.
PARMITER, Mr. Anthony De Clifton, FCA *1970;* 1 Landgate Yard, Well Lane, Stow on the Wold, CHELTENHAM, GLOUCESTERSHIRE, GL54 1DG.
PARMLEY, Mr. David George, BCom FCA *1976;* 40 Kenyons Lane, Lydiate, LIVERPOOL, L31 0BR.
PARNABY, Mr. Gary Alan, BSc(Hons) ACA *2001;* 26 Church Hams, Finchampstead, WOKINGHAM, BERKSHIRE, RG40 4XF.
PARNELL, Miss. Ceri-Anne, ACA *2007;* 17 Bronze Street, MARCH, CAMBRIDGESHIRE, PE15 8UJ.
PARNELL, Mr. David, FCA *1975;* 46 Chatsworth Drive, MANSFIELD, NOTTINGHAMSHIRE, NG18 4QT.
PARNELL, Mr. Hugh Robert, BA ACA *1978;* 22 St. Mary's View, SAFFRON WALDEN, ESSEX, CB10 2GF.
PARNELL, Mr. James David, BA(Hons) ACA *2003;* 117 Russell Drive, NOTTINGHAM, NG8 2BD.
PARNELL, Mrs. Louise Elizabeth, BA ACA *1995;* 10 Rickaby Close, WIRRAL, MERSEYSIDE, CH63 0EG.
PARNELL, Mr. Michael Kenneth, FCA *1965;* P.O.BOX CB 11989, NASSAU, BAHAMAS.
PARNELL, Miss. Michelle, ACA *2005;* 6 Ringland Lane, Easton, NORWICH, NORFOLK, NR9 5DL.
PARNELL, Mr. Shaun Stewart, ACA *2009;* 3 Ancar Road, South Wootton, KING'S LYNN, NORFOLK, PE30 3PS.
PARNELL, Mrs. Sherradan Victoria, BA LLB ACA CTA *2010;* Deloitte & Touche, 2 New Street Square, LONDON, EC4A 3BZ.
PARNELL, Mrs. Stephanie Louise, LLB ACA *2003;* 117 Russell Drive, NOTTINGHAM, NG8 2BD.
PARNELL, Mr. Stuart Alan, MEng ACA *1999;* 75 Campden Street, LONDON, W8 7EN.
•**PARNELL, Miss. Vanessa, FCA MAAT** *1995;* Thomas Westcott, London House, Fore Street, HOLSWORTHY, DEVON, EX22 6EB.
•**PARNELL, Miss. Victoria Heather, MA FCA** *1978;* (Tax Fac), Taxdore, Collingwood, 8 Oxshott Rise, COBHAM, KT11 2RN.
PARNESS, Mr. Paul, BSc FCA *1989;* (Tax Fac), E D & F Man Holdings Ltd Cottons Centre, Hays Lane, LONDON, SE1 2QE.
PARNHAM, Miss. Gayle Rebecca, BSc ACA *2005;* 6 Pollys Yard, NEWPORT PAGNELL, BUCKINGHAMSHIRE, MK16 8YU.
PARNHAM, Mr. Stuart, BSc ACA *2011;* 25 Warrels Grove, LEEDS, LS13 3NL.
PARNIS, Mr. Andrew William, ACA *2008;* U B S Warburg, 1-2 Finsbury Avenue, LONDON, EC2M 2PP.
PARNWELL, Mrs. Tracey Michelle, BCom ACA *2001;* 8 Hemmyng Corner, Quelm Park, Warfield, BRACKNELL, BERKSHIRE, RG42 2QH.
PARPA, Miss. Olivia, LLB ACA *2004;* Ifigenias 5, Aglangia, 2107 NICOSIA, CYPRUS.
PARPA, Ms. Tonia, BA ACA *1996;* 19 Amalias Str, 2014 NICOSIA, CYPRUS.
PARPAS, Mr. Christos, BSc ACA *2007;* 16 Chr-Kalaidji, 2015 NICOSIA, CYPRUS.
•**PARPERIS, Mr. Theodoros Costa, BSc ACA** *1991;* PricewaterhouseCoopers Limited, Julia House, 3 Themistocles Dervis Street, CY-1066 NICOSIA, CYPRUS.
PARR, Miss. Ailsa, ACA *2010;* 11 Prestwick Close, Ifield, CRAWLEY, WEST SUSSEX, RH11 0UH.
PARR, Mr. Alfred John, BA FCA *1965;* 5 Tremorvah Park, Swanpool, FALMOUTH, CORNWALL, TR11 5BE. (Life Member)
PARR, Mr. Andrew Neil, BSc FCA *1992;* La Ruette, La Ruette Lane, St. Martin's, GUERNSEY, GY4 6QW.
PARR, Miss. Anna-Marie, BSc ACA *2011;* 29 Highmarsh Crescent, MANCHESTER, M20 2LU.
PARR, Mr. Brenton Albert, LLB ACA *1993;* 2100 WEST LOOP SOUTH SUITE 1300, HOUSTON, TX 77027, UNITED STATES.
•**PARR, Miss. Christine Jean, FCA** *1977;* Parr & Company, Parsimony Towers, Brighton Road, Shermanbury, HORSHAM, WEST SUSSEX RH13 8HQ.

PARR, Mr. Christopher Martin, BA ACA *1992;* 45 Lincoln Way, COLCHESTER, CO1 2RJ.
PARR, Mr. Craig, MBA BSc FCA CFA *1989;* Ipsley House, Ipsley Church Lane, REDDITCH, WORCESTERSHIRE, B98 0TL.
PARR, Mrs. Elaine Gladys, MA FCA *1991;* The Wurly, Church Road Luthermuir, Laurencekirk, ABERDEEN, AB30 1YS.
PARR, Miss. Elizabeth Terry, BA ACA *1992;* 2 Forest View, BROCKENHURST, HAMPSHIRE, SO42 7YX.
PARR, Mr. Geoffrey Charles, MA FCA *1980;* Kitaoka Residence, 766-3 Ofusa, Koshigaya City, SAITAMA, 343-0027 JAPAN.
PARR, Mr. Ian Donald, BSc FCA *1963;* 24 Croft Road, Hurworth On Tees, DARLINGTON, DL2 2JF.
PARR, Mr. James Keith, MEng ACA *2000;* Salem Hospital, 665 Winter Street SE, PO Box 14001, SALEM, OR 97304, UNITED STATES.
•PARR, Mr. Jeffrey John, FCA *1973;* (Tax Fac), Chesapeake Associates Limited, Unit 5, Evans Business Centre, Jessop Close, Brunel Business Park, NEWARK NOTTINGHAMSHIRE NG24 2AG.
PARR, Mr. John Richard, BSc ACA *1988;* 9 Claremont Crescent, Meanwood, LEEDS, LS6 2BL.
PARR, Mr. John Taylor, FCA *1951;* Flat One, Owen Court, 2-12 Hollyfield Road, SUTTON COLDFIELD, WEST MIDLANDS, B75 7SG. (Life Member)
•①PARR, Mr. Julian Guy, FCA *1988;* PricewaterhouseCoopers LLP, 7 More London Riverside, LONDON, SE1 2RT. See also PricewaterhouseCoopers
•PARR, Mrs. Karen Louise, BSc FCA *1986;* Orchard House, Broomfallen Road, Scotby, CARLISLE, CA4 8DF.
PARR, Mrs. Kate Jane, BA(Hons) ACA *2001;* Woodacre Farm, Bleasdale, PRESTON, PR3 1UU.
PARR, Mr. Keith, FCA *1970;* 3 Yew Tree Place, LISS, GU33 7ET.
PARR, Miss. Kerry Maria, BA(Hons) ACA *2010;* 12 Snowberry Walk, BRISTOL, BS5 7DG.
PARR, Miss. Lauren, BA(Hons) ACA *2009;* 50 Silkstone Street, ST. HELENS, MERSEYSIDE, WA10 4PB.
PARR, Mrs. Lucy, BA(Hons) ACA *2003;* 19 Bridon Way, CLECKHEATON, WEST YORKSHIRE, BD19 5DF.
PARR, Mr. Martin Geoffrey, MBA BSc ACA *1980;* 1220 Chamboard Lane, HOUSTON, TX 77018, UNITED STATES.
PARR, Mr. Michael John, BSocSc ACA *2002;* Flat 27, Times Court, 24 Ravensbury Road, LONDON, SW18 4RZ.
PARR, Mr. Michael Keith, ACA *1995;* 8 Coed Gwydyr, TREFRIW, GWYNEDD, LL27 0JR.
PARR, Mr. Nicholas Robert, BA DipLP ACA *2000;* 9 Pilkington Avenue, Westlands, NEWCASTLE, ST5 3RA.
PARR, Mr. Nick Oliver Daniel, ACA *2008;* 24 Little Dimocks, LONDON, SW12 9JJ.
•PARR, Mr. Philip Henry Arthur, BSc FCA ATII *1982;* (Tax Fac), Moore Stephens LLP, 150 Aldersgate Street, LONDON, EC1A 4AB. See also Moore Stephens & Co
PARR, Miss. Rachel Clare, BSc ACA *1988;* 7 Eaton Rise, LONDON, W5 2HE.
PARR, Mr. Roger David, LLB FCA CTA *1988;* with Deloitte LLP, 1 Woodborough Road, NOTTINGHAM, NG1 3FG.
PARR, Mr. Ronald, BSc FCA *1971;* PO Box 783401, SANDTON, GAUTENG, 2146, SOUTH AFRICA.
PARR, Miss. Sarah Jane, BSc(Hons) ACA *2001;* 1 Smithy Court, WIGAN, WN3 6PS.
PARR, Mrs. Sharon Ann, BEng FCA TEP *1992;* Barclays Wealth, PO Box 671, GUERNSEY, GY1 3ST.
PARR, Mr. Simon Christopher, LLB ACA *2002;* Flat 105 Garand Court, Eden Grove, LONDON, N7 8EW.
PARR, Mr. Simon John, BSc ACA *1996;* Flat 11 Ashton Court, 94 Chatsworth Road, CROYDON, CR0 1HB.
•PARR, Mr. Timothy Francis Xavier, LLB FCA CTA *1986;* Baker Tilly Tax & Advisory Services LLP, 2 Whitehall Quay, LEEDS, LS1 4HG.
PARR, Mr. William David, FCA *1963;* 5 Mossley Court, Lyndhurst Avenue, Mossley Hill, LIVERPOOL, L18 8AR. (Life Member)
PARR-HEAD, Mr. Peter, FCA *1954;* The Malt House, The Street, South Stoke, READING, RG8 0JS. (Life Member)
PARRATT, Mr. Christopher Joseph, BA ACA *1986;* Church field House, Bicester Road, Oakley, AYLESBURY, BUCKINGHAMSHIRE, HP18 9QF.
PARRATT, Mr. Nicholas David, BA ACA *1995;* 9 Winchester House, Pavilion Way, MACCLESFIELD, CHESHIRE, SK10 3GB.
PARRETT, Mrs. Joanne, BA(Hons) ACA *2003;* 1&2 South Stour Cottage, Lower Mersham, ASHFORD, KENT, TN25 7HU.
•PARRETT, Mr. Nicholas John, ACA *2002;* Wilkins Kennedy, Greytown House, 221-227 High Street, ORPINGTON, BR6 0NZ.
PARRETT, Miss. Sophie Caroline, BSc ACA *1991;* 102 East Sheen Avenue, LONDON, SW14 8AU.
PARRETT-SMITH, Miss. Janet Elizabeth, BSc ACA CPA *1994;* 1511 South Pollard Street, ARLINGTON, VA 22204, UNITED STATES.
PARRIS, Mr. Adrian, BA ACA *1991;* Mead House, 8 Meadway, Oxshott, LEATHERHEAD, KT22 0LZ.
PARRIS, Mr. Andrew James, ACA CA(SA) *2009;* National Grid, National Grid House, Warwick Technology Park, Gallows Hill, WARWICK, CV34 6DA.
PARRIS, Mr. John, FCA *1958;* 5 Grange Gardens, Farnham Common, SLOUGH, SL2 3HL. (Life Member)
PARRIS, Mr. Rawle, MA ACA *1995;* 71 Moss Lane, PINNER, MIDDLESEX, HA5 3AZ.
PARRISH, Mr. Brian Walter, FCA *1960;* Lanark Cottage, Alton Lane, Four Marks, ALTON, HAMPSHIRE, GU34 5AL. (Life Member)
•PARRISH, Mr. Gabriel John, BA ACA *1986;* (Tax Fac), Fitzgerald and Law LLP, 8 Lincoln's Inn Fields, LONDON, WC2A 3BP.
PARRISH, Mr. James, FCA *1959;* Moorfield Bungalow, 15 Heaton Close, Baildon, SHIPLEY, BD17 5PL. (Life Member)
PARRISH, Mr. Keith John, BSc ACA *1989;* Bell House, Water Lane, Bishops Sutton, ALRESFORD, SO24 0AR.
PARRISH, Mr. Michael John, FCA *1971;* Flat 5, 22 Spencer Hill, Wimbledon, LONDON, SW19 4NY.
PARRISH, Mrs. Ruth Elizabeth, BA ACA *2006;* 116 Bromham Road, Biddenham, BEDFORD, MK40 4AH.
PARRISH, Miss. Vicky Louise, BSc ACA *2007;* 2 Constance Road, SUTTON, SURREY, SM1 4QG.
PARRISS, Mr. Terry Ralph, FCA *1961;* 329 Woodmill Lane, Swaythling, SOUTHAMPTON, SO18 2JJ.
•PARRITT, Mr. Clive Anthony, FCA CF FIIA FRSA *1966;* PRESIDENT MEMBER OF COUNCIL, Clive Parritt, 34 Eton Avenue, LONDON, NW3 3HL. See also Clive Parritt & Co
•PARROTT, Mr. Benjamin, BSc ACA *2000;* with PricewaterhouseCoopers, 101 Barbirolli Square, Lower Mosley Street, MANCHESTER, M2 3PW.
PARROTT, Mr. Bradley, ACA *2011;* Moore Stephens, 150 Aldersgate Street, LONDON, EC1A 4AB.
•PARROTT, Mr. Brian Michael, FCA *1956;* Brian M Parrott, Stonecroft, Beadon Road, SALCOMBE, TQ8 8LU.
PARROTT, Mr. Christopher, BSc ACA *2011;* Flat 5, 63-65 Hackney Road, LONDON, E2 7NX.
PARROTT, Mr. Gary Robert, BA ACA *1990;* 20 Gilbert Way, Finchampstead, WOKINGHAM, RG40 4HJ.
PARROTT, Mrs. Gemma Catherine, LLB ACA *1997;* 1 Rectory Court, Idmiston, SALISBURY, SP4 0AS.
•PARROTT, Mr. Graham William, BA ACA *1988;* (Tax Fac), Ernst & Young LLP, PO Box 9, Royal Chambers, St Julian's Avenue, St Peter Port, GUERNSEY GY1 4AF. See also Ernst & Young Europe LLP
PARROTT, Mr. John Donald, FCA *1962;* 323 Bramhall La, Davenport, STOCKPORT, SK3 8TE.
PARROTT, Mr. John Squire, FCA *1961;* PO Box 304, DARLING, WESTERN CAPE PROVINCE, 7345, SOUTH AFRICA.
PARROTT, Mr. Michael Colin, FCA *1964;* 6 Waverley Drive, South Wonston, WINCHESTER, HAMPSHIRE, SO21 3EF. (Life Member)
PARROTT, Mrs. Sara Elizabeth, ACA *1982;* 21 Berrycroft, Honley, HUDDERSFIELD, HD7 2BP.
PARROTT, Mr. Steven David, FCA *1976;* La Croute La Corbiere, Forest, GUERNSEY, GY8 0JG.
PARROTT, Mrs. Suzanne Kathryn, BSc ACA *2000;* 2 Dene Cottages, Warrington Road Great Budworth, NORTHWICH, CHESHIRE, CW9 6HB.
PARROTT, Mr. William James, MA ACA *1995;* 1 Manor Fields, Seale, FARNHAM, GU10 1HT.
PARRY, Miss. Abigail Victoria Leanne, ACA *2008;* 24 Post Office Road, Lingwood, NORWICH, NR13 4AR.
PARRY, Mr. Adrian Baskerville, FCA *1960;* 23 Vermont Crescent, IPSWICH, IP4 2ST. (Life Member)
PARRY, Mr. Alan Geoffrey, BSc ACA *1985;* 40 Hill View, Henleaze, BRISTOL, BS9 4PY.
PARRY, Mr. Alan Hugh, ACA *2005;* 12 Hampton Gate, Vierlanden, DURBANVILLE, WESTERN CAPE PROVINCE, 7550, SOUTH AFRICA.
PARRY, Mr. Alexander Toby Shedden, BA ACA *2002;* 43 Millfield Gardens, Nether Poppleton, YORK, YO26 6NZ.
PARRY, Miss. Alexis Jane, BSc ACA *2008;* 45 Meadow Court, Narborough, LEICESTER, LE19 3DX.
PARRY, Mrs. Aneta Maria, ACA *2009;* 106 Harlow Terrace, HARROGATE, NORTH YORKSHIRE, HG2 0PP.
PARRY, Mrs. Angela Joy, BSc ACA *1990;* 20 Nimrod Close, ST. ALBANS, HERTFORDSHIRE, AL4 9XY.
PARRY, Mr. Antony John, FCA *1991;* Ballacallow Glen Road, Colby, ISLE OF MAN, IM9 4PA.
PARRY, Mrs. Beatrice Elizabeth, LLB ACA *1985;* 40 Hill View, Henleaze, BRISTOL, BS9 4PY.
PARRY, Mr. Brian Dennis, BSc FCA *1981;* 45 Gilpin Avenue, LONDON, SW14 8QX.
PARRY, Mrs. Caroline, BSc ACA *1999;* 16 Yew Tree Avenue, Saughall, CHESTER, CH1 6HB.
PARRY, Mr. Chris Simon, BSc ACA *2004;* 43 Ravensbury Road, LONDON, SW18 4SA.
•PARRY, Mr. Christopher John, ACA *2009;* Howsons, Winton House, Stoke Road, STOKE-ON-TRENT, ST4 2RW. See also Howsons Accountants Limited
PARRY, Mrs. Clair, ACA *1999;* 25 Maes Gwalia, Sychdyn, MOLD, CLWYD, CH7 6RR.
•PARRY, Mrs. Claire Louise, ACA *2008;* Lakin Clark Limited, Delandale House, 37 Old Dover Road, CANTERBURY, KENT, CT1 3JF.
PARRY, Mr. David Andrew, MA ACA *2001;* First Floor, 88 Langthorne Street, LONDON, SW6 6JX.
PARRY, Mr. David John, BSc(Hons) ACA PGCE *2001;* 16 Yew Tree Avenue, Saughall, CHESTER, CH1 6HB.
PARRY, Mr. David Kim, BA ACA MBA *1992;* Sedbergh School, Lupton House, Back Lane, SEDBERGH, CUMBRIA, LA10 5BY.
PARRY, Mr. David Pryce, BSc ACA *1984;* Red Gables, 1 Mill Lane, Grove, WANTAGE, OXFORDSHIRE, OX12 7HU.
PARRY, Mrs. Deirdre Jane, BSc ACA *2003;* 53 Hartington Road, TWICKENHAM, TW1 3EL.
•PARRY, Mr. Derek Arthur, FCA MAE *1969;* Derek A Parry, 82 Tyne Crescent, Brickhill, BEDFORD, MK41 7UL.
PARRY, Mr. Edward David, BSc ACA *1996;* 34 Camberwell Grove, LONDON, SE5 8RE.
PARRY, Mrs. Felicity Anne, BA ACA *1992;* Sigma Kalon UK Ltd, Huddersfield Road, BATLEY, WEST YORKSHIRE, WF17 9XA.
PARRY, Mr. Glyn, BSc ACA *1992;* British Telecom BT Centre, 81 Newgate Street, LONDON, EC1A 7AJ.
PARRY, Mr. Glyn David, BSc(Econ) FCA *1995;* 42 Medway Road, IPSWICH, IP3 0QH.
PARRY, Mr. Graham Robert, BSc ACA *1980;* 10 Hill Close, Ness, NESTON, CH64 4ED.
PARRY, Mrs. Gwendoline, BA ACA *1988;* 31 Bedford Avenue, Worsley, MANCHESTER, M28 7GG.
PARRY, Mr. Hugh Archibald Pryce, FCA *1971;* 27 Pointers Hill, Westcott, DORKING, RH4 3PF. (Life Member)
PARRY, Mr. Hugh Pryce, FCA *1949;* 19 Cygnet Court, Caldecott Road, ABINGDON, OX14 5ET. (Life Member)
PARRY, Mr. Hugh Ranken, BSc ACA *1987;* In Bruggen 34, 8907 WETTSWIL, SWITZERLAND.
PARRY, Mr. Ian Huw, BSc FCA *1990;* HEFCE, Northavon House, Coldharbour Lane, BRISTOL, BS16 1QD.
PARRY, Mr. Ian Roger, BSc FCA *1999;* Red Sails, Douit Du Moulin, St Peter, GUERNSEY, GY7 9HP.
•PARRY, Mr. Ivan John, FCA *1990;* Trevor Beasley & Co Ltd, 25 Market Place, NUNEATON, WARWICKSHIRE, CV11 4EG. See also Beasley & Co Limited and Parry Ivan J
•PARRY, Mr. Iwan Rhys, BA ACA *2004;* A. Hughes-Jones Dyson & Co, Bryn Afon, Segontium Terrace, CAERNARFON, LL55 2PN.
PARRY, Mr. James, BSc ACA *2004;* 47 Waldron Road, LONDON, SW18 3TA.
•PARRY, Mrs. Jane, BA FCA ATII *1991;* (Tax Fac), PM+M Solutions for Business LLP, Greenbank Technology Park, Challenge Way, BLACKBURN, BB1 5QB. See also PM & M Corporate Finance Limited
PARRY, Miss. Jane Catherine, ACA *2011;* 5 Sutton Road, Howden, GOOLE, NORTH HUMBERSIDE, DN14 7DJ.
PARRY, Miss. Joan, FCA *1938;* Lower Flat, 5 Monks Road, LINCOLN, LN2 5HL. (Life Member)
PARRY, Miss. Joanne, LLB ACA *2009;* 24 Frank Large Walk, NORTHAMPTON, NN5 4UP.
PARRY, Mr. John David, BA ACA *1992;* 20 Nimrod Close, ST. ALBANS, AL4 9XY.
•PARRY, Mr. John Edward, BA ACA *1981;* 23 Chapel Lane, WILMSLOW, SK9 5HW.
PARRY, Mr. John Frederick Crawford, FCA *1965;* Church View The Mains, Giggleswick, SETTLE, NORTH YORKSHIRE, BD24 0AX.
•PARRY, Mr. John Howard, FCA *1970;* Peters Elworthy & Moore, Salisbury House, Station Road, CAMBRIDGE, CB1 2LA. See also PEM VAT Services LLP, PEM Corporate Finance LLP
PARRY, Mr. Keith Frowen, FCA *1964;* 10 Chatsworth Close, Almondbury, HUDDERSFIELD, HD5 8HX. (Life Member)
•PARRY, Mr. Kevin Allen Huw, MA FCA *1986;* 85 Cambridge Street, LONDON, SW1V 4PY.
PARRY, Mr. Laurence Edward, BA ACA *1991;* (Tax Fac), Yew Tree Farmhouse, Preston Road, Ribchester, PRESTON, PR3 3YD.
PARRY, Mrs. Lucy Alexandra, BSc ACA *2005;* 47 Warsash Road, Warsash, SOUTHAMPTON, SO31 9HW.
•PARRY, Mr. Malcolm, BA ACA *1990;* Parry Consulting, 20 Holly Avenue, Jesmond, NEWCASTLE UPON TYNE, NE2 2PY.
PARRY, Mr. Martin John, BSc ACA *1991;* 75 East Sheen Avenue, East Sheen, LONDON, SW14 8AX.
PARRY, Mr. Michael David, BA(Hons) ACA *2002;* V T Aerospace Ltd 1 Enterprise Way, Aviation Park Bournemouth International Airport Hurn, CHRISTCHURCH, DORSET, BH23 6BS.
PARRY, Dr. Michael John, FCA *1972;* Flat 3 Seapoint, 64 Banks Road, POOLE, BH13 7QF.
•PARRY, Mr. Owen Anderson, BA FCA *1955;* Owen A. Parry & Co, 14 Tavistock Road, Sketty, SWANSEA, SA2 0SL.
PARRY, Mr. Paul, BA FCA *1974;* Haystacks, Touch Road, Walmersley, BURY, LANCASHIRE, BL9 5QS.
•PARRY, Mr. Philip John, FCA *1974;* (Tax Fac), Parry & Co, Unit 1, Temple House Estate, 6 West Road, HARLOW, ESSEX CM20 2DU.
PARRY, Mr. Philip Robert, BA FCA *1956;* 30 Alexander Avenue, Papatoetoe, AUCKLAND 2025, NEW ZEALAND. (Life Member)
PARRY, Mr. Richard Nicholas, BSc FCA *1979;* Bramley Brown Heath Road, Christleton, CHESTER, CH3 7PN.
•PARRY, Mr. Robert, FCA *1972;* Robert Parry & Co Limited, Nat. Westminster Bank Chambers, 2 Dundas Street, Queensferry, DEESIDE, CH5 1SZ.
PARRY, Mr. Robert Griffith Pennant, FCA *1964;* 20 Dodonaea Court, DUNCRAIG, WA 6023, AUSTRALIA. (Life Member)
PARRY, Mr. Robert Spencer, BA FCA *1990;* with RSM Tenon Limited, York House, 20 York Street, MANCHESTER, M2 3BB.
•PARRY, Mr. Roger John, ACA FCCA *2009;* Thomas & Young LLP, 240-244 Stratford Road, Shirley, SOLIHULL, WEST MIDLANDS, B90 3AE. See also Thomas & Young
•PARRY, Mr. Roland George, ACA *2008;* (Tax Fac), Magee Gammon Partnership LLP, Henwood House, Henwood, ASHFORD, KENT, TN24 8DH. See also Magee Gammon Corporate Limited
PARRY, Mr. Ronald, FCA *1959;* 23 Howey Rise, FRODSHAM, WA6 6DN. (Life Member)
PARRY, Mrs. Sarah Louise, BSc ACA *1994;* Rookwood House, Woodbrook Road, ALDERLEY EDGE, CHESHIRE, SK9 7BY.
PARRY, Dr. Simon Nicholas, PhD BA FCA *1992;* Lime Tree House, North Road, Aspatria, WIGTON, CUMBRIA, CA7 3EN.
PARRY, Mrs. Stephanie Dawn, BSocSc ACA *1995;* Highfield, Rose Lane, Wheathampstead, ST. ALBANS, HERTFORDSHIRE, AL4 8RA.
PARRY, Mr. Stuart, BSc ACA *2003;* 7 Harmsworth Drive, STOCKPORT, CHESHIRE, SK4 4RP.
•PARRY, Mrs. Susan Mary, BSc ACA *1989;* Parry Business Services Limited, 28 Briarwood, Westbury on Trym, BRISTOL, BS9 3SS.
PARRY, Mrs. Suzanne Helen, BSc FCA *1989;* 39 Parkfields, Pen-y-Fai, BRIDGEND, MID GLAMORGAN, CF31 4NQ.
PARRY, Mr. Trevor Evan, FCA *1961;* 1 Sycamore Drive, BANBURY, OX16 9HF. (Life Member)
PARRY, Miss. Victoria, BSc ACA *2001;* 5 Branksome Road, LONDON, SW19 3AW.
PARRY, Mr. Vincent Hugh, MBA FCA *1975;* Tigeen, Hervines Road, AMERSHAM, BUCKINGHAMSHIRE, HP6 5HS.
PARRY, Ms. Vivienne Judith, BA ACA *1987;* 42 Margerison Road, ILKLEY, WEST YORKSHIRE, LS29 8QU.
•PARRY, Mr. William, MSc FCA *1991;* (Tax Fac), Parry & Co, Ynys Hir, Sandy Lane, RHOSNEIGR, GWYNEDD, LL64 5XA.
PARRY, Mr. William John, MA MSt ACA *2001;* 25 Berkeley Square, LONDON, W1J 6HN.

•**PARRY-RICHARDS, Mrs. Donna Marie, FCA** *1990;* GLF Richards & Co, Unit 8, Connect Business Village, 24 Derby Road, LIVERPOOL, L5 9PR.
PARRY-WINGFIELD, Mr. Maurice Andrew, BA FCA *1964;* (Tax Fac), 11 Montpelier Row, TWICKENHAM, TW1 2NQ. (Life Member)
PARS, Mr. Andrew, BA ACA *1992;* Garden Flat, 3 Buckland Crescent, LONDON, NW3 5DH.
PARSELL, Mr. Antony Clive, BSc ACA ATII *1987;* Anglian Home Improvements Unit 23, 23 Hurricane Way, NORWICH, NR6 6HE.
PARSELLE, Mr. Colin, BSocSc FCA *2000;* Crystal Holidays Kings House, 12-42 Wood Street, KINGSTON UPON THAMES, KT1 1JY.
•**PARSEY, Mrs. Katherine Mary, BA FCA** *1992;* (Tax Fac), Rose Cottage, Village Way, Little Chalfont, AMERSHAM, BUCKINGHAMSHIRE, HP7 9PX.
PARSEY, Mr. Michael Edward, FCA *1968;* Apartment B407, Residence de la Mer, 52 avenue Robert Soleau, 06600 ANTIBES, FRANCE.
PARSLIFFE, Mr. Andrew John, BA FCA *1980;* 7 Dupplin Terrace, PERTH, PH2 7DG.
PARSLIFFE, Mr. Simon James, MBA BA ACA *1987;* 6 Godwyn Gardens, FOLKESTONE, CT20 2JZ.
PARSLOE, Mr. John Stanley, FCA *1951;* 32 West Farm Road, Ogmore-by-Sea, BRIDGEND, Mid Glamorgan, CF32 0PU. (Life Member)
PARSLOW, Mr. Frederick Charles, FCA *1952;* 8 Herga Court, Stratford Road, WATFORD, WD17 4PA. (Life Member)
PARSON, Mr. Clive Graeme, FCA *1975;* 18 Joyce Close, CRANBROOK, TN17 3LZ.
PARSONAGE, Mrs. Jillian, BSc ACA *1990;* Gap Partnership Ashlyns Hall, Chesham Road, BERKHAMSTED, HERTFORDSHIRE, HP4 2ST.
PARSONAGE, Miss. Laura Mary, BA ACA *2007;* 20 Edward Street, Lower Weston, BATH, BA1 3BP.
PARSONAGE, Mr. Simon Kenneth, BA ACA *1982;* 10 Wyre Close, Valley Park, EASTLEIGH, SO53 4QR.
PARSONS, Mr. Adam Samuel, ACA *2011;* 51 Sheerstock, Haddenham, AYLESBURY, BUCKINGHAMSHIRE, HP17 8EZ.
PARSONS, Mr. Alan, BSc FCA *1973;* 30 Channel Road, CLEVEDON, BS21 7BY.
PARSONS, Miss. Amber Elizabeth Mary, MA ACA *2004;* Silchester International Investors Ltd Time & Life Building, 1 Bruton Street, LONDON, W1J 6TL.
•**PARSONS, Mrs. Andrea Maria, BSc ACA** *1995;* Calon, 17 Ford End, Denham, UXBRIDGE, MIDDLESEX, UB9 5AL.
PARSONS, Mr. Andrew, BSc ACA *2007;* Flat 4, 50 Coolhurst Road, LONDON, N8 8EU.
PARSONS, Mr. Andrew Colin, BSc ACA *1986;* Flat 102 Hudson House, Station Approach, EPSOM, KT19 8DL.
PARSONS, Mr. Andrew David, BA ACA *1993;* KPMG LLP, 345 Park Avenue, NEW YORK, NY 10154, UNITED STATES.
•**PARSONS, Mr. Andrew John, BSc FCA** *1979;* HW, 30 Camp Road, FARNBOROUGH, HAMPSHIRE, GU14 6EW. See also Haines Watts, HW Consulting and Haines Watts Consulting
PARSONS, Mr. Andrew Mark, BEng ACA *1992;* 83 Devonshire Road, Westbury Park, BRISTOL, BS6 7NH.
PARSONS, Mr. Andrew Raymond, BA ACA *1989;* Anchor Trust Burnbank House, Balliol Business Park Benton Lane, NEWCASTLE UPON TYNE, NE12 8EW.
PARSONS, Mr. Andrew Robert, FCA *1971;* 238B Kingston Road, STAINES, TW18 1PG.
PARSONS, Mrs. Angela Clare, ACA *2002;* 54 Effra Road, LONDON, SW19 8PP.
PARSONS, Mr. Anthony Edward, BSc ACA *1993;* 12 Latchett Road, LONDON, E18 1DJ.
PARSONS, Mr. Anthony John Matthew, BA ACA *1992;* Deutsche Bank, Winchester House, 1 Great Winchester Street, LONDON, EC2N 2DB.
PARSONS, Mr. Anthony William, FCA *1957;* 14 Fairhurst Drive, LEAMINGTON SPA, CV32 6HX. (Life Member)
•**PARSONS, Mr. Bernard Harold, FCA** *1967;* 46 Maple Drive, Denmead, WATERLOOVILLE, PO7 6QQ.
PARSONS, Mrs. Catherine Louise, BCom ACA *1986;* Pearson House, Whittington, CARNFORTH, LANCASHIRE, LA6 2NT.
PARSONS, Mr. Charles Geoffrey Carstairs, FCA *1977;* Waldron's Farm, Brinkworth, CHIPPENHAM, SN15 5DQ.
•**PARSONS, Mr. Charles Philip, BA FCA** *1982;* Hall Livesey Brown, 10 Nicholas Street, CHESTER, CH1 2NX.
PARSONS, Mrs. Charlotte Louise, BA ACA *1997;* Dairy Oast Chartwell Farm, Mapleton Road, WESTERHAM, TN16 1PS.
PARSONS, Mr. Christopher, BA ACA ACCA *1997;* 2 Pine Bank, Bishops Cleeve, CHELTENHAM, GLOUCESTERSHIRE, GL52 8JW.
PARSONS, Mr. Christopher, BA ACA *1998;* Climate Change Capital, 3 More London Riverside, LONDON, SE1 2AQ.
PARSONS, Mr. Christopher John, BSc ACA *2001;* 6 Carmelite Crescent, Eccleston, ST HELENS, WA10 5LP.
PARSONS, Mr. Colin James, FCA *1955;* 154 Valley Road, TORONTO M2L 1G4, ON, CANADA. (Life Member)
PARSONS, Mr. Conor James, MA ACA *2010;* Flat 4, 83 Abbey Road, LONDON, NW8 0AG.
PARSONS, Mr. Craig, BSc ACA *1996;* 26 Willow Court, Pool in Wharfedale, OTLEY, WEST YORKSHIRE, LS21 1RX.
•**PARSONS, Mr. Dale Nicholas, FCA** *1983;* (Tax Fac), Chalmers & Co (SW) Limited, 6 Linen Yard, South Street, CREWKERNE, SOMERSET, TA18 8AB.
PARSONS, Mr. David Anthony, ACA *2010;* 44 Waterloo Road, Bramhall, STOCKPORT, CHESHIRE, SK7 2NX.
PARSONS, Mr. David John, BSc FCA *1995;* 4 Truggan Close, Port Erin, ISLE OF MAN, IM9 6JR.
PARSONS, Mrs. Deborah Mary, BSc(Econ) ACA *1998;* 78 Selborne Road, LONDON, N14 7DG.
PARSONS, Mr. Denis Robert Alan, FCA *1973;* Holly House, Alexander Lane, Hutton, BRENTWOOD, ESSEX, CM13 1AG.
PARSONS, Mr. Derren Jonathan, BA ACA *1999;* Upper Ground Floor Flat, 54 Avenue Road, Highgate, LONDON, N6 5DR.
PARSONS, Mr. Edward Foster, BSocSc ACA CF *2001;* Candy & Candy Ltd, 100 Brompton Road, LONDON, SW3 1ER.
PARSONS, Mr. Geffrey, MBA BA FCA *1991;* Bnp Paribas, 10 Harewood Avenue, LONDON, NW1 6AA.
PARSONS, Mr. Gordon Lawrence, FCA *1983;* 35 Morrison Creek Crescent, OAKVILLE L6H 4C3, ON, CANADA.
•**PARSONS, Mr. Graham Jeremy, BSc ACA** *1998;* PricewaterhouseCoopers LLP, 1 Embankment Place, LONDON, WC2N 6RH. See also PricewaterhouseCoopers
PARSONS, Mr. Guy Thomas Ernest, CA *1974; (CA Scotland 1951);* 17 Lewes Road, HAYWARDS HEATH, WEST SUSSEX, RH17 7SP. (Life Member)
PARSONS, Mrs. Helen Elizabeth, ACA CTA *1982;* Cheyney Court, Bishops Frome, WORCESTER, HEREFORDSHIRE, WR6 5AS.
PARSONS, Mr. Howard Lewis, FCA *1958;* Highland, Westhill Village, Jurby Road, Ramsey, ISLE OF MAN, IM8 3TD.
PARSONS, Mr. Ian Douglas, BSc FCA *1981;* 37 Pooles Wharf Court, BRISTOL, BS8 4PB.
PARSONS, Mr. Ian Rexford, FCA *1962;* The Cleve South Street, Blewbury, DIDCOT, OXFORDSHIRE, OX11 9PR.
•**PARSONS, Mr. Ian William, ACA** *1991;* (Tax Fac), Ian Parsons, St John's Business Centre, St. Johns North, WAKEFIELD, WEST YORKSHIRE, WF1 3QA. See also Parsons & Co
PARSONS, Mrs. Irena, ACA ACCA *2009;* 27 Hill Street, ST HELIER, JE2 4UA.
•①**PARSONS, Miss. Jacqueline Ann, BSc ACA MABRP** *2005;* with Dodd & Co., Fifteen Rosehill, Montgomery Way, Rosehill Estate, CARLISLE, CA1 2RW.
•**PARSONS, Mr. James Arthur, FCA** *1983;* Kingly Brookes LLP, 415 Linen Hall, 162-168 Regent Street, LONDON, W1B 5TE.
PARSONS, Mr. James Thomas, BSc(Hons) ACA CTA *2003;* Second Floor Flat, 14 Beaufort Road Clifton, BRISTOL, BS8 2JZ.
PARSONS, Mr. Jason Ashley Michael, BSc ACA *2005;* 7 Pinnell Grove, Emersons Green, BRISTOL, BS16 7BJ.
PARSONS, Mrs. Jessica Naomi, ACA *2004;* 15 Hatch Mead, West End, SOUTHAMPTON, SO30 3NE.
PARSONS, Miss. Joanna Rebecca, BSc ACA *1997;* House A Floor 1, The Royal Bank of Scotland Plc, PO Box 1000, EDINBURGH, EH12 1HQ.
PARSONS, Sir John Christopher, KCVO MA FCA FIMC *1975;* The Old Rectory, Eydon, DAVENTRY, NN11 3QE.
PARSONS, Mr. John Richard, FCA *1969;* Mallards, 3 Mill Race, River, DOVER, KENT, CT17 0UZ.
PARSONS, Mr. Jon Roy, BSc(Hons) ACA *2004;* 27 Jordan Hill, OXFORD, OX2 8ET.
PARSONS, Mr. Jonathan, BSc ACA *2011;* Deepdene, The Warren, MAYFIELD, EAST SUSSEX, TN20 6UB.
PARSONS, Mr. Julian Edwin, BA ACA MBA MSI *1998;* 29 Avenue Egle, 78600 MAISONS LAFFITTE, FRANCE.
PARSONS, Miss. Kathryn Maree, ACA *2006;* 45 Epping Drive, FRENCHS FOREST, NSW 2086, AUSTRALIA.
PARSONS, Mr. Leslie Charles, FCA *1951;* 8 Tekels Way, CAMBERLEY, GU15 1HX. (Life Member)
PARSONS, Miss. Lucy Catherine Margaret, ACA *2008;* Flat 10, Old Theatre Court, 123 Park Street, LONDON, SE1 9ES.
PARSONS, Mr. Mark Leonard, BSc ACA *2001;* Flat 5, 21-22 Gosfield Street, LONDON, W1W 6HF.
PARSONS, Mr. Matthew, ACA *2008;* 84 Hazelwood Drive, ST. ALBANS, HERTFORDSHIRE, AL4 0UW.
PARSONS, Mr. Matthew Scott, BSc(Hons) ACA *2002;* Assurant Solutions, Assurant House, 6-12 Victoria Street, WINDSOR, SL4 1EN.
PARSONS, Mr. Michael David, BA(Hons) ACA *2011;* 42 Cresswell Grove, MANCHESTER, M20 2NH.
•**PARSONS, Mr. Michael Henry, FCA** *1974;* Mitchams Accountants Limited, 1 Cornhill, ILMINSTER, SOMERSET, TA19 0AD.
PARSONS, Mr. Michael Hewitt, FCA *1975;* 33 Rylett Road, LONDON, W12 9ST. (Life Member)
PARSONS, Mr. Michael Kenneth, FCA *1974;* Flat 26 Sharps Court, Cooks Way, HITCHIN, HERTFORDSHIRE, SG4 0JG.
PARSONS, Mr. Neil David, BA ACIB ACA *1997;* 13 Cooper Lane, Laceby, GRIMSBY, SOUTH HUMBERSIDE, DN37 7AY.
PARSONS, Mr. Niall Edward, BSc ACA *1993;* 9 West Temple Sheen, East Sheen, LONDON, SW14 7RT.
•**PARSONS, Mr. Nigel Reginald, BSc ACA** *1991;* Parker Hannifin Europe Sarl, La Tuiliere 6, CH 1163 ETOY, SWITZERLAND.
PARSONS, Miss. Penelope, BSc ACA *2006;* Quince Cottage Easton Town, Sherston, MALMESBURY, SN16 0LS.
•**PARSONS, Mr. Peter Frank, FCA** *1973;* with Deloitte LLP, 2 New Street Square, LONDON, EC4A 3BZ.
PARSONS, Mr. Peter John, FCA *1972;* Clover Cottage Freshfield Lane, Danehill, HAYWARDS HEATH, WEST SUSSEX, RH17 7HE.
PARSONS, Mr. Peter Leonard, FCA *1969;* Apartment 7, Knights House, 40 Four Oaks Road, SUTTON COLDFIELD, WEST MIDLANDS, B74 2UP.
PARSONS, Mr. Philip, BSc(Hons) ACA *2006;* 385 First Avenue, Apartment 15B, NEW YORK, NY 10010, UNITED STATES.
•**PARSONS, Mr. Philip Anthony, FCA** *1975;* Parsons & Co., Denendeh House, Mount Hermon Road, Palestine, ANDOVER, HAMPSHIRE SP11 7EW.
•**PARSONS, Mr. Philip Roger, FCA** *1993;* (Tax Fac), Clement Rabjohns, 111-113 High Street, EVESHAM, WR11 4XP. See also Clemrab LLP and Clement Rabjohns Limited
PARSONS, Miss. Rebecca Claudine, MSc BA ACA *1998;* Flat 3 Miles Court, 19 Miles Road Clifton, BRISTOL, BS8 2JB.
PARSONS, Mr. Richard John, BSc ACA *1992;* APPLEDOWN HOUSE, Noel Tatt Ltd Barton Business Park, New Dover Road, CANTERBURY, CT1 3TE.
•**PARSONS, Mr. Richard Keith, FCA** *1971;* AGHS Accounting & Taxation Services Limited, 14 Progress Business Centre, Whittle Parkway, SLOUGH, SL1 6DQ.
PARSONS, Mr. Robert Douglas, FCA *1955;* 31 Drew Gardens, GREENFORD, UB6 7QF. (Life Member)
PARSONS, Mr. Robert John, BSc ACA *1992;* 5 Victory Close, NEWTON ABBOT, DEVON, TQ12 2JJ.
•**PARSONS, Mr. Roger James, FCA** *1974;* Packwood Associates LLP, Cedar Court, Packwood Lane, Lapworth, SOLIHULL, B94 6AU.
•**PARSONS, Mr. Samuel Colin, FCA** *1989;* Munslows, 2nd Floor, Manfield House, 1 Southampton Street, LONDON, WC2R 0LR.
•**PARSONS, Mrs. Sarah Josephine, BA FCA** *1989;* (Tax Fac), SDP Financials Ltd, 28 Fordwich Drive, Frindsbury, ROCHESTER, KENT, ME2 3FA.
PARSONS, Mr. Shaun David Edward, MBA FCA *1970;* Winstone Glebe, CIRENCESTER, GL7 7LN.
PARSONS, Mr. Simon John, BSc ACA *2003;* 44 Cross Road, WATFORD, WD19 4DQ.
PARSONS, Mr. Simon Lawrence, BSc ACA *1994;* Codemasters Group Limited, Lower Farm House, Stoneythorpe, SOUTHAM, WARWICKSHIRE, CV47 2DL.
PARSONS, Mrs. Susannah Elizabeth, BA ACA *1995;* 9 West Temple Sheen, East Sheen, LONDON, SW14 7RT.
PARSONS, Mr. Timothy, ACA *2007;* 17 Shillington Road Meppershall, SHEFFORD, BEDFORDSHIRE, SG17 5ND.
PARSONS, Mrs. Victoria Ann, BSc ACA *2007;* 24 Watsons Walk, ST. ALBANS, HERTFORDSHIRE, AL1 1PD.
PARSONS-SMITH, Mr. Timothy, ACA *2008;* 34 Castle Hill, BERKHAMSTED, HERTFORDSHIRE, HP4 1HE.
PARSONSON, Mr. Ian Charles, BSc ACA *1990;* 46 Mexfield Road, LONDON, SW15 2RQ.
PARTAKIS, Mr. Michael Georgiou, FCA *1972;* 17 Bourne Street, Belgravia, LONDON, SW1 8JR.
PARTANEN, Miss. Sara Katja Emilia, ACA *2009;* 10 Anerley Station Road, LONDON, SE20 8PT.
PARTASSIDES, Mr. Costas, MSc BSc ACA *2003;* Galatariotis Building, 4th Floor, 11 Limassol Avenue, 2112 NICOSIA, CYPRUS.
PARTASSIDES, Miss. Maria, MSc BSc ACA *2005;* 17 Yianni Ritsou, 2332 NICOSIA, CYPRUS.
PARTELIDES, Mr. Polys George, MBA BSc ACA *1990;* Chemin des Ecaravez 16, 1092 BELMONT-SUR-LAUSANNE, SWITZERLAND.
•**PARTELLAS, Mr. Antonis Andrea, BSc FCA** *1987;* Alliott Partellas Kiliaris Ltd, 77 Strovolou Strovolos Center, Office 201, 2018 NICOSIA, CYPRUS.
PARTHASARATHY, Mr. Abhishekharee, ACA *2010;* Flat 61 Kenton Court, Kensington High Street, LONDON, W14 8NW.
PARTHASARATHY, Miss. Deepa Jagadish, MA ACA *1999;* 22 Tizzick Close, NORWICH, NR5 9HB.
PARTINGTON, Mr. Alan, BSc FCA *1979;* 34 Orchard Drive, Park Street, ST. ALBANS, AL2 2QG.
PARTINGTON, Mr. Andrew Stephen, BSc ACA *1997;* 33 Three Oaks Road, Wythall, BIRMINGHAM, B47 6HG.
PARTINGTON, Mr. Bryan Erik, LLB ACA *1983;* 2 Leinster Avenue, East Sheen, LONDON, SW14 7JP.
PARTINGTON, Mrs. Caroline Anne, BA ACA *1999;* Forresters House, 399 Stainland Road, Stainland, HALIFAX, HX4 9HF.
PARTINGTON, Miss. Catherine, ACA *2008;* 21 Bloemfontein Road, Shepherds Bush, LONDON, W12 7BH.
PARTINGTON, Mr. David John, BSc FCA *1975;* 28 Church Lane, Gawsworth, MACCLESFIELD, SK11 9QY.
PARTINGTON, Mr. Derek Woodfield, FCA *1951;* 28 Crossfield Drive, Worsley, MANCHESTER, M28 1GP. (Life Member)
PARTINGTON, Mr. Geoffrey, FCA *1969;* 32 Pinewood Road, FERNDOWN, BH22 9RR.
PARTINGTON, Mr. Graham, ACA *2011;* 2 Windover Close, BOLTON, BL5 1HR.
PARTINGTON, Miss. Helen, ACA *2009;* 28 Church Lane, Gawsworth, MACCLESFIELD, CHESHIRE, SK11 9QY.
PARTINGTON, Mr. Ian, FCA *1961;* 30 Wentworth Green, Eaton, NORWICH, NR4 6AE. (Life Member)
PARTINGTON, Mrs. Jacqueline Diana, BSc ACA *1981;* Linden End, Linden Gardens, LEATHERHEAD, KT22 7HB.
•**PARTINGTON, Miss. Jane Cressida, BA FCA** *1989;* (Tax Fac), 6 Meridian Place, MANCHESTER, M20 2QF.
PARTINGTON, Mr. Jason David, ACA *2010;* 14a Leopold Road, LONDON, W5 3PB.
PARTINGTON, Mr. John, FCA *1960;* The Hall House, 20 The High Street, Datchet, SLOUGH, SL3 9EQ. (Life Member)
PARTINGTON, Mr. John David, FCA *1961;* Kasteldreef 37, 3140 KEERBERGEN, BELGIUM.
PARTINGTON, Mr. Jonathan, BSc ACA *1993;* 80 Mosley Street, MANCHESTER, M2 3FX.
PARTIS, Mr. Anthony David, FCA *1970;* Home Waters, Riverside, Shaldon, TEIGNMOUTH, DEVON, TQ14 0DA.
PARTNER, Mr. Graham Robert, BA(Hons) ACA *2001;* (Tax Fac), with PricewaterhouseCoopers, West London Office, The Atrium, 1 Harefield Road, UXBRIDGE, UB8 1EX.
PARTON, Mr. Charles Joshua, BSc ACA *2011;* with Rees Pollock, 35 New Bridge Street, LONDON, EC4V 6BW.
PARTON, Mr. John, FCA *1963;* 7 Oxendon Road, Arthingworth, MARKET HARBOROUGH, LEICESTERSHIRE, LE16 8LA.
PARTON, Mr. Michael Neil, MA ACA *1991;* 95 Parkside Close, PO Box 30860, SEVEN MILE BEACH, GRAND CAYMAN, KY1 1204, CAYMAN ISLANDS.
PARTRIDGE, Mr. Andrew Arthur, FCA *1992;* 9 Castleton Road, Barnwood, GLOUCESTER, GL4 3GB.
PARTRIDGE, Mr. Charles Edward, BSc ACA *1994;* 24 Ashpole Spinney, NORTHAMPTON, NN4 9QB.
PARTRIDGE, Mr. Christopher Arthur, FCA *1982;* 2 Holly Orchard, STRATFORD-UPON-AVON, WARWICKSHIRE, CV37 6RJ.
PARTRIDGE, Mrs. Clare Margaret, BA ACA *2001;* 67 Haigh Lane, Hoylandswaine, SHEFFIELD, S36 7JQ.
PARTRIDGE, Miss. Emma Claire, BSc(Hons) ACA *2004;* 6211 Rosebriar Lane, CHARLOTTE, NC 28277, UNITED STATES.

•**PARTRIDGE, Mr. Gary, BSc ACA** *1992;* with PricewaterhouseCoopers, One Kingsway, CARDIFF, CF10 3PW.

PARTRIDGE, Mr. Geoffrey James, BSc ACA *1984;* 12 Clos Treoda, CARDIFF, CF14 6DL.

PARTRIDGE, Mr. Ian, BSc(Hons) ACA *2010;* 86 Shuttleworth Road, LONDON, SW11 3DE.

PARTRIDGE, Mr. Ian Claydon, BSc ACA *1989;* Vision Alert Automotive Ltd Unit 3, Victoria Industrial Park Victoria Road, LEEDS, LS14 2LA.

PARTRIDGE, Mr. John Francis, FCA *1961;* 6 Springfield Road, Castle Bromwich, BIRMINGHAM, B36 0DT. (Life Member)

PARTRIDGE, Dr. Julia Frances, BSc ACA *2004;* Kelda Group Ltd, Western House, Halifax Road, BRADFORD, BD6 2SZ.

PARTRIDGE, Mr. Keith Brian, BCom ACA *1995;* 52 Stanley Avenue, ROMFORD, RM2 5DR.

•**PARTRIDGE, Mrs. Louise Elizabeth Mary, MEng ACA** *1995;* Merryhill Accountancy Services Ltd, 73 High Street, Braunston, DAVENTRY, NORTHAMPTONSHIRE, NN11 7HS.

•**PARTRIDGE, Mr. Mark, BSc FCA** *1991;* (Tax Fac), Chariot House Ltd, Gunpowder House, 66/68 Great Suffolk Street, LONDON, SE1 0BL.

PARTRIDGE, Mr. Mark, ACA *2008;* 26 Fold Lane, Biddulph, STOKE-ON-TRENT, ST8 7SG.

PARTRIDGE, Mr. Michael John, FCA *1970;* Candle Dyke, Broadview Road, LOWESTOFT, NR32 3PL.

•**PARTRIDGE, Mr. Michael Richard, FCA** *1969;* Partridge & Co., The Old Malt House, The Green, Clipston, MARKET HARBOROUGH, LE16 9RS.

PARTRIDGE, Mr. Neil Russell, BA FCA *1979;* Apartment 10 Chellaston House, Toft Road, KNUTSFORD, CHESHIRE, WA16 9EB.

PARTRIDGE, Mr. Paul Kirwin, BA ACA *1995;* 130 Old Bath Road, CHELTENHAM, GLOUCESTERSHIRE, GL53 7DP.

PARTRIDGE, Mr. Peter Damian, BCom FCA *1955;* Cherith, Bull Lane, GERRARDS CROSS, SL9 8RD. (Life Member)

PARTRIDGE, Miss. Samantha Barbara, BA(Hons) ACA *2010;* 33 Marathon Avenue, Douglas, ISLE OF MAN, IM2 4JB.

•**PARTRIDGE, Mr. Steven John, BSc ACA** *1989;* PricewaterhouseCoopers, 7 More London Riverside, LONDON, SE1 2RT. See also PricewaterhouseCoopers LLP

PARTRIDGE, Mr. Thomas Richard, LLB ACA *2003;* with Deloitte LLP, Athene Place, 66 Shoe Lane, LONDON, EC4A 3BQ.

PARTRIDGE, Mr. William Francis, FCA *1959;* Homegrounds, Jesses Lane, Long Crendon, AYLESBURY, HP18 9AG. (Life Member)

PARVEZ, Mr. Mohsan, BCom FCA *1984;* c/o E A Juffali & Brothers, Corporate Office, P O Box 1049, JEDDAH, 21431, SAUDI ARABIA.

PARVIN, Ms. Barbara Ann, ACA *1979;* 26 Sandy Flatts Lane, MIDDLESBROUGH, CLEVELAND, TS5 7YY.

PARVIN, Mrs. Christine Elizabeth, BSc ACA *1996;* Sevenoaks Town Council, Town Council Offices, Bradbourne Vale Road, SEVENOAKS, KENT, TN13 3QG.

PARVIN, Mr. Donald, FCA *1959;* (Member of Council 1975 - 1977), Summers Reach, School Lane, Lindfield, HAYWARDS HEATH, WEST SUSSEX, RH16 2DX. (Life Member)

PARWANI, Mr. Jeremy, BA ACA *1994;* 200 East Randolph Street, 11th Floor, CHICAGO, IL 60601, UNITED STATES.

PARYLO, Mrs. Violetta Elizabeth, BA ACA *1993;* (Tax Fac), 22 Roughknowles Road, COVENTRY, CV4 8GX.

PASCAL, Mr. Irvin James, BA FCA *1988;* PO Box 526, Melrose Arch, MELROSE, 2076, SOUTH AFRICA.

PASCALL, Mr. Christopher John, FCA *1966;* West Wing, 15-16 Bermerside House, Greenroyd Close, HALIFAX, WEST YORKSHIRE, HX3 0JY. (Life Member)

PASCALL, Mr. Daniel Paul, BSc ACA *2000;* 7 Darwin Close, MARKET DRAYTON, TF9 3UT.

•**PASCALL, Mr. Ian Derek, FCA** *1979;* (Tax Fac), McCabe Ford Williams, Charlton House, Dour Street, DOVER, CT16 1BL.

PASCALL, Miss. Joanne Rae, BA ACA *2006;* Flat 45 Old Court House, 24 Old Court Place, LONDON, W8 4PD.

•**PASCAN, Mr. Paul Michael, BCom FCA** *1977;* 38 Hillcroft, DUNSTABLE, BEDFORDSHIRE, LU6 1TU.

•**PASCHALI, Mr. Paschalis, FCA** *1971;* Pascall & Co., 47 Park Way, Whetstone, LONDON, N20 0XN.

PASCHALIDOU, Ms. Sofia, BSc ACA *1995;* 9 Louki Akrita Street, Lakatamia, Archaggelos, 2333 NICOSIA, CYPRUS.

PASCHALIS, Mr. George Costa, BA(Econ) ACA *1996;* PO Box 21301, CY-1506 NICOSIA, CYPRUS.

PASCHALIS, Mr. Socrates Costa, BA(Hons) ACA *2000;* 27 Varnalis Street, Aglandjia 2112, Nicosia, 2112 NICOSIA, CYPRUS.

PASCO, Mr. Timothy Richard, BSc ACA *1996;* 16 Dawlish Avenue, LONDON, SW18 4RW.

PASCOE, Mr. Alan George, BA ACA *1978;* Anixter International Ltd, 1 York Road, UXBRIDGE, UB8 1RN.

PASCOE, Mr. Alexander James, BSc ACA *2004;* Pricewaterhousecoopers, 9 Greyfriars Road, READING, RG1 1JG.

PASCOE, Mr. Charles Lionel, BSc FCA *1983;* (Tax Fac), with BDO LLP, 55 Baker Street, LONDON, W1U 7EU.

PASCOE, Mr. Christopher Hugh, BSc FCA CPA *1975;* 130 Country Club Drive, HILLSBOROUGH, CA 94010, UNITED STATES.

•**PASCOE, Mr. Edward Trewhella, BA FCA** *1982;* Pryor Begent Fry & Co., 13/15 Commercial Road, HAYLE, TR27 4DE.

PASCOE, Mr. Graham Stephen, BA ACA *1986;* Willow Farm, Cocksford, Stutton, TADCASTER, NORTH YORKSHIRE, LS24 9NG.

PASCOE, John Hill, Esq CBE FCA *1955;* High Corner, 11 St Johns Close, Stratton, CIRENCESTER, GL7 2JA. (Life Member)

PASCOE, Mr. Jonathan Mark, BA ACA *1993;* Wightlink Ltd, Gunwharf Road, PORTSMOUTH, PO1 2LA.

•**PASCOE, Mr. Stephen Peter, BSc ACA** *1995;* Beechwood House, Narrow Lane, Downley, HIGH WYCOMBE, BUCKINGHAMSHIRE, HP13 5XP.

•**PASCOE, Mr. Trevor William, FCA CTA** *1968;* (Tax Fac), Dover Accountancy Ltd, 4 River Meadow, River, DOVER, KENT, CT17 0XA.

PASCUAL, Mr. Nick, BA ACA *1998;* 7 Mallard Place, TWICKENHAM, TW1 4SW.

PASCUAL, Mr. Torres Andrew, BA ACA *1986;* Court View, Hook Heath Road, WOKING, SURREY, GU22 0LB.

PASEA, Mr. Nigel Ashton Patrick, BSc FCA MBA *1983;* PO Box 506733, DUBAI, UNITED ARAB EMIRATES.

PASHA, Mr. Harold Charles, FCA *1971;* 4th Floor, 28 Margaret Street, LONDON, W1N 7LB.

•**PASHBY, Mr. Simon Mark, BA ACA** *1985;* KPMG LLP, Saltire Court, 20 Castle Terrace, EDINBURGH, EH1 2EG. See also KPMG Europe LLP

PASHIALI, Mr. Takis-Christoforos, MSc ACA *2009;* Flat 4, 60 Thornhill Road, LONDON, N1 1JY.

PASHIAS, Mr. Marios, BSc ACA ACCA *2009;* 13 Gladstonos street, Kaimakli, 1026 NICOSIA, CYPRUS.

PASHIAS, Mr. Savvas, LLB ACA *2005;* Flat 202, 4 Ioanni Megalemou Street, Strovolos, 2028 NICOSIA, CYPRUS.

PASHLEY, Mrs. Amie Louise, ACA *2007;* Bramble Barn La Rue Du Coin, Grouville, JERSEY, JE3 9QR.

•**PASHLEY, Mr. Mark Andrew, FCA** *1988;* Cooper Parry LLP, 14 Park Row, NOTTINGHAM, NG1 6GR.

PASHLEY, Mr. Michael, BA ACA *1986;* A R E A Property Partners (UK) Ltd, 1 Knightsbridge, LONDON, SW1X 7LX.

PASHLEY, Mr. Nigel James, BA ACA *1997;* 60 Heathfield Road, BROMLEY, BR1 3RW.

PASHLEY, Mr. Roger Leonard, FCA *1966;* 137a Brox Road, Ottershaw, CHERTSEY, SURREY, KT16 0LG. (Life Member)

PASHLEY, Mr. Stephen Roger, BA ACA *2000;* 23 Kettil'stoun Grove, LINLITHGOW, WEST LOTHIAN, EH49 6PP.

PASHOULIS, Mr. Marios Christaki, BSc ACA *1994;* Rachel 8 Strovolos, CY-2039 NICOSIA, CYPRUS.

PASK, Dr. Helen Jane, ACA *2010;* 38 Hanover Street, CARDIFF, CF5 1LS.

PASK, Mr. Simon David, ACA *1985;* 76 Murlough View, Dundrum, NEWCASTLE, COUNTY DOWN, BT33 0WE.

PASK, Mr. William Charles Wilson, MA ACA *1991;* 45 Beechcroft Manor, WEYBRIDGE, KT13 9NZ.

PASKINS, Mr. Howard Allan, BSc FCA *1977;* 9 Mount Pleasant Drive, Bransgore, CHRISTCHURCH, DORSET, BH23 8BZ.

PASKINS, Mr. Ian John, BA FCA *1981;* 25 Westfield Road, BISHOP'S STORTFORD, CM23 2RE.

PASKINS, Mr. Keith Terence, FCA *1969;* The Orchard, High Street, Taplow, MAIDENHEAD, SL6 0EX.

PASKINS, Mrs. Rosemary Ann, BA FCA *1981;* 16 Willoughby Drive, SOLIHULL, B91 3GB.

PASLEY, Mr. Robert Killigrew Sabine, BSc ACA *1991;* 60 Tana Road, Emmarentia, JOHANNESBURG, GAUTENG, 2195, SOUTH AFRICA.

PASQUILL, Mr. John Hilton, FCA *1964;* 33 Yewfield Crescent, DON MILLS M3B 2Y4, ON, CANADA. (Life Member)

•**PASRICHA, Mrs. Lesley Ann, BA FCA** *1976;* Lesley Pasricha, 8 Blanchard House, 28 Clevedon Road, TWICKENHAM, TW1 2TD.

PASRICHA, Mr. Niraj, FCA *1971;* 897 Ithaca Avenue, SUNNYVALE, CA 94087, UNITED STATES.

PASRICHA, Mr. Nitin, FCA *1972;* Pipit Wood, Kings Drive, MIDHURST, WEST SUSSEX, GU29 0BH.

PASS, Mr. Andrew James, BA FCA *1999;* 127 Crewe Road South, EDINBURGH, EH4 2NX.

PASS, Mr. Christopher Stuart, ACA *2009;* 36 Blighmont Crescent, SOUTHAMPTON, SO15 8RH.

PASS, Miss. Heather Elizabeth, MA BA ACA *2005;* (Tax Fac), 10 Makinen House, 49 Palmerston Road, BUCKHURST HILL, IG9 5NZ.

•**PASS, Mrs. Helen Lesley, BA FCA** *1987;* with Churchmill House Ltd, Churchmill House, Ockford Road, GODALMING, SURREY, GU7 1QY.

PASS, Mrs. Jacqueline Anne, BSc ACA MCIPD *1986;* 21 Highfield Close, Davenport, STOCKPORT, CHESHIRE, SK3 8UB.

PASS, Mr. John Richard Gibson, ACA *1981;* An Nead, 122 Main Road, Smalley, ILKESTON, DE7 6DS.

•**PASS, Mr. Johnathan David, MSc BA ACA** *1997;* with KPMG LLP, 1 The Embankment, Neville Street, LEEDS, LS1 4DW.

PASSA, Miss. Alexandra Ann, BSc ACA *2006;* Flat 42 Copsfield Court, 27-29 Woodford Road, LONDON, E18 2EF.

PASSAM, Mr. Mark Jonathan, BSc ACA *1989;* 8 Pinfold Close, Tutbury, BURTON-ON-TRENT, DE13 9NJ.

PASSANT, Miss. Margaret Fiona, BCom ACA *1986;* 17 Beachburn Way, Handsworth Wood, BIRMINGHAM, B20 2AU.

•**PASSEY, Mr. David Richard, BSc ACA** *1988;* Landau Morley LLP, Lanmor House, 370-386 High Road, WEMBLEY, MIDDLESEX, HA9 6AX.

PASSEY, Mr. Graham Francis, FCA *1967;* The Cottage, Ford Lane, Longdon, RUGELEY, WS15 4PJ.

PASSEY, Mrs. Ruth Mary, FCA *1990;* Harpin Ltd, PO Box 53, Nun Monkton, YORK, YO26 8WW.

PASSFIELD, Mr. Justin Brian, BA ACA *1989;* Odiam Farm, Stone, TENTERDEN, TN30 7JH.

PASSI, Mr. Vishu, ACA *2008;* 22 Harris Road, Beeston, NOTTINGHAM, NG9 4FB.

•**PASSINGHAM, Mrs. Amanda, ACA MAAT** *2002;* Halcyon Accountants & Business Adviser Ltd, PO Box 9953, LEICESTER, LE7 3UX.

PASSINGHAM, Mr. Matthew, ACA *2001;* (Tax Fac), 16 Ervin Way, Queniborough, LEICESTER, LE7 3TT.

PASSINGHAM, Mr. Neil, MBA BA ACA *1983;* 33 Wrights Way, South Wonston, WINCHESTER, SO21 3HE.

PASSMORE, Mr. Allan Gerald, BA ACA *1997;* Lloyds TSB Bank Plc, Canons House, Canons Way, BRISTOL, BS1 5LL.

PASSMORE, Mr. David John, ACA *2003;* Ground Floor Flat, 39 Cobbold Road, Willesden, LONDON, NW10 9SU.

PASSMORE, Mr. Edward, ACA *2010;* 3 Cheyne Close, AMERSHAM, BUCKINGHAMSHIRE, HP6 5LT.

PASSMORE, Mr. Guy Damien, BSc(Hons) ACA *2001;* 375 St. Albans Road West, HATFIELD, HERTFORDSHIRE, AL10 9RU.

PASSMORE, Mrs. Janet Mary, BSc ACA *1992;* 4 The Orchard, Bassett Green Village, SOUTHAMPTON, SO16 3NA.

PASSMORE, Mr. Mark David, LLB ACA *1999;* Raffine Nakameguro #103, 3-3-6 Nakameguro, Meguro, TOKYO, 153-0061 JAPAN.

•**PASSMORE, Mr. Mark Ian Weeks, MA FCA** *1977;* PWR Accountants Limited, 2 Beacon End Courtyard, London Road, Stanway, COLCHESTER, CO3 0NU.

PASSMORE, Mrs. Natalie Sophie, MA(Hons) ACA *2010;* Mulcaster House, Jersey New Waterworks Co, JERSEY, JE1 1DG.

PASSMORE, Richard Harry, Esq OBE FCA *1939;* Flat B5, Shirley Towers, Vane Hill Road, TORQUAY, TQ1 2BX. (Life Member)

PASSMORE, Mrs. Victoria Jane, BSc ACA *2001;* The Oaks, 38 The Causeway, Congresbury, BRISTOL, BS49 5DJ.

PASSWAY, Mr. Martin, BAcc ACA *1992;* Flat 2, 33 St Stephens Gardens, TWICKENHAM, TW1 2LT.

PASTAKIA, Mr. Kamal, BA ACA *1998;* 212 Glenview Avenue, TORONTO M4R 1R3, ON, CANADA.

PASTAKIA, Ms. Reena, BSc ACA *2001;* 54 Chapman Square, Wimbledon, LONDON, SW19 5QT.

PASTER, Mr. Leslie, BSc ACA *1990;* 7 Links Drive, Elstree, BOREHAMWOOD, HERTFORDSHIRE, WD6 3PP.

PASTUREL, Mrs. Michelle, ACA *2004;* Bay Tree Cottage 4 Les Ormes, La Rue Carree St. Brelade, JERSEY, JE3 8FJ.

PAT FONG, Mr. Victor Luke, ACA *2009;* Flat 104 Rossmore Court, Park Road, LONDON, NW1 6XZ.

PAT FONG, Mr. Yon Yan, BSc FCA *1963;* Coastal Road, Pointe Aux Sables, PORT LOUIS, MAURITIUS.

PATANI, Mr. Ashish Jayantilal, MSc BSc ACA *2005;* 31 Bourne End Road, NORTHWOOD, MIDDLESEX, HA6 3BP.

•**PATANI, Mr. Nitin Mohanlal, ACA FCCA** *2008;* Mccormack & Associates, Euro House, 1394-1400 High Road, LONDON, N20 9BH.

PATANI, Mr. Vishal Pankaj, BSc ACA *2005;* 11 Bromefield, STANMORE, HA7 1AA.

•**PATARA, Mr. Talwinder Singh, BSc(Hons) FCA FRSA** *1983;* (Tax Fac), T S Patara & Co Ltd, Financial House, 352 Bearwood Road, Bearwood, BIRMINGHAM, B66 4ET. See also Kensington Trading Co Limited, Patara & Co Limited

•**PATAS, Mr. Yusuf, BA ACA** *2004;* YP Finance Limited, Hawthorne House, 17A Hawthorne Drive, LEICESTER, LE5 6DL.

PATASHNIK, Mr. Paul Howard, FCA *1971;* Darlingtons, 48 High Street, EDGWARE, MIDDLESEX, HA8 7EQ.

PATCHETT, Mr. Edgar William, FCA *1965;* (Tax Fac), 33 Bigby High Road, BRIGG, DN20 9HB.

•**PATCHETT, Mr. George Fretigny, FCA** *1970;* Unit No 20035, Bel'Aire, SOMERSET WEST, C.P., 7130, SOUTH AFRICA.

•**PATCHING, Mr. Richard Colin, BA FCA** *1979;* PricewaterhouseCoopers, Dorchester House, 7 Church Street West, PO Box HM1171, HAMILTON HM EX, BERMUDA.

PATE, Mr. Andrew Nicholas, BA ACA *1986;* Bath & North East Somerset Council, The Guildhall, High Street, BATH, BA1 5AW.

PATE, Mr. Carl, BA ACA *1992;* Christmas Cottage, Birch Cross, Marchington, UTTOXETER, ST14 8NX.

PATE, Mr. Christopher David, ACA *1982;* 84 Hallow Road, WORCESTER, WR2 6BY.

•**PATE, Mr. Christopher Russell, FCA** *1971;* Trafalgar Accountancy & Tax Limited, Trafalgar House, 261 Alcester Road South, BIRMINGHAM, B14 6DT.

PATE, Mr. Jason, BSc ACA *1996;* 14 Ferndene Road, MANCHESTER, M20 4TT.

PATEL, Mrs. Aarti, BSc ACA *2006;* (Tax Fac), 44 Lodore Gardens, LONDON, NW9 0DR.

PATEL, Mr. Abdul Aziz, BSc ACA *1999;* 13 Pentland Road, DEWSBURY, WEST YORKSHIRE, WF12 9JR.

•**PATEL, Mr. Ahmed Dawood, FCA** *1971;* 47/121 Street, Off Khayaban-e-Mujahid, Phase 5, Defence Housing Authority, KARACHI 75500, PAKISTAN.

PATEL, Mr. Ajay, LLB ACA *1991;* (Tax Fac), Kingmaker House, 15 Station Road, Second Floor, Buyagigt Plc, NEW BARNET, HERTFORDSHIRE EN5 1NZ.

•**PATEL, Mr. Alay Bhupendra, BSc ACA CFA** *1998;* Ernst & Young LLP, 1 More London Place, LONDON, SE1 2AF. See also Ernst & Young Europe LLP

PATEL, Mr. Alay Chandrakant, ACA *2007;* 1 Parkside Road, NORTHWOOD, HA6 3HL.

•**PATEL, Miss. Alka, BA ACA** *1998;* 80 Orchard Gate, Sudbury, GREENFORD, UB6 0QP.

PATEL, Mrs. Alkaben Mahesh, BSc ACA *1985;* 29 The Avenue, PINNER, HA5 5BN.

•**PATEL, Mr. Amit, BSc ACA** *2007;* Farrell & Co Accountants Limited, 11 Amberside House, Wood Lane, Paradise Industrial Estate, HEMEL HEMPSTEAD, HERTFORDSHIRE HP2 4TP. See also Beginning 2 End Limited

PATEL, Mr. Amit, BSc ACA *2010;* 124 Northcote Road, LONDON, SW11 6QU.

PATEL, Mr. Amit, ACA *2008;* Flat 27 Ross Apartments, 23 Seagull Lane, LONDON, E16 1DE.

PATEL, Mr. Amit, BA ACA *2005;* 16 Briar Walk, Oadby, LEICESTER, LE2 5UF.

PATEL, Miss. Amita Vipinchandra, BA ACA *1989;* 5 rue J.P Beicht, Limpertsberg, L-1226 LUXEMBOURG, LUXEMBOURG.

PATEL, Miss. Amruta, BSc ACA *2010;* 71-73 Grove Road, ROMFORD, RM6 4PD.

PATEL, Mr. Anil, BSc(Econ) ACA *2001;* 49 Blossom Waye, HOUNSLOW, TW5 9HB.

•**PATEL, Mr. Anil Dahyabhai, BA(Hons) FCA** *2001;* AD Patel & Co Ltd, 3 Cromer Road, BIRMINGHAM, B12 9QP. See also Tax Accountants Ltd

PATEL, Mr. Anilkumar Indubhai, FCA *1974;* 11 Cuddington Park Close, BANSTEAD, SM7 1RF. (Life Member)

PATEL, Miss. Anita Sita, BA ACA *2003;* 18 Littleton Crescent, HARROW, MIDDLESEX, HA1 3SX.

PATEL, Mrs. Anitaben Anilkumar, BSc ACA *1989;* Woodlands, Shipley Bridge Lane, Copthorne, CRAWLEY, RH10 3JL.

PATEL, Mr. Anjay Vithalbhai, BA ACA *1990;* P.O.Box 86752, MOMBASA, KENYA.
PATEL, Mr. Anuj Raju, ACA *2008;* Flat 26 Raddon Tower, Dalston Square, LONDON, E8 3GN.
PATEL, Mr. Anup, BSc ACA *1991;* 30 Parkview Drive, MILLBURN, NJ 07041, UNITED STATES.
PATEL, Mr. Anup, BSc(Hons) ACA *2010;* Sleepy Hollow, Lynmouth Drive, Sully, PENARTH, SOUTH GLAMORGAN, CF64 5TP.
PATEL, Mr. Anup Ramesh, BSc ACA *1995;* GLG Partners LP, 1 Curzon Street, LONDON, W1J 5HB.
PATEL, Mr. Anup Ravidatta, FCA *1977;* P O Box 7116, TWEED HEADS SOUTH, NSW 2486, AUSTRALIA.
•PATEL, Mr. Anwer Hussaine, BA ACA *1991;* Prestons & Jacksons Partnership LLP, 364-368 Cranbrook Road, ILFORD, ESSEX, IG2 6HY. See also Prestons
PATEL, Mrs. Archana, BSc ACA *2010;* Flat 3 The Farmhouse, 205 Old Woking Road, WOKING, GU22 8JE.
PATEL, Mr. Arshad, BA FCA *1988;* Barnett Ravenscroft, 13 Portland Road, BIRMINGHAM, B16 9HN.
PATEL, Mr. Arun Vaghjibhai, FCA *1975;* 2 Empress Avenue, ILFORD, IG1 3DD.
PATEL, Mr. Arunkumar Vithalbhai, FCA *1971;* #604 - 3 Towering Heights Blvd., ST CATHARINES L2T 4A4, ON, CANADA. (Life Member)
•PATEL, Mr. Arvind Gangjibhai, FCA *1974;* Darvin & Co, 62 Redbridge Lane East, Redbridge, ILFORD, IG4 5EZ.
•PATEL, Mr. Arvind Motibhai, FCA *1975;* A.M. Patel & Co, 215B East Lane, WEMBLEY, HA0 3NG.
PATEL, Mr. Arvindkumar Hirabhai, FCA *1963;* 2307 Autumn Drive, TOMS RIVER, NJ 08755, UNITED STATES.
PATEL, Mrs. Asha, BSc ACA *2009;* 8 Lyndhurst Avenue, PINNER, MIDDLESEX, HA5 3XA.
PATEL, Miss. Asha Chimanbhai, BSc ACA *1994;* 201 Long Hill Drive, SHORT HILLS, NJ 07078, UNITED STATES.
PATEL, Mr. Ashank, BSc ACA *1994;* 3 Highbarrow Close, PURLEY, SURREY, CR8 2JX.
PATEL, Mr. Ashish, BSc ACA *1993;* 31 Harrow Fields Gardens, HARROW, HA1 3SN.
PATEL, Mr. Ashish Ashok, BSc(Hons) ACA *2000;* 66 Francklyn Gardens, EDGWARE, MIDDLESEX, HA8 8RZ.
•PATEL, Mr. Ashok Ranchhodbhai, ACA *1990;* (Tax Fac), Sharman Fielding, 9 University Road, LEICESTER, LE1 7RA.
PATEL, Mr. Ashok Shantilal, BSc ACA *1978;* 37 Killieser Avenue, LONDON, SW2 4NX.
•PATEL, Mr. Ashokkumar Dullabhbhai, BSc ACA *1992;* Ashcrofts, 34 Hartsbourne Drive, HALESOWEN, B62 8ST.
PATEL, Mr. Ashokkumar Kantibhai, FCA *1977;* 19 Nettleden Avenue, WEMBLEY, HA9 6DP.
PATEL, Mr. Ashvin Chandulal, ACA *1980;* AP Consultance Services, 6 Glencairn Court, Lansdown Road, CHELTENHAM, GLOUCESTERSHIRE, GL51 6QN.
PATEL, Mr. Ashwinkumar Janubhai, FCA *1972;* 7610 Greenbrier Circle, PORT ST LUCIE, FL 34986, UNITED STATES. (Life Member)
PATEL, Mr. Asif, MSc ACA *2001;* U B S Wealth Management, 1 Curzon Street, LONDON, W1J 5UB.
PATEL, Mr. Atul, BSc ACA *1992;* 1 Redshank Drive, MACCLESFIELD, CHESHIRE, SK10 2SN.
PATEL, Mr. Avinash, FCA *1970;* 28/441 Moo 5, Romyen Villa 1, Kukot, Lamlukka, PATHUMTHANI, 12130 THAILAND. (Life Member)
PATEL, Mrs. Avni Yogan, FCA *1985;* 5 Nightingale Park, Farnham Common, SLOUGH, SL2 3SN.
PATEL, Miss. Ayesha, BSc ACA *2005;* 50 Cambridge Road, Seven Kings, ILFORD, IG3 8LX.
PATEL, Mr. Badal, ACA *2008;* 3 The Croft, Sudbury Town, WEMBLEY, MIDDLESEX, HA0 3EQ.
•PATEL, Mr. Balvantkumar Bhikhabhai, FCA FCCA *1970;* John Cumming Ross Limited, 1st Floor, Kirkland House, 11-15 Peterborough Road, HARROW, MIDDLESEX HA1 2AX.
PATEL, Mr. Balwant Natubhai, FCA *1971;* (Tax Fac), 48 Hanover House, St. Johns Wood High Street, LONDON, NW8 7DY.
•PATEL, Mr. Bankim Chandulal, FCA *1979;* Higgins Fairbairn & Co, 1st Floor, 24/25 New Bond Street, LONDON, W1S 2RR. See also Bankim Patel & Co Ltd
PATEL, Miss. Beejal, ACA *2011;* 329 Durnsford Road, LONDON, SW19 8EF.
PATEL, Mr. Bejay, BSc ACA *2011;* Aashirwad, Monkton Road, Minster, RAMSGATE, KENT, CT12 4EF.
PATEL, Mr. Bhadresh, BSc ACA *1995;* 1B Wilfred Owen Close, LONDON, SW19 8SW.
•PATEL, Mr. Bhagubhai Purshottam, FCA *1963;* Green Sleeves, 3 Earleswood, Fairmile Lane, COBHAM, SURREY, KT11 2BZ.
PATEL, Mr. Bharat Arvindbhai, ACA *1982;* 21 South Lane, KINGSTON UPON THAMES, SURREY, KT1 2NJ.
PATEL, Mr. Bharat Jashbhai, ACA *1981;* 9 Russell Road, Moor Park, NORTHWOOD, MIDDLESEX, HA6 2LJ.
PATEL, Mr. Bharat Kumar Roajibhai, BSc FCA *1979;* 96 Midland Crescent S.E., CALGARY T2X 1P4, AB, CANADA.
•PATEL, Ms. Bharati, BSc ACA *1991;* Bharati Patel, 27b Priory Road, NEWBURY, RG14 7QS.
PATEL, Mr. Bharatkumar Ranchhodbhai, BSc FCA *1993;* 16 Sywell Avenue, LOUGHBOROUGH, LE11 4BU.
PATEL, Mr. Bhavesh, BSc ACA *2005;* 15 Dowding Way, Leavesden, WATFORD, WD25 7GA.
PATEL, Mr. Bhavin, ACA *2009;* 5 Forge Lane, FELTHAM, MIDDLESEX, TW13 6UR.
PATEL, Mrs. Bhavisha, BSc ACA *2007;* 5 Compton Gardens, ST. ALBANS, HERTFORDSHIRE, AL2 3HU.
PATEL, Miss. Bhavisha, ACA *2009;* Flat 1, 9 Wakley Street, LONDON, EC1V 7LT.
PATEL, Mr. Bhikhu Hirabhai, FCA *1973;* 81 Fursecroft, Brown Street, LONDON, W1H 5LG.
PATEL, Mr. Bhupendra Manubhai, BSc ACA *2007;* 7 Croyde Close, LEICESTER, LE5 4WG.
PATEL, Mr. Bhupesh, BSc(Hons) ACA *2003;* 58 Evington Drive, LEICESTER, LE5 5PD.
PATEL, Mr. Bhupesh Navin, BA ACA *1987;* 3407 Nirmal Court, MARIETTA, GA 30068-5319, UNITED STATES.
PATEL, Mr. Bijal, ACA *2008;* 1 Birch Grove, Kingswood, TADWORTH, SURREY, KT20 6QU.
PATEL, Miss. Bijal, BA(Hons) ACA *2003;* 322 Sherrard Road, Manor Park, LONDON, E12 6UF.
PATEL, Mr. Bijal Kirit, BSc ACA *2007;* 11 St. Andrews Drive, STANMORE, MIDDLESEX, HA7 2LY.
•PATEL, Miss. Bina Jashvantlal, BA ACA *1983;* (Tax Fac), B.J. Patel, 76 Buckingham Road, Bletchley, MILTON KEYNES, MK3 5HL.
PATEL, Mr. Bipin, BSc ACA *1987;* 58 Colebridge Avenue, Longlevens, GLOUCESTER, GL2 0RH.
PATEL, Miss. Chandni, BSc(Hons) ACA *2011;* 15 Heath Drive, SUTTON, SURREY, SM2 5RP.
•PATEL, Mr. Chandrakant Jiwabhai, FCA *1970;* C.J. Patel & Co, 112 Hamilton Avenue, ILFORD, IG6 1AB.
•PATEL, Mr. Chandrakant Vallabhbhai, FCA *1971;* Patel Khanderia & Co, 9 Hitherwood Drive, LONDON, SE19 1XA.
PATEL, Mr. Chandravadan Khushalbhai, FCA *1975;* 21 Arlington, Woodside Park, LONDON, N12 7JR.
PATEL, Mr. Chandulal Dalpatbhai, FCA *1971;* 66 Philbeach Gardens, LONDON, SW5 9EE.
PATEL, Mr. Chetansharan Bhailalbhai, FCA *1975;* 14 Sherington Avenue, Hatch End, PINNER, HA5 4DT. (Life Member)
PATEL, Mr. Chiraag, ACA *2008;* 19 Combemartin Road, LONDON, SW18 5PP.
PATEL, Mr. Chirag, BSc ACA *2010;* 55 Denchers Plat, Langley Green, CRAWLEY, WEST SUSSEX, RH11 7TR.
PATEL, Mr. Dai, BSc(Hons) ACA *2010;* 26 The Meadow Way, Harrow Weald, HARROW, MIDDLESEX, HA3 7BW.
•PATEL, Mrs. Dawn Michelle, BSc FCA *1992;* (Tax Fac), DN Consultancy Limited, Nakatcha, Over Wallop, STOCKBRIDGE, HAMPSHIRE, SO20 8HN.
PATEL, Mr. Devendra Narendra, FCA *1980;* Unit 5, 14 Salonika Street, THE GARDENS, NT 0820, AUSTRALIA.
PATEL, Miss. Devika, ACA *2008;* with PricewaterhouseCoopers AS LLP, 1 Embankment Place, LONDON, WC2N 6RH.
PATEL, Mr. Dhanji Harji, FCA *1972;* Hiral Yax Road, Post Madhaper Kutch (Bhuj), GUJRAT, INDIA.
PATEL, Mr. Dharmendra, BSc ACA *1995;* 118 Pepys Road, LONDON, SW20 8NY.
PATEL, Mr. Dharmesh Dhruvkumar, BSc ACA *1992;* Avanade Europe Services Ltd, Abbey House, 18-24 Stoke Road, SLOUGH, SL2 5AG.
PATEL, Mr. Dhaval, ACA *2011;* 21 Hadley Wood Rise, KENLEY, SURREY, CR8 5LY.
PATEL, Mr. Dhrupad, ACA *2009;* 4 Woodstock Avenue, SUTTON, SURREY, SM3 9EF.
PATEL, Mr. Dhruv Shamik, LLB(Hons) ACA *2010;* Mazars The Lexicon, 10-12 Mount Street, MANCHESTER, M2 5NT.
•PATEL, Mr. Dilip Dhirubhai, FCA *1984;* Assets Limited, Chiltern Chambers, St. Peters Avenue, Caversham, READING, RG4 7DH. See also Assets Outsourcing Limited
•PATEL, Mr. Dilipkumar Ramanbhai, FCA *1977;* (Tax Fac), Wormald & Partners, Redland House, 157 Redland Road, BRISTOL, BS6 6YE.
PATEL, Mrs. Dimple, BA(Hons) ACA *2000;* 10 Netherfield Road, LONDON, N12 8DP.
PATEL, Miss. Dina, ACA *2010;* 9 Marston Close, Oadby, LEICESTER, LE2 5WL.
PATEL, Mr. Dineshkumar Shanabhai, FCA *1976;* Delmonte, 4 Woodlands Avenue, Coombeside, NEW MALDEN, KT3 3UN.
PATEL, Miss. Dinta, BA(Econ) ACA *2002;* 6 Woodside Lane, LONDON, N12 8RB.
PATEL, Mr. Dipak, BSc FCA *1992;* (Tax Fac), 24 Breamore Crescent, DUDLEY, DY1 3DA.
PATEL, Mr. Dipak, BSc ACA *2010;* 13 Rees Drive, STANMORE, MIDDLESEX, HA7 4YN.
•PATEL, Mr. Dipak Madhavbhai, BA FCA FCCA *1991;* Allans The Accountants Ltd, 1st Floor, 21 Victoria Road, SURBITON, SURREY, KT6 4JZ.
•PATEL, Mr. Dipak Purusottam, BA ACA *1987;* (Tax Fac), Clenton Limited, 11 Old Court House, Old Court Place, LONDON, W8 4PD.
PATEL, Mr. Dipal Harshad, ACA *2009;* 39 Marlborough Road, LONDON, SW19 2HF.
PATEL, Mrs. Dipeeka, BA(Hons) ACA *2011;* 42 Welling Way, WELLING, KENT, DA16 2RT.
•PATEL, Mr. Dipen, BSc FCA *1987;* Eclipse Consultancy Limited, 9 Limes Road, BECKENHAM, KENT, BR3 6NS. See also Patson & Co
PATEL, Mr. Dipen Vijay, BSc ACA *2005;* Apartment 103 Eaton House, 38 Westferry Circus, LONDON, E14 8RN.
PATEL, Mr. Dipesh, BA ACA *1996;* GSK House CN7-197, 980 Great West Road, BRENTFORD, TW8 9GS.
PATEL, Mr. Dipesh, BSc ACA *2010;* 57 Hamilton Avenue, SUTTON, SURREY, SM3 9EA.
PATEL, Mr. Dipesh Anandilal, BSc(Econ) ACA MBA *2001;* 3202 era1Marathonnextgen, Ganpat Kadam Marg, Lower Parel, MUMBAI 400013, MAHARASHTRA, INDIA.
PATEL, Mr. Dipesh Narendra, BA ACA *2003;* 38 Church Way, SOUTH CROYDON, CR2 0JR.
PATEL, Mr. Dipit, BSc ACA *2007;* 48 Manor Close, LONDON, NW9 9HD.
PATEL, Miss. Falguni, BSc ACA *1991;* 127 Tiburon Boulevard, MILL VALLEY, CA 94941, UNITED STATES.
•PATEL, Mr. Farook Ahmed, BEng FCA *1993;* (Tax Fac), Riley Moss Limited, Riley House, 183-185 North Road, PRESTON, PR1 1YQ. See also Riley Moss Audit LLP
PATEL, Mrs. Gayatri, BSc ACA *2010;* 52 Dersingham Road, LONDON, NW2 1SL.
•PATEL, Mr. Girish, BSc ACA *1992;* GP & Co, 105 Streatfield Road, Kenton, HARROW, MIDDLESEX, HA3 9BL.
PATEL, Mr. Girish Keshavlal, FCA *1970;* P O Box 327, KISUMU, KENYA.
PATEL, Mrs. Gita, BSc FCA *1981;* The Junipers, Croydon Lane, BANSTEAD, SM7 3AT.
•PATEL, Mr. Gulam Mohamed Ismail, FCA *1979;* (Tax Fac), 46 Abbotswood Road, LONDON, SW16 1AW.
PATEL, Miss. Hajra, ACA *2008;* 87 Headingley Way, BOLTON, BL3 3EQ.
PATEL, Mr. Hamant Magan, BSc ACA *1992;* 30 Quebec Road, ILFORD, IG1 4TT.
PATEL, Mr. Hamesh, LLB ACA *2001;* 44 Chislehurst Road, CHISLEHURST, BR7 5LD.
PATEL, Miss. Hanisha Ashokkumar, BSc ACA *2006;* 19 Nettleden Avenue, WEMBLEY, MIDDLESEX, HA9 6DP.
PATEL, Mr. Harish Manubhai, BA ACA *1997;* Morgan Stanley, 25 Cabot Square, Canary Wharf, LONDON, E14 4QA.
PATEL, Mr. Harivadan Arvind, BA ACA *2008;* Flat 7, 17 Freeland Road, LONDON, W5 3HR.
PATEL, Miss. Harshika, BSc ACA *1998;* Barclays Capital, 5 North Colonnade, LONDON, E14 4BB.
•PATEL, Mr. Hasmuk, FCA *1985;* (Tax Fac), Hasmuk Patel & Co, Lalita Buildings, 378 Walsall Road, Perry Barr, BIRMINGHAM, B42 2LX.
PATEL, Mr. Hasmukh Ishverbhai, ACA *1980;* 19 Brittany Crescent, UNIONVILLE L3R 0R1, ON, CANADA.
PATEL, Miss. Heena, BSc ACA *2004;* Aviva UK Central Services, St. Helens, 1 Undershaft, LONDON, EC3P 3DQ.
•PATEL, Miss. Heena, BA ACA *1988;* Heena Patel BA ACA, 25 Burghley House, Somerset Road, LONDON, SW19 5JB.
PATEL, Miss. Heena Vasantlal, BSc(Hons) ACA *2009;* 76 Colombo Road, ILFORD, IG1 4RQ.
PATEL, Miss. Hemal, FCA *1993;* BNP Paribas, 10 Harewood Avenue, LONDON, NW1 6AA.
•PATEL, Mr. Hemal, BSc *1998;* Pretium Consulting Limited, 16 Martock Gardens, LONDON, N11 3GH.
PATEL, Mr. Hemant, ACA *2010;* 50 Spencer Road, WEMBLEY, MIDDLESEX, HA0 3SF.
•PATEL, Mr. Hemant Jayantilal, BSc ACA *1988;* Hemant Patel, The Manor House, 1028 Melton Road, Syston, LEICESTER, LE7 2NN.
PATEL, Mr. Himakshu Arvind, BSc ACA *1994;* 37 Ferndown, NORTHWOOD, HA6 1PH.
PATEL, Mr. Himanshu, BSc ACA *1993;* LM 500 Sp.zo.o., ul. 29 Listopada 18A (lok 3U), 00-465 WARSAW, POLAND.
•PATEL, Mr. Himatlal Vashrambhai, FCA *1980;* (Tax Fac), with RDP Newmans LLP, Lynwood House, 373/375 Station Road, HARROW, MIDDLESEX, HA1 2AW.
PATEL, Miss. Hinal, BSc(Hons) ACA *2011;* 9 Thurlby Road, WEMBLEY, MIDDLESEX, HA0 4RT.
PATEL, Mr. Hinesh, MSc BSc(Hons) ACA *2010;* 15 Glebelands Road, LEICESTER, LE4 2WB.
PATEL, Mr. Hiral Jagdish, BSc ACA *1995;* Peony Cottage, Pilton, PETERBOROUGH, PE8 5SN.
PATEL, Mr. Hiran, ACA *2011;* 16 Sandhurst Avenue, HARROW, MIDDLESEX, HA2 7AP.
•PATEL, Mr. Hiten, BSc ACA *1991;* 19 Marketstede, Hampton Hargate, PETERBOROUGH, PE7 8FA.
PATEL, Mr. Hiten, BSc ACA *2005;* 17 Dawlish Drive, PINNER, MIDDLESEX, HA5 5LL.
PATEL, Mr. Hiten Jitendra, BSc ACA *2004;* 14 Samian Gate, ST. ALBANS, HERTFORDSHIRE, AL3 4JW.
•PATEL, Mr. Hitesh, BA(Hons) ACA MBA *2002;* Integer Finance Limited, 32 Tilley Close, Thorpe Astley, Braunstone, LEICESTER, LE3 3TD.
PATEL, Mr. Hitesh Dinubhai, BSc ACA *1992;* Quantum Actions Ltd, 109 Burdon Lane, South Cheam, SUTTON, SM2 7BZ.
•PATEL, Mr. Hitesh Nathalal, BSc ACA *1993;* KPMG LLP, 15 Canada Square, LONDON, E14 5GL. See also KPMG Europe LLP
•PATEL, Mr. Hitesh Ramesh, BA(Hons) ACA CTA *1999;* Hitesh Patel, 14 Denehurst Gardens, WOODFORD GREEN, IG8 0PA.
PATEL, Mr. Hiteshkumar Rameshchandra, BSc ACA *1985;* Lucida Plc, 84 Grosvenors St, LONDON, W1K 6ZW.
PATEL, Mr. Hoshang Dinshaw, FCA *1958;* 77 Havelock Drive, BRAMPTON L6W 4C4, ON, CANADA. (Life Member)
•PATEL, Mr. Ilesh Narendrabhai, BA FCA *1986;* Ashlei Associates, 7 Heath Drive, SUTTON, SM2 5RP.
PATEL, Mr. Indubhai Bhailalbhai, FCA *1957;* 818 12th Cross 23RD Main, 2nd Phase JP Nagar, BANGALORE, INDIA. (Life Member)
PATEL, Mr. Jagjivan Vallabhbhai, FCA *1965;* 86 Sunita, 15th Floor, Cuffe Parade, GD Somani Marg, MUMBAI 400005, INDIA. (Life Member)
PATEL, Mrs. Jagruti, BA(Hons) ACA CTA *2000;* 91 Rustat Road, CAMBRIDGE, CB1 3QG.
PATEL, Mr. Jai Vijaykant, ACA *2009;* Pinaki, Oxhey Lane, PINNER, MIDDLESEX, HA5 4AN.
•PATEL, Mr. Jashwantkumar Nathubhai, BA FCA *1989;* (Tax Fac), Manorfive Ltd, 178 Westcotes Drive, LEICESTER, LE3 0SP.
PATEL, Mr. Jatin Jitendra, BA ACA *1997;* 35a Hermitage Road, KENLEY, CR8 5EA.
•PATEL, Mr. Jayantilal Govindbhai, BSc FCA *1977;* Jay Patel & Co, 278 Northfield Avenue, Ealing, LONDON, W5 4UB.
PATEL, Mr. Jayesh, ACA *1979;* 12 Court Parade, East Lane, WEMBLEY, HA0 3HX.
PATEL, Mr. Jayesh, ACA MAAT *2010;* 130 Ivanhoe Street, DUDLEY, WEST MIDLANDS, DY2 0YD.
•PATEL, Mr. Jayesh, BA ACA *1991;* (Tax Fac), Jacquards Limited, 2 Wannions Close, CHESHAM, BUCKINGHAMSHIRE, HP5 1YA.
PATEL, Mr. Jayesh, BSc ACA *1992;* 4 Hollyoaks, 21 Eastbury Avenue, NORTHWOOD, HA6 3LH.
PATEL, Mr. Jayesh Nareshkumar, BA ACA *1993;* 14 Copse Wood Way, NORTHWOOD, MIDDLESEX, HA6 2UE.
•PATEL, Mr. Jaykrishna Dineshbhai, BA ACA *1987;* Jay & Co, 12 Cherry Tree Close, Hughenden Valley, HIGH WYCOMBE, HP14 4LP.
PATEL, Mr. Jaymal, ACA *2008;* 4 Ruxton Close, COULSDON, CR5 2DY.
PATEL, Mr. Jaymin Balvantbhai, BA ACA *1993;* GTech Corporation, 10 Memorial Boulevard, PROVIDENCE, RI 02903, UNITED STATES.
PATEL, Miss. Jayoti, BSc ACA *1992;* Flat 7, 8 Millennium Drive, LONDON, E14 3GH.
PATEL, Mrs. Jayshree, BSc ACA MBA *1994;* 35 Littleton Road, HARROW, MIDDLESEX, HA1 3SY.

Members - Alphabetical PATEL - PATEL

•PATEL, Mrs. Jayshree Pankaj, ACA *1981;* VSP Limited, 23a Lyttleton Road, Hampstead Gardens Suburb, LONDON, N2 0DN.
PATEL, Miss. Jigna, BSc ACA *2009;* 82 Upton Lane, LONDON, E7 9LW.
PATEL, Mr. Jignesh Kirit, BSc ACA *1998;* Aristel Hotels, 4 Bryanston Street, Marble Arch, LONDON, W1H 7BY.
PATEL, Mr. Jiten, BSc ACA *2006;* 39 Gerard Road, HARROW, MIDDLESEX, HA1 2NE.
PATEL, Mr. Jiten, BSc ACA *2011;* 41 Clifton Avenue, WEMBLEY, MIDDLESEX, HA9 6BN.
PATEL, Mr. Jitendra Chhotabhai, BSc FCA *1985;* 3 Chelwood Close, COULSDON, SURREY, CR5 3EY.
PATEL, Mr. Jitendra Jethalal, BEng ACA *1995;* 19 Valley Drive, Kingsbury, LONDON, NW9 9NJ.
•PATEL, Mr. Jitesh, ACA FCCA *2011;* Red Emerald Ltd, Hadley House, 17 Park Road, High Barnet, BARNET, HERTFORDSHIRE EN5 5RY.
PATEL, Mr. Jitesh Natubhai, BA ACA *1996;* 21 Croham Park Avenue, SOUTH CROYDON, SURREY, CR2 7HN.
PATEL, Mrs. Joanne, BEng ACA *1993;* 85 Brooklands, Horwich, BOLTON, BL6 5RW.
•PATEL, Mr. Kailesh Gunvant, FCA *1990;* MCT Partnership, 1 Warner House, Harrovian Business Village, Bessborough Road, HARROW, HA1 3EX. See also Harrovian Business Services Limited
PATEL, Mrs. Kajal, BA ACA *2007;* 6 Hawlands Drive, PINNER, MIDDLESEX, HA5 1NT.
PATEL, Miss. Kalavati Bhikhabhai, BA ACA *1982;* 38 Stubbs Close, WELLINGBOROUGH, NORTHAMPTONSHIRE, NN8 4UQ.
PATEL, Miss. Kalpana, BSc(Hons) ACA *2009;* 17 Strone Road, LONDON, E7 8EX.
PATEL, Mr. Kalpesh, ACA *2011;* 71 Arnhem Drive, New Addington, CROYDON, CR0 0EE.
PATEL, Mr. Kamal Indravadan, BSc(Hons) ACA *2000;* 4 Grovelands Road, PURLEY, SURREY, CR8 4LA.
•PATEL, Mrs. Kamini, BSc ACA *1984;* PKIB Accounting LLP, 132 Leicester Road, LOUGHBOROUGH, LEICESTERSHIRE, LE11 2AQ.
PATEL, Mr. Kamlesh Chimanbhai, ACA *1991;* Ljustret 3, 193 41, SIGTUNA, SWEDEN.
PATEL, Mr. Kantilal Parbhoobhai, FCA *1973;* 1 Eurolie Street, NORTH BALWYN, VIC 3104, AUSTRALIA.
PATEL, Miss. Kapila, ACA *2008;* 34 Kennett Road, SLOUGH, SL3 8EE.
•PATEL, Mrs. Katharine, BSc ACA *1999;* Buzzacott LLP, 130 Wood Street, LONDON, EC2V 6DL.
PATEL, Mr. Kaushal Vinodroy, BSc ACA *1999;* 23 Knoll Drive, LONDON, N14 5LU.
PATEL, Mr. Kaushik Nagin, BA FCA CFA *1999;* 31 Tindall Mews, HORNCHURCH, ESSEX, RM12 4WW.
PATEL, Mr. Kavas Dara, FCA *1972;* C33 River Nest, 311 North Main Rd. Lane E, Koregaon Park, PUNE 411001, INDIA.
PATEL, Miss. Keshal Dinesh, MSc(Econ) ACA *2009;* 18 Forest Ridge, KESTON, BR2 6EQ.
•PATEL, Mr. Ketan, BSc ACA ATII *1991;* Ketan Patel & Co, A L'Avenier, 40a Britwell Road, Burnham, SLOUGH, SL1 8AQ.
PATEL, Mr. Ketu, BSc ACA *1999;* 66 Parkside Drive, WATFORD, WD17 3AX.
PATEL, Mr. Keval, LLB ACA *2001;* 36 Pine Grove, LONDON, SW19 7HE.
PATEL, Mr. Keyur, BSc ACA *2005;* 450 Larkshall Road, Chingford, LONDON, E4 9HH.
PATEL, Mr. Khageshchandra Kanubhai, ACA *1981;* 47 White Boulevard, THORNHILL L4J 5Z4, ON, CANADA.
PATEL, Mr. Khandubhai Parbhubhai, FCA *1975;* 47 Maidavale Crescent, Styverhale, COVENTRY, CV3 6GB.
PATEL, Mr. Kiran, LLB ACA *2010;* 72 Park Grove Road, LONDON, E11 4PU.
•PATEL, Mr. Kirankumar Dullabhbhai, BA FCA *1991;* (Tax Fac), Weston Kay, 73/75 Mortimer Street, LONDON, W1W 7SQ.
PATEL, Mr. Kirit, ACA *2008;* 39 Derwent Gardens, WEMBLEY, MIDDLESEX, HA9 8SG.
PATEL, Mr. Kirit Mohanlal, FCA *1982;* Commodore International Travel Ltd, 177 Shaftesbury Avenue, LONDON, WC2H 8JR.
PATEL, Mr. Kiritbhai Chandulal, BSc ACA *1979;* 5396 Bessborough Court, MISSISSAUGA L5M 5C5, ON, CANADA.
PATEL, Miss. Kreena, BSc ACA *2010;* 39 Marlborough Road, LONDON, SW19 2HF.
PATEL, Miss. Krishna, BSc ACA *2010;* 94 Fleetwood Road, LONDON, NW10 1NN.
PATEL, Miss. Krupa, ACA *2011;* 76 Pemdevon Road, West Croydon, CROYDON, CR0 3QP.
PATEL, Mrs. Krupa, BSc(Hons) ACA *2010;* 11 St. Andrews Drive, STANMORE, MIDDLESEX, HA7 2LY.
PATEL, Mr. Kunal, ACA *2009;* Jefferies International Ltd Vintners Place, 68 Upper Thames Street, LONDON, EC4V 3BJ.
PATEL, Mr. Kushal, BSc ACA *2004;* 26 Manland Way, HARPENDEN, HERTFORDSHIRE, AL5 4QS.
PATEL, Mr. Latish, BSc ACA *1991;* (Tax Fac), 132 Elm Drive, HARROW, HA2 7BZ.
PATEL, Miss. Leena, ACA *2011;* 18 Pinner Park Avenue, HARROW, MIDDLESEX, HA2 6LF.
PATEL, Miss. Lena, BSc(Hons) ACA *2010;* Post Office, 48-50 High Street Chesterton, CAMBRIDGE, CB4 1NG.
PATEL, Miss. Lena Vijanti, ACA *2009;* Nash Newsagents, 193 Rochdale Road, BURY, BL9 7BB.
PATEL, Miss. Lina, BA(Hons) ACA *2002;* 4 Wyndhurst Close, SOUTH CROYDON, SURREY, CR2 6EP.
PATEL, Mr. Madankumar Raojibhai, FCA *1969;* 67 Broomgrove Gardens, EDGWARE, HA8 5RH.
•PATEL, Mr. Mahendra Babubhai, FCA *1972;* (Tax Fac), Amey Kamp LLP, 310 Harrow Road, WEMBLEY, MIDDLESEX, HA9 6LL.
PATEL, Mr. Mahesh, BSc FCA *1994;* 48 Elm Park, STANMORE, HA7 4BJ.
PATEL, Mr. Mahesh, BA ACA *1991;* 8 The Chanters, Ellenbrook Grange, Worsley, MANCHESTER, M28 7XL.
PATEL, Mr. Mahesh Shivabhai, ACA *1980;* stables, 1 Grove Hill Road, HARROW, MIDDLESEX, HA1 3AA.
•PATEL, Mr. Manharbhai Chunibhai, FCA *1973;* M.C. Patel & Co, Hillingdon House, 386/388 Kenton Road, Kenton, HARROW, HA3 9DP.
PATEL, Mr. Manish, BA ACA *1997;* 52 Thorburn Road, NORTHAMPTON, NN3 3DA.
PATEL, Mr. Markand Jayminkumar, BSc ACA *2009;* 228 Basing Way, Finchley Central, LONDON, N3 3BN.
PATEL, Mr. Mayank, BSc(Econ) ACA *2002;* 248 Norbury Avenue, LONDON, SW16 3RN.
PATEL, Mr. Mayank, BSc ACA *1989;* 6 Rue Carnot, 78600 LE MESNIL LE ROI, FRANCE.
PATEL, Mr. Mayank Jashbhai, BSc ACA *1993;* SNAP Africa Advisory Service, PO Box 47945, NAIROBI, 00100, KENYA.
PATEL, Mr. Mayank Kumar, BSc(Econ) ACA *2001;* 22 Roman Way, CARSHALTON, SURREY, SM5 4EF.
PATEL, Mr. Mehulkumar Kanubhai, BSc ACA *1991;* 56 Stroudley Road, BRIGHTON, BN1 4BH.
PATEL, Mr. Mehulkumar Nalinkant, BA ACA *1990;* Unit 16, 25-31 Johnson Street, Chatswood, SYDNEY, NSW 2067, AUSTRALIA.
PATEL, Miss. Melissa, ACA *2009;* 12 Poplar Avenue, WALSALL, WS5 4EU.
PATEL, Mr. Mihir, ACA *2010;* 6 South Way, HARROW, MIDDLESEX, HA2 6EP.
PATEL, Miss. Minal, BSc ACA *2005;* 103 Quentin Road, LONDON, SE13 5DG.
PATEL, Mr. Minesh Praful, BA ACA *1991;* 8 Oakwood Drive, EDGWARE, HA8 9LF.
PATEL, Mr. Mitesh, BSc ACA *2007;* 14 Bridgewater Street, SALFORD, M3 7AS.
PATEL, Mr. Mitesh, ACA *2009;* E on UK Plc Westwood Way, Westwood Business Park, COVENTRY, CV4 8LG.
PATEL, Mr. Mitesh, BSc ACA *2010;* 10 Wilson Avenue, MITCHAM, SURREY, CR4 3JL.
PATEL, Mr. Mitesh Raj, ACA *2008;* Flat 84 Princess Park Manor, Royal Drive, LONDON, N11 3FP.
PATEL, Mr. Mithun, BSc ACA *2008;* 41 Hobart Drive, WALSALL, WS5 3NJ.
PATEL, Mr. Mitul, BA ACA *2003;* with Crouch Chapman, 62 Wilson Street, LONDON, EC2A 2BU.
PATEL, Mr. Mohammed Zubair, BA(Hons) ACA *2004;* 44 Thorold Road, ILFORD, IG1 4EX.
PATEL, Mr. Mohanlal Lallubhai, BA ACA *1989;* c/o COUNTRY HEARTH INN & SUITES, 1100 S JEFFERSON AVE, COOKEVILLE, TN 38506, UNITED STATES.
PATEL, Miss. Monna, ACA *2011;* 36 Hampton Road, ILFORD, ESSEX, IG1 1PT.
•PATEL, Mr. Mukesh Bhogilal, ACA *1982;* Giles Accounting Services Ltd, 7d Hill Avenue, AMERSHAM, BUCKINGHAMSHIRE, HP6 5BD.
•PATEL, Mr. Mukesh Mahendra, BA ACA *1987;* M M Patel & Co, 59 Carr Road, NORTHOLT, MIDDLESEX, UB5 4RB.
•PATEL, Mr. Mukund Rambhai Shivabhai, FCA *1974;* (Tax Fac), M.R.S. Patel & Co, Compton House, 20a Selsdon Road, SOUTH CROYDON, SURREY, CR2 6PA.
PATEL, Mr. Nahul Dilip, ACA *2009;* 8 Providence Drive, CURRAMBINE, WA 6028, AUSTRALIA.
PATEL, Miss. Namrata, ACA *2009;* Flat 2, 1 St. Cuthberts Road, LONDON, NW2 3QJ.
PATEL, Ms. Nandita, ACA *2011;* 4 Woodlands Avenue, NEW MALDEN, SURREY, KT3 3UN.
PATEL, Mr. Narendra, ACA *1980;* 3453 Marmac Crescent, MISSISSAUGA L5L 5A1, ON, CANADA.
•PATEL, Mr. Narendra Natwarlal, FCA *1965;* (Tax Fac), Naren Patel & Co, 126 Royal College Street, LONDON, NW1 0TA.
•PATEL, Mr. Narendrakumar Jashbhai, FCA *1980;* (Tax Fac), N.J. Patel & Co, 345 Bearwood Road, SMETHWICK, WEST MIDLANDS, B66 4DB.
•PATEL, Mr. Nareshchandra Rambhai, FCA *1973;* N.R. Patel & Co, 19 Hill Crescent, HARROW, HA1 2PW.
PATEL, Mr. Nayan Dahyabhai, BA ACA *1986;* 25 Polton Dale, SWINDON, SN3 5BN.
•PATEL, Mr. Neal Mahen, BSc FCA *2000;* (Tax Fac), BSG Valentine, Lynton House, 7/12 Tavistock Square, LONDON, WC1H 9BQ.
PATEL, Mrs. Nealam, BA(Econ) ACA *2000;* 129 Lichfield Grove, Finchley Central, LONDON, N3 2JL.
PATEL, Mr. Neel, BSc ACA *2007;* 54 Shillingford Close, LONDON, NW7 1HQ.
PATEL, Mr. Neel, ACA *2009;* 2 Ardross Avenue, NORTHWOOD, MIDDLESEX, HA6 3DS.
PATEL, Mr. Neel Rashmikant, BSc ACA *2004;* 145 Broomgrove Gardens, EDGWARE, HA8 5RJ.
PATEL, Mr. Neil, BSc ACA *2011;* 25 Preston Hill, HARROW, MIDDLESEX, HA3 9SB.
PATEL, Miss. Neva, BSc ACA *2010;* 24 Ware Road, HERTFORD, SG13 7HH.
PATEL, Mr. Nickesh, BA ACA *2005;* 115 Maxwell Gardens, ORPINGTON, BR6 9QT.
PATEL, Mr. Nikesh, ACA *2009;* 221 Chaplin Road, WEMBLEY, MIDDLESEX, HA0 4UR.
PATEL, Mr. Nikhil, ACA *2011;* 33 Northolme Gardens, EDGWARE, MIDDLESEX, HA8 5AY.
PATEL, Mr. Nilay Ramesh, BA ACA *1992;* William Hill, Greenside House, 50 Station Road, Wood Green, LONDON, N22 7TP.
PATEL, Mr. Nilesh, BA ACA *2006;* 4C Worcester Gardens, LONDON, SW11 6LR.
PATEL, Mr. Nilesh Chandubhai, BA ACA *1997;* 4028 Divot Court, DULUTH, GA 30097, UNITED STATES.
•PATEL, Mr. Nilesh Chimanbhai, FCA *1986;* (Tax Fac), Hakim Fry, 69-71 East Street, EPSOM, KT17 1BP. See also Barbican Services Limited
PATEL, Mr. Nilesh Raj, BSc ACA *2011;* Furze Cottage, Heathbourne Road, Bushey Heath, BUSHEY, WD23 1PD.
PATEL, Mr. Nimet, ACA *2011;* 179 High Street, Rainham, GILLINGHAM, KENT, ME8 8AY.
•PATEL, Mr. Nimish, BSc ACA *1991;* Re10 (UK) Plc, Albemarle House, 1 Albemarle Street, LONDON, W1S 4HA.
PATEL, Ms. Nina, BA ACA *2005;* 12 Hornbeam Close, Oadby, LEICESTER, LE2 4EQ.
PATEL, Mr. Niraj Mukund, BSc(Hons) ACA CF *2004;* 11 Maywater Close, Sanderstead, SOUTH CROYDON, SURREY, CR2 0RS.
PATEL, Mr. Niranjan Naranbhai, BSc FCA *1968;* 42A Village Road, ENFIELD, EN1 2ER. (Life Member)
•PATEL, Mrs. Niranjanaben Sureshchandra, FCA *1977;* 26 St. Georges Drive, Ickenham, UXBRIDGE, MIDDLESEX, UB10 8HW.
PATEL, Mr. Nish, ACA *2008;* 53 Scholars Road, LONDON, SW12 0PF.
PATEL, Miss. Nisha, ACA *2008;* 28 Hemp Walk, LONDON, SE17 1PF.
PATEL, Mr. Nishith, BSc ACA *1990;* 2a Mount Drive, Park Street, ST. ALBANS, HERTFORDSHIRE, AL2 2NY.
PATEL, Miss. Nishma, ACA *2010;* 19 Shetland Road, LEICESTER, LE4 6RS.
PATEL, Mr. Nitesh, ACA *2011;* 26 Colburn Way, SUTTON, SURREY, SM1 3AU.
PATEL, Mr. Nitil, BSocSc ACA *1999;* 6 Alfriston Road, LONDON, SW11 6NN.
PATEL, Mr. Nitin Amrut, ACA *2011;* 60 Beaumont Leys Lane, LEICESTER, LE4 2BA.
PATEL, Mr. Nitin Babubhai, BA ACA *1990;* 2 The Croft, Lower Road Fetcham, LEATHERHEAD, KT22 9FL.
PATEL, Miss. Nutan, ACA *2008;* 113 The Drive, ILFORD, ESSEX, IG1 3JD.
PATEL, Miss. Nutan, ACA *1992;* Lloyds TSB Bank, 10 Gresham Street, LONDON, EC2V 7AE.
PATEL, Mr. Palvesh, BA ACA *2006;* 12 Royal Avenue, WORCESTER PARK, SURREY, KT4 7JE.
•PATEL, Mr. Pankaj Rameshchandra, BSc ACA *1994;* (Tax Fac), P R Patel & Co, 2 Admiral House, Cardinal Way, HARROW, MIDDLESEX, HA3 5TE.
PATEL, Mr. Paras, ACA *2009;* Tanglewood Fairway Close, WOKING, SURREY, GU22 0LT.
PATEL, Mr. Paresh, BA ACA *1989;* 20 Ashbourne Avenue, HARROW, HA2 0JS.
PATEL, Mr. Paresh Jayendra, BA(Hons) ACA *2001;* 60 Sedley Grove Harefield, UXBRIDGE, MIDDLESEX, UB9 6JD.
PATEL, Mr. Parimal, FCA *1970;* Beethovenstraat 186-1, 1077 JX AMSTERDAM, NETHERLANDS.
PATEL, Mr. Parimal, BA FCA *1993;* 10 Woodside Road, NORTHWOOD, MIDDLESEX, HA6 3QE.
PATEL, Mr. Parimal Kantibhai, BA ACA *1984;* 71 Cherry Court, Acorn Walk, LONDON, SE16 5DY.
PATEL, Miss. Paru, BSc ACA *1990;* (Tax Fac), Pricewaterhousecoopers, 12 Plumtree Court, LONDON, EC4A 4HT.
PATEL, Mrs. Parul Suresh, BA ACA *1993;* 18 Fitzjames Avenue, CROYDON, CR0 5DH.
•PATEL, Mr. Pinakin Baldevbhai, ACA *1984;* APRP Ltd, 91 Sunnyhill Road, Streatham, LONDON, SW16 2UG.
•PATEL, Mr. Pinakin Thakorbhai, ACA *1982;* P.T. Patel & Co., Avad House, Belvue Road, NORTHOLT, UB5 5HY.
PATEL, Miss. Piya, BA ACA *2010;* 63 Lord Avenue, Clayhall, ILFORD, ESSEX, IG5 0HN.
PATEL, Mr. Piyush Ramanbhai, FCA *1988;* 29 Woodside Park Road, LONDON, N12 8RT.
•PATEL, Mr. Pradipkumar Durlabhbhai, MA DMS ACA CTA *1991;* (Tax Fac), Pradip D. Patel, 41 Warwick Road, New Southgate, LONDON, N11 2SD.
•PATEL, Mr. Praful, FCA *1982;* (Tax Fac), Chapmans Associates Limited, 3 Coombe Road, LONDON, NW10 0EB.
PATEL, Mr. Praful Chunilal, FCA *1975;* N. Jivanlal & Co. Pvt. Ltd., 2nd Floor, 50 Princess Street, MUMBAI 400 002, MAHARASHTRA, INDIA.
•PATEL, Mr. Praful Satilal, FCA *1978;* Portman & Co, 5 High Street, Hornsey, LONDON, N8 7PS.
PATEL, Mr. Pragnesh, BSc(Hons) ACA *2001;* 20 Baines Way, Grange Park, NORTHAMPTON, NN4 5DP.
PATEL, Mr. Prakash Kumar, BA ACA *1990;* 34 Freestone Place, The Woodlands, HOUSTON, TX 77382, UNITED STATES.
PATEL, Mr. Pramal Rajni, BA(Hons) ACA *2000;* 11 Grove Road, PINNER, HA5 5HW.
PATEL, Mr. Pramit, BSc ACA *2004;* 36A Windmill Road, Edmonton, LONDON, N18 1PA.
PATEL, Mr. Prasam, ACA *2010;* Foxgloves, Rickmansworth Road, Chorleywood, RICKMANSWORTH, HERTFORDSHIRE, WD3 5SB.
PATEL, Mr. Prashant, BSc(Hons) ACA *2001;* 20 Kenny Drive, CARSHALTON, SM5 4PH.
PATEL, Mr. Prashant Amrit, BSc ACA *1989;* 3 St Omer Ridge, Off St Omer Road, GUILDFORD, GU1 2DD.
•PATEL, Mr. Pravin Gordhanbhai, FCA *1977;* (Tax Fac), P G. Patel & Co, 48 Clarendon Gardens, WEMBLEY, HA9 7QN.
•PATEL, Mr. Pravinchandra Gandabhai, FCA *1976;* P. Patel, 71 Park Road, Great Sankey, WARRINGTON, WA5 3EA.
PATEL, Mr. Pritesh Ratilal, BSc ACA *1990;* Bank of America, Merrill Lynch Financial Centre, 2 King Edward Street, LONDON, EC1A 1HQ.
PATEL, Miss. Prithee, ACA *2007;* 74 Beverley Drive, EDGWARE, HA8 5NE.
PATEL, Miss. Priya, BSc ACA *2007;* Heldrew House, Tesco Stores Ltd Tesco House, Delamare Road Cheshunt, WALTHAM CROSS, HERTFORDSHIRE, EN8 9SL.
PATEL, Mr. Priyen, ACA *2008;* 26 Foxearth Road, SOUTH CROYDON, SURREY, CR2 8ED.
PATEL, Mr. Priyesh, BSc ACA *1993;* 87 Gordon Avenue, STANMORE, HA7 3QR.
PATEL, Mr. Puneet Bipin, ACA *2010;* 358a Wandsworth Bridge Road, LONDON, SW6 2TZ.
PATEL, Mr. Purav, ACA *2007;* North York Corporate Centre, 4100 Yonge Street, TORONTO M2P 2H3, ON, CANADA.
PATEL, Mr. Pushyant Shantilal, FCA *1973;* Westgate Healthcare Group Ltd, Churchill House, 137 Brent Street, LONDON, NW4 4DJ.
PATEL, Miss. Radha, BSc ACA *2009;* 92 Doncaster Road, LEICESTER, LE4 6JJ.
PATEL, Miss. Radhika, MA BSc ACA *2010;* 15 Alders Close, EDGWARE, MIDDLESEX, HA8 9QQ.
PATEL, Mr. Rahoel, BSc ACA *2010;* 15 Askew Road, NORTHWOOD, MIDDLESEX, HA6 2JE.
PATEL, Mr. Rahul, ACA *1980;* Portland Food & Wine, 15 London Street, LONDON, W2 1HL.
PATEL, Mr. Rahul Kumar Babubhai, BSc(Hons) ACA *2001;* 15 West View Road, ST. ALBANS, HERTFORDSHIRE, AL3 5JX.
•PATEL, Mr. Raj, BSc FCA *1989;* (Tax Fac), Patmans, 94 Brinkburn Gardens, EDGWARE, MIDDLESEX, HA8 5PP. See also F Winter & Co LLP and Nyman Linden
PATEL, Mr. Rajeep, BSc ACA *2000;* 7 Penwortham Road, SOUTH CROYDON, SURREY, CR2 0QU.

PATEL, Mr. Rajeev, BSc ACA *2006;* 15 The Avenue, NORTHWOOD, MIDDLESEX, HA6 2NJ.

•PATEL, Mr. Rajendra, ACA *1980;* Patens & Co Limited, 20a Selsdon Road, SOUTH CROYDON, SURREY, CR2 6PA.

PATEL, Mr. Rajendra Natubhai, FCA *1975;* Little Barn, Wych Hill Way, WOKING, GU22 0AE.

PATEL, Mrs. Rajendra Navnitbhai, MSc BA FCA CPA *1989;* 1983 Catrina Court, SAN JOSE, CA 95124-5500, UNITED STATES.

•PATEL, Mr. Rajendrakumar Chhotabhai, FCA *1985;* (Tax Fac), King & King, Roxburghe House, 273-287 Regent Street, LONDON, W1B 2HA.

•PATEL, Mr. Rajendrakumar Govind, FCA *1981;* (Tax Fac), Ashley King Limited, 68 St. Margarets Road, EDGWARE, MIDDLESEX, HA8 9UU.

PATEL, Mr. Rajesh, BSc ACA *1996;* 63 Grove Farm Park, NORTHWOOD, MIDDLESEX, HA6 2BQ.

PATEL, Mr. Rajesh, BA(Hons) ACA *2001;* 9 Lens Road, Forest Gate, LONDON, E7 8PU.

PATEL, Mr. Rajesh Bharat, BSc ACA *1999;* 23 Eden Way, BECKENHAM, KENT, BR3 3DN.

•PATEL, Mr. Rajesh V, ACA *1986;* Butler & Co LLP, 3rd Floor, 126-134 Baker Street, LONDON, W1U 6UE. See also Butler & Co

PATEL, Miss. Rajeshree Chandrakant, BEng FCA AMCT *1998;* 93 Gowan Avenue, LONDON, SW6 6RQ.

•PATEL, Mr. Rajnikant Chhotabhai, FCA FCCA *1974;* (Tax Fac), Inger & Company, 7 Redbridge Lane East, Redbridge, ILFORD, IG4 5ET.

PATEL, Mrs. Rajshree Sharadchandra, FCA *1978;* 3081 Hampton Court, CLEARWATER, FL 33714, UNITED STATES.

PATEL, Mrs. Rajul Kamlesh, BSc ACA *1992;* 134 Tanjong Rhu Road, #04-03 Lobby E, Pebble Bay, SINGAPORE 436920, SINGAPORE.

PATEL, Mr. Rakesh, BSc(Hons) ACA *2000;* 16 Wensley Road, HARROGATE, NORTH YORKSHIRE, HG2 8AQ.

PATEL, Mr. Rakesh, BA ACA *1995;* RAP Consult, 1A Winders Road, LONDON, SW11 3HE.

•PATEL, Mr. Rakesh Manubhai, BSc ACA *1992;* Harrison Bernstein Ltd, 10 Harmer Street, GRAVESEND, DA12 2AX.

PATEL, Miss. Raksha Raojibhai, ACA *1989;* 9 Granville Gardens, Norbury, LONDON, SW16 3LN.

•PATEL, Mr. Raman, BSc FCA *1984;* (Tax Fac), Berkeley-Tax Limited, Berkeley House, 5 Roman Way, BRACKNELL, RG42 7UT.

PATEL, Mr. Ramanbhai, FCA *1969;* 23 Manor Drive, Wembley Park, WEMBLEY, MIDDLESEX, HA9 8EB.

•PATEL, Mr. Ramesh Kashibhai, FCA *1973;* (Tax Fac), Patsons Accountancy Limited, Suraj Chambers, 53 Islington Park Street, LONDON, N1 1QB.

•PATEL, Mr. Rameshbhai Ambalal, FCA *1976;* Ramesh A. Patel & Co, 10 Harrow Place, Off Middlesex Street, LONDON, E1 7DB.

PATEL, Mr. Ramnik Ramji, FCA *1979;* 1 The Yews, Oadby, LEICESTER, LE2 5EF.

•PATEL, Mr. Ravindra Gordhanbhai, BCom FCA *1973;* (Tax Fac), Ravine & Co, 783 Harrow Road, WEMBLEY, HA0 2LP.

PATEL, Mr. Ravindra Harmanbhai, FCA *1984;* Shortlands, 19 Golf Side, South Cheam, SUTTON, SURREY, SM2 7HA.

PATEL, Miss. Reena, ACA *2008;* 5 Kelvin Close, EPSOM, KT19 9JE.

PATEL, Miss. Reena, ACA *2004;* 46 Tenby Road, EDGWARE, HA8 6DR.

PATEL, Mrs. Rekha, BA FCA *1990;* 11 Grassington Close, Friern Barnet, LONDON, N11 3FJ.

PATEL, Mrs. Reshma, ACA *1996;* 32 Ranelagh Gardens, ILFORD, ESSEX, IG1 3JR.

PATEL, Miss. Reshma, BA ACA *2002;* Flat 86, Grove End Gardens, Grove End Road, LONDON, NW8 9LP.

•PATEL, Miss. Rina, BA ACA *1997;* Patsons Accountancy Limited, Suraj Chambers, 53 Islington Park Street, LONDON, N1 1QB.

PATEL, Miss. Rinal, ACA *2009;* 27 The Fairoaks, Wakes Meadow, NORTHAMPTON, NN3 9UZ.

PATEL, Mr. Rinku, BA(Hons) FCA *2001;* (Tax Fac), 22 Hawthorn Road, SUTTON, SM1 4PF.

PATEL, Mr. Rishi, BSc ACA *2005;* 103 Quentin Road, LONDON, SE13 5DG.

PATEL, Mr. Ritesh, BA ACA *2004;* 65 Dorchester Road, WORCESTER PARK, SURREY, KT4 8NW.

PATEL, Mr. Ritesh Bhasker, ACA *2010;* 154 Laleham Road, STAINES, MIDDLESEX, TW18 2NX.

•PATEL, Mr. Rohit Shanabhai, ACA *1979;* (Tax Fac), R.S. Patel & Co, 43 Costons Avenue, GREENFORD, MIDDLESEX, UB6 8RJ.

PATEL, Mr. Rohitbhai Ambalal, MSc FCA *1973;* 17 Warren Avenue, Cheam, SUTTON, SM2 7QL. (Life Member)

•PATEL, Miss. Roma Chandrakant, BSc FCA *1995;* Trident Hotel, Nariman Point, MUMBAI 400 021, INDIA.

PATEL, Mr. Romil, MSc BSc ACA *2006;* 104-106 Holland Park Avenue, LONDON, W11 4UA.

PATEL, Mrs. Roopal, BSc ACA *2007;* 17 Cookson Road, LEICESTER, LE4 9WT.

PATEL, Miss. Roshni, ACA *2008;* E M I Music, Crown House, 72 Hammersmith Road, LONDON, W14 8UD.

PATEL, Miss. Rupal, ACA *2010;* Flat 10, Drake Court, 12 Swan Street, LONDON, SE1 1BH.

PATEL, Mr. Rupane, BSc(Econ) ACA *1998;* Canjayar, Tydecombe Road, WARLINGHAM, CR6 9LU.

PATEL, Mr. Rupesh, BSc ACA *2007;* 54 Seaford Close, RUISLIP, MIDDLESEX, HA4 7HN.

PATEL, Mrs. Rushina, ACA *2009;* 73 New Village Way, Churwell Morley, LEEDS, LS27 7GD.

•PATEL, Miss. Sabera, BSc ACA ATT *2003;* Sabera & Co, 126 Middlesex Street, LONDON, E1 7HY.

PATEL, Mr. Sailesh Vinubhai, BA ACA *1982;* P.O. Box 45139, NAIROBI, KENYA.

PATEL, Miss. Saleha, ACA *2011;* Alex Picot & Co, 95-97 Halkett Place, St. Helier, JERSEY, JE1 1BX.

PATEL, Miss. Salma, BA ACA *2005;* 454 Green Lane, ILFORD, IG3 9LF.

PATEL, Mr. Samant, BSc ACA *2003;* 101 Plashet Road, Upton Park, LONDON, E13 0RA.

PATEL, Mr. Samir Natwerlal, BSc ACA *1993;* 19 Dewhurst Road, LONDON, W14 0ET.

PATEL, Mr. Samirkumar Rasikchandra, BA(Hons) ACA *2004;* Eaglesfield House, Daventry Road, Norton, DAVENTRY, NORTHAMPTONSHIRE, NN11 5ND.

PATEL, Mr. Sandeep, BSc ACA *2003;* Flat 4, Chiltern House, 54-56 High Street, HARROW, MIDDLESEX, HA1 3LL.

PATEL, Mr. Sandip, BSc ACA *1998;* Whitegatye, Rickmansworth Road, NORTHWOOD, MIDDLESEX, HA6 2QY.

PATEL, Mr. Sandip Kumar, MEng ACA CTA *2002;* B U P A BUPA House, 15-19 Bloomsbury Way, LONDON, WC1A 2BA.

PATEL, Mr. Sanjai Hariprasad, MSc ACA *1992;* 43 Tresco Gardens, ILFORD, IG3 9NH.

PATEL, Mr. Sanjai Vinubhai, BA(Hons) ACA *2002;* 21 Cavendish Avenue, WOODFORD GREEN, IG8 9DA.

PATEL, Mr. Sanjay, BSc ACA *2007;* 59 Wakeley Hill, Penn, WOLVERHAMPTON, WV4 5RA.

PATEL, Mr. Sanjay, ACA *2011;* 7 Waterer Rise, WALLINGTON, SURREY, SM6 9DN.

PATEL, Mr. Sanjay, BA ACA *1996;* 21 Manor Road South, Hinchley Wood, ESHER, KT10 0PY.

PATEL, Mr. Sanjay, BSc ACA *1990;* 19 Gerard Road, HARROW, HA1 2ND.

PATEL, Mr. Sanjay Bhupendra, LLB ACA *1997;* 90 Totteridge Lane, LONDON, N20 8QQ.

PATEL, Mr. Sanjay Jayantilal, BSc ACA *1992;* 36 Beaminster Gardens, ILFORD, IG6 2BW.

PATEL, Mr. Sanjay Navin, BA ACA *2000;* 5 Copper Row, Tower Bridge Piazza, LONDON, SE1 2LH.

PATEL, Mr. Sanjay Ramesh, BSc ACA CFA *1999;* Oakley Capital, Incorporated Society of Valuers Auctioneers, 3 Cadogan Gate, LONDON, SW1X 0AS.

PATEL, Mr. Sanjay Suryakant, BSc ACA *1989;* 1 Abbots Lane, KENLEY, SURREY, CR8 5JB.

PATEL, Mr. Sanjiv, BA ACA *2007;* with MacIntyre Hudson, Peterbridge House, The Lakes, NORTHAMPTON, NN4 7HB.

PATEL, Mr. Santosh, BSc ACA *1992;* 9 Boston Gardens, LONDON, W7 2AN.

PATEL, Miss. Saraswati, BA ACA CTA *1991;* (Tax Fac), 28 Leigh Road, WALSALL, WS4 2DS.

PATEL, Mrs. Saroj, BSc ACA *1993;* 44 Gosling Grove, HIGH WYCOMBE, BUCKINGHAMSHIRE, HP13 5YS.

PATEL, Mr. Satish, BSc ACA *1982;* 10 Sheraton Close, Elstree, BOREHAMWOOD, WD6 3PZ.

PATEL, Mr. Savan, BSc ACA *2003;* 22 Northwick Park Road, HARROW, HA1 2NU.

PATEL, Mrs. Seema Mital, LLB ACA *2009;* 110 Aldrich Drive, Willen, MILTON KEYNES, MK15 9LU.

PATEL, Miss. Shachi, BSc ACA *2001;* 55 Galdana Avenue, BARNET, HERTFORDSHIRE, EN5 5JT.

PATEL, Mr. Shailen, BSc ACA *2006;* with PricewaterhouseCoopers LLP, 1 Hays Galleria, 1 Hays Lane, LONDON, SE1 2RD.

PATEL, Mr. Shailen, BA(Hons) ACA *2002;* Apartment 91 Berkeley Tower, 48 Westferry Circus, LONDON, E14 8RP.

•PATEL, Mr. Shailen Chandulal, BA FCA *1985;* (Tax Fac), with GBJ LLP, Sterling House, 27 Hatchlands Road, REDHILL, RH1 6RW.

•PATEL, Mr. Shailesh Bipinchandra, BSc ACA *1982;* 13 Woodbury Close, CROYDON, CR0 5PR.

•PATEL, Mr. Shailesh Virendra, BA ACA *1988;* Macilvin Moore Reveres LLP, 7 St John's Road, HARROW, HA1 2EY.

PATEL, Mrs. Shamim, BA ACA *1993;* Soregardsvagen 4, SE-36032 GEMLA, SWEDEN.

•PATEL, Mr. Shashi, BA ACA *1990;* (Tax Fac), Heywards, 6th Floor, Remo House, 310-312 Regent Street, LONDON, W1B 3BS.

PATEL, Mr. Shashin Navin, BSc ACA *1989;* 91 Chester Drive, HARROW, HA2 7PX.

PATEL, Mr. Shaylesh Vasant, BSc ACA *1994;* 49 Prebend Gardens, LONDON, W6 0XT.

PATEL, Miss. Sheena, BSc ACA *1994;* 30 St. Paul's Court, 146 Clapham Park Road, LONDON, SW4 7DE.

PATEL, Miss. Sheena, ACA *2007;* with Grant Thornton UK LLP, 30 Finsbury Square, LONDON, EC2P 2YU.

PATEL, Miss. Sheena, ACA *2009;* 23 Empire Square East, Empire Square, LONDON, SE1 4NB.

PATEL, Mrs. Sheena Nitinchandra, ACA *2010;* Pearson International - Sheena Patel - Finance Manager - 8th Floor, Edexcel, 190 High Holborn, LONDON, WC1V 7BH.

PATEL, Miss. Sheetal, BSc ACA CTA *1998;* 1 Westward Way, Kenton, HARROW, MIDDLESEX, HA3 0SE.

PATEL, Mr. Sheil Dilipkumar, BA ACA *1995;* Twinoaks, 1c Westbury Road, NORTHWOOD, MIDDLESEX, HA6 3DB.

PATEL, Mrs. Shibani, ACA *1995;* Mount Stewart Junior School, Carlisle Gardens, HARROW, MIDDLESEX, HA3 0JX.

PATEL, Miss. Shima, ACA *2009;* Flat 7 Thomas Frye Court, 30 High Street, LONDON, E15 2PS.

PATEL, Miss. Shivani, BSc ACA *2008;* 19 Leaholme Waye, RUISLIP, HA4 7RA.

PATEL, Miss. Simla, BSc ACA *1994;* 92 Dawlish Drive, Seven Kings, ILFORD, IG3 9EF.

PATEL, Mr. Sital Rajendra, BA ACA *2006;* 21 Hawthorn Road, BUCKHURST HILL, ESSEX, IG9 6JF.

PATEL, Mr. Siten Surendra, BSc(Econ) ACA *1999;* 1 Rossendale Close, ENFIELD, MIDDLESEX, EN2 9JQ.

PATEL, Mr. Sivani, BSc ACA *2007;* with KPMG LLP, Management Services Centre, 58 Clarendon Road, WATFORD, WD17 1DE.

PATEL, Mr. Sohael, MSc BSc ACA *2007;* 15 Askew Road, NORTHWOOD, HA6 2JE.

PATEL, Mrs. Sonal, BSc ACA *2002;* (Tax Fac), Flat B Welbeck Mansions, Inglewood Road, LONDON, NW6 1QX.

PATEL, Mrs. Sonal, BSc ACA *1995;* 350 S Fuller Avenue, Apt 3J, LOS ANGELES, CA 90036, UNITED STATES.

PATEL, Mr. Sujit Ashvinbhai, FCA *1979;* 60 Fairfax Avenue, EPSOM, KT17 2QT.

•PATEL, Mr. Suketu, FCA *1976;* Pool & Patel, P.O. Box 117, VICTORIA, SEYCHELLES. See also BDO International

PATEL, Mr. Sundeep Raman, BSc ACA *1995;* 29a Shelgate Road, LONDON, SW11 1BB.

PATEL, Mr. Sunil James, BEng ACA *1992;* with Grant Thornton UK LLP, Grant Thornton House, 22 Melton Street, Euston Square, LONDON, NW1 2EP.

PATEL, Miss. Sunita, BSc(Hons) ACA *2002;* 8 Cottam Green, Cottam, PRESTON, PR4 0AB.

•PATEL, Mr. Suresh Jashbhai, FCA *1976;* (Tax Fac), 26 St Georges Drive, Ickenham, UXBRIDGE, UB10 8HW.

PATEL, Mr. Surit Chhaganlal, BSc ACA *1996;* 4 Grantham Close, Brockley Hill, EDGWARE, HA8 8DL.

PATEL, Mr. Sushil, BSc(Hons) ACA *2010;* 7 Kingsmead Avenue, SUNBURY-ON-THAMES, MIDDLESEX, TW16 5HW.

PATEL, Miss. Swatal, BSc ACA *2007;* 121 Wards Wharf Approach, LONDON, E16 2ER.

PATEL, Miss. Sweta, BSc(Hons) ACA *2000;* 5 Langdon Close, CAMBERLEY, GU15 1AQ.

PATEL, Mrs. Taraneh, LLB ACA *2006;* First Floor Flat, 104 Holland Park Avenue, LONDON, W11 4UA.

PATEL, Mr. Tarunbhai, BEng ACA *2002;* 27 Briarwood Road, EPSOM, KT17 2LX.

PATEL, Mr. Tilesh Chimanbhai, BA ACA *1991;* AnnaKiri, 9 Kewferry Drive, NORTHWOOD, MIDDLESEX, HA6 2NT.

PATEL, Mrs. Tina, BA(Hons) ACA *2001;* 44 Glebelands Avenue, Newbury Park, ILFORD, ESSEX, IG2 7DN.

•PATEL, Miss. Tina, BA ACA CTA *2008;* 44 Chestnut Drive, Stretton Hall, Oadby, LEICESTER, LE2 4QX.

PATEL, Miss. Tina, ACA *2007;* with Grant Thornton UK LLP, 30 Finsbury Square, LONDON, EC2P 2YU.

PATEL, Ms. Tina, MA ACA *1997;* 24 Edmunds Walk, Hampstead Garden Suburb, LONDON, N2 0HU.

PATEL, Mrs. Tina, BSc ACA *2002;* 123 Northumberland Road, HARROW, MIDDLESEX, HA2 7RB.

PATEL, Mr. Truptesh, BA(Hons) ACA *2006;* Flat 8, 78 Meadowcourt Road, LONDON, SE3 9DP.

PATEL, Mr. Tushar, BSc ACA *1989;* 23 The Dene, WEMBLEY, HA9 7QS.

PATEL, Mr. Tushar Purushottam, BA ACA *1987;* 17 Poynings Road, LONDON, N19 5LH.

PATEL, Mr. Tushar Surendra, MSc ACA *2000;* Lloyds TSB Bank Plc, 10 Gresham Street, LONDON, EC2V 7AE.

•PATEL, Mr. Uday Vithalbhai, BA(Hons) ACA CTA *1993;* Kishens Limited, 3 Montpelier Avenue, BEXLEY, KENT, DA5 3AP.

PATEL, Miss. Ujal, ACA *2007;* North End House, Nugents Park, Hatchend, PINNER, MIDDLESEX, HA5 4RA.

•PATEL, Mr. Ullas Ambalal, BSc FCA *1977;* (Tax Fac), A.K. Patel & Co, 1 Coton Lane, Erdington, BIRMINGHAM, B23 6TP.

•PATEL, Mr. Umeshchandra Dahyabhai, MBA BSc FCA *1987;* (Tax Fac), Umesh Patel & Co, 1 Kings Court, Harwood Road, HORSHAM, RH13 5UR.

PATEL, Miss. Urva, BA ACA *2007;* 6 Midhurst Court, Hook Road, SURBITON, KT6 5AD.

PATEL, Mr. Vahid, ACA *2009;* 230 Skeffington Road, PRESTON, PR1 6RY.

PATEL, Mrs. Vandana, BSc ACA *1995;* 11 Balmoral Avenue, Friern Barnet, LONDON, N11 3QA.

PATEL, Mr. Vashit, BEng ACA *2000;* Hakuna Matata, Cobbetts Hill, WEYBRIDGE, KT13 0UA.

PATEL, Mr. Vikash, BA ACA *2007;* Flat 8 Milligan Lodge, 66a Hendon Lane, LONDON, N3 1JT.

•PATEL, Mr. Vikashkumar Vallabhbhai, BSc ACA *1997;* 45 Hungarton Drive, Syston, LEICESTER, LE7 2AU.

•PATEL, Mr. Vikram Shirishchandra, ACA *1991;* (Tax Fac), Vikram Patel, 168 Lavender Hill, Battersea, LONDON, SW11 5TG.

PATEL, Mr. Vinay, ACA *2008;* 2 Crowshott Avenue, STANMORE, MIDDLESEX, HA7 1JD.

PATEL, Mr. Vinay Somabhai, ACA *1980;* Sai Darshan, Nugents Park, PINNER, MIDDLESEX, HA5 4RA.

PATEL, Mr. Vineet, BSc ACA *1994;* 45 Moorfields, LONDON, EC2Y 9AE.

PATEL, Mr. Vinod Jasvant, BSc ACA *2007;* 58 Gopsall Street, Highfields, LEICESTER, LE2 0DL.

PATEL, Mr. Vinod Kumar, BSc ACA *1994;* 33 Pangbourne Drive, STANMORE, MIDDLESEX, HA7 4RA.

•PATEL, Mr. Vinod Rai, BSc FCA *1973;* V.R. Patel, 7 Greenway, HEMEL HEMPSTEAD, HERTFORDSHIRE, HP2 4QG.

•PATEL, Mr. Vinod Valjibhai, ACA *1981;* Freshfield Associates Ltd, 71a Knighton Way Lane, Denham, UXBRIDGE, UB9 4EH. See also Patel V.V. & Co

•PATEL, Mr. Vinodkumar Bhanabhai, BSc FCA *1981;* VBP & Co, 19 Morden Court Parade, London Road, MORDEN, SURREY, SM4 5HJ.

PATEL, Mr. Vipul, ACA *2008;* 402 St. Davids Square, LONDON, E14 3WQ.

•PATEL, Mr. Vipul Surendra, BSc ACA *1993;* (Tax Fac), Ropemaker Place, 25 Ropemaker Street, LONDON, EC2Y 9AN.

•PATEL, Mr. Viral, BA ACA *1994;* (Tax Fac), Virash Bach & Co Limited, 72 Lyndhurst Road, THORNTON HEATH, SURREY, CR7 7PW.

PATEL, Mr. Viren Jayantilal, BCom ACA *2003;* 17 Warden Road, SUTTON COLDFIELD, B73 5SB.

PATEL, Mr. Vishal, BSc(Hons) ACA *2011;* 47 Beverley Road, LONDON, SE20 8SH.

PATEL, Mr. Vishal, BA ACA *2008;* 12 Cotswold Gardens, LONDON, NW2 1QR.

PATEL, Mr. Vishal, ACA *2008;* 62 Holmwood Road, Cheam, SUTTON, SURREY, SM2 7JS.

PATEL, Mr. Vishal Ghanshyam, BSc ACA *2001;* Flat 1, 54 Keswick Road, LONDON, SW15 2JE.

PATEL, Miss. Yamini, ACA *2008;* 14 Roche Way, WELLINGBOROUGH, NORTHAMPTONSHIRE, NN8 5YD.

PATEL, Mr. Yashwant Purushottam, FCA *1971;* Lorentzen & Trifari CPA's PC, 209 Route 112, PORT JEFFERSON STATION, NY 11776, UNITED STATES.

PATEL, Mr. Yaxit, ACA *2009;* 86 Munster Avenue, HOUNSLOW, TW4 5BJ.

•PATEL, Mr. Yogan Apabhai, FCA *1983;* (Tax Fac), MacIntyre Hudson LLP, New Bridge Street House, 30-34 New Bridge Street, LONDON, EC4V 6BJ.

PATEL, Mr. Yogesh, BSc ACA *1999;* Suncourt House, 18-26 Essex Road, LONDON, N1 8LN.

PATEL, Mr. Yogesh Chandubhai, MBA BSc ACA *1980;* 17 Maryon Mews, Hampstead, LONDON, NW3 2PU.
PATEL, Mr. Yogesh Kumar, FCA *1975;* 86 Timberhill Drive, FRANKLIN PARK, NJ 08823, UNITED STATES.
PATEL, Mr. Yogeshchandra, ACA *1982;* 4 Ormonde Road, Moor Park, NORTHWOOD, MIDDLESEX, HA6 2EL.
PATEL, Mr. Yunus, ACA *2011;* 26 Norman Avenue, NUNEATON, WARWICKSHIRE, CV11 5NX.
•PATEL, Mr. Zafar-Altab Umarji, BSc ACA *1989;* PricewaterhouseCoopers, 1 Embankment Place, LONDON, WC2N 6RH. See also PricewaterhouseCoopers LLP
PATEL, Mr. Zainul Abedeen, BA ACA *2006;* 14 Glossop Street, Evington, LEICESTER, LE5 5HN.
PATEL, Miss. Zarin Homi, BSc FCA *1986;* 3 De Havilland Drive, Hazlemere, HIGH WYCOMBE, HP15 7FP.
PATEL, Mr. Zia Zane Ali, BSc ACA *2006;* C/O Marsh IAS Management Services (Bermuda) Ltd., 44 Church Street, HAMILTON HM12, BERMUDA.
•PATEL, Mr. Zubair Asad Ahmed, ACA *2002;* C/o KPMG Safi Al Mutawa, Rakan ower 18th Floor, Fahad Al Salam Street, P.O. Box 24 Safat 13001, Kuwait, KUWAIT CITY KUWAIT.
•PATEL, Mr. Zubin, BA ACA *1999;* Deloitte LLP, 2 New Street Square, LONDON, EC4A 3BZ. See also Deloitte & Touche LLP
PATEL, Mr. Zulfiqar Ahmed, ACA *2004;* 47/1 21st Street off:, Khayaban-E-Mujahid Phase 5, Defence Housing Authority, KARACHI 75500, PAKISTAN.
PATEL JUNIOR, Mr. Jayanti, BA(Hons) ACA *2011;* Quarry Hanger, Springbottom Lane, Bletchingley, REDHILL, RH1 4QZ.
PATELIA, Mr. Mitesh, ACA *2007;* 1 Barwick Drive, UXBRIDGE, MIDDLESEX, UB8 3UP.
•PATEMAN, Mr. Alan David, ACA FCCA *2009;* Segrave & Partners, Turnpike House, 1208/1210 London Road, LEIGH-ON-SEA, SS9 2UA.
PATEMAN, Dr. Andrew Glen, BSc(Hons) ACA *2003;* 7 Charville Court, Trafalgar Grove, LONDON, SE10 9AU.
PATEMAN, Mr. Colin John, FCA *1979;* GHL Insurance Services UK Limited, Chester House, Harlands Road, HAYWARDS HEATH, WEST SUSSEX, RH16 1LR.
•PATEMAN, Mr. Philip James, BA FCA *1996;* with KPMG LLP, Dukes Keep, Marsh Lane, SOUTHAMPTON, HAMPSHIRE, SO14 3EX.
PATEMAN, Mrs. Sarah, MA ACA *2006;* 11b Oaklands Avenue, SIDCUP, DA15 8NF.
PATEMAN, Mrs. Tamara Anne, BSc ACA *1997;* Hendrickson Europe Ltd, Sywell Airport, Sywell, NORTHAMPTON, NN6 0BN.
PATENALL, Mr. Roger Oliver, FCA *1970;* 10 Greta House, 60 Hardy Road, LONDON, SE3 7PA.
PATER, Mr. Alan, BA ACA *2002;* Asda Stores Ltd Asda House, Great Wilson Street, LEEDS, LS11 5AD.
PATER, Mrs. Caroline Mary, BSc(Hons) ACA *2002;* Applegarth, Arkendale Road, Ferrensby, KNARESBOROUGH, NORTH YORKSHIRE, HG5 0QA.
PATER, Miss. Caroline Mary, BSc FCA *1986;* (Tax Fac), with Fletcher & Partners, Crown Chambers, Bridge Street, SALISBURY, SP1 2LZ.
PATER, Mr. John Clayton, FCA *1960;* Middleton Farmhouse Middleton, Winterslow, SALISBURY, SP5 1QR. (Life Member)
PATERAS, Mr. Gregory, BSc(Hons) ACA *2004;* Littlewood Shop, Direct Home Shopping Limited, The Estuary, Commerce Park, Speke, LIVERPOOL L70 1AB.
•PATERNO, Mr. Nicholas Luigi, FCA *1991;* McBrides Accountants LLP, Nexus House, 2 Cray Road, SIDCUP, KENT, DA14 5DA. See also McBrides Corporate Finance Limited
PATERSON, Mr. Adrian Graham Bolam, MA FCA *1972;* 29 Nicholas Way, NORTHWOOD, HA6 2TR.
PATERSON, Mr. Alistair Bruce, BSc ACA *1994;* 389 Unthank Road, NORWICH, NR4 7QG.
PATERSON, Mr. Alistair James, BSc ACA *2001;* 49 Springfield Avenue, Horfield, BRISTOL, BS7 9QS.
PATERSON, Mr. Andrew, BA FCA *1981;* The Go-Ahead Group Plc, Go-Ahead House, 26-28 Addiscombe Road, CROYDON, CR9 5GA.
PATERSON, Mr. Andrew Julian, BA ACA *2003;* 10 The Avenue, Burton-upon-Stather, SCUNTHORPE, SOUTH HUMBERSIDE, DN15 9EU.
PATERSON, Mr. Andrew Neil, MChem ACA *2003;* 41/3 Shandon Crescent, EDINBURGH, EH11 1QF.
PATERSON, Mr. Angus Glencairn, BA ACA *2002;* Flat 6, 145a Balham Hill, LONDON, SW12 9DL.
PATERSON, Mr. Brian, BA ACA *1993;* Tandle View House, 2 Hollybrook, Chadderton, OLDHAM, OL1 2SY.
PATERSON, Mrs. Chloe Christina, BSc ACA *1995;* 25 Wood Lane, FLEET, HAMPSHIRE, GU51 3DX.
PATERSON, Mr. Christopher Douglas Mark, BA ACA *1999;* GSK Costache Negri Nr.1-5 Opera CenterSector5, 050552 BUCHAREST, ROMANIA.
PATERSON, Mr. Colin George, BSc ACA *1992;* 5 Thornly Park Avenue, PAISLEY, RENFREWSHIRE, PA2 7SB.
PATERSON, Mr. Daniel, BSc ACA *2003;* 57 Birmingham Road, Alvechurch, BIRMINGHAM, B48 7TB.
PATERSON, Mr. David Francis Joseph, MA FCA *1970;* 5A Greenview Gardens, 125 Robinson Road, MID LEVELS, HONG KONG ISLAND, HONG KONG SAR. (Life Member)
•PATERSON, Mr. David John, BSc ACA *1994;* Deloitte LLP, 2 New Street Square, LONDON, EC4A 3BZ. See also Deloitte & Touche LLP
PATERSON, Mr. Derrick Robert, BSc(Econ) FCA MICA *1981;* PO Box 441, GRAVESEND, KENT, DA12 9HP.
PATERSON, Mr. Douglas Gordon James, MA FCA *1968;* St Florian, 90 Evelyn Avenue, RUISLIP, HA4 8AJ.
PATERSON, Mr. Duncan, MSc FCA *1973;* Rosneath, Royce Way, West Wittering, CHICHESTER, WEST SUSSEX, PO20 8LN.
PATERSON, Mrs. Elizabeth Helen, BCom ACA *1991;* 23 Ravens Grove, Reedley, BURNLEY, BB10 2RD.
PATERSON, Mrs. Elizabeth Jennifer Rachel, BA ACA *1999;* 57 Birmingham Road, Alvechurch, BIRMINGHAM, B48 7TB.
PATERSON, Mr. Gary James, BA ACA *1987;* Penn Cottage Old Road, Buckland, BETCHWORTH, RH3 7DZ.
PATERSON, Mr. Ian Crawford, BA ACA *1999;* 92 George Lane, LONDON, SE13 6HL.
PATERSON, Mr. Ian James, BA BSc ACA *1988;* Aesop Brands Limited, 8-10 Lower James Street, LONDON, W1F9EL.
PATERSON, Mr. Ian Keith, FCA *1967;* Browns of Loughton Ltd, 199 High Road, LOUGHTON, IG10 1AA.
•PATERSON, Mr. Ian Michael, FCA *1988;* Cote Bank, Cuckfield Lane, Warninglid, HAYWARDS HEATH, WEST SUSSEX, RH17 5UB.
PATERSON, Mr. James David, BA ACA *1984;* 44 Walkington Drive, Market Weighton, YORK, YO43 3NR.
PATERSON, Mr. James Malcolm, LLB ACA *1999;* Cathcart Business Park, Spean Street, GLASGOW, G44 4BE.
•PATERSON, Miss. Janet Treacy, ACA ATII TEP *2002;* (Tax Fac), Charter Tax Consulting Limited, 11 St. James's Place, LONDON, SW1A 1NP.
PATERSON, Mr. John Alastair Cleland, FCA *1977;* The Long Barn, Ramsdean, PETERSFIELD, HAMPSHIRE, GU32 1RU.
PATERSON, Mr. John Malcolm, FCA *1962;* Oakland House, Slindon, STAFFORD, ST21 6LX. (Life Member)
PATERSON, Mrs. Karen Barbara, BSc ACA *1994;* 389 Unthank Road, NORWICH, NR4 7QG.
PATERSON, Ms. Katharine Anne, BSc(Hons) ACA *2001;* Anglo American, 20 Carlton House Terrace, LONDON, SW1Y 5AN.
•PATERSON, Mr. Kevin, FCA ATII *1983;* Ernst & Young LLP, 1 More London Place, LONDON, SE1 2AF. See also Ernst & Young Europe LLP
•PATERSON, Mrs. Lindsey Irene, MA ACA *1992;* PricewaterhouseCoopers LLP, 141 Bothwell Street, GLASGOW, G2 7EQ.
PATERSON, Mrs. Lorna Denise, LLB ACA *1999;* 12 Sayegh Street, St Heliers, AUCKLAND 1071, NEW ZEALAND.
PATERSON, Mr. Michael, BSc ACA *1991;* 15A Burleigh Road, West Bridgford, NOTTINGHAM, NG2 6FP.
PATERSON, Mr. Michael Stewart, BSc FCA *1973;* 28 Suffolk Street, HELENSBURGH, G84 9PA.
PATERSON, Mr. Nicholas James, BSc ACA CFE *1999;* PO Box 7124, Wellesley Street, AUCKLAND 1141, NEW ZEALAND.
PATERSON, Mr. Nigel Checkland, MBA FCA *1980;* 35 Sandy Lane, Charlton Kings, CHELTENHAM, GL53 9DG.
PATERSON, Mr. Phillip Edward, ACA *2008;* 17 Hyde Road, RICHMOND, TW10 6DU.
PATERSON, Mrs. Rajdip, BA(Hons) ACA *2002;* Unit 44, 20 Eve Street, Erskineville, SYDNEY, NSW 2043, AUSTRALIA.
PATERSON, Mr. Ralph Martin, BA ACA *1988;* with Deloitte LLP, 3 Rivergate, Temple Quay, BRISTOL, BS1 6GD.
PATERSON, Mr. Richard O'Donnell, MA FCA *1973;* Pound Hill House, Smith Street, West Kington, CHIPPENHAM, WILTSHIRE, SN14 7JG.
PATERSON, Mr. Robert Neil, LLB ACA CF *1979;* 16 Flanders Road, LONDON, W4 1NG.
•PATERSON, Mr. Rowland William Ormiston, FCA *1975;* (Tax Fac), Wellers, Stuart House, 55 Catherine Place, LONDON, SW1E 6DY.
PATERSON, Mr. Russell Cameron, BA ACA *1985;* Paterson Timber Ltd, 140 Elliot Street, GLASGOW, G3 8EX.
PATERSON, Mrs. Seema, BA ACA *1999;* 57 Str Aron Cotrus, Apt 21, Corpul A, BUCHAREST, ROMANIA.
PATERSON, Miss. Sheena Mary, ACA *1982;* 6 Adamson Gardens, West Didsbury, MANCHESTER, M20 2TQ.
PATERSON, Mrs. Sophie, BA(Hons) ACA *2011;* Mazars Tower Bridge House, St. Katharines Way, LONDON, E1W 1DD.
PATES, Mr. Martin Richard, BSc ACA *2001;* Flat 1 5 Highfield Close, LONDON, SE13 6US.
PATES, Mr. Thomas Vivian, BSc ACA *1979;* 3 Rubislaw View, ABERDEEN, AB15 4DD.
PATEY, Mrs. Jane Elizabeth, FCA *1977;* 157 Aston Cantlow Road, Wilmcote, STRATFORD-UPON-AVON, CV37 9XW.
PATEY, Miss. Louise Anne, ACA *2005;* 289 Link Road, CANVEY ISLAND, SS8 9YU.
PATEY, Mr. Stephen Ronald, BA ACA *1995;* 19 Compton Vale, Lower Compton, PLYMOUTH, PL3 5DX.
PATHAKJI, Miss. Swarupa Gaurang, BSc ACA *2005;* Duke Street Nations House, 103 Wigmore Street, LONDON, W1V 1QS.
PATHIRANA, Mr. Ruchira Senarath, LLB ACA *1997;* Flat 1, 39 Great Queen Street, LONDON, WC2B 5AA.
PATHIWILLE, Mr. Quintius Charindra, BSc ACA *2003;* Deloitte & Touche Llp, 66 Shoe Lane, LONDON, EC4A 3BQ.
PATHMANATHAN, Mr. Yogesh, ACA *2011;* 141 Shepherds Close, Romford, ROMFORD, RM6 5AJ.
PATHMANATHAN, Mr. Yohan, BSc ACA *1999;* 67 Bouverie Road, HARROW, HA1 4HD.
PATHMARAJAH, Mr. Allen Joseph, FCA *1963;* 17 Almond Crescent, SINGAPORE 677777, SINGAPORE.
PATIENCE, Mr. Kevin Stewart, BSc ACA *1992;* 1 Guestwick, TONBRIDGE, KENT, TN10 4HU.
PATIENCE, Mr. Michael John, BA FCA *1978;* Flat 3C, Cloudlands, 35-37 Plantation road, THE PEAK, HONG KONG ISLAND, HONG KONG SAR.
•PATIENT, Mr. Alan Stephen, FCA *1979;* Alan Patient & Co, 9 The Shrubberies, George Lane, South Woodford, LONDON, E18 1BD.
PATIENT, Mr. Benjamin George, BA(Hons) ACA *2001;* 14 Victoria Avenue, SURBITON, SURREY, KT6 5DW.
PATIENT, Mrs. Caroline Louise, BSc ACA *2003;* 130 Bassett Green Road, SOUTHAMPTON, SO16 3FG.
PATIENT, Mrs. Jacqueline Anne, BA ACA *1993;* Edmund Carr LLP, 146 New London Road, CHELMSFORD, CM2 0TT.
PATIENT, Mr. Simon, BA ACA *2000;* 6, Sistova Road, LONDON, SW12 9QT.
PATIKKI, Mrs. Katerina, BSc ACA *2008;* 3 Achilleos Street, Flat 301, Lycavitos, 1057 NICOSIA, CYPRUS.
PATMAN, Mr. Matthew Aldous, BSc ACA *2000;* 9 Radnor Road, TWICKENHAM, TW1 4NJ.
•PATMORE, Mr. Alan William, BSc FCA *1976;* Patmore & Co, Isabella Mews, The Avenue, Combe Down, BATH, BA2 5EH.
PATMORE, Mr. Anthony Harvey, FCA *1974;* Shaston Cottage, The Highlands, East Horsley, LEATHERHEAD, KT24 5BG.
PATMORE, Mr. James Herbert Frank, BA FCA *1960;* 7 Hawkenbury Way, LEWES, BN7 1LT. (Life Member)
PATMORE, Ms. Lynne Marie, BA ACA CTA *1988;* 9 Chalfont Road, OXFORD, OX2 6TL.
PATON, Mr. Andrew John, MSc BAcc ACA *2005;* 105 St. Johns Road, EDINBURGH, EH12 6NN.
PATON, Mr. Andrew Roger, FCA *1970;* Mill Cottage, Kings Mill Lane, South Nutfield, REDHILL, RH1 5NB.
PATON, Mrs. Ann Margaret, BA ACA *2003;* 64 Danvers Drive, Church Crookham, FLEET, HAMPSHIRE, GU52 0ZF.
PATON, Mrs. Caroline, BA ACA *2007;* Flat 2-6, 51 Linden Gardens, LONDON, W2 4HQ.
PATON, Miss. Catriona Jane, BSc(Hons) ACA *2001;* 82 Barringer Square, LONDON, SW17 8EE.
PATON, Mr. Christopher Vaughan, BSc ACA *1988;* with Deloitte LLP, Athene Place, 66 Shoe Lane, LONDON, EC4A 3BQ.
PATON, Mr. Colin John, MA(Hons) ACA *2004;* Apt 45C, 105 West 29th Street, NEW YORK, NY 10001, UNITED STATES.
PATON, Mr. Daryl Marc, BSc ACA *1991;* Easter House, Miles Lane, COBHAM, SURREY, KT11 2EF.
PATON, Mr. Duncan Barclay, FCA *1962;* PO Box 474, KNYSNA, 6570, SOUTH AFRICA. (Life Member)
PATON, Mrs. Elizabeth Lucy Mary, BSc ACA *2006;* Athene Place, Deloitte & Touche Llp, 66 Shoe Lane, LONDON, EC4A 3BQ.
PATON, Miss. Fiona Elizabeth, BSc ACA *1989;* PO Box 775, PC133 AL KHUWAIR, OMAN.
PATON, Mr. George Benjamin, MA ACA *1987;* 59 Cornwall Gardens, LONDON, SW7 4BE.
PATON, Mrs. Georgina Alice, MA ACA *1995;* Oxfordshire County Council Unipart House, Garsington Road Cowley, OXFORD, OX4 2GQ.
PATON, Mr. Jock Esmond, MA ACA *1978;* 27 Rosenau Road, Battersea, LONDON, SW11 4QN.
PATON, Miss. Kim Alexandra, BA ACA *2007;* 18 Burrage Road, REDHILL, SURREY, RH1 1TL.
PATON, Mr. Richard Edward, FCA *1965;* Mayflower Cottage, Barhatch Lane, CRANLEIGH, SURREY, GU6 7NH.
PATON, Mr. Robert Logan, BA ACA *1989;* 2 Sutherland Drive, West Bridgford, NOTTINGHAM, NG2 7BX.
PATON, Mr. Robert Thomas, BA ACA *1989;* Aon House, 30 Woodbourne Avenue, PEMBROKE HM 08, BERMUDA.
PATON, Mr. Timothy James, BSc FCA *1996;* 35 The Crescent, MAIDENHEAD, SL6 6AG.
PATON, Mrs. Tracey, BA ACA *2002;* A L D Ltd Oakwood Park, Lodge Causeway, BRISTOL, BS16 3JA.
PATOUX, Mr. John Lucien, FCA *1955;* Audley House, Stratford St.Mary, COLCHESTER, CO7 6JS. (Life Member)
PATPONG-PIBUL, Mr. Kitti, BSc FCA *1974;* 159/3 Soi Mahadlek 2, Rajadamri Road, BANGKOK 10330, THAILAND.
PATRICK, Mr. Charles Adam Simon, MA ACA *1995;* with KPMG LLP, One Snowhill, Snow Hill Queensway, BIRMINGHAM, B4 6GN.
PATRICK, Mr. Christopher John, BSc FCA *1977;* Dean Farmhouse, Aughton, Collingbourne Kingston, MARLBOROUGH, SN8 3SA.
PATRICK, Mr. David Andrew, MMath ACA *2006;* with National Audit Office, 1st Floor, 89 Sandyford Road, NEWCASTLE UPON TYNE, NE1 8HW.
PATRICK, Mrs. Deborah Leanne, MMath ACA *2004;* with Ernst & Young LLP, 100 Barbirolli Square, MANCHESTER, M2 3EY.
PATRICK, Mr. Fraser Malcolm, BSc(Hons) ACA *1998;* Shepherd Neame LTD, 17 Court Street, FAVERSHAM, KENT, ME13 7AX.
PATRICK, Mr. Ian Thomas, FCA *1973;* P.O. Box 1461, GEORGE TOWN, GRAND CAYMAN, KY1-1110, CAYMAN ISLANDS.
PATRICK, Mr. James Thomas, BSc ACA *2007;* Flat 3 Orpington Mansions, Orpington Road, LONDON, N21 3PJ.
PATRICK, Mr. John Richard, FCA *1975;* Lindos, White Rose Lane, WOKING, SURREY, GU22 7JS.
•PATRICK, Mr. Malcolm Leslie, FCA CTA *1973;* Malcolm Patrick, 170 Chesterton Road, CAMBRIDGE, CB4 1DA.
PATRICK, Mr. Peter Laurence, BA FCA *1972;* Amberley White Street Green, Boxford, SUDBURY, SUFFOLK, CO10 5JN.
PATRICK, Mr. Russell, BSc ACA *1992;* 36 Sandringham Road, COALVILLE, LE67 4PD.
PATRICK, Mr. Stephen Christopher, MA(Hons) ACA *2002;* Wolseley Plc Parkview, 1220 Arlington Business Park Theale, READING, RG7 4GA.
PATRICK, Mrs. Suzanne, BSc ACA *1988;* Chapel Farm, 24 Selby Road, Holme-On-Spalding-Moor, YORK, YO43 4ES.
PATRICK, Mr. William Desmond, FCA *1950;* 2 Graceland Court, Locker Street, Qui-si-Sana, SLIEMA SLM-11, MALTA. (Life Member)
PATRICKSON, Miss. Judith, FCA DChA *1986;* Ground Floor, 3 Holyrood Crescent, GLASGOW, G20 6HJ.
•PATRY, Mr. Maurice Robert Louis, FCA *1975;* (Tax Fac), Landlords Tax Services Limited, Davenport House, 16 Pepper Street, LONDON, E14 9RP.
PATSALIDES, Mr. Tassos, FCA *1980;* Patsalides & Co, 60 Larnacos Avenue, Flat 301, Aglantzia, 2101 NICOSIA, CYPRUS.
PATSALIDOU, Ms. Liza, ACA *2009;* 4 Ellados Street, Flat 301, Strovolos, 2003 NICOSIA, CYPRUS.
PATSALIDOU, Miss. Maria, BSc ACA *2005;* P.O. Box 4, 1142, 6309 LARNACA, CYPRUS.
•PATSTON-LILLEY, Mr. Gerald, FCA *1963;* (Tax Fac), Fairfax, 12 Malvern Close, SURBITON, KT6 7UG.
PATT, Mr. Alexander Laurence, FCA *1959;* 3 Seafield Road, LONDON, N11 1AR. (Life Member)
•PATT, Mr. Murray Philip, BA ACA *1996;* Hurst & Company Accountants LLP, Lancashire Gate, 21 Tiviot Dale, STOCKPORT, CHESHIRE, SK1 1TD.

PATTANAIK, Mr. Naga Bhushan, ACA *2011;* Flat 156, Quadrant Court, Empire Way, WEMBLEY, MIDDLESEX, HA9 0EQ.
•PATTANI, Mr. Jitendra, BSc FCA *1991;* Wilder Coe LLP, 233-237 Old Marylebone Road, LONDON, NW1 5QT. See also Wilder Coe
PATTAR, Mr. Taminder Singh, BSc ACA *2004;* 9 Hollington Way, Shirley, SOLIHULL, B90 4YD.
PATTEN, Miss. Anna Jane, MA ACA CTA MBA *1996;* High Grantley 39 Kippington Road, SEVENOAKS, KENT, TN13 2LL.
•PATTEN, Mr. Bernard Philip, FCA *1974;* (Tax Fac), Philip Patten & Co, 54 Oakington Avenue, Little Chalfont, AMERSHAM, HP6 6ST.
PATTEN, Miss. Karen, BSc ACA *2011;* 16 Coates Quay, CHELMSFORD, CM2 6HU.
•PATTEN, Mr. Nathan John, BSc ACA *2000;* 20 Brayburne Avenue, LONDON, SW4 6AA.
PATTEN, Mr. Nicholas John, BA ACA *1983;* Capita Commercial Services Pullman Place, Great Western Road, GLOUCESTER, GL1 3EA.
PATTEN, Mr. Shaun, LLB ACA *2001;* 103 Beechfield Avenue, BANGOR, COUNTY DOWN, BT19 7ZX.
PATTENDEN, Mrs. Catherine Janet, BSc(Hons) ACA *2004;* 22 Millholme Close, SOUTHAM, CV47 1FQ.
PATTENDEN, Mr. Mark Simon, LLB ACA *2001;* 56 Broad Lawn, LONDON, SE9 3XD.
PATTENDEN, Mr. Nicholas John, MSc ACA *1986;* 45 Station Road, THAMES DITTON, KT7 0PA.
PATTERN, Mr. Adrian Leonard, BSc ACA *1994;* 14 Broadacre Park, BROUGH, HU15 1LT.
•PATTERSON, Mr. Alan James, FCA *1981;* (Tax Fac), Greaves West & Ayre, 1-3 Sandgate, BERWICK-UPON-TWEED, TD15 1EW.
PATTERSON, Mr. Alfred John, FCA *1977;* 42 Oulder Hill Drive, Bamford, ROCHDALE, OL11 5LB.
PATTERSON, Mr. Andrew Robin William, BA ACA *1990;* 33 Roman Road, Birstall, LEICESTER, LE4 4BB.
PATTERSON, Mr. Daniel Mark, BA(Hons) ACA *2002;* 57 Woodheys Drive, SALE, CHESHIRE, M33 4JB.
PATTERSON, Mr. David Robert Mark, BA(Hons) ACA *2010;* 78 Bryansburn Road, BANGOR, COUNTY DOWN, BT20 3SB.
PATTERSON, Mr. Donald Albert, FCA MBA *1977;* P.O. Box 647, Meadowbridge P.O., KINGSTON 19, JAMAICA.
•PATTERSON, Mr. Donald Robert, BA ACA *1986;* (Tax Fac), Cyfri Cyfrifwyr Cyfyngedig, 23 College Street, LAMPETER, DYFED, SA48 7DY. See also Patterson, Jones & Evans
PATTERSON, Mrs. Frances, BSc ACA *1988;* 1 Cornes Close, WINCHESTER, HAMPSHIRE, SO22 5DS.
PATTERSON, Mr. Frank Derek, CBE RD FCA *1950;* Welcombe Cottage, 61 Meads Street, EASTBOURNE, BN20 7RN. (Life Member)
•PATTERSON, Mr. Frederick, BA FCA *1976;* (Tax Fac), Military House Limited, Military House, 24 Castle Street, CHESTER, CH1 2DS. See also Chester Accounting Services
PATTERSON, Mr. George Brian, FCA *1958;* 8 Pencarwick House, 11-15 Louisa Terrace, EXMOUTH, EX8 2BB. (Life Member)
PATTERSON, Mr. George Steven, MA FCA *1974;* 2 Rectory Gardens, Emley, HUDDERSFIELD, HD8 9RD.
PATTERSON, Mr. Gordon Donald, MA FCA *1993;* 46 Downs Way, Bookham, LEATHERHEAD, KT23 4BW.
PATTERSON, Mrs. Helen, BSc ACA *1995;* 80 Elmway, CHESTER LE STREET, COUNTY DURHAM, DH2 2LF.
PATTERSON, Mr. Ian Antony, ACA ACCA *2008;* (Tax Fac), 26 The Spinney, Sandal, WAKEFIELD, WEST YORKSHIRE, WF2 6JN.
PATTERSON, Mr. Ian Jocelyn, FCA *1953;* 22 Parkside Court, Baker Street, WEYBRIDGE, SURREY, KT13 8AG. (Life Member)
PATTERSON, Mr. Jeffrey Charles, BSc ACA *1985;* 2/41 Rockley Road, SOUTH YARRA, VIC 3141, AUSTRALIA.
PATTERSON, Ms. Joanne Lesley, ACA *2008;* 15 Barnbrough Street, LEEDS, LS4 2QY.
PATTERSON, Mr. John, BSc FCA *1974;* PO Box 278, NANOOSE BAY V9P 9J9, BC, CANADA.
PATTERSON, Mr. John Corner, FCA *1964;* 156 Whinneyfield Road, NEWCASTLE UPON TYNE, NE6 4RR. (Life Member)
PATTERSON, Mr. John Richard Spencer, FCA *1958;* Ash Tree House, Church Road, Fiddington, BRIDGWATER, SOMERSET, TA5 1JG. (Life Member)
PATTERSON, Mr. John Thomas Rutherford, MPhil BA FCA *1999;* 2 Hertfords Place, Chillesford, WOODBRIDGE, SUFFOLK, IP12 3SD.
PATTERSON, Mr. Jonathan Philip, BA FCA *1974;* 34 Queens Court, Alderham Close, SOLIHULL, B91 2PR.
PATTERSON, Miss. Kathryn Frances, ACA *2009;* 3/92 Ben Boyd Road, Neutral Bay, SYDNEY, NSW 2089, AUSTRALIA.
PATTERSON, Mr. Keith William, FCA *1956;* 1 Hatch Place, Lower Road, Cookham, MAIDENHEAD, BERKSHIRE, SL6 9EJ. (Life Member)
PATTERSON, Mr. Kenneth, VRD FCA *1957;* 4 Oakfield Terrace, Gosforth, NEWCASTLE UPON TYNE, NE3 4RQ. (Life Member)
PATTERSON, Mrs. Lauren Katherine Stewart, BSc FCA *2001;* 46 Attwood Drive, Arborfield, READING, RG2 9FE.
PATTERSON, Mr. Leslie Richard, FCA *1953;* 11 Kerrich Close, Dersingham, KING'S LYNN, PE31 6WG. (Life Member)
PATTERSON, Miss. Lucy Elisabeth, BA ACA *2007;* 25 Audley Gardens, LOUGHTON, ESSEX, IG10 2EL.
PATTERSON, Mr. Luke William, BSc ACA *2004;* 6 Matthew Street, DUNSTABLE, BEDFORDSHIRE, LU6 1SD.
PATTERSON, Mr. Mark, BA ACA *2002;* 116 Woodland Drive, WATFORD, WD17 3LB.
PATTERSON, Mr. Martin Stuart, BCom ACA *1986;* Nomura International plc, 25 Bank Street, LONDON, E14 5LE.
PATTERSON, Mr. Michael, BSc ACA *2006;* (Tax Fac), 31 Clover Drive, Etherley Dene, BISHOP AUCKLAND, COUNTY DURHAM, DL14 0TT.
PATTERSON, Mr. Michael Stewart, FCA *1954;* Flat 5, Spero Court, 15 Victoria Parade, BROADSTAIRS, CT10 1QS. (Life Member)
•PATTERSON, Mrs. Michelle, BSc(Hons) ACA *2005;* Legg & Co, 8 Greenrigg Close, Faverdale, DARLINGTON, COUNTY DURHAM, DL3 0EF.
PATTERSON, Mr. Neil Edward, BSc ACA *1992;* 4 South Drive, WOKINGHAM, RG40 2DH.
PATTERSON, Mr. Nicholas Martin, BA BSc FCA *1979;* 63 Squires Wood, Fulwood, PRESTON, PR2 9QA.
PATTERSON, Mr. Peter Desmond, BA ACA *1993;* Dunlop Aircraft Tyres Ltd, 40 Fort Parkway, BIRMINGHAM, B24 9HL.
PATTERSON, Mr. Robert Edmund William, BSc ACA *1994;* 10 Amherst Avenue, West Ealing, LONDON, W13 8NQ.
PATTERSON, Mrs. Sandra, BA ACA *1997;* 158a Welbeck Crescent, TROON, AYRSHIRE, KA10 6AW.
PATTERSON, Ms. Shalom Sarah, BA(Econ) ACA *2001;* 17 Bennerley Road, LONDON, SW11 6DR.
PATTERSON, Miss. Susan Elizabeth, ACA *1992;* 7 Buckbury Mews, DORCHESTER, DORSET, DT1 2TX.
PATTERSON, Mr. Thomas Roy, BSc FCA *1982;* 1 Cornes Close, WINCHESTER, HAMPSHIRE, SO22 5DS.
•PATTERSON, Mr. Timothy John, FCA *1966;* Tim Patterson, Ropewalk Cottage, Ropewalk, KINGSBRIDGE, DEVON, TQ7 1HH.
•PATTERSON, Mrs. Wendy, ACA FCCA *2009;* WSM Partners LLP, Pinnacle House, 17/25 Hartfield Road, Wimbledon, LONDON, SW19 3SE. See also Windsor Stebbing Marsh
PATTERSON, Mr. William Nigel, BSc FCA *1975;* 32 The Pagoda, MAIDENHEAD, SL6 8EU.
PATTESON, Mr. Anthony Ian, FCA *1971;* 1 The Fairway, NORTHWOOD, HA6 3DZ.
PATTESON, Mr. Colin George, FCA *1973;* 275 Bahia Point, NAPLES, FL 34103, UNITED STATES.
PATTESON, Mr. James Anthony George, BA ACA *2002;* 13 Kingston Drive, SALE, CHESHIRE, M33 2FS.
PATTESON-KNIGHT, Mrs. Fiona Christina, BSc ACA *1989;* Gadbrook House, Gadbrook Road, BETCHWORTH, RH3 7AH.
PATTICHIS, Mr. Constantinos, BA ACA *2011;* 48 Archimedous Street, Flat 102, Strovolos, NICOSIA, CYPRUS.
PATTIHI, Miss. Carolina, ACA *2010;* Flat 45, Longstone Court, 22 Great Dover Street, LONDON, SE1 4LB.
PATTINSON, Mr. Andrew, BA ACA *2003;* 3 Heather Court, Outwood, WAKEFIELD, WEST YORKSHIRE, WF1 3HF.
•PATTINSON, Mr. David, FCA *1979;* (Tax Fac), David Pattinson, 233 London Road, Balderton, NEWARK, NG24 3HA. See also Pattinson
•PATTINSON, Mr. Ian, FCA *1968;* 90-92 King Edward Road, NUNEATON, WARWICKSHIRE, CV11 4BB.
PATTINSON, Mr. John, FCA *1951;* Downwood, Sleepers Hill, WINCHESTER, SO22 4NA. (Life Member)
PATTINSON, Mr. Jonathan Michael, BA ACA *1997;* Homeloan Management Co, PO Box 12, SKIPTON, NORTH YORKSHIRE, BD23 2HL.
PATTINSON, Miss. Kate Alexandra, BSc ACA *2005;* with Albert Goodman LLP, Mary Street House, Mary Street, TAUNTON, TA1 3NW.
PATTINSON, Mr. Mark, MA FCA *1959;* Brynaport, Kishorn, STRATHCARRON, ROSS-SHIRE, IV54 8XB. (Life Member)
PATTINSON, Mrs. Melissa Anne, ACA *2005;* 1 Victory Drive, Swarland, MORPETH, NORTHUMBERLAND, NE65 9PA.
PATTINSON, Mr. Michael James, FCA *1967;* 8 Swallowtail Close, Pinewood, IPSWICH, IP8 3QX.
PATTINSON, Mr. Richard Mark, BA ACA *2005;* 1 Victory Drive, Swarland, MORPETH, NORTHUMBERLAND, NE65 9PA.
PATTINSON, Mr. Robin Craig, BSocSc ACA MBA *1995;* 6 Mere Court, TORONTO M4A 2J6, ON, CANADA.
PATTINSON, Miss. Sarah, BSc ACA *2009;* Chillcroft, 6a Stoney Brow, Roby Mill, SKELMERSDALE, WN8 0QE.
PATTISON, Mr. Andrew James, BSc ACA *1991;* WHYTETHORNE, WALPOLE AVENUE, CHIPSTEAD, CR5 3PN.
PATTISON, Mr. Benjamin Erik, ACA *2007;* 15 Tomlins Grove, LONDON, E3 4NX.
PATTISON, Mrs. Caroline Susan, BA ACA *1992;* 7 The Butts, Poulton, CIRENCESTER, GL7 5HY.
PATTISON, Mrs. Christine Elizabeth Katherine, FCA *1976;* 12 The Woods, TORQUAY, TQ1 2HS. (Life Member)
PATTISON, Mr. Clive Russell, BSc FCA *1974;* 5 Meadow Brow, ALDERLEY EDGE, SK9 7XD.
PATTISON, Mr. David Gavin, ACA *2009;* 25 Bronllwyn, Pentyrch, CARDIFF, CF15 9QL.
PATTISON, Mr. Donald Graham, FCA *1956;* Westbourne, 14 Castle Rise, South Cave, BROUGH, HU15 2ET. (Life Member)
PATTISON, Miss. Emma Jane, BEng ACA *1998;* 4 Birdwell Lane, Long Ashton, BRISTOL, BS41 9AJ.
PATTISON, Mr. George Edward Charles, ACA *2008;* Willowdene, Castle Street, Bletchingley, REDHILL, RH1 4QA.
PATTISON, Mr. Gordon Frederick, FCA *1966;* 1 Charles Street, LARGS, AYRSHIRE, KA30 8HJ.
PATTISON, Mr. Graham Neil, MA ACA *2000;* 40 Oakdene Road, SEVENOAKS, TN13 3HL.
PATTISON, Mr. Ian Frank, FCA *1966;* Hollybank, 81 Bramley Lane, Lightcliffe, HALIFAX, HX3 8NS.
PATTISON, Mr. Keith, BA ACA *1987;* 3 Knowlman Avenue, PYMBLE, NSW 2073, AUSTRALIA.
PATTISON, Miss. Marguerita Veronica, BA ACA *1986;* 91 Lake Crescent, ETOBICOKE M8V 1W2, ON, CANADA.
PATTISON, Mr. Mark Christopher, FCA *1976;* 14 Oaklands Way, Epsom Lane South, TADWORTH, SURREY, KT20 5SW.
PATTISON, Mr. Roger Harold Christopher, FCA *1957;* Danehurst Corner, Danehurst Crescent, HORSHAM, WEST SUSSEX, RH13 5HS. (Life Member)
PATTISON, Mrs. Suzanne Jane, BA ACA *1991;* Whytethorne, Walpole Avenue, CHIPSTEAD, CR5 3PN.
PATTISON, Mr. Sydney, FCA *1950;* P07, 41 Kirkstall Rd, CHORLEY, PR7 3JR. (Life Member)
PATTLE, Miss. Sheila Helen, BSc ACA *1983;* 44D Holland Park, LONDON, W11 3RP.
PATTNI, Mr. Aneel Kumar, BA ACA *2001;* 61 Lullingstone Lane, LONDON, SE13 6UH.
PATTNI, Miss. Anjali, BSc(Hons) ACA *2010;* Flat 32 Princess Park Manor, Royal Drive, LONDON, N11 3FL.
•PATTNI, Mr. Bharat, FCA *1976;* 1 Collets Brook, Bassetts Pole, SUTTON COLDFIELD, WEST MIDLANDS, B75 6LA.
PATTNI, Mr. Bhupatrai Narshidas, FCA *1966;* 75 The Parklands, BIRMINGHAM, B23 6LA.
PATTNI, Mr. Girish, ACA *1987;* Harish Finance Ltd, 16-20 Ealing Road, WEMBLEY, MIDDLESEX, HA0 4TL.
•PATTNI, Mr. Mahendra Maganlal, ACA *1980;* M. Pattni & Co, 21 Kingshill Drive, Kenton, HARROW, HA3 8TD.
•PATTNI, Mr. Nayan Narottam, ACA *1995;* Enpeyz Consulting Limited, Team House, St. Marys Road, WATFORD, WD18 0EE.
PATTNI, Mr. Rohit Chhotalal, BA ACA FCCA *1993;* 21 Dean Court, WEMBLEY, HA0 3PU.
PATTON, Mr. Nicholas, MA ACA *1985;* 36 Boyne Road, LONDON, SE13 5AW.
•PATTRICK, Mr. John Stanford, FCA *1970;* with Websters, Baker Street Chambers, 136 Baker Street, LONDON, W1U 6UD.
PATTRICK, Mr. Richard Mark Andrew, BA FCA *1987;* 9 Main Street, Ewerby, SLEAFORD, NG34 9PH.
PATWA, Mr. Mohammed, BA ACA *1992;* 4 Kent House, Stratton Close, EDGWARE, MIDDLESEX, HA8 6PR.
•PATWARI, Miss. Jagriti, ACA *2009;* (Tax Fac), Maroon Accounts Limited, 39 High Street, LEATHERHEAD, SURREY, KT22 8AE. See also Locum Accounting Limited
•PATWARI, Mr. Mohammed Abdul Wadud, FCA *1975;* (Tax Fac), Wadud Patwari & Co., 10 Tooting Bec Road, LONDON, SW17 8BD.
PAU, Mr. Anilkumar Haridas, BSc FCA *1984;* (Tax Fac), 5 Carnation Close, Shinfield, READING, RG2 9BZ.
•PAU, Mr. Mayur, BA(Hons) ACA MCSI *2001;* 31 Becmead Avenue, HARROW, MIDDLESEX, HA3 8HD.
PAU, Miss. Meera, BSc ACA *2005;* with PricewaterhouseCoopers LLP, 7 More London Riverside, LONDON, SE1 2RT.
PAU, Mr. Wai Sun, ACA *2007;* Flat F 29/F Block 4, South Horizons, AP LEI CHAU, HONG KONG SAR.
PAUK, Mr. Aaron, BSc(Hons) ACA *2010;* 7 Haddon Place, Staveley, CHESTERFIELD, DERBYSHIRE, S43 3NB.
PAUL, Mr. Adrian Robert, BSc FCA *1988;* 4 Highlands, NEWBURY, BERKSHIRE, RG14 6NZ.
PAUL, Mr. Allan Harvey, ACA *1980;* 5 Belvedere Court, West Harbour, AUCKLAND, NEW ZEALAND.
PAUL, Mr. Andrew Trevor, BSc(Hons) ACA *1999;* 191 Ryder Road, Kirby Firth, LEICESTER, LE3 6UZ.
PAUL, Miss. Anita, BA ACA *2000;* Flat 28 Angel Wharf, 168 Shepherdess Walk, LONDON, N1 7JL.
PAUL, Mr. Arun Kumar, FCA *1960;* 67 Midland Avenue, BEACONSFIELD H9W 4N9, QUE, CANADA. (Life Member)
PAUL, Mr. Bhupinderjeet Singh, BSc ACA *1995;* 45 Southbourne Gardens, RUISLIP, MIDDLESEX, HA4 9TY.
PAUL, Mr. Christopher, MBA FCA *1971;* P F M Associates Ltd Sir Peter Thompson House, 25 Market Close, POOLE, DORSET, BH15 1NE.
PAUL, Mr. Christopher Michael Kirkwood, MBA FCA *1974;* Flat 50 Lindsay Court, 15 Sherwood Park Road, SUTTON, SM1 2SN.
PAUL, Mr. Christopher Richard Thomas, ACA CA(SA) *2010;* 21 The Spinney, WATFORD, WD17 4QF.
•PAUL, Mr. David Graham, LLM BA FCA *1965;* (Tax Fac), Graham Paul Limited, 10-12 Dunraven Place, BRIDGEND, MID GLAMORGAN, CF31 1JD.
•PAUL, Mr. David John, MA FCA *1975;* David Paul, 5 Aldermary Road, BROMLEY, BR1 3PH.
PAUL, Mr. Dawood Nasir, FCA *1972;* House number.24/2 Street -20, Khayaban Tanzeem D.H.A. Phase -5, Karachi, KARACHI 705500, PAKISTAN. (Life Member)
PAUL, Miss. Flora, BA ACA *2010;* East Harting Farmhouse, East Harting Farm, East Harting, PETERSFIELD, HAMPSHIRE, GU31 5LU.
PAUL, Mr. Graham Edwin, BSc ACA *1991;* 62 Wickham Way, HAYWARDS HEATH, WEST SUSSEX, RH16 1UQ.
PAUL, Mr. Iain, BA ACA *1999;* A Bilbrough & Co. Ltd, 50 Leman Street, LONDON, E1 8HQ.
PAUL, Mr. James, ACA *2009;* 17b Ramsden Road, LONDON, SW12 8QX.
•PAUL, Ms. Jennifer Clare, BA ACA CTA *1991;* Jennifer Paul, 8 Southall Drive, Hartlebury, KIDDERMINSTER, WORCESTERSHIRE, DY11 7LD. See also Transfer Pricing Consultants Ltd
PAUL, Mr. Jeremy, BSc ACA *1992;* Argan Capital Advisors LLP, Monopolis House, 9 South Street, LONDON, W1K 2XA.
PAUL, Mr. John Murray Guy, FCA *1952;* The Grange, Stratford sub Castle, SALISBURY, SP4 6AE. (Life Member)
PAUL, Mr. John Rowland, MA FCA *1956;* 1 Heath Lodge, 32 Sussex Road, PETERSFIELD, GU31 4JZ. (Life Member)
•PAUL, Mr. Jose Roy, MBA BSc FCA *1995;* Joseph Paul & Co Ltd, 21 Oakleigh Road North, LONDON, N20 9HE.
PAUL, Mrs. Julia Margaret, FCA *1972;* Rivermeads, 8 Sutton Close, Cookham, MAIDENHEAD, SL6 9QU.
•PAUL, Mr. Julian Braithwaite, MA FCA *1970;* Julian Paul & Co., The Mount House, Brasted, WESTERHAM, KENT, TN16 1JB.
PAUL, Mrs. Karen Louise, BA ACA *1998;* Silverwood The Warren, Kingswood, TADWORTH, KT20 6PQ.
PAUL, Mrs. Lynn, BSc ACA *1989;* Orchard Croft, 41 Blackberry Lane, Four Marks, ALTON, GU34 5DF.
•PAUL, Mr. Malcolm Stephen, FCA *1974;* M.S. Paul, Henmead Hall, Staplefield Road, Cuckfield, HAYWARDS HEATH, WEST SUSSEX RH17 5HY.
PAUL, Mr. Michael Wilfred, MA FCA *1972;* 46 Ford Road, Wiveliscombe, TAUNTON, SOMERSET, TA4 2RE.

•**PAUL, Mr. Narinder, BSc FCA** *1982;* (Tax Fac), KPMG LLP, One Snowhill, Snow Hill Queensway, BIRMINGHAM, B4 6GN. See also KPMG Europe LLP

PAUL, Mr. Naveen, ACA *1987;* 8 Sequoia Park, Hatch End, PINNER, HA5 4BS.

•**PAUL, Mrs. Nicola Sarah, BA ACA** *1998;* with Deloitte LLP, PO Box 137, Regency Court, Glategny Esplanade, St Peter Port, GUERNSEY GY1 3HW.

PAUL, Mr. Nigel Anthony Lewis, BSc ACA *1978;* 3 The Paddock, Dirleton, NORTH BERWICK, EAST LOTHIAN, EH39 5AD.

•①**PAUL, Mr. Nigel Trevor, FCA** *1980;* Atherton Bailey LLP, Arundel House, 1 Amberley Court, Whitworth Road, CRAWLEY, WEST SUSSEX RH11 7XL. See also Stephens Paul

PAUL, Mr. Patrick Blackwell, CBE MA FCA *1974;* Flat 27B, 10-12 Po Shan Road, MID LEVELS, HONG KONG ISLAND, HONG KONG SAR.

PAUL, Mr. Patrick Robin David, BSc FCA *1971;* Haycroft, Sherborne, CHELTENHAM, GL54 3NB.

PAUL, Miss. Philippa Anna Carrel, ACA *2009;* 15 Malmstone Avenue, Merstham, REDHILL, RH1 3ND.

PAUL, Mr. Ranjit, ACA *2010;* 31 Langbourne Place, LONDON, E14 3WN.

PAUL, Mr. Richard Ewan, BSc ACA *1989;* 78 Sherard Court, 3 Manor Gardens, LONDON, N7 6FB.

PAUL, Mr. Richard James, BSc ACA *1991;* Orchard Croft, 41 Blackberry Lane, Four Marks, ALTON, GU34 5DF.

•**PAUL, Mr. Richard Jeremy, BA FCA** *1990;* Nyman Libson Paul, Regina House, 124 Finchley Road, LONDON, NW3 5JS.

PAUL, Mr. Richard Neil, BA FCA *1987;* 21 Almsford Avenue, HARROGATE, HG2 8HD.

PAUL, Mr. Robert James William, BA(Hons) ACA *2000;* Suffolk Food Hall, Wherstead Hall Peppers Lane, Wherstead, IPSWICH, IP9 2AB.

•**PAUL, Mr. Robert Simon, BSc ACA** *1992;* Nyman Libson Paul, Regina House, 124 Finchley Road, LONDON, NW3 5JS.

PAUL, Mr. Sashi, FCA *1972;* 7A Jersey Road, Strathfield, SYDNEY, NSW 2135, AUSTRALIA.

PAUL, Mr. Stephen James, BSc ACA *2010;* 14 Doudney Court, Bedminster, BRISTOL, BS3 4AP.

PAUL, Mr. Stephen William, BA(Hons) ACA *2010;* 5 Cube House, 5 Spa Road, LONDON, SE16 3GD.

PAUL, Mr. Thomas, FCA CTA *1969;* 164 Mortimer Road, SOUTH SHIELDS, TYNE AND WEAR, NE34 0RW.

•**PAUL, Mr. Viresh Kumar, FCA** *1978;* (Tax Fac), Paul & Co, 11-12 Freetrade House, Lowther Road, STANMORE, MIDDLESEX, HA7 1EP.

PAUL-FLORENCE, Mr. Grant Ian, BSc ACA *2000;* 1 Stevens Way, AMERSHAM, BUCKINGHAMSHIRE, HP7 0HF.

PAULDING, Mr. Richard John, FCA *1964;* 36 Littledown Drive, BOURNEMOUTH, BH7 7AQ.

PAULEY, Mr. Terence David, ACA *1995;* 15 Saville Close, Rednal, BIRMINGHAM, B45 8EN.

PAULEZ, Mr. Marc, ACA *1999;* 133 Forest Park Way, PORT MOODY V3H 5J4, BC, CANADA.

PAULGER, Ms. Jennifer Ann, MSc FCA *1974;* Serendipia, 34 Haciendas el Choco, Kilometro 3, SOSUA, PUERTO PLATA PROVINCE, DOMINICAN REPUBLIC.

PAULIAN, Mr. Gerard Thavanesan, ACA *1985;* 20 Jalan Bukit Desa 7, Taman Bukit Desa, 58100 KUALA LUMPUR, FEDERAL TERRITORY, MALAYSIA.

PAULINS, Mr. Karl Anthony, MBA BSc FCA *1986;* Rivendell, Park Lane, Lapley, STAFFORD, ST19 9JT.

PAULL, Mr. Charles Arthur, MPhil FCA *1970;* The Croft, Station Road, Tilbrook, HUNTINGDON, PE28 0JT. (Life Member)

PAULL, Mr. Joseph Denys, FCA *1948;* Sunlow Cottage, Manor Farm, Dockenfield, FARNHAM, SURREY, GU10 4HL. (Life Member)

PAULS, Mrs. Catherine Jane, BA ACA *2000;* 53 Wadham Road, LONDON, SW15 2LS.

PAULS, Mr. David Barrie, BA ACA *2000;* with PricewaterhouseCoopers LLP, 1 Embankment Place, LONDON, WC2N 6RH.

PAULSON, Mr. Gareth Stephen, BA ACA *2001;* 106 Southover Street, BRIGHTON, BN2 9UA.

PAULSON, Mr. James Gordon Henry, BSc ACA *2010;* 32 Highfield, Hatton Park, WARWICK, CV35 7TQ.

PAULSON, Mr. Michael John, BA FCA *1955;* 16 Hope Avenue, Handforth, WILMSLOW, SK9 3DL. (Life Member)

PAULSON-ELLIS, Mr. Michael Geoffrey Ellis, OBE MA FCA *1965;* 20/2 Royal Circus, EDINBURGH, EH3 6SS.

PAULUS, Mr. John Leo, BSc ACA *2010;* Flat 2, 14 De Parys Avenue, BEDFORD, MK40 2TW.

PAUN, Mr. Rajnikant Jagjivan, BSc FCA *1964;* 3904 Glamis Court, MISSISSAUGA L5L 3N5, ON, CANADA. (Life Member)

PAUS, Dr. Karl Christian, ACA *1991;* Vestengveien 4, N-1182 OSLO, NORWAY.

PAUSEY, Mr. Kenneth John, FCA *1951;* 72 Buckland Avenue, SLOUGH, SL3 7PH. (Life Member)

PAVELEY, Miss. Tracey, BSc ACA *2007;* with Baker & McKenzie LLP, 100 New Bridge Street, LONDON, EC4V 6JA.

PAVELIN, Mr. Laurence Arthur, CBE FCA *1968;* 18 Barberry Rise, PENARTH, CF64 2RB.

PAVER, Mr. Gary Neil, BA ACA *1992;* Ladywell Cottage Mill of Lumphart Oldmeldrum, INVERURIE, ABERDEENSHIRE, AB51 0EA.

PAVER, Mr. Mark Adrian, BSc ACA *1992;* 10 Meadow View, CHESTERFIELD, DERBYSHIRE, S40 3LT.

PAVER, Mr. Mark James, BA(Hons) ACA *2001;* 201 Seminary Avenue, YONKERS, NY 10704, UNITED STATES.

PAVER, Mr. Michael, BSc FCA *1979;* 27 Cavendish Meads, Sunninghill, ASCOT, SL5 9TB.

PAVEY, Mr. David William, FCA *1968;* Keepers Cottage, Slingsby, YORK, YO62 4AN. (Life Member)

PAVEY, Mr. Keith Henry, FCA *1964;* Rectory Barn Church Meadow, Oasthouse Field, Ivychurch, ROMNEY MARSH, TN29 0HJ.

PAVEY, Mr. Paul Bryan, BSc ACA *1997;* 10 Wanderdown Way, Ovingdean, BRIGHTON, BN2 7BX.

PAVIA, Mr. Michael James, FCA *1970;* (Member of Council 2004 - 2011), Tolt Coppice Farm Hill Grove, Lurgashall, PETWORTH, WEST SUSSEX, GU28 9EW.

PAVICIC, Miss. Helena, BA ACA *2010;* City Harbour, Flat 42, 8 Selsdon Way, LONDON, E14 9GR.

PAVIS, Mr. Craig Quinn, ACA *2008;* 228 St. Davids Square, LONDON, E14 3WE.

PAVITT, Mr. Richard George, FCA *1977;* Dr JH Burgoyne & Partners LLP, 11-12 Half Moon Court, Bartholomew Close, LONDON, EC1A 7HF.

PAVLIDES, Mr. George Pavlos Georgides, FCA *1977;* PO Box 20599, Hilton Area Post Office, 1660 NICOSIA, CYPRUS.

PAVLIDES, Miss. Mary Stella, BSc ACA *2003;* 229 Princes Avenue, LONDON, N13 6HH.

PAVLITSKI, Mr. Adrian Alexander, BA ACA *1988;* 15 Old North Road, ROYSTON, SG8 5DT.

PAVLOU, Miss. Chrystalla, BSc(Hons) ACA *2003;* Dikaiosynis 9, Kato Deftera, 2450 NICOSIA, CYPRUS.

PAVLOU, Mr. Evripides, BSc ACA *2011;* Panidos 1B, Oroclini, 7040 LARNACA, CYPRUS.

PAVLOU, Mr. Konstantinos, ACA *2011;* Lamprou Katsoni 7, 20300 LOUTRAKI, GREECE.

PAVLOU, Mr. Nicolas, BA ACA *2006;* KRISSOU 1 PALL HOUSE, FLAT 501, PALLOURIOTISSA, 1036 NICOSIA, CYPRUS.

PAVLOU, Mrs. Sarah Joanne, ACA *2008;* Finance, Inmarsat, 99 City Road, LONDON, EC1Y 1AX.

PAVLOU, Mr. Savvas, ACA *2011;* Photi Pitta 3, Agios Spyridonas, 3051 LIMASSOL, CYPRUS.

PAVLOVA, Miss. Olga Evgenievna, ACA *2002;* Building A 2nd floor, British Petroleum Co Plc, Chertsey Road, SUNBURY-ON-THAMES, MIDDLESEX, TW16 7LN.

PAVRI, Mr. Farrokh Noshir, FCA *1962;* 6/6 Brady Flats, Sorab Bharucha Road Colaba, MUMBAI 400005, INDIA.

PAVRI, Mr. Yezdi Noshir, MSc FCA *1979;* Deloitte & Touche LLP, Suite 1400, 181 Bay Street, TORONTO M5J 2V1, ON, CANADA.

PAVRI, Mr. Zareer Noshir, FCA CICBV *1971;* Business Valuations & Strategy Inc, 36 Toronto Street, Suite 850, TORONTO M5C 2C5, ON, CANADA.

PAW, Mr. Rakesh Vinodrai, BA ACA *2003;* 10a Kenneth Gardens, STANMORE, MIDDLESEX, HA7 3SD.

PAWLEY, Mr. Alex Shaun, ACA *2009;* Deloitte & Touche, 4 Brindley Place, BIRMINGHAM, B1 2HZ.

PAWLEY, Mr. Andrew Mark, MBA BA FCA *1990;* The Old Vicarage, 34 Northend, Batheaston, BATH, BA1 7ES.

PAWLEY, Dr. Susan Carol, BSc ACA *2002;* 1 Whitethorn Drive, Prestbury, CHELTENHAM, GLOUCESTERSHIRE, GL52 5LL.

•**PAWLOWSKI, Mr. Robert John, FCA** *1983;* (Tax Fac), Ronald Shaw & Co, Ashford House, 95 Dixons Green, DUDLEY, DY2 7DJ.

PAWLYN, Mr. Doyran Allen David, BSc FCA *1974;* Charlcote Steels Lane, Oxshott, LEATHERHEAD, KT22 0RF.

PAWSON, Mr. Christopher William Dalby, MSc BA(Hons) ACA *2002;* Goldman Sachs, Petershill, 1 Carter Lane, LONDON, EC4V 5ER.

PAWSON, Mr. Derek Leslie, FCA *1972;* 88 Bouverie Avenue, SALISBURY, SP2 8DX.

PAWSON, Mrs. Kay, BSc ACA *1995;* Colton Lodge, Meynell Road, Colton, LEEDS, LS15 9AQ.

PAWSON, Mr. Michael Andrew, BA ACA *1986;* Greenhous Remarketing Holsworth Park, Oxon Business Park Bicton Heath, SHREWSBURY, SY3 5HJ.

•**PAWSON, Mr. Michael Anthony, FCA** *1982;* Crawfords Accountants LLP, Stanton House, 41 Blackfriars Road, SALFORD, M3 7DB. See also Michael Pawson Ltd

•**PAWSON, Mr. Nicholas Charles, BA FCA** *1988;* with KPMG LLP, 15 Canada Square, LONDON, E14 5GL.

PAWSON, Mr. Nicholas Charles Thoresby, MA FCA *1977;* (Tax Fac), Haggas Hall, Weeton, LEEDS, LS17 0BH.

PAWSON, Mr. Philip Raymond, BA FCA *1981;* MEMBER OF COUNCIL, The Chantry, 412 Selby Road, Whitkirk, LEEDS, LS15 9BQ.

PAWSON, Mr. Roger Stewart, FCA *1967;* Bank Top House, Beech Tree Court, Baildon, SHIPLEY, BD17 5TB.

PAXTON, Mr. Adam Clive, ACA *2009;* Flat 150, 3 Limeharbour, LONDON, E14 9LU.

•**PAXTON, Mr. Ashley Charles, BSc FCA** *1996;* KPMG Channel Islands Limited, 20 New Street, St Peter Port, GUERNSEY, GY1 4AN.

PAXTON, Mr. Christopher James, MEng ACA *2003;* 9 Stuarts Green, STOURBRIDGE, DY9 0XR.

PAXTON, Mr. Graham John James, FCA ATII *1951;* Coastline, 42 Lammas Lane, PAIGNTON, DEVON, TQ3 2PX. (Life Member)

PAXTON, Miss. Margaret, MA BA(Hons) ACA *2011;* 14 Tudor Way, LONDON, W3 9AG.

PAY, Mr. Adrian, BA ACA *1994;* 1 Coleman Street, #07-04 The Adelphi, SINGAPORE 179803, SINGAPORE.

PAY, Mr. Christopher, ACA *2011;* 59 Cheylesmore Drive, Frimley, CAMBERLEY, SURREY, GU16 9BN.

PAY, Mrs. Deborah Eileen, BSc ACA *1983;* 112 High Street, Riseley, BEDFORD, MK44 1DF.

PAY, Mr. Jason Christopher, MSc ACA *1997;* 44 Osmaston Road, STOURBRIDGE, WEST MIDLANDS, DY8 2AL.

PAY, Miss. Kellie Louise, ACA *2006;* 39 Yew Tree Court, Chy Hwel, TRURO, CORNWALL, TR1 1AF.

PAY, Miss. Melanie, BSc ACA *2002;* 34 Algarve Road, LONDON, SW18 3EG.

PAY, Mr. Michael James, FCA *1996;* EMC Management Consultants Ltd, 49 Gildredge Road, EASTBOURNE, EAST SUSSEX, BN21 4RY.

PAY, Mr. Peter Ian Waterson, TD BA FCA *1985;* 2909 Morgan Drive, SAN RAMON, CA 94583, UNITED STATES.

PAY, Mr. Raymond Frederick, BSc ACA *1991;* 11 Bullfinch Close, WORCESTER, WR5 3SL.

PAY, Mr. Richard Stafford, BSc ACA *1992;* with PricewaterhouseCoopers, Royal Trust Tower, Suite 3000 TD Centre, Box 82, 77 King Street West, TORONTO M5K 1G8 ON CANADA.

•**PAYDON, Mr. Barry Harvey, FCA** *1970;* (Tax Fac), Barry Paydon Ltd, 28 Church Road, STANMORE, MIDDLESEX, HA7 4AW.

PAYER, Mr. Dominic Christopher, MA MSc FCA *1974;* 23A Thelda Avenue, Keyworth, NOTTINGHAM, NG12 5HU.

PAYLING, Mr. Antony Stephen, BA ACA *1989;* 11 Cavendish Road, RETFORD, DN22 7HD.

PAYLING, Ms. Catherine Mary, BA ACA *1992;* 1058 30th Street NW, WASHINGTON, DC 20007, UNITED STATES.

PAYLING, Mr. David Edward, MA ACA *2002;* 9 Exeter Road, LONDON, NW2 4SJ.

PAYLING, Mrs. Judith Catherine, FCA *1975;* Rosebank, 56 Quickley Lane, Chorleywood, RICKMANSWORTH, WD3 5AF.

PAYLING, Mr. Tony Steven, ACA *1993;* 18 Turnham Avenue, ROSANNA, VIC 3084, AUSTRALIA.

•**PAYLOR, Mr. Duncan John Graham, MA FCA** *1974;* Sochall Smith Limited, 3 Park Square, LEEDS, LS1 2NE.

PAYMAN, Mr. Robert Alan, FCA *1968;* Fairfax Coffee Ltd, 1 Regency Parade, LONDON, NW3 5EQ.

PAYN, Miss. Patricia Margaret, BA ACA *1987;* 59 Bond Street, MOSMAN, NSW 2088, AUSTRALIA.

PAYN, Mr. Richard Michael, MA ACA *1991;* 12 Pickhurst Green, BROMLEY, BR2 7QT.

PAYNE, Miss. Abigail Marie, BSc ACA *2006;* Lancashire County Council, County Hall, PRESTON, PR1 0LD.

PAYNE, Mr. Alan Douglas, BCom ACA *1993;* 8 Albion Street, LONDON, W2 2AS.

•**PAYNE, Mr. Alan Robert, FCA** *1977; (CA Scotland* Heywoods, Countrywide House, Knights Way, Battlefield Enterprise Park, SHREWSBURY, SY1 3AB.

PAYNE, Mr. Alan Thomas, BA FCA *1978;* Old Jockey Farmhouse, Old Jockey, Box, CORSHAM, SN13 8DJ.

PAYNE, Mr. Alan Tyson, FCA *1963;* The Coach House, 58A Main Street, Dundonald, KILMARNOCK, AYRSHIRE, KA2 9HG. (Life Member)

PAYNE, Miss. Alison Marie, MEng ACA *2002;* 9 Mallow Close, ELY, CAMBRIDGESHIRE, CB6 3WH.

PAYNE, Mr. Andrew Julian Chisholm, BA ACA CF FSI *1992;* Timbers Chase, Ruxbury Road, CHERTSEY, KT16 9NJ.

PAYNE, Mr. Andrew Nicolas, BSc ACA *1991;* The Flat Duke House, Duke Street, SKIPTON, NORTH YORKSHIRE, BD23 2HQ.

PAYNE, Mrs. Anne McLaren, BSc ACA *1992;* 39 Main Street, Cairneyhill, DUNFERMLINE, FIFE, KY12 8QT.

•**PAYNE, Mr. Anthony, FCA** *1979;* Payne & Co Accountants Limited, Holly Cottage, Over Lane, Almondsbury, BRISTOL, BS32 4DF.

PAYNE, Mr. Anthony Cyril, FCA *1965;* 35 Brackley, WEYBRIDGE, SURREY, KT13 0BL. (Life Member)

•**PAYNE, Mr. Anthony Tudor, FCA** *1977;* Tudor Payne & Co Ltd, 52 Parkstone Road, POOLE, DORSET, BH15 2PU.

PAYNE, Mr. Benjamin Richard, ACA *2001;* Goldman Sachs International, Peterborough Court, 133 Fleet Street, LONDON, EC4A 2BB.

PAYNE, Mr. Bradley Stuart, ACA *2000;* with Ernst & Young LLP, 1 More London Place, LONDON, SE1 2AF.

•**PAYNE, Mr. Brian Peter, FCA** *1975;* (Tax Fac), Brian Payne & Company, The Old Coach House, R/O 89-91 Mildmay Road, CHELMSFORD, CM1 0DS.

PAYNE, Mrs. Cheryl Jane, BA ACA *1994;* Harrop Lodge, 11 Harrop Road, Hale, ALTRINCHAM, CHESHIRE, WA15 9BU.

PAYNE, Mr. Christopher, ACA *2010;* 14 St. James Park, YEOVIL, SOMERSET, BA20 2EX.

PAYNE, Mr. Christopher, BA ACA *2009;* 101-811 West 7 Avenue, VANCOUVER V5T 1M5, BC, CANADA.

PAYNE, Mr. Christopher Cerdic, BA ACA *1998;* 42 Bradmore Way, COULSDON, SURREY, CR5 1PA.

PAYNE, Mr. Christopher John, ACA *1989;* 8 Japonica Close, WOKINGHAM, BERKSHIRE, RG41 4XJ.

PAYNE, Mr. Christopher Paul, BSc ACA *1988;* 1 Sweeting Street, WOODLANDS, WA 6018, AUSTRALIA.

PAYNE, Mr. Christopher Richard, BA ACA *1999;* Barley Cottage Broad Oak, Odiham, HOOK, RG29 1AH.

PAYNE, Ms. Clare Louise, BSc ACA *2000;* K B C Financial Products (UK) Ltd, 111 Old Broad Street, LONDON, EC2N 1FP.

•**PAYNE, Mr. Colin Geoffrey, FCA** *1977;* Hardcastle France, 30 Yorkersgate, MALTON, YO17 7AW.

•**PAYNE, Mrs. Dana Claire, BSc ACA** *1991;* (Tax Fac), Dana Payne Accountant ACA, 4 Cryfield Heights, COVENTRY, WEST MIDLANDS, CV4 7LA.

PAYNE, Mr. Darren Patrick, BSc ACA *1998;* 16 Strode Street, EGHAM, TW20 9BT.

•**PAYNE, Mr. David, BA ACA** *2003;* Turpin Barker Armstrong, Allen House, 1 Westmead Road, SUTTON, SURREY, SM1 4LA.

•**PAYNE, Mr. David, FCA** *1969;* David Payne, 60 The Green, EPSOM, SURREY, KT17 3JJ.

PAYNE, Mr. David Alexander, BEng ACA *2000;* with OMERS Private Equity, c/o Borealis Capital Corp, 6 New Street Square, New Fetton Lane, LONDON, EC4A 3BF.

•**PAYNE, Mr. David Andrew, FCA CIOT** *1980;* Baker Tilly Tax & Advisory Services LLP, 12 Gleneagles Court, Brighton Road, CRAWLEY, WEST SUSSEX, RH10 6AD.

•**PAYNE, Mr. David John, FCA** *1970;* David Payne, Sportsman Farm, St Michaels, TENTERDEN, TN30 6SY.

PAYNE, Mr. David John, BSc ACA *1989;* 46 Halifax Road, ENFIELD, MIDDLESEX, EN2 0PR.

•**PAYNE, Mr. David John Charles, FCA** *1977;* (Tax Fac), David J Payne Ltd, Room 42, 19b Moor Road, BROADSTONE, DORSET, BH18 8AZ.

PAYNE, Mr. David Michael, ACA *1998;* 7 St. Lukes Avenue, MAIDSTONE, KENT, ME14 5AN.

PAYNE, Mr. David Richard, BSc ACA *1992;* 21 Burdon Walk, Castle Eden, HARTLEPOOL, CLEVELAND, TS27 4FD.

•PECKHAM, Mr. Adrian Michael, BSc FCA *1988;* HPCA Limited, Station House, Connaught Road, Brookwood, WOKING, SURREY GU24 0ER. See also Herbert Parnell

PECKHAM, Mr. Stephen, BA ACA *1986;* Wedgewood, Dartnell Avenue, WEST BYFLEET, SURREY, KT14 6PJ.

PECKITT, Mr. Keith, BA FCA *1973;* 3 Baron Glade, Shipton Road, YORK, YO30 5FF.

PECKITT, Mr. Mark Andrew, BSc ACA *2003;* 9 Iona Way, WICKFORD, ESSEX, SS12 9QX.

PECKOVER, Mr. Nigel Jeffrey, BSc ACA *1991;* with KPMG LLP, 1 Waterloo Way, LEICESTER, LE1 6LP.

•PECOVER, Mr. Edward James, FCA *1969;* Abix Accounting, 20 Meare Estate, Wooburn Green, HIGH WYCOMBE, BUCKINGHAMSHIRE, HP10 0DX.

PEDDAR, Mr. Richard Granville, BSc FCA *1975;* Flat 1 Heath Mansions, Putney Heath Lane, LONDON, SW15 3JJ.

PEDDER, Mrs. Margaret Louise, FCA *1976;* 27 Vineyard Hill Road, LONDON, SW19 7JL.

•PEDDER, Mr. Matthew David, BA(Hons) ACA *2003;* The Martlet Partnership LLP, Martlet House, E1 Yeoman Gate, Yeoman Way, WORTHING, WEST SUSSEX BN13 3QZ.

PEDDER, Mr. Richard Vincent, FCA *1966;* Stone Lodge, 23 Westlands, PICKERING, YO18 7HJ. (Life Member)

PEDDER-SMITH, Mr. Samuel David, MSc BSc ACA *2010;* Flat 4, 11 Gloucester Avenue, LONDON, NW1 7AU.

•PEDDIE, Mr. Martin David, FCA *1983;* Menzies LLP, Victoria House, 50-58 Victoria Road, FARNBOROUGH, HAMPSHIRE, GU14 7PG.

PEDDLE, Mr. Alan Graham, BA FCA *1977;* with PricewaterhouseCoopers LLP, 1 Embankment Place, LONDON, WC2N 6RH.

PEDDLE, Miss. Sarah, BA(Hons) ACA *2011;* 6 Linden Avenue, RUISLIP, MIDDLESEX, HA4 8TW.

PEDELTY, Mrs. Stephanie, ACA *2011;* 8 Stanley Road, NORTHAMPTON, NN5 5DT.

•PEDEN, Mrs. Angela, BSc FCA *1993;* All About Business Limited, Audley House, Northbridge Rd, BERKHAMSTED, HERTFORDSHIRE, HP4 1EH.

PEDERSEN, Miss. Sara, BSc ACA *2003;* 20 Old Forge Road, Loudwater, HIGH WYCOMBE, BUCKINGHAMSHIRE, HP10 9TP.

PEDERZOLLI, Dr. Judith Ann, BSc ACA *2004;* with Peters Elworthy & Moore, Salisbury House, Station Road, CAMBRIDGE, CB1 2LA.

PEDGRIFT, Mr. Stephen Frederic, FCA *1970;* 3 Chemin du Bois de Ban, 1066 EPALINGES, SWITZERLAND. (Life Member)

PEDLAR, Mrs. Sarah Jayne, BA ACA *2004;* Walkers, 16-18 Devonshire Street, KEIGHLEY, WEST YORKSHIRE, BD21 2DG.

•PEDLER, Mr. Garth, FCA *1969;* (Tax Fac), Garth Pedler & Co, Hay Hill, TOTNES, TQ9 5LH.

PEDLEY, Mr. Anthony, BSc ACA *1981;* Layden Hall East Grinstead Road, North Chailey, LEWES, EAST SUSSEX, BN8 4DH.

PEDLEY, Mrs. Helen Mary, BSc FCA *1986;* Princes Exchange, Princes Square, LEEDS, WEST YORKSHIRE, LS1 4HY.

•PEDLEY, Mr. Joseph Anthony, FCA *1977;* Auker Rhodes Tax & Financial Planning Ltd, Sapphire House, Albion Mills, Albion Road, Greengates, BRADFORD WEST YORKSHIRE BD10 9TQ. See also Auker Rhodes Accounting Ltd

PEDLEY, Miss. Leah, BA ACA *1999;* 20 Carlton Road, LONDON, SW14 7RJ.

PEDLEY, Mr. Paul Louis, OBE BSc FCA *1979;* Tudor Lodge, Briardale Road, Willaston, NESTON, CH64 1TD.

PEDLEY, Mr. Roger Keith, FCA *1968;* 2 Deans Croft, Bramcote, NOTTINGHAM, NG9 3FL.

PEDLEY, Mr. Timothy John, ACA *1996;* 58 Roundwood Road, Nortenden, MANCHESTER, M22 4SF.

PEDLOW, Mr. Malcolm Howard, FCA *1952;* 28 Springfield Gardens, ELGIN, IV30 6XX. (Life Member)

PEDRE, Miss. Sara Elizabeth, MMath ACA *2003;* 24 Greyladies Gardens, Wat Tyler Road, LONDON, SE10 8AU.

PEDREIRA, Mrs. Paula, ACA *2009;* Rua dos Generais no 20, Futungo de Belas II, Luanda Sul, LUANDA, ANGOLA.

PEDRETTE, Mr. Andrew Charles, MA ACA CF *1996;* with Smith & Williamson Ltd, 25 Moorgate, LONDON, EC2R 6AY.

•PEDROPILLAI, Mr. Dunstan Ajith, MA FCA *1991;* PricewaterhouseCoopers LLP, Hays Galleria, 1 Hays Lane, LONDON, SE1 2RD. See also PricewaterhouseCoopers

PEDROZ, Mr. Nigel Orlando, MA ACA *1994;* 11 Gordon Avenue, East Sheen, LONDON, SW14 8DZ.

PEECH, Mrs. Esther Catrin, BA ACA *2002;* White Raven, Park Lane, ASHTEAD, SURREY, KT21 1EU.

PEECOCK, Mr. Bernard Joseph, BSc ACA *1992;* 279 Fir Tree Road, EPSOM, KT17 3LF.

•PEEK, Mr. Barry John Julian, MA FCA *1968;* Barry Peek & Co, Clock House, Stonham Parva, STOWMARKET, IP14 5JP.

•PEEK, Mr. David Richard, BSc ACA *1981;* Peter's Food Service Limited, Bedwas House Industrial Estate, Bedwas, CAERPHILLY, MID GLAMORGAN, CF83 8XP.

PEEK, Mr. Graham Henry, FCA *1973;* 132 Rue de la Roquette, 75011 PARIS, FRANCE. (Life Member)

PEEK, Mr. Reginald Alan, BSc ARCS ACA *1979;* Lamberts Healthcare Century Place, Lamberts Road, TUNBRIDGE WELLS, TN2 3EH.

PEEK, Mr. Richard Alan, BCom FCA *1960;* 31 Cecil Road, WESTON-SUPER-MARE, AVON, BS23 2NU. (Life Member)

PEEK, Mr. Robert, FCA *1975;* 6 Harlow Court, LEEDS, LS8 2JH.

PEEK, Miss. Stephanie, BSc ACA *2011;* 42 Mill Road, Lisvane, CARDIFF, CF14 0XL.

PEEKE, Mr. Edward Michael, BA ACA *2000;* David Webster Ltd Field House, Station Approach, HARLOW, CM20 2FB.

PEEL, Mrs. Caroline Frances, FCA *1978;* 40 Park Road, CAMBERLEY, SURREY, GU15 2SR.

PEEL, Mrs. Gemma Marie, LLB ACA *1998;* Lime Pictures, Campus Manor, Childwall, LIVERPOOL, L16 0JP.

PEEL, Mr. Ian Michael, FCA *1973;* 5 Bramley Close, New Mill, HOLMFIRTH, HD9 7NW. (Life Member)

PEEL, Miss. Irena Dawn, BSc ACA MBA *1996;* 45 Kenton Avenue, NEWCASTLE UPON TYNE, NE3 4SE.

PEEL, Miss. Joanna Victoria, ACA *2010;* 22 West Lea Drive, LEEDS, LS17 5BZ.

PEEL, Mrs. Katie Emma, BSc ACA *2007;* 9 Pasture Lane, Ruddington, NOTTINGHAM, NG11 6AE.

PEEL, Miss. Linda Margaret, ACA *1980;* Brooklands Cottage, Philpot Lane, Chobham, WOKING, GU24 8HE.

PEEL, Mr. Michael David, FCA *1969;* Windyridge, 64 Hawkstone Avenue, Guiseley, LEEDS, LS20 8ES.

•PEEL, Mr. Peter Graham, FCA *1976;* Porter Garland Limited, Portland House, Park Street, BAGSHOT, SURREY, GU19 5PG.

PEEL, Mr. Ronald, FCA *1951;* 64 Nailsea Park, Nailsea, BRISTOL, BS48 1BB. (Life Member)

PEEL, Mr. Timothy James Olatokunbo, BA ACA *1999;* Darling Park Tower 2, 201 Sussex Street, GPO Box 2650, SYDNEY, NSW 1171, AUSTRALIA.

PEEL, Mr. Wilfrid David, FCA *1968;* Apartment 14, Castle Keep, Scott Lane, WETHERBY, WEST YORKSHIRE, LS22 6NY.

•PEEL YATES, Mr. Charles William, FCA *1979;* 6B Clifftop House, Windmill Hill Road, GIBRALTAR, GIBRALTAR.

PEELING, Mr. Darren Mark, BA(Hons) FCA *2000;* with McBrides Accountants LLP, Nexus House, 2 Cray Road, SIDCUP, KENT, DA14 5DA.

PEELING, Mrs. Gillian, BA ACA *1990;* 16 Lackmore Gardens, Woodcote, READING, RG8 0SL.

PEER, Miss. Susan Catherine, LLB ACA *2005;* 133 Shirland Road, LONDON, W9 2EP.

PEERANI, Mr. Amin Mohamed, FCA *1975;* 32 Silver Ridge Court N.W., CALGARY T3B 4V5, AB, CANADA.

•PEERBAYE, Mr. Yousouf Ali, FCA *1975;* Y.A. Peerbaye, Richard House, 6th Floor, Remy Ollier Street, PORT LOUIS, MAURITIUS.

PEERBHOY, Mr. Ali Nawaz, BA ACA *1991;* Noor, 70 Woodland Way, Kingswood, TADWORTH, SURREY, KT20 6NW.

PEERBOCUS, Mrs. Shabnam Begum, MEng FCA *1995;* BDO DE CHAZAL DU MEE, 10 FRERE FELIX DE VALOIS STREET, PORT LOUIS, MAURITIUS.

PEERLESS, Mr. Darren, ACA *2009;* Auerbach Hope Epatra House, 58-60 Berners Street, LONDON, W1T 3JS.

PEERLESS, Mr. Edward John, BSc(Hons) ACA *2010;* 76 Ballater Road, LONDON, SW2 5QP.

PEERLESS, Mr. Simon Gideon Graham, MA FCA *1977;* 4 Porrington Close, CHISLEHURST, BR7 5RB.

PEERS, Mr. Bryan Cyril, FCA *1953;* 108 Coleherne Court, Old Brompton Road, LONDON, SW5 0ED. (Life Member)

PEERS, Mr. Donald Leslie, BA(Com) FCA *1964;* 34 Guffitts Rake, WIRRAL, MERSEYSIDE, CH47 7AD.

PEERS, Mr. John, BA ACA *1994;* Springfield, 19 Chester Road, Sutton Weaver, RUNCORN, WA7 3EE.

PEERS, Mrs. Maria Louise, BSc ACA *1991;* 3 Clouds, DUNS, BERWICKSHIRE, TD11 3BB.

PEERS, Mr. Mark Robert Ernest, BA ACA *1986;* (Tax Fac), Netherset Hey, Arrowe Brook Lane, Greasby, WIRRAL, CH49 3NY.

PEERS, Mr. Matthew Stephen, BA ACA *1999;* The Carphone Warehouse, 1 Portal Way, LONDON, W3 6RS.

PEERS, Mr. Neil Richard, BSc ACA *2000;* 200 Fernbank Road, ASCOT, SL5 8JX.

PEERS, Mr. Richard John, ACA *1999;* Faloria, Moulsford, WALLINGFORD, OXFORDSHIRE, OX10 9HR.

PEERS, Mr. Robert Martin, BA FCA ATII *2000;* 8 New Century Apartments, 55 Stubbins Lane Ramsbottom, BURY, BL0 0PP.

PEET, Mr. David Jonathan Frederick, BSc ACA *2010;* 26 Heathfield, CHISLEHURST, KENT, BR7 6AE.

PEET, Mr. Edward William James, BEng ACA *1996;* Redbrick Hillside, Odiham, HOOK, HAMPSHIRE, RG29 1HY.

PEET, Mr. John, FCA *1965;* 22 Carrwood, KNUTSFORD, WA16 8NE.

PEET, Mr. Lawrence Edwin, BSc ACA *1988;* 7 Saxstead Rise, LEEDS, LS12 4ND.

•PEET, Mr. Richard Martin, FCA *1973;* (Tax Fac), AVN Picktree Limited, Picktree House, The Barn, Tilford Road, FARNHAM, SURREY GU9 8HU.

PEEVOR, Mrs. Nicola Jane, ACA *2009;* Flat 2, 128 Earlsfield Road, LONDON, SW18 3DS.

PEGASIOU, Mr. Chrysis Mariou, MSc BA ACA *2003;* 38 Andreas Zisimopoulos street, 2402 Engomi, NICOSIA, CYPRUS.

PEGG, Mr. Anthony James, BA ACA *1983;* Lower Broadhurst Farm, 8 Broadhurst Lane, Wrightington, WIGAN, WN6 9RX.

PEGG, Miss. Sharon Elizabeth, BA ACA *1996;* (Tax Fac), 8 South Walsham Road, Acle, NORWICH, NR13 3EB.

PEGG, Miss. Suzanne Margaret, ACA *2009;* 16 Hunsdon Road, LONDON, SE14 5RE.

PEGG, Miss. Victoria, BSc ACA *2005;* 17 Mayfield Avenue, LONDON, W13 9UP.

PEGG, Mrs. Wendy, ACA *1979;* 40 Angelica, TAMWORTH, B77 3JZ.

PEGLER, Mr. Andrew Christopher, BA ACA *1997;* with Ernst & Young LLP, 1 More London Place, LONDON, SE1 2AF.

PEGLER, Mr. Jonathan Dahl, BSc FCA *1979;* Melbury House Lincoln Road, Chalfont St. Peter, GERRARDS CROSS, BUCKINGHAMSHIRE, SL9 9TQ.

PEGLER, Mr. Mark, BCom FCA *1993;* 7 Roman Grange, Little Aston, SUTTON COLDFIELD, WEST MIDLANDS, B74 3GA.

PEGLER, Mr. Michael John, BA(Hons) ACA *2001;* 65 Gloucester Road, RICHMOND, SURREY, TW9 3BT.

PEGLER, Mrs. Ruth, BSc ACA *1992;* 7 Roman Grange, SUTTON COLDFIELD, B74 3GA.

•PEGLER, Mr. Stephen Raymond, FCA *1967;* (Tax Fac), with Butterworth Jones, 80 Oxford Street, BURNHAM-ON-SEA, SOMERSET, TA8 1EF.

PEGRAM, Mr. Kevin John, BA ACA *2005;* 28/129 Bower Street, MANLY, NSW 2095, AUSTRALIA.

PEGRUM, Miss. Caroline Langdon, MA(Oxon) ACA *1997;* 51 Dudley Close, Tilehurst, READING, RG31 6JJ.

PEH, Miss. Siew Gaik, ACA *1991;* 21 Green Pastures, Heaton Mersey, STOCKPORT, SK4 3RB.

PEH, Miss. Siew Tin, ACA *1981;* 21 Green Pastures, Heaton Mersey, STOCKPORT, SK4 3RB.

PEILE, Mr. Michael, ACA *2007;* 7 Front Street, Fletchertown, WIGTON, CUMBRIA, CA7 1BQ.

PEIRANO, Mr. Paul Ambrose, ACA *1981;* 43 rue du Val Violet, 37300 JOUE LES TOURS, FRANCE.

PEIRCE, Mr. Adrian, BEng FCA *1999;* 51 Woodcote Road, Caversham, READING, RG4 7BB.

PEIRCE, Mrs. Amanda Jayne, BSc ACA *1989;* Western Power Distribution Ltd, Osprey Road, Sowton Industrial Estate, EXETER, EX2 7WP.

PEIRCE, Mr. Andrew, BA ACA *2002;* 114 Drumnich Wood, Portmarnock, DUBLIN 6, COUNTY DUBLIN, IRELAND.

PEIRCE, Mr. Arthur Randall Malcolm, FCA *1957;* (Tax Fac), Beechurst, Caddington Common, Markyate, ST. ALBANS, AL3 8QF. (Life Member)

PEIRCE, Mr. John Stephen, BSc ACA AMCT *1990;* Saga Group Ltd Enbrook Park, Sandgate High Street Sandgate, FOLKESTONE, CT20 3SE.

PEIRCE, Miss. Julie Ann, BSc ACA *1992;* 29 Oak Road, Hale, ALTRINCHAM, WA15 9JA.

PEIRSON, Mr. David Martin, BA ACA CTA TEP *2004;* (Tax Fac), with F.W. Smith Riches & Co, 15 Whitehall, LONDON, SW1A 2DD.

PEIRSON, Mr. Geoffrey John, FCA *1967;* Greenleaves, Braxted Road, Kelvedon, COLCHESTER, CO5 9BT.

PEIRSON, Mr. John Jeremy, FCA *1964;* 23 Market Place, Hingham, NORWICH, NR9 4AF.

PEJCINOVIC, Miss. Dina, ACA *1990;* 33 Newton Road, Ashton-On-Ribble, PRESTON, PR2 1DY.

PEJHAN-SYKES, Mrs. Visseh, MSc BA ACA *1990;* 1 Brookfield, Oxspring, SHEFFIELD, S36 8WG.

PEKAR, Mr. Juraj, ACA *2008;* 26 Candlemas Lane, BEACONSFIELD, BUCKINGHAMSHIRE, HP9 1AF.

PELANCONI, Mr. Justin Thomas, BSc ACA *2010;* 6 Godolphin Road, LONDON, W12 8JE.

PELCZER, Mr. Jeremy David, BA ACA *1983;* Bluff View Taunton Road, Ashcott, BRIDGWATER, SOMERSET, TA7 9BH.

PELCZER, Mr. Otto Hans Emmanuel, FCA *1953;* Octavia House, 28th October No 28, Agkleisides, 7571 LARNACA, CYPRUS. (Life Member)

PELECANI, Mr. Constantinos, ACA *2010;* 1 Komninon Street, Kapsalos, LIMASSOL, CYPRUS.

PELEKANOS, Mr. Andreas, BSc ACA *1998;* Amfitritis 31 App. 501, 2000 NICOSIA, CYPRUS.

•PELEKANOS, Mr. Chrisilios, BA(Econ) ACA *1996;* PricewaterhouseCoopers Limited, Julia House, 3 Themistocles Dervis Street, CY-1066 NICOSIA, CYPRUS.

•PELETIES, Mr. Panayiotis Andrea, BA FCA *1996;* KPMG, 14 Esperidon Street, 1087 NICOSIA, CYPRUS. See also KPMG Metaxas Loizides Syrimis

PELHAM, Mr. David Lucian, MA FCA *1970;* 39 Christchurch Avenue, LONDON, N12 0DG.

PELHAM, Mrs. Elizabeth Jane, BSc ACA *1995;* 16 Brampton Road, ST. ALBANS, HERTFORDSHIRE, AL1 4PS.

PELHAM, Miss. Kathryn, BSc ACA *2006;* E T X Capital Beaufort House, 15 St. Botolph Street, LONDON, EC3A 7DT.

PELL, Mr. Darren John, BSc ACA *1994;* Domestic & General Services Ltd Swan Court, 11 Worple Road, LONDON, SW19 4JS.

•PELL, Mr. Frederick Thomas Charles, FCA *1965;* Pells, 17 Newstead Grove, NOTTINGHAM, NG1 4GZ. See also T Wilford Pell & Company

PELL, Mr. Gavin Gerard Crompton, BSc ACA *1999;* Langstrasse 192, 8005 ZURICH, SWITZERLAND.

PELL, Mr. Gideon Anthony, BSc FCA *1983;* 61 Holbrook Drive, STAMFORD, CT 06906, UNITED STATES.

PELL, Mr. John Hopkins, FCA *1976;* East Wing, Saxby's, Cowden, EDENBRIDGE, TN8 7DU.

PELL, Dr. Jonathan David, BSc ACA *1997;* 19 Apley Way, Cambourne, CAMBRIDGE, CB3 6DF.

PELL, Mr. Michael Anthony, FCA *1987;* 7 Newfield Place, Hagley, STOURBRIDGE, DY9 0FB.

PELL, Mr. Steven Richard, BA ACA *2007;* Flat 5A, 28 Arkwright Road, LONDON, NW3 6BH.

•PELL, Mrs. Vivien Mary, BA ACA *1993;* JVP Consultants Limited, 19 Apley Way, Lower Cambourne, CAMBRIDGE, CB23 6DF.

•PELL-HILEY, Mr. Peter Francis, BA(Hons) FCA *1979;* Glen Grenaugh House, Harbour Road, Santon, ISLE OF MAN, IM4 1HF.

PELLAND, Mr. Jean-Sebastien, BCom ACA CFA *2005;* Top Floor, 44 South Hill Park, LONDON, NW3 2SJ.

PELLANDINI, Mr. Virgilio Angelo Gualtiero, MA MSc ACA *2010;* Virgilio Pellandini, Ret Utca 7, 1022 BUDAPEST, HUNGARY.

PELLANT, Mr. Roger Alfred, FCA *1960;* 30 Hurstleigh Drive, REDHILL, RH1 2AA.

PELLANT, Mr. Roger Ian, BSc FCA *1981;* 10 Chiddingstone Close, Senacre Wood, MAIDSTONE, ME15 8TP. (Life Member)

PELLATT, Mr. Franklin Thomas George, FCA *1950;* P.O. Box 137, SOUTHBROOM, NATAL SOUTH COAST, 4277, SOUTH AFRICA. (Life Member)

PELLEY, Mr. Ian Robertson, FCA *1963;* 32 Abbey Road, Westbury-on-Trym, BRISTOL, BS9 3QW.

PELLING, Mr. Benjamin James, BA ACA *2005;* 8 Paddock Farm, Coney Weston, BURY ST. EDMUNDS, SUFFOLK, IP31 1DS.

PELLING, Mr. Christopher Alan, FCA *1973;* 8 Paddock Farm, Coney Weston, BURY ST. EDMUNDS, SUFFOLK, IP31 1DS.

PELLING, Mr. Iain Searle, BA FCA *1986;* 46 Haslemere Avenue, LONDON, W13 9UJ.

•PELLING, Mr. John David, BA ACA *1989;* 17 Old Tollerton Road, Gamston, NOTTINGHAM, NG2 6NX.

PELLING, Mr. Melvin Keith, FCA *1959;* 72 Blairderry Road, Streatham Hill, LONDON, SW2 4SB. (Life Member)

PELLING, Mrs. Michelle Elizabeth, BSc(Hons) ACA *2003;* P.O. Box 689, Karen, 00502, NAIROBI, KENYA.

PELLING, Mr. Sean, BSc ACA *2001;* P.O.Box 689, Karen, NAIROBI, 00502, KENYA.

PELLOWE, Mr. Brian Mark, BSc ACA *1985;* 12 Melbourne Street, FAIRLIGHT, NSW 2094, AUSTRALIA.
PELLY, Mr. Nicholas James Michael, FCA *1972;* 30B Cedar Tower, President Park, Park View Tower, Sukhumvit Soi 24, BANGKOK, 10110 THAILAND.
PELTER, Mr. Mark Simon, BSc ACA *1991;* Mill Meadow, Church Road, Brasted, WESTERHAM, KENT, TN16 1HZ.
PELVANG, Mrs. Asa Elisabeth, ACA *1993;* 31 The Haydens, TONBRIDGE, TN9 1NS.
PEMBERTHY, Mr. Neil Michael, MA ACA *1996;* 20 Cyprus Road, EXMOUTH, DEVON, EX8 2EB.
PEMBERTON, Mr. Andrew Charles Thorburn, BSc ACA *1981;* St. Helier Parish Hall, PO Box 50, JERSEY, JE4 8PA.
PEMBERTON, Mr. Andrew Philip, FCA *1970;* Rosemary Cottage, Back Lane, Meriden, COVENTRY, CV7 7LD. (Life Member)
PEMBERTON, Ms. Caroline Amelia Sandys, BSc ACA *1992;* BROCKLAND, Sway Road, BROCKENHURST, HAMPSHIRE, SO42 7SG.
PEMBERTON, Mr. John, BSc ACA *2005;* Moss House, Plant Lane, Moston, SANDBACH, CW11 3PG.
•PEMBERTON, Mr. Mark Stephen, BSc ACA *1984;* with Carston & Co Limited, First Floor, Tudor House, 16 Cathedral Road, CARDIFF, CF11 9LJ.
PEMBERTON, Mr. Paul Graham, BMet ACA *1990;* D B Chenker, 72-80 Bourke Road, ALEXANDRIA, NSW 2015, AUSTRALIA.
PEMBERTON, Mr. Steven John, FCA *1979;* 23 Armistead Way, Cranage, CREWE, CW4 8FE.
PEMBERTON, Mr. Timothy Michael, BA(Hons) ACA *2001;* 12 Feathers Place, LONDON, SE10 9NE.
PEMBERTON, Miss. Vanessa, BSc ACA *1992;* 7 Heathlands Court, WOKINGHAM, BERKSHIRE, RG40 3AY.
PEMBERTON-PIGOTT, Mr. Jason Hugh, BA FCA *1973;* 21 Rowan Road, LONDON, W6 7DT.
PEMBERY, Mrs. Claire Fiona Attwood, BA ACA *1998;* 87 Gilbert Road, CAMBRIDGE, CB4 3NZ.
PEMBERY, Mrs. Fiona Louise, BSc(Hons) ACA *2002;* Bank Bungalow, Old Inn Lane, Fosdyke, BOSTON, LINCOLNSHIRE, PE20 2DE.
PEMBERY, Mrs. Julie Teresa, BSc ACA *1988;* Aspen Advisory Services, 44 Lowndes Street, LONDON, SW1X 9HX.
PEMBLE, Mrs. Alison Sian, BA ACA ATII *1987;* 17 Church Hayes Close, Nailsea, BRISTOL, BS48 4LY.
PEMBRIDGE, Mr. Kenneth John, FCA *1950;* 2 Pinetree Close, BROMYARD, HR7 4HL. (Life Member)
PEMBURY, Mr. Stephen Michael, BSc ACA *1979;* Hawkstone Management Serices Ltd, 44 Catherine Place, LONDON, SW1E 6HL.
•PENASA, Mr. Giovanni Vigilio, FCA *1980;* (Tax Fac), S. McCombie & Co, First Floor, 99 Bancroft, HITCHIN, SG5 1NQ.
PENBERTHY, Mr. Alan John, FCA *1969;* 37 Elphinstone Avenue, Flamingo Vlei, TABLE VIEW, 7441, SOUTH AFRICA.
•PENDARVES, Miss. Sarah, FCA CTA *1980;* Warwick Pendarves & Co, 38 Hound Road, Netley Abbey, SOUTHAMPTON, SO31 5FX.
PENDER, Mr. James, MMath ACA *2011;* 67b Bedford Hill, LONDON, SW12 9HA.
PENDER, Mrs. Janet Elizabeth, BA ACA *1980;* The End, 41 Valley Drive, Loose, MAIDSTONE, ME15 9TL.
PENDER, Mr. Mark Howard, BSc ACA *1982;* The West of England Ship Owners Insurance Services Ltd, 224-226 Tower Bridge Road, LONDON, SE1 2UP.
PENDERED, Mr. William Martin, BA ACA *1995;* Tatu Farm, Biddenden, ASHFORD, TN27 8JG.
PENDERGAST, Mr. John Neil, BSc FCA *1993;* Mourant, PO Box 87, 22 Grenville Street, St Helier, JERSEY, JE4 8PX.
PENDERGAST, Mrs. Sarah Louise, ACA *1995;* 3 Marmotier, La Rue De La Haye, St Martin, JERSEY, JE3 6UR.
PENDLEBURY, Mr. David Arthur, BA ACA *1985;* 16 Horseguards Way, MELTON MOWBRAY, LEICESTERSHIRE, LE13 0SU.
PENDLEBURY, Mr. Garry Charles Arthur, BA FCA *1975;* 80 Burley Lane, Quarndon, DERBY, DE22 5JR.
PENDLEBURY, Mrs. Rachel Lyn, BA(Hons) ACA *2000;* 58 Fenton Road, BOURNEMOUTH, BH6 5BU.
PENDLEBURY, Miss. Samantha Louise, BSc(Hons) ACA *2009;* 46 Webb Street, Horwich, BOLTON, BL6 5NS.
PENDLETON, Mr. Alistair Lee, BA ACA CF *2000;* LDC, 6th Floor, Interchange Place, Edmund Street, BIRMINGHAM, B3 2TA.
PENDLETON, Mrs. Galina, BAcc ACA *2003;* with Fauchier Partners Ltd, 72 Welbeck Street, LONDON, W1G 0AY.
•PENDLINGTON, Mr. Gregg Anthony, BA(Hons) ACA CF *2003;* Haines Watts Corporate Finance (NW), 1st Floor, Northern Assurance Buildings, Albert Square, 9-21 Princess Street, MANCHESTER M2 4DN.
PENDOCK, Mr. Simon Barry, FCA *1958;* 64 Chipstead Street, LONDON, SW6 3SS. (Life Member)
PENDRAY, Mr. Michael Antony, BA ACA *1982;* The Oaks, 123 Ullet Road, LIVERPOOL, L17 2AB.
•PENDRAY, Miss. Sheila Elizabeth, BSc FCA *1977;* Pendray & Co, The Hylands, 244 Chipstead Way, Woodmansterne, BANSTEAD, SM7 3LQ.
PENDRED, Mr. Oliver, MSc BSc ACA CTA *2006;* 6 Middle Avenue, FARNHAM, SURREY, GU9 8JL.
PENDRETH, Miss. Amy Clair, BA(Hons) ACA *2011;* Glenwood, Jail Lane, Biggin Hill, WESTERHAM, KENT, TN16 3AU.
PENDRICH, Mrs. Diana Susan, BA ACA *1992;* The Old Apple Tree, 197 Petersham Road, RICHMOND, TW10 7AW.
PENDRILL, Mr. Andrew Charles, BA ACA *1995;* JT International, 1 Rue De La Gabelle, 1211 GENEVA, SWITZERLAND.
PENDRILL, Prof. David, MSc BSc(Econ) LTCL FCA CTA *1966;* 20 Eider Close, BUCKINGHAM, MK18 1GL. (Life Member)
PENDRILL, Mr. Richard William, FCA *1962;* Boscobel, Sweetwater Lane, Wormley, GODALMING, GU8 5SS. (Life Member)
PENFOLD, Mr. Christopher Keith, ACA *2003;* Flat B101, 18 Hertsmere Road, LONDON, E14 4AY.
PENFOLD, Mr. David George, ACA *1979;* Deutsche Bank, Level 11, 126 Phillip Street, SYDNEY, NSW 2000, AUSTRALIA.
•PENFOLD, Mr. Gerard Michael, FCA *1982;* KPMG LLP, 15 Canada Square, LONDON, E14 5GL. See also KPMG Europe LLP
PENFOLD, Mr. Ian Jeremy, BSc FCA *1981;* 3 The Spinney, Grange Lane, Thurnby, LEICESTER, LE7 9QS.
•PENFOLD, Mr. John Stuart, FCA *1972;* with Turpin Barker Armstrong, Allen House, 1 Westmead Road, SUTTON, SURREY, SM1 4LA.
PENFOLD, Mr. Jonathan Mark, BA ACA *1988;* 45 High Street, Yardley Hastings, NORTHAMPTON, NN7 1ER.
PENFOLD, Mrs. Kerry, BSc ACA *2003;* Southern Finance Co Southern House, Shirley Road, SOUTHAMPTON, SO15 3EY.
•PENFOLD, Mrs. Maureen Bernadette, FCA *1987;* Kingston Smith LLP, 800 Uxbridge Road, HAYES, MIDDLESEX, UB4 0RS. See also Kingston Smith Limited Liability Partnership, Devonshire Corporate Services LLP and Kingston Smith Consulting LLP
PENFOLD, Mr. Neil Alexander James, BEng ACA *1999;* 1 West Street, 3302, NEW YORK, NY 10004, UNITED STATES.
PENFOLD, Mrs. Nicola Jacqueline, BSc ACA *1994;* 1 Chapel Lane, Wilstead, BEDFORD, MK45 3DH.
PENFOLD, Mr. Nigel Anton, BSc(Hons) ACA *2002;* Delta Park, Concorde Way, FAREHAM, PO155RL.
PENFOLD, Mr. Raymond Henry John, FCA *1952;* The Quickset, 38 The Ridgeway, LEATHERHEAD, KT22 9BH. (Life Member)
•PENFOLD, Mr. Robert Charles, FCA *1963;* R C Penfold, 238 Corbets Tey Road, UPMINSTER, ESSEX, RM14 2BL.
PENFOUND, Mr. Clive Spencer, FCA *1977;* BP International Ltd, Building 200, Chertsey Road, SUNBURY-ON-THAMES, MIDDLESEX, TW16 7LN.
PENFOUND, Miss. Laura Anne, ACA *2009;* 14 Johnson Street, HAWTHORN, VIC 3122, AUSTRALIA.
PENFOUND, Mrs. Lynsey Anne, FCA *1977;* Bellapaise, Hurstwood Lane, TUNBRIDGE WELLS, TN4 8YA.
PENG, Miss. Rui, ACA *2009;* Flat A 20/F, Block 19, Park Island, 8 Pak Lai Road, MA WAN, HONG KONG SAR.
PENG, Mr. Siwei, BSc ACA *2010;* FVP Credit Hybrid 8th Floor, J P Morgan Chase, 125 London Wall, LONDON, EC2Y 5AJ.
PENGELLEY, Mr. Martin Edwin, MA ACA *1984;* Capel Court Oast, Alders Road, Capel, TONBRIDGE, TN12 6SU.
PENGELLY, Mr. Andrew John, BEng ACA *1994;* 26 Surbiton Hill Park, SURBITON, KT5 8ES.
PENGELLY, Mr. Clive Eric, BSc FCA *1980;* (Tax Fac), with Grant Thornton UK LLP, Hartwell House, 55-61 Victoria Street, BRISTOL, BS1 6FT.
•PENGELLY, Mr. George Alistair, BA *1990;* 78 Upper Ratton Drive, EASTBOURNE, EAST SUSSEX, BN20 9DJ.
PENGELLY, Mr. Malcolm John, ACA *1984;* (Tax Fac), 1 Finch Way, Burghfield Common, READING, RG7 3XT.
PENGELLY, Mrs. Neil, BSc ACA *1985;* 56 Santos Wharf, EASTBOURNE, EAST SUSSEX, BN23 5UR.
PENGELLY, Mr. Richard Arthur, FCA *1974;* Seaways, Windmill, PADSTOW, CORNWALL, PL28 8RZ.
PENGILLY, Mr. Keith James, BSc ACA *1989;* 12 Peartree Close, Doddinghurst, BRENTWOOD, Essex, CM15 0TU.
PENGILLY, Mr. Martin David, BSc FCA *1992;* 42 Kissing Point Road, TURRAMURRA, NSW 2074, AUSTRALIA.
PENIKET, Mr. David John, BSc ACA *1995;* 26 Castle Hill, BERKHAMSTED, HERTFORDSHIRE, HP4 1HE.
PENISTON, Mr. Douglas James, BA ACA *1989;* Bosmere House 7 Nile Street, EMSWORTH, HAMPSHIRE, PO10 7EE.
PENISTON, John Norman, Esq MBE FCA *1939;* Port Sarde, 15 Chemin du Milieu, 1245 Collonge-Bellerive, GENEVA, SWITZERLAND. (Life Member)
PENK, Ms. Jacqueline Louise, BSc ACA *2000;* 65 Glaisdale Court, DARLINGTON, COUNTY DURHAM, DL3 7AE.
•PENKETH, Mr. Andrew, BSc FCA *1992;* Crowe Clark Whitehill LLP, St Bride's House, 10 Salisbury Square, LONDON, EC4Y 8EH. See also Horwath Clark Whitehill LLP and Crowe Clark Whitehill
PENKUL, Mr. Alexander Stewart, BA ACA *1994;* 35 Milliners Way, BISHOP'S STORTFORD, HERTFORDSHIRE, CM23 4GG.
PENLINGTON, Mr. Robert Ivan, FCA *1955;* 5 Meadow View Close, WAREHAM, BH20 4JQ. (Life Member)
PENMAN, Mr. Andrew Clark, BA ACA *1990;* 51 Straightsmouth, LONDON, SE10 9LB.
PENMAN, Mr. Jeffrey James, FCA *1965;* Sudels Farm, Darkinson Lane, Lea Town, PRESTON, PR4 0RJ.
•PENN, Mrs. Cheryl Amanda, FCA *1974;* Penn & Company LLP, Tordown, 5 Ashwell Lane, GLASTONBURY, BA6 8BG. See also Profitsevolution.co.uk Ltd
PENN, Mr. Edward Albert, FCA *1961;* 5 Glasshouse Lane, KENILWORTH, WARWICKSHIRE, CV8 2AH.
PENN, Mr. Giles Francis John, BSc ACA *1995;* Allerton House, Thurston Road, NORTHALLERTON, DL6 2NA.
PENN, Miss. Hannah, BSc ACA *2008;* 20 Williams Grove, Long Ditton, SURBITON, KT6 5RN.
•PENN, Mr. Jonathan Howard, BA FCA *1984;* (Tax Fac), Jonathan Penn and Company, Firs Farmhouse, Fishponds Way, Haughley, STOWMARKET, SUFFOLK IP14 3PJ. See also Jonathan Penn Limited
PENN, Mr. Joseph Jonathan, BCom FCA *1967;* Field House Lodge Mannings Lane Hoole Village, CHESTER, CH2 4EU.
①PENN, Miss. Lucinda Clare, ACA *2008;* with Francis Clark LLP, Vantage Point, Woodwater Park, Pynes Hill, EXETER, EX2 5FD.
PENN, Mr. Michael John, FCA *1967;* 10 Hall Park Hill, BERKHAMSTED, HP4 2NH. (Life Member)
•PENN, Mr. Michael Stuart, FCA *1972;* Penn & Company LLP, Tordown, 5 Ashwell Lane, GLASTONBURY, BA6 8BG. See also Profitsevolution.co.uk Ltd
PENN, Mr. Nicholas Robin Thomas, ACA MAAT *2001;* Avenue De Rumine 48, 1005 LAUSANNE, SWITZERLAND.
PENN, Miss. Nicola Tracie, BA ACA *1992;* 7 Abbey Gardens, CHERTSEY, SURREY, KT16 8RQ.
PENN, Mr. Nigel Francis, BSc FCA *1984;* Flat 3, The Balcony, 37 Esplanade Gardens, SCARBOROUGH, NORTH YORKSHIRE, YO11 2AW.
•①PENN, Mr. Stephen Richard, ACA *1980;* Simple Debt Solutions Limited, D T E House, Hollins Mount, BURY, LANCASHIRE, BL9 8AT.
PENN, Mr. Trevor Jeffery, FCA *1970;* 9 Mayfield Avenue, THORNTON-CLEVELEYS, LANCASHIRE, FY5 2HE.
PENN, Mr. William John Bannister, BA ACA *1981;* 35 Stuarts Green, Pedmore, STOURBRIDGE, DY9 0XR.
•PENN, Mrs. Zuzanka Daniella, FCA *1975;* (Tax Fac), Penn Accountants & Tax Consultants, Swale Folly, The Street, Doddington, SITTINGBOURNE, KENT ME9 0BG.
•PENN-NEWMAN, Mrs. Rosemary Elizabeth, FCA CF MBA *1987;* BTG Financial Consulting LLP, 41 Castle Way, SOUTHAMPTON, SO14 2BW. See also BTG McInnes Corporate Finance LLP and Begbies Traynor(Central) LLP
PENNANT-WILLIAMS, Mr. David Paul, ACA *2008;* 14 Columbine Close, Huntington, CHESTER, CH3 6BQ.
PENNELEGION, Miss. Anna, BSc ACA *1987;* 40Bis Avenue de Suffren, 75015 PARIS, FRANCE.
PENNELL, Mr. Alan Robert, BA(Hons) ACA *2001;* with Ernst & Young LLP, 1 More London Place, LONDON, SE1 2AF.
•PENNELLS, Mr. John Richard, FCA *1969;* Enclave, Wych Hill Way, WOKING, GU22 0AE.
PENNEY, Mr. Adrian Paul, BA ACA *1992;* 109 Western Road, BILLERICAY, ESSEX, CM12 9DT.
PENNEY, Mrs. Barbara Joan Kathleen, ACA *1981;* 4 Paxton Close, BASINGSTOKE, RG22 4UP.
PENNEY, Mr. Christopher Mark, BSc ACA *1990;* Morham Bank, Hop Garden Lane, SEVENOAKS, TN13 1PX.
PENNEY, Mr. Clive Edward, BSc FCA *1975;* Englefield, La Mazotte, Vale, GUERNSEY, GY3 5JN.
PENNEY, Mr. Darren Christopher, BA ACA *2006;* 61 Sydney Road, BEXLEYHEATH, DA6 8HQ.
PENNEY, Mr. John Hugh, FCA *1967;* Pantile Cottage, Broadwater Lane, Whistley Green, READING, RG10 0BQ.
PENNEY, Mrs. Katharine Anne Louise, MA ACA *1997;* (Tax Fac), 3 Cranford Rise, ESHER, KT10 9NG.
PENNEY, Mr. Mark Stephen, BA FCA *1980;* (Tax Fac), 8 Seton Drive, HOOK, HAMPSHIRE, RG27 9QS.
PENNEY, Mr. Matthew John, BSc ACA *1993;* 196 Banbury Road, STRATFORD-UPON-AVON, CV37 7HX.
PENNEY, Mr. Michael David, BA ACA *1992;* with PlanIT Services Limited, Lansdowne House, City Forum, 250 City Road, LONDON, EC1V 2QZ.
PENNEY, Mr. Nigel Francis, BA FCA *1984;* 51 Grasmere Road, Muswell Hill, LONDON, N10 2DH.
PENNEY, Mrs. Rebecca Anne, BA ACA *1995;* 196 Banbury Road, STRATFORD-UPON-AVON, CV37 7HX.
PENNEY, Mr. Simon Christopher, BA FCA *1973;* 77/29 Moo 6 Soi Layan 1, Cherngtalay, THALANG 83110, THAILAND.
•PENNEYCARD, Mr. Peter Kenneth, BA FCA *1975;* (Tax Fac), Treventon, Union Hill, ST COLUMB, TR9 6AR.
PENNIE, Mrs. Simone Sharon, BA ACA *1991;* The Yew Pinfarthings, Amberley, STROUD, GL5 5JQ.
•PENNIFOLD, Mr. Matthew John, FCA *1983;* (Tax Fac), Barrowby Accountants Limited, Kobia, Low Road, Barrowby, GRANTHAM, LINCOLNSHIRE NG32 1DJ. See also AIMS Matthew Pennifold Limited
PENNILL, Mr. David Roy, BSc ACA *1984;* 10 Kelvin Grove, CHESTER, CH2 2EL.
•PENNINGTON, Mr. Andrew John, ACA *1988;* (Tax Fac), Crossleys LLC, Portland House, Station Road, Ballasalla, ISLE OF MAN, IM9 2AE.
PENNINGTON, Mrs. Angela Mary, FCA *1985;* 6 Swarbrick Avenue, Grimsargh, PRESTON, LANCASHIRE, PR2 5JJ.
PENNINGTON, Mr. Chris, MA ACA *2000;* 5 Adel Park Gardens, LEEDS, LS16 8BN.
PENNINGTON, Mr. David, ACA CA(NZ) *2009;* 117 Stanlake Road, LONDON, W12 7HQ.
•PENNINGTON, Mr. David Ernest, FCA *1972;* Lewis Alexander & Connaughton, Second Floor, Boulton House, 17-21 Chorlton Street, MANCHESTER, M1 3HY. See also Lewis Alexander & Collins
•PENNINGTON, Mr. David Malcolm, FCA *1967;* David Pennington, Suite Four, The Old Station Business Park, Station Road, PERRANPORTH, CORNWALL TR6 0LH.
PENNINGTON, Miss. Debbie Louise, BA(Hons) ACA *2002;* 13 Matford Hill, Monkton Park, CHIPPENHAM, WILTSHIRE, SN15 3NX.
•PENNINGTON, Mr. Gordon, FCA *1970;* Gordon Pennington & Co, 1 Hall View Close, Gorstage, NORTHWICH, CW8 2GB.
PENNINGTON, Mrs. Helen, BSc ACA *2000;* 44a Bank Crest, Baildon, SHIPLEY, BD17 5HB.
•PENNINGTON, Mr. Ian Denzil, BSc ARCS FCA *1989;* with KPMG LLP, 3 Assembly Square, Britannia Quay, CARDIFF, CF10 4AX.
•PENNINGTON, Mr. Jack, FCA *1966;* J & D Pennington Limited, 30 Union Street, SOUTHPORT, MERSEYSIDE, PR9 0QE.
PENNINGTON, Mr. James Michael Edmonds, BA(Hons) ACA *2002;* 10 Jarvis Drive, Twyford, READING, RG10 9EW.
PENNINGTON, Miss. Julie Rebecca, BA ACA *2003;* with PricewaterhouseCoopers LLP, Benson House, 33 Wellington Street, LEEDS, LS1 4JP.
PENNINGTON, Mr. Keith Neil, BSc ARCS FCA *1983;* 6 Swarbrick Avenue, Grimsargh, PRESTON, PR2 5JJ.
•PENNINGTON, Mr. Malcolm Read, FCA *1971;* Pennington Hunter Limited, Stanhope House, Mark Rake, Bromborough, WIRRAL, MERSEYSIDE CH62 2DN. See also Pennington Williams
PENNINGTON, Mr. Mark Richard, BSc ACA *2005;* 27 Clockhouse Place, LONDON, SW15 2EL.

PENNINGTON, Mr. Michael, BA FCA ATII *1985;* First Intuition, County House, Conway Mews, LONDON, W1T 6AA.
PENNINGTON, Mr. Nigel John Lever, FCA *1969;* Apartment 5, 14 Beechwood Lane, DORCHESTER, DT13TP.
•**PENNINGTON, Mr. Richard Brian, FCA** *1981;* (Tax Fac), The Surrey Research Park, 30 Frederick Sanger Road, GUILDFORD, SURREY, GU2 7EF. See also Richard B. Pennington and Murray McIntosh O'Brien
PENNINGTON, Mr. Simon John, ACA *1981;* TR Services, 14 rue Ambroise Croizat, 77435 CROISSY BEAUBOURG, FRANCE.
PENNINGTON, Mr. Simon John, BSc ACA *1990;* 5 Catlins Place, Fairview Heights, NORTH SHORE CITY 0632, NEW ZEALAND.
PENNINGTON-BROOKFIELD, Mrs. Kerry Marie, ACA *2009;* 42a Melia House, 19 Lord Street, MANCHESTER, M4 4AX.
•**PENNINGTON LEGH, Mr. Peter Russell, FCA** *1973;* Vastern Manor, Vastern, Wootton Bassett, SWINDON, WILTSHIRE, SN4 7PB.
PENNOCK, Mrs. Helen, BA(Hons) ACA *2004;* Ryecroft Glenton, 32 Portland Terrace, NEWCASTLE UPON TYNE, NE2 1QP.
PENNOCK, Mrs. Helen Elizabeth, BSc ACA *1989;* 751 Warwick Road, SOLIHULL, B91 3DQ.
PENNOCK, Mr. James Nicholas, MA(Oxon) ACA *2002;* (Tax Fac), 36 Bramwell Street, SHEFFIELD, S3 7PA.
PENNY, Mr. Duncan John, MA FCA *1989;* XP Power, 401 Commonwealth Drive, Haw Par Technocentre, Lobby B, #02-02, SINGAPORE 149598 SINGAPORE.
PENNY, Mr. Ian Steven Elliott, BEng FCA *1992;* 95 Rosemullion Avenue, Tattenhoe, MILTON KEYNES, MK4 3AS.
•**PENNY, Miss. Jane, BA ACA CTA** *1991;* Lymm Tax Ltd, 6 Meadow View, LYMM, CHESHIRE, WA13 9AX. See also Beechwood Tax Services
PENNY, Mr. Jonathan Nicholas, BSc ACA *1993;* 21 St Michaels Street, ST. ALBANS, AL3 4SP.
PENNY, Mrs. Julia Suzanne, BA FCA *1989;* Wooben Hollybush Ride, Finchampstead, WOKINGHAM, BERKSHIRE, RG40 3QR.
PENNY, Mrs. Julie, BA ACA *1996;* 7 Northumberland Road, New Barnet, BARNET, HERTFORDSHIRE, EN5 1EF.
•**PENNY, Mr. Keith, FCA** *1969;* Priory Practice Limited, 1 Abbots Quay, Monks Ferry, BIRKENHEAD, CH41 5LH.
PENNY, Mrs. Leanne Marie, BSc ACA *2010;* 22 Ffordd Bryngwyn, Garden Village Gorseinon, SWANSEA, SA4 4EB.
•**PENNY, Miss. Linda Jane, BA FCA** *1982;* Wilkins Kennedy, Bridge House, London Bridge, LONDON, SE1 9QR.
PENNY, Mr. Mark Andrew, LLB ACA ACIS *1990;* 20 Hollywell Road, Knowle, SOLIHULL, B93 9JY.
PENNY, Mr. Michael William Harrison, BA FCA *1978;* Pinnacle, 6 St. Andrew Street, LONDON, EC4A 3AE.
•**PENNY, Miss. Miranda Jane Comyns, BA ACA** *1991;* (Tax Fac), PK Partners LLP, 22 The Quadrant, RICHMOND, SURREY, TW9 1BP. See also PK Audit LLP
PENNY, Mr. Richard Ralph, BEng ACA *1995;* Jacques Vert Plc, 46 Colebrooke Row, Islington, LONDON, N1 8AF.
PENNY, Mr. Stephen Michael, BSc ACA *1995;* 34 Smith Street, ROZELLE, NSW 2039, AUSTRALIA.
•**PENNY, Mr. Stuart Paul, BSc ACA** *2007;* Priory Practice Limited, 1 Abbots Quay, Monks Ferry, BIRKENHEAD, CH41 5LH.
PENNY, Miss. Susan Jane, BSc ACA *1988;* 33 Chase Avenue, Walton Park, MILTON KEYNES, MK7 7HE.
PENNYCOOK, Mr. Andrew Victor, ACA *1980;* 9 Briary Lodge, 56 The Avenue, BECKENHAM, BR3 5ES.
PENNYCOOK, Ms. Felicity Ann, BSc ACA *1984;* Mount Pleasant, Shawford, WINCHESTER, HAMPSHIRE, SO21 2AA.
PENNYCOOK, Mr. Richard John, BSc FCA *1988;* York House, Hodgson Lane, Upper Poppleton, YORK, YO26 6EA.
PENNYCOOK, Mr. Stephen Robert, ACA *1978;* 21 Redwoods, ADDLESTONE, SURREY, KT15 1JN.
PENNYCUICK, Mr. James, BSc ACA *2005;* Flat 7 Chartwell Court, 151 Brook Road, LONDON, NW2 7DW.
PENOLLAR, Mrs. Caroline Rebecca, BSc ACA *1992;* 6 Uplands Way, Riverhead, SEVENOAKS, TN13 3BN.
PENPRAZE, Mr. Stephen Andrew, BSc ACA *1997;* 36 Kendrey Gardens, TWICKENHAM, TW2 7PA.
PENROSE, Mr. Antony John, FCA *1962;* 1 Hollinhurst Avenue, Penwortham, PRESTON, PR1 0AE.
PENROSE, Mr. David Alfred, FCA *1955;* Rosewood, 22 Ashdale Park, WOKINGHAM, RG40 3QS. (Life Member)
PENROSE, Mr. Duncan, BA FCA *1978;* 107 Shaftesbury Way, TWICKENHAM, TW2 5RW.
PENROSE, Mr. Ian Richard, BSc ACA *1990;* Sportech Plc, 101 Wigmore Street, LONDON, W1U 1QU.
PENROSE, Mr. John Barton, FCA *1960;* Springfield House, Mill Road, Shiplake, HENLEY-ON-THAMES, RG9 3LW. (Life Member)
PENROSE, Mr. John Stuart, FCA *1971;* Greencroft, 566 Loose Road, Loose, MAIDSTONE, ME15 9UR.
PENROSE, Mr. Noel Richard, ACA *1981;* Dunvegan House, The Street, Shurlock Row, READING, RG10 0PR.
PENRY, Mr. John Rhys, BEng ACA *2004;* The Mount, Old Blandford Road, SALISBURY, SP2 8BZ.
•**PENSON, Mr. Alan Anthony, MA FCA** *1979;* Penson & Penson Limited, Fairfield House, Dodds Lane, CHALFONT ST. GILES, BUCKINGHAMSHIRE, HP8 4EL.
PENSON, Mr. Christopher James, BA ACA *1991;* 46 Shenstone Drive, Balsall Common, COVENTRY, CV7 7PH.
PENTALIOTIS, Mr. Aristos, BSc(Hons) ACA *2011;* P.O Box 50476, LIMASSOL, CYPRUS.
PENTALIOTIS, Mr. Yiangos, BSc ACA *2005;* P.O.Box 50476, 3605 LIMASSOL, CYPRUS.
PENTARIS, Mr. Savvas, BA(Econ) ACA *2001;* 1A Ayiou Evdokimou Street, 2055 STROVOLOS, CYPRUS.
PENTECOST, Miss. Charlotte Alexis, ACA *2009;* TFF 117 Gladstone Road, LONDON, SW19 1QS.
PENTECOST, Mr. Michael John, FCA *1975;* Manor Barn, Stoney Stoke, WINCANTON, BA9 8HY.
PENTELOW, Mr. Adam, BSc ACA *2009;* Flat B, 66 Leander Road, LONDON, SW2 2LJ.
PENTELOW, Miss. Imogen, BSc ACA *2011;* 51 Wagtail Close, SWINDON, SN3 5BL.
•**PENTELOW, Mr. Lindsay Roy, BA FCA** *1979;* (Tax Fac), Mazars LLP, The Pinnacle, 160 Midsummer Boulevard, MILTON KEYNES, MK9 1FF.
PENTELOW, Mr. Richard John, FCA *1970;* 31 Ferney Road, East Barnet, BARNET, HERTFORDSHIRE, EN4 8LA.
PENTER, Mr. Graham Michael, BA(Hons) ACA CTA *2009;* 5 Holifast Road, SUTTON COLDFIELD, B72 1AP.
PENTER, Mrs. Laura Louise, ACA *2009;* 5 Holifast Road, SUTTON COLDFIELD, WEST MIDLANDS, B72 1AP.
PENTIN, Mr. David John, LLB FCA *1959;* 16 St. Dunstans Terrace, CANTERBURY, CT2 8AX. (Life Member)
PENTLAND, Mr. Andrew Douglas, FCA *1980;* 37 Gainsborough Drive, Adel, LEEDS, LS16 7PE.
PENTLAND, Mrs. Teresa Anne, BSc ACA *1997;* 16 Edge Hill Road, Four Oaks, SUTTON COLDFIELD, WEST MIDLANDS, B74 4NU.
PENTLOW, Miss. Barbara Ann, MA ACA *1981;* 14 Larkbere Road, Sydenham, LONDON, SE26 4HB.
PENTNEY, Miss. Fiona Elizabeth Jean, BA ACA *1992;* Credit Suisse, 1 Raffles Link, SINGAPORE 039393, SINGAPORE.
PENTREATH, Mrs. Melony Claire, BA ACA *2002;* 11 Grosvenor Road, MANCHESTER, M16 8JP.
•**PENWARDEN, Mr. Clive Andrew, BA ACA** *1981;* PricewaterhouseCoopers LLP, 7 More London Riverside, LONDON, SE1 2RT. See also PricewaterhouseCoopers
PEOPLES, Mr. Garvin Brain Andrew, ACA *2011;* 2/9 Comely Bank Street, EDINBURGH, EH4 1BD.
•**PEPLINSKI, Mr. Paul, ACA** *1991;* PricewaterhouseCoopers Sp. z o.o., Al.Armii Ludowej 14, WARSAW, 00638, POLAND.
•**PEPLINSKI, Mr. Thomas, MA MEng ACA** *2002;* Financial Support for Schools, High Trees, Ty'r Winch Road, Old St. Mellons, CARDIFF, CF3 5UW.
PEPLOW, Mr. Nicholas Mark, BSc ACA *2006;* 6 Honey Lane, Cholsey, WALLINGFORD, OXFORDSHIRE, OX10 9NL.
•**PEPLOW, Mr. Nicholas Robert, BA FCA** *1980;* (Tax Fac), N R Peplow & Co Ltd, 2nd Floor, 150 Upper New Walk, LEICESTER, LEICESTERSHIRE, LE1 7QA.
PEPPER, Mr. Alexander Anthony William, BA FCA FRSA *1985;* Bowers, 7 Semaphore Road, GUILDFORD, GU1 3PS.
•①**PEPPER, Mr. Andrew John, BA ACA** *1994;* Hilco UK Ltd, 80 New Bond Street, LONDON, W1S 1SB.
•**PEPPER, Mr. David Ian, FCA** *1963;* (Tax Fac), with BDO LLP, 125 Colmore Row, BIRMINGHAM, B3 3SD.
PEPPER, Mr. David William, FCA *1970;* Hollyshaw, 14 Wynmore Avenue, Bramhope, LEEDS, LS16 9DE.
PEPPER, Mr. Frank, FCA *1953;* 3a Ewhurst Avenue, SOUTH CROYDON, SURREY, CR2 0DH. (Life Member)
PEPPER, Mr. Harry William Terry, BA ACA *1994;* 21 Burrough Court, Burrough on the Hill, MELTON MOWBRAY, LEICESTERSHIRE, LE14 2QS.
PEPPER, Mr. John Douglas, FCA *1954;* Field House, 5 Wentworth Way, Hunmanby, FILEY, YO14 0LA. (Life Member)
PEPPER, Mr. Jonathan James, BA ACA *2001;* 11 Chapel Close, Houghton-on-the-Hill, LEICESTER, LE7 9HT.
PEPPER, Mrs. Manjit, ACA CTA *1998;* 56 School Lane, Husborne Crawley, BEDFORD, MK43 0UZ.
PEPPER, Mr. Mark Deville, BA ACA *1986;* Longfield Chemicals Ltd, Weaver House Ashville Point, Sutton Weaver, RUNCORN, CHESHIRE, WA7 3FW.
PEPPER, Mr. Mark Edward, BA ACA *1989;* 21 Kimbers Drive, Burnham, SLOUGH, SL1 8JE.
PEPPER, Mr. Mark Godfrey Terry, BSc ACA *1995;* Pollies Hall, Withyham Road, Groombridge, TUNBRIDGE WELLS, KENT, TN3 9QL.
PEPPER, Mr. Matthew, BA ACA *1996;* 56 School Lane, Husborne Crawley, BEDFORD, MK43 0UZ.
•**PEPPER, Mr. Richard Anthony, FCA ATII** *1980;* Richard A. Pepper, 8 Apple Tree Close, PONTEFRACT, WEST YORKSHIRE, WF8 4RH.
PEPPER, Mr. Richard Mark, BSc ACA *1991;* Building 26, Best Avenue, MOSMAN, NSW 2088, AUSTRALIA.
PEPPER, Mr. Rodney Thomas Leslie, FCA *1963;* 31 Venator Place, WIMBORNE, BH21 1DQ. (Life Member)
•**PEPPER, Mr. Steven Gary, FCA** *1983;* Allotts, Sidings Court, Lakeside, DONCASTER, SOUTH YORKSHIRE, DN4 5NU.
PEPPERALL, Mr. Brian Robert, FCA *1958;* Wick House, Wick St Lawrence, WESTON-SUPER-MARE, BS22 7YJ. (Life Member)
PEPPERDAY, Mr. Anthony, ACA *2010;* Furze House, Westbrook, GILLINGHAM, DORSET, SP8 5DT.
•**PEPPIATT, Mr. Glenn Alan, BA FCA** *1978;* 85 Violet Lane, CROYDON, CR0 4HL.
PEPPIN, Mr. Nigel Garth, FCA *1970;* La Guermondiere, 35720 ST PIERRE DE PLESGUEN, FRANCE. (Life Member)
PERA, Mr. Gianpaolo Antonio, ACA *2009;* Marwyn, 11 Buckingham Street, LONDON, WC2N 6DF.
PERALTA, Mr. David James Francis, BA ACA *1998;* 3 Rendcomb Drive, CIRENCESTER, GLOUCESTERSHIRE, GL7 1YN.
PERAMAL, Ms. Dhaivanaighee, BA ACA *2006;* 52a Stanley Road, LONDON, E18 2NS.
PERCHARD, Mr. Simon Richard, BA ACA *1994;* Templar House, Volaw Trust, JERSEY, JE1 2TR.
PERCHARD, Mr. William John, BSc FCA *1975;* Casa dos Carvalhos, Barao de S. Joao, 8600 013 LAGOS, PORTUGAL.
PERCIVAL, Mr. Alan Dereck, FCA *1965;* 8 Kent Drive, Oadby, LEICESTER, LE2 4PN. (Life Member)
PERCIVAL, Mr. Alan Lester, FCA CTA *1961;* Wards End Old Farm, Moggie Lane, Adlington, MACCLESFIELD, SK10 4NY. (Life Member)
PERCIVAL, Mr. Anthony Henry, FCA *1963;* Lower Hall, Mill Road, Foxearth, SUDBURY, SUFFOLK, CO10 7JF. (Life Member)
PERCIVAL, Mr. Brian Joseph, FCA *1958;* 9 Reigate Drive, Attenborough, NOTTINGHAM, NG9 6AX. (Life Member)
PERCIVAL, Mr. Christopher Tom, MA FCA *1963;* 15 Gilesgate, DURHAM, DH1 1QW. (Life Member)
PERCIVAL, Mr. David, BA(Hons) ACA CTA *2000;* The Laurels, Warden Law Lane, SUNDERLAND, SR3 2PD.
PERCIVAL, Mrs. Dawn, BSc(Hons) ACA *2001;* Inland Revenue Mersey Bank House, Barbauld Street, WARRINGTON, WA1 1WA.
PERCIVAL, Mr. Ian Campbell, BA ACA *1987;* 5 The Green, EPSOM, KT17 3JP.
PERCIVAL, Mr. James Alan, ACA *2008;* K P M G Alteus House, 1 North Fourth Street, MILTON KEYNES, MK9 1NE.
PERCIVAL, Mr. James Owen, BA ACA *1996;* Jumeirah Group, P.O. Box 214159, DUBAI, UNITED ARAB EMIRATES.
•**PERCIVAL, Mr. James William, FCA** *1965;* (Tax Fac), James Percival, The Old Orchard, Otford Lane, Halstead, SEVENOAKS, TN14 7EE.
PERCIVAL, Mr. Jonathan Clive, BSc ACA *1995;* 6 Honeybourne Road, LONDON, NW6 1JJ.
PERCIVAL, Mrs. Karen Nicola, ACA *1995;* 6 Fergusson Avenue, Craigburn Farm, BLACKWOOD, SA 5051, AUSTRALIA.
PERCIVAL, Mrs. Lesley Ann, BSc ACA *1987;* St. Georges Hill Lawn Tennis Club, Warreners Lane, WEYBRIDGE, SURREY, KT13 0LL.
•**PERCIVAL, Mr. Michael Edward, FCA** *1979;* Lomas & Co., 28a Hardwick Street, BUXTON, DERBYSHIRE, SK17 6DH.
PERCIVAL, Mr. Peter William Scott, BA FCA *1964;* 16 Roland Way, LONDON, SW7 3RE.
PERCIVAL, Mr. Richard David, BA ACA ATII *1983;* WWRD United Kingdom Ltd., Wedgwood Drive Barlaston, STOKE-ON-TRENT, STAFFORDSHIRE, ST12 9ER.
PERCIVAL, Mr. Richard John, BA ACA *1982;* Flat 8, 62 Gloucester Avenue, LONDON, NW1 8JD.
PERCIVAL, Miss. Ruth Hannah, BSc ACA *1998;* 1 Claude Road, MANCHESTER, M21 8BZ.
PERCIVAL, Miss. Sally Claire, ACA *2010;* Linklaters, 1 Silk Street, LONDON, EC2Y 8HQ.
PERCIVAL, Mrs. Susan, BSc ACA *1982;* Westra Lodge, 114 Kippington Road, SEVENOAKS, TN13 2LN.
PERCY, Mr. Andrew James, BA(Hons) ACA *2000;* Unit 25, Basepoint Business Centre, Rivermead Drive, Westlea, SWINDON, WILTSHIRE SN5 7EX.
PERCY, Mr. Andrew Robert, ACA *2008;* Grant Thornton, PO Box 1044, GEORGE TOWN, GRAND CAYMAN, KY1-1102, CAYMAN ISLANDS.
•**PERCY, Mr. Brian Eric, BA FCA** *1981;* Seligman Percy, Hilton House, Lord Street, STOCKPORT, SK1 3NA.
PERCY, Miss. Elizabeth Clare, BA(Hons) ACA *2001;* 25 Knighton Drive, WOODFORD GREEN, IG8 0NY.
PERCY, Mr. Gronw, BSc ACA *1991;* 29 The Oaks, Llantwit Fardre, PONTYPRIDD, CF38 2EB.
PERCY, Dr. Jacquelyn Dorothy Ann, ACA *1991;* 149 Hulverstone Drive, Avondale, CHRISTCHURCH, NEW ZEALAND.
PERCY, Mr. James Crothers Habgood, MSc(Econ) ACA *2001;* 76 Cassiobury Drive, WATFORD, WD17 3AQ.
PERCY, Mr. John Graham, BSc ACA *1986;* Ungerer Ltd, Sealand Road, CHESTER, CH1 4LP.
PERCY, Mr. Mark Antony, LLB ACA *2006;* Ernst & Young Llp, 1 More London Place, LONDON, SE1 2AF.
PERCY, Mr. Mark Richard, BA ACA *1992;* Seymour Pierce Limited, 20 Old Bailey, LONDON, EC4M 7EN.
PERCY, Mr. Michael Hugh, FCA *1972;* Fortis Lease UK Limited, 5 Aldermanbury Square, LONDON, EC2V 7HR.
•**PERCY, Mr. Richard Charles St John, FCA** *1969;* Richard Percy Limited, Sandhills Farm, Braintree Road, Wethersfield, BRAINTREE, ESSEX CM7 4AG.
PERCY, Mr. Timothy John, ACA *1992;* 29 Tollhouse Way, Wombourne, WOLVERHAMPTON, STAFFORDSHIRE, WV5 8AF.
PERCY-ROBB, Mr. Michael Iain, BSc ACA *1990;* 159 Glen Park Ave, TORONTO M6B 2C8, ON, CANADA.
PERDEAUX, Mr. William, FCA *1966;* 42 Willow Green, INGATESTONE, ESSEX, CM4 0DQ.
PERDESI, Miss. Snita, BA ACA *1999;* Flat 11, Galleons View, 1 Stewart Street, LONDON, E14 3EX.
PERDONI, Mr. Giuseppe, BA ACA *1992;* The Old Coach House, 295 Waldegrave Road, TWICKENHAM, TW1 4SU.
PERDONI, Mr. Jonathan Talbot, ACA *2009;* 44 The Avenue, WEST WICKHAM, KENT, BR4 0DY.
•**PERDONI, Mr. Lino, FCA** *1990;* Hill Wooldridge & Co Limited, 107 Hindes Road, HARROW, MIDDLESEX, HA1 1RU.
PEREI, Mrs. Anna Margaret, BSc ACA *1998;* Old Blacknest Cottage Chiddingfold Road, Dunsfold, GODALMING, GU8 4PB.
PEREI, Mr. William Richard, BA ACA *1998;* Perei Group Ltd Sunbury House, 4 Christy Estate Ivy Road, ALDERSHOT, HAMPSHIRE, GU12 4TX.
PEREIRA, Mr. Alan Dennis, FCA *1975;* Santon Development Plc, 1st Floor, 21 Knightsbridge, LONDON, SW1X 7LY.
PEREIRA, Mr. Anthony Charles, BA ACA *1986;* 1st Floor Lot 6, Jalan 225 Section 51A, 46100 PETALING JAYA, MALAYSIA.
PEREIRA, Miss. Carol Ann, BA ACA *1989;* H Bauer Publishing Academic House, 24-28 Oval Road, LONDON, NW1 7DT.
PEREIRA, Mrs. Deborah Ann, BSc ACA *1990;* Tulbinger Kogel 60, Mauerbach, 3001 VIENNA, AUSTRIA.
PEREIRA, Mr. Dennis, FCA *1981;* 7 Lullington Garth, Woodside Park, LONDON, N12 7LT.
PEREIRA, Mr. Desmond Cajetan, BSc FCA *1989;* Apartment 19, 4 Maida Vale, LONDON, W9 1SP.
PEREIRA, Mr. Francis Richard, BSc FIA FCA *1997;* Flat 17 Westfield, 15 Kidderpore Avenue, Hampstead, LONDON, NW3 7SF.

PEREIRA, Mrs. Janice Belinda, MSc ACA *1996;* (Tax Fac), 780 Kenton Lane, HARROW, HA3 6AF.
PEREIRA, Mr. Keith, BSc ACA *2004;* 5c Queens Avenue, LONDON, N10 3PE.
PEREIRA, Mr. Lionel Ignatius Mathew, BCom ACA FCCA *2007;* 9 Oxford Avenue, Southgate, LONDON, N14 5AF.
PEREIRA, Miss. Maria-Elena, ACA *2010;* 140 Aldborough Road South, ILFORD, IG3 8HA.
PEREIRA, Mr. Rommel Philip, BSc ACA *1987;* Financial Services Compensation Scheme Ltd Lloyds Chambers, 1 Portsoken Street, LONDON, E1 8BN.
PEREIRA, Mr. Sean Steve, BSc(Econ) ACA *2001;* Flat 2, 56 Onslow Gardens, LONDON, SW7 3QA.
PEREIRA, Miss. Valentina Ann, ACA *1993;* 125 Paremoremo Road, Lucas Heights, NORTH SHORE CITY 0632, NEW ZEALAND.
•PEREIRA, Mr. Vivian Ambrose, BSc ACA *1985;* Deloitte LLP, Hill House, 1 Little New Street, LONDON, EC4A 3TR. See also Deloitte & Touche LLP
PERERA, Ms. Antalene Kushalani, ACA ACMA *1992;* Accounting, Peel District School Board, 5650 Hurontario Street, MISSISSAUGA L5R 1C6, ON, CANADA.
PERERA, Mr. Brandon Jayalath, FCA *1963;* (Tax Fac), Barham, Courtmead Road, Cuckfield, HAYWARDS HEATH, RH17 5LP.
PERERA, Mrs. Chanika Janitri, LLM ACA *2001;* Merrill Lynch Japan, Nihonbashi, 1 Chome Building, 1-4-1 Nihonbashi, Chuo Ku, TOKYO 103 8230 JAPAN.
PERERA, Miss. Dissanayakege Dilshara Prescila Trianka, ACA *2008;* Flat 8, Hertford Court, 45 Falcon Road, LONDON, SW11 2PH.
PERERA, Mr. Francis Gerard, ACA *1985;* (Tax Fac), Bramlyns, Colchester Road, Ardleigh, COLCHESTER, CO7 7NS.
PERERA, Mr. Joseph Lalith Thomas, ACA *2011;* 25 Elizabeth House, Exeter Close, WATFORD, WD24 4RE.
PERERA, Mr. Melvin Ralph, FCA *1965;* 4 Broke Court, GUILDFORD, SURREY, GU4 7HQ.
PERERA, Mr. Nalin Chrysantha, FCA *1967;* 32 Lofthouse Square, SCARBOROUGH M1W 2E2, ON, CANADA.
PERERA, Miss. Nirosha, BSc ACA *2007;* Deloitte & Touche, 2 New Street Square, LONDON, EC4A 3BZ.
PERERA, Mr. Osmund, FCA *1964;* 7 View Avenue, Langford, PERTH, WA 6147, AUSTRALIA.
PERERA, Miss. Renuka Bhadra, BSc(Hons) ACA *2001;* 105 Longmore Avenue, BARNET, HERTFORDSHIRE, EN5 1JU.
•PERERA, Mrs. Rohini Varuna, FCA *1970;* Mrs R V Perera, 484 Bideford Green, LEIGHTON BUZZARD, BEDFORDSHIRE, LU7 2TZ.
PERERA, Mr. Sanjiva, BSc(Econ) ACA *1999;* Flat 5 Princes House, 52 Kensington Park Road, LONDON, W11 3BN.
PERERA, Mr. Shamindra, BSc ACA *2007;* 7 Larch Close, LONDON, SW12 9SU.
PERERA, Mr. Terence Senaka, BA FCA *1994;* 10 Wheeler Avenue, OXTED, RH8 9LE.
PERERA, Miss. Visaka, BA ACA *2000;* Flat 6, Summerfield, 3 Freelands Road, BROMLEY, BR1 3AG.
PEREZ, Mr. Alfonso, ACA *1984;* 71 Heversham Road, BEXLEYHEATH, DA7 5BH.
•PEREZ, Mr. Lyndon Russell, FCA *1991;* RDP Newmans LLP, Lynwood House, 373/375 Station Road, HARROW, MIDDLESEX, HA1 2AW.
•PEREZ, Mr. Robert Barry, BA FCA *1988;* Silver Levene LLP, 37 Warren Street, LONDON, W1T 6AD.
PERFECT, Mr. Patrick Nicholas, BSc ACA *1992;* C/Candelero 4 16, El Ancla, El Puerto de Santa Maria, 11500 CADIZ, SPAIN.
•PERFITT, Mr. Angus John, BSc FCA *1986;* Perfitt Consultants Limited, Cornet Street, St. Peter Port, GUERNSEY, GY1 1LF.
PERHAM, Mr. John Nicholas, BA ACA *1982;* 139 Templeogue Road, Terenure, DUBLIN 6, COUNTY DUBLIN, IRELAND.
PERIASAMY, Mr. Raja Rajan, BSc ACA *2009;* 96 Jalan Setiabakti 9, Bukit Damansara, 50490 KUALA LUMPUR, FEDERAL TERRITORY, MALAYSIA.
PERINAYEGON, Mr. Clement Jayson, ACA CA(AUS) *2011;* Allmand Jones & Partners, 7/459 Collins Street, MELBOURNE, VIC 3000, AUSTRALIA.
PERINPANAYAGAM, Miss. Roshini, BSc ACA CTA *1994;* (Tax Fac), with PricewaterhouseCoopers LLP, Marlborough Court, 10 Bricket Road, ST. ALBANS, HERTFORDSHIRE, AL1 3JX.
PERIS, Ms. Ingrid Martha, BSc ACA *1993;* NAB, 500 Bourne Street, MELBOURNE, VIC 3000, AUSTRALIA.
•PERITON, Mr. Noel Macdonald, FCA *1971;* Noel M. Periton, 14 Claremont Avenue, ESHER, KT10 9JD.
PERIYAN, Mrs. Barbara Mary, BA ACA *1980;* 55 Buckingham Road, Heaton Moor, STOCKPORT, SK4 4RB.
PERIYASAMY, Mr. Krishnan, ACA *1983;* 19 Jalan 13/70A, Sri Hartamas, Off Jalan Duta 50480, KUALA LUMPUR, FEDERAL TERRITORY, MALAYSIA.
•PERKIN, Mr. Adam Richard North, FCA *1985;* Jolliffe Cork LLP, 33 George Street, WAKEFIELD, WEST YORKSHIRE, WF1 1LX. See also Jolliffe Cork Consulting Limited
PERKIN, Mrs. Frances Janet, BSc FCA *1977;* Bryaton Cottage Morwenstow, BUDE, CORNWALL, EX23 9SU.
PERKIN, Mr. James, BMus ACA DChA *2005;* 13 Craven Close, Gomersal, CLECKHEATON, BD19 4QZ.
PERKIN, Mr. Jeremy Nicholas Gilbert, BSc(Hons) ACA *2001;* 63 Orchard Road West, MANCHESTER, M22 4FD.
•PERKIN, Mr. Leon Melvin, FCA *1983;* (Tax Fac), Ballards Newman (Finchley) Limited, Apex House, Grand Arcade, Tally Ho Corner, LONDON, N12 0EH.
PERKIN, Mrs. Lynn Worth, BCom ACA *1987;* 8 Green Lane, Netherton, WAKEFIELD, WF4 4JD.
PERKIN, Mr. Roger Kitson, MA FCA *1974;* Hickens, Bore Place Lane, Chiddingstone, EDENBRIDGE, TN8 7AP.
PERKINS, Mr. Alexander Laurence, BA(Hons) ACA *2001;* 104 Lonsdale Drive, Rainham, GILLINGHAM, KENT, ME8 9HZ.
PERKINS, Mr. Andrew Keith, ACA *2009;* Flat 2105, Ontario Tower, 4 Fairmont Avenue, LONDON, E14 9JD.
•PERKINS, Mr. Anthony John, BA FCA *1983;* BDO LLP, 55 Baker Street, LONDON, W1U 7EU. See also BDO Stoy Hayward LLP
PERKINS, Mr. Anthony William, FCA *1952;* Cobwebs, 30 The Orchard, Milford-on-Sea, LYMINGTON, SO41 0SR. (Life Member)
PERKINS, Mr. Brendan Mark, MSc BA ACA *2010;* 18 Gambole Road, LONDON, SW17 0QJ.
•PERKINS, Mr. Brian Kenneth, FCA *1965;* Brian Perkins FCA, 11 Ilmington Close, Hatton Park, WARWICK, CV35 7TL.
PERKINS, Miss. Cara, BSc ACA *2011;* 8 Staunton Close, Castle Donington, DERBY, DE74 2XA.
PERKINS, Mrs. Caroline Anne, BSc ACA *1989;* 15 Birches Close, EPSOM, SURREY, KT18 5JG.
•PERKINS, Mrs. Caroline Helen, BA ACA *1986;* Perkins & Co, 20 Taylor Avenue, Kew, RICHMOND, TW9 4ED.
•PERKINS, Mrs. Catherine Ann, BA ACA *1991;* RJ & CA Perkins, Clemenstone Court, Clemenstone, COWBRIDGE, CF71 7PZ.
PERKINS, Miss. Cathryn Llywella, BA ACA *1994;* Specsavers Optical Group Ltd, La Villiaze Road, St. Andrew, GUERNSEY, GY6 8YP.
PERKINS, Mr. Charles Richard Ingram, BSc ACA *1992;* 11C Dragon View, 39 MAcdonnell Rd, MID LEVELS, HONG KONG SAR.
•PERKINS, Mr. Christopher Ashley, FCA *1972;* 7 Oakwood Avenue, BECKENHAM, BR3 6PT.
PERKINS, Mr. Christopher Matthew Harwood, ACA *1999;* 4 Grosvenor Place, LONDON, SW1X 7DL.
PERKINS, Mr. Daniel Kenneth James, ACA *2008;* 10 Berriedale Avenue, HOVE, EAST SUSSEX, BN3 4JH.
PERKINS, Mr. David Anthony, BA FCA *1979;* 10 Albion Place, NORTHAMPTON, NN1 1UD. (Life Member)
•PERKINS, Mr. David John, FCA *1977;* with John Swire & Sons Ltd, Swire House, 59 Buckingham Gate, LONDON, SW1E 6AJ.
PERKINS, Mr. David William, FCA *1972;* Flat 8, 24 Lowndes Square, LONDON, SW1X 9HE.
PERKINS, Mrs. Eloise Mary, BA(Hons) ACA *2002;* 51 Aranda Drive, DAVIDSON, NSW 2085, AUSTRALIA.
PERKINS, Mrs. Gail Danielle, MA ACA CTA *1991;* 1 White Hall Close, Somersham, HUNTINGDON, PE28 3EA.
PERKINS, Mr. Geoffrey, FCA *1962;* Foxleas, Main Street, Oxton, SOUTHWELL, NG25 0SD.
PERKINS, Mrs. Giovanna, MMath ACA *2010;* Pricewaterhousecoopers, 1 Embankment Place, LONDON, WC2N 6RH.
PERKINS, Miss. Jane Lesley, BSc ACA *1996;* 4 Dulverton Road, LEICESTER, LE3 0SA.
•PERKINS, Mr. John, FCA *1955;* Lithgow Perkins LLP, Crown Chambers, Princes Street, HARROGATE, HG1 1NJ.
PERKINS, Mr. John Anthony, ACA CA(SA) *2010;* Leadwood, 58 Cranley Road, Burwood Park, WALTON-ON-THAMES, SURREY, KT12 5BS.
PERKINS, Mr. John Basil, FCA *1954;* Richmond, Church Lane, Hagworthingham, SPILSBY, PE23 4LP. (Life Member)
PERKINS, Mr. John Douglas, BSc ACA *1998;* Le Rocher Le Gele Road, Castel, GUERNSEY, GY5 7LR.
PERKINS, Mr. John Michael, BSc ACA *1986;* (Tax Fac), Hazlems Fenton Palladium House, 1-4 Argyll Street, LONDON, W1F 7LD.
PERKINS, Mr. John Newitt, FCA *1959;* 85 Conifer Rise, Westone, NORTHAMPTON, NN3 3JY. (Life Member)
PERKINS, Mr. John Robert, FCA *1975;* 46 Broadway Avenue, HALESOWEN, B63 3DF.
•PERKINS, Mr. John Robert Hugh, FCA *1974;* Financial Direction, Unit 1C, Membury Logistics Centre, Ramsbury Road, Lambourn Woodlands, HUNGERFORD BERKSHIRE RG17 7TJ.
PERKINS, Mr. John Travers, FCA *1964;* 11 Merlin Court, Bembridge Gardens, RUISLIP, HA4 7EU. (Life Member)
PERKINS, Mr. Jonathan, BA ACA *2004;* 23 Galesbury Road, LONDON, SW18 2RL.
PERKINS, Miss. Katie Samantha, ACA *2009;* 58 Marshalls Road, Raunds, WELLINGBOROUGH, NORTHAMPTONSHIRE, NN9 6EU.
•PERKINS, Mr. Kevin Mark, FCA CTA *1987;* (Tax Fac), Deighan Perkins LLP, 6th Floor, Newbury House, 890-900 Eastern Avenue, ILFORD, ESSEX IG2 7HH.
PERKINS, Mrs. Louise, BA ACA *2003;* The Royal Bank of Scotland Plc, 280 Bishopsgate, LONDON, EC2M4RB.
PERKINS, Mr. Malcolm Courtney, FCA *1966;* Camellia Plc, Linton Park, Linton, MAIDSTONE, KENT, ME17 4AB.
PERKINS, Mr. Mark, BSc ACA *1991;* A2 Roqueville, 20 Blvd. Princesse Charlotte, MONTE CARLO, MC98000, MONACO.
•PERKINS, Mr. Martyn George, FCA *1972;* Martyn G Perkins, 166 Portland Street, SOUTHPORT, MERSEYSIDE, PR8 6RB.
•PERKINS, Mr. Matthew David, BA ACA *1998;* Deloitte LLP, 4 Brindley Place, BIRMINGHAM, B1 2HZ. See also Deloitte & Touche LLP
PERKINS, Mr. Michael Alan, FCA *1965;* Mandeville House, Cirencester Road, Minchinhampton, STROUD, GL6 9EQ.
PERKINS, Mr. Nicholas Michael, BD ACA ATII *1995;* Flat 1, 46 Islington Park Street, LONDON, N1 1PX.
•PERKINS, Mr. Richard Clive, FCA *1966;* (Tax Fac), Brookfield Realisation Ltd, 50 Brookfield Close, Hunt End, REDDITCH, WORCESTERSHIRE, B97 5LL.
•PERKINS, Mr. Richard Jonathan, BSc ACA *1987;* RJ & CA Perkins, Clemenstone Court, Clemenstone, COWBRIDGE, CF71 7PZ.
PERKINS, Mr. Rob Charles Arthur, BEng FCA CA(NZ) *1998;* Fisher & Paykel Appliances Limited, PO Box 58546, Botany, MANUKAU 2163, NEW ZEALAND.
PERKINS, Mr. Robert George, FCA *1972;* Les Corneilles Clos Des Grandes Mielles, Rue De La Ronde Cheminee, Castel, GUERNSEY, GY5 7GD. (Life Member)
PERKINS, Mr. Robert James, BSc ACA *2006;* 55 Birches Park Road, Codsall, WOLVERHAMPTON, WV8 2DT.
PERKINS, Mr. Roddy Trevor, BSc(Econ) ACA *1996;* 57 Sefton Road, WESTLEIGH, NSW 2120, AUSTRALIA.
PERKINS, Mr. Roger James, BSc FCA *1987;* Great Gables, Elm Close, Farnham Common, SLOUGH, SL2 3NA.
PERKINS, Mr. Russell John, BSc FCA *1977;* Apartment 2 Northcliffe House, Northfield Road, MINEHEAD, SOMERSET, TA24 5QH.
PERKINS, Mrs. Sarah Jane, BSc(Hons) ACA *2004;* 3 Upper Bere Wood, WATERLOOVILLE, HAMPSHIRE, PO7 7HX.
•PERKINS, Mrs. Sarah Jane, BA FCA CTA *1987;* Stoneleigh, Asenby, THIRSK, YO7 3QN.
PERKINS, Mr. Simon, BSc ACA *1992;* 39 Chancery Lane, #01-08 Villa Chancery, SINGAPORE 309568, SINGAPORE.
•PERKINS, Mr. Simon Donald, ACA *1988;* 23 Daphne Close, Great Notley, BRAINTREE, ESSEX, CM77 7YZ.
PERKINS, Mr. Simon Rhys, MA FCA *1990;* Flat 4, 24 Emerson Square, BRISTOL, BS7 0PP.
PERKINS, Mr. Stephen Edward, BSc(Hons) ACA *2000;* Mill House Cottage, The Street, Shalford, GUILDFORD, SURREY, GU4 8BS.
PERKINS, Mr. Thomas Daniel, BA ACA *2005;* Carteret 6 Portelet Drive, La Route de Noirmont St. Brelade, JERSEY, JE3 8JY.
PERKINS, Mr. Thomas Lee, BA(Hons) ACA *2004;* Hawthorn Church Road, Mersham, ASHFORD, TN25 6NS.
PERKINS, Mr. Timothy Richard, BA ACA *1997;* Man Group Plc Sugar Quay, Lower Thames Street, LONDON, EC3R 6DU.
•PERKS, Mr. Alan Trevor, BSc FCA *1988;* (Tax Fac), ATP Associates Limited, 7 Upper Aston, Claverley, WOLVERHAMPTON, WV5 7EE.
PERKS, Mr. Andrew Raymond, BSc ACA *1990;* Mizuho Corporate Bank, Bracken House, 1 Friday Street, LONDON, EC4M 9BT.
PERKS, Miss. Charlene Alison, ACA *2009;* Flat 3, 192 Hartfield Road, LONDON, SW19 3TQ.
•PERKS, Mr. Duncan Christopher, MSc FCA *1984;* Old Mill Accountancy LLP, The Old Rectory, South Walks Road, DORCHESTER, DORSET, DT1 1DT. See also Old Mill Audit LLP
PERKS, Mrs. Elizabeth Caroline, LLB ACA *2000;* with Ernst & Young LLP, 1 More London Place, LONDON, SE1 2AF.
PERKS, Mr. Ian Stephen James, BA ACA *1989;* Braeside, 103 Padfield Main Road, Padfield, GLOSSOP, SK13 1ET.
PERKS, Mr. Martin Vincent, BA ACA *1995;* PO Box 23287, House no.1, Valhalla Compound, Msasani Peninsula, DAR ES SALAAM, TANZANIA.
PERKS, Mr. Michael Leslie, BSc FCA *1979;* Riverview, The Strand, Lympstone, EXMOUTH, DEVON, EX8 5EY.
PERKS, Miss. Michaela Vivien, ACA *1992;* 69 Penrice Park, ST AUSTELL, CORNWALL, PL25 3NA.
PERKS, Mr. Peter John, MSc FCA *1959;* 2 Pearman Court, Singleton, CHICHESTER, WEST SUSSEX, PO18 0HB. (Life Member)
PERKS, Mr. Timothy Howard, BA ACA *1990;* Bowdown Farm, 40 Burys Bank Road, Greenham, THATCHAM, RG19 8DA.
•PERLIN, Mr. Howard Stephen, FCA *1970;* Howard Perlin, 66 Hawtrey Road, LONDON, NW3 3SS.
•PERLIN, Mr. Paul Leslie, FCA *1973;* (Tax Fac), Perlin Franco Ltd, Trojan House, 34 Arcadia Avenue, LONDON, N3 2JU.
PERLSTEIN, Mr. Pinkus, FCA FTII *1970;* 7 Moundfield Road, LONDON, N16 6DT.
PERMAL, Mrs. Bianca Gail, BSc(Hons) ACA *2003;* 34 Egerton Road, BERKHAMSTED, HERTFORDSHIRE, HP4 1DU.
PERMAL, Mr. Jaysen, BSc(Hons) ACA *2004;* 34 Egerton Road, BERKHAMSTED, HERTFORDSHIRE, HP4 1DU.
PERMAL, Mr. Rukshan, ACA *2008;* 29 Horseshoes Way, Brampton, HUNTINGDON, CAMBRIDGESHIRE, PE28 4TN.
PEROS, Miss. Helene, BSc ACA *2002;* Sega Europe Ltd, 27 Great West Road, BRENTFORD, TW8 9BW.
PEROTTI, Mr. Michael, ACA *1990;* Falcon Money Management, Beazley, 60 Great Tower Street, LONDON, EC3R 5AD.
PEROTTI, Ms. Paola, BSc ACA *1989;* 31 Canonbury Park North, LONDON, N1 2JU.
PERRAS, Miss. Gisele Huguette Martine, ACA *1988;* 22 Drayton Green, West Ealing, LONDON, W13 0JF.
PERREN, Mr. Ambros, FCA *1954;* Neuhausstrasse 17, 8044 ZURICH, SWITZERLAND. (Life Member)
PERREN, Mr. Brett, ACA CA(AUS) *2008;* 31 Van Gogh Court, Amsterdam Road, LONDON, E14 3UY.
PERREN, Mr. Paul Alexander, BSc FCA *1992;* 121 Discovery Drive, Kings Hill, WEST MALLING, ME19 4DS.
•PERREN, Mr. Richard Stuart, FCA *1984;* RPFCA Limited, The Counting House, 22 Bellrope Meadow, Thaxted, DUNMOW, ESSEX CM6 2FE.
PERRENS, Mr. Gary John, BA ACA *1993;* Westway Spicers Lane, Long Melford, SUDBURY, SUFFOLK, CO10 9JJ.
PERRET DU CRAY, Mrs. Florence, ACA *2002;* Isenhurst House, Isenhurst, Cross in Hand, HEATHFIELD, EAST SUSSEX, TN21 0TQ.
•PERRETT, Mr. Andrew Robert, BSc FCA *1986;* BDO LLP, 2 City Place, Beehive Ring Road, GATWICK, WEST SUSSEX, RH6 0PA. See also BDO Stoy Hayward LLP
•PERRETT, Mr. Darrell Russell, FCA *1971;* Russell & Co, 50 Bridge Road, Litherland, LIVERPOOL, L21 6PH.
•PERRETT, Mr. Michael Edward James, FCA *1981;* with BWCI Group, Albert House, South Esplanade, St. Peter Port, GUERNSEY, GY1 1AW.
PERRETT, Mr. Michael William Welford, MA FCA *1963;* 38 Crescent Road, Hale, ALTRINCHAM, CHESHIRE, WA15 9NA.
PERRETT, Mr. Peter William Russell, FCA *1960;* 28 Broadpark Road, Livermead, TORQUAY, TQ2 6UP.
PERRIAM, Miss. Andrea, BA ACA *1997;* AIG Building, 2-8 Altyre Road, CROYDON, SURREY, CR9 2LG.
•PERRIAM, Mr. Andrew John, BSc FCA CF DChA *1989;* (Tax Fac), Rothman Pantall LLP, Fryern House, 125 Winchester Road, Chandler's Ford, EASTLEIGH, HAMPSHIRE SO53 2DR.
PERRIAM, Mr. Christopher Paul, FCA *1957;* Sea of Pebbles, Madliena Hill, BAHAR LC-CAGHAQ, MALTA. (Life Member)
PERRIAM, Miss. Julia Samantha, BA ACA *1999;* 3 Highcroft Court, EXETER, EX4 4RW.
PERRIAM, Mr. Lee Martin, BSc ACA *1992;* 46 Carlton Road West, WESTGATE-ON-SEA, CT8 8PL.

PERRICOS, Mrs. Katherine Mary, MA ACA *1997;* 18 Trebor Avenue, FARNHAM, SURREY, GU9 8JH.
PERRIE, Mr. James Miller, BAcc CA *2007;* Fairfield House, 8 Brampton Road, Bramhall, STOCKPORT, CHESHIRE, SK7 3BS.
PERRIE, Mr. Martin William, ACA *2000;* BP Plc, The ICBT, Chertsey Road, SUNBURY-ON-THAMES, MIDDLESEX, TW16 7LN.
PERRIGO, Miss. Jillian, MBA ACA *1983;* PO Box 213820, DUBAI, UNITED ARAB EMIRATES.
PERRIMAN, Miss. Katherine, BSc ACA *2011;* Flat 7, 7 Eaton Cresent, Clifton, BRISTOL, BS8 2EJ.
PERRIN, Mr. Adrian Edward, FCA *1974;* PO BOX 0084, GLEN ERASMIA, KEMPTON PARK, GAUTENG, 1638, SOUTH AFRICA.
•**PERRIN, Mr. Andrew William, BA(Hons) FCA MCIArb** *1985;* 10 College Green, EASTBOURNE, EAST SUSSEX, BN21 2JT.
PERRIN, Mr. Barry Peter, BSc FCA AMCT *1989;* Balfour Beatty Ltd, 130 Wilton Road, LONDON, SW1V 1LQ.
PERRIN, Mr. John Stephen, MA FCA *1967;* Glebe House, South Tawton, OKEHAMPTON, EX20 2LJ. (Life Member)
•**PERRIN, Mr. Jonathan Paul, FCA CTA** *1980;* with RSM Tenon Audit Limited, 66 Chiltern Street, LONDON, W1U 4JT.
•**PERRIN, Mr. Mark Andrew, FCA** *1994;* Menzies LLP, Wentworth House, 4400 Parkway, Whiteley, FAREHAM, HAMPSHIRE PO15 7FJ.
PERRIN, Mr. Mark David, BA(Hons) ACA *2000;* The Order of St. John Care Trust, 11 Wellingore Hall Wellingore, LINCOLN, LN5 0HX.
PERRIN, Mr. Martin Henry Withers, MA ACA *1978;* 39 Station Road, THAMES DITTON, KT7 0PA.
PERRIN, Mr. Nicholas John, BA FCA *1986;* Treboro House Henley Road, Ullenhall, HENLEY-IN-ARDEN, B95 5NN.
PERRIN, Ms. Patricia Anne, BA ACA *1990;* Kidney Research UK Nene Hall, Peterborough Business Park Lynch Wood, PETERBOROUGH, PE2 6FZ.
PERRIN, Mr. Ross, BSc(Hons) ACA *2011;* 39 Station Road, THAMES DITTON, SURREY, KT7 0PA.
PERRIN, Ms. Sarah Jane, BA ACA *1993;* 92 Leander Road, LONDON, SW2 2LJ.
PERRIN, Mr. Stephen Charles, BCom ACA *1986;* Syngenta CP Ltd, CPC 4, Capital Park, Fulbourn, CAMBRIDGE, CB21 5XE.
PERRIN, Miss. Victoria, ACA *2010;* 1D, Claremont Avenue, CAMBERLEY, GU15 2DR.
PERRING, Mr. Antony William, BSc ACA *1993;* Bishops Cottage, Ginge, WANTAGE, OX12 8QR.
PERRING, Ms. Rowena Mary, BA ACA *1992;* The Rectory, Station Road, Pulham Market, DISS, NORFOLK, IP21 4TE.
PERRING, Mrs. Victoria Caroline, BA ACA *1993;* Bishops Cottage, Ginge, WANTAGE, OX12 8QR.
PERRINS, Mr. John Neville, FCA *1957;* (Tax Fac), 20 Blundell Drive, Birkdale, SOUTHPORT, PR8 4RG. (Life Member)
PERRINS, Mr. Matthew Frederick, BSc ACA *1999;* 5 Bridgewater Mews, Pandy, WREXHAM, CLWYD, LL12 8EQ.
PERRINS, Miss. Nicole Michelle, ACA *2007;* 420 Queslett Road, BIRMINGHAM, B43 7EL.
PERRINS, Mr. Robert, BSc ACA *1992;* Runnymede, Sandpit Hall Road, Chobham, WOKING, SURREY, GU24 8AN.
PERRINS, Miss. Sian, BA(Hons) ACA *2011;* Flat 15, Charcroft Court, Minford Gardens, LONDON, W14 0BX.
PERRINS, Mr. Timothy John Richard, BA ACA *1991;* The Beehive, City Place, Beehive Ring Road, London Gatwick Airport, GATWICK, WEST SUSSEX RH6 0PA.
PERRIS, Mr. John Derek, LLB ACA MCT *1991;* 83 Swan Avenue, BINGLEY, WEST YORKSHIRE, BD16 3PL.
PERROQUIN, Mrs. Karine, ACA *2000;* Bastadveien 95, 1387 ASKER, NORWAY.
PERROTT, Mr. Andrew Christopher, ACA MAAT *2005;* with Monahans, 38-42 Newport Street, SWINDON, SN1 3DR.
PERROTT, Mr. Donald Christopher, BSocSc ACA *2000;* 78 Fawe Park Road, Putney, LONDON, SW15 2EA.
PERROTT, Mr. Graham Laurence, BA FCA *1964;* Wood Royde, Sutcliffe Wood Lane, HALIFAX, WEST YORKSHIRE, HX3 8PS. (Life Member)
PERROTT, Mr. Hugh Richard Iliff, FCA *1969;* Gilletts Farm Oast, Water Lane, Smarden, ASHFORD, KENT, TN27 8QB.
PERROTT, Miss. Jennifer Elizabeth, MA(Hons) ACA *2000;* Harbourside, 10 Canons Way, BRISTOL, AVON, BS1 5LF.
PERROTT, Mrs. Julie Louise, ACA *2007;* 21 Salop Street, PENARTH, SOUTH GLAMORGAN, CF64 1HH.
PERROTT, Mr. Nicholas Edward John, BCom ACA *1995;* 1 Manor Cottage, Main Street Farrington Gurney, BRISTOL, BS39 6UB.
PERROTT, Mrs. Susan Caroline, BA(Hons) ACA *2001;* 1 Manor Cottages, Main Street, Farrington Gurney, BRISTOL, BS39 6UB.
PERRY, Mr. Adrian, BSc FCA *1986;* Daily Mail & General Trust, Northcliffe House, 2 Derry Street, LONDON, W8 5TT.
PERRY, Mr. Alan James, FCA *1967;* 29 King Edward's Road, South Woodham Ferrers, CHELMSFORD, CM3 5PQ.
PERRY, Mr. Alexander, BA ACA *2007;* 10 Pagoda Grove, LONDON, SE27 9BA.
PERRY, Mr. Andrew Bell, BA ACA *2001;* 46 Virginia Gardens, Great Sankey, WARRINGTON, WA5 8WN.
PERRY, Mrs. Anke, BSc ACA *2007;* 26 Mountfield Road, TUNBRIDGE WELLS, KENT, TN1 1SG.
PERRY, Miss. Anna, ACA *2011;* 20 Ramsthorn Grove, Walnut Tree, MILTON KEYNES, MK7 7ND.
PERRY, Miss. Carole Anne, BSc ACA *1994;* with PricewaterhouseCoopers LLP, 9 Greyfriars Road, READING, RG1 1JG.
PERRY, Miss. Caroline, BSc ACA *1994;* Finance, University of Bradford, Richmond Road, BRADFORD, WEST YORKSHIRE, BD7 1DP.
PERRY, Mr. Charles, MA ACA *2006;* Flat A, 3 Stockwell Terrace, LONDON, SW9 0QD.
PERRY, Mr. Christopher James, MEng ACA *2001;* Lapicida (SP) Ltd, St James Business Park, Grimbald Crag Close, KNARESBOROUGH, NORTH YORKSHIRE, HG5 8PJ.
PERRY, Mr. Christopher John, FCA *1973;* 30 Riverside Court, BIDEFORD, DEVON, EX39 2RZ.
PERRY, Mr. Christopher John, BSc(Hons) ACA *2002;* 54 Pine Grove, Brookmans Park, HATFIELD, HERTFORDSHIRE, AL9 7BW.
•**PERRY, Mr. Colin Charles, FCA** *1975;* (Tax Fac), Turner Peachey, Column House, London Road, SHREWSBURY, SY2 6NN.
PERRY, Mr. Colin Peter, FCA *1973;* 7 Chapman Crescent, Humberston, GRIMSBY, DN36 4UE.
PERRY, Mr. Darren Michael, BA(Hons) ACA DChA *2001;* Winter Rule Lowin House, Tregolls Road, TRURO, CORNWALL, TR1 2NA.
PERRY, Mr. David, BA ACA *2011;* Flat 8, Montana Building, Deals Gateway, LONDON, SE13 7QF.
PERRY, Mr. David Andrew, BSc(Econ) FCA *1970;* 7 Park Chase, GUILDFORD, GU1 1ES. (Life Member)
•**PERRY, Mr. David John, FCA** *1972;* Perry Douglass & Co, 4 Market Hill, Clare, SUDBURY, CO10 8NN.
PERRY, Mr. David Keith, MA ACA *1986;* 10 St. Leonards Road, SURBITON, SURREY, KT6 4DE.
PERRY, Mr. David Reginald, BSc FCA *1990;* 10022 East Stonecroft Drive, SCOTTSDALE, AZ 85255, UNITED STATES.
PERRY, Mrs. Debra Jayne, BSc FCA *1989;* 7 Woburn Close, NORTHWICH, CHESHIRE, CW9 8WT.
PERRY, Mr. Derek Alexander, FCA *1951;* Peartree Hall, Earls Colne, COLCHESTER, CO6 2JS. (Life Member)
PERRY, Mr. Douglas Scott, ACA *2008;* Clayton & Brewill Cawley House, 149-155 Canal Street, NOTTINGHAM, NG1 7HR.
PERRY, Mr. Edward Leddra, FCA *1965;* 13 Boskennal Drive, HAYLE, TR27 4QX.
PERRY, Miss. Elizabeth Ann, BA(Hons) ACA *2003;* Flat 18, St. Lawrence House, Melville Road, Edgbaston, BIRMINGHAM, B16 9NQ.
PERRY, Ms. Elizabeth Jane, BSc ACA *1985;* 12 Copthorn Avenue, BROXBOURNE, EN10 7RA.
PERRY, Miss. Emma Jayne, ACA *2010;* 8 Manor View, LONDON, N3 2SS.
PERRY, Miss. Eve Marie, BA(Hons) ACA *2002;* Ground Floor Flat, 120 Redland Road, BRISTOL, BS6 6QT.
PERRY, Miss. Fiona Jane, BSc ACA *2002;* U B S AG, 100 Liverpool Street, LONDON, EC2M 2RH.
PERRY, Miss. Gillian, BEng ACA *1999;* 9 Templeton Court, Manor Road, ST ALBANS, HERTFORDSHIRE, AL1 3FW.
PERRY, Mrs. Helen Jane, BA ACA *1996;* oakwood, 127 East Lane, West Horsley, LEATHERHEAD, SURREY, KT24 6LJ.
PERRY, Mr. Huw John, BSc ACA *1983;* ACTION FOCHILDREN ST DAVIDS COURT, 68A COWBRIDGE ROAD EAST, CARDIFF, CF11 9DN.
PERRY, Mr. Ian Andrew, BSc ACA *1987;* 15 Middle Lane Stoke Albany, MARKET HARBOROUGH, LEICESTERSHIRE, LE16 8QA.
PERRY, Miss. Jennifer Ellen, ACA BEng(Hons) *2009;* 36 The Sycamores, Bluntisham, HUNTINGDON, CAMBRIDGESHIRE, PE28 3XW.
PERRY, Miss. Joanna Mary Gordon, MA FCA *1982;* 665 Riddell Road, Glendowie, AUCKLAND, NEW ZEALAND.
PERRY, Mr. John, ACA *2008;* T & F(Eire) Limited, 9 Fitzwilliam Square, DUBLIN 2, COUNTY DUBLIN, IRELAND.
PERRY, Mr. John, FCA *1969;* The Lodge, Church Lane, Hackford, WYMONDHAM, NR18 9HN.
PERRY, Mr. John, BSc ACA *1979;* Valkenkamp 651, 3607 MP MAARSSEN, NETHERLANDS.
•**PERRY, Mr. John Andrew, BSc FCA** *1997;* with KPMG, KPMG Centre, 18 Viaduct Harbour Avenue, P.O. Box 1584, AUCKLAND 1140, NEW ZEALAND.
PERRY, Mr. John Andrew, BA ACA *1992;* Conquest Capital Group Pty Ltd, PO BOX H132, Australia Square, SYDNEY, NSW 1215, AUSTRALIA.
PERRY, Mr. John Henry, BA ACA *1989;* 43 Bathurst Close, BURNHAM-ON-SEA, TA8 2SZ.
•**PERRY, Mr. John William, FCA** *1973;* J.W. Perry & Co, 2nd Floor Hyde House, The Hyde, Edgware Road, LONDON, NW9 6LH.
•**PERRY, Mr. Jonathan Henry, FCA** *1974;* (Tax Fac), Mitchams Accountants Limited, 1 Cornhill, ILMINSTER, SOMERSET, TA19 0AD.
PERRY, Mr. Jonathan Peter Langman, FCA *1962;* Apuldram House, Dell Quay Road, CHICHESTER, WEST SUSSEX, PO20 7EE.
PERRY, Mr. Julian Ralph, JP BSc FCA ACIS *1981;* 82 Cliff Avenue, NORTHBRIDGE, NSW 2063, AUSTRALIA.
•**PERRY, Ms. Kate Louise, BA FCA** *1994;* (Tax Fac), Ramsay Brown and Partners, Ramsay House, 18 Vera Avenue, Grange Park, LONDON, N21 1RA.
PERRY, Mr. Laurence David George, BA FCA *1992;* with Deloitte LLP, Hill House, 1 Little New Street, LONDON, EC4A 3TR.
PERRY, Mr. Lionel George Raymond, FCA *1964;* 56 Carrant Road, Mitton, TEWKESBURY, GL20 8AD.
PERRY, Mrs. Louise Emma, BA ACA *1985;* (Tax Fac), 10 St Leonards Road, SURBITON, KT6 4DE.
PERRY, Mr. Mark Stephen, BSc(Hons) ACA *2000;* Daffodil Cottage Tandridge Lane, Tandridge, OXTED, SURREY, RH8 9NN.
•**PERRY, Mr. Matthew, BA ACA** *2003;* Haines Watts, Sterling House, 177-181 Farnham Road, SLOUGH, BERKSHIRE, SL1 4XP. See also HW Lee Associates LLP, Haines Watts London LLP, Haines Watts Slough LLP
PERRY, Mr. Michael, BA FCA *1974;* 42 Stivichall Croft, COVENTRY, CV3 6GN.
•**PERRY, Mr. Michael Anthony, FCA** *1980;* Badsell Manor, Badsell Road, Five Oak Green, TONBRIDGE, TN12 6QR.
•**PERRY, Mr. Michael David James, BSc FCA** *1992;* A.C. Mole & Sons, Stafford House, Blackbrook Park Avenue, TAUNTON, SOMERSET, TA1 2PX.
PERRY, Mr. Michael Jackson, BSc FCA *1987;* Garden flat, 4 Iddesleigh Road, Redland, BRISTOL, BS6 6YJ.
•**PERRY, Mr. Michael Joseph, FCA** *1980;* (Tax Fac), Michael J. Perry & Co, Flat 7, Castleham Court, 180 High Street, EDGWARE, MIDDLESEX HA8 7EX.
PERRY, Mr. Nathan Neil, FCA *1965;* 4 Petworth Drive, HORSHAM, WEST SUSSEX, RH12 5JH. (Life Member)
PERRY, Mr. Neil Adrian, BSc ACA *1983;* Balcony House, High Street, Sherston, MALMESBURY, SN16 0LH.
PERRY, Mr. Neil William, FCA *1985;* Helston Garages Ltd, 87 Meneage Street, HELSTON, CORNWALL, TR13 8RD.
PERRY, Mr. Nicholas John, FCA *1975;* Mayfield, Crocketts Lane, Lee Common, GREAT MISSENDEN, HP16 9JR.
PERRY, Mr. Nicholas John, MA ACA *1992;* 46 Carholme Road, LONDON, SE23 2HS.
PERRY, Mr. Nigel Ronald, BCom FCA *1964;* 17 Cranbourne Road, Oldswinford, STOURBRIDGE, DY8 1QZ. (Life Member)
PERRY, Mr. Paul James, BSc ACA *2004;* 3 Rye Croft, Trawden, COLNE, LANCASHIRE, BB8 8TH.
PERRY, Mr. Peter John, FCA *1960;* The Cotters17 Front Road, Woodchurch ASHFORD, Kent, TN26 3QB. (Life Member)
PERRY, Mr. Philip, BSc ACA *1982;* P.O.Box 5141, MBABANE, H100, SWAZILAND.
PERRY, Mr. Philip Charles, FCA *1955;* 9 Loire Close, ASHBY-DE-LA-ZOUCH, LE65 2QZ. (Life Member)
PERRY, Mr. Philip Martin, BSc ACA *1980;* Flat 101 Building 6, 198 Ziwei Road, ZHANGJIAGANG 201210, CHINA.
PERRY, Miss. Rachel, LLB ACA *2003;* Flat 8 Javelin Court Streatham Common North, LONDON, SW16 3HL.
•**PERRY, Mr. Richard, BA FCA** *1981;* (Tax Fac), McCranors Limited, Clifford House, 38-44 Binley Road, COVENTRY, CV3 1JA. See also McCranor Kirby Smale Limited
PERRY, Mr. Richard Anthony, BSc ACA *1981;* 3 Hunsdon, WELWYN GARDEN CITY, AL7 2PN.
PERRY, Mr. Richard John, FCA *1975;* Beech House, 4 The Paddock, Woodgates Lane, NORTH FERRIBY, HU14 3JU.
•**PERRY, Mr. Richard Michael Langman, FCA** *1974;* (Tax Fac), Morris Crocker, Station House, 50 North Street, HAVANT, PO9 1QU. See also Morris Crocker Limited
PERRY, Mr. Richard Nicholas, BSc ACA *1989;* 31 Lynton Road, LONDON, W3 9HL.
PERRY, Mr. Robert Anthony, BA ACA *2007;* 2547 N GREENVIEW AVE, CHICAGO, IL 60614, UNITED STATES.
•**PERRY, Mr. Robert Edward, BA ACA** *1981;* (Tax Fac), Robert Perry Limited, Parkside House, Old Stafford Road, Slade Heath. Near Coven, WOLVERHAMPTON, WV10 7PH.
PERRY, Mr. Robin, BA(Hons) ACA *2002;* Tirlebrook Cottage, Oxenton, CHELTENHAM, GLOUCESTERSHIRE, GL52 9SE.
PERRY, Mr. Rodney Charles Langman, FCA *1965;* (Member of Council 1984 - 1986), East Boldre House, East Boldre, BROCKENHURST, SO42 7WR.
PERRY, Mr. Roland Robert Joseph, BA ACA *1993;* Race Farm, Race Lane, Kingston Bagpuize, ABINGDON, OXFORDSHIRE, OX13 5AU.
PERRY, Mr. Rupert Grosvenor, BSc ACA *1994;* Heath Hall Cottage, Bowlhead Green, GODALMING, SURREY, GU8 6NW.
PERRY, Mr. Russell Christopher, FCA *1980;* Pathfinder Consulting International Ltd.Evergreen Hse, 68 Yew Tree Road, Southborough, TUNBRIDGE WELLS, TN4 0BN.
PERRY, Miss. Sara Jane, BSocSc ACA *1992;* 5 Linacre Crescent, CIRENCESTER, GLOUCESTERSHIRE, GL7 1WB.
PERRY, Mrs. Sarah Anne, BA(Hons) ACA *2002;* 4 Honeysuckle Close, Great Cambourne, CAMBRIDGE, CB23 5HS.
PERRY, Mrs. Sarah Catherine, MA ACA *2002;* Tirlebrook Cottage, Oxenton, CHELTENHAM, GLOUCESTERSHIRE, GL52 9SE.
PERRY, Mr. Sefton, BSocSc ACA *2000;* UEFA, ROUTE DE GENEVE 46, CH-1260 NYON2, GENEVA, SWITZERLAND.
PERRY, Mr. Shaun William, BA(Hons) ACA *1992;* The Crannog, 2 Linden Way, Ponteland, NEWCASTLE UPON TYNE, NORTHUMBERLAND, NE20 9DP.
PERRY, Mr. Simon James David, BA ACA *2006;* 48 Budgenor Lodge, Dodsley Lane Easebourne, MIDHURST, WEST SUSSEX, GU29 0AD.
•**PERRY, Mr. Simon Mark, BA ACA** *1994;* PricewaterhouseCoopers LLP, 1 Embankment Place, LONDON, WC2N 6RH. See also PricewaterhouseCoopers
•**PERRY, Mr. Simon Thomas, BA FCA** *1980;* Ernst & Young LLP, 1 More London Place, LONDON, SE1 2AF. See also Ernst & Young Europe LLP
PERRY, Mrs. Suzanne Michelle, BA(Hons) ACA MCT *2000;* Elsevier Finance SA, Espace de l'Europe 3, PO Box 333, CH-2002 NEUCHATEL, SWITZERLAND.
PERRY, Miss. Tanya, BSc ACA *2007;* 57 Meyrick Drive, Wash Common, NEWBURY, BERKSHIRE, RG14 6SY.
PERRY, Mr. Terence Anthony, ACA *2002;* 8 Recreation Ground Road, STAMFORD, LINCOLNSHIRE, PE9 1EN.
PERRY, Ms. Theresa, BA ACA *1986;* (Tax Fac), 6 Newark Crescent, AYR, KA7 4HP.
PERRY, Mr. Warwick Robert, ACA CA(NZ) *2009;* 121 Marlborough Crescent, SEVENOAKS, KENT, TN13 2HN.
PERRY, Mr. William Rees, BA ACA *2006;* 58 Charlton Road, SOUTHAMPTON, SO15 5FN.
PERRY, Mr. William Richard, BA(Hons) ACA *2003;* Tenant Services Authority, 1 Piccadilly Gardens, MANCHESTER, M1 1RG.
PERRY CROWN, Mrs. Gail, LLB ACA *2006;* 20 Parma Crescent, LONDON, SW11 1LT.
PERRYMAN, Mr. Brian Ernest, FCA *1959;* Arieniskill, High Hesket, CARLISLE, CA4 0HS. (Life Member)
PERRYMAN, Mr. Brian Leslie, FCA *1971;* 70 Springdale Road, BROADSTONE, BH18 9BY.
PERRYMAN, Mr. Francis Douglas, BCom FCA *1957;* 8 Henrietta Villas, Henrietta Road, BATH, BA2 6LX. (Life Member)
PERRYMAN, Mr. Roderick, FCA *1971;* Box 346, Crta.Cabo de La Nao, (Pla) 124-6, Javea, 03730 ALICANTE, SPAIN.
PERRYMENT, Mr. Ian Stuart, BSc ACA *1999;* 19 Mary Lane, North Waltham, BASINGSTOKE, RG25 2BY.
PERSAUD, Mr. Anand, BEng FCA *1993;* 6 Lintlaw Close, LEICESTER, LE4 7YH.

PERSAUD, Mr. Rabindranauth Tagore, BA FCA CF *1997;* 6 Lintlaw Close, Rushey Mead, LEICESTER, LE4 7YH.
PERSAUD, Mr. Samlall, ACA *1986;* 27 Dagwell Crescent, AJAX L1T 3M8, ON, CANADA.
PERSAUD, Mr. Stephen, BA ACA *1996;* 79 Heron Forstal Avenue, Hawkinge, FOLKESTONE, CT18 7PG.
PERSKY, Mr. Warren, BSc ACA AMCT *1990;* Meadow View, The Warren, RADLETT, HERTFORDSHIRE, WD7 7DU.
PERSSON, Mr. Henrik Johan Oskar, ACA *2009;* 72a Atlantic Road, LONDON, SW9 8PX.
PERSSON, Mr. Philip Martin, ACA *1986;* 18 Deepdene Avenue, DORKING, SURREY, RH4 1SR.
PERT, Miss. Barbara Ann, FCA *1969;* 5 Tansy Mead, Storrington, PULBOROUGH, RH20 4QJ. (Life Member)
PERT, Mr. Barry, BA ACA *1990;* The Chase, Mill Road, Kislingbury, NORTHAMPTON, NN7 4BB.
PERT, Mr. Julian Richard, BSc FCA *1991;* 1 Oaklands Way, FAREHAM, PO14 4LE.
PERTAUB, Mr. Michael Kevin, BSc ACA *2010;* 125 Colchester Road, LONDON, E10 6HD.
PERTUSINI, Mr. Miro Vittorio, BEng ACA *1998;* 52 Grandison Road, LONDON, SW11 6LW.
PERUMAL, Mr. Angelo Rohendra Ayam, BSc ACA *1995;* 4 Shaftesbury House, 16 Cayton Road, COULSDON, CR5 1LT.
•**PERVEZ, Mr. Ashar, BSc ACA** *2009;* IFA Accountancy Services Limited, 18 Clitheroe Road, MANCHESTER, M13 0GE.
•**PERVEZ, Mr. Hamid, ACA FCCA** *2008;* Hamid & Co, 35 Tintern Way, HARROW, MIDDLESEX, HA2 0RZ. See also Mr Hamid Pervez FCCA, ACA
PERVEZ, Mr. Rizwan, ACA *1997;* 2 Dobree Avenue, LONDON, NW10 2AE.
PERYER, Miss. Holly Juliet, BEng ACA *2002;* Indigo Vision 4-5 Charles Darwin House, Edinburgh Technopole Milton Bridge, PENICUIK, MIDLOTHIAN, EH26 0PY.
PESCATORE, Miss. Immacolata, BSc ACA *1994;* 53 Radcliffe Road, LONDON, N21 2SD.
•**PESCHARDT, Mr. John William Hagbarth, FCA** *1977;* (Tax Fac), 5 Fullers Grove, Fullers Hill, CHESHAM, BUCKINGHAMSHIRE, HP5 1LR.
PESCO, Mr. Mark Anthony John, BA ACA *1999;* La Grange La Rue Des Vallees, St. Martin, JERSEY, JE3 6BB.
PESCOTT, Mr. John Mcgregor, FCA *1967;* 2 Crossway, Tynemouth, NORTH SHIELDS, NE30 2LB.
PESCOTT-DAY, Mr. Anthony Alfred, FCA *1953;* 41 Fifth Cross Road, TWICKENHAM, TW2 5LJ. (Life Member)
PESCOTT FROST, Miss. Emma, BSc ACA *2007;* 1 Liberty Street, LONDON, SW9 0EE.
PESCUD, Mr. George Brian, FCA *1956;* (Tax Fac), Flat 1, Osborne Court, Osborne Road, SHEFFIELD, S11 9BB. (Life Member)
PESCUD, Mr. Trevor, FCA *1960;* Box Bush House, Marlpits Lane, Ninfield, BATTLE, TN33 9LD. (Life Member)
PESEZ, Mrs. Anne, MSc ACA *2007;* 20 Ashwell Park, HARPENDEN, HERTFORDSHIRE, AL5 5SG.
PESHALL, Mr. Edward Charles Eyre, MA ACA *1981;* 7 Broomhouse Dock, Carnwath Road, LONDON, SW6 3EH.
•**PESKETT, Mr. Simon John, BSc ACA** *1991;* Nexia Smith & Williamson Audit Limited, Portwall Place, Portwall Lane, BRISTOL, BS1 6NA. See also Nexia Audit Limited
PESLIKAS, Mr. Yiannis, BSc ACA *2006;* 18 Achilleos Street, 3016 LIMASSOL, CYPRUS.
PESSIAN-HAGHIGHI, Miss. Taraneh, BEng ACA *1993;* BACARDI, 267 Route de MEYRIN, 1217 GENEVA, SWITZERLAND.
•**PESTELL, Mr. John Philip, BA FCA CTA** *1982;* Pestell & Co, 2A Nicola Close, SOUTH CROYDON, SURREY, CR2 6NB.
PESTELL, Mrs. Lisa Marie, ACA *2005;* 37 Henry Tate Mews, LONDON, SW16 3HA.
PESTELL, Mr. Paul David, FCA *1993;* (Tax Fac), Thatched Cottage, Low Street, Ketteringham, WYMONDHAM, NORFOLK, NR18 9RY.
•**PESTER, Mrs. Lyndsay Margaret, BSc ACA** *2003;* with Sampson West, 34 Ely Place, LONDON, EC1N 6TD.
•**PESTER, Mr. Richard Giles, BA ACA** *1999;* Anchor Accounting Services Ltd, 67 Old Woking Road, WEST BYFLEET, SURREY, KT14 6LF.
PESTEREFF, Mr. Michael Nicholas, FCA *1967;* 26 Dobcroft Road, SHEFFIELD, S7 2LR.
PETCH, Mr. Barry Irvine, FCA *1957;* Chalet Saint-Georges, Le Hameau, 1936 VERBIER, SWITZERLAND. (Life Member)
PETCH, Mr. Jonathan David, BA ACA *1995;* Albertstr 101, 40233 DUSSELDORF, GERMANY.
PETCH, Mr. Matthew Scott Worley, BSc ACA *2004;* Sunset Cottage, Harrowbeer Lane, YELVERTON, PL20 6EA.
PETCHEY, Mr. Nigel Andrew, BSc ACA *1987;* 12 Lanes Close, Kings Bromley, BURTON-ON-TRENT, STAFFORDSHIRE, DE13 7JS.
•**PETER, Mr. Andre Colin, BSc FCA** *1992;* (Tax Fac), Andre Peter, First Floor, The Old Auction Rooms, Marine Walk Street, HYTHE, KENT CT21 5NW.
PETER, Mrs. Claire, BSc ACA *2003;* 28 Tolverne Road, Raynes Park, LONDON, SW20 8BR.
PETER, Mr. Damian Marc, ACA *2004;* 19 Woodbourne Square, Douglas, ISLE OF MAN, IM1 4DE.
•**PETER, Mr. Derek Robert, FCA** *1972;* Green & Peter, The Limes, 1339 High Road, Whetstone, LONDON, N20 9HR.
PETERKIN, Miss. Alexandra Jessie, BSc FCA *1986;* Lower Laggan House, Ballantrae, GIRVAN, AYRSHIRE, KA26 0JZ.
•**PETERMAN, Mr. David Michael, BA FCA** *1981;* (Tax Fac), Scarletts, Scarletts Lane, Wargrave, READING, RG10 9XD.
PETERMAN, Mr. Leslie, FCA *1952;* 55 Stanley Road, NORTHWOOD, HA6 1RH. (Life Member)
PETERPILLAI, Mrs. Kaiyathiri, BSc(Hons) ACA *2003;* 75 Preston Hill, Kenton, HARROW, HA3 9SQ.
PETERS, Mrs. Adele Louise, BSc(Hons) ACA *2003;* UBS Investment Bank, 100 Liverpool Street, LONDON, EC2M 2RH.
PETERS, Mr. Andrew James, FCA *1967;* T S M Agencies Ltd, 4th Floor Vantage House, 78 Leadenhall Street, LONDON, EC3A 3DH.
•①**PETERS, Mr. Andrew Philip, FCA** *1975;* Machan Gillan, Manaccan, HELSTON, CORNWALL, TR12 6HG.
PETERS, Mrs. Ann Octavia, BSc FCA *1996;* 77 Howards Wood Drive, GERRARDS CROSS, BUCKINGHAMSHIRE, SL9 7HS.
PETERS, Mrs. Anna-Louise, BSc ACA *2006;* 14 The Hall Way, Littleton, WINCHESTER, HAMPSHIRE, SO22 6QL.
•**PETERS, Mr. Anthony John, BA FCA** *1995;* Burwood (Pinner) Ltd, 17 Little Moss Lane, PINNER, MIDDLESEX, HA5 3BA.
PETERS, Mr. Brian Philip, FCA *1972;* 1 Brangwyn Avenue, Patcham, BRIGHTON, BN1 8XH.
PETERS, Mrs. Caroline Elizabeth, BA ACA *2003;* 37 Beaumont Terrace, Gosforth, NEWCASTLE UPON TYNE, NE3 1AS.
•**PETERS, Mrs. Caroline Maria, FCA** *1993;* Bird Luckin, 42a-42b High Street, DUNMOW, CM6 1AH. See also Peters & Wright
PETERS, Mr. Charles, BEng ACA *1995;* Scotts Grove House, Scotts Grove Road, Chobham, WOKING, SURREY, GU24 8DR.
•**PETERS, Mr. Christopher, FCA** *1971;* (Tax Fac), Peters & Co, 41A Mottram Old Road, STALYBRIDGE, SK15 2TF.
PETERS, Mr. Christopher James, MA FCA *1994;* 12 Henson Close, Radcliffe-on-Trent, NOTTINGHAM, NG12 2JQ.
PETERS, Mr. Christopher James, BA ACA *2000;* 227 Kings Road, KINGSTON UPON THAMES, SURREY, KT2 5JH.
PETERS, Mr. Christopher Leonard, BSc FCA *1990;* Floor 5 The Royal Bank of Scotland Plc 280 Bishopsgate, LONDON, EC2M 4RB.
PETERS, Mr. Ciaran, ACA *2009;* 3 Martineau Road, LONDON, N5 1NG.
PETERS, Mr. Colin Leslie, FCA *1968;* Oakbourne House, Chapel Row, READING, RG7 6QB.
PETERS, Mr. David, BSc ACA *1992;* 3 Denham Walk, Chalfont St. Peter, GERRARDS CROSS, BUCKINGHAMSHIRE, SL9 0EN.
PETERS, Mr. David, FCA *1977;* Woodbank, Longheys Lane, Dalton, WIGAN, WN8 7RT.
PETERS, Mr. David Ashmore, FCA *1969;* 1 Llwyneos, Penrhiwllan, LLANDYSUL, DYFED, SA44 5NT. (Life Member)
PETERS, Mr. David John Raymond, FCA *1966;* 25c Palace Court, LONDON, W2 4LP. (Life Member)
PETERS, Mr. Desmond Burie, FCA *1951;* 67 Gough Way, CAMBRIDGE, CB3 9LN. (Life Member)
•**PETERS, Miss. Elizabeth Helen, BSc FCA** *1989;* (Tax Fac), Ballard Dale Syree Watson LLP, Oakmoore Court, Kingswood Road, Hampton Lovett, DROITWICH, WORCESTERSHIRE WR9 0QH.
PETERS, Mrs. Fiona Janet, MA ACA *1992;* 5 Rosebridge Avenue, Castle Cove, SYDNEY, NSW 2069, AUSTRALIA.
PETERS, Mr. Gary Steven, BSc ACA *1988;* Sunnybank, Foxhill, HAYWARDS HEATH, RH16 4RF.
PETERS, Mr. Gerald John, FCA *1971;* Smestow Gate Cottage, Smestow, Swindon, DUDLEY, DY3 4PJ.
PETERS, Mrs. Gillian, BSc ACA *1983;* 17 Brookfield Close, Hunt End, REDDITCH, B97 5LL.
PETERS, Mrs. Isobel Louise, BA ACA *1998;* Hall Farm, Front Street, Topcliffe, THIRSK, YO7 3RJ.
PETERS, Mr. James Michael Collingwood, BA FCA *1998;* Ryders, The Avenue, Bucklebury, READING, RG7 6NH.
PETERS, Mr. James Richard Michael, BSc ACA *1992;* Goldman Sachs International Peterborough Court, 133 Fleet Street, LONDON, EC4A 2BB.
PETERS, Mr. James Stuart, FCA *1953;* 6 Castle Avenue, Mumbles, SWANSEA, SA3 4BA. (Life Member)
PETERS, Mrs. Janet, BSc ACA *1990;* 18 Grove Park, Fordham, ELY, CB7 5ND.
PETERS, Mr. Jason Daniel, BA ACA *1995;* Stuart Peters Ltd, 184-192 Drummond Street, LONDON, NW1 3HP.
PETERS, Mr. Jason Elliot, BSc(Hons) ACA *2000;* 38 Sunnyfield, LONDON, NW7 4RG.
PETERS, Mrs. Joanne, MA MPhil ACA *2002;* PricewaterCoopers, Freshwater Place, 2 Southbank Boulevard, SOUTHBANK, VIC 3006, AUSTRALIA.
PETERS, Mrs. Joanne Lisa, BSc ACA *1999;* 31 Sunnyfield, LONDON, NW7 4RD.
•**PETERS, Mr. John Andrew, BA FCA CTA** *1986;* Smith & Williamson (Bristol) LLP, Portwall Place, Portwall Lane, BRISTOL, BS1 6NA. See also Smith & Williamson Ltd
•**PETERS, Mr. John Fabian, FCA** *1968;* (Tax Fac), John F. Peters, 1 Peacewood Mews, Montville Drive, Les Vardes, St. Peter Port, GUERNSEY GY1 1BY.
PETERS, Mr. Jon, BA(Hons) ACA *2001;* 29 Kensington Gardens, BATH, BA1 6LH.
PETERS, Mr. Jonathan Steven, BSc ACA *1996;* Flat 170 Chiltern Court, Baker Street, LONDON, NW1 5SJ.
PETERS, Mrs. Karina Elizabeth, BA ACA *1993;* 12 Henson Close, Radcliffe-on-Trent, NOTTINGHAM, NG12 2JQ.
•**PETERS, Mr. Keith Leslie, FCA** *1977;* (Tax Fac), Law & Co, Pool House, Arran Close, 106 Birmingham Road, Great Barr, BIRMINGHAM B43 7AD.
PETERS, Mr. Lionel, FCA *1962;* 40 Berkeley Road, LONDON, NW9 9DG. (Life Member)
•**PETERS, Mr. Malcolm Gordon, ACA FCCA** *2011;* Kelsall Steele Limited, Woodlands Court, Truro Business Park, TRURO, CORNWALL, TR4 9NH.
•**PETERS, Mr. Martin, FCA** *1957;* EIS Advsors Limited, Millennium House, Victoria Road, Douglas, ISLE OF MAN, IM2 4RW.
•**PETERS, Mr. Matthew Charles Anthony, BA FCA** *1997;* MaxAim LLP, United Business Centre, 1 Mariner Court, Calder Park, WAKEFIELD, WEST YORKSHIRE WF4 3FL.
PETERS, Mr. Michael, BA(Hons) ACA *2009;* Rosemont, Hanney Road, Southmoor, ABINGDON, OXFORDSHIRE, OX13 5HT.
•**PETERS, Mr. Michael John, ACA** *1982;* West Wake Price LLP, 4 Chiswell Street, LONDON, EC1Y 4UP.
PETERS, Miss. Miranda Louise, BSc ACA *2010;* 195 Fox Lane, LONDON, N13 4BB.
PETERS, Mr. Neil, BSc ACA *1997;* 9 Thomson Lane, #27-07 Sky@Eleven, SINGAPORE 297726, SINGAPORE.
PETERS, Mr. Nicholas James, BA ACA *1992;* Barclays Bank Plc, 1 Churchill Place, LONDON, E14 5HP.
•**PETERS, Mr. Philip Michael, BSc FCA** *1985;* (Tax Fac), Whiting & Partners Limited, Garland House, Garland Street, BURY ST. EDMUNDS, SUFFOLK, IP33 1EZ.
PETERS, Mr. Richard Andrew, BA(Hons) ACA *2011;* 43 Eatonville Road, LONDON, SW17 7SH.
•**PETERS, Mr. Richard Burie, BA FCA** *1989;* PricewaterhouseCoopers (Vietnam) Ltd, 4th Floor Saigon Tower, 29 Le Duan Boulevard, District 1, HO CHI MINH CITY, VIETNAM.
•**PETERS, Mr. Richard James, FCA** *1972;* Newman Peters, 19 Fitzroy Square, LONDON, W1T 6EQ.
PETERS, Mr. Richard Wade, BSc FCA *1979;* Yew Tree House, 16 Main Street, PRESTON, LE15 9NJ.
PETERS, Mr. Robert Matt, BA ACA *1983;* 3 Pantiles Close, St. John's, WOKING, GU21 7PT.
PETERS, Mr. Robin, ACA *1979;* with Reeves & Co LLP, 37 St. Margarets Street, CANTERBURY, KENT, CT1 2TU.
PETERS, Miss. Sarah Katrina, BSc ACA *1985;* Brooklands Farm, Valewood Lane, Barns Green, HORSHAM, RH13 7QJ.
PETERS, Mr. Simon, BSc ACA *1996;* 41 Sole Farm Road Bookham, LEATHERHEAD, SURREY, KT23 3DW.
PETERS, Mr. Simon John, BA ACA *1994;* 66 Manchuria Road, LONDON, SW11 6AE.
PETERS, Ms. Siobhan, BA ACA *1997;* Home Office, 2 Marsham Street, LONDON, SW1P 4DF.
•**PETERS, Mrs. Sophie Elizabeth, BA ACA** *1988;* Sophie Peters, 33 Park Road, BURY ST. EDMUNDS, SUFFOLK, IP33 3QW.
PETERS, Mrs. Stephanie Clare, BSc FCA *1982;* 35 Beaver Road, Didsbury, MANCHESTER, M20 6SX.
PETERS, Mr. Stephen, BSc ACA *1992;* Alix Partners Ltd, 20 North Audley Street, LONDON, W1K 6WE.
PETERS, Mr. Stephen John, BSc ACA *1980;* 54 Brackendale Road, BOURNEMOUTH, BH8 9HZ.
PETERSEN, Mrs. Kathryn Elizabeth, BSc ACA *1988;* 71 Ridgeway, Wargrave, READING, RG10 8AS.
PETERSEN, Mr. Martin John, MA ACA *1979;* 70 Sutton Court Road, Chiswick, LONDON, W4 3EG.
PETERSEN, Mrs. Megan Haelie, BSc ACA *2010;* Flat C, 1 Haldon Road, LONDON, SW18 1QD.
PETERSEN, Miss. Tiffany Jayne, ACA *2010;* 20 Gardner Road, GUILDFORD, SURREY, GU1 4PG.
•**PETERSON, Mrs. Kathryn Vanda, ACA** *1991;* Turnpike Business Centre, Turnpike Road, Croesyceiliog, CWMBRAN, GWENT, NP44 2AG.
PETERSON, Mr. Terence Graham Grant, FCA *1949;* 10 The Cedars, Warford Park, Faulkners Lane, Mobberley, KNUTSFORD, CHESHIRE WA16 7RX. (Life Member)
PETERSON, Ms. Wendy, BA ACA MBA *1999;* 588 Franklin Street, WRENTHAM, MA 02093, UNITED STATES.
PETEVINOS, Mrs. Claire Louise, MA MEng ACA *2002;* 9 Carisbrooke Road, HARPENDEN, HERTFORDSHIRE, AL5 5QS.
PETHA, Mrs. Anne Cornelia, BA ACA *1989;* (Tax Fac), 9 Westernhay Road, LEICESTER, LE2 3HF.
PETHEN, Mr. David Keith, FCA *1960;* P.O. Box DV 759, DEVONSHIRE DV BX, BERMUDA. (Life Member)
PETHERBRIDGE, Miss. Sarah Ellen, BA ACA ATII *1993;* with Ernst & Young LLP, The Paragon, Counterslip, BRISTOL, BS1 6BX.
PETHERICK, Mr. Ian Stuart, FCA *1953;* 4 Colney Drive, Cringleford, NORWICH, NR4 7RH. (Life Member)
•**PETHERICK, Mr. Mark Julian, FCA** *1977;* (Tax Fac), Pethericks & Gillard Ltd, 124 High Street, Midsomer Norton, BATH, BA3 2DA.
PETHERS, Mr. Lee Robert, ACA *2008;* 16 Rosemary Avenue, Halfway, SHEERNESS, KENT, ME12 3HT.
PETHICK, Mrs. Jacqueline Jane, FCA *1982;* Stirtingale Farm, Corston View, Odd Down, BATH, BA2 2PJ.
•**PETHICK, Mr. Robert Ian Du Barry, BSc FCA** *1977;* SRP Accounts Limited, The Old Customs House, Torwood Gardens Rd, TORQUAY, TQ1 1EG.
PETHYBRIDGE, Mr. David, ACA *2011;* 58 Meadow Way, Caversham, READING, RG4 5LY.
PETITT, Mrs. Christina, BSc ACA *1995;* 2 Fryern Wood, CATERHAM, SURREY, CR3 5AR.
PETITT, Mr. John Derek, BA FCA *1978;* 34 Halls Lane, Waltham St Lawence, READING, RG10 0JD.
PETKAR, Mr. Ibrahim, ACA *2010;* 17 Bartlett Close, LONDON, E14 6LH.
PETKEN, Mr. Gavin Christopher, BA ACA *1997;* 15 Nightingale Close, RADLETT, HERTFORDSHIRE, WD7 8NT.
PETKOV, Mr. Vesselin Plamenov, ACA *2008;* (Tax Fac), Flat 2103 Landmark East Tower, 24 Marsh Wall, LONDON, E14 9DB.
PETLEY, Mr. David, BA ACA *1986;* Gurneys Solicitors, 6 Riverside Framlingham, WOODBRIDGE, SUFFOLK, IP13 9AG.
PETLEY, Mr. Richard William, MA FCA *1992;* 10 Chater Drive, Walmley, SUTTON COLDFIELD, B76 2BJ.
PETO, Mr. Christopher, ACA *2009;* 16 Holmesdale Road, DRONFIELD, DERBYSHIRE, S18 2FB.
PETO, Mrs. Judith Ann, BSc FCA *1981;* 58A Shelvers Way, TADWORTH, KT20 5QF.
•**PETRAKIS, Mr. Petros, MBA ACA** *1993;* PricewaterhouseCoopers Limited, City House, 6 Karaiskakis Street, CY-3032 LIMASSOL, CYPRUS.
PETRAS, Mr. Ioannis, ACA *2008;* Flat 68 Heathcroft, Hampstead Way, LONDON, NW11 7HL.
•**PETRASSI, Mr. David, ACA** *2009;* Francis James & Partners LLP, 1386 London Road, LEIGH-ON-SEA, ESSEX, SS9 2UJ.
PETRE, Mr. Edward Robert, BSc ACA *2002;* 54 Westcroft Square, LONDON, W6 0TA.
PETRELLA, Mr. Franco Joseph, FCA *1982;* 29 Northumberland Street, SALFORD, M7 4DQ.
PETRI, Mr. Arthur Charles David, FCA *1973;* Crossway House, Cliff Road, North Petherton, BRIDGWATER, SOMERSET, TA6 6PB.
PETRI, Mr. Dion Joseph, BSc ACA *1995;* Vine Tree House, Uckinghall, TEWKESBURY, GL20 6ES.
PETRICCIONE, Mr. Mario Stefano, BA ACA *1983;* (Tax Fac), 15 The Downsway, SUTTON, SURREY, SM2 5RL.

PETRIDES, Mr. Andreas, MSc BSc ACA *2010;* 174A Eirinis Megaro Petrides, Office 12, 3022 LIMASSOL, CYPRUS.
•**PETRIDES, Mr. Chrysanthos, BSc FCA** *1981;* Freemans, Solar House, 282 Chase Road, LONDON, N14 6NZ. See also Freemans Partnership LLP
PETRIDES, Mr. Ian, BA FCA *1989;* (Tax Fac), 63 Woodhurst Avenue, Petts Wood, ORPINGTON, BR5 1AS.
•**PETRIDES, Mr. Paul Bannerman, BA FCA** *1976;* Thomas Westcott, 47 Boutport Street, BARNSTAPLE, DEVON, EX31 1SQ.
PETRIDES, Mr. Petros, BSc ACA *2004;* 28 EVRIPIDOU STREET, 6036 LARNACA, CYPRUS.
PETRIDOU, Mrs. Constantia, BA ACA *2002;* PO BOX 24384, CY 1703 NICOSIA, CYPRUS.
PETRIDOU, Miss. Maria, BA ACA *2002;* Tweede Jan Van Der Heijdenstraat 107 (I&II), Floors 1&2, 1074 XT AMSTERDAM, NETHERLANDS.
PETRIE, Mr. Alasdair James Stewart, ACA *2010;* Flat 36, Crystal Wharf, 36 Graham Street, LONDON, N1 8GH.
PETRIE, Miss. Daisy Veronica, ACA *2011;* Pricewaterhousecoopers, 7 More London Riverside, LONDON, SE1 2RT.
PETRIE, Mr. David Martin, BSc ACA *1996;* 111 Queens Road, RICHMOND, SURREY, TW10 6HF.
PETRIE, Mr. Graham, BSc ACA *2001;* 26 Hamilton Drive, Cambuslang, GLASGOW, G72 8JQ.
PETRIE, Ms. Laura Anne, BCom ACA *1993;* Meadowbank House, 153 London Road, EDINBURGH, EH8 7AU.
PETRIE, Mr. Ross Grant, BSc ACA *1993;* White House Barn, Lapworth Street, Lowsonford, HENLEY-IN-ARDEN, WEST MIDLANDS, B95 5HJ.
PETRIE, Miss. Vivien Claire, BAcc ACA *2001;* 189 Hollin Lane, Middleton, MANCHESTER, M24 5WA.
PETROU, Mr. Antonis, BSc ACA *1994;* 43 Pericleous street, Flat 101, 2021 strovolos, NICOSIA, CYPRUS.
PETROU, Mr. Ioannis, MSc ACA *2006;* with PricewaterhouseCoopers, 268-270 Kifissias Avenue, Halandri, 15232 ATHENS, GREECE.
PETROU, Mr. Ioannis Charalambous, BSc ACA *1997;* 6 Festou Street, Strovolos, 2039 NICOSIA, CYPRUS.
•**PETROU, Mr. Kyriacos, BSc FCA** *1993;* (Tax Fac), Grosvenor Partners LLP, 6-7 Ludgate Square, LONDON, EC4M 7AS.
PETROU, Mr. Nikolai Andreas, BSc(Econ) ACA *2000;* PO Box 244, WAVERLEY, NSW 2024, AUSTRALIA.
PETROU, Mr. Peter, MSc ACA *1996;* Bergstrasse 62, 8706 MEILEN, SWITZERLAND.
•**PETROU, Mr. Peter, BSc FCA** *1993;* Nicholas Peters & Co, 18-22 Wigmore Street, LONDON, W1U 2RG.
•**PETROU, Mr. Stavros, BA ACA** *1992;* (Tax Fac), Petrou & Co, 4 Heddon Court, Cockfosters Road, BARNET, HERTFORDSHIRE, EN4 0DE.
PETROVIC, Mr. Nicholas, BSc ACA *2009;* 33 Brunswick Street, YORK, YO23 1EB.
PETRUSYK, Miss. Julia Mary, BSc ACA *1980;* 8 Deepdene, HASLEMERE, GU27 1RE.
•**PETSAS, Mr. Gregory Nicos, BSc FCA** *1994;* MGI Gregoriou & Co Ltd, Greg Tower, 7 Florina Street, P.O. Box 24854, 1304 NICOSIA, CYPRUS.
PETSAS, Mr. Ioannis, ACA *2009;* Ermes Department Stores Plc, PO Box 22273, 1584 NICOSIA, CYPRUS.
PETT, Mr. Christopher John, BSc FCA *1982;* Maison Neuve, 24140 SAINT MARTIN DES COMBES, FRANCE.
PETT, Mr. Colin Spencer, BSc FCA *1977;* The Magpies, 236A Springvale Road, Kings Worthy, WINCHESTER, SO23 7LF.
PETT, Mr. David Michael, FCA *1983;* Southlands, Rue Des Cotils, Mont A L'Abbe, St. Helier, JERSEY, JE2 3FJ.
PETT, Miss. Rebecca Elizabeth, BA ACA *2007;* with KPMG LLP, 15 Canada Square, LONDON, E14 5GL.
PETT, Mr. Roger Philip, BSc FCA *1977;* 11 Orchard Way, Send, WOKING, SURREY, GU23 7HS.
PETTEMERIDES, Mr. Yiannis, MA BA ACA *2005;* with K Treppides & Co. Ltd, Treppides Tower, 9 Kafkasou Street, Aglantzia, CY 2112 NICOSIA, CYPRUS.
PETTENGELL, Mrs. Samantha Jane, ACA *2000;* 25 Borough Road, DUNSTABLE, BEDFORDSHIRE, LU5 4BZ.
PETTENGELL, Miss. Tanya Louise, MEng ACA *2002;* #22-02 Regency Suites, 36 Kim Tian Road, SINGAPORE 169279, SINGAPORE.
PETTER, Mr. Rupert Simon Maclean, LLB ACA *1998;* 24175 Research Drive, FARMINGTON HILLS, MI 48335, UNITED STATES.
PETTER, Mr. Stephen Ronald, ACA *1982;* 12 Kenilworth Drive, WALTON-ON-THAMES, KT12 3JU.
PETTERSEN, Miss. Alice, BSc ACA *2010;* Top Flat, 60 Ritherdon Road, LONDON, SW17 8QG.
PETTERSSON, Miss. Lena Maria Erika, BA(Hons) ACA *2002;* 20 Gainsborough Road, SUDBURY, SUFFOLK, CO10 2HT.
PETTETT, Mr. Christopher Douglas, FCA *1971;* Benchstone, Lesser Lane, Combs, HIGH PEAK, SK23 9UZ.
PETTETT, Miss. Claire Marianne, BA ACA *2003;* 462 Goffs Lane, Goffs Oak, WALTHAM CROSS, HERTFORDSHIRE, EN7 5EN.
PETTETT, Ms. Nicola Mary, BSc ACA *1991;* 6 Greenfinch Way, HORSHAM, WEST SUSSEX, RH12 5HB.
PETTIE, Mr. Anthony Clive, FCA *1967;* 19 Norfolk Road, UXBRIDGE, MIDDLESEX, UB8 1BL. (Life Member)
•**PETTIFER, Mr. Matthew Christopher Alan, BA ACA CTA** *2002;* Staffords Cambridge LLP, CPC1, Capital Park, Fulbourn, CAMBRIDGE, CB21 5XE.
PETTIFER, Mrs. Michelle Kathryn, BSc(Hons) ACA *2002;* with Morris Lane, 31/33 Commercial Road, POOLE, DORSET, BH14 0HU.
PETTIFOR, Mr. Barry John, FCA *1982;* 30 Vicarage Road, Waresley, SANDY, BEDFORDSHIRE, SG19 3DA.
PETTIGREW, Mr. Andrew Hamish Hewitt, ACA *1982;* 77 Devonshire Road, Chiswick, LONDON, W4 2HU.
PETTIGREW, Mr. Duncan Macdonald, BA ACA *2000;* 72 Garden Street, MALDEN, MA 02148, UNITED STATES.
PETTIGREW, Mr. Guy Simon Charles, BSc ACA *1997;* 5 Wrights Walk, LONDON, SW14 8EU.
PETTIGREW, Miss. Suzanne Kirsten, BSc(Hons) ACA *2002;* 14 Lowick Place, Emerson Valley, MILTON KEYNES, MK4 2LP.
PETTINGALE, Miss. Louise Mary, BSc ACA *2010;* 11 Park Lane, South Yarra, MELBOURNE, VIC 3141, AUSTRALIA.
PETTINGELL, Mr. Charles, FCA *1970;* Pear Tree House, Hopperton, KNARESBOROUGH, NORTH YORKSHIRE, HG5 8NX.
PETTINGELL, The Revd. Hubert, FCA AKC *1954;* Chemin Du Pommier 22, 1218 Le Grand Saconnex, GENEVA, SWITZERLAND. (Life Member)
PETTINGER, Mr. Brian David, FCA *1970;* 7 Fairfax Road, Menston, ILKLEY, LS29 6EW.
•**PETTINGER, Mrs. Diane, BA FCA** *1992;* Business Advantage Limited, Douglas House, 24 Bridge Street, Slaithwaite, HUDDERSFIELD, HD7 5JN. See also Bamforth & Co
•**PETTINGER, Mr. John Healey, BA ACA** *1987;* 62 Ash Hill Drive, Shadwell, LEEDS, LS17 8JR.
PETTINGER, Mr. William, FCA *1976;* Bidston, Valley Road, Hughenden Valley, HIGH WYCOMBE, HP14 4PF.
PETTINICCHIO, Miss. Chiara, BSc ACA *2006;* with BDO LLP, 6th Floor, 3 Hardman Street, Spinningfields, MANCHESTER, M3 3AT.
PETTIT, Mr. Brian, FCA *1968;* Woodstock, Perrymead, BATH, BA2 5AY. (Life Member)
PETTIT, Miss. Emma, ACA *2011;* 2 Laurel Bank Mews, Blackwell, BROMSGROVE, WORCESTERSHIRE, B60 1PD.
PETTIT, Mr. Frederick George, FCA *1952;* 25 Brian Crescent, Southborough, TUNBRIDGE WELLS, TN4 0AP. (Life Member)
PETTIT, Mr. Gerard Vernon, FCA *1970;* 66 Burton Old Road, Streethay, LICHFIELD, WS13 8LF.
PETTIT, Mrs. Kirsty, BA ACA *2007;* with Price Bailey LLP, The Quorum, Barnwell Road, CAMBRIDGE, CB5 8RE.
PETTIT, Mr. Mark, ACA *2009;* Flat 6, 69 Greencroft Gardens, LONDON, NW6 3LJ.
•**PETTIT, Mr. Michael John, FCA** *1967;* Maurice Andrews, Grove House, 25 Upper Mulgrave Road, Cheam, SUTTON, SM2 7BE.
PETTIT, Mr. Philip John, BSc ACA JD *1990;* Deloitte LLP, 37th Floor, 1633 Broadway, NEW YORK, NY 10019, UNITED STATES.
PETTIT, Mr. Robert Stanley, BA ACA *1982;* Top Gear Unit 1 Gore Cross Business Park, Corbin Way Bradpole, BRIDPORT, DORSET, DT6 3UX.
PETTIT, Mr. Timothy John, BA ACA *1985;* Woodend, Munstead Heath Road, Bramley, GUILDFORD, GU5 0DD.
PETTIT, Mr. William David, FCA *1969;* Coldbrook House, Coldbrook, ABERGAVENNY, GWENT, NP7 9ST.
PETTITT, Mr. Andrew John, ACA *1989;* 45 Chatham Avenue, Hayes, BROMLEY, BR2 7QB.
PETTITT, Mr. Barry William, BA ACA *1997;* 40 Heath Lane, Bladon, WOODSTOCK, OX20 1SA.
•**PETTITT, Ms. Clare Louise, BA ACA** *1999;* with PricewaterhouseCoopers LLP, 1 Embankment Place, LONDON, WC2N 6RH.
PETTITT, Mr. David George, FCA *1963;* Cherry Trees, 4 Stevens Cross Close, SIDMOUTH, DEVON, EX10 9QJ. (Life Member)
PETTITT, Mr. Denby, BA ACA ATII *1984;* 82 Whitehall Place, ABERDEEN, AB25 2RZ.
PETTITT, Mr. Ian Roy, FCA *1969;* 3 Waterside Close, Darley Abbey, DERBY, DE22 1JT. (Life Member)
PETTITT, Mr. Robert Grant, MA FCA *1967;* Craddock Lodge, Craddock, CULLOMPTON, EX15 3LL. (Life Member)
PETTMAN, Mr. Douglas John, FCA *1953;* 96 Ashurst Road, Cockfosters, BARNET, EN4 9LG. (Life Member)
•**PETTMAN, Mrs. Katherine Zoe Vivian, BEng ACA** *1997;* (Tax Fac), Zoe Pettman, Broomfield, Cherry Gardens Hill, Groombridge, TUNBRIDGE WELLS, KENT TN3 9NY.
PETTMAN, Mr. Nigel Robert Anthony, FCA *1970;* The Old Farm, 26 Meriden Road, Hampton-In-Arden, SOLIHULL, B92 0BT.
PETTS, Mr. Alan James, BA ACA *1979;* 5 Bigstone Grove, Tutshill, CHEPSTOW, NP16 7EN.
PETTS, Mr. Gregory Wilfred, BA ACA *1991;* Pokerstars, Skandia House, King Edward Road, Onchan, ISLE OF MAN, IM3 1DZ.
PETTS, Mr. Ian Robert, MSc BSc ACA *2005;* No 6 Rue Alsace Lorraine, 06000 NICE, ALPES MARITIMES, FRANCE.
•**PETTS, Mrs. Lynn, FCA** *1973;* (Tax Fac), Millbank Financial Services Limited, 4th Floor, Swan House, 17-19 Stratford Place, LONDON, W1C 1BQ.
•**PETTY, Mr. Christopher Edward, FCA** *1974;* C.E. Petty & Co, 1 Effingham Court, Constitution Hill, WOKING, SURREY, GU22 7RX.
•**PETTY, Mr. Christopher John, FCA** *1972;* (Tax Fac), C J Petty Limited, 175 High Street, Brownhills, WALSALL, WS8 6HG.
•**PETTY, Mr. Ian Stewart, FCA** *1975;* (Tax Fac), Colston Bush, Lacemaker House, 5-7 Chapel Street, MARLOW, BUCKINGHAMSHIRE, SL7 3HN.
•**PETTY, Mrs. Maria Ines, ACA** *1983;* M I Petty, 4-6 Upper Green Avenue, Scholes, CLECKHEATON, WEST YORKSHIRE, BD19 6PD.
PETTY, Mr. Mark Jonathan, ACA *2009;* 168 Moselle Avenue, LONDON, N22 6EX.
PETTY, Mr. Robert William, FCA *1952;* Lindy Lou, 16 Rawdon Road, Horsforth, LEEDS, LS18 5DZ. (Life Member)
PETTYFER, Miss. Sarah, ACA *2009;* Flat 8, Calico Court, 41 Merton Road, LONDON, SW18 5SU.
PETYAN, Mr. Benjamin Paul, BA FCA *1974;* Olympic Varnish Co Ltd, The Dockyard, Brimscombe, STROUD, GL5 2TQ.
PETYT, Mr. Peter Edward, MA FCA CF *1990;* BDO Jawad Habib, PO Box 787, MANAMA, BAHRAIN.
PETZER, Mr. Bradley, ACA CA(SA) *2010;* 45 Brackley, WEYBRIDGE, SURREY, KT13 0BL.
PETZOLD, Miss. Christina Helen, MA ACA *2007;* 12 Alveston Drive, WILMSLOW, CHESHIRE, SK9 2GA.
PEVERETT, Mrs. Caroline Elizabeth, BA FCA *1995;* 26 Wilsthorpe Road, Breaston, DERBY, DE72 3EB.
•**PEXTON, Mr. Christopher John, FCA** *1979;* Coulthards Mackenzie, 9 Risborough Street, LONDON, SE1 0HF.
•**PEXTON, Mr. Peter Leslie, BSc FCA TEP** *1975;* (Tax Fac), Ganten Group, Städtle 22, LI-9490 VADUZ, LIECHTENSTEIN.
PEYSNER, Miss. Anna, ACA *2003;* with KPMG LLP, Quayside House, 110 Quayside, NEWCASTLE UPON TYNE, NE1 3DX.
PEYTON, Mr. Kevin Christopher Peter, FCA *1970;* 206 Raintree Lane, MALVERN, PA 19355, UNITED STATES.
PEYTON, Mr. Robert Henry, BA FCA *1972;* 5 Beech Grove, Nafferton, East Riding York, DRIFFIELD, NORTH HUMBERSIDE, YO25 4QR.
•**PEYTON, Mr. Timothy Christopher, FCA** *1973;* Peyton Tyler Mears, Middleborough House, 16 Middleborough, COLCHESTER, CO1 1QT.
PEZEILLIER, Miss. Nathalie Annette Marie, BA ACA *2004;* Hamworthy Heating Ltd, Fleets Corner, POOLE, DORSET, BH17 0HH.
PFEFFER, Mrs. Nadia Rachel, ACA *2007;* 48 Lynton Mead, LONDON, N20 8DJ.
PFEIL, Mr. John Christopher, MA ACA *1984;* All 3 Media Ltd, Berkshire House, 168-173 High Holborn, LONDON, WC1V 7AA.
PFLANZ, Mr. Edward Michael, FCA *1968;* Apartado De Correos 575, 29754, Competa, MALAGA, SPAIN.
•**PHADKE, Mr. Sanjeev Yeshwant, BSc FCA** *1982;* Butler & Co LLP, 3rd Floor, 126-134 Baker Street, LONDON, W1U 6UE. See also Butler & Co
PHAGURA, Mrs. Narinderjit, MSc(Eng) BA ACA *1993;* 25 Monksfield Avenue, Great Barr, BIRMINGHAM, B43 6AP.
PHAGURA, Mr. Rajbir Singh, BSc ACA *2006;* 20 Avebury Avenue, LUTON, LU2 7DT.
PHAIR, Miss. Rhonda Lorraine, MA FCA *1996;* 8 Cleaver Park, BELFAST, BT9 5HX.
PHAN, Mrs. Joyce Soo Yuen, ACA *1980;* 6001 Beach Road, Apartment #12-10, SINGAPORE 199589, SINGAPORE.
PHAN, Mr. Leong Kim, FCA *1979;* A-11-5 Mont Kiara Aman, Jalan Kiara 2, Mont Kiara, 50480 KUALA LUMPUR, FEDERAL TERRITORY, MALAYSIA.
PHAN, Mr. Steven Swee Kim, BSc ACA *1985;* with Ernst & Young, One Raffles Quay, North Tower, Level 18, SINGAPORE 048583, SINGAPORE.
PHANG, Mr. Alexius Kong Wong, ACA *1980;* Asiatic Land Developments Sdn Bhd, 12th Floor, 28 Wisma Genting, Jalan Sultan Ismail, 50250 KUALA LUMPUR, FEDERAL TERRITORY MALAYSIA.
PHANG, Miss. Oy Lin, BA ACA *1993;* No 5 Jalan 5/9 D, 46000 PETALING JAYA, SELANGOR, MALAYSIA.
PHARAOH, Mrs. Elaine Dawn, BA ACA *1992;* 32 Squires Bridge Road, SHEPPERTON, MIDDLESEX, TW17 0LB.
PHARO, Mr. George William Lewis, BSc(Econ) FCA *1961;* 68 Heathfield, ROYSTON, SG8 5BN. (Life Member)
•**PHEBY, Mr. John Bernard, FCA** *1968;* John B Pheby, 44 Flint Way, PEACEHAVEN, EAST SUSSEX, BN10 8GN.
PHELAN, Mr. Denis John, ACA *1997;* Seven Acres House, Seven Acres Lane, Great Hautbois, Coltishall, NORWICH, NR12 7JZ.
PHELAN, Mrs. Helen Louise, BA ACA *1995;* The Hollies, Slack Lane, Nether Heage, BELPER, DERBYSHIRE, DE56 2JU.
•**PHELAN, Mr. James Patric, FCA** *1970;* Home Farm House, 91 Main Street, Bushby, LEICESTER, LE7 9PL.
PHELAN, Mr. John Francis, FCA *1972;* Flat 2, Kennington Palace Court, Sancroft Street, LONDON, SE11 5UL.
PHELAN, Mrs. Lesley Anne, LLB FCA *1982;* (Tax Fac), Flat 2, Kennington Palace Court, Sancroft Street, LONDON, SE11 5UL.
PHELAN, Mr. Martin James, MA FCA *1980;* Underwood Gromford Lane, Snape, SAXMUNDHAM, SUFFOLK, IP17 1RD.
PHELAN, Mr. Patrick Justin, BSc ACA *1989;* York Villa, 34 Nursery Lane, WILMSLOW, CHESHIRE, SK9 5JQ.
PHELLAS, Mr. Demetris Glafkou, MSc BSc ACA *1979;* Cyprus Ports Authority, P.O. Box 2007, NICOSIA, CYPRUS.
PHELPS, Mrs. Clare Victoria, MChem ACA *2006;* 57 Hutton Grove, LONDON, N12 8DS.
•**PHELPS, Mr. David Simon, BSc ACA** *1994;* (Tax Fac), PricewaterhouseCoopers LLP, Cornwall Court, 19 Cornwall Street, BIRMINGHAM, B3 2DT. See also PricewaterhouseCoopers
PHELPS, Mr. Peter William, FCA *1957;* Hillcrest, Gravel Hill, LUDLOW, SY8 1QS. (Life Member)
PHELPS, Mrs. Philippa Lesley, FCA *1961;* 28 Courtleigh Avenue, Hadley Wood, BARNET, EN4 0HS. (Life Member)
PHELPS, Mr. Robert Charles Lewis, BA ACA *1980;* 27 Augustan Drive, Caerleon, NEWPORT, NP18 3DD.
PHELPS, Mr. Robin James, ACA *2008;* Flat 15, Hyperion House, Brixton Hill, LONDON, SW2 1HY.
PHELPS, Mr. Stephen William, BSc FCA *1978;* Park Hill, 59 Church Road, Abbots Leigh, BRISTOL, BS8 3QU.
PHELPS, Miss. Victoria Louise, BA(Hons) ACA *2002;* HSBC Level 3, 5 Emaar Square, DUBAI, PO Box 502, UNITED ARAB EMIRATES.
•**PHENIX, Mrs. Helen Louise, BSc ACA** *1991;* Hyperons Limited, 61 Greensleeves Avenue, BROADSTONE, DORSET, BH18 8BJ.
PHENIX, Mr. Paul Anthony, BSc FCA MBA *1971;* Baker Tilly Hong Kong Limited, 2nd Floor, 625 Kings Road, NORTH POINT, HONG KONG SAR.
•**PHIBBS, Mr. John Edward, FCA** *1974;* Afford Bond LLP, 31 Wellington Road, NANTWICH, CHESHIRE, CW5 7ED. See also Afford Astbury Bond LLP
PHIBBS, Mrs. Mary Catherine, BSc CA ACA *1983;* Ground Floor Flat, 17 Lincoln Road, LONDON, N2 9DJ.
PHIDIA, Mr. Christodoulos, BSc FCA *1990;* 36 Ledas Street, Aglantzia, 2115 NICOSIA, CYPRUS.
PHIDIA, Mr. Phidias Loizou, BSc ACA *1995;* 3 Acheloou Street, Strovolos, 2012 NICOSIA, CYPRUS.
PHILANIOTIS, Mr. Andreas, BA ACA *2002;* Flat 101 Zoe Court 12 Heras Street, 1061 NICOSIA, CYPRUS.
PHILANIOTOU, Miss. Ekaterini, BSc FCA *1994;* Rue du Tabellion 35, 1050 BRUSSELS, BELGIUM.

PHILBIN, Mr. Andrew Francis, BSc ACA *1993;* 8 Egerton Road, TWICKENHAM, TW2 7SH.
PHILBIN, Mr. John Nicholas, BCom FCA *1975;* 30 Airedale Avenue, Chiswick, LONDON, W4 2NW.
•**PHILBY, Mr. Mark, FCA** *1995;* Philbys Limited, Bank Chambers, 27a Market Place, Market Deeping, PETERBOROUGH, PE6 8EA.
PHILBY, Mr. Patrick Montague, BA FCA *1973;* Blandy & Blandy, 1 Friar Street, READING, RG1 1DA.
PHILCOX, Mr. James Alexander, BA(Hons) FCA *2001;* Chater House 26/F, 8 Connaught Road, CENTRAL, HONG KONG ISLAND, HONG KONG SAR.
PHILEBROWN, Mrs. Hilary Dion, MA ACA *1987;* 30 Marchbrook Circle, KANATA K2W 1A1, ON, CANADA.
PHILIP, Mr. Andrew, ACA *2011;* Flat 33, Batwa House, Varcoe Road, LONDON, SE16 3BF.
PHILIP, Mr. Colin James, BSc FCA *1975;* Oar Cottage, Homefield Road, Chorleywood, RICKMANSWORTH, HERTFORDSHIRE, WD3 5QJ.
PHILIP, Mr. David Royston, FCA *1975;* National Maritime Museum, Park Row, LONDON, SE10 9NF.
PHILIP, Mr. George Anthony, BSc FCA *1977;* 213 Ham Street, Ham, RICHMOND, TW10 7HF.
•**PHILIP, Mr. Ian Edward, FCA** *1973;* Lord Associates Limited, Caxton House, Old Station Road, LOUGHTON, ESSEX, IG10 4PE. See also Micromoney Limited
PHILIP, Mr. Jothi John, MSc ACA CISA *2011;* 31 Marquess Heights, Queen Mary Avenue, South Woodford, LONDON, E18 2FS.
PHILIP, Mr. Pramod Cherian, FCA FRSA *1995;* Little Down Cottage, Old Down Hill, Tockington, BRISTOL, BS32 4PA.
PHILIP, Mr. Timothy Neil, BSc ACA *2004;* 12 Churchfield Road, WALTON-ON-THAMES, KT12 2TF.
PHILIP, Mr. Truman Tilak, BSc FCA *1968;* 15 York Road, Bounds Green, LONDON, N11 2TH. (Life Member)
PHILIP-SMITH, Mr. John, BA FCA *1972;* Hackney Park, Mount Pleasant Lane, LYMINGTON, HAMPSHIRE, SO41 8LS.
PHILIP-SMITH, Mr. John Philipp, MC FCA *1963;* 41 Willow Court, Ackender Road, ALTON, GU34 1JW. (Life Member)
PHILIPPE, Miss. Anita Helene, BA(Hons) ACA *2004;* Les Pierres Des Haugard, 1 La Route de la Hougue Bie St. Saviour, JERSEY, JE2 7UA.
PHILIPPE, Miss. Donna Evelyn, BA ACA *2006;* 106 Glebelands Close, LONDON, N12 0AN.
PHILIPPIDES, Mr. Alexandros, ACA *2011;* Apartment 18, Hill Quays, 1 Jordan Street, MANCHESTER, LANCASHIRE, M15 4QU.
PHILIPPIDES, Mr. Demetrios, MSc ACA *2009;* 46 Vasileos Konstantinous IB, T.K 8021, PAFOS, CYPRUS.
PHILIPPIDOU, Ms. Anna, BSc FCA *1993;* 6 Festou Street, Strovolos, NICOSIA, 2039, CYPRUS.
PHILIPPIDOU, Miss. Panayiota, ACA *2004;* 5 AINEAS, AINEAS COURT, FLAT 301, LAKATAMIA, 2311 NICOSIA, CYPRUS.
PHILIPPOU, Mr. Agathoclis Savva, ACA *2009;* Agiou Nikolaou 1B, 8300 - Konia, PAPHOS, CYPRUS.
•**PHILIPPOU, Mr. Andreas, MBA BSc ACA** *2001;* Baker Tilly Klitou and Partners Ltd, 11 Bouboulinas Street, 1060 NICOSIA, CYPRUS.
PHILIPPOU, Mr. Andreas Joannou, BSc FCA *1964;* 20 Amalia Street, Dasoupolis, NICOSIA, CYPRUS.
PHILIPPOU, Miss. Angela, ACA *2011;* 5 A. Stavrides Street, Dasoupolis, TT2015 NICOSIA, CYPRUS.
PHILIPPOU, Mrs. Christina, ACA *2008;* with Deloitte LLP, Athene Place, 66 Shoe Lane, LONDON, EC4A 3BQ.
PHILIPPOU, Mr. Chrysostomos Costa, BSc ACA *1988;* 6 Andrea Vlami, Acropolis, Strovolos, 2008 NICOSIA, CYPRUS.
PHILIPPOU, Ms. Despina, BSc ACA *2002;* Eftaxias 5, 16672 VARI, GREECE.
•**PHILIPPOU, Mr. Eleftherios Nicolaou, FCA** *1982;* Deloitte Limited, 24 Spyrou Kyprianou Avenue, P.O.Box 21675 CY-1512, 1075 NICOSIA, CYPRUS.
PHILIPPOU, Ms. Phani, BSc ACA *2010;* 17 Geri Avenue, Geri Flat 204, 2200 NICOSIA, CYPRUS.
PHILIPPS, Mrs. Caroline Anne, BSc ACA ATII *1991;* (Tax Fac), Little Clarks, Thaxted Road, Little Sampford, SAFFRON WALDEN, CB10 2SA.
PHILIPPS, Mr. Charles Edward Lawrence, ACA *1983;* Dalham Hall, Dalham, NEWMARKET, SUFFOLK, CB8 8TB.
PHILIPPS, Mr. Richard Henry, BA ACA *1990;* 34 Murdoch Terrace, DUNBLANE, PERTHSHIRE, FK15 9JF.
PHILIPS, Mr. John Anthony, BA ACA *1982;* 98 Waterloo Road, SOUTHPORT, MERSEYSIDE, PR8 3AY.
PHILIPSON, Miss. Jennifer Mary, BA ACA *2007;* 5 Hardwick Avenue, Allestree, DERBY, DE22 2LN.
PHILIPSON, Mrs. Lucy Victoria, MA ACA *2001;* 204 Esplanade, SEACLIFF, SA 5049, AUSTRALIA.
PHILIPSON-STOW, Mr. Robert Nicholas, DL FCA *1963;* Priors Court, Long Green, GLOUCESTER, GL19 4QL. (Life Member)
PHILIS, Ms. Alexia, ACA CA(AUS) *2009;* 16 Macquarie Drive, Cherrybrook, SYDNEY, NSW 2126, AUSTRALIA.
PHILIS, Mr. Panayiotis Nicolaou, FCA *1971;* PN Philis & Co, 16 Macquarie Drive, CHERRYBROOK, NSW 2126, AUSTRALIA.
•**PHILLIP, Mr. Rhys Ap John, MA ACA** *1995;* Ernst & Young LLP, 1 More London Place, LONDON, SE1 2AF. See also Ernst & Young Europe LLP
PHILLIPPS, Mr. David Alan, FCA *1982;* 2 High Close, RICKMANSWORTH, HERTFORDSHIRE, WD3 4DZ.
PHILLIPS, Mr. Adam David, BSc ACA *2006;* Molson Coors Brewing Co(UK) Ltd, 137 High Street, BURTON-ON-TRENT, STAFFORDSHIRE, DE14 1JZ.
PHILLIPS, Mr. Adrian, ACA *2010;* 32 Plainsfield Street, MANCHESTER, M16 7HB.
PHILLIPS, Mr. Adrian Peter Wallace, FCA *1971;* 10 Longacre Court, 8 Newton Park Place, CHISLEHURST, KENT, BR7 5BF. (Life Member)
PHILLIPS, Mr. Alan Godfrey, FCA *1982;* 2 Loughbrow Park, HEXHAM, NORTHUMBERLAND, NE46 2QD.
PHILLIPS, Miss. Alexa, LLB ACA *2002;* Cobra (UK) Ltd Crossgate House, Cross Street, SALE, CHESHIRE, M33 7FT.
PHILLIPS, Mr. Alexander Wallace, FCA *1969;* 1 Berkley Road, BEACONSFIELD, HP9 2AY. (Life Member)
PHILLIPS, Miss. Alison Barbara, ACA *1992;* 1 Rhymers Gate, Wyton, HUNTINGDON, PE28 2JR.
PHILLIPS, Miss. Alison Mary, BA ACA *2001;* Older Peoples Commission for Wales, Cambrian Buildings, Mount Stuart Square, CARDIFF, CF10 5FL.
PHILLIPS, Miss. Amanda Joanne, BA ACA *2004;* 48 Fortis Green, LONDON, N2 9EL.
•**PHILLIPS, Mr. Andrew, FCA** *1973;* (Tax Fac), Whitehouse Ridsdale, 26 Birmingham Road, WALSALL, WS1 2LZ.
•**PHILLIPS, Mr. Andrew Goodwyn, BA FCA** *1990;* (Tax Fac), Tetlow & Smith, 1 Osborne Road, Jesmond, NEWCASTLE UPON TYNE, NE2 2AA.
PHILLIPS, Mr. Andrew Marcus, BA ACA *2010;* Ground Floor Flat, 51 Sherriff Road, LONDON, NW6 2AS.
PHILLIPS, Mr. Andrew Mark, MA FCA *1993;* The Duchy of Cornwall, The Old Rectory, Newton St Loe, BATH, BS2 9BU.
PHILLIPS, Miss. Ann Lloyd, BSc ACA *1989;* 38 Fieldway, Lindfield, HAYWARDS HEATH, RH16 2DD.
PHILLIPS, Mrs. Anna Marie, BA ACA *2000;* Deloitte & Touche Ltd Global House, High Street, CRAWLEY, WEST SUSSEX, RH10 1DL.
•**PHILLIPS, Mr. Anthony, ACA CA(SA)** *2008;* (Tax Fac), Exceed UK Limited, Bank House, 81 St Judes Road, Englefield Green, EGHAM, SURREY TW20 0DF.
PHILLIPS, Mr. Anthony, ACA *2009;* The Coach Holiday Warehouse Unit F-h, Pate Court St. Margarets Road, CHELTENHAM, GL50 4DY.
PHILLIPS, Mr. Anthony John, BSc FCA *1972;* Stile House, 17 Leighton Rd, Wingrave, AYLESBURY, HP22 4PA.
PHILLIPS, Mr. Anthony Peter, BA ACA *1985;* Smith Bilbrough & Co Ltd, 77 Gracechurch Street, LONDON, EC3V 0AG.
PHILLIPS, Mr. Anthony Pugh, FCA *1969;* Lightbounds, Wood Lane, UTTOXETER, STAFFORDSHIRE, ST14 8BE. (Life Member)
PHILLIPS, Mr. Arthur Edward, BA ACA ACMA *2011;* 85 Longmeads, TUNBRIDGE WELLS, KENT, TN3 0AU.
PHILLIPS, Mr. Arthur John, MA FCA *1973;* 611 Avenue du Marechal Juin, 92100 BOULOGNE, FRANCE.
PHILLIPS, Mr. Barry John, FCA *1969;* Ravenscroft St. Saviours Hill, St. Saviour, JERSEY, JE2 7LF.
PHILLIPS, Mr. Ben, ACA *2010;* Deloitte LLP, Athene Place 66 Shoe Lane, LONDON, EC4a 3BQ.
PHILLIPS, Mr. Brett Warwick James, BSc ACA *1986;* Portmeirion Group Plc, London Road, STOKE-ON-TRENT, STAFFORDSHIRE, ST4 7QQ.
PHILLIPS, Mrs. Caroline Jane, BA ACA *2005;* with BDO LLP, Kings Wharf, 20-30 Kings Road, READING, RG1 3EX.
PHILLIPS, Mrs. Caroline Wendy, BA ACA *1983;* Kiln Meadow, Sheet Hill, Plaxtol, SEVENOAKS, TN15 0PU.
PHILLIPS, Mrs. Catherine, ACA *2011;* Banérgatan 45, 115 22 STOCKHOLM, SWEDEN.
PHILLIPS, Miss. Catherine Jane, BA ACA *2003;* Flat 36 Bentahm House, 9 Falmouth Road, LONDON, SE1 4JY.
PHILLIPS, Miss. Charlotte Jayne, ACA *2008;* 35 Ferndene Road, LONDON, SE24 0AQ.
PHILLIPS, Miss. Cheryl Janet, ACA *2004;* Baytree Cottage, 18A Manor Road, BURNHAM-ON-SEA, SOMERSET, TA8 2AS.
PHILLIPS, Miss. Christina, BSc ACA *2011;* Flat J/65 Du Cane Court, Balham High Road, LONDON, SW17 7JX.
•**PHILLIPS, Mr. Christopher Charles Hugh, BA ACA** *1990;* Deloitte LLP, General Guisan-Quai 38, PO Box 2232, 8022 ZURICH, SWITZERLAND. See also Deloitte & Touche LLP
PHILLIPS, Mr. Christopher John, FCA *1975;* The Orchard Whittlebury House, 34 Church Way, Whittlebury, TOWCESTER, NORTHAMPTONSHIRE, NN12 8XS.
•**PHILLIPS, Mr. Christopher Mitchell, FCA** *1974;* 197 Berry Way, ANDOVER, SP10 3RY.
PHILLIPS, Miss. Claire, BA(Hons) ACA *2001;* 134 Valley Drive, CARLISLE, CA1 3TR.
PHILLIPS, Mrs. Clare Angela, BSc ACA *1995;* EC Drummond & Son, The Homme, Hom Green, ROSS-ON-WYE, HEREFORDSHIRE, HR9 7TF.
PHILLIPS, Miss. Clare April Jacqueline, BSc ACA *2007;* Flat 5, Nigel Court, Seymour Road, LONDON, N3 2NF.
PHILLIPS, Mr. Clarence Howard, FCA *1961;* Chy Gwyn, Tregenna Lane, CAMBORNE, TR14 7QT. (Life Member)
PHILLIPS, Mr. Craig, BSc ACA *2006;* 76 The Meadows, Marshfield, CARDIFF, CF3 2DY.
PHILLIPS, Mr. Dane Anthony, ACA *2010;* with Grant Thornton UK LLP, 30 Finsbury Square, LONDON, EC2P 2YU.
PHILLIPS, Mr. Daniel, BA(Hons) ACA *2000;* 28 Wykehurst House, Chaucer Way, LONDON, SW19 1UH.
PHILLIPS, Mr. Daniel, FCA *1958;* 19 Lancaster Grove, LONDON, NW3 4EX. (Life Member)
PHILLIPS, Mr. Daniel James, BSc ACA *2009;* 9 Brownlow Close, BARNET, HERTFORDSHIRE, EN4 8FE.
•**PHILLIPS, Mr. Darryl Clark Charles, BSc ACA** *1997;* with PricewaterhouseCoopers LLP, 1 Embankment Place, LONDON, WC2N 6RH.
PHILLIPS, Mr. David, BA FCA DChA *1982;* 'Norwood', 3 Manor Fields, Halam, NEWARK, NOTTINGHAMSHIRE, NG22 8DU.
PHILLIPS, Mr. David, BA ACA *1981;* with PKF (Isle of Man) LLC, PO Box 16, Analyst House, Douglas, ISLE OF MAN, IM99 1AP.
PHILLIPS, Mr. David James, MSc ACA *1980;* Park Villa, 91 Main Street, Uddingston, GLASGOW, G71 7EW.
PHILLIPS, Mr. David Jeremy, BA ACA *1983;* 11 Hillingdon Road, Whitefield, MANCHESTER, M45 7QQ.
•**PHILLIPS, Mr. David John, BSc FCA** *1974;* Waugh Haines Rigby Limited, 18 Miller Court, Severn Drive, Tewkesbury Business Park, TEWKESBURY, GLOUCESTERSHIRE GL20 8DN.
PHILLIPS, Mr. David John, BSc FCA *1973;* 15 Cherry Grove, PORT TALBOT, SA12 8UT.
PHILLIPS, Mr. David John, BSc ACA *1997;* Matthew Clark, Whitchurch Lane, BRISTOL, AVON, BS14 0JZ.
PHILLIPS, Mr. David John, BA FCA *1976;* Box 82722, SOUTHDALE, 2135, SOUTH AFRICA.
PHILLIPS, Mr. David Laurence, BA ACA *1991;* Rokko Court, 31 Carlton Road, Hale, ALTRINCHAM, CHESHIRE, WA15 8RH.
•**PHILLIPS, Mr. David Michael Havard, BA ACA** *1983;* PricewaterhouseCoopers LLP, 1 Embankment Place, LONDON, WC2N 6RH. See also PricewaterhouseCoopers
•**PHILLIPS, Mr. David Morgan, BSc FCA** *1980;* Young & Philllips Limited, Inspiration House, Williams Place, Cardiff Road, PONTYPRIDD, MID GLAMORGAN CF37 5BH.
PHILLIPS, Mr. David Morgan, BSc FCA *1977;* 5 Ffordd Camlas, High Cross Reach, High Cross, NEWPORT, GWENT, NP10 9LW.
PHILLIPS, Mr. David Osborne, ACA *1981;* 599 11th Avenue, 8 FL, NEW YORK, NY 10036, UNITED STATES.
PHILLIPS, Mr. David Owen, FCA *1969;* Apartado De Correos90, 03158 CATRAL, ALICANTE, SPAIN. (Life Member)
PHILLIPS, Mr. David Pugh, FCA *1960;* 38 Grasmere, TROWBRIDGE, BA14 7LL. (Life Member)
PHILLIPS, Mr. David Rhodri, ACA *2008;* Apartment 21, 24 Point Pleasant, LONDON, SW18 1GG.
PHILLIPS, Mr. David Wells, FCA *1956;* Lyndel, Bell Green Lane, Headley Heath, BIRMINGHAM, B38 0DJ. (Life Member)
PHILLIPS, Mr. Derek Ellis, FCA *1957;* 34 Pinewood Avenue, SEVENOAKS, TN14 5AF. (Life Member)
•**PHILLIPS, Mr. Derek Norman, FCA** *1984;* 10 Lawrence Crescent, RICHMOND, NORTH YORKSHIRE, DL10 5QE.
PHILLIPS, Mr. Derek Roy, FCA *1956;* Vitrsatile Plant Ltd, 14 Oakfield Drive, Formby, LIVERPOOL, L37 1NR.
PHILLIPS, Mr. Edwin George, FCA *1967;* Popeswood End, Popeswood Road, Binfield, BRACKNELL, RG42 4AD. (Life Member)
PHILLIPS, Ms. Elaine Lesley, BA ACA *1990;* 59 Bootham, YORK, YO30 7BT.
PHILLIPS, Mr. Ellis Reed, MA ACA *1997;* 7 Chaucer Road, LONDON, E11 2RE.
PHILLIPS, Mr. Emyr Maldwyn, BSc FCA *1993;* Glyndwr, Abermagwr, ABERYSTWYTH, DYFED, SY23 4AR.
PHILLIPS, Mrs. Erica Frances, BSc ACA *1992;* 14 Gardner Road, CHRISTCHURCH, BH23 2DZ.
PHILLIPS, Mr. Ewan Alastair, MA ACA *1990;* 89 Queens Road, RICHMOND, TW10 6HJ.
PHILLIPS, Mrs. Fiona Elizabeth, BSc ACA ATII *1990;* (Tax Fac), Tall Trees, Front Street, Naburn, YORK, YO19 4RR.
PHILLIPS, Mr. Gareth Morgan, ACA *2008;* Chequers House Chequers Lane, Eversley, HOOK, RG27 0NT.
PHILLIPS, Mr. Gareth Paul, BSc ACA *1992;* Flat 33H, Block 25, Park Island, 8 Paklai Road, MA WAN, NEW TERRITORIES HONG KONG SAR.
•**PHILLIPS, Mr. Gavin Mark, BSocSc ACA** *1997;* PricewaterhouseCoopers LLP, Hays Galleria, 1 Hays Lane, LONDON, SE1 2RD. See also PricewaterhouseCoopers
PHILLIPS, Mr. George Stephen, FCA *1944;* 71 Pearson Road, CLEETHORPES, DN35 0DR. (Life Member)
•**PHILLIPS, Mr. Graham Peter Nelson, BSc FCA** *1982;* PricewaterhouseCoopers LLP, Hays Galleria, 1 Hays Lane, LONDON, SE1 2RD. See also PricewaterhouseCoopers
PHILLIPS, Mr. Guy Robert, BA ACA *1996;* 27 Kings Road, HENLEY-ON-THAMES, OXFORDSHIRE, RG9 2DW.
PHILLIPS, Miss. Helen, BA(Econ) ACA *2011;* 6 Halford Road, LONDON, SW6 1JT.
•**PHILLIPS, Mrs. Helen Timothe, FCA** *1969;* Russell Phillips Ltd, 23 Station Road, GERRARDS CROSS, BUCKINGHAMSHIRE, SL9 8ES. See also Keen Phillips Ltd
PHILLIPS, Mr. Henry Michael James, ACA *2009;* Deloitte & Touche, PO Box 500, MANCHESTER, M60 2AT.
PHILLIPS, Mrs. Hilary Elizabeth, BSocSc ACA *1986;* 32 Shaplands, Stoke Bishop, BRISTOL, BS9 1AY.
PHILLIPS, Mr. Huw Alun, BA FCA CTA *1989;* 8 Chessfield Park, Little Chalfont, AMERSHAM, HP6 6RU.
PHILLIPS, Mr. Hywel Rhys, ACA *2008;* 135 Moorland Road, Sploff, CARDIFF, CF24 2LG.
PHILLIPS, Mr. I Peter Peter, OBE FCA *1968;* 5 Turner Drive, LONDON, NW11 6TX. (Life Member)
PHILLIPS, Mr. Ian, FCA *1961;* 5 The Croft, Carpenters Lane, CIRENCESTER, GLOUCESTERSHIRE, GL7 1EE.
•**PHILLIPS, Mr. Ian, FCA** *1980;* Duncan & Toplis, 14 London Road, NEWARK, NG24 1TW.
PHILLIPS, Mr. Ian Richard, BSc ACA *1994;* 29 Quartz Close, WOKINGHAM, RG41 3TS.
•**PHILLIPS, Mr. Ian Timothy, FCA** *1975;* Burton & Co, Sovereign House, Bradford Road, Riddlesden, KEIGHLEY, BD20 5EW.
PHILLIPS, Mr. Iwan Ceri, BSc ACA *2010;* Apartment 311, King Edwards Wharf, 25 Sheepcote Street, BIRMINGHAM, B16 8AB.
PHILLIPS, Miss. Jacqueline Maria, BA(Hons) ACA *2003;* 5 Chase Court Gardens, ENFIELD, MIDDLESEX, EN2 8DH.
PHILLIPS, Mr. James Brandon, BSc ACA *1995;* Bentinck Street, Farnworth, BOLTON, BL4 7EP.
PHILLIPS, Mr. James Edward Franklyn, MA ACA *1987;* 7 Broomfield Road, BECKENHAM, BR3 3QB.
PHILLIPS, Mr. James Edward Kyndon, ACA *2008;* Broadcom UK Ltd, 406 Science Park, Milton Road, CAMBRIDGE, CB4 0WW.
PHILLIPS, Mr. James Frederick, BA ACA *1982;* 2 The Grove, East Keswick, LEEDS, LS17 9EX.
PHILLIPS, Mrs. Jane Elizabeth Margaret, BA ACA ACCA *2000;* (Tax Fac), Niu Solutions, 45 Moorfields, LONDON, EC2Y 9AE.
PHILLIPS, Mrs. Janette May, FCA *1980;* (Tax Fac), 15 Ashtead Close, Walmley, SUTTON COLDFIELD, B76 1YH.
PHILLIPS, Mrs. Jayne Clare, BA(Hons) ACA *2003;* Bioprogress Technology Ltd, 15-17 Science Park Milton Road, CAMBRIDGE, CB4 0FQ.
PHILLIPS, Mr. Jeffrey John, FCA FCT *1968;* The Old Rectory, Cubley, ASHBOURNE, DE6 2EZ. (Life Member)

PHILLIPS, Miss. Jemma Ilva, ACA *2008;* 15 Basil Close, Earley, READING, RG6 5GL.
PHILLIPS, Ms. Jennifer Natalie Kyndon, BA ACA *2003;* 94 High Street, Harston, CAMBRIDGE, CB22 7QB.
PHILLIPS, Mr. John Bennett, FCA *1953;* Valhalla, Agneash, Laxey, ISLE OF MAN, IM4 7NP. (Life Member)
PHILLIPS, Mr. John Christopher, FCA *1958;* Willowgarth, Sunhill Lane, Topsham, EXETER, EX3 0BR. (Life Member)
PHILLIPS, Mr. John Clive, FCA *1951;* The Middle Wyke, The Wyke, SHIFNAL, TF11 9PP. (Life Member)
•PHILLIPS, Mr. John Irvine, BA ACA *1985;* John Phillips, 387 Chartridge Lane, CHESHAM, BUCKINGHAMSHIRE, HP5 2SL.
PHILLIPS, Mr. John Richard, BA FCA *1972;* 24 Pendwyallt Road, Coryton, CARDIFF, CF14 7EG.
PHILLIPS, Mr. John Richard, BSc ACA *1981;* Mercia Corporate Finance Ltd, 278 Ecclesall Road, SHEFFIELD, S11 8PE.
PHILLIPS, Mr. John Robert, BSc ACA *1979;* 89 Rosamond Avenue, Bradway, SHEFFIELD, S17 4LS.
•PHILLIPS, Mr. John Sidney, TD MA FCA *1974;* J.S. Phillips, Mill House, Dewlish, DORCHESTER, DORSET, DT2 7LT.
PHILLIPS, Mr. John Wilson, CBE MA FCA *1959;* Ash Hall, Ystradowen, COWBRIDGE, CF71 7SY.
PHILLIPS, Mr. Jonathan, MEng ACA *2003;* Russet Cottage, 4 Bridle Road, Whitchurch Hill, READING, RG8 7PR.
•ⒹPHILLIPS, Mr. Jonathan Guy Anthony, MA FCA *1978;* with Pricewaterhousecoopers, 12 Plumtree Court, LONDON, EC4A 4HT.
PHILLIPS, Mrs. Josephine Paula, BSc ACA *1989;* Cheltenham, Caenshill Road, WEYBRIDGE, KT13 0SW.
PHILLIPS, Mrs. Judith, FCA *1962;* 38 Grasmere, TROWBRIDGE, BA14 7LL.
PHILLIPS, Mrs. Julia Veronica, BA ACA *1990;* 46 Eltisley Avenue, Newnham, Cambridge, CAMBRIDGE, CAMBRIDGESHIRE, CB3 9JQ.
PHILLIPS, Mrs. Julie Hazel, BA ACA *1989;* 26 Lynn Street, Cwmbwrla, SWANSEA, SA5 8BB.
PHILLIPS, Ms. Juliet, BSc ACA *2000;* (Tax Fac), Flat B, 13 Fordwych Road, LONDON, NW2 3TN.
PHILLIPS, Mr. Justin Myles Jonathon, BA ACA *1992;* Opex Exhibition Services Ltd, 21 Highfield Road, Sandridge, ST. ALBANS, HERTFORDSHIRE, AL4 9BU.
PHILLIPS, Mrs. Karen Anne, MA ACA *1995;* 64 Overland Road, Mumbles, SWANSEA, SA3 4LL.
PHILLIPS, Mrs. Karen Louise, BAcc ACA *2006;* 154 West End Avenue, HARROGATE, NORTH YORKSHIRE, HG2 9BT.
PHILLIPS, Mr. Keith, FCA *1966;* 4 Strangford Court, Apperley Bridge, BRADFORD, WEST YORKSHIRE, BD10 9TJ. (Life Member)
•PHILLIPS, Mr. Keith, FCA *1987;* Duncan & Toplis, 18 Northgate, SLEAFORD, LINCOLNSHIRE, NG34 7BJ.
PHILLIPS, Mr. Keith Andrew, ACA *1980;* 193 Chartwell, Southill, WEYMOUTH, DORSET, DT4 9SP.
•PHILLIPS, Mr. Keith Arthur, FCA *1969;* (Tax Fac), Ingram & Terry Limited, Sullivan House, 72-80 Widemarsh Street, HEREFORD, HR4 9HG.
PHILLIPS, Mr. Kenneth, FCA *1947;* 168 Elwick Road, HARTLEPOOL, TS26 9NR. (Life Member)
PHILLIPS, Mr. Kenneth Charles, FCA *1955;* 2 Petersmead Close, TADWORTH, SURREY, KT20 5AR. (Life Member)
PHILLIPS, Miss. Kerri Louise, ACA *2004;* 32 Burnet Road, Bradwell, GREAT YARMOUTH, NORFOLK, NR31 8SL.
•PHILLIPS, Mr. Kevin John, MA FCA *1985;* Baker Tilly Tax and Advisory Services LLP, 25 Farringdon Street, LONDON, EC4A 4AB.
•PHILLIPS, Mr. Larry Michael, FCA *1979;* Goodman Jones LLP, 29-30 Fitzroy Square, LONDON, W1T 6LQ.
•PHILLIPS, Mr. Lawrence Anthony, FCA *1974;* Lawrence Phillips & Company, 42 Lipizzaner Fields, Whiteley, FAREHAM, HAMPSHIRE, PO15 7BH. See also Phillips Spyrou LLP
PHILLIPS, Mr. Leslie Ernest Stephen, FCA *1969;* 5 The Panney, Honeylands, EXETER, EX4 8QT. (Life Member)
PHILLIPS, Mrs. Lynda Mary, BSc FCA *1983;* 5 Brook Meadow, FAREHAM, PO15 5JH.
PHILLIPS, Mr. Marcus Andrew, BSc FCA *1991;* 20 Eaton Road, ILKLEY, WEST YORKSHIRE, LS29 9PU.
PHILLIPS, Mrs. Marilyn Jane, BA ACA *1989;* Pen-men-eth, 31 Horseshoe Walk, Bathwick, BATH, BA2 6DF.
PHILLIPS, Mrs. Marina Margaret, BA FCA DChA *1988;* 78 High Road, BUCKHURST HILL, IG9 5RP.
PHILLIPS, Mr. Mark, ACA *2009;* 12 Parkland Gardens, LEEDS, LS6 4PG.
PHILLIPS, Mr. Mark Christopher, MSc BA(Hons) ACA *2002;* The Cottage, Alderley, WOTTON-UNDER-EDGE, GL12 7QT.
PHILLIPS, Mr. Mark Edward, ACA *2008;* 17a Lower Redannick, TRURO, CORNWALL, TR1 2JW.
PHILLIPS, Mr. Mark Monteith, MA BSc(Econ) FCA CPA *1999;* 46616 Hampshire Station Drive, STERLING, VA 20165, UNITED STATES.
PHILLIPS, Mr. Mark Trevor, BA ACA *1993;* The Old Rectory, Main Street, Barwick In Elmet, LEEDS, LS15 4JR.
PHILLIPS, Miss. Maxine Lindsay, MA FCA *1988;* (Tax Fac), 6 Downs Mill, Frampton Mansell, STROUD, GL6 8JX.
PHILLIPS, Mrs. Melanie Kate, LLB ACA *1991;* Brenntag UK & Ireland Unit 1 Albion House, Rawdon Park Yeadon, LEEDS, LS19 7XX.
•PHILLIPS, Mr. Michael David Robert, BSc FCA *1979;* 23 Birches Lane, KENILWORTH, CV8 2AB.
PHILLIPS, Mr. Michael Douglas John, BA FCA *1970;* 15 The Park, CHELTENHAM, GL50 2SL. (Life Member)
PHILLIPS, Mr. Michael Eric John, FCA *1963;* 20 Glendale Crescent, ST AUSTELL, CORNWALL, PL25 3DD.
PHILLIPS, Mr. Michael Ian, ACA *1984;* 15 Norfolk Road, Great Neck, NEW YORK, NY 11020, UNITED STATES.
•PHILLIPS, Mr. Michael Jeremy, FCA *1982;* Phillips & Co., 52 The Chase, Newhall, HARLOW, ESSEX, CM17 9JA.
PHILLIPS, Mr. Michael John, BSc FCA *1980;* Quoins, Windmill Way, Lyddington, RUTLAND, LE15 9LY.
PHILLIPS, Mr. Michael John, MBA FCA *1977;* ISG Jackson Limited, Jackson House, 86 Sandy Hill Lane, IPSWICH, IP3 0NA.
PHILLIPS, Mr. Michael Lionel, FCA *1954;* 5th Floor, Berkeley Square House, Berkeley Square, LONDON, W1J 6BY. (Life Member)
PHILLIPS, Mr. Michael Scott, BSc ACA *1989;* Cheltenham, Caenshill Road, WEYBRIDGE, KT13 0SW.
PHILLIPS, Mr. Michael Sherman, BA ACA *1993;* 3 Onslow Close, WOKING, GU22 7AZ.
PHILLIPS, Mrs. Michelle Elizabeth, ACA *2008;* 56 Curzen Crescent, Kirk Sandall, DONCASTER, SOUTH YORKSHIRE, DN3 1PR.
PHILLIPS, Mr. Morgan Daniel, BA(Hons) ACA *2010;* 15 Teg Down Meads, WINCHESTER, HAMPSHIRE, SO22 5NF.
•PHILLIPS, Mr. Neil Christopher, BA FCA *1987;* (Tax Fac), Phillips Ltd, Kingsland House, Stafford Court, Stafford Park 1, TELFORD, SHROPSHIRE TF3 3BD.
PHILLIPS, Mr. Neil Paul, BA ACA *2008;* 701 Brickell Avenue Suite 2300, MIAMI, FL 33130, UNITED STATES.
PHILLIPS, Mr. Nicholas, BA ACA *1999;* 34/50 Aubin Street, NEUTRAL BAY, NSW 2089, AUSTRALIA.
•PHILLIPS, Mr. Nicholas Kennard, BSc FCA *1979;* N.K. Phillips, 30 Laneham Place, KENILWORTH, WARWICKSHIRE, CV8 2UN.
PHILLIPS, Mrs. Nicola Ann, BA ACA *1985;* Greenleaves, Milton Avenue, GERRARDS CROSS, SL9 8QN.
PHILLIPS, Mrs. Nicola Louise, BSc ACA *1998;* Pearson Plc Shell Mex House, 80 Strand, LONDON, WC2R 0RL.
PHILLIPS, Mr. Nigel John, BA ACA *1979;* 21 Paddock Close, Radcliffe-On-Trent, NOTTINGHAM, NG12 2BX.
PHILLIPS, Mr. Owen Rhodri, ACA *2008;* with Grant Thornton UK LLP, Grant Thornton House, 22 Melton Street, Euston Square, LONDON, NW1 2EP.
PHILLIPS, Mrs. Pamela Jane, LLB ACA *2004;* 134 Haydon Park Road, LONDON, SW19 8JT.
PHILLIPS, Mrs. Patricia Gail, BSc FCA *1986;* Culverwood Shinfield Road, Shinfield, READING, RG2 9BE.
PHILLIPS, Mr. Paul Haydn, BA(Hons) ACA *2003;* 134 Haydon Park Road, LONDON, SW19 8JT.
•PHILLIPS, Mr. Paul Jeremy, BA FCA *1984;* Brian Paul Limited, Chase Green House, 42 Chase Side, ENFIELD, MIDDLESEX, EN2 6NF.
PHILLIPS, Mr. Paul Nicholas, ACA *1982;* Hangar 89, Easyjet Airline Co Ltd, Airport Approach Road, LUTON, LU2 9PF.
PHILLIPS, Mr. Paul Raymond Joseph, BSS ACA *1991;* Intercontinental Hotels Group Plc Broadwater Park, North Orbital Road Denham, UXBRIDGE, MIDDLESEX, UB9 5HR.
PHILLIPS, Mrs. Penelope Margaret, BSc FCA *1978;* with Baker Tilly Tax & Advisory Services LLP, The Clock House, 140 London Road, GUILDFORD, SURREY, GU1 1UW.
PHILLIPS, Mr. Peter, FCA *1966;* Wistaria House, Coggeshall, COLCHESTER, CO6 1UF.
PHILLIPS, Mr. Peter Michael, ACA *1992;* 12 Huntingdon Gardens Horton Heath, EASTLEIGH, HAMPSHIRE, SO50 7FH.
PHILLIPS, Mr. Peter Sean, FCA FCT *1970;* Drift House, Astley, SHREWSBURY, SY4 4BP.
PHILLIPS, Mr. Peter Stuart, MA FCA *1979;* Old School, Church Hill, Finedon, WELLINGBOROUGH, NORTHAMPTONSHIRE, NN9 5NR.
PHILLIPS, Mr. Peter Warren, FCA *1955;* The Old Vicarage, Streatley, READING, RG8 9HX. (Life Member)
PHILLIPS, Mrs. Rachel Elizabeth, BA ACA *2001;* 88 Thatcham Avenue Kingsway, Quedgeley, GLOUCESTER, GL2 2BJ.
PHILLIPS, Miss. Rachel Louise, BSc ACA *2003;* 22 Chivalry Road, LONDON, SW11 1HT.
PHILLIPS, Miss. Rhianna, ACA *2011;* 222 Station Road, Knowle, SOLIHULL, B93 0ER.
PHILLIPS, Mr. Richard, BA ACA CF *2004;* with Grant Thornton UK LLP, 1 Whitehall Riverside, Whitehall Road, LEEDS, WEST YORKSHIRE, LS1 4BN.
PHILLIPS, Mr. Richard Adam Elliot, LLB ACA *2004;* 24 Speedwell Close, Abbeymead, GLOUCESTER, GL4 4GQ.
PHILLIPS, Mr. Richard Clive, BSc ACA *1992;* 17 Paines Lane, PINNER, MIDDLESEX, HA5 3DF.
PHILLIPS, Mr. Richard Gwyn, FCA *1966;* 10 Morlais Road, Margam, PORT TALBOT, SA13 2AT.
•PHILLIPS, Mr. Richard Horby, FCA *1968;* R.H. Phillips, Wychwood, 86 Kimpton Road Blackmore End, Wheathampstead, ST. ALBANS, AL4 8LX.
PHILLIPS, Mr. Richard James, MA ACA *1981;* Hornington Grange, Bolton Percy, YORK, YO23 7AT.
PHILLIPS, Mr. Richard John, BSc FCA *1975;* Flat 3 Athelstan Court, St. Thomas Park, LYMINGTON, SO41 9FB.
PHILLIPS, Mr. Richard Stephen, BSc ACA *1990;* Bedwen, Newtown, AMMANFORD, SA18 3TE.
PHILLIPS, Mr. Richard William, BA FCA *1984;* (Tax Fac), Flat 5, Shelbourne Place, 6a Lawn Road, BECKENHAM, BR3 1RH.
PHILLIPS, Mr. Robert, BA(Hons) ACA *2011;* Apartment 477, Orion Building, 90 Navigation Street, BIRMINGHAM, B5 4AJ.
PHILLIPS, Mr. Robert Brynley, MEng ACA *2002;* c/o Graceway Trading Ltd, PO Box 368, PROVIDENCIALES, TURKS AND CAICOS ISLANDS.
PHILLIPS, Mr. Robert Cornelius, BSc ACA *1987;* 26 Walnut Circle, Basking Ridge, NEW JERSEY, NJ 07920, UNITED STATES.
PHILLIPS, Mr. Robert Glen, BA ACA *2007;* Linear Park, Avon Street, BRISTOL, BS2 0PS.
PHILLIPS, Mr. Robert Glyn, BSc FCA *1973;* 23 Mead Way, Kirkburton, HUDDERSFIELD, HD8 0TG. (Life Member)
PHILLIPS, Mr. Robert Graham, BA(Hons) ACA *2010;* 144 Great Stone Road, MANCHESTER, M16 0HA.
PHILLIPS, Mr. Robert Leighton, FCA *1960;* Maeswenallt, Llangunnor Road, CARMARTHEN, SA31 2PA. (Life Member)
PHILLIPS, Mr. Robert William James, FCA *1977;* 31 Newbury Street, Lambourn, HUNGERFORD, RG17 8PB.
PHILLIPS, Mr. Robin Gareth, BSc ACA *1990;* Waitrose Ltd, Doncastle Road, BRACKNELL, RG12 8YA.
•PHILLIPS, Mr. Roderick John, ACA CA(SA) *2010;* Sable Accounting Ltd, Castlewood House, 77-91 New Oxford Street, LONDON, WC1A 1DG.
PHILLIPS, Mr. Roger, ACA *2011;* 6 Felstar Walk, Ashland Vale, MILTON KEYNES, BUCKINGHAMSHIRE, MK6 4BD.
PHILLIPS, Mr. Roger Simon Coltman, BSc ACA *1983;* Rotton Row, Furneux Pelham, BUNTINGFORD, SG9 0JP.
PHILLIPS, Ms. Rosamond Helen, BSc ACA *1999;* 22 Beaufort Road, Clifton, BRISTOL, BS8 2JY.
PHILLIPS, Mr. Ross Jonathan, BSc ACA *1978;* Chartered Institute of Public Relations, 52-53 Russell Square, LONDON, WC1B 4HP.
PHILLIPS, Mr. Rowland Thomas, BEng ACA *2007;* with KPMG LLP, 15 Canada Square, LONDON, E14 5GL.
•PHILLIPS, Mr. Roy Keith, FCA *1957;* Roy K. Phillips, 21 Spencers Close, Stanford-in-the-Vale, FARINGDON, OXFORDSHIRE, SN7 8NG.
PHILLIPS, Mrs. Rupa, BA ACA *2007;* 38 Hillbury Road, WARLINGHAM, CR6 9TA.
PHILLIPS, Mrs. Sarah Jane, BA ACA *1990;* 22d Leathermarket Street, LONDON, SE1 3HP.
PHILLIPS, Miss. Sarah Louise, BA(Hons) ACA *2003;* Latimer House Dunstall Road, Barton under Needwood, BURTON-ON-TRENT, STAFFORDSHIRE, DE13 8AX.
PHILLIPS, Ms. Sharon Julia, ACA *1989;* 9 Woodward Heights, GRAYS, ESSEX, RM17 5RR.
PHILLIPS, Mr. Simon Dennis, FCA *1988;* 6 Lodge Hill, Newtown, FAREHAM, HAMPSHIRE, PO17 6LQ.
PHILLIPS, Mr. Simon Edward, BSc ACA *2005;* 113 Selkirk Road, LONDON, SW17 0EW.
PHILLIPS, Mr. Simon Francis, FCA *1957;* Angel Sprints, Part Lane, Swallowfield, READING, RG7 1TB. (Life Member)
PHILLIPS, Mr. Stephen, ACA *1996;* 9 Orchard Court, 2 Kingswood Road, Shortlands, BROMLEY, BR2 0HH.
•PHILLIPS, Mr. Stephen James, FCA *1994;* Alex Picot, 95-97 Halkett Place, St. Helier, JERSEY, JE1 1BX. See also Alex Picot Ltd
PHILLIPS, Mr. Stephen Lloyd, MA FCA *1975;* Flat 2, The Mount, Trevor Road, Chirk, WREXHAM, CLWYD LL14 5HD.
•PHILLIPS, Mr. Stephen Rupert, BSc FCA *1985;* (Tax Fac), Phillips Dinnes Limited, Lyddons, Nailsbourne, TAUNTON, SOMERSET, TA2 8AF.
PHILLIPS, Mr. Steven John, BA ACA *2001;* 102 Brampton Road, ST. ALBANS, HERTFORDSHIRE, AL1 4PY.
PHILLIPS, Mr. Steven Norman, BSc FCA *1979;* Nestle Capital Advisers SA, Rue Entre-deux-Villes 10, 1814 LA TOUR DE PEILZ, VAUD, SWITZERLAND.
•PHILLIPS, Mr. Stuart, BSc ACA *2007;* Stuart Phillips, 154 West End Avenue, HARROGATE, NORTH YORKSHIRE, HG2 9BT.
PHILLIPS, Mr. Stuart David, BSc(Hons) ACA *2002;* 88 Thatcham Avenue Kingsway, Quedgeley, GLOUCESTER, GL2 2BJ.
•PHILLIPS, Mr. Stuart Martin, FCA CPA *1997;* PKF (Channel Islands) Ltd, PO Box 296, Sarnia House, Le Truchot, St Peter Port, GUERNSEY GY1 4NA. See also PKF Guernsey Ltd
PHILLIPS, Mrs. Susan Elizabeth, ACA *2004;* 33 Llys Llwyfen, Tregof Village, SWANSEA, SA7 0NF.
PHILLIPS, Ms. Tarn Denise, MA FCA *1980;* 3 Circus Street, Greenwich, LONDON, SE10 8SG.
PHILLIPS, Mr. Thomas Adam, BSc ACA *1989;* Floor 5 Dominions House Dominions Arcade, Queen StreetCardiff, CARDIFF, CF10 2AR.
PHILLIPS, Mr. Thomas John, BSc FCA *1979;* Yew Cottage, Station Road, Eynsford, DARTFORD, DA4 0ER.
PHILLIPS, Mr. Thomas Morgan, BSc FCA *1959;* 43 Anglers Reach, Grove Road, SURBITON, KT6 4EX. (Life Member)
PHILLIPS, Mr. Thomas William, FCA *1969;* 5 Maywell Drive, SOLIHULL, B92 0PR. (Life Member)
PHILLIPS, Mr. Tim, PhD MChem ACA *2011;* 226 Fordhouse Lane, Stirchley, BIRMINGHAM, B30 3AB.
PHILLIPS, Mr. Timothy Paul, FCA *1976;* Oaklea, Bryn Goodman, RUTHIN, CLWYD, LL15 1EL.
PHILLIPS, Mr. Timothy Piers Bennett, BA ACA *1996;* Hollywood Cottage Barrows Lane, Sway, LYMINGTON, SO41 6DE.
•PHILLIPS, Mr. Timothy Richard Harvey, BA FCA *1988;* Tim Phillips, The Steading, Knockmuir, AVOCH, ROSS-SHIRE, IV9 8RD.
PHILLIPS, Miss. Tracey Ann, BA ACA *1987;* Butlers Court County Combined School, Wattleton Road, BEACONSFIELD, BUCKINGHAMSHIRE, HP9 1RW.
PHILLIPS, Miss. Tracy Mary, BSc ACA *1993;* cobham house 16 Gillingham Road, GILLINGHAM, KENT, ME7 4RR.
PHILLIPS, Mr. Vernon Francis, FCA *1959;* 5 Troon Close, BEDFORD, MK41 8AY. (Life Member)
PHILLIPS, Miss. Victoria, BSc ACA *2011;* Flat 148 Delaware Mansions, Delaware Road, LONDON, W9 2LL.
PHILLIPS, Miss. Victoria Isabel, BA ACA CF *1996;* with Menzies LLP, Lynton House, 7-12 Tavistock Square, LONDON, WC1H 9LT.
PHILLIPS, Mr. Vincent, BA ACA *1987;* Tall Trees, Front Street, Naburn, YORK, YO19 4RR.
PHILLIPS, Mr. William Stephen, FCA *1967;* with Hobsons, Alexandra House, 43 Alexandra Street, NOTTINGHAM, NG5 1AY.
PHILLIPS-BAKER, Mr. Hugh, BA(Hons) ACA *2003;* (Tax Fac), Pantheon Financial Ltd, 5th Floor, Springfield House, 76 Wellington Street, LEEDS, LS1 2AY.
PHILLIPS-DAVIES, Mr. Paul Morton Alistair, MA ACA *1991;* Westmuir, 3 Essex Road, EDINBURGH, EH4 6LF.
PHILLIPS HAYES, Ms. Deborah Ann, BA ACA *1997;* 113 Ditton Hill, Long Ditton, SURBITON, SURREY, KT6 5EJ.
PHILLIPSON, Miss. Andrea, ACA *2011;* 7 Summerhill Drive, Lindfield, HAYWARDS HEATH, WEST SUSSEX, RH16 2AR.

PHILLIPSON, Mr. Christopher John Nicholas, BCom ACA *1981;* Langwith Draycote, RUGBY, WARWICKSHIRE, CV23 9RB.

•**PHILLIPSON, Mrs. Elaine, BSc ACA** *1987;* (Tax Fac), Elaine Philipson Ltd, Forest Way, Waste Lane, Kelsall, TARPORLEY, CHESHIRE CW6 0PE.

PHILLIPSON, Mr. Lawrence Stanley, FCA *1959;* Bracketts, 7 Summerhill Drive, HAYWARDS HEATH, RH16 2AR. (Life Member)

•**PHILLIS, Mr. Paul, ACA** *1992;* Paul Phillis & Co Limited, Unit 16, Leeway Estate, NEWPORT, GWENT, NP19 4SL.

PHILLPOT, Mr. Ian Gerald, BEng ACA *2003;* 5 Farm Close, Sutton, SUTTON, SURREY, SM2 5HZ.

PHILLPOTTS, Mr. Barrie John, FCA *1973;* Barley House, Foxearth, SUDBURY, CO10 7JH.

PHILOBBOS, Miss. Noha, BSc ACA *2006;* B D O Stoy Hayward, 3 Hardman Street, MANCHESTER, M3 3AT.

PHILP, Mr. Gregory Michael, BSocSc ACA *2000;* 9 Park View Sheepy Magna, ATHERSTONE, WARWICKSHIRE, CV9 3QT.

PHILP, Mr. Michael Paul, BA ACA *2005;* with PricewaterhouseCoopers LLP, 1 Embankment Place, LONDON, WC2N 6RH.

PHILP, Miss. Sally, BSc ACA *2008;* Woodstock, Surrey Gardens, Effingham, LEATHERHEAD, KT24 5HF.

PHILPIN, Mr. Monty Joseph Thomas, FCA *1964;* Efor Grug, High Street, FISHGUARD, DYFED, SA65 9AT.

PHILPOT, Mr. Joe, ACA *2011;* 69 Heather Road, Meltham, HOLMFIRTH, HD9 4HT.

•**PHILPOT, Mr. John David, FCA** *1973;* 197 Cooden Sea Road, Cooden, BEXHILL-ON-SEA, EAST SUSSEX, TN39 4TR.

PHILPOT, Mr. Michael Arthur, FCA *1953;* 47 Bucklesham Road, IPSWICH, IP3 8TW. (Life Member)

PHILPOT, Mr. Timothy Stephen Burnett, FCA *1972;* Ivinghoe, 9 Croft Avenue, DORKING, RH4 1LN. (Life Member)

PHILPOTT, Mr. Alan John, BA FCA *1955;* The Manor, Salford Road, Aspley Guise, MILTON KEYNES, MK17 8HZ. (Life Member)

PHILPOTT, Miss. Clare Louise, MSocSc BA ACA *1995;* 9a Queens Road, KENILWORTH, CV8 1UQ.

PHILPOTT, Mr. David James, BSc ACA *1992;* Le Daley, 1070 PUIDOUX, SWITZERLAND.

PHILPOTT, Mr. David John, FCA *1961;* 24 St. Luke's Road, BLACKPOOL, FY4 2EJ. (Life Member)

PHILPOTT, Mrs. Diana Elizabeth, MA ACA *1992;* Snape Hill House, Snape, BEDALE, DL8 2PU.

PHILPOTT, Ms. Gill, BSc(Hons) ACA CTA *2001;* (Tax Fac), 33 Longfields, WITHAM, ESSEX, CM8 2SN.

PHILPOTT, Mr. John Alan, MA FCA *1979;* with Ernst & Young LLP, 1 More London Place, LONDON, SE1 2AF.

PHILPOTT, Mr. Michael, FCA *1961;* 22 Bramley Avenue, FAVERSHAM, ME13 8NL.

•**PHILPOTT, Mr. Neil John Gordon, BSc ACA** *1996;* 24 Roughley Farm Road, SUTTON COLDFIELD, WEST MIDLANDS, B75 5RT.

•**PHILPOTT, Mr. Nicholas John, BA ACA** *1985;* 11 Kimbell Gardens, LONDON, SW6 6QG.

PHILPOTT, Mr. Raymond John, FCA *1981;* (Tax Fac), 14 Comfrey Close, RUSHDEN, NN10 0GL.

•**PHILPOTT, Mr. Shaun David, BSc FCA** *1991;* Steps for Success Ltd, 19 Quail Green, WOLVERHAMPTON, WV6 8DF.

PHILPOTT, Mr. Simon, BCom ACA *1999;* with Smith & Williamson Ltd, 25 Moorgate, LONDON, EC2R 6AY.

PHILPOTT, Mr. Stephen Nigel, BA ACA *2003;* 21 Mawbray Close Lower Earley, READING, RG6 3BZ.

•**PHILPOTT, Miss. Tessa Jane, BSc ACA** *1991;* Bailey Philpott Limited, 30 Medlicott Way, Swanmore, SOUTHAMPTON, SO32 2NE.

PHILPOTTS, Mrs. Rachel Ann, BSc ACA *1992;* 11 Gordon Street, CLONTARF, NSW 2093, AUSTRALIA.

PHILPOTTS, Mr. Timothy James, BSc FCA *1993;* 4130 Delbrook Avenue, NORTH VANCOUVER V7N 4A3, BC, CANADA.

PHILPS, Mrs. Bernice Constance Lilian, BA FCA *1986;* U R S Washington House, Birchwood Park Avenue Birchwood, WARRINGTON, WA3 6GR.

PHILPS-TATE, Mr. Duncan Edwards, BA ACA *1981;* with PricewaterhouseCoopers LLP, 1 Embankment Place, LONDON, WC2N 6RH.

PHIMISTER, Mr. Mark Andrew, BSc ACA *1993;* 43 Watchet Lane, Holmer Green, HIGH WYCOMBE, BUCKINGHAMSHIRE, HP15 6UF.

PHINN, Mrs. Nina Louise Bailey, BA ACA *2002;* Jupiter Asset Management, Cumberland House, 1 Victoria Street, HAMILTON HM11, BERMUDA.

PHINN, Mr. Richard Leslie, BA(Econ) ACA *2002;* Beecher Carlson, 2nd Floor Chevron House, 11 Church Street, HAMILTON, BERMUDA.

PHIPKIN, Mr. Anthony Peter, BSc ACA *1984;* Omnicom Finance Ltd, 239 Old Marylebone Road, LONDON, NW1 5QT.

PHIPP, Mrs. Esther Helen, BA ACA *2000;* Clarks Hill House, Wyck Beacon, Bourton-on-the-Water, CHELTENHAM, GL54 2NE.

PHIPP, Mr. Graham Neil, BSc ACA *1992;* 66 Thornhill Park, Streetly, SUTTON COLDFIELD, WEST MIDLANDS, B74 2LN.

PHIPPS, Mr. Alan John, BSc FCA *1974;* 43 Newberries Avenue, RADLETT, HERTFORDSHIRE, WD7 7EJ.

•**PHIPPS, Mr. David George, LLB ACA** *1995;* David Phipps Consultancy Limited, Thurlestone, 11 Hillcrest, Thornbury, BRISTOL, BS35 2JA.

•**PHIPPS, Mr. Eric William, BA FCA** *1986;* 1 Rowan Terrace, Courthope Villas, LONDON, SW19 4TF. See also Deloitte Touche Tohmatsu

•**PHIPPS, Mr. Ian, ACA** *1990;* Oury Clark, PO Box 150, Herschel House, 58 Herschel Street, SLOUGH, SL1 1HD.

•**PHIPPS, Mr. Jeremy William, BSc ACA** *1989;* 26 Hyde Vale, Greenwich, LONDON, SE10 8QH.

PHIPPS, Mr. Julian Gerard Powell, BSc ACA *1991;* Northgate Information Solution, Hillview House, 61 Church Road, Co Antrim, NEWTOWNABBEY, COUNTY ANTRIM BT36 7LQ.

PHIPPS, Mrs. Julie, BSc ACA *1980;* 41 Orchard Drive, DURHAM, DH1 1LA.

PHIPPS, Mr. Kenneth Carlyle, BA ACA *1979;* Yorks Farm, Watling Street, TOWCESTER, NN12 8EU.

PHIPPS, Miss. Lorna Jane, BSc ACA *1992;* 7 Nelson Road, BOURNEMOUTH, BH4 9JA.

PHIPPS, Mr. Mark Leslie, BSc ACA *1990;* 6 Inworth, Pendeford, WOLVERHAMPTON, WV9 5LE.

PHIPPS, Mr. Mark Richard, BA(Hons) ACA *2002;* Lul18, One International Finance Centre, 1 Harbour View Street, CENTRAL, HONG KONG ISLAND, HONG KONG SAR.

PHIPPS, Mr. Neil Robert, BSc ACA *1980;* Weymoor, Pitch Place, Thursley, GODALMING, GU8 6QW.

PHIPPS, Mr. Neil Stuart, BSc(Hons) ACA *2002;* with PricewaterhouseCoopers, 113-119 The Terrace, PO Box 243, WELLINGTON 6011, NEW ZEALAND.

PHIPPS, Mr. Peter Albert, FCA *1970;* 180 Walsall Road, Four Oaks, SUTTON COLDFIELD, B74 4RH.

•**PHIPPS, Mr. Peter John, FCA** *1973;* Phipps Henson McAllister, 22/24 Harborough Road, Kingsthorpe, NORTHAMPTON, NN2 7AZ.

PHIPPS, Mr. Robert Anthony, FCA *1959;* 25 Beacon Road, Wylde Green, SUTTON COLDFIELD, B73 5ST. (Life Member)

•**PHIPPS, Mr. Ross Andrew, ACA** *2007;* Phipps Henson McAllister, 22/24 Harborough Road, Kingsthorpe, NORTHAMPTON, NN2 7AZ.

PHIPPS, Mrs. Susannah, BA(Hons) ACA *2002;* 18 Winding Piece, Capel St. Mary, IPSWICH, IP9 2UZ.

PHIPPS, Mr. Timothy Keith, BA ACA *2008;* 28 Dordon Close, Shirley, SOLIHULL, B90 1AH.

PHIPPS, Mr. Timothy Normanby, FCA *1961;* Loubatiere Basse, Senergues, 12320 ST. CYPRIEN, FRANCE. (Life Member)

PHIPSON, Mr. Michael Oliver, BSc ACA *2004;* 11 The Orchard, LONDON, SE3 0QS.

•**PHIZACKERLEY, Miss. Stephanie Jane, BSc ACA** *1986;* Ernst & Young LLP, Apex Plaza, Forbury Road, READING, RG1 1YE. See also Ernst & Young Europe LLP

PHIZACKLEA, Mr. Michael Matthew, MBA FCA *1965;* 3 Melbourn Road, ROYSTON, SG8 7DB.

PHOENIX, Mr. Christopher John, FCA *1973;* Mount Pleasant Farm, Sturton-le-Steeple, RETFORD, NOTTINGHAMSHIRE, DN22 9HS.

PHOENIX, Mr. Stephen Patrick, BSc ACA *1986;* 39 Bowling Close, HARPENDEN, AL5 1QP.

PHOENIX, Mr. Tobias James, ACA *2008;* 119 Morley Avenue, LONDON, N22 6NG.

PHOON, Mr. Philip Choi Wai, BSc ACA *2010;* 27 Barons Keep, Gliddon Road, LONDON, W14 9AT.

PHOON, Mr. Waikien, ACA *2011;* Flat 14 da Vinci Torre, 77 Loampit Vale, LONDON, SE13 7FA.

PHOTIADES, Miss. Chloe, MSc BA ACA *2010;* 25 Thessalonikis Street, Platy Aglatzias, 2122 NICOSIA, CYPRUS.

PHOTINOS, Mr. Alexandros, ACA *2005;* 19 Athanasiou Diakou, Tatia Court, Apt 21, Mesa Yitonia, 4000 LIMASSOL, CYPRUS.

PHUA, Mr. Bob Cheng Loong, BA(Hons) ACA *2002;* 1 Winkfield Road, ASCOT, BERKSHIRE, SL5 7LX.

PHUA, Mr. San Chee, ACA *1982;* 32 Kerrie Road, GLEN WAVERLEY, VIC 3150, AUSTRALIA.

PHUAH, Mr. Eng Siew, ACA *1981;* 59 Orleans Way, Castle Hill, SYDNEY, NSW 2154, AUSTRALIA.

PHUNG, Miss. Chia-Yih, LLB ACA *2004;* U B S, 100 Liverpool Street, LONDON, EC2M 2RH.

PHUVANATNARANUBALA, Mr. Thirachai, BSc FCA *1978;* 445 Lad Prao 107, BANGKOK 10240, THAILAND.

PHYLACTOU, Mr. Theophylaktos, BA ACA *2009;* 13 Philopimenos, Mesa Yitonia, 4002 LIMASSOL, CYPRUS.

PHYTHIAN, Mr. John Paul, BSc ACA *2001;* Ivy Bank, 163 Thurstaston Road, Thurstaston, WIRRAL, MERSEYSIDE, CH61 0HQ.

PIALUCHA, Mrs. Malgorzata, FCA ACA *1992;* 40 Waldeck Road, LONDON, W13 8LZ.

•**PIANCA, Mr. Andrew John, FCA** *1975;* Crowe Clark Whitehill LLP, St Bride's House, 10 Salisbury Square, LONDON, EC4Y 8EH. See also Horwath Clark Whitehill LLP and Crowe Clark Whitehill

PIANCA, Mrs. Anne Rosemary, BA FCA *1975;* 96 Higher Drive, BANSTEAD, SURREY, SM7 1PQ.

PIASECKI, Mr. Michal, LLM BSc(Hons) ACA *2010;* Flat 3, Gainsborough Studios West, 1 Poole Street, LONDON, N1 5EA.

PIAT, Mr. Louis Andre, FCA *1968;* 3505 Cut Bank Cove, FORT WAYNE, IN 46804-6936, UNITED STATES.

PIATEK, Mr. Adam Mikolaj, BA ACA *1992;* Siemens, C/A Parsons Works Shields Road, NEWCASTLE UPON TYNE, NE6 2YL.

PIBWORTH, Miss. Ann Mary, FCA *1976;* 34a Solent Road, Hill Head, FAREHAM, HAMPSHIRE, PO14 3LD.

•**PICARDO, Mr. Ronald, FCA** *1973;* Ronald Picardo, 15 Woodridge Way, NORTHWOOD, HA6 2BE.

PICAZO, Mrs. Zinia Elena Noronha, LLB ACA *1999;* 305 West 72nd Street, #6B, NEW YORK, NY 10023, UNITED STATES.

PICCIRILLO, Mr. Paul John, ACA *2004;* 40 Village Road, ENFIELD, MIDDLESEX, EN1 2EN.

PICCOS, Mr. Chris, ACA MAAT *2011;* 149 Abbots Road, EDGWARE, MIDDLESEX, HA8 0RY.

PICHLER, Mr. Peter Joseph, BSc FCA *1974;* La Poste La Rue Du Flicquet St. Martin, JERSEY, JE3 6BP.

•**PICK, Mr. Douglas, FCA** *1974;* (Tax Fac), Walter Ridgway & Son Limited, Walter Ridgway & Son Ltd, 69 Flixton Road, Urmston, MANCHESTER, M41 5AN.

PICK, Mr. Graham John, ACA *1982;* 3 Hellier Drive, Wombourne, WOLVERHAMPTON, WV5 8AH.

PICK, Mrs. Helen Christina, BA(Hons) ACA *2001;* 108 Kerver Lane, Dunnington, YORK, YO19 5SH.

PICK, Mrs. Louise, BEng ACA *2005;* Cartref, Mill Lane, Holloway, MATLOCK, DERBYSHIRE, DE4 5AQ.

•**PICK, Mr. Robert Harry, MA FCA** *1977;* Moorfields Corporate Recovery LLP, 88 Wood Street, LONDON, EC2V 7QR.

PICK, Mr. Robert James, BA ACA *2003;* 5 Dugard Way, DROITWICH, WORCESTERSHIRE, WR9 8UX.

•**PICK, Mr. Robin Alexander, FCA** *1970;* R.A. Pick & Co, Cobham House, 9 Warwick Court, Grays Inn, LONDON, WC1R 5DJ.

PICK, Mr. Steven William, BSc(Hons) ACA *2001;* 108, Kerver Lane, Dunnington, YORK, YO19 5SH.

PICK, Mr. Trevor Gordon, FCA *1955;* 9 Heathwood, High Street, TADWORTH, KT20 5RB. (Life Member)

PICKANCE, Mr. Anthony Martin, BSc FCA *1977;* The Annexe West Park Farm, Rockbourne Road Sandleheath, FORDINGBRIDGE, HAMPSHIRE, SP6 1QG.

PICKANCE, Mr. Richard John Markwell, ACA *1970;* Maycroft, Tweed Lane, Boldre, LYMINGTON, HAMPSHIRE, SO41 8NF.

PICKARD, Mr. Alexander, BA(Hons) ACA *2010;* Balshaw Farm, The Green, Potten End, BERKHAMSTED, HERTFORDSHIRE, HP4 2QQ.

PICKARD, Mrs. Alexandra Ruth, BSc ACA *2006;* Derwent Close Cottage, Main Street, East Ayton, SCARBOROUGH, YO13 9HJ.

•**PICKARD, Mr. Antony James, BA FCA** *1989;* Orion Accountancy Limited, 30 Garners Road, Chalfont St. Peter, GERRARDS CROSS, BUCKINGHAMSHIRE, SL9 0EZ.

PICKARD, Mr. Bryan Milner, FCA *1960;* Box House, Bleke Street, SHAFTESBURY, SP7 8AH. (Life Member)

•**PICKARD, Mrs. Carolyn Mari, BSc FCA** *1989;* Orion Accountancy Limited, 30 Garners Road, Chalfont St. Peter, GERRARDS CROSS, BUCKINGHAMSHIRE, SL9 0EZ.

PICKARD, Mrs. Christine Margaret, BA ACA *1998;* 33 Ivymount Road, NEWCASTLE UPON TYNE, NE6 5RN.

•**PICKARD, Mr. Colin John, FCA** *1972;* Price Bailey Ltd, PO Box 511, 2nd Floor Elizabeth House, Les Ruetles' Brayes, St. Peter Port, GUERNSEY GY1 6DU. See also Price Bailey LLP, Price Bailey Private Client LLP and Colin Pickard & Company Limited

•**PICKARD, Mr. Dale, BA FCA** *1982;* Dale Pickard & Co, Bank House, 4 Wharf Rd, SALE, M33 2AF.

PICKARD, Mr. Damian Robert, BA FCA MCT *1990;* Cottesbrook Building, University of Northampton, Boughton Green Road, NORTHAMPTON, NN2 7AL.

PICKARD, Mr. David Hugh, BSc FCA *1981;* Cardiff International Airport, Rhoose, BARRY, SOUTH GLAMORGAN, CF62 3BD.

PICKARD, Mr. Edward, MA FCA *1971;* Bracken House Old Mugdock Road, Strathblane, GLASGOW, G63 9ET.

•**PICKARD, Mrs. Elizabeth Jenny Hayes, BA ACA** *2002;* Fraser Hayes Pickard, 7 Nimbus Way, Watnall, NOTTINGHAM, NG16 1FP.

PICKARD, Mrs. Erica Margaret, ACA *1984;* 36 Montague Avenue, SOUTH CROYDON, CR2 9NH.

PICKARD, Mr. Gary Charles, BSc FCA *1990;* 37 Kingsend, RUISLIP, MIDDLESEX, HA4 7DD.

PICKARD, Mr. Herbert Arthur, FCA *1974;* 6 Beckwith Close, Pannal Ash, HARROGATE, HG2 0BJ. (Life Member)

PICKARD, Mr. John Anthony, FCA *1961;* 3 Kirklees Close, Farsley, PUDSEY, LS28 5TF.

PICKARD, Mr. John Christopher, FCA *1962;* 7 Petra Tou Nerou, 8642 Amargeti Village, PAPHOS, CYPRUS. (Life Member)

PICKARD, Mr. John Lakin, BA ACA *1981;* SL Engineering Ltd, Temple Road, Aslackby, SLEAFORD, NG34 0HJ.

PICKARD, Sir John Michael, Kt FCA *1956;* Kingsbarn, Tot Hill, Headley, EPSOM, KT18 6PU. (Life Member)

PICKARD, Mr. Jon, BA ACA *1993;* Hutchison 3 G UK Ltd Star House, 20 Grenfell Road, MAIDENHEAD, SL6 1EH.

PICKARD, Mr. Jonathan Peter, ACA *1983;* Nutrition Centre Higher Nature Ltd, Burwash Common, ETCHINGHAM, TN19 7LX.

PICKARD, Mr. Keith William, BSc ACA CF *1993;* 15 Parkfield Avenue, East Sheen, LONDON, SW14 8DY.

•①**PICKARD, Mr. Martin Dominic, BSc FCA** *1987;* Mazars LLP, The Pinnacle, 160 Midsummer Boulevard, MILTON KEYNES, MK9 1FF.

PICKARD, Mr. Michael John, MA ACA *1991;* 28 Amiens Street, HAMPTON, VIC 3188, AUSTRALIA.

•**PICKARD, Mr. Paul Nigel, BSc FCA** *1984;* Deloitte LLP, 4 Brindley Place, BIRMINGHAM, B1 2HZ. See also Deloitte & Touche LLP

PICKEN, Mr. James Alexander, ACA *2011;* 20 Ormiston Crescent, BELFAST, BT4 3JP.

PICKEN, Mr. Jonathan Stephen, BSc FCA *1992;* BUPA Care Services, Bridge House, Outwood Lane, Horsforth, LEEDS, LS18 4UP.

PICKEN, Mrs. Ruth, ACA *1989;* Carillion Enterprise Limited, Defence Estates, Kingston Road, SUTTON COLDFIELD, B75 7RL.

PICKERING, Dr. Alistair Neil, ACA *1993;* 13 Upper Cranbrook Road, BRISTOL, BS6 7UW.

PICKERING, Mr. Andrew Edward, BSc ACA *1999;* Unit 3, 90 Champion Road, Tennyson Point, SYDNEY, NSW 2111, AUSTRALIA.

PICKERING, Mr. Andrew James, BSc ACA *1983;* Orchard House, 47 Worminghall Road, Oakley, AYLESBURY, HP18 9QU.

PICKERING, Mr. Andrew James, FCA *1982;* Cornermead, 21 Downs Avenue, EPSOM, KT18 5HQ.

PICKERING, Mr. Andrew Trevor, ACA *1986;* 8 Thornham Close, South Cave, BROUGH, HU15 2EQ.

PICKERING, Mrs. Belinda, BSc ACA *1988;* Myrtle Cottage, Emery Down, LYNDHURST, HAMPSHIRE, SO43 7EA.

PICKERING, Mr. Charles Edward, BA ACA *1995;* The School House, Smithy Lane, Willaston, NESTON, CH64 2UA.

PICKERING, Mr. Charles Roger, FCA *1968;* Via Mazzini 76, 20020 Ceriano Laghetto, MILAN, ITALY. (Life Member)

PICKERING, Miss. Claire Belinda, BSc ACA *1999;* 124 Ravensbury Road, LONDON, SW18 4RU.

PICKERING, Mrs. Clare, BA ACA *1996;* Home Farm Wellsborough Road Sheepy Parva, ATHERSTONE, CV9 3RF.

PICKERING, Dr. Clive Scott, BSc ACA *1997;* 42 Clive Road, Colliers Wood, LONDON, SW19 2JB.

PICKERING, Mr. Daniel Joseph, BSc ACA *2002;* 40 Graham Road, LONDON, SW19 3SR.
PICKERING, Mr. David Jonathan, BA ACA *1988;* Fareham Cottage Chilsham Lane, Herstmonceux, HAILSHAM, EAST SUSSEX, BN27 4QH.
PICKERING, Mr. David Owen, FCA *1966;* Meadow Foods Ltd, Marlston Court, Rough Hill, Marlston-cum-Lache, CHESTER, CH4 9JT.
PICKERING, Mr. Dean Graham, BA ACA *2002;* Flat 1 32 Eastway, LONDON, E9 5JB.
•PICKERING, Mrs. Denise, BA FCA *1982;* (Tax Fac), Pickering, 10 Oxford Street, MALMESBURY, SN16 9AZ.
PICKERING, Mr. Derek Gregory, BSc ACA *1979;* Grasmere, Woodlands Road East, VIRGINIA WATER, GU25 4PH.
PICKERING, Mrs. Emma Victoria, BSc ACA *2003;* 48 Beech Road, Hale, ALTRINCHAM, CHESHIRE, WA15 9HX.
•PICKERING, Mr. Gavin Lee, BSc ACA *1990;* Sovereign Payroll Services, First Floor Office, Wharf Road, Whaley Bridge, HIGH PEAK, DERBYSHIRE SK23 7AD.
PICKERING, Mr. Graham, FCA *1974;* P o Box 2438, Cramerview, JOHANNESBURG, GAUTENG, 2060, SOUTH AFRICA.
PICKERING, Mrs. Hilary Margaret, FCA *1976;* Gilberts Pendragon House, 65 London Road, ST. ALBANS, HERTFORDSHIRE, AL1 1LJ.
PICKERING, Mr. Iain, BA ACA *2005;* 35 Melbourne Grove, LONDON, SE22 8RG.
PICKERING, Mr. Ian, BSc ACA *1991;* 29 Mountserrat Road, BROMSGROVE, WORCESTERSHIRE, B60 2RU.
PICKERING, Mr. Ian, MA FCA *1980;* Avenue House, The Avenue, Aspley Guise, MILTON KEYNES, MK17 8HH.
PICKERING, Miss. Isla, BSc ACA *2007;* 10 Chime Square, ST. ALBANS, HERTFORDSHIRE, AL3 5JZ.
PICKERING, Mrs. Jane Nicola, BA ACA *1986;* Unit 12 Manchester Chambers, West Street, OLDHAM, OL1 1LF.
PICKERING, Miss. Joanne, ACA *2010;* 73 Sunnybrow, SUNDERLAND, SR3 1DQ.
•PICKERING, Mr. John Charles, FCA *1977;* Scrutton Bland, Sanderson House, Museum Street, IPSWICH, IP1 1HE.
•PICKERING, Mr. John Christopher Gordon, FCA *1971;* (Tax Fac), Pickerings, 48 South Street, ALDERLEY EDGE, SK9 7ES.
•PICKERING, Mr. John Philip, BA FCA *1983;* (Tax Fac), Flat 2, 47 Bennett Park, LONDON, SE3 9RA.
PICKERING, Mr. Jon, BA(Hons) ACA *2002;* 48 Beech Road, Hale, ALTRINCHAM, CHESHIRE, WA15 9HX.
•PICKERING, Mr. Jonathan Carrick, MA FCA *1982;* Echo Barn, 33 Echo Barn Lane, FARNHAM, GU10 4NG.
PICKERING, Miss. Katherine Louise, BA ACA *2007;* 75 San Juan Court, EASTBOURNE, EAST SUSSEX, BN23 5TP.
•PICKERING, Mrs. Kathryn Louise, BSc ACA *2007;* Kathryn Pickering, 15 Top Birches, ST. NEOTS, CAMBRIDGESHIRE, PE19 6BD.
•PICKERING, Mr. Keith Andrew, FCA CF *1987;* Catalyst Corporate Finance LLP, 21 The Triangle, NG2 Business Park, NOTTINGHAM, NG2 1AE.
PICKERING, Mrs. Laura, BA ACA *2005;* Aurora Fashions Services Limited, The Triangle, Stanton Harcourt Industrial Estate, Stanton Harcourt, WITNEY, OXFORDSHIRE OX29 5UX.
PICKERING, Mr. Martin Nigel, MA ACA *1986;* The Old Rectory, Wold Newton, LINCOLN, LN8 6BP.
PICKERING, Mr. Michael Ronald, FCA *1974;* 9 Osborne, TAMWORTH, STAFFORDSHIRE, B79 7SZ.
PICKERING, Mr. Neville, FCA *1957;* 28 Bayline Drive, POINT CLARE, NSW 2250, AUSTRALIA. (Life Member)
PICKERING, Mrs. Nicki, BSc ACA *2005;* 8 Baddesley Close, North Baddesley, SOUTHAMPTON, SO52 9DR.
PICKERING, Mr. Richard William, BEng ACA *2002;* c/o InterOil Australia, 60-92 Cook Street, Portsmith, CAIRNS, QLD 4870, AUSTRALIA.
PICKERSGILL, Miss. Andrea Claire, BSc(Hons) ACA *2003;* Flat 1, 16 Mansfield Road, READING, RG1 6AJ.
PICKERSGILL, Mr. David, FCA *1976;* Leeds Building Society, 105 Albion Street, LEEDS, LS1 5AS.
PICKERSGILL, Mrs. Janet Elizabeth, BSc ACA *1983;* Wellington House, 23 Canynge Road, Clifton, BRISTOL, BS8 3JZ.
PICKERSGILL, Mr. Nigel Henry, BSc FCA *1981;* Wellington House, 23 Canynge Road, Clifton, BRISTOL, BS8 3JZ.
PICKESS, Mr. Brian Arthur, FCA *1964;* 22 Temple Mill Island, Bisham, MARLOW, SL7 1SG.
PICKESS, Mrs. Dawn Helen, BA(Hons) ACA *2004;* 16 Hilltop Gardens, Spencers Wood, READING, RG7 1HQ.
PICKETT, Miss. Emma, BSc ACA *2007;* 2 Asia House, 82 Princess Street, MANCHESTER, M1 6BD.
•PICKETT, Mr. Graham Charles, BA FCA *1984;* Deloitte LLP, Global House, High Street, CRAWLEY, RH10 1DL. See also Deloitte & Touche LLP
PICKETT, Mrs. Isobel, BSc ACA *1999;* 37 The Rowans, Chalfont St. Peter, GERRARDS CROSS, BUCKINGHAMSHIRE, SL9 8SE.
PICKETT, Mr. Mark Jeremy, LLB ACA *1993;* Old Park Farm, 11 The Beeches, Fetcham, LEATHERHEAD, SURREY, KT22 9DT.
PICKETT, Mr. Michael Frederick, FCA *1952;* 15 Inchbrook Court, Inchbrook, Nailsworth, STROUD, GLOUCESTERSHIRE, GL5 5HQ. (Life Member)
PICKETT, Mr. Russell John, BSc ACA *2000;* 14 Orchard Way, OXTED, RH8 9DJ.
•PICKETT, Mr. William, BA ACA *1991;* Trans European Technology Laser House, 132-140 Goswell Road, LONDON, EC1V 7DY.
PICKFORD, Mrs. Amy Laura, BSc ACA *2004;* 52 Baker Avenue, Benson, WALLINGFORD, OXFORDSHIRE, OX10 6EQ.
PICKFORD, Mr. Andrew James, BA(Hons) ACA *2002;* 16 Weldon Road, ALTRINCHAM, CHESHIRE, WA14 4EH.
PICKFORD, Mr. Anthony Christian, FCA *1976;* Le Petit Fief Au Bret, Les Aubrets, St. Martin, GUERNSEY, GY4 6EX.
PICKFORD, Mr. Benjamin Dylan, BA ACA *2005;* with Deloitte LLP, 2 New Street Square, LONDON, EC4A 3BZ.
PICKFORD, Mr. Frank Thomas, FCA *1971;* Crown House, Eardington, BRIDGNORTH, WV16 5LB.
PICKFORD, Mr. Iorwerth Fergusson, BSc FCA *1972;* 8176 Collingwood Court, UNIVERSITY PARK, FL 34201, UNITED STATES.
PICKFORD, Mr. Michael Anthony, FCA *1965;* Ennismore, 54 West Street, REIGATE, RH2 9DB.
PICKFORD, Mr. Paul Anthony, BSc FCA *1993;* Wray Farm, 90 Raglan Road, REIGATE, RH2 0ET.
PICKFORD, Mr. Richard Henry George, BA(Hons) ACA *2004;* Nibelungenstr. 53, 80639 MUNICH, GERMANY.
PICKFORD, Mr. Roger, FCA *1962;* 97 Albert Road West, Heaton, BOLTON, BL1 5ED.
PICKFORD, Mr. Roger, FCA *1970;* 8 Troon Place, CARINDALE, QLD 4152, AUSTRALIA. (Life Member)
PICKFORD, Mrs. Sandra Dawn, MA ACA *2005;* 16 Weldon Road, ALTRINCHAM, CHESHIRE, WA14 4EH.
PICKFORD, Mr. Simon Hartley, ACA *1980;* 47 Wheats Avenue, Harborne, BIRMINGHAM, B17 0RH.
•PICKIN, Mr. Charles William, BA FCA *1994;* Harrison Jasper Limited, 3 The Close, Corseley Road, Groombridge, TUNBRIDGE WELLS, KENT TN3 9SE.
PICKLES, Mr. Andrew John Gardner, BSc ACA *1992;* Fitness First Ltd, 58 Fleets Lane, POOLE, DORSET, BH15 3BT.
PICKLES, Mr. Andrew Philip, FCA *1974;* 10 Sedgegarth, Thorner, LEEDS, LS14 3LB.
PICKLES, Mrs. Antonia Louise, BA ACA *1996;* Carradale, Hob Lane, Ripponden, SOWERBY BRIDGE, WEST YORKSHIRE, HX6 4LU.
PICKLES, Miss. Caroline Jane, MMath ACA *2006;* 7 The Brambles, Fulwood, PRESTON, PR2 9LR.
PICKLES, Mr. Christopher Hanley, BA ACA *1990;* 22 Greenmoor Avenue, LEEDS, LS12 5ST.
•PICKLES, Mr. David Anthony, FCA *1982;* Ashworth Moulds, 11 Nicholas Street, BURNLEY, BB11 2AL.
PICKLES, Mr. Graham, BSc ACA *1982;* 5 Hermitage Park, Fenay Bridge, HUDDERSFIELD, HD8 0JU.
PICKLES, Mr. Ian John, BA ACA *1998;* 47 Windsor Drive, Timperley, ALTRINCHAM, CHESHIRE, WA14 5AN.
PICKLES, Mr. James Francis, BSc FCA *1983;* 80 Ulleswater Road, LONDON, N14 7BT.
PICKLES, Mr. John Christopher, BA FCA *1979;* 36 St Georges Road, LONDON, N13 4AS.
•PICKLES, Mr. John Timothy Basil, FCA *1981;* (Tax Fac), Moore Stephens, P O Box 25, 26-28 Athol Street, Douglas, ISLE OF MAN, IM99 1BD. See also Moore Stephens Limited
PICKLES, Mr. Julian, BA ACA *2007;* 15 Milner Road, BRISTOL, BS7 9PQ.
PICKLES, Mr. Nicholas David, BSc FCA *1975;* Malibu Tristram Cliff, Polzeath, WADEBRIDGE, CORNWALL, PL27 6TP.
PICKLES, Mr. Richard John, BSc ACA *1995;* Hartley Gate Farmhouse, Hartley Road, CRANBROOK, KENT, TN17 3PT.
PICKLES, Mr. Robert Granville, FCA *1964;* Willow Tree House, Village Road, Coleshill, AMERSHAM, BUCKINGHAMSHIRE, HP7 0LR.
PICKLES, Mr. Roger Albert, BA ACA CTA *1986;* (Tax Fac), Tanglewood, Lunghurst Road, Woldingham, CATERHAM, SURREY, CR3 7EJ.
PICKLES, Miss. Sara Elizabeth, BA(Hons) ACA *2010;* with PricewaterhouseCoopers LLP, 1 Embankment Place, LONDON, WC2N 6RH.
PICKLES, Mrs. Sarah Helen, MA ACA AMCT *1989;* Willow House Silk Mill Lane, Winchcombe, CHELTENHAM, GL54 5HZ.
PICKSLEY, Mr. Brian Patrick, FCA *1964;* 4 Eastfield Close, Welton, LINCOLN, LN2 3NB.
PICKSTONE, Mr. Stephen, MSci ACA *2004;* 29 Church Lane, MIRFIELD, WEST YORKSHIRE, WF14 9HX.
PICKTHALL, Mr. Terence, FCA *1963;* 43 Cromwell Tower, Barbican, LONDON, EC2Y 8DD.
PICKUP, Mr. Alan William, FCA *1957;* 5 Fullerton Road, Hartford, NORTHWICH, CHESHIRE, CW8 1SR. (Life Member)
PICKUP, Mrs. Amanda Jane, LLB ACA *1989;* 14 King Edward Avenue, LYTHAM ST. ANNES, LANCASHIRE, FY8 1DP.
PICKUP, Mr. Andrew David, BA FCA *1996;* 33 Jubilee Way, Croston, LEYLAND, PR26 9HD.
PICKUP, Mr. David George Edward, BA FCA *1999;* N C L Smith & Williamson, 25 Moorgate, LONDON, EC2R 6AY.
PICKUP, Mr. Geoffrey, FCA *1938;* Saffrons Lodge Day Centre, 20 Saffrons Road, EASTBOURNE, EAST SUSSEX, BN21 1DU. (Life Member)
PICKUP, Mr. Harvey Eastwood, BA FCA *1975;* Pickup Investigative Accounting & Forensics Pty Ltd, 23 Emerald Tce, PERTH, WA 6005, AUSTRALIA.
PICKUP, Mr. Ian, ACA *2010;* 9 Ladyhouse Close, Milnrow, ROCHDALE, LANCASHIRE, OL16 4EB.
•PICKUP, Mr. Ian Christopher, BSc ACA DChA *1983;* Ian Pickup & Co, 123 New Road Side, Horsforth, LEEDS, LS18 4QD.
PICKUP, Mr. Ian Richard, FCA *1969;* 6 Nursteed Meadows, Nursteed, DEVIZES, SN10 3HL.
PICKUP, Mr. Jonathan Mark Spencer, BSc(Hons) ACA DChA *1990;* The Kings School, Cumberland Street, MACCLESFIELD, CHESHIRE, SK10 1DA.
PICKUP, Mrs. Mary Janet Somerville, FCA *1972;* 50b Huntenhull Lane, Chapmanslade, WESTBURY, BA13 4AS.
•PICKUP, Mr. Michael John John, FCA *1982;* PKW LLP, Cloth Hall, 150 Drake Street, ROCHDALE, LANCASHIRE, OL16 1PX.
PICKUP, Mr. Paul David, BA ACA *1989;* 4 Windermere Close, Gamston, NOTTINGHAM, NG2 6PQ.
•PICKUP, Mr. Roland, FCA *1969;* (Tax Fac), R. Pickup, Keepers Cottage, Sowerby Road, Sowerby, PRESTON, PR3 0TT.
PICKWELL, Mrs. Oriana, ACA *2002;* Delta Park, Coopervision Unit 8, Concorde Way, FAREHAM, HAMPSHIRE, PO15 5RL.
PICKWORTH, Mr. James Malcolm, BA ACA *1995;* Ask Restaurants Ltd, 5th Floor, 2 Balcombe, LONDON, NW1 6NW.
PICONE, Mr. Domenico, ACA *2011;* 12 Quick Street, LONDON, N1 8HL.
•PICOT, Mr. Rodney Alexander, FCA *1964;* Les Lauriers La Grande Route de St. Clement, St. Clement, JERSEY, JE2 6QN.
PICOT, Mr. Russell Clive, MA FCA *1982;* 2 St. Aubyns Avenue, Wimbledon, LONDON, SW19 7BL.
PICOT, Mr. Stephen Keith, BSc FCA *1974;* 7 Hillside Close, Disley, STOCKPORT, SK12 2DL.
PICTON, Mrs. Anna Elizabeth, MA ACA *2001;* 16 Roselands Court, Chester Road, Lavister, Rossett, WREXHAM, CLWYD LL12 0DD.
•PICTON, Mr. Brian Leslie, FCA *1962;* B L Picton, 4 Laburnum Road, SANDY, BEDFORDSHIRE, SG19 1HQ.
PICTON, Mr. David Stewart, BA(Hons) ACA *2003;* 5/53 Prince Albert Street, MOSMAN, NSW 2088, AUSTRALIA.
PICTON, Mr. Ernest William John, FCA *1956;* 51 Abbotshall Avenue, Southgate, LONDON, N14 7JU. (Life Member)
PICTON, Mr. James Bernard, BSc FCA *1982;* 17 Avery Road, Avery Park Haydock, ST.HELENS, MERSEYSIDE, WA11 0XA.
•PICTON, Mr. Jeffrey Maurice, LLB ACA *1983;* PricewaterhouseCoopers LLP, Hays Galleria, 1 Hays Lane, LONDON, SE1 2RD. See also PricewaterhouseCoopers
PICTON, Mrs. Katherine, BSc ACA *2004;* 5/53 Prince Albert Street, MOSMAN, NSW 2088, AUSTRALIA.
•PICTON, Mr. Neil Robert, FCA *1992;* Jervis Limited, 20 Harborough Road, Kingsthorpe, NORTHAMPTON, NN2 7AZ.
PICTON-PHILLIPPS, Mr. Peter Nicholas, MA ACA *1997;* with Ernst & Young, 18/F, Two International Finance Centre, 8 Finance Street, CENTRAL, HONG KONG ISLAND HONG KONG SAR.
PICTON-TURBERVILL, Mr. David, BA ACA *1992;* 7 Beaumont Mews, LONDON, W1G 6EB.
PIDD, Mr. Ian James, BCom ACA *1998;* 58 Bills Lane, Shirley, SOLIHULL, B90 2PE.
PIDD, Mrs. Jennifer Clare, BSc ACA *2002;* 58 Bills Lane, Shirley, SOLIHULL, B90 2PE.
PIDDINGTON, Mrs. Samantha Jane, BA ACA *1994;* Chapel Hatch Chapel Lane, Willington, TARPORLEY, CHESHIRE, CW6 0PH.
PIDGEON, Mr. Charles Willoughby, ACA *2010;* with PricewaterhouseCoopers LLP, 1 Embankment Place, LONDON, WC2N 6RH.
•PIDGEON, Mr. Christopher Milner Fosbrooke, FCA *1971;* (Tax Fac), C.M.F. Pidgeon, Sandaway, Daleside Park, Darley, HARROGATE, HG3 2PX.
PIDGEON, Mr. David Bryn, BSS ACA *1990;* 6/35 Normanby Street, BRIGHTON, VIC 3186, AUSTRALIA.
PIDGEON, Mr. Robert John, FCA *1968;* 4 Calstock Road, Woodthorpe, NOTTINGHAM, NG5 4FH. (Life Member)
PIECHOCZEK, Miss. Julia, ACA *2011;* Flat 5, 47 Effra Road, LONDON, SW2 1BZ.
PIECZYKOLAN, Miss. Magdalena, ACA *2011;* 51 Barnesdale Crescent, ORPINGTON, BR5 2AU.
PIEKARSKI, Mr. Stefan Zbygniew, ACA *2010;* 11 Park Avenue, Goldthorn Park, WOLVERHAMPTON, WV4 5AL.
PIEPKE, Mr. Dennis, BSc FCA *1977;* 10 Newland Close, Hatch End, PINNER, MIDDLESEX, HA5 4QP.
PIERCE, Mr. Andrew, ACA *2008;* Ropemaker Place, 25 Ropemaker St., LONDON, EC2Y 9AN.
PIERCE, Mr. Barry John, FCA *1959;* 4 West Farm, Osmington, WEYMOUTH, DT3 6EL. (Life Member)
PIERCE, Mr. Christopher, BA ACA CPA *1993;* 400/500 Campus Drive, FLORHAM PARK, NJ 07932, UNITED STATES.
PIERCE, Mr. Christopher James, MBA BSc FCA MCIM DipM AMCT *1976;* 34 Daws Hill Lane, HIGH WYCOMBE, HP11 1PU.
PIERCE, Mrs. Claire Louise, ACA *2007;* with Montpelier Professional (Lancashire) Limited, Charter House, Pittman Way, Fulwood, PRESTON, PR2 9ZD.
PIERCE, Mr. David James Michael, BA ACA *1992;* 78 Hamlet Gardens, LONDON, W6 0SX.
•PIERCE, Mr. David Richard, BA FCA *1978;* (Tax Fac), Hazlewoods LLP, Staverton Court, Staverton, CHELTENHAM, GLOUCESTERSHIRE, GL51 0UX.
PIERCE, Miss. Francesca Nicola, BMus ACA *2001;* BSKY B, Grant Way, ISLEWORTH, MIDDLESEX, TW7 5QD.
PIERCE, Mr. Graham Charles, BSc ACA *2001;* 66 Lausanne Road, LONDON, SE15 2JB.
PIERCE, Mrs. Helen Margaret, FCA *1994;* Burway Windsor Lane, Bomere Heath, SHREWSBURY, SY4 3LR.
PIERCE, Mr. James Robert, BSc ACA *2004;* with Brebners, The Quadrangle, 180 Wardour Street, LONDON, W1F 8LB.
PIERCE, Mr. John Charles, BA FCA *1979;* with Ernst & Young LLP, 1 More London Place, LONDON, SE1 2AF.
PIERCE, Miss. Julia Rosemary, BA ACA *1989;* 124 Faraday Road, LONDON, SW19 8PB.
PIERCE, Mrs. Julie Bridget, BSc ACA *1993;* 28 Queens Walk, Ealing, LONDON, W5 1TP.
PIERCE, Mr. Martin John, BA FCA *1984;* with Deloitte Middle East, Currency House, Building 1 Level 5, DIFC, PO Box 282056, DUBAI UNITED ARAB EMIRATES.
•ⒹPIERCE, Mr. Philip Edward, BA ACA *1997;* Baker Tilly Tax & Advisory Services LLP, 2 Whitehall Quay, LEEDS, LS1 4HG. See also Baker Tilly Restructuring and Recovery LLP
•PIERCE, Mr. Robert Kieran, BCom FCA *1972;* Kieran Pierce & Co, 15 Butterfield Park, Rathfarnham, DUBLIN 14, COUNTY DUBLIN, IRELAND.
PIERCE, Mr. Stuart John Duncan, BCom FCA *1972;* The Old Vicarage, Heytesbury, WARMINSTER, WILTSHIRE, BA12 0ES.
PIERCE-GROVE, Mr. Antony Terence, FCA *1964;* 24 Sheep Pasture Road, MADISON, CT 06443, UNITED STATES. (Life Member)
PIERCEY, Mr. Stephen Michael, BSc ACA *1990;* 22 Oldacres, MAIDENHEAD, SL6 1XJ.
PIERCY, Mr. Adam, ACA MAAT *2003;* 196 Spixworth Road, NORWICH, NR6 7EQ.
PIERCY, Mr. Arthur Frederick, BCom FCA *1965;* The Laurels, 8 Grange Meadows, Elmswell, BURY ST. EDMUNDS, SUFFOLK, IP30 9GE.

•PIERCY, Dr. Bernard Alan, BSc ACA *1995;* Taxassist Accountants, Hutchinson House, 21 Sandown Lane, Wavertree, LIVERPOOL, L15 7LQ.
PIERCY, Mr. David Edward, BSc ACA *1995;* 1 Forest Walk, BUCKLEY, CLWYD, CH7 3AZ.
•PIERCY, Mrs. Jean, FCA *1993;* Griffins, Griffins Court, 24-32 London Road, NEWBURY, RG14 1JX. See also Griffins Business Advisers LLP
•PIERCY, Mrs. Lynn Marie, BSc ACA *1996;* with PricewaterhouseCoopers LLP, 1 Embankment Place, LONDON, WC2N 6RH.
•PIERCY, Mr. Mark Wayne, BSc FCA *1983;* Piercy & Co, Tudor Lodge, The Drive, Hook Heath, WOKING, GU22 0JS.
PIERCY, Mr. Matthew Roy, BA ACA *1987;* Faris Barne Cottage, Faris Lane, Woodham, ADDLESTONE, KT15 3DW.
PIERCY, Mr. Nicholas James, BSc ACA *1992;* Compass Group Plc, Compass House, Guildford Street, CHERTSEY, SURREY, KT16 9BQ.
PIERCY, Mrs. Sally Ann, BA ACA *1990;* 33 Carpenders Close, HARPENDEN, HERTFORDSHIRE, AL5 3HN.
PIERCY, Mrs. Sarah Joanne, BSc ACA *2006;* with UHY Kent LLP, Thames House, Roman Square, SITTINGBOURNE, KENT, ME10 4BJ.
•PIERI, Mr. Chris, ACA *1993;* (Tax Fac), Kallis & Partners, Mountview Court, 1148 High Road, Whetstone, LONDON, N20 0RA.
PIERI, Ms. Marina, BSc ACA *2006;* with PricewaterhouseCoopers Limited, Julia House, 3 Themistocles Dervis Street, CY-1066 NICOSIA, CYPRUS.
PIERI, Miss. Mirto, BSc ACA *2011;* 5a-5b Stevenage Road, KNEBWORTH, HERTFORDSHIRE, SG3 6AN.
PIERIDES, Mr. George, BA ACA *2002;* 21 Kamelias Street, Ekali, 3110 LIMASSOL, CYPRUS.
PIERIDOU, Miss. Antigoni, MSc BA ACA *2005;* 6 Desdemonas Street, Larnaca Court 1, Office 203, 6016 LARNACA, CYPRUS.
PIERIS, Miss. Amanda, BSc ACA *2006;* 131 Albany Avenue, TORONTO M5R 3C5, ON, CANADA.
PIERLEONI, Mr. Marco Alessandro, MSc ACA *1992;* H M Land Registry, 32 Lincoln's Inn Fields, LONDON, WC2A 3PH.
PIERPOINT, Miss. Katherine, ACA *2008;* Plan-ItConstruction LTD, 4 Bishopgate, WIGAN, WN1 1NL.
•PIERRE, Mr. Antony David, BSc FCA *1982;* Baker Tilly Tax and Advisory Services LLP, 25 Farringdon Street, LONDON, EC4A 4AB. See also Baker Tilly Corporate Finance LLP
PIERRE, Mr. Claude Allain Guy, FCA *1971;* 49B Queen Mary Ave, FLOREAL, MAURITIUS.
PIERS, Mr. Philip Jeremy, BSc ACA *1995;* 53 Lancaster Road, Hindley, WIGAN, LANCASHIRE, WN2 3NJ.
PIERS, Mr. Pim, MA ACA CF *1996;* 12 Staunton Road, KINGSTON UPON THAMES, KT2 5TJ.
PIERSON, Miss. Catherine Emma, BSc ACA *2007;* 2/39 Waverley Street, BONDI JUNCTION, NSW 2022, AUSTRALIA.
PIERSON, Mr. Derek John, BA FCA *1972;* 113 Bow Lane, LONDON, N12 0JL.
PIERSSENE, Mr. Neil Christopher, BSc ACA *2005;* 72 Lowbrook Lane, Tidbury Green, SOLIHULL, B90 1QS.
PIESSE, Mr. Guy Michael, BA ACA *2007;* with BDO LLP, 55 Baker Street, LONDON, W1U 7EU.
PIETERSE, Mrs. Anissa Claire, BA(Hons) ACA *2004;* 38 The Paddocks, Normandy, GUILDFORD, SURREY, GU3 2HA.
PIETERSE, Mrs. Evelyn Catherine Mary, LLB ACA *2000;* 97 Manor Park, LONDON, SE13 5RQ.
PIETERSEN, Dr. Lloyd Keith, PhD MA BSc ACA *1980;* 7 The Brimbles, Northville, BRISTOL, BS7 0RU.
PIETERSZ, Miss. Ianthe Genevieve Rosanne, BSc ACA *1990;* 21D Reynolds Street, CREMORNE, NSW 2090, AUSTRALIA.
PIETERSZ, Mrs. Miriam Coralie, BSc ACA *1984;* Finlays Colombo PLC, P.O.Box 211, 186 Vauxhall Street, 00200 COLOMBO, SRI LANKA.
PIETKIEWICZ, Mr. Daniel, BSc ACA *2010;* Flat 34, Nonsuch House, 31 Chapter Way, LONDON, SW19 2RP.
PIETROBON, Miss. Manuela, ACA *2007;* Via Beato Angelico 8, Milano, VENICE, ITALY.
PIETRUNTI, Mr. Michael, BSc ACA *1988;* 4 Copley Way, TADWORTH, SURREY, KT20 5QS.
PIFF, Mrs. Jennifer Louise, BA ACA *2009;* 21 Colesbourne, CHELTENHAM, GLOUCESTERSHIRE, GL53 9NS.
PIFF, Mrs. Sally Ann, BSc ACA *1986;* 11 Proctor Road, Sprowston, NORWICH, NR6 7PF.
PIGEON, Mr. Robert Antony, FCA *1966;* 127 Chester Road, Hazel Grove, STOCKPORT, CHESHIRE, SK7 6HD.
PIGGOT, Mrs. Jane Elizabeth Louise, BSc ACA *1993;* Headmaster's House, Campbell College, Belmont Road, BELFAST, BT4 2ND.
PIGGOTT, Miss. Amy Joanne, BSc ACA *2005;* 14 Swan Terrace, WINDSOR, QLD 4030, AUSTRALIA.
•PIGGOTT, Mr. Andrew, BA FCA *1965;* (Tax Fac), Andrew Piggott, 10 Station Close, Leckhampton, CHELTENHAM, GLOUCESTERSHIRE, GL53 0AB.
PIGGOTT, Mrs. Chrissy, BSc(Hons) ACA *2010;* Flat 10 Nickleby House, George Row, LONDON, SE16 4UW.
PIGGOTT, Miss. Claire, BA ACA *1998;* 18 Mandrake Road, LONDON, SW17 7PT.
PIGGOTT, Mr. Dudley Frederick, FCA *1958;* 7 Donovan's Garden, Herongate, BRENTWOOD, Essex, CM13 3PX. (Life Member)
PIGGOTT, Mr. Richard Courtney, FCA *1968;* 72 Plymouth Place, LEAMINGTON SPA, CV31 1HW.
•PIGGOTT, Mr. Robert John, MA FCA *1993;* 2 Stanhope Road, ST. ALBANS, AL1 5BL.
PIGGOTT, Mrs. Sally Louise, BSc ACA *1992;* B N Y Mellon, 1 Whitehall Riverside, LEEDS, LS1 4BN.
PIGHTLING, Miss. Sarah Lynn, ACA *2001;* 42 Cardiff Road, NORWICH, NR2 3HS.
PIGOTT, Mr. Edward Sefton, MA ACA *1989;* 17 Burnaby Gardens, Chiswick, LONDON, W4 3DR.
PIGOTT, Mr. Gregory Michael, BSc(Econ) ACA *2000;* 37 Charlton Court Road Charlton Kings, CHELTENHAM, GLOUCESTERSHIRE, GL52 6JB.
PIJPER, Mr. Trevor John, ACA CA(SA) *2010;* 1 Carrick Drive, SEVENOAKS, KENT, TN13 3BA.
PIKE, Mr. Alexander James, BA ACA *2003;* 9 Hemmings Close, SIDCUP, KENT, DA14 4JR.
PIKE, Mr. Alistair Neil, BSc ACA *2006;* Tomdarroch, Tulliemet, PITLOCHRY, PERTHSHIRE, PH9 0PA.
PIKE, Mr. Andrew Stephen, BA ACA *1990;* Dimension Data Group UK, Dimension Data House, 2 Waterfront Business Park, FLEET, HAMPSHIRE, GU51 3QT.
PIKE, Mr. Anthony Frederick, ACA *2009;* 197 Huddersfield Road, MIRFIELD, WF14 9DQ.
PIKE, Mr. Anthony Noel, BCom FCA *1982;* 11, Herringshaw Croft, SUTTON COLDFIELD, B76 1HT.
PIKE, Mr. Brian David, FCA *1958;* 22 Dukes Wood, CROWTHORNE, RG45 6NF. (Life Member)
PIKE, Mrs. Cheryl Anne, BSc ACA *2005;* 107a Barry Avenue, BICESTER, OXFORDSHIRE, OX26 2HA.
PIKE, Mr. Christopher Paul Russell, BSc ACA *1995;* Chantwood Consultancy Ltd, Chantwood Mells Green, Mells, FROME, SOMERSET, BA11 3QE.
PIKE, Mr. Christopher Richard, BSc ACA *2005;* 2 Druce Wood, ASCOT, SL5 8NA.
PIKE, Mr. David Anthony, FCA *1978;* 343 Millview Place SW, CALGARY T2Y 2X6, AB, CANADA.
PIKE, Mr. David John, BSc(Hons) ACA *2002;* 414a Upper Richmond Road West, LONDON, SW14 7JX.
PIKE, Mr. David John, BSc FCA *1971;* 2b Lower Road, Edington, WESTBURY, BA13 4QN.
PIKE, Mr. David Kenneth, BA FCA *1986;* Willow House, 100 Sandford View, NEWTON ABBOT, DEVON, TQ12 2TH.
PIKE, Mr. David Robin, BSc FCA *1972;* with Ensors, Cardinal House, 46 St Nicholas Street, IPSWICH, IP1 1TT.
PIKE, Mrs. Elizabeth Anne, BSc ACA *1988;* Greystream, 3 Hare Lane End, Little Kingshill, GREAT MISSENDEN, HP16 0EX.
PIKE, Miss. Ellen, BSc(Hons) ACA *2009;* NBGI Private Equity, Old Change House, 128 Queen Victoria Street, LONDON, EC4V 4BJ.
PIKE, Mr. Elliott Lee, ACA *2009;* 45 Garthorne Road, LONDON, SE23 1EP.
PIKE, Miss. Emma Louise, ACA *2009;* 42 Waters Edge, Pewsham, CHIPPENHAM, WILTSHIRE, SN15 3GE.
•PIKE, Mr. Glyn Malcolm, FCA *1971;* Glyn Pike, 10 Mark Road, Hightown, LIVERPOOL, L38 0BH.
•PIKE, Mr. Graeme Kenneth, BA FCA CF *1983;* PricewaterhouseCoopers LLP, 1 Embankment Place, LONDON, WC2N 6RH. See also PricewaterhouseCoopers
•PIKE, Mr. Graeme Mark, FCA *1972;* Graeme M. Pike Ltd, 48 Prince Charles Avenue, CHATHAM, ME5 8EY.
PIKE, Mrs. Jane, BSc ACA *1990;* Grant Thornton Enterprise House, 115 Edmund Street, BIRMINGHAM, B3 2HJ.
PIKE, Mr. Jonathan Gordon, MA FCA *1994;* 7 Gorse Corner, Townsend Drive, ST. ALBANS, HERTFORDSHIRE, AL3 5SH.
PIKE, Mr. Jonathan Richard, MEng BA ACA *2004;* 5 Bardwell Road, ST. ALBANS, HERTFORDSHIRE, AL1 1RQ.
PIKE, Mrs. Lauren Kate, BA(Hons) ACA *2002;* 9 Hemmings Close, SIDCUP, KENT, DA14 4JR.
PIKE, Mrs. Linda Mary, BSc FCA *1986;* Sita UK Ltd Unit 301-304, Park Way Worle, WESTON-SUPER-MARE, AVON, BS22 6WA.
PIKE, Mr. Neil William, BA ACA *1999;* 12 Madden Street, North Balwyn, MELBOURNE, VIC 3104, AUSTRALIA.
•PIKE, Mr. Neville Douglas, BA ACA *1987;* Sackleford, Robin Hood Lane, Sutton Green, GUILDFORD, GU4 7QG.
PIKE, Mr. Norman, FCA *1962;* Barna House, Church Lane, Bradley, GRIMSBY, DN37 0AE. (Life Member)
PIKE, Mr. Oliver Edward, BA FCA *1976;* 24 Caistor Close, MANCHESTER, M16 8NW.
PIKE, Mr. Richard, BSc ACA *1980;* 195A Springvale Road, SHEFFIELD, S6 3NT.
PIKE, Mr. Richard Neil, LLB ACA ATII AMCT *1994;* British Sugar Plc, Sugar Way, PETERBOROUGH, PE2 9AY.
PIKE, Mr. Robert Alexander, BA ACA *2006;* 2 Wallis Gardens, Greenham Road, NEWBURY, BERKSHIRE, RG14 7SF.
•PIKE, Mr. Stephen Vincent, FCA *1981;* Bradshaw Johnson, 13 Bancroft, HITCHIN, HERTFORDSHIRE, SG5 1JQ. See also Bradshaw Johnson & Co
PIKE, Mr. William, BA FCA FRSA *1979;* Cranford Cottage Duck Street, Wendens Ambo, SAFFRON WALDEN, CB11 4JU.
PIKE, Mr. William Henry Roberts, FCA *1956;* Chestnut Croft, Cossall, NOTTINGHAM, NG16 2RW. (Life Member)
PIKIS, Mr. Angelos Michael, BSc FCA *1961;* 14 Lefkosias Str., 145 62 KIFISIA, GREECE.
PIKIS, Mr. Michael Angelos, BSc ACA *1995;* 194 Syngrou Avenue, 17671 ATHENS, GREECE.
PILAVAKIS, Mr. Marios Andrea, MBA MBS MPhil(Cantab) BA(Hons) ACA MCIM CF *2001;* 35 Nikou Pattichi Avenue, 3071 LIMASSOL, CYPRUS.
PILBEAM, Mr. Graeme James, BSc ACA *1993;* 26 Greenway, HORSHAM, RH12 2JS.
PILBEAM, Mr. Richard Henry, FCA *1965;* Westbury, 37a Courts Hill Road, HASLEMERE, SURREY, GU27 2PN. (Life Member)
•PILBROW, Mr. Nicholas David, FCA *1967;* Orion Network Consultants LLP, 12 Wootton Rivers, MARLBOROUGH, WILTSHIRE, SN8 4NH. See also Pilbrow N.D.
PILCH, Mrs. Natalie, BA(Econ) ACA *1998;* 63 Bronte Avenue Stotfold, HITCHIN, HERTFORDSHIRE, SG5 4FB.
PILCHER, Mr. Anthony Julian, FCA *1959;* The Garden House, Steventon, BASINGSTOKE, RG25 3BE. (Life Member)
•PILCHER, Mr. Grant Stanley, FCA ATII TEP *1991;* (Tax Fac), Larking Gowen, Faiers House, Gilray Road, DISS, IP22 4WR. See also Larking Gowen Limited
PILCHER, Mr. Jonathan Charles, BSc ACA *1992;* 101 Sandringham Road, SANDRINGHAM, VIC 3191, AUSTRALIA.
PILCHER, Mr. Michael Barrington Macdonald, FCA *1955;* The Hollies, Knapton Road, Mundesley, NORWICH, NR11 8LA. (Life Member)
PILCHER, Mr. Simon Charles, BSc ACA *1981;* 130-2979 Panorama Drive, COQUITLAM V3E 2W8, BC, CANADA.
PILCHER, Mr. Stephen Neil, ACA *1983;* Hayworthe House, Moody International, 2 Market Place, HAYWARDS HEATH, WEST SUSSEX, RH16 1DB.
PILCHER, Mr. Timothy James, BA ACA *1994;* Clarion Events, Earls Court Exhibition Centre, Warwick Road, LONDON, SW5 9TA.
•PILE, Miss. Elizabeth Anne, BA ACA *1992;* Elizabeth A Pile, Flat 2, 10 Frognal Gardens, LONDON, NW3 6UX.
PILE, Mrs. Jennifer Ruth, MMath ACA *2007;* 1 Hamilton Road, LONDON, SW19 1JD.
PILE, Mr. Philip, ACA *2010;* Fieldside, Oakdene Road, GODALMING, SURREY, GU7 1QF.
PILE, Miss. Sally Elizabeth, ACA *2007;* Lower West Apt #1, Smiling Hill, 7 Halfway Lane, SMITHS FL08, BERMUDA.
•PILGREM, Mr. Michael Anthony, MA ACA *1991;* FTI Consulting Limited, Davidson Building, 5 Southampton Street, LONDON, WC2E 7HA.
PILGRIM, Mr. Alan John Templer, BSc FCA *1976;* 44 Pepper Hill, Great Amwell, WARE, HERTFORDSHIRE, SG12 9RZ.
PILGRIM, Mr. Christopher, BSc ACA *1992;* 7 Glenwood Avenue, Bassett, SOUTHAMPTON, SO16 3PY.
•PILGRIM, Mr. Colin John, FCA *1968;* (Tax Fac), Clifford C. Palmer & Co, 61-67 Rectory Road, Wivenhoe, COLCHESTER, CO7 9ES.
PILGRIM, Mr. John Brian Neil, FCA *1961;* 7 Beeston Fields Drive, Beeston, NOTTINGHAM, NG9 3DB.
PILGRIM, Mr. Roger Granville, MA FCA *1982;* 55 Redington Road, Hampstead, LONDON, NW3 7RP.
PILIDES, Miss. Natasha, BA ACA *2006;* 8 Napoleontos Street, 1020 NICOSIA, CYPRUS.
•PILIDES, Mr. Phidias Kyriacou, FCA *1978;* PricewaterhouseCoopers Limited, Julia House, 3 Themistocles Dervis Street, CY-1066 NICOSIA, CYPRUS.
PILIPOVIC, Mrs. Latinka, ACA *2001;* 6 Egham Crescent, SUTTON, SURREY, SM3 9AL.
PILKINGTON, Mr. Anthony Philip William, BSc FCA *1975;* BookCheck Ltd, The Midway, Chalford Hill, STROUD, GLOUCESTERSHIRE, GL6 8EN.
PILKINGTON, Miss. Caroline, ACA *2008;* 44 Green Street, Chorleywood, RICKMANSWORTH, HERTFORDSHIRE, WD3 5QR.
PILKINGTON, Mrs. Caroline Elizabeth, BSc ACA *1997;* 9 Princes Road, SALE, CHESHIRE, M33 3EH.
•PILKINGTON, Mrs. Catherine Bernadette, BA ACA *1986;* Dunne & Pilkington Limited, 135 Towngate, LEYLAND, PR25 2LH.
PILKINGTON, Mrs. Clare Louise, BSc ACA *2001;* 24 Meadowcroft, Euxton, CHORLEY, PR7 6BU.
PILKINGTON, Mr. Gareth, BA ACA *2011;* 6 Huby Banks, Huby, LEEDS, LS17 0AH.
PILKINGTON, Miss. Gemma Marie, ACA *2011;* 12 Dene Way, Ashurst, SOUTHAMPTON, SO40 7BX.
PILKINGTON, Mr. Ian, BSc ACA *1989;* 308 Burnley Road, ACCRINGTON, LANCASHIRE, BB5 6HG.
PILKINGTON, Mr. John William, BA(Hons) ACA *2001;* 24 Meadowcroft, Euxton, CHORLEY, PR7 6BU.
PILKINGTON, Mr. Lee James, LLB ACA *2002;* 4 Ilford Way, Mobberley, KNUTSFORD, CHESHIRE, WA16 7GJ.
PILKINGTON, Mr. Leslie, FCA *1972;* 2 Lowther Court, Queens Promenade, BLACKPOOL, FY2 9NY.
PILKINGTON, Mr. Paul Timothy, MSc ACA *1995;* with PricewaterhouseCoopers LLP, 1 Embankment Place, LONDON, WC2N 6RH.
PILKINGTON, Mr. Peter John, FCA *1976;* The Cornerstone Practice, Shadsworth Surgery Shadsworth Road, BLACKBURN, BB1 2HR.
PILKINGTON, Mr. Richard David, MA BA BSc ACA *1992;* 403-60 rue William-Paul, VERDUN H3E 1N5, QC, CANADA.
PILKINGTON, Mr. Robert, BA ACA *2000;* UPS, 55 Glenlake Parkway NE, ATLANTA, GA 30328, UNITED STATES.
PILKINGTON, Mr. Ronald Vincent, FCA *1961;* 20 Gotts Park Crescent, LEEDS, LS12 2RP.
•PILKINGTON, Mr. Stephen, BSc ACA ATII *1986;* Dunne & Pilkington Limited, 135 Towngate, LEYLAND, PR25 2LH.
PILKINGTON, Mr. Timothy David, BSc ACA ATII MBA PGCE *1998;* Marlotlaan 1, 2594 CL DEN HAAG, NETHERLANDS.
PILL, Mr. Thomas Michael, BSc FCA *1976;* Sedgecombe, Garfield Road, CAMBERLEY, GU15 2JG.
PILLAI, Miss. Dushyanthy, BSc ACA *2002;* 7 Urban Mews, Hermitage Road, LONDON, N4 1AH.
PILLAI, Dr. Jayasheela, BA ACA *2005;* Deloitte & Touche Abbots House, Abbey Street, READING, RG1 3BD.
PILLAI, Mr. Ramesh, BSc(Hons) FCA CRP CA(MIA) ERM(IERP) *1991;* 66 Jalan BU 11/13, Bandar Utama, 47800 PETALING JAYA, SELANGOR, MALAYSIA.
PILLAI, Miss. Sothimalar Sash, ACA *2009;* 15 St. Johns Court St. Johns Road, ERITH, KENT, DA8 1NX.
PILLAI, Miss. Susheela Bridget, MSc ACA *2000;* RBS Bank Plc, 1 Princes Street, LONDON, EC2R 8PB.
PILLAR, Mrs. Anne Patricia, BSc ACA *1986;* 5 Larkswood, Kibworth Beauchamp, LEICESTER, LE8 0SB.
•①PILLAR, Mr. Christopher William, LLB FCA *1986;* 5 Larkswood, Kibworth, LEICESTER, LE8 0SB.
PILLAR, Mr. Mark Stephen, MA FCA *1985;* 3 Old Eagley Mews, BOLTON, BL1 7HR.
PILLER, Mr. Lee Robert, MA ACA *1992;* CESR, 11-13 Avenue De Friedland, 75008 PARIS, FRANCE.
PILLER, Mr. Richard Louis, FCA ATII *1984;* 7 Upshire Gardens, The Warren, BRACKNELL, RG12 9YZ.
PILLEY, Mr. Clive Richard, FCA *1982;* 43 Electric Avenue, WESTCLIFF-ON-SEA, ESSEX, SS0 9NN.

•**PILLEY, Mr. Martyn, BSc FCA CF** *1993;* with Cattaneo LLP, One Victoria Square, BIRMINGHAM, B1 1BD.

PILLING, Mr. Byron Alexander, ACA *2009;* 103 Randolph Avenue, LONDON, W9 1DL.

PILLING, Mr. Charles David, BCom FCA *1961;* 7 The Orchard, Albrighton, WOLVERHAMPTON, WV7 3RE. (Life Member)

PILLING, Mr. Christopher Mark, BSc ACA *2000;* Unit 1, 88a Kurraba Road, NEUTRAL BAY, NSW 2089, AUSTRALIA.

PILLING, Mr. Duncan Alexander Edward, BSc ACA *2010;* 71 Pinewood Drive, BIRMINGHAM, B32 4LF.

PILLING, Mr. John David Christopher, FCA *1961;* 12 Kiln Brow, Bromley Cross, BOLTON, BL7 9NR.

PILLING, Mr. Kenneth, FCA *1962;* 24 Wellfield Road, Culcheth, WARRINGTON, WA3 4JP.

PILLING, Mr. Michael, BA ACA *1990;* 25 Alexandra Road, TWICKENHAM, TW1 2HE.

PILLING, Mr. Michael William, BSc FCA *1975;* Deloitte & Touche, P.O.Box 1787 GT, One Capital Place, GEORGE TOWN, GRAND CAYMAN, KY1 1109 CAYMAN ISLANDS.

PILLING, Mrs. Rosemary June, FCA *1974;* with MacIntyre Hudson LLP, 31 Castle Street, HIGH WYCOMBE, BUCKINGHAMSHIRE, HP13 6RU.

PILLING, Mr. Steven Richard, BSc ACA *2010;* 31 Old Stack Yard, Village Road Great Barrow, CHESTER, CH3 7JE.

PILLING, Mr. Trevor Leon Harold, FCA *1965;* 5 Lycrome Lane, CHESHAM, HP5 3JY.

PILLINGER, Mr. Adrian Peter, BSc(Hons) ACA *2002;* Little Snoring Farm, Haroldslea Drive, HORLEY, SURREY, RH6 9PJ.

PILLINGER, Miss. Anna Margaret, BA ACA *2007;* 20A Caroline Height, 1 Link Road, HAPPY VALLEY, HONG KONG SAR.

PILLINGER, Mr. David James Albert, BA ACA *1988;* Copperfields, Clifford Manor Road, GUILDFORD, GU4 8AG.

PILLINGER, Mrs. Elizabeth, BA ACA *1988;* Copperfields, Clifford Manor Road, GUILDFORD, GU4 8AG.

PILLINGER, Miss. Jane Margaret, BA ACA *1989;* Elmfield House, Burgage, SOUTHWELL, NG25 0EP.

PILLINGER, Mr. Matthew James, LLB ACA *2004;* with RSM Tenon Limited, Vantage, Victoria Street, BASINGSTOKE, RG21 3BT.

PILLINGER, Mr. Richard, BSc ACA *2001;* 17 Audrey Street, BALGOWLAH, NSW 2093, AUSTRALIA.

•①**PILLMOOR, Mr. Alec David, ACA** *1982;* Baker Tilly Tax & Advisory Services LLP, 2 Humber Quays, Wellington Street West, HULL, HU1 2BN. See also Baker Tilly Restructuring and Recovery LLP and Debt Lifeboat Limited

•**PILLOW, Mrs. Jessica, BSc ACA** *2003;* (Tax Fac), Pillow May Ltd, Bremhill Grove Farmhouse, East Tytherton, CHIPPENHAM, WILTSHIRE, SN15 4LX.

PILOT, Mr. Denis-Claude, ACA CA(AUS) *2010;* Denis-Claude Pilot, Les Salines Pilot, BLACK RIVER, MAURITIUS.

PILOT, Mr. Joseph Marie Johan, ACA *2008;* C/o ENL Property, PO Box 47, REDUIT, MAURITIUS.

PILSWORTH, Mr. Andrew John, BA ACA MCT *2000;* 12 Sandale Close, Gamston, NOTTINGHAM, NG2 6QG.

PILSWORTH, Mr. Michael Edwin, FCA *1980;* 9 Lilac Avenue, Norwood Grange, Hull Bridge Road, BEVERLEY, HU17 9UT.

•**PIMBLETT, Mr. Roger David John, BA FCA** *1991;* Whyatt Pakeman Partners, Colkin House, 16 Oakfield Rd, Clifton, BRISTOL, BS8 2AP.

•**PIMBLOTT, Mr. Christopher, ACA CTA** *1980;* (Tax Fac), C Pimblott & Co, 341/343 Park Lane, MACCLESFIELD, SK11 8JR.

PIMENTA, Mr. Justin Paul, MA ACA *2000;* 4 Heenan Close, Frimley Green, CAMBERLEY, SURREY, GU16 6NQ.

PIMENTA, Mr. Robin, BSc ACA *1992;* 10 Carmelite Way, Hartley, LONGFIELD, KENT, DA3 8BP.

PIMENTIL, Mr. Stephen John, BA ACA *1982;* Pimentil, 3 Golf Road, Lundin Links, LEVEN, KY8 6BB.

•**PIMLOTT, Mr. Christopher John, BCom FCA** *1982;* Ernst & Young LLP, 725 South Figueroa Street, Suite 500, LOS ANGELES, CA 90017, UNITED STATES. See also Deloitte & Touche LLP

PIMLOTT, Mr. Kenneth George, FCA *1958;* Cloud Cottage Cloudside, Timbersbrook, CONGLETON, CW12 3QB. (Life Member)

PIMM, Mr. Anthony John, ACA *1984;* Sowley Cottage Farm, Marchington Cliff, UTTOXETER, STAFFORDSHIRE, ST14 8NB.

PIMM, Mr. David Anthony, BSc FCA *1984;* 48 Berrylands, SURBITON, KT5 8JU.

PIMM, Mr. Dennis Frank, FCA *1955;* 5 Ashford Gardens, COBHAM, KT11 3HN. (Life Member)

PIMM, Mr. Malcolm Arthur, FCA MBA *1965;* Avenue Orban 60, B-1150 BRUSSELS, BELGIUM.

PIMM, Mr. Nigel John, ACA *1990;* 21 Somerset Avenue, CHESSINGTON, KT9 1PW.

PIMPERTON, Mr. David, BEng ACA *1999;* 9 Thorntree Close, Ravenstone, COALVILLE, LEICESTERSHIRE, LE67 2JY.

PIMSTONE, Mr. Jaime David, BA ACA *1988;* 114 rue des Soeurs Grises Apt 402, MONTREAL H3C 2R1, QC, CANADA.

•**PINARD, Mrs. Jennifer Anne, BA FCA ATII** *1978;* Pinard & Co Limited, Berkley House, 18 Station Road, EAST GRINSTEAD, WEST SUSSEX, RH19 1DJ. See also Pinard Wright & Co Ltd

PINCHARD, Mr. John, BSc FCA *1979;* 5 Stocking Lane, Hughenden Valley, HIGH WYCOMBE, HP14 4NE.

PINCHARD, Mr. Michael Peter, FCA *1969;* Meadowside, St. Mary, JERSEY, JE3 3EJ.

PINCHBECK, Mr. Edward Roger, FCA *1974;* 8 Patterdale Way, Anston, SHEFFIELD, S25 4JS.

PINCHBECK, Mr. Simon Barrie, BA ACA *1999;* 70 Humberston Avenue, Humberston, GRIMSBY, SOUTH HUMBERSIDE, DN36 4SU.

PINCHEN, Miss. Catherine Christine, BSc ACA *1989;* 112 Annandale Road, Greenwich, LONDON, SE10 0JZ.

•**PINCHES, Mr. Michael John, FCA** *1955;* M.J. Pinches, 3 Rose Hill Arch Mews, Rose Hill, DORKING, RH4 2ER.

PINCHIN, Mr. Nicholas John, FCA *1975;* 8 Dryden Street, Grey Lynn, AUCKLAND 1021, NEW ZEALAND.

PINCHING, Mr. Scott Barry, BSc ACA *1994;* The Laurels, 4 Coltishall Road, Belaugh, NORWICH, NR12 8UX.

PINCKARD, Mr. Anthony Charles, MA FCA *1993;* 10 Beryl Road, West Kensington, LONDON, W6 8JT.

PINCKARD, Mr. John Moore, FCA *1954;* 27 Fieldgate Lane, KENILWORTH, CV8 1BT. (Life Member)

•**PINCKARD, Mr. Richard, BSc(Econ) FCA** *1987;* KPMG LLP, 15 Canada Square, LONDON, E14 5GL. See also KPMG Europe LLP

PINCKNEY, Mr. David Charles, MA FCA *1967;* Southcot House, Chapmanslade, WESTBURY, WILTSHIRE, BA13 4AU.

PINCOTT, Mr. Anthony Keith, MA FCA *1976;* 32 Belitha Villas, LONDON, N1 1PD.

•**PINCOTT, Miss. Antoinette Jean Marie, LLB FCA** *1988;* Stone Turn UK LLP, 85 Fleet Street, LONDON, EC4Y 1AE.

PINCOTT, Mr. Leslie Rundell, CBE FCA *1948;* 53 HUrlingham Court, Ranelagh Gardens, LONDON, SW6 3UP. (Life Member)

PINCOTT, Mr. Robin Michael, BSc FCA *1997;* Kingfisher Cottage Henley Road, Wargrave, READING, RG10 8HZ.

PINCUS, Mr. Barry Martin, FCA *1967;* 19 Willifield Way, LONDON, NW11 7XU.

PINDAR, Mr. Paul Richard Martin, BA ACA *1984;* Byron House, Bourneside, Wentworth, VIRGINIA WATER, GU25 4LZ.

PINDER, Mr. Andrew James, LLB ACA *2000;* 61 Clarendon Drive, LONDON, SW15 1AW.

•**PINDER, Mr. David, BSc FCA DChA** *1990;* David Pinder & Co Limited, 23 Lockyer Street, PLYMOUTH, PL1 2QZ.

PINDER, Mr. Gordon, FCA *1956;* 3 Ainsty Walk, CONSTANTIA, C.P., 7806, SOUTH AFRICA. (Life Member)

•**PINDER, Mr. Ian, BSc FCA** *1979;* A.C. Mole & Sons, Stafford House, Blackbrook Park Avenue, TAUNTON, SOMERSET, TA1 2PX.

PINDER, Mr. John Michael, FCA *1953;* Portville, Fleet Street, Gatehouse of Fleet, CASTLE DOUGLAS, DG7 2JT. (Life Member)

PINDER, Mr. John Richard, BA FCA *1976;* Methersham Manor, Hobbs Lane, Beckley, RYE, EAST SUSSEX, TN31 6TX.

•**PINDER, Mr. Jonathan Mark, BA FCA** *1991;* RSM Tenon Audit Limited, Sumner House, St. Thomas's Road, CHORLEY, LANCASHIRE, PR7 1HP. See also Tenon Audit Limited

PINDER, Miss. Kate, BSc ACA *2006;* with Ernst & Young LLP, 1 More London Place, LONDON, SE1 2AF.

PINDER, Mrs. Kathryn Alexandra, BSc FCA *1991;* The Old Rectory, Main Road, Burgh-On-Bain, MARKET RASEN, LN8 6JY.

PINDER, Mrs. Norah, FCA *1934;* 36 Kestor Lane, Longridge, PRESTON, PR3 3JX. (Life Member)

PINDER, Mr. Phillip Steven, BSc ACA *1987;* Benview East 17 Grahamsdyke Road, BO'NESS, WEST LOTHIAN, EH51 9EQ.

PINDER, Mr. Robert Graeme, BSc ACA *2003;* Lautrupvang 8, DK-2750 BALLERUP, DENMARK.

•**PINDER, Mr. Stephen John, FCA** *1975;* (Tax Fac), Angell Pinder Limited, 1 Victoria Street, DUNSTABLE, BEDFORDSHIRE, LU6 3AZ.

PINDORIA, Mr. Gopal Premji, LLB FCA *2000;* 48 Tewkesbury Gardens, LONDON, NW9 0QX.

PINDORIA, Mr. Mahesh Valji, BSc(Econ) FCA *1997;* 110 Northwick Avenue, HARROW, HA3 0AT.

PINDORIA, Mr. Ravji Kanji, BA ACA *1990;* (Tax Fac), Yakult UK Ltd, Artemis, Odyssey Business Park, West End Road, RUISLIP, MIDDLESEX HA4 6QE.

PINE, Mr. Anthony, LLB ACA *2003;* Lvl 4, 407 Pacific Highway, ARTARMON, NSW 2064, AUSTRALIA.

PINEDO, Mr. John Carlos, BA ACA *1993;* 24 Penshurst Road, Hackney, LONDON, E9 7DX.

•①**PINFIELD, Mr. Scott, BSc FCA** *1991;* Gillmoor House, Dukes Hill, Gill Bank Road, ILKLEY, WEST YORKSHIRE, LS29 0AZ.

PINFOLD, Miss. Corinna Jane, BA FCA *1988;* 17 Rolleston Crescent, Watnall, NOTTINGHAM, NG16 1JU.

PINFOLD, Mrs. Katharine Beatrice, MSc ACA *1994;* Camp Hill, Baldwins Gate, NEWCASTLE, STAFFORDSHIRE, ST5 5ES.

PING LEUNG, Mr. Wo, JP FCA *1982;* 52 Ma Kwu Lam Village, Shap Sze Heung, SAI KUNG, NEW TERRITORIES, HONG KONG SAR.

PINGEL, Mr. Kai, FCA *1999;* Ernst-Mittelbach-Ring 60, D-22455 HAMBURG, GERMANY.

PINGREE, Miss. Laura Clare, BSc ACA *2003;* Wyvern Heybrook Drive, Heybrook Bay, PLYMOUTH, PL9 0BW.

PINGREE, Mr. Timothy Robert, ACA *2002;* PO Box 965, 235 Ikorodu Road, ILUPEJU, LAGOS STATE, NIGERIA.

•**PINGUEY, Mr. Steven, BA FCA** *1989;* Armstrong Watson, Birbeck House, Duke Street, PENRITH, CA11 7NA.

PINHORN, Mr. David Anthony, BA ACA *1988;* 7 York Road, STOCKPORT, SK4 4PQ.

PINI, Mrs. Victoria Langley, BA(Hons) ACA *2004;* 62 Saffron Close, Chineham, BASINGSTOKE, RG24 8XQ.

•**PINION, Mr. Simon Leonard, ACA FCCA** *2009;* Taylor Viney & Marlow, 46-54 High Street, INGATESTONE, CM4 9DW.

PINION-JONES, Mrs. Wendy Jane, BSc ACA NTAAF *1998;* 8 Ossian Way, KINROSS, WA 6028, AUSTRALIA.

•**PINK, Mr. Alan David, MPhil BA FCA ATII** *1986;* (Tax Fac), Pink Consultants LLP, 44 The Pantiles, TUNBRIDGE WELLS, KENT, TN2 5TN.

PINK, Mr. Lawrence Martin, FCA *1961;* 1 Strand Close, Ashford, BARNSTAPLE, DEVON, EX31 4AE.

PINK, Mr. Martin, BA FCA *1963;* (Member of Council 1990 - 1993), Albertiweg 24, 22605 HAMBURG, GERMANY. (Life Member)

PINK, Mr. Michael Norman, BA(Hons) ACA *2004;* 18 Little Field, Staplehurst, TONBRIDGE, TN12 0SZ.

•①**PINK, Mr. Michael Robert, BCom FCA** *1987;* 5 Century Close, Flitwick, BEDFORD, MK45 1GB.

PINK, Mrs. Penelope Sarah Carwardine, ACA *2007;* 5 Wiluna Avenue, WHITE GUM VALLEY, WA 6162, AUSTRALIA.

PINK, Mr. Simon Richard Anthony, BA ACA *2000;* 1 Cromford Close, ORPINGTON, KENT, BR6 9QF.

PINK PROOPS, Mrs. Joan Allison, FCA *1966;* Oakhurst, Chapel Lane, Nettlebed, HENLEY-ON-THAMES, OXFORDSHIRE, RG9 5AW. (Life Member)

PINKERTON, Mrs. Philippa Mary, MA(Hons) ACA *2006;* 7/1 Learmonth Gardens, EDINBURGH, EH4 1HD.

PINKERTON-HIRON, Mr. Jonathan Richard, BSc ACA *2006;* Lloyds TSB Bank Plc, Tredegar Park, Pencarn Way, Duffryn, NEWPORT, GWENT NP10 8SB.

•**PINKHAM, Mr. David John, BA FCA** *1991;* (Tax Fac), Pinkham Blair, 87A High Street, The Old Town, HEMEL HEMPSTEAD, HERTFORDSHIRE, HP1 3AH.

PINKNEY, Mr. Andrew Charles, FCA *1981;* with PricewaterhouseCoopers LLP, 10-18 Union Street, LONDON, SE1 1SZ.

PINKNEY, Mrs. Nicola Claire, BSc ACA *1994;* 63 Goddard Place, LONDON, N19 5GT.

PINKNEY, Mr. Roger John, FCA *1972;* 13 Conway Road, Shirley, SOLIHULL, B90 4RE.

PINKS, Mr. Ian Peter, BA FCA *1977;* Barnhill House, Barnhill House Barn Hill, Hunton, MAIDSTONE, ME15 0QT.

PINKS, Mr. Simon Paul, ACA *1980;* Lil-Lets (UK) Ltd Radcliffe House, Blenheim Court, SOLIHULL, B91 2AA.

PINNEGAR, Mr. Ian Andrew, BA ACA *1990;* 26 Houghton Banks, Ingleby Barwick, STOCKTON-ON-TEES, CLEVELAND, TS17 5AL.

PINNELL, Mr. Anthony Charles Joseph, BA ACA *1993;* ul. Drawska 14 m.25, Ochota, WARSAW, 02-202, POLAND.

PINNELL, Mr. Charles John, MA FCA *1969;* Edifici Nordic 4A, Avda El Traves, AD 400 LA MASSANA, ANDORRA.

PINNELL, Mr. Gerard Stephen, BSc FCA *1991;* 16 Amberley Way, Wickwar, WOTTON-UNDER-EDGE, GL12 8LP.

PINNER, Mr. James Robert, BSc ACA *2002;* 100 Cannon Street, LONDON, EC4R 6EU.

•**PINNER, Mr. Michael Selby, BA ACA** *1991;* Errington Langer Pinner, Pyramid House, 956 High Road, Finchley, LONDON, N12 9RX.

•**PINNER, Mr. Roderick, FCA** *1968;* Pinner Darlington, Broughton House, 187 Wolverhampton Street, DUDLEY, DY1 3AD.

PINNEY, Mr. Graham Richard, BA ACA *1987;* 22 Ave. Des Muguets, B-1150 BRUSSELS, BELGIUM.

PINNEY, Mr. Michael, MA FCA *1970;* 25 Canterbury Road, Penn, WOLVERHAMPTON, WV4 4EQ. (Life Member)

PINNICK, Mr. Jeffrey Joseph, FCA *1959;* 34 Barnet Gate Lane, BARNET, EN5 2AB. (Life Member)

PINNINGTON, Miss. Emma Kate, BSc ACA *2005;* 36 Launceston Drive, Penketh, WARRINGTON, WA5 2ND.

PINNINGTON, Mr. Ian Harry, BA FCA *1974;* Shillingford, 4 Bucklow View, Bowdon, ALTRINCHAM, WA14 3JP.

PINNINGTON, Mrs. Katie, BSc ACA *1992;* 50 Overnhill Road, Downend, BRISTOL, BS16 5DP.

PINNOCK, Mr. Matthew Ian, ACA *2009;* 50a Horsecastle Farm Road, Yatton, BRISTOL, BS49 4BQ.

PINNOCK, Mr. Richard Mark, BSc ACA *1985;* AXA Real Estate 8th Floor, 155 Bishopsgate, LONDON, EC2M 3XJ.

•**PINNOCK, Mr. Robert Leonard, FCA** *1960;* Robert Pinnock, Tower House, High Street, Hurstpierpoint, HASSOCKS, WEST SUSSEX BN6 9RQ.

PINO, Mr. Roberto Alceste, BEng ACA *1992;* Stable Cottage, 4 Yew Tree Court, Poulton, CHESTER, CH4 9FH.

•**PINS, Mr. Anthony David, FCA** *1987;* Nyman Libson Paul, Regina House, 124 Finchley Road, LONDON, NW3 5JS.

PINS, Mr. Michael Allan, FCA *1958;* Flat C Dunholme Manor, 55 Manor Road, BOURNEMOUTH, BH1 3EP. (Life Member)

PINSENT, Mr. Oliver Clive, MA ACA *1989;* (Tax Fac), Cheddington, Quarry Close, Limpley Stoke, BATH, BA2 7FN.

PINSKER, Mr. Harry, FCA *1953;* 231 Princess Park Manor, Royal Drive, LONDON, N11 3FS. (Life Member)

PINSON, Mr. Andrew John, FCA *1978;* 5 Rushey Lane Boningale, Albrighton, WOLVERHAMPTON, WV7 3AZ.

PINSON, Mr. Robert Alan, BA FCA *1971;* Beech Grove House, 10 Barnfield Manor, Lodge Lane, Singleton, POULTON-LE-FYLDE, LANCASHIRE FY6 8LJ.

PINSON, Mr. Simon Morley, FCA *1974;* Pelloby Engineering Ltd Unit A, Halesfield 19, TELFORD, SHROPSHIRE, TF7 4QT.

PINTEAU, Mr. Malcolm, FCA *1967;* 403-1717 Wilmot Road, COWICHAN BAY V0R 1N1, BC, CANADA. (Life Member)

PINTO, Mr. Christopher Michael, ACA *2009;* Flat 149 Griffin Court, Black Eagle Drive Northfleet, GRAVESEND, DA11 9AP.

PINTO, Mr. Douglas Bazil Anthony, BA ACA *1982;* PO Box 44291, NAIROBI, 00100, KENYA.

PINTO, Mr. Maxwell Salustiano Crescencio, PhD ACA *1982;* 169 Morrison Avenue, TORONTO M6E 1M6, ON, CANADA.

PINTO, Mrs. Nasreen, BSc ACA *2009;* Flat 149, Griffin Court, Black Eagle Drive, Northfleet, GRAVESEND, KENT DA11 9AP.

PINTO, Mr. Ricky Allan Sydney, ACA *1988;* 2789 Quill Crescent, MISSISSAUGA L5N 2G8, ON, CANADA.

•**PINTON, Mr. Timothy John, FCA** *1975;* (Tax Fac), T.J. Pinton & Company, 15 Hazel Avenue, Cove, FARNBOROUGH, HAMPSHIRE, GU14 0HA.

PIOLI, Mr. Raymond Charles, MSc BSc FCA *1975;* 6 Chiltern Park, Thornbury, BRISTOL, BS35 2HX.

PIOLINI, Mr. Gianni, BA ACA *1993;* 41 Lytton Grove, LONDON, SW15 2HD.

PIPE, Mr. Alan Geoffrey, FCA *1971;* 3 Lower Cladswell Lane, Cookhill, ALCESTER, B49 5JY. (Life Member)

PIPE, Mr. Edward James, MSc BSc ACA *2008;* 101a East Hill, LONDON, SW18 2QB.

PIPE, Mr. Graham David, BA(Hons) ACA *2001;* Sunningdale, Bridekirk, COCKERMOUTH, CUMBRIA, CA13 0PE.

PIPE, Mr. Keeble Wilgress, FCA *1958;* 4 Forest Road, Chandler's Ford, EASTLEIGH, SO53 1LZ. (Life Member)

PIPE, Mr. Stephen David, MSc FCA *1988;* 3 Alwoodley Gates, LEEDS, LS17 8FB.

PIPE, Mrs. Vanessa Jane, FCA *1991;* Mirabelle, Rue Des Blanches Terres, St. Saviour, GUERNSEY, GY7 9LU.
PIPER, Mr. Andrew George, BCom FCA *1955;* 111 Widney Lane, SOLIHULL, B91 3LH. (Life Member)
PIPER, Mr. Andrew Michael, BSc ACA *1987;* 784 Wollaton Road, NOTTINGHAM, NG8 2AP.
PIPER, Mr. Bruce, BA ACA *1981;* 3 Woodroyd Gardens, Ben Rhydding, ILKLEY, LS29 8BU.
PIPER, Mr. Charles, FCA *1948;* 25 Stamford Road, Southbourne, BOURNEMOUTH, BH6 5DS. (Life Member)
PIPER, Mr. David Anthony George, FCA *1970;* 6 Oaken Coppice, ASHTEAD, KT21 1DL.
PIPER, Mr. Geoffrey Charles, FCA *1970;* 3 Coppens Green, WICKFORD, SS12 9PA.
PIPER, Mr. Geoffrey Steuart Fairfax, MA FCA *1968;* (Member of Council 2003 - 2007), 9 Leighton Hall, The Runnell, NESTON, CH64 3TQ.
PIPER, Miss. Hannah, BSc ACA *2011;* Flat 20, Lion Court, 28 Magdalen Street, LONDON, SE1 2EN.
PIPER, Mr. Harry Norman, FCA *1952;* Carrick, 11 Robb Place, CASTLE DOUGLAS, DG7 1LW. (Life Member)
•PIPER, Mr. Ian George Charles, BA FCA *1993;* Whiting & Partners, 41 St. Marys Street, ELY, CAMBRIDGESHIRE, CB7 4HF.
•PIPER, Mr. Jack Leon, FCA *1977;* (Tax Fac), King & King, Roxburghe House, 273-287 Regent Street, LONDON, W1B 2HA.
PIPER, Mr. James Paul, ACA ACCA *2008;* 14 Church Street, ST. ALBANS, HERTFORDSHIRE, AL3 5NQ.
•PIPER, Mr. John, FCA *1966;* SB Centre Ltd, 14 Somer Fields, LYME REGIS, DT7 3EL. See also Small Business Centre
PIPER, Mr. John Charles, BSc ACA *1986;* 8 Lodge Gate, Great Linford, MILTON KEYNES, MK14 5EW.
PIPER, The Revd. John Michael, MSc ACA *1978;* 114 Elgin Street, ASHTON-UNDER-LYNE, LANCASHIRE, OL7 9BQ.
PIPER, Mr. John Richard Sidney, FCA ATII *1975;* Sunflowers, Martineau Drive, DORKING, SURREY, RH4 2PN.
•PIPER, Ms. Julie Ann, BA FCA *1991;* Arram Berlyn Gardner, 30 City Road, LONDON, EC1Y 2AB.
PIPER, Mrs. Kathryn Victoria, BA(Hons) ACA *2001;* 11 Dighton Road, LONDON, SW18 1AN.
PIPER, Mr. Lloyd Charles, FCA *1967;* 23 Aldford Close, Bromborough, WIRRAL, CH63 0PT.
•PIPER, Mr. Malcolm John, FCA *1973;* Malcolm Piper & Company Limited, Business Services Centre, 446-450 Kingstanding Road, BIRMINGHAM, WEST MIDLANDS, B44 9SA.
PIPER, Mr. Mark Richard John, BSc ACA *1994;* Orchard House, Manningford Bruce, PEWSEY, WILTSHIRE, SN9 6JA.
PIPER, Mr. Michael John, BSc ACA *1985;* 1 Monks Wood, PETERSFIELD, HAMPSHIRE, GU32 2JP.
PIPER, Mrs. Penelope Elizabeth Jane, BSocSc ACA *2002;* Lodge Croft, Old Hall Lane, LICHFIELD, STAFFORDSHIRE, WS13 8PA.
PIPER, Mr. Peter John, BSc ACA *2006;* 32 Queens Drive, SURBITON, SURREY, KT5 8PN.
PIPER, Mr. Richard Gary, BSc ACA *1997;* Severn Trent Services Ltd Arley Drive, Birch Coppice Business Park Dordon, TAMWORTH, STAFFORDSHIRE, B78 1SA.
PIPER, Mr. Richard John, FCA *1970;* 31 Fitzmary Avenue, MARGATE, CT9 5EL.
PIPER, Mr. Richard John, MA FCA *1977;* Merryfield, St Georges Road, Bickley, BROMLEY, BR1 2LD.
PIPER, Mr. Terence Victor, FCA *1970;* 21 Basildon Avenue, Clayhall, ILFORD, IG5 0QE.
PIPER, Mr. Timothy Mark Burton, LLB FCA *1991;* PO Box 528, KENSINGTON PARK, SA 5068, AUSTRALIA.
PIPER, Mr. Tony Graham, BA ACA *1991;* Langdale House, 11 Marshalsea Road, LONDON, SE11EN.
PIPER, Mr. William John Courtney, MA ACA *1997;* Careers Wales West Head Office, Heol Nantyreos, Cross Hands, LLANELLI, DYFED, SA14 6RJ.
PIPES, Mr. Roger Albert, FCA *1967;* 91 The Green, Freethorpe, NORWICH, NR13 3AH.
PIPIKAKIS, Mrs. Alisha Gurmit, BA(Hons) ACA *2011;* 42 Hedgerow Walk, ANDOVER, HAMPSHIRE, SP11 6FD.
PIPPARD, Mr. Keith Richard, MA ACA *1978;* C/o Keenan & Associates, 2355 Crenshaw Boulevard, Suite 200, TORRANCE, CA 90501, UNITED STATES.
PIPPI, Miss. Polyxeni, ACA *2010;* 1-5 Adrastou Street, Ano Petralona, 11852 ATHENS, GREECE.
PIR MOHD, Mr. Eddy Rashdan, BA ACA *2008;* No. 9, Jalan 3/36, 42650 BANDAR BARU BANGI, MALAYSIA.
PIRA, Mr. Aminmohamed Roshanali, FCA *1975;* 7 Myers Boulevard, RICHMOND HILL L4C 0C2, ON, CANADA.
PIRACHA, Mr. Mahboob Ilahi, BSc ACA *1982;* Mumtaz Villa, Al-Mumtaz Cinema, Al-Mumtaz Road, Samanabad, LAHORE, PAKISTAN.
PIRAINO, Mr. Gerry Anthony, BA(Hons) ACA *2003;* 2 Kimblewick Lane, SPALDING, LINCOLNSHIRE, PE11 3GY.
PIRBHAI, Mr. Aftab Hussain, FCA *1968;* 1 Wentworth Park, LONDON, N3 1YE.
PIRES, Mr. David Christopher Day, ACA CA(SA) *2009;* 1 ALASSIA, HIGH GROVE UMGENI PARK, DURBAN, 4051, SOUTH AFRICA.
PIRIE, Mr. Edward, BA ACA *2009;* Flat 64 Perronet House, Princess Street, LONDON, SE1 6JS.
PIRIE, Miss. Jacqueline, BSc ACA *1990;* Millbank Cottage, Millbank, Udny, ELLON, ABERDEENSHIRE, AB41 6RY.
PIRIE, Mr. Kane Bruce, BSc ACA *1997;* Travel Republic Ltd, Clarendon House, 147 London Road, KINGSTON UPON THAMES, SURREY, KT2 6NH.
PIRIE, Mr. Philip Richard, BA FCA *1975;* 28 Arundel Terrace, Barnes, LONDON, SW13 8DS.
PIRIE, Mrs. Stella Jane, OBE BA FCA *1974;* The Towers, Entry Hill, BATH, BA2 5LU.
PIRIIE, Miss. Elizabeth Jane, BA ACA *1995;* 1 McKay Road, LONDON, SW20 0HT.
PIRILIDOU, Mrs. Katia, FCA *1980;* (Tax Fac), 5 Filopimenos Street, 3075 LIMASSOL, CYPRUS.
•PIRMOHAMED, Mr. Amir Gulamhussein, FCA *1982;* (Tax Fac), A.G. Pirmohamed & Co, 67 Lincoln Road, PETERBOROUGH, PE1 2SD.
PIROUET, Mr. David Robert, FCA *1977;* D.L.R.S Advisory Services Ltd, Le Ruisselet, Cap Verd, St Lawrence, JERSEY, JE3 1EL.
•PIROUET, Mr. John Edward, BSc ACA *2003;* Begbies Traynor (Channel Islands) Limited, Charles House, Charles Street, St. Helier, JERSEY, JE2 4SF.
•PIROUET, Mr. Malcolm Geffrard, BA ACA *1992;* with RSM Tenon Audit Limited, 66 Chiltern Street, LONDON, W1U 4JT.
PIROUET, Mr. Paul Dennis, BSc ACA CTA *2004;* Rawlinson & Hunter, P.O. Box 81 32 Pier Road, ST HELIER, JE4 8PW.
PIROUET, Mr. Richard John, FCA *1969;* La Colline, Mont Cambrai, St Lawrence, JERSEY, JE3 1JN.
PIRRIE, Mr. Andrew Richard, BA ACA *1990;* 1 McKay Road, LONDON, SW20 0HT.
PIRRIE, Mr. Stuart James, BSc ACA *2001;* 24 Beresford Road, SUTTON, SM2 6ER.
PIRZADA, Mr. Qasim Habib, BCom ACA *1997;* Qatar National Bank, PO Box 1000, DOHA, QATAR.
PISANO, Mrs. Louise Marie Susan, FCA *1987;* Birkett Long, Essex House, 42 Crouch Street, COLCHESTER, ESSEX, CO3 3HH.
•PISAVADI, Mr. Abdultaiyab, BSc FCA *1992;* Simmons Gainsford LLP, 5th Floor, 7-10 Chandos Street, Cavendish Square, LONDON, W1G 9DQ.
PISKORZ, Mr. Ryszard Jozef, BSc FCA *1980;* BNP Paribas Securities Services, 55 Moorgate, LONDON, EC2R 6PA.
PISLENSKI, Mr. Svetlin Emilov, MSc BSc ACA *2009;* 18 Taeping Street, LONDON, E14 9UN.
PISSARIDE, Mrs. Elisavet, BA ACA *2003;* Chloridos 3, Flat 31, Panthea, 4007 LIMASSOL, CYPRUS.
PISSARIDES, Mr. Kleanthis, BSc ACA *2005;* Lefkosias 41, APT 301, 2018 STROVOLOS, CYPRUS.
PISSARIDOU, Ms. Charlotte Louise, BSc FCA *1996;* 11 Kendal Close, REIGATE, RH2 0LR.
•PISSARRO, Mrs. Carolynn Pryse, FCA *1975;* (Tax Fac), Griffin Chapman, Blackburn House, 32a Crouch Street, COLCHESTER, CO3 3HH.
PISSI, Ms. Emilia, MA ACA *2001;* Hellenic Bank, Head Office, Corner Limassol & Athalassa Avenue, 1394 NICOSIA, CYPRUS.
•PISSOURIOS, Mr. Melinos Menelaos, BA FCA CF *1994;* SIS, 38 Karaiskaki Street, KANIKA Alexander Center, Block 1, Office 113 C/D, PC 3032 LIMASSOL CYPRUS.
PISTOL, Mr. Daniel Philip, FCA *1974;* 20 Dickerage Road, KINGSTON UPON THAMES, KT1 3SS.
PISTOL, Mr. Timothy Daniel, BA ACA *2004;* 6541 Deframe Court, ARVADA, CO 80004, UNITED STATES.
•PITAYANUKUL, Mr. Sangyai, MBA BSc FCA *1984;* (Tax Fac), P and Co LLP, Unit 13, 2 Artichoke Hill, LONDON, E1W 2DE. See also Pitayanukul & Co Ltd
PITCHACAREN, Miss. Natasha, ACA *2011;* 98 Ardrossan Gardens, WORCESTER PARK, SURREY, KT4 7AY.
PITCHER, Mr. Allan James, FCA *1971;* Beaconsfield, 53 Rakesmoor Lane, BARROW-IN-FURNESS, LA14 4LQ.
PITCHER, Mr. Anthony Arthur, BSc ACA *1986;* Le Petit Sentier La Rue de la Mare Ballam, St. John, JERSEY, JE3 4EJ.
PITCHER, Mrs. Betty Joyce, FCA *1968;* 33 Camfield Road, DARLINGTON, WA 6070, AUSTRALIA.
PITCHER, Mr. Julian Reginald, BSc FCA *1994;* 1 Prince William Close, Findon Valley, WORTHING, BN14 0AZ.
PITCHER, Mr. Martin Ramsey, BA FCA *1992;* Loft 4, 107 Clifton Street, LONDON, EC2A 4LG.
PITCHER, Mrs. Nicola Jane, FCA *1991;* 14 Bower Mount Road, MAIDSTONE, KENT, ME16 8AU.
PITCHER, Mr. Roy Liam, BSc FCA CTA TEP *1998;* Pentera Trust Co Ltd, Pentera Chambers, PO Box 79, Century Buildings, Patriotic Place, St Helier JERSEY JE4 8PS.
PITCHER, Mr. Scott Bryan, BCom ACA *2005;* Fairways, 8 La Maudelaine Estate, La Route Orange, St. Brelade, JERSEY, JE3 8GT.
PITCHER, Mr. Simon David, BA(Econ) ACA *1998;* 1 Parkfield, Chorleywood, RICKMANSWORTH, HERTFORDSHIRE, WD3 5AY.
PITCHERS, Mr. Matthew, MA ACA *2011;* 4 Morley Road, SOUTHPORT, MERSEYSIDE, PR9 9JS.
PITCHFORD, Mr. Geoffrey, FCA *1964;* 30 Lea Drive, Shepley, HUDDERSFIELD, HD8 8HA.
PITCHFORD, Miss. Jill Alison, BA(Hons) ACA *2000;* The White House, 2 Green Acres Road, DEVONSHIRE DV 08, BERMUDA.
•PITCHFORD, Mr. Kevin Michael, FCA *1970;* (Tax Fac), Kevin M Pitchford & Co, Building 67, Europa Business Park, Bird Hall Lane, Cheadle Heath, STOCKPORT SK3 0XA. See also Tax Support Limited and Kevin M Pitchford
•PITCHFORD, Mr. Steven Russell, ACA FCCA *2011;* 18 Woodthorpe Park Drive, Sandal, WAKEFIELD, WEST YORKSHIRE, WF2 6HZ.
PITERA, Miss. Anna, BA(Hons) ACA *2010;* Ul. Osiedlowa 28, 34-325 LODYGOWICE, POLAND.
PITFIELD, Mr. Barry Kenneth, BSc FCA CFP *1991;* X Ware Ltd, Le Grenier Grand Marche, La Route Des Camps, St. Martin, GUERNSEY, GY4 6AA.
PITHADIA, Mrs. Heena, BSc ACA *2005;* 9 Eaton Way, BOREHAMWOOD, HERTFORDSHIRE, WD6 4QJ.
PITHADIA, Mr. Priten, MEng ACA *2007;* 9 Eaton Way, BOREHAMWOOD, HERTFORDSHIRE, WD6 4QJ.
PITHER, Mrs. Jane Margaret Lacey, MA ACA *1983;* 881 Scott Hall Road, LEEDS, LS17 6HU.
PITHIA, Mr. Kantilal, BA ACA *1992;* 36 Barrow Point Avenue, PINNER, MIDDLESEX, HA5 3HF.
PITICK, Mr. David John, FCA *1963;* Midfields, First Field Lane, BRAUNTON, EX33 1ES. (Life Member)
PITKETHLY, Mr. Graeme David, BSc ACA *1991;* Unilever Plc Unilever House, 100 Victoria Embankment, LONDON, EC4Y 0DY.
PITKIN, Mr. Anthony William, FCA *1956;* COTTESLOE, Lascot Hill, WEDMORE, SOMERSET, BS28 4AE. (Life Member)
PITMAN, Mrs. April Dorothy, BSc ACA *1982;* IASB, 30 Cannon Street, LONDON, EC4M 6XH.
PITMAN, Miss. Carol Margaret, BSc ACA *1991;* 8 Chevening Court, Brasted Close, ORPINGTON, KENT, BR6 9UR.
PITMAN, Mr. Martyn Douglas, BSc ACA *1981;* 25 Provost Street, LONDON, N1 7NG.
PITMAN, Mrs. Victoria Rosemary, BSc ACA *1995;* 6 Lancaster Gardens, KINGSTON UPON THAMES, KT2 5NL.
•PITRAKKOU, Mr. George Nicholas, BA ACA *2004;* (Tax Fac), Flat B, 46 High Road, East Finchley, LONDON, N2 9PJ.
PITSILLIDES, Ms. Angela, ACA *2009;* 2 Coniscliffe Road, Palmers Green, LONDON, N13 5NW.
PITSILLIDES, Mr. Ioannis, BA(Hons) ACA *2003;* Agias Anastasias 11A, Kato Polemidia, 4156 LIMASSOL, CYPRUS.
PITSILLIDES, Mr. Vassilios, MSc BEng ACA *2005;* Elefsinas 16, Latsia, 2231 NICOSIA, CYPRUS.
PITSILLIS, Mr. George, ACA *2010;* Kavalas 2, 6047 LARNACA, CYPRUS.
PITSILLIS, Mr. Marios, BSc ACA *2010;* 2 J. Makriyianni, LARNACA, CYPRUS.
PITSILLOS, Mr. Charalambos Demetriou, ACA *2009;* 6 Patmou Street, PAFOS, CYPRUS.
PITSILLOS, Mr. Marios, ACA *1985;* 17 Meadowsweet Hill, Bingham, NOTTINGHAM, NG13 8TS.
•PITT, Mr. Andrew Michael, MA FCA *1977;* (Tax Fac), AM Pitt MA FCA, 14 Queen Square, BATH, BA1 2HN.
PITT, Mr. Bernard Joseph, FCA *1964;* 32 Church Meadow, Alpington, NORWICH, NR14 7NY.
PITT, Mrs. Caroline Louise, BA ACA *1999;* Birchfield, Shurlock Row, READING, RG10 0PN.
PITT, Mr. Clive Antony, BSocSc FCA *1989;* 1 Sketchley Manor Lane, Burbage, HINCKLEY, LE10 2NQ.
PITT, Mrs. Emma, BA ACA *2000;* 44 Bolton Gardens, TEDDINGTON, MIDDLESEX, TW11 9AY.
PITT, Mr. George Stanhope, FCA *1969;* 43 Ormside Way, REDHILL, RH1 2LG.
PITT, Mrs. Heather, LLB ACA *2010;* 46 Highlands Road, ANDOVER, HAMPSHIRE, SP10 2PZ.
PITT, Mr. Ian Geoffrey, BA(Hons) ACA *2006;* Wallflower Cottage High Street, Northleach, CHELTENHAM, GL54 3ES.
PITT, Mr. James Leslie, BA ACA *2009;* 17 Swanbrook, SWINDON, SN3 5AJ.
•PITT, Mrs. Joanne Mary, FCA *1983;* Frampton Pitt, 19 York Road, NORTHAMPTON, NN1 5QG.
•PITT, Mr. Martyn James, BA FCA *1982;* Kingscott Dix Limited, 60 Kings Walk, GLOUCESTER, GL1 1LA.
PITT, Mr. Michael John, BSc FCA *1979;* 97 St. Peters Avenue, Caversham, READING, RG4 7DP.
PITT, Mr. Nigel James, BSc FCA *1966;* 38 Manor Way, GUILDFORD, GU2 7RP.
PITT, Mr. Richard, BA(Hons) ACA *2011;* 10 Uxbridge Lane Kingsway, Quedgeley, GLOUCESTER, GL2 2EY.
PITT, Mr. Robert John, BSc ACA *2004;* Flat D, 1 Fieldway Crescent, LONDON, N5 1PU.
PITT, Miss. Rosemary Wentworth, MMath ACA *2010;* Apartment 28, New Hampton Lofts, 91 Branston Street, BIRMINGHAM, B18 6BF.
PITT, Mr. Rowland William Lloyd, FCA *1962;* 6 Ewloe Close, KIDDERMINSTER, DY10 1YJ. (Life Member)
PITT, Mr. Rupert Gordon, BSc ACA *1999;* 9 Linden Gardens, TUNBRIDGE WELLS, KENT, TN2 5QU.
PITT, Mr. Shaun Christopher William, BSc FCA *1974;* The Orchard, Red Lane, KENILWORTH, CV8 1PB.
PITT, Mr. Stephen, FCA CTA *1975;* Nicholson Hall Associates Ltd, 138 Westoe Road, SOUTH SHIELDS, TYNE AND WEAR, NE33 3PF.
PITT, Mr. Stewart, BSc ACA *1998;* Air Charter Service Millbank House, 171-185 Ewell Road, SURBITON, KT6 6AP.
PITT, Mr. William Harry, FCA *1961;* 23 Mascalls Park, Paddock Wood, TONBRIDGE, TN12 6LW.
PITT-JONES, Mrs. Keeley Claire, BSc(Hons) ACA *2004;* Whiteoaks, 17 London Road, Stanford Rivers, ONGAR, CM5 9PH.
PITT-JONES, Mr. Patrick Charles, BSc ACA ATII *1996;* Flat 56 Imperial Hall, 104-122 City Road, LONDON, EC1V 2NR.
PITT-LEWIS, Mr. Nicholas Herford, MA ACA *1979;* High Trees, 5 Broom Park, Broom Lane Langton Green, TUNBRIDGE WELLS, TN3 0RF.
PITT-PAYNE, Mr. Michael Georgee, FCA *1962;* 18 Church Way, Stone, AYLESBURY, HP17 8RG. (Life Member)
PITTA, Miss. Popi, BA ACA *2003;* 25 Ayiou Georgiou Street, Flat 202, Pallouriotissa, 1040 NICOSIA, CYPRUS.
PITTA, Miss. Yiolanda, MBA BA ACA *2002;* 4 Platonos Street, Mesa Yitonia, 4001 LIMASSOL, CYPRUS.
PITTAKAS, Mr. Andreas, ACA *2008;* 3 Kyrineias Street, Strovolos, 2008 NICOSIA, CYPRUS.
PITTAKAS, Mr. Stelios, ACA *2008;* 16A Elioudi Street, Ayios Dometios, 2364 NICOSIA, CYPRUS.
•PITTAL, Mr. Lee Elliott, BA FCA CTA *1993;* Nyman Libson Paul, Regina House, 124 Finchley Road, LONDON, NW3 5JS.
•PITTALIS, Mr. John Kyriacos, BSc FCA *1985;* (Tax Fac), K J Pittalis LLP, First Floor, Global House, 303 Ballards Lane, LONDON, N12 8NP.
PITTARD, Mr. Christian Alexander John, BSc ACA *1998;* Aberdeen Asset Management Plc Bow Bells House, 1 Bread Street, LONDON, EC4M 9HH.
PITTARD, Mr. Christopher John, BSc ACA *2000;* 173 Boardwalk Drive, TORONTO M4L 3X9, ON, CANADA.
PITTARD, Mrs. Sara Allicia, BA ACA *2000;* Horizon, Abbotts Hill, Pendomer, YEOVIL, SOMERSET, BA22 9PD.
•PITTAS, Mrs. Andreoulla Sophia, BSc FCA *1985;* PricewaterhouseCoopers Limited, Julia House, 3 Themistocles Dervis Street, CY-1066 NICOSIA, CYPRUS.
PITTAS, Mr. Charalambos, BSc ACA *2002;* 45 Stelios Kyriakides Street, 3080 LIMASSOL, CYPRUS.
PITTAS, Miss. Melanie Jade, ACA *2009;* 11 Gordon Road, BECKENHAM, KENT, BR3 3QE.

PITTAWAY, Mr. Kevin Mark, MSc BSc ACA *2007;* 24 Morden Road, LONDON, SW19 3BJ.
PITTAWAY, Mr. Nigel Clive, BSc FCA *1990;* 135 Windsor Street, PADDINGTON, NSW 2021, AUSTRALIA.
PITTAWAY, Mr. Paul Singleton, BSc FCA *1979;* 2 Harvest Close, Stoke Heath, BROMSGROVE, WORCESTERSHIRE, B60 3QS.
PITTMAN, Miss. Anna, BSc ACA *2003;* 2 Mary Rose Close, Chafford Hundred, GRAYS, ESSEX, RM16 6LY.
•PITTMAN, Mrs. Elizabeth Katherine, BSc ACA *1991;* Elizabeth Pittman Accountancy Limited, 8 Rectory Close, Swinford, LUTTERWORTH, LEICESTERSHIRE, LE17 6BR.
PITTMAN, Mr. Jamie William, BSc(Hons) ACA *2002;* 8 Rectory Close, Swinford, LUTTERWORTH, LEICESTERSHIRE, LE17 6BR.
PITTMAN, Mrs. Joanna Louise, BSc ACA DChA *2003;* with Sayer Vincent, 8 Angel Gate, City Road, LONDON, EC1V 2SJ.
PITTMAN, Mr. Robert Nicholas, FCA *1966;* 10 Oakdene, Burghfield Common, READING, RG7 3EW.
PITTMAN, Mr. William Francis, FCA *1968;* 12 The Ridings, EPSOM, KT18 5JQ.
•PITTOCK, Mr. Frederick, FCA *1955;* (Tax Fac), F. Pittock & Co, Tremlett Villa, London Road, Pitsea, BASILDON, SS13 2DB.
PITTOCK, Mr. John Spencer, FCA *1964;* Rosomna, Claremont Road, KILLINEY, COUNTY DUBLIN, IRELAND.
PITTOM, Mr. Thomas, FCA *1955;* Pine Trees, Little Heath Road, Fontwell, ARUNDEL, WEST SUSSEX, BN18 0SR. (Life Member)
PITTORINO, Mrs. Elizabeth Mary, ACA *1984;* 21 Avenue Princesse Grace, MC 98000 MONTE CARLO, MONACO.
PITTS, Mr. Christopher David, BSc ACA *1992;* 46 Nottingham Drive, ETOBICOKE M9A 2W5, ON, CANADA.
PITTS, Mrs. Julia Louise, BSc ACA *1993;* 2 Burrow Cottages, Broadclyst, EXETER, EX5 3HY.
•①PITTS, Mr. Julian Nigel Richard, BSc FCA *1987;* Begbies Traynor, Glendevon House, Hawthorn Park, Coal Road, LEEDS, LS14 1PQ. See also Begbies Traynor(Central) LLP and Begbies Traynor Limited
PITTS, Mrs. Maria Del Mar, BSc ACA *1994;* Dene House, Mile Path, WOKING, GU22 0JL.
PITTS, Mr. Matthew John, BSc ACA *1996;* Cedars, 1 Wynnstow Park, OXTED, RH8 9DR.
PITTS, Mr. Michael Anthony, BA FCA *1971;* 1 Marina Cottages, Willingdon Lane Jevington, POLEGATE, EAST SUSSEX, BN26 5QH.
•PITTS, Mr. Rodney Gordon, FCA *1981;* Rodney Pitts, 4 Fairways, 1240 Warwick Road, Knowle, SOLIHULL, B93 9LL.
PITZER, Mr. Glenn Robert Bruce, ACA CA(SA) *2010;* 18 Wellesley Crescent, TWICKENHAM, TW2 5RT.
PIWOWAR, Mrs. Jodie Louise, BA ACA *2005;* 170 Denham Way, Maple Cross, RICKMANSWORTH, HERTFORDSHIRE, WD3 9SR.
PIXTON, Mrs. Louise Ann, BSc ACA *1990;* Casa Hacienda II #401, 5-22 Hakushimakuken-cho, Naka-ku, HIROSHIMA, 730-0003 JAPAN.
PIYACHINAWAN, Miss. Phannarai, ACA *1986;* 21/143 Lad Prao Soi 15 Lad Prao Road, BANGKOK 10900, THAILAND.
•PIZER, Mr. Martyn Sydney, FCA *1980;* Simmons Gainsford LLP, 5th Floor, 7-10 Chandos Street, Cavendish Square, LONDON, W1G 9DQ.
PIZEY, Miss. Helen Sarah, BSc ACA *1994;* 9175 117th Street, DELTA V4C 6B5, BC, CANADA.
PIZEY, Mr. James, BA(Hons) ACA *2011;* 14 Meadow Way, WOKINGHAM, BERKSHIRE, RG41 2TH.
PIZZEY, Mr. Andrew James, BSocSc ACA *1996;* 7 Yewberry Way, Chandler's Ford, EASTLEIGH, HAMPSHIRE, SO53 4PE.
PIZZEY, Mrs. Gillian Dawn, BA ACA *1997;* 7 Yewberry Way, Chandler's Ford, EASTLEIGH, HAMPSHIRE, SO53 4PE.
PIZZEY, Mrs. Rachael Elizabeth, BCom ACA *1988;* W T Parker Group, 24-28 Moor Street, BURTON-ON-TRENT, STAFFORDSHIRE, DE14 3SX.
PLACE, Mr. Andrew George, MA FCA *1983;* 11 Branscombe Gardens, Winchmore Hill, LONDON, N21 3BP.
PLACE, Mr. Donald Hill, FCA *1970;* 6 John Henry Court, Pen-y-Maes Road, HOLYWELL, CLWYD, CH8 7BD.
PLACE, Mr. John Arthur, BSc FCA *1976;* 41 Woodward Road, Prestwich, MANCHESTER, M25 9TX.
PLACE, Mr. Richard John, BSc ACA *1990;* 31 Jacksons Road, Fendalton, CHRISTCHURCH, NEW ZEALAND.
•PLAHA, Mr. Satwant Singh, BA FCA *1988;* BDO LLP, 125 Colmore Row, BIRMINGHAM, B3 3SD. See also BDO Stoy Hayward LLP
PLAHAY, Mr. Kulvinder Singh, BSc(Econ) FCA *1993;* The Barn, 11 Mallory Place, Bowerhill, MELKSHAM, WILTSHIRE, SN12 6YB.
PLAISTED, Mr. Roger Peter, FCA *1973;* Basset Wood House, Stoke Row, HENLEY-ON-THAMES, RG9 5RB.
PLAISTOWE, Mr. William Ian David, MA FCA *1968;* (President 1992 - 1993) (Member of Council 1986 - 1999), Heybote, Ellesborough Road, Butlers Cross, AYLESBURY, HP17 0XF.
PLANE, Mr. David Maclachlan, ACA *1989;* 3464 Primera Ave., LOS ANGELES, CA 90068, UNITED STATES.
PLANE, Mr. Donald Edward, BSc ACA *1994;* with Mazars LLP, Regency House, 3 Grosvenor Square, SOUTHAMPTON, SO15 2BE.
PLANE, Mrs. Penelope Avis Jacques, BSc ACA *1987;* Le Petit Ponterrin La Rue Du Ponterrin, St. Saviour, JERSEY, JE2 7HP.
PLANE, Mr. Robin Francis, BSc ACA *1992;* 21 Phoenix Drive, Wateringbury, MAIDSTONE, ME18 5DR.
PLANT, Mr. Allan Geoffrey, FCA *1975;* 17 Well Hill, Minchinhampton, STROUD, GL6 9JE.
PLANT, Mr. Andrew John, BA ACA *1988;* Hillside Manor, Loxley, WARWICK, CV35 9JT.
PLANT, Mr. Christopher Boyd, BA FCA *1982;* 44 Bewdley Street, LONDON, N1 1HD.
PLANT, Mr. Graham George, FCA *1965;* 629 Rocha Brava, 8401-908, LAGOA, ALGARVE, PORTUGAL.
PLANT, Mrs. Hazel Ruth, BA ACA ATII *1998;* with Ernst & Young LLP, 1 Bridgewater Place, Water Lane, LEEDS, LS11 5QR.
PLANT, Miss. Joanne Helen, BSc ACA *1996;* (Tax Fac), 6 Skiathou, 2230 LATSIA, CYPRUS.
PLANT, Mr. John Charles, BCom FCA *1977;* 4361 Spruce Hill Lane, BLOOMFIELD, MI 48301, UNITED STATES.
PLANT, Mr. John Edward, FCA *1967;* 74 Irnham Road, Four Oaks, SUTTON COLDFIELD, B74 2TG.
PLANT, Mr. Jonathan Michael, BA ACA *2005;* 23 Haldon Way, WORKSOP, NOTTINGHAMSHIRE, S81 7RZ.
PLANT, Mrs. Judy Catherine, BA FCA *1982;* (Tax Fac), Saffery Champness, Lion House, 72-75 Red Lion Street, LONDON, WC1R 4GB.
PLANT, Mr. Keith Forrester, FCA *1959;* The Pyghtles, 9 Wappenham Road, Abthorpe, TOWCESTER, NORTHAMPTONSHIRE, NN12 8QU. (Life Member)
PLANT, Mr. Leslie Stephen, BSc ACA *1988;* 7047 Barrington Drive, CANFIELD, OH 44406, UNITED STATES.
PLANT, Mr. Lyndon Ernest Philip, ACA *2004;* Flat 4, Suffolk House, Queens Drive, LONDON, W3 0HN.
PLANT, Mr. Martin Robert, BA ACA *1999;* 22 Celandine, TAMWORTH, B77 1BG.
PLANT, Mr. Matthew Nigel, BA ACA *1994;* 17 Edlingham Close, South Gosforth, NEWCASTLE UPON TYNE, NE3 1RH.
•PLANT, Mr. Michael, FCA *1963;* Michael Plant FCA, 11 High Street, BALDOCK, SG7 6AZ.
PLANT, Mr. Michael Alan, BSc FCA *1973;* Derwen Deg Farm, Llechwedd, CONWY, LL32 8DQ.
PLANT, Mr. Noel, BA(Hons) ACA *2011;* Flat 115, Heron House Rushley Way, READING, RG2 0GJ.
PLANT, Mr. Percy Dallen, BSc FCA *1957;* La Grange, Vilary, 46150 CATUS, FRANCE. (Life Member)
PLANT, Mr. Peter Blurton, FCA *1965;* Hermits Hill, Reading Road, Burghfield Common, READING, RG7 3BH.
•PLANT, Mr. Peter James, BA ACA *1993;* Plant & Co, 17 Lichfield Street, STONE, STAFFORDSHIRE, ST15 8NA. See also Plant Peter J
PLANT, Mr. Peter John Mabane, FCA *1966;* The Walled Garden Well Lane, Repton, DERBY, DE65 6EY.
PLANT, Mr. Roger, BA ACA *1987;* Eastman Kodah Sarl, Route de Pre-Bois 29, CH1215 GENEVA, SWITZERLAND.
PLANT, Mr. Stephen David, ACA *1987;* Flat 81 Century Buildings, 14 St. Marys Parsonage, MANCHESTER, M3 2DE.
PLANT, Mr. Stephen Mark, ACA *1992;* 13 Greatford Road, Baston, PETERBOROUGH, PE6 9NR.
PLANT, Miss. Susan Lorraine, BA ACA *1993;* Fullex Locks Ltd, 18 First Avenue Pensnett Trading Estate, KINGSWINFORD, DY6 7NA.
PLANT, Mr. Terry, BSc(Hons) ACA *2004;* Anthony Collins Solicitors LLP, 134 Edmund Street, BIRMINGHAM, B3 2ES.
PLANT, Mr. William Allan, BA ACA *1989;* Eldon Court, Percy Street, NEWCASTLE UPON TYNE, TYNE AND WEAR, NE1 7YE.
PLANT, Mr. William John, MA FCA *1978;* 84 Dropmore Road, Burnham, SLOUGH, SL1 8AU.
•PLANTON, Mr. James Wesley, ACA *2002;* 4 Sextons Meadows, BURY ST. EDMUNDS, SUFFOLK, IP33 2SB.
•PLASKETT, Mr. John David, BSc FCA *1977;* robinson+co, Oxford Chambers, New Oxford Street, WORKINGTON, CA14 2LR. See also Robinson J.F.W. & Co
PLASKETT, Mrs. Sarah, BA ACA *2005;* 142 Carden Avenue, BRIGHTON, BN1 8NH.
PLASKITT, Mrs. Catherine, BA(Hons) ACA *2001;* Low Farm Howsham Lane, Searby, BARNETBY, SOUTH HUMBERSIDE, DN38 6DE.
•PLASKITT, Mr. Stephen Charles, BSc FCA CF *1994;* Tait Walker Advisory Services LLP, Bulman House, Regent Centre, Gosforth, NEWCASTLE UPON TYNE, NE3 3LS. See also Tait Walker Management Limited
•PLASKOW, Mr. Andrew Jay, FCA *1975;* Nyman Linden, 105 Baker Street, LONDON, W1U 6NY.
PLASOM-SCOTT, Mrs. Jane Mary, BA ACA *1986;* Prospect House, Helton, PENRITH, CUMBRIA, CA10 2QA.
PLASSARD, Mr. Jonathan, FCA *1996;* Great Oaks, Lubbock Road, CHISLEHURST, BR7 5LA.
•PLASTOW, Miss. Margaret Jean, FCA *1993;* Oxlade Limited, The Old Bakehouse, Holton, OXFORD, OX33 1PZ.
PLASTOW, Mr. Norman Peter, FCA *1973;* 2 Appletree Walk, BRAINTREE, CM7 1EE.
PLATAIS, Mr. Robert John, BA ACA *1985;* 243-245, Kennington Lane, LONDON, SE11 5QU.
PLATER, Mr. James Robert, FCA *1953;* 4 Tan-y-Llan, Tregynon, NEWTOWN, SY16 3HA. (Life Member)
•PLATER, Mrs. Karen Annette, BSc ACA *2000;* Avenue Fond Generet 30, Dion-Valmont, CHAUMONT-GISTOUX, BELGIUM.
PLATRITOU, Ms. Maria, BSc ACA *2006;* 13 Mnassiades Street, 1065, P.O.Box 21298, 1505, NICOSIA, CYPRUS.
PLATT, Mr. Adrian John, BSc ACA *1991;* 11 Freshwater Drive, Weston, CREWE, CW2 5GR.
•PLATT, Mr. Adrian Marc, BSc FCA *1989;* Platts, 643 Watford Way, Apex Corner Mill Hill, LONDON, NW7 3JR. See also Steinberg Platt
PLATT, Mr. Alan Joseph, BSc FCA *1975;* AJP Financial Management, Argoed, Pen y Cefn Road, Caerwys, MOLD, CLWYD CH7 5BH.
•PLATT, Mr. Anthony, ACA CA(SA) *2008;* abacus 73 Limited, 52 Lillibrooke Crescent, MAIDENHEAD, BERKSHIRE, SL6 3XG.
PLATT, Mr. Bryan Unsworth, FCA *1954;* 34 Redcar Road, BOLTON, BL1 6LL. (Life Member)
PLATT, Miss. Catherine Mary, MA FCA *1983;* 59 Brize Norton Road, Minster Lovell, WITNEY, OX29 0SG.
PLATT, Mr. Christopher Leonard, BSc ACA *1989;* 4a Grange Close, LEIGHTON BUZZARD, BEDFORDSHIRE, LU7 2PW.
PLATT, Miss. Clare Louise, BA ACA *2004;* 4 Cambridge Road, NOTTINGHAM, NG8 1FP.
•PLATT, Mr. Daniel Lloyd, FCA *1971;* SPW (UK) LLP, Gable House, 239 Regents Park Road, LONDON, N3 3LF.
PLATT, Mr. David John, FCA *1967;* 11 St. Giles Close, WINCHESTER, HAMPSHIRE, SO23 0JJ.
PLATT, Mr. Geoffrey Brian, FCA *1959;* 116 Main Street, Swanland, NORTH FERRIBY, NORTH HUMBERSIDE, HU14 3QR. (Life Member)
PLATT, Mr. Hamish, BSc ACA *1997;* Marks & Spencer Plc, The Point, North Wharf Road, LONDON, W2 1NW.
•PLATT, Mrs. Hazel Ann, LLB ACA *1996;* Baker Tilly Tax & Advisory Services LLP, The Pinnacle, 170 Midsummer Boulevard, MILTON KEYNES, MK9 1BP.
PLATT, Mr. Hugh Alexander, BA ACA *1995;* 4 Rue des Beaux Arts, 75006 PARIS, FRANCE.
PLATT, Mr. James Edward Nicholas, ACA *1980;* 44 Stephenson House, Bath Terrace, LONDON, SE1 6PR.
PLATT, Mr. John Camm, FCA *1961;* Meadows, Martyr Worthy, WINCHESTER, SO21 1DZ.
PLATT, Mr. John Langston, FCA *1970;* Church Farm House, The Street, Rotherwick, HOOK, RG27 9BG.
PLATT, Mr. John Trevor, ACA *1980;* Squirrels Wood, 1 Brow Close, Storrington, PULBOROUGH, RH20 4QE.
PLATT, Mr. Jonathon, BA ACA *1988;* 1 The Aisled Barn, The Green, Hilton, HUNTINGDON, PE28 9NA.
PLATT, Miss. Kathryn Anne, BA ACA *1998;* Silverburn Quarterbridge Road, Douglas, ISLE OF MAN, IM2 3RQ.
PLATT, Ms. Lanita Yvonne, ACA *2008;* 3736 Salloum Road, KELOWNA VT4 1E4, BC, CANADA.
PLATT, Mrs. Louise Amy, BSc ACA *1992;* 7 Hambleton Close, Burley Grange, OAKHAM, LE15 6FY.
PLATT, Mr. Malcolm Harold, BA FCA *1984;* 2004 MONTECITO TRL, SOUTHLAKE, TX 76092, UNITED STATES.
•PLATT, Mr. Mark Philip, FCA *1983;* Moore Stephens (North West) LLP, 110-114 Duke Street, LIVERPOOL, L1 5AG.
PLATT, Mr. Michael, BA FCA *1994;* Simarc Property Management Ltd Unit 4, Imperial Place Maxwell Road, BOREHAMWOOD, HERTFORDSHIRE, WD6 1JN.
PLATT, Mr. Michael John, BA FCA *1975;* 20 Thornsett Road, SHEFFIELD, S7 1NB.
•PLATT, Mr. Robin Douglas, FCA *1966;* Wits End, 4 Canal Cottages, Stanton St. Bernard, MARLBOROUGH, WILTSHIRE, SN8 4LS.
•PLATT, Mr. Roger Alan, BA FCA *1991;* Crowfoot and Company Limited, Lonsdale House, High Street, LUTTERWORTH, LEICESTERSHIRE, LE17 4AD.
PLATT, Mr. Roland Francis, FCA *1976;* Abbey Quilting Ltd, Selinas Lane, DAGENHAM, ESSEX, RM8 1ES.
•PLATT, Mr. Ronald Barrie, FCA *1976;* R.B. Platt & Co, Alpine House, 28 Church Road, Rainford, ST. HELENS, MERSEYSIDE WA11 8HE.
PLATT, Miss. Samantha Jane, BSc ACA *1992;* The Malt House, Bartington Hall Farm, Warrington Road, NORTHWICH, CW8 4QU.
PLATT, Mrs. Sarah Louise, BSc(Hons) ACA *2000;* 7 Saxon Way, Bradley Stoke, BRISTOL, BS32 9AR.
PLATT, Mr. Simon David John, BA FCA CPA *1984;* 60 State Street, 35th Floor, BOSTON, MA 02109, UNITED STATES.
•PLATT, Ms. Victoria Catherine, MA FCA CTA *1983;* (Tax Fac), Vicky Platt, 8 Moreton Avenue, HARPENDEN, HERTFORDSHIRE, AL5 2ET.
PLATT, Mr. William, ACA *2009;* 2 Tillers Close, STAINES, TW18 3AF.
PLATTEN, Mr. Michael John, ACA *2007;* General Healthcare Group, 4 Thameside Centre Kew Bridge Road, BRENTFORD, MIDDLESEX, TW8 0HF.
PLATTEN, Mr. Richard George, FCA *1957;* 46 Lower Street, Horning, NORWICH, NR12 8AA. (Life Member)
PLATTS, Mr. Alex, BA ACA *2010;* Homestead Farm, St. Peters Road, Arnesby, LEICESTER, LE8 5WJ.
•PLATTS, Mr. Graham John, BSc FCA *1975;* 17 Heath Road, St Leonards, RINGWOOD, BH24 2PZ.
PLATTS, Miss. Helen Jane, MA ACA *1988;* Wood Lawn, 36 Church Hill, Arnside, CARNFORTH, LA5 0DN.
PLATTS, Mr. John Stephen, MA ACA *1994;* 24 St. Mary's Road, LONDON, SW19 7BW.
PLATTS, Miss. Julie Christine, BSc ACA *1997;* 20 Shadwell Walk, Moortown, LEEDS, LS17 6EG.
PLATTS, Dr. Kathryn Elizabeth, BSc(Hons) ACA *2002;* Unit 2 Science Park Room U0204b, Sheffield Hallam University Registry, City Campus Howard Street, SHEFFIELD, S1 1WB.
PLATTS, Mr. Keith Gordon, FCA *1961;* 2 Carneton Close, Crantock, NEWQUAY, CORNWALL, TR8 5RY. (Life Member)
PLATTS, Mr. Leslie Michael, BA FCA *1979;* Long House Farm, Kermincham, CONGLETON, CW12 2LP.
PLATTS, Mr. Matthew Richard, BA ACA *2000;* 1/54 Church Street, BALMAIN, NSW 2041, AUSTRALIA.
•PLATTS, Mr. Nigel Landsbrough, MA FCA *1970;* 2 Briton Crescent, Sanderstead, SOUTH CROYDON, Surrey, CR2 0JE.
PLATTS, Mr. Phillip, BSc FCA *1975;* 35 Whitecroft, Nailsworth, STROUD, GL6 0NS.
PLATTS, Mr. Robert Charles, LLB ACA *2002;* Mill House St. Ives Road, Hemingford Grey, HUNTINGDON, CAMBRIDGESHIRE, PE28 9DX.
PLATTS-MARTIN, Miss. Susan Jane, LLB ACA *1987;* Oakhill House, Fidelity Investment Services Ltd, 130 Tonbridge Road Hildenborough, TONBRIDGE, TN11 9DZ.
•PLAVSIC, Mr. Alexander, BA ACA *1989;* KPMG LLP, 15 Canada Square, LONDON, E14 5GL. See also KPMG Europe LLP
PLAW, Mr. Anthony Charles, BSc ACA *1991;* (Tax Fac), 10 Lodge Road Writtle, CHELMSFORD, CM1 3HB.
PLAXTON, Mr. John Kirby, BSc ACA *1979;* 28 Norland Square, LONDON, W11 4PU.
PLAYER, Miss. Esmie Jayne, ACA *2010;* 10 Vera Road, BRISTOL, BS16 3EL.
PLAYER, Mr. John Colin, MSc ACA *1989;* Bokvagen 13B, 19141 SOLLENTUNA, SWEDEN.

PLAYFAIR, Mr. Roger James, BA ACA *1986;* The Wing, Sandford Lane, Woodley, READING, RG5 4SY.
•**PLAYFER, Mr. Guy Johnathan, BA ACA** *2003;* with Malthouse & Company Ltd, America House, Rumford Court, Rumford Place, LIVERPOOL, L3 9DD.
•**PLAYFOOT, Mr. Darrell James, FCA CTA** *1968;* with Begbies Playfoot, Old Printers House, Stone Street, CRANBROOK, KENT, TN17 3HF.
•**PLAYFOOT, Mr. Neville James, ACA CTA** *1994;* with Begbies Playfoot, Old Printers House, Stone Street, CRANBROOK, KENT, TN17 3HF.
PLAYFORD, Mr. Andrew Harley, ACA *1996;* 27 Hiddingh Ave, Newlands, CAPE TOWN, 7700, SOUTH AFRICA.
PLAYLE, Mr. David John, FCA *1976;* Immediate Transport Co Ltd, PO Box 4116, HORNCHURCH, RM12 4EL.
PLAYLE, Mrs. Margaret Sybil, BSc FCA *1992;* Bridgwater College, Bath Road, BRIDGWATER, SOMERSET, TA6 4PZ.
•**PLAYTER, Mrs. Susan, FCA** *1980;* Playter & Co, 18 Stinchar Drive, Badgers Copse, Chandlers Ford, EASTLEIGH, SO53 4QH.
PLEACE, Mr. Ian David, MSc FCA *1999;* 143 Sandringham Road, WORCESTER PARK, KT4 8UH.
PLEASANT, Ms. Joanne Margaret, MA ACA *2002;* 4 Ashmere Grove, LONDON, SW2 5UJ.
PLEASS, Mr. Christopher Anthony, BSc ACA *1994;* 71 Ashurst Road, North Finchley, LONDON, N12 9AU.
PLEASS, Mr. James Patrick John, BA FCA *1989;* Cotter House, Devonshaw, Powmill By Dollar, DOLLAR, CLACKMANNANSHIRE, FK14 7NH.
PLECH, Mr. Leszek Henry, BA ACA *1986;* Calle marina 44, 1st Floor B, 08005 BARCELONA, SPAIN.
PLEDGE, Mr. Brian Henry, FCA *1965;* Hawkwell Farmhouse, Maidstone Road, Pembury, TUNBRIDGE WELLS, TN2 4AG. (Life Member)
PLEDGE, Miss. Julie, BSc ACA *2000;* 6th Floor, Informa Global Markets (Europes) Ltd Phoenix House, 18 King William Street, LONDON, EC4N 7BP.
PLEDGE, Mr. Michael, FCA *1969;* 8 Mardleywood, WELWYN, AL6 0UX. (Life Member)
PLEDGER, Mr. Nicholas Frederick George, FCA *1973;* Willow Marsh, Riverside Road, Hoveton, NORWICH, NR12 8UD.
•**PLEDGER, Mr. Nigel George, FCA** *1964;* Witchert Associates Limited, 133 Sheerstock, Haddenham, AYLESBURY, BUCKINGHAMSHIRE, HP17 8EY.
PLENDER, Mr. William John Turner, BA FCA *1970;* 150 Camberwell Grove, LONDON, SE5 8RH.
PLENTY, Mr. Lloyd Samuel, BSc ACA *1986;* BNP Paribas, 787 Seventh Avenue, NEW YORK, NY 10019, UNITED STATES.
PLETNEVA, Ms. Galina, ACA *2011;* Bolshoi Karetny per. h. 18/1 app. 3, MOSCOW, RUSSIAN FEDERATION.
PLEVEY, Mrs. Anne Michelle, BSc(Hons) ACA *2000;* Rose Farm House, Church Fenton Lane, Ulleskelf, TADCASTER, LS24 9DW.
PLEWS, Mr. Jonathan Trevor Osborne, FCA *1971;* 236 Tullibardine Road, SHEFFIELD, S11 7GQ.
•**PLEWS, Mr. Robert, BEng ACA** *2003;* with BDO LLP, 55 Baker Street, LONDON, W1U 7EU.
•**PLEWS, Mr. Roderick Howard Maxwell, FCA** *1973;* PKF (UK) LLP, 2nd Floor, Fountain Precinct, Balm Green, SHEFFIELD, S1 2JA.
PLEWS, Mr. Timothy Edwin, FCA *1961;* Hall Green House, Iscoyd, WHITCHURCH, SHROPSHIRE, SY13 3AS.
PLEYDELL-BOUVERIE, Mr. Rupert William, FCA *1975;* Waverley House, Monkwood, ALRESFORD, SO24 0HB.
PLEYDELL-BOUVERIE, Mr. Simon, BA FCA *1955;* Castle House, Deddington, BANBURY, OX15 0TT. (Life Member)
PLIENMOLEE, Miss. Warisa, BSc ACA *2009;* 11 College Glen, MAIDENHEAD, SL6 6BL.
•**PLIMMER, Mr. Colin Marshall, ACA** *1980;* Tai-an, St Andrews Road, DINAS POWYS, CF64 4HB.
•**PLINSTON, Mr. John Anthony, FCA** *1971;* (Tax Fac), Daeche Dubois & Plinston, Mansfield House, 139 Shirley Road, CROYDON, CR0 7LR. See also John Plinston Limited, John Buckley Limited and Plinston Pallace
PLINT, Miss. Sheena Anne, BSc ACA *1997;* H M Revenue & Customs: Taxpayer Service, Longbrook House, New North Road, EXETER, EX4 4UD.
PLISKIN, Mrs. Emma Frances, BSc ACA *1999;* 169 Dugdale Hill Lane, POTTERS BAR, HERTFORDSHIRE, EN6 2DF.
PLISKIN, Mr. Gary Robert, MA FCA *1996;* 169 Dugdale Hill Lane, POTTERS BAR, HERTFORDSHIRE, EN6 2DF.
PLOW, Mr. Robert Michael, BA ACA *1998;* 105-153 Miller Street, NORTH SYDNEY, NSW 2060, AUSTRALIA.
PLOWDEN, The Hon. Francis John, BA FCA *1969;* 4 Highbury Road, LONDON, SW19 7PR.
PLOWMAN, Mr. Alan, BSc ACA *1980;* 65 Golden Square, TENTERDEN, TN30 6RN.
PLOWMAN, Mrs. Annsley Petula, BSc FCA *1993;* 28 Cronk Y Berry Drive, Douglas, ISLE OF MAN, IM2 6HL.
PLOWMAN, Mr. Barry, FCA *1990;* 67 Bridport Way, BRAINTREE, CM7 9FP.
PLOWMAN, Mr. David, BSc ACA *1990;* 23 Percheron Close, Impington, CAMBRIDGE, CB24 9YX.
PLOWMAN, Mrs. Diane Margaret, BSc ACA *1989;* 23 Percheron Close, Impington, CAMBRIDGE, CB24 9YX.
•**PLOWMAN, Mr. Stephen John, FCA** *1973;* Stephen Plowman FCA, 2 Sunflowers Close, Egerton Road, Pluckley, ASHFORD, KENT TN27 0PD.
PLOWRIGHT, Mr. Mark Jonathan, BSc ACA *1994;* 114 Bradford Road, Atworth, MELKSHAM, SN12 8HY.
•**PLOWS, Mr. John George, FCA** *1979;* (Tax Fac), John Plows, 30 Carlton Road, Caversham Heights, READING, RG4 7NT.
PLOWS, Mr. Richard Michael, BA ACA *1990;* ConocoPhillips Ltd, 2 Kingmaker Court, Warwick Technology Park, WARWICK, CV34 6DB.
•**PLUCK, Mrs. Deborah Janet, BA FCA** *1982;* Wenn Townsend, 30 St Giles', OXFORD, OX1 3LE. See also Wenn Townsend Accountants Limited
PLUCK, Mr. Mark, MA ACA *1996;* 42 St. Leonards Gardens, HOVE, EAST SUSSEX, BN3 4QB.
PLUCK, Mr. Martin James, BSc ACA *1992;* 18 Seymour Road, KINGSTON UPON THAMES, SURREY, KT1 4HW.
PLUCKNETT, Mr. Carl Derek, BSc ACA *1992;* 17 Lime Kiln Road, Tackley, KIDLINGTON, OXFORDSHIRE, OX5 3BW.
PLUEER, Mrs. Nadine Kaiulani, BA ACA *1995;* Weinbergstrasse 3, 8273 TRIBOLTINGEN, SWITZERLAND.
•**PLUMB, Mr. Alan Gordon, FCA** *1981;* A G Plumb, 10 South Road, SAFFRON WALDEN, CB11 3DH.
PLUMB, Alan Michael, Esq OBE BA FCA *1972;* Abicomms, 703 Sewha Building, 79-4 Garak-dong, Songpa-Gu, SEOUL, 138-160 KOREA REPUBLIC OF.
PLUMB, Ms. Anne-Marie, BSc ACA *1996;* with PricewaterhouseCoopers LLP, 101 Barbirolli Square, Lower Mosley Street, MANCHESTER, M2 3PW.
•**PLUMB, Mr. Barry Keith, FCA** *1970;* Arthur Daniels & Company, 227a West Street, FAREHAM, PO16 0HZ.
PLUMB, Mr. Christopher John, BSc FCA *1976;* 36 Selborne Close, PETERSFIELD, GU32 2JB.
•**PLUMB, Mr. David John, FCA** *1966;* D & S Plumb Accountants Limited, 19A/B Blackwell Business Park, Blackwell, SHIPSTON-ON-STOUR, WARWICKSHIRE, CV36 4PE.
PLUMB, Miss. Eleanor Marie, BA FCA *1991;* 48 Highfield Avenue, ALDERSHOT, GU11 3DA.
•**PLUMB, Mr. Gary Michael, BSc FCA ATII** *1985;* Taylor Dawson Plumb Limited, 2 King Street, NOTTINGHAM, NG1 2AS.
PLUMB, Miss. Gillian Elizabeth, BSc ACA *1995;* 78 Albany Road, WINDSOR, SL4 2QB.
PLUMB, Mr. Ian Colin, ACA *2008;* 32 Little Green, Elmswell, BURY ST. EDMUNDS, SUFFOLK, IP30 9FB.
PLUMB, Mr. Ian Philip, BSc ACA *2004;* Endless LLP, 4th Floor, The Chambers, 13 Police Street, MANCHESTER, M2 7LQ.
PLUMB, Mr. John Edward, FCA CTA *1961;* 'Tudor Cottage', 7 West Avenue, NEWCASTLE, STAFFORDSHIRE, ST5 0NB. (Life Member)
PLUMB, Mr. John Richard, BCom FCA *1983;* 39 Chiltern Road, Willoughby, SYDNEY, NSW 2068, AUSTRALIA.
PLUMB, Mr. Laurence Kenneth, ACA *2010;* Flat 11, Charlbert Court, Charlbert Street, LONDON, NW8 7BX.
PLUMB, Mrs. Louisa Jane, BA ACA *2005;* 3 Philip Drive, SALE, CHESHIRE, M33 3QY.
PLUMB, Miss. Louise, BA(Hons) ACA *2005;* (Tax Fac), 24 Manor Court, Swindon Village, CHELTENHAM, GL51 9SD.
•**PLUMB, Mr. Nicholas John, BA ACA** *1994;* KPMG LLP, Quayside House, 110 Quayside, NEWCASTLE UPON TYNE, NE1 3DX. See also KPMG Europe LLP
•**PLUMB, Mrs. Susan Elizabeth, BSc ACA** *1992;* HW, Old Station House, Station Approach, Newport Street, SWINDON, WILTSHIRE SN1 3DU. See also Haines Watts
PLUMBE, Mr. Michael, FCA *1954;* 6 Swan Terrace, HASTINGS, TN34 3HT. (Life Member)
PLUMBLY, Mr. Andrew George, BSc FCA *1990;* with PricewaterhouseCoopers LLP, 31 Great George Street, BRISTOL, BS1 5QD.
PLUMBLY, Mr. Andrew Mark, BA ACA *1992;* 97 Copt Heath Drive, Knowle, SOLIHULL, WEST MIDLANDS, B93 9PQ.
PLUMBLY, Mr. Andrew Philip, BA ACA *1986;* Ashridge Business School, Ashridge, BERKHAMSTED, HERTFORDSHIRE, HP4 1NS.
PLUMBRIDGE, Mr. Christopher Francis, BA ACA *1979;* 19 The Murreys, ASHTEAD, KT21 2LU.
PLUMBRIDGE, Mrs. Jacqueline Marie, BSc ACA *1978;* 19 The Murreys, ASHTEAD, KT21 2LU.
•**PLUME, Miss. Elizabeth Anne, ACA FCCA CTA** *2010;* Davisons Ltd, Lime Court, Pathfields Business Park, SOUTH MOLTON, DEVON, EX36 3LH.
PLUMER, Mr. Christian Charles, MEng FCA *1993;* Provident Insurance Plc, Blackwall, HALIFAX, HX1 2PZ.
PLUMLEY, Mr. Xavier Alexander, BA ACA *1988;* Ecovert F M Ltd Elizabeth House, 39 York Road, LONDON, SE1 7NQ.
PLUMLEY, Mrs. Zdenka, ACA *1992;* 16 King Edward's Gardens, LONDON, W3 9RG.
PLUMMER, Mr. Alan David, FCA *1970;* Postbox 480, Lone Hill, SANDTON, 2060, SOUTH AFRICA.
PLUMMER, Mr. Andrew John Bowen, BA ACA *1978;* Headway Adolescent Resources Limited, PO Box 52, CHEPSTOW, GWENT, NP16 5YE.
PLUMMER, Mr. Arthur William, FCA *1952;* 126 Grand Drive, HERNE BAY, CT6 8HT. (Life Member)
PLUMMER, Mr. Christopher Alan, FCA *1967;* 12405 Anjou Drive, Coldstream, VERNON V1B 1N5, BC, CANADA. (Life Member)
PLUMMER, Mr. Christopher Olaf, ACA *1989;* Romei Plummer, 3202C - 32nd Avenue, VERNON V1T 2M5, BC, CANADA.
•**PLUMMER, Mr. Clive Howard, FCA** *1977;* (Tax Fac), Mitchell Charlesworth, 5 Temple Square, Temple Street, LIVERPOOL, L2 5RH.
PLUMMER, Mr. David, FCA *1970;* Laurel Cottage, 12 North Road, SOUTH MOLTON, DEVON, EX36 3AZ. (Life Member)
•**PLUMMER, Mr. David, FCA** *1971;* Laburnum Consultants Ltd, 20 Laburnum Close, Chapeltown, SHEFFIELD, S35 1QU.
PLUMMER, Mr. David John, FCA *1965;* Whitehall Grange, Wiggington Road, YORK, YO32 2RJ.
PLUMMER, Mr. David Simon, BSc FCA *1996;* 25 Glebe View, Barlborough, CHESTERFIELD, S43 4WF.
•**PLUMMER, Mrs. Elizabeth Anne, BA FCA** *1978;* P O Box 1188 Montagu Pavilion 8 - 10 Queensway, GIBRALTAR, GIBRALTAR.
PLUMMER, Mrs. Emma Caroline, BA ACA *2000;* 22 St James Approach, ILUKA, WA 6028, AUSTRALIA.
PLUMMER, Mr. Jeremy James, MA ACA *1986;* 21 Bryanston Street, LONDON, W1H7PR.
PLUMMER, Mr. John George, FCA *1955;* 117 Langley Avenue, WORCESTER PARK, SURREY, KT4 8PD. (Life Member)
PLUMMER, Miss. Judith Kate, BA FCA *1987;* Walpole Farm, STANSTED, CM24 8TA.
PLUMMER, Mrs. Katharine Sara, FCA CTA TEP *1997;* with Davies Mayers Barnett LLP, Pillar House, 113-115 Bath Road, CHELTENHAM, GLOUCESTERSHIRE, GL53 7LS.
PLUMMER, Mr. Kevin John, MA ACA *1989;* Franz-Joseph-Strauss 24, 82041 OBERHACHING, GERMANY.
PLUMMER, Mr. Malcolm Winston, FCA *1972;* The Mews, Sandhills House, Southwood, Monkton, PRESTWICK, AYRSHIRE KA9 1UP. (Life Member)
PLUMMER, Mr. Michael William, BSc FCA *1976;* 19 Hurst Road, Milford on Sea, LYMINGTON, HAMPSHIRE, SO41 0PY.
•**PLUMMER, Mr. Oliver John, FCA** *1973;* (Tax Fac), Oliver Plummer & Co, 9 Seagrave Road, LONDON, SW6 1RP.
PLUMMER, Mr. Robert John, BSc ACA *1992;* 53 Victoria Road, BROMSGROVE, WORCESTERSHIRE, B61 0DW.
PLUMMER, Mr. Ronald Anthony, FCA *1961;* (Tax Fac), 2 Rue Honore Labande, MC98000 MONTE CARLO, MONACO. (Life Member)
PLUMPTON, Mr. Allan Lionel, FCA *1954;* 32 Amberley Drive, Goring-by-Sea, WORTHING, WEST SUSSEX, BN12 4QG. (Life Member)
PLUMPTON, Mr. Craig Salmo Kingsmill, BSc ACA *2003;* 11 Chatsworth Close, FAREHAM, PO15 5LS.
PLUMPTON, Mr. Gary, BSc ACA *1994;* Geo, Harmsworth House, 13-15 Bouverie Street, LONDON, EC4Y 8DP.
PLUMPTON, Mrs. Leanne Irene, BA ACA *2005;* Moore Stephens, 3 Saxon Way West, CORBY, NORTHAMPTONSHIRE, NN18 9EZ.
•**PLUMRIDGE, Mr. Brian Henry, FCA** *1961;* Radstock, Timber Yard, Churchfields, Stonesfield, WITNEY, OXFORDSHIRE OX29 8QZ.
PLUMRIDGE, Dr. Grant Spencer, MBBS ACA *1993;* Flat B, 13 Church Lane, LONDON, N8 7BU.
PLUMRIDGE, Mr. Ronald Charles, BA FCA *1985;* Higginsfield, Cholmondeley, MALPAS, SY14 8HE.
PLUMRIDGE, Mr. Stephen Robert, BA FCA *1984; (CA Scotland* 9 Coppergate Close, BROMLEY, KENT, BR1 3JG.
PLUMRIDGE, Mr. Troy, CA ACA *2009;* Flat 102 Lockwood House, Kennington Oval, LONDON, SE11 5TD.
PLUMTREE, Mrs. Jennifer Laura, ACA *2008;* 51 Manor Garth, Skidby, COTTINGHAM, NORTH HUMBERSIDE, HU16 5UF.
PLUMTREE, Mrs. Jenny Rebecca, BSc ACA *1996;* (Tax Fac), c/o Matthew Plumtree, Goltens, PO Box 2811, DUBAI, UNITED ARAB EMIRATES.
PLUMTREE, Mr. Jonathan, BSc FCA *1992;* The Sheiling, Bracknell Lane, Hartley Wintney, HOOK, RG27 8QP.
PLUMTREE, Mrs. Nicola, BA ACA *1993;* The Sheiling, Bracknell Lane, Hartley Wintney, HOOK, RG27 8QP.
PLUNKETT, Miss. Ciara Ann, BSc FCA *1995;* Lloyds TSB Bank Plc, 25 Gresham Street, LONDON, EC2V 7HN.
•**PLUNKETT, Mr. Ian James, FCA** *1974;* Bird Luckin limited, Aquila House, Waterloo Lane, CHELMSFORD, CM1 1BN.
•**PLUNKETT, Mr. Ian Robert, BA FCA** *1995;* BDO Corporate Finance (Middle East) LLP, DIFC, Gate Village 10, Level 03, Office 33, PO Box 125115 DUBAI UNITED ARAB EMIRATES.
PLUNKETT, Mrs. Kathryn Sarah, BA ACA *1999;* The Haven, Barden Road, Speldhurst, TUNBRIDGE WELLS, KENT, TN3 0QH.
PLUTHERO, Mr. John, ACA *1989;* Liberty House, 76 Hammersmith Road, LONDON, W14 8UD.
•**PNEH, Miss. Swee Mooi, ACA** *1982;* Musical Fidelity Ltd, 24-26 Fulton Road, WEMBLEY, MIDDLESEX, HA9 0TF. See also Robson & Co
PNG, Miss. Cheng Hwa, BSc ACA *2004;* Flat 4, 27 Cleveland Square, LONDON, W2 6DD.
PO, Mr. Chun Wong Danny, ACA *2007;* PricewaterhouseCoopers, 21/F Edinburgh Tower, 15 Queen's Road Central, CENTRAL, HONG KONG ISLAND, HONG KONG SAR.
PO, Mr. Kam Man William, ACA *2008;* Room 2302, CRE Building, 303 Hennessy Road, WAN CHAI, HONG KONG SAR.
POAD, Miss. Rebecca Ellen, MA(Hons) ACA *2010;* 30 Edwin Avenue, Guiseley, LEEDS, LS20 8QJ.
POCHANIS, Mr. Louis Michael, BSc ACA *1992;* Bank of Cyprus Group, Eurolife House, 4 Evrou Street, PO Box 21472, CY1599 STROVOLOS, CYPRUS.
POCHIN, Mr. Paul, ACA *2007;* PricewaterhouseCoopers LLP, 300 Madison Avenue, NEW YORK, NY 10017, UNITED STATES.
POCHKHANAWALA, Mr. Farhad Noshir, FCA *1976;* 111 Longwater Chase, UNIONVILLE L3R 4A9, ON, CANADA.
POCHKHANAWALA, Mr. Sorab Noshir, FCA *1971;* S N Pochkhanawala & Co, 86 Braeside Square, UNIONVILLE L3R 0A5, ON, CANADA.
POCHUN, Mr. Dinesh, MSc BEng ACA *2005;* 4 Grannum Road, VACOAS, MAURITIUS.
POCHUN PATEL, Mrs. Preeti Chandana, MEng ACA *2000;* 5 Bray Crescent, LONDON, SE16 6AN.
POCKETT, Mr. Ian Thomson, BA ACA *1996;* 2 Derwent Drive, Freckleton, PRESTON, PR4 1RT.
•**POCKNELL, Mr. Colin Michael, FCA** *1981;* (Tax Fac), Pocknells LLP, 46 Hullbridge Road, South Woodham Ferrers, CHELMSFORD, ESSEX, CM3 5NG. See also Segrave & Pocknell
POCKNEY, Mr. Penrhyn Charles Benjamin, FCA *1963;* Foxhill, Inkpen, HUNGERFORD, BERKSHIRE, RG17 9DE. (Life Member)
POCKSON, Mr. Jonathan Richard Hayward Hastings, MA MSc FCA *1973;* White Robin, 30 Clare Hill, ESHER, SURREY, KT10 9NB.
POCOCK, Mr. Andrew Edward, BA ACA *2006;* Flat 6, 82 Maida Vale, LONDON, W91PR.
POCOCK, Mr. Henry Charles, BSc ACA *2001;* Ernst & Young, 1 Colmore Square, BIRMINGHAM, B4 6HQ.
POCOCK, Mr. Iain Vyvyan, MA ACA *1992;* West Hill Elm Lane Copdock, IPSWICH, IP8 3ET.

POCOCK, Mr. John, FCA *1972;* 24 Boscobel Road, Cheswick Green, Shirley, SOLIHULL, B90 4JY.
POCOCK, Mr. Julian Neville, ACA *2008;* 1 The Farm, Littleton Panell, DEVIZES, SN10 4AX.
POCOCK, Miss. Kathryn Lynda, ACA *2001;* Critchleys Greyfriars Court, Paradise Square, OXFORD, OX1 1BE.
•POCOCK, Mr. Martin, BSc ACA *1983;* Pococks, 3 Thamesgate Close, Ham, RICHMOND, TW10 7YS.
POCOCK, Mrs. Michelle Odette, BA FCA *1999;* (Tax Fac), 24 South Hayes Copse, Landkey, BARNSTAPLE, EX32 0UZ.
POCOCK, Mr. Peter Bernard, FCA *1961;* 104 Hill Crest Drive, Molescroft, BEVERLEY, HU17 7JL.
POCOCK, Miss. Sarah Catherine, ACA *2009;* Top Floor, 48 Apsley Road, BRISTOL, BS8 2ST.
POCOCK, Mr. Simon James, BSc ACA *2002;* 35 Cody Close, Ash Vale, ALDERSHOT, HAMPSHIRE, GU12 5SJ.
PODD, Mr. Andrew Julian, BSc ACA *1991;* Spanish Oak House, 61 Albemarle Link, Springfield, CHELMSFORD, ESSEX, CM1 6AH.
PODD, Mrs. Elizabeth Frances Clare, BSc ACA *1992;* Spanish Oak House, 61 Albemarle Link, Beaulieu Park, CHELMSFORD, ESSEX, CM1 6AH.
PODD, Miss. Rachael Mary, LLB ACA *2004;* Travelex UK Ltd, 65 Kingsway, LONDON, WC2B 6TD.
PODD, Mr. Richard Geoffrey, MSci ACA *2005;* with PricewaterhouseCoopers LLP, 89 Sandyford Road, NEWCASTLE UPON TYNE, NE1 8HW.
PODESTA, Mr. Albert Louis, BSc FCA *1977;* 39 Kingsdale Avenue, Menston, ILKLEY, LS29 6QL.
PODESTA, Miss. Joanne, BSc(Hons) ACA *2002;* with Fairhurst, Douglas Bank House, Wigan Lane, WIGAN, WN1 2TB.
PODGORNEY, Mr. Stephen Elliot, BSc ACA *1985;* 3 Grand Drive, LEIGH-ON-SEA, ESSEX, SS9 1BG.
PODINARA, Miss. Alexia, BSc ACA *2006;* 2 Eleonon Street, 3112 LIMASSOL, CYPRUS.
PODLATI, Miss. Cornelia, BA ACA *2004;* Nikis 2, Aglantzia, 2102 NICOSIA, CYPRUS.
PODMORE, Mr. Daniel Mark, MSc ACA *2006;* 172 Crossbrook Street, Cheshunt, WALTHAM CROSS, HERTFORDSHIRE, EN8 8JY.
•PODMORE, Mr. Edward, FCA *1975;* (Tax Fac), Phil Dodgson & Partners Limited, 49 Chapeltown, PUDSEY, WEST YORKSHIRE, LS28 7RZ.
PODMORE, Mr. Ian Victor Stewart, MA(Hons) ACA CF *2000;* 10 Whornes Orchard, Upton St. Leonards, GLOUCESTER, GL4 8EE.
•PODMORE, Ms. Julia Barbara, BSc FCA *1990;* GCP Accountancy Services Limited, 54 Nelson Road, Crouch End, LONDON, N8 9RT.
PODMORE, Miss. Karen Louise, BSc ACA *2001;* 53 Meadow Close, LONDON, SW20 9JB.
PODMORE, Mr. Richard David, BA(Hons) ACA *2004;* Northgate Plc Norflex House, 20 Allington Way, DARLINGTON, COUNTY DURHAM, DL1 4DY.
POEL, Mr. Geoffrey Richard, MA FCA *1970;* Littlecroft, Mill Hill, Shenfield, BRENTWOOD, CM15 8EU. (Life Member)
•POELMAN, Mrs. Mary Lynn, BA ACA *1993;* PricewaterhouseCoopers, Thomas R. Malthusstraat 5, P O Box 90351, 1006 BJ AMSTERDAM, NETHERLANDS.
POERSCOUT-EDGERTON, Mr. Clive Eric, FCA *1955;* 28 Sidney Road, BECKENHAM, BR3 4QA. (Life Member)
POERSCOUT-EDGERTON, Mr. Robert John, BSc(Hons) ACA *2004;* Innovation Group, Yarmouth House, 1300 Parkway, Solent Business Park, Whiteley, FAREHAM PO15 7AE.
POFFLEY, Mr. Barry John, BSc ACA *1986;* 13 Main Road, Littleton, WINCHESTER, SO22 6PS.
POFFLEY, Mr. Colin Froome, FCA *1958;* Cole Crest, Sunnyhill, BRUTON, BA10 0NR. (Life Member)
POGSON, Mr. Christopher Eric, BA FCA *1995;* 60 Totton Road, THORNTON HEATH, CR7 7QR.
POGSON, Mr. Timothy Keith, BSc ACA *1994;* Flat 24B Visalia Garden, 48 Macdonnell Road, MID LEVELS, HONG KONG ISLAND, HONG KONG SAR.
POGUE, Mr. Ian George Stephen, BA ACA *1997;* 3a Waldron Road, LONDON, SW18 3TB.
POH, Mr. Benjamin Liong Ban, FCA *1983;* Poh & Tan, 19-1 Jalan 3/146, Bandar Tasik Selatan, 57000 KUALA LUMPUR, FEDERAL TERRITORY, MALAYSIA.
POH, Mr. Ee Chuan, BA ACA *1982;* Nippon Paint (Singapore) Co Pte, Ltd, 1 First Lok Yang Road, Jurong, SINGAPORE 629728, SINGAPORE.
POH, Miss. Evelyn Su Lin, BSc ACA *2001;* Shinagawa Prince Residence 716, Minato-ku Takanawa 4-10-31, TOKYO, 108-0074 JAPAN.
POH, Ms. Grace Li Hwa, BSc ACA *1993;* Flat 22E Rialto Building, 2 Landale Street, WAN CHAI, HONG KONG SAR.
POH, Mr. Seng Wei Edwin, ACA *2010;* Flat 5, 152 Goswell Road, LONDON, EC1V 7DW.
POH, Mr. Thomas Sim Tart, FCA *1976;* No 28B Northboro Road, TAKAPUNA 1309, NEW ZEALAND.
POHOOMULL, Miss. Vinnie, BSc ACA *2008;* PricewaterhouseCoopers, GPO Box 1331, MELBOURNE, VIC 3001 DX77, AUSTRALIA.
POI, Mr. Godwin Kpobari, BSc(Econ) FCA MBA *1989;* Plot 11 Road 12, Woji Federal Estate, PORT HARCOURT, NIGERIA.
POIGNAND, Mr. Richard Mark, BMus ACA *1998;* Flat 4 Fourth Floor Belvedere House, Belvedere Hill St. Saviour, JERSEY, JE2 7RP.
•POILE, Miss. Mary Alexandra, BSc FCA *1982;* Dutchmans, 3 Station Parade, Cherry Tree Rise, BUCKHURST HILL, ESSEX, IG9 6EU. See also Dutchmans Consultants Limited
POINGDESTRE, Mr. Nicholas Simon, FCA *1989;* 16 West Park Avenue, St. Helier, JERSEY, JE2 3PJ.
POINTEN, Mr. Robert John, BA ACA *2004;* Triumph Motorcycles Ltd, Dodwells Road, HINCKLEY, LE10 3BZ.
POINTER, Mr. Guy Robert, ACA *2009;* 10 Pound Place, Binfield, BRACKNELL, RG42 5HY.
POINTER, Mr. James Ross, ACA *2008;* 6 Rudkin Place, Fishbourne, CHICHESTER, WEST SUSSEX, PO18 8FH.
POINTER, Mr. Mark Robert, ACA *2009;* 32 Lydford Road, LONDON, W9 3LX.
POINTER, Mr. Michael Albert, FCA ATII *1959;* Spindles, 1 Pinecroft, Hutton, BRENTWOOD, ESSEX, CM13 2PG.
POINTING, Mr. Leslie John James, BSc FCA *1975;* 2 Sillswood, OLNEY, BUCKINGHAMSHIRE, MK46 5PL.
POINTON, Mrs. Janet Lesley, ACA *1982;* Grange School Bradburns Lane, Hartford, NORTHWICH, CHESHIRE, CW8 1LU.
POINTON, Prof. John, PhD BA BSc FCA *1975;* University of Plymouth, Drake Circus, PLYMOUTH, PL4 8AA.
POINTON, Mrs. Kerry Louise, BA ACA *2005;* 25 Tennant Place, Porthill, NEWCASTLE, STAFFORDSHIRE, ST5 8QP.
POINTON, Mr. Lee Andrew, BA ACA *1989;* Agco Ltd Abbey Park, Stareton, KENILWORTH, CV8 2TQ.
POINTON, Mr. Nicholas Matthew, LLB ACA *1996;* 28 Cleveland Gardens, LONDON, SW13 0AG.
POINTON, Miss. Rebecca, ACA *2011;* 22 Sunlea Crescent, Stapleford, NOTTINGHAM, NG9 7JP.
POINTON, Mr. Robert William, FCA *1977;* Monitor System (Electrical Engineers), 174 Chester Road, GreenBank, NORTHWICH, CHESHIRE, CW8 4AL.
POINTON, Mr. Russell Harry, BA(Hons) ACA *1992;* 12 Shambroook Road, Off Hammond Street Road, Cheshunt, WALTHAM CROSS, EN7 6WB.
POINTON, Mr. Stephen, ACA *2011;* 75 Barrington Avenue, HULL, HU5 4AZ.
•POINTON, Mr. William Samuel, BSc ACA *2000;* with Grant Thornton UK LLP, 30 Finsbury Square, LONDON, EC2P 2YU.
POIRRETTE, Mr. John Arnold, FCA *1957;* 7A Mossgiel Avenue, SOUTHPORT, PR8 2RE. (Life Member)
POIRRETTE, Mr. Jonathan Mark Arnold, FCA *1988;* 33 Theberton Street, Islington, LONDON, N1 0QY.
•POLA, Mr. Roberto Marco Francesco, FCA *1983;* Robert Pola, The Dormers, Low Road, Congham, KING'S LYNN, PE32 1AE. See also Jenemi Associates Ltd
POLACK, Mr. Gregory James, BSc ACA *1987;* Lloyds Banking Group plc, 25 Gresham Street, LONDON, EC2V 7HN.
POLAND, Mr. Andrew James, BA(Hons) ACA *2002;* 2 Woodgate Crescent, NORTHWOOD, HA6 3RB.
POLAND, Mrs. Emma, BA ACA *1998;* 31 Jervis Crescent, SUTTON COLDFIELD, B74 4PW.
POLAND, Mrs. Philippa Mary, BA FCA ATII *1995;* Black Moor Farm, Black Moor Road, Oxenhope, KEIGHLEY, BD22 9SR.
POLANYI, Mr. Thomas, ACA *1993;* Bossigasse 63, 1130 VIENNA, AUSTRIA.
•POLDING, Mr. Nicholas William, BSc ACA *1985;* P.B. Syddall & Co, Grafton House, 81 Chorley Old Road, BOLTON, BL1 3AJ.
•POLE, Mr. Christopher Joseph, ACA *1982;* (Tax Fac), Howell Davies Limited, 37a Birmingham New Road, WOLVERHAMPTON, WV4 6BL.
POLE, Mr. Christopher Robert, ACA *2003;* 6 Weston Close, Rearsby, LEICESTER, LE7 4DA.
POLE, Mr. Leslie Hammond, FCA *1954;* The Orchards, 40 School Lane, Woodhouse, LOUGHBOROUGH, LEICESTERSHIRE, LE12 8UJ. (Life Member)
POLES, Mr. Mark William, MA FCA *1998;* with KPMG LLP, Plym House, 3 Longbridge Road, Marsh Mills, PLYMOUTH, PL6 8LT.
POLEY, Mr. Lester Charles, FCA *1951;* 6 Warwick Court, 2 High Street, EMSWORTH, PO10 7AE. (Life Member)
•POLEY, Mr. Simon John, BSc FCA *1984;* (Tax Fac), Newton & Garner Limited, Building 2, 30 Friern Park, North Finchley, LONDON, N12 9DA.
POLEYKETT, Mrs. Lucy Anne, BA ACA *2006;* with Chantrey Vellacott DFK LLP, Russell Square House, 10-12 Russell Square, LONDON, WC1B 5LF.
POLEYKETT, Mr. Stephen John, BA(Hons) ACA *2001;* with MacIntyre Hudson LLP, New Bridge Street House, 30-34 New Bridge Street, LONDON, EC4V 6BJ.
•POLI, Mr. Elias, BSc ARCS FCA *1982;* Smithfield Accountants LLP, 117 Charterhouse Street, LONDON, EC1M 6AA.
POLICELLA, Mr. Vincent Remo Anthony, BSc FCA *1977;* 12 Main Street, Ormiston, TRANENT, EAST LOTHIAN, EH35 5HX.
POLISHCHUK, Mr. Rostislav, ACA *2008;* 36 Hanover Court, CAMBRIDGE, CB2 1JH.
POLITO, Mr. Charles Stephen, FCA *1969;* Shammar House, North Creake, FAKENHAM, NORFOLK, NR21 9LN.
POLKINGHORN, Mr. Christian, MEng ACA *2011;* 26 Holbeck Park Avenue, BARROW-IN-FURNESS, CUMBRIA, LA13 0RG.
POLKINGHORNE, Mr. James Patrick, LLB ACA *2007;* with HW, 174 Whiteladies Road, Clifton, BRISTOL, GLOUCESTERSHIRE, BS8 2XU.
POLKINGHORNE, Mrs. Joanne Elizabeth, ACA *2009;* 3a Broncksea Road, BRISTOL, BS7 0SE.
POLKINGHORNE, Mrs. Karen, BSc ACA *1987;* Games Workshop Ltd, Willow Road, NOTTINGHAM, NG7 2WS.
POLKINGHORNE, Mr. Michael James, MA ACA *1989;* Games Workshop Ltd, Willow Road, NOTTINGHAM, NG7 2WS.
POLKINGHORNE, Mr. Nicky, BSc ACA *2010;* 51 West Park, WADEBRIDGE, CORNWALL, PL27 6AW.
•POLLACK, Mr. Stephen, FCA *1973;* Civvals, 50 Seymour Street, LONDON, W1H 7JG. See also Civvals Ellam Ltd
POLLAK, Mr. Martin Frederick, FCA *1969;* 50 Mcintosh Drive, Suite 252, MARKHAM L3R 9T3, ON, CANADA.
POLLARD, Mr. Alan Michael Whitshed, FCA *1964;* The Old Station Masters House, Cliff Road, HYTHE, CT21 5XA. (Life Member)
POLLARD, Mr. Alexander Whitshed, BSc ACA *1997;* 56 Bovlevard Des Etats Unis, 78110 LE VESINET, FRANCE.
POLLARD, Miss. Ann-Marie Catherine, BA(Hons) ACA *2004;* 35 Woodstock, KNEBWORTH, SG3 6EA.
POLLARD, Mr. Bruce Waide, ACA *1981;* 6 Cambridgeshire Close, Warfield, BRACKNELL, RG42 3XW.
POLLARD, Mr. Christopher James, BA ACA *1985;* 26 Rose Walk, ST. ALBANS, HERTFORDSHIRE, AL4 9AF.
•POLLARD, Mr. Christopher Vincent, BSc FCA *1973;* Pollard Goodman, 49 High Street, Westbury on Trym, BRISTOL, BS9 3ED.
•POLLARD, Mrs. Claire Sylvia, ACA CTA *1985;* (Tax Fac), Tim Pollard Ltd, Creeds Farm, Elkington, NORTHAMPTON, NN6 6NJ.
POLLARD, Miss. Diana Mary, BSc ACA *1989;* 164 Duffy Street, AINSLIE, ACT 2602, AUSTRALIA.
POLLARD, Mrs. Elizabeth Helen, BA ACA *2008;* 7 Angers Close, CAMBERLEY, SURREY, GU15 1PU.
POLLARD, Miss. Fiona Katherine, BSc ACA *1993;* 21 Cautley Avenue, LONDON, SW4 9HX.
POLLARD, Mr. Frank Selwyn Martin, FCA *1961;* P.O. Box HM 1500, HAMILTON HMFX, BERMUDA. (Life Member)
POLLARD, Mr. Geoffrey, FCA *1968;* 6 Elgin Mews South, Maida Vale, LONDON, W9 1JZ.
POLLARD, Mr. Graham Nigel, BA ACA *1990;* 7 HAZELBANK AVENUE, NOTTINGHAM, NG3 3EY.
POLLARD, Miss. Hannah, ACA *2008;* 16 Guelder Road, NEWCASTLE UPON TYNE, NE7 7PN.
POLLARD, Mr. Harry, FCA *1934;* Rua Jose Linhares 154 Ap.304, Leblon, CEP 22430, CEP2233 RIO DE JANEIRO, BRAZIL. (Life Member)
POLLARD, Miss. Jacqueline, BSc ACA *1990;* North Meadow Cottage Brantridge Lane, Staplefield, HAYWARDS HEATH, WEST SUSSEX, RH17 6EW.
POLLARD, Mr. John, FCA *1939;* 4036 Ripple Road, WEST, VANCOUVER VFV 3K9, BC, CANADA. (Life Member)
POLLARD, Mr. John Bernard, FCA *1955;* 4 Trews Gardens, Kelvedon, COLCHESTER, CO5 9AQ. (Life Member)
POLLARD, Mr. John Reginald, BSc ACA *1985;* Frome Hall, Frome Hall Lane, STROUD, GL5 3JH.
POLLARD, Mr. Jonathan Howard Wrigley, FCA DChA *1971;* 73 Victoria Avenue, Grappenhall, WARRINGTON, WA4 2PE.
POLLARD, Mr. Jonathan James, BSc ACA *2002;* infomedia, 357 Warringah Road, FRENCHS FOREST, NSW 2086, AUSTRALIA.
POLLARD, Mr. Joseph Simon Martin, BSc FCA *1996;* 3 Alexandra Mews, LONDON, N2 9HA.
POLLARD, Mrs. Judith Ann, MA ACA *1981;* (Tax Fac), Warners Solicitors Bank House, Bank Street, TONBRIDGE, TN9 1BL.
POLLARD, Mr. Julian David, BA ACA *1989;* 7 High Street, Byfield, DAVENTRY, NORTHAMPTONSHIRE, NN11 6XQ.
•POLLARD, Mr. Keith Raymond, FCA *1973;* Keith Pollard, Provincial House, 1 Strand, TORQUAY, TQ1 2AA.
POLLARD, Miss. Lucinda Ruth, ACA *1997;* Mouchel Parkman Plc, West Hall, Parvis Road, WEST BYFLEET, SURREY, KT14 6EZ.
POLLARD, Mr. Martin Bernard, BA FCA *1969;* 3 Mount Close, KENLEY, CR8 5DP. (Life Member)
POLLARD, Mr. Matthew, ACA *2011;* Flat 8, William Winter Court, 3 Charles Haller Street, LONDON, SW2 2YP.
POLLARD, Mr. Matthew James, ACA *2008;* 43 Lathkill Street, MARKET HARBOROUGH, LEICESTERSHIRE, LE16 9EN.
•POLLARD, Mr. Michael, BSc FCA CTA *1961;* 12 Creighton Avenue, LONDON, N10 1NU.
POLLARD, Mr. Paul, BCom ACA *1993;* c/o Avery Dennison, #90/90 7th Main, Peenya Industrial Area, BANGALORE 560058, KARNATAKA, INDIA.
POLLARD, Mrs. Rebecca Ann, ACA *2007;* with Ernst & Young LLP, Compass House, 80 Newmarket Road, CAMBRIDGE, CB5 8DZ.
•POLLARD, Mr. Richard James, BA FCA *1989;* PricewaterhouseCoopers LLP, 1 Embankment Place, LONDON, WC2N 6RH. See also PricewaterhouseCoopers
POLLARD, Mr. Richard John, BSc ACA *1988;* Nu-Swift Ltd, Wistons Lane, ELLAND, HX5 9DT.
POLLARD, Mr. Richard Keith, BSc ACA *1993;* 3 Sykes Close, Swanland, NORTH FERRIBY, NORTH HUMBERSIDE, HU14 3GD.
POLLARD, Mr. Robert John, MSc FCA *1971;* 5 Calle Lobo, 29603 MARBELLA, SPAIN. (Life Member)
POLLARD, Mr. Ronald, FCA *1957;* 5 Northcliffe, Great Harwood, BLACKBURN, BB6 7PJ. (Life Member)
POLLARD, Miss. Sarah Fiona, BA ACA *1989;* 1 Allee des Hetres, 92410 VILLE D'AVRAY, FRANCE.
POLLARD, Mrs. Sarah-Jane, BSc ACA *2003;* 44 Cronks Hill Road, REDHILL, RH1 6LZ.
•POLLARD, Mr. Stuart William, ACA *2001;* SPD Accountants Limited, First Floor, Hampshire House, 169 High Street, SOUTHAMPTON, SO14 2BY. See also Hayhursts
•POLLARD, Mr. Thomas James Clive, FCA *1972;* James Pollard, The Old Farm, Trolliloes, Cowbeech, HAILSHAM, BN27 4QR.
POLLARD, Mr. Thomas Richard, ACA *2009;* Larchwood Machine Tools Ltd, 24 Browns Lane, Knowle, SOLIHULL, WEST MIDLANDS, B93 8BA.
•POLLARD, Mr. Timothy Noel, BA ACA *1986;* Tim Pollard Ltd, Creeds Farm, Elkington, NORTHAMPTON, NN6 6NJ.
POLLARD, Mr. Trevor Douglas, BSc ACA *1980;* Shimmerings, Riverside Road, Dittisham, DARTMOUTH, DEVON, TQ6 0HS.
POLLARD, Miss. Vicki Fay, ACA *1988;* 2 Whinney Field, HALIFAX, WEST YORKSHIRE, HX3 0NP.
POLLEDRI, Mr. Michael Anthony, FCA *1970;* Heron House, Hale Wharf, Ferry Lane, LONDON, N17 9NF.
POLLETT, Mr. Richard John, FCA *1970;* Residencia Ambassador Prk, C Martinez de la Rosa 2, Bloque 9-3-izda, 07180 SANTA PONSA, MALLORCA, SPAIN.
POLLETT, Mr. Ryan Jamie, BSc ACA *2004;* 245/102 Miller Street, PYRMONT, NSW 2009, AUSTRALIA.
POLLETT, Mr. William, BCom(Hons) ACA CFA *1992;* Montpelier House, 94 Pitts Bay Road, HAMILTON HM 08, BERMUDA.
POLLEY, Mr. Michael Stephen, FCA *1976;* 12 Denham Court, ATHERSTONE, CV9 1SD.

POLLEY, Miss. Rosemary Gillian Joy, MEng ACA *2005;* 38 Upham Park Road, LONDON, W4 1PG.
POLLINGER, Mrs. Catherine Mary, BSc FCA CTA *1992;* 15 Dyer Road, WOKINGHAM, RG40 5PG.
POLLINGER, Mr. Stephen Michael, BEng FCA *1998;* 15 Dyer Road, WOKINGHAM, RG40 5PG.
POLLINGTON, Miss. Julia, ACA *2006;* 116 Grosvenor Avenue, CARSHALTON, SURREY, SM5 3EP.
POLLINGTON, Mr. Robert Kenneth, FCA *1970;* 2 Taylor Avenue, Cringleford, NORWICH, NR4 6XY.
POLLINS, Mr. Jonathan Louis, BSc FCA *1970;* 6 Lullington Garth, LONDON, N12 7AS.
POLLINS, Mr. Martin, FCA CTA MBA *1964;* (Member of Council 1987 - 1996), 3 North Lodge, High Street, Newick, LEWES, EAST SUSSEX, BN8 4LY.
POLLINS, Mr. Simon Joseph, BA ACA *1989;* 3 Brabourne Heights, Marsh Lane, LONDON, NW7 4NU.
POLLITT, Miss. Clare, BA ACA *1999;* 18 Blue Ridge Close, Great Sankey, WARRINGTON, CHESHIRE, WA5 3GX.
POLLITT, Mr. David, BSc ACA *2007;* 34 Basin Approach, LONDON, E14 7JA.
POLLITT, Mr. Ian Anthony, BA ACA *1984;* Volvox Group Ltd, Volvox House, Gelderd Road, LEEDS, LS12 6NA.
POLLITT, Mrs. Jacqueline Sandra, BA ACA *1998;* The Old House, Buxton Road, Frettenham, NORWICH, NR12 7NJ.
POLLITT, Ms. Victoria, BA ACA *1992;* BUPA International, Russell Square, Russell Mews, BRIGHTON, BN1 2NR.
POLLITT-PIPKIN, Mr. Francis Dominic, FCA *1965;* Bellan House, Bryn Road, Gwernaffield, MOLD, CH7 5DE.
POLLOCK, Mr. Andrew John, FCA *1966;* 53 Penerley Road, LONDON, SE6 2LH.
POLLOCK, Mr. Andrew William, BSc ACA *1985;* 19 Rissington Drive, WITNEY, OX28 5FG.
•**POLLOCK, Mr. Angus John, BA ACA** *1989;* Deloitte LLP, Athene Place, 66 Shoe Lane, LONDON, EC4A 3BQ. See also Deloitte & Touche LLP
POLLOCK, Mrs. Ann Marie, BSc(Hons) ACA *2001;* 307 Bluejay Drive, Westwoods, HOCKESSIN, DE 19707, UNITED STATES.
POLLOCK, Mrs. Anne, FCA *1949;* Rose Ash House, SOUTH MOLTON, EX36 4RB. (Life Member)
•**POLLOCK, Mr. Anthony James, BSc FCA** *1983;* 8 Halfacre Close, Spencers Wood, READING, RG7 1DZ.
POLLOCK, Mr. Christopher Michael Gordon, BSc ACA *2001;* 307 Bluejay Drive, Westwoods, HOCKESSIN, DE 19707, UNITED STATES.
POLLOCK, Mr. David Timothy Campbell, BSc FCA CTA *1983;* Ormond House, 26-27 Boswell Street, LONDON, WC1N 3JZ.
POLLOCK, Mr. John Christopher, FCA RA *1964;* Birchwood House, 8 Dudsbury Crescent, FERNDOWN, DORSET, BH22 8JF.
POLLOCK, Mr. Jonathan James, MBA BA FCA AMCT *1979;* Cohen Cramer, 40 Great George Street, LEEDS, LS1 3DL.
POLLOCK, Mr. Kelvin Alexander, FCA *1952;* The Malthouse, Upper Street, Hollingbourne, MAIDSTONE, ME17 1UW. (Life Member)
POLLOCK, Mr. Peter Glen, MA FCA *1973;* LPA Group plc, Debden Road, SAFFRON WALDEN, CB11 4AN.
POLLOCK, Mr. Raymond, BA FCA *1968;* 32 Georgian Close, STANMORE, HA7 3QT. (Life Member)
•**POLLOCK, Mr. Robert Andrew, FCA** *1968;* Andrew Pollock, 3rd Floor, The Triangle, Exchange Square, MANCHESTER, M4 3TR.
POLLOCK, Mr. Robert Leslie, FCA *1960;* 51 Arbor Road, Croft, LEICESTER, LE9 3GB. (Life Member)
•**POLLOCK, Mr. Ronald Hugh, MA FCA** *1973;* AIMS - Ronald Pollock, 7 Ellison Road, Barnes, LONDON, SW13 0AD.
POLLOCK, Mrs. Susan Deborah, MA ACA *1987;* Burnbank, 44 Twatling Road, Barnt Green, BIRMINGHAM, B45 8HU.
POLLOCK, Mr. William Andrew Jackson, FCA *1980;* Closefield, Little Brickhill Lane, Great Brickhill, MILTON KEYNES, MK17 9AY.
POLLON, Mr. Peter Dominic, BA(Hons) ACA AMCT *1996;* Treasury Floor 8 Land Securities plc, 5 Strand, LONDON, WC2N 5AF.
POLSON, Mrs. Norma Frances, BA FCA *1983;* with Duncan Sheard Glass, Castle Chambers, 43 Castle St, LIVERPOOL, L2 9TL.
POLSON, Mr. Timothy James, LLB ACA *2005;* with Deloitte LLP, Hill House, 1 Little New Street, LONDON, EC4A 3TR.
•**POLUCK, Mr. Simon Clive, BA FCA** *1992;* BSG Valentine, Lynton House, 7/12 Tavistock Square, LONDON, WC1H 9BQ.
POLUS, Mr. Michael Alan, FCA *1965;* 183-191 Ballards Lane, Finchley, LONDON, N3 1LL. (Life Member)
POLYDORIDES, Mr. Michael, FCA *1969;* 11 Christou Christovasili, Green House 402, P.O. Box 50307, 3603 LIMASSOL, CYPRUS.
POLYDORIDES, Mr. Nikos, FCA *1976;* Flat 54 Arethousa Court, Kerkyras 3, Neapolis, 3107 LIMASSOL, CYPRUS.
•**POLYVIOU, Mr. Polyvios, BSc ACA** *1999;* P Polyviou & Partners Limited, Proteas House, 155 Arch. Makarios III Avenue, Office 202, 3026 LIMASSOL, CYPRUS. See also Mouzouris & Polyviou Limited
•**POLYVIOU, Mr. Polyvios, BSc FCA** *1992;* HLB Afxentiou Limited, Palaceview House, Corner of Prodromos St & Zinonos Kitieos, POBox 16006, CY-2085 NICOSIA, CYPRUS.
•**POLYVIOU, Mr. Savvas, BA ACA** *2001;* SPGM Limited, Galatariotis Building, 3rd Floor, 11 Limassol Avenue, 2112 NICOSIA, CYPRUS.
POMARIO, Mr. Sean Robert, ACA *2003;* 4200 Park Newport, Apt 217, NEWPORT BEACH, CA 92660, UNITED STATES.
POMEROY, Mr. Brian Walter, CBE MA FCA *1968;* 7 Ferncroft Avenue, LONDON, NW3 7PG.
POMEROY, Mrs. Catherine Ann, BA ACA *1999;* H142/1, Astrazeneca Alderley House, Alderley Park, MACCLESFIELD, CHESHIRE, SK10 4TF.
•**POMEROY, Mr. Colin Neill, BA FCA** *1987;* Brebners, Tubs Hill House, London Road, SEVENOAKS, KENT, TN13 1BL. See also Brebners Limited
POMEROY, Mr. John Victor, FCA *1961;* 89 Windsor Road, Chobham, WOKING, GU24 8LE. (Life Member)
POMEROY, Mrs. Julie Patricia, BSc ACA *1980;* The Shielings, Highgrove Gardens, Edwalton, NOTTINGHAM, NG12 4DF.
POMEROY, Mr. Lawrence Mark, BA ACA *2005;* with KPMG LLP, 1 The Embankment, Neville Street, LEEDS, LS1 4DW.
POMEROY, Mr. Simon Robert Valentine, MA FCA *1968;* Duddle Farm, Bockhampton, DORCHESTER, DT2 8QL.
POMERY, Mr. Nicholas Mark, BSc ACA *1987;* 37 Mayes Close, WARLINGHAM, CR6 9LB.
POMFRET, Mr. Andrew David, MA ACA FSI *1986;* Rathbones, 159 New Bond Street, LONDON, W1S 2UD.
POMFRET, Mrs. Ann, BSc FCA *1989;* 43 Macclesfield Road, WILMSLOW, CHESHIRE, SK9 2AJ.
•**POMFRET, Mr. David John, BSc FCA** *1979;* PKF (UK) LLP, Farringdon Place, 20 Farringdon Road, LONDON, EC1M 3AP.
POMFRET, Mrs. Jane Elizabeth, LLB ACA *1995;* with PricewaterhouseCoopers LLP, Cornwall Court, 19 Cornwall Street, BIRMINGHAM, B3 2DT.
•**POMFRET, Mrs. Julie Elizabeth, BA FCA** *1988;* Haines Watts (Lancashire) LLP, Northern Assurance Buildings, 9-21 Princess Street, MANCHESTER, M2 4DN.
POMFRET, Mr. Richard John, BEng ACA *1995;* 37 Stockley Crescent, Shirley, SOLIHULL, B90 3SW.
POMLETT, Mr. Timothy Frank, BA ACA *1978;* 40 Rowallan Road, SUTTON COLDFIELD, B75 6RH.
POMORTSEVA, Mrs. Elena, MA BA ACA *2006;* 11 Ardys Court, Loughton, MILTON KEYNES, MK5 8AH.
•**POMROY, Mr. Christopher Sherrard, BA FCA** *1980;* C S Pomroy & Co, Unit A1, Weltech Centre, Ridgeway, WELWYN GARDEN CITY, HERTFORDSHIRE AL7 2AA.
POMROY, Mr. Matthew William, ACA *2011;* Flat 5, Medlock House, 1 Slate Wharf, MANCHESTER, M15 4SW.
•**POMROY, Mr. Nicholas Stephen, BSc FCA** *1980;* Griffins, Griffins Court, 24-32 London Road, NEWBURY, RG14 1JX. See also Griffins Business Advisers LLP
POMROY, Mr. Patrick Leonard, BSc ACA *1992;* 1550 Innovation Way, HARTFORD, WI 53027, UNITED STATES.
PONCIA, Mr. Edmund Anthony, FCA *1960;* 15 Brueton Avenue, SOLIHULL, B91 3EN. (Life Member)
PONCIN, Mr. Gilles Joseph, MEng MSc ACA *2004;* 9 allée Scheffer, L-2520 LUXEMBOURG, LUXEMBOURG.
POND, Mr. Andrew, BSc FCA *1975;* Mollart Engineering Ltd, 106 Roebuck Road, CHESSINGTON, SURREY, KT9 1EU.
POND, Mr. Anthony William George, FCA *1960;* 22 Rope Walk, Bearley Park, MARTOCK, TA12 6HZ. (Life Member)
POND, Mr. Nigel Walter, BA ACA AMCT *1996;* 147 Buryfield Road, SOLIHULL, WEST MIDLANDS, B91 2AY.
POND, Mr. Richard Christopher, MA ACA *1990;* 10 Granville Road, Walmer, DEAL, CT14 7LU.
POND, Mr. Stephen Forder, BSc ACA *1994;* 20 Barker Way, Thorpe End, NORWICH, NR13 5EZ.
PONDER, Mr. Keith Ronald Morton, FCA *1975;* Furzefield House, Furzefield Road, BEACONSFIELD, BUCKINGHAMSHIRE, HP9 1PQ.
PONG, Mr. Chi Kwan, ACA *2007;* Flat D 9/F Block 3, Flora Garden, 7 Chun Fai Road, TAI HANG, HONG KONG ISLAND, HONG KONG SAR.
PONNAMBALAM, Mr. Prashantha Ajitkumar, MBA FCA *1983;* 93 Storey Street, Maroubra, SYDNEY, NSW 2035, AUSTRALIA.
PONNIAH, Mr. Bala Krishnan, FCA *1980;* Moore Stephens Associates & Co, Suite 5.2A, Level 5 Menara Pelangi No.2, Jalan Kuning Taman Pelangi, 80400 JOHOR BAHRU, JOHOR MALAYSIA.
PONNIAH, Mr. Thoolasydas, FCA *1980;* 2 Jalan Dato Menteri 1/1, 80100 JOHOR BAHRU, Johor, MALAYSIA.
PONNUSAMY, Miss. Sonia, MSc BA ACA *2007;* 93 Park Road, LONDON, W4 3ER.
PONS, Mr. Francis Joseph Ramon, ACA *1982;* (Tax Fac), Professional Fee Protection 5 Sylvan Court, Sylvan Way Southfields Business Park, BASILDON, SS15 6TH.
PONSONBY, Mr. Charles Ashley, MA FCA *1977;* Bankside Consultants, 1 Frederick's Place, LONDON, EC2R 8AE.
PONSONBY, Mr. John Piers, MA ACA *1997;* 9 Winchendon Road, LONDON, SW6 5DH.
PONT, Mr. Simon Geoffrey Donald, FCA *1977;* 31 Bliss Mill, CHIPPING NORTON, OXFORDSHIRE, OX7 5JR.
•**PONTEFRACT, Mr. Ian David, BSc FCA** *1991;* KPMG LLP, 15 Canada Square, LONDON, E14 5GL. See also KPMG Europe LLP
PONTIFEX, Mr. Charles Edward, BSc ACA *1981;* 219 Station Road, Knowle, SOLIHULL, B93 0PU.
PONTIN-MEDES, Mr. Richard, BA ACA *2007;* 4 Poole Ground, Highnam, GLOUCESTER, GL2 8NA.
PONTING, Mr. Adrian Nigel, BA ACA *1983;* 12 Vasey Close, Saxilby, LINCOLN, LN1 2WG.
•**PONTING, Mr. Alan Richard, ACA** *1992;* Hunt Johnston Stokes Ltd, 12-14 Carlton Place, SOUTHAMPTON, SO15 2EA.
PONTING, Mr. Andrew David, BA ACA *1998;* 27 Sackville Avenue, Hayes, BROMLEY, KENT, BR2 7JS.
PONTING, Mr. Curtis Scott, MBA BSc FCA *1993;* 3 The Hollands, WOKING, SURREY, GU22 7SP.
PONTING, Mrs. Helen Kathleen, BA ACA *1983;* 12 Vasey Close, Saxilby, LINCOLN, LN1 2WG.
PONTING, Miss. Jane Louise, BSc ACA *1995;* Beechwood, 60 Chislehurst Road, CHISLEHURST, KENT, BR7 5LD.
PONTING, Mrs. Penelope Joy, BSc FCA *1994;* 3 The Hollands, Montgomery Road, WOKING, GU22 7SP.
PONTING, Mr. Richard Michael, BSc ACA *1998;* 140 Fidlas Road, Llanishen, CARDIFF, CF14 ONE.
PONTING, Mr. Roger Brian, MBA ACA FCCA *2009;* 2 Bramble Cottages, Standon Green End, High Cross, WARE, HERTFORDSHIRE, SG11 1BW.
PONTING, Miss. Sarah Helen, ACA *2010;* 27 Radbourne Road, LONDON, SW12 0EA.
PONTONE, Mr. James David, BA ACA *2002;* 156 Southbridge Road, Victoria Dock, HULL, HU9 1QB.
POO, Mr. Denis Kooi Fatt, BSc ACA *1983;* 10 Jalan SS 2/38, 47300 PETALING JAYA, Selangor, MALAYSIA.
POOK, Mr. Laurence Alan, FCA *1978;* 9 Millers Quay House, Lower Quay Road, FAREHAM, PO16 0RH.
POOK, Mr. Mun Fee, ACA *1991;* 19 Jalan SS22/16, Damansara Jaya, 47400 PETALING JAYA, SELANGOR, MALAYSIA.
•**POOKIMLIFU, Mr. Li Kune Lan, ACA** *2007;* Ernst & Young, 9th Floor, Tower 1, NextTeracom, Cybercity, EBENE MAURITIUS.
POOL, Mr. Alastair Nigel, BA ACA *1990;* 201 Greenwood Avenue, SINGAPORE 286909, SINGAPORE.
•**POOL, Mr. Bernard Leon, FCA** *1970;* Pool & Patel, Maison La Rosiere, P.O. Box 117, VICTORIA, SEYCHELLES.
POOL, Mr. Bryan Anthony, BSc ACA *1981;* Limley House Main Street, Kirkby Malzeard, RIPON, NORTH YORKSHIRE, HG4 3SD.
POOL, Mr. Miles Antony, BSc FCA *1999;* 13 Russell Avenue, BEDFORD, MK40 3TE.
POOL, Miss. Rosemary, BSc ACA *2007;* EDF Training, 3rd Floor Cardinal Place, 80 Victoria Street, LONDON, SW1E 5JL.
POOL, Mr. Thomas Edward, BSc ACA *2010;* 19 Royal Avenue, MANCHESTER, M21 9EU.
POOL, Mr. Timothy Donald, BSc(Hons) ACA *2001;* 15/11 Harriette Street, Neutral Bay, SYDNEY, NSW 2089, AUSTRALIA.
POOLE, Mr. Adrian Christopher, BA FCA *1986;* with PricewaterhouseCoopers LLP, The Atrium, St. Georges Street, NORWICH, NR3 1AG.
•**POOLE, Mr. Alan Christopher, BA(Hons) ACA** *2002;* with James Cowper LLP, 3 Wesley Gate, Queens Road, READING, RG1 4AP.
POOLE, Mr. Andrew Arthur, BSc ACA *2003;* with Armstrong Watson, Fairview House, Victoria Place, CARLISLE, CA1 1HP.
POOLE, Mr. Andrew Charles William, BA ACA *1989;* 2 Old School End, Hook Norton, BANBURY, OX15 5QU.
POOLE, Mr. Andrew Colin, BA ACA *1988;* BGL Group Ltd, Pegasus House, Southgate Park, Bakewell Road, Orton Southgate, PETERBOROUGH PE2 6YS.
•**POOLE, Mr. Andrew Jonathan, BA FCA** *1987;* Tranter Lowe (Oakengates) Ltd, International House, 6 Market Street, Oakengates, TELFORD, SHROPSHIRE TF2 6EF.
POOLE, Mr. Andrew Robert, BSc FCA AMCT *1997;* 344 Boardwalk Place, LONDON, E14 5SF.
POOLE, Miss. Caroline Freda, BA ACA *1987;* Granthams, Petworth Road, Chiddingfold, GODALMING, SURREY, GU8 4UJ.
POOLE, Mr. Christopher Francis, MA ACA MSI CISA *2002;* JP Morgan, 14/F Capital Tower, 168 Robinson Road, SINGAPORE 068912, SINGAPORE.
POOLE, Mr. Christopher James, BA ACA *1998;* I P Access Ltd, 2020 Cambourne Business Park Cambourne, CAMBRIDGE, CB23 6DW.
POOLE, Mrs. Clair Alison, BCom ACA *1992;* 176 Waterloo Place, University of Manchester, Oxford Road, MANCHESTER, M13 9PL.
POOLE, Mr. Clive Vincent, BCom FCA *1980;* Lugwardine, 22 Mulroy Road, SUTTON COLDFIELD, B74 2PY.
•**POOLE, Mr. David Allan, BA ACA** *1980;* David Poole Accountants Ltd, Hemdean House, 39 Chapel Road, SOUTHAMPTON, SO30 3FG.
•**POOLE, Mr. David Eric, FCA** *1972;* 9 Branksome Road, NORWICH, NR4 6SN.
POOLE, Mrs. Emma Kay, BSc FCA *1995;* 37 Greenlands Road, STAINES, MIDDLESEX, TW18 4LR.
POOLE, Mrs. Fiona Elizabeth, BSc ACA *2002;* 67 Throgmorton Road, YATELEY, HAMPSHIRE, GU46 6FA.
POOLE, Mr. Gavin Michael, ACA CA(SA) *2009;* Henry Schein Inc, 135 Duryea Rd, MELVILLE, NY 11747, UNITED STATES.
POOLE, Mrs. Gillian Elizabeth, BSc ACA *2004;* The Rectory Plains Road, Wetheral, CARLISLE, CA4 8LA.
POOLE, Mr. Graham David Garden, FCA *1975;* 8 Lawley House, 37 Clevedon Road, TWICKENHAM, TW1 2TW.
POOLE, Mr. Ian Stuart, ACA *2007;* 76 Finchfield Lane, WOLVERHAMPTON, WV3 8ET.
•**POOLE, Mr. James Alan, BA FCA** *1981;* Alan Poole & Co, 51 Colwyn Drive, Knypersley, STOKE-ON-TRENT, ST8 7BJ.
POOLE, Mrs. Janet Anne, BSc ACA *1993;* 2137 N Dayton Street, CHICAGO, IL 60614, UNITED STATES.
POOLE, Mr. John Colin, MBA FCA *1964;* Wester Ballachraggan Steading, Amulree, DUNKELD, PERTHSHIRE, PH8 0EA. (Life Member)
POOLE, Mr. John Lawrence, MA ACA *1985;* 19 Beechwood Court, Stillorgan Road, BLACKROCK, COUNTY DUBLIN, IRELAND.
POOLE, Mrs. Katie Louise, BA(Hons) ACA *2000;* 9 Town Wells Court, North Anston, SHEFFIELD, S25 4FS.
POOLE, Mr. Kevin Lionel, FCA *1967;* 100 Sandpit Lane, ST. ALBANS, AL4 0BX. (Life Member)
POOLE, Ms. Louisa Jane, ACA *2001;* 3 Spinney Close, MARKET HARBOROUGH, LEICESTERSHIRE, LE16 9DY.
POOLE, Mr. Mark, BSc ACA *1990;* (Tax Fac), 25 Fullbrooks Avenue, WORCESTER PARK, KT4 7PE.
POOLE, Mr. Mark Alan, BSc ACA *2001;* Financial Services Centre, B O C Ltd Rother Valley Way, Holbrook, SHEFFIELD, S20 3RP.
POOLE, Mr. Martin, ACA *2010;* 12 Brooker Street, HOVE, EAST SUSSEX, BN3 3YX.
POOLE, Mr. Martin Arnold, MA FCA *1977;* Outer Reach Upper Wood Lane, Kingswear, DARTMOUTH, DEVON, TQ6 0DF.
POOLE, Mr. Martin Keith, BEng ACA *2000;* Apartment 15, 91 Branston Street, BIRMINGHAM, B18 6BF.
•**POOLE, Mr. Martyn Richard, BSc FCA** *1978;* (Tax Fac), Poole Mordant LLP, 35 City Business Centre, St Olav's Court, Rotherhithe, LONDON, SE16 2XB. See also Martyn Poole & Co
POOLE, Mr. Matthew John, BSc ACA *2001;* 13 Faircross Way, ST. ALBANS, HERTFORDSHIRE, AL1 4RT.
POOLE, Mr. Michael, BSc FCA *1975;* Gordons School, Bagshot Road, West End, WOKING, SURREY, GU24 9PT.

POOLE, Mr. Michael, BSc ACA *1993;* (Tax Fac), 169 Lichfield Court, Sheen Road, RICHMOND, SURREY, TW9 1AZ.

POOLE, Mr. Michael Andrew, BA FCA *1988;* 19 Sandale Close, Gamston, NOTTINGHAM, NG2 6QG.

POOLE, Mr. Michael John, BSc ACA *1990;* Flat 2, Berners Mansions, 34-36 Berners Street, LONDON, W1T 3LU.

•POOLE, Mr. Neill Paul, BA ACA *1989;* Alvarez & Marsal Asia Ltd, Rooms 1101-3, 11/F Mass Mutual Tower, 38 Gloucester Road, WAN CHAI, HONG KONG ISLAND HONG KONG SAR.

POOLE, Mr. Neville, FCA *1974;* 26 Redcliffe Drive, Wombourne, WOLVERHAMPTON, WV5 0JE. (Life Member)

POOLE, Mr. Peter William, FCA TEP *1984;* P O Box 765, Road Town, TORTOLA, VIRGIN ISLANDS (BRITISH).

POOLE, Mrs. Rachel Joanne, BA ACA *2007;* 24 Stonethwaite, NORTH SHIELDS, TYNE AND WEAR, NE29 6AS.

POOLE, Mr. Raymond Edward, FCA *1964;* with Vale & West, Victoria House, 26 Queen Victoria Street, READING, RG1 1TG. (Life Member)

POOLE, Mr. Richard Edwin, ACA *1978;* Cherry Tree Cottage, 12 Parkfields Farm, Tittensor Road, Barlaston, STOKE-ON-TRENT, ST12 9HQ.

POOLE, Mrs. Samantha Jayne, FCA *1987;* 3 Sheridan Way, Firwood Park, OLDHAM, OL9 9UY.

POOLE, Mrs. Sarah Lucy, BA ACA *1993;* 51 Shavian Blvd, LONDON N6G 2P1, ON, CANADA.

POOLE, Mr. Simon Hilliard, BSc ACA *1992;* 4 Haredale Road, Heme Hill, LONDON, SE24 0AF.

•POOLE, Mr. Stephen Anton, FCA *1977;* S. Poole & Co, 220 Barnet Road, POTTERS BAR, HERTFORDSHIRE, EN6 2SH.

POOLE, Mr. Steven Michael, BA ACA *2001;* 5 Myrtle Avenue, Bishopthorpe, YORK, YO23 2SD.

POOLE, Mr. Thomas, BSc ACA *1999;* 67 Throgmorton Road, YATELEY, HAMPSHIRE, GU46 6FA.

•POOLE, Mr. Trevor Barry, FCA *1966;* (Tax Fac), Trevor B. Poole, 109 Barnett Wood Lane, ASHTEAD, SURREY, KT21 2LR.

•POOLE, Mrs. Veronica, MSc FCA *1997;* Deloitte LLP, 2 New Street Square, LONDON, EC4A 3BZ. See also Deloitte & Touche LLP

POOLE-CONNOR, Mr. Murray, FCA *1961;* Furzefield House, Horsham Road, Cowfold, HORSHAM, WEST SUSSEX, RH13 8BU.

POOLER, Mr. Nicholas James, BSc(Hons) ACA *2010;* 47 St. Albans Avenue, CARDIFF, CF14 4AS.

POOLER, Mr. Simon Felix, BEng ACA *1993;* Montague Private Equity, 15th Floor, St James's House, Charlotte Street, MANCHESTER, M1 4DZ.

POOLER, Mrs. Victoria Jane, BA ACA *1993;* Cherry Tree House, Davey Lane, ALDERLEY EDGE, CHESHIRE, SK9 7NZ.

•POOLES, Mr. Christopher, FCA *1991;* BDO LLP, Kings Wharf, 20-30 Kings Road, READING, RG1 3EX. See also BDO Stoy Hayward LLP

POOLEY, Mr. Anthony John, MBA MSc FCA *1976;* 35 Turnoak Avenue, WOKING, GU22 0AJ.

•POOLEY, Mr. Bernard Bertram, FCA *1981;* Kelsall Steele Limited, Woodlands Court, Truro Business Park, TRURO, CORNWALL, TR4 9NH.

•POOLEY, Mr. David Henry, BA FCA *1985;* (Tax Fac), Pooleys, 45 Lemon Street, TRURO, TR1 2NS.

•POOLEY, Miss. Elizabeth Ann, FCA *1971;* Elizabeth Pooley, Norfolk House, Station Road, CHESHAM, HP5 1DH.

POOLEY, Mrs. Mandy, BSc ACA *1985;* 3 Coral Point, Dorset Lake Ave, POOLE, DORSET, BH14 8JD.

•POOLEY, Mr. Mark, BSc FCA *1994;* Hollingdale Pooley Limited, Bramford House, 23 Westfield Park, Clifton, BRISTOL, BS6 6LT.

•POOLEY, Mr. Martin Richard, MA FCA *1977;* M.R. Pooley, 91 Church Lane, Eaton, NORWICH, NR4 6NY.

POOLEY, Mr. Matthew Zenthon, MSc(Econ) ACA *1998;* Flat 7 Ristorante Il Portico, 314-316 Vauxhall Bridge Road, LONDON, SW1V 1AA.

POOLEY, Miss. Melissa Amy, ACA MAAT *2001;* 28 Vincent Close, Studlands Park, NEWMARKET, SUFFOLK, CB8 7AN.

POOLEY, Mr. Michael Lafone, FCA *1957;* Russett House, 1 Scamblers Mead, Penton Grafton, ANDOVER, SP11 0SR. (Life Member)

•POOLEY, Mrs. Nicola Louise, ACA *1990;* Top Spinney, Keeble Park, Perranwell Station, TRURO, CORNWALL, TR3 7NL.

POOLEY, Mr. Nigel John, ACA *1985;* 64 Victoria Road, DISS, NORFOLK, IP22 4JE.

POOLEY, Mr. Robert Guy, BEng ACA *1994;* 10 St Swithun Street, WINCHESTER, SO23 9JP.

•POOLEY, Mr. Stephen Richard, BA FCA *1973;* SR Pooley & Co, 56 Corner Farm Road, Staplehurst, TONBRIDGE, TN12 0PS.

POOLMAN, Mr. Andrew George, BA ACA *1979;* Avon House, 25 Abbey Row, MALMESBURY, WILTSHIRE, SN16 0AG.

POOLOOVADOO, Mr. Ashwin Soodarsham, BSc ACA *2007;* 9 Greenleas, Pembury, TUNBRIDGE WELLS, TN2 4NS.

POON, Mr. Andrew Yin Kwon, FCA *1969;* Flat 4B Hawthorn Garden, 70 to 70A Sing Woo Road, HAPPY VALLEY, HONG KONG ISLAND, HONG KONG SAR. (Life Member)

POON, Mr. Chee Keong, FCA *1975;* 23 Second Avenue, EPPING, NSW 2121, AUSTRALIA.

POON, Mr. Chi Yip, ACA *2006;* Flat D 10/F Block 2, Tsui Chuk Garden, Chuk Yuen, WONG TAI SIN, KOWLOON, HONG KONG SAR.

POON, Mr. Chi Leong Harry, ACA *2005;* Harry C.L. Poon, PO Box 9047, General Post Office, 2 Connaught Place, CENTRAL, HONG KONG ISLAND HONG KONG SAR.

POON, Mr. Chi Man, ACA *2010;* Room 319, Tin Hee House, Tin Ping Estate, SHEUNG SHUI, NEW TERRITORIES, HONG KONG SAR.

POON, Mr. Chun Man, ACA *2005;* Room 1103, Block 12, Heng Fa Chuen, CHAI WAN, HONG KONG ISLAND, HONG KONG SAR.

POON, Miss. Esther, BSc ACA *1985;* 46 Gloucester Mews, LONDON, W2 3HE.

POON, Mr. Ha Fung, ACA MBA *1993;* Flat F 17/F, Block 7, South Horizons, AP LEI CHAU, HONG KONG ISLAND, HONG KONG SAR.

POON, Mr. Hon Yin, ACA *2008;* ProBiz CPA Limited, 20/F, On Hong Commercial Building, 145 Hennessy Road, WAN CHAI, HONG KONG ISLAND HONG KONG SAR.

POON, Mr. Jonathan, MMath(Hons) ACA *2011;* 20 Wellington Avenue, Whalley Range, MANCHESTER, M16 8JG.

POON, Miss. Ka-Lai, ACA *2009;* Flat 8 Tudor Court, Church Road, EGHAM, TW20 9HZ.

POON, Mr. Kam Wah, ACA *2005;* Room 1802 18/F, Sunbeam Commercial Bldg, 469-471 Nathan Road, YAU MA TEI, KOWLOON, HONG KONG SAR.

POON, Mr. Kin Wo William, ACA *2008;* Flat D 38/F Sky Tower, The Arch, 1 Austin Road West, TSIM SHA TSUI, KOWLOON, HONG KONG SAR.

POON, Mr. Kok Ying Danny, ACA *2008;* Room 443, 18 Tsing Wun Road, TUEN MUN, HONG KONG SAR.

POON, Mr. Kui Ki Freddy, ACA *2005;* Rm 1402 Sun Hung Kai Centre, 30 Harbour Road, WAN CHAI, HONG KONG SAR.

POON, Mr. Lin Sing, ACA *2008;* DAH Chong Hong Holdings Ltd, 5/F Kai Cheung Road, KOWLOON BAY, KOWLOON, HONG KONG SAR.

POON, Mr. Mo Yiu, ACA *2008;* PH 15B, House 15, Forest Hill, 31 Lo Fai Road, TAI PO, NEW TERRITORIES HONG KONG SAR.

POON, Mr. Pak Wai, ACA *2007;* Room F, 37/F Tower 2, The Pacifica, 9 Sham Shing Road, CHEUNG SHA WAN, KOWLOON HONG KONG SAR.

POON, Ms. Po Hing Dorothy, ACA *2008;* Flat D, 18/F, Kwun Tien Mansion, Taikoo Shing, QUARRY BAY, HONG KONG SAR.

POON, Mr. Pui Wai Patrick, ACA *2005;* Flat 904 Block 2, Hong Lee Court, 22 Hong Lee Road, KWUN TONG, KOWLOON, HONG KONG SAR.

POON, Mr. Shik Kwong Stephen, ACA *2008;* Flat E 23/F, Block 28, Laguna City, KOWLOON TONG, KOWLOON, HONG KONG SAR.

•POON, Mr. Simon Yuen Choi, ACA *1985;* (Tax Fac), Farmiloes LLP, Winston Churchill House, 8 Ethel Street, BIRMINGHAM, B2 4BG.

POON, Mr. Siu Cheung, ACA *2005;* 3436 Puget Drive, VANCOUVER V6L 2T5, BC, CANADA.

POON, Mr. Steven Te Wen, BSc(Hons) ACA CTA *2001;* 24 Lancaster Drive, Isle of Dogs, LONDON, E14 9PT.

POON, Ms. Sui Ling, ACA *2008;* 23D Tower 2, Greenfields, No 1 Fung Kam Street, YUEN LONG, HONG KONG SAR.

POON, Ms. Suk Kuen, ACA *2008;* Flat C 6/F.Block 1, Ronsdale Garden, 25 Tai Hang Drive, TAI HANG, HONG KONG SAR.

POON, Mr. Tsz Hang, ACA *2008;* 23F Tower 2, Metro Town, 8 King Ling Road, TSEUNG KWAN O, NEW TERRITORIES, HONG KONG SAR.

POON, Mr. Wai Hoi Percy, ACA *2008;* 9th Floor, 464 Lockhart Road, WAN CHAI, HONG KONG SAR.

POON, Mr. Wing Cheung Peter, ACA *2005;* Poon & Co., Dominion Centre, 6th Floor, 43-59 Queen's Road East, WAN CHAI, HONG KONG ISLAND HONG KONG SAR.

POON, Mr. Wingfu, BSc ACA *1995;* 6 Gladesmore Road, Tottenham, LONDON, N15 6TB.

POON, Ms. Yee Wa Anita, ACA *2008;* 2504-2511, Windsor House, 311 Gloucester Road, CAUSEWAY BAY, HONG KONG SAR.

POON WONG, Mrs. Yuen Shan Teresa, ACA *2005;* Poon & Co., Dominion Centre, 6th Floor, 43-59 Queen's Road East, WAN CHAI, HONG KONG ISLAND HONG KONG SAR.

POONI, Mrs. Claire Patricia, BA ACA *1990;* Heart of England Foundation Trust, 45 Bordesley Green East, BIRMINGHAM, B9 5ST.

POONJA, Mr. Mohamed, MS FCA FCCA CIRA CFE *1992; (FCA Ireland 1976);* Poonja & Company, P O Box 1510, LOS ALTOS, CA 94023-1510, UNITED STATES.

POOPALASINGAM, Ms. Anitha, ACA *2008;* 5 Lorong 4/49D, 46050 PETALING JAYA, SELANGOR, MALAYSIA.

POOPALASINGAM, Mr. Rajasingam, FCA *1961;* 26/1 Macquire Street, Newstead, BRISBANE, QLD 4006, AUSTRALIA. (Life Member)

POORE, Mrs. Neelum, BA ACA *1992;* 22 Allington Drive, TONBRIDGE, TN10 4HH.

POORMAND, Mr. Maziar, BSc ACA *2005;* 25 Annington Road, LONDON, N2 9NB.

POORUN, Mr. Rajesh, BA ACA *2003;* (Tax Fac), 19 Buckland Avenue, SLOUGH, SL3 7PJ.

POOTHICOTE, Mr. John, MSc ACA *2010;* Flat 305 Wharfside Point South, 4 Prestons Road, LONDON, E14 9EL.

POP, Mrs. Hannah Claire, BMus ACA *2005;* with Deloitte LLP, 2 New Street Square, LONDON, EC4A 3BZ.

POPAT, Mr. Amit, BA ACA *2002;* 38 Clare Road, BRAINTREE, ESSEX, CM7 2PB.

POPAT, Mrs. Davinder, BA ACA *1994;* 19 Richardson Crescent, Cheshunt, WALTHAM CROSS, EN7 6WZ.

•POPAT, Mr. Harish Kabalal, BA ACA *1984;* HKP Kabason Limited, Kabason House, 30 Greenbank Drive, Oadby, LEICESTER, LE2 5RP.

POPAT, Mr. Harshadkumar Kantilal, FCA *1973;* 14 Shiremead, Elstree, BOREHAMWOOD, HERTFORDSHIRE, WD6 3JZ.

POPAT, Mr. Hitesh, BSc FCA *1990;* 2 Holly Court, Oadby, LEICESTER, LE2 4EH.

POPAT, Mr. Jayesh Hansraj, MA ACA *1995;* Cumberland Hotel, 1-3 St. Johns Road, HARROW, HA1 2EF.

POPAT, Mrs. Jyotshna Kiritkumar, FCA *1978;* Kashi Nivas, 65 Ashley Park Avenue, WALTON-ON-THAMES, KT12 1EU.

•POPAT, Ms. Kiran Kantilal, BSc(Hons) FCA CTA *1983;* Little Cheverel, 59 Carbery Avenue, LONDON, W3 9AB.

•POPAT, Mr. Kiritkumar Dhirajlal, FCA *1971;* (Tax Fac), K.D. Popat & Co, Kashi Nivas, 65 Ashley Park Avenue, WALTON-ON-THAMES, KT12 1EU.

POPAT, Mr. Netan, BSc ACA CISA *1999;* 71 Mandrake Road, Tooting Bec, LONDON, SW17 7PX.

•POPAT, Mr. Rajendra Nanalal, FCA *1980;* (Tax Fac), Lawrence & Co, 132/134 College Road, HARROW, HA1 1BQ.

POPAT, Mr. Rajnikant H, FCA *1977;* 1 Fontwell Close, HARROW, HA3 6DF.

POPAT, Mr. Ravi, BSc ACA *2010;* Oakleaf, Beresford Drive, BROMLEY, BR1 2DU.

POPE, Mr. Adrian Lee, BA(Econ) ACA *1996;* 4 Tenby Drive, Cheadle Hulme, CHEADLE, SK8 7BR.

POPE, Mr. Alexander BryanTimothy, BA(Hons) ACA *2010;* The Granary, East Road, WEYBRIDGE, SURREY, KT13 0LE.

•POPE, Mrs. Alison, ACA *1992;* The Davison Partnership, Reliance House, Moorland Road, Burslem, STOKE-ON-TRENT, ST6 1DP.

POPE, Miss. Alison, ACA *2008;* 9 Thorndike Way, BURNHAM-ON-SEA, SOMERSET, TA8 1QR.

POPE, Mrs. Alison Jane, BA ACA *2005;* with BDO LLP, 55 Baker Street, LONDON, W1U 7EU.

•POPE, Mrs. Andrea, BA ACA *1990;* Burton & Co, Sovereign House, Bradford Road, Riddlesden, KEIGHLEY, BD20 5EW.

•POPE, Mr. Andrew Charles, ACA *1984;* Montgomery McNally & Co, 4 Greenstede Avenue, EAST GRINSTEAD, WEST SUSSEX, RH19 3HZ.

POPE, Mr. Anthony James, BA ACA *1998;* Antony Hodari & Co, 34 High Street, MANCHESTER, M4 1AH.

POPE, Mrs. Brenda Yvonne, BSc ACA *1991;* 2 Clewer Park, WINDSOR, SL4 5HA.

•POPE, Mr. Brian Ronald, BA FCA *1982;* Kingston Smith LLP, Orbital House, 20 Eastern Road, ROMFORD, RM1 3PJ. See also Kingston Smith Limited Liability Partnership, Devonshire Corporate Services LLP and Kingston Smith Consulting LLP

POPE, Mr. Charles Simon Russell, MA ACA *1991;* Retain International Ltd, Suite 33, Beaufort Court, Admirals Way, LONDON, E14 9XL.

POPE, Mr. Christopher Miles, FCA *1966;* Oakfield Cottage, Overdale Road, Willaston, NESTON, CH64 1SZ. (Life Member)

POPE, Mr. David Rodney, FCA *1966;* 21 Rectory Road, Frampton Cotterell, BRISTOL, BS36 2BN.

POPE, Mr. Gordon Robert, FCA *1955;* Keepers Cottage, Muntham Farm, North End Findon, WORTHING, BN14 0RQ. (Life Member)

POPE, Mr. Ian Gordon, BA FCA *1982;* 2 Beta Road, LANE COVE, NSW 2066, AUSTRALIA.

POPE, Mr. James Legh, MA FCA *1973;* 9506 Marstan Road, PHILADELPHIA, PA 19118-2611, UNITED STATES.

POPE, Miss. Jennie Louise, ACA *2008;* 13 Trevelyan Road, LONDON, SW17 9LS.

•POPE, Mrs. Jennifer Margaret, MA ACA *1986;* Nyman Libson Paul, Regina House, 124 Finchley Road, LONDON, NW3 5JS.

•POPE, Mr. John Benjamin, MA FCA *1982;* (Tax Fac), Pope & Co, 1 Drayton Close, Swindon Village, CHELTENHAM, GL51 9QB.

POPE, Mr. John Charles, BA ACA *2005;* Hallidays Accountants Llp Riverside House, Kings Reach Road, STOCKPORT, CHESHIRE, SK4 2HD.

POPE, Mr. John Moreton, BEng ACA *1996;* Lee Associates, 5 Southampton Place, LONDON, WC1A 2DA.

POPE, Mrs. Judith Laura, BA ACA *1996;* Shell International Limited Shell Centre, York Road, LONDON, SE1 7NA.

•POPE, Mr. Keith, BSc FCA *1976;* (Tax Fac), Tax Solutions (North West) Limited, 35 Woodside Lane, Poynton, STOCKPORT, CHESHIRE, SK12 1BB.

POPE, Mrs. Kirstie Jane, BSc ACA *1994;* 5 Ethley Drive, Raglan, USK, GWENT, NP15 2FD.

POPE, Miss. Laura Jane, BSc(Hons) ACA *2011;* 167 Chessel Crescent, SOUTHAMPTON, SO19 4BT.

•POPE, Mr. Malcolm Philip, BA ACA *2004;* Shorts, 912 Ecclesall Road, SHEFFIELD, S11 8TR.

POPE, Mr. Mark, BSc ACA *2010;* 81 Long Beach Road, Longwell Green, BRISTOL, BS30 9XD.

POPE, Mr. Martin Edward, FCA *1967;* 27A Avenue De Miremont, 1206 GENEVA, SWITZERLAND. (Life Member)

POPE, Miss. Mary Angela, ACA *1982;* M. Pope Enterprises Ltd, P O Box 61755-8137, PAPHOS, CYPRUS.

POPE, Mr. Matthew Russell, BSc ACA CTA *1998;* (Tax Fac), 45 Woodvale Avenue, Cyncoed, CARDIFF, CF23 6SP.

POPE, Mr. Michael Frederick, BA FCA *1961;* with Reeves & Co LLP, 37 St. Margarets Street, CANTERBURY, KENT, CT1 2TU. (Life Member)

POPE, Mrs. Nia Rhiannon, BA ACA *2004;* 45 Woodvale Avenue, Cyncoed, CARDIFF, CF23 6SP.

POPE, Mr. Nicholas John, BSc ACA *1992;* 27 Mansionhouse Road, EDINBURGH, EH9 2JD.

POPE, Mr. Nigel Howard, BSc ACA *1990;* 17 Hawthorne Road, BROMLEY, BR1 2HN.

POPE, Mr. Peter, BA FCA *1950;* Woolley Barn Farm, Woolley Green, BRADFORD-ON-AVON, BA15 1TZ. (Life Member)

POPE, Mr. Robert Renton, FCA *1972;* Lower Roughway, TONBRIDGE, TN11 9SN.

POPE, Mr. Russell Charles, BSc FCA *1992;* 67a Warwick Road, BISHOP'S STORTFORD, HERTFORDSHIRE, CM23 5NL.

POPE, Mrs. Sandra Jane, BSc ACA *1987;* Wilton Old Farm, Beach, Bitton, BRISTOL, BS30 6NP.

POPE, Miss. Sarah Jane, BSc ACA *1995;* 21 Gladstone Terrace, Bulk Road, LANCASTER, LA1 1DW.

POPE, Ms. Sarah Joanne Elizabeth, BA ACA *1992;* (Tax Fac), with PricewaterhouseCoopers, 1 Embankment Place, LONDON, WC2N 6RH.

POPE, Mr. Simon Paul, MBA BSc FCA *1991;* Brandon Lodge, 31 Westcliffe Road, Shoreside Birkdale, SOUTHPORT, PR8 2BL.

POPE, Mrs. Sophie Hannah, ACA *2008;* 31 Melrose Street, NOTTINGHAM, NG5 2JP.

POPE, Mr. Stephen John, BSc ACA *1986;* Emirates Steel Industries, PO Box 9022, Mussafah, ABU DHABI, PO 9022, UNITED ARAB EMIRATES.

•POPE, Mr. Stewart Michael, FCA *1986;* Perrys, 32-34 St. Johns Road, TUNBRIDGE WELLS, KENT, TN4 9NT.

POPE, Mr. Timothy John, BA ACA *1992;* 51 Baldry Gardens, LONDON, SW16 3DL.
•**POPE, Mr. Timothy Patrick, FCA** *1970;* The Granary, East Road, WEYBRIDGE, SURREY, KT13 0LE.
•**POPE, Mr. William Michael John, FCA** *1957;* W.M.J. Pope, 54 Kings Avenue, Parkstone, POOLE, BH14 9QJ.
•**POPHAM, Mr. Andrew Jonathan, BA FCA** *1981;* PricewaterhouseCoopers LLP, 1 Embankment Place, LONDON, WC2N 6RH. See also PricewaterhouseCoopers
POPHAM, Mrs. Eileen, BSc ACA *1983;* 8 Balniel Gate, LONDON, SW1V 3SD.
POPHAM, Mr. Robert Michael Home, BA(Hons) ACA *2003;* Toedistrasse 78, 8800 THALWIL, SWITZERLAND.
POPKIN, Mr. Alexander Guy, MA ACA *1996;* (Tax Fac), with PricewaterhouseCoopers LLP, 31 Great George Street, BRISTOL, BS1 5QD.
POPKISS, Miss. Claire Lisa, ACA *2008;* Morris Owen, 43-45 Devizes Road, SWINDON, SN1 4BG.
POPKISS, Mr. Stephen Anthony, BSc ACA *1985;* Skanska ID UK Limited, Condor House, 10 St. Paul's Churchyard, LONDON, EC4M 8AL.
POPLE, Mr. Christopher John, ACA *1988;* 4 College Fields, Clifton, BRISTOL, BS8 3HP.
POPLE, Mr. David Michael, FCA *1969;* 51 Ham Green, Pill, BRISTOL, BS20 0HA.
•**POPLE, Mr. Ian Charles, ACA** *1986;* Lymore Partnership Limited, The Mount, Lymore Lane, Milford on Sea, LYMINGTON, HAMPSHIRE SO41 0TX.
•**POPLE, Mrs. Susan Jane, BSc FCA** *1980;* Lymore Partnership Limited, The Mount, Lymore Lane, Milford on Sea, LYMINGTON, HAMPSHIRE SO41 0TX.
POPLETT, Mr. Mark James, ACA *2009;* 59 St. Andrews Drive, Saxilby, LINCOLN, LN1 2PR.
POPOVICH, Mr. Mark, ACA *2011;* 53 Westfield Road, LEICESTER, LE3 6HU.
POPOWYCZ, Miss. Kerry, ACA *2008;* 4 Tansybrook Way, West Timperley, ALTRINCHAM, CHESHIRE, WA14 5ZB.
POPPE, Mr. John Wilfred, FCA *1972;* PO Box 27285, Shirley, CHRISTCHURCH 8640, NEW ZEALAND.
POPPITT, Mr. Marcus Simon, BSc ACA *2002;* with KPMG LLP, 100 Temple Street, BRISTOL, BS1 6AG.
POPPLE, Mr. Martin John, FCA *1963;* 17 Cameron Lane, Fernwood, NEWARK, NOTTINGHAMSHIRE, NG24 3GE.
POPPLE, Mr. Richard Dominic, BSc FCA FCILA MCMI FEUDI-ELAE *1987;* 19 Chepstow Ave, Berkeley Beverborne, WORCESTER, WR4 0EF.
POPPLESTON, Mr. Richard, BSc ARCS FCA *1995;* Equity Trust Group, 6 St Andrew Street, LONDON, EC4A 3AE.
POPPLESTONE, Mr. Harold, FCA *1950;* 1 Astoria Court, CURRAMBINE, WA 6028, AUSTRALIA. (Life Member)
POPPLETON, Mrs. Sarah Ghislaine, BSc ACA *1993;* Woodlands, East Common, HARPENDEN, AL5 1DG.
POPPLEWELL, Mr. Edmund James Bury, BA FCA *1994;* Siemens plc, Sir William Siemens Square, Frimley, CAMBERLEY, SURREY, GU16 8QD.
POPPLEWELL, Miss. Lynne, BA ACA *2007;* 3 Lowgarth, Yaddlethorpe, SCUNTHORPE, DN17 2UL.
POPPLEWELL, Mr. Martin James, LLB ACA *2007;* Notre Paradis Grand Fort Road, St. Sampson, GUERNSEY, GY2 4GZ.
•**POPPLEWELL, Mr. Noel, FCA** *1974;* (Tax Fac), Noel Popplewell & Co, 18 Vaughan Way, Connah's Quay, DEESIDE, CH5 4NG.
POR, Miss. Eileen Keng Khoon, BSc ACA *1980;* 38 Paines Lane, PINNER, HA5 3DB.
PORBUNDERWALLA, Mr. Anverali Mohamedali, FCA *1971;* A M Porbunderwalla, PO Box 40248, NAIROBI, 00100, KENYA.
PORCELLI, Mrs. Sophia So Yu, BSc FCA CFA *1992;* 9 Taman Serasi, #3-15, SINGAPORE 257720, SINGAPORE.
PORCH, Mr. Michael Garfield, BSc ACA *1989;* 38 Gerddi Quarella, BRIDGEND, MID GLAMORGAN, CF31 1LG.
PORCHERON, Mrs. Anne, BM ACA *1998;* 39 Alandale Drive, PINNER, HA5 3UP.
PORRITT, Mr. Brian Nigel, MA ACA *1985;* 16 Burgess Wood Road, BEACONSFIELD, BUCKINGHAMSHIRE, HP9 1EQ.
•**PORRITT, Mr. Christopher Simon, FCA** *1978;* Beever and Struthers, St George's House, 215-219 Chester Road, MANCHESTER, M15 4JE.
PORRITT, Mr. Darren, BSc ACA *1999;* 25 Beechfield, New Farnley, LEEDS, LS12 5QS.
PORRITT, Mr. Hugh Trevor, BSc FCA *1967;* Brooklyns, 5 The Hildens, Westcott, DORKING, RH4 3JX.
•**PORRITT, Mr. Nicholas Thomas Sam, MA ACA** *2000;* with Mazars LLP, Tower Bridge House, St. Katharines Way, LONDON, E1W 1DD.
PORRITT, Mr. Patrick James, BA ACA *1993;* 77 Elms Road, LONDON, SW4 9EP.
PORT, Mr. David John, BSc ACA *1992;* 600 West Chicago Avenue, Suite 300N, CHICAGO, IL 60654, UNITED STATES.
PORT, Mrs. Jill Marie, BA ACA *1987;* Far End Cottage, Shaw Lane, Kings Bromley, BURTON-ON-TRENT, STAFFORDSHIRE, DE13 7JQ.
•**PORT, Mr. Robin Michael, FCA** *1992;* Maynard Heady LLP, Matrix House, 12-16 Lionel Road, CANVEY ISLAND, ESSEX, SS8 9DE. See also Maynard Heady
•**PORTAL, Sir Jonathan Francis, Bt BCom FCA** *1979;* JP Associates, Burley Wood, Ashe, BASINGSTOKE, RG25 3AG.
PORTAS, Miss. Jane Louise, BSc FCA *1992;* with KPMG LLP, 15 Canada Square, LONDON, E14 5GL.
PORTAS, Mrs. Lisa Helen, BSc ACA *1995;* 15 Ashville Avenue, Eaglescliffe, STOCKTON-ON-TEES, TS16 9AU.
PORTCH, Mr. Julian John, LLB ACA *1996;* Ground Floor, 4 Westbury Mews, BRISTOL, BS9 3QA.
PORTCH, Mr. Martin Edward, FCA *1968;* Au Valades Chemin Des Sablons, Route De Vallabrix, St Quentin-La-Poterie, 30700 UZES, FRANCE. (Life Member)
PORTELLI, Mr. Mark Andrew, BA ACA *1990;* The Virtu Steamship Co Ltd, 8/10 Princess Elizabeth St, TA'XBIEX, MALTA.
•**PORTEOUS, Mr. Andrew Nigel, FCA** *1975;* Downend Cottage, Long Lane, Arreton, NEWPORT, ISLE OF WIGHT, PO30 2NT.
PORTEOUS, Mr. David, FCA *1961;* 74 Birchwood Avenue, SIDCUP, DA14 4JU.
PORTEOUS, Mr. Gavin, ACA *1979;* PO Box 11, AKAROA 7542, SOUTH ISLAND, NEW ZEALAND.
PORTEOUS, Mr. Graham Keith, FCA *1969;* The Stables, Elmhurst, Wood Road, Tettenhall, WOLVERHAMPTON, WV6 8LN. (Life Member)
PORTEOUS, Mr. Ian James, BSc ACA *1997;* 121 Rye Street, BISHOP'S STORTFORD, HERTFORDSHIRE, CM23 2HD.
•**PORTEOUS, Mr. Roger Malcolm, FCA** *1973;* Roger M. Porteous, 10 Windermere Road, Babbacombe, TORQUAY, TQ1 3RF.
PORTER, Mr. Adrian, ACA *2009;* 167 Frimley Green Road, Frimley Green, CAMBERLEY, SURREY, GU16 6JY.
PORTER, Mr. Alan John, BA FCA *1973;* Lu'shan, Millfield Road, Walberswick, SOUTHWOLD, IP18 6UD.
•**PORTER, Mrs. Andrea, BSc ACA** *1997;* BDO LLP, Kings Wharf, 20-30 Kings Road, READING, RG1 3EX. See also BDO Stoy Hayward LLP
PORTER, Mr. Andrew Boyd, BA ACA *1992;* Merrill Lynch Financial Centre, 2 King Edward Street, LONDON, EC1A 1HQ.
PORTER, Mr. Andrew James Blanchard, MA FCA *1994;* Australian Foundation Investment Company Ltd, GPO Box 2114, MELBOURNE, VIC 3001, AUSTRALIA.
PORTER, Mr. Andrew John, BSc ACA *1992;* 48 Elm Grove, MANCHESTER, M20 6PN.
PORTER, Mr. Andrew Jonathan, BSc ACA *1987;* 6 Fawcett Court, Fawcett Street, LONDON, SW10 9HW.
PORTER, Mrs. Angela Cynthia, BA ACA *1983;* 1 Strawberry Gardens, Seine Lane Enderby, LEICESTER, LE19 4PQ.
PORTER, Mrs. Annabel Jane, BSc ACA DipM *2001;* 1 Rotherfield Crescent, Hollingbury, BRIGHTON, BN1 8FF.
•**PORTER, Mr. Anthony Giles, BA FCA** *1989;* (Tax Fac), with Amherst & Shapland (Taunton & Wiveliscombe), Unit 2, Old Brewery Road, Wiveliscombe, TAUNTON, SOMERSET TA4 2PW.
PORTER, Mr. Antony, BSc FCA *1974;* 10 Atherton Road, Epsom, AUCKLAND 1023, NEW ZEALAND.
PORTER, Mr. Arthur Richard Ferguson, MA(Hons) ACA *2003;* 64 Chesson Road, LONDON, W14 9QU.
PORTER, Mrs. Catherine Margaret, MEng ACA AMCT ACIL *1991;* 53 Gartmoor Gardens, LONDON, SW19 6NX.
PORTER, Mr. Charles David Spencer, BA ACA *1991;* 58 Pinkneys Drive, MAIDENHEAD, SL6 6QE.
•**PORTER, Mrs. Clare Noelle, BA ACA** *2003;* (Tax Fac), Sage & Company Business Advisors Limited, 102 Bowen Court, St Asaph Business Park, ST. ASAPH, CLWYD, LL17 0JE.
PORTER, Mr. Colin George, FCA *1963;* Marlyns, Tugford, CRAVEN ARMS, SY7 9HS.
•**PORTER, Mr. David Antony, BSc FCA** *1988;* BDO LLP, 55 Baker Street, LONDON, W1U 7EU. See also BDO Stoy Hayward LLP
•**PORTER, Mr. David Charles, ACA FCCA** *1998;* Richardson Jones Limited, Mercury House, 19/21 Chapel Street, MARLOW, BUCKINGHAMSHIRE, SL7 3HN.
•**PORTER, Mr. David John, FCA** *1987;* Viewpoint Business Services Ltd, Suite 3, Unit 8, Kingsdale Business Centre, Regina Road, CHELMSFORD CM1 1PE.
PORTER, Mr. David Richard, FCA *1976;* 34A Eversleigh Road, BARNET, EN5 1ND.
PORTER, Mrs. Elizabeth Laurie, BSc FCA *1976;* 14 Lodge Drive, TRURO, CORNWALL, TR1 1TX.
PORTER, Mrs. Emma Jane, BA ACA *1994;* Manor Farm, Simpson, MILTON KEYNES, BUCKINGHAMSHIRE, MK6 3AH.
•**PORTER, Miss. Emma Sarah Louise, BSc ACA** *1997;* Aver Corporate Advisory Services Ltd, 21 York Place, EDINBURGH, EH1 3EN.
•**PORTER, Mr. Frederick Edward Oliver, MA ACA** *2005;* Clark Howes Auditing Solutions Limited, 2 Minton Place, Victoria Road, BICESTER, OXFORDSHIRE, OX26 6QB.
PORTER, Mr. Geoffrey Alan, FCA *1974;* 8 Chestnut Rise, BARROW-UPON-HUMBER, SOUTH HUMBERSIDE, DN19 7SG.
PORTER, Mr. Geoffrey William, BA FCA *1975;* (Tax Fac), 26 Spindlewood Close, Bassett, SOUTHAMPTON, SO16 3QD.
•**PORTER, Mr. Graham David, FCA** *1975;* (Tax Fac), with K M Business Solutions Limited, 4-6 Grimshaw Street, BURNLEY, LANCASHIRE, BB11 2AZ.
PORTER, Mrs. Gwynneth Mary, BSc FCA *1981;* 36 Grove Park, KNUTSFORD, WA16 8QA.
•**PORTER, Mr. Harold Keith, FCA JDipMA** *1957;* Harold K Porter & Co, Honor House, Honor End Lane, Prestwood, GREAT MISSENDEN, BUCKINGHAMSHIRE HP16 9QZ.
PORTER, Miss. Helen Sarah, BSc ACA *2004;* with Dutton Moore, 6 Silver Street, HULL, HU1 1JA.
PORTER, Mr. Iain, ACA *2010;* Flat 12 Tasman Court, 244 Westferry Road, LONDON, E14 3QJ.
PORTER, Mr. Ian, ACA *1981;* 33 Fortis Way, Salendine Nook, HUDDERSFIELD, HD3 3WW.
PORTER, Mr. Ian Charles Edward, BA ACA *1989;* 12 The Office Village, Romford Road, LONDON, E15 4EA.
PORTER, Mr. James Henry, BA ACA *2000;* 7 Franklands Drive, ADDLESTONE, KT15 1EQ.
PORTER, Mr. James John, LLB FCA *1970;* Tulip Tree House, Bagshot Road, Worplesdon Hill, WOKING, SURREY, GU22 0QY.
PORTER, Mr. James Robert Ian, BEng ACA *1999;* 318 Hillside Avenue, CHARLOTTE, NC 28209, UNITED STATES.
PORTER, Mr. Jeremy William, BA ACA *2009;* Flat 14, Badric Court, 5 Yelverton Road, LONDON, SW11 3SP.
PORTER, Mr. John Patrick Frederic, BA ACA *1986;* De Wittenkade 104A, 1051 AK AMSTERDAM, NETHERLANDS.
•**PORTER, Mr. Jonathan Howard, MA FCA** *1987;* (Tax Fac), AIMS - Jonathan Porter, 8 Bassett Dale, SOUTHAMPTON, SO16 7GT.
PORTER, Mrs. Julia Helen Caroline, BA ACA *1993;* The Thatched Cottage Meriden Road, Berkswell, COVENTRY, CV7 7BE.
PORTER, Mr. Julian, ACA *2011;* 147 Twickenham Road, Leytonstone, LONDON, E11 4BN.
•**PORTER, Mr. Justin, MSc BSc ACA** *2008;* Porters, 127 Fairacres, Prestwood, GREAT MISSENDEN, BUCKINGHAMSHIRE, HP16 0LF.
PORTER, Mr. Kelvin Robert, FCA *1974;* (Tax Fac), 18 Broad Field Road, Yarnton, KIDLINGTON, OXFORDSHIRE, OX5 1UL.
PORTER, Mrs. Linda Karen, BSc ACA *1988;* 56 Iveagh Close, Measham, SWADLINCOTE, DE12 7JL.
PORTER, Mrs. Lucie, BA ACA *1995;* (Tax Fac), Kildare, London Road, HOOK, RG27 9EQ.
PORTER, Mr. Luke Gareth, ACA *2008;* PKF (UK) Llp, Farringdon Place 20 Farringdon Road, LONDON, EC1M 3AP.
PORTER, Mr. Martin Reeves, MSc ACA *2004;* 12 Woodland Crescent, LONDON, SE16 6YP.
•**PORTER, Mr. Matthew, BSc FCA** *1987;* H W, Enterprise House, Timbrell Street, TROWBRIDGE, WILTSHIRE, BA14 8PL.
PORTER, Mr. Matthew Robert, BSc ACA *1991;* Santander UK Plc Santander House, 201 Grafton Gate East, MILTON KEYNES, MK9 1AN.
PORTER, Mr. Michael, BSc ACA *1993;* Chestnut House, 4 Gill Croft Court, Easingwold, YORK, YO61 3GX.
PORTER, Mr. Michael Jonathan, FCA *1968;* Crofton House, Wickfield, DEVIZES, SN10 5DU.
PORTER, Mr. Michael Lawrence, FCA *1960;* The Lodge, Station Road, Wargrave, READING, RG10 8EU.
PORTER, Mr. Michael William, BSc ACA *2002;* 611 South Titirangi Road, Titirangi, AUCKLAND, NEW ZEALAND.
PORTER, Mr. Nicholas James, BA ACA *2007;* 2 Moonhill Close, EXETER, EX2 8GA.
PORTER, Mr. Noil, BSc ACA *2000;* (Tax Fac), Flat 2, 12 Kidderpore Gardens, LONDON, NW3 7SR.
PORTER, Mr. Phillip Geoffrey, FCA *1974;* 15 Brackenwood Gardens, Portishead, BRISTOL, BS20 8FD.
•**PORTER, Mr. Richard James, BSc FCA** *1991;* PricewaterhouseCoopers LLP, 1 Embankment Place, LONDON, WC2N 6RH. See also PricewaterhouseCoopers
PORTER, Mr. Richard William, BCom ACA *1980;* White Thorn, The Warren, Ferring, WORTHING, WEST SUSSEX, BN12 5PQ.
PORTER, Mr. Robert, BSc ACA *2011;* Flat 7, 89 Park Hill, Clapham, LONDON, SW4 9NX.
PORTER, Mr. Robert, BA ACA *1981;* KPMG Poomchai Tax Ltd, 49F Empire Tower, 195 South Sathorn Road, BANGKOK 10120, THAILAND.
PORTER, Mr. Robert Charles, BSc ACA *1979;* 29 Bracken Gardens, LONDON, SW13 9HW.
PORTER, Mrs. Sarah Elizabeth, BSc ACA *1992;* Badgers Wood, Hanging Birch Lane, Horam, HEATHFIELD, EAST SUSSEX, TN21 0NT.
PORTER, Miss. Sarah Louise, BSc ACA *2006;* 124 Smisby Road, ASHBY-DE-LA-ZOUCH, LEICESTERSHIRE, LE65 2JN.
PORTER, Mr. Simon David Lynn, FCA *1977;* 1 Old Cottages Hardway, BRUTON, SOMERSET, BA10 0LW.
PORTER, Mr. Simon John, BA ACA *1985;* 15 Kendal Place, Putney, LONDON, SW15 2QZ.
PORTER, Mr. Simon Neil, MBA BSc ACA *1986;* Audio Visual Machines Ltd, 1-3 Old Lodge Place, St Margarets, TWICKENHAM, TW1 1RQ.
PORTER, Mr. Stanley, FCA *1956;* Nelson House, Station Road, CHIPPING CAMPDEN, GL55 6HY. (Life Member)
•**PORTER, Mr. Stephen Charles, FCA** *1980;* 18 Orakei Place, Welcome Bay, TAURANGA 3112, NEW ZEALAND.
PORTER, Mr. Stewart Charles, BSc FCA *1977;* Chasers Plaistow Road, Dunsfold, GODALMING, GU8 4PF.
PORTER, Mr. Terence George, BA FCA *1978;* 100 The Avenue, PINNER, HA5 5BJ.
•**PORTER, Mr. Timothy Henry Ralph, MA FCA** *1977;* The Manor, School Lane, Stapleton, LEICESTER, LE9 8JR.
PORTER, Mr. Timothy John, BSc ACA *1995;* 8 Saxon Road, WINCHESTER, SO23 7DJ.
PORTER, Mr. Trevor Ernest, FCA *1968;* 18 Edgewood Drive, Hucknall, NOTTINGHAM, NG15 6HY.
PORTER, Mr. Wayne, ACA CA(SA) *2009;* 5 Bullescroft Road, EDGWARE, MIDDLESEX, HA8 8RN.
PORTERGILL, Mr. Richard George, FCA *1964;* Abbey View, Henley Road, MARLOW, BUCKINGHAMSHIRE, SL7 2DQ. (Life Member)
PORTHOUSE, Ms. Sarah Louise, BSc ACA *2010;* Middle Flat, 9 Miranda Road, LONDON, N19 3RA.
•**PORTIS, Mr. Andrew Richard, FCA** *1972;* 3 Bay View Road, BROADSTAIRS, KENT, CT10 2EA.
PORTLOCK, Mr. David Maurice, FCA *1971;* 4 Lindley Farm Cottages, Cinder Lane, Lindley, OTLEY, NORTH YORKSHIRE, LS21 2QN.
PORTMAN, Mr. Frank, FCA *1959;* 56 Front Street, Whitburn, SUNDERLAND, SR6 7JF. (Life Member)
PORTMAN, Mr. Matthew Thomas, ACA *2007;* Rosie Lea, Castle Hill View, SIDMOUTH, EX10 9PP.
PORTMAN, Mr. Richard Harry, BSc MCMI FCA *1987;* (Tax Fac), 1A Claverdon Drive, Little Aston Park, SUTTON COLDFIELD, B74 3AH.
•**PORTMAN, Mrs. Sally Angela, BSocSc FCA** *1986;* Colin J B Spinks & Co Ltd, St James House, 65 Mere Green Road, SUTTON COLDFIELD, WEST MIDLANDS, B75 5BY.
•**PORTNOY, Mr. Martin Jacob, BA(Econ) ACA ATII** *1999;* Ernst & Young LLP, 100 Barbirolli Square, MANCHESTER, M2 3EY. See also Ernst & Young Europe LLP
PORTON, Mrs. Lesley Ann, BSc ACA *1992;* 29 Clayworth Road, Brunton Park, Gosforth, NEWCASTLE UPON TYNE, NE3 5AB.
PORTON, Mr. Martin Carl, BSc ACA *1991;* 29 Clayworth Road, Brunton Park Gosforth, NEWCASTLE UPON TYNE, NE3 5AB.
PORTSMOUTH, Mr. Charles Sinclair, BA FCA *1984;* 71 Grange Park Avenue, LONDON, N21 2LN.
PORTUPHY, Miss. Alice Ohui, MSc BSc ACA *2006;* 216 Malyons Road, LONDON, SE13 7XF.

PORTUS, Miss. Abigail, BCom ACA *2002;* 32 Riverslea Road, Binley, COVENTRY, CV3 1LD.
PORTWAY, Miss. Abigail, BSc ACA *2002;* 23 The Causeway, Burwell, CAMBRIDGE, CAMBRIDGESHIRE, CB5 0DU.
PORTWAY, Mrs. Rachel Jayne, BSc ACA *2001;* 4 Hen Parc Lane, Upper Killay, SWANSEA, SA2 7EY.
PORTWAY, Mr. Rhys Thomas, BSc(Hons) ACA *2001;* 4 Hen Parc Lane, Upper Killay, SWANSEA, SA2 7EY.
PORTWOOD, Mrs. Ann Elizabeth, ACA *1984;* 28 Wright Lane, Grange Farm, Oadby, LEICESTER, LE2 4TU.
PORTWOOD, Mrs. Ann Mary, BSc FCA *1987;* 42 Oakland Drive, WARRANDYTE, VIC 3113, AUSTRALIA.
POSANER, Mr. Peter Winston, BA FCA *1968;* 1526 Stratford Road, Hall Green, BIRMINGHAM, B28 9ET.
POSER, Mr. Daniel Henry, MA ACA *1992;* 20 Springfield Road, LONDON, NW8 0QN.
POSGATE, Mr. John Sidney Stapleton, FCA *1970;* 12 Reynolds Road, BEACONSFIELD, HP9 2NJ.
•**POSNANSKY, Mr. Nicholas Simon, FCA** *1972;* Sobell Rhodes LLP, Monument House, 215 Marsh Road, PINNER, MIDDLESEX, HA5 5NE. See also Mayfair Wealth Management Limited
POSNER, Mr. David Howard, FCA *1970;* 14 Glover Road, PINNER, HA5 1LF.
•**POSNER, Mr. Jack Leon, FCA** *1971;* LeonSchiller, 100 High Ash Drive, LEEDS, LS17 8RE.
•**POSNER, Mr. Jack Louis, FCA** *1954;* (Tax Fac), Posner Lyons, 38a Northiam, Woodside Park, LONDON, N12 7HA.
POSNER, Mr. Melvyn Malcolm, FCA *1966;* 3 Fletcher Street, WOOLLAHRA, NSW 2025, AUSTRALIA.
POSNETT, Mr. Mark William, BSc ACA *2004;* 47 Broadway, Houghton Conquest, BEDFORD, MK45 3LT.
•**POSPISIL, Mr. Stephen Paul, MA MBA ACA** *1985;* Sheepshead House, Lees Road, Brabourne Lees, ASHFORD, KENT, TN25 6QE.
POSSO, Mr. Maurice Henry, BSc FCA *1982;* 4/3 Jumpers, 1 Withams Road, GIBRALTAR, GIBRALTAR.
POST, Mr. Anthony Graham, FCA *1972;* C A C I Ltd, C A C I House, Avonmore Road, LONDON, W14 8TS.
POST, Mr. David Kenneth, BSc ACA *1989;* (Tax Fac), 17/F Tesbury Centre, 28 Queen's Road East, WAN CHAI, HONG KONG ISLAND, HONG KONG SAR.
POST, Mr. Geoffrey James, BA ACA *1990;* Church Hall, Church Road, Wormingford, COLCHESTER, CO6 3AZ.
POST, Mr. Jack Alfred Norman, FCA *1952;* 17 Pangbourne Hill, Pangbourne, READING, RG8 7AS. (Life Member)
POST, Mr. Simon Norman, BSc ACA *1990;* 5 Grimwood Road, TWICKENHAM, TW1 1BY.
POSTANS, Mr. Dean, ACA *2008;* 156c Sinclair Road, LONDON, W14 0NL.
POSTLE, Mr. Michael Geraint, LLB ACA *2000;* 12 Arundel Terrace, BRIGHTON, BN2 1GA.
POSTLETHWAITE, Mr. Alan, FCA *1950;* 29 Belmont Avenue, MIDDLESBROUGH, CLEVELAND, TS5 8EN. (Life Member)
POSTLETHWAITE, Miss. Chloe, ACA *2010;* Flat 3, 3 Blackpool Road, LYTHAM ST. ANNES, FY8 4EH.
•**POSTLETHWAITE, Mr. David, FCA** *1971;* (Tax Fac), Colston Bush, Lacemaker House, 5-7 Chapel Street, MARLOW, BUCKINGHAMSHIRE, SL7 3HN.
POSTLETHWAITE, Mrs. Deborah Ann, ACA *1983;* 112 Marine Parade, LEIGH-ON-SEA, ESSEX, SS9 2RH.
POSTLETHWAITE, Miss. Emma Marion, BA(Hons) ACA *2003;* 5 Carnegie Close, SALE, CHESHIRE, M33 5TN.
POSTLETHWAITE, Mr. Henry Charles, BSc ACA *2000;* Financial Services Authority, 25 North Colonnade, LONDON, E14 5HS.
POSTLETHWAITE, Mr. Philip, FCA *1970;* 11 Balfour Manor, Station Road, SIDMOUTH, DEVON, EX10 8XW.
POSTLETHWAITE, Mr. Richard Thomas Andrew, FCA *1983;* 1, King's Arms Yard, LONDON, EC2R 7AF.
POSTLETHWAITE, Mr. Timothy John, BSc FCA *1989;* 10 Railway Terrace, Kemble, CIRENCESTER, GL7 6AU.
POSTLOVA, Mrs. Irena, BSc ACA *1992;* Brackenfell, 12 Woodland Way, PURLEY, CR8 2HU.
POSTOLOVSKY, Mr. Vladimir, ACA *1997;* 78 Alleyn Road, LONDON, SE21 8AH.
•**POSTON, Mr. Christopher Michael, BSc FCA** *1992;* Royce Peeling Green Limited, The Copper Room, Deva Centre, Trinity Way, MANCHESTER, M3 7BG. See also RPG Services Limited
POSTONES, Mr. Trevor George, FCA *1971;* C/O, Howell Dunn & Co Beecher House, Station Street, CRADLEY HEATH, B64 6AJ.
•**POTAMITIS, Mr. Rois, BSc ACA** *1990;* BDO Limited, 146 Arch Makarios III Avenue, Alpha Tower, 4th FLoor PO Box 51681, CY-3507 LIMASSOL, CYPRUS. See also BDO Philippides Limited
POTE, Mr. Kenneth Charles, FCA *1955;* Cottage 211, Silvermine Village, Private Bag 1, Noordhoek, CAPE TOWN, 7975 SOUTH AFRICA. (Life Member)
POTEL, Mr. Marc, BSc ACA *1998;* 35 Platts Lane, LONDON, NW3 7NN.
POTEL, Mr. Solomon Stanton, FCA *1955;* 4 Denning Close, Hall Road, LONDON, NW8 9PJ. (Life Member)
POTHAST, Miss. Milou, BA ACA *2011;* Avenue du Premier-Mars 6, 2000 NEUCHATEL, SWITZERLAND.
POTHECARY, Miss. Holly, BSc ACA *2011;* 19 Perrett Way, Ham Green Pill, BRISTOL, BS20 0HX.
•**POTIER, Mr. Andre William, FCA** *1955;* PO Box 5, Goodleigh Road, BARNSTAPLE, EX32 7XU.
POTJEWIJD, Mr. Yme Alexander, BSc ACA *2000;* (Tax Fac), with PricewaterhouseCoopers LLP, 31 Great George Street, BRISTOL, BS1 5QD.
POTKINS, Mr. Martin, BSc FCA *1986;* The Barns at the Croft Cheneys Lane, Forncett St. Mary, NORWICH, NR16 1JT.
POTT, Mr. Derek Raymond, BA FCA *1967;* 9 Soi 18 Seri 2 Road, Ramkamhaeng Road (24), Hua Mark Bangkapi, BANGKOK, 10250, THAILAND.
POTT, Mrs. Helen Felicity, BSc ACA *1982;* 34 Judges Walk, NORWICH, NR4 7QF.
•**POTT, Mrs. Julie Maxine, BA FCA** *1991;* (Tax Fac), RMT Accountants and Business Advisors Limited, Unit 2, Gosforth Park Avenue, NEWCASTLE UPON TYNE, NE12 8EG. See also RMT Accountants and Business Advisors
POTT, Mr. Steven Anthony, BA ACA *2005;* Interpublic Ltd, 84 Eccleston Square, LONDON, SW1V 1PX.
POTTAGE, Mr. John Francis, MA FCA ATII MSI *1991;* The Laurels, 11 Burgess Wood Road South, BEACONSFIELD, HP9 1EU.
POTTAGE, Mr. Shaun David, BSc ACA *1995;* 33 Berrall Way, BILLINGSHURST, RH14 9PQ.
POTTER, Mr. Alan Ernest, FCA *1960;* 7 Rothermead, PETWORTH, WEST SUSSEX, GU28 0EW.
POTTER, Mr. Andrew, BSc ACA *2005;* 23 Bondgate, SELBY, NORTH YORKSHIRE, YO8 3LX.
POTTER, Mr. Andrew Richard, BA ACA *1994;* 528 Doverwood Drive, OAKVILLE L6H 6N4, ON, CANADA.
POTTER, Ms. Angela Jane, BA ACA *1988;* Ibbespen House, The Hollow, Child Okeford, BLANDFORD FORUM, DT11 8EX.
POTTER, Mr. Anthony William, FCA *1975;* 23 Upper Hill Rise, RICKMANSWORTH, WD3 7NU.
POTTER, Mr. Ashley Brian, BA ACA *1992;* Bnp Paribas, 10 Harewood Avenue, LONDON, NW1 6AA.
•**POTTER, Mr. Barry James, BA FCA** *1982;* HW, 30 Camp Road, FARNBOROUGH, HAMPSHIRE, GU14 6EW. See also HW Corporate Finance LLP, Haines Watts, HW Consulting and Haines Watts Consulting
POTTER, Mr. Ben, MA(Hons) ACA *2003;* 26 The Oval, HARROGATE, NORTH YORKSHIRE, HG2 9BA.
POTTER, Mrs. Bernadette Cheryl, BA ACA *1991;* 9 Willow Bridge Road, Canonbury, LONDON, N1 2LB.
POTTER, Ms. Carly, BA(Hons) ACA *2010;* 11 Meadow Way, HORLEY, SURREY, RH6 9JA.
•**POTTER, Mr. Charles Paul, BSc(Econ) FCA MLIA(Dip)** *1981;* Humphrey & Co, 7-9 The Avenue, EASTBOURNE, EAST SUSSEX, BN21 3YA.
POTTER, Miss. Cheryl Yvonne, BSc ACA *1995;* Mulberry Lodge, Old Avenue, WEYBRIDGE, KT13 0PS.
POTTER, Miss. Christine Diane, BA ACA *1992;* Nokia Siemens Networks, Locked Bag 34, Pyrmont, SYDNEY, NSW 2000, AUSTRALIA.
POTTER, Mr. Christopher Alan, MBA BA FCA CPA *1977;* 93 Ridge Hill Road, Maida Vale, PERTH, WA 6057, AUSTRALIA.
POTTER, Mr. Christopher Ian, BA(Hons) ACA *2003;* 18 Dewberry Close, BLYTH, NORTHUMBERLAND, NE24 3XJ.
•**POTTER, Mr. Christopher William, MA FCA** *1990;* PricewaterhouseCoopers LLP, Hays Galleria, 1 Hays Lane, LONDON, SE1 2RD. See also PricewaterhouseCoopers
POTTER, Mrs. Claire Louise, BSc ACA *1994;* Isode Limited, 5 Castle Business Village, 36 Station Road, HAMPTON, MIDDLESEX, TW12 2BX.
POTTER, Miss. Cynthia Elizabeth, FCA *1992;* c/o Saint & Co, Sterling House, Wavell Drive, Rosehill, CARLISLE, CA1 2SA.
POTTER, Mr. David Cameron, MA FCA *1975;* Campions, Tanyard Hill, Shorne, GRAVESEND, DA12 3EN.
POTTER, Mr. David Christopher, BSc FCA *1981;* 18 Harrowby Drive, Westlands, NEWCASTLE, ST5 3JE.
POTTER, Mrs. Denise, BA ACA *1986;* 37 Rookery Drive, Penwortham, PRESTON, PR1 9LU.
POTTER, Mrs. Diane Joy, BA ACA *1988;* Cambridge RF Limited, 10 Teversham Road, Fulbourn, CAMBRIDGE, CB21 5EB.
POTTER, Mr. Edward Marlin, ACA *2008;* Tudor House, 34 East Street, THAME, OXFORDSHIRE, OX9 3JT.
POTTER, Mr. Edwin, BA(Hons) FCA CTA *1971;* 3 Sopers Lane, Waterloo, POOLE, BH17 7EW. (Life Member)
POTTER, Mr. Graeme, BA FCA *1973;* 22 Hemmeberreg, L-5444 SCHENGEN, LUXEMBOURG.
•**POTTER, Mr. Graham Charles, BSc ACA** *1986;* Graham Potter & Co Limited, 3 Sandringham Road, Birkdale, SOUTHPORT, MERSEYSIDE, PR8 2JZ.
•**POTTER, Mr. Graham Henry, BSc ACA** *1983;* (Tax Fac), N.R. Barton & Co, 19-21 Bridgeman Terrace, WIGAN, WN1 1TD.
POTTER, Miss. Helen Elizabeth, BSc ACA *1989;* Wayside, Clandon Road, West Clandon, GUILDFORD, GU4 7UW.
POTTER, Mr. Iain Cameron, BSc ACA *2007;* Campions, Tanyard Hill, Shorne, DARTFORD, DA12 3EN.
POTTER, Mr. Ian, BEng ACA *1994;* The Gardener's Cottage, 11 Croysdale Terrace, Eggborough, GOOLE, NORTH HUMBERSIDE, DN14 0LF.
POTTER, Mr. Ian Roger, BA ACA *1994;* 17 Victoria Mill Drive, Willaston, NANTWICH, CW5 6RR.
•**POTTER, Mr. James Anthony, FCA** *1969;* (Tax Fac), Potter McGregor & Co., 89 Efflinch Lane, Barton under Needwood, BURTON-ON-TRENT, STAFFORDSHIRE, DE13 8EU.
POTTER, Mr. James Philip, BSc(Hons) ACA *2001;* with Ernst & Young, Level 28, AL Attar Bus Tower, Sheikh Zayed Road, P.O. Box 9267, DUBAI UNITED ARAB EMIRATES.
POTTER, Mr. Jason, BA(Hons) ACA *2011;* Flat 23, Harbour House, 150 Hotwell Road, BRISTOL, BS8 4UB.
POTTER, Mr. John Arthur, FCA *1961;* 86 Willow Way, Hale, FARNHAM, GU9 0NT.
•**POTTER, Mr. John Lionel, FCA** *1969;* 5 Brunswick Close, Lower Wick, WORCESTER, WR2 4DU.
•**POTTER, Mr. John Michael, BSc FCA** *1980;* (Tax Fac), Thomas Westcott, 26-28 Southernhay East, EXETER, DEVON, EX1 1NS.
POTTER, Mr. Jonathan Dominic, BCom ACA *1991;* 9 Willow Bridge Road, Canonbury, LONDON, N1 2LB.
•**POTTER, Mr. Keith Sydney, FCA** *1962;* K.S. Potter, 16 Peckarmans Wood, LONDON, SE26 6RY.
POTTER, Mr. Kenneth James, ACA *1981;* 18 Brimstone Close, ORPINGTON, BR6 7ST.
POTTER, Mrs. Lisa Jane, BCom(Hons) ACA *2003;* 26 The Oval, HARROGATE, NORTH YORKSHIRE, HG2 9BA.
POTTER, Miss. Louisa Dawn, BSc ACA *1999;* 19 Cunningham Hill Road, ST. ALBANS, HERTFORDSHIRE, AL1 5BX.
POTTER, Mr. Martin Julian Keith, BA ACA *1991;* Kleparivska Street 25, Apartment 22, 79007 LVIV, UKRAINE.
POTTER, Mrs. Mary Louise, BA ACA *1997;* 21 Clandon Road, GUILDFORD, SURREY, GU1 2DR.
POTTER, Mr. Matthew James, ACA *2009;* 3 Avonmore Gardens, LONDON, W14 8RU.
POTTER, Mr. Michael Adrian, FCA *1976;* Erkinholm House, Drove Road, LANGHOLM, DUMFRIESSHIRE, DG13 0JW.
POTTER, Mr. Michael Frederick, FCA *1976;* (Tax Fac), Channel 20-20, 20-20 House, 26/28 Talbot Lane, LEICESTER, LE1 4LR.
POTTER, Mr. Michael John William, BSc FCA *1976;* Blackhall Spinney, Blackhall Lane, SEVENOAKS, TN15 0HP.
POTTER, Mr. Neil, ACA *2009;* 21 Pearl Street, BATLEY, WEST YORKSHIRE, WF17 8HJ.
POTTER, Mr. Neil Anthony, BA(Hons) ACA *2001;* 36 Harding Avenue, Rawmarsh, ROTHERHAM, SOUTH YORKSHIRE, S62 7DN.
POTTER, Mr. Nicholas Charles, ACA *2009;* Flat 1, 163 Horn Lane, LONDON, W3 6PP.
POTTER, Mr. Nicholas John, BSc ACA *1997;* Spring Cottage, Winkfield Row, BRACKNELL, BERKSHIRE, RG42 6NE.
•**POTTER, Mrs. Pamela Margaret, FCA** *1977;* Michael Adamson & Co, 224 Ferry Road, Hullbridge, HOCKLEY, ESSEX, SS5 6ND.
POTTER, Mr. Paul David, BA ACA *1992;* 3029 Meadow Drive, NANAIMO U9R 3C6, BC, CANADA.
•**POTTER, Mr. Philip, FCA** *1972;* (Tax Fac), Philip Potter, 20 Egerton Road, Monton, Eccles, MANCHESTER, M30 9LR.
POTTER, Mr. Richard George, ACA *2008;* 3 Wood Mead, EPPING, ESSEX, CM16 6TD.
POTTER, Mr. Richard Vernon, BCom FCA *1960;* Carrera House, 76 South Road, Oundle, PETERBOROUGH, PE8 4BP. (Life Member)
POTTER, Mr. Richard William Grenville, FCA *1959;* Flat 1 Bridgefoot, London Road, ST. IVES, CAMBRIDGESHIRE, PE27 5EP. (Life Member)
•**POTTER, Mr. Robert John, FCA** *1976;* (Tax Fac), Potter & Co, 79 Friar Gate, DERBY, DE1 1FL. See also Potter Associates Ltd
POTTER, Mr. Robert John, BSc ACA *1993;* 28 Malcolm Drive, SURBITON, KT6 6QS.
POTTER, Miss. Rosemary Ann, BA ACA *1996;* Egererstrasse 3B, 82319 STARNBERG, GERMANY.
POTTER, Miss. Sarah, MA ACA *2011;* 24 South Island Place, LONDON, SW9 0DX.
POTTER, Miss. Sarah Jane, MEng ACA *2001;* 35 Charteris Road, LONDON, NW6 7EY.
POTTER, Mr. Sean Robert, ACA CA(SA) *2010;* 21 Ghyll Crescent, HORSHAM, WEST SUSSEX, RH13 6BG.
POTTER, Mrs. Sharon Louise, BA FCA *1980;* Olympus Avenue, Tachbrook Park, WARWICK, WARWICKSHIRE, CV34 6RJ.
POTTER, Mr. Simon Alexander Bailie, BA ACA *2010;* 14 St. Martins Close, Broadmayne, DORCHESTER, DORSET, DT2 8DG.
POTTER, Mr. Simon James, BA ACA *2001;* 1 Kestrel Close, Ash Vale, ALDERSHOT, GU12 5RS.
POTTER, Mrs. Sing Ying, BA ACA *2002;* Mazars Llp Times House, Throwley Way, SUTTON, SM1 4JQ.
POTTER, Mr. Stephen, ACA *1988;* The Hollies, Holly Lane, Alvechurch, BIRMINGHAM, B48 7HH.
POTTER, Mr. Stephen, FCA *1967;* 50 Temperley Road, LONDON, SW12 8QD. (Life Member)
•**POTTER, Mr. Stephen Dewar, FCA** *1983;* Carter Nicholls Limited, Victoria House, Stanbridge Industrial Park, Staplefield Lane, Staplefield, HAYWARDS HEATH WEST SUSSEX RH17 6AS.
POTTER, Mr. Stephen Edward, BCom ACA *1981;* I M I Plc, Lakeside, Solihull Parkway, Birmingham Business Park, BIRMINGHAM, B37 7XZ.
POTTER, Mr. Stephen John, ACA *1983;* 120 Bromham Road, Biddenham, BEDFORD, MK40 4AH.
•**POTTER, Mr. Stephen John, BA ACA** *1993;* Inspire Finance Partners LLP, 36 Lucerne Avenue, BICESTER, OXFORDSHIRE, OX26 3EL.
•**POTTER, Mr. Terence Sefton, BCom ACA** *1985;* (Tax Fac), with Sefton Potter Advisors Limited, 9 Wimpole Street, LONDON, W1G 9SR.
•**POTTER, Mr. Timothy James, BA FCA** *1993;* Hurst & Company Accountants LLP, Lancashire Gate, 21 Tiviot Dale, STOCKPORT, CHESHIRE, SK1 1TD.
POTTER, Mr. William David, BSc ACA *1995;* Trotwood The Firs, Odiham, HOOK, HAMPSHIRE, RG29 1PP.
•**POTTER, Mr. William Sydney, FCA** *1955;* Potter & Co, 79 Friar Gate, DERBY, DE1 1FL. See also Potter Associates Ltd
POTTICARY, Mr. Richard, BSc ACA *2006;* 10 Fernside Way, Wootton Bridge, RYDE, ISLE OF WIGHT, PO33 4QT.
•**POTTINGER, Mr. Thomas Charles Alston, BEng ACA** *2002;* (Tax Fac), Porter Garland Limited, Portland House, Park Street, BAGSHOT, SURREY, GU19 5PG.
•**POTTLE, Mr. Matthew Francis, BA ACA** *1988;* PricewaterhouseCoopers, BusinessCommunityCenter, Katerinska 40/466, 120 00 PRAGUE, CZECH REPUBLIC.
•**POTTON, Mr. Graham Reginald, FCA** *1972;* G.R. Potton & Co, 2 Harestone Valley Road, CATERHAM, SURREY, CR3 6HB.
•**POTTS, Mr. Andrew, FCA** *1986;* Moore Stephens LLP, 150 Aldersgate Street, LONDON, EC1A 4AB. See also Moore Stephens & Co
POTTS, Mr. Charles Norman, FCA *1948;* 247 Prenton Hall Road, PRENTON, CH43 3AQ. (Life Member)
POTTS, Mr. Christopher Brian, BSc ACA *2006;* with KPMG LLP, Arlington Business Park, Theale, READING, RG7 4SD.
POTTS, Mr. Daniel, BSc ACA *2007;* Jadaal, Roman Road, Maydensole, DOVER, CT15 5HP.
POTTS, Mr. Daniel James, ACA *2010;* Flat 1, 9a Moss Hall Crescent, LONDON, N12 8NY.
POTTS, Mr. David Clive, FCA *1972;* 4 Meadow Park, Cabus, PRESTON, PR3 1RE.

•POTTS, Mr. David Michael, FCA 1987; DMP Accounting, 5a Parkway, Porters Wood, ST. ALBANS, HERTFORDSHIRE, AL3 6PA.
•POTTS, Mr. David Robert, MA FCA 1977; Adams & Co Accountants Limited, 2 Millers Bridge, BOOTLE, MERSEYSIDE, L20 8LH.
POTTS, Mr. Derek, MA ACA 1985; 55 East Street, Coggeshall, COLCHESTER, CO6 1SJ.
•POTTS, Mr. Garry, FCA 1973; Baker Tilly Tax & Advisory Services LLP, Steam Mill, Steam Mill Street, CHESTER, CH3 5AN.
POTTS, Mr. Garry Raymond, MBA BA(Hons) ACA ACMA 2007; 40 Greenlands Road, STAINES, MIDDLESEX, TW18 4LR.
•POTTS, Mr. Graham, BA FCA 1988; Lerman Quaile, 56 Hamilton Square, BIRKENHEAD, MERSEYSIDE, CH41 5AS.
•POTTS, Mr. Graham Mark, BSc ACA CTA 1985; Wessex Commercial Solutions Ltd, Suite 29, Yeovil Innovation Centre, Barracks Close, Copse Road, YEOVIL SOMERSET BA22 8RN.
POTTS, Mr. Ian Garry Christopher, BSc ACA 2005; 17 Ellesmere Avenue, CHESTER, CH2 2DA.
POTTS, Mr. Ian William, FCA 1966; 18 Russley Green, WOKINGHAM, BERKSHIRE, RG40 3HT.
POTTS, Mr. James William, ACA 2011; 15 Thomas Street, Annfield Plain, STANLEY, COUNTY DURHAM, DH9 7SN.
POTTS, Mr. John David, FCA 1963; Ernest Thorpe Transport Ltd, Halifax Road, Thurgoland, SHEFFIELD, S35 7AJ.
POTTS, Mr. John Robinson, FCA 1952; Tilbury Cottage, 245 Darkes Lane, POTTERS BAR, EN6 1BZ. (Life Member)
POTTS, Mr. Jonathan David Barrington, BSocSc ACA 1988; 28 Langham Road, TEDDINGTON, MIDDLESEX, TW11 9HQ.
POTTS, Miss. Karen, ACA 1993; 36 Denning Mead, ANDOVER, HAMPSHIRE, SP10 3LG.
•POTTS, Mrs. Karen Marie, BSc FCA ATII 1993; East Lodge, Bedlars Green, Great Hallingbury, BISHOP'S STORTFORD, CM22 7TL.
POTTS, Miss. Lynne Davina, MBA BA ACA 1990; Greater Manchester Police, Chester House, Boyer Street, MANCHESTER, M16 0RE.
POTTS, Mr. Martin Terence, BSc FCA 1989; BPP Professional Education, 32 Colmore Circus Queensway, BIRMINGHAM, B4 6BN.
POTTS, Mr. Michael Charles, BA FCA 1981; 36 Chatsworth Drive, MARKET HARBOROUGH, LEICESTERSHIRE, LE16 8BS.
POTTS, Mr. Michael Stuart, DL FCA 1963; (Member of Council 1988 - 1992), Prospect House The Parade, Parkgate, NESTON, CH64 6SA.
POTTS, Mr. Neil Sydney, BSc FCA 1976; 28 Keswick Road, High Lane, STOCKPORT, SK6 8AP.
POTTS, Mr. Philip Ian Thomas, FCA 1963; Park Lodge Wold Road, BARROW-UPON-HUMBER, SOUTH HUMBERSIDE, DN19 7BT. (Life Member)
•POTTS, Mr. Raymond David, BSc(Hons) FCA 1979; (Tax Fac), Potts & Co, 6 Jacobs Yard, Middle Barton, CHIPPING NORTON, OXFORDSHIRE, OX7 7BY. See also Oxford Book-Keepers Limited
POTTS, Mr. Reginald Wilfred, FCA 1955; Tebbs Copyhold, Ismays Road, Ightham, SEVENOAKS, KENT, TN15 9BD. (Life Member)
POTTS, Mr. Simon Howard, ACA 1998; Group Finance (3rd Floor), Lloyds Register of Shipping, 71 Fenchurch Street, LONDON, EC3M 4BS.
POTTS, Dr. William Henry, ACA 1985; 59 St. Johns Road, SEVENOAKS, TN13 3NB.
•POTWOROWSKI, Mr. Tadeusz Krzysztof, FCA 1971; Copperfield, Wayside Gardens, GERRARDS CROSS, SL9 7NG.
POUCHER, Miss. Nicola Joanne, BA(Hons) ACA 2002; Ivy Cottage Main Road, Burgh-on-Bain, MARKET RASEN, LINCOLNSHIRE, LN8 6JY.
POUFOU, Miss. Mary, ACA 2010; 28 Ifigenias street, Acropolis, 2007 NICOSIA, CYPRUS.
•POUGNET, Mr. Jacques, FCA CF 1978; BDO De Chazal du Mee, P.O. Box 799, 10 Frere Felix, De Valois Street, PORT LOUIS, MAURITIUS.
•POULLIS, Mr. Christakis, FCA 1978; AIMS - Chris Poullis, 30 Tolworth Rise South, SURBITON, SURREY, KT5 9NN.
POULMAN, Mr. Stelios Renos, BA ACA 1989; National Grid Plc, Grand Buildings, 1-3 Strand, LONDON, WC2N 5EH.
POULOS, Mr. Arthur, MSc BSc ACA 2000; 43550 Thomas Creek Drive, SCIO, OR 97374, UNITED STATES.
POULOS, Mr. Paul Jason, ACA CA(AUS) 2010; 62b-62d Priory Road, LONDON, NW6 3RE.
POULSOM, Mr. Christopher Richard John, BSc(Hons) ACA 2001; 145 Knole Lane, BRISTOL, BS10 6JN.
•POULSOM, Mr. David Ambrose, BA ACA 1987; CWDC, 2nd Floor, City Exchange, 11 Albion Street, LEEDS, LS1 5ES.
POULSOM, Mr. David Frederick, FCA 1964; Campden Farm Cottage, Barton-on-the-Heath, MORETON-IN-MARSH, GLOUCESTERSHIRE, GL56 0PN. (Life Member)
POULSOM, Miss. Janette Elizabeth, BA ACA 1993; 102 Amherst Street, CAMMERAY, NSW 2062, AUSTRALIA.
POULSOM, Mrs. Verena Ann, BA ACA 1988; 81 Brooklands Crescent, Fullwood, SHEFFIELD, S10 4GF.
POULSON, Miss. Charlotte Louise, BA ACA 1992; 147 Stanley Road, CAMBRIDGE, CB5 8LF.
POULSON, Mr. Simon Mark, BSc ACA 1993; 43 Heol Y Coed, Rhiwbina, CARDIFF, CF14 6HQ.
POULTEN, Mr. Andrew William, BA ACA 1986; Grange Lodge, Rowton Lane, Rowton, CHESTER, CH3 6AT.
POULTEN, Mr. David John, BSc(Econ) ACA 2001; Barclays Capital, 1620 26th Street, Suite 2000N, SANTA MONICA, CA 90404, UNITED STATES.
POULTEN, Mrs. Julia Michelle, BSc ACA 1986; Grange Lodge, Rowton Lane, Rowton, CHESTER, CH3 6AT.
POULTER, Mr. Andrew David, BSc ACA 1980; 10 Burnalta Crescent, BURNSIDE, SA 5066, AUSTRALIA.
•POULTER, Mr. Anthony Malcolm, BA FCA 1973; Iliffe Poulter & Co., 1A Bonnington Road, Mapperley, NOTTINGHAM, NG3 5JR.
POULTER, Mr. Barrie, BSc ACA 1991; (Tax Fac), 18 Syke Cluan, IVER, SL0 9EH.
POULTER, Mr. Clifford Edwin, FCA 1967; Herricks, Poplar Close, Baughurst, TADLEY, RG26 5LH.
POULTER, Mr. David Walter, BSc ACA 1987; Reckitt Benckiser, 103-105 Bath Road, SLOUGH, SL1 3UH.
•POULTER, Mr. John Alfred, FCA CTA 1973; (Tax Fac), Rothman Pantall LLP, Avebury House, 6 St. Peter Street, WINCHESTER, HAMPSHIRE, SO23 8BN.
POULTER, Mr. Jonathan, ACA 2008; (Tax Fac), Rothman Pantall & Co Avebury House, 6 St. Peter Street, WINCHESTER, SO23 8BN.
POULTER, Miss. Julia, ACA 2008; P K F Accountants & Business Advisors Farringdon Place, 20 Farringdon Road, LONDON, EC1M 3AP.
POULTER, Mrs. Linda Jane, ACA 1992; 32 West Street, Over, CAMBRIDGE, CB24 5PL.
POULTER, Mr. Neil, BSc ACA 1994; Wogen Group Ltd, 4 The Sanctuary, LONDON, SW1P 3JS.
POULTER, Mr. Nicholas Robert, ACA 2009; 21 Windy Wood, GODALMING, SURREY, GU7 1XX.
POULTER, Mr. Nigel Mark, BA ACA 1986; 32 West Street, Over, CAMBRIDGE, CB24 5PL.
POULTER, Mrs. Rosalind, ACA 2008; 14 Westman Road, WINCHESTER, HAMPSHIRE, SO22 6DT.
POULTER, Mrs. Sandra, BA ACA 1995; 11 Knox Close, Church Crookham, FLEET, GU52 6TR.
POULTER, Mr. Steven Matthew, MA ACA ATII 1999; (Tax Fac), 22 Dover Road, SHEFFIELD, S11 8RH.
POULTNEY, Mr. Nigel Charles, BSc ACA 1981; Quadnetics Group plc, Haydon House, 5 Alcester Road, STUDLEY, WARWICKSHIRE, B80 7AN.
POULTON, Mr. Antony Robert James, FCA 1965; 3 Southlands Drive, Timsbury, BATH, BA2 0HB.
POULTON, Mr. Christopher Julian, BSc ACA 1986; 24 Russet Close, MARKET HARBOROUGH, LE16 7JA.
•POULTON, Mr. Clive James, FCA 1966; Evans & Co, 51 Brunswick Road, GLOUCESTER, GL1 1JS.
POULTON, Mr. Craig John, BA ACA 1986; Liverpool Victoria Friendly Society Ltd, Frizzell House, County Gates, BOURNEMOUTH, BH1 2NF.
POULTON, Mr. Derek William, FCA 1954; 15 Ratcliff Lawns, Southam, CHELTENHAM, GL52 3PA. (Life Member)
POULTON, Mr. Edward Matthew, BSc ACA 2010; Flat 1 Sprewell House, Lytton Grove, LONDON, SW15 2EU.
POULTON, Mr. Geoffrey Frederick, FCA 1960; Northend House, Woodford, BERKELEY, GLOUCESTERSHIRE, GL13 9JN. (Life Member)
POULTON, Miss. Hannah, ACA 1999; Cobra Holdings Plc, 110 Fenchurch Street, LONDON, EC3M 5JT.
POULTON, Mr. Jamie Dominic, BSc(Hons) ACA 2000; with Muras Baker Jones, Regent House, Bath Avenue, WOLVERHAMPTON, WV1 4EG.
POULTON, Mr. John Joseph, BSc ACA 1996; 39a Cherry Orchard, LICHFIELD, STAFFORDSHIRE, WS14 9AN.
POULTON, Mr. Malcolm John, MBA BSc ACA 1985; 1 Red House Drive, Red House Farm, WHITLEY BAY, NE25 9XL.
POULTON, Mrs. Margaret Mary, BA ACA 1984; 24 Russet Close, MARKET HARBOROUGH, LE16 7JA.
POULTON, Mrs. Rachel June, BSc ACA 1997; 39a Cherry Orchard, LICHFIELD, STAFFORDSHIRE, WS14 9AN.
•POULTON, Mr. Simon Nicholas, BA FCA CF 1980; Poulton & Co, 15 Oakdene, BEACONSFIELD, BUCKINGHAMSHIRE, HP9 2BZ. See also Starfield Management Ltd
POUND, Mr. Daniel Robert Dudley, BSc(Hons) ACA 2000; 38 Spencer Road, LONDON, SW18 2SW.
POUND, Mr. Dudley Clifford, FCA 1973; Great Warley Place, Great Warley Street, Great Warley BRENTWOOD, Essex, CM13 3JP.
POUND, Mr. John Adrian, BSc ACA 1994; 19 Howe Place, BRONXVILLE, NY 10708, UNITED STATES.
•POUND, Mr. Robert John, BSc(Econ) ACA 1999; with KPMG LLP, One Snowhill, Snow Hill Queensway, BIRMINGHAM, B4 6GN.
POUNDALL, Mr. Kevin, BSc ACA 1994; 5 Shardlow Close, STONE, ST15 8GA.
POUNDER, Mr. Daniel John, MChem ACA 2003; 16 Birley Road, LONDON, N20 0EZ.
•POUNDER, Mr. Ian Martin, FCA 1984; RNS, 50-54 Oswald Road, SCUNTHORPE, NORTH LINCOLNSHIRE, DN15 7PQ.
POUNDER, Mr. Stephen, BA ACA 1992; with Kingston Smith & Partners LLP, Devonshire House, 60 Goswell Road, LONDON, EC1M 7AD.
POUNDS, Mr. Colin George, FCA 1967; Padley Cottage Main Road, Nether Padley Grindleford, HOPE VALLEY, DERBYSHIRE, S32 2HE.
POUPARD, Mr. Patrick Vincent, MBA FCA 1971; 33 Tuffnells Way, HARPENDEN, AL5 3HA.
POUPAS, Mr. Andreas, BSc ACA 2011; 5 Anexartisias Street, Lymbia, Nicosia, 2566 NICOSIA, CYPRUS.
POURIAN, Ms. Lorita, BSc ACA 2004; 7 Burford Gardens, LONDON, N13 4LR.
POURKARIMI, Mrs. Deborah Jane, MA ACA DChA 1987; Youthnet UK, 50 Featherstone Street, LONDON, EC1Y 8RT.
•POUROS, Mr. George Theodorou, BSc FCA 1999; Grant Thornton, P.O. Box 23907, 1687 NICOSIA, CYPRUS.
•POVAH, Mr. David Glyn, FCA 1968; Ember Cottage, 12 Marine Crescent, SEAFORD, BN25 1DA.
POVAH, Miss. Karen, BSc ACA 1993; 24 Hallgate Close, Oakwood, DERBY, DE21 2QY.
POVALL, Miss. Michelle, ACA 2008; 2728 McKinnon Street, Apt 419, DALLAS, TX 75201, UNITED STATES.
POVER, Mrs. Nicola, BSc ACA 1994; St Antoni Maria Claret 35, pral. 2a, 08025 BARCELONA, SPAIN.
POVER, Miss. Pamela Victoria, BSc ACA CIOT 1985; 5 Dunham Rise, Racefield Road, ALTRINCHAM, WA14 2BB.
POVEY, Mr. Adrian Martin, BSc FCA 1991; Chamonix Estates Ltd, The Maltings, Hyde Hall Farm, Sandon, BUNTINGFORD, HERTFORDSHIRE SG9 0RU.
•POVEY, Mr. Alan Michael, ACA 1981; (Tax Fac), Povey Little, 12 Hatherley Road, SIDCUP, KENT, DA14 4DT. See also Complete Payroll Services Ltd
•ⒹPOVEY, Mr. Craig James, ACA 1993; Chantrey Vellacott DFK LLP, 35 Calthorpe Road, Edgbaston, BIRMINGHAM, WEST MIDLANDS, B15 1TS.
POVEY, Mr. Timothy Richard Michael, MA FCA 1996; 57 Canbury Park Road, KINGSTON UPON THAMES, KT2 6LQ.
POVOAS, Mr. Graham Stanley, FCA 1964; 17 Wilson Place, TWO ROCKS, WA 6037, AUSTRALIA.
POW, Miss. Amanda Louise, ACA 2010; 33 Hillbury Road, LONDON, SW17 8JT.
•POW, Mr. Andrew James, BA ACA 1992; The Hall Liddy Partnership, 12 St. John Street, MANCHESTER, M3 4DY. See also Hall Liddy
POWDRELL, Mr. Richard John, BSc ACA 1989; 3 Linden Road, Redbourn, ST ALBANS, AL3 7PL.
POWDRILL, Mr. Philip Eric, BSc FCA 1986; 57, Godwins Way, Stamford Bridge, YORK, YO41 1DA.
POWDRILL, Mr. Roger Arthur, FCA 1972; The Willows, Station Road, Woldingham, CATERHAM, SURREY, CR3 7DE.
POWE, Mr. Nicholas Talbot, ACA 1989; 97 Ilsham Road, TORQUAY, TQ1 2JD.
•POWE, Mrs. Sheena Durenda Isobel, ACA 1987; SP Accounting, Hermida, 97 Ilsham Road, Wellswood, TORQUAY, TQ1 2JD.
POWELL, Mr. Adam John Craigen, ACA 2008; 666 Greenwich St, Apt 932, NEW YORK, NY 10014, UNITED STATES.
•POWELL, Mr. Aidan James, BA FCA 1988; Holmes Widlake Limited, 3 Sharrow Lane, SHEFFIELD, S11 8AE.
POWELL, Mr. Alexander, BA(Hons) ACA 2011; 35 Wolds Rise, MATLOCK, DERBYSHIRE, DE4 3HJ.
POWELL, Miss. Alison, BSc(Econ) FCA 1998; 32 Craig House, Hartington Road, Ealing, LONDON, W13 8QJ.
POWELL, Mr. Alun Gwyn, BSc ACA 1990; 32 Alcester Road, POOLE, DORSET, BH12 2JW.
POWELL, Mrs. Andrea Jane, BSc ACA 1997; 19 Constitution Hill, IPSWICH, IP1 3RG.
POWELL, Mr. Andrew John, BSc ACA 1991; Pegasus House, 37-43 Sackville Street, LONDON, W1S 3DL.
POWELL, Mr. Anthony David, BSc ACA 1999; Amberley Cottage, 41b Waverley Lane, FARNHAM, GU9 8BH.
•POWELL, Mr. Anthony Wiseman, BA FCA FIMC 1977; 7 The Close, Muswell Avenue, LONDON, N10 2ED.
POWELL, Mr. Arwyn Morgan, BSc FCA 1979; Eyford, 181 Cyncoed Road, CARDIFF, CF23 6AH.
POWELL, Mr. Benjamin Miles, BA ACA 1999; Houghton Mifflin Harcourt Publishing Company, 222 Berkeley Street, BOSTON, MA 02116, UNITED STATES.
POWELL, Mr. Brian Christopher, BA FCA 1976; Rose Farm, Twemlow Lane, Cranage, CREWE, CW4 8EX.
POWELL, Mr. Bruce Lewis Hamilton, BA FCA 1978; Broadhatch House, Bentley, FARNHAM, GU10 5JJ.
POWELL, Miss. Catherine, BSc(Hons) ACA 2011; Apartment 20, 41 Essex Street, BIRMINGHAM, B5 4TT.
POWELL, Mrs. Chantal Marie France, BA ACA 1994; 57 Gloucester Road, HAMPTON, TW12 2UQ.
•POWELL, Mr. Christopher Charles, FCA 1968; Laverton Meadow House, Laverton, BROADWAY, WORCESTERSHIRE, WR12 7NA.
•POWELL, Mr. Christopher David, BA FCA 1990; Deloitte LLP, 1 City Square, LEEDS, WEST YORKSHIRE, LS1 2AL. See also Deloitte & Touche LLP
POWELL, Mr. Christopher David, FCA CIOT 1983; Institute of Chartered Accountants, Metropolitan House, 321 Avebury Boulevard, MILTON KEYNES, MK9 2FZ.
POWELL, Mr. Christopher James, MA BA ACA 2004; Pallinghurst Advisors LLP Floor 7, 54 Jermyn Street, LONDON, SW1Y 6LX.
•POWELL, Mr. Christopher John, BSc FCA 1977; Pharos Associates, PO Box 21, TEDDINGTON, MIDDLESEX, TW11 9SW.
POWELL, Mr. Christopher Michael Eric, BCom FCA 1980; 15 Earnley Road, HAYLING ISLAND, PO11 9SU.
POWELL, Mr. Christopher Miles, BSc ACA 1990; 57 Gloucester Road, HAMPTON, MIDDLESEX, TW12 2UQ.
POWELL, Mr. Christopher Robin, FCA 1965; Wickham House, 21 Grange Hill, Coggeshall, COLCHESTER, CO6 1RE.
POWELL, Mr. Christopher Stuart, ACA 2009; Flat 7, 391 Camden Road, LONDON, N7 0SH.
POWELL, Mr. Christopher Thomas, BA FCA 1974; 3 Bracebridge Close, Balsall Common, COVENTRY, CV7 7QJ.
POWELL, Mr. Cliff Lewis, ACA MAAT 1997; 5 Gloucester Road, HAMPTON, MIDDLESEX, TW12 2UQ.
POWELL, Mr. Darren Anthony, ACA 2010; A S G Accountancy Ltd, 17 St. Peters Terrace, BATH, BA2 3BT.
POWELL, Mr. Darren Roy, BSc ACA 2002; 31 Meadowgate, Worsley, MANCHESTER, M28 2RB.
POWELL, Mr. David, BSc ACA 2010; Flat 6 Chessing Court, Fortis Green, LONDON, N2 9ER.
POWELL, Mr. David, FCA 1951; Flat 8 Dorchester House, 29 Marsham Lane, GERRARDS CROSS, SL9 8HA. (Life Member)
•POWELL, Mr. David, ACA 1979; (Tax Fac), Booth Ainsworth LLP, Alpha House, 4 Greek Street, STOCKPORT, CHESHIRE, SK3 8AB.
POWELL, Mr. David Anthony, BSc ACA 1990; Reephenslei 33, Kontich, 2550 ANTWERP, BELGIUM.
POWELL, Mr. David Arthur, ACA 1982; 28 Villiers Crescent, ST. ALBANS, HERTFORDSHIRE, AL4 9HY.
POWELL, Mr. David Graham, BSc ACA 1986; 134 Rue de la Pisciculture, 01710 THOIRY, FRANCE.
POWELL, Mr. David John, BSc FCA 1984; 47 Taylor Street, BRAINTREE, MA 02184, UNITED STATES.
POWELL, Mr. David Joseph, BA ACA 1994; B3 Cable Solutions, Delaunays Road, MANCHESTER, M9 8FP.

POWELL, Mr. David Lawrence, BA ACA *1988;* Appletree House, The Green, North Deighton, WETHERBY, LS22 4EN.
•**POWELL, Mr. David Lyn, BSc ACA CTA** *1996;* Argenta Tax & Corporate Services Limited, Fountain House, 130 Fenchurch Street, LONDON, EC3M 5DJ.
POWELL, Mr. David Meredith, FCA *1970;* Kingwood House, Kingwood Common, HENLEY-ON-THAMES, RG9 5NB.
POWELL, Mr. David Middleton, BA ACA *1996;* SMS management and technology, 49/f, The Center, 99 Queens Road Central, CENTRAL, HONG KONG SAR.
POWELL, Mr. David Paul, BSc(Hons) ACA *2001;* Auditel, The Unit, Park Lane House, Park Lane, LEEDS, LS3 1AA.
POWELL, Mr. David Samuel, FCA *1963;* 84 Norton Road, STOURBRIDGE, WEST MIDLANDS, DY8 2AQ. (Life Member)
POWELL, Mr. David Waterman, MSc FCA *1972;* Berwin & Berwin Ltd, Roseville Road, LEEDS, LS8 5EE.
POWELL, Miss. Dawn Saw Liang, BA ACA *1989;* 91 Abbeville Road, Clapham Common, LONDON, SW4 9JL.
•**POWELL, Miss. Dilys Edith, MA FCA** *1986;* Archways, Alexandria Road, Sutton Scotney, WINCHESTER, HAMPSHIRE, SO21 3LF.
POWELL, Mr. Don Malcolm, ACA *1983;* 173 Station Road, Mickleover, DERBY, DE3 5FJ.
POWELL, Mr. Duncan Thomas Campbell, BA ACA *1996;* 1909 Toyon COurt, PLEASANTON, CA 94588, UNITED STATES.
POWELL, Mrs. Emma Jane, BSc ACA *2000;* Carmarthenshire County Council, 2 Spilman Street, CARMARTHEN, CARMARTHENSHIRE, SA31 1JP.
POWELL, Mr. Gareth Rhys, BSc ACA *1991;* BBC Wales, Broadcasting House, Llandaf, CARDIFF, CF5 2YQ.
POWELL, Mr. Gareth Rhys, ACA *2009;* with Gardners Accountants Ltd, Brynford House, Brynford Street, HOLYWELL, CLWYD, CH8 7RD.
POWELL, Mr. Gary James, BA ACA *1999;* Grosvenor, 70 Grosvenor Street, LONDON, W1K 3JP.
POWELL, Mr. George Christopher James, MA FCA *1979;* Brick Dock House, Saxmundham Road, ALDEBURGH, SUFFOLK, IP15 5PD.
POWELL, Mr. Graeme Huw Morgan, BSc(Econ) ACA *1990;* 56 Northcourt Avenue, READING, RG2 7HQ.
POWELL, Mr. Graham Ronald, BSc FCA *1965;* Nether House, Nether Green, Great Bowden, MARKET HARBOROUGH, LEICESTERSHIRE, LE16 7HF.
POWELL, Mr. Gregory James, BSc ACA FSI *1996;* Place de la Gare, La Rue Du Pont, Grouville, JERSEY, JE3 9BT.
•**POWELL, Mr. Gregory James, MA FCA** *1977;* PricewaterhouseCoopers LLP, Hays Galleria, 1 Hays Lane, LONDON, SE1 2RD. See also PricewaterhouseCoopers
POWELL, Mr. Gregory John, BSc ACA *1990;* 1 Harrow Road, FLEET, HAMPSHIRE, GU51 1JD.
POWELL, Miss. Heather Lynn, MPhil BSc ACA *1998;* 62 Orchard Drive, EDINBURGH, EH4 2DZ.
•**POWELL, Mrs. Heather Margaret, MA FCA** *1988;* Kingston Smith & Partners LLP, Devonshire House, 60 Goswell Road, LONDON, EC1M 7AD. See also Kingston Smith Limited Liability Partnership, Kingston Smith LLP, Devonshire Corporate Services LLP and Kingston Smith Consulting LLP
POWELL, Miss. Helen, BSc ACA *1990;* MGPA Japan LLC, 11F Sumitomo Fudosan Roppongi-dori Building, 7-18-18 Roppongi, Minato-ku, TOKYO, 106-0032 JAPAN.
POWELL, Miss. Helen Mary, BA ACA *1990;* 41 Downside Road, Risinghurst, OXFORD, OX3 8HP.
POWELL, Miss. Helen Victoria, BA ACA *2007;* Flat 4 Malling House, Abbey Park, BECKENHAM, BR3 1PZ.
POWELL, Ms. Holly, BSc(Hons) ACA *2010;* 2 Pellor Fields, Breage, HELSTON, CORNWALL, TR13 9UL.
POWELL, Mr. Ian, BA FCA *1989;* Apartment 2204 De Ricou, The Repulse Bay, 109 Repulse Bay Road, REPULSE BAY, HONG KONG ISLAND, HONG KONG SAR.
•①**POWELL, Mr. Ian Clifford, BA FCA** *1982;* PricewaterhouseCoopers LLP, 1 Embankment Place, LONDON, WC2N 6RH. See also PricewaterhouseCoopers
POWELL, Mr. Ian Donald, BSc FCA *1985;* Fernbank, Woodend Lane, HYDE, SK14 1DU.
•**POWELL, Mr. Ian Edward, MA ACA TEP** *1980;* (Tax Fac), Bush & Co, 2 Barnfield Crescent, EXETER, EX1 1QT. See also Westcountry Payroll Ltd
POWELL, Mr. James Ashley, BSc ACA *2009;* 64 Phoenix Way, CARDIFF, CF14 4PQ.
POWELL, Mr. Jamie Alan, BSc(Econ) ACA *2005;* V O S A Ellipse, Padley Road, SWANSEA, SA1 8AN.
POWELL, Mrs. Jane Christine, BSc(Hons) ACA CTA *2000;* 13 Beaulieu Road, PORTSMOUTH, PO2 0DN.
•**POWELL, Miss. Jean, FCA** *1978;* Feltons (Bham) Limited, 8 Sovereign Court, 8 Graham Street, BIRMINGHAM, B1 3JR.
POWELL, Mrs. Joanne Lisa, ACA *2001;* 12 Allerton Grange Gardens, Moortown, LEEDS, LS17 6LL.
POWELL, Mr. John, ACA *2010;* Flat 249, 14 St. George Wharf, LONDON, SW8 2LR.
•**POWELL, Mr. John Edward, FCA** *1966;* John E. Powell, 24 Colebrook Road, BRIGHTON, BN1 5JH.
POWELL, Mr. John Francis, FCA *1976;* Omega Underwriting Agents Ltd, 4th Floor, New London House, 6 London Street, LONDON, EC3R 7LP.
POWELL, Mr. John Frederick, FCA *1957;* Cleveland, 589a Warwick Road, SOLIHULL, B91 1AP. (Life Member)
POWELL, Mr. John George, BSc FCA DChA *1979;* 26 Bacons Drive, Cuffley, POTTERS BAR, EN6 4DU.
POWELL, Mr. John Lawrence, FCA *1962;* 9 St. Mary's Meadow, Wingham, CANTERBURY, CT3 1DF. (Life Member)
POWELL, Mr. John Walter, FCA *1949;* 5 Birch Tree Grove, SOLIHULL, B91 1HD. (Life Member)
•**POWELL, Mr. Jonathan Godfrey, BA FCA** *1978;* Kingdom Powell, The Greyhound, Back Street, Reepham, NORWICH, NR10 4SJ.
POWELL, Mr. Jonathan Richard Waring, BA ACA *1989;* The Great Barn, Plum Lane, Shipton-under-Wychwood, CHIPPING NORTON, OXFORDSHIRE, OX7 6DZ.
POWELL, Mr. Jonathan Robert, BSc ACA *1993;* Peter & Company Ltd, PO Box 84, CASTRIES, SAINT LUCIA.
POWELL, Mr. Julian, BA ACA *2005;* with Kingston Smith LLP, Devonshire House, 60 Goswell Road, LONDON, EC1M 7AD.
POWELL, Mrs. Julie Caroline, BA ACA *1988;* 48 Main Road, Drayton Parslow, MILTON KEYNES, MK17 0JS.
POWELL, Miss. Kate, BA(Hons) ACA *2002;* Deloitte & Touche 1 City Square, LEEDS, LS1 2AL.
•**POWELL, Mr. Kevin Stephen, FCA** *1987;* (Tax Fac), Knill James, One Bell Lane, LEWES, EAST SUSSEX, BN7 1JU.
•**POWELL, Mr. Laurie John, BSc FCA** *1987;* Gilroy & Brookes, Ground Floor, Interpower House, Windsor Way, ALDERSHOT, HAMPSHIRE GU11 1JG.
POWELL, Mr. Leighton John, BSc ACA *2007;* U B S Asset Management, 21 Lombard Street, LONDON, EC3V 9AH.
POWELL, Miss. Lisa, BSc ACA *2002;* Royal London, Alderley Road, WILMSLOW, CHESHIRE, SK9 1PF.
POWELL, Mrs. Lowri Sian, BSc ACA *2006;* 64 Phoenix Way, Birchgrove, CARDIFF, CF14 4PQ.
POWELL, Miss. Lucy Nicola, BA ACA *2004;* 7 Lilley Drive The Chase, Kingswood, TADWORTH, KT20 6JA.
POWELL, Mr. Luke, ACA *2010;* 31 Lowlands Avenue, SUTTON COLDFIELD, WEST MIDLANDS, B74 3QN.
POWELL, Miss. Lynne Elizabeth, BA ACA *1991;* 4A Dunton Road, Broughton Astley, LEICESTER, LE9 6NB.
POWELL, Mr. Malcolm Robert, BCom ACA *1998;* 4 Vale Row, LONDON, N5 1LL.
POWELL, Mr. Mark John, BSc ACA *2004;* 10 Cross Oak Road, BERKHAMSTED, HERTFORDSHIRE, HP4 3EH.
POWELL, Mr. Martin Derek, FCA *1968;* 20 Manorbier Road, BEDFORD, MK41 8PB.
POWELL, Mr. Martyn Richard, BA FCA *1987;* 18 Northgate Close, KIDDERMINSTER, DY11 6JW.
POWELL, Mr. Matthew David, BA ACA *1999;* 33 Tagg Wood View, Ramsbottom, BURY, LANCASHIRE, BL0 9XP.
POWELL, Mr. Maxwell John, FCA *1960;* Greenways, Whitehouse Lane, Codsall Wood, WOLVERHAMPTON, WV8 1QS. (Life Member)
POWELL, Mr. Michael Hugh, BSc FCA *1986;* 60 Chaparral Cove SE, CALGARY T2X 3L2, AB, CANADA.
POWELL, Mr. Michael John, ACA *1988;* Oorain, Earle Drive, Parkgate, NESTON, CH64 6RY.
POWELL, Mr. Michael Richard Hugh, FCA *1969;* Agrifuels Corporation, 6G Globe Telecom Plaza 1, Pioneer Madison St, Mandaloyong City, MANILA 1556, PHILIPPINES.
POWELL, Mr. Michael Robert, BA ACA CTA *1981;* 8 Kentmere Close, Gatley, CHEADLE, SK8 4RD.
POWELL, Miss. Moira Ann, BSc ACA *2001;* 125 Blair Athol Road, SHEFFIELD, S11 7GD.
POWELL, Mrs. Naomi Claire, BTh ACA *2005;* with Chris Duckett, Thorn Office Centre, Straight Mile Road, Rotherwas, HEREFORD, HR2 6JT.
•**POWELL, Mrs. Natalie Anne, ACA** *2002;* Natalie Powell ACA, 7 Shorefield Road, Marchwood, SOUTHAMPTON, SO40 4SR.
POWELL, Mrs. Natalie Jane, BA ACA *2002;* 21 Conway Drive, THATCHAM, BERKSHIRE, RG18 3AT.
POWELL, Mr. Nathan John, ACA *2008;* Friends Provident, Pixham End, DORKING, RH4 1QA.
•**POWELL, Mr. Neville Charles, BSc FCA** *1989;* Whitakers, Bryndon House, 5-7 Berry Road, NEWQUAY, TR7 1AD.
•**POWELL, Mr. Nicholas Charles, BSc ACA** *1990;* Ernst & Young LLP, Apex Plaza, Forbury Road, READING, RG1 1YE. See also Ernst & Young Europe LLP
POWELL, Miss. Nicola Jayne, BSc ACA *2005;* 86 High Street Wrestlingworth, SANDY, BEDFORDSHIRE, SG19 2EN.
POWELL, Mr. Nigel David, BA ACA *1987;* 49 Bladon Road, WOODSTOCK, OX20 1QD.
POWELL, Mrs. Pamela Anne, MA(Hons) FCA *1986;* Manor Barn, Sutton Lane, Elton, NOTTINGHAM, NG13 9LA.
POWELL, Mr. Philip Edwin, FCA *1975;* 6 Gravesend Gardens, TORPOINT, PL11 2HN.
POWELL, Mrs. Pippa Jane, BA ACA *2007;* Sagars Llp Gresham House, 5-7 St. Pauls Street, LEEDS, LS1 2JG.
•**POWELL, Mr. Richard Charles, BSc FCA** *1981;* KPMG LLP, St. James's Square, MANCHESTER, M2 6DS. See also KPMG Europe LLP
•**POWELL, Mr. Richard John, BA FCA** *1996;* MacIntyre Hudson LLP, Peterbridge House, The Lakes, NORTHAMPTON, NN4 7HB.
POWELL, Mr. Richard Mark, BSc ACA *1992;* 23 Wedderburn Road, HARROGATE, HG2 7QH.
POWELL, Mr. Richard Patrick, FCA *1968;* Primavera, Midlands Farm, St. Lawrence, JERSEY, JE3 1NN. (Life Member)
•**POWELL, Mr. Robert, BSc ACA** *2007;* Base Stone, 159 College Road, College Town, SANDHURST, BERKSHIRE, GU47 0RG.
POWELL, Mr. Robert Charles Phillips, FCA *1969;* 21 Heol Isaf, Radyr, CARDIFF, CF15 8AG. (Life Member)
POWELL, Mr. Robert Malcolm, BA ACA *2002;* 10 Harecastle Bank, STONE, STAFFORDSHIRE, ST15 8ZU.
•**POWELL, Mr. Robert William, FCA** *1980;* (Tax Fac), Robert Powell, A4 Spinnaker House, Spinnaker Road, Hempsted Lane, GLOUCESTER, GL2 5FD.
POWELL, Mr. Robin Clive, BA ACA CF *1991;* Laurel Farm, Brafferton, YORK, YO61 2NZ.
POWELL, Mr. Roger John, FCA *1973;* 2 Perry Mead, Eaton Bray, DUNSTABLE, BEDFORDSHIRE, LU6 2FA.
•**POWELL, Mr. Ronald Thomas William, FCA** *1974;* Powell & Co, 5 High Street, KINGTON, HEREFORDSHIRE, HR5 3AX.
POWELL, Mrs. Rosemary Margaret, BA ACA *1985;* 31 Ashwell Road, Whissendine, OAKHAM, LE15 7EN.
POWELL, Mr. Rufus John, BA ACA *1990;* Mill House The Ride, Ifold Loxwood, BILLINGSHURST, WEST SUSSEX, RH14 0TH.
POWELL, Mr. Russell Thomas, BA(Hons) ACA *2003;* 4 Leith Close, ASHBY-DE-LA-ZOUCH, LE65 1HN.
POWELL, Ms. Ruth Anne, FCA *1975;* parker and osborn ltd unit 1 expressway ind estate, bacebridge street aston, BIRMINGHAM, b64ne.
•**POWELL, Mrs. Sarah Alexandra Walwyn, BSc FCA DChA** *1979;* (Tax Fac), Powell & Co., Manor Cottage, Shamley Green, GUILDFORD, GU5 0UD.
POWELL, Mr. Scott Gordon, MPhil BA ACA *1996;* PO Box 28143, West Pender RPO, VANCOUVER V6C 3T7, BC, CANADA.
POWELL, Mr. Simon Philip, BSc ACA *2007;* 26 Quarry Way, Southwater, HORSHAM, WEST SUSSEX, RH13 9SU.
POWELL, Mr. Stephen, BSc FCA *1973;* 59 Rogersfield, Langho, BLACKBURN, BB6 8HD.
POWELL, Mr. Stephen John, BA FCA *1982;* Abney Gate, Hedsor Road, BOURNE END, SL8 5DH.
POWELL, Mr. Stephen John, FCA *1973;* 49 York Mews, ALTON, HAMPSHIRE, GU34 1JD.
POWELL, Mr. Stephen Mark, BSc ACA *2005;* 23 Ormonde Terrace, LONDON, NW8 7LR.
POWELL, Mr. Stephen Roy, BA ACA *1984;* Cressida, The Warren, Caversham, READING, RG4 7TQ.
POWELL, Mr. Stephen William, BA ACA *1999;* 17 Crouch Hall Lane, Redbourn, ST. ALBANS, HERTFORDSHIRE, AL3 7EQ.
POWELL, Mr. Steven George, ACA *1979;* 22 Wye Close, DROITWICH, WORCESTERSHIRE, WR9 8TE.
POWELL, Mrs. Susan, BSc(Hons) ACA *2002;* 105 Blenheim Road, Cheadle Hulme, CHEADLE, CHESHIRE, SK8 7BB.
POWELL, Mrs. Susannah Margaret, ACA *1991;* S G Hambros bank (Channel Islands) Limited, PO Box 78, 18 The Esplanade, St Helier, JERSEY, JE4 8PR.
POWELL, Miss. Suzannah, MA ACA *2006;* 45B Ravensbury Road, LONDON, SW18 4SA.
POWELL, Mrs. Teresa Mary, BSc ACA *2003;* 47 Beresford Crescent, NEWCASTLE, STAFFORDSHIRE, ST5 3RQ.
POWELL, Mr. Thomas St George, BSc ACA *1998;* 95 Richmond Road, ISLEWORTH, MIDDLESEX, TW7 7BS.
POWELL, Mr. Tim David, BA ACA *2007;* 14 rue Larrey, 75005 PARIS, FRANCE.
POWELL, Mr. Timothy, MEng ACA *2002;* Anchor Cottage, Weston Green, THAMES DITTON, SURREY, KT7 0JP.
POWELL, Mr. Timothy March, FCA *1972;* (Tax Fac), 15 Avenue Road, Astwood Bank, REDDITCH, WORCESTERSHIRE, B96 6AU.
POWELL, Mr. Timothy Martin, MA FCA *1980;* 34 Gorst Road, LONDON, SW11 6JE.
POWELL, Mr. Vernon David, FCA *1991;* 18 Sunny Bank Road, Helmshore, ROSSENDALE, BB4 4PF.
POWELL, Mr. Vic, BSc FCA *1971;* 523 Fulwood Road, SHEFFIELD, S10 3QB.
POWELL, Mr. William Tudor, FCA *1965;* Foye House, Cliffords Mesne, NEWENT, GL18 1JN. (Life Member)
POWELL-COOK, Mr. Neale Alan, MA ACA *1988;* Golden Acre Dairy Foods Ltd, 3000 Hillswood Drive, CHERTSEY, SURREY, KT16 0RS.
POWER, Mr. Alfred Michael David, FCA *1964;* 12 St. James Close, Pangbourne, READING, RG8 7AP.
POWER, Mr. Anthony Patrick, FCA *1965;* The Farmhouse, Craggs Lane Farm, Tunstall, RICHMOND, DL10 7RB.
POWER, Mr. Christopher Martin, BSc ACA *1986;* CLS Services, Exchange Tower, One Harbour Exchange Square, LONDON, E14 9GE.
POWER, Mr. Colin Lewis, FCA *1953;* Well Park, Lustleigh, NEWTON ABBOT, DEVON, TQ13 9TR. (Life Member)
•①**POWER, Mr. Dermot Justin, BSc FCA** *1976;* BDO LLP, 6th Floor, 3 Hardman Street, Spinningfields, MANCHESTER, M3 3AT. See also BDO Stoy Hayward LLP
POWER, Mr. Ian Derek, BA FCA *1989;* 5 Redhall House Close, EDINBURGH, EH14 1JN.
POWER, Mr. Ian John, BCom ACA *1996;* 15 Manland Avenue, HARPENDEN, HERTFORDSHIRE, AL5 4RG.
POWER, Mrs. Jennifer Hazel, BSc FCA *1987;* PO Box 7284, BRISBANE, QLD 4169, AUSTRALIA.
POWER, Mr. John Augustine, BCom FCA *1978;* 4 Cois Mara, DUNGARVON, COUNTY WATERFORD, IRELAND.
POWER, Mr. John Michael Joseph, BSc(Hons) ACA *2000;* Boskins, Newbiggin, CARNFORTH, LA6 2PL.
POWER, Mr. John Roger Le Poer, FCA *1957;* 55 Rusholme Road, Putney, LONDON, SW15 3LF. (Life Member)
POWER, Mr. Julian Timothy, BSc ACA *2001;* 8 Clare Mews, LONDON, SW6 2EG.
POWER, Mrs. Karen Lesley, BSc(Hons) ACA *2000;* 10 Abbey View Gardens, BATH, BA2 6DQ.
POWER, Mrs. Kimberly, BSc ACA *2001;* Hanalei, Carters Hill, Eadestown, RATHMORE, COUNTY KILDARE, IRELAND.
POWER, Mrs. Lydia, LLM BSc(Hons) ACA *2011;* 40 Mill Road, Tongwynlais, CARDIFF, CF15 7JP.
POWER, Mr. Michael John, FCA *1961;* 23A James Street, Victoria, ROTORUA 3010, BAY OF PLENTY, NEW ZEALAND.
POWER, Prof. Michael Kevin, PhD BA FCA *1987;* London School Of Economics, Department Of Accounting, & Finance, Houghton Street, LONDON, WC2A 2AE.
POWER, Mr. Michael Richard Parkes, MA ACA *1979;* Oakwood Farm, Shipley, HORSHAM, RH13 8PY.
•**POWER, Mr. Paul Graeme, FCA** *1969;* ETM Consulting Limited, The Old Stables, Hendal Farm, Groombridge, TUNBRIDGE WELLS, KENT TN3 9NU.
POWER, Mr. Robert Alexander, MA ACA *2004;* with Churchill & Co, Wessex Lodge, Billetfield, TAUNTON, SOMERSET, TA1 3NN.
•**POWER, Mr. Simon Christopher, FCA** *1990;* (Tax Fac), PRB Accountants LLP, Kingfisher House, Hurstwood Grange, Hurstwood Lane, HAYWARDS HEATH, WEST SUSSEX RH17 7QX. See also PRB Martin Pollins LLP and Movie Accounting LLP
•**POWER, Mr. Stephen John, FCA** *1974;* Power & Co, 12 Queen Eleanors Drive, Knowle, SOLIHULL, WEST MIDLANDS, B93 9LY.

POWER, Mr. William George Charles, BSc ACA *2009;* 3 Waterloo Place, TONBRIDGE, KENT, TN9 2SD.
POWERS, Mrs. Caroline, BA ACA *2004;* 2 Blakeney Drive, MANSFIELD, NOTTINGHAMSHIRE, NG18 4DN.
•POWERS, Mr. Keith Bernard, FCA *1995;* Keith Powers, P O Box 241, Sarisbury Green, SOUTHAMPTON, SO31 1DF.
POWICK, Mrs. Cheryl Lynne, BSc ACA *2003;* 43 Oak Apple Crescent, ILKESTON, DE7 4NZ.
POWIS, Mr. Aaron, BSc(Hons) ACA *2010;* 5 Sylvester Drive, Hilperton, TROWBRIDGE, BA14 7FG.
POWIS, Mr. George Mackenzie, FCA *1940;* 71 Kingsthorpe Park, Kenilworth Road, KENILWORTH, 7700, SOUTH AFRICA. (Life Member)
POWIS, Miss. Joanne Sarah, BSc(Hons) ACA *2000;* Walnut Tree Farm, 2 Prickwillow Road, Isleham, ELY, CAMBRIDGESHIRE, CB7 5RG.
POWIS, Mr. Paul Lionel, FCA *1962;* 16 Cherry Orchard, Old Wives Lees, CANTERBURY, CT4 8BQ. (Life Member)
•POWIS, Mr. Russell John, FCA *1969;* Innovation Professional Services LLP, Merlin House, Priory Drive, Langstone, NEWPORT, GWENT NP18 2HJ.
POWLES, Mr. Alan, FCA *1968;* Pendle Cottage, Merbach Hill, Bredwardine, HEREFORD, HR3 6DE.
POWLES, Mr. Christopher John, MA ACA *1989;* Westhouse, Southgreen, Kirtlington, KIDLINGTON, OXFORDSHIRE, OX5 3HJ.
POWLES, Mr. David Edwin, FCA *1972;* 8 Avenue Georges Digoy, 77500 CHELLES, FRANCE.
POWLES, Mr. David John, FCA *1961;* 3 West Coombe, Westbury-on-Trym, BRISTOL, BS9 2BA.
POWLEY, Mr. Allen James, BA ACA *1992;* 24 Dorey House, Brentford Lock, High Street, BRENTFORD, MIDDLESEX, TW8 8LD.
POWLEY, Mr. Andrew Mark, BSc ACA *2000;* 30 Montague Close, WOKINGHAM, BERKSHIRE, RG40 5PF.
POWLEY, Mrs. Barbara, BSc ACA *1987;* Black Rock, 33 King William Street, LONDON, EC4R 9AS.
POWLEY, Mr. Barry Alfred, FCA *1961;* 6 Watermeadow Close, Ormesby St Margaret, GREAT YARMOUTH, NR29 3NF. (Life Member)
POWLEY, Miss. Danielle Louise, BSc ACA *2006;* 45 Butler Drive, BRACKNELL, RG12 8DA.
POWLEY, Mr. Ian Walter, FCA *1971;* Ballacosney House, Baldhoon Road, Laxey, ISLE OF MAN, IM4 7QH.
POWLEY, Mrs. Joanna Faye, BSc ACA *2001;* 30 Montague Close, WOKINGHAM, BERKSHIRE, RG40 5PF.
POWLEY, Miss. Julia Hodgson, MA FCA *1980;* 25 Wigton Road, CARLISLE, CA2 7BB.
POWLEY, Mr. Roger Peter, FCA *1971;* Church Farm House, Bosham Lane, Bosham, CHICHESTER, WEST SUSSEX, PO18 8HL.
POWLEY, Miss. Sarah Elizabeth, BA ACA *1998;* World Vision UK Ltd Mapeley House, Opal Drive Fox Milne, MILTON KEYNES, MK15 0ZR.
•POWLING, Mr. Graham Mark, ACA *2003;* Platt Rushton LLP, Sutherland House, 1759 London Road, LEIGH-ON-SEA, ESSEX, SS9 2RZ. See also Sutherland Corporate Services Ltd
POWLING, Ms. Hazel Ann, BSc CertEd FCA *1996;* 21 Outwood Common Road, BILLERICAY, CM11 2NU.
POWLING, Mr. Kenneth John, FCA *1975;* Millstones, 17 Gidea Close, Gidea Park, ROMFORD, RM2 5NP.
POWLING, Mr. Nicholas Michael, BA FCA *1974;* 12817 Texas Sage Court, AUSTIN, TX 78732-2025, UNITED STATES.
POWLTON, Mr. John William, BA ACA *2007;* 12 Union Park, Annandale Road, Greenwich, LONDON, SE10 0JA.
POWNALL, Mr. Jonathan Nigel, MA ACA CISA *1995;* 21 Ingleby Way, CHISLEHURST, BR7 6DD.
POWNALL, Miss. Justine, BA ACA *2006;* 56 Dickens Street, ELWOOD, VIC 3184, AUSTRALIA.
•POWNALL, Mr. Mark Victor, BEng ACA *1996;* Baker Tilly Tax & Advisory Services LLP, 2 Whitehall Quay, LEEDS, LS1 4HG. See also Baker Tilly Corporate Finance LLP
POWNALL, Mr. Michael Granville, BA FCA *1986;* The Centre House, Swythamley Hall, MACCLESFIELD, CHESHIRE, SK11 0SN.
POWNALL, Mr. Steven Ellis, FCA *1981;* 26A Roundwood Lane, HARPENDEN, AL5 3BZ.
POWNE, Mrs. Christina Mary, BSc ACA *1986;* High Garth, Hebers Ghyll Drive, ILKLEY, WEST YORKSHIRE, LS29 9QH.
POWNE, Mr. Richard Alexander Ferrier, BA ACA *1982;* High Garth, Hebers Ghyll Drive, ILKLEY, WEST YORKSHIRE, LS29 9QH.
POWNEY, Mr. Ian George, BA ACA *1979;* 156 Crown Heights, Alencon Link, BASINGSTOKE, HAMPSHIRE, RG21 7TZ.
POWRIE, Mr. David, FCA *1959;* Flat 16, Tudor Grange, 83 Oatlands Drive, WEYBRIDGE, SURREY, KT13 9LN. (Life Member)
POWRIE, Mr. David Ernest, BSc ACA *1995;* 2/1 181 Kilmarnock Road, GLASGOW, G41 3JE.
•POWRIE, Mr. Dougal, BA FCA *1982;* Powrie Appleby LLP, Queen Anne House, 4 6 & 8 New Street, LEICESTER, LE1 5NR.
POWVALA, Mr. Khershed Manek, FCA *1964;* 211 Rambha, 66C L. Jagmohandas Marg, MUMBAI 400 006, INDIA.
•ⒾPOXON, Mr. Andrew, BSc ACA *1991;* Leonard Curtis Recovery Limited, Hollins Lane, BURY, LANCASHIRE, BL9 8DG. See also DTE Leonard Curtis Limited and Leonard Curtis Limited
POXON, Mr. Andrew John, BSc ACA *1998;* 10 Matthias Court, 119 Church Road, RICHMOND, TW10 6LL.
POYIADJI, Mr. Yiannos, BA ACA *2007;* Mercuria Energy Group Ltd, Nicolaides Sea View City, Arch. Makarios III & Kalogreon Corner 4, D1 4th Floor, 6016 LARNACA, CYPRUS.
•POYIADJIS, Mr. Ioannis Pavlou, FCA *1969;* (Tax Fac), Nexia Poyiadjis, 2 Sophouli St, Chanteclair House 8th Flr, P O Box 21814, 1513 NICOSIA, CYPRUS.
POYIADJIS, Mr. Savvas, BSc ACA CISA *2011;* 6 Omodous Street, 2037 STROVOLOS, CYPRUS.
•POYIADJIS, Miss. Susana, LLB ACA *2002;* Nexia Poyiadjis, 2 Sophouli St, Chanteclair House 8th Flr, P O Box 21814, 1513 NICOSIA, CYPRUS.
POYNDER, Mr. John Richard, FCA *1969;* Nutcrackers, Turnpike Hill, Withersfield, HAVERHILL, SUFFOLK, CB9 7RY.
•POYNER, Mr. Jonathan Shearer, BA(Econ) FCA *1978;* Thomas Westcott, 64 High Street, BIDEFORD, DEVON, EX39 2AN.
•POYNER, Mr. Philip Godber, ACA *1987;* IP-Config Limited, 12 Creek End, EMSWORTH, HAMPSHIRE, PO10 7EX.
POYNER, Miss. Sarah Elizabeth, BA ACA *1992;* 49 Bramfield Road, LONDON, SW11 6RA.
•POYNER, Mr. Stuart Anthony, MA FCA *1987;* KPMG, Naberezhnaya Tower Complex, Block C, 10 Presnenskaya Naberezhnaya, 123317 MOSCOW, RUSSIAN FEDERATION. See also KPMG Europe LLP and Firm created for CD only - see SJB
POYNTER, Miss. Emma Elizabeth, BSc ACA *2010;* flat 3, 37 Abbey Road, LONDON, NW8 0AT.
•POYNTER, Mr. Kieran Charles, BSc FCA *1975;* 15 Montpelier Mews, LONDON, SW7 1HB.
POYNTER, Mr. Lance Hamilton, FCA *1974;* 2 Billing Place, LONDON, SW10 9UN.
POYNTON, Mr. Anthony Bruce, BA ACA *1995;* 51 Oakfield Road, Long Stratton, NORWICH, NR15 2WB.
POYNTON, Mr. Darren William, BA ACA *1999;* 4 Charwood Close, Shenley, RADLETT, HERTFORDSHIRE, WD7 9LH.
POYNTON, Mr. John Edmund, BSc FCA CMC *1975;* 146 Elizabeth Avenue, AMERSHAM, BUCKINGHAMSHIRE, HP6 6RG.
POYNTON, Mrs. Kathleen Mary, FCA *1970;* Flat 16, Sunset Lodge, 30-32 The Avenue, POOLE, DORSET, BH13 6HG.
POYSER, Mr. David Charles, BA ACA *1988;* British Bankers Association, Pinners Hall, 105-108 Old Broad Street, LONDON, EC2N 1EX.
•POYSER, Mr. Edward Stephen, BA FCA CertPFS DChA *1976;* Eliment Hill Farm, Old Epperstone Road, Lowdham, NOTTINGHAM, NG14 7BZ.
POYSER, Mr. Eric Stanley, JP MA FCA *1951;* Hollyhurst, Priory Road, Thurgarton, NOTTINGHAM, NG14 7GW. (Life Member)
POYSER, Mrs. Jacqueline Ann, BA ACA *1989;* Sundial House, Altrincham Road, Styal, WILMSLOW, CHESHIRE, SK9 4JE.
POZZO, Mr. Neil, ACA *2010;* 14 Windmill Road, LONDON, SW18 2EU.
PRABHU, Mr. Ajit Chandrashekar, ACA *1983;* 10 Hartley Grove, SINGAPORE 457879, SINGAPORE.
PRABHU, Mr. Neelesh, ACA *2009;* Flat 1, 14 Bob Marley Way, LONDON, SE24 0LP.
PRACHAR, Mr. Ivan Miroslav, FCA *1956;* 14 Grove Leaze, BRADFORD-ON-AVON, BA15 1PH. (Life Member)
PRADHAN, Mr. Abinash, ACA *2006;* Sanepa Lalitpur, PO Box 3242, KATHMANDU, NEPAL.
PRADHAN, Mr. Karim Sadroodin, FCA *1976;* 16215 78 Street, EDMONTON T5Z 3K8, AB, CANADA.
PRADHAN, Mr. Rajaballi Khimji, FCA *1966;* VALHALLA, 1 Bowmans Close, Burnham, SLOUGH, BUCKINGHAMSHIRE, SL1 8LH.
PRADHAN, Mr. Rajiv, BSc ACA *1979;* Via Camparano 15, 6965 CADRO, SWITZERLAND.
•PRADITSMANONT, Mr. Songdej, BSc FCA *1967;* 193/136-137 Rajadapisek Road, Lake Rajada Office Complex, BANGKOK 10110, THAILAND.
PRAEM, Mr. Erik, FCA *1960;* 6 Green Hedges, 1 Riverdale Gardens, TWICKENHAM, TW1 2BU. (Life Member)
PRAGER, Mr. David Allan, ACA *1980;* 31/3 Rechov Hibner, 49400 PETACH TIKVA, ISRAEL.
PRAGER, Mr. Michael Edward, ACA *1980;* Hilltop, Rabley Heath, WELWYN, HERTFORDSHIRE, AL6 9UB.
PRAGNELL, Mr. Nigel John, FCA *1979;* with Grant Thornton UK LLP, 1 Dorset Street, SOUTHAMPTON, SO15 2DP.
PRAIN, Mr. Graham Lindsay, MA FCA *1970;* 17 Hylton Road, PETERSFIELD, HAMPSHIRE, GU32 3JY.
•PRAIS, Mr. Daniel, BA FCA *1992;* Crawfords Accountants LLP, Stanton House, 41 Blackfriars Road, SALFORD, M3 7DB. See also Daniel Prais Ltd
PRAJAPATI, Miss. Nita, ACA *2009;* 2 Spencer Road, WEMBLEY, MIDDLESEX, HA0 3SF.
PRAJAPATI, Mrs. Raksha Devant, BCom ACA *1996;* 62 St. Johns Avenue, Warley, BRENTWOOD, ESSEX, CM14 5DG.
PRAKASH, Mr. Om, ACA *2011;* C/O R.A.K. Ceramics India PVT. Ltd, P.B. No. 11 Adb Road, Ida Peddapuram, SAMALKOTA 533440, ANDHRA PRADESH, INDIA.
PRAKASH, Miss. Sita Sunaina, BSc(Hons) ACA *2011;* 11 Deans Way, EDGWARE, MIDDLESEX, HA8 9NG.
PRAKASH, Mr. Vinod, FCA *1965;* 267 MANDAKANI ENCLAVE, ALAKNANDA, NEW DELHI 110019, INDIA.
PRAMOJ, Mrs. Sophie Louise, BA ACA *2001;* 22 Paholyothin 37, BANGKOK 10900, THAILAND.
PRANCE, Mr. David William Michael, BA ACA *1984;* 9 Hanover Steps, St. Georges Fields, LONDON, W2 2YG.
PRANGLEY, Mr. Michael John, BSc ACA *1992;* B D O Stoy Hayward, 55 Baker Street, LONDON, W1U 7EU.
PRANGNELL, Miss. Elona, ACA *2011;* May Cottage High Street, Colne, HUNTINGDON, CAMBRIDGESHIRE, PE28 3ND.
PRANGNELL, Mr. Nicholas John, BSc ACA *1999;* The Pennfold, Church Meadow, Claypole, NEWARK, LINCOLNSHIRE, NG23 5AR.
•PRANKERD, Mr. Andrew Jonathan, BSc FCA *1984;* Roblins, 3 Deryn Court, Wharfedale Road, Pentwyn, CARDIFF, CF23 7HA.
PRASAD, Mr. Anil, BSc FCA *1981;* Life Fitness UK Ltd, Queen Adelaide, ELY, CAMBRIDGESHIRE, CB7 4UB.
PRASAD, Mr. Arjun, ACA *2009;* 9 Frognal Way, LONDON, NW3 6XE.
PRASAD, Mr. Parag, BSc ACA *2000;* 136 Basevi Way, LONDON, SE8 3JT.
•PRASANNA, Mr. Amit, MSc BA ACA *2006;* Georgiou & Prasanna LLP, 100 Pall Mall, St James, LONDON, SW1Y 5NQ.
PRASHAD, Mr. Shashi Amal, BSc(Hons) ACA *2003;* (Tax Fac), with KPMG LLP, 15 Canada Square, LONDON, E14 5GL.
PRASHAR, Mr. Amar, ACA *2008;* 126 Barnfield Wood Road, BECKENHAM, KENT, BR3 6SX.
PRASTITE, Ms. Georgia Eleftheriou, BA ACA *2009;* Vizantiou 2B, Tseri, 2480 NICOSIA, CYPRUS.
PRASTKA, Mr. Christopher Richard, BSc ACA *1987;* Ricoh UK Ltd, 1 Plane Tree Crescent, FELTHAM, TW13 7HG.
PRATCHETT, Mrs. Rhiannon Mair, BSc ACA *1996;* 48 Banc Gelli Las, BRIDGEND, MID GLAMORGAN, CF31 5DH.
PRATER, Mr. Mark William, BA ACA *1991;* Quantum Parters Group LLP, Foxs Barn, Fieldgate Drive, Kingsclere, NEWBURY, BERKSHIRE RG20 5SQ.
PRATER, Martin, Esq MBE FCA *1958;* 19 Hadley Close, Meopham, GRAVESEND, DA13 0NX. (Life Member)
PRATER, Mrs. Melanie Johanne, BA ACA *1993;* Fox's Barn, Fox's Lane, Kingsclere, NEWBURY, BERKSHIRE, RG20 5SQ.
PRATER, Mr. Peter John, BSc FCA *1977;* with QTAC Solutions Ltd, Kingsfield Lane, Longwell Green, BRISTOL, BS30 6DL.
PRATLEY, Mr. Derek Anthony, BA ACA *1993;* 630 W. Breckenridge Street, FERNDALE, MI 48220, UNITED STATES.
PRATLEY, Mrs. Janice, BSc ACA CTA *1987;* 87 Woodlands Grove, COULSDON, SURREY, CR5 3AP.
PRATLEY, Mr. Robert John, BSc ACA *1988;* Calle Infantas 15, Piso 1d, 28004 MADRID, SPAIN.
PRATS, Mr. Joan, ACA *2004;* Banco Santander, Santander UK Plc, 2-3 Triton Square, LONDON, NW1 3AN.
PRATT, Mr. Alan James, BA FCA *1978;* 100 King Street, SOUTHSEA, PO5 4EH.
PRATT, Mr. Alan Percy, FCA *1958;* 10 Grammar School Road, BRIGG, DN20 8AA. (Life Member)
PRATT, Mr. Alan Robert, FCA *1965;* 110A Twelfth Avenue, Morningside, DURBAN, KWAZULU NATAL, 4001, SOUTH AFRICA.
•PRATT, Mr. Andrew, BA ACA *1995;* 31 Peakirk Road, Deeping Gate, PETERBOROUGH, PE6 9AH.
PRATT, Mrs. Audrey Devereux, FCA *1944;* Warren Park Nursing Home, 66 Warren Road, LIVERPOOL, L23 6UG. (Life Member)
PRATT, Mr. Bernard, FCA *1952;* Sequoia, 15 Woodlands Drive, GRANTHAM, NG31 9DJ. (Life Member)
•PRATT, Mrs. Caroline Jane, MSc ACA *1987;* Caroline J Beresford Pratt ACA, The Manor House, High Street, BILLINGSHURST, WEST SUSSEX, RH14 9PH.
PRATT, Mr. Charles David, BSc ACA *1984;* Flat 31 Sovereign Court, The Strand Brighton Marina Village, BRIGHTON, BN2 5SH.
PRATT, Mrs. Christine Ann, FCA *1966;* 46 Eastwoods Road, HINCKLEY, LEICESTERSHIRE, LE10 1LH.
PRATT, Mr. Christopher, BA ACA *1987;* Newmason Properties Ltd, Victoria Mills, Salts Mill Road, SHIPLEY, WEST YORKSHIRE, BD17 7EF.
PRATT, Mr. David, BA ACA *2009;* K P M G Alteus House, 1 North Fourth Street, MILTON KEYNES, MK9 1NE.
PRATT, Mr. David Antony, BA ACA *1993;* Eschmann Equipment Unit G, Peter Road, LANCING, WEST SUSSEX, BN15 8TJ.
PRATT, Mr. Dean Raymond, BSc ACA *1989;* 17 Arnold Road, Stoke Golding, NUNEATON, CV13 6JG.
PRATT, Mr. Edward John, FCA *1964;* 31 Bullimore Grove, KENILWORTH, CV8 2QF.
PRATT, Mr. Gareth, BSc ACA *2008;* The Quartz, Apartment 71, 10 Hall Street, BIRMINGHAM, B18 6BN.
PRATT, Mr. George Henry, FCA *1952;* Lynthwaite, 45 Stainburn Road, WORKINGTON, CA14 1SW. (Life Member)
PRATT, Mr. Gordon Robert, ACA *1985;* Cherrygarth Shoreham Road, Otford, SEVENOAKS, TN14 5RW.
PRATT, Mr. Herbert, FCA *1953;* Sycamores, Blandford Road, Iwerne Minster, BLANDFORD FORUM, DORSET, DT11 8QN. (Life Member)
PRATT, Mr. Ian Derek, FCA *1980;* 3 Douglas Meadows, Scaldwell, NORTHAMPTON, NORTHAMPTONSHIRE, NN6 9JN.
•PRATT, Mr. Ian George, FCA *1981;* Wincroft Pratt Limited, 7 Forum Place, Fiddlebridge Lane, HATFIELD, HERTFORDSHIRE, AL10 0RN.
•PRATT, Mr. Ian Roger Mervyn, BA FCA *1987;* R.T.M Pratt + Co, Westerly Rhodyate, Blagdon, BRISTOL, BS40 7TR.
PRATT, Mr. James David, MA ACA CTA *2000;* with BDO LLP, 55 Baker Street, LONDON, W1U 7EU.
PRATT, Mr. Jeremy Richard, MA FCA *1974;* India Investment Partners Ltd, Cayzer House, 30 Buckingham Gate, LONDON, SW1E 6NN.
PRATT, Miss. Joanne, BEng ACA CF *2003;* 25 Anvil Court, Pity Me, DURHAM, DH1 5EL.
PRATT, Miss. Joanne, BSc ACA *2010;* 20 Park House Apartments, 11 Park Row, LEEDS, LS1 5HB.
•PRATT, Mr. John Peter, FCA *1968;* (Tax Fac), John Pratt & Co, Basford House, 29 Augusta Street, LLANDUDNO, Clwyd, LL30 2AE.
PRATT, Mr. Kenneth Charles, BA ACA *1986;* 18 Eddiscombe Road, LONDON, SW6 4UA.
PRATT, Mrs. Laura Elizabeth, ACA *2008;* 29 Princes Way, Hutton, BRENTWOOD, ESSEX, CM13 2JW.
PRATT, Mr. Malcolm James, BA ACA *2007;* St. Marys, Hillside Road, SIDMOUTH, DEVON, EX10 8JD.
•PRATT, Mr. Mark Wesley, BA FCA *1986;* Chargedeep Limited, 42 Shevington Moor, Standish, WIGAN, LANCASHIRE, WN6 0SA.
PRATT, Mr. Matthew, BSc ACA *2002;* 5 Cavendish Drive, Lawford, MANNINGTREE, CO11 2EX.
PRATT, Mr. Michael Anthony, FCA *1975;* 20 The Fairways, Rushmere St. Andrew, IPSWICH, IP4 5TN.
•PRATT, Mr. Michael John, BA(Econ) FCA *1980;* High Grove House, 3 High Grove, WORKINGTON, CUMBRIA, CA14 3JQ.
PRATT, Mr. Michael Jonathan, BSc FCA *1990;* 3 Near Crook, Thackley, BRADFORD, BD10 8WA.
PRATT, Mr. Michael Richard, BSc FCA *1989;* with Ashtead, Kings House, 36-37 King Street, LONDON, EC2V 8BB.
PRATT, Miss. Nicola Jane, BA ACA *2005;* Grahame Stowe Bateson, 5-7 Portland Street, LEEDS, LS1 3DR.

•PRATT, Mr. Norman Ward Josiah, LLB ACA *1982;* KPMG LLP, 15 Canada Square, LONDON, E14 5GL. See also KPMG Europe LLP
PRATT, Mr. Peter, FCA *1950;* St. Michaels, 71 Sandown Park, TUNBRIDGE WELLS, TN2 4RT. (Life Member)
PRATT, Mr. Robert Ian, BA(Hons) ACA *2002;* 8300 Manitoba Street, Appt 225, PLAYA DEL REY, CA 90293, UNITED STATES.
PRATT, Miss. Ruth, ACA *2011;* 14 The Maisonettes, Alberta Avenue, SUTTON, SM1 2LQ.
PRATT, Mr. Stephen John, BSc ACA *1992;* Knight Frank, 55 Baker Street, LONDON, W1U 8AN.
PRATT, Mr. Thomas Barrie, FCA *1967;* Mayroyd, 120 Hollins Lane, ACCRINGTON, LANCASHIRE, BB5 2JS.
PRATT, Mr. William John, ACA CFP *2001;* Church Cottage, Litton, RADSTOCK, BA3 4PW.
PRATT, Mr. William John, BSc ACA *1989;* Fenner Dunlop Europe, Marfleet Lane, Marfleet, HULL, HU9 5RA.
PRATTEN, Mrs. Anita Astrid, MA ACA *1994;* 23 Bowhay, Hutton, BRENTWOOD, ESSEX, CM13 2JX.
•PRATTEN, Mrs. Helen, BSc ACA *1993;* KPMG LLP, 55 Second Street, Suite 1400, SAN FRANCISCO, CA 94105, UNITED STATES.
PRATTEN, Mrs. Sarah Veronica, BSc ACA *1990;* Fircroft, Copt Hall Road, Ightham, SEVENOAKS, TN15 9DT.
PREADY, Mr. Gary Peter, BA ACA *2004;* with PricewaterhouseCoopers LLP, The Atrium, 1 Harefield Road, UXBRIDGE, UB8 1EX.
PREBBLE, Mr. Andrew Jeremy, BA ACA MBA *1983;* Orchard House, Roundwood Lane, HAYWARDS HEATH, RH16 1SJ.
•PREBBLE, Mr. Barrie, FCA ATII *1966;* 10 Peaks Hill, PURLEY, SURREY, CR8 3JE.
PREBBLE, Mr. Ian Harvey, BA ACA *1997;* 5 Beech House, 229 Sanderstead Road, Sanderstead SOUTH CROYDON, Surrey, CR2 0PH.
PREBBLE, Mr. Terence Stanley, FCA *1969;* 8 Marden Avenue, BROMLEY, BR2 7PX.
PRECHNER, Mr. Martin Stanley, FCA *1974;* Miller Hunter, 1 Phillip Street, Lippo Building #12-01, SINGAPORE 048692, SINGAPORE.
PRECIOUS, Mr. John Richard, FCA *1966;* Spindles, Hotley Bottom Lane, Prestwood, GREAT MISSENDEN, HP16 9PL. (Life Member)
PRECIOUS, Mr. Martin David, BA ACA CTA *1984;* (Tax Fac), Bowlers Green House, Bowlers Mead, BUNTINGFORD, HERTFORDSHIRE, SG9 9DE.
PRECIOUS, Ms. Susan Margaret, MA FCA *1979;* Mabey Holdings Ltd, Mabey House, Floral Mile, Twyford, READING, RG10 9SQ.
•PREDDY, Miss. Alice Cresten, FCA *1977;* Cresten Preddy - AIMS Accountants For Business, Firle Cottage, Chapel Lane, Iden Green, CRANBROOK, KENT TN17 4HQ. See also AIMS - Cresten Preddy
PREDDY, Ms. Catherine Jane, MSci ACA *2007;* 12 Morning Forest Ct, THE WOODLANDS, TX TX77381, UNITED STATES.
PREECE, Miss. Amy Elizabeth, BSc ACA *2002;* Finance Wales, Oakleigh House, Park Place, CARDIFF, CF10 3DQ.
PREECE, Mr. Andrew Richard, BSc ACA *1994;* The Mill, Drakes Farm, Ide, EXETER, EX2 9RL.
PREECE, Mr. Christopher, BSc ACA *2005;* Elderfield Cross Road, Belmont, SUTTON, SM2 6DJ.
PREECE, Mr. David, FCA *1975;* 30 Orion Crescent, Potters Green, COVENTRY, CV2 2FQ.
•PREECE, Mr. Glyn, MA FCA *1977;* Barron & Co, 175 Cole Valley Road, Hall Green, BIRMINGHAM, B28 0DG.
PREECE, Mr. Gregory Clarke, BSc FCA *1978;* 15 Karrington Heights, Dundonald, BELFAST, BT16 1XZ.
PREECE, Miss. Helen Elizabeth, BSc ACA *1991;* Prospects, 69 Honey End Lane, READING, RG30 4EL.
PREECE, Mr. James Douglas, BSc ACA *2003;* 3 River Court, SHEPPERTON, MIDDLESEX, TW17 9EZ.
PREECE, Miss. Karen Anne, BSc FCA *1986;* 49 St Francis Avenue, SOLIHULL, B91 1EB.
•PREECE, Mr. Kevin John, FCA *1986;* (Tax Fac), Rice & Co, Harance House, Rumer Hill Business Estate, Rumer Hill Road, CANNOCK, STAFFORDSHIRE WS11 0ET.
PREECE, Mrs. Linda Anne, BSc FCA *1979;* (Tax Fac), 4 Canford Cliffs Avenue, POOLE, BH14 9QN.
PREECE, Miss. Linda Mary, MMath ACA *2010;* Grant Thornton, 1 Westminster Way, OXFORD, OX2 0PZ.
•PREECE, Mr. Malcolm Nathan, BA FCA DChA *1980;* Price & Company, 30/32 Gildredge Road, EASTBOURNE, BN21 4SH.
PREECE, Mr. Peter James, FCA *1965;* C/O Fraud Squad, Auckland Central Police Station, Private Bag 92002, AUCKLAND 1001, NEW ZEALAND.
•ⓘPREECE, Mr. Ralph Stephen, FCA *1970;* Keldholme, Linton Lane, Linton, WETHERBY, LS22 4HL.
PREECE, Mr. Robert John, FCA *1974;* 63 St. Georges Road, CHELTENHAM, GLOUCESTERSHIRE, GL50 3DU.
•PREECE, Mr. Robert Stephen, FCA *1979;* Broomfield & Alexander Limited, Ty Derw, Lime Tree Court, Cardiff Gate Business Park, CARDIFF, CF23 8AB. See also B & A Associates
PREECE, Mr. Robert William James, BSc FCA *1992;* 20 Lindsay Square, Bessborough Gardens, LONDON, SW1V 3SB.
PREECE, Mr. Thomas William, BA ACA *1987;* 2 Friarsgate Close, LIVERPOOL, L18 2JL.
PREECE SMITH, Mr. Benjamin Tudur Llywelyn, BA ACA *1998;* Old Courthouse, High Street, FAIRFORD, GL7 4AD.
PREECE SMITH, Mrs. Melanie Jayne, BA ACA *1998;* Old Courthouse, High Street, FAIRFORD, GL7 4AD.
PREEDY, Miss. Amelia, PhD BSc ACA *2011;* Room 401, Falmouth Hall, Imperial College London, Princes Gardens, LONDON, SW7 1BA.
PREEDY, Miss. Nicola, BSc ACA *2000;* 19 Dodds Crescent, WEST BYFLEET, SURREY, KT14 6RT.
PREEDY, Mr. Richard James, ACA *2010;* Flat 2, 66 Albion Road, LONDON, N16 9PH.
PREEDY, Mr. Timothy George, FCA *1959;* 37 Essa Road, SALTASH, PL12 4EE. (Life Member)
PREEN, Mr. Martin John, BA ACA *1992;* Bourne Eau House, 30 South Street, BOURNE, LINCOLNSHIRE, PE10 9LY.
PREEST, Mr. Brenig, BSc FCA *2000;* 5 Millbrook Road, DINAS POWYS, SOUTH GLAMORGAN, CF64 4BZ.
PREEST, Mrs. Sarah Elizabeth, BSc ACA ACIArb *1995;* with Grant Thornton UK LLP, 11-13 Penhill Road, CARDIFF, CF11 9UP.
PREISS, Mr. Andrew Michael, BSc ACA *1987;* Girston, 13 Greenhead Drive, Utley, KEIGHLEY, BD20 6EZ.
PREMCHAND, Mr. Sushil Kishore, BA FCA *1971;* PRS Services AG, Strehlgasse 33, P.O. Box 2717, 8022 ZURICH, SWITZERLAND.
PREMPEH, Mr. Lovelace, BA FCA *1974;* PO Box AN 5401, ACCRA, GHANA.
PRENDECKI, Miss. Rosemary, MA ACA *2011;* Flat 20, Quain Mansions, Queen's Club Gardens, LONDON, W14 9TW.
•PRENDERGAST, Mr. Alan Charles, BA FCA *1984;* Alan C Prendergast Ltd, Leicester House, Castle Street, Hay-on-Wye, HEREFORD, HR3 5DF. See also Alan C. Prendergast
PRENDERGAST, Mr. John William, BEng ACA *1989;* 25 Anson Avenue, WEST MALLING, ME19 4RA.
PRENDERGAST, Mrs. Susan Phaik Suan, BMus ACA *1993;* 16 Llys Meillion, Llyswen, BRECON, POWYS, LD3 0US.
PRENDIVILLE, Miss. Marie Agnes, ACA *1991;* Killoughteen, NEWCASTLE WEST, LIMERICK, COUNTY LIMERICK, IRELAND.
PRENTICE, Mr. Christopher John, BSc ACA *1988;* Elmfield House, Burgage, SOUTHWELL, NG25 0EP.
PRENTICE, Mr. Colin, FCA *1978;* 58 Howard Close, NORWICH, NR7 0LE.
PRENTICE, Mr. Geoffrey William, FCA *1975;* Orchard House, Thatchers Lane, Tansley, MATLOCK, DE4 5FD.
PRENTICE, Mr. Jonathan Miles, MA ACA *1991;* Ernst & Young, The Ernst & Young Building, 680 George Street, SYDNEY, NSW 2000, AUSTRALIA.
PRENTICE, Mr. Jonathan Richard, BA(Hons) ACA *1987;* Mead House, Pyle Hill, Mayford, WOKING, GU22 0SR.
PRENTICE, Miss. Leanne Sarah, BSc ACA *2009;* Flat 1, 5-7 Hornsey Street, LONDON, N7 8GB.
PRENTICE, Mr. Mark David Stanley, FCA CFA CFE *1989;* 48 Poplar Road, Shalford, GUILDFORD, SURREY, GU4 8DJ.
•PRENTICE, Mr. Nicholas John, MA FCA CTA *1981;* with Ernst & Young LLP, 1 More London Place, LONDON, SE1 2AF.
PRENTICE, Mr. Ronald Edwin, FCA *1956;* 40 Church Road, Egginton, DERBY, DE65 6HP. (Life Member)
PRENTICE, Mr. Steven David, ACA MAAT *2009;* with Ellacotts LLP, Countrywide House, 23 West Bar Street, BANBURY, OXFORDSHIRE, OX16 9SA.
PRENTICE, Mr. Thomas Morton, BA(Hons) ACA *2002;* 6th Floor, 80-110 New Oxford Street, LONDON, WC1A 1HB.
PRENTIS, Mrs. Elizabeth Anne, BCom ACA *1987;* Benyons, North Road, Goudhurst, CRANBROOK, KENT, TN17 1AS.
PRENTIS, Mr. Henry Barrell, FCA *1969;* Caltofts, Broad Street, HARLESTON, NORFOLK, IP20 9AZ.
PRENTIS, Mr. Henry George, BSc(Hons) ACA *2002;* Caltofts, Broad Street, HARLESTON, NORFOLK, IP20 9AZ.
PRENTIS, Mr. Jonathan Paul, BA ACA *1987;* Booker Limited, Equity House, Irthlingborough Road, WELLINGBOROUGH, NORTHAMPTONSHIRE, NN8 1LT.
PRENTIS, Mr. Michael Jonathan, MA ACA *1982;* Benyons, North Road, Goudhurst, CRANBROOK, KENT, TN17 1AS.
•PRENTIS, Mr. Nigel Anthony, FCA *1974;* (Tax Fac), Prentis & Co LLP, 115c Milton Road, CAMBRIDGE, CB4 1XE. See also Prentis & Co
PRENTIS, Miss. Poppy, ACA *2008;* 46 St. Andrews Road, CAMBRIDGE, CB4 1DL.
PRESBURY, Mr. Brian Michael Henry, BSc FCA *1974;* 154 Arabella, PO Box 788, KLEINMOND, WESTERN CAPE PROVINCE, 7195, SOUTH AFRICA.
PRESCOT, Mr. Alastair John Vernon, BSc ACA *1984;* Netherwood House, 3 The Brow Church Road, Combe Down, BATH, BA2 5JL.
PRESCOTT, Mr. Alexander John, FCA *1959;* Woodview, Dacre, PENRITH, CA11 0HH. (Life Member)
PRESCOTT, Mr. Andrew James, BA(Hons) ACA *2001;* 2 Woodland Avenue, LYMM, CHESHIRE, WA13 0BJ.
PRESCOTT, Mr. Anthony Jeffrey, ACA *1986;* 8 Belvedere Road, Ainsdale, SOUTHPORT, PR8 2PA.
PRESCOTT, Mr. Charles Russell, FCA *1964;* 39 Wilmington Avenue, LONDON, W4 3HA.
PRESCOTT, Mr. Charles Stanley William, FCA *1978;* Fitch Ratings Limited, 30 North Colonnade, LONDON, E14 5GN.
PRESCOTT, Mr. David, ACA *2008;* Flat 2/B Sir John Lyon House, 8 High Timber Street, LONDON, EC4V 3PA.
PRESCOTT, Mrs. Elizabeth Anne, BA ACA *1997;* Braefoot, Longhorsley, MORPETH, NE65 8UU.
PRESCOTT, Mr. Francis Norman, LLB FCA *1963;* Summerlands, Kelleythorpe, DRIFFIELD, YO25 9DW. (Life Member)
PRESCOTT, Mr. George Andrew, BA FCA *1972;* 120 Sutton Court, Fauconberg Road, LONDON, W4 3EE.
PRESCOTT, Mrs. Janet, ACA *1984;* 47 West Hill, Portishead, BRISTOL, BS20 6LG.
PRESCOTT, Mr. Jeffrey, FCA *1984;* (Tax Fac), Berwin Leighton Paisner, Adelaide House, London Bridge, LONDON, EC4R 9HA.
PRESCOTT, Mr. Jeremy Malcolm, MA MSc FCA *1973;* 142 Court Lane, Dulwich, LONDON, SE21 7EB.
PRESCOTT, Mr. Neil, BA FCA *1990;* 51 Carkington Road, LIVERPOOL, L25 8TA.
PRESCOTT, Mr. Philip Henry, LLB ACA *1996;* 26 Station Road, AMERSHAM, BUCKINGHAMSHIRE, HP7 0BE.
PRESCOTT, Ms. Sarah Jane, BA ACA *2005;* C C H Association, 2 Ocean Way, CARDIFF, CF24 5TG.
PRESCOTT, Mrs. Susan, MA FCA *1992;* Brackens, Main Road, Knockholt, SEVENOAKS, TN14 7LQ.
PRESCOTT, Miss. Zoe Rebecca Elisabeth, ACA *2008;* 57A Doudney Court, William Street, BRISTOL, bs3 4ap.
•PRESKY, Mr. Howard Mark, FCA *1982;* (Tax Fac), Howard Presky Limited, 21 Bedford Square, LONDON, WC1B 3HH.
PRESKY, Mr. Oliver, BSc(Hons) ACA *2011;* Flat 6, Yale Court, Honeybourne Road, West Hampstead, LONDON, NW6 1JF.
PRESLAND, Mr. Peter Eric, LLB ACA *1979;* Mainvalley Limited, Rats Castle, Biddenden, ASHFORD, TN27 8DY.
PRESLEY, Miss. Katherine Rosemary, BA(Hons) ACA *2000;* with KPMG, 147 Collins Street, MELBOURNE, VIC 3000, AUSTRALIA.
•PRESS, Mr. Daniel Simon, BSc ACA *1999;* Belgrave Accountants, 5 Belgrave Gardens, St Johns Wood, LONDON, NW8 0QY.
PRESS, Mrs. Karen Michelle, BA ACA *2004;* 7 Squirrels Way, Earley, READING, RG6 5QT.
•PRESS, Mrs. Penelope Jane Arthurson, BSc FCA *1987;* SBM Resources, 48 Wycombe Road, Prestwood, GREAT MISSENDEN, BUCKINGHAMSHIRE, HP16 0PQ.
PRESS, Mrs. Sally, BSc ACA *2002;* 169 York Road, WOKING, SURREY, GU22 7XS.
PRESS, Mr. Steven Ross Sainfield, BA ACA *1979;* 61 Flood Street, LONDON, SW3 5SU.
PRESSBURG, Mr. Mark Andrew, BA ACA *1992;* 3 Cheyneys Avenue, Canons Park, EDGWARE, MIDDLESEX, HA8 6SA.
•PRESSDEE, Mr. Malcolm John, FCA *1970;* Timbers, 31 Chawkmare Coppice, BOGNOR REGIS, WEST SUSSEX, PO21 3SP.
PRESSDEE, Mr. Peter James, FCA *1970;* Dekan Consulting, 27 Duranta Street, BELLBOWRIE, QLD 4070, AUSTRALIA.
PRESSLAND, Mrs. Janet Elaine, FCA *1988;* Black Horse Cottage, 33 Milton Abbas, BLANDFORD FORUM, DT11 0BL.
PRESSLEY, Mr. Neville James, BA FCA *1970;* 25 Church Street, SHOREHAM-BY-SEA, WEST SUSSEX, BN43 5DQ.
PRESSWELL, Mr. Graeme Ian, BSc ACA *1984;* Poplars Farm, 41 The Green, Stotfold, HITCHIN, HERTFORDSHIRE, SG5 4AN.
PREST, Mr. Anthony Richard, BA FCA *1984;* Langley Cottage, 28 Dewlands Way, VERWOOD, BH31 6JN.
PREST, Mr. Joseph Sherwood, BA FCA *1972;* 20 Nottingham Place, LONDON, W1U 5NH. (Life Member)
PREST, Mr. Matthew Robert, BA ACA *1998;* 74 Endlesham Road, LONDON, SW12 8JL.
PREST, Mr. Michael Albert, ACA *2009;* Floor 4, Moore Stephens, 150 Aldersgate Street, LONDON, EC1A 4AB.
PREST, Mr. Neville Lyons, BSc FCA *1983;* Baliol Lodge, 63 Prior Park Road, Widcombe, BATH, BA2 4NF.
PRESTAGE, Mr. Robin William, FCA *1972;* Cowgill Holloway, 49 Peter Street, MANCHESTER, M2 3NG.
PRESTON, Mr. Alan, FCA *1962;* 55 Sharon Park Close, Grappenhall, WARRINGTON, WA4 2YN. (Life Member)
PRESTON, Mr. Alistair Lees, MSc BA ACA *1999;* 14 Westcombe Avenue, LEEDS, LS8 2BS.
PRESTON, Mr. Andrew Simon, BSc ACA *1996;* 24 Chester Road, CHIGWELL, IG7 6AJ.
•PRESTON, Mr. Anthony Clive Jellicoe, BA FCA *1975;* Griffiths Preston, Aldbury House, Dower Mews, 108 High Street, BERKHAMSTED, HERTFORDSHIRE HP4 2BL.
PRESTON, Mrs. Chivonne Li-Shan, MA MSc ACA *2002;* 5 Larkhall Rise, LONDON, SW4 6JB.
PRESTON, Miss. Christie, BA(Hons) ACA *2009;* Flat 6, 129 Whitechapel High Street, LONDON, E1 7PT.
PRESTON, Mrs. Christine Anne, BEng ACA *1997;* 25 Canada Way, LIPHOOK, HAMPSHIRE, GU30 7TD.
PRESTON, Mr. Christopher John, BA ACA *1995;* 66 Colomb Street, LONDON, SE10 9HA.
PRESTON, Mr. Christopher Trafford, FCA *1964;* 27 Gastard Lane, Gastard, CORSHAM, WILTSHIRE, SN13 9QP.
PRESTON, Mrs. Claire Elizabeth Jayne, BSc ACA *2005;* TiernayFedrick, 19 Trinity Square, LLANDUDNO, CONWY, LL30 2RD.
PRESTON, Miss. Claire Nicola, BA ACA *1994;* 9 Semley House, Semley Place, LONDON, SW1W 9QJ.
PRESTON, Mr. Colin John, BA ACA *1999;* 41 Churchfield Mansion, New Kings Road, LONDON, SW6 4RA.
PRESTON, Mr. Craig Thomas, BA ACA *1996;* 71 Crabtree Lane, HARPENDEN, HERTFORDSHIRE, AL5 5PX.
PRESTON, Mr. David, BSc ACA *1996;* 31 Whitchurch Lane, Shirley, SOLIHULL, WEST MIDLANDS, B90 1PB.
PRESTON, Mr. David Alan, FCA *1973;* 6 Misty Valley View, ROLEYSTONE, WA 6111, AUSTRALIA. (Life Member)
PRESTON, Mr. David Arthur, BSc FCA *1964;* Amadeus, Greenacres, Runfold, FARNHAM, GU10 1QH.
PRESTON, Mr. David Edward, BSc ACA *1993;* Mercator Trust Co. Ltd, PO Box 336, Anson Court, La Route des Camps, St Martin, GUERNSEY GY1 3UQ.
PRESTON, Mr. David Ian, ACA *2008;* 18 Place Philosophes, 1205 GENEVA, SWITZERLAND.
PRESTON, Mr. David James, BA ACA *1986;* Datel 4 Cinnamon Park, Crab Lane Fearnhead, WARRINGTON, WA2 0XP.
PRESTON, Mr. David Richard, BA FCA *1975;* 51 Valley Way, FAKENHAM, NORFOLK, NR21 8PH.
PRESTON, Mr. David William, BSc ACA *1993;* 82 Callow Hill Road, Alvechurch, BIRMINGHAM, B48 7LR.
PRESTON, Miss. Dawn Beverley, ACA *2008;* 6 Green Way, Nunthorpe, MIDDLESBROUGH, CLEVELAND, TS7 0DB.
PRESTON, Mrs. Estelle, BA ACA *1999;* 31 Whitchurch Lane, Shirley, SOLIHULL, WEST MIDLANDS, B90 1PB.
PRESTON, Mr. Gavin Shaun, BA ACA *1998;* Above Beck, Woodland Road, WINDERMERE, LA23 2AN.
PRESTON, Mrs. Gillian Leslie, MA ACA *2004;* 41 Monmouth Street, Topsham, EXETER, EX3 0AJ.
•PRESTON, Mr. Iain William, BSc FCA ATII *1989;* (Tax Fac), ICAP Plc, 2 Broadgate, LONDON, EC2M 7UR.
PRESTON, Miss. Jennifer, ACA *2009;* 10 Trinity Close, Gobowen, OSWESTRY, SHROPSHIRE, SY11 3NZ.
PRESTON, Mr. John, FCA *1955;* Grange House, Grange Avenue, Totteridge, LONDON, N20 8AD. (Life Member)

•**PRESTON, Mr. John David, BSc FCA FTII** *1982;* (Tax Fac), PricewaterhouseCoopers LLP, 7 More London Riverside, LONDON, SE1 2RT. See also PricewaterhouseCoopers
PRESTON, Mr. John Michael, FCA *1965;* 56 Wansunt Road, BEXLEY, DA5 2DJ.
PRESTON, Mrs. Julia Anne, BA ACA *1989;* JASMAQ Services, 898 Anketell Road, WA 6167 DI, WA 6167, AUSTRALIA.
PRESTON, Mrs. Karen Lee, BSc ACA *1996;* 4a Bridgegate North, The Pavilions Chester Business Park, CHESTER, CH4 9QH.
•**PRESTON, Mr. Kevin Henry Duncan, BSc FCA** *1982;* (Tax Fac), Amherst & Shapland Limited, 4 Irnham Road, MINEHEAD, SOMERSET, TA24 5DG.
PRESTON, Mrs. Lesley Anne, ACA *1983;* Finance Office, University of Warwick University House, Kirby Corner Road, COVENTRY, CV4 8UW.
•**PRESTON, Mr. Malcolm Hunter, BSc ACA** *1987;* (Tax Fac), PricewaterhouseCoopers LLP, 7 More London Riverside, LONDON, SE1 2RT. See also PricewaterhouseCoopers
PRESTON, Mrs. Margaret Susan, BA FCA CTA *1982;* Kennedy Institute of Rheumatology, 65 Aspenlea Road, LONDON, W6 8LH.
PRESTON, Mr. Mark David, BSc(Hons) ACA *2002;* Po Box 10516, Grand Cayman, GEORGE TOWN, KY1 1005, CAYMAN ISLANDS.
PRESTON, Mr. Martin Edward, FCA *1966;* Vue Des Hanois Rocque Poisson, St. Pierre Du Bois, GUERNSEY, GY7 9HW. (Life Member)
PRESTON, Mr. Martin Ernest, BSc ACA *1991;* 11 Osborne Gardens, WHITLEY BAY, NE26 3PG.
PRESTON, Mr. Michael David, MA FCA *1971;* 8 Abbey Road, ORANGEBURG, NY 10962, UNITED STATES.
PRESTON, Mr. Nicholas John, BA ACA *1996;* AXA Insurance, Ballam Road, LYTHAM ST. ANNES, FY8 4JZ.
•**PRESTON, Mr. Paul John, FCA CTA** *1971;* (Tax Fac), PJP Tax Consultancy Ltd, Longbridge Farm, WARWICK, CV34 6RB.
PRESTON, Mr. Raymond Eustace, FCA *1949;* 22 Copthorne Close, Oakley, BEDFORD, MK43 7SQ. (Life Member)
PRESTON, Mr. Richard Murray, FCA *1969;* Long Acre, Cobham Road, LEATHERHEAD, KT22 9SH.
PRESTON, Mr. Richard Timothy, MA ACA *1998;* Viking House, Foundry Lane, HORSHAM, RH13 5PX.
•**PRESTON, Mr. Robert John, FCA** *1970;* Southon & Co, 6 The Parade, EXMOUTH, EX8 1RL.
PRESTON, Mr. Robert Maurice, FCA *1968;* 47 Peaketon Avenue, Redbridge, ILFORD, ESSEX, IG4 5PG.
PRESTON, Mr. Robert Timothy Noah, BA ACA *2000;* #168 Emerald Forest, #2888 Hunan Road, Pudong, SHANGHAI 201315, CHINA.
PRESTON, Mrs. Samantha Joanne, BSc ACA *1998;* 4 Valeside, HERTFORD, SG14 2AR.
PRESTON, Mr. Simon Colin, BSc ACA *2006;* 14 Massams Lane, LIVERPOOL, L37 7BE.
•**PRESTON, Mr. Stephen John, FCA** *1971;* Prestons, The Old Stables, Ilex Farm, Handley Lane, Handley, Clay Cross CHESTERFIELD DERBYSHIRE S45 9AT.
PRESTON, Mr. Steven, ACA *2011;* Flat 4, Linfield, Grove Road, Headingley, LEEDS, LS6 2AB.
PRESTON, Mrs. Suzanne, BA FCA *1977;* 15 Upper Profit, Langton Green, TUNBRIDGE WELLS, TN3 0BZ.
•**PRESTON, Mrs. Suzanne Elizabeth, ACA FCCA** *2009;* Howsons, 50 Broad Street, LEEK, ST13 5NS. See also Howsons Accountants Limited
PRESTON, Mr. Timothy James, BA ACA CTA *2006;* The Kellogg Building, Talbot Road, Old Trafford, MANCHESTER, M16 0PU.
PRESTON, Mr. Timothy Michael, BA ACA *1997;* Apollo Fire Detectors Ltd, 36 Brookside Road, HAVANT, HAMPSHIRE, PO9 1JR.
•**PRESTON, Mr. William Brian, FCA** *1961;* William B. Preston, 1 Montrouge Crescent, EPSOM, KT17 3PB.
•**PRESTON, Mr. William Roger, FCA** *1974;* The Ollis Partnership Limited, 2 Hamilton Terrace, Holly Walk, LEAMINGTON SPA, WARWICKSHIRE, CV32 4LY.
PRESTWICH, Mrs. Anna Marie, BSc ACA *2001;* 6 Glendale Road, BURGESS HILL, WEST SUSSEX, RH15 0EJ.
•**PRESTWICH, Mrs. Katharine Esther, BA ACA** *1994;* CKP Services, Weavers Cottage, Porters Lane, Fordham Heath, COLCHESTER, CO3 9TX.
PRESTWICH, Mr. Philip James, BSc ACA *2006;* 139 Twentywell Lane, SHEFFIELD, S17 4QA.
PRESTWICH, Mr. Robert Geoffrey, FCA *1965;* 16 Sabden Close, Walmersley, BURY, BL9 5LR.
PRETLOVE, Miss. Anne Margaret, BA ACA *1990;* 10 Sandy Lane, LYMM, WA13 9HQ.
PRETORIUS, Mr. Gideon Petrus, ACA CA(SA) *2010;* Flat 1, 2 Cubitt Street, LONDON, WC1X 0LQ.
•**PRETTEJOHN, Mr. Philip Muir, FCA** *1973;* (Tax Fac), Rawlinson & Hunter, Lower Mill, Kingston Road, Ewell, EPSOM, KT17 2AE. See also Boroughs
PRETTY, Mr. Andrew Charles, ACA *2008;* 36 Uxbridge Road, KINGSTON UPON THAMES, KT1 2LL.
•**PRETTY, Mr. Charles Edmund, BSc FCA** *1976;* with Ernst & Young LLP, Wessex House, 19 Threefield Lane, SOUTHAMPTON, SO14 3QB.
PRETTY, Mrs. Sarah Elizabeth, BSc ACA *2003;* 36 Chapel Road, West End, SOUTHAMPTON, SO30 3FN.
PREUVENEERS, Mr. Simon Edward John, BA ACA *1999;* 18 London Terrace, Hackney Road, LONDON, E2 7SQ.
PREVATT, Mr. Francis Trevor, BSc FCA *1980;* 10 Young Pow Avenue, La Seiva, MARAVAL, TRINIDAD AND TOBAGO.
PREVEDELLO, Mr. Bruno, BSc ACA *1994;* Via G. Previati 47, 20149 MILAN, ITALY.
•**PREVETT, Mr. Anthony James, BSc FCA** *1974;* (Tax Fac), Revill Pearce, Stane House, Salmons Corner, Nr. Coggeshall, COLCHESTER, CO6 1RX. See also Brannans
PREVETT, Mr. Christopher Rex, BTech FCA *1977;* Leyenda Patria 3104, Apto. 10.02, MONTEVIDEO, 11300, URUGUAY.
PREVETT, Mr. Julien Edward George, FCA *1966;* 28 Paradise Walk, LONDON, SW3 4JL. (Life Member)
PREVEZER, Mr. David Simon James, BA ACA *2006;* Flat 77, Chandos Way, LONDON, NW11 7HF.
PREVEZER, Mr. Henry, FCA *1950;* 10 Willowdene, View Road Highgate, LONDON, N6 4DE. (Life Member)
•**PREVEZER, Mr. Jonathan Warren, BA FCA** *1981;* Citroen Wells, Devonshire House, 1 Devonshire Street, LONDON, W1W 5DR.
PREVIERO, Mr. Marco, BSc(Econ) ACA MBA *1997;* Frant Grange Church Lane, Frant, TUNBRIDGE WELLS, TN3 9DX.
•**PREVOST, Mr. John Peter Raymond, FCA** *1976;* (Tax Fac), C. B. Heslop & Co, 111 Milford Road, LYMINGTON, HAMPSHIRE, SO41 8DN.
PREW, Mr. Roger Vincent, FCA *1968;* The Old Cottage, Bath Road, Kiln Green, READING, RG10 9SE. (Life Member)
PREW, Mr. Simon Barry, MA ACA *1990;* 11 Nomansland, Wheathampstead, ST. ALBANS, HERTFORDSHIRE, AL4 8EJ.
PREW, Mr. William David, BA ACA *1996;* 44 Grove Road, WINDSOR, BERKSHIRE, SL4 1JQ.
PREYSER, Mr. Jacobus Francke, ACA CA(SA) *2008;* 14 Lindbergh Rise, Whiteley, FAREHAM, HAMPSHIRE, PO15 7HJ.
•**PRICE, Mr. Adrian, FCA** *1982;* Menzies LLP, Wentworth House, 4400 Parkway, Whiteley, FAREHAM, HAMPSHIRE PO15 7FJ.
•**PRICE, Mr. Adrian Robert Revill, FCA** *1987;* Pells, 17 Newstead Grove, NOTTINGHAM, NG1 4GZ. See also T Wilford Pell & Company
PRICE, Mr. Alan Harvey, FCA *1969;* Pollbreac, Coldwell, North Kessock, INVERNESS, IV1 3XQ.
PRICE, Mr. Alan Kenneth, BA FCA *1992;* 16 Rue Du Bassin De Thau, 34630 ST THIBERY, FRANCE.
PRICE, Mr. Alec Mitchell, FCA *1949;* 22 Deepdale Road, Wollaton, NOTTINGHAM, NG8 2FU. (Life Member)
PRICE, Mrs. Alison, BA ACA *2002;* 11 Salon Way, HUNTINGDON, CAMBRIDGESHIRE, PE29 6UG.
PRICE, Mrs. Amanda Jane, BSc ACA *2010;* 9 Amcotes Place, CHELMSFORD, CM2 9HZ.
PRICE, Mr. Andrew Christopher, BA ACA *2000;* Woodside Pockford Road, Chiddingfold, GODALMING, SURREY, GU8 4TP.
PRICE, Mr. Andrew Christopher, BA ACA *1996;* The Briars, 36 Pilkington Avenue, SUTTON COLDFIELD, B72 1LD.
PRICE, Mr. Andrew David, ACA *1996;* 5 Edwin Close, STAFFORD, ST17 9XN.
•**PRICE, Mr. Andrew David, BA FCA** *1990;* (Tax Fac), Andrew Price & Co Limited, Haldon House, 4 Castle Road, TORQUAY, TQ1 3BG.
PRICE, Mr. Andrew James, BA ACA *1989;* 47 Greenlee Drive, NEWCASTLE UPON TYNE, NE7 7GA.
PRICE, Mr. Andrew James, BA ACA *2006;* Colt Telecom Group, Beaufort House, 15 St. Botolph Street, LONDON, EC3A 7QN.
PRICE, Mr. Andrew John, MA ACA *1984;* Hardwick House, Twitchell Road, GREAT MISSENDEN, HP16 0BQ.
PRICE, Mr. Andrew Owen, BSc ACA *1992;* Minvers, Hedgehog Lane, HASLEMERE, GU27 2PJ.
PRICE, Mrs. Ann Arrol, BSc ACA *1979;* 18 Archer Road, PENARTH, CF64 3HW.
PRICE, Mrs. Anne Margaret, BA ACA *1993;* 30 Gresham Street, Dresdner Kleinwort, PO Box 52715, LONDON, EC2P 2XY.
PRICE, Mr. Anthony David, BSc ACA *1996;* Diageo Plc Lakeside Drive, Park Royal, LONDON, NW10 7HQ.
PRICE, Mr. Barnaby Valentine Walwyn, FCA *1966;* Lower Norchard Farm, Poepleton, PERSHORE, WR10 2EG. (Life Member)
•**PRICE, Mr. Barrie, FCA FCCA FBIM** *1959;* Eura Audit UK, John Aislabie Wing, Eva Lett House, 1 South Crescent, RIPON, NORTH YORKSHIRE HG4 1SN. See also Lishman Sidwell Campbell & Price LLP and Lishman Sidwell Campbell & Price Ltd
PRICE, Mr. Benedict James, BA ACA *1992;* Caffe Nero, 3 Neal Street, LONDON, WC2H 9QL.
PRICE, Mr. Brian Derek, FCA *1962;* (Member of Council 1987 - 1993), Banbury Community Transport Association Ltd, 17 Beaumont Business Centre Beaumont Close, BANBURY, OXFORDSHIRE, OX16 1TN. (Life Member)
PRICE, Mr. Brian Michael, FCA *1965;* 5 Arklow Court, Station Approach, Chorleywood, RICKMANSWORTH, WD3 5NF.
PRICE, Miss. Brigit Anne, MA MEng ACA *2000;* Caeronnen, Llantrithyd, COWBRIDGE, SOUTH GLAMORGAN, CF71 7UB.
PRICE, Mrs. Carli, BA ACA *2004;* 2 Lido Bay Court, La Route de St. Aubin, St. Helier, JERSEY, JE2 3SG.
PRICE, Mrs. Caroline Ann, BSc ACA *1982;* 1 Titchfield Close, BURGESS HILL, RH15 0RX.
PRICE, Mrs. Caroline Fiona, LLB ACA *1989;* 160 Burbage Road, LONDON, SE21 7AG.
PRICE, Miss. Catrin Elizabeth, BA ACA *2006;* Rua Ipero 63, Apt 21, Vila Madalena, SAO PAULO, 05439-020, BRAZIL.
PRICE, Mr. Cedric Harry, BSc FCA *1963;* Willow Lodge, Moddershall, STONE, ST15 8TJ.
PRICE, Miss. Ceri Jane, MSc ACA *1990;* 2 Hill Grove, Henleaze, BRISTOL, BS9 4RJ.
PRICE, Mr. Charles, BA ACA *2005;* 19 Stretton Mansions, Glaisher Street, Greenwich, LONDON, SE8 3JP.
PRICE, Mr. Christian Lee, BSc ACA *2001;* 27 Shakespeare Avenue, Hawarden, DEESIDE, CLWYD, CH5 3TB.
PRICE, Mr. Christopher, MA FCA *1995;* 743 Robinhood Circle, BLOOMFIELD HILLS, MI 48304, UNITED STATES.
PRICE, Mr. Christopher Daniel Alan, ACA *2008;* Basement, 49 Chesson Road, LONDON, W14 9QR.
PRICE, Mr. Christopher David, BA ACA *1981;* 14 Marlow Mill, Mill Road, MARLOW, BUCKINGHAMSHIRE, SL7 1QD.
PRICE, Mr. Christopher John, FCA *1973;* 17 Woodside Road, Ravenshead, NOTTINGHAM, NG15 9FX.
PRICE, Mr. Christopher John, BA ACA *2005;* Flat 94 The Maltings, 211 Ecclesall Road, SHEFFIELD, S11 8HP.
PRICE, Mr. Christopher Pendrell, BSc FCA *1984;* 33 Heathcote, TADWORTH, KT20 5TH.
PRICE, Mr. Christopher Ronald, BSc ACA *1987;* Epson UK Ltd Westside, London Road, HEMEL HEMPSTEAD, HERTFORDSHIRE, HP3 9TD.
PRICE, Mrs. Claire Margaret, BSc ACA *2000;* 12 Massewee, L-7670 REULAND, LUXEMBOURG.
PRICE, Mr. Colin Richard, MA FCA *1980;* 37 Ravensfield Gardens, EPSOM, KT19 0ST.
PRICE, Mr. Craig, BSc(Hons) ACA *2004;* 8 Queens Avenue, Douglas, ISLE OF MAN, IM1 4DA.
PRICE, Mr. Cyril Bertram, FCA *1937;* Villa Assumpta, 55 Tanner Road Wembley, PO Box 13266, CASCADES, 3202, SOUTH AFRICA. (Life Member)
PRICE, Mr. Dale Barry, BSc ACA *2010;* Control Techniques Drives Ltd, 79 Mochdre Industrial Estate Mochdre, NEWTOWN, POWYS, SY16 4LE.
PRICE, Mr. Darren Clive, BA ACA *1996;* 63 Beachampstead Road, Great Staughton, ST. NEOTS, PE19 5DX.
PRICE, Mr. David, BSc ACA *1996;* 45 Hodney Road, Eye, PETERBOROUGH, PE6 7YQ.
PRICE, Mr. David Anthony Huntley, BCom FCA CF *1990;* Hattan Street 1 Villa 18, Arabian Ranches, DUBAI, UNITED ARAB EMIRATES.
•**PRICE, Mr. David Edward, FCA FCCA CF** *1969;* (Tax Fac), Price Pearson Ltd, Finch House, 28-30 Wolverhampton Street, DUDLEY, DY1 1DB. See also Finch House Properties Limited
PRICE, Mr. David John, BSc ACA *1995;* 12 Mayfair Drive, Thornhill, CARDIFF, CF14 9EN.
PRICE, Mr. David John, BA ACA ATII *1984;* 10 Nightingale Court, Kelvedon Grove, SOLIHULL, WEST MIDLANDS, B91 2UG.
PRICE, Mr. David John, BSc FCA *1984;* 11 Brudenell Avenue, POOLE, BH13 7NW.
PRICE, Mr. David Jonathan, BA ACA *1998;* National Australian Bank, 800 Bourke Street, MELBOURNE, VIC 3008, AUSTRALIA.
PRICE, Mr. David Lester, MSocSc BA(Hons) ACA *2002;* with Ernst & Young LLP, 1 Colmore Square, BIRMINGHAM, B4 6HQ.
PRICE, Mr. David Michael, FCA *1972;* Corner Cottage Brook Lane, Neacroft, CHRISTCHURCH, DORSET, BH23 8JR.
•**PRICE, Mr. David Nigel, MA FCA ATII** *1982;* (Tax Fac), Nigel Price, Highfield, Green Lane, Appledore, BIDEFORD, DEVON EX39 1QZ.
PRICE, Mr. David Robert, BSc ACA *1983;* 1 Titchfield Close, BURGESS HILL, RH15 0RX.
PRICE, Mr. David Stewart, MA FCA *1964;* 118 Overdale, ASHTEAD, KT21 1PX.
PRICE, Mr. David William, BA ACA *1992;* 135 Avenell Road, Highbury, LONDON, N5 1BH.
PRICE, Mr. David William, BA ACA *1990;* 23 Orchard Road, Shalford, GUILDFORD, GU4 8ER.
PRICE, Mr. David Wyn, LLB ACA *1992;* 1 Foyle Road, Blackheath, LONDON, SE3 7RQ.
PRICE, Mr. Douglas Jonathan Charles, BA ACA *1990;* 2 Grasmere Avenue, LONDON, W3 6JU.
•**PRICE, Mr. Duncan, BA FCA** *1984;* DP Solutionz Limited, 1 The Old Drive, WELWYN GARDEN CITY, HERTFORDSHIRE, AL8 6TB.
•**PRICE, Mr. Edward Howe, FCA** *1952;* with Pitt Godden & Taylor, Brunel House, George Street, GLOUCESTER, GL1 1BZ.
PRICE, Mrs. Elisabeth, BSc ACA *1999;* 6 School Lane, Alvechurch, BIRMINGHAM, B48 7SB.
PRICE, Mrs. Elizabeth Ann, BA ACA *1983;* 9 Millbuie Street, ELGIN, MORAYSHIRE, IV30 6GE.
•**PRICE, Mrs. Ellen Anita, BA(Hons) ACA** *2001;* Cyfrifon Cadog Accounts, Trehelyg, Heol yr Orsaf, LLANGADOG, DYFED, SA19 9LS.
PRICE, Mr. Eric Rodney, BA ACA *1996;* 150 Repton Road, West Bridgford, NOTTINGHAM, NG2 7EL.
PRICE, Mr. Frederick Enoch, MA FCA *1961;* 3 Austen Place, Edgbaston, BIRMINGHAM, B15 1NJ. (Life Member)
PRICE, Mr. Gareth Craig, BA ACA *1991;* 48 Herbert March Close, Radyr Vale, Llandaff, CARDIFF, CF5 2TD.
PRICE, Mr. Gareth John, MA ACA ASI *1992;* Ty Rhosyn, 14a Crescent Close, COWBRIDGE, SOUTH GLAMORGAN, CF71 7EB.
PRICE, Mr. Gareth Rutherford, FCA *1982;* 23 Groves Lea, Mortimer, READING, RG7 3SS.
PRICE, Mr. Geoffrey Bernard, BSc FCA *1984;* Tanglewood, 15 Uplands Road, KENLEY, CR8 5EE.
PRICE, Mr. George William, FCA *1949;* Cherry Trees, Ashmore Green Road, Ashmore Green, THATCHAM, BERKSHIRE, RG18 9ES. (Life Member)
PRICE, Mr. Glyn Richard, FCA FIIA QICA *1970;* 20 Stanley Road, Kings Heath, BIRMINGHAM, B14 7NB.
PRICE, Mr. Graham James, FCA *1958;* 66 Park Mount, HARPENDEN, AL5 3AR. (Life Member)
PRICE, Mr. Gregory, BA ACA *2002;* 37 Walmington Fold, LONDON, N12 7LD.
PRICE, Mrs. Heather, BSc FCA *1977;* The Cedars Llanyre, LLANDRINDOD WELLS, POWYS, LD1 6DY.
PRICE, Miss. Heather Elizabeth, BSc ACA *1988;* 33a West Hill Avenue, EPSOM, KT19 8LE.
PRICE, Mrs. Helen, BSc ACA *2006;* with Muras Baker Jones, Regent House, Bath Avenue, WOLVERHAMPTON, WV1 4EG.
PRICE, Mrs. Helen Jane, BA ACA *1992;* Churchfields, Edlaston, ASHBOURNE, DERBYSHIRE, DE6 2DQ.
PRICE, Miss. Helen Jane, ACA *2009;* Flat 216, Latymer Court, Hammersmith Road, LONDON, W6 7JY.
PRICE, Mrs. Helen Zofia, BA ACA *2005;* 31 Wessex Gardens, Twyford, READING, RG10 0BA.
PRICE, Mr. Howard Gregson, FCA *1961;* 42 Towers Way, LEEDS, LS6 4PJ.
PRICE, Mr. Howard Philip Andrew, ACA *1990;* 11 Coval Road, LONDON, SW14 7RW.
PRICE, Mr. Humphrey James Montgomery, FCA *1966;* L S I Management Llp, 21 St. James's Square, LONDON, SW1Y 4JZ.
PRICE, Mr. Ian, ACA CTA *2004;* 6 Tir Wat, Mynydd Isa, MOLD, CLWYD, CH7 6SD.
•**PRICE, Mr. Ian John, ACA** *2006;* Griffiths Marshall, Beaumont House, 172 Southgate Street, GLOUCESTER, GL1 2EZ.

•PRICE, Mrs. Jacqueline, ACA *1979;* JP Accounting Services, 15 The Paddock, Newbold Verdon, LEICESTER, LE9 9NW.
PRICE, Miss. Jacqueline Amanda, BA(Hons) ACA CISA *2000;* Flat 2, 7 Pembroke Road, SEVENOAKS, TN13 1XR.
•PRICE, Mr. James Ian, BA(Hons) ACA CF *2002;* WKH, PO Box 501, The Nexus Building, Broadway, LETCHWORTH GARDEN CITY, HERTFORDSHIRE SG6 9BL.
PRICE, Miss. Janette, ACA *2011;* 18 Darris Road, INVERNESS, IV2 4DH.
PRICE, Mrs. Janice Ann, BA ACA *1988;* Wisteria 2 Park Street Kings Cliffe, PETERBOROUGH, NORTHAMPTONSHIRE, PE8 6XN.
PRICE, Miss. Jennifer Anne, BA ACA *1997;* Sara Lee Australia, 37 Ryde Road, Pymble, SYDNEY, NSW 2073, AUSTRALIA.
PRICE, Miss. Jennifer Louise, LLB ACA *2006;* 10 Shepherd Way, Taverham, NORWICH, NR8 6UD.
PRICE, Miss. Joanna Marilyn, BSc ACA *2005;* with W J James & Co Limited, Bishop House, 10 Wheat Street, BRECON, LD3 7DG.
PRICE, Mrs. Joanne, BA ACA *1998;* 6 Woolton Hill Road, Woolton, LIVERPOOL, L25 6HX.
PRICE, Mr. John, BA FCA *1964;* 302 Charlton Road, Brentry, BRISTOL, BS10 6JZ. (Life Member)
PRICE, Mr. John, FCA *1954;* Fairwinds, 6 Beaufort Avenue, Langland, SWANSEA, SA3 4NU. (Life Member)
•PRICE, Mr. John Bernard, MA FCA DChA *1980;* John Price, 1b Oxford Street, CHELTENHAM, GLOUCESTERSHIRE, GL52 6DT.
PRICE, Mr. John Clifford, BA FCA *1963;* 32 Birdrock Avenue, MOUNT MARTHA, VIC 3934, AUSTRALIA. (Life Member)
PRICE, Mr. John Daniel, ACA *2009;* Pandora, Pandora High Street, Claverley, WOLVERHAMPTON, WV5 7DR.
PRICE, Mr. John Edelsten, FCA *1956;* Oxted Place East, Broadham Green Road, OXTED, SURREY, RH8 9PF. (Life Member)
•PRICE, Mr. John Graham Vaughan, FCA *1975;* Graham Price, 18 Trotsworth Avenue, VIRGINIA WATER, GU25 4AL.
PRICE, Mr. John Henry, BEng ACA *1991;* 34 Elm Bank Gardens, LONDON, SW13 0NT.
•PRICE, Mr. John Lucas, MA FCA *1973;* (Tax Fac), John Price & Co Ltd, 18 Archer Road, PENARTH, SOUTH GLAMORGAN, CF64 3HW.
PRICE, Mr. John Michael Anthony, MA FCA *1966;* 38 Greenhill, Blackwell, BROMSGROVE, B60 1BL. (Life Member)
PRICE, Mr. John Nigel, BA FCA *1983;* Wayside, Noke Lane, ST. ALBANS, AL2 3NX.
PRICE, Mr. John Vernon, FCA *1953;* Penthouse, Bon Accord, 9 Victoria Avenue, SWANAGE, DORSET, BH19 1AJ. (Life Member)
•PRICE, Mr. Jonathan David, FCA *1995;* JD Price Consulting Ltd, 6 Isis Close, Long Hanborough, WITNEY, OXFORDSHIRE, OX29 8JN.
PRICE, Mr. Jonathan Hugh Vaughan, BA ACA *1995;* 30 Arthur Road, SOUTHAMPTON, SO15 5DY.
PRICE, Mr. Jonathan Stewart, BA ACA *1999;* Shawbrook Barn, Hayle Farm, Marle Place Road, Horsmonden, TONBRIDGE, KENT TN12 8DZ.
PRICE, Mrs. Kathryn, BA ACA *1984;* Brook House, 8 The Close, Bulkington, DEVIZES, WILTSHIRE, SN10 1SR.
PRICE, Miss. Katie Emma, ACA *2010;* 12 Hall Street, CHEADLE, CHESHIRE, SK8 1PJ.
PRICE, Mrs. Katie Susan, BA ACA *1992;* 23 Orchard Road, Shalford, GUILDFORD, GU4 8ER.
PRICE, Mr. Keith Eric, FCA *1961;* 1 Spring Bank, Bushmoor, CRAVEN ARMS, SHROPSHIRE, SY7 8DW. (Life Member)
PRICE, Mr. Kenneth Reginald, FCA *1963;* 36 Sandown Avenue, SWINDON, SN3 1QQ.
PRICE, Miss. Lauren Rebecca, BSc ACA *2006;* Flat C 1 Kennington Park Place, LONDON, SE11 4AS.
PRICE, Mr. Lee Michael, ACA *2007;* 5 Birdlip Close, WORCESTER, WR4 9JZ.
PRICE, Mr. Leighton Raymond John, FCA *1962;* 9 Parc Felindre, Mynyddygarreg, KIDWELLY, DYFED, SA17 4LX.
PRICE, Miss. Lesley Christina, BSc ACA *2007;* 14 Old Watling Street, CANTERBURY, KENT, CT1 2DX.
•PRICE, Ms. Linda, FCA *1986;* (Tax Fac), Parkhurst Hill Limited, Torrington Chambers, 58 North Road East, PLYMOUTH, DEVON, PL4 6AJ. See also Parkhurst Hill
PRICE, Mrs. Louise Anna, BSc ACA *2003;* 3 Westhorpe Road, LONDON, SW15 1QH.
PRICE, Mr. Luke Edward, BA(Hons) ACA *2004;* 18 Wellington House 398-400 Wilmslow Road, MANCHESTER, M20 3LU.
PRICE, Mrs. Mairead Bridget, BA ACA *1995;* 6 Sycamore Drive, Hollywood, BIRMINGHAM, B47 5QX.
PRICE, Miss. Margaret Amelia Anne, BSc ACA *1991;* Ty Maen Cottage Porthcawl Road, South Cornelly, BRIDGEND, MID GLAMORGAN, CF33 4RE.
PRICE, Mr. Mark, ACA MAAT *1996;* Dane Court, Copt Hill, Danbury, CHELMSFORD, CM3 4NW.
PRICE, Mr. Mark Adrian, BSocSc ACA *1984;* 25 Turnpike Way, Coven, WOLVERHAMPTON, WV9 5HY.
PRICE, Mr. Mark David, BSc ACA *1998;* 1 Underhill Close, MAIDENHEAD, SL6 4DS.
PRICE, Mr. Mark Gareth John, MA FCA *1995;* 21 Hyburn Close, Bricket Wood, ST. ALBANS, HERTFORDSHIRE, AL2 3QX.
•PRICE, Mr. Matthew Geoffrey, BA ACA *2003;* (Tax Fac), Alextra Accountants Limited, Units 12-14 Macon Court, Herald Drive, CREWE, CW1 6EA.
PRICE, Mr. Matthew John, BA ACA *1995;* 6 Long View, BERKHAMSTED, HERTFORDSHIRE, HP4 1BY.
PRICE, Mr. Matthew John, BSc ACA *2000;* 4 Finch Lane, AMERSHAM, BUCKINGHAMSHIRE, HP7 9NE.
PRICE, Mr. Matthew John, BSc FCA *1999;* Lady of Lourdes, Whitchurch, ROSS-ON-WYE, HEREFORDSHIRE, HR9 6DQ.
•PRICE, Mr. Matthew Richard, BSc ACA *2003;* Ernst & Young LLP, 1 More London Place, LONDON, SE1 2AF. See also Ernst & Young Europe LLP
PRICE, Mr. Maurice Neil, FCA *1973;* 39 Hartsbourne Drive, HALESOWEN, WEST MIDLANDS, B62 8ST.
•PRICE, Mr. Melvyn, FCA *1975;* 34 Avebury Gardens, SPALDING, PE11 2EN.
•PRICE, Mr. Michael John Edward, FCA *1973;* (Tax Fac), Price & Company, Meadsted House, 80 Jacklyns Lane, ALRESFORD, SO24 9LJ.
PRICE, Mrs. Michelle Etel Alice, BA ACA *1991;* PSE Consulting Ground Floor, 32 Candler Mews, Amyand Park Road, TWICKENHAM, TW1 3JF.
PRICE, Mrs. Nadia Ann, BSc ACA *2003;* 198 Juniper Way, Bradley Stoke, BRISTOL, BS32 0DR.
PRICE, Mr. Nathan Rhys, ACA *2008;* 13 Plas Taliesin, PENARTH, SOUTH GLAMORGAN, CF64 1TN.
PRICE, Mr. Neville Eric, FCA *1974;* 5 Drummond Drive, STANMORE, MIDDLESEX, HA7 3PF.
PRICE, Miss. Nia Cerys, BA ACA *1993;* Canterberry, 6 Peartree Road, Dibden Purlieu, SOUTHAMPTON, SO45 4AL.
•PRICE, Mrs. Nia Wynne, BEng ACA *2001;* (Tax Fac), DRP & Co, 6 St. Johns Court, Upper forest Way, SWANSEA, SA6 8QQ.
PRICE, Mr. Nicholas John, BA ACA *1991;* Close Brothers Group Plc, 10 Crown Place, LONDON, EC2A 4FT.
PRICE, Mr. Oliver Garth, BSc ACA *2006;* Flat 6, 112 Lansdowne Way, LONDON, SW8 2EE.
PRICE, Mr. Paul Leslie, BA FCA *1982;* 52 Manor Drive, LONDON, N20 0DX.
•PRICE, Mr. Peter Gordon, FCA *1969;* Peter Price & Co, 9 Broad Street, LLANDOVERY, DYFED, SA20 0AR.
PRICE, Mr. Peter William, FCA *1977;* 4 Aspen Close, HazelwoodSt. Mellons, CARDIFF, CF3 0BT.
•PRICE, Mr. Philip Colin, BA ACA CF FSI *1997;* Dow Schofield Watts Corporate Finance Limited, 7700 Daresbury Park, Daresbury, WARRINGTON, CHESHIRE, WA4 5BS.
•PRICE, Mr. Philip George, FCA *1976;* Price, 81 Park Square East, Jaywick, CLACTON-ON-SEA, ESSEX, CO15 2NP.
PRICE, Mr. Philip John, FCA *1959;* Batch Cottage, Elwell Street, Upwey, WEYMOUTH, DT3 5QF. (Life Member)
PRICE, Mrs. Philippa Louise, BSc ACA *1990;* L S G Sky Chefs UK Ltd, Pinfold Lane, Manchester Airport, MANCHESTER, M90 5XR.
PRICE, Mr. Phillip George, BA ACA *1982;* 3 Hawcroft, Longdon, RUGELEY, STAFFORDSHIRE, WS15 4QT.
PRICE, Mr. Phillip John, BSc FCA *1976;* Broadway House, Chartridge, CHESHAM, BUCKINGHAMSHIRE, HP5 2TT.
PRICE, Miss. Rachel Elizabeth, ACA *2008;* 188 Long Drive, RUISLIP, MIDDLESEX, HA4 0HU.
PRICE, Mr. Raymond Charles, FCA *1950;* 11 Regents Park, EXETER, EX1 2NT. (Life Member)
PRICE, Mr. Richard, ACA *2009;* 3 City Walk Apartments, 31 Perry Vale, LONDON, SE23 2AR.
PRICE, Mr. Richard Antony, BSc ACA *1990;* C M C UK Ltd Building One, Trident Industrial Park Glass Avenue, CARDIFF, CF24 5EN.
PRICE, Mr. Richard Duncan, BCom ACA *1989;* Wisteria, 2 Park Street, Kings Cliffe, PETERBOROUGH, NORTHAMPTONSHIRE, PE8 6XN.
PRICE, Mr. Richard Lionel Howroyd, FCA *1969;* 11 Dane Park, BISHOP'S STORTFORD, HERTFORDSHIRE, CM23 2PR.
PRICE, Mr. Richard Ralph, BSc FCA *1969;* 13 Victoria Grove, LONDON, W8 5RW.
•PRICE, Mr. Richard Stanley, BSc FCA *1988;* KPMG LLP, 15 Canada Square, LONDON, E14 5GL. See also KPMG Europe LLP
•PRICE, Mr. Richard William, BSc ACA *1996;* (Tax Fac), Zenon TTAS Limited, 51 The Stream, Ditton, AYLESFORD, KENT, ME20 6AG. See also Zenon Tax Limited, Zenon Transaction Services Limited and Zenon Training Services LLP
PRICE, Mr. Robert David, BSc ACA *1995;* 48 Quarry Hills Lane, LICHFIELD, STAFFORDSHIRE, WS14 9HL.
PRICE, Mr. Robert John, FCA *1976;* with Grant Thornton UK LLP, Enterprise House, 115 Edmund Street, BIRMINGHAM, B3 2HJ.
PRICE, Mr. Robert Matthew, BSc FCA *1999;* 951 Fell Street, Apt 606, BALTIMORE, MD 21231, UNITED STATES.
PRICE, Mr. Robin Mark Dodgson, LLB FCA *1982;* 71 Barrowgate Road, LONDON, W4 4QS.
•PRICE, Mr. Roger Charles, FCA *1974;* Roger Price Aims Accounting Beaconsfield, 36 Wattleton Road, BEACONSFIELD, HP9 1SE.
•PRICE, Mr. Ronald Dennis, FCA *1985;* (Tax Fac), Beak Kemmenoe, 1-3 Manor Road, CHATHAM, ME4 6AE.
PRICE, Mr. Russell, ACA *2010;* 4819 NE 142nd Street, Vancouver, WASHINGTON, WA 98686, UNITED STATES.
PRICE, Mr. Ryan John, ACA *2009;* with Mazars LLP, The Atrium, Park Street West, LUTON, LU1 3BE.
PRICE, Mrs. Sandra Frances, BSc FCA *1993;* 12 Durlston Close, Amington, TAMWORTH, STAFFORDSHIRE, B77 3QG.
PRICE, Ms. Sara, BA ACA *1991;* 4 Montagu Road, Datchet, SLOUGH, SL3 9DJ.
PRICE, Mrs. Sharon Kim, BA ACA *1991;* 22 Picton Way, Caversham, READING, RG4 8NJ.
•PRICE, Mr. Stephen David, BSc FCA *1977;* MH3 Marinascape, PO Box 23035, DUBAI, UNITED ARAB EMIRATES.
PRICE, Mr. Stephen John, BA(Hons) ACA *2001;* Equity Trust, 6 St Andrew Street, LONDON, EC4A 3AE.
PRICE, Mr. Stephen John, FCA *1976;* 11 Glebelands Road, WIRRAL, MERSEYSIDE, CH46 0PW.
PRICE, Mr. Stephen Nigel, ACA *1989;* 137 Brentwood Rd, Beaconsfield, MONTREAL H9W 4M6, QUE, CANADA.
PRICE, Mr. Steven Glenn, BSc ACA CTA *2000;* (Tax Fac), 79 Clyde Road, LONDON, N22 7AD.
•PRICE, Mr. Steven James, FCA *1990;* (Tax Fac), Mapperson Price, 286a High Street, DORKING, RH4 1QT.
PRICE, Mr. Stuart Andrew, BA(Hons) ACA *2002;* 14 Giffnock Avenue, MACQUARIE PARK, NSW 2113, AUSTRALIA.
PRICE, Mr. Stuart Robertson, BSc FCA *1996;* 35 Clifton Street, MILLSWOOD, SA 5034, AUSTRALIA.
PRICE, Mrs. Susan Ann, BSc ACA *1982;* 4 Aspen Close, HazelwoodSt. Mellons, CARDIFF, CF3 0BT.
PRICE, Ms. Susan Rachel Wilson, BA FCA CTA *1990;* 58 High Street, Long Crendon, AYLESBURY, BUCKINGHAMSHIRE, HP18 9AL.
PRICE, Mr. Sydney Stephen, FCA *1964;* 24 Wood Lane, Newhall, SWADLINCOTE, DE11 0LX. (Life Member)
PRICE, Mr. Thomas Adam James, ACA *2011;* 33 Westmount Apartments, Metropolitan Station Approach, WATFORD, WD18 7BE.
PRICE, Mr. Thomas Albert, FCA *1959;* 5 Elmroyd Close, POTTERS BAR, EN6 2EG. (Life Member)
PRICE, Mr. Thomas Richard Macbride, BSc(Hons) ACA *2002;* 36 Penn Place, Northway, RICKMANSWORTH, HERTFORDSHIRE, WD3 1QA.
•PRICE, Mr. Thomas Roger, FCA *1976;* Treetops, Herons Close, Copthorne, CRAWLEY, SURREY, RH10 3HF.
PRICE, Mr. Timothy Graham, BA ACA *1993;* 29 Lutley Mill Road, HALESOWEN, B63 4HX.
PRICE, Mr. Timothy James Walwyn, BSc ACA *1991;* 17 Kelvin Road, ALPHINGTON, VIC 3078, AUSTRALIA.
PRICE, Mr. Timothy Richard, BA(Hons) ACA *2001;* Waterstones Booksellers Ltd Royal House, Princes Gate Buildings 2-6 Homer Road, SOLIHULL, B91 3QQ.
PRICE, Mr. Trevor Sheldon, ACA *1988;* 49 Grand Avenue, CAMBERLEY, SURREY, GU15 3QJ.
PRICE, Mr. Tristan Robert Julian, MA MSc FCA *1992;* M P Evans Group Plc, 3 Clanricarde Gardens, TUNBRIDGE WELLS, TN1 1HQ.
•PRICE, Mr. Vaughan Jonathan, BSc FCA *1990;* PricewaterhouseCoopers GmbH, Elsenheimerstrasse 31-33, D-80687 MUNICH, GERMANY.
PRICE, Mrs. Victoria Louise, BA ACA *2002;* G V A Grimley Ltd, 3 Brindley Place, BIRMINGHAM, B1 2JB.
PRICE, Mr. Wilfred James, FCA *1951;* 61 Admiral's Walk, West Cliff Road, BOURNEMOUTH, DORSET, BH2 5HG. (Life Member)
•PRICE, Mr. William Evan, BSc FCA *1975;* Wm. E. Price & Co, Nyth Glyd, Ffrwd Road, Abersychan, PONTYPOOL, NP4 8PF.
PRICE, Mr. William Harold, LLB ACA *1987;* 2 Copthall Avenue, LONDON, EC2R 7DA.
PRICE, Winford Hugh Protheroe, Esq OBE FCA *1954;* 3 Oakfield Street, Roath, CARDIFF, CF24 3RD. (Life Member)
PRICHARD, Mr. Andrew John, FCA ATII *1993;* (Tax Fac), 61 Appletrees Crescent, BROMSGROVE, WORCESTERSHIRE, B61 0UD.
PRICHARD, Mrs. Claire Barbara, BSc ACA *2000;* 9 Wudgong St, MOSMAN, NSW 2088, AUSTRALIA.
PRICHARD, Mr. John Robert, FCA *1961;* Church House, Sellman Street, Gnosall, STAFFORD, ST20 0EP.
PRICHARD JONES, Mrs. Cecilia Jane, BA(Hons) ACA *2001;* The Coach House, 1 Southacre Drive, CAMBRIDGE, CB2 7EE.
PRICKETT, Mr. Adam, BA(Hons) ACA *2009;* 31 Captain Lees Road, Westhoughton, BOLTON, BL5 3UB.
PRICKETT, Mr. Daniel Ronald, LLB ACA *2003;* Pinder House, 249 Upper Third Street, MILTON KEYNES, BUCKINGHAMSHIRE, MK9 1DS.
PRICKETT, Mr. Neil, BA(Hons) ACA *2001;* 41 Glebe Road, Long Ashton, BRISTOL, BS41 9LJ.
PRICKETT, Mr. Peter John, MA FCA *1976;* Waterhouse Farm Waterhouse Lane, Bletchingley, REDHILL, RH1 4LU.
PRICKETT, Mr. Richard Other, FCA *1973;* Dingwood Park, LEDBURY, HEREFORDSHIRE, HR8 2JD.
PRIDAY, Mr. Nicholas Charles, BSc ACA *2000;* Aegis Media Ltd, 10 Triton Street, LONDON, NW1 3BF.
•PRIDDEN, Mr. John Leslie, ACA *1986;* Kintetsu World Express (UK) Ltd, Unit 2, 14 Newlands Drive, Colnbrook, SLOUGH, SL3 0DX.
•PRIDDEY, Mr. Stephen, MA FCA *1977;* Harrison Priddey & Co, 22 St John Street, BROMSGROVE, B61 8QY.
PRIDDING, Mr. John Alan, BSc FCA *1976;* 2 Badger Close, Fleckney, LEICESTER, LE8 8DF.
PRIDDIS, Mrs. Katie Jane, BA ACA *2001;* 7/122 Bower Street, MANLY, NSW 2095, AUSTRALIA.
PRIDDLE, Mr. Adrian John, BSc ACA *1996;* AJP Development Ltd, 6 Goldfinch Way, South Wonston, WINCHESTER, HAMPSHIRE, SO21 3SH.
PRIDDLE, Mr. Martin William, BA ACA *1985;* 79 Sonning Gardens, HAMPTON, TW12 3PN.
PRIDDLE-HIGSON, Miss. Fiona, MA MEng ACA *2011;* 21 College Gate, Townsend Street, DUBLIN 2, COUNTY DUBLIN, IRELAND.
PRIDE, Mr. James Charles, BSc FCA *1980;* 2 Spencer Road, Canford Cliffs, POOLE, BH13 7EU.
PRIDEAUX, Miss. Claire, ACA *2011;* with RSM Tenon Audit Limited, 2 Wellington Place, LEEDS, LS1 4AP.
PRIDEAUX, Mr. Ian Richard Scott, BSc ACA *1982;* 31 The Chase, LONDON, SW4 0NP.
•PRIDEAUX, Mr. Ian Robert Arkley, BA(Hons) ACA CTA *1997;* PricewaterhouseCoopers LLP, First Point, Buckingham Gate, London Gatwick Airport, GATWICK, WEST SUSSEX RH6 0NT. See also PricewaterhouseCoopers
PRIDEAUX, Mr. James, BCom ACA *1989;* 5th Floor 6750 Office Tower, Ayala Avenue, MAKATI CITY 1200, PHILIPPINES.
•①PRIDEAUX, Mr. Mark, BA FCA MABRP *1990;* Groby Lawn, Groby Road, ALTRINCHAM, CHESHIRE, WA14 2BJ.
•PRIDEAUX, Mrs. Rachael Elizabeth, BSc(Econ) ACA *2003;* Rachael Prideaux ACA, 64 Queens Crescent, BODMIN, CORNWALL, PL31 1QW.
PRIDGEON, Mrs. Emma Jane, BA ACA *1995;* 7 Calne Close, WIRRAL, MERSEYSIDE, CH61 4YB.
PRIDHAM, Mrs. Catherine Juliette, BSc ACA *1991;* 1 Standhill Cottage, Little Haseley, OXFORD, OXFORDSHIRE, OX44 7LP.
PRIDHAM, Mr. Michael Walter, BCom FCA *1977;* Bridge House, Bridge House Glenfaba Road, Raggatt Peel, ISLE OF MAN, IM5 3AB.

•PRIDHAM, Mrs. Rebecca Louise, BA ACA *2000;* (Tax Fac), Pridham Accountancy, Pear Tree House, Pebworth Road, Ullington, EVESHAM, WORCESTERSHIRE WR11 8QG. See also Rebecca L Pridham

PRIDMORE, Miss. Elizabeth Samar, ACA *2009;* 17 The Platt, Lindfield, HAYWARDS HEATH, WEST SUSSEX, RH16 2SY.

PRIDMORE, Mrs. Helen Elizabeth, BA ACA *1995;* 10 Exeforde Avenue, ASHFORD, MIDDLESEX, TW15 2EF.

•PRIDMORE, Mrs. Lynn Catherine, BA ACA *1986;* Royston Parkin Limited, 5 Railway Court, Ten Pound Walk, DONCASTER, SOUTH YORKSHIRE, DN4 5FB. See also RP Taxation Services Limited and Royston Parkin

PRIDMORE, Mr. Matthew, ACA *2011;* 65 Stone Court, CRAWLEY, WEST SUSSEX, RH10 7RX.

PRIDMORE, Mr. Richard Ian, BA ACA *1983;* 62 Tinshill Road, LEEDS, LS16 7DS.

•PRIDMORE, Mr. Wilfred John, FCA *1970;* (Tax Fac), Lamont Pridmore, 8 Stanger Street, KESWICK, CA12 5JU. See also Lamont Pridmore (South Cumbria) Limited, Lamont Pridmore Limited, Lamont Pridmore Limited, E.J. Williams & Co

PRIEBE, Mr. Christopher Cyril Kay, ACA *1993;* 43 Bloomfield Terrace, LONDON, SW1W 8PQ.

PRIEBS, Miss. Maria, MSc(Econ) BA ACA *2011;* 50 Aberdare Gardens, LONDON, NW6 3QA.

PRIEST, Mrs. Alicia Martha, BA ACA *1996;* 26 Cherry Tree Way, WITNEY, OXFORDSHIRE, OX28 1AJ.

PRIEST, Dr. Andrew, BSc(Hons) ACA *2004;* Unit 3, 34 Park Road, NAREMBURN, NSW 2065, AUSTRALIA.

PRIEST, Mr. Andrew Charles, FCA *1974;* Merryfield, Windmill Road, Sevenoaks Weald, SEVENOAKS, TN14 6PH.

PRIEST, Mr. David Peter, BCom FCA *1973;* 5 Gables Close, Chalfont St Peter, GERRARDS CROSS, SL9 0PR. (Life Member)

•PRIEST, Mr. Hayden Lee, BEng ACA *1995;* UHY Calvert Smith, 31 St Saviourgate, YORK, YO1 8NQ.

•PRIEST, Mr. Kenneth Peter, FCA *1971;* (Tax Fac), Kppbusiness Limited, 115 Huddersfield Road, OLDHAM, OL1 3NY.

PRIEST, Mr. Malcolm John, FCA *1980;* Greswolde Construction Ltd, Greswolde House, 197a Station Road, Knowle, SOLIHULL, WEST MIDLANDS B93 0PU.

PRIEST, Mr. Mark Andrew, BSc ACA *2000;* Flat A301, Gilbert Scott Building, Scott Avenue, LONDON, SW15 3SG.

PRIEST, Mr. Mark Anthony, BSc ACA *2010;* 86 Shuttleworth Road, LONDON, SW11 3DE.

PRIEST, Mr. Mark Derham, MEng ACA *2010;* Flat 3, 149 Goldhurst Terrace, LONDON, NW6 3EU.

PRIEST, Dr. Mark Richard, PhD BSc ACA *1997;* 2 West Hill Avenue, Chapel Allerton, LEEDS, LS7 3QH.

PRIEST, Mr. Martin Roy, FCA *1981;* (Tax Fac), Courtil LEssart, Tertre, Vale, GUERNSEY, GY3 5QF.

PRIESTLEY, Mr. Alexander Peter James, BA ACA *2007;* 65b Burlington Road, LONDON, SW6 4NH.

PRIESTLEY, Miss. Alison Mary, MBiochem ACA *2004;* Flat 17, 63 West Smithfield, LONDON, EC1A 9DY.

PRIESTLEY, Mr. Anthony John, FCA *1967;* Kempside, Orchard Mead, Painswick, STROUD, GLOUCESTERSHIRE, GL6 6YD. (Life Member)

PRIESTLEY, Mr. Brian John, FCA *1968;* 3 Bramham Drive Baildon, SHIPLEY, WEST YORKSHIRE, BD17 6SZ. (Life Member)

•PRIESTLEY, Mrs. Christine, BSc ACA *1992;* C Priestley & Co, 37 Minchenden Crescent, LONDON, N14 7EP.

PRIESTLEY, Mr. Christopher Richard, BSc FCA *1977;* 9 Kestrel Drive, Bingham, NOTTINGHAM, NG13 8QD.

PRIESTLEY, Mr. Graham Harry, FCA *1974;* 20 Moorside Drive, Drighlington, BRADFORD, BD11 1HD.

PRIESTLEY, Mr. Howard Lee, BA ACA *1998;* 42 Chester Road, Helsby, FRODSHAM, WA6 0EZ.

PRIESTLEY, Mr. Ian Robert, BSc ACA *1992;* 37 Minchenden Crescent, Southgate, LONDON, N14 7EP.

PRIESTLEY, Mrs. Jacqui Anne, MA ACA *1990;* 6 Dawson Drive, Westhill, ABERDEEN, AB32 6NS.

PRIESTLEY, Mrs. Jean Elaine, BSc ACA *1988;* Moore Stephens, 21/23 Clarendon Street, LONDONDERRY, BT48 7EP.

PRIESTLEY, Mr. John, FCA *1948;* 60 Bridle Road, PINNER, HA5 2SH. (Life Member)

PRIESTLEY, Mr. John Joseph, FCA *1951;* 35 Berry Hill Road, MANSFIELD, NG18 4RU. (Life Member)

PRIESTLEY, Mr. John Philip, BA FCA *1964;* Underwood, Underwood Road, ALDERLEY EDGE, SK9 7BR. (Life Member)

PRIESTLEY, Mr. Keith, FCA *1966;* 20 John Muir Gardens, DUNBAR, EAST LOTHIAN, EH42 1GA.

PRIESTLEY, Mrs. Linda, FCA *1969;* 20 John Muir Gardens, DUNBAR, EAST LOTHIAN, EH42 1GA.

PRIESTLEY, Mrs. Lisa Louise, ACA DChA *2002;* Asset Skills 2 The Courtyard, 48 New North Road, EXETER, EX4 4EP.

PRIESTLEY, Mr. Mark Richard, BSc ACA *1990;* 2 Old Farm Court Main Street, Grendon Underwood, AYLESBURY, HP18 0SU.

PRIESTLEY, Mr. Michael, FCA *1969;* 31 Hare Hill Road, LITTLEBOROUGH, OL15 9AD.

•PRIESTLEY, Mr. Nigel Benjamin, BA FCA *1995;* KPMG LLP, 15 Canada Square, LONDON, E14 5GL. See also KPMG Europe LLP

PRIESTLEY, Mr. Peter John, FCA *1968;* 14 Elm House, Old Hall Gardens, Old Hall Avenue, Littleover, DERBY, DE23 6EN. (Life Member)

PRIESTLEY, Mr. Richard Joseph, BA ACA *1993;* Westbury, Sleepers Hill, WINCHESTER, HAMPSHIRE, SO22 4NB.

PRIESTLEY, Mrs. Sally Jane, MBA LLB ACA *1998;* 4 Kettilstoun Crescent, LINLITHGOW, WEST LOTHIAN, EH49 6PR.

PRIESTLEY, Ms. Sarah, ACA *2007;* 31 Pares Close, WOKING, SURREY, GU21 4QL.

PRIESTLEY, Mr. Stephen Edward, FCA *1965;* 5 Hill End Close, Norwood Green, HALIFAX, HX3 8RH.

PRIESTLEY, Mr. Stephen Howard, FCA *1976;* 50 Kensington Drive, SHEFFIELD, S10 4NF.

•PRIESTMAN, Mr. Raymond, FCA *1987;* Evolution Business and Tax Advisors LLP, 10 Evolution, Wynyard Park, Wynyard, BILLINGHAM, CLEVELAND TS22 5TB.

PRIESTNALL, Mr. Jonathan Mark, LLB ACA CTA *2002;* The Gardens, Cotchers Lane, Saxton, TADCASTER, NORTH YORKSHIRE, LS24 9QA.

•PRIESTNER, Mr. Peter Neil, BA ACA *1996;* 10 Little Heath Lane, Dunham Massey, ALTRINCHAM, CHESHIRE, WA14 4TS.

PRIFTI, Mr. Andrew John, BA ACA *1994;* 31 St Augustines Avenue, BROMLEY, BR2 8AG.

PRIGGEN, Mr. John Edward Frederick, BSc(Econ) ACA *1997;* 4a Clarence Road, HARPENDEN, HERTFORDSHIRE, AL5 4AJ.

PRIGMORE, Mr. Mathew Alexander, BSc ACA *2001;* Flat 70, Ormonde Court, Upper Richmond Road, LONDON, SW15 6TP.

PRIKE, Mr. Christopher George, BA ACA *1983;* 16 Roundcroft, Romiley, STOCKPORT, SK6 4LL.

PRILL, Mr. Robert David, BSc(Hons) ACA *2002;* 8 Moorfield, Roe Green, Worsley, MANCHESTER, M28 2FL.

PRIMACK, Mrs. Tracey, BA ACA *1999;* 53 Shakespeare Road, LONDON, NW7 4BA.

PRIMAVESI, Mr. Stephen George, FCA *1948;* 18 Melbury Close, CHISLEHURST, KENT, BR7 5ET. (Life Member)

PRIME, Mr. Christopher John, ACA *2009;* 10 St. Johns Hill, READING, RG1 4EE.

PRIME, Mr. David Henry, ACA *2010;* 46 Providence Lane, Long Ashton, BRISTOL, BS41 9DJ.

PRIME, Mrs. Rebecca Marie, BA ACA *1995;* with RSM Tenon Limited, The Poynt Building, 45 Wollaton Street, NOTTINGHAM, NG1 5FW.

PRIME, Mr. Richard Percy, FCA *1963;* Parkside, The Green, Frant, TUNBRIDGE WELLS, KENT, TN3 9ED. (Life Member)

PRIME-MOORE, Mrs. Susan, ACA *2008;* 19 Peppercombe Road, EASTBOURNE, EAST SUSSEX, BN20 8JH.

PRIMETT, Mr. Christopher Donald, BSc ACA *1992;* Welland Medical Ltd, Unit 7-8, The Brunel Centre, Newton Road, CRAWLEY, RH10 9TU.

PRIMIC, Mr. Antony, ACA CA(SA) *2010;* 10 Wynton Grove, WALTON-ON-THAMES, SURREY, KT12 1LW.

•PRIMICERIO, Mr. Andrea, ACA *1999;* (Tax Fac), AccounTrust Ltd, Royalty House, 32 Sackville Street, Mayfair, LONDON, W1S 3EA. See also ITP Business Advisers Limited

PRIMROSE, Mr. Mark, ACA *2009;* A210 Le Capelain House Castle Quay, ST HELIER, JE2 3EA.

PRIMROSE, Mr. Nigel Edward, FCA *1978;* Hoth Cottage, Danegate, Eridge Green, TUNBRIDGE WELLS, TN3 9HU. (Life Member)

PRINCE, Mr. Adam Ralph, BSc ACA *1992;* 11 Green Lane, Burnham, SLOUGH, SL1 8DR.

PRINCE, Mr. Alan James, MBA BA FCA *1983;* Assicurazioni Generali S.P.A UK Branch, 100 Leman Street, LONDON, E1 8AJ.

PRINCE, Mr. Alastair Brian George, BA ACA *1991;* 15 Faulkland View, Peasedown St. John, BATH, BA2 8TG.

PRINCE, Mr. Anthony James, BA ACA *2003;* 62 Wroughton Road, LONDON, SW11 6BG.

PRINCE, Mr. Benjamin James, MSc ACA *2008;* 29 Richmond Road, CAMBRIDGE, CB4 3PP.

•PRINCE, Mr. Brian Warwick, FCA *1970;* with Somers Baker Prince Kurz LLP, 45 Ealing Road, WEMBLEY, HA0 4BA.

PRINCE, Mr. Colin, FCA *1960;* 25 Wynmore Avenue, Bramhope, LEEDS, LS16 9DD. (Life Member)

•PRINCE, Mr. Dale Austen, BA FCA *1990;* Austen Prince Limited, 59 St. Johns Hill, Shenstone, LICHFIELD, STAFFORDSHIRE, WS14 0JD.

PRINCE, Mr. David Gerald Joseph, BA FCA *1989;* Calle Fatiga 37, 11310 Sotogrande, CADIZ, SPAIN.

•PRINCE, Mr. David John, BCom ACA *1983;* Prince & Co, 23 Willes Road, LONDON, NW5 3DT. See also Prince David John

PRINCE, Mr. Derrick Walter, FCA *1955;* 34 Beverington Close, EASTBOURNE, BN21 2SB. (Life Member)

PRINCE, Mrs. Emma Jane Janice, BSc(Econ) ACA *2002;* 101 Westgate, CHICHESTER, WEST SUSSEX, PO19 3HB.

•PRINCE, Mr. Gary Kevin, ACA *1988;* G K Prince ACA, 151 Grove Road, HARPENDEN, HERTFORDSHIRE, AL5 1SY.

•PRINCE, Miss. Iris Ann, BSc FCA *1980;* (Tax Fac), Iris Prince B.Sc FCA, 23 Grove Crescent, Kingsbury, LONDON, NW9 0LS.

PRINCE, Mr. Keir James, BSc ACA *1992;* Flat 102 Whitehouse Apartments 9, Belvedere Road, LONDON, SE1 8YP.

•PRINCE, Mr. Mark Ashley Brian, BSc ACA *1999;* with KPMG LLP, 15 Canada Square, LONDON, E14 5GL.

PRINCE, Mr. Michael Eliot Gerald, MA FCA *1953;* 5 Knott Park House, Wrens Hill, Oxshott, LEATHERHEAD, SURREY, KT22 0HW. (Life Member)

PRINCE, Mr. Michael John, BSc FCA *1993;* 5 Chindit Close, Pulham Avenue, BROXBOURNE, EN10 7TL.

PRINCE, Mr. Philip Davies, ACA *1981;* The Old Dairy, Broadfield Road, SHEFFIELD, S8 0XQ.

•PRINCE, Mr. Philipp Nicholas Andre Martin, MA FCA *1995;* BDO LLP, 55 Baker Street, LONDON, W1U 7EU. See also BDO Stoy Hayward LLP

PRINCE, Mrs. Rachel Clare, BA ACA *2004;* Wolters Kluwer Health, Chowley Oak Business Park, Chowley Oak Lane, Tattenhall, CHESTER, CH3 9GA.

PRINCE, Mrs. Rachel Margaret, BA ACA *1989;* City of Coventry Whitley Abbey School, Abbey Road, COVENTRY, CV3 4BD.

PRINCE, Mrs. Rebecca Jill, BSc(Hons) ACA *2003;* with Dains LLP, Unit 306, Third Floor, Fort Dunlop, Fort Parkway, BIRMINGHAM B24 9FD.

PRINCE, Mr. Ross Anthony, MEng ACA *2006;* 49 Northwick Avenue, WORCESTER, WR3 7AS.

PRINCE, Miss. Sarah Elizabeth, ACA *2008;* 5 Filmer Lane, SEVENOAKS, KENT, TN14 5AG.

PRINCE, Mr. Stephen Christopher, BSc ACA *1998;* 14 Dagmar Road, WINDSOR, BERKSHIRE, SL4 1JL.

•PRINCE-WRIGHT, Mr. Kenneth Howard, FCA *1980;* 1 Basil Mansions, Basil Street, LONDON, SW3 1AP.

PRINCEP, Mr. Anthony, FCA *1948;* 22 Hornby Drive, NANTWICH, CHESHIRE, CW5 6JP. (Life Member)

PRINCEP, Mr. Oliver, BA ACA *1993;* Faculty of Management & Business, Manchester Metropolitan University, Aytoun Street, MANCHESTER, M1 3GH.

PRINCEP, Mrs. Sarah Louise, BA ACA *1996;* 6 Hill Drive, Whaley Bridge, HIGH PEAK, SK23 7BH.

PRING, Mr. Andrew John, FCA *1988;* Apartment 21, 8 Blue Lion Place, Long Lane, LONDON, SE1 4PU.

PRING, Mrs. Angela, ACA *1992;* Wingfield Hall, Hall Road, Wingfield, DISS, NORFOLK, IP21 5QX.

PRING, Mrs. Annabel Frances, BA FCA *1980;* Wombwell Homes, 23 - 25 Brunel Quays, Great Western Village, LOSTWITHIEL, CORNWALL, PL22 0JB.

•PRING, Mr. Brian John, FCA *1989;* (Tax Fac), Larking Gowen Ltd, Unit 1, Claydon Business Park, Great Blakenham, IPSWICH, IP6 0NL. See also Larking Gowen

PRING, Mr. James Marcus, BA ACA *1999;* 28 Kipling Avenue, BATH, BA2 4RB.

PRING, Mr. Kevin, BA ACA *1999;* 10 Connaught Drive, WEYBRIDGE, SURREY, KT13 0XA.

PRING, Mr. Michael Joseph, BA FCA *1961;* Stoneycroft, 22 Tinwell Road, STAMFORD, PE9 2SD.

•PRING, Mr. Peter Thomas, FCA *1987;* (Tax Fac), ABC 123 Limited, 41 Park Road, Freemantle, SOUTHAMPTON, SO15 3AW. See also AKP LTD

•PRING, Mrs. Susan Marie, FCA *1987;* RHP Partnership, Lancaster House, 87 Yarmouth Road, NORWICH, NORFOLK, NR7 0HF.

PRING, Mr. Thomas Neale, FCA *1960;* 34 Ballards Close, Mickleton, CHIPPING CAMPDEN, GL55 6TN. (Life Member)

PRINGLE, Mr. Andrew Lee, BA(Hons) ACA *2000;* Timpson House, Timpson Shoe Repairs Ltd Timpson House, Claverton Road Roundthorn Industrial Estate, MANCHESTER, M23 9TT.

•PRINGLE, Mrs. Anis, FCA *1977;* A. Pringle, P O Box 49561, NAIROBI, KENYA. See also KPMG Kenya

PRINGLE, Miss. Caroline, MBiochem ACA *2010;* 212 Milliners House, Eastfields Avenue, LONDON, SW18 1LP.

PRINGLE, Mrs. Caroline Mary Wadsworth, ACA MAAT *2009;* 3 Monterey Road, Walton Cardiff, TEWKESBURY, GLOUCESTERSHIRE, GL20 7RA.

PRINGLE, Miss. Claire, BSc ACA *2002;* 291 Milkwood Road, LONDON, SE24 0HE.

PRINGLE, Mr. Dodds Theodore, FCA *1989;* PO Box 342, TOOWONG, QLD 4066, AUSTRALIA.

PRINGLE, Mrs. Gail Karen, ACA *1996;* 17 Menteith View, DUNBLANE, FK15 0PD.

PRINGLE, Ms. Karen Jane, BSc ACA *1988;* Ernst & Young Llp, 1 More London Place, LONDON, SE1 2AF.

PRINGLE, Miss. Lorna Mary, BA ACA *1989;* 5 Evesham Terrace, St. Andrews Road, SURBITON, SURREY, KT6 4DS.

PRINGLE, Mr. Martin John, BSc ACA *1996;* 17 Menteith View, DUNBLANE, FK15 0PD.

PRINGLE, Mr. Robert Andrew, BA(Econ) ACA *2002;* 301/30 Warayama Place, ROZELLE, NSW 2039, AUSTRALIA.

PRINGLE, Mr. Robert Stewart, BA FCA *1988;* Convance CAPS Ltd, 6 Roxborough Way, MAIDENHEAD, BERKSHIRE, SL6 3UD.

PRINGLE, Mrs. Rosemary Jane, BSc FCA *1989;* Enniskillen House, Manor Road, PRINCES RISBOROUGH, BUCKINGHAMSHIRE, HP27 9DJ.

PRINGLE, Mrs. Ruth Emma, BSc ACA *2002;* 38 Union Road, ROCHDALE, LANCASHIRE, OL12 9QA.

PRINGLE, Miss. Sheila, BSc ACA *1994;* Pinacle Apartments, Oven Street, CANBERRA, ACT, AUSTRALIA.

PRINGLE, Mr. Stephen, LLB ACA *2006;* 9 Edgewood, Ponteland, NEWCASTLE UPON TYNE, NE20 9RY.

PRINJA, Mrs. Monica, BA ACA *1995;* 222 The Parkway, IVER, SL0 0RQ.

PRINS, Mr. Michiel Rutger, ACA CA(SA) *2010;* Koch Supply & Trading Co Ltd Fountain House, 130 Fenchurch Street, LONDON, EC3M 5DJ.

PRINT, Mr. John Howard, BA ACA *1986;* 84 St. Marks Road, HENLEY-ON-THAMES, RG9 1LW.

PRIOR, Mrs. Alexandra Charlotte, MSci ACA *2001;* White Lodge, Springfield Road, CAMBERLEY, GU15 1AB.

PRIOR, Mr. Andrew, BA ACA *1991;* Flat 42 Hardwick House, Masons Hill, BROMLEY, BR2 9GW.

PRIOR, Mr. Charles Campbell Leathes, FCA *1970;* Mill House, Woodspeen, NEWBURY, BERKSHIRE, RG20 8BT.

•PRIOR, Mr. David Brian, BA ACA *1988;* Independent Forensic Accounting Ltd, PO Box 158, LEEDS, LS8 5FF.

•PRIOR, Mrs. Emily Margaret, BSc ACA *2007;* (Tax Fac), Re:Accounts, 18 Highpoint, Lyonsdown Road, New Barnet, BARNET, HERTFORDSHIRE EN5 1LS.

PRIOR, Miss. Gemma, LLB ACA *2010;* 2 Hillside Apartments, Vauvert St. Peter Port, GUERNSEY, GY1 1NA.

PRIOR, Mr. James Anthony, ACA *2009;* 28 Salcombe Close, Chandler's Ford, EASTLEIGH, HAMPSHIRE, SO53 4PJ.

PRIOR, Mr. John David, BA FCA *1979;* 5 Walford Close, Bebington, WIRRAL, CH63 9HQ.

PRIOR, Mr. John Ernest Charles, FCA *1963;* Thorneywood, 1A Warwick Close, Aston Clinton, AYLESBURY, BUCKINGHAMSHIRE, HP22 5JF.

PRIOR, Mr. John Michael, FCA *1969;* Youngwood Farm, Youngwood Lane, Nailsea, BRISTOL, BS48 4NR.

PRIOR, Mr. Jonathan Wade, BSc FCA *1980;* The Willows, Belbroughton Road, Clent, STOURBRIDGE, DY9 9RA.

PRIOR, Mr. Julian Michael, BA ACA *1997;* 438 Riddell Road, GLENDOWIE, NEW ZEALAND.

PRIOR, Mrs. Karen Lesley, FCA *1985;* 16 Silcoates Avenue, Wrenthorpe, WAKEFIELD, WF2 0UP.

•PRIOR, Mr. Malcolm Beverley Charles, FCA *1974;* (Tax Fac), Malcolm Prior & Co, 4 Timber Lane, CATERHAM, SURREY, CR3 6LZ.

PRIOR, Mr. Mark, BA FCA *1996;* Top Floor Flat, 38 Merton Road, Wandsworth, LONDON, SW18 1QX.

PRIOR, Mr. Matthew, MA BSc ACA *2011;* 14 Rayleigh Road, WOODFORD GREEN, IG8 7HG.

PRIOR, Mr. Michael Ernest, BSc ACA *1995;* 172 Grosvenor Street, Wahroonga, SYDNEY, NSW 2076, AUSTRALIA.
PRIOR, Mr. Michael John, JP FCA *1966;* (Member of Council 1993 - 1999), 9 Gaddum Road, Bowdon, ALTRINCHAM, WA14 3PD.
PRIOR, Mr. Michael John, BA FCA *1991;* First Intuition, County House, Conway Mews, LONDON, W1T 6AA.
PRIOR, Miss. Michele Lesley, BA FCA *1985;* Be Happy at Work, PO Box 1054, BRADFORD, BD1 9JQ.
PRIOR, Mr. Nicholas Anthony, FCA *1973;* 4th Floor, 22 School Street, TAI HANG, HONG KONG ISLAND, HONG KONG SAR.
•**PRIOR, Mr. Nicholas John, BCom ACA** *1989;* Deloitte LLP, Athene Place, 66 Shoe Lane, LONDON, EC4A 3BQ. See also Deloitte & Touche LLP
PRIOR, Mrs. Nicola Kathryn, BSc ACA *1998;* 438 Riddell Road, GLENDOWIE, NEW ZEALAND.
•**PRIOR, Mr. Paul Stephen, BSc ACA** *1987;* (Tax Fac), Grant Thornton UK LLP, 4 Hardman Square, Spinningfields, MANCHESTER, M3 3EB. See also Grant Thornton LLP
PRIOR, Mr. Peter James, CBE DL BSc FCA *1947;* Highland, Holbach Lane, Sutton Saint Nicholas, HEREFORD, HR1 3DF. (Life Member)
PRIOR, Mr. Raymond Frank, MA ACA *1993;* Mercian Housing Association Ltd, Gee Business Centre, Holborn Hill, BIRMINGHAM, B7 5JR.
PRIOR, Mr. Robert Lloyd, BSc FCA *1975;* 8 Rogers Lane, Laleston, BRIDGEND, Mid Glamorgan, CF32 0LB.
PRIOR, Mr. Robin Frederick Lyndon, FCA *1969;* The Old Stocks, Sulgrave, BANBURY, OX17 2RX.
PRIOR, Mr. Rodney Francis Cunningham, FCA *1960;* 1 Surrey Heights, 29 Upper Brighton Road, SURBITON, SURREY, KT6 6QX. (Life Member)
PRIOR, Mr. Roger Jonathan, BA FCA *1980;* (Tax Fac), James Mason Ltd, Rixey Park, Kingsteignton Road, NEWTON ABBOT, DEVON, TQ13 0BY.
PRIOR, Mrs. Sarah Wilkes, BSc ACA *1989;* (Tax Fac), 8 Southern Road, LONDON, N2 9LE.
PRIOR, Miss. Shan Elizabeth, BA(Hons) ACA *2011;* 39 Ellesmere Road, Stockton Heath, WARRINGTON, WA4 6DZ.
PRIOR, Miss. Toni Marie, ACA *2008;* 56 Careys Wood, Smallfield, HORLEY, SURREY, RH6 9PB.
PRIOR, Mr. Tony, FCA *1971;* Fireworks Music Ltd, 28 Percy Street, LONDON, W1T 2DB.
PRIORE, Mr. Angelo, ACA *2010;* (Tax Fac), 38 Craven Street, LONDON, wc2n 5ng.
PRISMALL, Mr. Peter Arthur, FCA *1956;* 1 Holly Close, WALLINGTON, SURREY, SM6 0QB. (Life Member)
PRITCHARD, Mr. Adam Edward, BA ACA *2005;* 20 Linshiels Grove, Ingleby Barwick, STOCKTON-ON-TEES, CLEVELAND, TS17 0WF.
PRITCHARD, Mrs. Alexandra Jane, BSc ACA *2008;* 4 Belle Vue Grove, West Moors, FERNDOWN, BH22 0EF.
•**PRITCHARD, Mr. Alistair James, BSc FCA** *1999;* with Deloitte LLP, 1 Woodborough Road, NOTTINGHAM, NG1 3FG.
PRITCHARD, Mr. Andrew Simon, BSc FCA *1983;* Kidnal Grange, Kidnal, MALPAS, SY14 7DJ.
PRITCHARD, Mr. Anthony Brian, FCA *1972;* Terone, Easton, WELLS, BA5 1DZ. (Life Member)
•**PRITCHARD, Mrs. Caroline Mary, MA FCA** *1985;* Caroline Pritchard, 16 Huron Drive, LIPHOOK, GU30 7TZ.
PRITCHARD, Mrs. Catherine Dawn, BSc ACA *1990;* Gloucestershire County Council, Shire Hall, Westgate Street, GLOUCESTER, GL1 2TJ.
PRITCHARD, Miss. Cathryn, MSc ACA *2009;* 51A Cropley Street, LONDON, N1 7JB.
•**PRITCHARD, Mrs. Christine Janet, FCA** *1984;* Arthur Gait & Company, 18 Gold Tops, NEWPORT, NP20 5WJ.
PRITCHARD, Mr. David Alexander, FCA *1966;* Coppice Lodge, Lyth Hill, Bayston Hill, SHREWSBURY, SY3 0BS. (Life Member)
PRITCHARD, Mr. David Martin, BSc ACA *1988;* 43 Cefn Coed Avenue, Cyncoed, CARDIFF, CF23 6HF.
PRITCHARD, Mrs. Elizabeth Anne, BSc ACA *1990;* Colchester Global Investors Limited, Heathcoat House, 20 Savile Row, LONDON, W1S 3PR.
PRITCHARD, Miss. Emma Joanne, LLB ACA CTA *2002;* 252 Long Lane, Finchley, LONDON, N3 2RN.
•**PRITCHARD, Mr. Eric Richard, FCA** *1967;* (Tax Fac), Keelings Limited, Broad House, 1 The Broadway, Old Hatfield, HATFIELD, HERTFORDSHIRE AL9 5BG.
PRITCHARD, Mr. Francis Alan, FCA *1963;* 28 Chadwick Road, Urmston, MANCHESTER, M41 9RH.
PRITCHARD, Mr. Gary Michael, BSc ACA *1996;* 81 Florence Road, Wimbledon, LONDON, SW19 8TH.
PRITCHARD, Miss. Gill, BSc ACA *2003;* 4 Caledon Road, BEACONSFIELD, BUCKINGHAMSHIRE, HP9 2BX.
•**PRITCHARD, Mr. Glyndwr, FCA** *1970;* G Pritchard FCA, 6 County View, Clifton, BANBURY, OXFORDSHIRE, OX15 0PZ.
PRITCHARD, Mr. Gregory Forshaw, BSc FCA *1982;* Locksley Hall, Tennysons Lane, HASLEMERE, GU27 3AF.
PRITCHARD, Mr. Harry John Howard, BA ACA *1980;* Coverdale Baptist Church, Coverdale Christian Church, Coverdale Crescent, MANCHESTER, M12 4FG.
PRITCHARD, Mr. Hugh David, MA ACA *1995;* 37 Terrace Street, MONTPELIER, VT 05602, UNITED STATES.
PRITCHARD, Mr. Huw Brentnall, BA FCA FRSA *1986;* 6 Davema Close, CHISLEHURST, BR7 5QZ.
PRITCHARD, Mr. Huw Elis, BSc ACA *1984;* 25 Arbutus Drive, Coombe Dingle, BRISTOL, BS9 2PW.
PRITCHARD, Mr. Ian, BA ACA AMCT *1995;* 46 Millbrook Drive, SHENSTONE, STAFFORDSHIRE, WS14 0JL.
•**PRITCHARD, Mr. Ian, BA ACA** *1992;* BlueSky Consulting (Scotland) Limited, 9 McLauchlan Rise, Aberdour, BURNTISLAND, FIFE, KY3 0SS.
PRITCHARD, Mr. Ian Vincent, BSc FCA *1977;* Flexiload Ltd, 8 Allerton Road, RUGBY, CV23 0PA.
PRITCHARD, Mr. James Malcolm, ACA *2009;* 33 Welbeck Avenue, SOUTHAMPTON, SO17 1ST.
PRITCHARD, Mr. Jamie, BSc ACA *1996;* 19 Waverley Lane, FARNHAM, GU9 8BB.
PRITCHARD, Mr. John Anthony, FCA *1957;* 22 Hillcrest Ave, Great Barr, BIRMINGHAM, B43 6LX. (Life Member)
PRITCHARD, Mr. John Anthony Robert, BA ACA *1985;* Theokriotou 17, Peristeri, ATHENS, GREECE.
•**PRITCHARD, Mr. John Glyn, BSc FCA** *1973;* Hughes Parry & Co, 121 High Street, BANGOR, GWYNEDD, LL57 1NT.
PRITCHARD, Mr. John Michael, PhD BSc FCA *1985;* 16 Huron Drive, LIPHOOK, GU30 7TZ.
•**PRITCHARD, Mr. John Morris, BSc FCA** *1977;* (Tax Fac), W.J. Matthews & Son, 11 - 15 Bridge Street, CAERNARFON, LL55 1AB.
•**PRITCHARD, Mr. John Nicholas Dearn, FCA** *1970;* Nick Pritchard, 1 Church Street, STOURBRIDGE, WEST MIDLANDS, DY8 1LT.
•**PRITCHARD, Mr. Jon Charles, BSc ACA** *1993;* Barn Studios, Gaterounds Farm Parkgate Road, Newdigate, DORKING, RH5 5AJ.
•**PRITCHARD, Mrs. Kathleen Mary, FCA** *1957;* (Tax Fac), Worley Pritchard & Co, 34 Hydes Road, WEDNESBURY, WS10 9SY.
PRITCHARD, Mrs. Kathryn Jane, BSc FCA *1989;* with Bairstow & Atkinson, Carlton House, Bull Close Lane, HALIFAX, HX1 2EG.
PRITCHARD, Mr. Keith Holmes, FCA *1962;* 1 Emes Close, PERSHORE, WR10 1QY. (Life Member)
PRITCHARD, Dr. Kevin, PhD BSc ACA *2011;* 25 Grange Drive, Castle Donington, DERBY, DE74 2QU.
PRITCHARD, Mrs. Kirsten, BSc ACA *1997;* 96 Winterhill Road, MADISON, CT 06443, UNITED STATES.
•**PRITCHARD, Mrs. Leona Rose, BSc ACA** *2000;* 46 Millbrook Drive, Shenstone, LICHFIELD, STAFFORDSHIRE, WS14 0JL.
PRITCHARD, Mrs. Lucy Jane, BA ACA *1994;* 14 Manor Close, Drighlington, BRADFORD, BD11 1NP.
PRITCHARD, Mr. Mark, BSc ACA *1996;* Oxley Inc, 31 Business Park Drive, BRANFORD, CT 06405, UNITED STATES.
•**PRITCHARD, Mr. Michael Alexander Parry, BA FCA** *1982;* Michael Pritchard & Co, Nascot House, Church Lane, Wroxham, NORWICH, NR12 8SH.
PRITCHARD, Mr. Michael Andrew, BSc(Hons) ACA *2002;* 10 Coleraine Road, LONDON, N8 0QL.
PRITCHARD, Mr. Michael John Oulton, FCA *1971;* Rose Cottage, Wickham Heath, NEWBURY, BERKSHIRE, RG20 8PH.
PRITCHARD, Mr. Neil Bartley, BSc(Hons) FCA *2001;* 80 Park Road, New Barnet, BARNET, HERTFORDSHIRE, EN4 9QF.
PRITCHARD, Miss. Nicola, BA(Hons) ACA *2002;* 15 Hatherley Avenue, Crosby, LIVERPOOL, L23 0SD.
PRITCHARD, Miss. Nicola Dawn, BA ACA *1991;* The Granary Mill Lane, Aldridge, WALSALL, WS9 0NB.
PRITCHARD, Mr. Nigel, BSc ACA *1990;* (Tax Fac), 6 Vermuyden, Earith, HUNTINGDON, PE28 3QP.
PRITCHARD, Mr. Nigel George, BSc FCA *1980;* Haut Du Mont Farm, La Rue De L'aleval, St Peter, JERSEY, JE3 7ER.
PRITCHARD, Mr. Oliver Frank John, BA ACA *1987;* (Tax Fac), 55 Northumberland Place, LONDON, W2 5AS.
PRITCHARD, Mr. Paul James, MA MEng ACA *2002;* (Tax Fac), 13 Wells Close, SOUTH CROYDON, SURREY, CR2 7ZQ.
PRITCHARD, Mr. Reginald John, MA ACA *1981;* The British School, Chapel Lane, Blockley, MORETON-IN-MARSH, GLOUCESTERSHIRE, GL56 9BG.
PRITCHARD, Mr. Richard William Mortimer, ACA *1979;* M I N D in Haringey, Station House, 73c Stapleton Hall Road, LONDON, N4 3QF.
•**PRITCHARD, Mr. Robert Michael, BSc FCA** *1976;* (Tax Fac), Burnley & Evans Limited, 7 Centre Court, Vine Lane, HALESOWEN, WEST MIDLANDS, B63 3EB.
PRITCHARD, Mr. Robert Nigel, BA FCA *1991;* Terex, Central Boulevard, Prologis Park, COVENTRY, CV6 4BX.
PRITCHARD, Miss. Sally Victoria, ACA *2007;* (Tax Fac), Rose Cottage, Wickham Heath, NEWBURY, BERKSHIRE, RG20 8PH.
PRITCHARD, Mrs. Sarah Frances, BSc ACA *1991;* 21 Upper Bridge Street, Wye Near, ASHFORD, Kent, TN25 5AW.
PRITCHARD, Mrs. Sarah Louise, BA(Hons) ACA *2000;* 80 Park Road, New Barnet, BARNET, HERTFORDSHIRE, EN4 9QF.
PRITCHARD, Mrs. Selena Jane, BA ACA *1993;* 12 Miniva Drive, Walmley, SUTTON COLDFIELD, B76 2WT.
PRITCHARD, Mr. Simon David, BSc ACA *1989;* 16 Priory Lane, BRACKNELL, RG42 2JT.
PRITCHARD, Mr. Simon Francis Stephen, ACA *1997;* The Old Cross Keys, 37-38 Froxfield, MARLBOROUGH, SN8 3LD.
•**PRITCHARD, Mr. Stephen, FCA** *1977;* Stephen Pritchard & Co., 144 Folkestone Road, SOUTHPORT, MERSEYSIDE, PR8 5PP.
•**PRITCHARD, Mr. Stephen Guy, BSc FCA** *1983;* Menzies LLP, Wentworth House, 4400 Parkway, Whiteley, FAREHAM, HAMPSHIRE PO15 7FJ.
PRITCHARD, Mr. Timothy Charles, BSc FCA MBA *1980;* Cilfan, Pant Yr Afon, PENMAENMAWR, LL34 6BY.
•**PRITCHARD, Mrs. Tracey, BA FCA** *1997;* KPH Audit & Assurance Services Limited, 255 Poulton Road, WALLASEY, MERSEYSIDE, CH44 4BT. See also KBH Accountants Ltd
PRITCHARD, Mr. William Alexander, ACA *2009;* Flat 1 Grange Court Grange Street, ST. ALBANS, HERTFORDSHIRE, AL3 5NE.
PRITCHARD, Mr. William John, FCA *1950;* 3 Springside, Borthyn, RUTHIN, LL15 1NS. (Life Member)
PRITCHARD-WOOLES, Mrs. Ruth Suzanne, LLB FCA *1988;* 1 The Close, DUNMOW, CM6 1EW.
•**PRITCHET, Mrs. Jacqueline Ann, ACA** *1981;* Jackie Pritchet, 17 Ashley Close, Hightown, RINGWOOD, BH24 1QX.
PRITCHET, Mr. Stephen William, FCA *1980;* Jayesse Lodge, 17 Ashley Close, RINGWOOD, HAMPSHIRE, BH24 1QX.
•**PRITCHETT, Mr. Bruce Edward, BA ACA** *1986;* B&P Accounting Limited, Kingsley House, Church Lane, Shurdington, CHELTENHAM, GL51 5TQ. See also B & P Accounting Partnership
•**PRITCHETT, Mr. David Henry, BA FCA CTA MAE** *1973;* (Tax Fac), Pritchett & Co Limited, 16 Wynnstay Road, COLWYN BAY, CONWY, LL29 8NB.
PRITCHETT, Mr. Geoffrey Arthur, FCA *1960;* Lintorf Lodge, Main Road, Filby, GREAT YARMOUTH, NR29 3HY. (Life Member)
PRITCHETT, Mr. Nigel, FCA *1966;* 14 Vercourt, Little Aston, SUTTON COLDFIELD, B74 3XE.
•**PRITCHETT, Mr. Paul Arthur, BSc FCA** *1993;* Pritchett Consulting BSc FCA, 2 Sweep Close, Market Weighton, YORK, YO43 3NH.
PRITHIPAUL, Mr. Ashwin Kumar, BSc ACA *2003;* 8039 Merry Oaks Court, VIENNA, VA 22182, UNITED STATES.
PRIVETT, Mrs. Debra, BSc ACA *1981;* Samaras, Llandough, COWBRIDGE, CF71 7LR.
PRIVETT, Mr. James Michael, MMath ACA *2004;* 46 The Crescent, Haversham, MILTON KEYNES, MK19 7AN.
•**PRIVETT, Mrs. Nichola Kirsten, BA ACA** *2004;* The Stonebridge Partnership Ltd, 1 Chalkpit Terrace, DORKING, SURREY, RH4 1HX.
PRIZEMAN, Miss. Carol, ACA *2005;* 14 Desford Road, Kirby Muxloe, LEICESTER, LE9 2BB.
PROBERT, Mr. Andrew Charles, FCA *1975;* The Brew House, The Old Grammar School, Chuch Street, COWBRIDGE, SOUTH GLAMORGAN, CF71 7BB.
PROBERT, Mrs. Ann Elizabeth, BA ACA *2006;* Toronto Square, Toronto Street, LEEDS, WEST YORKSHIRE, LS1 2HJ.
PROBERT, Mr. Clive Michael Douglas, FCA *1967;* Cefn Bryn Cottage, Penmaen, SWANSEA, SA3 2HQ. (Life Member)
PROBERT, Miss. Helen Margaret, BSc FCA *1980;* (Tax Fac), with Alliotts, Imperial House, 15 Kingsway, LONDON, WC2B 6UN.
PROBERT, Mr. John Richard, BSc ACA *1998;* 464 Hatfield Road, ST. ALBANS, HERTFORDSHIRE, AL4 0XS.
PROBERT, Mrs. Julie Elizabeth, BSc ACA CTA *1995;* 464 Hatfield Road, ST. ALBANS, HERTFORDSHIRE, AL4 0XS.
PROBERT, Mrs. Kathryn Mary, BA ACA *1990;* (Tax Fac), Amberley, Greenway, Appleton, WARRINGTON, WA4 3AD.
PROBERT, Mr. Matthew David, ACA *2009;* 156 Mills Street, ALBERT PARK, VIC 3206, AUSTRALIA.
PROBERT, Mr. Simon, MChem ACA *2005;* Hartwell Plc Faringdon Road, Cumnor, OXFORD, OX2 9RE.
PROBERT, Mr. Stephen John, BA FCA CFA AMCT *1979;* Paget Consultancy Ltd, 1 Weedon Lane, AMERSHAM, BUCKINGHAMSHIRE, HP6 5QS.
PROBERT, Mr. Stephen William, ACA *1993;* Rio Ulla 16, 28660 BOADILLA DEL MONTE, SPAIN.
PROBERT, Mr. Trevor John, BSc FCA *1974;* (Tax Fac), 42 Rydal Gardens, WEMBLEY, MIDDLESEX, HA9 8RZ.
PROBETS, Ms. Karen Suzannah, ACA *1997;* Middle Penlean, Poundstock, BUDE, CORNWALL, EX23 0EE.
•**PROBITTS, Mr. Clive Miles, FCA** *1972;* Probitts & Co, No 1 Carrera House, Merlin Court, Gatehouse Close, AYLESBURY, BUCKINGHAMSHIRE HP19 8DP.
PROBY, Sir William Henry, CBE MA FCA *1975;* Elton Estates Co Ltd, Elton Hall, Elton, PETERBOROUGH, PE8 6SH.
•**PROBYN, Mrs. Susan Margaret, BA FCA** *1986;* Francis Clark LLP, Vantage Point, Woodwater Park, Pynes Hill, EXETER, EX2 5FD. See also Francis Clark Tax Consultancy Ltd
PROCKTER, Mr. Adrian David, LLB ACA *1985;* 47 Somerford Road, CIRENCESTER, GL7 1TP.
PROCKTER, Mr. Matthew Charles, MSc ACA *2005;* 11 Stonards Hill, LOUGHTON, ESSEX, IG10 3EH.
PROCOPIOU, Mr. George, BA ACA *2003;* European Commission - BRE2 8/385, Avenue d'Auderghem 19, 1040 BRUSSELS, BELGIUM.
PROCOPIOU, Mr. Stelios, BSc ACA *2004;* 7 Kazantzakis Street, Acropolis, 2007 NICOSIA, CYPRUS.
PROCOPIOU, Mr. Yiannakis, BSc ACA *2008;* 11 Socratous Street, 6036 LARNACA, CYPRUS.
PROCOPIS, Mrs. Sally Morven, BA ACA *1996;* 7A Lauderdale Road, LONDON, W9 1LT.
•**PROCTER, Mr. Andrew John, BL ACA** *2007;* (Tax Fac), Tyrrells Limited, 69 Princess Victoria Street, Clifton, BRISTOL, BS8 4DD.
PROCTER, Mr. Ian David, BSc ACA *1990;* 27 Reddish Lane, LYMM, CHESHIRE, WA13 9RU.
PROCTER, Mrs. Jane Elizabeth, BSc ACA *1992;* 153 Forres Road, SHEFFIELD, S10 1WF.
PROCTER, Mrs. Jennifer Linley, BSc ACA *2005;* 121 Wellington Road, WALLASEY, MERSEYSIDE, CH45 2NF.
PROCTER, Mr. John Rawsthorne, FCA *1977;* Weald & Downland Open Air Museum, Singleton, CHICHESTER, WEST SUSSEX, PO18 0EU.
PROCTER, Mr. Jonathan Michael, MA ACA *1994;* MSCI Barra SA, 8-10 rue de la Confederation, 1204 GENEVA, SWITZERLAND.
PROCTER, Mr. Mark, BSc ACA *1990;* 24 Recreation Road, GUILDFORD, GU1 1HQ.
•**PROCTER, Mr. Michael Sheriden Tuxworth, BSc FCA** *1974;* (Tax Fac), Reeves & Co LLP, Third Floor, 24 Chiswell Street, LONDON, EC1Y 4YX.
•**PROCTER, Mr. Michael William, BSc ACA FCCA** *2008;* Walkers Accountants Limited, 16-18 Devonshire Street, KEIGHLEY, WEST YORKSHIRE, BD21 2DG.
PROCTER, Mr. Neil William, FCA *1972;* North Staffs Tyre & Battery Ltd, Lightwood Road, STOKE-ON-TRENT, ST3 4JT.
PROCTER, Miss. Rebecca, BSc ACA *2011;* 9 Linden Crescent, KINGSTON UPON THAMES, SURREY, KT1 3DZ.
PROCTER, Mrs. Rebecca Mary, BSc FCA *1989;* 18 Redhill Grove, CHORLEY, LANCASHIRE, PR6 8TU.

PROCTER, Mr. Richard James Edward, BSc(Hons) ACA *2002;* 4 Amersham Road, HIGH WYCOMBE, BUCKINGHAMSHIRE, HP13 6PL.
PROCTER, Mr. Robert Elliott, MA ACA *2000;* 24 Pembroke Drive, Ponteland, NEWCASTLE UPON TYNE, NE20 9HS.
PROCTER, Mr. Robert Peter Tuxworth, MA MSci ACA *2003;* 4/12 Bogota Avenue, NEUTRAL BAY, NSW 2089, AUSTRALIA.
•PROCTER, Mr. Simon, BA ACA *1990;* (Tax Fac), Hopkins Allen Procter Limited, 4th Floor, St James House, Vicar Lane, SHEFFIELD, S1 2EX.
PROCTER, Mr. Stephen, MBE FCA *1967;* 23 Barnfield Road, PETERSFIELD, GU31 4DQ.
PROCTER, Mr. William, FCA *1954;* 21 Myrtle Terrace, DALTON-IN-FURNESS, LA15 8BU. (Life Member)
PROCTER, Mr. William Kenneth, FCA *1981;* Flat 26 Springalls Wharf Apartments, 25 Bermondsey Wall West, LONDON, SE16 4TL.
PROCTOR, Mr. Andrew Beauchamp, ACA CA(SA) *2009;* Singer Capital Markets Ltd, 1 Hanover Street, LONDON, W1S 1YZ.
PROCTOR, Mr. David Reginald, FCA *1961;* 60 Silverdale Rd., Ecclesall, SHEFFIELD, S11 9JL. (Life Member)
PROCTOR, Mrs. Elaine Ann, MSc ACA *1990;* 4 Hill Street, ASHBY-DE-LA-ZOUCH, LEICESTERSHIRE, LE65 2LS.
PROCTOR, Mrs. Elizabeth Rebecca, BSc ACA *1996;* 23 Orakei Road, Remuera, AUCKLAND 1050, NEW ZEALAND.
PROCTOR, Mrs. Emma Elizabeth Cooper, BSc(Hons) ACA *2002;* Highley Cottage, Gooseberry Lane, Ruyton Xi Towns, SHREWSBURY, SY4 1LG.
PROCTOR, Mr. Gary, LLB ACA *1998;* Law Offices of Gary E Proctor LLC, 8 E. Mulberry Street, BALTIMORE, MD 21202, UNITED STATES.
PROCTOR, Mr. Gary Alan, BA ACA *1994;* Glebe Farm, Mill Lane, Walkeringham, DONCASTER, SOUTH YORKSHIRE, DN10 4HY.
PROCTOR, Mr. George, FCA *1958;* 10 Kingston Drive, Whitley Lodge Estate, WHITLEY BAY, NE26 1JH. (Life Member)
PROCTOR, Mr. Gordon James, FCA *1981;* 26 Cosby Road, Littlethorpe, LEICESTER, LE19 2HF.
PROCTOR, Mr. Ian David Fraser, BA ACA *1992;* 21 Park Place, STIRLING, FK9 9JR.
PROCTOR, Mr. James Stephen, BA ACA *1984;* 24 Aylesby Close, KNUTSFORD, CHESHIRE, WA16 8AE.
PROCTOR, Miss. Jane Maria, ACA *2008;* 20 Keswick Drive, CHESTERFIELD, DERBYSHIRE, S41 8HP.
PROCTOR, Mrs. Li Jean, BSc ACA *2000;* (Tax Fac), Gerber Scientific, 1600 Park Avenue, Aztec West, Almondsbury, BRISTOL, BS32 4UA.
•PROCTOR, Mr. Mark, ACA DChA *2005;* Lovewell Blake LLP, 102 Prince of Wales Road, NORWICH, NORFOLK, NR1 1NY.
PROCTOR, Mr. Mark Stephen, BSc ACA *2005;* 9 London Street, Whittlesey, PETERBOROUGH, PE7 1BP.
PROCTOR, Mr. Matthew Frederick, BA ACA *1993;* Blaisdon, 4 Hill Street, ASHBY-DE-LA-ZOUCH, LEICESTERSHIRE, LE65 2LS.
•PROCTOR, Mrs. Patricia Anne, FCA *1990;* (Tax Fac), Fletcher & Partners, Crown Chambers, Bridge Street, SALISBURY, SP1 2LZ.
PROCTOR, Mr. Piers Christian Miles, LLB ACA *2002;* Fourways, 22 Highland Road, Nazeing, WALTHAM ABBEY, EN9 2PT.
•PROCTOR, Mr. Richard Norman, FCA CTA *1985;* (Tax Fac), Grant Thornton UK LLP, Kingfisher House, 1 Gilders Way, St James Place, NORWICH, NR3 1UB. See also Grant Thornton LLP
PROCTOR, Mr. Steven David, BSc ACA *1996;* FM3-52, 1900 Prairie City Road, FOLSOM, CA 95630, UNITED STATES.
•PROCTOR, Mrs. Susan, BSc FCA *1983;* Avantica Ltd, 3 The Grange, Flaxby, KNARESBOROUGH, NORTH YORKSHIRE, HG5 0RJ.
PRODGER, Mr. Michael John, FCA *1966;* 20 Lodge Avenue, EASTBOURNE, EAST SUSSEX, BN22 0JD. (Life Member)
•PRODROMIDES, Mr. Panos Socradi, MSc BA ACA *2001;* Nexia Poyiadjis, 2 Sophouli St, Chanteclair House 8th Flr, P O Box 21814, 1513 NICOSIA, CYPRUS.
PRODROMITIS, Mr. Stelios, BSc ACA *1991;* HLB Afxentiou Limited, Palaceview House, Corner of Prodromos St & Zinonos Kitieos, POBox 16006, CY-2085 NICOSIA, CYPRUS.
PRODROMOU, Mr. Alexandros, BA ACA *2004;* Kifissodotou 6, Lakatamia, 2335 NICOSIA, CYPRUS.
PRODROMOU, Mr. Andreas, FCA *1970;* Andreas Prodromou & Co, Prodromou Court, 54 Sittica Hanoum Street, P.O. Box 40163, 6301 LARNACA, CYPRUS.
PRODROMOU, Mr. George, ACA ACCA *2011;* Klistenous 12A, Kapsalos, 3087 LIMASSOL, CYPRUS.
PROFFIT, Mr. Philip Tony, FCA *1959;* 79 Landswood Park, Hartford, NORTHWICH, CHESHIRE, CW8 1NF. (Life Member)
•PROFFITT, Mr. Benjamin Joseph, BSc ACA *2007;* BDP Oribita Limited, Ioma House, Hope Street, Douglas, ISLE OF MAN, IM1 1AP.
PROFFITT, Mr. Michael Joseph, FCA *1976;* Renewable Energy Holdings Plc Isle of Man Assurance Ltd Ioma House Hope Street Douglas, ISLE OF MAN, IM1 1AP.
PROFFITT, Mr. Peter Raymond, FCA *1960;* 6 Alexandra Road, MINEHEAD, SOMERSET, TA24 5DR.
PROFFITT, Mr. Simon David, BSc FCA *1980;* Loros, Groby Road, LEICESTER, LE3 9QE.
PROKOPYSZYN, Mrs. Carol Louise, LLB ACA *1991;* 35 Katherine Drive, Toton, NOTTINGHAM, NG9 6JB.
PRONGER, Mr. Christopher James Tod, BA FCA *1965;* 10 Kingswood Avenue, BROMLEY, BR2 0NY.
PROOPS, Miss. Emma Louise, BA(Hons) ACA *2003;* 206 Gateshead Road, BOREHAMWOOD, WD6 5LL.
PROOST, Mr. Philip Andrew, BA ACA *1992;* 5 Ardilaun Road, LONDON, N5 2QR.
PROPHET, Mr. Andrew Michael, BA ACA *1996;* 27 Bradley Gardens, LONDON, W13 8HE.
•PROPHET, Miss. Gillian Mary, ACA *1985;* Prophet & Collinson, Tregolds, 20 Moorlands Road, Fishponds, BRISTOL, BS16 3LF.
PROPHET, Mr. Martin James, BA ACA *1999;* 204 Tilehouse Green Lane, Knowle, SOLIHULL, B93 9EJ.
PROSSER, Mr. Andrew James Mackenzie, BA ACA *1992;* Boots UK Fern House, 53-55 High Street, FELTHAM, MIDDLESEX, TW13 4HU.
PROSSER, Mr. Andrew Michael James, BSc FCA *1996;* Sanofi aventis Finance Department WW5, 1 Onslow Street, GUILDFORD, GU1 4YS.
PROSSER, Miss. Claire, BSc ACA *2004;* 27 Llys Eglwys, BRIDGEND, MID GLAMORGAN, CF31 5DT.
PROSSER, Mr. Craig, ACA *2011;* 28 West Lea Gardens, LEEDS, LS17 5DF.
•PROSSER, Mr. David Trevor, BSc FCA *1984;* PricewaterhouseCoopers LLP, 1 Embankment Place, LONDON, WC2N 6RH. See also PricewaterhouseCoopers
•PROSSER, Mr. Geoffrey George, FCA *1969;* John Crook & Partners, 255 Green Lanes, Palmers Green, LONDON, N13 4XE.
PROSSER, Mr. Ian Handley, FCA *1963;* 5 Ennismore Avenue, GUILDFORD, GU1 1SP.
PROSSER, Sir Ian Maurice Gray, Kt BCom FCA *1967;* 230 Bickenhall Mansions, Bickenhall Street, LONDON, W1U 6BW.
PROSSER, Mr. John Michael, MA FCA *1954;* 15 Euan Close, Gillhurst Road, BIRMINGHAM, B17 8PL. (Life Member)
PROSSER, Mrs. Louise, BSc(Econ) ACA *2003;* 14 Crane Close, Somersham, HUNTINGDON, CAMBRIDGESHIRE, PE28 3YG.
PROSSER, Miss. Marion, BA ACA *2006;* 88b Rhydypenau Road, CARDIFF, CF23 6PW.
•PROSSER, Mr. Mark Orde, FCA *1976;* CB Partnership, 119 Bury Old Road, Whitefield, MANCHESTER, M45 7AY.
PROSSER, Mr. Michael Trevelyan, BEng ACA *1993;* 73 Merlin Way, Mickleover, DERBY, DE3 5UJ.
PROSSER, Mr. Richard John Stobart, BSc FCA *1989;* Appleby Trust (Jersey) Ltd, P.O. Box 207, 13-14 Esplanade, ST. Helier, JERSEY, JE1 1BD.
PROSSER, Mr. Robert Edward, MA FCA *1975;* PricewaterhouseCoopers, Darling Park Tower 2, 201 Sussex Street, GPO Box 2650, SYDNEY, NSW 1171 AUSTRALIA.
PROSSER, Mr. Robert John, BSc FCA *1995;* (Tax Fac), 36 Mayditch Place, Bradwell Common, MILTON KEYNES, MK13 8DX.
PROTHERO, Mr. David Jonathan, ACA *2009;* 132 Harbut Road, LONDON, SW11 2RE.
PROTHERO, Mr. Graham, MA ACA *1987;* Development Securities Plc, Portland House, Bressenden Place, LONDON, SW1E 5DS.
PROTHEROE, Mr. David Jason Lloyd, MA FCA *1979;* Honeywell Control Systems Ltd, Honeywell House, Arlington Business Park, Downshire Way, BRACKNELL, BERKSHIRE RG12 1EB.
PROTHEROE, Mr. Denis John Gordon, FCA *1954;* 4 Westwood Close, BROMLEY, BR1 2JJ. (Life Member)
•PROTHEROE, Mr. John Robert Clement, BSc ACA *1987;* John Protheroe, 51 Beaufort Mansions, Beaufort Street, LONDON, SW3 5AF.
PROTHEROUGH, Mrs. Lisabeth Anne, BSc FCA *1991;* 3 Bourne Honour, Tonwell, WARE, HERTFORDSHIRE, SG12 0HW.
PROTO, Mr. Alan James, BA ACA *1991;* G M L Construction Ltd, Orchard House, Westerhill Road, Coxheath, MAIDSTONE, KENT ME17 4DH.
•PROTO, Mr. Peter Richard, FCA *1984;* (Tax Fac), Proto & Co, 41 Kingsmead Avenue, WORCESTER PARK, SURREY, KT4 8XA.
PROTOPAPAS, Mr. Emmanuel, BSc ACA *2011;* 175 Empire Square West, Empire Square, LONDON, SE1 4NL.
PROTTEY, Mr. Hans Oliver Edward, MEng ACA *2000;* 18 Ember Gardens, THAMES DITTON, SURREY, KT7 0LN.
PROTTO, Mr. Philippe Alexandre, ACA *2000;* Abbaye de Roseland, Kalinka 4, Boulevard Napoleon III, 06200 NICE, FRANCE.
PROUD, Mr. Andrew John, BEng CEng ACA *1999;* 3 Norman Terrace, Agamemnon Road, West Hampstead, LONDON, NW6 1BU.
PROUD, Mr. Christopher Wilfred Fredrick, BA ACA *1992;* Brambletye, Shepherds Lane, Lodsworth, PETWORTH, WEST SUSSEX, GU28 9BN.
PROUD, Mr. David Colin, BA ACA *2005;* 73 Magnolia Walk, EASTBOURNE, EAST SUSSEX, BN22 0ST.
PROUD, Mr. Kenneth Harold, FCA *1954;* Glaramara, 3 Greenslade Road, WALSALL, WS5 3QH. (Life Member)
PROUD, Mrs. Trudy Clare, ACA *2004;* 73 Magnolia Walk, Eastbourne, EASTBOURNE, BN22 0ST.
PROUDFOOT, Mr. Colin John, BA FCA *1986;* 6 St Hild Close, DARLINGTON, DL3 8LD.
PROUDFOOT, Mr. Frederick James, BSc FCA *1977;* Orchard House Cow Brow, Lupton, CARNFORTH, LA6 1PE.
PROUDFOOT, Mr. Ian William, BSc ACA *1996;* with KPMG, KPMG Centre, 18 Viaduct Harbour Avenue, P.O. Box 1584, AUCKLAND 1140, NEW ZEALAND.
PROUDFOOT, Mr. Keith Michael, BSc FCA *1979;* (Tax Fac), 12 Roseworth Crescent, NEWCASTLE UPON TYNE, NE3 1NR.
•PROUDFOOT, Mr. Michael Edward, ACA *1981;* Moore and Smalley LLP, Kendal House, Murley Moss Business Village, Oxenholme Road, KENDAL, CUMBRIA LA9 7RL.
PROUDLER, Mr. John Colin, FCA *1954;* Apartment 2, The Zetland, Marine Parade, SALTBURN-BY-THE-SEA, TS12 1BU. (Life Member)
PROUDLOCK, Mr. Michael John, BA FCA *1976;* Tendring House, 15 Greenhill Road, FARNHAM, GU9 8JP.
PROUDLOCK, Mr. Peter Drew, FCA *1972;* Te Moana, P.O. Box 192, OCHO RIOS, JAMAICA.
PROUDLOVE, Mrs. Caroline Amanda, BSc ACA *2001;* 19 Louring Bucket, Pantai 8, 59100 BANGSAR, MALAYSIA.
PROUDLOVE, Mr. Matthew Robert, BA ACA CF *2000;* 23 Gregory Avenue, Mapperley, NOTTINGHAM, NG3 6BW.
PROUDLOVE, Mr. Neil Harry, BSc(Hons) ACA *2000;* PricewaterhouseCoopers, Level 10, 1 Sentral, Jalan Travers, PO Box 10192, 50706 KUALA LUMPUR FEDERAL TERRITORY MALAYSIA.
PROUDLOVE, Mr. Richard, ACA *2009;* K P M G, 1 The Embankment, LEEDS, LS1 4DW.
PROUGHTEN, Mr. David James, MEng ACA *1990;* 33 Wick Avenue, Wheathampstead, ST. ALBANS, HERTFORDSHIRE, AL4 8QD.
PROUT, Mrs. Claire Elizabeth, BA ACA *1989;* Lostiford Cottage, Crockham Hill, EDENBRIDGE, TN8 6RD.
PROUT, Mr. John Christopher, BSc FCA *1978;* Richmond, Harnham Lane, Withington, CHELTENHAM, GL54 4DD.
PROUT, Mr. John Reginald, FCA *1949;* Silver Birches, 10 Oaks Road, CROYDON, CR0 5HL. (Life Member)
PROUT, Mr. Nigel John, BA ACA *1986;* 30 Le May Avenue, LONDON, SE12 9SU.
PROUTEN, Mrs. Pamela, BSc ACA ACMA *1993;* 8 Booth Rise, NORTHAMPTON, NN3 6HR.
PROVAN, Mr. David, FCA *1962;* Woodlands, Burtons Lane, CHALFONT ST. GILES, HP8 4BN. (Life Member)
PROVEST, Mrs. Rachel Claire, MA(Hons) ACA IAQ *2001;* c/o Savills Fideco Tower 81-85 Ham Nghi, HO CHI MINH CITY, District 1, VIETNAM.
PROVISOR, Mr. Stephen Brian, MA ACA *1982;* Revutski 46b, RA'ANANA, ISRAEL.
PROWER, Mr. Aubyn James Sugden, BTech ACA *1979;* Argent Estates Limited, 5 Albany Courtyard, LONDON, W1J 0HF.
PROWSE, Mr. Adam James, BSc(Hons) ACA *2010;* 15 Templecombe Mews, Oriental Road, WOKING, GU22 7DL.
•PROWTING, Mr. Kenneth David Jack, FCA *1964;* Prowting & Partners Limited, 6 West Park, Clifton, BRISTOL, BS8 2LT.
•PROWTING, Mr. Simon Craig, BA ACA *1994;* Prowting & Partners Limited, 6 West Park, Clifton, BRISTOL, BS8 2LT.
PRTAK, Mr. Dominic John, MA ACA *2004;* 30 Milton Road, WARE, SG12 0PZ.
PRUCHNIE, Mrs. Melinda Miriam Deborah, BSc FCA *1983;* 1 The Paddock, Cyncoed, CARDIFF, CF23 5JN.
PRUDDEN, Mrs. Vivienne Marie, BA FCA *1995;* 41 Seaview Estate, Netley Abbey, SOUTHAMPTON, SO31 5BQ.
PRUDHAM, Mrs. Catherine, BA ACA *1991;* 4 Carlton Road, BOLTON, BL1 5HU.
PRUE, Mr. Keith Adrian John, FCA *1982;* 289 Moody Street, No. 304, WALTHAM, MA 02453-5205, UNITED STATES.
PRUE, Mr. Nigel Leslie, BSc ACA *1997;* 49 Beach Road, Hartford, NORTHWICH, CHESHIRE, CW8 4BD.
PRUE, Mr. Norman John, FCA *1951;* 19 Rodborough Road, Dorridge, SOLIHULL, B93 8EE. (Life Member)
PRUST, Mr. Francis Charles, FCA *1968;* Millstones, Linton Hills Road, Linton, WETHERBY, WEST YORKSHIRE, LS22 4HQ. (Life Member)
PRUTTON, Mr. Jonathan Miles, BCom ACA *1989;* Energist Ltd 2 Park Pavilions, Clos Llyn Cwm Swansea Enterprise Park, SWANSEA, SA6 8QY.
PRVULOVICH, Mr. Richard, BA ACA *1991;* 68 Murrayfield Gardens, EDINBURGH, EH12 6DQ.
PRYCE, Mrs. Alison Mary, BSc ACA *1987;* 26A West Street, Welford, NORTHAMPTON, NN6 6HU.
PRYCE, Ms. Jennifer, ACA *2008;* 6 Haygarth, KNEBWORTH, HERTFORDSHIRE, SG3 6HE.
PRYCE, Mr. John Gareth, BSc ACA *1993;* Marks & Spencer Plc, Waterside House, 35 North Wharf Road, LONDON, W2 1NW.
PRYCE, Mr. Paul Anthony, ACA *1986;* C/- Stewarts Accountants, Level 7, 6 Underwood Street, SYDNEY, NSW 2000, AUSTRALIA.
PRYCE, Mr. Simon Charles Conrad, BSc ACA MSI *1988;* Hackers House, Junction Road, Churchill, CHIPPING NORTON, OXFORDSHIRE, OX7 6NW.
PRYCE, Mr. Timothy D G, MSc BA ACA *2006;* The Carbon Trust, 6th Floor, 5 New Street Square, LONDON, EC4A 3BF.
PRYDE, Mrs. Andrea, BSc ACA *2002;* First Floor, 30, Cannon Street, LONDON, EC4M 6XH.
•PRYDE, Mr. Geoffrey, FCA FCCA *1974;* Rawlinson Pryde & Partners, Argent House, 5 Goldington Road, BEDFORD, MK40 3JY. See also Rawlinson Pryde Limited
PRYER, Miss. Claire Louise, BSc ACA *2010;* Flat 1, Holly Lodge, 1 Oatlands Chase, WEYBRIDGE, SURREY, KT13 9RD.
PRYER, Mr. Robert Michael, BA(Hons) ACA *2001;* 18 Oakdale Drive, Chilwell, NOTTINGHAM, NG9 5LF.
PRYKE, Mrs. Gemma Fay, ACA *2009;* 48 Freehold Road, IPSWICH, SUFFOLK, IP4 5HY.
PRYKE, Mr. Kevin Geoffrey, ACA *2004;* 48 Freehold Road, IPSWICH, SUFFOLK, IP4 5LA.
PRYKMETA, Mr. Vladimir, BSc ACA *2009;* R G L Forensics Dashwood House, 69 Old Broad Street, LONDON, EC2M 1QS.
PRYNN, Mr. Benedict James, BA ACA *1992;* 143 John Ruskin Street, LONDON, SE5 0PQ.
PRYNN, Mr. Robert James, BSc ACA *1989;* Moto Hospitality Limited, PO Box 218, Toddington, DUNSTABLE, BEDFORDSHIRE, LU5 6QG.
PRYNNE, Mr. John William Gordon, FCA *1973;* Cruck Cottage, Church Road, Upper Farringdon, ALTON, GU34 3EG.
•PRYOR, Mr. Andrew Jonathan, MA FCA *1987;* Nexia Smith & Williamson Audit Limited, Portwall Place, Portwall Lane, BRISTOL, BS1 6NA. See also Smith & Williamson Ltd and Nexia Audit Limited
PRYOR, Mr. Thomas Robert, ACA *2010;* 2 Queensgate, 135 Queens Road, WEYBRIDGE, KT13 9UN.
PRYOR, Miss. Victoria Louise, BSc(Hons) ACA *2006;* Ageas Insurance Limited, Ageas House, Tollgate, Chandler's Ford, EASTLEIGH, HAMPSHIRE SO53 3YA.
PRYTHERCH, Mr. Antony David, BA ACA *1989;* 95 Ridgewood Drive, Pensby, WIRRAL, CH61 8RQ.
•PRZYBYCIN, Mrs. Joanne Michelle, BSc(Hons) ACA *2002;* JMP Accounting, 36a Warsash Road, Warsash, SOUTHAMPTON, SO31 9HX.
PRZYGRODZKA, Ms. Jennifer Ruth, MA ACA *1997;* 3320 Patterson Way, EL DORADO HILLS, CA 95762-4422, UNITED STATES.
PSALTIS, Mr. Demetris, BA FCA *1995;* 2 Zanettou Street, Flat 201, Ayios Andreas, CY1100 NICOSIA, CYPRUS.
PSALTIS, Mr. Kyriacos, BEng ACA *1999;* 30 Diogenous Street, Aglantzia, 2122 NICOSIA, CYPRUS.

•**PSALTIS, Mr. Marios, BSc FCA** *1996;* with PricewaterhouseCoopers, 268-270 Kifissias Avenue, Halandri, 15232 ATHENS, GREECE.
•**PSARA, Mr. Georgios Tasou, FCA** *1984;* GPMA Limited, Devon House, Church Hill, LONDON, N21 1LE.
PSOMATAKIS, Mr. Ioannis, ACA *2011;* Thoukididou 91, Agios Dimitrios, 17343 ATHENS, GREECE.
PTEROUDIS, Mr. Evangelos, ACA *2009;* P.O. Box 54341, 3723 LIMASSOL, CYPRUS.
PUA, Miss. Xiaowei, ACA *2009;* Barclays Capital, Level 47, Cheung Kong Centre, 2 Queens Road, CENTRAL, HONG KONG SAR.
PUCA, Dr. Claudio, ACA *2010;* (Tax Fac), Via Lamaticci 21, 60122 ANCONA, ITALY.
PUCCIO, Mr. Giuseppe, BA ACA *2005;* 160 Newland Gardens, HERTFORD, SG13 7WY.
PUCKETT, Mr. Stephen Ronald, BSc ACA *1986;* The Cottage, The Kings Drive, Burhill Park, WALTON-ON-THAMES, KT12 4BA.
PUCKNELL, Mr. James Martin, ACA *2008;* 65 Rowsby Court, Pontprennau, CARDIFF, CF23 8FG.
PUDDEFOOT, Miss. Amy, ACA *2010;* with PricewaterhouseCoopers, Royal Trust Tower, Suite 3000 TD Centre, Box 82, 77 King Street West, TORONTO M5K 1G8 ON CANADA.
PUDDICOMBE, Mr. Timothy Keith, ACA *1984;* Bukhatir Investments Group Limited, PO Box 88, SHARJAH, UNITED ARAB EMIRATES.
PUDDIFOOT, Mr. Raymond John, FCA *1975;* Rosemere, 14 Tudor Way, UXBRIDGE, UB10 9AB.
PUDDLE, Mr. David George Gordon, FCA *1977;* Hurst Farm, Burnt Oak Road, High Hurstwood, UCKFIELD, TN22 4AE.
PUDDLE, Mr. Joshua, BA ACA *2011;* Woodpeckers, Park Corner Drive, East Horsley, LEATHERHEAD, SURREY, KT24 6SE.
PUDDY, Mr. Stuart James, ACA *2009;* Flat 27 Palatine Place, 265 Palatine Road, MANCHESTER, M22 4ET.
PUDGE, Mr. Simon John, MA ACA *1981;* Merriton, Milland Lane, Milland, LIPHOOK, GU30 7JP.
PUDGE, Miss. Tessa Constance, ACA *2009;* 37 Chalcot Road, LONDON, NW1 8LP.
•**PUDNEY, Mr. Jeffrey John, BSc ACA** *1984;* (Tax Fac), Beechcroft Barn, Upton Lovell, WARMINSTER, WILTSHIRE, BA12 0JW.
PUDSCHEDL, Miss. Patricia, BA ACA *2009;* Zwinzstrasse 4-6 2/3/15, A - 1160 VIENNA, AUSTRIA.
PUGALIA, Mr. Chetan Kumar, ACA *1990;* 39 West Drive, SUTTON, SM2 7NB.
PUGH, Mr. Arthur John, BSc FCA *1976;* Grove House, Stoke St. Mary, TAUNTON, SOMERSET, TA3 5BX.
•**PUGH, Mr. Charles Desmond Bodenham, BSc FCA** *1975;* Charles D.B. Pugh, 2 Priory Walk, LONDON, SW10 9SP.
PUGH, Mr. Christopher Naunton, BSc ACA *1996;* 7 Brook Farm Close, BISHOP'S STORTFORD, CM23 4PT.
•**PUGH, Mr. David John, BCom FCA** *1975;* (Tax Fac), Daymar Ltd, 15 Partridge Way, Merrow Park, GUILDFORD, GU4 7DW.
PUGH, Mr. David Michael, BSc ACA *1995;* Kelstead, North View Road, BRIXHAM, DEVON, TQ5 9TT.
PUGH, Mr. David Richard, BSc FCA AMCT *1987;* Snowfield House, Sheraton Road, The Oakalls, BROMSGROVE, B60 2RT.
PUGH, Mr. David William, FCA *1975;* c/o The Argus Group, P.O. Box HM 1064, HAMILTON HMEX, BERMUDA.
PUGH, Mr. Dillwyn James, FCA *1960;* 8 Foxcombe Close, Swanmore, SOUTHAMPTON, SO32 2UJ. (Life Member)
PUGH, Mr. Francis Stewart Adlington, FCA *1932;* 10 Pendennis St, Riverside, LAUNCESTON, TAS 7250, AUSTRALIA. (Life Member)
PUGH, Mr. Gareth Alan David, BSc FCA *1978;* Saffron House Ferry Lane, Medmenham, MARLOW, BUCKINGHAMSHIRE, SL7 2EZ.
PUGH, Mr. Giles Adrian, BSc FCA *1992;* 2 Huntley Down, Milborne St. Andrew, BLANDFORD FORUM, DORSET, DT11 0LN.
PUGH, Mr. Graham David, BA ACA *2006;* Flat 34 Wimbledon Close, The Downs, LONDON, SW20 8HL.
PUGH, Mrs. Helen Jane, BSc ACA *1991;* 2 Huntley Down, Milborne St Andrew, BLANDFORD FORUM, DORSET, DT11 0LN.
PUGH, Mrs. Helen Rosemary, BA ACA *1998;* 46 Sydney Road, LONDON, W13 9EY.
PUGH, Mr. Howard, BA FCA *1972;* 30 Oakwood Drive, BINGLEY, WEST YORKSHIRE, BD16 4AH.
PUGH, Mr. Ian Richard, BA ACA *1989;* 22 Gatesmead, HAYWARDS HEATH, RH16 1SN.
PUGH, Mr. Ian Richard, BA(Hons) ACA *2002;* Emap Ltd Greater London House, Hampstead Road, LONDON, NW1 7EJ.
•**PUGH, Mr. James, MSc BEng ACA** *1995;* 5 McDowell Way, Narborough, LEICESTER, LE9 5RA.
PUGH, Miss. Jessica Maria, BSc ACA DChA *2003;* 92 Gleneldon Road, LONDON, SW16 2BE.
PUGH, Mrs. Joanne Sheila, ACA *1997;* 2 Brookside Gardens, Yockleton, SHREWSBURY, SY5 9PS.
PUGH, Mrs. Lisa, BA ACA *1990;* Snowfield House, 4 Sheraton Road, The Oakalls, BROMSGROVE, B60 2RT.
PUGH, Miss. Louise Nicola, BA ACA *1992;* 106 Victoria Avenue, PORTHCAWL, MID GLAMORGAN, CF36 3HA.
PUGH, Mr. Michael John, FCA *1967;* 21 Stanhopes, Limpsfield, OXTED, RH8 0TY. (Life Member)
•**PUGH, Mr. Neil, FCA** *1980;* (Tax Fac), Watts Gregory LLP, Elfed House, Oak Tree Court, Mulberry Drive, Cardiff Gate Business Park Pontprennau, CARDIFF CF23 8RS. See also Taxation Advice & Consultancy Ltd
PUGH, Mr. Nicholas David, MA ACA *2001;* 4 Gilmore Close, UXBRIDGE, MIDDLESEX, UB10 8DX.
PUGH, Mrs. Nicola Jane, BSc(Hons) ACA *2000;* 80 Waterside Road, GUILDFORD, SURREY, GU1 1RF.
PUGH, Mr. Oliver Michael, BSc FCA *1975;* BKAP Ltd, 3 High Street, Kinver, STOURBRIDGE, DY7 6HG.
•**PUGH, Mr. Peter Brandon, MA FCA** *1976;* (Tax Fac), Chapman Pugh, 4 Tregarne Terrace, ST. AUSTELL, CORNWALL, PL25 4BE.
PUGH, Mr. Raymond, FCA *1967;* 6 Garth Terrace, Bassaleg, NEWPORT, NP10 8LP.
PUGH, Miss. Rhian, BSc ACA *1998;* 2 Archer Road, PENARTH, SOUTH GLAMORGAN, CF64 3LS.
PUGH, Mr. Richard Henry Crommelin, DL LLB FCA *1951;* 4 Westlyn Close, MALVERN, WORCESTERSHIRE, WR14 2SJ. (Life Member)
PUGH, Mr. Richard Lloyd, TD ACA *1979;* Bronllwyn, North Road, WHITLAND, SA34 0BH.
PUGH, Mr. Richard William, LLB ACA *2010;* 117 Calder Drive, SUTTON COLDFIELD, WEST MIDLANDS, B76 1GG.
•**PUGH, Mr. Robert Mark Lewis, BA ACA** *1997;* PricewaterhouseCoopers LLP, Hays Galleria, 1 Hays Lane, LONDON, SE1 2RD. See also PricewaterhouseCoopers
PUGH, Mr. Stephen Crommelin, MA FCA *1983;* Adnams & Co Plc, Sole Bay Brewery, East Green, SOUTHWOLD, SUFFOLK, IP18 6JW.
PUGH, Mr. Stephen Geoffrey, BSc ACA *1998;* 80 Waterside Road, GUILDFORD, GU1 1RF.
PUGH, Mr. Steven Jeffrey, FCA *1973;* UNIT4 CODA Inc., 1000 Elm Street, Suite 801, MANCHESTER, NH 03101, UNITED STATES.
PUGH, Mr. Thomas James, BSc(Hons) ACA *2009;* 8f Dalebury Road, LONDON, SW17 7HH.
PUGH, Mrs. Tracey, BA ACA *1989;* 42 Headland Drive, DISCOVERY BAY, HONG KONG SAR.
PUGHE, Mr. David Michael Stephen, MA FCA *1991;* 27 rue des Orchidees, 98000 MONACO, MONACO.
•**PUGHE, Mr. Richard Neville Iain, MA ACA MAE** *1993;* Begbies Traynor (Central) LLP, 9th Floor, Bond Court, LEEDS, LS1 2JZ.
PUGSLEY, Mr. Bruce John Middleton, FCA *1966;* The Corner House, Clarendon Gardens, TUNBRIDGE WELLS, TN2 5LA.
PUGSLEY, Mr. Gary, ACA *2009;* 70 Daneville Road, LONDON, SE5 8SF.
PUGSLEY, Mr. Michael Neil, BA ACA *1998;* 68a Coast Road, REDCAR, CLEVELAND, TS10 3RD.
PUGSLEY, Mr. Richard Charles Vivian, ACA *1999;* 25 Heol y Cwm, Morganstown, CARDIFF, CF15 8FG.
PUGSLEY, Mr. Simon Colin, BA FCA *1996;* 17 Coulthard Close, TOWCESTER, NORTHAMPTONSHIRE, NN12 7BA.
PUI, Miss. Saw Hua, BSc ACA *1981;* Liechtensteinstrasse 12/TOP13, A-1090 VIENNA, AUSTRIA.
PULESTON, Mr. Andrew James, BSc ACA *1993;* Bostonia, Exeter Road, HONITON, DEVON, EX14 1AU.
•**PULFORD, Mr. John David, FCA** *1975;* (Tax Fac), John Pulford & Co Ltd, 21 Picksley Crescent, Holton le Clay, Grimsby, LINCOLNSHIRE, DN36 5DR.
PULFORD, Ms. Karen Jane, BSc FCA *1995;* 33 Holly Street, LEAMINGTON SPA, WARWICKSHIRE, CV32 4TT.
PULFORD, Mr. Piet James, BSc ACA *1980;* Highbridge Properties Plc, Berger House, 36-38 Berkeley Square, LONDON, W1J 5AE.
PULFORD, Mr. Richard Guy, MA MSc ACA MSI DipM *1997;* Downs House, 13 Higher Downs, ALTRINCHAM, CHESHIRE, WA14 2QL.
PULJIC, Miss. Danijela, BA(Hons) ACA *2002;* Flat 8, Harwood Court, Upper Richmond Road, LONDON, SW15 6JD.
PULL, Mr. William, MA FCA *1968;* Brook Farm, North Green, Pulham St. Mary, DISS, IP21 4XY. (Life Member)
PULLAN, Mr. Andrew David, BA ACA *1991;* 43 Oatlands Avenue, WEYBRIDGE, SURREY, KT13 9SS.
•**PULLAN, Mr. David John Smith, FCA** *1972;* David Pullan & Co, 24a Brook Street, ILKLEY, LS29 8DE.
•**PULLAN, Mr. David Michael, FCA** *1971;* David M. Pullan, Highfield House, Highfield Road, Idle, BRADFORD, BD10 8QY.
PULLAN, Mr. Gordon Waite, BSc FCA *1977;* Water Tower Nocton Road, Potterhanworth, LINCOLN, LN4 2DN.
•**PULLAN, Mr. Harry, FCA** *1962;* Ash Pullan, Epworth House, 25 City Road, LONDON, EC1Y 1AR.
•**PULLAN, Mr. Keith, ACA** *1982;* Pullan Barnes Limited, Stephenson House, Richard Street, Hetton-le-Hole, HOUGHTON LE SPRING, TYNE AND WEAR DH5 9HW.
•**PULLAN, Mr. Mark Jonathan, BSc ACA** *1999;* 23 Church Lane, Kirk Ella, HULL, HU10 7TA.
PULLAN, Mr. Nicholas John, BSc ACA *1999;* 1 Gardeners Close, Flitwick, BEDFORD, MK45 5BU.
PULLAN, Mrs. Nicola Elizabeth, FCA *1986;* (Tax Fac), 2 The Beanlands, Wanborough, SWINDON, SN4 0EJ.
PULLAN, Mr. Nigel Waite, BA FCA *1984;* 18 Firs Drive, HARROGATE, NORTH YORKSHIRE, HG2 9HB.
PULLAN, Mrs. Sarah Elizabeth, BA FCA *1983;* 18 Firs Drive, HARROGATE, NORTH YORKSHIRE, HG2 9HB.
PULLAN, Miss. Victoria, BSocSc ACA *2003;* Berkshire International Ltd, 95 Ewell Road, SURBITON, SURREY, KT6 6AH.
•**PULLAR, Mr. Simon Denis Hedley, BSc ACA** *1984;* (Tax Fac), Simon D H Pullar, Monks Tower, Honeywood Lane, Okewood Hill, DORKING, RH5 5PZ.
•**PULLEN, Mr. David, FCA** *1963;* (Tax Fac), David Pullen, 24 Katherine Drive, Toton, Beeston, NOTTINGHAM, NG9 6JB.
PULLEN, Mrs. Deborah Louise, BA ACA *1992;* 6 Blackthorn Road, Glenfield, LEICESTER, LE3 8QP.
PULLEN, Mr. Edward John, FCA *1954;* Sunnybank, 4 Anglebury Avenue, SWANAGE, DORSET, BH19 1QP. (Life Member)
PULLEN, Ms. Elise Michaela, ACA *2010;* Kedington, 12 New Road, Whitehill, BORDON, HAMPSHIRE, GU35 9AY.
PULLEN, Mrs. Fuzyunisa, BSc ACA *2005;* 10 Prospect Road, HUNGERFORD, BERKSHIRE, RG17 0JL.
PULLEN, Mr. Gareth Huw, MEng ACA *2003;* 12 Wasdale Close, West Bridgford, NOTTINGHAM, NG2 6RG.
PULLEN, Mr. Godfrey Thomas, FCA *1973;* 41 Morlais Road, Margam, PORT TALBOT, SA13 2AS.
PULLEN, Mr. Graham Douglas, BA FCA *1997;* 60 Redland Drive, Kirk Ella, HULL, HU10 7UY.
PULLEN, Mr. James Anthony, BSc ACA *1990;* Lands' End UK Limited, Lands' End Way, OAKHAM, LE15 6US.
PULLEN, Mrs. Jane Elizabeth, BSc FCA *1987;* (Tax Fac), Ipsen Ltd, 190 Bath Road, SLOUGH, SL1 3XE.
PULLEN, Ms. Jennifer Anne Louise, ACA *1995;* 563 Strathmere Court, WATERLOO N2T 2K2, ON, CANADA.
•**PULLEN, Mr. John Arthur, FCA** *1970;* (Tax Fac), Charles & Company Accountancy Ltd, 1st Floor, 16 Massetts Road, HORLEY, SURREY, RH6 7DE. See also Charles & Company(Services) Ltd, Hawthorns and Charles & Company
PULLEN, Miss. Kerry Ann, ACA *2008;* 44 Constable Road, CRAWLEY, WEST SUSSEX, RH10 5LP.
PULLEN, Miss. Laura, MA(Hons) ACA *2011;* Flat 869, Kestrel House, 2 St. George Wharf, LONDON, SW8 2AZ.
PULLEN, Mr. Mark Jonathan, BSc FCA *1997;* 40 Morland Road, CROYDON, SURREY, CR0 6NA.
PULLEN, Mr. Mark Reginald David, BSc ACA *1999;* 4 Goldcrest Way, Four Marks, ALTON, GU34 5FE.
PULLEN, Mr. Russell Watkins, FCA *1957;* 17 South Border, PURLEY, CR8 3LL. (Life Member)
•**PULLEN, Mr. Stephen John, FCA** *1984;* Booth Ainsworth LLP, Alpha House, 4 Greek Street, STOCKPORT, CHESHIRE, SK3 8AB.
PULLEN, Mr. Stuart Geoffrey, FCA *1973;* Attwood, 63A Greenway, Monkton Heathfield, TAUNTON, SOMERSET, TA2 8NQ. (Life Member)
PULLEN, Mr. Timothy Neil, BA ACA *2004;* 8 Jasmine Close, WOKINGHAM, RG41 3NQ.
•**PULLEY, Mr. Brian John, FCA** *1972;* (Tax Fac), Arundales, Stowe House, 1688 High Street, Knowle, SOLIHULL, B93 0LY.
PULLEY, Mr. Brian Robert, FCA *1958;* Friz Hill Lodge, Friz Hill, Walton, WARWICK, CV35 9HH. (Life Member)
PULLEY, Mr. Jonathan, BA ACA *1995;* 15 Blackdown Road, Knowle, SOLIHULL, B93 9HP.
PULLEY, Mrs. Sarah Emma, BSc ACA *1997;* 15 Blackdown Road, Knowle, SOLIHULL, B93 9HP.
PULLING, Mr. Nigel David, BA FCA *1984;* 4 Carlton Road, HARROGATE, HG2 8DD.
•**PULLINGER, Mr. Andrew Charles, FCA** *1981;* with Crowe Clark Whitehill LLP, Hatherton House, Hatherton Street, WALSALL, WS1 1YB.
PULLON, Mr. Martin James, LLB FCA *1982;* Kelowna, St Hilary, COWBRIDGE, CF71 7DP.
•**PULMAN, Mr. Ernest Wayne, FCA** *1972;* (Tax Fac), E Wayne Pulman & Co Ltd, 19 Church Street, MERTHYR TYDFIL, MID GLAMORGAN, CF47 0AY. See also Dexter Matthews Ltd
PULSFORD, Mr. Mark Patrick, ACA *2010;* 51 Cleaver Square, LONDON, SE11 4EA.
•**PULSFORD, Mr. Robert George, FCA** *1978;* Reddaway & Co, 30 St. Peter Street, TIVERTON, EX16 6NR.
•**PULVER, Mr. Nigel Roger, ACA** *1980;* NR Pulver & Co, Rear Office, 1st Floor, 43-45 High Road, BUSHEY, WD23 1EE.
PULZE, Mr. Paul, BEng ACA *2006;* Flat 4, 33 Hyde Park Square, LONDON, W2 2NW.
•**PUMFREY, Mr. David John, BSc FCA** *1995;* Simmons Gainsford LLP, 5th Floor, 7-10 Chandos Street, Cavendish Square, LONDON, W1G 9DQ.
PUMFREY, Mr. Mark Reginald, BA ACA *1983;* 36 Stevenage Road, LONDON, SW6 6ET.
PUMFREY, Mr. Oliver William Sheldon, ACA *2010;* Ground Floor Flat, 85 Sarsfeld Road, LONDON, SW12 8HT.
PUMPHREY, Mrs. Joanne, BSc ACA *2003;* C T C Marine Projects Ltd, Coniscliffe House, 9 Coniscliffe Road, DARLINGTON, COUNTY DURHAM, DL3 7EE.
PUMPHREY, Mr. John Richardson, RD FCA *1962;* La Grappe, Route de Berlou, 34360 PRADES SUR VERNAZOBRE, FRANCE. (Life Member)
PUN, Mr. David Yue Wah, ACA FCCA *1983;* 3 Old Peak Road, E3 Kam Yuen Mansion, MID LEVELS, HONG KONG ISLAND, HONG KONG SAR.
PUN, Mr. Geoffrey Wing Chuen, ACA *1979;* 33 Rue des Potiers, 31000 TOULOUSE, FRANCE.
PUN, Mr. Wing Mou, FCA *1975;* Flat C 39/F Tower 1, Scenecliff, 33 Conduit Road, MID LEVELS, HONG KONG ISLAND, HONG KONG SAR.
PUN LAI YUEN, Mr. Antoine Gilles Foong Lin, BSc(Econ) ACA *1998;* (Tax Fac), 26 Williams Grove, Long Ditton, SURBITON, KT6 5RN.
PUNCHARD, Mr. Alan, VRD FCA *1948;* 1 Hillwood Close, WARMINSTER, BA12 9QE. (Life Member)
PUNCHARD, Miss. Elizabeth Jane, BSc ACA *1979;* (Tax Fac), 30 Hanover Drive, FLEET, GU51 2TA.
PUNCHARD, Miss. Emma, BA ACA *2010;* 3 Biskra, Langley Road, WATFORD, WD17 4PF.
PUNCHIHEWA, Mr. Ruwan Charitha Gardiye, BSc ACA *1983;* 5660 Algonquin Way, SAN JOSE, CA 95138, UNITED STATES.
•**PUNGONG, Mr. Elias Pupesie Prombo, MSc FCA** *1996;* with PricewaterhouseCoopers, 366 rue Alfred-Marche, BP 2164, LIBREVILLE, GABON.
PUNIA, Mr. Raghuvinder Singh, ACA *1981;* PricewaterhouseCoopers, 21/F Edinburgh Tower, 15 Queen's Road Central, CENTRAL, HONG KONG ISLAND, HONG KONG SAR.
PUNJ, Miss. Seemar, ACA *2000;* 14 Thornton Avenue, LONDON, W4 1QG.
PUNJA, Mr. Aziz, BSc FCA *1975;* Stödjegränd 23, Rebro, 703 45 OREBRO, SWEDEN.
PUNNETT, Mrs. Joanna Lynne, BA ACA *1986;* 37 The Gowans, Sutton-On-The-Forest, YORK, YO61 1DL.
•**PUNT, Mr. David John, BSc FCA CF** *1998;* Baker Tilly & Co Limited, 25 Farringdon Street, LONDON, EC4A 4AB.
PUNT, Kenneth, Esq CBE FCA *1957;* 24 Endcliffe Hall Avenue, SHEFFIELD, S10 3EL. (Life Member)
•**PUNT, Mr. Richard Kenneth, BA ACA** *1992;* Deloitte LLP, Stonecutter Court, 1 Stonecutter Street, LONDON, EC4A 4TR. See also Deloitte & Touche LLP

PUNTER, Mr. Hayden William, BA ACA *2006;* 148a St. Pauls Road, LONDON, N1 2LL.
•**PUNTER, Mrs. Julie Carolyn, BSc ACA** *1981;* 7 Orchard Drive, Blackheath, LONDON, SE3 0QP.
PURBROOK, Mr. Clive, BA ACA *1981;* Glebe House, 38 High Street, Melbourn, ROYSTON, HERTFORDSHIRE, SG8 6DZ.
•**PURCELL, Mr. Cameron, BA FCA** *1997;* Alex Picot, 95-97 Halkett Place, St. Helier, JERSEY, JE1 1BX. See also Alex Picot Ltd
PURCELL, Mr. David Leo Patrick, FCA *1961;* Hale Farm Cottage, Hale Lane, The Hale, WENDOVER, BUCKINGHAMSHIRE, HP22 6QR. (Life Member)
PURCELL, Mr. Ian Turnbull, FCA *1972;* 69 Galtres Road, YORK, YO31 1JP.
PURCELL, Mr. Jamie, BSc ACA *2005;* Sportswift Ltd Century House, Brunel Road Wakefield 41 Industrial Estate, WAKEFIELD, WF2 0XG.
PURCELL, Mr. John, FCA *1961;* 35 Beck Lane, Collingham, WETHERBY, LS22 5BW. (Life Member)
•**PURCELL, Mr. Kieran, BSc ACA** *2008;* Apartment 18, 5 Tiltman Place, LONDON, N7 7EH.
PURCELL, Mr. Matthew Ian, BA ACA *1999;* The Cedars, Poolbridge Road, Blackford, WEDMORE, SOMERSET, BS28 4PA.
•**PURCELL, Mr. Michael Joseph Martin, ACA** *1984;* (Tax Fac), Purcells UK Limited, 342 Bloomfield Road, BATH, BA2 2PB.
PURCELL, Mr. Patrick John, FCA *1964;* Keepers Lodge, Penllyn, COWBRIDGE, CF71 7RQ.
PURCELL, Ms. Rachel, BA ACA *2004;* StoneTurn UK LLP, 85 Fleet Street, LONDON, EC4Y 1AE.
•**PURCELL, Mr. Roger Bernard Allan, MA FCA** *1969;* Roger Purcell LLP, 202 Old Brompton Road, LONDON, SW5 0BU.
PURCELL, Mr. Timothy Martin, BSc ACA *1988;* Paperlink Ltd, 356 Kennington Road, LONDON, SE11 4LD.
PURCELL, Mrs. Vanessa Sharon, BA ACA *2002;* The Cedars, Poolbridge Road, Blackford, WEDMORE, SOMERSET, BS28 4PA.
PURCHAS, Ms. Anna May Elizabeth, MA ACA *1996;* 100 Gloucester Road, BARNET, EN5 1NA.
PURCHASE, Mr. David Edward, BA FCA *1969;* Craig-y-Mor House, South Road, Sully, PENARTH, CF64 5SJ.
PURCHASE, Mr. Kenneth John, BSc ACA *1985;* 21 Framfield Road, Islington, LONDON, N5 1UU.
PURCHASE, Miss. Samantha Jayne, BSc ACA *2011;* 20 Whitehall Road, Penn, WOLVERHAMPTON, WEST MIDLANDS, WV4 5TA.
•**PURDHAM, Mr. Paul, FCA** *1981;* (Tax Fac), Paul Purdham, 26 Millers Hill, HOUGHTON LE SPRING, DH4 7AJ.
PURDIE, Mr. Andrew, MSc FCA *1992;* 20 Neville Road, LONDON, W5 1NN.
PURDON, Mr. David John, BCom FCA *1979;* Beechfield, Bathampton Lane, Bathampton, BATH, BA2 6SJ.
•**PURDY, Mr. Clive Robert, BA FCA** *1983;* (Tax Fac), DeVines Accountants Limited, DeVine House, 1299-1301 London Road, LEIGH-ON-SEA, ESSEX, SS9 2AD. See also De Vines and Atherton Bailey LLP
PURDY, Miss. Deborah Ann, BSc ACA *1993;* 30a Sherriff Road, West Hampstead, LONDON, NW6 2AU.
PURDY, Dr. Derek Ernest, FCA *1968;* Whitegates, 8 Highdown Avenue, Emmer Green, READING, RG4 8QS.
•**PURDY, Mr. Gary George, BSocSc FCA** *1984;* Baker Tilly UK Audit LLP, Hanover House, 18 Mount Ephraim Road, TUNBRIDGE WELLS, KENT, TN1 1ED. See also Baker Tilly Tax and Advisory Services LLP
PURDY, Miss. Jane Louise, BA ACA *1996;* 286 Dobbin Hill, SHEFFIELD, S11 7JG.
PURDY, Mr. John Charles Fairbairn, BA ACA *1987;* 46 Petley Road, LONDON, W6 9ST.
PURDY, Mr. John Douglas, FCA *1959;* Longmeadow, 123 Ilsham Road, TORQUAY, DEVON, TQ1 2HY. (Life Member)
PURDY, Mr. Keith Neil, ACA *1993;* (Tax Fac), 23 Rectory Way, Ickenham, UXBRIDGE, UB10 8BS.
PURDY, Mr. Richard George, LLB ACA *1994;* Internal Audit Dept, 3663 Manchester, Langley Road South, SALFORD, M6 6TZ.
PURDY, Mr. Robert Andrew, BSc ACA *1998;* 35 Kings Weston Road, Henbury, BRISTOL, BS10 7QT.
PURDY, Mr. Robert Joseph Balkan, ACA *2008;* 8 Highdown Avenue, Emmer Green, READING, RG4 8QS.
PUREWAL, Mrs. Harvinder, BA(Hons) ACA *2001;* 2e Hamilton Road, LONDON, W5 2EQ.
PUREWAL, Mr. Khushpal Singh, LLB DMS ACA MCMI *2003;* 49 Hallam Crescent, WOLVERHAMPTON, WV10 9YA.
•**PUREWAL, Mr. Parwinder Singh, BSc FCA** *1986;* PricewaterhouseCoopers LLP, 7 More London Riverside, LONDON, SE1 2RT. See also PricewaterhouseCoopers
PUREWAL, Mr. Sukhjinder Singh, BSc ARCS ACA *1997;* 7 Flavian Close, ST. ALBANS, AL3 4JX.
PURGAL, Mr. Jan, ACA *1992;* Vistra Group Management Ltd, 38 Esplanade, ST HELIER, JE1 4TR.
PURI, Mr. Abhay Kumar, FCA *1974;* P.O. Box 26367, ADLIYA, BAHRAIN. (Life Member)
PURI, Mr. Ajay Krishan, ACA *1982;* Indian Quotation Systems, Pvt Ltd, 16 Bhai Vir Singh Marg, NEW DELHI 110 001, INDIA.
PURI, Mr. Anupam, ACA *1996;* Bombardier, 505 Houston Centre, 63 Mody Road, TSIM SHA TSUI, KOWLOON, HONG KONG SAR.
PURI, Mr. Harkrishen Bir Singh, FCA *1986;* 9 Norfolk Road, BRIGHTON, BN1 3AA.
PURI, Mr. Hemant, ACA *1986;* 39 Sudbury Court Drive, HARROW, HA1 3SZ.
PURI, Mrs. Kamni Margaret, BA ACA *1991;* Oak Properties Ltd, 3 Benton Terrace, Jesmond, NEWCASTLE UPON TYNE, NE2 1QU.
PURI, Mr. Kundan Lal, FCA *1975;* 32 Longwood Gardens, Clayhall, ILFORD, IG5 0BA. (Life Member)
PURI, Mr. Lalit, ACA *1981;* Bahrain Airport Services, P.O. Box 22285, MANAMA, BAHRAIN.
PURI, Mr. Manoj, BSc ACA *1992;* Valucci Designs Ltd, 84 Commercial Road, LONDON, E1 1NU.
PURI, Mr. Pankaj, BA FCA *1986;* 1 Honeywell Place, TORONTO M2L 1Y2, ON, CANADA.
PURI, Miss. Punam, BSc(Hons) ACA *1997;* Brakelond, South Hill Avenue, HARROW, MIDDLESEX, HA1 3PB.
PURI, Mr. Raghav, ACA *2008;* 12 Friends Colony (West), Mathura Road, NEW DELHI 110065, INDIA.
PURI, Mr. Raj Kumar, FCA *1967;* House No 390, Sector 15-A, NOIDA 201301, UTTAR PRADESH, INDIA.
PURI, Mr. Rajan, BA ACA *1993;* 48 The Park, ST. ALBANS, HERTFORDSHIRE, AL1 4RY.
PURI, Mr. Rohit, ACA *2007;* c/o Mr Gyaneshwar Sharma, 401-403 4Floor Guardforce Centre, 3 Hok Yuen Street East, HUNG HOM, KOWLOON, HONG KONG SAR.
PURI, Mr. Santosh, ACA *2010;* 60a Beechwood Avenue, RUISLIP, HA4 6EH.
PURI, Mr. Vishal, BSc ACA *2000;* D-120 2nd floor, Defence Colony, NEW DELHI 110024, INDIA.
PURIE, Mr. Aroon, BSc FCA *1970;* Thomson Press (India) Ltd., K-Block, Connaught CircusP.O. Box 314, NEW DELHI 110011, INDIA.
PURKAYASTHA, Miss. Sohini, BSc ACA *2006;* 22 Augustus Close, ST. ALBANS, AL3 4JH.
PURKESS, Mrs. Linda Jean, BSc ACA *1988;* 1 Fairway Gardens, Rownhams, SOUTHAMPTON, SO16 8JJ.
PURKESS, Mr. Martin John, BA ACA *1992;* Huntingford Mill, Huntingford, WOTTON-UNDER-EDGE, GLOUCESTERSHIRE, GL12 8EX.
PURKESS, Mr. Neil Charles, BSc ACA *1988;* HSBC 4th Fl. Norwich House, Commercial Road, SOUTHAMPTON, SO15 1GX.
•**PURKESS, Mr. Simon, BSc ACA** *1992;* KPMG LLP, One Snowhill, Snow Hill Queensway, BIRMINGHAM, B4 6GN. See also KPMG Europe LLP
PURKIS, Miss. Jane Lydia, ACA *2009;* First Floor Flat, 103 Randolph Avenue, LONDON, W9 1DL.
•**PURKIS, Mr. John William, FCA** *1972;* (Tax Fac), Parlane Purkis & Co, 177 London Road, SOUTHEND-ON-SEA, SS1 1PW.
PURKIS, Mr. Justin James Edwin, BA FCA *1993;* Capita Life & Pensions, The Grange, Bishops Cleeve, CHELTENHAM, GLOUCESTERSHIRE, GL52 8YQ.
PURKIS, Mrs. Laura Emilia, FCA *1982;* 10 Denton Grove, WALTON-ON-THAMES, KT12 3HE.
PURKIS, Mr. Leonard Charles, FCA *1971;* PO BOX 5961, AUBURN, CA 95604, UNITED STATES.
PURKIS, Mrs. Michelle Yvonne, BA ACA *1990;* 9 Wentworth Close, Monkton Park, CHIPPENHAM, SN15 3XJ.
PURKIS, Mr. Richard Hugh Adrian, BA ACA MBA *1984;* 16 Marlborough Road, St Leonards, EXETER, EX2 4TJ.
PURKIS, Mr. Thomas Oliver, ACA *2009;* 45 Danehurst Street, LONDON, SW6 6SA.
•**PURNELL, Mr. Alan Gwynn, FCA** *1969;* with Harben Barker Limited, Drayton Court, Drayton Road, SOLIHULL, WEST MIDLANDS, B90 4NG.
PURNELL, Mr. Brian Frederick, BCom FCA *1966;* Apartado 3782, El Trigal, VALENCIA, VENEZUELA.
PURNELL, Miss. Caroline Elizabeth, BSc ACA *2001;* Flat B, 47 Larkfield Road, RICHMOND, SURREY, TW9 2PG.
•**PURNELL, Mr. Raymond Henry, FCA** *1970;* Trewoon, Poldhu Cove, Mullion, HELSTON, CORNWALL, TR12 7JB.
PURNELL, Mr. Richard, BA(Hons) ACA *2003;* Credit Suisse, 1 Cabot Square, LONDON, E14 4QJ.
PURNELL, Mr. Tim, BSc ACA *1988;* 106 Mornington Crescent, Fallowfield, MANCHESTER, M14 6DD.
•**PUROHIT, Mr. Sunil Kumud, BCom FCA** *1993;* Felstra Limited, Saunders House, 52-53 The Mall, LONDON, W5 3TA.
PURRETT, Mr. Michael John, FCA *1963;* 16 Spencer Lane, Bamford, ROCHDALE, OL11 5PE. (Life Member)
•**PURRINGTON, Mr. Michael, BA(Hons) ACA** *2002;* Ernst & Young LLP, 1 More London Place, LONDON, SE1 2AF. See also Ernst & Young Europe LLP
PURSE, Mr. David Christopher, FCA *1956;* Kingstree, 42 Kingsway, BOGNOR REGIS, WEST SUSSEX, PO21 4DL. (Life Member)
PURSE, Mr. Stephen John, BSc FCA *1978;* 36 Newry Road, TWICKENHAM, TW1 1PL.
PURSEHOUSE, Mr. John, FCA *1975;* Simpson (York) Ltd, PO BOX 289, YORK, YO19 5YL.
PURSELL, Mr. Robert John, BSc(Hons) ACA *2000;* Talk Talk - White Building, 11 Eversham Street, LONDON, W11 4AJ.
•**PURSER, Mr. David Keith, FCA** *1977;* (Tax Fac), Farmiloes LLP, Winston Churchill House, 8 Ethel Street, BIRMINGHAM, B2 4BG.
PURSER, Mr. Geoffrey, FCA *1986;* 69 High Street, LUTON, LU4 9JZ.
PURSER, Mr. Mark, JP BSc FCA *1988;* Lukoil Accounting & Finance Ltd, Rotunda Point, 11 Hartfield Crescent, LONDON, SW19 3RL.
PURSER, Mr. Philip, BSc ACA *2010;* 326 Bristol Road, BIRMINGHAM, B5 7SN.
•**PURSEY, Mr. Brian Patrick, MA ACA** *1979;* Oriel Accounting Ltd, Cheltenham House, Clarence Street, CHELTENHAM, GLOUCESTERSHIRE, GL50 3JR.
•**PURSEY, Mr. Malcolm Richard, BSc ACA** *1979;* Norfield House, Bank End Lane, High Hoyland, BARNSLEY, S75 4BB.
PURSEY, Mr. Richard Eric, FCA *1967;* Chippies, Broadlands Road, BURGESS HILL, WEST SUSSEX, RH15 0BG.
PURSEY, Miss. Sally Jane, BA ACA *1983;* with Thompson Jenner LLP, 1 Colleton Crescent, EXETER, EX2 4DG.
•**PURSGLOVE, Mr. Charles Norman Harold, FCA** *1969;* Military House Limited, Military House, 24 Castle Street, CHESTER, CH1 2DS. See also Chester Accounting Services
•**PURSGLOVE, Mr. Edward, ACA** *1982;* A. Hughes-Jones Dyson & Co, Bryn Afon, Segontium Terrace, CAERNARFON, LL55 2PN.
PURSGLOVE, Mrs. Justine Susanne, BSc ACA *1998;* 89a Chatburn Road, CLITHEROE, BB7 2AS.
PURSGLOVE, Mr. Philip Michael, BSc ACA *1993;* 69 Sussex Road, HARROW, HA1 4NN.
PURSSELL, Miss. Martine Elizabeth, ACA *1980;* PO Box HM 3221, HAMILTON HM PX, BERMUDA.
PURT, Mr. Alistair Charles, MA(Hons) ACA *2004;* Red Beech Cottage, Polecat Valley, HINDHEAD, SURREY, GU26 6BE.
PURTILL, Mr. Michael Edward, FCA *1974;* Quintessential Hotels Ltd, Wellington House, Cliffe Park, Morley, LEEDS, LS27 0RY.
PURTON, Mr. David John, FCA *1968;* 31 Kingfisher Way, HORSHAM, RH12 2LT. (Life Member)
PURUSHOTHAMAN, Ms. Kamenii, BA ACA *2010;* Pasir Ris, Street 71, Block 749, No.10-62, SINGAPORE 510749, SINGAPORE.
PURUSHOTHAMAN, Mr. Sanjay, ACA MBA *2005;* Sreevalsam 4 Buckland Road, READING, RG2 7SN.
PURVES, Mrs. Carolyn Mary, BSc ACA *1986;* 8 Grange Road, Highgate, LONDON, N6 4AP.
PURVES, Mr. Duncan, BSc FCA *1977;* Purves Philatelics, PO Box 95, TONBRIDGE, KENT, TN12 7PX.
PURVES, Mr. Ian Mckinnon, FCA *1977;* 158 Cirencester Road, Charlton Kings, CHELTENHAM, GL53 8DY.
PURVES, Ms. Judith Elizabeth, BCom FCA *1992;* 72 Pricefield Road, TORONTO M4W 1Z9, ON, CANADA.
PURVES, Mr. Nicholas Charles Hamilton, BSc ACA *1994;* RWC Partners, 60 Petty France, LONDON, SW1H 9EU.
•**PURVES, Mrs. Tiffany Ann, ACA CA(SA)** *2010;* About Finance Limited, 9 Danesfield, Ripley, WOKING, SURREY, GU23 6LS.
PURVIS, Mrs. Christine, LLB ACA *2002;* with Grant Thornton UK LLP, Grant Thornton House, 22 Melton Street, Euston Square, LONDON, NW1 2EP.
PURVIS, Mr. Christopher Keith, BA ACA *1993;* Achieve Global, Spencer House, 23 Sheen Road, RICHMOND, SURREY, TW9 1BN.
PURVIS, Mr. David James, BSc FCA *1975;* 10 The Maltings, ALNWICK, NORTHUMBERLAND, NE66 1YA. (Life Member)
PURVIS, Mr. Gordon James, BSc ACA *1993;* Schroders Ci Ltd, PO Box 334, GUERNSEY, GY1 3UF.
•**PURVIS, Mr. Graeme, BSc ACA** *1987;* Ratio Business Services Limited, 10 Mardley Hill, WELWYN, HERTFORDSHIRE, AL6 0TN.
PURVIS, Mrs. Janet Caroline, BA ACA *1989;* 25 Sauncey Avenue, HARPENDEN, HERTFORDSHIRE, AL5 4QR.
PURVIS, Ms. Jennifer Ann, BSc ACA *1995;* 15 Sheridan Road, LONDON, SW19 3HW.
•**PURVIS, Mr. John, LLB ACA** *1985;* John Purvis & Co, Riverbank House, 1 Putney Bridge Approach, Fulham, LONDON, SW6 3JD.
PURVIS, Mr. Julian Connor, BSc FCA *1984;* The Woodland Trust, Autumn Park, Dysart Road, GRANTHAM, NG31 6LL.
PURVIS, Mr. Mark David, BA(Hons) ACA *2000;* Urb. Playa Polarsol, Res. Alta Loma, Blq.B2 Bajo 5, 29649 MALAGA, SPAIN.
PURVIS, Mr. Michael, BSc ACA *1996;* 2 Fromelles Avenue, SEAFORTH, NSW 2092, AUSTRALIA.
•**PURVIS, Mr. Robin Alistair, BA FCA** *1979;* Glen C Rodger Limited, Cragside House, Heaton Road, NEWCASTLE UPON TYNE, NE6 1SE.
PURVIS, Mrs. Sarah Ann, BSc ACA *1993;* La Chaumiere Rue de la Girouette, St. Saviour, GUERNSEY, GY7 9NB.
PURVIS, Miss. Sarah Marie, ACA *2009;* 57 Highcroft Lane, WATERLOOVILLE, HAMPSHIRE, PO8 9PU.
•**PUSEY, Mrs. Amanda Jane, FCA** *1991;* Keith Graham, Suite 2, Wesley Chambers, Queens Road, ALDERSHOT, HAMPSHIRE GU11 3JD.
•**PUSEY, Mr. Simon Keith, BA FCA** *1991;* (Tax Fac), Keith Graham, Suite 2, Wesley Chambers, Queens Road, ALDERSHOT, HAMPSHIRE GU11 3JD.
PUSEY, Mr. Stephen John, BSc ACA *1998;* 19 Home Mead, Denmead, WATERLOOVILLE, HAMPSHIRE, PO7 6YE.
PUSHMAN, Mr. Antony John, FCA *1979;* Le Trais Carre, 67 La Ville Du Bocage, St. Peter, JERSEY, JE3 7YT.
PUSHPANATH, Mr. Shyam Sundar, MSc BSc ACA *2010;* Barclays Plc, Level 29, 1 Churchill Place, LONDON, E14 5HP.
PUSINELLI, Mr. David Charles, BA ACA *1980;* Woodhouse Farm, Ashford Hill, THATCHAM, RG19 8BA.
PUSSARD, Mr. Gerard, BA FCA *1974;* Bramshott, 6 Craneswater Park, SOUTHSEA, HAMPSHIRE, PO4 0NR.
PUST SHAH, Mrs. Susanne, ACA *2001;* 4 Clay Lane, HARROW, HA3 9EB.
PUTIH, Mr. Zainal Abidin, FCA *1972;* CIMB Group Holdings Berad, 12th Floor, Commerce Square, Jalan Semantan, Damansara Heights, 50490 KUALA LUMPUR FEDERAL TERRITORY MALAYSIA.
PUTLAND, Mr. Philip Harold, FCA *1956;* P.O.Box 41724, Craighall, JOHANNESBURG, GAUTENG, 2024, SOUTH AFRICA. (Life Member)
PUTMAN, Mr. Philip Michael, MA FCA *1976;* Mirembe, 6 Plough Close, Shillingford, WALLINGFORD, OX10 7EX.
PUTNAM, Mr. Edward George, BA FCA *1995;* 14 Prospect Place, HARROGATE, NORTH YORKSHIRE, HG1 1LB.
PUTNAM, Mr. Paul Thomas, BA ACA *1996;* Quarry Hill House, 44 Rectory Lane, Avening, TETBURY, GLOUCESTERSHIRE, GL8 8NN.
PUTNAM, Mrs. Rebecca Jane, BA ACA *1996;* Quarry Hill House, 44 Rectory Lane, Avening, TETBURY, GLOUCESTERSHIRE, GL8 8NN.
PUTNAM, Mr. Stephen Paul, FCA *1975;* Urb. Four Seasons, Los Flamingos, BQ 1 Apt 2A, 29679 BENAHAVIS, MALAGA, SPAIN.
PUTROS, Mr. Najib Sulaiman, FCA *1966;* P.O. Box 3213, Alwiya, BAGHDAD, IRAQ.
PUTSON, Mrs. Alison, BA(Hons) ACA *2000;* 15 Wetherby Road, LEEDS, LS8 2JU.
PUTT, Mr. Lee Desmond, ACA *2009;* Magnolia House, Wilby Road, Stradbroke, EYE, SUFFOLK, IP21 5JN.
PUTTICK, Mr. Matthew James, BA ACA *2004;* 9 Chantry Road, BRISTOL, BS8 2QF.
•**PUTTICK, Mr. Raymond Eric, BA FCA** *1982;* (Tax Fac), Easterbrook Eaton Limited, Cosmopolitan House, Old Fore Street, SIDMOUTH, DEVON, EX10 8LS.

QURESHI, Miss. Kokab Sadiq, BSc(Hons) ACA *2001;* C/O Qaiser Noor Level 12, The Royal Bank of Scotland Plc, 280 Bishopsgate, LONDON, EC2M 4RB.
QURESHI, Mr. Mahmud Ahmad, FCA *1972;* 243M Lahaore Cantt Co-Op, Housing Society, (LCCHS) Lahore Cantt, LAHORE, PAKISTAN.
QURESHI, Mr. Mohammad Sadiq, FCA *1971;* House No. 1134, Opposite Power Market, Street No. 41, Sector G 10/4, ISLAMABAD PAKISTAN. (Life Member)
QURESHI, Mr. Muhammad Uzair Saeed, BSc(Hons) ACA *2010;* 69 St. Josephs Drive, SOUTHALL, MIDDLESEX, UB1 1RP.
QURESHI, Mr. Munir Ahmed, FCA *1975;* Stanley House Industries(PVT) Ltd, Suite 205 Park Avenue, (Above Citibank), Pechs, KARACHI, SINDH PAKISTAN. (Life Member)
QURESHI, Mrs. Nagina, LLB ACA *2004;* 41 Coldharbour Lane, BUSHEY, WD23 4NU.
•QURESHI, Mr. Nisar Ahmed, FCA *1977;* (Tax Fac), Kirtley Qureshi & Co, 75 Herries Road, SHEFFIELD, S5 7AS.
QURESHI, Mr. Philip Craig, BA ACA *1994;* 7 Crownhill, West Buckland, WELLINGTON, TA21 9JJ.
QURESHI, Mr. Rizwan, MSc ACA *2002;* Abu Dhabi Investment Authority, 211 Corniche Street, PO Box 3600, ABU DHABI, UNITED ARAB EMIRATES.
QURESHI, Mrs. Saiqa, MA ACA *1996;* The Roost Harefield Farm, Harefield Drive, WILMSLOW, CHESHIRE, SK9 1NJ.
QURESHI, Mr. Sal, ACA *2008;* EDF Energy, 2nd Floor, Cardinal Place, 80 Victoria Street, LONDON, SW1E 5JL.
QURESHI, Mr. Sarmad Mehmood, BSc ACA CF *1998;* DP World, 16 Palace Street, LONDON, SW1E 5JQ.
•QURESHI, Mr. Shaikh Muhammed Hafeez, FCA *1970;* (Tax Fac), Hafeez & Co., 41 Willesden Lane, LONDON, NW6 7RF.
•QURESHI, Mr. Tariq Ayoob, FCA *1967;* Tariq Ayub Anwar & Co, 84-B-1 Gulberg III, LAHORE, PAKISTAN.
QURESHI, Mr. Usman, ACA *2007;* 15 Victoria Court, Howard Road, STANMORE, HA7 1DT.
QURESHI, Mr. Zeeshan Ahmad, FCA *1974;* A.F. Ferguson & Co, State Life Building 1C, Off I.I. Chundrigar Road, P.O. Box 4716, KARACHI 74000, PAKISTAN.
•QUY, Mr. Andrew James Mark, FCA *1968;* A.J.M. Quy, 343 Station Road, Dorridge, SOLIHULL, B93 8EY.
QUY, Mr. David George, FCA *1966;* 47 York Road, Cheam, SUTTON, SM2 6HL. (Life Member)
QUY, Miss. Louise Sophia, BA ACA *2004;* Elderfield Cross Road, Belmont, SUTTON, SURREY, SM2 6DJ.
QUYAM, Mr. Abul, BSc ACA *2009;* 47 Bradymead, LONDON, E6 6WN.
RAAFF, Mrs. Linda Maria Susan, BA FCA *1979;* 50A Sutherland Avenue, Biggin Hill, WESTERHAM, TN16 3HG.
RAATGEVER, Mr. Roger, ACA CA(SA) *2008;* Mgs House, Circular Road, Douglas, ISLE OF MAN, IM1 1BL.
RABADIA, Miss. Mina, Bsc ACA *2011;* 51 Kenton Park Avenue, HARROW, MIDDLESEX, HA3 8DS.
RABBAGE, Mr. Nigel James, BSc FCA *1983;* VP Plc, Central House, Beckwith Knowle, Otley Road, HARROGATE, HG3 1UD.
RABBANI, Mr. Samrand, BA ACA *2007;* Barclays Bank PLC, 3rd Floor Building No.6, Emaar Business Square, Burj Downtown, PO Box 1891, DUBAI UNITED ARAB EMIRATES.
RABBAT, Mr. Joseph George, FCA *1974;* 4 Down Yhonda, Moors Lane, Elstead, GODALMING, SURREY, GU8 6BN.
RABBITTS, Mrs. Tamsin Mary, BSc ACA *1993;* 32 The Ridings, Keyworth, NOTTINGHAM, NG12 5EF.
•ⒹRABET, Mr. Adrian John Denis, BSc FCA CFE MABRP TEP *1984;* (Tax Fac), Rabet & Co, 2 Old Farm Close, La Rue Du Mont Mado, St. John, JERSEY, JE3 4DS.
RABEY, Mr. Graham Eric, FCA *1989;* Bwci Group, PO Box 68, GUERNSEY, GY1 3BY.
RABHERU, Miss. Priya, ACA *2008;* 8 Abercorn Gardens, HARROW, MIDDLESEX, HA3 0PB.
RABHERU, Mr. Rakesh, BSc ACA *1992;* 76 Danetree Road, Ewell, EPSOM, SURREY, KT19 9RZ.
RABHERU, Mr. Snehal Vallabhdas, FCA *1980;* 16 Kingswood., Manor House Drive, NORTHWOOD, MIDDLESEX, HA6 2UJ.
RABIN, Mr. Adam Paul, BA ACA *1994;* 2 Woodfield Road, RADLETT, HERTFORDSHIRE, WD7 8JD.
RABIN, Mr. Alan Lionel, MA FCA *1958;* 12 Vivian Way, Finchley, LONDON, N2 0AE. (Life Member)
RABIN, Mr. Anthony Leon Philip, LLB FCA *1982;* 17 Collingwood Avenue, LONDON, N10 3EH.
RABIN, Mrs. Elizabeth Jane, BSc ACA *1995;* 2 Woodfield Road, RADLETT, WD7 8JD.
•RABIN, Mr. Franklyn Stuart, FCA *1965;* 15 Hill Hall, Theydon Mount, EPPING, ESSEX, CM16 7QQ.
•RABIN, Mr. Howard Sidney Michael, FCA *1970;* M. Rabin & Co., 22 Hillcrest Avenue, EDGWARE, HA8 8PA.
RABINDRAKUMAR, Miss. Geethanjali, MA ACA DChA *2002;* 13 Norbiton Avenue, KINGSTON UPON THAMES, KT1 3QR.
RABINDRAN, Mr. Ahilan, ACA *2009;* 2 Kenilworth Road, Cumnor, OXFORD, OX2 9QP.
•RABINOWITZ, Mr. David Phillip, BA ACA *1990;* 1 Ravens Close, Prestwich, MANCHESTER, M25 0FU.
•RABINOWITZ, Mrs. Diane Judith, MSc BSc FCA *1978;* 23 Freeland Park, Holders Hill Road, LONDON, NW4 1LP.
RABJOHN, Mr. Timothy John, BA FCA *1977;* Kane International Ltd Unit 11-12, Bridge Gate Centre Martinfield, WELWYN GARDEN CITY, HERTFORDSHIRE, AL7 1JG.
RABKIN, Mr. Harold David, FCA *1953;* 1/9 Hatanaim, Naveh Amirim, HERZLIYA, 46447, ISRAEL. (Life Member)
RABL, Mr. Preston Martin Charles, FCA *1973;* Winterbourne Manor, NEWBURY, BERKSHIRE, RG20 8AU.
RABONE, Mr. Robert, BSc ACA *1999;* University of Sheffield, Finance Dept, Western Bank, SHEFFIELD, S10 2TN.
RABONE, Mr. Robert James, MBA BSocSc ACA *1992;* 17 Sandy Lane, Codsall, WOLVERHAMPTON, WV8 1EN.
RABSTAFF, Mr. Leon David, JP FCA *1960;* 23 Hill House Close, Winchmore Hill, LONDON, N21 1LG.
RABY, Mr. Benjamin Arthur, FCA *1950;* 15 Chatsworth Road, WORKSOP, S81 0LQ. (Life Member)
RABY, Ms. Joanne, BA ACA *2005;* 25 Hartburn Road, NORTH SHIELDS, TYNE AND WEAR, NE30 3RH.
RABY, Miss. Joanne Elizabeth, MA ACA *2004;* A S L, Bury House, 31 Bury Street, LONDON, EC3A 5AG.
RABY, Mr. John Harold, BCom FCA *1976;* 18 Newbold Avenue, CHESTERFIELD, S41 7AR.
RABY, Mr. John Richard Martin, MBA LLB ACA ACIM *1992;* Oak Tree Barn, Netherwood, Skipton Road, ILKLEY, LS29 9RP.
RABY, Mr. Nicolas Leo, MA FCA *1986;* with PricewaterhouseCoopers LLP, 350 South Grand Avenue, LOS ANGELES, CA 90071, UNITED STATES.
•RABY, Mr. Paul, FCA *1961;* Paul Raby, 45 The Roundway, Morley, LEEDS, LS27 0JR.
RACE, Mr. Derek Colin, FCA *1975;* WOOLLEY BEVIS DIPLOCK LLP, 15 PRINCE ALBERT STREET, BRIGHTON, EAST SUSSEX, BN1 1HY.
RACE, Mr. Eric, FCA *1961;* Danny House New Way Lane, Hurstpierpoint, HASSOCKS, WEST SUSSEX, BN6 9BB.
RACE, Mr. Philip Stephen James, MSc ACA *2005;* Goldman Sachs, Petershill, 1 Carter Lane, LONDON, EC4V 5ER.
RACE JNR, Mr. Peter Frederick, BA(Hons) ACA *1999;* 2 Ashling Court, Tyldesley, MANCHESTER, M29 8QS.
RACHEL, Mr. Craig, ACA *2010;* 10 Albans Close, 14 Leigham Court Road, LONDON, SW16 2PJ.
RACHLIN, Mr. Christopher Martin, BSc FCA *1987;* 30 Mount Ararat Road, RICHMOND, SURREY, TW10 6PG.
RACHMAN, Mr. Marc George Ledingham, MSc ACA *1991;* C V C, 111 Strand, LONDON, WC2R 0AG.
RACHMAT, Mr. John Daniel, BSc ACA MBA *1994;* RBS Asia Securities Singapore, Level 21, One Raffles Quay, South Tower, SINGAPORE 048583, SINGAPORE.
RACKHAM, Miss. Annabel Katy, ACA *2010;* 92 Putney Park Lane, LONDON, SW15 5HN.
•ⒹRACKHAM, Mr. Douglas Nigel, MA FCA *1986;* with PricewaterhouseCoopers LLP, Pricewaterhousecoopers, 12 Plumtree Court, LONDON, EC4A 4HT.
RACKHAM, Mr. Edward, BA(Hons) ACA *2004;* with KPMG LLP, 100 Temple Street, BRISTOL, BS1 6AG.
RACKHAM, Mrs. Jane Hope, ACA *1991;* 10 Gainsborough Avenue, DARTFORD, DA1 3AS.
RACKSTRAW, Mr. Colin Albert, FCA *1961;* Bramble, 22 Willow Avenue, Booker, HIGH WYCOMBE, HP12 4QU.
RACKSTRAW, Mr. Mark Everington, BSc BCom ACA *1981;* 14 De Montfort Grove, HUNGERFORD, RG17 0DQ.
RACTLIFFE, Mr. Brian Arthur, FCA *1970;* 42 York Road, WEYBRIDGE, KT13 9DX.
RACTLIFFE, Miss. Gemma Clare, ACA *2008;* Flat 1, 99 Ashley Road, WALTON-ON-THAMES, KT12 1HH.
RADCLIFFE, Mrs. Deborah Ann, BSc ACA *1993;* 36 Rue de L'Independance, L8021 STRASSEN, LUXEMBOURG.
RADCLIFFE, Mr. Geoffrey Douglas, ACA *1989;* 36 Rue de L'Independance, Strassen, L8021 LUXEMBOURG, LUXEMBOURG.
RADCLIFFE, Mrs. Jessica Ruth, ACA *1991;* 8 Cavendish Rd, Crosby, LIVERPOOL, L23 6XB.
RADCLIFFE, Mr. John Robert, BA ACA *1983;* 185 Musters Road, West Bridgford, NOTTINGHAM, NG2 7DQ.
•RADCLIFFE, Mrs. Julie Ann, BA ACA *1989;* with KPMG LLP, St. James's Square, MANCHESTER, M2 6DS.
RADCLIFFE, Mr. Lee James, ACA *2008;* 8 Welsford Street, LONDON, SE1 5RA.
RADCLIFFE, Mr. Michael James, MA MEng ACA *2003;* with Ernst & Young LLP, 1 More London Place, LONDON, SE1 2AF.
RADCLIFFE, Mr. Peter Hirst, FCA *1962;* Morne House, Northbrook Avenue, WINCHESTER, SO23 0JW.
RADCLIFFE, Mr. Peter Howard, BA FCA *1970;* 30 Southern Wood, Cavendish Park, WORKSOP, S80 3DA.
RADCLIFFE, Mr. Richard Marcus Callister, BA ACA *1991;* The Walnuts Ingleby Road, Stanton-by-Bridge, DERBY, DE73 7HU.
RADCLIFFE, Mr. Robin Frederick Keppel, FCA *1963;* 8B Hoi Deen Court, 276 Gloucester Road, CAUSEWAY BAY, HONG KONG ISLAND, HONG KONG SAR. (Life Member)
RADCLIFFE, Mr. Steven James, BSc ACA *2006;* with Baker Tilly Tax & Advisory Services LLP, 3 Hardman Street, MANCHESTER, M3 3HF.
RADCLIFFE-CROW, Mrs. Charlotte Sarah, MEng ACA *2004;* 126 Cotterill Road, SURBITON, KT6 7UL.
RADCLYFFE, Mr. John Leslie, FCA *1970;* 26 Lyly Road, ALLAMBIE HEIGHTS, NSW 2100, AUSTRALIA.
•RADDAN, Mr. Mark Robert, MBA LLB ACA *2003;* KPMG LLP, 15 Canada Square, LONDON, E14 5GL.
RADFAR, Mr. Faramarz, BSc ACA *1986;* 19 Fulbeck Drive, Colindale, LONDON, NW9 5LH.
RADFORD, Mr. Adrian Charles, ACA *1984;* 17 Ryelands Close, CATERHAM, SURREY, CR3 5HY.
•RADFORD, Mr. Alan Clive, BA FCA DChA *1977;* (Tax Fac), Alan C Radford, Needham Cottage, Needham Green, Hatfield Broad Oak, BISHOP'S STORTFORD, HERTFORDSHIRE CM22 7JT.
RADFORD, Mr. Allan David, BSc ACA *1997;* 8 Pinecroft, Gidea Park, ROMFORD, RM2 6DG.
RADFORD, Mrs. Amanda Dawn, BSc ACA *1997;* Talk Talk Group, 11 Evesham Street, LONDON, W11 4AR.
RADFORD, Mr. Andrew William, ACA *2008;* Knoxbridge Oast House, Cranbrook Road, Frittenden, CRANBROOK, KENT, TN17 2BT.
RADFORD, Miss. Angela Gay, BA ACA *1991;* 6 Hanson Close, Weylea Farm, GUILDFORD, GU4 7NJ.
RADFORD, Mr. David Charles, BA FCA *1990;* 14 Oakway, Shortlands, BROMLEY, BR2 0LJ.
•RADFORD, Mr. David Michael, FCA *1969;* (Tax Fac), Thomas May & Co, Allen House, Newarke Street, LEICESTER, LE1 5SG.
•RADFORD, Mr. David Phillip, ACA MAAT *2004;* D & L Accountancy Services, 1 Mearns Place, CHELMSFORD, CM2 6TT.
RADFORD, Mrs. Eve Taylor, BSocSc ACA *1998;* (Tax Fac), 6 Copse Way, Finchampstead, WOKINGHAM, RG40 4EJ.
•RADFORD, Mr. Ian Lamond, FCA *1971;* Baker Tilly Isle of Man LLC, PO Box 95, 2a Lord Street, Douglas, ISLE OF MAN, IM99 1HP. See also Baker Tilly Bennett Roy LLC
RADFORD, Mr. Ian Peter, BA FCA *1980;* Network Technologies & Associates Ltd, 38 High Street, NEWMARKET, CB8 8LB.
RADFORD, Miss. Ingrid Susan, BA ACA *1984;* 14-110 Bay Road, Waverton, SYDNEY, NSW 2060, AUSTRALIA.
RADFORD, Miss. Jacqueline Margaret Mary, BSc ACA *1988;* 12 Corbett Street, DROITWICH, WR9 7BQ.
RADFORD, Miss. Jacqueline Mercedes, BA FCA *1993;* Deloitte & Touche Llp, 66 Shoe Lane, LONDON, EC4A 3BQ.
RADFORD, Mr. James Robert, BSc ACA *2007;* The Old Thatched Post Office, Sulhamstead Hill, Sulhamstead, READING, RG7 4DE.
RADFORD, Mr. James Thomas Hamilton, ACA *2010;* 15/14 Waterloo Street, CARLTON, VIC 3053, AUSTRALIA.
RADFORD, Mr. John, BA ACA *1985;* 26 Nottingham Road, Gotham, NOTTINGHAM, NG11 0HG.
RADFORD, Mr. John, BSc FCA *1975;* Monksmead, 16 Abbotswood, Speen, PRINCES RISBOROUGH, BUCKINGHAMSHIRE, HP27 0SR.
RADFORD, Mr. Julian Alexander, BA ACA *1992;* Tourism Asset Holdings Ltd, Level 28, 123 Pitt Street, SYDNEY, NSW 2000, AUSTRALIA.
RADFORD, Mr. Julian David, BSc(Hons) ACA *2001;* 37 Shoesmith Lane, Kings Hill, WEST MALLING, ME19 4FF.
RADFORD, Mr. Kevin, BA ACA *2007;* Michael A Jarvis & Co Edenthorpe, Grove Road, ROTHERHAM, SOUTH YORKSHIRE, S60 2ER.
RADFORD, Mrs. Lauren Anne, BSc ACA *2005;* Bridgwater House, Sedgemoor District Council Bridgwater House, King Square, BRIDGWATER, SOMERSET, TA6 3AR.
RADFORD, Mrs. Meredith, ACA *2008;* 47 Oaklea, Ash Vale, ALDERSHOT, HAMPSHIRE, GU12 5HP.
RADFORD, Mr. Michael Gordon Victor, FCA *1958;* Field Barn, Church street, Micheldever, WINCHESTER, SO21 3DB. (Life Member)
RADFORD, Mr. Patrick, FCA *1969;* 11 Stewart, TADWORTH, SURREY, KT20 5TU.
RADFORD, Mr. Peter, FCA *1972;* Squirrels, The Ridge, Cold Ash, THATCHAM, RG18 9HY.
RADFORD, Mr. Peter Gordon, BSc FCA *1981;* Maison Bordeaux Rue de Havre, Vale, GUERNSEY, GY3 5LZ.
RADFORD, Mr. Peter John, BSc ACA *1985;* 10 Somerset Grove, Warfield Green, BRACKNELL, RG42 3TN.
RADFORD, Mr. Richard, ACA *2010;* Flat 31, Building 36, Marlborough Road, LONDON, SE18 6XD.
•RADFORD, Mr. Robert James, FCA *1981;* The Rowleys Partnership Limited, 6 Dominus Way, Meridian Business Park, LEICESTER, LE19 1RP. See also Rowleys Partnership LLP
RADFORD, Mr. Robert Michael, FCA *1966;* 2 Birch Lea Redhill, NOTTINGHAM, NG5 8LT. (Life Member)
RADFORD, Mr. Roy, FCA *1939;* 75 Southernhay Road, LEICESTER, LE2 3TP. (Life Member)
•RADFORD, Mr. Samuel Charles, BSc FCA *1980;* Venture Alliance Corporate Finance Ltd, 18 Chinthurst Park, Shalford, GUILDFORD, GU4 8JH.
RADFORD, Mrs. Sarah Jane, BSc FCA *1989;* C4 Pine Court, 5 Old Peak Road, MID LEVELS, HONG KONG ISLAND, HONG KONG SAR.
•RADFORD, Mr. Simon Malcolm, FCA *1981;* La Marmotte Le Mont Gras D'Eau, St. Brelade, JERSEY, JE3 8ED.
RADFORD, Mr. William James, FCA *1973;* Birch Grove, NEWTONMORE, INVERNESS-SHIRE, PH20 1BD.
RADFORTH, Mrs. Shirley Ching-Yui, MPhys ACA *2004;* 48 Forster Road, GUILDFORD, GU2 9AF.
RADHAKRISHNAN, Mr. Kripa, BSc ACA *1981;* Collins Stewart Ltd, 9th Floor, 88 Wood Street, LONDON, EC2V 7QR.
RADHAKRISHNAN, Miss. Radhika Dilruha, BSc ACA *1995;* Twentieth Century Fox Film Co Ltd, 31-32 Soho Square, LONDON, W1D 3AP.
•RADIA, Mr. Paresh, BA FCA *1992;* RDP Newmans LLP, Lynwood House, 373-375 Station Road, HARROW, MIDDLESEX, HA1 2AW.
•RADIA, Mr. Pradip Jethalal, FCA *1976;* Parker Randall, 4-7 Floor Shehnez Towers, 30 Louis Pasteur St, PORT LOUIS, MAURITIUS.
RADIA, Mr. Ramesh, BA ACA *1987;* 35 Copse Wood Way, NORTHWOOD, MIDDLESEX, HA6 2TZ.
RADIA, Mr. Rameshchandra Babulal, FCA *1973;* Environmental Storage Solutions Ltd, 19-21, Leyland Trading Estate, Irthlingborough Road, WELLINGBOROUGH, NORTHAMPTONSHIRE NN8 1RS.
•RADIA, Mr. Romil Sudhir, BSc ACA *2001;* PricewaterhouseCoopers, 7 More London Riverside, LONDON, SE1 2RT. See also PricewaterhouseCoopers LLP
RADIA, Mr. Shailen, ACA *2011;* 401 London Road, LEICESTER, LE2 3JU.
RADIA, Miss. Sheena, ACA *2009;* 2a Eastbury Avenue, NORTHWOOD, MIDDLESEX, HA6 3LG.
RADIA, Mrs. Shivani Ramankant, BA(Hons) ACA *2001;* with Deloitte LLP, Hill House, 1 Little New Street, LONDON, EC4A 3TR.
RADIA, Mr. Sushilkumar Chandulal, BSc FCA *1982;* Westminster Homecare Ltd Symal House, Edgware Road, LONDON, NW9 0HU.
•RADIA, Mr. Yogesh Dhirajlal, FCA *1988;* (Tax Fac), 45 Hawthorn Drive, North Harrow, HARROW, HA2 7NU.
RADIC, Mr. Daniel, ACA *1998;* with KPMG Croatia d.o.o, Eurotower 17th Floor, Ivana Lucica 2a, 10 000 ZAGREB, CROATIA.
RADIC, Mrs. Gordana, ACA *1998;* Mlinovi 64, 10000 ZAGREB, CROATIA.

Members - Alphabetical RADICE - RAI

RADICE, Mr. Mark Justin, BA ACA *1992;* 60 Santos Road, LONDON, SW18 1NS.
RADIN-AMIR, Ms. Dewi Izza Suhana Binti, BA ACA *2005;* Petronas (Group Finance Department), Level 55 Tower 1, Petronas Twin Towers, 50088 KUALA LUMPUR, FEDERAL TERRITORY, MALAYSIA.
RADLETT, Mr. Stephen John, MA FCA *1993;* (Tax Fac), Esso Petroleum Co Ltd, Mailpoint 16, Ermyn Way, LEATHERHEAD, SURREY, KT22 8UX.
RADLEY, Mr. Daren Scott, BSc(Econ) ACA *1996;* 1091 Stillwood Circle, LITITZ, PA 17543, UNITED STATES.
RADLEY, Mrs. Helen Rachel, ACA *1986;* 14 Greenway, Campton, SHEFFORD, SG17 5BN.
RADLEY, Mr. Howard Malcolm, FCA *1961;* Howard M. Radley, P.O.Box 1644, Independence Square 11, NETANYA, 42115, ISRAEL.
RADLEY, Mr. Jeremy Paul, BSc ACA *1994;* Chemin de la Fin 15, CH1295 TANNAY, VAUD, SWITZERLAND.
RADLEY, Miss. Julie Claire, BA ACA *1998;* Beach End, 10 Woodlands Glade, BEACONSFIELD, BUCKINGHAMSHIRE, HP9 1JZ.
RADLEY, Mr. Neil Andrew, BA ACA *1987;* Barclays Bank Plc, 1 Churchill Place, LONDON, E14 5HP.
RADLEY, Mrs. Pamela, BSc ACA *2003;* 5 Lidgett Rise, Skelmanthorpe, HUDDERSFIELD, HD8 9BF.
•**RADLEY-SEARLE, Mr. David Michael, ACA** *1989;* Grant Thornton Spain, Jose Abascal 56, 28003 MADRID, SPAIN.
RADMALL, Mrs. Faye, ACA *2009;* 20 Meadow Way, Latchingdon, CHELMSFORD, CM3 6LH.
RADNOR, Mr. Michael Andrew, BCom ACA *1979;* 16 Arlington Road, CHEADLE, CHESHIRE, SK8 1LW. (Life Member)
RADOMSKY, Mr. Binyamin, ACA *2008;* P.O.Box 247, Yishuv Elazar, 90942 GUSH ETZION, ISRAEL.
RADOSE, Mrs. Lynn, BSc ACA *2006;* 11 Fleeming Close, LONDON, E17 5BB.
RADULSKI, Mr. George Bernard, ACA *1982;* Central Bank of the U.A.E, PO BOX 448, DUBAI, UNITED ARAB EMIRATES.
RADWANSKI, Mr. Philip John, BSc ACA *1992;* 14 Diana Way, Corfe Mullen, WIMBORNE, BH21 3XE.
RADWAY, Mr. James Edward, ARCS ACA *2003;* with PricewaterhouseCoopers Ltd, 252 Veer Savarkar Marg, Shivaji Park Dadr, MUMBAI 400028, MAHARASHTRA, INDIA.
RADWELL, Mr. Matthew Gerard, ACA *2010;* 18-20 North Road, Alconbury Weston, HUNTINGDON, CAMBRIDGESHIRE, PE28 4JR.
RAE, Mr. Alastair Frame, BSc ACA *1998;* 37 Festing Road, LONDON, SW15 1LW.
RAE, Mr. Alistair Kynoch, ACA *1983;* 45 Lilyville Road, LONDON, SW6 5DP.
RAE, Mr. David Richard, BSc FCA *2000;* 62 Hawkhurst Way, WEST WICKHAM, KENT, BR4 9PF.
RAE, Mrs. Emily Frances, BA ACA *1992;* 31 Quernmore Road, LONDON, N4 4QT.
RAE, Mr. Frank Anthony, MA ACA *1981;* 417 Canterbury Crescent, OAKVILLE L65 5K8, ON, CANADA.
RAE, Mr. Graham Keith, BEng ACA *1991;* 29 Reynolds Road, BEACONSFIELD, BUCKINGHAMSHIRE, HP9 2NJ.
RAE, Mrs. Helen Louise, ACA *2008;* 13 Buristead Road, Great Shelford, CAMBRIDGE, CB22 5EJ.
RAE, Mr. Ian Kenyon, MA ACA *1993;* (Tax Fac), with PricewaterhouseCoopers LLP, 1 Embankment Place, LONDON, WC2N 6RH.
RAE, Miss. Jennifer Helen, BEng ACA *1994;* 5 Springfield Lane, ABERDEEN, AB15 8JE.
•**RAE, Mr. Michael Neill, ACA** *1981;* Classique Consultants LTD, 4 Frere Street, LONDON, SW11 2JA.
RAE, Mr. Neil, BA ACA *1998;* 1 Park Avenue, LONDON, SW14 8AT.
RAE, Mr. Nicholas Leslie Peter, FCA *1987;* 41 Bradway Road, SHEFFIELD, S17 4QQ.
RAE, Mrs. Paula Jane, BA ACA *1992;* 9 Queens Road, ABERDEEN, AB15 4YL.
RAE, Mr. Richard Anthony, BA ACA *1987;* Woodside House, Woodside Road, Wootton Bridge, RYDE, ISLE OF WIGHT, PO33 4JR.
RAE, Mr. Roger Stuart, BA ACA *1996;* 11 Lammas Road, Cheddington, LEIGHTON BUZZARD, LU7 0RY.
RAE, Mrs. Sarah Ann, MA BA ACA *1993;* 127 Teddington Park Road, TEDDINGTON, MIDDLESEX, TW11 8NG.
RAE, Mr. Stephen William James, BA(Hons) ACA *2011;* 66 Easter Warriston, EDINBURGH, EH7 4QY.
RAE, Mr. Stewart David, FCA *1974;* with Financial & Taxation Consultants Limited, 40 Southernhay East, EXETER, EX1 1PE.
RAEBURN, Mr. Philip Michael, FCA *1970;* Le Mauguillard, 16390 LAPRADE, FRANCE. (Life Member)
RAEBURN, Mr. Stuart Ian, FCA *1968;* 8 Skeena Hill, LONDON, SW18 5PL.
RAESIDE, Mrs. Samantha Jacqueline, BSc ACA *2005;* Sutton Barn, Sutton Baron Road, Borden, SITTINGBOURNE, KENT, ME9 8LH.
RAETTIG, Mr. Jonathan Paul, BSc FCA *1999;* Bryntirion, 56 Savage Lane, SHEFFIELD, S17 3GW.
RAETTIG, Mr. Max Donald, FCA *1949;* 46 Derrymore Road, Willerby, HULL, HU10 6ET. (Life Member)
•**RAFFAN, Mr. Richard Keith, BA FCA** *1971;* (Tax Fac), Keith Raffan & Co Limited, 2nd Floor, 36 Great Russell Street, LONDON, WC1B 3QB.
RAFFAY, Mr. Francis Robert, BSc ACA *1987;* Rawlinson & Hunter, PO Box 83, JERSEY, JE4 8PW.
RAFFE, Mrs. Julie Elaine, FCA *1986;* 6 Amberley Way, Lower Plenty, MELBOURNE, VIC 3093, AUSTRALIA.
RAFFERTY, Miss. Elizabeth Anne, BA(Hons) ACA *2009;* 9f Allanfauld Road, Seafar, Cumbernauld, GLASGOW, G67 1EX.
RAFFERTY, Mr. James Francis, FCA *1969;* 1 Valley Road, Weaverham, NORTHWICH, CW8 3PP.
RAFFERTY, Mr. John Andrew, BA FCA *1990;* Begbies Traynor, 340 Deansgate, MANCHESTER, M3 4LY.
RAFFERTY, Mrs. Laura, MA ACA *2002;* The Ethical Property Foundation, 56-64 Leonard Street, LONDON, EC2A 4LT.
RAFFERTY, Mr. Martin Graham, BA ACA *1990;* 4 Ullswater Drive, ALDERLEY EDGE, CHESHIRE, SK9 7WB.
RAFFERTY, Mr. Paul, BA ACA *1988;* 17 Frensham Grove, BRADFORD, BD7 4AN.
RAFFERTY, Mr. Simon Mark, BSc ACA *1998;* 201 Coptain House, Eastfields Avenue, Wandsworth, LONDON, SW18 1JX.
RAFFERTY, Mr. Stephen James, BEng ACA *2001;* 23 Pegasus Place, ST. ALBANS, HERTFORDSHIRE, AL3 5QT.
RAFFLE, Mrs. Elizabeth Briony, BA ACA *1990;* 1 Carnarvon Road, Redland, BRISTOL, BS6 7DP.
•**RAFFLE, Mrs. Georgina, BA ACA** *1990;* (Tax Fac), Georgina Raffle, Warringtons, Gelsmoor Road, Coleorton, COALVILLE, LEICESTERSHIRE LE67 8JF.
RAFFLE, Mrs. Jennifer Maria, ACA *1989;* Cramond House, Regent Road, ALTRINCHAM, WA14 1RR.
RAFFLE, Mr. Paul, BSc FCA *1989;* 420 Wando Park Boulevard, MOUNT PLEASANT, SC 29464, UNITED STATES.
RAFFLE, Mr. Timothy David, MA ACA *1988;* Cramond House, Regent Road, ALTRINCHAM, CHESHIRE, WA14 1RR.
RAFFRAY, Mr. Alain Joseph Henri, FCA *1956;* Sant Jordi D'Alfama, L'Ametlla de Mar, 43860 TARRAGONA, SPAIN. (Life Member)
RAFFRAY, Mr. Andre Robert Georges, FCA *1962;* Coastal Road, CAP MALHEUREUX, MAURITIUS. (Life Member)
RAFFRAY, Mr. Didier Marcel Joseph, LLB ACA *1996;* 23 Trelawn Road, LONDON, E10 5QD.
RAFFRAY, Mr. Jacques Joseph, FCA *1970;* PO Box 136, Riverclub, SANDTON, GAUTENG, 2146, SOUTH AFRICA.
RAFI, Mr. Khalid, FCA *1968;* A.F. Ferguson & Co, State Life Building 1C, Off I.I. Chundrigar Road, P.O. Box 4716, KARACHI 74000, PAKISTAN.
RAFIQ, Mr. Asif, BA ACA *2009;* 21 Deeds Grove, HIGH WYCOMBE, BUCKINGHAMSHIRE, HP12 3NT.
RAFIQ, Mr. Muhammad, FCA *1971;* 122-C New Muslim Town, LAHORE, PAKISTAN. (Life Member)
RAFIQ, Mr. Muhammad Ateeq, ACA FCCA *2008;* 32 Gade Close, HAYES, MIDDLESEX, UB3 3PY.
RAFIQ, Mr. Nasir, BA ACA *2006;* with HW Controls & Assurance LLP, Sterling House, 97 Lichfield Street, TAMWORTH, STAFFORDSHIRE, B79 7QF.
•**RAFIQUE, Mr. Haroon, BSc ACA** *1992;* Meer & Co, 1 Cochrane House, Admirals Way, Canary Wharf, LONDON, E14 9UD. See also Tailored Tax Solutions LLP
RAFTERY, Mr. Andrew David, BA ACA *2002;* 4 Raven Close, SANDBACH, CHESHIRE, CW11 1SF.
RAFTERY, Mr. Michael Paul, FCA *1966;* 2001-837 West Hastings Street, VANCOUVER V6C 3N7, BC, CANADA.
RAFTERY, Mr. Patrick John, FCA *1958;* 18 Bourton Croft, SOLIHULL, WEST MIDLANDS, B92 8BE. (Life Member)
RAFTERY, Mr. Paul, BSc ACA *1996;* Divisional Financial Controller - Aerospace, Mubadala Development Company, 3rd Floor - Mamoura B Building, PO Box 45005, ABU DHABI, UNITED ARAB EMIRATES.
RAGAB, Mr. Mohammed Zarrough, FCA *1967;* P.O. Box 454, TRIPOLI, LIBYAN ARAB JAMAHIRIYA.
•**RAGG, Mr. James Charlton, LLB FCA FCIE DChA** *1996;* Blue Spire South LLP, Cawley Priory, South Pallant, CHICHESTER, WEST SUSSEX, PO19 1SY.
RAGG, Mr. Simon Christopher, BA ACA *1990;* 12 Carlton Terrace, NEWCASTLE UPON TYNE, NE2 4PD.
RAGGETT, Mr. Andrew Thurston, BSc ACA *1998;* 1 Belmont Crescent, SWINDON, SN1 4EY.
RAGGETT, Mr. Daniel Charles, ACA *2009;* 94 Crescent Drive, ORPINGTON, KENT, BR5 1BE.
RAGGETT, Mr. David Arthur, BA ACA *1992;* 45 Goose Green, HOOK, HAMPSHIRE, RG27 9QY.
RAGGETT, Mr. David Nicholas, BEng ACA *1992;* 77 Folly Road, WYMONDHAM, NORFOLK, NR18 0QR.
•**RAGGETT, Mrs. Jennifer Diane, BA ACA** *1992;* J Raggett Accounting, 1 Belmont Crescent, SWINDON, SN1 4EY.
RAGGETT, Mr. Jonathan Michael, MA ACA *2002;* with PricewaterhouseCoopers LLP, 1 Embankment Place, LONDON, WC2N 6RH.
RAGGETT, Mr. Richard John, MA ACA *1987;* Middle Barton, North Petherwin, LAUNCESTON, CORNWALL, PL15 8LR.
RAGHAVAN, Mr. Ramabadran Veera, FCA *1968;* 41 Hollywood Town Sadahalli Post, Devanahalli Taluk, BANGALORE 562110, INDIA. (Life Member)
RAGHAVAN, Mr. Satish, MA(Cantab) ACA CTA *2010;* HSBC, 8 Canada Square, Canary Wharf, LONDON, E14 5AE.
RAGHU, Mr. Bharat Deo Persaud, ACA *1982;* (Tax Fac), East Anglia Care Homes Ltd., Sutherlands 136 Norwich Rd, WYMONDHAM, NORFOLK, NR15 0SX.
RAGHU, Mr. Kevin Maniram, BSc ACA *2000;* 14/73 Darley Road, MANLY, NSW 2095, AUSTRALIA.
•**RAGHVANI, Mr. Govind Kanji, BSc FCA CTA FPC** *1986;* 26 Briar Road, Kenton, HARROW, MIDDLESEX, HA3 0DR.
RAGLESS, Mrs. Andrea Michelle, BA ACA *2005;* 59 Wilga Road, WELWYN, HERTFORDSHIRE, AL6 9PT.
RAGNAUTH, Mr. Reimell Tagenath, MA ACA *2001;* Specialist Insulation Ltd, 10 Euro Court Oliver Close, GRAYS, RM20 3EE.
RAGOOWANSI, Mr. Avinash Hiranand, BSc ACA *2002;* Burj Residence 4, Apartment 402, POBOX 126230, Dubai, UAE, DUBAI UNITED ARAB EMIRATES.
RAGUNATHER, Mr. Surendra, BEng ACA *1996;* 49 Lincoln Park, AMERSHAM, BUCKINGHAMSHIRE, HP7 9HD.
•**RAHA, Miss. Bipasha, BA(Hons) ACA** *2004;* 15 Southway, Totteridge, LONDON, N20 8EB.
RAHAMAN, Mr. Alexander, BA ACA *1999;* Kirkman House, 12-14 Whitfield Street, LONDON, W1T 2RF.
RAHAMAN, Mr. Mohamed Imtiyaz, MBA MEng BSc ACA *1999;* Imtiyaz Rahaman, Pearl Qatar, Parcel 6 Saban Tower D, Apartment 1708, DOHA, QATAR.
RAHEEM, Mr. Muhammad Abdur, BSc ACA *1989;* 113b Burdon Lane, SUTTON, SURREY, SM2 7DB.
RAHIM, Mr. Imran Abdul, BSc(Econ) ACA *1999;* 38 Lofting Road, LONDON, N1 1ET.
RAHIM, Mr. Karim Kassamali, FCA *1975;* 141 Barber Greene Road, TORONTO M3C 3Y5, ON, CANADA.
RAHIM, Mr. Khalid, MA ACA *1985;* House No. 53(new) 276(old), Road No. 16(new) 27(old), Dhanmondi R/A, DHAKA, BANGLADESH.
RAHIM, Mr. Mohammed Iqbal Jaffer, FCA *1971;* Galana Petroleum Ltd, P.O Box 120620, DUBAI, UNITED ARAB EMIRATES.
RAHIM, Mr. Mohammed Naieem, BSc ACA *2000;* 85 Duckworth Lane, BRADFORD, WEST YORKSHIRE, BD9 5EX.
RAHIM, Mr. Mohd Asrul Ab, ACA *2008;* No. 24 Jalan Jeriji U8/76B, Seksyen U8 Bukit Jelutong, 40150 SHAH ALAM, MALAYSIA.
•**RAHIM, Mr. Razahusein Mohamed, FCA** *1980;* R.M. Rahim & Co., 164 Lincoln Road, PETERBOROUGH, PE1 2NW.
RAHIMI, Mrs. Catherine Louise, BSc ACA *2003;* 5 Millers Meadow Close, LONDON, SE3 9ED.
RAHIMTOOLA, Mr. Zahid, ACA *1993;* 4201 H Juniper Lane, PALO ALTO, CA 94306, UNITED STATES.
RAHKA, Mr. Ronnie Albert, ACA *2008;* Idrottsgatan 24 B 35, 00250 HELSINKI, FINLAND.
RAHMAN, Mr. Abdul, FCA *1966;* 178/A Sindhi Muslim Cooperative Housing Society, KARACHI 74400, PAKISTAN.
RAHMAN, Mr. Ataur, BSc ACA *2009;* 14 MacDonald Road, LONDON, E7 0HE.
RAHMAN, Mr. Enamur, BSc ACA *2008;* Aitch Group Holdings Ltd, 88 Snakes Lane East, WOODFORD GREEN, ESSEX, IG8 7HX.
RAHMAN, Mr. Fakhir Ahmad, ACA *1982;* 167-C III P.E.C.H.S, KARACHI 75400, PAKISTAN.
RAHMAN, Mr. Habibur, BSc ACA *2008;* 10 The Coral Reef Club, PO Box 31118, SEVEN MILE BEACH, GRAND CAYMAN, KY1 1205, CAYMAN ISLANDS.
RAHMAN, Mr. Hafi, BA ACA *2000;* 13 Berridge Mews, LONDON, NW6 1RF.
RAHMAN, Mr. Iqbalur, FCA *1980;* House 19 Road 3 Block K, Baridhara, DHAKA, BANGLADESH.
RAHMAN, Miss. Jenita, BSc ACA *2003;* Flat 22, Parkview Court, 15 Broomhill Road, LONDON, SW18 4JG.
RAHMAN, Mr. Kazaur, ACA *2009;* 384 Southbury Road, ENFIELD, MIDDLESEX, EN3 4JJ.
RAHMAN, Mr. Khalid, FCA *1982;* C/O Pakistan Petroleum Limited, 4th Floor PIDC House, Dr Ziauddin Ahmed Road, KARACHI 755000, PAKISTAN.
•**RAHMAN, Mr. Khandaker Mahboobul Aarefeen, BSc ACA FCCA** *2010;* Rahman & Co Ltd, 7 Meadows Bridge, Parc Menter, Cross Hands, LLANELLI, DYFED SA14 6RA.
•**RAHMAN, Mr. Md Rezaur, FCA** *1970;* Rahman & Co., 3 Narcissus Road, LONDON, NW6 1TJ.
RAHMAN, Mr. Mir Habibur, FCA *1975;* 15 Claremont Road, Hadley Wood, BARNET, HERTFORDSHIRE, EN4 0HR.
RAHMAN, Mr. Mizanur, BSc(Hons) ACA *2011;* 66 Rosebery Avenue, LONDON, N17 9SA.
RAHMAN, Mr. Mohammad Adnan, BSc ACA *2006;* 5 Parkfield Road, HARROW, HA2 8LA.
RAHMAN, Mr. Mohammad Mahbubur, BSc ACA *2002;* 15 Fortune Street, BOLTON, BL3 2QZ.
•**RAHMAN, Mr. Mohammed, MSc BCom ACA** *2006;* Azadi & Company Limited, 765 Pershore Road, Selly Park, BIRMINGHAM, B29 7NY. See also TT(Midlands) Limited
•**RAHMAN, Mr. Mohammed Rafiq, BSc FCA** *1992;* KPMG LLP, One Snowhill, Snow Hill Queensway, BIRMINGHAM, B4 6GN. See also KPMG Europe LLP
RAHMAN, Mr. Muhammed Saleem, FCA *1967;* 46-F Gulberg II, LAHORE, PAKISTAN.
•**RAHMAN, Mr. Mujibur, FCA** *1971;* KWSR & Co, 136 Merton High Street, LONDON, SW19 1BA.
RAHMAN, Mr. Navees, BSc ACA *2006;* 22 Leamore Street, LONDON, W6 0JZ.
RAHMAN, Mr. Rezaur, FCA *1956;* Interspace Communications Ltd, 11 Waterloo Place, LONDON, SW1Y 4AU. (Life Member)
RAHMAN, Mr. Riazur, FCA *1974;* W.Rahman Jute Mills Ltd., 52 Motijheel C-A, DHAKA 1000, BANGLADESH.
RAHMAN, Miss. Rosanna, BSc ACA *2010;* 77 Valleyfield Road, LONDON, SW16 2HX.
RAHMAN, Miss. Sabina Akhtar, BSc ACA *2004;* 86 Bow Field, HOOK, HAMPSHIRE, RG27 9SA.
RAHMAN, Mr. Salman Shahid, BSc FCA *1994;* 230 Coombe Lane, LONDON, SW20 0QT.
•**RAHMAN, Mr. Sheikh Anisur, BSc(Hons) ACA ATT CTA** *2006;* (Tax Fac), Serco, 133 Nork Way, BANSTEAD, SURREY, SM7 1HR.
•**RAHMAN, Mr. Shelim, BA(Hons) ACA** *2003;* Beever and Struthers, St George's House, 215-219 Chester Road, MANCHESTER, M15 4JE.
•**RAHMAN, Mrs. Susan, BSc FCA** *1997;* KWSR & Co, 136 Merton High Street, LONDON, SW19 1BA.
RAHMAN, Mr. Tareq Razaur, ACA *1979;* 17 Kalianna Street, HARRISON, ACT 2914, AUSTRALIA.
RAHMAN, Mr. Umar, ACA *2010;* 98 Bromley Common, BROMLEY, BR2 9PF.
RAHMAN, Mr. Usman Ghani, FCA *1996;* 272/FF, Street #12, DHA Phase IV, LAHORE, PAKISTAN.
RAHMAN, Miss. Yasmeen, BSc ACA *2001;* 95 Radstock Road, READING, RG1 3PR.
•**RAHMAT-SAMII, Mr. Gholam-Reza, MSc ACA** *1985;* (Tax Fac), Reza Samii, 5 Calico Row, Plantation Wharf, Battersea, LONDON, SW11 3YH.
RAHMATOVA, Ms. Nazira, LLM LLB ACA *2010;* Environmental Resources Management Ltd Exchequer Court, 33 St. Mary Axe, LONDON, EC3A 8AA.
•**RAHMATULLAH, Mr. Mohammed, FCA FCCA MBA** *1989;* (Tax Fac), Danmirr Consultants, 170 Church Road, MITCHAM, SURREY, CR4 3BW.
RAI, Miss. Devina, LLB ACA *2004;* A B N Amro Bank NV, 250 Bishopsgate, LONDON, EC2M 4AA.
RAI, Mr. Dilraj Singh, BSc ACA *2010;* Langano House, Winkfield Road, ASCOT, BERKSHIRE, SL5 7LP.
RAI, Mr. Furqan Ahmad, ACA *2008;* 20 Welford Place, COVENTRY, CV6 5NZ.

•RAI, Mr. Gobind Singh, MEng ACA *1998;* AMG Accountancy Services, 76 Woodthorne Road South, Tettenhall, WOLVERHAMPTON, WV6 8SL.
RAI, Mr. Hardip Singh, MA ACA *1993;* 26 Priory Road, RICHMOND, TW9 3DF.
RAI, Mr. Jaskaran Singh, BA ACA *2008;* 37 Moorcroft Road, Moseley, BIRMINGHAM, B13 8LT.
RAI, Miss. Neelam, BSc ACA *2011;* 60 Headingley Road, Handsworth, BIRMINGHAM, B21 9QD.
RAI, Miss. Pritisha, ACA *2011;* Flat 37 Chatsworth Court, Granville Road, ST. ALBANS, HERTFORDSHIRE, AL1 5BQ.
RAI, Mr. Sandeep Gurdev Singh, BSc ACA *2003;* 23 Donnington Road, HARROW, MIDDLESEX, HA3 0NB.
RAI, Miss. Sapna Julie, ACA *2009;* 24 Francis Close, HITCHIN, HERTFORDSHIRE, SG4 9EJ.
RAI, Miss. Sharandeep Kaur, ACA *2008;* 20 Cornwell Close, TIPTON, DY4 8TU.
•RAI, Mr. Shaukat, FCA *1976;* S. Ray & Co, 52 Royston Park Road, Hatch End, PINNER, HA5 4AF.
RAI, Mr. Suresh Vikra Chandra, MSc FCA *1976;* Scientific Computers, Jubilee House, Jubilee Walk, CRAWLEY, WEST SUSSEX, RH10 1LQ.
•RAI, Ms. Sutinder, BA FCA DChA *1992;* Raise Associates Limited, 10th Floor, 3 Hardman Street, Spinning Fields, MANCHESTER, M3 3HF.
•RAIBLE, Mr. Hans-Peter, ACA *2009;* Äussere Sulzbacher Straße 100, 90491 NURNBERG, GERMANY.
•RAIBLE, Mrs. Silvia, ACA *2006;* Volbehrstr. 27, 90491 NUERNBERG, GERMANY.
RAICAR, Mr. Rajan, BA ACA *1993;* 2a Chequer Street, ST. ALBANS, HERTFORDSHIRE, AL1 3XZ.
RAICHOORA, Mr. Rajan Prataprai, BSc ACA *1990;* 5 Wildwood, NORTHWOOD, MIDDLESEX, HA6 2DB.
RAICHURA, Mr. Arun, ACA *1982;* 2 Albany Close, BUSHEY, WD23 4SG.
RAICHURA, Miss. Fejal, BA ACA *2007;* 54 Park Drive, Sunningdale, ASCOT, SL5 0BE.
•RAICHURA, Mr. Rashmikant Narbheram, FCA *1977;* (Tax Fac), Alan Rush & Co., 1349/1353 London Road, LEIGH-ON-SEA, SS9 2AB.
RAICHURA, Mr. Rikki, ACA *2011;* 163 Uxbridge Road, HARROW, MIDDLESEX, HA3 6DG.
•RAICHURA, Mr. Sanjay Chunilal Chhaganlal, ACA *1980;* (Tax Fac), Haines Watts, Interwood House, Stafford Avenue, HORNCHURCH, ESSEX, RM11 2ER.
RAICHURA, Mr. Trishul, BSc(Hons) ACA *2010;* 203 Gleneagles Avenue, LEICESTER, LE4 7YJ.
RAIJI, Mr. Vasant Naishadh, FCA *1948;* 6A Rockside, 112 Walkeshwar Road, MUMBAI 400006, INDIA. (Life Member)
RAIKES, Mrs. Anne, MA FCA *1975;* Blackrock Investment Management, 33 King William Street, LONDON, EC4R 9AS.
RAIKES, Mrs. Elizabeth Constance, MPhil BA ACA *1995;* Marine South, Thatcher Avenue, TORQUAY, TQ1 2PD.
RAIKES, Mr. Fred, ACA *2011;* The Ridge, Colemans Hatch, HARTFIELD, EAST SUSSEX, TN7 4EH.
RAIKES, Mr. Jason Alexander, BSc ACA *1993;* Wood Cottage, Wood Road, Ashill, ILMINSTER, SOMERSET, TA19 9NR.
RAIKUNDALIA, Mrs. Jaimi, BA(Hons) ACA *2004;* 23 Shepperton Close, Great Billing, NORTHAMPTON, NN3 9NT.
RAILTON, Mr. David Vaughan Hedley, MA FCA *1978;* 6 Trearddur Court, Trearddur Bay, HOLYHEAD, GWYNEDD, LL65 2TW.
RAILTON, Mr. Paul Howard Neil, BA ACA *1996;* 4 Cliff Road, HESSLE, HU13 0HB.
•RAIMBACH, Mr. John Michael Scott, BSc ACA *1985;* Goodman Derrick Llp, 90 Fetter Lane, LONDON, EC4A 1PT.
RAIMOND, Dr. Paul, PhD BA FCA MBA *1972;* Larram Gyll, The Coombe, Streatley, READING, RG8 9QL.
RAINBIRD, Miss. Alison Jane, BSc ACA *1989;* ABB Ltd, Daresbury Park, Daresbury, WARRINGTON, WA4 4BT.
RAINBOW, Mrs. Caroline Jane, BA ACA *1990;* Audit Commission, Room 301, County Hall, Cauldwell Street, BEDFORD, MK41 8AP.
RAINBOW, Mr. David Spencer, MA ACA *1994;* 45 Park Avenue, BEDFORD, MK40 2NF.
RAINBOW, Mr. John William, FCA *1948;* 7 Wentworth Court, Wellesley Road, TWICKENHAM, TW2 5SH. (Life Member)
RAINBOW, Miss. Julie Dawn, ACA *1993;* The Utile Engineering Co Ltd, New Street, Irthlingborough, WELLINGBOROUGH, NORTHAMPTONSHIRE, NN9 5UG.
•RAINBOW, Mrs. Samantha Jane, BA ACA *1994;* Kenneth Easby LLP, Oak House, Market Place, 35 North End, BEDALE, NORTH YORKSHIRE DL8 1AQ.
•RAINBOW, Mr. Stanley William, FCA *1963;* Highfield House, Great Whittington, NEWCASTLE UPON TYNE, NE19 2HP.
RAINCOCK, Mr. Toby John Dawson, BEng ACA *2002;* 16 Cullerne Close Ewell, EPSOM, SURREY, KT17 1XY.
RAINE, Mr. Charles Peter Everton, MA MSc FCA *1976;* Water Farm House, Stowting, ASHFORD, KENT, TN25 6BA.
RAINE, Mr. Daniel Paul, LLB ACA *2002;* 35 Martins Wood, Chineham, BASINGSTOKE, HAMPSHIRE, RG24 8TR.
RAINE, Mrs. Jennifer Rosemary, BSc ACA *1989;* 104 High Street, Stetchworth, NEWMARKET, Suffolk, CB8 9TJ.
•RAINE, Mrs. Judith, BSc FCA *1975;* J. Raine, 25 Barlows Road, Edgbaston, BIRMINGHAM, B15 2PN.
RAINE, Mr. Richard Denby, MBA BA FCA *1979;* 19 Madrid Road, LONDON, SW13 9PF.
RAINE, Miss. Sarah Elizabeth, MA ACA *1998;* 38 Fairfield South, KINGSTON UPON THAMES, KT1 2UW.
RAINE, Mr. Stephen Michael, BSS FCA *1975;* 25 Barlows Road, Edgbaston, BIRMINGHAM, B15 2PN.
RAINER, Mr. Alan Richard Ivan, MA BD FCA *1967;* 38 Essex Court, Essex Close, LUTON, LU1 3EL.
RAINER, Mrs. Majda, BA ACA *2003;* 98 Castellain Mansions, Castellain Road, LONDON, W9 1HB.
RAINER, Mr. Michael James, BA ACA *1993;* Flat 98 Castellain Mansions, Castellain Road, LONDON, W9 1HB.
RAINES, Mr. Thomas Guy, FCA *1958;* 59 Meadlands, Burnholme, YORK, YO31 0NR. (Life Member)
RAINEY, Mr. Charles Anthony, BSc ACA *1992;* 48 Dalewood, Ballyhenry Road, NEWTOWNABBEY, COUNTY ANTRIM, BT36 5WR.
RAINEY, Mr. Duncan John, ACA *2008;* Deloitte & Touche Llp, 3 Rivergate, BRISTOL, BS1 6GD.
RAINEY, Mr. Graham John Holmes, FCA *1964;* Bates Moor Farm, Foulsham, DEREHAM, NR20 5RS.
RAINEY, Mr. John Steven, BA FCA *1991;* HHB Communications Ltd, 73-75 Scrubs Lane, LONDON, NW10 6QU.
RAINEY, Mr. Leslie Vernon, FCA *1945;* 3 Latches Walk, AXMINSTER, DEVON, EX13 5DQ. (Life Member)
RAINEY, Mr. Robert Edward Holmes, MA FCA *1993;* 24 Byron Road, LONDON, W5 3LL.
•RAINEY, Mr. William, BSc FCA *1978;* 19 Little Fryth, Hollybush Ride, Finchampstead, WOKINGHAM, RG40 3RN.
RAINFORD, Mrs. Ann Elizabeth, ACA *1988;* 4 Fernyhalgh Court, Fulwood, PRESTON, PR2 9NJ.
RAINFORD, Mr. Bruce Alan James, LLB ACA *1999;* Flat 4, 68 Epsom Road, GUILDFORD, GU1 3PB.
RAINFORD, Mrs. Leigh, ACA *2008;* 3 Standale Rise, PUDSEY, WEST YORKSHIRE, LS28 7JL.
RAINFORD, Mr. Philip, BA ACA *1982;* 9 Collingwood Drive, Beaumont Park, HEXHAM, NE46 2JA.
RAINGOLD, Mr. Gerald Barry, FCA *1969;* 12 Marston Close, LONDON, NW6 4EU.
RAINS, Mrs. Gaynor, BA ACA *1999;* 10 Pentre Close, Ashton, CHESTER, CH3 8BR.
RAINSBURY, Mr. David John, FCA *1970;* 2 Kings Drive, Marple, STOCKPORT, SK6 6NQ.
RAINSFORD, Mr. Frank Christopher, FCA *1962;* Low Leas House, Lea, MATLOCK, DE4 5JR.
RAINSFORD, Mr. Mark Andrew, BA ACA *2007;* Chemin de Prelaz 42B, 1260 NYON, VAUD, SWITZERLAND.
•RAINSFORD, Mrs. Valerie Maud, FCA *1966;* (Tax Fac), Rainsford & Co, Low Leas House, Lea, MATLOCK, DE4 5JR.
•RAINSFORD, Miss. Vanessa Louise, BA FCA *1997;* V.L. Rainsford, 31b Thirsk Road, Battersea, LONDON, SW11 5SU.
RAINTON, Mr. Eric David, FCA *1967;* Flour Mills of Nigeria plc, P.O. Box 341, 2 Old Dock Road, APAPA, NIGERIA.
•RAISBECK, Mr. Murray Alexander, BSc ACA *2003;* with KPMG LLP, 100 Temple Street, BRISTOL, BS1 6AG.
RAISHBROOK, Mr. Neil, BSc ACA *1985;* with Cookson Group plc, 165 Fleet Street, LONDON, EC4A 2AE.
•RAISHBROOK, Mr. Terence Frederick, FCA *1970;* T.F. Raishbrook, 28 Highsted Road, SITTINGBOURNE, KENT, ME10 4PS.
RAISTRICK, Mrs. Anne Louise, BCom FCA *1996;* (Tax Fac), Godfrey Holland Ltd Venture House, 341 Palatine Road, MANCHESTER, M22 4FY.
RAISTRICK, Mrs. Fiona Jayne, BSc(Hons) ACA *2001;* with BDO LLP, 55 Baker Street, LONDON, W1U 7EU.
RAISTRICK, Mr. John, FCA *1966;* 10 Jacqueline Close, Grundisburgh, WOODBRIDGE, IP13 6UZ.
•RAISTRICK, Mr. Paul, ACA *1988;* Wilkinson & Partners, Victoria Mews, 19 Mill Field Road, Cottingley Business Park, Cottingley, BINGLEY WEST YORKSHIRE BD16 1PY.
RAITHATHA, Mr. Jiten, BA ACA *1993;* 9 Turks Close, Hillingdon, UXBRIDGE, UB8 3JH.
RAITHATHA, Mr. Marcus Kantilal, BA ACA *1990;* 14 Kingscote Road, LONDON, W4 5LJ.
•RAITHATHA, Mr. Prakash Chunilal, ACA *1982;* Prakash Raithatha & Co, 11 Grove Farm Park, NORTHWOOD, HA6 2BQ.
RAITHATHA, Mr. Rajesh Mansukhlal, BA ACA MBA *1999;* Brakelond, South Hill Avenue, HARROW, MIDDLESEX, HA1 3PB.
RAITHATHA, Mr. Sandeep, BSc ACA *2000;* 23 Elm Drive, HARROW, MIDDLESEX, HA2 7BS.
RAITZ, Mr. Gerald Norman, FCA *1951;* 3 The Rise, EDGWARE, HA8 8NS. (Life Member)
RAIZADA, Mr. Bimal Kishore, FCA *1968;* Ranbaxy Laboratories Ltd, L32/7 Dlf City Phase II, Gurgaon, HARYANA 122002, INDIA.
•RAIZADA, Miss. Neena, ACA *2008;* Matrix, 112/113 Cumberland House, 80 Scrubs Lane, LONDON, NW10 6RF.
RAJ, Mr. Amrit, BSc(Hons) ACA *2011;* S A B Miller S A B Miller House, Church Street West, WOKING, GU21 6HS.
RAJ, Miss. Anita, ACA *2008;* 54 Sydenham Park Road, LONDON, SE26 4DL.
RAJ PANDEY, Mr. Santosh, ACA MBA *2007;* Flat 205 Lower Mast House, Mast Quay, LONDON, SE18 5NF.
RAJA, Mr. Adnan, BSc ACA *2010;* Marsh Ltd, 1 Tower Place West, LONDON, EC3R 5BU.
RAJA, Mr. Ahmad Shafi, ACA *1986;* Noble Drilling (Canada) Ltd, 4th Floor, Baine Johnston Centre, 10 Fort William Place, ST JOHN'S A1C 1K4, NF CANADA.
RAJA, Mrs. Almas Akhtar, BA ACA *1985;* 2a Kings Road, UXBRIDGE, UB8 2NW.
RAJA, Mr. Anil Devchand, FCA *1965;* Raja Building, Biashara Street, P.O. Box 30590, NAIROBI, KENYA. (Life Member)
RAJA, Mrs. Anjali, ACA *2008;* with KPMG LLP, 15 Canada Square, LONDON, E14 5GL.
RAJA, Mr. Binoy, BSc ACA *1998;* 13 Amberden Avenue, LONDON, N3 3BJ.
RAJA, Mr. Himanshu Haridas, LLB ACA *1991;* Church Farm, Church Road, Little Gaddesden, BERKHAMSTED, HERTFORDSHIRE, HP4 1NZ.
RAJA, Mr. Ibrar, BSc ACA *2011;* Two Roofs, Holcombe Hill, Mill Hill, LONDON, NW7 4ES.
RAJA, Mr. Ketan Nathalal, BSc FCA *1994;* 15 Montpelier Rise, Golders Green, LONDON, NW11 9SS.
•RAJA, Mr. Mahendra Khimjibhai, FCA *1973;* (Tax Fac), Raja & Co, Aknam, 56 Chorley New Road, BOLTON, BL1 4AP.
RAJA, Mr. Mitul, ACA *2010;* 9 Marston Close, Oadby, LEICESTER, LE2 5WL.
•RAJA, Mr. Muhammad Afzal, FCA *1974;* (Tax Fac), M A Raja & Co, 20 Bowring Drive, Parkgate, NESTON, CH64 6ST.
RAJA, Mr. Mukesh Chhotalal, BSc ACA *1993;* 27 Westmorland Road, HARROW, HA1 4PL.
•RAJA, Mr. Rajnikant Kakubhai, FCA *1973;* (Tax Fac), R.K. Raja & Co, 21 Whitehouse Way, LONDON, N14 7LX.
RAJA, Mr. Shreyash Praful, MA ACA *1995;* Coblantra Ltd, PO Box 41619, NAIROBI, 00100, KENYA.
RAJA, Mr. Tushar Keshavlal, BSc FCA *1977;* 27 Kings Avenue, SANDWICH, CT13 9PH.
•RAJA, Mr. Vinaykumar Mohanlal, FCA *1975;* Clarke Henning LLP, 10 Bay Street, Suite 801, TORONTO M5J 2R8, ON, CANADA.
•RAJA, Mr. Vipinchandra Mohanlal, FCA *1975;* V R Accountants Limited, Vipin Raja & Co, 100 College Road, HARROW, MIDDLESEX, HA1 1BQ.
RAJA-BROWN, Ms. Sarah Frances, MA ACA *1991;* Church Farm, Church Road, Little Gaddesden, BERKHAMSTED, HERTFORDSHIRE, HP4 1NZ.
RAJABALEE, Mr. Salim, ACA *2010;* DDB Europe, 12 Bishops Bridge Road, LONDON, W2 6AA.
RAJABALI, Mr. Mohamed Hussein, BA ACA *2000;* po box 118736, DUBAI, UNITED ARAB EMIRATES.
RAJABALLY, Miss. Mariam Bibi, LLB ACA *2010;* 29 Chestnut Grove, ILFORD, ESSEX, IG6 3AS.
RAJADHYAKSHA, Mr. Robin, MSc ACA *1997;* 9 Penrhyn Avenue, PYMBLE, NSW 2073, AUSTRALIA.
RAJAGOPAL, Mr. Ramaswamy, MBA MSc ACA *1978;* Unit 61, 94-96 Alfred Street South, MILSONS POINT, NSW 2061, AUSTRALIA.
RAJAGOPALAN, The Revd. Siva Kumar, MTh BSc ACA *1993;* 36 Sidney Road, Wood Green, LONDON, N22 8LU.
RAJAH, Mrs. Anna-Marie, BA ACA *2001;* 52 Hedley Road, ST. ALBANS, HERTFORDSHIRE, AL1 5JP.
RAJAH, Mr. Sujee, ACA *2009;* 14 Nursery Grove, LINCOLN, LN2 1RS.
RAJAKUMAR, Mr. Inbaraj, BCom ACA *2008;* Lorne Stewart Plc Stewart House, Kenton Road, HARROW, MIDDLESEX, HA3 9TU.
•RAJAN, Mr. Benoy Thomas, BAcc FCA *1997;* (Tax Fac), BTR Accountancy, 2 Hornsby Square, Southfields Business Park, BASILDON, ESSEX, SS15 6SD.
RAJAN, Mr. Duraiswamy Gunaseela, FCA *1965;* Chitra, 110 Chamiers Road, CHENNAI 600028, INDIA.
RAJAN, Mr. Duraiswamy Saradhi, ACA *1995;* Chitra, 110 Chamiers Road, CHENNAI 600 028, INDIA.
RAJANAYAGAM, Mrs. Sharmila Lalani, ACA *2010;* 22 Sunningdale Avenue, FELTHAM, MIDDLESEX, TW13 5JT.
RAJANI, Mr. Dipesh, LLB ACA *2003;* with Ernst & Young LLP, 1 Colmore Square, BIRMINGHAM, B4 6HQ.
•RAJANI, Mr. Mukesh Gopaldas, FCA *1981;* PricewaterhouseCoopers LLP, 1 Embankment Place, LONDON, WC2N 6RH. See also PricewaterhouseCoopers
RAJANI, Miss. Niriksha, BSc ACA *2009;* 21 Sunnydene Lodge, Sunnydene Gardens, WEMBLEY, MIDDLESEX, HA0 1AT.
•RAJANI, Mr. Pankaj Keshavlal, BA FCA CF *1988;* Macilvin Moore Reveres LLP, 7 St John's Road, HARROW, HA1 2EY.
•RAJANI, Mrs. Rajeshri, BSc ACA *1994;* with R Rajani & Co Ltd, Midland House, 50-52 Midland Road, WELLINGBOROUGH, NN8 1LU.
RAJANI, Mr. Rameshchandra Haridas, FCA *1966;* 19 The Deerings, HARPENDEN, AL5 2PF. (Life Member)
RAJARAI, Mr. Romesh, ACA *1983;* M C F I Ltd, Chausse Tromelin, PORT LOUIS, MAURITIUS.
RAJARAM, Mrs. Charu, FCA *1973;* Flat A, Langford Grove, 2 Langford Gardens, BANGALORE 560025, INDIA.
RAJARATNAM, Miss. Narishta, BSc ACA *2006;* Flat 7, 50-52 Denbigh Street, LONDON, SW1V 2EU.
RAJARATNAM, Mr. Prashanth, BSc ACA *2002;* 16 SS 21/42, Damansara Utama, 47400 PETALING JAYA, SELANGOR, MALAYSIA.
RAJARATNAM, Mr. Rameswaran, BEng ACA *1994;* 185 Jalan 5/46, 46000 PETALING JAYA, MALAYSIA.
RAJASEKARAN, Mr. Prahalathan, BSc ACA *1994;* 27 Coolgardie Avenue, CHIGWELL, IG7 5AX.
RAJASINGHAM, Miss. Rajivalochana, BA ACA *1997;* Royal Bank of Scotland, 90-100 Southwark Street, LONDON, SE1 0SW.
RAJESH, Mr. Rahul, BA ACA *2006;* 88 Leonard Street, Apt 622, NEW YORK, NY 10013, UNITED STATES.
RAJESPARAN, Mr. Nimalan, BA ACA *2010;* 20 Falmouth Road, LONDON, SE1 4JQ.
RAJKUMAR, Mr. Thiagarajah, BSc FCA *1984;* 63 Kewferry Road, NORTHWOOD, MIDDLESEX, HA6 2PQ.
RAJPAL, Mr. Ajay, ACA *1999;* 22 Brookmans Avenue, Brookmans Park, HATFIELD, HERTFORDSHIRE, AL9 7QJ.
RAJPAR, Mr. Anverali Mohamedali, FCA *1962;* Seaforth General Agencies Ltd, Missions to Seamen Annexe, Bandari Road, Kurasini, PO Box 9313, DAR ES SALAAM TANZANIA.
RAJPUT, Miss. Seema, BA ACA *1994;* 2612 West Tyson Avenue, TAMPA, FL 33611, UNITED STATES.
RAJU, Mr. Harinder, MSc ACA *2003;* 72 Blenheim Crescent, LUTON, LU3 1HD.
•RAJUDIN, Mr. Abu Bakar, FCA *1980;* Abu Bakar Rajudin & Co, Suite A Resorts Business Suites, 18-2 Jalan Kampung Attap, 50460 KUALA LUMPUR, FEDERAL TERRITORY, MALAYSIA.
RAJUDIN, Mr. Muhammad Harris Imran, ACA *2009;* No.3 Lorong Damansara Endah, Damansara Heights, 50490 KUALA LUMPUR, FEDERAL TERRITORY, MALAYSIA.
RAJUNARAYANAN, Mr. Raghav, MSc ACA *2011;* Flat 435, Neutron Tower, 6 Blackwall Way, LONDON, E14 9GW.
RAJVANSHI, Mr. Rohit, BA ACA *2000;* KPMG, Level 32, Emirates Towers, Sheikh Zayed Road, PO Box 3800, DUBAI UNITED ARAB EMIRATES.
RAJWANI, Mr. Karim, BA FCA *1990;* 1468 Ferncrest Road, OAKVILLE L6H 7W2, ON, CANADA.

RAKE, Sir Michael Derek Vaughan, KT FCA *1972;* BT Group plc, BT Centre, 81 Newgate Street, LONDON, EC1A 7AJ.
RAKER, Mr. Peter James, BSc ACA *1999;* 139 St Augustines Avenue, Thorpe Bay, SOUTHEND-ON-SEA, SS1 3JE.
•RAKESTRAW, Mrs. Sarah Jane, BA(Hons) ACA *2004;* Braken Limited, 28 Edward Gardens, Martinscroft, WARRINGTON, WA1 4QT. See also Braken
RAKHA, Mr. Javid Khaled, BAcc ACA *1999;* 14 Egerton Road South, MANCHESTER, M21 0YP.
RAKHECHA, Mrs. Anshu, ACA *2010;* Flat 3, 18 Tapton House Road, SHEFFIELD, S10 5BY.
RAKOWICZ, Mr. Zygmunt Jozef, BSc(Econ) ACA *1999;* Flat 5 Gladstone Court, 97 Regency Street, LONDON, SW1P 4AL.
RAKUSHINA, Miss. Irina, BA ACA *2006;* Orange St. James Court, Great Park Road Bradley Stoke, BRISTOL, BS32 4QJ.
RALFS, Mr. John, BSc ACA *2006;* Marney, Munday Dean Lane, MARLOW, SL7 3BU.
RALLEY, Mr. Paul Dylan, BA FCA *1999;* 1st Floor, Legal & General Assurance Society Ltd Knox Court, 10 Fitzalan Place, CARDIFF, CF24 0TL.
RALLI, Mr. Stephen Demetrius, FCA *1974;* 4115 Dahoon Holly CT, BONITA SPRINGS, FL 34134, UNITED STATES.
RALLS, Mr. Malcolm Harry, FCA *1964;* c/o BCL Ltd, PO Box 3, SELEBI-PIKWE, BOTSWANA.
•RALLS, Mr. Steven Philip, BA FCA *1990;* Abu Dhabi Accountability Authority, Financial Audit and Professional Regulation, PO Box 435 4th Floor, Falcon Tower, Hamdan Street, ABU DHABI UNITED ARAB EMIRATES.
•RALPH, Mr. Adrian Charles, BSc ACA CTA *1997;* A C Ralph Ltd, c/o The Old Police Station, Whitburn Street, BRIDGNORTH, SHROPSHIRE, WV16 4QP.
RALPH, Miss. Alexandra, ACA *2004;* 22 Prospect Road, SEVENOAKS, TN13 3UA.
RALPH, Mr. Charles Philip, BA ACA *1988;* Horsley Manor, Nupend, Horsley, STROUD, GLOUCESTERSHIRE, GL6 0PY.
RALPH, Mr. Daniel Oliver, BEng ACA *1997;* Raedore, Sale Green, DROITWICH, WORCESTERSHIRE, WR9 7LP.
RALPH, Mrs. Delaram, BA ACA *2002;* Flat 12 Mayfield Mansions, 94 West Hill, LONDON, SW15 2YB.
RALPH, Mr. Duncan Stewart, ACA *1986;* Hatfield, The Avenue, TAUNTON, TA1 1ED.
RALPH, Mr. Edward John, MA ACA *2002;* Flat 12 Mayfield Mansions, 94 West Hill, LONDON, SW15 2YB.
RALPH, Mr. Graham Christopher, ACA *1994;* Redwings House, Park View Road, PINNER, HA5 3YF.
RALPH, Mr. Ian Peter, BSc ACA *1984;* (Tax Fac), 467 Streetbrook Road, SOLIHULL, B91 1LA.
RALPH, Mrs. Joanne Margaret, BSc ACA *1991;* Inzlingerstrasse 184, CH-1425 RIEHEN, SWITZERLAND.
RALPH, Mr. John Benjamin, ACA *2008;* Flat 6 Winchester Court, Castlegate, RICHMOND, TW9 2LQ.
RALPH, Mr. Jonathan, ACA *1987;* Broomlea, Racecourse Lane, Cotebrook, TARPORLEY, CW6 9EF.
RALPH, Mr. Michael, ACA *2009;* Apartment 15 Hanover Mill, Hanover Street, NEWCASTLE UPON TYNE, NE1 3AB.
RALPH, Mr. Michael Nicholas Haley, BSc ACA *1997;* Barclays Capital, 5 North Colonnade, LONDON, E14 4BB.
RALPH, Mr. Nicholas Anthony, BEng ACA *2002;* 46 Newmill Gardens, Miskin, PONTYCLUN, MID GLAMORGAN, CF72 8RX.
RALPH, Mr. Nicholas Thomas James, FCA *1973;* 25 Settler's Ridge Way, OTTAWA K2J 4V3, ON, CANADA.
RALPH, Mrs. Nicola Ann, BSc ACA *2005;* 21 Kylemilne Way, STOURPORT-ON-SEVERN, WORCESTERSHIRE, DY13 9NA.
RALPH, Mr. Philip Pyman, BA FCA *1958;* Oak Tree House, Warboys Road, KINGSTON-UPON-THAMES, KT2 7LS. (Life Member)
RALPH, Mr. Simon Edwin, BA ACA *1996;* Acergy, 200 Hammersmith Road, LONDON, W6 7DL.
RALPH, Mr. Stephen, ACA *2005;* 21 Kylemilne Way, STOURPORT-ON-SEVERN, WORCESTERSHIRE, DY13 9NA.
RALPH-BOWMAN, Mr. Joshua Nathan, LLB ACA *2002;* 3 Parkthorne Road, LONDON, SW12 0JN.
RALPHS, Ms. Susan Mary, BA ACA *1991;* Ethical Property Co Plc, The Old Music Hall, 106-108 Cowley Road, OXFORD, OX4 1JE.
RALSTON, Miss. Jemma, BA ACA *2010;* 47 Elms Crescent, LONDON, SW4 8QE.
RAM, Miss. Lauren Vanessa, ACA *2009;* 31 Langford Lane, Burley in Wharfedale, ILKLEY, LS29 7EH.
RAM, Mr. Raja, BA ACA *1995;* 50 St. Marys Road, Long Ditton, SURBITON, KT6 5EY.
RAM, Mr. Rajesh, ACA *2009;* Binnewith News, 57 St. Peters Street, CANTERBURY, CT1 2BE.
RAM, Mrs. Sarah Louise, BEd ACA *1996;* 50 St. Marys Road, Long Ditton, SURBITON, KT6 5EY.
RAMA, Mr. Amit Hasmukhlal, ACA *2005;* 6 Hunters Meadow, Dulwich Wood Avenue, LONDON, SE19 1HX.
RAMACHANDRAN, Mr. Ruban, MEng ACA *1998;* 36 Blinco Grove, CAMBRIDGE, CB1 7TS.
RAMACHANDRAN, Miss. Ruby, BA(Hons) ACA *2003;* Invesco, 30 Finsbury Square, LONDON, EC2A 1AG.
RAMACHANDRAN, Mr. Rupak, BSc(Hons) ACA *2011;* Flat 4, Davinia Court, 23-25 Priory Avenue, HIGH WYCOMBE, BUCKINGHAMSHIRE, HP13 6SQ.
RAMACHANDRAN, Miss. Shanthi, BA ACA *1992;* 3198 KINROSS CIRCLE, OAK HILL, VA 20171, UNITED STATES.
RAMADAN, Mr. Rafick Jamie, BA ACA *1999;* 2 Milo Gardens, LONDON, SE22 8LU.
RAMADOSS, Mr. Murali, ACA *2011;* 21 Garrick Road, GREENFORD, MIDDLESEX, UB6 9HT.
RAMAGE, Mr. Andrew Philip, BSc ACA *1990;* Helvetica, Level 6, 10a Prospect Hill, Douglas, ISLE OF MAN, IM1 1EJ.
RAMAGE, Mr. John Michael Victor, BA ACA *1992;* Ellwood House, Crowell, CHINNOR, OX39 4RP.
•RAMAGE, Mr. Neil William, ACA *2010;* Sycamore Accountancy Services Limited, 29 Blenheim Road, Moseley, BIRMINGHAM, B13 9TY.
RAMAGE, Mr. Rognvald Hunter Percy, FCA *1969;* 203 Two Oceans Beach, 18 Bay Road, Mouille Point, CAPE TOWN, 8005, SOUTH AFRICA.
RAMAGE, Miss. Sarah-Jane, MA ACA *2004;* 136 Court Farm Road, NEWHAVEN, EAST SUSSEX, BN9 9HB.
RAMALINGAM, Mr. Shayantharam, MA ACA *2002;* 10 Whitelands Crescent, LONDON, SW18 5QY.
•RAMALINGUM, Mr. Richard, FCA *1982;* (Tax Fac), Richard Ramalingum & Co, 30 West Gardens, Ewell Village, EPSOM, SURREY, KT17 1NE.
RAMAN, Mr. Kariamanikkam, FCA *1966;* 13 The Ryde, HATFIELD, AL9 5DQ. (Life Member)
RAMAN, Miss. Rajni, BSc ACA *2000;* 66 Grove Vale Avenue, Great Barr, BIRMINGHAM, B43 6BZ.
RAMAN, Mr. Ravi, FCA *1973;* 33 Psrn Jelapang 7, 30100 IPOH, MALAYSIA.
RAMANAN, Mr. Ramakrishnan, ACA ACMA *2009;* Flat C, 37 Woodford Avenue, ILFORD, ESSEX, IG2 6UF.
•RAMANATHAN, Mr. Gopal, RA(NL) FCA *1975;* KPMG Accountants N.V., Laan van Langerhuize 1, 1186 DS Amstelveen, P O Box 74500, 1070 DB AMSTERDAM, NETHERLANDS. See also KPMG Europe LLP
RAMANATHAN, Mrs. Tracey Elizabeth, BA(Hons) ACA *2001;* 109 Nevay Road, Mirama, WELLINGTON 6022, NEW ZEALAND.
RAMANI, Miss. Gouree, BSc ACA *2002;* 75 Grosvenor Gardens, WOODFORD GREEN, ESSEX, IG8 0BD.
RAMANI, Mr. Yathiraja, BSc ACA *1999;* 2 Glenwood Gardens, ILFORD, ESSEX, IG2 6XT.
RAMASWAMI, Miss. Gayathri, BSc ACA *2002;* 21 Jalan Anak Patong, SINGAPORE 489336, SINGAPORE.
RAMBAUT, Mr. Peter Richard, BSc FCA *1979;* Honey Barrett, 53 Gildredge Road, EASTBOURNE, EAST SUSSEX, BN21 4SF.
RAMBOCUS, Mr. Prem, FCA *1977;* International Financial Services Ltd, IFS Court, 28 Cybercity, EBENE, MAURITIUS.
RAMBOCUS, Mr. Reshan Kirti, ACA *1995;* c/o India Management Services Ltd, 7th Floor Nexteracom Tower 1, Cybercity, EBENE, MAURITIUS.
RAMBOCUS, Mr. Rubysen, BA ACA *1992;* Apartment C1, Residences Corps De Garde, 29 Avenue Farquar, QUATRE-BORNES, MAURITIUS.
RAMCHANDANI, Mr. Diraj, MEng ACA *2007;* UBS Investment Bank, 2 Finsbury Avenue, LONDON, EC2M 2PP.
RAMCHANDANI, Mr. Neil, ACA *2009;* Natwest, 1 Princes Street, LONDON, EC2R 8BP.
RAMDANY, Mr. Indranil, MSc BSc ACA *2010;* 24 Tharp Road, WALLINGTON, SM6 8LE.
RAMDAURSINGH, Mr. Geerja Shankar, FCA CF *1989;* 14 Bathfield Street, PORT LOUIS, MAURITIUS.
RAMDEEN, Mr. Darrin, ACA *2008;* 39a Pymmes Green Road, LONDON, N11 1DE.
•RAMDENEE, Miss. Sharon, BA ACA *2007;* Sharon Ramdenee, Deburg Edwards Street, FLOREAL, MAURITIUS.
•RAMDENY, Mr. Virrsing, ACA FCCA *2010;* Suite G12 St James Court, St Denis Street, PORT LOUIS, MAURITIUS.
RAMDIN, Mrs. Ameenah Bibi, ACA FCCA *2011;* BDO De Chazal du Mee, P.O. Box 799, 10 Frere Felix, De Valois Street, PORT LOUIS, MAURITIUS.
RAMDIN, Miss. Nazrah Banaun, ACA ACMA *2010;* BDO Associates, PO Box 18, The Creole Spirit, Quincy Street, VICTORIA, SEYCHELLES.
RAMDIN, Mr. Roni Laxman Singh, MSci ACA *2003;* La Maison, 144 Foxley Lane, PURLEY, CR8 3NE.
RAMESH, Mr. Sivagnanam, ACA *1990;* 1 Moncorvo Close, LONDON, SW7 1NQ.
RAMGOOLAM, Mr. Shailendra, BA ACA *1995;* Ernst & Young, 20th Floor, Newton Tower, Sir William Newton Street, PORT LOUIS, MAURITIUS.
RAMIREZ-ESPAIN, Mrs. Sunette, BA(Hons) ACA *2002;* 8 Rose Joan Mews, 96 Fortune Green Road, West Hampstead, LONDON, NW6 1DS.
RAMJAN, Mrs. Naseem, MA ACA *2006;* 45 Morley Road, LONDON, E10 6LJ.
RAMJEEOWAN, Mr. Vikaash, BA ACA *2005;* 142 Crosse Courts, BASILDON, ESSEX, SS15 5JE.
•RAMJI, Mr. Fatehali Gulamhussein, FCA FCCA CTA *1972;* Fairman Law, Fairman Law House, 1-3 Park Terrace, WORCESTER PARK, SURREY, KT4 7JZ. See also Fairman Davis
RAMKHELAWON, Miss. Anjaala, ACA FCCA ACCA *2004;* 26 Beamish Road, LONDON, N9 7JA.
RAMLI, Mr. Feroz Razi, ACA *2008;* 11 Jalan Kelawar 6/4H, 40000 SHAH ALAM, MALAYSIA.
RAMLI, Mr. Mohd Rafizi, BEng ACA *2003;* A405 Kyoto Garden Condominium, Persiaran Bukit Jaya, 68000 AMPANG, SELANGOR, MALAYSIA.
RAMLI, Mr. Muhamad Faizul Bin, BA(Hons) ACA *2003;* Internal Audit Department, Abu Dhabi Investment Authority, PO Box 3600, 211 Corniche Street, ABU DHABI, UNITED ARAB EMIRATES.
RAMLOCHUN, Miss. Leena, BSc ACA *2005;* Flat 60 Stamford Court, Goldhawk Road, LONDON, W6 0XD.
RAMM, Mr. Andrew Terence, BA ACA *1990;* 55 High Street, Eye, PETERBOROUGH, PE6 7UX.
•RAMM, Mr. David Geoffrey, BA ACA *1993;* Ernst & Young Europe LLP, 1 More London Place, LONDON, SE1 2AF.
•RAMM, Mr. Louis, BA FCA *1971;* Ramm Louis & Co, Fifth Floor, Kingmaker House, Station Road, New Barnet, BARNET HERTFORDSHIRE EN5 1NZ. See also Pinnacle Freelance Services Limited
RAMNANI, Miss. Neeta Murli, BSc ACA *1998;* 143 Blackbrook Lane, BROMLEY, BR1 2HL.
RAMNANI, Mr. Sham Murli, BSc ACA *2001;* 143 Blackbrook Lane, BROMLEY, BR1 2HL.
RAMNATH, Mr. Indar Errol, ACA *1981;* 1A St. Margaret's Junction, CLAXTON BAY, TRINIDAD AND TOBAGO.
RAMNAUTH, Miss. Rigvi, FCA *1993;* 6 St. Leonards Road, LONDON, W13 8PW.
RAMOORTHY, Ms. Natasha, ACA CA(SA) *2010;* 91B Boundary Road, St Johns Wood, LONDON, NW8 0RG.
RAMOUTAR, Miss. Leah, BSc ACA *2006;* 102 Dover House Road, LONDON, SW15 5AT.
•RAMPERSAD, Mr. Ishri Harribaran, FCA *1971;* I.H. Rampersad & Co, 4 Aruac Road, VALSAYN, TRINIDAD AND TOBAGO.
RAMPERSAUD, Miss. Cindy, BA ACA MBA *1993;* 22 Mountfield Road, LONDON, N3 3NE.
RAMPHUL, Miss. Lekha, ACA *2009;* 29 Brymay Close, LONDON, E3 2SY.
•RAMPHUL, Mr. Tejwansing, ACA FCCA *2011;* KPMG, 9 Allee Scheffer, L-2520 LUXEMBOURG, LUXEMBOURG.
RAMPLING, Mr. David William, BA FCA *1984;* Great Holland Mill, Little Clacton Road, Great Holland, FRINTON-ON-SEA, CO13 0EU.
RAMROOP, Mrs. Shreya, LLB ACA *2001;* The Spinney Bridle Lane, Loudwater, RICKMANSWORTH, HERTFORDSHIRE, WD3 4JA.
•RAMSAY, Mr. Alan Stuart, BA FCA *1987;* 6 Court Lane Gardens, LONDON, SE21 7DZ.
RAMSAY, Mr. Albert Edward, FCA *1961;* 74 Woolacombe Road, LIVERPOOL, L16 9JQ. (Life Member)
RAMSAY, Mr. Alexander John, MEng ACA *1997;* Siemens Protection Devices Ltd, P.O. Box 8, North Farm Road, HEBBURN, TYNE AND WEAR, NE31 1LX.
RAMSAY, Mrs. Caroline Frances, MA ACA *1988;* RSA, 6th Floor, Leadenhall Court, 1 Leadenhall Street, LONDON, EC3V 1PP.
•RAMSAY, Mrs. Charlotte Clare Zoe, BSc ACA *1998;* Self Assessment Taxation Services, The Barn, The Old Farm House, Pewit Lane, NANTWICH, CHESHIRE CW5 7PP.
RAMSAY, Mr. David, FCA *1966;* 6 Elm Close, Groby, LEICESTER, LE6 0ES.
RAMSAY, Mrs. Elizabeth Anne, BA ACA *1994;* High Close, Leazes Lane, HEXHAM, NORTHUMBERLAND, NE46 3AZ.
RAMSAY, Miss. Fiona Claire, BA ACA *1992;* Orchard End Lower Farm Road, Effingham, LEATHERHEAD, KT24 5JL.
RAMSAY, Mrs. Fiona Jane, LLB ACA *1988;* 150/3 Soi 20, Sukhumvit, BANGKOK, 10110, THAILAND.
RAMSAY, Mr. Francis Fawcus, FCA *1951;* Akaroa, 25 Freelands, Mendlesham, STOWMARKET, IP14 5TW. (Life Member)
RAMSAY, Mr. Graeme John, BSc FCA *1993;* 18 Valley Road, RICKMANSWORTH, HERTFORDSHIRE, WD3 4DS.
RAMSAY, Mr. Ian Ross Mcgregor, BSc FCA *1978;* Platinum Securities Company Ltd, 22nd Floor, Standard Chartered Bank Building, 4 Des Voeux Road, CENTRAL, HONG KONG SAR.
RAMSAY, Mr. John, BA ACA *1982;* St Annaweg 5, 4112 FLUEH, SWITZERLAND.
RAMSAY, Mr. Peter James Sired, BSc FCA *1996;* Xstrata (Schweiz) AG, Bahnhofstrasse 2, PO Box 102, 6301 ZUG, SWITZERLAND.
RAMSAY, Mr. Richard Alexander Macgregor, MA FCA *1976;* Richard Ramsay Ltd, The Little Priory, Sandy Lane, Nutfield, REDHILL, RH1 4EJ.
RAMSAY, Mr. Robert Andrew, BSc ACA *2005;* 6B/8 Sutherland Street, CREMORNE, NSW 2090, AUSTRALIA.
RAMSAY, Mr. Scot Hunter Anderson, BSc ACA ACIArb *1995;* 5 Alpha Place, BISHOP'S STORTFORD, CM23 2HN.
•RAMSAY, Mr. Stephen Norman, BSc FCA *1973;* Ramsay & Co, 28 Carpenters Wood Drive, Chorleywood, RICKMANSWORTH, WD3 5RJ.
RAMSAY, Mr. Stuart Donald, BEng ACA *2007;* Flat 2305, West Tower, 1 Pan Peninsula Square, LONDON, E14 9HG.
RAMSAY, Miss. Valerie, FCA *1972;* 1 Vicarage Cottages, Wilbees Road, Arlington, POLEGATE, EAST SUSSEX, BN26 6RU. (Life Member)
•RAMSAY, Mr. William Alexander, ACA *1986;* Deloitte LLP, Hill House, 1 Little New Street, LONDON, EC4A 3TR. See also Deloitte & Touche LLP
RAMSBOTTOM, Mr. Andrew Bernard, MA BCom ACA MSI *1984;* Tilney Fund Management, Royal Liver Building, Pier Head, LIVERPOOL, L3 1NY.
•RAMSBOTTOM, Mr. George Loynd, FCA *1975;* (Tax Fac), G L Ramsbottom & Co Ltd, Kenmore, Bolton Road, Bradshaw, BOLTON, BL2 3EU.
RAMSBOTTOM, Mr. Howard Duncan, BSc ACA *1986;* Al Salam Tower, Floor 38, PO Box 502666, DIC, DUBAI, UNITED ARAB EMIRATES.
RAMSBOTTOM, Mrs. Karen Rachel, BSc ACA *2005;* 58 Appledore Gardens, Lindfield, HAYWARDS HEATH, WEST SUSSEX, RH16 2EU.
RAMSBOTTOM, Mr. Paul Michael, BA FCA *1989;* Pennon Group Plc, Peninsula House, Rydon Lane, EXETER, EX2 7HR.
RAMSBOTTOM, Mr. Peter, FCA *1966;* 5 High Meadows, Thornhill, DEWSBURY, WF12 0PH.
•RAMSBOTTOM, Mr. Philip, FCA *1973;* 21 Lanark Road, LONDON, W9 1DE.
RAMSDALE, Mr. Charles Albert John, FCA *1958;* 37 Aspen Drive, VERWOOD, BH31 6TE. (Life Member)
RAMSDALE, Mr. Jonathan James, BEng ACA *1996;* 36, New Road, BROXBOURNE, EN10 7LW.
RAMSDALE, Mr. Robert Wyatt, BSc FCA *1983;* Bend-Or Cottage, 35 Rosemary Lane, Rowledge, FARNHAM, SURREY, GU10 4DD.
RAMSDALE, Mr. Simon Francis, BA ACA *1996;* 54 Walson Way, STANSTED, CM24 8EU.
RAMSDALE, Mr. Stephen Thomas, BSc ACA *2002;* Swan Hotel (Newbybridge) Ltd, Newby Bridge, ULVERSTON, CUMBRIA, LA12 8NB.
RAMSDALE, Mr. Timothy Max, BSc ACA *2011;* 9 Pelham Road, BECKENHAM, BR3 4SQ.
RAMSDEN, Mr. Carl Ian, BSc ACA *2001;* 74 Moss Road, Winnington, NORTHWICH, CW8 4BL.
RAMSDEN, Miss. Catherine Anne, BA ACA *2005;* 31 Byde Street, HERTFORD, SG14 3AR.
RAMSDEN, Mr. David Anthony, BA ACA *1996;* 62 Camborne Avenue, LONDON, W13 9QZ.

RAMSDEN, Mr. David John, BA(Hons) ACA *2003;* Heathfield, Steepways, HINDHEAD, SURREY, GU26 6PG.
RAMSDEN, Mr. David Michael James, MA(Hons) MBA ACA *2003;* 9 Woodcroft, WAKEFIELD, WF2 7LS.
RAMSDEN, Mr. Edward John, BSc ACA *1997;* 88 High Street, LEWES, EAST SUSSEX, BN7 1XN.
RAMSDEN, Mr. Ian, BA(Hons) ACA *2002;* 30 Dartington Road Platt Bridge, WIGAN, LANCASHIRE, WN2 5BE.
RAMSDEN, Mr. Jonathan Edward, BA ACA *1990;* 6301 Fitch Path, NEW ALBANY, OH 43054, UNITED STATES.
RAMSDEN, Mr. Kevin Malcolm, MA ACA *1999;* White House, Hoe Lane, Nazeing, WALTHAM ABBEY, ESSEX, EN9 2RG.
RAMSDEN, Miss. Leanne Rebecca, BA(Hons) ACA *2009;* 3 Pinfold Road, ORMSKIRK, L39 4AB.
RAMSDEN, Mrs. Lucy, BSc ACA *2003;* Heathfield, Steepways, HINDHEAD, SURREY, GU26 6PG.
RAMSDEN, Mr. Mark Andrew, BA FCA *1990;* ZAO PricewaterhouseCoopers Audit, White Square Office Center, 10 Butyrsky Val, 125047 MOSCOW, RUSSIAN FEDERATION.
RAMSDEN, Mrs. Natasha Jane, LLB ACA *1996;* 62 Camborne Avenue, LONDON, W13 9QZ.
RAMSDEN, Mr. Noel, BA FCA *1981;* The Priory, Freefolk, WHITCHURCH, Hampshire, RG28 7NL.
RAMSDEN, Mr. Paul Michael, ACA *2009;* 21 Durham Close, DUKINFIELD, CHESHIRE, SK16 5JR.
RAMSDEN, Mrs. Penelope Jane, BA ACA *2000;* 17 Chapel Hill, Clayton West, HUDDERSFIELD, HD8 9NH.
RAMSDEN, Mr. Richard Nigel, BSc ACA *1997;* 200 West Street, 22nd Floor, NEW YORK, NY 10282-2198, UNITED STATES.
RAMSDEN, Mr. Toby Daniel, BSc ACA *1999;* Trillium Partners Ltd, 8 Grafton Street, LONDON, W1S 4EL.
RAMSDEN, Mr. Zachary John, BA FCA *1992;* with Gilbert Allen & Co, Churchdown Chambers, Bordyke, TONBRIDGE, TN9 1NR.
RAMSEY, Mr. Alan Charles, FCA *1970;* 21 Eastway, Urmston, MANCHESTER, M41 8SG.
RAMSEY, Mrs. Amanda Jane, BA ACA *2001;* 23 Somerville Green, LEEDS, LS14 6AY.
RAMSEY, Mrs. Heather Christine Elaine, BCom ACA *1988;* 11 Lingfield Road, Wimbledon Village, LONDON, SW19 4QA.
RAMSEY, Mr. Julian Michael, BA(Hons) ACA *2001;* with Ernst & Young LLP, 1 More London Place, LONDON, SE1 2AF.
RAMSEY, Miss. Julie, BSc ACA *2001;* 25 Eyhurst Avenue, Elm Park, HORNCHURCH, ESSEX, RM12 4RB.
RAMSEY, Mr. Karl David, BA ACA *1998;* 54 Woodleigh Avenue, LEIGH-ON-SEA, ESSEX, SS9 4JB.
RAMSEY, Mrs. Kelly, BA ACA *2003;* 20 Haddricks Mill Road, NEWCASTLE UPON TYNE, NE3 1QL.
•RAMSEY, Mr. Martin, ACA *2009;* with Grant Thornton UK LLP, Enterprise House, 115 Edmund Street, BIRMINGHAM, B3 2HJ.
•RAMSEY, Mr. Michael Stephen, FCA *1973;* (Tax Fac), Michael S Ramsey Ltd, 9 Bridge Street, NEWCASTLE EMLYN, DYFED, SA38 9DX. See also Topline Ltd
RAMSEY, Mrs. Nina Frances, BA(Hons) ACA *2001;* 106 Shankbridge Road, Kells, BALLYMENA, COUNTY ANTRIM, BT42 3NJ.
RAMSEY, Mr. Paul, BA ACA *2003;* R H K Chartered Accountants & Business Advisers Coburg Hous, 1 Coburg Street, GATESHEAD, TYNE AND WEAR, NE8 1NS.
RAMSEY, Mr. Richard David, BSc ACA *1997;* Ace Group The Ace Building 100 Leadenhall Street, LONDON, EC3A 3BP.
RAMSEY, Mr. Simon, FCA *1957;* 15 Throgmorton Hall, Old Sarum, SALISBURY, SP4 6BQ. (Life Member)
RAMSEY, Mr. Stephen Richard Leslie, LLB FCA *1989;* 6 Draper House, 1 Chiltern Road, SUTTON, SURREY, SM2 5QP.
RAMSEY, Mr. Steven James, BSc ACA *2007;* Origin Energy, Level 45, Australia Square, 264-278 George Street, SYDNEY, NSW 2000 AUSTRALIA.
RAMSEY, Mr. Stuart Ian Robert, BA FCA *1989;* Minster Law Solicitors, Alexander House, Hospital Fields Road, Fulford Industrial Estate, Fulford, YORK YO10 4DZ.
•RAMSHAW, Mr. David Shaun, BSc FCA *1982;* (Tax Fac), Ramshaw & Co Ltd, 2nd Floor, Yarm House, Roseworth Crescent, Gosforth, NEWCASTLE UPON TYNE NE3 1NR.
RAMSHAW, Miss. Emma, ACA *2011;* Holeys, 15-17 North Park Road, HARROGATE, NORTH YORKSHIRE, HG1 5PD.
RAMSHAW, Mr. Ian David, BA FCA *1993;* 4 Ponsonby Drive, PETERBOROUGH, PE2 9RZ.
RAMSKILL, Mrs. Gaynor Louise, BA(Hons) ACA *2002;* 18 Ruvigny Gardens, LONDON, SW15 1JR.
RAMSKILL, Mr. Timothy St John, BA(Hons) ACA *2002;* 18 Ruvigny Gardens, Putney, LONDON, SW15 1JR.
RAMSTEDT, Mr. Christopher John, ACA *1979;* Rees Bradley Hepburn Ltd Diddington Farm, Diddington Lane Meriden, COVENTRY, CV7 7HQ.
RAMTOOLA, Mr. Mohammad Nassir, FCA *1987;* 7A Volcy de La Faye, BEAU BASSIN, MAURITIUS.
RAMTOOLA, Mr. Mohammad Shah Nawaz, BA ACA *2007;* Flat 109 A Hampton Lodge, Gracepark Road, Drumcondra, DUBLIN 9, COUNTY DUBLIN, IRELAND.
RAMTOOLA, Mr. Mohammad Yacoob Ayoob, FCA CF *1980;* BDO De Chazal du Mee, P.O. Box 799, 10 Frere Felix, De Valois Street, PORT LOUIS, MAURITIUS.
RAMU, Mr. Ravi, ACA *1985;* 15/4 Primrose Road, BANGALORE 560025, INDIA.
RANA, Mr. Ali Shahid, ACA AMIChemE ACGI *2005;* Barclays Capital, 5 North Colonnade, LONDON, E14 4BB.
•RANA, Mr. Azhar Mushtaq, MBA BSc FCA *1988;* Littlejohn LLP, 1 Westferry Circus, Canary Wharf, LONDON, E14 4HD.
RANA, Ms. Jaishree, ACA *1984;* Greythorne, Grays Road, Westerham Hill, WESTERHAM, TN16 2HX.
RANA, Mrs. Jasveera Kaur, BSc ACA *1994;* 5 Ellerman Avenue, TWICKENHAM, TW2 6AA.
RANA, Mr. Liaquatali, FCA *1974;* 272 Martin Street, MILTON L9T 2R6, ON, CANADA.
RANA, Mr. Major Singh, BA ACA CTA AMCT *1994;* (Tax Fac), 4 Benson Avenue, Goldthorn Park, WOLVERHAMPTON, WV4 5HB.
•RANA, Mr. Manbhinder, BA ACA *1989;* Deloitte LLP, Hill House, 1 Little New Street, LONDON, EC4A 3TR. See also Deloitte & Touche LLP
RANA, Mr. Minesh Jayantilal, BSc ACA *2005;* 83 Dorchester Way, HARROW, MIDDLESEX, HA3 9RD.
RANA, Mr. Mohammad Adil Pervaiz, MA BA ACA *2002;* 2 Latimer Close, PINNER, MIDDLESEX, HA5 3RB.
RANA, Mr. Nadeem Faiz, ACA *1981;* 4 Janine Drive, NORTH EASTON, MA 02356, UNITED STATES.
•RANA, Mr. Parmjit, BSc ACA *1992;* Rana Chartered Accountants, 140 High Street, SMETHWICK, WEST MIDLANDS, B66 3AP.
RANA, Mr. Pramod, BA ACA *1996;* 90 Colchester Road, LEICESTER, LE5 2DG.
RANA, Mr. Sanjeev Singh, BSc ACA *1999;* 68 Admiralty Way, TEDDINGTON, TW11 0NN.
RANA, Mr. Sarbjit, MEng ACA *1992;* with KPMG LLP, 15 Canada Square, LONDON, E14 5GL.
•RANA, Mr. Zaka Elahi, FCA *1981;* 27 Old Gloucester Street, LONDON, WC1N 3AF.
RANADIVE, Mr. Ketan Anil, ACA *1994;* 52 Meyer Road, Apt 12-54 Equatorial Apartments, SINGAPORE 437875, SINGAPORE.
RANAVAYA, Mr. Manoj, BA ACA *2006;* 31 Imperial Heights, Queen Mary Avenue, LONDON, E18 2FJ.
RANAWAKE, Mr. Armin Guy Ariya, MA ACA *1993;* Lexicon Partners, 1 Paternoster Square, LONDON, EC4M 7DX.
RANAWEERA, Mr. Keith Amara, BSc ACA *2010;* 9 Thorold Close, SOUTH CROYDON, SURREY, CR2 8SA.
RANCE, Dr. Stephanie Jane, BA(Hons) ACA *2001;* Threeways, Sleepers Hill, WINCHESTER, HAMPSHIRE, SO22 4ND.
•RANCHHOD, Mr. Dilip Mohan, BA ACA *1990;* (Tax Fac), Hothi Cash & Carry Ltd, 31-37 Park Royal Road, LONDON, NW10 7LQ.
RANCOMBE, Mr. Digby Benedict, BSc ACA *2003;* 16 Queen Street, HENLEY-ON-THAMES, OXFORDSHIRE, RG9 1AP.
RAND, Mr. Alan John, BSc(Econ) ACA *2004;* Jardine Lloyd Thompson Ltd Jardine House, 6 Crutched Friars, LONDON, EC3N 2PH.
•RAND, Mr. Andrew Stanes, BA FCA *1990;* (Tax Fac), Stanes Rand & Co, 10 Jesus Lane, CAMBRIDGE, CB5 8BA. See also Stanes Rand LLP
RAND, Mr. Jonathan David, MA MEng ACA *2001;* (Tax Fac), 192 Uxbridge Road, Hampton Hill, HAMPTON, MIDDLESEX, TW12 1BG.
RAND, Miss. Louise Frances, BSc(Hons) ACA *2003;* 29 Allendale Road, Earley, READING, RG6 7PD.
RAND, Mr. Nicholas Arthur, FCA *1966;* The Hive, Honey Lane, Woodbury Salterton, EXETER, DEVON, EX5 1PQ.
RAND, Mr. Peter John, FCA *1976;* 61 Kingswood Road, TADWORTH, KT20 5EF.
RAND, Mr. Richard John, FCA *1965;* Cherrytree Cottage, The Common, Silchester, Silchester, READING, RG7 2PH. (Life Member)
RANDAL, Mr. Eric Maynard, FCA *1969;* 5 Grantley Place, Bradley Manor, HUDDERSFIELD, HD2 1LZ.
RANDALL, Mr. Adrian John Laurence, BSc(Econ) FCA FCIE *1968;* PO Box 263W, WORTHING, CHRIST CHURCH, BARBADOS.
RANDALL, Mr. Aidan Christopher, BA ACA *1988;* 1 Scotland Road, BUCKHURST HILL, ESSEX, IG9 5NP.
RANDALL, Mrs. Alexandra Emma, BSc ACA *1993;* Gownfold Farm, Kirdford, BILLINGSHURST, WEST SUSSEX, RH14 0LW.
RANDALL, Mrs. Alsion Edna, BA FCA *1987;* (Tax Fac), with Whittingham Riddell LLP, Belmont House, Shrewsbury Business Park, SHREWSBURY, SY2 6LG.
RANDALL, Mr. Andrew Brian, BEng ACA *1999;* 213 Rathmines Rd, HAWTHORN EAST, VIC 3123, AUSTRALIA.
RANDALL, Mr. Barry David, BA ACA *1995;* 30 The Mall, SURBITON, SURREY, KT6 4EQ.
RANDALL, Mrs. Becki Tanya, BSc ACA *2000;* 30 Stratford Drive, Wooburn Green, HIGH WYCOMBE, BUCKINGHAMSHIRE, HP10 0QH.
RANDALL, Miss. Caroline Jane, LLB ACA *2000;* 11 Riverside Drive Apt 15ME, NEW YORK, NY 10023, UNITED STATES.
•RANDALL, Mr. Clive Whitby, FCA *1973;* Fairway, The Common, Kinsbourne Green, HARPENDEN, HERTFORDSHIRE, AL5 3PE.
RANDALL, Mr. David John, BSc ACA *1998;* 83 Clayton Hall Road, Cross Hills, KEIGHLEY, BD20 7TA.
•RANDALL, Mr. David Michael, FCA *1976;* Brookwood House, Walworth Road, Picket Piece, ANDOVER, HAMPSHIRE, SP11 6LU.
RANDALL, Mr. David Rex, BA FCA *1971;* 1 Park Close, Whittlebury, TOWCESTER, NORTHAMPTONSHIRE, NN12 8XE. (Life Member)
RANDALL, Miss. Elaine, BSc ACA *2001;* 4 Deva Close, ST. ALBANS, HERTFORDSHIRE, AL3 4JS.
RANDALL, Ms. Emily Kate, BSc ACA *2010;* P.O. Box 905, GEORGE TOWN, GRAND CAYMAN, KY1-1103, CAYMAN ISLANDS.
RANDALL, Miss. Emma Jane, BA ACA *2007;* 8 Waters Avenue, Carlton Colville, LOWESTOFT, SUFFOLK, NR33 8BJ.
RANDALL, Mr. Frederick John, FCA *1963;* Walnut Tree House, Ladywood, DROITWICH, WR9 0AL. (Life Member)
•RANDALL, Mr. Gary Robert, ACA *1990;* Ward Randall Limited, The Parade, LISKEARD, CORNWALL, PL14 6AF. See also Tax Processing Limited
RANDALL, Mr. Gerald Martin, MA FCA *1972;* 6 Hurst Park, MIDHURST, WEST SUSSEX, GU29 0BP. (Life Member)
•RANDALL, Mr. Graham James, FCA *1974;* PKF (UK) LLP, 16 The Havens, Ransomes Europark, IPSWICH, IP3 9SJ.
RANDALL, Mrs. Helen Jane, BSc ACA *1998;* 12 Furniss Avenue, Dore, SHEFFIELD, S17 3QL.
RANDALL, Mrs. Helen Louisa, BSc ACA *2005;* 21 Orchard Road, Mortimer, READING, RG7 3QN.
RANDALL, Mr. Ian Leslie, BA ACA *1981;* 23 Greenway, CHISLEHURST, KENT, BR7 6JQ.
RANDALL, Mr. James, BA(Hons) ACA CTA *2003;* 5 Dunoon Gardens, Devonshire Road, LONDON, SE23 3NH.
RANDALL, Mr. James Edward, BA(Hons) ACA *2003;* 8 Vernon Court, London Road, ASCOT, BERKSHIRE, SL5 8DS.
RANDALL, Mr. James William, BSc ACA *2007;* 12 Channel Crescent, DERBY, DERBYSHIRE, DE24 1AQ.
RANDALL, Mr. Jeremy Anthony Philip, BSc(Hons) ACA *1991;* Stratton Lodge, Beckets Lane, Nailsea, BRISTOL, BS48 4LT.
RANDALL, Mr. John Alexander, FCA *1967;* (Tax Fac), with Ballard Dale Syree Watson LLP, Oakmoore Court, Kingswood Road, Hampton Lovett, DROITWICH, WORCESTERSHIRE WR9 0QH.
RANDALL, Mr. John David, BEng ACA *1993;* Way Farmhouse, Way Hill, Minster, RAMSGATE, KENT, CT12 4HS.
RANDALL, Mr. John Gurney, FCA *1961;* Le titien, 4 Quai Jean-Charles Rey, 98000 MONACO, MONACO. (Life Member)
RANDALL, Mr. John Harold, FCA *1973;* 83 Manning Road, WOOLLAHRA, NSW 2025, AUSTRALIA.
RANDALL, Mrs. Julie Langhorne, BA ACA *1988;* Vero Software Plc Hadley House, Bayshill Road, CHELTENHAM, GLOUCESTERSHIRE, GL50 3AW.
•RANDALL, Mr. Justin, FCA *1990;* Jeffreys Henry LLP, Finsgate, 5-7 Cranwood Street, LONDON, EC1V 9EE.
RANDALL, Mrs. Karen Margaret, BSc ACA *1985;* Owlpen Hall, Owlpen, DURSLEY, GLOUCESTERSHIRE, GL11 5BX.
•RANDALL, Mr. Kenneth John, BSc FCA *1984;* Llewelyn Davies, Bank House, St.James Street, NARBERTH, PEMBROKESHIRE, SA67 7BX.
•RANDALL, Mr. Kevin Andrew, BSc ACA CTA *2007;* (Tax Fac), LMW Limited, Riverside View, Basing Road, Basing, BASINGSTOKE, HAMPSHIRE RG24 7AL.
RANDALL, Mrs. Margaret Lesley, BA ACA *1980;* 3 Devonshire Park, READING, RG2 7DX.
•RANDALL, Mr. Mark Jonathan, BA FCA *1995;* Randall Management Services Limited, 12 Furniss Avenue, Dore, SHEFFIELD, S17 3QL.
RANDALL, Mr. Martin Keith, BA ACA *1987;* Jacks Platt, Duddleswell, UCKFIELD, TN22 3JR.
RANDALL, Mr. Maurice, FCA *1972;* 20 Ashdene Road, Ash, ALDERSHOT, HAMPSHIRE, GU12 6TB.
RANDALL, Mr. Michael Bince, FCA *1972;* 12 Lancaster Drive, BROADSTONE, DORSET, BH18 9EJ.
•RANDALL, Mrs. Pamela Marion, FCA *1973;* (Tax Fac), P.M. Randall & Co, PO Box 131, Harold Hill, ROMFORD, ESSEX, RM3 9LZ.
•RANDALL, Mr. Paul, BA ACA *2005;* Royce Peeling Green Limited, 15 Buckingham Gate, LONDON, SW1E 6LB.
RANDALL, Dr. Paula Louise, BSc ACA *1995;* 100 Commercial Road, Rhydyfro Pontardawe, SWANSEA, SA8 4SS.
•RANDALL, Mr. Peter George, BA FCA *1982;* (Tax Fac), RNV Limited, 21-23 West Street, Oundle, PETERBOROUGH, PE8 4EJ.
RANDALL, Mrs. Rachel Clare, LLB ACA *2003;* 4 Lime Tree Road, NORTH WALSHAM, NORFOLK, NR28 9DY.
•RANDALL, Mr. Robert Andrew, ACA *1980;* (Tax Fac), R.A. Randall, 166 Kempshott Lane, Kempshott, BASINGSTOKE, RG22 5LA.
•RANDALL, Mr. Ross Woolfrey, FCA *1957;* (Tax Fac), Framecall Ltd, 21 Clarence Road, Kew Gardens, RICHMOND, TW9 3NL.
RANDALL, Mrs. Sarah Louise, ACA MAAT *2010;* 27 Lyndhurst Drive, BASINGSTOKE, HAMPSHIRE, RG22 4QT.
RANDALL, Mr. Stuart Alan, BSc FCA *1973;* 17 Belgravia Gardens, Aylestone Hill, HEREFORD, HR1 1RB.
RANDALL, Mr. Trevor Neil, BA(Hons) FCA *1965;* 18 Somerton Gardens, Earley, READING, RG6 5XG.
RANDALL, Mr. William George, FCA *1951;* 8 Glenmount Way, Thornhill, CARDIFF, CF14 9HS. (Life Member)
RANDALL-PALEY, Mrs. Sarah Jane, FCA *1993;* 2 Churchfield Barn, Tunstall, CARNFORTH, LANCASHIRE, LA6 2RH.
•RANDELL, Mr. Francis John, BSc FCA *1975;* 36 Westgate Road, NEWBURY, BERKSHIRE, RG14 6AU.
RANDELL, Mr. Gordon John, ACA *1987;* 48 Malin Close, SOUTHAMPTON, SO16 8BX.
RANDELL, Mrs. Kathleen Moira, BTech ACA *1982;* 36 Westgate Road, NEWBURY, RG14 6AU.
•RANDELL, Mr. Mark Benjamin, BA ACA *2001;* with PricewaterhouseCoopers, 7 More London Riverside, LONDON, SE1 2RT.
RANDERIA, Mr. Minocher Edulji, FCA *1962;* 70 The Avenue, Kew, RICHMOND, TW9 2AH.
•RANDERIA, Mr. Zubin Paul, BEng FCA *1995;* PricewaterhouseCoopers LLP, Pricewaterhousecoopers, 12 Plumtree Court, LONDON, EC4A 4HT. See also PricewaterhouseCoopers
RANDEVA, Mrs. Harbir Kaur, BA ACA *1998;* 8 Portsmouth Avenue, THAMES DITTON, SURREY, KT7 0RT.
RANDHAWA, Mr. Gursharan Jit Singh, MA ACA MBA *1994;* 26 Heaton Drive, Edgbaston, BIRMINGHAM, B15 3LW.
RANDHAWA, Mrs. Rajveer Kaur Chahal, BSc(Hons) ACA *2011;* 33 Cranbourne Avenue, Ettingshall Park, WOLVERHAMPTON, WV4 6RJ.
RANDHAWA, Mrs. Rupinderjit Kaur, BSc ACA *2000;* 18 Blagdon Road, NEW MALDEN, SURREY, KT3 4AE.
RANDHAWA, Mrs. Sarah Jane, BA ACA *2005;* 937 4th Street, Apt 10, SANTA MONICA, CA 90403, UNITED STATES.
•RANDLE, Mr. Adrian Edward, BA FCA *1983;* (Tax Fac), 3 St. Anthonys, 30 Christchurch Road, CHELTENHAM, GLOUCESTERSHIRE, GL50 2PL.
RANDLE, Mr. Alister Neil, BCom ACA *1995;* Flat 4 Coach House Court, 27 Highgate Avenue, LONDON, N6 5SJ.
RANDLE, Mrs. Angela Alexandra Maria, MSc BCom FCA *1986;* 31 Evergreen Way, STOURPORT-ON-SEVERN, WORCESTERSHIRE, DY13 9GH.

RANDLE, Miss. Helen Elizabeth, BSc ACA *1989;* Budget Insurance, Pegasus House, Bakewell Road, Orton Southgate, PETERBOROUGH, PE2 6YS.
•**RANDLE, Mr. Ian, FCA** *1988;* The Ollis Partnership Limited, 2 Hamilton Terrace, Holly Walk, LEAMINGTON SPA, WARWICKSHIRE, CV32 4LY.
•**RANDLE, Mr. Jaiye Kofolaran, FCA** *1970;* JK Randle & Co, XKPMG House, King Ologunkuntere Street, Park View Estate, Ikoyi, LAGOS NIGERIA.
RANDLE, Mr. Jaiye Kofolaran, BA(Hons) ACA *2009;* 40 Cheyne Court, LONDON, SW3 5TR.
RANDLE, Mrs. Judith Mary, BSc FCA *1980;* Flat 1B Celeste Court, 12 Fung Fai Terrace, HAPPY VALLEY, HONG KONG SAR.
RANDLE, Mr. Martin Charles, BSc FCA *1978;* Flat 1B Celeste Court, 12 Fung Fai Terrace, HAPPY VALLEY, HONG KONG SAR.
RANDLE, Mr. Matthew James, MEng ACA *2008;* 8 Chariot Way, CAMBRIDGE, CB4 2GY.
RANDLE, Mr. Michael George, FCA *1974;* 31 Evergreen Way, STOURPORT-ON-SEVERN, WORCESTERSHIRE, DY13 9GH.
RANDLE, Mr. Paul Henry, BSc ACA *1996;* 4 Forest Grove Edwardsville, TREHARRIS, MID GLAMORGAN, CF46 5NG.
RANDLE, Mr. Peter Michael, FCA *1968;* 11 Harvest Way, Ashgate, CHESTERFIELD, DERBYSHIRE, S42 7JX.
RANDLES, Mr. Christopher Mark, BA ACA *1993;* 8 Chestnut Close, Sychdyn, FLINT, CH7 6RP.
•**RANDLES, Mr. David Frank, BA FCA** *1978;* (Tax Fac), D & J Randles Limited, 203 Askern Road, Bentley, DONCASTER, SOUTH YORKSHIRE, DN5 0JR.
RANDLES, Mr. Julian Norman Cyril, BSc ACA *1996;* 2nd floor, O'Gorman House, 37 Ixworth Place, LONDON, SW3 3QH.
RANDLES, Mrs. Kay, BSc ACA *1991;* 1 Wesley Close, Parkgate, NESTON, CH64 6TW.
RANDLES, Mr. Michael Richard, MEng ACA *2001;* 62 Hillcrest, WEYBRIDGE, SURREY, KT13 8EB.
RANDLES, Mr. Philip John, BA ACA *1994;* Kawneer UK Ltd, Astmoor Road, Astmoor Industrial Estate, RUNCORN, CHESHIRE, WA7 1QQ.
RANDLESOME, Mr. David John, FCA *1978;* 14 Wakes Colne, WICKFORD, ESSEX, SS11 8XY.
•**RANDOLPH, Mr. Ian Anthony, FCA** *1968;* (Tax Fac), Montpelier Audit Limited, Montpelier House, 62-66 Deansgate, MANCHESTER, M3 2EN. See also Montpelier Professional (West End) Ltd
RANDS, Mrs. Caroline Joy, BA ACA *2004;* Willoughby (542) Limited, North Lodge Farm, Widmerpool Lane, Widmerpool, NOTTINGHAM, NG12 5QE.
•**RANDS, Mr. Edward Charles, BSc FCA** *1992;* Cooper Parry LLP, 1 Colton Square, LEICESTER, LE1 1QH.
RANDS, Mr. Ian Jonathan, BA(Hons) ACA *2000;* 1 Dalby Grove, Sothall, SHEFFIELD, S20 2PX.
RANDS, Mrs. Lynda Wallace, BSc ACA *2000;* 1 Dalby Grove, Sothall, SHEFFIELD, S20 2PX.
RANDS, Mr. Michael Anthony, FCA *1975;* The Old Nurseries, The Old Nurseries Cheapside, Waltham, GRIMSBY, SOUTH HUMBERSIDE, DN37 0HU.
RANDS, Mr. Peter Geoffrey Graham, FCA *1961;* 1 Court Cottages, Old Worcester Road, Waresley, KIDDERMINSTER, WORCESTERSHIRE, DY11 7XS.
RANEVA-GURSAHANI, Mrs. Ralitza Kirilova, ACA *2008;* Beechwood House, Berry Lane, Chorleywood, RICKMANSWORTH, HERTFORDSHIRE, WD3 5ED.
RANFORD, Mr. Paul Frederick, FCA *1977;* Bacombe Beeches Ellesborough Road, Wendover, AYLESBURY, BUCKINGHAMSHIRE, HP22 6ES.
RANGARAJAN, Mr. Krishnamoorthy, FCA *1968;* 10 Lansdowne Road, Wimbledon, LONDON, SW20 8AR. (Life Member)
RANGE, Mr. Dudley Lawrence, FCA *1953;* 1 Holsart Close, TADWORTH, KT20 5EJ. (Life Member)
•**RANGELEY, Mr. Robert David Alexander, FCA** *1974;* (Tax Fac), R.D. Rangeley FCA, Abbey House, 25 Clarendon Road, REDHILL, RH1 1QZ.
RANINGA, Mr. Hatal, BSc ACA AMCT *2001;* Flat 5 2 Archie Street, LONDON, SE1 3JT.
•**RANIWALA, Mr. Asif, BSc ACA** *2000;* AZR Limited, 79 College Road, HARROW, MIDDLESEX, HA1 1BD.
•**RANIWALA, Mr. Zaffer Fazleabbas Hassanali, FCA** *1968;* (Tax Fac), AZR Limited, 79 College Road, HARROW, MIDDLESEX, HA1 1BD.
RANIWALA, Mr. Zoeb Fazleabbas, MBA FCA *1970;* Logistics Plus UK Ltd, 22-26 Eastern Road, ROMFORD, ESSEX, RM1 3PJ.
RANKIN, Mr. Brian Kenneth, FCA *1961;* 22 Gordon Avenue, Greasby, WIRRAL, CH49 1SH.
RANKIN, Ms. Caroline Jill, MA ACA *1999;* 114 Princes Road, BUCKHURST HILL, IG9 5DX.
RANKIN, Mr. Charles Stuart Brian, FCA *1966;* 767 Walkern Street, QUESNEL V2J 2J8, BC, CANADA. (Life Member)
RANKIN, Mr. David Alexander, FCA *1982;* Michaelmas Cottage, Stoke Wood, Stoke Poges, SLOUGH, SL2 4BA.
RANKIN, Mr. Gavin Niall, LLB ACA *1989;* 206 Hammersmith Grove, LONDON, W6 7HG.
•**RANKIN, Mr. Ian Thomas, FCA** *1959;* (Tax Fac), Ian Rankin & Co, 4 Blades Close, LEATHERHEAD, KT22 7JY.
•**RANKIN, Mr. Richard Andrew, BA ACA CF** *1999;* Armstrong Watson, First Floor East, Bridge Mills, Stramongate, KENDAL, CUMBRIA LA9 4UB.
RANKIN, Mrs. Stephanie Mary, BA FCA *1989;* Haleys Chartered Accountants, Thomas House, Pope Lane, Whitestake, PRESTON, PR4 4AZ.
RANKIN, Mrs. Trudy Elaine, BSc FCA *1991;* 4 Albert Cottages, London Road Hartley Wintney, HOOK, RG27 8RN.
•**RANN, Mr. Adrian Christopher Dale, BSc FCA** *1978;* James Cowper LLP, Mill House, Overbridge Square, Hambridge Lane, NEWBURY, BERKSHIRE RG14 5UX. See also JC Payroll Services Ltd
RANN, Mr. James Mytton, BSc FCA *1990;* 3 Letheren Place, EASTBOURNE, BN21 1HL.
RANN, Mr. Robert Thomas Jonathan, BSc ACA *1992;* 21 Ealing Park Gardens, LONDON, W5 4EX.
RANNARD, Mrs. Amanda Jane, BSc ACA *1994;* 4 St Peters Way, Mickle Trafford, CHESTER, CH2 4EJ.
RANNARD, Mrs. Sarah Louise, ACA *2011;* 17 Brambling Drive, BACUP, OL13 9QJ.
RANS, Mr. Saul Anderson, BA ACA *1995;* 1 Powys Gardens, LEICESTER, LE2 2DS.
•**RANSCOMBE, Mr. Stephen Christopher, ACA** *1979;* Stephen C Ranscombe & Co, Tigh Ceilidh, NAIRN, IV12 5NX.
RANSFORD, Mr. Ian, ACA *1995;* 9 West End Road, Epworth, DONCASTER, DN9 1LA.
RANSLEY, Ms. Kerry Angela, MA BA(Hons) ACA *2002;* with PricewaterhouseCoopers, 1 Embankment Place, LONDON, WC2N 6RH.
RANSLEY, Mr. Paul, BSc ACA *1990;* 40 Harefield Avenue, Cheam, SUTTON, SM2 7NE.
•**RANSLEY, Mr. Thomas Luke, BSc FCA** *1983;* 212 Brooklands Road, WEYBRIDGE, SURREY, KT13 0RJ.
RANSOM, Miss. Joanna Mary, ACA *1980;* 8 Elmbank Avenue, Arkley, BARNET, EN5 3DS.
•**RANSOM, Mr. Jonathan Peter, BSc FCA** *1980;* (Tax Fac), Jon Ransom, Office 7a, Unit 16, Dinan Way Trading Estate, Concorde Road, EXMOUTH DEVON EX8 4RS.
RANSOM, Mr. Peter Alan, BA ACA *1986;* 25 Kelham Hall Drive, Wheatley, OXFORD, OX33 1SL.
RANSOM, Mr. Richard William, BA FCA *1980;* The White House, 235 Nottingham Road, Borrowash, DERBY, DE72 3FR.
RANSOM, Mr. Robert Stephen, FCA *1957;* Rampyndene, High Street, Burwash, ETCHINGHAM, TN19 7EH. (Life Member)
RANSOME, Mr. David Peter, BSc ACA *1992;* Silver Birches, Stinchcombe Hill, DURSLEY, GL11 6AQ.
RANSOME, Mr. Edward, BA ACA *2011;* Flat 8, 1 Marshall St, LEEDS, LS11 9AB.
RANSOME, Mrs. Ellen Ruth, BA ACA *2006;* 21 Napier Crescent, Laverstock, SALISBURY, SP1 1PJ.
RANSOME, Miss. Hilary Katie, BA ACA *2005;* Procter & Gamble UK, Cobalt 12A, Silver Fox Way, Cobalt Business Park, NEWCASTLE UPON TYNE, NE27 0QW.
RANSOME, Mr. Michael William, FCA *1972;* (Tax Fac), with John Swire & Sons Ltd, Swire House, 59 Buckingham Gate, LONDON, SW1E 6AJ.
•**RANSOME, Mr. Neal John, MA FCA CF** *1984;* PricewaterhouseCoopers LLP, 80 Strand, LONDON, WC2R 0AF. See also PricewaterhouseCoopers
RANSOME, Mr. Peter John, FCA *1958;* Bethany, Chequers Lane, TADWORTH, KT20 7RB. (Life Member)
RANSOME, Mrs. Sarah Elizabeth Ann, MA BA ACA *1993;* 15 Willis Road, CAMBRIDGE, CB1 2AQ.
•**RANSON, Mr. Christopher Gordon, BVSc MRCVS ACA** *2004;* CGR Sussex Ltd, 1 Naseby Cottages, Fletching, UCKFIELD, EAST SUSSEX, TN22 3TB. See also ZXCV 27 Ltd
RANSON, Mr. Damian James, MA ACA *1999;* Jesmond Mersea Road, Abberton, COLCHESTER, CO5 7NS.
RANSON, Mr. David Antony, BSc ACA *1997;* Flat 2, 5 Roderick Road, LONDON, NW3 2NN.
RANSON, Mr. David Charles, FCA *1979;* 2a Norfolk Hill, Grenoside, SHEFFIELD, S35 8QB.
•**RANSON, Mr. David John, BSc FCA** *1980;* D.J. Ranson, 17 Willets Rise, Shenley Church End, MILTON KEYNES, MK5 6JW.
RANSON, Mr. Geoffrey, BSc(Hons) ACA *2001;* 24 Fink Hill, Horsforth, LEEDS, LS18 4DH.
RANSON, Miss. Helen Jane, BA ACA *1986;* 27 Speldhurst Road, Chiswick, LONDON, W4 1BX.
RANSON, Mrs. Linda Ann, FCA *1990;* 25 Newell Rise, Claydon, IPSWICH, IP6 0AQ.
•①**RANSON, Mr. Mark Nicholas, BA FCA MABRP** *1993;* Baker Tilly Restructuring & Recovery LLP, 2 Whitehall Quay, LEEDS, LS1 4HG. See also Baker Tilly Tax and Advisory Services LLP
•**RANSON, Mr. Michael John, ACA** *1979;* 38 Coopers Green, BICESTER, OXFORDSHIRE, OX26 4XJ.
RANSON, Mr. Michael Leonard, JP FCA *1971;* 6 North Jesmond Avenue, Jesmond, NEWCASTLE UPON TYNE, NE2 3JX.
RANSON, Mr. Paul Nigel, BEng ACA *1999;* K P M G 1 Forest Gate, Tilgate Forest Business Centre Brighton Road, CRAWLEY, WEST SUSSEX, RH11 9PT.
RANSON, Miss. Rachel, MSci ACA *2006;* West Corporation Ltd, PO Box 16, Analyst House, Douglas, ISLE OF MAN, IM99 1AP.
RANSON, Mr. Stephen, BSc FCA MBA *1993;* Archers, London Road, Newport, SAFFRON WALDEN, ESSEX, CB11 3PN.
RANSON, Mr. Thomas Edward, BSc ACA *1990;* Kirchstrasse 1, 13129 BERLIN, GERMANY.
•**RANSTED, Mr. David Andrew, BA FCA** *1981;* (Tax Fac), Reed Ransted, Finance House, 522 Uxbridge Road, PINNER, MIDDLESEX, HA5 3PU.
RANSTED, Mr. Dennis Reginald, FCA *1952;* 95 Herne Hill Road, Herne Hill, LONDON, SE24 0AY. (Life Member)
RANWELL, Mr. Martin Elliott, FCA *1961;* Tucker Brook House, 1 Tuckers Brook, Modbury, IVYBRIDGE, DEVON, PL21 0UT.
RAO, Mr. Addanki Ramachandra, FCA *1953;* 345 Station Road, WINSFORD, CW7 3DQ. (Life Member)
RAO, Mr. Arshad Amin, ACA *1992;* 317 Great West Road, HOUNSLOW, TW5 0DE.
RAO, Mr. Omair Abid, ACA *2010;* 33 Bolton Road, CHESSINGTON, KT9 2JF.
RAO, Mr. Parry, BA ACA *1992;* 1 The Dell, Sandwich Road Nonington, DOVER, CT15 4HQ.
RAO, Mr. Paul Kasina, MA BA ACA *2008;* with Mazars LLP, The Atrium, Park Street West, LUTON, LU1 3BE.
RAO, Mr. Purandar, ACA *1995;* Ernst & Young, One Raffles Quay, North Tower Level 18, SINGAPORE 048583, SINGAPORE.
RAO, Ms. Vasudha, BSc ACA ATII *1988;* QBE Group Investor Relations Level 2 82 Pitt Street, SYDNEY, NSW 2000, AUSTRALIA.
RAO, Mrs. Venkata Devikarani, BSc ACA *1989;* 304 Curtner Rd, FREMONT, CA 94539, UNITED STATES.
RAPAZZINI, Mr. Adrian Colin, FCA *1969;* 12 Westmead, LONDON, SW15 5BQ.
RAPAZZINI, Mr. Robert Michael, FCA *1962;* Via Sauli Sant'Alessandro, 16/B, 20127 MILAN, ITALY. (Life Member)
RAPER, Mr. Christopher William, MA FCA *1987;* Camoy Lodge, Hunstanton Hall, Church Road, HUNSTANTON, NORFOLK, PE36 6JS.
RAPER, Mr. Duncan, ACA *1981;* Orchard House, Lane Close, Horley, BANBURY, OX15 6BH.
RAPER, Mrs. Elizabeth Sarah, BSc ACA *1989;* Peach Tree Lodge, Marton, Marton Cum Grafton, YORK, YO51 9QY.
RAPER, Mr. Martin, BA FCA *1977;* Pricewaterhousecoopers, 89 Sandyford Road, NEWCASTLE UPON TYNE, NE1 8HW.
•**RAPER, Mrs. Michelle, ACA ACCA** *2011;* Rostrons, St Peter's House, Cattle Market Street, NORWICH, NR1 3DY. See also Rostron & Partners
•**RAPER, Mr. Peter David, FCA** *1977;* Whittingtons Business Services Ltd, 1 High Street, GUILDFORD, SURREY, GU2 4HP.
RAPER, Mr. Simon, BSc(Hons) ACA *2001;* Area 3B, Department for Environment Food & Rural Affairs (D E F R A), Nobel House 17 Smith Square, LONDON, SW1P 3JR.
RAPER, Miss. Vicky Louise, ACA *2011;* 27 Park View Court, 215 Devons Road, LONDON, E3 3AN.
•**RAPERPORT, Mr. Hugh Simon Anthony, FCA MBA** *1972;* Sandes, 45 Arden Road, LONDON, N3 3AD.
RAPHAEL, Mr. David Howard Gordon, FCA *1964;* 14 Lytton Road, Observatory, CAPE TOWN, 7925, SOUTH AFRICA.
RAPHAEL, Mr. Harry, FCA *1953;* Kfar Hittim, LOWER GALILEE, 15280, ISRAEL. (Life Member)
RAPHAEL, Mr. Norman Barry, FCA *1955;* 49 Kingston Hill Place, KINGSTON UPON THAMES, KT2 7QY. (Life Member)
•**RAPHAEL, Mr. Peter, FCA** *1975;* Cranford Consulting (Alderney) Limited, Moonshine, Barrack Masters Lane, Route Des Carrieres, Alderney, GUERNSEY GY9 3YD.
RAPHAEL, Mr. Terence Patrick, FCA *1972;* 6625 180 St, SURREY V3S 8C3, BC, CANADA. (Life Member)
RAPINET, Mrs. Linda, BSc FCA *1988;* 32 Conduit Road, SHEFFIELD, S10 1EW.
RAPLEY, Mr. Alistair, FCA *1975;* Amalgamated Metal Trading Ltd, 55 Bishopsgate, LONDON, EC2N 3AH.
RAPLEY, Mr. Ian Andrew, ACA *1992;* 47 Oakleigh Park South, LONDON, N20 9JR.
RAPLEY, Mr. Justin William, BSc(Hons) ACA *2009;* 9 Phillips Close, Headley, BORDON, GU35 8LY.
RAPONI, Mrs. Julie Anne, BSc ACA *1998;* 11 Crowell Way, Walton-Le-Dale, PRESTON, PR5 4LG.
RAPOPORT, Mr. David Roderick, FCA *1975;* 3 Brassey Hill, OXTED, SURREY, RH8 0ES.
RAPPITT, Miss. Emily Julia, BA ACA *1998;* 62 Tranmere Road, LONDON, SW18 3QJ.
RAPPITT, Mr. Roy James Benjamin, FCA *1952;* 153 Ongar Road, BRENTWOOD, ESSEX, CM15 9DL. (Life Member)
RAPPORT, Mrs. Claire Tina, BSc(Hons) ACA *2009;* with Smith & Williamson Ltd, 25 Moorgate, LONDON, EC2R 6AY.
RAPPORT, Mr. Oliver Edward Guy, BSc ACA *2006;* 9 Tarrant Place, LONDON, W1H 1AD.
RAPPS, Mr. Richard, BSc ACA *2010;* Sunridge, Woodbury Salterton, EXETER, EX5 1PR.
RAPSON, Mr. Andrew Mark, BSc ACA *2008;* 54 Mossvale Drive, WAKERLEY, QLD 4154, AUSTRALIA.
RAPSON, Mr. Bernard David, MA ACA *1986;* Bank Cottage, Old Forge Lane, PRESTON CAPES, NORTHAMPTONSHIRE, NN11 3TD.
RAQUIB, Mr. Muhammad Abdur, FCA *1983;* Canopius Holdings UK Limited, Lloyds of London Insurance Lloyds Building, 1 Lime Street, LONDON, EC3M 7HA.
RARATY, Dr. David Guy Jerome, PhD FCA *1994;* with National Audit Office, 157-197 Buckingham Palace Road, Victoria, LONDON, SW1W 9SP.
RASAENDIRAN, Miss. Rajini, ACA *2008;* 34 Grangeway Gardens, ILFORD, ESSEX, IG4 5HN.
RASANAYAGAM, Mr. Sabanayagam, FCA *1959;* 81-8 Kynsey Road, 8 COLOMBO, SRI LANKA. (Life Member)
RASANESAN, Miss. Rathi, ACA *2009;* 42 Arundel Drive, HARROW, MIDDLESEX, HA2 8PR.
RASCHE, Mr. Charles William, BSc FCA *1976;* Airedale Pilgrims Way, Chew Stoke, BRISTOL, BS40 8TT.
RASCHEN, Mr. Henry David, TD BCom FCA *1983;* H S B C, Level 28, 8-16 Canada Square, LONDON, E14 5HQ.
•**RASCHID, Mr. Neville Ewart, MA ACA** *1983;* Kennard Cousins and Associates Limited, 8 Little Trinity Lane, LONDON, EC4V 2AN.
RASH, Mr. Christopher John Roland, BA ACA *1991;* 3 Lovett's Place, LONDON, SW18 1LA.
RASH, Mr. Malcolm Ernest, FCA *1970;* 46 West Street, Kings Cliffe, PETERBOROUGH, PE8 6XA.
RASHEED, Mr. Mohammed Anwar, ACA *2008;* Flat 59 Ashleigh Court, 29 Loates Lane, WATFORD, WD17 2PJ.
RASHEED, Mr. Qamar, FCA *1982;* PO BOX 450044, DUBAI, UNITED ARAB EMIRATES.
RASHID, Mr. Abdul Rauf, BSocSc ACA *1996;* Ernst & Young, Level 23A Menara Milenium, Pusat Bandar Damansara, 50490 KUALA LUMPUR, FEDERAL TERRITORY, MALAYSIA.
RASHID, Mr. Ahsan, FCA *1965;* 4 Forest Laneway, Apartment 1106, TORONTO M2N 5X8, ON, CANADA.
RASHID, Miss. Alina, ACA *2009;* No 13 Jalan Memanah 13/55D, Laman Seri, 40100 SHAH ALAM, SELANGOR, MALAYSIA.
RASHID, Mr. Aminoor, ACA *2008;* 4 Banastre Drive, NEWTON-LE-WILLOWS, MERSEYSIDE, WA12 8BE.
RASHID, Mr. Amir, FCA *1973;* 8-B Block H, Gulberg -2, LAHORE, PAKISTAN.
RASHID, Mr. Halimur, MSc ACA *2010;* 30 Upper Holt Street, Earls Colne, COLCHESTER, CO6 2PG.
RASHID, Mr. Hammad, ACA *2007;* Descon Chemicals Ltd, Descon Headquarters, 18 km Ferozepur Road, LAHORE 53000, PAKISTAN.

RASHID, Mr. Haroon, BA ACA *1997;* Rose Cottage, Chellow Lane, BRADFORD, WEST YORKSHIRE, BD9 6AS.
RASHID, Mr. Haroun, FCA *1975;* Heritage Developments, A-403 Gulberg Arcade, 38G Gulberg-2, LAHORE, PAKISTAN.
RASHID, Mr. Harun, ACA *2008;* Porterbrook Leasing Company Limited, Ivatt House, 7 The Point, Pride Park, DERBY, DE24 8ZS.
•**RASHID, Mr. Hassan Akhtar, FCA** *1984;* Barker Maule Limited, 27/33 Castle Gate, NEWARK, NOTTINGHAMSHIRE, NG24 1BA.
RASHID, Mr. Humain, BCom ACA *1998;* 202 Walmley Ash Road, SUTTON COLDFIELD, B76 1XJ.
RASHID, Mr. Khalil, BSc ACA *1998;* (Tax Fac), Grainger Trust plc, Citygate, St. James Boulevard, NEWCASTLE UPON TYNE, NE1 4JE.
RASHID, Mr. Nadeem, FCA *1984;* Al Tayer Group, P.O.Box 2623, DUBAI, UNITED ARAB EMIRATES.
RASHID, Mr. Nasar, BA ACA *1992;* 210 Westbury Avenue, Wood Green, LONDON, N22 6RU.
RASHID, Mr. Pervaiz, FCA MBA *1966;* World Bank (J11176), 1818 H StreetNW, WASHINGTON, DC 20433, UNITED STATES.
•**RASHID, Mr. Rahmatullah, BSc ACA** *1988;* 17 Norford Way, ROCHDALE, OL11 5QS.
RASHID, Mr. Raza Ali, ACA *1987;* 5472 Freshwater Drive, MISSISSAUGA L5M 0J8, ON, CANADA.
RASHID, Mr. Sajid, MSc BA ACA *2001;* 25 Devonshire Park, READING, RG2 7DX.
RASHID, Miss. Salma Shireen, ACA *2009;* (Tax Fac), Almas, 4a Durham Road, LUTON, LU2 0RB.
RASHID, Mr. Sheheryar, BSc(Hons) ACA *2010;* 4 School Street, OLDHAM, OL8 1SE.
•**RASHID, Mr. Tariq, FCA** *1986;* T. Rashid, 20 Sundew Court, Elmore Close, WEMBLEY, HA0 1YY.
RASHLEIGH, Mr. Jonathan Michael Vernon, FCA *1973;* The Old Piggery, Thorns Lane, Underbarrow, KENDAL, CUMBRIA, LA8 8HF. (Life Member)
•**RASHLEIGH, Mrs. Karen Patricia, FCA** *1974;* 02Vie Ltd, 43 Oxshott Way, COBHAM, SURREY, KT11 2RU.
RASKINA, Mr. Lloyd Gerard, ACA *1980;* Lloyd G Raskina CA, 5 McIntosh Drive, Suite 218, MARKHAM L3R 8C7, ON, CANADA.
RASLAN, Mr. Ahmad Johan, BSc FCA *1984;* PricewaterhouseCoopers, P.O.Box 10192, Level 10 1 Sentral, Jalan Travers, 50470 KUALA LUMPUR, FEDERAL TERRITORY MALAYSIA.
•**RASMUSSEN, Mr. Anders Charles, BSc ACA** *1992;* Grant Thornton UK LLP, Kingfisher House, 1 Gilders Way, St James Place, NORWICH, NR3 1UB. See also Grant Thornton LLP
RASMUSSEN, Mr. Phillip John, BSc ACA *1995;* Lagreach, Botany Bay, TINTERN, MONMOUTHSHIRE, NP16 6NJ.
RASOULY, Mr. David, BSc FCA *1987;* 54 Elmstead Avenue, WEMBLEY, HA9 8NY.
RASSOU, Mr. Michel Patrice, MSc ACA *1996;* 7 Freesia Close, Platterkloof 3, Parow, CAPE TOWN, 7500, SOUTH AFRICA.
•**RASTALL, Mr. Walter Guy, BA FCA** *1966;* (Tax Fac), W.G.Rastall, Crest Acre House, Sedbury Lane, Tutshill, CHEPSTOW, NP16 7DU.
RASTRICK, Mr. Robert, FCA *1975;* 33 Bright Meadow, Half Way, SHEFFIELD, S20 4SY.
•**RASUL, Mr. Munaver Hussain, BSc FCA CTA** *1981;* Munaver Rasul, Entrance 2a, Part 1st Floor, Crossford Court, Dane Road, SALE CHESHIRE M33 7BZ.
RASZPLA, Mr. Marian Jan, BCom FCA *1977;* Stop-choc Limited, Banbury Avenue, SLOUGH, SL1 4LR.
RATANSI, Mr. Mahendra, FCA *1969;* 167 Kingshill Drive, Kenton, HARROW, HA3 8QT. (Life Member)
RATCHFORD, Mr. Martin, BA(Hons) ACA *2001;* The Mill House, Evegate Water Mill Station Road, Smeeth, ASHFORD, TN25 6SY.
RATCLIFF, Mr. Kenneth Maurice, BSc FCA *1975;* Brahe, 57 Fox Dene, GODALMING, SURREY, GU7 1YG.
RATCLIFF, Mr. Martin James, BSc(Hons) ACA *2004;* 5 Ormonde Road, Horsell, WOKING, SURREY, GU21 4RZ.
•**RATCLIFFE, Mr. Alan George, FCA** *1974;* (Tax Fac), Katonah, 6 The Gateway, Woodham, WOKING, GU21 5SL. See also Ratcliffe & Co
•**RATCLIFFE, Mr. Andrew Nicholas, MA ACA** *1980;* MEMBER OF COUNCIL, PricewaterhouseCoopers LLP, 7 More London Riverside, LONDON, SE1 2RT. See also Andrew Ratcliffe
RATCLIFFE, Mr. Anthony James, BSc ACA *1989;* Hepworth Hall, The Street, Hepworth, DISS, IP22 2PS.
RATCLIFFE, Mr. Anthony John, FCA *1968;* Waterside, Blacksmiths Lane, Newton Solney, BURTON-ON-TRENT, DE15 0SD.
RATCLIFFE, Dr. Charles, PhD MA BA ACA *2009;* UK Greetings Ltd, Mill Street East, DEWSBURY, WEST YORKSHIRE, WF12 9AW.
RATCLIFFE, Mr. Christopher Charles, BSc FCA *1992;* 31 The Limes, Harston, CAMBRIDGE, CB22 7QT.
RATCLIFFE, Mr. David, FCA *1955;* 17 Chartridge Lane, CHESHAM, BUCKINGHAMSHIRE, HP5 2JL. (Life Member)
RATCLIFFE, Mr. David Eastham, BA FCA *1969;* Topstreet Farmhouse, 28 Crabtree Lane, HARPENDEN, AL5 5NU. (Life Member)
RATCLIFFE, Mrs. Elizabeth Anne, BSc ACA *1990;* 1906 Old Ballard Farm Road, CHARLOTTESVILLE, VA 22901, UNITED STATES.
RATCLIFFE, Miss. Frances Susan, BCom ACA *1986;* 18 Earlswood Road, Birches Head, STOKE-ON-TRENT, ST1 6UF.
RATCLIFFE, Mr. Freddie, ACA *2009;* 64 Gallon Close, LONDON, SE7 8SY.
RATCLIFFE, Mr. Gareth John, BA ACA *1998;* 29 Park Copse, Horsforth, LEEDS, LS18 5UN.
•**RATCLIFFE, Mr. Gerard Nicholas, BSc FCA** *1990;* Debtmatters Limited, Mansell House, Aspinall Way, Middlebrook Business Park, BOLTON, BL6 6QQ. See also Unique Debt Solutions Ltd
•**RATCLIFFE, Mr. John, BA ACA** *1978;* PricewaterhouseCoopers LLP, 7 More London Riverside, LONDON, SE1 2RT. See also PricewaterhouseCoopers
RATCLIFFE, Mr. John Nigel, FCA *1974;* 28 Littlethorpe Hill, Hartshead, LIVERSEDGE, WF15 8AZ.
RATCLIFFE, Mr. Neill Edward, FCA *1953;* Shawfield, Maidens Grove, HENLEY-ON-THAMES, RG9 6EX. (Life Member)
RATCLIFFE, Mr. Nicholas Paul, BA ACA *1998;* Associated Newspapers Ltd Northcliffe House, 2 Derry Street, LONDON, W8 5TT.
RATCLIFFE, Mr. Nicholas Simon, BA ACA *1988;* 1 Parakeet Place, BURLEIGH WATERS, QLD 4220, AUSTRALIA.
RATCLIFFE, Mr. Nigel Terence, BSc ACA *1989;* (Tax Fac), 20 Farriers Close, EPSOM, SURREY, KT17 1LS.
RATCLIFFE, Mr. Paul, ACA *1980;* Taunusstr 9, 63594 HASSELROTH, GERMANY.
RATCLIFFE, Mr. Peter, FCA *1973;* 22 Hilltop Avenue, WILMSLOW, SK9 2JE.
RATCLIFFE, Mr. Peter Gervis, BA FCA *1972;* 1433 Nathan Lane, VENTURA, CA 93001, UNITED STATES.
RATCLIFFE, Miss. Rebecca, ACA *2011;* 8 Empire Avenue, MANLY WEST, QLD 4179, AUSTRALIA.
•**RATCLIFFE, Mr. Richard Charles, BA FCA** *1993;* Grant Thornton, PO Box 307, 3rd Floor, Exchange House, 54-58 Athor Street, Douglas ISLE OF MAN IM99 2BE.
RATCLIFFE, Miss. Sarah Elizabeth, BSc ACA *1989;* 59b Grange Road, SUTTON, SM2 6SP.
RATCLIFFE, Mr. Simon Richard, BA ACA *1992;* 4 Little Lane, HOLMFIRTH, HD9 1QF.
RATCLIFFE, Miss. Sophie, ACA *2010;* with Deloitte LLP, 1 City Square, LEEDS, WEST YORKSHIRE, LS1 2AL.
RATCLIFFE, Mr. William Michael, FCA *1971;* 21 Wentworth Way, Bletchley, MILTON KEYNES, MK3 7RW. (Life Member)
RATE, Mr. Anthony Gilbert, FCA *1975;* N T N Bearings (UK) Ltd, 11 Wellington Crescent, Fradley Park, LICHFIELD, STAFFORDSHIRE, WS13 8RZ.
RATES, Mrs. Carol Ada, BA ACA *1995;* 9 Woodyard Lane, LONDON, SE21 7BH.
RATES, Mr. Clive Leslie, BSc(Econ) ACA *1995;* Villa 203, Cordoba Oasis Village, PO Box 61834, RIYADH, 11575, SAUDI ARABIA.
•**RATFORD, Mr. Alan George, FCA** *1970;* (Tax Fac), Alan Ratford & Co, 20 School Lane, Herne, HERNE BAY, CT6 7AL.
RATFORD, Mr. Michael Christopher, BSc ACA *1983;* Renishaw Plc, New Mills, WOTTON-UNDER-EDGE, GL12 8JR.
RATFORD, Mr. Stephen Frank, FCA *1957;* 136 Worrin Road, Shenfield, BRENTWOOD, CM15 8JN.
RATFORD, Mr. William Frederick, FCA *1955;* West Lawn, Chapel Lane, Burley, RINGWOOD, HAMPSHIRE, BH24 4DJ. (Life Member)
RATH, Mr. James Winston, MA FCA *1972;* 28 Alba Gardens, Golders Green, LONDON, NW11 9NR. (Life Member)
RATH, Mr. Paul Joseph, BA ACA *1982;* 15931 Ellendale Court, CYPRESS, TX 77429, UNITED STATES.
RATHBONE, Mr. Adam, MSc ACA *1997;* HJ Heinz Europe Ltd, South Building, Hayes Business Park, HAYES, UB4 8AL.
RATHBONE, Mr. David, BA ACA *1994;* 21 Barker Way, Thorpe End, NORWICH, NR13 5EZ.
•**RATHBONE, Mr. David, FCA** *1978;* Slimming World, Clover Nook Ind Est, Somercotes, ALFRETON, DE55 4SW.
RATHBONE, Mr. Francis Peter, MA ACA *1980;* 29 Cumberland Avenue, GUILDFORD, GU2 9RQ.
RATHBONE, Mr. Julian Benson, MA ACA *1998;* Old Hall, Woodhouse Lane, Marchwiel, WREXHAM, CLWYD, LL13 0ST.
RATHBONE, Mr. Mark Leslie Lyle, ACA *1999;* with PricewaterhouseCoopers LLP, 17-00 PWC Building, 8 Cross Street, SINGAPORE 048424, SINGAPORE.
RATHBONE, Mr. Matthew, BA ACA *1988;* 6 Weavers Field, Girton, CAMBRIDGE, CB3 0XB.
RATHBONE, Mr. Nicholas William, MA ACA *2002;* 194 Salthouse Road, Jackfield, TELFORD, SHROPSHIRE, TF8 7LP.
RATHBONE, Mr. Paul Benedict, BA *1988;* 27 Old Deer Park Gardens, RICHMOND, TW9 2TN.
RATHINAVEL, Mr. Kannan, ACA *2010;* 85 Heigham Road, LONDON, E6 2JJ.
RATHJEN, Mr. Ian Thomas, JP BSc FCA *1957;* 9 Kimmerghame Place, EDINBURGH, EH4 2GD. (Life Member)
RATHMELL, Mr. Michael, BSc ACA *2011;* 67 Westbury Road, BRADFORD, WEST YORKSHIRE, BD6 3NQ.
RATHORE, Mr. Ali, BA(Econ) ACA *2003;* BHP Billiton, 1360 - Post Oak Blvd, HOUSTON, TX 77056, UNITED STATES.
RATHOUR, Ms. Sheila, BA ACA *1993;* Standard Chartered, 1 Basinghall Avenue, LONDON, EC2V 5DD.
RATIBB, Mr. Jamie Reginald, ACA *2009;* 72 Buckley Road, Lillington, LEAMINGTON SPA, WARWICKSHIRE, CV32 7QQ.
•**RATIGAN, Mr. Paul Andrew, BSc FCA** *1989;* (Tax Fac), Ratigan & Co Ltd, 43 South Avenue, BUXTON, DERBYSHIRE, SK17 6NQ.
RATKI, Mrs. Dorothy, MA FCA *1978;* 20 Jameson Drive, CORBRIDGE, NE45 5EX.
•**RATKI, Mr. Michael, FCA DChA** *1976;* Pinder & Ratki, 7 Lansdowne Terrace, Gosforth, NEWCASTLE UPON TYNE, NE3 1HN.
RATLEDGE, Mr. Alan John, FCA *1963;* Ghyllside, Netherghyll Lane, Cononley, KEIGHLEY, BD20 8PB. (Life Member)
RATLEDGE, Mr. Martin Richard, FCA *1959;* Ladybeck, Tirril, PENRITH, CA10 2JF. (Life Member)
RATNAGE, Mr. Ian Clay, FCA *1973;* Rio Tinto Plc, 6 St. James's Square, LONDON, SW1Y 4JU.
RATNAGE, Mr. Jonathan David, BA ACA *1987;* Chesterfield & North Derbyshire Royal Hospital, Chesterfield Road Calow, CHESTERFIELD, DERBYSHIRE, S44 5BL.
RATNAGE, Mr. Julian Thomas, BSc ACA *1983;* 70 St. Albans Road, KINGSTON UPON THAMES, SURREY, KT2 5HH.
•**RATNAM, Mr. Edward Indran, BSc FCA** *1977;* Edward Ratnam FCA, 23 Chetwynd Park, Rawnsley, CANNOCK, STAFFORDSHIRE, WS12 0NZ.
RATNAM, Mr. Seshadri, FCA *1973;* Amba Bhavani, 164 Sarjapur Road, 1st Block, Kuramangala, BANGALORE 560034, INDIA. (Life Member)
RATNASWAMY, Dato' Jeyaraj, FCA *1981;* MustaphaRaj, E-33-05 Dataran 32, No 2 Jalan 19/1, 46300 PETALING JAYA, SELANGOR, MALAYSIA. See also Rabinraj & Partners
RATNAYAKA, Mr. Don Nishan, ACA *2010;* 126 Queens Walk, RUISLIP, MIDDLESEX, HA4 0NS.
RATRA, Mrs. Sarah, BA ACA *1999;* 38685 Pickering Court, FREMONT, CA 94536, UNITED STATES.
RATSEY, Mr. Michael Brinton, MA ACA *1984;* 36 Maiden Castle Road, DORCHESTER, DT1 2ES.
RATTA, Mr. Tajinderpal Singh, BSc ACA *1998;* Fursecroft, Flat 6 Fursecroft, George Street, LONDON, W1H 5LF.
RATTAN, Mr. Aditya, ACA *1985;* daiwa securities, 10th floor 3 north avenue, maker maxity bandra east, MUMBAI 400051, MAHARASHTRA, INDIA.
RATTAN, Mr. Jastej Singh, ACA *2009;* 3 Boulters Lock, Giffard Park, MILTON KEYNES, MK14 5QR.
•**RATTAN, Mr. Ramesh Kumar, FCA** *1970;* R.K. Rattan, 51 Paxford Road, WEMBLEY, HA0 3RQ.
RATTAN, Mr. Vivek, BSc(Econ) ACA *1983;* G E Commercial Finance, 30 Berkeley Square, LONDON, W1J 6EX.
RATTANSEY, Mr. Aly Noormahomed, FCA *1968;* House 19A, Street 2, Sector F-8/3, ISLAMABAD 44000, PAKISTAN. (Life Member)
•ⒹRATTEN, Mr. Christopher, BA ACA** *1998;* RSM Tenon Limited, Arkwright House, Parsonage Gardens, MANCHESTER, M3 2LF.
RATTENBURY, Mr. John Harold Alan, FCA *1969;* Myrtle Cottage, Gassons Lane, SOMERTON, SOMERSET, TA11 6HW.
RATTENBURY, Mr. Neil William, BSc ACA *1991;* 31 Stewart Road, HARPENDEN, HERTFORDSHIRE, AL5 4QE.
RATTI, Miss. Kerti, BA ACA *2005;* 187 Waller Road, Telegraph Hill, LONDON, SE14 5LX.
RATTI, Miss. Sujata, BSc ACA *2001;* Plaza Asensio Magraner, Perez no1 13a, 46022 VALENCIA, SPAIN.
RATTIGAN, Mr. Liam, BA ACA *2003;* Flat C, 128 Salusbury Road, LONDON, NW6 6PB.
•**RATTIGAN, Mrs. Lynn Stacey, BSc ACA** *1990;* Ernst & Young LLP, 1 More London Place, LONDON, SE1 2AF. See also Ernst & Young Europe LLP
RATTNER, Mr. Eytan, BSc ACA *1990;* 158 Maplin Way, Thorpe Bay, SOUTHEND-ON-SEA, SS1 3ND.
RATTRAY, Mr. Andrew, BA ACA *1990;* Birchall Blackburn Solicitors, Merchant House, 38-46 Avenham Street, PRESTON, PR1 3BN.
RATTRAY, Miss. Hannah Louise, BA(Hons) ACA *2002;* 7 Cavendish Road, ST. ALBANS, HERTFORDSHIRE, AL1 5EF.
RATTRAY, Mr. James Stephen, FCA *1964;* 59 Chantry View Road, GUILDFORD, GU1 3XU.
RAUBENHEIMER, Mrs. Danellahanna Yang, BSc(Hons) ACA *2003;* Sumaya, Undershore Road, LYMINGTON, HAMPSHIRE, SO41 5SA.
RAUCH, Mr. Joseph Peter, FCA *1963;* Cherry Tree Cottage, The Close, Wonersh, GUILDFORD, GU5 0PA.
RAUCHENBERG, Dr. Richard Paul, BSc ACA *2010;* 6 Styvechale Avenue, COVENTRY, CV5 6DX.
RAUZ, Mr. Qavi-Ul-Amin, BSc ACA *1992;* 1908/1 Kings Cross Road, RUSHCUTTERS BAY, NSW 2011, AUSTRALIA.
RAVAL, Mr. Chetan, BSc(Econ) ACA *2002;* 9 Laburnum Court, STANMORE, MIDDLESEX, HA7 4JP.
RAVAL, Miss. Deepa, BSc(Hons) ACA *2002;* 19 Pinner Park Gardens, HARROW, MIDDLESEX, HA2 6LQ.
•**RAVAL, Mr. Maunik Manharbhai, ACA** *2011;* JMR Financial Consultancy Ltd, Flat 5, Embassy Court, 76 Kenton Road, HARROW, MIDDLESEX HA3 8BB.
RAVAL, Mr. Pradipkumar, FCA *1981;* 9 Woodstone Court, DANBURY, CT 06811-3400, UNITED STATES.
RAVAL, Mr. Punal, BSc ACA *2009;* 42 Homerton Road, LUTON, BEDFORDSHIRE, LU3 2UL.
RAVAT, Mr. Hamid, BA ACA *1995;* 4 Clumber Road, LEICESTER, LE5 4FH.
RAVAT, Mr. Imran, ACA *2009;* 105 Plashet Road, LONDON, E13 0RA.
RAVAT, Mr. Nitin Savji, BSc FCA *1999;* with BG Group plc, 100 Thames Valley Park Drive, READING, RG6 1PT.
RAVDEN, Mr. David Bernard, FCA *1973;* 57 Queens Grove, LONDON, NW8 6EN.
RAVEN, Mr. Christopher Alan Norman, FCA *1967;* White Cottage, Marine Drive, Widemouth Bay, BUDE, CORNWALL, EX23 0AQ.
•**RAVEN, Mr. Colin John, FCA** *1974;* (Tax Fac), F.W. Berringer & Co, Lygon House, 50 London Road, BROMLEY, BR1 3RA.
•**RAVEN, Mr. Gary John, FCA** *1991;* (Tax Fac), Barrons, Monometer House, Rectory Grove, LEIGH-ON-SEA, ESSEX, SS9 2HN. See also Barrons Limited
RAVEN, Mr. George Sidney, FCA *1969;* 225 Darkes Lane, POTTERS BAR, EN6 1BX.
RAVEN, Mr. John Edwin, FCA *1973;* 11b Central Way, Cranbourne Hall, Winkfield, WINDSOR, BERKSHIRE, SL4 4UB. (Life Member)
RAVEN, Mr. Mark Clifford, BA FCA *1984;* 17 Nunnery Way, Clifford, WETHERBY, WEST YORKSHIRE, LS23 6SL.
RAVEN, Mr. Michael John, BA FCA *1983;* HSBC Bank USA, Group Risk IT, 9/F One HSBC Center, BUFFALO, NY 14203, UNITED STATES.
•**RAVEN, Mr. Neil Walter, FCA** *1981;* Griffin Chapman, Blackburn House, 32a Crouch Street, COLCHESTER, CO3 3HH.
RAVEN, Mr. Peter Leo, MBE FCA FCT *1962;* Ballyin Garden House, Lismore, WATERFORD, COUNTY WATERFORD, IRELAND. (Life Member)
•**RAVEN, Mr. Peter Micheal, FCA** *1981;* (Tax Fac), Peter M. Raven, The White House, 318 Manchester Road, West Timperley, ALTRINCHAM, CHESHIRE WA14 5NB.
RAVEN, Mr. Timothy Charles Henry, BA ACA *2005;* 51a Perham Road, LONDON, W14 9SP.

RAVENDRAN, Mr. Rajapakiam, ACA *1986;* PO Box 6180, EAST PERTH, WA 6892, AUSTRALIA.
RAVENHILL, Mr. Simon Philip, BA FCA *1989;* The Mount, Brantfell Road, Bowness-On-Windermere, WINDERMERE, LA23 3AE.
RAVENSCROFT, Mr. Alan Peter, BSc FCA *1956;* Oakengates, 37 Forest View, North Chingford, LONDON, E4 7AU. (Life Member)
RAVENSCROFT, Mr. Andrew Mark, BA ACA *1999;* 45 Elizabeth Avenue, La Route Orange St. Brelade, JERSEY, JE3 8GR.
RAVENSCROFT, Mrs. Candy Ann, BA FCA *1989;* Pook Pit Cottage, Whitegates Lane, WADHURST, TN5 6QG.
RAVENSCROFT, Mr. Frank Alan, FCA *1950;* 15 Chesham Road, WILMSLOW, SK9 6EZ. (Life Member)
RAVENSCROFT, Mr. Kenneth James, BSc FCA *1963;* 34 Firs Crescent, Freshfield Formby, LIVERPOOL, L37 1PT.
RAVENSCROFT, Mr. Michael Ronald, BA ACA *1991;* Pook Pit Cottage, Whitegates Lane, WADHURST, TN5 6QG.
RAVENSCROFT, Mr. Pelham Francis, BA FCA *1955;* Oakwoods Farmhouse, Selborne, ALTON, GU34 3BS. (Life Member)
RAVENSCROFT, Mr. Raymond, FCA *1947;* Glenville, Salters Lane, Lower Moore, PERSHORE, WR10 2PQ. (Life Member)
RAVENSCROFT, Mr. Richard Anthony, FCA *1968;* Warren Cottage, Hophurst Lane, Crawley Down, CRAWLEY, RH10 4LJ.
RAVENSDALE, Mr. Robert Cyril, FCA *1954;* 56 Ladywood Avenue, BELPER, DERBYSHIRE, DE56 1HT. (Life Member)
RAVER, Mr. Harold Mark, FCA *1972;* S J Phillips Ltd, 139 New Bond Street, LONDON, W1S 2TL.
RAVI, Mr. Vikram, BSc ACA *2004;* 15 The Warren, BILLERICAY, ESSEX, CM12 0LW.
RAVID, Mr. Barak, BSc ACA *1999;* with KPMG LLP, 55 Second Street, Suite 1400, SAN FRANCISCO, CA 94105, UNITED STATES.
RAVINDRAN NAIR, Miss. Ramya, MSc ACA *2007;* Flat 204, Belvedere Heights, 199 Lisson Grove, LONDON, NW8 8HZ.
RAVIPRAKASH, Miss. Gajendri, ACA *2010;* 12 Southwell Gardens, LONDON, SW7 4RL.
RAVIPRAKASH, Miss. Gayathri, ACA *2011;* 55 Jalan Limau Manis, Bangsar Park, 59000 KUALA LUMPUR, MALAYSIA.
RAVJI, Miss. Bhavista, BSc ACA *2010;* 24 Milverton Gardens, ILFORD, ESSEX, IG3 8DS.
RAW, Mr. Christopher James, JP BSocSc FCA *1999;* 17 Copperbeech Close, Harborne, BIRMINGHAM, B32 2HT.
RAW, Mr. Gordon James Donald, BSc ACA *1988;* Charles Letts & Co Ltd, Thornybank Industrial Estate, DALKEITH, EH22 2NE.
RAW, Mr. James Robert Foster, FCA *1960;* 2 Old Farm Court, Comberton Road, Toft, CAMBRIDGE, CB3 7WH. (Life Member)
RAW, Mrs. Joanne Lesley, BSocSc ACA *2001;* 17 Copperbeech Close, Harborne, BIRMINGHAM, B32 2HT.
RAW, Mr. Thomas Spensley, FCA *1952;* 5 Manor Road, DARLINGTON, DL3 8ET. (Life Member)
RAWAL, Mr. Hemang, BA ACA *2002;* 53 Orchard Grove, Kenton, HARROW, HA3 4QR.
•**RAWAL, Mr. Sudhir, FCA** *1987;* HW Lee Associates LLP, New Derwent House, 69-73 Theobalds Road, LONDON, WC1X 8TA.
•**RAWAT, Mr. Ayoob Mamode Hossen, FCA** *1975;* Cabinet Comptable - Ayoob Rawat, 37/39 Avenue Dumas, 1206 GENEVA, SWITZERLAND.
RAWAT, Mr. Omar Ajum, ACA *1981;* Finacc, 3rd Floor PCL Building, 43 Sir William Newton Street, PORT LOUIS, MAURITIUS.
RAWCLIFFE, Mr. Gerald Richard, MA ACA *1987;* 69 Grove Avenue, LONDON, N10 2AL.
RAWCLIFFE, Mr. James Maurice, BA ACA *1994;* PO BOX 1567, GEORGETOWN, GRAND CAYMAN, KY1-1110, CAYMAN ISLANDS.
RAWCLIFFE, Mr. James Overbury, FCA *1953;* 45 Rosalyn Court, FREDONIA, NY 14063, UNITED STATES. (Life Member)
RAWCLIFFE, Mr. Michael, BA ACA *2010;* 72a Cambridge Street, LONDON, SW1V 4QQ.
RAWCLIFFE, Mr. Roger Capron, MA FCA TEP *1960;* The Malt House, Bridge Street, Castletown, ISLE OF MAN, IM9 1ET. (Life Member)
RAWCLIFFE, Mr. Thomas Mawdsley, BA FCA *1952;* 17 Southwood Park, Southwood Lawn Road, LONDON, N6 5SG. (Life Member)
RAWDON SMITH, Ms. Christine Amanda, BSc ACA *1992;* 72 Monument Street, PETERBOROUGH, PE1 4AG.
•**RAWI, Mr. Radwan Al, FCA** *1974;* (Tax Fac), Rawi & Co LLP, 128 Ebury Street, LONDON, SW1W 9QQ.
RAWJI, Mr. Amin-Mohamed Aziz Kurji, BSc ACA *1989;* 9 Alderdale Grove, WILMSLOW, SK9 1BP.
RAWJI, Mrs. Masuma, BBA ACA *2009;* Flat 42 Cherry Court, 621 Uxbridge Road, PINNER, MIDDLESEX, HA5 3PS.
•**RAWKINS, Mr. Robert Michael, FCA** *1971;* with RSM Tenon Audit Limited, Sumner House, St. Thomas's Road, CHORLEY, LANCASHIRE, PR7 1HP.
RAWLA, Miss. Chandni, ACA *2009;* Flat 11B, Dimple Court, 26 Theatre Road, KOLKATA 700017, WEST BENGAL, INDIA.
RAWLE, Mr. James Alexander, BA ACA *1986;* Mumbleys Cottage, Mumbleys Lane, kINGTON, Thornbury, BRISTOL, BS35 3JZ.
RAWLE, Mr. John Edward, FCA *1968;* (Tax Fac), with Reeves & Co LLP, 37 St. Margarets Street, CANTERBURY, KENT, CT1 2TU.
RAWLENCE, Mr. Simon Edward Fitzgerald, MA FCA *1972;* Flat 3, Charnwood House, 11 Charnwood Road, SALISBURY, WILTSHIRE, SP2 7HT.
RAWLES, Mr. Matthew, BSc ACA *2006;* 701 Stonehouse Park, Sperry Way, STONEHOUSE, GLOUCESTERSHIRE, GL10 3UT.
•**RAWLIN, Mrs. Catherine Mary, FCA MAE MCIArb CFE** *1989;* RGL LLP, 8th Floor, Dashwood, 69 Old Broad Street, LONDON, EC2M 1QS.
RAWLING, Dr. Alan John, ACA *1989;* Audit Commission, Nicholson House, Lime Kiln Close, Stoke Gifford, BRISTOL, BS34 8SU.
RAWLING, Mrs. Alison Helen, BA(Hons) ACA *2004;* 39 Rushton Drive, MIDDLEWICH, CW10 0NJ.
RAWLING, Mrs. Ann Elizabeth, BSc ACA *1993;* Location Code SHM 338, Santander UK Plc Santander House, 201 Grafton Gate East, MILTON KEYNES, MK9 1AN.
RAWLING, Mr. Jonathan Martin, LLB FCA *2000;* Zurich Financial Services, The Gate Building, DIFC, PO BOX 50389, DUBAI, UNITED ARAB EMIRATES.
RAWLING, Mr. Mark, BSc ACA *2005;* Flat 8 Claughton Court 60 Russet Drive, ST. ALBANS, HERTFORDSHIRE, AL4 0AS.
RAWLINGS, Mr. Alex, ACA *2009;* Flat 115 The High, Streatham High Road, LONDON, SW16 1HA.
RAWLINGS, Mrs. Carolyn, BSc FCA *1989;* British Petroleum Co Ltd, 4 Longwalk Road Stockley Park, UXBRIDGE, MIDDLESEX, UB11 1FE.
•**RAWLINGS, Mr. Colin Clifford, BA FCA** *1994;* Deloitte LLP, Hill House, 1 Little New Street, LONDON, EC4A 3TR. See also Deloitte & Touche LLP
•**RAWLINGS, Mr. Derek Charles, BSc FCA CF** *1997;* Rawlinson & Hunter, Eighth Floor, 6 New Street Square, New Fetter Lane, LONDON, EC4A 3AQ.
RAWLINGS, Mr. Jamie, BA ACA *1999;* Gabled Cottage Byron Road, Twyford, READING, RG10 0AE.
RAWLINGS, Mr. John Graham, BSc ACA *1990;* 9 Sandringham Gardens, Muscliff, BOURNEMOUTH, DORSET, BH9 3QW.
RAWLINGS, Mr. Jonathan Geoffrey, ACA *2008;* Flat 21 North Contemporis, 20 Merchants Road Clifton, BRISTOL, BS8 4HH.
RAWLINGS, Mrs. Katherine Emma, BSc ACA *2000;* 6 Old Nursery View, Kennington, OXFORD, OX1 5NT.
RAWLINGS, Mr. Kevin Hedley, BA ACA *1999;* Caparo Plc, Caparo House, Popes Lane, OLDBURY, WEST MIDLANDS, B69 4PJ.
•**RAWLINGS, Mrs. Lynda Alison, ACA** *1992;* Ellay, Maple Court, Quarry Lane, Cricket Hill, YATELEY, HAMPSHIRE GU46 6XW.
RAWLINGS, Mrs. Margaret, BSc FCA CIOT *1991;* Summerfield House, Upper Wield, ALRESFORD, HAMPSHIRE, SO24 9RT.
RAWLINGS, Mr. Mark Anthony, BA ACA *1992;* 3 Stanbrook Road, Belmont, HEREFORD, HR2 7ZA.
•**RAWLINGS, Mr. Mark Anthony, BA ACA** *1986;* (Tax Fac), Mark Rawlings, Summerfield House, Upper Wield, ALRESFORD, SO24 9RT.
RAWLINGS, Miss. Melanie, BA ACA *2003;* with Deloitte LLP, Mountbatten House, 1 Grosvenor Square, SOUTHAMPTON, SO15 2BZ.
RAWLINGS, Mrs. Nicola Jane, LLB ACA *2001;* Oakwood, East Harting, PETERSFIELD, HAMPSHIRE, GU31 5NF.
RAWLINGS, Mr. Nigel Charles, BSc ACA *1987;* 31 Shalbourne Rise, CAMBERLEY, SURREY, GU15 2EJ.
RAWLINGS, Mr. Nigel Keith, BSc FCA *1980;* Broadoak, 18 Hollin Lane Styal, WILMSLOW, SK9 4JH.
RAWLINGS, Miss. Rebecca Daisy, MA ACA *2000;* 67 rue de Crequi, 69006 LYON, FRANCE.
RAWLINGS, Mr. Robin Ian, FCA *1958;* 7 Draycott Drive, # 19-02, SINGAPORE 259421, SINGAPORE. (Life Member)
•**RAWLINGS, Mr. Stephen Bruce, BA ACA** *1986;* (Tax Fac), Wootton Manor Farm, Westwell Lane, Charing, ASHFORD, TN27 0DU.
•**RAWLINGS, Mr. Stuart Andrew, BA FCA** *1980;* (Tax Fac), Rawlings Professionals Ltd, Craven House, Lansbury Estate, 102 Lower Guildford Road, Knaphill, WOKING SURREY GU21 2EP.
RAWLINS, Mr. Alun Parry, BSc FCA *1981;* 5 Clos Brynderi, Rhiwbina, CARDIFF, CF14 6NN.
RAWLINS, Mr. Anthony Stephen, FCA *1977;* 193 Sopwith Cresent, Merley, WIMBORNE, BH21 1SR.
RAWLINS, Mr. Christopher Edward, MA FCA *1973;* 27 Silverdale Close, SHEFFIELD, S11 9JN.
RAWLINS, Miss. Donna Kathryn, BA ACA *2006;* 40 Colonel Grantham Avenue, AYLESBURY, BUCKINGHAMSHIRE, HP19 9AP.
RAWLINS, Mr. Malcolm Julian, BSc ACA *1979;* Financial Services Authority, 25 North Colonnade, LONDON, E14 5HS.
RAWLINS, Mr. Peter Jeremy, BA FCA *1967;* Conyers Place, 2 West Courtyard, Hornby, BEDALE, NORTH YORKSHIRE, DL8 1DG.
RAWLINS, Miss. Rhianna Jane, MSc BSc(Hons) ACA *2010;* 78a Barkham Ride, Finchampstead, WOKINGHAM, BERKSHIRE, RG40 4ET.
RAWLINS, Mr. Steven Clive, BCom FCA *1989;* Brackens Forest Road, East Horsley, LEATHERHEAD, KT24 5BA.
RAWLINSON, Mr. Anthony Paul, BA ACA *1982;* Shepherds Hill Hall, 13 Shepherds Hill, LONDON, N6 5QJ.
RAWLINSON, Mr. Barry, FCA *1975;* The Orchard, Primrose Lane, Highburton, HUDDERSFIELD, HD8 0QY.
RAWLINSON, Mr. Charles Frederick Melville, MA FCA FCT *1958;* (Member of Council 1995 - 1997), The Old Forge, Arkesden, SAFFRON WALDEN, CB11 4EX. (Life Member)
•**RAWLINSON, Mr. David John, FCA FCCA** *1974;* Rawlinson Pryde & Partners, Argent House, 5 Goldington Road, BEDFORD, MK40 3JY. See also Rawlinson Pryde Limited
RAWLINSON, Mrs. Emma Jane, BA ACA *2006;* Copley Cottage, Singleton Road, Weeton, PRESTON, PR4 3PA.
RAWLINSON, Mr. Henry Thomas, BA ACA *1988;* Woodlands, Bates Hill, Ightham, SEVENOAKS, TN15 9BG.
RAWLINSON, Mr. Jonathan Mark, BSc ACA *1990;* The East Wing Crosland Hill Hall, 7 Crosland Hill Road, HUDDERSFIELD, HD4 5NX.
RAWLINSON, Mr. Keith Burton, FCA *1958;* 13 Winchester Drive, Norris Hill Park, STOCKPORT, SK4 2NU. (Life Member)
RAWLINSON, Mr. Kenneth, FCA *1968;* 10 The Dunterns, ALNWICK, NORTHUMBERLAND, NE66 1AL.
RAWLINSON, Mrs. Nicola Jane, BA ACA *1994;* 94 Kelmscott Road, LONDON, SW11 6PT.
•**RAWLINSON, Mr. Paul Stephen, MA ACA** *1986;* PricewaterhouseCoopers LLP, 1 Embankment Place, LONDON, WC2N 6RH. See also PricewaterhouseCoopers
RAWLINSON, Mr. Robert Gerrard, FCA *1954;* 71 Greenacres, Fulwood, PRESTON, PR2 7DB. (Life Member)
RAWLINSON, Mr. Stephen Anthony, BA FCA *1977;* Spinney Hill House, Sharnbrook Road, Souldrop, BEDFORD, MK44 1EX.
•**RAWLINSON, Mr. Stuart Charles, FCA** *1975;* Northpoint Accountants, 61a High Street, ALTON, HAMPSHIRE, GU34 1AB.
RAWLINSON, Mr. Terence, FCA *1961;* Orion, 11 Ingrams Road, Tetney, GRIMSBY, DN36 5LW. (Life Member)
RAWLINSON, Mr. William Giles, BA BSc ACA *1994;* The Shire, O'Keys Lane, Fernhill Heath, WORCESTER, WR3 8RL.
RAWNSLEY, Mr. Paul Michael, BA ACA *1996;* 2a Corner Gate Daisy Hill, Westhoughton, BOLTON, BL5 2SE.
RAWORTH, Mr. Paul John Basil, FCA *1968;* 1 Brandy Mount, Cheriton, ALRESFORD, SO24 0QQ. (Life Member)
•**RAWSE, Mr. John Malcolm, FCA** *1964;* Rawse Varley & Co, Lloyds Bank Chambers, Hustlergate, BRADFORD, BD1 1UQ.
RAWSON, Mr. Daniel, MChem MSci ACA *2011;* Rolls-Royce Plc Jubilee House, 4 St. Christophers Way Pride Park, DERBY, DE24 8JY.
RAWSON, Ms. Emma, DPhil BSc(Hons) ACA *2011;* 1c Moreland Cottages, Fairfield Road, LONDON, E3 2QN.
RAWSON, Mr. Gordon, BSc ACA *1980;* Eversley, Heath Road, Skircoat Green, HALIFAX, HX3 0BU. (Life Member)
RAWSON, Mr. Jonathan Ralph, ACA *1980;* with Debson & Co., Galley House, Second Floor, Moon Lane, BARNET, HERTFORDSHIRE EN5 5YL.
RAWSON, Mr. Kenneth, FCA *1952;* Strathmore, The Homestead, Menston, ILKLEY, LS29 6PB. (Life Member)
RAWSON, Mr. Michael John, FCA *1973;* 580 Fulwood Road, SHEFFIELD, S10 3QE.
•**RAWSON, Mr. Nicholas, FCA** *1992;* (Tax Fac), Knill James, One Bell Lane, LEWES, EAST SUSSEX, BN7 1JU.
RAWSON, Mr. Paul Edwin, BA(Hons) ACA *2000;* 46 Lichfield Lane, MANSFIELD, NOTTINGHAMSHIRE, NG18 4RE.
RAWSON, Mr. Philip Andrew James, BA ACA *1989;* 11355 Enyart Road, LOVELAND, OH 45140, UNITED STATES.
RAWSON, Miss. Samantha Maria, BSc ACA *1991;* 1 Lee Fair Court, Tingley, WAKEFIELD, WF3 1UH.
RAWSTHORN, Mr. David James, MA ACA *1985;* Moor House, Heads Nook, CARLISLE, CA8 9BX.
RAWSTORNE, Miss. Victoria Ann, BA FCA *1985;* 119 Cowper Road, LONDON, W7 1EL.
RAWSTRON, Mr. Michael John, FCA *1963;* 71 Clarence Road, Bickley, BROMLEY, BR1 2DD. (Life Member)
RAWSTRON, Mr. Richard, MEng ACA *2006;* 25 North Cross Road, LONDON, SE22 9ET.
RAWSTRON, Mr. Ronald Freeman, FCA *1962;* The Penthouse, 39 Sunningdale Court, LYTHAM ST. ANNES, LANCASHIRE, FY8 3UP.
•**RAY, Mr. Alan Charles, FCA** *1978;* (Tax Fac), FSP (UK) Ltd, 87 Firs Park Avenue, Winchmore Hill, LONDON, N21 2PU.
RAY, Mr. Andrew John, BSc ACA *1978;* 41 Beech Bank, Unthank Road, NORWICH, NR2 2AL.
RAY, Mr. Atri Narayan, ACA *1985;* 378 Sugar Maple Lane, RICHMOND HILL L4C 4C4, ON, CANADA.
•**RAY, Mr. Brian Edward, FCA** *1968;* Brian E Ray, 30 Old Sneed Avenue, Stoke Bishop, BRISTOL, BS9 1SE.
RAY, Mr. Christopher, FCA *1971;* (Tax Fac), 178 Hanging Lane, Northfield, BIRMINGHAM, B31 5DN. (Life Member)
•**RAY, Mr. Damon, BCom FCA** *1968;* 20 Victoria Road, MARLOW, BUCKINGHAMSHIRE, SL7 1DW.
RAY, Mr. Daniel, BA ACA *2005;* 3 Tinbridge Oast, Canterbury Road, FAVERSHAM, KENT, ME13 9LJ.
•**RAY, Mr. David William, FCA** *1970;* David Ray, 4 Walk Mill, Dalston, CARLISLE, CA5 7QW.
RAY, Mr. Derek Frank, FCA JDipMA *1960;* 7 Sevenoaks Avenue, Ainsdale, SOUTHPORT, PR8 2PT. (Life Member)
RAY, Mr. Devarshi, ACA *2011;* 64 Lightcliffe Road, LONDON, N13 5PW.
RAY, Mr. Eamon, BSc ACA *2011;* 95 Highview Gardens, POTTERS BAR, HERTFORDSHIRE, EN6 5PL.
RAY, Edward Ernest, Esq CBE BCom FCA *1950;* (President 1982 - 1983) (Member of Council 1973 - 1988), Southgate, Wiveton Road, Blakeney, HOLT, NR25 7NJ.
RAY, Ms. Elaine, ACA *2005;* Flat 6 The Woodlands, Aberdeen Park, LONDON, N5 2BB.
RAY, Mr. Henry Kenneth Wakelin, BSc ACA *1997;* Contractors Bonding Limited, Tower One Level 8, Shortland Centre, 51 Shortland, AUCKLAND, NEW ZEALAND.
RAY, Mrs. Jacqueline Clare, LLB ACA *2006;* Newstyle Enterprise Ltd, 11 Short Wyre Street, COLCHESTER, CO1 1LN.
RAY, Mr. Jayanta Prasanna, MPhil BA ACA *1999;* Flat 18, Manor Court, Aylmer Road, LONDON, N2 0PJ.
RAY, Mrs. Joanne Mary, BA ACA *1988;* (Tax Fac), Fernbank Lavender Hall Lane, Berkswell, COVENTRY, CV7 7BN.
RAY, Mr. John Stewart, FCA *1969;* Birchley, 2 West End Farm, Long Marston Road, Cheddington, LEIGHTON BUZZARD, BEDFORDSHIRE LU7 0RS.
RAY, Mr. Jonathan Edgar, FCA *1996;* #30 1035 64th Ave SE, CALGARY T2H 2J7, AB, CANADA.
•**RAY, Mr. Justin Sebastian Anthony, BSc FCA CF** *1996;* 31 Cavendish Road, OXFORD, OX2 7TN.
RAY, Mr. Kalyan, BCom FCA FSI *1978;* 95 Highview Gardens, POTTERS BAR, EN6 5PL.
RAY, Mr. Mark William, BA ACA *1989;* Gerstekamp 17, 7231 BJ WARNSVELD, NETHERLANDS.
RAY, Mr. Matthew Alexander, BA ACA *2007;* 8 Aulton Place, LONDON, SE11 4AG.
RAY, Mr. Michael Edward, BSc ACA *1988;* 24 St Stephens Avenue, ST. ALBANS, AL3 4AD.
RAY, Mr. Michael John, FCA *1972;* 3 Johnston Close, Rogerstone, NEWPORT, NP10 0AY. (Life Member)
RAY, Mr. Neil, FCA *1971;* Schlumberger plc, 10 Duchess St, LONDON, W1G 9AB.
RAY, Mr. Peter William, BA ACA *1989;* 3 Clevedon Mansions, Cambridge Road, TWICKENHAM, TW1 2JA.

RAY, Miss. Sarah Karen, MSc BA ACA *1998;* 33 Hathaway Green Lane, STRATFORD-UPON-AVON, WARWICKSHIRE, CV37 9HX.
RAY, Mr. Stephen Anthony, LLB ACA *1985;* 34 Llansannor Drive, Anchor Court, CARDIFF, CF10 4AW.
RAY, Mr. Stephen Bruce, BA ACA *1988;* 26th Floor Portland House, Bressenden Street, LONDON, SW1E 5BG.
RAY, Mr. Stephen Douglas, BA ACA *1987;* Linpac Group Ltd, 3180 Park Square, Birmingham Business Park, BIRMINGHAM, B37 7YN.
RAY, Mr. Subir Kumar, FCA *1969;* 32 Newport Drive, PRINCETON JUNCTION, NJ 08550, UNITED STATES.
RAY, Mr. Sukhendu, FCA *1951;* 6B Sonali Appartments, 8/2A Alipore Park Road, CALCUTTA 700 027, INDIA. (Life Member)
RAY, Mr. Sunandan, ACA *1983;* 320 Southdown Road, Lloyd Harbor, NEW YORK, NY 11743, UNITED STATES.
RAY, Mr. Supriya Kinkar, BA ACA *1996;* 1 Redmarley Road, CHELTENHAM, GLOUCESTERSHIRE, GL52 5GA.
RAY, Miss. Tania Alys, BA ACA *2010;* with PKF Australia Ltd, Level 10, 1 Margaret Street, SYDNEY, NSW 2000, AUSTRALIA.
RAY, Mr. Thomas William, FCA *1974;* 26 Astwick Road, Stotfold, HITCHIN, SG5 4AT.
•**RAY, Mr. Utpal Kumar, FCA** *1979;* Pracserve Limited, Falcon House, 257 Burlington Road, NEW MALDEN, KT3 4NE. See also SME Accountancy Limited
RAY-JOHNSON, Mrs. Karen Louise, BSc ACA *1998;* 44 Yurilla Drive Bellevue Heights, ADELAIDE, SA 5050, AUSTRALIA.
RAY-JONES, Mr. Philip Raymond, FCA *1971;* (Tax Fac), 6 Senga Road, HACKBRIDGE, SURREY, SM6 7BQ. (Life Member)
RAYBOULD, Mrs. Amanda Jayne, BSc ACA *1994;* 151 Little Sutton Lane, SUTTON COLDFIELD, WEST MIDLANDS, B75 6SW.
RAYBOULD, Mr. Michael Trevor, BSc ACA *1995;* 22 Mirfield Road, SOLIHULL, B91 1JD.
RAYBOULD, Mrs. Philippa Gail, ACA *1986;* 18 Grayshott Close, BROMSGROVE, WORCESTERSHIRE, B61 8PT.
RAYDEN, Mr. Christopher Michael, BA ACA *1998;* 35 Beech Avenue, Gatley, CHEADLE, SK8 4LS.
RAYEN, Mr. Sampath, ACA *1994;* 5852 Greensboro Drive, MISSISSAUGA L5M 5S9, ON, CANADA.
RAYER, Mr. John Bernard, FCA *1972;* B D O Stoy Hayward, 55 Baker Street, LONDON, W1U 7EU.
RAYERS, Mrs. Catherine Joy, BA FCA *1988;* Holly Tree Cottage, Eccups Lane, Morley Green, WILMSLOW, CHESHIRE, SK9 5NZ.
RAYFIELD, Mr. Ashley Barron James, FCA *1972;* El-Monte House, 5 Buckeridge Avenue, TEIGNMOUTH, TQ14 8LX.
RAYFIELD, Mr. Martin James, BSc ACA *1982;* Peterscourt, Walkern Road, Benington, STEVENAGE, HERTFORDSHIRE, SG2 7LN.
RAYFIELD, Mr. Thomas James, ACA *2009;* Whitehall, Knightons Lane, Dunsfold, GODALMING, SURREY, GU8 4NY.
RAYKUNDALIA, Mr. Sanjiv Rasiklal, BA ACA *1993;* Quorn House, Lunghurst Road, Woldingham, CATERHAM, SURREY, CR3 7EJ.
•**RAYLAND, Mr. Neill Antony, BA FCA** *1987;* Kirk Newsholme Ltd, 4315 Park Approach, Thorpe Park, LEEDS, LS15 8GB.
RAYMAN, Dr. Robert Anthony, PhD BCom FCA *1963;* 178 Alwoodley Lane, LEEDS, LS17 7PF.
•①**RAYMENT, Mr. Christopher Kim, BSc ACA** *1982;* BDO LLP, 125 Colmore Row, BIRMINGHAM, B3 3SD. See also BDO Stoy Hayward LLP
RAYMENT, Mr. Ian Leslie, BCom ACA *1982;* 20 Princeton Road, TORONTO M8X 2E2, ON, CANADA.
RAYMENT, Mr. Jeremy Noel, FCA *1990;* with Menzies LLP, Heathrow Business Centre, 65 High Street, EGHAM, SURREY, TW20 9EY.
RAYMENT, Mr. Leonard Francis, FCA *1967;* 131 High Road, North Weald, EPPING, CM16 6EA.
RAYMENT, Mr. William Edward, BSc ACA *1987;* PO Box 2084, NEW FARM, QLD 4005, AUSTRALIA.
RAYMER, Mr. Garth Anthony, FCA *1967;* Woodwards House, Cooks Hill, Wick, PERSHORE, WR10 3PA.
•**RAYMOND, Mr. Anthony James, MA FCA** *1972;* Little Place, 38 Beaucroft Lane, Colehill, WIMBORNE, BH21 2PA.
RAYMOND, Mr. Ellis, FCA *1972;* The KBSP Partnership, Harben House Harben Parade Finchley Road, LONDON, NW3 6LH. (Life Member)
•**RAYMOND, Mr. Jonathan Barrett, BSc FCA CTA** *1994;* Barrett ATS Limited, 1 Ellis Barn, The Old Dairy, Badbury, SWINDON, SN4 0EU.
RAYMOND, Mr. Michael, FCA *1965;* 44 Malthouse Square, BEACONSFIELD, HP9 2LE.
RAYMOND, Mr. Michael Gordon, BSc ACA *1980;* Forest Edge, Hangersley Hill, RINGWOOD, BH24 3JS.
RAYMOND, Miss. Miriam, ACA *2008;* 17 Russell Road, BUCKHURST HILL, IG9 5QJ.
RAYMOND, Mr. William George, FCA *1964;* (Tax Fac), Clos de L'Ecluse, Sark, GUERNSEY, GY9 0SF.
RAYMONT, Mr. Nicholas, BSc FCA *1975;* 11 Ainsworth Place, CAMBRIDGE, CB1 2PG.
RAYNER, Mr. Andrew Piers Courtauld, MA FCA *1968;* PO Box 125, HANA, HI 96713, UNITED STATES.
RAYNER, Mr. Anthony Wellesley, FCA *1950;* 4 Lansdown Gardens, Chillerton, NEWPORT, Isle of Wight, PO30 3HJ. (Life Member)
RAYNER, Mr. Benjamin Thomas William, ACA *1993;* (Tax Fac), Scotsdale Nursery & Garden Centre Ltd, 120 Cambridge Road, Great Shelford, CAMBRIDGE, CB22 5JT.
RAYNER, Mrs. Catriona, BA ACA *1979;* 75 Greenwich South Street, LONDON, SE10 8NT.
RAYNER, Mr. Christopher William, BA(Hons) ACA *2004;* Bell Cottage, The High Street, Limpsfield, OXTED, RH8 0DR.
•**RAYNER, Mrs. Clair Louise, ACA DChA** *2002;* McCabe Ford Williams, Bank Chambers, 1 Central Ave., SITTINGBOURNE, ME10 4AE.
RAYNER, Mrs. Fiona Jane, BA ACA *1992;* Wellfield, High Bank Lane, Lostock, BOLTON, LANCASHIRE, BL6 4DT.
RAYNER, Mr. Graham Mark, BA(Hons) ACA *2001;* 2 Vale Drive, HORSHAM, WEST SUSSEX, RH12 2JX.
•**RAYNER, Mrs. Heather Gillian, BSc FCA DChA** *1980;* with MacIntyre Hudson LLP, Euro House, 1394 High Road, Whetstone, LONDON, N20 9YZ.
RAYNER, Mr. Iain Rob, BA FCA *1997;* St. James's Place, 1 Tetbury Road, CIRENCESTER, GLOUCESTERSHIRE, GL7 1FP.
•**RAYNER, Mr. Jeremy Paul, BA ACA CTA AMCT** *1992;* PricewaterhouseCoopers LLP, 101 Barbirolli Square, Lower Mosley Street, MANCHESTER, M2 3PW. See also PricewaterhouseCoopers
RAYNER, Miss. Joanne Carolyn, BA ACA *1997;* 5 Greenways, Digswell, WELWYN, HERTFORDSHIRE, AL6 0EE.
RAYNER, Mr. John Nicholas, BA ACA *1987;* KPMG AG, Wirtschaftsprüfungsgesellschaft, Emil-von-Behring-Strasse 2, 60439 FRANKFURT AM MAIN, GERMANY.
RAYNER, Mr. John Peter, BSc FCA *1976;* 29 Norval Road, WEMBLEY, HA0 3TD. (Life Member)
RAYNER, Mrs. Kay, FCA CTA *1996;* 2 Rose Grove, Ainsworth Chase, BURY, BL8 2UJ.
RAYNER, Mr. Keith Mackay, BSc FCA *1986;* 1 Carolina Place, Finchampstead, WOKINGHAM, RG40 4PQ.
RAYNER, Mr. Lee Hamilton, MA ACA *1997;* with PricewaterhouseCoopers LLP, Pricewaterhousecoopers, 12 Plumtree Court, LONDON, EC4A 4HT.
•**RAYNER, Mr. Mark, FCA** *1982;* (Tax Fac), Keens Shay Keens MK, Sovereign Court, 230 Upper Fifth Street, MILTON KEYNES, MK9 2HR.
RAYNER, Mr. Mark David, BSc ACA *1998;* Room 4436 BBC White City, British Broadcasting Corporation White City, 201 Wood Lane, LONDON, W12 7TS.
RAYNER, Mr. Mark Royston, BA ACA *1991;* Weydown House, Weydown Road, HASLEMERE, SURREY, GU27 1DS.
•**RAYNER, Mr. Martin John, BA ACA** *1998;* Wilds Limited, Lancaster House, 70-76 Blackburn Street, Radcliffe, MANCHESTER, M26 2JW.
RAYNER, Mr. Neil Firth, ACA *2009;* 96 Coniston Road, DEWSBURY, WEST YORKSHIRE, WF12 7EB.
RAYNER, Mr. Paul Adrian, BA FCA *1987;* 48 Kilham Lane, WINCHESTER, HAMPSHIRE, SO22 5QD.
RAYNER, The Revd. Paul Anthony George, BA BD FCA *1964;* 36 Amberley Road, BUCKHURST HILL, ESSEX, IG9 5QW.
RAYNER, Mr. Paul Edward, BSc ACA *1993;* (Tax Fac), 68 Habgood Road, LOUGHTON, ESSEX, IG10 1HE.
RAYNER, Mr. Paul Michael, MA ACA *2003;* Maple House Main Road, Boreham, CHELMSFORD, CM3 3JF.
RAYNER, Miss. Penelope Jane, BA ACA *1991;* PO Box 106094, AUCKLAND 1143, NEW ZEALAND.
RAYNER, Mrs. Selina, BSc ACA *2000;* 33 Cambridge Cottages, RICHMOND, SURREY, TW9 3AY.
RAYNER, Mrs. Sonia Claire, BA ACA *2000;* 50 Finch Lane, Appley Bridge, WIGAN, LANCASHIRE, WN6 9DT.
RAYNES, Ms. Alison Margaret, BA ACA *1982;* 13 Hallside Park, KNUTSFORD, CHESHIRE, WA16 8NQ.
RAYNES, Miss. Lorna Michell, BA ACA *2006;* 51 Upper Way, FARNHAM, SURREY, GU9 8RL.
•**RAYNES, Mr. Robert Vaughan Marriott, FCA** *1976;* Robert Raynes, Bridleway Cottage, 85 Priors Hill, Wroughton, SWINDON, SN4 0RL.
RAYNES, Mr. William Robert, FCA *1970;* Rogan Cottage, Church Street, Tansley, MATLOCK, DE4 5FE.
•**RAYNEY, Mr. Peter Cyril, FCA CTA(Fellow)** *1981;* (Tax Fac), Peter Rayney Tax Consulting Limited, 91 Eighth Avenue, LUTON, LU3 3DP. See also Price Pearson Ltd
•**RAYNOR, Mr. Andrew Paul, BA FCA** *1981;* RSM Tenon Limited, 66 Chiltern St, LONDON, W1U 4JT. See also Premier Strategies Limited
RAYNOR, Mr. Hubert George, FCA *1962;* (Tax Fac), 16 Beechfield, BANSTEAD, SURREY, SM7 3RG.
RAYNOR, Mr. John Robert, ACA *2010;* 2 Stocking Way, LINCOLN, LINCOLNSHIRE, LN2 4FX.
RAYNOR, Mrs. Karen Jane, BA FCA *1981;* The Manor House, Ollerton Road, Little Carlton, NEWARK, NOTTINGHAMSHIRE, NG23 6BX.
RAYNOR, Mr. Michael James, LLB ACA *2001;* 208 / 2 Wentworth Street, SYDNEY, NSW 2095, AUSTRALIA.
RAYNOR, Mrs. Pamela Rose, BSc FCA *1977;* Conde Nast Publications Ltd Vogue House, 1-2 Hanover Square, LONDON, W1S 1JU.
RAYNOR, Mrs. Shirley Barbara, FCA *1977;* 84 Winsley Hill, Limpley Stoke, BATH, BA2 7FA.
RAYNSFORD, Mr. Andrew Charles, BSc ACA *2004;* Airedale Business Centre, Lawkholme Lane, KEIGHLEY, WEST YORKSHIRE, BD21 3JQ.
RAYNSFORD, Miss. Tania Suzanne, BSc ACA *1997;* 28 Beacon Hill, WOKING, SURREY, GU21 7QR.
RAYSON, Mr. David John, FCA *1975;* Cromford Group Ltd, Old Rectory Taghole Lane, Mugginton Weston Underwood, ASHBOURNE, DERBYSHIRE, DE6 4PN.
RAYSON, Mr. Lee, BSc ACA *1995;* 37 Turnberry Drive, NUNEATON, CV11 6TT.
RAYSON, Miss. Sian Louise, BA(Hons) ACA *2002;* 18 Butlers & Colonial Wharf, LONDON, SE1 2PX.
RAYTON, Mr. Michael Antony, FCA *1958;* 2 Beechwood Rise, Douglas, ISLE OF MAN, IM2 5NE. (Life Member)
RAYVADERA, Miss. Anoli Arvind, BSc ACA *2002;* 13 Dornfell Street, LONDON, NW6 1QN.
RAYWORTH, Mrs. Elizabeth Claire, BA ACA *1997;* 3 St. Lawrence Park, CHEPSTOW, NP16 6DP.
RAZA, Mr. Atif, ACA *1983;* PO Box 200121, DOHA, QATAR.
RAZA, Ms. Saman, BA(Hons) ACA *2001;* P.O. Box 60279, DUBAI, UNITED ARAB EMIRATES.
RAZA, Mr. Zohaib Hassan, ACA *2010;* Flat 102 Falaknaz building Al Barsha 1, DUBAI, UNITED ARAB EMIRATES.
RAZAK, Mr. Kamal Mohamed Abdul, FCA *1970;* 13 Clare Close, Elstree, BOREHAMWOOD, HERTFORDSHIRE, WD6 3NJ. (Life Member)
RAZINA, Miss. Tanya, BA ACA *2004;* Ground Floor Flat, 81 Fernhead Road, LONDON, W9 3EA.
RAZNICK, Mr. Stephen Ivan, FCA *1972;* 10 Hill Hall, Theydon Mount, EPPING, CM16 7QQ.
RAZVI, Mrs. Asimah, BA ACA *2002;* 2 Mount Nod Road, Streatham, LONDON, SW16 2LQ.
RAZVI, Mr. Saleem, BSc ACA *1992;* 30/F Standard Chartered Tower, Milennium City 1, 388 Kwun Tong Road, KWUN TONG, KOWLOON, HONG KONG SAR.
RAZWI, Mr. Sayad Hassan Raza, ACA *1980;* 25 Church Road, HAYES, UB3 2LB.
•**RAZZAQ, Mr. Abdur, FCA** *1974;* A. Razzaq & Company, Suite #40 3rd floor, landmark Plaza, Jail Road, LAHORE, PAKISTAN.
RAZZAQ, Mr. Imran, BA FCA MBA *1994;* 34 Gosberton Road, LONDON, SW12 8LF.
RDULTOWSKI, Mr. Filip Dominik, BSc ACA *2009;* Pl Powstancow Slaskich 15 m 25, 53-329 WROCLAW, POLAND.
REA, Mrs. Agnieszka, BSc ACA *2003;* Clocktower House London Road, Rake, LISS, GU33 7JJ.
REA, Mrs. Eleanor Katrina, BA ACA *1991;* Bohermore, BAGENALSTOWN, COUNTY CARLOW, IRELAND.
REA, Mrs. Felice Kirsten, BSc ACA ATII *1992;* Torquil Clark Holdings Plc, St. Marks Church Hall, Chapel Ash, WOLVERHAMPTON, WV3 0TZ.
REA, Mr. James Keith, MA ACA CTA *2004;* 30 Tivoli Road, LONDON, N8 8RE.
REA, Mr. Jason Edward George, MBA FCA *1989;* 14 Rue Du Laboratoire, L-1911 LUXEMBOURG, LUXEMBOURG.
•**REA, Mr. Marcus Roger, BA ACA** *1997;* Deloitte LLP, Athene Place, 66 Shoe Lane, LONDON, EC4A 3BQ. See also Deloitte & Touche LLP
REA, Mr. Mark Anthony, BA FCA *1981;* 40 Broadwalk, WILMSLOW, SK9 5PL.
•**REA, Mr. Nicholas Laurence Sinclair, BA ACA** *1995;* PricewaterhouseCoopers LLP, 7 More London Riverside, LONDON, SE1 2RT. See also PricewaterhouseCoopers
•**REA, Mr. Nigel, ACA** *2003;* Mitchells Grievson Limited, Kensington House, 3 Kensington, BISHOP AUCKLAND, COUNTY DURHAM, DL14 6HX.
•**REA, Mr. Norman Thomas, BA FCA** *1973;* (Tax Fac), Norman T. Rea, 41 Plantation Rd, AMERSHAM, HP6 6HL.
REA, Mr. Peter Beaumont, FCA *1958;* 42 Woodville Drive, PORTSMOUTH, PO1 2TG. (Life Member)
REA, Mr. Shawn Lawrence, ACA CA(SA) *2011;* 37 Tollington Park, Islington, LONDON, N4 3QP.
REA, Mr. Steven James, BA(Hons) ACA *2003;* Clocktower House London Road, Rake, LISS, GU33 7JJ.
•**REA-PALMER, Mr. Bruce John, FCA** *1973;* Breavis Consultants, Boissiere, St Andre Nord, 47360 MONTPEZAT D'AGENAIS, FRANCE.
•**READ, Mr. Alan Charles, BSc ACA** *1992;* Ashford Read, Unit 4, Basepoint Enterprise Centre, Andersons Road, SOUTHAMPTON, SO14 5FE.
•**READ, Mr. Alexander David, BEng ACA** *2000;* Clearview Book Keeping & Accountancy Services, Little Brockley, Broadway, Shipham, WINSCOMBE, SOMERSET BS25 1UF. See also Clearview
READ, Mr. Andrew, BA ACA *1982;* 51 St. Peters Road, STOWMARKET, SUFFOLK, IP14 1LE.
READ, Mr. Andrew Richard, MA ACA *1995;* Langham Hall Hong Kong Limited, 3602 The Center, 99 Queens Road, CENTRAL, HONG KONG ISLAND, HONG KONG SAR.
READ, Mr. Benjamin Stevenson, BSc(Hons) ACA *2000;* 14 Tolverne Road, LONDON, SW20 8RA.
READ, Mr. Christopher John, BSc ACA *2006;* 45 Peplins Way, Brookmans Park, HATFIELD, HERTFORDSHIRE, AL9 7UR.
READ, Mr. Christopher Keith, BA FCA *1989;* 6 Parkview Court, 19 Cambridge Park, TWICKENHAM, TW1 2JF.
READ, Miss. Claire Frances, BA ACA *2004;* 25 Spindletree Drive, Oakwood, DERBY, DE21 2DG.
READ, Mr. Damon Frederick, ACA *1996;* Greenacre Hill Close, Wingfield, LEIGHTON BUZZARD, BEDFORDSHIRE, LU7 9QJ.
READ, Mr. Darren Robert, BA ACA *1995;* 15 Danbury Street, LONDON, N1 8LD.
•**READ, Mr. David Arthur, ACA** *1983;* (Tax Fac), Gatley Read, Prince of Wales House, 18/19 Salmon Fields Business Village, Royton, OLDHAM, OL2 6HT.
READ, Mr. David Houghton, BA ACA *1999;* 2 Church Hayes Drive, Nailsea, BRISTOL, BS48 4LX.
•**READ, Mr. David Leck, BSc ACA** *1985;* Ernst & Young LLP, 1 More London Place, LONDON, SE1 2AF. See also Ernst & Young Europe LLP
READ, Mr. Derek John, FCA *1957;* 76 Preston Road, YEOVIL, BA20 2DR. (Life Member)
READ, Mrs. Elaine, BSc ACA *2005;* 5 Brick Kiln Barns, Chaul End Road Caddington, LUTON, LU1 4AT.
READ, Mr. Eric John, MA FCA *1978;* 92 Harberton Road, LONDON, N19 3JP.
READ, Mr. Eric Stephen, BSc FCA *1974;* Willowmay Hooke Road, East Horsley, LEATHERHEAD, KT24 5DY.
•**READ, Mrs. Fiona Anne, FCA** *1981;* MWS, Kingsridge House, 601 London Road, WESTCLIFF-ON-SEA, ESSEX, SS0 9PE.
READ, Mr. Gareth Bowen, ACA *2010;* 15 Ennerdale Road, Stubbington, FAREHAM, HAMPSHIRE, PO14 2DS.
READ, Miss. Gemma Elizabeth, ACA *2009;* Hazelwoods Staverton Court, Staverton, CHELTENHAM, GLOUCESTERSHIRE, GL51 0UX.
READ, Mr. Geoffrey John, BSc ACA *1997;* 23 Trematon Place, TEDDINGTON, MIDDLESEX, TW11 9RH.
READ, Mr. Graham Calton, BSc(Hons) ACA *2002;* ul. Stanczyka 10/84, Malopolska, 30-124 KRAKOW, POLAND.
READ, Miss. Helen Joanna, MA ACA *1996;* Royal Bank of Scotland, 90-100 Southwark Street, LONDON, SE1 0SW.

READ, Mr. Ian Charles, BSc FCA *1978;* Pfizer Inc, 235 East 42nd Street, 23rd Floor 2, NEW YORK, NY 10017, UNITED STATES.
READ, Mr. James, ACA *2007;* 47 Harcourt Drive, Hillarys, PERTH, WA 6025, AUSTRALIA.
READ, Mr. James Christopher, FCA *1975;* Stirling Cottage, Glebe Lane, Abinger Common, DORKING, SURREY, RH5 6JQ.
READ, Mr. Jason Martin, BSc ACA *1998;* 3 Wilkinson Avenue, KINGS LANGLEY, NSW 2147, AUSTRALIA.
•READ, Mr. Jeremy Duncan Andrew, BSc ACA *1997;* Baker Tilly UK Audit LLP, The Pinnacle, 170 Midsummer Boulevard, MILTON KEYNES, MK9 1BP. See also Baker Tilly Tax and Advisory Services LLP
READ, Miss. Joanna, ACA *2011;* 33 Vale Drive, HORSHAM, WEST SUSSEX, RH12 2JU.
READ, Miss. Joanne Denise, ACA *2001;* 8 Massey Close, Hardingstone, NORTHAMPTON, NN4 6DW.
READ, Mr. John Brooke, BA FCA *1979;* 23 Trafalgar Road, Eaton Ford, ST. NEOTS, CAMBRIDGESHIRE, PE19 7NA.
READ, Mr. John Desmond, FCA *1976;* 11 Squirrels Green, Bookham, LEATHERHEAD, KT23 3LE.
READ, Sir John Emms, Kt FCA *1948;* Flat 68, 15 Portman Square, LONDON, W1H 9LL. (Life Member)
READ, Mr. John Penwarden, FCA *1957;* St Anne's, 11 Turner Close, Hampstead Garden Suburb, LONDON, NW11 6TU. (Life Member)
READ, Mr. Jonathan, BSc ACA *2009;* Flat 9, Norfolk House, Trig Lane, LONDON, EC4V 3QQ.
READ, Mrs. Judith Ann, FCA *1968;* 41 Casterbridge Road, DORCHESTER, DT1 2AH.
READ, Mr. Julian Edward James, BSc ACA *1992;* 54 St. Albans Avenue, LONDON, W4 5JR.
READ, Mrs. Karin, BA FCA *1982;* 64 Barnet Gate Lane, Arkley, BARNET, EN5 2AD.
READ, Miss. Katherine Susan, BSc ACA *2007;* 10 Church View, Long Marston, TRING, HERTFORDSHIRE, HP23 4QB.
READ, Mr. Kevin Charles, BEng ACA *1998;* 16b Barnsbury Terrace, LONDON, N1 1JH.
READ, Mr. Kevin Ronald, BSc ACA *1989;* 15 Valley Road, Chandler's Ford, EASTLEIGH, HAMPSHIRE, SO53 1GQ.
•READ, Mrs. Lesley Anne, FCA *1982;* Read Business Consulting Ltd, Leys House, Alveston, STRATFORD-UPON-AVON, WARWICKSHIRE, CV37 7QT.
READ, Mrs. Lisa Frances, ACA *1997;* Acorns The Glade, Hutton, BRENTWOOD, CM13 2JL.
READ, Miss. Lorna Jane, ACA *2008;* 18 High Street, Washingborough, LINCOLN, LN4 1BG.
READ, Mrs. Louise, BSc ACA *2000;* JCRegulatory Authority, 2nd Floor, Salisbury House, 1-9 Union Street, St. Helier, JERSEY JE2 3RF.
READ, Mr. Martin Lester, BSc(Hons) ACA *2001;* 47 Rudloe Road, LONDON, SW12 0DR.
READ, Mr. Martin Philip, FCA *1974;* Ashby House, 45 Petitor Road, TORQUAY, TQ1 4QF.
READ, Mr. Matthew Edward, BSc ACA *2003;* 18 Halford Road, RICHMOND, SURREY, TW10 6AP.
READ, Miss. Melanie, LLB ACA *2006;* 5 Shepherds Walk, Oakley, BASINGSTOKE, RG23 7BF.
•READ, Mr. Michael John, FCA *1973;* (Tax Fac), MJR Taxation Services Limited, 1 Cobden Road, SEVENOAKS, KENT, TN13 3UB.
READ, Mr. Michael John, BA ACA AMCT *1992;* Morgan Crucible The Quadrant, 55-57 High Street, WINDSOR, SL4 1LP.
READ, Ms. Monica Susan, BSc ACA *1988;* South West Water Plc, Peninsula House, Rydon Lane, EXETER, EX2 7HR.
READ, Mr. Neil Michael, LLB ACA *2002;* Flat 6 Broughton House, 28-30 Bullar Road, SOUTHAMPTON, SO18 1GS.
READ, Mr. Nicholas Edward, FCA *1986;* 466 Lexington Avenue, NEW YORK, NY 10017, UNITED STATES.
READ, Mr. Nicholas Kenneth Paul, BA ACA *1998;* 2 Dun Park, Kirkintilloch, GLASGOW, G66 2DU.
READ, Mr. Nigel Howard, BA(Hons) ACA *2003;* with BDO LLP, Arcadia House, Maritime Walk, Ocean Village, SOUTHAMPTON, SO14 3TL.
READ, Mr. Paul Graham, FCA *1973;* 2095 Lake Shore Blvd West, Suite 217, ETOBICOKE M8V 4G4, ON, CANADA.
•READ, Mr. Paul John, BA FCA *1986;* Acorn Accounting Solutions Limited, Shrover Cottage, Denmead, WATERLOOVILLE, HAMPSHIRE, PO7 6HN.
READ, Mr. Paul William, BA(Hons) ACA *2002;* Woods House, River Way, HARLOW, ESSEX, CM20 2DP.
READ, Mr. Peter, ACA *2008;* 35 Oakfield Street, Roath, CARDIFF, CF24 3RE.
•READ, Mr. Peter Graham, BSc FCA *1979;* KPMG LLP, 15 Canada Square, LONDON, E14 5GL. See also KPMG Europe LLP
READ, Ms. Rachel, MA ACA *1996;* Cuckoo Farm, West Anstey, SOUTH MOLTON, EX36 3PN.
READ, Mrs. Rebecca Elizabeth, BSc ACA *2007;* 23 Oakdene, COTTINGHAM, NORTH HUMBERSIDE, HU16 5AS.
READ, Mr. Richard, ACA CA(SA) *2010;* 34 Orford Gardens, TWICKENHAM, TW1 4PL.
READ, Mr. Richard James, LLB ACA *1992;* 14 Oaklands, Somerford Road, CIRENCESTER, GLOUCESTERSHIRE, GL7 1FA.
READ, Mr. Richard Michael Hodgson, BSc FCA *1961;* Holmlea, Bradford Place, PENARTH, CF64 1AF.
READ, Mr. Robert John Lythgoe, FCA *1959;* 36 Bateman Drive, OTTAWA K2G 5H2, ON, CANADA. (Life Member)
READ, Miss. Sharon Joy, ACA *2011;* 9 Wood End Road, HARPENDEN, HERTFORDSHIRE, AL5 3EE.
READ, Mr. Simon Geoffrey, FCA *1971;* The Old White Hart, Downend, Horsley, STROUD, GL6 0PF. (Life Member)
READ, Mr. Stephen Mark, BSc ACA *1995;* Scarlet Cottage Mill Lane Witton, NORWICH, NR13 5DS.
•READ, Mr. Stephen Robert, FCA *1978;* (Tax Fac), Read & Co, 3c Sopwith Crescent, Hurricane Way, WICKFORD, ESSEX, SS11 8YU.
READ, Mr. Stuart Noel, BA ACA *2006;* 645 Stockton Street, Apartment 202, SAN FRANCISCO, CA 94108, UNITED STATES.
READ, Mrs. Susan Mary, BA BSc ACA *1981;* 8 Clarewood Drive, CAMBERLEY, GU15 3TE.
READ, Mrs. Susannah Marian, BA ACA *1998;* Little Brockley, Broadway, Shipham, WINSCOMBE, BS25 1UF.
•READE, Miss. Barbara Mary Hamilton, FCA CTA AMCT *1974;* (Tax Fac), Barbara M H Reade & Co, May Tree Hollow, 10 Crownfields, SEVENOAKS, KENT, TN13 1EF. See also Beta Ways Limited
READE, Dr. Brian, MSc ACA *2001;* Saltgate, 22-24 Seale Street, St. Helier, JERSEY, JE2 3QG.
READE, Mr. Brian Stanley, FCA *1970;* Copshall Oast, Butchers Lane, Three Oaks, Guestling, HASTINGS, EAST SUSSEX TN35 4LT.
READE, Mrs. Catherine Jane, BSc ACA *1993;* Diocese of St. Edmundsbury & Ipswich, 4 Cutler Street, IPSWICH, IP1 1UQ.
READE, Mr. James Walter, BA ACA *2005;* Victoria University, Robert Stout Building, Salamanca Road, WELLINGTON 6021, NEW ZEALAND.
READER, Mr. Adam Jon, ACA *1996;* 9 Drayton Avenue, POTTERS BAR, EN6 2LF.
•READER, Mr. Carl Stuart, ACA FCCA *2010;* Dennis & Turnbull Limited, Swatton Barn, Badbury, SWINDON, SN4 0EU. See also Dennis & Turnbull Holdings Limited
READER, Mr. Craig Vivian, BA ACA *1980;* New Pond Farm, New Pond Hill, Cross in Hand, HEATHFIELD, EAST SUSSEX, TN21 0LX.
READER, Mrs. Emma Louise, BSc ACA *1997;* 24 The Uplands, HARPENDEN, HERTFORDSHIRE, AL5 2PQ.
•READER, Mr. Gary John Charles, BSc ACA *1988;* KPMG LLP, Two Financial Center, 60 South Street, BOSTON, MA 02111, UNITED STATES.
READER, Mr. James William, BEng ACA *1996;* Provident Insurance Plc, Blackwall, HALIFAX, WEST YORKSHIRE, HX1 2PZ.
READER, Mr. Marcus, BA(Hons) ACA *2001;* Dovecote House, Hall Lane, Haughton, TARPORLEY, CHESHIRE, CW6 9RH.
READER, Mr. Michael, MA FCA *1981;* (Tax Fac), The Barn, Ryecroft, Scholes, HOLMFIRTH, HD9 1ST.
READER, Mr. Michael William, FCA *1970;* 33 Northvale Close, KENILWORTH, CV8 2EN.
READER, Mr. Neil William, MSc BSc ACA MRICS PgDip *1986;* Pricewaterhousecoopers, 33 Wellington Street, LEEDS, LS1 4JP.
READER, Mrs. Suzanne Carole, BA ACA *2003;* 5 Osborne Grove, NOTTINGHAM, NG5 2HE.
READER, Mr. Terence Edward, BSc FCA *1977;* 3 Moat House, Uplees Road Oare, FAVERSHAM, ME13 0QT.
READHEAD, Mr. Robert Henry William, BA ACA *2009;* 45 Queenstown Road, LONDON, SW8 3RG.
READHEAD, Mr. Simon Michael, BSc ACA *2002;* 10/39 Belmont Avenue, WOLLSTONECRAFT, NSW 2065, AUSTRALIA.
READING, Anthony John, Esq MBE FCA *1966;* 16 Heatherside Gardens, Farnham Common, SLOUGH, SL2 3RR.
READING, Ms. Jane, BSc FCA *1993;* 3 Mary Cross Close, TRING, HP23 6QL.
READING, Mr. Michael Richard, FCA *1962;* The Forge House, Church Road, Claverdon, WARWICK, CV35 8PB.
READING, Mr. Patrick Alistair, BSc FCA *1975;* 42 Hamilton Quay, EASTBOURNE, EAST SUSSEX, BN23 5PZ.
READINGS, Mr. Nicholas Beresford, FCA *1976;* 5 Churchwell Avenue, Easthorpe, Kelvedon, COLCHESTER, CO5 9HN.
READINGS, Mrs. Pamela Ann, ACA *1978;* 5 Churchwell Avenue, EasthorpeKelvedon, COLCHESTER, CO5 9HN.
READMAN, Mr. Conrad Mark, ACA *1990;* 19 St.Helena Road, COLCHESTER, CO3 3BA.
READMAN, Mrs. Elizabeth Jane, BA ACA *1991;* 15 Wrelton Hall Gardens, Wrelton, PICKERING, NORTH YORKSHIRE, YO18 8PF.
READMAN, Mr. Frank, FCA *1964;* 51a Main Street, Bishopstone, AYLESBURY, HP17 8SH. (Life Member)
READMAN, Guy, Esq OBE DL FCA *1963;* 21 Graham Park Road, Gosforth, NEWCASTLE UPON TYNE, NE3 4BH. (Life Member)
READMAN, Mr. William Leslie, FCA *1980;* 10 Shrewsbury Close, Church Green Little Benton, NEWCASTLE UPON TYNE, NE7 7YS.
READSHAW, Mr. Kenneth Ian, BA ACA *1993;* School House, Horsehouse, LEYBURN, DL8 4TS.
•READY, Mrs. Charlotte, ACA *2008;* C Ready Limited, The Oast, Stone Green Farm, Mersham, ASHFORD, KENT TN25 7HE.
READYHOUGH, Mr. Stuart Paul, BSc ACA *1998;* 37 Pot House Road, BRADFORD, WEST YORKSHIRE, BD6 1UE.
•REAH, Mr. Christopher, BA FCA ATII *1991;* Joseph Miller & Co, Floor A, Milburn House, Dean Street, NEWCASTLE UPON TYNE, NE1 1LE.
REAH, Mr. Daniel Lee, BA ACA *2008;* 3 Manor House, East Grinstead Road, LINGFIELD, RH7 6NE.
REAL, Miss. Caroline Victoria, BA ACA *2005;* 23 Hill Road, Theydon Bois, EPPING, CM16 7LX.
REALE, Miss. Nicola, BA ACA *2011;* 4 Monkton House, Wolfe Crescent, LONDON, SE16 6SS.
REALF, Miss. Annabel Louise, ACA *2004;* PricewaterhouseCoopers, 125 High Street, BOSTON, MA 02110, UNITED STATES.
REAMES, Mr. Rodney Charles Dudley, MA MBA FCA *1973;* Field House Coed-yr-Ynys Road, Llangynidr, CRICKHOWELL, POWYS, NP8 1NA.
REANEY, Ms. Avis Janet, BEd FCA DChA *1985;* PO Box 16880, Hornby, CHRISTCHURCH 8441, NEW ZEALAND.
REANEY, Mr. James Anthony, FCA *1968;* River View, Thorney Road, Kingsbury Episcopi, MARTOCK, SOMERSET, TA12 6BB. (Life Member)
REAP, Mr. Donald Wentworth, BA FCA *1956;* 135 Eastcote Road, RUISLIP, HA4 8BJ. (Life Member)
REARDEN, Mr. Michael Gaunt, FCA *1970;* Brooklands House, Halstock, YEOVIL, BA22 9QU.
REARDON, Mr. Gary, BSc ACA *1996;* 3 Rydon Street, Islington, LONDON, N1 7AL.
REASON, Mrs. Heather Louise, BA FCA CTA *1985;* (Tax Fac), with PricewaterhouseCoopers LLP, 1 Embankment Place, LONDON, WC2N 6RH.
REASON, Mrs. Jane Margaret, MA ACA *1989;* Apartado 2271, Quinta do Lago, 8135-024 ALMANCIL, ALGARVE, PORTUGAL.
REASON, Mr. Ross George, MA ACA *1987;* Robinson College, CAMBRIDGE, CB3 9AN.
REASON, Mr. William Matthew, FCA *1952;* 2 Cedar Hythe, CHapel Brampton, NORTHAMPTON, NN6 8BG. (Life Member)
REAST, Mr. John Ernest, FCA *1973;* Hidcote Vale, Hidcote Boyce, CHIPPING CAMPDEN, GLOUCESTERSHIRE, GL55 6LT. (Life Member)
•REAST, Mr. Peter Barradell, FCA *1971;* (Tax Fac), P.B. Reast, 78 Cedar Road, Mickleton, CHIPPING CAMPDEN, GLOUCESTERSHIRE, GL55 6SZ.
REAST, Miss. Rebecca Jane, MA BA ACA *1993;* GOAL Kenya, Nyangumi Road, Kilimani, NAIROBI, KENYA.
REAVELL, Mr. Fraser Moore, FCA *1971;* 25 Cromwell Road, BASINGSTOKE, RG21 5NR.
•REAVES, Mr. Kenneth David, FCA *1962;* Douglas & Reaves, Dundock, 15 Ancrum Bank, Eskbank, DALKEITH, MIDLOTHIAN EH22 3AY.
•REAY, Mr. Alan, FCA *1971;* AIMS - Alan Reay, 3 Hartley Avenue, WHITLEY BAY, NE26 3NS.
REAY, Mr. Clive Jonathan Forster, FCA *1974;* Hammercombe, Hill Road, HASLEMERE, GU27 2NH.
REAY, Mr. David Michael, ACA *1991;* 52 Coledale Meadows, CARLISLE, CA2 7NZ.
REAY, Miss. Elspeth Lucy, ACA *2010;* The Cottage Carberry Tower, Carberry, MUSSELBURGH, MIDLOTHIAN, EH21 8PY.
REAY, Mr. Ian Arthur Jeremy, BSc ACA *1993;* 14 Tangmere Grove, KINGSTON-UPON-THAMES, KT2 5GT.
REAY, Mr. Joseph James, BSc(Hons) ACA *2008;* 18 Hill Road, BARROW-IN-FURNESS, CUMBRIA, LA14 4HA.
REAY, Mr. Martin Paul, BA(Hons) ACA *2002;* 42 L'Arbre Crescent, Whickham, NEWCASTLE UPON TYNE, NE16 5YH.
REAY, Mr. Michael John, BA ACA *1989;* 53 High Street, Silsoe, BEDFORD, MK45 4EP.
REAY, Mrs. Susan Margaret, BA ACA *2005;* 1a Olivedale Road, LIVERPOOL, L18 1DD.
•REAY, Mr. William Stephen, LLB ACA *2001;* Smith Craven, 18 South Street, CHESTERFIELD, DERBYSHIRE, S40 1QX.
REBBECK, Mr. Brian, MA FCA *1970;* 2 Laurel Lane, Craigavad, HOLYWOOD, COUNTY DOWN, BT18 0JT. (Life Member)
•REBBECK, Mr. David John, ACA *1982;* Rebbeck & Company, Bramley Cottage, 45 Haconby Lane, Morton, BOURNE, LINCOLNSHIRE PE10 0NP.
•REBBETTS, Mr. Christopher John, FCA *1979;* Wilder Coe, Gloucester House, Church Walk, BURGESS HILL, RH15 9AS.
REBEIRO, Mr. Wilfred Allan, FCA *1958;* 3 Lambs Meadow, WOODFORD GREEN, ESSEX, IG8 8QD. (Life Member)
•REBELLO, Mr. Trevor Peter, FCA *1972;* (Tax Fac), Rebello & Co, 200 Brighton Road, PURLEY, CR8 4HB.
REBOLLINI, Mr. Thomas, BA(Hons) ACA *2002;* with Ernst & Young, PO Box 136, ABU DHABI, UNITED ARAB EMIRATES.
RECORD, Anthony, Esq MBE FCA *1964;* WCR Ltd, Woodcote House, 15 Highpoint, Henwood, ASHFORD, KENT TN24 8DH.
RECORD, Mr. Guy Charles, BSc ACA *1992;* 28 Marlborough Crescent, SEVENOAKS, KENT, TN13 2HP.
RECORD, Mrs. Jacqueline Alexandra, BSc ACA *1991;* C/o Mr Chris Record, IBM, PO Box 27242, Arenco Tower, Dubai Media City, DUBAI UNITED ARAB EMIRATES.
•RECORD, Mrs. Jennefer, LLB ACA *1997;* Credor Point Ltd, Arford Lodge, Bowcott Hill, Headley, BORDON, HAMPSHIRE GU35 8DF.
•RECORDON, Mr. Ian Charles, FCA FCMA *1970;* Ian Recordon, 25A Bromfelde Road, LONDON, SW4 6PP.
REDBURN, Mr. Timothy John, FCA *1977;* Little Abbots, Snower Hill Road, BETCHWORTH, RH3 7AQ.
REDCLIFFE, Ms. Charlotte, BA ACA ATII *1991;* Centrica Plc, Millstream, Maidenhead Road, WINDSOR, BERKSHIRE, SL4 5GD.
REDCLIFFE, Mr. Neil Graham Morgan, BSc FCA MBA *1985;* Currencies Direct, 51 Moorgate, LONDON, EC2R 6BH.
REDD, Mr. Andrew, MChem ACA *2003;* 6 Compton Road, Lindfield, HAYWARDS HEATH, WEST SUSSEX, RH16 2JZ.
REDDAN, Miss. Hannah, ACA *2004;* 55 Kingswood Chase, LEIGH-ON-SEA, ESSEX, SS9 3BB.
REDDAWAY, Mrs. Claire Marie, BA(Hons) ACA *2001;* 8 Oaklands Park, Hatherleigh Road, OKEHAMPTON, EX20 1LN.
REDDAWAY, Mr. Joshua John, BA ACA *2005;* 7a Loubet Street, LONDON, SW17 9HD.
REDDECLIFFE, Miss. Jocelyn Mary, BSc ACA *1990;* 4 Swallow Court, Clayton-Le-Woods, CHORLEY, PR6 7NZ.
REDDEN, Mr. Alan Raymond, BA FCA *1988;* (Tax Fac), Old Granary Poplar Farm, Wormald Green, HARROGATE, NORTH YORKSHIRE, HG3 3NJ.
•REDDEN, Mr. Alfred Edward, FCA *1973;* Alfred E Redden FCA, 42 Drylla, DINAS POWYS, SOUTH GLAMORGAN, CF64 4UL.
REDDICK, Miss. Allison May, BSc ACA *2006;* with Ernst & Young LLP, 1 More London Place, LONDON, SE1 2AF.
REDDICK, Miss. Joanne, ACA *2009;* 6 Bevington Walk, Patchway, BRISTOL, BS34 5NY.
•REDDIHOUGH, Mr. Malcolm Paul, FCA *1981;* (Tax Fac), Littlejohn LLP, 1 Westferry Circus, Canary Wharf, LONDON, E14 4HD.
REDDING, Mrs. Helen Louise, ACA *1999;* Henry Schein, Whatman House, St. Leonards Road, Allington, MAIDSTONE, KENT ME16 0PF.
REDDING, Mrs. Lucy, BSc ACA *1999;* with PricewaterhouseCoopers LLP, Exchange House, Central Business Exchange, Midsummer Boulevard, MILTON KEYNES, MK9 2DF.
REDDING, Mr. Michael Charles, ACA *1983;* 3 Alzey Gardens, HARPENDEN, AL5 5SZ.

•**REES, Mr. Peter Malcolm Tait, FCA** *1973;* Speechleys, Princes Chambers, 23 Wynnstay Road, COLWYN BAY, CLWYD, LL29 8NT.
REES, Mr. Philip Thomas John, MSc BA ACA *2003;* with Deloitte LLP, Athene Place, 66 Shoe Lane, LONDON, EC4A 3BQ.
•**REES, Mr. Phillip Aubrey, MA FCA** *1968;* Rees Beaufort & Co, 38 Beaufort Avenue, Langland, SWANSEA, SA3 4PB.
REES, Mr. Richard Charles, BA ACA *1990;* 7 High Grove, ST. ALBANS, AL3 5SU.
REES, Mr. Richard John, BSc ACA *2001;* 43 Cambrian Drive, Marshfield, CARDIFF, CF3 2TE.
•**REES, Mr. Richard Jonathan Owen, BSc FCA** *1996;* (Tax Fac), Carston & Co Limited, First Floor, Tudor House, 16 Cathedral Road, CARDIFF, CF11 9LJ. See also Sullivans Associate Limited and Carston & Co (Cardiff) Limited
REES, Mr. Robert Christopher, BSc FCA *1982;* 95 Cole Park Rd, TWICKENHAM, TW1 1HX.
REES, Mr. Robert Maitland, FCA *1975;* 103 Hampstead Way, Hampstead Garden Suburb, LONDON, NW11 7LR.
REES, Mrs. Sandra Diane, BSc FCA *1990;* Zepler building 59 Room 1225, University of Southampton, University Road, SOUTHAMPTON, SO17 1BJ.
•**REES, Mrs. Sharan Carole, FCA** *1976;* David M Rees & Associates Limited, Hawkswick House, Hawkswick, Harpendon Road, ST. ALBANS, HERTFORDSHIRE AL3 6JG.
REES, Mr. Simon David, BA ACA *1981;* S G Petch Ltd, McMullen Road, DARLINGTON, COUNTY DURHAM, DL1 1XZ.
•**REES, Mr. Simon Philip, BSc FCA CTA** *1982;* (Tax Fac), Rees Pollock, 35 New Bridge Street, LONDON, EC4V 6BW.
•**REES, Mrs. Sonya Faye, BA(Hons) ACA CIOT** *2004;* (Tax Fac), Dixon Wilson, 22 Chancery Lane, LONDON, WC2A 1LS.
REES, Miss. Stephanie Louise, BSc ACA *2011;* 4 Navy Street, Clapham, LONDON, SW4 6EZ.
REES, Mr. Stephen, BSc ACA *2011;* 27 Pepper Drive, BURGESS HILL, WEST SUSSEX, RH15 9UZ.
REES, Mr. Stephen Patrick, DL FCA *1960;* Nyth Cariad, 13 Queens Lofts, Princess Street, LLANELLI, SA15 2TW. (Life Member)
REES, Mr. Steven Christopher, BSc ACA *1998;* 78 Aldwickbury Crescent, HARPENDEN, HERTFORDSHIRE, AL5 5SE.
REES, Mr. Steven Peter, BA ACA *1990;* 17 Glebelands, Penshurst, TONBRIDGE, TN11 8DN.
REES, Mr. Thomas, BA ACA *2005;* Bank of America, Chester Business Park, CHESTER, CH4 9FB.
REES, Mr. Thomas Henry, BA ACA *1993;* 56 Fawe Park Road, LONDON, SW15 2EA.
REES, Mr. Thomas Matthew, BSc ACA *2010;* 6 Long Ayres, Caldecotte, MILTON KEYNES, MK7 8HF.
REES, Mr. Timothy Player, ACA *1979;* Friends Provident Axa Centre Bristol, Brierly Furlong Stoke Gifford, BRISTOL, BS34 8SW.
REES, Mr. Trevor Aston, FCA *1970;* Flat 8, Lissenden, 1 Burton Road, Branksome Park, POOLE, BH13 6DS.
•**REES, Mr. Trevor Meirion Emlyn, BA FCA** *1984;* KPMG LLP, St. James's Square, MANCHESTER, M2 6DS. See also KPMG Europe LLP
REES, Prof. William Page, PhD MBA FCA *1976;* Business School, 29 Buccleuch Street, EDINBURGH, EH8 9JS.
•**REES-PULLEY, Mr. Richard, FCA FTII** *1978;* 24 Stonehill Road, East Sheen, LONDON, SW14 8RW.
REES-STEER, Mr. Peter James, BSc ACA *1992;* Apartment 407 The Rotunda, 150 New Street, BIRMINGHAM, B2 4PA.
REESE, Mr. Adrian Marc, BSc ACA *2000;* Morgan Stanley, 46th Floor, International Commerce Centre, 1 Austin Road, TSIM SHA TSUI, KOWLOON HONG KONG SAR.
REESE, Miss. Anne, MSc ACA *2006;* Avenida Claveles 42B - B, 07193 PALMANYOLA, SPAIN.
REESE, Mrs. Bernadine Kathleen, ACA *2000;* 1 Foxwarren, HAYWARDS HEATH, RH16 1EN.
•**REESE, Mr. Nigel Martin, FCA** *1971;* Nigel M Reese FCA, 48 Dalkeith Grove, STANMORE, HA7 4SF.
REESE, Mr. Trevor Ellison, BA FCA *1994;* (Tax Fac), 6 Hilton Grove, West Kirby, WIRRAL, CH48 5HB.
REEVE, Mr. Alan, FCA *1957;* Redwood, 6 Horton Close, MAIDENHEAD, SL6 8TP. (Life Member)
•①**REEVE, Mrs. Annette, BSc(Hons) ACA** *2002;* with Varden Nuttall Limited, Release House, Heap Bridge, BURY, LANCASHIRE, BL9 7JR.
REEVE, Mr. Brian Henry, FCA *1958;* 163 New Village Road, COTTINGHAM, HU16 4ND. (Life Member)
•**REEVE, Mrs. Cheryl Anne, BSc ACA** *1996;* Cheryl Reeve, 4 Ennion Close, Soham, ELY, CB7 5GU.
•**REEVE, Mr. Christopher, ACA FCCA** *2009;* Gascoynes Limited, 15 Whiting Street, BURY ST. EDMUNDS, SUFFOLK, IP33 1NX.
REEVE, Mr. David, MA MEng ACA *2000;* 62 Surley Row Emmer Green, READING, RG4 8NB.
•**REEVE, Mr. David Martin, ACA** *1980;* David Reeve, Harvern, Colber Lane, Bishop Thornton, HARROGATE, HG3 3JR.
REEVE, Mrs. Emma, BSc ACA *1987;* 326 A Street, Unit 6C, BOSTON, MA 02210, UNITED STATES.
REEVE, Mr. Geoffrey Arnold, FCA *1957;* 100 Patching Hall Lane, CHELMSFORD, CM1 4DB. (Life Member)
REEVE, Mr. Hayden James, BA ACA *2000;* 16 Australian Avenue, SALISBURY, SP2 7JT.
REEVE, Miss. Helen Katherine, ACA *2008;* 60 Franche Court Road, LONDON, SW17 0JU.
REEVE, Mrs. Hilary Thatcher Bunting, MA FCA *1993;* 118 St Andrews Road, HENLEY-ON-THAMES, RG9 1PL.
REEVE, Mrs. Jean Faith, FCA *1958;* Timbers, 2 Eastmoor Farm Cottages, Moor Street Rainham, GILLINGHAMKent, ME8 8QE. (Life Member)
REEVE, Mr. John, FCA *1955;* Longmeadows, 70 Elwyn Road, MARCH, PE15 9DB. (Life Member)
REEVE, Mr. John, FCA *1967;* Cliff Dene, 24 Cliff Parade, LEIGH-ON-SEA, SS9 1BB.
REEVE, Mr. John Richard, BA FCA *1975;* Family Assurance Friendly, Society Ltd, 17 West Street, BRIGHTON, BN1 2RL.
REEVE, Mrs. Julie, BSc ACA *2005;* 1 Grove Avenue, HARPENDEN, HERTFORDSHIRE, AL5 1EU.
REEVE, Mr. Malcolm, BSc(Econ) ACA *1979;* 5800 Sylvia Avenue, TARZANA, CA 91356, UNITED STATES.
REEVE, Mr. Michael Arthur Ferard, MBE MA FCA *1963;* 138 Oakwood Court, Abbotsbury Road, LONDON, W14 8JS.
REEVE, Mr. Nathan Spencer, MA CA ACA *1998;* Ontario Power Generation, 700 University Avenue, H7-G27, TORONTO M5G 1X6, ON, CANADA.
•**REEVE, Mr. Nicholas James, FCA CF** *1973;* Smith & Williamson (Bristol) LLP, Portwall Place, Portwall Lane, BRISTOL, BS1 6NA. See also Smith & Williamson Ltd
REEVE, Mr. Nicholas John, MA ACA *1981;* Chestnut Cottage, Church Lane, PINNER, HA5 3AA.
REEVE, Mr. Patrick Harold, BA ACA *1985;* 17 Albion Street, LONDON, W2 2AS.
REEVE, Mr. Paul, FCA *1969;* 55 Clyst Valley Road, Clyst St Mary, EXETER, EX5 1DE. (Life Member)
REEVE, Mr. Paul, BA ACA *2005;* 1 Grove Avenue, HARPENDEN, HERTFORDSHIRE, AL5 1EU.
•**REEVE, Mr. Peter Malcolm, FCA** *1977;* Lyndoe Reeve, 34/36 Maddox Street, LONDON, W1S 1PD.
REEVE, Mr. Peter William, FCA *1968;* 19 Lower Church Road, BENFLEET, SS7 4DL.
•**REEVE, Mr. Philip John, FCA** *1984;* Leggatt Bell, 14 Railway Street, CHELMSFORD, CM1 1QS.
REEVE, Mrs. Philippa, FCA *1963;* Apartado Correos 255, Orihuela Costa, 03189 ALICANTE, SPAIN.
REEVE, Miss. Rachel Elizabeth, ACA *2006;* 29 Sperling Drive, HAVERHILL, SUFFOLK, CB9 9SG.
REEVE, Ms. Sally-Anne, BA ACA *1984;* 23 Addington Court, Horseguards, EXETER, EX4 4UY.
REEVE, Mr. Simon, BA ACA *1992;* EPS Plc, Riverside House, New Mill Road, ORPINGTON, KENT, BR5 3QA.
REEVE, Mr. Stuart Edward, BA ACA *1988;* Byways, Rye Lane, Otford, SEVENOAKS, KENT, TN14 5JF.
REEVE, Mrs. Vanessa Jane, BA ACA *1996;* Croydon High School for Girls, Old Farleigh Road, SOUTH CROYDON, CR2 8YB.
REEVE, Miss. Vanessa Jane, LLB ACA *2004;* with BDO LLP, 55 Baker Street, LONDON, W1U 7EU.
•**REEVE-TUCKER, Mr. Charles Stanley, FCA** *1977;* (Tax Fac), Reeves & Co LLP, Third Floor, 24 Chiswell Street, LONDON, EC1Y 4YX.
REEVE-TUCKER, Mr. Stephen John, BA(Econ) FCA *1978;* Barclays Bank Plc, 1 Churchill Place, LONDON, E14 5HP.
REEVE-TUCKER, Mr. William Lovell, FCA *1974;* Glewstone Court Hotel, Glewstone, ROSS-ON-WYE, HR9 6AW.
•**REEVES, Mr. Adam David, BA ACA** *1992;* Adam Reeves, 1st Floor Offices, Allied House, Bryn Lane, Wrexham Industrial Estate, WREXHAM LL13 9UT.
REEVES, Mr. Andrew Frank, FCA *1975;* Andrew Reeves Estate Agents, 77-79 Ebury Street, LONDON, SW1W 0NZ.
REEVES, Mr. Andrew James, BA ACA *1992;* 36 Alton Street, ROSS-ON-WYE, HR9 5AG.
REEVES, Mr. Andrew Robert, MSci ACA *2005;* 60 Lysia Street, LONDON, SW6 6NG.
REEVES, Mr. Anthony Alexander, BSc FCA *1983;* Arocomet Tower Cranes Regus House, Victory Way Crossways Business Park, DARTFORD, DA2 6QD.
REEVES, Miss. Anya Jane, ACA *1983;* 10 Orchard Road, St Margarets, TWICKENHAM, TW1 1LY.
REEVES, Mr. Arthur John, ACA *1986;* Powdermill Farm, Littleton Lane, Winford, BRISTOL, BS40 8HE.
REEVES, Mr. Austin Sirrell, BSc FCA *1960;* Fernhill, Laugharne, CARMARTHEN, SA33 4SJ. (Life Member)
REEVES, Mr. Benjamin, BSc ACA *1989;* Unit 12, 33 Mitchell Street, MCMAHONS POINT, NSW 2060, 2060, AUSTRALIA.
REEVES, Mrs. Catherine Jane, ACA *2008;* with Deloitte LLP, Athene Place, 66 Shoe Lane, LONDON, EC4A 3BQ.
•**REEVES, Mr. Clive Michael, FCA ATII** *1962;* Michael Reeves & Co, 12 Harmsworth Way, Totteridge, LONDON, N20 8JU.
REEVES, Mr. Colin Boyd Meredith, FCA *1971;* PO Box 1089, FOURWAYS, GAUTENG, 2055, SOUTH AFRICA.
REEVES, Mr. David Bertram, FCA *1961;* 37 Michleham Down, LONDON, N12 7JJ. (Life Member)
REEVES, Mr. David Edward, MA ACA *1981;* 62 High Street, Thurlby, BOURNE, PE10 0EE.
REEVES, Mr. David Sidney, FCA *1961;* Lane House, 9 The Avenue, Chobham, WOKING, GU24 8RU. (Life Member)
REEVES, Mrs. Deborah Jayne, BA ACA *1985;* Lime Tree House, 4 Lime Avenue, Wheathampstead, ST. ALBANS, HERTFORDSHIRE, AL4 8LG.
REEVES, Miss. Diana Mary, BA ACA *1992;* PO Box 30497 Budaiya Post Office, BUDAIYA, BAHRAIN.
REEVES, Mr. Duncan Charles, BA FCA *1967;* 51 Highfield, LETCHWORTH GARDEN CITY, HERTFORDSHIRE, SG6 3PY. (Life Member)
REEVES, Mr. Duncan James, MPhys ACA *2005;* 14 Lord Reith Place, BEACONSFIELD, BUCKINGHAMSHIRE, HP9 2GE.
REEVES, Mrs. Elizabeth, LLB ACA *2000;* 11 Tudorville Road, Bebington, WIRRAL, CH63 2HT.
REEVES, Mr. Ernest John, FCA *1959;* Woodpeckers, Brook Lane, Brocton, STAFFORD, ST17 0TZ. (Life Member)
REEVES, Mr. Gerald Alan, BA ACA *1989;* 7 Clovelly Way, ORPINGTON, KENT, BR6 0WD.
REEVES, Mr. Graham Barry, ACA *1979;* Moore Stephens, 150 Aldersgate Street, LONDON, EC1A 4AB.
REEVES, Mr. Graham Trevor, ACA *1980;* 17 Raglan Close, Chandlers Ford, EASTLEIGH, SO53 4NH.
•**REEVES, Mr. Gwyn, BSc ACA** *1983;* G. Reeves, 11 Percy Terrace, Beltring Road, TUNBRIDGE WELLS, TN4 9RH.
REEVES, Mrs. Jackie, BSc ACA *2001;* Parkfields Farm, Bramshall Road, Kiddlestitch, UTTOXETER, STAFFORDSHIRE, ST14 5BD.
REEVES, Mr. James Clifford, MA BA(Hons) ACA *2002;* Charlton House, Hollow Lane, Dormansland, LINGFIELD, SURREY, RH7 6NS.
REEVES, Miss. Jane, ACA *1992;* 1 Coopers Close East Wellow, ROMSEY, SO51 6AZ.
•**REEVES, Mrs. Janet Dorothy, FCA** *1977;* JR, Avondale, Ellesmere Road, Wem, SHREWSBURY, SY4 5TU.
REEVES, Mr. John Leslie, BSc ACA *1979;* 14 Fowey Close, Chandlers Ford, EASTLEIGH, SO53 4SQ.
REEVES, Mr. John Maxwell, BA FCA *1983;* Bank House, Main Street, Sicklinghall, WETHERBY, WEST YORKSHIRE, LS22 4BD.
REEVES, Mr. John Terence, MBA FCA *1971;* Parkwood Farm, Cryals Road, Brenchley, TONBRIDGE, KENT, TN12 7HN. (Life Member)
REEVES, Mrs. Karen Jane, FCA *1984;* Beresford, Cliveden Mead, MAIDENHEAD, BERKSHIRE, SL6 8HE.
REEVES, Mrs. Katherine Dawn, BSc ACA *1997;* with KPMG, KPMG Centre, 18 Viaduct Harbour Avenue, P.O. Box 1584, AUCKLAND 1140, NEW ZEALAND.
REEVES, Mrs. Kathryn Jane, BA ACA *1990;* John Lawson Wild & Co, 150 Drake Street, ROCHDALE, OL16 1PX.
REEVES, Miss. Katie Samantha, BA(Hons) ACA *2009;* 6 Chipchase Mews, NEWCASTLE UPON TYNE, NE3 5RH.
REEVES, Mr. Kenneth Leslie, FCA *1960;* Longmynd, Tanpit Lane, Easingwold, YORK, YO61 3HD. (Life Member)
REEVES, Mr. Kevin David, BA ACA *1987;* PricewaterhouseCoopers, Darling Park Tower 2, 201 Sussex Street, GPO Box 2650, SYDNEY, NSW 1171 AUSTRALIA.
REEVES, Mrs. Laura Jane, MA BA(Hons) ACA *2002;* Charlton House, Hollow Lane, Dormansland, LINGFIELD, SURREY, RH7 6NS.
REEVES, Mr. Martin Adam, MA ACA *1996;* 49 Fitzroy Road, LONDON, NW1 8TP.
REEVES, Mr. Michael, ACA *2011;* 1 Meadow Court, Ponteland, NEWCASTLE UPON TYNE, NE20 9RA.
•**REEVES, Mr. Michael Harry, ACA CF** *1989;* Clearwater Corporate Finance LLP, 7th Floor, Chancery Place, 50 Brown Street, MANCHESTER, M2 2JT.
REEVES, Mr. Michael John, FCA *1965;* Flat 5 Sans Souci, 48 Leigh Park Road, LEIGH-ON-SEA, SS9 2DU.
REEVES, Mr. Nigel Janbret Frank, FCA *1971;* Browns Temple Dairy Wynnstay Hall Estate, Ruabon, WREXHAM, CLWYD, LL14 6LA.
REEVES, Mrs. Patricia Ann, BA ACA *1991;* Adam Reeves Chartered Accountants, Allied House, Bryn Lane, Wrexham Industrial Estate, WREXHAM, CLWYD LL13 9UT.
REEVES, Mr. Paul Bernard Joseph, ACA *2006;* African Mining Services(Sarl), Villa MAEVA 7 Porte 139, Cite Du Niger 2, BAMAKO, BPE 5410, MALI.
REEVES, Mr. Paul Nicholas, BA ACA *1989;* 3B Stanhope Road, CROYDON, CR0 5NS.
REEVES, Mr. Paul William James, BA ACA *1979;* Queens Spinney, Ashurst Road, Ashurst, TUNBRIDGE WELLS, KENT, TN3 9SU.
REEVES, Mrs. Pauline Marion, LLB ACA *1999;* 14 Beech Way, TWICKENHAM, TW2 5JT.
REEVES, Mr. Peter James, FCA *1965;* The Retreat, 40 North Furzeham Road, BRIXHAM, DEVON, TQ5 8BD. (Life Member)
REEVES, Mr. Peter Michael, MSc FCA *1968;* 1 St. Keyna Avenue, HOVE, BN3 4PN.
•**REEVES, Mr. Peter Thomas, FCA** *1977;* Peter Reeves, The Old Orchard, Sandy Lane, Southmoor, ABINGDON, OXFORDSHIRE OX13 5HX.
REEVES, Mr. Richard Ivan, BSc FCA *1975;* 44 Hillcrest Rise, LEEDS, LS16 7DL.
REEVES, Mr. Richard John, FCA *1967;* Langelinie, 221 Vicarage Hill, BENFLEET, SS7 1PG.
REEVES, Mr. Richard John, MA ACA *1998;* 224 Stanley Hill, AMERSHAM, BUCKINGHAMSHIRE, HP7 9ES.
•**REEVES, Mr. Roy Arnold, FCA** *1976;* (Tax Fac), JR, Avondale, Ellesmere Road, Wem, SHREWSBURY, SY4 5TU.
REEVES, Mr. Sacha Alexander James, MA ACA *2002;* United Kingdom Debt Management Office, Eastcheap Court, 11 Philpot Lane, LONDON, EC3M 8UD.
•**REEVES, Mrs. Sarah Jane, BA(Hons) ACA** *1996;* Springtide Accountancy Ltd, 21 Lentune Way, LYMINGTON, HAMPSHIRE, SO41 3PE. See also Reeves Sarah
REEVES, Mrs. Sarah Leonora Mary, BSc ACA *1991;* 7 Mount Field, FAVERSHAM, ME13 8SZ.
REEVES, Mr. Simon Mark, BA ACA *1990;* with Burberry Ltd, Horseferry House, Horseferry Road, LONDON, SW1P 2AW.
REEVES, Mr. Steven Paul, BA(Hons) ACA *2001;* Hewitt Associates, Parkside House, Ashley Road, EPSOM, SURREY, KT18 5BS.
REEVES, Mr. Steven Robert, BA ACA *1986;* Lime Tree House, 4 Lime Avenue, Blackmore End, Wheathampstead, ST. ALBANS, HERTFORDSHIRE AL4 8LG.
REEVES, Mr. Steven Victor, ACA *1991;* Parkfields Farm, Bramshall Road, Kiddlestitch, UTTOXETER, ST14 5BD.
REEVES, Mrs. Susan Eleanor, MA FCA *2001;* 11 Church Crescent, LONDON, N3 1BE.
REEVES, Mr. Thomas, BSc ACA *2011;* 36 Gerard Road, ALCESTER, B49 6QQ.
REEVES, Mr. Trevor Charles, BSc ACA *1979;* 2 Windsor Court, FARMINGTON, CT 06032, UNITED STATES.
REEVES, Mrs. Victoria, ACA *2006;* 6 Midfield House, LASSWADE, MIDLOTHIAN, EH18 1ED.
REEVES-HALL, Mrs. Samantha Claire, BSc ACA *2002;* 508 E 61st street, SAVANNAH, GA 31405, UNITED STATES.
REEVY, Mr. Joseph Charles, MSc BA FCA MAE *1983;* 9 Howell Road, EXETER, EX4 4LG.
REFFIN, Mr. Gordon Trasler, FCA *1952;* 1 High Street, Catworth, HUNTINGDON, CAMBRIDGESHIRE, PE28 0PF. (Life Member)
•**REGAL, Mr. Richard Neill, MBA FCA** *1985;* (Tax Fac), 5170 Maris Ave, Apt 300, ALEXANDRIA, VA 22304-1965, UNITED STATES.
REGAN, Mr. Andrew William, BA ACA *1987;* Andrew Marr International Ltd, Livingstone Road, HESSLE, NORTH HUMBERSIDE, HU13 0EE.
REGAN, Mr. Anthony, FCA *1963;* 2 Old Forge Way, SIDCUP, DA14 4QL.
REGAN, Mr. Bryan Charles, FCA *1982;* Hybu Cig Cymru-Meat Promotion Wales, PO Box 176, ABERYSTWYTH, DYFED, SY23 2YA.

REGAN, Mr. Cennydd Geraint, BSc(Hons) ACA *2001;* The Royal Bank of Scotland, 4th Floor, 2 St. Philips Place, BIRMINGHAM, B3 2RB.
REGAN, Mr. Charles Joseph, BSc FCA *1974;* 3 Framfield Close, Woodside Park, LONDON, N12 7HH.
REGAN, Miss. Claire Elizabeth, ACA *2008;* with Towers & Gornall, Suites 5 & 6, The Printworks, Hey Road, Barrow, CLITHEROE LANCASHIRE BB7 9WB.
REGAN, Mrs. Dianne Michele, ACA *1985;* 16 Adlington Drive, SANDBACH, CW11 1DX.
REGAN, Mr. Fergus Thomas, BA ACA *1993;* 516 Bloomfield Road, HOBOKEN, NJ 07030, UNITED STATES.
REGAN, Mr. Francis Edward, FCA *1961;* Cavalier Lodge, Woodland Hills, Madeley, CREWE, CW3 9HN. (Life Member)
REGAN, Mr. Geoffrey, BA ACA *1980;* 176 Kings Hall Road, BECKENHAM, BR3 1LJ.
•REGAN, Mrs. Jennifer, BA FCA *1982;* Jenny Regan, Ffoslas, Penuwch, TREGARON, DYFED, SY25 6RA.
REGAN, Mrs. Jenny Patricia, BA ACA *1999;* with Ernst & Young LLP, 1 More London Place, LONDON, SE1 2AF.
REGAN, Mrs. Joanna Mary, BSc ACA *1989;* Plas Coch Bridge Road, Old St. Mellons, CARDIFF, CF3 6UY.
•REGAN, Mrs. Joanne, FCA *1996;* Evolution Audit LLP, 10 Evolution, Wynyard Park, BILLINGHAM, CLEVELAND, TS22 5TB.
REGAN, Mr. John, BSc ACA *1984;* (Tax Fac), Baltic Publications Ltd, Baltic Business Centre, Saltmeadows Road, GATESHEAD, TYNE AND WEAR, NE8 3AH.
REGAN, Mr. John Francis Peter, BA ACA *1995;* 31 Gordon Road, LONDON, E11 2RA.
REGAN, Mr. John Patrick, BCom FCA *1969;* PO Box 31516, SEVEN MILE BEACH, GRAND CAYMAN, CAYMAN ISLANDS.
REGAN, Miss. Kerry Elizabeth, BSc ACA *1997;* 10 Barbourne Terrace, WORCESTER, WR1 3JS.
REGAN, Mr. Laurence Peter, FCA *1961;* 18 Riffhams, Thriftwood, BRENTWOOD, ESSEX, CM13 2TW. (Life Member)
•REGAN, Mr. Martin, BA FCA *1983;* Crowe Clark Whitehill LLP, Carrick House, Lypiatt Road, CHELTENHAM, GLOUCESTERSHIRE, GL50 2QJ. See also Horwath Clark Whitehill LLP and Crowe Clark Whitehill
REGAN, Mr. Maurice David Brian Campbell, FCA *1960;* 19 Gerrard Road, LONDON, N1 8AY. (Life Member)
REGAN, Mr. Michael Anthony, FCA *1961;* 36 Rouse Gardens, Dulwich, LONDON, SE21 8AF. (Life Member)
REGAN, Mr. Michael John, FCA *1974;* Tara Signs Ltd, St. Peters Place, Western Road, LANCING, WEST SUSSEX, BN15 8SB.
REGAN, Mr. Nicholas Andrew, BSc ACA *1990;* Plas Coch Bridge Road, Old St. Mellons, CARDIFF, CF3 6UY.
REGAN, Mr. Patrick Charles, BSc ACA *1992;* Flat 27 Discovery Dock Apartments East, 3 South Quay Square, LONDON, E14 9RU.
REGAN, Mr. Paul Christopher, BSc ACA *1989;* PO Box HM, 3109, HAMILTON HM NX, BERMUDA.
REGAN, Mr. Russell Jude, BBS ACA *1991;* 30/44 Bent Street, NEUTRAL BAY, NSW 2089, AUSTRALIA.
REGAS, Mr. Constantinos, MEng ACA *2010;* National Audit Office, 157-197 Buckingham Palace Road, LONDON, SW1W 9SP.
REGELOUS, Ms. Stefka, ACA CF *1996;* 16 Flanders Road, LONDON, W4 1NG.
REGEN, Mr. David, BSc ACA *1996;* 8 Norfolk Avenue, COLLAROY, NSW 2097, AUSTRALIA.
REGENT, Mr. Christopher Philip, BEng ACA *2001;* 26 Park Hill, HARPENDEN, HERTFORDSHIRE, AL5 3AT.
REGER, Mr. David Michael, BSc ACA *1979;* Bernard Mathews Ltd, Great Witchingham Hall, Lenwade, NORWICH, NR9 5QD.
REGESTER, Mr. Michael Paul Stearn Dinsmored, FCA *1965;* 613 Crescent Avenue, GLENSIDE, PA 19038, UNITED STATES.
REGGIO, Mr. Italico Paul Amedeo, BEng ACA *1995;* with IBM, 76 Upper Ground, South Bank, LONDON, SE1 9PZ.
REGIS, Miss. Charmain, BA(Hons) ACA *2002;* Financial TImes, 59/F 99 Queens Road, CENTRAL, HONG KONG ISLAND, HONG KONG SAR.
REGISTER, Miss. Lynsey Clare, BA(Hons) ACA *2004;* Hermes Pensions Management Ltd Lloyds Chambers, 1 Portsoken Street, LONDON, E1 8HZ.
REGLAR, Miss. Kate Elizabeth, BA ACA CTA *2005;* Etosha Lodge, Vinneys Close, BROCKENHURST, SO42 7AB.
•REGNAULD, Mr. Nicholas John, BSc FCA FCCA *1977;* J.C. Barker & Co, 6 Richmond Terrace, Shelton, STOKE-ON-TRENT, STAFFORDSHIRE, ST1 4ND.
REGNIER, Mrs. Jane, BA ACA *1999;* 11 Wheatlands Road East, HARROGATE, NORTH YORKSHIRE, HG2 8PX.
REGO, Mr. Christopher James, BSc(Hons) ACA *2004;* 88 Kimberley Avenue, Nunhead, LONDON, SE15 3XH.
•REGO, Mr. Philip Daniel, FCA *1987;* BDO LLP, Emerald House, East Street, EPSOM, SURREY, KT17 1HS. See also BDO Stoy Hayward LLP
REHAAG, Mr. Godfrey Claude, MA FCA CTA *1973;* Lower Cadham Farmhouse, Jacobstowe, OKEHAMPTON, DEVON, EX20 3RB.
REHLON, Mr. Amandeep Singh, BA ACA *2004;* 23 Minstrel Gardens, SURBITON, SURREY, KT5 8DD.
REHMAN, Mr. Ameer, ACA *2009;* 96 Faraday Drive, Shenley Lodge, MILTON KEYNES, MK5 7HQ.
REHMAN, Mrs. Beth Ann, ACA *1997;* Gesegnetmattstr. 6, 6006 LUZERN, SWITZERLAND.
REHMAN, Mr. Fasih, ACA *2007;* Gesegnetmattstrasse 6, 6006 LUZERN, SWITZERLAND.
•REHMAN, Mr. Fiaz Ur, MBA FCA *1992;* Bailey Watts, Meridian House, 62 Station Road, LONDON, E4 7BA.
REHMAN, Mr. Jameel Ur, FCA *1967;* 88 Ataturk Block, New Garden Town, LAHORE 54600, PAKISTAN.
REHMAN, Miss. Marine, BA ACA *2010;* 112 Bellingdon Road, CHESHAM, BUCKINGHAMSHIRE, HP5 2HF.
REHMAN, Mr. Sarfaraz Ahmed, ACA *1983;* 1/ll Khayaban - e - Shujaat, Phase V, Defence Housing Authority, KARACHI, PAKISTAN.
REHMAN, Mr. Shafik, FCA *1965;* 15 Eskaton Gardens, DHAKA 1000, BANGLADESH.
REHMANI, Mr. Hadi Mohammed Karim, FCA *1970;* H.M.K. Rehmani, Farmaniyeh Rouhani St., Koy Ferdos No 32, TEHRAN, 19547, IRAN.
•REHNCY, Mr. Jasdev Singh, FCA *1980;* (Tax Fac), RehncyShaheen, 1276-1278 Greenford Road, GREENFORD, MIDDLESEX, UB6 0HH.
•REICH, Mr. Martin Jeremy, BSc ACA *1987;* Martin J. Reich & Co, 41 Boyne Ave, LONDON, NW4 2JL.
REICHEL, Mr. Eric Paul, FCA *1976;* Arboressence, Rue de l'Eglise, 59143 LEDERZEELE, FRANCE.
REICHELT, Mr. Graham John, BEng ACA *1995;* 413 Grand Street, Apt F1004, NEW YORK, NY 10002, UNITED STATES.
•REICHWALD, Mrs. Anna Catherine, BSc ACA *1987;* A.C.Reichwald, 239 Richmond Road, TWICKENHAM, TW1 2NN.
REICHWALD, Mr. Ian Edward, BSc(Econ) FCA *1979;* 239 Richmond Road, Marble Hill Park, TWICKENHAM, TW1 2NN.
REID, Mr. Adam Alastair, ACA *2009;* The Wooste, 6 Hill Rise, Elloughton, BROUGH, NORTH HUMBERSIDE, HU15 1JG.
REID, Mrs. Alison Anne, MA ACA *1983;* Linacre College, St. Cross Road, OXFORD, OX1 3JA.
REID, Mr. Allan Martin Russell, MA FCA *1974;* 38 Christchurch Road, WINCHESTER, SO23 9SU.
•REID, Mr. Allan McLean, FCA *1980;* (Tax Fac), McLean Reid, 1 Forstal Road, AYLESFORD, ME20 7AU.
REID, Miss. Alyson, BA ACA *2007;* 20 Sandringham Gardens, LEEDS, LS17 8DD.
REID, Miss. Amanda Anne, BSc ACA *2005;* East Midlands Electricity Plc, 1 Woolsthorpe Close, NOTTINGHAM, NG8 3JP.
REID, Mrs. Amanda Jane, BSc ACA *1992;* PO Box 2163, WOODRIDGE, WA 6041, AUSTRALIA.
REID, Mr. Andrew David, BSc ACA *1995;* Finance Department, Bristol Airport, BRISTOL, BS48 3DY.
REID, Mr. Andrew Michael, MA MBA FCA *1979;* University of Cambridge: Finance Division, The Old School, Trinity Lane, CAMBRIDGE, CB2 1TS.
REID, Mr. Andrew Stewart, BSc ACA *1992;* Friarsgate, 1011 Stratford Road, SOLIHULL, B90 4EB.
REID, Mr. Andrew William, BA FCA MCT *1992;* Nomura International Plc, 1 Angel Lane, LONDON, EC4R 3AB.
REID, Mr. Andy James, ACA *2010;* 2 Harland Street, IPSWICH, IP2 8JU.
REID, Mr. Anthony Arthur, FCA *1975;* Blue Shutters, 12 Palm Ridge, Royal Westmorland, ST JAMES, BARBADOS.
REID, Mr. Anthony Edward, BSc FCA *1974;* Luxury Timepieces (UK) Ltd, 13-15 Hurlingham Business Pk, Sulivan Road, LONDON, SW6 3DU.
REID, Mr. Brian John, FCA *1965;* 16/18 Lansell Road, TOORAK, VIC 3142, AUSTRALIA.
REID, Mrs. Caroline Elizabeth, BA FCA *1984;* with Anderson Barrowcliff, Waterloo House, Teesdale South, Thornaby Place, STOCKTON-ON-TEES, TS17 6SA.
REID, Miss. Catherine Jane, BA ACA *2006;* with Grant Thornton UK LLP, 1 Whitehall Riverside, Whitehall Road, LEEDS, WEST YORKSHIRE, LS1 4BN.
REID, Mr. Charles, BSc ACA *2010;* Rose House, 15 West Common Way, HARPENDEN, HERTFORDSHIRE, AL5 2LH.
REID, Mr. Charles Cochrane, BSc ACA *1992;* 10 Heights Close, LONDON, SW20 0TH.
REID, Mr. Charles Douglas, FCA *1974;* 17 Tilehouse Road, GUILDFORD, GU4 8AP.
•REID, Mr. Christopher, FCA *1978;* (Tax Fac), Chris Reid Ltd, 42 Brook Street, LONDON, W1K 5DB. See also Reid Chris and Zeros Ltd
REID, Mr. Christopher Ean, ACA *1993;* 40 Trevelyan Way, BERKHAMSTED, HERTFORDSHIRE, HP4 1JH.
REID, Mr. Christopher Paul, BA ACA *2005;* 14 Coulter Road, LONDON, W6 0BL.
•REID, Mr. Colin Stewart, BSc FCA CTA *1997;* Burgess Hodgson, Camburgh House, 27 New Dover Road, CANTERBURY, CT1 3DN.
REID, Mr. Colin William, BSc ACA *1980;* PO Box 32162, Seven Mile Beach, GEORGE TOWN, GRAND CAYMAN, KY1-1208, CAYMAN ISLANDS.
REID, Mr. Damian Hugh, BSc ACA *1988;* 5th Floor, 55 Baker Street, LONDON, W1U 8AN.
•REID, Mr. Daniel Charles William, MA ACA *2004;* Donald Reid Limited, Prince Albert House, 20 King Street, MAIDENHEAD, BERKSHIRE, SL6 1DT. See also Coyne Butterworth (Dorchester) Limited
•REID, Mr. David Maurice, BSc FCA *1990;* 36 Jackson Place, TORONTO M6P 1T6, ON, CANADA.
•REID, Mr. David Michael, BSc FCA *1970;* (Tax Fac), David Reid Accountancy Ltd, Unit 4, The Bardfield Centre, Braintree Road, Great Bardfield, BRAINTREE ESSEX CM7 4SL. See also David Reid Audit And Accountancy Ltd
REID, Miss. Dawn Margaret, BSc ACA *1990;* Poppy Cottage, Brackenhill, Cawood, SELBY, YO8 3TU.
REID, Mrs. Deborah Karen, BA ACA *1985;* University of Central Lancashire Adelphi Building, Fylde Road, PRESTON, LANCASHIRE, PR1 2HE.
REID, Mr. Donald Peter, FCA *1964;* Garden Reach, Gibraltar Lane, Cookham Dean, MAIDENHEAD, SL6 9TR. (Life Member)
REID, Mr. Duncan Murray, BSc ACA *1989;* 96 Wise Lane, LONDON, NW7 2RD.
•REID, Mr. Ewan David, FCA CTA *1993;* (Tax Fac), 27a Elwood, HARLOW, CM17 9QJ.
REID, Miss. Fiona McNair, BA(Hons) ACA *2002;* 15 Henderson Avenue, GUILDFORD, SURREY, GU2 9LP.
•REID, Mrs. Frances Mary, BSc FCA *1988;* (Tax Fac), HW Associates, Portmill House, Portmill Lane, HITCHIN, HERTFORDSHIRE, SG5 1DJ.
REID, Mr. Francis Henry Marcus, BA ACA *1985;* 94 Hambalt Road, LONDON, SW4 9EJ.
•REID, Mr. Francis Patrick Andrew, FCA *1978;* Granary Accounting Ltd, The Granary, Wheatlands Manor, Park Lane, Finchampstead, WOKINGHAM BERKSHIRE RG40 4QL.
•REID, Mr. George McGrimmon, BSc FCA *1991;* Ernst & Young LLP, Ten George Street, EDINBURGH, EH2 2DZ. See also Ernst & Young Europe LLP
•REID, Mr. Graeme Charles, BSc FCA *1988;* G.C. Reid & Co, 57 Hull Road, COTTINGHAM, NORTH HUMBERSIDE, HU16 4PT.
REID, Mr. Graham Alexander, FCA *1962;* (Tax Fac), 66 Avenue Terlinden, B1310 LA HULPE, BELGIUM.
REID, Mr. Graham Charles, FCA *1970;* Mitchery Farm House, Mitchery Lane, Rattlesden, BURY ST. EDMUNDS, SUFFOLK, IP30 0SS. (Life Member)
REID, Mr. Graham Matheson, BSc ACA CF *1991;* Integrated Capital Solutions, National Australia Bank, Level 23, 255 George Street, SYDNEY, NSW 2000 AUSTRALIA.
REID, Miss. Hannah, BSc ACA *2004;* with Ernst & Young LLP, 1 Colmore Square, BIRMINGHAM, B4 6HQ.
REID, Mr. Ian, FCA *1973;* 59 Canadian Bay Road, MOUNT ELIZA, VIC 3930, AUSTRALIA.
REID, Mr. Ian Clive, BA ACA CTA *1992;* (Tax Fac), The Counting House, 4 Mount Beacon Place, BATH, BA1 5SP.
REID, Mr. James, BEng ACA *2007;* Apt 1102 Oakwood Apartments Roppongi Central 3-8-5 Roppongi Minato-ku, TOKYO, 106-0032 JAPAN.
REID, Mr. James John, BSc ACA *2005;* 20 Arne Grove, ORPINGTON, KENT, BR6 9TT.
REID, Mr. James Richard Arthur, FCA *1958;* 4 Greenwood Close, FAREHAM, PO16 7UF. (Life Member)
REID, Miss. Janie, BSc ACA *2006;* 2 Peartree Avenue, LONDON, SW17 0JG.
REID, Miss. Joanna Mary, BA ACA *2007;* (Tax Fac), 114 Woodmansterne Road, Streatham, LONDON, SW16 5UQ.
REID, Mrs. Joanne, BSc ACA *2003;* 16 Shepherds Way, HARPENDEN, HERTFORDSHIRE, AL5 3HF.
REID, Mr. John, BCom FCA *1956;* 68 Porters Road, KENTHURST, NSW 2156, AUSTRALIA. (Life Member)
•①REID, Mr. John Charles, MA ACA *1985;* Deloitte LLP, Saltire Court, 20 Castle Terrace, EDINBURGH, EH1 2DB. See also Deloitte & Touche LLP
REID, Mr. John Mcdonald, BA FCA *1972;* #1002, 1717 Bayshore Drive, British Columbia, VANCOUVER V6G 3H3, BC, CANADA. (Life Member)
REID, Mr. John Steele Thorney, FCA *1973;* Fox Financial Training, Fox House, Southend Bradfield, READING, RG7 6ER.
REID, Mr. John Wilson, FCA *1958;* 8405 Riverside Drive, POWELL, OH 43065, UNITED STATES. (Life Member)
REID, Mr. Jonathan, BEng ACA *2002;* Flat 15 Nathan House, Reedworth Street, LONDON, SE11 4PG.
REID, Mr. Jonathan, BSc ACA *2001;* 28 Stanley Road, WORTHING, WEST SUSSEX, BN11 1DT.
REID, Miss. Judith Louise, BSocSc ACA *2002;* 3 Venice Court Wake Green Park, BIRMINGHAM, B13 9YL.
•REID, Mrs. Kathryn Ann, BSc FCA *1987;* Baker Tilly UK Audit LLP, Elgar House, Holmer Road, HEREFORD, HR4 9SF. See also Baker Tilly Tax and Advisory Services LLP
REID, Mr. Keith, BA FCA *1977;* Buces, Mendlesham, STOWMARKET, SUFFOLK, IP14 5NR.
REID, Mr. Kenneth Edward John, BSc ACA *1994;* 23 Adelaide Street, Balgowlah Heights, SYDNEY, NSW 2093, AUSTRALIA.
REID, Mr. Kevin Richard, FCA *1983;* PricewaterhouseCoopers, Darling Park Tower 2, 201 Sussex Street, GPO Box 2650, SYDNEY, NSW 1171 AUSTRALIA.
REID, Miss. Kirsten Margaret Cray, BA FCA *1991;* Room 223, The Innovation Centre, 1 Evolution Park Haslingden Road, BLACKBURN, BB1 2FD.
REID, Mrs. Louise, BA ACA *2002;* 7 Birkdale Close, Molehill Road, WHITSTABLE, KENT, CT5 3PY.
•REID, Mr. Malcolm, FCA *1957;* Malcolm Reid & Co, Caudle Street, High Street, HENFIELD, WEST SUSSEX, BN5 9DQ.
REID, Mr. Malcolm Gwilym, BTech FCA *1975;* 13 Meadowside, WALTON-ON-THAMES, SURREY, KT12 3LS.
REID, Mr. Mark Anthony, ACA *1980;* EGRET HOUSE, JUMBY BAY, LONG ISLAND, ANTIGUA AND BARBUDA.
REID, Mr. Martin Paul, BSc ACA *1995;* 23 Holly Court, Blackthorn Manor, Oadby, LEICESTER, LE2 4EH.
REID, Mr. Maxwell Jonathan, BA ACA *1991;* The Old Mill, Millhouse Lane, Millhouse Green, SHEFFIELD, S36 9NU.
•REID, Mr. Michael Charles, ACA *1981;* Goodin Reid & Co, 7 Woodside Road, NEW MALDEN, KT3 3AH.
REID, Mr. Michael John, MA FCA *1976;* 49 Waldemar Avenue, LONDON, W13 9PZ.
REID, Mr. Michael William John, FCA *1959;* Crabtree Hall, Mill Lane, Lower Beeding, HORSHAM, RH13 6PX. (Life Member)
•REID, Miss. Morag Elspeth, PhD BSc ACA *2002;* Morag Reid, Blackhillock, Glenbuchat, STRATHDON, ABERDEENSHIRE, AB36 8TQ.
REID, Mr. Morgan Bernardine Gerard, BSc FCA *1978;* Kiruna, 11 Heath Close, HINDHEAD, GU26 6RX.
REID, Mr. Neville Christopher, BA ACA *1986;* Poplar Harca Unit 3 Quebec Wharf, 14 Thomas Road, LONDON, E14 7AF.
REID, Mr. Nicholas Timothy John, BSc ACA *1992;* 11 Dewhurst Road, LONDON, W14 0ET.
REID, Mr. Nigel James Hamilton, ACA *1982;* Flat 3d No.5 Parkvale, Parkvale Village, Discovery Bay, LANTAU ISLAND, NEW TERRITORIES, HONG KONG SAR.
REID, Mrs. Nina Rose, BA(Hons) ACA *2000;* Domino UK Ltd, Trafalgar Way, Bar Hill, CAMBRIDGE, CB23 8TU.
REID, Mr. Norman George, FCA *1940;* Hill House, RR1, LINDSAY K9V 4R1, ON, CANADA. (Life Member)
•REID, Mr. Paul, BA ACA *2000;* Resolve Cambridge Ltd, Tyburn House, Station Road, Oakington, CAMBRIDGE, CB24 3AH.
•REID, Mr. Richard Harry, FCA *1980;* (Member of Council 2006 - 2010), KPMG LLP, 15 Canada Square, LONDON, E14 5GL. See also KPMG Europe LLP

REID, Mr. Richard Michael, BA ACA *1982;* Ravenswood, Stanley Road, Battledown, CHELTENHAM, GLOUCESTERSHIRE, GL52 6PB.
REID, Mr. Robert Alan Bowen, ACA *1980;* 3 Baydon Drive, READING, RG1 6JB.
REID, Mr. Ronald James, MA FCA *1980;* Ackleton Manor, Folley Road, Ackleton, WOLVERHAMPTON, WV6 7JL.
REID, Mrs. Sarah Louise, BA ACA *1995;* The Old School House School Lane, Baslow, BAKEWELL, DERBYSHIRE, DE45 1RZ.
REID, Mr. Sean Neil, BEng ACA *1992;* 17 Mimosa Street, Fulham, LONDON, SW6 4DS.
REID, Mr. Simon David, BSc FCA *1993;* Oakley House Headway Business Park, 3 Saxon Way West, CORBY, NORTHAMPTONSHIRE, NN18 9EZ.
REID, Mr. Stephen, BA ACA *2011;* Flat 71, Catalpa Court, Hither Green Lane, LONDON, SE13 6TG.
REID, Mr. Stephen Anderson, BCom ACA *1998;* 6 Locksley Gardens, Winnersh, WOKINGHAM, BERKSHIRE, RG41 5NZ.
REID, Mr. Steven Robert, BA ACA *1990;* 7 Jennings Close, St James Park Long Ditton, SURBITON, KT6 5RB.
REID, Mr. Stuart John, MEng ACA *1993;* 2 Hawthorn Gardens, WHITLEY BAY, NE26 3PQ.
REID, Mr. Stuart Kenneth, BSc ACA *2008;* 13 Bryn Dewi Sant, Miskin, PONTYCLUN, MID GLAMORGAN, CF72 8TJ.
REID, Miss. Susan Alice, BA ACA *1992;* 10 Fortescue Drive, Shenley Church End, MILTON KEYNES, MK5 6BJ.
•REID, Miss. Susan Morrison, BSc FCA *1982;* Rock House, Blazefield, HARROGATE, HG3 5DP.
•REID, Mrs. Tabitha Belinda, BCom ACA *2004;* 9 Abbey Road, BOURNE END, BUCKINGHAMSHIRE, SL8 5NZ.
REID, Prof. Walter, MA FCA *1961;* 17 Burghley Road, LONDON, SW19 5BG. (Life Member)
REID, Mr. William Marston, BA(Hons) ACA *2011;* Flat 24, Oxford Court, Queens Drive, LONDON, W3 0HH.
•REID-MARR, Mr. Godfrey, FCA *1963;* Fourwood Services Limited, 18 Cedar Drive, Barming, MAIDSTONE, KENT, ME16 9HD.
REIDY, Mr. Jeremiah Stephen, BSc ACA *1991;* 19b Hermitage Road, Edgbaston, BIRMINGHAM, B15 3UP.
•REIFER, Mr. Abraham, FCA CTA *1980;* (Tax Fac), Reifer & Co, 23 Craven Walk, LONDON, N16 6BS.
REILLY, Mr. Alan William, BSc ACA *1986;* 14 Carleton Gardens, POULTON-LE-FYLDE, FY6 7PB.
REILLY, Mrs. Alison Jane, BSc ACA *1992;* 46 Alric Avenue, NEW MALDEN, KT3 4JN.
REILLY, Mr. Benjamin, MA BSc(Hons) ACA *2011;* Flat 2, 5 Eckstein Road, LONDON, SW11 1QE.
REILLY, Mr. Brian John, FCA *1974;* 23 Karen Road, Illiondale, EDENVALE, 1609, SOUTH AFRICA.
REILLY, Mr. Christopher John, BSc ACA *2010;* 60 Victoria Court, New Street, CHELMSFORD, CM1 1GP.
REILLY, Mr. Christopher John, BA FCA *1988;* Cazenove Capital Management Ltd, 12 Moorgate, LONDON, EC2R 6DA.
REILLY, Mr. David Joseph, BA FCA FTII *1990;* with Grant Thornton UK LLP, Grant Thornton House, 22 Melton Street, Euston Square, LONDON, NW1 2EP.
REILLY, Mr. Howard Neil, BA ACA *1980;* The Little Thatch Galtons Lane, Belbroughton, STOURBRIDGE, DY9 9TS.
REILLY, Mr. Jakob, BA ACA *2002;* 67 South Street, EPSOM, SURREY, KT18 7PY.
REILLY, Miss. Jane Carmel, BSc ACA *2005;* 1 The Meadows, Maghull, LIVERPOOL, L31 6EY.
REILLY, Mrs. Jill Anita, BSc ACA *1990;* 2GA07, Glaxosmithkline Pharmaceuticals (Ware) Ltd, Park Road, WARE, HERTFORDSHIRE, SG12 0DP.
REILLY, Mr. John, BA ACA *2007;* with PricewaterhouseCoopers LLP, Marlborough Court, 10 Bricket Road, ST. ALBANS, HERTFORDSHIRE, AL1 3JX.
REILLY, Mr. Mark, BSc ACA *1996;* Johnson Matthey Plc, Orchard Road, ROYSTON, HERTFORDSHIRE, SG8 5HE.
•REILLY, Miss. Mary Margaret, BA FCA *1979;* Deloitte LLP, 2 New Street Square, LONDON, EC4A 3BZ. See also Deloitte & Touche LLP
•REILLY, Mr. Peter Alexander, BA FCA *1990;* (Tax Fac), Edwards Rowley & Co, 168A Hoylake Road, Moreton, WIRRAL, CH46 8TQ.
REILLY, Mr. Sidney Hugh, FCA *1958;* 1 Edgewood Court, Sacriston, DURHAM, DH7 6XH. (Life Member)
REILLY, Mr. Stephen Hugh, MA ACA *1988;* Tir Onnen, Five Roads, LLANELLI, DYFED, SA15 4NB.
REILLY, Mrs. Tracy, ACA *2003;* 257A Levers Road, Matua, TAURANGA 3110, BAY OF PLENTY, NEW ZEALAND.
REILLY, Dr. William Mark, ACA *1990;* (Tax Fac), Glaxo Smithkline, 6/F The Headquarters Building, #168 Tibet Road (M), SHANGHAI 200001, CHINA.
REIMER, Mr. Stephen Peter Thomas, FCA *1976;* SR Management Services Ltd, 52 Milton Crescent, EAST GRINSTEAD, RH19 1TN.
•REIMERS, Mr. Herbert Koert Oskar, ACA *2006;* T Smalle Weer 2, 2265EB LEIDSCHENDAM, NETHERLANDS.
REINDEL, Mr. Matthew, BA ACA *1996;* 202 Kim Seng Road #34-07, SINGAPORE 239496, SINGAPORE.
REINECKE, Mr. Daniel John, ACA CA(SA) *2009;* 11c Lansdowne Road, LONDON, SW20 8AN.
•REINECKE, Mr. Marc, ACA *2007;* BDO LLP, 55 Baker Street, LONDON, W1U 7EU. See also BDO Stoy Hayward LLP
REINECKE, Mrs. Melanie Tracey Margaret, ACA CA(SA) *2009;* 23 Kew Crescent, SINGAPORE 466213, SINGAPORE.
REIS, Mr. Reni Miguel, ACA *2008;* 15 Harrier Way, BRACKNELL, BERKSHIRE, RG12 8AU.
•REIS, Mrs. Sarah Francine, BSc FCA ATII CFE *2000;* Lucas Reis Limited, Landmark House, Station Road, Cheadle Hulme, CHEADLE, CHESHIRE SK8 7BS.
REISER, Mr. Michael Bernard, BSc FCA *1972;* Newalls, Batts Bridge Road, Maresfield, UCKFIELD, TN22 2HJ. (Life Member)
•REISMAN, Mr. Melvyn Stanley, BSc ACA *1983;* Reisman & Co, 63 High Road, Bushey Heath, BUSHEY, WD23 1EE.
•REISS, Mr. Martin, BSc FCA *1961;* 9 De Walden Court, 85 New Cavendish Street, LONDON, W1W 6XD.
REITH, Mr. Colin John, MSc ACA *1985;* Holme Park Stud, Hinxworth Road, Ashwell, BALDOCK, SG7 5HY.
REITH, Mrs. Deborah Jayne, LLB ACA *1999;* (Tax Fac), 5 Studdridge Court, Stokenchurch, HIGH WYCOMBE, BUCKINGHAMSHIRE, HP14 3UL.
REITZE, Mr. Darran, ACA *2011;* 3 Bermudiana Road, HAMILTON HM11, BERMUDA.
•RELF, Mr. Clive Neil, FCA *1980;* (Tax Fac), Reeves & Co LLP, 37 St. Margarets Street, CANTERBURY, KENT, CT1 2TU.
•RELF, Mrs. Julie Dawn, BA(Hons) ACA *2003;* Applause Accountancy Services Ltd, 60 Beamish View, BIRTLEY, COUNTY DURHAM, DH3 1RS. See also Applause Accountancy Services
RELF, Mr. Paul David, FCA *1985;* 48 Wyles Road, CHATHAM, KENT, ME4 6LD.
RELF, Mr. Stephen John, MPhil BA ACA CTA *2002;* 60 Beamish View, Birtley, CHESTER LE STREET, COUNTY DURHAM, DH3 1RS.
RELLEEN, Mr. Christopher John, BSc FCA *1972;* 3 Claygate Lodge Close, Claygate, ESHER, KT10 0PS.
•RELPH, Mr. Neil Andrew, ACA *1981;* Rouse Audit LLP, 55 Station Road, BEACONSFIELD, BUCKINGHAMSHIRE, HP9 1QL. See also Rouse Partners LLP
RELTON, Mrs. Elizabeth Margaret, PhD ACA *1991;* 43 St. Georges Road, SEVENOAKS, KENT, TN13 3ND.
RELTON, Mr. Peter Edward, BA ACA *1993;* Heath Farm Ponsongath, Coverack, HELSTON, CORNWALL, TR12 6SQ.
REMEDIOS, Mr. Eugene Francis, MSc ACA *1984;* 3 Coronation Avenue, CRONULLA, NSW 2230, AUSTRALIA.
•REMEDIOS, Mr. Oscar Francis, BA FCA CISA *1992;* 8 Laurel Terrace, WELLESLEY HILLS, MA 02481-7515, UNITED STATES.
REMEDIOS, Ms. Yvette Isis Judith, BA ACA *1990;* 52 Crown Walk, WEMBLEY, HA9 8HU.
REMINGTON, Mr. David Graham, FCA *1973;* 14 Abbots Close, GUILDFORD, GU2 7RW.
•REMINGTON, Mr. David William, BA ACA *1992;* Jon Child & Co, 107 Oldham Street, MANCHESTER, M4 1LW.
REMINGTON, Mr. Michael, ACA *2009;* 15 Maple Leaf Drive, SIDCUP, DA15 8WG.
REMINGTON, Mr. Philip John, BA ACA *1982;* 4 Church Lane, Kimpton, HITCHIN, HERTFORDSHIRE, SG4 8RP.
REMNANT, Lord James Wogan, CVO FCA *1955;* 53a Northfield End, HENLEY-ON-THAMES, OXFORDSHIRE, RG9 2JJ. (Life Member)
REMNANT, Mr. Luke, BSc(Hons) ACA *2000;* with Deloitte LLP, Global House, High Street, CRAWLEY, RH10 1DL.
REMNANT, The Hon. Philip John, CBE MA ACA *1979;* Ham Farm House, Ham Lane, Baughurst, TADLEY, RG26 5SD.
REN, Mrs. Xue Jie, MSc ACA *2009;* Pierhead Lock, Flat 31, 416 Manchester Road, LONDON, E14 3FD.
RENAGHAN, Mr. James Michael, MA FCA *1986;* S J Bargh Ltd Hornby Road, Caton, LANCASTER, LA2 9JA.
•RENAK, Mr. Leigh Maurice, BA FCA *1981;* Your Business Partners Limited, Bowmans House, Bessemer Drive, STEVENAGE, HERTFORDSHIRE, SG1 2DL.
RENAUD, Ms. Jane Caroline, BSc ACA *1990;* 8 Croham Manor Road, SOUTH CROYDON, SURREY, CR2 7BE.
RENAUD, Mr. Jean-Pierre Cecil, ACA *1994;* Madresfield House, Rectory Lane, Madresfield, MALVERN, WR13 5AB.
RENAUD, Mr. Sonny James, FCA *1979;* 43 Highgate Crescent, WINNIPEG R2N 1T8, MB, CANADA.
RENAUT, Mr. Edward Toby, BSc ACA *2010;* 11 Meadow Way, HORLEY, SURREY, RH6 9JA.
RENDALL, Mr. Lee, BSc ACA *1989;* Bonhams, 101 New Bond Street, LONDON, W1S 1SR.
RENDALL, Mr. Michael James Ledger, BSc ACA *1989;* The Oast House, Lower Church Farm, Speldhurst, TUNBRIDGE WELLS, TN3 0NJ.
RENDALL, Mr. Peter Alan, BSc ACA *1992;* 70 Concord Road, WESTFORD, MA 01886, UNITED STATES.
RENDALL, Mr. Peter Frank, BA ACA *1997;* 94 Cornerswell Road, PENARTH, SOUTH GLAMORGAN, CF64 2WB.
RENDALL, Mr. Richard James Spencer, FCA *1973;* Trerice Farm, Burlawn, WADEBRIDGE, CORNWALL, PL27 7LE.
•RENDALL, Mr. Stephen Charles, BSc FCA *1983;* Ivan Rendall & Co, Torre Lea House, 33 The Avenue, YEOVIL, BA21 4BN. See also Rendalls Limited
RENDALL, Mr. Thomas Moinet, BA FCA *1965;* 4 Pipe Aston Barns, Pipe Aston, LUDLOW, SHROPSHIRE, SY8 2HG.
RENDALL, Mr. Timothy, BA ACA *1992;* 111B Greenvale Drive, GREENVALE, VIC 3059, AUSTRALIA.
RENDELL, Mr. Charles Ian, BSc FCA *1991;* 31 Harmer Green Lane, Digswell, WELWYN, AL6 0AS.
RENDELL, Mr. Colin James, FCA *1956;* Queen Elizabeth Cottage, 42 Broadtown, SWINDON, SN4 7RE. (Life Member)
RENDELL, Mr. John Austin, BSc FCA *1977;* Candover, Old Park, DEVIZES, WILTSHIRE, SN10 5JR.
•①RENDELL, Mr. Julian Clive, BA FCA *1981;* Rendell & Co, 125 Portway, WELLS, BA5 2BR. See also Rendell Thompson
RENDELL, Mrs. Kathryn Patricia, BA ACA *1983;* 24 Red House Lane, Westbury On Trym, BRISTOL, BS9 3RZ.
RENDELL, Mr. Patrick Edward, FCA *1961;* Three Oaks Cottage Sandy Lane, Dockenfield, FARNHAM, GU10 4EQ. (Life Member)
RENDELL, Mr. Paul John, BSc ACA *1984;* Tellermate Ltd, Unit 15 Leeway Industrial Estate, NEWPORT, GWENT, NP19 4SL.
RENDELL, Mr. Peter Jocelyn Parminter, FCA *1975;* Peter Rendell Chartered Accountants, PO Box 7333, Taradale, NAPIER 4141, NEW ZEALAND.
RENDELL, Dr. Richard William, PhD BSc ACA *1983;* 11 Tytherington Park Road, Tytherington, MACCLESFIELD, CHESHIRE, SK10 2EL.
RENDLE, Mr. Peter John, BEng ACA *2007;* Lower Mellguards, Park Road, TIVERTON, DEVON, EX16 6AU.
•①RENDLE, Mr. Richard Paul, FCA *1982;* R P Rendle & Co Limited, No 9 Hockley Court, Hockley Heath, SOLIHULL, WEST MIDLANDS, B94 6NW. See also R P Rendle & Co
•RENDLE, Mr. Robert, FCA *1957;* R.Rendle, 38 Antonio Nani Street, TA'XBIEX XBX 1086, MALTA.
RENDU, Mrs. Clare Louise, BSc ACA *2006;* 141 High Street, Bitton, BRISTOL, BS30 6HQ.
RENEL, Mr. Marie Gilbert Michel-Ange, BSc ACA *1987;* 22 Rue Weistroffer, L 1898 KOCKLESCHEUER, LUXEMBOURG.
RENFORD, Dr. Raymond Kevin, FCA ACMA CPA *1954;* 27 Leah Street, 34403 HAIFA, ISRAEL. (Life Member)
RENFREW, Mr. Gavin Stuart Dobbie, BSc(Hons) ACA *2001;* 28 Convent Close, HITCHIN, HERTFORDSHIRE, SG5 1QN.
RENFREW, Mr. Stewart Lennox, BA ACA *1989;* 17 The Granary, Wynyard, BILLINGHAM, TS22 5QG.
RENGANATHAN, Mrs. Sashi Kala Devi, ACA CPA *1981;* Sashi Kala Devi Associates, 31 Cantonment Road, SINGAPORE 089747, SINGAPORE.
•RENGERT, Mr. Christopher, FCA *1961;* (Tax Fac), C. Rengert & Company Limited, 24 High Street, SAFFRON WALDEN, CB10 1AX. See also Chequers Tax Bureau Limited
RENGOS, Mr. Nicholas John, MA ACA *2010;* Flat 3 Victoria House Epsom Road, LEATHERHEAD, SURREY, KT22 8TB.
RENISON, Mr. Philip Anthony John, BA ACA *2002;* 86 Kennington Avenue, Bishopston, BRISTOL, BS7 9ES.
RENISON, Mrs. Sally, BSc ACA *2003;* 86 Kennington Avenue, Bishopston, BRISTOL, BS7 9ES.
RENNARD, Mr. Paul Anthony, BSc ACA *1985;* Soha Housing, Royal Scot House, 99 Station Road, DIDCOT, OX11 7NN.
RENNELLS, Mr. Graham John, FCA *1987;* with Batchelor Coop Ltd, The New Barn, Mill Lane, Eastry, SANDWICH, CT13 0JW.
RENNIE, Mr. Adrian James, BSc ARCS ACA *1993;* 2-4 Rue Eugene Ruppert, Vertigo Buildings, Polaris, LUXEMBOURG, LUXEMBOURG.
RENNIE, Mr. Alan, BA ACA *2011;* Flat 932 Whitehouse Apartments, 9 Belvedere Road, LONDON, SE1 8YW.
•RENNIE, Mr. Alexander Donald, BAcc ACA CTA *2002;* Fiveoaks Accountancy Services, Fiveoaks, Gatelawbridge, THORNHILL, DUMFRIESSHIRE, DG3 5EA.
RENNIE, Mr. Duncan Thomas, BSc(Hons) ACA *2004;* 2nd Floor, Universities Superannuation Scheme Ltd Royal Liver Building, Pier Head, LIVERPOOL, L3 1PY.
RENNIE, Mrs. Gail Marie, BSc ACA *1993;* Brock House, 2A Brockhurst Way, NORTHWICH, CHESHIRE, CW9 8AP.
RENNIE, Mr. Gavin Alexander Howieson, BA ACA *1989;* 73 Armour Hill, Tilehurst, READING, RG31 6JH.
RENNIE, Mrs. Helen Elizabeth, MBChB ACA *2002;* 24 West Street, LEICESTER, LE1 6XQ.
RENNIE, Mrs. Hilary Jane, ACA *1992;* 39 West Drive, Sonning, READING, RG4 6GE.
RENNIE, Mrs. Kim Michelle, BSc ACA *1990;* 15 Connaught Road, HARPENDEN, HERTFORDSHIRE, AL5 4TW.
RENNIE, Ms. Melanie Louise, BA ACA *2002;* 3 Wheatleys, ST. ALBANS, HERTFORDSHIRE, AL4 9UE.
RENNIE, Mr. Paul David, ACA *1981;* White Lodge, Les Grupieaux, St Peter, JERSEY, JE3 7ED.
RENNIE, Mr. Peter David, BSc ACA *1991;* Redwood House, 39 West Drive, Sonning, READING, RG4 6GE.
RENNIE, Miss. Vicky, BSc ACA *2010;* 39 Cavendish Road, ST. ALBANS, HERTFORDSHIRE, AL1 5EF.
RENNIE, Mr. Vincent James, BA ACA *1981;* Zurich Financial Services UK Life Centre, Station Road, SWINDON, SN1 1EL.
RENNISON, Mrs. Carole Margaret, BSc ACA *1986;* Fernbank, How Lane, Chipstead, COULSDON, CR5 3LT.
RENNISON, Mr. John Robert Alexander, BSc ACA *1987;* Moor House Lower Road, Hardwick, AYLESBURY, BUCKINGHAMSHIRE, HP22 4DZ.
•RENNISON, Mr. Mark Martin, BA FCA *1986;* Fernbank, How Lane, Chipstead, COULSDON, SURREY, CR5 3LT.
RENNISON, Ms. Yvonne, MA ACA CTA *1995;* (Tax Fac), 184 Cannock Road, Westcroft, WOLVERHAMPTON, WV10 8QP.
RENNIX, Miss. Catherine Louise, BAcc ACA *2000;* 15 Cliveden Crescent, BELFAST, BT8 6ND.
RENNOCKS, Mr. John Leonard, FCA *1967;* Crown Acre, Queens Drive, Oxshott, LEATHERHEAD, KT22 0PB.
RENNOCKS, Mrs. Rachel Jayne, ACA *2008;* Lucentum Ltd, Kensal House, 77 Springfield Road, CHELMSFORD, CM2 6JG.
RENOUF, Mrs. Louise, BA ACA *1993;* Deo Juvante, Ruette de Saumarez, Castel, GUERNSEY, GY5 7TJ.
RENSHALL, Mr. James Michael, CBE MA FCA *1957;* (Member of Council 1986 - 1990), New House, Staunton-on-Wye, HEREFORD, HR4 7LW. (Life Member)
RENSHAW, Mr. Andrew Frazer, ACA *1987;* Emil Klumpp-Str 17, 74321 BIETIGHEIM-BISSINGEN, GERMANY.
RENSHAW, Mr. Charles Stanley, FCA *1952;* Arwynfa, Panteg Cross, Croeslan, LLANDYSUL, SA44 4SL. (Life Member)
RENSHAW, Mr. Jamie, BA ACA *2010;* 71 Wagstaff Lane, Jacksdale, NOTTINGHAM, NG16 5JL.
RENSHAW, Mr. Keith Andrew, BSc ACA *1985;* Finance Shared Service Centre, B A E Systems, Glascoed, USK, GWENT, NP15 1XL.
RENSHAW, Mr. Matthew, BA ACA *2010;* 99 Campden Crescent, CLEETHORPES, SOUTH HUMBERSIDE, DN35 7UG.
RENSHAW, Mr. Peter James, FCA *1971;* Greenaway, Warren Drive, Kingswood, TADWORTH, KT20 6PZ.
RENSHAW, Mr. Simon James, MSc BA ACA *2006;* 20 Fitzalan Road, LONDON, N3 3PD.
RENSHAW, Mr. William George, FCA *1973;* 28 Foxhall Close, COLWYN BAY, CLWYD, LL29 8RT. (Life Member)
RENSHAW AMES, Mrs. Elizabeth Kay, BA FCA *1984;* 97 Howards Lane, LONDON, SW15 6NZ.
RENTON, Mr. Adam John, BA ACA *1997;* (Tax Fac), Flat 3 The Cooperage, 6 Gainsford Street, LONDON, SE1 2NG.

RENTON, Mr. Colin Harrison, FCA *1956;* 59 Park Place, Park Parade, HARROGATE, NORTH YORKSHIRE, HG1 5NS. (Life Member)
RENTON, Mr. Daniel Paul, BEng BCom ACA CF *1997;* 12 Gateland Drive, Shadwell, LEEDS, LS17 8HU.
RENTON, Mr. David Jonathan, BA ACA *1996;* 14 Craigwell Drive, SUNDERLAND, SR3 2TR.
RENTON, Mr. Elliot Paul, BA FCA *1994;* London Luton Airport Operations Ltd, Navigation House, Airport Way, LUTON, LU2 9LY.
RENTON, Mrs. Joanne Elizabeth, BSc(Hons) ACA *2001;* Unit 37, 20 Eve Street, ERSKINEVILLE, NSW 2043, AUSTRALIA.
RENTON, Ms. Lindsey-Jane, BSc ACA *1999;* Darville Lodge, Station Road, Lower Heyford, BICESTER, OXFORDSHIRE, OX25 5PD.
RENTON, Mr. Mark, MA ACA *1984;* 61 North Street, RYE, NY 10580, UNITED STATES.
•RENTON, Mr. Stephen Norman, FCA *1975;* Renton & Co, Chalkwell Park House, 700 London Road, WESTCLIFF-ON-SEA, SS0 9HQ.
RENTON, Mrs. Susan Mary, BSc ACA *2006;* with Grosvenor Group Limited, 70 Grosvenor Street, LONDON, W1K 3JP.
RENTOUL, Mr. James Alexander, MA ACA *1979;* 42 Hartington Road, LONDON, W4 3TX.
•RENTSCH, Mr. Stephen Anthony, BA FCA *1993;* BBA Limited, Beachside Business Centre, La Rue du Hocq, St Clement, JERSEY, JE2 6LF.
RENVOIZE, Mr. Jaime Alexander, BSc ACA *1998;* 13 St. Leonards Road, SURBITON, KT6 4DE.
•RENVOIZE, Mr. Stephen Ronald, BA ACA *1981;* S R Renvoize Limited, St Edmunds House, 1 Arwela Road, FELIXSTOWE, IP11 2DG.
RENWICK, Mr. Andrew, BSc ACA *1993;* 16 Queens Road, BRENTWOOD, Essex, CM14 4HE.
RENWICK, Mrs. Beverley Dawn, BA ACA *1992;* 12 Morven Road, SUTTON COLDFIELD, B73 6NB.
RENWICK, Mr. David John Frederick, BA ACA *1986;* 18 Central Rd, Rossmoyne, PERTH, WA 6148, AUSTRALIA.
RENWICK, Mr. Geoffrey Owen Norman, FCA *1961;* Verity, 3 West Avenue, Middleton On Sea, BOGNOR REGIS, PO22 6EF.
RENWICK, Mr. Graham Andrew, BSc ACA *1993;* 2 Lime Tree Drive, Brandesburton, DRIFFIELD, NORTH HUMBERSIDE, YO25 8RQ.
RENWICK, Mr. John Stuart, FCA *1964;* 131 Church Lane, Marple, STOCKPORT, SK6 7LD. (Life Member)
RENWICK, Mr. Keith Victor, FCA *1985;* 12 Third Avenue, Charmandean, WORTHING, BN14 9NZ.
RENWICK, Mr. Paul, ACA *1994;* 2 Rye Close, SLEAFORD, LINCOLNSHIRE, NG34 7BT.
•RENWICK, Mr. Robert Hugh, FCA *1967;* R.H. Renwick, 121-123 High Street, NORTHALLERTON, DL7 8PQ.
RENWICK, Mr. Stephen George, BA FCA CPFA *1991;* 25 Winton Terrace, EDINBURGH, EH10 7AT.
REOCH, Mrs. Annabel Hardman, MA ACA *2004;* Apartment 16a, 101 Amies Street, LONDON, SW11 2JW.
REOCH, Miss. Eleanor, BA ACA *2006;* with Deloitte Middle East, Currency House, Building 1 Level 5, DIFC, PO Box 282056, DUBAI UNITED ARAB EMIRATES.
RESHAD, Mr. Reza, MSc BSc ACA *2010;* 20a Hilgrove Road, LONDON, NW6 4TN.
RESNEKOV, Mr. David Ian, BSc FCA *1984;* 2 Chapel Gardens, BRISTOL, BS10 7DF.
RESTALL, Mrs. Sarah Elizabeth, MA ACA *2010;* 66 Auckland Road, POTTERS BAR, HERTFORDSHIRE, EN6 3HS.
•RESTELL, Mrs. Imogen Harriet, ACA *2002;* JJ Accountancy Ltd, 41 Alma Way, FARNHAM, SURREY, GU9 0QN.
RET, Mr. Daniel Marcus, FCA *1997;* Virgin Media, Bartley Way, HOOK, HAMPSHIRE, RG27 9UP.
RETCHAKAN, Miss. Varah, MA ACA CPA *1993;* 1615 Greenleaf Oaks Drive, SUGARLAND, TX 77479, UNITED STATES.
•RETHINASAMY, Dr. Peter, FCA *1966;* P Rethinasamy & Co, Kompleks Skomk, Block A 2nd Floor, Jalan Mahkamah, PO Box 117, 36008 DR TELUK INTAN PERAK MALAYSIA.
•RETOUT, Mr. Paul Gerard, FCA *1984;* (Tax Fac), Retout Capel & Co, Unit 4, Ffordd yr onnen, Lon Parcwr Business Park, RUTHIN, CLWYD LL15 1NJ.
RETOUT, Mr. Peter Anthony, FCA ACIS *1969;* 13 Alder Gardens, BEXHILL-ON-SEA, EAST SUSSEX, TN39 5JY. (Life Member)
RETTER, Mr. Simon, BSc ACA *2007;* Stonebrook, Woodbury Salterton, EXETER, EX5 1PS.
RETTKE-GROVER, Mr. Ralph Frederick, BSc ACA *1988;* 32 Westhorpe Road, Putney, LONDON, SW15 1QH.
•REUBEN, Mr. Howard Robert, FCA *1972;* (Tax Fac), Montpelier Audit Limited, Montpelier House, 62-66 Deansgate, MANCHESTER, M3 2EN. See also Montpelier Professional (West End) Ltd
REUBERSON, Mrs. Emma Louise, PhD BSc ACA *2005;* 16 Tithing Road, FLEET, HAMPSHIRE, GU51 1GG.
REUSCH, Mr. Thomas Christof, BA ACA *1999;* 3 The Avenue, POTTERS BAR, HERTFORDSHIRE, EN6 1EG.
REUSS, Mr. Nicholas Benedict, FCA *1974;* 29/4 The One Villas, Moo 6, Najomtien, CHON BURI 20250, THAILAND. (Life Member)
REUTTER, Miss. Alison, BA ACA *2011;* Kegelgasse, 21/23, 1030 VIENNA, AUSTRIA.
•REVEL-CHION, Mr. Gary, BSc FCA *1984;* (Tax Fac), Gary Revel-Chion, 35 Benett Drive, HOVE, EAST SUSSEX, BN3 6US.
•REVELL, Mr. Bradley James, MA FCA *1996;* Resort Solutions Ltd, St. Marys House, St. Marys Road, MARKET HARBOROUGH, LEICESTERSHIRE, LE16 7DS.
REVELL, Mr. Christopher James, ACA *2009;* 4 Enderby Close, Bentley Heath, SOLIHULL, B93 8LW.
REVELL, Mrs. Elizabeth Margaret, FCA *1975;* ICDP Ltd, 5 The Hen House, Oldwich Lane West, Chadwick End, SOLIHULL, B93 0BJ.
REVELL, Miss. Joanne Elizabeth, BA ACA *2008;* 4 Yellow Brook Close, Aspull, WIGAN, LANCASHIRE, WN2 1ZH.
REVELL, Mr. John Kenneth, ACA *1978;* Stone Villa, 55 Cobbold Street, IPSWICH, IP4 2DN.
REVELL, Mrs. Nicola, BSc ACA *1996;* Littlewoods Shop Direct Home Shopping Ltd Skyways House, Speke Road Speke, LIVERPOOL, L70 1AB.
REVENOK, Miss. Natalia, ACA *2008;* P.O. Box 54027, 3720 LIMASSOL, CYPRUS.
REVERES, Mr. Michael Brian, FCA *1964;* 4 Snaresbrook Drive, STANMORE, MIDDLESEX, HA7 4QW. (Life Member)
•REVILL, Mr. David, FCA *1977;* Pugsley Revill, 18 High West Street, DORCHESTER, DT1 1UW.
REVILL, Miss. Debbie Anne, BSc ACA *2003;* Flat A, 10-11 Rheidol Terrace, LONDON, N1 8NT.
REVILL, Mr. Ian, BA FCA *1977;* 11 Kevan Drive, Send, WOKING, GU23 7BU.
•REVILL, Mr. Philip Andrew, BA FCA *1983;* The P&A Partnership, 93 Queen Street, SHEFFIELD, S1 1WF.
REVILL, Mr. Stewart, FCA *1970;* (Tax Fac), 71 Rundle Road, Nether Edge, SHEFFIELD, S7 1NW.
•REVILL, Mr. Timothy John, BA FCA *1974;* Fabrica de Cerveza Kettal SL, Avda de los Cortijos 8, Sotogrande, 11310 SAN ROQUE, SPAIN.
REVILLE, Mr. Andrew Michael Maxwell, BSc ACA *2004;* BNP Paribas Internal Audit, 5 Aldermanbury Square, LONDON, EC2V 7HR.
REVILLE, Mr. Edward, FCA *1953;* 28 Newton Road, Knowle, SOLIHULL, WEST MIDLANDS, B93 9HN. (Life Member)
•REVIS, Mrs. Catherine, FCA *1997;* Fiander Tovell LLP, Stag Gates House, 63/64 The Avenue, SOUTHAMPTON, SO17 1XS.
REVITT, Miss. Charlotte Sarah, ACA *2011;* 4 Hoults Lane, Greetland, HALIFAX, WEST YORKSHIRE, HX4 8HN.
REW, Mr. Christopher John, FCA *1970;* 20 Woodfield Rise, BUSHEY, WD23 4QS.
REW, Mr. Christopher John, BMus ACA *1988;* 105 South Road, TAUNTON, SOMERSET, TA1 3EA.
•REW, Mr. Graham Timothy, BSc FCA *1989;* Hazlewoods LLP, Staverton Court, Staverton, CHELTENHAM, GLOUCESTERSHIRE, GL51 0UX.
REW, Mr. John Leslie, BSc ACA *2000;* 90 Nelson Road, LONDON, SW19 1HX.
REW, Mr. Paul, MA ACA *1993;* Hillcroft, School Lane, Little Horkesley, COLCHESTER, CO6 4DN.
•REW, Mr. Paul Francis, BSc FCA *1978;* Clayton, Ruxley Crescent, Claygate, ESHER, KT10 0TX.
REWSTON, Mrs. Elaine Katherine, BSc ACA *2003;* 29 Armistead Way, Cranage, CREWE, CW4 8FE.
REX, Mr. Norman, FCA *1960;* 46 Calver Crescent, GRIMSBY, DN37 9EX. (Life Member)
REXWINKEL, Miss. Helen Nicole, BA ACA *2006;* Flat 10 Halcyon Place, Keswick Road, LONDON, SW15 2DL.
REXWORTHY, Mr. Simon James, MA ACA *2002;* 25 Glenthorne Road, KINGSTON UPON THAMES, SURREY, KT1 2UB.
REY, Mr. Alfred Joseph Gerard Robert Alain, BSc ACA *1986;* 41C Queen Mary Avenue, FLOREAL, MAURITIUS.
REY, Mr. David, BA FCA *2000;* 40 Milton Drive, Poynton, STOCKPORT, CHESHIRE, SK12 1EY.
REY, Mr. Olivier, MEng ACA *2011;* with PricewaterhouseCoopers LLP, 1 Embankment Place, LONDON, WC2N 6RH.
REY, Mr. Simon Pierre, BA ACA *1982;* c/o Ireland Blyth Ltd, P.O. Box 58, PORT LOUIS, MAURITIUS.
•REYERSBACH, Mr. John Quentin, BSc FCA *1981;* (Tax Fac), John Reyersbach & Co, The Old Post Office, High Street, Hartley Wintney, HOOK, HAMPSHIRE RG27 8NZ.
•REYES, Mr. Stephen Joseph, BSc ACA *1988;* (Tax Fac), Deloitte Limited, PO Box 758, Merchant House, 22-24 John Mackintosh Square, GIBRALTAR, GIBRALTAR.
REYFORD, Mr. Joseph Christian Alain, FCA *1988;* Marks & Clerk, 90 Long Acre, LONDON, WC2E 9RA.
REYLAND, Mrs. Deborah Louise, ACA CTA *2000;* (Tax Fac), F L Memo Ltd, 185 Park Street, LONDON, SE1 9DY.
•REYNAERT, Mr. Paul Anthony, MA ACA *1980;* (Tax Fac), Kingscott Dix Limited, 60 Kings Walk, GLOUCESTER, GL1 1LA.
•REYNARD, Mr. John Anthony, LLB FCA *1985;* 3 Greenmount Lane, Heaton, BOLTON, BL1 5JF.
REYNARD, Miss. Michelle Claire, ACA *2004;* 90b Kaye Lane, HUDDERSFIELD, HD5 8XU.
REYNARD, Mr. Thomas Paul, MEng ACA *2010;* Flat 2, 763 Wandsworth Road, LONDON, SW8 3JG.
REYNER, Mr. Liam James, BSc ACA *2005;* Flat 8 Ocean Wharf, 60 Westferry Road, LONDON, E14 8LN.
REYNIERS, Mr. Christopher James, ACA *2008;* with PricewaterhouseCoopers LLP, 1 Embankment Place, LONDON, WC2N 6RH.
•REYNOLDS, Mr. Adrian Nigel, BA FCA *1985;* Duncan & Toplis, 5 Resolution Close, Endeavour Park, BOSTON, LINCOLNSHIRE, PE21 7TT.
REYNOLDS, The Revd. Adrian Robert, BSc(Hons) ACA *1993;* 63 Brokesley Street, LONDON, E3 4QJ.
REYNOLDS, Mr. Alan Walter, FCA *1969;* Aloys Schneider Strasse 2, 54568 GEROLSTEIN, GERMANY.
REYNOLDS, Mrs. Alexandra, BA ACA *2006;* 10 Brumfield Road, EPSOM, SURREY, KT19 9PA.
REYNOLDS, Mr. Andrew David Finch, BA ACA ACT *1988;* Expotel Hotel Reservations St. James House, 192 Wellington Road North, STOCKPORT, CHESHIRE, SK4 2RZ.
REYNOLDS, Mr. Andrew John, MA ACA *2002;* V T B Bank, 14 Cornhill, LONDON, EC3V 3ND.
REYNOLDS, Mr. Andrew Joseph, BSc ACA *1994;* Industrieparken 31, 2750 BALLERUP, DENMARK.
REYNOLDS, Mr. Andrew Stephen, BSc ACA *1991;* The Old Wheelhouse, 2 Fairfield Way, Chillington, KINGSBRIDGE, DEVON, TQ7 2LS.
REYNOLDS, Mr. Anthony, BA FCA *1976;* Suite 11a, Design Works, William Street, GATESHEAD, TYNE AND WEAR, NE10 0JP.
REYNOLDS, Mr. Anthony Norman, FCA *1970;* 64 The Hamlet, Leek Wootton, WARWICK, CV35 7QW.
REYNOLDS, Mr. Anthony Robert, FCA *1961;* 43 Nutfields, Redwell Lane, Ightham, SEVENOAKS, TN15 9EA. (Life Member)
REYNOLDS, Mr. Antony Clifton, BSc ACA *1995;* with PricewaterhouseCoopers, Edifici Caja De Madrid, Avinguda Diagonal, 640 7a Planta, 08017 BARCELONA, SPAIN.
•REYNOLDS, Mr. Benjamin Robert, BSc(Hons) ACA *2002;* TGFP Limited, Fulford House, Newbold Terrace, LEAMINGTON SPA, WARWICKSHIRE, CV32 4EA.
REYNOLDS, Mr. Brett Wilson, ACA *2008;* 12 Woodside Avenue, Hersham, WALTON-ON-THAMES, SURREY, KT12 5LG.
REYNOLDS, Mrs. Carla Jayne, BSc ACA *2006;* Orchard House, Weights Lane, REDDITCH, WORCESTERSHIRE, B97 6RG.
REYNOLDS, Mr. Christopher Glenn, FCA *1972;* Stowaway Cottage Madeira Road, Littlestone, NEW ROMNEY, KENT, TN28 8QX.
REYNOLDS, Mr. Christopher Ian, BSc ACA *1999;* Ravensburgh, Hexton, HITCHIN, HERTFORDSHIRE, SG5 3JN.
REYNOLDS, Mr. Christopher Patrick Myles, FCA *1970;* Bridgwater Bros Holdings Ltd, Hamilton House, 39 Kings Road, HASLEMERE, SURREY, GU27 2QA.
REYNOLDS, Mr. Clifford Francis, MA FCA *1969;* Pentypark Lodge, Spittal, HAVERFORDWEST, PEMBROKESHIRE, SA62 5QN. (Life Member)
REYNOLDS, Mr. Daniel Thomas, BSc(Hons) ACA *2009;* 12 Victoria House Park Heights, St. Johns Road St. Helier, JERSEY, JE2 3TG.
REYNOLDS, Mr. David Alan, ACA CTA *2002;* (Tax Fac), 8 Westminster Drive, Cheadle Hulme, CHEADLE, CHESHIRE, SK8 7QX.
•REYNOLDS, Mr. David John, FCA *1972;* Goldwyns Limited, Rutland House, 90-92 Baxter Avenue, SOUTHEND-ON-SEA, SS2 6HZ.
•REYNOLDS, Mr. David Joseph, BA FCA *1980;* D.J. Reynolds & Co, 15 Alverton Street, PENZANCE, CORNWALL, TR18 2QP.
REYNOLDS, Mr. David Michael, BA ACA *1985;* 16 Golden Crescent, Everton, LYMINGTON, SO41 0LL.
REYNOLDS, Mrs. Deborah Helen, BA ACA *1994;* 2184 Saratoga Lane, GLENDORA, CA 91741, UNITED STATES.
REYNOLDS, Mrs. Debra Margaret, BA ACA *1993;* 8 Sherwood Road, Chandler's Ford, EASTLEIGH, HAMPSHIRE, SO53 5DE.
•REYNOLDS, Mr. Donald Sylvester, FCA *1970;* 8 Russell Heights, KINGSTON 8, JAMAICA.
REYNOLDS, Ms. Donna, BA ACA *1992;* 49 Valleyfield Road, LONDON, SW16 2HS.
REYNOLDS, Mr. Duncan Alistair Scott, BA ACA *1994;* 94 Jalan Lim Tai See, SINGAPORE 268429, SINGAPORE.
REYNOLDS, Mrs. Elizabeth Elizabeth, BSc ACA *1994;* 32 Lotus Avenue, SINGAPORE 277615, SINGAPORE.
REYNOLDS, Miss. Elizabeth May, BSc ACA *2006;* 14 Sydney Road, SMETHWICK, WEST MIDLANDS, B67 5QQ.
REYNOLDS, Mrs. Fiona Elaine, BSc ACA *1990;* 93 Pen-y-Dre, Rhiwbina, CARDIFF, CF14 6EL.
REYNOLDS, Miss. Frances Harriet, BSc ACA *1984;* 16 Barker Road, SUTTON COLDFIELD, B74 2NY.
REYNOLDS, Mr. Gareth Powell, MA FCA *1991;* University Hospital of Wales, Finance, 5th Floor Brecknock House, Heath Park, CARDIFF, CF14 4XW.
REYNOLDS, Mr. George, BA(Hons) ACA *2002;* Bridgwater Holdings Ltd Hamilton House, 39 Kings Road, HASLEMERE, GU27 2QA.
REYNOLDS, Mr. Glen, BA ACA *1990;* 26 Poppyfields, Horsford, NORWICH, NR10 3SR.
REYNOLDS, Ms. Glenys, BA ACA *1988;* 83 Crowborough Lane, Kents Hill, MILTON KEYNES, MK7 6JN.
REYNOLDS, Mr. Graeme Keith, MA ACA *2003;* 14 Brook Lane, TONBRIDGE, TN9 1PU.
REYNOLDS, Mr. Graeme Malcolm, MBA BA ACA *1993;* 7 An den Aessen, Ehnen, L-5418 WORMELDANGE, LUXEMBOURG.
REYNOLDS, Mr. Graham Marshall John, BA ACA *1999;* with PricewaterhouseCoopers, 8 Princes Parade, St Nicholas Place, LIVERPOOL, L3 1QJ.
REYNOLDS, Mrs. Hannah, BA ACA *1994;* 154 Broom Road, TEDDINGTON, MIDDLESEX, TW11 9PQ.
REYNOLDS, Mr. Hugh Barrett, MA FCA *1985;* 97 Muswell Avenue, Muswell Hill, LONDON, N10 2EJ.
•REYNOLDS, Mr. Hugh Michael Peter, FCA *1976;* (Tax Fac), 36 Brook End, Longdon, RUGELEY, STAFFORDSHIRE, WS15 4PN.
•REYNOLDS, Mr. James Alan, FCA *1972;* (Tax Fac), Alan Reynolds & Co Ltd, Walnut House, 34 Rose Street, WOKINGHAM, BERKSHIRE, RG40 1XU.
REYNOLDS, Mr. James Julius Saul, FCA *1951;* 15 Burlington Park House, Dennis Lane, STANMORE, HA7 4LA. (Life Member)
•REYNOLDS, Mr. James Keith, FCA CTA *1982;* Keith Reynolds Associates, Ground Floor, 135 Bermondsey Street, LONDON, SE1 3UW. See also Upper Street Accounts Ltd
REYNOLDS, Mrs. Jennifer, BSc ACA *1983;* 5 Shawbury Village, Shustoke Coleshill, BIRMINGHAM, B46 2RU.
REYNOLDS, Mrs. Jennifer, BSc ACA *2001;* Pasture View, 58 Central Avenue, BEVERLEY, NORTH HUMBERSIDE, HU17 8LN.
REYNOLDS, Mrs. Jennifer Angela, BA(Hons) ACA *2004;* Unit 1, Harlequin Office Park, Fieldfare, Emersons Green, BRISTOL, BS16 7FN.
REYNOLDS, Mr. Jeremy Howard Newland, LLB FCA *1978;* 38 Park Drive, Sheen, LONDON, SW14 8RD.
REYNOLDS, Ms. Jill, BA ACA *1989;* Twinn Accountants, Suite 4, East Barton Barns, East Barton Road, Great Barton, STOWMARKET SUFFOLK IP14 2QY.
REYNOLDS, Mrs. Joanna Helen, BA ACA *1995;* 41 Kellerton Road, LONDON, SE13 5RB.
REYNOLDS, Mrs. Joanne Louise, BSc ACA CTA *1997;* Cargill PLC, Knowle Hill Park, Fairmile Lane, COBHAM, KT11 2PD.
REYNOLDS, Mr. John Carl, FCA *1956;* 21 Verlands Road, Preston, WEYMOUTH, DT3 6BY. (Life Member)

•REYNOLDS, Mr. John Hartley, FCA *1963;* J.H. Reynolds, 2 Insole Gardens, CARDIFF, CF5 2HW.
•REYNOLDS, Mr. John William, FCA *1970;* Reynolds & Co, 4 Thorpe Hall Close, Thorpe Bay, SOUTHEND-ON-SEA, SS1 3SQ.
REYNOLDS, Mr. Joseph, ACA MAAT *2009;* 60 The Street, Upchurch, SITTINGBOURNE, ME9 7EU.
REYNOLDS, Mr. Justin David George, BSc ACA *1996;* Reedham House, Manns Hill, Burghfield Common, READING, RG7 3BD.
REYNOLDS, Mrs. Kate, BA ACA CTA *2001;* Halcyon, 15 Stoke Row Road, Peppard Common, HENLEY-ON-THAMES, OXFORDSHIRE, RG9 5EJ.
REYNOLDS, Mrs. Lisa Joanne, BA ACA *1993;* 76 Coronation Drive, SINGAPORE 269613, SINGAPORE.
REYNOLDS, Dr. Lucy Antonia Fitzherbert, MSc BSc ACA ATII AKC *1990;* 72 Ferndale Road, LONDON, SW4 7SE.
REYNOLDS, Ms. Maria Antoinette, BA ACA *1991;* Aegis Group Plc, 180 Great Portland Street, LONDON, W1W 5QZ.
•REYNOLDS, Mr. Mark, FCA *1976;* (Tax Fac), Fitzpatrick & Kearney Ltd, 10 Marcus Square, NEWRY, COUNTY DOWN, BT34 1AE. See also Fitzpatrick & Kearney
REYNOLDS, Mr. Martin, BSc ACA *1995;* Barclays Capital, L28, One Raffles Quay, South Tower, SINGAPORE 048583, SINGAPORE.
REYNOLDS, Mr. Martyn Deane, FCA *1978;* 8 Cox Close, Bidford-on-Avon, ALCESTER, B50 4EF.
REYNOLDS, Mr. Matthew, BA ACA *1996;* 50 Marshall Avenue, BOGNOR REGIS, WEST SUSSEX, PO21 2TW.
REYNOLDS, Mr. Matthew Colin, BSc ACA *2005;* 134 Fenside Avenue, COVENTRY, CV3 5NJ.
REYNOLDS, Mr. Michael Barry, FCA *1971;* Jose Ortega y Gasset 90 3° ctro izqda, 28006 MADRID, SPAIN.
REYNOLDS, Mr. Michael Joseph, BSc FCA *1994;* 10 Sandy Lane, TEDDINGTON, TW11 0DR.
•REYNOLDS, Mr. Michael McKenzie, BA ACA *2003;* DPC Accountants Limited, Vernon Road, STOKE-ON-TRENT, ST4 2QY.
•REYNOLDS, Mr. Michael Stanley, FCA *1962;* (Tax Fac), Michael S. Reynolds, 14 Great Thrift, ORPINGTON, BR5 1NG.
REYNOLDS, Mr. Michael Thomas, BSc ACA *1983;* 185 Adel Lane, LEEDS, LS16 8BY.
•REYNOLDS, Mrs. Michele Jane, ACA *1983;* M Reynolds, 42 Temple Rhydding Drive, Baildon, SHIPLEY, WEST YORKSHIRE, BD17 5PU.
•REYNOLDS, Mr. Neil Anthony William, BSc ACA *1987;* (Tax Fac), West Reynolds, 42 Windmill Street, GRAVESEND, KENT, DA12 1BA.
REYNOLDS, Mr. Nicholas, BA ACA *2006;* Flat 6, Atlantic House, 51-57 Upper Richmond Road, LONDON, SW15 2RD.
REYNOLDS, Mr. Nicholas David, BSc(Hons) ACA *2002;* with ICAEW, Metropolitan House, 321 Avebury Boulevard, MILTON KEYNES, MK9 2FZ.
REYNOLDS, Mr. Nicholas Jeffrey, FCA *1968;* 27 The Stables, Runshaw Hall, Euxton, CHORLEY, LANCASHIRE, PR7 6HQ.
•REYNOLDS, Mr. Nigel Hugh, BSc ACA *1994;* PricewaterhouseCoopers LLP, 1 Embankment Place, LONDON, WC2N 6RH. See also PricewaterhouseCoopers
•REYNOLDS, Mr. Nigel Philip, FCA *1974;* (Tax Fac), Reynolds & Company, Meridian House, 7 The Avenue, Highams Park, LONDON, E4 9LB.
REYNOLDS, Mr. Norman Donald, FCA *1949;* 29 Kempsford Close, REDDITCH, WORCESTERSHIRE, B98 7YS. (Life Member)
REYNOLDS, Miss. Pamela Mary, ACA *1982;* 2 Springfields, Coleshill, BIRMINGHAM, B46 3EG.
REYNOLDS, Mr. Patrick Ernest, FCA *1968;* North House, 198 High Street, TONBRIDGE, KENT, TN9 1BE.
•REYNOLDS, Mr. Peter Kinsey, LLB FCA *1985;* (Tax Fac), Dyke Ruscoe & Hayes Limited, 110 Corve Street, LUDLOW, SHROPSHIRE, SY8 1DJ.
REYNOLDS, Mrs. Pui-Ah, FCA *1973;* 4837 Angus Drive, VANCOUVER V6J 4J6, BC, CANADA. (Life Member)
REYNOLDS, Miss. Rebecca Lucy, BSc ACA *2005;* 39 Lodge Farm Drive, NORWICH, NR6 7LP.
•REYNOLDS, Mr. Robert, ACA *1978;* M. Wasley Chapman & Co, 3 Victoria Square, WHITBY, NORTH YORKSHIRE, YO21 1EA.
REYNOLDS, Mr. Robert Andrew, BSc ACA *2005;* 36 Briarmeadow Drive, Thornhill, CARDIFF, CF14 9FB.
•REYNOLDS, Mr. Robert Dennis, BA FCA *1991;* Wilkins Kennedy FKC Limited, Stourside Place, 35-41 Station Road, ASHFORD, KENT, TN23 1PP. See also W K Finn-Kelcey & Chapman Limited
REYNOLDS, Mr. Robert Edward, BA ACA *2005;* c/o Weir Minerals, 1 Marden Street, ARTARMON, NSW 2064, AUSTRALIA.
•REYNOLDS, Mr. Robert James, BA FCA *1978;* Reynolds & Co, Square Root Business Centre, 102-116 Windmill Road, CROYDON, CR0 2XQ.
REYNOLDS, Mrs. Roselle Ann, BSc(Hons) ACA *2000;* Cains Accounting Services Ltd, Third Floor, St Georges Court, Douglas, ISLE OF MAN, IM1 1EE.
REYNOLDS, Mr. Sam Jonathan, BA ACA *2003;* 5 Priory Road, WILMSLOW, CHESHIRE, SK9 5PS.
REYNOLDS, Mrs. Sarah Catherine, BA ACA *1998;* Avenue de la chapelle 2, 1200 Woluwe St Lambert, 1200 BRUSSELS, BELGIUM.
REYNOLDS, Mrs. Sau King Jenny, BSc ACA *1992;* 76 Hindemith Gardens, Old Farm Park, MILTON KEYNES, MK7 8PW.
REYNOLDS, Mr. Shaun, BA ACA *2006;* with Deloitte LLP, Athene Place, 66 Shoe Lane, LONDON, EC4A 3BQ.
REYNOLDS, Mr. Shawn Kevin, BSc ACA *2000;* with PKF (UK) LLP, Farringdon Place, 20 Farringdon Road, LONDON, EC1M 3AP.
REYNOLDS, Miss. Sheila Mary, BSc ACA *1986;* 84 Priory Road, Hornsey, LONDON, N8 7EY.
REYNOLDS, Ms. Shelley Leticia, BSc ACA *1999;* Luddesdown House Henley Street, Luddesdown, GRAVESEND, DA13 0XB.
REYNOLDS, Mr. Simon, ACA *2008;* Group Accounts, Kronospan Ltd, Chirk, WREXHAM, CLWYD, LL14 5NT.
•REYNOLDS, Mrs. Sonia Jane, ACA CTA *1990;* Moulds & Co Ltd, Unit 10, York Road Estate, WETHERBY, WEST YORKSHIRE, LS22 7SU.
REYNOLDS, Mr. Stephen, FCA *1963;* 5 White Oak Close, Marple, STOCKPORT, SK6 6NT.
REYNOLDS, Mr. Stephen John, MA ACA *1989;* Polmennor House, Polmennor Road, Heamoor, PENZANCE, TR20 8UW.
REYNOLDS, Mr. Stephen Keith, BA ACA *1982;* 5 Shawbury Village, Shawbury Ln, Coleshill, BIRMINGHAM, B46 2RU.
•REYNOLDS, Mr. Stephen William Michael, BSc FCA *1977;* S.W.M. Reynolds, Morar, 20 Delavor Road, Heswall, WIRRAL, MERSEYSIDE CH60 4RW.
•REYNOLDS, Mr. Steven Mark, BA ACA *2000;* Steve Reynolds, Suite 125, 6 The Broadway, Mill Hill, LONDON, NW7 3LL.
REYNOLDS, Mr. Thomas Kenneth, ACA *2011;* 112 Fell Road, WESTBURY, WILTSHIRE, BA13 2GP.
•REYNOLDS, Mr. Timothy Edward, FCA *1968;* (Tax Fac), KCL Management Services Ltd, Kinchyle, Church Lane, Great Holland, FRINTON-ON-SEA, ESSEX CO13 0JS.
REZA, Mr. Mehdee, BA(Hons) FCA *1994;* International Commercial Centre, 1 Austin Road West, TSIM SHA TSUI, KOWLOON, HONG KONG SAR.
REZAIFARD, Miss. Pantea, BSc ACA *1994;* 11 Ormonde Rise, BUCKHURST HILL, ESSEX, IG9 5QQ.
REZLER, Mr. Rodney James, MSc FCA *1975;* 17 Shepherds Close, LONDON, N6 5AG.
REZMER, Ms. Katarzyna Wanda, BSc ACA *1992;* 3722 Heritage Colony Drive, MISSOURI CITY, TX 77459, UNITED STATES.
RHEAD, Mr. David Michael, FCA CCMI *1961;* 20 Buckton Close, Four Oaks, SUTTON COLDFIELD, B75 5TF. (Life Member)
RHEAD, Mr. Robert John, ACA *2008;* The Windrush, Poolhouse Road, Wombourne, WOLVERHAMPTON, WV5 8AZ.
RHENIUS, Mr. Theodore, FCA *1956;* 2186 Belgrave Court, BURLINGTON L7P 3R5, ON, CANADA. (Life Member)
RHIND, Mrs. Caroline Margaret, BA ACA *1999;* QBE, 82 Pitt Street, SYDNEY, NSW 2000, AUSTRALIA.
•RHIND, Mr. Kevin John, FCA *1985;* (Tax Fac), Kevin J Rhind, Corner Cottage, Heath Road, Hempstead, NORWICH, NR12 0SH.
RHIND, Mr. Mark, LLB ACA *1990;* 73a High Street, SIDCUP, KENT, DA14 6DW.
•RHIND-TUTT, Ms. Nicola Ann, ACA MAAT *2003;* Nicola Rhind -Tutt ACA MAAT, 9 Castle Mount, Tisbury, SALISBURY, WILTSHIRE, SP3 6PP.
RHOADES, Mrs. Anne Louise, BA FCA *1993;* 68 Goddard Avenue, SWINDON, SN1 4HS.
RHOADES, Mr. Leslie Malcolm, FCA *1962;* 14 Brocklehurst Drive, Prestbury, MACCLESFIELD, SK10 4JD.
RHOADES, Mr. Simon Charles Hardy, BPharm ACA *1997;* Greenhills Asset Management Limited, 7 Portman Mews South, LONDON, W1H 6HY.
RHOADS, Mr. Terry Edward, FCA *1973;* 27 Winterberry Way, Caversham, READING, RG4 7XA.
RHODDA, Mr. Owain Bryn, ACA *2009;* 6 St. Jude Street, LONDON, N16 8JT.
RHODEN, Miss. Joanne Lesley, BSc FCA *2000;* 8E/5 Tambua Street, PYRMONT, NSW 2009, AUSTRALIA.
RHODEN, Dr. Philip Keith, MA ACA *2001;* 91 St. Johns Road, HEMEL HEMPSTEAD, HP1 1QG.
•RHODES, Mr. Andrew Max, FCA *1976;* Sobell Rhodes LLP, Monument House, 215 Marsh Road, PINNER, MIDDLESEX, HA5 5NE.
•RHODES, Mr. Anthony Charles Edward, FCA *1974;* Mark J Rees, Granville Hall, Granville Road, LEICESTER, LE1 7RU.
RHODES, Mr. Anthony Joseph Morgan, FCA *1959;* 3/131 Morala Avenue, RUNAWAY BAY, QLD 4216, AUSTRALIA. (Life Member)
RHODES, Mr. Barton James Daniel, BSocSc ACA *1999;* 67 Engadine Street, LONDON, SW18 5BZ.
RHODES, Mr. Ben Alexander Alan, BA ACA *2007;* Flat D 18 Marmora Road, LONDON, SE22 0RX.
RHODES, Mr. Christopher James, BA ACA *1999;* Partnership Assurance, Sackville House, 143-149 Fenchurch Street, LONDON, EC3M 6BN.
RHODES, Mr. Christopher Stuart, BSc ACA *1990;* Nationwide House, Nationwide Bldg Soc, SWINDON, SN38 1NW.
RHODES, Mrs. Claire Helen, BSc ACA *2007;* 48 Redwood, Westhoughton, BOLTON, BL5 2RU.
RHODES, Mr. David Arthur, FCA *1958;* 6 Dovedale Road, LEICESTER, LE2 2DJ. (Life Member)
RHODES, Mr. Denis Charles, FCA *1957;* 607 Cindy Drive, WELLINGTON, FL 33414, UNITED STATES. (Life Member)
RHODES, Ms. Emma, PhD BEng ACA *2007;* 52 Castle Street, Caergwrle, WREXHAM, CLWYD, LL12 9DS.
RHODES, Mrs. Evelyn Rose, BSc ACA *1983;* 3 Greenglade Road, BELAIR, SA 5052, AUSTRALIA.
RHODES, Mr. Geoffrey Stuart, FCA *1975;* The Old Manse, Main Street, Beeford, DRIFFIELD, YO25 8AY.
•ⒹRHODES, Mr. Geoffrey William, FCA *1971;* Begbies Traynor, 2/3 Pavilion Buildings, BRIGHTON, BN1 1EE. See also Begbies Traynor(Central) LLP and Begbies Traynor Limited
RHODES, Mrs. Hanna Nabila, BA ACA *2009;* 51 Buckland Way, WORCESTER PARK, KT4 8NT.
•RHODES, Miss. Helen Claire, BSc ACA *2002;* HR Accountancy, 25 High Meadows, Greetland, HALIFAX, WEST YORKSHIRE, HX4 8QF.
RHODES, Mr. Ian, FCA *1965;* The Coach House, St. Veep, LOSTWITHIEL, CORNWALL, PL22 0PA.
RHODES, Mrs. Jacqueline Mary, BSc ACA *1996;* The Pines, Woodlands Park, Hopwell Road, Draycott, DERBY, DE72 3SD.
•RHODES, Mr. John Derek, BA FCA *1989;* Alex Picot, 95-97 Halkett Place, St. Helier, JERSEY, JE1 1BX. See also Alex Picot Ltd
RHODES, Mr. John Frederic, FCA *1966;* Rycroft, 37 Bingley Road, Heaton, BRADFORD, BD9 6HL.
•RHODES, Mr. John Graham, BSc FCA *1975;* J.G. Rhodes, Lodge Park, Hortonwood 30, TELFORD, SHROPSHIRE, TF1 7ET.
•RHODES, Mr. John Howard, FCA *1969;* (Tax Fac), Rhodes & Co, 7 Richmond Bridge House, 419 Richmond Road, TWICKENHAM, TW1 2EX.
RHODES, Mr. John Stephen, BSc FCA *1991;* 14 Wellmans Meadow, Kingsclere, NEWBURY, RG20 5HJ.
•RHODES, Mr. Jonathan, BSc FCA *1984;* (Tax Fac), Walter Hunter & Co Limited, 24 Bridge Street, NEWPORT, GWENT, NP20 4SF.
RHODES, Mr. Jonathan David, BA(Hons) ACA *2000;* Oakdene Leathley Road, Menston, ILKLEY, WEST YORKSHIRE, LS29 6DP.
RHODES, Mr. Jonathan Edward, BEng ACA *2004;* 19 Tutnall Drive, Hockley Heath, SOLIHULL, WEST MIDLANDS, B94 6SA.
RHODES, Miss. Karen Marie, BA ACA *1999;* c/o Mr Rohit Rajvanshi, KPMG LEVEL 32, EMIRATES TOWERS, DUBAI, 3800, UNITED ARAB EMIRATES.
•RHODES, Mr. Karl Tristan, BSc FCA *1990;* Hope Agar, 24a Marsh Street, Rothwell, LEEDS, LS26 0BB. See also Hope Agar Limited
RHODES, Mr. Kenneth Robert, ACA *2009;* The Old Manse, Main Street, Beeford, DRIFFIELD, NORTH HUMBERSIDE, YO25 8AS.
RHODES, Mr. Kevin Paul, FCA *1976;* 29 Kingshayes Road, Aldridge, WALSALL, WS9 8RT.
RHODES, Miss. Laura, ACA *2009;* 21 Borrowdale Croft, Yeadon, LEEDS, LS19 7FN.
RHODES, Mr. Marcus James, BSc ACA *1987;* Calle Bolivar 3, Sotogrande, 11310 CADIZ, SPAIN.
RHODES, Mr. Mark, MA ACA *1998;* Sadlers Wells Theatre, Rosebery Avenue, LONDON, EC1R 4TN.
RHODES, Mr. Mark Anthony, ACA MAAT CIA AMCT *1996;* GPO Box 1453, BRISBANE, QLD 4001, AUSTRALIA.
•RHODES, Mr. Martin Harold, FCA *1977;* HHG Business Services Ltd, Hill House, Shelton Road, Upper Dean, HUNTINGDON, CAMBRIDGESHIRE PE28 0NQ.
•RHODES, Mr. Martin Jack, ACA *1986;* M J Rhodes & Co, First Floor, 8 Poole Hill, BOURNEMOUTH, BH2 5PS.
RHODES, Mr. Matthew Paul, BEng ACA *2007;* Flat 3, 162 West Hill, LONDON, SW15 3SR.
RHODES, Mr. Michael, BSc ACA *2005;* 11 The Paddock, Elton, CHESTER, CH2 4PT.
RHODES, Mr. Neil, BSc ACA *1993;* 3 Leslie Lane, NEW CANAAN, CT 06840, UNITED STATES.
RHODES, Mr. Paul Andrew, MA BSc CA ACA *2001;* 3 Dolby Crescent, AJAX L1Z 0E1, ON, CANADA.
RHODES, Mr. Paul Martin, BSc ACA *1985;* 1 Walden Avenue, Arborfield, READING, RG2 9HR.
RHODES, Mr. Peter Geoffrey, ACA *2008;* Pricewaterhousecoopers, 1 Embankment Place, LONDON, WC2N 6RH.
RHODES, Mr. Peter Graham, BEng ACA *1993;* 61 Williams Grove, St James Park, SURBITON, SURREY, KT6 5RP.
RHODES, Mr. Philip, FCA *1973;* 7 Buckfast Close, MANCHESTER, M21 0RY.
RHODES, Mr. Phillip Baverstock, FCA *1969;* 12 Peterborough Villas, LONDON, SW6 2AT.
RHODES, Mrs. Rachel Clare, BA ACA *1997;* 20 Cedars Road, BECKENHAM, KENT, BR3 4JF.
RHODES, Mrs. Rachel Louise, ACA *1993;* 29 The Moorings, Apperley Bridge, BRADFORD, BD10 0UH.
•RHODES, Mr. Richard Spencer, BA ACA *1987;* (Tax Fac), Feltons, 12 Sheet Street, WINDSOR, SL4 1BG. See also Pumphrey Dasalo Limited, Feltons Limited, LW Feltons Limited
•RHODES, Mrs. Sharon, BA ACA *1989;* HHG Business Services Ltd, Hill House, Shelton Road, Upper Dean, HUNTINGDON, CAMBRIDGESHIRE PE28 0NQ.
RHODES, Mrs. Sophie Caroline, BA(Hons) ACA *2001;* with Deloitte LLP, 4 Brindley Place, BIRMINGHAM, B1 2HZ.
RHODES, Mr. Stephen Graham, BA ACA *1986;* 1 Scarborough Close, Cheam, SUTTON, SM2 7EA.
•RHODES, Mr. Stephen Keith, BSc FCA *1977;* S. Keith Rhodes BSc FCA, 14 Limetree Gardens, Lowdham, NOTTINGHAM, NG14 7DJ.
•RHODES, Mr. Stephen Robert, BCom FCA *1976;* Rhodes Clarke & Co, 42 Market Street, Eckington, SHEFFIELD, S21 4JH. See also RCC Processing Limited
•RHODES, Mr. Steven Lewis, FCA *1984;* (Tax Fac), Bennett Verby LLP, 7 St Petersgate, STOCKPORT, CHESHIRE, SK1 1EB. See also De La Wyche Baker Limited
RHODES, Mr. William Whitteron, FCA *1960;* Quietways, 7 Burley Dr, Quarndon, DERBY, DE22 5JT.
RHYDDERCH, Mr. David Anthony, BA ACA *2006;* The UK Drainage Network Ltd The Chapel Pinewood Court, Coleshill Road Marston Green, BIRMINGHAM, B37 7HG.
RHYMER, Mr. Alastair St John, BSc ACA *1994;* Flat 5 Earls House, 10 Strand Drive, RICHMOND, SURREY, TW9 4DZ.
RHYMER, Mrs. Nicola Jayne, ACA *1991;* building 2, Royal Caribbean Cruise Building 2, Aviator Park Station Road, ADDLESTONE, KT15 2PG.
RHYS, Mr. David Benjamin Lewellin, BA(Hons) FCA *2001;* with KPMG, 8/F Prince's Building, 10 Chater Road, CENTRAL, HONG KONG ISLAND, HONG KONG SAR.
RHYS, Mr. Huw Daniel Wade, BA ACA *2011;* 21 Mount Park Crescent, LONDON, W5 2RN.
RHYS, Mr. Jonathan William, BSc ACA *1993;* Thorntree Farm Thorpe Road, Carlton, STOCKTON-ON-TEES, CLEVELAND, TS21 1DT.
•RHYS, Mr. Mark Geraint, BSc FCA MBA *1988;* Deloitte LLP, Hill House, 1 Little New Street, LONDON, EC4A 3TR. See also Deloitte & Touche LLP
RHYS, Mr. Mark Struan, LLB ACA *2002;* Shell International, Shell Centre, York Road, LONDON, SE1 7NA.

RHYS, Mr. Owen Mark Lewellin, FCA *1964;* Apartado 28.3009, Santa Barbara, HEREDIA, 3009, COSTA RICA.
RHYS-DAVIES, Mr. Andrew Charles, FCA *1970;* Price & Pierce Softwoods Ltd, Cavendish House, 40 Goldsworth Road, WOKING, GU21 1JT.
RHYS-DAVIES, Mr. Mark Iorwedd, BA FCA *1975;* Ballea Castle, Carrigaline, CORK, COUNTY CORK, IRELAND. (Life Member)
RIALAS, Mr. Kyriakos, MA ACA *1990;* Miroforon 11, Strovolos, 2055 NICOSIA, CYPRUS.
RIAZ, Mr. Rashid, BA ACA ACCA *2010;* 167 Ali Block, Ittefaq Town, Mansoora, LAHORE, PUNJAB, PAKISTAN.
RIAZ, Mrs. Shahin Nouraina, FCA *1981;* Audit Commission Nickalls House, Metrocentre, GATESHEAD, TYNE AND WEAR, NE11 9NH.
RIAZ, Mr. Sheikh Mohammad Umar, ACA *2008;* 30 Privett Road, GOSPORT, HAMPSHIRE, PO12 3SU.
•RIAZI, Mr. Amir Akbar Michael, MMath ACA *2007;* Time Business Services, 5 Acacia Road, EASTBOURNE, EAST SUSSEX, BN22 0TW.
RIBBONS, Mr. Kenneth James, BSc ACA *1988;* West Lothian Civic Centre, Howden South Road, LIVINGSTON, WEST LOTHIAN, EH54 6FF.
RIBCHESTER, Mr. Alan, FCA *1968;* 18 Springwell Avenue, North End, DURHAM, DH1 4LY.
RIBCHESTER, Mrs. Rebecca Julie, ACA *2008;* 15 South Crescent, DURHAM, DH1 4NF.
RIBCHESTER, Mr. Robert William, ACA *2007;* (Tax Fac), 15 South Crescent, DURHAM, DH1 4NF.
RIBEIRO, Mr. Daniel Odarlai, ACA *1981;* PO BOX 2569, ACCRA, GHANA.
RIBET, Miss. Eleanor Madeleine, BA(Hons) ACA *2001;* 50a Arundel Square, LONDON, N7 8AP.
RIBY, Mr. Andrew, BA FCA *1980;* 5 Fal Paddock, Mansfield Woodhouse, MANSFIELD, NOTTINGHAMSHIRE, NG19 9RW.
RIBY, Mr. Robert, ACA *2008;* 414 West Carriage House, Royal Carriage Mews, LONDON, SE18 6GB.
RICE, Mr. Adam Michael James, BSc ACA *1990;* Kingsmead, Old Mead Road, Henham, BISHOP'S STORTFORD, CM22 6JQ.
RICE, Mr. Andrew Clive, ACA *1994;* J O Hambro Capital Management Group, Ryder Court, 14 Ryder Street, LONDON, SW1Y 6QB.
RICE, Mr. Andrew John, FCA *1975;* Central YMCA, 112 Great Russell Street, LONDON, WC1B 3NQ.
RICE, Mr. Andrew Philip, BSc ACA *1982;* Via del Carso 5, 20063 CERNUSCO SUL NAVIGLIO, MI, ITALY.
•RICE, Miss. Beverley E, BA FCA *1996;* Robinson Rice Associates Ltd, 49 Station Road, Ainsdale, SOUTHPORT, MERSEYSIDE, PR8 3HH. See also Robinson Rice Associates
RICE, Mr. Charles Dennis, FCA *1954;* 88 Lakeside Drive, Roath Park, CARDIFF, CF23 6DG. (Life Member)
RICE, Mrs. Christine Marjorie, BSc ACA *1978;* Timber Wharf, Groundwork, 42-50 Worsley Street, MANCHESTER, M15 4LD.
RICE, Mr. Colin Frederick, FCA *1978;* 39 Loveridge Close, ANDOVER, SP10 5ND.
RICE, Mr. Colum, BA ACA *1995;* PricewaterhouseCoopers, Private Bag 92162, AUCKLAND 1142, NEW ZEALAND.
•RICE, Mr. David, FCA *1970;* Rice Associates Ltd, Market Chambers, 3-4 Market Place, WOKINGHAM, BERKSHIRE, RG40 1AL.
•RICE, Mr. David Arthur, FCA *1974;* (Tax Fac), Belmont Services (Southwest) Limited, 117 The Ridgeway, Plympton, PLYMOUTH, PL7 2AA.
RICE, Mr. David Charles, FCA *1978;* 16 Warren Mead, BANSTEAD, SM7 1LU.
RICE, Mr. David Francis, ACA CA(SA) *2010;* 9 Harveur Court, 145 Graham Road, LONDON, SW19 3SL.
•RICE, Mrs. Eleanor Ann, FCA *1976;* Eleanor Rice Ltd, 13 Buckingham Road, NEWBURY, RG14 6DH.
RICE, Mrs. Emma, BSc ACA *2004;* 39 Sinclair Drive, Longford, COVENTRY, CV6 6QX.
RICE, Mr. Gareth, BA ACA *1992;* 7 Monkstone Rise, Rumney, CARDIFF, CF3 3LW. (Life Member)
RICE, Ms. Gill, BSc ACA ATII *1985;* (Tax Fac), Pond House, Patmore End, Ugley, BISHOP'S STORTFORD, CM22 6JA.
RICE, Miss. Helen Louise, ACA *2009;* Ernst & Young Ltd RMZ Infinity Tower C 3rd Floor Old Madras Road K R Puram, BANGALORE 560016, INDIA.
RICE, Mrs. Julie Ann, BEd ACA *1991;* 16 Smithland Court, Greens Norton, TOWCESTER, NN12 8DA.
•RICE, Miss. Julie Ann, MPhil BA ACA *1998;* BDO LLP, 55 Baker Street, LONDON, W1U 7EU. See also BDO Stoy Hayward LLP
RICE, Mr. Kieran, BA ACA *1990;* B P P Holdings Plc, Aldine House, 142-144 Uxbridge Road, LONDON, W12 8AA.
•RICE, Mr. Kirk Andrew Stephen, BSc FCA *1982;* (Tax Fac), Kirk Rice LLP, The Courtyard, High Street, ASCOT, BERKSHIRE, SL5 7HP.
RICE, Miss. Lynn, BSc ACA CPA *1980;* (Tax Fac), with PricewaterhouseCoopers LLP, 31 Great George Street, BRISTOL, BS1 5QD.
RICE, Mr. Mark Jonathan, BSc ACA *1990;* 16 Peronne Avenue, Clontarf, SYDNEY, NSW 2093, AUSTRALIA.
RICE, Mr. Mark William, BSc(Hons) ACA *2001;* 7 Yew Tree Close, EVESHAM, WORCESTERSHIRE, WR11 1YR.
RICE, Mr. Michael Arthur, ACA *1982;* 75 Thame Road, Warborough, WALLINGFORD, OX10 7EA.
RICE, Mr. Michael Ernest, FCA *1959;* Wiltshire Cottage, Monks Alley, Binfield, BRACKNELL, RG42 5NY. (Life Member)
RICE, Mr. Nicholas Graham, BA ACA *2004;* Flat 8 Nickelby House, 33 South Ealing Road, LONDON, W5 4QT.
RICE, Mr. Paul Martin, BSc ACA *1997;* 37 Coulstock Road, BURGESS HILL, RH15 9XH.
RICE, Mr. Philip John, FCA *1973;* PO Box 11728, DOHA, QATAR.
RICE, Miss. Rebecca Louise, ACA MAAT *2010;* 5 Llain y Felin, Rhosbodrual, CAERNARFON, GWYNEDD, LL55 2BG.
•RICE, Mr. Robert John, FCA *1953;* R J Rice, 144 Cromwell Way, KIDLINGTON, OXFORDSHIRE, OX5 2LJ.
RICE, Miss. Sarah Louise, BA ACA *2002;* Deloitte & Touche Llp, 66 Shoe Lane, LONDON, EC4A 3BQ.
•RICE, Mr. Stephen Euston, BA ACA *1983;* (Tax Fac), Iverley Management Services Limited, Iverley Lodge, 186 Norton Road, Iverley, STOURBRIDGE, WEST MIDLANDS DY8 2RT.
RICE, Mr. Thomas, BA ACA *1991;* Scica Pack UK Ltd, Oakwood House, 82 Eastmount Road, DARLINGTON, COUNTY DURHAM, DL1 1LA.
RICE, Mr. William Robert, ACA *2008;* Hondecoeterstraat 24-2, 1071LS AMSTERDAM, NETHERLANDS.
•RICH, Mr. Andrew Gavin, BA FCA DChA *1995;* H W Fisher & Company, Acre House, 11-15 William Road, LONDON, NW1 3ER. See also H W Fisher & Company Limited
RICH, Mr. Andrew Peter, MA(Hons) ACA *2002;* Vision Capital Group Ltd, 54 Jermyn Street, LONDON, SW1Y 6LX.
RICH, Mr. Andrew Philip, FCA *1973;* Sandholme, Sandholme Lane, Leven, BEVERLEY, HU17 5LW.
RICH, Mr. Anthony George Ledger, FCA *1960;* 48 Nicola Close, SOUTH CROYDON, SURREY, CR2 6NB. (Life Member)
RICH, Mr. Donald, FCA *1954;* (Member of Council 1981 - 1990), 134 Crewe Road, NANTWICH, CHESHIRE, CW5 6JS. (Life Member)
RICH, Mr. Ernest Albert, FCA *1961;* 1 Cricket Way, WEYBRIDGE, KT13 9LP.
RICH, Miss. Holly, ACA *2009;* 7 Maple Lodge, 40-44 Roding Lane, BUCKHURST HILL, ESSEX, IG9 6GQ.
RICH, Mr. Jonathan Marc, BSc ACA *2010;* Fortis House, Hammers Lane, LONDON, NW7 4DJ.
RICH, Mr. Mark Andrew, BSc ACA *1998;* 18 Heath Road, Ramsden Heath, BILLERICAY, CM11 1NA.
RICH, Mrs. Nasreen, MPhil ACA *1995;* 24 Kenilworth Avenue, OXFORD, OX4 2AN.
RICH, Nigel Mervyn Sutherland, Esq CBE MA FCA *1971;* Segro Plc Cundard House, 15 Regent Street, LONDON, SW1Y 4LR.
RICH, Ms. Rananda Anne, MA(Cantab) ACA *2000;* PO BOX 206, DEE WHY, NSW 2099, AUSTRALIA.
RICH, Mr. Roy Thomas, BSc FCA *1963;* Elmhurst Fairstead Hall Road, Fairstead, CHELMSFORD, CM3 2AU.
•RICH, Mr. Russell Marc, FCA *1991;* Lubbock Fine, Russell Bedford House, City Forum, 250 City Road, LONDON, EC1V 2QQ.
RICH, Mrs. Sally Jacqueline, BSc ACA *1989;* The Old Laundry, STANSTED, ESSEX, CM24 8TJ.
RICH, Mr. Simon Donald, BSc FCA *1989;* XL Group plc, XL House, 1 Bermudiana Road, HAMILTON HM08, BERMUDA.
RICH, Mr. Stephen Anthony, FCA *1969;* 28 Bentcliffe Court, LEEDS, LS17 6SY.
RICHARD, Mr. David Vaughan, BSc ACA *2009;* Deloitte LLP Athene Place, 66 Shoe Lane, LONDON, EC4A 3BQ.
RICHARD, Ms. Janet Margaret, BSc ACA *1987;* 189 Green Lanes, SUTTON COLDFIELD, B73 5LX.
RICHARDS, Mr. Adam Charles, BSc ACA *1998;* 3 Castle Hill, DAVENTRY, NORTHAMPTONSHIRE, NN11 4AQ.
RICHARDS, Mr. Adrian Henry Rainford, FCA *1968;* Bicton House, Bicton, SHREWSBURY, SY3 8EQ.
RICHARDS, Mr. Adrian John, FCA *1965;* Unit 14 Crofty Industrial Estate, Crofty, SWANSEA, SA4 3RS.
•ⓘRICHARDS, Mr. Adrian Nicholas, BSc ACA *1988;* Grant Thornton UK LLP, 30 Finsbury Square, LONDON, EC2P 2YU. See also Grant Thornton LLP
•RICHARDS, Mr. Alan David, ACA *1981;* (Tax Fac), McEwan Wallace, 68 Argyle Street, Birkenhead, WIRRAL, CH41 6AF. See also Premier Payroll Centre Limited
RICHARDS, Mr. Alun, BSc FCA MCLIP *1977;* (Tax Fac), 2 Chinthurst Park, Shalford, GUILDFORD, GU4 8JH.
RICHARDS, Mr. Andrew, BSc ACA *2002;* 21 Penmynydd, Gorseinon, SWANSEA, SA4 4PT.
RICHARDS, Mr. Andrew David, BSc ACA *1992;* Altium Capital Ltd, 30 St. James's Square, LONDON, SW1Y 4AL.
•RICHARDS, Mr. Andrew Henry, BSc FCA *1986;* (Tax Fac), Francis Clark LLP, Vantage Point, Woodwater Park, Pynes Hill, EXETER, EX2 5FD. See also Francis Clark Tax Consultancy Ltd
RICHARDS, Mr. Andrew James, BSc ACA *2005;* 157 Wigan Road, Standish, WIGAN, WN6 0AG.
RICHARDS, Mr. Andrew Paul, BSc FCA *1993;* (Tax Fac), 1 Rustic Cottages, Tandridge Lane, OXTED, RH8 9NJ.
RICHARDS, Miss. Ann Mary, BSc ACA *1988;* 58 Elmwood Drive, Ewell, EPSOM, KT17 2NN.
RICHARDS, Ms. Anna, BSc ACA CTA *2003;* with PricewaterhouseCoopers LLP, Exchange House, Central Business Exchange, Midsummer Boulevard, MILTON KEYNES, MK9 2DF.
RICHARDS, Mrs. Anna Celia Louise, BSc ACA *2007;* 57 Ray Park Avenue, MAIDENHEAD, SL6 8DZ.
•RICHARDS, Ms. Anna Marie, ACA *2008;* Richards Associates Limited, Suite 10 & 11, Hawkesyard Hall, Armitage Road, RUGELEY, STAFFORDSHIRE WS15 1PU.
RICHARDS, Mrs. Anne-Louise, BA ACA *1997;* Kjeksla 3B, 1397, Nesøya, 1397 OSLO, NORWAY.
RICHARDS, Mr. Anthony John, BA ACA *2002;* 7 Broxash Road, LONDON, SW11 6AD.
•RICHARDS, Mr. Anthony William, FCA *1971;* Thistleholme House, Taylors Green, Warmington, PETERBOROUGH, PE8 6TG.
•RICHARDS, Mr. Brian, BSc FCA *1977;* (Tax Fac), Richards & Co., Owners Business Centre, High Street, Newburn, NEWCASTLE UPON TYNE, NE15 8LN.
RICHARDS, Mr. Carl Damian, BSc ACA *2002;* 125 Bradford Road, BOURNEMOUTH, BH9 3PL.
RICHARDS, Mrs. Carol Anne, BA ACA *1994;* St Phillips Point, Baker Tilly Third & Fourth Floors, City Plaza Temple Row, BIRMINGHAM, B2 5AF.
RICHARDS, Ms. Carol Margaret, BSc ACA *1982;* BC Hydro, 11th Floor, 333 Dunsmuir, VANCOUVER V6B 5R3, BC, CANADA.
RICHARDS, Miss. Caroline Ann, BA ACA *2006;* with Burgess Hodgson, Camburgh House, 27 New Dover Road, CANTERBURY, CT1 3DN.
RICHARDS, Mrs. Caroline Ann, BSc ACA *1990;* (Tax Fac), 15 Barnbrook Road, Knowle, SOLIHULL, B93 9PW.
RICHARDS, Mrs. Catherine Allingham, BA ACA *1998;* 11 Norlands Park, WIDNES, CHESHIRE, WA8 5BH.
RICHARDS, Mrs. Cathrin Mary, BA ACA *1992;* (Tax Fac), 7 Woodgate Close, Charlton Kings, CHELTENHAM, GLOUCESTERSHIRE, GL52 6UW.
RICHARDS, Mr. Christopher Arthur, BSc ACA *1985;* Roxton Consultancy Services Ltd, Roxton, 54 Murton Lane, Newton, SWANSEA, SA3 4TR.
RICHARDS, Mr. Christopher Murray, BA ACA *1980;* 3 Kidbrooke Grove, Blackheath, LONDON, SE3 0PG.
RICHARDS, Mrs. Claire, MA FCA *1992;* 133 Turney Road, Dulwich, LONDON, SE21 7JB.
RICHARDS, Mrs. Claire Michelle, BA ACA *2000;* 22 Crabtree Way, Old Basing, BASINGSTOKE, HAMPSHIRE, RG24 7AS.
RICHARDS, Mr. Clive, FCA *1968;* Myrtle House, Ambleston, HAVERFORDWEST, SA62 5QY.
RICHARDS, Mr. Clive Walter, FCA *1957;* 3 Harene Crescent, Kirby Muxloe, LEICESTER, LE9 2HS. (Life Member)
RICHARDS, Mr. Colin Bryan, BSc ACA *1995;* 25 Uplands Way, SEVENOAKS, TN13 3BW.
RICHARDS, Mr. Colin Edward George, BA FCA *1980;* (Tax Fac), 26 Bishops Close, STRATFORD-UPON-AVON, CV37 9ED.
RICHARDS, Mr. David, ACA *2008;* 276/102 Miller Street, PYRMONT, NSW 2009, AUSTRALIA.
RICHARDS, Mr. David, ACA *2010;* KPMG, Level 13, 10 Shelley Street, SYDNEY, NSW 2000, AUSTRALIA.
RICHARDS, Mr. David Clive, FCA *1968;* 21 Redlake Drive, STOURBRIDGE, WEST MIDLANDS, DY9 0RX.
RICHARDS, Mr. David Hugh, BSc ACA *1986;* Les Fontaines, Rue de la Mare, Castel, GUERNSEY, GY5 7AS.
•RICHARDS, Mr. David John, BA ACA *1990;* (Tax Fac), Pearson May, 37 Great Pulteney Street, BATH, BA2 4DA.
RICHARDS, Mr. David John, FCA *1975;* 54 Sussex Street, BRIGHTON, VIC 3186, AUSTRALIA.
•RICHARDS, Mr. David Michael, FCA *1973;* D.M. Richards, 17 Whittington Road, Norton, STOURBRIDGE, DY8 3DB.
•RICHARDS, Mr. David William, MA FCA *1979;* J L Simpson Ltd, Hunters, Headley Road, Grayshott, HINDHEAD, SURREY GU26 6DL.
RICHARDS, Mr. David William Ryman, MA ACA *1992;* (Tax Fac), Standard Chartered Bank, 1 Basinghall Avenue, LONDON, EC2V 5DD.
RICHARDS, Mrs. Deborah Lesley, BA FCA *1991;* 20 Stevens Road, Pedmore, STOURBRIDGE, DY9 0XA.
RICHARDS, Mr. Derek Pointon, FCA *1960;* 5 Falcons Court, MUCH WENLOCK, SHROPSHIRE, TF13 6BF.
RICHARDS, Mrs. Doreen Frances, FCA *1970;* 4 Fairview Close, Llansamlet, SWANSEA, SA7 9SE.
RICHARDS, Mr. Douglas John, BSc ACA ACT *1992;* Richmond, 75 Windsor Road, GERRARDS CROSS, SL9 7NL.
RICHARDS, Mr. Edward Ian, BA FCA *2001;* 40 Boroimhe Cedars, SWORDS, COUNTY DUBLIN, IRELAND.
RICHARDS, Mr. Edwin David Charles, BSc(Econ) FCA *1989;* 5 Chaucers Lane, WOODSTOCK, OXFORDSHIRE, OX20 1SR.
RICHARDS, Mrs. Elizabeth Anne, BA ACA *1988;* 23 Cavendish Avenue, HARROGATE, HG2 8HY.
RICHARDS, Miss. Emma Louise, BSc ACA *2007;* Dains LLP, Gibraltar House, First Avenue, Centrum One Hundred, BURTON-ON-TRENT, STAFFORDSHIRE DE14 2WE.
RICHARDS, Miss. Emma Louise, BSc(Hons) ACA *2006;* 4/1 Neptune Street, COOGEE, NSW 2034, AUSTRALIA.
RICHARDS, Ms. Fiona Catherine Margaret, BA ACA *1992;* 97 St. Marks Avenue, SALISBURY, SP1 3DW.
RICHARDS, Mr. Gary, MSc ACA *2003;* 3 St. Barts Close, ST. ALBANS, HERTFORDSHIRE, AL4 0BY.
•RICHARDS, Mr. Gary Alan, FCA *1985;* TaxAssist Accountants - Gary Richards, 714 London Road, Larkfield, AYLESFORD, KENT, ME20 6BL.
RICHARDS, Mr. Gavin John, ACA *1999;* 8a The Drive, WEST WICKHAM, KENT, BR4 0EP.
RICHARDS, Mr. Geoffrey Clement, BSc FCA *1978;* E on UK Plc Westwood Way, Westwood Business Park, COVENTRY, CV4 8LG.
RICHARDS, Mr. Geoffrey Stanley, FCA *1965;* Birchmead, Nevill Gate, TUNBRIDGE WELLS, TN2 5ES.
RICHARDS, Mr. George, MSc BA ACA *2006;* 134 Munster Road, LONDON, SW6 5RD.
RICHARDS, Mr. Graham Edward, ACA *1980;* 2 The Malthouse, Farleigh Bridge, East Farleigh, MAIDSTONE, KENT, ME16 9NB.
RICHARDS, Mrs. Heather Marie, BSc ACA *1992;* Richmond, 75 Windsor Road, GERRARDS CROSS, SL9 7NL.
RICHARDS, Ms. Helen, BA ACA *1994;* The Walt Disney Company (Germany) GmbH, Kronstadter Str. 9, 81677 MUNICH, GERMANY.
RICHARDS, Mr. Howard James, BSc ACA *1990;* Hayfellside, Hayclose Lane, New Hutton, KENDAL, LA8 0AG.
RICHARDS, Mr. Hywel, MEng ACA *2011;* Upper Maisonette, 18 Remington Street, LONDON, N1 8DH.
RICHARDS, Mr. Ian David, BCom ACA *1990;* 48 Silverdale Avenue, Red Hill, WORCESTER, WR5 1PX.
RICHARDS, Mr. Ian Warwick, BSc ACA *1988;* Apartment 184 Liberty Place, 26-38 Sheepcote Street, BIRMINGHAM, B16 8JZ.
RICHARDS, Mr. Ivor Bryan, BSc FCA *1961;* Flat 30, Fifteen Grand Avenue, HOVE, BN3 2NG.
RICHARDS, Mr. Ivor Mark, BA FCA *1990;* 18 Oakwood Drive, ST. ALBANS, AL4 0XD.
RICHARDS, Mrs. Jacqueline, ACA *1983;* Ashwood House, 15 The Burrow, Ash Hill, WOLVERHAMPTON, WV3 9DD.
RICHARDS, Mrs. Jacqueline Denise, BA ACA *1989;* 73 Sir Alfreds Way, SUTTON COLDFIELD, B76 1ET.

RICHARDS, Mr. James Craig, BSc ACA *1997;* Upper Sydenhurst Cottage, Mill Lane, Chiddingfold, GODALMING, SURREY, GU8 4SJ.
RICHARDS, Mrs. Jane Elizabeth, FCA *1987;* The Limes, Ash Hill, WOLVERHAMPTON, WV3 9DR.
•**RICHARDS, Mr. Jason David, BA ACA** *1993;* Deloitte LLP, Athene Place, 66 Shoe Lane, LONDON, EC4A 3BQ. See also Deloitte & Touche LLP
RICHARDS, Mr. Jason Lovell, BA FCA *1993;* 1751 Silverwood Terrace, LOS ANGELES, CA 90026, UNITED STATES.
RICHARDS, Mr. Jason Neville Timothy, BSS ACA MIOD *1993;* 4 Dr Crawfords Close Windmill Road, Minchinhampton, STROUD, GLOUCESTERSHIRE, GL6 9EZ.
•**RICHARDS, Mr. Jeremy Brian, BSc ACA** *2000;* Jeremy Richards Limited, 1 Eastwood, Harry Weston Road, Binley Business Park, COVENTRY, CV3 2UB.
RICHARDS, Mr. John Arthur, FCA *1957;* 6 Top Yard Farm, Burnmill Road, Great Bowden, MARKET HARBOROUGH, LE16 7JB. (Life Member)
RICHARDS, Mr. John Clifford, FCA *1966;* Amberwood House, Blackbush Road, Milford-on-Sea, LYMINGTON, SO41 0PB.
RICHARDS, Mr. John Desmond, BCom FCA *1950;* 15 Tyrells Close, Springfield, CHELMSFORD, CM2 6BT. (Life Member)
•**RICHARDS, Mr. John Edward, BA ACA** *1987;* John Richards Accountancy Services, Westgate House, 134-136 Westgate, GUISBOROUGH, NORTH YORKSHIRE, TS14 6NB.
RICHARDS, Mr. John Llewelyn, MA ACA *1983;* PO Box 90259, KLEIN WINDHOEK, NAMIBIA.
•Ⓓ**RICHARDS, Mr. John Parry, FCA** *1971;* Little Renby, Boars Head, CROWBOROUGH, TN6 3HE.
RICHARDS, Mr. John William Anthony, FCA *1950;* 18 Rue Du Golf, 03200 VICHY, FRANCE. (Life Member)
•**RICHARDS, Mrs. Jula Muriel Gaved, BA ACA** *1989;* FD Accounting Solutions, New Nutwalls, Aylesbeare, EXETER, EX5 2JL. See also Management Accounting Solutions
RICHARDS, Miss. Julie Marie, BSc ACA *2010;* Porthygan Farm, Marchwiel, WREXHAM, CLWYD, LL13 0TP.
RICHARDS, Mrs. Karen Elizabeth, BA ACA *1987;* Roxton, 54 Murton Lane, Newton, SWANSEA, SA3 4TR.
RICHARDS, Mrs. Kathryn Joanne, BA ACA *1999;* 31 Old Hall Road, SALE, M33 2HT.
•**RICHARDS, Mr. Keith Spenser, BA ACA** *1986;* (Tax Fac), The Barn, Church Lane, Sibthorpe, NEWARK, NG23 5PN.
•**RICHARDS, Mr. Keith Thomas John, BA FCA CF** *1993;* Keith Richard Limited, 12 Turbary Gardens, TADLEY, HAMPSHIRE, RG26 4HS.
RICHARDS, Mrs. Kelly Frances, ACA *2009;* 21 Evergreen Close, Three Legged Cross, WIMBORNE, DORSET, BH21 6SH.
•**RICHARDS, Mr. Kenneth John, FCA** *1963;* Rohans Auditors (UK) Ltd, Rohans House, 92-96 Wellington Road South, STOCKPORT, CHESHIRE, SK1 3TJ.
RICHARDS, Mr. Kevin James, FCA *1973;* 6 Chandler Drive, Penn, WOLVERHAMPTON, WV4 5NH.
RICHARDS, Miss. Lauren Alexina, ACA *2008;* 9 Cwrt ty Mawr, CAERPHILLY, MID GLAMORGAN, CF83 3EQ.
RICHARDS, Miss. Lavinia Marie, LLB ACA *2004;* 7 Pymgate Drive, Heald Green, CHEADLE, CHESHIRE, SK8 3TR.
RICHARDS, Miss. Leonie, BSc ACA *2003;* High View, Clay Street, Whiteparish, SALISBURY, SP5 2ST.
RICHARDS, Mrs. Lorraine Carole, BA ACA *1986;* 9 Farriers Way, UCKFIELD, TN22 5BY.
RICHARDS, Miss. Marion Elizabeth, BSc ACA *1995;* 3 Old Dairy Cottages, Ibstone, HIGH WYCOMBE, HP14 3YW.
RICHARDS, Mr. Mark Charles Oliver, BA ACA *1988;* Assa Abloy UK Ltd Portebello Works, School Street, WILLENHALL, WV13 3PW.
RICHARDS, Mr. Mark Edward James, BSc ACA *2007;* 12 Peregrine Way, Heath Hayes, CANNOCK, STAFFORDSHIRE, WS11 7JX.
RICHARDS, Mr. Mark John, MEng ACA *2003;* 6a Highgrove Way, RUISLIP, MIDDLESEX, HA4 8EA.
RICHARDS, Mr. Mark Julian, ACA *1982;* PO Box 31698, Kyalami, JOHANNESBURG, 1684, SOUTH AFRICA.
RICHARDS, Mr. Martin Basil, FCA *1975;* Barnshaw Cottage, Pepper Street, Mobberley, KNUTSFORD, WA16 6JH.
•**RICHARDS, Mr. Martin Jonathan, BA ACA** *1995;* One 2 One Accountants Ltd, The School House, 108 Bedminster Down Road, BRISTOL, BS13 7AF.
RICHARDS, Mr. Matthew John, BSc ACA *2001;* 1 Hodgetts Drive, HALESOWEN, WEST MIDLANDS, B63 1ET.
RICHARDS, Mrs. Melanie Jane, BA ACA *1995;* 9 Berrington Drive, East Horsley, LEATHERHEAD, KT24 5ST.
RICHARDS, Mr. Michael James Russell, BSc ACA *1991;* Arran Isle Limited, Premier Way Lowfields Business Park, ELLAND, HX5 9HF.
RICHARDS, Mr. Michael Roy, FCA *1973;* Spruce Cottage, Newbridge, Cadnam, SOUTHAMPTON, SO40 2NW.
RICHARDS, Mr. Mike James, BA ACA *2005;* 10 Needham Drive, Cranage, CREWE, CW4 8FB.
RICHARDS, Mr. Neil Kevin, BA ACA *1992;* 9 The Willows, Parbrook, BILLINGSHURST, WEST SUSSEX, RH14 9WL.
RICHARDS, Mr. Nicholas Guy, BA ACA *1992;* 6 Charterhouse Close, Nailsea, BRISTOL, BS48 4PU.
RICHARDS, Mrs. Nicola Jane, BA(Hons) ACA *2000;* Via Nino Bixio 21, 21054 FAGNANO OLONA, ITALY.
RICHARDS, Mrs. Nicola Marie, BA ACA *2002;* St. Merryn Meat Ltd, Talgarrick House, Victoria Business Park, Roche, ST. AUSTELL, CORNWALL PL26 8LX.
•**RICHARDS, Mrs. Pamela Vanessa Roberta, FCA** *1975;* (Tax Fac), 34 Queensmill Road, LONDON, SW6 6JS. See also Richards P.V.R. Mrs
•**RICHARDS, Miss. Patricia Anne, BA FCA DChA** *1987;* Wyatt Morris Golland & Co, Park House, 200 Drake Street, ROCHDALE, OL16 1PJ.
RICHARDS, Mr. Paul, BSc ACA *2006;* 284b Archway Road, Highgate, LONDON, N6 5AU.
RICHARDS, Mr. Paul James, ACA *2008;* Mitchell Charlesworth Centurion House, 129 Deansgate, MANCHESTER, M3 3WR.
RICHARDS, Mr. Peter, FCA *1972;* Wenallt, West Parade, CRICCIETH, LL52 0EN. (Life Member)
RICHARDS, Mr. Peter Anthony Joyner, BSc FCA *1978;* with KPMG Audit plc, 15 Canada Square, LONDON, E14 5GL.
RICHARDS, Mr. Peter Brookhouse, FCA *1973;* 14 rue Georges Vigor, 94230 CACHAN, FRANCE.
RICHARDS, Mr. Peter Josef, FCA *1949;* Little Hayfield Rowden Mill Lane Stourton Caundle, STURMINSTER NEWTON, DORSET, DT10 2JT. (Life Member)
RICHARDS, Mr. Peter Robin, FCA *1968;* with Clement Rabjohns, 111-113 High Street, EVESHAM, WR11 4XP.
•**RICHARDS, Mr. Philip David Edward, BEng ACA ATII** *1994;* Deloitte LLP, Abbots House, Abbey Street, READING, RG1 3BD. See also Deloitte & Touche LLP
RICHARDS, Mr. Philip John, BA ACA *1985;* Ashlea, Presteigne Road, KNIGHTON, LD7 1HY.
RICHARDS, Mr. Philip Roger, BSc ACA *1993;* with PricewaterhouseCoopers Inc, PO Box 2799, CAPE TOWN, C.P., 8000, SOUTH AFRICA.
RICHARDS, Mrs. Rachel, BSc ACA *1999;* DSA Electrical, Electron House, West Hanningfield Road, Great Baddow, CHELMSFORD, CM2 8JT.
RICHARDS, Mrs. Rachel Marie, BA ACA *1995;* Beech House Church Hill Thorner, LEEDS, LS14 3EG.
RICHARDS, Mr. Ralph Henry Arthur, FCA *1951;* (Tax Fac), 20 Homestead Gardens, Frenchay, BRISTOL, BS16 1PH.
RICHARDS, Mr. Richard William Thomas, FCA *1968;* Paddock View, Poling, ARUNDEL, BN18 9PT.
RICHARDS, Mr. Robert Brian, FCA *1963;* 4 Royal Crescent, BATH, BA1 2LR.
•**RICHARDS, Mr. Robert Iestyn, FCA FCCA CTA** *1993;* The Richards Sandy Partnership Limited, 6 Edgar Street, WORCESTER, WR1 2LR.
RICHARDS, Mr. Robert Mark, BA(Hons) ACA *2006;* 94 Avenue Road, Winslow, BUCKINGHAM, MK18 3DB.
•**RICHARDS, Mr. Rodney Sebastian Wilson, MA FCA** *1984;* Rodney S. W. Richards, 3 Shaftesbury Villas, Allen Street, LONDON, W8 6UZ.
RICHARDS, Mr. Ronald Jack, FCA *1950;* Hadley Cottage, 17 Copp Hill Lane, BUDLEIGH SALTERTON, EX9 6DT. (Life Member)
RICHARDS, Mrs. Rosemary Anne, BA FCA *1989;* The Orchard House, Wiston, HAVERFORDWEST, DYFED, SA62 4PW.
RICHARDS, Mr. Russell Martin Perren, FCA *1971;* PO Box-F-42322, 43 Shoreline, Doubloon Road, FREEPORT, GRAND BAHAMA ISLAND, BAHAMAS.
RICHARDS, Mr. Samuel Kenneth Carroll, FCA *1965;* 15 Clos y Hebog, Thornhill, CARDIFF, CF14 9JL.
RICHARDS, Mrs. Sarah Katharine, BSc ACA *1994;* 25 Bankart Avenue, Oadby, LEICESTER, LE2 2DD.
RICHARDS, Ms. Sharon Dawn, BSc ACA *1988;* 15 Hibiscus Place, CHERRYBROOK, NSW 2126, AUSTRALIA.
RICHARDS, Mrs. Sharon Elizabeth, BSc ACA *1992;* 26 The Mount, Badgers Mount, BILLERICAY, CM11 1HD.
RICHARDS, Mr. Simon Anthony, MA FCA *1980;* Heathercombe House, Drayton St. Leonard, WALLINGFORD, OXFORDSHIRE, OX10 7BG.
RICHARDS, Mr. Simon Leonard Christopher, MEng FCA *1991;* 15 Barnbrook Road, Knowle, SOLIHULL, WEST MIDLANDS, B93 9PW.
RICHARDS, Miss. Sonya Lorraine, BSc FCA *1995;* Yattendon Investment Trust Plc, Burnt Hill, Yattendon, THATCHAM, RG18 0UX.
RICHARDS, Mr. Stephen Andrew, BSc ACA *1997;* 8 Durham Road, Pitstone, LEIGHTON BUZZARD, BEDFORDSHIRE, LU7 9JZ.
RICHARDS, Mr. Stephen Graham, BSc ACA *1991;* with Ing Bank Nv, 60 London Wall, LONDON, EC2M 5TQ.
RICHARDS, Mr. Stephen John, BSc ACA *1995;* 10 Ashford Road, Cricklewood, LONDON, NW2 6TP.
•**RICHARDS, Mr. Stephen John, MA FCA ATII** *1986;* (Tax Fac), Price Firman, Prince Consort House, Albert Embankment, LONDON, SE1 7TJ.
RICHARDS, Mr. Stephen Malcolm, FCA *1974;* The Old Livery, Draycote Farm, Draycote, RUGBY, CV23 9RB.
•**RICHARDS, Mr. Steven Mark, BA FCA** *1986;* (Tax Fac), BSN Associates Limited, 3b Swallowfield Courtyard, Wolverhampton Road, OLDBURY, WEST MIDLANDS, B69 2JG. See also BSN Associates Holdings Limited
RICHARDS, Miss. Susan, BA ACA *1992;* 73 Selwyn Avenue, RICHMOND, SURREY, TW9 2HB.
RICHARDS, Mrs. Suzanne Helen, BSc ACA *2001;* 12 Stuart Road, NEWBURY, RG14 6QX.
RICHARDS, Mr. Thomas Christopher, BA ACA *2002;* 47 Ormeley Road, LONDON, SW12 9QF.
RICHARDS, Mr. Thomas Llewelyn, BA(Econ) ACA *1999;* Pricewaterhousecoopers, 12 Plumtree Court, LONDON, EC4A 4HT.
•**RICHARDS, Mr. Timothy Roy, FCA** *1953;* (Tax Fac), Richards & Co, The Dormer House, 159 Rough Common Road, CANTERBURY, CT2 9BS.
RICHARDS, Mr. Trevor Richard, BSc ACA *1993;* 34 Whitehill Place, VIRGINIA WATER, SURREY, GU25 4DG.
RICHARDS, Miss. Victoria Jacqueline, MA ACA *2004;* with Moore Stephens LLP, 150 Aldersgate Street, LONDON, EC1A 4AB.
RICHARDS, Mr. Wilfred Eric, FCA *1951;* Eastleigh House, First Drive, Dawlish Road, TEIGNMOUTH, TQ14 8TJ. (Life Member)
RICHARDS, William Samuel Clive, Esq OBE DL FCA FCMA FCMI *1961;* (Member of Council 1995 - 1999), Clive Richards & Co, Lower Hope, Ullingswick, HEREFORD, HR1 3JF.
RICHARDS, Mrs. Yvonne, BA ACA *1990;* (Tax Fac), Lark Rise, Stocking Lane, Hughenden Valley, HIGH WYCOMBE, BUCKINGHAMSHIRE, HP14 4NE.
RICHARDS-CLARKE, Miss. Judith, BA(Hons) ACA *2002;* 12 Gurney Court Road, ST. ALBANS, HERTFORDSHIRE, AL1 4RL.
RICHARDSON, Mr. Adam, BSc ACA *2004;* 45 Alexandra Road, RICHMOND, TW9 2BT.
RICHARDSON, Mr. Adrian, ACA *2009;* Flat 14, Lexington, 42 Chorlton Street, MANCHESTER, M1 3HW.
RICHARDSON, Mr. Alan, BA ACA *2002;* 7 Southlands Drive, LEEDS, LS17 5NZ.
•**RICHARDSON, Mr. Alan, MSc FCA** *1976;* Baker Tilly UK Audit LLP, 25 Farringdon Street, LONDON, EC4A 4AB. See also Slater Maidment
•**RICHARDSON, Mr. Alexander Bernard, MA FCA** *1985;* P O BOX 20613, MANAMA, BAHRAIN.
•**RICHARDSON, Mrs. Alison, BSc ACA** *2002;* Richardsons Financial Group Limited, 30 Upper High Street, THAME, OXFORDSHIRE, OX9 3EZ.
RICHARDSON, Mrs. Alison Jane, ACA *1986;* Ridding Bungalow, Roundfields, Stockton Brook, STOKE-ON-TRENT, ST9 9PG.
RICHARDSON, Mr. Andrew James, BA ACA *1987;* 11 Nelson Road, LONDON, N8 9RX.
•**RICHARDSON, Mr. Andrew James Grenville, BA FCA** *1984;* AJR & Co Ltd, 1 Sandhill Farm, Middle Claydon, BUCKINGHAM, MK18 2LD. See also AJR & Co
RICHARDSON, Mr. Andrew Shaw, BA ACA *1990;* 62/6A-19F11 Duong Quang Trung, Quan Go Vap, HO CHI MINH CITY, VIETNAM.
RICHARDSON, Mrs. Angela Mary, FCA *1971;* 28 Waverley Gardens, STAMFORD, PE9 1BH. (Life Member)
RICHARDSON, Miss. Anne, BSc ACA *1990;* 11 Blue Ridge Close, Great Sankey, WARRINGTON, WA5 3GX.
•**RICHARDSON, Mr. Anthony John, BA ACA** *2002;* Ford Campbell Corporate Finance LLP, Bass Warehouse, 4 Castle Street, Castlefield, MANCHESTER, M3 4LZ.
RICHARDSON, Mr. Ben Peter, ACA *2007;* Flat 5, 68 Elmbourne Road, Tooting, LONDON, SW17 8JJ.
RICHARDSON, Mr. Benjamin, MA ACA *2001;* Aldhams Bromley Road, Lawford, MANNINGTREE, CO11 2NE.
RICHARDSON, Mr. Benjamin George, MA ACA *2002;* 33 Ennismore Avenue, Chiswick, LONDON, W4 1SE.
RICHARDSON, Miss. Beverley Jayne, ACA *1991;* Warrington Volkswagen, Milner Street, WARRINGTON, WA5 1AD.
RICHARDSON, Mr. Brian, FCA *1964;* 34B Benington Road, Aston, STEVENAGE, SG2 7DY. (Life Member)
RICHARDSON, Mr. Brian Edwin, FCA *1961;* 180-1405 Lorne Park Road, Unit 180, MISSISSAUGA L5H 3B2, ON, CANADA. (Life Member)
RICHARDSON, Mr. Brian Ernest, FCA *1958;* Quarry House, GUNNISLAKE, CORNWALL, PL18 9ND. (Life Member)
•**RICHARDSON, Mr. Brian Keith, FCA** *1972;* 38 Branscombe Road, Stoke Bishop, BRISTOL, BS9 1SN.
RICHARDSON, Mr. Brian Laurence, FCA *1957;* 42 Lady Byron Lane, Copt Heath, SOLIHULL, B93 9AU.
RICHARDSON, Mrs. Camilla Jane, BSc ACA *1999;* 30 Hearnville Road, Balham, LONDON, SW12 8RR.
•**RICHARDSON, Mrs. Carol Anne, ACA** *2004;* The Bungalow, Wold House Farm, Trundlegate, South Newbald, YORK, YO43 4TN.
RICHARDSON, Mrs. Caroline Jane, BSc ACA *1998;* Deutsche Knowledge Services Pts Ltd, Net Quad Center, 31st Street cor 4th Avenue, E-Square Zone, Crescent Park West, Bonificiao Global City TAGUIG CITY TA4 METRO MANILA PHILIPPINES.
RICHARDSON, Mrs. Catherine Margaret, BA FCA *1978;* 24 Old Malt Way, Horsell, WOKING, GU21 4QD.
RICHARDSON, Miss. Catherine Mary, FCA *1962;* 18 St. Johns Court, Howden, GOOLE, NORTH HUMBERSIDE, DN14 7BE. (Life Member)
RICHARDSON, Mr. Charles Austen, MA ACA CTA *1999;* 2 Vale Row, LONDON, N5 1LL.
RICHARDSON, Mr. Charles Bulmer, FCA *1951;* 35 Postern Close, Bishop's Wharf, YORK, YO23 1JF. (Life Member)
RICHARDSON, Mr. Charlie Howard, BSc ACA *2005;* Penguin Books Ltd, 80 Strand, LONDON, WC2R 0RL.
•**RICHARDSON, Mrs. Charlotte Diana, BA ACA** *1993;* PricewaterhouseCoopers LLP, 1 Embankment Place, LONDON, WC2N 6RH. See also PricewaterhouseCoopers
RICHARDSON, Mr. Christopher Mark, BA FCA *1982;* 28 Lebanon Park, TWICKENHAM, TW1 3DG.
RICHARDSON, Mr. Christopher Nigel, BA FCA *1974;* 41 Lynton Drive, Hillside, SOUTHPORT, PR8 4QG.
RICHARDSON, Mrs. Claire Juliet, BA(Hons) ACA *2001;* with Deloitte LLP, Mountbatten House, 1 Grosvenor Square, SOUTHAMPTON, SO15 2BZ.
RICHARDSON, Mr. Clifford Paul, FCA *1977;* 12 Mill Close, Great Bardfield, BRAINTREE, ESSEX, CM7 4RJ.
RICHARDSON, Mr. Clive John, BA FCA *1978;* 8 Cote Green Road, Marple Bridge, STOCKPORT, SK6 5EH.
RICHARDSON, Mrs. Constance Evelyn, ACA *1991;* 16 Kinga Crescent, BURNS BEACH, WA 6028, AUSTRALIA.
•**RICHARDSON, Mr. Craig Stuart, BA ACA CF** *1993;* Dow Schofield Watts Corporate Finance Limited, Marsh Lane, PRESTON, PR1 8UQ. See also Dow Schofield Watts Transaction Services LLP
RICHARDSON, Mr. Daniel James, BSc ACA *1999;* 56 North Eyot Gardens, Hammersmith, LONDON, W6 9NL.
•**RICHARDSON, Mr. David, FCA** *1975;* (Tax Fac), David Richardson & Co, 4a London Road, STROUD, GL5 2AG.
•**RICHARDSON, Mr. David Edward, FCA** *1981;* Trenfield Williams, The Old Railway Station, Sea Mills Lane, Stoke Bishop, BRISTOL, BS9 1FF. See also Trenfield Williams Ltd
RICHARDSON, Mr. David Gordon, BA FCA *1987;* Haselbury House, Water Lane, Radwinter, SAFFRON WALDEN, CB10 2TX.
RICHARDSON, Mr. David Hedley, BSc FCA FRSA *1975;* Flat 56, Circus Lodge, Circus Road, LONDON, NW8 9JN.
•**RICHARDSON, Mr. David Henry, FCA** *1977;* Laverick Walton & Co, Unit A1 Marquis Court, Team Valley, GATESHEAD, TYNE AND WEAR, NE11 0RU.

RICHARDSON, Mr. David James Murray, BSc ACA *1985;* Rensburg Sheppards Investment Management Ltd, 2 Gresham Street, LONDON, EC2V 7QN.
RICHARDSON, Mr. David Mark, MBA LLB FCA *1988;* 9 Bryn Grove, Hest Bank, LANCASTER, LA2 6EX.
RICHARDSON, Mr. David Michael, BA ACA *1995;* Moores Furniture Group Ltd Unit 350, Thorp Arch Estate, WETHERBY, WEST YORKSHIRE, LS23 7DD.
RICHARDSON, Mr. David Michael, FCA *1979;* with Mark J Rees, Granville Hall, Granville Road, LEICESTER, LE1 7RU.
RICHARDSON, Mr. Denis, FCA *1967;* 38 Longmeadow, Cheadle Hulme, CHEADLE, SK8 7ER.
RICHARDSON, Mr. Denis Ian, FCA *1948;* 26 Rosetree Avenue, Birstall, LEICESTER, LE4 4LS. (Life Member)
RICHARDSON, Miss. Diana Mary, BSc ACA *1984;* 10 Emsworth Road, HAVANT, PO9 2SS.
RICHARDSON, Mr. Douglas Paul, FCA *1970;* 4 Maple Close, Willand, CULLOMPTON, EX15 2SP.
•RICHARDSON, Mr. Edward Andrew, BSc ACA *1994;* (Tax Fac), Richardsons, 99 London Street, READING, RG1 4QA.
RICHARDSON, Miss. Elisabeth Anne, BA FCA *1982;* 13 Mount Hermon Close, WOKING, GU22 7TU.
RICHARDSON, Mrs. Ellen Jane, FCA CTA *1986;* Haselbury House, Water Lane, Radwinter, SAFFRON WALDEN, CB10 2TX.
RICHARDSON, Mr. Eric John, FCA *1958;* 91 Marland Fold, Marland, ROCHDALE, OL11 4RF. (Life Member)
•RICHARDSON, Mr. Eric Keith, BSc FCA *1971;* Richardson & Co, Summerville, 65 Daisy Bank Rd, Victoria Pk, MANCHESTER, M14 5QL.
RICHARDSON, Mrs. Fiona Jayne, BA ACA *1999;* 40 Great Innings North, Watton at Stone, HERTFORD, SG14 3TD.
RICHARDSON, Mr. Francis John, BA ACA *1998;* 15 Love Lane, CANTERBURY, CT1 1TZ.
RICHARDSON, Mr. Geoffrey, FCA *1956;* 173 Golf Links Road, West Parley, FERNDOWN, BH22 8BX. (Life Member)
RICHARDSON, Mr. Geoffrey Paul, BCom ACA *1986;* 420 Oak Road, MATCHAM, NSW 2250, AUSTRALIA.
RICHARDSON, Mr. George Michael, MA FCA *1963;* Killaloe, Hollybank Road, Hook Heath, WOKING, GU22 0JN.
RICHARDSON, Mr. Giles Harvey Roberts, BSc ACA *2002;* 309 Chapelier House, Eastfields Avenue, LONDON, SW18 1LR.
RICHARDSON, Mr. Gordon Cameron, BSc ACA *1986;* Shelfield Lodge, 22 Henbury Road, Westbury-On-Trym, BRISTOL, BS9 3HJ.
•RICHARDSON, Mr. Graham Oram, BSc FCA *1982;* Deloitte LLP, 2 New Street Square, LONDON, EC4A 3BZ. See also Deloitte & Touche LLP
RICHARDSON, Mr. Grahame, FCA *1957;* Church Farm House, Main Street, Stillington, YORK, YO61 1JS. (Life Member)
RICHARDSON, Mr. Guy Harvey, ACA *2009;* 65 Walmer Close, ROMFORD, RM7 8QH.
RICHARDSON, Miss. Hannah, BA ACA *2005;* Corporate Finance, B D O Stoy Hayward, 55 Baker Street, LONDON, W1U 7EU.
RICHARDSON, Mr. Harry Thomas, FCA *1971;* Silverlea, The Vale, LONDON, N14 6HN.
RICHARDSON, Mrs. Helen Joanna, BMus ACA *1985;* Willinghurst Farmhouse, Guilford Road, Shamley Green, GUILDFORD, SURREY, GU5 0SU.
•RICHARDSON, Mr. Howard Frederick, FCA *1970;* 67 Windermere Road, BRADFORD, WEST YORKSHIRE, BD7 4BB.
RICHARDSON, Mr. Hugh Denys, FCA *1969;* Tall Cedars, Courtlands Hill, Pangbourne, READING, RG8 7BE. (Life Member)
RICHARDSON, Mr. Hugh Francis, MA FCA *1973;* 13 Rotherfield Road, HENLEY-ON-THAMES, OXFORDSHIRE, RG9 1NR.
RICHARDSON, Mr. Iain Charles, ACA *1986;* Americka 22, PRAGUE, VINOHRADY, CZECH REPUBLIC.
RICHARDSON, Mr. Iain Stuart, BA ACA CF *1998;* Tait Walker, Bulman House, Regent Centre, Gosforth, NEWCASTLE UPON TYNE, NE3 3LS.
•RICHARDSON, Mr. Ian, BSc FCA *1979;* Hall & Co, 59 The Avenue, SOUTHAMPTON, SO17 1XS.
RICHARDSON, Mr. Ian Michael, BA ACA *1991;* Stehlin & Hostag Ltd Unit D/4 Linkmel Close, Longwall Avenue Queens Drive Industrial Estate, NOTTINGHAM, NG2 1NA.
RICHARDSON, Mr. Ian Robert, FCA *1973;* La Tenue, La Rue De La Vallee, St Mary, JERSEY, JE3 3DL.
RICHARDSON, Mr. Ian Stuart, ACA CA(SA) *2008;* 32 Sun Street, Isleham, ELY, CAMBRIDGESHIRE, CB7 5RU.
•RICHARDSON, Mrs. Jacqueline Anne, ACA *1978;* Beachview, 199 Cooden Drive, BEXHILL-ON-SEA, EAST SUSSEX, TN39 3AE.
RICHARDSON, Mr. James, ACA *2011;* Flat 7, 39 Netherhall Gardens, LONDON, NW3 5RL.
RICHARDSON, Mr. James Alexander, BSc ACA *1997;* 2 Hatch Lane, Wormley, GODALMING, SURREY, GU8 5UX.
RICHARDSON, Mr. James Andrew, BA ACA *2000;* 81 Monkhams Drive, WOODFORD GREEN, ESSEX, IG8 0LD.
•RICHARDSON, Mr. James Ernest, FCA *1962;* James Richardson, Sirama, Little Boundes Close, TUNBRIDGE WELLS, TN4 0RS.
•RICHARDSON, Mr. James Luke, BA(Hons) ACA *2004;* Metric Accountants Ltd, 85B Bedford Road, East Finchley, LONDON, N2 9DB.
RICHARDSON, Mr. James Peter Charles, BSc ACA *2007;* J W T, 1 Knightsbridge Green, LONDON, SW1X 7NW.
RICHARDSON, Mrs. Jane Amanda, BSc FCA *1984;* La Grande Rue La Grande Rue, St. Mary, JERSEY, JE3 3BD.
RICHARDSON, Miss. Jane Mary, BA ACA *1981;* 18 Rathgar Avenue, DUBLIN 6, COUNTY DUBLIN, IRELAND.
RICHARDSON, Mrs. Jane Miranda, FCA *1970;* The Coach House, 13 Rotherfield Road, HENLEY-ON-THAMES, OXFORDSHIRE, RG9 1NR. (Life Member)
•RICHARDSON, Mrs. Jennifer Mary, FCA *1991;* (Tax Fac), Jennifer M Richardson Limited, 43A High Street, Newington, SITTINGBOURNE, KENT, ME9 7JR.
RICHARDSON, Mr. Jeremy Bruce, BA ACA *1996;* Mulberry Court Ockley Road, Ewhurst, CRANLEIGH, GU6 7QF.
RICHARDSON, Mr. Jeremy Charles, FCA *1976;* Advantage House, Business Link 19 Ridgeway, Quinton Business Park Quinton, BIRMINGHAM, B32 1AL.
RICHARDSON, Mr. Jeremy Edward, BSc ACA *1994;* Denting Stanley Plc Stanley House, 151 Dale Street, LIVERPOOL, L2 2JW.
RICHARDSON, Ms. Joanna, BSc ACA *1994;* Eastbrook House, Back Street, Thornborough, BUCKINGHAM, MK18 2DH.
RICHARDSON, Miss. Joanna Mary, ACA *2008;* with Kenneth Easby LLP, Hanover House, 13 Victoria Road, DARLINGTON, COUNTY DURHAM, DL1 5SF.
RICHARDSON, Miss. Joanne Amanda, BA ACA *2004;* Flat 5, 166 Arden Street, Coogee, SYDNEY, NSW 2034, AUSTRALIA.
•RICHARDSON, Mrs. Joanne Claire, BSc ACA *2006;* Richardson Business Services, 29 Bolton Road North, Edenfield, BURY, LANCASHIRE, BL0 0HB.
RICHARDSON, Mr. John, FCA *1952;* 7 Oaks Avenue Hayfield, HIGH PEAK, DERBYSHIRE, SK22 2JU. (Life Member)
•RICHARDSON, Mr. John, FCA *1964;* Glen Avon, 57 Booth Road, Waterfoot, ROSSENDALE, LANCASHIRE, BB4 9BP.
RICHARDSON, Mr. John D'arcy, BA FCA *1970;* 63 Langdon Avenue, Bedgrove, AYLESBURY, HP21 9UW. (Life Member)
RICHARDSON, Mr. John David, BSc ACA *1991;* 23 Deep Spinney Biddenham, BEDFORD, MK40 4QJ.
RICHARDSON, Mr. John Edgar, FCA *1941;* 13 Albery Crescent, AJAX L1S 2Y2, ON, CANADA. (Life Member)
RICHARDSON, Mr. John Kenneth, FCA *1954;* 4 Barber Drive, CRANLEIGH, GU6 7DG. (Life Member)
•RICHARDSON, Mr. John Martin Gerald, BSc ACA *1995;* Temporal Lennon & Company Limited, Suite 1A, Realtex House, Leeds Road, Rawdon, LEEDS LS19 6AX. See also JMGR Limited
RICHARDSON, Mr. John Nicholas Michael, FCA *1975;* 1 St, Bruno Flats, Charters Road, SUNNINGDALE, BERKSHIRE, SL5 9QB.
RICHARDSON, Mr. John Peter, BA ACA *2005;* Les Autelets Rue Du Clos, St. Sampson, GUERNSEY, GY2 4FN.
•RICHARDSON, Mr. Jonathan, BA ACA *1994;* (Tax Fac), PricewaterhouseCoopers LLP, 1 Embankment Place, LONDON, WC2N 6RH. See also PricewaterhouseCoopers
RICHARDSON, Mr. Jonathan Charles, BA ACA *1987;* 24 Foxcote Way, Walton, CHESTERFIELD, S42 7NP.
RICHARDSON, Mr. Joseph Sarto, BSc ACA *1979;* 14 Haining Road, KINGSTON 10, JAMAICA.
RICHARDSON, Miss. Josie Eloise, LLB ACA *2004;* Beverlac, Leeds Road, Pool in Wharfedale, OTLEY, WEST YORKSHIRE, LS21 3BR.
•RICHARDSON, Mrs. Judith Anne, FCA *1979;* (Tax Fac), Larking Gowen, King Street House, 15 Upper King Street, NORWICH, NR3 1RB.
RICHARDSON, Mr. Julian Paul De Rougemont, FCA JDipMA *1954;* Old Croft Cottage, Hookhouse Lane, Dunsfold, GODALMING, GU8 4LR. (Life Member)
RICHARDSON, Mrs. Justine, BA ACA *2000;* PO Box 484, PORT MORESBY, PAPUA NEW GUINEA.
RICHARDSON, Ms. Kate Louise, BA ACA *2006;* 155 New Chester Road, WIRRAL, MERSEYSIDE, CH62 4RB.
RICHARDSON, Mrs. Katharine Jane, BSc ACA *1992;* Norwest House, Redwood Lane, Medstead, ALTON, HAMPSHIRE, GU34 5PE.
•RICHARDSON, Mrs. Katherine Ann, FCA *1990;* PWR Accountants Limited, 2 Beacon End Courtyard, London Road, Stanway, COLCHESTER, CO3 0NU.
RICHARDSON, Mr. Keith John, BSc ACA *1984;* Robinson's Barn, Green Common Farm, Green Common Lane, Westhoughton, BOLTON, BL5 3BN.
RICHARDSON, Mr. Kenneth Gordon, FCA *1954;* 3 The Fir Trees, Anlaby, HULL, HU10 7DQ. (Life Member)
•RICHARDSON, Mr. Kenneth Larry, FCA *1965;* (Tax Fac), K L Richardson & Co, 20 South Close, CANNOCK, WS11 1EH.
RICHARDSON, Mr. Kevin Francis, FCA *1977;* 14 Burbidge Grove, SOUTHSEA, PO4 9RR.
RICHARDSON, Miss. Linda, BA ACA *1998;* College Gates, GORMANSTON, COUNTY MEATH, IRELAND.
•RICHARDSON, Mrs. Linda Louise, FCA ATII *1977;* (Tax Fac), Menzies LLP, Heathrow Business Centre, 65 High Street, EGHAM, SURREY, TW20 9EY.
RICHARDSON, Mrs. Louise Joanna, BSc ACA *1983;* Mencap, Canon Lodge, Canon Street, TAUNTON, SOMERSET, TA1 1SW.
RICHARDSON, Mr. Luke, BSc ACA *2006;* with Hillier Hopkins LLP, 2a Alton House Office Park, Gatehouse Way, AYLESBURY, BUCKINGHAMSHIRE, HP19 8YF.
RICHARDSON, Mrs. Lynn Christina, BSc FCA *1978;* 33 Doveridge Road, Hall Green, BIRMINGHAM, B28 0LT.
•RICHARDSON, Mr. Malcolm Raymond, FCA *1966;* M R Richardson, Four Ways, Rake Lane, ULVERSTON, CUMBRIA, LA12 9NG.
RICHARDSON, Mr. Mark, MMath ACA *2007;* 71 Lyndhurst Way, LONDON, SE15 4PT.
RICHARDSON, Mr. Mark, BSc ACA *1979;* Bristol Infracare Lift LTD, Castlemead, Lower Castle Street, BRISTOL, BS1 3AG.
RICHARDSON, Mr. Mark Alexander, MA ACA *2003;* Barclays Capital, 4th Floor, 5 North Colonnade, Canary Wharf, LONDON, E14 4BB.
RICHARDSON, Mr. Mark Allington, BSc FCA *1978;* Western Group, PO Box 157, LEATHERHEAD, SURREY, KT24 9BE.
RICHARDSON, Mr. Mark Edward, BSc(Hons) ACA *2003;* 24 Reddington Way, BRENTWOOD, WA 6153, AUSTRALIA.
•RICHARDSON, Mr. Mark John Edmund, BA ACA *2000;* Mark Richardson, 25 Valerie Court, Bath Road, READING, RG1 6HP.
RICHARDSON, Mr. Martin, ACA *2011;* 2 Simmons Court, GUILDFORD, GU1 1DJ.
RICHARDSON, Mr. Martin, MEng ACA *2004;* 1 Appold Street, Deutsche Bank, PO Box 135, LONDON, EC2A 2HE.
RICHARDSON, Mr. Martin Allen, FCA *1964;* 3 Navey Hall Circle, Niagara-on-the-Lake, ONTARIO L0S1J0, ON, CANADA. (Life Member)
RICHARDSON, Mr. Martin James, BSc(Hons) ACA CTA *2002;* (Tax Fac), with Grant Thornton UK LLP, 1-4 Atholl Crescent, EDINBURGH, EH3 8LQ.
RICHARDSON, Mr. Martin Willaume, BSc FCA *1979;* Douceville Farm, Mont Cochon, St. Helier, JERSEY, JE2 3JB.
RICHARDSON, Mr. Matthew John De Rougemont, BA ACA *1989;* Abbey National Treasury Services Plc, 2 Triton Square, Regents Place, LONDON, NW1 3AN.
RICHARDSON, Mr. Matthew Neil, ACA *2006;* Zolfo Cooper (BVI) Limited, P.O. Box 4571, 2nd Floor Palm Grove House, TORTOLA, VG1110, VIRGIN ISLANDS (BRITISH).
•RICHARDSON, Mrs. Melanie Jane, BA(Hons) FCA *2000;* Swindells LLP, New Olives, High Street, UCKFIELD, EAST SUSSEX, TN22 1QE.
RICHARDSON, Dr. Michael, ACA *1990;* The Granary, Aston Common Farm, Worksop Road, SHEFFIELD, S26 2AE.
RICHARDSON, Mr. Michael Charles, FCA *1964;* St. Vincents, Addington, WEST MALLING, ME19 5BW. (Life Member)
RICHARDSON, Mr. Michael James, BSc(Hons) FCA *2001;* 17 Barnes Avenue, Dronfield Woodhouse, DRONFIELD, S18 8YF.
RICHARDSON, Mr. Michael John, FCA *1960;* 19 Mount Harry Road, SEVENOAKS, TN13 3JJ.
RICHARDSON, Mr. Michael Thomas, FCA *1977;* Wise Insurance Services Ltd, 168 Croydon Road, BECKENHAM, KENT, BR3 4DE.
•RICHARDSON, Mr. Michael Thomas, FCA *1982;* Richardson Swift Ltd, 11 Laura Place, BATH, BA2 4BL.
RICHARDSON, Mr. Michael William John, BA ACA *1996;* 4 Spinney Gardens, ESHER, KT10 8BY.
RICHARDSON, Mrs. Natalie Anne, BA ACA *1992;* 5 Craiglea, Causeway Head, STIRLING, FK9 5EE.
RICHARDSON, Mr. Neil, BSc ACA *2010;* 16 The Oaks, LEEDS, LS10 4GZ.
RICHARDSON, Mr. Neil Peter, MSc ACA *2000;* Park Lodge, Ugley Green, BISHOP'S STORTFORD, HERTFORDSHIRE, CM22 6HL.
RICHARDSON, Mr. Neville Brian, BA FCA *1980;* Co-operative Insurance Society Ltd, Miller Street, MANCHESTER, M60 0AL.
RICHARDSON, Mr. Paul, BA(Hons) ACA *2002;* 96 Albert Road West, BOLTON, BL1 5ED.
RICHARDSON, Mr. Paul, BSc ACA *1992;* 2 Harvest Close, Strensall, YORK, YO32 5SA.
RICHARDSON, Mr. Paul, BA FCA *1973;* 1439 The Links Dr, OAKVILLE L6M 2N9, ON, CANADA.
RICHARDSON, Mr. Paul, BA ACA *1985;* Reed Elsevier, 1-3 Strand, LONDON, WC2N 5JR.
RICHARDSON, Mr. Paul William, BA FCA *1985;* 1 Dunlin Close, Poynton, STOCKPORT, SK12 1JS.
RICHARDSON, Mr. Paul Winston George, BA ACA *1984;* WPP Group USA, 125 Park Avenue, NEW YORK, NY 10017, UNITED STATES.
RICHARDSON, Mr. Peter, BSc FCA *1992;* 19 Madeira Park, TUNBRIDGE WELLS, TN2 5SX.
RICHARDSON, Mr. Peter David, ACA *1994;* 19 Colston Avenue, SHERBROOKE, VIC 3789, AUSTRALIA.
RICHARDSON, Dr. Peter David, PhD MA ACA *2010;* 41 Cornwallis Avenue, TONBRIDGE, KENT, TN10 4ER.
RICHARDSON, Mr. Philip, FCA *1964;* The Leys, Melford Road, SUDBURY, SUFFOLK, CO10 1XT. (Life Member)
RICHARDSON, Mr. Philip David, MA ACA MEng(Cantab) *2007;* Flat 130 Rembrandt Court, 6 Stubbs Drive, LONDON, SE16 3EQ.
RICHARDSON, Ms. Rachel, BA ACA *1998;* 37 East Parade, ILKLEY, WEST YORKSHIRE, LS29 8JP.
RICHARDSON, Mrs. Rebecca, ACA *2011;* 65 Walmer Close, ROMFORD, RM7 8QH.
RICHARDSON, Mr. Robert, BCom FCA *1957;* 121 Edge Hill Darras Hall, Ponteland, NEWCASTLE UPON TYNE, NE20 9JS. (Life Member)
RICHARDSON, Mr. Robert David, FCA *1966;* Little Orchard, 41 Cornwallis Avenue, TONBRIDGE, TN10 4ER.
RICHARDSON, Mr. Robert Mary, BBS ACA *1980;* Robert Richardson & Co, The Citadel, Old Clare Street, LIMERICK, COUNTY LIMERICK, IRELAND.
RICHARDSON, Mr. Russell John, ACA *1993;* 118C Mansfield Road, Hampstead, LONDON, NW3 2JB.
RICHARDSON, Mrs. Ruth Drysdale, BA FCA *1972;* 13 Poyle Road, GUILDFORD, SURREY, GU1 3SL. (Life Member)
RICHARDSON, Miss. Samantha, BSc(Hons) ACA *2000;* 44 Ullswater Road, Urmston, MANCHESTER, M41 8PW.
RICHARDSON, Mrs. Sarah Louise, BSc(Hons) ACA *2000;* Computype Incorporated, Oslo Road, HULL, HU7 0YN.
RICHARDSON, Miss. Sian Gillian Prout, FCA *1975;* Park Row Developments, 6 Back Royal Parade, HARROGATE, NORTH YORKSHIRE, HG2 0QA.
RICHARDSON, Mr. Simon David, ACA *2010;* Flat 25, Spur House, The Crescent, MAIDENHEAD, BERKSHIRE, SL6 6FL.
RICHARDSON, Mr. Simon Mark, BA(Econ) ACA *2003;* Pricewaterhousecoopers, Savannah House, 3 Ocean Way, SOUTHAMPTON, SO14 3TJ.
RICHARDSON, Mrs. Stephanie Lucy, BA ACA *2005;* 58 Bridge Street, Golborne, WARRINGTON, WA3 3QB.
RICHARDSON, Mr. Stephen Alan, MSci ACA *2003;* C/O Justine Richardson, PricewaterhouseCoopers, PO Box 484, PORT MORESBY, PAPUA NEW GUINEA.
RICHARDSON, Mr. Stephen Clive, FCA *1968;* 41 The Maltings, Carpenters Lane, TONBRIDGE, TN11 0DQ.
RICHARDSON, Mr. Stephen James, BSocSc ACA *2004;* 9/122 Bower Street, MANLY, NSW 2095, AUSTRALIA.
RICHARDSON, Mr. Stephen John, BSc ACA *1993;* 52 Quinton Close, Hatton Park, WARWICK, CV35 7TN.
RICHARDSON, Mr. Stephen Laurence, FCA *1984;* 10 Meon Close, TADWORTH, KT20 5DN.
•RICHARDSON, Mr. Steven, FCA *1983;* HW, Floor 11, Cale Cross House, 156 Pilgrim Street, NEWCASTLE UPON TYNE, NORTHUMBERLAND NE1 6SU. See also Haines Watts

RICHARDSON, Mr. Steven John, MA ACA *1986;* 21 East Sheen Avenue, LONDON, SW14 8AR.
RICHARDSON, Mr. Steven Robert, BSc FCA ACT *1995;* Zurich Insurance Co The Zurich Centre 3000b, Parkway Whiteley, FAREHAM, PO15 7JZ.
RICHARDSON, Mrs. Susan, BA ACA *1984;* 3 Woodside, HEXHAM, NE46 1HU.
RICHARDSON, Mrs. Susan, BA ACA *2005;* 7 Southlands Drive, Moortown, LEEDS, LS17 5NZ.
•**RICHARDSON, Mrs. Susan Christina, BSc ACA** *1988;* S. C. Telfer, 24 High Street, Holme-on-Spalding Moor, YORK, YO43 4HL.
RICHARDSON, Ms. Susan Lynne, BSc ACA *1990;* Finance Section, University of Aberdeen, Kings College, ABERDEEN, AB24 3FX.
RICHARDSON, Mr. Tim, ACA *2008;* with BDO LLP, 55 Baker Street, LONDON, W1U 7EU.
•**RICHARDSON, Mr. Timothy, FCA** *1974;* Mitchell Meredith Limited, The Exchange, Fiveways, Temple Street, LLANDRINDOD WELLS, POWYS LD1 5HG.
•**RICHARDSON, Mr. Timothy John, BA ACA** *1989;* (Tax Fac), Trafalgar Accounting and Taxation Services LLP, 8 Emsons Close, Linton, CAMBRIDGE, CB21 4NB.
RICHARDSON, Mr. Timothy John David, BSc ACA *1993;* 96 Riverside Road, GISBORNE 4010, NEW ZEALAND.
RICHARDSON, Mr. Tobias Charles, LLB ACA *2000;* Arcus Infrastructure, 6 St Andews Street, LONDON, EC4A 3AE.
RICHARDSON, Mrs. Tracey, BSc(Hons) ACA *2001;* 14 Priory Gardens, STAMFORD, LINCOLNSHIRE, PE9 2EG.
RICHARDSON, Miss. Tracy Anne, BA ACA *1995;* Capital & Regional Terminal House, 52 Grosvenor Gardens, LONDON, SW1W 0AU.
RICHARDSON, Mrs. Victoria, BSc ACA *2000;* 18 Lund Road, Worrall, SHEFFIELD, S35 0AN.
RICHARDSON, Mrs. Victoria, BSc ACA CTA *2006;* 18 Bourne Road, CAMBRIDGE, CB4 1UF.
RICHARDSON, Mrs. Victoria Anne, BSc(Hons) ACA *2001;* Financial Services Authority, 25 North Colonnade, LONDON, E14 5HS.
RICHARDSON, Mr. Walter John, BA FCA *1963;* 8 Glazedale Avenue, Royton, OLDHAM, OL2 5TS. (Life Member)
RICHARDSON, Mr. William James, BA FCA *1998;* Pricewaterhousecoopers, 33 Wellington Street, LEEDS, LS1 4JP.
RICHARDSON, Miss. Zoe, BA ACA *2007;* with Baker Tilly UK Audit LLP, 12 Gleneagles Court, Brighton Road, CRAWLEY, WEST SUSSEX, RH10 6AD.
RICHARDSON, Mrs. Zoe Victoria, MA BA(Hons) ACA *2002;* Suite 207 Butlers Wharf Building, 36 Shad Thames, LONDON, SE1 2YE.
RICHARDSON BROWN, Ms. Anna, BSc ACA *2005;* 27 Fitzwilliam Road, LONDON, SW4 0DW.
RICHARDSON BROWN, Mr. Scott James, BA FCA *2000;* 27 Fitzwilliam Road, LONDON, SW4 0DW.
RICHARDSON HILL, Mr. Jeffrey George, FCA *1963;* 74 Westbury Road, NORTHWOOD, HA6 3BZ.
RICHART, Miss. Gillian Mary, BEng ACA *2002;* 29 Scotts Lane, BROMLEY, BR2 0LL.
RICHBELL, Mr. Mark James, BA(Hons) ACA *2009;* 872 London Lane, VALPARAISO, IN 46383, UNITED STATES.
RICHBELL, Miss. Patricia Lesley, ACA *1983;* 86 Nevill Road, LONDON, N16 0SX.
RICHDALE, Mrs. Amy, MA ACA *1996;* Flat A, 11 Gledhow Gardens, LONDON, SW5 0AY.
•**RICHENS, Mr. Brian Neil, FCA** *1974;* MacIntyre Hudson LLP, Equipoise House, Grove Place, BEDFORD, MK40 3LE.
RICHENS, Mr. Gavin Peter, ACA *2008;* 2 Eddison Street, Farsley, PUDSEY, WEST YORKSHIRE, LS28 5BX.
•**RICHENS, Mr. Nigel John, BA FCA** *1979;* (Member of Council 2001 - 2007), PricewaterhouseCoopers LLP, 101 Barbirolli Square, Lower Mosley Street, MANCHESTER, M2 3PW. See also PricewaterhouseCoopers
RICHER, Mr. Charles Martin, FCA *1952;* APARTMENT, 8 Mayfield Grange, Little Trodgers Lane, MAYFIELD, EAST SUSSEX, TN20 6BF. (Life Member)
RICHERBY, Mrs. Emma Louise, ACA *2008;* 5 Stefan Close, PLYMOUTH, PL9 9RS.
RICHES, Mr. Adam Stanford, BA(Hons) ACA AKC *2009;* 1 Windmill Close, Aldbourne, MARLBOROUGH, SN8 2DN.
RICHES, Mr. Brian George, FCA JDipMA *1970;* 90 Higher Drive, BANSTEAD, SM7 1PQ.
RICHES, Mr. Christopher, ACA *1980;* 31 Westgate, Scotton, GAINSBOROUGH, LINCOLNSHIRE, DN21 3QY.
•**RICHES, Miss. Janice Rosemary, FCA** *1982;* Kingston Smith LLP, Devonshire House, 60 Goswell Road, LONDON, EC1M 7AD. See also Kingston Smith Limited Liability Partnership, Devonshire Corporate Services LLP and Kingston Smith Consulting LLP
RICHES, Mr. Jonathan Henry, ACA *1995;* 86 Moffats Lane, Brookmans Park, HATFIELD, HERTFORDSHIRE, AL9 7RW.
RICHES, Mr. Julian Mark, BSc ACA *1988;* 1063 Sunflower Circle, WESTON, FL 33327, UNITED STATES.
RICHES, Mrs. Karen Ann, BA ACA *1993;* 71 Eton Rise, Eton College Road, LONDON, NW3 2DA.
•**RICHES, Mr. Keith Ian, FCA** *1970;* Riches Consulting, Little Coombe, Longfield Road, DORKING, SURREY, RH4 3DE.
RICHES, Mr. Neil Simon, BA(Hons) ACA *2010;* Flat 7, 8 Eaton Crescent, BRISTOL, BS8 2EJ.
RICHES, Mr. Paul Henry, BSc ACA *1991;* Loreley, Police Row, Therfield, ROYSTON, SG8 9QE.
RICHES, Mrs. Tina Elizabeth, BA ACA CTA *1982;* (Tax Fac), 1 New Road, Burwell, CAMBRIDGE, CB25 0BY.
RICHEY, Mrs. Carol Annette, MA ACA *1985;* Oakwood House Bridle Path, Ewshot, FARNHAM, GU10 5BW.
RICHFORD, Mr. Adam Nathaniel, BA ACA ACT *2001;* GECC (Funding) Ltd, 30 Berkeley Square, LONDON, W1J 6EX.
RICHINGS, Mr. Anthony Keith, FCA *1964;* 36A Ferry Road, KETTERING, TAS 7155, AUSTRALIA. (Life Member)
RICHINGS, Mrs. Claire Alicia, BSc(Hons) ACA *2002;* 11 Forbes Close, Abbeymead, GLOUCESTER, GL4 5GE.
RICHINGS, Miss. Gwyneth Eluned, ACA *2006;* Flat 703 Chart House, 6 Burrells Wharf Square, LONDON, E14 3TW.
•**RICHINGS, Mrs. Julie, BA ACA** *1997;* (Tax Fac), 8 Blandford Avenue, LUTON, LU2 7AX.
RICHINGS, Mr. Paul David, BA FCA *1996;* 21 Starrock Road, COULSDON, SURREY, CR5 3EH.
RICHINGS, Miss. Zoe, BSc ACA *2000;* 26 Strathmore Road, LONDON, SW19 8DB.
•**RICHMAN, Mr. Marcus, FCA ATII** *1979;* (Tax Fac), Richman & Co, 293 Kenton Lane, HARROW, HA3 8RR.
RICHMAN, Mr. Philip Geoffrey, ACA *2009;* 112 Grosvenor Road, Maghull, LIVERPOOL, L31 5NW.
RICHMOND, Mr. Adrian Alastair, BSc ACA *1997;* Argyll Partners Limited, 15 South Molton Street, LONDON, W1K 5QR.
RICHMOND, Mr. Alec John, BSc FCA FIIA *1983;* 10 Kingsland Drive, Dorridge, SOLIHULL, B93 8SP.
RICHMOND, Mr. Andrew David, BA FCA *1994;* Suite 247 Linen Hall, 162-168 Regent Street, LONDON, W1B 5TB.
RICHMOND, Mrs. Barbara Mary, BSc FCA *1984;* Apartment 1003, 8 Dean Ryle Street, LONDON, SW1P 4DA.
•**RICHMOND, Mr. Charles Lynton, BA ACA** *1990;* KPMG LLP, 15 Canada Square, LONDON, E14 5GL. See also KPMG Europe LLP
RICHMOND, Mr. Chris, BA ACA *2006;* Flat 3A Block 46, Coastline Villa, DISCOVERY BAY, NEW TERRITORIES, HONG KONG SAR.
RICHMOND, Mr. Christopher, BA ACA *2003;* Morgan Stanley, Level 39 Chifley Tower, 2 Chifley Square, SYDNEY, NSW 2000, AUSTRALIA.
•**RICHMOND, Mr. David Andrew, BA(Hons) FCA** *1988;* Robertshaw Myers, Number 3, Acorn Business Park, Keighley Road, SKIPTON, NORTH YORKSHIRE BD23 2UE. See also Robertshaw & Myers
RICHMOND, Mr. Denis George, FCA *1959;* Herne Farm House, Park Drive, Rustington, LITTLEHAMPTON, BN16 3DZ. (Life Member)
RICHMOND, Mr. Duncan Andrew, ACA ACGI BEng(Hons) *2009;* National Audit Office, 157-197 Buckingham Palace Road, LONDON, SW1W 9SP.
RICHMOND, Mr. Gerard Stuart, FCA *1962;* Apartado 84, 38400 Puerto de la Cruz, 38400 TENERIFE, CANARY ISLANDS, SPAIN. (Life Member)
RICHMOND, Mrs. Gillian Linda, BA ACA *1995;* Dormans, Ridgeway, OTTERY ST. MARY, DEVON, EX11 1DY.
RICHMOND, Mr. Ian Harry, BA ACA *1987;* 27 Malmsey Close, TEWKESBURY, GL20 5FH.
•**RICHMOND, Mr. Ian Victor, BA FCA** *1982;* Ian Richmond Limited, Chapel Ash House, 6 Compton Road, WOLVERHAMPTON, WV3 9PH. See also Ian Richmond
RICHMOND, Mrs. Joanne Marie, BSc ACA *2002;* 22 Kitchener Street, BALGOWLAH, NSW 2093, AUSTRALIA.
RICHMOND, Mr. John Anthony, BA ACA *1996;* Flat 2, 23 Southey Road, LONDON, SW9 0PD.
RICHMOND, Mr. John Derek, ACA *1981;* 48 Greenan Road, NEWRY, COUNTY DOWN, BT34 2PZ.
RICHMOND, Mr. John Gordon, FCA *1954;* 18 Sandygate Park Crescent, SHEFFIELD, S10 5TW. (Life Member)
RICHMOND, Mr. John Lewis, BA FCA *1994;* with Chantrey Vellacott DFK LLP, Russell Square House, 10-12 Russell Square, LONDON, WC1B 5LF.
RICHMOND, Mr. Jonathan Carne, FCA *1976;* Welbeck Management Ltd, P.O. Box HM 2446, HAMILTON HMJX, BERMUDA.
RICHMOND, Mr. Kenneth, FCA *1954;* 44 North Church Street, FLEETWOOD, FY7 6AX. (Life Member)
RICHMOND, Mr. Mark, BA ACA *1992;* 118 Caldy Road, WIRRAL, MERSEYSIDE, CH48 1LW.
RICHMOND, Mr. Mark Andrew, BSc ACA *1994;* 12 Westpark Drive, DARLINGTON, COUNTY DURHAM, DL3 0TB.
RICHMOND, Mr. Mark William, BA ACA *2007;* Bnp Paribas, 10 Harewood Avenue, LONDON, NW1 6AA.
RICHMOND, Miss. Michelle Ann, BA(Hons) ACA *2003;* 29 Amis Avenue, New Haw, ADDLESTONE, SURREY, KT15 3ET.
RICHMOND, Mr. Paul James, BSc ACA *1990;* Right Training Ltd, Spring Water House, 1 Sybron Way, CROWBOROUGH, TN6 3DZ.
RICHMOND, Mr. Paul Robert, ACA *2008;* 28 Lambert Avenue, LEEDS, LS8 1NH.
RICHMOND, Mr. Philip Anthony, BCom ACA *2001;* 5 Summer Lane, SHEFFIELD, S17 4AJ.
RICHMOND, Mrs. Rachel Catherine, BSc(Hons) ACA *2004;* BT Global Services, PP 113, Moortown Telephone Exchange, 87 Stainburn Drive, LEEDS, LS17 6LZ.
RICHMOND, Mr. Robert Paul, BA ACA *1993;* 2231 Austin Court, BURLINGTON L7L 6V5, ON, CANADA.
RICHMOND, Mr. Robin, MBA FCA *1969;* Coppey Holt, 6 Upper Ferry Lane, Callow End, WORCESTER, WR2 4TL.
RICHMOND, Mr. Timothy Stewart, MBE TD DL FCA CCMI *1970;* Huthwaite International Hoober House, Hoober, ROTHERHAM, SOUTH YORKSHIRE, S62 7SA.
RICHOLD, Mr. Scott Jeffery, BSc(Hons) ACA *2011;* Unit 12, 67 Evans Street, FRESHWATER, NSW 2096, AUSTRALIA.
•**RICHTER, Miss. Marzena Elizabeth, MSc ACA** *1993;* Staniszewski & Richter Sp. z.o.o., ul.Lwowska 10/21, 00-658 WARSAW, POLAND.
RICKABY, Mr. Robert John Mayors, MBA BA FCA *1963;* The Old Vicarage, Hunstanworth, CONSETT, DH8 9UF. (Life Member)
RICKABY, Miss. Sally Ann, BSc ACA *2000;* Compass Point Business Services (East Coast) Ltd, East Lindsey District Council Tedder Hall, Manby Park, LOUTH, LINCOLNSHIRE, LN11 8UP.
RICKARD, Mr. Adrian, BA ACA *1991;* 727 Clarence Street, WESTFIELD, NJ 07090, UNITED STATES.
RICKARD, Mr. Charles Anthony, BCom ACA *2000;* 23 Meriden Road, Hampton-in-Arden, SOLIHULL, B92 0BS.
RICKARD, Mr. Christopher Colin, BSc FCA *1975;* (Tax Fac), 37 The Mount, Fetcham, LEATHERHEAD, KT22 9EG.
RICKARD, Mr. Christopher John, BA ACA *1983;* The Beeches, Straight Mile, Ampfield, ROMSEY, HAMPSHIRE, SO51 9BB.
•**RICKARD, Mr. David, BA FCA** *1977;* Flat 2, 3 Market Yard Mews, LONDON, SE1 3TJ.
RICKARD, Miss. Deborah May, BSc ACA *2005;* Hodgsons, 48 Arwenack Street, FALMOUTH, CORNWALL, TR11 3JH.
RICKARD, Mr. Edward Martin, BSc ACA *2002;* 44 Lickey Rock, Marlbrook, BROMSGROVE, WORCESTERSHIRE, B60 1HF.
RICKARD, Mr. John Dale, BA ACA *1979;* 15 Slaidburn Avenue, Silverdale Estate, NOTTINGHAM, NG11 7FT.
RICKARD, Mr. Michael Alan, FCA *1975;* 18 Achilles Close, Chineham, BASINGSTOKE, RG24 8XB.
RICKARD, Mr. Paul James, BSc ACA *2003;* TradeRisks, 21 Great Windsor Street, LONDON, EC2N 2JA.
RICKARD, Mr. Philip John, FCA *1975;* 11 Cheesemans Green Lane, ASHFORD, TN25 7EX. (Life Member)
RICKARD, Miss. Ruth Anna, ACA *2008;* Flat 2, 19 Anson Road, LONDON, NW2 3UX.
•**RICKARDS, Mr. Alistair, ACA FCCA** *2009;* with Sterlings Ltd, Lawford House, Albert Place, LONDON, N3 1QA.
RICKARDS, Mr. Anthony Peter, FCA *1959;* 113 Selhurst Close, Wimbledon, LONDON, SW19 6AY.
RICKARDS, Mr. Stephen David John, BSc ACA CTA *1987;* with Zurich Financial Service UK Life, UK Life Centre, Station Road, SWINDON, SN1 1EL.
RICKEARD, Miss. Tamsin Jane, BA ACA *1994;* 92 Kilravock Street, LONDON, W10 4HY.
RICKELS, Mr. Martyn Christopher, BSc ACA *2006;* 20 Albert Road, Grappenhall, WARRINGTON, CHESHIRE, WA4 2PG.
①**RICKELTON, Ms. Lisa Jane, MA ACA** *2004;* with FTI Consulting Limited, 322 Midtown, High Holborn, LONDON, WC1V 7PB.
RICKERBY, Mr. Iain, BSc FCA CTA *1992;* 6 Nursery Gardens, ST.IVES, CAMBRIDGESHIRE, PE27 3NL.
RICKERBY, Mrs. Susan Mary, ACA *1989;* 11 Hazelbury Drive, North Common Warmley, BRISTOL, BS30 8UF.
RICKERS, Mr. Simon, BEng ACA *1993;* (Tax Fac), International Power Senator House, 85 Queen Victoria Street, LONDON, EC4V 4DP.
RICKETT, Mr. David Ian, BSc ACA *1987;* 54 The Ridgway, SUTTON, SURREY, SM2 5JU.
•**RICKETT, Mr. Julian Clive, BSc FCA** *1991;* PricewaterhouseCoopers LLP, The Atrium, St. Georges Street, NORWICH, NR3 1AG. See also PricewaterhouseCoopers
RICKETTS, Mr. Andrew Stephen, BSc ACA *2007;* Flat C, 34 Bromley Grove, BROMLEY, BR2 0LN.
RICKETTS, Mr. Antony Francis William, BSc ACA *1991;* 1820 Laurel Ridge Drive, RENO, NV 89523, UNITED STATES.
•**RICKETTS, Mr. Brian George, BCom FCA** *1983;* PKF (UK) LLP, 5 Temple Square, Temple Street, LIVERPOOL, L2 5RH.
•**RICKETTS, Mr. Christopher Mark Walker, BSc FCA** *1983;* (Tax Fac), Ricketts & Co Limited, 43 Bugle Street, SOUTHAMPTON, SO14 2AG.
•**RICKETTS, Mr. Dominic Harford, BSc ACA** *1992;* PricewaterhouseCoopers LLP, 300 Madison Avenue, NEW YORK, NY 10017, UNITED STATES. See also PricewaterhouseCoopers
•**RICKETTS, Mrs. Gemma Katie, ACA** *2001;* Harrison Black Limited, Pyle House, 137 Pyle Street, NEWPORT, ISLE OF WIGHT, PO30 1JW.
RICKETTS, Mr. Graham, ACA *2008;* 25 Farringdon Street, LONDON, EC4A 4AB.
RICKETTS, Mrs. Karen Elaine, BA ACA *1994;* 2 Church Farm Barns, Church Lane Oving, AYLESBURY, BUCKINGHAMSHIRE, HP22 4HG.
RICKETTS, Mrs. Katherine, BSocSc ACA *2000;* 46 Snake Lane Alvechurch, BIRMINGHAM, B48 7NL.
RICKETTS, Miss. Louise Clare, ACA *2009;* 22 St. Augustines Park, RAMSGATE, CT11 0DE.
RICKETTS, Mr. Mark, BA ACA *1998;* 13 Innox Hill, FROME, SOMERSET, BA11 2LW.
RICKETTS, Mr. Mark John, BSc ACA *1987;* Holly Lodge, 39 Beck Lane, BINGLEY, BD16 4DD.
RICKETTS, Mr. Michael Francis Roger, BA FCA *1975;* 40 The Willows, FRODSHAM, WA6 7QS.
RICKETTS, Mr. Michael Godfrey, FCA *1966;* 11 Langmead Close, Eggbuckland, PLYMOUTH, PL6 5TB.
•**RICKETTS, Mr. Piers Harford, BA ACA** *1997;* KPMG LLP, 15 Canada Square, LONDON, E14 5GL.
RICKETTS, Miss. Rebekah Suzanne, BCom ACA *2007;* Kaplan, Baskerville House, Broad Street, BIRMINGHAM, B1 2ND.
RICKETTS, Mrs. Suzanne, BSc FCA CTA *1988;* 7 Place du Commerce, 75015 PARIS, FRANCE.
•**RICKETTS, Mr. Timothy Walker, BSc ACA** *1988;* Avonglen Limited, 2 Venture Road, Southampton Science Park, Chilworth, SOUTHAMPTON, SO16 7NP.
RICKITT, Mr. Peter Edward, FCA CF MSI *1969;* Mill House, Cuddington Lane, Cuddington, NORTHWICH, CW8 2SY.
•**RICKLER, Ms. Janet Ann, FCA** *1985;* Alwyns LLP, Crown House, 151 High Road, LOUGHTON, ESSEX, IG10 4LG.
RICKLESS, Mr. Victor, FCA *1962;* 34 Dalebrook Court, Stumperlowe Crescent Road, SHEFFIELD, S10 3PQ.
RICKMAN, Mr. Jeremy Peter, BSc ACA *1992;* 93 Robsart Road, KENILWORTH, IL 60043, UNITED STATES.
•**RICKMAN, Mr. Leonard, FCA** *1958;* Leonard Rickman Accountancy Services Limited, Devonshire House, Manor Way, BOREHAMWOOD, HERTFORDSHIRE, WD6 1QQ.
•**RICKS, Mr. Frederick Nigel, FCA** *1982;* Nigel Ricks & Company Limited, Rose Villa, 42 Glebe Street, LOUGHBOROUGH, LEICESTERSHIRE, LE11 1JR.
RICKUS-WILKES, Mr. Theo James, MA ACA *2001;* 115 Hayward Road, THAMES DITTON, SURREY, KT7 0BF.

RICKWOOD, Mr. Neil Duncan, MSc ACA *2000;* 23 Craiston Way, CHELMSFORD, CM2 8ED.
RICKWOOD, Mr. Peter Robin, FCA *1967;* Arcturus Securities Ltd, Coltwood House, 2 Tongham Road, Runfold, FARNHAM, SURREY GU10 1PH.
RICKWOOD, Miss. Victoria, BSc ACA *2009;* 56 Colemans Moor Lane, Woodley, READING, RG5 4BT.
RICKWORD, Mrs. Freda Wei-Chin, BSc FCA *1972;* 50 Draycott Park, #23-01 Draycott Tower, SINGAPORE 259396, SINGAPORE. (Life Member)
RICKWORD, Mr. Ian Percy, MA FCA *1972;* 50 Draycott Park, 23-01 Draycott Tower, SINGAPORE 259396, SINGAPORE. (Life Member)
RIDAL, Mr. Philip Martin, BEng FCA *1979;* British Waterways, 64 Clarendon Road, WATFORD, WD17 1DA.
RIDD-JONES, Mrs. Chantall Sylvette Florence, BSc(Hons) ACA *2000;* Islip House, Chapel Hill, Islip, KETTERING, NORTHAMPTONSHIRE, NN14 3JP.
RIDD-JONES, Mr. Gary Royston, BA ACA *1999;* (Tax Fac), 10 Bowood Road, LONDON, SW11 6PE.
RIDD-JONES, Mrs. Jessica Sarah Jane, BSc ACA *1999;* 10 Bowood Road, LONDON, SW11 6PE.
RIDD-JONES, Mr. Stuart Benjamin, BSc ACA *1999;* The Coach House Wentworth Farm, Great Harrowden, WELLINGBOROUGH, NORTHAMPTONSHIRE, NN9 5AD.
RIDDALL, Mr. Alan Stuart, FCA *1963;* Mill View Magdalen Laver, ONGAR, CM5 0DR. (Life Member)
RIDDELL, Mr. David William, BA ACA *1997;* The Blackstone Group, 40 Berkeley Square, LONDON, W1J 5AL.
RIDDELL, Mrs. Emma Estelle, BSc ACA *2000;* 4 Marquis Lane, HARPENDEN, HERTFORDSHIRE, AL5 5AA.
RIDDELL, Mr. Geoffrey Martin, BA ACA *1982;* Zurich Financial Services, 24-27F One Island East, 18 Westlands Road, QUARRY BAY, HONG KONG SAR.
RIDDELL, Mrs. Heidi Ruth, ACA *2001;* Ernst & Young Building, 11 Mounts Bay Road, PERTH, WA 6000, AUSTRALIA.
RIDDELL, Mr. Hugh Michael, BA FCA *1980;* Hamilton Corporate Finance Ltd, 1 St. Andrew's Hill, LONDON, EC4V 5BY.
RIDDELL, Mr. Ian, BAcc ACA CTA *2001;* 71 Cove Circle, Cove Bay, ABERDEEN, AB12 3DG.
RIDDELL, Mr. James Renwick, BEng FCA *1953;* Flat 1, Lambridge House, London Road West, BATH, BA1 7HY. (Life Member)
RIDDELL, Mr. Michael Ian, BSc ACA *2005;* Interroute Communications Ltd Wallbrook Building, 195 Marsh Wall, LONDON, E14 9SG.
RIDDELL, Mr. Stuart James, FCA *1969;* 4 Whitehill Close, NEWTON ABBOT, TQ12 6QY.
RIDDELL, Mr. Warren Peter, MA BA FCA GAICD *1982;* GPO Box 1383, SYDNEY, NSW 2001, AUSTRALIA.
RIDDELL-WEBSTER, Mr. Thomas William, BSc ACA *1988;* 14 Larnach Road, LONDON, W6 9NX.
RIDDELSDELL, Mr. Michael Edward, FCA *1952;* 1 Chapel House, Brays Lane, AMERSHAM, HP6 5SN. (Life Member)
RIDDICK, Mr. Steven Keith, BCom FCA *1987;* The Hawthorns, Tewkesbury Road, Twigworth, GLOUCESTER, GL2 9PQ.
RIDDIFORD, Mr. Timothy John, FCA *1966;* Pinewood, 73A Pashley Road, EASTBOURNE, BN20 8EA. (Life Member)
RIDDINGTON, Mr. Derek Walter, FCA *1956;* 1st Floor Suite, 159 Blendon Road, BEXLEY, DA5 1BT. (Life Member)
RIDDINGTON, Mr. Steven Graham, BSc ACA *1996;* 15 Locksley Drive, FERNDOWN, DORSET, BH22 8JU.
RIDDIOUGH, Mrs. Gillian, BSc ACA ATII *1996;* with PKF (UK) LLP, Pannell House, 6 Queen Street, LEEDS, LS1 2TW.
RIDDIOUGH, Mr. James Harry, MA ACA CF *1992;* 74 Fordhook Avenue, Ealing Common, LONDON, W5 3LR.
•RIDDLE, Mr. Brian John, FCA *1968;* Birch Riddle & Co Limited, Pond House, Weston Green, THAMES DITTON, SURREY, KT7 0JX.
RIDDLE, Mr. David, ACA *2011;* 30 Radnor Road, Horfield, BRISTOL, BS7 8QY.
RIDDLE, Mr. Ellison James John, MSc ACA *2002;* 36 Belvoir House, 181 Vauxhall Bridge Road, LONDON, SW1V 1ER.
RIDDLE, Mr. Gordon Henry, FCA *1971;* 6 Eccleston Road, SOUTH SHIELDS, TYNE AND WEAR, NE33 3BS.
RIDDLE, Mr. Jonathan Rowlatt Huber, BA ACA *1987;* 39 Marriott Grove, Sandal, WAKEFIELD, WF2 6RP.
RIDDLE, Miss. Marion Eleanor, BA ACA *2003;* Pricewaterhousecoopers Llp, Hays Galleria, 1 Hays Lane, LONDON, SE1 2RD.
•RIDDLE, Mr. Rodney Keith, FCA *1971;* (Tax Fac), R.K. Riddle, 121 Imperial Way, ASHFORD, KENT, TN23 5HT.
RIDDLES, Mr. John, FCA *1957;* 6 Sheepfair, LEWES, EAST SUSSEX, BN7 1QH. (Life Member)
RIDDLESTON, Mr. Mark John, BA FCA *1999;* FremantleMedia Group Limited, 1 Stephen Street, LONDON, W1T 1AL.
RIDDLESTON, Mr. Martyn Bryan, BA(Hons) ACA *2000;* Finance Office, University of Leicester, University Road, LEICESTER, LE1 7RH.
RIDDY, Mr. Alan Michael, BSc ACA *1983;* The Willows, Well Lane, Mollington, CHESTER, CH1 6LD.
•RIDEAL, Mr. John Fraser, BA FCA *1977;* Kite & Company, 9 Clive House, 80 Prospect Hill, REDDITCH, B97 4BS. See also Kite & Co Accountants Limited
RIDEHALGH, Mr. David Brian, FCA *1963;* Poole House, The Square, Whalley, CLITHEROE, BB7 9SU.
RIDEHALGH, Mr. David Nicholas, FCA *1985;* 20 Beauty Point Road, MOSMAN, NSW 2088, AUSTRALIA.
RIDEHALGH, Mr. Frank, FCA *1964;* Prestbury Management Limited, Prestbury House, 46 Bury New Road, Prestwich, MANCHESTER, M25 0JU.
RIDEHALGH, Mr. Mark, ACA *2011;* 12 Belvedere Road, Ainsdale, SOUTHPORT, MERSEYSIDE, PR8 2PA.
RIDEOUT, Mrs. Heather Jane, BSc ACA *1992;* Ranikhet Farm, Park Corner, Freshford, BATH, BA2 7UQ.
RIDEOUT, Mr. Matthew Benedict, BA ACA *1993;* 25 Harwood Close, Tewin, WELWYN, HERTFORDSHIRE, AL6 0LF.
RIDER, Mr. David Alan, BA ACA *1988;* C/O Egypt Mailbag, British Petroleum Co Plc, 20 Canada Square, LONDON, E14 5NJ.
RIDER, Mr. David John, MBA MSc BSc FCA *1985;* 26 Petersfield, CHELMSFORD, CM1 4EP.
RIDER, Mr. Edward, BA FCA CTA *1963;* Clarendon, Claridge Gardens, Dormansland, LINGFIELD, RH7 6HZ.
RIDER, Mr. Frederick, FCA *1938;* 5 High View Lane, SOUTHAMPTON SN01, BERMUDA. (Life Member)
RIDER, Mr. Howard John, BSc FCA *1970;* 8 Red House Close, BEACONSFIELD, HP9 1XU.
RIDER, Mr. Ian Martin, FCA *1975;* 174 Oak Tree Lane, Bournville, BIRMINGHAM, B30 1TX.
RIDER, Mr. John Francis, FCA *1964;* 5 Lynton Gardens, Bush Hill Park, ENFIELD, EN1 2NF.
RIDER, Mr. Mark John, BSc ACA *2001;* 20 Celtic Avenue, BROMLEY, BR2 0RU.
RIDER, Mr. Maurice George, FCA *1955;* 6 Shipgate Street, CHESTER, CH1 1RT. (Life Member)
RIDER, Mr. Neil Christopher, BSc FCA *1976;* c/- Trinity, 230 Hampden Road, CRAWLEY, WA 6009, AUSTRALIA.
RIDER, Mr. Robert Andrew, BSc ACA *1979;* 16 St. James Terrace, WINCHESTER, HAMPSHIRE, SO22 4PP.
RIDER, Mr. Stuart Granville, MA FCA *1976;* 6 Golfers View, Finchley Park, LONDON, N12 9JX.
•RIDER, Mr. Timothy John, FCA *1964;* T.J. Rider, 36 Oaken Lane, Claygate, ESHER, KT10 0RG.
•RIDEWOOD, Mr. Gary Spencer, BSc ACA *1991;* GSR Consultancy (UK) Limited, Leigh Cottage, Mount Road, DINAS POWYS, SOUTH GLAMORGAN, CF64 4DG.
•RIDGE, Mr. Anthony Michael, FCA *1962;* J.F. Mallabar & Co, 24a West Street, EPSOM, KT18 7RJ.
RIDGE, Mrs. Catherine Mary, ACA *1995;* 14a Polwarth Terrace, EDINBURGH, EH11 1ND.
RIDGE, Mr. Charles, BSc ACA *1990;* Birch Cottage Green Road, Horsmonden, TONBRIDGE, TN12 8JS.
RIDGE, Mr. Darren John, BA ACA *2003;* Boots the Chemists Ltd, PO Box 94, NOTTINGHAM, NG2 3AA.
•RIDGE, Mrs. Elizabeth Mary, BSc FCA *1976;* Bryan and Ridge, The Gatehouse, 2 Devonhurst Place, Heathfield Terrace, LONDON, W4 4JD.
RIDGE, Mr. Ian David, BA ACA *1997;* 14a Polwarth Terrace, EDINBURGH, EH11 1ND.
RIDGE, Mrs. Jennifer Jane, ACA *1979;* Norfolk Lodge, Park Lane, Finchampstead, WOKINGHAM, BERKSHIRE, RG40 4PT. (Life Member)
RIDGE, Michael John, Esq OBE FCA *1958;* 42 Dolphin Court, Cliff Road, EASTBOURNE, BN20 7XF. (Life Member)
•RIDGE, Mr. Nicholas Benedict, BA FCA ATII *1976;* Bryan and Ridge, The Gatehouse, 2 Devonhurst Place, Heathfield Terrace, LONDON, W4 4JD. See also Nicholas Ridge, CTA and Brian and Ridge
RIDGE, Mr. Paul Graham, BSc FCA *1987;* 173 Shepherds Drive, CHERRYBROOK, NSW 2126, AUSTRALIA.
RIDGE, Mr. Peter, FCA *1966;* The White House, Old Perry Street, CHISLEHURST, BR7 6PL.
RIDGE, Mr. Timothy, BSc ACA *1999;* 10 Park Road, BECKENHAM, KENT, BR3 1QD.
RIDGEON, Mr. David Howard, MA ACA *1979;* International Insurance Co of Hannover Novell House, 1 Arlington Square Downshire Way, BRACKNELL, RG12 1WA.
RIDGER, Mr. Giles Philip, BA ACA *1986;* IPC UK Ltd, Elscot House, Arcadia Avenue, Finchley, LONDON, N3 2JE.
RIDGEWAY, Mr. Alan Brian, BA ACA *1992;* Live Nation Ltd, Regent Arcade House, 19-25 Argyll Street, LONDON, W1F 7TS.
•RIDGEWAY, Mr. John Weston, ACA *1980;* J.W. Ridgeway & Co, 106a High Street, CHESHAM, HP5 1EB.
RIDGEWAY, Mr. Kevin Stuart, BSc ACA *1993;* Stainless Steel Fasteners Ltd, Broombank Road, CHESTERFIELD, DERBYSHIRE, S41 9QJ.
RIDGEWAY, Mr. Lewis, FCA *1974;* 1212 SUNCAST LANE SUITE 1, EL DORADO HILLS, CA 95762, UNITED STATES.
RIDGEWELL, Mr. Nicholas John, BA FCA *1991;* 48 Wilberforce Avenue, ROSE BAY, NSW 2029, AUSTRALIA.
RIDGLEY, Mrs. Celia Helen, BA FCA *1988;* Wellfield House, Caps Lane, Cholsey, WALLINGFORD, OXFORDSHIRE, OX10 9HF.
RIDGLEY, Mr. Giles Andrew, BA ACA *1996;* Rolls Royce plc, PO Box 31, DERBY, DE24 8BJ.
RIDGWAY, Mrs. Bethan, PhD BSc ACA *2011;* Tryweryn Cottage, St. Brides Lane, SAUNDERSFOOT, DYFED, SA69 9HL.
RIDGWAY, Mr. George, FCA *1972;* (Member of Council 1994 - 2002), Alma House, Station Road, ATTLEBOROUGH, NORFOLK, NR17 2AS. (Life Member)
RIDGWAY, Mr. Graham Martin, BA FCA *1982;* 42 Broadlake, Willaston, NESTON, CHESHIRE, CH64 2XB.
•RIDGWAY, Mr. Ian James, BSc FCA MBA *1994;* Spring House, La Ferme Du Marais, La Rue Du Pont, St. Mary, JERSEY, JE3 3AH.
RIDGWAY, Mrs. Julia Anne, BSc ACA DChA *1994;* with Sayer Vincent, 8 Angel Gate, City Road, LONDON, EC1V 2SJ.
RIDGWAY, Miss. Kara Louise, ACA *2008;* 33 James Close, MARLOW, BUCKINGHAMSHIRE, SL7 1TS.
RIDGWAY, Mr. Malcolm Walter, FCA *1959;* 4 Mill Bank, LYMM, WA13 9DG. (Life Member)
•RIDGWAY, Mr. Michael Andrew Joseph, BSc FCA *1977;* Michael J. Ridgway, Avenue du Maelbeek 7 bte 11, 1000 BRUSSELS, BELGIUM.
RIDGWAY, Mr. Nigel, BA ACA *1982;* 10 Albion Place, EXETER, EX4 6LH.
RIDGWAY, Mr. Richard Kingsley, FCA *1967;* 749 Ridge Road, DURBAN, KWAZULU NATAL, 4001, SOUTH AFRICA. (Life Member)
RIDGWELL, Miss. Amanda, ACA *2010;* 45 Goodwood Grove, YORK, YO24 1ER.
•RIDGWELL, Mr. Terence, ACA *1979;* 6 Catherines Close, WEST DRAYTON, UB7 7PB.
•RIDING, Mr. David Stanley, FCA *1969;* David S Riding FCA, Sherwood House, Division Lane, BLACKPOOL, FY4 5DZ.
•RIDING, Mr. Ian David, BSc FCA *1983;* (Tax Fac), JPH Ltd, 112-114 Whitegate Drive, BLACKPOOL, FY3 9XH.
RIDING, Mrs. Karen Ann, BSc ACA *1991;* (Tax Fac), 55 The Rydings, Langho, BLACKBURN, LANCASHIRE, BB6 8BQ.
•RIDING, Mr. Philip Alan, FCA *1983;* (Tax Fac), Barlow Andrews LLP, Carlyle House, 78 Chorley New Road, BOLTON, BL1 4BY. See also Beech Business Services Limited
RIDING, Mr. Steven Edward, BSc ACA *1991;* 10 Gladeside, Jersey Farm, ST. ALBANS, HERTFORDSHIRE, AL4 9JA.
RIDING, Mr. Tom Livsey, FCA *1955;* 4 Copthorne Crest, Copthorne, SHREWSBURY, SY3 8RU. (Life Member)
•RIDINGS, Mr. James, FCA *1973;* P.B. Syddall & Co, Grafton House, 81 Chorley Old Road, BOLTON, BL1 3AJ.
RIDINGS, Mr. John Gordon, FCA *1970;* 35 York Place, HARROGATE, NORTH YORKSHIRE, HG1 5RH.
RIDINGS, Mr. Nicholas Andrew, BA ACA *1987;* Avocet Hardware Ltd Brookfoot Industrial Estate, Brookfoot, BRIGHOUSE, WEST YORKSHIRE, HD6 2RW.
RIDLER, Mr. David Andrew, BA ACA *1997;* 34 Hay Street, PERTH, PH1 5HS.
RIDLER, Mr. Stephen John, BA ACA *1985;* Bourton House Lonsdale Court Great Rollright, CHIPPING NORTON, OXFORDSHIRE, OX7 5RB.
RIDLEY, Mr. Andrew, BA(Hons) ACA *2006;* 4/1 Neptune Street, COOGEE, NSW 2034, AUSTRALIA.
RIDLEY, Mrs. Carmen, BSc ACA *1999;* 14 Balmoral Avenue, SANDRINGHAM, VIC 3191, AUSTRALIA.
RIDLEY, Miss. Catherine Judith, BSc ACA *2011;* 15 Baldwyn Gardens, LONDON, W3 6HJ.
RIDLEY, Mr. Craig Mark, BSc ACA *1998;* Waterman Group Plc, Pickfords Wharf, Clink Street, LONDON, SE1 9DG.
RIDLEY, Mr. David Anthony, FCA *1978;* 6 Upper Golf Links Road, BROADSTONE, BH18 8BU.
RIDLEY, Mr. David James, BA ACA *1984;* 27 Kelso Place, LONDON, W8 5QG.
RIDLEY, Mr. David John, BA ACA *1980;* 71 Fairholme Avenue, ROMFORD, RM2 5UR.
RIDLEY, Miss. Hayley, BA ACA *2011;* 41 Charnock Drive, SHEFFIELD, S12 3HD.
RIDLEY, Miss. Helen Louise, ACA *2008;* Opsec Security Ltd, 40 Phoenix Road, Crowther District 3, WASHINGTON, TYNE AND WEAR, NE38 0AD.
RIDLEY, Mr. Ian Christopher, FCA *1975;* Cock Inn Uckfield Road, Ringmer, LEWES, BN8 5RX.
RIDLEY, Mr. James Edward, MMath ACA *2002;* 14 Balmoral Avenue, Sandringham, MELBOURNE, VIC 3191, AUSTRALIA.
RIDLEY, Mr. Jocelyn Thomas Dixon, MA MSc ACA *2004;* Cofan Ltd, The Compasses, Littley Green, CHELMSFORD, CM3 1BU.
RIDLEY, Mr. John Charles, BA ACA *1994;* Forest Laboratories UK Ltd Riverbridge House, Anchor Boulevard Crossways Business Park, DARTFORD, DA2 6SL.
RIDLEY, Mr. John Henry Wallace, BSc FCA *1975;* 52 Park Lane, BEWDLEY, DY12 2EU.
RIDLEY, Mr. Jonathan, BEng ACA *2003;* 5 Vale Court, Pembroke Vale, BRISTOL, BS8 3DN.
RIDLEY, Mr. Matthew John, ACA *2000;* 93 The edge, Clowes Street, MANCHESTER, M3 5ND.
RIDLEY, Mr. Michael John, BSc FCA *1995;* 1 Sutton Drove Cottages, Sutton Drove, SEAFORD, EAST SUSSEX, BN25 3NG.
RIDLEY, Mr. Michael Leslie, BSc FCA *1975;* Epsom College, Accounts Department, College Road, EPSOM, SURREY, KT17 4JQ.
RIDLEY, Miss. Nicola, BSc ACA *1995;* Thomas of York Ltd The Bakers Yard, Sawmill Lane Helmsley, YORK, YO62 5DQ.
RIDLEY, Mr. Paul Richard, FCA ATII *1971;* Paul Ridley & Associates, Pantons Coach House, The Street, Dallington, HEATHFIELD, EAST SUSSEX TN21 9NH.
RIDLEY, Mr. Peter Robinson, BA ACA *1982;* 206 Ashley Gardens, Emery Hill Street, LONDON, SW1P 1PA.
RIDLEY, Mr. Philip Ian, BA ACA *1987;* 16 Elmfield Road, Gosforth, NEWCASTLE UPON TYNE, NE3 4AY.
RIDLEY, Mr. Richard Nicholas, FCA *1963;* Paines Corner, Broad Oak, HEATHFIELD, EAST SUSSEX, TN21 8UT.
RIDLEY, Mr. Roy, BA FCA *1983;* 7 Kelso Drive, The Priory's, Preston Grange, NORTH SHIELDS, NE29 9NS.
RIDLEY, Mr. Stephen, MA BA(Hons) ACA *2011;* 28 Beverley Road, WHITLEY BAY, TYNE AND WEAR, NE25 8JH.
RIDLEY, Mr. William Patrick, MA BA FCA *1962;* 15D John Spencer Square, LONDON, N1 2LZ. (Life Member)
RIDLEY-THOMAS, Mr. Christopher Iain, BSc ACA *1992;* with KPMG LLP, Box 10426 Pacific Centre, 777 Dunsmuir Street, VANCOUVER V7Y 1K3, BC, CANADA.
RIDOUT, Mr. Christopher Charles, FCA *1974;* Apartment 2, Historic Royal Palaces, Hampton Court Palace, EAST MOLESEY, KT8 9AU.
RIDOUT, Miss. Clare Elizabeth, BA ACA *1994;* 223 Helensburgh Road, Helensburgh, DUNEDIN 9001, NEW ZEALAND.
RIDOUT, Mr. John Mark Crue, BSc ACA *1996;* Block C, 1st Floor, Astown Gate, DUBLIN 15, COUNTY DUBLIN, IRELAND.
RIDOUT, Mr. John Scott, MA FCA *1977;* 32 Fauconberg Road, LONDON, W4 3JU.
RIDOUT, Mr. Philip Michael, BA ACA *1992;* 77 Monks Avenue, BARNET, EN5 1DA.
RIDOUT, Mr. Robert James, BSc ACA *2004;* 28 Mafeking Place, Chapeltown, SHEFFIELD, S35 2UT.
RIDOUT, Mr. Thomas Geoffrey, BA(Hons) ACA *2002;* 80 Westfield Road, Caversham, READING, RG4 8HJ.
RIDSDALE, Mr. Glenn David, BA ACA *1988;* 4 Margrove Chase, Lostock, BOLTON, BL6 4NN.
RIEDEL, Mrs. Linda, BA ACA *2004;* 12 Henley Road, SOUTHSEA, HAMPSHIRE, PO4 0HS.
•RIEDEN, Mrs. Vivien Margaret, BSc ACA CTA *1983;* Vivien M. Hirst, 4 White Rose Lane, Lower Bourne, FARNHAM, GU10 3NG.

RIEDER, Miss. Jemma Louise, BSc ACA *2009;* 9 Trinity Court, South Lane, HESSLE, HU13 0TN.

RIEKIE, Mr. Maxwell Francis, BA FCA *1982;* 266 Dobcroft Road, Ecclesall, SHEFFIELD, S11 9LJ.

RIEKSTINS, Mr. Juris, BSc FCA *1975;* 18 Pymers Mead, Dulwich, LONDON, SE21 8NQ.

RIEMER, Miss. Bianca, BSc ACA *2007;* 22 Ufford Street, LONDON, SE1 8QD.

RIESCO, Miss. Polly, BA ACA *2004;* B P P Holdings Plc Aldine House, 142-144 Uxbridge Road, LONDON, W12 8AA.

RIESE, Mr. Mark Edwin, BCom FCA *1985;* Urban Living, 68 Marylebone Lane, LONDON, W1U 2PQ.

RIETKERK, Mr. James Dirk, BA ACA *1989;* 78 Blackheath Park, Blackheath, LONDON, SE3 0ET.

RIETKERK, Mrs. Victoria Sarah, MA ACA *1991;* Christ's College LTD, 4 St Germans Place Blackheath, LONDON, SE3 0NJ.

RIEUPEYROUX, Ms. Helen Louise, BA(Hons) ACA *2002;* 5 Brambledene Close, WOKING, SURREY, GU21 3HE.

•RIEVELEY, Mr. Antony Paul, BA ACA *1995;* KPMG Ltd, Chemin De-Normandie 14, 1211 GENEVA, SWITZERLAND. See also KPMG Europe LLP

RIFAAT, Mr. Osman Cherif, MA ACA *1998;* OCR Consulting Ltd, Flat 8, 93 Belgrave Road, Pimlico, LONDON, SW1V 2BQ.

RIFKIND, Miss. Caroline Emma, BA(Hons) ACA *2001;* with PricewaterhouseCoopers LLP, Pricewaterhousecoopers, 12 Plumtree Court, LONDON, EC4A 4HT.

RIGAS, Mr. Savvas, BSc ACA *2002;* 7 Aulidos Street, Mesa Yitonia, 4002 LIMASSOL, CYPRUS.

RIGAUDBARRETT, Mr. Ian James, FCA *1963;* Leverets Walk, Niton Road, Rookley, VENTNOR, ISLE OF WIGHT, PO38 3NR.

RIGBY, Mr. Adam John Guthrie, BA ACA *2010;* 50 Chevet Lane, WAKEFIELD, WEST YORKSHIRE, WF2 6JD.

RIGBY, Mr. Andrew Peter, BA ACA *1982;* KYC Limited, Hough Hole House, Hough Hole, Rainow, MACCLESFIELD, CHESHIRE SK10 5UW.

RIGBY, Mr. Andrew Pryce, BA FCA *1980;* 6 Lodge Drive, WESTON-SUPER-MARE, BS23 2TY.

RIGBY, Mr. Anthony David, BSc(Hons) ACA *2001;* 79 High Road, LOUGHTON, IG10 4JE.

RIGBY, Mrs. April Sarah Jane, BSc ACA *1987;* Bridfield House, Lambridge Wood Road, HENLEY-ON-THAMES, RG9 3BP.

•RIGBY, Mr. Barry Arthur, BA ACA *1980;* John Goulding & Co Ltd, 4 Southport Road, CHORLEY, LANCASHIRE, PR7 1LD.

RIGBY, Mr. Brian Keith, BA(Com) FCA *1959;* 11 Stetchworth Road, Walton, WARRINGTON, WA4 6JQ. (Life Member)

RIGBY, Ms. Carol Gabrielle Reed, MA FCA *1988;* 2704 Flintridge Court, MYERSVILLE, MD 21773, UNITED STATES.

RIGBY, Mr. David Keith, BA ACA *1987;* Bridfield House, Lambridge Wood Road, HENLEY-ON-THAMES, RG9 3BP.

RIGBY, Mr. Dominic Alexander, BSc ACA *1999;* Flat 1B, Sunrise House, 27 Old Bailey Street, CENTRAL, HONG KONG ISLAND, HONG KONG SAR.

RIGBY, Mr. Edwin Allan, FCA *1977;* Garry White & Co, 24 James Street, EBBW VALE, GWENT, NP23 6JG.

RIGBY, Miss. Gemma, LLB ACA *2009;* 4 Brewery Bond, Duke Street, NORTH SHIELDS, TYNE AND WEAR, NE29 6EQ.

RIGBY, Mr. Geoffrey Thomas, BA FCA *1980;* Newgate Farm, Turn VIllage, Edenfield, BURY, BL0 0RN.

RIGBY, Mr. Graeme Michael Hildred, ACA *2001;* PO Box 749, Kyalami Estates, 1684, JOHANNESBURG, GAUTENG, SOUTH AFRICA.

•RIGBY, Mr. Graham Kenneth, BSc ACA *1999;* CLB Coopers, Ship Canal House, 98 King Street, MANCHESTER, M2 4WU.

RIGBY, Mr. Graham Lakin, FCA *1964;* Magnolia Cottage, 4 Fulmer Place Farm, Fulmer Road, Fulmer, SLOUGH, SL3 6HP. (Life Member)

•RIGBY, Mr. Guy Anthony, FCA *1976;* Smith & Williamson Ltd, 25 Moorgate, LONDON, EC2R 6AY.

RIGBY, Mr. James Antony, BSc ACA *1999;* 22 Mill Green Road, WELWYN GARDEN CITY, HERTFORDSHIRE, AL7 3XF.

RIGBY, Mr. James Douglas, BCom ACA *2005;* with Deloitte LLP, 1 City Square, LEEDS, WEST YORKSHIRE, LS1 2AL.

RIGBY, Mrs. Jennifer Ann, BA ACA *1981;* Hough Hole House, Hough Hole, Rainow, MACCLESFIELD, SK10 5UW.

RIGBY, Mr. John Alan, FCA *1958;* Rosebank, Westbrook, Boxford, NEWBURY, RG20 8DH. (Life Member)

RIGBY, Mr. John Leslie, FCA *1977;* 53 Orchard Court, Black Bull Lane, Fulwood, PRESTON, PR2 3LB.

•①RIGBY, Mr. Jonathan Paul, BSc ACA *1997;* Rigby Lennon & Co, 20 Winmarleigh Street, WARRINGTON, WA1 1JY.

RIGBY, Mr. Jonathon, BSc ACA *1993;* U B S, 1 Finsbury Avenue, LONDON, EC2M 2PP.

RIGBY, Miss. Judith Anne, BA ACA *1993;* 12 Meadowside, FRODSHAM, WA6 7BY.

RIGBY, Ms. Julia, BSc ACA *1986;* 23 Thirsk Road, LONDON, SW11 5SU.

RIGBY, Mrs. Karen Sarah, BSc FCA ATII *1988;* Chemin des Macherettes 3, 1172 BOUGY-VILLARS, SWITZERLAND.

•RIGBY, Mr. Keith Michael, ACA *1989;* The LK Partnership LLP, Rowan House, Hill End Lane, ST. ALBANS, HERTFORDSHIRE, AL4 0RA.

RIGBY, Mr. Michael, BA FCA *1994;* 45 Duchy Road, HARROGATE, NORTH YORKSHIRE, HG1 2HB.

RIGBY, Mr. Michael Graham Neil, BA ACA *1983;* 25 Aberaman, Emmer Green, READING, RG4 8LD.

RIGBY, Mr. Michael Harry, FCA *1956;* 12 Gateways, GUILDFORD, GU1 2LF. (Life Member)

RIGBY, Mr. Neil Michael, BSc ACA *1993;* 1 Coles Farm, Chequers Lane, WATFORD, WD25 0GL.

RIGBY, Mr. Oliver James, BSc ACA *2006;* Daniel Stewart & Company, Becket House, 36 Old Jewry, LONDON, EC2R 8DD.

RIGBY, Mr. Peter Wesley, BA ACA *1980;* Methodist Colleges and Schools, Methodist Church House, 25 Marylebone Road, LONDON, NW1 5JR.

RIGBY, Mr. Richard Peter, BA FCA *1990;* International Air Transport Association, 33 Route de l'Aeroport, PO Box 416, 1215 GENEVA, SWITZERLAND.

RIGBY, Mrs. Sarah Elizabeth Louise, BA ACA *1991;* Woodhouse Cottage, Main Street, Thorganby, YORK, YO19 6DB.

RIGBY, Mr. Stephen John, BA ACA *1987;* The West of England Insurance Services (Luxembourg) SA, Tower Bridge Court, 224-226 Tower Bridge Road, LONDON, SE1 2UP.

RIGBY, Mr. Stuart James, BA FCA *1987;* J P Knight Limited, The Admiral's Offices, Main Gate Road, The Historic Dockyard, CHATHAM, ME4 4TZ.

RIGBY, Miss. Victoria Therese, BA ACA *2004;* 47 Bamford Close, RUNCORN, CHESHIRE, WA7 5NT.

RIGBY-HALL, Mrs. Siobhan Claire Mary, BSc ACA *1991;* 537 Steamboat Road, GREENWICH, CT 06830, UNITED STATES.

RIGBY-JONES, Mr. Peter John, BA ACA *1981;* Court Cottage, Coldharbour Road, Pyrford, WOKING, GU22 8SJ.

RIGDEN, Miss. Claire, ACA *2009;* 353 Beaver Lane, ASHFORD, KENT, TN23 5PQ.

RIGDEN, Mr. Darren James, BSc ACA *2002;* with Crowe Clark Whitehill LLP, 10 Palace Avenue, MAIDSTONE, KENT, ME15 6NF.

RIGDEN, Mr. Denis George, FCA *1953;* Apartment 8, Holland Court, Willow Close, Poynton, STOCKPORT, CHESHIRE SK12 1PL. (Life Member)

RIGDEN, Mrs. Louisa, BSc ACA *1997;* 72 Nailcote Avenue, Tile Hill, COVENTRY, CV4 9GL.

RIGDEN, Mr. Stephen Peter, BCom ACA *1987;* (Tax Fac), 72 Nailcote Avenue, COVENTRY, CV4 9GL.

RIGELSFORD, Mr. Kenneth George, BSc FCA *1979;* 14 Glebelands Ave, South Woodford, LONDON, E18 2AB.

RIGG, Mr. Ben James, BA ACA *2006;* with Grant Thornton UK LLP, 30 Finsbury Square, LONDON, EC2P 2YU.

RIGG, Mr. Bryan John, MA ACA *1989;* Atterbury House, 1 The High Street, Welford, NORTHAMPTON, NN6 6HT.

RIGG, Mr. Christian Alexander, BA(Hons) ACA *2001;* 59 Bramhall Drive, High Generals Wood, Rickleton, WASHINGTON, TYNE AND WEAR, NE38 9DE.

RIGG, John Christopher, Esq OBE MA FCA *1976;* 113 Laudersdale Tower, Barbican, LONDON, EC2Y 8BY.

RIGG, Miss. Katie Elizabeth, BSc ACA *2010;* 40 Grange Way, SANDBACH, CHESHIRE, CW11 1ES.

RIGG, Mr. Malcolm Gerald, BSc FCA *1974;* 4 The Vale, HARTLEPOOL, TS26 0AA.

RIGG, Mr. Michael Philip, BCom FCA *1983;* 47 Petts Wood Road, ORPINGTON, BR5 1JU.

RIGG, Mr. Scott James, ACA *2008;* K P M G Llp, 15 Canada Square, LONDON, E14 5GL.

RIGG, Miss. Tracy Diane, BA(Hons) ACA *2001;* 3 Egbert Road, WIRRAL, MERSEYSIDE, CH47 5AH.

RIGGALL, Mr. Michael, FCA *1971;* Meadowview Aldworth Road, Upper Basildon, READING, RG8 8NG.

RIGGOTT, Mrs. Cheryl Karen, ACA *2000;* with Grant Thornton UK LLP, Enterprise House, 115 Edmund Street, BIRMINGHAM, B3 2HJ.

RIGGS, Mr. Andrew Simon, MBA BSc FCA *1993;* The Old Bakery, Hawkesbury Road, Hillesley, WOTTON-UNDER-EDGE, GLOUCESTERSHIRE, GL12 7RD.

RIGGS, Mr. Eoin, ACA *2003;* 101a Bancroft, HITCHIN, HERTFORDSHIRE, SG5 1NB.

RIGGS, Mr. Nicholas Stephen, BCom ACA *2001;* with Deloitte LLP, Abbots House, Abbey Street, READING, RG1 3BD.

RIGHTON, Mr. Ben John, ACA *2009;* 24 Chorley Road, Parbold, WIGAN, WN8 7AL.

RIGHTON, Mrs. Caroline, ACA *2009;* 20 Parsonage Close, Upholland, SKELMERSDALE, WN8 0JL.

RIGHTON, Mr. Philip Anthony, BA ACA *1979;* Hostombe Group Ltd, Minalloy House, Regent Street, SHEFFIELD, S1 3NJ.

RIGHTON, Mr. Timothy Paul, BSc(Hons) ACA *2009;* 20 Parsonage Close, Upholland, SKELMERSDALE, WN8 0JL.

RIGLEY, Mr. James William, FCA *1976;* 235 Melton Road, Edwalton, NOTTINGHAM, NG12 4DB.

RIGNELL, Mr. Dudley James, FCA *1954;* 7 Queen Square, BRIGHTON, BN1 3FD. (Life Member)

RIGNEY, Mr. Paul Harvey, BSc ACA *1987;* Royce Peeling Green Limited, The Copper Room Deva Centre Trinity Way, MANCHESTER, m3 7bg.

RIKHY, Mr. Naveen, BA ACA *1998;* KPMG LLP, 345 Park Avenue, NEW YORK, NY 10154, UNITED STATES.

RIKHY, Mr. Paramraj Singh, FCA *1974;* 1755 York Avenue, Apt 22G, NEW YORK, NY 10128, UNITED STATES.

RILETT, Mr. Peter John David, MBA FCA *1972;* Grange Fell, Leigh Woods, BRISTOL, BS8 3PX.

RILEY, Mrs. Alison Patricia, BSc(Econ) ACA CTA *1989;* (Tax Fac), U B S AG, 100 Liverpool Street, LONDON, EC2M 2RH.

RILEY, Dr. Andrew, ACA *2011;* 11 Peterhouse Drive, OTLEY, WEST YORKSHIRE, LS21 1DS.

RILEY, Mr. Andrew, BA ACA *1998;* 3 Blackshaw Drive Great Sankey, WARRINGTON, WA5 8TJ.

•RILEY, Mr. Andrew Charles, BSc ACA *1990;* Howsons, 20 Moorland Road, Burslem, STOKE-ON-TRENT, ST6 1DW. See also Howsons Accountants Limited

RILEY, Mr. Andrew Colin, BA ACA *1992;* 18 Kinghorn Park, MAIDENHEAD, BERKSHIRE, SL6 7TX.

RILEY, Mr. Andrew Luke, BA FCA *1995;* 20 Humber Road, Blackheath, LONDON, SE3 7LT.

•RILEY, Mrs. Angela Kathryn, BSc FCA *1982;* (Tax Fac), Riley & Co Limited, 52 St.Johns Lane, HALIFAX, HX1 2BW.

RILEY, Mr. Anthony John, BA ACA *1993;* 187 Wigan Road, Standish, WIGAN, WN6 0AE.

RILEY, Mr. Barrington Marshall, BA FCA *1977;* 35 Oldfield Way, WIRRAL, MERSEYSIDE, CH60 6RH.

RILEY, Mr. Benjamin, BA ACA *2011;* Flat 1, 8 Edgedale Road, SHEFFIELD, S7 2BQ.

RILEY, Mrs. Brenda Ann, FCA *1984;* 20 Chadfield Road, Duffield, BELPER, DE56 4DU.

RILEY, Mr. Bruce Michael, BA ACA *1997;* RBS Global Banking and Markets, 135 Bishopsgate, LONDON, EC2M 3UR.

RILEY, Mr. Carl Terence, FCA *1973;* 8th Floor, George Davies Solicitors Llp, 1 New York Street, MANCHESTER, M1 4AD.

RILEY, Mr. Christopher George, BSc FCA *1977;* Rowan House, 9A Acacia Drive, Thorpe Bay, SOUTHEND-ON-SEA, SS1 3JU.

RILEY, Mr. Ciaran John, BA ACA *2009;* 245 Upper Marshall Street, BIRMINGHAM, B1 1LP.

RILEY, Mr. Daniel Foster, BA ACA *2007;* 6 Station Approach, Burley in Wharfedale, ILKLEY, WEST YORKSHIRE, LS29 7PS.

RILEY, Mr. David, FCA *1968;* Corner Cottage, 37 Mucklestone, MARKET DRAYTON, SHROPSHIRE, TF9 4DN.

RILEY, Mr. David Brian, BA FCA *1992;* Mille Vues, Rue de la Falaise, St. Martin, GUERNSEY, GY4 6UN.

RILEY, Mr. David James, BSc ACA *2005;* Pieter Baststraat 31-3, 1071TV AMSTERDAM, NETHERLANDS.

•RILEY, Mr. David Neil, ACA *1978;* (Tax Fac), Clough Tomblin & Co, Nat.Westminster Bank Chmbrs, The Grove, ILKLEY, LS29 9LS.

•RILEY, Mr. David Richard, BSc ACA *1988;* haysmacintyre, Fairfax House, 15 Fulwood Place, LONDON, WC1V 6AY.

RILEY, Mr. Derek Brian, FCA *1954;* P.O. Box 781540, SANDTON, GAUTENG, 2146, SOUTH AFRICA. (Life Member)

RILEY, Mr. Edward John, BSc ACA *1983;* Langland, Broad Lane, Tanworth-In-Arden, SOLIHULL, WARWICKSHIRE, B94 5HX.

RILEY, Mr. Edward Peter, BA ACA *1993;* TURNERSTRASSE 22, CH-8472 SEUZACH, SWITZERLAND.

RILEY, Mrs. Elizabeth Ann, BA ACA *2005;* 32 Vienna Road, Edgeley, STOCKPORT, CHESHIRE, SK3 9QH.

•RILEY, Mrs. Elizabeth Jane, ACA *1986;* (Tax Fac), Evolvement, 12 The Vinery, New Longton, PRESTON, PR4 4YB.

RILEY, Mr. Geoffrey Haigh, FCA *1964;* Habasco International Ltd, Stafford Mills, Milnsbridge, HUDDERSFIELD, HD3 4JD.

RILEY, Mr. Graeme, BA ACA *1992;* 5 Fillingham Way, HATFIELD, HERTFORDSHIRE, AL10 9GE.

RILEY, Mrs. Guro Farnes, MSc ACA *1997;* Locker & Riley Ltd, 42-50, Bancrofts Road, South Woodham Ferrers, CHELMSFORD, CM3 5UQ.

RILEY, Miss. Gwenan, BSc ACA *2002;* 98 Nicholson Road, Khandallah, WELLINGTON, NEW ZEALAND.

•RILEY, Ms. Helen Doone, LLB FCA CTA *1979;* (Tax Fac), with Grant Thornton UK LLP, 1-4 Atholl Crescent, EDINBURGH, EH3 8LQ.

RILEY, Miss. Helen Elizabeth, BA(Hons) ACA *2003;* 14 Syddal Crescent, Bramhall, STOCKPORT, CHESHIRE, SK7 1HS.

RILEY, Mr. Ian, ACA *2010;* 7 Rivington Hall Close, Ramsbottom, BURY, LANCASHIRE, BL0 9YL.

RILEY, Mr. Jack, FCA *1952;* 17 Canford Drive, Allerton, BRADFORD, BD15 7AR. (Life Member)

RILEY, Mrs. Jacqueline Anne Louise, BSc ACA *1988;* 13 Heralds Place, LONDON, SE11 4NP.

RILEY, Mr. James Martin, BA FCA *1991;* 19 Westwood Way, Boston Spa, WETHERBY, WEST YORKSHIRE, LS23 6DX.

RILEY, Mrs. Jane, BSc ACA *1998;* 2 Chelsea Cottages, Priory Road, ASCOT, SL5 8DU.

RILEY, Miss. Jane Fiona, BSc ACA *1989;* 1 Blenheim Close, WATFORD, WD19 4QN.

RILEY, Mr. John Christopher William, MA FCA *1961;* 202 Rivermead Court, Ranelagh Gardens, LONDON, SW6 3SG. (Life Member)

RILEY, Mr. John Damian, BA ACA *1994;* 1st Floor Power House, MacGregor (G B R) Ltd Power House, Silverlink, WALLSEND, TYNE AND WEAR, NE28 9ND.

RILEY, Mr. John David, FCA *1968;* Rhinsdale, The Ridge, Linton, WETHERBY, LS22 4HJ.

RILEY, Mr. John Edward, JP FCA *1965;* 46 Meadow Rise, Blackmore, INGATESTONE, CM4 0QY.

RILEY, Mr. John Frederick, FCA *1957;* 1 The Orchards, Little Kingshill, GREAT MISSENDEN, HP16 0EA. (Life Member)

RILEY, Mr. John Michael Joseph, FCA *1974;* 288 Leigh Road, Worsley, MANCHESTER, M28 1LH.

RILEY, Mr. John Raynor, FCA *1964;* Box 296, BOWEN ISLAND V0N 1G0, BC, CANADA.

RILEY, Mr. Jonathan, MSc BA ACA *2004;* Flat 29 Saffron House, 7 Woodman Mews, RICHMOND, TW9 4AP.

RILEY, Mr. Jonathan, LLB ACA *2005;* 20 Kingscroft, Kings Avenue, LONDON, SW4 8ED.

RILEY, Mr. Jonathan Mark, BSc ACA *1988;* St. Marys Cottage, Pinewoods Road, Longworth, ABINGDON, OXFORDSHIRE, OX13 5HG.

RILEY, Miss. Karen Michelle, ACA *1993;* 3 William Street, BERKHAMSTED, HP4 2EL.

RILEY, Mr. Kenneth John, FCA *1960;* 71 Gladstone Avenue, TWICKENHAM, MIDDLESEX, TW2 7PS. (Life Member)

RILEY, Miss. Kristen Sanchia, ACA *2005;* 33 Parsonage Way, Linton, CAMBRIDGE, CB21 4YL.

RILEY, Mr. Leigh Winston, FCA *1975;* 68 Moor End, Spondon, DERBY, DE21 7EE.

RILEY, Ms. Lesley Marie, BA ACA *1997;* 1 Watchung Avenue, MONTCLAIR, NJ 07043, UNITED STATES.

RILEY, Miss. Marian Linda, BSc ACA *1991;* Rockfield House, Flagg, BUXTON, SK17 9QS.

RILEY, Mrs. Marie, BA ACA *2004;* Wilkinson Hardware Stores Ltd, JK House PO Box 20, Roebuck Way Manton Wood, WORKSOP, NOTTINGHAMSHIRE, S80 3YY.

•RILEY, Mr. Mark Pearce, FCA *1979;* Atherton Bailey LLP, 28-30 High Street, GUILDFORD, SURREY, GU1 3HY. See also Riley Mark & Co

RILEY, Mr. Martin James, BSc FCA *1987;* Lloyds Banking Group, 125 Shaftesbury Avenue, LONDON, WC2H 8AD.

RILEY, Mr. Martin Rupert, MA FCA *1969;* The Lime House, Leckhampstead, BUCKINGHAM, MK18 5NY.

RILEY, Mr. Matthew, ACA *2011;* 151 Grove Lane, Cheadle Hulme, CHEADLE, CHESHIRE, SK8 7NG.

RILEY, Mr. Matthew James, MA ACA *2003;* 33 Percy Road, Handbridge, CHESTER, CH4 7EY.

Members - Alphabetical

RILEY - RISLEY

RILEY, Mr. Michael Austin, BA ACA *1989;* 12 West Park Avenue, LEEDS, LS8 2HG.
RILEY, Mr. Michael Bernard, FCA *1971;* 7 Pastures Avenue, Littleover, DERBY, DE23 4BE.
RILEY, Mr. Michael Bruce, FCA *1967;* Chelliapur Richmond Avenue, St. Peter Port, GUERNSEY, GY1 1QQ.
•RILEY, Mr. Michael John, BA(Hons) ACA *1988;* (Tax Fac), M J Riley & Co, 22 Church Street, KIDDERMINSTER, DY10 2AW. See also Rilis Limited
•RILEY, Mr. Nicholas Edward, MBA FCA *1989;* Libcus Limited, Wye House, Water Street, BAKEWELL, DERBYSHIRE, DE45 1EW.
•RILEY, Mr. Peter George Campbell, FCA *1971;* Crossley & Davis, 348-350 Lytham Road, BLACKPOOL, FY4 1DW. See also Campbell Crossley & Davis
RILEY, Mr. Peter James Holland, BA ACA *1986;* Jardine Matheson Ltd, 48th Floor, Jardine House, CENTRAL, HONG KONG ISLAND, HONG KONG SAR.
RILEY, Mr. Peter Lawrence, FCA *1970;* Landings, 50 Yealm Road, Newton Ferrers, PLYMOUTH, DEVON, PL8 1BQ.
•RILEY, Mr. Peter William, ACA *1980;* (Tax Fac), Peter Riley, 21 New Road, BRIXHAM, TQ5 8NB.
RILEY, Mr. Philip, BA ACA *2001;* 12 Mountfield Road, TUNBRIDGE WELLS, TN1 1SG.
RILEY, Mr. Philip Ian, BA FCA *1987;* (Tax Fac), Ashdown, Hollow Lane, Dormansland, LINGFIELD, RH7 6NS.
RILEY, Mr. Philip John, BA ACA *1985;* Northwood, Patterdale Road, WINDERMERE, CUMBRIA, LA23 1NQ.
RILEY, Mrs. Philippa Joy Curwen, MA ACA *1985;* 4 Cruikshank Lea, College Town, SANDHURST, BERKSHIRE, GU47 0FX.
RILEY, Mr. Phillip John, BA ACA *2010;* 8 Ashbourne Avenue, Douglas, ISLE OF MAN, IM2 1NW.
RILEY, Mr. Robert Edward, FCA *1960;* 74 Bramley Lane, Hipperholme, HALIFAX, HX3 8NW. (Life Member)
RILEY, Mr. Robert Kenneth Thomas, BSc ACA *1989;* 5 Nascot Road, WATFORD, WD17 4RD.
RILEY, Miss. Rosemary Penelope, MA FCA *1988;* Fern Bank, Kissing Tree Lane, Alveston, STRATFORD-UPON-AVON, WARWICKSHIRE, CV37 7QS.
RILEY, Miss. Ruth Mary, BA ACA *1993;* 25 Round Wood, Penwortham, PRESTON, PR1 0BN.
RILEY, Mrs. Sarah Jane, BSc ACA MSI *2002;* 4 Bardney Avenue, Golborne, WARRINGTON, WA3 3TQ.
RILEY, Mrs. Saranna Grace Clare, BSc ACA *2004;* Wentway House, Buckham Thorns Road, WESTERHAM, KENT, TN16 1ET.
RILEY, Mr. Simon James Temple, BSc FCA *1990;* 102 Heythorp Street, Southfields, LONDON, SW18 5BX.
RILEY, Mr. Simon Paul Andrew, BSc ACA *2003;* Les Corvais, 2 La Rue de la Patente, St. Lawrence, JERSEY, JE3 1HS.
•RILEY, Mr. Stephen, BA ACA *1984;* Evolvement, 12 The Vinery, New Longton, PRESTON, PR4 4YB.
RILEY, Mrs. Susan Jane, ACA *1989;* 5 Nascot Road, WATFORD, WD17 4RD.
•RILEY, Mr. Terence David, ACA *2004;* Ward Goodman (Wareham) Limited, 18 West Street, WAREHAM, DORSET, BH20 4JX.
RILEY, Mr. Thomas David, BSc ACA *2003;* 4 Paris Avenue, Winstanley, WIGAN, WN3 6FA.
•RILEY, Mr. William Laurence, BA FCA *1983;* Dyke Yaxley Limited, 1 Brassey Road, Old Potts Way, SHREWSBURY, SY3 7FA.
RILEY-SMITH, Mr. Alexander William Anthony, FCA *1971;* Allton Group, Po Box 4, Ure Bank, RIPON, HG4 1JE.
RIMELL, Mr. James Edward, BSc ACA *2005;* Albion, Bury Lane, WOKING, GU21 4RP.
RIMELL, Mrs. Katie Louise, ACA *2010;* 106 Wigorn Road, SMETHWICK, WEST MIDLANDS, B67 5HF.
RIMELL, Mr. Matthew Liam, MEng ACA *2007;* 106 Wigorn Road, SMETHWICK, WEST MIDLANDS, B67 5HF.
RIMELL, Miss. Sarah, BSc ACA *2007;* with BDO LLP, 125 Colmore Row, BIRMINGHAM, B3 3SD.
RIMER, Mr. Mark, BSc ACA *2006;* The Court House, Chenies, RICKMANSWORTH, HERTFORDSHIRE, WD3 6EU.
•RIMER, Mrs. Nicola Clare, BSc ACA *2004;* Salisbury Accounting & Payroll Services, Sunrize House, Downton, SALISBURY, SP5 3JJ.
•RIMINGTON, Mr. Christopher Laurence, FCA *1975;* (Tax Fac), Rimingtons, 14 Hill Brow, Kirk Ella, HULL, HU10 7PP.
RIMINGTON, Mr. David Blackett, MA FCA *1973;* 26 St. Bernards Road, SOLIHULL, B92 7BB.
RIMINGTON, Mr. Richard John, FCA *1952;* 29 Sunbury Avenue, Mill Hill, LONDON, NW7 3SL. (Life Member)
RIMINGTON, Mr. Stephen Brian, BA ACA *1990;* 71 Lingfield Avenue, KINGSTON UPON THAMES, KT1 2TL.
RIMMER, Miss. Barbara, BSc ACA *1987;* 28 Chapel Lane, Halebarns, ALTRINCHAM, WA15 0HN.
RIMMER, Mr. Christopher Alban, TD FCA ARPS *1964;* 65 Pear Tree Way, WELLINGTON, SOMERSET, TA21 9AB.
RIMMER, Mr. Christopher John, BA ACA *1992;* Fidelity International Limited, 25 Cannon Street, LONDON, EC4M 5TA.
RIMMER, Mr. Christopher William, BSc ACA *1992;* Fleet Estate Office, Manor Farm Holbeach Hurn, SPALDING, LINCOLNSHIRE, PE12 8LR.
•RIMMER, Mrs. Clare Frances, BSc FCA *1983;* (Tax Fac), Rimmer Case Partnership, Fir Tree House, Truemans Way, Hawarden, DEESIDE, CLWYD CH5 3LS. See also Clare F. Rimmer FCA
RIMMER, Mrs. Deborah Claire, BSc ACA *1998;* Route De La Chaniaz 5, 1807 BLONAY, SWITZERLAND.
RIMMER, Mr. John Charles Parry, BSc FCA *1973;* Moore Green, 22 Friars Street, SUDBURY, SUFFOLK, CO10 2AA.
RIMMER, Mr. John Edward, FCA *1954;* 3 Killicks Hill, PORTLAND, DORSET, DT5 1JW. (Life Member)
•RIMMER, Mr. Jonathan, BSc ACA *1993;* (Tax Fac), James Holyoak & Parker Limited, 1 Knights Court, Archers Way, Battlefield Enterprise Park, SHREWSBURY, SHROPSHIRE SY1 3GA.
•RIMMER, Mr. Keith, FCA *1968;* K Rimmer Services Ltd, 15 Condon Road, Barrow upon Soar, LOUGHBOROUGH, LEICESTERSHIRE, LE12 8NQ.
RIMMER, Mr. Kenneth Henry, BA FCA *1958;* 4 Green Bower Drive, BROMSGROVE, WORCESTERSHIRE, B61 0UN. (Life Member)
RIMMER, Mr. Malcolm Robert, MA ACA *1985;* (Tax Fac), 2 Allee des Jonquilles, 78630 ORGEVAL, FRANCE.
RIMMER, Mr. Malcolm Thomas, FCA *1959;* 21 Grenville Crescent, Bromborough, WIRRAL, MERSEYSIDE, CH63 0JT. (Life Member)
RIMMER, Mr. Michael John, BSc ACA *2006;* 41 Barley Road, Thelwall, WARRINGTON, CHESHIRE, WA4 2EZ.
RIMMER, Mr. Peter Richard, FCA *1993;* 14 Elmsett Close, Saxonfield, Great Sankey, WARRINGTON, WA5 3RX.
RIMMER, Miss. Sophie, BSc(Hons) ACA *2011;* 86 Marshall Court, Marshall Square, SOUTHAMPTON, SO15 2PG.
RIMMER, Mr. Stephen Charles, BA ACA *1985;* Rua Otavio Correa 391 Apt 4, Urca, RIO DE JANEIRO, 22291-180, BRAZIL.
RIMMINGTON, Mr. David Anthony, BEng ACA *1994;* 57 Swann Lane, Cheadle Hulme, CHEADLE, SK8 7HR.
RIMMINGTON, Mr. Richard Leon Edgar, BA(Econ) FCA *1968;* 27 Cleveland Road, STOCKPORT, SK4 4BS.
RINALDI, Miss. Santina, BA(Hons) ACA *2003;* ILCHESTER ESTATES, The Estate Office, Melbury Sampford, DORCHESTER, DORSET, DT2 0LF.
RINBERG, Mr. Richard Jonathan, BSc ACA *1978;* 55 Ahad Ha'Am, RA'ANANA, 43210, ISRAEL.
RINDERER, Mr. Thomas Alfred, ACA *2009;* Bismarckstr. 77, 70197 STUTTGART, GERMANY.
RING, Mrs. Alison Ruth, LLB FCA *1991;* 7 Henrys Avenue, WOODFORD GREEN, IG8 9RB.
RING, Mr. Andrew John, ACA *2009;* 22 Shearman Road, LONDON, SE3 9HX.
RING, Mr. Christopher John, ACA *1980;* Rensburg Sheppards Investment Management Ltd, 2 Gresham Street, LONDON, EC2V 7QN.
RING, Mr. Jamie Patrick, BSc ACA *2007;* 88 Spinney Road, Keyworth, NOTTINGHAM, NG12 5NG.
RING, Mr. John Paul, BSc FCA *1991;* Flat 1/B, Vincent House, Vincent Square, Westminster, LONDON, SW1P 2NB.
RING, Mr. Mark Robert, FCA *1991;* 4 Woodland Drive, Old Catton, NORWICH, NR6 7AX.
RING, Mr. Richard Peter, BA ACA *1997;* Apetito Ltd, Canal Road, TROWBRIDGE, BA14 8RJ.
•RING, Mr. Rory Robert, FCA *1973;* Ring, 443 C Queen Street E, TORONTO M5A 1T6, ON, CANADA.
RINGER, Mrs. Amanda Maria, BA ACA *1994;* Carisbrooke Shipping Ltd Bridge House, 38 Medina Road, COWES, ISLE OF WIGHT, PO31 7DA.
RINGHAM, Miss. Catherine Mary, BA ACA *1992;* Brasenose Farmhouse, Oxford Road, Steeple Aston, BICESTER, OXFORDSHIRE, OX25 5QG.
RINGHAM, Mr. Paul Michael, BSc ACA *1995;* 28 The Hall, Foxes Dale, Blackheath, LONDON, SE3 9BE.
RINGHAM, Mr. Steven Paul, BA ACA *2001;* Yew Tree Cottage Down End, Chieveley, NEWBURY, RG20 8TS.
RINGROSE, Miss. Aleeta, ACA *2011;* Flat 805, Collingwood House, Dolphin Square, LONDON, SW1V 3NG.
•RINGROSE, Mr. Charles Howard, BA FCA *1996;* Barber Harrison & Platt, 2 Rutland Park, SHEFFIELD, S10 2PD.
RINGROSE, Mr. Christopher James, FCA *1968;* Lindum Lodge, Orchard Close, Risby, BURY ST. EDMUNDS, IP28 6QL.
RINGROSE, Mr. Christopher Jude, BSc ACA *1998;* African Century Ltd, 42 Queen Annes Gate, LONDON, SW1H 9AP.
•RINGROSE, Mr. Mark William Francis, BSc FCA *1987;* Farrar Smith Limited, 2 Woodside Mews, Clayton Wood Close, LEEDS, LS16 6QE.
RINGROSE, Mr. Nigel John Carter, FCA *1964;* 11 Rue du Belvedere, 56400 AURAY, FRANCE.
RINGROSE, Mr. Paul Andrew, BSc ACA *1990;* Brightpoint Asia Pacific, PO Box 6012, FRENCHS FOREST, NSW 1640, AUSTRALIA.
RINGROSE, Mr. Robert Hollingworth, BA FCA *1978;* 15 Napier Avenue, LONDON, SW6 3PS.
RINGROW, Miss. Caroline Sarah, ACA *2008;* Anglo American Plc Anglo American House, 20 Carlton House Terrace, LONDON, SW1Y 5AN.
RINGROW, Mr. David Colin, BA FCA *1976;* Moonrakers, Pit Farm Road, GUILDFORD, GU1 2JL.
•RINGROW, Mr. Peter Randolph William, FCA *1977;* Vale & West, Victoria House, 26 Queen Victoria Street, READING, RG1 1TG.
RINGSHALL, Miss. Joanna Elizabeth, BA ACA *1985;* The Grange, Battenhall Avenue, WORCESTER, WR5 2HN.
RINGWOOD, Mr. George, FCA *1951;* 26 Dower Chase, Escrick, YORK, NORTH YORKSHIRE, YO19 6JF. (Life Member)
RINK, Mr. Andrew Charles, BA ACA *1993;* 53 Oakwood Lane, Bowdon, ALTRINCHAM, CHESHIRE, WA14 3DL.
RINK, Mr. Denis John, FCA *1953;* 14 Harefield, Hinchley Wood, ESHER, KT10 9TQ. (Life Member)
RINKOFF, Mrs. Ilana Rosalind, BA ACA *1990;* 34a Chiltern Avenue, BUSHEY, WD23 4QB.
RINSLER, Mrs. Ann Linda, BSc ACA *1979;* 73 Woodlands Road, SURBITON, SURREY, KT6 6PW.
RINTOUL, Mr. Graeme Forbes, BSc ACA *1991;* 22 Acacia Road, HAWTHORNDENE, SA 5051, AUSTRALIA.
RINTOUL, Mr. Kevin James, MA ACA *1996;* Iron Mountain, Whitelan House, Alderstone Business Park, MacMillan Road, LIVINGSTON, WEST LOTHIAN EH54 7DF.
RINTOUL, Mrs. Nicola Jane, ACA *1995;* 20 Rookswood Lane, Rockbeare, EXETER, EX5 2LG.
RINTOUL, Mr. Toby, BSc(Hons) ACA *2000;* Johnston Carmichael, 7 - 11 Melville Street, EDINBURGH, EH3 7PE.
RINTOUL-HOAD, Mr. Oliver, ACA *2009;* Virgin Media First Floor, 90 Long Acre, LONDON, WC2E9RA.
RINU, Mr. George, ACA *2010;* 20 Thrifts Mead, Theydon Bois, EPPING, ESSEX, CM16 7NF.
RIO SIXTO, Miss. Patricia, ACA *2008;* 35 Elmers Court, Post Office Lane, BEACONSFIELD, BUCKINGHAMSHIRE, HP9 1QF.
RIODA, Mr. Peter James, MSc ACA *1999;* Sanne Group, 13 Castle Street, ST HELIER, JE4 5UT.
RIORDAN, Mr. James Ian Killorn, FCA *1958;* Flat 5, Braemar House, 33 Bidston Road, Oxton, PRENTON, MERSEYSIDE CH43 6UH. (Life Member)
RIORDAN, Mr. Michael, BComm ACA *2004;* 44 Helena Road, LONDON, E13 0DU.
•RIORDAN, Mr. Timothy Michael, FCA *1978;* (Tax Fac), Launceston Limited, 2 Barley Fields, Dark Lane, East Grafton, MARLBOROUGH, WILTSHIRE SN8 3DR.
RIORDAN-WILLIAMS, Miss. Emma Claire, BA ACA *2007;* 72 Strathmore Road, BRISTOL, BS7 9QJ.
RIP, Mr. Martin Raymond, LLB ACA *1999;* 4771 Woodrow Crescent, NORTH VANCOUVER V7K 3A6, BC, CANADA.
RIPLEY, Mrs. Alison Fiona, BA ACA *1990;* Garden Flat, 50 Fairhazel Gardens, West Hampstead, LONDON, NW6 3SJ.
RIPLEY, Mrs. Claire Anne, ACA MAAT *2003;* 15 Birch View, CHESTER LE STREET, DH2 2XP.
RIPLEY, Mr. Giles Oscar Rene, BSc(Hons) ACA *2000;* P A News Ltd, 292 Vauxhall Bridge Road, LONDON, SW1V 1AE.
RIPLEY, Mrs. Helen, BA ACA FCCA *1995;* 16 Westfield, SELBY, YO8 9DH.
RIPLEY, Ms. Helen, ACA *1995;* 8 Astley Drive, WHITLEY BAY, TYNE AND WEAR, NE26 4AE.
RIPLEY, Mr. Joel Charles, BA ACA *2000;* Norbeck Cottage, Leyfield Farm, High Moor Road, North Rigton, LEEDS, LS17 0AA.
RIPLEY, Mr. Mark Neil, BSc(Hons) ACA *2010;* 4 Wichling Close, CANTERBURY, KENT, CT2 7QR.
RIPLEY, Mr. Owen, FCA *1959;* 50 Acorn Ridge, Walton, CHESTERFIELD, S42 7HE. (Life Member)
RIPLEY, Mr. Paul Francis, BSc ACA *2003;* 87 Old Woolwich Road, LONDON, SE10 9PP.
•RIPLEY, Mr. Stanley George, FCA *1937;* 11 Chesterton Avenue, SEAFORD, EAST SUSSEX, BN25 3RL. (Life Member)
RIPPE, Mr. Craig Nicholas, ACA CFA *2001;* 1-6 Lombard Street, LONDON, EC3V 9JU.
RIPPE, Mr. David, BA FCA *1970;* 5 Knapp Ridge, LEDBURY, HR8 1BJ.
RIPPETH, Mrs. Jacqueline, MBA BSc FCA *1986;* Cambridge Assessment, 1 Hills Road, CAMBRIDGE, CB1 2EU.
RIPPIN, Mr. Stephen, BA(Hons) ACA *2004;* 5 Beech Farm Drive, Tytherington, MACCLESFIELD, CHESHIRE, SK10 2ES.
RIPPINGALE, Mr. Simon John, BCom FCA CTA *1977;* (Tax Fac), Parson's Piece, Church Lane, COLCHESTER, ESSEX, CO3 4DX.
RIPPON, Miss. Claire Louise, ACA *2009;* 3 The Newlands, Alabaster Lane Cromford, MATLOCK, DERBYSHIRE, DE4 3QJ.
RIPPON, Mr. Duncan Thomas, BA FCA *1976;* Oaklands, 1 Long Lane, Fradley, LICHFIELD, WS13 8NS.
RIPPON, Mr. George John Wheatley, FCA *1970;* 2 Beacon Close, PENRITH, CUMBRIA, CA11 8QH.
RIPPON, Mr. Nigel Lee, BA ACA *1995;* 5 Moatfield, YORK, YO10 3PT.
RIPPON, Mr. Thomas, BA ACA *2011;* 61 Green Lane, Eccleshall, STAFFORD, ST21 6BB.
RISBEY, Mr. John David, FCA *1968;* 4 Dell Court, Dell Road, GRAYS, ESSEX, RM17 5JS.
RISBY, Mrs. Clare Una, FCA *1977;* Mill Cottage, Newbridge, Colemans Hatch, HARTFIELD, TN7 4ES.
RISBY, Mrs. Helen Louise, ACA *2002;* 74 Stubley Mill Road, LITTLEBOROUGH, LANCASHIRE, OL15 8SE.
RISBY, Mr. Simon Peter, BA ACA *1992;* 23 Julius Road, Bishopston, BRISTOL, BS7 8EU.
RISDALE, Mr. Philip Edward, BA ACA *1985;* 92 Hillview Road, Carlton, NOTTINGHAM, NG4 1LD.
RISDON, Mr. Michael Francis, BSc ACA *1986;* 3 Swallow Wood, FAREHAM, PO16 8UF.
RISDON, Mr. Richard Edward Ross, FCA *1961;* Drysdale Nurse & Co, 35 Purlieu Way, Theydon Bois, EPPING, CM16 7EH.
•RISEBOROUGH, Mr. John Leslie, FCA *1973;* Field View House, 3 Horses Head, Upton, NORWICH, NR13 6AZ.
RISELEY, Mr. Clifford Frederick, FCA *1956;* 67 Hamilton Road, Cockfosters, BARNET, EN4 9HD. (Life Member)
RISELEY, Mr. John Eric, FCA *1962;* 7 Coundon Court, KILLINEY, COUNTY DUBLIN, IRELAND.
RISEMAN, Mr. David Warren, FCA *1969;* 50 Crosby Road, WESTCLIFF-ON-SEA, ESSEX, SS0 8LG.
RISHI, Mr. Sahil Nath, BA(Hons) ACA *2009;* Flat 2, 26 Yukon Road, LONDON, SW12 9PU.
•RISHIRAJ, Mr. Ashwani Kumar, BA FCA *1993;* Luckmans Duckett Parker Limited, 44-45 Queens Road, COVENTRY, CV1 3EH.
RISHWORTH, Mrs. Joanne Elizabeth, BSc ACA CTA *2003;* 105 Main Road, Higher Kinnerton, CHESTER, CH4 9AJ.
RISHWORTH, Mr. John Richard, FCA *1970;* 117 Winchester Road, Four Marks, ALTON, HAMPSHIRE, GU34 5HU.
RISHWORTH, Mr. Michael James, BSc ACA *2003;* 105 Main Road Higher Kinnerton, CHESTER, CH4 9AJ.
RISHWORTH, Mr. Norman, FCA *1966;* 1141 Pintail Drive, QUALICUM BEACH V9K 1C8, BC, CANADA.
RISING, Mr. William Stanley, BA FCA *1977;* 8400 Majestic Lake Court, Texas, MONTGOMERY, TX 77316, UNITED STATES.
RISINO, Mr. Anthony John, PhD MSc BEng ACA *1998;* 10 Broughton Close, Grappenhall-Heys, WARRINGTON, CHESHIRE, WA4 3DR.
RISK, Mrs. Lynda Ann, BSc ACA *1991;* 42 Riddings Lane, Hartford, NORTHWICH, CW8 1NA.
RISLEY, Mr. Allan David, ACA *1980;* Morris Feinmann House, 178 Palatine Road, MANCHESTER, M20 2YW.
RISLEY, Mr. Steven Donald, ACA *1983;* 36 Kings Walden Rise, STEVENAGE, SG2 0JX.

•RISON, Mr. Robin Donald, FCA *1977;* Kelmscott Consulting Limited, 43 Kelmscott Road, Harborne, BIRMINGHAM, B17 8QW.
RISSBROOK, Mr. Anthony Edward, BSc ACA *1992;* Co-operative Travel Management 5 Hargreaves Court, Dyson Way Staffordshire Technology Park, STAFFORD, ST18 0WN.
RISSBROOK, Mr. John Timothy, FCA *1965;* Whiston Grange, Albrighton, WOLVERHAMPTON, WV7 3BU. (Life Member)
•RISSBROOK, Mrs. Susan Mary, BSc ACA *1992;* (Tax Fac), PricewaterhouseCoopers LLP, Cornwall Court, 19 Cornwall Street, BIRMINGHAM, B3 2DT. See also PricewaterhouseCoopers
RISSEN, Mr. Daniel, LLB ACA *2006;* 13 Watling Mansions, Watling Street, RADLETT, WD7 7NA.
•RISSEN, Mr. Howard Theo, FCA *1976;* (Tax Fac), The Business Orchard Consultancy Limited, 3a Chestnut House, Farm Close, Shenley, RADLETT, HERTFORDSHIRE WD7 9AD.
RISSIK, Mr. Angus Hawker, BEng ACA *2001;* 50 Chatto Road, LONDON, SW11 6LL.
RISSO, Mr. James Alexander Clunes, BSc ACA *1995;* Victor Chandler Intl, Leanse Place, 50 Town Range, GIBRALTAR, GIBRALTAR.
RIST, Mr. Martin Jonathan, BA FCA *1971;* Southdown Cottage, Southdown Road, Shawford, WINCHESTER, SO21 2BX.
RIST, Mrs. Wendy Jane, BA ACA *1992;* 28 St. Mary Street, MONMOUTH, GWENT, NP25 3DB.
RITACCA, Miss. Rosalynd Amy Louise, ACA *2009;* 63 Dollis Hill Avenue, Cricklewood, LONDON, NW2 6QU.
RITCHENS, Miss. Joanne, ACA *2009;* 5 Ullswater Close, BRISTOL, BS30 5XR.
RITCHIE, Mr. Alan Francis, FCA *1963;* 5 Swan Court, York Road, HARROGATE, NORTH YORKSHIRE, HG1 2QH.
RITCHIE, Mr. Alan Peter, FCA CPFA *1966;* 45 Crutchfield Lane, WALTON-ON-THAMES, KT12 2QY.
RITCHIE, Mr. Alexander Charles Smail, BSc ACA *2003;* 21 Belvedere Square, LONDON, SW19 5DJ.
RITCHIE, Mrs. Carol Ann, BA ACA ATII *1985;* 34 Hob Hey Lane, Culcheth, WARRINGTON, WA3 4NW.
RITCHIE, Mrs. Caroline Mary, BSc ACA *1997;* Durfold, Durfold Hill, Warnham, HORSHAM, RH12 3RY.
RITCHIE, Mrs. Claire Susan, ACA *1987;* Tudor Lodge, 89 Weald Road, SEVENOAKS, TN13 1QJ.
RITCHIE, Mr. David Alan Teviotdale, FCA *1956;* 6 Aspen Close, Willand, CULLOMPTON, DEVON, EX15 2ST. (Life Member)
RITCHIE, Mr. David James, BA ACA *1993;* Scuffits, Elphicks Farm, West Street, Hunton, MAIDSTONE, KENT ME15 0SB.
RITCHIE, Mr. Duncan Smail, FCA *1972;* Old Werretts, Castle Combe, CHIPPENHAM, WILTSHIRE, SN14 7HH. (Life Member)
RITCHIE, Mr. Duncan Stuart, FCA *1977;* 4 Manor Barns Lane, Finchampstead, WOKINGHAM, BERKSHIRE, RG40 3TQ.
RITCHIE, Mrs. Glenda Tracey, BA ACA *1992;* 20 Godstone Road, OXTED, RH8 9JT.
RITCHIE, Mr. Graham Alistair, BA ACA *1999;* Spencer's Cottage, 1 New Cottages, Bendish, HITCHIN, SG4 8JD.
RITCHIE, Mr. Guy Charles, BA ACA *1989;* 157 Humber Road, LONDON, SE3 7EG.
RITCHIE, Mr. Hamish Smail, FCA *1968;* 24 Warren Way, Digswell, WELWYN, HERTFORDSHIRE, AL6 0DH.
RITCHIE, Miss. Helen Margaret, BA ACA *1991;* 6 Deansgate Lane, Formby, LIVERPOOL, L37 3LG.
RITCHIE, Mr. James Gordon, FCA *1962;* Flat 7, Hesketh Manor, 12 Hesketh Road, SOUTHPORT, PR9 9PD. (Life Member)
RITCHIE, Mr. Jason Victor, ACA MAAT *2004;* 1-3 Baines Street, CLIFTON BEACH, QLD 4879, AUSTRALIA.
RITCHIE, Mr. John, BA ACA *1993;* with PricewaterhouseCoopers LLP, 32 Albyn Place, ABERDEEN, AB10 1YL.
•RITCHIE, Mr. John Alan, FCA *1965;* John Ritchie, Downsview, 1 Brambles, HASSOCKS, BN6 8EQ.
RITCHIE, Mr. John Fraser, BA ACA *1992;* 91 Kirklake Road, Formby, LIVERPOOL, L37 2DA.
RITCHIE, Mr. John Scott, FCA *1975;* Hunters Lodge, 20 Godstone Road, OXTED, RH8 9JT.
RITCHIE, Mr. Jonathan Allan, BA(Hons) ACA *2001;* 7 Relton Terrace, WHITLEY BAY, TYNE AND WEAR, NE25 8DY.
RITCHIE, Miss. Kate, ACA *2011;* 62c Belsize Park Gardens, LONDON, NW3 4NE.
RITCHIE, Mr. Keith Archibald, BA ACA *1984;* Tudor Lodge, 89 Weald Road, SEVENOAKS, TN13 1QJ.
RITCHIE, Mrs. Lai-Shen, FCA MCT *1974;* LR Associates Ltd, 72 Albemarle Road, BECKENHAM, BR3 5HR.
RITCHIE, Mr. Malcolm, BSc ACA *1982;* 12 Town End View, HOLMFIRTH, HD9 1AX.
RITCHIE, Mr. Neil, BCom ACA *1986;* 56 Higher Lane, LYMM, CHESHIRE, WA13 0BG.
RITCHIE, Mr. Neil James, BA ACA ACCA *1997;* Dyson Ltd, Tetbury Hill, MALMESBURY, SN16 0RP.
RITCHIE, Mr. Niall Macgregor, FCA *1977;* Flat 9 Chateau Royal, La Rue Vardon Grouville, JERSEY, JE3 9HT.
RITCHIE, Miss. Rachel Catherine, MA ACA *1989;* 23 Lavant Road, CHICHESTER, WEST SUSSEX, PO19 5RA.
RITCHIE, Miss. Samantha Jane, BSc ACA *1991;* Avaya UK Avaya House, Cathedral Hill, GUILDFORD, SURREY, GU2 7YL.
RITCHIE, Mr. Stanley Arthur, FCA *1951;* The Old Orchard, 52 Anderwood Drive, Sway, LYMINGTON, HAMPSHIRE, SO41 6AW. (Life Member)
•RITCHIE, Mr. Stuart David, FCA ATII *1990;* (Tax Fac), Ritchie Phillips LLP, The Old Granary, Field Place Estate, Field Place, Broadbridge Heath, HORSHAM WEST SUSSEX RH12 3PB.
RITCHIE, Mrs. Susan Amanda, LLB ACA *1994;* 2nd Floor - Edinburgh Building, University of Sunderland, Chester Road, SUNDERLAND, SR1 3SD.
RITCHIE, Mr. Timothy James, BA ACA *2006;* 50 Spring Thyme Fold, LITTLEBOROUGH, LANCASHIRE, OL15 8DJ.
RITCHIE, Miss. Victoria Louise, BA ACA *1992;* Flat E103, 12 Hertsmere Road, LONDON, E14 4AE.
•RITCHIE, Mr. William James, BSc FCA *1990;* Bill Ritchie FCA, 18 Westbury Road, CROYDON, CR0 2ES.
•RITCHIE, Mr. William Neil, FCA *1969;* 2 Acacia Road, HAMPTON, TW12 3DS.
RITCHIE, Mr. William Robin Smail, BSc(Hons) ACA *2001;* Monitor, 4 Matthew Parker Street, LONDON, SW1H 9NP.
RITCHLEY, Mr. Martin Howard, FCA *1969;* The Beeches, 1 Abberton Way, COVENTRY, WEST MIDLANDS, CV4 7HF.
RITCHLEY, Miss. Suzannah, ACA *2011;* Flat 19 Helsby Court, Pollitt Drive, LONDON, NW8 8JQ.
RITSON, Mrs. Christine Ann, BSc ACA *1995;* 197 Darras Road, Darras Hall, Ponteland, NEWCASTLE UPON TYNE, NE20 9AF.
RITSON, Mrs. Lisa Jane, BA ACA *2006;* 4 Bradley Street, Crookes, SHEFFIELD, S10 1PB.
RITSON, Ms. Ru-Ying Helen, ACA *2011;* Flat 2, 87 Cleaveland Road, SURBITON, SURREY, KT6 4AJ.
RITTER, Mr. Daniel, ACA *2011;* 12 Hayeley Drive, Bradley Stoke, BRISTOL, BS32 8AE.
RITTER, Mr. Michael John, BSc ACA *1996;* 11 All Saints Villas Road, CHELTENHAM, GLOUCESTERSHIRE, GL52 2HB.
•RITZEMA, Mr. Gary, BA ACA *1992;* (Tax Fac), O'Reilly, Ullswater House, Duke St, PENRITH, CA11 7LY. See also O'Reilly N.T. & Partners
RITZEMA, Mrs. Joanne Lesley, BA ACA *1997;* The Barn, Chapel Burn, Nether Denton, BRAMPTON, CA8 2LY.
RIVERS, Miss. Anna Marie, BA BSc ACA *1999;* 192 The Moors, KIDLINGTON, OX5 2AD.
RIVERS, Mr. Anthony Malcolm Warner, BA FCA *1972;* Prudential Plc, Governors House, Laurence Pountney Hill, LONDON, EC4R 0HH.
RIVERS, Mr. Dominic, BSc ACA *2004;* Dulux Decorator Centre Manchester Road, West Timperley, ALTRINCHAM, CHESHIRE, WA14 5PG.
RIVERS, Mrs. Emma Claire, BSc ACA *2000;* Seniah Honey Lane, Angmering, LITTLEHAMPTON, WEST SUSSEX, BN16 4AB.
RIVERS, Mr. Graham Paul, BSc ACA *1999;* Seniah Honey Lane, Angmering, LITTLEHAMPTON, WEST SUSSEX, BN16 4AB.
RIVERS, Mrs. Nicoleta, ACA *2011;* 96 Northfield Road, THATCHAM, BERKSHIRE, RG18 3EN.
RIVERS, Mr. Paul Edward, MA FCA *1981;* Fox Cottage, 1A Abingdon Road, Tubney, ABINGDON, OX13 5QL.
RIVETT, Mr. Andrew, BA FCA *1988;* 11 Carden Crescent, BRIGHTON, BN1 8TQ.
RIVETT, Miss. Caroline Jane, BSc ACA *1993;* 124 St. Georges Avenue, LONDON, N7 0AH.
RIVETT, Mr. David Geoffrey, FCA *1958;* The Meads, The Common, Dunsfold, GODALMING, GU8 4LE. (Life Member)
RIVETT, Mr. Eric Lionel, FCA *1958;* 32 Old Park Ridings, Grange Park, LONDON, N21 2ES. (Life Member)
RIVETT, Miss. Natalie, BSc ACA *2009;* 122 Perry Street, Crayford, DARTFORD, KENT, DA1 4RL.
•RIVETT, Mr. Nicholas William, FCA *1971;* (Tax Fac), N.W. Rivett, 41 Thompson Avenue, COLCHESTER, CO3 4HW.
•RIVETT, Mr. Philip George, BSc ACA *1979;* PricewaterhouseCoopers LLP, 7 More London Riverside, LONDON, SE1 2RT. See also PricewaterhouseCoopers
RIVIERE, Mr. David John, MA FCA *1982;* 4 The Droveway, HAYWARDS HEATH, WEST SUSSEX, RH16 1LL.
RIVIERE, Mrs. Elizabeth Anne, MSc BA ACA *1985;* 4 The Droveway, HAYWARDS HEATH, WEST SUSSEX, RH16 1LL.
RIVIERE, Mr. Peregrine Douglas Gonzague, BA ACA *1997;* Garford House, Garford Road, OXFORD, OX2 6UY.
RIX, Mr. Alexander Spencer Christopher, MA ACA *1988;* 6 Meynell Crescent, Hackney, LONDON, E9 7AS.
RIX, Mr. Barnaby Harwood, BSc(Hons) ACA *2001;* 6 Keene Fields, Linton, CAMBRIDGE, CB21 4AA.
RIX, Miss. Caroline, BSc ACA *2011;* Flat 25, Bennets Courtyard, Watermill Way, LONDON, SW19 2RW.
RIX, Mrs. Catherine Louise, BSc(Hons) ACA *2004;* 41 Park Road North, NEWTON-LE-WILLOWS, MERSEYSIDE, WA12 9TA.
RIX, Mr. Christopher S, BSc ACA CTA PGCE *2002;* 36 The Parchments, NEWTON-LE-WILLOWS, MERSEYSIDE, WA12 0DY.
RIX, Mr. David Geoffrey Andrew, BA ACA *1988;* 39 The Avenue, HERTFORD, SG14 3DR.
RIX, Mr. David Hilaire, BSc(Econ) FCA *1975;* 18 Siegfried Walk, BINGLEY, WEST YORKSHIRE, BD16 3QF.
RIX, Mr. Eric Rodway, BA FCA *1964;* Field House, Pettiwell, Garsington, OXFORD, OX44 9DB.
RIX, Mr. Ian John, BA ACA *1990;* The Barn, Lychgate Lane, Aston Flamville, HINCKLEY, LE10 3AQ.
RIX, Mr. Jeremy Hugh Rodway, BSc ACA *1990;* B U P A Care Services, Bridge House, Outwood Lane, Horsforth, LEEDS, LS18 4UP.
RIX, Mr. John Edward, MA FCA *1964;* Carrer De Les Mimoses 28, Can Macia, 08810 SANT PERE DE RIBES, SPAIN. (Life Member)
RIX, Mr. John George Rodway, FCA *1956;* Wodehouse, Liphook Road, Headley, BORDON, HAMPSHIRE, GU35 8RF. (Life Member)
RIX, Mrs. Julie Lorraine, BSc ACA *1992;* The Barn, Lychgate Lane, Aston Flamville, HINCKLEY, LE10 3AQ.
RIX, Mrs. Lesley Ann, BA ACA *2002;* 36 The Parchments, NEWTON-LE-WILLOWS, WA12 0DY.
RIX, Mr. Martin Paul, MA FCA *1998;* Moore Stephens, Office 303, 7 Kamenskaya Street, 630099 NOVOSIBIRSK, RUSSIAN FEDERATION.
RIX, Mr. Stewart, BSc FCA *1990;* Cable & Wireless UK, Worldwide House, Western Road, BRACKNELL, BERKSHIRE, RG12 1RW.
RIXON, Mr. Mark John, BSc ACA *2010;* 15 Devonshire Gardens, Tilehurst, READING, RG31 6FW.
RIYAT, Mrs. Sheetal, BSc ACA CTA *2004;* 8 Westbury Lodge Close, PINNER, MIDDLESEX, HA5 3FG.
•RIZAN, Mrs. Patricia Mary, FCA *1982;* (Tax Fac), Patricia Rizan, 21 Chervil Way, Burghfield Common, READING, RG7 3YX.
RIZK, Miss. Farida Jane, BA ACA *1996;* 20 Thiam Siew Avenue, SINGAPORE 436857, SINGAPORE.
RIZVI, Mr. Feroz, FCA *1979;* ICI Pakistan Ltd, 5 West Wharf, KARACHI, PAKISTAN.
RIZVI, Mr. Irfan Mehdi, ACA *2010;* Flat 23, Clarinet Court, 19 Symphony Close, EDGWARE, MIDDLESEX, HA8 0EH.
RIZVI, Mr. Syed Fida Ali, BSc ACA *2003;* Flat F, 8 Blackburnes Mews, LONDON, W1K 2LG.
•RIZVI, Mr. Syed Masroor Mehdi, FCA *1984;* Rizvi & Co, Wonea House, 2 Richmond Road, ISLEWORTH, MIDDLESEX, TW7 7BL.
RIZVI, Mr. Syed Samar Abbas, BA ACA *2004;* Lloyds TSB Bank Plc, 5th Floor, 25 Gresham Street, LONDON, EC2V 7HN.
RIZVI, Mr. Syed Zafar Husain, FCA *1978;* Das Holding LLC, PO BOX 33811, ABU DHABI, UNITED ARAB EMIRATES.
RIZVI, Mr. Wasi Abbas, ACA *2009;* 11 Westview Close, LONDON, W10 6QZ.
RIZVI, Miss. Yusra, ACA *2010;* 31 Grove Road, NORTHWOOD, MIDDLESEX, HA6 2AP.
RIZWANULLAH, Mr. Muhammad, FCA *1974;* 615 Seventh Avenue, New Hyde Park, NEW YORK, NY 11040, UNITED STATES.
RIZZO, Mr. Michael Albert Vincent, BA ACA *2001;* Flat 5, Santa Marija Apartments, Olive Street, The Gardens, ST JULIANS STJ1955, MALTA.
•ROACH, Mr. David Andrew, MA FCA *1981;* PricewaterhouseCoopers S.a.r.l., 400 route d'Esch, B P 1443, L-1014 LUXEMBOURG, LUXEMBOURG.
ROACH, Mr. Geoffrey Leslie, FCA *1966;* 2 Yew Tree Close, Curzon Park, CALNE, WILTSHIRE, SN11 0JP. (Life Member)
ROACH, Mrs. Janet Lesley, BSc ACA *1991;* 18 Aylesbury Grove, Middleton, MANCHESTER, M24 2TG.
ROACH, Miss. Joanna Katharine, MA ACA *1997;* 179 Thomas Street, BRIGHTON EAST, 3187, AUSTRALIA.
•ROACH, Mr. John Roger Murray, FCA TEP *1969;* (Tax Fac), John Roger Murray Roach, 1 St. Andrew's Drive, Holmes Chapel, CREWE, CW4 7DN.
ROACH, Mr. Mark John, LLB ACA CTA *2002;* 5 Temple Road, CROYDON, CR0 1HU.
ROACH, Mr. Matthew David, BSc(Econ) ACA *1996;* Exeter & Devon Airport Ltd Exeter Airport, Clyst Honiton, EXETER, EX5 2BD.
•ROACH, Mr. Nicolas James, BSc ACA *1996;* Northbrook Park, FARNHAM, SURREY, GU10 5EU.
ROACH, Mr. Paul Vyvyan, BA FCA *1981;* P O Box 625, KABUL, AFGHANISTAN.
ROACH, Mrs. Sarah, BA ACA *2005;* 24 Fullaford Park, BUCKFASTLEIGH, DEVON, TQ11 0NJ.
•ROACH, Mr. Thomas William, BSc ACA *2000;* Winter Rule LLP, Lowin House, Tregolls Road, TRURO, CORNWALL, TR1 2NA. See also Francis Clark LLP
ROACH, Mr. Tom Edward, BSc ACA *1996;* 5 Church Path Road, Pill, BRISTOL, BS20 0EE.
•ROACH, Mr. William Graham Dunstan, FCA *1966;* 14 Tynedale Close, Oadby, LEICESTER, LE2 4TS.
ROADNIGHT, Mr. Nicholas John, FCA *1977;* 7 Wellswood Gardens, ROWLAND'S CASTLE, PO9 6DN.
ROADS, Mr. Robin Warner Stanwell, FCA *1962;* 2 North Lodge, Ealing Green, LONDON, W5 5QU. (Life Member)
ROADS-MERRY, Mr. Alan John, BA ACA *1978;* 58 Daniel Way, Silver End, WITHAM, CM8 3SS.
ROAN, Mrs. Jemma Lucy, BSc ACA *2005;* 7 Linden Road, ROMSEY, SO51 8DA.
ROARTY, Mrs. Suzanne Louise, BCom ACA *1992;* Duntally, CREESLOUGH, COUNTY DONEGAL, IRELAND.
ROAST, Mr. Charles William, BSc ACA *1996;* 38 Dewhurst Road, LONDON, W14 0ES.
•ROBACK, Mr. Barry Peter, FCA *1975;* Barry Roback & Co, 17 Parkside Drive, EDGWARE, MIDDLESEX, HA8 8JU. See also Privilege Accounts Limited
ROBACK, Mr. Jonathan Nicholas, BA ACA *1995;* 3 Old Hall Close, PINNER, HA5 4ST.
ROBARTS, Mr. Charles James, BSc ACA *1989;* Network Rail, Kings Place, 90 York Way, LONDON, N1 9AG.
ROBARTS, Mr. John James William, BA FCA *1996;* ZAO Deloitte & Touche CIS, 5 Lesnaya Street, Building B, 125047 MOSCOW, RUSSIAN FEDERATION.
ROBARTS, Mr. Michael, FCA *1968;* Priory Farm, Balscote, BANBURY, OXFORDSHIRE, OX15 6JL.
ROBB, Miss. Alison Jane, BSc FCA *1994;* Group Strategy & Planning A2, Nationwide Building Society, Pipers Way, SWINDON, WILTSHIRE, SN38 1NW.
ROBB, Mr. Christopher Michael, FCA *1972;* Henley Gap Chilcroft Lane, Kingsley Green, HASLEMERE, GU27 3LZ.
ROBB, Mr. Douglas Stewart, BA ACA *2000;* 1 Burnbrae Drive, EDINBURGH, MIDLOTHIAN, EH12 8AS.
ROBB, Miss. Fiona Mackenzie, BA ACA *1992;* 86 Cranworth Gardens, Stockwell, LONDON, SW9 0NT.
•ROBB, Mrs. Georgina Alison, BSc ARCS FCA *1995;* Deloitte LLP, 2 New Street Square, LONDON, EC4A 3BZ. See also Deloitte & Touche LLP
ROBB, Mrs. Gillian Fiona, BSc ACA *1991;* (Tax Fac), 166 Sheen Road, RICHMOND, TW9 1XD.
ROBB, Mr. Hector Ian Samuel, BSc FCA *1974;* Delichon House, Park Lane, Hatherton, NANTWICH, CW5 7QG.
ROBB, Miss. Jennifer Lynn Houston, BSc ACA *1996;* 40 Belle Vue Road, HENLEY-ON-THAMES, OXFORDSHIRE, RG9 1JG.
•ROBB, Mrs. Linda Christine, BSc FCA *1984;* Robb & Co, 26 Mayes Close, WARLINGHAM, CR6 9LB.
ROBB, Mrs. Lynne, BSc ACA *1990;* 8 Old Bury Hill House, Old Bury Hill, Westcott, DORKING, SURREY, RH4 3JU.
ROBB, Mr. Matthew Peter, MA ACA *2001;* Robb & Co Gainsborough House, 14 Burnett Road, SUTTON COLDFIELD, B74 3EJ.
ROBB, Mr. Morris David, MA ACA CPA *1986;* 63 Cranston Road, Forest Hill, LONDON, SE23 2HA.

ROBB, Mr. Nicholas James Arden, BSc ACA CF *1984;* 1 Enderley Road, CLAYFIELD, QLD 4011, AUSTRALIA.
•**ROBB, Mr. Paul David, BSc ACA** *1989;* KPMG LLP, 15 Canada Square, LONDON, E14 5GL. See also KPMG Europe LLP
ROBB, Mr. Richard Bruce Duncan, BSc FCA *1975;* Briscoe House, 28 Church Street, Bathford, BATH, BA1 7RS.
•**ROBB, Mr. Stuart James, FCA** *1985;* Baker Tilly Tax & Advisory Services LLP, Lancaster House, 7 Elmfield Road, BROMLEY, BR1 1LT.
•**ROBB, Mr. Thomas Morgan, BA ACA** *2003;* PricewaterhouseCoopers LLP, 7 More London Riverside, LONDON, SE1 2RT. See also PricewaterhouseCoopers
ROBB, Mrs. Valerie Elizabeth, BSc ACA *1994;* Wildlife, Baldromma Moar, Lonan, ISLE OF MAN, IM4 6AG.
ROBBIE, Mr. David Andrew, MA ACA *1990;* Rexam Plc, 4 Millbank, LONDON, SW1P 3XR.
ROBBIE, Mr. Steven, BA ACA *1999;* 4 Balkaithly Farm Cottages, Dunino, ST ANDREWS, FIFE, KY16 8LU.
ROBBINGS, Mr. Adam Scott, BSc(Hons) ACA CMA *1999;* 202 N 42nd Street, SEATTLE, WA 98103, UNITED STATES.
ROBBINS, Mr. Allan, BSc ACA *2004;* 19 Chartwell Close, CROYDON, CR0 2AW.
ROBBINS, Mr. Andrew, BSc ACA *1993;* 16 Goldacre Close, Whitnash, LEAMINGTON SPA, WARWICKSHIRE, CV31 2TW.
ROBBINS, Mr. Andrew, BSc ACA *2002;* Floor 2, Barclays Bank Plc, PO Box 190, LEEDS, LS1 5WU.
•**ROBBINS, Mr. Anthony Thomas, FCA** *1978;* (Tax Fac), Tony Robbins FCA Limited, 8 Redwood Close, West End, SOUTHAMPTON, SO30 3SG.
ROBBINS, Mr. Christopher John, FCA *1972;* Camellia, Gorse Hill Road, VIRGINIA WATER, SURREY, GU25 4AU.
•**ROBBINS, Mr. Denis Cooper, FCA** *1973;* Robbins Partnership, 176 Monton Road, Monton, Eccles, MANCHESTER, M30 9GA.
ROBBINS, Mrs. Diane Lilian, ACA *1979;* Oakdene, 32 Robert Street, Lower Gornal, DUDLEY, DY3 2AY.
ROBBINS, Mr. Gerald James, BA FCA *1959;* 9 Doctor Crawford's Close, Windmill Road, Minchinhampton, STROUD, GL6 9EZ. (Life Member)
ROBBINS, Miss. Helen, ACA *2009;* 21 Marlborough Gardens, Hedge End, SOUTHAMPTON, SO30 2AS.
ROBBINS, Mr. Hugh Charles, BSc ACA *1994;* Lane End, 23 Driffield, CIRENCESTER, GLOUCESTERSHIRE, GL7 5PY.
ROBBINS, Mr. Ian Edward, BSc ACA *2005;* 23 Braeside Avenue, LONDON, SW19 3PU.
ROBBINS, Mr. Jonathan Rowland Meirion, BA ACA *2005;* 41 Kincora Grove, CLONTARF, COUNTY DUBLIN, IRELAND.
ROBBINS, Mr. Julian Simon, FCA *1974;* 28 Westbury Road, Finchley, LONDON, N12 7NX.
ROBBINS, Mrs. Karen Lorraine, BSS ACA *1991;* 14 Walsingham Gardens, Stoneleigh, EPSOM, KT19 0LU.
ROBBINS, Mrs. Karen Marie, BA(Hons) ACA *2001;* H B Accountants Amwell House, 19 Amwell Street, HODDESDON, HERTFORDSHIRE, EN11 8TS.
ROBBINS, Miss. Laura Catherine, BSc ACA CTA *2006;* (Tax Fac), 99 Stanmer Villas, BRIGHTON, BN1 7HN.
ROBBINS, Mr. Martin Louis Michael, FCA *1963;* 45 Wyddial Road, BUNTINGFORD, HERTFORDSHIRE, SG9 9AT.
ROBBINS, Mr. Michael, BA ACA *2000;* 2 Jersey Avenue, CHELTENHAM, GLOUCESTERSHIRE, GL52 2SZ.
ROBBINS, Mr. Paul Edward, BSc ACA *1981;* 53 Laurel Drive, Eccleston, ST. HELENS, MERSEYSIDE, WA10 5JB.
ROBBINS, Mr. Paul John Gilbert, BA ACA CTA *1990;* (Tax Fac), 9 Broad Gap, Bodicote, BANBURY, OX15 4DE.
ROBBINS, Mr. Peter, BSc FCA *1990;* 62 Azalea Drive, TROWBRIDGE, BA14 9GG.
ROBBINS, Mr. Peter James, BSc ACA *1989;* 25 Edwina Drive, POOLE, DORSET, BH17 7JG.
ROBBINS, Mr. Philip Mark, BSc ACA *1994;* Provident Financial Management Services Ltd, 1 Godwin Street, BRADFORD, BD1 2SU.
ROBBINS, Mr. Reginald Michael, FCA *1970;* 123 Mayals Road, Mayals, SWANSEA, SA3 5DH.
ROBBINS, Mrs. Rhian Elizabeth, BSc ACA *2002;* 20 Meadow Hill, St Davids Manor, Church Village, PONTYPRIDD, MID GLAMORGAN, CF38 1RX.
ROBBINS, Mr. Stephen Frederick, BSc ARCS ACA CTA *1993;* (Tax Fac), Credit Suisse, 20 Columbus Courtyard, LONDON, E14 4DA.
ROBBINS, Mr. Stuart John, BA FCA *1985;* 171 Higham Lane, NUNEATON, WARWICKSHIRE, CV11 6AN.
ROBBINS-CHERRY, Mr. Nicholas John, ACA *1996;* 18 Tymawr, Caversham, READING, RG4 7XR.
ROBBIRT, Miss. Karen Mary, BSc ACA ATII *1988;* The Old School House, Frensham, FARNHAM, SURREY, GU10 3EQ.
ROBBS DE LA HOYDE, Mr. Paul Frederick John, BEng ACA *1994;* 29 Springhead, TUNBRIDGE WELLS, KENT, TN2 3NY.
ROBER, Mr. Gustav, BSc ACA *2003;* Diploma PLC, 12 Charterhouse Square, LONDON, EC1M 6AX.
ROBERSON, Mr. Richard Arthur, FCA *1977;* Seltten, Hamm Court, WEYBRIDGE, KT13 8YE.
ROBERSON, Mr. Simon John Lewis, FCA *1976;* 48 Glebe Hyrst, SOUTH CROYDON, Surrey, CR2 9JF.
•**ROBERT, Mr. Gregory George, FCA** *1981;* Lince Salisbury, Avenue House, St Julian's Ave, St Peter Port, GUERNSEY, GY1 1WA. See also BKR Lince Salisbury Limited
•①**ROBERT, Mr. Ian, BSc FCA MIPA MABRP** *1990;* Kingston Smith & Partners LLP, Devonshire House, 60 Goswell Road, LONDON, EC1M 7AD. See also Kingston Smith Limited Liability Partnership
ROBERT, Mrs. Nicola Claire, BA ACA DChA *1994;* Folly Cottage, Wenden Road, Arkesden, SAFFRON WALDEN, ESSEX, CB11 4HB.
ROBERT, Mrs. Sarah, BA ACA *1992;* with James Cowper LLP, 3 Wesley Gate, Queens Road, READING, RG1 4AP.
ROBERT-SMITH, Robert Courtice, Esq MBE TD JP FCA *1947;* 4 Burlington Road, LEICESTER, LE2 3DD. (Life Member)
ROBERTJOHNS, Mr. Peter Henry, FCA *1973;* Eavesmere, North Road, Kingsland, LEOMINSTER, HR6 9RX.
ROBERTON, Mr. Ian David, ACA *2008;* KPMG, P.O. Box 493, Century Yard, Cricket Square, GEORGE TOWN, KY1-1106 CAYMAN ISLANDS.
ROBERTS, Mrs. Abiola Natalie, BSc ACA *2003;* 47 Berwick Road, BOREHAMWOOD, WD6 4BG.
•**ROBERTS, Mr. Adrian Lewis, BCom ACA** *2000;* Ernst & Young LLP, City Gate West, Toll House Hill, NOTTINGHAM, NG1 5FY. See also Ernst & Young Europe LLP
ROBERTS, Mr. Adrian Mark, BCom ACA *1988;* 12 Steps Close, Pinhoe, EXETER, EX1 3QH.
•**ROBERTS, Mr. Alan, FCA** *1985;* (Tax Fac), Alan Roberts & Company Limited, Chartered Chambers, 294 Balby Road, Balby, DONCASTER, SOUTH YORKSHIRE DN4 0QF.
ROBERTS, Mr. Alan, FCA *1976;* 57 Rake Hill, BURNTWOOD, WS7 9DE.
•①**ROBERTS, Mr. Alan John, MSc FCA MABRP** *1992;* Begbies Traynor (Channel Islands) Limited, Charles House, Charles Street, St. Helier, JERSEY, JE2 4SF. See also Begbies Traynor(Central) LLP
ROBERTS, Mr. Aled, FCA *1978;* The Dutch Barn, Houghs Lane, Higher Walton, WARRINGTON, WA4 5GZ.
ROBERTS, Mr. Aled Francis, BA ACA *1987;* 1001 Frankston-Flinders Road, SOMERVILLE, VIC 3912, AUSTRALIA.
•**ROBERTS, Mr. Aled Owen, BA ACA** *2007;* Salisbury & Company Business Solutions Limited, Irish Square, Upper Denbigh Road, ST. ASAPH, CLWYD, LL17 0RN.
ROBERTS, Mrs. Alison Janet, BSc ACA *1991;* Timber Tops, 39 Eghams Wood Road, BEACONSFIELD, HP9 1JX.
•**ROBERTS, Mr. Alistair Dominic, BSc(Hons) ACA CTA** *2003;* (Tax Fac), Littlejohn LLP, 1 Westferry Circus, Canary Wharf, LONDON, E14 4HD.
•**ROBERTS, Mr. Allen Christopher George, FCA** *1972;* The Hill Farm Orchard End, Wyesham, MONMOUTH, GWENT, NP25 3TG.
ROBERTS, Mr. Alwyn, BA FCA *1964;* 6 Lupin Close, ACCRINGTON, BB5 4SD. (Life Member)
•**ROBERTS, Mrs. Amanda Louise Rumbelow, ACA FMAAT** *2002;* Blueworm, Winnington Hall, Winnington, NORTHWICH, CHESHIRE, CW8 4DU.
•**ROBERTS, Mr. Andrew, FCA** *1985;* BSR Bespoke, Linden House, Linden Close, TUNBRIDGE WELLS, KENT, TN4 8HH.
•**ROBERTS, Mr. Andrew, FCA CF** *1977;* Anlo Associates LLP, 15 Windmill Street, Brill, AYLESBURY, BUCKINGHAMSHIRE, HP18 9SZ.
ROBERTS, Mr. Andrew, BSc FCA *1979;* 260 West 54th Street, Apt 45C, NEW YORK, NY 10019, UNITED STATES.
•**ROBERTS, Mr. Andrew, BSc FCA** *1985;* Grugeon Reynolds Limited, Rutland House, 44 Masons Hill, BROMLEY, BR2 9JG.
ROBERTS, Mr. Andrew James, ACA *2010;* Twin Oaks, Beech Drive, Kingswood, TADWORTH, SURREY, KT20 6PS.
ROBERTS, Mr. Andrew John, BCom FCA *1976;* 9 De Montfort Road, Streatham, LONDON, SW16 1NF.
ROBERTS, Mr. Andrew Nicholas, BSc FCA *1981;* PO Box 160837, BIG SKY, MT 59716-0837, UNITED STATES.
ROBERTS, Mr. Andrew Philip, BA FCA *1980;* 7 Lindsay Square, LONDON, SW1V 3SB.
ROBERTS, Mr. Andrew Steven, BA(Hons) ACA *2011;* 90 Cambridge Road, SOUTHPORT, MERSEYSIDE, PR9 9RH.
ROBERTS, Mr. Andrew William, ACA *1983;* The Old Vicarage, 7 Tong Lane, Tong Village, BRADFORD, BD4 0RR.
ROBERTS, Mrs. Angela Marie, BSc ACA *1990;* Arden House Arden Road, Dorridge, SOLIHULL, B93 8LJ.
ROBERTS, Miss. Ann Lloyd, BSc ACA *1980;* 39 Maes-Y-Coed Road, Heath, CARDIFF, CF14 4HB.
ROBERTS, Mrs. Ann Louise, BA ACA *1992;* Honeysuckle Cottage, Sewell Lane, Sewell, DUNSTABLE, BEDFORDSHIRE, LU6 1RP.
ROBERTS, Mrs. Annette Louise, ACA *1992;* Khandallah House, High House Road, ST BEES, CUMBRIA, CA27 0BY.
ROBERTS, Mrs. Annie, ACA *2001;* 35 Sandy Lane, Church Crookham, FLEET, GU52 8BX.
ROBERTS, Mrs. Annika Jane, BA ACA *1993;* 3 Birkfield Park, Rumbling Bridge, KINROSS, KY13 0QR.
ROBERTS, Mr. Anthony John, FCA *1964;* Chasemore, Ockenden Lane, Cuckfield, HAYWARDS HEATH, RH17 5LD. (Life Member)
ROBERTS, Mr. Anthony Philip, BA ACA *1981;* Devon County Council: Finance Services, County Hall, Topsham Road, EXETER, EX2 4QJ.
ROBERTS, Mr. Antony Steven James, BA ACA *1988;* Arboretumlaan 31, 3080 TERVUREN, BELGIUM.
•**ROBERTS, Mr. Arthur George, FCA** *1972;* (Tax Fac), Keen Dicey Grover, Bathurst House, 50 Bathurst Walk, IVER, SL0 9BH.
•**ROBERTS, Miss. Barbara Elizabeth, BSc FCA** *1973;* (Tax Fac), BE Roberts & Co, 3 Kirkleas Road, SURBITON, SURREY, KT6 6QJ. See also Roberts B.E.
•**ROBERTS, Mr. Barry, FCA** *1976;* Cotterell Partnership Limited, The Curve, 83 Tempest Street, WOLVERHAMPTON, WV2 1AA.
ROBERTS, Miss. Beverly Louise, BA ACA *1999;* 26 Palmer Avenue, Abbeymead, GLOUCESTER, GL4 5BH.
•**ROBERTS, Mr. Brian John, FCA** *1979;* (Tax Fac), Brian Roberts & Co, 7/8 Raleigh Walk, Brigantine Place, CARDIFF, CF10 4LN. See also Northcliffe Accountancy Services Limited
ROBERTS, Mr. Brian Peter, BA ACA *1980;* HBOS plc, 5th Floor Premier House, Charterhall Drive, CHESTER, CH99 3AN.
ROBERTS, Mr. Brian Vivian, BSc FCA *1976;* 5 Tyddyn Gwaun, Laleston, BRIDGEND, MID GLAMORGAN, CF32 0LN.
•**ROBERTS, Mr. Bruce Simon Spearing, BA FCA** *1995;* Bruce Roberts & Co Limited, 18 Ruabon Road, WREXHAM, LL13 7PB.
ROBERTS, Mr. Brynmor, BSc FCA *1977;* 7 Rodeheath Close, WILMSLOW, SK9 2DL.
ROBERTS, Mr. Carl, BSc ACA *2006;* 188 Lawnhurst Avenue, MANCHESTER, M23 9RQ.
ROBERTS, Miss. Carol Anne, BA ACA *1988;* 23 Park View, Felton, MORPETH, NE65 9DQ.
•**ROBERTS, Miss. Caroline Christine, BA ACA** *1999;* Beavis Morgan LLP, 82 St. John Street, LONDON, EC1M 4JN.
ROBERTS, Mrs. Caroline Lesley, BSc ACA *1987;* Uned Cyngor Ariannol, Gwynedd Council, Shirehall Street, CAERNARFON, GWYNEDD, LL55 1SH.
ROBERTS, Miss. Catherine Elizabeth, BSc ACA *1994;* Flat 6 Greener Court, 156 Worple Road, LONDON, SW20 8QA.
ROBERTS, Mr. Charles Anthony, FCA *1971;* Flat 4, 11 Arundel Gardens, LONDON, W11 2LN.
ROBERTS, Mr. Charles Anthony, FCA *1958;* (Tax Fac), 41 Broadwater, Lower Kings Road, BERKHAMSTED, HERTFORDSHIRE, HP4 2AH.
ROBERTS, Mr. Charles Nesfield, ACA MRICS *2000;* Eurohypo, 90 Long Acre, LONDON, WC2E 9RA.
ROBERTS, Miss. Cheryl Ann, BSc(Hons) ACA *2001;* 2 Horkesley Road, Boxted, COLCHESTER, ESSEX, CO4 5HS.
ROBERTS, Mr. Chris Matthew, ACA *2009;* Nominet Minerva House, Edmund Halley Road, OXFORD, OX4 4DQ.
•**ROBERTS, Mrs. Christine, BA ACA** *1992;* Christine Clark, 6 Rowan Grove, Huyton With Roby, LIVERPOOL, L36 5XX.
•**ROBERTS, Mr. Christopher, BA FCA** *1975;* (Tax Fac), Nairne Son & Green, 477 Chester Road, MANCHESTER, M16 9HF.
ROBERTS, Mr. Christopher Dathan, BA ACA *1996;* 238 Alwyn Road, Bilton, RUGBY, CV22 7RR.
ROBERTS, Mr. Christopher Edward, BA ACA *1986;* Archways, Station Road, BRAMPTON, CA8 1EX.
ROBERTS, Mr. Christopher Howard, BSc ACA *2001;* 25 Gwydrin Road, LIVERPOOL, L18 3HA.
ROBERTS, Mr. Christopher John, BSc FCA *1989;* 5 Glenda Close, Warsash, SOUTHAMPTON, SO31 9HQ.
ROBERTS, Mr. Christopher Michael, BSc FCA *1983;* The Old Chapel, East Street, THAME, OX9 3JS.
ROBERTS, Mr. Christopher William, MA BA ACA *2011;* 47 Mansfield Street, Bedminster, BRISTOL, BS3 5PS.
ROBERTS, Dr. Claire Helen, MSc ACA *2004;* with Deloitte LLP, Abbots House, Abbey Street, READING, RG1 3BD.
ROBERTS, Mrs. Clare, BSc ACA *2000;* Detica Ltd, Surrey Research Park, GUILDFORD, SURREY, GU2 7YP.
ROBERTS, Mr. Clive Timothy, BA FCA *1991;* Elm Cottage, Bowling Bank, WREXHAM, CLWYD, LL13 9RY.
•**ROBERTS, Mr. Clive William, BSc FCA** *1979;* Dauman & Co Limited, 9 Station Parade, Uxbridge Road Ealing Common, LONDON, W5 3LD.
ROBERTS, Miss. Coleen Jane, BA ACA *1993;* The Tannery, 207 Drub Lane, Drub, CLECKHEATON, BD19 4BZ.
•**ROBERTS, Mr. Colin David, ACA** *1995;* Baker Tilly UK Audit LLP, The Clock House, 140 London Road, GUILDFORD, SURREY, GU1 1UW. See also Baker Tilly Tax and Advisory Services LLP
ROBERTS, Mr. Colin John, FCA *1964;* Lansdowne, Watford Road, NORTHWOOD, HA6 3PP.
ROBERTS, Mr. Cyril Lloyd, FCA *1980;* 4 Beechfield Drive, LEIGH, LANCASHIRE, WN7 3JB.
ROBERTS, Mr. Daniel, BA ACA *2008;* The Stylo Building, Flat 46, 5 Freehold Street, NORTHAMPTON, NN2 6BF.
ROBERTS, Mr. Daniel James, BSc ACA CFA *1998;* Gartmore Investment Management Gartmore House, 8 Fenchurch Place, LONDON, EC3M 4PB.
ROBERTS, Mr. Daryl Eric, BA(Hons) ACA *2001;* 35 Causeway Crescent, Totton, SOUTHAMPTON, SO40 3AX.
ROBERTS, Mr. David, BSc ACA *2006;* 23 Guildford Grove, LONDON, SE10 8JY.
ROBERTS, Mr. David, BA ACA *1987;* Oaklands, Dr Crouch's Road, Eastcombe, STROUD, GL6 7EA.
ROBERTS, Mr. David Alexander Glyn, BSc(Hons) ACA *2001;* Midland Steel Traders Ltd, Nortrac Works, Shadon Way, Portobello Industrial Estate, BIRTLEY, COUNTY DURHAM DH3 2SW.
ROBERTS, Mr. David Arnold, FCA *1982;* 71 Joseph Banks Drive, Whitby, PORIRUA 5024, NEW ZEALAND.
ROBERTS, Mr. David Benjamin, BSc ACA *1993;* Thatched Cottage Rake Lane, Milford, GODALMING, GU8 5AB.
ROBERTS, Mr. David Benjamin Turton, BA FCA *1999;* BP Exploration Operating Co Ltd, 1-4 Wellheads Avenue Dyce, ABERDEEN, AB21 7PB.
•**ROBERTS, Mr. David Brian, FCA** *1976;* (Tax Fac), Roberts Toner LLP, Melbourne House, 44-46 Grosvenor Street, STALYBRIDGE, CHESHIRE, SK15 2JN.
ROBERTS, Mr. David Charles, MA ACA *1980;* 1 Berkley Road, LONDON, NW1 8XX.
ROBERTS, Mr. David Clive, FCA *1972;* Pengarreg House, Llangibby, USK, NP15 1NN.
ROBERTS, Mr. David Edward, ACA *2002;* with Johnsons Accountants Limited, 2 Hallgarth, PICKERING, NORTH YORKSHIRE, YO18 7AW.
ROBERTS, Mr. David Edward Knee, ACA *1983;* 27 Whitelands Avenue, Chorleywood, RICKMANSWORTH, WD3 5RE.
ROBERTS, Mr. David Edwin, BA ACA *1993;* 35 Northleigh Grove, Eneurys Park, WREXHAM, LL11 2HQ.
ROBERTS, Mr. David Gareth, FCA *1961;* 18 Grenville Meadows, LOSTWITHIEL, PL22 0JS. (Life Member)
•**ROBERTS, Mr. David Gareth, BA FCA** *1986;* (Tax Fac), Fountain Accountancy Limited, Great Western House, The Sidings, Chester Street, Saltney, CHESTERFIELD CH4 8RD.
•**ROBERTS, Mr. David Geoffrey, BCom FCA** *1970;* Boyd Roberts & Co, The Tallett, Ewen, CIRENCESTER, GLOUCESTERSHIRE, GL7 6BU.
ROBERTS, Mr. David Gordon, BSc FCA MCT *1994;* 40 Broadfern Road, Knowle, SOLIHULL, B93 9DD.
•**ROBERTS, Mr. David Graham, FCA** *1972;* Pritchard Roberts & Co, 108A Lammas Street, CARMARTHEN, SA31 3AP.
•**ROBERTS, Mr. David Graham, FCA** *1976;* (Tax Fac), Roberts & Co (Accountants) Ltd, 2 Tower House, HODDESDON, EN11 8UR.

ROBERTS, David Griffith, Esq OBE FCA *1957;* 33 Ffordd Tan'r Allt, ABERGELE, LL22 7DQ. (Life Member)
ROBERTS, Mr. David Ian, BSc ACA *1993;* Chiene & Tait, 61 Dublin Street, EDINBURGH, EH3 6NL.
ROBERTS, Mr. David John, BCom ACA *1991;* 9 Bransholme Drive, YORK, YO30 4XN.
ROBERTS, Mr. David John, FCA *1973;* 24 Eastmont Road, Hinchley Wood, ESHER, KT10 9AZ.
•ROBERTS, Mr. David Lewis, BSc *1991;* Strover Leader & Co, Barry House, 20/22 Worple Road, Wimbledon, LONDON, SW19 4DH.
ROBERTS, Mr. David Lloyd, BSc ACA *2005;* Apartment 21, The Chambers, 2-6 Booth Street, MANCHESTER, M2 4AT.
ROBERTS, Mr. David Mark, BSc FCA *2001;* Arundales, Stowe House, 1688 High Street, Knowle, SOLIHULL, WEST MIDLANDS B93 0LY.
ROBERTS, Mr. David Matthew, FCA *1976;* Via Lorenzo di Credi 9, 20149 MILAN, ITALY.
•ROBERTS, Mr. David Nicholas, FCA *1972;* Roberts & Co, 136 Kensington Church Street, LONDON, W8 4BH.
ROBERTS, Mr. David Norton, MA FCA *1979;* 31 Beeches Walk, CARSHALTON, SURREY, SM5 4JS.
ROBERTS, Mr. David Philip, BSc ACA *1994;* Box Barn, Frouds Close, Childrey, WANTAGE, OXFORDSHIRE, OX12 9NT.
ROBERTS, Mr. David Richard, FCA *1957;* 3 Broadway, LONDON, N14 6PJ. (Life Member)
•ROBERTS, Mr. David Rodger, BA FCA *1978;* Tax and Accounts Shop Limited, 12 Hibel Road, MACCLESFIELD, CHESHIRE, SK10 2AB. See also TaxAssist Accountants
•ROBERTS, Mr. David Stuart, BSc FCA *1989;* DMC Accounting, Olympic House, 63 Wallingford Road, UXBRIDGE, UB8 2RW.
ROBERTS, Mr. David William, BCom ACA *1997;* 17 Brookside Close, Baglan, PORT TALBOT, WEST GLAMORGAN, SA12 8EN.
ROBERTS, Mr. David William, BSc FCA *1956;* Way of the Wind, 45 Dome Hill, CATERHAM, CR3 6EF. (Life Member)
•ROBERTS, Mr. David Wyn, MA FCA *1986;* Littlejohn LLP, 1 Westferry Circus, Canary Wharf, LONDON, E14 4HD.
ROBERTS, Mrs. Davina, BSc ACA *1992;* The Old Vicarage, Llangynog, CARMARTHEN, DYFED, SA33 5BS.
•ROBERTS, Mrs. Deborah Ann, FCA *1990;* DA Roberts Accountancy Services Limited, 41 Newbury Drive, DAVENTRY, NORTHAMPTONSHIRE, NN11 0WQ.
•ROBERTS, Miss. Debra Jane, BSc ACA *1990;* Murrell Consultancy Limited, 39 Manor Road, SUTTON COLDFIELD, B73 6EE.
ROBERTS, Ms. Diane Elisabeth, BA ACA *1985;* Santander UK Plc, 3 Princess Way, REDHILL, RH1 1SR.
ROBERTS, Mrs. Dianne, BSc ACA *1992;* Elv Cottage, Sandy Lane, Great Boughton, CHESTER, CH3 5UL.
ROBERTS, Mr. Edward, FCA *1969;* Villa 232/ 36 Racecourse Road, Cardinia Waters Retirement Village, PAKENHAM, VIC 3810, AUSTRALIA. (Life Member)
ROBERTS, Mr. Edward Matthew Giles, BA FCA *1989;* Upper Walland Farm, Shovers Green, WADHURST, TN5 6NE.
•ROBERTS, Mr. Edward Nicholas, BA ACA *1990;* Hodson Lewis, The Flint House, Heath Farm Business Centre, Tut Hill, Fornham All Saints, BURY ST. EDMUNDS SUFFOLK IP28 6LG.
ROBERTS, Mr. Edwin William, FCA FRSA *1962;* Spanish Lodge, Fitzgeorge Avenue, NEW MALDEN, SURREY, KT3 4SH.
•ROBERTS, Mr. Eifion, BSc ACA *1992;* (Tax Fac), Cobham Murphy Limited, 116 Duke Street, LIVERPOOL, L1 5JW.
ROBERTS, Mrs. Elaine, BSc(Hons) ACA *2001;* 41 Hansford Square, BATH, BA2 5LH.
ROBERTS, Mrs. Elaine Sarah, BSc FCA *1995;* 22 Volunteer Close, Wootton, NORTHAMPTON, NN4 6SB.
ROBERTS, Miss. Eloise, ACA *2011;* Unit 6, Quarry Master Drive, Pyrmont, SYDNEY, NSW 2009, AUSTRALIA.
ROBERTS, Mr. Eric Alan, BCom FCA *1955;* 86 Riddlesdown Road, PURLEY, CR8 1DD.
ROBERTS, Mr. Evan John Dudley, FCA *1970;* 2 Brecon Road, Pontardawe, SWANSEA, SA8 4PA.
•ROBERTS, Mrs. Fiona Christina, BA FCA *1989;* Hilton Sharp & Clarke, 30 New Road, BRIGHTON, BN1 1BN.
ROBERTS, Mrs. Fiona Shelagh, BA ACA *2001;* Swallows Cottage Booths Hall Road, Worsley, MANCHESTER, M28 1LB.
ROBERTS, Mrs. Francesca, BEng ACA *1994;* 396 Wokingham Road, Earley, READING, RG6 7HX.
ROBERTS, Mr. Francis George, FCA *1953;* 27 Heath Drive, POTTERS BAR, HERTFORDSHIRE, EN6 1EV. (Life Member)
ROBERTS, Mr. Gareth, ACA *2011;* Oakcroft, Bridgewater Road, WEYBRIDGE, SURREY, KT13 0EL.
ROBERTS, Mr. Gareth, BA ACA *2010;* 4 Woolmer Close, Birchwood, WARRINGTON, WA3 6UU.
ROBERTS, Mr. Gareth Howell, BA ACA *1993;* European Court of Auditors, 16 rue Alcide de Gasperi, L-1615 LUXEMBOURG, LUXEMBOURG.
ROBERTS, Mr. Gareth Huw, LLB ACA *2005;* Flat 60 Vanguard House, 70 Martello Street, LONDON, E8 3QQ.
ROBERTS, Mr. Gareth Morgan, BSc ACA *2000;* 2104, AL THURAYA TOWER1, PO BOX 500113, DUBAI MEDIA CITY, DUBAI, 500113 UNITED ARAB EMIRATES.
ROBERTS, Mr. Gareth Peter, BSc ACA *1997;* 18 Maslen Road, ST. ALBANS, HERTFORDSHIRE, AL4 0GT.
•ROBERTS, Mr. Gary, ACA *1997;* Business & Tax Solutions Limited, Watergate House, 85 Watergate Street, CHESTER, CH1 2LF.
ROBERTS, Mr. Gavin James, ACA CA(AUS) *2011;* Heogh Capital Partners, 5 Young Street, LONDON, W8 5EH.
ROBERTS, Miss. Gemma Louise, BA ACA *2009;* 8 The Dell, Penn, HIGH WYCOMBE, BUCKINGHAMSHIRE, HP10 8ED.
ROBERTS, Mr. Geoffrey, ACA *1960;* 33 Hillhead Park, BRIXHAM, TQ5 0HG. (Life Member)
ROBERTS, Mr. Geoffrey John, BSc FCA *1957;* Flat 7, 26 Greenhill, WEYMOUTH, DT4 7SG. (Life Member)
ROBERTS, Mr. George David, FCA *1964;* P.O.Box N8336, NASSAU, BAHAMAS. (Life Member)
ROBERTS, Mr. George Edward, FCA *1964;* 54 Manchester Road, Chapel-en-le-Frith, HIGH PEAK, DERBYSHIRE, SK23 9TH. (Life Member)
ROBERTS, Mr. George Norman, FCA *1952;* 22 Meadow Road, Finchfield, WOLVERHAMPTON, WV3 8EZ. (Life Member)
ROBERTS, Mrs. Gillian, MA ACA *1993;* Moat Farm House, Kettle Green Road, MUCH HADHAM, HERTFORDSHIRE, SG10 6AE.
ROBERTS, Ms. Glenda Jane, BA(Hons) ACA *2002;* 39 Woodleigh Gardens, Streatham, LONDON, SW16 2SX.
ROBERTS, Mr. Graeme, ACA *2008;* Alter Domus (Jersey) Limited, Union House Union Street, ST HELIER, JE2 3RF.
ROBERTS, Mr. Graham, ACA *2007;* with PricewaterhouseCoopers LLP, 1 Embankment Place, LONDON, WC2N 6RH.
ROBERTS, Mr. Graham Charles, BA FCA *1984;* The British Land Co Ltd, York House, 45 Seymour Street, LONDON, W1H 7LX.
ROBERTS, Mr. Graham John, ACA *2007;* 18 Skardale Gardens, Austin Farm, PLYMOUTH, PL6 5UT.
ROBERTS, Mr. Graham Philip, BA ACA *1989;* 2 Valley Road, Simmondley, GLOSSOP, SK13 6YN.
•ROBERTS, Mr. Gryffydd Elwyn, MA FCA *1982;* PricewaterhouseCoopers LLP, Cornwall Court, 19 Cornwall Street, BIRMINGHAM, B3 2DT. See also PricewaterhouseCoopers
ROBERTS, Mr. Guy Nicholas, BA(Hons) ACA *2000;* 12645 West Airport BLVD Sugar Land, HOUSTON, TX 77478, UNITED STATES.
ROBERTS, Mrs. Helen Claire, BA ACA *1991;* with Egan Roberts Limited, Glenfield House, Philips Road, BLACKBURN, BB1 5PF.
ROBERTS, Miss. Helen Elizabeth, BSc ACA *2007;* 13 Abercrombie Street, LONDON, SW11 2JB.
ROBERTS, Mrs. Helen Elizabeth, BSc ACA *1997;* Citigroup, Citigroup Centre, Canada Square, Canary Wharf, LONDON, E14 5LB.
ROBERTS, Ms. Helen Janet, BSc ACA *1992;* 194 Roberts Wharf, Neptune Street, LEEDS, LS9 8DX.
ROBERTS, Mrs. Hilary Anne, MA ACA *1985;* Orchard House, Chapel Road, Kempsford, FAIRFORD, GL7 4EQ.
ROBERTS, Mr. Hugh Benedict Polmear, BSc FCA *1986;* WHILEWORTH, 42 Hamilton Road, HIGH WYCOMBE, BUCKINGHAMSHIRE, HP13 5BJ.
ROBERTS, Mr. Ian, BA ACA *1998;* 7 Cross Road, WEYBRIDGE, SURREY, KT13 9NX.
ROBERTS, Mr. Ian David, BA(Hons) ACA *2007;* 24 Newlaithes Road, Horsforth, LEEDS, LS18 4LG.
ROBERTS, Mr. Ian David, BSc ACA *1999;* Twin Peaks, 40 D'Abernon Drive, Stoke D'Abernon, COBHAM, SURREY, KT11 3JD.
ROBERTS, Mr. Ian Jeremy, BSc ACA *1987;* 18 Colescroft Hill, PURLEY, CR8 4BB.
ROBERTS, Mr. Ian Lloyd, BA ACA *2004;* 70 Northfield Court, SHEFFIELD, S10 1QR.
ROBERTS, Mr. Ian Paul Hartin, FCA *1974;* Le Mouret, 32100 CONDOM, FRANCE.
ROBERTS, Mr. Ian Pennell, ACA *1981;* Naille, Upper Swainswick, BATH, BA1 8BX.
•ROBERTS, Mr. Ian Vaughan, FCA *1974;* Hicks Randles Limited, 7 Grove Park Road, WREXHAM, CLWYD, LL12 7AA.
ROBERTS, Mr. Ioan William, BSc ARCS ACA *1999;* 9 Chalford Road, LONDON, SE21 8BX.
ROBERTS, Mrs. Irina, LLB ACA *2001;* 75a Wargrave Road, Twyford, READING, RG10 9PD.
ROBERTS, Mr. Iwan Lewis, ACA *2009;* Church View High Street, Llandrillo, CORWEN, CLWYD, LL21 0TL.
ROBERTS, Mr. James, ACA *2010;* No 51 Street 135, Sangkat Toul Tompoung 1, Khan Chamkarmorn, PHNOM PENN, CAMBODIA.
•ROBERTS, Mr. James Alan, FCA *1976;* McDade Roberts Accountants Limited, 316 Blackpool Road, Fulwood, PRESTON, PR2 3AE.
ROBERTS, Mr. James Allen, LLB ACA *2005;* with Grant Thornton UK LLP, 11-13 Penhill Road, CARDIFF, CF11 9UP.
•ROBERTS, Mr. James Arthur, BCom FCA *1979;* BDO LLP, 2 City Place, Beehive Ring Road, GATWICK, WEST SUSSEX, RH6 0PA. See also BDO Stoy Hayward LLP
ROBERTS, Mr. James Matthew, ACA *2009;* 21 Briars Close, Long Lawford, RUGBY, WARWICKSHIRE, CV23 9DW.
ROBERTS, Mr. James Matthew Arthur, BA(Hons) ACA *2004;* Horatio Investments, Unit 1 Landmark House, Wirrall Park Road, GLASTONBURY, SOMERSET, BA6 9FR.
ROBERTS, Mr. James Nigel Scott, BSc(Hons) ACA *2002;* Abbey Farmhouse, Mundham, NORWICH, NR14 6EL.
•ROBERTS, Miss. Jane, BA FCA *1986;* (Tax Fac), Hills & Burgess, 20 Bridge Street, LEIGHTON BUZZARD, LU7 1AL.
•ROBERTS, Mrs. Janet Margaret, BA FCA *1989;* Janet Roberts, 112 - 114 St. Marys Road, MARKET HARBOROUGH, LEICESTERSHIRE, LE16 7DX.
ROBERTS, Miss. Janet McKenzie, BSc ACA *2010;* 4 Ellesmere Grove, CHELTENHAM, GLOUCESTERSHIRE, GL50 2QQ.
•ROBERTS, Mrs. Jennifer, FCA *1971;* Ashworth Moulds, 11 Nicholas Street, BURNLEY, BB11 2AL.
ROBERTS, Miss. Jennifer Rosemary Ford, BA ACA *1995;* 75 Gowan Avenue, LONDON, SW6 6RH.
ROBERTS, Mr. Jeremy Edward, ACA *2002;* 28 ST Peters Close, Ditton, AYLESFORD, ME20 6PG.
ROBERTS, Mr. Jeremy Guy, BA ACA *2003;* 22 Fernside Avenue, LONDON, NW7 3BD.
ROBERTS, Mrs. Jill Elizabeth, BMus ACA *1992;* 9 Hickton Drive, ALTRINCHAM, WA14 4LZ.
ROBERTS, Ms. Jitka, ACA *2005;* The Old Wesleyan Chapel, Briestfield Road, Briestfield, DEWSBURY, WEST YORKSHIRE, WF12 0NR.
ROBERTS, Mrs. Joan, FCA *1969;* 60 Gledhow Wood Road, LEEDS, LS8 4BZ.
•ROBERTS, Mrs. Joan Lucille, FCA *1972;* (Tax Fac), Joan L. Freiwald & Co, 60 Pangbourne Drive, STANMORE, HA7 4RB.
ROBERTS, Miss. Joanne, BA ACA *1995;* 23 D'Abernon Drive, Stoke D'Abernon, COBHAM, SURREY, KT11 3JE.
ROBERTS, Miss. Joanne, BSc ACA *2003;* 322 Wick Road, BRISTOL, BS4 4HU.
ROBERTS, Mr. John Anthony, FCA *1964;* The Ferns, Broc Hill Way, Brocton, STAFFORD, ST17 0UB.
•ROBERTS, Mr. John Arthur, FCA *1980;* (Tax Fac), Roberts & Co (Accountants) Ltd, 2 Tower House, HODDESDON, EN11 8UR.
ROBERTS, Mr. John Bernard, ACA *2009;* 224 Upper Batley Low Lane, BATLEY, WEST YORKSHIRE, WF17 0JF.
•ROBERTS, Mr. John Brian, FCA FCCA *1969;* Roberts Redman, 27 St Johns Avenue, LEATHERHEAD, KT22 7HT.
ROBERTS, Mr. John Christopher, BSc ACA *2008;* with PricewaterhouseCoopers LLP, 1 East Parade, SHEFFIELD, S1 2ET.
ROBERTS, Mr. John Christopher, FCA *1969;* 31 Rookery Lane, Great Totham, MALDON, CM9 8DF.
ROBERTS, Mr. John Clarke, BSc FCA *1987;* The Old Vicarage, Coldharbour, DORKING, SURREY, RH5 6HG.
ROBERTS, Mr. John Evan, ACA *1981;* M V A Consultancy Ltd, Dukes Court, Duke Street, WOKING, SURREY, GU21 5BH.
ROBERTS, Mr. John Garmon, FCA *1971;* Holy Trinity Church, Carlton Road, REDHILL, RH1 2BX.
ROBERTS, Mr. John Gregory, FCA *1958;* Thira, Kings Court, 133 Kings Acre Road, HEREFORD, HR4 0SP. (Life Member)
ROBERTS, Mr. John Henry, BA FCA CTA *1979;* with PricewaterhouseCoopers LLP, 1 Embankment Place, LONDON, WC2N 6RH.
ROBERTS, Mr. John Hilmer, FCA *1960;* 12 Larkhill Lane, Formby, LIVERPOOL, L37 1LX.
ROBERTS, Mr. John Laing, MA FCA *1967;* 44 Greenbank Drive, Ashgate, CHESTERFIELD, S40 4BX.
ROBERTS, Mr. John Mark, BSc ACA *1995;* Hawthorn House, Heddington, CALNE, SN11 0PF.
ROBERTS, Mr. John Merfyn, MSc BSc ACA *1980;* CQS Management, 5th Floor, 33 Grosvenor Place, LONDON, SW1X 7HY.
ROBERTS, Mr. John Michael, MA ACA *1997;* 18 Kings Road, Crosby, LIVERPOOL, L23 7TW.
•ROBERTS, Mr. John Michael, FCA *1980;* 60 St. Marys Road, WEYBRIDGE, KT13 9PZ.
ROBERTS, Mr. John Richard, MSc ACA *2005;* 37 Fidlers Walk, Wargrave, READING, RG10 8BA.
ROBERTS, Mr. Jonathan David, BA ACA *2010;* 2 Springside Court, Josephs Road, GUILDFORD, GU1 1BT.
ROBERTS, Mr. Jonathan Luke, LLB ACA *2004;* 90 Bonsall Road, Erdington, BIRMINGHAM, B23 5SY.
ROBERTS, Mr. Jonathan Mark, BSc ACA *2006;* 440 N McClurg Ct, Apt 1208, CHICAGO, IL 60611, UNITED STATES.
ROBERTS, Mr. Jonathan Paul, BSc(Hons) ACA *2001;* PricewaterhouseCoopers, Freshwater Place, 2 Southbank Boulevard, Southbank, MELBOURNE, VIC 3006 AUSTRALIA.
•ROBERTS, Mr. Jonathan Warwick, BSc FCA CTA *1991;* Jonathan W. Roberts, Blackford Barn, Pillerton Priors, WARWICK, CV35 0PE.
ROBERTS, Mr. Jonathan Christopher George, MA ACA *2009;* 6 Stonehouse, Lower Basildon, READING, RG8 9NQ.
ROBERTS, Mr. Joseph William, FCA *1994;* Halcyon, 19 Grape Bay Drive, PAGET PG06, BERMUDA.
ROBERTS, Mr. Julian Victor Frow, BA FCA *1984;* 27 Fairway, Merrow, GUILDFORD, GU1 2XJ.
ROBERTS, Mrs. Julie Susan, BA ACA *1995;* 4 Delvesridge Road, Darley, HARROGATE, NORTH YORKSHIRE, HG3 2RD.
ROBERTS, Mr. Justin James, BSc ACA *2003;* 10 Winfrith Road, LONDON, SW18 3BD.
ROBERTS, Miss. Karen Margaret, BA ACA *1990;* 132 Purves Road, LONDON, NW10 5TG.
ROBERTS, Mrs. Kate Jane, LLB ACA *2004;* 50 Newton Court, LEEDS, LS8 2PH.
•ROBERTS, Mr. Keith, BA FCA *1985;* (Tax Fac), Egan Roberts Limited, Glenfield House, Philips Road, BLACKBURN, BB1 5PF.
•ROBERTS, Mr. Keith Andrew, ACA *1989;* KAR Accountancy Services Limited, 11 Benedict Green, Warfield, BRACKNELL, RG42 3DW. See also Bruton Charles
ROBERTS, Mr. Keith Nicholson, FCA *1959;* 7 Sluysken Road, HOUT BAY, 7806, SOUTH AFRICA. (Life Member)
•ROBERTS, Mr. Kenneth Sidney, FCA *1976;* Shipleys LLP, 10 Orange Street, Haymarket, LONDON, WC2H 7DQ.
ROBERTS, Mr. Kenneth Stanley, FCA *1970;* Erewhon, 11 The Mount, Noak Hill, ROMFORD, ESSEX RM5 7LJ.
ROBERTS, Mr. Kenneth Thomas, FCA *1952;* 19 Montserrat, West Parade, BEXHILL-ON-SEA, TN39 3DS. (Life Member)
ROBERTS, Mr. Kern, BA(Hons) ACA *2004;* 20 Great Woodcote Park, PURLEY, CR8 3QS.
ROBERTS, Mrs. Kirsty Marie, ACA *2011;* 33 Summerfield Close, OSWESTRY, SHROPSHIRE, SY11 2YA.
ROBERTS, Mrs. Kristina Jane, BA ACA *1993;* 8 Chichester Street, CHESTER, CH1 4AD.
ROBERTS, Miss. Lauren Hayley, BSc ACA *2010;* Flat 61, 15 Portman Square, LONDON, W1H 6LJ.
ROBERTS, Mr. Lawrence John Desmond, BA FCA *1976;* 25 Newlands, Langton Green, TUNBRIDGE WELLS, TN3 0DB.
•ROBERTS, Mr. Lee, ACA *1991;* The Mulberry, Sheethanger Lane, Felden, HEMEL HEMPSTEAD, HERTFORDSHIRE, HP3 0BQ.
•ROBERTS, Mrs. Lesley Karen, BA ACA *1988;* Ernst & Young LLP, 1 More London Place, LONDON, SE1 2AF. See also Ernst & Young Europe LLP
ROBERTS, Mrs. Lisa Anne, BA(Hons) ACA *2000;* Anchor Cottage Bowbridge Lane, Prestbury, CHELTENHAM, GLOUCESTERSHIRE, GL52 3BJ.
ROBERTS, Miss. Lisa Jayne, BA(Hons) ACA *2002;* 76 Fennel Close, MAIDSTONE, ME16 0FG.
ROBERTS, Mrs. Lorraine, LLB ACA *2004;* 139 Carden Avenue, BRIGHTON, BN1 8NH.
ROBERTS, Mrs. Louisa, BSc ACA *2011;* (Tax Fac), Thomas Westcott, 64 High Street, BIDEFORD, DEVON, EX39 2AR.
ROBERTS, Mrs. Louisa Elisabeth, BA(Hons) ACA *2004;* 6 Cae Gwyn, Llanferres, MOLD, CLWYD, CH7 5SL.
ROBERTS, Ms. Louise Joan, BA ACA *1992;* 86 Craiglockhart Drive South, Otterburn Park, EDINBURGH, EH14 1JY.

ROBERTS, Mrs. Louise Teresa, BSc ACA *1990;* Faculty of Social & Human Sciences, University of Southampton, University Road, SOUTHAMPTON, SO17 1BJ.
ROBERTS, Mrs. Madeleine Jayne, ACA *2007;* Deloitte & Touche, 1 City Square, LEEDS, LS1 2AL.
ROBERTS, Mrs. Madeline, BA ACA *1998;* BMSP, Uxbridge Business Park, Sanderson Road, UXBRIDGE, MIDDLESEX, UB8 1DH.
ROBERTS, Mr. Mark, BA ACA *1993;* 45 Southfield, Balderton, NEWARK, NOTTINGHAMSHIRE, NG24 3QB.
ROBERTS, Mr. Mark Andrew, BSc ACA *1992;* GPO Box 1777, ADELAIDE, SA 5001, AUSTRALIA.
ROBERTS, Mr. Mark Charles, BSc ACA *1987;* 5 Mallard Way, Lavernock Park, PENARTH, CF64 5FG.
ROBERTS, Mr. Mark Edward, BSc ACA *1990;* IBM UK Ltd, 76 Upper Ground, South Bank, LONDON, SE1 9PZ.
ROBERTS, Mr. Mark Edward, BSc ACA *1990;* 3 Kingsley Close, Sandal, WAKEFIELD, WF2 7EB.
ROBERTS, Mr. Mark George, BSc ACA *1989;* 17 Connaught Drive, WEYBRIDGE, SURREY, KT13 0XA.
•ROBERTS, Mr. Mark John, FCA *1979;* M J Roberts Associates Ltd, Regency House, Kings Place, BUCKHURST HILL, ESSEX, IG9 5EB.
ROBERTS, Mr. Martin, ACA *2007;* 19 Sneezum Walk, WITHAM, ESSEX, CM8 1US.
ROBERTS, Mr. Martin George, BA ACA *2002;* J S Wright & Co Ltd, 16 Portland Street, BIRMINGHAM, B6 5RX.
ROBERTS, Mr. Martyn James, BSc ACA *1993;* Woolworths Limited, 1 Woolworths Way, BELLA VISTA, NSW 2153, AUSTRALIA.
•ROBERTS, Mr. Martyn John, BSc ACA CTA *2000;* Willow Accountancy, Willow Cottage, Valley Road, WOTTON-UNDER-EDGE, GLOUCESTERSHIRE, GL12 7NP.
•ROBERTS, Mr. Matthew John, ACA FCCA *2009;* Kirby and Haslam Limited, 11 King Street, KING'S LYNN, NORFOLK, PE30 1ET.
ROBERTS, Mr. Matthew John Christopher, BA FCA *1986;* 21 Downside Road, GUILDFORD, SURREY, GU4 8PH.
ROBERTS, Mr. Matthew Leigh, BA ACA *2000;* 104 York Road, WOKING, GU22 7XS.
ROBERTS, Mrs. Maureen Josephine, ACA *1983;* Jessimine Cottage, West End Road, Norton, DONCASTER, SOUTH YORKSHIRE, DN6 9DH.
ROBERTS, Mr. Meirion, LLB FCA *1965;* Hafan, Borth-Y-Gest, PORTHMADOG, LL49 9TW.
ROBERTS, Miss. Melanie Jane, BA(Hons) ACA *2009;* 7 Duxbury Gardens, CHORLEY, PR7 3JZ.
ROBERTS, Mr. Melvyn, FCA *1975;* 11 Ashwood Road, Disley, STOCKPORT, SK12 2EL.
ROBERTS, Mr. Mervyn Keith, BSc ACA *1979;* 215 Chester Road, Grappenhall, WARRINGTON, WA4 2QB.
ROBERTS, Mr. Meurig Wyn, BSc FCA *1983;* (Tax Fac), 99 Kingsdown Avenue, SOUTH CROYDON, SURREY, CR2 6QL.
ROBERTS, Mr. Michael Alan, FCA *1954;* 26 Limetree Crescent, COCKERMOUTH, CA13 9HW. (Life Member)
ROBERTS, The Revd. Michael Anthony, FCA *1964;* 12 Little Meadow End, Nailsea, BRISTOL, BS48 4LS. (Life Member)
ROBERTS, Mr. Michael Antony, BA ACA *1999;* Swallows Cottage Booths Hall Road Worsley, MANCHESTER, M28 1LB.
ROBERTS, Mr. Michael Christopher, BSc FCA *1988;* 15 Henley Close, SUTTON COLDFIELD, B73 5LU.
ROBERTS, Mr. Michael Curig, FCA *1961;* The Old Granary, Church Farm, Little Gaddesden, HEMEL HEMPSTEAD, HERTFORDSHIRE, HP4 1NZ.
ROBERTS, Mr. Michael David, BSc ACA *1995;* Nuvia Ltd Building A, Kelburn Court Birchwood, WARRINGTON, WA3 6TW.
ROBERTS, Mr. Michael David, BA ACA *1981;* 26 Curzon Road, BIRKENHEAD, MERSEYSIDE, CH42 8PH.
ROBERTS, Mr. Michael De-Villamar, FCA *1973;* 25 Main St, Elloughton, BROUGH, HU15 1JN.
ROBERTS, Mr. Michael Guist, MBE FCA *1966;* Ridgeview Estate Winery, Upper Furzefield, Fragbarrow Lane, Ditchling Common, HASSOCKS, WEST SUSSEX BN6 8TP.
ROBERTS, Mr. Michael Leslie, FCA *1969;* 8 Southfield Rise, CHELTENHAM, GL53 9LJ.
ROBERTS, Mr. Michael Lloyd, MA FCA *1998;* Thomson Reuters, Monmouth House, 58-64 City Road, LONDON, EC1Y 2AL.
ROBERTS, Mr. Michael Stewart, BSc FCA *1972;* West Styles, The Mount, Highclere, NEWBURY, BERKSHIRE, RG20 9PS.
ROBERTS, Mr. Michael William, MA FCA *1974;* 124 Aldersgate Street, LONDON, EC1A 4JQ.
•ROBERTS, Mr. Michael William, FCA *1956;* (Tax Fac), MW Roberts & Co, 8 Kings Oak, COLWYN BAY, CLWYD, LL29 6AJ.
ROBERTS, Mr. Miles William, BEng ACA *1992;* Moat Farm House, Kettle Green Road, MUCH HADHAM, HERTFORDSHIRE, SG10 6AE.
ROBERTS, Mr. Nathan John, BA ACA *1995;* H B O S Terra Nova House, Pierhead Street, CARDIFF, CF10 4PB.
ROBERTS, Mr. Neal Anthony, LLB ACA *1984;* Darbys Church Road, Cookham, MAIDENHEAD, SL6 9PR.
ROBERTS, Mr. Neil, BSc ACA *1997;* 39 Womersley Road, LONDON, N8 9AP.
ROBERTS, Mr. Neil Andrew Thomas, BA ACA *1997;* 10 Chantry Road, Thornbury, BRISTOL, BS35 1ER.
ROBERTS, Mr. Neil Martin, BSc ACA *2006;* with PricewaterhouseCoopers LLP, 101 Barbirolli Square, Lower Mosley Street, MANCHESTER, M2 3PW.
•ROBERTS, Mr. Neil Michael, BA FCA *1997;* Wright Vigar Limited, Chancery Court, 34 West Street, RETFORD, NOTTINGHAMSHIRE, DN22 6ES. See also Camamile Limited
ROBERTS, Mr. Neville James, FCA *1974;* Guernsey Financial Services, PO Box 128, GUERNSEY, GY1 3HQ.
•ROBERTS, Mr. Nicholas, BA ACA *1989;* Taylor Roberts, Unit 9B, Wingbury Business Village, Upper Wingbury Farm, AYLESBURY, HP22 4LW.
ROBERTS, Mr. Nicholas Edward, BCom ACA *2003;* Villa 96, Al Nakheel Villas, Al Sufouh 1, DUBAI, 114569, UNITED ARAB EMIRATES.
ROBERTS, Mr. Nicholas Elis Vaughan, BSc ACA *1992;* Texaco Ltd, 1 Westferry Circus, LONDON, E14 4HA.
ROBERTS, Mr. Nicholas Luca Andrew, BSc ACA *2010;* 178 Cavendish Road, LONDON, SW12 0DA.
ROBERTS, Mr. Nick, BSc ACA *2009;* Petlers, East Street, Rusper, HORSHAM, WEST SUSSEX, RH12 4RE.
ROBERTS, Mrs. Nicola Ann, BCom ACA *1990;* 9 Long Close, Botley, OXFORD, OX2 9SG.
ROBERTS, Mrs. Nicola Jayne, BA ACA *1999;* Caerphilly County Borough Council, Penallta House, Tredomen Park, Ystrad Mynach, HENGOED, MID GLAMORGAN CF82 7PG.
ROBERTS, Mr. Nigel John, BSc ACA *1990;* 39 Eghams Wood Road, BEACONSFIELD, BUCKINGHAMSHIRE, HP9 1JX.
ROBERTS, Mr. Nigel Joseph Edge, BSc FCA *1987;* THE BENBOW GROUP LTD, BRADLEY MILL, NEWTON ABBOT, DEVON, TQ12 1NF.
ROBERTS, Mr. Norman Stuart, FCA *1970;* N. S. Roberts Consultancy, 32 South Lodge Crescent, ENFIELD, MIDDLESEX, EN2 7NP.
ROBERTS, Mrs. Omobolanle, BA(Hons) ACA *2001;* 23 Glenview Road, BROMLEY, BR1 2QQ.
ROBERTS, Mr. Owain Llewelyn, BSc ACA *2010;* 9 Jellicoe Court, Schooner Way, CARDIFF, CF10 4AJ.
ROBERTS, Mr. Owen Anthony, MA(Hons) ACA *2001;* Omnicom Management Europe Ltd., 239 Old Marylebone Road, LONDON, NW1 5QT.
ROBERTS, Mr. Owen Graham, FCA *1972;* 2 Orchard Grove, MAIDENHEAD, SL6 6DR. (Life Member)
•ROBERTS, Mr. Paul, FCA *1961;* Dunn & Ellis, St Davids Building, Lombard Street, PORTHMADOG, GWYNEDD, LL49 9AP.
ROBERTS, Mr. Paul Anthony, LLM LLB ACA *1990;* Forgebank, Eridge Road, Groombridge, TUNBRIDGE WELLS, TN3 9NJ.
ROBERTS, Mr. Paul Barry, FCA *1964;* 4 Higher Green, BEAMINSTER, DT8 3SE. (Life Member)
ROBERTS, Mr. Paul John, MEng ACA *1995;* Multipart Solutions Limited, Logistics House Buckshaw Avenue, CHORLEY, PR6 7AJ.
ROBERTS, Mr. Paul Leslie, BA ACA *1986;* 27 Sandy Lane, Stretford, MANCHESTER, M32 9DB.
ROBERTS, Mr. Paul Richard, BSc(Hons) ACA *2001;* with Deloitte LLP, 1 City Square, LEEDS, WEST YORKSHIRE, LS1 2AL.
ROBERTS, Mr. Paul Timothy, BA ACA *1984;* Bishop Lodge, 2 William Stumpes Close, MALMESBURY, SN16 9LD.
ROBERTS, Mr. Paul William, BA ACA *1992;* 19 Lambie Drive, MANUKAU 2104, NEW ZEALAND.
ROBERTS, Mrs. Paula Anne, BA ACA *2003;* 83 Glenavon Road, PRENTON, MERSEYSIDE, CH43 0RD.
ROBERTS, Mrs. Penelope Anne, BA ACA *1986;* Unit 2, 11 Fishermans Hill, HAMILTON CR 04, BERMUDA.
ROBERTS, Mr. Peter, FCA *1976;* 11a Holbein Close, DRONFIELD, S18 1QH.
ROBERTS, Mr. Peter, FCA *1954;* 4 Milestone Drive, Dunchurch Road, RUGBY, CV22 6SR. (Life Member)
ROBERTS, Mr. Peter, BSc FCA *1977;* 8 Cannee Chase, KIRKCUDBRIGHT, DUMFRIESSHIRE, DG6 4DB.
ROBERTS, Mr. Peter Alexander Windsor, MA FCA *1971;* The Coach House, 50 Hough Green, CHESTER, CH4 8JQ. (Life Member)
ROBERTS, Mr. Peter Ashley, BSc FCA MAE FCILA *1977;* Cunningham Lindsey, 2nd Floor, Apex Plaza, Forbury Road, READING, RG1 1AX.
•ROBERTS, Mr. Peter Collingwood, FCA *1973;* P.C. Roberts & Co, P.O.Box 561, PMB 6803 International, Commercial Central, GIBRALTAR, GIBRALTAR.
ROBERTS, Mr. Peter Gordon, FCA *1956;* 10 The Moorings, HINDHEAD, SURREY, GU26 6SD. (Life Member)
ROBERTS, Mr. Peter James, FCA *1979;* 72 Bargate, GRIMSBY, DN34 4SR.
ROBERTS, Mr. Peter John, FCA *1975;* Standard Chartered, 1 Basinghall Avenue, LONDON, EC2V 5DD.
•ROBERTS, Mr. Peter John, BSc FCA *1985;* Roberts & Co (Bristol) Limited, 24 High Street, Chipping Sodbury, BRISTOL, BS37 6AH.
ROBERTS, Mr. Peter Kenneth, FCA *1975;* Seven Trees, 16 Alcester Road, Brooklands, SALE, M33 3QP.
ROBERTS, Mr. Peter Mark, BSc ACA *2005;* 36 Maes Berea, BANGOR, GWYNEDD, LL57 4TQ.
•ROBERTS, Mr. Philip John, FCA *1975;* Beever and Struthers, St George's House, 215-219 Chester Road, MANCHESTER, M15 4JE.
•ROBERTS, Mr. Philip Michael, FCA *1981;* (Tax Fac), Albert J. Pope, Unit 4 Westfield Court, Third Avenue, Westfield Inds Est, Midsomer Norton, RADSTOCK BA3 4XD.
ROBERTS, Mr. Philip William, FCA *1977;* 41 Brimstage Road, Heswall, WIRRAL, CH60 1XE.
ROBERTS, Mrs. Philippa Mary, BSc ACA *1982;* Ffridd, Nant Bwlch Yr Haiarn, TREFRIW, LL27 0JB.
•ROBERTS, Mr. Phillip Howard, FCA *1972;* Roberts & Co, 136 Kensington Church Street, LONDON, W8 4BH.
ROBERTS, Mr. Piers Ben, ACA CTA *2004;* J P Morgan Asset Management, 20 Finsbury Street, LONDON, EC2Y 9AQ.
•ROBERTS, Mrs. Rachel Jane Scott, BSc ACA *1989;* (Tax Fac), Rachel Roberts, Brookfield, Thorpe Road, MELTON MOWBRAY, LEICESTERSHIRE, LE13 1SH.
ROBERTS, Mr. Richard Allan, BA ACA *1993;* Flat 4 17 Clyde Road, MANCHESTER, M20 2NJ.
ROBERTS, Mr. Richard Andrew, BA BSc FCA *1972;* North End Farm, Ingersley Vale, Bollington, MACCLESFIELD, SK10 5BP.
•ROBERTS, Mr. Richard Andrew, BSc ACA *1990;* (Tax Fac), Hill & Roberts, 1 Tan-Y-Castell, Dog Lane, RUTHIN, LL15 1DQ.
ROBERTS, Mr. Richard Anthony, BA ACA *1990;* 183 Cambridge Road, HITCHIN, SG4 0JP.
ROBERTS, Mr. Richard Edwin Stace, FCA *1959;* The Pines, Tangmere Road, Tangmere, CHICHESTER, WEST SUSSEX, PO20 2HW.
ROBERTS, Mr. Richard Gilbert, FCA *1953;* 139 Southchurch Boulevard, Thorpe Bay, SOUTHEND-ON-SEA, SS2 4UR. (Life Member)
ROBERTS, Mr. Richard Guyton, FCA *1950;* 65 Oakbury Drive, Preston, WEYMOUTH, DORSET, DT3 6JG. (Life Member)
ROBERTS, Mr. Richard John, BA FCA *1988;* Orchard View, South Farm Close, Rodmell, LEWES, BN7 3HW.
ROBERTS, Mr. Richard Lloyd, FCA *1981;* 1 Tai Glo, Steeple Lane, BEAUMARIS, GWYNEDD, LL58 8EJ.
ROBERTS, Mr. Richard Thomas Howard, FCA *1964;* No 3 Glen Chess, Loudwater Lane, RICKMANSWORTH, WD3 4HQ.
ROBERTS, Mr. Robert, BSc FCA *1977;* Bodafon, Benllech, TYN-Y-GONGL, LL74 8RU.
ROBERTS, Mr. Robert John Michael, FCA *1951;* Little Nethertons, New England Lane, Sedlescombe, BATTLE, EAST SUSSEX, TN33 0RP. (Life Member)
ROBERTS, Mrs. Rosanna Elizabeth, LLB ACA CTA *2005;* The Elms, Guildford Road, WOKING, GU22 7UT.
•ROBERTS, Miss. Rosemary Anne, ACA *1987;* Roberts & Co, The Pheasants, Digging Lane, Fyfield, ABINGDON, OXFORDSHIRE OX13 5LY.
ROBERTS, Mr. Roy Stuart, ACA *2006;* 50 The Vale, BASILDON, ESSEX, SS16 4RL.
ROBERTS, Mr. Roydon Alexander, BSc FCA *1976;* 5 Crystal Avenue, Heath, CARDIFF, CF23 5QJ.
ROBERTS, Mr. Rupert Alexander Leslie, FCA *1954;* Longbarn House, 106a High Street, Brant Broughton, LINCOLN, LN5 0SA. (Life Member)
ROBERTS, Miss. Ruth, MEng ACA *2011;* Flat 11 Travers House, 127 Dalmeny Avenue, LONDON, N7 0JJ.
ROBERTS, Mrs. Sally Ann, BSocSc ACA *2003;* Gatehouse, North Duffield, SELBY, NORTH YORKSHIRE, YO8 5DB.
ROBERTS, Mr. Sam, BSc ACA *2006;* 5 Cheltenham Court, Dexter Close, ST. ALBANS, HERTFORDSHIRE, AL1 5WB.
ROBERTS, Mrs. Sarah, BSc ACA *1996;* 3 Mangholes Cottages, Acre, Haslingden, ROSSENDALE, BB4 5TZ.
ROBERTS, Mrs. Sarah Elizabeth, BA ACA *1991;* Three Gables, High Street, CHIPPING CAMPDEN, GL55 6AG.
•ROBERTS, Mrs. Sarah Jayne, BSc ACA *2003;* J.L. Winder & Co., 125 Ramsden Square, BARROW-IN-FURNESS, LA14 1XA.
ROBERTS, Mrs. Sarah Jean, FCA *1985;* with Clement Rabjohns, 111-113 High Street, EVESHAM, WR11 4XP.
ROBERTS, Mrs. Sharon Mary, BSc FCA *1987;* 6 Hillwood Road, SUTTON COLDFIELD, B75 5QL.
•ROBERTS, Mrs. Sheila Jean, MA ACA *1998;* SJR Associates, 5 Rodens Close, Rossett, WREXHAM, CLWYD, LL12 0EZ.
ROBERTS, Mrs. Shelley, ACA *2001;* Unit 8, 17 Shell Cove Road, NEUTRAL BAY, NSW 2089, AUSTRALIA.
•ROBERTS, Mrs. Sian, BSc ACA *1982;* TierneyFedrick, 19 Trinity Square, LLANDUDNO, GWYNEDD, LL30 2RD.
ROBERTS, Mrs. Stephanie Marion, BSc ACA *1999;* Discovery Court, Bournemouth & Poole Primary Care, Discovery Court Business Centre 551-553 Wallisdown Road, POOLE, DORSET, BH12 5AG.
ROBERTS, Mr. Stephen Edward, BSc ACA *1989;* Fujifilm Image COlorants Ltd, PO Box 42, MANCHESTER, M9 8ZS.
ROBERTS, Mr. Stephen Jamie, ACA *2009;* Woodbine Dark Lane, Lathom, ORMSKIRK, L40 5TR.
ROBERTS, Mr. Stephen Leslie, BCom ACA *1986;* WidneyManufacturing UK Ltd, Plume Street, Aston, BIRMINGHAM, B6 7SA.
ROBERTS, Mr. Stephen Mark, ACA *2008;* The Kyte Group Ltd Business Design Centre, 52 Upper Street, LONDON, N1 0QH.
ROBERTS, Mr. Stephen Paul, BA(Hons) FCA *1996;* 3 Elderberry Cottages, Willow Green Otterburn, NEWCASTLE UPON TYNE, NE19 1LJ.
ROBERTS, Mr. Steven, BA ACA *1995;* 3 Platt Lane, RYE, NY 10580, UNITED STATES.
ROBERTS, Mr. Steven Harrison, BA(Econ) FCA *1959;* 65 Beacon Way, RICKMANSWORTH, HERTFORDSHIRE, WD3 7PB. (Life Member)
ROBERTS, Mr. Steven James, ACA *2009;* 234 Hamilton Street, Atherton, MANCHESTER, M46 0AZ.
ROBERTS, Mr. Steven John, BA ACA *1989;* 112 Church Road, Wick, BRISTOL, BS30 5PD.
ROBERTS, Mr. Steven Mark, BSc ACA *1992;* with BTG Financial Consulting LLP, 340 Deansgate, MANCHESTER, M3 4LY.
•ROBERTS, Mr. Steven Michael, BA ACA *1997;* PricewaterhouseCoopers, Marie-Curie-Strasse 24-28, D-60439 FRANKFURT AM MAIN, GERMANY. See also PricewaterhouseCoopers GmbH
ROBERTS, Mr. Stuart Conrad, ACA *1995;* 36 Charlecote Gardens, Boldmere, SUTTON COLDFIELD, B73 5LS.
ROBERTS, Mr. Stuart David, MA ACA *2003;* 77 Ridge Road, LONDON, N8 9NP.
ROBERTS, Mr. Stuart Kurt, BSc ACA *1986;* 22 St. Bernards Road, SUTTON COLDFIELD, B72 1LE.
ROBERTS, Mrs. Susan, BSc ACA *1989;* 14 Chiltern Close Sandiway, NORTHWICH, CHESHIRE, CW8 2NE.
ROBERTS, Mrs. Suzanne, MSc ACA *2005;* 2 Albion Grove, SALE, CHESHIRE, M33 7TJ.
ROBERTS, Miss. Suzanne, MA(Cantab) ACA *2006;* 22 Dovecote Gardens, LONDON, SW14 8PN.
ROBERTS, Mrs. Suzanne Melody, ACA MAAT *1996;* Mole House 63 Pelhams Walk, ESHER, SURREY, KT10 8QA.
ROBERTS, Ms. Tamara, LLB ACA *2000;* Ridgeview Estate Winery Limited, Upper Furzefied Ditchling Common, Ditchling, HASSOCKS, WEST SUSSEX, BN6 8TP.
ROBERTS, Mr. Thomas Alan, BA FCA *1973;* 12 Tennyson Avenue, CHESTERFIELD, DERBYSHIRE, S40 4SW.
ROBERTS, Mr. Thomas Edward, BA ACA *2004;* 167 Holmley Lane, Coal Aston, SHEFFIELD, S18 3DA.
ROBERTS, Mr. Timothy Edward, BA FCA *1983;* 4 Medway Crescent, ALTRINCHAM, CHESHIRE, WA14 4UB.
ROBERTS, Mr. Timothy Guy, FCA *1983;* Honeycroft, 1 Gaddum Road, Bowdon, ALTRINCHAM, WA14 3PD.

ROBERTS, Mr. Timothy John, FCA DChA *1977;* The Goldsmiths Company, Goldsmiths Hall, Foster Lane, LONDON, EC2V 6BN.
ROBERTS, Mr. Timothy Roland, BSc ACA *2001;* 1 Slieau Curn Park, Kirk Michael, ISLE OF MAN, IM6 1EH.
ROBERTS, Mrs. Tizzie Nicola, MA MRCVS ACA VetMB *1998;* 17 Denistone Road, EASTWOOD, NSW 2122, AUSTRALIA.
ROBERTS, Mrs. Tracy, BSc ACA *1989;* 65 Evelyn Drive, PINNER, HA5 4RL.
ROBERTS, Mr. Trevor Alan, FCA *1976;* 92 Broadmarsh Lane, Freeland, WITNEY, OXFORDSHIRE, OX29 8QR.
•**ROBERTS, Mr. Trevor Ian, BSc FCA** *1986;* 5 Honey Hill, Emberton, OLNEY, BUCKINGHAMSHIRE, MK46 5LT.
ROBERTS, Mr. Trevor Spurring, MA FCA *1966;* 80 Osmaston Road, Prenton, BIRKENHEAD, CH42 8LP.
ROBERTS, Mrs. Uta Irene, BSc ACA *1981;* Ty Wytach, 60 Heol Fawr, Nelson, TREHARRIS, CF46 6NP. (Life Member)
ROBERTS, Mrs. Victoria Anne, MA ACA *2001;* Deutsche Bank AG, 1 Great Winchester Street, LONDON, EC2N 2EQ.
ROBERTS, Miss. Victoria Jane, BA ACA *1998;* A D M Cocoa Classic Couverture, 10 Estuary Banks, Speke, LIVERPOOL, L24 8RB.
ROBERTS, Mr. William, ACA *2009;* Flat 57 Balin House, Long Lane, LONDON, SE1 1YH.
ROBERTS, Mr. William, BA ACA *2004;* 23 Henge Way, Portslade, BRIGHTON, BN41 2EP.
ROBERTS, Mr. William David, BSc ACA *2007;* Flat 3, Egerton Court, 4 Old Brompton Road, South Kensington, LONDON, SW7 3HT.
•**ROBERTS, Mr. William Harry, FCA** *1962;* W.H. Roberts & Co, The Old Rectory, Church Lane, Hoby, MELTON MOWBRAY, LE14 3DR.
ROBERTS, Mr. William Jeremy, BSc ACA *1998;* 10 Longley Road, FARNHAM, SURREY, GU9 8LZ.
ROBERTS, Mr. William Mark, BSc FCA *1990;* Sundog Energy Fairfield House Stony Cove Lane, North Lakes Business Park Flusco, PENRITH, CUMBRIA, CA11 0BT.
ROBERTS, Mr. William Morys, MA FCA *1961;* Pound Hall, The Green, Long Melford, SUDBURY, SUFFOLK, CO10 9DX. (Life Member)
ROBERTS, Mrs. Yolanda Jane, MPhil BSc(Hons) ACA *2002;* Oakwood House, 153 Malvern Road, WORCESTER, WR2 4LN.
ROBERTS, Mrs. Zoe Michelle, BSc ACA CTA *2002;* (Tax Fac), with Barber Harrison & Platt, 2 Rutland Park, SHEFFIELD, S10 2PD.
ROBERTS-TRUMAN, Mrs. Angharad, BSc ACA *2009;* Gelli Cottage Tramway Road, Gellinudd Pontardawe, SWANSEA, SA8 3HW.
ROBERTSHAW, Mrs. Emma Kate, BSc ACA *1999;* Hagthorn Farm Pennypot Lane, Chobham, WOKING, GU24 8DG.
ROBERTSHAW, Mr. John Desmond, MA FCA *1957;* Parsonage Farm, Chiddingly, LEWES, BN8 6HF. (Life Member)
ROBERTSHAW, Mr. John Rees, FCA *1969;* 1 Stoney Butts Lane, Barkisland, HALIFAX, HX4 0EX. (Life Member)
•**ROBERTSON, Mr. Adrian William Snowdon, FCA** *1972;* Snowdon Robertson & Co, The Old Pheasant, Parmoor, Hambleden, HENLEY-ON-THAMES, RG9 6NH.
ROBERTSON, Mrs. Ailsa Margaret, BA FCA *1982;* Westfield House, Highfields, Westoning, BEDFORD, MK45 5EN.
ROBERTSON, Mr. Alan David, FCA CTA *1970;* 1 Woodpeckers, Southwater, HORSHAM, WEST SUSSEX, RH13 9AA.
•**ROBERTSON, Mr. Alan Trantor, MA FCA** *1975;* Clement Keys, 39/40 Calthorpe Road, Edgbaston, BIRMINGHAM, B15 1TS.
•**ROBERTSON, Mr. Alastair David, ACA** *1984;* Ernst & Young, Via Wittgens 6, 20123 MILAN, ITALY. See also Ernst & Young Europe LLP
•①**ROBERTSON, Ms. Amanda Sheila Mary, BA FCA** *1985;* 30 Westley Crossing, Six Mile Bottom, NEWMARKET, SUFFOLK, CB8 0UB.
ROBERTSON, Miss. Amelia, MEng ACA *2006;* Little Oast, Battle Lane, Marden, TONBRIDGE, KENT, TN12 9DF.
ROBERTSON, Mr. Andrew, MMath ACA *2011;* 74b Kelmscott Road, LONDON, SW11 6PT.
ROBERTSON, Mr. Andrew David Giles, BSc(Hons) ACA *2004;* 25 Broadview Close, Kings Worthy, WINCHESTER, SO23 7FL.
ROBERTSON, Mr. Andrew Gallantry, BSc ACA *1999;* 46 Cleveland Avenue, LONDON, W4 1SW.
ROBERTSON, Mr. Andrew John Stuart, BA FCA *1977;* Ecometals Limited, 111 Buckingham Palace Road, LONDON, SW1W 0SR.
ROBERTSON, Mr. Andrew Michael, BSc ACA *1982;* Westfield House, Highfields, Westoning, BEDFORD, MK45 5EN.
ROBERTSON, Mr. Andrew Stephen, BSc ACA *1992;* 1 Shalden Park Farm Cottages, Avenue Road Shalden, ALTON, GU34 4DS.
ROBERTSON, Mrs. Ann Kathleen, BSc ACA *1993;* 716 33 Cox Blvd, MARKHAM L3R 8A6, ON, CANADA.
ROBERTSON, Mr. Anthony Steven Craig, BSc ACA *1995;* 98 Tuihana Drive, PAPAMOA 3118, NEW ZEALAND.
ROBERTSON, Mr. Benedict Sebastian, BA ACA *1996;* 60 Llandaff Road, CARDIFF, CF11 9NL.
ROBERTSON, Mr. Benjamin Michael, MA ACA *1996;* 1 Ainger Road, LONDON, NW3 3AR.
ROBERTSON, Mr. Brian Noel Alexander, BA ACA *1986;* 29 Spencer Road, EAST MOLESEY, KT8 0SP.
ROBERTSON, Mr. Bruce William, BA ACA *1992;* 39/150 Wigram Road, GLEBE, NSW 2037, AUSTRALIA.
ROBERTSON, Mrs. Catherine Ann, BA ACA *1994;* 4 Shetland Close, Cinnamon Brow, WARRINGTON, WA2 0UW.
ROBERTSON, Mrs. Christine Ruth, BSc ACA *1983;* Little Round Hill, Tinkers Castle Road, Seisdon, WOLVERHAMPTON, WV5 7HF.
•**ROBERTSON, Mr. Christopher David, BCom ACA** *1994;* Deloitte LLP, 4 Brindley Place, BIRMINGHAM, B1 2HZ. See also Deloitte & Touche LLP
ROBERTSON, Mrs. Clare Gillian Mary, BA ACA *2004;* 36 Beverley Crescent, TONBRIDGE, TN9 2RD.
ROBERTSON, Mr. Cornelius, BSc FCA *1981;* Europaring 49, 64521 GROSS-GERAU, GERMANY.
•**ROBERTSON, Mr. Craig Kirkpatrick, BA(Hons) ACA** *2001;* Abacus Accountancy Services (Lancs) Limited, 28 The Esplanade, Rishton, BLACKBURN, BB1 4BL.
ROBERTSON, Mr. Daniel, LLB ACA CTA *2002;* 62b St. Johns Wood High Street, LONDON, NW8 7SH.
ROBERTSON, Mr. Daniel, BA ACA *2007;* 16 Bankside, Charlton Road Singleton, CHICHESTER, WEST SUSSEX, PO18 0HT.
ROBERTSON, Mr. David Balfour, BA FCA *1980;* Viridor Waste Management Ltd, Great Western House, Station Approach, TAUNTON, SOMERSET, TA1 1QW.
ROBERTSON, Mr. David Iain, BSocSc ACA *1990;* University of Birmingham, Finance Office, Edgbaston, BIRMINGHAM, B15 2TT.
•**ROBERTSON, Mr. David James, BA FCA** *1993;* Anderson Barrowcliff LLP, Waterloo House, Thornaby Place, Thornaby on Tees, STOCKTON-ON-TEES, CLEVELAND TS17 6SA. See also Anderson Barrowcliff
ROBERTSON, Mr. David Maitland, BA ACA *1983;* 7 St. John's Road, CLEVEDON, BS21 7TG.
ROBERTSON, Miss. Donna Margaret Olivia, BA ACA *2009;* 14 Holmwood Road, Cheam, SUTTON, SM2 7JR.
ROBERTSON, Mr. Douglas Grant, BA FCA *1979;* Blackmore Grange, Blackmore End, Hanley Swan, WORCESTER, WR8 0EE.
ROBERTSON, Mr. Duncan, BA ACA *1991;* 103 Brownlow Road, Bowes Park, LONDON, N11 2BN.
ROBERTSON, Dr. Duncan Andrew, DPhil FCA MInstP CPhys CSci *1999;* 12a Morrell Avenue, OXFORD, OX4 1NE.
•**ROBERTSON, Mrs. Elizabeth Mary, MA FCA** *1985;* (Tax Fac), Creaseys LLP, 12 Lonsdale Gardens, TUNBRIDGE WELLS, KENT, TN1 1PA.
ROBERTSON, Mrs. Elizabeth Naomi, MA ACA *1993;* Icas Ltd Radlett House, 93-95 West Hill Aspley Guise, MILTON KEYNES, MK17 8DT.
ROBERTSON, Mr. Eric Graeme, JP FCA *1957;* 324 Tadcaster Road, YORK, YO24 1HF. (Life Member)
ROBERTSON, Mr. Ewan John, BA ACA *1993;* 47 Greenbank Crescent, EDINBURGH, EH10 5TD.
ROBERTSON, Mr. Gareth James, BA ACA *1999;* 36 Cresswell Grove, West Didsbury, MANCHESTER, M20 2NH.
ROBERTSON, Mr. Geoffrey Stuart, BSc(Econ) ACA *1998;* 239 Victoria Road, LONDON, N22 7XH.
ROBERTSON, Mr. Gordon, BA(Hons) ACA *2001;* 38 Calembeena Avenue, HUGHESDALE, VIC 3166, AUSTRALIA.
ROBERTSON, Mr. Gordon Alan, BA ACA *1994;* 16 Wymer Street, NORWICH, NR2 4BJ.
ROBERTSON, Mr. Graham, BSc FCA *1978;* 15A Queens Gate Place, LONDON, SW7 5NX.
ROBERTSON, Mr. Graham Leslie, BSc ACA *1981;* Briarwood, Knightsbridge Road, CAMBERLEY, GU15 3TS.
ROBERTSON, Mr. Harry Mackinnon, MA BA ACA *1979;* 28a Tongdean Avenue, HOVE, EAST SUSSEX, BN3 6TN.
ROBERTSON, Mr. Iain James, MA(Oxon) ACA *2000;* 36 Beverley Crescent, TONBRIDGE, KENT, TN9 2RD.
ROBERTSON, Mr. Ian, BSc FCA *1977;* 7 Airedale Aveune, HAWTHORN EAST, VIC 3123, AUSTRALIA.
•**ROBERTSON, Mr. Ian, FCA** *1985;* Brewster & Brown, 129 New Bridge Street, NEWCASTLE UPON TYNE, NE1 2SW.
ROBERTSON, Mr. Ian George, BSc ACA *1995;* Insight Medical Research Ltd, 11-13 Charterhouse Buildings, LONDON, EC1M 7AP.
ROBERTSON, Mr. Ian Peter, BA ACA *1994;* Simla House, 36 Dry Hill Park Road, TONBRIDGE, TN10 3BU.
ROBERTSON, Miss. Isobel Strachan, MA FCA *1978;* Squirrels Leap, Apperley Dene, STOCKSFIELD, NE43 7SB.
ROBERTSON, Ms. Jacqueline Margaret, BAcc ACA *1996;* 30C Ngaumatau Road, Point Howard, LOWER HUTT 5013, NEW ZEALAND.
ROBERTSON, Ms. Jahneata, ACA *2008;* ground floor, 13 Holmewood Road, LONDON, SW2 3RP.
ROBERTSON, Mr. James, MA FCA MIPA FABRP *1976;* 54 The Vineyard, RICHMOND, SURREY, TW10 6AT. (Life Member)
ROBERTSON, Mr. James Binnie, BEng ACA *1999;* Flat 53 Drive Mansions, Fulham Road, LONDON, SW6 5JD.
ROBERTSON, Ms. Jane Helen, BA ACA *1995;* 1 B Tedder Road, WINSTON PARK, KWAZULU NATAL, 3610, SOUTH AFRICA.
ROBERTSON, Mr. John Binnie, FCA *1967;* Silverbirches, The Street, Stoke By Clare, SUDBURY, CO10 8HP. (Life Member)
•**ROBERTSON, Mr. John Duguid, FCA** *1966;* Robertson & Co, 169 Spencefield Lane, LEICESTER, LE5 6GG.
ROBERTSON, Mr. John Lund, FCA *1969;* 47 Proctors Rd, WOKINGHAM, RG40 1RP.
ROBERTSON, Ms. Judith, FCA *1974;* 9 Beechfield Close, BOREHAMWOOD, HERTFORDSHIRE, WD6 4NT.
ROBERTSON, Miss. Karen Mae, BA ACA *1987;* 93 St John's Avenue, GORDON, NSW 2072, AUSTRALIA.
ROBERTSON, Mr. Keith James, BA FCA *1993;* Rue Du Conseil General 11, 1205 GENEVA, SWITZERLAND.
ROBERTSON, Mrs. Laura Jane, BSc ACA *1992;* 27 Stoke Park Road, Bishopstoke, EASTLEIGH, SO50 6BQ.
ROBERTSON, Mrs. Lauren, BA ACA *1992;* Parkhill Mackie & Co, 60 Wellington Street, GLASGOW, G2 6HJ.
•**ROBERTSON, Mr. Macrae Philip, BSc FCA** *1987;* Robertson Milroy & Co, Coopers House, 65 Wingletye Lane, HORNCHURCH, RM11 3AT. See also Robertson Milroy Limited
ROBERTSON, Mr. Martin Graham, BA FCA *1981;* Walsall Housing Group, Tameway Tower, Bridge Street, WALSALL, WS1 1JZ.
ROBERTSON, Mr. Matthew Alexander, BA ACA *2003;* 32 Drewstead Road, LONDON, SW16 1AB.
ROBERTSON, Mr. Neil Charles, MA ACA *1984;* 16 Barmstedt Drive, OAKHAM, LE15 6RG.
ROBERTSON, Mr. Nicholas Antony Norman Stuart, MA FCA *1975;* The Old Rectory, Thorpe Malsor, KETTERING, NN14 1JS.
ROBERTSON, Mrs. Nicola Jane, BA ACA *2005;* 1 Bittell Court, Bittell Road, Barnt Green, BIRMINGHAM, B45 8LU.
ROBERTSON, Mr. Nigel James, MA FCA *1967;* Elmdown, Skirmett, HENLEY-ON-THAMES, RG9 6SR.
ROBERTSON, Mrs. Pamela Ann, BA ACA *1988;* 336 High Road, Leavesden, WATFORD, WD25 7EQ.
ROBERTSON, Mrs. Paula Kim, BA ACA *1988;* 16 Barmstedt Drive, OAKHAM, LE15 6RG.
ROBERTSON, Mr. Peter Anthony, LLB ACA *2007;* (Tax Fac), 74 Hogshill Lane, COBHAM, KT11 2AL.
ROBERTSON, Mr. Peter Thomas, BSc ACA *1994;* Dailycer Ltd Fourth Avenue, Deeside Industrial Park, DEESIDE, CLWYD, CH5 2NR.
ROBERTSON, Miss. Rachel Elizabeth, ACA *2009;* 7 Grosvenor Drive, Littleover, DERBY, DE23 3UQ.
ROBERTSON, Mr. Richard Andrew Fairweather, FCA *1974;* 6 Gurney Way, CAMBRIDGE, CB4 2ED.
ROBERTSON, Mrs. Sarah Elizabeth, ACA *2010;* Top Floor Flat, 2 Chantry Road, BRISTOL, BS8 2QD.
ROBERTSON, Miss. Sarah Louise, BA ACA *2007;* 33 Hunter Road, SOUTHSEA, PO4 9DL.
ROBERTSON, Miss. Sarahjane, BA ACA *1996;* 36 Northwood End Road Haynes, BEDFORD, BEDFORDSHIRE, MK45 3QB.
ROBERTSON, Mr. Scott Alexander, BA(Hons) ACA *2010;* 37 Quaypoint, Lime Kiln Road, BRISTOL, BS1 5AD.
ROBERTSON, Mr. Shaun Archibald, BCom FCA CTA *1995;* (Tax Fac), 1 Herbert Mews, Tulse Hill, LONDON, SW2 2YF.
ROBERTSON, Mr. Steven Andrew, ACA *1993;* Xchanging Claims Services, 34 Leadenhall Street, LONDON, EC3A 1AX.
ROBERTSON, Mr. Struan John, BA ACA *2007;* with BDO LLP, 2 City Place, Beehive Ring Road, GATWICK, WEST SUSSEX, RH6 0PA.
ROBERTSON, Mr. Stuart James, ACA *2008;* 66 The Shires, ST. HELENS, MERSEYSIDE, WA10 3XL.
ROBERTSON, Mr. Stuart James, BA(Hons) ACA *2003;* G J Johnson & Sons Ltd, Unit 7, Trinity Court, Brunel Road, Totton, SOUTHAMPTON SO40 3WX.
ROBERTSON, Mr. Stuart John, BSc FCA *1986;* Gleddoch House, Stockcroft Road, Balcombe, HAYWARDS HEATH, WEST SUSSEX, RH17 6LG.
ROBERTSON, Mrs. Susan, BSc ACA *1986;* Local Solution, Mount Vernon Green, Hall Lane, LIVERPOOL, L7 8TF.
ROBERTSON, Miss. Susan Mary, BA FCA *1990;* Cherwell, Knowl Hill, WOKING, SURREY, GU22 7HL.
ROBERTSON, Mr. Terence James, FCA *1974;* 49 Chiltern Drive, Charvil, READING, RG10 9QF.
ROBERTSON, Mr. Thomas Crawford, BA FCA *1974;* 23 Newton Road, Tankerton, WHITSTABLE, CT5 2JD.
ROBERTSON, Mr. Timothy, FCA *1958;* The Coppice, Abbots Way, Hodnet, MARKET DRAYTON, TF9 3NQ. (Life Member)
ROBERTSON, Mr. Torquhil Francis, MA FCA *1975;* Sinclair Robertson, 8 Holyrood Street, LONDON, SE1 2EL.
ROBERTSON, Miss. Valerie Siobhan, ACA *2008;* Network Rail Infrastructure Ltd Kings Place, 90 York Way, LONDON, N1 9AG.
ROBERTSON, Miss. Victoria Elizabeth, BA(Hons) ACA *2001;* 9 Smyrna Road, LONDON, NW6 4LY.
ROBERTSON-ADAMS, Mr. Donald Henry, FCA *1975;* Bryngwrg, Beulah, NEWCASTLE EMLYN, DYFED, SA38 9QR.
•**ROBERTSON-KELLIE, Mr. Julian Alexander, BA ACA** *1990;* Ernst & Young LLP, 1 More London Place, LONDON, SE1 2AF. See also Ernst & Young Europe LLP
ROBEY, Mrs. Dawn Zoe, MA ACA *1987;* Financial Reporting Council Aldwych House, 71-91 Aldwych, LONDON, WC2B 4HN.
ROBEY, Mr. Edward Peter, FCA *1954;* 23 Marconi Close, HELSTON, CORNWALL, TR13 8PD. (Life Member)
ROBEY, Mr. Patrick Alexander, BSc ACA *1985;* 35 Oathall Road, HAYWARDS HEATH, RH16 3EG.
ROBEY, Mr. Peter, BA(Hons) ACA *2010;* 118 Gosport Road, LEE-ON-THE-SOLENT, HAMPSHIRE, PO13 9DP.
ROBEY, Mr. Peter William, BSc ACA *1981;* 154 Church Street, NORTHPORT, NY 11768, UNITED STATES.
ROBEY, Mr. Quentin Edward, BA FCA *1974;* 34 Homefield Road, Chiswick, LONDON, W4 2LW.
ROBIN, Mr. Craig Illis, ACA *1979;* Primrose Marketing Ltd Unit 6, Berber Business Centre Kitchener Road, HIGH WYCOMBE, BUCKINGHAMSHIRE, HP11 2TD.
ROBIN, Mr. Peter, BSc FCA *1979;* Robin Associates, 16 Sandy Lodge Road, RICKMANSWORTH, HERTFORDSHIRE, WD3 1LJ.
ROBINETTE, Mr. Giles Andrew David, BCom FCA *1988;* 22a Caldwell Street, LONDON, SW9 0EL.
ROBINS, Mr. Andrew James, BA(Hons) ACA *2001;* 48 Puddingstone Drive, ST. ALBANS, HERTFORDSHIRE, AL4 0GY.
ROBINS, Mr. Andrew Stephen, MA FCA *1992;* RBC International Wealth Planning, Fourth Floor, The Quadrangle, Imperial Square, CHELTENHAM, GL50 1PZ.
ROBINS, Mr. Dominic John, BSc(Hons) ACA *2002;* 12 Leacey Mews, Churchdown, GLOUCESTER, GL3 1PD.
ROBINS, Mrs. Heather Margaret, FCA *1978;* The Cowshed, Great Nineveh, Nineveh Lane, Benenden, CRANBROOK, TN17 4LG.
•**ROBINS, Mr. Ian David, BA ACA** *1994;* 10 Montagu Road, Formby, LIVERPOOL, L37 1LA.
ROBINS, Mr. Kenneth Lamerton, FCA *1947;* c/o Mr K Robins, Redmoor House, Down Road, TAVISTOCK, DEVON, PL19 9AF. (Life Member)
ROBINS, Mrs. Lisa Jane, BA ACA *1997;* 16 Engliff Lane, Pyrford, WOKING, SURREY, GU22 8SU.

ROBINS, Mr. Michael George, FCA *1969;* Milford Hall, Milford, Baschurch, SHREWSBURY, SY4 2JU. (Life Member)
ROBINS, Mr. Neil Stewart, MSc ACA *2004;* 4 Roman Drive, LEEDS, LS8 2DR.
ROBINS, Mr. Nicholas Calamada, BSc ACA *1993;* 16 Engliff Lane, WOKING, SURREY, GU22 8SU.
ROBINS, Mr. Nicholas David Turner, FCA *1972;* Redmoor House, Down Road, TAVISTOCK, PL19 9AF.
ROBINS, Mr. Paul Ashcroft, BSc FCA *1980;* Maesderwen, Penperlleni, PONTYPOOL, GWENT, NP4 0AJ.
ROBINS, Mr. Paul Ian, BSc ACA *1992;* 79 Trafalgar Road, HORSHAM, WEST SUSSEX, RH12 2QJ.
ROBINS, Mr. Peter Anthony, FCA *1958;* 10 Braids Walk, Kirk Ella, HULL, HU10 7PD. (Life Member)
ROBINS, Mr. Richard Hilton, BSc FCA *1994;* 1467 Rifle Range Road, EL CERRITO, CA 94530, UNITED STATES.
ROBINS, Mrs. Susan Mary, ACA *1983;* Wycombe Abbey School Cloister House, Abbey Way, HIGH WYCOMBE, BUCKINGHAMSHIRE, HP11 1PE.
ROBINS, Mrs. Tanya, ACA *1994; (CA Scotland* Portsmouth Football Club Ltd, Fratton Park, Frogmore Road, PORTSMOUTH, HAMPSHIRE, PO4 8RA.
ROBINS, Miss. Tessa Louise, BSc FCA *1995;* National Bank House Level 11, 170-187 Featherston Steet, WELLINGTON 6014, NEW ZEALAND.
ROBINS, Mr. Timothy Mark, BA ACA *1990;* 26 Penlington Court, NANTWICH, CHESHIRE, CW5 6SB.
•ROBINSKI, Mr. Tadeusz Edward, BA ACA *1997;* Poselska 29, 03-931 WARSAW, POLAND.
ROBINSON, Mr. Adam Peter, BA ACA *2005;* 35 Somerdale Grove, LEEDS, LS13 4SD.
ROBINSON, Mr. Adam Worsley, BA ACA *1988;* G.P.O Box 161, CENTRAL, HONG KONG ISLAND, HONG KONG SAR.
•ROBINSON, Mr. Alan Arthur Macleod, FCA *1965;* Alan A.M. Robinson, New Glenmore, Sliders Lane, Furners Green, UCKFIELD, EAST SUSSEX TN22 3RU.
ROBINSON, Mr. Alan George, FCA *1973;* 3 Tivoli Place, ILKLEY, LS29 8SU.
ROBINSON, Mr. Alan Paul, ACA *1979;* Driftwood, Rosevine, Portscatho, TRURO, TR2 5EW.
ROBINSON, Mr. Alan Steven, BA FCA *1991;* Kirkstone House, Pex Hill, WIDNES, CHESHIRE, WA8 5QW.
ROBINSON, Mr. Alan William, BSc FCA *1991;* 16 Fairlawn Grove, Chiswick, LONDON, W4 5EH.
ROBINSON, Mr. Alfred William, FCA *1967;* 33 Ethelburga Road, Harold Wood, ROMFORD, RM3 0QR. (Life Member)
ROBINSON, Mrs. Alison Jane, FCA *1993;* with Grant Thornton UK LLP, 30 Finsbury Square, LONDON, EC2P 2YU.
•ROBINSON, Mrs. Alison Mary, ACA *1989;* A M Robinson, 3 Hospital Cottages, Crescent Road, BRENTWOOD, ESSEX, CM14 5JA.
•ROBINSON, Mrs. Alison Ruth, BCom ACA *1990;* (Tax Fac), Saffery Champness, Sovereign House, 6 Windsor Court, Clarence Drive, HARROGATE, HG1 2PE.
ROBINSON, Mr. Alistair James, BA ACA *1996;* The Old School House, 2 Eastfield Road, Westbury-On-Trym, BRISTOL, BS9 4AD.
ROBINSON, Mr. Alvin David, BA FCA *1967;* 120 Old Birmingham Rd, Marlbrook, BROMSGROVE, B60 1DH. (Life Member)
ROBINSON, Mrs. Amanda Jane, BA FCA *1992;* Cummins Ltd, St. Andrews Road, HUDDERSFIELD, HD1 6RA.
ROBINSON, Miss. Andrea Michelle, BSc ACA *2004;* 81 Gordon Road, LONDON, E11 2RA.
•ROBINSON, Mr. Andrew, ACA *1993;* 35 Lysander Way, Cottingley, BINGLEY, WEST YORKSHIRE, BD16 1WF.
ROBINSON, Mr. Andrew, BSc ACA *1992;* 280 Bishopsgate, LONDON, EC2M 4AA.
•ROBINSON, Mr. Andrew Craig, ACA *1996;* Armstrong Watson, Milburn House, Hexham Business Park, Burn Lane, HEXHAM, NORTHUMBERLAND NE46 3RU.
ROBINSON, Mr. Andrew David, BSc ACA CF *2003;* Tanglewood, Stortford Road, Hatfield Heath, BISHOP'S STORTFORD, CM22 7DL.
ROBINSON, Mr. Andrew David Firth, MA FCA *1986;* Cherry Trees, Hooke Road, East Horsley, LEATHERHEAD, KT24 5DX.
•ROBINSON, Mr. Andrew James, BSc FCA *1992;* A J Robinson & Co, Saddleworth Business Centre, Huddersfield Road, Delph, OLDHAM, OL3 5DF.
ROBINSON, Mr. Andrew John, ACA *2009;* Flat 2 Les Chenes Court, La Route de Maufant St. Saviour, JERSEY, JE2 7HX.
ROBINSON, Mr. Andrew John, FCA *1971;* 4 Clumber Close, Poynton, STOCKPORT, SK12 1PG.
ROBINSON, Mr. Andrew John, BSc ACA *1992;* Kincraigie, Over Ross Street, ROSS-ON-WYE, HEREFORDSHIRE, HR9 7AU.
•ROBINSON, Mr. Andrew Mark, BA ACA *1986;* Humphrey & Co, 7-9 The Avenue, EASTBOURNE, EAST SUSSEX, BN21 3YA.
ROBINSON, Mr. Andrew Nicholas, BA ACA *1980;* 85 Deacon Road, KINGSTON UPON THAMES, KT2 6LS.
•ROBINSON, Mr. Andrew Paul, BCom FCA *1992;* (Tax Fac), A P Robinson LLP, 107 Cleethorpe Road, GRIMSBY, SOUTH HUMBERSIDE, DN31 3ER.
ROBINSON, Mr. Andrew Peter Lyles, MSci ACA *2007;* 2 Vine Farm Road, POOLE, DORSET, BH12 5EN.
ROBINSON, Mr. Andrew Stewart, BSc ACA *2006;* 34 Huckford Road, Winterbourne, BRISTOL, BS36 1DU.
ROBINSON, Mr. Andrew Stuart, BA ACA TEP *1992;* Russell Cooke Solicitors, 2 Putney Hill, LONDON, SW15 6AB.
•ROBINSON, Mr. Andrew William, FCA *1983;* A.W. Robinson, P O Box 3800, DUBAI, UNITED ARAB EMIRATES.
ROBINSON, Mrs. Angela Ellis, BSc ACA *1992;* Moore Stephens, 150 Aldersgate Street, LONDON, EC1A 4AB.
•ROBINSON, Mrs. Ann Katrina, BA ACA *1995;* (Tax Fac), Ann K Robinson, 13b Market Place, Caistor, MARKET RASEN, LINCOLNSHIRE, LN7 6TW. See also Book Manager Limited
ROBINSON, Miss. Anna, BA(Hons) ACA *2009;* 17 Tay Close, OAKHAM, LE15 6JR.
ROBINSON, Mrs. Anne, BSc FCA *1984;* 45 High Meadow, Tollerton, NOTTINGHAM, NG12 4DZ.
•ROBINSON, Mrs. Annika Jane, BSc ACA *1991;* Enterprise Solutions (England) Ltd, March House, 44 The Avenue, TADWORTH, KT20 5AT. See also Enterprise Solutions Ltd
ROBINSON, Mr. Anthony, MA FCA *1962;* 44 Inverness Street, LONDON, NW1 7HB.
ROBINSON, Mr. Anthony David, MMath ACA *2005;* Kaplan Financial Alan House, 5 Clumber Street, NOTTINGHAM, NG1 3ED.
ROBINSON, Mr. Anthony Gordon, BA ACA *1997;* with Deloitte LLP, 4 Brindley Place, BIRMINGHAM, B1 2HZ.
ROBINSON, Mr. Anthony John, ACA FMAAT *2004;* 77 Princes Reach, Ashton-on-Ribble, PRESTON, PR2 2GB.
ROBINSON, Mr. Anthony Leake, BA FCA *1970;* 57 Bottrells Lane, CHALFONT ST. GILES, BUCKINGHAMSHIRE, HP8 4EY.
ROBINSON, Mr. Anthony Lee, ACA *1986;* C/o Mumtalakat, P.O. Box 820, MANAMA, BAHRAIN.
ROBINSON, Mr. Antony James, FCA *1972;* Priory Gardens Main Street, Hampole, DONCASTER, SOUTH YORKSHIRE, DN6 7ET.
•ROBINSON, Mr. Antony Stephen, FCA *1980;* J.P.B. Harris & Co, 54 St. Marys Lane, UPMINSTER, ESSEX, RM14 2QT. See also JPB Harris & Co Ltd
ROBINSON, Mr. Arthur Edward Steward, FCA *1961;* 64 Brookside, London Road, HERTFORD, SG13 7LL. (Life Member)
•ROBINSON, Mr. Arthur Sydney, FCA *1956;* A.S. Robinson, 17 Ingham Close, Bradshaw, HALIFAX, HX2 9PQ.
ROBINSON, Mr. Avi Karel, ACA *2008;* Cairn Financial Advisers LLP, 61 Cheapside, LONDON, EC2V 6AX.
ROBINSON, Mr. Barry Alexander, FCA *1955;* 2 Marton Court, Cawston, RUGBY, WARWICKSHIRE, CV22 7SW. (Life Member)
ROBINSON, Mr. Barry John, BA ACA *2005;* Flat 1, 23 Millgate Lane, MANCHESTER, M20 2SD.
ROBINSON, Mr. Ben, ACA *2001;* (Tax Fac), Cobwebs Main Street, Elvington, YORK, YO41 4AG.
ROBINSON, Mr. Benjamin Paul, BA ACA *2006;* Place du Cirque 4, 1205 GENEVA, SWITZERLAND.
ROBINSON, Mr. Boyd, BSc ACA *1996;* 26 Shackleton Way, SHREWSBURY, SY3 8SW.
ROBINSON, Mr. Brian, BA FCA *1982;* 7 Acle Burn, NEWTON AYCLIFFE, DL5 4XB.
•ROBINSON, Mr. Brian John, FCA *1975;* B.J. Robinson, 10 Bishops Avenue, Llandaff, CARDIFF, CF5 2HJ.
ROBINSON, Miss. Bridie, BSc ACA *2003;* with Grant Thornton UK LLP, 1 Whitehall Riverside, Whitehall Road, LEEDS, WEST YORKSHIRE, LS1 4BN.
ROBINSON, Mr. Bruce William, MA(Oxon) FRGS ACA MSI *1979;* Hawkesfoot House, 1 Panorama, Cape Hawke, FORSTER, NSW 2428, AUSTRALIA.
•ROBINSON, Mr. Bryan George, BSc FCA ATII *1989;* Holeys, Stuart House, 15/17 North Park Road, HARROGATE, HG1 5PD. See also Holeys Limited
ROBINSON, Miss. Bryony Charlotte, BSc(Hons) ACA *2003;* 12 Anson Close, RINGWOOD, BH24 1XN.
ROBINSON, Miss. Carol Ann, BA ACA AMCT *1997;* Flat 107 Block A, 27 Green Walk, LONDON, SE1 4TT.
•ROBINSON, Mrs. Caroline Anne, ACA *1992;* Robinson, 9 Costins Walk, BERKHAMSTED, HERTFORDSHIRE, HP4 2WG.
ROBINSON, Mrs. Catherine Ann, BSc ACA *1999;* 2 New Church Road, Boldmere, SUTTON COLDFIELD, WEST MIDLANDS, B73 5RT.
ROBINSON, Mrs. Catherine Julie Louise, BSc ACA *1997;* Maple Tree House, Cranleigh Road, Wonersh, GUILDFORD, SURREY, GU5 0PB.
ROBINSON, Mr. Charles Edward, BA ACA *2005;* ISIS Equity Partners, Bank House, 8 Cherry Street, BIRMINGHAM, B2 5AN.
ROBINSON, Mr. Charles Francis, MA FCA *1970;* 520 Rodes Drive, CHARLOTTESVILLE, VA 22903, UNITED STATES.
ROBINSON, Mr. Charles William Guy, BSc ACA *1981;* Portland, Goytside Road, CHESTERFIELD, S40 2PH.
ROBINSON, Mrs. Christina Edna, BSc ACA *1981;* Surfs Edge, West Rae Road, Polzeath, WADEBRIDGE, CORNWALL, PL27 6ST.
ROBINSON, Mr. Christopher Charles, BSc ACA *1984;* 4 Damson Way, ST. ALBANS, AL4 9XU.
ROBINSON, Mr. Christopher David, BSc ACA *1997;* Lindens 1a Hare Hill Close Pyrford, WOKING, SURREY, GU22 8UH.
•ROBINSON, Mr. Christopher Eric, BA ACA *1992;* QX Accounting Services Ltd, Castle Chambers, Off Mill Bridge, SKIPTON, NORTH YORKSHIRE, BD23 1NJ.
•ROBINSON, Mr. Christopher James, FCA *1973;* Sproull & Co, 31-33 College Road, HARROW, MIDDLESEX, HA1 1EJ.
ROBINSON, Mr. Christopher Michael, FCA *1976;* 255 Middle Patent Road, Bedford, NEW YORK, NY 10506, UNITED STATES.
ROBINSON, Mr. Christopher Paul, BSc ACA *1989;* 2 St Germans Place, LONDON, SE3 0NH.
ROBINSON, Mr. Christopher Peter, BA ACA *1982;* St Aidans House, Lidgett Lane, Skelmanthorpe, HUDDERSFIELD, HD8 9AQ.
ROBINSON, Mr. Christopher Philip, BA FCA *1969;* Galley Hill Cottage, Galley Hill, Selborne, ALTON, GU34 3LN.
ROBINSON, Mr. Christopher Stopford, BA ACA *1985;* 17 Old Oak Avenue, COULSDON, CR5 3PG.
ROBINSON, Mrs. Claire, BSc ACA CTA *1990;* The Old Cottages, Church Road, Swanmore, SOUTHAMPTON, HAMPSHIRE, SO32 2PU.
ROBINSON, Miss. Claire, ACA *2011;* 8 Yukon Road, Balham, LONDON, SW12 9PU.
ROBINSON, Mrs. Claire Elizabeth, BSc ACA *1995;* The Well House, Park Lane, Walton, LUTTERWORTH, LEICESTERSHIRE, LE17 5RQ.
ROBINSON, Mrs. Clare, BSc ACA *1994;* Hare House, 16 Kelvedon Road, Coggeshall, COLCHESTER, CO6 1RG.
ROBINSON, Miss. Clare Patricia, BSc FCA *1984;* 54 Somerset Road, Edgbaston, BIRMINGHAM, B15 2PD.
ROBINSON, Ms. Clare Vosper, BA ACA *2007;* Flat C, 27 Albert Road, LONDON, N4 3RR.
ROBINSON, Mr. Colin Graham, FCA *1971;* 34 Warrington Road, IPSWICH, IP1 3QU.
ROBINSON, Mr. Colyn Sydney, BA ACA *1981;* Berakah House, Kent Road, CHICHESTER, WEST SUSSEX, PO19 7NH.
ROBINSON, Mr. Craig Hunter, MA ACA *1989;* 101 Summerleys Road, PRINCES RISBOROUGH, HP27 9QA.
ROBINSON, Mr. Darryl, BSc ACA *1998;* 29 Back Lane, Whixley, YORK, YO26 8BG.
•ROBINSON, Mr. David, FCA *1982;* Haywood & Co., 24-26 Mansfield Road, ROTHERHAM, S60 2DR.
ROBINSON, Mr. David, BA ACA *1979;* 40 South Audley Street, LONDON, W1K 2PR.
ROBINSON, Mr. David, FCA *1971;* Pear Tree Cottage, Arram Road, Leconfield, BEVERLEY, HU17 7NP.
•ROBINSON, Mr. David, LLB ACA *1984;* Odyssey Accounting and Tax Services, 167 Ramsden Road, LONDON, SW12 8RF.
ROBINSON, Mr. David Alan, FCA *1966;* 98a Tadcaster Road, YORK, YO24 1LT.
ROBINSON, Mr. David Alexander, FCA *1977;* 99 High Street, Girton, CAMBRIDGE, CB3 0QQ.
ROBINSON, Mr. David Alfred Edward, BSc FCA *1973;* 3 Lebanon Park, TWICKENHAM, TW1 3DE. (Life Member)
ROBINSON, Mr. David Anthony, FCA *1961;* 6 Parrys Grove, Stoke Bishop, BRISTOL, BS9 1TT. (Life Member)
ROBINSON, Mr. David Anthony, BA(Hons) ACA *2002;* 43 Leasway, WESTCLIFF-ON-SEA, ESSEX, SS0 8PA.
ROBINSON, Mr. David Arthur, BSc ACA *1978;* Downs View Old Station Road, Itchen Abbas, WINCHESTER, HAMPSHIRE, SO21 1BA.
ROBINSON, Mr. David Arthur Thomas, FCA *1970;* Alvar Strategic Solutions LLP, 19 Friths Drive, REIGATE, SURREY, RH2 0DS.
ROBINSON, Mr. David Foster, BA FCA *1959;* Luards, Ulting Lane, Langford, MALDON, CM9 6QB. (Life Member)
ROBINSON, Mr. David Francis, MA FCA *1965;* Tuck Mill, Usk Road, Shirenewton, CHEPSTOW, GWENT, NP16 6BU.
ROBINSON, Mr. David Frank, FCA *1973;* 62 Smugglers Way, Barns Green, HORSHAM, WEST SUSSEX, RH13 0JY.
•ROBINSON, Mr. David Howard, FCA *1973;* (Tax Fac), Howard & Co, Bridge House, High Street, Horam, HEATHFIELD, TN21 0EY.
ROBINSON, Mr. David James, MA FCA *1971;* 4 The Hayles Donkey Lane Ashford Carbonel, LUDLOW, SHROPSHIRE, SY8 4DA.
ROBINSON, Mr. David James, BSc ACA *2000;* Hypo Real Estate Bank International, 30 St. Mary Axe, LONDON, EC3A 8BF.
ROBINSON, Mr. David James Ian, BA ACA *2008;* (Tax Fac), Arnold Hill & Co Craven House, 16 Northumberland Avenue, LONDON, WC2N 5AP.
ROBINSON, Mr. David Jeremy, MBA ACA *2002;* Ramsey Robinson Solicitors Mallan House, Bridge End Industrial Estate, HEXHAM, NORTHUMBERLAND, NE46 4DQ.
•ROBINSON, Mr. David John, FCA *1981;* 56 Butt Lane, Milton, CAMBRIDGE, CB24 6DG.
•ROBINSON, Mr. David John, FCA *1967;* D J. Robinson, 58 Peartree Walk, Cheshunt, WALTHAM CROSS, EN7 6RE.
ROBINSON, Mr. David John, BA(Hons) ACA *2004;* 2 Riverside Drive, Summerseat, BURY, LANCASHIRE, BL9 5QX.
ROBINSON, Mr. David John, BSc ACA *2011;* Apartment 19, 50 George Street, BIRMINGHAM, B3 1PP.
ROBINSON, Mr. David John, FCA *1963;* 4 Druids Close, West Parley, FERNDOWN, DORSET, BH22 8RU. (Life Member)
ROBINSON, Mr. David John, MSc BA FCA ATII *1991;* (Tax Fac), 63 Beech Grove, Stanwix, CARLISLE, CA3 9BL.
•ROBINSON, Mr. David John Lyles, FCA *1981;* Hope Shaw Ltd, 21 The Old Yarn Mills, Westbury, SHERBORNE, DT9 3RQ.
ROBINSON, Mr. David Michael, BA ACA *1981;* Inglenook, 10 Hillside Road, RADLETT, WD7 7BH.
•ROBINSON, Mr. David Nicholas, MA FCA *1982;* The Barn, Shaftenhoe End, Barley, ROYSTON, HERTFORDSHIRE, SG8 8LE.
ROBINSON, Mr. David Payne, BSc ACA *1988;* Mayfield Thorns Close, Whiteleaf, PRINCES RISBOROUGH, BUCKINGHAMSHIRE, HP27 0LU.
•ROBINSON, Mr. David Raymond, BA FCA *1972;* Robinson Stopford Limited, 30 West Avenue, EXETER, DEVON, EX4 4SE.
ROBINSON, Mr. David Stanley, BA ACA *1998;* 6 Vale Drive, Hampton Vale, PETERBOROUGH, PE7 8EP.
ROBINSON, Mrs. Deborah Jane, BSc ACA *1993;* 33 Snowdrop Garth, Holme-On-Spalding-Moor, YORK, YO43 4DW.
ROBINSON, Mr. Dennis Edwin, FCA *1958;* 35 Hedge End, Barnham, BOGNOR REGIS, WEST SUSSEX, PO22 0JP. (Life Member)
ROBINSON, Mr. Derek Arthur, FCA *1976;* 7 Park Way, RICKMANSWORTH, WD3 7AU. (Life Member)
•ROBINSON, Mr. Derek Curtis, BA FCA *1988;* S V Bye, New Garth House, Upper Garth Gardens, GUISBOROUGH, TS14 6HA.
ROBINSON, Mr. Derek John, FCA *1973;* 17 Old Palace Lane, RICHMOND, TW9 1PG.
ROBINSON, Mrs. Diana Elizabeth Deborah, BSc ACA *1983;* The Beacon School, Amersham Road, Chesham Bois, AMERSHAM, BUCKINGHAMSHIRE, HP6 5PF.
ROBINSON, Mr. Dominic Nicholas Yeoman, BA ACA *1980;* The Old Coach House, Upper Brighton Road, SURBITON, KT6 6JY.
•ROBINSON, Mr. Douglas, FCA *1974;* (Tax Fac), with Hope Agar Limited, 24a Marsh Street, Rothwell, LEEDS, LS26 0BB.
ROBINSON, Mr. Douglas James, MA ACA CTA *2003;* Flat 3 29/F, Block B Ventris Place, 19-23 Ventris Road, HAPPY VALLEY, HONG KONG SAR.
ROBINSON, Mr. Douglas Richard, ACA *1994;* KINCH ROBINSON LIMITED, 83 WILKINSON STREET, SHEFFIELD, S10 2GJ.
ROBINSON, Mrs. Eleni, BSc ACA CTA *1996;* (Tax Fac), 11 Highlands Road, BARNET, EN5 5AA.
ROBINSON, Mrs. Elisabeth Ann, BA ACA *1986;* 1 The Halyards, Satchell Lane, Hamble, SOUTHAMPTON, SO31 4HQ.
ROBINSON, Miss. Elkie, BA ACA *2007;* 42 Sycamore Park, Brandon, DURHAM, DH7 8PR.

ROBINSON, Miss. Emma Jane, MA BA ACA *2009;* 62 Smugglers Way, Barns Green, HORSHAM, WEST SUSSEX, RH13 0JY.
•**ROBINSON, Mr. Fergus David, BA ACA** *1992;* Sinclair & Co (Accountants) Ltd, 7 Portland Road, Edgbaston, BIRMINGHAM, B16 9HN.
ROBINSON, Mrs. Fiona, FCA *1987;* Springfield, Hall Park Road, Walton, WETHERBY, LS23 7DQ.
•**ROBINSON, Mr. Francis, BSc ACA** *1990;* (Tax Fac), Mitchells, Suite 4, Parsons House, Parsons Road, WASHINGTON, TYNE AND WEAR NE37 1EZ.
ROBINSON, Mr. Frank Edward Starte, MA FCA *1973;* 9 Bourne Grove, ASHTEAD, SURREY, KT21 2NX. (Life Member)
ROBINSON, Mr. Frederick, FCA *1939;* 143 Liverpool Road, Beckerstaffe, ORMSKIRK, L39 0EQ. (Life Member)
ROBINSON, Mr. Frederick Alan, FCA *1956;* 405-9280 Salish Court, BURNABY V3J 7J8, BC, CANADA. (Life Member)
ROBINSON, Mr. Frederick Vaughan, FCA *1978;* 9 Orchard Avenue, NEW MALDEN, KT3 4JU.
•**ROBINSON, Mr. Gary, MSc BSc ACA** *2008;* Stewart & Co Accountancy Services Ltd, Knoll House, Knoll Road, CAMBERLEY, SURREY, GU15 3SY. See also Stewart & Co
ROBINSON, Mr. Gary, BSc ACA *1993;* 6 Stuart Green, EDINBURGH, EH12 8YF.
•**ROBINSON, Mr. Gary Brian, BA FCA** *1993;* Alpha Accountancy Evesham Limited, 35 Badsey Road, Willersey, BROADWAY, WORCESTERSHIRE, WR12 7PR.
ROBINSON, Mr. Gary Thomas, BA ACA *1999;* 90 Battersea High Street, LONDON, SW11 3HP.
ROBINSON, Mr. Gavin James, BSc FCA *1990;* Wellington House, 4b Cassington Road, EYNSHAM, OXFORDSHIRE, OX29 4LF.
ROBINSON, Miss. Gemma, ACA *2008;* Flat 13, Stapleford Lodge, 33a Bycullah Road, ENFIELD, MIDDLESEX, EN2 8FH.
ROBINSON, Mr. Geoffrey, FCA *1954;* 11 Hadendale, CRADLEY HEATH, B64 7JW. (Life Member)
ROBINSON, Mr. Geoffrey, LLB ACA CTA *1981;* with Deloitte LLP, Abbots House, Abbey Street, READING, RG1 3BD.
ROBINSON, Mr. Geoffrey Robert Anthony, BA FCA *1998;* 11 Stuart Road, Wimbledon Park, LONDON, SW19 8DJ.
ROBINSON, Mr. Geoffrey Wroughton, MA FCA *1972;* 3A Brunswick Gardens, Kensington, LONDON, W8 4AS.
ROBINSON, Mr. George, ACA *2011;* Flat 527, Ben Jonson House, Barbican, LONDON, EC2Y 8NH.
ROBINSON, Mr. George Edward, BSc FCA *1978;* Financial Services Authority, 25 The North Colonnade, LONDON, E14 5HS.
ROBINSON, Mr. Gerald Norman, FCA FMAAT *1963;* (Member of Council 1998 - 2005), 15 Cyncoed Crescent, CARDIFF, CF23 6SW. (Life Member)
•**ROBINSON, Mr. Gerard Paul, FCA** *1981;* Roddis Taylor Robinson, Unit 6, Acorn Business Park, Woodseats Close, SHEFFIELD, S8 0TB.
ROBINSON, Mr. Giles Philip, MEng ACA *2007;* Quince Cottage Easton Town, Sherston, MALMESBURY, SN16 0LS.
ROBINSON, Mr. Glenn, BSc ACA *1992;* 15 Pack Horse Road, Melbourne, DERBY, DE73 8EG.
ROBINSON, Mr. Gordon Bourne, BSc FCA *1977;* 27 Redpath Drive, FALKIRK, FK2 8QL.
ROBINSON, Mr. Graeme Michael, ACA *2009;* 16 Cheyne Gardens, LIVERPOOL, L19 3PH.
ROBINSON, Mr. Graeme Neal, BA FCA *1977;* The Lypiatts, Lansdown Road, CHELTENHAM, GLOUCESTERSHIRE, GL50 2JA.
ROBINSON, Mr. Graham Alan, FCA *1977;* 82 Isis Avenue, BICESTER, OXFORDSHIRE, OX26 2GS.
ROBINSON, Mr. Graham Peter, FCA *1964;* 39 St. James Gardens, WESTCLIFF-ON-SEA, SS0 0BU.
•**ROBINSON, Mr. Graham Timothy, MA ACA CTA AMCT** *2000;* PricewaterhouseCoopers LLP, 1 Embankment Place, LONDON, WC2N 6RH. See also PricewaterhouseCoopers
•**ROBINSON, Mr. Guy, BA FCA** *1981;* Christopher Guy Accountants Limited, Sovereign House, 37 Middle Road, Park Gate, SOUTHAMPTON, SO31 7GH. See also Stressfree Bookkeeping Limited
ROBINSON, Mr. Harry Charles, BSc FCA *1964;* 30 Ridings Avenue, Winchmore Hill, LONDON, N21 2EL.
ROBINSON, Mrs. Heather Elaine, BA ACA *1998;* 19 Raglan Road, BANGOR, COUNTY DOWN, BT20 3TL.
ROBINSON, Miss. Helen, BSc ACA *2010;* Baker Tilly Festival Way, Festival Park, STOKE-ON-TRENT, ST1 5BB.

ROBINSON, Miss. Helen, ACA *1993;* with PKF (UK) LLP, Pannell House, 159 Charles Street, LEICESTER, LE1 1LD.
ROBINSON, Mrs. Helen Ann Elizabeth, BSc ACA CTA *1979;* (Tax Fac), Cedarwood, 5 Harmer Dell, Harmer Green, WELWYN, HERTFORDSHIRE, AL6 0BE.
ROBINSON, Mrs. Hilary Anne, LLB FCA *1984;* (Tax Fac), Kodak Ltd, Hemel One, Boundary Way, HEMEL HEMPSTEAD, HERTFORDSHIRE, HP2 7YU.
ROBINSON, Mr. Howard Charles Alfred, BSc FCA *1978;* Spring Well Farm, Chesterton, BICESTER, OX26 1TW.
ROBINSON, Mr. Hugh James Francis, BSc FCA *1982;* School House Kake Street, Waltham, CANTERBURY, CT4 5SD.
ROBINSON, Mr. Hugo Edward William, MA ACA *1999;* Flat 3, 10 Abbeville Road, LONDON, SW4 9NJ.
•**ROBINSON, Mr. Ian, BSc FCA** *1973;* (Tax Fac), 23 Courtlands Avenue, HAMPTON, TW12 3NS. See also Ian Robinson
ROBINSON, Mr. Ian, BSc ACA *1989;* 11 Ercall Lane, Wellington, TELFORD, SHROPSHIRE, TF1 2DY.
ROBINSON, Mr. Ian, ACA *2011;* 2 Totland Close, Great Sankey, WARRINGTON, WA5 3JW.
•**ROBINSON, Mr. Ian, BSc FCA** *1991;* MaxAim LLP, United Business Centre, 1 Mariner Court, Calder Park, WAKEFIELD, WEST YORKSHIRE WF4 3FL.
ROBINSON, Mr. Ian, BA ACA *1996;* 25 Avenue Matignon, 75008 PARIS, FRANCE.
ROBINSON, Mr. Ian Claude Melville, FCA *1977;* 25 Nash Avenue, Perton, WOLVERHAMPTON, WV6 7SS.
•**ROBINSON, Mr. Ian George, BA FCA** *1972;* 74 Brookmans Avenue, Brookmans Park, HATFIELD, AL9 7QQ.
ROBINSON, Mr. Ian Harold Musgrave, FCA *1950;* The Vicarage Cottage, Arncliffe, SKIPTON, BD23 5QD. (Life Member)
ROBINSON, Mr. Ian James, MA ACA *1995;* 2 Lower Barford Cottages, Bramshaw, LYNDHURST, SO43 7JN.
ROBINSON, Mr. Ian Kenneth, BA ACA *1996;* Liverpool Volkswagen, Derby Road, LIVERPOOL, L20 1AB.
ROBINSON, Mr. Ian Michael, FCA *1969;* 47 Apsley Road, Clifton, BRISTOL, BS8 2SN.
ROBINSON, Mr. Ian Philip, BA FCA *1996;* The Old Reading Rooms, High Street, Laxton, NEWARK, NG22 0NX.
ROBINSON, Mr. Ian William, FCA *1968;* Riverway Sparepenny Lane, Eynsford, DARTFORD, DA4 0JJ.
ROBINSON, Mrs. Ingrid, BSc(Hons) ACA *2003;* 4 Stevenson Crescent, POOLE, BH14 9NU.
ROBINSON, Mr. James, BSc ACA *2007;* 22 Carmarthen Road, CHELTENHAM, GLOUCESTERSHIRE, GL51 3LA.
ROBINSON, Mr. James Edward Manning, BSc ACA *2006;* with Kensington Management Group Ltd, 2nd Floor Genesis Building, PO Box 10027, GEORGE TOWN, GRAND CAYMAN, KY1-1001 CAYMAN ISLANDS.
•**ROBINSON, Mr. James Ian, ACA FCCA** *2008;* Princecroft Willis LLP, Towngate House, 2-8 Parkstone Road, POOLE, DORSET, BH15 2PW. See also PW Business Solutions
ROBINSON, Mr. James Ian, BA ACA *1995;* with KPMG LLP, 37 Albyn Place, ABERDEEN, AB10 1JB.
ROBINSON, Mr. James Peyton, BSc FCA *1980;* Manor Farm House, North Waltham, BASINGSTOKE, RG25 2BS.
ROBINSON, Mr. James Scott, BA(Hons) ACA *2001;* 2A York Terrace, NORTH SHIELDS, NE29 0EF.
•**ROBINSON, Mrs. Janet, BSc FCA** *1977;* (Tax Fac), Janet Robinson & Co, Victoria Loft, Hill Furze, Bishampton, PERSHORE, WR10 2NB.
ROBINSON, Mrs. Jayne Lesley, BA ACA *1989;* Kevin Beare & Co Forest House, 3-5 Horndean Road, BRACKNELL, BERKSHIRE, RG12 0XQ.
ROBINSON, Mr. Jeff Fordham, BSc ACA *2001;* 45 Woodcote Side, EPSOM, SURREY, KT18 7HB.
ROBINSON, Miss. Jennifer, BSc ACA *2011;* St. Aidans House, Lidgett Lane, Skelmanthorpe, HUDDERSFIELD, HD8 9AQ.
ROBINSON, Mrs. Jennifer Ann, BA ACA ATII *1999;* 43 Crescent Road, BURGESS HILL, WEST SUSSEX, RH15 8EH.
ROBINSON, Mrs. Jennifer Ann, ACA *2008;* Kingscott Dix, 60 Kings Walk, GLOUCESTER, GL1 1LA.
ROBINSON, Mrs. Jennifer Isabel Anne, BA ACA *1992;* 209 Ladies Mile Road, BRIGHTON, BN1 8TF.
ROBINSON, Miss. Jessica, BSc ACA *2006;* 3 Tivoli Place, ILKLEY, WEST YORKSHIRE, LS29 8SU.
ROBINSON, Miss. Jill, BSc ACA *1987;* STA Travel Ltd, Priory House, 6 Wrights Lane, LONDON, W8 6TA.

•**ROBINSON, Mrs. Jillian Ann, BA FCA** *1982;* 750 City Road, SHEFFIELD, S2 1GN.
ROBINSON, Miss. Joanna Carole, BSc ACA *2001;* 4 South Ridge, NEWCASTLE UPON TYNE, NE3 2EJ.
ROBINSON, Mrs. Joanna Helen, BA ACA *1997;* Paradise Cottage, Forthampton, GLOUCESTER, GL19 4RB.
ROBINSON, Mrs. Joanne, BSc ACA *1992;* 1 IMPASSE DE LA PALANQUE, 31490 BRAX, FRANCE.
ROBINSON, Mrs. Joanne Elizabeth, ACA *2007;* 10 Clent Gardens, LIVERPOOL, L31 0BB.
ROBINSON, Dr. John, FCA *1989;* Stemcor Ltd Citypoint, 1 Ropemaker Street, LONDON, EC2Y 9ST.
ROBINSON, Mr. John, MMath ACA *2009;* 35 Morton Close, LONDON, E1 2QT.
ROBINSON, Mr. John Anthony, BSc(Econ) FCA *1995; (FCA Ireland 1972);* Riverview, Quayside, Queens Avenue, CHRISTCHURCH, DORSET, BH23 1BZ.
ROBINSON, Mr. John Anthony, BSc ACA CTA *1996;* Kidde Limited, Mathisen Way, Poyle Road, Colnbrook, SLOUGH, SL3 0HB.
ROBINSON, Mr. John Benedict Stuart, BSc ACA *1984;* Butterfield Bank (GSY) Ltd, PO Box 25, Regency Court, St. Peter Port, GUERNSEY, GY1 1WW.
ROBINSON, Mr. John David, BA FCA *1977;* Spring Barn, 1 The Harrows, East Morton, KEIGHLEY, WEST YORKSHIRE, BD20 5WE.
ROBINSON, Mr. John Douglas, FCA *1968;* 2 Burnham Rise, Emmer Green, READING, RG4 8XJ. (Life Member)
•**ROBINSON, Mr. John Edward, FCA** *1993;* Akintola Williams Deloitte, 235 Ikorodu Road, Ilupeju, PO Box 965, Marina, LAGOS NIGERIA.
•**ROBINSON, Mr. John Edwin, FCA** *1970;* (Tax Fac), Tanglewood, Stortford Road, Hatfield Heath, BISHOP'S STORTFORD, HERTFORDSHIRE, CM22 7DL.
ROBINSON, Mr. John James, FCA *1974;* 42 Axwell Park Road, Axwell Park, BLAYDON-ON-TYNE, NE21 5PB.
ROBINSON, Mr. John Keith, FCA *1955;* Northfield House, High Harrington, WORKINGTON, CA14 4LH. (Life Member)
ROBINSON, Mr. John Lee, BA ACA *1986;* The Village House, High Street, NEWPORT, CB11 3PF.
ROBINSON, Mr. John Lloyd, FCA *1966;* Ratefield Farm, Kimbolton, LEOMINSTER, HEREFORDSHIRE, HR6 0JB. (Life Member)
ROBINSON, Mr. John Neil, MA ACA *1979;* Cedarwood, 5 Harmer Dell, Harmer Green, WELWYN, HERTFORDSHIRE, AL6 0BE.
ROBINSON, Mr. John Philip, FCA *1954;* Cherry Cottage, 6 The Briars, HESSLE, HU13 9BE. (Life Member)
ROBINSON, Mr. John Robert, FCA *1965;* Hartfield, Orestan Lane, Effingham, LEATHERHEAD, KT24 5SL. (Life Member)
ROBINSON, Mr. John Rowland, MA FCA *1973;* 24 Blythswood South, Osborne Road, Jesmond, NEWCASTLE UPON TYNE, NE2 2BG.
ROBINSON, Mr. John Stewart, FCA *1991; (ACA Ireland 1986);* (Tax Fac), Robinson Stewart & Co., 7 Granard Business Centre, Bunns Lane, Mill Hill, LONDON, NW7 2DQ.
ROBINSON, Mr. John William, FCA *1952;* 54 Belper Road, West Hallam, ILKESTON, DE7 6GY. (Life Member)
ROBINSON, Mr. John William, MA FCA *1976;* 3/81 Grafton Street, BONDI JUNCTION, NSW 2022, AUSTRALIA.
•**ROBINSON, Mr. Jonathan Howard, FCA** *1982;* (Tax Fac), Hart Shaw LLP, Europa Link, Sheffield Business Park, SHEFFIELD, S9 1XU.
ROBINSON, Mr. Joseph Keith, BSc FCA *1992;* Frog Hall, 19a Quarlton Drive, Hawkshaw, BURY, LANCASHIRE, BL8 4JY.
ROBINSON, Mrs. Judith, BSc FCA *1992;* 41 Penmaen Bod Eilias, Clifftops, Old Colwyn, COLWYN BAY, CLWYD, LL29 8BL.
ROBINSON, Ms. Judith Anne, MSc ACA *1987;* Manchester Grammar School, Old Hall Lane, MANCHESTER, M13 0XT.
ROBINSON, Miss. Judith Yvonne, BA ACA *1993;* 6 Glengarven Close, WASHINGTON, TYNE AND WEAR, NE38 0DY.
ROBINSON, Miss. Julie, BSc ACA *1994;* First Floor Flat, 52 Geraldine Road, LONDON, SW18 2NT.
ROBINSON, Mrs. Karen Ann, ACA *1984;* 42 Victoria Road, Hale, ALTRINCHAM, CHESHIRE, WA15 9AB.
ROBINSON, Mrs. Karen Zoe, BSc(Hons) ACA *2001;* 24 Fellows Lane, Harborne, BIRMINGHAM, B17 9TP.
ROBINSON, Miss. Katharine, BA ACA *2003;* with KPMG LLP, 1 The Embankment, Neville Street, LEEDS, LS1 4DW.
ROBINSON, Miss. Katharine, BA(Hons) ACA *2011;* Emohym, Little London, Oakhill, RADSTOCK, BA3 5AU.

ROBINSON, Miss. Katherine Elizabeth, BSc ACA *2010;* 8 Ketcher Green, Binfield, BRACKNELL, BERKSHIRE, RG42 5TA.
ROBINSON, Mr. Keith, FCA *1956;* 41 Sandygate Park, SHEFFIELD, S10 5TZ. (Life Member)
•**ROBINSON, Mr. Keith, FCA** *1972;* K. Robinson, Willowcroft, Brasted Chart, WESTERHAM, TN16 1LX.
•**ROBINSON, Mr. Keith, BA FCA** *1973;* 54 Mount Leven Road, YARM, CLEVELAND, TS15 9RJ.
ROBINSON, Mr. Keith Andrew, BSc ACA *1994;* 79 Chalvington Road, Chandler's Ford, EASTLEIGH, SO53 3EG.
ROBINSON, Mr. Keith O'Dwyer, MA FCA *1971;* 53 Cole Park Road, TWICKENHAM, TW1 1HT.
ROBINSON, Miss. Kelly, BA(Hons) ACA *2011;* 58 Melstock Road, SWINDON, SN25 1XF.
ROBINSON, Mr. Kenneth Alan, FCA *1973;* Cortijo El Canuelo, Aptdo 87 Guadiaro, 11311 CADIZ, SPAIN.
ROBINSON, Mr. Kenneth Alfred, FCA *1960;* Barnston, Cooks Lane, Raymonds Hill, AXMINSTER, EX13 5SQ. (Life Member)
ROBINSON, Mr. Kenneth Anthony Marlow, FCA *1962;* Jardin Des Raisies, La Rue Des Raisies, St. Martin, JERSEY, JE3 6AT.
ROBINSON, Mr. Kim Edward, ACA *2008;* with KPMG LLP, 15 Canada Square, LONDON, E14 5GL.
ROBINSON, Mrs. Kristi, BSc(Hons) ACA *2001;* Christmas Cottage, St Georges Avenue, WEYBRIDGE, KT13 0BS.
ROBINSON, Miss. Laura Emily, BSc ACA *2009;* Jenkin, Loweswater, COCKERMOUTH, CUMBRIA, CA13 0RU.
ROBINSON, Mr. Leslie Anthony, FCA *1975;* Oaklands Trinity Road, Kingsbury, TAMWORTH, STAFFORDSHIRE, B78 2LA.
ROBINSON, Mrs. Linda Susan, FCA *1981;* 2 The Grange Long Acres Close, Coombe Dingle, BRISTOL, BS9 2RD.
ROBINSON, Miss. Louise, BA ACA *1997;* 75 Palmerston Road, LONDON, SW19 1PB.
ROBINSON, Miss. Lucy Clare, BA(Hons) ACA *2001;* 36 Dryden Road, Wimbledon, LONDON, SW19 8SG.
ROBINSON, Mrs. Lucy Constance, BA ACA *1989;* Hull John Roe Ltd, Henry Boot Way, Priory Park East, HULL, HU4 7DY.
ROBINSON, Mrs. Lynda Maxine, BSc ACA *1997;* Old Doctors Cottage, Old Doctors Street, Tottington, BURY, BL8 3ND.
ROBINSON, Mrs. Lynn Frances, BSc ACA *1992;* 43 Northcroft, Wooburn Green, HIGH WYCOMBE, HP10 0BP.
ROBINSON, Miss. Lynne, MA BA ACA *2003;* 61 Hosack Road, LONDON, SW17 7QW.
ROBINSON, Mr. Malcolm Stewart, MA FCA *1974;* 14 Alderley Close, Duston, NORTHAMPTON, NN5 6XG.
•**ROBINSON, Mrs. Margaret, BSc FCA** *1976;* M. Robinson, 10 Greet Park Close, SOUTHWELL, NG25 0EE.
ROBINSON, Miss. Margot-Veronique, BA ACA *2005;* Fools Syke House, Hesketh, Nr Rimington, Gisburn, CLITHEROE, LANCASHIRE BB7 4JH.
ROBINSON, Mrs. Marie-Claire, BSc ACA *1999;* 31 Sibley Avenue, HARPENDEN, HERTFORDSHIRE, AL5 1HF.
ROBINSON, Mr. Mark, FCA *1976;* Surfs Edge, West Rae Road, Polzeath, WADEBRIDGE, CORNWALL, PL27 6ST.
•**ROBINSON, Mr. Mark, BSc ACA** *1997;* GMR Accounting Limited, Castle Court, 41 London Road, REIGATE, RH2 9RJ.
ROBINSON, Mr. Mark Anthony, BA ACA *1993;* 12 Canfold Cottages, Bookhurst Road, CRANLEIGH, SURREY, GU6 7DR.
ROBINSON, Mr. Mark Charles, ACA *2007;* 12 Centurion Way, BASINGSTOKE, RG22 4TL.
•**ROBINSON, Mr. Mark Graham, ACA** *1987;* Mark Robinson, Trullwell, Box, STROUD, GLOUCESTERSHIRE, GL6 9HD.
•**ROBINSON, Mr. Mark Stephen, BA(Hons) FCA** *2000;* Mark Robinson, 36 Queen Victoria Avenue, HOVE, EAST SUSSEX, BN3 6WN.
ROBINSON, Mr. Martin, BA FCA *1986;* Braemar Group Plc, Richmond House, Heath Road, Hale, ALTRINCHAM, CHESHIRE WA14 2XP.
ROBINSON, Mr. Martin Claude, FCA *1977;* 2 Clumps Road, Lower Bourne, FARNHAM, SURREY, GU10 3HF.
ROBINSON, Mr. Martin Edward, LLB ACA CTA *2002;* (Tax Fac), 16 Polwarth Grove, EDINBURGH, EH11 1LY.
ROBINSON, Mr. Matthew James, BSc ACA *2011;* 33 Freshwater Drive, ASHTON-UNDER-LYNE, LANCASHIRE, OL6 9SH.
ROBINSON, Mr. Matthew James, BSc *2000;* 10 Downes Court, LONDON, N21 3PS.
ROBINSON, Mr. Matthew John, ACA *2008;* 20 Southridge Road, WIRRAL, MERSEYSIDE, CH61 8RJ.
ROBINSON, Mr. Matthew Phillip, BSc ACA *2004;* 106 Fellows Lane, BIRMINGHAM, B17 9TX.

ROBINSON, Mr. Matthew Seymour, BA ACA *1986;* finnCap Ltd, 60 New Broad Street, LONDON, EC2M 1JJ.
ROBINSON, Mr. Matthew Stephen, BCom ACA *1996;* 5 Sion Place, BATH, BA2 6ES.
ROBINSON, Mrs. Maureen Ann, BA ACA *1997;* Victorian House Main Street, Mareham-le-Fen, BOSTON, LINCOLNSHIRE, PE22 7RW.
ROBINSON, Mr. Maxwell Mackenzie, BSc FCA *1977;* Cobdown, Copt Hall Road, Ightham, SEVENOAKS, TN15 9DU.
ROBINSON, Mr. Michael, BSc ACA *1995;* West Barn, Hillside, La Route Des Cotes Du Nord, Trinity, JERSEY, JE3 5BJ.
ROBINSON, Mr. Michael Albert, FCA *1962;* 5 Oak Drive, Seisdon, WOLVERHAMPTON, WV5 7ET. (Life Member)
ROBINSON, Mr. Michael Derek, FCA *1984;* with Baker Tilly Tax and Accounting Limited, 1210 Centre Park Square, WARRINGTON, WA1 1RU.
ROBINSON, Mr. Michael Edward, MA FCA *1968;* 32 Kent Road, EAST MOLESEY, KT8 9JZ.
ROBINSON, Mr. Michael Francis, FCA *1960;* 21 Foley Road, Claygate, ESHER, KT10 0LU. (Life Member)
ROBINSON, Mr. Michael Hedley, FCA *1976;* 15 Thorncliffe Road, OXFORD, OX2 7BA.
ROBINSON, Mr. Michael John, BSc FCA *1979;* 2 The Grange, Long Acres Close, Coombe Dingle, BRISTOL, BS9 2RD.
ROBINSON, Mr. Michael John, BSc FCA *1963;* 36 Trevelyan Way, BERKHAMSTED, HP4 1JH. (Life Member)
ROBINSON, Mr. Michael John, FCA *1970;* P.O. Box 19, KALORAMA, VIC 3766, AUSTRALIA.
•ROBINSON, Mr. Michael Mark, FCA *1963;* Galleon Chambers, 3 Connaught Avenue, FRINTON-ON-SEA, CO13 9PN.
ROBINSON, Mr. Michael Philip, ACA *1987;* 39 Causeway Head Road, Dore, SHEFFIELD, S17 3DS.
ROBINSON, Mr. Michael Stuart, BSc ACA *1990;* 2 Peter Avenue, OXTED, SURREY, RH8 9LG.
•ROBINSON, Mr. Michael Stuart, MA ACA *1988;* KPMG LLP, 15 Canada Square, LONDON, E14 5GL. See also KPMG Europe LLP
•ROBINSON, Mr. Michael Winston, BA FCA *1985;* PricewaterhouseCoopers LLP, Exchange House, Central Business Exchange, Midsummer Boulevard, MILTON KEYNES, MK9 2DF. See also PricewaterhouseCoopers
ROBINSON, Mrs. Michelle Anne, BSc ACA *1991;* 64 Oakwood Road, SUTTON COLDFIELD, B73 5EQ.
•ROBINSON, Mrs. Michelle Louise, ACA *2002;* MLR Accountancy, Hold House Farm Cottage, Ponteland, NEWCASTLE UPON TYNE, NE20 9TS.
ROBINSON, Mr. Neil David, BSc ACA *2008;* 12 Private Road, Sherwood, NOTTINGHAM, NG5 4DB.
ROBINSON, Mr. Neil John, MA(Hons) ACA *2004;* 19 Holden Avenue, MANCHESTER, M16 8TA.
ROBINSON, Mr. Nicholas, BA ACA *2006;* 7 Winifred Street, SWINDON, SN3 1RT.
ROBINSON, Mr. Nicholas James, MA ACA MBA *1997;* 14 Hurricane Way, ABBOTS LANGLEY, HERTFORDSHIRE, WD5 0TF.
ROBINSON, Mrs. Nicola Anne, BSc FCA *1994;* West Barn, Hillside La Route des Cotes, du Nord Trinity, JERSEY, JE3 5BJ.
ROBINSON, Mrs. Nicola Jane, BSc FCA CTA *1980;* (Tax Fac), Horsemill Barn, Mill Lane, Frittenden, CRANBROOK, TN17 2DT.
ROBINSON, Mr. Nigel Francis, BSc ACA *1995;* Central Asia Metals Ltd, 4-5 Park Place, LONDON, SW1A 1LP.
ROBINSON, Mr. Nigel James, BSc FCA *1977;* Nore Hill House, Barnard Road, Chelsham, WARLINGHAM, CR6 9QE.
ROBINSON, Mr. Nigel John, ACA *1993;* Floor 5, Entrance 3, Bolshoy Savvinsky Per. 11, MOSCOW, RUSSIAN FEDERATION.
ROBINSON, Mr. Nigel Tozer, BA ACA *1988;* I N G, 60 London Wall, LONDON, EC2M 5TQ.
ROBINSON, Mrs. Nina Firdaus, BA ACA CISA *1991;* 18 Greenway, Appleton, WARRINGTON, WA4 3AD.
ROBINSON, Mr. Norman Alan, FCA *1957;* 30 Islestone Drive, North Sunderland, SEAHOUSES, NE68 7XB. (Life Member)
ROBINSON, Mr. Oliver John, ACA *2001;* Avocent International Limited, Avocent House, Shannon Free Zone, SHANNON, COUNTY CLARE, IRELAND.
ROBINSON, Mr. Patrick Michael Whitmore, FCA *1962;* Penleigh, Bradford Road, SHERBORNE, DT9 6BS. (Life Member)
ROBINSON, Mr. Paul, ACA *2011;* Flat 2, 3 Pond Road, Blackheath, LONDON, SE3 9JL.
ROBINSON, Mr. Paul David, BA ACA *1988;* 358 Barkham Road, WOKINGHAM, BERKSHIRE, RG41 4DL.
ROBINSON, Mr. Paul Geoffrey, FCA *1971;* P.O. Box 1734, HONEYDEW, 2040, SOUTH AFRICA.
•ROBINSON, Mr. Paul James, BSc FCA *1980;* Robconsult Limited, 3 Tunnel Hill Mews, Knock Lane, Blisworth, NORTHAMPTON, NN7 3DA. See also J.R. Watson & Co and Robinson Consulting
ROBINSON, Mr. Paul James, ACA *1984;* Pipeline Induction Heat Ltd The Pipeline Centre, Trans Britannia Industrial Estate Farrington Road, BURNLEY, BB11 5SW.
ROBINSON, Mr. Paul Philip, BA FCA *1977;* 7 Edgeway, WILMSLOW, SK9 1NH.
ROBINSON, Ms. Pauline, ACA FCCA *2010;* with Anderson Barrowcliff LLP, Waterloo House, Thornaby Place, Thornaby on Tees, STOCKTON-ON-TEES, CLEVELAND TS17 6SA.
ROBINSON, Mrs. Penelope Ann, BA ACA *1978;* Lavender Cottage, Bathampton, BATH, BA2 6ST.
ROBINSON, Mr. Peter, FCA *1961;* 2 Nascot Gardens, Aughton, SHEFFIELD, S26 3RZ. (Life Member)
ROBINSON, Mr. Peter Arthur, FCA *1963;* 5 Curven Edge, Helmshore, ROSSENDALE, BB4 4LP.
ROBINSON, Mr. Peter David, BSc ACA *1989;* Croft House, Kilncroft, SELKIRK, TD7 5AQ.
ROBINSON, Mr. Peter Edward, BSc FCA *1978;* (Tax Fac), Findings, Woodlands Close, BROMLEY, BR1 2BD.
•ROBINSON, Mr. Peter Graham, FCA *1967;* (Tax Fac), Chandley Robinson Ltd, 33 Church Road, Gatley, CHEADLE, CHESHIRE, SK8 4NG.
ROBINSON, Mr. Peter Greville, FCA *1951;* 12 Park View Lodge, East Street, FAVERSHAM, KENT, ME13 8AY. (Life Member)
ROBINSON, Mr. Peter James John, FCA MBA *1970;* 43 Frankfield Rise, TUNBRIDGE WELLS, TN2 5LF.
ROBINSON, Mr. Peter John, BSc FCA *1978;* 15 Avon Way, LONDON, E18 2AR.
ROBINSON, Mr. Peter John, BSc ACA *1979;* 6 Mannix Place, QUAKERS HILL, NSW 2763, AUSTRALIA.
ROBINSON, Mr. Peter Laurie, BA ACA *1979;* 5 Silverdale Grove, LEEDS, LS20 8BA.
•ROBINSON, Mr. Peter Leslie, MA FCA *1982;* Hardwickes, Etruria Old Road, STOKE-ON-TRENT, ST1 5PE.
ROBINSON, Mr. Peter Tero, MA ACA *1990;* 3 Hermitage Close, Claygate, ESHER, KT10 0HH.
ROBINSON, Mr. Philip, BSc ACA *1988;* 19 Claremont Road, SOUTHPORT, MERSEYSIDE, PR8 4DY.
ROBINSON, Mr. Philip, BSc(Hons) ACA *2002;* Wren Properties Ltd, 696 Wilmslow Road, Didsbury, MANCHESTER, M20 2DN.
ROBINSON, Mr. Philip, MA ACA *1996;* 83 Replingham Road, LONDON, SW18 5LU.
ROBINSON, Mr. Philip Brian, FCA *1963;* 14 Shotesham Road, Poringland, NORWICH, NR14 7LG. (Life Member)
ROBINSON, Mr. Philip David, BSc FCA *1987;* Springfield Hall Park Road, Walton, WETHERBY, LS23 7DQ.
ROBINSON, Mr. Philip Hugh Stafford, BSc FCA *1977;* 8 Wellington Terrace, WHITBY, NORTH YORKSHIRE, YO21 3HF.
ROBINSON, Mr. Philip John, BA(Hons) ACA *2006;* with PricewaterhouseCoopers, PO Box 21144, BMB Centre 9th Floor, Diplomatic Area, MANAMA, BAHRAIN.
ROBINSON, Mr. Philip Matthew, BA ACA *2000;* 152 Benhill Road, LONDON, SE5 7LZ.
ROBINSON, Mrs. Philippa Jane, BSc FCA *1978;* Findings, Woodlands Close, BROMLEY, BR1 2BD.
•ROBINSON, Mr. Phillip David, FCA *1973;* (Tax Fac), 6 Huddersfield Road, Shelley, HUDDERSFIELD, HD8 8HJ.
ROBINSON, Mrs. Rachel, BA(Hons) ACA *2003;* 11 Stuart Road, Wimbledon Park, LONDON, SW19 8DJ.
•ROBINSON, Mrs. Rachel Margaret, HND FCA *1993;* MCT Partnership, 1 Warner House, Harrovian Business Village, Bessborough Road, HARROW, HA1 3EX. See also Harrovian Business Services Limited
•ROBINSON, Mr. Raymond, FCA *1977;* Gibbons Mannington & Phipps, 82 High Street, TENTERDEN, KENT, TN30 6JG.
ROBINSON, Mr. Reginald Stuart, BA FCA *1976;* 19 Jay Close, Oakwood, WARRINGTON, WA3 6QJ.
ROBINSON, Mr. Richard, BA(Hons) ACA *2004;* 12 Silver Birches, WOKINGHAM, BERKSHIRE, RG41 4YZ.
ROBINSON, Mr. Richard Anthony, BSc ACA *1989;* The Old Police House, 24 Petersfield Road, Buriton, PETERSFIELD, HAMPSHIRE, GU31 5RZ.
ROBINSON, Mr. Richard Anthony, FCA MBA *1970;* Birches House Birches Lane, Gomshall, GUILDFORD, SURREY, GU5 9QR.
ROBINSON, Mr. Richard Daniel, MA(Hons) ACA *2003;* Oaktree Capital Management, 27 Knightsbridge, LONDON, SW1X 7LY.
•ROBINSON, Mr. Richard Graham, FCA *1973;* Anderson Barrowcliff LLP, Waterloo House, Thornaby Place, Thornaby on Tees, STOCKTON-ON-TEES, CLEVELAND TS17 6SA. See also Anderson Barrowcliff
ROBINSON, Mr. Richard John Arundell, FCA DChA *1974;* Tanglewood, Parklands South Drive, Tehidy, CAMBORNE, TR14 0EZ.
•ROBINSON, Mr. Richard William, BA FCA *2001;* MacMahon Leggate Ltd, Charter House, 18-20 Finsley Gate, BURNLEY, LANCASHIRE, BB11 2HA.
ROBINSON, Mr. Robert Barrie, FCA CTA *1956;* 5 Wharfe Grove, WETHERBY, WEST YORKSHIRE, LS22 6HA. (Life Member)
ROBINSON, Mr. Robert Eldred, MSc BEng ACA *2010;* Snipe House, ALNWICK, NORTHUMBERLAND, NE66 2JD.
ROBINSON, Mr. Robert George, BSc FCA *1975;* 240 Hesketh Lane, Tarleton, PRESTON, PR4 6RH.
•ROBINSON, Mr. Robert William, FCA *1981;* (Tax Fac), Robert W. Robinson, 58 Coppice Farm Road, Penn, HIGH WYCOMBE, HP10 8AH.
•ROBINSON, Mr. Robin Edward, FCA *1970;* 91 Lyndhurst Avenue, Mossley Hill, LIVERPOOL, L18 8AR.
ROBINSON, Mr. Ronald, FCA *1972;* 36 Leicester Road, MARKFIELD, LEICESTERSHIRE, LE67 9RE.
•ROBINSON, Mr. Ronald, BA FCA *1974;* R. Robinson, Broadstones Farm, Mill Brow, Marple, STOCKPORT, SK6 5DG.
ROBINSON, Mr. Russell Colin, MSc BA ACA *1979;* Mile Edge, Fairmile, HENLEY-ON-THAMES, RG9 2JU.
ROBINSON, Mrs. Ruth Anne, BA ACA *1980;* (Tax Fac), 23 The Churchills, Highweek, NEWTON ABBOT, TQ12 1QN.
ROBINSON, Mr. Samuel, BA ACA *1996;* SVG Advisers Limited, Centrium, 61 Aldwych, LONDON, WC2B 4AE.
ROBINSON, Mrs. Sanaya Homi, BSc ACA MCT *1988;* Sycamore House Devonshire Farm, 84 Aylesbury Road, Bierton, AYLESBURY, BUCKINGHAMSHIRE, HP22 5DL.
ROBINSON, Ms. Sandra, BA ACA *1992;* (Tax Fac), 2 Simms Cottage, Braintree Road, Wethersfield, BRAINTREE, ESSEX, CM7 4BX.
ROBINSON, Mrs. Sara Joanne, BEng ACA *1995;* 91 Lakewood Road, Chandler's Ford, EASTLEIGH, HAMPSHIRE, SO53 5AD.
ROBINSON, Miss. Sarah Anne, BA ACA *1999;* Level 1, The Bond, 30 Hickson Road, MILLERS POINT, NSW 2000, AUSTRALIA.
ROBINSON, Mrs. Sarah Doris, BSc FCA PGCE *1999;* (Tax Fac), with Mazars LLP, 37 Frederick Place, BRIGHTON, BN1 4EA.
ROBINSON, Mrs. Sarah Eve, ACA *2004;* 63 Larivane Meadows, Andreas, ISLE OF MAN, IM7 4JF.
ROBINSON, Miss. Sarah Jane, BSc ACA *2001;* 41 Cromwell Avenue, Reddish, STOCKPORT, SK5 6GA.
ROBINSON, Mrs. Sarah Margaret Anne, BA ACA *1989;* 9 Berkeley Lodge, Sandal Road, NEW MALDEN, SURREY, KT3 5AW.
ROBINSON, Mrs. Shauna, ACA *2000;* 14 Coppershell, Gastard, CORSHAM, SN13 9PZ.
ROBINSON, Mr. Simon Charles, BA FCA *1990;* RBS plc, 135 Bishopsgate, LONDON, EC2M 3UR.
ROBINSON, Mr. Simon Edward, BSc ACA *2004;* 17 Brockridge Lane, Frampton Cotterell, BRISTOL, BS36 2HU.
•ROBINSON, Mr. Simon Nigel, FCA *1988;* Wall and Partners, 3 & 5 Commercial Gate, MANSFIELD, NG18 1EJ.
•ROBINSON, Mr. Simon William, BCom FCA DChA *1987;* Shipleys LLP, 3 Godalming Business Centre, Woolsack Way, GODALMING, SURREY, GU7 1XW.
ROBINSON, Miss. Sophie Louise, ACA *2010;* 1 Whalley Avenue, Chorlton cum Hardy, MANCHESTER, M21 8TU.
ROBINSON, Miss. Stacey, ACA *2009;* with RSM Tenon Limited, Ferryboat Lane, SUNDERLAND, SR5 3JN.
ROBINSON, Miss. Stephanie Jane, BA ACA *2006;* G400 Alderley House, Alderley Park, MACCLESFIELD, CHESHIRE, SK10 4TF.
ROBINSON, Mr. Stephen, BSc ACA *1989;* 11 Brownhill Crescent, Rothley, LEICESTER, LE7 7LA.
ROBINSON, Mr. Stephen Andrew, BA ACA *1999;* Financial Services Authority, 25 North Colonnade, Canary Wharf, LONDON, E14 5HS.
ROBINSON, Mr. Stephen Beresford, MA BSc FCA FCMA *1986;* (Tax Fac), Esco Europe Distribution SA, Zoning Industriel, Rue Des Fours A Chaux, B-7080 FRAMERIES, BELGIUM.
ROBINSON, Mr. Stephen James, ACA *2006;* with Coates and Partners Limited, 51 St. John Street, ASHBOURNE, DERBYSHIRE, DE6 1GP.
•ROBINSON, Mr. Stephen John, BA FCA *1990;* Grant Thornton UK LLP, Grant Thornton House, Kettering Parkway, Kettering Venture Park, KETTERING, NORTHAMPTONSHIRE NN15 6XR. See also Grant Thornton LLP
ROBINSON, Mr. Stephen Leonard, BSc ACA *1996;* September Lodge, Mile Path, WOKING, GU22 0JX.
ROBINSON, Mr. Stephen Maurice, ACA *1983;* with Champion Accountants LLP, 4 Nile Close, Nelson Court Business Centre, Riversway, PRESTON, PR2 2XU.
ROBINSON, Mr. Stephen Paul, BSc ACA *1988;* 18 Greenway, Appleton, WARRINGTON, WA4 3AD.
ROBINSON, Mr. Steven Allan, BA ACA *2005;* 24a Spencer Walk, LONDON, SW15 1PL.
ROBINSON, Mr. Steven Paul, BA ACA ATII *1991;* 226 Godstow Road, OXFORD, OX2 8PH.
ROBINSON, Mr. Stewart, ACA *2008;* Arran House Northfields, Barmby Moor, YORK, YO42 4DN.
ROBINSON, Mr. Stuart Rhys, BA ACA *1997;* 20 Crimicar Lane, Fulwood, SHEFFIELD, S10 4FB.
ROBINSON, Ms. Susan Ann, BA ACA *1992;* (Tax Fac), 43 The Gower, Thorpe, EGHAM, SURREY, TW20 8UB.
ROBINSON, Ms. Susan Claire, ACA *1990;* 20 Beauty Point Road, MOSMAN, NSW 2088, AUSTRALIA.
ROBINSON, Miss. Susan Jane, ACA *2002;* Apartment 111 Vantage Quay, 5 Brewer Street, MANCHESTER, M1 2ER.
•ROBINSON, Miss. Susan Mary, BA FCA FCIE DChA MCMI *1985;* (Tax Fac), Reeves & Co LLP, Montague Place, Quayside, Chatham Maritime, CHATHAM, KENT ME4 4QU.
ROBINSON, Miss. Suzanne, BA(Hons) ACA *2003;* 3 Clyde Road, Bluff Hill, NAPIER 4110, NEW ZEALAND.
•ROBINSON, Mrs. Suzanne Catherine, BSc ACA *1997;* Ernst & Young LLP, 1 Bridgewater Place, Water Lane, LEEDS, LS11 5QR. See also Ernst & Young Europe LLP
ROBINSON, Mr. Terry John, FCA *1967;* 34 Burkes Road, BEACONSFIELD, HP9 1PN.
ROBINSON, Mr. Thomas, BSc ACA *2011;* First Floor Flat, 338 Old York Road, Wandsworth, LONDON, SW18 1SS.
ROBINSON, Mr. Thomas Alexander, BA ACA *2007;* Well Lane End, Wardlow'n'Tideswell, DERBY, SK17 8RP.
ROBINSON, Mr. Tim Bradbury, MSc BSc ACA *2002;* 40 Tantallon Road, LONDON, SW12 8DG.
ROBINSON, Mr. Tim David, BSocSc ACA *1999;* Mars Horsecare UK Ltd, 29 Old Wolverton Road Old Wolverton, MILTON KEYNES, MK12 5PZ.
ROBINSON, Mr. Tim Edward, ACA *2008;* 11 Gordon Road, BECKENHAM, KENT, BR3 3QE.
•ROBINSON, Mr. Timothy James, BSc FCA *1991;* Wallace Williams Austin Ltd, 57 Cowbridge Road East, CARDIFF, CF11 9AE.
ROBINSON, Mr. Timothy James, BSc FCA *1985;* 59 Gibson Square, LONDON, N1 0RA.
ROBINSON, Mr. Timothy Mark, BA ACA *1997;* Warth & Klein Grant Thornton AG, Rosenstr 47, 40479 DUSSELDORF, GERMANY.
ROBINSON, Mr. Timothy Philip, BSc ACA *1986;* Stanegates, Leazes Lane, HEXHAM, NE46 3BA.
ROBINSON, Mr. Timothy Scott, BSc ACA *1993;* 1a Moor Park Road, NORTHWOOD, MIDDLESEX, HA6 2DL.
•ROBINSON, Mr. Tony Ian, BSc FCA *1981;* Forrester Boyd, 26 South Saint Mary's Gate, GRIMSBY, NORTH LINCOLNSHIRE, DN31 1LW.
•ROBINSON, Miss. Tracey Jane, ACA *1992;* Robinson Financial Consultancy Ltd, 31 Elmswood Gardens, Sherwood, NOTTINGHAM, NG5 4AY.
ROBINSON, Mr. Vaughan Bartley, BSc(Hons) ACA *2002;* Flat 151, The Perspective, 100 Westminster Bridge Road, LONDON, SE1 7XB.
ROBINSON, Mr. William Alfred, BSc ACA *1979;* 71 Peters Road, Locks Heath, SOUTHAMPTON, SO31 6EL.
•ROBINSON, Mr. William Charles Frederick, FCA *1968;* Robinson & Co, 5 Pinehurst, SEVENOAKS, TN14 5AQ.
•ROBINSON, Mr. William Ernest, FCA *1974;* Sovereign Business Services Ltd, 7 Portland Terrace, NEWCASTLE UPON TYNE, NE2 1QQ.
ROBINSON, Mr. William Ian, FCA *1971;* Highdown Amberley, ARUNDEL, BN18 9LZ.

ROBINSON, Mrs. Zoe Victoria, BA ACA *1999;* 7 Southlands Close, Badsworth, PONTEFRACT, WEST YORKSHIRE, WF9 1AU.
ROBINSON-PRICE, Mr. Keston, BSc ACA *2002;* Camwood Limited, 4 Broadgate, LONDON, EC2M 2DA.
ROBINSON-WELSH, Mr. Phillip Dennis, BA ACA *1993;* 7 Parklands, Cholmeley Park, LONDON, N6 5FE.
ROBJOHNS, Mr. Graham, BSc FCA *1989;* Medebank, 42 Chelmsford Road, Shenfield, BRENTWOOD, CM15 8RJ.
ROBLIN, Mr. Gareth David, BA FCA *1984;* The Hyde, Spinfield Lane, MARLOW, SL7 2LB.
ROBLIN, Mr. John Anthony, FCA *1962;* 12 West Orchard Crescent, Llanaff, CARDIFF, CF5 1AR. (Life Member)
•ROBLIN, Mr. Lynn Anthony, BA ACA DChA *1987;* (Tax Fac), Roblins, 3 Deryn Court, Wharfedale Road, Pentwyn, CARDIFF, CF23 7HA.
ROBLIN, Mr. Lynn Francis, BA FCA *1956;* Hillside, Sully Road, PENARTH, CF64 2TQ. (Life Member)
ROBLIN, Mrs. Nia Helen, BSc ACA *1986;* 45 Heath Park Avenue, CARDIFF, CF14 3RF.
ROBOTHAM, Ms. Fleur Ann, BA ACA *1992;* 25 Abinger Road, Chiswick, LONDON, W4 1EU.
ROBOTHAM, John Michael, Esq OBE FCA *1957;* Brickwall Farm House, Kiln Lane, Clophill, BEDFORD, MK45 4DA. (Life Member)
ROBOTHAM, Mr. Paul Stephen, BA FCA *1991;* 5 Decimus Place, Calverley Park Gardens, TUNBRIDGE WELLS, KENT, TN1 2JX.
ROBOTHAM, Mr. Roger James, BSc ACA *1986;* 2 Farm Place, LONDON, W8 7SX.
•ROBOTHAM, Mrs. Sally Patricia, FCA *1994;* Johnson Tidsall, 81 Burton Road, DERBY, DE1 1TJ.
ROBOTHAM, Mrs. Stephanie Helen, BSc ACA *1996;* 6 Wugga Place, CHAPEL HILL, QLD 4069, AUSTRALIA.
ROBOTTOM, Mr. Christopher David, BSc ACA *1999;* 101 John O'Gaunt Road, KENILWORTH, WARWICKSHIRE, CV8 1DY.
ROBOTTOM, Mr. John Dennis, FCA *1965;* PO Box 1168, HIGHLANDS NORTH, 2037, SOUTH AFRICA. (Life Member)
ROBOTTOM, Ms. Karen Jane, ACA CA(SA) *2010;* 1 The Hopkiln, Church Street Harvington, EVESHAM, WORCESTERSHIRE, WR11 8PB.
•ROBSHAW, Mr. David John, MSc FCA *1969;* D J R Associates, 1 Bowden Way, Failand, BRISTOL, BS8 3XA.
ROBSHAW, Mr. Grant David, ACA *2008;* 9 Lancaster Road, BRISTOL, BS2 9UP.
ROBSHAW, Mr. Michael, FCA *1972;* Hill-Side Cottage, 139 Whitstable Road, CANTERBURY, CT2 8EQ. (Life Member)
ROBSHAW, Mr. Terence Ian, FCA *1969;* Walsall Hospice Bentley Health Centre, Churchill Road, WALSALL, WS2 0BA.
ROBSON, Mr. Aidan Paul, BSc ACA *2005;* with Endless LLP, 3 Whitehall Quay, LEEDS, LS1 4BF.
ROBSON, Mr. Alan George, FCA *1959;* The Willows, Woolsington Park South, NEWCASTLE UPON TYNE, NE13 8BJ. (Life Member)
ROBSON, Mr. Alan Lewis, FCA *1958;* Tolmans, 13 Warren Lane, East Dean Friston, EASTBOURNE, BN20 0EW. (Life Member)
ROBSON, Mr. Alan Peel, BSc FCA *1958;* Mellstock, Graemsdyke Road, BERKHAMSTED, HP4 3LX. (Life Member)
•ROBSON, Mr. Andrew Harold, FCA *1979;* with Robson Laidler LLP, Fernwood House, Fernwood Road, Jesmond, NEWCASTLE UPON TYNE, NE2 1TJ.
ROBSON, Mr. Andrew Stephen, BA FCA *1984;* Holford House, North Chailey, LEWES, BN8 4DT.
ROBSON, Mrs. Angela Shireen, BA ACA *1986;* Beaconsfield House, Market Place, Hingham, NORWICH, NORFOLK, NR9 4AF.
ROBSON, Mrs. Ann Sylvia, BA FCA *1981;* (Tax Fac), Ballandaine, Slaley, HEXHAM, NE47 0BQ.
ROBSON, Mr. Barnaby, ACA *2008;* with KPMG LLP, 15 Canada Square, LONDON, E14 5GL.
ROBSON, Miss. Catherine Ruth, PhD BSc(Hons) ACA *2009;* 14 Conway Close, Euxton, CHORLEY, LANCASHIRE, PR7 6NT.
ROBSON, Mr. Charles Thomas Alexander, BSc(Hons) FCA CFE *2000;* KPMG Level 17, Saba Tower 1, Jumeirah Lakes Towers, PO Box 346038, DUBAI, UNITED ARAB EMIRATES.
ROBSON, Mr. Christopher Edward, BSc FCA *1988;* 75 Bradfield Road, Lindfield, SYDNEY, NSW 2070, AUSTRALIA.
ROBSON, Mr. Christopher Harvey, BA ACA *2008;* Pricewaterhousecoopers, 33 Wellington Street, LEEDS, LS1 4JP.
•ROBSON, Mr. Christopher Robert, BA FCA *1981;* Ryecroft Glenton, 32 Portland Terrace, Jesmond, NEWCASTLE UPON TYNE, NE2 1QP.
ROBSON, Mr. David Anthony, BCom ACA *1990;* Ratcliffe College, Fosse Way, Ratcliffe on the Wreake, LEICESTER, LEICESTERSHIRE, LE7 4SG.
ROBSON, Mr. David Arthur, BA ACA *1992;* 13 Bradwell Drive, Heald Green, CHEADLE, SK8 3BX.
ROBSON, Mr. David Charles, MA FCA MIPD *1982;* 28 Joyberry Drive, Oldswinford, STOURBRIDGE, DY8 2EF.
•ROBSON, Mr. David Robert, FCA *1963;* David R. Robson, 143 Sidecliff Road, Roker, SUNDERLAND, SR6 9NE.
ROBSON, Mr. David Spencer, BA ACA *1979;* Dampfaergevej, 16 5 dor 2, 2100 KOBENHAVN, DENMARK.
ROBSON, Miss. Dawn, BA ACA *1999;* 28 Manor Road, TADCASTER, NORTH YORKSHIRE, LS24 8HP.
ROBSON, Miss. Deborah Jane, ACA *1997;* 39 School Road, Highfields, DURSLEY, GLOUCESTERSHIRE, GL11 4PA.
ROBSON, Mr. Denis Anthony, FCA *1955;* Bast House Manchester Road, Walmersley, BURY, BL9 5LZ. (Life Member)
ROBSON, Mr. Derrick Joseph, FCA CA(SA) *1962;* 201 Magaliesberg, Cnr Mitchell St & Fife Ave, Berea, JOHANNESBURG, GAUTENG, 2198 SOUTH AFRICA.
ROBSON, Mr. Donald Gillery, FCA *1956;* The Coach House, The Park, Swanland, NORTH FERRIBY, HU14 3LU. (Life Member)
ROBSON, Mr. Edward Simon, BSc ACA *1980;* 19/6 M6 Tambon Bpohng, Soi Huay Yai Mook, BANG LAMUNG 20150, CHONBURI PROVINCE, THAILAND.
ROBSON, Mr. Eric Stewart, FCA *1960;* 31 Orchard Road, Skidby, COTTINGHAM, HU16 5TL. (Life Member)
•ROBSON, Ms. Fiona, BA ACA *1993;* (Tax Fac), The Alnwick Accountants Ltd, 16 Bondgate Without, ALNWICK, NORTHUMBERLAND, NE66 1PP.
ROBSON, Mrs. Frances Amanda, BSc FCA *1992;* 14 Warwick Crescent, HARROGATE, HG2 8JA.
ROBSON, Mr. Geoffrey John, FCA *1966;* 769 Durham Road, Lowfell, GATESHEAD, NE9 6PL. (Life Member)
ROBSON, Mr. Geoffrey Miles Chalmers, BSc(Econ) ACA *1999;* Ingle Cottage, Inglestone Common, BADMINTON, AVON, GL9 1BS.
•ROBSON, Mr. Geoffrey William, MA FCA *1984;* Quantum Accountancy Services Limited, The Quadrus Centre, Woodstock Way, Boldon Business Park, BOLDON COLLIERY, TYNE AND WEAR NE35 9PF.
ROBSON, Mr. Graham David, BEng CEng ACA *1999;* 136 A Marlow Bottom, MARLOW, BUCKINGHAMSHIRE, SL7 3PP.
•ROBSON, Mr. Ian Charles, BA FCA *1990;* DNG Dove Naish, 14 Cottesbrooke Park, Heartlands Business Park, DAVENTRY, NORTHAMPTONSHIRE, NN11 8YL.
•ROBSON, Mr. Ian Peter, BSc FCA *1981;* Robson & Co Limited, Kingfisher Court, Plaxton Bridge Road, Woodmansey, BEVERLEY, NORTH HUMBERSIDE HU17 0RT.
ROBSON, Mr. James, Bsc ACA *2011;* Flat 11, 50 Fitzjohns Avenue, LONDON, NW3 5LT.
ROBSON, Mrs. Jane Wendy, BA ACA *1986;* 15 Anglesey Drive, Poynton, STOCKPORT, CHESHIRE, SK12 1BT.
ROBSON, Mr. Jason, BA ACA *1990;* 16 Ware Point Drive, LONDON, SE28 0HL.
•ROBSON, Miss. Jill, BA(Hons) ACA *2003;* 13 Williams Road, DIANELLA, WA 6059, AUSTRALIA.
ROBSON, Mrs. Jocelyn Sarah Frances, BA(Hons) ACA *2001;* 91 High Street, Melbourn, ROYSTON, HERTFORDSHIRE, SG8 6AA.
ROBSON, Mr. John Edmund, BA ACA *1983;* 45 Sterne Street, LONDON, W12 8AB.
•ROBSON, Mr. John Sutherland, MA FCA *1968;* (Tax Fac), John Robson, PO Box 56958, Muswell Hill Broadway, LONDON, N10 9AY.
ROBSON, Ms. Julia Helen, ACA *2009;* 33 Briarbank Terrace, EDINBURGH, EH11 1SU.
ROBSON, Mrs. Julie Elisabeth, FCA *1980;* Morris & Co Chester House, Lloyd Drive, ELLESMERE PORT, CH65 9HQ.
•ROBSON, Mrs. Karen Margaret, BA ACA *1984;* (Tax Fac), Robsons, 1a Sykes Grove, HARROGATE, HG1 2DB.
•ROBSON, Mr. Keith, FCA *1969;* Keith Robson, 117 Roman Road, MIDDLESBROUGH, CLEVELAND, TS5 5QB.
•①ROBSON, Mr. Keith Edward Michael, FCA *1975;* with Royce Peeling Green Limited, The Copper Room, Deva Centre, Trinity Way, MANCHESTER, M3 7BG.
ROBSON, Miss. Kerry Helen, ACA *2009;* 5 Hereford Road, LONDON, E11 2EA.
ROBSON, Mrs. Louise Clare, BA ACA *1998;* 24 Woodend Drive, ASCOT, SL5 9BG.
ROBSON, Mr. Malcolm Henry, BA ACA *1985;* Morston Assets Limited, Morston House, Jacobs Place, High Street, HOLT, NORFOLK NR25 6BH.
ROBSON, Mr. Mark David, BSc FCA *1987;* 27 Richmond Place, TUNBRIDGE WELLS, TN2 5JZ.
ROBSON, Mr. Mark Donald, BSc(Hons) ACA *2001;* 6 Braeside, Mouseyhaugh, HEXHAM, NORTHUMBERLAND, NE48 1BJ.
ROBSON, Mr. Mark Jonathan, BA ACA *1987;* 4 Ambrose Place, WORTHING, WEST SUSSEX, BN11 1PZ.
ROBSON, Mr. Mark Philip William, BA FCA *1983;* 14 Bathgate Road, Wimbledon, LONDON, SW19 5PN.
ROBSON, Mr. Martin, BSc ACA *2000;* 3 Jersey Court, Irton, SCARBOROUGH, NORTH YORKSHIRE, YO12 4RT.
ROBSON, Mr. Michael, FCA *1972;* 1 Brooks Close, Burton Latimer, KETTERING, NN15 5PX.
ROBSON, Mr. Michael Timothy, BA ACA *1986;* 5 Arbor Court, Heath Road, HAYWARDS HEATH, WEST SUSSEX, RH16 3BQ.
•ROBSON, Mr. Neil Jonathan, BSc FCA *1993;* Talbot Hughes McKillop LLP, 6 Snow Hill, LONDON, EC1A 2AY.
ROBSON, Mr. Nigel Edward, FCA *1969;* Far Rockaway, Durford Wood, PETERSFIELD, GU31 5AW. (Life Member)
ROBSON, Mr. Norman John, BA FCA *1974;* 54 Baring Road, BEACONSFIELD, BUCKINGHAMSHIRE, HP9 2NE.
ROBSON, Mr. Oran Kenneth Hindhaugh, BSc ACA *1997;* 73 Hartley Avenue, Monkseaton, WHITLEY BAY, NE26 3NS.
ROBSON, Mr. Paul, ACA *2011;* 86 Harford Street, MIDDLESBROUGH, CLEVELAND, TS1 4PP.
ROBSON, Mr. Paul Anthony, BSc FCA *1994;* 66 Thrupp Close, Castlethorpe, MILTON KEYNES, MK19 7PL.
ROBSON, Mr. Paul John, BA ACA *1997;* Procter & Gamble, Route de Saint Georges, 1213 PETIT LANCY, SWITZERLAND.
ROBSON, Mr. Peter, BA ACA *1986;* 19 Victoria Springs, Holmfirth, HUDDERSFIELD, HD9 2NB.
ROBSON, Mr. Peter David, FCA *1969;* 18 St. Georges Crescent, DROITWICH, WORCESTERSHIRE, WR9 8BX.
ROBSON, Mr. Peter Stephen, BA ACA *1991;* 4 Glengarry Way, Friars Cliff, CHRISTCHURCH, BH23 4EQ.
•ROBSON, Mr. Philip Anthony, FCA *1982;* Joseph Miller & Co, Floor A, Milburn House, Dean Street, NEWCASTLE UPON TYNE, NE1 1LE.
•ROBSON, Mr. Philip Martyn, BSc FCA *1990;* (Tax Fac), Jackson Robson Licence Limited, 33/35 Exchange Street, DRIFFIELD, NORTH HUMBERSIDE, YO25 6LL. See also Jackson Robson Licence
ROBSON, Mr. Richard William, MEng ACA *2005;* Flat 5, 46 Stanhope Road, LONDON, N6 5AJ.
•ROBSON, Mr. Robert Elliott, FCA *1953;* Chipchase Robson & Co, 3 Springfield Park, DURHAM, DH1 4LS.
ROBSON, Mrs. Ruth, BA ACA *1992;* Wellbank, 15 Kings Avenue, MORPETH, NORTHUMBERLAND, NE61 1HX.
ROBSON, Mr. Scott Michael, BEng ACA *2003;* 17 Highview Gardens, UPMINSTER, RM14 2YU.
ROBSON, Mr. Shaun, FCA *1986;* Tor Coatings Ltd, Portobello Ind Estate, Birtley, CHESTER LE STREET, DH3 2RE.
ROBSON, Mr. Simon Kenneth Geoffrey, BA ACA *1998;* 88 Manchuria Road, Battersea, LONDON, SW11 6AE.
ROBSON, Mr. Steven Gordon, BSc ACA *1990;* Ankkurisaarentie 15D, ESPOO, 02160, FINLAND.
ROBSON, Mr. Stuart Ian, BSc FCA *1984;* with Ashtead, Kings House, 36-37 King Street, LONDON, EC2V 8BB.
ROBSON, Mr. Timothy Dougal, BA ACA *1997;* Apartment 401, Mandel House, Eastfields Avenue, Wandsworth, LONDON, SW18 1JU.
ROBSON, Mr. William Henry Mark, BSc ACA *1988;* Thorntons Plc Thornton Park, Somercotes, ALFRETON, DERBYSHIRE, DE55 4XJ.
ROBSON BROWN, Mr. Jeremy Simon, BA ACA *1999;* 25 Barrow Road, CAMBRIDGE, CB2 8AP.
ROBY, Miss. Emma Christine, BSc ACA *2001;* Lockheed Martin UK Insys Ltd Reddings Wood, Ampthill, BEDFORD, MK45 2HD.
ROBY, Mr. John Christopher, FCA *1972;* 116 School Road, Hockley Heath, SOLIHULL, B94 6RB.
•ROBY, Mrs. Nicola Marie, ACA FCCA *2009;* Warings, Bedford House, 60 Chorley New Road, BOLTON, BL1 4DA. See also Warings Business Advisers LLP
ROBY, Mr. Steven John, BSc ACA *1996;* 72 Earls Lane, Cippenham, SLOUGH, SL1 5TD.
ROCH, Mr. John David, FCA *1969;* 39 Pine Croft, Chapeltown, SHEFFIELD, S35 1EB.
ROCHA, Mr. Michael Alberto, MA ACA *1999;* Brand Finance, 3rd Floor 56 Haymarket, LONDON, SW1Y 4RN.
ROCHE, Mrs. Charlotte Louisa, BSc ACA *2004;* 119 Elm Road, KINGSTON UPON THAMES, KT2 6HY.
•ROCHE, Mr. Christopher Philip, ACA *1978;* Roche & Co, Barnswood, 64 Orton Lane, Wombourne, WOLVERHAMPTON, WV5 9AW.
ROCHE, Mr. Dale, BSc ACA *2005;* (Tax Fac), 9 Tees Green, Colden Common, WINCHESTER, SO21 1UL.
ROCHE, Sir David O'Grady, Bt FCA *1974;* 20 Lancaster Mews, LONDON, W2 3QE.
ROCHE, Ms. Elizabeth Susan, BSc ACA *1998;* West Barn, Dartford Road, Horton Kirby, DARTFORD, DA4 9JF.
ROCHE, Mr. Francis John, FCA *1975;* 20 Sea Road, WALLASEY, CH45 0JU.
ROCHE, Mr. Gary William, BCom ACA *1989;* 110 N Federal Highway, Apt 1412, FORT LAUDERDALE, FL 33301, UNITED STATES.
ROCHE, Mr. Gerard Michael, BSc ACA *1986;* The Copse Rectory Close, Skelbrooke, DONCASTER, SOUTH YORKSHIRE, DN6 8GA.
ROCHE, Mr. Howard Bartholomew, BA ACA *1984;* 4 Tilmore Gardens, PETERSFIELD, GU32 2JQ.
ROCHE, Mrs. Jane, FCA *1994;* 16 Whalley Road, Hale, ALTRINCHAM, WA15 9DF.
•ROCHE, Mrs. Janet Elizabeth, ACA *1991;* 7 Ingswell Avenue, Notton, WAKEFIELD, WEST YORKSHIRE, WF4 2NG.
ROCHE, Mr. Peter Charles Kenneth, FCA *1970;* Field House, 20 Leigh Hill Road, COBHAM, KT11 2HX.
•ROCHE, Mr. Richard Anthony, FCA ATII *1989;* (Tax Fac), Roches, 40 Locks Heath Centre, Centre Way, Locks Heath, SOUTHAMPTON, SO31 6DX.
ROCHE, Mr. Simon Patrick, BSc(Hons) ACA *2003;* 12 Cranwich Avenue, LONDON, N21 2BB.
ROCHE, Mr. William Peter, BSc ACA *2010;* 14 Highfield Road, Mellor, STOCKPORT, CHESHIRE, SK6 5AL.
•ROCHE-SAUNDERS, Mr. Richard David Kyle, FCA *1971;* Roche-Saunders & Co, 34 The Watton, BRECON, POWYS, LD3 7EF.
ROCHESTER, Mr. Cyril, FCA *1963;* Red Cottage, Brackendene Drive, GATESHEAD, NE9 6DP. (Life Member)
ROCHESTER, Mr. Mervyn Alan, FCA *1981;* Barons Property Management Ltd, 114 Stanpit, CHRISTCHURCH, DORSET, BH23 3ND.
•ROCHESTER, Mr. Stephen Gordon, FCA *1982;* (Tax Fac), Rochesters LLP, 3 Caroline Court, 13 Caroline Street, St Pauls Square, BIRMINGHAM, B3 1TR. See also Rochesters Audit Services Limited
ROCHFORD, Mr. David William, BSc ACA *1996;* 18 Nevill Road, HOVE, BN3 7BQ.
ROCHFORD, Mr. Edward Arthur Byran, FCA *1970;* White House, Bettws Newydd, USK, NP15 1JN. (Life Member)
ROCHFORD, Mr. John Michael, ACA *1988;* Retail Brands Limited, Second Floor 1 Imperial Place, BOREHAMWOOD, HERTFORDSHIRE, WD6 1JN.
•ROCHMAN, Mr. Paul Henry, FCA *1966;* (Tax Fac), Rochman Goodmans, 29 Barrett Road, Fetcham, LEATHERHEAD, KT22 9HL.
ROCK, Mr. Daniel Peter, BSc ACA *2009;* Flat 6, 61 The Avenue, RICHMOND, TW9 2AL.
ROCK, Mr. Graham Arthur, FCA *1959;* 3 Swindell Road, STOURBRIDGE, DY9 0TN. (Life Member)
ROCK, Mr. Jonathan David, BA ACA *1998;* 6 Nailsworth Close, Blackpole, WORCESTER, WR4 9XQ.
ROCK, Mr. Joseph Anthony, MA BA(Hons) ACA *1996;* PO Box 6140, Rivonia, JOHANNESBURG, 2128, SOUTH AFRICA.
ROCK, Mr. Philip Paul, BEng ACA *1992;* 47 Northumberland Avenue, LONDON, E12 5HA.
ROCK, Miss. Samantha, BSc ACA *2006;* Minerva Plc, 42 Wigmore Street, LONDON, W1U 2RY.
ROCK REES, Dr. Cassandra Fernanda, MEng ACA *2007;* 25 Dapps Hill, Keynsham, BRISTOL, BS31 1ES.
•ROCKALL, Mr. David John, FCA *1962;* D.J.Rockall, 14 MacLean Close, Abington, NORTHAMPTON, NN3 3DJ.
ROCKE, Mr. David Michael, BA ACA *1993;* Enstar Limited, PO Box HM2267, HAMILTON HMJX, BERMUDA.

Members - Alphabetical ROCKE - ROE

ROCKE, Mr. Timothy Rohan, MA ACA *1995;* Les Tourneurs, La Chapelle Haute Grue, 14140 LIVAROT, NORMANDY, FRANCE.
•ROCKER, Mr. Antony Michael, BSc FCA *1991;* KPMG LLP, 15 Canada Square, LONDON, E14 5GL. See also KPMG Europe LLP
ROCKER, Mr. Michael Douglas, BSc ACA *1987;* 54 Home Close, Greens Norton, TOWCESTER, NN12 8AY.
ROCKETT, Mr. Matthew Ian, BSc(Hons) ACA *2001;* 7 Trent Walk, Welton Grange, BROUGH, NORTH HUMBERSIDE, HU15 1GF.
•ROCKETT, Mr. Nicholas Anthony, FCA *1978;* (Tax Fac), Rockett & Co, 16 Rickmansworth Road, NORTHWOOD, HA6 1HA.
ROCKETT, Mr. William James Trevethen, BA FCA *1988;* Netik LLC, Broken Wharf House, 2 Broken Wharf, High Timber Street, LONDON, EC4V 3DT.
•ROCKEY, Mrs. Edwina Tamsin, BA FCA *1989;* (Tax Fac), Sheppard Rockey & Williams Ltd, Sannerville Chase, Exminster, EXETER, EX6 8AT. See also Edwina Rockey
ROCKLIN, Mr. Robert David, BSc FCA *1987;* Rubicon West Plc, 1 Marylebone Mews, LONDON, W1G 8PU.
ROCYN JONES, Miss. Gemma, BA ACA *2006;* Flat 3 73 Monkton Street, LONDON, SE11 4TX.
ROCYN-JONES, Mr. Leighton, FCA *1969;* 47 Park Road, Keynsham, BRISTOL, BS31 1DE.
RODAK, Miss. Krysia, BA ACA *1987;* Route Des Grands Champs 13, 1278 LA RIPPE, SWITZERLAND.
RODAN, Miss. Moira Elizabeth, BA(Hons) ACA *2010;* Orrys Mount, Ballaragh Road, Laxey, ISLE OF MAN, IM4 7PE.
•RODAWAY, Mr. Adrian Christopher, BA FCA DChA *1990;* HPH, 21 Victoria Avenue, HARROGATE, HG1 5RD.
RODAWAY, Mr. Neil, BSc ACA FCIS *1990;* 81 Valley Parade, Glen Iris, MELBOURNE, VIC 3146, AUSTRALIA.
RODBOURN, Mr. Daniel, MChem ACA *2007;* 77 High Kingsdown, BRISTOL, BS2 8EP.
RODBOURN, Mr. Stephen, ACA *2002;* Colmarerstrasse 31, CH-4055 BASEL, SWITZERLAND.
•RODD, Mr. Ian Michael, BSc ACA FCCA *2008;* Ward Goodman Limited, 4 Cedar Park, Cobham Road, Ferndown Industrial Estate, WIMBORNE, DORSET BH21 7SF. See also Ward Goodman
RODD, Mr. Ian Michael, BA ACA *1986;* 12 Conway Close, Euxton, CHORLEY, PR7 6NT.
RODD, Mr. Nicholas Anthony, BEng ACA *1997;* Bristow Helicopters Ltd, Redhill Aerodrome, Kings Mill Lane, REDHILL, RH1 5JZ.
RODD, Mr. Philip Bruce, BSc ACA *1993;* 37 A Winsome Park, 42 Conduit Road, MID LEVELS, HONG KONG SAR.
RODDA, Mr. James, BA FCA *1971;* 22 Redding Drive, AMERSHAM, BUCKINGHAMSHIRE, HP6 5PX. (Life Member)
RODDAM, Mr. Louis Daniel, BA(Hons) ACA *2001;* 37a Esmond Gardens, South Parade, LONDON, W4 1JT.
RODDE, Mrs. Katharine Mary, BSc ACA *1992;* 4 Rue Baillou, 75014 PARIS, FRANCE.
RODDEN, Mr. Stuart James, BSc ACA *1996;* Aurelian Property Finance LTd Priory House Priory Street, USK, NP15 1BJ.
RODDICK, Mr. Luke, ACA *2009;* Flat 8 25 Cromwell Road, HOVE, EAST SUSSEX, BN3 3EB.
RODDICK, Mrs. Sophie, BA ACA *2009;* 28 Maple Gardens, HOVE, EAST SUSSEX, BN3 7JU.
RODDIS, Mr. Eric, FCA *1955;* 5 Hilltop Way, Southwood, Dronfield, DRONFIELD, S18 1YL. (Life Member)
RODDIS, Mr. Simon James Edward, BA ACA *1993;* The Old Farmhouse, 36 High Street, Easton on the Hill, STAMFORD, LINCOLNSHIRE, PE9 3LN.
•RODDISON, Mr. John, FCA *1977;* Brown McLeod Limited, 51 Clarkegrove Road, SHEFFIELD, SOUTH YORKSHIRE, S10 2NH.
RODE, Mr. Paul, BA(Hons) ACA *2002;* 4839 Elester Drive, SAN JOSE, CA 95124, UNITED STATES.
RODEL-DUFFY, Mr. Mark Laurence Frank, FCA *1982;* Voicenet Solutions Unit 2, Bell Business Park Smeaton Close, AYLESBURY, BUCKINGHAMSHIRE, HP19 8JR.
RODEN, Mr. Ernest Victor, FCA *1954;* 4 Ellesmere Drive, Aintree Sefton, LIVERPOOL, L10 2JR. (Life Member)
RODEN, Mr. Frank Gerald, BSc ACA *1992;* Brookside, La Rue Du Huquet, St. Martin, JERSEY, JE3 6HE.
RODEN, Mr. Gary David, BSc FCA *1986;* Derwent House, Icehouse Wood, OXTED, SURREY, RH8 9DW.
•RODEN, Mr. James Vincent, BA ACA *2002;* Garratts Wolverhampton Limited, 29 Waterloo Road, WOLVERHAMPTON, WV1 4DJ.
•RODEN, Mr. Michael John, BA ACA *1979;* KPMG LLP, 15 Canada Square, LONDON, E14 5GL. See also KPMG Europe LLP
RODEN, Mr. Paul Andrew, BSc ACA *1989;* Crowshaw House, Little Scotland, Blackrod, BOLTON, BL6 5JJ.
RODEN, Mr. Philip George, BSc FCA *1974;* 67 Wellman Croft, BIRMINGHAM, B29 6NR.
RODER, Mr. Jens, BSc FCA *1972;* Furesovej 71, 2830 VIRUM, DENMARK.
RODER, Mr. Stephen Bernard, BSc FCA *1982;* 1B Evergreen Gardens, 18 Shouson Hill Road, SHOUSON HILL, HONG KONG ISLAND, HONG KONG SAR.
RODERICK, Mr. Alun Rhys, BSc ACA MBA *1995;* Anglo American Plc Anglo American House, 20 Carlton House Terrace, LONDON, SW1Y 5AN.
RODERICK, Mr. David Vivian, BSc(Econ) ACA *1997;* 13 Eastover Close, Westbury on Trym, BRISTOL, BS9 3JQ.
RODERICK, Mr. Joseph Alan John, FCA ACII *1975;* Wesleyan Assurance Society, Colmore Circus, BIRMINGHAM, B4 6AR.
RODERICK, Mr. Stephen John Charles, BSc ACA ATII *1992;* Nair & Co, Whitefriars, Lewins Mead, BRISTOL, BS1 2NT.
RODERICK, Mr. Timothy Clive Lumley, BA ACA *1992;* Friars Pool Station Road, Otford, SEVENOAKS, KENT, TN14 5QU.
RODFORD, Mrs. Emma Louise, BSc ACA *1997;* 65 Bangalore Street, LONDON, SW15 1QF.
RODGER, Mr. Christopher John, FCA *1988;* Leonard Curtis D T E House, Hollins Lane, BURY, BL9 8DG.
RODGER, Mr. Euan, BEng ACA *2007;* Unit 205, 2 Wentworth Street, MANLY, NSW 2095, AUSTRALIA.
RODGER, Mr. Graham Carl, FCA *1970;* Berwyn, 3 Oakway, Heswall, WIRRAL, CH60 3SP.
RODGER, Mr. Irvine Neil, MA ACA *1992;* Flat 405, Pacific Wharf, 165 Rotherhithe Street, LONDON, SE16 5QF.
RODGER, Mr. John Harley, FCA *1959;* 60 Bradway Road, SHEFFIELD, SOUTH YORKSHIRE, S17 4QU. (Life Member)
RODGER, Mr. Peter Robert Charles, BSc FCA CTA *1977;* 16 Links Road, Flackwell Heath, HIGH WYCOMBE, BUCKINGHAMSHIRE, HP10 9LY.
RODGER, Mr. Simon Harley, BSc ACA *1992;* 1 Birch Glade, Park Place, Ashton Keynes, SWINDON, SN6 6PX.
RODGER, Mr. Timothy Charles, BA ACA *1998;* 3 Aston Grove Cottage, Cold Aston, CHELTENHAM, GLOUCESTERSHIRE, GL54 3BJ.
RODGERS, Mr. Adrian, BSc FCA FCT *1978;* ARC Solutions, 1 Oaks Coppice, Horndean, WATERLOOVILLE, HAMPSHIRE, PO8 9QR.
RODGERS, Mrs. Amanda Cecelia, BSc FCA *1978;* Havenwood House, Broad Road, Hambrook, CHICHESTER, PO18 8RF.
RODGERS, Mrs. Andrea Lorraine, BA ACA *1996;* Camel, BEQUIA, SAINT VINCENT AND THE GRENADINES.
RODGERS, Mr. Andrew Ian, BA ACA *1999;* Flat 9, 20 Mauldeth Road, Heaton Moor, STOCKPORT, SK4 3NE.
RODGERS, Miss. Arwen Elizabeth, ACA *2009;* Flat 2 Chalice Court, Deanery Close, LONDON, N2 8NU.
RODGERS, Mrs. Beverley, BA ACA *2004;* 3 Paxton Close, Cottenham, CAMBRIDGE, CB24 8XP.
RODGERS, Mrs. Brigid Marie, BA ACA *1983;* 21 Ramillies Avenue, Cheadle Hulme, CHEADLE, CHESHIRE, SK8 7AQ.
RODGERS, Mrs. Carol Elizabeth, BSc ACA *1987;* Metta, Valley Lane, Meopham, GRAVESEND, KENT, DA13 0DQ.
•RODGERS, Mr. Christopher John, BSc FCA *1980;* with KPMG LLP, 15 Canada Square, LONDON, E14 5GL.
RODGERS, Mr. Colin John, FCA *1975;* Sion View, Green Lane, Kirby Wiske, THIRSK, NORTH YORKSHIRE, YO7 4ET.
•RODGERS, Mr. Derrick Thomas, FCA *1953;* D.T. Rodgers, 3 Ruscote, Cross Oak Road, BERKHAMSTED, HP4 3NA.
RODGERS, Mr. Frederick Clive, FCA CTA AMCT *1990;* Heather Bank, 6 Burston Gardens, Lingfield Road, EAST GRINSTEAD, RH19 2HD.
RODGERS, Mr. Henry James, FCA *1968;* 48 Butt Lane, Allesley, COVENTRY, CV5 9EZ.
RODGERS, Mrs. Joanne Carol, BMus ACA *1992;* 3 Pear Tree Way, Crowle, WORCESTER, WR7 4SB.
RODGERS, Mr. John Brian, MSc FCA *1956;* 1 Lincoln Circus, The Park, NOTTINGHAM, NG7 1BG. (Life Member)
RODGERS, Mr. Jonathan Paul, MA FCA *1991;* Tindall Riley Marine Ltd, Regis House, 45 King William Street, LONDON, EC4R 9AS.
RODGERS, Mrs. Judith Anne, FCA *1965;* 169 Nanpantan Road, Nanpantan, LOUGHBOROUGH, LE11 3YB.
RODGERS, Mr. Kevin, BA ACA *1980;* Flat 1 Victoria Court, 2 Aromire Street, IKOYI, NIGERIA.
RODGERS, Mrs. Lisa Jane, BA ACA *1999;* Perkins Engines, PETERBOROUGH, PE1 5NA.
RODGERS, Miss. Louise Karen, MChem ACA *2009;* 127 Fairacres, Prestwood, GREAT MISSENDEN, BUCKINGHAMSHIRE, HP16 0LF.
•RODGERS, Mr. Martin Bruce, FCA *1972;* Baker Tilly Tax & Advisory Services LLP, The Clock House, 140 London Road, GUILDFORD, SURREY, GU1 1UW. See also Baker Tilly Restructuring and Recovery LLP
RODGERS, Mrs. Mary-Jane, ACA CA(SA) *2010;* 5 Bendemeer Road, Putney, LONDON, SW15 1JX.
RODGERS, Mr. Michael, ACA *1987;* Highfield, Lyeway Lane, Ropley, ALRESFORD, SO24 0DW.
RODGERS, Mr. Michael Charles, BA ACA *1984;* 41 Dock Street, VICTORIA V8V 1Z9, BC, CANADA.
RODGERS, Mr. Paul Leslie, BSc FCA *1989;* Meadow Sweet The Common, East Hanningfield, CHELMSFORD, CM3 8AH.
RODGERS, Mr. Peter William, BA FCA *1976;* 7 Aldiss Close, SWAFFHAM, PE37 7UG.
RODGERS, Mr. Philip Michael, FCA *1964;* Grove House, Bells Road, Belchamp Walter, SUDBURY, CO10 7AR. (Life Member)
RODGERS, Mr. Philip Nicholas, BA FCA *1984;* Tythe Cottage, Church Lane, GODSTONE, SURREY, RH9 8BL.
RODGERS, Mrs. Sheila Mary, BA ACA *1985;* 68 Aldwickbury Crescent, HARPENDEN, AL5 5SE.
RODGERS, Mr. Simon, BA ACA *2001;* 175 Deepwater Road, Castle Cove, SYDNEY, NSW 2069, AUSTRALIA.
RODGERS, Dr. Simon Jon, PhD MBiochem ACA *2004;* 3 Paxton Close, Cottenham, CAMBRIDGE, CB24 8XP.
RODGERS, Mr. Stephen, FCA *1974;* 37 Ashfield Park, Whickham, NEWCASTLE UPON TYNE, NE16 4SQ.
RODHAM, Mr. Thomas Peter, ACA *2009;* 31 Broom Mills Road, Farsley, PUDSEY, WEST YORKSHIRE, LS28 5GR.
RODHOUSE, Mr. Matthew John, ACA *1983;* The Old Brew House, 2 Northampton Rd, Litchborough, TOWCESTER, NN12 8JB.
RODICK, Mrs. Carolyn Lesley, BSc ACA *1990;* 4 Wensleydale Close, Maghull, LIVERPOOL, L31 8DR.
•RODICK, Mr. David James, BA(Hons) ACA ACMA *2007;* Tax Matters Accountants Ltd, 259 Edleston Road, CREWE, CHESHIRE, CW2 7EA.
RODIN, Mr. Ian Jonathan, BSc ACA *1984;* Ernst & Young, PO Box 7878, Waterfront Place, 1 Eagle Street, BRISBANE, QLD 4001 AUSTRALIA.
RODIN, Mr. Sam, FCA *1940;* 20 Holders Hill Crescent, LONDON, NW4 1ND. (Life Member)
RODLEY, Mr. James William Eric, BA ACA *1989;* The Vicarage, St. Clements Road, BOURNEMOUTH, BH1 4DZ.
RODLEY, Mr. Kevin Cyril, FCA *1951;* C/O David Wong, HR1 - 10 -1 Riana Green Condo, Jalan Tropicana Utara, 47410 PETALING JAYA, SELANGOR, MALAYSIA. (Life Member)
RODMELL, Mrs. Catherine Anne Gibson, BSc ACA *1986;* 41 Jubilee Road, Formby, LIVERPOOL, L37 2HT.
•RODNEY, Mr. David Howard, FCA *1970;* (Tax Fac), Citroen Wells, Devonshire House, 1 Devonshire Street, LONDON, W1W 5DR.
•RODNEY, Mr. Peter Allan, FCA *1974;* (Tax Fac), Bright Grahame Murray, 131 Edgware Road, LONDON, W2 2AP.
RODNEY-SMITH, Mrs. Katherine Rhiannon, BSc ACA *1999;* 44 Kingsway, LONDON, SW14 7HW.
RODNEY-SMITH, Mr. Martin, FCA *1968;* Rodney-Smith & Partners, 2 Ringwould Cottage, Back Street Ringwould, DEAL, CT14 8HN.
•RODRIGUES, Mr. Adrian, FCA *1987;* H.G.Field & Co, 2 Guildford Street, CHERTSEY, KT16 9BQ.
RODRIGUES, Mr. Einstein Carlos Xavier, BA FCA *1995;* Basement Flat, 17 Chancellors Street, LONDON, W6 9RN.
RODRIGUES, Mrs. Elizabeth Jane, MSci ACA *2002;* 1 Marina Avenue, Beeston, NOTTINGHAM, NG9 1HB.
RODRIGUES, Mr. Francisco Joao, BSc ACA *1983;* 93 West Road, Avondale, HARARE, ZIMBABWE.
RODRIGUES, Mr. Francisco Xavier, BSc FCA *1994;* 32 Beresford Avenue, Tolworth, SURBITON, KT5 9LJ.
RODRIGUES, Miss. Joanna Elisabeth Stefanie, BSocSc ACA *1999;* Back Lane Farmhouse Back Lane, Kingston, STURMINSTER NEWTON, DORSET, DT10 2DT.
RODRIGUES, Miss. Joanne May, BSc ACA *2000;* 29th Floor, Menara Bumiputra Commerce, 11 Jalan Raja Laut, P.O Box 10063, 50704 KUALA LUMPUR, FEDERAL TERRITORY MALAYSIA.
RODRIGUES, Mr. Joaquim Cordeiro, FCA ACMA *1999;* 6 Pepper Street, LONDON, E14 9RB.
RODRIGUES, Mrs. Karen, ACA *1993;* Suite 3 Shenley Pavillions, Chalkdell Drive Shenley Wood, MILTON KEYNES, BUCKINGHAMSHIRE, MK5 6LB.
RODRIGUES, Ms. Maria Luiza, BSc ACA *1999;* South Hawke Lodge The Ridge, Woldingham, CATERHAM, SURREY, CR3 7AX.
RODRIGUES, Mr. Mario Antonio, BSc FCA *1984;* 36 Wycombe Street, EPPING, NSW 2121, 2121, AUSTRALIA.
RODRIGUES, Mrs. Petronella Nicolasina, FCA ACMA *1999;* 6 Pepper Street, LONDON, E14 9RB.
RODRIGUES, Mr. Raymond Roy, BA FCA *1994;* 79 Fragata Calle, PANAMA CITY, PANAMA.
RODRIGUES, Mr. Selwyn Mario Pius, BSc ACA *1986;* 224 Ferme Park Road, LONDON, N8 9BN.
•RODRIGUES-PEREIRA, Mr. Robert Brian, FCA *1969;* Halliwell & Horton, 29 Burnley Road East, Waterfoot, ROSSENDALE, BB4 9AG.
RODRIGUEZ, Mrs. Anne Elizabeth, BA ACA *1994;* 17 The Drive, Mardley Heath, WELWYN, AL6 0TW.
RODRIGUEZ, Mrs. Wendy Jean Carol, BSc ACA *1993;* 6 Lynton Grove, Timperley, ALTRINCHAM, CHESHIRE, WA15 7LS.
RODRIGUEZ-SOLIS, Mrs. Yanina Marisol, MSc ACA *2007;* 35 Hampden Way, LONDON, N14 5DJ.
•RODWAY, Mr. Alan James, FCA *1967;* (Tax Fac), The Tax People Limited, Apple Pie Cottage, Woodside Road, Chiddingfold, GODALMING, GU8 4RA.
RODWAY, Mr. Nigel David, ACA *1984;* 164 Old Winton Road, ANDOVER, SP10 2DS.
RODWAY, Mr. Timothy John, BSc FCA *1983;* Berkeley Homes (Oxford & Chiltern) Ltd Berkeley House, Abingdon Science Park Barton Lane, ABINGDON, OXFORDSHIRE, OX14 3NB.
RODWAY, Mrs. Valerie Ann, BSc ACA *1989;* 44 Buckingham Road West, STOCKPORT, SK4 4BA.
RODWELL, Miss. Amy, BA ACA *2009;* 45 Kingsmead Road, LEICESTER, LE2 3YE.
RODWELL, Ms. Chania Jade, BA ACA *2000;* 23A Rosemead Road, HORNSBY, NSW 2077, AUSTRALIA.
RODWELL, Mr. David Peter, BEng ACA *1997;* 17 Enville Road, Bowdon, ALTRINCHAM, CHESHIRE, WA14 2PF.
RODWELL, Mrs. Katharine Anne, BSocSc ACA *2000;* 17 Enville Road, Bowdon, ALTRINCHAM, CHESHIRE, WA14 2PF.
RODWELL, Mr. Keith James, FCA *1965;* 4 Malthouse Lane, West Ashling, CHICHESTER, PO18 8DZ. (Life Member)
RODWELL, Mr. Patrik Robert Gosta, BA FCA FSI *1994;* 14 Belmont Grove, Lewisham, LONDON, SE13 5DW.
RODZYNSKI, Mr. Andrew Christopher, ACA *2008;* 2 Cranbrook Drive, Kennington, OXFORD, OX1 5RR.
ROE, Mrs. Anne Elizabeth, BSc ACA CTA *1993;* Rabobank International London Branch, Thames Court, 1 Queenhithe, LONDON, EC4V 3RL.
ROE, Mr. Barry Stephen, BTech ACA *1979;* Loxley House, 32 Beck Street, Digby, LINCOLN, LN4 3NE. (Life Member)
ROE, Mr. Darren, BA ACA *2003;* 15 Kent Close, Royston, BARNSLEY, SOUTH YORKSHIRE, S71 4FB.
ROE, Mr. David James, BSc ACA *1993;* SAMPI SpA, Via Amerigo Vespucci 1, 55100 ALTOPASCIO, TUSCANY, ITALY.
ROE, Mr. David Michael, BA ACA *1985;* Ofquest Limited, Irton House, Warpsgrove Lane, Chalgrove, OXFORD, OX44 7TH.
ROE, Mr. David William, BSc FCA *1975;* Coombehurst Wonham Way, Peaslake, GUILDFORD, SURREY, GU5 9PA.
ROE, Mr. George Samuel, BA ACA *2005;* 6 The Avenue, HASLEMERE, GU27 1JT.
ROE, Mr. Ian, BA ACA *1988;* Yew Tree Cottage, How Caple, HEREFORD, HR1 4TA.
ROE, Mr. James Brian, BSc FCA *1975;* Bere Marsh House, Shillingstone, BLANDFORD FORUM, DORSET, DT11 0QY.
ROE, Mr. James Peter Norton, BSc ACA *2003;* 59 Lugtrout Lane, SOLIHULL, WEST MIDLANDS, B91 2SB.
ROE, Mr. John Patrick William, ACA *1983;* Meadow-View, Mill Road, Nassington, PETERBOROUGH, PE8 6QA.

ROE, Mr. Jonathan Caldwell, BA ACA *1981;* 5 Cottenham Park Road, LONDON, SW20 0RX.

ROE, Mr. Julian James Benedict, BSc FCA *1992;* 8 Leeward Gardens, Wimbledon, LONDON, SW19 7QR.

ROE, Mr. Magnus, ACA *2009;* 55 Meyer Road, #07-03, The Seafront on Meyer, SINGAPORE 437978, SINGAPORE.

ROE, Mr. Matthew Steven, ACA *2011;* 12 Caledonia Place, Clifton, BRISTOL, BS8 4DJ.

ROE, Miss. Nicola Louise, BA(Hons) ACA *2004;* Flat 6 Bramley Court, 19 Orchard Grove, ORPINGTON, BR6 0AT.

•ROE, Mr. Peter Howard, FCA *1963;* (Tax Fac), 21 Lucombe Way, New Earswick, YORK, YO32 4DS.

ROE, Mr. Peter Stephen, BA FCA *1984;* 1 Chesterfield Close, Littler Lane, WINSFORD, CW7 2NS.

ROE, Mr. Richard Keith, BA(Hons) FCA CTA *1981;* 62 Firs Road, Edwalton, NOTTINGHAM, NG12 4BX.

ROE, Miss. Sarah Marie, BSc ACA *2010;* 22 Halstead Avenue, MANCHESTER, M21 9FT.

ROE, Mr. Timothy Michael, BSc ACA *1989;* 2A Kenley Road, LONDON, SW19 3JQ.

ROE, Mrs. Victoria Julie, ACA *2008;* 8 Cameron Lane, Fernwood, NEWARK, NOTTINGHAMSHIRE, NG24 3GE.

ROEBUCK, Miss. Fiona Elizabeth, BA(Hons) ACA *2011;* 27 Avonmore Gardens, LONDON, W14 8RU.

•ROEBUCK, Mr. Geoffrey Stuart, FCA *1971;* Connelly & Co Limited, Permanent House, 1 Dundas Street, HUDDERSFIELD, HD1 2EX.

•ROEBUCK, Mr. James, FCA *1970;* J Roebuck & Co, 148 Droylsden Road, Audenshaw, MANCHESTER, M34 5SJ.

ROEBUCK, Miss. Janet, ACA MAAT *1995;* 59 Woodburn Square, Whitley Lodge, WHITLEY BAY, NE26 3JD.

•ROEBUCK, Mr. Richard Christopher Russell, FCA *1974;* Roebuck & Co, 165 Bournville Lane, Bournville, BIRMINGHAM, B30 1LY.

ROEBUCK, Mr. Simon Charles Albany, MA ACA *1994;* Flying Pig Publishing, 3 Basset Place, FALMOUTH, CORNWALL, TR11 2SS.

•ROFE, Mr. Colin, FCA *1969;* Colin Rofe & Company, 12 Hatherley Road, SIDCUP, DA14 4BG.

ROFE, Mr. Michael John, BA ACA *2002;* with Simpson Wreford & Partners, Suffolk House, George Street, CROYDON, CR0 0YN.

ROFF, Mr. Andrew Harvey, BSc ACA *2006;* 37 Essex Road, LONDON, W3 9JA.

•ROFF, Mr. Jeremy Nicholas, FCA CTA TEP *1982;* J N Roff & Co, Swinholme Farm, Bowes, BARNARD CASTLE, COUNTY DURHAM, DL12 9NB.

ROFF, Mr. John Bayliss, FCA *1963;* Malt House Farm Bungalow, Queen Street, Sandhurst, CRANBROOK, KENT, TN18 5HR.

ROFF, Mr. Michael Dyson, FCA *1959;* Deeside, 20 Chapel Road, ALDERLEY EDGE, SK9 7DU. (Life Member)

ROFF, Mrs. Susan Moira, BSc ACA *1986;* 79 High Street, GODSTONE, RH9 8DT.

ROFFE, Mr. Ronald John Cawley, FCA *1952;* May Cottage, Church Lane, Witley, GODALMING, GU8 5PW. (Life Member)

ROFFEY, Mr. Derek Charles, BSc ACA *1987;* Hogeweg 41 hs, 1098 BX AMSTERDAM, NETHERLANDS.

ROFFEY, Mr. Paul Richard, BA ACA *1992;* 48 Rudthorpe Road, Horfield, BRISTOL, BS7 9QG.

ROFFEY, Mrs. Stephanie Joanne, BSc ACA *1993;* 48 Rudthorpe Road, BRISTOL, BS7 9QG.

ROGAN, Mr. David Christopher, BSc ACA *1986;* Brathay House, Broad Walk, Prestbury, MACCLESFIELD, SK10 4BR.

ROGAN, Mr. Haydn, BA(Hons) ACA *2001;* (Tax Fac), Apartment 66, The Wentwood, 76 Newton Street, MANCHESTER, M1 1EE.

ROGAN, Mr. Paul Bernard, FCA *1976;* 79 Forest Road, Annesley Woodhouse Kirkby-in-Ashfield, NOTTINGHAM, NG17 9HA. (Life Member)

ROGAN, Miss. Shirley Anne, BA ACA *2005;* with Ernst & Young LLP, Apex Plaza, Forbury Road, READING, RG1 1YE.

•ROGBEER, Mr. Arvin, ACA *2007;* Moore Stephens Mauritius, 6th Floor, Newton Tower, Sir William Newton Steet, PORT LOUIS, MAURITIUS. See also Moore Stephens

ROGBEER, Mr. Chandradutt, ACA *2008;* H Ramnarain Building, Mer Rouge, PORT LOUIS, MAURITIUS.

•ROGBEER, Mrs. Rubeenna, ACA *2008;* Moore Stephens Mauritius, 6th Floor, Newton Tower, Sir William Newton Steet, PORT LOUIS, MAURITIUS. See also Moore Stephens

ROGER, Mr. Paul Barry, BA(Hons) ACA *2001;* 59 Culmstock Road, LONDON, SW11 6LY.

ROGERS, Mr. Alan Edwin, MA ACA *1988;* Laycock Farm, Northcote Road, Langho, BLACKBURN, BB6 8BG.

ROGERS, Mr. Alan Michael, BSc ACA *1983;* The Poplars, Orchard Road, Kelvedon, COLCHESTER, CO5 9NA.

ROGERS, Mrs. Alison May, BSc ACA *1988;* 12 Ballencrieff Steading, LONGNIDDRY, EAST LOTHIAN, EH32 0QH.

•ROGERS, Mrs. Alison Veronica, BA ACA *1989;* Alison Rogers Limited, 4 Longborough Close, REDDITCH, WORCESTERSHIRE, B97 5QN.

ROGERS, Miss. Amy Louise, ACA *2004;* 31 Great Lane, Frisby on the Wreake, MELTON MOWBRAY, LEICESTERSHIRE, LE14 2PB.

ROGERS, Mr. Andrew James, BA(Hons) ACA *2000;* with Deloitte LLP, Athene Place, 66 Shoe Lane, LONDON, EC4A 3BQ.

ROGERS, Mr. Andrew James, FCA *1974;* 78 Merewood Road, BEXLEYHEATH, KENT, DA7 6PQ.

•ROGERS, Mr. Andrew Mitchell, FCA *1968;* A M Rogers, Yorkshire House, 7 South Lane, HOLMFIRTH, HD9 1HN.

ROGERS, Mr. Andrew Paul, BA ACA *1999;* 19 Primrose Drive, Thornbury, BRISTOL, BS35 1UP.

ROGERS, Mr. Andrew Richard, BSc ACA *1994;* Rothend, New House Lane, Ashdon, SAFFRON WALDEN, ESSEX, CB10 2LX.

ROGERS, Mrs. Anne Caroline, MA ACA *1982;* Grey Roofs, Box, Minchinhampton, STROUD, GL6 9HD.

ROGERS, Mrs. Anne Christine, BA ACA *1990;* Kingsmead, 24 Detillens Lane, Limpsfield, OXTED, SURREY, RH8 0DJ.

ROGERS, Mr. Anthony Cannington, FCA *1969;* Quinces, Hosey Common Road, WESTERHAM, TN16 1PP.

ROGERS, Mr. Anthony Charles, ACA *1980;* 565 Huntington Road, Huntington, YORK, YO32 9PY.

ROGERS, Mr. Anthony Christopher, MA FCA *1971;* Le Tourtel, Rue des Marettes, St Martin, GUERNSEY, GY4 6JW. (Life Member)

ROGERS, Mr. Anthony Colin, FCA *1967;* Flat 90, 4001 Old Clayburn Road, ABBOTSFORD V3G 1C5, BC, CANADA.

•ROGERS, Mr. Bernard Alexander, BA FCA *1986;* Kenilworth Accountancy Limited, Bank Gallery, 13 High Street, KENILWORTH, WARWICKSHIRE, CV8 1LY.

ROGERS, Mr. Bernard Cedric James, MA FCA *1963;* Spindrift, Higher Sea Lane, Charmouth, BRIDPORT, DT6 6BB. (Life Member)

ROGERS, Mr. Bruce, FCA *1968;* 65 Spitalfields, YARM, TS15 9HL.

•ROGERS, Mr. Bryan Keith Humphrey, FCA *1957;* Bryan K H Rogers, 1 Cranleigh Gardens, Sanderstead, SOUTH CROYDON, Surrey, CR2 9LD.

•ROGERS, Mr. Carl Stanley, FCA *1971;* Rogers Paulley Limited, Arclight House, 3 Unity Street, BRISTOL, BS1 5HH. See also Palley Rogers

ROGERS, Mrs. Caroline Jane, BSc ACA *2001;* 8 Wynnstow Park, OXTED, RH8 9DR.

•ROGERS, Mrs. Catherine Margaret, BSc FCA *1991;* N.R. Barton & Co, 19-21 Bridgeman Terrace, WIGAN, WN1 1TD.

•ROGERS, Mrs. Christina, BSc ACA CTA *1990;* (Tax Fac), L M Griffiths & Co, 4 Goat Street, HAVERFORDWEST, DYFED, SA61 1PX.

ROGERS, Mr. Christopher Charles, BA FCA *1961;* 7 The Avenue, Laleham, STAINES, TW18 2SE.

ROGERS, Mr. Christopher Charles Bevan, BA ACA *1986;* The Mill House, Turville, HENLEY-ON-THAMES, RG9 6QL.

ROGERS, Mr. Christopher Mark, BA ACA *1990;* British American Tobacco, Globe House, 4 Temple Place, LONDON, WC2R 2PG.

•ROGERS, Mr. Christopher Michael Catesby, TD BSc FCA *1976;* St. James's Church, 197 Piccadilly, LONDON, W1J 9LL.

•ROGERS, Mr. Clive John, BSc FCA *1990;* CJR Accountants Limited, Oxford House, 8 Church Street, Arnold, NOTTINGHAM, NG5 8FB.

ROGERS, Mr. Colin John, MA FCA *1983;* 7 Luckley Road, WOKINGHAM, RG41 2ES.

ROGERS, Mr. Cyril Walter, FCA *1965;* 7 Bayham Road, TUNBRIDGE WELLS, KENT, TN2 5HR.

ROGERS, Mr. David, FCA *1973;* Tower House, Freston, IPSWICH, IP9 1AD. (Life Member)

ROGERS, Mr. David, FCA *1967;* Rose Cottage, High Onn, Church Eaton, STAFFORD, ST20 0AX.

ROGERS, Mr. David Antony John, FCA *1970;* 9 Brockhurst Park, Marldon, PAIGNTON, DEVON, TQ3 1LB. (Life Member)

ROGERS, Mr. David Charles, FCA *1954;* 11 Dalloway Road, ARUNDEL, WEST SUSSEX, BN18 9HJ. (Life Member)

ROGERS, Mr. David Charles, FCA *1969;* 45 Church Lane, Darley Abbey, DERBY, DE22 1EX.

ROGERS, Mr. David Charles, FCA *1974;* Wood View, Withinlee Road, Prestbury, MACCLESFIELD, CHESHIRE, SK10 4AT.

ROGERS, Mr. David Frederick Swiffin, BChD ACA *1991;* 29 North Shore Road, HAYLING ISLAND, PO11 0HL.

•ROGERS, Mr. David George, FCA *1981;* David Rogers FCA, The Old Malt House, Church Street, BROSELEY, SHROPSHIRE, TF12 5DA.

ROGERS, Mr. David John, FCA *1974;* Redburn Partners Llp, 75 King William Street, LONDON, EC4N 7BE.

•ROGERS, Mr. David Michael, BA FCA *1988;* D Rogers & Co Limited, St. Edith's View, High Street, Kemsing, SEVENOAKS, KENT TN15 6NA.

ROGERS, Mr. David Paul, BSc ACA *2010;* 130 Malthouse Lane, Earlswood, SOLIHULL, WEST MIDLANDS, B94 5SA.

ROGERS, Mr. David Paul, ACA *2008;* 4 The Forge Mews, Wilmslow Road, Withington, MANCHESTER, M20 4AW.

ROGERS, Mr. David Stephen, BA ACA *2010;* 30 Ranleigh Walk, HARPENDEN, HERTFORDSHIRE, AL5 1SR.

•ROGERS, Mr. Dean Warren, BA FCA *1992;* KPMG LLP, 15 Canada Square, LONDON, E14 5GL. See also KPMG Europe LLP

ROGERS, Mr. Dennis William, FCA *1963;* Cedar Gables, Hatfield Road, WITHAM, CM8 1EN.

ROGERS, Mr. Derek Ronald, BSc ACA *1979;* 14285 W Kirkwall Ct, LIBERTYVILLE, IL 60048-4837, UNITED STATES.

ROGERS, Mr. Dominic Mark, BSc(Hons) ACA *2000;* 69 Swinburne Road, ABINGDON, OXFORDSHIRE, OX14 2HF.

ROGERS, Mr. Edward William, ACA *1981;* High Ridge, Wolverton Road, Norton Lindsey, WARWICK, CV35 8JL.

ROGERS, Miss. Emily, BA ACA *2006;* Unit 111, 152 Campbell Parade, BONDI BEACH, NSW 2026, AUSTRALIA.

ROGERS, Mr. Fergal James, ACA *2011;* 2/9 Comely Bank Street, EDINBURGH, EH4 1BD.

•ROGERS, Mr. Francis John, ACA *1979;* (Tax Fac), Rogers, 20 St. Georges Close, TODDINGTON, BEDFORDSHIRE, LU5 6AT.

ROGERS, Mr. Frederick George, FCA *1957;* 23 Kings Gardens, Cranham, UPMINSTER, RM14 1LA. (Life Member)

ROGERS, Mr. Gareth, BSc ACA *2004;* Barn Piece, 31 Knightwood Park, Chandlers Ford, EASTLEIGH, SO53 4HP.

•ROGERS, Mr. Geoffrey, FCA *1969;* Geoffrey Rogers, Metropolitan House, 37 The Millfields, Stonehouse, PLYMOUTH, PL1 3JB.

ROGERS, Mr. George Edward, FCA *1952;* L'arche Var, Maison de Retraite, Avenue du 8 Mar 1945, 83120 SAINT MAXIME, FRANCE. (Life Member)

•ROGERS, Mr. George William, FCA *1972;* George Rogers & Co., 12 Landor Road, Knowle, SOLIHULL, B93 9HZ.

ROGERS, Mr. Graham John, BA FCA *1969;* Claires Court School, 1 College Avenue, MAIDENHEAD, BERKSHIRE, SL6 6AW.

ROGERS, Mr. Guy Christopher, BA ACA *2008;* The Stags, Footes Lane, St. Peter Port, GUERNSEY, GY1 2UF.

ROGERS, Mrs. Hazel Ann, MA ACA *1983;* 7 Luckley Road, WOKINGHAM, RG41 2ES.

ROGERS, Mrs. Helen, MBA BSc FCA *1992;* (Tax Fac), 85 Frenchay Road, OXFORD, OX2 6TF.

ROGERS, Miss. Helen Jane, ACA *2008;* 53 Langholme Drive, YORK, YO26 6AH.

ROGERS, Mrs. Helen Joy, BSc ACA *1990;* Charnbrook, Hawthorne Road, BROMLEY, BR1 2HN.

•ROGERS, Mrs. Helen Louise, BSc(Hons) ACA MAAT *2001;* Marypark Farmhouse, Marypark Farm, Marypark, BALLINDALLOCH, BANFFSHIRE, AB37 9BG.

ROGERS, Miss. Helen Louise, ACA *1992;* 7 Ladbroke Road, EPSOM, KT18 5BG.

ROGERS, Miss. Helen Myfanwy, BA ACA *2007;* Flat 3, 64 Granville Park, LONDON, SE13 7DX.

ROGERS, Mr. Hugh Phillip, MA FCA *1974;* 24 Lime Avenue, Duffield, BELPER, DE56 4DX.

ROGERS, Mr. Iain Michael, BA ACA *1994;* (Tax Fac), Peters Elworthy & Moore, Salisbury House, 3 Salisbury Villas, CAMBRIDGE, CB1 2LA.

ROGERS, Mr. Ian Terence, MA FCA *1973;* 18 Hillcroft Crescent, Ealing, LONDON, W5 2SQ.

ROGERS, Mr. James George, MA FCA *1978;* 39 Bare Avenue, Bare, MORECAMBE, LANCASHIRE, LA4 6BD.

•ROGERS, Mr. James Neave, BA FCA *1988;* Grant Thornton UK LLP, 1-4 Atholl Crescent, EDINBURGH, EH3 8LQ. See also Grant Thornton LLP

ROGERS, Mr. James Norman, FCA *1950;* 3 Sandhurst Way, Lydiate, LIVERPOOL, L31 4DR. (Life Member)

ROGERS, Mr. James William, BA ACA *1998;* 39 Schooner Close, Isle of Dogs, LONDON, E14 3GG.

ROGERS, Mrs. Jane Elizabeth, BSc ACA *1989;* Dreycote, Quarry Park Road, STOURBRIDGE, WEST MIDLANDS, DY8 2RE.

ROGERS, Mrs. Jane Linda, BSc ACA *1994;* 47 Hillrise Avenue, Sompting, LANCING, WEST SUSSEX, BN15 0LU.

ROGERS, Mrs. Janet Elizabeth, BSc ACA *1982;* Upper Knightsbridge Farm Cottage, Newbury Road, Headley, THATCHAM, BERKSHIRE, RG19 8LA.

ROGERS, Mr. Jason Francis Basil, BA FCA ATII *1993;* Cedar Cottage, Watts Road, THAMES DITTON, KT7 0BX.

ROGERS, Mr. John, FCA *1969;* 49 East Sheen Avenue, LONDON, SW14 8AR.

ROGERS, Mr. John Andrew, BCom ACA *1993;* 1 Oldfold Park, MILLTIMBER, ABERDEENSHIRE, AB13 0JW.

ROGERS, Mr. John David Michael, FCA *1963;* Brunton House, Austwick, LANCASTER, LA2 8DE.

ROGERS, Mr. John Henry Wilson, FCA *1960;* Bryn Coch, Mountain Road, Trimsaran, KIDWELLY, SA17 4EU. (Life Member)

ROGERS, Mr. John Keith, FCA *1981;* 31 Fairfield, INGATESTONE, CM4 9ER.

ROGERS, Mr. John Murray, FCA *1959;* 53 Parklands, WOTTON-UNDER-EDGE, GLOUCESTERSHIRE, GL12 7NR. (Life Member)

ROGERS, Mr. John Terence, FCA *1967;* 232 Leigham Court Road, LONDON, SW16 2RB.

ROGERS, Mr. Jonathan Mark, BA ACA *1995;* 16th Floor, 4 King Sreet West, TORONTO M5H 1B6, ON, CANADA.

ROGERS, Miss. Julie Mary, ACA *1984;* 5 Aldersyde, Birstall, BATLEY, WF17 9PU.

ROGERS, Mrs. Justine Claire, MBChB ACA *2004;* GE Healthcare, Pollards Wood, Nightingales Lane, CHALFONT ST. GILES, BUCKINGHAMSHIRE, HP8 4SP.

•ROGERS, Ms. Karen Louise, BSc FCA *1987;* 7 Heol y Deri, CARDIFF, CF14 6HA.

ROGERS, Mrs. Karen Marie Stochholm, FCA *1992;* Serious Fraud Office, Elm House, 10-16 Elm Street, LONDON, WC1X 0BJ.

ROGERS, Miss. Katharine Jane, BA(Hons) ACA *2011;* 24 Constantine Road, WITHAM, ESSEX, CM8 1HL.

ROGERS, Mrs. Kathleen Maria, BSc ACA *1992;* RBS Insurance, Churchill Court, Westmoreland Road, BROMLEY, BR1 1DP.

•ROGERS, Miss. Kathryn Michelle, BA(Hons) ACA *2002;* KR Accountancy, Bank Bottom Farm, Broadhead Road, Turton, BOLTON, LANCASHIRE BL7 0JN.

ROGERS, Mrs. Katie, BA ACA *2006;* 37 High Street, Sandridge, ST. ALBANS, HERTFORDSHIRE, AL4 9DD.

•ROGERS, Mr. Kenneth Albert, LLB FCA *1966;* (Tax Fac), Proud Goulbourn, 608 Liverpool Road, Irlam, MANCHESTER, M44 5AA. See also Proud Goulbourn Accountants Ltd

ROGERS, Mr. Lee Ashley, BA FCA *1999;* Caprice, Highgate Lane, Whitworth, ROCHDALE, LANCASHIRE, OL12 8SL.

•ROGERS, Mr. Lewis John, BSc FCA *1981;* Young & Co, Bewell House, Bewell Street, HEREFORD, HR4 0BA.

ROGERS, Miss. Lynne Denise, BA ACA *1986;* 34 Old Butt Lane, Talke, STOKE-ON-TRENT, ST7 1NL.

ROGERS, Mr. Malcolm Sidney Richard, FCA ATII *1969;* Pine Reach, Church Street, Weedon Bec, Weedon, NORTHAMPTON, NN7 4PL. (Life Member)

ROGERS, Mr. Mark Andrew, MA FCA *1982;* Grey Roofs, Box, Minchinhampton, STROUD, GL6 9HD.

ROGERS, Mr. Mark Andrew, BSc FCA *1997;* 2 Shaftesbury Close, DAWLISH, DEVON, EX7 9PZ.

ROGERS, Mr. Mark Peter, BSc ACA *1997;* SPTI, 10202 West Washington Blvd, CULVER CITY, CA 90232, UNITED STATES.

ROGERS, Mr. Martin Ian, BSc ACA *1994;* 6 Lulworth Avenue Goffs Oak, WALTHAM CROSS, HERTFORDSHIRE, EN7 5LQ.

•ROGERS, Mr. Martin John, BSc FCA *1980;* Mazars LLP, Cartwright House, Tottle Road, NOTTINGHAM, NG2 1RT.

ROGERS, Mr. Michael John, FCA *1964;* MRMA, MRM Office Park, 10 Village Road, KLOOF, 3610, SOUTH AFRICA. See also Michael Roger & Maingard

ROGERS, Mr. Michael Jonathan, BA(Hons) ACA *2010;* 4 Ditchford Close, Wootton, NORTHAMPTON, NN4 6AY.

ROGERS, Mr. Michael Thomas, BSc FCA *1980;* Risk Services Llc, 1800 Second Street Suite 909, SARASOTA, FL 34236, UNITED STATES.

ROGERS, Mr. Michael Vincent, FCA *1973;* 32 Signal Road, Ramsey, HUNTINGDON, CAMBRIDGESHIRE, PE26 1NG.
ROGERS, Mr. Murray William, BA ACA *2006;* Data Connection Ltd, 100 Church Street, ENFIELD, MIDDLESEX, EN2 6BQ.
•ROGERS, Mr. Neil Derek, ACA *1984;* (Tax Fac), Rogers & Company, Suite E, 102A Longstone Road, EASTBOURNE, BN21 3SJ.
ROGERS, Mr. Neil Graham, BA ACA *1987;* SGS SA, 1 Place Des Alpes, P.O. Box 2152, 1211 1 GENEVA, SWITZERLAND.
ROGERS, Mr. Neil William Charles, BSc ACA *2002;* Jark Recruitment, 8 Commercial Road, DEREHAM, NORFOLK, NR19 1AE.
•ROGERS, Mr. Nicholas Anthony, BA ACA CF *1987;* James Cowper LLP, 3 Wesley Gate, Queens Road, READING, RG1 4AP. See also JC Payroll Services Ltd
ROGERS, Mr. Nicholas James, BSc ACA *1989;* 35 Rectory Road, BECKENHAM, BR3 1HL.
ROGERS, Mr. Nicholas Moreton, FCA *1978;* 3 Ridgewood, Knoll Hill, Sneyd Park, BRISTOL, BS9 1QZ.
ROGERS, Mr. Nigel Foster, FCA *1984;* Stadium Group plc, Brenda Road, HARTLEPOOL, TS25 2BQ.
ROGERS, Mr. Nigel Harold John, FCA *1975;* The Underwriter Insurance Co Ltd, 117 Fenchurch Street, LONDON, EC3M 5DY.
ROGERS, Mr. Paul Andrew, BA ACA *2004;* KPMG, 10 Shelley Street, SYDNEY, NSW 2000, AUSTRALIA.
ROGERS, Mr. Paul Anthony, BSc ACA *2001;* 41 Celandine Way, CHIPPENHAM, WILTSHIRE, SN14 6XH.
ROGERS, Mr. Paul Michael, BSc FCA *1994;* Devonshires Solicitors, 30 Finsbury Circus, LONDON, EC2M 7DT.
ROGERS, Mr. Paul Robert, BA FCA *1989;* 2 Zig Zag Road, KENLEY, CR8 5EL.
ROGERS, Mr. Peter Ernest, FCA *1962;* Saffron House, Wendens Ambo, SAFFRON WALDEN, CB11 4JS.
ROGERS, Mr. Peter John, MA FCA *1979;* 1759 Chastain Parkway East, PACIFIC PALISADES, CA 90272, UNITED STATES.
ROGERS, Mr. Peter Lloyd, CBE LLB FCA *1973;* Fairfield House, Fairbourne, COBHAM, KT11 2BT.
ROGERS, Mr. Peter Mervyn, FCA *1979;* (Tax Fac), 2 St. Peters Road, MALVERN, WORCESTERSHIRE, WR14 1QS.
ROGERS, Mr. Philip Julian, BSc ACA *1998;* 5 Russet Glade, Burghfield Common, READING, RG7 3DZ.
ROGERS, Mr. Philip Timo, BSc ACA *1995;* SCI Entertainment Group PLC, 1 Hartfield Road, LONDON, SW19 3RU.
ROGERS, Mr. Phillip, ACA *2011;* Wayside The Ridgeway, Lamphey, PEMBROKE, DYFED, SA71 5PB.
ROGERS, Mr. Richard Anthony, BA ACA *1996;* 4/363 Pittwater Road, NORTH MANLY, NSW 2100, AUSTRALIA.
ROGERS, Mr. Richard Stewart, FCA *1973;* La Fideliere, Le Chefresne, 50410 PERCY, FRANCE.
ROGERS, Mr. Robert Charles, MA ACA *1985;* Lower Moor House, Oaksey, MALMESBURY, WILTSHIRE, SN16 9TW.
ROGERS, Mr. Robert Stephen, BSc ACA *1987;* 3 Gilian Road, CARDIFF, CF5 2PZ.
ROGERS, Mr. Robert William, MA ACA *1985;* SEB Enskilda, 2 Cannon Street, LONDON, EC4M 6XX.
ROGERS, Mr. Ronald Hugh, FCA *1934;* Rua Dez De Novembro 429, SAO PAULO, 04644-080 SP, BRAZIL. (Life Member)
ROGERS, Mr. Ronald John, FCA *1976;* 60 Flinders Street, ADELAIDE, SA 5000, AUSTRALIA.
ROGERS, Mr. Ross, BA(Hons) ACA *2003;* 133 Wheatfield Way, CHELMSFORD, CM1 2RB.
ROGERS, Mr. Roy Arthur, FCA *1954;* 38 The Walk, POTTERS BAR, EN6 1QE. (Life Member)
ROGERS, Ms. Sarah Ann, BA ACA *1994;* Tate Gallery, Millbank, LONDON, SW1P 4RG.
ROGERS, Mr. Shaun Patrick, BA ACA *1983;* Montoya Ltd, 2 Wellesley Parade, Godstone Road, WHYTELEAFE, SURREY, CR3 0BL.
ROGERS, Mr. Simon Jonathan, BA ACA *2002;* with KPMG LLP, 1 The Embankment, Neville Street, LEEDS, LS1 4DW.
ROGERS, Mr. Simon Nicholas, ACA *2008;* Tesco Stores Ltd Progress House, Shires Park, WELWYN GARDEN CITY, HERTFORDSHIRE, AL7 1GB.
ROGERS, Mr. Stanley, FCA *1951;* 132 Coniston Road, Tettenhall, WOLVERHAMPTON, WV6 9DU. (Life Member)
ROGERS, Mrs. Stephanie Anne, BSc ACA *1995;* Ong Plc, Minns Business Park, OXFORD, OX2 0JB.
ROGERS, Mr. Stephen, BSc FCA *1978;* Churchby House Church Street, Kirkby Malzeard, RIPON, NORTH YORKSHIRE, HG4 3RT.
ROGERS, Mr. Stephen, MA FCA *1972;* 1 Ashley Close, Earley, READING, RG6 5QY.
ROGERS, Mr. Steven Richard, ACA *1980;* 9 Halifax Close, Marske By Sea, REDCAR, TS11 6NP.
ROGERS, Mr. Stuart James, BA ACA *1997;* 15 Hill View Spencers Wood, READING, RG7 1QB.
ROGERS, Mr. Stuart Keith, BSc ACA ACII MIIA *1984;* 101 Godfrey Way, DUNMOW, CM6 2SQ.
ROGERS, Mrs. Susan, MEng BSc ACA CTA *1995;* (Tax Fac), 7 Blackstone Close, REDHILL, RH1 6BG.
ROGERS, Mrs. Susan Jane, BSc ACA *1983;* 195 Harvey Road, Redlynch, CAIRNS, QLD 4870, AUSTRALIA.
ROGERS, Miss. Suzanne, ACA *1993;* 258 Henley Road, Caversham, READING, RG4 6LS.
ROGERS, Mr. Timothy Charles, BA ACA *1988;* 1 Cupstone Close, East Morton, KEIGHLEY, BD20 5JA.
ROGERS, Mr. Timothy Duncan, MA MPhil ACA *2001;* 12 Forthringham Drive, Monifieth, DUNDEE, DD5 4SN.
ROGERS, Miss. Victoria Emma, BSc ACA *2001;* 7 Steerforth Street, LONDON, SW18 4HH.
ROGERS, Miss. Wendy Fiona, BSc ACA *1992;* Fulbrook House, 14 West End, Weston Turville, AYLESBURY, HP22 5TT.
ROGERS, Mr. William Michael, BA FCA *1979;* 10 Causeway Glade, SHEFFIELD, S17 3EZ.
ROGERS, Miss. Zoe Louise, BSc(Hons) ACA *2001;* 3 Barclay Gardens (off Walkern Road), STEVENAGE, HERTFORDSHIRE, SG1 3BF.
ROGERS-JONES, Miss. Eva, FCA *1970;* Cwm, Llanarmon yn Ial, MOLD, CH7 4QD. (Life Member)
ROGERSON, Mr. Andrew Francis, FCA *1974;* Rua dos Aimores 1862 Ap1606, Lourdes, MG Brasil, BELO HORIZONTE, 30140-072, BRAZIL.
ROGERSON, Mr. Duncan Fraser, BSc ACA *1996;* 11 Old Rydon Ley, EXETER, EX2 7UA.
ROGERSON, Mr. James, ACA *2008;* 2 Wood Chat Court, CHORLEY, LANCASHIRE, PR7 2RF.
ROGERSON, Mr. Mark William, BSc ACA *1989;* 26 Beverley Rise, ILKLEY, WEST YORKSHIRE, LS29 9DB.
ROGERSON, Mr. Michael Anthony, FCA *1965;* Plum Tree Cottage, Newnham Road, NEWNHAM, HAMPSHIRE, RG27 9AE.
•ROGERSON, Mr. Michael Paul, BA ACA ATII *1990;* CW Energy LLP, 4th Floor, 40 Queen Street, LONDON, EC4R 1DD. See also CW Energy Tax Consultants Ltd
•ROGERSON, Mr. Peter, BA FCA *1974;* The Birches, Church Road, Westoning, BEDFORD, MK45 5JW.
ROGERSON, Mr. Philip Graham, FCA *1968;* Flat 1 Providence Tower, Bermondsey Wall West, LONDON, SE16 4US.
ROGERSON, Mr. Sydney, FCA *1953;* 45 Cross Lane, Marple, STOCKPORT, SK6 6DJ. (Life Member)
ROGERSON, Mr. Timothy Ian, BA ACA *1989;* Ernst & Young Becket House, 1 Lambeth Palace Road, LONDON, SE1 7EU.
•ROGERSON, Mr. Timothy Miles, BSc FCA *1997;* Timothy M Rogerson, 18 Saxon Way, ROMSEY, HAMPSHIRE, SO51 5PT.
ROGG, Mr. Dudley Julian, FCA *1974;* BHC - Grosvenor Hospitals Group Ltd, 87 Watford Way, Hendon Central, LONDON, NW4 4RS.
•ROGGER, Mrs. Josephine Ruth, FCA *1974;* Rogger & Co, 5 Grass Park, Finchley, LONDON, N3 1UB.
•ROGOFF, Mr. Samuel, MBA FCA ATII *1972;* (Tax Fac), Sam Rogoff & Co Limited, 2nd Floor, 167-169 Great Portland Street, LONDON, W1W 5PF.
•ROGOL, Mr. Peter Jonathan, BA FCA *1980;* Goodman Jones LLP, 29-30 Fitzroy Square, LONDON, W1T 6LQ.
•ROGOVE, Mr. Albert Ivor, FCA *1960;* Eppy Limited, 101 White Lion Street, LONDON, N1 9PF.
•ROGOVE, Mr. Ivan John, BA ACA *1995;* Eppy Limited, 101 White Lion Street, LONDON, N1 9PF.
ROHATGI, Mr. Pradip Krishna, BSc FCA *1969;* Olympus Apartments, 512, Altamount Road, MUMBAI 400026, INDIA.
ROHIT, Mr. Anish, ACA *2008;* 17 Browning Road, PRESTON, PR1 5SH.
ROISER, Mr. David Walter, FCA *1961;* Tudor Management Consultants Ltd, 8 Windsor Close, Rustington, LITTLEHAMPTON, WEST SUSSEX, BN16 3TJ.
ROJAS, Mr. Pablo, ACA *1995;* 27 Chestnut Avenue, WOKINGHAM, BERKSHIRE, RG41 3HW.
ROKADIA, Mr. Kassam, BSc ACA *2008;* 26 Prebendal Drive, Slip End, LUTON, LU1 4JW.
ROKED, Mr. Faruk Hussein Ahmed, BA ACA *1989;* P O Box 211184, DUBAI, UNITED ARAB EMIRATES.
ROLAND-PRICE, Mr. Andy, MEng ACA *2006;* Flat 1, 45 Dulwich Road, LONDON, SE24 0NJ.
ROLES, Mr. Kenneth Austen, MA ACA *1987;* Marlborough House, Gretton Fields, Gretton, CHELTENHAM, GL54 5HJ.
•ROLES, Mr. Kenneth Brian, FCA *1982;* (Tax Fac), Bland Baker, 21 Lodge Lane, GRAYS, RM17 5RY.
ROLFE, Mrs. Catherine Emma Joan, BA ACA *1986;* Le Villot Coach House, La Rue Du Flicquet, St. Martin, JERSEY, JE3 6BP.
ROLFE, Mr. Christopher Derek, BA FCA *1981;* Linacre, Ridgeway Road, TORQUAY, TQ1 2HL.
ROLFE, Mr. David Mathew, BA ACA *2001;* 26 Morlais, Emmer Green, READING, RG4 8PQ.
ROLFE, Miss. Eleanor Lucy, ACA *2011;* 19 St. Johns Road, LEATHERHEAD, SURREY, KT22 8SE.
ROLFE, Mr. Eric Martin, BSc FCA *1978;* 63 Sketty Road, ENFIELD, EN1 3SF.
ROLFE, Mr. Ian Peter, ACA *2008;* Murco Petroleum Ltd, 4 Beaconsfield Road, ST. ALBANS, HERTFORDSHIRE, AL1 3RH.
ROLFE, Mr. James Michael, BA(Hons) ACA *2003;* with RSM Tenon Limited, International House, 66 Chiltern Street, LONDON, W1U 4JT.
ROLFE, Mrs. Jane Elizabeth, BSc ACA *1996;* with KPMG, 147 Collins Street, MELBOURNE, VIC 3000, AUSTRALIA.
ROLFE, Mr. Mark Edward, BCom FCA *1984;* 8 The Paddock, GODALMING, SURREY, GU7 1XD.
ROLFE, Mr. Michael Lawrence, FCA *1974;* 19 Wroughton Road, LONDON, SW11 6BE.
ROLFE, Mr. Neil John, BSc ACA *2001;* with Ernst & Young LLP, 1 More London Place, LONDON, SE1 2AF.
ROLFE, Mr. Philip Hugh, BA FCA *1985;* 1 Woodfield Road, PETERBOROUGH, PE3 6HD.
•ROLFE, Mrs. Susan Jane, MA FCA *1990;* (Tax Fac), Banham Graham, 28 Longs Business Park, Englands Lane, Gorleston, GREAT YARMOUTH, NORFOLK NR31 6NE. See also Banham Graham Corporate Limited
ROLISON, Mr. Paul Terence, ACA *1982;* Yellowspring Plc 1 Aurum Court, Sylvan Way Southfields Business Park, BASILDON, SS15 6TH.
ROLLASON, Mr. David Anthony, FCA *1968;* The Pippins, 30 Barrow Road, Burton-on-the-Wolds, LOUGHBOROUGH, LE12 5TB.
ROLLASON, Mr. Garrick Brian, BA BCom ACA *2004;* 27 Cowper St, Brighton, VICTORIA, VIC 3186, AUSTRALIA.
ROLLASON, Mr. Martin Christopher, BSc ACA *1982;* Flat 7 Richmond Court, Redlake Rd, Pedmore, STOURBRIDGE, DY9 0RY.
•ROLLASON, Mrs. Melanie Anne, BA ACA *2002;* Rollason Accountancy Limited, 26 Langdale Drive, ASCOT, BERKSHIRE, SL5 8TQ.
ROLLASON, Mr. Michael John, FCA *1971;* 10 Orchard End, Cleobury Mortimer, KIDDERMINSTER, WORCESTERSHIRE, DY14 8BA.
ROLLASON, Mr. Stephen David, BSc ACA *1991;* 7 Montgomery Road, Enham Alamein, ANDOVER, HAMPSHIRE, SP11 6HB.
•ROLLASON, Mr. William Peter, MA ACA *1987;* 97 Chesterton Road, LONDON, W10 6ET.
ROLLE, Mr. Alex, BCom ACA *1996;* U B S, 1 Finsbury Avenue, LONDON, EC2M 2PP.
ROLLER, Mr. Michael Roy David, MA ACA *1989;* The Red House Wilsford, Amesbury, SALISBURY, SP4 7BL.
ROLLIN, Miss. Amy, ACA *2011;* 16 New Street, Ackworth, PONTEFRACT, WEST YORKSHIRE, WF7 7JF.
•ROLLIN, Mr. Charles Austin Noble, FCA *1968;* (Tax Fac), Greenhow & Co, Montague House, 258 Kings Road, READING, RG1 4HP.
ROLLIN, Mr. Charles Timothy Hardey, FCA *1971;* 149 Bury Street, RUISLIP, HA4 7TQ. (Life Member)
ROLLINGS, Mr. Geoffrey Gordon, FCA ACA *1952;* 64 Chestnut Road, Cimla, NEATH, SA11 3NU. (Life Member)
•ROLLINGS, Mrs. Georgina Rachel, MA ACA CPA *2000;* Starfish Accounting, Littledene, Ellington Road, MAIDENHEAD, BERKSHIRE, SL6 0AX.
ROLLINGS, Mr. Mark Andrew, BSc FCA *1987;* 25 Chenies Avenue, Little Chalfont, AMERSHAM, BUCKINGHAMSHIRE, HP6 6PP.
ROLLINGS, Mr. Steven John, BCom ACA *1999;* 34 Metchley Lane, Harborne, BIRMINGHAM, B17 0HS.
ROLLINS, Mr. Edward John, BSc ACA *1992;* 25 Edwards Close, WATERLOOVILLE, PO8 8RJ.
ROLLINS, Mr. Mark, BEng ACA *1990;* 1 Old Glebe Pastures, Peopleton, PERSHORE, WR10 2HQ.
ROLLINS, Mr. Thomas Edward, FCA *1962;* Hathaway Cottage, 9 Althorp Gardens, PERSHORE, WR10 1RY.
•ROLLINSHAW, Mr. Richard Mark, BA ACA *1999;* c/o Price Waterhouse Coopers LLP, Level 40, Emirates Towers Offices, PO Box 11987, DUBAI, UNITED ARAB EMIRATES. See also PricewaterhouseCoopers LLP
ROLLINSON, Mr. Ian David, BA(Hons) ACA *2003;* Kellogg Co of GB Ltd The Kellogg Building, Talbot Road Old Trafford, MANCHESTER, M16 0PU.
ROLLINSON, Mr. Mark, ACA *2008;* Coors Brewers Ltd, 137 High Street, BURTON-ON-TRENT, STAFFORDSHIRE, DE14 1JZ.
ROLLINSON, Mrs. Rachel Jane, BSc ACA *2003;* Acacta Ltd York Biocentre, Innovation Way Heslington, YORK, YO10 5NY.
ROLLINSON, Miss. Sarah Louise, BA ACA PGCE *2004;* Flat B 112 Thornlaw Road, LONDON, SE27 0SB.
•ROLLISON, Mr. Peter Graham, FCA *1983;* AVN Petersons Limited, Church House, 94 Felpham Road, BOGNOR REGIS, WEST SUSSEX, PO22 7PG.
•ROLLISTON, Mr. Guy Charles, FCA *1980;* (Tax Fac), Hartley Fowler LLP, Pavilion View, 19 New Road, BRIGHTON, EAST SUSSEX, BN1 1EY.
ROLLO, Mr. Gary, MEng ACA *2000;* 16 Woodland Street, BALGOWLAH HEIGHTS, NSW 2093, AUSTRALIA.
ROLLO, Mrs. Rachel Sarah, ACA *2009;* Meridian House, Farringdon Street, LONDON, EC4A 4HL.
ROLLO GARDNER, Ms. Claire Louise, BSc FCA *1998;* National Audit Office, 89 Sandyford Road, NEWCASTLE UPON TYNE, NE1 8HW.
•ROLLS, Mr. Andrew Edisto, BSc ACA *1981;* Andrew Rolls, 3 Pound Lane, LEAMINGTON SPA, WARWICKSHIRE, CV32 7RT.
ROLLS, Mrs. Ann Elizabeth, BSc FCA *1976;* 3 Pound Lane, LEAMINGTON SPA, CV32 7RT.
ROLLS, Mr. Christopher Peter, BSc ACA *1985;* 13 Pine Drive, Finchampstead, WOKINGHAM, RG40 3LD.
ROLLS, Mr. Edmund James, FCA *1969;* 11 Robert Close, Little Venice, LONDON, W9 1BY.
ROLLS, Mrs. Efthalia Anne Alice, BA(Hons) ACA *2000;* 101 St. Pauls Wood Hill, ORPINGTON, KENT, BR5 2SS.
ROLLS, Mrs. Lindsay Barbara, BA ACA *1983;* Our Lady Of Charity, Fairlight, The Avenue, ASCOT, BERKSHIRE, SL5 7LY.
ROLLS, Mr. Richard John, BSc ACA *1992;* 11 Halloughton Road, SOUTHWELL, NOTTINGHAMSHIRE, NG25 0LP.
•ROLLS, Mrs. Sarah Jane, MPhil BSc ACA *2003;* with KPMG LLP, 15 Canada Square, LONDON, E14 5GL.
ROLPH, Miss. Amanda Jane, BSc ACA *2007;* 106a Peabody Road, FARNBOROUGH, GU14 6DY.
ROLPH, Mr. Anthony Graham Charles, FCA *1962;* Mill Cross, 43 Mill Lane, SHOREHAM-BY-SEA, BN43 5NA. (Life Member)
ROLPH, Miss. Catherine Jane, ACA *2009;* Flat 9 Cambridge House, Cambridge Gardens, TUNBRIDGE WELLS, TN2 4SB.
•ⒹROLPH, Mr. David Alan, BSc FCA *1978;* Moore Stephens LLP, 150 Aldersgate Street, LONDON, EC1A 4AB. See also Moore Stephens & Co
ROLPH, Mrs. Joanne Nicola, BSc ACA *1993;* 1611 Copperas Cove, Lakes Of Parkway, HOUSTON, TX 77077, UNITED STATES.
ROLPH, Mr. John Bernard, FCA *1968;* The Old House, 72 Chapel Road, Dersingham, KING'S LYNN, NORFOLK, PE31 6PN.
ROLPH, Mr. John Richard, BSc FCA *1975;* (Tax Fac), The Old Vicarage, High Street, Laxton, NEWARK, NOTTINGHAMSHIRE, NG22 0NX. (Life Member)
ROLPH, Mr. Robert William, BA(Hons) ACA *2002;* Liverpool Victoria Friendly Society Ltd, County Gates, BOURNEMOUTH, BH1 2NF.
ROLPH, Mr. Terence John, FCA *1969;* 25 Dale Road, LEIGH-ON-SEA, ESSEX, SS9 2RQ.
ROLPH, Mrs. Tessa Jeannette, BSc ACA *1981;* The Old Vicarage High Street, Laxton, NEWARK, NOTTINGHAMSHIRE, NG22 0NX.
ROLT, Mr. Clive Anthony Gerard, BA ACA *1988;* 10 Culloden Road, ENFIELD, EN2 8QB.
•ROLT, Mr. Henry Ernest Adrian, FCA *1951;* Rolt Harrison & Hewitt, 110/112 Lancaster Road, BARNET, EN4 8AL.
ROLT, Mr. Jeremy Charles, ACA *1986;* 4 Sycamore Close, St Ippollyts, HITCHIN, SG4 7SN.
•ROLT, Mr. Nicholas Lewis Evelyn, BA FCA *1973;* 16Ter Avenue du Docteur, Faugeroux, Le Parc du Perreux, 94170 LE PERREUX-SUR-MARNE, FRANCE.

ROMAIN, Mr. Gary Carl, BA ACA *1999;* Flat 137 Discovery Dock Apartments West, 2 South Quay Square, LONDON, E14 9LT.
ROMAINE, Mr. Charles Aubrey, BSc FCA *1984;* with BDO LLP, 55 Baker Street, LONDON, W1U 7EU.
•ROMAN, Mr. Roderick Andrew Charles, BSc ACA *1987;* Ernst & Young LLP, 1 More London Place, LONDON, SE1 2AF. See also Ernst & Young Europe LLP
•ROMANOVITCH, Miss. Sacha Veronica, MA ACA *1994;* Grant Thornton UK LLP, Grant Thornton House, 22 Melton Street, Euston Square, LONDON, NW1 2EP. See also Grant Thornton LLP
ROMANOVSKAYA, Miss. Vera, MA ACA *2011;* 206a Friern Road, LONDON, SE22 0BA.
•ROMANS, Mr. Christopher David, BSocSc ACA *1994;* PricewaterhouseCoopers LLP, Cornwall Court, 19 Cornwall Street, BIRMINGHAM, B3 2DT. See also PricewaterhouseCoopers
ROMANS, Mr. David Charles, BA FCA *1982;* PricewaterhouseCoopers, 2 Southbank Boulevard, Southbank, MELBOURNE, VIC 3006, AUSTRALIA.
ROMANS, Miss. Shelley Ann, BA FCA *1983;* (Tax Fac), with Fiander Tovell LLP, Stag Gates House, 63/64 The Avenue, SOUTHAMPTON, SO17 1XS.
ROMANSKI, Miss. Margaret Ann Christine, MA ACA *1986;* Designers Guild Unit 3 Latimer Place, 3 Latimer Place, LONDON, W10 6QT.
ROMARY, Mr. John Gerald Robert, FCA *1960;* 44 Polmear Parc, PAR, PL24 2AU. (Life Member)
ROMAYA, Miss. Nadia, ACA *2007;* 210 Bowring Park Road, Merseyside, LIVERPOOL, L14 3NR.
ROME, Mr. Andrew Michael, BSc FCA *1987;* Revolution Consulting Ltd, 21 Meadowfield, BRADFORD-ON-AVON, BA15 1PL.
ROME, Mrs. Joanne Kathleen Mary, ACA *1993;* Shaw Head Farm, Easton, Longtown, CARLISLE, CA6 5RS.
•ROME, Mr. John Jack, FCA *1965;* (Tax Fac), Benjamin Kay & Brummer, York House, Empire Way, WEMBLEY, HA9 0QL. See also BKB Services Limited
ROME, Mr. Richard Leslie, FCA *1972;* KPMG Phoomchai Audit Ltd, 50-51 Floors Empire Tower, 195 South Sathorn Road, BANGKOK 10120, THAILAND.
ROMEO, Mr. Nathan, ACA *2009;* 115 Canterbury Leys, TEWKESBURY, GLOUCESTERSHIRE, GL20 8BP.
ROMER-LEE, Mr. Alexander Knyvett, FCA *1980;* AKRL Ltd, Nunns Orchard, Whiteparish, SALISBURY, SP5 2RJ.
ROMER-LEE, Mr. Peter Thornycroft, BA FCA *1965;* Denton House, Weston Road, Upton Grey, BASINGSTOKE, RG25 2RJ.
ROMINIYI, Mrs. Adebukunola, BA ACA *2010;* 3 Tawney Road, Thamesmead, LONDON, SE28 8EE.
ROMNEY, Mr. Kenneth Owen, BA FCA *1977;* Chesnara Plc, Harbour House, Port Way, Ashton-on-Ribble, PRESTON, PR2 2PR.
ROMYN, Mr. Timothy William, FCA *1973;* with Grant Thornton UK LLP, The Explorer Building, Fleming Way, Manor Royal, CRAWLEY, WEST SUSSEX RH10 9GT.
RONA, Mr. Daniel Pablo, BA ACA *1994;* 49 Culmstock Road, LONDON, sw11 6ly.
RONALD, Miss. Fiona Louise, BA ACA *2010;* Deloitte & Touche Stonecutter Court, 1 Stonecutter Street, LONDON, EC4A 4TR.
•RONALD, Mrs. Sharon Ann, ACA ATII *1995;* (Tax Fac), Berkeley Hall Limited, Vallis House, 57 Vallis Road, FROME, SOMERSET, BA11 3EG.
RONALDSON, Mr. Adam Channing, BA ACA *1989;* 4 Fulford Close, NORWICH, NR4 6AL.
RONALDSON, Miss. Susan Helen, MSc BA ACA *2004;* with National Audit Office, 157-197 Buckingham Palace Road, Victoria, LONDON, SW1W 9SP.
RONAN, Mrs. Elizabeth Sybil Louise, BSc ACA *1990;* Rhosilli, Wellington Heath, LEDBURY, HEREFORDSHIRE, HR8 1NB.
RONAN, Miss. Michelle Nicole, BA(Hons) ACA *2004;* with BDO LLP, 55 Baker Street, LONDON, W1U 7EU.
•RONAN, Mr. Paul Antony, BA FCA *1990;* G. Spratt Accountancy Limited, 3 Abbeylands, High Street, DUNBAR, EH42 1EH.
RONAYNE, Mr. Peter James, BSc ACA *1982;* Share Registrars Limited, Suite E First Floor, 9 Lion and Lamb Yard, FARNHAM, GU9 7LL.
RONCHETTI, Miss. Eliana, ACA *2011;* 10 Eton Square, Eton, WINDSOR, BERKSHIRE, SL4 6BG.
RONCHETTI, Mr. Marc, BSc ACA *2003;* 22 New Road, Croxley Green, RICKMANSWORTH, HERTFORDSHIRE, WD3 3EP.
RONCHETTI, Mrs. Myfanwy, BSc ACA *2003;* 22 New Road, Croxley Green, RICKMANSWORTH, HERTFORDSHIRE, WD3 3EP.
RONDELLI, Mr. Roberto, ACA *2010;* with PricewaterhouseCoopers LLP, 1 Embankment Place, LONDON, WC2N 6RH.
•ⒹRONES, Mr. Richard Jeffrey, BA FCA *1993;* ThorntonRones Ltd, 311 High Road, LOUGHTON, ESSEX, IG10 1AH.
RONEY, Mr. Jonathan Michael, BSc ACA *2003;* Citco Trustees (Cayman) Limited, 89 Nexus Way, Camana Bay, PO Box 31106, SEVEN MILE BEACH, KY1-1205 CAYMAN ISLANDS.
RONEY, Mr. Stephen James, BSc(Hons) ACA *2004;* PO box 1034GT, Close Brothers (Cayman) Limited, GEORGE TOWN, GRAND CAYMAN, CAYMAN ISLANDS.
•RONKOWSKI, Mr. Philip Konrad, FCA CTA *1980;* (Tax Fac), Ronkowski & Hall Ltd, 12 Westgate, Baildon, SHIPLEY, WEST YORKSHIRE, BD17 5EJ.
RONSON, Mr. Denis, FCA *1954;* 26 Rhodesway, Hoghton, PRESTON, PR5 0JY. (Life Member)
•RONSON, Mr. George Robertson, FCA *1971;* George Ronson FCA, 11 Healy Drive, ORPINGTON, KENT, BR6 9LB.
ROOBOTTOM, Mr. Colin Douglas, FCA *1954;* Brooklands, Barrow Lane, Tarvin, CHESTER, CH3 8JF. (Life Member)
ROOD, Mr. David Leonard, FCA *1970;* 122 Crumpfields Lane, REDDITCH, WORCESTERSHIRE, B97 5PW.
ROODENBURGH, Mr. Alan Derek, BA ACA *1984;* 7 Wallace Fields, EPSOM, KT17 3AX.
ROODHOUSE, Mr. Jonathan, BA ACA *2002;* 1 Hopkin Close, GUILDFORD, SURREY, GU2 9LS.
ROOHI LARIJANI, Mrs. Michele Elizabeth, BSc FCA *1993;* (Tax Fac), Woodstock, Jollyboys Lane South, Felsted, DUNMOW, ESSEX, CM6 3LR.
ROOK, Mr. Alan, FCA *1965;* 39 The Ridgeway, Fetcham, LEATHERHEAD, SURREY, KT22 9BE.
ROOK, Ms. Caroline Yook Lin, BSc FCA *1987;* 130 Ocean Park Blvd, #533, SANTA MONICA, CA 90405, UNITED STATES.
•ROOK, Ms. Fiona, BSc ACA *1995;* My Business Centre Ltd, Bridge House, 25 Fore Street, OKEHAMPTON, DEVON, EX20 1DL.
•ROOK, Mrs. Jane Alison, FCA *1980;* (Tax Fac), George Arthur Limited, York House, 4 Wigmores South, WELWYN GARDEN CITY, HERTFORDSHIRE, AL8 6PL.
ROOK, Mr. Jeremy Thomas, MSc BSc FCA *1972;* Lopen Farmhouse, Church Street, Lopen, SOUTH PETHERTON, TA13 5JX.
ROOK, Mr. Jonathan William, BA ACA *2010;* Hillcrest, Potters Bank, DURHAM, DH1 3RR.
•ROOK, Mr. Peter Philip, FCA *1981;* (Tax Fac), George Arthur Limited, York House, 4 Wigmores South, WELWYN GARDEN CITY, HERTFORDSHIRE, AL8 6PL.
ROOKE, Mr. Andrew Michael, BA ACA *1986;* 9725 Industrial Drive, BRIDGEVIEW, IL 60455, UNITED STATES.
ROOKE, Mr. Andrew Paul, BSc FCA *1988;* 2532 S. Oak Knoll Ave, SAN MARINO, CA 91108, UNITED STATES.
ROOKE, Miss. Annette Marie, BSc(Hons) ACA *2004;* 81 Ivy Street, Rainham, GILLINGHAM, KENT, ME8 8BH.
ROOKE, Mr. Charles Leonard Edward, MA FCA *1976;* Rivendell, Cranley Road, GUILDFORD, GU1 2JS.
ROOKE, Mr. David Philip, MBA FCA *1965;* 27 Deneside, East Dean, EASTBOURNE, EAST SUSSEX, BN20 0HY.
ROOKE, Mr. Gavin Alan, BA(Hons) ACA *2010;* Flat 4, 87 Shirland Road, LONDON, W9 2EL.
•ROOKE, Mr. Graham Colin, FCA *1986;* Peplows, Sterling House, Wavell Drive, Rosehill, CARLISLE, CA1 2SA.
ROOKE, Mr. Martin Mansfield, BA FCA *1978;* 1 Whitehall Way, Perry, HUNTINGDON, PE28 0DL.
ROOKE, Mr. Patrick, BA ACA *2011;* 8 Reginald Road, NORTHWOOD, MIDDLESEX, HA6 1EE.
ROOKE, Mr. Paul Matthew, BA ACA *2004;* Rensburg Sheppards Investment Management Limited, 61 Napier Street, SHEFFIELD, SOUTH YORKSHIRE, S11 8HA.
ROOKE, Mr. Peter Robert, BSc ACA *1979;* 2 Ringmore Drive, Merrow Park, GUILDFORD, GU4 7DQ.
ROOKE, Mr. Philip Anthony, BA ACA *1996;* 7 Howard Gardens, GUILDFORD, SURREY, GU1 2NX.
ROOKE, Miss. Sophie Melanie, BSc ACA *1998;* with PricewaterhouseCoopers LLP, 1 Embankment Place, LONDON, WC2N 6RH.
ROOKE, Mr. Stuart Thomas, FCA *1970;* 7 Augusta Court, ROUSE HILL, NSW 2155, AUSTRALIA. (Life Member)
ROOKE, Mrs. Susan Elizabeth, BSc ACA *1984;* 2 Ringmore Drive, Merrow Park, GUILDFORD, GU4 7DQ.
•ROOKE, Mr. Timothy James, BSc ACA *1994;* Ernst & Young LLP, 1 More London Place, LONDON, SE1 2AF. See also Ernst & Young Europe LLP
ROOKE, Miss. Virginia Elizabeth, BSc(Hons) ACA *2000;* European Directories Building 10 Chiswick Park, 566 Chiswick High Road, LONDON, W4 5XS.
ROOKER, Mr. Malcolm Loyn, LLB ACA *1990;* Brookleigh Milley Road, Waltham St. Lawrence, READING, RG10 0JR.
ROOKES, Mr. Ben, BSc ACA *2005;* 5 Maple View, NOTTINGHAM, NG11 7GE.
ROOKES, Mr. Peter David, BA FCA *1995;* 11 Lysander Way, Cottingley, BINGLEY, WEST YORKSHIRE, BD16 1WF.
ROOKS, Mr. Anthony Peter Gordon, ACA *1994;* Hi! Hotels International, Gremi de Cirugians i Barbers 48-3A, Poligono Son Rossinyol, 07009 PALMA DE MALLORCA, SPAIN.
ROOKS, Mr. Michael Alexander Blake, ACA *2009;* 6 Ryland Road, LONDON, NW5 3EA.
ROOKS, Mr. Stewart John, BSc ACA *2005;* 123 Shenley Road, LONDON, SE5 8NF.
•ROOKYARD, Mr. Graham Leonard, FCA *1975;* Kirby Rookyard Limited, 1 Castle Court, St. Peters Street, COLCHESTER, CO1 1EW.
ROOLEY, Mr. David Arthur, FCA *1957;* Celyn, ABERDOVEY, LL35 0HF. (Life Member)
ROOME, Mrs. Belinda Jane, BSc ACA *1992;* 5 Earl Richards Road North, EXETER, EX2 6AQ.
ROOME, Mr. Charles McCrea, BSc ACA *2009;* The Duchies, Mill Lane, Pirbright, WOKING, SURREY, GU24 0BT.
ROOME, Mrs. Clare Angela, ACA *2002;* 21 Hawcliffe Road, Mountsorrel, LOUGHBOROUGH, LE12 7AQ.
ROOME, Mr. David, BSc ACA *2011;* 12 Ingleby Close, SWADLINCOTE, DERBYSHIRE, DE11 9SE.
ROOME, Mr. Harry Mccrea, BSc FCA *1979;* The Duchies, Mill Lane, Pirbright, WOKING, GU24 0BT. (Life Member)
ROOME, Mrs. Joanne Elizabeth, MBA BA ACA *1993;* 2 Wellington Court, Spencers Wood, READING, RG7 1BN.
ROOME, Mr. John William Joseph, BA FCA *1985;* Spindles, 60 Brattle Wood, SEVENOAKS, TN13 1QU.
ROOME, Mr. Martin Paul, BSc FCA *1995;* with RSM Tenon Audit Limited, Cedar House, Breckland, Linford Wood, MILTON KEYNES, MK14 6EX.
ROOMES, Mrs. Sara Eleanor, BA ACA ATII *1990;* 27 Rue de la Ferme, 92200 NEUILLY-SUR-SEINE, FRANCE.
ROONEY, Mr. Andrew John, MA ACA *1985;* Structured Portfolio Management Level 4, 135 Bishopsgate, LONDON, EC2M 3UR.
•ⒹROONEY, Mr. Chris Bryan, BA ACA *2000;* with PricewaterhouseCoopers LLP, Benson House, 33 Wellington Street, LEEDS, LS1 4JP.
ROONEY, Mrs. Deborah, ACA *2008;* 11 Willow Court, CLONDALKIN Dublin 22, COUNTY DUBLIN, IRELAND.
•ROONEY, Mr. Kevin Dennis, BA FCA *1990;* with RSM Tenon Audit Limited, Tenon House, Ferryboat Lane, SUNDERLAND, SR5 3JN.
ROONEY, Mrs. Lesley-Ann Russell, MLitt BSc ACA *1995;* 3 Balta Crescent, Cambuslang, GLASGOW, G72 8TS.
•ROONEY, Mr. Martin James, BSc FCA *1978;* (Tax Fac), F.W. Smith Riches & Co, 15 Whitehall, LONDON, SW1A 2DD.
ROONEY, Mr. Paul Gerald, BA FCA ATII *1993;* European Commission, DG Markt, Unit F3, Rue de Spa 2, B-1049 BRUSSELS, BELGIUM.
ROONEY, Miss. Sarah Kay, BA(Hons) ACA *2004;* Johnson Cleaners UK Limited, Lydia House, Puma Court, Kings Business Park, Kings Drive, PRESCOT MERSEYSIDE L34 1PJ.
ROOP, Mr. Dalvir Singh, BSc ACA *2003;* 61 Church Road, Heston, HOUNSLOW, MIDDLESEX, TW5 0LU.
ROOPE, Mr. Dominic, ACA *2011;* Harbour View, Southgate Road, LONDON, N1 3JF.
ROOPRAI, Mrs. Jaspal, ACA *1986;* with Arram Berlyn Gardner, 30 City Road, LONDON, EC1Y 2AB.
ROOS, Mr. Lachlan James, ACA CA(AUS) *2008;* 20 Wellfields, LOUGHTON, ESSEX, IG10 1NX.
ROOS, Mr. Stefan Maurice, BSc ACA *1981;* 30 The Fairway, NORTHOLT, UB5 4SL.
•ROOSE, Miss. Alison Elizabeth, BA(Hons) ACA *1994;* 7 Brandon Road, PO Box 658, STANLEY, FIQQ 1ZZ, FALKLAND ISLANDS.
ROOSEBOOM, Ms. Carla, ACA *2003;* 12 Devonshire Avenue, JOHANNESBURG, GAUTENG, 2196, SOUTH AFRICA.
•ROOT, Mr. Christopher David, BSc FCA *1990;* AAA Tax & Accounting Services Limited, Chambers Business Centre, Chapel Road, Hollinwood, OLDHAM, LANCASHIRE OL8 4QQ. See also AMR Accounting Services Limited
ROOT, Mr. Christopher Dennis, BSc ACA *1983;* Holmewood, Lamplugh Road, COCKERMOUTH, CUMBRIA, CA13 0DP.
ROOT, Mrs. Jane Yvette, BA ACA *1992;* Level 21 GBM Finance Change Management, H S B C, 8-16 Canada Square, LONDON, E14 5HQ.
ROOT, Mr. Jonathan Stanley, BA ACA *1990;* 9 Field House Drive, OXFORD, OX2 7NT.
ROOT, Mr. Martin Richard, BA FCA *1985;* 3F3.M5.01, U B S Warburg, 1-2 Finsbury Avenue, LONDON, EC2M 2PP.
ROOT, Mr. Nigel Ronald, BA FCA *1978;* 3 Ruskin Gardens, Ealing, LONDON, W5 1NZ.
•ROOT, Mr. Paul Derek, BA FCA *1987;* Hope Jones, Dunlop House, 23a Spencer Road, NEW MILTON, BH25 6BZ. See also Root P.D.
ROOT, Mrs. Stephanie Kate, BA ACA *1983;* Netherdowns, 15 Elmlea Avenue, Stoke Bishop, BRISTOL, BS9 3UU.
ROOT, Mr. Stephen Edmund Thomas, BSc ACA *1989;* 21 Dovercourt Gardens, STANMORE, HA7 4SJ.
ROOTE, Mr. John Alan, LLB ACA *1990;* 20 Egerton Road, Queen's Park, BOURNEMOUTH, BH8 9AY.
ROOTH, Mrs. Jeannette, FCA *1996;* Constellation Europe Ltd Constellation Park, Kings Weston Lane Avonmouth, BRISTOL, BS11 9FG.
•ROOTS, Mr. Ewart Haldane, BA FCA *1988;* Ewart Roots, Trethullan Cottage, Trethullan, Sticker, ST. AUSTELL, CORNWALL PL26 7EH.
•ROOZE, Mr. David Peter, FCA *1973;* D.P. Rooze, 122 Glenfield Frith Drive, Glenfield, LEICESTER, LE3 8PS.
ROPER, Miss. Alison, BSc ACA *2006;* 37 Craiglee Drive, CARDIFF, CF10 4BN.
ROPER, Mr. Anthony Dillingham, FCA *1961;* 20 Howards Thicket, GERRARDS CROSS, BUCKINGHAMSHIRE, SL9 7NX. (Life Member)
•ROPER, Mr. Christopher, BA ACA *1980;* with Notts Ltd, 38 Rothesay Road, LUTON, LU1 1QZ.
ROPER, Mr. David Alexander, BSc FCA *1977;* Melrose Plc Leconfield House, Curzon Street, LONDON, W1J 5JA.
•ROPER, Mr. David Andrew, MA FCA *1986;* PricewaterhouseCoopers LLP, 101 Barbirolli Square, Lower Mosley Street, MANCHESTER, M2 3PW. See also PricewaterhouseCoopers
•ROPER, Mr. David Anthony, BSc FCA CTA *1980;* (Tax Fac), Lambert Roper & Horsfield Limited, The Old Woolcombers Mill, 12-14 Union Street South, HALIFAX, WEST YORKSHIRE, HX1 2LE.
ROPER, Mr. David Charles, FCA *1952;* 4 Hillwood Common Road, SUTTON COLDFIELD, B75 5QJ. (Life Member)
•ROPER, Mr. David William, BA FCA CF *1986;* Smith & Williamson Ltd, Portwall Place, Portwall Lane, BRISTOL, BS1 6NA.
ROPER, Miss. Elizabeth, ACA *2011;* Hawthorne Cottage Trinity Manor, La Route de la Trinite Trinity, JERSEY, JE3 5JP.
ROPER, Miss. Gillian Ann, BA ACA *1992;* Hildesheimer Weg 24, D-22459 HAMBURG, GERMANY.
•ROPER, Mr. Graham, BA FCA *1985;* Cresswells Accountants LLP, Barclays Bank Chambers, 12 Market Street, HEBDEN BRIDGE, WEST YORKSHIRE, HX7 6AA.
•ROPER, Mr. Ian, BA ACA *1990;* (Tax Fac), Ian Roper & Company, 37 Fore Street, SIDMOUTH, DEVON, EX10 8AQ.
ROPER, Mr. John Stuart, FCA *1956;* 58 Roberts Close, Stratton, CIRENCESTER, GL7 2RP. (Life Member)
•ROPER, Mr. Jonathan Paul, BA ACA *1985;* (Tax Fac), McKellens Ltd, 11 Riverview, The Embankment Business Park, Heaton Mersey, STOCKPORT, CHESHIRE SK4 3GN. See also McKellens Outsourcing LLP
ROPER, Mr. Keith William, FCA *1950;* with Lambert Roper & Horsfield Limited, The Old Woolcombers Mill, 12-14 Union Street South, HALIFAX, WEST YORKSHIRE, HX1 2LE.
ROPER, Mr. Lee Andrew, ACA *2004;* 144 Parkway, WELWYN GARDEN CITY, HERTFORDSHIRE, AL8 6HP.
ROPER, Mr. Malcolm Thomas, LLB FCA *1963;* 43 Grove Avenue, Coombe Dingle, BRISTOL, BS9 2RP.
ROPER, Mr. Mark Niven, BSc ACA *2003;* 29 Greenways, Walton, CHESTERFIELD, S40 3HF.
•ROPER, Mr. Michael William, FCA *1963;* 25 Court Hey Drive, Court Hey, LIVERPOOL, MERSEYSIDE, L16 2NB.

ROPER, Mrs. Sarah, ACA *2007;* 2 Derwent Road, BRADFORD, WEST YORKSHIRE, BD2 4HR.
ROPER, Mrs. Sarah-Jane, BSc ACA *2003;* Alma Cottages, 20 Under Lane, Grotton, OLDHAM, OL4 5RJ.
•ROPER, Mr. Simon, ACA FCCA *2010;* Fuller Accountants Limited, The Counting House, Church Farm Business Park, Corston, BATH, BA2 9AP.
ROPER, Mr. Stephen Dawson, BA FCA *1978;* 89 Discovery Drive, Kings Hill, WEST MALLING, KENT, ME19 4DJ.
ROPER, Mr. Stephen John, BA FCA *1970;* Lavendale House, Broomfield Park, ASCOT, SL5 0JS. (Life Member)
ROPER, Miss. Victoria, BA ACA *2006;* with National Audit Office, 157-197 Buckingham Palace Road, Victoria, LONDON, SW1W 9SP.
ROPNER, Mr. Henry, ACA *2008;* F F P Services Ltd, 15 Suffolk Street, LONDON, SW1Y 4HG.
ROSA, Mr. Ricardo Horacio, MA ACA *1981;* Chemin de Blandonnet 10, 1214 VERNIER, SWITZERLAND.
ROSBROOK, Mrs. Janet Mary, BSc FCA *1981;* (Tax Fac), 10 Hudson View, TADCASTER, NORTH YORKSHIRE, LS24 8JE.
ROSBROOK, Mr. Paul James, BSc FCA *1998;* Millwood Designer Homes, Bordyke End, East Street, TONBRIDGE, KENT, TN9 1HA.
ROSCHER, Mrs. Julia Louise, BA ACA *1988;* La Belle Epoque, 60 King Street, KNUTSFORD, CHESHIRE, WA16 6DT.
ROSCOE, Dr. David, BSc ACA *1997;* 15 Cambridge Avenue, Crosby, LIVERPOOL, L23 7XN.
ROSCOE, Mr. Neil Howard, BSc FCA *1982;* 720 Comanche Court, WALNUT CREEK, CA 94598, UNITED STATES.
ROSCOE, Mr. Stephen James, BA ACA *1989;* Agresso Ltd St. Georges Hall, St. Georges Hill Easton-in-Gordano, BRISTOL, BS20 0PX.
ROSCOE, Miss. Tracy Ann, BSc ACA *1991;* 1 Middlefield Drive, Binley, COVENTRY, CV3 2UZ.
ROSCORLA, Mr. Paul Adrian, MSc FCA *1974;* Paul Roscorla Associates Limited, 125 Peperharow Road, GODALMING, SURREY, GU7 2PW.
•ROSCOW, Mr. Vaun Hedley, FCA *1974;* with Colman Whittaker & Roscow, The Close, Queen Square, LANCASTER, LA1 1RS.
ROSCROW, Mr. Peter Donald, ACA *1989;* 74 Highbury Park, LONDON, N5 2XE.
ROSE, Mr. Adam Walter Patrick, BSc(Hons) ACA *2010;* Flat A 5/F, 6 Hillwood Road, Jordan, TSIM SHA TSUI, KOWLOON, HONG KONG SAR.
ROSE, Mr. Alan Thomas, FCA *1972;* 4 Thurlstone Road, RUISLIP, HA4 0BS.
ROSE, Ms. Alison Margaret, BA ACA *1994;* 21 Calbourne Road, Balham, LONDON, SW12 8LW.
ROSE, Mrs. Alison Virginia, FCA *1974;* 55 Priory Road, Kew, RICHMOND, TW9 3DQ.
•ROSE, Mr. Alistair John Balfour, BA FCA *1982;* PricewaterhouseCoopers LLP, 1 Embankment Place, LONDON, WC2N 6RH. See also PricewaterhouseCoopers
ROSE, Mrs. Amanda Lucy, ACA *2006;* 19 Broom Close, Darton, BARNSLEY, SOUTH YORKSHIRE, S75 5PZ.
ROSE, Mr. Andrew David, BSc ACA *1983;* 1 Gills Hill Lane, RADLETT, HERTFORDSHIRE, WD7 8DB.
ROSE, Mr. Andrew David, ACA *1989;* Motorola Ltd Radio Network Solutions Group, Viables Industrial Estate Jays Close, BASINGSTOKE, RG22 4PD.
•ROSE, Mr. Andrew Simon, FCA CF *1984;* Sterling Corporate Finance LLP, 12 York Place, LEEDS, LS1 2DS.
ROSE, Mr. Angus Frederick, FCA *1973;* Red Lodge, Warren Road, KINGSTON UPON THAMES, SURREY, KT2 7HN.
ROSE, Mrs. Anne Mary, BA ACA *1986;* The Chestnuts, Middle Lane, Nether Broughton, MELTON MOWBRAY, LE14 3HD.
•ROSE, Mr. Anthony, FCA *1973;* Fisher Sassoon & Marks, 43-45 Dorset Street, LONDON, W1U 7NA.
•ROSE, Mr. Anthony David, BA(Hons) ACA CTA *2000;* (Tax Fac), Intelligent Tax Solutions LLP, New Broad Street House, 35 New Broad Street, LONDON, EC2M 1NH.
ROSE, Mr. Anthony John, FCA *1975;* 34 Myrtle Avenue, RUISLIP, MIDDLESEX, HA4 8RZ.
ROSE, Mr. Anthony Nicholas Franchot, MA ACA *1981;* 10 Powis Gardens, LONDON, W11 1JG.
ROSE, Mr. Anthony Stuart, BSc ACA *1991;* 2 Elevation Avenue, BALGOWLAH HEIGHTS, NSW 2093, AUSTRALIA.
ROSE, Mr. Barrie David, BCom FCA *1953;* 110 Bloor Street West, Suite 905, TORONTO M5S 2WY, ON, CANADA. (Life Member)
ROSE, Mr. Barry, FCA *1956;* 8 Church Street, WHITSTABLE, CT5 1PJ. (Life Member)
•ROSE, Mr. Barry Stephen, FCA *1975;* B S Rose & Co, Milford Lodge, 38a Talbot Avenue, Talbot Woods, BOURNEMOUTH, BH3 7HZ.
ROSE, Miss. Carly Anne, ACA *2010;* 26 Annesley Road, NEWPORT PAGNELL, BUCKINGHAMSHIRE, MK16 0BB.
ROSE, Miss. Catherine Isabel, ACA *1984;* 8 Old French Horn Lane, HATFIELD, AL10 8AJ.
ROSE, Mr. Charles George Ian, FCA *1956;* Woodland Cottage, 70 Bell Barn Road, Stoke Bishop, BRISTOL, BS9 2DG. (Life Member)
ROSE, Mr. Christopher Ian, BSc ACA *2002;* 3 Mill Court, DEREHAM, NORFOLK, NR19 1UX.
ROSE, Mr. Christopher Paul, FCA *1999;* Hitachi Data Systems Sefton Park, Bells Hill Stoke Poges, SLOUGH, SL2 4HD.
ROSE, Mr. Colin Leslie, FCA *1954;* Waldeck House, Chapel Lane, Minchinhampton, STROUD, GLOUCESTERSHIRE, GL6 9DL. (Life Member)
ROSE, Mr. Danny, MPhys ACA *2011;* 11 Thorney Mill Road, IVER, BUCKINGHAMSHIRE, SL0 9AQ.
ROSE, Mr. David, BSc ACA *1987;* Level 8, 108 St Georges Terrace, PERTH, WA 6000, AUSTRALIA.
•ROSE, Mr. David Alan, FCA *1976;* David A. Rose & Co, Unit 404 Centennial Avenue, Centennial Park, Elstree, BOREHAMWOOD, HERTFORDSHIRE WD6 3TN. See also Rose David A. & Co
ROSE, Mr. David Ellis, FCA *1978;* 10 Church Crescent, LONDON, N3 1BG.
ROSE, Mr. David Jonathan, BA ACA *1990;* 17 Northwick Close, WORCESTER, WR3 7EF.
ROSE, Mr. David Paul, FCA *1975;* 38 Fieldhouse Close, LONDON, E18 2RJ. (Life Member)
ROSE, Miss. Deborah Ann, MSc ACA *2003;* 135 The Avenue, Alwoodley, LEEDS, LS17 7PA.
ROSE, Mr. Dennis Leonard, FCA *1957;* 11 Beaulieu Drive, PINNER, HA5 1NB. (Life Member)
ROSE, Mr. Dennis William, FCA *1963;* Anchor Point, Marine Crescent, WHITSTABLE, KENT, CT5 2QL. (Life Member)
•ROSE, Mr. Douglas Charles, FCA *1972;* (Tax Fac), DDR Securities Limited, 22 New Upperton Road, EASTBOURNE, EAST SUSSEX, BN21 1NU.
•ROSE, Mrs. Elizabeth, FCA ATT *1974;* Elizabeth Rose FCA ATT, 12 Forest Dean, FLEET, HAMPSHIRE, GU51 2UQ.
ROSE, Miss. Elizabeth Frances, BA ACA *2011;* Flat 23, Florin Court, 6-9 Charterhouse Square, LONDON, EC1M 6ET.
•ROSE, Mrs. Elizabeth Sarah, MA ACA *1992;* 20 Stubbs Wood, Chesham Bois, AMERSHAM, BUCKINGHAMSHIRE, HP6 6EY.
ROSE, Mr. Geoffrey Edward, FCA *1953;* Clock Tower Cottage, The Abbey, Ixworth, BURY ST.EDMUNDS, IP31 2HQ. (Life Member)
ROSE, Mr. Geoffrey Wilfrid, FCA *1962;* Meadowlands, Coxcombe Lane, Chiddingfold, GODALMING, GU8 4QF.
ROSE, Mr. Gordon Stanley, FCA *1955;* Little Kingshaw, West Street, Winterbourne Kingston, BLANDFORD FORUM, DORSET, DT11 9AX. (Life Member)
•ROSE, Mr. Harvey John, FCA *1969;* with Arram Berlyn Gardner, 30 City Road, LONDON, EC1Y 2AB.
ROSE, Mrs. Helen, BA ACA *2005;* 110 Middleton Hall Road, BIRMINGHAM, B30 1DG.
ROSE, Miss. Helen Claire, BSc FCA *1990;* Lloyds TSB Bank Plc, 25 Gresham Street, LONDON, EC2V 7HN.
ROSE, Mrs. Helena, BSc ACA *2006;* 12 King Cup Drive, Huntington, CANNOCK, STAFFORDSHIRE, WS12 4WB.
ROSE, Mr. Ian Simon, BA(Econ) ACA *1996;* (Tax Fac), 2 Grove Cottages, Harrogate Road, LEEDS, LS17 7DY.
•ROSE, Mr. James Robert, ACA *2008;* Pearson May, 5 Wicker Hill, TROWBRIDGE, BA14 8JS.
•ROSE, Mrs. Jane Belinda, BSc ACA *1982;* Jane B Rose, Growle Abbey, High Road, Briston, MELTON CONSTABLE, NORFOLK NR24 2JH.
ROSE, Mrs. Jane Louise, BSc ACA *1996;* 2 Blakes Field Drive, Barnt Green, BIRMINGHAM, WORCESTERSHIRE, B45 8JT.
•ROSE, Mr. Jeffrey Sydney, FCA *1966;* (Tax Fac), J.S. Rose & Co, Fiosam House, 25 Station Road, New Barnet, BARNET, EN5 1PH.
ROSE, Mrs. Jennifer Louise, ACA *2009;* 43 Pytha Fold Road, Withington, MANCHESTER, M20 4UR.
ROSE, Miss. Joanna Louise, BSc ACA *2005;* 11 Kelsey Close, MAIDENHEAD, SL6 3YW.
ROSE, Mr. Joel Gerald, FCA *1956;* 3 Ashley Close, Bookham, LEATHERHEAD, KT23 3QJ. (Life Member)
•ROSE, Mr. John Douglas, FCA *1981;* RFW Rutherfords Ltd, Ardenham Court, Oxford Road, AYLESBURY, BUCKINGHAMSHIRE, HP19 8HT.
ROSE, Mr. John Haydn, FCA *1969;* 80 Scenic Ridge Crescent, N.w., CALGARY T3L 1V2, AB, CANADA.
ROSE, Mr. John Reginald, FCA *1953;* 36 Cranedown, LEWES, BN7 3NA. (Life Member)
ROSE, Mr. John William, FCA *1961;* 12 Thornhill Road, LONDON, N1 1HW.
ROSE, Mr. Jonathan, ACA *1981;* Prospect House, 121 Bury Old Road, WHITEFIELD, M45 7AY.
ROSE, Mr. Jonathan Andrew William, FCA *1969;* The Pump House, Colemere, ELLESMERE, SY12 0QL.
ROSE, Mrs. Judith Anne, BSc ACA *2001;* 2 Olde Forde Close, Brixworth, NORTHAMPTON, NN6 9XF.
ROSE, Mr. Julian Alexander, BA ACA *1995;* 6380 Aviation Way, WEST CHESTER, OH 45069, UNITED STATES.
ROSE, Mr. Julian Edward, BSc ACA *2003;* 360 W34th St, Apt 14N, NEW YORK, NY 10001, UNITED STATES.
ROSE, Mrs. Katharine Louise, BSc ACA *2003;* 25 Chesterton Avenue, HARPENDEN, HERTFORDSHIRE, AL5 5ST.
ROSE, Mrs. Kathryn Margaret, BSc ACA *1995;* 43 Riverside Walk, Strensall, YORK, YO32 5RZ.
ROSE, Mr. Keith Martin, FCA *1959;* 24 Berne Avenue, NEWCASTLE, STAFFORDSHIRE, ST5 2QJ. (Life Member)
ROSE, Mr. Kevin Granville, BA ACA ACT *1992;* Christies, 8 King Street, LONDON, SW1Y 6QT.
ROSE, Mr. Lawson Robert, BEng BCom ACA *2001;* Shire plc, Hampshire Int Business Park, Chineham, BASINGSTOKE, HAMPSHIRE, RG24 8EP.
ROSE, Mr. Leonard Paul, FCA *1968;* Flat 29 The Boat House, Waterside Marina Brightlingsea, COLCHESTER, CO7 0GA.
•ROSE, Mr. Marcus John, FCA CTA *1995;* (Tax Fac), Austral Ryley Limited, 416-418 Bearwood Road, SMETHWICK, WEST MIDLANDS, B66 4EZ.
•ROSE, Miss. Marie-Anne, BSc ACA *1986;* Marie-Anne Rose Limited, Bay Tree Cottage, Crabbswood Lane, Sway, LYMINGTON, SO41 6EQ.
ROSE, Mr. Mark Neville Andrew, BSc ACA *1990;* Court St. Lawrence, Llangovan, MONMOUTH, MONMOUTHSHIRE, NP25 4BT.
ROSE, Mr. Matthew Saul, MA FCA *1992;* (Tax Fac), 7 Townsend Avenue, LONDON, N14 7HH.
•①ROSE, Mr. Melvyn Laurence, FCA *1972;* Elliot Woolfe & Rose, Equity House, 128-136 High Street, EDGWARE, MIDDLESEX, HA8 7TT. See also Lentongate Ltd
•①ROSE, Mr. Michael, ACA *1994;* M1 Insolvency LLP, Cumberland House, 35 Park Row, NOTTINGHAM, NG1 6EE.
ROSE, Mr. Michael John, BSc ACA *1989;* 32 High Street, Potterspury, TOWCESTER, NORTHAMPTONSHIRE, NN12 7PQ.
ROSE, Miss. Michele, FCA *1994;* 53 Prospect Road, WOODFORD GREEN, ESSEX, IG8 7NA.
ROSE, Miss. Michelle, LLB ACA *2010;* 102 Marshall Crescent, STOURBRIDGE, DY8 5TA.
•ROSE, Mr. Nathan Paul, ACA *2008;* Fisher Sassoon & Marks, 43-45 Dorset Street, LONDON, W1U 7NA.
ROSE, Mr. Nicholas Paul, BSc ACA *2000;* 2 Olde Forde Close, Brixworth, NORTHAMPTON, NORTHAMPTONSHIRE, NN6 9XF.
ROSE, Mr. Nicholas Stephen, BSc FCA *1984;* NC1-014-22-05, 200 S. COLLEGE STREET, CHARLOTTE, NC 28255, UNITED STATES.
•ROSE, Mr. Paul William, FCA *1972;* (Tax Fac), Turner & Partners, 8 The Crescent, WISBECH, CAMBRIDGESHIRE, PE13 1EN.
•ROSE, Mrs. Pauline Jane, BSc ACA *1988;* 45 Sussex Gardens, Hucclecote, GLOUCESTER, GL3 3SP.
ROSE, Mr. Peter John, BSc FCA *1979;* Les Anguillieres, La Rocque, St Pierre Du Bois, GUERNSEY, GY7 9LS.
ROSE, Mr. Peter Leslie, BA FCA *1972;* 107 Main Street, Newtown Linford, LEICESTER, LEICESTERSHIRE, LE6 0AF.
ROSE, Mr. Peter Michael, MA ACA *1984;* 24 Town Street, Holbrook, BELPER, DE56 0TA.
ROSE, Mr. Philip, FCA *1951;* 12 The Callenders, Heathbourne Road, Bushey Heath, BUSHEY, HERTFORDSHIRE, WD23 1PU. (Life Member)
ROSE, Mr. Philip William, BA FCA *1977;* Gardenways, Blackpot Lane, Oundle, PETERBOROUGH, PE8 4AT.
ROSE, Mr. Phillip Ramon, FCA *1976;* 10 Moorside Road, SALFORD, M7 3PJ.
ROSE, Mr. Richard, BSc ACA *1998;* 21 Pine Hill, EPSOM, SURREY, KT18 7BH.
•ROSE, Mr. Richard, BA FCA ATII *1992;* BDO LLP, 125 Colmore Row, BIRMINGHAM, B3 3SD. See also BDO Stoy Hayward LLP
ROSE, Mr. Richard Anthony, BSc ACA *1996;* Bracken Lodge, Old Bury Hill, DORKING, RH4 3JU.
ROSE, Mr. Richard Dennis, FCA *1965;* Overdale, St. Nicholas Hill, LEATHERHEAD, SURREY, KT22 8NE.
•①ROSE, Mr. Robert Geoffrey, FCA *1976;* (Tax Fac), Larking Gowen, King Street House, 15 Upper King Street, NORWICH, NR3 1RB. See also Larking Gowen Limited
ROSE, Mr. Robert Hugh, FCA *1959;* Promasidor, PO Box 2458, CRAMERVIEW, 2060, SOUTH AFRICA. (Life Member)
•ROSE, Mr. Roger, FCA *1970;* R Rose & Co Ltd, 213 Derbyshire Lane, Norton Lees, SHEFFIELD, S8 8SA.
ROSE, Mr. Samuel Anthony, FCA *1962;* 106 Cecil Road, Hale, ALTRINCHAM, CHESHIRE, WA15 9NU.
ROSE, Mrs. Sarah Jane, BSc ACA *2001;* 15 Rockliffe Avenue, BATH, BA2 6QP.
ROSE, Miss. Shelley Leanne, BA ACA *2007;* Grace Bay Club, Grace Bay Road, PROVIDENCIALES, TURKS AND CAICOS ISLANDS.
ROSE, Miss. Silvie Louise, BA(Hons) ACA *2010;* 45 Brockenhurst Gardens, LONDON, NW7 2JY.
ROSE, Mr. Simon Robert, BSc ACA *2006;* 55 Lodge Lane, LONDON, N12 8JG.
ROSE, Mr. Stanley, FCA *1967;* 31 The Green, Southgate, LONDON, N14 6EN.
ROSE, Mrs. Stephanie May, BSc ACA *1993;* 44 Murrayfield Gardens, EDINBURGH, EH12 6DF.
ROSE, Mr. Stephen George, BA ACA *1990;* 30 Kewferry Road, NORTHWOOD, MIDDLESEX, HA6 2PB.
•ROSE, Mr. Stephen John, FCA *1984;* S.J. Rose & Co, 2 Oak Lodge, 6 Oak Lodge Drive, WEST WICKHAM, KENT, BR4 0RQ.
•ROSE, Mr. Stephen Patrick, MSc FCA *1979;* Lakin Rose Limited, Pioneer House, Vision Park, Histon, CAMBRIDGE, CB24 9NL.
ROSE, Mr. Stewart, BA ACA *2003;* Key Source Ltd, North Heath Lane Industrial Estate, HORSHAM, WEST SUSSEX, RH12 5QE.
•ROSE, Mrs. Suzanne June, BA ACA *1988;* SOE Building 83, Cranfield University College Road, Cranfield, BEDFORD, MK43 0AL.
•ROSE, Miss. Suzanne Michelle, MA ACA CTA *1999;* Dixon Wilson, 22 Chancery Lane, LONDON, WC2A 1LS.
•ROSE, Mr. Trevor, FCA CTA *1989;* (Tax Fac), Crossley & Co, Star House, Star Hill, ROCHESTER, KENT, ME1 1UX. See also Fortisratio Limited, First Payroll & Accounting
ROSEFF, Mr. Benjamin Bruce, FCA *1972;* 20 Coldharbour Close, HENLEY-ON-THAMES, OXFORDSHIRE, RG9 1QF.
ROSEFF, Ms. Joanna, MSc ACA *1994;* 2 Pelting Road, Priddy, WELLS, BA5 3BA.
ROSEFF, Mr. William, BSc FCA *1975;* Hillside (New Media), Festival Way, STOKE-ON-TRENT, STAFFORDSHIRE, ST1 5SH.
ROSEN, Miss. Alison Gay, BSc ACA *1992;* Langdale, 44 Little Bushey Lane, Bushey, WATFORD, WD2 3JX.
ROSEN, Mr. Daniel Bruce, MA FCA ATII *1989;* Cable & Wireless, 26 Red Lion Square, LONDON, WC1R 4HQ.
ROSEN, Mr. Ellis David, BA ACA *1992;* 21 Fullwell Avenue, ILFORD, ESSEX, IG6 2HA.
ROSEN, Mrs. Louise, BA ACA *2005;* 223 Hale Drive, LONDON, NW7 3EH.
ROSEN, Mrs. Mandy Hayley, BA ACA *1989;* 44 Lodge Avenue, Elstree, BOREHAMWOOD, WD6 3ND.
ROSEN, Mr. Michael, BSc FCA *1977;* 56 Roundmead Avenue, LOUGHTON, IG10 1PZ.
•ROSEN, Mr. Michael, FCA *1982;* Gerald Kreditor & Co, Hallswelle House, 1 Hallswelle Road, LONDON, NW11 0DH.
ROSEN, Mr. Neil David, MA FCA CTA *1986;* AMC Plc, 55 Bishopsgate, LONDON, EC2N 3AH.
ROSEN, Mr. Paul Jeremy, ACA *1990;* Maurice Phillips Group Plc, 1 Old Parkbury Lane Colney Street, ST. ALBANS, HERTFORDSHIRE, AL2 2EB.
ROSEN, Mr. Paul McKee, ACA *2009;* Flat 9, The Clock House, 83 Tweedy Road, BROMLEY, BR1 1RP.
•ROSEN, Mr. Stephen, FCA *1972;* (Tax Fac), DTE Business Advisory Services Limited, Park House, 26 North End Road, LONDON, NW11 7PT.
ROSEN, Ms. Susan Lynn, BA ACA *1991;* 39 Gordon Street, PADDINGTON, NSW 2021, AUSTRALIA.

ROUGIER-CHAPMAN, Mr. Alwyn Spencer Douglas, FCA *1963;* 919 Thornapple River Dr S.E., GRAND RAPIDS, MI 49301, UNITED STATES. (Life Member)
ROULLIER, Mr. John Harry, FCA *1953;* 40 Bourne End Road, NORTHWOOD, HA6 3BS. (Life Member)
•ROULSTON, Mr. Christopher James, MSc BA FCA *1981;* Howarth Corporate Finance Limited, 64 Wellington Street, LEEDS, LS1 2EE.
ROULSTON, Mrs. Elizabeth Sally, BSc ACA *1984;* Westville House, Carters Lane, Middleton, ILKLEY, WEST YORKSHIRE, LS29 0DQ.
•ROULSTONE, Mr. John Arthur, BSc FCA *1977;* John Roulstone, 12 Silver Street, Chacombe, BANBURY, OXFORDSHIRE, OX17 2JR.
ROUMBIES, Mr. Gregory, ACA CA(SA) *2008;* 10 Lowther Mansions, Church Road, LONDON, SW13 9HT.
ROUNCE, Mr. Jonathan Neil, FCA *1975;* The Petersham Group, 333 Petersham Road, RICHMOND, SURREY, TW10 7DB.
ROUND, Mr. Andrew John, BA ACA *1985;* 77 High Street, Landbeach, CAMBRIDGE, CB25 9FR.
ROUND, Mr. Ben, BSc ACA *2006;* Aero Engine Controls, Shaftmoor Lane, Hall Green, BIRMINGHAM, B28 8SW.
ROUND, Mr. Brian Henry, FCA *1972;* Oaklea, New Road, Hanley William, TENBURY WELLS, WORCESTERSHIRE, WR15 8QT.
ROUND, Mr. Christopher Frank, BA ACA *1987;* 11 Lytton Park, COBHAM, KT11 2HB.
ROUND, Mrs. Claire, BSocSc ACA *2001;* with PKF (UK) LLP, New Guild House, 45 Great Charles Street, BIRMINGHAM, B3 2LX.
ROUND, Mr. David Matthew, ACA *2009;* 33 Middlehill Road, WIMBORNE, DORSET, BH21 2SB.
ROUND, Miss. Debra, BSc ACA *2004;* 9/8 Kenilworth Street, Bondi Junction, SYDNEY, NSW 2022, AUSTRALIA.
•ROUND, Mr. Gordon, FCA *1983;* Round Numbers Limited, The Maples, Fydell Court, ST. NEOTS, CAMBRIDGESHIRE, PE19 1UJ.
•ROUND, Mr. Iain Edward, BSc FCA *1993;* Beever and Struthers, St George's House, 215-219 Chester Road, MANCHESTER, M15 4JE.
•ROUND, Mr. Jonathan Paul, BSc FCA *1997;* Jonathan Round Accountancy Services Ltd, 14-15 Regent Parade, HARROGATE, NORTH YORKSHIRE, HG1 5AW. See also Round Hall Limited
ROUND, Mr. Michael Andrew, BSc ACA *1983;* Lukes, The Common, MARLBOROUGH, SN8 1DL.
ROUND, Mr. Stephen John, BSc(Econ) FCA *1975;* 9 Healey Hall Farm, Shawclough Road, ROCHDALE, LANCASHIRE, OL12 7HA.
ROUNDELL, Mr. Ian John, BSc ACA *1990;* Credit Suisse Group, Paradeplatz 8, PO Box 1, CH 8070 ZURICH, SWITZERLAND.
ROUNDS, Mr. Thomas Edward, ACA *2008;* Flat 22 City View Apartments, 207 Essex Road, LONDON, N1 3PH.
•ROUNSEFELL, Mr. Terence Martin, FCA *1971;* (Tax Fac), T M Rounsefell FCA, 8 Alexandra Close, CREDITON, DEVON, EX17 2DY.
ROUNTHWAITE, Mr. Francis Anthony, BA FCA *1966;* Brookside House, Truggist Lane, Berkswell, COVENTRY, CV7 7BX. (Life Member)
ROUNTREE, Mr. Robert James, BA ACA *1986;* Lazard Freres, 121 Boulevard Haussmann, 75008 PARIS, FRANCE.
ROUNTREE, Miss. Sarah Victoria Ann, BA LLB ACA *2002;* with KPMG LLP, 15 Canada Square, LONDON, E14 5GL.
ROURKE, Mr. Barry John, FCA *1973;* 9 Woodcote Valley Road, PURLEY, CR8 3AL.
ROURKE, Mr. Brian, FCA ATII *1960;* with Stonebridge Stewart, Daryl House, 76a Pensby Road, Heswall, WIRRAL, CH60 7RF.
•ROURKE, Mr. Kevin Henry, FCA *1975;* Kevin H Rourke, 35 Hillington Road, SALE, M33 6GQ. See also Sale Accounting Services Limited
ROURKE, Mr. Matthew Joseph, LLB ACA *1996;* Court House, Rectory Lane, Sutton Valence, MAIDSTONE, KENT, ME17 3BS.
ROURKE, Mr. Sean Joseph, FCA *1974;* Pirin Holdings Ltd, Sage House, New Ford Road, WALTHAM CROSS, HERTFORDSHIRE, EN8 7PG.
ROUS, Mr. John, BA ACA *1979;* Clovelly Estate Co Ltd, The Estate Office, Clovelly, BIDEFORD, DEVON, EX39 5SY.
ROUS, Mr. Simon Nicholas, ACA *1985;* 15 Well Street, BURY ST. EDMUNDS, SUFFOLK, IP33 1EQ.
ROUSE, Mr. Christopher John, FCA *1972;* 18 Sarsen Close, SWINDON, SN1 4LA.
•ROUSE, Mr. David George, FCA *1967;* David G.Rouse, 18 Four Pools Road, EVESHAM, WR11 1EF.
ROUSE, Mr. Gary Paul, ACA *1995;* (Tax Fac), with BDO LLP, 125 Colmore Row, BIRMINGHAM, B3 3SD.
•ROUSE, Mr. Geoffrey Frederick Roland, ACA *1980;* (Tax Fac), Sandison Rouse & Co, Richmond House, 48 Bromyard Road, St Johns, WORCESTER, WR2 5BT.
ROUSE, Mr. Ian Rudolph, FCA *1961;* Gyddiuns, 10 Pound Close, Banham, NORWICH, NR16 2SY. (Life Member)
ROUSE, Mr. James Edward, BEng ACA *1997;* Flat 6, Brunswick Court, Darlaston Road, Wimbledon, LONDON, SW19 4LF.
ROUSE, Mr. John Stephen, BSc FCA *2000;* 4 Kingsdale Grove, Chellaston, DERBY, DE73 5NX.
ROUSE, Mr. John William, FCA *1974;* 31A Rhondda Grove, Bow, LONDON, E3 5AP. (Life Member)
ROUSE, Mr. Nicholas Clive Morfey, MA ACA *1991;* The Royal Bank Of Scotland, 135 Bishopsgate, LONDON, EC2M 3UR.
ROUSE, Mr. Nigel Clifford, BSc FCA *2000;* P.O. Box CB 11720, NASSAU, BAHAMAS.
ROUSE, Mr. Paul Michael Francis, BSc(Hons) ACA *2004;* Blue Crest Capital Management Ltd, 40 Grosvenor Place, LONDON, SW1X 7AW.
ROUSE, Mr. Philip James Arthur, BA ACA *1988;* The Yews, Upton Cheyney, BRISTOL, BS30 6NH.
ROUSE, Mr. Robert David, FCA *1966;* 25 Island View, Coast Road, Malahide, DUBLIN, COUNTY DUBLIN, IRELAND. (Life Member)
ROUSE, Mr. Robert Eric, ACA *1982;* 23 Manor Farm Meadow, East Leake, LOUGHBOROUGH, LE12 6LL.
ROUSE, Mrs. Sandra Jane, FCA *1974;* 23 Manor Farm Meadow, East Leake, LOUGHBOROUGH, LE12 6LL.
ROUSE, Mr. Scott Paul, ACA *2005;* with WKH, PO Box 501, The Nexus Building, Broadway, LETCHWORTH GARDEN CITY, HERTFORDSHIRE SG6 9BL.
•ROUSE, Mr. Steven John, FCA FCCA *1983;* (Tax Fac), John S Ward & Co LLP, 1 London Road, KETTERING, NN16 0EF. See also John s. Ward & Co
ROUSOS, Mr. Louis, ACA *2010;* 11 Pittalou Street, 3117 LIMASSOL, CYPRUS.
ROUSOU, Mr. James, BSc FCA *1971;* Tamarind, Quarrywood Road, MARLOW, BUCKINGHAMSHIRE, SL7 1RE. (Life Member)
ROUSOUNELI, Ms. Despina, BA ACA *2007;* Pindou 44A, Agia Paraskevi, ATHENS, GREECE.
•ROUSSAK, Mr. Malcolm, BCom FCA *1972;* Malcolm Roussak & Co., 52 Bury Old Road, Whitefield, MANCHESTER, M45 6TL.
ROUSSET, Mr. Marie Joseph Eugene Yves, ACA *1984;* Lawrence Wharf, 301a Rotherhithe Street, LONDON, SE16 5EY.
ROUSSIS, Mr. Marios, ACA *2007;* 34 PRINGIPISSIS ALEXIAS STREET, LIMASSOL, CYPRUS.
ROUSSOS, Mr. Nicholas, MSIT BSc ACA *2007;* 3 Grammou Street, Flat 32, Akropoli, CY-2006 NICOSIA, CYPRUS.
ROUSSOT, Mrs. Caroline, LLB ACA *2000;* Hammerson Plc, 10 Grosvenor Street, LONDON, W1K 4BJ.
ROUTLEDGE, Mr. Alan Stanley, FCA *1959;* 10 Woodland Grove, Westbury-on-Trym, BRISTOL, BS9 2BB. (Life Member)
ROUTLEDGE, Mrs. Helen Elizabeth, BSc ACA *1986;* London Borough of Newham, Housing Services, Bridge House, 320 High Street, LONDON, E15 1EP.
ROUTLEDGE, Mr. Jon Peter, BA(Hons) ACA *2010;* 7 Aydon Gardens, NEWCASTLE UPON TYNE, NE12 8WE.
•ROUTLEDGE, Mr. Paul, FCA *1975;* AbacusHouse.com LLP, Abacus House, Wickhurst Lane, Broadbridge Heath, HORSHAM, RH12 3LY.
ROUTLEDGE, Mr. Rex Thompson, FCA *1953;* 25 Spring Gardens Mount, KEIGHLEY, BD20 6LJ. (Life Member)
ROUTLEDGE, Mr. Richard John, BA ACA *1989;* 6 Clutha Road, STOCKPORT, CHESHIRE, SK3 8TY.
ROUTLEDGE, Mr. Robert Alfred, FCA *1973;* Oat Barns, Newchapel Road, LINGFIELD, SURREY, RH7 6BJ.
ROUTLEDGE, Mr. Stephen Crighton, LLB ACA *1990;* Manor Barn, Shepton Montague, WINCANTON, SOMERSET, BA9 8JB.
•ROUTLEDGE, Mr. Steven Mark, BSc ACA *1992;* Deloitte LLP, Athene Place, 66 Shoe Lane, LONDON, EC4A 3BQ. See also Deloitte & Touche LLP
•ROUTLEDGE, Mrs. Trudi Ann, BSc FCA *1992;* (Tax Fac), BJCA Limited, Rumwell Hall, Rumwell, TAUNTON, SOMERSET, TA4 1EL. See also BJ Dixon Walsh Limited
ROUTS, Ms. Sarah Ann Mary, BSc ACA *1992;* 8 Beauchamp Road, TWICKENHAM, TW1 3JD.
•ROUVAS, Mr. Antonis, FCA *1996;* Hellenic Bank, Head Office, PO Box 24747, 1394 NICOSIA, CYPRUS.
ROUX, Miss. Isabelle, MSc ACA *2007;* 76 C Culverden Road, Balham, LONDON, SW12 9LS.
•ROUX, Mr. John, FCA *1975;* John Roux, 25 Old Woods Hill, TORQUAY, TQ2 7NR.
ROUZEL, Mr. Alan Keith, FCA *1974;* (Tax Fac), 88 Montrose Avenue, EDGWARE, MIDDLESEX, HA8 0DR.
ROVIRA, Mr. Michael John, FCA *1965;* 1 Dince Hill Close, Whimple, EXETER, EX5 2TE.
ROW, Mr. Andrew George Stephen, BSc ACA *1988;* 4 Forrest Close, Shrivenham, SWINDON, SN6 8AP.
ROW, Mr. Iain John, MSci ACA *2005;* 15 Silverthorne Loft Apartments, 400 Albany Road, LONDON, SE5 0DJ.
ROW, Ms. Marion Jane, BSc FCA *1986;* Hawthorn Cottage, The Village, Finchampstead, WOKINGHAM, RG40 4JU.
ROWAN, Mr. Francis Thomas, FCA *1957;* The Cottage, Timbermede, Kings Road, Silchester, READING, RG7 2NP. (Life Member)
ROWAN, Mr. Geoffrey Charles Leacroft, BA FCA *1976;* 27 Crieff Road, LONDON, SW18 2EB.
•ROWAN, Mr. Kevin Christopher, BCom ACA *1988;* (Tax Fac), Account Ability, 4 Gibbs Hill, Headcorn, ASHFORD, KENT, TN27 9UD.
ROWAN, Mr. Logan, MSc BA ACA *2008;* Peabody Trust, Minster Court, 45-47 Westminster Bridge Road, LONDON, SE1 7JB.
ROWAN, Mr. Philip Adrian, BSc FCA *1987;* 230 Coal Clough Lane, BURNLEY, BB11 4DH.
ROWAN, Mr. Steven David, LLB ACA *1988;* Edwards Angell Palmer & Dodge Dashwood House, 69 Old Broad Street, LONDON, EC2M 1QS.
•ROWAN, Mrs. Susan Margaret, BSc FCA *1984;* Rowan & Co, 4 Gibbs Hill, Headcorn, ASHFORD, KENT, TN27 9UD. See also Account Ability
ROWBERRY, Mr. Brian Timothy, FCA *1955;* Willow Creek, Bodenham Moor, HEREFORD, HR1 3HS. (Life Member)
ROWBERRY, Mr. Duncan John, BA ACA *1984;* 2 Morris Rise, Chineham, BASINGSTOKE, HAMPSHIRE, RG24 8LD.
ROWBERRY, Mr. Edward John, BA ACA *2000;* 7 Cornwall Road, BRISTOL, BS7 8LJ.
ROWBERRY, Mrs. Rebecca Anne, MA ACA *2000;* 19 Hereford Road, HARROGATE, NORTH YORKSHIRE, HG1 2NW.
ROWBERRY, Mr. William Michael, BA ACA *2003;* 256 Worple Road, LONDON, SW20 8RH.
ROWBOTHAM, Mr. Brian, BA FCA *1977;* 7 Dundee Court, 73, Wapping High Street, LONDON, E1W 2YG.
ROWBOTHAM, Mr. Brian William, FCA *1954;* Robins' Mount, 46 Alma Road, REIGATE, SURREY, RH2 0DN. (Life Member)
•ROWBOTHAM, Mr. Christopher Guy, FCA *1963;* Davies Rowbotham & Co, 1 St Lawrence Court, 81 High Street, Chobham, WOKING, GU24 8LX.
ROWBOTHAM, Miss. Cressida Sisile, ACA *2008;* 100 Broom Park, TEDDINGTON, MIDDLESEX, TW11 9RR.
ROWBOTHAM, Mr. Jaime Bann, MA ACA *2006;* Flat 1, 15 Primrose Gardens, LONDON, NW3 4UJ.
ROWBOTHAM, Mrs. Sarah Jane, MSc ACA *2005;* 5 Charter Buildings, Catherine Grove, LONDON, SE10 8BB.
ROWBOTHAM, Mr. Sean Anthony, BSc FCA MBA *1989;* 110 Tuffnells Way, HARPENDEN, HERTFORDSHIRE, AL5 3HW.
ROWBOTTOM, Mrs. Karen, FCA *1982;* 14 Oldacre Close, SUTTON COLDFIELD, B76 1WF.
ROWBOTTOM, Mrs. Katherine Jane, BSc ACA *1999;* 15 Meadows Road, Heald Green, CHEADLE, SK8 3RF.
ROWBOTTOM, Mr. Peter Graham, ACA *1979;* 14 Oldacre Close, SUTTON COLDFIELD, WEST MIDLANDS, B76 1WF.
ROWBOTTOM, Mrs. Rachelle, ACA *2004;* (Tax Fac), Barber Harrison & Platt, 2 Rutland Park, SHEFFIELD, S10 2PD.
ROWBURY, Mr. Timothy James, BA FCA *1978;* 25 Priestley Drive, Larkfield, AYLESFORD, ME20 6TX.
ROWCLIFFE, Mr. Tom James, BA ACA *2006;* 2 Oxford Cottages, 30 Potters Lane, Send, WOKING, SURREY, GU23 7AH.
ROWCROFT JAMES, Mrs. Rosemary Helen Parry, BA ACA *1995;* 110 Linceslade Grove, Loughton, MILTON KEYNES, MK5 8BL.
ROWDEN, Mr. Dennis Cyril, ACA *1979;* 149 Grand Drive, HERNE BAY, CT6 8HU.
•ROWDEN, Mr. Jonathan Bruce, BA ACA *1983;* Rowdens Ltd, Unit 3E, Vinnetrow Business Park, Vinnetrow Road, Runcton, CHICHESTER WEST SUSSEX PO20 1QH.
ROWDEN, Mr. Jonathan Christopher, BA ACA *1993;* with PricewaterhouseCoopers LLP, 1 Embankment Place, LONDON, WC2N 6RH.
ROWDEN, Miss. Laura Louise, ACA *2010;* 162b Tressillian Road, Brockley, LONDON, SE4 1XY.
•ROWDEN, Mrs. Penelope Ann, ACA *1987;* (Tax Fac), Rowdens Ltd, Unit 3E, Vinnetrow Business Park, Vinnetrow Road, Runcton, CHICHESTER WEST SUSSEX PO20 1QH.
ROWE, Mrs. Aimee Lynda, BA(Hons) ACA *2003;* The Association of Chartered Certified Accountants, 29 Lincoln's Inn Fields, LONDON, WC2A 3EE.
ROWE, Mr. Andrew Sutherland, FCA *1959;* The Mansion, Harrold, BEDFORD, MK43 7BJ. (Life Member)
ROWE, Mr. Anton Edward Richard, BSc ACA *1992;* Danisco Animal Nutrition, Ailesbury Court, High Street, MARLBOROUGH, WILTSHIRE, SN8 1AA.
ROWE, Mr. Christopher David, FCA *1966;* Nether Pound Cottage, Preston Bagot, Henley-In-Arden, SOLIHULL, B95 5ED.
ROWE, Miss. Clare Elizabeth, BA ACA *1996;* 32 Belmore Gardens, Wollaton, NOTTINGHAM, NG8 4GG.
ROWE, Mr. Colin William, FCA *1976;* 4 Wallers Hoppet, LOUGHTON, IG10 1SP.
ROWE, Mr. David, ACA *1994;* Unit 45 Offerton Industrial Estate, Hempshaw Lane, STOCKPORT, CHESHIRE, SK2 5TJ.
•ROWE, Mr. David Andrew, BA ACA *1993;* WBV Limited, Woodfield House, Castle Walk, NEATH, SA11 3LN. See also D A & C M Rowe Limited
•ROWE, Mr. David John, BSc ACA *1986;* Talbot Hughes McKillop LLP, 6 Snow Hill, LONDON, EC1A 2AY.
ROWE, Mr. David John, BSc ACA *2003;* 17 Basin Street, PRINCETON, NJ 08540, UNITED STATES.
ROWE, Mr. David Michael, BA ACA *1981;* Middle Stoodley, Lee Bottom Road, TODMORDEN, OL14 6HD.
ROWE, Mr. David Philip, BA ACA *2004;* SW1-E522, Capital One Bank (Europe) Plc Trent House, Station Street, NOTTINGHAM, NG2 3HX.
ROWE, Mr. Edward Lloyd, ACA *2008;* 16 Addison Road, TUNBRIDGE WELLS, TN2 3GG.
ROWE, Miss. Esther Carys, BSc ACA *2000;* 63a Ha'penny Bridge Way, HULL, HU9 1HD.
ROWE, Mr. Frederick William, FCA *1952;* 6 Eastwick Drive, Bookham, LEATHERHEAD, KT23 3PP. (Life Member)
ROWE, Dr. Gaynor Louise, BSc ACA *2001;* 25 Fernihough Close, WEYBRIDGE, SURREY, KT13 0UY.
ROWE, Mr. George Colin, FCA *1951;* 75 Copandale Road, BEVERLEY, HU17 7BN. (Life Member)
•ROWE, Mr. Geraint Anthony, BSc FCA CF *1997;* Gambit Corporate Finance LLP, 3 Assembly Square, Britannia Quay, Cardiff Bay, CARDIFF, CF10 4PL.
ROWE, Mr. Graham Vincent, FCA FCCA *1969;* Oaktree Cottage, Keele Road, Keele, NEWCASTLE, STAFFORDSHIRE, ST5 5AL.
ROWE, Mr. Gregory Stephen, ACA *1999;* Old Plough Southgate, Cawston, NORWICH, NR10 4HY.
ROWE, Mrs. Heather Jean, MA FCA *1980;* 199 Gilesgate, DURHAM, DH1 1QN.
ROWE, Mrs. Helen Sian, BA BSc ACA *2003;* 23 Newlyn Avenue, Stoke Bishop, BRISTOL, BS9 1BP.
ROWE, Mr. Ian Clive, BSc ACA *1989;* 13 Wallace Crescent, CARSHALTON, SURREY, SM5 3SU.
ROWE, Mrs. Isobel Jennifer, ACA *1996;* Albert Goodman Mary Street House, Mary Street, TAUNTON, SOMERSET, TA1 3NW.
ROWE, Mr. James Matthew Bevington, BSc(Hons) ACA *2002;* 23 Newlyn Avenue, Stoke Bishop, BRISTOL, BS9 1BP.
•ROWE, Mr. James Winston, FCA *1968;* Leftley Rowe & Company, The Heights, 59-65 Lowlands Road, HARROW, MIDDLESEX, HA1 3AW. See also Mountsides Limited
ROWE, Mr. Jeremy Alexander, BSc ACA *2011;* 19 Woodburn Close, LONDON, NW4 2NF.
•ROWE, Mr. Jeremy Franklin, FCA *1987;* 443 Livesey Branch Road, BLACKBURN, BB2 5BX.
ROWE, Mr. John Charles, FCA *1974;* 331 De Haer Road, WA 6167 DI, WA 6167, AUSTRALIA.
ROWE, Mr. John George, MA BA ACA *2005;* Internal Audit Room 2nd Floor, Network Rail Ltd, 1 Eversholt Street, LONDON, NW1 2DN.

•**ROWE, Mr. John Neil, FCA CTA** *1988;* (Tax Fac), Francis Clark, Francis Clark LLP, Sigma House, Oak View Close, Edginswell Park, TORQUAY TQ2 7FF. See also Francis Clark LLP
ROWE, Mr. Julian Austen, MA ACA *1998;* Flat 5 The Cedars, 8 Westgate Road, BECKENHAM, BR3 5DY.
ROWE, Mr. Julian William Richard, ACA *2008;* Horsley Bridge International Ltd, 4 Cork Street, LONDON, W1S 3LG.
ROWE, Mr. Keith Frederick Anthony, FCA *1962;* 52a Brook Avenue North, NEW MILTON, BH25 5HQ.
ROWE, Mr. Kenneth Alan, BA ACA *1989;* 55 Whitcliffe Lane, RIPON, HG4 2LB.
ROWE, Mr. Kenneth James, FCA *1950;* 12 Tainters Brook, UCKFIELD, TN22 1UQ. (Life Member)
ROWE, Mr. Kenneth James, BA(Hons) ACA *2004;* Flat 2, 12 Hungerford Road, LONDON, N7 9LX.
ROWE, Mr. Kevan, BA FCA *1977;* (Tax Fac), 25 Wanstead Close, Poulner, RINGWOOD, BH24 1SJ.
ROWE, Mrs. Louise Frances, BSc ACA *2007;* 22 Glebelands, Exminster, EXETER, EX6 8AR.
ROWE, Mr. Mark, ACA *2003;* 1 Foscote Rise, BANBURY, OXFORDSHIRE, OX16 9XS.
•**ROWE, Mr. Michael, ACA CA(AUS)** *2008;* APT Partnership LLP, 44 The Pantiles, TUNBRIDGE WELLS, KENT, TN2 5TN.
ROWE, Mr. Nicholas Charles, LLB FCA *1983;* Royal Bank of Scotland, ABN AMRO Tower, 88 Philip Street, SYDNEY, NSW 2000, AUSTRALIA.
ROWE, Mr. Nicholas David, BSc(Econ) FCA *2001;* 9 William Belcher Drive, St. Mellons, CARDIFF, CF3 0NZ.
ROWE, Mr. Nicholas Denton, MA ACA *1985;* Woodmancote Farmhouse, Woodmancote, EMSWORTH, PO10 8RD.
•**ROWE, Mr. Oliver, BA ACA** *2003;* with CW Fellowes Limited, Templars House, Lulworth Close, Chandlers Ford, EASTLEIGH, SO53 3TL.
ROWE, Mr. Peter John, FCA *1958;* 39 Homewood Road, ST. ALBANS, AL1 4BG. (Life Member)
ROWE, Mr. Peter Thomas, BSc ACA *2007;* 7 Jupiter Way, Abbeymead, GLOUCESTER, GL4 5JE.
ROWE, Miss. Philippa Jane, ACA *2010;* Flat 7, Tavistock House, Rosebury Square, WOODFORD GREEN, ESSEX, IG8 8NT.
ROWE, Mr. Richard Jonathan, BSc FCA *1971;* Puffin Cottage, Headland Road, Carbis Bay, ST.IVES, CORNWALL, TR26 2NU.
•**ROWE, Mrs. Rosalind, ACA** *1979;* (Tax Fac), PricewaterhouseCoopers LLP, Hays Galleria, 1 Hays Lane, LONDON, SE1 2RD. See also PricewaterhouseCoopers
•**ROWE, Mr. Sean David, ACA** *1995;* Sean Rowe Limited, 169 New London Road, CHELMSFORD, CM2 0AE.
ROWE, Mr. Simon George, FCA *1975;* 117 Gregories Road, BEACONSFIELD, BUCKINGHAMSHIRE, HP9 1HZ.
•**ROWE, Mr. Stephen, BSc FCA** *1984;* PricewaterhouseCoopers LLP, Cornwall Court, 19 Cornwall Street, BIRMINGHAM, B3 2DT. See also PricewaterhouseCoopers
ROWE, Mr. Steven, ACA *2011;* 4 Woodhall Close, BURY, LANCASHIRE, BL8 1HQ.
ROWE, Mr. Steven Howard, FCA *1972;* Flat 8, Beechwood Hall, Regents Park Road, LONDON, N3 3AT.
ROWE, Mrs. Susannah Catherine, BSc ACA *1997;* Heathy View, Hatchet Close, Hale, FORDINGBRIDGE, HAMPSHIRE, SP6 2NF.
ROWE, Mr. William James, BSc ACA *1989;* 22 Avenue Gardens, TEDDINGTON, TW11 0BH.
ROWE, Mr. William Patrick, BA ACA *1989;* 6 Lime Grove, LONDON, W12 8EA.
ROWE-HAM, Sir David Kenneth, GBE FCA *1962;* 140 Piccadilly, LONDON, W1J 7NS.
ROWE-HAM, Mr. Gerald, BSc ACA *2001;* BlueCrest Capital Management, 7th floor, Rue Vallin 2, 1201 GENEVA, SWITZERLAND.
•**ROWELL, Mr. Anthony John, ACA** *1979;* Tony Rowell, 1a Middle Way, LEWES, EAST SUSSEX, BN7 1NH.
ROWELL, Mr. David Frederick, MA MBA FCA *1981;* 3 Gill Close, Addingham, ILKLEY, LS29 0TG.
ROWELL, Mr. David Robert, BSc FCA *1980;* Apartment 1401, 18 Leftbank, MANCHESTER, M3 3AL.
ROWELL, Mr. Graham Michael, ACA *1988;* Bosch Rexroth Ltd, 15 Cromwell Road, ST. NEOTS, CAMBRIDGESHIRE, PE19 2ES.
ROWELL, Mrs. Heather Margaret, BSc FCA *1975;* Worshipful Company of Masons, 22 Cannon Hill, LONDON, N14 6LG.
ROWELL, Mr. Jack, OBE LLD MA FCA *1964;* Middlehill House, Middlehill, Box, CORSHAM, SN13 8QS.
ROWELL, Mr. Jonathan Grant, BSc FCA *1993;* 31 Coutts Crescent, COLLAROY, NSW 2097, AUSTRALIA.
ROWELL, Mr. Matthew David, BA ACA *2006;* 17 Abberley Grove, STAFFORD, ST17 4FE.
•**ROWELL, Mr. Peter William, FCA CTA** *1977;* (Tax Fac), Lewis Rowell, 20 Springfield Road, CRAWLEY, WEST SUSSEX, RH11 8AD.
ROWELL, Mr. Robert Henry, ACA *1983;* 7 Rue Maréchal Ney, 34170 CASTELNAU-LE-LEZ, FRANCE.
ROWELL, Mr. Simon Allen, BA ACA *1980;* PO Box 291, HUNTERS HILL, NSW 2110, AUSTRALIA.
ROWELL, Mr. Stephen James, BA ACA *1994;* 24 Cannons Meadow, Tewin, WELWYN, AL6 0JU.
ROWELL, Mr. Sydney David, BCom FCA *1972;* 25 Raglan Road, DUBLIN 4, COUNTY DUBLIN, IRELAND.
ROWEN, Mrs. Victoria Claire, ACA *2008;* Staffords C P C, 1 Capital Park Fulbourn, CAMBRIDGE, CB21 5XE.
ROWES, Mr. Peter Graham, BSc FCA *1954;* 14 Spicer Lodge, Enville Street, STOURBRIDGE, WEST MIDLANDS, DY8 1BS. (Life Member)
ROWETT, Mrs. Pauline Hildred, BSc ACA *1985;* Tilquhillie Cottage, BANCHORY, AB31 6LE.
ROWLAND, Mrs. Amanda Ann, BSc ACA *1995;* Heinemann Educational Books Halley Court, Jordan Hill Business Park Banbury Road, OXFORD, OX2 8EJ.
•**ROWLAND, Mr. Anthony Bernard, FCA** *1977;* (Tax Fac), Norrie Gibson & Co Ltd, Grosvenor House, 102 Beverley Road, HULL, HU3 1YA.
ROWLAND, Mr. Anthony Edward, FCA *1955;* 63 Stourton Road, Ainsdale, SOUTHPORT, PR8 3PL. (Life Member)
ROWLAND, Mr. Anthony John, LLB ACA CFA *2000;* Ambrian Partners Ltd Old Change House, 128 Queen Victoria Street, LONDON, EC4V 4BJ.
ROWLAND, Mr. Anthony Stephen, BSc ACA *1991;* 11 Warkton Lane, KETTERING, NN15 5AB.
•**ROWLAND, Mrs. Barbara Mary, BSc FCA** *1988;* Barbara Rowland Limited, Summer House, Knowle Hill, EVESHAM, WR11 7EL. See also Rowland Barbara
•**ROWLAND, Mr. Christopher Charles, PhD MA ACA** *1988;* PricewaterhouseCoopers LLP, Hays Galleria, 1 Hays Lane, LONDON, SE1 2RD. See also PricewaterhouseCoopers
ROWLAND, Mr. Christopher David, BSc ACA *2006;* Lend Lease, PO Box 67914 20 Triton Street, LONDON, nw1w 8su.
ROWLAND, Mr. David Mark, MSc ACA *1983;* 2 Mount Pleasant, Stoke Goldington, NEWPORT PAGNELL, BUCKINGHAMSHIRE, MK16 8LL.
ROWLAND, Mr. Dennis Charles, FCA *1970;* Flat 8 Grasmere Court, 3 Cedar Gardens, SUTTON, SURREY, SM2 5EQ.
ROWLAND, Mrs. Diane, BA ACA *1999;* 77 Pentrebane Street, CARDIFF, CF11 7LP.
ROWLAND, Mr. Donald Stewart, FCA *1950;* 9 Victoria Court, CHESTER, CH2 2BA. (Life Member)
ROWLAND, Mr. Eric John, BA ACA *2003;* 28b Altenburg Gardens, LONDON, SW11 1JJ.
ROWLAND, Miss. Fiona Louise, BA ACA *1995;* Bourne House, Queen Street, Gomshall, GUILDFORD, SURREY, GU5 9LY.
ROWLAND, Mr. Graham Edward, FCA *1975;* 8 Rollo Road, Hextable, SWANLEY, KENT, BR8 7RD. (Life Member)
ROWLAND, Mr. Ian Eric, BSc(Hons) ACA CTA *2000;* with Grant Thornton UK LLP, 4 Hardman Square, Spinningfields, MANCHESTER, M3 3EB.
ROWLAND, Mr. Ian Peter, BA ACA *1989;* 31 Hook Hill, SOUTH CROYDON, CR2 0LB.
ROWLAND, Miss. Joanne Louise, ACA *2006;* Mini Clipper Ltd, Billington Road, LEIGHTON BUZZARD, BEDFORDSHIRE, LU7 4AT.
ROWLAND, Mr. John David, BA ACA *2005;* Alchemy Partners Llp, 25 Bedford Street, LONDON, WC2E 9ES.
ROWLAND, Mr. John Garth, FCA *1968;* Red Gables, South Crescent, RIPON, NORTH YORKSHIRE, HG4 1SW. (Life Member)
ROWLAND, Mr. John Richard, FCA *1975;* 40 Parkside Drive, WATFORD, WD17 3AX.
ROWLAND, Mrs. Julie Claire, BSc ACA *1988;* 11 Warkton Lane, Barton Seagrave, KETTERING, NORTHAMPTONSHIRE, NN15 5AB.
ROWLAND, Mr. Justin Matthew, BEng ACA *1993;* E D F Trading Markets Ltd, 80 Victoria Street, Cardinal Place, LONDON, SW1E 5JL.
ROWLAND, Mrs. Katherine Louise, MSc ACA *1996;* The Juice Corporation, Hornby Street Ltd, 2-16 Bury New Road, MANCHESTER, M8 8FR.
ROWLAND, Mrs. Lynn Suzanne, BSc ACA *1988;* 10 Belvedere Grove, Wimbledon Village, LONDON, SW19 7RL.
ROWLAND, Mr. Mark Andrew, BSc FCA ATII *1992;* (Tax Fac), Flat 12, Windmill Rise, 40 Windmill Hill, ENFIELD, MIDDLESEX, EN2 7AW.
ROWLAND, Mr. Martin Andrew, FCA *1970;* Saxons, New Road, Ridgewood, UCKFIELD, TN22 5TG.
ROWLAND, Mr. Martin Christopher, BSc ACA *1998;* LDC 1st Floor, One Forbury Square, READING, RG1 3BB.
ROWLAND, Mr. Matthew, BSc ACA *2006;* (Tax Fac), 14 Lord Avenue, ILFORD, ESSEX, IG5 0HP.
ROWLAND, Mr. Michael Louis, FCA *1962;* Lynwood House, Lyne Lane, Lyne, CHERTSEY, KT16 0AN.
•**ROWLAND, Mr. Neil, FCA** *1979;* (Tax Fac), Meadows & Co, 1 Kings Court, Kettering Parkway, KETTERING, NORTHAMPTONSHIRE, NN15 6WJ.
ROWLAND, Mr. Philip Barry, BA ACA *2000;* 66 Willifield Way, LONDON, NW11 7XT.
ROWLAND, Mr. Philip James, BSc ACA *1992;* Blick Rothenberg, 12 York Gate, LONDON, NW1 4QS.
ROWLAND, Mr. Phillip David, BEng ACA *1996;* 9 Aire Close, MORECAMBE, LA3 3SA.
ROWLAND, Mr. Reginald Charles Frederick, FCA *1960;* 7 Prestwick Drive, Blundellsands, LIVERPOOL, L23 7XB. (Life Member)
ROWLAND, Mr. Robert Lyndon, FCA *1958;* Furzefield, Clappers Lane, Fulking, HENFIELD, WEST SUSSEX, BN5 9NJ. (Life Member)
ROWLAND, Mr. Roger Sargeant, FCA *1957;* Pigeon Cottage, Murcott, KIDLINGTON, OX5 2RE. (Life Member)
•**ROWLAND, Mrs. Rosemary Helen, BSc(Hons) FCA** *2001;* (Tax Fac), Howard Worth, Drake House, Gadbrook Park, NORTHWICH, CHESHIRE, CW9 7RA.
ROWLAND, Mr. Stephen, BSc ACA *1983;* (Tax Fac), Elvetham Business Solutions Limited, 45 Kingsley Square, FLEET, HAMPSHIRE, GU51 1AH.
ROWLAND, Mr. Stuart Henry, FCA *1966;* 17 St. Wilfrids Close, Kibworth Beauchamp, LEICESTER, LE8 0PY.
ROWLAND, Mrs. Teresa Clare, BSc ACA *1997;* 1 Brendon Drive, ESHER, SURREY, KT10 9EQ.
ROWLAND, Ms. Tracey Elizabeth, BSc FCA *1991;* 13 East Road, Barton Stacey, WINCHESTER, SO21 3RZ.
ROWLAND-HILL, Mr. John Duncan, FCA *1971;* 12 North Meadow Road, Cricklade, SWINDON, SN6 6LU.
ROWLAND-HILL, Miss. Judith Ann, BA ACA *2000;* 21 Earlsmead Crescent, Cliffsend, RAMSGATE, CT12 5LQ.
ROWLANDS, Mr. Andrew, BA ACA *2000;* 2 Tudor Road, SOUTHPORT, MERSEYSIDE, PR8 2RY.
ROWLANDS, Miss. Anne Justine, PhD MA ACA *1996;* 5 Heydons Close, ST. ALBANS, HERTFORDSHIRE, AL3 5SF.
•**ROWLANDS, Mr. Anthony Joseph, BSc FCA** *1975;* (Tax Fac), AJ Rowlands & Co, Suite 17, 4th Floor, 1 Crown Square, Church Street East, WOKING SURREY GU21 6HR.
ROWLANDS, Mrs. Choo Swee, BMus ACA *1994;* 15a Leboh Lasam, 30350 IPOH, Perak, MALAYSIA.
ROWLANDS, Mr. Christopher John, MA FCA *1977;* 24 Northumberland Road, Redland, BRISTOL, BS6 7BB.
ROWLANDS, Mr. Colin John, BSc ACA *1999;* OpenBet Ltd, Building 9 Chiswick Park, 566 Chiswick High Road, LONDON, W4 5XT.
ROWLANDS, Mr. David George, FCA *1956;* Halgabron Cottage, Pednor Road, CHESHAM, HP5 2SS. (Life Member)
ROWLANDS, Mr. David Gummer, FCA *1966;* 203 Southport Road, ORMSKIRK, L39 1LU.
ROWLANDS, Mr. David Hedley, BSc ACA *2002;* 34 Jubilee Road, Knowle, BRISTOL, BS4 2LP.
ROWLANDS, Mr. James Edward, BA(Hons) ACA *2001;* 34 Blackcurrant Drive, Long Ashton, BRISTOL, BS41 9FP.
ROWLANDS, Mrs. Jennifer Louise, BSc FCA *1990;* 28 Prowse Avenue, Bushey Heath, BUSHEY, WD23 1LA.
ROWLANDS, Mr. John Edward, ACA *2008;* Benfield Greig Group Plc, 55 Bishopsgate, LONDON, EC2N 3BD.
ROWLANDS, Mrs. Katie Victoria, BSc(Hons) ACA *2000;* Royal & Sunalliance, PO Box 144, LIVERPOOL, L69 3EN.
ROWLANDS, Mr. Kevin, BSc ACA *1987;* 23 North Road, Midsomer Norton, RADSTOCK, BA3 2QB.
ROWLANDS, Mr. Marc Neil, BA ACA *1998;* 8 Bedford Road, ST. ALBANS, HERTFORDSHIRE, AL1 3BQ.
ROWLANDS, Miss. Sally, BSc(Hons) ACA *2002;* 40 Montclaire Avenue, BLACKWOOD, GWENT, NP12 1EF.
ROWLANDS, Mr. Stuart Charles, BSc FCA *1978;* 3 Rue Mathias Perrang, 8160 BRIDEL, LUXEMBOURG.
ROWLANDS, Mr. Thomas Arthur, FCA *1962;* Aptfold Lea, Paxford, CHIPPING CAMPDEN, GL55 6XL. (Life Member)
ROWLANDS, Mr. Trefor Huw, MA ACA *1989;* Unilever Unilever House, Springfield Drive, LEATHERHEAD, KT22 7GR.
ROWLANDSON, Mr. James Collingwood, FCA *1972;* 2581 de Miniac, MONTREAL H4S1E5, QC, CANADA.
ROWLANDSON, Mr. John, FCA *1951;* 243 Lobelia Terrace, Welcome Bay, TAURANGA 3112, NEW ZEALAND. (Life Member)
ROWLANDSON, Mr. Richard Graham St John, FCA *1964;* 73 West Common, HARPENDEN, AL5 2LD.
ROWLATT, Mrs. Christine, BSc ACA *1979;* Shotts Farm, Malvern Road, Staunton, GLOUCESTER, GL19 3NZ.
ROWLATT, Mr. Rafe Napier, FCA *1955;* Wood Green Cottage, Astley, STOURPORT-ON-SEVERN, DY13 0RU. (Life Member)
ROWLEDGE, Mr. Michael, BSc FCA *1978;* 19 Thetford Gardens, Wednesfield, WOLVERHAMPTON, WV11 1TR.
•**ROWLEDGE, Mr. Ralph Edgar, FCA** *1965;* Smith Cooper Livery Place, 35 Livery Street, BIRMINGHAM, B3 2PB.
ROWLES, Mr. Arthur Leonard, FCA *1954;* c/o Mr M Rowles, MRM, Cedar House, Vine Lane, Hillingdon, UXBRIDGE MIDDLESEX UB10 0NF. (Life Member)
•**ROWLES, Mr. Graham John, FCA** *1959;* Westbrook, 11 Glebe Road, Long Ashton, BRISTOL, BS41 9LJ.
•**ROWLES, Mr. Maurice John, FCA** *1969;* Griffiths & Co, 97a High Street, LYMINGTON, HAMPSHIRE, SO41 9AP. See also Rowles & Co
ROWLES, Mrs. Suzanne, BSc ACA *1992;* 18 Riversmill, DURSLEY, GLOUCESTERSHIRE, GL11 5GG.
ROWLETT, Mr. Julian David, BA ACA *1991;* 55 Swanmore Road, Boscombe East, BOURNEMOUTH, BH7 6PD.
ROWLETT, Mr. Michael Edward, FCA *1967;* Chalcott New Road, Shiplake, HENLEY-ON-THAMES, OXFORDSHIRE, RG9 3LA. (Life Member)
ROWLETT, Mr. Robert Alan, FCA *1966;* 153 Bloxham Road, BANBURY, OXFORDSHIRE, OX16 9JU.
ROWLEY, Mr. Allan John, MPhil BSc ACA *1996;* Barlandhu, Fairclose Drive, Littleton, WINCHESTER, HAMPSHIRE, SO22 6QW.
ROWLEY, Ms. Andrea Justine, BSc ACA *1993;* 32 Kingston Road, MANCHESTER, M20 2RZ.
ROWLEY, Mr. Andrew Duncan, BSc ACA *1979;* Watering Farm, Yaxham Road, DEREHAM, NR19 1JQ.
ROWLEY, Miss. Anna-Marie, MA ACA *2005;* Independent Regulator of NHS Foundation Trust, 4 Matthew Parker Street, LONDON, SW1H 9NP.
ROWLEY, Mr. Christopher Andrew, BA ACA *1997;* Source8, 5 Hobart Place, LONDON, SW1W 0HU.
ROWLEY, Mr. Christopher Charles, FCA *1957;* UHURU, 189 Railway Road, TORBAY, WA 6330, AUSTRALIA. (Life Member)
ROWLEY, Mr. Christopher James, BSc ACA *2011;* 64 Curzon Avenue, Birstall, LEICESTER, LE4 4AD.
ROWLEY, Mr. Colin, FCA *1965;* Meadowspring, Undershore Road, Walhampton, LYMINGTON, SO41 5SB.
ROWLEY, Mr. David Arthur, FCA *1971;* Caparo Tube Components, PO Box 14, OLDBURY, B69 4NN.
ROWLEY, Mr. David Roger, BA FCA *1960;* 12 Schlassgewan, L-5364 SCHRASSIG, LUXEMBOURG. (Life Member)
ROWLEY, Miss. Eileen Mary, BCom ACA *1986;* 12 Blagdens Close, LONDON, N14 6DE.
ROWLEY, Mr. Gordon William, FCA *1952;* Magnolia Cottage, 114 Clarence Road, Four Oaks, SUTTON COLDFIELD, B74 4AU. (Life Member)
ROWLEY, Miss. Helen Louise, BSc ACA *1994;* A & N Media Finance Services Ltd, PO Box 6795, St Georges Street, LEICESTER, LE1 1ZP.
ROWLEY, Mr. James Eric, FCA *1969;* 6 Bay View Court, La Route de St. Aubin, St. Helier, JERSEY, JE2 4ZZ. (Life Member)
ROWLEY, Mr. Jonathan David, MA ACA *1997;* UBS, 1 Finsbury Avenue, LONDON, EC2M 2PP.
ROWLEY, Mr. Jonathan James Graham, MSc FCA *1971;* Betton Farm House, MARKET DRAYTON, SHROPSHIRE, TF9 4AD.
ROWLEY, Mr. Keith Andrew, BSc ACA *1990;* 4 Mabett Close, Arborfield, READING, RG2 9FF.

ROWLEY, Mr. Lee Anthony, MA ACA *2011;* Flat 3, 66 Dyne Road, LONDON, NW6 7DS.
ROWLEY, Mr. Leslie Graham, MA FCA *1976;* 78 Starlight Crescent, RICHMOND HILL L4C 4X6, ON, CANADA.
•**ROWLEY, Mr. Michael John, BSc FCA** *1992;* KPMG LLP, One Snowhill, Snow Hill Queensway, BIRMINGHAM, B4 6GN. See also KPMG Europe LLP
ROWLEY, Mr. Neil James, ACA *2008;* 231 Ladbroke Grove, LONDON, W10 6HG.
ROWLEY, Mrs. Pamela Ann, BSc ACA *1990;* 16 Ashbourne Drive, Desborough, KETTERING, NN14 2XG.
•**ROWLEY, Mr. Paul David, BA ACA** *1997;* Cooper Parry LLP, 3 Centro Place, Pride Park, DERBY, DE24 8RF.
•**ROWLEY, Mr. Peter Michael, MA FCA** *1978;* 79 Weirdale Avenue, Whetstone, LONDON, N20 0AJ.
ROWLEY, Mr. Philip Edward, BSc FCA *1977;* The Mill, High Street, Whitchurch-On-Thames, READING, RG8 7DG.
•**ROWLEY, Mr. Richard George, FCA** *1970;* Apperley Rowley & Co, Bell House, Bell Street, Great Baddow, CHELMSFORD, CM2 7JS.
ROWLEY, Mr. Stephen Gavin, BA ACA CIA *1995;* 1051 Kilmore Road, RIDDELLS CREEK, VIC 3431, AUSTRALIA.
•**ROWLEY, Mrs. Sylvia May, FCA** *1983;* Mrs S.M. Rowley FCA, 223 Fullingdale Road, NORTHAMPTON, NN3 2QH.
ROWLEY, Mr. Thomas James, BA(Hons) ACA *2004;* 14 Charter Road, Hale, ALTRINCHAM, CHESHIRE, WA15 9RL.
ROWLING, Mr. Christopher John, BCom ACA *1996;* 150 Danube Drive, PITTSBURGH, PA 15209, UNITED STATES.
ROWLING, Mr. Keith Peter, BSc FCA *1988;* The Orchard, Annables Lane, HARPENDEN, HERTFORDSHIRE, AL5 3PJ.
ROWLINSON, Mr. Colin Mark, BCom ACA *1991;* Apartment 318, 21-33 Worple Road, LONDON, SW19 4BJ.
ROWLINSON, Mrs. Suzanne Jean, FCA *1993;* 208 Tonbridge Road, Wateringbury, MAIDSTONE, KENT, ME18 5NU.
ROWLSTON, Mr. Nicholas, ACA *2001;* 3 Lakeshore Drive, HAMMOND B4B 1S6, NS, CANADA.
ROWNEY, Mr. Charles Michael, BSc ACA *1993;* 3 Flint Cottages, Jevington, POLEGATE, BN26 5QF.
•**ROWNTREE, Mr. Alan Thomas, MBE FCA** *1969;* (Tax Fac), Beever and Struthers, Central Buildings, Richmond Terrace, BLACKBURN, BB1 7AP.
ROWSE, Mr. David Alan, ACA *1978;* The Cornmill, Stoke St. Milborough, LUDLOW, SHROPSHIRE, SY8 2EJ.
ROWSE, Mr. Victor, BA(Hons) ACA *2004;* Flat 18D, Ivy on Belchers, 26 Belcher Street, SAI YING POON, HONG KONG ISLAND, HONG KONG SAR.
ROWSELL, Miss. Abigail, ACA *2010;* Creaseys Llp, 12-16 Lonsdale Gardens, TUNBRIDGE WELLS, TN1 1PA.
ROWSELL, Mr. Benjamin James, BSc ACA *2003;* 45 Druid Hill, BRISTOL, BS9 1EH.
•**ROWSELL, Mrs. Cheryl Anne, FCA** *1980;* (Tax Fac), Gibbons Mannington & Phipps, 24 Landgate, RYE, EAST SUSSEX, TN31 7LJ.
ROWSELL, Mr. Kenneth Harry Theodore, FCA *1955;* Picardy, 2 Lammas Lane, ESHER, KT10 8NY. (Life Member)
ROWSELL, Mr. Lynton John, BSc ACA *1999;* 3466 Lilly Avenue, LONG BEACH, CA 90808, UNITED STATES.
ROWSON, Dr. David, PhD FCA *1991;* Town Farm, High Street, Tibshelf, ALFRETON, DERBYSHIRE, DE55 5NY.
ROWSON, Mr. Ian Michael, BSc ACA *1987;* 6 Potters Lane, ELY, CAMBRIDGESHIRE, CB7 4BX.
ROWSON, Mr. Richard James Christopher, BSc ACA *1992;* Milbank Tower, 21 - 24 Millbank, LONDON, SW1P 4QP.
ROWSON, Mr. Rupert John, BA ACA *2001;* K P M G Llp, 15 Canada Square, LONDON, E14 5GL.
•**ROWSON, Mr. Stuart Anthony, FCA** *1989;* Venthams Limited, Millhouse, 32-38 East Street, ROCHFORD, SS4 1DB.
ROWSWELL, Miss. Ann, MA ACA *1982;* Inglewood, Bowling Alley, Oving, AYLESBURY, HP22 4HD.
ROWSWELL, Mr. Geoffrey Graham, FCA *1953;* Chapins, Kings Arms Hill, ARUNDEL, BN18 9BT. (Life Member)
•**ROXBURGH, Mr. Andrew Campbell, MSc ACA ATII** *1981;* Roxburgh Consulting Limited, 9 Valley Court, Craig Road, STOCKPORT, SK4 2AW. See also CHCA Limited
ROXBURGH, Mr. Douglas Selwyn, BA FCA CTA TEP *1971;* (Tax Fac), Flat 24, Tewit Well Gardens, 1 Tewit Well Road, HARROGATE, NORTH YORKSHIRE, HG2 8JG.
ROXBURGH, Mr. Gerald Ralph, FCA *1971;* PT CORROCOAT INDONESIA, Jl Cakung Cilincing KM. 1 No 7, PO Box 1404/JKT, JAKARTA, 13910, INDONESIA.
ROXBURGH, Miss. Helen, MA MSci ACA *2006;* 4 Lidgett Park View, LEEDS, LS8 1HF.
ROXBURGH, Mr. Joseph Lindsay, BSc ACA *1997;* The Bureau Le Quai Bisson, Le Boulevard St. Brelade, JERSEY, JE3 8JT.
ROXBURGH, Mrs. Marion Rosamund, BSc FCA *1982;* Little Croft, Woodland Rise, SEVENOAKS, KENT, TN15 0HY.
ROXBURGH, Mr. Thomas George, ACA CA(AUS) *2009;* Standard Chartered, 1 Basinghall Avenue, LONDON, EC2V 5DD.
ROXBY, Miss. Gemma Louise, ACA *2009;* 15 Taverner Close, POOLE, DORSET, BH15 1UP.
•**ROY, Mr. Andrew Steven, FCA** *1973;* Baker Tilly Isle of Man LLC, PO Box 95, 2a Lord Street, Douglas, ISLE OF MAN, IM99 1HP. See also Baker Tilly Bennett Roy LLC
ROY, Mr. Arnab, BSc ACA *1992;* 17/2 Ritchie Road, CALCUTTA 700 019, INDIA.
ROY, Mr. Arno, BSc ACA *1980;* Chemin du Daillard 23, 1071 CHEXBRES, VAUD, SWITZERLAND.
•**ROY, Mr. Ashoke, FCA** *1970;* Ashoke Roy, 3rd Floor, Baroda Bank Building, Sir William Newton St, PORT LOUIS, MAURITIUS.
ROY, Mr. Ashwin, MA ACA *2000;* Citigroup Venture Capital International, 33 Cavendish Square, LONDON, W1G 0PW.
ROY, Mr. Bejoy Krishna, FCA *1973;* 77 Burleigh Gardens, LONDON, N14 5AJ.
ROY, Mr. Biresh, BSc ACA *1991;* Flat 56, Chelsea Gate Apartments, 93 Ebury Bridge Road, LONDON, SW1W 8RB.
ROY, Mr. Edward Martin, BSc ACA *1995;* Roys (Wroxham) Ltd, Hoveton, NORWICH, NR12 8DB.
ROY, Mr. George Cunningham, MA ACA *1984;* Chez M. Philippe Boucher, Anse des Cayes, SAINT BARTHELEMY, F-97133, GUADELOUPE.
ROY, Mr. Hitendra Nath, FCA *1960;* 656 Tubman Crescent, OTTAWA K1V 8L6, ON, CANADA. (Life Member)
ROY, Mrs. Julie Ann, BA ACA *1982;* 2 Mill Park Gardens, Mildenhall, BURY ST. EDMUNDS, SUFFOLK, IP28 7FE.
ROY, Mrs. Kate Alicia, BSc(Hons) ACA ATII *1999;* 17 Lyons Fold, SALE, CHESHIRE, M33 3GU.
ROY, Mr. Kevin, ACA *1997;* villa 12 cluster 14, jumeirah islands, dubai, DUBAI, 74207, UNITED ARAB EMIRATES.
ROY, Mr. Krishna Pada, FCA *1961;* 172 Rashbehari Avenue, Flat No 503, CALCUTTA 700029, INDIA. (Life Member)
ROY, Mrs. Mahyra, ACA *1997;* villa 12 cluster 14, DUBAI, UNITED ARAB EMIRATES.
ROY, Mr. Marcus, BA(Hons) ACA *2003;* 2 Carbery Avenue, LONDON, W3 9AL.
ROY, Mr. Niall Andrew Chisholm, FCA *1971;* Centriforce Products Ltd, 14-16 Derby Road Kirkdale, LIVERPOOL, L20 8EE.
ROY, Mr. Nikhilesh Chandra, FCA *1962;* Flat 8, No. 10 Judges Court Road, KOLKATA 700027, WEST BENGAL, INDIA.
ROY, Mr. Peter, FCA *1968;* PO Box 6911, Coffs Harbour Plaza, COFFS HARBOUR, NSW 2450, AUSTRALIA.
ROY, Mr. Pinaki Ranjan, FCA *1960;* Mangal Chhaya 5th Floor, 15th Road, Bandra West, MUMBAI 400050, MAHARASHTRA, INDIA. (Life Member)
ROY, Mr. Piyush, ACA *2011;* PO Box 4254, City Tower 2, Sheikh Zayed Road, DUBAI, 4254, UNITED ARAB EMIRATES.
ROY, Mr. Prannoy Lal, BSc FCA *1975;* NDTV, Archana Complex, W 17, Greater Kailash I, NEW DELHI 110048, INDIA.
ROY, Miss. Priyadarshini, MSc BA ACA *2011;* 33A Surrey Lane, WAPPINGERS FALLS, NY 12590, UNITED STATES.
ROY, Ms. Purbasha, MEng ACA *2002;* SSAFA Forces Help, 19 Queen Elizabeth Street, LONDON, SE1 2LP.
ROY, Mr. Robert Stewart, FCA *1974;* Sulby Edge, Mount Auldyn, Ramsey, ISLE OF MAN, IM8 3PJ. (Life Member)
ROY, Mr. Robin, BA ACA *1992;* 196 Greys Road, HENLEY-ON-THAMES, OXFORDSHIRE, RG9 1QU.
•**ROY, Mrs. Susan Jennifer Ruth, BSc FCA** *1991;* (Tax Fac), Gardiners Limited, Hutton House, Dale Road, Sheriff Hutton, YORK, YO60 6RZ.
ROY, Mr. Udayan, ACA *1997;* with Ernst & Young, (P.O. Box N3231), Sassoon House, Shirley & Victoria, NASSAU, BAHAMAS.
ROY CHOUDHURY, Mr. Jayanta, FCA *1972;* D2/2003, Vasant Kunj, NEW DELHI 110 070, INDIA.
ROY CHOUDHURY, Mrs. Sesi, ACA *2008;* 22 Hillside Crescent, NORTHWOOD, MIDDLESEX, HA6 1RW.
ROY CHOWDHURY, Mr. Sandip Narayan, FCA MBA *1992;* 74 Wise Lane, LONDON, NW7 2RG.
ROY-CHOWDHURY, Mr. Sanjay, BSc ACA *1992;* 24 St. Leonards Road, SURBITON, SURREY, KT6 4DE.
ROYAL, Mr. Adam Alexander Malcolm, ACA *2009;* 1 Colombo Square, Worsdell Drive, GATESHEAD, TYNE AND WEAR, NE8 2DF.
ROYAL, Mrs. Anne-Marie, BA ACA *2007;* Hafodneddyn, LLANDEILO, DYFED, SA19 7AE.
ROYAN, Mr. John Brent, BA ACA *1993;* Longdown Management Limited, The Estate Office, Longdown, Marchwood, SOUTHAMPTON, SO40 4UH.
ROYAN, Mrs. Tracey Elizabeth, BSc ACA *1992;* Longdown Management Ltd, The Estate Office, Longdown, Marchwood, SOUTHAMPTON, SO40 4UH.
ROYCE, Mr. Brian Vivian, FCA *1950;* 23 West Drive, Cheam, SUTTON, SM2 7NB. (Life Member)
•**ROYCE, Mr. David Lester, BA FCA** *1985;* Ernst & Young LLP, 1 More London Place, LONDON, SE1 2AF. See also Ernst & Young Europe LLP
•**ROYCE, Mr. Harry, FCA** *1960;* H. Royce, 6 Filleigh, 2 Barry Rise, Bowdon, ALTRINCHAM, CHESHIRE WA14 3JS.
ROYCE, Mrs. Mary May, FCA *1958;* 34 Glenrosa Street, Fulham, LONDON, SW6 2QZ. (Life Member)
•**ROYCE, Ms. Susan Jane, MA FCA** *1991;* Susan J Royce, Flat 29, Speed House, Barbican, LONDON, EC2Y 8AT.
ROYCHOUDHURI, Mr. Ranjit, BA ACA *1993;* 21 Mansfield Avenue, Quorn, LOUGHBOROUGH, LE12 8BD.
ROYDE, Mr. Daniel Akiba, FCA *1969;* 4 Castlefield Avenue, SALFORD, M7 4GQ.
ROYDEN, Mrs. Fiona Esther, MA ACA *1997;* 6 Vale Drive, BARNET, HERTFORDSHIRE, EN5 2ED.
ROYDS, Mrs. Hana, ACA *2001;* 19 The Smithy, Bramley, TADLEY, HAMPSHIRE, RG26 5AY.
ROYDS-JONES, Miss. Johane Elizabeth, BA ACA *2006;* 61D Whitehall Park, LONDON, N19 3TW.
ROYER, Mr. Antoine, ACA *2008;* Flat B, 40 Osborn Street, LONDON, E1 6TD.
ROYLANCE, Mrs. Celeste Karen, BA ACA *1998;* Eastington House, High Street, Iron Acton, BRISTOL, BS37 9UQ.
ROYLANCE, Mr. Jonathan Kingsley, ACA *1996;* Audit New Zealand Level 8 St Pauls Square, 45 Pipitea Street, Thorndon PO Box 99, WELLINGTON 6140, NEW ZEALAND.
•**ROYLANCE, Mr. Julian Mark, BSc ACA** *1982;* Corporate Audit Solutions, Georges Court, Chestergate, MACCLESFIELD, SK11 6DP. See also Corporate Accountancy Solutions Ltd
•**ROYLE, Mr. John Cartwright, BCom FCA** *1968;* (Tax Fac), Royles (Heaton Moor) Ltd, 18 Heaton Gardens, 25 Heaton Moor Road, STOCKPORT, CHESHIRE, SK4 4LT. See also Royles
ROYLE, Mr. John Charles, FCA *1955;* 6 Primrose Court, Primrose Valley, ST.IVES, TR26 2ED. (Life Member)
•**ROYLE, Mr. Jonathan, MA FCA** *1983;* (Tax Fac), Fitzpatrick Royle, 16 Stirling Drive, NORTH SHIELDS, NE29 8DJ.
ROYLE, Mr. Marcus, BSc(Hons) ACA *2004;* 44 Oakland Avenue, Haslington, CREWE, CW1 5PB.
•**ROYLE, Mr. Michael Saint John, BA(Hons) FCA** *1996;* Grundy Anderson & Kershaw Limited, 123-125 Union Street, OLDHAM, OL1 1TG.
ROYLE, Mrs. Sarah, BSc ACA *2006;* 34 Medbourne Road, Hallaton, MARKET HARBOROUGH, LEICESTERSHIRE, LE16 8UH.
ROYLE, Mr. Simon William, BSc ACA *1990;* Golden Properties Ltd, Suite 500, 1177 West Hastings Street, VANCOUVER V6E 2K3, BC, CANADA.
ROYNON-JONES, Mr. Robert Edward, BCom FCA *1988;* Les Buissonnets La Rue de la Hougette, St. Clement, JERSEY, JE2 6LD.
ROYOU, Ms. Jocelyne Sue, BA ACA *1993;* Sherwood House, 80 The Street, Rockland All Saints, ATTLEBOROUGH, NR17 1UX.
ROYS, Mrs. Rebecca Jayne, ACA *2010;* 46 Walsingham Road, Woodthorpe, NOTTINGHAM, NG5 4NW.
•**ROYSE, Mr. Howard William Stanley, BSc ACA** *1986;* Howard Royse Limited, 11 Warren's Way, Tacolneston, NORWICH, NR16 1DH. See also Silverghost Consultancy Ltd
ROYSTON, Mr. Allan Braid, BA(Hons) ACA *2004;* 39 Dorset Drive, BUCKSHAW VILLAGE, PR7 7DN.
ROYSTON, Mr. David Christopher Sheridan, BA ACA *1995;* Well Cottage High Street, Hawkesbury Upton, BADMINTON, AVON, GL9 1AU.
ROYSTON, Mr. David Michael, BA FCA *1991;* 18 Park Mount Avenue, Baildon, SHIPLEY, BD17 6DS.
ROYSTON, Mrs. Karen Louise, BSc ACA *1995;* Elizabethan Cottage, Brook End, Luckington, CHIPPENHAM, WILTSHIRE, SN14 6PJ.
ROYSTON, Mr. Peter Ronald, FCA *1954;* 96 Admirals Walk, West Cliff Road, BOURNEMOUTH, DORSET, BH2 5HF. (Life Member)
ROYSTON, Mr. Richard Anthony, BA FCA CPA CFE *1982;* 60 Island Avenue, MADISON, CT 06443, UNITED STATES.
ROYSTON, Mr. Richard Sykes, BA ACA *1993;* 2 Park Lane, Herongate, BRENTFORD, CM13 PPJ.
ROYSTON, Mrs. Sarah Louise, BSc ACA *2005;* 3 Plover Close, CHATTERIS, PE16 6PP.
ROZALI-WATHOOTH, Mr. Johan Ariffin, BSc ACA CFA *2004;* 11 Jalan SS19/3C, 47500 SUBANG, SELANGOR, MALAYSIA.
ROZARIO, Mr. Clive Joseph Lawrence, FCA *1959;* (Tax Fac), 14 St. Georges Drive, WESTCLIFF-ON-SEA, SS0 0SS. (Life Member)
ROZARIO, Mr. Mark Victor, BSc FCA *1990;* Ground Floor Block A Mines Waterfront Business Park, No. 3 Jalan Tasik, Mines Resort City, 43300 SERI KEMBANGAN, MALAYSIA.
ROZARIO, Miss. Michelle, BA(Hons) ACA *2011;* Top Floor Flat, 34 Bennett Park, LONDON, SE3 9RB.
ROZEN, Mr. Henri Willy, FCA *1960;* 18 Buffalo Road, Emmerentia 2195, JOHANNESBURG, SOUTH AFRICA. (Life Member)
ROZENBROEK, Mr. John, BSc ACA *1994;* Damson Cottage 49 Smithy Brow Croft, WARRINGTON, WA3 7DA.
ROZIER, Mr. David John, ACA *2010;* 20 Burford Gardens, CARDIFF, CF11 0AP.
ROZIER, Miss. Leanne Dawn, BA ACA *2007;* 42 Blake Close, WELLING, KENT, DA16 3NS.
ROZOU, Mrs. Paraskevi, BA FCA *1986;* Eilenau 106, 22089 HAMBURG, GERMANY.
•**RUANE, Mr. Denis, FCA** *1965;* C.A. Hunter & Partners, Britannia Chambers, George Street, ST. HELENS, MERSEYSIDE, WA10 1BZ.
RUANE, Mr. Edward Owen, BA ACA *1998;* 4 Elm Road, Sherborne St. John, BASINGSTOKE, HAMPSHIRE, RG24 9JL.
RUBACK, Mr. Daniel David, BSocSc ACA *2005;* Smiths Detection Inc, 2202 Lakeside Blvd, EDGEWOOD, MD 21040, UNITED STATES.
RUBACK, Mr. David Philip, MSc FCA *1975;* 54 High View, PINNER, HA5 3PB.
•**RUBACK, Mr. Sidney Martin, FCA** *1974;* (Tax Fac), SMR Business & Tax Associates Limited, 25 Woodhall Gate, PINNER, MIDDLESEX, HA5 4TN.
RUBAKUMAR, Mr. Sivasubramaniam, MEng BA ACA *2003;* (Tax Fac), 57 High Worple, HARROW, MIDDLESEX, HA2 9SX.
•**RUBENSTEIN, Mr. Raymond Alan, FCA** *1982;* (Tax Fac), Parker Cavendish, 28 Church Road, STANMORE, HA7 4XR. See also Parker Cavendish Limited
RUBERY, Mr. Ian Stewart, BA ACA *1989;* 42 Mill Hill, Baginton, COVENTRY, CV8 3AG.
RUBIDGE, Miss. Tina Michelle, BA(Hons) ACA *2001;* (Tax Fac), 20 Mayfield Road, SUTTON, SURREY, SM2 5DT.
RUBIE, Mr. Alastair Edward, FCA *1969;* 7 Doran Drive, REDHILL, RH1 6AX.
RUBIN, Mr. Daniel Robert, BA FCA *1973;* Dune London, 9 Hatton Street, LONDON, NW8 8PL.
•①**RUBIN, Mr. David Antony, FCA** *1982;* (Tax Fac), David Rubin & Partners LLP, Pearl Assurance House, 319 Ballards Lane, North Finchley, LONDON, N12 8LY. See also David Rubin & Partners
RUBIN, Mr. Leslie Reuben, FCA CTA *1961;* 11 Greenacre Walk, LONDON, N14 7DB. (Life Member)
RUBINS, Mr. Jeffrey, FCA FSI *1969;* Cairnmuir, Hargate Drive, Hale, ALTRINCHAM, CHESHIRE, WA15 0NL. (Life Member)
RUBINS, Mr. Michael Stuart, BCom ACA *1983;* 20 Alder Grove, POULTON-LE-FYLDE, LANCASHIRE, FY6 8EH.
RUBINSTEIN, Mr. Daniel, ACA *2011;* 1 Butterstile Avenue, Prestwich, MANCHESTER, M25 9JR.
•**RUBINSTEIN, Mr. Michael Jack, BSc ACA** *1985;* RWF Rubinstein, 171 Bury New Road, Whitefield, MANCHESTER, M45 6AB.
RUBNER, Mr. Nathaniel, BSc FCA *1980;* Flat 1, 20 Fitzjohns Avenue, LONDON, NW3 5NA.
RUBNER, Miss. Sally Ann, BSc ACA *1992;* Chandler Insurance Management Ltd, PO Box 1854 GT, GEORGE TOWN, GRAND CAYMAN, KY1-1110, CAYMAN ISLANDS.
RUCK, Ms. Clare Elizabeth, BA ACA *1995;* 45 Thorparch Road, LONDON, SW8 4SX.
RUCK, Mrs. Rebecca Jane, BSc ACA *1992;* Caer Ffynnon, Denbigh Road, MOLD, CH7 1BL.

RUCK KEENE, Mr. David Kenneth Lancelot, FCA *1974;* Troy, Old London Road, Ewelme, WALLINGFORD, OX10 6PY.

RUCKER, Mr. William John, BSc ACA *1987;* with Lazard, 50 Stratton Street, LONDON, W1J 8LL.

•RUCKLIDGE, Mr. James Francis, BSc FCA *1970;* (Tax Fac), Rucklidge & Co, Blakes Farm, Ashurst, STEYNING, BN44 3AN.

RUDA, Mr. Edgar Elias, BCom FCA *1950;* 158 Sandringham Drive, DOWNSVIEW M3H 1E3, ON, CANADA. (Life Member)

RUDD, Mr. Adrian Bramwell, LLB FCA *1988;* Woodside Cottage Grouse Road, Colgate, HORSHAM, WEST SUSSEX, RH13 6HT.

RUDD, Mr. Andrew Alan, BSc(Hons) ACA *2003;* 22 Nightingale Way, Butterworth Gardens, Gillibrands, CHORLEY, LANCASHIRE, PR7 2RS.

RUDD, Sir Anthony Nigel Russell, Kt FCA *1968;* Stonell, 23 Royal Scot Road, Pride Park, DERBY, DE24 8AJ.

RUDD, Mr. Brian Anthony, FCA *1971;* 40 Saltwater Avenue, NOOSAVILLE, QLD 4566, AUSTRALIA.

RUDD, Mrs. Catherine Anne, ACA *2002;* 31 Hollycroft Avenue, LONDON, NW3 7QJ.

RUDD, Mrs. Charlotte Helena, BA(Hons) ACA *2000;* 2 Amwell Lane, Wheathampstead, ST. ALBANS, AL4 8DZ.

•RUDD, Mr. Daniel John, BA(Hons) ACA *2001;* Coastal Accountants Ltd, Unit C, Oxford Court, Cambridge Road, Granby Industrial Estate, WEYMOUTH DORSET DT4 9GH. See also Daniel Rudd Associates

RUDD, Mr. Edward Thomas, BA ACA *2002;* 31 Hollycroft Avenue, LONDON, NW3 7QJ.

RUDD, Mr. Ian Harrison, BSc FCA ATII *1976;* 5 Dunholme Close, Aykley Heads, DURHAM, DH1 5WB.

RUDD, Mr. John Graham Russell, DL FCA *1966;* Hilton Lodge, Hilton, DERBY, DE65 5FP. (Life Member)

RUDD, Mr. Marcus John, ACA *1990;* The Lindens Drayton Lane Horsford, NORWICH, NR10 3AN.

•RUDD, Mr. Michael John, FCA CTA *1985;* Four Oaks Taxation & Accounting Services Limited, Suite D, Astor House, 282 Lichfield Road, SUTTON COLDFIELD, WEST MIDLANDS B74 2UG.

•RUDD, Mr. Nigel Arnold, FCA *1971;* RHP Partnership, Lancaster House, 87 Yarmouth Road, NORWICH, NORFOLK, NR7 0HF.

RUDD, Mr. Peter Jonathan, ACA *1993;* 26 Queens Road, NEWPORT, ISLE OF WIGHT, PO30 1EZ.

RUDD, Mr. Robert Walrond, FCA *1974;* 64 Ashworth Mansions, Grantully Road, Maida Vale, LONDON, W9 1LW.

•RUDD, Mr. Steven Graham, BA FCA *1996;* (Tax Fac), Larking Gowen, King Street House, 15 Upper King Street, NORWICH, NR3 1RB.

RUDD, Mr. Warren Dean, BCom ACA *2008;* 28f Thorney Crescent, LONDON, SW11 3TT.

RUDDELL, Mr. Geoffrey Frith, BA ACA *1996;* 4 Tangier Wood, TADWORTH, SURREY, KT20 6AG.

•RUDDEN, Mr. Stephen James, FCA *1978;* (Tax Fac), 206 Chesterfield Drive, Riverhead, SEVENOAKS, TN13 2EH. See also Sheppard J.B. & Co

RUDDERHAM, Mr. Keith Peter, MA ACA *1982;* 21 Craigwell Avenue, RADLETT, WD7 7ET.

RUDDICK, Miss. Ann Michelle, BSc ACA *2005;* 65 Pennine View, CARLISLE, CA1 3GX.

•RUDDICK, Mr. Brian, FCA *1973;* (Tax Fac), S.W.Frankson & Co, Bridge House, 119-123 Station Road, HAYES, MIDDLESEX, UB3 4BX.

RUDDICK, Mr. Ian William, FCA *1969;* 32 Woodend Drive, ASCOT, SL5 9BG.

RUDDICK, Mr. Jonathan, ACA CA(AUS) *2009;* Level 30 Westpac House, 91 King William Street, ADELAIDE, SA 5000, AUSTRALIA.

RUDDICK, Mrs. Kelly, BSc ACA *2005;* 4 Turstin Drive, FLEET, HAMPSHIRE, GU51 1GF.

RUDDICK, Mr. Neil Jon, BA ACA *2006;* 4 Turstin Drive, FLEET, HAMPSHIRE, GU51 1GF.

RUDDLE, Mr. Guy Reginald, ACA CA(SA) *2010;* 46 Buttermere Drive, LONDON, SW15 2HW.

RUDDOCK, Miss. Carol Henrietta Grevile, BSc FCA *1977;* 40 Spencer Road, Strawberry Hill, TWICKENHAM, TW2 5TQ.

RUDDOCK, Mr. Geoffrey John, FCA *1969;* 10 Vimiera Close Brockhill Village Norton, WORCESTER, WR5 2QP.

RUDDOCK, Mr. Ian Edwin, BSc ACA CF *1992;* River Cottage, Deans Mill, Ardingly Road, Lindfield, HAYWARDS HEATH, WEST SUSSEX RH16 2QY.

RUDDOCK, Mr. Jon Paul, BA ACA *2006;* 24 Hemming Way, NORWICH, NR3 2AF.

•RUDDOCK, Mr. Paul Geoffrey, FCA *1972;* (Tax Fac), with HWEA Ltd, 8 Hopper Way, Diss Business Park, DISS, NORFOLK, IP22 4GT.

RUDDOCK, Mrs. Sarah Margaret, BA ACA *1992;* (Tax Fac), Flat 180, 9 Albert Embankment, LONDON, SE1 7HG.

•RUDDOCK-BROYD, Mr. James Grevile, FCA *1960;* James G Ruddock-Broyd, 2 Mayfield Lodge, 28 Brackley Road, BECKENHAM, KENT, BR3 1RQ.

RUDDUCK, Mr. Mark Jeremy, BSc ACA *1992;* 12 Douglas Road, HARPENDEN, HERTFORDSHIRE, AL5 2EW.

RUDDY, Mrs. Alexandra Kirsty, LLB ACA *2003;* Unit 6, Fremont Perle, La Route Du Mont Mado, St. John, JERSEY, JE3 4DN.

RUDDY, Mr. Andrew Ian, BSc ACA *2001;* Unit 6, Fremont Perle, La Route Du Mont Mado, St. John, JERSEY, JE3 4DN.

RUDDY, Mrs. Clare Mary, BSc ACA *1996;* 11 Seafields, Warrenpoint, NEWRY, COUNTY DOWN, BT34 3TG.

•RUDDY, Mr. John Michael, FCA *1966;* (Tax Fac), J.M. Ruddy, Long Acre, Pattingham, WOLVERHAMPTON, WV6 7AD.

RUDDY, Mr. Sean, FCA *1981;* 137 Coppice Drive, Parklands, NORTHAMPTON, NN3 6NQ.

RUDEBECK, Mr. Howard Alan, FCA *1970;* Beedon House, Beedon, NEWBURY, rg20 8sw.

RUDEBECK, Mr. Victor, ACA *2010;* F T I Consulting, 322 High Holborn, LONDON, WC1V 7PB.

RUDERHAM, Mr. Gradleigh Talbot, BSc(Hons) ACA *2001;* 57 Roth Walk, LONDON, N7 7RJ.

RUDGE, Mr. Andrew Charles, BSc ACA *1993;* Basement Flat, 46 Wilbury Road, HOVE, EAST SUSSEX, BN3 3PA.

•RUDGE, Mrs. Carol Anne, BSc FCA *1987;* Grant Thornton UK LLP, Grant Thornton House, 22 Melton Street, Euston Square, LONDON, NW1 2EP. See also Grant Thornton LLP

RUDGE, Mr. Christopher, BSc ACA *2011;* 2 Edinburgh Road, Keadby, SCUNTHORPE, SOUTH HUMBERSIDE, DN17 3DN.

RUDGE, Mr. Christopher John, ACA *1979;* Cemetery Lodge Lincoln Hill, Ironbridge, TELFORD, SHROPSHIRE, TF8 7NY.

•RUDGE, Mr. John Foster, FCA *1967;* Summerhayes, Compass House, 6 Billetfield, TAUNTON, SOMERSET, TA1 3NN.

RUDGE, Mr. Jonathan Harold, MA FCA *1974;* 20 Blackthorne Close, SOLIHULL, B91 1PF.

RUDGE, Mrs. Kate, ACA *2011;* St. Edwards School, Woodstock Road, Summertown, OXFORD, OX2 7NN.

RUDGE, Miss. Madeleine Emily, ACA *2009;* Finning International Inc, 1000-666 Burrard Street, VANCOUVER V6E 1P2, BC, CANADA.

•RUDGE, Mr. Malcolm Arthur, FCA *1973;* (Tax Fac), 18 Baldwin Way, Swindon, DUDLEY, DY3 4PF.

•RUDGE, Mr. Paul Anthony, BSc FCA *1988;* (Tax Fac), Rudge & Co Ltd, Bordesley Hall, The Holloway, Alvechurch, BIRMINGHAM, B48 7QA. See also Reginald J Coade & Co Limited

RUDGE, Dr. Peter Jay, PhD MEng ACA *2007;* 19 Holmwood Crescent, LEEDS, LS6 4NL.

RUDGE, Mr. Peter John Harrington, FCA *1957;* Flat 5 Milieu, 371 Lonsdale Road, LONDON, SW13 9PY. (Life Member)

RUDGE, Mrs. Sarah Jane, BSc ACA *2003;* 58 Maney Hill Road, SUTTON COLDFIELD, WEST MIDLANDS, B72 1JS.

RUDGE, Mr. Stanley Bickerton, FCA *1964;* 19 Murdoch Road, WOKINGHAM, RG40 2DQ. (Life Member)

RUDGE, Mr. William Bickerton, BSc ACA *2003;* 51a Beauchamp Road, LONDON, SW11 1PG.

RUDICH, Mr. Daniel Yehudi, BSc ACA *2005;* (Tax Fac), Hassans, International Law Firm, 57/63 Line Wall Road, P.O. Box 199, GIBRALTAR, GIBRALTAR.

RUDKIN, Dr. Christopher Julian, PhD BSc ACA *2005;* Third Floor Bldg 200, British Petroleum Co Plc, Chertsey Road, SUNBURY-ON-THAMES, MIDDLESEX, TW16 7LN.

RUDKIN, Mrs. Deborah, MA ACA *1999;* Hereford House, Hereford Street, BOLTON, BL1 8JB.

RUDKIN, Mr. John Gordon, BA ACA *1994;* Flat 8 Tradewind Heights, 167 Rotherhithe Street, LONDON, SE16 5GW.

RUDKIN, Mr. Kevin John, ACA *1984;* Capel Court Plc, 1 Balkerne Hill, COLCHESTER, CO3 3FG.

RUDKIN, Mr. Thomas John, BSc ACA *1999;* 8 Eversley Road, MANCHESTER, M20 2FG.

RUDKINS, Mr. Ian Frederick, BSc FCA *1988;* 14 Upland Road, BILLERICAY, CM12 0JP.

RUDLAND, Mr. Terence John, FCA *1977;* Watson & Hillhouse Ltd, 51 White House Road, IPSWICH, IP1 5NT.

RUDLING, Miss. Patricia Ann, BA ACA *1989;* 4 Durdham Park, Redland, BRISTOL, BS6 6XA.

•RUDLOFF, Mr. Grant Adrian, FCA *1998;* Auker Rhodes Professional Services LLP, Sapphire House, Albion Road, Greengates, BRADFORD, WEST YORKSHIRE BD10 9TQ. See also Auker Rhodes Tax & Financial Planning Ltd

RUDMAN, Mr. Austin Alan Henry, BSc ACA *1995;* Ernst & Young, P.O. Box 140, MANAMA, BAHRAIN.

RUDMAN, Mr. Brian Reginald, FCA *1956;* 4 Churchfields Drive, Bovey Tracey, NEWTON ABBOT, TQ13 9RU. (Life Member)

RUDMAN, Mr. John Franklin, FCA *1981;* 43 King Ina Road, SOMERTON, TA11 6LA.

RUDMAN, Mr. Philip John, BSc(Hons) ACA *2001;* 2 Whitewater Rise, HOOK, RG27 9EN.

RUDNICK, Mr. Errol Stephen, BCom ACA *1982;* Business Design Centre, 52 Upper Street, LONDON, N1 0QH.

RUDOLF, Mr. Gerald Anthony, BA FCA *1977;* Industrial Fasteners Ltd, Waterwells Drive, Waterwells Business Park, Quedgeley, GLOUCESTER, GL2 2FR.

RUDOLPH, Mrs. Frances Elizabeth, MA ACA *1994;* 7 Merton Hall Road, LONDON, SW19 3PP.

RUDOLPH, Mr. Guy Richard Giles, BSc ACA *1995;* The Coach House, Broadhayes, Stockland, HONITON, DEVON, EX14 9EL.

RUDOLPH, Mr. James Duncan, BA ACA *1993;* 7 Merton Hall Road, LONDON, SW19 3PP.

RUDOLPH, Mr. Simon de Villiers, BA ACA *1986;* Flat 25b, 127 Repulse Bay Road, REPULSE BAY, Hong Kong Island, HONG KONG SAR.

RUDRUM, Mrs. Gemma Jane, BA ACA *2004;* 20 Bowden Close, Coombe Dingle, BRISTOL, BS9 2RW.

RUDZINSKI, Mr. Alexander Peter Marek, BCom ACA *1999;* 6 Chantry Road, Moseley, BIRMINGHAM, B13 8DW.

RUELL, Mr. Christopher John William, BSc ACA *1999;* 322 Midtown, High Holborn, LONDON, WC1V 7PB.

RUELLAN, Miss. Samantha Jayne Anne, LLB(Hons) ACA *1999;* La Chenais, 3 La Ville Des Chenes, St. John, JERSEY, JE3 4BG.

RUELLE, Mr. Paul John, BSc ACA *1995;* 7 Heol y Brenin, PENARTH, SOUTH GLAMORGAN, CF64 3HR.

RUELLE, Mrs. Yvonne Michelle, BSc ACA *1993;* 7 Heol y Brenin, PENARTH, SOUTH GLAMORGAN, CF64 3HR.

RUFF, Mr. Cameron Robert William, FCA *1998;* 4 West Hill, EPSOM, SURREY, KT19 8HR.

RUFFLE, Mr. Adrian Christopher, FCA *1968;* 41 Wood Ride, Petts Wood, ORPINGTON, BR5 1QA.

RUFFLE, Mr. Brian Dudley, FCA *1958;* Binnenkruierstraat 16, 1911 XL UITGEEST, NETHERLANDS. (Life Member)

•RUFFLE, Mr. David, FCA *1973;* 35 The Comp, Eaton Bray, DUNSTABLE, LU6 2DH.

RUFFLE, Mr. John Cousins, BA ACA *2003;* Virgin Atlantic Airways Ltd The Office, Manor Royal, CRAWLEY, WEST SUSSEX, RH10 9NU.

RUFFLE, Mrs. Josie Anna, BSc(Hons) ACA *2001;* with Deloitte LLP, 2 New Street Square, LONDON, EC4A 3BZ.

•RUFFLES, Mr. Mark John, BA FCA *1985;* Mark J Ruffles & Co, 4 Baron Court, Werrington, PETERBOROUGH, PE4 7ZE.

RUFFLES, Miss. Suzannah Elizabeth, MMath ACA *2007;* Baker Street Entertainment Ltd, 25 Weymouth Street, LONDON, W1G 7BP.

•RUFFONI, Mr. Peter Conrad, FCA *1984;* (Tax Fac), Conrad Ruffoni, Suite 14, Kent House, Old Bexley Business Park, 19 Bourne Road, BEXLEY KENT DA5 1LR.

RUFFY, Mr. Maurice James, FCA *1962;* 27 Conifers, WEYBRIDGE, KT13 9TJ.

RUGG, Mr. Robin John, FCA *1957;* 1300 Maple Ridge, SAINT-LAZARE J7T 2K9, QUE, CANADA. (Life Member)

•RUGGLES, Miss. Amanda Jane, BSc FCA *1999;* Gilberts, Pendragon House, 65 London Road, ST. ALBANS, AL1 1LJ.

RUGGLES, Mr. David Sidney, FCA *1969;* 17 Roedich Drive, Taverham, NORWICH, NR8 6RB.

RUGHANI, Mr. Mehul Chandulal, BA ACA *2002;* 20 Audley Gardens, ILFORD, IG3 9LB.

RUGHANI, Miss. Seema, BA ACA *1992;* (Tax Fac), 122b Trent Gardens, Southgate, LONDON, N14 4QG.

RUGHANI, Ms. Sophie R, BA FCA AMCT *1993;* 26 Hillcrest Road, LOUGHTON, ESSEX, IG10 4QQ.

RUGHWANI, Miss. Reshma, MA ACA *1994;* 205 West End Avenue, Apt 27P, NEW YORK, NY 10023, UNITED STATES.

RUGMAN, Mr. Francis Michael Barclay, FCA *1967;* 7 St. Martin's Road, LONDON, SW9 0SP. (Life Member)

RUGMAN, Ms. Jennifer Ann, BA ACA *1986;* Hollybank, Seal Hollow Road, SEVENOAKS, TN13 3RZ.

RUIA, Mr. Anil Kumar, LLB ACA *1980;* Botraco Limited, 1 Mayfair Mews, Mersey Road, Didsbury, MANCHESTER, M20 2JX.

RUIA, Miss. Nikita, ACA *2011;* Flat 4, Winsley Court, 37 Portland Place, LONDON, W1B 1QG.

RUIZ, Mr. George Walter, ACA *1995;* 95 Inderwick Road, Crouch End, LONDON, N8 9LA.

•RUIZ, Mr. Paul Christopher Raymond, BSc ACA *1990;* KPMG, 10 Shelley Street, SYDNEY, NSW 2000, AUSTRALIA.

RUIZ, Mrs. Tracy, BA ACA *1995;* 9 Balmeg Hill, The Peak at Balmeg No 3-13, SINGAPORE 119916, SINGAPORE.

RUKAVINA, Mrs. Robyn Mary McCombe, BSc ACA *1998;* 85a Leigham Court Road, LONDON, SW16 2NR.

RUKSKUL, Miss. Kakai, BSc ACA *1980;* 907AChina Merchants Tower, Shun Tak Centre, 168-200 Connaught Road, CENTRAL, HONG KONG SAR.

RULE, Mr. Benjamin Rupert, ACA *2008;* Flat 3, 2-5 Denton Street, LONDON, SW18 2JR.

•RULE, Mr. Daniel, MA BBS ACA *2002;* McCambridge Duffy LLP, Templemore Business Park, Northland Road, Derry, LONDONDERRY, BT48 0LD. See also McCambridge Duffy

RULE, Mrs. Emma Louise, ACA *2006;* 23 Cedar Road, PAIGNTON, DEVON, TQ3 2DB.

RULE, Mr. John Eric, FCA *1957;* 24 Swallowfield Park, Swallowfield, READING, RG7 1TG. (Life Member)

RULE, Mrs. Lindsay Dawn, MA ACA *2006;* (Tax Fac), Compass Centre, Nelson Road, HOUNSLOW, MIDDLESEX, TW6 2GW.

•RULE, Mr. Michael, FCA *1979;* Moore Stephens (South) LLP, The French Quarter, 114 High Street, SOUTHAMPTON, HAMPSHIRE, SO14 2AA.

RULEMAN, Mrs. Gillian, BA ACA *1984;* 17 Crossfield Drive, Worsley, MANCHESTER, M28 1GP.

RULTEN, Miss. Claire Ann, BSc ACA *1992;* (Tax Fac), 94 Cowley Road, Mortlake, LONDON, SW14 8QB.

RULTON, Ms. Taryn Ella Frances, BSc ACA *2005;* 375 Manningham Road, DONCASTER, VIC 3108, AUSTRALIA.

RUMBELOW, Mrs. Amanda Doreen, BA ACA *1983;* 9 Richmond Court, WISBECH, PE13 1LR.

RUMBLE, Mr. Jonathan James, ACA *2007;* 24 Canterbury Way, NUNEATON, CV11 6FY.

RUMBLE, Mr. Mark Colin, BA FCA *1996;* 34 Park Way, LONDON, N20 0XP.

RUMBLE, Mr. Michael Douglas, BA ACA *1980;* 94a Purley Downs Road, SOUTH CROYDON, Surrey, CR2 0RB.

RUMBLE, Ms. Paige Ellen, MA ACA CFE *1990;* Financial Reporting Council Aldwych House, 71-91 Aldwych, LONDON, WC2B 4HN.

RUMBLES, Mrs. Anne, BSc ACA *1978;* 11 Brook End Close, Henley in Arden, SOLIHULL, B95 5JE.

RUMBLOW, Miss. Kirsty, ACA *2009;* 36 Mill Gate, Ackworth, PONTEFRACT, WEST YORKSHIRE, WF7 7PQ.

RUMBOLD, Mr. Charles Anton, BA ACA *1986;* Barclays Capital, 745 Seventh Avenue, NEW YORK, NY 10019, UNITED STATES.

RUMBOLL, Mr. Christopher Richard, ACA *2001;* 39 Redgrave Road, LONDON, SW15 1PX.

RUMBOLL, Mr. Robin Ernest Richard, FCA *1965;* Windsor House, St. Lawrence, JERSEY, JE3 1NL.

RUMFORD, Miss. Tarita Marie Rebekah, BSc(Hons) ACA *2003;* 12 Parsonage Street, CAMBRIDGE, CB5 8DN.

RUMGAY, Mr. Jock Andrew Hugh, BA ACA *1996;* 11 Mordaunt Street, Brixton, LONDON, SW9 9RD.

RUMINS, Mr. John Sandford, BA FCA *1959;* 3 Lyle Park, SEVENOAKS, TN13 3JX. (Life Member)

RUMLEY, Mrs. Bridget Vivien, FCA *1991;* Lime Kiln Farm, Tilden Chapel Lane, Smarden, ASHFORD, KENT, TN27 8QN.

RUMLEY, Mr. James George Gary Jan, BSc ACA *1994;* 2 Hampden Road, Flitwick, BEDFORD, MK45 1HX.

RUMLEY, Mr. John Eric, BSc ACA *1994;* 5 Middle Lane, TEDDINGTON, MIDDLESEX, TW11 0HQ.

•RUMMINGS, Mr. Neil John, BSc(Econ) ACA *2000;* with PricewaterhouseCoopers LLP, One Kingsway, CARDIFF, CF10 3PW.

•RUMMINS, Mr. Julian Philip, BA FCA *1987;* Littlejohn LLP, 1 Westferry Circus, Canary Wharf, LONDON, E14 4HD.

RUMMINS, Mr. Mark Adam, BSc ACA *1998;* Flat 5, Edenthorpe Lodge, 7 St. Johns Road, EASTBOURNE, EAST SUSSEX, BN20 7JA.
RUMP, Mr. Gerard Alexander, BSc ACA *1992;* Baetenburg 93, 1852 TT HEILOO, NETHERLANDS.
•**RUMPH, Mr. Alan, FCA** *1968;* (Tax Fac), Alan Rumph & Co, Jubilee House, Altcar Road, Formby, LIVERPOOL, L37 8DL.
RUMSAM, Mr. Robin Bruce, FCA *1975;* 56 Purlieu Way, Theydon Bois, EPPING, CM16 7EH.
RUMSEY, Mrs. Carole, BA ACA MCT *1987;* International Power Senator House, 85 Queen Victoria Street, LONDON, EC4V 4DP.
RUMSEY, Mr. David William, BSc ACA *1989;* Brambles, Sorrell Green, Wyverstone, STOWMARKET, IP14 4TS.
•**RUMSEY, Mrs. Helen Rachel, BSc ACA** *1998;* Helen Rumsey, 18 Plough Close, DAVENTRY, NORTHAMPTONSHIRE, NN11 0NX.
•**RUMSEY, Mrs. Helen Selena, FCA DChA** *1990;* Ensors, Cardinal House, 46 St Nicholas Street, IPSWICH, IP1 1TT.
RUMSEY, Mr. Michael, BSc ACA *1986;* 10 Farrer Road #08-05, Waterfall Gardens, SINGAPORE 268822, SINGAPORE.
RUMUN, Mrs. Malgorzata, BSc ACA *1991;* Greenford Depot, Greenford Rd, GREENFORD, MIDDLESEX, UB6 9AP.
RUNACRES, Mr. Peter, BA ACA *1998;* 95 Alexandra Avenue, SOUTH YARRA, VIC 3141, AUSTRALIA.
•**RUNACRES, Mr. Peter George, FCA ACMA** *1966;* 8 Waldegrave Road, BROMLEY, BR1 2JP.
RUNC, Mrs. Carolyn Ann, FCA *1969;* Vice-Chancellor's Office Building 41, Cranfield University College Road, Cranfield, BEDFORD, MK43 0AL.
RUNCIE, Mr. Simon Alexander, BSc ACA *1998;* Flat 3 Torri Katur, Triq In-Nemes, SWIEQI, MALTA.
RUNDELL, Mr. Ian, BA ACA *1999;* (Tax Fac), 140 Bishops Road, LONDON, SW6 7AS.
RUNDELL, Mr. Paul Frederick, BA FCA MCT *1978;* 35 Baring Road, BEACONSFIELD, BUCKINGHAMSHIRE, HP9 2NB.
RUNDELL, Miss. Rebecca Lydia Joy, MA ACA *2010;* 35 Baring Road, BEACONSFIELD, BUCKINGHAMSHIRE, HP9 2NB.
RUNDLE, Mr. David Christopher, MA ACA *2005;* Fidelity Investments Ltd Beech Gate, Millfield Lane Lower Kingswood, TADWORTH, SURREY, KT20 6RP.
RUNDLE, Mr. John David, BCom ACA ATII *1989;* (Tax Fac), 15 Highcroft, Claverdon, WARWICK, CV35 8LH.
RUNDLE, Mr. Jonathan Michael, BA(Hons) ACA *2001;* 41 Exe Vale Road, EXETER, DEVON, EX2 6LF.
RUNDLE, Mr. Mark Christopher, BSc ACA *1981;* Bankfield House, 41 Lanner Hill, Lanner, REDRUTH, CORNWALL, TR16 6DB.
RUNDLE, Mr. Phillip Wayne, FCA ACA *1987;* Benson Partners, 14 Audrey Crescent, GLEN IRIS, VIC 3146, AUSTRALIA. See also Moore Stephens
RUNDLE, Mrs. Sheila, BSc(Hons) FCA *2001;* 23 Kirkwood Drive, DURHAM, DH1 4FF.
RUNDLE-EDWARDS, Mrs. Alison Morwenna, BSc ACA *2007;* Pentire House, 5 Burghley Court, Winterbourne, BRISTOL, BS36 1LR.
RUNHAM, Miss. Jayne Elizabeth, BA ACA *1989;* 22 Alnwick Road, Bloxwich, WALSALL, WS3 3XD.
RUNNACLES, Mr. Matthew Robert, BEng ACA *1998;* 10 Waddling Lane, Wheathampstead, ST. ALBANS, HERTFORDSHIRE, AL4 8FD.
•**RUNNACLES, Mr. Stephen Murray, FCA** *1980;* Ensors, Cardinal House, 46 St Nicholas Street, IPSWICH, IP1 1TT.
RUNNALLS, Mr. Adam, BA(Hons) ACA *2011;* 128 Sunnymead Avenue, GILLINGHAM, ME7 2EB.
RUNNEGAR, Mr. Antony James, BSc ACA *1996;* (Tax Fac), 48 Wertheim Way, HUNTINGDON, PE29 6UX.
RUNTON, Mrs. Dainylle Marie, BCom ACA *1992;* The Stables, Great Chatwell House Barns, Great Chatwell, NEWPORT, SHROPSHIRE, TF10 9BJ.
RUOCCO, Mr. Carlo Michael, BA ACA *1985;* 200 West 60th Street, Apt 9F, NEW YORK, NY 10023, UNITED STATES.
RUOCCO, Miss. Frances Luisa, BA ACA *2010;* 7/80 Murdoch Street, CREMORNE, NSW 2090, AUSTRALIA.
RUOCCO, Mr. Paul George, BSc FCA *1981;* Ashleigh, 56 The Avenue, SALE, CHESHIRE, M33 4QA.
RUOCCO, Mr. Salvatore, BSocSc ACA *2005;* (Tax Fac), 17 Manor Drive, ESHER, KT10 0AU.
•**RUPAL, Mr. Raj Gopal, BSc FCA** *1980;* (Tax Fac), R.G. Rupal Ltd, 30 Fernhall Drive, ILFORD, IG4 5BW.
RUPALL, Mr. Tarlochan Singh, BSc ACA *1985;* BNP Paribas, 787 Seventh Ave, NEW YORK, NY NY 10019, UNITED STATES.
RUPANGA, Mr. Masimba Shingai, ACA CA(SA) *2011;* 50 Chancelot Road, Abbey Wood, LONDON, SE2 0ND.
RUPANI, Mr. Rajen Dhirajlal, ACA *1984;* 1 Eastglade, Eastbury Avenue, NORTHWOOD, MIDDLESEX, HA6 3LD.
RUPANI, Mr. Rajesh Dhirajlal, ACA *1978;* 98 Shaftesbury Avenue, Kenton, HARROW, MIDDLESEX, HA3 0RE.
RUPANI, Mr. Ruchir, BA ACA *2010;* 111a Manchester Road, WILMSLOW, SK9 2JH.
•**RUPAREL, Mr. Ravi, BSc FCA** *1998;* Counting Tree Limited, 118 Massingberd Way, LONDON, SW17 6AH.
RUPARELIA, Miss. Deepa, ACA *2009;* 5 The Gateway, WATFORD, WD18 7HW.
RUPARELIA, Mr. Rishit, BA(Hons) ACA *2001;* 31 Bishop Ramsey Close, RUISLIP, MIDDLESEX, HA4 8GY.
•**RUPARELLIA, Mr. Sachin Prabhudas, ACA FCCA** *2009;* MCT Partnership, 1 Warner House, Harrovian Business Village, Bessborough Road, HARROW, HA1 3EX.
•**RUPP, Mr. Christopher David, FCA** *1972;* (Tax Fac), Rupp & Fraser, 7 St. Paul's Road, NEWTON ABBOT, TQ12 2HP.
RUPP, Mr. Peter Martin, BSc FCA *1993;* Deloitte Touche Tohmatsu, Woodside Plaza Level 14, 240 St Georges Terrace, PERTH, WA 6000, AUSTRALIA.
RUPPING, Mr. Johannes Gerhardus, ACA CA(SA) *2011;* Re10(UK) plc, Albemarle House, 1 Albemarle Street, LONDON, W1S 4HA.
RUSBY, Mr. Peter Grenville, BSc ACA *1979;* Chapel House Farm, Grindlow, Great Hucklow, BUXTON, SK17 8RJ.
RUSBY, Mr. Timothy John, BA FCA *1984;* Flat 2, Grosvenor Lodge, 980 High Road, LONDON, N20 0QG.
RUSBY, Mr. William Mitchell, BA(Econ) FCA *1970;* 28 Brookmill Close, Colwall, MALVERN, WR13 6HY.
RUSCH, Mr. Henry Maximilian, BSc ACA *1984;* 161 Station Road Earl Shilton, LEICESTER, LE9 7GF.
RUSCOE, Mr. Antony Myles, BA FCA *1965;* 21 Sycamore Close, Endmoor, KENDAL, LA8 0NY. (Life Member)
RUSCOE, Mr. Peter Alan, FCA *1969;* Bryn Tirion, 44 Church Walks, LLANDUDNO, GWYNEDD, LL30 2HL.
•**RUSDEN, Mr. Clive Melville, FCA** *1983;* Christchurch Accountants LLP, 3 The Paddock, 73a Mudeford, CHRISTCHURCH, DORSET, BH23 3NJ.
RUSDEN, Mrs. Heather Jane, BSc ACA *1991;* Hestow Barton, Ideford, Chudleigh, NEWTON ABBOT, DEVON, TQ13 0BH.
•**RUSDEN, Mrs. Saron Rowena, FCA** *1983;* Saron Rusden, 3 The Paddock, 73a Mudeford, CHRISTCHURCH, BH23 3NJ. See also Christchurch Accountants LLP
RUSE, Mr. Brian Edward, FCA *1967;* Flat 3, Montague Mansions, 3 Victoria Quadrant, WESTON-SUPER-MARE, SOMERSET, BS23 2QB.
•**RUSE, Mr. Clive John, BSc ACA** *1985;* Stephenson Harwood, 1 Finsbury Circus, LONDON, EC2M 7SH.
RUSH, Mrs. Alison Clare, BA ACA *1995;* Rymer Farm, Barnham, THETFORD, IP24 2PP.
RUSH, Mrs. Amanda, BEd ACA *1994;* Three Oaks, Kew Lane, Bursledon, SOUTHAMPTON, SO31 8DD.
RUSH, Mr. Charles Jocelyn, MSc BA ACA *2009;* 63 New Road, WOODSTOCK, OXFORDSHIRE, OX20 1PA.
•**RUSH, Mr. David James, ACA** *1995;* Deloitte LLP, Hill House, 1 Little New Street, LONDON, EC4A 3TR. See also Deloitte & Touche LLP
RUSH, Mrs. Lesley, ACA *1990;* 20 Glenda Crescent, New Costessey, NORWICH, NR5 0AZ.
RUSH, Miss. Lucianne Emma, BA ACA ACCA *1998;* 1 Beverston, TETBURY, GLOUCESTERSHIRE, GL8 8TT.
RUSH, Mr. Peter David, MA ACA *1997;* Harrods Ltd, Grant Way, Syon Lane, ISLEWORTH, TW7 5QD.
RUSH, Mr. Peter Joyce, FCA *1955;* Ford Lane Barn, Troutbeck, WINDERMERE, LA23 1LB. (Life Member)
RUSH, Mrs. Sarah, BSc ACA *2003;* Mole End Moreton Close, Churt, FARNHAM, GU10 2JP.
•**RUSH, Mr. Timothy James, BSc ACA** *1998;* with KPMG LLP, 15 Canada Square, LONDON, E14 5GL.
RUSHBROOKE, Mr. Anthony Philip, FCA *1963;* Lady Park, Burrator Road, Dousland, YELVERTON, DEVON, PL20 6NF.
RUSHBROOKE, Miss. Rachel Claire, BA(Hons) ACA *2011;* 6 Acre Road, Cowling, KEIGHLEY, WEST YORKSHIRE, BD22 0FN.
RUSHBY, Miss. Carol Anne, ACA *1984;* 117 Spencer Road, MOSMAN, NSW 2088, AUSTRALIA.
RUSHBY, Mr. Colin Bruce, FCA *1975;* Apple Trees, 14 Landguard Manor Road, SHANKLIN, ISLE OF WIGHT, PO37 7HZ.
RUSHBY, Mr. Ian Leslie, BSc FCA *1974;* B P Plc, 1 St. James's Square, LONDON, SW1Y 4PD.
RUSHBY, Mr. John Andrew, BA ACA *1994;* 1 The Coppice, Tonteg, PONTYPRIDD, CF38 1TH.
•**RUSHD, Mr. Asad Ali, FCA** *1976;* (Tax Fac), Asad A. Rushd & Co, 74 Walton Road, HARROW, HA1 4UU.
RUSHDEN, Mrs. Nicola Jane, BA FCA DChA *1992;* Susan Field Chartered Accountant, 70 Royal Hill, LONDON, SE10 8RF.
RUSHE, Mrs. Rachel Clare, BA ACA *1998;* 4 Silwood Close, WINCHESTER, SO22 6EN.
•**RUSHEN, Mr. John William, FCA** *1978;* Wayside, Kings Copse Road, Blackfield, SOUTHAMPTON, SO45 1XF.
•**RUSHEN, Mr. Keith Douglas, MA FCA CTA** *1984;* (Tax Fac), Robinson Rushen, 47 Queen Anne Street, LONDON, W1G 9JG.
RUSHENT, Mr. Paul Julian, BA ACA *1983;* 11 Cogdean Way, Corfe Mullen, WIMBORNE, BH21 3XD.
RUSHTON, Mr. Christopher Charles St John, BA FCA *1979;* (Tax Fac), with KPMG LLP, 15 Canada Square, LONDON, E14 5GL.
RUSHTON, Mr. Christopher John, FCA *1971;* 34 Woodside, HARROGATE, NORTH YORKSHIRE, HG1 5NG.
RUSHTON, Mr. David Steven, BSc ACA *1993;* 28 Christchurch Hill, LONDON, NW3 1JL.
RUSHTON, Miss. Elizabeth Jane, BA ACA *2005;* with BDO LLP, 55 Baker Street, LONDON, W1U 7EU.
RUSHTON, Mr. Frederick Neil, FCA *1963;* Andalucia 175, San Borja, LIMA, 44, PERU.
RUSHTON, Mr. James Keith, BA FCA *1993;* 3 Holme View Park, Upperthong, HOLMFIRTH, HD9 3HS.
•**RUSHTON, Mr. James Stuart, BSc FCA** *1990;* Baker Tilly Tax & Advisory Services LLP, Festival Way, Festival Park, STOKE-ON-TRENT, ST1 5BB. See also Baker Tilly UK Audit LLP
RUSHTON, Mrs. Joanne Frances Louise, BA ACA *1993;* 54 New Street, ALTRINCHAM, WA14 2QP.
•**RUSHTON, Mr. John Richard Albert, MA FCA** *1984;* 28 Park Avenue, SALE, CHESHIRE, M33 6HE.
RUSHTON, Mrs. Karen Elizabeth, BA ACA *1992;* Rectory Cottage, 1 Resthaven Road, Wootton, NORTHAMPTON, NN4 6LR.
RUSHTON, Mrs. Kathleen Ann, BA(Econ) ACA *1997;* Kaplan Financial St. James Buildings, 79 Oxford Street, MANCHESTER, M1 6FQ.
RUSHTON, Mrs. Kathryn Elizabeth, BSc ACA *2004;* with PricewaterhouseCoopers LLP, 80 Strand, LONDON, WC2R 0AF.
RUSHTON, Mr. Michael James, MEng ACA *1997;* 84 Wylde Green Road, SUTTON COLDFIELD, B72 1HH.
RUSHTON, Mr. Michael John, BSc FCA *1992;* Rectory Cottage 1 Resthaven Road Wootton, NORTHAMPTON, NN4 6LR.
RUSHTON, Mr. Paul, BA ACA *2000;* 9 Lazell Gardens, BETCHWORTH, RH3 7BF.
•**RUSHTON, Mr. Peter Shaun, BA FCA** *1995;* (Tax Fac), The Accounts Company.Com Ltd, Unit 1 City Point, 156 Chapel Street, MANCHESTER, M3 6BF. See also Taxassist Direct Manchester
RUSHTON, Mr. Richard Alan, FCA *1962;* 19 Queens Road, Hale, ALTRINCHAM, CHESHIRE, WA15 9HF.
RUSHTON, Mr. Ronald Frederick, FCA *1964;* 5 Winsfield Rd, Hazel Grove, STOCKPORT, SK7 6ES.
RUSHTON, Mrs. Sally Elizabeth Anne, BSc ACA *1996;* 41 St Johns Park, Blackheath, LONDON, SE3 7JW.
RUSHTON, Mrs. Shella, BSc FCA *1985;* Luccombe, Old Long Grove, Seer Green, BEACONSFIELD, BUCKINGHAMSHIRE, HP9 2QH.
RUSHTON, Mr. Stephen Mark, BSc ACA *1995;* SCOFF Food Ltd Unit 5, Kingston Garden Services Unit 5, The Ashway Centre Elm Crescent, KINGSTON UPON THAMES, SURREY, KT2 6HH.
RUSHTON, Mrs. Victoria Elaine, LLB ACA *2001;* High Street, TONBRIDGE, KENT, TN9 1JP.
RUSHTON, Mr. Wayne, ACA *2003;* 27/125 Wellington Street, PERTH, WA 6004, AUSTRALIA.
RUSHTON, Miss. Wendy Maureen Shirley, BSc FCA *1977;* 7 Kenworthy Lane, Northenden, MANCHESTER, M22 4FJ.
RUSHTON-TURNER, Mr. John Martin, LLB ACA *1990;* (Tax Fac), 4 The Gables, Vale of Health, LONDON, NW3 1AY.
RUSHWORTH, Mrs. Anne Louise, BSc ACA *1993;* D B M T Ltd, Crown House, 151 High Road, LOUGHTON, ESSEX, IG10 4LF.
RUSHWORTH, Mr. Martin William Forster, ACA *1983;* 7 Braeside Gardens, WIRRAL, CH49 6LR.
RUSHWORTH, Mr. Paul Edward, BA ACA *2007;* 6 Ivy Graham Close, MANCHESTER, M40 3AS.
RUSHWORTH, Mr. Richard Eric Lyon, FCA *1973;* 6 Lucerne Mews, LONDON, W8 4ED.
RUSHWORTH, Mr. Richard Paul, BSc ACA *1989;* EDF Energy Plc, 49 Southwark Bridge Road, LONDON, SE1 9HH.
RUSHWORTH, Mr. Stephen John, MBA FCA CTA *1983;* (Tax Fac), 5 Clarence Drive, COALVILLE, LEICESTERSHIRE, LE67 4PF.
RUSK, Mr. Simon, ACA CA(AUS) *2008;* Business Environment Group Ltd, 12 Groveland Court, LONDON, EC4M 9EH.
•**RUSKELL, Miss. Diane Jane, BSc FCA** *1990;* (Tax Fac), Ruskells Limited, The Tall House, 29a West Street, MARLOW, BUCKINGHAMSHIRE, SL7 2LS. See also Ruskells
RUSKIN, Mrs. Sandra Ann, FCA *1970;* 19 Goodwell Lea, Brancepeth, DURHAM, DH7 8EN.
RUSLING, Mr. Alan Henry, FCA *1961;* 32 Laidon Avenue, Wistaston, CREWE, CW2 6RU. (Life Member)
RUSLING, Mr. Andrew, LLB ACA *2007;* 1 Northgate Place, Northgate, HESSLE, NORTH HUMBERSIDE, HU13 9AB.
•**RUSMAN, Mr. David Jacob, BA FCA** *1975;* (Tax Fac), Cook Sutton, Tay Court, Blounts Court Road, Sonning Common, READING, RG4 9RS.
RUSS, Mr. Darren Mark, BSc ACA *1994;* Skandia Life Assurance Co Ltd, Skandia House, Portland Terrace, SOUTHAMPTON, SO14 7EJ.
RUSS, Miss. Lucy Ann, BA ACA *2009;* 4 Heysham House, 52 Park Place, CHELTENHAM, GLOUCESTERSHIRE, GL50 2RA.
RUSS, Mr. Neil Andrew, BEng ACA *1999;* Archdale House, 87 Wanlip Road, Syston, LEICESTER, LEICESTERSHIRE, LE7 1PB.
RUSSAM, Mr. Charles Michael, FCA *1970;* Brookside, 37 Tathall End, Hanslope, MILTON KEYNES, MK19 7NF.
RUSSAM, Mr. John Michael, FCA *1954;* 33 Dominion Avenue, LEEDS, LS7 4NW. (Life Member)
RUSSE, Mr. Anthony James, BA(Hons) CertBibSt FCA *1957;* 22 Beaumont Close, WESTON-SUPER-MARE, BS23 4LL. (Life Member)
RUSSEL-FISHER, Mr. Robin John, BA ACA *1984;* South End House, 10 West Rd, Bowdon, ALTRINCHAM, WA14 2LA.
RUSSELL, Mr. Adam Christopher, ACA *2007;* Brookfield Main Road, Ballaugh, ISLE OF MAN, IM7 5EQ.
RUSSELL, Mrs. Adele Kate, BA(Hons) ACA *2010;* 58b Beulah Road, LONDON, E17 9LQ.
RUSSELL, Mr. Alan John, BA ACA *1998;* Inchcape Shipping Services Unit 5a-8 Retail Park, Fleming Road Chafford Hundred, GRAYS, RM16 6EW.
RUSSELL, Mr. Alan Roy, FCA *1969;* Baytree, Nyetimber Lane, West Chiltington, PULBOROUGH, WEST SUSSEX, RH20 2ND.
RUSSELL, Ms. Alison Helen, BMus ACA *1991;* John Muir Trust, Tower House, Station Road, PITLOCHRY, PERTHSHIRE, PH16 5AN.
RUSSELL, Mrs. Alison Lynn, BA ACA *1998;* Kenmare, Camden Park, TUNBRIDGE WELLS, TN2 5AA.
•**RUSSELL, Mr. Alistair Robert James, BA FCA** *1996;* Gibson Booth, New Court, Abbey Road North, Shepley, HUDDERSFIELD, HD8 8BJ.
•**RUSSELL, Mr. Allan, FCA** *1981;* (Tax Fac), TTR Barnes Limited, 3-5 Grange Terrace, Stockton Road, SUNDERLAND, SR2 7DG. See also TTR Barnes Financial Services Limited
RUSSELL, Mr. Allan, FCA *1963;* 18 Lapstone Gardens, Kenton, HARROW, HA3 0ED.
RUSSELL, Mr. Allan Phillip, BA ACA *1985;* 55 Manchester Road, Greenfield, OLDHAM, OL3 7ES.
RUSSELL, Mr. Andrew Christopher, BSc ACA *2004;* Ashbrook, Long Lane, Wistow, SELBY, NORTH YORKSHIRE, YO8 3FY.
•**RUSSELL, Mr. Andrew James, ACA** *1982;* Millington & Russell Limited, Sovereign House, 4 Machon Bank, SHEFFIELD, S7 1GP. See also The Tax Return Service(Sheffield) Ltd
RUSSELL, Mr. Andrew Neville, FCA *1963;* Burrswood, Hugletts Lane, HEATHFIELD, EAST SUSSEX, TN21 9BX.
RUSSELL, Mr. Andrew Paul, BSc(Hons) ACA *2000;* 66 Littleton Street, LONDON, SW18 3SY.

•RUSSELL, Mr. Andrew Ronald, BSc ACA 2007; Russell & Co Partnership LLP, Station House, Station Approach, East Horsley, LEATHERHEAD, SURREY KT24 6QX.
RUSSELL, Mrs. Angela May, BA FCA CPA 1992; 14 The Drey, Darras Hall, Ponteland, NEWCASTLE UPON TYNE, NE20 9NS.
RUSSELL, Mr. Angus Charles, ACA 1979; Westwood Court, Crooksbury Road, Tilford, FARNHAM, SURREY, GU10 2AY.
RUSSELL, Miss. Anne Fiona, MA ACA 1992; 42 Dewhurst Road, LONDON, W14 0ES.
•RUSSELL, Mr. Barry John, ACA 1984; The Old Vicarage, Down Ampney, CIRENCESTER, GLOUCESTERSHIRE, GL7 5QW.
RUSSELL, Mr. Barry Keith, FCA 1971; 9 Regent Place, HEATHFIELD, EAST SUSSEX, TN21 8TJ.
•RUSSELL, Mr. Benjamin James, BSc ACA 2007; HBD Accountancy Services LLP, Gladstone House, 2 Church Road, Wavertree, LIVERPOOL, L15 9EG.
RUSSELL, Mr. Brian Peter, FCA 1974; Dunromin, Coutanche, St. Peter Port, GUERNSEY, GY1 2TU.
•RUSSELL, Mr. Brian Vernon, FCA 1987; Profit Ability North East Limited, Unit 1, Meadowfield Court, Meadowfield, Ponteland, NEWCASTLE UPON TYNE NE20 9SD. See also Russell Brian
•RUSSELL, Mrs. Caroline Anne, BA FCA 1982; Calebs Brook, Plaistow Road, Kirdford, BILLINGSHURST, WEST SUSSEX, RH14 0JY.
RUSSELL, Miss. Caroline Marie, ACA 2001; 42 Hillcrest, LONDON, N21 1AT.
RUSSELL, Mr. Charles Adrian, MSc BSc FCA 1979; Aixtron Ltd Buckingway Business Park, Anderson Road Swavesey, CAMBRIDGE, CB24 4FQ.
RUSSELL, Miss. Charlotte Louise, BSc ACA 2007; 12 Tranby Lane, Anlaby, HULL, HU10 7DS.
RUSSELL, Mrs. Christine Savill, BA ACA 1986; Bristol City Council Amelia Court, Pipe Lane, BRISTOL, BS1 5AA.
RUSSELL, Mr. Christopher, FCA 1976; Active Management, Third Floor, Natwest House, Le Truchot, St. Peter Port, GUERNSEY GY1 1WD.
RUSSELL, Mr. Christopher Howard, MBA BA FCA 1985; Russell Court, 55 Russell Hill Road, PURLEY, SURREY, CR8 2LL.
RUSSELL, Mr. Christopher James, BSc ACA CTA 2002; (Tax Fac), 13 Highfield Park, RHYL, CLWYD, LL18 3NH.
RUSSELL, Mr. Christopher John, FCA 1973; 2 Mill Barn, Boverton, LLANTWIT MAJOR, SOUTH GLAMORGAN, CF61 1UB.
RUSSELL, Mr. Christopher John, FCA 1957; The Old Rectory, Yaverland, SANDOWN, ISLE OF WIGHT, PO36 8QW. (Life Member)
RUSSELL, Mr. Christopher Mark, BA ACA 2005; (Tax Fac), Victrex, Hillhouse Industrial Site, Fleetwood Road North, THORNTON-CLEVELEYS, LANCASHIRE, FY5 4QD.
•RUSSELL, Mr. Clive John, ACA 1985; Phillip A Roberts, 9/10 Hampshire Terrace, PORTSMOUTH, HAMPSHIRE, PO1 2QF.
RUSSELL, Mr. Clive Samuel, FCA 1963; 60 Northway, LONDON, NW11 6PA.
•RUSSELL, Mr. Colin, ACA FCCA DChA 2008; BPU Limited, Radnor House, Greenwood Close, Cardiff Gate Business Park, CARDIFF, CF23 8AA.
RUSSELL, Mr. Colin David, BSc ACA 1992; 39 Chessfield Park, Little Chalfont, AMERSHAM, BUCKINGHAMSHIRE, HP6 6RU.
RUSSELL, Mr. Craig, BSc FCA 1978; 58 Dawstone Road, WIRRAL, MERSEYSIDE, CH60 0BS.
RUSSELL, Mr. David, BSc ACA 1982; 25 Park Road, Welton, BROUGH, HU15 1NW.
•RUSSELL, Mr. David Archibald, BA ACA 1991; PricewaterhouseCoopers LLP, 7 More London Riverside, LONDON, SE1 2RT. See also PricewaterhouseCoopers
RUSSELL, Mr. David Edward, BCom ACA 1995; IG Group Cannon Bridge 25, Dowgate Hill, LONDON, EC4R 2YA.
RUSSELL, Mr. David Michael, LLB ACA 1997; 30 Palmerston Road, LONDON, SW14 7PZ.
RUSSELL, Mr. David Stephen, FCA 1969; Wheelwrights Cottage, Pershore Road, Upton Snodsbury, WORCESTER, WR7 4NR. (Life Member)
RUSSELL, Mr. Dermot Michael, MA ACA 1989; P D Ports Plc, 17-27 Queen Square, MIDDLESBROUGH, CLEVELAND, TS2 1AH.
RUSSELL, Mr. Donald Ridley, FCA 1956; 3 The Quantocks, Dibden Purlieu, SOUTHAMPTON, SO45 5QU. (Life Member)
•RUSSELL, Mrs. Donna-Maria, BA ACA 1986; Russell Associates Ltd, 40 Birchdale Gardens, Chadwell Heath, ROMFORD, RM6 4DU. See also Garside & Co LLP
RUSSELL, Mr. Edward Anthony, FCA 1959; 44 Cauldwell Place, SOUTH SHIELDS, TYNE AND WEAR, NE34 0SA. (Life Member)
RUSSELL, Mr. Edward James, BSc ACA 2006; Telereal Bastion House, 140 London Wall, LONDON, EC2Y 5DN.
RUSSELL, Mr. Edward Oliver, BA ACA 1997; Little Craigo House, Craigo, MONTROSE, ANGUS, DD10 9JT.
RUSSELL, Miss. Elizabeth Helen, ACA 2006; with KPMG Channel Islands Limited, 20 New Street, St Peter Port, GUERNSEY, GY1 4AN.
RUSSELL, The Revd. Eric Watson, FCA 1962; 20 Slater Road, Bentley Heath, SOLIHULL, B93 8AG.
RUSSELL, Mr. Frank Hamilton, FCA 1959; Shurlock Row, 25 Danes Way, Oxshott, LEATHERHEAD, KT22 0LU. (Life Member)
RUSSELL, Mr. Gary David, BSc FCA 1992; Falcon House, 67A Kings Road, BERKHAMSTED, HP4 3BP.
RUSSELL, Mr. Geoffrey Charles, FCA 1975; 11 Cranstar Apartments, Hilgrove Road, NEWQUAY, CORNWALL, TR7 2QW.
RUSSELL, Mr. Geoffrey Thomas, BSc FCA 1977; Woodlands Bathroom Furniture Ltd, 11-12 Parkside Industrial Estate, Hickman Avenue, WOLVERHAMPTON, WV1 2EN.
RUSSELL, Mr. Gerald William, FCA 1973; PRESIDENT MEMBER OF COUNCIL, The White House, Castle Road, WEYBRIDGE, KT13 9QN.
RUSSELL, Mrs. Hazel Victoria, BA FCA 1983; 26 Church Road, Warsash, SOUTHAMPTON, SO31 9GD.
RUSSELL, Mrs. Helen, BSc ACA 1990; 15 Eastbury Road, Thornbury, BRISTOL, BS35 1DR.
RUSSELL, Mrs. Helen Barbara, BA ACA 1992; 40 Hamlet Street, Annerley, BRISBANE, QLD 4121, AUSTRALIA.
RUSSELL, Mr. Henry, BA ACA 2006; with KPMG LLP, 15 Canada Square, LONDON, E14 5GL.
RUSSELL, Mr. Howard Benjamin, FCA 1967; 6 Cottons Field, Dry Drayton, CAMBRIDGE, CB23 8DG.
RUSSELL, Mr. Ian Campbell, BSc ACA 1983; 88 Forest Glade, Highams Park, LONDON, E4 9RJ.
RUSSELL, Miss. Jacqueline Anne, BA ACA 1995; 1 Archway Street, Barnes, LONDON, SW13 0AS.
RUSSELL, Miss. Jacqueline Yvette, BSc ACA 1993; 77 Kenilworth Avenue, Southcote, READING, BERKSHIRE, RG30 3EH.
RUSSELL, Mr. James Francis, BSc ACA 2002; 5 Cordwainers Court, Black Horse Lane, YORK, YO1 7NE.
RUSSELL, Mr. James Frederick, FCA 1964; Dene Cottage, 3 Main Street, Mapperley, ILKESTON, DE7 6BY.
•RUSSELL, Mr. James Robert, BSc(Hons) ACA FCCA MCIM FCMA 2007; (Tax Fac), Gorrie Whitson Limited, 18 Hand Court, LONDON, WC1V 6JF.
RUSSELL, Mrs. Jane Anne, BSc ACA 1989; 1 Parc Castell-y-Mynach, Creigiau, CARDIFF, CF15 9NU.
RUSSELL, Mrs. Janet Marion, BA ACA 1995; The March House, Edgehill, BANBURY, OXFORDSHIRE, OX15 6DJ.
RUSSELL, Mr. Jason Paul, BSc(Hons) ACA 2002; Johnstone Kemp Tooley Limited, Solo House, The Courtyard London Road, HORSHAM, WEST SUSSEX, RH12 1AT.
RUSSELL, Mrs. Jennifer Anne, FCA 1963; 2 Rowdens Road, WELLS, SOMERSET, BA5 1TU.
RUSSELL, Miss. Jennifer Mary, MChem ACA 2010; 76 Hubert Grove, LONDON, SW9 9PD.
•RUSSELL, Mr. John Alan, FCA 1956; Cocke Vellacott & Hill, Unit 3, Dock Offices, Surrey Quays Road, Surrey Quays, LONDON SE16 2XU.
RUSSELL, Mr. John Alan, FCA 1955; 9 Queensway, Poynton, STOCKPORT, CHESHIRE, SK12 1JG. (Life Member)
RUSSELL, Mr. John Harry, FCA 1949; 442 Bromsgrove Road, Hunnington, HALESOWEN, B62 0JL. (Life Member)
RUSSELL, The Hon. John Hugo Trenchard, FCA 1973; Ringstead Farm Ringstead, DORCHESTER, DORSET, DT2 8NF.
•RUSSELL, Mr. John Oliver, FCA 1970; (Tax Fac), J.O. Russell, 38 Leathway, Ormesby St. Margaret, GREAT YARMOUTH, NR29 3QA.
RUSSELL, Mr. John Whitmore, FCA 1967; 18 Bank Street, LUTTERWORTH, LE17 4AG.
RUSSELL, Mr. Jonathan, MA ACA 2006; Flat 31 Masefield Court, Leicester Road, BARNET, HERTFORDSHIRE, EN5 5DA.
RUSSELL, Mr. Jonathan Gavin, MSc BSc ACA 2005; with KPMG LLP, Arlington Business Park, Theale, READING, RG7 4SD.
•RUSSELL, Mr. Jonathan Michael, FCA 1981; ReesRussell LLP, 37 Market Square, WITNEY, OXFORDSHIRE, OX28 6RE. See also Keen Phillips Ltd and ReesRussell Taxation Services Limited
RUSSELL, Mr. Joseph, BSc ACA 2000; 1 Moore St, COOGEE, NSW 2034, AUSTRALIA.
RUSSELL, Mr. Julian Leslie, BA FCA 1995; 26 Grays Lane, HITCHIN, HERTFORDSHIRE, SG5 2HH.
RUSSELL, Miss. Karen Jackalyn, ACA 1989; 22 Manor Drive, LONDON, N14 5JJ.
RUSSELL, Miss. Karen Lee, BCom ACA 1987; 42 Belsize Square, LONDON, NW3 4HN.
•RUSSELL, Mr. Kevin John, ACA CTA FCIE 1985; (Tax Fac), Stewardship Services (UK E T) Ltd Oakwood House, Oakwood Hill Industrial Estate Oakwood Hill, LOUGHTON, IG10 3TZ.
RUSSELL, Mrs. Kirsty, BA ACA 2005; 55 Westerdale, WALLSEND, TYNE AND WEAR, NE28 8UB.
RUSSELL, Mrs. Lauren April, BSc ACA 2006; 353a Manchester Road, NORTHWICH, CHESHIRE, CW9 7NL.
•ⒹRUSSELL, Mr. Laurence George, BA FCA 1993; with Albert Goodman LLP, Mary Street House, Mary Street, TAUNTON, TA1 3NW.
RUSSELL, Mrs. Lesley Gillian, MA ACA 2002; (ACA Ireland 1993); Deloitte LLP, 2 New Street Square, LONDON, EC4A 3BZ. See also Deloitte & Touche LLP
RUSSELL, Miss. Lynn, ACA 2004; with Ernst & Young LLP, 1 Bridgewater Place, Water Lane, LEEDS, LS11 5QR.
RUSSELL, Mrs. Marion Elaine, BSc ACA 1993; Jasmine Cottage, Poole Keynes, CIRENCESTER, GLOUCESTERSHIRE, GL7 6EG.
RUSSELL, Mr. Mark David, BSc ACA 1986; 9 Garendon Way, Groby, LEICESTER, LE6 0YR.
RUSSELL, Mr. Mark Graham, BA ACA 1988; The Maersk Company Ltd, Maersk House, Braham Street, LONDON, E1 8EP.
RUSSELL, Mr. Mark Harvey, BSc ACA 1995; 45 Woodhall Gate, PINNER, MIDDLESEX, HA5 4TY.
RUSSELL, Mr. Mark Wonham, BA FCA 1989; with Ernst & Young LLP, The Paragon, Counterslip, BRISTOL, BS1 6BX.
•RUSSELL, Mr. Martin John Pinion, FCA 1982; with Ernst & Young LLP, 1 More London Place, LONDON, SE1 2AF.
RUSSELL, Mrs. Mary Louise, ACA 1992; 18 Croft Road, EVESHAM, WORCESTERSHIRE, WR11 4NE.
RUSSELL, Mr. Matthew, MA BSc ACA 2002; 37 Tees Close, Chandler's Ford, EASTLEIGH, HAMPSHIRE, SO53 4RU.
RUSSELL, Mr. Matthew John, ACA 2003; Schröderstrasse 6, 69120 HEIDELBERG, GERMANY.
RUSSELL, Mr. Michael, BSc ACA 1992; 2 Forester Avenue, KNUTSFORD, CHESHIRE, WA16 8LB.
RUSSELL, Mr. Michael Alan, FCA 1971; Little Franchise, Spring Lane, Burwash, ETCHINGHAM, EAST SUSSEX, TN19 7HY.
RUSSELL, Mr. Michael Anthony, BSc(Hons) ACA 2002; 11 Cumberland Grove, STOCKTON-ON-TEES, TS20 1NT.
•RUSSELL, Mr. Michael Charles, FCA 1981; Michael Russell, Waterloo House, Don Street, JERSEY, JE2 4TQ.
•RUSSELL, Mr. Michael Graham, FCA 1990; Bright Brown Limited, Exchange House, St. Cross Lane, NEWPORT, ISLE OF WIGHT, PO30 5BZ.
•RUSSELL, Mr. Michael John, BSc ACA 1990; Brown Russell Ltd, 71a and 71c High Street, HEATHFIELD, EAST SUSSEX, TN21 8HU.
RUSSELL, Mr. Michael Jonathan, FCA 1969; 216 Streetsbrook Road, SOLIHULL, B91 1HF.
RUSSELL, Mr. Michael William, BSc ACA MCT 1993; Spring Cottage Cleavers Lane, Old, NORTHAMPTON, NN6 9RG.
RUSSELL, Mr. Neil Neil, BSc FCA 1982; 40 Kidbrooke Grove, Blackheath, LONDON, SE3 0LG.
RUSSELL, Mr. Nicholas David, BA ACA 1993; 24 Overdale, DORKING, SURREY, RH5 4BS.
RUSSELL, Mrs. Nicola Anne, BSc ACA 1994; 32 Oasthouse Drive, FLEET, HAMPSHIRE, GU51 2UL.
•RUSSELL, Mrs. Nicola Jane, BA ACA ATII 1982; Nicola J Russell, 27 Valley Road, RICKMANSWORTH, WD3 4DT.
RUSSELL, Mr. Paul Anthony, BSc ACA 2004; Wedlake Bell, 52 Bedford Row, LONDON, WC1R 4LR.
•RUSSELL, Mr. Paul Barry, BA ACA 1997; BDO LLP, Arcadia House, Maritime Walk, Ocean Village, SOUTHAMPTON, SO14 3TL. See also BDO Stoy Hayward LLP
RUSSELL, Mr. Peter, BSc ACA 1989; Musters Cottage, Wiverton Hall, Wiverton, NOTTINGHAM, NG13 8GU.
RUSSELL, Mr. Peter Andrew, FCA 1983; 27 Valley Road, RICKMANSWORTH, HERTFORDSHIRE, WD3 4DT.
RUSSELL, Mr. Peter Brian, BEng ACA MCT 1993; Kenmare, Camden Park, TUNBRIDGE WELLS, TN2 5AA.
RUSSELL, Mr. Peter James, ACA 1984; Chase de Vere Financial Services, 11 Seven Dials, BATH, BA1 1EN.
RUSSELL, Mr. Peter John, BSc FCA 1994; 4 Northdown Close, Penenden Heath, MAIDSTONE, KENT, ME14 2ER.
RUSSELL, Mr. Peter John, FCA 1959; 26 Worcester Avenue, Kings Hill, WEST MALLING, ME19 4FL.
RUSSELL, Mr. Peter Neil, ACA 1978; 7 Grove Road, UXBRIDGE, UB8 1QR.
RUSSELL, Mr. Peter Owen, BSc FCA 1973; Norwich Business School, University of East Anglia, Earlham Road, NORWICH, NR4 7TJ.
RUSSELL, Mr. Peter Powell, FCA 1952; 2 Royston Close, Friston, EASTBOURNE, BN20 0EY. (Life Member)
RUSSELL, Mr. Peter Walter, BA ACA 1980; Tudor Rose, 1 Molember Court, Molember Road, EAST MOLESEY, KT8 9NF.
RUSSELL, Mr. Philip William, BA ACA 1988; Flat 4, Meadhurst, Queens Place, ASCOT, BERKSHIRE, SL5 7JA.
RUSSELL, Mr. Richard Paul, BA ACA 2005; 10 Brackendale Grove, HARPENDEN, HERTFORDSHIRE, AL5 3EJ.
RUSSELL, Mr. Richard Paul, MSc ACA 1992; 11 Marica Street, BELLBOWRIE, QLD 4070, AUSTRALIA.
RUSSELL, Mr. Richard Scott, MA BA FCA 1999; 44 Bradford Road, Stanningley, PUDSEY, WEST YORKSHIRE, LS28 6DD.
•RUSSELL, Mr. Robert Haran, BA FCA 1993; (Tax Fac), Med Act, 36 Lancaster Road, Wimbledon, LONDON, SW19 5DD.
RUSSELL, Mr. Robert James, BA ACA 2002; 3 Gunnersbury Way, Nuthall, NOTTINGHAM, NG16 1QD.
RUSSELL, Mr. Robert Johnston, FCA 1960; 17, Hampden Hill, BEACONSFIELD, HP9 1BP. (Life Member)
RUSSELL, Mr. Robert Michael, BCom FCA 1966; Dykes Bank House, 2 Lower Bromstead Lane, Moreton, NEWPORT, SHROPSHIRE, TF10 9DQ.
RUSSELL, Mr. Robin Charles, MA MBA FCA 1961; Waterside, Lower Road, Bemerton, SALISBURY, SP2 9NP. (Life Member)
RUSSELL, Mr. Robin Leslie Dorrien, MA ACA 1979; Fitz Farm Fitz, Bomere Heath, SHREWSBURY, SY4 3AS.
•RUSSELL, Mrs. Samantha Mary Genevieve, BSc FCA 1997; Mazars LLP, Tower Bridge House, St. Katharines Way, LONDON, E1W 1DD.
RUSSELL, Miss. Sarah Irene, BA ACA 2004; 22 Lionel Mansions, Haarlem Road, LONDON, W14 0JH.
RUSSELL, Mrs. Sarah Louise, BSc(Hons) ACA 2001; 12 Bay View Road, CABLE BAY 0420, NEW ZEALAND.
RUSSELL, Mr. Simon Gordon, BSc(Hons) ACA 2001; Grant Thornton Hartwell House, 55-61 Victoria Street, BRISTOL, BS1 6FT.
RUSSELL, Mr. Simon John, BSc FCA CF 1998; Hawkpoint Partners Ltd, 41 Lothbury, LONDON, EC2R 7AE.
RUSSELL, Mr. Simon Mark, FCA 1975; 510 Quails End, POWELL, OH 43065, UNITED STATES.
RUSSELL, Mr. Simon Richard Nicholas, ACA 1986; Utopia Furniture Group, Springvale Avenue, BILSTON, WEST MIDLANDS, WV14 0GL.
RUSSELL, Mr. Stanley, FCA 1950; Kingarth, 31 Front Street, Whitburn, SUNDERLAND, SR6 7JB. (Life Member)
RUSSELL, Mr. Stephen Antony, BA FCA 1993; Apartment 504, 545 Sanctuary Drive, LONGBOAT KEY, FL 34228, UNITED STATES.
RUSSELL, Mr. Stephen Barrie, FCA 1971; 9 The Close, Upton, NEWARK, NG23 5SS.
•RUSSELL, Mr. Stephen Clark, FCA 1979; White Cottage, Wolverton Fields, Norton Lindsey, WARWICK, CV35 8JN.
RUSSELL, Mr. Stephen David, ACA 1981; with RSM Tenon Limited, 1 Hollinswood Court, Stafford Park 1, TELFORD, SHROPSHIRE, TF3 3DE.
•RUSSELL, Mr. Stephen Paul, FCA 1977; Steve Russell and Associates, Paddock Hill House, Sacombe Green, Sacombe, WARE, HERTFORDSHIRE SG12 0JH.
RUSSELL, Mr. Steven Charles, BA ACA 1984; 36 Navigation Road, YORK, YO1 9UG.
•RUSSELL, Mr. Steven John, BSc FCA 1993; PricewaterhouseCoopers LLP, Pricewaterhousecoopers, 12 Plumtree Court, LONDON, EC4A 4HT. See also PricewaterhouseCoopers
•RUSSELL, Mr. Stewart Scott, FCA 1997; 2 Redan Road, KAITAIA 0441, NEW ZEALAND.
RUSSELL, Mr. Stuart Alistair, BA ACA 2003; 42 Stretton Avenue, BLACKPOOL, FY4 4AQ.
RUSSELL, Mr. Stuart Ralph, FCA 1972; Petham Cottage, Rectory Lane, Ightham, SEVENOAKS, TN15 9AJ.

RUSSELL, Miss. Suzanne Evangeline Frances, BA(Hons) ACA *2000;* 102 Lawson Street, PADDINGTON, NSW 2021, AUSTRALIA.
RUSSELL, Mr. Thomas, ACA *2011;* Abbott Mead Vickers B B D O Ltd, 151 Marylebone Road, LONDON, NW1 5QE.
RUSSELL, Mr. Thomas Macdonald, FCA CTA *1969;* St. Rose Sway Road, Pennington, LYMINGTON, HAMPSHIRE, SO41 8LR. (Life Member)
RUSSELL, Mr. Thomas Peter, BA ACA *2005;* 34 Schulhaustrasse, 8706 MEILEN, SWITZERLAND.
RUSSELL, Mr. Thomas Wetherall, FCA *1947;* 16 Huskards, Waldegrave Gardens, UPMINSTER, ESSEX, RM14 1UP. (Life Member)
RUSSELL, Mr. Timothy, MEng ACA *2007;* (Tax Fac), Flat 13, Flat 9-16 Acuba House, Acuba Road, LONDON, SW18 4QS.
RUSSELL, The Hon. Valentine Francis-Xavier Michael, MA FCA *1964;* 207 W.86th Street Apt.515A, NEW YORK, NY 10024, UNITED STATES.
RUSSELL, Mrs. Vanessa Siobhan, BSc ACA *1996;* 23 Yew Tree Road, TUNBRIDGE WELLS, TN4 0BD.
RUSSELL, Mr. Vincent Harvey, BA ACA *1998;* 20 Bellevue Road, LONDON, SW13 0BJ.
RUSSELL, Miss. Virginia, ACA *2008;* Flat 10, Eastwell House, Weston Street, LONDON, SE1 4DH.
RUSSELL GRANT, Mr. Geoffrey Hamilton, FCA *1968;* Heath House Crayes Green, Layer Breton, COLCHESTER, CO2 0PN.
RUSSELL-SMITH, Mrs. Helen Catherine, BSc ACA *2002;* with Deloitte LLP, Athene Place, 66 Shoe Lane, LONDON, EC4A 3BQ.
RUSSELL-SMITH, Mr. Paul Henry, FCA *1954;* 24 Meadway, EPSOM, KT19 8JZ. (Life Member)
RUSSELL-SMITH, Mr. Peter James, BSc ACA *2007;* 12 The Ridgeway, BRACKNELL, RG12 9QU.
•RUSSELL-SMITH, Mrs. Susanna Gibson, FCA *1971;* (Tax Fac), Susanna Russell-Smith FCA, 249 Upper Richmond Road, Putney, LONDON, SW15 6SW.
•RUSSETT, Mrs. Barbara Joan, FCA *1972;* (Tax Fac), Barbara J. Russett, Lamara, 29 Duporth Bay, ST AUSTELL, CORNWALL, PL26 6AF.
RUSSON, Miss. Clare Brenda, ACA *2008;* 119 Hallchurch Road, DUDLEY, DY2 0TQ.
RUST, Miss. Annaliese, BA ACA *2011;* 10 Sandhurst Avenue, IPSWICH, IP3 8DU.
RUST, Mr. Jonathan Simon David Anthony, BA ACA *1998;* 17 Hayton Close, LUTON, LU3 4HD.
RUST, Miss. Lucille Anne Marie, BA ACA *2005;* 13 Merrills Way, Ingoldmells, SKEGNESS, LINCOLNSHIRE, PE25 1JN.
RUST, Mr. Martyn Ronald, FCA *1970;* 2Mount Dale View, ROLEYSTONE, WA 6111, AUSTRALIA. (Life Member)
•RUST, Mr. Marvin Paul, BSc ACA *1990;* Deloitte LLP, 2 New Street Square, LONDON, EC4A 3BZ. See also Deloitte & Touche LLP
RUST, Mr. Neil Kenneth, BA ACA *1990;* September House Lewes Road, Blackboys, UCKFIELD, EAST SUSSEX, TN22 5LF.
RUST, Mr. Richard Alan Hayden Mark, BA ACA *1998;* 151 Old Bedford Road, LUTON, BEDFORDSHIRE, LU2 7EF.
RUST, Miss. Sara Katrine, ACA *2010;* (Tax Fac), Apple Cottage, Cage End, Hatfield Broad Oak, BISHOP'S STORTFORD, HERTFORDSHIRE, CM22 7HT.
RUST, Mr. Stephen Andrew, BSc ACA *1992;* The Studio, 98 Fellows Road, LONDON, NW3 3JG.
RUSTED, Mr. Philip William, FCA *1974;* Oakcroft, 15 The Heath, Chaldon, CATERHAM, CR3 5DJ.
RUSTED, Mr. Richard Mark, BSc ACA *1995;* 30 Wingfield Street, BUNGAY, NR35 1EZ.
RUSTELL, Mrs. Georgianna, MPhil ACA *2010;* K P M G Arlington Business Park, Theale, READING, RG7 4SD.
•RUSTEM, Mr. Sumer Suat, FCA *1972;* Sumer Rustem & Co, Ecevit Sokak No 58, Gonyeli, PO Box 6, LEFKOSA MERSIN 10, TURKEY.
RUSTEN, Mr. Paul Ivar, BCom ACA *1984;* C/O IFC, 14th floor, 1 Pacific Place, 88 Queensway, ADMIRALTY, HONG KONG ISLAND HONG KONG SAR.
RUSTOMJI, Mr. Sohrab, FCA *1972;* 14 Hartshill Close, Off Sweetcroft Lane, UXBRIDGE, UB10 9LH.
RUSTON, Mr. Kenneth, FCA *1954;* Flat 14, Chadbrook Crest, Richmond Hill Road, BIRMINGHAM, B15 3RL. (Life Member)
RUSTON, Mr. Richard Allpress, FCA *1974;* Rushtons Engineering Co Ltd, Brampton Road, HUNTINGDON, PE29 3BS.
•RUSTRICK, Mr. Sean Michael, FCA *1989;* Perrys, 32-34 St. Johns Road, TUNBRIDGE WELLS, KENT, TN4 9NT.
RUTA, Miss. Helen, BSc ACA *2004;* Sulzer (UK) Pumps Ltd, Manor Mill Lane, LEEDS, LS11 8BR.
RUTENBERG-HOUCHEN, Mrs. Inga, ACA *1985;* The Brackens, 53 Ripley Avenue, Minster Lovell, WITNEY, OX29 0RP.
RUTHEN-GOUGH, Mrs. April Elaine, ACA *1998;* 1 Kipling Road, ALTON, GU34 1UD.
RUTHERFORD, Mrs. Abigail Louise, BA ACA *1991;* Downe Hall, Cudham Road, ORPINGTON, KENT, BR6 7LE.
RUTHERFORD, Mr. Andrew McLeod, BSc ACA *1992;* 157 Trent Boulevard, West Bridgford, NOTTINGHAM, NG2 5BX.
RUTHERFORD, Mr. Colin Harry Cecil, OBE FCA *1950;* C.A.Cigarrera Bigott Sucs., Apartado No.186, CARACAS, 1010-A, VENEZUELA. (Life Member)
RUTHERFORD, Mr. Craig, BA(Hons) ACA *2003;* Eaga Partnership House, Regent Farm Road, NEWCASTLE UPON TYNE, NE3 3AF.
•RUTHERFORD, Mr. Darren George Nicholas Thomas, FCA *1994;* 11 Westerkirk, Southfield Lea, CRAMLINGTON, NE23 6NA.
RUTHERFORD, Mr. Derek Thomas Jones, CBE FCA *1953;* 3 Berkeley Gardens, BURY ST.EDMUNDS, IP33 3JW. (Life Member)
RUTHERFORD, Mr. Duncan Maxwell, ACA *2008;* 30 Finsbury Square, LONDON, EC2P 2YU.
RUTHERFORD, Mr. Iain Stuart, BA ACA *1991;* 3 Meadowsweet Hill, Bingham, NOTTINGHAM, NG13 8TS.
RUTHERFORD, Miss. Joanne Cecilia, BSc ACA *2002;* 67 Cobden Road, BRIGHTON, BN2 9TJ.
RUTHERFORD, Mr. John Alexander, BCom FCA *1972;* Wyndales Cottage, Symington, BIGGAR, ML12 6JU.
RUTHERFORD, Mr. John David, FCA *1975;* John Good & Sons Ltd, Maritime House, Kingston Street, HULL, HU1 2DB.
RUTHERFORD, Mr. John Heslop, BCom FCA *1955;* 113 Rennies Mill Road, ST JOHN'S A1B 2P2, NF, CANADA. (Life Member)
RUTHERFORD, Mr. John Wonham, FCA *1978;* 19 Orchard Way, Stoke Goldington, NEWPORT PAGNELL, BUCKINGHAMSHIRE, MK16 8PE.
RUTHERFORD, Mrs. Judith, BA ACA *1991;* Biocity Nottingham Ltd, Pennyfoot Street, NOTTINGHAM, NG1 1GF.
RUTHERFORD, Mrs. Judith Marie, BSc ACA *1998;* 31 Oakwood Road, Chandler's Ford, EASTLEIGH, HAMPSHIRE, SO53 1LW.
RUTHERFORD, Mr. Julian Michael, BSc ACA *1997;* 47, Chigwell Park Drive, CHIGWELL, IG7 5BD.
•①RUTHERFORD, Miss. Katharine Josefa, FCA *1982;* 27 Kingsbridge Road, BISHOP'S STORTFORD, CM23 2AE.
RUTHERFORD, Mrs. Margaret Helen, BA ACA *1988;* Inglewood, 65 Beckwith Road, Dulwich, LONDON, SE24 9LQ.
RUTHERFORD, Mr. Mark Andrew, BSc ACA *2007;* 26 Allonby Mews, Shankhouse, CRAMLINGTON, NORTHUMBERLAND, NE23 3BJ.
RUTHERFORD, Mr. Martin Richard Paul, ACA *2005;* 12 Southmount, BRIGHTON, BN1 7BD.
RUTHERFORD, Mr. Matthew Stewart, ACA *1990;* SAS Institute GmbH, In der Neckarhelle 162, 69118 HEIDELBERG, GERMANY.
RUTHERFORD, Mr. Michael Paul, BA ACA *1996;* 218 Wards Wharf Approach, LONDON, E16 2EQ.
RUTHERFORD, Mrs. Tonia Catherine, BA ACA *1994;* Mere House Farm, Baddiley, NANTWICH, CW5 8BS.
RUTHNUM, Mr. Ambeekhavadee, FCA *1977;* 1062 BRAVAR DRIVE, MANOTICK K4M 1G3, ON, CANADA.
RUTHVEN, Miss. Anne Whitehead, MA ACA *1984;* Westenriederstraße 16, D-80331 MUNICH, GERMANY.
RUTHVEN, Mr. Michael John, FCA *1965;* 4 Cold Harbour Lane, GRANTHAM, LINCOLNSHIRE, NG31 9EW.
RUTHVEN, Miss. Sarah, ACA *2011;* 12 Chestnut Walk, WORTHING, WEST SUSSEX, BN13 3QL.
RUTLAND, Mr. Daniel Peter, BSocSc ACA *2003;* 38 Chestnut Close Rushmere St. Andrew, IPSWICH, IP5 1ED.
RUTLAND, Mr. Ian Victor, ACA *2008;* 106 Boundaries Road, LONDON, SW12 8HQ.
RUTLAND, Mr. James Michael Norris, BSc(Hons) ACA *2002;* 160 Hamlet Gardens, LONDON, W6 0TR.
RUTLAND, Mr. Michael Raymond, BSc ACA *1992;* 13 Northumberland Place, TEIGNMOUTH, DEVON, TQ14 8BZ.
RUTLAND, Mr. Simon Christopher John, ACA *2009;* Flat 9, 39 Craven Hill Gardens, LONDON, W2 3EA.
RUTLEDGE, Mr. Arran, LLB ACA MBA *2003;* 16 Cheltenham Park, BELFAST, BT6 0HR.
RUTLEDGE, Ms. Hannah Francoise, BA ACA *1996;* U B S AG, 100 Liverpool Street, LONDON, EC2M 2RH.
RUTLEDGE, Mr. Michael Howard, BA ACA *1987;* 56 Nassau Road, Barnes, LONDON, SW13 9QE.
•RUTLEDGE, Mr. Neil Michael, BA ACA *1990;* Grant Thornton UK LLP, Grant Thornton House, 22 Melton Street, Euston Square, LONDON, NW1 2EP. See also Grant Thornton LLP
RUTT, Mr. Christopher Stewart, BSc ACA *2007;* Man Group Plc, Sugar Quay, Lower Thames Street, LONDON, EC3R 6DU.
RUTT, Mr. Jabez James, BA ACA *2000;* 93 Villiers Avenue, SURBITON, KT5 8BE.
•RUTT, Mr. Michael Logan, FCA *1981;* (Tax Fac), ML and JP Rutt, 7 Shepherds Fold, Holmer Green, HIGH WYCOMBE, HP15 6XZ.
RUTT, Miss. Sarah Jane, LLB ACA *2004;* 16 The Exchange, Queen Street, HITCHIN, HERTFORDSHIRE, SG4 9TY.
RUTTEMAN, Mr. John Peter, BSc ACA *1997;* #14 - 303 Pandan Valley Condo, 3 Pandan Valley, SINGAPORE 597627, SINGAPORE.
RUTTEMAN, Mr. Paul Johannes, CBE BSc FCA *1964;* (Member of Council 1979 - 1988 1990 - 1992 1996 - 2002), 5 Alleyn Road, Dulwich, LONDON, SE21 8AB.
RUTTEMAN, Mr. Philip Charles, ACA *2010;* 5 Alleyn Road, LONDON, SE21 8AB.
RUTTER, Mr. Andrew Phillip, MSc BSc ACA *2005;* with KPMG LLP, One Snowhill, Snow Hill Queensway, BIRMINGHAM, B4 6GN.
RUTTER, Mrs. Catherine, BA(Hons) ACA *2004;* B P P Holdings Plc, Aldine House, 142-144 Uxbridge Road, LONDON, W12 8AA.
RUTTER, Miss. Fiona Jane, BA ACA *2002;* 28 Ellerton Road, LONDON, SW18 3NN.
•RUTTER, Mr. Garry Thomas, BA FCA *1983;* Ormerod Rutter Limited, The Oakley, Kidderminster Road, DROITWICH, WORCESTERSHIRE, WR9 9AY.
•RUTTER, Mrs. Geraldine Ann, BSc ACA *1991;* PricewaterhouseCoopers LLP, Cornwall Court, 19 Cornwall Street, BIRMINGHAM, B3 2DT. See also PricewaterhouseCoopers
RUTTER, Mr. Graham Paul, BSc ACA *1983;* Pork Farms Ltd Dunsil Drive, Queens Drive Industrial Estate, NOTTINGHAM, NG2 1LU.
RUTTER, Mr. James Edgar, BSc FCA *1954;* 35 Naples Drive, Westlands, NEWCASTLE, ST5 2QD. (Life Member)
RUTTER, Mrs. Jean, BSc(Hons) ACA *2002;* 26 Pinewood Close, Kingston Park, NEWCASTLE UPON TYNE, NE3 2YB.
RUTTER, Mr. Keith, BSc ACA *1992;* 3 Rosehall Terrace, FALKIRK, FK1 1PY.
RUTTER, Mr. Kevin, BSc ACA *1991;* 159 Moor Green Lane, Moseley, BIRMINGHAM, B13 8NT.
RUTTER, Mr. Matthew James, BSc ACA *2008;* 40 Hardens Mead, CHIPPENHAM, WILTSHIRE, SN15 3AE.
RUTTER, Miss. Melissa Louise, BA(Hons) ACA *2010;* 4 Retford Close, BURY, LANCASHIRE, BL8 1XG.
RUTTER, Mr. Paul Terence, ACA *1983;* 123 Raedwald Drive, BURY ST.EDMUNDS, IP32 7DG.
RUTTER, Mr. Philip John, FCA *1950;* 21 Conduit Lane, BRIDGNORTH, WV16 5BW. (Life Member)
RUTTER, Mrs. Sophie Louise, MA ACA *2001;* 33 Parklands Way, HARTLEPOOL, TS26 0AP.
RUTTERFORD, Mr. Stephen John, BSc ACA *1993;* 16 Winterbank Close, SUTTON-IN-ASHFIELD, NOTTINGHAMSHIRE, NG17 1LS.
RUTTLEY, Mr. Neil Christopher, BA ACA *2007;* 25 Havelock Street, SPALDING, LINCOLNSHIRE, PE11 2YL.
RUVIGNY, Mrs. Kumudini Nelun, MA ACA *1986;* 38 Chartfield Avenue, LONDON, SW15 6HG.
RUVIGNY, Mr. Rupert Francis James Henry, BA ACA *1986;* 10th floor, Brompton Asset Management Ltd, 1 Knightsbridge Green, LONDON, SW1X 7QA.
RUYGROK, Miss. Claudia, ACA *2011;* 12 Jelf Road, LONDON, SW2 1BH.
RUYGROK, Mr. Peter Alaric, FCA *1969;* 13 Salisbury Road, RICHMOND, TW9 2JB.
RUZICKA, Mr. Giulio, BSc ACA *2003;* Via Calcinaia 23, 00139 ROME, ITALY.
RUZZON, Mr. Alberto, ACA *2010;* (Tax Fac), Flat 15/3, 20 Bryanston Street, LONDON, W1H 7EF.
RWEZAHURA, Mr. Philip, FCA *1972;* P O Box 32501, DAR ES SALAAM, TANZANIA. (Life Member)
RYALL, Miss. Caroline Elizabeth, ACA *1982;* 39 James Avenue, SANDOWN, ISLE OF WIGHT, PO36 9NH.
RYALL, Ms. Deborah Clare, ACA *1993;* 2 Lye Common, Christian Malford, CHIPPENHAM, WILTSHIRE, SN15 4BH.
RYALL, Miss. Jennifer Kendrick, BA ACA *1991;* Royal Academy of Arts Burlington House, Piccadilly, LONDON, W1J 0BD.
RYALLS, Mrs. Sarah Rebecca, BSc ACA *1992;* British Library, Boston Spa, WETHERBY, WEST YORKSHIRE, LS23 7BQ.
RYAN, Mr. Adam, BA ACA *2003;* 126 Henleaze Road, BRISTOL, BS9 4LB.
RYAN, Mr. Adrian, BA ACA AITI *2002;* 6 Woodberry Lawn, Castleredmond, MIDLETON, COUNTY CORK, IRELAND.
RYAN, Mr. Adrian Noel, ACA *1996;* 32 Christchurch Road, East Sheen, LONDON, SW14 7AA.
RYAN, Mr. Alan Martin, BSc FCA *1976;* Pendragon Financial Servces Ltd Crown Works, Luton Street, KEIGHLEY, WEST YORKSHIRE, BD21 2LE.
RYAN, Mrs. Alicia Marie, BSc ACA *1990;* Greggs Plc, Fernwood House, Clayton Road, NEWCASTLE UPON TYNE, NE2 1TL.
RYAN, Mr. Andrew James, ACA *2010;* Flat 10 Chaucer House, 59 Poets Road, LONDON, N5 2SH.
RYAN, Mr. Andrew Patrick, BEng ACA *1999;* Fen Farm Fen Lane, Hitcham, IPSWICH, IP7 7NL.
RYAN, Mr. Anthony Laurence, FCA *1968;* Craigellachie, 184 Willingdon Road, EASTBOURNE, EAST SUSSEX, BN21 1TT. (Life Member)
RYAN, Mr. Chad, BSc ACA *1997;* 12 Strathearn Road, NORTH BERWICK, EAST LOTHIAN, EH39 5BZ.
RYAN, Mrs. Christine Janice, BSc ACA *1996;* 12 Strathearn Road, NORTH BERWICK, EAST LOTHIAN, EH39 5BZ.
RYAN, Mr. Clayton Michael, ACA *2007;* 5th Floor Minories House, 2 - 5 Minories, LONDON, EC3N 1BJ.
•RYAN, Mr. Clifford Anthony, ACA *1990;* (Tax Fac), Cliff Ryan, 4F Shirland Mews, LONDON, W9 3DY.
RYAN, Mr. Daniel Joseph, BA ACA *1993;* Wall Garth, Coombe End, KINGSTON UPON THAMES, SURREY, KT2 7DQ.
RYAN, Mr. David Edward, FCA *1968;* Leathes Cottage, Borrowdale, KESWICK, CUMBRIA, CA12 5UY.
RYAN, Mr. David Garvin, BSc ACA *2005;* 1st floor, Barclays Capital, 5 North Colonnade, LONDON, E14 4BB.
RYAN, Mr. David Michael, BSc FCA *1978;* 19 Greenleafe Drive, Barkingside, ILFORD, IG6 1LN.
RYAN, Mr. James Patrick, BA(Hons) ACA *2009;* Centrica Plc Millstream, Maidenhead Road, WINDSOR, SL4 5GD.
RYAN, Mrs. Janet Margaret, BA ACA *1994;* Ash Tree Cottage, Wonston, WINCHESTER, SO21 3SJ.
RYAN, Mrs. Joanne Kelly, BSc ACA *2005;* 126 Henleaze Road, BRISTOL, BS9 4LB.
RYAN, Mr. John Benedict, BA(Econ) FCA *1977;* 508Soi 16, Sor Thoranin, Huay Kwang, BANGKOK 10320, THAILAND.
RYAN, Mr. John Patrick, BA ACA *1989;* 128 Carrs Mill, DONABATE, COUNTY DUBLIN, IRELAND.
RYAN, Mr. Joseph, BSc BEng ACA AMCT *1992;* Medicover, C/o Belro Medical S.A, Waterloo Office Park Building M, 1410 WATERLOO, BELGIUM.
RYAN, Mr. Joseph Edmond, FCA *1974;* 58 Buckingham Way, WALLINGTON, SM6 9LT.
RYAN, Mr. Joseph Mary, BCom ACA *1981;* Hillcrest House, South Douglas Road, CORK, COUNTY CORK, IRELAND.
RYAN, Miss. Julia, BSc ACA *1994;* 27 Elsynge Road, Wandsworth, LONDON, SW18 2HR.
RYAN, Mr. Kevin James, FCA *1962;* Bilsdale Priory, Chop Gate, MIDDLESBROUGH, TS9 7HY. (Life Member)
RYAN, Ms. Linda Claire, MBA BSc ACA *1988;* 40 Sylvan Road, WALTHAM, MA 02451, UNITED STATES.
RYAN, Miss. Lisa Anne, BA ACA *2009;* with Wilkins Kennedy, Bridge House, London Bridge, LONDON, SE1 9QR.
RYAN, Mrs. Margaret Ellen, BSc ACA *2003;* Fen Farm Fen Lane, Hitcham, IPSWICH, IP7 7NL.
RYAN, Mrs. Margaret Iona, BSc ACA *1989;* Savannah, Lindale Close, VIRGINIA WATER, SURREY, GU25 4NT.
RYAN, Mr. Mark Philip, BA ACA *1981;* Flat 6 Aran Lodge, 10 Woodchurch Road, LONDON, NW6 3PN.
RYAN, Mr. Martyn, BSc FCA *1984;* Genesis Investment Management LLP, 21 Knightsbridge, LONDON, SW1X 7LY.
•RYAN, Mr. Matthew Alexander, BSc ACA *2002;* (Tax Fac), PricewaterhouseCoopers LLP, Cornwall Court, 19 Cornwall Street, BIRMINGHAM, B3 2DT. See also PricewaterhouseCoopers
RYAN, Mr. Matthew John, MA ACA *2011;* 17 Oatlands Chase, Shinfield, READING, RG2 9FY.
RYAN, Mr. Michael Francis, FCA *1961;* Keyes Cottage, 10 Copthorne Road, Croxley Green, RICKMANSWORTH, HERTFORDSHIRE, WD3 4AE. (Life Member)

•**RYAN, Mr. Nicholas James, BA ACA** *1994;* Ryan Consulting, Halasto UTCA 21, 1039 BUDAPEST, HUNGARY.
RYAN, Mr. Nicholas James, BA ACA *1998;* 55 Shaftesbury Road, LONDON, N19 4QW.
RYAN, Mr. Paul Christopher, BA ACA *1990;* Stoneleigh, 47 Elvaston Road, HEXHAM, NE46 2HD.
RYAN, Mr. Paul Simeon, BA FCA *1978;* 1 Manor Farm Barns 34A The Street Snailwell, NEWMARKET, CB8 7LX.
•**RYAN, Ms. Penelope Anne, MA FCA FRSA DChA** *1980;* P A Ryan MA(Ed) FCA DChA, 66 Fountain Road, LONDON, SW17 0HQ.
RYAN, Mr. Peter James Esperson, FCA *1974;* Duelguide Management Services Limited 57 Grosvenor Street, LONDON, W1K 3JA.
RYAN, Mr. Philip James, FCA *1976;* Wellington Lodge Pottery Lane Inkpen, HUNGERFORD, BERKSHIRE, RG17 9QA.
RYAN, Mr. Philip James, BSc FCA *1995;* 4 Yellow Brook Close, Aspull, WIGAN, LANCASHIRE, WN2 1ZH.
RYAN, Mr. Robert, FCA *1975;* 108 Bulkington Lane, NUNEATON, CV11 4SB.
RYAN, Mr. Robert Anthony, BSc FCA *1989;* 12 Bishopdale Close, Great Sankey, WARRINGTON, WA5 3DF.
RYAN, Prof. Robert James, FCA *1975;* Raybarrow Cottage, Nettleton Shrub, Nettleton, CHIPPENHAM, WILTSHIRE, SN14 7NN.
•**RYAN, Mrs. Sharon Rosemary, ACA** *1989;* (Tax Fac), Sharon R Ryan, 1 The Limes, Priory Road, SHANKLIN, ISLE OF WIGHT, PO37 6SB.
RYAN, Mr. Simon, BA(Hons) ACA *2002;* 3 Chretien Road, Northenden, MANCHESTER, M22 4ES.
RYAN, Mr. Stephen, BSc ACA *1983;* 5 Lilian Street, NUNAWADING, VIC 3131, AUSTRALIA.
RYAN, Mr. Tim, MEng ACA *2001;* 2710 baker street apartment#1, SAN FRANCISCO, CA 94123, UNITED STATES.
RYAN-BELL, Mr. Peter John, BA ACA *1992;* 113 Broomwood Road, LONDON, SW11 6JU.
RYANS, Mr. Matthew Alistair Angus, MEng ACA *2001;* RSA Consulting Ltd, The Melon Ground, Hatfield Park, HATFIELD, HERTFORDSHIRE, AL9 5NB.
RYANS, Mr. Peter Graham, FCA *1980;* 1 The Willows, Hambleton, SELBY, YO8 9GU.
RYBA, Ms. Caroline Anne, MA FCA *1989;* Cambridgeshire County Council, RES 1211, Shire Hall, CAMBRIDGE, CB3 0AP.
RYBAK, Mr. Martin, BA(Hons) ACA *2002;* 61 Cotswold Avenue, RAYLEIGH, SS6 8AN.
RYBCZAK, Mr. Myron, MA FCA *1980;* The Hollies, 3 Central Avenue, Borrowash, DERBY, DE72 3JZ.
RYBURN, Mr. Donald McNair, FCA MBA MCMI *1989;* 11 Tooke Road, Minchinhampton, STROUD, GLOUCESTERSHIRE, GL6 9DA.
RYCE, Mr. Dermot Michael Walter, FCA *1976;* 48 Kingswear Road, RUISLIP, HA4 6AY.
RYDALL, Mrs. Sylvia Elizabeth, FCA *1965;* 12 Rosemary Close, WHITEHAVEN, CUMBRIA, CA28 6JH.
RYDE, Mr. Matthew Charles, BSc ACA *2002;* 130 Carlton Road, REIGATE, RH2 0JF.
RYDER, Mr. Andrew James, BSc(Hons) ACA *2002;* 94 Hurst Lane, EAST MOLESEY, KT8 9DY.
RYDER, Mr. Andrew John, BSc ACA CF *1997;* with PKF (UK) LLP, 2nd Floor, Fountain Precinct, Balm Green, SHEFFIELD, S1 2JA.
RYDER, Mr. Anthony Charles, MA FCA *1962;* Alders Croft, South Moreton, DIDCOT, OX11 9AD. (Life Member)
RYDER, Mr. David, BA FCA *1979;* 100 Ivy Park Road, Ranmoor, SHEFFIELD, S10 3LD.
RYDER, Mr. Edward Charles, ACA *2008;* Route de St Georges 47, 1213 PETIT LANCY, SWITZERLAND.
RYDER, Mrs. Fiona Victoria, BA(Hons) ACA *2001;* 94 Hurst Lane, EAST MOLESEY, SURREY, KT8 9DY.
•**RYDER, Mr. Geoffrey Winston, FCA** *1970;* (Tax Fac), Faust Loveday Bell LLP, 5 Curfew Yard, Thames Street, WINDSOR, BERKSHIRE, SL4 1SN.
•**RYDER, Mr. Graham Ian, FCA** *1961;* Graham I. Ryder, 120 Ashton Road, Denton, MANCHESTER, M34 3JE.
RYDER, Mr. Mark Stephen, BSc ACA *1984;* Patton Grange Farm House, Bourton, MUCH WENLOCK, SHROPSHIRE, TF13 6JW.
RYDER, Mr. Michael James, FCA *1970;* 5 Tennis Corner, Churnet View Road, Oakamoor, STOKE-ON-TRENT, ST10 3AE.
RYDER, Mr. Neill Timothy, MA ACA *2001;* 31 North Road, BERKHAMSTED, HERTFORDSHIRE, HP4 3DU.
RYDER, Mr. Oliver James, BSc ACA *1995;* PLOT 6 AVIGNON ESTATE, VALLEY ROAD, HOUT BAY, CAPE TOWN, WESTERN CAPE PROVINCE, 7806 SOUTH AFRICA.
RYDER, Mr. Phillip George, BA FCA *1966;* Wychwood, Theobalds Road, BURGESS HILL, RH15 0SX. (Life Member)
RYDER, Mrs. Rebecca Jane, ACA *2009;* 24 Bradley Road, Patchway, BRISTOL, BS34 5LE.
•**RYDER, Mr. Roger Kevin, BSc ACA** *1993;* Slaney & Co, Portland House, 3 Queen Street, WORKSOP, NOTTINGHAMSHIRE, S80 2AW.
•**RYDER, Mr. Simon Denis, BA FCA** *1992;* KPMG LLP, 15 Canada Square, LONDON, E14 5GL. See also KPMG Europe LLP
RYDER, Mr. Stephen, BA ACA *1983;* 6 Birch Lea, Three Bridges, CRAWLEY, RH10 8AR.
RYDER, Mrs. Zoe Leeanne, BSc(Hons) ACA *2001;* 31 North Road, BERKHAMSTED, HERTFORDSHIRE, HP4 3DU.
RYDON, Mrs. Holly Jane, MPhil BSc ACA *1998;* 97 Bromley Heath Road, Downend, BRISTOL, BS16 6HZ.
RYDQVIST, Mr. Craig Ivan, BSc(Hons) ACA *2001;* 11 Beaulieu Gardens, LONDON, N21 2HR.
•**RYE, Mr. Julien Thomas, BSc ACA** *1988;* BDO LLP, 6th Floor, 3 Hardman Street, Spinningfields, MANCHESTER, M3 3AT. See also BDO Stoy Hayward LLP
RYE, Mr. Keith John, BSc FCA FCCA *1979;* ATC Ukraine, 7th Floor, 48 Bohdana Khmelnytskogo Street, 01030 KYIV, UKRAINE.
RYE, Miss. Suzanne Elizabeth, BSc ACA *1989;* 2 Narrow Lane, WARLINGHAM, CR6 9HY.
RYELL, Mr. David Edward, BSc ACA *1997;* 36 Overdale, DORKING, SURREY, RH5 4BS.
RYGALSKA, Mrs. Christina Mary Louise, BSc ACA *1993;* Holly House Bath Lane, BUCKINGHAM, MK18 1DX.
RYKERS, Mr. Nicholas Bruce, ACA CA(NZ) *2009;* 71a Fitzjohns Avenue, Hampstead, LONDON, NW3 6PD.
RYLANCE, Mrs. Alison Mary, BA ACA *1992;* 19 Galahad Crescent, CASTLE HILL, NSW 2154, AUSTRALIA.
RYLANCE, Mr. David William, BSc(Hons) ACA *2004;* F305, Astrazeneca Alderley House, Alderley Park, MACCLESFIELD, CHESHIRE, SK10 4TF.
RYLANCE, Mr. Edward Paul Haywood, BSc ACA *1993;* Pathside, 12 Chestnut Close, AMERSHAM, HP6 6EQ.
RYLANCE, Mr. Mark Philip John, ACA *1988;* Vines Farm Cottage, Chalkhouse Green Road, Kidmore End, READING, RG4 9AP.
RYLAND, Mr. Anthony John Stuart, FCA *1952;* 79 Bilton Road, RUGBY, CV22 7AW. (Life Member)
RYLAND, Mr. Christopher Michael, BSc FCA *1971;* 60 Old Coast Road, KORORA, NSW 2450, AUSTRALIA. (Life Member)
RYLAND, Mr. Richard Hamilton, BSc ACA *1982;* 3 Hither Mead, Frampton Cotterell, BRISTOL, BS36 2SJ.
•**RYLAND, Mr. Stuart Antony, BSc ACA DChA** *1990;* Ryland Consulting Limited, 5 Yeading Avenue, Rayners Lane, HARROW, MIDDLESEX, HA2 9RL. See also Ryland Consulting
RYLAND-DAY, Mrs. Maire Camille, BSc(Hons) ACA *2000;* Care of Andrew Day Egypt Asset, B G Group Plc, 100 Thames Valley Park Drive, READING, RG6 1PT.
RYLANDS, Mr. Hugh John Joseph, BA ACA *1980;* Oak Farm, Oak Lane, Marton, MACCLESFIELD, CHESHIRE, SK11 9HE.
RYLATT, Mrs. Caroline Elizabeth Armes, BSc FCA *1987;* Romm 5168 White City Building, 201 Wood Lane, LONDON, W12.
•**RYLATT, Mrs. Claire, BSc ACA AMCT** *2005;* Cooper Rylatt LLP, 6 Teasel Drive, ELY, CAMBRIDGESHIRE, CB6 3WJ.
•**RYLATT, Mr. James Jonathan Charles, BSc ACA** *2004;* Cooper Rylatt LLP, 6 Teasel Drive, ELY, CAMBRIDGESHIRE, CB6 3WJ.
RYLE, Mr. Cameron, BA FCA *1967;* Jagoes Mill, KINSALE, COUNTY CORK, IRELAND.
RYLE, Mr. Stuart John, FCA *1976;* The Conifers, Leafy Grove, KESTON, BR2 6AH.
RYLETT, Mr. Colin Lee, BA ACA *1995;* 97 Mather Road, SHEFFIELD, S9 4GR.
RYLEY, Mr. Brian Edward, FCA *1951;* 26 Villiers Road, West Bridgford, NOTTINGHAM, NG2 6FR. (Life Member)
RYLEY, Mr. Derrick John, BCom ACA *1986;* PricewaterhouseCoopers, 26/F Office Tower A, Beijing Fortune Plaza, 23 Dongsanhuan North Road, Chaoyang District, BEIJING 100020 CHINA.
RYMAN, Mrs. Caroline Rebecca, BSc ACA *1996;* Crown Clark Whitehill & Co, St. Brides House, 10 Salisbury Square, LONDON, EC4Y 8EH.
•**RYMAN, Mr. Stephen Blandford, FCA** *1978;* Shipleys LLP, 10 Orange Street, Haymarket, LONDON, WC2H 7DQ.
RYMASZEWSKI, Mr. Bohdan Konrad, BSc ACA *1986;* 36 Dean Moor Road, Hazel Grove, STOCKPORT, SK7 5LL.
RYMELL, Ms. Samantha Claire, BA ACA *2002;* U N W Llp, Citygate, St. James Boulevard, NEWCASTLE UPON TYNE, NE1 4JE.
RYMILL, Miss. Diane Susan, BSc ACA *1989;* 1 Grosvenor Avenue, Streetly, SUTTON COLDFIELD, B74 3PB.
RYN, Mr. Robert Bernard, FCA *1972;* GPO Box 1615, SYDNEY, NSW 2001, AUSTRALIA.
RYNINKS, Mr. Brian Preston, ACA CA(SA) *2010;* Merrywood, Hampton-on-the-Hill, WARWICK, CV35 8QR.
RYNTJES, Mr. Simon David, BSc ACA *1997;* 335 Porter Street, TEMPLESTOWE, VIC 3106, AUSTRALIA.
RYVES, Mr. Alun Thomas Mckellar, BA ACA *1988;* 3 Tower Meadows, SWAFFHAM, NORFOLK, PE37 7LT.
SAADAT-LAJEVARDY, Miss. Shiva, BSc ACA *1992;* Flat 16 Abbotsbury House, 139 Abbotsbury Road, LONDON, W14 8EN.
SAADE, Mr. Abdallah Ibrahim, BSc ACA *1991;* 3rd floor Centria Building, 2908 Prince Mohammad Bin Abdulaziz Road, Tahlia, RIYADH, PO Box 250, SAUDI ARABIA.
SAADETIAN, Mr. Setrak Kevork, FCA *1968;* Veinard Gelingen Limited, 109 Georgiou Griva Digeni, Aegean Building, 1st Floor Office 101, 3101 LIMASSOL, CYPRUS.
•**SAADY, Mr. Stephen Jon, FCA** *1974;* (Tax Fac), SJS Tax Limited, Symal House, Suite C2, 423 Edgware Road, LONDON, NW9 0HU. See also SJS Tax Consultancy
SABA, Miss. Clare Elisabeth, BA ACA *1999;* RPS Group plc, Centurion House, 85 Milton Park, Milton, ABINGDON, OX14 4RY.
SABA, Mrs. Eilish, BA(Hons) ACA *2000;* 39 Grandison Road, Battersea, LONDON, SW11 6LS.
SABARATNAM, Mr. Siva, BSc(Hons) ACA *2000;* 28 Park Mansions, Prince Of Wales Drive, LONDON, SW11 4HQ.
SABELL, Mr. Nigel, BCom ACA *1982;* 35 Woodrow Crescent, Knowle, SOLIHULL, B93 9EF.
SABETI, Mr. Amir Farhad, MSc BA FCA *1999;* 6A Harold Avenue, GREENWICH, CT 06830, UNITED STATES.
SABEY, Mr. Mark James, BA ACA *2003;* Ferrari UK, 275 Leigh Road, SLOUGH, SL1 4HF.
SABEY, Mr. Martin Alfred John, FCA *1968;* La Valette, La Ruette, St. Lawrence, JERSEY, JE3 1HT.
SABEY, Mr. Warwick Norman Francis, FCA *1970;* Beechwood, Holly Bank Rd, WOKING, GU22 0JW.
SABHARWAL, Mr. Anil, MA FCA *1976;* 340 East 50th Street, NEW YORK, NY 10022, UNITED STATES.
SABHARWAL, Mr. Deepak, FCA *1971;* 3 Woodhall Avenue, LONDON, SE21 7HL.
SABHARWAL, Mr. Harish Hampton, MA ACA *1997;* 43 Dorchester Road, WEYBRIDGE, SURREY, KT13 8PE.
SABHARWAL, Mr. Mukesh, ACA *1985;* 44 MALDIVES CRESCENT, BRAMPTON L6P 1L3, ON, CANADA.
SABHARWAL, Mr. Naveen, BA ACA *2002;* 26 Wentworth Road, Wollaston, STOURBRIDGE, WEST MIDLANDS, DY8 4SB.
SABHARWAL, Miss. Neena, MA MSc ACA *2003;* Apartment 59 Becquerel Court, School Square, LONDON, SE10 0QY.
SABHARWAL, Mr. Rajiv, FCA *1981;* 100, Pall Mall, LONDON, SW1Y 5NQ.
SABHARWAL, Mrs. Usha, BCom ACA *1980;* Whitestones, Old Mill Road, Denham, UXBRIDGE, UB9 5AW.
SABHLOK, Mr. Varun, BSc ACA *1984;* 237 Arcadia Road #01-01, SINGAPORE 289844, SINGAPORE.
SABIN, Mr. John Richard, FCA *1971;* 4 Kielder Close, Narborough, LEICESTER, LE19 3YW.
SABIN, Mr. Mark Rowland, BA ACA *1990;* The White Cottage, 132 Kippington Road, SEVENOAKS, KENT, TN13 2LW.
SABIN, Mr. Trevor Thomas, FCA *1963;* 2 Allendale Avenue, Attenborough, Beeston, NOTTINGHAM, NG9 6AN.
•**SABINE, Mr. Peter Graham, FCA** *1971;* Peter Sabine & Co, 17 Keble Place, LONDON, SW13 8HJ.
SABLES, Mr. Michael James, BSc ACA *1999;* 3 Sylvan Ridge, SANDHURST, GU47 8QT.
SABOOWALA, Miss. Nafisa, BA ACA MBA *1994;* 35 Theobald Road, Walthamstow, LONDON, E17 8JQ.
SABWANI, Mr. Waqas, ACA FCCA *2011;* Flat 6 Fairwood Court, 33 Fairlop Road, LONDON, E11 1BJ.
SABZWARI, Mr. Wajid Ali, FCA *1970;* 7 Tariq Block, New Garden Town, LAHORE, PAKISTAN.
SACCO, Mrs. Vivienne Amanda, BSc ACA *1997;* Ardoch House, Glenhead, DUNBLANE, PERTHSHIRE, FK15 9PD.
SACERDOTI, Mr. Daniel David, BA ACA *2007;* 25 Manor House Drive, LONDON, NW6 7DE.
SACERDOTI, Mr. Simon Emanuel, MA ACA *1997;* 12 Biddulph Road, LONDON, W9 1JB.
SACH, Mr. Colin Francis, BSc FCA CF *1981;* Watchmaker Court, 33 St John's Lane, LONDON, EC1M 4DB.
SACH, Mrs. Katherine Louise, BA(Hons) ACA *2002;* 1 Chestnut Way, Newton Poppleford, SIDMOUTH, DEVON, EX10 0DL.
SACHAK, Miss. Rukaiya, BSc ACA *1988;* 6 Athena Close, Byron Hill Road, HARROW, HA2 0JB.
SACHDEV, Mr. Chetan, ACA *2011;* 6 Highbury Road, LEICESTER, LE4 6FT.
•**SACHDEV, Mr. Mahesh, BA(Hons) ACA** *2001;* RDP Newmans LLP, Lynwood House, 373-375 Station Road, HARROW, MIDDLESEX, HA1 2AW.
SACHDEV, Mr. Mitan Dinesh, BSc ACA *2009;* 9 Irvine Avenue, HARROW, MIDDLESEX, HA3 8QE.
SACHDEV, Mr. Neil Shalen, ACA *2009;* 20 Wolstonbury, LONDON, N12 7BA.
•**SACHDEV, Mr. Ripan, FCA** *1986;* (Tax Fac), Sachdevs, 63 Cromwell Lane, Westwood Heath, COVENTRY, CV4 8AQ.
SACHDEV, Miss. Sejal, BA ACA *1993;* 3 Mayhall Farm, Copperkins Lane, AMERSHAM, HP6 5RG.
SACHEDINA VIRANI, Mrs. Najma, BA(Hons) ACA *2004;* 3033 Riverbrooke Ct, ATLANTA, GA 30339, UNITED STATES.
•**SACHER, Mr. Brad Jonathan, ACA CA(AUS)** *2011;* (Tax Fac), TaxCo Global Limited, 38 Wigmore Street, LONDON, W1U 2RU.
SACHO, Mr. Zwi Yosef, CA(SA) *2006;* Flat 1 Ray Court, Golders Green Road, LONDON, NW11 9LX.
SACHS, Mrs. Kathryn, BSS ACA *1978;* Henriette-Herz-Ring 110, 21035 HAMBURG, GERMANY.
•**SACKER, Mr. Laurence, FCA CF** *1981;* UHY Hacker Young LLP, Quadrant House, 4 Thomas More Square, LONDON, E1W 1YW. See also UHY Corporate Finance Limited
•**SACKETT, Mr. Malcolm Thomas, ACA** *2005;* Stephen Hill Partnership Limited, 139-141 Watling Street, GILLINGHAM, KENT, ME7 2YY. See also Stephen Hill Partnership (Holdings) Limited
SACKETT, Mr. Rex Wilton, FCA *1968;* 31 Chiltern Park, Thornbury, BRISTOL, BS35 2HX.
SACKEY, Mr. James Ebenezer, BSc ACA *2001;* Box 307, 253 College Street, TORONTO M5T1R5, ON, CANADA.
SACKMAN, Mr. Alan, FCA *1965;* 10 Lake View, EDGWARE, HA8 7RU. (Life Member)
•**SACKMAN, Mr. Malcolm, BA FCA CTA** *1998;* Sackman & Co Limited, Unit L32, MK Two Business Centre, Barton Road, Water Eaton, MILTON KEYNES MK2 3HU.
•**SACKS, Mr. Alan Leon Barry, FCA** *1965;* (Tax Fac), Alan Sacks & Co, Little Red Court, 7 St. Ronans Close, Hadley Wood, BARNET, HERTFORDSHIRE EN4 0JH. See also ASCA Limited and ASCA Limited
•**SACKS, Mr. Andrew Marc, BA ACA** *1995;* 71 High Ash Avenue, LEEDS, LS17 8RX.
SACKS, Mrs. Eve Gillian, BA ACA ATII *1999;* Rathbone Brothers plc, 159 New Bond Street, LONDON, W1S 2UD.
SACKS, Mr. John Harvey, LLB FCA *1968;* with JSA Consultancy Services, Atlas Chambers, 3 Field Court, Gray's Inn, LONDON, WC1R 5EP.
SACKS, Mr. Leon Joseph, BSc FCA *1976;* Baker & Mckenzie, 1111 Brickell Avenue, 17th Floor, MIAMI, FL 33131, UNITED STATES.
•**SACKS, Mr. Stephen Howard, FCA** *1981;* Shears & Partners Limited, 88 Edgware Way, EDGWARE, MIDDLESEX, HA8 8JS.
SACKWILD, Mr. Gerald, FCA *1967;* 154 Howard Drive, LETCHWORTH GARDEN CITY, HERTFORDSHIRE, SG6 2DE.
SACRANIE, Mr. Bashir, FCA *1969;* 21 Thistle Road, Newlands, CAPE TOWN, 7700, SOUTH AFRICA.
•**SACRANIE, Mr. Farouk Mahomed, FCA** *1969;* P O Box 2629, BLANTYRE, MALAWI.
SACRANIE, Mr. Shahin Akbar, ACA *1985;* 17 Woodlands, LONDON, NW11 9QJ.
SADARANGANI, Mr. Dinesh Bhagwan, ACA *1995;* 7th Floor Flat F Block 10, South Horizons, AP LEI CHAU, HONG KONG ISLAND, HONG KONG SAR.
SADD, Mr. Michael John Gower, FCA *1951;* Southease, Copyhold Lane, Cuckfield, HAYWARDS HEATH, WEST SUSSEX, RH17 5EB. (Life Member)
SADD, Mr. Nigel William, FCA *1956;* 3254 Windrift Circle, MEMPHIS, TN 38125, UNITED STATES. (Life Member)
SADD, Mr. Philip James Gower, FCA *1972;* Kendal Cottage, Woodfield Lane, Stutton, IPSWICH, IP9 2ST.

SADD, Mr. Robert Llewelyn, FCA *1955;* 11 Park Meadow, HATFIELD, AL9 5HA. (Life Member)
•**SADDIQUE, Mr. Muhammad, FCA** *1982;* Ray (Accountants) Mcr Ltd, 78 Dickenson Road, Rusholme, MANCHESTER, M14 5HF. See also Ray (Accountants) Ltd
•**SADDLETON, Mr. William, FCA** *1972;* William Saddleton, 94 Cowper Road, HARPENDEN, AL5 5NH.
•**SADEK, Mr. Anis Fernando, BA FCA** *1981;* P O Box 4254, 1001 City Tower 2, Sheikh Zayed Road, DUBAI, UNITED ARAB EMIRATES.
SADEK, Mr. Faisal, BA ACA *1997;* 5 Mill View Gardens, CROYDON, CR0 5HW.
SADEK, Mr. Mohamed Zakaria, ACA CA(SA) *2009;* 103 Sama Residence, DUBAI, UNITED ARAB EMIRATES.
SADHRA, Miss. Sharanjeet Kaur, BA ACA *2005;* 14 Rhapsody Crescent, Warley, BRENTWOOD, CM14 5GD.
•**SADHU, Mr. Amar Nath, MA FCA** *1970;* Professor, Indian Institute of Technology, 73/1A Palm Avenue, KOLKATA 700 019, INDIA.
SADHU, Mr. Mitesh, BSc ACA *2010;* 5 Wood End Way, NORTHOLT, MIDDLESEX, UB5 4QQ.
SADHWANI, Ms. Dimple Murli, BSc ACA *2004;* c/o Grandwood Limited, Suite 2A, International House, Bell Lane, GIBRALTAR, GIBRALTAR.
SADIKALI, Mr. Shamuun, FCA *1970;* 10 Ballinger Way, NORTHOLT, MIDDLESEX, UB5 6FG.
SADIKOT, Mr. Aunali Ibrahim, FCA *1975;* 43 Boxmoor Road, HARROW, HA3 8LH.
SADILINE, Mr. Igor, ACA *2001;* 16 Drayton Gardens, LONDON, W13 0LQ.
SADIQ, Mr. Liaqat Ali, BA FCA *1989;* 22 Shortwood Avenue, STAINES, TW18 4JL.
•**SADIQ, Mr. Muhammad, BA FCA ATII** *1972;* (Tax Fac), Sadiq Metcalfe & Co., 94 Dickenson Road, MANCHESTER, M14 5HJ.
SADIQ, Mr. Muhammed Shahid, BCom FCA *1980;* A.F. Ferguson & Co, P.I.A. Building, 49 Blue Area, P.O. Box 3021, ISLAMABAD, PAKISTAN.
SADIQ, Miss. Sabrina, BSc ACA *2005;* 21 Pendrell Road, LONDON, SE4 2PB.
SADIQ, Mr. Shahid, BSc ACA *2001;* 16 Aldin Avenue, SLOUGH, SL1 1RS.
•**SADIQ AKBAR, Mr. Mohamed Tariq, FCA** *1979;* Ernst & Young, P.O. Box 140, MANAMA, BAHRAIN.
SADIQUE, Mr. Waseem, FCA *1978;* Four Trees, Nightingales Lane, CHALFONT ST. GILES, BUCKINGHAMSHIRE, HP8 4SF.
SADLEIR, Mr. Hugh Vennor Morris, MA ACA *2010;* 28 Oswyth Road, LONDON, SE5 8NH.
SADLEIR, Mr. William Hugh Granby, BSc FCA *1970;* Lads House, Lynes Yard, Bishops Cannings, DEVIZES, SN10 2LS.
•**SADLER, Mrs. Ailsa Clare, BA ACA** *2001;* Ailsa Sadler Ltd, 4 Shaftesbury Avenue, Chandler's Ford, EASTLEIGH, HAMPSHIRE, SO53 3BS.
SADLER, Mr. Alan Peter, BA ACA *1990;* Improvement Development Agency, 76-86 Turnmill Street, LONDON, EC1M 5LG.
SADLER, Mr. Anthony Graham, BA ACA *1981;* 2 Astons Road, NORTHWOOD, MIDDLESEX, HA6 2LD.
SADLER, Mr. Anthony James, BA ACA *1990;* Holly Cottage, 25 North Road, Chavey Down, ASCOT, SL5 8RP.
SADLER, Mrs. Christina Mary, FCA *1987;* Easton College Farms Ltd PO Box 5, Easton, NORWICH, NR9 5DX.
SADLER, Mr. Christopher Richard, BA ACA *1995;* Berghaus Limited, 12 Colima Avenue, Sunderland Enterprise Park, SUNDERLAND, SR5 3XB.
SADLER, Mr. Colin Ian, BSc(Econ) FCA *1963;* 49 Gurdon Road, Grundisburgh, WOODBRIDGE, IP13 6XA.
SADLER, Mr. David Albert, FCA *1962;* 16 St. Ronan's Circle, Peterculter, ABERDEEN, AB14 0NE. (Life Member)
SADLER, Mr. David John, FCA *1971;* Westwood, Westfield Lane, Woodborough, NOTTINGHAM, NG14 6EP.
SADLER, Mr. David Robert, BA FCA *1993;* 43 The Ridgeway, Fetcham, LEATHERHEAD, SURREY, KT22 9BE.
•**SADLER, Mrs. Dianne Louise, ACA** *1994;* Oaken Accountancy Services, Fairfields, Oaken Lane, Oaken, WOLVERHAMPTON, WV8 2BD.
SADLER, Mr. Douglas George, FCA *1955;* 7 Langford Road, Withington, MANCHESTER, M20 1QA. (Life Member)
•**SADLER, Mr. Graham Edward Joseph, FCA** *1974;* (Tax Fac), Sadler Davies & Co LLP, 25A Essex Road, DARTFORD, DA1 2AU.
SADLER, Ms. Heather Elizabeth, BA ACA *1993;* 23 Queensway, NORTH SHIELDS, NE30 4NB.
SADLER, Mr. Iain William, BA ACA *1999;* 28 Henry Street, Windsor, MELBOURNE, VIC 3181, AUSTRALIA.
•**SADLER, Mr. Ian Frank, LLB ACA** *1989;* Deloitte LLP, Hill House, 1 Little New Street, LONDON, EC4A 3TR. See also Deloitte & Touche LLP
SADLER, Mr. James, FCA *1971;* Fayrefield Foods Ltd, Englesea House, Barthomley Road, CREWE, CW1 5UF.
•**SADLER, Mr. James Anthony, FCA** *1961;* James A. Sadler, 13 Fountain Place, Barbourne, WORCESTER, WR1 3HW.
•**SADLER, Ms. Jane Miriam, MBA ACA** *1985;* 3a May Lam Mansions, 2 Sing Woo Crescent, HAPPY VALLEY, HONG KONG SAR.
SADLER, Miss. Julie, BSc FCA *1994;* 10 Walpole Lodge, 5-7 Culmington Road, LONDON, W13 9NP.
SADLER, Mrs. Karen Kimberley, BA ACA *1999;* Stable Cottage Main Street, Thorganby, YORK, YO19 6DA.
SADLER, Mrs. Katherine Jane, ACA *1989;* 8 Oaks Drive, SUTTON COLDFIELD, B75 5AP.
SADLER, Mr. Keith John, BA ACA *1986;* 3 Clifton High Grove, Stoke Bishop, BRISTOL, BS9 1TU.
SADLER, Mr. Lee Antony, FCA *1992;* 26 Watercombe Heights, YEOVIL, BA20 2TB.
SADLER, Miss. Rachel Kay, BA ACA *1996;* WPNSA, Osprey Quay, PORTLAND, DORSET, DT5 1SA.
•**SADLER, Mr. Richard James, ACA** *1999;* Accountancy Solutions Online Limited, 12 St. Anthonys Avenue, HEMEL HEMPSTEAD, HERTFORDSHIRE, HP3 8HQ.
•**SADLER, Mr. Robert Alistair, BSc FCA** *1991;* (Tax Fac), Robert Sadler & Company, Hargroves Cycles, 30b Southgate, CHICHESTER, WEST SUSSEX, PO19 1DP.
•**SADLER, Mr. Robert Ian, FCA** *1971;* The Red Cottage, 29 Colbert Avenue, SOUTHEND-ON-SEA, SS1 3BH.
SADLER, Mr. Sean Anthony, BA ACA *1987;* Ivydene, Leicester Road, Ravenstone, COALVILLE, LE67 2AR.
SADLER, Mr. Stephen Paul, BSc(Econ) ACA *1997;* Buckleaze Farm, Buckleaze, PEWSEY, WILTSHIRE, SN9 5NY.
SADLER, Mr. Steven, BSc ACA *1994;* 25 Egerton Drive, Hale, ALTRINCHAM, WA15 8EF.
SADLER, Mr. Steven Arthur, BSc ACA *1980;* 1 Dyer Road, WOKINGHAM, RG40 5PG.
SADLER, Mr. Terrance John Frederick, BA ACA *1985;* Redcot, Grange Road, Bromley Cross, BOLTON, BL7 9AU.
SADLER, Mr. Thomas, BSc(Hons) ACA *2003;* with National Audit Office, 157-197 Buckingham Palace Road, Victoria, LONDON, SW1W 9SP.
SADLER, Mr. Timothy, MSc ACA *1981;* 16 Virginia Drive, Penn, WOLVERHAMPTON, WV4 5PS.
SADLER, Mr. Timothy Martyn, BA ACA *2001;* 11 Oxlease Close, ROMSEY, HAMPSHIRE, SO51 7HA.
SADLER, Miss. Victoria Jane, MSc BA(Hons) ACA *2003;* 15 Lockyer House, The Platt, LONDON, SW15 1EE.
•**SADLIER, Miss. Rachael Jennifer, FCA** *1977;* R Sadlier, 22 Heather Close, Whittoncroft, ISLEWORTH, MIDDLESEX, TW7 7PR.
•**SADOFSKY, Mr. Melvyn Warren, FCA** *1971;* (Tax Fac), MWS Business Management Limited, 6 Earls Court, Priory Park East, HULL, HU4 7DY.
SADOWSKI, Miss. Sarah Marie, BSc ACA *2006;* 18 Clift Road, BRISTOL, BS3 1RZ.
•**SADRA, Mr. Kamiljit Singh, BA FCA** *1991;* (Tax Fac), Majainah Sadra Limited, 2 Martin House, 179/181 North End Road, LONDON, W14 9NL.
SADRANI, Miss. Ami, BA(Hons) ACA *2010;* 3 Heritage Court, Gibbet Hill, COVENTRY, CV4 7HD.
SADUR, Mr. Khalid Mohammad Khalleck, BSc ACA *1999;* 13 Yorkshire Gardens, LONDON, N18 2LD.
•**SAEED, Mrs. Fiza Ann, BA ACA** *1994;* Kimeon Limited, 7 Peregrine Way, Wimbledon, LONDON, SW19 4RN. See also Kimeon Accountants
SAEED, Mr. Khalid, FCA *1964;* 7 Peregrine Way, Wimbledon, LONDON, SW19 4RN.
SAEED, Mr. Mohammed Umair, BSc ACA *2011;* 139 Lansdowne Road, CARDIFF, CF5 1PS.
SAEED, Mr. Oneib, BSc ACA *2001;* Flat 10 Projection West, Merchants Place, READING, RG1 1ET.
SAEED, Mrs. Pamela, FCA *1968;* 7 Peregrine Way, LONDON, SW19 4RN.
SAEED, Mr. Rifat, FCA *1974;* 80D, Phase 1, Defence Housing Authority, LAHORE, PAKISTAN.
SAEED, Miss. Safia, MSc BA(Hons) ACA *2009;* 1 Shelton Drive, Ainsdale, SOUTHPORT, MERSEYSIDE, PR8 2TE.
SAEED, Mr. Saquib, MA ACA *1999;* 18 Samels Court, South Black Lion Lane, LONDON, W6 9TL.
SAEED, Mr. Yusaf Mian, ACA *1983;* 188 Scotch Corner Upper Mall, LAHORE, PAKISTAN.
SAEED MOHAMMED, Mr. Akhtar Ali, ACA *2006;* 2nd Floor, Addax Tower, Seef District, MANAMA, 11939, BAHRAIN.
SAER, Mr. David Richard Ernest, FCA *1968;* 1 Cutts Close, Brinkworth, CHIPPENHAM, WILTSHIRE, SN15 5BB.
SAFDAR, Mr. Zahid Muraad, ACA *2009;* 44 Young Street, DERBY, DE23 6NB.
SAFFER, Mr. Alan, BA FCA *1982;* 3 Heathfield Road, BUSHEY, WD23 2LH.
•**SAFFER, Mr. Michael Jonathan, BCom FCA** *1974;* (Tax Fac), Michael J Saffer & Co, Northern House, 87 Town Street, Horsforth, LEEDS, LS18 5BP.
SAFIER, Mr. Boaz, BSc ACA *2004;* Flat 5 Tower Court, 1a Canonbury Street, LONDON, N1 2US.
SAGAR, Mr. Lance, MPhys(Hons) ACA *2010;* 47 Hill Crest Drive, BEVERLEY, NORTH HUMBERSIDE, HU17 7JL.
SAGAR, Mrs. Louise Jane, BSc(Hons) ACA *2000;* 23 St. Catherines Road, HARROGATE, NORTH YORKSHIRE, HG2 8JZ.
SAGAR, Miss. Mandy Louise, BA ACA *1992;* Ernst & Young LLP, Room 4444, 8484 West Park Drive, MCLEAN, VA 22102, UNITED STATES.
•**SAGAR, Mr. Paul, FCA** *1974;* Sagar & Co, 2 Ambleside Close, STONE, STAFFORDSHIRE, ST15 8FU.
SAGAR, Mr. Richard Francis, JP FCA *1957;* 42 Dunderdale Avenue, NELSON, BB9 0AR. (Life Member)
SAGAYAM, Miss. Sheila Christine, BA ACA *1994;* 29 Kings Drive, SINGAPORE 266396, SINGAPORE.
SAGAYAM, Miss. Theresa Ann, BA ACA *1994;* New Broad Street House, 35 New Broad Street, LONDON, EC2M 1NH.
SAGE, Mr. Alexander, BA FCA *1998;* 2 Cunningham Avenue, ST. ALBANS, HERTFORDSHIRE, AL1 1JL.
SAGE, Mr. Brian William, FCA *1956;* 72 Orchard Close, Fetcham, LEATHERHEAD, KT22 9JB. (Life Member)
SAGE, Mr. Charles Lyndon, BSc ACA *1992;* 15A Caerphilly Road, Bassaleg, NEWPORT, NP10 8LE.
•**SAGE, Mr. Colin, BSc FCA** *1973;* CS Taxation and Accountancy Limited, 41 High Cross Drive, Rogerstone, NEWPORT, GWENT, NP10 9AB.
•**SAGE, Mr. David Alan, BSc FCA** *1986;* 24a Alma Square, LONDON, NW8 9QA.
SAGE, Miss. Hilary Suzanne, FCA *1976;* The Disabilities Trust, 32 Market Place, BURGESS HILL, WEST SUSSEX, RH15 9NP.
SAGE, Mr. Joe, BSc ACA *2004;* Garden Flat, 119 Greencroft Gardens, LONDON, NW6 3PE.
SAGE, Mr. Morley Andrew, LLB FCA *1987;* Stovax (Holdings) Limited, Falcon Road, Sowton Industrial Estate, EXETER, EX2 7LF.
SAGE, Mr. Richard Anthony, MA FCA *1992;* Rzeczycza 26, 66-614 MASZEWO, POLAND.
SAGE, Mr. Richard Peter, BSc(Hons) ACA *2000;* 37A Cheapside, Horsell, WOKING, SURREY, GU21 4JQ.
SAGE, Mr. Robert Bernard, FCA *1974;* 1 Springfield Cottages, Shipston Road, STRATFORD-UPON-AVON, WARWICKSHIRE, CV37 8LU.
SAGE, Mr. Robert Ian, MA FCA *1987;* 14 Hasker Street, LONDON, SW3 2LG.
SAGE, Mr. Roderick Noel Anthony, FCA *1976;* (Tax Fac), No. 97 Kadoorie Avenue, HO MAN TIN, KOWLOON, HONG KONG SAR.
SAGE, Mrs. Sarah-Helen, BSc ACA *1997;* 48 Emet Lane, Emersons Green, BRISTOL, BS16 7BX.
•**SAGER, Mr. Aron Mier, FCA** *1967;* Sager & Co., 7 Water End Close, BOREHAMWOOD, HERTFORDSHIRE, WD6 4PW.
SAGGAR, Mr. Ashish, BSc ACA *2009;* 1 Tollhouse Lane, WALLINGTON, SM6 9PA.
SAGGAR, Mrs. Ritu, BSc ACA *1995;* with C P Waites, 24 St Cuthberts Way, DARLINGTON, DL1 1GB.
SAGGAR, Mrs. Ruchi Parmar, BSc ACA *2007;* 1 Tollhouse Lane, WALLINGTON, SURREY, SM6 9PA.
SAGGAR, Mr. Sachin, ACA *2008;* 58 Southover, Woodside Park, LONDON, N12 7ES.
SAGGU, Mr. Ranjit Singh, BSc ACA *2000;* 32 St. Peters Way Chorleywood, RICKMANSWORTH, HERTFORDSHIRE, WD3 5QE.
SAGHIR, Mr. Rehan Qaid, ACA *1992;* Eli Lilly Asia Inc. Thailand Branch, Thanapoom Tower 14th Floor, 1550 New Petchburi Road, Makasan Rachtavee, BANGKOK 10400, THAILAND.
SAGLANI, Miss. Mita, ACA *2008;* 9 The Crescent, WIGSTON, LEICESTERSHIRE, LE18 1HW.
•**SAGOO, Mrs. Fiona Gwendoline, LLB ACA** *1999;* (Tax Fac), FGS Accountancy & Taxation, 39 Woodland Way, Theydon Bois, EPPING, ESSEX, CM16 7DY.
SAGOO, Miss. Harkiran, MA BMedSc ACA *2011;* 62 Brewers Square, BIRMINGHAM, B16 0PN.
•**SAGOO, Mr. Sukhdev Singh, MSc ACA** *1979;* CSJ Financial Solutions Limited, 122 High Street, Acton, LONDON, W3 6QX.
•**SAHA, Mr. Ajit Kumar, FCA** *1968;* A.K.Saha & Co, 40 Highcliffe Gardens, ILFORD, IG4 5HR.
SAHA, Mr. Debashish Mintu, BA ACA *1988;* Eden Financial Ltd Moorgate Hall, 155 Moorgate, LONDON, EC2M 6XB.
SAHA, Mr. Dipak, BA ACA *2007;* 2 Gold Street, Apt 4111, NEW YORK, NY 10038, UNITED STATES.
SAHA, Miss. Lipi Aba, BA(Hons) ACA *2003;* 105 Atkins Road, LONDON, SW12 0AL.
SAHA, Mr. Manik Krishnendu, BSc ACA *2006;* 129 Wellesley Road, ILFORD, ESSEX, IG1 4LN.
SAHA, Mr. Mantu Lal, FCA *1975;* 82 Badessa Circle, THORNHILL L4J 6E5, ON, CANADA. (Life Member)
SAHA, Mr. Ricki Anirudh, ACA *2011;* 40 Highcliffe Gardens, ILFORD, ESSEX, IG4 5HR.
SAHA, Mrs. Shalini, BSc ACA *2006;* 129 Wellesley Road, ILFORD, ESSEX, IG1 4LN.
•**SAHA, Mr. Sukumar Chandra, ACA FCCA** *2010;* Plus Minus Ltd, C/6, 417 Wick Lane, Fish Island, LONDON, E3 2JG.
SAHA, Mr. Tamal, BA ACA *1994;* Riso 610 Centennial Avenue, Centennial Park Elstree, BOREHAMWOOD, HERTFORDSHIRE, WD6 3TJ.
•**SAHA, Miss. Tanuka, BSc(Hons) ACA** *2004;* N Saha & Co Limited, Flat 21 Parade Mansions, Hendon Central, LONDON, NW4 3JR.
SAHADEVAN, Mr. Sajit, BCom ACA *1991;* (Tax Fac), 36 Meadow Rise, Blackmore, INGATESTONE, CM4 0QY.
SAHAI, Mr. Anil, FCA *1974;* UBS International Inc, 1285 Avenue of the Americas, 19th Floor, NEW YORK, NY 10019, UNITED STATES.
SAHAI, Mr. Neel, BA(Hons) ACA *2001;* Minerva Financial Services Ltd, PO Box 218, JERSEY, JE4 8SD.
SAHAI, Mr. Romi, BSc(Econ) ACA *2001;* Apartment 401, Travo A, The Views, P.O.Box 126227, DUBAI, 126227 UNITED ARAB EMIRATES.
SAHAI, Mr. Umesh, FCA *1969;* Fairlawn, La Vieille Charriere, Trinity, JERSEY, JE3 5AT.
•**SAHAMI, Mr. Firooz, BSc FCA** *1970;* (Tax Fac), Finac Services Ltd, 16 Charles II Street, LONDON, SW1Y 4QU.
•**SAHAY, Mr. Arjun, FCA** *1985;* ASA & Co, Regent House Business Centre, 24/25 Nutford Place, Marble Arch, LONDON, W1H 5YN.
SAHGAL, Ms. Nandita, BCom ACA MSI *2000;* Seymour Pierce Limited, 20 Old Bailey, LONDON, EC4M 7EN.
SAHIN, Mr. Huseyin, ACA *2008;* Flat 15, Gaysley House, Hotspur Street, LONDON, SE11 6TS.
SAHNEY, Mrs. Anupa, BA ACA *1992;* 6 Manavi Apartments, 36 Ridge Road, MUMBAI 400006, MAHARASHTRA, INDIA.
•**SAHNI, Mr. Barinder Singh, FCA** *1973;* Sahni & Co Limited, 55 Maresfield Gardens, LONDON, NW3 5TE. See also Accountancy, Taxation & Secretarial Services Ltd, Hampstead Accountants Ltd and UK Tax Returns Ltd
SAHNI, Mr. Manjit Singh, FCA *1972;* The Croft, 26 Great North Road, Highgate, LONDON, N6 4LU.
SAHNI, Mr. Ranjit, MA ACA *2010;* 55 Maresfield Gardens, LONDON, NW3 5TE.
SAHOTA, Mr. Ajvinder Singh, BA(Hons) ACA *2003;* 21 Thorburn Road, NORTHAMPTON, NN3 3DA.
•**SAHOTA, Mr. Amritpal Singh, BA ACA ATII** *1988;* Darwins, 54 Batchworth Lane, NORTHWOOD, MIDDLESEX, HA6 3HG.
SAHOTA, Mr. Gurdeep, BSc ACA *2010;* 62 Himley Crescent, WOLVERHAMPTON, WV4 5DE.
SAHOTA, Mr. Gurmit Singh, MA BA ACA *2007;* 72 Chalgrove Crescent, ILFORD, IG5 0LU.
•**SAHOTA, Mr. Jasbinder Singh, FCA** *1994;* Deloitte LLP, Athene Place, 66 Shoe Lane, LONDON, EC4A 3BQ. See also Deloitte & Touche LLP
SAHOTA, Mr. Kalbir Singh, BSc ACA *2007;* with HSBC Bank plc, 62-76 Park Street, LONDON, SE1 9DZ.
•ⓘ**SAHOTA, Mr. Sabia Singh, BSc FCA FABRP** *1994;* BBK Partnership, 1 Beauchamp Court, Victors Way, BARNET, HERTFORDSHIRE, EN5 5TZ.

SAHOTA, Mrs. Sukhjinder, BA ACA *1992;* 3 Ravenswood Park, NORTHWOOD, HA6 3PR.
SAHU, Mr. Peter, BEng ACA *1993;* Veritas Asset Management (UK) Ltd Elizabeth House, 39 York Road, LONDON, SE1 7NQ.
SAICH, Mrs. Margaret Anna, BA(Hons) ACA *2003;* with PricewaterhouseCoopers LLP, 80 Strand, LONDON, WC2R 0AF.
SAID, Mr. Abdul Malek Bin Mohamed, BSc ACA *1999;* 27 Jalan Rabung U8/40, Bukit Jelutong, 40150 SHAH ALAM, MALAYSIA.
SAID, Mr. Faraz Raza, MSc BSc ACA *2003;* PO BOX 212697, DUBAI, UNITED ARAB EMIRATES.
SAID, Mr. Shaqeel Ahmed, LLB ACA *1998;* No. 2a Setia Murni, Bukit Damansara, 50490 KUALA LUMPUR, FEDERAL TERRITORY, MALAYSIA.
SAID, Mr. Usman, FCA *1968;* 1-E-II Gulberg-III, LAHORE, PAKISTAN.
SAIDEMAN, Mr. Seymour Geoffrey, FCA *1960;* 10 Oak Lodge Close, STANMORE, MIDDLESEX, HA7 4QB. (Life Member)
SAIDI, Mr. Wan Shahriman, BSc ACA *1993;* 40 Jalan USJ 11/3L, UEP, 47610 SUBANG, SELANGOR, MALAYSIA.
SAIDI, Miss. Wan Shamila, BSc ACA *1998;* Level 21 Tower Two, Petronas Twin Towers, Kuala Lumpur City Centre, 50088 KUALA LUMPUR, FEDERAL TERRITORY, MALAYSIA.
•SAIFUDDIN, Mr. Akhter, ACA *1982;* Saifuddin & Co, 62 Widmore Road, BROMLEY, BR1 3BD.
SAIFULLAH, Mrs. Shamim, FCA *1977;* 59 Limesdale Gardens, EDGWARE, HA8 5HY.
SAIGAL, Mr. Anish, ACA FCCA *2009;* Barclays Capital, 10 South Colonnade, LONDON, E14 4PU.
SAIGAR, Mr. Ali-Asgar Mustafa, BSc(Hons) ACA *2009;* 29 Ffordd Brynhyfryd, Old St. Mellons, CARDIFF, CF3 5XE.
SAILES, Mr. Tony, FCA *1970;* 8 Holt Park Avenue, LEEDS, LS16 7RA.
SAINI, Miss. Katrina, MBA ACA *2006;* 655 S Fair Oaks Ave #P313, SUNNYVALE, CA 94086, UNITED STATES.
SAINI, Mr. Vikas, ACA *2010;* 2 Stanhope Road, SLOUGH, SL1 6JS.
SAINS, Miss. Elizabeth Claire, MA ACA *2001;* 32 Colchester Road, White Colne, COLCHESTER, CO6 2PN.
SAINSBURY, Mr. Adam, ACA *2011;* 44 Highfield Road, DERBY, DERBYSHIRE, DE22 1GZ.
SAINSBURY, Mr. Andrew, MMath(Hons) ACA *2011;* 12 Lentworth Drive, Scotforth, LANCASTER, LA1 4RJ.
•SAINSBURY, Mr. Andrew Keith, FCA *1980;* Treasury Accounting Limited, The Old Treasury, 7 Kings Road, SOUTHSEA, HAMPSHIRE, PO5 4DJ.
•SAINSBURY, Mr. Ian Leicester, FCA *1973;* Ian Sainsbury, 62 Branksome Hill Road, BOURNEMOUTH, BH4 9LG.
SAINSBURY, Mr. Jeffrey Paul, FCA *1966;* Computershare Investor Services Plc Vintners Place, 68 Upper Thames Street, LONDON, EC4V 3BJ.
SAINSBURY, Mr. John Seymour, FCA *1972;* 9 Ribstone Road, Cox Green, MAIDENHEAD, SL6 3HJ.
SAINSBURY, Mr. Richard Frank Newton, FCA *1970;* 4 Pytchley Drive, Long Buckby, NORTHAMPTON, NN6 7PL.
SAINSBURY, Mr. Robert Nicholas, BSc ACA *1996;* Huntfield House, Diddies Road, Stratton, BUDE, CORNWALL, EX23 9DW.
SAINT, Mr. David Julian, BSc ACA *1992;* 3 Old Dairy Cottages, Ibstone, HIGH WYCOMBE, HP14 3YW.
SAINT, Mr. Michael Boulton, FCA *1969;* The Pennines, Croft Ends, APPLEBY-IN-WESTMORLAND, CUMBRIA, CA16 6JW.
SAINT, Mr. Oliver Jackson, FCA *1960;* Jackson Saint & Co Limited, 86A Victoria Road, DEVONPORT 0624, NEW ZEALAND.
SAINT, Mr. Tim, BSc FCA *1979;* 9 Skye Close, MAIDSTONE, KENT, ME15 9SJ.
SAITH, Mr. Vijay Kumar, MA FCA *1970;* 14 Dane Court, WOKING, SURREY, GU22 8SX. (Life Member)
SAJAN, Mr. Amyn, BSc(Hons) ACA *2003;* Pricewaterhousecoopers Llp, 1 Hays Lane, LONDON, SE1 2RD.
SAJBENOVA, Miss. Eva, BSc ACA *2011;* 16 Marshalls Close, EPSOM, KT19 8HZ.
•SAJID, Mr. Adnan Amer, ACA MBA *2000;* Sajid & Sajid Limited, 26 Dover Street, Mayfair, LONDON, W1S 4LY.
SAJID, Miss. Lubna, BSc(Hons) ACA *2005;* 17 Sawley Drive, Cheadle Hulme, CHEADLE, CHESHIRE, SK8 7QA.
SAKAI, Miss. Haru, ACA *2009;* 33 Ambergate Street, LONDON, SE17 3RY.
SAKAMOTO, Mr. Shintaro, ACA *1999;* 4204 1-3-1 MINAMI-AOYAMA, MINATO-KU, TOKYO, 107-0062 JAPAN.
SAKER, Mr. Hitendra, FCA *1964;* (Tax Fac), 142 Darland Avenue, GILLINGHAM, KENT, ME7 3AS.
SAKER, Ms. Julia Ann, BSc(Hons) ACA *2001;* 5 Priestlands Close, HORLEY, RH6 8GG.
•SAKER, Miss. Nicola Catherine, BA ACA *1994;* Life Management Services, 69 Littleton Street, LONDON, SW18 3SZ.
SAKKOS, Mr. Dimitrios, MSc ACA *2011;* 5 Thalias Street, Vouliagmeni, 16671 ATHENS, GREECE.
SAKLANI, Mr. Mahesh Chandra, BA FCA *1974;* 53 Worple Road, Wimbledon, LONDON, SW19 4LA. (Life Member)
SAKLOW, Mr. Alex James, BSc ACA *2007;* with BDO LLP, 55 Baker Street, LONDON, W1U 7EU.
SAKS, Mr. Matthew Peter, BA ACA *2003;* 11 rue Ledru-Rollin, Casselardit, 31300 TOULOUSE, FRANCE.
SAKSENA, Mr. Devesh, BA ACA *2003;* Willows, Love Lane, Long Ditton, SURBITON, SURREY, KT6 5EB.
SAKSIDA, Mrs. Megan Jennifer, ACA *1994;* Residenza Ponti, 231 Milano 2, Segrate, 20090 MILAN, ITALY.
SALAH, Mrs. Farah, BA ACA *2010;* 39 Wintersdale Road, LEICESTER, LE5 2GR.
SALAHUDDIN, Mr. Muhammad, FCA *1966;* 5B Hospital Street Phase II, Defense Housing Authority, KARACHI, PAKISTAN. (Life Member)
SALAHUDDIN, Miss. Saira, BSc ACA *2009;* 4341 Tantallon Lane, Apt #108, MEMPHIS, TN 38125, UNITED STATES.
SALAKAEVA, Ms. Veronika, BA ACA *2007;* House 19 Flat 109, Kalimashkina Street, MOSCOW, RUSSIAN FEDERATION.
SALAM, Miss. Sheema, BA ACA *2009;* 55 Henrietta Street, MANCHESTER, M16 9PN.
SALAMAN, Mrs. Claire Elizabeth, LLB ACA *2005;* Globe OP, Grand Buildings, 1-3 Strand, LONDON, WC2N 5HR.
SALAMI, Mr. Ayodele Rafiu, MSc ACA *1990;* 27 Hill Street, LONDON, W1J 5LP.
SALAMONE, Mrs. Pembe, BA FCA *1994;* Sedley Ricchard Laurence Voulters, Kendal House, 1 Conduit Street, LONDON, W1S 2XA.
SALCEDO, Mrs. Emma, ACA *2007;* 31 Osier Fields, East Leake, LOUGHBOROUGH, LEICESTERSHIRE, LE12 6QG.
SALDANA, Miss. Asuncion, BA ACA *2003;* 4 Maryfield Place, BONNYRIGG, MIDLOTHIAN, EH19 3BQ.
SALDANA, Miss. Renata, BA ACA *2005;* Craven Cottage, 16 Craven Terrace, Sale, MANCHESTER, M33 3GA.
•SALDANHA, Mr. Joseph Manuel, BA FCA *1977;* Joe Saldanha & Co, 164 Rochdale Road, Royton, OLDHAM, OL2 6QF.
SALDANHA, Miss. Rachel, ACA *2010;* Apartment 2, 19 Court Street, Uppermill, OLDHAM, OL3 6HD.
SALDIN, Mr. Erasmon Pernamo, BSc FCA *1970;* Eden Gardens, 428/89 Samagi Mawatha, Hokandara South, 10118 HOKANDARA, SRI LANKA.
•SALE, Mr. Christopher John Norman, BSc ACA *1981;* (Tax Fac), 24 Upper Hall Park, BERKHAMSTED, HERTFORDSHIRE, HP4 2NP.
SALE, Mr. Dereck Courtney, FCA *1966;* Dereck C. Sale, 4015 Cormack Crescent, PRINCE GEORGE V2N 5K8, BC, CANADA.
SALE, Mr. Iain Duncan, MEng ACA *1992;* 157 Moor Green Lane, Moseley, BIRMINGHAM, B13 8NT.
SALE, Mr. Ian David, MA FCA *1973;* 1201-552 Wellington St West, TORONTO M5V 2V5, ON, CANADA.
•SALE, Mr. Michael Derek, BSc FCA DChA *1982;* (Tax Fac), M.D. Sale & Co, 7 Carlisle Road, Birkdale, SOUTHPORT, PR8 4DJ.
SALE, Ms. Nicola Jane, BSc ACA *1993;* 16 Rose Avenue, Horsforth, LEEDS, LS18 4QE.
SALE, Mr. Timothy, MA ACA *1990;* Welton Farm House, Welton, NEWCASTLE UPON TYNE, NE18 0LJ.
SALEEM, Mr. Imran, ACA *1995;* P.O.Box 71902, DUBAI, UNITED ARAB EMIRATES.
SALEEM, Mr. Mohammad Kamran, BSc ACA CFA *1996;* 25 Tamarack Circle, TORONTO M9P 3T9, ON, CANADA.
SALEEM, Mr. Umar, FCA *1995;* PO Box 283735, DUBAI, UNITED ARAB EMIRATES.
SALEEM, Mr. Zahid Husain, FCA *1969;* 28 Broad Common Estate, Osbaldeston Road, Stoke Newington, LONDON, N16 6NB.
•SALEEMI, Mr. Mohammad Ashfaq, FCA *1983;* (Tax Fac), Saleemi Associates, 792 Wickham Road, CROYDON, SURREY, CR0 8EA.
SALEEMI, Mr. Salman Ahmed, ACA *2005;* 5726 Slate Valley Court, MISSOURI CITY, TX 77459, UNITED STATES.
SALEH, Mr. Ebrahim Ismail, FCA *1981;* 12 Hove Park Road, HOVE, BN3 6LA.
SALEH, Mr. Kamel Magdy, ACA *1990;* Deloitte & Touche., 95 C Merghany Street, CAIRO, 11341, EGYPT.
•SALEH, Mr. Sassoon, FCA *1980;* Sassoon Saleh, 13 Woodward Avenue, LONDON, NW4 4NU.
SALEM, Mr. Elyas Manzur, MA FCA *1979;* 1 Olympic Drive, SOUTH BARRINGTON, IL 60010, UNITED STATES.
SALES, Mr. Adrian Paul Alan, BA ACA *1989;* c/o Albourne America LLC, 105 Rowayton Avenue, NORWALK, CT 06853, UNITED STATES.
•SALES, Mr. Christopher, FCA *1981;* JVSA Accountants, 20 Derby Street, ORMSKIRK, LANCASHIRE, L39 2BY.
SALES, Mr. Christopher Hedley, FCA *1967;* 4 Pomeroy Close, AMERSHAM, BUCKINGHAMSHIRE, HP7 9BW.
SALES, Miss. Jessica, BSc ACA *2011;* 79a Noel Road, LONDON, N1 8HE.
SALES, Miss. Joanna Phyllis, BSc FCA DipM *1999;* Chantrey Vellacott D F K Russell Square House, 10-12 Russell Square, LONDON, WC1B 5LF.
SALES, Mr. John Arthur, FCA *1959;* 18 Aprilwood Close, Woodham, ADDLESTONE, SURREY, KT15 3SX.
SALES, Mr. Nicholas Simon, BSc(Hons) ACA *2001;* 28 Harston Road, Newton, CAMBRIDGE, CB22 7PA.
SALES, Mr. Paul David, BSc ACA *2007;* Edwards & Keeping Unity Chambers, 34 High East Street, DORCHESTER, DORSET, DT1 1HA.
SALES, Mr. Roger Brian, BCom FCA *1974;* The Hermitage, 29 Cumberland Street, WOODBRIDGE, IP12 4AH.
SALES, Mr. Stephen Anthony, BSc ACA CFA *1998;* The Barn, Ightham Court, Fen Pond Road, Ightham, SEVENOAKS, KENT TN15 9JF.
•SALFORD, Mr. Carlo Peter, BSc FCA *1969;* Carlo Salford, Via Passo Di Fargorida 6, 20148 MILAN, ITALY.
SALH, Miss. Kalveer Kaur, ACA *2008;* with Ernst & Young LLP, The Paragon, Counterslip, BRISTOL, BS1 6BX.
SALH, Miss. Sharandeep Kaur, BSc ACA *2005;* 76 Eastern Avenue, Monkton Park, CHIPPENHAM, SN15 3LW.
SALIH, Mr. Abdulelah Abdulrazzak, BA FCA MBA *1972;* with PricewaterhouseCoopers, P O Box 3075, Ruwi, 112 MUSCAT, OMAN.
SALIM, Mr. Ali Ben, BSc ACA MBA *2005;* Flat 13, 5 Hardman Road, KINGSTON UPON THAMES, KT2 6ST.
SALIM, Mr. Ataf, BSc ACA *2007;* 7 Heol Miaren, BARRY, SOUTH GLAMORGAN, CF63 1FA.
SALIM, Mr. Javed, BSc ACA *2003;* with Vantis Group Ltd, 3rd Floor, Crown House, 151 High Road, LOUGHTON, IG10 4LG.
•SALIM, Mr. Suhail, BSc ACA ATII *1991;* 41 Sarsfeld Road, LONDON, SW12 8HR.
SALINGER, Mr. Michael Lawton, FCA *1971;* 39 Broadfields Avenue, EDGWARE, HA8 8PF.
•SALISBURY, Mr. Andrew John, BA FCA *1992;* with Ernst & Young LLP, PO Box 9, Royal Chambers, St Julian's Avenue, St Peter Port, GUERNSEY GY1 4AF.
SALISBURY, Mrs. Cari, BA ACA *2006;* Sully Partnership, 8 Unity Street, BRISTOL, BS1 5HH.
SALISBURY, Mr. Francis John, BA ACA *1979;* 3 Taylor Drive, Bramley, TADLEY, RG26 5XB.
SALISBURY, Mr. Graham John, ACA *2009;* 34a Kings Lane, South Heath, GREAT MISSENDEN, BUCKINGHAMSHIRE, HP16 0QY.
•SALISBURY, Mr. Jeremy Charles, MBA FCA *1991;* Salisbury & Co, Irish Square, Upper Denbigh Road, ST. ASAPH, CLWYD, LL17 0RN. See also Salisbury & Company Business Solutions Limited
SALISBURY, Mr. Julian Charles, MSc ACA *1999;* 59 Blackheath Park, LONDON, SE3 9SQ.
SALISBURY, Mr. Keith William, BSc ACA *1995;* Dingle House, The Hampsons, Off Belmont Road, Bromley Cross, BOLTON, BL7 9QR.
SALISBURY, Mr. Martin Ian, BSc ACA *1992;* 62 Dial Hill Road, CLEVEDON, AVON, BS21 7EW.
SALISBURY, Mrs. Melanie Faith, BSc ACA *1990;* 1 Newby Drive, LEYLAND, PR25 5ST.
SALISBURY, Mr. Paul Harold Winston, FCA *1972;* Bramblewod Barn, 6 Church Fields, Wixford, ALCESTER, WARWICKSHIRE, B49 6DY.
SALISBURY, Mr. Raymond Ralph, FCA *1959;* Latchi, Les Damouttes, St Peter Port, GUERNSEY, GY1 1ZN. (Life Member)
SALISBURY, Mr. Richard Lloyd, BA ACA *1990;* 1 Newby Drive, Leyland, PRESTON, PR25 5ST.
SALISBURY, Mr. Robert Michael, BSc ACA *1995;* 42A Kheam Hock Road, SINGAPORE 298810, SINGAPORE.
•SALISBURY, Mr. Roger Maxim, ACA *1979;* Roger M. Salisbury, Cedar Cottage, Denham Lane, Chalfont St Peter, GERRARDS CROSS, SL9 0QQ.
•SALISBURY-JONES, Mr. Peter Gordon, FCA *1976;* Clark & Deen LLP, Benson House, Suite D, 98-104 Lombard Street, BIRMINGHAM, B12 0QR.
SALKELD, Mr. Adam Luke, BSc ACA *2010;* 7/80 Murdoch Street, CREMORNE, NSW 2090, AUSTRALIA.
SALKELD, Mr. Andrew, MSc BSc ACA *2011;* The Old Hall Back Lane, Bramham, WETHERBY, WEST YORKSHIRE, LS23 6QR.
•SALKELD, Mrs. Catherine, BA ACA *1981;* Yorkshire Financial Management Limited, The Old Hall, Bramham, WETHERBY, WEST YORKSHIRE, LS23 6QR.
SALKELD, Mr. Ian, BA ACA *1980;* 14 Cornard Road, SUDBURY, SUFFOLK, CO10 2XA.
SALKELD, Mr. John Graham, MA FCA *1965;* Farm Hill House, Armsworth, ALRESFORD, SO24 9RJ.
SALKIE, Mr. Stephen, FCA *1975;* 27 Wentworth Court, Higher Lane, Whitefield, MANCHESTER, M45 7UZ.
SALKIN, Mr. Daniel, BA ACA *1992;* 20 Hillingdon Road, Whitefield, MANCHESTER, M45 7QN.
SALLABANK, Miss. Amy, ACA *2010;* Flat 6 Prospect House, Arcade Steps St. Peter Port, GUERNSEY, GY1 1JZ.
SALLEH, Mr. Mohammed Bakke, BSc FCA *1983;* 33 Cangkat Datuk Sulaiman, Ttdi Hills, Taman Tun Dr. Ismail, 60000 KUALA LUMPUR, FEDERAL TERRITORY, MALAYSIA.
SALLIN, Mr. Mark, BA ACA *2004;* Dechra Veterinary Products, Sansaw Business Park, Hadnall, SHREWSBURY, SY4 4AS.
SALLIS, Mr. Gerald Heber, FCA *1963;* 5 Hartford Road, Hartley Wintney, HOOK, RG27 8QW. (Life Member)
SALLIS, Miss. Julie Susan, LLB FCA *1985;* 20 Campbell Gardens, Arnold, NOTTINGHAM, NG5 8RY.
SALLITT, Mr. Henry William Baines, BSc ACA *1987;* Apple Tree Cottage, Newtown Common, NEWBURY, RG20 9DA.
SALLOUMIS, Mr. Demetris, ACA *2011;* Meletiou Metaxaki 44, Anglos Nicolaos, LIMASSOL, CYPRUS.
SALLOWS, Mr. Benton, FCA *1998;* 17, Harbour Way, ST. LEONARDS-ON-SEA, TN38 8EP.
•SALLOWS, Mr. Daniel Edward, FCA *1991;* (Tax Fac), Gibbons Mannington & Phipps, 20-22 Eversley Road, BEXHILL-ON-SEA, EAST SUSSEX, TN40 1HE.
SALLOWS, Mr. James Robert, BA ACA *2000;* 20 Cooks Road, AYLESBURY, BUCKINGHAMSHIRE, HP19 7GD.
SALMAN, Mr. Ahmad Makhdoom, ACA FCCA *2011;* Saudi Arabian Airlines, PO Box 620, CC: 612 Loc: 130, Building 8 3rd floor, Saudi City Khalidiya Dist, JEDDAH 21231 SAUDI ARABIA.
SALMAN, Mrs. Deborah Ellen, BSc FCA *1991;* with Lewis Golden & Co, 40 Queen Anne Street, LONDON, W1G 9EL.
SALMAN, Miss. Hoda, MSc BSc ACA *2006;* c/o Rafic Salman, Marwan Elmdakkah bldg., Block B 3rd floor, Al Fawwara District, JABALPUR, LEBANON.
SALMAN, Mr. Mohammad Abid, FCA *1968;* 62 WOBURN AVENUE, TORONTO M5M 1K6, ON, CANADA. (Life Member)
SALMAN, Mr. Shaikh Ahmed, ACA *2010;* House No 10, Popular Avenue Phase 6, Defence Housing Authority, KARACHI 75500, PAKISTAN.
SALMON, Mr. Andrew Alfred, BSc ACA *1988;* Arbuthnot Banking Group Plc, Arbuthnot House, 20 Ropemaker Street, LONDON, EC2Y 9AR.
•SALMON, Mr. Andrew Michael, BEng ACA *1999;* Websters, Baker Street Chambers, 136 Baker Street, LONDON, W1U 6UD.
•SALMON, Mr. Brian Edward, BSc ACA *1993;* (Tax Fac), Sabre Management Services Limited, Anglo International House, Lord Street, Douglas, ISLE OF MAN, IM1 4LN.
SALMON, Miss. Carol Jane, BA ACA *1990;* 7 Clos Cwm Creunant, Pontprennau, CARDIFF, CF23 8LA.
•SALMON, Mr. Christopher David, BA ACA *1994;* Francis James & Partners LLP, 1386 London Road, LEIGH-ON-SEA, ESSEX, SS9 2UJ.
SALMON, Mr. Christopher Mark, BSc ACA *1982;* Valley View Cottage, Les Ruettes, St Andrew, GUERNSEY, GY6 8UG.
•SALMON, Mr. Derek Harry, FCA *1953;* (Tax Fac), D H Salmon, 25 Mayfield Drive, KENILWORTH, CV8 2SW.
SALMON, Miss. Emma, BA(Hons) ACA *2010;* 70 Kingsley Way, LONDON, N2 0EN.
SALMON, Mr. Giles Pollock, BCom FCA *1995;* 43 St. Marys Grove, LONDON, W4 3LN.
SALMON, Mr. Graham William, FCA *1979;* Beever & Struthers St. Georges House, 215-219 Chester Road, MANCHESTER, M15 4JE.
SALMON, Mrs. Helen Margaret, BA ACA *1991;* Toad Hall, Wymondham Road, Hethel, NORWICH, NR14 8EU.

SALMON, Miss. Hilary Jane, BA ACA *1979;* 46 Leaside Avenue, Muswell Hill, LONDON, N10 3BU.
SALMON, Mr. Ian Stewart, JP FCA *1958;* 29 Carlton Hill, St. John's Wood, LONDON, NW8 0JX. (Life Member)
SALMON, Mr. John, BA FCA *1976;* Rag Whistle, Jolly Tar Lane, Coppull, CHORLEY, PR7 4BJ.
SALMON, Mr. John Adrian, FCA *1973;* Box 6047, Erinvale Estate, SOMERSET WEST, WESTERN CAPE PROVINCE, 7130, SOUTH AFRICA. (Life Member)
SALMON, Mr. John Christopher Russell, FCA *1971;* A-17-3A Menjalara 18, 6 Lebuh Menjalara, 52200 KUALA LUMPUR, FEDERAL TERRITORY, MALAYSIA.
SALMON, Mr. John Howard, FCA *1968;* Brookside, 18 Mymms Drive, Brookmans Park, HATFIELD, AL9 7AF.
SALMON, Mr. John James William, FCA *1952;* 33 Speer Rd, THAMES DITTON, KT7 0PJ. (Life Member)
SALMON, Mr. Michael Stephen, BA ACA *2004;* Deloitte & Touche Llp, 3 Rivergate, BRISTOL, BS1 6GD.
SALMON, Miss. Nicola, ACA *2011;* 106 Boundaries Road, LONDON, SW12 8HQ.
•**SALMON, Mr. Peter, FCA** *1964;* Salmon & Co, PO Box 71, Farnham Royal, SLOUGH, SL2 3SH.
SALMON, Mr. Peter Robert George, BSc ACA *2002;* 25 Newlyn Drive, Ashton-in-Makerfield, WIGAN, WN4 9PW.
SALMON, Mrs. Rachel Clare, BA ACA *2000;* 25 Newlyn Drive, Ashton-in-Makerfield, WIGAN, LANCASHIRE, WN4 9PW.
SALMON, Miss. Rebecca Ann, BA(Hons) ACA *2011;* 43 Reachview Close, Camden, LONDON, NW1 0TY.
SALMON, Mr. Richard Andrew, BSc FCA *1996;* Ernst & Young LLP Becket House, 1 Lambeth Palace Road, LONDON, SE1 7EU.
SALMON, Mr. Richard Guy, FCA *1970;* PO Box 892, KERIKERI 0245, BAY OF ISLANDS, NEW ZEALAND. (Life Member)
•**SALMON, Mr. Roy Charles, FCA** *1969;* Salmon & Co, 4 Buckingham Place, Bellfield Road, HIGH WYCOMBE, HP13 5HQ.
•**SALMON, Mr. Rupert Edward Fitzjohn, FCA** *1960;* (Tax Fac), with Websters, Baker Street Chambers, 136 Baker Street, LONDON, W1U 6UD.
SALMON, Mr. Ryan Alan, BA ACA *1999;* 16 Barn Croft Drive, Lower Earley, READING, RG6 3WE.
SALMON, Mr. Stephen James, FCA *1970;* Garden Cottage, Wappingthorn Farm Lane, Horsham Road, STEYNING, WEST SUSSEX, BN44 3AG.
SALMON, Mr. Steven Kenneth, BA ACA *1985;* Valley Farm Hanbury Road, Hanbury, BROMSGROVE, WORCESTERSHIRE, B60 4HJ.
SALMON, Mrs. Susan Jane, BSc ACA *2002;* 22 Brookfield Drive, Wolvey, HINCKLEY, LEICESTERSHIRE, LE10 3LT.
SALMON, Mr. Thomas Guy Maunder, BA ACA *2003;* 138 Hydethorpe Road, LONDON, SW12 0JD.
SALMON, Mr. Timothy John, BA FCA *1985;* Woodside, Slines Oak Road, Woldingham, CATERHAM, CR3 7BH.
SALMOND, Mr. Richard Robert, BA ACA *1995;* Wootton Grange Farm House, Wootton, BRIDGNORTH, SHROPSHIRE, WV15 6EB.
SALMONS, Mr. David Colin, BSc FCA *1996;* 65 Fleet Street, Freshfields Bruckhaus Deringer Llp, PO Box 561, LONDON, EC4Y 1HS.
SALMONS, Ms. Esther Ann, ACA *2003;* 171 Church Road, Shoeburyness, SOUTHEND-ON-SEA, SS3 9HA.
SALOLE, Mr. Anthony Ronald, FCA *1972;* Canadian Institute of C.A., 277 Wellington Street West, TORONTO M5V 3H2, ON, CANADA.
•**SALOMON, Mr. Gareth, ACA** *2008;* G Salomon & Co, 89 Hullah Lane, WREXHAM, CLWYD, LL13 9AT.
•**SALSAC, Mr. Alan John, BA BSc ACA** *1987;* Axis Fiduciary, 4th Floor Unicorn Centre, 18N Frere Felix de Valois Street, PORT LOUIS, MAURITIUS.
•**SALT, Mr. Alan Charles, FCA** *1961;* Alan Salt, Rose Croft, Fauls Green, Fauls, WHITCHURCH, SHROPSHIRE SY13 2AS.
SALT, Mr. Bruce, BSc ACA *1992;* 15 Morris Grove, Kirkstall, LEEDS, LS5 3EZ.
SALT, Mr. Derek Arthur, FCA *1971;* 40 Harestone Valley Road, CATERHAM, CR3 6HD.
SALT, Mr. Giles John, BSc ACA *1995;* M & I Materials, Hibernia Way, Trafford Park, MANCHESTER, M32 0ZD.
SALT, Miss. Helen Marie, ACA *2008;* 34 Pleasant Drive, BILLERICAY, CM12 0JL.
SALT, Mr. John Russell Gregory, ACA *1981;* 16 Birkett Drive, Belmont Road, BOLTON, LANCASHIRE, BL1 7DE.
SALT, Mr. Jonathan Martyn, BSc ACA *1988;* Nolan Baptist & Bond, Whitehall House, Sandy Lane, NEWCASTLE, STAFFORDSHIRE, ST5 0LZ.
•**SALT, Mrs. Joy, BSc FCA** *1992;* Howard Painter & Company Ltd, 26 Sansome Walk, WORCESTER, WR1 1LX. See also Sargent Services LLP
SALT, Mrs. Kathryn, BSc ACA *1986;* 4 Willow Bank, Bagslate Moor Road, ROCHDALE, LANCASHIRE, OL11 5YJ.
SALT, Mr. Malcolm Ross, FCA *1957;* Glenross, Rolfe Lane, NEW ROMNEY, TN28 8JP. (Life Member)
SALT, Mrs. Malini, BA ACA *1992;* 5 Borden Way, Hollins, BURY, BL9 8QF.
SALT, Mrs. Megumi Claire, BCom ACA *2001;* 12 Laburnum Road, BIRMINGHAM, B30 2BA.
SALT, Mr. Richard Martin, BSc ACA *2010;* 98 Combe Road, GODALMING, GU7 3SL.
SALT, Mr. Roger, MBA BA ACA *1982;* 55 Ashford Road, Dronfield Woodhouse, DRONFIELD, S18 8RT.
SALT, Mr. Steven, BA ACA *2008;* 66 Longmeadow Drive, DUDLEY, DY3 3QR.
SALT, Mr. William, BCom FCA *1964;* 1 The Paddock, Scholes Village, ROTHERHAM, S61 2XA.
SALTARICHE, Mr. Lewis, BA(Hons) ACA *2001;* 34 Acre Moss Lane, MORECAMBE, LANCASHIRE, LA4 4NA.
SALTER, Mr. Andrew Kershaw, BSc ACA *1987;* Investec Bank (UK) Ltd, 2 Gresham Street, LONDON, EC2V 7QP.
SALTER, Mr. David Andrew, MA FCA *1994;* Coastline Housing Ltd, Ferris House, Dolcoath Avenue, CAMBORNE, CORNWALL, TR14 8SD.
SALTER, Mr. David Ian, BSc FCA *1970;* 1 Coates Cottages, Greinton, BRIDGWATER, SOMERSET, TA7 9BW.
SALTER, Mr. Edward John, ACA *2011;* Flat 12, 71d Drayton Park, LONDON, N5 1DG.
•**SALTER, Mr. Gary, FCA** *1983;* Milsted Langdon LLP, Motivo House, Alvington, YEOVIL, SOMERSET, BA20 2FG.
SALTER, Miss. Jennifer Ann, BA ACA *2008;* 18 Grange Avenue, Breaston, DERBY, DE72 3BX.
SALTER, Mr. Jeremy Whitton, FCA *1968;* 3 Woodbourne Dr, Claygate, ESHER, KT10 0DR. (Life Member)
SALTER, Mr. John Arthur Philip, MA FCA *1956;* 7 Church Row, Hampstead, LONDON, NW3 6UT. (Life Member)
SALTER, Mr. Jonathan David, BSc ACA *1992;* 29 Blackbrook Lane, BROMLEY, BR2 8AU.
•**SALTER, Mrs. Kathleen Ann, FCA** *1977;* Premier Tax Consultancy Ltd, Calico House, Calico Lane, Furness Vale, HIGH PEAK, DERBYSHIRE SK23 7SW.
•**SALTER, Mr. Keith James, FCA** *1974;* Salter & Co, 34 Byron Avenue, LONDON, E18 2HQ.
•**SALTER, Mr. Kevin Nigel, FCA FTII** *1978;* (Tax Fac), Glover Stanbury & Co, 30 Bear Street, BARNSTAPLE, DEVON, EX32 7DD. See also BBS Computing Ltd
•**SALTER, Mrs. Margaret Anne, BA ACA** *1987;* PJE, 3 Oakfield Court, Oakfield Road, Clifton, BRISTOL, BS8 2BD.
SALTER, Mr. Mark, BSc ACA *1993;* 31 Denning Road, LONDON, NW3 1ST.
SALTER, Mr. Mark David, ACA *2009;* 8 Barberi Close, OXFORD, OXFORDSHIRE, OX4 4GF.
SALTER, Mr. Michael Anthony John, FCA *1969;* Shepherds Hall Heol Hir, Thornhill, CARDIFF, CF14 9UD.
SALTER, Mr. Peter Cecil, BSc FCA *1974;* 75 High Street, MARLBOROUGH, WILTSHIRE, SN8 1HF.
SALTER, Mr. Richard Stephen, FCA *1967;* Hunstrete Cottage, Hunstrete, Pensford, BRISTOL, BS39 4NT.
SALTER, Mr. Robert Edward, FCA *1970;* High Rigg D'Urton Lane, Broughton, PRESTON, PR3 5LE.
SALTER, Mr. Steven William, FCA *1975;* 27 Branch Hill Rise, Charlton Kings, CHELTENHAM, GL53 9HN.
SALTER, Mrs. Victoria Isaline Louise, BEng ACA *2003;* Portal Fund Administration Ltd, 2nd Floor, Belgravia House, 34-44 Circular Road, Douglas, ISLE OF MAN IM1 1AE.
SALTMARSH, Mr. Henry Reginald, FCA *1969;* 25 Westgate Street, BURY ST. EDMUNDS, SUFFOLK, IP33 1QG.
SALTMARSH, Mr. Philip David, BA FCA *1965;* 106 Broadwood Avenue, RUISLIP, HA4 7XT. (Life Member)
SALTMARSH, Mr. Richard Malcolm, FCA *1960;* R.M.Saltmarsh, P.O. Box 21145, Orchard Park P.O., KELOWNA VIY 9N8, BC, CANADA.
SALTMER, Mr. Thomas Christopher, ACA *2008;* 114 Beaconsfield Road, HASTINGS, EAST SUSSEX, TN34 3TN.
•**SALTON, Miss. Sarah Elizabeth, BSc ACA** *2006;* Hurst & Company Accountants LLP, Lancashire Gate, 21 Tiviot Dale, STOCKPORT, CHESHIRE, SK1 1TD.
•**SALTRICK, Mrs. Caroline Rosemary, BA FCA** *1982;* Saltrick & Saltrick Limited, 5 The Glasshouse Studios, Fryern Court Road, Burgate, FORDINGBRIDGE, HAMPSHIRE SP6 1QX.
•**SALTRICK, Mr. Christopher James, FCA** *1980;* Saltrick & Saltrick Limited, 5 The Glasshouse Studios, Fryern Court Road, Burgate, FORDINGBRIDGE, HAMPSHIRE SP6 1QX.
SALUJA, Mr. Amit, LLB ACA *2004;* 23 Kilburn Close, Bramcote Moor, Beeston, NOTTINGHAM, NG9 3FG.
SALUJA, Mr. Manoj Kumar, ACA *1984;* 38 Alexandra Road, HOUNSLOW, TW3 4HN.
SALUJA, Mr. Sudhir, BCom ACA *1979;* 601 Sethi Bhawan., 7 Rajendra Place, NEW DELHI 110008, INDIA.
•**SALUVEER, Mr. Martin Alexander, MA FCA** *1992;* Deloitte LLP, 2 New Street Square, LONDON, EC4A 3BZ. See also Deloitte & Touche LLP
•**SALVAGE, Mr. Martin Richard, FCA** *1975;* M R Salvage Limited, 7-8 Eghams Court, Boston Drive, BOURNE END, BUCKINGHAMSHIRE, SL8 5YS.
SALVIDIO, Mr. Ascanio, ACA *2009;* Viale Bruno Bouozzi, 32, 58091 ROME, ITALY.
SALVIN, Mr. Peter, BA ACA *2006;* 36 Vicarage Lane, Stubbington, FAREHAM, HAMPSHIRE, PO14 2LA.
SALWAN, Mr. Parveen Kumar, ACA *1994;* B-26 Greater Kailash Enclave Part II, NEW DELHI 110048, CAPITAL TERRITORY OF DELHI, INDIA.
SALWAY, Mr. Keith John, BCom FCA *1970;* Lime Tree Cottage, Burford Street, LECHLADE, GL7 3AR.
SALWAY, Mr. Mark John, BSc(Hons) ACA DChA *2000;* 11 Tall Oaks, Lyoth Lane, Lindfield, HAYWARDS HEATH, WEST SUSSEX, RH16 2QD.
SALZEDO, Mrs. Catherine Jane, BA FCA *1993;* Tunstall House, Tunstall, CARNFORTH, LANCASHIRE, LA6 2QW.
SALZEDO, Mr. Simon Lopez, BA FCA *1994;* Brick Court Chambers, 7-8 Essex Street, LONDON, WC2R 3LD.
SALZEN, Ms. Fiona, LLB ACA *1986;* 52 Blacket Place, EDINBURGH, EH9 1RJ.
SALZMAN, Mr. David Gavin, ACA *1993;* Po Box 1065, Woodstock, CAPE TOWN, WESTERN CAPE PROVINCE, 7915, SOUTH AFRICA.
SALZMAN, Miss. Emily, BSc ACA *2006;* Westwood The Green, Oaksey, MALMESBURY, SN16 9TL.
SAM, Mr. Andrew Kobina, MCMI BSc FCA *1989;* PO Box 9721, Kotoka International Airport, ACCRA, GHANA.
SAM, Mr. Kok-Weng, ACA *2000;* with PricewaterhouseCoopers LLP, 17-00 PWC Building, 8 Cross Street, SINGAPORE 048424, SINGAPORE.
SAM YUE, Mr. Wong Voon Moye, ACA *1979;* P O Box R668, Royal Exchange, SYDNEY, NSW 1225, AUSTRALIA.
SAM YUE, Mr. Wong Yuet Moye, BSc ACA *1986;* 32/333 Bulwara Road, ULTIMO, NSW 2007, AUSTRALIA.
SAMA, Mr. Nakul, ACA *2010;* 66 Godfrey Avenue, TWICKENHAM, TW2 7PF.
•**SAMAD, Mr. Abdul, BA(Hons) ACA** *2007;* Bay Accountants Ltd, 215 Bacchus Road, BIRMINGHAM, B18 4RE. See also Yasbar Services Limited
SAMAD, Mr. Bilal Abdus, ACA ACCA *2009;* Novartis Pharma Pakistan Limited, 15 West Wharf Road, PO Box 100, KARACHI, PAKISTAN.
SAMAD, Mr. Muhammed Habibus, FCA CTA *1965;* House 52 Flat 5A Road 2, DOHS Banani, DHAKA 1206, BANGLADESH.
•**SAMAD, Mrs. Tanzeela, BA ACA** *2008;* Tanzeela Samad, 2 Hawksnest Gardens East, Alwoodley, LEEDS, LS17 7JQ.
SAMANI, Mr. Akhil Jayant, ACA *2009;* 7 Shale End, NORTHAMPTON, NN5 6BL.
SAMANI, Mr. Milan, BA ACA *2006;* 1 Pickwick Place, HARROW, HA1 3BG.
•**SAMANI, Mr. Naresh Shamji, FCA** *1976;* H W Fisher & Company, Acre House, 11-15 William Road, LONDON, NW1 3ER. See also H W Fisher & Company Limited
SAMANI, Mr. Pravin Popatlal, ACA *1982;* 83 Copse Wood Way, NORTHWOOD, MIDDLESEX, HA6 2TX.
SAMANI, Mr. Ronal Anilkumar, MSc BSc(Hons) ACA *2001;* AMS Properties Ltd, P.O. Box 10713, NAIROBI, 00100, KENYA.
SAMANIDOU, Ms. Kiriaki, BSc ACA *1998;* 2 Davis Close, MARLOW, BUCKINGHAMSHIRE, SL7 1SY.
SAMANTA, Mr. Sutanu, BSc(Econ) ACA *1996;* 28 Eyot Gardens, LONDON, W6 9TN.
•**SAMAR, Mr. Raza Ullah, MBA BA(Hons) ACA FCCA** *2007;* (Tax Fac), RUS & Company (UK) Ltd, 1190a - 1192 Stratford Road, Hall Green, BIRMINGHAM, B28 8AB. See also Rus & Company
SAMARAS, Mr. Christos Stavrou, FCA *1980;* 5 Elias Street, Ayios Vasilios, 2049 STROVOLOS, CYPRUS.
SAMARASINGHE, Miss. Sathya Ravindi, BSc(Hons) ACA *2010;* 1 Winifred Terrace, Great Cambridge Road, ENFIELD, MIDDLESEX, EN1 1HH.
•**SAMARATUNGA, Mr. Punsri Samantha, BSc ACA** *1992;* PricewaterhouseCoopers LLP, Hays Galleria, 1 Hays Lane, LONDON, SE1 2RD. See also PricewaterhouseCoopers
SAMARAWEERA, Miss. Piumi, BSc ACA *2006;* 20 Coburg Gardens, Clayhall, ILFORD, ESSEX, IG5 0PP.
SAMBANTHAR, Mr. Rajaratnam Thirugnana, FCA *1953;* 3 Laluan Canning, Taman Ipoh, 31400 IPOH, MALAYSIA. (Life Member)
SAMBRIDGE, Mr. Nicholas Paul, BA ACA *1993;* 61 Quintonside, Grange Park, NORTHAMPTON, NN4 5AD.
SAMBROOK, Mr. Andrew William, LLB ACA *1992;* PO Box 904, EAST DORSET, VT 05253, UNITED STATES.
SAMBROOK, Mr. Duncan James, MA MSci ACA *2005;* 3A Crabtree Lane, Fulham, LONDON, SW6 6LP.
SAMBROOK, Mr. Matthew Richard, BSocSc ACA *2001;* 433 West 16th Street, NORTH VANCOUVER V7M 1V1, BC, CANADA.
SAMELS, Miss. Nicola Ruth, BSc ACA *1991;* 6 Durlings Orchard, Ightham, SEVENOAKS, KENT, TN15 9HW.
SAMENGO-TURNER, Mr. Joseph Paul, FCA *1977;* WELFENALLEE 34, 13465 BERLIN, GERMANY.
SAMENGO-TURNER, Mr. Peter Anthony, ACA *1980;* 65 Grandison Road, LONDON, SW11 6LT.
SAMI, Mr. Mohammed Ahmed, ACA *2010;* The Bungalow, Llantrisant Road, Groesfaen, PONTYCLUN, MID GLAMORGAN, CF72 8NJ.
SAMI, Mr. Muhammad Noman, BCom ACA *2010;* 2 Maison Des Hougues, Well Road St. Peter Port, GUERNSEY, GY1 1WS.
•**SAMJI, Mr. Abdulmohamed Mohamedali Premji, FCA** *1970;* (Tax Fac), Samjis, 4 Fulwood Court, Kenton Rd, HARROW, HA3 8AA.
SAMJI, Mr. Mohamed Alibhai, FCA *1975;* 35 Lee Anne Court, RR2 Box 1A7, WOODBRIDGE L4L 8L3, ON, CANADA.
SAMJI, Miss. Roxana, BSc ACA *2007;* Flat 11, 27 William Road, LONDON, NW1 3EY.
•**SAMJI, Mr. Sadrudin Noordin, FCA** *1978;* (Tax Fac), Thurston Watts & Co, 39-41 North Road, LONDON, N7 9DP.
SAMMANTHAN, Mr. Sheranjiv, BCom ACA *1996;* PricewaterhouseCoopers, P.O.Box 10192, Level 10 1 Sentral, Jalan Travers, 50470 KUALA LUMPUR, FEDERAL TERRITORY MALAYSIA.
SAMME, Mr. Geoffrey Richard, BSc(Econ) ACA *1995;* 6 Weyhill Close, MAIDSTONE, ME14 5SQ.
SAMMES, Mr. Christopher Leonard, ACA *1982;* 37 Main Avenue, NORTHWOOD, MIDDLESEX, HA6 2LH.
SAMMONS, Mrs. Constance Beryl, FCA *1966;* 12 Priory View, CASTLE CARY, SOMERSET, BA7 7DX. (Life Member)
SAMMONS, Mr. Graham Edwin George, FCA *1966;* One Step Away, Hawford Wood, Ombersley, DROITWICH, WORCESTERSHIRE, WR9 0EZ.
SAMMONS, Mr. Philip Michael, BA ACA *1984;* 5A Sugardock, 4 Distillery Drive, PYRMONT, NSW 2009, AUSTRALIA.
SAMMONS, Mr. Richard Douglas, FCA *1979;* 12 Hengist Way, BROMLEY, BR2 0NS.
SAMMUT, Mr. Manuel, MSc BA ACA *2006;* Flat 4, Fleet House, 6 Victory Place, LONDON, E14 8BG.
•**SAMOTHRAKIS, Mrs. Deborah Mary, BSc FCA** *1978;* (Tax Fac), Tester Accountancy & Bookkeeping Ltd, 34 Fairoak Road, CARDIFF, CF24 4PY.
SAMPAT, Mr. Bimal, ACA *2010;* 106 Cherry Orchard Road, CROYDON, CR0 6BA.
SAMPEY, Mrs. Catherine Anne, BSc ACA CTA *1990;* The Royal Bank of Scotland Plc, Group Taxation, Business House F, Ground Floor, RBS Gogarburn, PO Box 1000 EDINBURGH EH12 1HQ.
SAMPHIER, Mr. Charles Arthur, FCA *1966;* Plovers Barron, Higher Village, Westleigh, BIDEFORD, EX39 4NN.
SAMPLE, Mrs. Loredana Anna-Maria, BA ACA *1987;* 125 Benslow Lane, HITCHIN, SG4 9RA.
SAMPLE, Mr. Mark John, BSc FCA *1989;* 9 Marylebone Lane, LONDON, W1U 1HL.
SAMPLES, Mrs. Sandra Jane, FCA *1981;* JOHN WHITEHEAD BUILDING FINANCE DEPT, De Montfort University, The Gateway, LEICESTER, LE1 9BH.
•**SAMPSON, Mr. Arthur Roy, FCA** *1975;* Bramley Place Limited, Bramley Place, Orchard Road, 45 The Scarr, NEWENT, GLOUCESTERSHIRE GL18 1DQ.

SAMPSON, Mr. Charles David, VRD DSC FCA *1939;* Gaydon, Baggrow, Aspatria, WIGTON, CA7 3QH. (Life Member)
SAMPSON, Mr. Christopher Graham Ayerst, BA FCA *1982;* Teacheractive Ltd Victoria House, 126 Colmore Row, BIRMINGHAM, B3 3AP.
SAMPSON, Miss. Danielle, BA ACA *2005;* 14 Sandpits Road, RICHMOND, TW10 7DT.
SAMPSON, Mr. Douglas, ACA *2009;* 150 Ferndale Road, LONDON, SW4 7SA.
•SAMPSON, Mrs. Eileen Ann, BSc ACA *1983;* Delamere, 9 Glendyke Road, Allerton, LIVERPOOL, L18 9TD.
•SAMPSON, Mrs. Elizabeth Jane, BSc(Econ) ACA *1999;* ESampson, 59 Heyes Lane, ALDERLEY EDGE, CHESHIRE, SK9 7LA.
SAMPSON, Mrs. Emma Lucy, BCom ACA *2009;* Flat 5 Fitzjohns House, 46 Fitzjohns Avenue, LONDON, NW3 5LU.
SAMPSON, Mr. Gareth John, ACA CA(SA) *2008;* The Wessex Group, Jewry House, 13 Jewry Street, WINCHESTER, HAMPSHIRE, SO23 8RZ.
SAMPSON, Mr. Geoffrey Howard, ACA *1982;* Allergan Inc., 2525 Du Pont Drive, IRVINE, CA 92612, UNITED STATES.
SAMPSON, Mr. Graeham Stuart, BA ACA *1999;* 59 Heyes Lane, ALDERLEY EDGE, CHESHIRE, SK9 7LA.
SAMPSON, Mr. John Alexander, FCA *1968;* 3 Crossways, BERKHAMSTED, HP4 3NH.
SAMPSON, Mr. Jonathan, BA FCA *1995;* 154 Chellaston Road, Shelton Lock, DERBY, DE24 9DY.
SAMPSON, Mr. Julian Walter, BA ACA *1990;* 27 Lower Kenwood Avenue, Oakwood, ENFIELD, EN2 7LT.
SAMPSON, Mrs. Julie Ann, BSc ACA CTA *1991;* Dundrie, 9 Northumberland Road, LEAMINGTON SPA, WARWICKSHIRE, CV32 6HE.
•SAMPSON, Mr. Michael Anthony, BSc FCA APFS *1978;* (Tax Fac), Sampson West, 34 Ely Place, LONDON, EC1N 6TD.
•SAMPSON, Mr. Michael Oliver, FCA *1967;* (Tax Fac), M.O. Sampson & Co, 42 Kew Court, Richmond Road, KINGSTON UPON THAMES, SURREY, KT2 5BF.
SAMPSON, Mr. Paul Thomas, BCom FCA CTA *1974;* 34 Mansfield Road, READING, RG1 6AJ.
SAMPSON, Mr. Phillip Kerwan, ACA *2008;* 118 Wordsworth Avenue, PENARTH, SOUTH GLAMORGAN, CF64 2RQ.
SAMPSON, Mrs. Rebecca Margaret, MA(Hons) ACA *2002;* The Farmhouse on the Green, Upper Quinton, STRATFORD-UPON-AVON, CV37 8SX.
•SAMPSON, Mr. Roy Leonard, FCA *1981;* Spring House, Springfield Road, Bickley, BROMLEY, BR1 2LJ.
SAMPSON, Mr. Stephen David, BA ACA *1985;* Alliance Boots, 2 The Heights Brooklands, WEYBRIDGE, SURREY, KT13 0NY.
•SAMPSON, Mr. Stephen Robert, FCA *1986;* with Ashdown Hurrey LLP, 20 Havelock Road, HASTINGS, EAST SUSSEX, TN34 1BP.
SAMPSON, Mr. Stephen Samuel, FCA *1983;* 15 Stratton Street, Mayfair, LONDON, W1J 8LQ.
SAMPSON, The Revd Canon Terence Harold Morris, FCA *1964;* Edificio Balcon de San Miguel, Avenida de Alicante 17/19, San miguel de Salinas, 03193 ALICANTE, SPAIN. (Life Member)
SAMRA, Mr. Bilraj Singh, BSc(Hons) ACA *2002;* 23 Francis Drive, Cawston, RUGBY, WARWICKSHIRE, CV22 7FS.
SAMRA, Mr. Harbant Singh, BSc ACA *1999;* 232 Langley Road, Langley, SLOUGH, SL3 7EF.
SAMRA, Miss. Jasmine Kaur, BA(Hons) ACA *2001;* 8 Ardys Court, Loughton, MILTON KEYNES, MK5 8AH.
SAMRA, Mrs. Mandhese, BSc ACA *1999;* Manor House Lutterworth Road, Bitteswell, LUTTERWORTH, LE17 4RX.
SAMRA, Mr. Parminder Singh, BSc ACA *2011;* 1 Admirals Way, ROWLEY REGIS, WEST MIDLANDS, B65 8BL.
SAMRA, Ms. Rainuka, BSc ACA *2003;* 28 Ferndale Avenue, HOUNSLOW, TW4 7ES.
SAMRA, Miss. Randeep Kaur, BSc ACA *2008;* 14 Broadway Road, LEICESTER, LE5 5TA.
SAMRA, Mr. Sukhjeevan Singh, LLB ACA *2003;* 16c North Road, BERKHAMSTED, HERTFORDSHIRE, HP4 3DU.
•SAMRAH, Mr. Paul Edward Marshall, BSc FCA *1986;* (Tax Fac), Kingston Smith LLP, Surrey House, 36-44 High Street, REDHILL, RH1 1RH. See also Kingston Smith Limited Liability Partnership, Devonshire Corporate Services LLP and Kingston Smith Consulting LLP
SAMS, Mr. Christopher James, BSc ACA *1996;* Rowland Homes Stanifield House, Stanifield Lane Farington, LEYLAND, PR25 4UA.
SAMS, Mr. David William Ian, PhD BSc ACA MCT *1999;* 21A Danbury Street, LONDON, N1 8LE.
SAMS, Mr. Gordon, FCA *1959;* 6 Cloverdale, Wildwood, STAFFORD, ST17 4QJ. (Life Member)
SAMS, Mr. Jonathan, BSc FCA *1987;* 10 Hummersknott Avenue, DARLINGTON, DL3 8LG.
SAMS, Mr. Mark Andrew, ACA *1993;* 12 Albany Road, West Bergholt, COLCHESTER, CO6 3LB.
SAMS, The Revd. Michael Charles, FCA *1957;* 13 Hound Close, ABINGDON, OX14 2LU. (Life Member)
•SAMSON, Mr. David, FCA *1972;* Armstrong Watson, Central House, 47 St Pauls Street, LEEDS, LS1 2TE.
SAMSON, Mr. Harvey Jack, BA ACA *1982;* 11 Parkhill Road, Hale, ALTRINCHAM, WA15 9JX.
SAMSON, Mrs. Judith Margaret, BA ACA *1986;* 11 Parkhill Road, Hale, ALTRINCHAM, WA15 9JX.
SAMSON, Mrs. Lucy Jane, BA ACA *2001;* Stone Settle, Frogmore, KINGSBRIDGE, DEVON, TQ7 2NR.
•SAMSON, Mr. Richard, BSc ACA *1992;* Richard Samson, 21 Coldharbour Lane, LONDON, SE5 9NR.
SAMTANI, Miss. Ashwina Bihari, BSc ACA *2000;* with PricewaterhouseCoopers LLP, 1 Embankment Place, LONDON, WC2N 6RH.
SAMTER, Mr. Daniel John, FCA *1975;* 7 Sunnyvale Road, MIDDLE DURAL, NSW 2158, AUSTRALIA.
SAMUDA, Mr. Richard Markham D'Aguilar, FCA *1972;* The Old Vicarage, Church Lane, Aston Cantlow, SOLIHULL, WEST MIDLANDS, B95 6JB.
SAMUEL, Mrs. Alison Oralia, MA ACA *1984;* 26 Irving Mews, LONDON, N1 2FP.
SAMUEL, Mr. Christopher John Loraine, MA ACA *1984;* Washington House, 26 Irving Mews, LONDON, N1 2FP.
SAMUEL, Mr. David Lawrence, FCA *1987;* (Tax Fac), Fimalac, 30 North Colonnade, LONDON, E14 5GN.
SAMUEL, Mr. Gareth Douglas, BSc CA ACA MBA *1982;* 5 Boylson Place, CROMER HEIGHTS, NSW 2099, AUSTRALIA.
SAMUEL, Mr. Job Albert Thiagaraj, BSc FCA *1961;* 52 Lakeland Drive, ETOBICOKE M9V 1N1, ON, CANADA. (Life Member)
SAMUEL, Mr. John Anthony, FCA *1972;* Willowby Lodge, Meavy Lane, YELVERTON, DEVON, PL20 6AL.
SAMUEL, Mr. John Graham, BSc FCA *1968;* 19 Crown Lane, CHISLEHURST, KENT, BR7 5PL. (Life Member)
SAMUEL, Mr. John William Young Strachan, BA FCA *1981;* Charnwood, Easby Drive, ILKLEY, WEST YORKSHIRE, LS29 9AZ.
SAMUEL, Mr. Michael Richard, FCA *1972;* 7 Rutland Gardens, CROYDON, CR0 5ST.
•SAMUEL, Mr. Philip Michael, BA FCA *1990;* Beaumonts, 8 Navigation Court, Calder Park, WAKEFIELD, WEST YORKSHIRE, WF2 7BJ.
SAMUEL, Mr. Simon Robert, BSc ACA *1992;* Peach End, St. Chloe, Amberley, STROUD, GLOUCESTERSHIRE, GL5 5AP.
•SAMUEL, Mr. Stephen, FCA *1971;* Stephen Samuel & Co, 141 Stanmore Hill, STANMORE, MIDDLESEX, HA7 3ED.
SAMUEL, Mr. Steven Paul, BA ACA *1986;* Cygnia Technologies Unit2, Roway Lane, OLDBURY, B69 3EH.
SAMUEL, Mr. Thattacherril George, FCA *1969;* 104 Locust Road, Briarcliff Manor, NEW YORK, NY 10510, UNITED STATES.
SAMUEL, Mr. William Meredith, BSc FCA *1976;* 23 Cross Street, LONDON, N1 2BH.
SAMUEL, Mr. William Nicholas, ACA *2008;* with BDO LLP, 55 Baker Street, LONDON, W1U 7EU.
•SAMUELS, Mr. Adam Bernard Andrew, BA ACA *1986;* AS Collaborative Consulting Ltd, 12 Park Mount, HARPENDEN, HERTFORDSHIRE, AL5 3AR. See also Switchcourt Limited
SAMUELS, Mr. Alan William, ACA *2010;* Flat 20 Dawn Court, Bakers Close, ST. ALBANS, HERTFORDSHIRE, AL1 5FH.
SAMUELS, Mr. Jason, BA(Hons) ACA *2010;* 26 Morgan Gardens, Aldenham, WATFORD, WD25 8BF.
SAMUELS, Ms. Juliet, BA ACA *1990;* 27 Chrysostom Street, North Beach, PERTH, WA 6020, AUSTRALIA.
•SAMUELS, Mr. Keith, ACA *1989;* Tax Beans & Law Ltd, 111 Stratford Road, Wolverton, MILTON KEYNES, MK12 5LW.
SAMUELS, Mr. Malcolm Stanley, FCA *1965;* Flat 7, Littleberry Court, 5 St. Vincents Lane, LONDON, NW7 1EN. (Life Member)
SAMUELS, Mr. Montague Ivor, BSc FCA *1960;* 11 Linden Lea, Hampstead Garden Suburb, LONDON, N2 0RF. (Life Member)
•SAMUELS, Mr. Paul Nathan, BA FCA *1983;* Heywards, 6th Floor, Remo House, 310-312 Regent Street, LONDON, W1B 3BS.
•SAMUELS, Mr. Peter Trevor, FCA CF *1972;* Samuels Corporate Limited, The Old Forge, 36A West Street, REIGATE, SURREY, RH2 9BX.
•SAMUELS, Mr. Stephen, BCom FCA *1978;* S. Samuels & Co, 205 Bury Old Road, Prestwich, MANCHESTER, M25 1JF.
SAMUELS, Mr. Steven Bailey, FCA *1975;* 11 Queen Mary Avenue, HOVE, EAST SUSSEX, BN3 6XG.
SAMUELSON, Mr. Jonathan Wylie, FCA *1980;* 1 Maytrees, Loom Lane, RADLETT, WD7 8AW.
SAMUELSSON, Mrs. Shamala, ACA *1992;* Batsmansv. 36, S-192 48 SOLLENTUNA, SWEDEN.
SAMWAYS, Mr. Roy, BA FCA *1978;* Alnwick Farm House, Long Marston, TRING, HP23 4RA.
SAMWAYS, Mr. Stephen Anthony, BA ACA MBA *1996;* International Personal Finance Plc, 3 Leeds City Office Park, Meadow Lane, LEEDS, LS11 5BD.
SAMWAYS, Mrs. Tracey Anne, BA ACA *1997;* 8 Cairn Garth, Guiseley, LEEDS, LS20 8QP.
SAMWELL, Mr. Stanley David, FCA *1954;* Chapel House, The Platt, AMERSHAM, BUCKINGHAMSHIRE, HP7 0HX. (Life Member)
SAMWORTH, Mr. Robert James, FCA *1951;* Rivendell, Kings Lane, Chipperfield, KINGS LANGLEY, WD4 9EN. (Life Member)
SAMYANI, Mr. Sohail, BSc ACA *2004;* 41 Nonsuch Walk, SUTTON, SM2 7LG.
SAN, Miss. Joceline Chooi-Yin, FCA *1977;* 1b Parsifal Road, LONDON, NW6 1UG.
SAN, Mr. Kin Cheong, BA ACA *1986;* No 1 Jalan 22/36, 46300 PETALING JAYA, SELANGOR, MALAYSIA.
SAN, Mr. Mun Kwong, FCA *1970;* 85 Livingstone Avenue, PYMBLE, NSW 2073, AUSTRALIA.
SAN, Ms. Sek Chean, ACA *2011;* Flat 49, Sherard Court, 3 Manor Gardens, LONDON, N7 6FB.
SAN, Miss. Vivienne Wai Yin, FCA *1969;* 9 Nathan Road, 18-03 Regency Park, SINGAPORE 248730, SINGAPORE.
•SAN-JUAN MARTIN, Mr. Eugenio, FCA *1975;* Altash Consultants & Partners Ltd, Shaw House, Pegler Way, CRAWLEY, WEST SUSSEX, RH11 7AF.
SAN MARTIN, Mr. Sebastian Andres, LLB ACA *2006;* Pricewaterhousecoopers Llp, 1 Hays Lane, LONDON, SE1 2RD.
SANATHRA, Mr. Ajay, BSc ACA *2006;* with Deloitte Middle East, Currency House, Building 1 Level 5, DIFC, PO Box 282056, DUBAI UNITED ARAB EMIRATES.
SANCHEZ, Mr. Guillermo, ACA *2009;* 4 Archway Mews, Putney, LONDON, SW15 2PE.
SANCHEZ, Mr. Paul Nicholas, FCA *1974;* September House, 187 The Street, West Horsley, LEATHERHEAD, KT24 6HR.
•SANCHEZ MONTES, Mr. Michael James, BSc ACA *2002;* ASE Audit LLP, Rowan Court, Concord Business Park, MANCHESTER, M22 0RR.
SANCHEZ SALAN, Miss. Carolina Ascension, ACA *2001;* 12 Hillcrest Road, LONDON, W5 1HW.
SANCHO, Mr. Gerald Eugene, BA FCA *1963;* 104 Woodford Street, Newtown, PORT OF SPAIN, TRINIDAD AND TOBAGO.
SANCTIS, Mr. Sylvan, FCA *1972;* 2 Strafford Road, HOUNSLOW, TW3 3EN.
SANDALL, Mr. Michael, FCA *1980;* Went Farm House, Langton Road, Speldhurst, TUNBRIDGE WELLS, TN3 0NR.
•SANDALL, Mr. Nicholas John, MA ACA *1989;* Deloitte LLP, Stonecutter Court, 1 Stonecutter Street, LONDON, EC4A 4TR. See also Deloitte & Touche LLP
•SANDBACH, Mr. Anthony John Clifton, FCA *1978;* 139 Westley Road, BURY ST. EDMUNDS, SUFFOLK, IP33 3SE.
SANDBACH, Mr. Peter Worsley, FCA *1955;* 84 Little Sutton Lane, Four Oaks, SUTTON COLDFIELD, B75 6PE. (Life Member)
•SANDBACH, Mr. Richard Paul Stainton, BA FCA DChA *1981;* Moore Stephens, Rutland House, Minerva Business Park, Lynch Wood, PETERBOROUGH, PE2 6PZ.
SANDBACH, Mr. Ross Martin, BSc ACA *2005;* 3 Hubbard Close, Twyford, READING, BERKSHIRE, RG10 0XU.
SANDE, Ms. Sonia, MA ACA *1998;* Ernst & Young LLP, 5 Times Square, NEW YORK, NY 10036, UNITED STATES.
SANDELL, Miss. Katy Holly, ACA *2009;* 12/35 Moruben Road, MOSMAN, NSW 2088, AUSTRALIA.
SANDELL, Mr. Paul, BSc(Hons) ACA *2009;* 38 Teazlewood Park, LEATHERHEAD, SURREY, KT22 7JQ.
SANDELL, Mr. Robert Laurie, MA FCA *1965;* 56 Dale Street, Chiswick, LONDON, W4 2BZ. (Life Member)
SANDELLS, Mr. David, FCA *1970;* (Tax Fac), 55 Parkdale Road, Paddington, WARRINGTON, WA1 3EN.
SANDEMAN, Mr. Angus William, MA ACA *1990;* 83 Warwick Park, TUNBRIDGE WELLS, KENT, TN2 5ET.
SANDEMAN, Ms. Sian Elizabeth, BA ACA *1990;* 83 Warwick Park, TUNBRIDGE WELLS, KENT, TN2 5ET.
SANDER, Mr. Jonathan David, BA(Hons) ACA *2002;* Flat 14, Balmoral Court, Priory Field Drive, EDGWARE, MIDDLESEX, HA8 9QT.
•SANDERCOMBE, Mr. Martin Stafford, FCA *1965;* Ashdens, Pennyroyal, Stour Lane, Stour Row, SHAFTESBURY, DORSET SP7 0QJ.
SANDERS, Mr. Alec Harold, FCA *1974;* Titteringdales, Pye Lane, Grasmere, AMBLESIDE, CUMBRIA, LA22 9RQ.
SANDERS, Miss. Anne Judith, MA(Hons) ACA *2000;* 110 Norbiton Avenue, KINGSTON UPON THAMES, KT1 3QP.
SANDERS, Mr. Anthony Martin, BA ACA *1980;* 149 Tamworth Road, SUTTON COLDFIELD, B75 6DY.
SANDERS, Mr. Ben, BEng ACA *2004;* 15 Crutchfield Lane, WALTON-ON-THAMES, SURREY, KT12 2QY.
SANDERS, Mr. Blake, ACA *2009;* 8 Dombey Close, ROCHESTER, ME1 2JA.
SANDERS, Mr. Christopher James, BSc ACA *2007;* 28 Graham Road, LONDON, W4 5DR.
SANDERS, Mr. Colin Southern, BA ACA *1989;* Flat 22A Block 1 Provident Centre 21 Wharf Road, NORTH POINT, HONG KONG SAR.
•SANDERS, Mr. Damian Robert, BA ACA *1989;* Deloitte LLP, PO Box 500, 2 Hardman Street, MANCHESTER, M60 2AT. See also Deloitte & Touche LLP
•SANDERS, Mr. David, BSc FCA *1978;* Sanders Swinbank Limited, 7 Victoria Road, DARLINGTON, DL1 5SN.
SANDERS, Mr. David, FCA *1973;* OMRON EUROPE B.V., WEGALAAN 69, 2132 JD HOOFDDORP, NETHERLANDS.
•SANDERS, Mr. David Andrew, BA FCA *1993;* (Tax Fac), Sheen Stickland LLP, 4 High Street, ALTON, HAMPSHIRE, GU34 1BU.
SANDERS, Mr. Derren, BSc ACA *1998;* 31 Wyndham Wood Close, Fradley, LICHFIELD, STAFFORDSHIRE, WS13 8UZ.
SANDERS, Mr. Geoffrey Turner, FCA *1954;* 12 St.Martins Road, Finham, COVENTRY, CV3 6EU. (Life Member)
SANDERS, Mr. Guy Nicholas, FCA *1983;* Maple House, 1 Maple Drive, Lower Road, Bookham, LEATHERHEAD, SURREY KT23 4AX.
SANDERS, Miss. Heather, BA ACA *2002;* Apartment 82, 7 Romana Square, ALTRINCHAM, CHESHIRE, WA14 5QG.
SANDERS, Mr. Ian Aelwin, MA FCA *1986;* PricewaterhouseCoopers, 9th Floor, East Tower, Abu Dhabi Trade Centre, ABU DHABI, 45263 UNITED ARAB EMIRATES.
SANDERS, Mr. Ian Mark, FCA CF *1999;* with Smith & Williamson Ltd, Portwall Place, Portwall Lane, BRISTOL, BS1 6NA.
SANDERS, Mr. Ian Stuart, FCA *1970;* Aibel Oleo & Gas Ltda, Rodavia Amaral Peixoto, Km 167, Estr. da Fazenda São José da Mutum 180, MACAE, 27973-030 BRAZIL.
•SANDERS, Mrs. Jacqueline Rachel, BA ACA *1993;* JS2 Limited, 1 Crown Square, Church Street East, WOKING, SURREY, GU21 6HR.
SANDERS, Mr. James, BSc ACA *2004;* 3/11 Birriga Road, BELLEVUE HILL, NSW 2023, AUSTRALIA.
•SANDERS, Mr. James Alastair, MA FCA *1982;* The Cedars, Doveleys Manor Park, Rocester, UTTOXETER, STAFFORDSHIRE, ST14 5BZ.
SANDERS, Mr. James William Ashton, MA ACA *1997;* Lloyds, 10 Gresham Street, LONDON, EC2V 7AE.
SANDERS, Mr. Jan Charles, BA ACA *1998;* St. Georges Hill, New House Lane, REDHILL, RH1 5RE.
•SANDERS, Mrs. Jennifer Ann, BSc ACA *1990;* Catalyst Corporate Finance LLP, 21 The Triangle, NG2 Business Park, NOTTINGHAM, NG2 1AE.
SANDERS, Mr. John Anthony, FCA MAAT *1999;* C/O British Embassy, DOHA, PO Box 3, QATAR.
SANDERS, Mr. John Edward, BA FCA *1992;* Rosehill House, Rosehill Drive, BRIDGNORTH, SHROPSHIRE, WV16 5BP.
SANDERS, Mr. John Joseph, BA ACA *1996;* MacFarlane & Co Cunard Building, Water Street, LIVERPOOL, L3 1DS.
•SANDERS, Mr. John Michael, FCA *1960;* (Tax Fac), J.M. Sanders, Badgers Croft, Hive Road, Bushey Heath, BUSHEY, WD23 1JG. See also J.M. Sanders & Co
SANDERS, Ms. Judith Ann, MA ACA *1993;* Chemin Des Prés Doraux 20, 1297 FOUNEX, VAUD, SWITZERLAND.
SANDERS, Mrs. Julia Katherine, BA ACA *1989;* 18 Woodland Road, SEWICKLEY, PA 15143, UNITED STATES.

SAPRA, Mr. Rishi, ACA *2009;* 151 Woodcock Hill, HARROW, MIDDLESEX, HA3 0NZ.
SAPRA, Miss. Shailesh, ACA *2009;* 54 Englewood Road, LONDON, SW12 9NY.
SAPRA, Mrs. Sonia, BA ACA *1993;* 55 London Road, STANMORE, HA7 4PA.
SAPSFORD, Mrs. Alison Kay, BSc ACA *1997;* 112 Mortlake Road, RICHMOND, SURREY, TW9 4AS.
SAPSFORD, Mr. Anthony Paul, ACA *1979;* 11 The Mile, Pocklington, YORK, YO42 2HQ.
SAPSFORD, Mr. John Dennis Patrick, FCA *1975;* 1306 Groucher Street, PACIFIC PALISADES, CA 90272, UNITED STATES.
SAPSFORD, Mrs. Roxana, BSc ACA *2004;* with PricewaterhouseCoopers LLP, Pricewaterhousecoopers, 12 Plumtree Court, LONDON, EC4A 4HT.
SAPTE, Mr. David Rodney Fitzroy, FCA *1970;* Chellaston House, Love Lane, KINGS LANGLEY, WD4 9HN. (Life Member)
•SARA, Mr. Derek Richard Tomlin, FCA *1972;* (Tax Fac), Farmiloes LLP, Winston Churchill House, 8 Ethel Street, BIRMINGHAM, B2 4BG.
•SARA, Mr. Nigel Dennis, FCA *1973;* Nigel D. Sara, 12 Paulton Drive, Bishopston, BRISTOL, BS7 8JJ.
SARAF, Mr. Rakesh, FCA *1974;* D8/2 Vasant Vihar, NEW DELHI 110057, INDIA.
SARAGOSSI, Mr. Mark, ACA *1983;* 3 Hurst Place, NORTHWOOD, HA6 2JS.
•SARAI, Mr. Jaskamal Singh, BA ACA *1996;* PricewaterhouseCoopers LLP, The Atrium, 1 Harefield Road, UXBRIDGE, UB8 1EX. See also PricewaterhouseCoopers
SARAIVA, Mrs. Rosa Marina Da Silva, ACA *2004;* Rua Ponta Delgada, No 4 - 1dto, 2790-398 QUEIJAS, PORTUGAL.
SARAKAKIS, Mr. Dimitrios, ACA *2011;* 57 17th November Street, Cholargos, 15562 ATHENS, GREECE.
SARALIS, Mr. James David, BSc ACA *2004;* The Reddings The Common, Woolaston, LYDNEY, GL15 6NT.
SARAN, Dr. Mohinder Pal Singh, DPhil ACA *2010;* Premier Place, The Royal Bank of Scotland Plc Premier Place & A Half, 2 Devonshire Square, LONDON, EC2M 4BA.
•SARAN, Mr. Tejinder Singh, BSc ACA *2000;* Accumen Business Consultancy Limited, The Quadrant Business Centre, 3 The Quadrant, COVENTRY, CV1 2DY.
SARANGI, Mr. Ashley, BA ACA *2002;* 186 Ashby Road, BURTON-ON-TRENT, DE15 0LB.
SARAVANAMUTTU, Mr. Rohan Ratnanayagam, BSc ACA *1983;* 9 St. Wilfrids Road, BARNET, HERTFORDSHIRE, EN4 9SB.
SARAWAGI, Mr. Amit Kumar, ACA *2010;* with PricewaterhouseCoopers, Royal Trust Tower, Suite 3000 TD Centre, Box 82, 77 King Street West, TORONTO M5K 1G8 ON CANADA.
SARAYIAH, Miss. Camilla, BSc FCA *1999;* 48B Melrose Avenue, LONDON, NW2 4JS.
SARBICKI, Mr. Martin Jan, BA FCA *1977;* 7 Marlborough Road, Ealing, LONDON, W5 5NY.
SARDA, Mr. Sandip, ACA *2010;* Exel Middle East FZE Office, 726 Phase 4A East Wing, Dubai Aiport Free Zone, DUBAI, 54528, UNITED ARAB EMIRATES.
SARDA, Mr. Subhash Chandra, FCA *1974;* 998 Chestnut Hill Road, MARIETTA, GA 30064, UNITED STATES.
SARDANA, Miss. Ruchi, BSc ACA *2011;* 145 Sydenham Hill, LONDON, SE23 3PH.
SARDAR, Mr. Jakaria, BSc ACA *2010;* 37 Hennessy Road, LONDON, N9 0XB.
SARDAR, Mr. Omar Saeed, BA ACA *2006;* Flat 507, Holly Court, John Harrison Way, LONDON, SE10 0BL.
SARDAR, Mr. Samiullah, ACA *1995;* Afren Plc Kinnaird House, 1 Pall Mall East, LONDON, SW1Y 5AU.
SARDHARWALA, Mr. Elyasali Badruddin, FCA *1963;* 11 Samian Gate, ST. ALBANS, AL3 4JW.
SARDON, Mr. Mohamed Sukarno, BSc ACA *1982;* Ernst & Young, Level 23A Menara Milenium, Pusat Bandar Damansara, 50490 KUALA LUMPUR, FEDERAL TERRITORY, MALAYSIA.
SAREEN, Mr. Inmark Ditlev, MSc ACA *2000;* 166 Court Lane, LONDON, SE21 7ED.
SAREEN, Mr. Michael Antony, FCA CTA *1980;* Welland House, Cobbaton, Chittlehampton, UMBERLEIGH, DEVON, EX37 9RZ.
SAREEN, Mr. Vipin, ACA *1984;* Flat K, 80 Eaton Square, LONDON, SW1W 9AP.
SARESSALO, Mr. Mikko Juhana, ACA *2002;* (Tax Fac), K P M G Llp, 15 Canada Square, LONDON, E14 5GL.
SARFO, Mr. Claude Kwasi, BA ACIB ACA MBA AMSI *1996;* 29 Nuffield Drive, DROITWICH, WORCESTERSHIRE, WR9 0DJ.
SARFRAZ, Mr. Javed, ACA *1979;* 3 Wokingham Road, READING, RG6 1LE.
SARGEANT, Mr. Andrew, ACA *1980;* USA Risk Group Of Vermont, PO Box 306, MONTPELIER, VT 05601, UNITED STATES.
SARGEANT, Miss. Emma Claire, BSc ACA *2010;* A-8-5, Damaipuri Condominium, JLN Chin HWA, Chateau Garden, 30250 IPOH, PERAK MALAYSIA.
SARGEANT, Miss. Emma Jane, BA(Hons) ACA *2011;* 108 Salters Road, NEWCASTLE UPON TYNE, TYNE AND WEAR, NE3 3UP.
•SARGEANT, Mr. Gary Andrew, FCA *1982;* (Tax Fac), Gary Sargeant + Company, 5 White Oak Square, London Road, SWANLEY, BR8 7AG.
SARGEANT, Mr. Ian Charles, FCA *1968;* The Spinney, Farnham Road Ewshot, FARNHAM, SURREY, GU10 5AU. (Life Member)
•SARGEANT, Mr. Ian Gordon, BA FCA *1983;* Deloitte LLP, 1 City Square, LEEDS, WEST YORKSHIRE, LS1 2AL. See also Deloitte & Touche LLP
SARGEANT, Mr. John, BA FCA *1973;* 1 Rue Louis Pouey, 92800 PUTEAUX, FRANCE.
SARGEANT, Miss. Katy Jane, BA(Hons) ACA *2001;* Room 1.70 Electronic and Electrical Engineering, University of Leeds, Woodhouse Lane, LEEDS, LS2 9JT.
SARGEANT, Mrs. Linda Joan, BSc FCA *1978;* 66 Shipton Road, YORK, YO30 5RQ.
SARGEANT, Mr. Mark Simon, MA ACA *1997;* Garden Flat, 66a Edith Road, LONDON, W14 9AR.
•SARGEANT, Mrs. Mary Anne, BA ACA ATII *2001;* MA Partners LLP, 2 Cyprus Court, Queens Square, ATTLEBOROUGH, NORFOLK, NR17 2AE.
SARGEANT, Mr. Michael, BSc FCA TEP *1993;* Gerenstrasse 32, CH 8602 WANGEN BEI DUBENDORF, SWITZERLAND.
SARGEANT, Mr. Neville, FCA *1961;* 60 Highway, FISH HOEK, 7975, SOUTH AFRICA. (Life Member)
SARGEANT, Mr. Paul Stuart, BA ACA *2007;* 23 Siloam Place, IPSWICH, SUFFOLK, IP3 0FA.
SARGEANT, Mr. Peter Francis, FCA *1967;* Fishers Cottage, Combe Lane, Chiddingfold, GODALMING, GU8 4XN.
SARGEANT, Mr. Philip Mark Jellett, BSc ACA *2006;* 10a Gorse Lane, HERNE BAY, CT6 7BE.
•SARGEANT, Mr. Raymond Michael, FCA *1967;* R M Sargeant, 13 Fairgreen, Cockfosters, BARNET, EN4 0QS.
SARGEANT, Mr. Sydney Reginald Francis, FCA *1972;* YaYa Towers Ltd, PO Box 76440, NAIROBI, 00508, KENYA.
SARGENT, Mr. Adrian Boyd, BA ACA *1995;* Man Truck & Bus Ltd Frankland Road, Blagrove, SWINDON, SN5 8YU.
SARGENT, Mr. Alex James, BA ACA *1994;* 103 Highbury Park, LONDON, N5 1UB.
•SARGENT, Mr. Alfred Charles, BA FCA *1962;* (Tax Fac), Sargent & Co, 37 Albury Drive, PINNER, MIDDLESEX, HA5 3RL.
•SARGENT, Mrs. Alison Grace, BSc FCA *1979;* Sargent & Co, 194b Addington Road, Selsdon, SOUTH CROYDON, SURREY, CR2 8LD.
SARGENT, Mr. David George, FCA *1969;* London Waste Ltd, The Ecopark, Advent Way, Edmonton, LONDON, N18 3AG.
SARGENT, Mr. Geoffrey Frank, FCA *1960;* Dryden Associates, P O Box 61, Alderney, GUERNSEY, GY9 3JT.
SARGENT, Mr. Graham, FCA *1970;* 25 Charterhouse Road, ORPINGTON, KENT, BR6 9EJ.
SARGENT, Mr. Graham Antony, BA FCA *1980;* 20 St. Laurence Road, BIRMINGHAM, B31 2AX.
SARGENT, Mr. John Gerald, FCA *1950;* 120 Tyrone Avenue, Greenside East, JOHANNESBURG, GAUTENG, 2193, SOUTH AFRICA. (Life Member)
•SARGENT, Mr. Jonathan, FCA *1979;* Stewart Fletcher and Barrett, Manor Court Chambers, 126 Manor Court Road, NUNEATON, CV11 5HL. See also SFB Consultants Limited
SARGENT, Mr. Maurice Edwin, FCA *1966;* 8 Greenlands Close, BURGESS HILL, RH15 0AR.
SARGENT, Mr. Michael Gregory, FCA *1966;* 43a Church Road, Altoft, NORMANTON, WEST YORKSHIRE, WF6 2NN.
SARGENT, Mrs. Miranda, BA ACA *1990;* Treyford Cottage, Warren Corner, Ewshot, FARNHAM, GU10 5AT.
•SARGENT, Mr. Orlando Gorham, BSc ACA *1991;* with HW Lee Associates LLP, New Derwent House, 69-73 Theobalds Road, LONDON, WC1X 8TA.
•SARGENT, Mr. Paul, FCA *1982;* Albert Goodman LLP, Mary Street House, Mary Street, TAUNTON, TA1 3NW.
SARGENT, Mr. Peter Bertram James, BSc(Econ) FCA *1957;* 13 East Ridgeway, Cuffley, POTTERS BAR, EN6 4AW. (Life Member)
SARGENT, Mr. Robert George, FCA *1972;* 7 Washingborough Road, Heighington, LINCOLN, LN4 1QW.
SARGENT, Mr. Rodger David, BSc ACA *1997;* 11 Beaufort Close, Lynden Gate, LONDON, SW15 3TL.
•SARGENT, Mrs. Sarah-Jane, BSc FCA *1987;* with Moore Stephens, 12/13 Alma Square, SCARBOROUGH, YO11 1JU.
•SARGENT, Mr. Shaun William, BA FCA *1994;* Streets LLP, Tower House, Lucy Tower Street, LINCOLN, LINCOLNSHIRE, LN1 1XW. See also Streets Audit LLP, Streets Whitmarsh Sterland and SMS Corporate Partner Unlimited
SARGENT, Mr. Stephen Clive, BSc FCA *1979;* Spinney End, 5 Harcourt Spinney, Market Bosworth, NUNEATON, CV13 0LH.
SARGISON, Mr. David Stephen, BSc ACA *1979;* PO Box 414, Savannah, GEORGE TOWN, GRAND CAYMAN, KY1-1502, CAYMAN ISLANDS.
SARIF, Mr. Irwin Peter, BSc ACA *1982;* 8 Talbot Road, LONDON, N6 4QR.
SARIKHANI, Mr. Ali-Reza, BSc FCA *1971;* Oakbank, Courtenay Ave, Kenwood, LONDON, N6 4LR.
SARIN, Miss. Anushka, BSc(Hons) ACA *2010;* Flat 14, West Court, Great West Road, HOUNSLOW, TW5 0TL.
SARJANT, Mrs. Amanda Louise, ACA *1993;* Suva Taylors Lane, Bosham, CHICHESTER, WEST SUSSEX, PO18 8QQ.
•SARJANT, Mr. David, FCA *1970;* (Tax Fac), David Sarjant & Co, Suite 21, Oliver House, Hall Street, CHELMSFORD, CM2 0HG.
SARJANT, Mr. Mark Richard, BA ACA *1992;* Suva, Taylors Lane, Bosham, CHICHESTER, WEST SUSSEX, PO18 8QQ.
•SARJEANT, Mr. Richard John, BSc FCA *1973;* WH Parker, 174 High Street, Harborne, BIRMINGHAM, B17 9PP.
SARKAR, Mr. Anando, BA(Hons) ACA *2002;* 1125 Maxwell Lane, Apartment 342, HOBOKEN, NJ 07030, UNITED STATES.
SARKAR, Mr. Bidesh, BSc ACA *1994;* 21 Hampden Road, LONDON, N10 2HP.
SARKAR, Miss. Bipasha, MEng ACA *2011;* 20 Nexus Court, 10 Kirkdale Road, LONDON, E11 1HB.
SARKAR, Mr. Kiron Chandra, FCA *1977;* Castleturvin, Athenry, GALWAY, COUNTY GALWAY, IRELAND.
SARKAR, Mr. Pradyot Kumar, FCA *1950;* As - 3/2 - Phase 1, Golf Green Urban Complex, CALCUTTA 700045, INDIA. (Life Member)
SARLL, Mrs. Janet Margaret, BA ACA *1981;* 23 Colonels Walk, The Ridgeway, ENFIELD, MIDDLESEX, EN2 8HN.
SARLL, Ms. Sarah Isobelle, BSc ACA MBA *1988;* 59 Westover Road, Downley, HIGH WYCOMBE, HP13 5HX.
SARMAD, Mrs. Javaria, ACA FCCA *2010;* 23 Dartnell Park Road, WEST BYFLEET, SURREY, KT14 6PN.
•SARNA, Mr. Naresh Kumar, FCA *1985;* Chancellers, 38/39 Bucklersbury, HITCHIN, SG5 1BG.
SARNA, Miss. Sonja Maria, BA ACA *1993;* British Telecom Kelvin House, 123 Judd Street, LONDON, WC1H 9NP.
SARNA, Mr. Surinder, ACA *1979;* 3 Quarry Bank, LIGHTWATER, SURREY, GU18 5PE.
SAROIA, Mr. Jabran Samuel, ACA FCCA *2011;* House No J30, Street No 03, Friends Colony, Misrial Road, RAWALPINDI 44000, PAKISTAN.
SARPASH, Mr. Hamid, BA FCA *1974;* 31 Havenbrook Blvd, TORONTO M2J 1A3, ON, CANADA.
SARRAU, Mrs. Carolyn Patricia, BA ACA CTA *2001;* (Tax Fac), 11 Browning Road, HARPENDEN, HERTFORDSHIRE, AL5 4TS.
SARSBY, Mr. John Charles Anthony, FCA *1969;* Seven Acres, Doncombe Lane, North Colerne, CHIPPENHAM, SN14 8QP.
SARSFIELD, Mr. Patrick Lucan, BA ACA *1992;* 87 Alt Road, Formby, LIVERPOOL, L37 6DD.
SARSFIELD, Mr. Vincent Gerard, BSc FCA *1987;* Little Lowes Fold, Heath Lane, Lowton, WARRINGTON, WA3 2SJ.
SARSON, Mr. David Peter, ACA *1979;* 30 Lambridge Wood Road, HENLEY-ON-THAMES, RG9 3BS.
SARSON, Mrs. Jeni Miriam, BA FCA *1983;* The Point, Reading Road North, FLEET, GU51 4HP.
SARSON, Mr. Michael Robert, ACA *1980;* Extrastaff Ltd, The Gate House, Alban Park, Hatfield Road, ST. ALBANS, HERTFORDSHIRE AL4 0JJ.
SARSON, Mr. Timothy James, ACA *1989;* Gothic Cottage Grove Hill, Dedham, COLCHESTER, CO7 6DX.
SARSON, Mr. Timothy James, BA(Hons) ACA *2002;* with KPMG LLP, 15 Canada Square, LONDON, E14 5GL.
•SARTIN, Mr. Scott John, ACA *2003;* (Tax Fac), Charlton Baker Limited, 1 Fordbrook House, Fordbrook Business Centre, Marlborough Road, PEWSEY, SN9 5NU. See also Charlton Baker
SARTORI, Mrs. Lindsay Marguerite Ann, BA ACA *1985;* 45 Beech Street, LONDON, EC2Y 8AD.
SARUP, Mr. Deepak, FCA *1981;* c/o Siam Commercial Bank, 9 Ratchadapisek Road, BANGKOK, 10900, THAILAND.
SARVANADA, Miss. Roshini, BA ACA *2005;* Siemens, Sir William Siemens Square, Frimley, CAMBERLEY, SURREY, GU16 8QD.
SARWAL, Mr. Arun Kumar, FCA *1983;* 130a Kew Road, RICHMOND, TW9 2AU.
SARWAL, Mr. Prodaman Kumar, FCA *1976;* 28 Atwood Avenue, Kew Gardens, RICHMOND, TW9 4HG.
SARWAR, Mr. Aftab, ACA *2010;* 134 Lansdowne Road, ILFORD, IG3 8NQ.
SARWAR, Mr. Natheem, MSc BA ACA *1997;* 4 Bollinwood Chase, WILMSLOW, CHESHIRE, SK9 2DF.
SASIDARAN, Mr. Naveen, ACA *2009;* Block 175 #07-857 Yishun Avenue 7, SINGAPORE 760175, SINGAPORE.
SASIDEVAN, Mr. Santharajah, ACA *1994;* 100 Greystoke Drive, RUISLIP, MIDDLESEX, HA4 7YW.
SASS, Miss. Beverley Jane, BA ACA *1997;* 35 Stella Street, Collaroy Plateau, SYDNEY, NSW 2097, AUSTRALIA.
SASSEN, Mr. Antony Phillip, BSc ACA *2001;* with PKF (UK) LLP, 4th Floor, 3 Hardman Street, MANCHESTER, M3 3HF.
SASSEN, Mrs. Elizabeth, BSc ACA *2005;* 14 Greenwood Place, Eccles, MANCHESTER, M30 9EX.
SASSIE, Miss. Elizabeth Anne, BSc ACA *1989;* Ground Floor Flat, 108 Huddleston Road, LONDON, N7 0EG.
SASSIENIE, Mr. Neville Naphtali, FCA *1955;* High Hill Cottage, Bulstrode Lane, Felden, HEMEL HEMPSTEAD, HP3 0BP. (Life Member)
SASSOON, Mrs. Carol, BA ACA *1988;* 7 Rowan Walk, Hampstead Garden Suburb, LONDON, N2 0QJ.
SASSOON, Mr. Eldon David, BA(Com) FCA *1963;* 6 Nethercroft Court, Grey Road, ALTRINCHAM, WA14 4BZ.
•SASSOON, Mr. Isaac David, FCA *1987;* I Sassoon & Co, 79 Windmill Lane, BUSHEY, WD23 1NE.
SASSOON, Lord James Meyer, KT MA FCA *1980;* 4 Chelsea Park Gardens, LONDON, SW3 6AA.
•SASSOON, Mr. Mark Robert, BA FCA *1989;* Mark Sassoon, 8 Sheraton Close, Elstree, BOREHAMWOOD, WD6 3PZ.
SASSOON, Mr. Ronald Joseph, FCA *1960;* Flat 3, 25 Belsize Park, LONDON, NW3 4DU.
SASSOULAS, Mr. Claude, ACA *1993;* Tata Communications France, 131 avenue charles de gaulle, 92200 NEUILLY-SUR-SEINE, FRANCE.
SASTRI, Mrs. Anita, FCA *1969;* 3181 Bayview Avenue, Unit No. 711, TORONTO M2K 2Y2, ON, CANADA.
SATARIANO, Mr. Luke, ACA *2002;* 122 Msida Valley Road, B'KARA BKR 9024, MALTA.
SATCHELL, Mr. John Hildebrand, FCA *1961;* St Cross House, 134 St. Cross Road, WINCHESTER, HAMPSHIRE, SO23 9RJ. (Life Member)
SATCHELL, Mr. Paul James, BA ACA *2005;* 27 Dalby Road, LONDON, SW18 1AW.
SATCHITHANANDA, Mr. Ananda Krishna, FCA *1979;* 59 Badgery Avenue, HOMEBUSH, NSW 2140, AUSTRALIA.
SATCHWELL, Mr. Paul, BSc ACA *2005;* 16 Hamble Close, Desford, LEICESTER, LE9 9HH.
SATCHWELL, Mr. Terry, FCA *1974;* Urschel International Ltd Unit D, Tiber Way Meridian Business Park, LEICESTER, LE19 1QP.
SATCHWILL, Mrs. Katherine Fiona, BSc ACA *1987;* 7 Autumn Walk, Wargrave, READING, RG10 8BS.
SATCHWILL, Mr. Peter Christopher, BSc ACA *1981;* 7 Autumn Walk, Wargrave, READING, RG10 8BS.
SATE, Mr. Derek James, FCA *1950;* 112 Dove Park, PINNER, HA5 4EE. (Life Member)
•SATER, Mr. Paul Edward Roisen, ACA *1995;* Ernst & Young LLP, 1 More London Place, LONDON, SE1 2AF. See also Ernst & Young Europe LLP
SATHYASEELAN, Mr. Zak, ACA *2009;* 6b The Mall, LONDON, N14 6LN.
SATIZABAL, Mr. Daniel, BA ACA *2004;* Lambourn, Shore Road, Hesketh Bank, PRESTON, PR4 6XQ.
SATNARINE, Mr. Gregory Kumar, BSc ACA *1992;* Hinduja Bank Switzerland Ltd, Place De La Fusterie 38IS, 1211 GENEVA, SWITZERLAND.
SATO, Miss. Satomi, MA ACA *1994;* 15 Belbroughton Road, OXFORD, OX2 6UZ.

•SATOW, Mrs. Claire Elspeth, MA ACA *1986;* Stancroft Capital Ltd, 18-20 Bride Lane, LONDON, EC4Y 8JP.
•①SATOW, Mr. Frederick Charles, BA ACA *1986;* MacIntyre Hudson LLP, Moorgate House, 201 Silbury Boulevard, MILTON KEYNES, MK9 1LZ.
SATSANGI, Mr. Rahul, BSc ACA *2006;* Rutland Partners, 15 Regent Street, LONDON, SW1Y 4LR.
SATSANGI, Miss. Satyesh Anita, BA ACA *1991;* 64 Chiswick Green Studios, 1, Evershed Walk, LONDON, W4 5BW.
•SATTAR, Mr. Abdul, FCA *1974;* Sattar & Co, 95 Oldham Road, ROCHDALE, LANCASHIRE, OL16 5QR.
SATTAR, Mr. Imran, BSc ACA *2007;* 55B Mitcham Lane, Streatham, LONDON, SW16 6LW.
SATTAR, Mr. Muhammad Abdus, FCA *1966;* Islamic Development Bank, P.O. Box 5925, JEDDAH, 21432, SAUDI ARABIA.
SATTAR, Miss. Nasrin, BSc ACA *2005;* 15 Jubilee Street, LUTON, LU2 0EA.
SATTAR, Mr. Osman Abdul, BSc ACA *2006;* Financial Services Authority, 25 North Colonnade, LONDON, E14 5HS.
•SATTAR, Mr. Sikander Abdul, BA ACA *1987;* KPMG, Edificio Monumental, Av. Praia da Vitoria 71-A-11o, 1069-006 LISBON, PORTUGAL.
•SATTERLEY, Mr. Mark David, ACA *1997;* Mark Satterley, 58 Clyde Avenue, EVESHAM, WORCESTERSHIRE, WR11 3FE.
SATTERTHWAITE, Mr. Michael, BA ACA *1994;* 4 Croft Court, Finningley, DONCASTER, SOUTH YORKSHIRE, DN9 3PJ.
SATTIANAYAGAM, Miss. Premila, ACA *2011;* 3 Old Horsham Road, Southgate, CRAWLEY, WEST SUSSEX, RH11 8PD.
SATYENDRA, Mr. Andrew Karunalingam, BA ACA *1988;* 14 Kerferd Road, GLEN IRIS, VIC 3146, AUSTRALIA.
SAUCE, Mr. Paul Christopher, BA(Hons) ACA *2003;* 25 Thetford Road, Great Sankey, WARRINGTON, WA5 3EQ.
SAUJANI, Miss. Vishali, BSc(Hons) ACA *2011;* Flat 22, 59 Bunhill Row, LONDON, EC1Y 8QW.
SAUL, Mr. Adrian Christopher, BSc ACA *1986;* Diageo Plc Lakeside Drive, Park Royal, LONDON, NW10 7HQ.
SAUL, Mr. David Israel, BSc(Econ) ACA *1996;* 8 Jesmond Way, STANMORE, MIDDLESEX, HA7 4QR.
SAUL, Mr. Ian, BA FCA *1994;* Vopak Terminal Teesside Ltd, Seal Sands, MIDDLESBROUGH, CLEVELAND, TS2 1UA.
•①SAUL, Mr. Mark Ashley, FCA MIPA FABRP *1991;* Ashway Accountants Limited, Willow Garth, Field House Close, WETHERBY, WEST YORKSHIRE, LS22 6UD.
SAUL, Mrs. Nicola Jane, BA ACA *1991;* Willow Garth, 1 Field House Close, Linton Hills, WETHERBY, LS22 6UD.
SAUL, Mr. Thomas James Bycroft, MA ACA *1994;* Southwood Scar Hill, Minchinhampton, STROUD, GL6 9AH.
SAULTER, Mr. Daniel Mark, BSc ACA *2005;* 46 Murrills Road, Purdis Farm, IPSWICH, IP3 8US.
SAUNBY, Mr. Jonathan Edward, BMus ACA *1998;* 23 Farbailey Close, CHESTER, CH4 7QH.
SAUNDER, Mrs. Bhanumathy, BCom FCA ACA *2011;* 48 Kneller Gardens, ISLEWORTH, MIDDLESEX, TW7 7NW.
SAUNDER, Mr. David Pasmore, MA FCA *1977;* St. Aldates Parish Centre, 40 Pembroke Street, OXFORD, OX1 1BP.
SAUNDERS, Mr. Alain, BA ACA *1985;* 37 Vernon Avenue, PEACEHAVEN, EAST SUSSEX, BN10 8RT.
SAUNDERS, Mr. Alan John, BSc ACA *1989;* (Tax Fac), 40 Albany Road, WORCESTER, WR3 8EY.
SAUNDERS, Mrs. Alison Penelope Helen, BSc ACA *1988;* 27 Dovedale, Thornbury, BRISTOL, BS35 2DU.
SAUNDERS, Miss. Andrea Louise, ACA *2008;* Tredavoe Old Village, Willand, CULLOMPTON, DEVON, EX15 2RW.
SAUNDERS, Mr. Andrew Christopher William, ACA *2008;* 49 Moreton Terrace, LONDON, SW1V 2NS.
•SAUNDERS, Mr. Andrew David, BSc ACA *1985;* Andrew Saunders, Scotchcoultard, HALTWHISTLE, NORTHUMBERLAND, NE49 9NH.
•SAUNDERS, Mr. Andrew William, FCA MAE *1980;* Plummer Parsons Accountants Limited, 5 North Street, HAILSHAM, BN27 1DQ. See also Plummer Parsons
SAUNDERS, Miss. Anna Claire, BSc ACA *1999;* Cisco Systems, 9-11 New Square, FELTHAM, MIDDLESEX, TW14 8HA.
SAUNDERS, Mr. Anthony James, FCA *1981;* 31 Jubilee Road, WATERLOOVILLE, PO7 7RD.
SAUNDERS, Mr. Anthony Michael, BA ACA *2005;* 58 Wilkinson Street, SHEFFIELD, S10 2GJ.
SAUNDERS, Mr. Anthony Peter, MA FCA *1980;* Piazza Stefano Jacini 5, Palazzo A Interno 10, 00191 ROME, ITALY.
•SAUNDERS, Mrs. Birgitt, ACA ACCA *2011;* Stanley Yule Ltd, 79 Church Hill, Northfield, BIRMINGHAM, B31 3UB.
SAUNDERS, Mrs. Christine Judith, FCA *1977;* (Tax Fac), with Saffery Champness, Fox House, 26 Temple End, HIGH WYCOMBE, HP13 5DR.
SAUNDERS, Mr. Christopher, ACA *2009;* Flat 2 Bosworth House, 87 Havisham Drive, SWINDON, SN25 1BQ.
SAUNDERS, Mr. Clive, FCA *1966;* Newton House Martley Road, Lower Broadheath, WORCESTER, WR2 6QG.
SAUNDERS, Mr. Clive John, FCA *1973;* 37 Thorpland Avenue, Ickenham, UXBRIDGE, UB10 8TW. (Life Member)
SAUNDERS, Mr. Daniel John, BA ACA *2001;* 13 Wisley Road, LONDON, SW11 6NF.
•SAUNDERS, Mr. David Brian, ACA *1989;* Ellacotts LLP, Countrywide House, 23 West Bar Street, BANBURY, OXFORDSHIRE, OX16 9SA.
SAUNDERS, Mr. David Bruce, BA ACA *1992;* 74 High Street, Wootton, RYDE, PO33 4PR.
SAUNDERS, Mr. David John, BEng FCA *1994;* 16 Regal Close, Ealing, LONDON, W5 2SB.
SAUNDERS, Mr. David Melville James, FCA *1966;* 32 Wynnewood Lane, STAMFORD, CT 06903, UNITED STATES.
SAUNDERS, Mr. David Richard, ACA *1986;* 45 Beaverhall Drive, NORTH YORK M2L 2C8, ON, CANADA.
SAUNDERS, Mr. David Robert, BSc ACA *2010;* 17 The Grove, Chelworth, MALMESBURY, WILTSHIRE, SN16 9SS.
SAUNDERS, Mrs. Debra Anne, BSc ACA *2006;* with Wilkins Kennedy, Gladstone House, 77-79 High Street, EGHAM, TW20 9HY.
SAUNDERS, Mr. Edward Harvey, ACA *1996;* 5 Windermere Avenue, ASHBY-DE-LA-ZOUCH, LE65 1FA.
SAUNDERS, Mrs. Eleanor Caroline, BA ACA *2000;* 1661 Dasmarinas Avenue, MAKATI CITY, METRO MANILA, PHILIPPINES.
SAUNDERS, Mr. Garry Clifton, FCA *1971;* 20 Albany Hill, TUNBRIDGE WELLS, TN2 3RX.
SAUNDERS, Mr. Gavin Ross, BA ACA *1995;* 83 Maze Hill, Greenwich, LONDON, SE10 8XQ.
•SAUNDERS, Mr. Graham Paul Cavendish, MA FCA *1981;* Keens Shay Keens Limited, Christchurch House, Upper George Street, LUTON, LU1 2RS.
SAUNDERS, Miss. Grainne, BCom ACA *1991;* PO Box 62, GLADESVILLE, NSW 1675, AUSTRALIA.
SAUNDERS, Mr. Hugh Andrew, BSc ACA *2004;* Flat 15, Percy Laurie House, 217 Upper Richmond Road, LONDON, SW15 6SY.
SAUNDERS, Mr. Hugh Martin, MA FCA *1967;* Hursley, Trevone, Nr Padstow, PADSTOW, CORNWALL, PL28 8QX.
SAUNDERS, Mr. Hugh Richard, BA ACA *2001;* 29 Station Road, RADLETT, WD7 8JY.
SAUNDERS, Mr. Iain William, BCom FCA *2000;* 8860 East Chaparral Road, Suite 100, SCOTTSDALE, AZ 85250, UNITED STATES.
SAUNDERS, Mr. Ian Austen, BSc ACA *1995;* Old Church House, Marsh Green, EDENBRIDGE, TN8 5PT.
SAUNDERS, Mr. Ivan Derek, BSc FCA *1960;* Nashdom, Ashwood Road, WOKING, GU22 7JN. (Life Member)
SAUNDERS, Mrs. Jacqueline Barbara, BSc ACA *1993;* 63 York Gardens, WALTON-ON-THAMES, KT12 3EN.
•SAUNDERS, Mrs. Jacqueline Noreen, BA FCA DChA *1980;* Allotts, The Old Grammar School, 13 Moorgate Road, ROTHERHAM, SOUTH YORKSHIRE, S60 2EN.
SAUNDERS, Mr. Jason Peter, ACA *2006;* 26 Little Bookham Street, Bookham, LEATHERHEAD, SURREY, KT23 3AQ.
SAUNDERS, Mr. Jeffrey Alastair, BA FCA *1978;* 3 High Pewley, GUILDFORD, SURREY, GU1 3SH.
SAUNDERS, Mr. Jocelyn Arthur, BA(Econ) ACA *2002;* Flat 3, 66 Upper Richmond Road, Putney, LONDON, SW15 2RP.
SAUNDERS, Mrs. Jodie Shane, LLB ACA *1999;* 35 Bramley Green Road Bramley, TADLEY, HAMPSHIRE, RG26 5UE.
SAUNDERS, Mr. John Nicholas, BA FCA *1974;* Arundel, Church Bank, Shotley Bridge, CONSETT, DH8 0NW.
SAUNDERS, Ms. Joy E, ACA *2007;* Flat 42 Nonsuch House, 31 Chapter Way, LONDON, SW19 2RP.
SAUNDERS, Miss. Katherine Elizabeth, BSc ACA *2004;* with PricewaterhouseCoopers LLP, 9 Greyfriars Road, READING, RG1 1JG.
SAUNDERS, Miss. Kathryn, ACA *2010;* 3 High Pewley, GUILDFORD, SURREY, GU1 3SH.
SAUNDERS, Mrs. Katrina Jane, BA ACA *1996;* 9 Dorking Road, TUNBRIDGE WELLS, KENT, TN1 2LN.
•SAUNDERS, Mr. Keith Anthony, FCA *1980;* Keith Saunders, Fairview, 22 Ottershaw Park, Ottershaw, CHERTSEY, KT16 0QG.
SAUNDERS, Mr. Kenneth Cecil, FCA *1952;* 72 Laburnum Crescent, Allestree, DERBY, DE22 2GR. (Life Member)
SAUNDERS, Mr. Kenneth Henry Arthur, FCA *1962;* 36 Hillhouse Drive, BILLERICAY, ESSEX, CM12 0BA. (Life Member)
SAUNDERS, Mr. Kenneth John, FCA *1959;* 2 Barnfield, St Michaels, TENTERDEN, TN30 6NH. (Life Member)
•SAUNDERS, Mr. Kenneth William John, FCA CTA *1961;* Simpson Wreford & Co, Wellesley House, Duke of Wellington Avenue, Royal Arsenal, LONDON, SE18 6SS. See also Pure FD Limited
SAUNDERS, Mr. Kiaran Francis, BEng ACA *1999;* 21 Marney Road, LONDON, SW11 5EW.
SAUNDERS, Mrs. Laura Judith, BSc ACA *2005;* 27 Dowding Close, Woodley, READING, RG5 4NL.
SAUNDERS, Mr. Leon, BSc ACA *2006;* Flat B, 36 Overstone Road, LONDON, W6 0AB.
SAUNDERS, Mr. Mark, BEng FCA CTA *1993;* 73 Firecrest Road, BASINGSTOKE, RG22 5UL.
SAUNDERS, Mr. Mark Adrian, BSc(Hons) ACA *2002;* Flat 7, Gainsborough Court, 164-170 Kingston Road, Ewell, EPSOM, SURREY KT19 0SE.
SAUNDERS, Mr. Mark Ian, BA ACA *1993;* 3 The Woodlands, Harlestone Road, NORTHAMPTON, NN5 6NW.
•SAUNDERS, Mr. Mark Richard, BA FCA *1979;* Wilder Coe LLP, 233-237 Old Marylebone Road, LONDON, NW1 5QT. See also Wilder Coe
SAUNDERS, Mr. Martin Henry, FCA *1967;* 20 Highlands Park, Seal, SEVENOAKS, KENT, TN15 0AQ. (Life Member)
SAUNDERS, Mr. Maurice Roy, FCA *1968;* IFS International Corporate Services, 40 Townshend Road, LONDON, NW8 6LE.
•SAUNDERS, Mrs. Maxine Frances Kay, BA FCA *1991;* Deloitte LLP, Athene Place, 66 Shoe Lane, LONDON, EC4A 3BQ. See also Deloitte & Touche LLP
•SAUNDERS, Mr. Michael David, FCA *1972;* (Tax Fac), 6 Kings Drive, Littleover, DERBY, DE23 6EU.
SAUNDERS, Mr. Michael Ernest, BA FCA *1964;* 12 Brettenham Crescent, IPSWICH, IP4 2UB.
SAUNDERS, Mr. Michael Herbert, FCA *1959;* Milestone Cottage, Upottery, HONITON, EX14 9QT. (Life Member)
SAUNDERS, Mr. Michael John, FCA *1971;* Watermill House, Watermill Lane, Nettleham, LINCOLN, LN2 2PQ.
•SAUNDERS, Mr. Michael Peter, FCA *1967;* M.P. Saunders & Co., 2nd Floor, Walsingham House, 1331-1337 High Road, Whetstone, LONDON N20 9HR.
SAUNDERS, Mr. Michael Stephen, BSc ACA *1995;* William Grant & Sons Ltd, Customer Service Centre, Phoenix Crescent, Strathclyde Business Park, BELLSHILL, LANARKSHIRE ML4 3AN.
SAUNDERS, Mr. Michael-John, BCom ACA *1987;* M3 Consulting, Dashwood House, 69 Old Broad Street, LONDON, EC2M 1QS.
•SAUNDERS, Mr. Miles Antony, BSc FCA *1992;* PricewaterhouseCoopers LLP, 9 Greyfriars Road, READING, RG1 1JG. See also PricewaterhouseCoopers
SAUNDERS, Mr. Nicholas John, FCA *1962;* 2 Bledlow Cottages, Perry Lane, Bledlow, PRINCES RISBOROUGH, HP27 9QT.
SAUNDERS, Mr. Norman Stanley, FCA *1955;* 3 Golden Pightle, Style Loke, Barford, NORWICH, NR9 4AX. (Life Member)
SAUNDERS, Mr. Owen Glyn Thomas, BA ACA *1999;* 9 Holmeswood, 46 Worcester Road, SUTTON, SURREY, SM2 6GE.
SAUNDERS, Mrs. Patricia Elaine, FCA *1977;* with Fitzgerald Mithia, Newgate House, 431 London Road, CROYDON, CR0 3PF.
SAUNDERS, Mr. Paul Andrew, BEng ACA *1999;* Jansen-Cilag Ltd, 50-100 Holmers Farm Way, HIGH WYCOMBE, BUCKINGHAMSHIRE, HP12 4EG.
•SAUNDERS, Mr. Paul Barry, FCA *1973;* (Tax Fac), Saunders & Co, 29 Harcourt Street, LONDON, W1H 4HS.
SAUNDERS, Mr. Paul Bowman, BA ACA *1992;* 63 Reservoir Road, Elburton, PLYMOUTH, PL9 8NL.
•SAUNDERS, Mr. Peter James Alan, BSc ACA CPA *1993;* Deloitte LLP, 2 New Street Square, LONDON, EC4A 3BZ. See also Deloitte & Touche LLP
SAUNDERS, Mr. Philip, BSc ACA *2011;* 87 Nickleby Road, CHELMSFORD, ESSEX, CM1 4XG.
•SAUNDERS, Mr. Philip Kevin, BA ACA *1989;* Philip Saunders BA ACA, 6 Vyvyans Terrace, Praze, CAMBORNE, CORNWALL, TR14 0LD.
SAUNDERS, Mr. Richard Charles Meredith, BSc ACA *1993;* 116 The Street, Puttenham, GUILDFORD, GU3 1AU.
SAUNDERS, Mr. Richard Philip, BSc ACA *2000;* 92 Park Rise, HARPENDEN, HERTFORDSHIRE, AL5 3AN.
SAUNDERS, Mr. Robert Brian, BSc ACA *1991;* The Grange Eglwys Nunnydd, Margam, PORT TALBOT, WEST GLAMORGAN, SA13 2PS.
SAUNDERS, Mr. Roger Philip, BA ACA *1989;* Child Maintenance & Enforcement Commission, PO Box 239, HOLBECK, LEEDS, WEST YORKSHIRE, LS11 1EB.
SAUNDERS, Mr. Roger Ward, FCA *1968;* 12 Newman Close, HORNCHURCH, ESSEX, RM11 2TD.
SAUNDERS, Mrs. Sally Alexandra, BSc(Hons) ACA *2001;* Sharomis Old Vicarage Lane, Quarndon, DERBY, DE22 5JB.
SAUNDERS, Mrs. Sarah Louise, FCA *1990;* 122 Mitchley Avenue, SOUTH CROYDON, SURREY, CR2 9HH.
SAUNDERS, Mrs. Sharon, BSc ACA *1997;* 23 Tollerton Lane, Tollerton, NOTTINGHAM, NG12 4FP.
SAUNDERS, Miss. Sharon Amanda, BSc ACA *1996;* 4 Rye Field, ASHTEAD, KT21 2EH.
SAUNDERS, Mrs. Simona Janet, BSc ACA AMCT *1997;* 6 Boltons Lane, Binfield, BRACKNELL, RG42 4UB.
SAUNDERS, Mr. Stanley Leo, FCA *1960;* 29 Averill Close, BROADWAY, WORCESTERSHIRE, WR12 7RA. (Life Member)
SAUNDERS, Mr. Stephen Frederick, FCA *1966;* Oast Cottage, South Street, Boughton-under-Blean, FAVERSHAM, KENT, ME13 9NR. (Life Member)
SAUNDERS, Ms. Tanya, ACA CA(SA) *2008;* 15 Lime Avenue, Measham, SWADLINCOTE, DERBYSHIRE, DE12 7NG.
•SAUNDERS, Mr. Terence James, BA FCA *1981;* Baker Tilly Tax & Advisory Services LLP, The Pinnacle, 170 Midsummer Boulevard, MILTON KEYNES, MK9 1BP. See also Baker Tilly UK Audit LLP
SAUNDERS, Mr. Timothy, MA ACA *1987;* Beckets Place, Marksbury, BATH, BA2 9HP.
•SAUNDERS, Mrs. Vanessa Ann, BA(Hons) ACA *2003;* Saunders Accounting, 34 Shaftesbury Mount, Blackwater, CAMBERLEY, SURREY, GU17 9JR.
SAUNDERS, Mr. Wesley Ken Stephen, ACA *2009;* Flat 458 Anchor House, Smugglers Way, LONDON, SW18 1EX.
SAUNDERS, Mr. William Paul, FCA *1977;* BDO Spencer Stewart Zambia, P.O. Box 35139, LUSAKA, 10101, ZAMBIA.
SAUNDERS-DAVIES, Mr. Christopher Gwyn, BSc FCA *1972;* The Island, ROMSEY, SO51 0HP.
SAUNDERS-DAVIES, Mr. Mark Adrian Robert, FCA *1973;* 19 Jalan Durian, Jagakarsa, JAKARTA, 12620, INDONESIA.
•SAUNDERS-JONES, Mrs. Kathryn Rebecca, BSc(Hons) FCA *2000;* W J James & Co Limited, Bishop House, 10 Wheat Street, BRECON, LD3 7DG.
SAUNDERSON, Miss. Catherine Elizabeth, BSc ACA *2007;* 6 Voltaire, Ennerdale Road, RICHMOND, TW9 3PQ.
SAUNDERSON, Mr. Clive Robert Edwin, FCA *1984;* Ernst & Young, 18/F, Two International Finance Centre, 8 Finance Street, CENTRAL, HONG KONG ISLAND HONG KONG SAR.
SAUNDERSON, Mr. Colin Macrae, BA(Hons) FCA *1961;* 12 Cedar Road, ST.IVES, CAMBRIDGESHIRE, PE27 6TL. (Life Member)
SAUNDERSON, Mr. David James, MA ACA *1979;* Longacre, Haverhill Road, Stapleford, CAMBRIDGE, CB22 5BX.
SAUNDERSON, Mr. David Paul, BSc FCA *1987;* 23 Raine Way, Oadby, LEICESTER, LE2 4UB.
•SAUNDERSON, Mr. Ian Horton, BA ACA *1988;* with Berg Kaprow Lewis LLP, 35 Ballards Lane, LONDON, N3 1XW.
SAUNDERSON, Mrs. Judith Elizabeth Sharon, MA ACA *1999;* 1 Kites Nest Cottages, Swinhay, WOTTON-UNDER-EDGE, GLOUCESTERSHIRE, GL12 7PH.
SAUNDERSON, Mr. Keith Horton, FCA *1950;* Appledore, Rays Hill, Horton Kirby, DARTFORD, DA4 9DB. (Life Member)
SAUNDERSON, Mr. Mark, LLB ACA *2004;* Deloitte & Touche, 2 New Street Square, LONDON, EC4A 3BZ.
SAUNDERSON, Dr. Thomas Robert, PhD BSc(Hons) ACA *2002;* 7 Cricketers Way, CHATTERIS, PE16 6UR.
SAUNT, Mr. Timothy Patrick Gatty, BA ACA *1982;* Coats Plc, 1 The Square, Stockley Park, UXBRIDGE, MIDDLESEX, UB11 1TD.

SAUNTER, Mr. Michael Peter, BA ACA *1995;* Warner Music, 28 Kensington Church Street, LONDON, W8 4EP.
SAUNTER, Mrs. Pauline Jean, BSc ACA *1994;* 45 Cumberland Park, LONDON, W3 6SX.
SAUTTER, Mr. Mark Desmond, BSc ACA *1991;* 14a Campden Hill Gardens, LONDON, W8 7AY.
SAVADIA, Mr. Nitin Devchand, ACA *1979;* (Tax Fac), 52 Hillbury Avenue, HARROW, MIDDLESEX, HA3 8EW.
•**SAVAGE, Mr. Adrian Carleton, FCA** *1981;* AC Savage & Co, 275 High Street, NORTHALLERTON, DL7 8DW.
SAVAGE, Mr. Adrian George Logsdaile, BA ACA *1991;* 168b Hatfield Road, ST. ALBANS, HERTFORDSHIRE, AL1 4JD.
SAVAGE, Mrs. Alison Mary, BA ACA *1990;* Fielders Farmhouse, Sherfield English Lane, Plaitford, ROMSEY, SO51 6EJ.
SAVAGE, Mr. Andrew Jeremy, BA ACA *1990;* I P C Media Blue Fin Building, 110 Southwark Street, LONDON, SE1 0SU.
SAVAGE, Mr. Barry David, BA ACA *1983;* 8 Stubbs Close, SALFORD, M7 3BD.
SAVAGE, Mr. Christopher Henry, FCA *1957;* Chalfont House, 10 Marine Drive, Barton on Sea, NEW MILTON, HAMPSHIRE, BH25 7EG. (Life Member)
SAVAGE, Mr. Christopher Terence, BSc FCA MSI *1977;* J P Morgan Chase Bank, 20 Moorgate, LONDON, EC2R 6DA.
SAVAGE, Mr. David Luke, ACA *2010;* 88 Shirland Road, LONDON, W9 2EQ.
SAVAGE, Mr. David Ralph, FCA *1981;* Halcyon Days Studio Unit 9, Brymill Industrial Estate Brown Lion Street, TIPTON, DY4 9EG.
SAVAGE, Mr. Geoffrey Nigel, FCA *1977;* 54 Park Meadow, HATFIELD, HERTFORDSHIRE, AL9 5HB.
SAVAGE, Mr. George Campbell, MA ACA *1992;* 169 Slad Road, STROUD, GLOUCESTERSHIRE, GL5 1RG.
SAVAGE, Mr. Gerald, FCA *1955;* 4 Heythrop Close, Whitefield, MANCHESTER, M45 7YB. (Life Member)
SAVAGE, Mr. Graham Ronald, FCA *1966;* 46 Maze Green Road, BISHOP'S STORTFORD, HERTFORDSHIRE, CM23 2PJ. (Life Member)
SAVAGE, Dr. Hannah Elizabeth, ACA *2008;* 2 Alma Street, LEEK, STAFFORDSHIRE, ST13 8EH.
•**SAVAGE, Mrs. Helen Claire, BSc FCA** *1992;* Claire Savage, 37 Olney Road, Emberton, OLNEY, BUCKINGHAMSHIRE, MK46 5BX.
SAVAGE, Mr. Iain Albert Walter, BA FCA *1976;* Foray Motor Group Ltd, Telford Road, Churchfields, SALISBURY, SP2 7PF.
SAVAGE, Mr. Ian David, BA ACA *1997;* 9 Carpenters Wood Drive, Chorleywood, RICKMANSWORTH, HERTFORDSHIRE, WD3 5RH.
SAVAGE, Mr. Ian Paul, BA ACA *1996;* 320 8th Ave Apt 2L, BROOKLYN, NY 11215-3038, UNITED STATES.
•**SAVAGE, Ms. Jacqueline Elizabeth Franziska, BA FCA** *1980;* (Tax Fac), Alvery Ltd, Capital Business Centre, Suite 126, 22 Carlton Road, SOUTH CROYDON, SURREY CR2 0BS.
SAVAGE, Mr. James David Grant, MA ACA *2005;* Barclays Ventures, 7th Floor, United Kingdom House, 180 Oxford Street, LONDON, W1D 1EA.
SAVAGE, Mr. James Frederick, BSc ACA *1994;* Headland Capital Partners Limited, 1301 AIA, 1 Connaught Road, CENTRAL, HONG KONG ISLAND, HONG KONG SAR.
SAVAGE, Mr. Jamie Mark, BSc(Hons) ACA *2004;* 17 Holyhead Close, Callands, WARRINGTON, WA5 9RN.
•**SAVAGE, Mr. John, MA ACA** *1988;* Le Trocadero, 43 Avenue de Grande Bretagne, 98000 MONACO, MONACO.
SAVAGE, Mr. John Richard, BA FCA *1976;* Primrose Bank, Brooks Lane, Bosley, MACCLESFIELD, SK11 0PU.
SAVAGE, Mr. Joseph Henderson, ACA *1991;* 32 Woodhouse Road, HOVE, BN3 5NE.
SAVAGE, Mr. Keir John, MA ACA *2000;* with PricewaterhouseCoopers, Dorchester House, 7 Church Street West, PO Box HM1171, HAMILTON HM EX, BERMUDA.
SAVAGE, Mr. Kenneth, BA ACA *1989;* Perrys Group Ltd, 500 Pavilion Drive, NORTHAMPTON, NN4 7YJ.
•**SAVAGE, Mr. Leo, BSc FCA** *1976;* (Tax Fac), White Horse, York Way Fort George, St. Peter Port, GUERNSEY, GY1 2SY.
SAVAGE, Miss. Lindsay Sarah, ACA *2009;* 77 Melton Gardens, Edwalton, NOTTINGHAM, NG12 4BJ.
SAVAGE, Mr. Luke, BEng ACA *1988;* 71 Lee Road, Blackheath, LONDON, SE3 9EN.
SAVAGE, Mrs. Marianne Dorothy, FCA *1973;* PO Box 180, WULGURU, QLD 4811, AUSTRALIA.
SAVAGE, Mr. Mark Anthony William, BSc ACA *1990;* 8 Gardenia Grove, Up Hatherley, CHELTENHAM, GL51 3HR.
SAVAGE, Mr. Mark Brian, ACA *2008;* 5 Sorting Lane, BASINGSTOKE, HAMPSHIRE, RG24 9TD.
SAVAGE, Mr. Mark John, BA FCA *1992;* (Tax Fac), with Mazars LLP, The Atrium, Park Street West, LUTON, LU1 3BE.
SAVAGE, Mr. Martyn Godfrey, FCA *1978;* Accident Exchange, Alpha, 1 Hams Hall National Distribution Park, Canton Lane, Coleshi, BIRMINGHAM B46 1GA.
SAVAGE, Mr. Matthew Paul, BSc ACA *2003;* with KPMG LLP, 15 Canada Square, LONDON, E14 5GL.
SAVAGE, Mr. Michael John, BA FCA *1972;* 1f St. Marys Court, La Rue Piette, Castel, GUERNSEY, GY5 7AA.
SAVAGE, Mr. Oliver, BSc ACA *2006;* 3 Tabor Close, Harlington, DUNSTABLE, BEDFORDSHIRE, LU5 6PF.
SAVAGE, Mr. Paul Jonathan, MA MSc ACA *1992;* 3 Grange Avenue, WOODFORD GREEN, IG8 9JT.
•**SAVAGE, Mr. Paul Reginald, FCA** *1975;* (Tax Fac), P R Savage & Company Limited, 3a Warwick Road, BEACONSFIELD, BUCKINGHAMSHIRE, HP9 2PE.
SAVAGE, Mr. Paul Vincent, BA FCA *1984;* 3 Wilstrop Farm Road, Copmanthorpe, YORK, YO23 3RZ.
•**SAVAGE, Mrs. Rachael Ann, BSc ACA** *2002;* Simplified Accounting Limited, 34 Brackley Road, TOWCESTER, NORTHAMPTONSHIRE, NN12 6DJ.
SAVAGE, Mr. Richard Alexander James, BA ACA *2002;* 41 Pageant Road, ST. ALBANS, HERTFORDSHIRE, AL1 1NB.
SAVAGE, Mr. Richard David, MA FCA *1987;* Pricewaterhousecoopers, Tower 2 Darling Park, 201 Sussex Street, SYDNEY, NSW 2000, AUSTRALIA.
SAVAGE, Mr. Robert Edwin John, BA ACA *1992;* Greenpark Capital, Cassini House, 57-59 St. James's Street, LONDON, SW1A 1LD.
SAVAGE, Mrs. Sandra, BSc ACA DChA *1984;* with Bolton & Co, 14 Warrington Street, ASHTON-UNDER-LYNE, OL6 6AS.
SAVAGE, Mr. Steven, BA ACA *1988;* Perenco Holdings, 10 Duke of York Square, LONDON, SW3 4LY.
SAVAGE, Mr. Steven, BA ACA *1996;* 77 Scott Street, YORK, YO23 1NR.
SAVAGE, Mr. Stuart, ACA *2011;* 326 Bolton Road, Kearsley, BOLTON, BL4 8NQ.
SAVAGE, Mrs. Susan Jane, BSc FCA *1982;* Ivy House, Great Asby, APPLEBY-IN-WESTMORLAND, CUMBRIA, CA16 6HD.
SAVAGE, Mr. Timothy John, BSc ACA *1988;* The Capital Partnership, 11 Upper Grosvenor Street, LONDON, W1K 2NB.
SAVAGE-ROBERTS, Ms. Katarina, ACA *2009;* 32 Pine Avenue, WEST WICKHAM, KENT, BR4 0LW.
SAVAGE-ROBERTS, Mr. Michael John, BSc(Hons) ACA *2001;* 32 Pine Avenue, WEST WICKHAM, BR4 0LW.
SAVALA, Mr. Craig Lloyd, MA(Hons) ACA *2002;* Apt 2101 Colonnades, 30 Glen Street, MILSON'S POINT, NSW 2061, AUSTRALIA.
SAVANI, Mr. Iqbal, BA ACA *1997;* 18 Berry Hill, STANMORE, HA7 4XS.
SAVEALL, Mr. Regan Barry, ACA *1994;* Zone Vision, 105-109 Salusbury Road, LONDON, NW6 6RG.
SAVELLI, Mr. Gianluca, ACA *2010;* 39 Draycott Place, Flat 7, LONDON, SW3 2SH.
SAVERY, Mr. Barry John, MSc FCA *1968;* Whitewings, Chalfont Lane, Chorleywood, RICKMANSWORTH, WD3 5PR.
SAVERY, Mrs. Joanne Margaret, BCom ACA *1995;* 3 Westover Gardens, Westbury-on-Trym, BRISTOL, BS9 3LE.
SAVERY, Mr. John Lawrence, BSc ACA *1991;* 12 Thistledown Road, Horsford, NORWICH, NR10 3ST.
SAVERY, Mr. John William, FCA *1966;* 45 St. Dunstans Road, LONDON, W6 8RE.
SAVERY, Mr. Mark Richard, BSc ACA *2005;* 2 Swallowfield Gardens, Theale, READING, RG7 5AD.
SAVI, Mr. John Peter, FCA *1976;* P.za Gozzano 15, 10132 TORINO, ITALY.
SAVIDENT, Mr. Simon Allan, FCA *1996;* Guernsey Trust Company Ltd, PO Box 140, Manor Place, St Peter Port, GUERNSEY, GY1 4EW.
SAVIDGE, Mr. Paul, LLB ACA *2004;* 33 The Glebe, Ewhurst, CRANLEIGH, SURREY, GU6 7PY.
SAVIDGE, Mr. Stuart, MA ACA *2001;* CB Richard Ellis Investors, 21 Bryanston Street, LONDON, W1H 7PR.
SAVILE, Mr. George Keith Wrey, FCA *1974;* with Mazars LLP, Tower Bridge House, St. Katharines Way, LONDON, E1W 1DD.
SAVILE, Mr. Robert Victor, ACA *1979;* Springfields, Main Street, Hannington, NORTHAMPTON, NN6 9SU.
•**SAVILL, Mr. David Charles, LLB FCA** *1988;* (Tax Fac), Bishop Fleming, Stratus House, Emperor Way, Exeter Business Park, EXETER, EX1 3QS.
SAVILL, Mr. Oliver, BA ACA *2010;* Flat 2, Grosvenor Court, Irving Road, LONDON, W14 0JU.
SAVILL, Mr. Roger Stewart, FCA *1958;* 7 Manor Road, TAUNTON, TA1 5BB.
SAVILLE, Mr. Elliott Paul, MA ACA CTA *1993;* 91 College Hill Road, HARROW, HA3 7BT.
SAVILLE, Mr. Eric Geoffrey, BA ACA *1986;* 21 Ribby Avenue, Kirkham, PRESTON, PR4 2BU.
SAVILLE, Mr. Ian Leslie, BA FCA *1986;* Corwen, 22 West Way, PINNER, HA5 3NX.
•**SAVILLE, Ms. Julie Elizabeth, BSc ACA** *1993;* Arcadis A Y H Plc, 10 Furnival Street, LONDON, EC4A 1YH.
•①**SAVILLE, Mr. Michael Edward George, LLB FCA** *1985;* Begbies Traynor Limited, 340 Deansgate, MANCHESTER, M3 4LY. See also Begbies Traynor(Central) LLP
SAVILLE, Mr. Paul, BA ACA *1985;* 2 Millers Meadow Close, LONDON, SE3 9ED.
SAVILLE, Mr. Peter Denny, FCA *1953;* 3 Cross Lane, West Mersea, COLCHESTER, CO5 8HN. (Life Member)
SAVILLE, Mr. Philip Charles, BA ACA *1989;* 701 King Street W #1012, TORONTO M5V 2W7, ON, CANADA.
•**SAVILLE, Mr. Rafael Aryeh, BA ACA** *2001;* H W Fisher & Company, Acre House, 11-15 William Road, LONDON, NW1 3ER. See also H W Fisher & Company Limited
SAVILLE, Mr. Selwyn Michael, LLB FCA *1964;* 476 Street Lane, LEEDS, LS17 6HA. (Life Member)
SAVILLE, Mr. Terence Neil, FCA *1977;* Sherwood, 62 Archer Road, FOLKESTONE, CT19 5SA.
SAVILLE SNEATH, Mr. Christopher Anthony, BA ACA *1994;* Notting Hill Media Ltd, Park House, 206-208 Latimer Road, LONDON, W10 6QY.
SAVIN, Mrs. Angela Margaret, BSc ACA ATII *1989;* Grubstrasse 14, Bietingen, 78244 GOTTMADINGEN, GERMANY.
SAVIN, Mr. Werner Ernst Udo, BA ACA *1988;* Suntech Power International Ltd, Mühlentalstr. 36, 8200 SCHAFFHAUSEN, SWITZERLAND.
•**SAVJANI, Mr. Avnish Kumar, BA FCA** *1984;* Buzzacott LLP, 130 Wood Street, LONDON, EC2V 6DL. See also Fiscal Solutions Ltd
•**SAVJANI, Mr. Nilesh Dayalji, FCA CF** *1990;* Wags LLP, Richmond House, Walkern Road, STEVENAGE, HERTFORDSHIRE, SG1 3QP.
SAVJANI, Mrs. Nisha, BA ACA *1992;* 3 Clare Close, Elstree, BOREHAMWOOD, WD6 3NJ.
SAVJANI, Mr. Ramesh Haridas, FCA *1977;* Hannover House, P.O.Box 2126, BLANTYRE, MALAWI.
SAVJANI, Mr. Satish Haridas, BSc ACA *1982;* 16 Chancerygate Business Centre, Whiteleaf Road, HEMEL HEMPSTEAD, HERTFORDSHIRE, HP3 9HD.
SAVJANI, Mr. Snehal, BA ACA *1994;* 84 Coledale Drive, STANMORE, MIDDLESEX, HA7 2QF.
SAVLA, Mr. Bhavin, BSc ACA *2002;* 63 Woodlands, HARROW, MIDDLESEX, HA2 6EJ.
•**SAVLA, Mr. Hiten Panachand, BSc ACA** *1994;* Greenaways, 19 Kingswood Way, SOUTH CROYDON, SURREY, CR2 8QL.
•**SAVOMY, Mr. Naraidoo, FCA FCCA CTA** *1997;* Anderson Ross LLP, Waltham Forest Business Centre, 5 Blackhorse Lane, LONDON, E17 6DS. See also Interbusiness Services Ltd
SAVORY, Mr. Charles Edward, ACA *2009;* Bridge Cottage, Thorpland, FAKENHAM, NORFOLK, NR21 0HD.
SAVORY, Ms. Margaret Anne, MA MPhil MSc FCA *1995;* with BDO LLP, Kings Wharf, 20-30 Kings Road, READING, RG1 3EX.
•**SAVORY, Mr. Nigel Rudolph, FCA** *1977;* Grant Thornton UK LLP, Kingfisher House, 1 Gilders Way, St James Place, NORWICH, NR3 1UB. See also Grant Thornton LLP
SAVORY, Mr. Peter John, FCA *1972;* Corry House, Dalwood, AXMINSTER, DEVON, EX13 7HJ. (Life Member)
SAVVA, Mr. Andreas, BA ACA *2005;* 90 Evagora Laniti Street, EKALI, 3111 LIMASSOL, CYPRUS.
•**SAVVA, Mr. Andreas Achilleos, FCA** *1972;* Grant Thornton, P.O. Box 23907, 1687 NICOSIA, CYPRUS. See also Costouris, Michaelides & Co(Overseas)
SAVVA, Mr. Avraam, FCA *1966;* 85 Ashbourne Road, Ealing, LONDON, W5 3DH. (Life Member)
•**SAVVA, Mr. George P, MA ACA** *2002;* KPMG, P O Box 40075, 6300 LARNACA, CYPRUS. See also KPMG Metaxas Loizides Syrimis
SAVVA, Miss. Louiza, MSc ACA *2011;* 6 Panayias Tinou Street, Strovolos, 2020 NICOSIA, CYPRUS.
SAVVA, Miss. Maria, ACA *2006;* 8 Aftakrateras, Theodoras Street, 8020 PAPHOS, CYPRUS.
SAVVA, Mr. Paris, BA ACA *2007;* 25 Sporadon Street, Anthoupoli, 2303 NICOSIA, CYPRUS.
SAVVA, Mr. Savvas, ACA *2011;* Flat 11, 9 Kalymnou Street, Strovolos, 2002 NICOSIA, CYPRUS.
•**SAVVA, Mr. Savvas Antoniou, MBA BSc ACA** *1988;* (Tax Fac), AJ & S Associates Ltd, 289a High Street, WEST BROMWICH, WEST MIDLANDS, B70 8ND. See also AJ & Associates
SAVVA, Mr. Savvas Christou, LLB FCA DipFS *1997;* Ul. Gen. Maczka 84, 05-082 JANOW, POLAND.
SAVVA, Mr. Xenophon, MPhil BSc ACA *2009;* 8 Athalassas Street, Aglanjia, 2109 NICOSIA, CYPRUS.
SAVVAS, Mr. Nicholas Alexander, BSc ACA *2003;* 2 Henleaze Park Drive, BRISTOL, BS9 4LH.
SAVVIDES, Mr. Adamos, ACA *2008;* Lamias 12 Flat 103, Rita Court 36, 2001 STROVOLOS, CYPRUS.
SAVVIDES, Ms. Argyro, BSc ACA *2006;* 44 Tempon street Flat 202 Egkomi, 2408 NICOSIA, CYPRUS.
SAVVIDES, Mr. Charis, BA ACA *2008;* 27 Fediou Street, CY 3075 LIMASSOL, CYPRUS.
SAVVIDES, Mr. Christos, MA FCA CTA *1992;* P. O. Box 54447, 3724 LIMASSOL, CYPRUS.
SAVVIDES, Mr. Constantinos, BSc ACA CF *1993;* Petrolina (Holdings) Public Ltd, 1 Kilkis Street, 6015 Larnaca, PO Box 40162, 6301 LARNACA, CYPRUS.
SAVVIDES, Mr. Emilios, BA ACA *1990;* 8 AMAZONON LATSIA, 2236 NICOSIA, CYPRUS.
SAVVIDES, Mr. Filios, BSc ACA *1992;* P.O Box 16299, 2087 NICOSIA, CYPRUS.
•**SAVVIDES, Mr. Frixos, FCA** *1978;* PKF Savvides & Co Ltd, Meliza Court, 4th & 7th Floor, 229 Arch Makorious III Avenue, 3105 LIMASSOL, CYPRUS.
•**SAVVIDES, Mr. George, FCA** *1984;* Savvides Audit Limited, Loucaides Court, 3 Makarios Avenue, 4th Floor, Mesa Geitonia, 4000 LIMASSOL CYPRUS. See also Christodoulides Shakallis & Co
SAVVIDES, Mr. George, BA ACA *2004;* (Tax Fac), 23 Souliou Street, 3016 LIMASSOL, CYPRUS.
•**SAVVIDES, Mr. Savvas Epiphaniou, FCA** *1972;* (Tax Fac), Savvas E Savvides Ltd, Pelekanos Court 21, 12 Prometheus Str, Office 102, PO Box 28743, 2082 NICOSIA CYPRUS.
SAVVIDOU, Ms. Barbara, BSc ACA *2003;* 24 Germanou Patron Street, Engomi, 2414 NICOSIA, CYPRUS.
SAVVIDOU, Mrs. Soteroulla, ACA FCCA *2010;* 8 Amazonon Street, Latsia, 2236 NICOSIA, CYPRUS.
SAW, Miss. Bee Leng, BSc ACA *1989;* 20 Jalan Jelita, SINGAPORE 278344, SINGAPORE.
SAW, Miss. Beng Kim, BSc FCA AMCT *1987;* 61 Fairfax Avenue, Ewell, EPSOM, KT17 2QQ.
SAW, Mr. Chang Jiann, FCA *1983;* 2A Lorong Bukit Sepanggar 3/4A, Taman Bukit Sepanggar, 88450 KOTA KINABALU, SABAH, MALAYSIA.
SAW, Mr. Kok Peng, BSc ACA *1992;* 28-18-C Gurney Beach Resort Condo, Persiaran Gurney, Georgetown, 10450 PENANG, MALAYSIA.
SAW, Miss. Mary Biq Shyuan, FCA *1972;* (Tax Fac), Camperdown, Sycamore Road, AMERSHAM, BUCKINGHAMSHIRE, HP6 6BB.
SAW, Mrs. Min Choo, ACA *1998;* 9 Solok Slim 1, Slim Villas, 11600 JELUTONG, MALAYSIA.
SAWARD, Mr. Geoffrey William, MA FCA Fifs *1988;* 3 Albion Court, Meltham, HOLMFIRTH, HD9 5JB.
SAWARD, Miss. Hannah Kate, MA ACA *2000;* Flat 1 Walnut Court, The Hill Wheathampstead, ST. ALBANS, HERTFORDSHIRE, AL4 8PL.
SAWARD, Mrs. Joanna Elizabeth, BA ACA *1993;* with Davis Grant LLP, Treviot House, 186-192 High Road, ILFORD, ESSEX, IG1 1LR.
SAWBRIDGE, Mr. Edward Henry Ewen, MA FCA *1979;* Longwood, Kings Road, Sunninghill, ASCOT, SL5 0AG.
SAWBRIDGE, Ms. Karen Elizabeth, BSc ACA *1991;* Leisureplex Ltd, Alfa Building, Euxton Lane, Euxton, CHORLEY, LANCASHIRE PR7 6AF.
SAWBRIDGE, Mr. Matthew John, BSc ACA *1997;* Hollyoak House Kettlemore Lane, Sheriffhales, SHIFNAL, SHROPSHIRE, TF11 8RG.

SAWBRIDGE, Mr. Neil John, BA ACA *1991;* (Tax Fac), 11 Lakewood Road, Chandler's Ford, EASTLEIGH, HAMPSHIRE, SO53 1ER.
•**SAWDON, Mrs. Audrey Jean, BSc FCA** *1983;* (Tax Fac), Dawkins Lewis & Soar, 4 Cowdown Business Park, Micheldever, WINCHESTER, SO21 3DN. See also DLS Accounting Services Ltd
•**SAWDON, Mr. Paul Kenneth, BA ACA** *1992;* KPMG LLP, 15 Canada Square, LONDON, E14 5GL. See also KPMG Europe LLP
SAWE, Mrs. Kimberley, ACA *2008;* K P M G Edward VII Quay, Navigation Way Ashton-on-Ribble, PRESTON, PR2 2YF.
SAWERS, Mr. Robert Keith, FCA *1959;* 19 Siskin Road, Uppingham, OAKHAM, LE15 9UL. (Life Member)
SAWERS, Mr. Samuel, ACA *2011;* Flat 27, Stubbs House, Erasmus Street, LONDON, SW1P 4DY.
SAWEY, Mr. Declan Patrick, BSc FCA MCT CFA *1991;* Shaheed Tower, Khalid Bin Waleed Street, Sharq, P.O. Box 23982, SAFAT, 13100 KUWAIT.
SAWFORD, Miss. Nicola Mary, BA ACA *1989;* Serle Court Chambers, 6 New Square, LONDON, WC2A 3QS.
•**SAWHNEY, Mr. Kanwarbir Singh, BSc FCA** *1988;* K S Sawhney, 104 Britannic Park, 15 Yew Tree Road, Moseley, BIRMINGHAM, B13 8NF.
SAWHNEY, Mr. Swapan, BA ACA *1986;* WESTRIDGE, Westridge Otham Lane, Bearsted, MAIDSTONE, ME15 8SJ.
SAWIN, Miss. Margot, BSc ACA *2007;* Flat 1 Poulett Lodge, Cross Deep, TWICKENHAM, TW1 4QJ.
•**SAWIN, Mr. Witold Karol, BSc FCA** *1980;* Sawin & Edwards, 15 Southampton Place, LONDON, WC1A 2AJ.
SAWJANI, Mrs. Hena, BSc ACA *2007;* 5 Cassander Place, PINNER, MIDDLESEX, HA5 4QS.
SAWJANI, Miss. Kalpa Kishorilal Ranchhoddas, MSc BSc ACA *2003;* 51 Lady Aylesford Avenue, STANMORE, MIDDLESEX, HA7 4FG.
SAWLE, Mr. Frederick Christopher, BSc(Econ) FCA *1972;* Woodmans Lodge, Orchard Hill, BIDEFORD, DEVON, EX39 2RA.
SAWREY, Mr. Philip Stephen, BA ACA *1986;* 9 Craigleith Gardens, EDINBURGH, EH4 3JW.
SAWTELL, Mr. Christopher Hugh Charles, MEng ACA *2011;* 89 Streathbourne Road, LONDON, SW17 8RA.
SAWTELL, Mr. George Edward, FCA *1953;* 26 Swallowdale, Wightwick, WOLVERHAMPTON, WV6 8DT. (Life Member)
SAWTELL, Mr. George Robert, LLB ACA *1992;* Inmarsat, 99 City Road, LONDON, EC1Y 1AX.
SAWYER, Mrs. Catherine, ACA *2011;* Endicot, Church Road, Boreham, CHELMSFORD, CM3 3EP.
SAWYER, Mr. Christopher Charles, BA FCA *1986;* 27 Rusland Avenue, ORPINGTON, KENT, BR6 8AT.
SAWYER, Mr. Christopher Lionel, BSc ACA *1991;* Watson Wyatt Westgate, 120-130 Station Road, REDHILL, RH1 1WS.
SAWYER, Mr. Colin Paul, FCA *1969;* Le Ser, 31420 PEYROUZET, FRANCE.
SAWYER, Mr. Daniel David, BA ACA *2003;* 57 Shaftesbury Road, BRIGHTON, BN1 4NF.
•**SAWYER, Mr. David Alexander, BSc FCA** *1981;* 53 Devon Road, BEDFORD, MK40 3DF.
SAWYER, Ms. Elizabeth Jane, BA FCA *1992;* with KPMG LLP, 15 Canada Square, LONDON, E14 5GL.
SAWYER, Miss. Helen, ACA *2007;* 15 Burnham Close, Cheadle Hulme, CHEADLE, CHESHIRE, SK8 6DN.
SAWYER, Mr. John Patrick, FCA *1975;* Flat 4, 35 Kent Gardens, West Ealing, LONDON, W13 8BU.
SAWYER, Mr. Mark Stephen, BA FCA *1985;* (Tax Fac), 11 Hills View, NEWENT, GL18 1SG.
SAWYER, Miss. Melanie, ACA *2011;* Flat 6 Boundary House, 224-226 St. Margarets Road, TWICKENHAM, TW1 1NW.
SAWYER, Mr. Philip Leslie, BSc ACA *1988;* Weinmanngasse 15, 8700 ZURICH, SWITZERLAND.
SAWYER, Mr. Reginald Harry, FCA FCMA JDipMA *1947;* Flat 8 Devere Gardens, 47-49 South Promenade, LYTHAM ST.ANNES, FY8 1LZ. (Life Member)
SAWYER, Mr. Tom, BA ACA *2005;* 5 Blandford Road, BECKENHAM, BR3 4NE.
SAWYER, Mr. William, BSc ACA *2004;* 67 Western Road, LONDON, W5 5DT.
•**SAWYER, Mr. William Hall, FCA** *1983;* J.N Straughan & Co, Fram Well House, Framwelgate, DURHAM, DH1 5SU.
SAWYERS, Mrs. Carole Ann, BSc FCA *1981;* The Fremantle Trust Woodley House, 64-65 Rabans Close Rabans Lane Industrial Area, AYLESBURY, BUCKINGHAMSHIRE, HP19 8RS.
SAXBY, Mr. Andrew James, BA FCA *1982;* with Lubbock Fine, Russell Bedford House, City Forum, 250 City Road, LONDON, EC1V 2QQ.
SAXBY, Mr. Duncan Alastair, FCA CTA *1989;* Flat 6, Carlton Gate, 6 West Overcliff Drive, BOURNEMOUTH, BH4 8AA.
SAXBY, Mr. John Christopher Leslie, FCA *1957;* The Orchards, Kenn Road, Kenn, CLEVEDON, BS21 6TS. (Life Member)
•**SAXBY, Mr. Nicholas Syred, FCA** *1988;* (Tax Fac), Saxbys, Maple House, Rookery Road, Monewden, WOODBRIDGE, SUFFOLK IP13 7DD. See also Saxby Limited
SAXBY-SOFFE, Mr. Richard Nigel, BA FCA *1975;* The Knowle, Spithurst Road, Barcombe, LEWES, EAST SUSSEX, BN8 5EF.
SAXEL, Mrs. Hannah Claire, ACA *2008;* 38 Tower Hill, WITNEY, OXFORDSHIRE, OX28 5ES.
SAXELBY, Mr. John Michael, MSc FCA *1968;* 5 Knightlow Close, KENILWORTH, CV8 2PX. (Life Member)
SAXENA PORIA, Miss. Vandana, BA ACA *1997;* B14 Swan lake, 324 North Main Road, Koregaon Park, PUNE 411001, INDIA.
•**SAXON, Mr. Anthony Alfred, FCA** *1976;* (Tax Fac), Saxon & Co, Kings Chambers, Queens Cross, DUDLEY, DY1 1QT. See also Saxons Limited
SAXON, Miss. Hollie Anne, ACA *2008;* 13 Rutland Avenue, Withington, MANCHESTER, M20 1JD.
•**SAXON, Mr. John Christopher, FCA** *1986;* Saxon & Co, Crowley, 85 Hope Road, SALE, M33 3AW. See also Moffatt & Co
SAXON, Mr. John Stuart, FCA *1974;* 19 Park Close, Glen Vine, ISLE OF MAN, IM4 4HB.
•**SAXON, Mr. Timothy John, FCA** *1977;* (Tax Fac), T.J. Saxon, 43 Hagley Road, STOURBRIDGE, DY8 1QR.
SAXTON, Miss. Helen Florence, BA ACA *2007;* 20 Thornaby Court, Craiglee Drive, CARDIFF, CF10 4BD.
SAXTON, Mr. Jonathan, BSc(Hons) ACA *2002;* 40 Jackson Road, LONDON, N7 6EE.
•**SAXTON, Mr. Paul Anthony, BA ACA** *1981;* Elwell Watchorn & Saxton LLP, 14 Queensbridge, NORTHAMPTON, NN4 7BF.
SAXTON, Mr. Peter William Harley, BSc ACA *1982;* Ducklake House, Springhead, Ashwell, BALDOCK, SG7 5LL.
•**SAXTON, Mr. Timothy Lewis, BSc FCA** *1986;* Leigh Saxton Green, Clearwater House, 4-7 Manchester Street, LONDON, W1U 3AE.
SAY, Mr. Geoffrey Michael, BA ACA *1991;* Cranfield University, Defence Academy, Shrivenham, SWINDON, SN6 8LA.
•**SAYAGH, Miss. Abigail, BA(Hons) ACA** *2002;* (Tax Fac), Abigail Sayagh, Britannic House, 17 Highfield Road, LONDON, NW11 9LS.
SAYCE, Mr. Anthony David, ACA *2009;* 69 Rosebery Crescent, NEWCASTLE UPON TYNE, NE2 1EX.
SAYCE, Mr. Ian Paul, BCom ACA *1996;* 91 Trafalgar Road, SMETHWICK, B66 3SA.
SAYE, Dr. Samantha Ellen, ACA *2008;* Tax Department, Zurich Financial Services UK Life Centre, Station Road, SWINDON, SN1 1EL.
SAYED, Mr. Bilal Nehal, BA ACA *2008;* 240 Eastern Avenue, ILFORD, ESSEX, IG4 5AB.
SAYED, Mrs. Eva, FCA *1958;* 16 St Oswalds Road, Knuzden, BLACKBURN, BB1 2DS. (Life Member)
SAYED, Mr. Rizwan Hassan, FCA *1984;* (Tax Fac), with PricewaterhouseCoopers LLP, Marlborough Court, 10 Bricket Road, ST. ALBANS, HERTFORDSHIRE, AL1 3JX.
SAYER, Mr. Brian Nicholas, BSc ACA *1988;* Zest Aromatics Gallamore Lane Industrial Estate, Gallamore Lane, MARKET RASEN, LN8 3HA.
•**SAYER, Miss. Catherine Lois, BA FCA DChA** *1983;* Sayer Vincent, 8 Angel Gate, City Road, LONDON, EC1V 2SJ.
SAYER, Mr. Christopher Andrew, MA ACA *1983;* Penthouse B, 103-121 Barkston Gardens, LONDON, SW5 0EX.
•**SAYER, Mr. David Anthony, BA FCIB ACA** *1981;* KPMG LLP, 15 Canada Square, LONDON, E14 5GL. See also KPMG Europe LLP
SAYERS, Mr. Adrian, ACA *2008;* 6 Old Farm Close, Knotty Green, BEACONSFIELD, BUCKINGHAMSHIRE, HP9 2TH.
•**SAYERS, Mr. Andrew John, BA FCA** *1990;* KPMG LLP, 15 Canada Square, LONDON, E14 5GL. See also KPMG Europe LLP
•**SAYERS, Mrs. Anne Louise, LLB ACA** *2000;* with BDO LLP, 55 Baker Street, LONDON, W1U 7EU.
SAYERS, Mr. David George, FCA ACMA *1972;* The Maples, Horsell Vale, WOKING, GU21 4QU.
SAYERS, Mr. Gary Richard, ACA *2009;* QBE Insurance Group, 82 Pitt Street, SYDNEY, NSW 2000, AUSTRALIA.
SAYERS, Mr. Ian Robert, BA ACA *1995;* Association of Investment Trust Companies, 21-24 Chiswell Street, LONDON, EC1Y 4YY.
SAYERS, Mrs. Jane Beverley, BA FCA *1987;* Brand Rule Ltd, 47 Grace Gardens, CHELTENHAM, GLOUCESTERSHIRE, GL51 6QE.
SAYERS, Mr. Jeremy John, FCA *1963;* 74 Waldemar Avenue, LONDON, SW6 5LU.
SAYERS, Mr. John Michael, BA(Hons) ACA *2000;* 2201 Akasaka Tameike Tower, Akasaka 2 Chome, Minato Ku, TOKYO, 1070052 JAPAN.
SAYERS, Mrs. Julie Ann, BSc ACA *1991;* The Cherries, Loxwood Road, Rudgwick, HORSHAM, RH12 3DW.
•**SAYERS, Mrs. Karen Patricia, BA ACA** *1989;* (Tax Fac), Karen Sayers Limited, 29 Silver Street, Colerne, CHIPPENHAM, WILTSHIRE, SN14 8DY.
•**SAYERS, Mrs. Pamela Joyce, ACA** *1992;* Smith & Williamson Ltd, 25 Moorgate, LONDON, EC2R 6AY.
SAYERS, Mr. Paul, ACA *2004;* DPC Media Limited Holed Stone Barn, Stisted Cottage Farm Hollies Road, Bradwell, BRAINTREE, CM77 8DZ.
•**SAYERS, Mr. Philip Anthony, BSc ACA** *1993;* with PricewaterhouseCoopers LLP, 1 Embankment Place, LONDON, WC2N 6RH.
SAYERS, Mr. Richard Anthony, FCA *1974;* 29 North Way, Houghton On The Hill, LEICESTER, LE7 9HR.
SAYERS, Mr. Robert Malcolm, FCA *1980;* 26 Dorian Drive, Cheapside, ASCOT, SL5 7QL.
SAYERS, Mrs. Stephanie Jane, BA ACA *1986;* Moorside, 1 Cawder Ghyll, SKIPTON, NORTH YORKSHIRE, BD23 2QG.
SAYERS, Mr. Timothy Myles Cubitt, BSc ACA *1988;* 58 Skene Street, NEWTOWN, VIC 3220, AUSTRALIA.
SAYLE, Mr. Paul John, BA ACA *2006;* Crossley Accountants PO Box 1, Ballasalla, ISLE OF MAN, IM99 6AB.
SAYNOR, Mr. Kristian Michael, BA(Hons) ACA *2002;* 29 Pasture View, Sherburn in Elmet, LEEDS, LS25 6LZ.
SAYNOR, Mrs. Sara Louise, BA ACA *1995;* 138 Rectory Road, SUTTON COLDFIELD, WEST MIDLANDS, B75 7RS.
SAYSELL, Mr. Christopher Mark, BA ACA *1986;* Lisle House, 3 Ferrers Hill Farm, Pipers Lane Markyate, ST. ALBANS, HERTFORDSHIRE, AL3 8QG.
SAYSON, Mrs. Divinia Rosal, ACA *1990;* La Seda de Barcelona S.A., Av Remolar 2, 08820 EL PRAT DE LLOBREGAT, CATALONIA, SPAIN.
SAYWELL, Miss. Emma, BA ACA *2005;* 9 Bread and Meat Close, WARWICK, CV34 6HF.
SAYWELL, Mr. John Anthony Telfer, JP BA FCA *1964;* 2 Cumberland Road, RICHMOND, SURREY, TW9 3HQ. (Life Member)
•**SAZAN, Mr. Abdul Mohamed Akbarali Ismail, FCA** *1977;* (Tax Fac), Sazan & Company, 93 Crayford Road, Crayford, DARTFORD, DA1 4AS.
SCADDEN, Ms. Laura, ACA *2007;* 30 Gleneagles Drive, STAFFORD, ST16 3XF.
SCADDEN, Mr. Paul Vincent, ACA *1979;* 1/8 MONTE CASSINO PLACE, BIRKDALE 0626, NEW ZEALAND.
SCADE, Mr. Andrew, MEng ACA *2000;* 127 Mount Street, Coogee, SYDNEY, NSW 2034, AUSTRALIA.
SCADE, Mr. John Charlton, FCA *1977;* Calle Creta 6, 28420 PARQUELAGOS, SPAIN.
SCAIFE, Mr. Andrew John, BA(Hons) ACA *2001;* 20 Whitebridge Close, NEWCASTLE UPON TYNE, NE3 2DN.
SCAIFE, Miss. Anne Elizabeth, BSc FCA *1993;* Cook Trotter Limited 3 Sceptre House, Hornbeam Square North Hornbeam Park, HARROGATE, NORTH YORKSHIRE, HG2 8PB.
SCAIFE, Mr. Carl, BA ACA *2007;* U B S, 100 Liverpool Street, LONDON, EC2M 2RH.
SCAIFE, Mr. David Richard, MBA BSc ACA *1991;* 26 Durvale Court, Dore, SHEFFIELD, S17 3PT.
•**SCAIFE, Mr. Joseph Hargreaves, BA FCA DChA** *1995;* Bishop Fleming, 16 Queen Square, BRISTOL, BS1 4NT.
SCAIFE, Mrs. Leonora Maria, BSc ACA *1998;* London & Scandinavian Metallurgical Co Ltd, Fullerton Road, ROTHERHAM, SOUTH YORKSHIRE, S60 1DL.
SCAIFE, Mrs. Muriel Adrienne, BSc ACA *1994;* Home Cottage, 20 Church Street, Holme, PETERBOROUGH, PE7 3PB.
SCAIFF, Mr. Nicholas Charles, BSc ACA *1994;* 59 Duke St, FORESTVILLE, NSW 2087, AUSTRALIA.
SCALES, Mr. Matthew, FCA *1978;* 66 Ernest Road, HORNCHURCH, RM11 3JW.
SCALES, Mr. Michael, BSc ACA *2006;* Olde School House Wignall Street, Lawford, MANNINGTREE, CO11 2JJ.
•**SCALES, Mr. Philip Ray, FCA** *1976;* Fairbank, 32 Woodmansterne Lane, BANSTEAD, SM7 3HE.
SCALES, Mr. Rupert Derek Cameron, BA ACA *2000;* Asenby Hall Farm Asenby, THIRSK, NORTH YORKSHIRE, YO7 3QR.
SCALES, Mr. Westleigh James, ACA *2005;* Apple Tree House, 11 Hill Top Close, MARKET HARBOROUGH, LE16 9DE.
SCALES, Mr. William Peter Johnston, FCA *1964;* Brookes Cottage, Southrop, LECHLADE, GL7 3PG. (Life Member)
SCALESE, Mr. Ettore, ACA *2007;* Via Villoresi 8, 20021 BOLLATE, ITALY.
SCALLAN, Mr. James, BSc ACA *2007;* 48c Whistlers Avenue, LONDON, SW11 3TS.
SCALLON, Mr. Michael, BSc ACA *2000;* 3 Harebell Drive, MELTON MOWBRAY, LEICESTERSHIRE, LE13 0FR.
•**SCALLY, Mrs. Julie Elaine, ACA** *1990;* (Tax Fac), Beckenham Business Services Ltd, 3 Mackenzie Road, BECKENHAM, KENT, BR3 4RT.
SCALLY, Mr. Steven Antony, BSc ACA *1997;* 3 Mackenzie Road, BECKENHAM, BR3 4RT.
SCAMAN, Mr. Martin James, BA ACA *1980;* JSS (LR) Ltd, 17-21 Church Road, Wimbledon, LONDON, SW19 5DQ.
SCAMP, Mr. Edward John, FCA *1975;* Dafferns LLP, 1 Eastwood Business Village, Harry Weston Road, COVENTRY, CV3 2UB.
SCAMPION, Mr. John Matthew, MA ACA *1982;* Cheddleton House, West Road, Prestwich, MANCHESTER, M25 3FB.
SCANDRETT, Mrs. Caroline Alma, BSc FCA *1979;* St. Ronans Lea, Upper Brailes, BANBURY, OX15 5AT.
SCANDRETT, Mr. Craig Michael Leonard, ACA *2008;* 7 St. Peters Road, Boughton-under-Blean, FAVERSHAM, KENT, ME13 9TA.
SCANDRETT, Mrs. Julie Ann, BSc ACA *1993;* 75 The Paddock, Stokesley, MIDDLESBROUGH, CLEVELAND, TS9 5PN.
SCANE, Mr. Robert Andrew, ACA *2005;* 18 Millards Close, Hilperton Marsh, TROWBRIDGE, WILTSHIRE, BA14 7UN.
SCANES, Mr. Mark Harvey, FCA *1974;* PO Box 1857, TOOWONG, QLD 4066, AUSTRALIA.
SCANLAN, Miss. Alexandra Anne, MBA BSc(Hons) ACA *1993;* 45 Lucas Street, LONDON, SE8 4QH.
SCANLAN, Mr. Michael John, ACA *1990;* HMRC Criminal Investigation, PO Box 4247, CARDIFF, CF14 8EU.
•**SCANLAN, Mr. William Andrew, FCA** *1975;* (Tax Fac), Gutteridge Scanlan, 5 High View Close, Hamilton Office Park, Hamilton, LEICESTER, LE4 9LJ.
•**SCANLON, Mr. Christopher Peter, BA ACA** *1994;* (Tax Fac), Fintech Associates Limited, Ballards, Jobs Lane, MAIDENHEAD, BERKSHIRE, SL6 9TX.
SCANLON, Mr. Dominic, ACA *2009;* 108 Murray Road, LONDON, W5 4DA.
SCANLON, Mr. James, BA ACA *2000;* Ernst & Young LLP, 5 Times Square, NEW YORK, NY 10036, UNITED STATES.
SCANLON, Mr. Patrick Mark, BSc ACA *1991;* 6 Le Jardin Du Val, 78860 ST NOM LA BRETECHE, FRANCE.
SCANLON, Ms. Rebecca Clare, BSc ACA *2006;* 4 Partridge Close, BASINGSTOKE, HAMPSHIRE, RG22 5UT.
SCANLON, Mr. Richard John, BSc ACA *1987;* Ways Cottage Lime Grove, West Clandon, GUILDFORD, SURREY, GU4 7UT.
SCANLON, Mrs. Susan Hilary, BSc ACA *1987;* Ways Cottage Lime Grove, West Clandon, GUILDFORD, SURREY, GU4 7UT.
SCANNELL, Mrs. Elizabeth Jane, BSc ACA *2004;* 53b Ongar Road, LONDON, SW6 1SH.
SCANNELL, Mr. Jerome Eugene, MBE BA FCA *1972;* Calle Freixa 51, 08021 BARCELONA, SPAIN. (Life Member)
•**SCANNELL, Ms. Mary, BEd ACA** *1992;* Scannell & Associates, 180 Piccadilly, LONDON, W1J 9HF.
SCANNELL, Mr. Matthew Patrick, BA ACA *2004;* 53b Ongar Road, LONDON, SW6 1SH.
SCANNELL, Mr. Patrick John, BSc FCA *1977;* Currian, Manaccan, HELSTON, CORNWALL, TR12 6HN.
SCAPENS, Mr. Ian Lloyd, BA ACA *1999;* 30 Parkfield Road, Cheadle Hulme, CHEADLE, CHESHIRE, SK8 6EX.
SCAPENS, Prof. Robert William, PhD *1968;* Accounting & Finance Group, Manchester Business School, University of Manchester, MANCHESTER, M15 6PB.
•**SCARAMANGA, Mrs. Lorraine Sedgewick, LLB FCA** *1984;* Alpha Tankers & Freighters, 354 Syngrou Avenue, 17674 ATHENS, GREECE.

SCARBOROUGH, Mr. Glenn David Paul, ACA *1987;* Aston Barclay PLC, Chelmsford Car Auction, Drovers Way, CHELMSFORD, CM2 5PP.
SCARBOROUGH, Mr. Howard Edward, BSc(Econ) ACA *1990;* 6 St. Andrews Street, LONDON, EC4A 3AE.
SCARBOROUGH, Mr. John Menzies, FCA *1967;* Le Hurel, La Rue Du Tas de Geon, Trinity, JERSEY, JE3 5AN.
SCARBOROUGH, Mr. Paul, BA ACA *1992;* (Tax Fac), 1 Abbey Road, Well End, BOURNE END, SL8 5NZ.
SCARBOROUGH, Mr. Timothy William Walter, FCA *1962;* PO Box 551, CONSTANTIA, 7848, SOUTH AFRICA.
SCARBOROUGH, Mr. Tom, BSc ACA *2006;* with Merrill Lynch Europe Plc, 2 King Edward Street, LONDON, EC1A 1HQ.
SCARBROUGH, Mrs. Louise Jayne, ACA *2006;* 70 Ter Rue De Tourcoing, 59223 RONCQ, FRANCE.
SCARFE, Mr. Peter, FCA *1951;* (Member of Council 1973 - 1977), Rosedale, 6 Newmarket Road, Cringleford, NORWICH, NR4 6UE. (Life Member)
SCARGILL, Mr. John Royston, FCA JDipMA *1955;* 31 Trinity Drive, Holme, CARNFORTH, LA6 1QL. (Life Member)
SCARGILL, Mr. Peter, MBA BA FCA *1985;* United Water International, P O Box 1875, ADELAIDE, SA 5001, AUSTRALIA.
•SCARGILL, Mr. Stewart, FCA *1981;* (Tax Fac), A. Macdonald & Co, 21 Parliament Street, HULL, HU1 2BL.
SCARIA, Mr. Thomas, FCA ACA *2011;* Sama Residence, Po Box 12928, DUBAI, UNITED ARAB EMIRATES.
SCARISBRICK, Mr. John George, LLB FCA *1980;* 1a Oakwood Court, LEEDS, LS8 2PQ.
SCARISBRICK, Mrs. Natasha, BA ACA *2005;* 112 Bachelor Lane, Horsforth, LEEDS, LS18 5NF.
SCARLES, Mr. Nicholas Richard, MA LLM FCA ATII CPA *1988;* Mills Folly Hawthorn Lane, Farnham Common, SLOUGH, SL2 3TE.
SCARLES, Mr. Ronald Michael, FCA *1957;* Penn Lodge, Church Road, Penn, HIGH WYCOMBE, BUCKINGHAMSHIRE, HP10 8NU. (Life Member)
SCARLES, Ms. Virginia Ann, ACA *1988;* 48 Chenies Avenue, AMERSHAM, HP6 6PP.
SCARLETT, Miss. Clare Elaine, BSc ACA *1989;* Coombe Lodge, 88 White Hill, Kinver, STOURBRIDGE, DY7 6AU.
SCARLETT, Mr. James Henry, FCA *1957;* 8 Sherwood Glen, SHEFFIELD, S7 2RB. (Life Member)
SCARLETT, Mr. Marcus Adrian, MA ACA *1979;* Marex Group Limited, 155 Bishopgate, LONDON, EC2M 3TQ.
•SCARLETT, Mr. Michael, FCA *1974;* (Tax Fac), Michael Scarlett & Co, 66 Norman Road, ST. LEONARDS-ON-SEA, EAST SUSSEX, TN38 0EJ.
SCARLETT, Mr. Michael George, FCA *1976;* Sienna, Chapel Lane, Bodenham, HEREFORD, HR1 3HR.
•SCARR, Mr. Craig Anthony, BSc FCA *1990;* Mazars LLP, The Atrium, Park Street West, LUTON, LU1 3BE.
SCARR, Dr. James Richard Hadley, ACA *2008;* Connolly Consulting, Unit 7, Arlington Court, Whittle Way, Arlington Business Park, STEVENAGE HERTFORDSHIRE SG1 2FS.
SCARR, Mr. Michael Jonathon, BA ACA *1990;* 11 Forest Drive, Rickleton, WASHINGTON, TYNE AND WEAR, NE38 9JD.
SCARROTT, Mr. Richard James, BSc ACA *1993;* 1000 Lakeside Building 1000, Lakeside North Harbour Western Road, PORTSMOUTH, PO6 3EN.
SCARSBROOK, Miss. Keeley Jo, BSc ACA *2003;* St. George Plc, St. George House, 76 Crown Road, TWICKENHAM, TW1 3EU.
SCARSELLA, Mr. Mark Joseph, ACA *2010;* Flat 1, 36 Philbeach Gardens, LONDON, SW5 9EB.
SCASE, Mr. Melvyn Robert, FCA *1972;* 30 Beresford Gardens, HOUNSLOW, TW4 5HW. (Life Member)
SCATTERGOOD, Mr. Jodi, BSc ACA *2010;* The Compass Centre Meridian 2nd floor North., Heathrow Airport Northern Perimeter Road, HOUNSLOW, MIDDLESEX, TW6 2JA.
SCAWN, Mr. Michael Vincent, FCA *1962;* C/o Mrs Scawn, Steep Hill House, Steep Hill, Chobham, WOKING, GU24 8SZ. (Life Member)
•SCHACHTER, Mr. Michael, FCA *1977;* Michael Sinclair, Trafalgar House, Grenville Place, Mill Hill, LONDON, NW7 3SA.
SCHACTER, Mr. Peter, FCA *1971;* 110 rue des Grands Champs, 75020 PARIS, FRANCE. (Life Member)
SCHADE, Ms. Barbel, MA FCA *1992;* 82 Mill Lane, Fordham, ELY, CB7 5NQ.
SCHAEFER, Miss. Jessica, BA ACA MBA *2011;* Rohrkampstr.13, 48165 MUNSTER, GERMANY.
SCHAEFFER, Mrs. Charlotte, BSc ACA *1996;* Tall Pines Fawke Common, Underriver, SEVENOAKS, TN15 0SP.
SCHAFFER, Mr. Mark Harold, FCA *1987;* 3 Priory Close, Totteridge, LONDON, N20 8BB.
SCHAFFER, Mrs. Nicola, BSc ACA *1985;* 3 Priory Close, Totteridge, LONDON, N20 8BB.
•SCHAJER, Mr. Marcel-Louis, FCA *1972;* with Sinclairs Carston Ltd, 32 Queen Anne Street, LONDON, W1G 8HD.
SCHAJER, Mr. Philip Emmanuel, BA(Hons) ACA *2002;* 20 Miriam HaChashmonait, 71724 MODI'IN, ISRAEL.
SCHALLER, Mr. Clive Alan, BA ACA *1979;* 16 Hillcrest Road, LOUGHTON, IG10 4QQ.
•SCHANSCHIEFF, Simon George, Esq OBE FCA *1962;* S.G. Schanschieff FCA, Rushworth, Church Farm, Church Brampton, NORTHAMPTON, NN6 8BN.
SCHAPIRA, Mr. Jonathan Joseph, ACA *1980;* Cable Finance Ltd, Fofriame House, 35-37 Brent Street, LONDON, NW4 2EF.
SCHAPIRA, Miss. Tracy, BA ACA *2006;* Apartment 2, 24 Lower Richmond Road, LONDON, SW15 1JP.
SCHAVERIEN, Mr. Robert Lewis, BSc FCA *1979;* 31 Kendall Road, CASTLE COVE, NSW 2069, AUSTRALIA.
SCHECHTER, Mr. Mark, BA FCA *1994;* 8 Abbots Place, BOREHAMWOOD, WD6 5QP.
SCHECK, Mr. Martin Nicholas, BSc ACA *1983;* International Capital Market Association, Talacker 29, CH-8022 ZURICH, SWITZERLAND.
•SCHEERMANN, Mr. Steven Anthony, FCA *1970;* (Tax Fac), Scheermann & Partners, 31b Lyndhurst Road, LONDON, NW3 5PB.
SCHEFER, Mr. Steven David Anthony, BSc ACA PGCE *1998;* 78 Nayland Street, Sumner, CHRISTCHURCH 8081, NEW ZEALAND.
SCHEIJDE, Mr. Leonardus George Nicolaas, ACA CA(SA) *2008;* 27 Guildown Road, GUILDFORD, GU2 4EU.
SCHEIJDE, Mrs. Sarah Ann, BSc ACA *1991;* 27 Guildown Road, GUILDFORD, GU2 4EU.
SCHEINER, Mr. Michael, BSc FCA *1964;* P O Box 105, 30550 BINYAMINA, ISRAEL.
SCHELLEKENS, Mrs. Susanna Marion, BSc ACA *1994;* Gaston Gate Cottage, Guildford Road, CRANLEIGH, SURREY, GU6 8QZ.
SCHENCK, Mr. John Charles, BCom ACA *1982;* 1A Lincoln Way, Rainhill, PRESCOT, L35 6PH.
SCHEUER, Mr. Edward John, MBA ACA *1992;* 3132 Lewiston Avenue, BERKELEY, CA 94705, UNITED STATES.
SCHEURER, Mr. Eric Robert, ACA CA(SA) *2008;* No 126, Mail Boxes Etc, 235 Earls Court Road, LONDON, SW5 9FE.
SCHICK, Ms. Adelheid, ACA *1994;* 157 Hamlet Gardens, Hammersmith, LONDON, W6 0TR.
•SCHICK, Mr. Stephen Edward, BCom FCA *1974;* (Tax Fac), Stephen Schick, 31 Abbey Gardens, LONDON, NW8 9AS.
•SCHICK-MAIER, Mr. Allon, BA ACA *1986;* ASM Accounting Services Limited, 21 Culverlands Close, STANMORE, HA7 3AG. See also ASM Company Secretaries Limited, Payroll Services Limited
SCHICKNER, Mr. David Ian, MA ACA *1987;* Hans Hemberger Strasse 15, 63150 HEUSENSTAMM, GERMANY.
SCHIEBLER, Miss. Jade, ACA *2008;* 1-4 Crewe Close, Albany, NORTH SHORE CITY 0632, NEW ZEALAND.
SCHIEL, Mr. Michael John, FCA *1978;* Bosch Rexroth Ltd, 15 Cromwell Road, ST. NEOTS, PE19 2ES.
SCHIFF, Mrs. Zsuzsanna, ACA *1999;* 24 Wentworth Park, Finchley, LONDON, N3 1YG.
SCHIJVESCHUURDER, Mr. Abraham Daniel, FCA *1976;* KPMG Somekh Chaikin, 17 Ha'arba'a Street, TEL AVIV, 64739, ISRAEL.
SCHILD, Mr. Julian Dominic, MA ACA *1987;* Champery Investments Ltd, Unit 1, Hampstead West, 224 Iverson Road, LONDON, NW6 2HL.
SCHILIZZI, Mrs. Anne Magdalene, BA ACA CTA *1982;* with The TACS Partnership, Graylaw House, Mersey Square, STOCKPORT, CHESHIRE, SK1 1AL.
SCHILIZZI, Mrs. Louise Jordan, BCom ACA *1995;* Mathinna, The Coombe, Streatley on Thames, West Berkshire, READING, RG8 9QL.
SCHILIZZI, Mr. Peter Miles, BA ACA *1983;* Arcon Housing Association, 12 Lloyd Street, MANCHESTER, M2 5ND.
SCHILIZZI, Mr. Stephen John, BA ACA *1995;* Alamy Ltd, Units 6 & 8, 127 Milton Park, Milton, ABINGDON, OXFORDSHIRE OX14 4SA.
•SCHILLER, Mr. Edwin Harvey, FCA *1964;* 4 The Mews, Ringley Drive, Whitefield, MANCHESTER, M45 7HT.
•SCHILLER, Mr. Michael Frank, BSc FCA *1975;* (Tax Fac), Ainsleys, Suite 2, 40 Compton Rise, PINNER, MIDDLESEX, HA5 5HR. See also Alef Tuf Limited
SCHILLER, Mr. William Francis, BA ACA *1990;* Liverpool Victoria Friendly Society Ltd, County Gates, BOURNEMOUTH, BH1 2NF.
SCHILLING, Mr. Michael George, BSc ACA *2009;* #06-03 The View @ Meyer, 46 Meyer Road, SINGAPORE 437871, SINGAPORE.
•SCHINDLER, Mr. Joachim, ACA *1995;* KPMG Deutsche Treuhand Group, Klingelhoferstrasse 18, 10785 BERLIN, GERMANY. See also KPMG AG Wirtschaftsprufungsgesellschaft
•SCHINDLER, Mr. Richard Franz, FCA *1983;* (Tax Fac), Gargate Mill, St Peters Valley, JERSEY, JE3 7EG.
•SCHINELLA, Mrs. Ceri Diane, BA ACA *1987;* Ceri Schinella, 74 The Maultway, CAMBERLEY, SURREY, GU15 1QF.
•SCHIZAS, Mr. Constantinos, BSc ACA *1997;* Moore Stephens Stylianou & Co, Iris Tower, Office 602, 5B Archbishop Makarios Avenue, 1302 NICOSIA, CYPRUS.
SCHIZAS, Mr. Yiannos, BA ACA *2009;* 2 Simis Street, Lakatamia, 2302 NICOSIA, CYPRUS.
SCHLEE, Mr. Robin Lawrence Matthew, MA ACA *1979;* Orchardside, 7a Pilgrims Way, GUILDFORD, GU4 8AB.
SCHLESINGER, Mr. Thomas Edward, BSc FCA *1977;* 6 North Head, West Road, Milford-on-Sea, LYMINGTON, SO41 0LX.
SCHMID, Miss. Grainne Anne, ACA *2008;* Nidelbadstr 65, 8803 RUESCHLIKON, SWITZERLAND.
SCHMID, Mr. Maxwell Kenneth, ACA *2010;* 12 Radipole Road, LONDON, SW6 5DL.
SCHMIDT, Mr. Dwight, ACA *2009;* FLAT 9, 33 Longridge Road, LONDON, SW5 9SD.
SCHMIDT, Mr. Glen Kevin Manfred, BSc ACA *1989;* Ubersbach 72, 8362 SOCHAU, AUSTRIA.
SCHMIDT, Ms. Nina, ACA *1999;* 102 Brambletye Park Road, REDHILL, RH1 6EJ.
SCHMIDT, Miss. Tammy, ACA *2011;* PO Box 394, FERNIE V0B 1M0, BC, CANADA.
SCHMIDT-SOLTAU, Mr. Nils Soren, ACA *2008;* Blick Rothenberg, 12 York Gate, LONDON, NW1 4QS.
SCHMUTTERMEIER, Ms. Laura Helene, ACA *2010;* Flat 6, Coleridge Court, Blythe Road, LONDON, W14 0PH.
•SCHNABEL, Mr. Udo, ACA *1997;* Tannenweg 1, 31535 HELSTORF, GERMANY.
SCHNAIER, Mr. Martin Charles, BCom ACA *2003;* 127 Kingston Road, EPSOM, SURREY, KT17 2HA.
SCHNECK, Mr. Lawrence Alistair, BSc(Econ) ACA *2001;* 5-15-8, Higashinakano, Nakano-ku, TOKYO, 164-0003 JAPAN.
SCHNEIDER, Mrs. Claire Lynne, BA ACA *1993;* Fasanenweg 1, 85540 HAAR BEI MUNCHEN, GERMANY.
SCHNEIDER, Mr. David Arthur Charles, LLB FCA *1975;* 2 Dalkeith Grove, STANMORE, HA7 4SG.
•ⓘSCHNEIDER, Mr. Ian, BSc FCA *1987;* PricewaterhouseCoopers, Emaar Square, Building 4 Level 8, PO Box 11987, DUBAI, UNITED ARAB EMIRATES. See also PricewaterhouseCoopers LLP
ⓘSCHNEIDERMAN, Mr. Robert, BSc ACA *1989;* Capital Merchants Limited, 14 Snaresbrook Drive, STANMORE, MIDDLESEX, HA7 4QW.
SCHNELLEN, Mr. James, FCA *1953;* P O Box 487, SIMONS TOWN, SOUTH AFRICA. (Life Member)
•SCHOEB, Mrs. Georgina, BSc ACA *2002;* Peninsula Accounting, 66 Sandtoft Road, LONDON, SE7 7LR.
SCHOEMAN, Mr. Johan Coenraad, ACA CA(SA) *2010;* 6a Hurley Close, WALTON-ON-THAMES, SURREY, KT12 1LP.
SCHOFIELD, Mr. Alan Donald, BA ACA *1991;* Silverlink Holdings Ltd Stockbridge House, Stockbridge, NEWCASTLE UPON TYNE, NE1 2HJ.
SCHOFIELD, Mr. Andrew Charles, BCom ACA *1981;* 14 Thicknall Rise, West Hagley, STOURBRIDGE, DY9 0LQ.
SCHOFIELD, Mr. Andrew Peter, FCA *1975;* 45 Tilehouse Green Lane, Knowle, SOLIHULL, WEST MIDLANDS, B93 9EZ.
•SCHOFIELD, Mr. Anthony William, BA FCA *1982;* 5 Bishops Road, HOVE, BN3 6PQ.
SCHOFIELD, Miss. Cheryl Ann, ACA *2011;* 3 Rock Gardens, Europa Rd, GIBRALTAR, GIBRALTAR.
SCHOFIELD, Mrs. Gaye, BSc ACA *1992;* Finance Department, College of Law, Braboeuf Manor, Portsmouth Road, GUILDFORD, GU3 1HA.
SCHOFIELD, Mrs. Gillian Maureen, FCA *1971;* 25 Queen's Crescent, OSSETT, WF5 8AU.
SCHOFIELD, Miss. Gillian Ruth, BSc ACA *1996;* 3 Hannaford Road, BLACKWOOD, SA 5051, AUSTRALIA.
SCHOFIELD, Mr. Gordon Frank, FCA *1955;* 47 Woodfield Road, Cheadle Hulme, CHEADLE, SK8 7JT. (Life Member)
SCHOFIELD, Miss. Hannah, ACA *2009;* Compass Group UK Parklands Court, 24 Parklands Rednal, BIRMINGHAM, B45 9PZ.
•ⓘSCHOFIELD, Mr. Ian Christopher, FCA *1980;* PKF (UK) LLP, Pannell House, 6 Queen Street, LEEDS, LS1 2TW.
SCHOFIELD, Mr. Jack, FCA *1951;* 15 Park Road, DEWSBURY, WF13 4LQ. (Life Member)
SCHOFIELD, Mrs. Janette Margaret, BA ACA *1993;* Nicholas Zorab Estate Agents, 18 Market Place, ROMSEY, SO51 8NA.
SCHOFIELD, Miss. Jenny Elizabeth, MSc ACA *2006;* 9 Ilkley Drive, Urmston, MANCHESTER, M41 8DB.
•SCHOFIELD, Mr. Jeremy Mark Dominic, LLB FCA *1992;* PricewaterhouseCoopers LLP, 1 Embankment Place, LONDON, WC2N 6RH. See also PricewaterhouseCoopers
•SCHOFIELD, Mr. John, BA ACA *1986;* N.R. Barton & Co, 19-21 Bridgeman Terrace, WIGAN, WN1 1TD.
SCHOFIELD, Mr. John Alexander, BSc ACA *1994;* with Peel Holdings Plc, The Dome, The Trafford Centre, MANCHESTER, M17 8PL.
SCHOFIELD, Mr. John Anthony, FCA *1958;* 40 Newall Hall Park, OTLEY, LS21 2RD. (Life Member)
SCHOFIELD, Mr. John David, BSc FCA *1975;* 7 Hawth Way, SEAFORD, EAST SUSSEX, BN25 2NG. (Life Member)
SCHOFIELD, Mr. John Michael, LLB ACA *2002;* Auto Trader House, Auto Traders Danehill, Lower Earley, READING, RG6 4UT.
•SCHOFIELD, Mr. Jonathan Hugh, BA ACA CF *1986;* Dow Schofield Watts Corporate Finance Limited, 7700 Daresbury Park, Daresbury, WARRINGTON, CHESHIRE, WA4 5BS.
•SCHOFIELD, Miss. Katie, BSc ACA *1992;* (Tax Fac), Leon Charles Ltd, 247 Gray's Inn Road, LONDON, WC1X 8QZ.
•SCHOFIELD, Mr. Mark, BA FCA *1982;* (Tax Fac), Haworths Holdings Ltd, The Old Tannery, Eastgate, ACCRINGTON, LANCASHIRE, BB5 6PW. See also Haworths Limited and Haworths
SCHOFIELD, Mr. Martin Howard, FCA *1974;* Norwood Farmhouse, Hiscott, BARNSTAPLE, EX31 3JS.
SCHOFIELD, Mrs. Mary Elizabeth, LLB ACA *2000;* 23 Branksome Road, NORWICH, NR4 6SW.
SCHOFIELD, Mr. Michael Gregory, BSc ACA CTA *1983;* (Tax Fac), 15 Alder Close, Newton-With-Scales, PRESTON, PR4 3TQ.
SCHOFIELD, Mr. Michael James, MA BA ACA *2003;* 20 Hollytree Road, LIVERPOOL, L25 5PA.
SCHOFIELD, Mr. Paul Anthony, ACA *1979;* Reid Atkinson Ltd, Eden Works, Colne Road, Kellbrook, BARNOLDSWICK, BB18 6SH.
•SCHOFIELD, Mr. Paul Jonathon, BA FCA *1994;* Deloitte LLP, 3 Victoria Square, Victoria Street, ST. ALBANS, HERTFORDSHIRE, AL1 3TF. See also Deloitte & Touche LLP
•SCHOFIELD, Mr. Peter John, FCA *1968;* Schofields Partnership LLP, 6th Floor, Dean Park House, Dean Park Crescent, BOURNEMOUTH, BH1 1HP.
SCHOFIELD, Mr. Raymond, FCA *1972;* 6 Whitham Close, Off Westwood Way Boston Spa, WETHERBY, LS23 6DU.
•SCHOFIELD, Mr. Richard, BSc ACA *1992;* 196 Bramhall Lane South, Bramhall, STOCKPORT, CHESHIRE, SK7 3AA.
SCHOFIELD, Mr. Richard Michael, BA FCA *1991;* Rishworth School, Rishworth, SOWERBY BRIDGE, WEST YORKSHIRE, HX6 4QA.
SCHOFIELD, Mr. Robert Anthony, BA ACA *1996;* 22 Wychwood Avenue, Knowle, SOLIHULL, B93 9DG.
SCHOFIELD, Miss. Ruth Carol, BCom ACA *1992;* 3 Pilmuir Grove, BALERNO, MIDLOTHIAN, EH14 7FD.
SCHOFIELD, Mr. Simon, MA ACA ATII *1998;* 2B Helena Road, Ealing, LONDON, W5 2RA.
SCHOFIELD, Mr. Stephen Arthur, BSc FCA *1976;* 9 Lyndon Mead Sandridge, ST. ALBANS, HERTFORDSHIRE, AL4 9EX.
SCHOFIELD, Mrs. Susan Jane, FCA *1988;* 35 Progress Road, LEIGH-ON-SEA, SS9 5PR.
SCHOFIELD, Mr. Timothy, LLB ACA *1987;* 20 Lymbourn Road, HAVANT, HAMPSHIRE, PO9 2SL.
SCHOLEFIELD, Mrs. Alison Marie, BA ACA *1987;* 11928 Sunwood Place, DELTA V4E 2X6, BC, CANADA.
•SCHOLEFIELD, Miss. Amy-Joanne, BA(Hons) ACA *2003;* Long & Co.(Harrogate), 17 Wensley Road, HARROGATE, NORTH YORKSHIRE, HG2 8AQ.

SCHOLEFIELD, Mr. Andrew, BA ACA *1984;* Dragon Cottage, Dragons Green Road, Shipley, HORSHAM, WEST SUSSEX, RH13 8GG.
•**SCHOLEFIELD, Mr. Andrew Graham, BSc FCA** *1990;* Abraxas Corporate Finance Limited, 4 Croft Gardens, Grappenhall Heys, WARRINGTON, WA4 3LH.
SCHOLEFIELD, Mr. Richard, BA ACA *1995;* W/3, Standard Life Assurance Co Standard Life House, 30 Lothian Road, EDINBURGH, EH1 2DH.
SCHOLEFIELD, Mr. Richard Alan, FCA *1958;* The Poplars, Reeds Brow, Rainford, ST.HELENS, MERSEYSIDE, WA11 8PD. (Life Member)
SCHOLES, Mr. Anthony John, BA ACA *1991;* Stoke City Football Club, The Britannia Stadium, Stanley Matthews Way, STOKE-ON-TRENT, ST4 4EG.
SCHOLES, Ms. Caroline Elisabeth, BSc ACA *1989;* 4 Jalan Gallagher, Bukit Tunku, 50480 KUALA LUMPUR, FEDERAL TERRITORY, MALAYSIA.
SCHOLES, Mr. David, FCA *1973;* 11 Abbey Grove, Adlington, CHORLEY, PR6 9QB.
SCHOLES, Mr. John, BA FCA *1976;* 9 Walcot Square, LONDON, SE11 4UB.
SCHOLES, Miss. Pamela Ann, BA ACA *1981;* 74 Artillery Mansions, 75 Victoria Street, LONDON, SW1H 0HZ.
•**SCHOLES, Mr. Peter Thomas, FCA** *1981;* Parry Scholes & Co Ltd, A9 Trem Y Duffryn, Colomendy Industrial Estate, Rhyl Road, DENBIGH, CLWYD LL16 5TA.
SCHOLES, Mr. Richard Thomas, FCA *1969;* 37 Doneraile Street, LONDON, SW6 6EW.
SCHOLEY, Mr. Bryan Duncan, BA ACA *1986;* Styal Cottage, Village Rd, Christleton, CHESTER, CH3 7AT.
SCHOLEY, Mr. Geoffrey Michael, FCA *1956;* The Garden House, 5c Breary Lane, Bramhope, LEEDS, LS16 9AD. (Life Member)
SCHOLEY, Mr. Michael David, BSc FCA *1992;* 45 Oatlands Avenue, WEYBRIDGE, SURREY, KT13 9SS.
SCHOLFIELD, Mr. Brian Beaumont, FCA *1978;* Worleys Farm, Worleys Lane, Upper Culham, READING, RG10 8PA.
•**SCHOLL, Mr. Jeremy Simon, ACA** *1986;* (Tax Fac), Jeremy Scholl & Company, 20-21 Jockey's Fields, LONDON, WC1R 4BW.
SCHOLLAR, Mr. Richard Gareth, BSc ACA *2001;* 2 Beaver Drive, EASTLEIGH, HAMPSHIRE, SO50 8NA.
SCHOLTZ, Mr. Adrian, BA(Hons) ACA *2002;* with KPMG LLP, 15 Canada Square, LONDON, E14 5GL.
SCHOMBERG, Mr. Raymond, MA FCA *1957;* 27 Gloucester Circus, LONDON, SE10 8RY. (Life Member)
SCHOMMARZ, Mr. Herman Gunther, ACA CA(SA) *2008;* with MAS Luxembourg, 6C rue Gabriel Lippmann, L-5365 MUNSBACH, LUXEMBOURG.
SCHONBERG, Mr. Anders Stenseng, BSc ACA *1999;* C/Bori i Fontesta, 6-2, 08021 BARCELONA, SPAIN.
SCHONBERG, Mr. Jacob, FCA *1972;* Nachal Zavitan 6/2, 99634 BEIT SHAMESH, ISRAEL.
•**SCHONBERGER, Mr. Paul Christopher, FCA** *1980;* Thorne Lancaster Parker, 8th Floor, Aldwych House, 81 Aldwych, LONDON, WC2B 4HN.
SCHOON, Mr. Andrew Aitchison, BA ACA *1998;* Brierleigh, Upper Sutherland Road, Lightcliffe, HALIFAX, HX3 8NT.
SCHOONRAAD, Miss. Natalie Jane, ACA MAAT *2010;* PKF Australia Ltd, Level 10, 1 Margaret Street, SYDNEY, NSW 2000, AUSTRALIA.
SCHOPP, Mr. Lee Darren, BSc ACA *1996;* Milton Villas, 27 Dunstable Road, Toddington, DUNSTABLE, LU5 6DS.
SCHORAH, Mr. George Milford, BA ACA *1992;* Ebenried Nr 156, 90584 ALLERSBERG, GERMANY.
SCHOTT, Miss. Isabella, BA(Hons) ACA *2010;* 35 St. Mary Abbots Terrace, LONDON, W14 8NX.
•**SCHOTTLER, Mr. Klaus, CA ACA CA(SA)** *2008;* (Tax Fac), ACT Yorkshire Limited, Roundhay Chambers, 199 Roundhay Road, LEEDS, LS8 5AN.
SCHRAGGER, Mr. Rodney, BA ACA *1979;* Second Nature Ltd, 10 Malton Road, LONDON, W10 5UP.
SCHREIBER, Mr. Cyril, FCA CTA *1962;* 107 Waterfall Road, New Southgate, LONDON, N11 1BT. (Life Member)
SCHROD, Mr. Keith Alan, BSc ACA *1986;* 337 Osborne Road, HORNCHURCH, RM11 1HW.
SCHROEDER, Mrs. Eileen Jane, MA ACA *1999;* 59 Victory Road, LONDON, SW19 1HP.
SCHROEDER, Miss. Kelly, BSc ACA *2005;* 8 Bulford Road, Johnston, HAVERFORDWEST, DYFED, SA62 3EU.
SCHROEDER, Mr. Marek Aleksander Stanislaw, BA ACA *1982;* University of Birmingham, Dept of Accounting & Finance, Edgbaston, BIRMINGHAM, B15 2TT.
SCHROTER, Mr. Michael Raymond, BA FCA *1967;* Apartment 2G, 25 Belmont Hills Drive, WARWICK WK 06, BERMUDA.
SCHRUM, Mr. Michael, MSc ACA *1997;* 29 Pitts Bay Road, PEMBROKE HM06, BERMUDA.
•**SCHRYBER, Mr. Irving David, FCA** *1958;* Irving D. Schryber, Flat 3, Opal Court, 120 Regents Park Road, LONDON, N3 3HY.
SCHUBERT, Mrs. Alison Christine, BSc ACA *1991;* 23 Elm Place, WINDSOR, VIC 3181, AUSTRALIA.
SCHUCH, Miss. Pamela Jane, BA(Hons) ACA *2002;* Flat 2, 25 Gwendolen Avenue, Putney, LONDON, SW15 6ET.
SCHUELER, Mr. Matthias, ACA *2008;* 34 Ecclesbourne Apartments, 64 Ecclesbourne Road, LONDON, N1 3GG.
SCHUETTE, Mr. Nicolas, MSc ACA *2003;* Flat C 21/F Tower 3, Pacific Palisades, 1 Braemar Road, NORTH POINT, HONG KONG ISLAND, HONG KONG SAR.
SCHULENBURG, Mr. Erich Coetzee, ACA CA(SA) *2008;* Postnet Suite #168, Private Bag X11, Birnam Park, JOHANNESBURG, 2015, SOUTH AFRICA.
SCHULER, Mr. Martin Alexander, FCA *1968;* Lanebridge Investment Management Ltd, The Coach House, Fulsham Hall, Alderley Road, WILMSLOW, CHESHIRE SK9 1QA.
SCHULTEN, Mr. Christopher Francis, BA FCA *1977;* Ryecroft, Sheerwater Road, WEST BYFLEET, KT14 6AQ.
•**SCHULZ, Miss. Nicola Jayne, BSc ACA** *2006;* 102 Nags Head Hill, BRISTOL, BS5 8QL.
SCHULZE, Ms. Grit, BA ACA *2007;* 115 Abbey Road, BRISTOL, BS9 3QJ.
•**SCHUMAN, Mr. Martin Paul, FCA** *1977;* (Tax Fac), Martin Schuman Accountancy Ltd, 13 Oakfields, WALTON-ON-THAMES, SURREY, KT12 1EG.
•**SCHUMAN, Mr. Norman, FCA** *1963;* (Tax Fac), Norman Stanley, Suite 1R10, Elstree Business Centre, Elstree Way, BOREHAMWOOD, HERTFORDSHIRE WD6 1RX.
•**SCHUMAN, Mr. Richard John, FCA** *1975;* Norman Stanley, Suite 1R10, Elstree Business Centre, Elstree Way, BOREHAMWOOD, HERTFORDSHIRE WD6 1RX.
SCHUR, Mr. Anthony Erwin, MA FCA *1978;* 57 Cumberland Street, WOODBRIDGE, SUFFOLK, IP12 4AQ. (Life Member)
SCHUTZ, Mrs. Phyllipa Kathryn Amanda, MA(Hons) ACA *2004;* with BDO LLP, 55 Baker Street, LONDON, W1U 7EU.
•**SCHUZ, Mr. Michael, BSc FCA** *1990;* Alan Cooper Saunders Angel, Kenton House, 666 Kenton Road, HARROW, HA3 9QN.
SCHUZ, Mr. Stephen, BA ACA *1986;* 301 Derbyshire Lane, SHEFFIELD, S8 8SG.
SCHWABE, Mr. Jurgen, ACA CA(SA) *2010;* 18 Stanhope Road, CROYDON, CR0 5NS.
SCHWABE, Mrs. Naomi, ACA CA(SA) *2010;* 18 Stanhope Road, CROYDON, CR0 5NS.
•**SCHWALBE, Mr. Howard, ACA** *2000;* HAS Ltd, Prince Albert House, 2b Mather Avenue, Prestwich, MANCHESTER, M25 0LA.
SCHWARTZ, Mr. Anthony Alan, FCA *1961;* 191 Lake Road West, Roath Park, CARDIFF, CF23 5PN.
SCHWARTZ, Mr. Vincent Anthony, FCA *1972;* Broadlands, 2 Broadway Close, Chilcompton, RADSTOCK, SOMERSET, BA3 4EJ.
SCHWARZ, Miss. Andrea Claudia, MA BA(Hons) ACA *2001;* 4229 Thursley Road, WILMINGTON, NC 28412, UNITED STATES.
•**SCHWARZ, Mr. Jonathan N, BSc FCA** *1973;* Cohen Arnold, New Burlington House, 1075 Finchley Road, Temple Fortune, LONDON, NW11 0PU. See also Cohen Arnold & Co
•①**SCHWARZMANN, Mr. Dan Yoram, ACA** *1987;* PricewaterhouseCoopers LLP, Pricewaterhousecoopers, 12 Plumtree Court, LONDON, EC4A 4HT. See also PricewaterhouseCoopers
SCHWARZMANN, Mrs. Jennifer Ann, BA ACA *1995;* Longcote, Tanglewood Close, STANMORE, MIDDLESEX, HA7 3JA.
SCHWEIGER, Mr. Mark Alexander Harry, BCom ACA *2001;* 33 Carlton Road, Hale, ALTRINCHAM, CHESHIRE, WA15 8RH.
SCHWENK, Mr. Simon Francis, BSc ACA *1994;* 40 Broadway, CAMBERWELL, VIC 3124, AUSTRALIA.
SCIALO, Mr. Francesco, BA ACA ATII *1987;* 170 Bromley Road, BECKENHAM, BR3 6PG.
SCIAMA, Mr. Michael Ernest, BSc ACA *1983;* Westbourne, Rappax Road, Hale, ALTRINCHAM, WA15 0NT.
SCICLUNA, Mr. Martin Anthony, BCom FCA *1977;* (Member of Council 1991 - 1995), Parkways, Little Heath Lane, Potten End, BERKHAMSTED, HP4 2RX.
SCIVER, Mr. Richard James, BA ACA *1989;* Island House, Downside Common Road, Downside, COBHAM, SURREY, KT11 3NU.
SCIVIER, Miss. Ruth Anne, BSc FCA *1977;* Northacre, Deerleap Road, Westcott, DORKING, RH4 3LE.
SCLAVERANO, Mr. Peter Victor, FCA *1956;* (Tax Fac), 42 Maplehurst Road, CHICHESTER, WEST SUSSEX, PO19 6RP. (Life Member)
SCOBBIE, Mr. Alastair, ACA *2009;* Flat 6, 27 McDonald Crescent, FALKIRK, STIRLINGSHIRE, FK2 9FN.
SCOBBIE, Mr. Martyn David, BSc ACA *1995;* 22 Beech Road, Stockton Heath, WARRINGTON, WA4 6LT.
SCOBIE, Mr. Andrew, ACA *2011;* 72 Broxash Road, LONDON, SW11 6AB.
SCOBLE, Mr. Timothy James, ACA *1981;* Guoco Leisure Executive Offices, Royal Horse Guards Hotel, 2 Whitehall Court, LONDON, SW1A 2EJ.
•**SCODIE, Mr. Laurence, FCA** *1972;* Laurence Scodie, P.O. Box 11194, 35B Flower Lane, LONDON, NW7 2JG.
•**SCODIE, Mr. Michael, FCA** *1971;* (Tax Fac), Scodie Deyong LLP, 85 Frampton Street, LONDON, NW8 8NQ.
SCOFFIELD, Mr. Darren Tony, BSc ACA *1999;* 20 Gracechurch Street, LONDON, EC3V 0AF.
SCOFFIELD, Mr. Ian Michael, BSc ACA *1995;* 42 Brook Road, TWICKENHAM, TW1 1JE.
SCOFFIELD, Mr. Stephen John, BA FCA DChA *1984;* Broomhayes School & Children's Centre, Kingsley Lodge, Alverdiscott Road, BIDEFORD, DEVON, EX39 4PL.
SCOFIELD, Mr. Julian Nicholas, BA(Hons) ACA *2000;* Hewitt Hall Cottage High Street, Dedham, COLCHESTER, CO7 6HJ.
SCOGGINS, Mr. Sean Michael, BSc ACA *2005;* Moelis & Company, 1st Floor, Condor House, 10 St. Paul's Churchyard, LONDON, EC4M 8AL.
SCOLES, Miss. Louise, BSc ACA *2000;* 149 Morningside Drive, EDINBURGH, EH10 5NR.
SCOLES, Mr. Martin Peter, BCom ACA *1984;* 2 Bigstone Meadow, Tutshill, CHEPSTOW, GWENT, NP16 7JU.
SCOLLEN, Mrs. Anne Josephine, BSc ACA *1993;* 15 The Glen, ENFIELD, MIDDLESEX, EN2 7BZ.
•**SCOLTOCK, Mr. Michael Gerard David, BSc FCA TEP** *1988;* Blick Rothenberg, 12 York Gate, Regent's Park, LONDON, NW1 4QS.
SCONCE, Mrs. Anne Elizabeth, BA ACA *2005;* 28 Hill View Avenue, Helsby, FRODSHAM, WA6 0ES.
SCOONES, Mr. Roy Ernest, FCA *1956;* Wychwood, High Road, Fobbing Village, STANFORD-LE-HOPE, SS17 9JJ. (Life Member)
SCOPE, Mrs. Rebecca, BA ACA *2002;* Robert Bewick House, Burton Hospital N H S Trust Queens Hospital, Belvedere Road, BURTON-ON-TRENT, STAFFORDSHIRE, DE13 0RB.
SCOPES, Mr. John Lancelot, FCA *1953;* 19 Pickers Green, Lindfield, HAYWARDS HEATH, RH16 2BS. (Life Member)
SCOPES, Mr. Jonathan Emrys, BSc ACA *1982;* 35 Bowerfold Lane, STOCKPORT, CHESHIRE, SK4 2LT.
SCORDI, Ms. Niki Ioannou, BSc ACA *1992;* 42 Thorpebank Road, LONDON, W12 0PQ.
SCORE, Mr. Terry Anthony, ACA *1992;* 60 Grove Avenue, YEOVIL, SOMERSET, BA20 2BE.
SCORE, Mr. Timothy, BA ACA *1985;* 11 Park Town, OXFORD, OX2 6SN.
•**SCORER, Mr. Michael Fred, FCA** *1975;* City Financial Trust Limited, 33 Waring Drive, Green Street Green, ORPINGTON, BR6 6DN.
SCORER, Mr. Simon, BSc ACA *2010;* The Bank of England, Threadneedle Street, LONDON, EC2R 8AH.
SCORER, Mr. William, FCA *1958;* 3 West View Glade, Clonee, DUNBOYNE, COUNTY MEATH, IRELAND. (Life Member)
SCOREY, Mr. Douglas, FCA *1961;* 25 Bury Road, GOSPORT, PO12 3UE.
SCOREY, Mr. Mark Robert, BA ACA *1998;* South Barn Appledram Barns, Birdham Road, CHICHESTER, WEST SUSSEX, PO20 7EQ.
SCOT-SIMMONDS, Mr. Nicholas John, FCA *1977;* Coney Green, Kemerton, TEWKESBURY, GLOUCESTERSHIRE, GL20 7HY.
SCOTCHMER, Mr. David William, FCA *1961;* 2 Church Close, Caldecott, MARKET HARBOROUGH, LE16 8RN. (Life Member)
SCOTCHMER, Mr. Patrick, BA ACA *2007;* 91 Urban Road, SALE, CHESHIRE, M33 7TS.
SCOTCHMER, Mr. Robert Bruce, FCA *1973;* 19 Paramount Court, University Street, LONDON, WC1E 6JP.
SCOTHERN, Mr. John Charles, MSc FCA *1981;* Alma Place, Hillesley Road, Kingswood, WOTTON-UNDER-EDGE, GLOUCESTERSHIRE, GL12 8RU.
SCOTLAND, Miss. Joanne, BSc ACA *2002;* 33 All Saints Road, CHELTENHAM, GL52 2EY.
SCOTT, Mr. Alan Leslie, FCA *1959;* 8 Sunbury Gardens, Mill Hill, LONDON, NW7 3SG. (Life Member)
SCOTT, Mr. Alastair John Catton, BA ACA *1990;* Warkworth House, Warkworth, BANBURY, OX17 2AG.
SCOTT, Mr. Alexander, ACA *2008;* (Tax Fac), 6 Pursers Cross Road, LONDON, SW6 4QX.
SCOTT, Mr. Alexander, BA ACA *2006;* Flat 2 Newton House, Granville Park, LONDON, SE13 7EA.
SCOTT, Mr. Alexander Gordon, ACA *2009;* 160 Rupert Street, NORWICH, NR2 2AX.
SCOTT, Mr. Alistair Graham, MA ACA *1989;* Corporate Financial Analysis, The Royal Bank of Scotland Plc, 280 Bishopsgate, LONDON, EC2M 4RB.
SCOTT, Mr. Alistair Kerr, BA FCA *1973;* 7 Tanwood Close, SOLIHULL, B91 3JX.
SCOTT, Mrs. Amanda Mary, BA ACA *1990;* 13 Woodrush Glade, Adambrae Park, LIVINGSTON, WEST LOTHIAN, EH54 9JY.
SCOTT, Mr. Andrew, BA FCA *1983;* 79 Westwood Drive, AMERSHAM, HP6 6RR.
SCOTT, Mr. Andrew Charles, BSc FCA *1975;* 'Bogartowse', 5a Minto Road, SHEFFIELD, S6 4GJ.
SCOTT, Mr. Andrew Christopher, FCA *1967;* 40 Seaway Avenue, Friars Cliff, CHRISTCHURCH, DORSET, BH23 4EX. (Life Member)
SCOTT, Mr. Andrew Hillyer, FCA *1976;* Lower Lye, East Knoyle, SALISBURY, SP3 6AQ.
SCOTT, Mr. Andrew James Moffat, MA ACA *1992;* Travelex UK Ltd, 65 Kingsway, LONDON, WC2B 6TD.
SCOTT, Mr. Andrew McNair, MA(Oxon) ACA *2005;* Man Valuation Services Limited, Man Group Plc Sugar Quay, Lower Thames Street, LONDON, EC3R 6DU.
SCOTT, Mr. Andrew Munro, BA FCA MCT *1993;* Heatherfield House, Copsewood Lane, Stone Allerton, AXBRIDGE, SOMERSET, BS26 2NS.
SCOTT, Mr. Andrew Neil, BSc ACA *1992;* 13 Plymouth Road, PENARTH, CF64 3DA.
•**SCOTT, Mr. Andrew Paul, FCA** *1974;* with Williamson Morton Thornton LLP, 47 Holywell Hill, ST. ALBANS, HERTFORDSHIRE, AL1 1HD.
SCOTT, Mr. Andrew Peter, BSc FCA *1985;* 38 Spa Drive, Sapcote, LEICESTER, LE9 4FN.
SCOTT, Mr. Angus Keith, BSc FCA *1992;* OPTIMUS HOUSE, PROSPECT ROAD ARNHALL BUSINESS PARK WESTHILL, ABERDEEN, AB32 6FE.
SCOTT, Mrs. Anna Jane, ACA *2008;* 11 Craggwood Road, Horsforth, LEEDS, LS18 4RW.
SCOTT, Mrs. Anne, BSc FCA *1983;* Bela House, Knott Hill, Whassett, MILNTHORPE, CUMBRIA, LA7 7DN.
SCOTT, Mr. Anthony, BCom FCA *1956;* 24 Oak Tree Road, Eccleston, ST. HELENS, MERSEYSIDE, WA10 5LH. (Life Member)
SCOTT, Mr. Anthony Arnold Lennard, FCA *1964;* Shute Park Farm, Liverton, NEWTON ABBOT, DEVON, TQ12 6JB.
SCOTT, Mr. Anthony Douglas, FCA *1957;* 2 Oakfield Road, HARPENDEN, HERTFORDSHIRE, AL5 2NE. (Life Member)
•**SCOTT, Mr. Anthony Norman, FCA FCCA FCMA** *1995;* SWAT UK Limited, 36 Montpelier Street, BRIGHTON, BN1 3DL.
SCOTT, Mr. Austin John, BSc(Hons) ACA *2002;* 15 Francis Street, FAIRLIGHT, NSW 2094, AUSTRALIA.
SCOTT, Miss. Beatrice Lewis, FCA *1947;* 4 Rutland Lodge, Clifton Road, LONDON, SW19 4QZ. (Life Member)
SCOTT, Mr. Benjamin Andrew Clifford, ACA *2008;* 6 Woodlands Road, Pownall Park, WILMSLOW, CHESHIRE, SK9 5QB.
•**SCOTT, Mrs. Brenda Joyce, BSc FCA** *1975;* B.J. Scott, High Barn, Hunters Meadow, Great Shefford, HUNGERFORD, RG17 7EQ.
•①**SCOTT, Mr. Brian Andrew, FCA** *1980;* Johnson Tidsall, 81 Burton Road, DERBY, DE1 1TJ.
SCOTT, Mr. Brian Donald, FCA *1960;* 57 Iberian Way, CAMBERLEY, GU15 1LZ. (Life Member)
•**SCOTT, Mr. Brian Godfrey, FCA** *1980;* (Tax Fac), Graham Paul Limited, 10-12 Dunraven Place, BRIDGEND, MID GLAMORGAN, CF31 1JD.
SCOTT, Miss. Caroline Helen, BSc ACA *2010;* 13 Beverley Court, Breakspears Road, LONDON, SE4 1UN.
SCOTT, Mrs. Caroline Jane, ACA *1987;* 26 Stapleton Road, BUDE, CORNWALL, EX23 8TS.

SCOTT, Dr. Caroline Mary, BSc DIC ACA *2002;* Tattersalls Ltd, Terrace House, NEWMARKET, SUFFOLK, CB8 9BT.
SCOTT, Mrs. Chani, ACA *1992;* 2 Hamilton Mews, Cavendish Crescent North, NOTTINGHAM, NG7 1AY.
SCOTT, Mr. Charles Thomas, FCA *1972;* Chase Manor Farm, Lickfold Road, Fernhurst, HASLEMERE, GU27 3JA.
SCOTT, Mr. Charles William, BSc FCA MBA *1996;* 33 Berks Hill, Chorleywood, RICKMANSWORTH, HERTFORDSHIRE, WD3 5AJ.
SCOTT, Mr. Chris Alexander Marquis, MA ACA *2004;* Flat 4, 696a High Road, Leytonstone, LONDON, E11 3AJ.
SCOTT, Mr. Christopher Charles, MEng(Hons) ACA *2011;* Daleside, Exton Lane, Exton, EXETER, EX3 0PP.
SCOTT, Mr. Christopher David, BA(Hons) ACA *2001;* 5 Alnwick View, West Park, LEEDS, LS16 5RP.
SCOTT, Mr. Christopher John, MA ACA *1994;* Telford College of Arts & Technology Haybridge Road, Wellington, TELFORD, SHROPSHIRE, TF1 2NP.
SCOTT, Mr. Christopher Malcom, BSc ACA *1991;* 6 Westbourne Gardens, TROWBRIDGE, BA14 9AW.
SCOTT, Mr. Christopher Richard, BA ACA *1997;* Crow Plain Oast House, Jarmons lane, Crow Plain, Collier Street, TONBRIDGE, KENT TN12 9PU.
SCOTT, Mr. Clive Anthony, FCA *1966;* (Tax Fac), 36 Kings Road, BERKHAMSTED, HP4 3BD. (Life Member)
•SCOTT, Mr. Colin Alan, BSocSc FCA *1985;* 19 Sycamore Way, Brantham, MANNINGTREE, ESSEX, CO11 1TL.
SCOTT, Mr. Colin Peter James, FCA MCT *1978;* Summerfield, Wayside Road, BASINGSTOKE, HAMPSHIRE, RG23 8BH.
SCOTT, Mr. Daniel Richard, BA ACA *2007;* 6 Finchwell Rise, SHEFFIELD, SOUTH YORKSHIRE, S13 9DS.
SCOTT, Mr. Darryl, MPhys ACA *2010;* 27 Lime Close, Penwortham, PRESTON, PR1 0PL.
SCOTT, Mr. David Alan, MSci ACA *2002;* 47 Marian Drive, GATESHEAD, TYNE AND WEAR, NE10 0TJ.
SCOTT, Mr. David Albert, BSc FCA *1976;* The Cottage, Quarry Park Road, Pedmore, STOURBRIDGE, DY8 2RE.
SCOTT, Mr. David Andrew Campbell, BA FCA *1992;* The Homewood, Portsmouth Road, ESHER, SURREY, KT10 9JL.
SCOTT, Mr. David Crosfield Garratt, ACA *1978;* John Henry Group Station Road, Longstanton, CAMBRIDGE, CB24 3DS.
•SCOTT, Mr. David Douglas, BA ACA *1992;* Deloitte LLP, Athene Place, 66 Shoe Lane, LONDON, EC4A 3BQ. See also Deloitte & Touche LLP
SCOTT, Mr. David Jeffery Milton, BA(Hons) ACA *2001;* K P M G St. Nicholas House, 31 Park Row, NOTTINGHAM, NG1 6FQ.
•SCOTT, Mr. David John, BA ACA *1988;* (Tax Fac), Harold Everett Wreford LLP, 1st Floor, 44-46 Whitfield Street, LONDON, W1T 2RJ.
SCOTT, Mr. David John, FCA *1970;* Apt 12, 9 Sheftel Street, 75234 RISHON LEZION, ISRAEL.
SCOTT, Mr. David Michael, MA BA FCA CTA *1988;* (Tax Fac), 23 Saxon Way, Willingham, CAMBRIDGE, CB24 5UR.
SCOTT, Mr. David Richard Alexander, CBE FCA *1977;* 25 Moreton Place, LONDON, SW1V 2NL.
•SCOTT, Mr. David Thomas, FCA *1972;* David Scott & Co, 15 Colburn Avenue, NEWTON AYCLIFFE, COUNTY DURHAM, DL5 7HX. See also Tax Credit Strategies LLP
•SCOTT, Mr. David Vincent, FCA *1980;* David Scott, 440 Carnation Lane, Bowerhill, MELKSHAM, WILTSHIRE, SN12 6RD.
SCOTT, Mrs. Deirdre, BSc ACA *1994;* Diageo, 5 Lochside Way, EDINBURGH, EH12 9DT.
•SCOTT, Mr. Derek Andrew, MA FCA *1960;* D.A. Scott, 1 Merryhill Park, Belmont, HEREFORD, HR2 9SS.
SCOTT, Mr. Derek Anthony, BA FCA *1978;* Flat 7 Grayson House, Beech Grove, HARROGATE, NORTH YORKSHIRE, HG2 0ER.
SCOTT, Mr. Derek John, FCA *1955;* 44 Three Cuppes Lane, SALISBURY, SP1 1ER. (Life Member)
SCOTT, Mr. Donald Owen, FCA *1969;* 79 Pams Way, Ewell, EPSOM, KT19 0HN.
SCOTT, Mr. Duncan McLaren, BSc ACA *1989;* ENSTAR LIMITED, 3RD FLOOR WINDSOR PLACE, 18 QUEEN ST, HAMILTON HM11, BERMUDA.
SCOTT, Mrs. Elise, BSc ACA *1996;* 32 Acorn Way, Pool in Wharfedale, OTLEY, WEST YORKSHIRE, LS21 1TY.
SCOTT, Dr. Elizabeth Mary, PhD MA ACA *1991;* 16 Rue Héierchen, ZAE Robert Steichen, L-4940 BASCHARAGE, LUXEMBOURG.
SCOTT, Ms. Fiona Anne, MA ACA ASIP *1993;* Scott Translation Services, 3 St. Clair Terrace, EDINBURGH, EH10 5NW.
SCOTT, Mrs. Frances Stewart, MA ACA *1982;* Bank of Scotland, 150 Fountainbridge, EDINBURGH, EH3 9PE.
SCOTT, Mr. Francesc-John, BSc ACA *2004;* 8 Erskine Close, Bewbush, CRAWLEY, RH11 8GL.
SCOTT, Miss. Francesca, BA(Hons) ACA *2010;* 88c Taybridge Road, LONDON, SW11 5PZ.
SCOTT, Mr. Gareth James, BSc ACA *2000;* 9 Petrie Way, LONDONDERRY, BT48 8PW.
SCOTT, Mr. Gary, BA ACA *1995;* 40A Wright Street, Mt Cook, WELLINGTON 6002, NEW ZEALAND.
SCOTT, Mr. Gary James, BA FCA *1977;* 9 Wellhouse Way, Penistone, SHEFFIELD, SOUTH YORKSHIRE, S36 8HW.
SCOTT, Mr. Gavin, BA FCA *1993;* 17 Pinewood Close, Scarisbrick, SOUTHPORT, PR8 5LL.
SCOTT, Mr. Geoffrey Leonard, FCA *1980;* Ropemaker Place, 25 Ropemaker Street, LONDON, EC2Y 9AN.
SCOTT, Mr. Geoffrey Ralph, FCA *1974;* Business Systems Development, Hillcrest, Congleton Edge, CONGLETON, CW12 3NB.
SCOTT, Mr. George, FCA *1963;* White Bear House, 149 London Road, Stanford Rivers, ONGAR, ESSEX, CM5 9QF.
SCOTT, Miss. Georgina Jane, BSc ACA *2000;* Flat 10 The Red House, 49-53 Clerkenwell Road, LONDON, EC1M 5RS.
SCOTT, Mr. Graeme, BA ACA *1988;* New Hall Place, Old Hall Street, LIVERPOOL, MERSEYSIDE, L69 3HS.
SCOTT, Mr. Graeme Nicholas, BSc ACA *1995;* First Assist Legal Expenses Insurance Ltd, Norfolk House, Wellesley Road, CROYDON, CR0 1LH.
SCOTT, Ms. Hannah Elizabeth, ACA *2007;* 22a Lower Golf Links Road, BROADSTONE, DORSET, BH18 8BH.
SCOTT, Mr. Harold Arthur, FCA *1973;* 4 White Oaks Close, FERNDOWN, DORSET, BH22 9FF.
SCOTT, Mr. Harvey John, BSc(Hons) ACA *2001;* with Deloitte LLP, Saltire Court, 20 Castle Terrace, EDINBURGH, EH1 2DB.
SCOTT, Mrs. Hazel, BSc ACA *1989;* Quadriga Health & Safety Ltd, 318 Kings Road, READING, RG1 4JG.
SCOTT, Mrs. Helen Marie, MMath ACA *2005;* 26 Greenhill Avenue, LIVERPOOL, L18 6HT.
SCOTT, Mrs. Hilary Ann, BSc FCA *1989;* Cherry Bank, Ogdens, FORDINGBRIDGE, HAMPSHIRE, SP6 2PZ.
SCOTT, Miss. Hilary Anne, BA ACA *1996;* 328 London Road, WOKINGHAM, RG40 1RD.
SCOTT, Mrs. Hilary Ruth, BSc ACA *1992;* 57 Churchill Avenue, COTTINGHAM, HU16 5NJ.
SCOTT, Mr. Howard Martin, BA FCA FTII *1970;* Tara House, Pyrton, WATLINGTON, OXFORDSHIRE, OX49 5AP.
SCOTT, Mr. Howard Paul, BA ACA *1985;* 27 Maplefield, Park Street, ST. ALBANS, AL2 2BE.
SCOTT, Mr. Iain Henry, BSc ACA *1998;* Arcadia Group Ltd, Colegrave House, 70 Berners Street, LONDON, W1T 3NL.
SCOTT, Mr. Iain Parker, BSc ACA *1989;* Highland & Universal Investments Ltd, Suite B1 Highland House, St. Catherines Road, PERTH, PH1 5RY.
SCOTT, Mr. Ian, BSc ACA *1980;* Glen Doone, Bull Lane, GERRARDS CROSS, SL9 8RF.
•SCOTT, Mr. Ian, BA FCA DChA *1990;* Saint & Co., 12-13 Church Street, WHITEHAVEN, CA28 7AY.
•SCOTT, Mr. Ian Anthony, BA ACA *1990;* Ernst & Young LLP, 1 More London Place, LONDON, SE1 2AF. See also Ernst & Young Europe LLP
•SCOTT, Mr. Ian Paul, FCA *1966;* (Tax Fac), I.P. Scott, 81 Hawes Lane, WEST WICKHAM, BR4 0DF.
SCOTT, Mr. Ian Russell, FCA *1973;* 116 Broadwater Street West, WORTHING, BN14 9DJ.
SCOTT, James Alexander, Esq OBE MA MSc FCA *1965;* Southbrook, Shrubs Hill, Chobham, WOKING, GU24 8ST.
•SCOTT, Mr. James Brendan, FCA FCCA *1971;* 10 Tiverton Drive, SALE, CHESHIRE, M33 4RJ.
•SCOTT, Mr. James Christopher, FCA *1982;* HW, Sterling House, 22 St. Cuthberts Way, DARLINGTON, COUNTY DURHAM, DL1 1GB. See also Haines Watts
SCOTT, Mr. James Richard, BCom ACA *1992;* 15 Little Fryth, Finchampstead, WOKINGHAM, BERKSHIRE, RG40 3RN.
SCOTT, Mr. Jamie Robert, BSc(Hons) ACA *2011;* 29 Savernake Road, AYLESBURY, BUCKINGHAMSHIRE, HP19 9LR.
•SCOTT, Mr. Jeremy Lloyd, FCA *1977;* PricewaterhouseCoopers LLP, 7 More London Riverside, LONDON, SE1 2RT. See also PricewaterhouseCoopers
SCOTT, Mr. Jeremy Peter Malcolm, ACA *1979;* 50 Kings Hill, Beech, ALTON, GU34 4AN.
SCOTT, Mrs. Jill Elizabeth, BA ACA *1989;* 18 Foxtails, FLEET, GU51 5AE.
SCOTT, Mrs. Joanne, BSc(Hons) ACA *2003;* 3 Copthall Cottages The Hill, CRANBROOK, KENT, TN17 3HR.
SCOTT, Ms. Joanne Elizabeth, BA ACA *1991;* 52 Highfield Close, Davenport, STOCKPORT, CHESHIRE, SK3 8UB.
•SCOTT, Mr. John, FCA *1971;* with Scott Vevers Ltd, 65 East Street, BRIDPORT, DORSET, DT6 3LB.
SCOTT, Mr. John Anthony, FCA *1965;* 12 Rue de la Chandelle de Bois, Le Petit Chevallon, Geay, 17250 CHARENTE MARITIME, FRANCE.
SCOTT, Mr. John Armour, MA FCA *1971;* The Glebe House, Law Road, NORTH BERWICK, EH39 4PL.
SCOTT, Mr. John Carter, BA ACA *1987;* 35 Bellemere Road, Hampton In Arden, SOLIHULL, B92 0AN.
SCOTT, Mr. John Edward, BA ACA *1985;* Oxford Venture Management Ltd, Unit 2, Oakfield Industrial Estate, Stanton Harcourt Road, Eynsham, WITNEY OXFORDSHIRE OX29 4TS.
SCOTT, Mr. John Malcolm, ACA *1981;* 13 Beaker Close, Smeeton Westerby, LEICESTER, LE8 0RT. (Life Member)
SCOTT, Mr. John Richard William, FCA *1974;* 12 Reeds Buildings, Northgate Street, BURY ST. EDMUNDS, SUFFOLK, IP33 1HU.
SCOTT, Mr. John Robert, FCA *1953;* 7 Bridge Farm Drive, Maghull, LIVERPOOL, L31 9AL. (Life Member)
SCOTT, Mr. John Stearn, FCA *1967;* Three Elms, Common Gate Road, Chorleywood, RICKMANSWORTH, HERTFORDSHIRE, WD3 5NZ.
SCOTT, Mr. John William Arthur, FCA FCCA *1964;* Thirlstone, Newby Bridge, ULVERSTON, CUMBRIA, LA12 8NE.
SCOTT, Mr. Jonathan Cape, MA ACA *1992;* 93 Macdonald Road, LIGHTWATER, GU18 5XZ.
SCOTT, Mr. Jonathan Keeling, BCom FCA AMCT *1993;* 62 Camelot Road, SPARTA, NJ 07871, UNITED STATES.
SCOTT, Mr. Jonathan Mark, BCom ACA *1990;* 4 Research Drive, BETHEL, CT 06801, UNITED STATES.
SCOTT, Mr. Jonathan Mark, BA ACA *1997;* 28 Warwick Road, New Barnet, BARNET, EN5 5EH.
SCOTT, Mr. Jonathan Paul, BSc ACA *1988;* National Car Parks Ltd, Whitgift Centre, CROYDON, CR0 1LP.
SCOTT, Mr. Jonathan Paul, BSc ACA *1991;* 6 Bowers Way, HARPENDEN, AL5 4EW.
SCOTT, Mr. Jonathan Wylie, MA ACA *2003;* Cambridge City Council, 2nd Floor, Lion House, Lion Yard, CAMBRIDGE, CB2 3NA.
SCOTT, Mr. Joseph, FCA *1950;* 1 Sunset Crescent, Kalamunda, KALAMUNDA, WA 6076, AUSTRALIA. (Life Member)
SCOTT, Mrs. Julia Rachel, BSc ACA *2001;* 6 Redcliffe place, LONDON, SW10 9DD.
SCOTT, Mrs. Julie Catherine, BA ACA *1986;* 8 Folkestone Road, Harnham, SALISBURY, SP2 8JP.
•SCOTT, Mr. Justin Joseph, LLB ACA CTA *1997;* (Tax Fac), SMP Accounting and Tax Limited, PO Box 227, Clinch's House, Lord Street, Douglas, ISLE OF MAN IM99 1RZ.
SCOTT, Miss. Karen Jeness, ACA *1997;* Abbeystead, Penenden Heath Road, Penenden Heath, MAIDSTONE, KENT, ME14 2DE.
SCOTT, Mrs. Kate, BSc ACA *1991;* 758 Landsborough Maleny Road, BALD KNOB, QLD 4552, AUSTRALIA.
•SCOTT, Mrs. Katherine, BA(Hons) ACA *2002;* Katherine Scott Limited, 1 Landseer Drive, Marple Bridge, STOCKPORT, CHESHIRE, SK6 5BL.
SCOTT, Mrs. Katherine Mary, BSc ACA *1993;* The Grange, Elmbridge, DROITWICH, WEST MIDLANDS, WR9 0DA.
SCOTT, Mrs. Katie Louise, BA ACA *2006;* with PKF (UK) LLP, St Hughs, 23 Newport, LINCOLN, LN1 3DN.
SCOTT, Mr. Keith, MA ACA *1996;* 7 Sir Lancelot Close, Chandler's Ford, EASTLEIGH, HAMPSHIRE, SO53 4HJ.
SCOTT, Mr. Keith, FCA *1958;* Linnet House, Twittenside, Penfold Way, STEYNING, WEST SUSSEX, BN44 3TW. (Life Member)
SCOTT, Mr. Keith David, BA FCA *1965;* 827 Asa Gray Drive, Apt 357, ANN ARBOR, MI 48105, UNITED STATES. (Life Member)
•SCOTT, Mr. Kenneth, FCA *1978;* (Tax Fac), Willis Scott, 27/28 Frederick Street, SUNDERLAND, SR1 1LZ. See also Willis Scott Group and JM Accountancy Ltd
•SCOTT, Mr. Kenneth Michael, FCA *1972;* with Mercer & Hole Trustees Limited, Gloucester House, 72 London Road, ST. ALBANS, AL1 1NS.
SCOTT, Miss. Kirsty, ACA *2011;* 15 Holyhead Court, Anglesea Road, KINGSTON UPON THAMES, SURREY, KT1 2ES.
•SCOTT, Mrs. Lisa Helen, ACA *1987;* Lisa Scott, 22 St Augustines Road, LONDON, NW1 9RN.
SCOTT, Miss. Louise Amanda, BSc ACA *1995;* Fairlands Lunghurst Road, Woldingham, CATERHAM, CR3 7EJ.
SCOTT, Miss. Louise Frances, BA ACA *2006;* 5 Gorselands Close, Ash Vale, ALDERSHOT, GU12 5EF.
SCOTT, Mr. Malcolm, LLB FCA *1964;* 11 Belgravia Road, WAKEFIELD, WF1 3JP. (Life Member)
SCOTT, The Revd Canon Malcolm Kenneth Merrett, FCA *1953;* 10 The Ring, Little Haywood, STAFFORD, ST18 0TP. (Life Member)
SCOTT, Ms. Mandy Ellen, BA ACA *1987;* Chapel House, Langford, LECHLADE, GLOUCESTERSHIRE, GL7 3LW.
SCOTT, Mr. Marcus John, BA FCA *1995;* The Old Post Office, Bridge Street, Wistow, HUNTINGDON, PE28 2QA.
SCOTT, Miss. Margaret Anne, MEng ACA *2004;* with Deloitte LLP, PO Box 500, 2 Hardman Street, MANCHESTER, M60 2AT.
SCOTT, Mrs. Margaret Mary Mue, BA ACA *1991;* 1 Grange Wood, Grammar School Lane, West Kirby, WIRRAL, MERSEYSIDE, CH48 8BU.
SCOTT, Ms. Margot, BA FCA *1994;* 218 Whitehall Road, GATESHEAD, TYNE AND WEAR, NE8 4PU.
SCOTT, Mr. Mark David, BA ACA *1984;* 9 Church Wood Avenue, Far Headingley, LEEDS, LS16 5LF.
SCOTT, Mr. Mark Joseph, BEng ACA *1993;* Chinewood, Moor Lane, Downley, HIGH WYCOMBE, BUCKINGHAMSHIRE, HP13 5YP.
•SCOTT, Mr. Mark Leonard, ACA *1986;* Abacuss Limited, Wakefield House, Cardigan Road, MARLBOROUGH, WILTSHIRE, SN8 1LB.
SCOTT, Mr. Mark William, FCA *1974;* Flat 3, 89 Warrington crescent, LONDON, W9 1EH.
SCOTT, Mr. Martin Donald, MA ACA *1990;* 32 Rose Street, LONDON, WC2E 9ET.
SCOTT, Miss. Mary, ACA *2010;* 86 WILKIE RD, #02-05, SINGAPORE 228096, SINGAPORE.
SCOTT, Mr. Mathew Robert, BA ACA *1997;* (Tax Fac), with KPMG LLP, Plym House, 3 Longbridge Road, Marsh Mills, PLYMOUTH, PL6 8LT.
SCOTT, Mr. Matthew, BSc ACA *1995;* The Vale Gasden Copse, Witley, GODALMING, GU8 5QE.
SCOTT, Mr. Matthew James, MA ACA *2010;* 6 Finchwell Rise, SHEFFIELD, SOUTH YORKSHIRE, S13 9ds.
SCOTT, Mr. Matthew Robert, BSc ACA *2004;* 24a Longton Grove, LONDON, SE26 6QE.
SCOTT, Miss. Melanie, LLB ACA *2006;* (Tax Fac), Blue Crest Capital Management Ltd, 40 Grosvenor Place, LONDON, SW1X 7AW.
SCOTT, Mr. Michael Andrew, BSc ACA *1988;* The Commercial Bank of Qatar (Q.S.C.), Commercialbank Plaza, Majlis Al Tawoun Street, West Bay Area, P.O.Box 4166, DOHA QATAR.
•SCOTT, Mr. Michael Howard, BEng FCA *1976;* (Tax Fac), Michael H. Scott & Company, 107 Kenton Road, Kenton, HARROW, HA3 0AN.
SCOTT, Mr. Michael Iain, BA ACA *1992;* 2 Birkdale Close, Edwalton, NOTTINGHAM, NG12 4FB.
SCOTT, Mr. Michael Ian, BSc(Hons) ACA *2003;* 3 Copthall Cottages, The Hill, CRANBROOK, KENT, TN17 3HR.
SCOTT, Mr. Michael James, MA FCA *1968;* The Old Vicarage, Old Warden, BIGGLESWADE, SG18 9HQ.
•SCOTT, Mr. Michael James, FCA *1978;* Moore Stephens (South) LLP, City Gates, 2-4 Southgate, CHICHESTER, WEST SUSSEX, PO19 8DJ. See also Moore Secretaries Limited
SCOTT, Mr. Michael James, ACA *1984;* Birchwood, Lake Road, VIRGINIA WATER, SURREY, GU25 4PP.
•SCOTT, Mr. Michael John, FCA *1983;* Michael J. Scott, 68 Heath Row, BISHOP'S STORTFORD, CM23 5DF.
SCOTT, Mr. Michael John, BA ACA *1999;* Peregrine, 14 Falconwood, East Horsley, LEATHERHEAD, SURREY, KT24 5EG.
SCOTT, Mr. Michael John, BSc ACA *1999;* Norman & Underwood Ltd The Freeschool Building, 170 Scudamore Road, LEICESTER, LE3 1HP.

SCOTT, Mr. Michael John, FCA *1968;* Austhorpe Farm, Ewerby Thorpe, SLEAFORD, NG34 9PR.
SCOTT, Mr. Michael William, BA(Hons) ACA *2011;* 277 Lyham Road, LONDON, SW2 5NS.
SCOTT, Mr. Miles, ACA *1986;* Derbyshire County P C T Park Hill, Egginton, DERBY, DE65 6GU.
SCOTT, Mr. Murray John, BA ACA *1989;* 5 Middle Drive, BEACONSFIELD, BUCKINGHAMSHIRE, HP9 2AF.
SCOTT, Mr. Neil, BA ACA *1984;* 17 Woodlands, Gosforth, NEWCASTLE UPON TYNE, NE3 4YN.
•**SCOTT, Mr. Neil Simon, BA ACA** *1978;* Neil Scott & Company, 107 Kenton Road, Kenton, HARROW, HA3 0AN.
SCOTT, Mr. Neville Conor, BSc ACA *1992;* 1 Thalia Close, LONDON, SE10 9NA.
SCOTT, Mr. Neville Duncan, ACA CA(SA) *2009;* Mourant Phoenix House, 18 King William Street, LONDON, EC4N 7BP.
SCOTT, Mr. Nicholas Graeme, BSc FCA *1990;* 17 Ranmoor Road, SHEFFIELD, S10 3HG.
SCOTT, Mr. Nicholas John Dring, BSc(Hons) ACA *2003;* E.A.Dring (Farms)Ltd, Pelhams Land Farm, Chapel Hill, LINCOLN, LN4 4QG.
SCOTT, Mr. Nicholas Roger, BSc ACA *1997;* 2 Wonford Road, EXETER, EX2 4EQ.
SCOTT, Mr. Nicholas Stephen, BSc ACA *1997;* 14 Halton Way Kingsway, Quedgeley, GLOUCESTER, GL2 2BB.
SCOTT, Miss. Nicola, ACA *2008;* A207, 107 Beach Street, PORT MELBOURNE, VIC 3207, AUSTRALIA.
SCOTT, Miss. Nicola Anne, BA ACA *1993;* Roman Hill House Mersea Road, Blackheath, COLCHESTER, CO2 0BX.
SCOTT, Mr. Nigel Anthony, BA ACA *1984;* 98 Fabis Drive, Clifton Grove, NOTTINGHAM, NG11 8NZ.
•**SCOTT, Mr. Nigel Glazier, FCA** *1974;* (Tax Fac), Overdale, Bay View Road, Port Erin, ISLE OF MAN, IM9 6LG.
SCOTT, Mr. Oliver Lawrence, BSc ACA *2002;* 20 Smith Avenue, Allambie Heights, SYDNEY, NSW 2100, AUSTRALIA.
SCOTT, Mr. Paul, BA ACA *2009;* 32 High Street, Carlby, STAMFORD, LINCOLNSHIRE, PE9 4LX.
SCOTT, Mr. Paul Branch, FCA *1968;* Ringlaan 24A, B 3560 LUMMEN, BELGIUM.
SCOTT, Mr. Paul Michael, ACA MBA *1991;* Meadowlands, Nuthurst St, Nuthurst, HORSHAM, RH13 6LH.
•**SCOTT, Mr. Peter, FCA** *1982;* Harben Barker Limited, 112 High Street, Coleshill, BIRMINGHAM, WEST MIDLANDS, B46 3BL.
SCOTT, Mr. Peter, BA FCA *1979;* Alsbridge Plc, 22-24 Ely Place, LONDON, EC1N 6TE.
SCOTT, Mr. Peter, BA ACA *1984;* 35 Church Street, Barford, WARWICK, CV35 8BS.
SCOTT, Dr. Peter, ACA *1988;* 8 Alford Road, West Bridgford, NOTTINGHAM, NG2 6GJ.
SCOTT, Mr. Peter Alistair Sinclair, MA MSc FCA *1969;* Water UK, 1 Queen Annes Gate, LONDON, SW1H 9BT.
SCOTT, Mr. Peter John, FCA *1961;* 12 Howard Lane, Boughton, NORTHAMPTON, NN2 8RS.
SCOTT, Mr. Peter John, BA FCA *1973;* 23 Brockwell, Oakley, BEDFORD, MK43 7TD.
SCOTT, Mr. Peter Michael, MA ACA *2005;* 8 Mervan Road, LONDON, SW2 1DS.
SCOTT, Mr. Peter Neville, FCA *1966;* Flat 24, Overstrand Mansions, Prince of Wales Drive, LONDON, SW11 4EZ.
SCOTT, Mr. Philip Gordon, MA ACA *2009;* 32 Thirsk Road, LONDON, SW11 5SX.
SCOTT, Mr. Phillip William, BSc(Hons) ACA *2002;* 26 Greenhill Avenue, LIVERPOOL, L18 6HT.
SCOTT, Miss. Phillipa Lucy, BSc(Hons) ACA *2002;* Finance Department, Queen Mary University of London, 327 Mile End Road, LONDON, E1 4NS.
SCOTT, Mr. Piran Andrew, BSc(Hons) ACA *2003;* 22 Burlington Road, Portishead, BRISTOL, BS20 7BE.
SCOTT, Miss. Rachael Nicole, BSc ACA *2009;* Glen Doone, Bull Lane, GERRARDS CROSS, BUCKINGHAMSHIRE, SL9 8RF.
•**SCOTT, Mrs. Rachel Elizabeth, BA ACA** *1992;* (Tax Fac), Rachel E. Scott & Co, The Old Vicarage, Wellington, HEREFORD, HR4 8AU.
•**SCOTT, Miss. Rebecca Briony, LLB ACA** *2005;* Mazars LLP, The Atrium, Park Street West, LUTON, LU1 3BE.
SCOTT, Mrs. Rebecca Kathryn, BSc ACA *2006;* 14 Grosvenor Avenue, Breaston, DERBY, DE72 3AB.
SCOTT, Mr. Richard Antony Cargill, MA FCA AMCT *1983;* 8 Folkestone Road, SALISBURY, SP2 8JP.
SCOTT, Mr. Richard Ian, BA ACA *1995;* Dunsley Orchard, London Road, TRING, HERTFORDSHIRE, HP23 6HA.
SCOTT, Mr. Richard John, FCA *1970;* Fulshaw Court, Mill Road, MARLOW, BUCKINGHAMSHIRE, SL7 1QB.
SCOTT, Mrs. Rinda, BA FCA *1996;* 24/50 Ellenborough Street, LYNEHAM, ACT 2602, AUSTRALIA.
SCOTT, Mr. Robert, BSc ACA *2011;* 64 Ratcliff Lawns, Southam, CHELTENHAM, GLOUCESTERSHIRE, GL52 3NT.
SCOTT, Mr. Robert Charles, BEng ACA *2004;* KPMG, 10 Shelley Street, SYDNEY, NSW 2000, AUSTRALIA.
SCOTT, Mr. Robert James, MSci ACA *2010;* Milsco Harrington Way, Bermuda Park, NUNEATON, CV10 7SH.
SCOTT, Mr. Robert James, BSc ACA *1999;* 14 Imperial Way, ASHFORD, KENT, TN23 5HB.
•**SCOTT, Mr. Robert Peter, ACA** *1979;* Thornhill Scott Ltd, Albert Buildings, 49 Queen Victoria Street, LONDON, EC4N 4SA.
SCOTT, Mr. Robert Stuart, FCA *1972;* 3 Osborne, TAMWORTH, STAFFORDSHIRE, B79 7SZ.
SCOTT, Mr. Rory John, BSc ACA *1988;* PO Box 670, WILLOUGHBY, NSW 2068, AUSTRALIA.
SCOTT, Mrs. Rosalind Heather, MA FCA *1986;* with PricewaterhouseCoopers LLP, 1 Embankment Place, LONDON, WC2N 6RH.
SCOTT, Mr. Roy Leonard, FCA *1954;* 2 Crossways, Shenfield, BRENTWOOD, Essex, CM15 8QX. (Life Member)
SCOTT, Mr. Russell Malcolm Craig, FCA *1970;* Cotswold Coombe, Draycott, Claverley, WOLVERHAMPTON, WV5 7EA.
SCOTT, Mrs. Sara, FCA *1964;* 4 Heath Road, READING, RG6 1ND. (Life Member)
•**SCOTT, Mrs. Sharon Ann, FCA** *1988;* 38 Spa Drive, Sapcote, LEICESTER, LE9 4FN.
SCOTT, Mr. Simon Edward, BA ACA *1992;* 806 Riverside Avenue, SCOTIA, NY 12302, UNITED STATES.
SCOTT, Mr. Simon Lloyd, FCA *1961;* 9c Yuan Ching Road, No 06-30 Parkview Mansions, SINGAPORE 618645, SINGAPORE.
SCOTT, Mr. Simon Robert Alan, BSc ACA *1985;* 147 Tolmers Road, Cuffley, POTTERS BAR, EN6 4JP.
SCOTT, Mrs. Sonia Elaine, BSc(Hons) ACA *1994;* 2 Corn Mill Mews, Whalley, CLITHEROE, BB7 9ST.
SCOTT, Mr. Stephen, FCA *1976;* 68 Camberley Drive, ROCHDALE, LANCASHIRE, OL11 4BA.
SCOTT, Mr. Stephen, BA ACA *2007;* 25 Kielder Close, Killingworth, NEWCASTLE UPON TYNE, NE12 6TE.
•**SCOTT, Mr. Stephen Lindsay, FCA** *1969;* (Tax Fac), S.L. Scott, 235 New London Road, CHELMSFORD, CM2 9AA.
SCOTT, Mr. Stephen Michael, BA ACA *1988;* 27 Avondale Road, Ponteland, NEWCASTLE UPON TYNE, NE20 9NA.
SCOTT, Mr. Steven John, ACA *2009;* 49 Wembley Avenue, WHITLEY BAY, TYNE AND WEAR, NE25 8TA.
SCOTT, Mr. Steven Paul, BA ACA *1994;* 29 St Peter's Road, CHELMSFORD, CM1 2SR.
SCOTT, Mr. Stuart Mark Gill, FCA *1975;* Westways, 6 Leeds Road, SELBY, YO8 4HX. (Life Member)
SCOTT, Mrs. Susan Catherine, FCA *1975;* Flat 3, 89 Warrington Crescent, LONDON, W9 1EH.
SCOTT, Mrs. Susan Margaret, FCA *1974;* 9 Herschell Road, LEIGH-ON-SEA, ESSEX, SS9 2NH.
SCOTT, Mr. Sydney Arthur, FCA *1965;* Stoneacre, 78 High Street, Irchester, WELLINGBOROUGH, NN29 7AB.
SCOTT, Mr. Thomas Arundel Andrew, FCA *1974;* 266 Lorong Maarof, 59000 KUALA LUMPUR, FEDERAL TERRITORY, MALAYSIA.
SCOTT, Mr. Thomas Leonard, FCA *1966;* 5 Hoopern Avenue, Pennsylvania, EXETER, EX4 6DN.
SCOTT, Mr. Thomas Michael, BEng ACA *2003;* 8 Heenan Close, Frimley Green, CAMBERLEY, SURREY, GU16 6NQ.
SCOTT, Mr. Thomas Richard, BSc FCA *1999;* Le Colombier Manor La Grande Route de St. Laurent, St. Lawrence, JERSEY, JE3 1NF.
•**SCOTT, Mr. Timothy James, BA ACA** *2005;* with Hurst & Company Accountants LLP, Lancashire Gate, 21 Tiviot Dale, STOCKPORT, CHESHIRE, SK1 1TD.
SCOTT, Dr. Timothy John, BA ACA CTA *1996;* Flat 3, 76 Sloane Street, LONDON, SW1X 9SF.
SCOTT, Mrs. Victoria Ann, BSc ACA *2004;* Flat 13, Collette Court, Eleanor Close, LONDON, SE16 6PW.
SCOTT, Mr. Wade Ashely, ACA CA(SA) *2010;* 5514 N Charles Street, BALTIMORE, MD 21210, UNITED STATES.
•**SCOTT, Mr. Walter, FCA AITI** *1968;* Walter Scott, 3 Clonard Avenue, Sandyford Road, DUBLIN 16, COUNTY DUBLIN, IRELAND.
•**SCOTT, Mr. Walter Michael, BA FCA** *1959;* F.P.Leach & Co, Northumbria House, 62/64 Northumbria Drive, Henleaze, BRISTOL, BS9 4HW.
SCOTT, Mr. Warren Michael, BSc ACA *1988;* Stable Cottage, Furnace Place, Killinghurst Lane, HASLEMERE, SURREY, GU27 2EJ.
SCOTT, Mr. William, BA ACA *1986;* 3 St. Clare Drive, COLCHESTER, CO3 3TA.
SCOTT, Mr. William Joseph, BA FCA *1986;* 73 Arundel Road, KINGSTON UPON THAMES, SURREY, KT1 3RY.
•**SCOTT, Mr. William Robert, FCA** *1966;* (Tax Fac), Hawkins Scott, Wyvern House, 55-61 Frimley High Street, Frimley, CAMBERLEY, SURREY GU16 7HJ.
•**SCOTT-BAIRD, Mr. John Hugh, FCA** *1969;* (Member of Council 1997 - 1998), Scott Baird & Co., Ardbeg, Drominane, KILLEAGH, COUNTY CORK, IRELAND.
SCOTT-BARRETT, Mr. Alexander John, MA ACA *1982;* The Old Rectory, Stutton, IPSWICH, IP9 2SE.
SCOTT-BAYFIELD, Miss. Penelope Samantha Juliette, BSc ACA *1998;* Conde Nast Publications Ltd, Vogue House, 1-2 Hanover Square, LONDON, W1S 1JU.
SCOTT BOOTH, Ms. Clare, BA FCA DChA *1991;* 12 Salvia Gardens, GREENFORD, UB6 7PG.
SCOTT-GALL, Mr. Ian Harold, BSc FCA *1974;* Oakfields House, East Garston, HUNGERFORD, RG17 7HD.
SCOTT-GATTY, Mr. James Alexander, BA ACA *1984;* Cheviot Asset Management Ltd, 90 Long Acre, LONDON, WC2E 9RA.
SCOTT-KERR, Miss. Fiona Margaret, ACA *2009;* (Tax Fac), 2012 Saint Louis Drive, HONOLULU, HI 96816-2024, UNITED STATES.
SCOTT LEACH, Mrs. Jacqueline, BA ACA *1996;* Ancien Chemin De Pignans, 83660 CARNOULES, FRANCE.
SCOTT-LEE, Mrs. Tara Marie, BSc ACA *2005;* Basement Flat, 51 Pembridge Villas, LONDON, W11 3ES.
SCOTT PLUMMER, Mr. Patrick Joseph, MA FCA *1969;* Mainhouse House, KELSO, ROXBURGHSHIRE, TD5 8AA. (Life Member)
SCOTT-PRIESTLEY, Mrs. Trina, BSc ACA *2007;* East Appleton Farm, East Appleton, RICHMOND, NORTH YORKSHIRE, DL10 7QE.
SCOTT-SMITH, Mrs. Emma, BA ACA *1996;* with KPMG LLP, Management Services Centre, 58 Clarendon Road, WATFORD, WD17 1DE.
SCOTT-SMITH, Mr. Stephen Jeffrey, BA FCA *1976;* Woolpack Cottage, Hawkes Lane, Chedworth, CHELTENHAM, GL54 4AH.
SCOTT-WALTON, Mr. David William, BA ACA CPA *1989;* P.O. Box 4015, One Carrier Place, FARMINGTON, CT 06034-4015, UNITED STATES.
SCOTT WARREN, Mr. Jonathan Michael, FCA *1976;* Rougemont, College Hill, St Helier, JERSEY, JE2 4RX.
SCOTT WARREN, Mr. Timothy, ACA *1979;* Jardin du Foret, Mont du Ouaisne, St Brelade, JERSEY, JE3 8AW.
SCOTT-WEBB, Mr. Jonathan, BSc ACA *2007;* Flat 82 Delaware Mansions, Delaware Road, LONDON, W9 2LJ.
SCOTT-WEBB, Mr. Thomas James, MA FCA *1971;* 10 Gordon Place, LONDON, W8 4JD.
•**SCOTTON, Mr. Geoffrey, FCA** *1977;* Geoffrey Scotton FCA, 29 Stoneleigh Park, WEYBRIDGE, SURREY, KT13 0DZ.
SCOURFIELD, Mr. Bryn James, BA FCA *1959;* Flat 7 Kingshill Court, Stow Hill, NEWPORT, GWENT, NP20 4DT. (Life Member)
SCOURFIELD, Mr. David Anthony, ACA *1989;* 18 Clos y Cwarra, CARDIFF, CF5 4QT.
SCOURFIELD, Mrs. Inga Thomasin, BSc ACA *1999;* 9 Victoria Road, HITCHIN, SG5 2LS.
SCOURLOCK, Miss. Lynne Marie, BA(Econ) ACA *2001;* 14 Mareshall Avenue, Warfield, BRACKNELL, BERKSHIRE, RG42 2QU.
SCOVELL, Mrs. Gemma Louise, ACA *2009;* 76 Wainwright Gardens, Hedge End, SOUTHAMPTON, SO30 2NF.
•**SCOVELL, Mr. Martin Gilbert, FCA** *1964;* Scovells, Mennadews, Windlesham Road, Chobham, WOKING, SURREY GU24 8SY.
SCOVELL, Mrs. Monica Gabrielle, LLB FCA *1973;* Thomas' Cottage, Northleigh, COLYTON, EX24 6BL.
SCOWCROFT, Mr. Brian Kenneth, BA ACA *1981;* Kingmoor Park Properties, The Marketing Suite, Unit D, Barron Way, Kingmoor Business Park, CARLISLE CA6 4SJ.
SCOWCROFT, Mrs. Louisa, BA ACA *2006;* Myrfield, Lench Road, ROSSENDALE, BB4 7JH.
SCOWCROFT, Mr. Michael Jon, BSc ACA *1998;* Linden Homes Southern Ltd, 14 Bartram Road, Totton, SOUTHAMPTON, SO40 9PP.
SCOWEN, Mr. James Allan, MA ACA *2000;* N M Rothschild & Sons Ltd, PO Box 185, LONDON, EC4P 4DU.
SCOWSILL, Mr. Jeremy Mark, BSc ACA *1983;* Tuddenham House, Main Road, Tuddenham, IPSWICH, IP6 9BZ.
SCRACE, Mr. Anthony, BSc FCA *1978;* Willowdale, 57 Rooksbury Road, ANDOVER, HAMPSHIRE, SP10 2LP.
•**SCRACE, Mrs. Elizabeth Brady, BA FCA** *1977;* Brady Scrace Limited, Willowdale, 57 Rooksbury Road, ANDOVER, HAMPSHIRE, SP10 2LP.
SCRAFTON, Mr. Derek, FCA *1959;* Paderova House, 34A Arkwright RoadSanderstead, SOUTH CROYDONSurrey, CR2 0LL. (Life Member)
SCRAGG, Mr. Kevin Paul, BA ACA *1992;* Lakehouse, Padeswood, MOLD, CH7 4JD.
SCRASE, Mrs. Vivien Kathryn, BSc ACA *1987;* Conegar, Fenway, Steeple Aston, BICESTER, OXFORDSHIRE, OX25 4SS. (Life Member)
•**SCREATON, Mr. Brian, FCA** *1971;* Screaton & Co, 49 Station Street, ATHERSTONE, CV9 1DB. See also Harris & Screaton Ltd
SCREATON, Mr. Neil William, ACA *2010;* 1 Meadow Gardens, Baddesley Ensor, ATHERSTONE, WARWICKSHIRE, CV9 2DA.
SCREAWN, Mr. Graham Philip, BSc ACA *1991;* Greenroofs, 7 Kings Close, Bramhall, STOCKPORT, SK7 3BN.
SCREAWN, Mrs. Janet Elizabeth, BA ACA *1992;* Chester House, 68 Chestergate, MACCLESFIELD, CHESHIRE, SK11 6DY.
SCREECH, Mr. Andrew Frederick, BSc(Hons) ACA *2002;* Lansdowne Farm, Dean Road Stewkley, LEIGHTON BUZZARD, BEDFORDSHIRE, LU7 0ET.
SCREEN, Dr. Andrew, BDS ACA *2011;* 28 Drovers Way, Radyr, CARDIFF, CF15 8GG.
SCREEN, Mr. Darren, BEng ACA *1999;* South Street Asset Management, 80 South Audley Street, LONDON, W1K 1JH.
SCREETON, Mrs. Natasha Louise, BSc(Hons) ACA *2002;* Morrell Middleton, 3 Cayley Court, George Cayley Drive, YORK, YO30 4WH.
SCREETON, Ms. Samantha Jane, LLB ACA *1999;* BP Exploration Operating Co Ltd, 1-4 Wellheads Avenue Dyce, ABERDEEN, AB21 7PB.
SCREWVALA, Mr. Zubin, MSc BSc ACA *2006;* 23a Blackheath Road, LONDON, SE10 8PE.
SCRIBBINS, Mrs. Margaret, BSc ACA *1984;* Orchard House, Holywell Hill, ST. ALBANS, AL1 1BX.
SCRIBBINS, Mr. Philip Woodley, FCA *1960;* 31 Okeley Lane, TRING, HP23 4HD. (Life Member)
SCRIMGEOUR, Mr. Alastair James, BSc FCA *1982;* 5 Elswick Street, LONDON, SW6 2QR.
SCRIMGEOUR, Mr. Anthony John Carron, MSc FCA *1967;* 4 Rue Mercerie, 05100 BRIANCON, FRANCE. (Life Member)
SCRIMGEOUR, Mr. Gordon Vernon, FCA *1971;* 3303 W. 9th Avenue, SPOKANE, WA 99224, UNITED STATES.
SCRIMGEOUR, Mr. Hugh Carron, BA FCA *1976;* 1 Teignmouth Road, LONDON, NW2 4HR.
SCRIMSHAW, Mr. Arthur Gilbert, FCA *1935;* The Lawns, 1a Knighton Rise, Oadby, LEICESTER, LEICESTERSHIRE, LE2 2RF. (Life Member)
SCRIMSHAW, Mr. John Christopher, MA ACA *2002;* 3/853 High Street, RESERVOIR, VIC 3073, AUSTRALIA.
SCRIMSHIRE, Mrs. Helen Lesley, BSc ACA *1993;* Kingspan Insulation Ltd, Pembridge, LEOMINSTER, HR6 9LA.
SCRIVEN, Ms. Eleanor Marie, BSc ACA *1997;* Derbyshire County Council, County Offices, MATLOCK, DERBYSHIRE, DE4 3AG.
SCRIVEN, Mr. Graham, FCA *1967;* Pinewood, The Meadows, Kingstone, UTTOXETER, ST14 8QE.
SCRIVEN, Mrs. Jane Rankin, MA ACA *1995;* 5 Maclean Walk, Pitreavie Castle, DUNFERMLINE, FIFE, KY11 8TX.
SCRIVEN, Mr. Jeremy Mark Richard, BA ACA *1991;* 8 Gleneagles Close, WIRRAL, MERSEYSIDE, CH61 5YF.
SCRIVEN, Mr. John Geoffrey, FCA *1959;* 134 Pack Lane, Kempshott, BASINGSTOKE, RG22 5HP. (Life Member)
SCRIVEN, Mr. Martin James Wynne, FCA *1968;* Holes Beck House, Hartlington, SKIPTON, BD23 5EE.
SCRIVEN, Mr. Robert Anthony, BA FCA *1992;* Cairn Energy Plc Clydesdale Bank Plaza, 50 Lothian Road, EDINBURGH, EH3 9BY.
•**SCRIVENER, Mr. David Paul, ACA MAAT** *2002;* Ensors, Cardinal House, 46 St Nicholas Street, IPSWICH, IP1 1TT.
SCRIVENER, Mrs. Karina, BA ACA *2004;* Ormiston Children & Families Trust, 333 Felixstowe Road, IPSWICH, IP3 9BU.
SCRIVENER, Mr. Michael, BSc ACA *2009;* 100 Nelson Road, IPSWICH, IP4 4DU.

SCRIVENER, Miss. Nenette, BSc BA(Hons) ACA *2001;* Goodmans Cottage Welford Road, South Kilworth, LUTTERWORTH, LE17 6DY.
SCRIVENS, Mr. David James, MSc BSc(Hons) ACA *2002;* 79 Evans Wharf, HEMEL HEMPSTEAD, HERTFORDSHIRE, HP3 9WN.
SCRIVENS, Mr. Gary Stuart, BSc ACA *2001;* (Tax Fac), 28 Wavell Road, MAIDENHEAD, SL6 5AD.
SCRIVENS, Mr. Martin John, BSc ACA *1980;* Ropemaker Place, 25 Ropemaker Street, LONDON, EC2Y 9AN.
SCRIVENS, Mr. Martyn, MA FCA *1981;* Lloyds TSB Bank plc, 48, Chiswell Street, LONDON, EC1Y 4XX.
SCRIVENS, Mr. Neil James, BSc(Hons) ACA *2001;* 5 Leslie Road, Streetly, SUTTON COLDFIELD, B74 3BS.
SCRIVENS, Mr. Philip Joseph, FCA *1948;* 1 Walnut Close, Milton, DERBY, DE65 6WA. (Life Member)
•**SCRIVINS, Mr. David Robert, BA(Hons) FCA CTA DChA TEP** *1987;* Clark Brownscombe Limited, 2 St. Andrews Place, Southover Road, LEWES, EAST SUSSEX, BN7 1UP.
SCRIVINS, Mrs. Deborah Louise, FCA ATII *1990;* with Clark Brownscombe Limited, 8 The Drive, HOVE, EAST SUSSEX, BN3 3JT.
SCROPE, Miss. Hermione Catherine, FCA *1973;* 4 Rectory Gardens, Church Road Thurston, BURY ST. EDMUNDS, IP31 3TH.
SCROPE, Mr. Tom Oscar, BSc ACA MBA *1998;* Minit Group 6th Floor, 40 Bruton Street, LONDON, W1J 6QZ.
SCROWSTON, Mr. Michael John, BSc ACA *1981;* 25 Manor Garth, Wigginton, YORK, YO32 2WZ.
•**SCROXTON, Mr. Jonathan Mark, FCA** *1973;* Oppenheim Scroxton Limited, 52 Great Eastern Street, LONDON, EC2A 3EP. See also Think Map Corporation Limited
SCRUBY, Mr. Basil Thomas Richard, FCA *1958;* Data Financial Services Ltd, The Barn, Hambleden, HENLEY-ON-THAMES, OXFORDSHIRE, RG9 6RT.
•**SCRUTON, Mr. Andrew Edward Charles, MA ACA** *1991;* A.E.C Scruton, 271 State Street, BROOKLYN, NY 11201, UNITED STATES.
SCRUTON, Mr. Grahame Richard, BA FCA *1989;* 32 Kendal Avenue, EPPING, CM16 4PR.
SCRUTON, Miss. Rebecca, BSc(Hons) ACA *2009;* Flat 4, 10 Marlborough Road, RICHMOND, TW10 6JR.
SCRUTON, Mr. Robert, MSc FCA *1977;* OneSavings Bank Plc, Reliance House Sun Pier, CHATHAM, ME4 4ET.
SCRUTON, Mr. Timothy Andrew, BA ACA *2006;* 55 Coleshill Road, TEDDINGTON, TW11 0LL.
SCRUTTON, Mr. Anthony Muir, FCA *1958;* 10 Admiral Square, Chelsea Harbour, LONDON, SW10 0UU. (Life Member)
•**SCRUTTON, Mrs. Carolyn Mary, BSc FCA** *1978;* (Tax Fac), Scruttons, 2A Bickerton Road, Headington, OXFORD, OX3 7LS.
•**SCRUTTON, Mr. Hugh Geoffrey, FCA** *1964;* Scruttons, 2A Bickerton Road, Headington, OXFORD, OX3 7LS.
•**SCUDAMORE, Mr. Stephen John, MA FCA** *1977;* KPMG, 235 St George's Terrace, PERTH, WA 6000, AUSTRALIA.
SCUDDER, Miss. Janna, BA ACA *2004;* 7 The Marlinespike, SHOREHAM-BY-SEA, WEST SUSSEX, BN43 5RD.
SCUFFELL, Miss. Caroline, BSc ACA *2006;* 4 Blackbush Avenue, Chadwell heath, ROMFORD, RM6 5TU.
SCULL, Mr. Adam John, BA(Hons) ACA *2000;* 39 Comber Street, Paddington, SYDNEY, NSW 2021, AUSTRALIA.
•**SCULL, Mr. Nicholas John, BA FCA** *1994;* (Tax Fac), The Nook, Low Road, Kirby Grindalythe, MALTON, NORTH YORKSHIRE, YO17 8DH.
•**SCULLARD, Mr. Christopher Derrick Peter, BSc ACA** *2002;* Scullard & Co Ltd, 14 Vetchwood Gardens, West Timperley, ALTRINCHAM, CHESHIRE, WA14 5ZG.
SCULLION, Mrs. Emma Joanne, BSc ACA *1997;* 44 Hazelwood Road, Duffield, BELPER, DERBYSHIRE, DE56 4AA.
SCULLION, Mr. Neil Francis, BSc(Hons) ACA CPA *2000;* 349 Norfolk Street, Unit R, CAMBRIDGE, MA 02139, UNITED STATES.
SCULLION, Mr. Paul Adam, BSc ACA *2006;* St. Merryn Meat Ltd, Talgarrek House, Victoria Business Park, Roche, ST. AUSTELL, CORNWALL PL26 8LX.
SCULLION, Mrs. Rebecca Ellen, BA ACA *1993;* 43 Bondgate Green Lane, RIPON, NORTH YORKSHIRE, HG4 1QQ.
•**SCULLY, Mr. James, FCA** *1981;* Hobsons, Alexandra House, 43 Alexandra Street, NOTTINGHAM, NG5 1AY.
SCULLY, Mrs. Joanne Louise, BA ACA *1998;* Sattenham Cottage, Rake Lane, Milford, GODALMING, SURREY, GU8 5AB.
SCULLY, Mrs. Nicola Jane, BA ACA *1993;* 38 Bramble End, Alconbury, HUNTINGDON, PE28 4EZ.
SCULLY, Mr. Oliver Hugh, BA ACA *1999;* Sattenham Cottage, Rake Lane, Milford, GODALMING, SURREY, GU8 5AB.
SCULLY, Mr. Paul, BA(Hons) ACA *2004;* with PricewaterhouseCoopers, 101 Barbirolli Square, Lower Mosley Street, MANCHESTER, M2 3PW.
SCULLY, Mr. Robert James, ACA *1979;* Greenshields, 2 St. Loes Pitch, Off Culver Hill, Amberley, STROUD, GLOUCESTERSHIRE GL5 5BB.
SCURLOCK, Mr. Peter Frederick, FCA *1959;* 130 Dorridge Road, Dorridge, SOLIHULL, B93 8BN. (Life Member)
SCURR, Mr. John Edward, ACA *1978;* 55 Cherry Wood Crescent, Fulford, YORK, YO19 4QL.
SCURR, Mr. Richard John, BSS FCA *1977;* HSBC Holdings Plc, Level 39, 8 Canada Square, Canary Wharf, LONDON, E14 5HQ.
•**SCURR, Mr. Stephen John, FCA** *1971;* Blue Spire South LLP, Cawley Priory, South Pallant, CHICHESTER, WEST SUSSEX, PO19 1SY.
•**SCURRAH, Mr. Robert James, BCom FCA** *1973;* R.J. Scurrah, 8 Bonds Lane, Elswick, PRESTON, PR4 3ZE.
SCURRAH WHITTON, Mrs. Christine, BA ACA *1986;* 34 Karamu Street, Ngaio, WELLINGTON 6035, NEW ZEALAND.
•**SCURRY, Mr. George Martin, BSc FCA** *1982;* (Tax Fac), George Scurry & Co, Suite B, Western House, St James Place, CRANLEIGH, SURREY GU6 8RL.
SCUTT, Mr. Brian Percy Hugh, BSc FCA *1964;* 31 Rivershill, Watton-at-Stone, HERTFORD, SG14 3SD. (Life Member)
SCUTT, Mr. Gerald Arthur Tom, TD FCA *1948;* Lawnswood, Ashley Road, Shortlanesend, TRURO, TR4 9DT. (Life Member)
SCUTT, Mrs. Michelle Louise, BA ACA *2005;* 13 Foxholes Avenue, HERTFORD, SG13 7JG.
SCUTT, Mr. Phillip James, ACA *2008;* 8 Collington Street, Beeston, NOTTINGHAM, NG9 1FJ.
SCUTT, Mrs. Rachel, ACA *2008;* 23 Boleyn Close, Maidenbower, CRAWLEY, WEST SUSSEX, RH10 7QJ.
SCUTTER, Mr. Adrian Keith, LLB FCA *1974;* Skippetts Cottage, Behind Hayes Lane, South Cheriton, TEMPLECOMBE, SOMERSET, BA8 0BP.
SCUTTER, Mr. Darren, BSc ACA *2000;* Caravan Parks Division, Bourne Leisure Group Ltd, 1 Park Lane, HEMEL HEMPSTEAD, HERTFORDSHIRE, HP2 4YL.
SE, Mr. Kuo Shen, ACA *2010;* BDO, Suite 18-04 Level 18, Menara Maa, No 15 Julan Dato, Abdullah Tahir, 80300 JOHOR BAHRU MALAYSIA.
SEABORNE, Miss. Helen Rachel, BSc ACA *1992;* 8 Meadows Crescent, LOCHGILPHEAD, ARGYLL, PA31 8AG.
•**SEABOURNE, Miss. Fay Theresa, FCA** *1994;* Bright Brown Limited, Exchange House, St. Cross Lane, NEWPORT, ISLE OF WIGHT, PO30 5BZ.
SEABOURNE, Mrs. Mary Elizabeth, BA FCA *1987;* Burnt Oak Farmhouse, Ashford Road, Bethersden, ASHFORD, KENT, TN26 3BQ.
SEABOURNE, Mrs. Shelley, ACA *1997;* 2a Maxwell Road, CONGLETON, CHESHIRE, CW12 3HY.
SEABRIDGE, Mr. Stephen James, FCA *1978;* (Tax Fac), with McCabe Ford Williams, 2 The Links, HERNE BAY, KENT, CT6 7GQ.
•**SEABRIGHT, Mr. David Eaton, FCA** *1970;* David E Seabright & Co (Nailsea) Limited, 126a High Street, Nailsea, BRISTOL, BS48 1AH. See also David E Seabright & Co (Nailsea) Limited
SEABROOK, Mr. James Gustav, BA ACA *1994;* 37 Balmaringa Avenue, South Turramurra, SYDNEY, NSW 2074, AUSTRALIA.
•**SEABROOK, Mr. Jeffery Charles, FCA** *1968;* J.C. Seabrook, 56 Woodland Way, WEST WICKHAM, BR4 9LR.
SEABROOK, Mr. John Philip Antony, BA ACA *1978;* 16 Les Liots, 37220 RILLY SUR VIENNE, FRANCE.
SEABROOK, Mr. Timothy James, FCA *1964;* Dippenhall Management, Cleveland House, 3 Abbotts Close, Abbotts Ann, ANDOVER, HAMPSHIRE SP11 7NP.
SEABROOKE, Mr. George, BSc ACA *2007;* 35 Hollybush Lane, HARPENDEN, HERTFORDSHIRE, AL5 4AY.
SEABROOKE, Mrs. Jane Ann, FCA *1974;* Clock House, 121 Roman Road, Birstall, LEICESTER, LE4 4BF.
SEABROOKE, Mrs. Victoria, BSc ACA *2006;* 35 Hollybush Lane, HARPENDEN, HERTFORDSHIRE, AL5 4AY.
SEABURY, Mr. David Holland, BSc ACA *1991;* 2 Freshfield Gardens, Freshfield Road, Formby, LIVERPOOL, L37 3HW.
SEACHOY, Miss. Finola Sukanya, BA ACA *2011;* 4 Warwick Place, LONDON, W5 5PS.
SEAFORD, Mr. Paul, ACA *1978;* 15 Longchamp Drive, ELY, CAMBRIDGESHIRE, CB7 4QL.
SEAGER, Mr. Anthony Edward, MA FCA *1965;* Allendale, Kingston Avenue, East Horsley, LEATHERHEAD, SURREY, KT24 6QT. (Life Member)
SEAGER, Mr. Craig Darren, BA ACA *1998;* Falles Motor Group Ltd, Bagot Road, St Saviour, JERSEY, JE1 1BP.
SEAGER, Mr. Daniel David Vernon, BA ACA *2009;* 35 Landsburg Road, CANVEY ISLAND, SS8 8HW.
SEAGER, Ms. Susan Judith, LLB ACA *2001;* 3 Manston Way, ST. ALBANS, HERTFORDSHIRE, AL4 0AG.
SEAGER-SMITH, Mr. Eric John, BSc ACA *1990;* Feketerigo u.3, H1029 BUDAPEST, HUNGARY.
SEAGERS, Mrs. Phillippa Jane, BA ACA *1991;* Bramleys, The Street, Bredfield, WOODBRIDGE, SUFFOLK, IP13 6AZ.
SEAGRAVE, Mr. Malcolm David, BSc ACA *1996;* The Croft, Rawson Avenue, HALIFAX, WEST YORKSHIRE, HX3 0JP.
SEAGRAVE, Miss. Marian Susan, FCA *1953;* 2B High Beech, SOUTH CROYDON, Surrey, CR2 7QB. (Life Member)
SEAGRAVE, Mr. Steven Peter, BSc ACA *1997;* (Tax Fac), with ICAEW, Metropolitan House, 321 Avebury Boulevard, MILTON KEYNES, MK9 2FZ.
SEAGREAVES, Mr. Terence John, BA ACA *2005;* 15 Stirling Crescent, Sherdley Park, ST HELENS, WA9 3TY.
SEAGROVE, Mr. David Martin, MA ACA *1982;* 385 Ham Green, Holt, TROWBRIDGE, BA14 6PX.
•**SEAH, Mr. Cheoh Wah, ACA** *1980;* Seah & Associates, Suite 15.05 Level 15, City Square Office Tower, 106-108 Jalan Wong Ah Fook, 80000 JOHOR BAHRU, MALAYSIA. See also SQ Associates and SQ Morison
SEAH, Mr. Manfred Kok Khong, BSc ACA CF MBA *1990;* c/o WhiteRock Medical Company Pte Ltd, 138 Cecil Street, 03-01 Cecil Court, SINGAPORE 069538, SINGAPORE.
SEAH, Miss. May Geok Mui, MA ACA *1993;* Flat 4A, 4th Floor Alpine Court, 12 Kotewall Road, MID LEVELS, HONG KONG ISLAND, HONG KONG SAR.
SEAH, Miss. Sook Ping, BSc ACA *2006;* 20 Coniston Road, LONDON, N10 2BP.
SEAL, Mr. David, BA(Hons) ACA *2004;* 11 Widecombe Way, LONDON, N2 0HJ.
SEAL, Mr. Douglas Cyril, FCA *1971;* 12 Holmesdale Road, SEVENOAKS, TN13 3XL.
SEAL, Mrs. Elizabeth Janet Nicola, BA ACA *1998;* ViiV Healthcare 12th Floor, Glaxo Smithkline Plc G S K House, 980 Great West Road, BRENTFORD, TW8 9GS.
SEAL, Mrs. Kristy Louise, BSc ACA *2002;* 65 Newbridge Road, Ambergate, BELPER, DERBYSHIRE, DE56 2GS.
•**SEAL, Mr. Matthew Ian, BA(Econ) ACA** *1998;* with Ernst & Young LLP, 1 More London Place, LONDON, SE1 2AF.
SEAL, Mr. Michael, FCA *1971;* 30 Spencer Drive, Hampstead Garden Suburb, LONDON, N2 0QX.
•**SEAL, Mr. Paul John, FCA CTA TEP** *1974;* (Tax Fac), P.J. Seal, 5 Beechbank Drive, Thorpe End Gardens, Gt Plumstead, NORWICH, NR13 5BW.
SEALE, Mr. Andrew Fayle, BSc ACA *1987;* 128 St. Cross Road, WINCHESTER, HAMPSHIRE, SO23 9RJ.
SEALE, Mr. Christopher John, BSc ACA *2007;* 2002/1 Hosking Place, SYDNEY, NSW 2000, AUSTRALIA.
SEALE, Mr. Frederick Hermon, FCA *1949;* 14 Britten Close, HYTHE, CT21 4SG. (Life Member)
SEALE, Mr. Matthew Lucien, BA ACA *1994;* Kentech International Limited, Office G05, Ibn Battuta Gate, PO Box 27062, DUBAI, 27062 UNITED ARAB EMIRATES.
SEALE, Mr. Michael John, FCA *1958;* The Woodlands, Quarry Road, Morley, ILKESTON, DE7 6DJ. (Life Member)
•**SEALE, Mr. Robert Mark, BA ACA** *1991;* KPMG LLP, 15 Canada Square, LONDON, E14 5GL. See also KPMG Europe LLP
SEALEY, Mr. Adrian, BSc ACA *1994;* Cummins Turbo Technologies Ltd, St. Andrews Road, HUDDERSFIELD, HD1 6RA.
•**SEALEY, Mr. Alan Gerald, BA ACA** *1994;* David Poole Accountants Ltd, Hemdean House, 39 Chapel Road, SOUTHAMPTON, SO30 3FG.
SEALEY, Mr. Colin Robert, FCA *1961;* 8 Thornfield Road, MIDDLESBROUGH, CLEVELAND, TS5 5LB. (Life Member)
SEALEY, Mr. Ian, MA MEng ACA *2010;* Flat 606, Colorado Building, Deals Gateway, LONDON, SE13 7RD.
SEALEY, Mr. John Malcolm, FCA *1962;* Willow House, Ouse Lane, Hickling, NORWICH, NR12 0YP.
SEALEY, Mr. Oliver, ACA *2009;* K P M G, 1 Canada Square, LONDON, E14 5AG.
SEALEY, Mr. Paul Andrew, BA ACA *1988;* T G Jeary Ltd Agricentre, Clarke Avenue, CALNE, SN11 9BS.
SEALEY, Mr. Philip Andre, MA BSc FCA *1975;* Voyage Ltd Garrick House, 2 Queen Street, LICHFIELD, STAFFORDSHIRE, WS13 6QD.
SEALEY, Mr. Timothy John, BA ACA *1988;* 3 Durham Road, LONDON, N2 9DP.
•**SEALS, Mr. Russell, FCA** *1967;* (Tax Fac), Seals King & Co Limited, 17 Brunts Street, MANSFIELD, NOTTINGHAMSHIRE, NG18 1AX.
SEALY, Mr. John Marcus, BEng FCA *1996;* 26 Ewellhurst Road, Clayhall, ILFORD, IG5 0PD.
SEALY, Mr. Nicholas John Elliot, FCA *1971;* Timber Hill, Chertsey Road, Chobham, WOKING, GU24 8JF.
SEAMAN, Mr. Barrie Michael, FCA *1966;* 23 Clifton Road, NEWBURY, RG14 5JS.
SEAMAN, Mr. Charles Richard Henry, FCA *1962;* 9 Burlington Court, George V Avenue, WORTHING, BN11 5RG.
SEAMAN, Miss. Claire, ACA *2010;* Bromhead Chartered Accountants Harscombe House, 1 Darklake View Estover, PLYMOUTH, PL6 7TL.
SEAMAN, Mr. Darryl Rodney, BSc(Hons) ACA *2001;* 2 Drovers Mead, Warley, BRENTWOOD, ESSEX, CM14 5WH.
•**SEAMAN, Mr. David Neil, BSc FCA** *1990;* Three Lines Management Limited, Unit 17, Sandleheath Industrial Estate, FORDINGBRIDGE, HAMPSHIRE, SP6 1PA.
SEAMAN, Miss. Helen Louise, BA ACA *2010;* 54b Keston Road, LONDON, SE15 4JB.
SEAMAN, Ms. Helen Rosemary, ACA *1992;* 15 Mercers Avenue, BISHOP'S STORTFORD, HERTFORDSHIRE, CM23 4AG.
SEAMAN, Mr. Howard Reginald, ACA *1983;* 14 Seaview Drive, HAPPY VALLEY, SA 5159, AUSTRALIA.
•**SEAMAN, Mr. Jonathan David, BA FCA** *2000;* Mazars LLP, Tower Bridge House, St. Katharines Way, LONDON, E1W 1DD.
SEAMAN, Mr. Nicholas Richard Motum, BA ACA *2007;* 11 Brockwell Park Gardens, LONDON, SE24 9BL.
•**SEAMAN, Mr. Peter William, FCA** *1969;* Peter W. Seaman, 32 Offley Road, SANDBACH, CHESHIRE, CW11 1GY.
SEAMAN, Mr. Ronald Keith, FCA *1957;* 8 St. Clements Way, Bishopdown, SALISBURY, SP1 3FF. (Life Member)
SEAMAN, Mrs. Susan Catherine, BA FCA *1992;* Sagars Llp Gresham House, 5-7 St. Pauls Street, LEEDS, LS1 2JG.
SEAMAN, Mr. Thomas, MBiochem ACA *2010;* 2 Woodsome Lodge, WEYBRIDGE, SURREY, KT13 0DH.
SEAMAN, Mr. Thomas James Paul, ACA MAAT *1998;* 5 Carylls Meadow, West Grinstead, HORSHAM, WEST SUSSEX, RH13 8HW.
SEAMAN, Mr. Thomas Phillip, BA ACA *2010;* 1 Crows Lane, Woodham Ferrers, CHELMSFORD, CM3 8RR.
SEAMARK, Mrs. Gail Victoria, BSc ACA *2007;* with Smith & Williamson Ltd, Portwall Place, Portwall Lane, BRISTOL, BS1 6NA.
•**SEAMARK, Mr. Martin John Prothero, FCA** *1978;* Seamark Forensic Services Limited, Stella House, 82 Greenway Road, TAUNTON, SOMERSET, TA2 6LE.
SEAR, Mr. Hugh Edward, FCA *1967;* The Brackens, 1 Lynwood Avenue, EPSOM, KT17 4LQ.
SEAR, Mr. John Frederick, FCA *1973;* 157 Minerva Way, WELLINGBOROUGH, NN8 3TS.
SEAR, Mr. Phillip Charles Clutton, BA FCA ATCL *1980;* 68 Appledore Gardens, Lindfield, HAYWARDS HEATH, RH16 2EU.
SEARANCKE, Miss. Rebecca, ACA *2010;* 263 Ringleas, Cotgrave, NOTTINGHAM, NG12 3PS.
SEARANCKE, Mrs. Shailina Chandrakant, BSc ACA *2004;* 11 Greenway Rise, Gulf Harbour, WHANGAPARAOA 0930, NEW ZEALAND.
•**SEARBY, Mr. David Neville, FCA** *1972;* Searby & Co, Princes House, Wright Street, HULL, HU2 8HX.
•**SEARBY, Miss. Elizabeth Morena, BSc FCA** *1993;* UHY Hacker Young, 22 The Ropewalk, NOTTINGHAM, NG1 5DT. See also UHY Hacker Young LLP
•**SEARBY, Mrs. Gail Diane, FCA** *1972;* Searby & Co, Princes House, Wright Street, HULL, HU2 8HX.
SEARBY, Mr. John Philip, ACA *1985;* 5 Borodale, Kirkwick Avenue, HARPENDEN, HERTFORDSHIRE, AL5 2QW.
SEARBY, Mr. Robert Anthony, BA ACA *1981;* 5 Spinfield Lane West, MARLOW, BUCKINGHAMSHIRE, SL7 2DB.

SEARING, Miss. Lucy, BA ACA *2002;* Appleby, 13-14 Esplanade, St Helier, JERSEY, JE1 1BD.
SEARLE, Mr. Adrian Derek, FCA *1974;* 122 Thorkhill Road, THAMES DITTON, KT7 0UW.
SEARLE, Miss. Carol Anne, BA ACA *1987;* Waterfall Cottage, 7 Basnetts Wood, Endon, STOKE-ON-TRENT, ST9 9DQ.
•SEARLE, Mr. Christopher John, BA FCA *1985;* BDO LLP, 55 Baker Street, LONDON, W1U 7EU. See also BDO Stoy Hayward LLP
SEARLE, Mr. Colin Frederick John, BSc ACA *1996;* Le Vigne Haut, 12220 PEYRUSSE LE ROC, AVEYRON, FRANCE.
•SEARLE, Mr. David John, BA FCA *1979;* (Tax Fac), Baker Tilly Tax and Advisory Services LLP, 25 Farringdon Street, LONDON, EC4A 4AB. See also Slater Maidment
SEARLE, Miss. Deborah, ACA *2008;* 91 Thamesmead, WALTON-ON-THAMES, SURREY, KT12 2SJ.
SEARLE, Mr. Derek Christopher, BSc FCA *1964;* 14 The Mount, MALTON, YO17 7ND. (Life Member)
SEARLE, Mr. Dickon William John, BA(Hons) FCA *2001;* 11 Evesham Road North, REIGATE, RH2 9DW.
SEARLE, Mr. Dominic Geoffrey, MA(Oxon) ACA *1999;* 47 Elmstead Lane, CHISLEHURST, BR7 5EG.
SEARLE, Mr. Fraser Wyman, BA ACA *1989;* 92 Creighton Avenue, LONDON, N10 1NT.
SEARLE, Mr. Gary Anthony, BSc ACA *1996;* 65 The Meadows, Hanham, BRISTOL, BS15 3PB.
SEARLE, Mr. Graham Steven, FCA *1987;* Ecclesiastical Insurance Group Beaufort House, Brunswick Road, GLOUCESTER, GL1 1JZ.
SEARLE, Mr. Ian David Marc, MSc FCA *1974;* 8 Denmark Mews, HOVE, EAST SUSSEX, BN3 3TX.
•SEARLE, Mr. James Francis, FCA *1962;* (Tax Fac), James F. Searle Limited, 176 Spixworth Road, NORWICH, NR6 7EQ.
SEARLE, Mr. John, FCA *1968;* Eastside Cottage, 20 Beech Road, REIGATE, SURREY, RH2 9LR. (Life Member)
SEARLE, Mr. John Bennett, FCA *1978;* No 16 Associates Limited, 16 Martins Drive, WOKINGHAM, RG41 1NY.
SEARLE, Mr. John Richard, BCom ACA CTA *1997;* 136 Royal Worcester Crescent, BROMSGROVE, WORCESTERSHIRE, B60 2TR.
SEARLE, Mrs. Julie Louise, BPharm ACA *2001;* 136 Royal Worcester Crescent, BROMSGROVE, WORCESTERSHIRE, B60 2TR.
SEARLE, Miss. Katherine Clare, MSc BSc ACA *2005;* with PricewaterhouseCoopers LLP, Abacus House, Castle Park, CAMBRIDGE, CB3 0AN.
•SEARLE, Mr. Kenneth Henry, FCA *1952;* Searle & Co, Camelot, 32 Diddington Lane, Hampton in Arden, SOLIHULL, B92 0BZ.
SEARLE, Mrs. Lisa Jayne, BA ACA *1993;* Le Vigne Haut, 12220 PEYRUSSE LE ROC, FRANCE.
SEARLE, Mrs. Margaret Anne, BA ACA *1995;* 10 Airedale Road, Balham, LONDON, SW12 8SF.
SEARLE, Mr. Philip Andrew, BA ACA *1990;* 52 Chestnut Avenue, LOS GATOS, CA 95030, UNITED STATES.
SEARLE, Mr. Philip John, ACA *1986;* 22 Epsom Road, CRAWLEY, WEST SUSSEX, RH10 6LU.
•SEARLE, Mrs. Rachel Karen, ACA FCCA MAAT *2009;* T P Lewis & Partners (BOS) Limited, 10 Church Street, WEDMORE, SOMERSET, BS28 4AB.
•SEARLE, Mr. Richard Michael, BSc FCA *1993;* BDO Limited, PO Box 180, Place du Pre, Rue du Pre, St Peter Port, GUERNSEY GY1 3LL.
SEARLE, Mr. Robert, ACA *2011;* 6 The Mount Apartments, La Rue de la Petite Falaise, Trinity, JERSEY, JE3 5AR.
SEARLE, Mr. Robert, BA(Hons) ACA *2000;* 76 Felpham Way, BOGNOR REGIS, WEST SUSSEX, PO22 8QU.
SEARLE, Mr. Robert George, FCA *1971;* 60E MARINE TERRACE, FREMANTLE, WA 6160, AUSTRALIA.
SEARLE, Miss. Rona Sian Teague, BSc ACA *1986;* (Tax Fac), The Walt Disney Company Limited, 3 Queen Caroline Street, Hammersmith, LONDON, W6 9PE.
SEARLE, Mr. Russell Anthony, BSc ACA *1999;* Chyderus, 69 College Way, Gloweth, TRURO, CORNWALL, TR1 3RX.
SEARLE, Mrs. Shona Claire, BSc ACA CTA *1993;* (Tax Fac), 3 Merdon Close, Chandler's Ford, EASTLEIGH, HAMPSHIRE, SO53 1EF.
SEARLE, Mr. Stanley Richard, FCA CPFA *1952;* 2 Parkstone Close, BEDFORD, MK41 8BD. (Life Member)
•SEARLE, Mr. Wayne Richard, BA ACA *1995;* Abacus 114 Limited, 24a Main Street, Saltby, MELTON MOWBRAY, LEICESTERSHIRE, LE14 4QW.
SEARLES, Mr. Graham Arthur, FCA *1973;* Avenue Cancio Montarela 210, Dept 201, LIMA, 09, PERU.
SEARLES, Mr. John, BEng ACA *1993;* British Energy Barnett Way, Barnwood, GLOUCESTER, GL4 3RS.
•SEARS, Mr. Alan, FCA *1959;* Alan Sears, 2 Hartsbourne Park, 180 High Road, Bushey Heath, BUSHEY, WD23 1SD.
SEARS, Mr. Mark-Anthony, BEng ACA ACT *1994;* SEB Merchant Banking, 10640 STOCKHOLM, SWEDEN.
SEARS, Mr. Philip Alan, FCA *1963;* 84 Knowle Avenue, BLACKPOOL, FY2 9UU. (Life Member)
SEARS, Mr. Roy Stanley, BCom FCA *1959;* 37 Broadhurst, ASHTEAD, KT21 1QD. (Life Member)
SEARY, Mr. David, BA ACA *1992;* 2 Riverside, Hendon, LONDON, NW4 3TX.
SEATON, Mr. Anthony Derek, BSc ACA *1983;* 9 Troutbeck Drive, BRIERLEY HILL, DY5 3YU.
SEATON, Mrs. Barbara Jadwiga, BSc ACA *1982;* with KPMG LLP, One Snowhill, Snow Hill Queensway, BIRMINGHAM, B4 6GN.
SEATON, Mrs. Emma Victoria, MA(Oxon) ACA CTA *2003;* 34 Well Close, Leigh, TONBRIDGE, TN11 8RQ.
SEATON, Mr. James Gareth, BA ACA *1993;* QGC, Level 28, 275 George Street, BRISBANE, QLD 4001, AUSTRALIA.
SEATON, Mrs. Jane, BSc ACA *1983;* N O A H Enterprise, 141 Park Street, LUTON, LU1 3HG.
SEATON, Mr. John Neil, ACA FCMA *2007;* Springfield, Welford Road, South Kilworth, LUTTERWORTH, LEICESTERSHIRE, LE17 6EA.
•SEATON, Mrs. Karen, BA ACA *1990;* Johnsons Accountants Limited, 2 Hallgarth, PICKERING, NORTH YORKSHIRE, YO18 7AW.
SEATON, Mr. Michael David, BSc ACA *1999;* (Tax Fac), Pricewaterhousecoopers, 1 Embankment Place, LONDON, WC2N 6RH.
SEATON, Mr. Peter, FCA *1958;* 10 Cambridge Road, Barnes, LONDON, SW13 0PG. (Life Member)
SEATON, Mr. Roger John, FCA *1972;* 23 Greenhill Park, BARNET, EN5 1HQ.
SEAVER, Mr. Richard Patrick Kingsley, BA FCA *1977;* 20 Probyn Road, Ikoyi, LAGOS, NIGERIA.
SEAVOR, Mr. Graeme, BA ACA *2010;* 24 Dalston Street, Denton Holme, CARLISLE, CA2 5JW.
•SEAWARD, Mr. Alan Rex, FCA *1959;* A.R.Seaward, 32 Palmersfield Road, BANSTEAD, SURREY, SM7 2LD.
SEAWARD, Miss. Carla, BSc ACA *2011;* 15 Gower Road, STONE, STAFFORDSHIRE, ST15 8NZ.
SEAWARD, Mrs. Christine Ann, ACA *1985;* Coan Aalin, Greeba Bridge, St Johns, ISLE OF MAN, IM4 3LD.
•SEAWARD, Mrs. Hilary Jean, MA FCA *1990;* Hilary Seaward Limited, 9 Sherlock Road, CAMBRIDGE, CB3 0HR.
SEAWARD, Mr. John, BSc FCA *1986;* Tudor Griffiths Group, Wood Lane, ELLESMERE, SHROPSHIRE, SY12 0HY.
SEAWARD, Mr. Julian Lloyd, MA ACA *1982;* TDR Capital LLP, 1 Stanhope Gate, LONDON, W1K 1AF.
SEAWARD, Mr. Martyn Peter, ACA *2002;* 34 Fairways Crescent, CARDIFF, CF5 3EA.
•ⒹSEAWARD, Mr. Paul Adrian, FCA *1984;* PKF (Isle of Man) LLC, PO Box 16, Analyst House, Douglas, ISLE OF MAN, IM99 1AP. See also Northwest Trust Company Limited
SEBARATNAM, Mr. Rohan Michael, BSc ACA *1999;* with Deloitte LLP, Athene Place, 66 Shoe Lane, LONDON, EC4A 3BQ.
SEBASTIAN, Mr. Peter Anthony, ACA *2008;* 49 Willifield Way, LONDON, NW11 7XU.
SEBASTIAN, Mr. Stephen, ACA *1988;* 31 Elm Grove, SOUTHEND-ON-SEA, SS1 3EY.
SEBBA, Mr. Henryk Ilan, MA ACA *2003;* 3675 Conifer Court, BOULDER, CO 80304-1522, UNITED STATES.
SEBBA, Mr. Mark Jonathan, FCA *1973;* 9 Pembroke Villas, The Green, RICHMOND, TW9 1QF.
SEBBA, Mr. Neil, BSc ACA *2004;* 237 Uxbridge Road, Mill End, RICKMANSWORTH, HERTFORDSHIRE, WD3 8DP.
SEBIRE, Mr. David John, TD FCA *1966;* Mill Farm, Wood Lane, Horton, BRISTOL, BS37 6PG.
SECCOMBE, Mr. Alan David, BSc ACA *1992;* Pricewaterhousecoopers, 2 Eglin Road, SUNNINGHILL, SOUTH AFRICA. See also PricewaterhouseCoopers Inc
SECCOMBE, Mr. Benjamin Geoffrey Fraser, LLB ACA *2007;* Homes & Communities Agency, St. Georges House, Kingsway, Team Valley Trading Estate, GATESHEAD, TYNE AND WEAR NE11 0NA.
SECCOMBE, Mr. Colin John, BSS FCA *1977;* Dovecote House, Dovecote Farm, CHESTER LE STREET, DH2 2NQ.
•SECCOMBE, Mr. David Alan, FCA *1981;* D A Seccombe FCA, Boyden House, 6a Avenue Road, STRATFORD-UPON-AVON, WARWICKSHIRE, CV37 6UW.
SECCOMBE, Mrs. Fiona, BSc ACA *2007;* Homes and Communities Agency, Kingsway Team Valley, GATESHEAD, TYNE AND WEAR, NE11 0NA.
SECCOMBE, Mr. James Thomas, BA ACA *2007;* 11 Englefield Road, LONDON, N1 4LJ.
SECCOMBE, Mr. Jonathan Paul, BSc ACA *1990;* 3 Huntsmans Meadow, ASCOT, SL5 7PF.
•SECCOMBE, Miss. Penney, BA(Hons) ACA *2002;* Service Charge Assurance Ltd, Salatin House, 19 Cedar Road, SUTTON, SURREY, SM2 5DA.
SECCOMBE, Mrs. Rachel Louise, MBA BA ACA *1985;* Betula, Great Rough, Newick, LEWES, BN8 4HY.
•SECKEL, Mr. Trevor John, FCA *1976;* TJS Consultants, Ridgeway, Westfield, Hoe Lane, Abinger Hammer, DORKING SURREY RH5 6RS.
•SECKER, Mr. Alan, FCA *1962;* Alan Secker & Co., 209 Albury Drive, PINNER, MIDDLESEX, HA5 3RH.
SECKER, Mr. Gordon Paul Alec, BSc(Hons) ACA *2001;* with PKF (UK) LLP, East Coast House, Galahad Road, Beacon Park, Gorleston, GREAT YARMOUTH NORFOLK NR31 7RU.
SECKER, Mr. Mark David, BSc ACA CPA *1996;* with Ernst & Young, 303 Almaden Boulevard, SAN JOSE, CA 95110, UNITED STATES.
SECKER, Mr. Philip, ACA *2009;* with Nyman Libson Paul, Regina House, 124 Finchley Road, LONDON, NW3 5JS.
SECKER, Mr. Stephen Bruce, BSc FCA *1993;* Village Farm House, Main Street, Newton on Derwent, YORK, YO41 4DA.
•SECKER, Dr. Stuart John, BA ACA *2002;* KPMG LLP, 15 Canada Square, LONDON, E14 5GL. See also KPMG Europe LLP
SECKINGER, Mrs. Sharon Lesley, LLB ACA *2001;* 1512 Windsor Court, NAPERVILLE, IL 60565, UNITED STATES.
SECKINGTON, Miss. Claire Marie, BSc ACA *2002;* 99 High Street, Winslow, BUCKINGHAM, MK18 3DG.
SECKLEY, Miss. Jenieveve, BA ACA *2005;* 17 Sellincourt Road, Tooting, LONDON, SW17 9RX.
•SECRETT, Mr. Philip James, MEng ACA *1998;* Grant Thornton UK LLP, 30 Finsbury Square, LONDON, EC2P 2YU. See also Grant Thornton LLP
SECTOR, Mr. Richard Frederick, BA ACA *1992;* The Gables, 3 Claremont Gardens, MARLOW, BUCKINGHAMSHIRE, SL7 1BP.
•SECULAR, Mr. Leslie, FCA *1977;* True Partners Consulting (UK) LLP, 68 Lombard Street, LONDON, EC3V 9LJ.
SEDANI, Mr. Ketan, BCom ACA *1996;* Signet Group Plc, 15 Golden Square, LONDON, W1F 9JG.
SEDANI, Mr. Nitin Kantilal, BSc ACA *1995;* The Oaks, One Pin Lane, Farnham Common, SLOUGH, SL2 3RA.
SEDCOLE, Mr. Cecil Frazer, FCA *1952;* Beeches, Tyrrells Wood, LEATHERHEAD, KT22 8QH. (Life Member)
SEDCOLE, Mr. James, FCA *1949;* 1 Gypsy Lane, Great Amwell, WARE, SG12 9RL. (Life Member)
SEDDON, Mr. Andrew David, BA ACA *1986;* Leicestershire Health Headquarters, Gwendolen Road, LEICESTER, LE5 4QF.
SEDDON, Mrs. Anita Jane, ACA *1986;* with CLB Coopers, Ship Canal House, 98 King Street, MANCHESTER, M2 4WU.
SEDDON, Mrs. Catriona Louise, BA(Hons) ACA *2003;* Shipleys Llp, 3 Godalming Business Centre Wool Sack Way, GODALMING, GU8 6JE.
SEDDON, Mr. Christopher David, BSc ACA *1999;* 51 Briony Avenue, Hale, ALTRINCHAM, WA15 8PZ.
SEDDON, Mrs. Claire Louise, BSc ACA *1999;* (Tax Fac), 51 Briony Avenue, Hale, ALTRINCHAM, WA15 8PZ.
•SEDDON, Mr. David Clive, MSc BA FCA *1983;* (Tax Fac), Seddon Smith Limited, Milton House, Gatehouse Road, AYLESBURY, BUCKINGHAMSHIRE, HP19 8EA.
SEDDON, Mr. David William, LLB FCA *1970;* 25 Southvale Road, Blackheath, LONDON, SE3 0TP.
•SEDDON, Mr. Graham Robert, ACA MAAT *2001;* Menzies LLP, Victoria House, 50-58 Victoria Road, FARNBOROUGH, HAMPSHIRE, GU14 7PG.
SEDDON, Mr. Guy, BA ACA *1994;* 32 Ernle Road, Wimbledon, LONDON, SW20 0HJ.
SEDDON, Mr. John, FCA *1967;* 7 Tithebarn Drive, Parkgate, NESTON, CH64 6RG. (Life Member)
SEDDON, Mr. John Dunbar, BA ACA *1986;* 77 Lawn Road, LONDON, NW3 2XB.
SEDDON, Mr. Joseph, FCA *1954;* 59 Scarisbrick Road, Rainford, ST.HELENS, MERSEYSIDE, WA11 8JN.
•SEDDON, Mr. Michael James, BA ACA *1991;* Wilds Limited, Lancaster House, 70-76 Blackburn Street, Radcliffe, MANCHESTER, M26 2JW.
SEDDON, Mr. Nigel Francis, BSc ACA *1989;* 100 Gowan Avenue, LONDON, SW6 6RG.
SEDDON, Mr. Nigel Ralph, BSc ACA *1990;* Shandon Lodge, 14 Tarvin Road, Littleton, CHESTER, CH3 7DG.
SEDDON, Mr. Norman, BSc FCA *1971;* Sunholme, 36 Rutland Drive, HARROGATE, HG1 2NX. (Life Member)
SEDDON, Mr. Paul, BA FCA *1994;* R S M Tenon Ltd, 2 Wellington Place, LEEDS, LS1 4AP.
SEDDON, Mr. Philip John, ACA *1985;* Rossendale Borough Council, Room 222, Kingfisher Business Centre, Futures Park, BACUP, LANCASHIRE OL13 0BB.
•SEDDON, Mr. Richard James, BSc FCA *1975;* (Tax Fac), Richard Seddon, 4 Hardy Drive, Bramhall, STOCKPORT, SK7 2BW.
SEDDON, Mr. Ronald Kelsall, BA FCA *1960;* (Tax Fac), 9 Dorset Road, ALTRINCHAM, CHESHIRE, WA14 4QN. (Life Member)
SEDGLEY, Mrs. Anna Katherine Lucy, ACA *1998;* 3 Stout Road, PRINCETON, NJ 08540, UNITED STATES.
SEDGLEY, Mr. Peter John, BSc ACA *1982;* 32 Ermelo Road, Gumdale, BRISBANE, QLD 4154, AUSTRALIA.
SEDGLEY, Mr. Robert Alan, BA ACA *1988;* 3 Stout Road, PRINCETON, NJ 08540, UNITED STATES.
•SEDGWICK, Mrs. Caroline Suzanne, BSc ACA *1987;* (Tax Fac), Caroline Sedgwick, 163 Powder Mill Lane, TWICKENHAM, TW2 6EQ.
SEDGWICK, Mr. Christopher Edward, JP FCA *1956;* 33 Beach Crescent, LITTLEHAMPTON, WEST SUSSEX, BN17 5NT. (Life Member)
SEDGWICK, Mr. Christopher John, BA BBS FCA *1969;* 38 Hartington Road, Chiswick, LONDON, W4 3UB.
SEDGWICK, Mr. Christopher John, FCA *1970;* Glebe Cottage, Auld Petty, INVERNESS, IV2 7JH.
SEDGWICK, Miss. Claire Louise, BA(Hons) ACA *2004;* After Glory Limited, 32 Kirklees Street, Tottington, BURY, LANCASHIRE, BL8 3NJ.
SEDGWICK, Miss. Elaine, BSc ACA *2007;* Skipton Bldg Society, 15 Market Place, KENDAL, CUMBRIA, LA9 4TP.
•SEDGWICK, Mr. Graham Harvey, FCA *1968;* Stuff Ltd, PO Box 417, 2nd Floor Abbott Building, Waterfront Drive, ROAD TOWN, TORTOLA ISLAND VIRGIN ISLANDS (BRITISH). See also Vigilate Financial Services Ltd
SEDGWICK, Mr. John, BA ACA *1985;* Cool Milk House, Cool Milk at School Ltd, Kingsley Road, LINCOLN, LN6 3TA.
SEDGWICK, Mr. Jonathan Wylie, ACA *1985;* 41 Foxham Road, LONDON, N19 4RR.
SEDGWICK, Mrs. Louisa, BSc ACA *1999;* 4 Wakefield Mews, BOLTON, BL7 9DR.
SEDGWICK, Mr. Richard Alen, BA ACA *1985;* 17 Kitwood Drive, Lower Earley, READING, RG6 3TA.
SEDGWICK, Mr. Roger Frank, FCA *1974;* 26 Eastwood Drive, KIDDERMINSTER, DY10 3AW.
SEDGWICK, Miss. Sarah Melanie, BA ACA *1992;* The Garth, High Lane, HASLEMERE, SURREY, GU27 1BD.
•SEDGWICK, Mrs. Susan Margaret, BSc FCA *1980;* (Tax Fac), Watson Buckle LLP, York House, Cottingley Business Park, BRADFORD, BD16 1PE.
SEDGWICK, Mr. Timothy John, BSc ACA *1981;* 9 Ivy Court, ILKLEY, WEST YORKSHIRE, LS29 9TX.
SEDGWICK, Mrs. Tracy Elizabeth, BSc(Hons) ACA CTA *2000;* 18 Royal Troon Mews, WAKEFIELD, WF1 4JL.
SEDLEY, Mr. Douglas Richard, FCA *1962;* 6 Rochester Court, 82 Holders Hill Road, LONDON, NW4 1LT.
SEDMAN, Mr. Barrie, FCA *1961;* 210 Station Road, New Waltham, GRIMSBY, DN36 4PH.
SEDWELL, Mr. Christopher John, BA(Hons) ACA *2004;* 6 Cheshires Way, Saighton, CHESTER, CH3 6BB.

SEDWELL, Mrs. Melanie, BSc ACA *2003;* 6 Cheshires Way, Saighton, CHESTER, CH3 6BB.
SEE, Ms. Doreen Lay In, BSc ACA *1989;* 1 Belmont Close, LONDON, N20 8QT.
SEE, Mr. Ian Hua Yen, ACA *1981;* Ian See & Co, Suite1602 Bangkok Bank Building, 18 Bonham Strand West, SHEUNG WAN, HONG KONG ISLAND, HONG KONG SAR.
SEE, Mr. Thuan Po, BSc ACA *2002;* 31A BU 11/9, Bandar Utama, 47800 PETALING JAYA, SELANGOR, MALAYSIA.
SEE, Mr. Thuan Un, BSc ACA *2004;* H S B C Holdings Plc, Level 18, 8 Canada Square, LONDON, E14 5HQ.
SEE, Mr. Wee Chuan, ACA *2011;* 59, PJU 1A/ 1F, Ara Damansara, 47301 PETALING JAYA, SELANGOR, MALAYSIA.
SEEBOO, Miss. Kira Kristel, BSc ACA *2010;* 104 Electra House, Falcon Drive, CARDIFF, CF10 4RD.
SEECHURN, Mr. James, ACA *2011;* 39 Wallace Fields, EPSOM, SURREY, KT17 3AX.
SEED, Miss. Caroline Ann, BA ACA *1998;* 2/ 5 Tower Street, MANLY, NSW 2095, AUSTRALIA.
SEED, Mr. Craig Arthur, BSc ACA *2000;* 16 Leyburn Avenue, HALIFAX, HX3 8NX.
SEED, John Desmond, Esq OBE FCA *1954;* 14 Abbey Mill, Shirleys Drive, Prestbury, MACCLESFIELD, CHESHIRE, SK10 4XY. (Life Member)
SEED, Mr. John Keith, FCA *1962;* 121 Whittingham Lane, Broughton, PRESTON, PR3 5DD. (Life Member)
SEED, Mr. Nicholas James Seys, MA LLB FCA *1968;* 84 Sylvan Valleyway, TORONTO M5M 4M3, ON, CANADA. (Life Member)
SEED, Mr. Nigel Peter, BCom ACA *1992;* 1 Priory Road, WILMSLOW, CHESHIRE, SK9 5PS.
SEED, Mr. Oliver Brian, BA ACA *2006;* 1 Beech House, Weetwood Lane, LEEDS, LS16 5TZ.
SEED, Mr. Peter David, BSc ACA *1991;* Hathaway, 19 Wood Ride, Petts Wood, ORPINGTON, KENT, BR5 1PZ.
SEED, Mrs. Sheila, BSc ACA *1984;* 6 Salisbury Place, WINDERMERE, LA23 1EQ.
SEEDALL, Mr. Jonathan Raymond, ACA *2009;* 53 Brotherston Drive, BLACKBURN, LANCASHIRE, BB2 4FJ.
SEEDHOUSE, Mr. Robin Duncan John, BSc ACA *1987;* National Heritage Memorial Fund, 7 Holbein Place, LONDON, SW1W 8NR.
•**SEEDS, Mr. Kevin William, FCA** *1976;* K.W. Seeds, 3 Leche Croft, BELPER, DERBYSHIRE, DE56 0DD.
SEEFF, Mr. Geoffrey Michael, PhD FCA *1970;* 32c Churchfields, LONDON, E18 2QZ.
•**SEEKINGS, Mrs. Alison Dawn, MA FCA CTA** *1991;* Grant Thornton UK LLP, 101 Cambridge Science Park, Milton Road, CAMBRIDGE, CB4 0FY. See also Grant Thornton LLP
SEEKINGS, Mr. David John Emmott, BA ACA *1993;* 2411 Newport Court, OSHKOSH, WI 54904, UNITED STATES.
SEEKINGS, Mrs. Deborah, BSc ACA *1990;* 2411 Newport Court, OSHKOSH, WI 54904, UNITED STATES.
SEELAN, Mr. Surendran, BSc ACA *2006;* 2 Jalan 5/41, 46000 PETALING JAYA, MALAYSIA.
•**SEELEY, Mr. David William, BA FCA** *1980;* (Tax Fac), D. Seeley & Company, 40 Bear Hill, Alvechurch, BIRMINGHAM, B48 7JX.
SEELEY, Mrs. Karen, BA ACA *2005;* 111 Greenhaze Lane, Great Cambourne, CAMBRIDGE, CB23 5EF.
•**SEELEY, Mr. Keith, FCA** *1973;* Target Consulting Limited, Lawrence House, Lower Bristol Road, BATH, BA2 9ET. See also Target Winters Limited
SEELEY, Mr. Raymond Michael Scott, FCA *1968;* Buckleigh House, Portsmouth Road, Milford, GODALMING, GU8 5DP.
SEELEY, Mrs. Susan Jayne, BSc ACA *1983;* 40 Bear Hill, Alvechurch, BIRMINGHAM, B48 7JX.
SEELEY, Miss. Tanya, BSc ACA *1993;* 38a Berrymede Road, LONDON, W4 5JD.
SEELY, Mr. David Hugh, FCA *1971;* 33 Dunstal Field, Cottenham, CAMBRIDGE, CB24 8UH.
SEEMUNGAL-DASS, Mrs. Catherine Maree, FCA *1990;* PO Box 3376, RED HILL ROCKHAMPTON, QLD 4701, AUSTRALIA.
SEER, Mr. Obaid Farrukh, ACA *2008;* P O Box 136, Ernst & Young, 11th floor Al Gaith Tower, Hamdan Street, ABU DHABI, UNITED ARAB EMIRATES.
SEERA, Mrs. Penelope Jane, BA ACA *2001;* 114 Marshalswick Lane, ST. ALBANS, HERTFORDSHIRE, AL1 4XE.
SEERA, Mrs. Sarabjit Kaur, BSc(Hons) ACA *2003;* 25 Berkeley Avenue, HOUNSLOW, TW4 6LE.
SEERATUN, Miss. Nideshnee, BA ACA *2009;* Ernst & Young Block D, Apex Plaza Forbury Road, READING, RG1 1YE.
•**SEERUNGUM, Mr. Naressen, ACA FCCA** *2008;* N Seerungum & Co, 25 Vicarage Lane, ILFORD, ESSEX, IG1 4AG. See also Startax Accountancy Services Ltd
SEERY, Mr. Ivan Christopher, BA ACA *1988;* with KPMG LLP, 15 Canada Square, LONDON, E14 5GL.
SEERY, Mr. Joseph Patrick, BBS ACA *1995;* Classon House, Dundrum Business Park, DUNDRUM Dublin 14, COUNTY DUBLIN, IRELAND.
•**SEERY, Mr. Michael Thomas, FCA** *1976;* Magnet Associates Ltd, 4 Brookes Lane, Whalley, CLITHEROE, LANCASHIRE, BB7 9RG.
•**SEET, Mr. Joe Lip Poh, FCA** *1977;* Sigma Partnership, 45-47 Cornhill, LONDON, EC3V 3PF. See also Sigma 2002 LLP
SEET, Ms. Karolyn Cher Min, BSc(Hons) ACA *2000;* 53a Hillside Drive, SINGAPORE 549002, SINGAPORE.
SEET, Mr. Keong Huat, FCA *1969;* 7 Tanjong Rhu Road No. 06-03, The Waterside, SINGAPORE 436887, SINGAPORE.
SEET, Mr. Quee Leong, FCA *1979;* QL Seet & Company, 60 Albert Street, #08-01 Albert Complex, SINGAPORE 189969, SINGAPORE.
SEETOHUL, Miss. Karishma, BSc ACA *2004;* Flat 7, Glenavon Lodge, 46 Park Road, BECKENHAM, KENT, BR3 1QD.
SEEVARATNAM, Mr. Ranjeevan, BSc FCA *1974;* Apt 4\6 Station Court, 19 Station Road, 6 COLOMBO, SRI LANKA.
SEEVARATNAM, Mr. Theivendran, BSc FCA *1964;* 57 Finlayson Street, ROSANNA, VIC 3084, AUSTRALIA.
SEEVENESERAJAH, Miss. Gajani Nayagi, BA ACA *2002;* 3 Jalan 5/15, 46000 PETALING JAYA, SELANGOR, MALAYSIA.
SEEYAVE, Mr. Gilbert Louis Kim Fa Cheh, ACA *1989;* (Tax Fac), BDO De Chazal du Mee, P.O. Box 799, 10 Frere Felix, De Valois Street, PORT LOUIS, MAURITIUS.
SEEYAVE, Miss. Pauline Sybille Cheh, MA(Cantab) BA ACA *2000;* 26 John Kennedy Ave, FLOREAL, MAURITIUS.
•**SEFERIS, Mr. Christodoulos Constantinou, BCom FCA** *1986;* Ernst & Young, 11 KLM National Road, Athens Lamia, Metamorphosi, PC 14451 ATHENS, GREECE. See also Ernst & Young Europe LLP
SEFI, Mr. Michael Richard, FCA *1970;* Highfield House, Crossbush, ARUNDEL, BN18 9PQ.
SEFTEL, Mr. David Arnold, BA ACA *1986;* Britannia Row Ltd, 35 Britannia Row, LONDON, N1 8QH.
SEFTEL, Mr. Harold Harris, FCA *1955;* Flat 53 Darwin Court, Gloucester Avenue, LONDON, NW1 7BQ. (Life Member)
SEFTON, Mr. David, FCA *1966;* 3 Bas Etang, 86470 LAVAUSSEAU, FRANCE.
SEFTON, Mr. Kevin Simon, MA FCA ATII *1998;* 4000rpm TX Ltd Linton House, 39-51 Highgate Road, LONDON, NW5 1RT.
SEFTON, Mrs. Lucinda Jane, BSc ACA *1995;* (Tax Fac), with PricewaterhouseCoopers LLP, 1 Embankment Place, LONDON, WC2N 6RH.
SEFTON, Dr. Mark John, BSc(Hons) ACA *2002;* Topza, Sherborne Road, Sherborne St. John, BASINGSTOKE, HAMPSHIRE, RG24 9LP.
•**SEFTON, Mr. Simon Jerome, ACA** *1993;* (Tax Fac), Scodie Deyong LLP, 85 Frampton Street, LONDON, NW8 8NQ.
SEGAL, Mrs. Alexandra Charlotte, BSc FCA *1974;* (Tax Fac), 17 Spencer Road, POOLE, DORSET, BH13 7ET.
SEGAL, Mrs. Amanda Heather, ACA *2002;* (Tax Fac), 2 Beechmeads, Leigh Hill Road, COBHAM, SURREY, KT11 2JX.
SEGAL, Mr. Barrie David, FCA *1968;* 97a Pimlico Road, LONDON, SW1W 8PH.
SEGAL, Mr. Bernard Harold, BA ACA *1986;* 201 Sheen Lane, LONDON, SW14 8LE.
•**SEGAL, Mr. Colin Graham, FCA FCCA** *1971;* 4 Myrtleside Close, NORTHWOOD, HA6 2XH.
•**SEGAL, Mr. David Ashley, BA ACA** *1989;* (Tax Fac), David Ashley & Co, PO Box 716, BOREHAMWOOD, WD6 9GD.
SEGAL, Mrs. Helen Hester, MSc BA ACA *1999;* Haweswater House, United Utilities, Lingley Green Avenue, Lingley Mere Business Park, Great Sankey, WARRINGTON WA5 3LP.
•**SEGAL, Mr. Ian Howard, FCA** *1980;* with Nyman Libson Paul, Regina House, 124 Finchley Road, LONDON, NW3 5JS.
SEGAL, Mr. Mark Jeremy, BA ACA *1988;* 51 Dorset Drive, EDGWARE, HA8 7NT.
SEGAL, Mr. Mark Kevin, BA ACA *2004;* 1a Ashley Close, LONDON, NW4 1PH.
SEGAL, Mr. Matthew Nicholas, BA(Hons) ACA *2001;* Frederick's Restaurant, Camden Passage, LONDON, N1 8EG.
SEGAL, Mr. Melvyn, FCA *1980;* 69 Belmont Lane, STANMORE, HA7 2QA.
SEGAL, Mr. Nicholas Elliot, BSc FCA MBA *1978;* Frederick's, 106 Islington High Street, LONDON, N1 8EG.
SEGAL, Mr. Peter David, FCA *1967;* 15 Gilston Road, LONDON, SW10 9SJ. (Life Member)
SEGAL, Mr. Richard Lawrence, BA ACA *1988;* 7 Ingram Avenue, LONDON, NW11 6TG.
SEGAL, Mr. Sanjeev, BA FCA *1996;* 6 Anstruther Road, BIRMINGHAM, B15 3NN.
SEGAL, Mr. Sidney, FCA *1952;* 3 Pavillion Lodge, Lower Road, HARROW, HA2 0DZ. (Life Member)
•**SEGAL, Mr. Steven Louis, BSc(Econ) ACA** *1987;* Forensic Accounting Solutions, 315 Regents Park Road, Finchley, LONDON, N3 1DP.
SEGARAJASINGAM, Mr. Nagalingam, BSc FCA *1967;* 1 Westall Terrace, Leeming, PERTH, WA 6149, AUSTRALIA.
SEGAT, Mr. Anil Singh, BA FCA *1979;* PCI, 15215 Boulder Trail, ROSEMOUNT, MN 55068, UNITED STATES.
SEGER, Mr. Roy Henry William, MA FCA *1976;* Ciria, Classic House, 174-180 Old Street, LONDON, EC1V 9BP.
SEGLIAS, Miss. Joan Kathleen, FCA *1954;* 35 Canford Road, LONDON, SW11 6PB. (Life Member)
SEGRE, Mr. Michael Anthony, FCA *1965;* 19 Lymden Gardens, REIGATE, RH2 7HX.
SEGUSS, Mr. Anthony John, FCA *1970;* 1206 - 195 21st. Street, WEST VANCOUVER V7V 4A4, BC, CANADA.
SEHGAL, Mr. Hermit Singh, ACA *2009;* 95 Balmoral Drive, HAYES, MIDDLESEX, UB4 0DB.
SEHGAL, Mrs. Purnima, BA(Hons) ACA *2000;* 5 Charleswood, Whitebridge Park, Gosforth, NEWCASTLE UPON TYNE, NE3 5LZ.
SEHMER, Mr. Charles James, FCA *1965;* Witley Court, Petworth Road, Wormley, GODALMING, GU8 5TR. (Life Member)
SEHMI, Mr. Harminder Singh, ACA *1987;* Springhill, Spring Hill, Longworth, Oxon, ABINGDON, OXFORDSHIRE OX13 5HL.
SEHMI, Mr. Sandeep Singh, MSc ACA *1995;* 42 Melody Road, LONDON, SW18 2QF.
SEIDLER, Mr. Andrew Francis, BA ACA ATII *1998;* (Tax Fac), 9 Beauforts, Englefield Green, EGHAM, SURREY, TW20 0DW.
SEIDMAN, Mr. Julian Steven, BA FCA *1982;* MAYFLY HOUSE, Longparish, ANDOVER, HAMPSHIRE, SP11 6PZ.
SEIFERT, Mr. Jonathan Lewis, BA ACA *2002;* Ashley Bank, South View Road, Pinner Hill, PINNER, HA5 3YB.
SEIFERT, Mr. Malcolm John, FCA *1968;* PO Box 330, PINNER, HA5 3WA.
SEIFERT, Mr. Martin Keith, BA FCA *1994;* N.M. Rothschild & Sons Ltd, New Court, St Swithins Lane, LONDON, EC4P 4DU.
SEIFERT, Mr. Robert Morris, BA(Hons) ACA *2002;* Ashley Bank, South View Road, PINNER, HA5 3YB.
•**SEIFERT, Mr. Stephen Neil, BA FCA** *1992;* Elliot Woolfe & Rose, Equity House, 128-136 High Street, EDGWARE, MIDDLESEX, HA8 7TT. See also Lentongate Ltd
SEIPEL, Mr. John Philip, FCA *1965;* 694/696 Freemans Drive, COORANBONG, NSW 2265, AUSTRALIA.
SEITLER, Mr. Benjamin, FCA *1958;* Retail Property Investments Ltd, 4 The Cottages Deva Centre, Trinity Way, SALFORD, M3 7BE.
•**SEITLER, Mr. Martin Peter, BA FCA** *1989;* M. Seitler & Co, Unit 4, The Cottages, Deva Centre, Trinity Way, SALFORD M3 7BE. See also Manchester Accountancy Services Limited
SEJPAL, Mr. Manhar Ranchhoddas, FCA *1980;* c/o 70 Streatham Vale, LONDON, SW16 5TD.
•**SEJPAL, Mr. Mukesh Ranchhoddas, FCA** *1979;* (Tax Fac), 34 Rofant Road, NORTHWOOD, HA6 3BE.
SEJPAL, Mr. Sanket, BSc ACA *2010;* 18 Sandown Way, NORTHOLT, MIDDLESEX, UB5 4HZ.
SEKE, Mrs. Sarah Pauline, BA(Hons) ACA *2009;* 95 Highmarsh Crescent, NEWTON-LE-WILLOWS, MERSEYSIDE, WA12 9WE.
SEKHA, Mr. Kamran, ACA CPA *2002;* 2 Eltham Avenue, SLOUGH, SL1 5TH.
SEKHON, Mrs. Gurjit Kaur, BA ACA *1991;* Xstrata Services UK Ltd Panton House, 25 Haymarket, LONDON, SW1Y 4EN.
SEKHON, Mr. Navdeep, ACA *2009;* Flat 32 Woodpecker Close, HATFIELD, HERTFORDSHIRE, AL10 9ET.
SEKHON, Ms. Sukhminder Kaur, BSc(Econ) ACA CTA *1993;* 11 Stanway Gardens, LONDON, W3 9ST.
SELA, Mr. Owen Thomas Kelaart, BSc FCA *1963;* 38 Sandbourne Crescent, WILLOWDALE M2J 3A6, ON, CANADA. (Life Member)
SELBEY, Mr. Thomas Norman Hunter, FCA *1967;* Avda. Francia 18, Puebla Aida 13G, Urb. Mijas Golf, Mijas Costa, 29650 MALAGA, SPAIN. (Life Member)
SELBY, Mr. Andrew Keith, ACA *1993;* 1190 Oakton Lane, NAPERVILLE, IL 60540, UNITED STATES.
SELBY, Mr. Andrew Stuart, ACA *1982;* Edinburgh Woollen Mill Ltd, Waverley Mills, LANGHOLM, DUMFRIESSHIRE, DG13 0EB.
SELBY, Miss. Anna, ACA *2011;* The Manor House, 5 The Close, Odiham, HOOK, RG29 1FE.
SELBY, Mr. Christopher Richard, FCA *1968;* Town Farmhouse, St. Tudy, BODMIN, CORNWALL, PL30 3NW.
SELBY, Mr. Daniel, FCA ACCA *1994;* 84 Temple Fortune Lane, Hampstead Garden Surbub, LONDON, NW11 7TX.
SELBY, Mrs. Felicity Susan, BSc ACA *1994;* 25 Alsthorpe Road, OAKHAM, LEICESTERSHIRE, LE15 6FD.
SELBY, Miss. Gemma, ACA *2011;* 40 Manor Park Avenue, PONTEFRACT, WEST YORKSHIRE, WF8 2PX.
SELBY, Mr. Hugo Charles Hurford, BA(Hons) ACA *2003;* 257 Eversleigh Road, LONDON, SW11 5XS.
SELBY, Mr. Ian Robert, BSc ACA *1992;* 9 Coppice Way, Hedgerley, SLOUGH, SL2 3YL.
SELBY, Mr. John David, BSc ACA *1981;* 30 Rosebury Square, Repton Park, WOODFORD GREEN, ESSEX, IG8 8GT.
SELBY, Mrs. Lindsey Joy, BSc(Econ) ACA *1998;* 20 Sprigs Road, Hampton Hargate, PETERBOROUGH, PE7 8FT.
•**SELBY, Mr. Mark Ilya, BEng** *1996;* Ashgates Corporate Services Ltd, 5 Prospect Place, Millennium Way, Pride Park, DERBY, DE24 8HG.
SELBY, Mr. Nicholas, BA ACA *2010;* 35 Kings Court, BISHOP'S STORTFORD, HERTFORDSHIRE, CM23 2AB.
SELBY, Miss. Rebecca Mary, ACA *2009;* 26 Hedley Street, Gosforth, NEWCASTLE UPON TYNE, NE3 1DL.
SELBY, Mr. Robert Clive, BSc ACA *1982;* Manor House, Main Street, Askrigg, LEYBURN, NORTH YORKSHIRE, DL8 3HQ.
SELBY, Mr. Robert John, BA(Hons) ACA *2002;* 20 Sprigs Road, Hampton Hargate, PETERBOROUGH, PE7 8FT.
SELDEN, Mr. David Michael, BA FCA FRSA *1992;* The White Lodge, Lodge Hill Road, Lower Bourne, FARNHAM, SURREY, GU10 3RD.
•**SELDEN, Mr. Jeffrey Robert, BSc ACA** *1997;* Nexia Smith & Williamson Audit Limited, 1 Bishops Wharf, Walnut Tree Close, GUILDFORD, SURREY, GU1 4RA. See also Smith & Williamson Ltd and Nexia Audit Limited
SELDEN, Mrs. Rachel, ACA *2009;* 28 Clos y Gog, Broadlands, BRIDGEND, MID GLAMORGAN, CF31 5FP.
SELDEN, Mrs. Shirley Anne, BSc ACA *1998;* 21 The Grove, WOKING, GU21 4AF.
•**SELDON, Mr. Mark George Kennison, FCA** *1968;* Mark Seldon & Co, 10 Sherwood Close, Lily Hill, BRACKNELL, RG12 2SB.
•**SELDON, Mr. Robert Duncan, MEng ACA** *1990;* Deloitte LLP, 1 City Square, LEEDS, WEST YORKSHIRE, LS1 2AL. See also Deloitte & Touche LLP
SELF, Mr. Anthony Charles, BA ACA *1999;* Ernst & Young New Zealand, 41 Shortland Street, PO Box 2146, AUCKLAND, NEW ZEALAND.
SELF, Mr. David Keith, BSc ACA *1985;* Monkton Insurance Services Ltd, P.O. Box MP 11383, GEORGETOWN, GRAND CAYMAN, KY1-1009, CAYMAN ISLANDS.
SELF, Miss. Fiona Jane, BSc ACA *2002;* Landmark House, Experian Way NG2 Business Park, NOTTINGHAM, NOTTINGHAMSHIRE, NG80 1ZZ.
SELF, Mrs. Heather, MA FCA CTA(Fellow) *1984;* (Tax Fac), McGrigors Solicitors Century House, 5 Old Bailey, LONDON, EC4M 7BA.
SELF, Mr. Michael John, BCom ACA *1982;* PO BOX 2542, LONEHILL, GAUTENG, 2062, SOUTH AFRICA.
•**SELF, Mr. Philip, ACA** *1991;* Haines Watts, Airport House, Purley Way, CROYDON, CR0 0XZ.
SELF, Mr. Robert John Charles, BSc ACA *2005;* #40-02, Icon Tower 1, 10 Gopeng Road, SINGAPORE 078878, SINGAPORE.
SELFIN, Ms. Yael, BSc ACA *2001;* with PricewaterhouseCoopers LLP, 1 Embankment Place, LONDON, WC2N 6RH.
•**SELFRIDGE, Mr. Iain McKenzie, BSc FCA** *1993;* PricewaterhouseCoopers LLP, 1 Embankment Place, LONDON, WC2N 6RH. See also PricewaterhouseCoopers
SELIG, Mr. Darren Mark, MEng ACA *1996;* 34 Brookland Hill, Hampstead Garden Suburb, LONDON, NW11 6DX.

•**SELIG, Mr. Jason Henry, BA ACA CTA DChA** *1994;* (Tax Fac), Lopian Gross Barnett & Co, 6th Floor, Cardinal House, 20 St. Marys Parsonage, MANCHESTER, M3 2LG.
SELIGMAN, Mr. Mark Donald, MA ACA *1981;* Credit Suisse First Boston (Europe) Ltd, 20 Columbus Courtyard, LONDON, E14 4DA.
•**SELIGMAN, Mr. Philip Michael, FCA CTA** *1980;* (Tax Fac), Seligman Percy, Hilton House, Lord Street, STOCKPORT, SK1 3NA.
SELIGMAN, Mr. Roderick Julian Richard, MBA BA ACA *1980;* World Productions Ltd, Lasenby House, 32 Kingly Street, LONDON, W1B 5QQ.
•**SELIGMANN, Mr. Ryan, ACA CA(SA)** *2009;* Seles Limited, 17 St. Marys Road, LONDON, NW11 9UE.
SELKIRK, Mr. Andrew Robert Logan, MA FCA *1968;* 9 Nassington Road, LONDON, NW3 2TX.
SELKIRK, Mr. Iain Alexander, FCA *1965;* PO Box 96, Flat 14, Malvern House, Abbey Road, MALVERN, WORCESTERSHIRE WR14 3HG.
SELKIRK, Mr. James Robert, BSc ACA *1998;* 6 59-61 Finlayson Street, LANE COVE, NSW 2066, AUSTRALIA.
SELL, Mrs. Catherine Susan, BA ACA *1989;* The Wilf Ward Family Trust, Westgate House, 5 Westgate, PICKERING, NORTH YORKSHIRE, YO18 8BA.
SELLAHEWA, Mr. Pemil Rangika, ACA ACMA *2009;* 15 Amberlea Court, CASTLE HILL, NSW 2154, AUSTRALIA.
SELLAR, Mr. Fred, FCA *1954;* 47 Augusta Street, GRIMSBY, DN34 4TX. (Life Member)
SELLAR, Mr. Nigel Anthony, BSc ACA *1980;* Yew Tree House, Brobury, HEREFORD, HR3 6DX.
SELLAR, Mr. Sidney Jack, FCA *1954;* 17 Heron Close, GRIMSBY, LINCOLNSHIRE, DN32 8PP. (Life Member)
SELLAR, Mr. Tim, BA FCA *1992;* Unit 401Level 3A Uptown 1, Jalan SS 21/58, Damansara Uptown, 47400 PETALING JAYA, MALAYSIA.
SELLARS, Mr. Antony Paul, BSc ACA *1998;* 81a avenue du polo, Woluwe-St-Pierre, 1150 BRUSSELS, BELGIUM.
SELLARS, Mr. Bruce Charles, FCA *1948;* 62 Hangleton Way, HOVE, EAST SUSSEX, BN3 8EQ. (Life Member)
•**SELLARS, Mr. Christopher, ACA** *1992;* Mackenzie Spencer Limited, 61 Huntley Road, Ecclesall, SHEFFIELD, S11 7PB.
SELLARS, Mr. Christopher James, MPhys ACA *2001;* 7 Chapel Lane, WILMSLOW, CHESHIRE, SK9 5HZ.
SELLARS, Miss. Fiona Gabrielle, BA ACA *2006;* Toronto Vale Tynwald Road Peel, ISLE OF MAN, IM5 1JL.
SELLARS, Dr. Irene Yousept, ACA *2009;* with KPMG LLP, 1 The Embankment, Neville Street, LEEDS, LS1 4DW.
SELLARS, Mr. Julian Scott, BSc(Hons) FCA *2000;* 1 Mill Lane, Pannal, HARROGATE, HG3 1JX.
SELLARS, Miss. Melissa Jane, BA ACA *1995;* 1-3 Strand, LONDON, WC2N 5EH.
SELLARS, Mr. Paul, BA FCA *1978;* White House, Withyham, HARTFIELD, TN7 4BT.
SELLATURAY, Mr. Haresh, BSc ACA *2007;* 55 Russell Road, Moor Park, NORTHWOOD, HA6 2LP.
•**SELLENS, Mr. Keith, FCA** *1984;* (Tax Fac), Sellens French, 93/97 Bohemia Road, ST. LEONARDS-ON-SEA, EAST SUSSEX, TN37 6RJ.
SELLERS, Mr. Andrew Graham, BSc ACA *1992;* The Old Vicarage, 13 Church Street, Bishop Middleham, FERRYHILL, COUNTY DURHAM, DL17 9AF.
SELLERS, Mr. Calvin Lee, BA ACA *1993;* 77 Twickenham Road, TEDDINGTON, TW11 8AL.
SELLERS, Mr. James Anthony, MA FCA *1997;* 497 London Road, Davenham, NORTHWICH, CHESHIRE, CW9 8NA.
SELLERS, Mr. Mark David, BA ACA *2001;* 18 Kilvert Drive, SALE, CHESHIRE, M33 6PN.
SELLERS, Mr. Michael John Wadsworth, FCA *1966;* Flat 1 Fairseat House, 302 High Street, Boston Spa, WETHERBY, WEST YORKSHIRE, LS23 6AJ. (Life Member)
SELLERS, Mr. Michael Warren, FCA *1965;* Rua Jacques de Oliveira Neves 43, Porto de Mos, 8600 373 LAGOS, PORTUGAL.
•**SELLERS, Mr. Neil David, BA ACA** *1988;* Sellers & Co Ltd, 2a Brookfield Avenue, Bredbury, STOCKPORT, CHESHIRE, SK6 1DF.
SELLERS, Mr. Richard Ian, FCA *1939;* 23 Farm Close, RINGWOOD, BH24 1RZ. (Life Member)
SELLERS, Mr. Robin David, ACA *1984;* 4 Boytons Acre, SAFFRON WALDEN, ESSEX, CB11 4FS.
SELLERS, Mr. Rodney Horrocks, OBE BSc(Econ) FCA FRSA *1970;* Stonecroft, 3 Lostock Junction Lane, Lostock, BOLTON, BL6 4JR.
•**SELLERS, Mr. Stephen, BSc FCA** *1984;* (Tax Fac), Grant Sellers Limited, Bank Court, Manor Court, VERWOOD, DORSET, BH31 6DY. See also Grant & Co Associates Limited
SELLERS, Mrs. Suneeta, BA ACA *1998;* 22 Ravenswood Road, BRISTOL, BS6 6BN.
SELLEY, Mr. Graham Peter, ACA *2005;* 11 Buckholt Way Brockworth, GLOUCESTER, GL3 4RH.
•**SELLEY, Mr. Peter Frederick, BSc FCA** *1977;* (Tax Fac), Peter F Selley & Co, 84 Belleville Road, LONDON, SW11 6PP.
SELLIS, Mr. Mark, BSc FCA *1995;* 17 Tavistock Avenue, LONDON, NW7 1GA.
SELLORS, Mr. Gordon Lucian, FCA *1966;* 12 Britannia House, Marina Bay, GIBRALTAR, POB 622, GIBRALTAR.
SELLORS, Mr. Michael Walmsley, FCA *1966;* 21 Borth Avenue, Offerton, STOCKPORT, CHESHIRE, SK2 6AJ.
SELLS, Mr. Edward Andrew Perronet, FCA *1971;* 9 Warwick Square, LONDON, SW1V 2AA.
SELLWOOD, Mr. Darren James, BA ACA *1998;* 16 Mill Drive, HENFIELD, WEST SUSSEX, BN5 9RY.
SELLWOOD, Mr. David John, FCA *1959;* 139 Cooden Drive, BEXHILL-ON-SEA, EAST SUSSEX, TN39 3AJ. (Life Member)
SELLYN, Mr. Laurence Gabriel, MA FCA *1975;* Gildan Activewear, 600 De Maisonneuve Blvd West, 33rd Floor, MONTREAL H3A 3J2, QC, CANADA.
SELMAN, Mr. Barry Neil, BCom ACA *1991;* 2 Glebe Cottage, Selham, PETWORTH, WEST SUSSEX, GU28 0PW.
SELMAN, Miss. Janice Nicola, MA ACA *1985;* 66 Chelsea Gate, 93 Ebury Bridge Road, LONDON, SW1W 8RB.
SELMAN, Mr. Roger Malcolm, FCA *1966;* Selman Associates LLP, 5 Vineries Bank, Milespit Hill, Mill Hill, LONDON, NW7 2RP.
SELMES, Mrs. Zoe, BA ACA *1999;* 3 Osier Way, Great Cambourne, CAMBRIDGE, CB23 6GB.
SELMON, Mr. Peter, FCA *1953;* 36 St. Thomas Drive, PINNER, HA5 4SS. (Life Member)
SELSBY, Mr. David John, ACA *1984;* 23 Bancroft Road, Maidenbower, CRAWLEY, WEST SUSSEX, RH10 7WS.
SELVAKUMAR, Mrs. Pamathy, ACA *1998;* 31a Brandville Gardens, Barkingside, ILFORD, IG6 1JG.
SELVARAJAH, Mr. Jeysan, BSc(Hons) ACA *2011;* 67 Pleasant Way, WEMBLEY, MIDDLESEX, HA0 1DQ.
•**SELVARAJAH, Mr. Ravindran, ACA** *1991;* (Tax Fac), A.R. Consulting Limited, 57 Abbots Lane, KENLEY, SURREY, CR8 5JG. See also AR Consulting
SELVARAJAH, Miss. Sarasavi, MA FCA CTA *1986;* (Tax Fac), Throgmorton UK Ltd, 42 Portman Road, READING, RG30 1EA.
SELVARAJAH, Mr. Varan, ACA *2008;* 27 Cumberland Close, AYLESBURY, BUCKINGHAMSHIRE, HP21 7HH.
SELVARATNAM, Mr. Raghavan, BSc ACA *2010;* 14 Tamarind Yard, LONDON, E1W 2JT.
SELVEY, Mr. John, BSc(Hons) ACA *2002;* 3936 48th St, Sunnyside, NEW YORK, NY 11104, UNITED STATES.
•**SELVEY, Mr. Peter, BA FCA** *1991;* KPMG LLP, Altius House, 1 North Fourth Street, MILTON KEYNES, MK9 1NE. See also KPMG Europe LLP
SELWOOD, Mr. Gary Edward, BSc ACA *1990;* 97 Bluebell Way, Bamber Bridge, PRESTON, PR5 6XQ.
•**SELWOOD, Mr. Ian, ACA MAAT DChA** *1991;* Randall & Payne LLP, 79 Promenade, CHELTENHAM, GLOUCESTERSHIRE, GL50 1PJ.
SELWOOD, Mr. John Malcolm, ACA *1992;* The Larches, Littlebourne Road, CANTERBURY, KENT, CT3 4AF.
SELWOOD, Mrs. Lisa Anne, BSc ACA *1995;* Villa O 109, Palm Jumeirah, DUBAI, PO 487317, UNITED ARAB EMIRATES.
SELWOOD, Miss. Rebecca, BSc ACA *2006;* 48 Kipling Drive, LONDON, SW19 1TW.
SELWOOD, Mr. Thomas Roland, BA(Hons) ACA *2003;* 34 Blakestone Drive, NORWICH, NR7 0LF.
SELWOOD, Mrs. Tracey Helen, LLB ACA *2000;* 12 Royal Field Close Hullavington, CHIPPENHAM, WILTSHIRE, SN14 6DY.
•**SELWYN, Mr. David Stewart, FCA** *1979;* H W Fisher & Company, Acre House, 11-15 William Road, LONDON, NW1 3ER. See also H W Fisher & Company Limited
SELWYN, Mr. Geoffrey, BCom FCA *1965;* 32 St. Marys Avenue, NORTHWOOD, HA6 3AZ.
SELWYN, Mr. Jeffrey Michael, FCA *1960;* The Pines, 2 Totteridge Village, LONDON, N20 8JP. (Life Member)
•**SELWYN, Mr. Julian Glyn, BA ACA** *1982;* Selwyns, Hillside, Letton Close, BLANDFORD FORUM, DORSET, DT11 7SS.
SELWYN, Mr. Michael Allan Simon, BSc ACA *1978;* Paramount Pictures Australia, P.O. Box 4040, SYDNEY, NSW 2001, AUSTRALIA.
SELWYN, Mr. Peter Mark, BA ACA *1997;* 17 Kingswell Ride, Cuffley, POTTERS BAR, HERTFORDSHIRE, EN6 4LH.
•**SELWYN, Mr. Russell Morley, FCA** *1979;* Harris & Trotter LLP, 65 New Cavendish Street, LONDON, W1G 7LS.
•**SELWYN-SMITH, Mr. Paul Alexander, BSc FCA** *1981;* 89 Mitchell Street, Brooklyn, WELLINGTON 6021, NEW ZEALAND.
SELZER, Mrs. Elizabeth Margaret, BA ACA *1983;* 20 Danes Court, St. Edmunds Terrace, St. Johns Wood, LONDON, NW8 7QR.
SELZER, Mr. Jonathan, MA MSc ACA *1979;* Exxon Mobil House, Mail Point 37, Ermyn Way, LEATHERHEAD, SURREY, KT22 8UX.
SEMARD, Miss. Alexandra Maria Felisa, ACA *2008;* 312 Maurice Duplessis, GATINEAU J9J3L8, QC, CANADA.
SEMARK, Mr. Roy Edward, FCA *1962;* 15 Aston Bury Manor, Aston, STEVENAGE, SG2 7EG.
SEMBI, Mr. Jasvinder, BSc ACA *2008;* 1 Woodside Road, PURLEY, CR8 4LQ.
SEMERE, Mr. Abel, ACA *2010;* Flat 12, Benson Court, Hartington Road, LONDON, SW8 2EX.
SEMIKHODSKI, Mr. Igor Alexandre, BSc(Hons) FCA *2001;* Meadow Brook, 1b Oatlands Drive, WEYBRIDGE, SURREY, KT13 9NA.
SEMKE, Mr. Philip Roland, BA ACA *1993;* 10 Northcote Road, SOUTHSEA, PO4 0LH.
SEMMENS, Mrs. Helen Mary, BSc ACA *1994;* Soleco Uk Limited, Florette House, Wood End Lane, LICHFIELD, STAFFORDSHIRE, WS13 8NF.
SEMP, Mr. Malcolm, BSc FCA *1988;* 33 Park Lane, Whitefield, MANCHESTER, M45 7HL.
SEMPLE, Mr. Adam Thomas, BA ACA *2003;* with PricewaterhouseCoopers LLP, Benson House, 33 Wellington Street, LEEDS, LS1 4JP.
SEMPLE, Miss. Francesca, ACA *1995;* 8 Hogarth Road, HOVE, EAST SUSSEX, BN3 5RG.
SEMPLE, Mr. Iain, ACA *2009;* with PricewaterhouseCoopers LLP, Erskine House, 68-73 Queen Street, EDINBURGH, EH2 4NH.
SEMPLE, Mr. Ian Chalmers, MA FCA *1956;* Chemin de la Buchille 16, CH-1630, BULLE, SWITZERLAND. (Life Member)
•**SEMPLE, Mr. Mark Andrew, BA ACA** *1999;* Ernst & Young LLP, 1 More London Place, LONDON, SE1 2AF. See also Ernst & Young Europe LLP
SEMPLE, Mr. Thomas Stevenson, FCA *1954;* Great Beats, Kilve, BRIDGWATER, SOMERSET, TA5 1SS. (Life Member)
SEMPLE-PIGGOT, Ms. Maureen Ann, BSc ACA *1983;* 126 Leighton Road, LONDON, NW5 2RG.
SEMPRINI, Mr. Christopher William Jose, ACA *1980;* 31 Highfield Avenue, ALDERSHOT, HAMPSHIRE, GU11 3BZ.
SEN, Mr. Abhijit, FCA *1969;* 27A Asutosh Chowdhury Avenue, Ballygonge, KOLKATA 700 019, INDIA.
SEN, Mr. Aditya Kumar, MA LLB FCA *1976;* (Tax Fac), 29 Woodstock Road, LONDON, NW11 8ES.
SEN, Mr. Anannya, MSc ACA *2003;* Flat B, 9th Floor, Comfort Mansions, Wong Nai Chung Road, HAPPY VALLEY, HONG KONG.
SEN, Mr. Biswa Bikash, FCA *1974;* B B Sen Associates, Mercantile Buildings, 9 Lal Bazaar Street, Block B, 1st Floor, CALCUTTA 700 001 INDIA.
SEN, Mr. Kallol, BA ACA *2010;* 13D, King William Walk, LONDON, SE10 9JH.
SEN, Ms. Linnet, BSc ACA *1992;* Flat 26, Oakley House, 103 Sloane Street, LONDON, SW1X 9PP.
SEN, Mr. Peter, ACA *2011;* Flat 19, Moorings House, Tallow Road, BRENTFORD, MIDDLESEX, TW8 8EL.
SEN, Mr. Siva Prasad, FCA *1976;* 7 Bangalow Avenue, BEECROFT, NSW 2119, AUSTRALIA.
•**SEN, Mr. Subrata, FCA** *1974;* (Tax Fac), Ross Edwards, 70 Claremont Road, SURBITON, KT6 4RH.
SEN-GUPTA, Mr. Anirudha, ACA *1981;* 111 Constance Road, Whitton, TWICKENHAM, TW2 7HX.
SEN GUPTA, Mr. Subimal, FCA *1970;* 29 Jalan Utara, 46200 PETALING JAYA, SELANGOR, MALAYSIA.
SENA, Mrs. Heather Mary, BSc ACA *1993;* Forest Ridge, Bagshot Road, ASCOT, BERKSHIRE, SL5 9JL.
SENBANJO, Miss. Omokorede Adeola Abisola, BA ACA *2006;* 14 Moorholme, WOKING, GU22 7QZ.
SENDER, Mr. Richard Paget, BSc ACA *1992;* The Stowage, Laddingford, MAIDSTONE, KENT, ME18 6BY.
SENEVIRATNE, Mr. Kirthi NilkamalEhelapola, FCA *1970;* Tudor Lodge, Old Marsh Lane, Dorney Reach, MAIDENHEAD, SL6 0DZ.
SENG, Mr. Timothy Vanna, ACA *2009;* Flat 73 Townshend Court, Townshend Road, LONDON, NW8 6LD.
SENGUPTA, Miss. Adity, LLB ACA *1998;* Brocas Dene, Tilford Road, FARNHAM, SURREY, GU9 8JA.
SENGUPTA, Mrs. Munisha, BA ACA *2001;* 55a Long Drive, RUISLIP, MIDDLESEX, HA4 0HN.
SENGUPTA, Ms. Piya, BA(Hons) ACA *2003;* Flat 37 Road Courtyard, 60 Devonshire Drive, LONDON, SE10 8LQ.
•**SENGUPTA, Mr. Raja, ACA** *1990;* Equal IP Ltd, 60 Park Road, BECKENHAM, KENT, BR3 1QH.
SENIOR, Mr. Adrian, FCA *1974;* 464-466 Manchester Road, Stocksbridge, SHEFFIELD, S36 2DU.
SENIOR, Mr. Andrew James, MA ACA *1982;* (Tax Fac), 9 Summerhouse Road, Stoke Newington, LONDON, N16 0NA.
SENIOR, Mr. Barrie Allan, FCA *1980;* 5 Hollingwood Gate, ILKLEY, LS29 9PP.
SENIOR, Mrs. Charlotte, ACA *2009;* 1 Haycroft, BISHOP'S STORTFORD, HERTFORDSHIRE, CM23 5JL.
SENIOR, Mr. David Christopher Vincent, BSc ACA *1999;* Flat 6 Wellington Court, 116 Knightsbridge, LONDON, SW1X 7PL.
SENIOR, Mr. David Harold, FCA *1952;* 10 Mount Road, EVESHAM, WORCESTERSHIRE, WR11 3HE. (Life Member)
SENIOR, Mr. Gordon Stanley, FCA *1963;* 3 Firbeck, Harden, BINGLEY, BD16 1LP. (Life Member)
SENIOR, Dr. Helen Jane, FCA *1988;* Braemar, 11 Victoria Gardens, SAFFRON WALDEN, ESSEX, CB11 3AF.
•**SENIOR, Mrs. Helen Jayne, BA ACA** *1991;* Helen J Senior, The Azaleas, Norchard Lane, Crossway Green, STOURPORT-ON-SEVERN, WORCESTERSHIRE DY13 9SN.
SENIOR, Mr. Ian Elliott, FCA CPA CISA CIA *2000;* 23 Main Street, HOLMDEL, NJ 07733, UNITED STATES.
•**SENIOR, Mr. Ian James, ACA** *1982;* Ian J. Senior, 18 Market Place, Chapel-en-le-Frith, HIGH PEAK, SK23 0EN.
SENIOR, Mrs. Jacqueline Helen, ACA *2004;* with G & E Professional Services Limited, Arabesque House, Monks Cross Drive, Huntington, YORK, YO32 9GW.
SENIOR, Miss. Joanne Louise, ACA *2008;* 26 Porterbush Road, Mulbarton, NORWICH, NR14 8GL.
SENIOR, Mr. John Davy, BA FCA *1986;* Friars Mead Pershore Road, EVESHAM, WORCESTERSHIRE, WR11 2PQ.
SENIOR, Mrs. Karen Jane, BSc ACA *1998;* 30 Valley Road, LOUGHBOROUGH, LE11 3PZ.
•**SENIOR, Mr. Keith Frederick, MA FCA** *1985;* Jacobs Allen, 59 Abbeygate Street, BURY ST. EDMUNDS, SUFFOLK, IP33 1LB. See also is business ltd
•**SENIOR, Mr. Kevin William, LLB FCA** *1985;* Ernst & Young LLP, 1 More London Place, LONDON, SE1 2AF. See also Ernst & Young Europe LLP
SENIOR, Mr. Mark Andrew, BSc ACA *1988;* 7 Winton Road, Bowdon, ALTRINCHAM, CHESHIRE, WA14 2PE.
•**SENIOR, Mr. Michael George, ACA** *1999;* Bright Partnership, Yarmouth House, Trident Business Park, Daten Avenue, Birchwood, WARRINGTON WA3 6BX.
SENIOR, Mr. Michael Thomas, FCA *1971;* 7 Faustina Drive, ASHFORD, KENT, TN23 3QW.
SENIOR, Mr. Paul, MEng ACA *2001;* 65a Cottonmill Lane, ST. ALBANS, HERTFORDSHIRE, AL1 2ET.
SENIOR, Mr. Peter Julian, BSc ACA *1990;* 34 Wood Street, Skelmanthorpe, HUDDERSFIELD, HD8 9BN.
•**SENIOR, Mr. Robert Maxwell, FCA** *1979;* 1 Greenacres Drive, Otterbourne, WINCHESTER, SO21 2HE.
SENKOWSKY, Miss. Alexia, MA ACA *1997;* Oberer Batterieweg 61, CH 4059 BASEL, SWITZERLAND.
SENN, Mrs. Sharon Elizabeth, BSc ACA *1987;* 36 Robert Moffatt, High Legh, KNUTSFORD, WA16 6PS.
SENN, Mr. Stanley Alfred, FCA *1951;* 1003-25 Scrivener Sq, TORONTO M4W 3Y6, ON, CANADA. (Life Member)
•**SENN, Mr. Timothy James, BA ACA** *1987;* Senn & Co, 36 Robert Moffat, High Legh, KNUTSFORD, CHESHIRE, WA16 6PS.
•**SENNETT, Mr. Barry Rodney, FCA** *1964;* (Tax Fac), Bronsens, 6 Langdale Court, WITNEY, OXFORDSHIRE, OX28 6FG.

SENNIK, Mr. Nitul, BSc(Econ) ACA *2010;* Deloitte LLP, Plot 64518, Fairgrounds office park, PO Box 778, GABORONE, PO Box 778 BOTSWANA.
•**SENNIK, Mr. Yoginder Pall, FCA** *1976;* Y.P.Sennik, P.O. Box 45551, NAIROBI, KENYA.
SENNITT, Mrs. Joanne Victoria, BEng ACA *1993;* Scion Investment Group LLP, 50 Broadwick Street, LONDON, W1F 7AG.
•**SENNITT, Mrs. Karen Andrea, FCA CTA** *1992;* (Tax Fac), Karen A Sennitt FCA CTA, 181a Knapp Lane, Ampfield, ROMSEY, HAMPSHIRE, SO51 9BT.
SENNITT, Mr. Owen Stephen Alexander, BSc ACA *1990;* 20 Westbourne Crescent, CARDIFF, CF14 2BL.
•**SENOGLES, Mr. Geoffrey, BA(Hons) FCA MAE** *1994;* LBC Investigative Accounting (Suisse) sarl, Route de St-Cergue 15, CH-1260 NYON, SWITZERLAND.
SENTANCE, Mr. Paul Roger, FCA *1973;* Woodlea, 20 High Hurst Close, Newick, LEWES, EAST SUSSEX, BN8 4NJ.
•**SENTANCE, Mr. Raymond George Arthur, FCA** *1967;* Raymond Sentance & Co, 4 Dunsmore, The Hoe, Carpenders Park, WATFORD, WD19 5AU.
SENTANCE, Mr. Robert Frank, BA FCA *1978;* Robins Bottom Cottage, Stubbs Hill, Iping, MIDHURST, GU29 0PJ.
SENTER, Mr. David John, ACA *1980;* 105 Parkfields Road, BRIDGEND, MID GLAMORGAN, CF31 4BL.
SEOW, Ms. Jean Lin, PhD MSc BA ACA *1992;* Block 148, Tampines Avenue 5, Apt 04-292, SINGAPORE 521148, SINGAPORE.
SEOW, Mr. Kuan Yeow, ACA *1999;* 1640 Notre Dame Dr, MOUNTAIN VIEW, CA 94040, UNITED STATES.
SEPHTON, Mr. James Arthur, FCA *1970;* Frogmore Grange, Frog Lane, Balsall Common, COVENTRY, CV7 7FP.
•**SEPHTON, Mr. Marcus Julian d'Alton, BA ACA** *1982;* with KPMG LLP, 15 Canada Square, LONDON, E14 5GL.
SEPHTON, Mr. Noel Alan, BSc ACA *1983;* 16 Clare Drive, Highfields Caldecote, CAMBRIDGE, CB23 7UY.
SEQUEIRA, Mr. Julius Orlando, FCA *1975;* 71 Farnaby Road, BROMLEY, BR1 4BN. (Life Member)
SEQUEIRA, Miss. Ortanza, BSc ACA *2011;* 12 Costa Loizou Street, Latsia, 2222 NICOSIA, CYPRUS.
SEQUEIRA, Mr. Zepherino Martin, BSc ACA *1986;* 44 Mandrake Road, LONDON, SW17 7PT.
•**SEQUERRA, Mr. Sam, BA(Hons) ACA** *2001;* R L & Associates Limited, Unit 9 Acorn Business Park, Woodseats Close, SHEFFIELD, S8 0TB. See also CFC Accountancy Services Ltd
SERAPIGLIA, Mrs. Stephanie Susan, BSc(Hons) ACA *2000;* Spotless Group, 13 rue Madeleine Michelis, 92200 NEUILLY-SUR-SEINE, FRANCE.
SERBAN, Miss. Madalina Ruxandra, ACA *2002;* Flat B, 16 Crediton Hill, LONDON, NW6 1HP.
SERCK-HANSSEN, Mr. Eilif, BA ACA MBA *1993;* Laureate Education, 650 S. Exeter Street, BALTIMORE, MD 21202, UNITED STATES.
SERCOMBE, Dr. Elizabeth Anne, BA ACA *2001;* 16 Chute Street, EXETER, EX1 2BZ.
SERCOMBE, Mr. Robert Clifford, LLB FCA *1975;* 499 Malpas Road, NEWPORT, GWENT, NP20 6NA.
SERCOMBE, Mr. Stephen James, BA ACA *1985;* Theatre for a Change, PO Box 31739, Capital City, LILONGWE, MALAWI.
•**SERFATY, Mr. Mesod William, BA FCA** *1970;* (Tax Fac), Serfaty & Co, Suite 4 1st Floor, 123 Main Street, GIBRALTAR, GIBRALTAR.
SERFATY, Mr. Moses, BA(Econ) ACA *2001;* with BDO LLP, 55 Baker Street, LONDON, W1U 7EU.
SERFIOTIS, Mr. George, ACA *2009;* Iroon Polemikou Naftikou 1, Vranas, PO Box 2653, 19007 MARATHON, ATTICA, GREECE.
SERFONTEIN, Mr. Johannes Frederick Van Blerk, ACA CA(SA) *2010;* 15 Southdean Gardens, LONDON, SW19 6NT.
SERGANT, Mr. Maurice Joseph, FCA *1954;* 27 Riverbank Road, Ramsey, ISLE OF MAN, IM8 3PR. (Life Member)
SERGEANT, Miss. Harriet, BA BA(Hons) ACA *2011;* Malthouse Cottage, Swelling Hill, Ropley, ALRESFORD, HAMPSHIRE, SO24 0DA.
SERGEANT, Mr. James John Holroyd, MA ACA *1996;* 10 Albemarle Street, LONDON, W1S 4HH.
SERGEANT, Mr. Michael Robert, BA ACA *1988;* Flat 12 Whitehall Place, Thoroughfare, WOODBRIDGE, SUFFOLK, IP12 1FB.
SERGEANT, Mrs. Sarah Jane, MA(Hons) ACA *2001;* Compass Group Plc, Compass House, Guildford Street, CHERTSEY, SURREY, KT16 9BQ.
SERGEANT, Mr. Warren, BComm ACA *2010;* 349 Earlsfield Road, LONDON, SW18 3DG.
•**SERGENT, Mr. Aidan William, BA FCA** *1984;* (Tax Fac), Sergents, 4 Leyland Street, PRESCOT, MERSEYSIDE, L34 5QP.
SERGHIDES, Miss. Joanna, BCom ACA *2009;* 68 Brook Green, LONDON, W6 7BE.
•**SERGI, Mr. Michael Demetrios, BA(Hons) ACA** *2001;* (Tax Fac), Priory Practice Limited, 1 Abbots Quay, Monks Ferry, BIRKENHEAD, CH41 5LH.
SERGIOU, Mr. Charalambos, BSc ACA *2006;* 24 Antistaseos Street, Dromolaxia, 7020 LARNACA, CYPRUS.
SERGIOU, Mr. Markellos, ACA *2010;* 8 Kalvou Street, 2023 NICOSIA, CYPRUS.
SERIES, Mr. Ronald Charles, ACA CA(SA) *2009;* Flat 14 The Oaks, 84-86 Wimbledon Hill Road, LONDON, SW19 7PB.
SERJEANT, Mrs. Caroline Louise, BSc FCA *1992;* The Vine, Nether Winchendon, AYLESBURY, BUCKINGHAMSHIRE, HP18 0DY.
SERJEANT, Mrs. Catherine Helen, BSc ACA *1994;* 44 Gras Lawn, EXETER, EX2 4SS.
SERJEANT, Mr. James Prosper, BA ACA *1991;* The Vine, Nether Winchendon, AYLESBURY, BUCKINGHAMSHIRE, HP18 0DY.
•**SERJEANT, Mr. Peter George, BSc FCA** *1981;* Francis Clark, Vantage Point, Woodwater Park, Pynes Hill, EXETER, EX2 5FD. See also Francis Clark LLP
SERKIN, Mr. Stanley, FCA *1964;* Penthouse 2, Admirals Place, 24-27 The Leas, WESTCLIFF-ON-SEA, ESSEX, SS0 7BF. (Life Member)
SERLUI, Mr. Leslie, FCA *1965;* 28 Beechcroft Avenue, Golders Green, LONDON, NW11 8BL.
SERMON, Mr. Christopher Leslie, BSc ACA *1985;* Troodos, Crowder Terrace, WINCHESTER, SO22 4PT.
SERMON, Mr. Michael George, FCA *1958;* Le Jardin de la Fontaine, Water Lanes, St. Peter Port, GUERNSEY, GY1 2ED. (Life Member)
SERRANO, Miss. Noelia, BA ACA DChA *2006;* Flat 21 Albert Barnes House, New Kent Road, LONDON, SE1 6PH.
SERRANO-DAVEY, Mrs. Susana, BA ACA *2005;* 2a Thompsons Close, HARPENDEN, HERTFORDSHIRE, AL5 4ES.
•**SERRAO, Mr. David Michael, FCA** *1971;* D.M. Serrao, P.O. Box WK 705, WARWICK WK BX, BERMUDA.
•**SERRUYA, Mr. Charles David, JP BA ACA** *1981;* Baker Tilly (Gibraltar) Limited, Regal House, Queensway, PO Box 191, GIBRALTAR, GIBRALTAR.
SERVANTE, Mr. Graham Paul, BSc ACA *1991;* CGP Ltd Eccle Riggs Hall, Foxfield Road, BROUGHTON-IN-FURNESS, LA206BN.
SERVI, Mr. Andrea, ACA *2008;* 9a Philbeach Gardens, LONDON, SW5 9DY.
SERVICE, Mr. Andrew Alexander, ACA *2009;* 148 West Main Street, DARVEL, AYRSHIRE, KA17 0EZ.
SERVICE, Mr. Graham Andrew, BA FCA *1973;* Eagle Lodge, Mile Path, Hook Heath, WOKING, GU22 0JX.
SERVICE, Miss. Lorna Jane, BSc ACA *1992;* 47 Langmuir Avenue, IRVINE, KA11 2DS.
•**SERVICE, Mr. Thomas Nicholas Mckinlay, FCA** *1978;* Juxon House, 100 St Paul's Churchyard, LONDON, EC4M 8BU.
SERVINI, Mr. Simon Daniel, BA ACA *2006;* 2 Egham Street, CARDIFF, CF5 1FQ.
SESHADRI, Mr. Ram Narayan, ACA *2010;* 52 Wolsey Grove, EDGWARE, MIDDLESEX, HA8 0PJ.
•**SESSIONS, Mrs. Lee Anne, FCA** *2000;* Quay Business Advice Limited, 1 Town Quay Wharf, Abbey Road, BARKING, ESSEX, IG11 7BZ.
SETCHELL, Mr. David Lloyd, MA FCA *1963;* South Hayes, Sandy Lane Road, CHELTENHAM, GL53 9DE. (Life Member)
•**SETCHELL, Mr. James Henry, BSc ACA** *2001;* (Tax Fac), Midsummer Consultants, 28 Parsonage Street, CAMBRIDGE, CB5 8DN.
SETCHELL, Mr. Roger William, BA ACA *1994;* 1 Soden Place, Longworth, ABINGDON, OXFORDSHIRE, OX13 5EY.
SETCHFIELD, Mrs. Hannah, ACA *2009;* 65 Cavendish Way, GRANTHAM, LINCOLNSHIRE, NG31 9FN.
•①**SETCHIM, Mr. Richard Victor Yerburgh, MA FCA** *1982;* PricewaterhouseCoopers LLP, Pricewaterhousecoopers, 12 Plumtree Court, LONDON, EC4A 4HT. See also PricewaterhouseCoopers
SETH, Mr. Anil, FCA *1967;* M-10 Greater Kailash Part 1, NEW DELHI 110048, INDIA. (Life Member)
SETH, Mr. Gaurav, BA ACA *2006;* Tesco Stores Ltd Tesco House, Delamare Road Cheshunt, WALTHAM CROSS, HERTFORDSHIRE, EN8 9SL.
SETH, Mr. Prakash Chander, FCA *1967;* III-J-33, Lajpat Nagar, NEW DELHI 110024, INDIA. (Life Member)
SETH, Mr. Rahoul Kumar, FCA *1976;* 1870 Jackson Street, #504, SAN FRANCISCO, CA 94109, UNITED STATES.
SETH, Mr. Sandip, ACA *1987;* 19 Colt Lane, BELL CANYON, CA 91307, UNITED STATES.
SETH, Mr. Sanjay, BA ACA *1996;* 23 Wadebridge Avenue, Baguley, MANCHESTER, M23 9LS.
SETH, Mr. Toby John, BA FCA *1991;* 52 Pensford Avenue, RICHMOND, SURREY, TW9 4HP.
•**SETHI, Mr. Harash Pal, FCA** *1977;* Cornelius Barton & Co, Mitre House, 44-46 Fleet Street, LONDON, EC4Y 1BN.
•**SETHI, Mr. Ramesh Kumar, FCA** *1977;* R.K. Sethi & Co, 140 Springwell Road, HOUNSLOW, TW5 9BP.
SETHI, Mrs. Samidha Simmi, BSc ACA *1995;* 20 The Holdings, HATFIELD, HERTFORDSHIRE, AL9 5HQ.
SETHI, Mr. Sanjive, BSc ACA *1995;* 6 Harefield Road, Hornsey, LONDON, N8 8QY.
SETHI, Mr. Shailandra, BA ACA *1992;* 20 The Holdings, HATFIELD, HERTFORDSHIRE, AL9 5HQ.
SETHI CAKIR, Mrs. Boo, BSc ACA *1990;* 49 Hartland Road, LONDON, NW1 8DB.
SETHIA, Mr. Akshay, BEng ACA *1993;* 1-3-22-401 Minami Azabu, Minato-ku, TOKYO, 106-0047 JAPAN.
SETHIA, Mr. Chandra Kumar, BA ACA *1995;* Royal London Asset Management Ltd, 55 Gracechurch Street, LONDON, EC3V 0UF.
•**SETHIA, Mr. Indra Kumar, FCA** *1968;* I.K. Sethia, 6 Arundel Road, SUTTON, SURREY, SM2 7AD.
SETHNA, Mr. Harry M K, MBA FCA *1982;* 10033 Tummel Falls, BRISTOW, VA 20136-1929, UNITED STATES.
•**SETHNA, Mr. Zal Cawas, BSc ACA** *2002;* Thorne Lancaster Parker, 8th Floor, Aldwych House, 81 Aldwych, LONDON, WC2B 4HN.
SETHU, Mr. Amir, BEng ACA *2003;* 85 Parkstone Avenue, HORNCHURCH, RM11 3LP.
SETIA, Mr. Atul, BSc ACA *1991;* 6 Selvage Lane, Mill Hill, LONDON, NW7 3SP.
SETO, Mr. Man Fai, ACA *2009;* Room 201 Two Grand Tower, 625 Nathan Road, MONG KOK, KOWLOON, HONG KONG SAR.
•**SETON, Mr. Paul, BSc FCA** *1976;* Spenser Wilson & Co, Equitable House, 55 Pellon Lane, HALIFAX, WEST YORKSHIRE, HX1 5SP.
SETON, Mrs. Paula Louise, BSc ACA *1997;* 15 Mill View Close, Ewell, EPSOM, SURREY, KT17 2DW.
SETTER, Mr. Anthony John, FCA *1969;* Cottonwood, Pleamore Cross, Sampford Arundel, WELLINGTON, TA21 9QE.
SETTERINGTON, Mr. Christopher Michael David, MA ACA *1979;* Weedon Hill House, Buckingham Road, Weedon, AYLESBURY, BUCKINGHAMSHIRE, HP22 4DP.
SETTERS, Mr. Alan David, ACA *1980;* 148 Ringwood Road, St Ives, RINGWOOD, BH24 2NS.
SETTLE, Mrs. Amanda Caroline, ACA *2007;* 133 Godstone Road, CATERHAM, CR3 6RF.
SETTLE, Mr. James, BA(Hons) ACA *2004;* 34 Albert Street, Ramsbottom, BURY, LANCASHIRE, BL0 9EL.
SETTLE, Mr. John Laurence, FCA *1952;* 75 Homesea House, Green Road, SOUTHSEA, HAMPSHIRE, PO5 4DQ. (Life Member)
SETTLE, Ms. Kara Louise, BMus ACA *2002;* 31 Blenheim Gardens, WALLINGTON, SURREY, SM6 9PJ.
SETTLE, Mrs. Louise Elizabeth, BA ACA *1997;* Orchard House, 1a Red House Lane, WALTON-ON-THAMES, SURREY, KT12 1EF.
SETTLE, Mr. Richard John, BA ACA *1997;* Orchard House, 1a Red House Lane, WALTON-ON-THAMES, SURREY, KT12 1EF.
SETTLE, Mr. Stephen Nicholas Charles, MA FCA *1986;* 62 Swiss View, #07-01 La Suisse 1, SINGAPORE 288063, SINGAPORE.
SETTON, Ms. Louise Jennie, BA ACA *1992;* Eaton Manor, Lightfoot Lane, Eaton, TARPORLEY, CHESHIRE, CW6 9AF.
SEVENICH, Mrs. Geraldine, BA ACA *1996;* 1 Portland Square, LONDON, E1W 2QR.
SEVENOAKS, Mr. Matthew Frederick George, BSc ACA *2009;* 302 Kenton Road, HARROW, MIDDLESEX, HA3 8DF.
SEVERE, Mr. David Stephan, BEng ACA *2010;* Flat 392 Russell Court, Woburn Place, LONDON, WC1H 0NH.
SEVERN, Mr. Gary Martin, BA ACA CTA *2003;* Saddle Hall Farm, Bradshaw, HALIFAX, HX2 9PD.
SEVERN, Mr. John Michael, BSc ACA *1989;* 3 Countryman Way, MARKFIELD, LE67 9QL.
SEVERN, Mrs. Lois Tyndale, BSc ACA *1986;* 51 Coniston Avenue, Headington, OXFORD, OX3 0AW.
•**SEVERN, Mr. Paul Andrew, ACA** *2007;* Price & Company, 30/32 Gildredge Road, EASTBOURNE, BN21 4SH.
SEVERS, Miss. Lynne Joanne, BSc(Hons) ACA *2002;* 39 Cotswold Drive, Gonerby Hill Foot, GRANTHAM, LINCOLNSHIRE, NG31 8GE.
SEVERS, Mr. Matthew David James, BA(Hons) ACA *2004;* 4 Redesmere Drive, Cheadle Hulme, STOCKPORT, SK8 5JY.
SEVILLE, Mrs. Vivien Ruth, BSc ACA *1993;* 29 Waterloo Gardens, ASHTON-UNDER-LYNE, OL6 9RD.
•**SEVITT, Mr. Neil Philip, BA FCA** *1984;* RSM Tenon Audit Limited, 2 Wellington Place, LEEDS, LS1 4AP.
•**SEVKET, Mr. Sinasi, FCA** *1973;* Silver Sevket & Co, 16 Bromley Road, BECKENHAM, KENT, BR3 5JE.
SEW, Mr. Simon Joseph, BSc ACA *1997;* FLAT B 26 FLOOR TOWER 2, THE PALAZZO, 28 LOK KING STREET, SHA TIN, HONG KONG SAR.
SEW, Mr. Yon Kuan, ACA *1984;* 92 Jalan Haji Alias, SINGAPORE 268566, SINGAPORE.
SEWARD, Miss. Claire, BSc(Hons) ACA *2002;* (Tax Fac), 24 Northampton Road, Higham Ferrers, RUSHDEN, NORTHAMPTONSHIRE, NN10 8AW.
SEWARD, Mr. Michael John, BSc ACA *1991;* 5 Carlton Road, HARROGATE, NORTH YORKSHIRE, HG2 8DD.
SEWARD, Mr. Peter John, FCA *1956;* Lantern Cottage, Little Comberton, PERSHORE, WR10 3EH. (Life Member)
SEWARD, Mr. Robert Anthony Peter, MSc BA ACA *2004;* 2 Martin Close, BILLERICAY, ESSEX, CM11 2BZ.
SEWELL, Miss. Alison Walker, MA MSc ACA *1995;* 99 Hadlow Road, TONBRIDGE, KENT, TN9 1QE.
SEWELL, Mr. Allan, FCA *1969;* Edenwood, 44 Longlands Road, CARLISLE, CA3 9AE. (Life Member)
SEWELL, Mr. Barry, ACA *2004;* Royal & Sunalliance Plantation Place, 30 Fenchurch Street, LONDON, EC3M 3BD.
SEWELL, Mr. Brian Geoffrey Richard, BA FCA *1978;* Shorts, 6 Fairfield Road, CHESTERFIELD, DERBYSHIRE, S40 4TP.
SEWELL, Mr. David, BSc ACA *2006;* Flat 56 Kelday Heights, 2 Spencer Way, LONDON, E1 2PW.
SEWELL, Mr. David John, FCA *1978;* 98 Banstead Road South, SUTTON, SM2 5LH.
•**SEWELL, Mr. David John Elliott, FCA DChA** *1981;* haysmacintyre, Fairfax House, 15 Fulwood Place, LONDON, WC1V 6AY.
SEWELL, Mr. David Martin, BSc ACA *1993;* Starlings Barn, Chestnut Road, Sutton Benger, CHIPPENHAM, WILTSHIRE, SN15 4RP.
SEWELL, Mr. David Norman, BA ACA *1991;* Bow Bells House, 1 Bread Street, LONDON, EC4M 9HH.
SEWELL, Mr. Dennis John, BA FCA *1971;* Hays House, Herringfleet Road, St. Olaves, GREAT YARMOUTH, NORFOLK, NR31 9HJ. (Life Member)
SEWELL, Mr. Geoffrey Victor, FCA *1974;* 106 Station Road, Kegworth, DERBY, DE74 2FR.
SEWELL, Mr. Grahame Terence, FCA *1974;* Lynx House, Lynx Hill, East Horsley, LEATHERHEAD, KT24 5AX.
•**SEWELL, Mr. Grahame William, BA FCA** *1983;* Armstrong Watson, Bute House, Montgomery Way, Rosehill, CARLISLE, CA1 2RW.
SEWELL, Mrs. Helen, ACA *2009;* 5 St. Georges Villas, TRURO, CORNWALL, TR1 3NL.
•**SEWELL, Mrs. Jacqueline Ann, BSc ACA** *1986;* Jacqueline Sewell, 4 School Road, Twyford, WINCHESTER, SO21 1QQ.
•**SEWELL, Mr. James Paul, BA(Hons) ACA CTA** *2006;* Wright Vigar Limited, 5/6 Clover House, Boston Road, SLEAFORD, LINCOLNSHIRE, NG34 7HD.
SEWELL, Mr. Jeremy Paul, ACA *1991;* 168 Worlds End Lane, Chelsfield Park, ORPINGTON, KENT, BR6 6AS.
SEWELL, Mr. Joseph Barron, FCA *1939;* 37 Hogback Wood Road, BEACONSFIELD, HP9 1JT. (Life Member)
SEWELL, Mrs. Klara-Jane, BA ACA *1991;* 168 Worlds End Lane, Chelsfield Park, ORPINGTON, KENT, BR6 6AS.
SEWELL, Miss. Laura Ann, BSc ACA *2010;* 16 Arthington Close, Tingley, WAKEFIELD, WF3 1BT.
SEWELL, Mr. Nicholas Allan, BA ACA *2007;* 38d Edward Street, NORTH SYDNEY, NSW 2060, AUSTRALIA.
SEWELL, Mr. Peter Robert, BA FCA *1974;* 1 Victoria Terrace, LIVERPOOL, L15 5BH.
SEWELL, Mr. Robert James, BA FCA *1977;* The Homestead, Cautherly Lane, Great Amwell, WARE, SG12 9SN.
SEWELL, Mr. Robert Peter, BSc FCA *1990;* 17 St. Omer Road, GUILDFORD, GU1 2DA.

•**SEWELL, Mr. Robin George, FCA** *1972;* (Tax Fac), Midgley Snelling, Ibex House, Baker Street, WEYBRIDGE, SURREY, KT13 8AH.
•**SEWELL, Mr. Sidney John, FCA** *1966;* (Tax Fac), Sewell & Co, Rafters, 31 Luton Avenue, BROADSTAIRS, CT10 2DH.
SEWELL, Mr. Stuart Paul, BSc ACA MBA *1999;* with KPMG LLP, One Snowhill, Snow Hill Queensway, BIRMINGHAM, B4 6GN.
SEWELL, Mr. Timothy Michael, BA ACA *1982;* (Tax Fac), 46 Williams Way, RADLETT, WD7 7HB.
SEWELL, Mr. Timothy William, BSc ACA *1994;* Valad Property Group, 64 North Row, LONDON, W1K 7DA.
•**SEWELL, Mrs. Victoria Jane, BSc ACA** *1997;* with KPMG LLP, Plym House, 3 Longbridge Road, Marsh Mills, PLYMOUTH, PL6 8LT.
SEWRAJ, Miss. Hemlata Sadhna, BA ACA *1994;* Bank of Mauritius, Sir William Newton St, PORT LOUIS, MAURITIUS.
SEWRAJ, Miss. Reena, ACA *2008;* 30 River Court, Apartment 1912, Jersey City, NEW JERSEY, NJ 07310, UNITED STATES.
SEXTON, Mr. Bryan, FCA *1973;* 15 Shakespeare Road, BIRCHINGTON, KENT, CT7 9ET.
•**SEXTON, Mr. Carl Stewart, BA ACA** *1996;* Andromeda Telematics Limited, Unit 6, Byfleet Technical Centre, Canada Road, Byfleet, WEST BYFLEET SURREY KT14 7JX.
SEXTON, Ms. Elizabeth, BSc ACA *1994;* 172 Brox Road, Ottershaw, CHERTSEY, KT16 0LQ.
SEXTON, Mr. Geoffrey, BSc FCA *1976;* Beaverbrooks Adele House, 32-34 Park Road, LYTHAM ST. ANNES, FY8 1RE.
SEXTON, Mr. James Michael Henry, FCA *1969;* 8 Seaway Avenue, Friars Cliff, CHRISTCHURCH, BH23 4EX. (Life Member)
SEXTON, Mr. Michael James, BA ACA *2007;* Top Floor Flat, 23 Dorville Crescent, LONDON, W6 0HH.
SEXTON, Mrs. Morag Margaret, BSc ACA *1984;* Wood End, The Ridge, EPSOM, SURREY, KT18 7EP.
•**SEXTON, Mr. Richard George, BSc FCA** *1984;* PricewaterhouseCoopers LLP, 1 Embankment Place, LONDON, WC2N 6RH. See also PricewaterhouseCoopers AS LLP, Richard Sexton and PricewaterhouseCoopers
SEXTON, Mr. Robert Edward, BA ACA *1999;* 3 College Fields, BRISTOL, BS8 3HP.
•**SEXTON, Mr. Stuart, ACA MAAT** *2006;* Gateway Advisors Limited, 4 York Place, LEEDS, LS1 2DR.
SEXTON, Mrs. Tracy Ann, BA ACA *1995;* 3 Morris Close, Leyland, PRESTON, PR25 3FD.
SEYDERHELM, Mr. Peter Douglas, BSc ACA *1991;* 8 Danegeld Place, STAMFORD, LINCOLNSHIRE, PE9 2AF.
•**SEYED MOKHTASSI, Mr. Mir Saeid, BSc FCA CTA** *1987;* Sterling Partners LLP, Grove House, 774-780 Wilmslow Road, Didsbury, MANCHESTER, M20 2DR. See also Sterling Pay Limited and Sterling Informia Limited
SEYLER, Mr. Ivor Graham, FCA *1965;* 31 Harold Road, Minnis Bay, BIRCHINGTON, CT7 9NA.
SEYMOUR, Mr. Anthony Eric, FCA *1966;* Briary Bank, 11 Dome Hill, CATERHAM, CR3 6EE.
SEYMOUR, Mr. Christopher David, BA ACA *1999;* 10 Crimicar Lane, SHEFFIELD, S10 4FB.
SEYMOUR, Mr. Clive Howard, FCA *1964;* 2 Enys Road, EASTBOURNE, BN21 2DE.
•**SEYMOUR, Mr. David John, ACA** *1989;* Masons Audit Limited, 4 Hadleigh Business Centre, 351 London Road, Hadleigh, BENFLEET, ESSEX SS7 2BT.
SEYMOUR, Mr. David Ralph, FCA *1968;* 110 Bromedale Avenue, Mulbarton, NORWICH, NR14 8GZ.
SEYMOUR, Mrs. Deborah Clare, BA ACA *1990;* 23 Mycenae Road, LONDON, SE3 7SF.
SEYMOUR, Mrs. Elizabeth Tamsin, ACA *1991;* 4 Meadow View, New Road, Lutton, IVYBRIDGE, DEVON, PL21 9RH.
SEYMOUR, Mr. Gerald Marcus, BA ACA *1998;* Waldman Diamonds (WDC) Israel Ltd, Yahalom Bldg Suite 874-883, 21 Tuval St, 52531 RAMAT GAN, ISRAEL.
SEYMOUR, Mr. Guy Mark, BA ACA *1985;* 86 Wainfleet Road, Burgh le Marsh, SKEGNESS, LINCOLNSHIRE, PE24 5AH.
SEYMOUR, Mrs. Jacqueline Mary, BSc ACA *1995;* Foxcovert House, Goring Heath, READING, RG8 7SN.
SEYMOUR, Mrs. Joanne Lucy, BA ACA *1994;* Langside House North Road, Bretherton, LEYLAND, PR26 9AY.
•**SEYMOUR, Mr. Jonathan Philip, BA ACA** *1991;* Kingston Smith LLP, 800 Uxbridge Road, HAYES, MIDDLESEX, UB4 0RS. See also Kingston Smith Limited Liability Partnership, Devonshire Corporate Services LLP and Kingston Smith Consulting LLP
SEYMOUR, Mrs. Kim Suzanne, BSc(Econ) ACA *2001;* 44 Billington Gardens, Hedge End, SOUTHAMPTON, SO30 2RY.
SEYMOUR, Miss. Laura, ACA *2010;* American Express Europe Ltd, Sussex House, Civic Way, BURGESS HILL, WEST SUSSEX, RH15 9AQ.
SEYMOUR, Mrs. Linda Jane, BSc ACA *1988;* 11 Anglesmede Way, PINNER, HA5 5SS.
•**SEYMOUR, Mr. Malcolm Baillie John, MBA BSc FCA** *1972;* White's House, Compton Bassett, CALNE, SN11 8RE.
SEYMOUR, Mr. Paul Richard, BA ACA *1988;* 14 Campanula Drive, Meadow Brook, Rogerstone, NEWPORT, NP10 9JG.
SEYMOUR, Miss. Rebecca Anne, MA BA(Hons) ACA *2010;* Aldermore, 1st Floor Block B, Western House, Lynch Wood, PETERBOROUGH, PE2 6FZ.
SEYMOUR, Mr. Roger Greville, FCA *1976;* 1 Fir Tree Close, Epsom Downs, EPSOM, KT17 3LD.
SEYMOUR, Mr. Timothy, MA ACA *1997;* 30 Highwoods Drive, MARLOW, BUCKINGHAMSHIRE, SL7 3PY.
SEYMOUR-DOWD, Mr. Sean, BA ACA *2010;* Stand No 2374, Thabo Mbeki Road, PO Box 30942, LUSAKA, ZAMBIA.
SEYMOUR MEAD, Mr. Tom, BEng ACA *2005;* Flat 3 159 Balham Hill, LONDON, SW12 9DJ.
SEYMOUR-TAYLOR, Mr. Thomas James, BA ACA *2008;* with Pricewaterhousecoopers, King Faisal Foundation Building, PO Box 8282, RIYADH, 11482, SAUDI ARABIA.
SEYMOUR-WILLIAMS, Mr. Jonathan Tippet, MA FCA *1982;* Farleaze Farm, Farleaze, MALMESBURY, SN16 0LB.
SEYS LLEWELLYN, Miss. Cerys, MChem ACA *2011;* 7 St. Dunstans Court, 113 Totteridge Road, HIGH WYCOMBE, BUCKINGHAMSHIRE, HP13 6EY.
SEYYAD, Mr. Amir Abbas, BA ACA *1996;* 33 Elmcroft Avenue, Wanstead, LONDON, E11 2DU.
SFONDRINI, Mrs. Anna, ACA *2008;* 20 Selwyn Court, Church Road, RICHMOND, SURREY, TW10 6LR.
SHAAH, Mr. Taalibhusain, MA ACA *1991;* 5 Sandown Road, ESHER, SURREY, KT10 9TT.
SHAARI, Mr. Mohammad Zainal, FCA *1988;* Khazanah Nasional Berhad, Level 33 Tower 2, Petronas Twin Towers, Kuala Lumpur City Centre, 50088 KUALA LUMPUR, FEDERAL TERRITORY MALAYSIA.
SHAARI, Ms. Noor Asma, BSc ACA *2004;* Felda Palm Industries SDN BHD, 4th Floor, Balaifelda, Jalan Gurney Satu, 54000 KUALA LUMPUR, FEDERAL TERRITORY MALAYSIA.
•**SHABABI, Mr. Arash, BA FCA** *1995;* A & A Accounting Services Ltd, 2 Acorn Grove, Kingswood, TADWORTH, SURREY, KT20 6QT.
SHABARUDDIN, Mr. Amir Abdillah, BSc ACA *2011;* 124 Pinggir Zaaba, Taman Tun Dr Ismail, 60 000 KUALA LUMPUR, FEDERAL TERRITORY, MALAYSIA.
•**SHABBIR, Mr. Ghulam, FCA** *1972;* (Tax Fac), Shabbir & Co, 248 Brockley Road, LONDON, SE4 2SF.
•**SHABBIR, Mr. Muhammed, ACA FCCA** *2010;* (Tax Fac), Armstrongs Accountancy Ltd, 1 & 2 Mercia Village, Torwood Close, Westwood Business Park, COVENTRY, CV4 8HX.
SHABI, Mr. Cyrus Jonathan Mark, MA ACA *1991;* 1 Old Park Avenue, LONDON, SW12 8RH.
•**SHABIR, Mr. Mohammed, BSc FCA** *1995;* Portland Business Consulting Ltd, 16th Floor, Portland House, Bressenden Place, LONDON, SW1E 5RS.
SHACALLIS, Mr. Demetris John, BSc ACA *1997;* 12 Pasikratous Street, Acropolis, 2008 STROVOLOS, CYPRUS.
SHACKCLOTH, Mr. Richard, BA ACA *1999;* with PricewaterhouseCoopers, 2 Southbank Boulevard, Southbank, MELBOURNE, VIC 3006, AUSTRALIA.
SHACKELL, Mr. Clive Ernest, BSc ACA *1994;* Merton College, Merton Street, OXFORD, OX1 4JD.
SHACKELL, Mr. Ian Richard Charles, BA FCA *1980;* Let Alliance Ltd, 19 Grosvenor Street, CHESTER, CH1 2DD.
•**SHACKLEFORD, Mr. Tony Dean, BA FCA** *1989;* Shacklefords Limited, 3 Essex Road, Four Oaks, SUTTON COLDFIELD, WEST MIDLANDS, B75 6NR.
SHACKLETON, Mr. Andrew David, BSc ACA *2003;* 7B, 7 Coleshill Place, Bradwell Common, MILTON KEYNES, MK13 8DF.
SHACKLETON, Mr. Anthony James, BA ACA *2004;* Oaktree Capital Management, 27 Knightsbridge, LONDON, SW1X 7LY.
SHACKLETON, Mrs. Elaine Joy, BSc FCA *1982;* 37 Woodhall Drive, Dulwich, LONDON, SE21 7HJ.
SHACKLETON, Mrs. Emma Charlotte, BA ACA *2001;* 22 Buckingham Grove, Timperley, ALTRINCHAM, CHESHIRE, WA14 5AH.
•**SHACKLETON, Mr. Frank Michael, BSc FCA** *1979;* RSM Tenon Audit Limited, The Hamlet, Hornbeam Park, HARROGATE, NORTH YORKSHIRE, HG2 8RE.
SHACKLETON, Mr. Ian Mark, BA FCA *1982;* 37 Woodhall Drive, Dulwich, LONDON, SE21 7HJ.
•**SHACKLETON, Mr. John David, BA FCA** *1976;* Shackleton & Co, 8 Huxley Drive, Bramhall, STOCKPORT, SK7 2PH.
SHACKLETON, Mrs. Judith Mary, BSc FCA *1991;* 28 Kingswood Avenue, BROMLEY, BR2 0NY.
SHACKLETON, Mrs. Julie Ann, ACA *1995;* Yew Tree Cottage, Burford Road, Shipton-under-Wychwood, CHIPPING NORTON, OXFORDSHIRE, OX7 6DW.
SHACKLETON, Mrs. Laura Marie, BCom ACA *2003;* Parkstone House, Little Common Lane, Bletchingley, REDHILL, RH1 4QG.
•**SHACKLETON, Mrs. Marilyn Freda, FCA** *1976;* (Tax Fac), Shackleton & Co, 8 Huxley Drive, Bramhall, STOCKPORT, SK7 2PH.
SHACKLETON, Mr. Michael Payton, BA ACA *2001;* 22 Buckingham Grove, Timperley, ALTRINCHAM, WA14 5AH.
SHACKLETON, Mr. Paul Robert, BSc ACA *1999;* Parkstone House, Little Common Lane, Bletchingley, REDHILL, RH1 4QG.
SHACKLETON, Mr. Timothy Robert, BSc FCA *1981;* 11 Charles Street, Queensbury, BRADFORD, WEST YORKSHIRE, BD13 2HS.
SHACKLEY, Mr. Donald William, BSc ACA ATII *1994;* Flat 35 China Court, Asher Way, LONDON, E1W 2JF.
SHACKLOCK, Mr. Kenneth Harvey, FCA *1953;* 11 Acacia Drive, MALDON, CM9 6AW. (Life Member)
SHACKLOCK, Mr. Timothy Anthony, FCA *1980;* Gleacher Shacklock LLP, Cleveland House, 33 King Street, LONDON, SW1Y 6RJ.
SHACKLOCK, Mr. Timothy James, BSc ACA *1987;* 26 Moore Street, Rozelle, SYDNEY, NSW 2039, AUSTRALIA.
SHACKLOCK, Mr. Toby Marcus John, BSc ACA *1993;* 3 Northumberland Avenue, AYLESBURY, BUCKINGHAMSHIRE, HP21 7HG.
SHACKSHAFT, Miss. Elizabeth Ann, BSc ACA *2004;* with Barclays plc, 1 Churchill Place, Canary Wharf, LONDON, E14 5HP.
SHADBOLT, Mr. David Henry, FCA *1970;* 11 Ty Gwyn Crescent, CARDIFF, CF23 5JL.
SHADBOLT, Mr. David William, FCA *1976;* 25 Palemeadow Road, BRIDGNORTH, WV15 6BE.
SHADBOLT, Mr. Marcus John, MSc ACA *1997;* Vermillon, C405 Lufthansa Centre, 50 Liangmaqiao Road, P.R.C, BEIJING 100016, CHINA.
•**SHADBOLT, Mr. Vivian Roger, BSc FCA** *1995;* with RSM Tenon Audit Limited, Charterhouse, Legge Street, BIRMINGHAM, B4 7EU.
SHADBOLT, Mr. William John, FCA *1959;* 69 Larkholme Lane, FLEETWOOD, FY7 8AU. (Life Member)
SHADDICK, Mr. Mark, MA FCA *1985;* Church House, Church Street, Bidford-on-Avon, ALCESTER, WARWICKSHIRE, B50 4DA.
•**SHADDICK, Mr. Peter Brian, BA ACA** *1990;* Shaddick Smith LLP, Bank Chambers, 7 Market Street, LEIGH, LANCASHIRE, WN7 1ED. See also Shaddick Consultancy Services Ltd
SHADDOCK, Mr. Crispin, BA FCA *1978;* Dewhurst, 36 Belle Vue Road, EXMOUTH, DEVON, EX8 3DN.
SHADDOCK, Mr. Richard Frederick, FCA *1952;* 37A Knoll Road, BEXLEY, DA5 1AY. (Life Member)
SHADFORD, Miss. Lynn, MA ACA *1987;* 22 The Quarry, Alwoodley, LEEDS, LS17 7NH.
SHADFORTH, Mr. Christopher James, BSc ACA *1997;* 23 Pearl Road, CLOVERDALE, WA 6105, AUSTRALIA.
•**SHADWELL, Mr. David John, BSc(Hons) ACA** *2002;* Moore Stephens, P O Box 25, 26-28 Athol Street, Douglas, ISLE OF MAN, IM99 1BD.
SHADWELL, Mrs. Natasha, ACA *2010;* with Monahans, Clarks Mill, Stallard Street, TROWBRIDGE, BA14 8HH.
SHADWELL, Mrs. Pui-See, BSc(Hons) ACA *2003;* 3 River Dhoo Court, Old Castletown Road, Douglas, ISLE OF MAN, IM1 5AU.
SHAER, Mr. David, FCA *1972;* 86 Cliffsea Grove, LEIGH-ON-SEA, SS9 1NQ.
•**SHAFAR, Mr. Brian Martin, FCA** *1972;* Alexander Bursk, Parkgates, Bury New Road, Prestwich, MANCHESTER, M25 0JW.
SHAFFER, Mr. Andrew, BSc ACA *2011;* 36 Craigwell Road, Prestwich, MANCHESTER, M25 0FE.
•**SHAFFER, Mr. Anthony Louis, FCA** *1959;* Shaffers, 90 Moorlands Drive, Shirley, SOLIHULL, B90 3RE.
SHAFFER, Mr. Geoffrey Saul, BA FCA *1974;* (Tax Fac), 36 Craigwell Road, Prestwich, MANCHESTER, M25 0FE.
SHAFFER, Mr. Stephen Leslie, FCA *1971;* Aluf Simchoni 5/15, kiryat Shmuel, 92505 JERUSALEM, ISRAEL.
SHAFFI, Mr. Mohammed Aksan Upali, BSc ACA *1993;* 19 Meadway Drive, WOKING, SURREY, GU21 4TA.
SHAFI, Mr. Nadeem, FCA *1994;* Ernst & Young, P.O. Box 74, SAFAT, 13001, KUWAIT.
SHAFI, Mr. Omar Farid, BSc ACA *1997;* 11 Kinnerton Street, LONDON, SW1X 8EA.
SHAFI, Mr. Waseem Ahmed, BSc ACA *2005;* 27 Jenner Road, LONDON, N16 7SB.
SHAFI, Mrs. Yasmin Rebecca, BSc ACA *1997;* 1st Floor Castle House, I Deal Castle House, 37-45 Paul Street, LONDON, EC2A 4LS.
SHAFIE, Mr. Mohammad Romzi, BSc ACA *2004;* No 56 Jalan BSJ 5, Taman Bukit Segar Jaya 2, 43200 CHERAS, FEDERAL TERRITORY, MALAYSIA.
•**SHAFIER, Mr. Lawrence Edward, FCA** *1989;* Haslers, Old Station Road, LOUGHTON, ESSEX, IG10 4PL.
•**SHAFIQ, Mr. Shahid, BA ACA** *1981;* Shafiq & Co, 1 Lark Street, BOLTON, BL1 2UA.
SHAFIQUE, Mr. Salahuddin Mohammed, FCA *1974;* 5 Clarence Road, WALLINGTON, SURREY, SM6 0EW.
SHAFIQUE, Mr. Sofian, BA ACA *2005;* 19 Burford Gardens, LONDON, N13 4LR.
SHAFRAN, Mr. Michael Alan, BSc FCA *1960;* Longbourne, 11 Totteridge Common, Totteridge, LONDON, N20 8LR. (Life Member)
SHAFRAN, Ms. Victoria Constance, BSc ACA *1993;* 16 Greenhalgh Walk, LONDON, N2 0DJ.
SHAFTESLEY, Mr. Colin Stuart, BA FCA FHKSA *1988;* PricewaterhouseCoopers, Prince's Building, 22/F, 10 Chater Road, CENTRAL, HONG KONG ISLAND HONG KONG SAR.
SHAFTO, Miss. Catharine Vanessa, BA ACA *1998;* 79 Halsbury Road, Westbury Park, BRISTOL, BS6 7ST.
•**SHAFTO, The Revd. Robert James, MA BTh FCA** *1961;* OJK (Audit) Limited, 19 Portland Place, LONDON, W1B 1PX. See also O J Kilkenny & Co Ltd
SHAH, Mrs. Aarti, BSc ACA *2004;* 13 Mount Drive, HARROW, MIDDLESEX, HA2 7RW.
SHAH, Ms. Aarti Rameshchandra, MChem ACA *2005;* 13308 Lake George Lane, TAMPA, FL 33618, UNITED STATES.
•**SHAH, Mr. Aashish, BA ACA** *1997;* Ashdene Accountancy Limited, 17 Thorndene Avenue, LONDON, N11 1ET.
SHAH, Mr. Aashish, BSc ACA *2000;* 30 Chase Way, Southgate, LONDON, N14 5DE.
SHAH, Mr. Aashit Kiran Hirji, BA ACA *1989;* 3 Links Drive, Elstree, BOREHAMWOOD, HERTFORDSHIRE, WD6 3PP.
SHAH, Mr. Abhinav Kumar, BSc(Hons) ACA *2001;* 2 Willoughby Road, LONDON, NW3 1SA.
SHAH, Mr. Adarsh, BA ACA *2010;* 68 Carlton Avenue, HARROW, MIDDLESEX, HA3 8AY.
SHAH, Mr. Adarsh, BSc ACA *1999;* 86 Hartland Drive, EDGWARE, MIDDLESEX, HA8 8RH.
SHAH, Miss. Adelita Adriana, BA ACA *2005;* 23 West Street, Upton, NORTHAMPTON, NN5 4EP.
SHAH, Mr. Ahmed, BSc ACA *2011;* Flat 6, 169 George Street, LONDON, W1H 5LA.
SHAH, Mr. Ajitkumar Premchand Jiveraj, FCA *1971;* 25 Riverside Drive, PO Box 42435-00100, NAIROBI, KENYA.
SHAH, Mr. Akhil, BSc ACA *1990;* 184 Ealing Road, WEMBLEY, MIDDLESEX, HA0 4QD.
SHAH, Mrs. Akshi C, BSc ACA *2007;* 50 Walmington Fold, Woodside Park, LONDON, N12 7LL.
SHAH, Mr. Alkesh Suryakant, BSc ACA *2004;* (Tax Fac), 8 Arlington Road, Southgate, LONDON, N14 5AR.
SHAH, Mr. Alok Ramniklal, OM BSc ACA MSI *2001;* 16 Cranbourne Court, Briar Close, LONDON, N2 0SD.
SHAH, Mrs. Alpa, BSc(Hons) ACA *2002;* 42 Woodside Avenue, LONDON, N12 8AX.
SHAH, Mrs. Alpa N, BSc(Hons) ACA *2000;* 14 Huntsmans Gate, South Bretton, PETERBOROUGH, PE3 9AU.
SHAH, Mr. Amar, BSc ACA *2008;* 55 Wentworth Avenue, LONDON, N3 1YN.
SHAH, Mr. Amit, BSc ACA *2004;* 12 sovereign court, unwin way, STANMORE, MIDDLESEX, ha71fh.
SHAH, Mr. Amit, ACA *2009;* 8 Dollis Avenue, LONDON, N3 1TX.
SHAH, Mr. Amit Mulji, LLB FCA *1984;* 34 Drax Avenue, Wimbledon, LONDON, SW20 0EJ.
•**SHAH, Mr. Amit Ratilal, ACA FCCA** *2009;* Nyman Libson Paul, Regina House, 124 Finchley Road, LONDON, NW3 5JS.
SHAH, Mr. Amrish, BA ACA *1992;* 44 Grange Close, WATFORD, WD17 4HQ.

•**SHAH, Mr. Amrish Kanubhai, BSc FCA** *1984;* with Grant Thornton UK LLP, Churchill House, Chalvey Road East, SLOUGH, SL1 2LS.

SHAH, Mr. Anandbabu Dineshkumar, BA(Hons) ACA *2001;* 27 Flint Way, ST. ALBANS, AL3 6DU.

SHAH, Mr. Aneet, BSc FCA *1994;* 53 Ridge Lane, WATFORD, WD17 4SX.

SHAH, Mr. Anil Kumar Laxmichand, BSc FCA *1977;* Fisatex (K) Ltd., Post Box 41285, NAIROBI, 00100, KENYA.

•**SHAH, Mr. Anilkumar Jayantilal, FCA** *1973;* A J Shah & Company, 8 Pinner View, HARROW, HA1 4QA.

SHAH, Mr. Anish, BSc(Hons) ACA *2010;* 6 Newnham Way, Kenton, HARROW, MIDDLESEX, HA3 9NT.

SHAH, Mr. Anish, BSc ACA *2006;* 14 Eastern Avenue, PINNER, MIDDLESEX, HA5 1NP.

SHAH, Miss. Anisha, BSc ACA *2010;* 17 Dukes Avenue, HARROW, MIDDLESEX, HA1 1XP.

SHAH, Miss. Anisha Hematlal, ACA *2010;* 45 Hillside Gardens, EDGWARE, MIDDLESEX, HA8 8HA.

SHAH, Miss. Anjali, BSc ACA *2005;* 2 Royston Park Road, Hatch End, PINNER, HA5 4AD.

SHAH, Miss. Anjana, BA ACA *1991;* 12 Chantry Close, Kenton, HARROW, MIDDLESEX, HA3 9QZ.

SHAH, Mr. Anjul Mansukhlal, BSc ACA *1999;* 79 Springfield Mount, Kingsbury, LONDON, NW9 0SD.

SHAH, Mr. Ankit, ACA *2011;* 16 Lancaster Road, Didsbury, MANCHESTER, M20 2QU.

SHAH, Mr. Anuj, BSc ACA *1998;* 1 Northolm, EDGWARE, HA8 9RL.

SHAH, Miss. Anuksha, ACA *2009;* Deloitte & Touche Hill House, 1 Little New Street, LONDON, EC4A 3TR.

SHAH, Mr. Anup, BSc ACA *1994;* Metropolitan Housing Trust Ltd Cambridge House, 109 Mayes Road, LONDON, N22 6UR.

•**SHAH, Mr. Anup, BSc ACA CF** *1992;* Deloitte LLP, Athene Place, 66 Shoe Lane, LONDON, EC4A 3BQ. See also Deloitte & Touche LLP

SHAH, Mr. Anup Zaverchand, ACA *1981;* Safiri Textiles Ltd., P. O. Box 70656-00400, NAIROBI, KENYA.

SHAH, Mrs. Anupa Tanna, BSc ACA *2004;* CCI Chambers, 32 Dinshaw Wachha Road, Churchgate, MUMBAI 400020, MAHARASHTRA, INDIA.

SHAH, Miss. Arpna, ACA *2008;* Flat 209, 6 Naoroji Street, LONDON, WC1X 0GD.

SHAH, Mr. Arun Harakhchand Meghji, BSc FCA *1977;* Weingeist Ltd, 15 Station Parade, Cockfosters, BARNET, HERTFORDSHIRE, EN4 0DL.

SHAH, Mr. Arvind Kumar Velji, FCA *1974;* (Tax Fac), 50 Craigweil Avenue, RADLETT, HERTFORDSHIRE, WD7 7EY.

•**SHAH, Mr. Arvind Raichand, FCA** *1983;* Elliotts Shah, 2nd Floor, York House, 23 Kingsway, LONDON, WC2B 6UJ.

SHAH, Miss. Asha, ACA *2007;* Flat 16 Ballota Court, 1 Fortune Avenue, EDGWARE, MIDDLESEX, HA8 0FD.

SHAH, Mr. Ashik Pethraj, BA ACA *1994;* Virgin Management Ltd The School House, 50 Brook Green, LONDON, W6 7RR.

SHAH, Mr. Ashit Gulabchand, ACA *2007;* 38 The Hollies, Oakleigh Park North, LONDON, N20 9HD.

•**SHAH, Mr. Ashok Kawas, BSc FCA** *1983;* (Tax Fac), Ash & Co Accountants Ltd, Acorn House, 74-94 Cherry Orchard Road, CROYDON, SURREY, CR9 6DA.

SHAH, Mr. Ashok Vaghji Karamshi, FCA *1974;* 2 Haywood Park, RICKMANSWORTH, HERTFORDSHIRE, WD3 5DR.

SHAH, Mr. Ashokkumar Maganlal, ACA *1978;* 43 Whiteleaf Crescent, SCARBOROUGH M1V 3G1, ON, CANADA.

•①**SHAH, Mr. Ashvinkumar Meghji Karman, FCA** *1973;* (Tax Fac), KLSA LLP, 28-30 St John's Square, LONDON, EC1M 4DN.

•**SHAH, Mr. Ashvinrai Govindji Shamat, FCA** *1966;* (Tax Fac), Walters Shah, Unit B, 15 Bell Yard Mews, LONDON, SE1 3TY.

SHAH, Mr. Ashwin Motichand, ACA *1982;* Tudor House, 185 Kenton Road, Kenton, HARROW, MIDDLESEX, HA3 0EY.

SHAH, Dr. Atul Keshavji, PhD BSc ACA *1986;* 9 Redmill, COLCHESTER, ESSEX, CO3 4RT.

SHAH, Mr. Avinash, FCA *1965;* Avinash Shah & Co, P O Box 48716, NAIROBI, 00-100, KENYA. (Life Member)

SHAH, Mr. Baijul Arun, BSc FCA *1995;* 8 Hillside Rise, NORTHWOOD, HA6 1RR.

SHAH, Mr. Bakul Ramji, BSc ACA *1987;* 19 Highview Ave, EDGWARE, HA8 9TX.

SHAH, Mrs. Baldip Kaur, ACA *2005;* 11 Eaves Close, ADDLESTONE, SURREY, KT15 2BF.

SHAH, Mrs. Bansi, BA ACA *2005;* 52 Byron Avenue, LONDON, E18 2HQ.

SHAH, Miss. Bansi, BSc ACA *2010;* Bakkavor Pizza, 10-21 Forward Drive, HARROW, HA3 8NT.

SHAH, Miss. Beena, BSc ACA *1993;* 20 Corey Court, SAN RAMON, CA 94583, UNITED STATES.

SHAH, Mr. Bhagesh, ACA *2009;* 7 Eustace Road, ROMFORD, RM6 6JR.

SHAH, Mr. Bharat, BA ACA FCCA *2009;* 11 High Street, WEMBLEY, HA9 8DD.

SHAH, Mr. Bharat Hirji, ACA *1983;* P C Harrington Formwork Ltd, 19 Witley Gardens, SOUTHALL, MIDDLESEX, UB2 4ES.

•**SHAH, Mr. Bharat Punja Merag, FCA** *1977;* Bharat Shah & Co, 786 London Road, THORNTON HEATH, SURREY, CR7 6JB.

SHAH, Mrs. Bharti, BSc ACA *1993;* 41 Edgwarebury Lane, EDGWARE, MIDDLESEX, HA8 8LJ.

SHAH, Mr. Bhavesh, BSc(Econ) ACA *1996;* 44 Ringwood Way, Winchmore HIll, LONDON, N21 2QX.

SHAH, Mr. Bhavin Bimal, BA ACA *1998;* 24 Uxendon Crescent, WEMBLEY, HA9 9TN.

SHAH, Mr. Bhavin Chandrakant, BSc ACA *1996;* 35 Old Orchard Road, RIVERSIDE, CT 06878, UNITED STATES.

SHAH, Mr. Bhavin Manish, ACA *2008;* Flat 9 Latimer Place, 40 Eastbury Avenue, NORTHWOOD, MIDDLESEX, HA6 3FD.

SHAH, Mr. Bhavin Shantilal, BA ACA *1996;* 4 River Close, RETFORD, NOTTINGHAMSHIRE, DN22 6TE.

SHAH, Mrs. Bhavini, BSc FCA *1999;* Talbot Underwriting Ltd 8th floor, 60 Threadneedle Street, LONDON, EC2R 8HP.

SHAH, Mrs. Bhavna, BSc ACA *1992;* 44 Grange Close, WATFORD, WD17 4HQ.

SHAH, Mr. Bhupesh Devraj, BSc ACA *1990;* Gudsons, 230 Regents Park Road, LONDON, N3 3HP.

SHAH, Mrs. Bibi Shamim, ACA *1979;* (Tax Fac), 68 Devonshire Road, LONDON, SW19 2EF.

SHAH, Mr. Bijal, BSc ACA *1992;* 43375 Hay Road, ASHBURN, VA 20147, UNITED STATES.

•①**SHAH, Mr. Bijal Ramniklal, BSc ACA** *1990;* Shasens & Re10 (South East) Ltd, 165 High Street, RICKMANSWORTH, HERTFORDSHIRE, WD3 1AY. See also Shasens

SHAH, Mr. Bijal Ratilal, BSc ACA *1993;* National Pharmacy Association, Mallinson House, 40-42 St. Peters Street, ST. ALBANS, HERTFORDSHIRE, AL1 3NP.

SHAH, Mr. Bijesh Mansukhlal, BSc ACA *1994;* Steelwool (Africa) Ltd, PO Box 10105 (GPO), NAIROBI, 00100, KENYA.

SHAH, Mr. Bimal, BA ACA ATII *1989;* (Tax Fac), 2 East Towers, PINNER, HA5 1TL.

SHAH, Mr. Bimal, LLB ACA *2000;* 262 Sandridge Road, ST. ALBANS, HERTFORDSHIRE, AL1 4AJ.

SHAH, Mrs. Bindi, ACA *2005;* 7 Uxendon Crescent, WEMBLEY, MIDDLESEX, HA9 9TW.

SHAH, Mr. Binit, BSc ACA *2011;* Flat 51, Moineau, The Concourse, LONDON, NW9 5UR.

SHAH, Miss. Binni Navin, BSc ACA *1995;* 89 Kilkenny Circle, WA 6152 ERFORD, WA 6152, AUSTRALIA.

SHAH, Mr. Bipin Chandra, BSc ACA *1992;* 9 Beaufort Avenue, HARROW, HA3 8PF.

SHAH, Mr. Biren, BA FCA *1995;* with Deloitte LLP, Stonecutter Court, 1 Stonecutter Street, LONDON, EC4A 4TR.

SHAH, Mr. Chandrakant Gosar Meghan, FCA *1965;* 13 Brampton Grove, HARROW, HA3 8LD. (Life Member)

•**SHAH, Mr. Chandrakant Hansraj Kalidas, FCA** *1969;* Ashford & Partners, 2nd Floor, Kings House, 202 Lower High Street, WATFORD, WD17 2EH.

SHAH, Mr. Chandrakant Velji, FCA *1968;* The Regal Press Kenya Ltd, P.O. Box 46166, NAIROBI, 00100 GPO, KENYA. (Life Member)

•**SHAH, Mr. Chandrakirti Liladhar, FCA** *1974;* Chandra Shah & Co, 64 Belmont Lane, STANMORE, MIDDLESEX, HA7 2PZ.

•**SHAH, Mrs. Chandrikaben, FCA** *1976;* Shah Dodhia & Co, 173 Cleveland Street, LONDON, W1T 6QR.

SHAH, Mrs. Charulata Ramchand, FCA *1975;* 33019 Brockway Street, UNION CITY, CA 94587, UNITED STATES.

•**SHAH, Mr. Chetan, BSc ACA** *1992;* 25 Friern Mount Drive, LONDON, N20 9DP.

SHAH, Mr. Chinan, BA ACA *2002;* 6 Abbots Place, BOREHAMWOOD, HERTFORDSHIRE, WD6 5QP.

SHAH, Mr. Chirag Ratilal, BEng ACA *2005;* 168 Crescent Road, New Barnet, BARNET, EN4 9RS.

•**SHAH, Mr. Darsh Kirtikumar, BSc(Hons) ACA** *2002;* Adler Shine LLP, Aston House, Cornwall Avenue, LONDON, N3 1LF.

SHAH, Mrs. Darshana, BSc ACA *1991;* 8A Derwent Avenue, PINNER, HA5 4QJ.

SHAH, Mr. Deep Arunkumar, MBA BSc ACA *2007;* 51 Lady Aylesford Avenue, STANMORE, MIDDLESEX, HA7 4FG.

SHAH, Miss. Deepa, BA ACA *2001;* 22, Elm Drive, HARROW, HA2 7BS.

•**SHAH, Mr. Deepak Kantilal Amritlal, BSc FCA CF** *1983;* P O Box 39112, NAIROBI, 623, KENYA.

SHAH, Mr. Dharam, BSc(Hons) ACA *2009;* 20 Kenton Avenue, SOUTHALL, MIDDLESEX, UB1 3QF.

SHAH, Mr. Dharmesh, BSc ACA *1995;* 32 Coleshill Place, Bradwell Common, MILTON KEYNES, MK13 8DN.

SHAH, Mr. Dhiraj Kapurchand, BSc(Hons) ACA *2010;* 27 Manor Road, HARROW, MIDDLESEX, HA1 2PF.

•**SHAH, Mr. Dhirajlal Fulchand, FCA** *1986;* (Tax Fac), D.S. & Co, DS House, 306 High Street, CROYDON, CR0 1NG.

SHAH, Mr. Dhirajlal Lakhamshi, FCA *1970;* 24 Kingshill Avenue, HARROW, HA3 8JU.

•**SHAH, Mr. Dhiren Meghji, FCA** *1976;* 21 Hillbury Avenue, Kenton, HARROW, HA3 8EP.

SHAH, Mr. Dhirendra Mulji, BSc ACA *1992;* Baring Investment Services Ltd, 155 Bishopsgate, LONDON, EC2M 3XY.

•**SHAH, Mr. Dhiresh Jayantilal, BSc ACA ATII** *1989;* (Tax Fac), KPMG LLP, 15 Canada Square, LONDON, E14 5GL. See also KPMG Europe LLP

SHAH, Miss. Dhruti, BSc ACA *2011;* 46 Norwood Drive, HARROW, MIDDLESEX, HA2 7PE.

SHAH, Mr. Dhruv Arvind, ACA *2009;* 9 Hallam Gardens, PINNER, HA5 4PT.

SHAH, Mr. Dilip, MA ACA *2001;* 69 Barn Way, WEMBLEY, MIDDLESEX, HA9 9NP.

SHAH, Mr. Dilip Kumar, ACA *1981;* 265 Woodcock Hill, HARROW, HA3 0PG.

SHAH, Mr. Dilip Raichand, FCA *1972;* P.O. Box 42130, NAIROBI, GPO 00100, KENYA.

•**SHAH, Mr. Dilipkumar Rasiklal, BSc FCA** *1973;* Chapmans Associates Ltd, 3 Coombe Road, LONDON, NW10 0EB.

SHAH, Miss. Dimple, BSc ACA *2007;* 79 Carlton Avenue East, WEMBLEY, HA9 8LZ.

SHAH, Miss. Dina Vinodrai, ACA *1987;* 4 Marlborough, 38/40 Maida Vale, LONDON, W9 1RW.

SHAH, Mr. Dinashlal, FCA *1972;* P O Box 39427, Parklands, NAIROBI, 00623, KENYA. (Life Member)

•**SHAH, Mr. Dinesh Ambalal, BCom FCA** *1975;* (Tax Fac), A.M. Shah & Sons, 211 Signal House, 16 Lyon Road, HARROW, HA1 2AQ.

•**SHAH, Mr. Dineshchandra Mulchand, FCA** *1973;* D.M. Shah, 3 Alicia Avenue, Kenton, HARROW, HA3 8HW.

•**SHAH, Mr. Dineshkumar Depar, BA FCA** *1978;* Peer Roberts Limited, The Pavilion, 56 Rosslyn Crescent, HARROW, MIDDLESEX, HA1 2SZ.

SHAH, Mr. Dineshkumar Zaverchand, FCA *1968;* 187 Kenton Lane, HARROW, HA3 8TL. (Life Member)

SHAH, Mrs. Dipa, BSc ACA *1999;* 10 Regents Close, RADLETT, HERTFORDSHIRE, WD7 7DB.

SHAH, Miss. Dipa, LLB ACA *2003;* 6 Crawford Gardens, Palmers Green, LONDON, N13 5TD.

SHAH, Mr. Dipak Fulchand, ACA *1985;* P.O. BOX 48527, NAIROBI, 00100, KENYA.

SHAH, Mr. Dipak Keshavlal, MBA BSc ACA *1982;* 38 Eastbury Road, NORTHWOOD, HA6 3AW.

•**SHAH, Mr. Dipak Kumar, ACA** *1983;* D. Shah & Co, 40 Annesmere Grove, STANMORE, MIDDLESEX, HA7 1PA.

•**SHAH, Mr. Dipakkumar Umedchand, FCA** *1977;* Nielsens, 453 Cranbrook Road, ILFORD, ESSEX, IG2 6EW.

SHAH, Mr. Dipan Chandrakant, BSc ACA *2004;* Flat 10 Lime Court, Gayton Road, HARROW, HA1 2YD.

SHAH, Mr. Dipan Mahendra, MBA BA ACA CTA *2006;* (Tax Fac), with PricewaterhouseCoopers LLP, 1 Embankment Place, LONDON, WC2N 6RH.

SHAH, Mr. Dipan Raichand, BSc ACA *1992;* Nyali Cinemax, PO Box 82675, MOMBASA, 80100, KENYA.

SHAH, Mr. Dipen, BSc ACA *1992;* 11 Chestnut Avenue, NORTHWOOD, MIDDLESEX, HA6 1HR.

SHAH, Mr. Dipen, BSc(Hons) ACA *2001;* Icorelate Ltd (MBE), Unit 115, 113 High Street, RUISLIP, MIDDLESEX, HA4 8JN.

SHAH, Mr. Dipen, BSc(Econ) ACA *2001;* Ashwell Dental Surgery, 44 High Street, Ashwell, BALDOCK, HERTFORDSHIRE, SG7 5NR.

SHAH, Mr. Dipen Shantilal Jeshang, BSc FCA *1998;* Allied Irish Banks Plc, St. Helen's, 1 Undershaft, LONDON, EC3A 8AB.

SHAH, Mr. Dipesh, ACA *2009;* 47 Sedgecombe Avenue, HARROW, HA3 0HW.

SHAH, Mrs. Dipika Kantilal, BPharm ACA *1994;* Cavendish House, Reenglass Road, STANMORE, MIDDLESEX, HA7 4NT.

•**SHAH, Mr. Dipun Velji, BSc FCA** *1995;* (Tax Fac), DVS Tax Limited, 13 Hillbury Avenue, Kenton, HARROW, MIDDLESEX, HA3 8EP. See also Tuson & Partners Limited

SHAH, Mr. Divya Kishorchandra, BSc ACA *1993;* 322 Anchorage Drive, MINDARIE, WA 6030, AUSTRALIA.

SHAH, Mr. Fagun, BSc ACA *1999;* 30 Deane Croft Road, PINNER, HA5 1SR.

SHAH, Mr. Hamun, BA(Hons) ACA *2001;* 4 Rixon Close, NORTHAMPTON, NN3 3PF.

•**SHAH, Mr. Harish Hirji, ACA FCCA** *2008;* (Tax Fac), Mccormack & Associates, Euro House, 1394-1400 High Road, LONDON, N20 9BH.

SHAH, Mr. Harish Motichand, FCA *1982;* 22 Brookdene Drive, NORTHWOOD, MIDDLESEX, HA6 3NS.

•**SHAH, Mr. Harish Raichand, FCA** *1977;* PKF Kenya, Jubilee Insurance Building, 3rd Floor, Moi Avenue, PO Box 90553, MOMBASA 80100 KENYA. See also KLSA LLP, KLSA Taxation Services Limited

SHAH, Mr. Harris Rajnikant, BSc ACA *1994;* 12 Bramley Road, LONDON, N14 4HR.

SHAH, Mrs. Harsha, BSc ACA *1993;* 11 Anthorne Close, POTTERS BAR, EN6 1RW.

SHAH, Mr. Harshil, BSc ACA *2006;* Orbit Engineering Ltd, PO Box 13476 - 00800, NAIROBI, KENYA.

•**SHAH, Mr. Hasmukh Devshi Vrajpal, FCA** *1975;* H.D. Shah & Co, 2 The Avenue, WEMBLEY, MIDDLESEX, HA9 9QJ.

SHAH, Miss. Hema, ACA *2011;* 21 Sedgecombe Avenue, HARROW, MIDDLESEX, HA3 0HW.

SHAH, Miss. Hemali, ACA *2011;* 10 Hall Farm Close, STANMORE, MIDDLESEX, HA7 4JT.

SHAH, Mr. Hemel Arvinlal, BSc ACA *1998;* (Tax Fac), Congress House, 14 Lyon Road, HARROW, MIDDLESEX, HA1 2EN.

SHAH, Mr. Hemendra Laxmidas, ACA *1980;* Deloitte Haskins & Sells, 12 Dr Annie Besant Road, Opp. Shiv Sagar Estate, Worli, MUMBAI 400 018, INDIA.

SHAH, Mr. Hemendra Natwerlal, BSc FCA *1978;* 4454 Autumnwood Lane, VICTORIA V8X 4V8, BC, CANADA.

SHAH, Mr. Hilesh Chandrakant, BA(Hons) ACA *2003;* 13 Alicia Close, HARROW, HA3 8HP.

SHAH, Mr. Hillen, BA ACA *1992;* 22 St. Leonards Avenue, LONDON, E4 9QX.

SHAH, Mr. Hiten, BSc FCA *1995;* 50 London Road, STANMORE, MIDDLESEX, HA7 4NU.

SHAH, Mr. Hitesh, BSc ACA *2005;* Link Financial Outsourcing Ltd, Camelford House, 89 Albert Embankment, LONDON, SE1 7TP.

•**SHAH, Mr. Hitesh Chandra, FCA** *1988;* Flemmings, 76 Canterbury Road, CROYDON, SURREY, CR0 3HA.

SHAH, Mr. Hitesh Dhanji, BA ACA *1984;* 57 Crosthwait Circle, Tapping, PERTH, WA 6065, AUSTRALIA.

SHAH, Mr. Hursh, BA(Econ) ACA *2002;* The British Land Co Ltd York House, 45 Seymour Street, LONDON, W1H 7LX.

SHAH, Mr. Indukumar Ambalal, FCA FTII *1973;* Tanglewood, Ashdown Place, FOREST ROW, RH18 5LP.

SHAH, Mr. Jai Rajni, BSc ACA *2007;* 36 Gorseway, HATFIELD, HERTFORDSHIRE, AL10 9GS.

SHAH, Mr. Jaimin, ACA *2008;* 35 Icknield Way, LUTON, LU3 2BT.

SHAH, Mr. Jaimin Jayantilal, BSc ACA *1992;* 41 Edgwarebury Lane, EDGWARE, MIDDLESEX, HA8 8LJ.

SHAH, Mrs. Jaishri, ACA *1983;* 1 Airfield Park, Donnybrook, DUBLIN 4, COUNTY DUBLIN, IRELAND.

SHAH, Miss. Jalpa, ACA *2009;* 122 Prince George Avenue, LONDON, N14 4TA.

SHAH, Mr. Janak Bhaichand, FCA *1973;* 776 Kilbirnie Drive, NEPEAN K2J 0M3, ON, CANADA.

SHAH, Mr. Jay, BSc ACA *2010;* Apartment 1302, Twin Towers, Baniyas Road, Deira, PO Box 46482, DUBAI UNITED ARAB EMIRATES.

•**SHAH, Mr. Jay Kantilal, BSc ACA** *1992;* Kajaine Limited, First Floor, Alpine House, Unit 2, Honeypot Lane, LONDON NW9 9RX. See also Knav UK Limited

•**SHAH, Mr. Jayendra, ACA** *1986;* (Tax Fac), Montpelier Professional (West End) Ltd, 58/60 Berners Street, LONDON, W1T 3JS.

•**SHAH, Mrs. Jayshree, BSc ACA** *1999;* Jen Consulting Ltd, 30 Deane Croft Road, PINNER, MIDDLESEX, HA5 1SR.

SHAH, Mr. Jayu Amratlal, BA ACA *1993;* Chevron Australia Pty ltd, 250 St. Georges Terrace, PERTH, WA 6000, AUSTRALIA.

SHAH, Mr. Jinal, BA ACA *2002;* Flat 11, Harestone Court, 45 Normanton Road, SOUTH CROYDON, SURREY, CR2 7AF.

SHAH, Mr. Jinesh, BSc ACA *1987;* 69 Highland Drive, BUSHEY, WD23 4HH.

SHAH, Mr. Jinit, ACA *2008;* 4 Glebe Crescent, HARROW, MIDDLESEX, HA3 9LD.

SHAH, Mr. Jiten Jayendrakumar, BSc ACA *2008;* 54 Whitchurch Gardens, EDGWARE, HA8 6PD.

•**SHAH, Mr. Jitendra Meghji, FCA** *1973;* (Tax Fac), J.M. Shah & Company, 24 Old Bond Street, LONDON, W1S 4AP.

SHAH, Mr. Jitesh, BSc ACA *1991;* with PricewaterhouseCoopers-Qatar LLC, PO Box 6689, Tornado Tower, West Bay, DOHA, QATAR.

SHAH, Miss. Julie Mahendra, BSc ACA *2004;* with PricewaterhouseCoopers LLP, The Atrium, 1 Harefield Road, UXBRIDGE, UB8 1EX.

SHAH, Miss. Kajal, BSc ACA *2006;* 16 The Hollies, Christchurch Avenue, HARROW, MIDDLESEX, HA3 8NX.

•**SHAH, Mr. Kalpesh Navinchandra, ACA FCCA** *2007;* KNS Limited, 11 Trinity Close, NORTHWOOD, MIDDLESEX, HA6 2AF.

•**SHAH, Mr. Kamal Somchand, BA ACA ATII** *1986;* KSEG, Belfry House, Champions Way, Hendon, LONDON, NW4 1PX.

SHAH, Mr. Kamalkumar Devshi Shamat, FCA *1971;* P.O. BOX 80899-80100, MOMBASA, KENYA.

SHAH, Mr. Kamalnayan Popatlal Ranmal, BSc ACA *1981;* 13 Moor Park Road, NORTHWOOD, MIDDLESEX, HA6 2DL.

SHAH, Mr. Kamil, BSc(Hons) ACA *2010;* 68 Hartland Drive, EDGWARE, MIDDLESEX, HA8 8RH.

•**SHAH, Mr. Kanaiyalal Kashalchand Jagjivan, FCA** *1967;* (Tax Fac), RBS Accountants Limited, Suite 16, Beaufort Court, Admirals Way, LONDON, E14 9XL. See also PAAM THIRTEEN LIMITED

SHAH, Mrs. Kanta Ratilal, FCA *1975;* 7 The Avenue, WEMBLEY, HA9 9QH.

•**SHAH, Mr. Kanubhai Nagindas, FCA** *1967;* (Tax Fac), K.N. Shah & Co, 232a Northolt Road, HARROW, MIDDLESEX, HA2 8DU.

SHAH, Mr. Kapoor Devchand, FCA *1970;* 15 Engel Park, Mill Hill, LONDON, NW7 2HE.

SHAH, Mr. Kaushik, BSc FCA FCMA *1984;* 105 Fleetside, WEST MOLESEY, KT8 2NQ.

SHAH, Mr. Kaushik Bhimji, MBS FCA *1975;* Mabati Rolling Mills Ltd, PO Box 271, Athi River, NAIROBI, 00204, KENYA.

•**SHAH, Mr. Kaushik Kanji, BA FCA** *1984;* (Tax Fac), Deitch Cooper, 54-58 High Street, EDGWARE, HA8 7EJ.

SHAH, Mr. Kaushik Muljibhai, BA FCA IMC *1982;* Pramerica Real Estate Investores Ltd, Grand Buildings, 1-3 Strand, LONDON, WC2N 5HR.

SHAH, Mr. Kavit, BSc ACA *2002;* 46 Jubilee Drive, RUISLIP, MIDDLESEX, HA4 0PQ.

SHAH, Mr. Kavit, BSc ACA *2010;* Flat 14, The Galleries, 9 Abbey Road, LONDON, NW8 9AQ.

SHAH, Mr. Kekul, BSc ACA *2006;* 65 Du Cros Drive, STANMORE, MIDDLESEX, HA7 4TL.

SHAH, Mr. Kenil, BSc ACA *2008;* with Mazars LLP, Tower Bridge House, St. Katharines Way, LONDON, E1W 1DD.

SHAH, Mr. Ketan, BSc ACA *1992;* 77 Hartland Drive, EDGWARE, MIDDLESEX, HA8 8RJ.

•**SHAH, Mr. Ketan, BSc FCA MBA** *1995;* Tax Assist Accountants, 121 Dugdale Hill Lane, POTTERS BAR, HERTFORDSHIRE, EN6 2DS.

SHAH, Mr. Ketan Bhupendra, BSocSc ACA *1996;* J P Morgan Chase, 10 Aldermanbury, LONDON, EC2V 7RF.

•**SHAH, Mr. Ketan Dipchand, BA FCA** *1991;* KLSA LLP, 28-30 St John's Square, LONDON, EC1M 4DN. See also KLSA Taxation Services Limited

SHAH, Mr. Ketan Kantilal, BSc ACA *2006;* CB Richard Ellis, St. Martins Court, 10 Paternoster Row, LONDON, EC4M 7HP.

•**SHAH, Mr. Ketan Kumar, BSc FCA** *1996;* with RBS Accountants Limited, Suite 16, Beaufort Court, Admirals Way, LONDON, E14 9XL.

SHAH, Mr. Ketan Pravin, BA(Hons) ACA *2001;* (Tax Fac), with BDO LLP, 55 Baker Street, LONDON, W1U 7EU.

SHAH, Mr. Ketul Chandulal, BSc ACA *2010;* Flat 4, Block C, 27 Green Walk, LONDON, SE1 4TQ.

SHAH, Mr. Ketul Shantilal, BSc ACA *2004;* P.O.Box 28226, 00200, NAIROBI, 00200, KENYA.

SHAH, Mr. Keval Ashok, BSc ACA *2008;* 27 Kembla Circle, MADELEY, WA 6065, AUSTRALIA.

SHAH, Mr. Keval Manilal, BSc(Econ) ACA *1995;* 92 Waterfall Road, LONDON, N14 7JT.

SHAH, Mr. Khilan, ACA *2009;* with Ernst & Young LLP, 1 More London Place, LONDON, SE1 2AF.

SHAH, Mr. Khilan Rameshlal, BSc(Hons) ACA *2001;* 39 Elm Park, STANMORE, MIDDLESEX, HA7 4AU.

SHAH, Mr. Khilan Yashvant, BSc(Econ) ACA *2002;* Tax Computer Systems Ltd, Centurion House, London Road, STAINES, MIDDLESEX, TW18 4AX.

SHAH, Miss. Khilna, BSc ACA *2011;* 37 Benton Road, ILFORD, ESSEX, IG1 4AU.

SHAH, Miss. Khiloni Arun, ACA *2009;* Flat 12, Nash Court, 2 Nash Way, Kenton, HARROW, MIDDLESEX HA3 0ST.

SHAH, Mr. Khwaja Mansoor Mukhtar, FCA *1956;* 22A Central Avenue, Defence Housing Authority, Phase II, KARACHI, PAKISTAN. (Life Member)

SHAH, Mr. Kinner, BSc ACA *2006;* 114 Green Lane, EDGWARE, MIDDLESEX, HA8 8EJ.

SHAH, Mr. Kiran, BSc FCA *1976;* Kiran Shah, C/O Printpak S.A., 88 Route de Frontenex, 1208 GENEVA, SWITZERLAND.

SHAH, Mr. Kiran Navinchandra, BA ACA *1996;* 12 Bulmer Gardens, HARROW, MIDDLESEX, HA3 0PA.

SHAH, Mr. Kiren Narshi, BA ACA *1985;* Fairbourne, 74 Gordon Avenue, STANMORE, HA7 3QS.

•**SHAH, Mr. Kirit Nataverlal, ACA** *1980;* 85 Shirland Road, LONDON, W9 2EL.

SHAH, Mr. Kirtan Amichand, BSc ACA *2005;* Flat 53 Solomons Court, 451 High Road, LONDON, N12 0AW.

SHAH, Mr. Kirti Ratilal, BA ACA *1991;* Laing Investment Management Services Ltd Allington House, 150 Victoria Street, LONDON, SW1E 5LB.

•**SHAH, Mr. Kishorilal, BSc(Econ) ACA** *1986;* (Tax Fac), PK Audit LLP, 22 The Quadrant, RICHMOND, SURREY, TW9 1BP. See also PK Partners LLP

•**SHAH, Mrs. Kokila, ACA** *1982;* (Tax Fac), 21 Hillbury Avenue, HARROW, MIDDLESEX, HA3 8EP.

SHAH, Mrs. Kosha, ACA *2009;* Flat 4, Greenhill Mansions, 11 Gayton Road, HARROW, MIDDLESEX, HA1 2HQ.

SHAH, Mr. Krishan, BA ACA *2010;* Flat 8 Axis Court, High Mead, HARROW, MIDDLESEX, HA1 2TJ.

SHAH, Mrs. Krishna, BSc ACA *1991;* P.O. Box 1157, NAIROBI, 00606, KENYA.

SHAH, Miss. Krishna, BSc ACA *2007;* 29 Lindsay Drive, Kenton, HARROW, HA3 0TA.

SHAH, Mr. Kumar, MA ACA *2003;* 80 Shakespeare Road, LONDON, W7 1LS.

SHAH, Mr. Kunjal Kantilal, BA ACA *1997;* Cavendish House, Reenglass Road, STANMORE, MIDDLESEX, HA7 4NT.

•**SHAH, Mr. Lalit, ACA** *1988;* Thakrar Coombs & Co, The Dairy House, Moneyrow Green, Holyport, MAIDENHEAD, SL6 2ND.

SHAH, Miss. Lina, BSc ACA *1994;* 6 Bourne End Road, NORTHWOOD, MIDDLESEX, HA6 3BS.

•**SHAH, Mr. Mahendra Nemchand, FCA** *1972;* M N. Shah, PO Box 59832, City Square Post Office, NAIROBI, KENYA.

SHAH, Mr. Maheschandra Raichand Punja, FCA *1976;* 27 Tyrone Road, Thorpe Bay, SOUTHEND-ON-SEA, SS1 3HE.

SHAH, Mr. Mahesh Shantilal, BA ACA *1990;* (Tax Fac), The Gate House, 1 Devonshire Road, Hatch End, HARROW, HA5 4LY.

SHAH, Mr. Maheshkumar Vaghji, BA FCA *1978;* 68 Hartland Drive, EDGWARE, MIDDLESEX, HA8 8RH.

•**SHAH, Mr. Manesh, BA ACA** *1991;* P.S.J. Alexander & Co, 1 Doughty Street, LONDON, WC1N 2PH. See also Abott Secretaries Ltd, Patel, Shah & Joshi

SHAH, Mr. Manish Hansraj, BA ACA *1982;* 1 St. Martins, Repton House, Batchworth Lane, NORTHWOOD, MIDDLESEX, HA6 2BP.

SHAH, Mr. Manish Ratilal, MBA BSc FCA *1993;* Deloitte LLP, Athene Place, 66 Shoe Lane, LONDON, EC4A 3BQ. See also Deloitte & Touche LLP

SHAH, Mr. Manoj Dinubhai, BSc ACA *1993;* 39 Jellicoe Gardens, STANMORE, MIDDLESEX, HA7 3NS.

SHAH, Dr. Manoj Kantilal, ACA *1991;* Shanta Nivas, Sandy Lane, NORTHWOOD, HA6 3ES.

SHAH, Mr. Manshukhlal, FCA *1977;* 10 Lyon Meade, STANMORE, MIDDLESEX, HA7 1JA.

SHAH, Mr. Mansoor Ahmed, FCA *1974;* 4 Santos Road, LONDON, SW18 1NS.

SHAH, Mr. Mansukhlal Kanji Shamat, BA FCA *1966;* 5 Windermere Avenue, WEMBLEY, HA9 8SH.

SHAH, Mrs. Meera, BA(Econ) ACA *2004;* 13 Dovedale Avenue, HARROW, MIDDLESEX, HA3 0DX.

SHAH, Miss. Meera Mohanlal, BSc ACA *1997;* 7 Myddleton Close, STANMORE, MIDDLESEX, HA7 4WL.

SHAH, Mr. Mehul, BSc FCA *1996;* 62 Medway Court, Judd Street, LONDON, WC1H 9QZ.

SHAH, Mrs. Melina, ACA *1996;* 4 Wensley Close, Friern Barnet, LONDON, N11 3GU.

SHAH, Mr. Mihir, ACA *2011;* Flat 2, Lime Court, Gayton Road, HARROW, MIDDLESEX, HA1 2YD.

•**SHAH, Mr. Milan Chandrakant, BSc ACA** *2007;* 19 Fitzroy Square, LONDON, W1T 6EQ.

•**SHAH, Mrs. Minakshi Narendra, FCA** *1984;* Shah And Shin, 42a The Broadway, Joel Street, NORTHWOOD, MIDDLESEX, HA6 1PA.

SHAH, Mrs. Minal, BSc ACA *1986;* Europcar UK Ltd, Aldenham Road, BUSHEY, WD23 2QQ.

SHAH, Mr. Minal Nalin, MA ACA CFA *2001;* with PricewaterhouseCoopers, 1 Embankment Place, LONDON, WC2N 6RH.

SHAH, Mrs. Mita, BA ACA *1992;* 8 Hillside Gardens, EDGWARE, HA8 8HE.

•**SHAH, Mrs. Mita Rajni, FCA CTA** *1984;* Chamberlains UK LLP, 173-175 Cleveland Street, LONDON, W1T 6QR.

SHAH, Mr. Miten Amichand, MSc BSc(Hons) ACA *2010;* 36 Crowshott Avenue, STANMORE, MIDDLESEX, HA7 1HX.

SHAH, Mr. Mitesh Ratilal, BA ACA *1993;* 12 St. Mirren Court 28 Richmond Road New Barnet, BARNET, HERTFORDSHIRE, EN5 1SD.

•**SHAH, Mr. Muhammed Parvez, ACA** *2010;* Saga Business Solutions Limited, Unit 5, 20 High Street, LONDON, E15 2PP.

•**SHAH, Mr. Mukesh Keshavji, BSc ACA** *1982;* FisherEase Limited, Acre House, 3-5 Hyde Road, WATFORD, WD17 4WP.

SHAH, Mr. Mukesh Liladhar, ACA *1982;* 21 Bulmer Gardens, Kenton, HARROW, MIDDLESEX, HA3 0PA.

SHAH, Mr. Mukesh Nathoobhai, ACA *1980;* 66 Avondale Avenue, North Finchley, LONDON, N12 8EN.

SHAH, Mr. Mukeshkumar Keshavlal, ACA *1980;* 22 Sedgecombe Avenue, HARROW, MIDDLESEX, HA3 0HL.

SHAH, Miss. Mumta Shantilal, ACA *2008;* 26 Nathans Road, WEMBLEY, MIDDLESEX, HA0 3RX.

•**SHAH, Mr. Murtaza Ali, BA ACA** *2006;* Cameron & Associates Ltd, 35-37 Lowlands Road, HARROW, MIDDLESEX, HA1 3AW.

•**SHAH, Mr. Nalin Govindji, FCA** *1981;* 11 Longcrofte Road, EDGWARE, HA8 6RR.

SHAH, Mr. Nalin Mansukhlal, FCA *1973;* Deloitte Haskins & Sells, 12 Dr Annie Besant Road, Opp Shiv Sagar Estate, MUMBAI 400 018, INDIA.

•①**SHAH, Mr. Naresh Devchand Pethraj, FCA** *1978;* Lubbock Fine, Russell Bedford House, City Forum, 250 City Road, LONDON, EC1V 2QQ.

SHAH, Mrs. Navdeep Kaur, MSc ACA *2004;* 27 Flint Way, ST. ALBANS, HERTFORDSHIRE, AL3 6DU.

SHAH, Mr. Naveed, BSc ACA MSI *1998;* Flat 8, 36 Frognal, LONDON, NW3 6AG.

•**SHAH, Mr. Navinchandra Chhaganlal, BSc FCA** *1962;* Abott Secretaries Ltd, 1 Doughty Street, LONDON, WC1N 2PH.

•**SHAH, Mr. Navinchandra Dharamshi, FCA ATII** *1979;* (Tax Fac), Vinshaw Limited, 1 Promenade Chambers, 1-8 Edgwarebury Lane, EDGWARE, MIDDLESEX, HA8 7JZ.

SHAH, Mr. Navnitlal Maganlal, FCA *1974;* 12 Southbrook Grove, Great Lever, BOLTON, BL3 2DN. (Life Member)

•**SHAH, Mr. Nayan Manilal, FCA** *1976;* N.M. Shah & Co., Miller House, Rosslyn Crescent, HARROW, MIDDLESEX, HA1 2RZ.

SHAH, Mr. Nayan Premchand Hirji, BA ACA ATII *1992;* 46 Milner Drive, TWICKENHAM, TW2 7PJ.

SHAH, Mr. Neal, BA ACA *2006;* 203/188 Chalmers Street, SURRY HILLS, NSW 2010, AUSTRALIA.

•**SHAH, Mr. Neel Kamal, BSc(Econ) ACA** *2002;* (Tax Fac), Ashford & Partners, 2nd Floor, Kings House, 202 Lower High Street, WATFORD, WD17 2EH.

SHAH, Mr. Neer, BSc ACA *2006;* 55 Anglesmede Crescent, PINNER, MIDDLESEX, HA5 5ST.

SHAH, Mr. Neeraj, BSc(Econ) ACA CF *1996;* KPMG, Private Bag 9, Parkview, JOHANNESBURG, GAUTENG, 2122 SOUTH AFRICA.

SHAH, Miss. Neeta, BSc ACA *2007;* 45 Tudor City Place, Apartment 1211, NEW YORK, NY 10017, UNITED STATES.

SHAH, Mr. Neil Ashok, ACA *2009;* 213 Kenton Lane, Kenton, HARROW, MIDDLESEX, HA3 8TL.

SHAH, Mr. Neil Devchand, BSc ACA *2010;* 3 Bosworth Road, BARNET, HERTFORDSHIRE, EN5 5LZ.

SHAH, Mr. Neten Hirji, BSc ACA *1987;* 150 Beverley Drive, Queensbury, EDGWARE, HA8 5ND.

SHAH, Mr. Nickil Ramesh, BSc ACA *1995;* 30 Cissbury Ring North, Woodside Park, LONDON, N12 7AN.

SHAH, Mr. Nihit Anilbhai, ACA *2004;* ADIA, P.O. BOX 3600, ABU DHABI, UNITED ARAB EMIRATES.

SHAH, Mr. Nikunj Nalin, BSc ACA *1994;* 21A RED, ADIA 211 Corniche, PO Box 3600, ABU DHABI, UNITED ARAB EMIRATES.

SHAH, Miss. Nilam Mansukhlal, BSc ACA *2006;* 11 Prescelly Place, Edgware, HARROW, HA8 6DH.

•**SHAH, Mr. Nilesh, FCA** *1978;* (Tax Fac), Elliotts Shah, 2nd Floor, York House, 23 Kingsway, LONDON, WC2B 6UJ.

•**SHAH, Mr. Nilesh, BA FCA ATII** *1984;* (Tax Fac), Blick Rothenberg, 12 York Gate, Regent's Park, LONDON, NW1 4QS.

SHAH, Mr. Nilesh M, ACA *1984;* Rajni Shah & Company, P O Box 14843, NAIROBI, 00800, KENYA.

SHAH, Mr. Nilesh Prabhulal, FCA *1977;* 38 Foxleys, Carpenders Park, WATFORD, WD19 5DE.

•**SHAH, Mr. Nileshkumar Harakchand, BA ACA** *1982;* (Tax Fac), Ashmar & Co (London) Ltd, Marlborough House, 159 High Street, Wealdstone, HARROW, MIDDLESEX HA3 5DX.

SHAH, Mr. Nileshkumar Nathoo, ACA *1981;* Abbey Stockbrokers Ltd, Kingfisher House, Radford Way, BILLERICAY, ESSEX, CM12 0GZ.

SHAH, Mrs. Nima, MSc BSc ACA *2003;* Egerton Capital, 2 George Yard, Lombard Street, LONDON, EC3V 9DH.

SHAH, Mr. Nimish Jethalal, BSc ACA *1991;* 8a Derwent Avenue, PINNER, MIDDLESEX, HA5 4QJ.

SHAH, Miss. Nirali, BSc ACA *2005;* KPMG, Private Bag 9, Parkview, JOHANNESBURG, GAUTENG, 2122 SOUTH AFRICA.

SHAH, Mr. Nishal Kantilal, MEng ACA *2004;* 83 London Road, STANMORE, MIDDLESEX, HA7 4PB.

SHAH, Miss. Nisheeta Subhash, BSc ACA *2004;* 8 Fortnums Acre, STANMORE, HA7 3NU.

SHAH, Mr. Nishith Gautam, BSc ACA *1996;* P.O. Box 44173, NAIROBI, 00100, KENYA.

SHAH, Miss. Nishma, BSc ACA *2010;* 36 St. Marys Crescent, ISLEWORTH, MIDDLESEX, TW7 4NA.

SHAH, Miss. Nishma, BSc ACA *2009;* Little Oak, 3 Donnay Close, GERRARDS CROSS, BUCKINGHAMSHIRE, SL9 7PZ.

•**SHAH, Mr. Nitesh Bhagwanji, BSc ACA** *1994;* (Tax Fac), Nittin Accountancy Services Limited, 50 Bullescroft Road, EDGWARE, HA8 8RW.

SHAH, Mr. Nitesh Ratilal, BSc FCA *1988;* Nitesh R. Shah, PO Box 14571, NAIROBI, 00800, KENYA.

SHAH, Mr. Nitin Hirji, FCA *1977;* 23295 Caminito Marcial, LAGUNA HILLS, CA 92653, UNITED STATES.

•**SHAH, Mr. Nitin Premchand, ACA** *1983;* (Tax Fac), N.P. Shah & Company, Unit A2 Livingstone Court, 55 Peel Road, Wealdstone, HARROW, HA3 7QT.

•**SHAH, Mr. Nyandra Panachand, FCA** *1976;* N.P. Shah & Co, 26 Willowcourt Avenue, Kenton, HARROW, MIDDLESEX, HA3 8ES.

SHAH, Mr. Omar Syed, BSc(Hons) ACA *2003;* 26 Newark Way, LONDON, NW4 4JL.

SHAH, Ms. Pallvee, MSc LLB ACA CTA *2004;* 5 The Fairway, NORTHWOOD, HA6 3DZ.

SHAH, Mrs. Palvi, ACA *2009;* Flat 14 Roxborough Heights, College Road, HARROW, MIDDLESEX, HA1 1GN.

SHAH, Miss. Palvi Dalichand, BA ACA *2007;* Flat 3, 8 Cosway Street, LONDON, NW1 5NR.

SHAH, Mr. Pankaj, ACA *1979;* PO Box 10827, NAIROBI, 00400, KENYA.

•**SHAH, Mr. Pankaj, ACA** *1982;* (Tax Fac), Kajaine Limited, First Floor, Alpine House, Unit 2, Honeypot Lane, LONDON NW9 9RX.

SHAH, Mr. Pankaj Baburaj, BA ACA *1983;* 24 Davenham Avenue, NORTHWOOD, HA6 3HQ.

•**SHAH, Mr. Pankaj Kantilal, BA ACA ATII** *1987;* S P K Shah & Co Ltd, 216 Melton Road, LEICESTER, LE4 7PG.

•**SHAH, Mr. Pankaj Nathalal, FCA** *1983;* (Tax Fac), Lubbock Fine, Russell Bedford House, City Forum, 250 City Road, LONDON, EC1V 2QQ.

SHAH, Mr. Paras, BSc ACA *2007;* Flat 6 Winterberry Court, 71 Woodside Park Road, LONDON, N12 8LA.

SHAH, Mr. Paras Amritlal, BA ACA *1997;* 801 Bay Street, Suite 1501, TORONTO M5S 1Y9, ON, CANADA.

SHAH, Mr. Paraskumar, BA(Hons) ACA *2002;* 89 Woodgrange Avenue, LONDON, N12 0PT.

•**SHAH, Mr. Paresh Bhimji Khimji, BSc FCA** *1975;* Parker Cavendish, 28 Church Road, STANMORE, HA7 4XR. See also Parker Cavendish Limited

•**SHAH, Mr. Paresh L, FCA** *1980;* (Tax Fac), Paresh Shah Ltd, 128 Malvern Gardens, HARROW, MIDDLESEX, HA3 9PG.

SHAH, Mr. Paresh Raichand, BSc ACA *1982;* Toscafund Assett Management Ltd, 90 Long Acre, LONDON, WC2E 9RA.

SHAH, Mr. Parit Narendra, LLB ACA *2003;* P.O.Box 22001, postal code 00400 - Tom Mboya, NAIROBI, KENYA.

SHAH - SHAH Members - Alphabetical

SHAH, Miss. Parita, ACA *2009;* Flat 180 Dorset House, Gloucester Place, LONDON, NW1 5AH.

SHAH, Mr. Piyush Mepa Kanji, FCA *1976;* Deltion Ltd, Swan House, 203 Swan Road, FELTHAM, MIDDLESEX, TW13 6LL.

SHAH, Ms. Poonam, BSc ACA *2008;* 5 Cowley Close, SOUTH CROYDON, SURREY, CR2 8LU.

•**SHAH, Mr. Pradeep Motichand, FCA** *1985;* DAS UK Limited, 1st Floor, Windsor House, 1270 London Road, LONDON, SW16 4DH.

•**SHAH, Mr. Pradip Kumar, BA FCA** *1984;* (Tax Fac), PK Shah & Co Ltd, 60 Fairlands Avenue, THORNTON HEATH, SURREY, CR7 6HA.

SHAH, Mr. Pradip Kumar Mohanlal, FCA *1976;* 30 Pasture Close, North Wembley, WEMBLEY, HA0 3JE.

SHAH, Mrs. Prafula Hirji, FCA *1974;* P.O. Box 39296, NAIROBI, KENYA.

SHAH, Mr. Prakash, BSc ACA *1998;* 29 Grasmere Avenue, WEMBLEY, HA9 8TB.

•**SHAH, Mr. Praphulchandra Raichand, FCA** *1975;* (Tax Fac), Elliotts Shah, 2nd Floor, York House, 23 Kingsway, LONDON, WC2B 6UJ.

•**SHAH, Mr. Prashant Dhirajlal, BSc FCA** *1988;* KPMG Audit, 7 Bvd Albert Einstein, B.P. 41125, Cedex 3, 44311 NANTES, FRANCE. See also KPMG S.A.

SHAH, Mr. Pravin Chimanlal, FCA *1979;* 6522 East Broadway, BURNABY V5B 2Y5, BC, CANADA.

SHAH, Mr. Pravinchandra Bharmal karamshi, FCA *1977;* 47 Southover, Woodside Park, LONDON, N12 7JG.

SHAH, Miss. Preena, ACA *2008;* 34 West Avenue, LONDON, N3 1AX.

SHAH, Miss. Preety, ACA *2008;* 3 Greville Drive, BIRMINGHAM, B15 2UU.

SHAH, Miss. Priya, BSc ACA *1999;* 27 Briar Road, HARROW, MIDDLESEX, HA3 0DP.

SHAH, Miss. Priya Nalin, BA ACA AMCT *1998;* 40 Acacia Close, STANMORE, MIDDLESEX, HA7 3JR.

SHAH, Mr. Priyan, LLB ACA *2004;* with Barclays Capital, 5 North Colonnade, Canary Wharf, LONDON, E14 4BB.

SHAH, Mr. Priyesh, ACA *1994;* 35 Kenton Park Crescent, HARROW, HA3 8TZ.

SHAH, Mr. Priyesh Shantilal, BSc ACA *1996;* Unit 401, Glenealy Tower, 1 Glenealy, CENTRAL, HONG KONG ISLAND, HONG KONG SAR.

SHAH, Mr. Pulin, FCA *1977;* One Wentworth Avenue, LONDON, N3 1YA.

SHAH, Mr. Purvesh Bimalkumar, BSc ACA *2010;* P.O.Box 40732 - 00100, GPO, NAIROBI, KENYA.

SHAH, Mrs. Rachel, ACA *1986;* Manor Barn, Hawling, CHELTENHAM, GL54 5TA.

SHAH, Ms. Radhika Panachand, BSc ACA *1993;* 11 Chestnut Avenue, NORTHWOOD, HA6 1HR.

SHAH, Mr. Rahul, BA ACA *1998;* Deutsche Bank, PO Box 504902, DIFC, DUBAI, UNITED ARAB EMIRATES.

SHAH, Mr. Rahul Jagmohan, BSc FCA *1996;* 55 East Towers, PINNER, MIDDLESEX, HA5 1TN.

SHAH, Mr. Raj, BSc ACA *2011;* 19 Mount Drive, HARROW, MIDDLESEX, HA2 7RW.

SHAH, Mr. Rajan, BSc ACA *1995;* 14 Drew Gardens, GREENFORD, UB6 7QG.

SHAH, Mr. Rajan, BSc ACA *1991;* Leotel Lines House, 78 High Street, STEVENAGE, HERTFORDSHIRE, SG1 3DW.

SHAH, Mr. Rajan Dalichand, MPhil BSc ACA *1995;* Capwell Industries Limited, PO Box 746, THIKA, KENYA.

•**SHAH, Mr. Rajan Shantilal, FCA** *1986;* (Tax Fac), Raj Shah & Co, 46 Heddon Court Avenue, BARNET, HERTFORDSHIRE, EN4 9NG.

SHAH, Mr. Rajeev Maganlal, BSc ACA IMC *1992;* Baring Investment Services Ltd, 155 Bishopsgate, LONDON, EC2M 3XY.

SHAH, Mr. Rajen, BA ACA *1993;* Apartment 844, Ritz-Carlton Executive Residences, DIFC, PO Box 482032, DUBAI, UNITED ARAB EMIRATES.

SHAH, Mr. Rajen Gulabchand, BSc ACA *1996;* Ecstacy Ltd, PO Box 10177, NAIROBI, KENYA.

•**SHAH, Mr. Rajendra, BSc FCA** *1991;* Mccormack & Associates, Euro House, 1394-1400 High Road, LONDON, N20 9BH.

•**SHAH, Mr. Rajendra Tejpar, BA ACA** *1986;* Hammonds Consultants Ltd, 21 The Broadwalk, Pinner Road, HARROW, MIDDLESEX, HA2 6ED. See also Hammonds Ltd

•**SHAH, Mr. Rajesh Hiralal, FCA** *1982;* (Tax Fac), Litchfields, 5 Luke Street, LONDON, EC2A 4PX.

SHAH, Mr. Rajesh Keshavlal, BSc FCA *1982;* (Tax Fac), PricewaterhouseCoopers, Rahimtulla Tower, Upper Hill Road, PO Box 43963, NAIROBI, 00100 KENYA.

SHAH, Mr. Rajesh Lalji, BSc ACA *1986;* 9 Westward Way, HARROW, MIDDLESEX, HA3 0SE.

SHAH, Mr. Rajesh Natwerlal, ACA *1986;* (Tax Fac), 37 Edgwarebury Lane, EDGWARE, HA8 8LJ.

SHAH, Mr. Rajiv, ACA *2008;* 11 Hill Road, HARROW, MIDDLESEX, HA1 2PN.

SHAH, Mr. Rajiv, BA ACA *1992;* 44 Appletree Walk, Garston, WATFORD, WD25 0DE.

SHAH, Mr. Rajiv Surendra, BA ACA *1993;* P.O. Box 1255, NAIROBI, 00621, KENYA.

SHAH, Mr. Rajnikant Narshi, FCA *1972;* 13395 Paloma Drive, ORLANDO, FL 32837, UNITED STATES.

SHAH, Mr. Raju, ACA *2009;* Clear Channel Outdoor, 33 Golden Square, LONDON, W1F 9JT.

SHAH, Mr. Raju, MEng ACA *2003;* 41 Lamorna Grove, STANMORE, MIDDLESEX, HA7 1PH.

SHAH, Mr. Raju Amritlal, BA ACA *2008;* 157 Fairlands Avenue, THORNTON HEATH, SURREY, CR7 6HJ.

SHAH, Mr. Rajul, BA FCA *1998;* 172 Kenton Lane, Kenton, HARROW, HA3 8SU.

SHAH, Mr. Rakesh, BSc FCA *1990;* 18 Bowness Drive, HOUNSLOW, TW4 7BL.

SHAH, Mrs. Rakhee, BSc(Econ) ACA *1998;* 100 The Fairway, WEMBLEY, MIDDLESEX, HA0 3TJ.

SHAH, Miss. Rakhee Praful, ACA *2009;* P.O Box 18200606, Sarit Centre, NAIROBI, KENYA.

SHAH, Miss. Raksha, BSc ACA ATII *1987;* Flat 5, Katrina Court, 845 Harrow Road, WEMBLEY, MIDDLESEX, HA0 2PL.

•**SHAH, Mr. Ramakant Ratilal, FCA** *1970;* R.R. Shah & Co, 78 Wembley Park Drive, WEMBLEY, HA9 8HB.

•**SHAH, Mr. Rameshchandra Manilal Dharamshi, BCom FCA** *1968;* (Tax Fac), Chamberlains UK LLP, 173-175 Cleveland Street, LONDON, W1T 6QR.

SHAH, Mr. Rameshchandra Virpal, FCA *1972;* 24 Becmead Avenue, HARROW, MIDDLESEX, HA3 8EY. (Life Member)

SHAH, Mr. Ramniklal Dharamshi, BSc FCA *1977;* 1 Fenstanton Avenue, LONDON, N12 9HA.

•**SHAH, Mr. Ramniklal Sojpar, ACA** *1984;* Nagaria & Co, 21 Alverstone Road, NEW MALDEN, SURREY, KT3 4BA. See also Accountancy Services (New Malden) Limited

SHAH, Mr. Rashmikant Bharmal, FCA *1977;* P O Box 46979, NAIROBI, 0100, KENYA.

•**SHAH, Mr. Rashmikant Ratilal, BA ACA** *1989;* Rashmi Shah & Co, 62 Bertram Road, Hendon, LONDON, NW4 3PP.

SHAH, Mr. Rashmin, BA FCA AMCT *1987;* Hazelwood, Cansiron Lane, Cowden, EDENBRIDGE, TN8 7EE.

SHAH, Mr. Rasik Narshi Panachand, FCA *1974;* 11 Eaves Close, New Haw Road, ADDLESTONE, SURREY, KT15 2BF.

•**SHAH, Mr. Rasiklal Ladhabhai, ACA** *1986;* (Tax Fac), DSJ Partners LLP, 2nd Floor, 1 Bell Street, LONDON, NW1 5BY. See also Vital Accounting Limited

SHAH, Ms. Reena, BA ACA *1998;* 45C Muswell Road, LONDON, N10 2BS.

SHAH, Mrs. Reena, LLB ACA *2002;* 20 Langland Drive, PINNER, HA5 4SA.

SHAH, Mr. Reenit, BSc ACA *2009;* 43 College Road, WEMBLEY, MIDDLESEX, HA9 8RN.

SHAH, Miss. Rena, BSc ACA *2007;* Adersbacher Strasse 37, 74889 SINSHEIM, GERMANY.

SHAH, Miss. Reshma Kiran, BA(Hons) ACA *2002;* 213 Albury Drive, PINNER, MIDDLESEX, HA5 3RH.

SHAH, Miss. Reshma Mansukhlal, BA(Econ) ACA *2002;* Tullow Oil Plc, Building 11, Chiswick Park, 566 Chiswick High Road, LONDON, W4 5YS.

•**SHAH, Mr. Riaz Ali, BSc ACA** *1988;* Ernst & Young LLP, 1 More London Place, LONDON, SE1 2AF. See also Ernst & Young Europe LLP

SHAH, Mr. Ricky, MEng ACA *2006;* 44 Byron Avenue, BOREHAMWOOD, HERTFORDSHIRE, WD6 2BN.

SHAH, Mr. Rikesh, BA FCA *2000;* 7 Redfern Gardens, ROMFORD, RM2 6PY.

SHAH, Ms. Rima, BSc ACA *2003;* Flat 17 Duke Shore Wharf, 106 Narrow Street, LONDON, E14 8BU.

SHAH, Mrs. Rina, BSc ACA *1998;* 21 Manor Park Gardens, EDGWARE, HA8 7NB.

SHAH, Mr. Rishi, ACA *2005;* 12 Kettlewell Close, LONDON, N11 3FB.

SHAH, Mr. Rishi, BSc ACA *2006;* 105 Arlington Road, Southgate, LONDON, N14 5BA.

SHAH, Miss. Rishma, ACA *2009;* 83 Church Drive, HARROW, MIDDLESEX, HA2 7NR.

SHAH, Mrs. Rita, BA(Hons) ACA *2001;* 67 Jackson Road, BARNET, HERTFORDSHIRE, EN4 8UU.

SHAH, Mr. Ritesh Keshavji, BSc ACA *1991;* 245 Park Avenue, NEW YORK, NY 10167, UNITED STATES.

•**SHAH, Mr. Ritish, ACA** *1989;* 97 Selborne Road, Southgate, LONDON, N14 7DE.

•**SHAH, Mr. Rizwan Ul-Hassan, BA(Hons) ACA** *2003;* (Tax Fac), Jafferies, 134a Maybury Road, WOKING, SURREY, GU21 5JR. See also Jafferies Financial Management Ltd

SHAH, Mr. Ronal, ACA *2009;* Baker Tilly, 25 Farringdon Street, LONDON, EC4A 4AB.

SHAH, Mrs. Roopal, BA ACA *1995;* 4334 East Angela Drive, PHOENIX, AZ 85032, UNITED STATES.

SHAH, Mr. Rumit, BSc ACA *1984;* 32 The Drive, NORTHWOOD, HA6 1HP.

•**SHAH, Mr. Rumit Kantilal, BEng ACA** *1994;* Aanand Nivas, Manor Way, POTTERS BAR, HERTFORDSHIRE, EN6 1EE.

SHAH, Mr. Rupen, ACA *2010;* 9 Castleton Avenue, WEMBLEY, MIDDLESEX, HA9 7QH.

SHAH, Mr. Rupen, BSc ACA *2003;* Victoria Furnitures Ltd, P O BOX 10827, NAIROBI, 00400, KENYA.

SHAH, Mr. Rupesh, BSc ACA *2005;* Gatehouse Bank Plc, 125 Old Broad Street, LONDON, EC2N 1AR.

SHAH, Mr. Rushabh, BSc(Eng) ACA *2000;* 33 Orchard Court, Portman Square, LONDON, W1H 6LF.

SHAH, Mr. Sachin, BSc(Hons) ACA *2011;* 15 Gallus Close, LONDON, N21 1JR.

•**SHAH, Mr. Sailesh Premchand, MA FCA** *1987;* Flemmings, 76 Canterbury Road, CROYDON, SURREY, CR0 3HA.

SHAH, Mr. Sajeel, ACA *2009;* 2 Royston Park Road, PINNER, MIDDLESEX, HA5 4AD.

SHAH, Mrs. Saloni, BA ACA *1997;* 4 Milne Field, Hatch End, PINNER, HA5 4DP. (Life Member)

SHAH, Mr. Sameer Rameshchandra, MSc ACA *2006;* 24 Becmead Avenue, HARROW, MIDDLESEX, HA3 8EY.

SHAH, Mr. Sameet, BSc ACA *2006;* Integrix Sports Group Limited, Unit 1, Colonial Business Park, Colonial Way, WATFORD, WD24 4PR.

SHAH, Mr. Samir, MSc FCA *1995;* 21 Windsor Avenue, EDGWARE, HA8 8SR.

SHAH, Mr. Samir, BA ACA *1996;* 42 Roderick Road, LONDON, NW3 2NL.

SHAH, Mr. Samir Pravin, BSc ACA *1992;* 1 Aldridge Avenue, EDGWARE, HA8 8TA.

SHAH, Mr. Samir Rasik, BSc FCA *2000;* 11 Eaves Close, ADDLESTONE, KT15 2BF.

•**SHAH, Mr. Samir Vinodchandra, BSc(Econ) ACA** *2002;* Capitax Financial Limited, Devonshire House, 582 Honeypot Lane, STANMORE, MIDDLESEX, HA7 1JS.

•**SHAH, Mr. Sandip, MSc ACA** *1987;* KPMG LLP, 15 Canada Square, LONDON, E14 5GL. See also KPMG Europe LLP

SHAH, Mrs. Sangeeta, BSc ACA *2006;* Flat 1, 135 Three Colt Street, LONDON, E14 8AP.

SHAH, Mr. Sanjay, BA(Hons) FCA *1990;* Duchy House, 28 Duchy Road, BARNET, HERTFORDSHIRE, EN4 0HN.

SHAH, Mr. Sanjay, BSc ACA *1993;* 2 Layton Street, WELWYN GARDEN CITY, HERTFORDSHIRE, AL7 4FF.

SHAH, Mr. Sanjay Babubhai, BSc FCA *1968;* Mayfair Gardens A-13, Little Gibbs Road, MUMBAI 400 006, INDIA.

SHAH, Mr. Sanjay Chandrikan, MA ACA *1999;* 27 Hillview Road, PINNER, MIDDLESEX, HA5 4PB.

•**SHAH, Mr. Sanjay Gosar, BSc FCA** *1981;* (Tax Fac), William Evans & Partners, 20 Harcourt Street, LONDON, W1H 4HG.

SHAH, Mr. Sanjay Premchand, BSc ACA *1993;* 78 Highview Avenue, EDGWARE, HA8 9UA.

•**SHAH, Mr. Sanjay Rameshchandra, LLB ACA CTA** *2000;* (Tax Fac), PricewaterhouseCoopers LLP, 7 More London Riverside, LONDON, SE1 2RT. See also PricewaterhouseCoopers

SHAH, Mr. Sanjay Ramji, FCA *1978;* 6 Michleham Down, Woodside Park, LONDON, N12 7JN.

SHAH, Mr. Sanjeev Madhusudan, BA(Hons) ACA *2002;* 24 Ridge Lane, WATFORD, WD17 4TD.

SHAH, Mr. Sanjiv Mohanlal, BSc(Econ) FCA MCIM *1984;* (Tax Fac), Whitecroft, Lynwood Heights, RICKMANSWORTH, WD3 4ED.

SHAH, Mr. Sanjiv Nemish, BSc ACA *1986;* 26 Jolly Maker Chambers 2, 225 Nariman Point, MUMBAI 400021, INDIA.

SHAH, Mr. Sarad C H, ACA *1984;* 5 Handel Close, EDGWARE, MIDDLESEX, HA8 7QZ.

SHAH, Mr. Sarit, BSc ACA *1998;* 170 Belsize Road, LONDON, NW6 4BJ.

SHAH, Mrs. Satchi, BA ACA *2006;* 9 The Avenue, WEMBLEY, MIDDLESEX, HA9 9QH.

SHAH, Mr. Satish, FCA *1973;* Satish Shah, PO Box 82675, MOMBASA, KENYA.

•**SHAH, Mr. Satish Anandji, FCA** *1979;* Ashfords Accountants Ltd, 1378 Leeds Road, BRADFORD, WEST YORKSHIRE, BD3 8NE.

•**SHAH, Mr. Satishchandra Baburaj, FCA** *1975;* (Tax Fac), Shah Dodhia & Co, 173 Cleveland Street, LONDON, W1T 6QR. See also Chamberlains UK LLP

•**SHAH, Mr. Satishchandra Z, FCA** *1978;* (Tax Fac), S. Shah & Co., 17 Lovatt Close, EDGWARE, HA8 9XG.

SHAH, Mr. Savan Himatlal, BSc ACA *2004;* Oaktree Capital Management, 27 Knightsbridge, LONDON, SW1X 7LY.

SHAH, Mr. Sawan Shashikant, ACA *2008;* PO Box 30983, NAIROBI, 00100, KENYA.

SHAH, Mr. Shafqat Hussain, FCA *1966;* 9Q 9th East Street, Phase 1 DHA, KARACHI, PAKISTAN.

•**SHAH, Mr. Shakunt Vinodrai, BSc ACA CTA** *1991;* (Tax Fac), KLSA LLP, 28-30 St John's Square, LONDON, EC1M 4DN. See also KLSA Taxation Services Limited

SHAH, Mr. Shalil Nilam, BSc(Hons) ACA *2010;* 92 Norton Road, WEMBLEY, MIDDLESEX, HA0 4RF.

SHAH, Mr. Shamil, BSc ACA *2003;* with Deutsche Bank AG, CIB Global Markets, Winchester House, 1 Great Winchester Street, LONDON, EC2N 2DB.

SHAH, Mr. Shamir, BSc(Hons) ACA *2010;* 9 Little Cedars, LONDON, N12 8TH.

SHAH, Mr. Shamit Rajnikant, BA ACA *1995;* 31B Paine Court, KARRINYUP, WA 6018, AUSTRALIA.

SHAH, Mr. Shanti, ACA *1981;* Oak Lodge, 28a Sand Lodge Way, NORTHWOOD, MIDDLESEX, HA6 2AS.

SHAH, Mr. Shantilal Kanjibhai, FCA *1961;* Flat 18, Graham White House, Warneford Road, HARROW, MIDDLESEX, HA3 9JH. (Life Member)

•**SHAH, Mr. Shantilal Khimji, FCA** *1970;* Shah Patel & Company, Laxmi Plaza, Biashara Street, PO Box 41652, NAIROBI, 00100 KENYA.

SHAH, Mr. Shashinkumar Kanji, BSc ACA *1983;* Wood Rising, Kewferry Drive, NORTHWOOD, MIDDLESEX, HA6 2NT.

SHAH, Mr. Sheelan, ACA *2010;* 17 Lansdowne Road, LONDON, N3 1ET.

SHAH, Miss. Sheelan, BSc ACA *2003;* 21 Manor Court, Bonnersfield Lane, HARROW, MIDDLESEX, HA1 2LD.

SHAH, Ms. Sheena, BSc ACA *1995;* PO Box 47945, NAIROBI, KENYA.

SHAH, Mrs. Sheetal, BSc ACA *1999;* 17 Bishops Avenue, NORTHWOOD, MIDDLESEX, HA6 3DQ.

SHAH, Mrs. Sheetal, ACA *2010;* 71 Nibthwaite Road, HARROW, MIDDLESEX, HA1 1TD.

SHAH, Miss. Sheetal, BSc ACA *2007;* 211 Corniche Street, P O Box 3600, ABU DHABI, UNITED ARAB EMIRATES.

•**SHAH, Mr. Shirish Amratlal, FCA** *1982;* SPW (UK) LLP, Gable House, 239 Regents Park Road, LONDON, N3 3LF.

SHAH, Mr. Shitul Mansukhlal, BSc ACA *1991;* Flat 13 Seymour Court, Eversley Park Road, LONDON, N21 1JG.

SHAH, Miss. Shraya Mahendrakumar, BSc ACA *2004;* 19 West Avenue, Finchley, LONDON, N3 1AU.

SHAH, Miss. Shreya S, BSc ACA *2011;* 45 Craigweil Drive, STANMORE, MIDDLESEX, HA7 4TT.

SHAH, Mr. Shrikesh Praful, MBA BA(Hons) DIC FCA *2001;* 8 Churchill Avenue, Kenton, HARROW, HA3 0AY.

SHAH, Mr. Shripal, BSc ACA *2010;* 1 Conyers Close, Hersham, WALTON-ON-THAMES, KT12 4NG.

•**SHAH, Mr. Shuja Bakht, FCA** *1964;* S.B.Shah & Co., 97 Brim Hill, LONDON, N2 0EZ.

•**SHAH, Mr. Siddharth Kantilal, BSc ACA ATII** *1979;* (Tax Fac), S P K Shah & Co Ltd, 216 Melton Road, LEICESTER, LE4 7PG.

SHAH, Mr. Sidharth, ACA *2010;* 1 Conyers Close, Hersham, WALTON-ON-THAMES, SURREY, KT12 4NG.

SHAH, Mr. Sinesh Ramesh, MSc BSc ACA *2003;* 6 Fairway Close, HARPENDEN, HERTFORDSHIRE, AL5 2NN.

SHAH, Mr. Siral, BSc ACA *2007;* 22 Lakenheath, LONDON, N14 4RN.

SHAH, Miss. Sneh, ACA *2006;* 25 Morland Road, HARROW, MIDDLESEX, HA3 9LU.

SHAH, Miss. Sneh Ashok, BSc ACA *2007;* 2 Haywood Park, Chorleywood, RICKMANSWORTH, WD3 5DR.

SHAH, Miss. Sneha, ACA *2010;* with PricewaterhouseCoopers AS LLP, 1 Embankment Place, LONDON, WC2N 6RH.

SHAH, Mr. Snehal Suresh, BSc(Econ) ACA *2002;* 12 Christchurch Gardens, Kenton, HARROW, HA3 8NR.

SHAH, Mr. Snehar, BEng ACA CFA *1999;* P. O. Bx 20730, NAIROBI, KENYA.

SHAH, Mr. Sobakchand Zaverchand, FCA *1974;* PO BOX 39282, NAIROBI, 00623, KENYA.

•**SHAH, Mr. Sohin Mansukhlal, BSc FCA** *1997;* 107 Ducks Hill Road, NORTHWOOD, HA6 2SQ.
SHAH, Mrs. Sonal, BSc ACA *1995;* 65 East 93rd Street, Apt 2a, NEW YORK, NY 10128, UNITED STATES.
SHAH, Miss. Sonal, ACA *2009;* 133 Spring Grove Crescent, HOUNSLOW, TW3 4DA.
SHAH, Mrs. Sonal, BA(Hons) ACA CTA *2003;* 14 Mayfield Avenue, HARROW, HA3 8EU.
SHAH, Miss. Sonia, LLB ACA *2003;* 28 Court House Gardens, West Finchley, LONDON, N3 1PX.
•**SHAH, Miss. Sonia Indu, BSc ACA FCCA CTA** *2003;* Brooms Professional Services Limited, Broom House, 39-43 London Road, Hadleigh, BENFLEET, ESSEX SS7 2QL.
•**SHAH, Mr. Subhash Chimanlal, FCA** *1975;* (Tax Fac), Castle Ryce, The Clockhouse, 87 Paines Lane, PINNER, MIDDLESEX, HA5 3BY.
SHAH, Mr. Sudhirkumar Ratilal, FCA *1973;* 35 Buckingham Drive, EAST BRUNSWICK, NJ 08816, UNITED STATES.
SHAH, Ms. Sujal, BSc ACA *2001;* 13 Oakleigh Park North, Whetstone, LONDON, N20 9AN.
•**SHAH, Mrs. Sumitra, BA FCA** *1992;* Flemmings, 76 Canterbury Road, CROYDON, SURREY, CR0 3HA.
•**SHAH, Mr. Sundip, BSc ACA** *1986;* Sundip Shah BSc (Econ) ACA, 135 Northwood Way, NORTHWOOD, MIDDLESEX, HA6 1RF.
SHAH, Mr. Suneer, BSc ACA *2002;* 1 Sedgecombe Avenue, HARROW, MIDDLESEX, HA3 0HW.
SHAH, Mr. Sunil, BA(Hons) ACA *2010;* 62 Draycott Avenue, HARROW, MIDDLESEX, HA3 0BU.
SHAH, Mr. Sunil Dinker Laxmichand, BSc ACA *1993;* 32 Brownlow Road, Tamboerskloof, CAPE TOWN, 8001, SOUTH AFRICA.
SHAH, Mr. Sunil Kirit, BSc ACA *1997;* 44 Gyles Park, STANMORE, HA7 1AW.
SHAH, Mr. Sunil Premchand, BSc ACA *1986;* 97 Green Lane, EDGWARE, HA8 8EL.
SHAH, Miss. Swati, BSc ACA *1997;* Flat 14 Florence Mansions, Vivian Avenue, LONDON, NW4 3UY.
SHAH, Mr. Syed Mohamed Akhtar, BSc FCA *1977;* 9 Rosebery Road, Langley Vale, EPSOM, KT18 6AF.
SHAH, Mr. Syed Imran Ali, ACA *2011;* Flat 212 Raphael House, 250 High Road, ILFORD, IG1 1YS.
SHAH, Mrs. Tejal, BSc ACA *2005;* 114 Green Lane, EDGWARE, MIDDLESEX, HA8 8EJ.
SHAH, Miss. Tejal, BSc ACA *2004;* 1 Gladys Road, LONDON, NW6 2PU.
•**SHAH, Mr. Terence Rajnikant, BSc ACA** *1993;* with PricewaterhouseCoopers LLP, 1 Embankment Place, LONDON, WC2N 6RH.
SHAH, Mr. Trishul, BSc ACA *2006;* Norwegian Barn Edgwarebury Lane, Elstree, BOREHAMWOOD, HERTFORDSHIRE, WD6 3RG.
SHAH, Mr. Tushar Amritlal, ACA *1980;* 1 Manor Close, Kingsbury, LONDON, NW9 9HD.
SHAH, Mr. Tushar Amritlal, BSc ACA *1982;* 56 Hillbury Avenue, HARROW, HA3 8EW.
SHAH, Mr. Tushin, MA ACA *2006;* 9 East Crescent, New Southgate, LONDON, N11 3AR.
SHAH, Mr. Udian Amritlal, FCA *1976;* Rolled Steel Products Ltd, PO Box 2400, IBADAN, NIGERIA.
SHAH, Miss. Vaishali Chandrakant, BA ACA *1998;* P. O. Box 85234, MOMBASA, COAST PROVINCE, KENYA.
SHAH, Mr. Vijal Premchand, BSc ACA *1993;* (Tax Fac), 6 Holt Road, WEMBLEY, MIDDLESEX, HA0 3PS.
•**SHAH, Mr. Vijay Manubhai, FCA** *1977;* Orbital Insurance Services Ltd, 180 London Road, KINGSTON UPON THAMES, SURREY, KT2 6QW.
•**SHAH, Mr. Vikram Navnitlal, FCA** *1978;* ST-Partnership, Mandeville House, 45-47 Tudor Road, HARROW, HA3 5PQ.
SHAH, Mr. Vimal, BA ACA *1991;* 34 Landra Gardens, LONDON, N21 1RT.
•**SHAH, Mr. Vimal Navin, MA ACA** *1996;* P.S.J. Alexander & Co, 1 Doughty Street, LONDON, WC1N 2PH. See also Abott Secretaries Ltd, Patel, Shah & Joshi
SHAH, Mr. Vinaychandra Lalji Nathoo, FCA *1977;* K Waterhouse Ltd, Unit 22 Sheraton Business Centre, Wadsworth Close, Perivale, GREENFORD, MIDDLESEX UB6 7JB. (Life Member)
•**SHAH, Mr. Vinodkumar Depar, BSc FCA** *1980;* Gill Peer & Company Limited, 13 Alwyn Close, Elstree, BOREHAMWOOD, HERTFORDSHIRE, WD6 3LF. See also Gill Peer & Co
•**SHAH, Mr. Vinodkumar Devchand Pethraj, FCA** *1977;* Vinod Shah, 25 Montpelier Rise, WEMBLEY, MIDDLESEX, HA9 8RG.
•**SHAH, Mr. Vipin Ambalal, BSc FCA** *1980;* (Tax Fac), Aakabeni & Co Ltd, 25 Croham Manor Road, SOUTH CROYDON, SURREY, CR2 7BJ.
•**SHAH, Mr. Vipin Shantilal, FCA** *1975;* (Tax Fac), V.S. Shah & Co, 3 Lakenheath, Oakwood, LONDON, N14 4RJ.
•**SHAH, Mr. Vipool Khetshi Nathoobhai, MA FCA** *1977;* (Tax Fac), Godley & Co., Congress House, 14 Lyon Road, HARROW, MIDDLESEX, HA1 2EN.
SHAH, Mr. Viral, ACA *2011;* 3 Annette Close, HARROW, MIDDLESEX, HA3 7BG.
SHAH, Mr. Vishal, ACA *2009;* 42 Westbury Road, LONDON, N12 7PD.
SHAH, Mr. Vishal Mansukh, MSc BCom ACA CIOT *2002;* 27 Charmian Avenue, STANMORE, HA7 1LL.
SHAH, Mr. Yashovardhan, BA ACA *2007;* 22 Jubilee Road, Perivale, GREENFORD, UB6 7HZ.
SHAH, Mr. Yul, BSocSc ACA *1997;* c/o Norwegian Church Aid, P.O.Box 30703, LUSAKA, ZAMBIA.
SHAH-COULON, Miss. Mala, BA ACA *2000;* with ERNST & YOUNG GLOBAL, Becket House, 1 Lambeth Palace Road, LONDON, SE1 7EU.
SHAHA, Mr. Mark, MSc BA ACA *2006;* 156 Manor Grove, RICHMOND, TW9 4QG.
SHAHABI, Mr. Akbar Khosro, FCA *1972;* 170 Avenue Victor Hugo, 75116 PARIS, FRANCE. (Life Member)
•**SHAHABUDDIN, Mr. Kazi, FCA** *1975;* Shahabuddin & Co Limited, Lombard Chambers, Ormond Street, LIVERPOOL, L3 9NA. See also SMS Abacus & Co Ltd
•**SHAHABUDDIN, Mr. Kazi Furkan, BSc(Econ) FCA** *1991;* SMS Abacus & Co Ltd, Rowlandson House, 289-293 Ballards Lane, LONDON, N12 8NP. See also Shahabuddin & Co Limited
•**SHAHABUDDIN, Mr. Kazi Imran, BA(Hons) ACA** *2003;* Shahabuddin & Co Limited, Lombard Chambers, Ormond Street, LIVERPOOL, L3 9NA.
SHAHAR, Ms. Mazatul Aini, BA ACA *2004;* Capital Markets & Advisory, Level 20 Menara Bank Pembangunan, Jalan Sultan Ismail, 50724 KUALA LUMPUR, FEDERAL TERRITORY, MALAYSIA.
SHAHBANDI, Mrs. Elham, BSc(Hons) ACA *2000;* 22 Farm Way, BUCKHURST HILL, ESSEX, IG9 5AH.
SHAHDADPURI, Mr. Deepak, LLB FCA MBA *1996;* BCP Advisors Pvt Ltd, 11-B Nirmal, Nariman Point, MUMBAI 400021, INDIA.
•**SHAHEEDEE, Mr. Rashed Ahmad, FCA** *1972;* Rashed Shaheedee & Co, Chytel House, 160-164 Mile End Road, LONDON, E1 4LJ. See also Shaheedee Rashed
SHAHEEDEE, Miss. Safina Afroz, BSc ACA *2004;* 20 Cannon Lane, PINNER, MIDDLESEX, HA5 1HL.
SHAHEEN, Miss. Nabila, BA(Econ) ACA *2002;* 2 Carpenters Way, ROCHDALE, LANCASHIRE, OL16 4XU.
SHAHEEN, Mr. Rahan Ahmad, MBA BSc ACA *1993;* Apartment 730, Point West, 116 Cromwell Road, LONDON, SW7 4XH.
SHAHID, Mr. Abdul, BA(Hons) ACA *2004;* 9 Maplewood Close, MANCHESTER, M9 8NW.
SHAHID, Mr. Kazi Mamun, BA ACA *1999;* Flat 1, 27 Blakesley Avenue, Ealing, LONDON, W5 2DN.
SHAHID, Ms. Momina, ACA *2011;* Flat 198, Ability Place, 37 Millharbour, LONDON, E14 9DF.
SHAHID, Mr. Sharjeel, ACA *2001;* 100 Cover Drive, Street 26, Phase VI, DHA, KARACHI, SINDH PAKISTAN.
SHAHMIR, Mr. Farrokh, MBA BA FCA *1984;* 21 Granby Avenue, HARPENDEN, HERTFORDSHIRE, AL5 5QP.
•**SHAHMOON, Mr. Ran Charles, ACA** *1996;* (Tax Fac), Levy Cohen & Co, 37 Broadhurst Gardens, LONDON, NW6 3QT.
SHAHRABANI, Mr. Ezra, FCA *1969;* 77/79 Great Eastern Street, LONDON, EC2A 3HU.
SHAHRIARI, Mr. Afshin Ferydoon, BSc ACA *2006;* Flat 62, Charlbert Court, Mackennal Street, LONDON, NW8 7DB.
SHAHSAVARI, Mr. Mehrdad, FCA *1973;* 113 Falls Church Court, FRANKLIN, TN 37064, UNITED STATES.
SHAHZAD, Mr. Nabeel, ACA *2011;* Flat 8, Bulwer Court, Bulwer Court Road, Leytonstone, LONDON, E11 1DB.
•**SHAIDA, Mr. Farrukh Mohammed, BSc(Econ) ACA** *1995;* Quantum, 208 Redbridge Lane East, ILFORD, ESSEX, IG4 5BH. See also Quantum ATS Limited
•**SHAIK, Mr. Abdul Aziz, BSc ACA** *1981;* (Tax Fac), Shaik & Co Ltd, 1145 Oldham Road, Newton Heath, MANCHESTER, M40 2FU. See also Accounting & Business Services Limited
SHAIKH, Mr. Kumail, ACA *2010;* C/O Shahid Shaikh, KPMG Al Fozan and Al Sadhan, Al Dainy Plaza, Madinah Road, P.O Box 55078, JEDDAH 21534 SAUDI ARABIA.
SHAIKH, Mr. Mazin, BSc(Hons) ACA *2011;* 23 Parkland Road, WOODFORD GREEN, ESSEX, IG8 9AP.
•**SHAIKH, Mr. Mohommad, FCA** *1968;* (Tax Fac), Shaikh & Co, 174 Canterbury Road, CROYDON, SURREY, CR0 3HE.
SHAIKH, Mr. Naheed Akhtar, BA FCA *1978;* 61 Blewbury Rd, East Hagbourne, DIDCOT, OX11 9LE.
SHAIKH, Mr. Raheel, MSc BSc ACA *2007;* 41 Swyncombe Avenue, Ealing, LONDON, W5 4DR.
•**SHAIKH, Mr. Salimullah, FCA** *1970;* S Shaikh, 19 Faber Gardens, Hendon, LONDON, NW4 4NP.
SHAIKH, Miss. Samiha, ACA *2011;* 23 Parkland Road, WOODFORD GREEN, ESSEX, IG8 9AP.
•**SHAIKH, Mr. Shahid Hanif, ACA** *1980;* KPMG Al Fozan Al Sadhan, PO Box 55078, JEDDAH, 21534, SAUDI ARABIA. See also KPMG Europe LLP
SHAIKH, Mr. Tabassum Hanif, FCA *1983;* Al Tayer Group, P O Box 2623, DUBAI, UNITED ARAB EMIRATES.
SHAIKH, Mr. Yasser, ACA *2011;* 319 Great West Road, HOUNSLOW, TW5 0DE.
SHAIKH, Mr. Zaki Ahmed, BCom FCA *1961;* Ibrahim Shaikh & Co, 259-260 Panorama Centre, Fatima Jinnah Road, KARACHI 74400, PAKISTAN.
SHAIL, Mr. Richard, FCA *1968;* Swiftbow Ltd, Drumochter, Wickham Bishops, WITHAM, CM8 3JL.
SHAILI, Miss. Joanna, LLB ACA *2007;* 4 Parthenon Street, Livadia, 7060 LARNACA, CYPRUS.
SHAIN, Mr. Jonathan, BEng ACA *2004;* Flat 29 Straffan Lodge, 1-3 Belsize Grove, LONDON, NW3 4XE.
SHAJANI, Mr. Salim Abdulla, FCA *1974;* 19 Parfield Drive, TORONTO M2J 1C1, ON, CANADA.
SHAKALLI, Miss. Maria Eleni, BSc ACA *2003;* Flat 202, 18 Etolon Street, Ayios Andreas, 1101 NICOSIA, CYPRUS.
SHAKALLIS, Mr. Loizos, FCA *1969;* 19 Halkidos Street, CY 6031 LARNACA, CYPRUS. (Life Member)
SHAKERIFAR, Mr. Farhad, FCA *1981;* Cutler & Gross, 209 Old Marylebone Road, LONDON, NW1 5QT.
SHAKESBY, Mr. Anthony Jonathan, BSc ACA *1982;* 90 Atlantic Close, SOUTHAMPTON, SO14 3TB.
SHAKESPEARE, Mrs. Alison Jean, MA FCA *1997;* Leicester Grammar School London Road, Great Glen, LEICESTER, LE8 9FL.
SHAKESPEARE, Miss. Anne Muriel Carter, BA(Hons) ACA *2002;* (Tax Fac), Walnut Tree Farm, Pandy, ABERGAVENNY, NP7 8ED.
SHAKESPEARE, Mr. John Wallace, FCA *1955;* Drws y Coed, Bron Eifion, CRICCIETH, GWYNEDD, LL52 0SA. (Life Member)
•**SHAKESPEARE, Mr. Justin, BA ACA** *2000;* with KPMG LLP, Arlington Business Park, Theale, READING, RG7 4SD.
SHAKIR-KHALIL, Mr. Tarique, BSc ACA *1996;* with PricewaterhouseCoopers, 63 rue de Villiers, 92208 NEUILLY SUR SEINE CEDEX, FRANCE.
SHAKOOR, Mr. Javed, FCA *1971;* 35/2 Khayaban-e-rahat Phase 6, Defence Housing Authority, KARACHI 75500, PAKISTAN.
SHALE, Mrs. Margaret Susan, BA FCA *1980;* Farrer & Co LLP, 65-66 Lincoln's Inn Fields, LONDON, WC2A 3LH.
SHALET, Mr. Stanley Alan, FCA *1959;* Flat 5 Admirals Place, 24-27 The Leas, WESTCLIFF-ON-SEA, SS0 7BF. (Life Member)
SHALIT, Mr. David Manuel, FCA *1953;* Flat 8 Stavordale Lodge, 10-12 Melbury Road, LONDON, W14 8LW. (Life Member)
SHALL, Mr. Alexander Thomas, BEng ACA *2011;* 10a Hampstead Hill Gardens, LONDON, NW3 2PL.
SHALLCROSS, Mr. Michael Graham, MA ACA ATII MIAP *1982;* Conflict & Change, 2a Streatfeild Avenue, East Ham, LONDON, E6 2LA.
SHALLCROSS, Mr. Ralph Charles, FCA *1965;* with A. Macdonald & Co, 21 Parliament Street, HULL, HU1 2BL.
SHALLIKER, Mr. Robert Edward, BA ACA *1998;* 1 Kings Road, Formby, LIVERPOOL, L37 4BB.
SHALLISH, Mrs. Sarah Elizabeth, BSc ACA *1994;* Commerce House The Street, Grundisburgh, WOODBRIDGE, SUFFOLK, IP13 6TD.
SHALLOW, Mr. Michael St John, MA FCA *1979;* Felsham Hall, Felsham, BURY ST.EDMUNDS, IP30 0QN.
SHALOM, Mrs. Caroline Emma, BSc ACA *1998;* Blenheim Cottage, Flyford Flavell, WORCESTER, WR7 4BS.
SHALOM, Mr. David Michael, BA ACA *1992;* 9 Valley Road, CHEADLE, SK8 1HY.
SHAM, Miss. Clara Pui Wah, MSc BSc ACA *2006;* 51 Seren Park Gardens, LONDON, SE3 7RP.
SHAM, Mr. Daniel Sui Leung, BA ACA *1981;* 42/F Central Plaza, 18 Harbour Road, WAN CHAI, HONG KONG ISLAND, HONG KONG SAR.
•**SHAM, Mrs. Fowziah, FCA** *1982;* Westmere Services Limited, 15 Burleigh Gardens, LONDON, N14 5AH.
SHAM, Mr. Hon Lung Francis, ACA *2008;* Francis HL Sham & Co, Room 1416, 14/F, Hollywood Plaza, 610 Nathan Road, MONG KOK KOWLOON HONG KONG SAR.
SHAMANNA, Mr. Nanjappa, FCA *1970;* PO Box 50751, DUBAI, 50751, UNITED ARAB EMIRATES. (Life Member)
SHAMASH, Mr. Andrew, BA ACA *2000;* 33 Marlborough Avenue, EDGWARE, MIDDLESEX, HA8 8UT.
•**SHAMASH, Mr. David Naim, MA FCA** *1972;* 3rd Floor, 12/13 Conduit Street, LONDON, W1S 2XQ.
SHAMBROOK, Mr. Andrew John, BSc(Hons) ACA *2002;* ICI Paints, Wexham Road, SLOUGH, SL2 5DS.
SHAMIM, Mr. Rashad, BSc ACA *1996;* Flat 3 Cavendish Court, 9 Birkenhead Avenue, KINGSTON UPON THAMES, KT2 6NJ.
SHAMMASIAN, Mr. George Armen, BEng ACA *2007;* 2 Ploutarchou Street, Flat 301, Engomi, 2406 NICOSIA, CYPRUS.
SHAMMAT, Mr. Kinan, BSc ACA *2010;* with PricewaterhouseCoopers LLP, 1 Embankment Place, LONDON, WC2N 6RH.
SHAMP, Mr. Alan John, BSc FCA *1978;* Stanley House, Stoneage Lane, Dunkerton, BATH, BA2 8AS.
•**SHAMSI, Mrs. Rasheeda Ambereen, BSc FCA** *1997;* (Tax Fac), A Shamsi & Co, 11 Stone Close, TAUNTON, SOMERSET, TA1 4YG.
SHAMSIE, Mr. Afzaal Hussain, FCA *1981;* 3810 Lynn Regis Court, FAIRFAX, VA 22031, UNITED STATES.
SHAMSUDDIN, Miss. Aasha Meliza, MA BA ACA *1998;* 53 Shrubbery Road, Streatham, LONDON, SW16 2AS.
SHAMSUDDIN, Mr. Ahmad Khairi, BA(Hons) ACA *2002;* PROKHAS SDN BHD, Level 12, Bangunan Setia 1, 15 Lorong Dungun, Damansara Heights, 50490 KUALA LUMPUR FEDERAL TERRITORY MALAYSIA.
SHAMSUDDIN, Mr. Doni, BA ACA *2002;* No 801 4-3-1, Shirakawa, Koto-Ku, TOKYO, 135-0021 JAPAN.
SHAMTOOB, Mr. Fariborz, BSc ACA *1983;* 44 Deacons Hill Road, Elstree, BOREHAMWOOD, WD6 3LH.
SHANAHAN, Mr. Mark Edward, ACA *1997;* A P V UK Ltd 2 City Place, Beehive Ring Road London Gatwick Airport, GATWICK, WEST SUSSEX, RH6 0PA.
SHANAHAN, Mr. Patrick, FCA *1960;* 74A Higher Drive, PURLEY, CR8 2HF. (Life Member)
SHANBHAG, Mr. Sandeep, BSc(Hons) ACA *2004;* 109 Edenfield Gardens, WORCESTER PARK, KT4 7DX.
SHANBURY, Mr. Clifford Eric, LLB FCA *1969;* 33 Chiltern Avenue, BUSHEY, WD23 4PX.
SHAND, Mr. Alastair John, MA MEng ACA *1993;* 7 Fulwith Gate, HARROGATE, NORTH YORKSHIRE, HG2 8HS.
SHAND, Ms. Carol Robyn, ACA *1996;* Flat 41 Speed House, Barbican, LONDON, EC2Y 8AT.
•**SHAND, Mr. James David Alexander, BSc FCA CF** *1989;* VFD Ltd, Magdalen Centre, Robert Robinson Avenue, OXFORD, OX4 4GA. See also Vfdnet
•**SHAND, Mr. John Philip, FCA** *1977;* (Tax Fac), Townends Accountants Limited, 7-9 Cornmarket, PONTEFRACT, WEST YORKSHIRE, WF8 1AN. See also Townends
SHAND, Mr. Richard Edward, FCA *1975;* Novum, Hopper Way, DISS, NORFOLK, IP22 4GT.
SHANE, Mrs. Helen, ACA *2009;* 14 Longcroft Drive Barton-le-Clay, BEDFORD, MK45 4SF.
SHANE GOODHAND, Mrs. Mayuri Vinod, BA(Hons) ACA *2001;* 10 Western Gardens, NOTTINGHAM, NG8 5GP.
SHANGHAVI, Mr. Sunil, ACA *1987;* Connection Europe Limited, 26 Calthorpe Road, Edgbaston, BIRMINGHAM, B15 1RP.
SHANKAR, Mr. Naresh, FCA *1975;* Via del Fosso di, Fioranello 35, 00134 ROME, ITALY.
SHANKARDASS, Mr. Arun Baldev, FCA FCT *1975;* 74 Buckingham Avenue, Whetstone, LONDON, N20 9DH.
SHANKER, Mrs. Shiamala, BA ACA *1982;* 48 Greenridge Crescent, SINGAPORE 598936, SINGAPORE.
SHANKLAND, Mr. David, FCA *1960;* Hove To, 124 Pencisely Road, CARDIFF, CF5 1DR. (Life Member)

•**SHANKLEY, Mr. David Michael, FCA** *1987;* Shankley Enterprises Limited, 32 Market Place, KENDAL, CUMBRIA, LA9 4TN.
SHANKS, Miss. Christine, BSc ACA *1997;* 46 Quainton Road, Waddesdon, AYLESBURY, BUCKINGHAMSHIRE, HP18 0LP.
SHANKS, Mr. Geoffrey David, MBA FCA FCII *1979;* 247 Preston Road, BRIGHTON, BN1 6SE.
•**SHANKS, Mr. Ian James, FCA** *1975;* Ian J. Shanks FCA, 25 Lancaster Avenue, South Woodford, LONDON, E18 1QF.
•**SHANKS, Mr. James Douglas Douglas, BA FCA** *1988;* (Tax Fac), Chancery (UK) LLP, Chancery Pavilion, Boycott Avenue, Oldbrook, MILTON KEYNES, MK6 2TA.
SHANKS, Mr. Michael Jonathan, BA ACA *2000;* 3 Nellington Road, Rusthall, TUNBRIDGE WELLS, TN4 8SH.
•**SHANKS, Mr. Neil David George, FCA** *1992;* Stubbs Parkin South, 28 Cheshire Street, MARKET DRAYTON, SHROPSHIRE, TF9 1PF. See also Stubbs Parkin & South
SHANKS, Mr. Richard Vincent, FCA *1971;* 22 Priorfields, ASHBY-DE-LA-ZOUCH, LE65 1EA.
SHANKS, Mr. William, MA BA ACA *2011;* 22 Priorfields, ASHBY-DE-LA-ZOUCH, LEICESTERSHIRE, LE65 1EA.
SHANKSTER, Miss. Jane Kelly, BSc ACA *1993;* Arthur Road Landscapes, 3 Faraday Road, LONDON, SW19 8PE.
SHANLEY, Mr. Leon James, BA ACA *1993;* 7 Headleigh Road, NEWQUAY, TR7 2HJ.
•**SHANLEY, Mrs. Nicola Michele, ACA** *1991;* 1310-2-1-2 Tsukuda, Chuo-ku, TOKYO, 104-0051 JAPAN.
SHANMUGAM, Mr. Bala, BSc ACA *1997;* 40 Bridge Way, TWICKENHAM, TW2 7JJ.
SHANMUGAM, Mrs. Roma, BSc ACA *1999;* Exxonmobil House, Ermyn Way, LEATHERHEAD, SURREY, KT22 8UX.
SHANMUGANATHAN, Mr. Nijegan, BEng ACA *2009;* 19 Highway Road, MAIDENHEAD, BERKSHIRE, SL6 5AE.
SHANMUGANATHAN, Miss. Priya, ACA *1999;* 14 Callowhill Avenue, RICHMOND HILL L4B 4G1, ON, CANADA.
SHANMUGANATHAN, Mr. Suresh, BA ACA *2003;* Pricewaterhousecoopers, 1 Embankment Place, LONDON, WC2N 6RH.
SHANMUGARATNAM, Miss. Sivani, BSc ACA *1999;* 23 Ethelbert Place, RIDGEWOOD, NJ NJ 07450, UNITED STATES.
SHANN, Mr. David James, BA ACA *1999;* Acacia Cottage, Cragg Wood Drive, Rawdon, LEEDS, LS19 6LG.
SHANNAHAN, Mr. Justin Michael, BA ACA *1991;* Rolls-Royce Plc, PO Box 31, DERBY, DE24 8BJ.
SHANNON, Miss. Alayne, MA BA ACA *2005;* 44 Twyning Road, Stirchley, BIRMINGHAM, B30 2XY.
SHANNON, Mrs. Caroline Elizabeth, MA ACA *1989;* Glen Clova, Bonfield Road, Strathkinness, ST ANDREWS, FIFE, KY16 9RP.
SHANNON, Mr. Colin Edgar, FCA *1967;* 38 Suffolk Street, HELENSBURGH, G84 9PD. (Life Member)
SHANNON, Mr. George Russell, MA FCA *1988;* Wellman International, Newfield Road, OLDBURY, WEST MIDLANDS, B69 3ET.
SHANNON, Mr. Henry John, BCom FCA *1976;* The Golden Horseshoe Ltd., 102 Lower Baggot Street, DUBLIN 2, COUNTY DUBLIN, IRELAND.
SHANNON, Mr. John Richard, MA FCA *1971;* (Tax Fac), 9 Ellerby Street, LONDON, SW6 6EX.
SHANNON, Mrs. Kelly Jane, BSc ACA *2004;* 3 The Priory, St. Andrews Park, NORWICH, NR7 0GJ.
SHANNON, Mr. Mark James, BEng ACA *1998;* Windrush, 53 The Uplands, GERRARDS CROSS, SL9 7JQ.
SHANNON, Mr. Richard, BSc ACA *1991;* 16 Brinklow Way, HARROGATE, HG2 9JW.
SHANNON, Mr. Stephen, ACA *1982;* Manesty, Common Wood, KINGS LANGLEY, HERTFORDSHIRE, WD4 9BA.
SHANNON, Mr. Toby Richard, ACA *1985;* Howard de Walden Estates Ltd, 23 Queen Anne Street, LONDON, W1G 9DL.
•**SHANSON, Mr. Alan, FCA** *1957;* Bryal Commercial & Financial Facilities Ltd, Flat 6, 71 Park Road, New Barnet, BARNET, EN4 9QD.
SHAO, Mr. Shuai, ACA *2008;* 20 Brownfield Street, LONDON, E14 6NE.
•**SHAPCOTT, Miss. Kimberley Faye, ACA** *2008;* M J Shapcott & Company Limited, Charter House, Wyvern Court, Stanier Way, Wyvern Business Park, DERBY DE21 6BF.
•**SHAPCOTT, Mr. Melvin James, FCA** *1980;* M J Shapcott & Company Limited, Charter House, Wyvern Court, Stanier Way, Wyvern Business Park, DERBY DE21 6BF.
SHAPCOTT, Mr. Peter William St George, FCA *1954;* 27 Wadham Drive, Frenchay, BRISTOL, BS16 1PF. (Life Member)
•**SHAPIRO, Mr. Anthony, BA FCA** *1978;* Shapiro Dymant & Co, 17 Cawkwell Close, CHELMSFORD, CM2 6SG. See also October Marketing Limited
•**SHAPIRO, Mrs. Barbara, FCA** *1979;* (Tax Fac), A-spire Business Partners Limited, 32 Byron Hill Road, HARROW, MIDDLESEX, HA2 0HY.
•**SHAPIRO, Mr. David, BA ACA** *1987;* (Tax Fac), Edwards Veeder LLP, Alex House, 260-268 Chapel Street, SALFORD, M3 5JZ.
•**SHAPIRO, Mr. Jeffrey Israel Joseph, FCA** *1964;* (Tax Fac), with Sterlings Ltd, Lawford House, Albert Place, LONDON, N3 1QA.
SHAPIRO, Mr. Philip Mark, FCA *1967;* 2 Vardon Drive, WILMSLOW, CHESHIRE, SK9 2AQ. (Life Member)
SHAPLAND, Mr. Richard Guy, FCA *1960;* 49 Tregenver Road, FALMOUTH, TR11 2QP. (Life Member)
•**SHAPLAND, Mrs. Rosemary Jean, BSc ACA** *1992;* PricewaterhouseCoopers LLP, First Point, Buckingham Gate, London Gatwick Airport, GATWICK, WEST SUSSEX RH6 0NT. See also PricewaterhouseCoopers
SHAPTER, Mr. Martyn John, BSc FCA *1992;* Tui Travel Plc Crawley Business Quarter, Fleming Way, CRAWLEY, WEST SUSSEX, RH10 9QL.
SHAR, Mr. Saleemullah, BA ACA *2010;* Flat 1018, Block 10 Defence Garden, Apartments, DHA Phase 1, KARACHI, SINDH PAKISTAN.
SHARDLOW, Mrs. Claire Elizabeth, ACA *2006;* Hunter Jones Alton & Co, 36 Bridge Street, BELPER, DERBYSHIRE, DE56 1AX.
SHARDLOW, Mr. Richard Joseph, BSc(Hons) ACA *2003;* 3 Waverley Drive, TUNBRIDGE WELLS, TN2 4RX.
SHARE, Mr. Peter John, FCA *1972;* 31 Oakleigh Dr, Codsall, WOLVERHAMPTON, WV8 1JP.
SHARE, Mr. Stanley Richard Seymour, FCA *1973;* 12 Crown Walk, Oakington Avenue, WEMBLEY, HA9 8HU.
•**SHAREEF, Mr. Naeem Mohammed, BA FCA** *1992;* (Tax Fac), Shareef & Co Ltd, 18-22 Stoney Lane, Yardley, BIRMINGHAM, B25 8YP.
•**SHARER, Mr. Adam Elliot, ACA** *1999;* Fox Sharer LLP, Britannic House, 17 Highfield Road, LONDON, NW11 9LS.
SHARFF, Mr. Matthew James, BA(Hons) ACA *2001;* Ladbrokes Ltd Imperial House, Imperial Drive, HARROW, HA2 7JW.
SHARIATMADARI, Mr. Shahriar, BSc ACA *1993;* 54 Park View Gardens, LONDON, NW4 2PN.
SHARIEFF, Ms. Taha, ACA *2010;* Flat 46 Galleons View, 1 Stewart Street, LONDON, E14 3EX.
•**SHARIF, Mr. Ashfaq, BA FCA CTA** *1991;* (Tax Fac), PB Associates, 2 Castle Business Village, Station Road, HAMPTON, MIDDLESEX, TW12 2BX.
•**SHARIF, Mrs. Louise Jane, BA(Hons) FCA FCIE** *1990;* Louise Sharif, The White Hart, 80 Main Road, Hackleton, NORTHAMPTON, NN7 2AD.
SHARIF, Mr. Mazin, BSc ACA *1992;* 2 McCraes Walk, Wargrave, READING, RG10 8LN.
SHARIF, Mr. Mohammed Taqi, FCA *1975;* 5517 YELLOW RAIL COURT, FAIRFAX, VA 22032, UNITED STATES.
SHARIF, Mr. Nazar, BSc ACA *1995;* 3 Longfield Drive, LONDON, SW14 7AU.
SHARIFF, Mr. Aftab Mohamed, ACA FCCA *2005;* 69 Stretton Road, CROYDON, CR0 6ET.
SHARIFF, Miss. Farah Adiba, MChem ACA *2006;* 3 Waylett Place, WEMBLEY, MIDDLESEX, HA0 3BH.
•**SHARIFF, Mr. Mehboob Hussein, FCA CPA(K)** *1982;* Manohar lall & Rai, P O Box 42027 - 00100, NAIROBI, KENYA.
SHARIFF, Mr. Mohamed Habib, FCA *1977;* 211 Gariepy Crescent, EDMONTON T6M 1C2, AB, CANADA.
SHARIFF, Mr. Shuaib Sadruddin, BSc FCA *1983;* 10 Mortimer Crescent, AJAX L1T 3Y1, ON, CANADA.
SHARIFF, Miss. Suha Mumtaz, ACA *2010;* 47A Cambridge Street, Pimlico, LONDON, SW1V 4PR.
SHARIFF, Mr. Zulfikar Hassamali, FCA *1975;* 123 Fresno Place N.E., CALGARY T1Y 6Y2, AB, CANADA.
•**SHARIFI, Mr. Ali Akbar, BEng FCA CF** *1994;* Grant Thornton UK LLP, 4 Hardman Square, Spinningfields, MANCHESTER, M3 3EB. See also Grant Thornton LLP
SHARIPOV, Mr. Sharof, ACA *2008;* Flat 37 187 East India Dock Road, LONDON, E14 0EF.
•**SHARKEY, Mr. Andrew Beck, BA FCA** *1986;* Andrew B Sharkey Limited, Jasmine Cottage, Rowland, BAKEWELL, DERBYSHIRE, DE45 1NR.
•**SHARKEY, Mr. Brendan Michael, FCA** *1981;* MacIntyre Hudson LLP, Euro House, 1394 High Road, Whetstone, LONDON, N20 9YZ.
SHARKEY, Mr. David John, LLB ACA *1985;* 13 Dungarvan Avenue, LONDON, SW15 5QU.
SHARKEY, Mr. John Patrick, BA ACA *1989;* Mercia Group Ltd Best House Grange Business Park, Enderby Road Whetstone, LEICESTER, LE8 6EP.
SHARKEY, Mr. Kevin Patrick, BA ACA *2006;* Sharkey & Co Ltd, Vincent Court, Hubert Street, Aston Lock, BIRMINGHAM, B6 4BA.
•**SHARKEY, Mrs. Melanie Ann Menzies, FCA** *1965;* (Tax Fac), Rumford & Co, Conex House, 148 Field End Road, Eastcote, PINNER, MIDDLESEX HA5 1RJ.
SHARKEY, Mr. Stuart Graeme, FCA *1973;* 14 Wyke Oliver Road, Preston, WEYMOUTH, DT3 6BW.
SHARLAND, Mr. David Ian, MA BA ACA *1985;* Citigroup Global Markets Ltd, Citigroup Centre, 33 Canada Square, Canary Wharf, LONDON, E14 5LB.
SHARLAND, Mr. Richard Samuel, FCA *1967;* Carters Court, Dalwood, AXMINSTER, DEVON, EX13 7ED.
SHARLAND, Mr. Robert Edgar, FCA *1940;* 1 Fishers Heron, East Mills, FORDINGBRIDGE, SP6 2JR. (Life Member)
SHARLAND, Mr. Stephen John, BSc ACA *1992;* 181 Glengrove Avenue West, TORONTO M4R 1P4, ON, CANADA.
•**SHARMA, Mr. Adarsh Kumar Dev Prakash Gurbux Rai, FCA** *1981;* (Tax Fac), Andrew Sharma & Co, Wembley Point, 2nd Floor, 1 Harrow Road, WEMBLEY, MIDDLESEX HA9 6DE.
SHARMA, Mr. Ajay, BA ACA *1998;* 41 Blandford Road, LONDON, W4 1DX.
SHARMA, Miss. Alaknanda, BSc(Hons) ACA *2001;* 74 Caerphilly Road, Heath, CARDIFF, CF14 4AG.
SHARMA, Miss. Alka, ACA *1993;* Flat 26 Avenue Mansions, Finchley Road, LONDON, NW3 7AX.
SHARMA, Mr. Alok Kumar, BSc ACA *1992;* Maplecroft, Upper Warren Avenue, Caversham, READING, RG4 7EB.
SHARMA, Mr. Alvin, MBA BSc ACA CFA *1997;* 17 Croach Crescent, TORONTO M1S 4H9, ON, CANADA.
•**SHARMA, Mr. Amit, BEng ACA** *1999;* Goodman Jones LLP, 29-30 Fitzroy Square, LONDON, W1T 6LQ.
SHARMA, Mr. Amitabh, BSc FCA *1993;* Gibbs + Dandy Limited, P.O. 17 226 Dallow Road, LUTON, LU1 1JG.
SHARMA, Mr. Anikait, ACA *2008;* Apartment 305 Firestone House, Clayponds Lane, BRENTFORD, TW8 0GW.
SHARMA, Mr. Anil, BA ACA *1999;* 121 Wentworth Road, LONDON, NW11 0RJ.
•**SHARMA, Mrs. Anugrah, BSc FCA** *1990;* (Tax Fac), A & N (Haslemere) Limited, Aruna House, 2 Kings Road, HASLEMERE, SURREY, GU27 2QA.
SHARMA, Mr. Arun, ACA *1985;* 507 Bhikaiji Cama Bhawan, Bhikaiji Cama Place, NEW DELHI 110066, INDIA.
SHARMA, Mr. Arun Kumar, BSc ACA *1982;* 15 Greystoke Park Terrace, Ealing, LONDON, W5 1JL.
SHARMA, Mr. Ashani Kumar, BSc FCA *1998;* 3408 Whitetail Avenue, SIMI VALLEY, CA CA93063, UNITED STATES.
SHARMA, Mr. Ashishkumar, ACA *1993;* AGA Khan Fund for Economic Development, Aiglemont, 60270 GOUVIEUX, FRANCE.
•**SHARMA, Mr. Atul, BSc BCom ACA ACCA DChA** *2007;* GKP Partnership Ltd, 109-110 Viglen House, Alperton Lane, WEMBLEY, MIDDLESEX, HA0 1HD. See also CPL Audit Limited and AMP & Partners Limited
SHARMA, Mr. Atul Bhushan, ACA *1993;* 104 Chiranjiv Tower, 43 Nehru Place, NEW DELHI 110019, INDIA.
SHARMA, Mr. Atul Kumar, BSc ACA *1991;* 6 Bracondale, ESHER, SURREY, KT10 9EN.
SHARMA, Mr. Avinash Kumar, BSocSc ACA *2002;* 21 Beaumont Road, Springbank, CHELTENHAM, GL51 0LP.
•**SHARMA, Mr. Brij Kishor, ACA** *2009;* Brij K Sharma, 175 Old Surrey Lane, RICHMOND HILL L4K 2P5, ON, CANADA.
SHARMA, Mrs. Elizabeth Clare, BA(Hons) ACA *2001;* 51 Hartington Road, TWICKENHAM, TW1 3EL.
SHARMA, Miss. Girija Nupur, BSc ACA *2003;* 15 Charlbert Court, Charlbert Street, LONDON, NW8 7BX.
SHARMA, Mr. Hari-Har, ACA *1995;* 12 Oldfield Close, Earley, READING, RG6 1HP.
SHARMA, Mr. Harminder Kumar, BA ACA *1986;* 11 Church Road, Osterley, ISLEWORTH, TW7 4PL.
•**SHARMA, Mr. Hira Lal, MBA MEng FCA ATII** *1992;* BDO LLP, 55 Baker Street, LONDON, W1U 7EU. See also BDO Stoy Hayward LLP
SHARMA, Mr. Jagdish Kumar, FCA *1966;* 190 Broadway, Dobbs Ferry, NEW YORK, NY 10522, UNITED STATES.
SHARMA, Miss. Kavita, BSc(Hons) ACA *2002;* The Rose Cottage Icknield Street, Beoley, REDDITCH, WORCESTERSHIRE, B98 9AJ.
•**SHARMA, Mr. Kewal Krishan, FCA** *1967;* Mazars, 133 Cecil Street, 15-02 Keck Seng Tower, SINGAPORE 069535, SINGAPORE.
•**SHARMA, Mrs. Kim, ACA** *2001;* Inspired Accounting Ltd, 24 Gardenia Drive, Allesley, COVENTRY, CV5 9BN.
SHARMA, Mr. Manmohan Shiv Parshad, ACA *1982;* 4 Bluebell Crescent, NORWICH, NR4 7LE.
SHARMA, Miss. Naomi Lynn, BA ACA *1994;* 32 Grebe Road, BICESTER, OXFORDSHIRE, OX26 6WG.
•**SHARMA, Mr. Naveen Kumar, BA(Hons) ACA CF** *2000;* KPMG LLP, 15 Canada Square, LONDON, E14 5GL.
SHARMA, Mr. Nirmal, ACA ACMA *2011;* Blakeney, Derby Road, HASLEMERE, SURREY, GU27 1BP.
SHARMA, Mr. Paul Krishan, BA ACA *1989;* Financial Services Authority, 25 North Colonnade, Canary Wharf, LONDON, E14 5HS.
SHARMA, Mr. Pradeep Kumar, LLB ACA *1981;* 64 Amanda Court, SLOUGH, SL3 7TE.
SHARMA, Mr. Prashant, MEng ACA *2003;* 305 Haydons Road, LONDON, SW19 8TX.
SHARMA, Mr. Praveen, BA ACA *1986;* Quevelda, Quakers Walk, Winchmore Hill, LONDON, N21 2DE.
SHARMA, Mr. Prithvi Nath, ACA *1990;* 5/12 Sector 2, Rajendra Nagar, Sahibabad, GHAZIABAD 201005, INDIA.
SHARMA, Mr. Puneet Kumar, BA(Hons) ACA *2002;* 22 Chapel Market, Islington, LONDON, N1 9EN.
SHARMA, Mr. Rahul, FCA *1982;* Best At Travel, Worldwide House, 10 Berners Mews, LONDON, W1T 3AP.
SHARMA, Mr. Rajeev, BSc ACA *1989;* 18 Cranbourne Drive, PINNER, MIDDLESEX, HA5 1BZ.
•**SHARMA, Mr. Rajesh, FCA** *1984;* Smith & Williamson Ltd, 25 Moorgate, LONDON, EC2R 6AY.
SHARMA, Mr. Rajesh Kumar, BA(Hons) ACA *2004;* 1 Tilston Road, WALLASEY, CH45 4QG.
•**SHARMA, Mr. Rajnish Kumar, BA ACA** *1984;* R.K. Sharma, 22 Bisley Road, STROUD, GL5 1HE.
SHARMA, Mr. Ramendra Paul, BSc FCA *1999;* Northland Les Landes, Vale, GUERNSEY, GY3 5JQ.
SHARMA, Mr. Ravi, BA ACA *1982;* 230 Cranbrook Road, ILFORD, IG1 4UT.
SHARMA, Mr. Ravi, BSc ACA *2006;* 79 Park Avenue, SOUTH SHIELDS, NE34 8QL.
SHARMA, Mrs. Ruby, FCA *1994;* with Ernst & Young, 5 Times Square, NEW YORK, NY 10036, UNITED STATES.
SHARMA, Mrs. Ruth, BSc ACA *2004;* 2 Mackintosh Square, 546 Wellingborough Road, NORTHAMPTON, NN3 3HZ.
•**SHARMA, Mr. Sanjay, ACA FCCA** *2011;* Deloitte Touche Tohmatsu Private India Ltd, 12 Dr Annie Besant Road, Opp Shiv Sagar Estate, Worli, MUMBAI 400018, INDIA.
SHARMA, Mr. Sanjib, BA ACA *1997;* 3 Tanner Street, LONDON, SE1 3LE.
SHARMA, Mr. Satish Dev, MSc ACA *2010;* Flat E, 40 Exmouth Market, LONDON, EC1R 4QE.
SHARMA, Miss. Shashi Kiran, BSocSc ACA CTA *2002;* Conoco Ltd Conocophillips Centre, 2 Kingmaker Court Warwick Technology Park Gallows Hill, WARWICK, CV34 6DB.
•**SHARMA, Mr. Shyam Kumar, FCA** *1976;* Sharma & Co., 5 St. Denys Road, Portswood, SOUTHAMPTON, SO17 2GN.
•**SHARMA, Mr. Shyam Sunder, ACA** *1980;* with Leftley Rowe & Company, The Heights, 59-65 Lowlands Road, HARROW, MIDDLESEX, HA1 3AW.
•**SHARMA, Mr. Sudheer Kumar, FCA** *1984;* S.K. Sharma & Co, Gable House, Black Pond Lane, Farnham Common, SLOUGH, SL2 3EN.
SHARMA, Mr. Sumesh Kumar, BSc ACA *1998;* 27 Northpoint Square, 175 Camden Road, LONDON, NW1 9AW.
SHARMA, Mrs. Sunita, BSc ACA *1992;* 16-03 1 Tanjong Rhu Road, SINGAPORE 4326879, SINGAPORE.
SHARMA, Miss. Surekha, BSc ACA *2011;* 169 Jersey Road, Osterley, ISLEWORTH, MIDDLESEX, TW7 4QJ.
•**SHARMA, Mr. Surender, FCA** *1975;* S. Sharma & Co, 42 Kathleen Ave, WEMBLEY, HA0 4JH.
SHARMA, Mr. Viren Chandra, MSc ACA *2004;* 209 Peppard Road, Emmer Green, READING, RG4 8TS.

SHARMA, Mr. Vishawdeep, BA ACA *1990;* 105 Copse Wood Way, NORTHWOOD, MIDDLESEX, HA6 2TU.
SHARMA, Mr. Vivek, MA BA ACA MSI *2000;* (Tax Fac), 11 Rope Street, LONDON, SE16 7TE.
SHARMA, Mr. Vivek, ACA *2009;* Flat 102, Russell Court, Woburn Place, LONDON, WC1H 0LP.
SHARMA, Mr. Vivek Mohan, BSc ACA *2005;* 73 Fonda Meadows, Oxley Park, MILTON KEYNES, MK4 4TT.
SHARMA-STOREY, Mr. David Andrew, BSc(Hons) ACA *2001;* 16 Rodmarton Street, LONDON, W1U 8BH.
SHARMAN, Mrs. Alison Ruth, BA ACA *1989;* 12 Churwell Avenue, Heaton Mersey, STOCKPORT, CHESHIRE, SK4 3QE.
SHARMAN, Mr. Alistair Richard Norris, BCom ACA *1987;* Flint Ink (UK) Ltd, Vauxhall Industrial Estate, Ruabon, WREXHAM, CLWYD, LL14 6HU.
SHARMAN, Miss. Beverley, BSc ACA *2011;* 16 Dawson Road, BROMSGROVE, WORCESTERSHIRE, B61 7JF.
SHARMAN, Mr. Carl John, FCA MCT *1995;* Pricewaterhousecoopers, 1 Embankment Place, LONDON, WC2N 6RH.
SHARMAN, Lord Colin Morven, OBE FCA *1966;* Baverstock House Baverstock, Dinton, SALISBURY, SP3 5EN.
SHARMAN, Ms. Hilary Jane, BSc ACA *1992;* 12 Town Hill Road, SMITHS FL07, BERMUDA.
•**SHARMAN, Mr. Ian, BSc FCA** *1973;* Garth House, Bollinway, Hale, ALTRINCHAM, CHESHIRE, WA15 0NY.
SHARMAN, Mr. Ian Michael, MA ACA *2006;* 3321 NE Hoona Dr, BEND, OR 97701, UNITED STATES.
SHARMAN, Mr. John, FCA *1964;* 55 Lucks Lane, Buckden, ST. NEOTS, PE19 5TQ.
SHARMAN, Mrs. Katherine Mary, BA FCA *1972;* The Garden Cottage, Birthwaite Hall, Darton, BARNSLEY, SOUTH YORKSHIRE, S75 5JS.
SHARMAN, Mr. Kevin Mark, BSc(Hons) ACA *2001;* 14 Street Farm Lane, Ixworth, BURY ST. EDMUNDS, SUFFOLK, IP31 2JF.
SHARMAN, Miss. Louise Michelle, BSc ACA *1996;* Woodfordes, Stoke St. Mary, TAUNTON, SOMERSET, TA3 5BY.
SHARMAN, Miss. Lucinda Emma Joanna, BA ACA *2004;* 51 Scott Farm Close, THAMES DITTON, KT7 0AN.
SHARMAN, Mr. Martin Leslie, BSc FCA *1990;* 55 Hepworth Road, Oak Farm, Binley, COVENTRY, CV3 2XJ.
SHARMAN, Mr. Matthew James, BA ACA *1995;* 43 Milliners Way, St Michael's Mead, BISHOP'S STORTFORD, CM23 4GG.
SHARMAN, Mr. Neil, BSc ACA ATII *1979;* (Tax Fac), Brit Insurance, 55 Bishopsgate, LONDON, EC2N 3AS.
•**SHARMAN, Mr. Neil William, BSc ACA** *1990;* Neil Sharman, 91 Manchester Road, Slaithwaite, HUDDERSFIELD, HD7 5HP.
SHARMAN, Mr. Nicholas Peter, BA FCA *1993;* Highways Agency Corporate Centre, 123 Buckingham Palace Road, LONDON, SW1W 9HA.
•**SHARMAN, Mr. Patrick Michael, FCA** *1982;* (Tax Fac), Yew Tree House, Pardshaw, COCKERMOUTH, CA13 0SP.
•**SHARMAN, Mr. Paul, ACA** *1982;* Paul Sharman Limited, 33 Watling Close, Bracebridge Heath, LINCOLN, LN4 2BD.
•**SHARMAN, Mr. Paul David, LLB ACA** *1990;* (Tax Fac), The Sharman Partnership, 4 Coronation Road, Crosby, LIVERPOOL, L23 3BJ.
SHARMAN, Mr. Peter Russell, BA ACA *1994;* Park View, Long Newnton, TETBURY, GL8 8RH.
SHARMAN, Mr. Richard Charles, MA ACA *2005;* Flat C, 32 Queens Road, HARROGATE, NORTH YORKSHIRE, HG2 0HB.
SHARMAN, Mr. Richard George Lonsdale, FCA *1968;* Bay Cottage, Kingsland, Newdigate, DORKING, SURREY, RH5 5DB.
•**SHARMAN, Mr. Richard John, BA ACA** *1992;* KPMG Europe LLP, 15 Canada Square, LONDON, E14 5GL. See also KPMG LLP
SHARMAN, Mr. Robert Paul, BSc ACA *1995;* GlobeOp Financial Services Ltd, 1-3 Strand, Trafalgar Square, LONDON, WC2N 5HR.
SHARMAN, Mrs. Sarah Amanda, BA ACA *2002;* 5 Linnet Avenue, WHITSTABLE, KENT, CT5 4TN.
SHARMAN, Mr. Steven, BSc ACA *1992;* 102 114th Terr NE, ST PETERSBURG, FL 33716, UNITED STATES.
SHARMAN, Mrs. Susan Jane, BA FCA *1983;* Albury Farm, Gracious Pond Road, Chobham, WOKING, SURREY, GU24 8HJ.
SHARMAN, Mr. Timothy, ACA *1986;* Albury Farm Gracious Pond Road, Chobham, WOKING, SURREY, GU24 8HJ.
•**SHARMAN, Mr. Timothy Scott, BA(Hons) ACA** *1996;* Martin Greene Ravden LLP, 55 Loudoun Road, St John's Wood, LONDON, NW8 0DL.
•**SHARNOCK, Mr. Philip John, FCA** *1975;* (Tax Fac), Sharnock & Co, First Floor, 8B Lonsdale Gardens, TUNBRIDGE WELLS, KENT, TN1 1NU.
SHARP, Mr. Alan Donald, BCom ACA *1993;* 253 Lower Richmond Road, RICHMOND, TW9 4LU.
SHARP, Mr. Alexander Nicholas Pattinson, ACA *2008;* 15B, Denver Road, LONDON, N16 5JL.
SHARP, Miss. Amanda-Jane, BSc ACA *2007;* Advantage Insurance Company Limited, PO Box 1429, The Old Bank 17/21 Cannon Lane, GIBRALTAR, GIBRALTAR.
SHARP, Mr. Andrew Gordon, FCA *1971;* 5 Arethousis Street, 6031 LARNACA, CYPRUS.
SHARP, Mrs. Anne Cecilia, BA ACA *1987;* Laterna Cresta Drive, Woodham, ADDLESTONE, SURREY, KT15 3SW.
SHARP, Mrs. Anneke Jane Louisa, ACA *2003;* with Ernst & Young LLP, Apex Plaza, Forbury Road, READING, RG1 1YE.
SHARP, Mr. Anthony Raymond Buckley, ACA *1981;* 14 Hillbury Road, LONDON, SW17 8JT.
SHARP, Mr. Barry John, MSc FCA *1967;* The Old Orchard, Bekesbourne Lane, Bekesbourne, CANTERBURY, CT4 5DY. (Life Member)
SHARP, Mr. Benjamin Lloyd, MSci ACA *2003;* Merrill Lynch Financial Centre, 2 King Edward Street, LONDON, EC1A 1HQ.
SHARP, Ms. Caroline Frances, BA ACA DChA *2002;* 55 Canberra Road, LONDON, SE7 8PF.
SHARP, Miss. Catrin, BA ACA *1992;* 9D Westbourne Park Road, LONDON, W2 5PX.
SHARP, Mr. Charles Ernest, FCA *1950;* 17 Carlton Crescent, Kamo, WHANGAREI, NEW ZEALAND. (Life Member)
SHARP, Ms. Christine Patricia, BA ACA *1979;* 68 Brondesbury Road, LONDON, NW6 6BS.
SHARP, Mr. Christopher David, ACA *2009;* 24 Witham Croft, SOLIHULL, B91 3FB.
SHARP, Mr. Christopher James, BSc ACA *2009;* Flat 3, 21 Springfield Road, LONDON, SW19 7AL.
SHARP, Mr. Christopher James, BA ACA *2001;* 3 Dagden Road, Shalford, GUILDFORD, GU4 8DD.
SHARP, Mr. Christopher Patrick, BSc ACA *1990;* Hedges, Jackmans Lane, WOKING, SURREY, GU21 7RL.
•**SHARP, Mr. Clifford John Kent, FCA** *1975;* Clifford Sharp & Co, 42 Park Road, BURGESS HILL, WEST SUSSEX, RH15 8ET. See also Clifford Sharp & Co Ltd
SHARP, Mr. Colin Winston, FCA *1969;* 220 St. Johns Road, TUNBRIDGE WELLS, KENT, TN4 9XD. (Life Member)
SHARP, Mr. Daniel, BA ACA *2007;* with Man Group plc, Riverbank House, 2 Swan Lane, LONDON, EC4R 3AD.
SHARP, Mr. David, FCA *1969;* 4 Tannery Close, Slinfold, HORSHAM, RH13 0RW.
•**SHARP, Mr. David Anthony, BA FCA** *1991;* Rouse Audit LLP, 55 Station Road, BEACONSFIELD, BUCKINGHAMSHIRE, HP9 1QL. See also Rouse Partners LLP
SHARP, Mr. David Edwin, FCA *1972;* Moore Stephens, 3 Saxon Way West, CORBY, NORTHAMPTONSHIRE, NN18 9EZ.
SHARP, Mr. Dominic John, BA ACA *1993;* 36 Tufton Court, Tufton Street, Westminster, LONDON, SW1P 3QH.
SHARP, Mr. Douglas David, LLB ACA *1983;* Sciens Capital Limited 4th Floor, 25 Berkeley Square, LONDON, W1J 6HN.
SHARP, Mr. Edward James Kingsley, FCA *1959;* 60 Orchard Road, Tewin, WELWYN, AL6 0HN. (Life Member)
SHARP, Ms. Ellen Elizabeth, BSc ACA *2011;* Apartment 820, Manor Mills, Ingram Street, LEEDS, LS11 9BT.
SHARP, Mrs. Emma Claire, BA ACA *1994;* Toutley Hall Bungalow, Old Forest Road, WOKINGHAM, RG41 1JA.
SHARP, Mr. Ernest Henry, FCA *1953;* Flat 36, Tufton Court, Tufton Street, Westminster, LONDON, SW1P 3QH. (Life Member)
SHARP, Mr. Geoffrey Dennis, FCA *1960;* 22 Inglewood, WOKING, GU21 3HX. (Life Member)
SHARP, Mr. Giles Henry, BSc ACA *2000;* Eaga Partnership House, Regent Farm Road, NEWCASTLE UPON TYNE, NE3 3AF.
SHARP, Ms. Hazel Anne, BA ACA *1988;* 20 Weald Way, CATERHAM, CR3 6EG.
SHARP, Mr. Howard Graham, BA ACA *1982;* 2 Ayot House, Ayot St. Lawrence, WELWYN, HERTFORDSHIRE, AL6 9BP.
SHARP, Mr. Hugo Benedict, BA ACA *2003;* 72 Park Avenue East, EPSOM, SURREY, KT17 2NY.
SHARP, Mr. Huw Richards, BSc ACA *1992;* Scotsbridge Les Petites Capelles Road, St. Sampson, GUERNSEY, GY2 4GX.
SHARP, Mr. Ivo Johnathan Peter, BA ACA *2009;* Ashley House, Henfield Club, Cagefoot Lane, HENFIELD, WEST SUSSEX, BN5 9HD.
SHARP, Ms. Jacqui Belinda, BSc ACA *1994;* 48 Church Lane, LYMINGTON, SO41 3RD.
SHARP, Mr. James, ACA *2009;* 26 Hamilton Road, TWICKENHAM, TW2 6SN.
SHARP, Mr. James Roger, MA FCA *1973;* Broad Lee House, Combs, Chapel-en-le-Frith, High Peak, SK23 9XA.
SHARP, Mr. Jason Philip, BA ACA *1997;* 2 Cross Keys Drive, Whittle-le-Woods, CHORLEY, PR6 7TF.
SHARP, Mr. Jeremy Peter, BA ACA *1994;* The Royal Bank of Scotland Plc, 135 Bishopsgate, LONDON, EC2M 3UR.
SHARP, Mr. Jeremy Richard Carling, MA ACA *1993;* 178a Ember Lane, EAST MOLESEY, KT8 0BS.
SHARP, Mrs. Jody Lyn, ACA *1983;* St. Peter & St. James Home & Hospice North Common Road, North Chailey, LEWES, EAST SUSSEX, BN8 4ED.
SHARP, Mr. John, FCA *1963;* 3 Lower Meadow, Turton, Edgworth, BOLTON, BL7 0DQ. (Life Member)
SHARP, Mr. John Alan, ACA *2008;* 79 Amersham Road, Caversham, READING, RG4 5BP.
•**SHARP, Mr. John Campbell, BA ACA** *1986;* Sharp Consulting (UK) Ltd, 182 White Hill, CHESHAM, BUCKINGHAMSHIRE, HP5 1AZ.
•**SHARP, Mr. John Michael Irvin, BSc FCA** *1986;* 27 Warrender Park Terrace, EDINBURGH, EH9 1EE.
SHARP, Mr. Jonathan Michael Keith, BA ACA *2010;* 99 College Place, LONDON, NW1 0DR.
SHARP, Mr. Jonathan William, BA ACA *1991;* 36 St. Marys Grove, LONDON, W4 3LN.
SHARP, Miss. Julie Diane, BSc ACA *1986;* 6 Hull Close, Cheshunt, WALTHAM CROSS, HERTFORDSHIRE, EN7 6XG.
SHARP, Miss. Kathryn Elizabeth, MA FCA *1997;* 15, Woodland Avenue, HOVE, BN3 6BH.
SHARP, Mr. Kenneth Charles, BSc FCA *1974;* Elleron Rambledown Lane, West Chiltington, PULBOROUGH, WEST SUSSEX, RH20 2NW.
SHARP, Mr. Kevin Ian, BA ACA *1987;* Downlands Liability Management, DLM House, Lyons Way, WORTHING, WEST SUSSEX, BN14 9RX.
•**SHARP, Mr. Leslie Henry Anderton, FCA** *1976;* (Tax Fac), Merkler Sharp & Co., Crown Lodge, Crown Road, MORDEN, SURREY, SM4 5BY.
SHARP, Mrs. Louise Claire, BA ACA *1999;* 14 Back Lane, Wool, WAREHAM, BH20 6LS.
SHARP, Miss. Mary Bernadette, PhD ACA *1989;* The Barn House, Old Station Road, Hampton-in-Arden, SOLIHULL, B92 0EY.
SHARP, Mr. Michael Alan, FCA *1974;* Orchard Cottage, 34a The Avenue, TADWORTH, KT20 5AT.
SHARP, Mr. Michael John, FCA *1963;* 30 Earlsfield Road, HYTHE, CT21 5PE. (Life Member)
SHARP, Mr. Michael John Perry, BSc FCA *1973;* Orchard End, Holyrood Lane, Ledsham, South Milford, LEEDS, LS25 5LL.
SHARP, Mrs. Michelle, MA ACA *1993;* Molescroft, 178a Ember Lane, EAST MOLESEY, KT8 0BS.
SHARP, Mrs. Miranda Esther Susanna, BA ACA *2004;* with Deloitte LLP, 2 New Street Square, LONDON, EC4A 3BZ.
SHARP, Miss. Natalie, BSc ACA *2010;* 24 Whitmore Road, HARROW, MIDDLESEX, HA1 4AB.
SHARP, Miss. Nicola Margaret, ACA *1987;* 13 Caernarvon, Frimley, CAMBERLEY, SURREY, GU16 8YQ.
SHARP, Mr. Paul Antony, BSc FCA *1981;* 20 Brassey Hill, Limpsfield, OXTED, RH8 0ES.
SHARP, Mr. Paul John, FCA *1978;* (Tax Fac), William Kendrick & Sons Ltd, Tasker Street, WALSALL, WS1 3QW.
SHARP, Mr. Peter, FCA *1967;* Torgersens Somerford Buildings, Norfolk Street, SUNDERLAND, SR1 1EE.
•**SHARP, Mr. Peter John, FCA** *1978;* (Tax Fac), Wellers, 8 King Edward Street, OXFORD, OX1 4HL. See also Wellers Contractors Limited
SHARP, Mr. Philip Arthur, BSc FCA *1983;* Ticketmaster Systems Ltd East Court Riverside, Campbell Road, STOKE-ON-TRENT, ST4 4DA.
SHARP, Mr. Philip Denis, FCA *1973;* Chaselands House, Lydlinch, STURMINSTER NEWTON, DORSET, DT10 2HU.
SHARP, Mr. Ralph Julian, FCA *1973;* 126 Manor Park, LONDON, SE13 5RH.
SHARP, Mr. Robert Walter, FCA *1964;* 34 Briardene, DURHAM, DH1 4QU. (Life Member)
•**SHARP, Mr. Robert William, BA FCA** *1985;* Herald Trust Company Limited, Herald House 8 Hill Street, ST HELIER, JE4 9XB.
SHARP, Mrs. Ruth, ACA *2008;* 67 Linton Crescent, LEEDS, LS17 8PZ.
SHARP, Mr. Simon Lister, BSc ACA *1994;* 4634 Avenue De Lorimier, MONTREAL H2H 2B5, QC, CANADA.
SHARP, Mr. Stanley Herbert, FCA *1952;* 13 Courtleigh Avenue, Hadley Wood, BARNET, EN4 0HT. (Life Member)
SHARP, Mr. Stephen Daniel, BA ACA *2006;* 26 Riverside View, OTTERY ST. MARY, DEVON, EX11 1YA.
SHARP, Mr. Steven Laurence, BSc(Hons) ACA *2002;* Flat 3 Sandrock Molyneux Drive, WALLASEY, MERSEYSIDE, CH45 1JS.
SHARP, Mr. Steven Robert, FCA *1982;* 168 Ember Lane, ESHER, KT10 8EJ.
SHARP, Mr. Stuart, ACA *2009;* Q B E, 88 Leadenhall Street, LONDON, EC3A 3BP.
SHARP, Mr. Thomas Frederick, MA FCA *1953;* Davyhulme House, Davyhulme Road, Urmston, MANCHESTER, M41 8QD.
SHARP, Mr. Thomas Leslie, ACA CPFA *2003;* 1 Pullin Court, BRISTOL, BS30 8YL.
SHARP, Mr. Timothy Joseph, BSc(Hons) ACA *2004;* 43 Bowling Green Road, STOURBRIDGE, DY8 3TY.
SHARP, Mrs. Valerie Jane, ACA *1984;* 19 Porlock Drive, Gilmorton, LUTTERWORTH, LE17 5PE.
SHARP, Mrs. Wendy Jill, BSc ACA *1990;* Hedges, Jackmans Lane, St Johns, WOKING, GU21 7RL.
SHARPE, Miss. Alexandra, BA ACA *2010;* 76a Kingsgate Road, LONDON, NW6 4LA.
SHARPE, Mr. Alistair Jonathan, BA ACA *1995;* Flat 3, 24 Elsworthy Road, LONDON, NW3 3DL.
•**SHARPE, Mr. Andrew Holland, BA FCA** *1985;* AHS & Co Limited, 5 Spinney Close, Douglas, ISLE OF MAN, IM2 1NF.
•**SHARPE, Mrs. Angela Victoria, FCA** *1973;* 25 Merrow Croft, GUILDFORD, SURREY, GU1 2XH.
SHARPE, Mrs. Ann Louise, BA ACA *1985;* with Grant Thornton UK LLP, 4 Hardman Square, Spinningfields, MANCHESTER, M3 3EB.
SHARPE, Mr. Anthony John, BSc ACA *1990;* 67 Millbrook Road, CROWBOROUGH, TN6 2SB.
•**SHARPE, Mrs. Carol, BSc ACA** *1991;* Wilson Sharpe & Co, 27 Osborne Street, GRIMSBY, NORTH LINCOLNSHIRE, DN31 1NU.
SHARPE, Mrs. Carolyn, BSc ACA *2007;* 6, Newstead Road Greenside Newcastle Great Park, NEWCASTLE UPON TYNE, NE13 9AX.
SHARPE, Mr. Christopher Ian, BSc ACA *2007;* with Zolfo Cooper LLP, 10 Fleet Place, LONDON, EC4M 7RB.
SHARPE, Mr. Christopher John, ACA *2009;* 7 Middletons Field, LINCOLN, LN2 1QP.
•**SHARPE, Mr. David Kelvin, BA FCA CF** *1986;* Pierce C A Ltd, Mentor House, Ainsworth Street, BLACKBURN, BB1 6AY. See also Pierce Group Limited
SHARPE, Mr. Donald Francis, FCA *1956;* 3 Hall Gate, LONDON, NW8 9PG. (Life Member)
SHARPE, Mr. Donald Honore, FCA *1965;* Deacon View, Chilcomb, WINCHESTER, HAMPSHIRE, SO21 1HR. (Life Member)
SHARPE, Mrs. Emily Jayne, ACA *2004;* 21 Gresford Close, Woolley Grange, BARNSLEY, SOUTH YORKSHIRE, S75 5QR.
SHARPE, Mr. Frank Arthur, FCA *1970;* Porto do Paraiso - Loja O, Rua Direita, Praia Da Luz, 8600 - 160 LAGOS, ALGARVE, PORTUGAL.
SHARPE, Mr. Gareth Jonathan, ACA *2006;* 18 Woodhall Drive, PINNER, MIDDLESEX, HA5 4TQ.
SHARPE, Mr. Geoffrey David, BSc ACA *1995;* 58 Sandringham Road, SWINDON, SN3 1HX.
•**SHARPE, Mr. Geoffrey Victor John, FCA** *1966;* Sharpe Perry & Co., 8 Spring Grove, Woburn Sands, MILTON KEYNES, MK17 8RY.
SHARPE, Mr. Graham Robertson, BA ACA *1986;* Old Keysford Hall, Treemans Road, Horsted Keynes, HAYWARDS HEATH, WEST SUSSEX, RH17 7EA.
SHARPE, Mr. Guy William, FCA *1964;* 7A Learmonth Terrace, EDINBURGH, EH4 1PQ. (Life Member)
•**SHARPE, Mrs. Hilary Frances, BSc FCA** *1989;* (Tax Fac), PKF (UK) LLP, 4th Floor, 3 Hardman Street, MANCHESTER, M3 3HF.
•**SHARPE, Mr. Ian Michael, ACA** *1991;* Old Mill Accountancy LLP, The Old Mill, Park Road, SHEPTON MALLET, SOMERSET, BA4 5BS. See also Old Mill Audit LLP
SHARPE, Mr. John Richard, FCA *1967;* Bridge House, The Marsh, Weobley, HEREFORD, HR4 8RP.

SHARPE, Mr. John Thornhill, BCom FCA *1964;* 18 Parkwood, Elmley Castle, PERSHORE, WR10 3HT.
SHARPE, Mrs. Karen, BA FCA *1995;* Hay's Galleria, 1 Hay's Lane, LONDON, SE1 2RD.
SHARPE, Mr. Matthew, BSc ACA *2010;* 188 Scotter Road, SCUNTHORPE, SOUTH HUMBERSIDE, DN15 7EQ.
SHARPE, Mr. Matthew David, BA(Hons) ACA *2002;* (Tax Fac), 6 Newstead Road, NEWCASTLE UPON TYNE, NE13 9AX.
SHARPE, Mr. Neil Stuart, FCA *1973;* 11 Tait Place, TILLICOULTRY, FK13 6RU.
•**SHARPE, Mr. Nigel Philip, FCA** *1974;* N P Sharpe, 84 Nettleham Road, LINCOLN, LN2 1RR.
•**SHARPE, Mr. Paul, FCA** *1982;* Townends, Carlisle Chambers, Carlisle Street, GOOLE, DN14 5DX. See also Townends Accountants Limited
SHARPE, Mr. Peter James, BSc ACA *1992;* Deutsche Bank, PO Box 135, LONDON, EC2A 2HE.
SHARPE, Dr. Peter Rhys, BSc FCA *1999;* 5 Jumbuck Court, GLADSTONE, QLD 4680, AUSTRALIA.
SHARPE, Mr. Peter William Ian, ACA *2008;* Flat 9, 26-28 Belvedere Road, LONDON, SE19 2HW.
•**SHARPE, Mr. Philip James, BSc FCA** *1993;* Sheen Stickland LLP, 4 High Street, ALTON, HAMPSHIRE, GU34 1BU.
SHARPE, Mr. Philip John, BSc ACA *1997;* 61 High Street, Guilden Morden, ROYSTON, HERTFORDSHIRE, SG8 0JR.
SHARPE, Mrs. Rebecca Jane, BSc ACA *1996;* Flat 15D, Tower 3, Parc Palais, 18 Wylie Road, KINGS PARK, KOWLOON HONG KONG SAR.
SHARPE, Mr. Robert Ballard, FCA *1961;* 30 Gainsborough Drive, SHERBORNE, DORSET, DT9 6DR. (Life Member)
SHARPE, Mr. Robin Alexander Honore, BSc FCA *1997;* Hillside Cottage, Pitcot Lane, Owslebury, WINCHESTER, HAMPSHIRE, SO21 1LR.
SHARPE, Mr. Russell David, BA(Hons) ACA *2003;* 16 Cranwells Lane, Farnham Common, SLOUGH, SL2 3GW.
SHARPE, Mrs. Sharon Margaret, BSc ACA *2001;* 144 Missenden Acres, Hedge End, SOUTHAMPTON, SO30 2AQ.
SHARPE, Mrs. Sheila Christine, FCA *1963;* 1 Maypole Close, SAFFRON WALDEN, ESSEX, CB11 4DB.
SHARPE, Mr. Timothy William Faulkner, BSc FCA *1980;* 85 Merrow Woods, Merrow, GUILDFORD, GU1 2LJ.
SHARPE, Mr. William John, FCA *1970;* 32b King Richard Place, Browns Bay, AUCKLAND 0630, NEW ZEALAND.
SHARPEN, Mr. Tim, MA(Cantab) ACA *2009;* 18 Waller Road, LONDON, SE14 5LA.
SHARPER, Mr. Ian David, ACA *2000;* 21 Fir Leaze, Nailsea, BRISTOL, BS48 4DH.
•**SHARPIN, Mrs. Linda Jane, BA FCA** *1988;* Linda J. Sharpin, Mayfield House, 2 Ganghill, GUILDFORD, GU1 1XE.
SHARPINGTON, Mrs. Miranda, BSc ACA *1985;* 3 Mulberry Court, Holmer Green, HIGH WYCOMBE, HP15 6TF.
SHARPLES, Mr. Adam Dominic, BSc ACA *1984;* 4 King Edwards Road, RUISLIP, HA4 7AJ.
SHARPLES, Mr. Andrew David, LLB ACA *1986;* 37 Park Gates Drive, Cheadle Hulme, CHEADLE, SK8 7DD.
SHARPLES, Mr. Antony, BSc ACA *1996;* 7 Woodbines Avenue, KINGSTON UPON THAMES, KT1 2AZ.
SHARPLES, Mr. Christopher John, BA(Hons) ACA *2010;* 3 Whalley Road, Wilpshire, BLACKBURN, BB1 9PJ.
SHARPLES, Mr. Christopher Richard, BA ACA *1985;* 19 Goldsmith Way, CROWTHORNE, RG45 7QP.
•**SHARPLES, Mr. David Allan, BA ACA** *1989;* Moore & Sharples Limited, 37 Warner Street, ACCRINGTON, LANCASHIRE, BB5 1HN.
SHARPLES, Mr. David John, ACA *1985;* Astley Lodge Breach Oak Lane, Corley, COVENTRY, CV7 8AU.
SHARPLES, Mr. Geoffrey, FCA *1963;* 29 Bayley Hills, NEWPORT, TF10 8JG.
•**SHARPLES, Mrs. Gillian, LLB ACA** *1984;* 4 Hambledon Close, Little Sutton, ELLESMERE PORT, CH66 4YF.
SHARPLES, Mr. Michael Craig, ACA *1982;* Exel Middle East, P O Box 54528, DUBAI, UNITED ARAB EMIRATES.
SHARPLES, Mr. Stephen, BA ACA *1979;* 3/4 Fiddlers Court, 5 Walls Street, GLASGOW, G1 1PA.
SHARPLES, Mr. Thomas Frederick, FCA *1959;* Blåsutvägen 25 1tr, 12136 JOHANNESHOV, SWEDEN. (Life Member)
•**SHARPLEY, Mr. James Mark, FCA** *1983;* Smailes Goldie, Regents Court, Princess Street, HULL, HU2 8BA.
SHARPSTONE, Mr. Lewis Edward, BSc FCA *1985;* 10960 Wilshire Blvd, Suite 700, LOS ANGELES, CA 90024, UNITED STATES.
SHARRATT, Mrs. Emma Tracey, ACA *1993;* 5c Dinorben Avenue, FLEET, HAMPSHIRE, GU52 7SG.
SHARRATT, Miss. Helen, BSc ACA *1995;* Flat 6 Earlsleigh, 27 Groby Road, ALTRINCHAM, CHESHIRE, WA14 2BQ.
SHARRATT, Mrs. Helen Kay, BSc ACA *2003;* 122 Newgate Street, Chasetown, BURNTWOOD, WS7 8TX.
SHARRATT, Mr. John, BSc ACA *2005;* 33 Cowan Way, WIDNES, CHESHIRE, WA8 9BJ.
•**SHARRATT, Mrs. Julie Patricia, BSc FCA** *1992;* (Tax Fac), Crystal Clear Accountancy Limited, 11 Whitehall Drive, Hartford, NORTHWICH, CHESHIRE, CW8 1SJ.
SHARROCK, Mr. David Morris, BA ACA *1995;* 5 Heritage Gardens, Wilmslow Road, Didsbury, MANCHESTER, M20 5HJ.
•**SHARROCK, Mr. Duncan Geoffrey, FCA** *1980;* CFW, 1 Sterling Court, Loddington, KETTERING, NN14 1RZ.
SHARROCK, Mr. John Bryan, FCA *1960;* Sealine Apartments, Flat 1, Triq San Giraldu, ST PAULS BAY SPB3313, MALTA. (Life Member)
SHARROCK, Mr. Jon Stewart, BSc ACA *1996;* 7 Victoria Avenue, Didsbury, MANCHESTER, M20 2GY.
SHARROCK, Mrs. Kate Victoria, BSc ACA *1996;* 5 Heritage Gardens, Didsbury, MANCHESTER, M20 5HJ.
SHARROCK, Mrs. Lynne, BA(Hons) ACA *2003;* 88B Whitley Crescent, WIGAN, WN1 2PU.
SHARROCK YATES, Ms. Susan, BA ACA *1985;* 17 Coalecroft Road, Putney, LONDON, SW15 6LW.
SHARROCKS, Mr. Ian, ACA *2008;* Flat 5, Hamson Court, Brickfields, HARROW, MIDDLESEX, HA2 0JG.
SHARROCKS, Mr. Paul Robert, MA(Cantab) ACA *2006;* with KPMG LLP, 15 Canada Square, LONDON, E14 5GL.
SHARRON, Mr. William, FCA *1958;* Barrie, Compton Avenue, LONDON, N6 4LB. (Life Member)
SHARROTT, Mr. Richard Frank, FCA *1964;* Sharrott.net Ltd, 183 Windermere Avenue, NUNEATON, WARWICKSHIRE, CV11 6HW.
SHARVILL, Mr. Andrew James, BSc ACA CTA *2006;* 14 Ethelburt Avenue, SOUTHAMPTON, SO16 3DD.
SHARVILL, Mrs. Joanna, ACA *2009;* 14 Ethelburt Avenue, SOUTHAMPTON, SO16 3DD.
•**SHASHA, Mr. Jonathan Choua, BA FCA** *1980;* Brookside, Knutsford Road, Mobberley, KNUTSFORD, WA16 7BE.
SHASHA, Mrs. Ruth, BSc ACA *1989;* 25 Cavendish Road, SALFORD, M7 4WP.
SHASHOUA, Mr. Salim Jacob, FCA *1968;* Salim Shashoua, Oberneuhofstrasse 1, CH-6341 BAAR, SWITZERLAND.
•**SHASTRI, Mr. Rohit, FCA** *1982;* Wilkins Kennedy, Cecil House, 52 St Andrew Street, HERTFORD, SG14 1JA.
SHATTOCK, Mr. Michael Rodney, BA FCA *1969;* Clipsam, 28 Oak Road, COBHAM, KT11 3BA.
SHAUGHNESSY, Mr. Colin, BA FCA *1985;* 7 Cleveland Avenue, Linthorpe, MIDDLESBROUGH, TS5 7RR.
SHAUL, Mr. Jonathan, BSc ACA *1990;* NBC Tower, 9th Floor, CHICAGO, IL 60611, UNITED STATES.
•**SHAUL, Mr. Richard John Leslie, BSc FCA** *1984;* (Tax Fac), Chandlers, 85-87 Bayham Street, LONDON, NW1 0AG.
•**SHAUL, Mr. William, BA FCA** *1987;* (Tax Fac), KPMG LLP, 15 Canada Square, LONDON, E14 5GL. See also KPMG Europe LLP
SHAUNAK, Mr. Kishen Daljet, BSc(Econ) ACA *2004;* Shaunaks Limited, Shaunak House, Netham Road, Redfield, BRISTOL, BS5 9PQ.
SHAUNAK, Mr. Rajeev, BSc ACA *2000;* 23 Wood Lane, ISLEWORTH, MIDDLESEX, TW7 5EF.
•**SHAUNAK, Mr. Rakesh, ACA** *1980;* MacIntyre Hudson LLP, New Bridge Street House, 30-34 New Bridge Street, LONDON, EC4V 6BJ.
SHAVE, Mr. Harry William Reid, MA ACA *2010;* 72a Greenwich South Street, LONDON, SE10 8UN.
•**SHAVE, Mr. Martin David Reid, FCA** *1979;* (Tax Fac), Simpson & Co (Accountants) Limited, 21 High Street, LUTTERWORTH, LEICESTERSHIRE, LE17 4AT.
SHAVE, Mr. Richard Andrew, BSc ACA *1999;* with BDO LLP, 55 Baker Street, LONDON, W1U 7EU.
SHAW, Mr. Adam Dominic Bradley, BSc ACA *1996;* 90 Felsham Road, LONDON, SW15 1DQ.
SHAW, Mr. Adrian David, BSc FCA *1999;* with The London Stock Exchange Plc, 10 Paternoster Square, LONDON, EC4M 7LS.
SHAW, Mr. Adrian Fazackerley, BSc ACA *1991;* 5 Chemin de Cretely, La Tour de Peilz, 1814 VAUD, SWITZERLAND.
SHAW, Ms. Alison Mary, ACA *2008;* University House, University of Warwick University House, Kirby Corner Road, COVENTRY, CV4 8UW.
SHAW, Mr. Alistair Philip Raymond, BSc ACA *2004;* Dove House, High Street, Hatfield Broad Oak, BISHOP'S STORTFORD, HERTFORDSHIRE, CM22 7HH.
SHAW, Mrs. Andrea, BA ACA *1990;* The Possums, 6C Eastbury Avenue, NORTHWOOD, HA6 3LG.
SHAW, Mr. Andrew, BSc ACA *2005;* with Deloitte LLP, 4 Brindley Place, BIRMINGHAM, B1 2HZ.
SHAW, Mr. Andrew, FCA *1976;* 5 Spring Street, Hollingworth, HYDE, SK14 8NQ.
SHAW, Mr. Andrew, ACA *2011;* 88 Bridle Lane, SUTTON COLDFIELD, B74 3HF.
SHAW, Mr. Andrew, ACA *2008;* 56 Dukewood Road, Clayton West, HUDDERSFIELD, HD8 9HF.
SHAW, Mr. Andrew Charles, BSc FCA *1983;* BTG Tax, Charles House, Charles Street, St. Helier, JERSEY, JE2 4SF.
SHAW, Mr. Andrew Glyn, BA ACA *1994;* 2 Summerfield Grove, Lepton, HUDDERSFIELD, HD8 0BQ.
SHAW, Mr. Andrew Hank, BA ACA *1993;* Drapers, Fletching, UCKFIELD, TN22 3TB.
SHAW, Mr. Andrew James, ACA *2009;* Flat A/203, Gilbert Scott Building, Scott Avenue, LONDON, SW15 3SG.
SHAW, Mr. Andrew John, BEng ACA *2002;* with KPMG LLP, 1 The Embankment, Neville Street, LEEDS, LS1 4DW.
•**SHAW, Mr. Andrew Nigel, BA FCA** *1983;* (Tax Fac), Kingston Smith LLP, Devonshire House, 60 Goswell Road, LONDON, EC1M 7AD. See also Kingston Smith Limited Liability Partnership, Devonshire Corporate Services LLP and Kingston Smith Consulting LLP
•**SHAW, Mr. Andrew Rhead, FCA** *1974;* (Tax Fac), Andrew R Shaw, Windsmoor, School Lane, Chittering, CAMBRIDGE, CB25 9PW.
SHAW, Mrs. Ann Elizabeth, BSc FCA *1978;* (Member of Council 2007 - 2011), Parkfoot Holiday Homes Ltd, Mingulay, Farleton, LANCASTER, LA2 9LF.
SHAW, Mr. Anthony, BA FCA *1962;* 3 The Ash Grove, Timperley, ALTRINCHAM, WA15 6JX. (Life Member)
SHAW, Mr. Anthony Vause, FCA *1959;* (Tax Fac), Zilverberkenlei 86, 2930 BRASSCHAAT, BELGIUM.
SHAW, Mr. Antony Edward, FCA *1950;* 4 Glebe Close, Empingham, OAKHAM, LEICESTERSHIRE, LE15 8QF. (Life Member)
SHAW, Mr. Antony Jonathan, BSc FCA *1992;* 14 Hayes Barton, Pyrford, WOKING, GU22 8NH.
•**SHAW, Mr. Ashley Mark, BSc FCA** *1986;* (Tax Fac), Leigh Philip & Partners, 1/6 Clay Street, LONDON, W1U 6DA.
SHAW, Mrs. Audrey Angeline, BA ACA *1986;* 7 Deer Park, HENFIELD, BN5 9JQ.
SHAW, Mr. Barry David, BSc ACA *1998;* Glenmore, Five Oaks Road, Slinfold, HORSHAM, WEST SUSSEX, RH13 0RQ.
SHAW, Mr. Benjamin Ewan, BA ACA *1999;* 7 Clifton Hill, LONDON, NW8 0QE.
SHAW, Mr. Benjamin Paul, BSc ACA *2010;* 24 Elmwood Close, Walton, WAKEFIELD, WEST YORKSHIRE, WF2 6LP.
SHAW, Mr. Brian, FCA *1953;* Woodfield House, 3 The Knowle, Beech Hill Road, Headley Down, GRAYSHOTT, HAMPSHIRE GU35 8DP. (Life Member)
SHAW, Mr. Bryan Douglas, FCA *1947;* 16 Norwich Road, Horsham St.Faith, NORWICH, NR10 3LB. (Life Member)
SHAW, Mrs. Catherine Jane, BSc ACA *2006;* 159 Manchester Road, ACCRINGTON, LANCASHIRE, BB5 2NY.
SHAW, Mr. Christopher Leslie, BSc FCA *1996;* with Baines Jewitt, Barrington House, 41-45 Yarm Lane, STOCKTON-ON-TEES, CLEVELAND, TS18 3EA.
SHAW, Miss. Claire, BA(Hons) ACA *2011;* Zurich Financial Services UK Life Centre, Station Road, SWINDON, SN1 1EL.
SHAW, Mr. Clive Michael, FCA *1966;* Grey Cedars, Cartworth Road, HOLMFIRTH, HD9 2RQ.
•**SHAW, Mr. Colin Richard, BSc FCA** *1988;* Cooper Parry LLP, 14 Park Row, NOTTINGHAM, NG1 6GR.
•**SHAW, Mr. Colin Wallace, FCA** *1967;* with BBK Partnership, 1 Beauchamp Court, Victors Way, BARNET, HERTFORDSHIRE, EN5 5TZ.
SHAW, Mr. Darren Alexander, BA ACA *1996;* Nahal Elal 6/1, 99622 RAMAT BEIT SHEMESH, ISRAEL.
SHAW, Mr. David, BSc ACA *2005;* 12 Tewkesbury Close, LOUGHTON, ESSEX, IG10 3NT.
•**SHAW, Mr. David, BCom FCA** *1974;* David Shaw, 9 Gorsty Hill Close, Balterley, CREWE, CW2 5QS.
•**SHAW, Mr. David Adam, BSc FCA** *1992;* (Tax Fac), A Shaw & Co Ltd, 21 Bushy Park Road, TEDDINGTON, MIDDLESEX, TW11 9DQ.
SHAW, Mr. David Andrew, FCA *1967;* with Monahans, Lennox House, 3 Pierrepont Street, BATH, BA1 1LB.
SHAW, Mr. David Baxter, FCA *1959;* (Member of Council 1993 - 2003), Kireka House, 527 Fulwood Road, SHEFFIELD, S10 3QB.
SHAW, Mr. David Brian, BA ACA *1985;* 48 Dane Avenue, BARROW-IN-FURNESS, LA14 4JY.
•**SHAW, Mr. David Hamilton, BSc FCA** *1985;* (Tax Fac), Shaw Austin Limited, 45 City Road, CHESTER, CH1 3AE.
•**SHAW, Mr. David Harry, FCA** *1972;* D.H.Shaw, 7 Chapel Row, Wilsden, BRADFORD, BD15 0EQ.
SHAW, Mr. David John, FCA *1968;* 8955 E. Voltaire Drive, SCOTTSDALE, AZ 85260, UNITED STATES. (Life Member)
SHAW, Mr. David John, BA ACA *1982;* 6 Clare Park, AMERSHAM, HP7 9HW.
•**SHAW, Mr. David Lawrence, FCA** *1974;* 66 Richborne Terrace, LONDON, SW8 1AX.
•**SHAW, Mr. David Richard, BSc FCA** *1988;* Hardwickes, Etruria Old Road, STOKE-ON-TRENT, ST1 5PE.
SHAW, Mr. David William, FCA *1970;* H T C Plant Ltd, Grange Mill Lane, SHEFFIELD, SOUTH YORKSHIRE, S9 1HW.
•**SHAW, Mr. Dennis Ian, MA FCA** *1962;* Ian Shaw, Mandalay, Chelmsford Road, Felsted, DUNMOW, CM6 3EP.
SHAW, Mr. Derek, BA ACA *1987;* Chloride Group Plc, 23 Lower Belgrave Street, LONDON, SW1W 0NR.
SHAW, Mr. Derek Steven Colin, BA ACA *1990;* 4 Templewood Gate, Farnham Common, SLOUGH, SL2 3EX.
SHAW, Mr. Edward James, BSc ACA *2006;* 14 Holmefield, SALE, CHESHIRE, M33 3AN.
SHAW, Mr. Edwin Alan, FCA *1960;* The Beechings, 2 Castle Nurseries, CHIPPING CAMPDEN, GLOUCESTERSHIRE, GL55 6JT.
SHAW, Mrs. Elizabeth Ann, BA FCA *1998;* 10 Shakespeare Road, HARPENDEN, HERTFORDSHIRE, AL5 5ND.
SHAW, Mrs. Elizabeth Anne, MA FCA *1986;* Max-Högger-Strasse 80, Postfach, CH8098 ZURICH, SWITZERLAND.
SHAW, Mrs. Elizabeth Anne, BCom ACA *1997;* 22 Stoneyflatts Park, SOUTH QUEENSFERRY, WEST LOTHIAN, EH30 9YL.
SHAW, Mrs. Emma Elizabeth Jane, BSc ACA *2003;* 10a Woodside Avenue, Hersham, WALTON-ON-THAMES, KT12 5LQ.
SHAW, Mr. Gareth, BSc ACA *1996;* Masterlease (UK), International House, Bickenhill Lane, BIRMINGHAM, B37 7HQ.
•**SHAW, Mr. Gary David, BA ACA** *2000;* with PricewaterhouseCoopers, Benson House, 33 Wellington Street, LEEDS, LS1 4JP.
SHAW, Mr. George Thomas, FCA *1966;* 6 Clos De Le Ruette, La Villette, St Martins, GUERNSEY, GY4 6QF. (Life Member)
•**SHAW, Mr. Graham, FCA** *1976;* (Tax Fac), Graham Shaw, 2 St Paul's Close, CLITHEROE, BB7 2NA.
SHAW, Mr. Graham Neil Akeroyd, FCA *1984;* Wilken Telecommunications, (kenya Ltd), P. O. Box 49428, Gpo 00100, NAIROBI, KENYA.
SHAW, Mr. Graham Philip, MA FCA ATII *1991;* (Tax Fac), Goldman Sachs International, Peterborough Court, 133 Fleet Street, LONDON, EC4A 2BB.
SHAW, Mr. Harold Malcolm, FCA *1957;* 37 Curzon Park South, CHESTER, CH4 8AA. (Life Member)
SHAW, Miss. Helen Clare, ACA *2008;* 1 Woodlands, Pirbright Road Normandy, GUILDFORD, GU3 2HT.
SHAW, Miss. Helen Jane, ACA *2010;* with Deloitte LLP, Hill House, 1 Little New Street, LONDON, EC4A 3TR.
SHAW, Mr. Henry, FCA *1952;* 18a Hartsbourne Avenue, Bushey Heath, BUSHEY, WD23 1JL. (Life Member)
SHAW, Mr. Herbert Cedric, FCA *1935;* Rose Cottage., Hackness, SCARBOROUGH, YO13 0JW. (Life Member)
SHAW, Mr. Howard, FCA *1960;* 1 Hathersage Drive, GLOSSOP, SK13 8RG.
SHAW, Mr. Howard John Brook, BA ACA *1991;* Tecni-Form Ltd, Goldstone Lane, HOVE, EAST SUSSEX, BN3 7BU.
SHAW, Mr. Howard Stephen, BSc ACA *1982;* D L A Piper Rudnick Gray Cary UK St. Pauls Place, 121 Norfolk Street, SHEFFIELD, S1 2JX.
•**SHAW, Mr. Ian, BA FCA** *2000;* 34 Rutherford Way, Bushey Heath, BUSHEY, WD23 1NJ.

SHAW, Mr. Ian Gordon, FCA *1965;* (Tax Fac), 5 South Road, The Park, NOTTINGHAM, NOTTINGHAMSHIRE, NG7 1EB.
SHAW, Mr. Ian Richard, FCA *1961;* Easton House, The Old School 38 Herd Street, MARLBOROUGH, SN8 1UN.
SHAW, Mr. James, BSc ACA *2007;* with Target Consulting Limited, Lawrence House, Lower Bristol Road, BATH, BA2 9ET.
•SHAW, Mr. James Leslie, ACA *1979;* (Tax Fac), Rothman Pantall LLP, 24 Park Road South, HAVANT, HAMPSHIRE, PO9 1HB. See also South Coast Accounting Services Limited
•ⒹSHAW, Mr. James Paul, FCA *1976;* Myers Clark Limited, Iveco House, Station Road, WATFORD, WD17 1DL. See also Bluedome Finance Limited
SHAW, Mrs. Jane Elizabeth, BA ACA *1989;* Johnson & Johnson Ltd, 1-4 Foundation Park Roxborough Way, MAIDENHEAD, SL6 3UG.
•SHAW, Mrs. Jane Hilary, BA ACA *1991;* Accountancy Services (Batley) Limited, 21 Henrietta Street, Batley, BATLEY, WEST YORKSHIRE, WF17 5DN.
SHAW, Miss. Jane Louise, BSc ACA *1988;* Calle Rovello 239, Les Tres Cales, 43860 L' AMETLLA DE MAR, SPAIN.
SHAW, Miss. Jane Margaret, BA CA ACA *1988;* 54 Valleyview Court, KLEINBURG L0J 1C0, ON, CANADA.
SHAW, Mrs. Janet Rose, BSc ACA *1984;* 6 Kirkton Road, WESTHILL, AB32 6LF.
SHAW, Mr. Jason, ACA *2007;* Unlimited, 123 Whitecross Street, LONDON, EC1Y 8JJ.
SHAW, Mr. Jeffrey Leonard, FCA *1967;* 97 Ennerdale Road, Kew, RICHMOND, SURREY, TW9 2DN. (Life Member)
SHAW, Mr. Jeremy James, FCA *1965;* Hylton, Felbrigg Road, Roughton, NORWICH, NORFOLK, NR11 8PA.
SHAW, Mr. Jeremy William Jonathon, BSc ACA *1987;* Castweazel Manor, Biddenden, ASHFORD, KENT, TN27 8EW.
SHAW, Mr. John, ACA CA(NZ) *2010;* 36a Burnbury Road, LONDON, SW12 0EJ.
SHAW, Mr. John Alexander, BSc FCA *1976;* 200 W. Springfield Street, Unit 1, BOSTON, MA 02118, UNITED STATES.
SHAW, Mr. John Bernard, FCA *1952;* 78 Gloucester Street, Winchcombe, CHELTENHAM, GLOUCESTERSHIRE, GL54 5LX. (Life Member)
•ⒹSHAW, Mr. John David, BSc ACA *2001;* PO BOX 138, FRODSHAM, CHESHIRE, WA6 1AY. See also Totality Solutions Ltd
SHAW, Mr. John Howard, MA FCA *1966;* 4 The Paddox, OXFORD, OX2 7PN.
•SHAW, Mr. John Joseph, BA(Hons) FCA DChA *1979;* (Tax Fac), Bentleys, Hazlemere, 70 Chorley New Road, BOLTON, BL1 4BY.
SHAW, Mr. John Julian St Clair, FCA *1958;* Linnets, Shute Road, Kilmington, AXMINSTER, EX13 7ST. (Life Member)
SHAW, Mr. John Patrick, BA FCA *1969;* 8 Plaxton Court, SCARBOROUGH, NORTH YORKSHIRE, YO12 6QT.
SHAW, Mr. John Richard, BCom FCA *1975;* Garden Flat, 4 Camden Terrace, LONDON, NW1 9BP.
SHAW, Mr. Jonathan Alan, BA FCA *1984;* 6 Springhill, Higher Hurdsfield, MACCLESFIELD, SK10 2PH.
SHAW, Mr. Jonathan Richard, BA ACA *1995;* Flat 21A Block 5 Coastal Skyline, 12 Tung Chung Waterfront Road, TUNG CHUNG, HONG KONG SAR.
SHAW, Mr. Joseph Bryan, FCA *1972;* 108 Middleton Lane, Winwick, WARRINGTON, WA2 8NA.
SHAW, Mr. Julian, BA ACA *1994;* Simon & Schuster (UK) Ltd, 222 Gray's Inn Road, LONDON, WC1X 8HB.
SHAW, Miss. Julie Ann, BSc ACA *1997;* Anglers Oast Church Lane, West Farleigh, MAIDSTONE, ME15 0DT.
SHAW, Miss. Karen, ACA *2007;* 4 Elizabeth Avenue, Milton of Campsie, GLASGOW, G66 8HT.
SHAW, Mrs. Karen Beverley, BSc ACA *1986;* 104 Harley Close, Dothill, TELFORD, TF1 3LF.
SHAW, Mr. Keith, FCA *1969;* 47 Petersfield, CHELMSFORD, CM1 4EP.
SHAW, Mr. Keith Graham, FCA *1970;* 5 Hawfield Bank, ORPINGTON, BR6 7TA.
SHAW, Mr. Kenneth Michael, FCA *1968;* 10 The Paddocks, PENARTH, CF64 5BW.
•SHAW, Mr. Kevan Graham, BA ACA *1991;* 100 Acorn Drive, Stannington, SHEFFIELD, S6 6ES.
SHAW, Mr. Kevin Michael, BSc ACA *2007;* 60 Jericho Road, Balderton, NEWARK, NOTTINGHAMSHIRE, NG24 3GT.
SHAW, Mr. Kieran Patrick, BCom ACA *2001;* 22 Stoneyflatts Park, SOUTH QUEENSFERRY, EH30 9YL.
SHAW, Mr. Kristian Stuart, MSci ACA *2006;* 38 Green Lane, ST. ALBANS, HERTFORDSHIRE, AL3 6EY.
SHAW, Mr. Lance Glenn Bridgman, FCA *1974;* Underbeeches, Underhill Park Road, REIGATE, RH2 9LX.
•SHAW, Mrs. Laura Jane, BA ACA *2005;* PKF (UK) LLP, 8th Floor, Helmont House, Churchill Way, CARDIFF, CF10 2HE.
SHAW, Mrs. Laura Rhona Rowansey, MA ACA *1998;* Britannia Building Society, Britannia House, Cheadle Road, LEEK, ST13 5RG.
SHAW, Mr. Leon Paul, FCA *1956;* Flat 8 James Court, 23 Devonshire Gardens, MARGATE, KENT, CT9 3AE. (Life Member)
SHAW, Miss. Lisa Jane, BCom ACA *1995;* 12 Highlands, Burley in Wharfedale, ILKLEY, WEST YORKSHIRE, LS29 7SA.
SHAW, Mr. Louis Raymond, FCA *1957;* 32 Regency House, 269 Regents Park Road, LONDON, N3 3JZ. (Life Member)
SHAW, Miss. Louisa Jane, BEng ACA *2003;* Meadows Cottage, Eccups Lane, WILMSLOW, CHESHIRE, SK9 5NZ.
SHAW, Miss. Louise Elizabeth Jane, BSc ACA *2004;* 509/5 Warayama Place, ROZELLE, NSW 2039, AUSTRALIA.
SHAW, Mr. Malcolm Selwyn, FCA *1957;* The Nash, Love Lane, Marnhull, STURMINSTER NEWTON, DT10 1PT. (Life Member)
SHAW, Mr. Malcolm Stuart, FCA *1970;* Walnut House, 12 Woodlands Road, HARROGATE, NORTH YORKSHIRE, HG2 7AY.
SHAW, Mr. Mark, BA ACA *1990;* Le Moulin, Rue de la Fontaine Ste Martin, 60300 BOREST, FRANCE.
SHAW, Mr. Mark Glenn Bridgman, FCA *1971;* Amalgamated Financial Services, The Lodge, Odell, BEDFORD, MK43 7BB.
•SHAW, Mr. Mark James, BA(Hons) ACA ACCA CF *2006;* BDO LLP, 55 Baker Street, LONDON, W1U 7EU. See also BDO Stoy Hayward LLP
SHAW, Mr. Mark Nicholas, BA FCA *1993;* 1 Harewood Close, YORK, YO30 5XQ.
SHAW, Mr. Mark William Edward, BSc ACA *1999;* Bureside House, North River Road, GREAT YARMOUTH, NORFOLK, NR30 1TA.
•ⒹSHAW, Mr. Martin Andrew, BSc FCA *1979;* Refresh Recovery Limited, West Lancashire Investment Centre, Maple View, Whitemoss Business Park, SKELMERSDALE, LANCASHIRE WN8 9TG.
SHAW, Mr. Martin Gee, BSc FCA MCT *1991;* 1 Little Acre, Townsend Drive, ST. ALBANS, HERTFORDSHIRE, AL3 5SG.
•SHAW, Mr. Martin Thomas, BSc FCA *1984;* Via Giacomo 16, CH 6911 CAMPIONE, SWITZERLAND.
SHAW, Mr. Martin Warwick, BEng FCA *1993;* Fletchers Farm, Water Street, Brindle, CHORLEY, PR6 8NH.
SHAW, Mr. Martyn Alan, BSc FCA *1978;* (Tax Fac), 10 Chapel Road, REDHILL, RH1 1HH.
•SHAW, Mr. Matthew John, BSc FCA FCCA *1994;* Holborn Accountancy Tuition Limited, 12 Cock Lane, LONDON, EC1A 9BU.
SHAW, Miss. Melanie Nicola, BA ACA *2006;* Tate & Lyle Ltd, Sugar Quay, Lower Thames Street, LONDON, EC3R 6DQ.
SHAW, Mr. Michael, LLB ACA MBA *2003;* 2308 North Gilinger Road, LAFAYETTE, PA 19444, UNITED STATES.
SHAW, Mr. Michael David, FCA *1969;* 29 Garstang Road East, POULTON-LE-FYLDE, LANCASHIRE, FY6 8HJ. (Life Member)
SHAW, Mr. Michael John, BSc ACA *1981;* (Tax Fac), 69 Avoncroft Rd, Stoke Heath, BROMSGROVE, B60 4NG.
SHAW, Lord Michael Norman, FCA *1945;* Duxbury Hall, LIVERSEDGE, WF15 7NR. (Life Member)
SHAW, Mrs. Natalie Amanda, BSc ACA *1996;* BI Group Plc, Unit 1 First Avenue, Maybrook Industrial Estate, Minworth, SUTTON COLDFIELD, B76 1BA.
SHAW, Mr. Neil Anthony, MA ACA *1992;* 4 MIN y DDOL, Penyffordd, CHESTER, CH4 0JB.
SHAW, Mr. Nicholas David, FCA *1970;* 4 The Saltings, SEATON, DEVON, EX12 2XW.
SHAW, Miss. Nicola Jane, BSc ACA *2002;* 10 Chesterton Drive, STRATFORD-UPON-AVON, WARWICKSHIRE, CV37 7LG.
•SHAW, Mr. Nigel, ACA *1980;* Fisher Michael, Boundary House, 4 County Place, New London Road, CHELMSFORD, CM2 0RE.
SHAW, Miss. Patricia Jane, FCA *1976;* Cappellen, 17 Carlton Avenue, WILMSLOW, SK9 4EP.
•SHAW, Mr. Paul, BA FCA *1980;* Beever and Struthers, St George's House, 215-219 Chester Road, MANCHESTER, M15 4JE.
SHAW, Mr. Paul Andrew, BSc ACA *1995;* City Learning Ltd, 4 Chiswell Street, LONDON, EC1Y 4UP.
SHAW, Mr. Paul Jonathan, BSc ARCS ACA MCT *1993;* No 9 Highland Ridge, MIDDLE COVE, NSW 2068, AUSTRALIA.
•SHAW, Mr. Peter, FCA *1974;* (Tax Fac), Crossley & Davis, 52 Chorley New Road, BOLTON, BL1 4AP.
SHAW, Mr. Peter, BBS FCA *1974;* Flat 8 Collingwood Mount, 4 Collingwood Rise, CAMBERLEY, GU15 1BY.
SHAW, Mr. Peter George, FCA *1975;* 2 Chesham Road, WILMSLOW, SK9 6HA.
SHAW, Mr. Peter George, FCA *1958;* 14 Draycott Road, Southmoor, ABINGDON, OX13 5BY. (Life Member)
•SHAW, Mr. Peter Holme, BSc FCA *1975;* Shaws ATS Limited, Mingulay, Farleton, LANCASTER, LA2 9LF.
•SHAW, Mr. Peter James, ACA *1992;* Peter Shaw, 1 Radcliffe Gardens, Radcliffe Lane, PUDSEY, WEST YORKSHIRE, LS28 8BG.
SHAW, Mr. Peter Laurence, MA ACA *2006;* EME Capital, 83 Piccadilly, LONDON, W1J 8QA.
SHAW, Mr. Peter Robert, BSc ACA *1987;* (Tax Fac), Maersk UK Limited, Maersk House, Beagle House, Braham Street, LONDON, E1 8EP.
SHAW, Mr. Peter Robin, BA ACA *1987;* Saga Group Ltd Enbrook Park, Sandgate High Street Sandgate, FOLKESTONE, CT20 3SE.
SHAW, Mr. Peter William, FCA *1962;* George Hotel, 41-49 St. Georges Road, CHELTENHAM, GLOUCESTERSHIRE, GL50 3DZ.
SHAW, Mr. Philip Duncan, FCA *1964;* Banks House, Smallhythe Road, Smallhythe, TENTERDEN, TN30 7NG.
SHAW, Mr. Philip Martin, BA ACA *1992;* 6 Ribbledale Close, MANSFIELD, NG18 3GW.
SHAW, Mr. Phillip James, ACA *2002;* 28 King George Crescent, WALSALL, WS4 1EG.
SHAW, Miss. Rachael Mary, BA(Hons) ACA *2010;* 29 Quentin Road, LONDON, SE13 5DQ.
SHAW, Mrs. Rachel Helen, BA ACA *2002;* 25 Bowers Way, HARPENDEN, HERTFORDSHIRE, AL5 4EP.
SHAW, Miss. Rebecca Ilana, BA ACA *1992;* University of Greenwich, Old Royal Naval College, Park Row, GREENWICH, SE10 9LS.
SHAW, Miss. Rebekah Elizabeth, BMus ACA *2003;* 52 Trefoil Close, Huntington, CHESTER, CHESHIRE, CH3 6DZ.
SHAW, Mr. Richard Charles Julian, ACA FCCA *2008;* 23 Damson Way, ST. ALBANS, HERTFORDSHIRE, AL4 9XU.
•SHAW, Mr. Richard Gardner, FCA CTA *1977;* (Tax Fac), Richard G Shaw Limited, The Granary, Caldewell Farm Barns, Pershore Road, Stoulton, WORCESTER PARK WR7 4RL.
SHAW, Mr. Richard Geoffrey, BA(Hons) ACA *2000;* Hammerson Plc, 10 Grosvenor Street, LONDON, W1K 4BJ.
SHAW, Mr. Richard Gordon Ryrie, BA ACA *1999;* Lazard, 50 Stratton Street, LONDON, W1J 8LL.
SHAW, Mr. Richard James, BSc ACA *2006;* Flat 1, 171 Inderwick Road, LONDON, N8 9JR.
SHAW, Mr. Richard Martin, ACA *2009;* 9 Blue Haze Close, PLYMOUTH, PL6 7HR.
SHAW, Mr. Richard Stirling, BA ACA *1982;* Silvan House, Hibbert Road, MAIDENHEAD, BERKSHIRE, SL6 1UT.
SHAW, Mr. Richard William, FCA *1970;* 50 N Plum Grove Road, Apt 705E, PALATINE, IL 60067, UNITED STATES.
•SHAW, Mr. Robert, BSc ACA *1981;* Macilvin Moore Reveres LLP, 7 St John's Road, HARROW, HA1 2EY.
SHAW, Mr. Robert John, BA ACA *1999;* Haslers, Old Station Road, LOUGHTON, ESSEX, IG10 4PL.
SHAW, Mr. Robert Malcolm, BSc ACA *1997;* Hertswegenstraat 66, 3080 TERVUREN, BELGIUM.
SHAW, Mr. Robert Michael, FCA *1966;* 11 Westminster Road, POOLE, BH13 6JQ. (Life Member)
SHAW, Mr. Robert Sean Peter, ACA *1985;* 21 Jackson Road, WYLAM, NORTHUMBERLAND, NE14 8EL.
•SHAW, Mr. Robert William George, FCA *1990;* Robert Shaw FCA, 5 Thorley Hill, BISHOP'S STORTFORD, HERTFORDSHIRE, CM23 3ND.
SHAW, Mr. Roderick Brian, FCA *1966;* 316/2 New Quay Promenade, Docklands, MELBOURNE, VIC 3008, AUSTRALIA. (Life Member)
SHAW, Mr. Roger David, FCA *1973;* Leda Support Services Ltd, 74 Kirkgate, LEEDS, LS2 7DJ.
SHAW, Mr. Roger Malcolm, BA FCA *1967;* 24 Acacia Drive, Thorpe Bay, SOUTHEND-ON-SEA, SS1 3JX. (Life Member)
•SHAW, Mr. Ronald, FCA *1961;* Newfield & Co, 2 Broadwaters Drive, Hagley, STOURBRIDGE, DY9 0JU.
SHAW, Mr. Ronald, FCA *1966;* Flat 4, Princess Park Manor, Royal Drive, New Southgate, LONDON, N11 3FL.
SHAW, Miss. Rosemary Jane, BA ACA *1992;* 3 Old Tollerton Road, Gamston, NOTTINGHAM, NG2 6NX.
SHAW, Mr. Ryan Andrew, BSc ACA *1996;* 25 Toulon Avenue, WENTWORTH FALLS, NSW 2782, AUSTRALIA.
SHAW, Mrs. Sarah Elizabeth, BSc ACA *1997;* 40 Middleton Road, ILKLEY, WEST YORKSHIRE, LS29 9EX.
SHAW, Miss. Sarah Jayne, BA(Hons) ACA *2003;* 5 Spring House Close, Ashgate, CHESTERFIELD, DERBYSHIRE, S42 7PD.
SHAW, Mr. Simon Andrew, BSc ACA *1993;* 8 The Fold, Lothersdale, KEIGHLEY, WEST YORKSHIRE, BD20 8HD.
SHAW, Mr. Simon James, BA ACA *1998;* Eggborough Plant, Saint Gobain Glass UK Ltd Weeland Road, Eggborough, GOOLE, NORTH HUMBERSIDE, DN14 0FD.
SHAW, Mr. Simon James Blouet, BA ACA *1990;* Church House, Catherington Lane, WATERLOOVILLE, PO8 0TE.
SHAW, Mr. Simon James Lowther, BA ACA *1988;* Unit 8 Hightown, White Cross Industrial Estate, LANCASTER, LA1 4XS.
SHAW, Mr. Simon John, ACA *1983;* 66 Liverpool Road, Birkdale, SOUTHPORT, PR8 4BB.
SHAW, Mr. Simon Richard, BSc ACA *1999;* 23 Upcroft Avenue, EDGWARE, HA8 9RA.
SHAW, Miss. Stephanie Anne, BSc ACA *1994;* 18 Westvale Road, Timperley, ALTRINCHAM, WA15 7RN.
•SHAW, Mr. Stephen, FCA *1972;* Stephen Shaw Accountancy Services Limited, 9 Blue Haze Close, PLYMOUTH, PL6 7HR.
SHAW, Mr. Stephen Dominic, BSc(Hons) ACA *2007;* Flat 71 The Worcestershire, St. Andrews Road, DROITWICH, WORCESTERSHIRE, WR9 8DW.
SHAW, Mr. Stephen Paul, BSc ACA *2006;* Kesa Electricals Plc, 22-24 Ely Place, LONDON, EC1N 6TE.
SHAW, Mrs. Susan Angela, BSc ACA *1993;* Skills for Care Ltd, Albion Court, 5 Albion Place, LEEDS, LS1 6JL.
•SHAW, Mrs. Susan Elizabeth, BSc ACA CTA *1989;* (Tax Fac), with Smith & Williamson Ltd, Old Library Chambers, 21 Chipper Lane, SALISBURY, SP1 1BG.
SHAW, Mrs. Susan Elizabeth, FCA *1973;* Clarte, Les Cherfs, La Ruette Des Corneilles, Castel, GUERNSEY, GY5 7HG.
SHAW, Mrs. Susan Elizabeth, BSc FCA *1989;* 45 Meeting House Close, East Leake, LOUGHBOROUGH, LE12 6HY.
SHAW, Miss. Suzanne Elisabeth, BSc ACA *1989;* Brantwood Southstoke Lane, Southstoke, BATH, BA2 7DN.
SHAW, Mr. Timothy Goodwin, FCA CTA *1973;* 35 Bernard Gardens, LONDON, SW19 7BE.
SHAW, Mr. Timothy John, BA ACA CTA *2002;* 27 Ashburn Road, STOCKPORT, CHESHIRE, SK4 2PU.
•SHAW, Mr. Timothy Martin, ACA *1991;* (Tax Fac), Blick Rothenberg, 12 York Gate, Regent's Park, LONDON, NW1 4QS.
•SHAW, Mr. Timothy Michael, BA ACA *1990;* The Possums, 6C Eastbury Avenue, NORTHWOOD, HA6 3LG.
•SHAW, Mrs. Tracy Jane, BSc FCA *1984;* (Tax Fac), T J Shaw, 6 Cherrington Manor Court, Cherrington, NEWPORT, TF10 8PA. See also The Integrity Partnership Ltd
SHAW, Mr. Trevor Derek, BSc FCA *1992;* RSM Tenon Cedar House Breckland, Linford Wood, MILTON KEYNES, MK14 6EX.
SHAW, Mr. Vee Fong, BSc FCA *1959;* Shaw and Sons Ltd, 16th Floor, Fairmont House, 8 Cotton Tree Drive, CENTRAL, HONG KONG ISLAND HONG KONG SAR. (Life Member)
SHAW, Miss. Victoria, ACA MAAT *2011;* 38 Holyrood Close, Caversham, READING, RG4 6PZ.
SHAW, Mr. Vincent, BA ACA *2006;* 45 Wentworth Avenue, Emley, HUDDERSFIELD, HD8 9XR.
SHAW, Mr. William, FCA *1971;* 3 Fairbourne Close, Callands, WARRINGTON, WA5 9RR.
SHAW, Mr. William James Edward, BSc ACA *1993;* 44 Werter Road, LONDON, SW15 2LJ.
SHAW-BROWN, Mr. Patrick James Cameron, BSc ACA *2010;* 28 Camborne Road, LONDON, SW18 4BJ.
SHAW STEWART, Mr. David Hugh, MA ACA *1981;* McInroy & Wood Ltd, Easter Alderston, Alderston, HADDINGTON, EAST LOTHIAN, EH41 3SF.
SHAWCROFT, Ms. Alison Jane, BSc ACA *1996;* Gue de Ray, 49390 PARCAY LE PINS, FRANCE.
•SHAWCROSS, Mr. David Robert, BSc FCA *1992;* Anderson Barrowcliff LLP, Waterloo House, Thornaby Place, Thornaby on Tees, STOCKTON-ON-TEES, CLEVELAND TS17 6SA. See also Anderson Barrowcliff
SHAWCROSS, Mr. John Edward, FCA *1963;* 14 St.Brannocks Road, Cheadle Hulme, CHEADLE, SK8 7LA. (Life Member)
SHAWCROSS, Miss. Karen, BSc ACA *2002;* Flat 25, 70 Mariner Avenue, BIRMINGHAM, B16 9EQ.

SHAWCROSS, Mr. Robert Edward Newlove, FCA *1961;* (Tax Fac), with Anderson Barrowcliff, Waterloo House, Teesdale South, Thornaby Place, STOCKTON-ON-TEES, TS17 6SA.
SHAWE, Miss. Joanna Lucy, ACA *2009;* 9 Oakleafe Drive, Pontprennau, CARDIFF, CF23 8AL.
SHAWKAT, Mrs. Denise, BA ACA *1991;* 20 Hollybush Lane, HARPENDEN, HERTFORDSHIRE, AL5 4AT.
SHAWKAT, Mr. Haydar Suham, BEng ACA *1992;* 20 Hollybush Lane, HARPENDEN, HERTFORDSHIRE, AL5 4AT.
•SHAWKI, Mr. Ahmed Mostafa, PhD FCA MBA *1982;* Mostafa Shawki & Co, 153 Mohamed Farid St., Bank Misr TowerP.O.Box 2095, CAIRO, 11511, EGYPT.
•SHAWYER, Mr. David Martin, FCA *1975;* (Tax Fac), David Shawyer & Co Ltd, 6 Lodge Place, Thunder Lane, NORWICH, NR7 0LA.
SHAWYER, Mr. Gideon, BA ACA *2007;* 11 Alacross Road, LONDON, W5 4HS.
SHAWYER, Mr. James Sebastian, BA FCA *1978;* 14 Fox Close, Wigginton, TRING, HP23 6ED.
SHAWYER, Mr. Jonathan Philip, ACA *2010;* 21 Noyna Road, LONDON, SW17 7PQ.
•SHAWYER, Mr. Michael, FCA *1980;* Monahans, 38-42 Newport Street, SWINDON, SN1 3DR.
SHAWYER, Mr. Peter Michael, BA FCA *1976;* 73 Park Lane, BROXBOURNE, EN10 7PG.
SHAWYER, Mr. Robin Nicholas Scott, MA FCA *1975;* Windle Trust International, 37a Oxford Road, Cowley, OXFORD, OX4 2EN.
SHAY, Mr. Ian, FCA *1968;* Hatton Green, The Street, Salcott, MALDON, CM9 8HL.
SHAY, Mr. Ian Lawton, ACA *1983;* 9 Warwick Crescent, HARROGATE, NORTH YORKSHIRE, HG2 8JA.
SHAYA, Mr. Albert Moses, FCA *1969;* 39 Templars Avenue, LONDON, NW11 0NU. (Life Member)
SHAYA, Mr. Saadi Dawood, BA FCA *1963;* P.O.Box FL 346, FLATTS, BERMUDA. (Life Member)
SHE, Mr. Shing Pang, ACA *2009;* Flat 11C Blk 1, Marble Gardens, 33 Marble Road, NORTH POINT, HONG KONG ISLAND, HONG KONG SAR.
SHEA, Miss. Amanda Jane, BSc ACA *1997;* The Croft, Rawson Avenue, HALIFAX, WEST YORKSHIRE, HX3 0JP.
SHEA, Mr. Andrew John, MA ACA *2000;* 19 Chisbury Close, Forest Park, BRACKNELL, RG12 0TX.
SHEA, Mr. Christopher William, MA ACA *1979;* 34 Earls Road, TUNBRIDGE WELLS, TN4 8EE.
SHEA, Miss. Erica Katherine, ACA *2008;* 109 St. Thomas's Road, LONDON, N4 2QJ.
•SHEA, Mr. John Brian, LLB FCA *1979;* (Tax Fac), Shea & Co Limited, 105 Stansted Road, LONDON, SE23 1HH.
•SHEA, Mr. Kenneth Peter, FCA *1966;* Kenneth P Shea & Co, 25 Durnford Close, Norden, ROCHDALE, OL12 7RX.
SHEA, Mrs. Margaret Louise, FCA *1982;* (Tax Fac), 42 Corney Rd, Chiswick, LONDON, W4 2RA.
SHEA, Mr. Paul, BSc ACA *2009;* 2 Cromer Road, CHEADLE, CHESHIRE, SK8 2AX.
SHEAF, Miss. Lesley Janet, BA ACA *1979;* Wyndeham Press Group Ltd, 14c Bentalls Complex, Colchester Road, Heybridge, MALDON, ESSEX CM9 4NW.
SHEAF, Miss. Susan Elizabeth, BSc ACA *1995;* 50 Daines Way, SOUTHEND-ON-SEA, SS1 3PQ.
SHEAHAN, Mr. Benedict Robert, MSc BA FCA *1990;* 8 Ridgeway Road, Long Ashton, BRISTOL, BS41 9EU.
SHEAHAN, Mr. Daniel Edward, MSc BA(Hons) ACA *2001;* Park House Kirklees Hall, Kirklees, BRIGHOUSE, HD6 4HD.
SHEAHAN, Mrs. Jade Caroline, BSc(Hons) ACA *2001;* Park House Kirklees Hall, Kirklees, BRIGHOUSE, WEST YORKSHIRE, HD6 4HD.
•SHEAHAN, Mr. John Joseph, BCom FCA *1981;* John J. Sheahan & Co, Blackwater House, Mallow Business Park, MALLOW, COUNTY CORK, IRELAND.
SHEAHAN, Mr. Nicholas, ACA CA(AUS) *2010;* Flat 108a, Queens Court, Queensway, LONDON, W2 4QR.
SHEAIL, Mr. Nigel Malcolm, BSc ACA *1990;* Mattenweg 2, Pfeffingen, BL 4148 BASEL LAND, SWITZERLAND.
SHEAMAN, Mr. George William, FCA *1963;* Cedargrove, 40C Braemar Place, ABERDEEN, AB10 6ER. (Life Member)
SHEAR, Mr. Alexander Michael, MA ACA ATII AIIT *2000;* (Tax Fac), with Crowe Clark Whitehill LLP, St Bride's House, 10 Salisbury Square, LONDON, EC4Y 8EH.
•SHEAR, Mr. Daniel Marc, MA FCA CF *1993;* Berg Kaprow Lewis, 35 Ballards Lane, LONDON, N3 1XW.
SHEARAN, Mr. Michael John, MA FCA *1992;* (Tax Fac), with Grant Thornton UK LLP, 3140 Rowan Place, John Smith Drive, Oxford Business Park South, OXFORD, OX4 2WB.
SHEARD, Mr. Andrew Philip Snell, BA ACA *1990;* (Tax Fac), D H Industries Ltd, Sullivan House, Fenton Way, Southfields Business Park, BASILDON, ESSEX SS15 6TD.
SHEARD, Mr. Anthony John, LLB FCA ATII *1983;* 7201 Hannum Ave, CULVER CITY, CA CA 90230, UNITED STATES.
•SHEARD, Mr. Bryan Charles, BA FCA *1987;* Gibbons, Netherall Chambers, 2 Curzon Street, MARYPORT, CUMBRIA, CA15 6LL. See also Gibbons & Company
•SHEARD, Mr. Charles Simon Beaumont, ACA *1982;* Forrest Burlinson, 20 Owl Lane, DEWSBURY, WEST YORKSHIRE, WF12 7RQ. See also Accounting Management Services Ltd
SHEARD, Mr. Frederick John, FCA *1956;* 12 Foxglove Road, Almondbury, HUDDERSFIELD, HD5 8LW. (Life Member)
•SHEARD, Mr. Graham, BTech FCA *1975;* (Tax Fac), WHS Accountants Limited, Elmville House, 305 Roundhay Road, LEEDS, LS8 4HT.
SHEARD, Miss. Harriet, BSc ACA *2011;* West House, Glen Tramman, Lezayre, Ramsey, ISLE OF MAN, IM7 2AR.
•SHEARD, Mr. James Edward, BSc ACA *1990;* BS Tax and Accountancy Limited, Phoenix House, 2 Huddersfield Road, STALYBRIDGE, CHESHIRE, SK15 2QA. See also TaxAssist Accountants - James Sheard
SHEARD, Mr. John Paul, ACA *1989;* 42 Serpentine Road, FAREHAM, PO16 7EB.
SHEARD, Mrs. Julia Catherine, BSc ACA *1990;* Prospection, Tunstead Lane, Greenfield, OLDHAM, OL3 7NY.
SHEARD, Mr. Kenneth, FCA *1952;* 3 Hill Grove, Oakes, HUDDERSFIELD, HD3 3TL. (Life Member)
SHEARD, Mr. Matthew David George, BSc(Hons) ACA *2000;* 2 The Nook, Holbrook, BELPER, DERBYSHIRE, DE56 0TT.
SHEARD, Mr. Philip Arthur, BSc FCA *1975;* Sandwell Metropolitan Borough Council, PO Box 2374, OLDBURY, B69 3DE.
SHEARD, Mrs. Rachel Jane, MA ACA *2000;* 2 Harlech Grove, Lodge Moor, SHEFFIELD, S10 4NP.
SHEARD, Mr. Richard Anthony, FCA *1968;* Undercliffe House, 35 Dunford Road, Holmfirth, HUDDERSFIELD, HD9 2DR. (Life Member)
SHEARD, Mr. Simon Alexander Blakeley, BA ACA *1992;* The Basement Flat, 75 Cornwall Gardens, LONDON, SW7 4AZ.
•SHEARER, Mr. Andrew Charles, BSc FCA *1982;* (Tax Fac), Andrew Shearer, Town House, 16-18 Town Street, Horsforth, LEEDS, LS18 4RJ.
SHEARER, Mrs. Ann-Marie, BA FCA *1987;* 64 Sovereign Crescent, Titchfield Common, FAREHAM, PO14 4LU.
SHEARER, Mr. Anthony Patrick, FCA *1971;* 10 Napier Road, LONDON, W14 8LQ.
•SHEARER, Mr. Brian Robert, MA *1973;* 40 Langside Crescent, Southgate, LONDON, N14 7DR.
SHEARER, Mr. Donald MacSween, MBA BA ACA *1986;* 54 Milford Close, Walkwood, REDDITCH, B97 5PZ.
SHEARER, Mrs. Fiona Jean, ACA *2000;* 6 The Heronry, WALTON-ON-THAMES, SURREY, KT12 5AT.
SHEARER, Mrs. Joan Wilson, MA ACA *1991;* 25 Edgehill Road Bearsden, GLASGOW, G61 3AA.
SHEARER, Miss. Kirsten Louise, ACA *2008;* 21 Derby Road, POULTON-LE-FYLDE, FY6 7AF.
SHEARER, Miss. Laura Ann, ACA *2010;* K P M G, 1-2 Dorset Rise, LONDON, EC4Y 8EN.
SHEARER, Mr. Richard, ACA CA(SA) *2008;* 6 The Heronry, Hersham, WALTON-ON-THAMES, SURREY, KT12 5AT.
•SHEARER, Mrs. Sarah Elizabeth, BSc ACA *2003;* Emmaus Accountants Ltd, Westmead House, Westmead, FARNBOROUGH, HAMPSHIRE, GU14 7LP. See also Footprints Accountancy Ltd
SHEARER, Mr. Stanley, FCA *1968;* DERRINSALLAGH, BALLYBROPHY, PORTLAOISE, COUNTY LAOIS, IRELAND.
SHEARER, Mr. Wayne Ernest, BCom ACA *2003;* 108 Barton Road, Hawthorne, HAWTHORNE, QLD 4171, AUSTRALIA.
SHEARGOLD, Mrs. Bridget Louise, BSc(Hons) ACA *2000;* Balmedie, 208 Annandale Street, Annandale, SYDNEY, NSW 2038, AUSTRALIA.
SHEARING, Mrs. Amanda Caroline, FCA *1976;* 18 Onslow Road, Burwood Park, WALTON-ON-THAMES, KT12 5BB.
SHEARING, Mr. Andrew Geoffrey, BA(Hons) ACA *2001;* 66 Silverburn Drive, Oakwood, DERBY, DE21 2JH.
SHEARING, Mr. David Anthony, FCA *1975;* Maurice Turnor Gardner Llp, 201 Bishopsgate, LONDON, EC2M 3AB.
SHEARING, Mrs. Lynn Marie, BA ACA *2003;* 1 Maidenhair, Biddick Woods, HOUGHTON LE SPRING, DH4 7TL.
SHEARING, Mr. Mark Paul, ACA *2008;* with Grant Thornton UK LLP, Kingfisher House, 1 Gilders Way, St James Place, NORWICH, NR3 1UB.
SHEARING, Mr. Robert Dean, ACA CA(AUS) *2008;* 67 Mortimer Court, Abbey Road, LONDON, NW8 9AD.
SHEARING, Mr. William Robert, FCA *1953;* 23 Royston Avenue, Orton Longueville, PETERBOROUGH, PE2 7AA. (Life Member)
SHEARMAN, Mr. Andrew James, FCA *1975;* 35 Hawthorne Court, Ryefield Crescent, NORTHWOOD, MIDDLESEX, HA6 1LS.
SHEARMAN, Mrs. Jayne Anne, BSc FCA *1995;* 15 High Farm Meadow, Badsworth, PONTEFRACT, WF9 1PB.
SHEARMAN, Mrs. Karen Fiona, MA FCA *1995;* Group Audit, Zurich Financial Services UK Life Centre, Station Road, SWINDON, SN1 1EL.
SHEARMAN, Mrs. Katy Helen, BSc ACA *2003;* 16 Helmsdale, WOKING, SURREY, GU21 3HT.
SHEARMAN, Mr. Peter, BSc FCA *1992;* 15 High Farm Meadow, Badsworth, PONTEFRACT, WEST YORKSHIRE, WF9 1PB.
SHEARN, Mr. David Anthony, FCA *1965;* (Tax Fac), 8 St. Marks Road, Midsomer Norton, RADSTOCK, BA3 2EN. (Life Member)
•SHEARS, Mrs. Helen Carlene, BSc ACA DChA *2004;* H S Accounting, 47 All Hallows Road, Preston, PAIGNTON, DEVON, TQ3 1DX.
SHEARS, Mr. James Charles, BSc FCA *2000;* Adelaide Cottage, The Green, Ellington, HUNTINGDON, CAMBRIDGESHIRE, PE28 0AQ.
SHEARS, Mr. Kevin Reginald Park, MA FCA *1956;* 21 Great Ellshams, Holly Lane, BANSTEAD, SM7 2BA. (Life Member)
SHEARS, Mr. Mark Andrew, BSc FCA *1994;* 215 Musters Road, West Bridgford, NOTTINGHAM, NG2 7DT.
•SHEARS, Mr. Richard John, FCA ATII *1972;* Richard Shears, Parallel House, 32 London Road, GUILDFORD, SURREY, GU1 2AB.
SHEARS, Mr. Stephen John, BSc ACA *1999;* Merlin Entertainments Ltd, 3 Market Close, POOLE, DORSET, BH15 1NQ.
SHEARS, Mr. Trevor Halliday, OBE FCA *1973;* Elmfield Lodge, 35 Elmfield Road, Gosforth, NEWCASTLE UPON TYNE, NE3 4BA. (Life Member)
SHEARSBY, Mr. Mark John, ACA *2009;* Apartment 108 Oyster Wharf, 18 Lombard Road, LONDON, SW11 3RR.
SHEASBY, Dr. Christopher Edmund, PhD BSc ACA *2005;* M & A Partners, 7 The Close, NORWICH, NR1 4DJ.
SHEASBY, Mr. John Michael, FCA *1959;* The Red House, Old Beaconsfield Road, Farnham Common, SLOUGH, SL2 3LR. (Life Member)
SHEATH, Mr. Christopher Gorden, BA FCA *1982;* Unit D, 1 Willis Way, POOLE, BH15 3SS.
SHEATH, Mr. Stuart Roy, BA ACA *1996;* 111 London Road, BIGGLESWADE, BEDFORDSHIRE, SG18 8EE.
SHEATH, Mrs. Vivien Anne, ACA *1982;* Fairways Care (UK) Ltd, Fairways House, Mount Pleasant Road, SOUTHAMPTON, SO14 0QB.
•SHEATHER, Mr. John Donald, BSc FCA *1992;* (Tax Fac), McCabe Ford Williams, Charlton House, Dour Street, DOVER, CT16 1BL.
•SHECKLESTON, Mr. Thomas James, MA FCA *1982;* The Pavilion Apartments, 56/25 Love Street, BULIMBA, QLD QLD 4171, AUSTRALIA.
•SHEDD, Mr. Clive Leonard, FCA *1977;* Clive Shedd & Co, 232 Sladepool Farm Road, Highters Heath, BIRMINGHAM, B14 5EE.
SHEDD, Mr. John Wilfred, FCA *1952;* 9 Prince Henrys Close, EVESHAM, WR11 4NW. (Life Member)
SHEDEL, Mr. Bryan Edmund, FCA *1958;* 50 Willow Green, INGATESTONE, CM4 0DH. (Life Member)
SHEEHAN, Mrs. Anne Loretta, BA ACA *1985;* 8 Valleyview Close, Highwoods, COLCHESTER, CO4 9UN.
SHEEHAN, Mr. Brendan John Patrick, BSc ACA *1989;* 5 Sutherland Crescent, CHIPPENHAM, WILTSHIRE, SN14 6RS.
SHEEHAN, Mrs. Catherine Joy, FCA *1983;* 88 Goswell End Road, Harlington, DUNSTABLE, BEDFORDSHIRE, LU5 6NX.
SHEEHAN, Mr. Daniel, ACA *2009;* 5 High Street, Crowle, SCUNTHORPE, SOUTH HUMBERSIDE, DN17 4LD.
SHEEHAN, Mr. Daniel Francis, MBA BA FCA *1982;* Balquhidder, River Gardens, Bray, MAIDENHEAD, BERKSHIRE, SL6 2BJ.
SHEEHAN, Mr. David, BSc ACA *1998;* 62 Priestfields, LEIGH, LANCASHIRE, WN7 2RG.
•SHEEHAN, Mr. John Paul, FCA *1981;* (Tax Fac), WKH, PO Box 501, The Nexus Building, Broadway, LETCHWORTH GARDEN CITY, HERTFORDSHIRE SG6 9BL.
SHEEHAN, Miss. Katrina Margaret, BCom FCA *1977;* 40 Lower Churchtown Road, DUBLIN 14, COUNTY DUBLIN, IRELAND.
SHEEHAN, Mr. Mark David, BA(Hons) ACA *2002;* 13 Stanley Road, Portslade, BRIGHTON, BN41 1SW.
SHEEHAN, Mr. Matthew Alexander, BA ACA *2006;* Flat 4, 112 East Dulwich Road, LONDON, SE22 9AT.
SHEEHAN, Mr. Robin James, BA ACA *2002;* 16 Ridge Road, LONDON, N21 3EA.
SHEEHY, Miss. Dervla, BA ACA *1993;* 41 Sandycove Road, Sandycove, DUBLIN, COUNTY DUBLIN, IRELAND.
SHEEHY, Mr. John Anthony, BA ACA *1989;* St. Mannelier, La Rue de St. Mannelier, St. Saviour, JERSEY, JE2 7HJ.
•SHEEHY, Mr. Martin James, ACA ACCA DChA *2008;* Fish Partnership LLP, The Mill House, Boundary Road, Loudwater, HIGH WYCOMBE, BUCKINGHAMSHIRE HP10 9QN.
SHEEHY, Mr. Stuart David, BA ACA *1992;* Chandlers, 28 Upper Holt Street, Earls Colne, COLCHESTER, ESSEX, CO6 2PG.
SHEEKEY, Mrs. Dawn Anne, BA ACA *1992;* 6 Saulfland Drive, CHRISTCHURCH, DORSET, BH23 4QN.
•SHEEKEY, Mr. Duncan Arthur, FCA *1984;* Platt Rushton LLP, Sutherland House, 1759 London Road, LEIGH-ON-SEA, ESSEX, SS9 2RZ. See also Sutherland Corporate Services Ltd
SHEEKEY, Mr. Geoffrey Leslie, FCA *1970;* 29 Mead Walk, HULL, HU4 6XE.
•SHEEKEY, Mr. Ian Charles, FCA *1987;* Hugh Davies & Co Limited, 35 Chequers Court, Brown Street, SALISBURY, SP1 2AS.
•SHEEN, Mr. Mark Richard Churchill, BA FCA *1989;* (Tax Fac), Barlow Andrews LLP, Carlyle House, 78 Chorley New Road, BOLTON, BL1 4BY. See also Beech Business Services Limited
SHEENA, Mr. Abraham Albert, FCA *1961;* 1 Greenacres, Bushey Heath, BUSHEY, WD23 1RF.
SHEENA, Mrs. Claudia Martine, BSc ACA *1997;* 20 Highwood Grove, LONDON, NW7 3LY.
SHEER, Mr. Gary John, ACA *1984;* 17 Franklin Road, Portslade, BRIGHTON, BN41 1AF.
•SHEER, Mr. John Rodney, MA FCA *1983;* PricewaterhouseCoopers LLP, 1 Embankment Place, LONDON, WC2N 6RH. See also PricewaterhouseCoopers
SHEERAN, Ms. Gillian Yvonne, ACA *2005;* 17 Butterworth Court, 1 Pendennis Road, LONDON, SW16 2SS.
SHEERAN, Mr. John Gerard, BSc ACA *1990;* Prologue Capital LLP, Greensand House Plumpton Lane, Plumpton, LEWES, EAST SUSSEX, BN7 3AD.
SHEERAN, Mr. Nicholas James, BA ACA *1997;* 17 Everard Road, BEDFORD, MK41 9LD.
SHEERAN, Miss. Rebecca, LLB ACA *2007;* Flat 2, 147 Alderney Street, LONDON, SW1V 4HD.
SHEERIN, Mrs. Elizabeth Mary, BSc ACA *1991;* 4 Southgate Wood, MORPETH, NORTHUMBERLAND, NE61 2EN.
•SHEEZAN, Mr. Mohammad, BSc(Hons) ACA CTA *2009;* Tax4You.co.uk Limited, Castle Court, 41 London Road, REIGATE, SURREY, RH2 9RJ.
SHEFFER, Mr. Derek Alfred, BA FCA *1966;* Lorne Cottage, Navarino Court, High Street, LYMINGTON, SO41 9AE.
SHEFFER, Mr. Nicholas David, MBA FCA *1980;* 61 Belgrave Gardens, LONDON, NW8 0RE.
SHEFFIELD, Mr. Alan, BA(Hons) ACA *2009;* 7 Orleigh Cross, NEWTON ABBOT, DEVON, TQ12 2FX.
SHEFFIELD, Mr. Alexander Charles Winter, MA ACA *2002;* The Old Rectory, Dunton, BUCKINGHAM, MK18 3LW.
SHEFFIELD, Mrs. Audra Jane, BSc ACA *1991;* The Willows, Wall Hill, CONGLETON, CHESHIRE, CW12 4TE.
SHEFFIELD, Mr. Jonathan Richard, BSc ACA *2002;* 82 North Hinksey Lane, OXFORD, OX2 0LY.
SHEFFIELD, Mr. Peter John Kirkham, BSc FCA *1980;* Wood Bros Furniture Ltd, London Road, WARE, HERTFORDSHIRE, SG12 9QH.
•SHEFFRIN, Mr. Robert Anthony, FCA MCSI *1982;* MEMBER OF COUNCIL, 83 South Downs Road, Bowdon, ALTRINCHAM, CHESHIRE, WA14 3DZ.
•SHEH, Mr. Michael Pui Hung, BSc ACA *1984;* Warwick Hotel, 1776 Grant Street, DENVER, CO 80203, UNITED STATES.

SHEHZAD, Mr. Aamer, ACA ACCA *2010;* Flat 8, Bulwer Court, Bulwer Court Road, LONDON, E11 1DB.
•SHEIBANI, Mr. Bijan, FCA *1971;* Bijan Sheibani, 18C Radisson Plaza, Al Makthoum Street, PO Box 51130, DUBAI, UNITED ARAB EMIRATES.
SHEIK FAREED, Mr. Shabbir Ahmad, BA(Econ) FCA *2000;* 23 Dunnock Avenue, Clayton Heights, BRADFORD, BD6 3XH.
SHEIKH, Mr. Asiam, BSc ACA *1999;* 35A Fairhazel Gardens, LONDON, NW6 3QN.
SHEIKH, Mr. Asim Jamil, FCA *1992;* with Ernst & Young, Al Faisaliah Office Tower, Level 14, PO Box 2732, RIYADH, 11461 SAUDI ARABIA.
SHEIKH, Mr. Babar Hameed, BSc ACA MBA *2000;* 3504 Maplewood Avenue, LOS ANGELES, CA 90066, UNITED STATES.
SHEIKH, Mr. Faheem, Ba BA(Hons) ACA *2011;* 29 Keston Road, THORNTON HEATH, SURREY, CR7 6BT.
SHEIKH, Mr. Faisal, BA ACA *1997;* 18 Marston Close, LONDON, NW6 4EU.
SHEIKH, Mr. Fazlur Rahman, LLB FCA *1960;* House No 418, Street No 12, Sector F-10/2, ISLAMABAD, PAKISTAN. (Life Member)
SHEIKH, Mr. Furrukh Mehmood, ACA *2009;* 41 Haworth Road, BRADFORD, WEST YORKSHIRE, BD9 5PB.
SHEIKH, Mr. Hasan Tauqeer, ACA *2011;* 129 Cambridge Street, OLDHAM, OL9 7BY.
SHEIKH, Miss. Humaira, BSc ACA *1995;* 103 Delamere Road, LONDON, W5 3JP.
SHEIKH, Mr. Ina'Am Ellahi, FCA *1973;* Riaz Ahmad & Co, 10B St Marys Park, Main Boulevard, Gulberg III, LAHORE, PAKISTAN.
SHEIKH, Mr. Kamran Iftikhar, ACA *2009;* (Tax Fac), with PricewaterhouseCoopers LLP, Pricewaterhousecoopers, 12 Plumtree Court, LONDON, EC4A 4HT.
SHEIKH, Mr. Khalid Mahboob, FCA *1967;* Zonienboslaan 23, B-3090 OVERIJSE, BELGIUM. (Life Member)
SHEIKH, Mr. Mohamed Imran, MA ACA *1996;* 41 Mitchley Avenue, PURLEY, CR8 1BZ.
SHEIKH, Mr. Mohammed Saleem, FCA *1975;* 85 Rochfords Gardens, SLOUGH, SL2 5XA.
SHEIKH, Mr. Mohammed Wasim, BSc ACA *1997;* 15 Lowlands Avenue, Tettenhall, WOLVERHAMPTON, WV6 9PA.
SHEIKH, Mr. Muhammad Saeed, FCA *1965;* BP Pakistan Exploration & Production, Bahria Complex Maulvi, Tameez Uddin Road, KARACHI, PAKISTAN.
SHEIKH, Mr. Muhammed Usman, BSc(Hons) ACA *2001;* 19 Kent Close, UXBRIDGE, MIDDLESEX, UB8 1XR.
SHEIKH, Mr. Nadim-Ul Hassan, BSc FCA *1995;* The Royal Bank of Scotland Plc, 280 Bishopsgate, LONDON, EC2M 4RB.
SHEIKH, Mr. Rizwan Khalid, BA ACA *1992;* Barclays Bank Plc, 5 North Colonnade, Canary Wharf, LONDON, E14 4BB.
SHEIKH, Mr. Tanweer, ACA *2011;* 11 Griffin Close, LONDON, NW10 1LL.
SHEIKH-ANENE, Mrs. Aisha Iqbal, BSc(Hons) ACA *2003;* 151 Second Avenue, DAGENHAM, ESSEX, RM10 9EA.
SHEILS, Miss. Margaret Ann, BA ACA *1984;* T'Gallant, Halls Lane, Waltham St Lawrence, READING, RG10 0JD.
SHEINMAN, Mr. David Nigel Jeremy, BA ACA *1988;* Merchant Property Group, 6 Torriano Mews, LONDON, NW5 2RZ.
SHEK, Mr. Kenny, MEng ACA *2003;* Flat 13A, Block 1 Site 9, Whampoa Garden, HUNG HOM, KOWLOON, HONG KONG SAR.
SHEK, Mr. Kwok Man, ACA *2008;* Flat H 59/ FloorTower 5, Metro Town, 8 King Ling Road, TSEUNG KWAN O, NEW TERRITORIES, HONG KONG SAR.
SHEK, Mr. Rocky, ACA *2007;* Rocky Shek & Co, Room 901, Yip Fung Building, 9/F No 2, D'Aguilar Street, CENTRAL HONG KONG ISLAND HONG KONG SAR.
SHEK, Mr. Stanley Chi Ping, BSc ACA *1993;* 68 Tintagel Court, 201 St. JOhn Street, LONDON, EC1V 4LZ.
SHEK, Ms. Wai Kuen, ACA *2008;* Flat E6.Floor, Block 2, Provident Centre, 23 Wharf Road, NORTH POINT, HONG KONG ISLAND HONG KONG SAR.
•SHEKLE, Mr. Hadleigh James, BA FCA *1997;* Deloitte LLP, 2 New Street Square, LONDON, EC4A 3BZ. See also Deloitte & Touche LLP
•SHELBOURNE, Mr. Christopher John, MA FCA *1987;* Wright Vigar Limited, 15 Newland, LINCOLN, LN1 1XG. See also Camamile Limited and Camamile Associates Ltd
SHELDON, Mr. Allan Ernest, BSc ACA *1981;* Geneva Centre for Security Policy, Avenue de la Paix 7bis, PO box 1295, CH - 1211 GENEVA, SWITZERLAND.
SHELDON, Mr. Andrew George, BA ACA *1991;* 20 Swains Lane, Flackwell Heath, HIGH WYCOMBE, BUCKINGHAMSHIRE, HP10 9BU.
SHELDON, Mrs. Anne Crosbie, BA ACA *1988;* Tupperware International Holdings B.V, Avenue Reverdil 12, 1260 NYON, SWITZERLAND.
SHELDON, Mr. David, BA MSt ACA *2003;* 3 Rannoch Court, 26 Adelaide Road, SURBITON, KT6 4TE.
SHELDON, Miss. Gwyneth Barbara, BSc ACA *1993;* 69 Selby Grove, Shenley Church End, MILTON KEYNES, MK5 6BT.
SHELDON, Mr. Jack Cecil, FCA *1961;* 4 Northfield Hall, 59 North Road, Highgate, LONDON, N6 4BJ.
SHELDON, Mr. John Basil Robertson, MA FCA *1971;* Midland Industrial Leasing Ltd, 17 Cowley Street, LONDON, SW1P 3LZ.
SHELDON, Mr. John Richard, MA FCA *1981;* Brookwood FarmhouseWater Lane, Headcorn ASHFORD, Kent, TN27 9JR.
SHELDON, Mr. Jonathan Paul, BA ACA *1999;* (Tax Fac), Old Post Office Station Road, Portbury, BRISTOL, BS20 7TN.
SHELDON, Mr. Jonathan Richard, MA FCA CFA *1982;* The Health Foundation, 90 Long Acre, LONDON, WC2E 9RA.
SHELDON, Miss. Leanne, BA ACA *2006;* Tribal Group Plc, 87-91 Newman Street, LONDON, W1T 3EY.
•SHELDON, Mr. Leslie Kieran, FCA *1975;* Suite D, Four Oaks Taxation & Accounting Services Ltd Unit 4, Astor House 282 Lichfield Road, SUTTON COLDFIELD, B74 2UG.
SHELDON, Miss. Nikki, ACA *2007;* 31 Heyford Way, HATFIELD, HERTFORDSHIRE, AL10 0AT.
SHELDON, Mr. Paul Godfrey Ellis, FCA *1967;* 72 Quinta Drive, BARNET, HERTFORDSHIRE, EN5 3BE. (Life Member)
SHELDON, Mr. Peter, FCA *1964;* Flat 8 Denver Court, 132 Hendon Lane, LONDON, N3 3RH.
SHELDON, Mr. Raymond, FCA *1967;* 4 King Edward Bay Apartments, Sea Cliff Road, Onchan, ISLE OF MAN, IM3 2JE.
SHELDON, Mr. Richard John, BSc ACA *2000;* 3 Bond Close, Knockholt, SEVENOAKS, KENT, TN14 7NB.
SHELDON, Mr. Richard Sirr, FCA *1953;* Rest Harrow, Woodgreen, FORDINGBRIDGE, HAMPSHIRE, SP6 2BD. (Life Member)
SHELDON, Mr. Richard Stephen, BA ACA *1988;* 21 O'Connors Lane, OLD TAPPEN, NJ 07675, UNITED STATES.
SHELDON, Mr. Ricky John, BA *1988;* Holly Farm, Broad Lane, Sproston, CREWE, CW4 7LT.
SHELDON, Mr. Roger Norman, FCA *1968;* 43 Quilp Drive, CHELMSFORD, CM1 4YA.
SHELDON, Mr. Ronald Frank, FCA *1973;* Sheridan, Wood Way, Farnborough Park, ORPINGTON, BR6 8LS.
•SHELDON, Mr. Simon, BSc FCA *1991;* THS Accountants Limited, The Old School House, Leckhampton Road, CHELTENHAM, GLOUCESTERSHIRE, GL53 0AX.
SHELDON, Mr. Simon James, BA ACA *1992;* Resource Information Service Unit 4-7 Gateway House, 8 Milverton Street, LONDON, SE11 4AP.
SHELDON, Mr. Stephen Richard, BA FCA *1977;* H M Revenue & Custom: Serious Civil Inve, 101 Victoria Street, BRISTOL, BS1 6BG.
SHELDON, Mrs. Susan Jean, BA ACA *1984;* Kings Manor Farm, FRESHWATER, ISLE OF WIGHT, PO40 9TL.
SHELDON, Mr. Tom, BA ACA *2006;* Seymour Pierce Limited, 20 Old Bailey, LONDON, EC4M 7EN.
SHELDON, Mr. William Mcmichael, FCA *1966;* Bryn Celyn, 27 Tysoe Close, Hockley Heath, SOLIHULL, B94 6QG.
SHELDRAKE, Miss. Helen Kristen, BSc ACA *2008;* 37 Renaissance Drive, Churwell Morley, LEEDS, LS27 7GB.
SHELEMAY, Ms. Claire, ACA *2009;* Flat 1, 54 Station Road, LONDON, NW4 3SX.
SHELFORD, Mrs. Emma Elizabeth, BSc ACA *2006;* 10 Leppoc Road, LONDON, SW4 9LT.
SHELFORD, Mr. Thomas William Joseph, LLB ACA *2006;* Bowmark Capital Llp, 3 St. James's Square, LONDON, SW1Y 4JU.
•SHELL, Mr. Stephen, BA FCA *1988;* The Studio Practice Limited, Holly House, 2 Hardy Close, Swarland, MORPETH, NORTHUMBERLAND NE65 9PG.
SHELLARD, Mr. Andrew John, BA ACA *1996;* Barclays Capital 5 North Colonnade, LONDON, E14 4BB.
SHELLARD, Mr. Craig Anthony, BSc ACA *1998;* Zennor, Amhurst Hill, SEVENOAKS, KENT, TN13 3DS.
SHELLARD, Mr. David Edmund, FCA *1972;* Courtleet, Cranley Road, WALTON-ON-THAMES, SURREY, KT12 5BZ.
SHELLARD, Mr. Graham David, FCA *1976;* 135 Lake Road West, Roath Park, CARDIFF, CF23 5PJ.
SHELLEY, Mrs. Adeline, ACA *2006;* Room 579 Victoria Block, Metropolitan Police New Scotland Yard, 8-10 Broadway, LONDON, SW1H 0BG.
SHELLEY, Miss. Catherine Jane, MA ACA *1989;* Flat 19 Great Jubilee Wharf, 78 Wapping Wall, LONDON, E1W 3TH.
SHELLEY, Mr. Christopher John, ACA *2008;* 21 Sandhurst Avenue, SURBITON, KT5 9BS.
SHELLEY, Mr. Daniel, BA ACA *2011;* 10 Main Street, Buckshaw Village, CHORLEY, PR7 7AQ.
SHELLEY, Mr. Geoffrey David, FCA *1968;* 5479 Piping Rock Drive, BOYNTON BEACH, FL 33437, UNITED STATES.
•SHELLEY, Mrs. Geraldine Anne, BSc FCA MPMI *1990;* (Tax Fac), AIMS - Geraldine Shelley FCA, 45 Kimberley Road, Nuthall, NOTTINGHAM, NG16 1DA.
SHELLEY, Mr. Jonathan, MA ACA *2006;* with PricewaterhouseCoopers LLP, 32 Albyn Place, ABERDEEN, AB10 1YL.
•SHELLEY, Mr. Jonathan, BSc ACA *2007;* Jonathan Shelley & Co, 15 Alconbury Close, BOREHAMWOOD, HERTFORDSHIRE, WD6 4QG.
SHELLEY, Mr. Martin, BSc ACA *2011;* Tilly Whim, Poldown, Breage, HELSTON, CORNWALL, TR13 9NN.
SHELLEY, Mr. Miles Colin, BA ACA *1987;* 20 Tuffnells Way, HARPENDEN, AL5 3HQ.
SHELLEY, Mr. Neil Robert, BA ACA *2010;* 23 Whitehall Road, MANCHESTER, M20 6RY.
•SHELLEY, Mr. Ronald Charles, FCA *1952;* 59 The Drive, EDGWARE, MIDDLESEX, HA8 8PS.
SHELLEY, Mrs. Sharon Joy, BA ACA *1993;* Limnis 2, Royal Ris Complex, 7041 OROKLINI, CYPRUS.
•SHELLEY, Mr. Stephen Michael, FCA *1982;* (Tax Fac), Wenn Townsend, Gosditch House, 5 Gosditch Street, CIRENCESTER, GL7 2AG. See also Wenn Townsend Accountants Limited
SHELMERDINE, Mr. Bruce Bernard, BSc ACA *1992;* 4 Yester Drive, CHISLEHURST, BR7 5LR.
SHELMERDINE, Miss. Katie Louise, BA ACA *2006;* 34A MINNIEDALE, SURBITON, SURREY, KT5 8DH.
SHELMERDINE, Mr. Mark Edward Alexander, FCA *1968;* 2700 Neilson Way, Suite 1428, SANTA MONICA, CA 90405, UNITED STATES.
SHELMERDINE, Miss. Nicola Susan, BA ACA *1981;* Lower Pempwell House, Stoke Climsland, CALLINGTON, PL17 8LN.
SHELMERDINE, Miss. Rosalyn Ann, BSc FCA *1987;* Unicredit Bank AG, Moor House, 120 London Wall, LONDON, EC2Y 5ET.
SHELTER, Mr. Howard David, FCA *1970;* 33 Chestnut Close, Oakwood, LONDON, N14 4SD.
SHELTON, Mr. Andrew James, BA FCA *2000;* with Hart Shaw LLP, Europa Link, Sheffield Business Park, SHEFFIELD, S9 1XU.
SHELTON, Mr. Anthony Joseph, BA FCA *1976;* 90a Millway, LONDON, NW7 3JJ.
SHELTON, Miss. Deborah, BSc ACA *1987;* Bramble Cottage, 5 Moorfield Farm, Bradshaw Road Honley, HOLMFIRTH, HD9 6RJ.
SHELTON, Mr. Gary Robert, FCA *1980;* 34 Brookdene Avenue, Oxhey, WATFORD, WD19 4LF.
SHELTON, Mrs. Jane Nicola, BSc ACA *1989;* The Core Technology Facility, 46 Grafton Street, MANCHESTER, M13 9NT.
SHELTON, Mr. Laurie John, LLB ACA *2003;* 16, Romans Close, GUILDFORD, GU1 2ST.
SHELTON, Mr. Lennox Harvey St John, FCA *1958;* 200 Pennsylvannia Avenue, FALLS CHURCH, VA 22046, UNITED STATES. (Life Member)
SHELTON, Mr. Mark Michael, BA ACA *1992;* 81 Woodstock Road, OXFORD, OX2 6HL.
•SHELTON, Mr. Mark William, BSc FCA *1992;* The Moore Scarrott Partnership LLP, Calyx House, South Road, TAUNTON, SOMERSET, TA1 3DY.
SHELTON, Mr. Neil Robert, BA ACA *1999;* 8 Melody Lane, LONDON, N5 2BQ.
SHELTON, Mr. Richard James, FCA *1993;* Stumpwell Lodge Beacon Hill, Penn, HIGH WYCOMBE, BUCKINGHAMSHIRE, HP10 8NJ.
SHELTON, Mr. Richard Paul Penrose, BA FCA *1977;* 44 Nelson Road, NEW MALDEN, SURREY, KT3 5EB.
SHELTON, Mr. Robin Turner, FCA *1969;* Kings Willow, Lower Green, Towersey, THAME, OXFORDSHIRE, OX9 3QP.
SHELTON, Mr. William Robert, BA ACA *1985;* Lowfield Farm, Beamsley, SKIPTON, BD23 6HN.
SHELTON-SMITH, Mrs. Christine Marjory, FCA *1966;* 15 Corfe Close, ASHTEAD, KT21 2HA.
SHELVEY, Mrs. Julie Elizabeth Thurston, ACA *1993;* 3 Daybell Close, Morton, SOUTHWELL, NOTTINGHAMSHIRE, NG25 0US.
SHEMYAKINA, Miss. Iryna, ACA *2009;* 10 Langweidstrasse, 9000 ST GALLEN, SWITZERLAND.
SHEMYAKINA, Mrs. Tetyana, MSc ACA *2004;* 24A Glifadas street, Germasogeia, CY-4046 LIMASSOL, CYPRUS.
SHEN, Miss. Harriet, BSc ACA *2010;* Flat 6, 6 Observatory Mews, LONDON, E14 3AZ.
SHEN, Miss. Hongbo, ACA *2011;* Flat A, 7 Kingscourt Road, LONDON, SW16 1JA.
SHEN, Mr. Michael Tik Kin, BA FCA *1977;* Sun Sun, 79 Haverstock Hill, LONDON, NW3 4SL.
SHEN, Mr. Siguo, MPhil FCA *1996;* Flat 2B, 11 Vista Avenue, La Vista, LANTAU ISLAND, NEW TERRITORIES, HONG KONG SAR.
SHEN, Ms. Yanli, ACA *2010;* FOSS China, Rm.1105Science&Technology Tower, No.5Zhong Guan Cun South Street, BEIJING 100081, CHINA.
SHEN, Miss. Yiping, MSc ACA *2010;* 3 Williamson Close Mortimer, READING, RG7 3UJ.
SHEN, Mrs. Yu E, ACA MIPA *2010;* Unit C 12/ F, Goldsun Building, 109 Ti Yu Road West, GUANGZHOU 510620, GUANGDONG PROVINCE, CHINA.
•SHENKER, Mr. Michael Martin, BSc FCA *1979;* (Tax Fac), Shenkers LLP, 5 Wellesley Court, Apsley Way, LONDON, NW2 7HF.
•SHENKER, Mrs. Reva Suzanne, FCA *1983;* Shenkers LLP, 5 Wellesley Court, Apsley Way, LONDON, NW2 7HF.
SHENKMAN, Mr. Phillip Howard, BEng ACA *2004;* 2 Mon Desir, Les Quennevais Drive, La Route Orange, St. Brelade, JERSEY, JE3 8GN.
SHENNAN, Mr. Peter John, BA FCA *1977;* 191 Brookdale Avenue South, Greasby, WIRRAL, CH49 1SR.
SHENOY, Mr. Arun Michael, FCA *1964;* 26660 Egrets Landing Drive, Unit 201, BONITA SPRINGS, FL 34134, UNITED STATES. (Life Member)
SHENOY, Mr. Sailesh, MSc BSc ACA *2011;* Flat 33 Edison Building, 20 Westferry Road, LONDON, E14 8LU.
SHENTON, Mr. Alan Newman, LLB FCA ATII *1985;* Letus, 13 Walton Avenue, HENLEY-ON-THAMES, OXFORDSHIRE, RG9 1LA.
SHENTON, Mrs. Alison Lesley, BA FCA *1996;* Highbury, La Grande Route De St. Clement, St. Clement, JERSEY, JE2 6QN.
•SHENTON, Mrs. Denise, ACA *1991;* The Old Thatch, Sandy Lane, Baddeley Edge, STOKE-ON-TRENT, ST2 7LS.
SHENTON, Mrs. Joanne, BA ACA *1999;* 161b Mountnessing Road, BILLERICAY, ESSEX, CM12 0EE.
SHENTON, Mr. John Gerard, ACA *1981;* 3214 Kenya Place, VICTORIA V8P 3V1, BC, CANADA.
SHENTON, Mr. Paul Henry, BSc FCA *1979;* 25 Gilmais, Great Bookham, LEATHERHEAD, KT23 4RP.
•SHENTON, Mr. Paul Kenneth, BCom FCA *1969;* Armstrong Rogers & Co, 18 Etnam Street, LEOMINSTER, HR6 8AQ.
SHENTON, Mr. Timothy, FCA *1979;* 31 Grange Road, BUSHEY, WD23 2LQ.
•SHEPARD, Mrs. Sally Joanne, BSc ACA *1987;* Sally Shepard, Hopesay, 8 Glebe Close, Moulsford, WALLINGFORD, OX10 9JA.
SHEPHARD, Miss. Claire Elizabeth Deane, BA ACA *1998;* 315 Finch Street, BALLARAT EAST, VIC 3350, AUSTRALIA.
SHEPHARD, Mr. Garth, BA ACA *1997;* Opus Corporate Finance LLP, 1 Bell Yard, LONDON, WC2A 2JR.
SHEPHARD, Ms. Pamela Ann, BA ACA *1995;* (Tax Fac), 31 Nene Way, Hilton, DERBY, DE65 5HX.
•SHEPHARD, Mr. Peter William, FCA *1974;* (Tax Fac), Peter W Shephard, 2 Brinsley Close, SOLIHULL, WEST MIDLANDS, B91 3FR.
SHEPHARD, Mr. Richard, BSc ACA *1985;* 18 Beckside Close, RD4, HAMILTON, NEW ZEALAND.
SHEPHEARD, Miss. Amy Philippa, ACA *2010;* 3 Kenville Road, Kennington, OXFORD, OX1 5PJ.
•SHEPHEARD, Mr. Martin Richard, FCA *1973;* Shepheard Accounting, Westview, Hayes Lane, Slinfold, HORSHAM, WEST SUSSEX RH13 0SJ.
SHEPHEARD, Mr. Richard Arthur, FCA *1965;* 1 Ivy Lane, FARNHAM, SURREY, GU9 7PQ.
SHEPHERD, Miss. Alice Katherine, BSc ACA *2006;* 104 Woolgreaves Drive, WAKEFIELD, WEST YORKSHIRE, WF2 6DT.
•SHEPHERD, Mr. Andrew David, FCA *1989;* 18 St. Anns Road, FAVERSHAM, KENT, ME13 8RH.
SHEPHERD, Mr. Andrew Norman, BCom ACA *1993;* 39 Oulder Hill Drive, Oulder Hill, ROCHDALE, LANCASHIRE, OL11 5LB.
•SHEPHERD, Mr. Andrew Paul, BA FCA *1983;* (Tax Fac), Couch Bright King & Co, 91 Gower Street, LONDON, WC1E 6AB.

•**SHEPHERD, Mrs. Anne Elizabeth, FCA** *1975;* (Tax Fac), Shepherd Accountancy Ltd, 27 Nursery Close, HOOK, RG27 9QX.
•**SHEPHERD, Mr. Anthony Carson, FCA** *1970;* Shepherd & Company, Old London House, High Street, Stoke Row, HENLEY-ON-THAMES, RG9 5QL.
SHEPHERD, Mr. Brian, FCA *1967;* Porch Cottage, York Road, Sheriff Hutton, YORK, YO60 6RG.
•**SHEPHERD, Mr. Christopher John, BA ACA** *1995;* Blick Rothenberg, 12 York Gate, Regent's Park, LONDON, NW1 4QS.
SHEPHERD, Mr. Christopher Malcolm, ACA *2009;* 13 Ladybrook Avenue, Timperley, ALTRINCHAM, CHESHIRE, WA15 6DT.
SHEPHERD, Mrs. Claire, BSc(Hons) ACA *2009;* (Tax Fac), Cargill Plc, Witham St. Hughs, LINCOLN, LN6 9TN.
SHEPHERD, Mr. Dale Keith, BA(Hons) ACA *2001;* Airport Central Level 8, 203 Coward Street, MASCOT, NSW 2020, AUSTRALIA.
SHEPHERD, Mr. David Charles, FCA *1963;* 19 Mingle Lane, Stapleford, CAMBRIDGE, CB22 5SY. (Life Member)
•**SHEPHERD, Mr. David Charles, BSc FCA CTA** *1991;* Epsom Accounting Limited, 93 High Street, EPSOM, KT19 8DR.
SHEPHERD, Mr. David John, PhD MSc FCA *1976;* Eli Lilly & Co Erlwood Manor, London Road, WINDLESHAM, GU20 6PH.
SHEPHERD, Mr. Donald Henry, FCA *1955;* 72 Pier Avenue, SOUTHWOLD, IP18 6BL. (Life Member)
•**SHEPHERD, Mr. Edward Michael, FCA** *1975;* PKF (UK) LLP, 2nd Floor, Fountain Precinct, Balm Green, SHEFFIELD, S1 2JA.
SHEPHERD, Miss. Ellen, MMath ACA *2006;* Pricewaterhousecoopers Llp, 80 Strand, LONDON, WC2R 0AF.
SHEPHERD, Mr. Gary Paul, BSc ACA *2005;* with Ernst & Young LLP, 1 Colmore Square, BIRMINGHAM, B4 6HQ.
SHEPHERD, Mrs. Gwyneth, BA ACA *1983;* 37 West Meadows Road, SUNDERLAND, SR6 7TU.
SHEPHERD, Mrs. Heather Louise, BSc(Hons) ACA *2011;* 225 Torridon Road, LONDON, SE6 1RF.
SHEPHERD, Miss. Helen, BA(Hons) ACA PgDip *2011;* 26 Church Meadow Road, Rossington, DONCASTER, SOUTH YORKSHIRE, DN11 0YD.
SHEPHERD, Mr. Ian David Kerr, MA FCA *1983;* 86 Beckenham Place Park, BECKENHAM, BR3 5BT.
SHEPHERD, Mr. James, BSc ACA *2002;* with PricewaterhouseCoopers, 31 Great George Street, BRISTOL, BS1 5QD.
SHEPHERD, Mr. James William, BSc(Hons) ACA *2010;* Mousley Hill Farm Mousley End, Hatton, WARWICK, CV35 7JF.
SHEPHERD, Miss. Jane Nicola, ACA *1979;* (Tax Fac), Woodside, 2 Cedar Mews, HOCKLEY, SS5 4RZ.
SHEPHERD, Miss. Joanna Elizabeth Rachel, LLB ACA *2004;* The Orchard, Swabs Lane, Cropwell Bishop, NOTTINGHAM, NG12 3BL.
SHEPHERD, Mrs. Joanne Claire, BA ACA CTA *1999;* Leaseplan UK Ltd, 165 Bath Road, SLOUGH, SL1 4AA.
SHEPHERD, Mr. John, BSc FCA *1975;* Gillotts Hall, Gillotts Farm, Cinder Hill Lane, Chadderton, OLDHAM, OL1 2SU.
SHEPHERD, Mr. John Barlow, FCA *1972;* Care Ltd, 14 Nursery Court Kibworth Harcourt, LEICESTER, LE8 0EX.
SHEPHERD, Mr. John Bramley, FCA *1953;* Bramley House, Whin Hill Road, Bessacarr, DONCASTER, SOUTH YORKSHIRE, DN4 7AF. (Life Member)
SHEPHERD, John Fletcher, Esq OBE FCA *1958;* 3 Grenville Close Stokenham, KINGSBRIDGE, DEVON, TQ7 2SY. (Life Member)
•**SHEPHERD, Mr. John Kenneth, FCA** *1962;* (Tax Fac), John K Shepherd FCA, 33 Beechwood Avenue, MELTON MOWBRAY, LEICESTERSHIRE, LE13 1RT.
SHEPHERD, Mr. Jonathan Ashley, MEng ACA *2000;* Cotswold Outdoor Ltd Unit 11, Kemble Business Park Crudwell, MALMESBURY, SN16 9SH.
SHEPHERD, Mr. Jonathan Mark, LLB ACA *1994;* 38 Langton Way, LONDON, SE3 7TJ.
SHEPHERD, Miss. Judith Ann, BA FCA AMCT *1987;* City & Guilds of London Institute, 1 Giltspur Street, LONDON, EC1A 9DD.
SHEPHERD, Miss. Kate Isabel, BA ACA *2006;* 3 Trinity Road, STROUD, GLOUCESTERSHIRE, GL5 2HX.
SHEPHERD, Mrs. Katherine Jane, BA ACA *1997;* Ridsdale, School Lane, Collingham, WETHERBY, WEST YORKSHIRE, LS22 5BQ.
SHEPHERD, Mrs. Katy Elizabeth, BA(Hons) ACA *2004;* with CK, No 4 Castle Court 2, Castlegate Way, DUDLEY, WEST MIDLANDS, DY1 4RH.
SHEPHERD, Mrs. Kelly, BA ACA *2002;* 34 Lundy Drive, ELLESMERE PORT, CH65 9JS.
SHEPHERD, Miss. Lindsey Anne, ACA *2007;* 34 Seathwaite Road, Farnworth, BOLTON, BL4 0QY.
SHEPHERD, Miss. Louise Ellen, BA ACA *1999;* 39 Chatterton Road, LONDON, N4 2EA.
SHEPHERD, Mr. Marcus Owen, BSc ACA *1991;* 64 Clarence Road, TEDDINGTON, MIDDLESEX, TW11 0BW.
SHEPHERD, Mrs. Mary Anne, BSc ACA *1999;* with Blick Rothenberg, 12 York Gate, Regent's Park, LONDON, NW1 4QS.
SHEPHERD, Mr. Michael Robert Charles, BSc ACA *1993;* 24 Grove Wood Hill, COULSDON, CR5 2EL.
SHEPHERD, Mr. Neil, ACA *1982;* Corner Cottage, 1 Rectory Lane, Mulbarton, NORWICH, NR14 8AG.
SHEPHERD, Mr. Neil, ACA *2008;* 35a Station Road, STUDLEY, B80 7JU.
SHEPHERD, Mr. Neil Harvey, BA FCA *1992;* 39 Empress Avenue, WOODFORD GREEN, IG8 9DZ.
SHEPHERD, Mr. Nicholas John, BA ACA *1995;* 27 Kerwin Drive, SHEFFIELD, S17 3DG.
•**SHEPHERD, Mr. Peter Antony, BA FCA** *1986;* Anderson & Shepherd, Shepson House, Stockwell Street, LEEK, STAFFORDSHIRE, ST13 6DH.
SHEPHERD, Mr. Peter David, BCom ACA *1986;* 10 Mirfield Road, SOLIHULL, B91 1JD.
•**SHEPHERD, Mr. Philip Anthony, BSc ACA** *1988;* PricewaterhouseCoopers LLP, 7 More London Riverside, LONDON, SE1 2RT. See also PricewaterhouseCoopers
•**SHEPHERD, Mr. Philip Eric, FCA** *1983;* with Grant Thornton UK LLP, 1 Dorset Street, SOUTHAMPTON, SO15 2DP.
SHEPHERD, Mr. Philip William, BSc ACA *1995;* 8 The Mount, ALTRINCHAM, CHESHIRE, WA14 4DX.
•**SHEPHERD, Mr. Richard James, BA FCA** *1971;* (Tax Fac), Shepherd Smail, Northway House, The Forum, CIRENCESTER, GLOUCESTERSHIRE, GL7 2QY.
SHEPHERD, Mr. Richard John, BEng ACA *1991;* 17 Wollescote Drive, Hillfield, SOLIHULL, WEST MIDLANDS, B91 3YN.
SHEPHERD, Mr. Roger Alan, BA ACA *1992;* Business Control Solutions Plc, Churchgate, New Road, PETERBOROUGH, PE1 1TT.
SHEPHERD, Mr. Roger Colston, MA FCA *1970;* Roslin Barn, Chillerton, NEWPORT, Isle of Wight, PO30 3HG. (Life Member)
SHEPHERD, Mr. Roger Edward, BSc FCA *1964;* 62 Bentmeadows, Falinge, ROCHDALE, OL12 6LF.
SHEPHERD, Miss. Sandra, ACA *1982;* Pedlars Halt, Sharperton, MORPETH, NORTHUMBERLAND, NE65 7AE.
SHEPHERD, Miss. Sarah, ACA *2011;* 6 Ducaine Apartments, Merchant Street, LONDON, E3 4PG.
SHEPHERD, Miss. Sarah Emelie, ACA *2007;* 1 Roff Avenue, BEDFORD, MK41 7TF.
SHEPHERD, Miss. Sarah Jane, ACA *2005;* 1 Scott Walk, Bridgeyate, BRISTOL, BS30 5WB.
SHEPHERD, Mr. Simon James, MA FCA *1982;* 37 Tower Road North, Heswall, WIRRAL, CH60 6RS.
SHEPHERD, Mr. Simon Welton, BCom ACA *2001;* 25 Meadowview, HUNGERFORD, BERKSHIRE, RG17 0YY.
SHEPHERD, Mr. Steven Peter, LLB ACA *2002;* with UNESCO, BOC, 7 Place Fontenoy, 75007 PARIS, FRANCE.
SHEPHERD, Mrs. Susan Caroline, BSc FCA *1992;* 17 Northcliffe Close, WORCESTER PARK, KT4 7DS.
SHEPHERD, Thomas Julian Durrant, Esq OBE FCA *1952;* 1369 El Hito Circle, PACIFIC PALISADES, CA 90272, UNITED STATES. (Life Member)
•**SHEPHERD, Mr. William John, FCA** *1960;* W J Shepherd, 33 West Road, Bowdon, ALTRINCHAM, CHESHIRE, WA14 2LA.
•**SHEPHERD, Mr. William Ralph, ACA CTA** *1983;* (Tax Fac), Shepherd & Co, 1st Floor, 4 Fisher Street, CARLISLE, CA3 8RN.
SHEPHERD-BARRON, Mr. Andrew John, BA ACA *1985;* The Old Vicarage, The Green, Leigh, TONBRIDGE, TN11 8QJ.
SHEPHERD-THEMISTOCLEOUS, Miss. Helen Louise, BA ACA *1994;* (Tax Fac), 7 Millbrook Close, Blewbury, DIDCOT, OXFORDSHIRE, OX11 9QL.
SHEPHERDSON, Mr. John, FCA *1978;* (Tax Fac), 128 Cranbrook Avenue, HULL, HU6 7ST.
SHEPHERDSON, Mr. John Roger, FCA *1960;* Holly Cottage, 237 Westella Road, West Ella, HULL, HU10 7SD. (Life Member)
SHEPLEY, Mr. Sebastian Anthony, BSc ACA *1993;* Roxel Group, La Boursidiere - Immeuble Jura, 92357 LE PLESSIS-ROBINSON, FRANCE.
SHEPLEY-CUTHBERT, Mr. David Charles, FCA *1969;* Moors House, Hook Norton, BANBURY, OX15 5LS.
SHEPPARD, Mr. Andrew Michael, BA ACA *1991;* 1 Barton Lane Cottages, Barton Lane, Barton, NEW MILTON, BH25 7PP.
SHEPPARD, Mr. Andrew Michael, BA ACA *1997;* 10 Talbot Road, Dibden Purlieu, SOUTHAMPTON, SO45 4PN.
SHEPPARD, Mr. Andrew Peter Day, BSc FCA *1978;* The School House, Church Road, Little Waldingfield, SUDBURY, SUFFOLK, CO10 0SP.
SHEPPARD, Miss. Audrey Crampton, BA FCA CTA *1949;* 50 Sandfield Road, Arnold, NOTTINGHAM, NG5 6QB. (Life Member)
•**SHEPPARD, Mrs. Barbara Lyn, FCA** *1970;* (Tax Fac), Barbara L. Sheppard, 23 Brookdene Drive, NORTHWOOD, HA6 3NS.
SHEPPARD, Mrs. Christine, BSc ACA *1995;* 10 Athol Road, Whalley Range, MANCHESTER, M16 8QN.
SHEPPARD, Mr. Christopher Kenneth, BA(Hons) ACA *2000;* 4 Gomer Close, Codicote, HITCHIN, HERTFORDSHIRE, SG4 8XP.
SHEPPARD, Mrs. Claire Emma, BSc ACA *2003;* 5 Castleton Court, MARLOW, BUCKINGHAMSHIRE, SL7 3HW.
SHEPPARD, Mr. Darren Wayne, BSc ACA *1997;* Little Changes, Blundens Corner, Stoke by Nayland, COLCHESTER, ESSEX, CO6 4RA.
SHEPPARD, Mr. David Gwyn, FCA *1977;* 38 Paines Lane, PINNER, HA5 3DB.
SHEPPARD, Mr. David Leigh Alban, BA FCA *1977;* 21 Avenue Rd, BISHOP'S STORTFORD, CM23 5NT.
•**SHEPPARD, Mr. Derrick Richard Adam, FCA** *1967;* (Tax Fac), Derrick Sheppard & Co, Orchard House, Back Lane, Garboldisham, DISS, IP22 2SD.
SHEPPARD, Mr. Donald Edwin, FCA *1974;* 21 Bridge Street, RICHMOND, DL10 4RW.
SHEPPARD, Mrs. Faye Donna, BSc ACA *2006;* 7 Stapleford Close, CHIPPENHAM, WILTSHIRE, SN15 3FZ.
SHEPPARD, Mrs. Gail Anne, BA ACA *1996;* 3 Nunthorpe Gardens, Nunthorpe, MIDDLESBROUGH, CLEVELAND, TS7 0GA.
SHEPPARD, Mr. Garth Stephen, FCA *1964;* 23 Church Street, Lees, OLDHAM, OL4 5DB.
SHEPPARD, Dr. Helen, MA ACA *2004;* 3 The Chestertons, Bathampton, BATH, BA2 6UJ.
SHEPPARD, Mr. Huw William, BSc ACA *2002;* 21 Garth Olwg, Gwaelod-y-Garth, CARDIFF, CF15 9HW.
•**SHEPPARD, Mr. Ian Francis, FCA** *1974;* (Tax Fac), Sheppards Accountants Limited, 22 The Square, The Millfields, PLYMOUTH, PL1 3JX.
SHEPPARD, Mr. John, BSc(Hons) ACA *2000;* A & JM Sheppard Limited, 4 Mill Street, ABERDARE, MID GLAMORGAN, CF44 8NA.
•**SHEPPARD, Mr. John Kenneth, FCA** *1971;* (Tax Fac), F.C.R. Moule & Co, Westminster Buildings, Theatre Square, NOTTINGHAM, NG1 6LG.
SHEPPARD, Mr. Jonathan Lance, BSc FCA *1976;* 7 Borrowdale Close, CARDIFF, CF23 5LQ.
•**SHEPPARD, Mr. Julian Mark, FCA** *1983;* Sheppard and Co, International House, George Curl Way, SOUTHAMPTON, SO18 2RZ.
SHEPPARD, Mrs. Kelly Amanda, BA(Hons) ACA *2002;* 1 Fiddlers Close, GREENHITHE, KENT, DA9 9QT.
SHEPPARD, Mr. Kenneth John, FCA *1961;* Vectis, Trindles Road, South Nutfield, REDHILL, RH1 4JL.
SHEPPARD, Mr. Kevin John, BSc ACA *2002;* 1 Holifast Road, SUTTON COLDFIELD, WEST MIDLANDS, B72 1AP.
SHEPPARD, Mr. Leslie Roy, FCA *1962;* 'Lantern Cottage', 62 Southleigh Road, Denvilles, HAVANT, PO9 2QJ. (Life Member)
•**SHEPPARD, Mr. Mark, FCA** *1993;* with KPMG LLP, 1 Forest Gate, Brighton Road, CRAWLEY, WEST SUSSEX, RH11 9PT.
SHEPPARD, Mr. Mark Brian Birch, BA ACA *1997;* 21 Brompton Square, LONDON, SW3 2AD.
SHEPPARD, Mr. Matthew Laurence, BSc ACA *1999;* 91c Blackheath Hill, LONDON, SE10 8TJ.
SHEPPARD, Mr. Matthew Patrick, MA FCA *1976;* 75 Soundview Lane, NEW CANAAN, CT 06840-2732, UNITED STATES.
SHEPPARD, Mr. Michael Aspinwall, BCom FCA *1954;* 110 Causeway Head Road, Dore, SHEFFIELD, S17 3DW. (Life Member)
•**SHEPPARD, Mr. Michael David, BSc ACA** *1994;* Grant Thornton UK LLP, Enterprise House, 115 Edmund Street, BIRMINGHAM, B3 2HJ. See also Grant Thornton LLP
SHEPPARD, Mr. Michael James, BSc ACA *2005;* Korsåsliden 116, 421 47, Vastra Frolunda, GOTHENBURG, SWEDEN.
SHEPPARD, Mr. Nigel Philip, BSc ACA *1985;* 38 The Hedgerows, BISHOP'S STORTFORD, CM23 5FD.
SHEPPARD, Mr. Paul, MA FCA *1978;* with Audit Inspection Unit, Financial Reporting Council, 5th Floor, Aldwych House, 71-91 Aldwych, LONDON WC2B 4HN.
•**SHEPPARD, Mr. Peter Michael, BSc FCA** *1986;* (Tax Fac), Whittingham Riddell LLP, Belmont House, Shrewsbury Business Park, SHREWSBURY, SY2 6LG.
SHEPPARD, Mrs. Rebecca Mary, BA ACA *2003;* The Laurels Tite Hill, Englefield Green, EGHAM, TW20 0NJ.
SHEPPARD, Mr. Reginald Thomas, FCA *1976;* (Tax Fac), Birchsyde, 70 Luccombe Road, Upper Shirley, SOUTHAMPTON, SO15 7RU.
SHEPPARD, Mr. Richard Michael, BSc ACA *1996;* Deutsche Bank, 1 Great Winchester Street, LONDON, EC2N 2DB.
SHEPPARD, Mr. Steven Robert, BA FCA ACA *1984;* 20 Chequers Croft, Hilton, HUNTINGDON, PE28 9PD.
SHEPPARD, Mr. Thomas, BA(Hons) ACA *2011;* 38 St. Johns Road, Caversham, READING, RG4 5AL.
•**SHEPPARD, Mr. William John, FCA** *1973;* Forresters, 8 Gayton Road, Lower Heswall, WIRRAL, CH60 8PE.
SHEPPARDSON, Mr. Nicholas Charles, BA ACA *1983;* Chess Partnership, 14a Ganton Street, LONDON, W1F 7QT.
SHEPPEARD, Mr. Charles Thomas, ACA CA(AUS) *2011;* 16 Treport Street, Earlsfield, LONDON, SW18 2BP.
SHEPPECK, Mr. Anthony John, CBE FCA *1965;* Swanland House, Ellesborough Road, Butlers Cross, AYLESBURY, BUCKINGHAMSHIRE, HP17 0XH. (Life Member)
SHEPPY, Miss. Jocelyn Mary, BSc ACA *1992;* 43 Marble Hill Close, TWICKENHAM, TW1 3AY.
SHEPPY, Mr. Timothy James, BA ACA *1991;* 6 Cornmill Close Elmley Castle, PERSHORE, WORCESTERSHIRE, WR10 3JH.
•**SHEPSTONE, Miss. Nicola Jane, BA(Hons) ACA** *1997;* with PricewaterhouseCoopers, Sixty Circular Road, Douglas, ISLE OF MAN, IM1 1SA.
SHER, Miss. Ching Man, BA ACA *1999;* Flat 6B Block 10 PROVIDENT CENTER, WHARF ROAD, NORTH POINT, HONG KONG SAR, HONG KONG SAR.
SHER, Mr. Gary Lewis, BSc ACA *2006;* Westside, 55 Priory Road, LONDON, NW6 3NG.
SHER, Mr. Gideon Marc, ACA *2010;* with Rayner Essex LLP, Tavistock House South, Tavistock Square, LONDON, WC1H 9LG.
SHER, Mr. Sean Ryan, BA(Hons) ACA *2003;* Flat 6 Limeleaf Court, 214 Hale Lane, EDGWARE, MIDDLESEX, HA8 9PX.
SHER, Mr. Steven Richard, ACA *1998;* 5 The Park, Golders Hill Park, LONDON, NW11 7SR.
SHER, Mr. William Wing Hong, BSc ACA *2007;* Flat D 32/F 1 Star Street, WAN CHAI, HONG KONG SAR.
SHERANI, Mr. Mohamed Abid, MBA ACA *1983;* 53-B 4th Sunset Street, Phase 2 Ext DHA, KARACHI 75500, PAKISTAN.
SHERAR, Mr. Andrew John, ACA *1983;* 6 Becky Street, KULUIN, QLD 4558, AUSTRALIA.
SHERATON, Miss. Amanda Louise, LLB ACA *1999;* with Deloitte LLP, 3 New Street Square, LONDON, EC4A 3BT.
SHERATON, Mr. Michael Karl, BA ACA *1988;* Salvus House, Sunderland Marine Mutual Insurance Co Ltd Salvus House, Aykley Heads, DURHAM, DH1 5TS.
SHERAZEE, Mr. Aly, FCA *1963;* Woodlands, Green Dene, East Horsley, LEATHERHEAD, SURREY, KT24 5RG. (Life Member)
SHERAZEE, Mr. Tarek, BA ACA *1993;* Cheery Tree Cottage, Abinger Common, DORKING, SURREY, RH5 6LW.
SHERBURN, Mr. Andrew David, MA ACA *1987;* 35 High Street, Kippax, LEEDS, LS25 7AF.
SHERBURN, Mr. Geoffrey, FCA *1971;* 8 Marbury Drive, West Timperley, ALTRINCHAM, WA14 5BE. (Life Member)
SHERER, Prof. Michael Leslie Joseph, MA FCA *1975;* 116 Ernest Road, Wivenhoe, COLCHESTER, CO7 9LJ.
•**SHERET, Mr. William Allen, FCA** *1967;* (Tax Fac), W.A. Sheret, Meadowcroft, Yarm Road, Hilton, YARM, TS15 9LF.
•**SHERFIELD, Mr. Mark Andrew, FCA** *1987;* BDO LLP, 55 Baker Street, LONDON, W1U 7EU. See also BDO Stoy Hayward LLP
•**SHERGILL, Mr. Gurdev Singh, BSc FCA** *1979;* G.S. Shergill, 30 Bell Road, WALSALL, WS5 3JW.
SHERGILL, Mr. Kuldip Singh, MEng ACA *1999;* 85 Erskine Hill, LONDON, NW11 6HJ.

SHERGILL, Mr. Raminder Singh, BA(Hons) ACA *2002;* 39 Chestnut Close, Oakwood, LONDON, N14 4SD.

SHERICK, Mr. Nathaniel Grant David, FCA *1970;* 108-20-1 Millennium Tower, Gurney Drive, 10250 PENANG, MALAYSIA. (Life Member)

SHERICK, Mrs. Siew Yen, FCA *1977;* 108-20-1 Millenium Tower, Gurney Drive, 10250 PENANG, MALAYSIA.

•**SHERIDAN, Mr. Alan Peter, BSc ACA** *1989;* (Tax Fac), Sheridan Brooks Limited, Sheridan Brooks Ltd, 176 Brighton Road, COULSDON, SURREY, CR5 2NF.

•**SHERIDAN, Miss. Alison Jane, BSc FCA** *1999;* Littlejohn LLP, 1 Westferry Circus, Canary Wharf, LONDON, E14 4HD.

SHERIDAN, Mrs. Alison Jayne, BA(Hons) ACA *2003;* 6A Rosebery Street, MOSMAN, NSW 2088, AUSTRALIA.

SHERIDAN, Mr. Andrew Philip, MA ACA *1992;* 76 Laurel Street, SYDNEY, NSW 2068, AUSTRALIA.

SHERIDAN, Mr. David Martin, BSc ACA *1978;* (Member of Council 1993 - 1996), 9 Lynton Avenue, ST. ALBANS, AL1 5PD.

SHERIDAN, Mr. Farrell, BA BA(Hons) ACA *2011;* 1 Princes Way, BAGSHOT, SURREY, GU19 5QU.

•**SHERIDAN, Ms. Hayley, BSc ACA** *1991;* (Tax Fac), The Campbell Parker Partnership Limited, 2 City Limits, Danehill, Lower Earley, READING, RG6 4UP.

SHERIDAN, Mr. Jonathan James Edward, BSc(Hons) ACA *2001;* 6A Rosebery Street, MOSMAN, NSW 2088, AUSTRALIA.

SHERIDAN, Mr. Jonathan Patrick James, BSc ACA *1997;* 17 Lavenham Road, LONDON, SW18 5EZ.

SHERIDAN, Mr. Julius, FCA *1953;* 26/8 Alexandroni Street, NETANYA, 42467, ISRAEL. (Life Member)

•**SHERIDAN, Mr. Michael Kenneth, FCA** *1972;* Sheridan Strategic Services Limited, Oakways, Tubbs Lane, Highclere, NEWBURY, BERKSHIRE RG20 9PQ.

SHERIDAN, Mr. Peter, BA ACA *1991;* 6 Sixty Acre Close, Failand, BRISTOL, BS8 3UH.

SHERIDAN, Mrs. Rebecca Claire, BA ACA *1983;* Cottage Farm, 50 High Street, Claverham, BRISTOL, BS49 4NE.

SHERIDAN, Mr. Richard Martin, ACA *2008;* 10 The Close, Alwoodley, LEEDS, LS17 7RD.

•**SHERIDAN, Mrs. Sarah Melissa, BA FCA** *1998;* 101 Park Road, Hale, ALTRINCHAM, CHESHIRE, WA15 9JU.

SHERIDAN, Mr. Stephen Lance, BA ACA *1990;* 11 Kiln Gardens, Hartley Wintney, HOOK, HAMPSHIRE, RG27 8RG.

SHERIDAN JOHNSON, Mr. Frederick Peter, BA FCA *1974;* PO Box 70192, DAR ES SALAAM, TANZANIA.

SHERIFF, Mrs. Audrey Linda Ann, FCA *1975;* Ravensworth, 51 Pilkington Avenue, SUTTON COLDFIELD, B72 1LD.

SHERIFF, Mr. Benjamin John, MPhil BA ACA *2005;* 12 High Mount, Station Road, LONDON, NW4 3SS.

SHERIFF, Mr. Eusuf Omar, BA ACA *1986;* 14 Ruxley Lane, EWELLSurrey, EPSOM, KT19 0JA.

SHERIFF, Mr. John Arnold, FCA *1974;* 51 Pilkington Avenue, SUTTON COLDFIELD, B72 1LD.

SHERIFF, Mr. Paul Nigel, BEng ACA *1996;* 27 Stonor, HENLEY-ON-THAMES, OXFORDSHIRE, RG9 6HB.

•**SHERIFF, Mr. Rodney Arthur, BA ACA** *2001;* Flat 902, Block 1, Europlaza, GIBRALTAR, GIBRALTAR.

SHERLEY, Mr. Paul Simon, MA FCA *1997;* 30 Whitehead Way, AYLESBURY, BUCKINGHAMSHIRE, HP21 8LR.

•**SHERLING, Mr. Andrew Mark, FCA** *1977;* Andrew M Sherling FCA, 100 Green Lane, EDGWARE, HA8 8EJ.

SHERLING, Mr. Clive Richard, BSc FCA *1973;* Lincoln House, Woodside Hill, Chalfont Heights, GERRARDS CROSS, SL9 9TF.

•**SHERLING, Mr. Graham Charles, FCA** *1976;* Graham Sherling and Co Limited, 36 The Avenue, Hatch End, PINNER, MIDDLESEX, HA5 4EY.

SHERLOCK, Mr. Andrew Michael, BA ACA *1994;* Church Farm House, Idbury, CHIPPING NORTON, OXFORDSHIRE, OX7 6RU.

SHERLOCK, Mr. Ciaran Francis, ACA *2008;* Bentley Jennison Charter House, Legge Street, BIRMINGHAM, B4 7EU.

SHERLOCK, Mr. Donald Joseph, FCA *1954;* 13 The Oaks, Walton-le-Dale, PRESTON, PR5 4LT. (Life Member)

SHERLOCK, Mr. Edward Steven, MA ACA *1994;* 34 Clarewood Drive, CAMBERLEY, GU15 3TE.

•**SHERLOCK, Mrs. Estelle Gaye, BSc ACA** *1982;* (Tax Fac), DMC Partnership, Yew Tree House, Lewes Road, FOREST ROW, RH18 5AA.

SHERLOCK, Mr. Ian Montague, BA FCA *1983;* 73 Queens Avenue, Meols, WIRRAL, CH47 0LT.

SHERLOCK, Mr. James Frederick, FCA *1960;* 41 The Yews Stoughton Park, Oadby, LEICESTER, LE2 5EF. (Life Member)

SHERLOCK, Mr. Mark Christopher, BA(Hons) ACA CFA *2001;* Hermes Pensions Management Ltd Lloyds Chambers, 1 Portsoken Street, LONDON, E1 8HZ.

SHERLOCK, Mr. Mark David, BA ACA *1997;* with Brebners, The Quadrangle, 180 Wardour Street, LONDON, W1F 8LB.

SHERLOCK, Mr. Peter Joseph, FCA *1958;* West End House, Thenford, BANBURY, OX17 2BX. (Life Member)

SHERLOCK, Miss. Rebecca Clare, BSc ACA *2005;* 2/63A Ramsgate Avenue, NORTH BONDI, NSW 2026, AUSTRALIA.

SHERLOCK, Mr. Robert Andrew Charles, BA ACA *1989;* Hollands, Shaftesbury Road, WOKING, GU22 7DT.

SHERLOCK, Mr. Robert Anthony, BSc ACA *1997;* Flat 43, Voltaire Buildings, Earlsfield, LONDON, SW18 4FQ.

•**SHERMAN, Mr. Anthony Max, FCA** *1969;* A M Sherman & Co Limited, 199 Roundhay Road, LEEDS, LS8 5AN.

SHERMAN, Mr. Antony, BA FCA *1983;* Motor Insurers Bureau Linford Wood House, 6-12 Capital Drive Linford Wood, MILTON KEYNES, MK14 6XT.

SHERMAN, Mr. Hyman Arnold, FCA *1954;* Suite 717 738 Third Avenue S.W., CALGARY T2P 0G7, AB, CANADA.

SHERMAN, Mr. Ian Samuel, BA ACA *2000;* 8118 Highland Bluff Drive, SUGARLAND, TX 77479, UNITED STATES.

SHERMAN, Mr. Ian Walter, FRCS FCA *1976;* Westwood, 4 Burrell Road, BIRKENHEAD, CH42 8NH.

SHERMAN, Mr. Jamie, BSc ACA *2011;* 52 Longsands Road, ST. NEOTS, CAMBRIDGESHIRE, PE19 1TA.

SHERMAN, Mr. Maurice, FCA *1945;* 7 Vaughan Avenue, LONDON, NW4 4HT. (Life Member)

SHERMAN, Mr. Oliver Leo, BSc ACA *2010;* 75 Rephidim Street, LONDON, SE1 4XD.

SHERMAN, Mr. Paul, ACA *1988;* 12301 NW 39th Street, CORAL SPRINGS, FL 33065, UNITED STATES.

SHERMAN, Mr. Paul Roger, FCA *1971;* 39 Marjorams Avenue, LOUGHTON, IG10 1PU.

SHERMAN, Mr. Raymond Thomas, FCA *1970;* Celandine, 9 Cot Lane, Biddenden, ASHFORD, TN27 8JB.

SHERMAN, Mr. Stephen Paul, FCA *1976;* 25 Henderson Road, LONDON, SW18 3RR.

SHERMER, Mr. Warren Bruce, BA ACA *1992;* GNE Pullman House, Treefield Industrial Estate Gelderd Road, LEEDS, LS27 7JU.

SHERPA, Mrs. Karen Maria, BA ACA *1996;* 25 Haigh Moor Road, Tingley, WAKEFIELD, WEST YORKSHIRE, WF3 1EE.

SHERRARD, Mr. Eustace Patrick Garnet, FCA *1975;* 20 Western Gardens, LONDON, W5 3RU.

SHERRARD, Mr. Nicholas Richard, MA FCA *1978;* 110 St Albans Avenue, Chiswick, LONDON, W4 5JR.

SHERRATT, Mr. John Peter Edward, MA FCA *1975;* 63 Narbonne Avenue, LONDON, SW4 9JP.

SHERRATT, Mr. Matthew Neil, BEng ACA *2006;* 46 Birchtree Drive, Cheddleton, LEEK, STAFFORDSHIRE, ST13 7FE.

SHERRELL, Mr. David Roy, BA ACA *2000;* Mayflower Cottage, Brentor, TAVISTOCK, DEVON, PL19 0LU.

•**SHERREY, Mr. Andrew Edward Siviter, FCA** *1975;* Andrew E.S. Sherrey, Laburnum House, Adams Hill, Clent, STOURBRIDGE, DY9 9PS.

•**SHERREY, Mr. Charles Anthony, FCA** *1975;* Charles A. Sherrey F.C.A., Falcons Rest, Fairfield Lane, Wolverley, KIDDERMINSTER, DY11 5QJ.

SHERRIFF, Mrs. Hannah Elizabeth, BSc ACA *1998;* 2A Copse Avenue, Caversham, READING, RG4 6LX.

SHERRIFF, Mr. Jeffrey Craig, ACA CA(NZ) *2010;* J M Finn & Co Ltd, 4 Coleman Street, LONDON, EC2R 5TA.

SHERRIFF, Mr. John Denis, BSc ACA *1986;* Turner House, 44 Munster Road, Fulham, LONDON, SW6 4EW.

SHERRIFFS, Mr. Duncan Charles, BA(Hons) ACA *2002;* The Garth, 6 Greenhill Road, FARNHAM, GU9 8JN.

SHERRING, Mr. Peter James, FCA *1962;* 2 Blake Close, ST. ALBANS, AL1 5SG. (Life Member)

•**SHERRINGTON, Mr. David, BSc FCA** *1982;* (Tax Fac), Sherrington & Co, 16 Gold Tops, NEWPORT, GWENT, NP20 4PH. See also Peter Price & Company(Pontypool) Limited

SHERRINGTON, Mr. Howard Dudley, LLB FCA *1958;* NSC Programming Ltd, 49 Piccadilly, MANCHESTER, M1 2AP.

SHERRINGTON, Mr. James David, BSc(Hons) ACA *2003;* 3rd Floor Clareville House, 26-27 Oxendon Street, LONDON, SW1Y 4EL.

SHERRINGTON, Mr. John James Marshall, LLB ACA *1988;* 23 Ballingdon Road, LONDON, SW11 6AJ.

SHERRY, Mr. Andrew Paul, ACA *1986;* P.O. Box 88, Dostyk 36, ALMATY 050010, KAZAKHSTAN.

SHERRY, Miss. Helen, MA(Hons) ACA *2003;* 33 Ilminster Gardens, LONDON, SW11 1PJ.

SHERRY, Mr. Hugh, BA ACA *1987;* 89 Edgedale Road, Nether Edge, SHEFFIELD, S7 2BR.

SHERRY, Mr. John, FCA *1958;* Best Wishes, Box No 628, La Piramide Local 11, Avda Dr Meca, Pto De Mazarron, 30860 MURCIA SPAIN. (Life Member)

SHERRY, Miss. Margaret Yvonne, BA ACA *1980;* Ceuta Healthcare Ltd, 41 Richmond Hill, BOURNEMOUTH, BH2 6HS.

SHERRY, Mr. Michael Gabriel, MA FCA FTII CTA *1981;* (Member of Council 1999 - 2009), (Tax Fac), Temple Tax Chambers, 3 Temple Gardens, Temple, LONDON, EC4Y 9AU.

SHERRY, Mr. Patrick Michael, BCom FCA *1972;* 97 Silverdale Avenue, WALTON-ON-THAMES, KT12 1EJ. (Life Member)

SHERRY, Miss. Rachel, ACA *2010;* 1st and 2nd Floor Maisonette, 312 Queenstown Road, LONDON, SW8 4LT.

SHERRY, Mr. Steven, ACA *2009;* 6c South Terrace, SURBITON, KT6 6HT.

SHERWILL, Mr. Jason De Beauvoir, FCA *1980;* Maison de Bas La Rue Des Truchots, St. Andrew, GUERNSEY, GY6 8UD.

SHERWIN, Mr. Christopher Charles, FCA *1965;* 15 Meadow Bank, MOFFAT, DUMFRIESSHIRE, DG10 9LR.

SHERWIN, Mr. David Michael Weldon, ACA *1980;* 35A Oakfield Road, ASHTEAD, SURREY, KT21 2RD.

SHERWIN, Mr. Michael, BA FCA *1984;* 42 Carisbrooke Drive, Mapperley Park, NOTTINGHAM, NG3 5DS.

SHERWIN, Mrs. Susan Anne, BA ACA *1979;* 1 Regent Road, Kirkheaton, HUDDERSFIELD, HD5 0LW.

SHERWOOD, Mr. Andrew Kenneth, BSc ACA *1994;* 42 Blackfriars, YARM, TS15 9HG.

•**SHERWOOD, Mrs. Anny Kirkegaard, BA ACA** *1980;* (Tax Fac), Barnsdale Grange, The Avenue, Exton, OAKHAM, LEICESTERSHIRE, LE15 8AH.

SHERWOOD, Mr. Ben, ACA *2009;* 34 Elmgrove Road, FARNBOROUGH, HAMPSHIRE, GU14 7RD.

SHERWOOD, Ms. Bree Amy, BA ACA *2006;* 93 Harwood Road, NORWICH, NR1 2NQ.

SHERWOOD, Mr. Brian Douglas, MA FCA *1980;* 40 Hobart Road, CAMBRIDGE, CB1 3PU.

SHERWOOD, Mrs. Carolyn Louise, BA ACA *1998;* 1 Rosemary Nook, Rosemary Hill Road, Little Aston, SUTTON COLDFIELD, B74 4HS.

SHERWOOD, Mr. Charles Maxwell, FCA *1967;* Clay Pitts House, Much Birch, HEREFORD, HR2 8HX. (Life Member)

SHERWOOD, Mr. David Andrew, BSc ACA *1993;* 5A - 7250 West Saanich Road, BRENTWOOD BAY V8M 0A3, BC, CANADA.

•**SHERWOOD, Mrs. Jennifer Elizabeth, ACA** *2004;* Larkings (S.E) LLP, 31 St. Georges Place, CANTERBURY, KENT, CT1 1XD.

•**SHERWOOD, Mr. John Seton, FCA** *1967;* (Tax Fac), JS Sherwood, West Cottage, Newborough End, Newborough, BURTON-ON-TRENT, STAFFORDSHIRE DE13 8SR. See also John Sherwood & Co

SHERWOOD, Mr. Julian Alexander James, BSc FCA *1973;* 23 Berkeley Road, LONDON, N8 8RU.

SHERWOOD, Mr. Justin William, BA ACA *2001;* 7 Thornberry Meadows, Barry's Boreen, FERMOY, COUNTY CORK, IRELAND.

SHERWOOD, Miss. Margaret Jill, FCA *1963;* 6 St. Johns Road, NEWPORT, Isle of Wight, PO30 1LN. (Life Member)

SHERWOOD, Mrs. Marie Dianne, BSc(Hons) ACA *2001;* 7 Broomhall Road, WOKING, SURREY, GU21 4AP.

SHERWOOD, Mr. Neil Martin, BSc ACA *1993;* 1 Rosemary Nook, Rosemary Hill Road, Little Aston, SUTTON COLDFIELD, B74 4HS.

SHERWOOD, Mr. Paul, BSc ACA *1995;* 7 Kingswood Place, LONDON, SE13 5BU.

SHERWOOD, Mr. Paul Alexander, BA ACA *1999;* 31 Sowell Street, BROADSTAIRS, CT10 2AU.

SHERWOOD, Mr. Peter Graham, FCA *1958;* 12 Bluecoat Pond, Christs Hospital, HORSHAM, WEST SUSSEX, RH13 0NW. (Life Member)

SHERWOOD, Mr. Richard Stuart, FCA *1968;* 4 Bridge Road, EMSWORTH, HAMPSHIRE, PO10 7DS.

SHERWOOD, Mr. Robert, FCA *1958;* Lilac Cottage, 39 Vine Street, Billingborough, SLEAFORD, LINCOLNSHIRE, NG34 0QE. (Life Member)

SHERWOOD, Mrs. Susannah Jane, BA FCA *1989;* 14 Belgravia Gardens, HEREFORD, HR1 1RB.

SHERWOOD, Mr. Timothy Robin, BSc ACA *1987;* 15 Wyndale Close, HENLEY-ON-THAMES, OXFORDSHIRE, RG9 1BA.

•**SHETH, Mr. Bharat Rasiklal, FCA** *1982;* B. R. Sheth & Co, 15 Rosecroft Walk, PINNER, HA5 1LJ.

•**SHETH, Mr. Dhiren, BEng ACA** *1993;* P O Box 46711-00100, NAIROBI, KENYA.

SHETH, Miss. Kalpana Pravin, BSc ACA MBA *1998;* 270 Radford Road, Radford, COVENTRY, CV6 3BU.

SHETH, Mr. Narendra Amritlal, FCA *1972;* 2075 Blacksmith Lane, OAKVILLE L6M 3A3, ON, CANADA. (Life Member)

SHETH, Mr. Rajendra, FCA *1981;* BSI House, British Standards Institution, 389 Chiswick High Road, LONDON, W4 4AL.

SHETH, Mr. Rajesh Chiman, BSc ACA *1996;* 21 Kilncroft, HEMEL HEMPSTEAD, HERTFORDSHIRE, HP3 8HH.

SHETH, Mr. Sanjay, BSc ACA *2001;* 15 Courtens Mews, STANMORE, MIDDLESEX, HA7 2SP.

SHETH, Mr. Sushil, BA ACA *2010;* The Moorings Heatherlands Road, Chilworth, SOUTHAMPTON, SO16 7JB.

•**SHETH, Mr. Vipul Pravinchandra, BA ACA ATII** *1995;* (Tax Fac), Sheth & Co, 270-272 Radford Road, COVENTRY, CV6 3BU. See also E-accounting Solutions Limited

•**SHETLY, Mr. David Lewis, FCA** *1966;* (Tax Fac), James Todd & Co Limited, Nos 1 & 2 The Barn, Oldwick, West Stoke Road, Lavant, CHICHESTER WEST SUSSEX PO18 9AA.

SHEW, Mr. Anthony Harold, FCA *1974;* PO Box 21, 29692 SAN LUIS DE SABINILLAS, MALAGA, SPAIN.

•**SHEW, Mr. Edmund Jeffrey, FCA FCCA CTA FCMI** *1960;* (Member of Council 1989 - 1995), (Tax Fac), North West Accounting Services Ltd, 46 Crank Road, Billinge, WIGAN, LANCASHIRE, WN5 7EZ.

•**SHEWARD, Mr. Paul, BA ACA** *1996;* PricewaterhouseCoopers LLP, 300 Madison Avenue, NEW YORK, NY 10017, UNITED STATES. See also PricewaterhouseCoopers

SHEWARD, Mr. Robert Edward, ACA *1988;* Robert Sheward, Rowans, Old Odiham Road, ALTON, HAMPSHIRE, GU34 4BU. (Life Member)

SHEWRING, Mr. David John, BSc ACA *1994;* with Ernst & Young, Ernst & Young Building, 8 Exhibition Street, MELBOURNE, VIC 3000, AUSTRALIA.

•**SHEWRING, Mr. Joseph Alan, FCA** *1959;* Shewrings, 17 Tynewydd Drive, Castleton, CARDIFF, CF3 2SB.

SHEWRING, Mr. Mark, ACA *2008;* 24 Summerhill Grove, ENFIELD, EN1 2HY.

SHEWRY, Mr. Thomas David, BSc FCA *1998;* Zurich Insurance, 1 Gladiator Way, FARNBOROUGH, HAMPSHIRE, GU14 6GB.

SHI, Mrs. Chen, ACA *2011;* Room 301 Building 47, Tiantongdongyuan, No3 Changping District, BEIJING 102218, CHINA.

SHI, Miss. Margaret, BSc ACA *2011;* CCG Investor Relations, Unit 918-920, 91F, Shanghai Central Plaza, 381 Middle Huaihuai Road, SHANGHAI 200020 CHINA.

SHI, Mr. Siaw Seng, BSc FCA *1961;* 217-7600 Moffatt Rd, RICHMOND V67 3V1, BC, CANADA. (Life Member)

SHIACH, Mr. Gordon, FCA *1944;* 37 Greenacres, Wetheral, CARLISLE, CA4 8LD. (Life Member)

SHIACH, Miss. Lynne Elizabeth, ACA *2009;* 32 Manchester Road, BARNOLDSWICK, LANCASHIRE, BB18 5PR.

SHIAFKOU, Mr. Antonio John, BA ACA *1988;* 66 Langham Gardens, Grange Park, LONDON, N21 1DJ.

SHIAKALLI, Mrs. Ioanna, BSc ACA *2000;* 9 Aigiou Street, Strovolos, 2027 NICOSIA, CYPRUS.

•**SHIAKALLIS, Mr. Nicholas, BA(Econ) ACA** *1999;* Shiakallis & Co Audit Services Ltd, 44-46 Acropolis Avenue, 1st Floor Office 101, CY2012 NICOSIA, CYPRUS.

SHIAKKAS, Mr. Panayiotis, BA ACA *1993;* Napa Plaza Hotel, PO Box 30305, 5343 AYIA NAPA, CYPRUS.

SHIAMISHIS, Mr. Andreas Nicolaou, BA FCA *1992;* 41 Imittou Street, Holargos, 15561 ATHENS, GREECE.

SHIAMMOUDIS, Mr. George, ACA *2009;* 20 Kyvelis Street, 6041 LARNACA, CYPRUS.

•**SHIAMMOUTIS, Mr. Antonis Ioannou, BSc FCA** *1998;* KPMG, 14 Esperidon Street, 1087 NICOSIA, CYPRUS. See also KPMG Metaxas Loizides Syrimis

SHIATIS, Mr. Andreas Michael, BSc ACA *1992;* 1 Hophurst Drive, Crawley Down, CRAWLEY, RH10 4XA.
•**SHIATIS, Mr. Christakis Panayiotou, FCA** *1973;* 177 Leoforos Stamatas, Rodopoli, 14572 ATHENS, GREECE.
SHIATIS, Mrs. Krishna, BSc ACA *1995;* 1 Hophurst Drive, Crawley Down, CRAWLEY, RH10 4XA.
SHIATIS, Mr. Savvas, BSc(Econ) FCA *2000;* Sophouli Street 1a, Engomi, 2402 NICOSIA, CYPRUS.
SHIEH, Mr. Peter Yue Shan, BSc ACA *1990;* 32G Tower 17, South Horizons, Ap Lei Chau, AP LEI CHAU, HONG KONG ISLAND, HONG KONG SAR.
SHIEKH, Mr. Mohommed Tariq, FCA *1975;* C/O Private Office SBKAN, PO box 44044, Khalidaya, ABU DHABI, 44044, UNITED ARAB EMIRATES.
SHIELD, Miss. Helen, BA ACA *2011;* 5 Wolverley Road, SOLIHULL, B92 9HN.
SHIELD, Mrs. Helen Marie, PhD BSc(Hons) ACA DChA *2002;* St. Albans School, Abbey Gateway, ST. ALBANS, HERTFORDSHIRE, AL3 4HB.
•**SHIELD, Miss. Nicola Jane Elizabeth, BSc ACA** *1999;* PricewaterhouseCoopers LLP, 1 Embankment Place, LONDON, WC2N 6RH. See also PricewaterhouseCoopers
SHIELD, Mr. Peter Charles, BSc ACA *1980;* South Park, Chargrove Lane Up Hatherley, CHELTENHAM, GLOUCESTERSHIRE, GL51 4XD.
SHIELDS, Mr. Alastair Brian Roderick, ACA *2008;* 179 Maidenhead Road, WINDSOR, BERKSHIRE, SL4 5EZ.
SHIELDS, Miss. Amanda Louise, BA ACA *1989;* 28 Broomsleigh Street, Hampstead, LONDON, NW6 1QH.
•**SHIELDS, Mr. Barry Joseph Mark, FCA** *1977;* (Tax Fac), Harold Smith, Unit 32, Llys Edmund Prys, St. Asaph Business Park, ST. ASAPH, LL17 0JA.
SHIELDS, Miss. Gail, ACA *2010;* Freshwaterplace level 19, 2 Southbank Boulevard, SOUTHBANK, VIC 3006, AUSTRALIA.
SHIELDS, Mr. John Malcolm, FCA *1966;* 7 Ashurst Lodge, 145 Highbury Grove, LONDON, N5 1HN.
SHIELDS, Mr. Martin David, MEng ACA *2000;* 48 Williams Way, RADLETT, HERTFORDSHIRE, WD7 7HB.
SHIELDS, Mr. Matthew David, MSc BA(Hons) ACA *2002;* 28 Tivy Dale Close, Cawthorne, BARNSLEY, SOUTH YORKSHIRE, S75 4ET.
SHIELDS, Mr. Oliver Elliot, MSc ACA *2002;* 1738 West Belmont Apt 3R, CHICAGO, IL 60657, UNITED STATES.
SHIELDS, Mr. Paul Anthony, ACA *2005;* 9 Penrith Road, SUNDERLAND, SR5 1RG.
SHIELDS, Mr. Peter, FCA *1972;* 11 Dartnell Park Road, WEST BYFLEET, KT14 6PN.
SHIELDS, Miss. Rebecca Jane, ACA *2006;* 1402 Lincoln Road, PETERBOROUGH, PE4 6LS.
SHIELDS, Mr. Ryan, ACA CA(AUS) *2009;* Flat 2, 15 - 17 Hornton St, LONDON, W8 7NP.
SHIELDS, Miss. Susan, BA ACA *2008;* Flat b, 11 Cavendish Road, LONDON, SW12 0BH.
SHIELS, Mr. Andrew John, MA ACA *1998;* 41 Belsize Avenue, LONDON, N13 4TL.
•**SHIELS, Mr. Gary Shaun Leonard, FCA** *1981;* PricewaterhouseCoopers LLP, Cornwall Court, 19 Cornwall Street, BIRMINGHAM, B3 2DT. See also PricewaterhouseCoopers
SHIELS, Ms. Laura Jane, ACA *2008;* 20 Flaxman Croft, Copmanthorpe, YORK, YO23 3TU.
SHIERS, Mr. Clifford Michael, BA ACA *1993;* 30 Keats Way, Cottam, PRESTON, PR4 0NL.
•**SHIERS, Mr. Paul Thomas, BSc ACA CTA** *1986;* (Tax Fac), Pitt Godden & Taylor, Brunel House, George Street, GLOUCESTER, GL1 1BZ.
•**SHIERSON, Mr. Malcolm Brian, BSc FCA** *1975;* Whitegates, 195 Moor Lane, Woodford, STOCKPORT, SK7 1PF.
SHILDRICK, Mr. Simon David, BA ACA *2002;* 44 Jay Close, Lower Earley, READING, RG6 4HE.
SHILL, Ms. Anna Mary, BA(Hons) FCA ATII *1991;* 6 Church Terrace, BURES, SUFFOLK, CO8 5ED.
SHILL, Mr. David Anthony, BSc ACA *1987;* 52 Simcoe Close SW, CALGARY T3H 4N4, AB, CANADA.
SHILL, Mr. John Heath, FCA *1954;* Cotteswold, Leckhampton Hill, CHELTENHAM, GL53 9QH. (Life Member)
SHILL, Mrs. Marion Agnes, MA(Hons) ACA *1991;* 52 Simcoe Close SW, CALGARY T3H 4N4, AB, CANADA.
SHILLAKER, Mr. Michael John, BSc ACA *1997;* Flat 5, 30 Wadham Gardens, LONDON, NW3 3DP.
•**SHILLING, Mr. Andrew, BA FCA CTA** *1993;* Rawlinson & Hunter, Eighth Floor, 6 New Street Square, New Fetter Lane, LONDON, EC4A 3AQ.
SHILLING, Mr. Raymond Trevor, BA ACA *1982;* 13 Regent Street, LONDON, SW1Y 4LR.
SHILLING, Mr. Stephen James, BSc(Hons) ACA *2000;* 152 Knighton Church Road, South Knighton, LEICESTER, LE2 3JL.
SHILLINGFORD, Mr. James Hugh, MA ACA *1979;* 59 Doughty Street, LONDON, WC1N 2JT.
•**SHILLINGFORD, Mrs. Sarah Louise, BSc ACA** *1992;* Deloitte LLP, 2 New Street Square, LONDON, EC4A 3BZ. See also Deloitte & Touche LLP
•**SHILLINGLAW, Mr. Ian, ACA** *1986;* Higgisons, Higgison House, 381/383 City Road, LONDON, EC1V 1NW.
•**SHILLINGLAW, Mr. Peter, FCA** *1975;* (Tax Fac), Stephen Hill Mid Kent Ltd, 44 High Street, NEW ROMNEY, KENT, TN28 8BZ.
SHILLINGLAW, Mr. Robert William, MA ACA *1998;* 15 Raymer Close, ST. ALBANS, HERTFORDSHIRE, AL1 3QH.
SHILLINGTON, Mrs. Joanna Katherine Margaret, MA ACA *2002;* Airs, 7 Tribe Road #1, PAGET DV04, BERMUDA.
•**SHILLITO, Mr. James Robert, BSc FCA CF** *1997;* Shillito Partners LLP, 43-45 Portman Square, LONDON, W1H 6HN.
SHILLITO, Mr. Jonathan, ACA *2010;* 37a Crouch Hill, LONDON, N4 4AP.
SHILLITO, Mr. Richard John, MA ACA *1995;* 47 Salisbury Gardens, NEWCASTLE UPON TYNE, NE2 1HP.
SHILSTON, Mr. Andrew Barkley, MA ACA MCT *1980;* Rolls-Royce, 65 Buckingham Gate, LONDON, SW1E 6AT.
SHILSTON, Miss. Nichola Jayne, BA ACA *1993;* (Tax Fac), 8 The Dene, SEVENOAKS, TN13 1PB.
SHILTON, Mr. Jason Edward, BSc ACA *1997;* 24 Broadhill Road, Kegworth, DERBY, LEICESTERSHIRE, DE74 2DQ.
SHILTON, Mr. Michael Sean, BA ACA *2004;* 92 Muncaster Road, LONDON, SW11 6NU.
SHILTON, Mr. Wesley Vincent, BAcc ACA *2002;* 88 Lancaster Road, BLACKPOOL, FY3 9ST.
SHIMELL, Mr. Maurice, BA FCA *1974;* with Ernst & Young LLP, 1 More London Place, LONDON, SE1 2AF.
SHIMELL, Mr. Simon Andrew, ACA *2009;* Valance Carruthers Coleman Priest Greencoat House, Francis Street, LONDON, SW1P 1DH.
•**SHIMMIN, Mr. Andrew Paul, BA FCA** *1983;* Shimmin Wilson & Co, 13-15 Hope Street, Douglas, ISLE OF MAN, IM1 1AQ.
SHIMMIN, Mr. Christopher John, BSc ACA *1982;* 81 Brondesbury Road, LONDON, NW6 6BB.
SHIMMIN, Mr. Edward Ramsey, BSc ACA CFE *2000;* 1 Northside Piers, Apt 4A, BROOKLYN, NY 11211, UNITED STATES.
SHIMMIN, Mrs. Kelly Anne, BSc ACA *2004;* 5 Old School View, Eyreton Lea Crosby, ISLE OF MAN, IM4 4DA.
SHIMWELL, Mr. Lee Michael, ACA *2001;* Orchard House Bridgnorth Road, Stourton, STOURBRIDGE, DY7 5BJ.
SHIMWELL, Dr. Susan Jane, PhD BSc ACA *2006;* County Treasurers Department Derbyshire County Council, PO Box 2, MATLOCK, DERBYSHIRE, DE4 3AH.
SHIN, Mr. Dong-Joon, BEng ACA *1993;* 475 Hunter Road, RIDGEWOOD, NJ 07450, UNITED STATES.
•**SHIN, Mr. Yoke Luen, FCA** *1978;* Shah And Shin, 42a The Broadway, Joel Street, NORTHWOOD, MIDDLESEX, HA6 1PA.
SHIN KOY SIEN, Miss. Marilyn, ACA *2009;* 15 Hengest Avenue, ESHER, KT10 0BP.
SHINDLER, Mr. David Lawrence, ACA *1984;* 4 Berkeley Close, Elstree, BOREHAMWOOD, HERTFORDSHIRE, WD6 3JN.
SHINDLER, Mrs. Michelle, BSc ACA *2007;* 18 Babington Road, LONDON, NW4 4LD.
SHINER, Mr. Brendan Niall, BA ACA *1985;* Culver House, Giddynap Lane, Amberley, STROUD, GLOUCESTERSHIRE, GL5 5BA.
SHINER, Mr. Peter James, BA ACA *1990;* 88 Rutland Gardens, LONDON, N4 1JR.
SHING, Miss. Anita Yuen-Kiu, MA FCA *1986;* FLAT G 12/F TOWER 6, LAGUNA VERDE, HUNG HOM, HONG KONG SAR.
•**SHING, Mr. Chi, ACA** *1993;* All Accountancy, 377 Edgware Road, LONDON, W2 1BT.
SHING, Mr. Hang Kwong, ACA *2007;* Alan H.K.Shing & Co, Unit B 15/F, Kiu Yin Commercial Building, WAN CHAI, HONG KONG ISLAND, HONG KONG SAR.
SHING, Mr. Kai Chiu, ACA *2005;* Flat 9E Stage One, Boland Court, 10 Broadcast Drive, KOWLOON CITY, KOWLOON, HONG KONG SAR.
SHING, Miss. Serena, BSc(Hons) ACA *2011;* Flat 9E Stage 1, Boland Court, 10 Broadcast Drive, KOWLOON TONG, HONG KONG SAR.
SHINGLER, Mr. Anthony Durrant, FCA *1965;* Aldertree, 109 Lower Street, Horning, NORWICH, NR12 8PF. (Life Member)
SHINGLER, Mr. David, BA FCA *1980;* with E.J. Williams & Co, 31 Lonsdale Street, CARLISLE, CA1 1BJ.
SHINGLER, Mr. Philip James, BEng ACA *1996;* 39 Grand Avenue, CAMBERLEY, SURREY, GU15 3QJ.
•**SHINGLETON, Mrs. Amanda Katharine, BSc ACA** *1986;* Davison & Shingleton, Boundary House, 91-93 Charterhouse Street, LONDON, EC1M 6HR.
SHINN, Miss. Claire Louise, BA ACA *2006;* Chalk Pit Cottage, Coombe Bissett, SALISBURY, SP5 4LH.
•**SHINN, Mr. David John Brooklyn, FCA** *1985;* (Tax Fac), 39 Ashdown Avenue, Rottingdean, BRIGHTON, BN2 8AH.
SHINN, Mr. Philip Andrew, BSc ACA *1991;* 5 Rothesay Avenue, RICHMOND, SURREY, TW10 5EB.
•**SHINNICK, Mr. John Michael, FCA** *1983;* Grant Thornton UK LLP, 4 Hardman Square, Spinningfields, MANCHESTER, M3 3EB. See also Grant Thornton LLP
SHINNIE, Mr. Damon Scott, BCom ACA *1994;* 19 Mariner Avenue, BIRMINGHAM, B16 9DF.
SHINTON, Mr. John, FCA *1960;* Kingsnorth, 17 Oak Drive, Seisdon, WOLVERHAMPTON, WV5 7ET.
SHINTON, Miss. Natalie Anne, MMath ACA *2005;* Tesco Stores Ltd, Tesco House, Delamare Road, Cheshunt, WALTHAM CROSS, HERTFORDSHIRE EN8 9SL.
SHIOUFTAS, Mr. Demetris, ACA *2008;* Demosthenous 9, Aradippou, 7103 LARNACA, CYPRUS.
SHIPILLIS, Miss. Elena, BA ACA *2005;* Flat 301, 9 Ellados Street, Acropolis, 2003 NICOSIA, CYPRUS.
SHIPLEY, Mr. Andrew James, BA ACA *1993;* Orchard House York Road Green Hammerton, YORK, YO26 8BN.
SHIPLEY, Mr. Anthony John, FCA *1971;* 25 Church Street, STONE, ST15 8BW. (Life Member)
SHIPLEY, Mr. David Charles, MA FCA *1969;* Saddlebole, Mottram Road, ALDERLEY EDGE, SK9 7JF.
SHIPLEY, Miss. Emma-Louise, ACA MAAT *2003;* Unit 6, 101A St. Georges Cresent, Drummoyne, SYDNEY, NSW 2047, AUSTRALIA.
SHIPLEY, Mr. Grant Martin, BSc ACA *1988;* 20 Bevere Close, WORCESTER, WR3 7QH.
SHIPLEY, Miss. Hannah Nadira, ACA *2008;* Flat 2, 55 Bedford Road, LONDON, SW4 7RH.
SHIPLEY, Miss. Jenny Grace, BSc ACA *2005;* 155 Burley Wood Crescent, LEEDS, LS4 2QJ.
SHIPLEY, Mr. John Kenneth, BSc ACA *1979;* Mill House, Trehaddle, TRURO, CORNWALL, TR4 8RN.
SHIPLEY, Mr. John Richard, BSc(Hons) ACA *2001;* Home Garth Carr Lane, Broomfleet, BROUGH, NORTH HUMBERSIDE, HU15 1RH.
SHIPLEY, Mr. John Waterhouse, BCom FCA *1972;* The Laurels, 1 Knights Hill, Barr Common, WALSALL, WS9 0TG.
SHIPLEY, Miss. Lisa, BA ACA CTA *2006;* with Deloitte LLP, 2 New Street Square, LONDON, EC4A 3BZ.
•**SHIPLEY, Mrs. Nicola, ACA** *2002;* Smailes Goldie, Regents Court, Princess Street, HULL, HU2 8BA.
SHIPLEY, Mrs. Pamela Jayne, BSc ACA *2005;* 51 Tarry Hill, Swineshead, BOSTON, LINCOLNSHIRE, PE20 3LW.
SHIPLEY, Mr. Peter, ACA *2011;* 12 St. Margarets Drive, Craig-y-don, LLANDUDNO, LL30 1YD.
SHIPLEY, Mr. Robert Elliott, FCA *1971;* 31 Wellard Road, BOX HILL SOUTH, VIC 3128, AUSTRALIA. (Life Member)
SHIPLEY, Mr. Robert James, FCA *1958;* Clove Cottage, Clove Farm, Longdown, EXETER, DEVON, EX6 7SB. (Life Member)
SHIPLEY, Mr. Stephen Robert, FCA *1975;* 69 Wychwood Avenue, Knowle, SOLIHULL, B93 9DL.
•**SHIPLEY, Mr. Thomas John, BSc FCA** *1982;* (Tax Fac), McCabe Ford Williams, Charlton House, Dour Street, DOVER, CT16 1BL.
SHIPMAN, Miss. Amanda Jane, BA ACA FRSA *1983;* 119 Ladbroke Road, LONDON, W11 3PR.
SHIPMAN, Mr. Daniel Bryan, BCom ACA *1993;* The Copse, 3 Dunnockswood, Alsager, STOKE-ON-TRENT, ST7 2XU.
SHIPMAN, Mr. Michael Robert, MA FCA *1972;* 19 Framfield Road, LONDON, N5 1UU. (Life Member)
SHIPMAN, Mrs. Sara, BSc FCA *1989;* 33 Fennyland Lane, KENILWORTH, WARWICKSHIRE, CV8 2RS.
SHIPP, Dr. Darrin John, PhD MA ACA *1996;* 32 Hutton Close, BRISTOL, BS9 3PT.
SHIPP, Mr. Donald Albert, FCA *1971;* 6 Thorneycroft Close, Kingswood, MAIDSTONE, KENT, ME17 3BF.
SHIPP, Mrs. Jacqueline Clare, BSc ACA CTA *1995;* Burges Salmon LLP, One Glass Wharf, BRISTOL, BS2 0ZX.
•**SHIPP, Mr. John Vernon, BSc FCA** *1986;* with Ernst & Young, The Ernst & Young Building, 680 George Street, SYDNEY, NSW 2000, AUSTRALIA.
SHIPP, Mr. Martin William, BSc ACA *2003;* 5 Williams Grove, Long Ditton, SURBITON, SURREY, KT6 5RN.
SHIPP, Mr. Robert William, MSc BA FCA *2000;* with Ernst & Young LLP, 1 Colmore Square, BIRMINGHAM, B4 6HQ.
SHIPP, Mr. Thomas Henry Neale, FCA *1952;* 64 Metcalfe Road, CAMBRIDGE, CB4 2DD. (Life Member)
•**SHIPPAM, Mr. Frank Michael Earle, BSc FCA DChA** *1996;* MA Partners LLP, 7 The Close, NORWICH, NORFOLK, NR1 4DJ.
SHIPPERLEE, Mr. James, BA ACA *2007;* with Matrix Private Equity Partners, 1 Vine Street, LONDON, W1J 0AH.
SHIPPEY, Mrs. Antonia Fay, BSc ACA *2001;* 26 Bradbourne Street, LONDON, SW6 3TE.
SHIPPEY, Mr. Thomas Adam, BSc ACA *1999;* 26 Bradbourne Street, LONDON, SW6 3TE.
SHIPPIN, Mrs. Lucinda, BSc ACA *2001;* 8 Beresford Road, KINGSTON UPON THAMES, SURREY, KT2 6LR.
SHIPPIN, Mr. Nicholas Paul, BA ACA *1996;* 8 Beresford Road, KINGSTON UPON THAMES, SURREY, KT2 6LR.
SHIPSEY, Mrs. Fiona Jill, BA ACA *1991;* Home Farm Easton Town, Sherston, MALMESBURY, WILTSHIRE, SN16 0PS.
SHIPSEY, Mr. John Francis, MBA BA ACA *1991;* Dyson Ltd, Tetbury Hill, MALMESBURY, WILTSHIRE, SN16 0RP.
SHIPTON, Mr. Craig Michael, BA ACA *2005;* unit 2 24-26 Malcolm st Hawthorne, BRISBANE, QLD 4151, AUSTRALIA.
SHIPTON, Mr. Derek, FCA *1953;* 701 East Seminary Ave., TOWSON, MD 21286-1440, UNITED STATES. (Life Member)
SHIPTON, Mr. Jonathan Mark, BSc ACA CF *1996;* Moor End, Harlow Pines, HARROGATE, HG3 1PZ.
SHIPTON, Mr. Matthew Guy, BA(Hons) ACA *2010;* Flat 1/A Lanark Mansions, 12 Lanark Road, LONDON, W9 1DB.
SHIPWAY, Mr. Andrew Michael, BSc ACA *1997;* Flat 17 Dorchester House, 8 Strand Drive, RICHMOND, SURREY, TW9 4DX.
SHIPWAY, Mrs. Carol Anne, FCA *1975;* Oak House, Main Street, Gawcott, BUCKINGHAM, MK18 4HZ.
SHIPWAY, Mr. Paul Michael, BA(Hons) ACA *2003;* 43 Ashdown Close, Chandler's Ford, EASTLEIGH, HAMPSHIRE, SO53 5QF.
SHIPWAY, Mr. Roger Andrew, FCA *1971;* Aries, Fringford Road, Caversfield, BICESTER, OX27 8TH.
•**SHIRAZ, Mr. Mohammed, BA(Hons) ACA** *2003;* Mohammed Shiraz, 23 Abbotsfield Court, MANCHESTER, M8 0AW.
SHIRAZI, Mr. Shahbaz Abdulrasul Bamdad, FCA *1975;* P.O. Box 213591, DUBAI, UNITED ARAB EMIRATES.
SHIRCLIFF, Miss. Katherine Marianne, BA ACA *1987;* 31 College Lane, BURY ST. EDMUNDS, SUFFOLK, IP33 1QE.
SHIRE, Mr. Roderick John, FCA *1971;* 37 Watson Avenue, ROSE PARK, SA 5067, AUSTRALIA.
•ⓘ**SHIRES, Mr. Edward Mark, BA FCA** *1981;* PricewaterhouseCoopers LLP, Donington Court, Pegasus Business Park, Castle Donington, DERBY, DE74 2UZ. See also PricewaterhouseCoopers
SHIRES, Mr. Martin, BSc ACA *1982;* Doulieu, Rue A L'Or, St. Saviour, GUERNSEY, GY7 9XS.
SHIRET, Mr. Anthony Lance, BA ACA *1982;* Monkenholt, Hadley Green Road, BARNET, EN5 5PR.
SHIRLAW, Mr. Marc Clive Watton, BA ACA *1984;* W E R Storage Ltd, Richmond Street, WEST BROMWICH, B70 0DD.
SHIRLEY, Mr. Brian Anthony, FCA *1969;* Wraxall Vineyard, Wraxall, SHEPTON MALLET, SOMERSET, BA4 6RQ.
•**SHIRLEY, Mr. David John, FCA** *1980;* (Tax Fac), N.R. Barton & Co, 19-21 Bridgeman Terrace, WIGAN, WN1 1TD.
SHIRLEY, Mr. Gregory Michael, BA ACA *1999;* Broad Lane Farm, Broad Lane, North Curry, TAUNTON, SOMERSET, TA3 6EE.
SHIRLEY, Mr. James Stewart, BSc FCA *1977;* Brocklehurst Nursing Home, 65 Cavendish Road, Withington, MANCHESTER, M20 1JG. (Life Member)
SHIRLEY, Mr. Martin John, FCA *1964;* Burnham House, The Street, Bredgar, SITTINGBOURNE, ME9 8EX.
SHIRLEY, Mr. Paul Christopher, BA ACA *1990;* 51 Hillhouse Close, BILLERICAY, CM12 0BB.

SHIRLEY, Mr. Philip, FCA *1939;* 30 Kirk Street, Kincardine, ALLOA, FK10 4PT. (Life Member)

•**SHIRLEY, Mr. Philip Evelyn, BA ACA** *1980;* (Tax Fac), P.E. Shirley LLP, 24 Lime Street, LONDON, EC3M 7HS.

SHIRLEY, Mr. Richard John, FCA *1977;* Bambara, Maybury Hill, WOKING, GU22 8AF.

SHIRLEY, Mr. Richard Kenneth, FCA *1972;* 63A Aylesford Street, LONDON, SW1V 3RY.

•**SHIRLEY, Mr. Roger Anthony, BSc FCA MCT** *1971;* Conocophillips, 2 Portman Street, LONDON, W1H 6DU.

SHIRLEY, Mr. Roy David, BA ACA *1979;* 13 Zetland Avenue, GILLINGHAM, Kent, ME7 3AE.

SHIRLEY, Mr. Timothy Paul, BSc(Hons) ACA *2005;* Clinicenta Ltd Hampden House Monument Business Park, Warpsgrove Lane Chalgrove, OXFORD, OX44 7RW.

SHIRTCLIFF, Mr. Richard Andrew, FCA *1963;* Hollandoak, Underriver, SEVENOAKS, KENT, TN15 0SH.

SHIRTCLIFFE, Mr. Andrew Graham Charles, BSc ACA *2004;* 11 Lindore Road, Clapham, LONDON, SW11 1HJ.

SHIRTCLIFFE, Mr. Christopher Charles, FCA *1968;* Tankards, Quarry Road, OXTED, RH8 9HE. (Life Member)

SHIRTCLIFFE, Miss. Lisa Jane, BSc ACA *1997;* Joshua Agency Plc, 79 Wells Street, LONDON, W1T 3QN.

•**SHIRTCLIFFE, Mr. Stephen James, BA(Hons) ACA** *2004;* (Tax Fac), Shirtcliffe & Co Limited, 668 Woodborough Road, Mapperley, NOTTINGHAM, NG3 5FS.

SHIRTCLIFFE, Mr. William James, BSc ACA *2006;* 11 Lindore Road, LONDON, SW11 1HJ.

SHIRVELL, Mr. Warren David, BSc(Hons) ACA MSI *1993;* Mondrian Investment Partners Ltd, 5th Floor, 10 Gresham Street, LONDON, EC2V 7JD.

SHIRVILLE, Mrs. Nadia, ACA *2010;* 9a Belitha Villas, LONDON, N1 1PE.

SHIU, Mr. Ka Wing Geoffrey, ACA *2005;* Flat G 17th Floor Block II, Academic Terrace, 101 Pokfulam Road, POK FU LAM, HONG KONG ISLAND, HONG KONG SAR.

SHIU, Ms. Shuk Ching, ACA *2007;* Flat 2809, Block B, Kornhill, QUARRY BAY, HONG KONG ISLAND, HONG KONG SAR.

SHIU, Ms. Suk Kwan, ACA *2008;* Hospital Authority, Flat 4A, Finance Dep., Admin. Building, Kwong Wah Hospital, 25 Waterloo Road YAU MA TEI KOWLOON HONG KONG SAR.

SHIVRAM, Mr. Vikram, ACA *2009;* Flat 408 Chetna Apartments, JP Road 7 Bungalows, Andherhi-West, MUMBAI 400053, MAHARASHTRA, INDIA.

SHLAPAK, Miss. Yulia, ACA *2009;* Apt 102, Othonos and Amalias (and Zinonos) Street, Heroes Square 25, 3032 LIMASSOL, CYPRUS.

SHOAIB, Mr. Mohammad, BA ACA *1989;* IMI plc, Lakeside, Solihull Parkway, Birmingham Business Park, BIRMINGHAM, B37 7XZ.

SHOARD, Mrs. Kerri Sheena, BA(Hons) ACA *2001;* with KPMG LLP, 1 The Embankment, Neville Street, LEEDS, LS1 4DW.

SHOBBROOK, Mr. David Gordon, BA FCA *1974;* 270 Kempshott Lane, Kempshott, BASINGSTOKE, RG22 5LS.

SHOESMITH, Mr. Colin Michael, BA ACA *1983;* 68 Binswood Avenue, LEAMINGTON SPA, CV32 5RY.

SHOESMITH, Mr. David Edward, MA FCA *1969;* (Tax Fac), Liverpool John Moores, University Business School, 98 Mount Pleasant, LIVERPOOL, L3 5UZ.

SHOESMITH, Mr. David Martin, BA ACA *1984;* 17 Beech Walk, Adel, LEEDS, LS16 8NY.

•**SHOESMITH, Mrs. Elaine Rosemary, FCA** *1975;* Shoesmiths, Suites 1 & 2, Ground Floor, 54 Hagley Road, Edgbaston, BIRMINGHAM B16 8PE. See also Shoesmiths Business Solutions Ltd

SHOESMITH, Mr. James Francis, FCA *1967;* 1 Park Leys, DAVENTRY, NORTHAMPTONSHIRE, NN11 4AS. (Life Member)

SHOESMITH, Miss. Lisa Naomi, BA(Hons) ACA *2001;* Old Mast House, The Square, ABINGDON, OXFORDSHIRE, OX14 5AR.

SHOHAM, Mr. Nicholas, BA(Hons) ACA *2004;* 37 Linkside, LONDON, N12 7LE.

•**SHOHET, Mr. Philip Samuel David, FCA** *1969;* 203 Goring Road, Goring-by-Sea, WORTHING, BN12 4PA.

SHOHID, Mr. Abdul, BSc(Hons) ACA *2001;* 7 Rotherfield Road, CARSHALTON, SURREY, SM5 3DN.

SHOKER, Mrs. Gurjit Kaur, BA ACA *2010;* 23 Stableford Close, BIRMINGHAM, B32 3XL.

SHOKER, Miss. Karenjeet, ACA *2010;* 41 Westbury Lodge Close, PINNER, MIDDLESEX, HA5 3FG.

SHOLAY, Mr. Mervyn Krisnen, ACA *2009;* Flat 105, Basque Court, Garter Way, LONDON, SE16 6XE.

SHOLICAR, Mrs. Julie Ann, BA ACA *1988;* Anderson & Co Sumpter House, 8 Station Road Histon, CAMBRIDGE, CB24 9LQ.

SHOLLEY, Ms. Kathryn, ACA *2007;* 1/14A Mays Street, Devonport, NORTH SHORE 0624, NEW ZEALAND.

•**SHONCHHATRA, Mr. Ashvinkumar M, FCA** *1982;* (Tax Fac), Ashon Limited, Sental House, 66 Waldeck Road, Strand on the Green, LONDON, W4 3NU.

SHONCHHATRA, Mr. Rikhil, ACA *2007;* 8 Second Avenue, WEMBLEY, MIDDLESEX, HA9 8QF.

•**SHONE, Miss. Amanda Jane, ACA** *2002;* (Tax Fac), AJ Shone & Co, Ashley House, Unit 3, Brickfields Business Park, GILLINGHAM, DORSET SP8 4PX.

SHONE, Miss. Cathrine Anne, BA ACA *1989;* 32 Albert Road, RICHMOND, TW10 6DP.

SHONE, Mr. Christopher Martin, MA ACA *1987;* 3 Balchraggan, Abriachan, INVERNESS, IV3 8LD.

SHONE, Mr. John Anthony, BSc ACA *1981;* Templeton, Cedar Road, COBHAM, KT11 2AE.

SHONE, Mrs. Karen Patricia, BA ACA *1989;* Beeson End Orchard, Beeson End Lane, HARPENDEN, HERTFORDSHIRE, AL5 2AB.

SHONE, Mrs. Marcella Jane, MA ACA *1990;* (Tax Fac), Dickinson Dees One Trinity Gardens, Broad Chare, NEWCASTLE UPON TYNE, NE1 2HF.

SHONE, Mrs. Penelope Rosemary, BSc FCA *1978;* Little Orchard, Jeffries Lane, Goring-by-Sea, WORTHING, WEST SUSSEX, BN12 4PS.

SHONE, Mrs. Ruth Elizabeth, MA ACA *1996;* 24 Park Drive, LONDON, SW14 8RD.

SHONE, Mr. Simon John, ACA *1982;* Barnes Brow, Newton Hall Lane, Mobberley, KNUTSFORD, CHESHIRE, WA16 7LW.

SHONE, Mr. Stephen, BSc FCA *1982;* Beeson End Orchard, Beeson End Lane, HARPENDEN, HERTFORDSHIRE, AL5 2AB.

SHONE, Miss. Susan, BA ACA *1989;* 14 Willow Crescent, Hawarden, DEESIDE, CH5 3QT.

SHONFIELD, Mr. John Kenneth Charles, FCA *1968;* 10 Hassock Wood, KESTON, BR2 6HX. (Life Member)

SHONFIELD, Mr. Paul Andrew, BA ACA *1982;* Mentmore Court, 109 September Way, STANMORE, MIDDLESEX, HA7 2SF.

SHONN, Mr. Jonathan, BA FCA *1997;* 46 Great Bushey Drive, LONDON, N20 8QL.

SHOOBRIDGE, Mr. Peter James, ACA *1991;* 9550 S Eastern Avenue, Suite 253, LAS VEGAS, NV 89144, UNITED STATES.

•**SHOOMAN, Mr. Peter Joseph, FCA** *1971;* Rehov Axelrod 10, Apartment 15, Ramat Aviv Hachadasha, 69634 TEL AVIV, ISRAEL.

SHOOTER, Mr. Alan, FCA *1968;* 8 Sherwood Rd, Hendon, LONDON, NW4 1AD. (Life Member)

SHOOTER, Mr. Christopher John, BSc ACA *1986;* 76 Rosebery Road, Muswell Hill, LONDON, N10 2LA.

•**SHOOTER, Mr. John Brian, BSc FCA** *1997;* Mannac, MGS House, Circular Road, Douglas, ISLE OF MAN, IM1 1BL.

•**SHOOTER, Mr. Richard Graham, FCA** *1976;* (Tax Fac), Trouble Shooter, 39 Castle Street, LEICESTER, LE1 5WN.

SHOPLAND, Ms. Rachael Jane, BSc ACA *1997;* Goldman Sachs Peterborough Court, 133 Fleet Street, LONDON, EC4A 2BB.

SHORE, Miss. Anna Louise, MSc BSc ACA *2005;* 49 Emmanuel Road, LONDON, SW12 0HN.

•**SHORE, Mrs. Anne Charles, MA(Hons) ACA** *2001;* Shore Accountancy Services, Frew Toll Cottage, Thornhill, STIRLING, FK8 3QU.

•**SHORE, Mr. Charles Nicholas, BA FCA** *1978;* (Tax Fac), Frank Hirth plc, 236 Gray's Inn Road, LONDON, WC1X 8HB.

SHORE, Mr. Frank, BA FCA *1971;* Old Manor, Quality Street, REDHILL, RH1 3BB.

SHORE, Mr. Laurence Charles, FCA CTA *1992;* (Tax Fac), 17 Gorway Gardens, WALSALL, WS1 3BJ.

SHORE, Mr. Michael Howard, ACA CA(SA) *2008;* Arnewood Lodge, 223 Everton Road, Hordle, LYMINGTON, HAMPSHIRE, SO41 0HE.

SHORE, Mr. Michael John, BA(Hons) ACA *2001;* McKinnon & Clarke Ltd Claymore House, Carnegie Campus Enterprise Way, DUNFERMLINE, FIFE, KY11 8PY.

SHORE, Mr. Richard Cameron, BSc ACA *2002;* 87 Queensgate, NORTHWICH, CHESHIRE, CW8 1DU.

SHORE, Mr. Robert, BSc ACA *2005;* 14 Forest Glen, CHERRYBROOK, NSW 2126, AUSTRALIA.

SHORE, Mr. Stephen Peter, BSc ACA *1993;* Lanwades House, Moulton Road, Kennett, NEWMARKET, SUFFOLK, CB8 7PX.

SHORE, Miss. Tamarin Sophie Alicia, BA ACA *2004;* 13 Althea Street, LONDON, SW6 2RX.

•**SHORES, Mr. David Neville Waite, FCA** *1958;* D.N.W. Shores, Hillrise, Hare Lane, Hordle, LYMINGTON, SO41 0GE. See also DS Management Consultants Ltd

SHOREY, Mrs. Wendy, ACA *2003;* 6 Galt Close, WICKFORD, ESSEX, SS12 9SG.

SHORNEY, Mr. Jonathan Andrew, BA ACA *2005;* 31 Four Acres Close, Nailsea, BRISTOL, BS48 4YF.

SHORNEY, Mr. Mark James, BA ACA *1988;* 5 Sandy Lane, SINGAPORE 437322, SINGAPORE.

SHORROCK, Mr. Daniel, BA ACA *2011;* 73 Rydal Crescent, Worsley, MANCHESTER, M28 7JD.

SHORROCK, Mr. Edward Daniel, BSc FCA *1999;* Bakerplatt, PO Box 842, 2 Mulcaster Street, St Helier, JERSEY, JE4 0US.

SHORROCK, Mr. John Parker, BA FCA *1971;* Plane Tree House, Lomas Lane, Balladen, ROSSENDALE, BB4 6HU.

SHORROCK, Mr. Matthew John, LLB ACA *2001;* 109 Bents Road, SHEFFIELD, S11 9RH.

SHORROCKS, Mr. Richard George, BSc FCA *1991;* The Wine Society, Gunnels Wood Road, STEVENAGE, HERTFORDSHIRE, SG1 2BT.

SHORT, Mrs. Alice Elizabeth Wesley, MSci ACA *2010;* Flat A, 16 Strathblaine Road, LONDON, SW11 1RJ.

SHORT, Mrs. Alison Margaret, BSc ACA *1991;* Viaduct House, 168 Barnsley Road, Denby Dale, HUDDERSFIELD, HD8 8TS.

•**SHORT, Mr. Andrew Christopher, BA FCA** *1981;* Saleport Limited, Merewood, Pond Road, WOKING, SURREY, GU22 0JZ.

SHORT, Mr. Anthony William, FCA *1968;* 5 Whitestones, Stocksmoor, HUDDERSFIELD, HD4 6XQ.

SHORT, Mrs. Audrey Mary, FCA *1952;* Poldens, Church Lane, Ruishton, TAUNTON, TA3 5LL. (Life Member)

SHORT, Mr. Bryan Charles Beebee, FCA *1973;* West Field House Swannells Wood, Studham, DUNSTABLE, BEDFORDSHIRE, LU6 2QB.

SHORT, Mr. Carl, BA FCA *1986;* Graceland, Darnley Drive, TUNBRIDGE WELLS, KENT, TN4 0TH.

SHORT, Mrs. Catherine Barron, MA ACA *1992;* 10 Egmont Road, NEW MALDEN, SURREY, KT3 4AS.

SHORT, Mr. Christopher David, BA ACA *1986;* Brammer plc, Claverton Court, Claverton Road, Wythenshawe, MANCHESTER, M23 9NE.

SHORT, Mrs. Claire, ACA *2009;* 60 Central Drive, Swanton Morley, DEREHAM, NORFOLK, NR20 4LD.

SHORT, Mr. David James, BSc(Hons) ACA *2003;* 2 Bellingham Drive, REIGATE, RH2 9BB.

SHORT, Mrs. Dawn, ACA *1986;* 6 Cardinal Close, Abbey Farm, North Walbottle, NEWCASTLE UPON TYNE, NE15 9XE.

SHORT, Mrs. Deborah Jane, BA ACA *1998;* 10 Monks Drive, Eye, PETERBOROUGH, PE6 7WG.

SHORT, Ms. Dianne Elsie, ACA *1984;* Gorno Grove, Strathmiglo, CUPAR, KY14 7SE.

SHORT, Dr. Eleri, PhD BSc ACA *2011;* 24 Cole Street, LONDON, SE1 4YH.

•**SHORT, Mrs. Elizabeth Anne, FCA** *1984;* Spenser Wilson & Co, Equitable House, 55 Pellon Lane, HALIFAX, WEST YORKSHIRE, HX1 5SP.

•**SHORT, Miss. Francesca Fiona Mirella, BSc ACA** *1990;* KPMG LLP, 15 Canada Square, LONDON, E14 5GL. See also KPMG Europe LLP

SHORT, Mr. Gary Redvers, BSc ACA *1993;* 64 Warren Road, LEIGH-ON-SEA, ESSEX, SS9 3TS.

SHORT, Mr. Iain David, ACA *2009;* 52 L'Arbre Crescent, Whickham, NEWCASTLE UPON TYNE, NE16 5YJ.

SHORT, Mr. Ian George, ACA *1981;* (Tax Fac), Copper Beeches, 112 Crewe Road, NANTWICH, CW5 6JS.

•**SHORT, Mr. Ian George, MA FCA** *1982;* Kevin Loy Limited, Victoria Buildings, High Street, TAIN, ROSS-SHIRE, IV19 1AE.

SHORT, Miss. Jacqueline Angela, BA ACA *2010;* Pricewaterhousecoopers Abacus House, Castle Park, CAMBRIDGE, CB3 0AN.

SHORT, Mr. James Edward, BSc ACA *2002;* 54 Alaska Apartments, 22 Western Gateway, Royal Victoria Docks, LONDON, E16 1BW.

SHORT, Mrs. Janet Marie, ACA *1990;* Copper Beeches, 112 Crewe Road, NANTWICH, CW5 6JS.

SHORT, Mr. Jason Ian, MA ACA ATII *1996;* 1 Whitecroft Close, BECKENHAM, BR3 3AN.

•**SHORT, Mr. John Robert, FCA** *1977;* The Jamesons Partnership Limited, 92 Station Road, CLACTON-ON-SEA, CO15 1SG.

SHORT, Miss. Louise Mary, ACA MAAT *2005;* 4 Ashridge Drive, BEDFORD, MK41 0QE.

SHORT, Mr. Mark Andrew, ACA *1984;* Highcliffe, Long Lane, Southowram, HALIFAX, HX3 9UD.

SHORT, Mr. Mark Andrew, ACA *2008;* 19 Sandy Lane, Hucknall, NOTTINGHAM, NG15 7GR.

•**SHORT, Mr. Martin John, BA ACA** *1982;* M Short & Co LLP, 7 Waterloo Road, WHITSTABLE, KENT, CT5 1BP. See also Shorts (Management Consultants) Ltd

SHORT, Mr. Martin Paul, BA ACA *1993;* 2 Cheltenham Way, Whitehall Park, CLEETHORPES, DN35 0UG.

SHORT, Mr. Michael Edward, BSc FCA *1966;* 47 Brantwood Drive, PAIGNTON, DEVON, TQ4 5HY. (Life Member)

SHORT, Mrs. Nicola Jane, MA ACA *1994;* Credit Suisse Securities USA LLC, Eleven Madison Avenue - 25th Floor, NEW YORK, NY 10010, UNITED STATES.

SHORT, Mr. Paul Fanuel, BSc ACA *2004;* 124 Eastworth Road, CHERTSEY, SURREY, KT16 8DS.

•**SHORT, Mr. Paul Richard, BA FCA CF** *1982;* (Tax Fac), Lambert Chapman LLP, 3 Warners Mill, Silks Way, BRAINTREE, ESSEX, CM7 3GB.

•**SHORT, Mr. Paul Trevor, FCA** *1978;* (Tax Fac), Moore Stephens & Co, 150 Aldersgate Street, LONDON, EC1A 4AE. See also Moore Stephens LLP

SHORT, Mr. Peter Alexander, BSc FCA *1979;* 154 The Drive, RICKMANSWORTH, HERTFORDSHIRE, WD3 4DH.

SHORT, Mr. Peter Mark Iain, BA FCA *1999;* Suncroft 25 Thorpe Road Easington, PETERLEE, COUNTY DURHAM, SR8 3UA.

SHORT, Miss. Rachel Elizabeth, BSc(Hons) ACA *2008;* 1 Marlborough Avenue, High Harrington, WORKINGTON, CUMBRIA, CA14 4NW.

SHORT, Mr. Richard Thomas, ACA *2007;* Apartment S2 Zion Chapel, George Street, WAKEFIELD, WF1 1LG.

SHORT, Mr. Richard Vickery, MA FCA *1985;* 104 Maplin Way, Thorpe Bay, SOUTHEND-ON-SEA, SS1 3NB.

SHORT, Mr. Robert William, BSc ACA *1997;* 89 Langham Road, TEDDINGTON, TW11 9HG.

SHORT, Mr. Thomas Aidan, ACA *2010;* 102 Drakefield Road, LONDON, SW17 8RR.

SHORT, Mr. Thomas Edmund, FCA *1972;* 2 Merriefield Close, BROADSTONE, BH18 8DG.

SHORT, Mrs. Tracey Joan, FCA *1996;* Whinbarrow House, Hayton, Aspatria, WIGTON, CUMBRIA, CA7 2PJ.

SHORTER, Mr. Andrew Timothy, MEng ACA *2004;* Mayflower, Beacon View Road, Elstead, GODALMING, SURREY, GU8 6DT.

SHORTER, Mr. Graham John, BA ACA *2005;* 19 Westfield Green, Tockwith, YORK, YO26 7RE.

SHORTER, Mr. Graham Martin, MA FCA *1981;* 36 Price's Way, BRACKLEY, NORTHAMPTONSHIRE, NN13 6NR.

SHORTER, Mrs. Jaclyn Dawn, BSc ACA *2005;* 19 Westfield Green, Tockwith, YORK, YO26 7RE.

SHORTER, Mr. Stephen James, ACA *2010;* 56a Harleyford Road, LONDON, SE115AY.

SHORTHOUSE, Mr. Barry, MA FCA *1978;* 7 Broadlands Croft, Owlthorpe, SHEFFIELD, S20 6SZ.

SHORTHOUSE, Mr. Christopher Mark, BA ACA *2005;* with Telefonica O2 Europe plc, 260 Bath Road, SLOUGH, SL1 4DX.

SHORTHOUSE, Mrs. Lisa, ACA MAAT *2011;* 19 Sycamore Close, Wattisham Airfield, IPSWICH, IP7 7SG.

SHORTHOUSE, Mr. Peter James, BSc ACA *1991;* 5 Ashley Street, TAMARAMA, NSW 2026, AUSTRALIA.

SHORTHOUSE, Mrs. Valentine Jillian, BCom ACA *1992;* Cott Hayes, Branscombe, SEATON, DEVON, EX12 3BH.

SHORTLAND, Mr. Christopher David, BA(Hons) ACA *2002;* A O N Ltd, 8 Devonshire Square, LONDON, EC2M 4PL.

SHORTLAND, Mr. Michael James, BA ACA *1997;* with Duncan & Toplis, 3 Castlegate, GRANTHAM, LINCOLNSHIRE, NG31 6SF.

SHORTLAND, Mr. Timothy James, BCom ACA *1998;* 85 Greenfield Road, Flitton, BEDFORD, MK45 5DR.

SHORTLEY, Miss. Hannah Joy, ACA *2009;* 24 Ladygrove Drive, GUILDFORD, SURREY, GU4 7FA.

SHORTMAN, Mr. Gary Edward, BA ACA *1999;* 13 Paignton Avenue, CHELMSFORD, CM1 7NS.

•**SHORTRIDGE, Mr. Andrew Lancaster, MBA ACA** *1991;* (Tax Fac), St. John Ambulance St. John House, 5 Broadfield Close, SHEFFIELD, S8 0XN.

•**SHORTRIDGE, Mr. Anthony John, BTech ACA** *1980;* (Tax Fac), A J Shortridge Limited, Wessex House, Teign Road, NEWTON ABBOT, DEVON, TQ12 4AA.

•**SHORTT, Mr. Dermot Owen, BSc FCA** *1989;* 65 Camp Road, GERRARDS CROSS, BUCKINGHAMSHIRE, SL9 7PF.

SHORTT, Mr. Michael Brian, BA FCA *1969;* Hannington House, Ibworth Lane, Hannington, TADLEY, RG26 5TY. (Life Member)

SHOTT, Mrs. Lesley Anne, BSc ACA *1982;* Little Court, London Road, Ryarsh, WEST MALLING, KENT, ME19 5AH.

•**SHOTTER, Ms. Magdalena, ACA CA(SA)** *2010;* ATS Accounting & Tax Solutions, 6 Corfield Close, Finchampstead, WOKINGHAM, BERKSHIRE, RG40 4PA.

SHOTTER, Mr. Peter Robert Surtees, FCA *1965;* 48 Simonstown Road, Sunny Cove, FISH HOEK, 7975, SOUTH AFRICA. (Life Member)

SHOTTON, Mr. Anthony David, BA ACA *1988;* 50 Hoop Lane, LONDON, NW11 7NH.

SHOTTON, Mr. Anthony David, BA ACA *2007;* 1 Pether Avenue, BRACKLEY, NORTHAMPTONSHIRE, NN13 6NJ.

SHOTTON, Miss. Gayle, BSc ACA *1993;* 54 Achray Drive, FALKIRK, STIRLINGSHIRE, FK1 5UN.

SHOTTON, Mr. Kenneth John, FCA *1969;* 15 Merlynn, Devonshire Place, EASTBOURNE, EAST SUSSEX, BN21 4AQ. (Life Member)

SHOTTON, Mr. Kevin, BA ACA *2006;* 11 Waldridge Close, Mayfield, WASHINGTON, TYNE AND WEAR, NE37 1SU.

SHOTTON, Mr. Norman Bernard, FCA *1961;* 7 Rue Blaise Pascal, LE MESNIL, 78320 ST. DENIS, FRANCE. (Life Member)

SHOTTON, Mr. Steven John, BA ACA *1987;* Kingston Tech Europe Ltd, Kingston Court, Brooklands Close, SUNBURY-ON-THAMES, MIDDLESEX, TW16 7EP.

SHOTTON, Mr. Timothy, BSc FCA *1987;* QInvest, PO Box 26222, DOHA, QATAR.

SHOUKRY, Mr. Kamal, FCA *1970;* 28 Samir Mukhtar Street, Ard El Golf, Merghani - Heliopolis, CAIRO, 11341, EGYPT. (Life Member)

SHOULER, Mr. Michael Howard, FCA *1969;* Cornerstone Church, Blucoat Wollation Park Campus, Wollaton, NOTTINGHAM, NG8 1GA.

SHOULTS, Mr. Kenneth John, FCA *1977;* 10 Essex Road, ENFIELD, EN2 6TZ.

•**SHOVELL, Mr. Kenneth Leonard, MA ACA** *1990;* 64 Adam & Eve Mews, LONDON, W8 6UJ.

•**SHOWAN, Mr. Richard David Lewis, BA FCA** *1984;* Rothman Pantall LLP, 10 Romsey Road, EASTLEIGH, HAMPSHIRE, SO50 9AL.

SHOWELL, Mr. Ian, MA ACA *2003;* 30 St. Michaels Crescent, PINNER, MIDDLESEX, HA5 5LG.

SHOWELL, Mr. Richard, BSc(Hons) ACA *2005;* with BDO Corporate Finance (Middle East) LLP, DIFC, Al Fattan Currency Tower, Floor 33 East, PO Box 506802, DUBAI UNITED ARAB EMIRATES.

SHOWELL, Mr. Steven, BA(Hons) ACA *2002;* Laneside House, 9 Poles Lane, Otterbourne, WINCHESTER, HAMPSHIRE, SO21 2DS.

SHOWERS, Mrs. Hannah Jayne, ACA *2011;* 10 Penybryn View, Incline Top, Bradley Gardens, MERTHYR TYDFIL, MID GLAMORGAN, CF47 0GB.

SHRAGER, Mr. James, ACA *2011;* Flat 7, 57a Lisson Street, LONDON, NW1 5DA.

SHREEVE, Miss. Heidi, BA ACA *1998;* 230 East Moor's Lane, Ringwood Road, St Leonards, RINGWOOD, HAMPSHIRE, BH24 2SB.

SHREEVE, Mr. Michael David, BA ACA FCIPD *1985;* 32 Church Hill, NEWHAVEN, EAST SUSSEX, BN9 9LY.

SHREEVE, Mr. Timothy Mark, ACA *2009;* Netherfield, Ashdown Road, FOREST ROW, EAST SUSSEX, RH18 5BN.

SHRIER, Mr. Morris, caba FCA *1948;* 4 Garson House, Gloucester Terrace, LONDON, W2 3DG. (Life Member)

SHRIMPTON, Mr. David Everard, FCA *1967;* 21 Foxgrove Avenue, BECKENHAM, KENT, BR3 5BA.

SHRIMPTON, Mr. Donald Richard, BA FCA *1975;* 2 Hill Gardens, Streatley, READING, RG8 9QF.

SHRIMPTON, Mr. Edward Paul, ACA *1980;* Arena Leisure Plc, 408 Strand, LONDON, WC2R 0NE.

SHRIMPTON, Miss. Helen Clare, BA(Hons) ACA *2010;* 17 Sunnybank Road, Greetland, HALIFAX, WEST YORKSHIRE, HX4 8JP.

SHRIMPTON, Mrs. Lindsey Marie, ACA *2003;* Charities Aid Foundation, Kings Hill, WEST MALLING, ME19 4TA.

SHRINGARPURE, Mr. Atul Jagannath, BEng ACA *1993;* (Tax Fac), 27 Braithwaite Gardens, STANMORE, HA7 2QG.

SHRIVES, Dr. Philip Jonathan, PhD MAcc BA ACA *1983;* 14 Ramshaw Close, Little Benton Haydon Grange, NEWCASTLE UPON TYNE, NE7 7GP.

SHROFF, Mr. Byram Phiroze, ACA *1980;* Deloitte Haskins & Sells, 12 Dr Annie Besant Road, Opp Shiv Sagar Estate, MUMBAI 400 018, INDIA. See also Ferguson A.F. & Co and Billimoria S.B. & Co

•**SHROFF, Mr. Cusrow Phiroze, FCA** *1981;* Shroff & Associates, Flat 52 5t Floor, Goolestan Building, (Besides Mahalaxmi Temple), 34 Bhulabhai Desai Road, MUMBAI 400 026 INDIA.

•**SHROFF, Mr. Jimmy, BA ACA** *1988;* Shroff Accountancy Services, Excel House, 1 Hornminster Glen, HORNCHURCH, RM11 3XL. See also Kase Accountancy Services Limited

•**SHRUBB, Mr. Christopher John, FCA FCCA** *1980;* (Tax Fac), Hamlyns LLP, Sundial House, 98 High Street, Horsell, WOKING, SURREY GU21 4SU.

SHRUBSALL, Mr. Roger Francis, FCA *1964;* 18 Hillcrest Road, ORPINGTON, BR6 9AW.

SHU, Miss. Pei Yi, ACA *2004;* Flat E 2/F, Tower 2, Robinson Place, 70 Robinson Road, MID LEVELS, HONG KONG ISLAND HONG KONG SAR.

SHU, Ms. Wai Fong, ACA *2007;* Flat D 11/F Block 3, Cascades, 93 Chung Hau Street, HO MAN TIN, KOWLOON, HONG KONG SAR.

SHU, Miss. Wanting, ACA *2008;* Flat C3-802 No.8 Xin Guang Road Gao Xing District, CHENGDU 610041, CHINA.

SHUAI, Mr. Raymond, MEng ACA CFA *2007;* 29 Ullswater Crescent, LONDON, SW15 3RG.

SHUENYANE, Mr. Khumo, BSocSc ACA *1995;* P O Box 715, MELROSE ARCH, GAUTENG, 2076, SOUTH AFRICA.

SHUET, Mr. Kai Him, ACA *2005;* Flat A 10/F, Hang Po Building, 6-8 Mercury Street, NORTH POINT, HONG KONG ISLAND, HONG KONG SAR.

SHUFFREY, Mrs. Caroline, JP BSc ACA FCT *1979;* 19 Westmoreland Road, Barnes, LONDON, SW13 9RZ.

•**SHUFFREY, Mr. John Roderick, BA FCA DChA** *1980;* Saffery Champness, Lion House, Red Lion Street, LONDON, WC1R 4GB.

SHUKER, Mr. John Robert, ACA CA(NZ) *2011;* with PricewaterhouseCoopers LLP, 1 Embankment Place, LONDON, WC2N 6RH.

•**SHUKLA, Mr. Ashok Parshuram, FCA** *1970;* Ash Pullan, Epworth House, 25 City Road, LONDON, EC1Y 1AR.

SHUKLA, Mr. Ashutosh, ACA BEng(Hons) *2010;* 31 Holmead Road, LONDON, SW6 2JD.

SHUKLA, Mr. Jayant Amritanand, ACA *1982;* C-11 Dewanshree Apts., 30 Ferozeshah Rd., NEW DELHI 110001, INDIA.

SHUKLA, Mr. Nalin, BSc ACA *1995;* 5 Maytree Road, Hiltingbury, Chandler's Ford, EASTLEIGH, HAMPSHIRE, SO53 5RT.

SHUKLA, Mr. Pinakin Mayashanker, FCA *1974;* 195 Edgwarebury Lane, EDGWARE, HA8 8QJ.

SHUKLA, Mr. Rahul Rajendra, BSc ACA *2009;* 27 Heath Lodge, High Road Bushey Heath, BUSHEY, WD23 1NR.

SHUKLA, Mr. Satinder Singh, BSc ACA *1999;* 142 Aldborough Road South, ILFORD, ESSEX, IG3 8HA.

SHUKLA, Mr. Sukh Dev, FCA *1973;* 56 Broomfield Avenue, Palmers Green, LONDON, N13 4JP. (Life Member)

SHUKLA, Miss. Vatsala, FCA *1991;* B-35, IFS Apartments, Mayur Vihar Phase I, NEW DELHI 110091, INDIA.

•**SHULMAN, Mr. Keith John, FCA** *1968;* Keith J. Shulman, 11 Harley Court, High Road Whetstone, LONDON, N20 0QD.

•**SHULMAN, Mr. Michael Alan, FCA** *1966;* Jade Securities Limited, Acre House, 11/15 William Road, LONDON, NW1 3ER.

•**SHULMAN, Mr. Neville, CBE FCA** *1962;* Shulman & Company, 52 Redington Road, Hampstead, LONDON, NW3 7RS.

•**SHUM, Mr. Chi Kit, BCom FCA** *1966;* C.K. Shum & Co, 20/F, 88 Lockhart Road, WAN CHAI, HONG KONG ISLAND, HONG KONG SAR.

SHUM, Miss. Ina Chee Man, MEng ACA *2001;* 46/F Manhattan Place, 23 Wang Tai Road, KOWLOON BAY, KOWLOON, HONG KONG SAR.

SHUM, Mr. Kai Shing, ACA *2008;* Hutchison Ports China, c/o Hongkong International, Terminal 4, Container Port Road South, KWAI CHUNG, KOWLOON HONG KONG SAR.

SHUM, Ms. Lai Fong, ACA *2008;* Vincent Mak & Company, Room 1617-18, Star House, 3 Salisbury Road, TSIM SHA TSUI, KOWLOON HONG KONG SAR.

SHUM, Mr. Lok To, ACA *2007;* Flat C 39/F Block 11, Villa Esplanada, 8 Nga Ying Chau Street, TSING YI, NEW TERRITORIES, HONG KONG SAR.

SHUM, Mr. Lun Kwong Stewart, BSc ACA *1993;* P.O. Box No. 28552, Gloucester Road Post Office, WAN CHAI, HONG KONG ISLAND, HONG KONG SAR.

SHUM, Mr. Man To, ACA *2007;* 3A Heng Fa Villa, 100 Shing Tai Road, SHAU KEI WAN, HONG KONG SAR.

SHUM, Ms. Yin, ACA *2008;* Unit 1715 17/ Floor, Block N Kornhill, QUARRY BAY, HONG KONG ISLAND, HONG KONG SAR.

SHUMATE, Miss. Deanne, ACA *1992;* 3 Greencroft Cottages, Mount Nugent, CHESHAM, HP5 2XJ.

SHUPINSKI, Ms. Andrea Mary, ACA *1984;* Reult Na Mara, 63 Hyde Road, Dalkey, DUBLIN, COUNTY DUBLIN, IRELAND.

SHURMER, Mrs. Alison Deana, BSc(Hons) ACA *2002;* 30 Highclere, ASCOT, SL5 0AA.

SHUTE, Mr. Kenneth Telford, FCA *1964;* Cobblers, High Park Avenue, East Horsley, LEATHERHEAD, KT24 5DD.

SHUTE, Mrs. Louise Ann, ACA *2004;* Mamas & Papas Ltd, Colne Bridge Road, HUDDERSFIELD, HD5 0RH.

•**SHUTE, Mr. Mark Reginald, BA FCA** *1997;* Glover Stanbury & Co, 30 Bear Street, BARNSTAPLE, DEVON, EX32 7DD.

SHUTER, Mr. Donald Alan, BSc ACA *1987;* Broome Cottage, 11 St. Marys Way, Chalfont St. Peter, GERRARDS CROSS, SL9 9BL.

SHUTT, Lord David Trevor, FCA *1969;* Woodfield, 197 Saddleworth Road, Greetland, HALIFAX, WEST YORKSHIRE, HX4 8LZ.

SHUTT, Mr. Thomas Huw, MSc ACA *2004;* Avon Rubber Plc, Corporate Headquarters, Hampton Park West, Semington Road, MELKSHAM, WILTSHIRE SN12 6NB.

SHUTTE, Mr. Malcolm David Neale, FCA *1961;* Rookwood, Rushmere Lane, Denmead, WATERLOOVILLE, HAMPSHIRE, PO7 6HA. (Life Member)

SHUTTER, Mr. Nicholas John, BA FCA *1987;* Rubens, Station Road, Flax Bourton, BRISTOL, BS48 1UA.

SHUTTLEWOOD, Miss. Katie, BA ACA *2006;* Universal Pictures International Entertainment Ltd, Prospect House 80-110 New Oxford Street, LONDON, WC1A 1HB.

SHUTTLEWORTH, Mr. David Andrew, BSc ACA *1982;* 8 Elmbridge Avenue, SURBITON, SURREY, KT5 9EX.

SHUTTLEWORTH, Mr. David Mark, BSc ACA *1989;* C/O Du, PO Box 502666, DUBAI, UNITED ARAB EMIRATES.

SHUTTLEWORTH, Mr. Edward Neil, ACA *1982;* 17 Boyle Street, Balgowlah, SYDNEY, NSW 2093, AUSTRALIA.

SHUTTLEWORTH, Mr. Hugh Ashton John, FCA *1973;* Suite 44, 60 Westbury Hill, Westbury-on-Trym, BRISTOL, BS9 3UJ.

SHUTTLEWORTH, Mr. John Fergusson, FCA *1951;* 64 Brim Hill, LONDON, N2 0HQ. (Life Member)

SHUTTLEWORTH, Mr. Kristian John, BA(Hons) ACA *2002;* with Deloitte LLP, 1 City Square, LEEDS, WEST YORKSHIRE, LS1 2AL.

SHUTTLEWORTH, Mr. Mark, ACA *2010;* 8 Cedar Close, Hutton, BRENTWOOD, ESSEX, CM13 1NE.

SHUTTLEWORTH, Mr. Michael Kay, FCA *1968;* 16 Burnt Acre, Chelford, MACCLESFIELD, CHESHIRE, SK11 9SS.

SHUTTLEWORTH, Mr. Philip, BA ACA *1996;* 29 Ponsonby Place, LONDON, SW1P 4PS.

SHUTTLEWORTH, Mr. Thomas Charles, BSc ACA *2005;* 13 Woodstock Road South, ST. ALBANS, HERTFORDSHIRE, AL1 4QL.

SI, Mr. Shun Wang, ACA *2008;* with PricewaterhouseCoopers, 33/F Cheung Kong Center, 2 Queen's Road, CENTRAL, HONG KONG ISLAND, HONG KONG SAR.

SIA, Mr. Chin Hoe, ACA FCCA *2011;* F-10-05 Metropolitan Sq, Jalan PJU 8/1, Damansara Perdana, 47820 PETALING JAYA, SELANGOR, MALAYSIA.

SIA, Ms. Cindy Siew Nyuk, FCA *1984;* 38 Jalan Pinang, Leisure Farm Resort, 81560 GELANG PATAH, JOHOR, MALAYSIA.

SIA, Miss. Joanna Hui Ling, BSc ACA *2010;* 11 Lorong Chelagi, Damansara Heights, 50490 KUALA LUMPUR, FEDERAL TERRITORY, MALAYSIA.

SIAH, Mr. Siong Kuang, BSc ACA *1993;* V-Logic Limited, Room 1003-5, 10/F Phase One, Modern Terminals, Berth One, KWAI CHUNG KOWLOON HONG KONG SAR.

SIAMBARTAS, Mr. Charalambos, FCA *1980;* 3 Laerti, 2028 STROVOLOS, CYPRUS.

SIAN, Dr. Sukhvinder, PhD MSc BSc ACA *1992;* 22 Topiary Square, Stanmore Road, RICHMOND, TW9 2DB.

SIAW, Mr. Ai Yao, BSc FCA *1990;* c/o Labuan Re, 8th Floor Bangunan Malaysian Re, 17 Lorong Dungun, Damansara Heights, 50490 KUALA LUMPUR, FEDERAL TERRITORY MALAYSIA.

SIAW, Miss. Liuh Yee, BSc ACA *2005;* 9 Rambai Road, #02-02 Sunshine Regency, SINGAPORE 424352, SINGAPORE.

SIAW, Mr. Shin Kon, ACA *1980;* Jalan Aman No8, Mampang Prapatan, JAKARTA, INDONESIA.

•**SIBA, Mr. Miroslav, FCA** *1973;* (Tax Fac), Siba & Co, 308 High Street, CROYDON, CR0 1NG.

SIBAL, Mr. Viven, BSc ACA *2005;* 15 Kingsley Avenue, HOUNSLOW, TW3 4AE.

SIBANDA, Mr. Kurai Watida, ACA *2010;* 24 Holloway Road, MARKHAM L35 4P2, ON, CANADA.

SIBBALD, Mr. Ian, BA FCA *1994;* 11 Primrose Close, Marston Moretaine, BEDFORD, MK43 0UR.

SIBBALD, Mr. James Lawson, BCom FCA *1960;* 25 Drum Brae Park, EDINBURGH, EH12 8TF. (Life Member)

•**SIBBALD, Mr. Philip, FCA** *1977;* S Y Accountancy Services Ltd, Unit 6D Planet Business Centre, Planet Place, West Moor, NEWCASTLE UPON TYNE, NE12 6DY.

SIBCY, Mrs. Eileen Patricia, FCA *1966;* (Tax Fac), Whitcliff Cottage, Richards Castle, LUDLOW, SY8 4EL.

SIBERT, Mrs. Doreen Marie, BSc ACA *1996;* 28 Bracken Avenue, LONDON, SW12 8BH.

SIBLEY, Mr. Alan John, BSc ACA *1983;* 11 Downesway, ALDERLEY EDGE, CHESHIRE, SK9 7XB.

SIBLEY, Mr. Earl, BA ACA *1997;* One Wellstones, WATFORD, HERTFORDSHIRE, WD17 2AE.

SIBLEY, Mrs. Emma Claire, BSc ACA *1998;* Sycamore House Hollybush Lane, Burghfield Common, READING, RG7 3JL.

SIBLEY, Mr. Geoffrey William, FCA *1948;* 55 Springfield Road, Linslade, LEIGHTON BUZZARD, LU7 2QS. (Life Member)

•**SIBLEY, Mr. James William, FCA** *1977;* (Tax Fac), King Freeman, 1st Floor, Kimberley House, Vaughan Way, LEICESTER, LE1 4SG.

SIBLEY, Mr. Michael Ian, MEng ACA *2009;* Flat 1, St. Johns Hill Court, 144-146 St. John's Hill, LONDON, SW11 1SN.

SIBLEY, Mr. Nicholas Theobald, FCA *1965;* Le Moulin des Barres, 06480 LA COLLE SUR LOUP, FRANCE.

SIBLEY, Mr. Philip James, BA(Hons) ACA *2002;* Chartis Memsa Insurance Company Limited, The Gate West Wing 11th Floor DIFC, PO Box 117719, DUBAI, UNITED ARAB EMIRATES.

SIBSON, Mr. Ian Daniel, FCA *1963;* 12 Southwood, MAIDSTONE, KENT, ME16 9EB. (Life Member)

SIBSON, Mr. John Andrew William, FCA *1969;* 9 Cullen Close, Castle View, NEWARK, NG24 1DF.

SIBSON, Mr. Peter Timothy, BSc ACA *1996;* 20 Comiston Drive, EDINBURGH, EH10 5QP.

SICE, Mr. Timothy Robert, BA ACA *1987;* Hamblings, Church Road, Ham, RICHMOND, SURREY, TW10 5HG.

SICELY, Mr. Michael John, BA ACA *1992;* Heath Lodge Park Road, Albury, GUILDFORD, GU5 9DF.

•**SIDA-PAGE, Mrs. Helen Veronica, FCA** *1990;* Helen Sida Ltd, Bramble Cottage, Middle Road, Denton, HARLESTON, NORFOLK IP20 0AJ.

SIDAT HUMPHREYS, Mrs. Kamar, LLM BA LLB ACA *1992;* OAMI, avenida de Europa 4, E-03008 ALICANTE, ALICANTE, SPAIN.

•**SIDAWAY, Mr. George Frederick, BCom FCA** *1952;* F.E. Sidaway Son & Co, 5-6 Long Lane, ROWLEY REGIS, B65 0JA.

•**SIDAWAY, Mr. Jeremy Frederick John, BA FCA** *1987;* (Tax Fac), Sidaways Limited, Unit 5, Providence Court, Pynes Hill, EXETER, EX2 5JL.

SIDAWAY, Mrs. Lorraine Olive, BA ACA *1997;* 3 Hazelhurst Drive, Bollington, MACCLESFIELD, CHESHIRE, SK10 5QT.

•**SIDAWAY, Mrs. Sarah Anne, BSc FCA** *1987;* Sidaways Limited, Unit 5, Providence Court, Pynes Hill, EXETER, EX2 5JL.

SIDBURY, Mr. David Julian, FCA *1958;* 36 Chandos Ave., LONDON, N20 9DX. (Life Member)

SIDDALL, Mrs. Adrienne Helen, BSc ACA *1986;* Field Head, Leeds Road, Lightcliffe, HALIFAX, HX3 8SD.

SIDDALL, Mr. Alan, BSc FCA *1976;* 8 Penmaes, Pentyrch, CARDIFF, CF15 9QS.

SIDDALL, Mr. Peter John, FCA *1966;* 77 Lowther Road, LONDON, SW13 9NP.

SIDDALL, Mr. Richard Michael, ACA *2009;* 54 Green Acres, Penistone, SHEFFIELD, S36 6DB.

SIDDALL, Mr. Stuart James, FCA *1975;* A C T Ltd, 51 Moorgate, LONDON, EC2R 6BH.

SIDDERS, Mrs. Anne Lesley, BA ACA *1984;* 17 Beech Way, Wheathampstead, ST. ALBANS, AL4 8LY.

SIDDERS, Mr. Martin John, BSc FCA *1983;* 17 Beech Way, Wheathampstead, ST. ALBANS, HERTFORDSHIRE, AL4 8LY.

SIDDIKY, Mr. Daneel Ahmed, BSc ACA *2007;* 5 Denoon Terrace, DUNDEE, DD2 2EL.
SIDDIQ, Mr. Omar, BSc ACA *2000;* 17 SS1/ 35, 47300 PETALING JAYA, SELANGOR, MALAYSIA.
SIDDIQI, Mr. Ahmed Ahsan, ACA ACCA *2009;* VP Financial Institutions, Global Banking & Markets, The Royal Bank of Scotland, Dubai International Financial Centre, Gate Village 4 Level 2, PO Box 506655 DUBAI UNITED ARAB EMIRATES.
•**SIDDIQI, Mr. Amir, BSc ACA ACCA** *2005;* (Tax Fac), Sidikies, 1-3 Sun Street, LONDON, EC2A 2EP.
SIDDIQI, Mr. Asif, FCA *1972;* 18 Claire Gardens, STANMORE, MIDDLESEX, HA7 4EH.
SIDDIQI, Mr. Asim Ahmed, MSc BSc ACA *2008;* 31 Eve Road, ISLEWORTH, MIDDLESEX, TW7 7HS.
•**SIDDIQI, Mr. Fareeduddin, FCA** *1970;* 44 Russell Road, Moor Park, NORTHWOOD, MIDDLESEX, HA6 2LR.
SIDDIQI, Mr. Favad Khalid, BA ACA *1996;* 20 Kenwyn Road, LONDON, SW20 8TR.
•**SIDDIQI, Mr. Mohammad Akram, FCA** *1976;* Akram Siddiqi & Co, 58 Almond Way, MITCHAM, SURREY, CR4 1LN.
SIDDIQI, Mr. Mohammed Shafiq, FCA *1965;* Penketh, Mount Park Road, HARROW, MIDDLESEX, HA1 3LB. (Life Member)
SIDDIQI, Mr. Muhammad Nadeem, ACA *1981;* Collierbridge Properties, 127 Trinity Road, LONDON, SW17 7HJ.
SIDDIQI, Miss. Naima Piya Murad, LLB ACA *2006;* Flat 1, 12 Riverdale Road, TWICKENHAM, TW1 2BS.
SIDDIQI, Mr. Naveed, BA ACA *1993;* PO Box 57568, DUBAI, UNITED ARAB EMIRATES.
SIDDIQI, Dr. Naveed Iqbal, MBBS ACA *1995;* Flat 120, Berkeley Court, Marylebone Road, LONDON, NW1 5NE.
SIDDIQI, Mr. Saadat, FCA *1977;* The World Bank, 1818 H Street NW, WASHINGTON, DC 20433, UNITED STATES.
SIDDIQI, Mr. Salman Zafar, ACA *1992;* 401 DD, Phase IV, D.H.A, LAHORE, PAKISTAN.
SIDDIQI, Ms. Yasmin, BSc ACA ATII *1998;* Flat 6, 46 Queens Gardens, Baywater, LONDON, W2 3AA.
SIDDIQI, Mr. Zafarul Hameed, FCA *1977;* PO Box 215686, DUBAI, 215686, UNITED ARAB EMIRATES.
SIDDIQI, Ms. Zainab, ACA MBA *2010;* 54 Corringway, LONDON, W5 3AD.
SIDDIQUE, Mrs. Alyia, BSc ACA *1996;* 9 Broadlea Crescent, BRADFORD, BD5 8PE.
SIDDIQUE, Mr. Amir, BA ACA *2003;* 1 Anthony Way, SLOUGH, SL1 5PG.
SIDDIQUE, Mrs. Sadia, BA(Hons) ACA *2003;* 3 William Street, Hurstead, ROCHDALE, OL16 2SF.
•**SIDDIQUI, Mr. Abdul Mabood, FCA** *1964;* Reddy Siddiqui & Kabani, Park View, 183-189 The Vale, LONDON, W3 7RW. See also Reddy Siddiqui
SIDDIQUI, Mr. Abu Nasar Altaf Hussain, FCA *1968;* Rahman Rahman Huq, 9 Mohakhali Commercial Area, 11th & 12th Floors, DHAKA 1212, BANGLADESH.
SIDDIQUI, Ms. Adeeba Sahar, BSocSc ACA *2001;* 32 Seymour Road, SLOUGH, SL1 2NY.
SIDDIQUI, Mr. Amer Jawed, BA(Hons) ACA *2002;* PO Box 63392, ABU DHABI, UNITED ARAB EMIRATES.
SIDDIQUI, Mr. Anwar Ahmad, FCA *1972;* 185 Hillside Drive, BOLINGBROOK, IL 60440, UNITED STATES.
SIDDIQUI, Mr. Asim, ACA *1994;* Ernst & Young Ford Rhodes Sidat Hyder, 6th Floor Progressive Plaza, Beaumont Road, KARACHI 75530, PAKISTAN.
SIDDIQUI, Mr. Ayaz Yousuf, ACA *1985;* 2 The Dell, WALTHAM ABBEY, EN9 3YD.
SIDDIQUI, Miss. Faiza Ghayas, BSc(Econ) ACA *1999;* PO Box 215759, DUBAI, UNITED ARAB EMIRATES.
SIDDIQUI, Mr. Farhan-Ul-Haq, ACA *2003;* Flat 38 Building 41 Avenue 44 Hillat Abdulsaleh 444 (Fort Garden-Villa 14), MANAMA, BAHRAIN.
SIDDIQUI, Mr. Fayyaz Yousuf, ACA *1982;* P. O. 21529 VIVA, Al Waleed Tower, Next to CityCentre, Seef District, MANAMA, BAHRAIN.
SIDDIQUI, Mr. Ghazali Asim, BSc ACA *2000;* with BDO LLP, 2 City Place, Beehive Ring Road, GATWICK, WEST SUSSEX, RH6 0PA.
•**SIDDIQUI, Mr. Haroon Saeed, FCA** *1972;* Emirates Flight Catering LLC, PO Box 22525, DUBAI, UNITED ARAB EMIRATES.
SIDDIQUI, Miss. Humera, BA ACA *1994;* 2 Farmhouse Close, Pyrford, WOKING, SURREY, GU22 8LR.
SIDDIQUI, Mr. Iqbal Ahmad, FCA *1971;* Tadman Hornstein, 1325 Kenaston Blvd, WINNIPEG R3P 2P2, MB, CANADA.
SIDDIQUI, Mr. Irfan, ACA *1979;* Meezan Bank Limited, Meezan House, C-25 Estate Avenue SIRE, Karachi, KARACHI, PAKISTAN.
SIDDIQUI, Mr. Irfan Husain, FCA *1963;* 7 Route De St. Loup, 1290 Versoix, GENEVA, SWITZERLAND. (Life Member)
SIDDIQUI, Mr. Khursheed Ahmad, BSc FCA ACMA *1961;* Falkenweg 14, 40764 LANGENFELD, GERMANY. (Life Member)
SIDDIQUI, Mr. Mohammad Nazim Uddin, BA ACA *2005;* 15 Broadwalk, South Woodford, LONDON, E18 2DL.
•**SIDDIQUI, Mr. Mohammed Imran, BSc ACA** *1996;* (Tax Fac), Accounting For You, 4 Morrab Gardens, ILFORD, ESSEX, IG3 9HL.
•**SIDDIQUI, Mr. Mohammed Javed, FCA** *1973;* (Tax Fac), Charterhouse (Accountants) LLP, 88-98 College Road, HARROW, MIDDLESEX, HA1 1RA. See also White Hart Associates LLP
•**SIDDIQUI, Mr. Omar Faruq, BSc ACA** *2004;* Reddy Siddiqui & Kabani, Park View, 183-189 The Vale, LONDON, W3 7RW. See also Reddy Siddiqui
SIDDIQUI, Mr. Ovais Sultan Maurice, BSc(Econ) ACA *1998;* 61a Queens Road, CHELMSFORD, CM2 6HB.
SIDDIQUI, Miss. Saba, BSc ACA *1993;* 5164 Cottonwood Lane, SALT LAKE CITY, UT 84117, UNITED STATES.
SIDDIQUI, Mr. Salman, ACA *2011;* Flat 6, Basle House, Albert Square, LONDON, E15 1HH.
SIDDIQUI, Mr. Salman, BA ACA *2006;* 39 Bispham Road, LONDON, NW10 7HB.
SIDDIQUI, Mr. Salman Hussain, BSc ACA *1998;* 71 Street 23 Khayaban-e-Badar Phase 6 Defence Housing Authority, KARACHI 75500, PAKISTAN.
•**SIDDIQUI, Mrs. Seema Halim, FCA** *1994;* Reddy Siddiqui & Kabani, Park View, 183-189 The Vale, LONDON, W3 7RW. See also Reddy Siddiqui
SIDDIQUI, Mr. Shamim Ullah, FCA *1966;* 25 Palliser Road, LONDON, W14 9EB. (Life Member)
SIDDIQUI, Mr. Shamimur Rahman, FCA *1974;* Binzagr Company, P.O. Box 54, JEDDAH, 21411, SAUDI ARABIA.
SIDDIQUI, Mrs. Syeda Tahira Batool Tahir, MSc BA(Hons) ACA *2002;* 18 Bargate Close, NEW MALDEN, SURREY, KT3 6BQ.
SIDDLE, Mr. Christopher, BA FCA *1984;* Provincial House, Northumberland Street, NEWCASTLE UPON TYNE, NE1 7PW.
SIDDLE, Mrs. Jane Ann, BA ACA *1993;* NEL Fund Managers Limited Akenside Studios, Akenside Developments Ltd, 3 Akenside Hill, NEWCASTLE UPON TYNE, NE1 3UF.
SIDDLE, Mr. Keith, FCA *1969;* 10 Meeson Meadows, MALDON, CM9 6YS. (Life Member)
SIDDLE, Mr. Richard James, BA ACA *1999;* (Tax Fac), Kirkstone, Carlisle Road, BRAMPTON, CUMBRIA, CA8 1ST.
SIDDLE, Mr. Richard Stewart, BSc ACA *2002;* 51 Hutton Gate, HARROGATE, NORTH YORKSHIRE, HG2 9QG.
SIDDLE, Mr. Roger, PhD FCA *1976;* 3 Elmslack Lane, Silverdale, CARNFORTH, LA5 0RX. (Life Member)
SIDDONS, Mr. Alan Herbert, FCA *1958;* 1 Heather Close, Brocton, STAFFORD, ST17 0TG. (Life Member)
SIDDONS, Mr. Benjamin Charles Reid, FCA *1969;* Knapp House, Sparrowhawk Close, Ewshot, FARNHAM, SURREY, GU10 5TJ.
SIDDONS, Mr. Ernest George, FCA *1960;* 220 Hillcrest Road, PITTSBURGH, PA 15238, UNITED STATES.
SIDDONS, Mr. Ian, FCA *1965;* Chalermphrakiat Rama 9 Road, Moobaan Ladawan, House 333/24, Nongbon, Prawet, BANGKOK 10250 THAILAND.
SIDDONS, Mr. Jonathan Ian, BSc ACA *1991;* Ul. Wojewodzka 23, 05-510 KONSTANCIN-JEZIORNA, POLAND.
SIDDONS, Mrs. Moira Katharine, FCA *1977;* Flat 123 Shakespeare Tower, Barbican, LONDON, EC2Y 8DR.
SIDDONS, Mr. Peter Robert, MA FCA *1968;* Topleigh Cottage, Graffham, PETWORTH, GU28 0PA. (Life Member)
SIDDONS, Mrs. Susan Linda, FCA *1976;* Green Acres, Station Lane, Birkenshaw, BRADFORD, BD11 2JE.
SIDDORNS, Mr. Andrew David, BSc ACA *2006;* 5 Ravendale, Spencer Road, BROMLEY, BR1 3SX.
SIDE, Mr. Neville, BA ACA *2006;* Farm Side, Homedean Road, Chipstead, SEVENOAKS, KENT, TN13 2RU.
SIDEBOTHAM, Mr. John Harvey, BEng ACA *1998;* 26 Old Leicester Road, Wansford, PETERBOROUGH, PE8 6JR.
SIDEBOTTOM, Mr. Alan, FCA *1955;* 62 Alan Road, Heaton Moor, STOCKPORT, SK4 4DF. (Life Member)
•**SIDEBOTTOM, Mr. Alan Mark, BA FCA** *1993;* Garbutt & Elliott LLP, Arabesque House, Monks Cross Drive, Huntington, YORK, YO32 9GW. See also G & E (Holdings) Ltd and Garbutt & Elliott Limited
SIDEBOTTOM, Ms. Alison Betty, BA ACA *1988;* 9 Rue Waldteufel, 67000 STRASBOURG, FRANCE.
SIDEBOTTOM, Mr. Arnold Kenneth, FCA *1955;* West Winds, Bryning Lane, Warton, PRESTON, PR4 1TN. (Life Member)
SIDEK, Mr. Mohd Zakhir Siddiqy, LLB ACA *1993;* A-32-1 & 13 Menara UOA Bangsar 5 Jalan Bangsar Utama 1, 59000 KUALA LUMPUR, FEDERAL TERRITORY, MALAYSIA.
SIDELL, Mr. Andrew John, MSci ACA *2011;* Dionex Holding GmbH, Part of Thermo Fisher Scientific, Am Woerzgarten 10, 65510 IDSTEIN, GERMANY.
SIDELL, Mrs. Katherine Jane, MEng ACA *2006;* 101 Meriton Road, Handforth, WILMSLOW, CHESHIRE, SK9 3HD.
SIDELL, Mr. Peter Andrew, BSc ACA *2006;* 31 Jersey Drive, Winnersh, WOKINGHAM, RG41 5GQ.
•**SIDERY, Mr. Gerald James, ACA** *1981;* Sidery & Co, Ashfield, Wrexham Road, CHESTER, CH4 7QQ.
SIDERY, Mr. Richard David, BSc FCA FCMA *1973;* 49 Burnaby Gardens, Chiswick, LONDON, W4 3DR.
SIDES, Mr. Robert Brian William, BSc ACA *1991;* 2 Longley Drive, Worsley, MANCHESTER, M28 2TP.
SIDEY, Mrs. Kate Louise, BA ACA *2005;* Johnson + Johnson Consumer Services Eame Ltd, Foundation Park Roxborough Way, MAIDENHEAD, SL6 3UG.
SIDGWICK, Mr. David, BA ACA *1998;* 50 Salisbury Place, Langton Road, LONDON, SW9 6UW.
SIDGWICK, Mrs. Katie Anna, LLB ACA *2009;* 24 Mossbank Grove, DARLINGTON, COUNTY DURHAM, DL1 2TS.
SIDHU, Miss. Amrita, BA ACA *2010;* Flat 34, Heritage Court, 15 Warstone Lane, BIRMINGHAM, B18 6HP.
SIDHU, Miss. Chandandeep, BSc ACA *2006;* 19 Woodstock Avenue, SOUTHALL, MIDDLESEX, UB1 2QN.
SIDHU, Mr. Gursewak Singh, FCA *1988;* 1/85 Normanby Road, KEW, VIC 3101, AUSTRALIA.
SIDHU, Mr. Harbir Singh, BSc(Hons) ACA *2000;* 82 The Mall, LONDON, N14 6LP.
•**SIDHU, Mr. Harperbean Singh, BSc(Hons) ACA MBA** *2003;* Ernst & Young LLP, 1 More London Place, LONDON, SE1 2AF. See also Ernst & Young Europe LLP
SIDHU, Miss. Kiranjeet Kaur, ACA ACCA *2002;* State Street Bank & Trust Co, 525 Ferry Road, EDINBURGH, EH5 2AW.
SIDHU, Mr. Mandip Singh, BCom ACA *1999;* 11 Lascelles Road, SLOUGH, SL3 7PN.
SIDHU, Mr. Manoj, BSc ACA *1991;* 21 Belmore Avenue, HAYES, UB4 0RB.
SIDHU, Miss. Pavandip Kaur, ACA *2008;* 19 Highgrove, Westwood Heath, COVENTRY, CV4 8JJ.
SIDHU, Mr. Raman Singh, ACA *1983;* 606-B The Aralias, DLF Golf Links, DLF Phase V, GURGAON 122 002, HARYANA, INDIA.
•**SIDHU, Mr. Rupinder Singh, BSc ACA** *1997;* 516 Great West Road, HOUNSLOW, TW5 0TQ.
SIDHU, Mrs. Sabrina, BSc ACA *2005;* 17 David Avenue, GREENFORD, MIDDLESEX, UB6 8HG.
SIDHU, Miss. Simran Kaur, ACA *2009;* EDF Energy Renewables, 52 Grosvenor Gardens, LONDON, SW1W 0AU.
SIDHU, Mrs. Tracy Jane, BSc ACA *1991;* Satwell Consultancy Services Ltd, Stoke Poges Lane, STOKE POGES, BUCKINGHAMSHIRE, SL2 4NP.
SIDI, Mr. Richard Marcel, BA ACA *1990;* The Boathouse, Clappersgate, AMBLESIDE, CUMBRIA, LA22 9LE.
SIDIQUE, Mr. Malique Firdauz, BSc ACA *2005;* 45 Cosedge Crescent, CROYDON, CR0 4DN.
SIDLIN, Mr. Mark Howard, FCA *1990;* 22 Larchwood Close, BANSTEAD, SURREY, SM7 1HE.
SIDNEY, Mr. Paul Colin, MA ACA *1999;* 89 Bramfield Road, LONDON, SW11 6PZ.
SIDOLI, Dr. Fabio, MEng ACA *2009;* 43 Courthope Road, LONDON, NW3 2LE.
SIDWELL, Mr. David Hugh, MA ACA *1978;* 25 Central Park West, Apt 20J, NEW YORK, NY 10023, UNITED STATES.
•**SIDWELL, Mr. Graham Robert, BSc FCA** *1979;* 1 Stanley Mansions, Park Walk, LONDON, SW10 0AG.
SIDWELL, Mr. John, BA ACA *1986;* Flat 4, 12 Fawcett Street, LONDON, SW10 9JD.
SIENKIEWICZ, Mrs. Teresa, MA BSc FCA *1976;* 28 Newbury Gardens, EPSOM, KT19 0NU.
SIEW, Mr. Chen Yei, BA(Hons) ACA *2001;* 75 Jalan Waras 3, Taman Connaught, Cheras, 56000 KUALA LUMPUR, FEDERAL TERRITORY, MALAYSIA.
SIEW, Mr. Mun Wai, FCA *1983;* 1/226A Kooyong Road, Toorak, MELBOURNE, VIC 3142, AUSTRALIA.
SIEW, Mr. Richard Peng Kong, ACA *1982;* Lot 450, 59 Jalan Pelangi Pagi, Country Heights, 43000 KAJANG, SELANGOR, MALAYSIA.
SIEW, Mr. Rick Ah Fah, FCA *1979;* P O Box 61, CHATSWOOD, NSW 2057, AUSTRALIA.
SIEW, Miss. Sau Chan, ACA *1984;* E1-22-1 BUKIT UTAMA 1, 3 CHANGKAT BUKIT UTAMA, BANDAR UTAMA, 47800 PETALING JAYA, SELANGOR, MALAYSIA.
SIEW, Miss. Shan Lyn, ACA *2009;* 7 Jalan SS 22/3, Damansara Utama, 47400 PETALING JAYA, MALAYSIA.
SIEW, Mr. Yew Tuck, ACA *1981;* 23 Jalan SS7/ 4, Kelana Jaya, 47301 PETALING JAYA, SELANGOR, MALAYSIA.
SIFORD, Mr. Neil Edward, BSc ACA *1990;* 47 Strickland Street, SOUTH PERTH, WA 6151, AUSTRALIA.
•**SIFRI, Mr. Camille Charles, FCA** *1984;* PricewaterhouseCoopers, SNA Building 5th Floor, PO Box 11-3155, Tabaris Square, BEIRUT, LEBANON.
•**SIGANPORIA, Mr. Aspy Nariman, FCA** *1973;* Civvals Ltd, 50 Seymour Street, LONDON, W1H 7JG. See also Civvals Ellam Ltd and Civvals
•**SIGANPORIA, Mr. Nauzer Nariman, BA FCA** *1981;* H W Fisher & Company Limited, Acre House, 11/15 William Road, LONDON, NW1 3ER. See also H.W. Fisher & Company
SIGGERS, Ms. Lesley Anne, BA ACA *1992;* Marie Curie Cancer Care Camelford House, 87-90 Albert Embankment, LONDON, SE1 7TP.
SIGGERS, Mr. Paul Francis, ACA MPMI *1979;* Two Hoots, 38 Cranford Drive, Holybourne, ALTON, GU34 4HJ.
SIGGS, Mrs. Elizabeth Joyce, BSc FCA *1990;* 23 Station Road, Balsall Common, COVENTRY, CV7 7FN.
SIGLER, Mr. Michael James, BA FCA *1970;* 28 Richmond Road, LONDON, SW20 0PQ.
•**SIGLEY, Mr. Michael Paul, FCA** *1976;* Davies Sigley, Dresden House, The Strand, Longton, STOKE-ON-TRENT, ST3 2PD.
SIGMUND, Mr. John, BA ACA *1990;* 61 Fairfield Road, Bow, LONDON, E3 2QA.
SIK, Mr. Gary Siu Kwan, BA ACA *1992;* 9D Hilltop Mansion, 60 Cloudview Road, NORTH POINT, HONG KONG ISLAND, HONG KONG SAR.
SILAS, Mr. Charles Frederick, FCA *1961;* Flat 15, Wohl Lodge, Ravenscroft Avenue, LONDON, NW11 0SB. (Life Member)
SILBER, Mr. Adrian Giles, BSc FCA *1980;* 18 Barlows Road, BIRMINGHAM, B15 2PL.
SILBERSTEIN, Mr. Joel Messod, ACA CA(SA) *2008;* European Goldfields Limited, Level 3 11 Berkeley Street, LONDON, W1J 8DS.
SILBURN, Mr. Henry Charles, FCA *1955;* PO Box 68072, Bryanston, SANDTON, GAUTENG, 2021, SOUTH AFRICA. (Life Member)
•**SILCOCK, Mr. Charles John Francis, MA ACA** *1983;* PricewaterhouseCoopers LLP, 7 More London Riverside, LONDON, SE1 2RT. See also PricewaterhouseCoopers
SILCOCK, Mrs. Fiona Karen Ann, MA FCA FABRP *1983;* (Member of Council 2007 - 2009), Homecroft, Colne Road, Somersham, HUNTINGDON, CAMBRIDGESHIRE, PE28 3DQ.
•**SILCOCK, Mr. Graham James Greer, FCA** *1961;* PO BOX 902, NAIROBI, 00502, KENYA.
SILCOCK, Mr. Ian, FCA *1974;* 31 Marlborough Way, ASHBY-DE-LA-ZOUCH, LE65 2NN.
SILCOCK, Mr. Martin James, BSc ACA *1989;* Anglian Water Services Ltd Anglian House Ambury Road South, HUNTINGDON, CAMBRIDGESHIRE, PE29 3NZ.
•**SILCOCK, Mr. Michael John, FCA ASFA** *1971;* West Wake Price LLP, 4 Chiswell Street, LONDON, EC1Y 4UP.
SILCOCK, Mrs. Nicola Catherine, ACA *2001;* Investec Bank, 1st Floor, 100 Grayston Drive, Sandton, JOHANNESBURG, 2196 SOUTH AFRICA.
•**SILCOCK, Mr. Stuart Andrew, FCA** *1972;* Lawford & Co, Creek Lights, 23 Cliff Parade, LEIGH-ON-SEA, ESSEX, SS9 1AS. See also Lawfords Consulting Limited
SILCOCK, Mrs. Victoria Louise, BA(Hons) ACA *2010;* 11 Knowsley Grove, Horwich, BOLTON, BL6 6EZ.
SILCOCKS, Mr. Trevor Beresford, FCA *1955;* The Quest, Glen Avenue, Abbots Leigh, BRISTOL, BS8 3SD. (Life Member)
•**SILINS, Miss. Zinaida Biruta, FCA** *1985;* (Tax Fac), Zinaida Silins FCA, Hybank, 12 Old Road, Walgrave, NORTHAMPTON, NN6 9QW.
•**SILK, Mr. Antony Peter, FCA** *1972;* (Tax Fac), Silk & Co, 23 Havelock Road, HASTINGS, TN34 1BP.
SILK, Mr. Derek John, FCA *1964;* 67a Red Lane, Burton Green, KENILWORTH, WARWICKSHIRE, CV8 1PA.

SILK, Mrs. Frances, BSc ACA *1987;* Hatherton House, The Old Rectory, Admaston, RUGELEY, STAFFORDSHIRE, WS15 3NL.
SILK, Mr. Frederick Charles Ziervogel, FCA *1959;* 80 Front Street E, Suite 602, TORONTO M5E 1T4, ON, CANADA. (Life Member)
SILK, Mr. James Douglas, BSc ACA *1992;* 11 Mace Terrace, OAKURA 4314, TARANAKI, NEW ZEALAND.
SILK, Mr. Jon Stanley, BA ACA *1986;* Hatherton House, The Old Rectory, Admaston, RUGELEY, STAFFORDSHIRE, WS15 3NL.
SILLANDY, Mr. Paul William, BSc ACA *1989;* 3 Park Road, Bramcote, NOTTINGHAM, NG9 3LA.
SILLARS, Mr. Anthony Geoffrey, FCA *1975;* 8 High Green, Gainford, DARLINGTON, DL2 3DL.
SILLARS, Mr. Ian Wilson, BSc FCA *1976;* Brigade Electronics Plc, Brigade House, Unit 2, Horton Kirby Trading Estate, Station Road, South Darenth DARTFORD DA4 9BD.
SILLARS, Mr. Michael Gordon, FCA *1970;* 34 West Green, Heighington Village, NEWTON AYCLIFFE, DL5 6PE.
SILLARS, Mr. Tristan Richard Gordon, BSc ACA *2006;* Moorstones Ruebury Lane, Osmotherley, NORTHALLERTON, NORTH YORKSHIRE, DL6 3BG.
SILLE, Mr. Richard Anthony, BSc(Hons) ACA *2001;* 4 Creggan Lea, Port St Mary, ISLE OF MAN, IM9 5BD.
SILLETT, Mrs. Caroline Hazel, BSc ACA *1997;* Little Furnace Farm, Colemans Hatch, HARTFIELD, EAST SUSSEX, TN7 4EH.
SILLITO, Miss. Jane, MA(Hons) ACA *2011;* 139 Englefield Road, Islington, LONDON, N1 3LH.
SILLITOE, Mrs. Elizabeth Claire, BA ACA *2005;* 27 Uppermill Drive, Burnage, MANCHESTER, M19 1RU.
•**SILLS, Mr. Andrew John, BA ACA** *2000;* with KPMG LLP, 1 The Embankment, Neville Street, LEEDS, LS1 4DW.
SILLS, Mr. Christopher Darlington, FCA *1964;* 65 Dunsmure Road, LONDON, N16 5PT.
SILLS, Mr. Colin Anthony, FCA *1973;* 3 Moss Close, Moss Lane, Garstang, PRESTON, PR3 1NG.
SILLS, Mrs. Emily Claire, ACA *2009;* Flat 16, 207 Lavender Hill, LONDON, SW11 5SD.
SILLS, Miss. Kimberley, BA(Hons) ACA *2010;* 5 Lake View Close, North Hykeham, LINCOLN, LN6 9SW.
SILLS, Mrs. Melanie Jane, BSc ACA *1985;* 35 Baytree Walk, WATFORD, WD17 4RX.
SILLS, Mr. Michael Robert Thatcher, FCA *1960;* Avenue des Vienu Amis 4, 1410 WATERLOO, BELGIUM. (Life Member)
SILLS, Mr. Michael Thatcher, BSc ACA *1991;* Ernst & Young, Route de Chancy 59, CH 1213 GENEVA, SWITZERLAND.
SILLS, Mr. Peter John, FCA *1968;* 12 Burlingham Avenue, West Kirby, WIRRAL, MERSEYSIDE, CH48 8AP. (Life Member)
SILLS, Mrs. Sarah Elizabeth, BSc FCA *1993;* 23 Dunkirk Drive, Brockhill Village, Norton, WORCESTER, WR5 2SG.
SILMAN, Mr. Anthony Stephen Charles, BSc FCA *1978;* McCann Erickson, Highlands Road, Shirley, SOLIHULL, WEST MIDLANDS, B90 4WE.
SILSBURY, Miss. Rachel Naomi, BSc ACA *2009;* 83 Wilton Crescent, SOUTHAMPTON, SO15 7QG.
•**SILVA, Miss. Bianca Kamala, BA ACA DChA** *1988;* MacIntyre Hudson LLP, 31 Castle Street, HIGH WYCOMBE, BUCKINGHAMSHIRE, HP13 6RU.
SILVA, Mrs. Dhanitha Nayanee, BEng FCA *1996;* 29 Verran Road, CAMBERLEY, GU15 2ND.
SILVA, Mr. Paul, BA(Hons) ACA *2010;* 64b West End, Silverstone, TOWCESTER, NORTHAMPTONSHIRE, NN12 8UY.
SILVER, Mr. Adam, BA(Hons) ACA *2001;* 39 Midholm, LONDON, NW11 6LL.
•**SILVER, Mr. Alan John, FCA** *1972;* (Tax Fac), A-spire Business Partners Limited, 32 Byron Hill Road, HARROW, MIDDLESEX, HA2 0HY.
SILVER, Mrs. Alexandra Claire, BSc ACA *2002;* Flat 14, 307 Upper Richmond Road, LONDON, SW15 6SS.
SILVER, Miss. Amanda Jane, ACA *2009;* 32 Aldwell Close, Wootton, NORTHAMPTON, NN4 6AX.
SILVER, Mr. Andrew Paul David, BSc FCA *1991;* Bjerkelundsveien 47B, 1358 JAR, NORWAY.
SILVER, Mrs. Caroline Louise, BA ACA *1988;* 29 Kings Road, RICHMOND, SURREY, TW10 6EX.
SILVER, Mr. Charles Edward, MSc BSc ACA *2006;* Flat 3 Paveley Court, 30 Langstone Way, LONDON, NW7 1GR.
SILVER, Mr. David Alan, BA(Hons) ACA *1991;* 107 Cherry Hinton Road, CAMBRIDGE, CB1 7BS.
SILVER, Mr. David Stephen, BSc ACA *1997;* Flat 10, Eagle Wharf East, 35 Narrow Street, LONDON, E14 8DP.
SILVER, Mr. Geoffrey Stephen, BSc ARCS ACA *1996;* 111 East Dulwich Grove, LONDON, SE22 8PU.
•**SILVER, Mr. Gordon Robert, FCA** *1973;* (Tax Fac), with Cartwrights Audit Limited, Regency House, 33 Wood Street, BARNET, EN5 4BE.
SILVER, Miss. Lisa Amanda, BSc ACA *2002;* Flat 20, Etchingham Court, Etchingham Park Road, LONDON, N3 2EA.
SILVER, Mr. Mark James, BSc ACA *2004;* 31 Queensmill Road, Fulham, LONDON, SW6 6JP.
SILVER, Mr. Mark Jonathan, BSc ACA *1986;* 29 Kings Road, RICHMOND, SURREY, TW10 6EX.
•**SILVER, Mr. Mervyn Scott, FCA** *1970;* PMM Services Limited, Flat 4, 7 Gordon Avenue, STANMORE, MIDDLESEX, HA7 3QE.
•**SILVER, Mr. Michael Alan, FCA** *1971;* Maurice Apple, 3rd Floor, Marlborough House, 179-189 Finchley Road, LONDON, NW3 6LB. See also Maco Administration Ltd
•**SILVER, Mr. Mordechai, FCA** *1975;* Lord & Co, 31 Waterpark Road, SALFORD, M7 4FT.
SILVER, Mr. Paul Anthony, BA(Econ) ACA *1998;* 26 Beechcroft Avenue, LONDON, NW11 8BL.
•**SILVER, Mr. Peter John, FCA FRSA** *1972;* (Tax Fac), Silver & Co, The Hollies, 16 St. Johns Street, BRIDGNORTH, SHROPSHIRE, WV15 6AG.
•**SILVER, Mr. Philip Edward, BSc ACA** *1992;* Pennington Silver Limited, 30 Union Street, SOUTHPORT, MERSEYSIDE, PR9 0QE. See also Pennington Silver
SILVER, Mr. Richard Alexander, LLB FCA *1995;* 20 Wolstonbury Road, HOVE, EAST SUSSEX, BN3 6EJ.
SILVER, Mr. Robert, BA ACA *1999;* 6 Valley View, BARNET, HERTFORDSHIRE, EN5 2NY.
SILVER, Mr. Roy Myer, FCA *1969;* P.O. Box 1148, Sea Point, CAPE TOWN, C.P., 8060, SOUTH AFRICA.
SILVERBECK, Mr. Andrew David, MA ACA *1994;* The Orchard, 12 Barham Avenue, Elstree, BOREHAMWOOD, HERTFORDSHIRE, WD6 3PN.
SILVERLEAF, Mrs. Nicola Mary, ACA *1979;* The Old Byre, 86 High Street, Hinxton, SAFFRON WALDEN, ESSEX, CB10 1QY.
SILVERMAN, Mr. Brian Geoffrey, FCA *1961;* 21 Claybury, BUSHEY, WD23 1FS.
SILVERMAN, Mr. David Elliott, FCA *1972;* 10A/8 Nitza Boulevard, NETANYA, 42262, ISRAEL.
•**SILVERMAN, Mr. Irving, FCA** *1957;* (Tax Fac), Irving Silverman, 52 Mayflower Lodge, Regents Park Road, LONDON, N3 3HX.
•**SILVERMAN, Mr. Justin Andrew, FCA** *1979;* Silvermans AP Limited, 2 Castleham Court, 180 High Street, EDGWARE, MIDDLESEX, HA8 7EX.
•**SILVERMAN, Mr. Lynn Russell, BA FCA** *1982;* HW, Pacific Chambers, 11-13 Victoria Street, LIVERPOOL, MERSEYSIDE, L2 5QQ. See also Haines Watts
SILVERMAN, Mr. Martin Barry, FCA *1967;* 25 Malvern Mews, LONDON, NW6 5PT.
SILVERMAN, Mrs. Mary Anne, BA ACA *1990;* 35 Dowsefield Lane, LIVERPOOL, L18 3JG.
SILVERMAN, Mr. Michael Alan, FCA *1970;* 16 Clearwater Place, Long Ditton, SURBITON, SURREY, KT6 4ET.
SILVERMAN, Mr. Robert David, ACA *1992;* Cardiff Pinnacle Insurance Management Services Plc, Pinnacle House Stangate Crescent, BOREHAMWOOD, HERTFORDSHIRE, WD6 2XX.
SILVERMAN, Mr. Vivian Howard, FCA *1974;* 78 Lakes Lane, BEACONSFIELD, BUCKINGHAMSHIRE, HP9 2JZ.
SILVERS, Mr. Graham Lewis, BSc FCA *1977;* 7 Athol Road, Bramhall, STOCKPORT, SK7 1BR.
SILVERSTEIN, Mr. Adrian, FCA *1955;* Martin Motors (Highgate) Ltd, Unit 4, Broadbent Close, Highgate High Street, LONDON, N6 5JW.
SILVERSTONE, Mr. Howard Martin, BA FCA CPA CFE *1985;* 10 Lucerne Court, CHERRY HILL, NJ 08003, UNITED STATES.
SILVERSTONE, Mr. John David, BBS FCA *1977;* Bacta Alders House, 133 Aldersgate Street, LONDON, EC1A 4JA.
•**SILVERTON, Mr. Dennis Alfred, FCA** *1966;* Haysom Silverton & Partners Ltd, Norfolk House Centre, 82 Saxon Gate West, MILTON KEYNES, MK9 2DL.
SILVERWOOD, Mr. Kevin, BSc ACA *2003;* Computer 2000 Unit 5 Intec, 2 Wade Road, BASINGSTOKE, HAMPSHIRE, RG24 8NE.
SILVESTER, Mr. Anthony William, LLB FCA *1975;* 12 Coleshill Road, SUTTON COLDFIELD, B75 7AA.
•**SILVESTER, Mrs. Christine Marie, BSc ACA** *1991;* Silvester Parker & Co LLP, The Spinney, Beausale, WARWICK, CV35 7NU.
SILVESTER, Mr. Dominic Francis Michael, BSc ACA *1986;* Enstar Limited, Windsor Place, 3rd Floor, 18 Queen Street, HAMILTON HM 11, BERMUDA.
SILVESTER, Mr. Eric George, FCA *1962;* 35 The Grove, Ickenham, UXBRIDGE, UB10 8QJ. (Life Member)
SILVESTER, Mr. Francis Stanley, FCA *1966;* 2 Sands Farm Drive, Burnham, SLOUGH, SL1 7LD.
SILVESTER, Mr. Graham William, FCA *1975;* 1 Woodleyes Crescent, STAFFORD, ST17 4RE.
SILVESTER, Mr. Iain Charles, BSc ACA *1990;* Picco Chip Designs Ltd, Riverside Buildings, 108 Walcot Street, BATH, BA1 5BG.
SILVESTER, Mrs. Juliet Anne Rosemary, BSc ACA *1989;* Ben Mead Middlehill, Box, CORSHAM, SN13 8QD.
SILVESTER, Mr. Nicholas James, BA ACA *2000;* La Villanelle, Le Chemin Des Maltieres, Grouville, JERSEY, JE3 9EB.
SILVESTER, Mr. Peter, FCA *1958;* Sizergh View, Burton Road, Oxenholme, KENDAL, LA9 7EP. (Life Member)
•**SILVESTER, Mr. Roger Brian, FCA** *1969;* Khaniwara, Little Green, Mells, FROME, BA11 3QZ.
SILVESTER, Miss. Ruth, BA ACA *1998;* 17 Pinewood Drive, Caversham, READING, RG4 7LJ.
SILVESTER, Mr. Simon John, BSc FCA *1977;* Forge House, College Street, Ullesthorpe, LUTTERWORTH, LE17 5BU.
SILVESTER, Mr. Stephen, BSc ACA *2009;* 88 Cumberland Street, The Rocks, SYDNEY, NSW 2001, AUSTRALIA.
SILVEY, Mr. Stephen John, BSc FCA *1990;* 77 Halfway Bush Road, DUNEDIN 9076, NEW ZEALAND.
SIM, Miss. Agnes Lee Yong, FCA *1984;* Unit 5, 37-41 Glen Park Road, BAYSWATER, VIC 3153, AUSTRALIA.
SIM, Miss. Ah Luan, ACA *1985;* 3A Jalan Sayang, SINGAPORE 418624, SINGAPORE.
SIM, Mrs. Alison Jane, BSc FCA *1978;* E.on Ruhrgas UK E & P Ltd, 129 Wilton Road, LONDON, SW1V 1JZ.
SIM, Mr. Angus John Frederic, MA ACA *1996;* Hill Croft, Shoppe Hill, Dunsfold, GODALMING, SURREY, GU8 4LN.
SIM, Mr. Ban Tek, FCA *1972;* 18 Chancery Hill Road, SINGAPORE 309658, SINGAPORE.
SIM, Mr. Bingley Kia Miang, BCom FCA CF *1990;* 86 Jalan Bu 10/6, Bandar Utama, 47800 PETALING JAYA, SELANGOR, MALAYSIA.
SIM, Miss. Chi Wei, MBA BSc ACA *2004;* No 5 Jalan TR 9/1, Tropicana Golf & Country Resort, 47410 PETALING JAYA, SELANGOR, MALAYSIA.
SIM, Mr. David Robert, BA(Hons) ACA *2003;* Hill House Rose Hill, Grundisburgh, WOODBRIDGE, SUFFOLK, IP13 6TG.
SIM, Miss. Gek Hoon Amy, LLB ACA *1992;* 64 Oxhey Road, WATFORD, WD19 4QQ.
•**SIM, Mr. George Edward, MA FCA** *1984;* Sim Kapila, St. George's House, 14-17 Wells Street, LONDON, W1T 3PD.
SIM, Mr. Jerome Churt Loon, BSc(Econ) ACA *1993;* 47 Lorong Lintang Park Selatan 4, 93200 KUCHING, SARAWAK, MALAYSIA.
SIM, Mr. Kevin, BEng ACA *2007;* Barclays Bank Plc, 1 Churchill Place, LONDON, E14 5HP.
SIM, Mr. Kevin Kia Ju, BSc ACA *1990;* 31 Jalan Setia Nusantara U13/22Q Setia Eco Park Section U13, 40170 SHAH ALAM, MALAYSIA.
•**SIM, Mr. Kon Fah, ACA** *1987;* Moores Rowland, 701 Sunning Plaza, 10 Hysan Avenue, CAUSEWAY BAY, HONG KONG ISLAND, HONG KONG SAR.
SIM, Mr. Kui Hock, FCA *1976;* 569 1st Floor, Jalan Upper Chawan, 93300 KUCHING, SARAWAK, MALAYSIA.
•**SIM, Mr. Michael Cher Khuan, FCA FCCA** *1991;* (Tax Fac), M.Sim & Co, 233 Princes Gardens, LONDON, W3 0LU.
SIM, Miss. Pearl Ai Lian, FCA *1969;* 10 Toh Close, SINGAPORE 507995, SINGAPORE.
SIM, Mr. Peter William John, BSc FCA *1980;* (Tax Fac), Coquet Lea, 16 De Merley Road, MORPETH, NE61 1HZ.
SIM, Mr. Puay Huat, BA FCA *1982;* PO Box 1271, QVB, SYDNEY, NSW 1230, AUSTRALIA.
SIM, Mr. Roger James, BSc ACA *1990;* 3472 Meadowlark Ln, Prairie Grove, CRYSTAL LAKE, IL 60012, UNITED STATES.
SIM, Miss. Siew Boi, BA ACA *1987;* 5a Dunbar Walk, SINGAPORE 459276, SINGAPORE.
SIM, Mr. Stuart William, FCA *1975;* Old Fanshawe Vicarage, Off Fanshawe Lane, Siddington, MACCLESFIELD, SK11 9PP.
SIM, Mr. Ti, ACA CA(AUS) *2011;* 568-9-36 9th Floor, Kompleks Mutiara, 3 and 1/2 Miles, Jalan Ipoh, 51200 KUALA LUMPUR, MALAYSIA.
SIM, Miss. Valerie Margaret, BSc ACA *1999;* 11 West Kilbride Road, DALRY, AYRSHIRE, KA24 5DY.
•**SIMANS, Mr. Louis, FCA** *1968;* Lou Simans & Co, 35 Court Road, SOUTHPORT, MERSEYSIDE, PR9 9ET.
SIMCOX, Mr. Andrew James, BA FCA *1981;* 53 Ashley Drive South, Ashley Heath, RINGWOOD, BH24 2JP.
•**SIMCOX, Mr. David, BSc ACA** *1978;* (Tax Fac), Walter Wright, 89 High Street, Hadleigh, IPSWICH, IP7 5EA. See also Walter Wright Consultancy Ltd
•**SIMCOX, Mr. Joseph Richard Maurice, FCA** *1982;* (Tax Fac), Lonsdale & Marsh, Orleans House, Edmund Street, LIVERPOOL, L3 9NG.
SIMCOX, Mr. Piers, BSc(Econ) ACA *2002;* 92 Kingscourt Road, LONDON, SW16 1JB.
SIMCOX, Mr. Timothy Simon, FCA *1995;* 8 Park Drive, Swanwick, ALFRETON, DE55 1AH.
SIME, Mr. Alan, BCom FCA *1988;* Pitt Cottage, Blymhill Lawn, SHIFNAL, STAFFORDSHIRE, TF11 8LT.
•**SIME, Mr. Andrew Charles Moncur, FCA FCCA ATII** *1967;* Andrew C.M. Sime, 6 The Courtyard(The Farmhouse), The Outwoods, Burbage, HINCKLEY, LEICESTERSHIRE LE10 2UD. See also Moncur Charles & Co Ltd
SIME, Mrs. Elizabeth Jane, ACA *2008;* 131 Tavistock Road, FLEET, GU51 4EE.
SIME, Mr. Peter Ernest Miller, MA MSc FCA FSI *1979;* The Barn, Haffenden Quarter, Smarden, ASHFORD, KENT, TN27 8QR.
SIME, Mr. Robert, BSc ACA *2009;* 131 Tavistock Road, FLEET, GU51 4EE.
SIMEONS, Mr. Peter Charles Creighton, FCA *1977;* Red Gables, Nightingales Lane, CHALFONT ST. GILES, BUCKINGHAMSHIRE, HP8 4SR.
SIMISTER, Mr. Brian Philip, LLB FCA *1965;* 30 The Verlands, COWBRIDGE, CF71 7BY.
•**SIMISTER, Mr. Christopher Paul, BA FCA MBA** *1984;* Planning & Control Solutions Limited, 17 Beachburn Way, Handsworth Wood, BIRMINGHAM, B20 2AU.
SIMISTER, Mr. Malcolm, BA FCA *1980;* 3 Goodwin Street, GLEN IRIS, VIC 3146, AUSTRALIA.
SIMJANOSKI, Mrs. Larissa, BSc ACA *1993;* PO Box 179R, REDLYNCH, QLD 4870, AUSTRALIA.
SIMKIN, Mr. Anthony Nicholas, FCA *1978;* 10 Riverview Grove, Chiswick, LONDON, W4 3QJ.
SIMKIN, Mr. Craig, ACA *2002;* Meditor Capital Management Ltd, Tower 42, International Financial Centre, 25 Old Broad Street, LONDON, EC2N 1HQ.
SIMKIN, Mr. Jon Paul, BSc ACA *2003;* 20 Putney Wharf Tower, Brewhouse Lane, LONDON, SW15 2JQ.
SIMKIN, Miss. Kelly, BSc(Hons) ACA *2010;* Flat 6 Mount Lodge, 102 Clapham Park Road, LONDON, SW4 7BH.
SIMKIN, Mr. Robert Andrew, BSc ACA *1988;* Argent Partners Limited, New Broad Street House, 35 New Broad Street, LONDON, EC2M 1NH.
SIMKINS, Mr. Daniel Richard, MA ACA *2001;* c/o MAF Kenya, Wilson Airport, PO Box 21123, NAIROBI, 00505, KENYA.
•**SIMKINS, Mr. Matthew William, BSc FCA MIFT DChA** *1992;* The Old Hop Kiln, 1 Long Garden Walk, FARNHAM, GU9 7HY.
•**SIMKINS, Mr. Nicholas Jon, BSocSc FCA** *1992;* Chantrey Vellacott DFK LLP, 35 Calthorpe Road, Edgbaston, BIRMINGHAM, WEST MIDLANDS, B15 1TS.
SIMKINS, Mr. Paul Charles, LLB FCA *1986;* with ICAEW, Metropolitan House, 321 Avebury Boulevard, MILTON KEYNES, MK9 2FZ.
SIMKISS, Mrs. Pamela Louise, ACA *1985;* 2 Charles Dickens Close, DROITWICH, WR9 7HW.
•**SIMLER, Mr. Gerald Joseph, FCA ATII** *1958;* (Tax Fac), Lewis-Simler, 83 Baker Street, LONDON, W1U 6AG. See also The Simlers Partnership
SIMM, Mr. Andrew Grant, BSc FCA *2001;* 517 Church Road, Smithills, BOLTON, LANCASHIRE, BL1 5RE.
SIMM, Mr. Brian, MBA FCA *1976;* 58 Darlow Drive, STRATFORD-UPON-AVON, WARWICKSHIRE, CV37 9DG.
SIMM, Mr. Fraser Murray, FCA *1972;* 5 Manor Park, StowSelkirkshire, GALASHIELS, TD1 2RD.
•**SIMM, Mrs. Jenifer Harley, MA FCA** *1972;* (Tax Fac), Jenifer H Simm, Tun Mead, Gussage All Saints, WIMBORNE, BH21 5ET.
SIMM, Mr. Jonathan David, BA ACA CF *1993;* Altitude Partners, International House, George Curl Way, SOUTHAMPTON, SO18 2RZ.

•SIMM, Mr. Michael, BA ACA *1986;* Simm Associates, Hillside Cottage, Agneash, Lonan, ISLE OF MAN, IM4 7NS. See also Simm Michael
SIMMERS, Mr. Paul Richard, BA ACA *1994;* 34 Mitchell Road, ORPINGTON, BR6 9TP.
SIMMESTER, Miss. Jodi, ACA *2011;* 12 Suddaby Close, HULL, HU9 3RG.
•SIMMONDS, Mr. Andrew Keith John, BSc FCA *1977;* MEMBER OF COUNCIL (Member of Council 1997 - 2001), Deloitte LLP, 2 New Street Square, LONDON, EC4A 3BZ. See also Deloitte & Touche LLP
•SIMMONDS, Mrs. Ann Elaine, ACA *1985;* with Whitley Stimpson LLP, Penrose House, 67 Hightown Road, BANBURY, OXFORDSHIRE, OX16 9BE.
SIMMONDS, Mr. Anthony, FCA *1967;* Frog Place, The Woods, NORTHWOOD, MIDDLESEX, HA6 3EY.
SIMMONDS, Mr. Antony Guy Richard, FCA *1965;* Penny Cottage, Hinton Martell, WIMBORNE, BH21 7HD. (Life Member)
•SIMMONDS, Miss. Barbara Ann, MA FCA *1980;* Barbara A. Simmonds, 3 Cotton Row, Plantation Wharf, Battersea, LONDON, SW11 3UG.
SIMMONDS, Mr. Brian John, FCA *1970;* 22 Culverlands Close, STANMORE, MIDDLESEX, HA7 3AG.
SIMMONDS, Mr. Bruce Norman, FCA *1968;* 3 Park Crescent, Frenchay, BRISTOL, BS16 1PD. (Life Member)
SIMMONDS, Ms. Caroline Rebecca, BA ACA *1985;* 21 Robinson Road, Boars Hill, Wootton, OXFORD, OX1 5LE.
SIMMONDS, Mrs. Catherine Anne Louise, LLB ACA *2006;* 46 Viking, BRACKNELL, BERKSHIRE, RG12 8UL.
SIMMONDS, Miss. Catherine Helen, BA ACA *2005;* 99 Clarence Road, LONDON, SW19 8QB.
SIMMONDS, Mr. Geoffrey Emanuel, FCA *1956;* 49A Townshend Road, LONDON, NW8 6LJ. (Life Member)
•SIMMONDS, Mr. Geoffrey Michael, FCA *1966;* Simmonds & Co, 23 Links Way, NORTHWOOD, HA6 2XA.
•SIMMONDS, Mr. Gerard Vaughan Charles, BSc ACA *1992;* Affinity Accountancy, 44 Charlbury Road, OXFORD, OX2 6UX. See also Affinity Accountancy Services Limited
SIMMONDS, Mr. Graham Martin, FCA *1963;* 2 West Park Lane, Goring-by-Sea, WORTHING, WEST SUSSEX, BN12 4ER.
SIMMONDS, Mr. Ian David, BSc ACA *1994;* 1 Ash Close, HOVE, EAST SUSSEX, BN3 6QS.
•SIMMONDS, Mr. Ian Roger, BA FCA *1980;* with RSM Tenon Audit Limited, Sumner House, St. Thomas's Road, CHORLEY, LANCASHIRE, PR7 1HP.
SIMMONDS, Miss. Jackie, BSc ACA *1996;* Pinecroft 71a Long Ashton Road Long Ashton, BRISTOL, BS41 9HW.
•SIMMONDS, Mr. James Austen, BA(Hons) FCA *2000;* UHY Hacker Young LLP, 110 Nottingham Road, Chilwell, NOTTINGHAM, NG9 6DQ.
SIMMONDS, Mr. John, FCA *1970;* Richmond House, Walkern Road, STEVENAGE, HERTFORDSHIRE, SG4 9AZ.
•SIMMONDS, Mr. John Anthony Edward, FCA *1968;* (Tax Fac), J A E Simmonds & Company Ltd, 24 Garth Road, SEVENOAKS, KENT, TN13 1RU.
SIMMONDS, Mr. John Antony, FCA *1958;* Branca Azul, Lot 32, Montinhos Da Luz, 8600 - 125 LAGOS, PORTUGAL. (Life Member)
SIMMONDS, Mr. John Philip, BSc FCA *1980;* 28 Woodstock Avenue, LONDON, NW11 9SL.
SIMMONDS, Mr. Kerry Francis, BA ACA *1984;* Orchard Lodge, 14a High Street, Woodford Halse, DAVENTRY, NORTHAMPTONSHIRE, NN11 3RQ.
SIMMONDS, Mrs. Linda Jane, MA ACA CTA *1992;* June Cottage, Dornafield Road, Ipplepen, NEWTON ABBOT, DEVON, TQ12 5SH.
SIMMONDS, Mrs. Lisa Dawn, BSc(Hons) ACA *2004;* 8 Minnow Close, Oakhurst, SWINDON, WILTSHIRE, SN25 2HW.
SIMMONDS, Mr. Mark Oakley, BSc ACA *1993;* 2 Glendower House, Clifton Down, BRISTOL, BS8 3BP.
SIMMONDS, Mr. Michael, FCA *1964;* Pipkin, Grove Heath, Ripley, WOKING, GU23 6EU. (Life Member)
SIMMONDS, Mr. Michael Gary, LLB ACA *1992;* 35 Bareena Road, AVALON, NSW 2107, AUSTRALIA.
SIMMONDS, Mr. Michael John, BEng ACA *1995;* Risk Capital Partners LLP, 9 Grafton Mews, LONDON, W1T 5HZ.
•SIMMONDS, Mr. Neil Sancho, BSc ACA *1998;* Smith & Williamson Ltd, 25 Moorgate, LONDON, EC2R 6AY. See also Nexia Audit Limited
SIMMONDS, Mr. Peter John, FCA *1973;* Cleveland House 109 Pack Lane, BASINGSTOKE, HAMPSHIRE, RG22 5HH.
SIMMONDS, Mr. Peter John, FCA *1953;* Stoney Croft, Houndscroft, Rodborough Common, STROUD, GL5 5DF. (Life Member)
SIMMONDS, Mr. Ronald Kimberley, FCA *1979;* Lazard Freres & Co Ltd, 30 Rockefeller Center, NEW YORK, NY 10020, UNITED STATES.
SIMMONDS, Mr. Thomas Peter, FCA *1976;* Av Prof Frederico Herman Jr 199 ap 241B, Alto de Pinheiros, SAO PAULO, 05459-010 SP, BRAZIL.
SIMMONS, Mr. Alan Richard Martin, FCA *1949;* 55 Wayland Avenue, BRIGHTON, BN1 5JL. (Life Member)
SIMMONS, Mrs. Beverley Ann, MA ACA *1982;* Knowle, 13 Lemmington Way, HORSHAM, RH12 5JG.
SIMMONS, Mr. Brian Edward, FCA *1961;* Starlings, Barn Close, Kingston, LEWES, BN7 3PH.
SIMMONS, Mr. Christopher Andrew, BA(Hons) ACA *2003;* 57 Gaskarth Road, LONDON, SW12 9NN.
•SIMMONS, Mr. Christopher Timothy, FCA *1977;* Mitchell Rodrigues & Co Limited, Suite 14, Zeal House, 8 Deer Park Road, LONDON, SW19 3GY.
SIMMONS, Mrs. Clare Marie, BA ACA *1989;* 29 Clewley Drive, Pendeford, WOLVERHAMPTON, WV9 5LB.
SIMMONS, Mr. Colin Ian, ACA *2002;* Sideways, 7 Pond Road, Bramley, TADLEY, HAMPSHIRE, RG26 5UJ.
SIMMONS, Mr. Colin Thomas, BSc ACA *1988;* 5a Harewood Place, WARRIEWOOD, NSW 2102, AUSTRALIA.
SIMMONS, Mr. David Alan, FCA *1972;* 27 Ossulton Way, LONDON, N2 0DT.
SIMMONS, Mr. David Alastair, BA ACA *1988;* Charter Limited 7th Floor, 322 High Holborn, LONDON, WC1V 7PB.
SIMMONS, Mr. David Mark, BA FCA *1999;* with RSM Tenon Limited, Arkwright House, Parsonage Gardens, MANCHESTER, M3 2LF.
SIMMONS, Mr. Dennis Owen, FCA *1953;* Chissom, Claycastle, Haselbury Plucknett, CREWKERNE, TA18 7PE. (Life Member)
SIMMONS, Mrs. Emma Lucy, BA ACA *2004;* 62 Firs Road, West Mersea, COLCHESTER, CO5 8NL.
SIMMONS, Mrs. Gillian Patricia, BSc(Econ) ACA *1995;* 26 Hill Village Road, SUTTON COLDFIELD, WEST MIDLANDS, B75 5BA.
SIMMONS, Mrs. Helen Elizabeth, BSc ACA *1991;* 44 Connaught Road, Brookwood, WOKING, GU24 0HE.
SIMMONS, Mr. Iain Goodway, BA ACA *2009;* 29 Windy Arbour, KENILWORTH, WARWICKSHIRE, CV8 2AT.
•SIMMONS, Mr. James, FCA *1978;* Bishop Simmons Limited, Mitre House, School Road, Bulkington, BEDWORTH, WARWICKSHIRE CV12 9JB.
SIMMONS, Mrs. Janet Elizabeth, BSc ACA *1989;* 61 Madeira Park, TUNBRIDGE WELLS, KENT, TN2 5SX.
SIMMONS, Miss. Jennifer, BA(Hons) ACA *2010;* 17a Suttons Lane, Deeping Gate, PETERBOROUGH, PE6 9AA.
SIMMONS, Mrs. Jill, BA ACA *2005;* 6 Egglestone Drive, Eaglescliffe, STOCKTON-ON-TEES, CLEVELAND, TS16 0GF.
•SIMMONS, Mr. John Howard, FCA *1970;* The KBSP Partnership, Harben House, Harben Parade, Finchley Road, LONDON, NW3 6LH. See also Stardata Business Services Limited
SIMMONS, Mr. John Richard, FCA *1981;* 3 Surrey Close, Burbage, HINCKLEY, LE10 2NY.
SIMMONS, Mr. Jonathan, BSc CA ACA *1995;* with PricewaterhouseCoopers, Royal Trust Tower, Suite 3000 TD Centre, Box 82, 77 King Street West, TORONTO M5K 1G8 ON CANADA.
SIMMONS, Mr. Kevin, BSc FCA *1985;* 41 The Avenue, SUTTON, SM2 7QA.
•SIMMONS, Mr. Kevin Peter, FCA CF *1982;* Mazars LLP, The Lexicon, Mount Street, MANCHESTER, M2 5NT.
SIMMONS, Miss. Lian Christina, BSc ACA *1986;* 22 Silverston Way, STANMORE, HA7 4HR.
SIMMONS, Mr. Malcolm, FCA *1959;* 216 Evesham Road, STRATFORD-UPON-AVON, CV37 9AS.
SIMMONS, Mr. Mark, BEng *1999;* Five Gables, The Street, Witnesham, IPSWICH, IP6 9HG.
SIMMONS, Mr. Mark Andrew, BSc FCA *1993;* (Tax Fac), 23 The Avenue, WEMBLEY, HA9 9QH.
SIMMONS, Mr. Martin John, BA ACA *1992;* 3 Foxes Walk, Charvil, READING, RG10 9TX.
SIMMONS, Mrs. Merilyn Jane, BSc FCA *1978;* 5 Great Bounds Drive, TUNBRIDGE WELLS, KENT, TN4 0TP.
SIMMONS, Mr. Nicholas Karl, BA ACA *1992;* 6 Kinsella Gardens, LONDON, SW19 4UB.
•SIMMONS, Mr. Paul David Hamilton, ACA *1989;* Haines Watts, Sterling House, 177-181 Farnham Road, SLOUGH, BERKSHIRE, SL1 4XP. See also Chakko Harris
•SIMMONS, Mr. Paul Jonathan, BA FCA *1992;* (Tax Fac), Nagler Simmons, 5 Beaumont Gate, Shenley Hill, RADLETT, HERTFORDSHIRE, WD7 7AR.
SIMMONS, Mr. Paul Martin, BA(Hons) ACA *2011;* 29 Moss Bank Road, ST.HELENS, MERSEYSIDE, WA11 7DD.
SIMMONS, Mr. Philip Louis, FCA *1966;* Flat 20 Caenwood Court, Hampstead Lane, LONDON, N6 4RU.
•SIMMONS, Mr. Richard Barry, BA FCA *1975;* UHY Hacker Young (S.E) Ltd, 168 Church Road, HOVE, EAST SUSSEX, BN3 2DL. See also UHY Hacker Young
SIMMONS, Richard John, Esq CBE BSc FCA *1971;* BDP Media Group Ltd, 1 Hurst Avenue, Highgate, LONDON, N6 5TX.
SIMMONS, Dr. Richard Stanley, PhD MSc BA FCA *1985;* 1st Floor, 60 Po Wah Yuen, Yung Shue Wan, LAMMA ISLAND, NEW TERRITORIES, HONG KONG SAR.
SIMMONS, Mr. Spencer Mark, FCA *1982;* 30 Broomhill Road, WOODFORD GREEN, IG8 9HD.
•SIMMONS, Mr. Stephen, BSc FCA *2000;* Company Contracts and Services Limited, 11 The Shrubberies, George Lane, LONDON, E18 1BD.
SIMMONS, Mrs. Susan, BSc ACA *1983;* 1 Townhead Court, Melmerby, PENRITH, CUMBRIA, CA10 1HG.
SIMMONS, Mr. Thomas Bernard Frederick, FCA *1965;* Thomas Simmons, 12 Halland Close, CRAWLEY, WEST SUSSEX, RH10 1SD. (Life Member)
SIMMS, Mr. Andrew David, BSc(Hons) ACA *2004;* Universal Music, 364-366 Kensington High Street, LONDON, W14 8NS.
SIMMS, Mr. Andrew James, BSc ACA *1999;* 9a Hatherley Lane, CHELTENHAM, GL51 6PN.
SIMMS, Mr. Andrew John, BA ACA *1995;* 9 Park Road, GUILDFORD, GU1 4PH.
SIMMS, Mrs. Anne Margaret, BSc ACA *1989;* Birmingham Midshires ; Margin & Volume Team, P.O. Box 81 Pendeford Business Park Wobaston Road, WOLVERHAMPTON, WV9 5HZ.
SIMMS, Mr. Derek John, BSc FCA *1977;* G V A Grimley 3 Brindley Place, BIRMINGHAM, B1 2JB.
SIMMS, Mrs. Fiona Helen, BA ACA *1990;* 51 Manor Rise, LICHFIELD, WS14 9RF.
SIMMS, Mr. Greig Thomas, ACA *2008;* (Tax Fac), 25 Tredegar Road, LONDON, E3 2EH.
SIMMS, Mrs. Janet Ruth, BSc ACA *1996;* 92 Chestnut Avenue, WEST WICKHAM, BR4 9EX.
•SIMMS, Mr. Michael Edward, ACA *1997;* Moore Stephens LLP, 150 Aldersgate Street, LONDON, EC1A 4AB. See also Moore Stephens & Co
•SIMMS, Mr. Richard Frank, BSc FCA *1995;* F A Simms & Partners Ltd Insol House, 39 Station Road, LUTTERWORTH, LE17 4AP.
•SIMMS, Mr. Richard Henry, FCA *1961;* Simms Hanson, 51 Windy Arbour, KENILWORTH, WARWICKSHIRE, CV8 2BB.
SIMMS, Mr. William Richard, BA ACA FSI *1985;* Bestridge, Hillview Road, Claygate, ESHER, SURREY, KT10 0TU.
SIMNOCK, Mr. Clive, BA(Hons) FCA *1984;* 607 Main Avenue, Suite 200, NORWALK, CT 06851, UNITED STATES.
•SIMNOCK, Mr. Paul, FCA CTA *1977;* Martin Greene Ravden LLP, 55 Loudoun Road, St John's Wood, LONDON, NW8 0DL. See also MGR Audit Limited
SIMON, Mr. Andrew Douglas, ACA *2009;* Flat B23a Herbal Hill Gardens, 9 Herbal Hill, LONDON, EC1R 5XB.
SIMON, Mr. Charles Anthony, BA ACA *1979;* Cary House, South Cary Lane, CASTLE CARY, BA7 7ER.
•SIMON, Mr. Christopher Michael Alister, FCA *1964;* C.M.A. Simon, 13 Malt House Close, Old Windsor, WINDSOR, BERKSHIRE, SL4 2SD.
SIMON, Mr. Clive Norman, FCA *1970;* Les Martins Farm, Les Martins, St. Pierre Du Bois, GUERNSEY, GY7 9AN.
SIMON, Mr. Colin Terence Maitland, FCA *1972;* Flat 75, 47-49 Westbourne Grove, LONDON, W2 4UA.
SIMON, Mr. Daniel Conrad Henry, MA FCA *1976;* 25 West Hill Park, Highgate, LONDON, N6 6ND. (Life Member)
•SIMON, Mr. David George, FCA *1974;* 7 Nicholas Way, NORTHWOOD, HA6 2TR.
•SIMON, Mr. Elliot Bernard, BA FCA *1977;* Baker Tilly Tax & Advisory Services LLP, 3 Hardman Street, MANCHESTER, M3 3HF. See also Baker Tilly UK Audit LLP
•SIMON, Mr. Gary Ian, BSc FCA CITP FBCS *1982;* 32 Hill Crescent, Totteridge, LONDON, N20 8HD.
SIMON, Mr. Howard Philip, FCA *1977;* 7 Lynnbank Road, Calderstones, LIVERPOOL, L18 3HE.
SIMON, Mr. John Daniel, BSc ACA *1980;* Templefield, 4 Fairy Road, WREXHAM, LL13 7PR.
SIMON, Mr. Jonathan Barret, BSc FCA *1982;* 8 Longmans Lane, Cottingham, HULL, HU16 4EA.
SIMON, Mr. Julian Louis, BSc ACA *1997;* Dovelawn Management Limited, Osterley, Heathbourne Road, Bushey Heath, BUSHEY, WD23 1PD.
SIMON, Mr. Kenneth Adam, BA FCA *1988;* 4 Spenser Avenue, WEYBRIDGE, SURREY, KT13 0ST.
•SIMON, Mr. Michael Jonathan, MA CA FCA *1984;* Simon Silver-Myer, 8 Durweston Street, LONDON, W1H 1EW.
SIMON, Miss. Michelle, ACA *2009;* 2 Reddings Close, LONDON, NW7 4JL.
SIMON, Mr. Peter William, FCA *1971;* Ashfield, Bottom Lane, Seer Green, BEACONSFIELD, HP9 2UH.
•SIMONDS, Mr. Andrew Mark, BSc FCA *1987;* PricewaterhouseCoopers KFT, Wesselenyi u 16, BUDAPEST, H-1077, HUNGARY.
SIMONDS, Mr. Colin Duncan, FCA *1974;* 7 Chesterfield Road, Chiswick, LONDON, W4 3HG.
•SIMONDS, Mr. Colin Stuart, FCA *1974;* Help the Aged York House, 207-221 Pentonville Road, LONDON, N1 9UZ.
SIMONDS, Mr. Gavin Napier, FCA *1980;* Danehill, Lower Earley, READING, RG6 4BP.
SIMONDS, Mr. Geoffrey Charles, FCA *1977;* 7 Harding Close, Upperhaugh Rawmarsh, ROTHERHAM, S62 7HD.
SIMONDS, Miss. Rebecca Kate, BSc ACA MBA *1993;* Top Floor Flat, 8 Frognal Lane, LONDON, NW3 7DU.
SIMONIS, Mr. Kevin David, BSc ACA *1998;* 52 Station Road, Stoke Mandeville, AYLESBURY, BUCKINGHAMSHIRE, HP22 5UA.
SIMONITSCH, Mr. Tom, MSc BA ACA *2011;* Flat 5, 117 Ifield Road, LONDON, SW10 9AS.
•SIMONS, Mr. Alan William, BSc FCA *1982;* Alan W Simons Limited, Hillview Business Centre, 2 Leybourne Avenue, BOURNEMOUTH, BH10 6HF. See also Alan W Simons & Co
•SIMONS, Mr. Anthony Victor, BA FCA *1982;* (Tax Fac), Richard Anthony & Company, 13 Station Road, Finchley, LONDON, N3 2SB.
SIMONS, Mrs. Belita Joy, BA ACA *1980;* Belita J. Simons, 31 Elmbank Avenue, BARNET, HERTFORDSHIRE, EN5 3DU.
SIMONS, Ms. Catriona Ruth, BA ACA *1998;* The Guinness Trust, 17 Mendy Street, HIGH WYCOMBE, BUCKINGHAMSHIRE, HP11 2NZ.
SIMONS, Mr. David Albert, FCA *1973;* Cumbrian Developments Ltd, 13 Vicarage Lane, Ennerdale Bridge, CLEATOR, CUMBRIA, CA23 3BE.
SIMONS, Mr. David Edmund Frederick, MA FCA *1967;* Blue Cedars, Wayside Gardens, GERRARDS CROSS, SL9 7NG. (Life Member)
•SIMONS, Mr. Gavin Ronald Maurice, FCA *1974;* (Tax Fac), MWS, Kingsridge House, 601 London Road, WESTCLIFF-ON-SEA, ESSEX, SS0 9PE.
SIMONS, Mrs. Helen Emma, BA(Hons) ACA ACCA *2002;* 19 Millison Grove, Shirley, SOLIHULL, WEST MIDLANDS, B90 4UN.
SIMONS, Mr. Hugh Sellick, MA FCA *1984;* with Grant Thornton UK LLP, 30 Finsbury Square, LONDON, EC2P 2YU.
SIMONS, Mr. Jason Alexander, BSc ACA *2010;* Stevenstone Guest House, 2 Stevenstone Road, EXMOUTH, DEVON, EX8 2EP.
SIMONS, Mr. John Russell, FCA *1955;* Vivary Gate, 27 Mount Street, TAUNTON, TA1 3QF. (Life Member)
•SIMONS, Mr. Jonathan Geoffrey, FCA *1977;* Jonathan G. Simons, Office No 1, Paris House, Market Square, RUGELEY, WS15 2BL. See also A.K. Papadamou & Co
SIMONS, Mrs. Katherine Clare, BCom ACA *1989;* The White House, Coombe Hill Road, EAST GRINSTEAD, WEST SUSSEX, RH19 4LY.
SIMONS, Mr. Keith Nicholas, MA FCA MBCS *1973;* Dell Cottage, Dog Kennel Lane, Chorleywood, RICKMANSWORTH, WD3 5EL.
SIMONS, Mr. Kevin Paul, BA ACA *1987;* The White House, Coombe Hill Road, EAST GRINSTEAD, WEST SUSSEX, RH19 4LY.
SIMONS, Mr. Martin Edward, BSc FCA *1954;* 24 Granard Avenue, LONDON, SW15 6HJ. (Life Member)
SIMONS, Mr. Martin John, BSc ACA *1991;* 6A Osborne Road, Winton, BOURNEMOUTH, BH9 2JL.
SIMONS, Mr. Matt James, MA ACA *1994;* 18 Enborne Road, NEWBURY, BERKSHIRE, RG14 6AH.

•**SIMONS, Mr. Peter James, BSc FCA ATII** *1993;* Moore Stephens, Kings House, 40 Billing Road, NORTHAMPTON, NN1 5BA.
•**SIMONS, Mr. Richard Alan, BSc ACA** *1983;* (Tax Fac), Deben Financial Services Ltd, 270 Colchester Road, IPSWICH, IP4 4QX.
•**SIMONS, Mr. Richard Ivan, FCA** *1974;* Richard Anthony & Company, 13 Station Road, Finchley, LONDON, N3 2SB. See also RA Payroll Services Ltd
SIMONS, Mr. Robert Geoffrey, BSc FCA *1977;* 52 Fairford Avenue, LUTON, LU2 7ER.
SIMONS, Mr. Robin Francis, FCA *1966;* #7, Avenue des Papalins, MC 98000 MONACO, MONACO.
SIMONS, Mr. Steven, BSc ACA *2000;* 18 Stoatley Rise, HASLEMERE, SURREY, GU27 1AF.
SIMONS, Mr. Timothy John, BSc ACA *1992;* 8 Fern Way, Scarcroft, LEEDS, WEST YORKSHIRE, LS14 3JJ.
SIMONS, Mr. Victor Emanuel, FCA *1968;* Dubbeldamsweg Zuid 274, 3312 KS DORDRECHT, NETHERLANDS.
•**SIMOU, Mr. Stephen, BA FCA** *1990;* Citroen Wells, Devonshire House, 1 Devonshire Street, LONDON, W1W 5DR.
SIMOU, Mr. Theo Christofis, BA FCA *1994;* with KPMG LLP, 15 Canada Square, LONDON, E14 5GL.
SIMPKIN, Mr. David Anthony, FCA *1962;* Long Bank Barn, 8 Wymeswold Road, Rempstone, LOUGHBOROUGH, LE12 6RN.
SIMPKIN, Mr. Ian Richard Holroyd, MA FCA *1984;* Restharrow, Ballfield Road, GODALMING, GU7 2HE.
SIMPKIN, Mr. Nicolas Guy, BSc ACA *1996;* 44 Clarence Road, TEDDINGTON, MIDDLESEX, TW11 0BW.
SIMPKIN, Mr. Terence John, ACA *1979;* Ghyll Cottage, Casterton, CARNFORTH, CUMBRIA, LA6 2SA.
SIMPKIN, Mr. Timothy, BEng ACA *2001;* 3 Claremont Road, TEDDINGTON, MIDDLESEX, TW11 8DH.
SIMPKINS, Mr. Andrew John, FCA *1969;* 2946 Cohansey Drive, SAN JOSE, CA 95132, UNITED STATES. (Life Member)
•**SIMPKINS, Mr. Colin, FCA** *1972;* C & S Associates Ltd, 3 Wessex Way, Highworth, SWINDON, SN6 7NT.
•**SIMPKINS, Mr. John, BSc FCA** *1975;* (Tax Fac), John Simpkins & Co, 12 Stake Lane, FARNBOROUGH, HAMPSHIRE, GU14 8NP.
SIMPKINS, Mr. John Charles, MA FCA *1978;* Golford Place, Tenterden Road, Golford, CRANBROOK, KENT, TN17 3PA.
SIMPKINS, Mrs. Judith Mary, BSc FCA *1977;* 19 St. Andrews Road, MALVERN, WORCESTERSHIRE, WR14 3PR.
SIMPKINS, Mr. Mark Philip, BSc ACA *1990;* 8 Rodeheath Close, WILMSLOW, SK9 2DL.
•**SIMPSON, Mr. Adrian, FCA** *1985;* Simpson & Associates (Accountants) Limited, 23 Browning Avenue, BOURNEMOUTH, DORSET, BH5 1NR.
SIMPSON, Mr. Adrian Charles, BSc ACA *1987;* Rowlinson Constructions Ltd London House, London Road South Poynton, STOCKPORT, CHESHIRE, SK12 1YP.
SIMPSON, Mr. Adrian Keith, BSc ACA *1998;* 1 Ambervale Close, Littleover, DERBY, DE23 3YB.
SIMPSON, Mr. Adrian Lyndon, BSc FCA *1988;* 23 Caxmere Drive, Wollaton, NOTTINGHAM, NG8 1GG.
SIMPSON, Mr. Adrian Richard, BSc ACA *1982;* 11 Alder Close, Englefield Green, EGHAM, SURREY, TW20 0LU.
SIMPSON, Mr. Alan John, FCA *1967;* Mirador, 28 The Rath, MILFORD HAVEN, SA73 2QA. (Life Member)
SIMPSON, Mr. Alan Prestwood, MA ACA *1989;* 2377 S Youngfield Way, LAKEWOOD, CO 80228, UNITED STATES.
SIMPSON, Mr. Alec John, BA ACA *1997;* Waverley, Pershore Road, Eckington, PERSHORE, WORCESTERSHIRE, WR10 3AP.
SIMPSON, Mr. Alexander David Robert, BA ACA *2007;* 22 Parkfield Drive, Tyldesley, MANCHESTER, M29 8QJ.
SIMPSON, Mr. Alexander Harvey, BA ACA *1994;* Allens Arthur Robinson, Deutsche Bank Place, Corner Hunter and Phillip Streets, SYDNEY, NSW 2000, AUSTRALIA.
SIMPSON, Mr. Alexander James Arthur, BA ACA *2005;* with Ernst & Young LLP, 1 More London Place, LONDON, SE1 2AF.
SIMPSON, Ms. Alison Jane, BA ACA *1997;* 26 Spencer Walk, LONDON, SW15 1PL.
SIMPSON, Miss. Alison Marina, BSc ACA *1996;* KPMG Hong Kong, 8/F Princes Building, CENTRAL, HONG KONG ISLAND, HONG KONG SAR.
SIMPSON, Miss. Amanda Jane, ACA *2009;* 31 Ringwood Road, Headington, OXFORD, OX3 8JB.
SIMPSON, Mrs. Amanda Rhean, MA ACA *1999;* 146 Rakau Road, Hataitai, WELLINGTON 6021, NEW ZEALAND.
SIMPSON, Mrs. Amy Louise, BA ACA AMCT *1998;* 6 Finwood Road, Rowington, WARWICK, CV35 7DH.
SIMPSON, Mr. Andrew David, BSc ACA *2007;* Andreas Stihl Ltd Stihl House, Stanhope Road, CAMBERLEY, GU15 3YT.
SIMPSON, Mr. Andrew Honeyman, BA ACA *1986;* 173b Central Road, MORDEN, SURREY, SM4 5SP.
SIMPSON, Mr. Andrew Howard, BA ACA *1998;* 3 Toller Road, Quorn, LOUGHBOROUGH, LEICESTERSHIRE, LE12 8AH.
SIMPSON, Mr. Andrew John, MA ACA *1991;* Pinetree Barns, Harts Lane, Bawburgh, NORWICH, NR9 3LT.
SIMPSON, Mr. Andrew Mark, BA(Hons) ACA *2000;* 23 Birchwood Avenue, Woodlands Park, North Gosforth, NEWCASTLE UPON TYNE, NE13 6PZ.
SIMPSON, Mr. Andrew Roger, FCA *1962;* P O Box 2794, PORT ALFRED, EASTERN CAPE, 6170, SOUTH AFRICA.
•**SIMPSON, Mrs. Angela Fay, ACA FCCA** *2008;* Walkers Accountants Limited, 16-18 Devonshire Street, KEIGHLEY, WEST YORKSHIRE, BD21 2DG.
•**SIMPSON, Miss. Anne Elizabeth, BA FCA** *1985;* PricewaterhouseCoopers LLP, Hays Galleria, 1 Hays Lane, LONDON, SE1 2RD. See also PricewaterhouseCoopers
SIMPSON, Mrs. Anne-Marie, BSc ACA *1995;* Mallards, Moulsford, WALLINGFORD, OX10 9HR.
SIMPSON, Mr. Antony Geoffrey, BSc ACA *1991;* 7 Knightthorpe Court, Burns Road, LOUGHBOROUGH, LE11 4NP.
SIMPSON, Mr. Bryan, FCA *1959;* Ashbyrne House, 13 Birch Grove, SPALDING, PE11 2HL. (Life Member)
SIMPSON, Miss. Caroline, BA ACA *2007;* 25 High Road, Cotton End, BEDFORD, MK45 3AA.
SIMPSON, Miss. Caroline Ann, BA ACA *1981;* The Cottage, Goldberdon, CALLINGTON, PL17 7ND. (Life Member)
SIMPSON, Miss. Catherine Ann Howarth, BA(Hons) ACA *2002;* Bells Mills House, Bells Mills, EDINBURGH, EH4 3DG.
•**SIMPSON, Mr. Charles Haddon McBratney, MSc ACA CF** *1988;* (Tax Fac), Saffery Champness, Lion House, Red Lion Street, LONDON, WC1R 4GB.
SIMPSON, Mr. Chris, MChem ACA *2009;* with PKF (UK) LLP, 4th Floor, 3 Hardman Street, MANCHESTER, M3 3HF.
SIMPSON, Mr. Christopher David, BSc FCA *1974;* 96 Mount View Road, LONDON, N4 4JX.
SIMPSON, Mr. Christopher Graham, BA ACA *1987;* 1755 Broadway, NEW YORK, NY 10019, UNITED STATES.
SIMPSON, Mr. Christopher Jay, BSc ACA *2005;* Simmons & Simmons Citypoint, 1 Ropemaker Street, LONDON, EC2Y 9SS.
SIMPSON, Miss. Claire Luan, BSc ACA *1999;* with KPMG LLP, Edward VII Quay, Navigation Way, Ashton-on-Ribble, PRESTON, PR2 2YF.
SIMPSON, Mr. Craig Jonathan, ACA CTA AIIT *1998;* with Ernst & Young LLP, 1 Colmore Square, BIRMINGHAM, B4 6HQ.
•**SIMPSON, Mr. Dale Howard, FCA** *1973;* (Tax Fac), Thomas Westcott, 26-28 Southernhay East, EXETER, DEVON, EX1 1NS.
SIMPSON, Mr. David, BSc FCA *1977;* 5 Geary House, Mendip Way, STEVENAGE, HERTFORDSHIRE, SG1 6GX.
SIMPSON, Mr. David Alan, MA ACA *1986;* 28 Keynshambury Road, CHELTENHAM, GL52 6HB.
SIMPSON, Mr. David Anthony, BA ACA *1990;* KMR Group, Ealing Gateway, 26-30 Uxbridge Road, LONDON, W5 2BP.
SIMPSON, Mr. David Anthony, MA FCA *1996;* with BDO LLP, 55 Baker Street, LONDON, W1U 7EU.
•**SIMPSON, Mr. David Broadbent, FCA** *1953;* D.B. Simpson, Prospect House, Prospect Street, HUDDERSFIELD, HD1 2NU.
•**SIMPSON, Mr. David Donald Lionel, BSc ACA** *1999;* with KPMG LLP, Altius House, 1 North Fourth Street, MILTON KEYNES, MK9 1NE.
SIMPSON, Mr. David Headon, MA FCA *1966;* 1 South Terrace, DARLINGTON, COUNTY DURHAM, DL1 5JA. (Life Member)
SIMPSON, Mr. David Lawrence, BA ACA *1992;* 11 Redes Close, HOOK, RG27 9UX.
SIMPSON, Mr. David Michael, BA FCA *1967;* 2A Eglinton Park, DUN LAOGHAIRE, COUNTY DUBLIN, IRELAND. (Life Member)
SIMPSON, Mr. David Robert, ACA *1985;* 1 Rose Gardens, Woodgates Road East Bergholt, COLCHESTER, CO7 6RH.
SIMPSON, Mr. David Stuart, FCA *1970;* Telepara, 1 Shillingridge Park, Frieth Road, MARLOW, BUCKINGHAMSHIRE, SL7 2QX. (Life Member)
SIMPSON, Mr. David William, BSc(Econ) ACA FRSA DChA *1980;* Beacondawn Limited, 43a Uxbridge Road, LONDON, W12 8LA.
SIMPSON, Mr. Denis Akers, FCA *1953;* Coryton, 8 Bull Hill, FOWEY, PL23 1BZ. (Life Member)
•**SIMPSON, Mr. Derek Ewan, BSc FCA** *1991;* The P&A Partnership, 69 Buchanan Street, GLASGOW, G1 3HL.
SIMPSON, Mr. Derrick John, BCom ACA *2007;* Flat 32 Wheel House, 1 Burrells Wharf Square, LONDON, E14 3TA.
SIMPSON, Mr. Donald, FCA *1954;* 6 Hillside Road, ST AUSTELL, CORNWALL, PL25 4DW. (Life Member)
SIMPSON, Mr. Edward Barnaby Russell, MA ACA *1999;* Carbon Trust 6th Floor, 5 New Street Square, LONDON, EC4A 3BF.
SIMPSON, Mr. Edward Harvey, BSc FCA *1962;* 80 The Ryde, HATFIELD, AL9 5DL. (Life Member)
SIMPSON, Miss. Eleanor, BA ACA *2010;* 32a Colestown Street, LONDON, SW11 3EH.
SIMPSON, Mrs. Elizabeth, BA ACA *1998;* 1 Ambervale Close, Littleover, DERBY, DE23 3YB.
SIMPSON, Miss. Elizabeth, LLB ACA CTA *2002;* with Deloitte LLP, 1 City Square, LEEDS, WEST YORKSHIRE, LS1 2AL.
SIMPSON, Mr. Gareth Andrew, ACA *2008;* Group Accounts & Taxation, Hutchison Whampoa Limited, Hutchison House 22/F, 10 Harcourt Road, CENTRAL, HONG KONG SAR.
SIMPSON, Mr. Geoffrey, BSc ACA *1988;* Hillcrest, Springfield Park, DURHAM, DH1 4LS.
SIMPSON, Mr. Geoffrey William, MBA BA FCA *1976;* 17 Westray Close, Bramcote Moor, NOTTINGHAM, NG9 3GP.
SIMPSON, Mr. George Basil, FCA *1942;* Hoopers Farm Chardstock, AXMINSTER, DEVON, EX13 7BY. (Life Member)
SIMPSON, Mr. Gordon Iain, BCom ACA *1984;* Isentry Limited, Unit 2 The Square Industrial Units Grampound Road, TRURO, CORNWALL, TR2 4DS.
SIMPSON, Mr. Gordon Stanley, FCA *1951;* Silver Birches, Stanford Hill, LYMINGTON, SO41 8DE. (Life Member)
•**SIMPSON, Mr. Graham Cooper, FCA** *1969;* (Tax Fac), Percy Gore & Co, 39 Hawley Square, MARGATE, KENT, CT9 1NZ.
SIMPSON, Mr. Gregory Paul, BSc ACA *1992;* 73 Ottways Lane, ASHTEAD, KT21 2PS.
•**SIMPSON, Mr. Gregory Robert, BSc ACA** *1998;* with KPMG LLP, 15 Canada Square, LONDON, E14 5GL.
SIMPSON, Mr. Harry, BBLS ACA *2010;* 67 Merrion Road, Ballsbridge, DUBLIN 4, COUNTY DUBLIN, IRELAND.
SIMPSON, Mrs. Helen Grace, MA ACA *1993;* 38 Finsbury Park Road, LONDON, N4 2JX.
SIMPSON, Mrs. Helen Mary, BSc(Hons) ACA *2002;* 6 Tanners Row, WOKINGHAM, BERKSHIRE, RG41 4EL.
•**SIMPSON, Mrs. Helen Vanessa, BA ACA** *1990;* 19 Egerton Drive, Hale, ALTRINCHAM, WA15 8EF.
SIMPSON, Mr. Heward Nigel Clair, MA FCA *1976;* with ICAEW, Metropolitan House, 321 Avebury Boulevard, MILTON KEYNES, MK9 2FZ.
SIMPSON, Mr. Hinton Stuart, BSc FCA *1979;* 17 Wood Crescent, Rogerstone, NEWPORT, NP10 0AL.
SIMPSON, Mr. Ian, FCA *1971;* The Laurels, Birchwood Grove Road, BURGESS HILL, RH15 0DL. (Life Member)
•**SIMPSON, Mr. Ian Brian, BSc ACA** *2002;* Humphrey & Co, Curtis House, Third Avenue, HOVE, EAST SUSSEX, BN3 2PD.
SIMPSON, Mr. Ian David, FCA FCMA *1964;* Virginia Lodge, 8a Croft Road, EVESHAM, WORCESTERSHIRE, WR11 4NE.
SIMPSON, Mr. Ian Patrick, FCA *1966;* 9 Grandfield Crescent, Radcliffe-on-Trent, NOTTINGHAM, NG12 1AN.
•**SIMPSON, Mr. Ian Stanley, FCA** *1976;* (Tax Fac), Goldwyns Limited, Rutland House, 90-92 Baxter Avenue, SOUTHEND-ON-SEA, SS2 6HZ.
SIMPSON, Mr. Jack Mitchell, FCA *1968;* 21 Cumberlands, KENLEY, CR8 5DX.
SIMPSON, Mr. James Allen, FCA *1968;* 15 St. Marys Close, SOUTHAM, CV47 1EW. (Life Member)
SIMPSON, Mr. James Lonsdale, BSc ACA *1999;* Flat 21, Cavendish Mansions, Mill Lane, LONDON, NW6 1TE.
SIMPSON, Mr. James Robert, BA ACA *1982;* 15 Veronica Road, LONDON, SW17 8QL.
•**SIMPSON, Mrs. Jenny, BSc FCA DChA** *1994;* 7 Reid Avenue, Bearsden, GLASGOW, G61 3DR.
SIMPSON, Mr. Jeremy Charles, BSc FCA *1992;* Invesco Asset Management Pacific Limited, 41/F, Citibank Tower, 3 Garden Road, CENTRAL, HONG KONG ISLAND HONG KONG SAR.
SIMPSON, Mr. Jeremy John Cobbett, BA ACA *1996;* Smiths Medical International Limited, HYTHE, KENT, CT21 6JL.
•**SIMPSON, Mr. John Allwood, BA ACA** *1984;* J A Simpson & Co Ltd, 48 Bredbury Green, Romiley, STOCKPORT, SK6 3DN.
SIMPSON, Mr. John Charles, MSc BA FCA *1978;* 9 Chestnut Avenue, Boston Spa, WETHERBY, LS23 6EE.
SIMPSON, Mr. John Colin, FCA *1968;* Ruthavon, Granby Road, Bradwell, HOPE VALLEY, DERBYSHIRE, S33 9HU. (Life Member)
SIMPSON, Mr. John Derek, FCA *1957;* 12 Cobbett's Way, WILMSLOW, SK9 6HN. (Life Member)
SIMPSON, Mr. John Edward, BA(Hons) ACA *2004;* 3 Wallace Circle, LONDONDERRY, NH 03053, UNITED STATES.
•**SIMPSON, Mr. John Hart, FCA** *1980;* JHS Associates, 37 Cricklewood Drive, Penshaw, HOUGHTON LE SPRING, TYNE AND WEAR, DH4 7EA.
SIMPSON, Mr. John Keith, FCA *1950;* 129 Lovelace Drive, Pyrford, WOKING, GU22 8RZ. (Life Member)
SIMPSON, Mr. Jonathan, BSc ACA *1999;* 3 Pickwick Drive, Blundeston, LOWESTOFT, NR32 5BX.
SIMPSON, Mr. Jonathan Paul, BSc ACA *2002;* 10 Kepstorn Road, LEEDS, LS16 5HL.
SIMPSON, Mr. Joseph Patrick, BCom ACA *1993;* 14 Tara Green, Ballymoney, Gorey, WEXFORD, COUNTY WEXFORD, IRELAND.
SIMPSON, Miss. Julie Fiona, BSc ACA *1989;* 74 Camden Park, TUNBRIDGE WELLS, KENT, TN2 5BB.
SIMPSON, Mr. Justin Anthony, ACA BBusSci *2011;* 19 Whittingstall Road, LONDON, SW6 4EA.
SIMPSON, Miss. Katey Nicolina, BA ACA *1995;* 1 Myrtle Cottages, Stoke Canon, EXETER, EX5 4AP.
SIMPSON, Miss. Kathryn, ACA *2008;* 9/3 Powderhall Rigg, EDINBURGH, EH7 4GG.
SIMPSON, Mrs. Katy, BCom ACA *1999;* 95 Wood Lane, Harborne, BIRMINGHAM, B17 9AY.
•**SIMPSON, Mr. Kenneth Gordon, BSc ACA** *1990;* Richard Sexton & Co, St. Margaret's, 3 Manor Road, COLCHESTER, CO3 3LU.
SIMPSON, Mr. Kevin John, BA(Hons) ACA *2003;* Room 1/440, Ford Motor Co Ltd Eagle Way, Great Warley, BRENTWOOD, CM13 3BW.
SIMPSON, Miss. Laura Jane, BSc ACA *1995;* 25 Evelyn Road, LONDON, SW19 8NU.
SIMPSON, Mr. Lawrence Elliott, BCom ACA *1999;* 6 Sergison Road, HAYWARDS HEATH, WEST SUSSEX, RH16 1HS.
SIMPSON, Mr. Lee John, BA ACA *2005;* 8, Silver Birch Close, BOLTON, BL6 4GF.
SIMPSON, Mr. Leslie Gordon Richard, FCA *1954;* 10 Brimstone Close, Chelsfield, ORPINGTON, BR6 7ST. (Life Member)
•**SIMPSON, Mr. Lyndon Acford, FCA** *1977;* Simpson & Co (Accountants) Limited, 21 High Street, LUTTERWORTH, LEICESTERSHIRE, LE17 4AT.
SIMPSON, Mr. Malcolm, FCA *1965;* Glenridding, Elm Bank Road, WYLAM, NE41 8HT.
SIMPSON, Mr. Mark, ACA *2009;* 115 Buckler Court, Eden Grove, LONDON, N7 8GQ.
•**SIMPSON, Mr. Mark Bellas, ACA** *1983;* Respirex International, Unit F, Kingsfield Business Centre Philanthropic Road, REDHILL, SURREY, RH1 4DP.
SIMPSON, Mr. Mark Jeremy, BA FCA *1981;* 1 St. Cuthberts Close, Englefield Green, EGHAM, TW20 0QN.
SIMPSON, Mr. Mark Richard, BSc ACA *1987;* The Whitehouse, 26 Church Walk, ATHERSTONE, CV9 1AJ.
SIMPSON, Mr. Martyn James, BSc ACA *1989;* 20 Benenden Green, ALRESFORD, SO24 9PF.
SIMPSON, Mrs. Mary Jane, BA ACA *1986;* Holly House, 22 High Street, Long Buckby, NORTHAMPTON, NN6 7RD.
SIMPSON, Mr. Maurice, FCA *1950;* 3 The Drive, Roman RoadBirstall, LEICESTER, LE4 4BL. (Life Member)
•**SIMPSON, Mrs. Melinda Jayne, BSc ACA** *1985;* Chantrey Vellacott DFK LLP, Town Wall House, Balkerne Hill, COLCHESTER, CO3 3AD.
•**SIMPSON, Mr. Michael, BA FCA** *1986;* PricewaterhouseCoopers, Sixty Circular Road, Douglas, ISLE OF MAN, IM1 1SA.
SIMPSON, Mr. Michael, BSc ACA *2010;* 4 Union Road, Deepcut, CAMBERLEY, GU16 6TE.
SIMPSON, Mr. Michael Anthony, BA ACA *1982;* 38 The Street, Brundall, NORWICH, NR13 5LJ.

SIMPSON, Mr. Michael Harry Trevor, FCA *1960;* Hawthorn Cottage, 26 Gardeners Way, St. Issey, WADEBRIDGE, PL27 7RN. (Life Member)
SIMPSON, Mr. Neil, ACA *2003;* 80a Lincroft Crescent, Chapel Fields, COVENTRY, CV5 8GU.
•SIMPSON, Mr. Neil Ferguson, MA FCA *1978;* (Tax Fac), Neil Simpson & Co, 12 Church Road, Bengeo, HERTFORD, SG14 3DP.
SIMPSON, Miss. Nicola, BA(Hons) ACA *2001;* with Deloitte LLP, Athene Place, 66 Shoe Lane, LONDON, EC4A 3BQ.
SIMPSON, Mr. Norman, BSc FCA *1974;* 1 Stanmore Gardens, RICHMOND, TW9 2HN.
SIMPSON, Mr. Patrick David, BA(Hons) ACA *2000;* Hypovereinsbank Moor House, 120 London Wall, LONDON, EC2Y 5ET.
SIMPSON, Mr. Paul, BA ACA *1999;* Carphone Warehouse Northbank House, 1 Siemens Road Irlam, MANCHESTER, M44 5AH.
SIMPSON, Mr. Paul Anthony, BA ACA *2003;* 2 Rockliffe Road, BATH, BA2 6QN.
SIMPSON, Mr. Paul Ernest, BA ACA *1982;* 67 Coniston Avenue, TUNBRIDGE WELLS, TN4 9SR.
SIMPSON, Mr. Paul Michael, MA ACA *1983;* Hawling House, Hawling, CHELTENHAM, GLOUCESTERSHIRE, GL54 5TA.
SIMPSON, Mr. Paul Simon, BA ACA *1995;* 14 Langwith Avenue, Collingham, WETHERBY, LS22 5DD.
•SIMPSON, Mrs. Paula Ellen, BA FCA *1993;* Simpson Accountants Limited, 24 Oxfield Park Drive, Old Stratford, MILTON KEYNES, MK19 6DP.
SIMPSON, Mr. Peter David, MA MBA FCA *1989;* 30 Rotherwood Road, LONDON, SW15 1JZ.
•SIMPSON, Mr. Peter Geoffrey, ACA *2004;* Bache Brown & Co Ltd, Swinford House, Albion Street, BRIERLEY HILL, WEST MIDLANDS, DY5 3EE. See also Swinford House LLP
SIMPSON, Dr. Peter James, PhD ACA MInstP CPhys *2000;* with PricewaterhouseCoopers LLP, 1 Embankment Place, LONDON, WC2N 6RH.
SIMPSON, Mr. Peter Robert Freeman, FCA *1976;* Hillside Farmhouse, Sissinghurst, CRANBROOK, TN17 2JH.
SIMPSON, Mr. Peter Ronald, FCA *1972;* 2992 Chippewa Avenue, SIMI VALLEY, CA 93063, UNITED STATES.
SIMPSON, Mr. Philip, LLB ACA *2006;* Flat 2, 2 Holmbush Road, LONDON, SW15 3LE.
SIMPSON, Mr. Richard Grant, BA ACA *1997;* Welbeck Investment Management, 49 Welbeck Street, LONDON, W1G 9XN.
•SIMPSON, Mr. Richard Neil, MA ACA *1981;* (Tax Fac), haysmacintyre, Fairfax House, 15 Fulwood Place, LONDON, WC1V 6AY.
SIMPSON, Robert Bazeth Blyth, Esq OBE FCA *1937;* Flat 67, Seabright, West Parade, WORTHING, BN11 3QU. (Life Member)
SIMPSON, Mr. Robert Gordon, BCom FCA *1968;* 5 Wensley Road, LEEDS, LS7 2LX. (Life Member)
SIMPSON, Mr. Robert Ian, FCA *1969;* NONE, NONE.
SIMPSON, Mr. Robert Leonard, FCA *1963;* 33 Copthorne Road, Croxley Green, RICKMANSWORTH, WD3 4AB.
•SIMPSON, Mr. Robert Mark, BA ACA *1987;* (Tax Fac), Simpson Burgess Nash Ltd, Ground Floor, Maclaren House, Lancastrian Office Centre, Talbot Road, Old Trafford MANCHESTER M32 0FP. See also Dialmode (328) Limited
SIMPSON, Miss. Roberta May, BA ACA *2006;* Flat B, 8 Northiam Street, Hackney, LONDON, E9 7HQ.
SIMPSON, Mr. Robin Henry, BBS FCA *1978;* 67 Merrion Road, DUBLIN 4, COUNTY DUBLIN, IRELAND.
SIMPSON, Mr. Robin Jonathan, BSc ACA *2006;* 5 Emmbrook Vale, WOKINGHAM, BERKSHIRE, RG41 1PW.
SIMPSON, Mr. Roderick Nicholas Priestley, MA ACA CF *1987;* Room 703, Lloyds of London Insurance Lloyds Building, 1 Lime Street, LONDON, EC3M 7HA.
SIMPSON, Mr. Roger, FCA *1975;* 15 Meltham Close, Heaton Mersey, STOCKPORT, SK4 3BD.
SIMPSON, Mr. Ronald, FCA *1960;* 6 High Street, Broom, BIGGLESWADE, SG18 9NP. (Life Member)
SIMPSON, Mr. Ronald Peter, FCA *1953;* 492 Ringwood Road, FERNDOWN, BH22 9AZ. (Life Member)
SIMPSON, Mr. Russell Edward, BA(Hons) ACA *2010;* Flat 2, Shiplake Court, Leconfield Road, LONDON, N5 2SB.
SIMPSON, Mr. Russell Grant, BA(Hons) ACA *2002;* 21 Laurel Gardens, LONDON, W7 3JG.
SIMPSON, Mr. Samuel Jon, LLB ACA *1999;* Broadchapel, Lochmaben, LOCKERBIE, DUMFRIESSHIRE, DG11 1RL.
SIMPSON, Mrs. Sandra Jane Penelope, BSc ACA *1990;* Hillcrest, Springfield Park, DURHAM, DH1 4LS.
SIMPSON, Mrs. Sara, BSc ACA *1996;* 128 Hesketh Lane, Tarleton, PRESTON, PR4 6AS.
SIMPSON, Ms. Sarah, BA ACA *1993;* c/o Imani Development, PostNet Suite No 303, Private Bag x 15, SOMERSET WEST, 7129, SOUTH AFRICA.
SIMPSON, Mrs. Sarah Anne, BSc ACA *2003;* with KPMG LLP, Quayside House, 110 Quayside, NEWCASTLE UPON TYNE, NE1 3DX.
SIMPSON, Mrs. Shirley Anna, MA FCA *1992;* Broadland Housing Association, Norwich City Football Club, Jarrold Strand, Carrow Road, NORWICH, NR1 1HU.
•SIMPSON, Mr. Stanley John, FCA *1973;* S.J. Simpson, Anchor & Hope Cottage, 1 Cove Hill, Perranarworthal, TRURO, CORNWALL TR3 7QQ.
•SIMPSON, Mr. Stephen John, BA FCA *1988;* with PricewaterhouseCoopers LLP, 2 Humber Quays, Wellington Street West, HULL, HU1 2BN.
SIMPSON, Mr. Steven John, BA FCA *1983;* 49 Moor Park Court, NORTH SHIELDS, TYNE AND WEAR, NE29 8AH.
SIMPSON, Mr. Steven Norman, BA ACA *1988;* Responsive Engineering, Kingsway South, Team Valley, GATESHEAD, TYNE AND WEAR, NE11 0JL.
SIMPSON, Mr. Stuart Campbell, BA ACA *1995;* The Old Bank, Giggs Hill Road, THAMES DITTON, SURREY, KT7 0BT.
SIMPSON, Mr. Stuart Harris, BA FCA *1983;* A C L Packaging Solutions Ltd Unit F, Argent Court Hook Rise South, SURBITON, KT6 7NL.
SIMPSON, Mrs. Susan Angela, BA ACA *2004;* 39 Radnormere Drive, Cheadle Hulme, CHEADLE, CHESHIRE, SK8 5JS.
SIMPSON, Mr. Terence Colin Frank, FCA *1962;* Beckett, Manor Road, Goring, READING, RG8 9ED. (Life Member)
SIMPSON, Mr. Thomas, ACA *2009;* Flat 5 Normanhurst, Vera Road, LONDON, SW6 6QN.
SIMPSON, Mr. Thomas, MEng ACA *2011;* 98 Hewlett Road, CHELTENHAM, GLOUCESTERSHIRE, GL52 6AR.
SIMPSON, Mr. Thomas Alexander, BA ACA *1984;* 26 Templecombe Drive, Springfield HeightsSharples, BOLTON, BL1 7LT.
SIMPSON, Mr. Tom, BSc ACA *2007;* Wanganui 38 Causie Drive, La Rue de Causie St. Clement, JERSEY, JE2 6SR.
•SIMPSON, Mr. Tommie, BSc FCA *1991;* Torr Waterfield Ltd, Park House, 37 Clarence Street, LEICESTER, LE1 3RW. See also TMH Simpson Limited
SIMPSON, Mr. William, ACA *2008;* with Smith & Williamson (Bristol) LLP, Portwall Place, Portwall Lane, BRISTOL, BS1 6NA.
SIMPSON, Mr. William Anthony Hamish, MA FCA *1980;* Nachmittagsweg 6, 30539 HANOVER, GERMANY.
SIMPSON, Mr. William Gerald, BA ACA *2003;* with Grant Thornton UK LLP, 4 Hardman Square, Spinningfields, MANCHESTER, M3 3EB.
SIMPSON, Mr. William Henry Kenneth, BSc FCA *1978;* Le Petit Manoir, Le Neuf Chemin, St John, JERSEY, JE3 4EH.
SIMPSON, Mr. William Russell, BCom FCA *1950;* Rua Mira Serra 32, Galamares, 2710, SINTRA, PORTUGAL. (Life Member)
SIMPSON CARDWELL, Mrs. Nicola Samantha, BSc ACA *1993;* Oakwood Church Lane, Grayshott, HINDHEAD, SURREY, GU26 6LY.
SIMPSON-DENT, Mr. Jonathan Andrew, BA FCA *1993;* Carisbrook, 19 Briar Walk, Putney, LONDON, SW15 6UD.
•SIMPSON-PRICE, Mrs. Dianne Elizabeth, BSc ACA *1983;* (Tax Fac), Baker Tilly UK Audit LLP, Hartwell House, 55-61 Victoria Street, BRISTOL, BS1 6AD.
SIMPSON-SCOTT, Miss. Vivien Louise, ACA *2011;* 20 Briar Road, Hethersett, NORWICH, NR9 3FG.
SIMS, Mr. Adam Duncan, BEng ACA *1992;* Laburnum House Kitty Frisk, Corbridge Road, HEXHAM, NORTHUMBERLAND, NE46 1UN.
SIMS, Mr. Andrew Brian, BSc ACA *1990;* Level 15, Menara Prudential, 10 Jalan Sultan Ismail, 50250 KUALA LUMPUR, FEDERAL TERRITORY, MALAYSIA.
SIMS, Mr. Andrew Brodie, BSc(Hons) ACA *2011;* Park Fauld Barn, Durdar, CARLISLE, CA5 7LJ.
SIMS, Mr. Andrew John Hugh Macintyre, BSc ACA *1997;* Alexander Gallo Holdings LLC, 2700 Centennial Tower, 101 Marietta Street, ATLANTA, GA 30303, UNITED STATES.
SIMS, Mr. Andrew Mitford, FCA *1974;* Ashdene, 85a Oakhill Road, SEVENOAKS, KENT, TN13 1NU.
SIMS, Mrs. Carolyn, BSc ACA *1992;* 15 Ridgmont Road, ST. ALBANS, HERTFORDSHIRE, AL1 3AG.
SIMS, Miss. Catherine Jane, BSc ACA *1992;* The Old Granary, East Street, West Chiltington, PULBOROUGH, WEST SUSSEX, RH20 2JY.
SIMS, Mr. Christopher John, MA FCA *1981;* 21 Davis Close, Barrs Court, BRISTOL, BS30 7BU.
SIMS, Mr. David, MA FCA *1979;* 1 Heathfield, COBHAM, KT11 2QY.
•SIMS, Mr. David Barry, BSc ACA *1986;* R T Marke & Co Limited, 69 High Street, BIDEFORD, DEVON, EX39 2AT.
SIMS, Mrs. Emma Jane, ACA *2006;* 18 Avalon Road, BRISTOL, BS5 8RX.
SIMS, Mrs. Fiona Margaret, BSc ACA *1987;* Lodge Farm Uppingham Road, Skeffington, LEICESTER, LE7 9YE.
SIMS, Mr. Frank, BA FCA *1970;* Birchdale, 24 Oakland Place, BUCKHURST HILL, IG9 5JZ. (Life Member)
SIMS, Mr. Gary David, BA ACA *1991;* The Orchard, 66 Norton Road, LETCHWORTH GARDEN CITY, SG6 1AE.
•SIMS, Mr. Gerald, FCA *1986;* Accounting Associates Ltd, 3 Whitears Way, Kingsteignton, NEWTON ABBOT, DEVON, TQ12 3HQ.
SIMS, Mr. Guy Rohan, BSc ACA *1993;* 3 Manor Farm Court, Cottenham, CAMBRIDGE, CB24 8RD.
SIMS, Mr. Hugh Greville, FCA *1961;* 7 Fallowfields, Oulton, LOWESTOFT, SUFFOLK, NR32 4WQ. (Life Member)
SIMS, Mr. Jack, ACA *2011;* 133 Northstand Apartments, Highbury Stadium Square, LONDON, N5 1FL.
SIMS, Mr. John Andrew, BSc ACA *1995;* 101 COLONIAL RIDGE NORTH, MOORESTOWN, NJ 08057, UNITED STATES.
•SIMS, Mr. Julian Leslie, ACA CTA *1991;* (Tax Fac), Hunt Johnston Stokes Ltd, 12-14 Carlton Place, SOUTHAMPTON, SO15 2EA.
SIMS, Miss. Karen, BSc ACA *1993;* 34 Little Lullaway, BASILDON, ESSEX, SS15 5JH.
•SIMS, Mr. Keith James, FCA *1968;* F.E. Sidaway Son & Co, 5-6 Long Lane, ROWLEY REGIS, B65 0JA.
SIMS, Ms. Lorna Jean, ACA *2006;* with Chantrey Vellacott DFK LLP, Russell Square House, 10-12 Russell Square, LONDON, WC1B 5LF.
SIMS, Mrs. Margaret Jean, BSc ACA *1988;* The Norfolk Truffle Co, Park Farm, 23 High Green, Brooke, NORWICH, NR15 1HR.
SIMS, Mr. Mark David, ACA CA(SA) *2008;* 13A York Street, TWICKENHAM, TW1 3JZ.
SIMS, Mr. Mark Lewis, ACA *2010;* 68 Friezland Lane, Brownhills, WALSALL, WEST MIDLANDS, WS8 7AR.
SIMS, Mrs. Mary Elizabeth, FCA *1975;* Lantern House, Wildmoor Lane, Sherfield-on-Loddon, HOOK, HAMPSHIRE, RG27 0HJ.
SIMS, Mr. Michael John, BSc ACA *1997;* Old Town House, 3 Tyllwyd Road, NEWPORT, NP20 4LS.
SIMS, Mr. Michael Peter, FCA *1975;* Capital Tower, Waterloo Road, LONDON, SE1 8RT. (Life Member)
SIMS, Mr. Neil, BA(Hons) ACA *2003;* Haven House, Bradbourne, ASHBOURNE, DE6 1PB.
SIMS, Neville William, Esq MBE FCA *1957;* (Member of Council 1981 - 1999), 15 Westminster Crescent, Cyncoed, CARDIFF, CF23 6SE.
SIMS, Mr. Nicholas Richard, BSc ACA *1997;* 10 Norbury Avenue, WATFORD, WD24 4PJ.
SIMS, Mr. Nigel Philip Benford, BSc ACA *1987;* Lodge Farm, Uppingham Road, Skeffington, LEICESTER, LE7 9YE.
SIMS, Mr. Robert Leslie, MSci ACA *2009;* 58 The Willows, Bradley Stoke, BRISTOL, BS32 8HJ.
SIMS, Mr. Stephen John Petter, FCA *1968;* 22 Hookway, CREDITON, EX17 3PU.
SIMS, Mrs. Tracey Ann, ACA *2009;* 7 Ashcombe, ROCHFORD, SS4 1SW.
SIMSON, Mr. Daniel Michael Nicolas, MA FCA JDipMA *1958;* Flat 20, Pegasus Court, Station Road, BROADWAY, WORCESTERSHIRE, WR12 7DE. (Life Member)
SIMSON, Mrs. Marie-Therese Dominique, BSc ACA *1988;* 60 Stile Hall Gardens, Chiswick, LONDON, W4 3BU.
•SIMSON, Mr. Wallace, FCA *1949;* Wallace Simson, 4 Holland Close, STANMORE, MIDDLESEX, HA7 3AN.
SIN, Ms. Ai Chie, BSc ACA *2006;* Flat 73 Settlers Court, 17 Newport Avenue, LONDON, E14 2DG.
SIN, Mr. Benson, BSc ACA *2005;* with PKF (UK) LLP, Farringdon Place, 20 Farringdon Road, LONDON, EC1M 3AP.
SIN, Mrs. Jane Patricia, BSc FCA *1992;* The Mauritius Commercial Bank Ltd, Sir William Newton, PORT LOUIS, TQ1 1DE, MAURITIUS.
SIN, Mr. Ka Ming Camon, ACA *2008;* HOUSE 31 PALM SPRING VILLA, 3800 LONG DONG AVENUE, PUDONG 201210, CHINA.
SIN, Miss. Nicole Wai Chin, BSc ACA *1997;* No.33 Jalan Taman Pantai, Bukit Pantai, 59100 KUALA LUMPUR, FEDERAL TERRITORY, MALAYSIA.
SIN, Mr. Sai Kit Martin, ACA *2007;* Flat G 10 Floor Block 2, Tsing Yi Garden, TSING YI, NT, HONG KONG SAR.
SIN, Mr. To Sang, BA ACA *1992;* 17 Kent Road, KOWLOON TONG, KOWLOON, HONG KONG SAR.
SIN, Ms. Tse Ming Monica, ACA *2008;* Rm.E 22/F Tower 10, Le Point, Tiu King Leng, TSEUNG KWAN O, NEW TERRITORIES, HONG KONG SAR.
SIN, Mr. Wai Sang, BA ACA *1990;* 17 Kent Road, KOWLOON TONG, KOWLOON, HONG KONG SAR.
SIN, Miss. Wan Lin, MPhil BSc ACA *2004;* Block 104A Ang Mo Kio St 11 #07-69, SINGAPORE 560104, SINGAPORE.
SIN, Ms. Wing Hung, ACA *2007;* Flat B3, 11th Floor, Block B, Po Wing Building, 235 - 241 Yee Kuk Street, SHAM SHUI PO KOWLOON HONG KONG SAR.
SIN, Mr. Yiu Sang, BSc ACA *1991;* 29A Goldwin Heights, 2 Seymour Road, MID LEVELS, HONG KONG ISLAND, HONG KONG SAR.
SIN, Mr. Yuen Ko Terence, ACA *2005;* 11/F, Ka Wah Bank Ctr, 232 Des Vozus Road, CENTRAL, HONG KONG ISLAND, HONG KONG SAR.
SIN FAI LAM, Mr. Andre, FCA *1973;* Swan Cottage, Low Road, Norton Subcourse, NORWICH, NR14 6SD. (Life Member)
SIN YAN TOO, Mr. Denis Patrick Siow Yive Cheong, FCA *1992;* Sparrow Lane, Pope Hennessey Street, CUREPIPE, MAURITIUS, MAURITIUS.
SINAGINA, Miss. Tatjana, ACA *2010;* Flat 3 Mayfair Court, Mersey Road, MANCHESTER, M20 2PY.
SINAGOLA, Mrs. Susan Joy, MA FCA *1983;* 48 Sunnybank Road, Bowdon, ALTRINCHAM, WA14 3PW.
SINAI, Mr. James, ACA *2008;* 52 Neale Close, LONDON, N2 0LF.
SINAI, Mr. Sagar Ashwin, ACA *2011;* Berg Kaprow Lewis, 35 Ballards Lane, LONDON, N3 1XW.
SINCLAIR, Mr. Alistair James, BA FCA *1975;* 200 Avenue des Sommets, Apartment 1801, Ile des Soeurs, VERDUN H3E 2B4, QUE, CANADA.
SINCLAIR, Mr. Alistair James Richard, BA(Hons) ACA *2010;* Commercial Finance (Floor 2), McDonalds Restaurants Ltd, 11-59 High Road, LONDON, N2 8AW.
SINCLAIR, Mrs. Andrea Jane, BSc ACA *1984;* Artemis Trustees Ltd, PO Box 100, Sydney Vane House, St. Peter Port, GUERNSEY, GY1 2HU.
SINCLAIR, Dr. Andrew, PhD BSc(Hons) ACA *2001;* 13 Valley Drive, SEVENOAKS, TN13 1EG.
SINCLAIR, Mr. Andrew Paul, ACA *1991;* Malojo, Restronguet Point, Feock, TRURO, CORNWALL, TR3 6RB.
SINCLAIR, Mr. Charles James Francis, BA FCA *1974;* 6 Highbury Road, LONDON, SW19 7PR.
•SINCLAIR, Mr. Christopher Gill, BA FCA *1972;* Chris Sinclair Accountants Limited, 17 Upper Batley Low Lane, BATLEY, WEST YORKSHIRE, WF17 0AP. See also It Adds Up Ltd
SINCLAIR, Mrs. Clare-Louise, ACA *2008;* 53 Treachers Close, CHESHAM, BUCKINGHAMSHIRE, HP5 2HD.
•SINCLAIR, Mr. David, FCA *1978;* Wheawill & Sudworth, P.O. Box B30, 35 Westgate, HUDDERSFIELD, HD1 1PA.
•SINCLAIR, Mr. David Grant, FCA CF *1972;* Sinclair UK Associates Limited, Roman House, 296 Golders Green Road, LONDON, NW11 9PT. See also Axiom Capital Limited
SINCLAIR, Mr. David Joseph, BSc ARCS ACA *1987;* Glenthorne, 39 Stanhope Road, CROYDON, SURREY, CR0 5NS.
•SINCLAIR, Mr. David Mark, FCA *1991;* Hillbrow, 106 Paynesfield Road, Tatsfield, WESTERHAM, KENT, TN16 2BQ.
•SINCLAIR, Mr. Deryck Allan Peter, FCA *1970;* (Tax Fac), Sinclair & Co, 10 Colson Road, CROYDON, CR0 6UA.
SINCLAIR, Mr. Duncan Morrall, FCA *1971;* The Paddocks, Howe Green, HERTFORD, SG13 8LH.
SINCLAIR, Mrs. Elizabeth Ann, BA ACA MITI *1991;* Fairview, Wych Hill, WOKING, SURREY, GU22 0EU.

SINCLAIR, Mr. Eric Thomas, BA ACA *1982;* 13 Stapleton Avenue, Heaton, BOLTON, BL1 5ES.
SINCLAIR, Mr. Gilbert Menzies Ross Greenwood, FCA *1966;* Inyanga, 2 Thornbury Heights, chandlers Ford, EASTLEIGH, SO53 5DQ. (Life Member)
SINCLAIR, Mr. Hugh Alastair, FCA *1967;* Granby House, Main Street, Granby, NOTTINGHAM, NG13 9PQ.
SINCLAIR, Mr. Hunter, FCA *1970;* Church Cottage, Tregynon, NEWTOWN, POWYS, SY16 3EH.
SINCLAIR, Mr. Iain Richard, MSc ACA *2005;* 3 Purley Place, LONDON, N1 1QA.
SINCLAIR, Mr. James Rory, BSc ACA *1992;* 10 The Paddock, GUILDFORD, GU1 2RQ.
SINCLAIR, Mr. Jared Conan, BSc ACA *1998;* Hillview 5a Cheney Close Binfield, BRACKNELL, BERKSHIRE, RG42 4HF.
SINCLAIR, Mr. Jeremy Mark, BA ACA *2007;* 40 Sugden Road, LONDON, SW11 5EF.
SINCLAIR, Mr. John, BSc FCA *1974;* Anglemoss Ltd, The Hall, Great Finborough, STOWMARKET, SUFFOLK, IP14 3EF.
•**SINCLAIR, Mr. Jonathan Harris, FCA FABRP** *1991;* Sinclair Harris, 46 Vivian Avenue, Hendon Central, LONDON, NW4 3XP.
SINCLAIR, Mrs. Joy Marian, BSc ACA *1982;* 4 Muirfield, Nunthorpe, MIDDLESBROUGH, CLEVELAND, TS7 0JN.
SINCLAIR, Mr. Keith, BA ACA *1984;* PricewaterhouseCoopers Sp. z o.o., Al.Armii Ludowej 14, WARSAW, 00638, POLAND.
SINCLAIR, Mr. Keith Law Grant, FCA *1963;* 16b Bellevue Road, AYR, KA7 2SA.
SINCLAIR, Miss. Kirsty, ACA *1995;* 8 Sentry Close, Wootton, NORTHAMPTON, NN4 6RT.
SINCLAIR, Mrs. Lisa Jane, ACA *1998;* 85 Dornden Drive, Langton Green, TUNBRIDGE WELLS, TN3 0AG.
SINCLAIR, Mrs. Louise Susan, MA ACA *1989;* Lynbourn Faris Lane, Woodham, ADDLESTONE, KT15 3DJ.
•**SINCLAIR, Mr. Malcolm Eugene, FCA** *1991;* Barnbrook Sinclair Limited, 1 High Street, Knaphill, WOKING, SURREY, GU21 2PG. See also The Barnbrook Sinclair Partnership LLP
SINCLAIR, Miss. Maria Pieta, ACA *2010;* 8 Picton Street, Kingsmead, MILTON KEYNES, MK4 4EH.
SINCLAIR, Mrs. Marilyn Joan, BA ACA *1980;* 3 Chevington Drive, STOCKPORT, SK4 3RF. (Life Member)
SINCLAIR, Mr. Mark, BSc ACA *1992;* Raven Russia (Service Company) Ltd, PO Box 522, GUERNSEY, GY1 6EH.
SINCLAIR, Mr. Mark Christopher, BSc ACA *1999;* 34 Creswell, HOOK, HAMPSHIRE, RG27 9TG.
SINCLAIR, Mr. Mark Sean, BSc ACA *1996;* GMO ALM, H S B C, 8-14 Canada Square, LONDON, E14 5HQ.
SINCLAIR, Mr. Maxim Alexander, BA FCA *1969;* Lawn Cottage, Bitchet Green, Seal, SEVENOAKS, KENT, TN15 0ND. (Life Member)
•**SINCLAIR, Mr. Michael Nathan, FCA** *1974;* (Tax Fac), Kingston Smith LLP, Orbital House, 20 Eastern Road, ROMFORD, RM1 3PJ. See also Kingston Smith Limited Liability Partnership, Devonshire Corporate Services LLP and Kingston Smith Consulting LLP
SINCLAIR, Mrs. Nicola Annette, BSc ACA *1990;* Co-Operative Insurance Society, Miller Street, MANCHESTER, M4 4DY.
SINCLAIR, Mr. Patrick Malcolm Mann, BA ACA *2001;* Foremans Cottage Coldrey Farm, Lower Froyle, ALTON, HAMPSHIRE, GU34 4ND.
SINCLAIR, Mr. Paul Jonathan, BA ACA *1991;* 131 Cassiobury Drive, WATFORD, WD17 3AH.
SINCLAIR, Mr. Paul Leonard, MA FCA MRICS *1983;* with PricewaterhouseCoopers LLP, 1 Embankment Place, LONDON, WC2N 6RH.
•**SINCLAIR, Mr. Richard, FCA** *1972;* Richard A. Sinclair, 122 Lickhill Road, STOURPORT-ON-SEVERN, DY13 8SF.
•**SINCLAIR, Mr. Robert Archibald Gilchrist, FCA** *1973;* Artemis Trustees Ltd, PO Box 100, Sydney Vane House Admiral Park, St Peter Port, GUERNSEY, GY1 3EL.
SINCLAIR, Mr. Robert James, BA ACA *2010;* 21 Parma Crescent, LONDON, SW11 1LT.
SINCLAIR, Mr. Robert Neil, FRICS FCA *1974;* Robert Neil & Co, 56 Grosvenor Street, LONDON, W1K 3HZ.
SINCLAIR, Mr. Robin Lewis, BA FCA *1991;* with Deloitte LLP, Saltire Court, 20 Castle Terrace, EDINBURGH, EH1 2DB.
SINCLAIR, Mr. Ronald Thomas, BSc FCA *1978;* 5 Gregory Avenue, Romiley, STOCKPORT, SK6 3JZ.
SINCLAIR, Mr. Thomas Stanley, ACA *2009;* British Sky Broadcasting Ltd, New Horizons Court 1, Grant Way, ISLEWORTH, MIDDLESEX, TW7 5QD.
•**SINCLAIR, Mr. Walter Isaac, FCA** *1959;* (Tax Fac), Walter Sinclair & Co, 81 Wembley Park Drive, WEMBLEY, HA9 8HE. See also Walter Sinclair
SINCLAIR-BROWN, Mr. Frederick John, BCom ACA *1986;* Rudge House, Itchel Lane, Crondall, FARNHAM, SURREY, GU10 5PR.
•**SINDAHA, Mr. Saba Yousef, ACA** *1982;* Deloitte & Touche (M.E.), P.O.Box 990, Bin Ghanem Tower, Hamdan Street, ABU DHABI, UNITED ARAB EMIRATES.
SINDALL, Mr. Andrew John, BSc FCA *1982;* Romany, 100 Oakhill Road, SEVENOAKS, TN13 1NU.
•**SINDEN, Mr. Alan Jeremy, FCA** *1980;* (Tax Fac), Saxby & Sinden Limited, 18 High Street, BUDLEIGH SALTERTON, DEVON, EX9 6LQ.
SINDEN, Mr. David Alan, BA FCA *1981;* 4 Hill House Gardens, Cringleford, NORWICH, NR4 7RB.
SINDEN, Mr. David John, MA FCA *1979;* 86 Cornwall Road, SUTTON, SURREY, SM2 6DS.
SINDEN, Mrs. Janis Sylvia, BA FCA *1990;* (Tax Fac), 10 Colson Road, CROYDON, CR0 6UA.
SINDEN, Mr. Michael Peter George, FCA *1961;* 20 Chilton Lane, RAMSGATE, KENT, CT11 0LQ.
SINDEN, Mr. Nicholas George, BSc ACA *1999;* 6 Christchurch Road, LONDON, SW14 7AA.
SINDEN, Mr. Robert Ian, BSc ACA *2010;* Lord Coutanche House 66-68 Esplanade, Deloitte & Touche, PO Box 403, JERSEY, JE4 8WA.
•**SINDERSON, Mrs. Alison Noelle, LLB FCA** *1988;* Hamlet House, 7 Langham Road, Bowdon, ALTRINCHAM, CHESHIRE, WA14 2HT.
SINDERSON, Mr. Ian Charles, BCom ACA *1987;* Hamlet House, 7 Langham Road, Bowdon, ALTRINCHAM, CHESHIRE, WA14 2HT.
SINDHAR, Miss. Mandeep Kaur, ACA *2011;* 65 Manor Drive, Upton, WIRRAL, MERSEYSIDE, CH49 6LG.
•**SINDLE, Mr. Graham James, FCA** *1974;* (Tax Fac), Thomas Westcott, Queens House, New Street, HONITON, DEVON, EX14 1BJ.
•**SINEL, Miss. Alexandra Moira, BSc FCA** *1991;* Valeur Accountancy Limited, Oaklands, La Rue de la Frontiere, St Mary, JERSEY, JE3 3EG.
SINEL, Mrs. Allyson Janice, ACA *1988;* Solitaire, La Commune, St Saviour, JERSEY, JE2 7HS.
SINEY, Mr. Paul, MEng ACA *1999;* Flat 2, 88 Kings Road, RICHMOND, TW10 6EE.
•**SINFIELD, Mr. John Kenneth, FCA** *1975;* Streets, Fairways, A1/A428 Interchange, Wyboston Lakes, Great North Road, BEDFORD BEDFORDSHIRE MK44 3BZ. See also Streets Whitmarsh Sterland
SINFIELD, Mr. Jonathan Leslie, FCA *1980;* 55 Townsend Lane, HARPENDEN, AL5 2RE.
SINFIELD, Miss. Laura, MA ACA *2006;* 35 Burgh Street, LONDON, N1 8HG.
•**SINFIELD, Mr. Michael John, FCA** *1973;* (Tax Fac), Petersons Accountants Limited, 28 High Street, WITNEY, OXFORDSHIRE, OX28 6RA.
SINFIELD, Mr. Paul Maurice Keith, BA ACA *1998;* 20 Henty Close, Battersea, LONDON, SW11 4AH.
•**SING, Mr. Wilfred Wei Pei, FCA** *1973;* Simmons Gainsford LLP, 5th Floor, 7-10 Chandos Street, Cavendish Square, LONDON, W1G 9DQ.
SINGER, Mr. Andrew Bruce, FCA *1970;* 3 Clevis Hill, PORTHCAWL, CF36 5NT.
SINGER, Mr. Andrew Peter, BA ACA *1981;* 13 Cambridge Road North, LONDON, W4 4AA.
SINGER, Mr. Daniel Charles, BSc ACA *2007;* Flat 9, Hanover House, 6 Olive Shapley Avenue, MANCHESTER, M20 6QG.
SINGER, Mr. Darren David, BA ACA *1995;* Mindshare, 101 St Martins Lane, LONDON, WC2N 4DB.
•**SINGER, Mr. Gordon Michael, BA ACA** *1988;* PricewaterhouseCoopers LLP, Benson House, 33 Wellington Street, LEEDS, LS1 4JP. See also PricewaterhouseCoopers
SINGER, Mr. Jeffrey Michael Ralph, MA FCA CF *2000;* C/Rossello 220 3-1, 08008 BARCELONA, SPAIN.
SINGER, Mr. John Howard, FCA *1970;* 62 Woodhall Gate, PINNER, MIDDLESEX, HA5 4TL. (Life Member)
SINGER, Miss. Lynsey Dryhurst, BSc ACA *2010;* Burleigh Manor Peel Road, Douglas, ISLE OF MAN, IM1 5EP.
SINGER, Mr. Mark David, BSc ACA *1987;* Headlamp Management Ltd, 33 Hawkshead Drive, Knowle, SOLIHULL, WEST MIDLANDS, B93 9QE.
•**SINGER, Mr. Maurice, FCA TEP** *1973;* Browne Craine Associates Limited, Burleigh Manor, Peel Road, Douglas, ISLE OF MAN, IM1 5EP.
SINGER, Mr. Michael Richard, BA ACA *2004;* Ace Group The Ace Building, 100 Leadenhall Street, LONDON, EC3A 3BP.
SINGER, Mr. Nigel David, JP FCA *1971;* 9 Brewery Wharf, Castletown, ISLE OF MAN, IM9 1ES.
•**SINGER, Mr. Stuart, BSc FCA** *1986;* Ramsay Brown and Partners, Ramsay House, 18 Vera Avenue, Grange Park, LONDON, N21 1RA.
SINGER, Mr. Thomas Daniel, BSc ACA *1987;* 242 Sheen Lane, East Sheen, LONDON, SW14 8RL.
SINGERTON, Mr. Kevin Ward, BSc ACA *1980;* 1 Greystones Close, Mardy, ABERGAVENNY, GWENT, NP7 6JZ.
SINGH, Mr. Agni Vijay, MSc BSc ACA *2007;* 36 Silver Oaks Avenue, DLF 1, GURGAON 122001, HARYANA, INDIA.
•**SINGH, Mr. Amanjit, ACA** *1995;* Kajaine Limited, First Floor, Alpine House, Unit 2, Honeypot Lane, LONDON NW9 9RX. See also Knav UK Limited
SINGH, Mr. Amardeep, MPhil BA ACA *1998;* 51 Stanhope Gardens, ILFORD, IG1 3LQ.
•**SINGH, Mr. Amarjit, MA ACA** *2000;* Ernst & Young LLP, 1 More London Place, LONDON, SE1 2AF. See also Ernst & Young Europe LLP
SINGH, Mr. Aneil Kumar, BA ACA *1997;* Dumbreeze House, Ormskirk Road, Knowsley Village, PRESCOT, L34 8HB.
SINGH, Mrs. Anjali, BSc(Hons) ACA *2011;* 3 River Road, Caversham, READING, RG4 7EH.
SINGH, Mr. Anup Valmiki, MA FCA *1994;* 2777 Clara Smith Place, SAN JOSE, CA 95135, UNITED STATES.
SINGH, Mr. Anurag, ACA *2008;* 22 Stonehall Avenue, ILFORD, ESSEX, IG1 3SH.
SINGH, Mr. Arindra, FCA *1973;* 14 Finchley Road, ETOBICOKE M9A 2X5, ON, CANADA.
SINGH, Mr. Balbinder Dhinsay, BA ACA *2004;* with KPMG LLP, Arlington Business Park, Theale, READING, RG7 4SD.
•**SINGH, Mr. Balbir, MSc BSc(Hons) FCA CTA AIIT PGCE TEP** *1992;* (Tax Fac), Richard Anthony & Company, 13 Station Road, Finchley, LONDON, N3 2SB.
SINGH, Mr. Baljit, BA ACA *1999;* 46 Allhallows, BEDFORD, MK40 1LN.
SINGH, Mr. Bedi Ajay, BSc FCA *1985;* 7 Coveview Drive, RANCHO PALOS VERDES, CA 90275, UNITED STATES.
SINGH, Mrs. Belinder Kaur, BSc(Econ) ACA *2002;* 3 Ebrington Road, Kenton, HARROW, MIDDLESEX, HA3 0LP.
SINGH, Mr. Bhagwant, BSc FCA *1988;* 27 Granby Road, STEVENAGE, SG1 4AR.
•**SINGH, Mr. Bhupinderpal, ACA** *1982;* JSP Accountants Limited, First Floor, 10 College Road, HARROW, MIDDLESEX, HA1 1BE. See also The Dinsdale Young Practice Ltd
SINGH, Mr. Charles Wesley, BSc ACA *1991;* 30 Chislehurst Avenue, North Finchley, LONDON, N12 0HU.
SINGH, Mr. Damien, ACA MAAT *2010;* 806/1-15 Francis Street, DARLINGHURST, NSW 2000, AUSTRALIA.
SINGH, Mr. Darpan Shah, ACA MBA *1997;* Ceejay House 9 To 10/f, Dr. Annie Besant Road, MUMBAI 400018, INDIA.
•**SINGH, Mr. Deldar Tony, BSc ACA** *2000;* Euro Asia Capital Ventures Ltd, 26 Cypress Avenue, WELWYN GARDEN CITY, HERTFORDSHIRE, AL7 1HN. See also Arcturus Securities & Investments Limited
SINGH, Mr. Digvijay, FCA *1975;* C-2 Maharani Bagh, NEW DELHI 110 065, INDIA.
SINGH, Mr. Gurjinder, BA ACA MBA *2009;* 3 Midhurst Close, CRAWLEY, RH11 0BS.
•**SINGH, Mr. Gurjit, BSc ACA** *1994;* GS, 2 Woodfarm Road, Rouken Glen, GLASGOW, G46 7JJ.
•**SINGH, Mr. Gursharan Hardeyal, BA FCA** *1988;* Chuhan & Singh Partnership Limited, 81 Borough Road, MIDDLESBROUGH, TS1 3AA.
•**SINGH, Mr. Harant Pal, FCA** *1984;* Spiers & Company, 72 Fielding Road, Chiswick, LONDON, W4 1DB.
SINGH, Mr. Harbaksh, ACA *1992;* 129 Bassett Avenue, SOUTHAMPTON, SO16 7EP.
SINGH, Mr. Harleen, BEng ACA *1994;* Toggwilerstrasse 17, 8706 MEILEN, SWITZERLAND.
SINGH, Mr. Harpal, MA BA(Hons)Oxon ACA AMCT *2000;* (Tax Fac), Lloyds Register, 71 Fenchurch Street, LONDON, EC3M 4BS.
SINGH, Mr. Harpartap, LLB ACA *2001;* 4 Sandleford Drive, Elstow, BEDFORD, MK42 9GN.
SINGH, Mr. Harsharan Francis William Jeeves, BSc ACA CTA *2004;* (Tax Fac), with Eacotts Limited, Grenville Court, Britwell Road, Burnham, SLOUGH, SL1 8DF.
SINGH, Mr. Herinder, BA ACA *1993;* 1 Wharf Terrace, Deodar Road, Putney, LONDON, SW15 2JZ.
SINGH, Mr. Inderjit, BA ACA *1999;* 167 Framingham Road, SALE, CHESHIRE, M33 3RQ.
SINGH, Mr. Inderneel, BSc ACA *2010;* Tetworth Hall, Cheapside Road, ASCOT, BERKSHIRE, SL5 7QW.
SINGH, Mr. Ishminder, ACA *2008;* 72 Coombe Lane West, KINGSTON UPON THAMES, SURREY, KT2 7DA.
SINGH, Mr. Ishwin, ACA *2010;* Flat 4, 87 Hatton Garden, LONDON, EC1N 8QQ.
SINGH, Mr. Jagdev, ACA *1983;* 16 JALAN 5/10F, 46000 PETALING JAYA, MALAYSIA.
SINGH, Mr. Jasdip, ACA *2011;* 125 Salisbury Avenue, BARKING, ESSEX, IG11 9XP.
SINGH, Mr. Jaswinder Judge, BSc ACA *1998;* 40 Victoria Road, Hanham, BRISTOL, BS15 3QH.
SINGH, Mr. Jayvinder, BA(Hons) ACA *2004;* 485 Rochdale Road, Middleton, MANCHESTER, M24 2GN.
SINGH, Mr. Jeevan, BA ACA *2011;* 42 Reddings Road, Moseley, BIRMINGHAM, B13 8LN.
•**SINGH, Mr. Joga, BSc ACA** *1995;* PricewaterhouseCoopers LLP, Cornwall Court, 19 Cornwall Street, BIRMINGHAM, B3 2DT. See also PricewaterhouseCoopers
SINGH, Mr. Jugdeep, BSc ACA *2001;* Flat 185 Berberis House, Highfield Road, FELTHAM, MIDDLESEX, TW13 4GS.
•**SINGH, Mr. Jutinder, BA ACA** *1996;* JS Gulati & Co Ltd, 4 Peter James Business Centre, Pump Lane, HAYES, MIDDLESEX, UB3 3NT.
SINGH, Mr. Kaka, ACA FCCA FCMA FCPA *2010;* 9 Woo Mon Chew Road, SINGAPORE 455060, SINGAPORE.
SINGH, Mr. Kamaljit, BA ACA *1982;* 13 Deer Leap, LIGHTWATER, GU18 5PF.
SINGH, Mr. Keelan, ACA *2009;* 51 Endymion Road, LONDON, SW2 2BU.
•**SINGH, Mr. Kultaran, FCA** *1974;* HSKS Limited, 18 St. Christophers Way, Pride Park, DERBY, DE24 8JY.
•**SINGH, Mr. Kulwant, BSc ACA** *1989;* 9 Upland Road, Selly Park, BIRMINGHAM, B29 7JR.
SINGH, Mr. Mandip, BSc ACA *2005;* 30 Belvoir Vale Grove, Bingham, NOTTINGHAM, NG13 8QZ.
SINGH, Mr. Mohinder Shah, FCA *1966;* D-93, Panchsheel Enclave, NEW DELHI 110017, INDIA.
SINGH, Miss. Mohini, BA ACA *1993;* Flat 18 Gauri Apartments, 3 & 4 Rajesh Pilot Lane, NEW DELHI 110011, INDIA.
•**SINGH, Mr. Mukhtiar, BA ACA** *2007;* Sohans, 44a Bradford Street, WALSALL, WEST MIDLANDS, WS1 3QA.
SINGH, Mr. Nakesh, ACA *2011;* 1 Kestrel Avenue, Moormede Park, STAINES, MIDDLESEX, TW18 4RU.
SINGH, Mr. Navneet, FCA *1974;* The Bank of New York Mellon, 3 North Avenue 3rd Floor, Maker Maxity, Bandra Kurla Complex, MUMBAI 400051, INDIA.
SINGH, Miss. Nina, BSc(Econ) ACA *2002;* 26 Dersingham Road, LONDON, NW2 1SL.
•**SINGH, Mr. Peter Mota, FCA** *1974;* 3 Plymbridge Gardens, Plympton, PLYMOUTH, PL7 4HQ.
SINGH, Mr. Prabhjot, BSc ACA *2001;* c/o, 61 Hampton Lane, SOLIHULL, B91 2QD.
SINGH, Mr. Prabhmeet, ACA *2008;* 10 Priory Hill, WEMBLEY, MIDDLESEX, HA0 2QF.
SINGH, Miss. Prachi, BSc ACA *2010;* 23 The Drive, Fulwood, PRESTON, PR2 8FF.
SINGH, Mr. Rabindra, BEng ACA *2009;* 37 Brazier Crescent, NORTHOLT, MIDDLESEX, UB5 6FB.
•**SINGH, Miss. Raemy, BCom ACA** *2001;* Forward Financials Ltd, Kemp House, 152-160 City Road, LONDON, EC1V 2NX.
SINGH, Mr. Rahul, ACA BEng(Hons) *2010;* Flat 12, Pyramid House, 952 High Road, North Finchley, LONDON, N12 9RX.
SINGH, Mr. Raymond, ACA *1994;* 6674 Foxcroft Court, CHINO, CA 91710, UNITED STATES.
SINGH, Mr. Reshpal, MA ACA CTA *1994;* 4 Michael Drive, Edgbaston, BIRMINGHAM, B15 2EL.
SINGH, Mr. Rickinder, BSc ACA *1993;* 113 Elgar Avenue, SURBITON, KT5 9JS.
•**SINGH, Mr. Rupendra, FCA** *1975;* KPMG, DLF Building No 10, 8th Floor, Tower B DLF Cyber City, Phase 2, GURGAON 122 002 HARYANA INDIA.
SINGH, Mrs. Ruth, BSc(Econ) ACA *1999;* Croucher Needham Hope Agar, 27 St. Cuthberts Street, BEDFORD, MK40 3JG.
SINGH, Miss. Ruth Chandra, ACA *2008;* Flat 7, 17 Freeland Road, LONDON, W5 3HR.
SINGH, Mrs. Sally Marie, BSc ACA *2003;* with PricewaterhouseCoopers LLP, Cornwall Court, 19 Cornwall Street, BIRMINGHAM, B3 2DT.
•**SINGH, Mr. Satpal, ACA** *2008;* SAT & Co, 331 Torbay Road, HARROW, MIDDLESEX, HA2 9QD.

SINGH, Mr. Shalinder, ACA *2011;* 65 Roxy Avenue, ROMFORD, RM6 4AW.
•**SINGH, Mr. Sudhir, BSc ACA DChA** *1991;* Baker Tilly Tax & Advisory Services LLP, 1st Floor, 46 Clarendon Road, WATFORD, WD17 1JJ. See also Baker Tilly UK Audit LLP
SINGH, Mr. Sukhjit, BSc ACA *1995;* Starshine Associates Ltd, 51 Stanhope Gardens, ILFORD, IG1 3LQ.
SINGH, Mr. Varinder, FCA *1974;* 53 Chiltern Road, SUTTON, SURREY, SM2 5QU.
SINGH, Mr. Vijay, ACA *2008;* 8 Broadway, Duffield, BELPER, DERBYSHIRE, DE56 4BT.
SINGH POONI, Mr. Pritpal, ACA *2011;* 28 Tingle View, LEEDS, LS12 6LJ.
SINGH PUREWAL, Mr. Inderjeet, BSc(Hons) ACA *2002;* 4 Lawson Court, Farsley, PUDSEY, WEST YORKSHIRE, LS28 5GS.
SINGHAL, Mr. Brij Mohan, FCA *1979;* PO Box 37377, DOHA, QATAR.
SINGHAL, Ms. Deepika, ACA *2009;* 15 Bellflower Road, Hamilton, LEICESTER, LE5 1TS.
SINGHAM, Mr. Jeremy, BA(Hons) ACA *2010;* 11 Fairfield Avenue, RUISLIP, MIDDLESEX, HA4 7PG.
•**SINGHANIA, Mrs. Sarita, ACA** *2007;* Singhania Associates, 25 Lodge Close, HUNTINGDON, CAMBRIDGESHIRE, PE29 6GR.
SINGHERA, Mr. Jagdip Singh, BSc(Hons) ACA *2001;* 39 North View, PINNER, HA5 1PT.
•①**SINGLA, Mr. Surjit Kumar, FCA** *1973;* Singla & Co Ltd, 12 Devereux Court, LONDON, WC2R 3JJ.
SINGLETON, Mr. Andrew Morten, MBA BA ACA *1994;* Lealands Barn, Station Road, Groombridge, TUNBRIDGE WELLS, EAST SUSSEX, TN3 9NB.
SINGLETON, Mr. Colin Robert, BSc ACA *2003;* Flat 71 Antrim Mansions, Antrim Road, LONDON, NW3 4XL.
SINGLETON, Miss. Deborah Elizabeth, BSc ACA *1992;* 72 Clapham Common West Side, LONDON, SW4 9AX.
•**SINGLETON, Mr. Edwin, BA FCA** *1974;* Wallwork Nelson & Johnson, Chandler House, 7 Ferry Road Office Park, Riversway, PRESTON, PR2 2YH.
•**SINGLETON, Mr. Gareth Mark, BSc ACA** *2002;* PKF (UK) LLP, Century House, St James Court, Friar Court, DERBY, DE1 1BT.
SINGLETON, Mr. Glynn Lee, FCA *1970;* Apple Trees, Froggatt, Calver, HOPE VALLEY, DERBYSHIRE, S32 3ZA.
SINGLETON, Mr. Jeffrey Philip, ACA CA(AUS) *2010;* 78 Rue Mademoiselle, 75015 PARIS, FRANCE.
SINGLETON, Mrs. Kathryn Ann, BSc ACA *1997;* Barclays Bank Plc, UK Retail Banking, Level 25, 1 Churchill Place, LONDON, E14 5HP.
SINGLETON, Mr. Keir Graham, BA ACA *2006;* Mid Elm Cottage, Elm Road, Penn, HIGH WYCOMBE, BUCKINGHAMSHIRE, HP10 8LF.
SINGLETON, Dr. Kevin Alan, ACA *1986;* H S B C, 8-16 Canada Square, LONDON, E14 5HQ.
SINGLETON, Mr. Leslie McBride, FCA *1972;* Bury Barn Cottage, Bury Farm Bury Road, Pleshey, CHELMSFORD, CM3 1HB.
SINGLETON, Mrs. Lisa Jayne, BSc(Hons) ACA *2003;* 44 Park Road, Duffield, BELPER, DERBYSHIRE, DE56 4GR.
SINGLETON, Mr. Luke, BSc ACA *2007;* 6 Kendal Drive, Flitwick, BEDFORD, MK45 1NW.
•**SINGLETON, Mr. Michael Henry Tilbury, FCA** *1959;* Michael Singleton, 7 Rudry Road, Lisvane, CARDIFF, CF14 0SN. See also Singleton MHT
•**SINGLETON, Mr. Nigel John, FCA** *1984;* B D & M Limited, Skies, 20 St. Martinsfield, Martinstown, DORCHESTER, DORSET DT2 9JU.
SINGLETON, Mr. Paul, BSc ACA *2003;* Flat 5, 24 New Wharf Road, LONDON, N1 9RR.
•**SINGLETON, Mr. Paul Charles, FCA** *1976;* Paul C. Singleton, Riverdale, 89 Graham Road, SHEFFIELD, S10 3GP. See also Paul C. Singleton Ltd
SINGLETON, Mr. Paul James, BSc ACA *1996;* 15 Kingsway Avenue, Broughton, PRESTON, PR3 5JN.
SINGLETON, Mr. Richard Brian, ACA *1995;* La Hure (Godfrey) Hougue Anthan, St. Pierre Du Bois, GUERNSEY, GY7 9BN.
SINGLETON, Mrs. Rosina Susan, BSc ACA *1989;* British Jewellery Giftware & Finishing Federation, 10 Vyse Street Hockley, BIRMINGHAM, B18 6LT.
SINGLETON, Miss. Sharon Joan, BA(Hons) ACA *2002;* with KPMG LLP, Arlington Business Park, Theale, READING, RG7 4SD.
SINGLETON, Mr. Steven David, BSc ACA *1997;* 23 Poppyfields, Hesketh Bank, PRESTON, PR4 6TJ.
SINGLETON, Mr. Stuart, BA ACA *1989;* Pensbury, Cotherstone, BARNARD CASTLE, COUNTY DURHAM, DL12 9PQ.
•**SINGLETON, Mrs. Susan Lucy, BA ACA** *1983;* Susan Singleton, 475 Whirlowdale Road, Whirlow, SHEFFIELD, S11 9NH.
SINGLETON, Mr. Thomas Giles, BA ACA *1990;* 3 Elm Grove, Hoylake, WIRRAL, MERSEYSIDE, CH47 3DL.
SINGLETON-GREEN, Mr. Brian, MA FCA *1976;* with ICAEW, Chartered Accountants' Hall, Moorgate Place, LONDON, EC2P 2BJ.
SINH, Mr. Gopal, MSc ACA *1986;* PO Box 1485, TOOMBUL, QLD 4012, AUSTRALIA.
SINHA, Mr. Amit Ranjan, BEng FCA *1998;* Flat 901/902, Supreme Residency, 14th Road Bandra (W), MUMBAI 400 050, INDIA.
SINHA, Miss. Angeli, LLB ACA *2005;* Flat 4, 133 Hamilton Terrace, LONDON, NW8 9QR.
SINHA, Mr. Jonathan, BSc ACA *1995;* Knollbury House, Undy, CALDICOT, GWENT, NP26 3BX.
SINHA, Mr. Raj, BSc ACA *2000;* Jasmine Leaf 7 Villa 5, Al Barari, DUBAI, 74429, UNITED ARAB EMIRATES.
SINHA, Mr. Raj Narayan, FCA *1963;* 135 Webster Road, Scarsdale, NEW YORK, NY 10583-5848, UNITED STATES.
•**SINHA, Mr. Sudhir Kumar, ACA** *2010;* Sudhir Sinha & Co, 2 Silver Street, CARDIFF, CF24 0LG.
SINHA, Mr. Tej Narayan, FCA *1973;* 40 Belsize Court, Wedderburn Road, LONDON, NW3 5QH.
SINJAKLI, Mr. Mark David, BA ACA *2005;* with Zolfo Cooper LLP, The Zenith Building, 26 Spring Gardens, MANCHESTER, M2 1AB.
SINKER, Mr. David Tennant, OBE MA FCA *1964;* 10 Church Lane, Fulbourn, CAMBRIDGE, CB21 5EP. (Life Member)
SINKER, Mr. Nigel Dalcour, MA FCA *1976;* 7 Westfield Road, RUGBY, CV22 6AS.
SINKER, Mr. Patrick Andrew Charles Chisolm, FCA *1967;* The Orchard, 3 Alexandra Road, WHITSTABLE, KENT, CT5 4LR.
•**SINKINSON, Mrs. Gillian Mary, BA ACA** *1979;* Gill Sinkinson, Fairview, 16 Wickwar Road, Kingswood, WOTTON-UNDER-EDGE, GLOUCESTERSHIRE GL12 8RF.
SINKINSON, Mr. John Miles, BA ACA *1983;* 19a Stokewood Road, BOURNEMOUTH, BH3 7NA.
SINNADURAI, Mr. Vallipuram, BSc FCA *1958;* Charter House, 65/2 Sir Chittampalam A Gardiner Mawatha, 2 COLOMBO, SRI LANKA. (Life Member)
•**SINNETT, Mrs. Diane, BSc ACA** *1988;* Tricom Services Limited, 22 High Street, BUCKINGHAM, MK18 1NU.
SINNETT, Mr. Paul Martin, BA ACA *1984;* Mill Croft Barn, Water Stratford Road, Tingewick, BUCKINGHAM, MK18 4PD.
•**SINNETT, Mr. Stephen James, FCA** *1980;* Sinnett & Co, 61-63 Church Street, Caversham, READING, RG4 8AX.
SINNETT-THOMAS, Mr. Kevin Melvyn, BA(Hons) ACA *2000;* 15 Bridge Road, NOTTINGHAM, NG8 2DG.
SINNOTT, Mr. Martin Anthony, BA ACA *2005;* Morgan Stanley International, 25 Cabot Square, LONDON, E14 4QA.
SINODOROU, Mr. Sinos George, FCA *1961;* 10 Louroutsiatis Court, Const. Kalogera Street, 302 LARNACA, CYPRUS. (Life Member)
SINTON, Mr. Alastair Paul, BSc ACA *1995;* 44 Abbott Road, North Curl Curl, SYDNEY, NSW 2099, AUSTRALIA.
SINTON, Mr. Charles Blair Ritchie, FCA *1973;* The Penthouse, 7 Avior, 10 Longworth Drive, MAIDENHEAD, BERKSHIRE, SL6 8XA.
SINTRAT, Miss. Claire, BBA ACA *2011;* Flat 15, Claremont Heights, 70 Pentonville Road, LONDON, N1 9PR.
SINYOR, Dr. Alan David, MA BA ACA ATII *1996;* 2 Grosvenor Gardens, LONDON, NW11 0HG.
SION, Miss. Elin, MEng ACA *2011;* Apartment G, 188 Hall Lane, MANCHESTER, M23 1NB.
SIONG SIN, Mr. Ken Keean Cheong, BSc ACA CPA *1995;* International Federation of Accountants, 545 Fifth Ave, 14th Floor, NEW YORK, NY 10017, UNITED STATES.
SIOW, Mr. Chai Khun, FCA *1974;* No. 9 Jalan Kantan 3, Ambang Botanic, KLANG, MALAYSIA. (Life Member)
SIOW, Mr. Chern Ik, BA ACA *1981;* 32 Jalan Layang 3, Taman Perling, 81200 JOHOR BAHRU, Johor, MALAYSIA.
SIOW, Mr. Sak Sung, FCA *1979;* Terasys Australia Pty Ltd, Lvl 5, 97 Pacific Highway, NORTH SYDNEY, NSW 2060, AUSTRALIA.
SIOW HON TING, Mr. Gilles Khin Fah, BSc(Econ) FCA *2001;* 3 Beechwood Close, Western Road, East Finchley, LONDON, N2 9JA.
SIOW-HON-TING, Miss. Nadine F L, BSc ACA *2006;* 2/2 18 Woodlands Drive, GLASGOW, G4 9EH.
SIOW HON TING, Mr. Vivian Sem Fah, BSc ACA *2002;* with PricewaterhouseCoopers LLP, 1 Embankment Place, LONDON, WC2N 6RH.
SIPPY, Miss. Janet Elaine, BSocSc ACA *1997;* 50 Lanercost Road, LONDON, SW2 3DN.
SIPPY, Miss. Veena Lorraine, BA ACA *1996;* 16 Fairview Road, LONDON, SW16 5PY.
SIRETT, Mr. Thomas William, Ma BA ACA *2009;* Yew Tree House, High Street, Wanborough, SWINDON, WILTSHIRE, SN4 0AE.
SIRHAN, Mr. Tareq Rebhi, MA(Hons) ACA *2002;* 9 Wool Road, LONDON, SW20 0HN.
SIRIVONGSE, Mr. Boonprasom, ACA *1980;* 660/1Soi Sirimongkhol(Senikhom 16), Senikhom 2 (Paholyothin 32) Road, Lad Yao, BANGKOK 10900, THAILAND.
SIRS, Mr. Ben, BA(Hons) ACA *2002;* with Ernst & Young LLP, Citygate, St James' Boulevard, NEWCASTLE UPON TYNE, NE1 4JD.
SISK, Mr. Stuart Jonathan, BA ACA *2002;* 17 Cranford Avenue, Church Crookham, FLEET, GU52 6QU.
•**SISKIN, Mr. Colin Howard, BA FCA CTA** *1976;* C.H. Siskin & Co, Mulberry Cottage, Church Lane, PINNER, HA5 3AA.
•**SISKIND, Mr. Leonard Jeffrey, BA FCA** *1984;* Hazlems Fenton LLP, Palladium House, 1-4 Argyll Street, LONDON, W1F 7LD.
SISLEY, Mr. Robert David, BSc ACA *1995;* 1 Fremlins Road, Bearsted, MAIDSTONE, KENT, ME14 4HA.
•**SISMAN, Mr. Gary, BSc ACA** *1989;* The Red Sky Partnership Ltd, Red Sky House, Fairclough Hall, Halls Green, Weston, HITCHIN HERTFORDSHIRE SG4 7DP. See also Clark & Co Accountants Ltd and Gary Sisman
SISMEY, Mr. Richard George, BA ACA *1992;* 3 Caradon Place, VERWOOD, DORSET, BH31 7PW.
SISODIA, Mr. Mrunal, BA ACA *1996;* Flat 4, Beaconsfield Lodge, 101 Aberdeen Park, LONDON, N5 2BP.
SISODIA, Mr. Rambhai Parbat, ACA *1979;* 22 Lulworth Avenue, Osterly, HOUNSLOW, MIDDLESEX, TW5 0TZ.
SISODIA, Mr. Vijay Viram, ACA *2008;* 19 Arnald Way, Houghton Regis, DUNSTABLE, BEDFORDSHIRE, LU5 5UN.
SISODIYA, Mr. Ranjit, BEng ACA *1992;* 1 Salisbury Road, HUNGERFORD, BERKSHIRE, RG17 0LG.
SISSON, Mrs. Amanda Helen, BA ACA *1999;* 23 High Street, Walkern, STEVENAGE, HERTFORDSHIRE, SG2 7PA.
•**SISSON, Mr. David, FCA CTA** *1981;* Richardson Nutt Limited, Unit 7, Stadium Business Court, Millennium Way, Pride Park, DERBY DE24 8HP.
SISSON, Mr. Jonathan Michael, FCA *1974;* 2 Orwell Road, NORWICH, NR2 2ND.
SISSON, Mr. Mark David, ACA *2008;* Jaeger House, 5 Clanricarde Gardens, TUNBRIDGE WELLS, TN1 1PE.
•**SISSONS, Mr. Damien Stephen John, BA FCA** *1993;* (Tax Fac), Waters & Atkinson, The Old Court House, Clark Street, MORECAMBE, LA4 5HR.
SISSONS, Mr. Nigel Keith, BCom ACA *1983;* 37 Willow Bank Road, Alderton, TEWKESBURY, GL20 8NJ.
SITARAM, Mr. Nagaraj, FCA *1962;* Little Court, The Planks, SWINDON, SN3 1QP. (Life Member)
•**SITCH, Mr. David Charles, FCA** *1961;* (Tax Fac), K.A.Jeffries & Company, 18 Melbourne Grove, LONDON, SE22 8RA.
SITHAMPARANATHAN, Mr. Nivan, ACA *2009;* 14 Ullswater Road, DUNSTABLE, BEDFORDSHIRE, LU6 3PX.
SITHANEN, Mr. Tevindren, ACA *2009;* No8 Dr Harel, QUATRE-BORNES, MAURITIUS.
SITHOLE, Mr. Samuel, ACA *2001;* P O Box 5540, Rivonia, SANDTON, GAUTENG, 2128, SOUTH AFRICA.
SITHOLE, Miss. Tendai Doreen, BSc(Hons) ACA *2011;* 63 Russell Street, READING, RG1 7XG.
SITT, Mr. William Hock Seng, FCA *1977;* 20A SHIRLEY AVENUE, MOUNT PLEASANT, WA 6153, AUSTRALIA.
SITU, Mr. Xing, MSc BA ACA *2009;* Flat 14 Aurora Building, 164 Blackwall Way, LONDON, E14 9NZ.
SIU, Mr. Clement Ka-Kui, BSc ACA *2006;* C5 Butler Towers, 1-3 Boyce Road, JARDINE'S LOOKOUT, HONG KONG ISLAND, HONG KONG SAR.
SIU, Mr. Dominic Man Kit, BEng ACA MCT *1989;* Block 122 Toa Payoh Lorong 2, #04-14, SINGAPORE 310122, SINGAPORE.
SIU, Mr. Fun To, BSc ACA *1991;* Room 2713 27/FUn Shing House, Un Chau Estate SHAM SHUI PO, Kowloon, HONG KONG SAR.
SIU, Mr. Ka Chi Eric, ACA *2008;* Suites 1203-4 12/F. Li Po Chun Chambers, 189 Des Voeux Road, CENTRAL, HONG KONG ISLAND, HONG KONG SAR.
SIU, Mr. Kai Chun, ACA *2005;* Flat E 39/F, Tower 3 The Grandiose, 3 Tong Chun Street, TSEUNG KWAN O, NEW TERRITORIES, HONG KONG SAR.
SIU, Mr. Kin Wai, ACA *2007;* 66/F Central Plaza, 18 Harbour Road, WAN CHAI, HONG KONG ISLAND, HONG KONG SAR.
SIU, Ms. Kithar, BSc ACA *1992;* Flat F 8/F Tower 11, Ocean Shores, 88 O King Road, SAI KUNG, HONG KONG SAR.
SIU, Mr. Kwok Keung, ACA *2007;* Flat A 25/F Block 1, Academic Terrace, 101 Pok Fu Lam Road, CENTRAL, HONG KONG SAR.
SIU, Mr. Kwok Ming, ACA *2008;* Flat D, 48th Floor, Tower 6, Residence Oasis, TSEUNG KWAN O, NEW TERRITORIES HONG KONG SAR.
SIU, Mr. Leung Wah, ACA *2008;* Unit F Floor 22 Tower 5, Prima Villa, 8 Chui Yan Street, SHA TIN, NEW TERRITORIES, HONG KONG SAR.
SIU, Mr. Man Kun, ACA *2008;* Flat B 12/F Tower 1, Lake Silver, 599 Sai Sha Road, Ma On Shan, SHA TIN, NEW TERRITORIES HONG KONG SAR.
SIU, Mr. Ping Kwong, ACA *2007;* Flat D 31st Floor, No 2 Park Road, MID LEVELS, HONG KONG SAR.
SIU, Mr. Simon Michael, BA(Hons) ACA *2002;* with Deloitte LLP, Hill House, 1 Little New Street, LONDON, EC4A 3TR.
SIU, Mr. Stephen Andrew, BA(Hons) ACA *2002;* with Ernst & Young, 5 Times Square, NEW YORK, NY 10036, UNITED STATES.
SIU, Ms. Tracy Wai-Han, LLB ACA *2002;* British Telecom Faraday Building, 1 Knightrider Street, LONDON, EC4V 5BT.
•**SIU, Mr. Wai Keung, BA FCA** *1983;* W.K. Sui, 8th Floor, Prince's Building, CENTRAL, Hong Kong Island, HONG KONG SAR. See also KPMG
SIU, Mr. Wai Man, ACA *2005;* 39/F West Tower, Shun Tak Centre, 200 Connaught Roadl, CENTRAL, HONG KONG ISLAND, HONG KONG SAR.
SIU, Ms. Wai Yee, ACA *2008;* Flat C 16/F, Man King Building, 3 Hing Wo Street, ABERDEEN, HONG KONG SAR.
SIU, Mr. Yue Wa Logan, ACA *2008;* Edwin Cheung & Siu, Room A, 7/F, China Overseas Building, 139 Hennessy Road, WAN CHAI HONG KONG ISLAND HONG KONG SAR.
SIVA, Mrs. Ambika, BSc FCA *1992;* 3 Lyndhurst Court, WEST PENNANT HILLS, NSW 2125, AUSTRALIA.
SIVA-PRAKASAM, Mr. Christopher Nesakumar, BSc ACA *1990;* (Tax Fac), 110 Woodside Road, LONDON, N22 5HS.
SIVAGNANARATNAM, Mr. Haran, BSc ACA *1998;* 11 Ontario Avenue, ROSEVILLE, NSW 2069, AUSTRALIA.
SIVAGNANASINGHAM, Mr. Ponnambalam, BSc FCA *1967;* Flat A 12F, Tower 3, Robinson Heights, 8 Robinson Road, MID LEVELS, HONG KONG ISLAND HONG KONG SAR. (Life Member)
SIVAKUMARAN, Mr. Hari, ACA *2011;* 3 Branksome Way, NEW MALDEN, SURREY, KT3 3AX.
SIVANITHY, Mr. Rajanbabu, BSc ACA *1994;* 68 Chartfield Avenue, Putney, LONDON, SW15 6HQ.
•**SIVAPALAN, Mr. Kanapathipillai, FCA** *1984;* Siva Palan & Co., 69-75 Boston Manor Road, BRENTFORD, MIDDLESEX, TW8 9JJ.
SIVAPRAGASAM, Mr. Shanmugathaas, ACA *2008;* 82 Amos Street, WESTMEAD, NSW 2145, AUSTRALIA.
SIVAPUNNIYAN, Miss. Malathy, BSc ACA *2005;* with PricewaterhouseCoopers LLP, 1 Embankment Place, LONDON, WC2N 6RH.
SIVARAJAH, Miss. Bhrraveenthi, BA ACA *2005;* Flat 61, Voltaire Buildings, 330 Garratt Lane, LONDON, SW18 4FQ.
SIVARAJAH, Mr. Ganesh, ACA *2009;* 1 Persiaran Titwangsa 2, 53200 KUALA LUMPUR, FEDERAL TERRITORY, MALAYSIA.
SIVARAJAH, Mr. Jeysen, BSc ACA *2007;* 3 Orchard Close, LONDON, SW20 9HU.
SIVARAM, Mr. Nagaraj, FCA *1984;* Ernst & Young, One Raffles Quay, North Tower, Level 18, SINGAPORE 048583, SINGAPORE.
SIVASOTHY, Miss. Ramani, BSc ACA *1982;* Flat 3, 7 Lyndhurst Gardens, LONDON, NW3 5NS.
SIVATHASAN, Miss. Nirupa, MSci ACA *2007;* 13 Derwent Court, Eleanor Close, LONDON, SE16 6PS.
SIVATHONDAN, Mr. Krishan, BSc(Hons) ACA *2011;* 8 Heddon Road, Cockfosters, BARNET, HERTFORDSHIRE, EN4 9LD.
SIVAYOGAN, Mr. Sivasubramanian, FCA *1964;* 8 Oakham Drive, BROMLEY, BR2 0XE. (Life Member)
SIVERS, Mr. Ronald George, FCA *1964;* 15 Wessex Avenue, NEW MILTON, BH25 6NG.

SIVITER, Mr. Adam James, BSc ACA AMCT *1996;* 32 Sevenoaks Drive, BOURNEMOUTH, BH7 7JQ.
SIVITER, Miss. Claire Suzanne, BSc ACA *1999;* 9 Saffron Drive, CHRISTCHURCH, BH23 4LP.
SIVITER, Mr. David Hubert John, FCA *1963;* Tesfa House, Heathfield Road, Burwash, ETCHINGHAM, EAST SUSSEX, TN19 7HL. (Life Member)
•**SIVLAL, Mr. Inderjith Soorajlal, ACA FCCA** *2008;* Gerald Kreditor & Co, Hallswelle House, 1 Hallswelle Road, LONDON, NW11 0DH.
SIVORN, Miss. Kelly Marie, BSc ACA *2008;* 51 Keswick Crescent, PLYMOUTH, PL6 8SL.
SIVYER, Mr. Andrew John, BA(Hons) ACA *2002;* 6 Flowers Piece, Ashampstead, READING, RG8 8SG.
SIVYER, Mrs. Fiona Jane, BSc ACA *1991;* Le Roudier RN89, 24110 SAINT ASTIER, FRANCE.
•**SIVYER, Mr. Mark Anthony, ACA** *1991;* Brookes Sivyer Limited, The Old Chapel, High Street, East Hoathly, LEWES, EAST SUSSEX BN8 6DR.
SIZELAND, Mr. Edward William, BA FCA *1998;* Cofunds Ltd Dorset House, 25 Duke Street, CHELMSFORD, CM1 1HL.
SIZER, Mrs. Anna, BCom ACA *2003;* 9 Westcar Lane, Hersham, WALTON-ON-THAMES, KT12 5ER.
SIZER, Mr. Graham Kevin, BSc ACA *1996;* Crakehall House The Green, Crakehall, BEDALE, NORTH YORKSHIRE, DL8 1HS.
SIZER, Miss. Rachel, BSc ACA *2007;* Basement Flat, 24 Abbotsford Road, BRISTOL, BS6 6HB.
SIZOVA, Mrs. Elena, ACA *2011;* Yasenevaya 36-2-27, 115597 MOSCOW, RUSSIAN FEDERATION.
SJOBLOM, Miss. Cara Louise, ACA *2009;* 5 Villas of the Galleon, PO Box 30009, SEVEN MILE BEACH, GRAND CAYMAN, KY1-1201, CAYMAN ISLANDS.
SKAANILD, Mrs. Hannah Mary, BA(Hons) ACA *2001;* 87c Syta, Wilanow, 02-987 WARSAW, POLAND.
SKAIFE, Mr. Howard, BSc FCA *1975;* 19 Belle Vue Avenue, Scholes, LEEDS, LS15 4AD.
SKAILES, Mrs. Alexandra Sarah, BA FCA DChA *1992;* Washbrook Grange, Pigeons Lane, Washbrook, IPSWICH, SUFFOLK, IP8 3HQ.
•**SKAILES, Mr. Duncan James Anthony, BSc FCA** *1991;* PricewaterhouseCoopers LLP, 7 More London Riverside, LONDON, SE1 2RT. See also PricewaterhouseCoopers
•**SKAILES, Mr. Jonathan Toby Strickland, BSc FCA** *2000;* Lower Ground Floor Flat, 8 St. Georges Square, LONDON, SW1V 2HP.
SKALIOTIS, Mr. Loukis, BSc ACA *1990;* 19 Severis Ave, P.O.Box 21724, 1512 NICOSIA, CYPRUS.
SKAN, Mr. John Oliver Frank, FCA *1958;* 8 Homewood, CRANLEIGH, GU6 7HS. (Life Member)
SKAN, Mr. Trevor, FCA *1962;* Whispers, 112 Pauntley Rd., Mudeford, CHRISTCHURCH, BH23 3JL. (Life Member)
SKANTHAN, Miss. Suhanya, BSc ACA *1994;* 68 Chartfield Avenue, LONDON, SW15 6HQ.
SKAPOULLIS, Mr. Christos Michael, MSc BSc ACA *2001;* 74 Myrras Str., Laiki Lefkothea, 3115 LIMASSOL, CYPRUS.
SKARPARI KELESHI, Miss. Maria, BSc FCA *1994;* Group Finance, Hellenic Bank Ltd, POBOX 24747, 1394 NICOSIA, CYPRUS.
•**SKARPARIS, Mr. Christakis, BSc FCA** *1992;* (Tax Fac), Chris Skarparis & Co Ltd, 2nd Floor, 10(b) Aldermans Hill, Palmers Green, LONDON, N13 4PJ.
SKEA, Miss. Katie, BSc ACA *2004;* 2 Bracken Close, Rhind Street, BODMIN, CORNWALL, PL31 2FL.
•**SKEAT, Mr. Hans Peter, BSc FCA** *1988;* Bosworth Business Management Limited, 37 Northumberland Avenue, Market Bosworth, NUNEATON, WARWICKSHIRE, CV13 0RJ.
SKEAT, Mrs. Victoria Louise, BSc ACA *2000;* 5 Blandford Road, ST. ALBANS, HERTFORDSHIRE, AL1 4JP.
SKEATES, Mr. Alan John, FCA *1981;* (Tax Fac), Steeles, 2-3 Norwich Business Park Whiting Road, NORWICH, NR4 6DJ.
SKEATES, Mr. Graham, FCA *1974;* 3053 Great North Road, WOLLOMBI, NSW 2325, AUSTRALIA.
SKEATES, Mr. Robert, ACA *2011;* 14 Chaucer Grove, CAMBERLEY, SURREY, GU15 2XZ.
SKEATS, Mr. Graham Frank, BA ACA *1986;* Level 2, The Royal Bank of Scotland Plc, 280 Bishopsgate, LONDON, EC2M 4RB.
SKED, Mr. Duncan Alexander, ACA *1994;* 2 Cheyne Park Drive, WEST WICKHAM, KENT, BR4 9LQ.
SKEDD, Mrs. Alison Jane, BSc FCA *1990;* Cote House, Upper North Wraxall, CHIPPENHAM, WILTSHIRE, SN14 7AG.
SKEDGEL, Mrs. Louisa Katie, BSc ACA *2002;* 158 Station Road, Kings Norton, BIRMINGHAM, B30 1DB.
•**SKEDGEL, Mr. Mark Nicholas, BSc ACA** *2001;* with PricewaterhouseCoopers LLP, Cornwall Court, 19 Cornwall Street, BIRMINGHAM, B3 2DT.
•**SKEELES, Mr. John William, FCA** *1964;* (Tax Fac), Skeeles & Zanini, 1a Bearton Green, HITCHIN, SG5 1UN.
SKEET, Mr. Christopher Richard, ACA CA(SA) *2010;* 11 Clevedon, WEYBRIDGE, SURREY, KT13 0PJ.
SKEET, Mr. Christopher Roland, BA ACA *1996;* 24 Weston Road, THAMES DITTON, SURREY, KT7 0HN.
•**SKEET, Mr. David James, FCA** *1974;* Steele Robertson Goddard, 28 Ely Place, LONDON, EC1N 6AA.
SKEET, Mr. Eric Edmund, FCA *1949;* 19 High Street, Sanquhar, DUMFRIES, DG4 6DJ. (Life Member)
SKEET, Mr. Matthew James, BA ACA *1998;* 39 Thompson Street, WILLIAMSTOWN, VIC 3016, AUSTRALIA.
SKEET, Mrs. Sophie Victoria, BEng ACA *2000;* 39 Thompson Street, WILLIAMSTOWN, VIC 3016, AUSTRALIA.
•**SKEETE, Mr. John Wendell, FCA** *1972;* PKF Professional Services Inc, P O Box 201, Laborie Street, CASTRIES, SAINT LUCIA.
SKEGGS, Mr. Peter Michael, BA FCA FCT *1976;* 13 Riverside, Lower Hampton Road, SUNBURY-ON-THAMES, TW16 5PW.
SKEGGS, Mr. Robert Alexander, BSc FCA *1995;* Horseracing Betting Levy Board, 25 Wilton Road, LONDON, SW1V 1LW.
SKELCHY, Mr. Anthony Joseph, FCA *1961;* PKF, 9th Floor, MCB Plaza, No 6 Changkat Raja, Chulan, 50200 KUALA LUMPUR FEDERAL TERRITORY MALAYSIA.
SKELDING, Mr. Neville Richard, FCA *1971;* 1457 Warwick Road, Knowle, SOLIHULL, B93 9LU. (Life Member)
SKELDING, Mr. Simon William Edward, BA(Hons) ACA *2003;* CMP Medica Ltd, 8th Floor, Ludgate House, 245 Blackfriars Road, LONDON, SE1 9UY.
SKELDING, Mr. William Edward, FCA *1962;* Arbury House, Newnham Way, Ashwell, BALDOCK, SG7 5PN. (Life Member)
SKELLON, Miss. Sarah-Louise, BA ACA *2007;* 34 Burnham Road, SCUNTHORPE, SOUTH HUMBERSIDE, DN15 7HG.
•**SKELLS, Mrs. Rachel Marion, BA FCA** *1997;* (Tax Fac), Whittle & Partners LLP, Century House South, North Station Road, COLCHESTER, CO1 1RE.
•**SKELLUM, Mr. David Kenneth, JP FCA** *1968;* 69 Sunnybank Road, Wyldegreen, SUTTON COLDFIELD, WEST MIDLANDS, B73 5RL.
SKELLUM, Mr. Mark Andrew, BSc(Hons) ACA *2002;* 10 Darnick Road, SUTTON COLDFIELD, WEST MIDLANDS, B73 6PE.
SKELLUM, Mrs. Naomi Ruth, BSc ACA *2004;* William Mitchell Sinkers Ltd Tram Way, Oldbury Road, SMETHWICK, B66 1NY.
SKELLUM, Ms. Nicola Hilary, BSc(Hons) ACA *2004;* 17 Beresford Drive, SUTTON COLDFIELD, WEST MIDLANDS, B73 5QZ.
SKELLY, Ms. Helena Anne, ACA *1999;* 10 Norman Avenue, St Margarets, TWICKENHAM, TW1 2LY.
SKELLY, Dr. John Francis, PhD BSc ACA *2006;* 42 Hillside Road, LIVERPOOL, L18 2ED.
SKELLY, Mr. Robert, ACA *1981;* Dalton House, Dalton, NEWCASTLE UPON TYNE, NE18 0AA.
SKELLY, Mrs. Stephanie Netta Elizabeth, BSc ACA *1999;* 31 Wentworth Avenue, Finchley, LONDON, N3 1YA.
•**SKELTON, Mr. Charles Craig, MEng ACA** *2002;* with PricewaterhouseCoopers, 1 Embankment Place, LONDON, WC2N 6RH.
SKELTON, Mrs. Charlotte Louise, LLB ACA *2001;* 47 Swiss Avenue, CHELMSFORD, ESSEX, CM1 2AD.
SKELTON, Mr. James Alan, BA ACA *1993;* B & Q Plc, 1 Hampshire Corporate Park, Chandler's Ford, EASTLEIGH, HAMPSHIRE, SO53 3YX.
SKELTON, Mr. John, BA FCA *1974;* Beazer Homes USA Inc, 1000 Abernathy Road, Suite 1200, ATLANTA, GA 30328, UNITED STATES.
SKELTON, Mr. Joseph Osmotherley, BCom FCA *1953;* Church Close, 48 Rectory Lane, WOODSTOCK, OX20 1UQ. (Life Member)
SKELTON, Mr. Julian Miles, BA ACA *1992;* 25 Dale Avenue, STRATFORD-UPON-AVON, WARWICKSHIRE, CV37 7EN.
•**SKELTON, Mr. Malcolm James, BA ACA** *1992;* (Tax Fac), MJS Accountancy Services (Fangfoss) Limited, Hillcroft, Fangfoss, YORK, YO41 5QJ.
•**SKELTON, Mr. Mark Gerard, ACA CA(AUS)** *2011;* with Zolfo Cooper LLP, 10 Fleet Place, LONDON, EC4M 7RB.
SKELTON, Mr. Mervyn Alexander, BSc ACA *1984;* Townsend McCormack Ltd, Anlaby House, 35 Boundary Street, LONDON, E2 7JQ.
SKELTON, Mr. Nathaniel Stephen, BA FCA ATII *1982;* 15 Con Owl Close, Helmsley, YORK, YO62 5DU.
SKELTON, Mr. Nigel Keith, BSc FCA *1982;* 9 Brockhampton, Downhead Park, MILTON KEYNES, MK15 9BT.
SKELTON, Mr. Peter John Struan, BA ACA *1984;* The New Bungalow, Croome Hall, Pontshill, ROSS-ON-WYE, HR9 5TB.
SKELTON, Mr. Peter Stephen, FCA *1956;* Glen Morven, Forest Drive, Kingswood, TADWORTH, SURREY, KT20 6LQ. (Life Member)
SKELTON, Mr. Peter William, FCA *1965;* 3 Chiltern Way, Huntington, YORK, YO32 9RS.
•**SKEPPER, Mr. Richard Nigel, BSc FCA** *1982;* Adjutant Ltd, 8 The Braid, CHESHAM, BUCKINGHAMSHIRE, HP5 3LU.
SKERMER, Mrs. Madeleine Mary, FCA *1947;* Dystlegh Grange, 40 Jacksons Edge Road, Disley, STOCKPORT, CHESHIRE, SK12 2JL. (Life Member)
SKERN, Miss. Elizabeth, BBA ACA *2006;* 26 Robinia Drive, HULL, HU4 6QN.
SKERRATT, Mr. Nicholas, ACA *2007;* 3 Gews Farm Barns, St. Just, PENZANCE, CORNWALL, TR19 7AJ.
SKERRETT, Mr. Robert Mark, BA ACA *2002;* Bradburys Hammerpond Road, Plummers Plain, HORSHAM, WEST SUSSEX, RH13 6PE.
SKERRITT, Mr. Nicholas Richard, FCA *1980;* Go-Exit Ltd, T/A King William IV, Heacham Road, Sedgeford, HUNSTANTON, NORFOLK PE36 5LU.
SKERTCHLY, Mr. Paul Clifford, BSc ACA *1989;* Dormer Cottage, Hardwick Close, Oxshott, LEATHERHEAD, SURREY, KT22 0HZ.
SKETCHLEY, Mr. Peter Trevor, FCA *1953;* 15 Spinney Drive, Collingtree, NORTHAMPTON, NN4 0NG. (Life Member)
SKETCHLEY, Mr. William Bennett, FCA *1969;* Leith Hill Place Farmhouse, Leith Hill Lane, Holmbury St Mary, DORKING, RH5 6LY.
SKETT, Mr. John Charles, FCA *1953;* 26 South Street, Port William, NEWTON STEWART, DG8 9SG. (Life Member)
SKEY, Mr. Christopher Robert, ACA *2009;* 14 Danesbury Close, Billinge, WIGAN, LANCASHIRE, WN5 7UD.
SKIBENES, Mr. Joachim, ACA *2010;* Fagertunveien 121, 1358 JAR, NORWAY.
SKIDMORE, Mrs. Carolyn Elaine, BA ACA *1989;* 10 Bayview Road, ABERDEEN, AB15 4EY.
SKIDMORE, Mr. John Fletcher, BA ACA *1993;* 5 Downey Grove, Penpedairheol, HENGOED, MID GLAMORGAN, CF82 8LE.
SKIDMORE, Mr. Jonathan, BSc ACA *1986;* Fircroft College, 1018 Bristol Road Selly Oak, BIRMINGHAM, B29 6LH.
SKIDMORE, Mr. Jonathan Patrick, MA FCA ATII *1994;* 32 The Robins, BRACKNELL, RG12 8BU.
SKIDMORE, Mr. Neil Rayner, FCA *1954;* Buttermere, 14 Telford Gardens, Brewood, STAFFORD, ST19 9ED. (Life Member)
SKIDMORE, Mr. Robert William, BSc ACA *1986;* 10 Bayview Road, ABERDEEN, AB15 4EY.
•**SKILBECK, Mr. Peter Godfrey, FCA** *1971;* Humphrey & Co, 7-9 The Avenue, EASTBOURNE, EAST SUSSEX, BN21 3YA.
SKILBECK, Mr. Thomas Beynac, FCA *1975;* 49 Walton Street, LONDON, SW3 2HT.
SKILBECK, Miss. Victoria Jane, BA ACA *2000;* Rose Court, 92 Rumbush Lane, Dickens Heath Village, Shirley, SOLIHULL, WEST MIDLANDS B90 1FH.
•**SKILL, Mr. Simon Christopher Robert, ACA** *1982;* Higson & Co, White House, Wollaton St, NOTTINGHAM, NG1 5GF.
SKILLEND, Mrs. Renee Patricia, FCA *1951;* 26 Foxes Dale, LONDON, SE3 9BQ. (Life Member)
SKILLETT, Ms. Kim, ACA BEng(Hons) *2011;* 12a Ashburnham Close, Bitterne, SOUTHAMPTON, SO19 7AT.
SKILLMAN, Mr. Stephen John, BSc ACA *1995;* Apartment 260 Metro Central Heights, 119 Newington Causeway, LONDON, SE1 6BX.
•**SKILTON, Mr. Andrew Martin, ACA** *1982;* Brewers, Bourne House, Queen Street, Gomshall, GUILDFORD, SURREY GU5 9LY.
SKILTON, Mrs. Catherine Jane, BSc ACA *2004;* with Ernst & Young LLP, 1 More London Place, LONDON, SE1 2AF.
SKILTON, Mr. Daniel, BSc ACA *2011;* 38 Clare Cottages, Bletchingley, REDHILL, RH1 4RE.
SKILTON, Mr. Edwin, BA ACA *1997;* 41 Landford Road, Putney, LONDON, SW15 1AQ.
SKILTON, Mr. Joe, ACA *2011;* 471a Kingston Road, LONDON, SW20 8JP.
•**SKINGLE, Mr. David Nevile, FCA** *1961;* (Tax Fac), David N Skingle, 8 Glengarry Way, Friars Cliff, CHRISTCHURCH, BH23 4EQ.
•**SKINGLEY, Mr. Julian James, BA ACA** *1999;* Ernst & Young LLP, 1 More London Place, LONDON, SE1 2AF. See also Ernst & Young Europe LLP
•**SKINNER, Mr. Alan Kenneth, FCA** *1970;* Green Hayes, Forest Road, Pyrford, WOKING, GU22 8LU.
SKINNER, Mr. Alexander Michael George, FCA *1995;* 66 Memorial Avenue, CHRISTCHURCH, NEW ZEALAND.
SKINNER, Mr. Andrew Merrick, BSc(Hons) ACA *2002;* 30 Thornby Avenue, SOLIHULL, WEST MIDLANDS, B91 2BJ.
SKINNER, Mrs. Carole Ann, FCA *1980;* 5 Sycamore Avenue, UPMINSTER, ESSEX, RM14 2HR.
SKINNER, Mr. Charles David, LLB FCA *1984;* Apartment 5, Magnolia Villa, La Route de St. Aubin, St. Lawrence, JERSEY, JE3 1LW.
SKINNER, Mr. Charles Edward, BSc ACA *2002;* 80 White Lodge Close, ISLEWORTH, MIDDLESEX, TW7 6TR.
SKINNER, Mr. Christopher Hugh, BA(Hons) ACA *2004;* with Deloitte LLP, Athene Place, 66 Shoe Lane, LONDON, EC4A 3BQ.
SKINNER, Mr. Christopher Martin, MA FCA *1975;* Star Meadow, Zeal Monachorum, CREDITON, DEVON, EX17 6DF.
•**SKINNER, Mr. Christopher Paul, ACA** *1981;* Chris Skinner, 27 Albatross Way, DARLINGTON, COUNTY DURHAM, DL1 1DN.
SKINNER, Mr. Christopher Phillip, BA ACA *2007;* 10 Evergreen Close, Hempstead, GILLINGHAM, ME7 3QY.
•**SKINNER, Mr. David John, FCA** *1973;* Wernham Wallace Skinner & Co, Summit House, 2A Highfield Road, DARTFORD, DA1 2JY.
•**SKINNER, Mr. Derek James, FCA** *1969;* Skinner & Co, The Old Vicarage, 10 Church Street, RICKMANSWORTH, HERTFORDSHIRE, WD3 1BS.
SKINNER, Mr. Edward, ACA *2011;* First Floor Flat, 18 Kingdon Road, LONDON, NW6 1PH.
SKINNER, Mrs. Elinor Ann, MA ACA *2002;* 85 Gomm Road, LONDON, SE16 2TY.
SKINNER, Miss. Gail Margaret, BSc ACA *1993;* 8\5 Boat Green, Canonmills, EDINBURGH, EH3 5LL.
SKINNER, Mr. Gordon James, FCA *1975;* 14 Bosley Close, CHRISTCHURCH, DORSET, BH23 2HQ.
SKINNER, Mrs. Helen, BA ACA *2006;* 67 Church Road, SUTTON COLDFIELD, B73 5RQ.
SKINNER, Mr. Howard Charles, FCA *1978;* with MacIntyre Hudson LLP, Equipoise House, Grove Place, BEDFORD, MK40 3LE.
SKINNER, Miss. Jenny Susan, BSc ACA *2009;* 1 Belinus Drive, BILLINGSHURST, WEST SUSSEX, RH14 9BX.
SKINNER, Mr. John Alexander, BA FCA *1976;* 15 Stanley Road, Hoylake, WIRRAL, MERSEYSIDE, CH47 1HN.
SKINNER, Mr. John Bruce, FCA *1973;* 126 Gloucester Road, KINGSTON UPON THAMES, SURREY, KT1 3QN.
SKINNER, Mr. Jonathan Nigel, BSc ACA *1982;* 1 Southlands Close, Badsworth, PONTEFRACT, WF9 1AU.
SKINNER, Mrs. June Margaret, BA ACA *1989;* 116a Church Side, EPSOM, SURREY, KT18 7SY.
SKINNER, Mr. Kevin, MSc BSc ACA *2006;* 4 Halford Court, HATFIELD, HERTFORDSHIRE, AL10 9NB.
SKINNER, Mr. Kevin Douglas, BA(Hons) ACA *2003;* Wellbrow, Patrick Street, Peel, ISLE OF MAN, IM5 1BP.
SKINNER, Miss. Laura Jane, ACA *2008;* 7 Belle Vue Road, COLCHESTER, ESSEX, CO1 1XA.
SKINNER, Miss. Leanne Rosemary, BSc ACA *2010;* 364 Lords Wood Lane, CHATHAM, KENT, ME5 8JT.
SKINNER, Mr. Mark William, BA(Hons) ACA *2001;* Craig Cottage, Reigate Hill, REIGATE, RH2 9PJ.
SKINNER, Mr. Martin Robert, BSc ACA *1994;* 53 Priests Lane, Shenfield, BRENTWOOD, ESSEX, CM15 8BX.
SKINNER, Mr. Michael Edward George, DPhil BSc ACA *2005;* 4 Waltham Close, West Bridgford, NOTTINGHAM, NG2 6LE.
SKINNER, Mr. Michael James, FCA *1987;* 2 Friendship Way, Old Bracknell Lane East, BRACKNELL, RG12 7SG.
SKINNER, Mr. Neill Jonathan, BA FCA *1996;* 13 Mason Close, ELLESMERE PORT, CH66 2GU.
•**SKINNER, Mr. Owen Stephen, FCA** *1982;* Reeves & Co LLP, Third Floor, 24 Chiswell Street, LONDON, EC1Y 4YX. See also F W Stephens Taxation Limited

SKINNER, Mr. Paul Hindley, FCA *1965;* Tyn Llan, Llanfairmathafarneithaf, TYN-Y-GONGL, LL74 8NT. (Life Member)
SKINNER, Mr. Peter John, FCA *1957;* Maple House, 20 Common Road, Bressingham, DISS, IP22 2AX. (Life Member)
SKINNER, Mr. Peter Ross, MA FCA *1958;* 5 Homecolne House, Louden Road, CROMER, NR27 9EF. (Life Member)
SKINNER, Mr. Peter Thomas, BCom ACA *1989;* 15 Albert Road, ALTON, GU34 1LP.
SKINNER, Miss. Polly Sian, BSc(Hons) ACA *2010;* 81 Ratcliffe Court, Barleyfields, BRISTOL, AVON, BS2 0FD.
SKINNER, Miss. Rebecca Marie, ACA *2005;* 21 Birchwood, Chineham, BASINGSTOKE, HAMPSHIRE, RG24 8TY.
SKINNER, Mr. Richard Adrian, BSc ACA *1981;* Fawside House, Allenheads, HEXHAM, NORTHUMBERLAND, NE47 9HR.
SKINNER, Mr. Richard Gordon, BSc FCA *1956;* 26 Hayes Road, BROMLEY, BR2 9AA. (Life Member)
SKINNER, Mr. Richard Michael Mark, BEng ACA *1989;* Voith Turbo Ltd, 6 Beddington Farm Road, CROYDON, CR0 4XB.
SKINNER, Mr. Robert David Nigel, FCA *1981;* Llwyncelyn Court, Pantmawr Road, CARDIFF, CF14 7TB.
SKINNER, Mr. Robert Michael, FCA *1975;* 4 Oaklands Avenue, WEST WICKHAM, BR4 9LE.
SKINNER, Mr. Simon John Norman, FCA *1969;* 24 Friday Street Warnham, HORSHAM, RH12 3QX.
SKINNER, Mr. Stephen John, MA FCA *1981;* Chelton Ltd, The Chelton Centre, Fourth Avenue, MARLOW, BUCKINGHAMSHIRE, SL7 1TF.
SKINNER, Miss. Suzanne K, BA ACA *1992;* 15 Hilbre Road, WIRRAL, MERSEYSIDE, CH48 3HA.
SKINNER, Mr. Timothy John, FCA *1975;* 10 Whitsbury Close, BOURNEMOUTH, BH8 0NX.
SKIPP, Mr. Richard John, BSc ACA *1992;* P A Consulting Group Cambridge Technology Centre, Back Lane Melbourn, ROYSTON, HERTFORDSHIRE, SG8 6DP.
SKIPPER, Mr. Kevin John, BA ACA *1992;* 27 Streatham Place, Bradwell Common, MILTON KEYNES, MK13 8RH.
•**SKIPPER, Mr. Paul Arthur Rees, BSc FCA** *1988;* (Tax Fac), FBL Services Limited, Bridge House, 25 Fiddle Bridge Lane, HATFIELD, HERTFORDSHIRE, AL10 0SP. See also HBB Audit Limited and Ian Pratt Limited
SKIPPER, Mr. Stephen Mark, BA FCA *1980;* Drayton House, The Green, Pulham Market, DISS, NORFOLK, IP21 4SU.
SKIPPER, Mr. Steven David, BSc ACA *1989;* 22 Audubon, KIRKLAND H9J 3Y6, QUE, CANADA.
SKIPTON, Mr. Colin Richard, FCA *1975;* 5 Gallows Drive, West Parley, FERNDOWN, DORSET, BH22 8RH.
SKIPWITH, Mr. Mark, BSc FCA *1969;* 2 School Lane, Itchen Abbas, WINCHESTER, SO21 1BE.
SKIRROW, Mr. Christopher William Michael, BSc ACA *1979;* PricewaterhouseCoopers, White Square Office Center, 10 Butyrsky Val, 125047 MOSCOW, RUSSIAN FEDERATION.
SKIRROW, Mr. Michael Philip, BA ACA *1982;* 71 High Lane East, West Hallam, ILKESTON, DE7 6HW.
SKIRROW, Mr. Richard Ian, BSc ACA *1980;* 5 High Street, Claverley, WOLVERHAMPTON, WV5 7DR.
SKIRVING, Mr. Peter Henry, BSc FCA *1976;* 1500 909 -11th Avenue S.W., CALGARY T2R 1N6, AB, CANADA.
SKITCH, Mrs. Sharon Joanne, ACA CA(SA) *2009;* 10 Camplin Street, LONDON, SE14 5QY.
SKITT, Mr. Martin James, ACA *2007;* 47 Rushbrooke Close, HIGH WYCOMBE, BUCKINGHAMSHIRE, HP13 7QW.
•**SKITTLES, Mr. Terence Ian, FCA** *1988;* Numis Limited, 1st Floor, Brook House, Mount Pleasant, CROWBOROUGH, EAST SUSSEX TN6 2NE.
SKOKOVA, Miss. Tatiana, BSc ACA *2007;* Agios Panteleimonos 2, Diamond C, Apartment 201, Agios Athanasios, 4102 LIMASSOL, CYPRUS.
SKOLAR, Mr. Alexander James, BSc ACA *1998;* 20 Crouch Hall Lane, Redbourn, ST. ALBANS, HERTFORDSHIRE, AL3 7EQ.
•**SKOLNICK, Mr. Ian Nathan, FCA** *1975;* (Tax Fac), Ian Skolnick & Co, Langley House, Park Road, LONDON, N2 8EX.
SKORDI, Ms. Georgoulla, BA FCA *1996;* 76 Abinger Road, LONDON, W4 1EX.
SKORDIS, Mr. Daniel, ACA CA(SA) *2010;* Oak Cottage, 34 Cuckoo's Knob, Wootton Rivers, MARLBOROUGH, WILTSHIRE, SN8 4NR.
SKOULDING, Mr. Peter Iain Maynard, BSc ACA *1993;* 11 Beaufort View, Luckington, CHIPPENHAM, SN14 6GS.
SKOUROS, Mr. Argyris, BA ACA *2005;* 2 Romanou Street, Tlais Tower, 2nd Floor, 1070 NICOSIA, CYPRUS. (Life Member)
SKRASTIN, Mr. Mark, MA ACA *1993;* 100 Tyrell Street, Nedlands, PERTH, WA 6009, AUSTRALIA.
SKRBA, Miss. Mirjana, ACA *2009;* 79a-79b Patshull Road, LONDON, NW5 2LE.
SKRY, Mrs. Angela Caroline, BA ACA *1993;* Practical Law Company Ltd, 19 Hatfields, LONDON, SE1 8DJ.
SKRZYPCZAK, Ms. Kristin Helen, MSc FCA ATII *1991;* 12, Burnaby Gardens, LONDON, W4 3DT.
•**SKRZYPECKI, Mr. Anthony Stefan Mark, BSc ACA** *1984;* PricewaterhouseCoopers LLP, 7 More London Riverside, LONDON, SE1 2RT. See also PricewaterhouseCoopers
SKUSE, Mr. Benjamin, BSc ACA MBA *1998;* 2 Haven Close, Portsmouth Road, ESHER, SURREY, KT10 9AH.
SKUSE, Mrs. Emma Victoria, BSc ACA *2001;* Zurich Financial Services, The Grange, Bishops Cleeve, CHELTENHAM, GLOUCESTERSHIRE, GL52 8XX.
SKUSE, Peter Christopher Bright, Esq LLB FCA *1973;* H B Clark & Co (Successors) Ltd, Westgate Brewery, WAKEFIELD, WEST YORKSHIRE, WF2 9SW.
SKYNER, Mr. Leo, BA ACA *2001;* 70 Wheat Sheaf Close, LONDON, E14 9UY.
SLACK, Mr. Albert Roylance, FCA *1965;* 34 Welton Drive, WILMSLOW, SK9 6HE. (Life Member)
•**SLACK, Mr. Andrew Michael, BSc FCA** *1974;* with Land and Rural Business, Woodlands, Westfield Road, Oakley, BEDFORD, MK43 7SU.
SLACK, Mr. Andrew Neil, MEng ACA *2003;* 208 - 1445 Marpole Avenue, VANCOUVER V6H 1S5, BC, CANADA.
SLACK, Mrs. Barbara Jane, BA ACA *1991;* Doric, 33 Cley Hall Drive, SPALDING, PE11 2EB.
SLACK, Mr. David Granville, BA FCA *1988;* Lindisfarne, 1 Fons George Road, TAUNTON, TA1 3JU.
SLACK, Mr. Edward Guy, FCA *1974;* Newsouth Innovations Pty Ltd, Rupert Myers Building, UNSW, SYDNEY, NSW 2052, AUSTRALIA.
SLACK, Mr. Edwin, FCA *1961;* 30 Reid Park Road, Jesmond, NEWCASTLE UPON TYNE, NE2 2ES. (Life Member)
SLACK, Mr. Ian David, BA FCA *1996;* Les Sables Blancs, Le Mont A la Brune, St. Brelade, JERSEY, JE3 8FL.
SLACK, Ms. Jessica Rosemary, BA ACA *2005;* Manor Office, West End, MARAZION, CORNWALL, TR17 0EF.
SLACK, Mr. John Stuart Anderson, BSc FCA *1975;* The British International School, Bintaro sektor IX, Jalan Raya Jombang, Ciputat, JAKARTA, 15227 INDONESIA.
•**SLACK, Mr. Kevin, FCA** *1982;* (Tax Fac), Mabe Allen LLP, 50 Osmaston Road, DERBY, DE1 2HU.
SLACK, Mr. Matthew James, BA ACA *2002;* Kingdom Bank Ltd Mere Way, Ruddington Fields Business Park Ruddington, NOTTINGHAM, NG11 6JS.
SLACK, Mr. Nicholas Mark Victor, BSc ACA *1991;* Hylands Farmhouse, Buckland Newton, DORCHESTER, DT2 7BS.
SLACK, Miss. Philippa, BSc ACA *2007;* 1B/28 Woods Parade, FAIRLIGHT, NSW 2094, AUSTRALIA.
SLACK, Prof. Richard Edwin, MA ACA *1989;* 9 Woodbine Avenue, NEWCASTLE UPON TYNE, NE3 4EU.
•**SLACK, Mr. Robert Myles, FCA** *1953;* R.M. Slack, 278 Skinburness Road, Skinburness, WIGTON, CA7 4QU.
SLACK, Mr. Stuart, FCA *1968;* Flat 43, Regatta House, 32 Twickenham Road, TEDDINGTON, MIDDLESEX, TW11 8AZ. (Life Member)
SLACK, Mr. William John Walton, BA ACA *1996;* Ocean Equities Limited, 3 Copthall Avenue, LONDON, EC2R 7BH.
SLADDEN, Mr. James, ACA *2010;* 106a Ashley Gardens, Thirleby Road, LONDON, SW1P 1HJ.
•**SLADDEN, Mr. Nicholas Paul, FCA DChA** *1995;* Baker Tilly Tax & Advisory Services LLP, Hanover House, 18 Mount Ephraim Road, TUNBRIDGE WELLS, KENT, TN1 1ED. See also Baker Tilly UK Audit LLP
SLADDIN, Mr. Philip, BSc ACA *1991;* PricewaterhouseCoopers AG, Olof-Palme-Strasse 35, 60439 FRANKFURT AM MAIN, GERMANY.
SLADE, Mr. Alastair James Temple Walker, BSc ACA *1994;* 95 Joo Chiat Place, SINGAPORE 427820, SINGAPORE.
SLADE, Mr. Andrew Lee, ACA *2006;* UK Coal Plc Harworth Park, Blyth Road Harworth, DONCASTER, SOUTH YORKSHIRE, DN11 8DB.
SLADE, Mrs. Ann, BA ACA *1999;* 7 Heath Mews, Ripley, WOKING, GU23 6EH.
•**SLADE, Mr. David James, BSc FCA** *1977;* 187 Rednal Road, Kings Norton, BIRMINGHAM, B38 8EA.
SLADE, Mr. Dennis Edwin, FCA *1956;* Kings Cottage, Dean Street, East Farleigh, MAIDSTONE, ME15 0PR. (Life Member)
SLADE, Mr. Douglas Colin, BSc FCA *1984;* I N G Lease (UK) Ltd Redcentral, 60 High Street, REDHILL, RH1 1NY.
•**SLADE, Miss. Emma Alicia Suzanne, BA ACA** *1995;* with RSM Tenon Audit Limited, 66 Chiltern Street, LONDON, W1U 4JT.
SLADE, Miss. Emma Clare, MSc ACA *2005;* 78 Empire Square East, Empire Square, LONDON, SE1 4NB.
SLADE, Miss. Hayley, BSc ACA *2002;* 43 Ethelfleda Road Hockley, TAMWORTH, STAFFORDSHIRE, B77 5HS.
•**SLADE, Ms. Janet Margaret, BSc FCA DChA** *1983;* Charity Commission, PO Box 1227, LIVERPOOL, L69 3UG.
SLADE, Mr. John Edward, FCA *1967;* 27 Aston Way, EPSOM, KT18 5LZ.
SLADE, Mr. John Ewart, BA FCA *1961;* Burnhayes, Cotmaton Road, SIDMOUTH, DEVON, EX10 8QT.
SLADE, Mr. Jonathan Barclay, FCA *1973;* 5 Grosvenor House, 127 Church Street, MALVERN, WORCESTERSHIRE, WR14 2BA.
SLADE, Mr. Jonathan Thomas Charles, BSc ACA MCT *1992;* 6 Woodlands, HARPENDEN, HERTFORDSHIRE, AL5 3BY.
SLADE, Mr. Keith Frederick John, FCA *1949;* Flat 8, Elgar Mews, Ednall Lane, BROMSGROVE, WORCESTERSHIRE, B60 2DB. (Life Member)
SLADE, Mr. Kenneth John, FCA *1971;* Garreglwyd, Cenarth, NEWCASTLE EMLYN, DYFED, SA38 9RB.
SLADE, Mrs. Lorraine, BA ACA *2002;* 7 Grove Road, TRING, HERTFORDSHIRE, HP23 5HA.
SLADE, Mr. Mark, BSc *2002;* 7 Grove Road, TRING, HERTFORDSHIRE, HP23 5HA.
SLADE, Mr. Mark Frederick, BA ACA *2005;* 5 Newman Drive, Branston, BURTON-ON-TRENT, STAFFORDSHIRE, DE14 3DZ.
SLADE, Mr. Michael John, BA ACA *1986;* 7 Deramore Drive, YORK, YO10 5HW.
•**SLADE, Mr. Michael Robert, ACA CA(NZ)** *2010;* Accounting Kiwi Ltd, 24 Finchley Road, WESTCLIFF-ON-SEA, ESSEX, SS0 8AE.
•**SLADE, Mr. Neville James Kimber, BA FCA** *1990;* 8 Warrender Road, CHESHAM, BUCKINGHAMSHIRE, HP5 3NE.
SLADE, Mr. Nigel Ronald, FCA *1971;* Arcadia Group Ltd, Cavendish House, 13 Portland Square, BRISTOL, BS2 8ST.
SLADE, Mr. Peter Frederick, BCom FCA *1963;* 1 Green Meadow, Little Heath, POTTERS BAR, EN6 1LL. (Life Member)
SLADE, Mr. Philip Anderson, FCA *1947;* 5 Hill Court, Chattenden, ROCHESTER, ME3 8LH. (Life Member)
SLADE, Mr. Richard Paul, BA ACA *1995;* 29 Dower Park, WINDSOR, BERKSHIRE, SL4 4BG.
SLADE, Mr. Robin Joseph, BA ACA *1985;* 69 Spring Grove, LOUGHTON, IG10 4QE.
SLADE, Mr. Roger James, FCA *1970;* 37 Chilbolton Avenue, WINCHESTER, SO22 5HE.
SLADE, Mr. Stewart William, BSc ACA *1979;* 65 Moorlands, WELWYN GARDEN CITY, AL7 4QJ.
SLADE, Mr. Tristan Rowland, BSc ACA *2005;* 9/14-16 Victoria Parade, MANLY, NSW 2095, AUSTRALIA.
SLADE, Mr. William James, BSc ACA *2002;* Lea View Pilning Street, Tockington, BRISTOL, BS32 4LR.
SLADER, Mr. David John, BA ACA *1988;* 149 Mostyn Road, Merton Park, Wimbledon, LONDON, SW19 3LS.
SLADER, Mr. Kenneth William, FCA *1959;* 120 Lower Cross Road, Bickington, BARNSTAPLE, EX31 2PJ. (Life Member)
SLAGEL, Mr. Paul Leon, BCom FCA *1981;* 89 The Drive, RICKMANSWORTH, WD3 4DY.
•**SLANEY, Mr. Arnold Keith, BA FCA** *1955;* Little Ovens, Church Lane, West Drayton, RETFORD, NOTTINGHAMSHIRE, DN22 8EB.
•**SLANN, Mr. Anthony, FCA** *1971;* Anthony Slann, 52A Walsall Road, Aldridge, WALSALL, WS9 0JL.
SLARK, Miss. Andrea Dawn, BA FCA *1987;* 14A OAKS AVENUE, CREMORNE, NSW 2090, AUSTRALIA.
SLASKA, Dr. Natalia, ACA *2011;* 2 Mercers Place, Hammersmith, LONDON, W6 7BZ.
SLATE, Mr. Liam, BSc ACA *2007;* Cross View Cottage High Street, Saul, GLOUCESTER, GL2 7LW.
SLATE, Mrs. Maxine Hannah, BSc ACA *2006;* 82 Fairdene Road, COULSDON, SURREY, CR5 1RF.
SLATER, Mr. Alexander James, ACA *2009;* 48 Canada Street, STOCKPORT, CHESHIRE, SK2 6EF.
SLATER, Mr. Andrew Edward, BA ACA *1997;* 44 Monsell Road, LONDON, N4 2EJ.
SLATER, Mrs. Anita Carole, BSc ACA *1996;* Hazelrue, Holyport Road, MAIDENHEAD, BERKSHIRE, SL6 2HA.
SLATER, Mrs. Anne Valerie Lydia, BA ACA *1998;* 10 Dunmore Road, LONDON, SW20 8TN.
SLATER, Mr. Anthony Charles, BA ACA *1992;* 3 Woodside, KNUTSFORD, CHESHIRE, WA16 8BX.
SLATER, Mr. Ben, BA ACA *2005;* 2a Cornwall Grove, LONDON, W4 2LB.
SLATER, Mr. Brett, MSc ACA *1992;* Flat 5, 23 Glenluce Road, LONDON, SE3 7SD.
SLATER, Mr. Brian Malcolm, FCA *1981;* 15 Larkfield Close, Greenmount, BURY, BL8 4QJ.
•**SLATER, Mr. Christopher Mark, ACA** *1981;* Royce Peeling Green Limited, The Copper Room, Deva Centre, Trinity Way, MANCHESTER, M3 7BG. See also RPG Holdings Limited
SLATER, Miss. Clair-Marie, BSc ACA *1993;* Flat 2, 44 Mount Sion, TUNBRIDGE WELLS, KENT, TN1 1TJ.
SLATER, Mrs. Claire, BSc ACA *1989;* 191 Elmer Road, Middleton on sea, BOGNOR REGIS, PO22 6JA.
SLATER, Miss. Claire Rosalind, BSc(Hons) ACA *2004;* 128 Kingsway, WOKING, GU21 6NR.
•**SLATER, Mr. Colin David, FCA** *1967;* (Tax Fac), Burgess Hodgson, Camburgh House, 27 New Dover Road, CANTERBURY, CT1 3DN.
SLATER, Mr. Darren William Garfield, ACA *2005;* 2 Howard Close, Fair Oak, EASTLEIGH, SO50 7AG.
SLATER, Mr. David Alan, FCA *1979;* Wentworth, Alrewas Rd, Kings Bromley, BURTON-ON-TRENT, DE13 7HP.
SLATER, Mr. David Alan, BSc ACA *1992;* 10 Parkside, Upton, NORTHAMPTON, NN5 4EQ.
•**SLATER, Mr. Edward, FCA** *1974;* Westbury Consultancy UK Ltd, 12 Westbury Drive, BRENTWOOD, CM14 4JZ.
SLATER, Mr. Edward Quentin, BA ACA *2002;* Reef Estates Limited, 14 Little Portland Street, LONDON, W1W 8BN.
•**SLATER, Mrs. Elizabeth Rosemary, FCA** *1975;* Slater Johnstone, 3 Thimble Lane, Knowle, SOLIHULL, WEST MIDLANDS, B93 0LY.
SLATER, Mrs. Fiona Diane, BSc ACA *2004;* 5 Albion Crescent, CHALFONT ST. GILES, BUCKINGHAMSHIRE, HP8 4EU.
•**SLATER, Mr. Frederick Charles, FCA** *1974;* (Tax Fac), Slater Johnstone, 3 Thimble Lane, Knowle, SOLIHULL, WEST MIDLANDS, B93 0LY.
SLATER, Mr. Gareth Ferguson, BSc ACA *2002;* 44 Blackcurrant Drive, Long Ashton, BRISTOL, BS41 9FP.
SLATER, Mr. Gavin Michael, BSc ACA *2002;* 39 Southwood Gardens, Cookham, MAIDENHEAD, BERKSHIRE, SL6 9EB.
•**SLATER, Mr. Geoffrey David, ACA** *1986;* (Tax Fac), Watson Associates, 30-34 North Street, HAILSHAM, EAST SUSSEX, BN27 1DW.
SLATER, Mr. Geoffrey Robert, FCA *1960;* Ferndown, Kinders Crescent, Greenfield, OLDHAM, OL3 7JQ. (Life Member)
SLATER, Mr. Geoffrey Stephen, FCA *1949;* 5 Hasells Courtyard, Westgate Street, Long Melford, SUDBURY, SUFFOLK, CO10 9DR. (Life Member)
•**SLATER, Mr. Gerald Robert, MBE BSc ACA** *1982;* (Tax Fac), Ernst & Young, P.O. Box 91873, TRIPOLI, LIBYAN ARAB JAMAHIRIYA.
SLATER, Mr. Gordon Edward, BA ACA *1997;* Macquarie Bank Citypoint, 1 Ropemaker Street, LONDON, EC2Y 9HD.
SLATER, Mr. Gregg Nicholas, BCom ACA *1999;* 10 Deeley Close, BIRMINGHAM, B15 2NR.
SLATER, Mr. Iain Gordon, BSc ACA *1993;* 43 Sinnels Field, Shipton-under-Wychwood, CHIPPING NORTON, OX7 6EJ.
SLATER, Mr. Iain Robert, BSc ACA *1992;* Manor House, Swineshead, BEDFORD, MK44 2AF.
SLATER, Mr. Ian Gordon, BSc ACA *1998;* 421 Watling Street, RADLETT, HERTFORDSHIRE, WD7 7JG.
SLATER, Mr. Ian James, BSc ACA *2003;* 10 Stepping Stones Bidford-on-Avon, ALCESTER, WARWICKSHIRE, B50 4PH.
SLATER, Mrs. Jacqueline, BSc ACA *2005;* The Haven, White House Lane, Jacob's Well, GUILDFORD, SURREY, GU4 7PT.
•**SLATER, Miss. Jacqueline Suzanne, FCA** *1968;* (Tax Fac), J.S. Slater, The Old House, 28 Bradford Street, SHIFNAL, TF11 8AU.
SLATER, Mr. James Derrick, FCA *1953;* Field House, Alderbrook, Smithwood Common, CRANLEIGH, SURREY, GU6 8QU. (Life Member)
SLATER, Mr. John Arthur Glascock, FCA *1967;* Flat 22, Hamilton Court, Hamilton Road, LONDON, W5 2EJ.

SLATER, Mr. Julian Christopher, ACA *1981;* Korn Ferry Whitehead Mann Ryder Court, 14 Ryder Street, LONDON, SW1Y 6QB.
•**SLATER, Mrs. Katherine Ann, BCom FCA** *1990;* with KPMG LLP, One Snowhill, Snow Hill Queensway, BIRMINGHAM, B4 6GN.
•**SLATER, Mrs. Katherine Anne, MA ACA** *2001;* Katherine Slater ACA, 29 Lime Street, RUSHDEN, NORTHAMPTONSHIRE, NN10 6DY.
SLATER, Mr. Kenneth Frederick, FCA *1953;* 125 Hallam Grange Rise, SHEFFIELD, S10 4BE. (Life Member)
SLATER, Miss. Lucy, BSc(Hons) ACA *2010;* Scottish & Southern Energy Plc, 55 Vastern Road, READING, RG1 8BU.
SLATER, Mr. Michael David, BA ACA *1984;* 12 Goldfinch Avenue, Churchlands, PERTH, WA 6018, AUSTRALIA.
SLATER, Mr. Michael John, BSc FCA *1970;* 10 B2 Amarilla Bay, Costa Del Silencio, 38630 TENERIFE, CANARY ISLANDS, SPAIN.
SLATER, Mr. Michael John, BSc ACA *1993;* Schellenstrasse 19, 8708 MANNEDORF, SWITZERLAND.
SLATER, Mr. Michael Keith, BSc(Hons) ACA *2000;* South Hill Cottage, 220 Town Lane, Whittle-le-Woods, CHORLEY, PR6 8AJ.
•**SLATER, Mr. Nigel, BSocSc ACA** *1993;* Deloitte LLP, Stonecutter Court, 1 Stonecutter Street, LONDON, EC4A 4TR. See also Deloitte & Touche LLP
SLATER, Mr. Norman Higson, FCA *1959;* 640 Newchurch Road, ROSSENDALE, BB4 9HG. (Life Member)
•**SLATER, Mr. Paul, ACA CA(SA)** *2009;* PricewaterhouseCoopers, 1 Embankment Place, LONDON, WC2N 6RH. See also PricewaterhouseCoopers LLP
•**SLATER, Mr. Paul, FCA** *1970;* (Tax Fac), Paul Slater & Co, 1 Washington Street, NORTHAMPTON, NN2 6NL.
SLATER, Mr. Paul Nolan, BSc ACA *1996;* 29 Newcomen Road, TUNBRIDGE WELLS, TN4 9PA.
SLATER, Mr. Peter Charles, BA ACA *1983;* 61 West Common, HARPENDEN, HERTFORDSHIRE, AL5 2LD.
SLATER, Mr. Peter Finlay, FCA *1960;* 6 Old Hay Close, Dore, SHEFFIELD, S17 3GQ. (Life Member)
SLATER, Mr. Philip Howard, MSc BSc FCA *1973;* Old Dairy Cottage Main Road, Walhampton, LYMINGTON, HAMPSHIRE, SO41 5RE.
SLATER, Miss. Rachel Melanie, ACA *2009;* 14 Laurel Gardens, Greenham, THATCHAM, RG19 8XU.
SLATER, Miss. Rebecca Jane, BSc ACA *1989;* 14 Wilton Avenue, LONDON, W4 2HY.
SLATER, Mr. Richard Anthony, FCA *1966;* Saxons, Chard Road, AXMINSTER, DEVON, EX13 5ED.
SLATER, Mr. Richard Craig Alan, MBA BA FCA *1988;* Westleigh, Stannage Lane, Churton, CHESTER, CH3 6LE.
SLATER, Mr. Robert John, BSc ACA *2007;* with BDO LLP, 125 Colmore Row, BIRMINGHAM, B3 3SD.
SLATER, Mrs. Sally, ACA MAAT *1997;* 49 Dorset Avenue, Shaw, OLDHAM, OL2 7EG.
SLATER, Mr. Scott Matthew, BSc ACA *2005;* The Old School House, 1 Long Road, Framingham Earl, NORWICH, NR14 7RY.
•**SLATER, Mr. Stephen Derek, BA(Hons) ACA** *1992;* RMT Accountants and Business Advisors Limited, Unit 2, Gosforth Park Avenue, NEWCASTLE UPON TYNE, NE12 8EG. See also RMT Accountants and Business Advisors
•**SLATER, Mr. Stephen John, FCA** *1981;* Butler & Co (Bishops Waltham) Limited, Avalon House, Waltham Business Park, Brickyard Road, Swanmore, SOUTHAMPTON SO32 2SA. See also Butler & Co
SLATER, Mr. Stephen Michael, BSc FCA *1982;* 5 The Haydens, TONBRIDGE, KENT, TN9 1NS.
•**SLATER, Mr. Stephen Peter, FCA** *1991;* (Tax Fac), Slaters, Lymore Villa, 162a London Road, Chesterton, NEWCASTLE, STAFFORDSHIRE ST5 7JB.
SLATER, Mr. Steven Frederick, BA ACA *1995;* The Venus, Bovis Lend Lease Ltd, 1 Old Park Lane Urmston, MANCHESTER, M41 7HG.
SLATER, Mr. Steven Roger, BSc ACA *2005;* 3 Bexhill Drive, Amington, TAMWORTH, STAFFORDSHIRE, B77 3AL.
SLATER, Mr. Steven Thomas, BA ACA *2009;* Navis Agere, Unit 1 Beaufort House, Beaufort Court, Sir Thomas Longley Road, Medway City Estate, ROCHESTER ME2 4FB.
SLATER, Mrs. Sue Helen, BA ACA *1983;* 61 West Common, HARPENDEN, HERTFORDSHIRE, AL5 2LD.
SLATER, Mr. Timothy David Wishart, FCA *1957;* 69 High Street, Odiham, HOOK, HAMPSHIRE, RG29 1LB. (Life Member)
SLATER, Mr. Timothy Giles, BA ACA *1999;* with Grant Thornton UK LLP, 30 Finsbury Square, LONDON, EC2P 2YU.
•**SLATER, Mr. Timothy William, BSc ACA** *1991;* (Tax Fac), Harmer Slater Limited, Salatin House, 19 Cedar Road, SUTTON, SURREY, SM2 5DA. See also Service Charge Assurance Ltd
SLATER, Mr. Toby Paul, BSc ACA *2005;* British Gas Plc, 30 The Causeway, STAINES, MIDDLESEX, TW18 3BY.
SLATER, Mrs. Wendy Jane, ACA *1983;* Wentworth, Alrewas Road, Kings Bromley, BURTON-ON-TRENT, DE13 7HP.
SLATOR, Mr. Michael Barton, BCom FCA *1972;* 26 Withey Close West, Stoke Bishop, BRISTOL, BS9 3SX.
SLATOR, Mr. Richard Anthony, BA FCA *1972;* 27 Fallowfield Drive, Barton-Under-Needwood, BURTON-ON-TRENT, DE13 8DH.
•①**SLATOR, Mr. Thomas, MA ACA** *1979;* Maccallum Slator, Claverton House, Love Lane, CIRENCESTER, GL7 1YG.
SLATTER, Mr. Benjamin St Pierre, BA ACA *1999;* Rutland Partners LLP, Cunard House, 15 Regent Street, LONDON, SW1Y 4LR.
•**SLATTER, Mrs. Claire Elizabeth, ACA FCCA** *2010;* Manningtons, 7-9 Wellington Square, HASTINGS, EAST SUSSEX, TN34 1PD.
SLATTER, Miss. Claire Jacqueline, ACA MAAT BBusSci *2006;* Hunting Plc, 3 Cockspur Street, LONDON, SW1Y 5BQ.
SLATTER, Mr. David Martin, FCA *1964;* 36 Thames Village, Hartington RoadChiswick, LONDON, W4 3UE.
SLATTER, Mr. Keith William, FCA *1959;* 116 Reddown Road, COULSDON, CR5 1AL.
SLATTER, Mr. Raymond John, MPhil FCA *1989;* Harrow Hill Farm Shipston Road, Long Compton, SHIPSTON-ON-STOUR, CV36 5JR.
SLATTERY, Mr. Barry John, BA ACA ACII *1994;* 21 Beckenham Road, WEST WICKHAM, BR4 0QR.
SLATTERY, Mr. Jonathan Christopher, BDS ACA *1992;* 8 Hill Top Avenue, WILMSLOW, CHESHIRE, SK9 2JE.
SLATTERY, Mr. Paul Francis, BA ACA *1994;* 11 Stamford Road, OAKHAM, LEICESTERSHIRE, LE15 6HZ.
SLATTERY, Mr. Peter John, BA(Hons) ACA *2004;* Dungan Management Services Limited, 2nd Floor, 7 West Centre, Bath Street, St. Helier, JERSEY JE2 4ST.
SLAUGHTER, Mr. Andreas Michael Rogers Heimers, BSc ACA *1979;* Mitterteicherstr 11, 81549 MUNICH, GERMANY.
SLAUGHTER, Mrs. Caroline Elizabeth, BA ACA *1992;* Alderley House H166, Astrazeneca Alderley House, Alderley Park, MACCLESFIELD, CHESHIRE, SK10 4TF.
SLAUGHTER, Mr. David Charles Ellis, BSc ACA *1990;* Citigroup Centre, 33 Canada Square, LONDON, E14 5LB.
SLAUGHTER, Miss. Jane Carol, BSc ACA *1990;* 14 Kingscote Road, LONDON, W4 5LJ.
SLAVEN, Miss. Alison Jane, BSc(Econ) ACA *1997;* 128 West End Avenue, HARROGATE, NORTH YORKSHIRE, HG2 9BT.
SLAVIN, Miss. Adele Christine, MA ACA *1995;* Flat 3 Woodhayes, Woodlands Road, WEST BYFLEET, KT14 6BF.
SLAVIN, Mr. Alan, FCA *1958;* Greyfor, Aldenham Grove, RADLETT, HERTFORDSHIRE, WD7 7BN. (Life Member)
SLAVIN, Mr. Jeffrey Robert, FCA *1975;* Fragrance Oils (Int) Ltd, Eton Hill Industrial Estate, Eton Hill Road, Radcliffe, MANCHESTER, M26 2FR.
•**SLAVIN, Mr. Laurence Mark, FCA** *1985;* (Tax Fac), Ramsay Brown and Partners, Ramsay House, 18 Vera Avenue, Grange Park, LONDON, N21 1RA.
SLAVIN, Mr. Philip Simon, BSc ACA *2000;* Westfield Shoppingtowns Limited, 71 High Holborn, LONDON, WC1V 6EA.
SLAWTHER, Mr. Gary Michael, BA ACA FCT *1991;* Financial Risk Advisory Limited, 115 Walton Road, Stockton Heath, WARRINGTON, WA4 6NT.
SLAY, Mr. Stephen Derek, BA ACA *2010;* 38 Oliver Road, Cowley, OXFORD, OX4 2JF.
SLAYDEN, Miss. Beth Anna, ACA *2009;* 85 Park Avenue South, LONDON, N8 8LX.
SLAYTOR, Mr. John Singleton, FCA *1996;* 44 Euroka Street, WAVERTON, NSW 2060, AUSTRALIA.
SLEAP, Mr. Jeremy Ronald, FCA *1977;* Boyes Turner Abbots House, Abbey Street, READING, RG1 3BD.
•**SLEAP, Mr. William Bruce Dimoline, BA FCA** *1991;* Bristow Burrell, 4 Riverview, Walnut Tree Close, GUILDFORD, GU1 4UX.
SLEAT, Mr. Kenneth William, FCA *1979;* 2 Camden Park, TUNBRIDGE WELLS, TN2 4TW.
SLEATER, Mr. William, FCA FCII FCILA *1964;* Infinity House, South County Office Park, Leopardstown, DUBLIN 18, COUNTY DUBLIN, IRELAND.
SLEATH, Mr. Craig, BA ACA *1995;* 35 High Street, Barkway, ROYSTON, HERTFORDSHIRE, SG8 8EA.
SLEATH, Mr. David John Rivers, BSc FCA *1985;* Cunard House, 15 Regent Street, LONDON, SW1Y 4LR.
SLEATH, Mr. Dennis William, FCA *1967;* Lynden House, 53 Swingbridge Street, Foxton, MARKET HARBOROUGH, LEICESTERSHIRE, LE16 7RH.
SLEATOR, Mr. Lorcan Jude, BA ACA *1995;* Oakwood House, Curraghmore, MULLINGAR, COUNTY WESTMEATH, IRELAND.
•**SLEAVE, Mr. Leonard Ian, BSc FCA** *1975;* Rossmore, Ridgeway, Horsell, WOKING, GU21 4QR.
SLEDMERE, Mr. Peter Robert, FCA *1973;* Tanglewood, Church Road, Otley, IPSWICH, IP6 9NP.
•**SLEE, Mrs. Amy Louise, FCA** *2000;* Crowe Morgan, 8 St. George's Street, Douglas, ISLE OF MAN, IM1 1AH.
SLEE, Mr. Brian Richard, BA ACA *1987;* Imperial Tobacco Ltd: West Pdo, PO Box 76, NOTTINGHAM, NG7 5PL.
SLEE, Mr. Harry, FCA *1953;* Crockers Ash, Broad Walk, Prestbury, MACCLESFIELD, SK10 4BR. (Life Member)
SLEE, Mr. Rodney, FCA *1969;* 73 Galsworthy Road, CHERTSEY, KT16 8EP.
SLEE, Mr. Roy Kenneth Folland, FCA *1988;* 9 Vincent Close, Duston, NORTHAMPTON, NN5 6YA.
SLEEMAN, Mr. Anthony John, MA ACA *2010;* Brook Cottage, Sychem Lane, Five Oak Green, TONBRIDGE, KENT, TN12 6TT.
SLEEMAN, Mr. Benjamin Hywel, MSc BSc ACA *2010;* 1 Chartwell Court, New Cut, CHATHAM, ME4 6DS.
SLEEMAN, Mr. John Keith, BSc FCA *1974;* 35 Berkeley Square, LONDON, W1J 5BF.
SLEEMAN, Mrs. Sandra Louise, BSc ACA *1996;* with PricewaterhouseCoopers LLP, Cornwall Court, 19 Cornwall Street, BIRMINGHAM, B3 2DT.
SLEEP, Mr. Paul Marshall, FCA *1969;* PO Box 10400, GEORGETOWN, GRAND CAYMAN, KY1-1004, CAYMAN ISLANDS.
SLEEP, Mr. Peter George, BA FCA *1989;* 13 Lancaster Park, RICHMOND, SURREY, TW10 6AB.
SLEEP, Miss. Sally Anne, BSc ACA *1987;* 48 Aylesbury Road, Aston Clinton, AYLESBURY, BUCKINGHAMSHIRE, HP22 5AH.
SLEET, Mr. Harry Anthony, BSc ACA *1995;* 5 Stanford Close, HASSOCKS, WEST SUSSEX, BN6 8JN.
SLEETH, Mr. Philip John, BA FCA *1981;* Grovelands House, Moulton, BARRY, CF62 3AB.
SLEGG, Mrs. Nicola Susanna, FCA *1999;* Field House Highfield Lane, Great Ryburgh, FAKENHAM, NORFOLK, NR21 7AL.
SLEIGH, Mr. Andrew Peter, BA FCA *1989;* Kier North West Keir House, 4 Windward Drive Speke, LIVERPOOL, L24 8QR.
SLEIGH, Mr. Geoffrey Colin, FCA *1963;* Swan Hill, Llynclys, OSWESTRY, SY10 9QB.
SLEIGH, Mr. Matthew James Noel, ACA *1990;* 60 Oakleigh Park North, LONDON, N20 9AS.
SLEIGH, Mr. Michael John, FCA *1972;* Orchard Gate, Queens Road, OSWESTRY, SY11 2HY.
SLEIGH, Mr. Richard Edward, BA(Hons) ACA *2002;* 901 Izumi Garden Residence, Roppongi 1-5-3, Minato-Ku, TOKYO, 1060032 JAPAN.
SLEIGH-JOHNSON, Dr. Nigel Victor, FCA *1987;* with ICAEW, Chartered Accountants' Hall, Moorgate Place, LONDON, EC2P 2BJ.
SLEIGHT, Miss. Alison, BSc(Hons) ACA *2000;* 9 Newson Street, IPSWICH, IP1 3NY.
SLEIGHT, Mr. Mark James, BSc FCA *2000;* (Tax Fac), 32 Pentland Road, Dronfield Woodhouse, DRONFIELD, DERBYSHIRE, S18 8ZQ.
SLEIGHTHOLME, Mr. Ian Clifford William, BA ACA *1995;* Hollies Cottage, Hollies Common, Gnosall, STAFFORD, ST20 0JD.
SLEIGHTHOLME, Mr. John Joseph, BSc ACA *2002;* LCCG, Dewhurst Row, Bamber Bridge, PRESTON, PR5 6BB.
SLENEY, Mrs. Amanda Sarah Louise, BA ACA *1993;* St Georges Quarter Unit 9, New North Parade, HUDDERSFIELD, WEST YORKSHIRE, HD1 5JP.
SLESS, Mr. Henry John, BA ACA *1980;* Hideaway, Quarry Wood, MARLOW, BUCKINGHAMSHIRE, SL7 1RF.
SLEVIN, Mr. Damian, BSc ACA *1990;* 55 Green End Street, Aston Clinton, AYLESBURY, HP22 5EX.
SLEVIN, Mr. David John, BSc FCA *1995;* The Milton Group Ltd, Unit 4, Station Approach, Borough Green, SEVENOAKS, KENT TN15 8AD.
SLEVIN, Mr. Richard John, ACA *2008;* 12 Hadley Place, WEYBRIDGE, KT13 0SH.
SLIM, Mr. Adam James, MA ACA *1998;* with PKF (UK) LLP, Farringdon Place, 20 Farringdon Road, LONDON, EC1M 3AP.
SLIM, Mr. Alfred, FCA *1971;* 2 Roger Close, Romiley, STOCKPORT, CHESHIRE, SK6 3DJ.
SLIMMING, Mr. Paul, BA ACA *2007;* 11F Sumitomo Fudosan Roppongi Dori Bldg 7-18-18 Roppongi Minato-ku, TOKYO, 106-0032 JAPAN.
SLINGER, Mrs. Alison Jane, BSc ACA *1991;* 234 Norwood Gardens, SOUTHWELL, NG25 0DS.
SLINGER, Miss. Arabella Claire Felicity, MA ACA *1997;* Penfida Partners LLP, 1 Carey Lane, LONDON, EC2V 8AE.
SLINGER, Mrs. Helen Louise, BSc(Hons) ACA *2003;* with PricewaterhouseCoopers LLP, Benson House, 33 Wellington Street, LEEDS, LS1 4JP.
SLINGER, Mrs. Janet Mary, FCA *1973;* 6 Royal Park, Grosvenor Road, SOUTHPORT, MERSEYSIDE, PR8 2HS.
SLINGER, Mrs. Joanne, BA(Hons) ACA *2003;* Carole Nash Insurance Consultants, Trafalgar House, 110 Manchester Road, ALTRINCHAM, CHESHIRE, WA14 1NU.
SLINGER, Mr. Mark, LLB ACA *2004;* 38 Woodstock Road, SHEFFIELD, S7 1HB.
SLINGER, Mr. Mark David, LLB ACA *2002;* 9 Oak Road, SALE, CHESHIRE, M33 2FD.
•**SLINGSBY, Mr. Arthur Geoffrey, FCA ACA** *1966;* A.G.Slingsby & Co, Quinton Cottage, Kitesnest Lane, Whiteshill, STROUD, GL6 6BQ.
SLINGSBY, Mr. Jonathan Malcolm, FCA *1975;* Larchfield, Barncroft, Appleshaw, ANDOVER, SP11 9BU.
SLINN, Mr. Trevor James Martin, ACA *1983;* 59 Hawkhurst Way, BEXHILL-ON-SEA, TN39 3SN.
SLIPPER, Mr. James Andrew, BSc ACA *1996;* Gresham L L P, 1 South Place, LONDON, EC2M 2GT.
SLIPPER, Mr. John Charles Crichton, BSc ACA *1993;* Amberfield House, Amber Lane, Chart Sutton, MAIDSTONE, KENT, ME17 3SF.
SLOAN, Mr. Benjamin James, ACA *2002;* Sotham Engineering Services Ltd, The Granary, Home End, Fulbourn, CAMBRIDGE, CB21 5BS.
SLOAN, Mr. Christopher, FCA *1963;* with Heywood Shepherd, 1 Park Street, MACCLESFIELD, CHESHIRE, SK11 6SR.
SLOAN, Mr. James Ferguson, FCA *1958;* 5331 Malibu Court, CAPE CORAL, FL 33904, UNITED STATES. (Life Member)
SLOAN, Mr. Jeremy Alan, MA ACA *1994;* 39 Foster Street, PARKSIDE, SA 5063, AUSTRALIA.
SLOAN, Mr. John Anthony, FCA *1980;* 47 Maple Street, Suite L 15, SUMMIT, NJ 07901, UNITED STATES.
SLOAN, Mr. Neil Thomas Alexander, MChem ACA *2007;* with KPMG, 147 Collins Street, MELBOURNE, VIC 3000, AUSTRALIA.
SLOAN, Mr. Peter, FCA *1966;* 50 South Park Road, Gatley, CHEADLE, SK8 4AN.
•**SLOAN, Mrs. Sarah Forbes, LLB(Hons) ACA** *2001;* The A9 Partnership, Abercorn School, Newton, BROXBURN, WEST LOTHIAN, EH52 6PZ.
SLOAN, Mr. Sean William, BSc(Hons) FCA *2001;* (Tax Fac), 65 Montonmill Gardens, Eccles, MANCHESTER, M30 8BQ.
SLOAN, Mr. Simon Royston, MEng ACA *2010;* 222 Cockett Road, Cockett, SWANSEA, SA2 0FN.
SLOANE, Mr. Brian George Roger, FCA *1970;* Sea Haze, 21 Marine Drive West, West Wittering, CHICHESTER, WEST SUSSEX, PO20 8HH.
SLOBOM, Mr. David Laurence, FCA *1964;* Little Tudors, 44 Marshals Drive, ST. ALBANS, AL1 4RQ. (Life Member)
SLOCOCK, Mr. Jason Rupert, BSc ACA *1996;* with PricewaterhouseCoopers LLP, 7 More London Riverside, LONDON, SE1 2RT.
•**SLOCOMBE, Mr. Daniel Terence, BA ACA** *2000;* Moore Stephens, 30 Gay Street, BATH, BA1 2PA.
SLOCOMBE, Mr. John Clive, FCA *1960;* 3 Cyncoed Crescent, Cyncoed, CARDIFF, CF23 6SW.
SLOGGETT, Miss. Tina, ACA *1980;* 66 Varney Rd, Warners End, HEMEL HEMPSTEAD, HP1 2LR.
SLOLEY, Mr. Alexander John, BEng ACA *1997;* Halls Farm, Church Lane, Osmington, WEYMOUTH, DORSET, DT3 6EW.
SLOMAN, Mr. Andrew George, BA ACA *1999;* 50 Stray Park, Yealmpton, PLYMOUTH, PL8 2HF.
SLOMAN, Mr. Ian Stanley, BSc ACA *1992;* Albury, Terrys Lane, Cookham, MAIDENHEAD, BERKSHIRE, SL6 9RT.
SLOMAN, Mrs. Sandra Janet, BSc(Hons) ACA *2002;* Moonrakers Rydes Hill Road, Chittys Common, GUILDFORD, SURREY, GU2 9UQ.

SLOMAN, Mr. Steven Paul, BSc ACA *1993;* C/0 PricewaterhouseCoopers, Sumitomo Fudosan, Shiodome Hamarikyu, Bldg 8-21-1, Ginza, Chuo-ku TOKYO 104-0061 JAPAN.
•**SLONEEM, Mr. Jeffrey, FCA** *1969;* (Tax Fac), Harold Everett Wreford LLP, 1st Floor, 44-46 Whitfield Street, LONDON, W1T 2RJ.
SLOPER, Mr. Edward, FCA *1969;* Woodend, The Ridge, Little Baddow, CHELMSFORD, CM3 4RU.
SLOPER, Mr. Richard, BA(Hons) ACA *2002;* 38 Bamfield Place, Isle of dogs, LONDON, E14 9YA.
SLOSS, Miss. Barbara Elizabeth Maude, ACA *2009;* Acxiom, 17 Hatfields, LONDON, SE1 8DJ.
SLOTEMA, Mrs. Jennie Louise, BSc ACA *2001;* 38 Llanedeyrn Road, Penylan, CARDIFF, CF23 9DY.
SLOTEMA, Mr. Sander Hugo, BSc ACA *2000;* 802 Bamboo Grove, 82 Kennedy Road, WAN CHAI, HONG KONG ISLAND, HONG KONG SAR.
SLOW, Mr. Jonathan Mark, BA ACA *1999;* 8 Brussels Road, LONDON, SW11 2AF.
SLOWE, Mr. Philip John, FCA *1975;* 31 College Close, Longridge, PRESTON, PR3 3AX.
SLOWE, Mr. Robert Leon, FCA *1960;* c/o J.Leon & Co Ltd, J Leon & Company Ltd, 32 Hampstead High Street, LONDON, NW3 1JQ.
•**SLUCKIS, Mr. Ian, BA FCA** *1983;* (Tax Fac), Freedman Frankl & Taylor, Reedham House, 31 King Street West, MANCHESTER, M3 2PJ.
SLUMBERS, Mrs. Jill Elizabeth, BCom ACA *1986;* Winfield, The Warren, East Horsley, LEATHERHEAD, KT24 5RH.
SLUMBERS, Mr. Martin Richard, BSc ACA *1985;* Deutsche Bank, Winchester House, 1 Great Winchester Street, LONDON, EC2N 2DB.
SLUPEK, Mr. Jonathan, BA ACA *2011;* 78 Greenham Road, LONDON, N10 1LP.
•**SLY, Mr. Christopher David, BA ACA** *2002;* York Sly Limited, Charterhouse, 5 Hill Rise View, BROMSGROVE, WORCESTERSHIRE, B60 1GA. See also York Sly
SLYFIELD, Mr. Christopher Charles Eric, FCA *1972;* Sandness, The Close, GODALMING, SURREY, GU7 1PQ.
•**SMAIL, Mr. Adam Trevor Kelly, FCA** *1973;* Shepherd Smail, Northway House, The Forum, CIRENCESTER, GLOUCESTERSHIRE, GL7 2QY.
SMAIL, Mr. Adam Trevor Nicholas, MEng ACA *2005;* with Hazlewoods LLP, Windsor House, Barnett Way, Barnwood, GLOUCESTER, GL4 3RT.
•**SMAIL, Mr. Christopher John, BSc FCA DChA** *1983;* Seaview, 2 Bamford Grove, Didsbury, MANCHESTER, M20 2FF.
SMAIL, Mrs. Lee Nadine, BSc ACA MBA *1996;* Oaktree House, St Charles Road, SPENNYMOOR, DL16 6JY.
SMAILES, Mr. David Norman, BSc FCA *1991;* Mid Foresterseat, Pluscarden, ELGIN, MORAYSHIRE, IV30 8TZ.
SMAILES, Mr. David Roy, FCA *1978;* 57 Fulwood Walk, LONDON, SW19 6RB.
SMAILES, Mrs. Lyndsay Anne, BA ACA *1992;* Mid Foresterseat, Pluscarden, ELGIN, MORAYSHIRE, IV30 8TZ.
SMAILES, Miss. Nicola Emma, ACA *2009;* 1 Eckstein Road, LONDON, SW11 1QE.
SMAILES, Mr. Norman, BA ACA *1994;* Jessamine Cottage, 1 Langford Road, Burley-in-Wharfedale, ILKLEY, LS29 7NL.
SMAILS, Mr. William Peter, FCA *1956;* 23 Basil Green, Orton Longueville, PETERBOROUGH, PE2 7AW. (Life Member)
SMAL, Mr. Karol Zygmunt, FCA *1973;* 9 Grove Lane, KINGSTON-UPON-THAMES, KT1 2SU.
SMALE, Mr. Adrian, BSc ACA *2007;* 189 Kingsdown Avenue, SOUTH CROYDON, SURREY, CR2 6QS.
SMALE, Mrs. Caroline, BSc FCA *1992;* with Bishop Fleming, Stratus House, Emperor Way, Exeter Business Park, EXETER, EX1 3QS.
SMALE, Mr. David, MA BA ACA *2003;* 258 Dunford Road, HOLMFIRTH, HD9 2RR.
SMALE, Mr. Dennis Harold, FCA *1952;* Shenstone, South Grove, Kilham, DRIFFIELD, NORTH HUMBERSIDE, YO25 4SL. (Life Member)
SMALE, Mrs. Georgina Louise, BSc ACA *2004;* American Express Europe Ltd Belgrave House, 76 Buckingham Palace Road, LONDON, SW1W 9AX.
SMALE, Miss. Jenny Anne, BA ACA *2010;* Specific Media 10th Floor, 1 St. Giles High Street, LONDON, WC2H 8AG.
SMALE, Mr. John Leslie James, FCA *1955;* Long Orchard, Dalditch Lane, BUDLEIGH SALTERTON, EX9 7AH. (Life Member)
SMALE, Mr. Ralph John, MBA BA FCA *1992;* Maple House, 149 Tottenham Court Road, LONDON, W1T 7BN.
•**SMALE, Mr. Simon Jonathan, BSc FCA** *1992;* Robson & Co Limited, Kingfisher Court, Plaxton Bridge Road, Woodmansey, BEVERLEY, NORTH HUMBERSIDE HU17 0RT. See also RBA Accountancy Limited
SMALES, Mr. David Andrew, BA ACA *1995;* Aecorn Group, 20 Carlson Court, Sutie 800, TORONTO M9W 7K6, ON, CANADA.
SMALL, Mr. Andrew, BSc ACA *2011;* 14 Keswick Road, Cringleford, NORWICH, NR4 6UG.
SMALL, Mr. Andrew, FCA *1991;* 29 Douglas Road, Horfield, BRISTOL, BS7 0JE.
SMALL, Mr. Angus James, LLB ACA *1992;* 59 Balham Park Road, Balham, LONDON, SW12 8DZ.
SMALL, Mr. Brian Michael, BSc FCA *1981;* Salwarpe House, Salwarpe, DROITWICH, WR9 0AH.
SMALL, Mr. Clive James, ACA *1978;* Quatford Grange Quatford, BRIDGNORTH, SHROPSHIRE, WV15 6QJ.
SMALL, Mr. Daniel Ben, BA ACA *2002;* 45 Spoonhill Road, Stannington, SHEFFIELD, S6 5PA.
•**SMALL, Mr. David Angus, BA ACA** *1984;* Financial Forensics LLP, 6 Snow Hill, LONDON, EC1A 2AY.
SMALL, Mrs. Elizabeth Mary, ACA *1983;* 15 Richmond Drive, SCUNTHORPE, SOUTH HUMBERSIDE, DN16 3NP.
•**SMALL, Mrs. Frances Elizabeth, FCA** *1974;* Redland Business Consultancy Limited, 4 Branksome Road, Redland, BRISTOL, BS6 7LL.
•**SMALL, Mr. Francis David, MA FCA** *1982;* Ernst & Young LLP, 1 More London Place, LONDON, SE1 2AF. See also Ernst & Young Europe LLP
SMALL, Mr. Gerard William, BA FCA *1990;* Audit Commission, 411 The Heath Business & Technical Park, RUNCORN, CHESHIRE, WA7 4QX.
•**SMALL, Mr. James Donald, FCA** *1956;* J.D. Small, 7 Niall Close, Edgbaston, BIRMINGHAM, B15 3LU.
•**SMALL, Mr. Julian Philip, BSc FCA** *1991;* Deloitte LLP, 2 New Street Square, LONDON, EC4A 3BZ. See also Deloitte & Touche LLP
SMALL, Mr. Mark Calita, BA ACA *2003;* 2 Carpenters Way, ROCHDALE, LANCASHIRE, OL16 4XU.
•**SMALL, Mr. Matthew George, ACA** *2007;* (Tax Fac), Berkeley Hall Marshall Limited, 6 Charlotte Street, BATH, BA1 2NE.
SMALL, Mr. Michael, PhD MPhys(Hons) ACA *2006;* 23 Third Avenue, GLASGOW, G44 4TH.
SMALL, Mrs. Nicola, LLB ACA CTA *2003;* 119 Laleham Road, SHEPPERTON, MIDDLESEX, TW17 0AA.
SMALL, Mr. Peter Lawson, FCA *1968;* Cobbetts, 56 Woodland Road, Patney, DEVIZES, SN10 3RG.
•**SMALL, Mr. Richard Ealey, BSc FCA** *1981;* Richard Small & Co, 24 Central Precinct, Winchester Road, Chandlers Ford, EASTLEIGH, SO53 2GA.
SMALL, Mr. Richard Ernest John, BA ACA *2001;* Hermann Raddatz weg 8, 40489 DUSSELDORF, GERMANY.
SMALL, Mrs. Shona Margaret, BMet ACA *1987;* Nottingham Council for Voluntary Service, 7 Mansfield Road, NOTTINGHAM, NG1 3FB.
SMALL, Mr. Simon Ashley, MA ACA *1986;* 6 Rowley Close, Edingale, TAMWORTH, STAFFORDSHIRE, B79 9LN.
SMALL, Mr. Steven Howard, BSc FCA *1979;* 18 Marquis Avenue, NEWCASTLE UPON TYNE, NE5 1YF.
SMALL, Mr. Steven Murray, BA FCA *1980;* 5 Sunset Place, SINGAPORE 597354, SINGAPORE.
SMALL, Mrs. Wendy Patricia, BSc ACA *1987;* Babcock 4 S Ltd Bay Tree Avenue, Kingston Road, LEATHERHEAD, KT22 7UE.
SMALLBONE, Mr. Gary Bryan, BSc FCA *1993;* 1 Beaurepaire Close, Bramley, TADLEY, HAMPSHIRE, RG26 5DT.
SMALLBONE, Mr. Timothy Charles, BSc ACA *1992;* Four Oaks Hall Drive, Bramhope, LEEDS, LS16 9JE.
SMALLER, Mr. Adrian Mark, BSc ACA *1991;* Flat A/28, Parliament View Apartments, 1 Albert Embankment, LONDON, SE1 7XH.
SMALLER, Mr. David, BSc ACA *1990;* 44 Clos Des Ormes, La Verte Rue, St. Lawrence, JERSEY, JE3 1JJ.
SMALLEY, Mr. Fraser John, BSc ACA *1997;* 12 McAuley Parade, PACIFIC PINES, QLD 4211, AUSTRALIA.
SMALLEY, Mr. Ian Christopher, BSc FCA *1989;* 23 Town Street, Rawdon, LEEDS, LS19 6PU.
SMALLEY, Mr. James David, BSc ACA *2002;* with Mazars LLP, Sixth Floor, Times House, Throwley Way, SUTTON, SURREY SM1 4JQ.
SMALLEY, Mr. John William, BSc(Hons) ACA *2001;* 300 Inu Pl, KULA, HI 96790, UNITED STATES.
SMALLEY, Mr. Michael, ACA *1983;* (Tax Fac), 3 Townwell Lane, Irchester, WELLINGBOROUGH, NN29 7AH.
SMALLEY, Mrs. Monica, LLB ACA *1999;* 629 Luzon Avenue, TAMPA, FL 33606, UNITED STATES.
SMALLEY, Mr. Oliver James, BSc ACA *2004;* Keller Court, Route De Coudre, St. Peters, GUERNSEY, GY7 9DL.
SMALLEY, Mr. Robert Anthony, BSc ACA *2001;* 1 Carlbury Close, ST. ALBANS, AL1 5DR.
•**SMALLMAN, Mr. Robin Charles, BA FCA** *1984;* 148 Strines Road, Strines, STOCKPORT, CHESHIRE, SK6 7GA.
•**SMALLMAN, Mr. Roger Charles Bruno, FCA** *1969;* Roger Smallman & Co Limited, 30A Bedford Place, SOUTHAMPTON, SO15 2DG. See also Bedford Place Tax Shop Limited
SMALLPEICE, Mr. Charles Peter, JP BA FCA *1963;* 1 Osborne Court, NORWICH, NR2 2NN. (Life Member)
•**SMALLWOOD, Mrs. Alison Margaret Felicite, ACA** *1984;* Thorne Widgery Accountancy Ltd, 33 Bridge Street, HEREFORD, HR4 9DQ. See also TW Business Solutions LLP and Thorne Widgery & Jones LLP
SMALLWOOD, Mrs. Felicity Joan, BSc ACA *1979;* 49 Channel View Road, Campbells Bay, AUCKLAND, NEW ZEALAND.
SMALLWOOD, Mr. Ian Malcolm, BCom ACA *1988;* 21 Highfield Crescent, WILMSLOW, SK9 2JL.
SMALLWOOD, Mr. John Charles Thaine, FCA *1972;* Rua Dr Shigeo Mori 1073, Cidade Universitaria, Campinas, 13084-080 SAO PAULO, BRAZIL.
SMALLWOOD, Mr. Malcolm Philip, FCA *1979;* Calle Espana 6, Ventanicas, Mojacar Playa, ALMERIA, SPAIN.
SMALLWOOD, Mr. Matthew John, BSc ACA *1999;* Apartment 4071, 2727 Revere Street, HOUSTON, TX 77098, UNITED STATES.
SMALLWOOD, Mr. Neil McNaughton, BSc ACA *1983;* Fiba Tech Industries Ltd, Willmotts Business park, Waterlip, SHEPTON MALLET, SOMERSET, BA4 4RN.
SMALLWOOD, Mr. Paul, MA BA FCA *1994;* 18 Newquay Close, NUNEATON, CV11 6FH.
SMALLWOOD, Mr. Roger John, FCA *1975;* 43 Clifford Road, Copcut, DROITWICH, WR9 8UR.
SMALLWOOD, Mr. Steven Charles, BA FCA *1980;* 8 Wymondley Grove, Trentham, STOKE-ON-TRENT, ST4 8TW.
SMALLWOOD-ROSE, Mrs. June, BA FCA *1983;* 43 Linthurst Newtown, Blackwell, BROMSGROVE, WORCESTERSHIRE, B60 1BS.
SMARDON, Mr. Andrew Robert, MA ACA *2004;* Critchleys Greyfriars Court, Paradise Square, OXFORD, OX1 1BE.
SMARIDGE, Mr. Roger Nicholas, FCA *1970;* The Old Manor House, Petersfield Road, Ropley, ALRESFORD, HAMPSHIRE, SO24 0DX.
SMART, Mr. Adrian Paul, ACA *1997;* 32 Epping Grove, Sothall, SHEFFIELD, S20 2GL.
SMART, Mr. Alan George, FCA *1952;* Little Orchard, Dittisham, DARTMOUTH, TQ6 0HS. (Life Member)
SMART, Mr. Alasdair John Douglas, FCA *1987;* Inglenook, Waterside, Greenfield, OLDHAM, OL3 7DP.
•**SMART, Mr. Andrew Peter, ACA** *2008;* MurraYoung Limited, 15 Home Farm, Luton Hoo Estate, LUTON, LU1 3TD.
SMART, Mr. Brian Trevor, FCA *1961;* 79 Midland Rd, Raunds, WELLINGBOROUGH, NN9 6JF. (Life Member)
SMART, Mr. Campbell Anderson, FCA *1963;* Crossways, 39 Windsor Road, Radyr, CARDIFF, CF15 8BQ.
SMART, Miss. Caroline Margaret, MA ACA *1989;* 5 Somerset Road, TEDDINGTON, TW11 8RT.
SMART, Miss. Christianne Fiona, BSc ACA *1997;* Top Flat, 48 Willoughby Road, LONDON, NW3 1RU.
SMART, Mr. Christopher, BSc ACA *2005;* 9 East View, New Road, Luddendenfoot, HALIFAX, WEST YORKSHIRE, HX2 6QY.
SMART, Mr. Christopher Joffre Thomas, BA(Hons) ACA *2010;* 14 La Ville Au Roi, La Rue de Trachy, St. Helier, JERSEY, JE2 3JR.
•**SMART, Mr. Christopher Stephen Kaye, BSc FCA CTA** *1980;* (Tax Fac), Volans Limited, 10 Blenheim Terrace, LEEDS, LS2 9HX.
SMART, Mr. Clive Frederick, MA FCA *1954;* Shemshia, Ffordd Cynlas, Benllech, TYN-Y-GONGL, LL74 8SP. (Life Member)
•**SMART, Mr. David Alan, BSc FCA** *1986;* Smith & Williamson Ltd, 25 Moorgate, LONDON, EC2R 6AY.
•**SMART, Mr. David Alexander, BA FCA** *1973;* DA Smart & Co, 1 Sharnden Manor, Mayfield, MAYFIELD, EAST SUSSEX, TN20 6PY.
•**SMART, Mr. David Michael, FCA** *1966;* Smart & Co., 17 Liverpool Road, WORTHING, BN11 1SU.
SMART, Mrs. Elizabeth Gail, BA ACA *1995;* 20 Elliswick Road, HARPENDEN, AL5 4TP.
•**SMART, Mr. Ernest Leslie, LLB FCA** *1984;* The A9 Partnership (Highland) Ltd, Elm House, Cradlehall Business Park, INVERNESS, IV2 5GH.
SMART, Miss. Fiona Jane Conway, MEng ACA *2001;* 39 Lysias Road, LONDON, SW12 8BW.
SMART, Mr. Frederick Bryan, FCA *1975;* 1 Castle Gate Way, Castle Hill, BERKHAMSTED, HP4 1LH.
SMART, Mr. Gregory Paul, BA ACA *1981;* 8 Home Acre, Little Houghton, NORTHAMPTON, NN7 1AG.
SMART, Miss. Helen Frances, ACA *2009;* 39 Bilsdale Road, HARTLEPOOL, CLEVELAND, TS25 2AH.
SMART, Mr. Hugh Christopher, BSc ACA FCT *1987;* 17th Floor, 125 Broad Street, LONDON, EC2N 1AR.
•**SMART, Mr. Ian Victor, BSc FCA CF** *1986;* Grant Thornton UK LLP, Grant Thornton House, 22 Melton Street, Euston Square, LONDON, NW1 2EP. See also Grant Thornton LLP
SMART, Mr. James Arundell, FCA *1973;* Financial Reporting Council, Audit Inspection Unit, 5th Floor, Aldwych House, 71-91 Aldwych, LONDON WC2B 4HN.
SMART, Mr. Jeremy Lionel Lambert, MA ACA *1997;* 5 Manor Road, ST. ALBANS, HERTFORDSHIRE, AL1 3ST.
SMART, Mr. John Gerard Wernicke, FCA *1968;* Gazebo, Trolver Croft, Feock, TRURO, TR3 6RT.
•**SMART, Mr. John Watkin, BA ACA** *1983;* John Smart, Delfan, New Park Terrace, Treforest, PONTYPRIDD, CF37 1TH.
SMART, Mrs. Karen Jane, BA ACA *1996;* 14 Springfield Road, Pamber Heath, TADLEY, RG26 3DL.
SMART, Mr. Kim Andrew, FCA *1974;* 14 La Ville Au Roi, Rue De Trachy, St Helier, JERSEY, JE2 3JR.
SMART, Mrs. Laura Jane, BA ACA ATII *1994;* (Tax Fac), 793 Ripponden Road, Moorside, OLDHAM, OL1 4SQ.
SMART, Mr. Malcolm, FCA *1965;* 153 Green Road, Moseley, BIRMINGHAM, B13 9XA.
SMART, Mrs. Marion Doreen, BSc ACA *1990;* Dunraven, Harewood Road, CHALFONT ST. GILES, BUCKINGHAMSHIRE, HP8 4UB.
SMART, Mr. Michael Anthony, FCA *1976;* The Old Mill, Shoreham, SEVENOAKS, TN14 7RP.
SMART, Mr. Michael John, BSc ACA *1990;* 793 Ripponden Road, Moorside, OLDHAM, OL1 4SQ.
SMART, Ms. Nicola Jane Mary, BA BSc ACA *1996;* Smart Human Logistics, Avenida Dr Arce 12, Portal B 2A, 28002 MADRID, SPAIN.
SMART, Mr. Nigel William Alan, FCA *1972;* 1976 rue Perodeau, VAUDREUIL-DORION J7V 8P7, QC, CANADA.
•**SMART, Mr. Philip, BSc ACA** *1996;* KPMG LLP, 15 Canada Square, LONDON, E14 5GL. See also KPMG Europe LLP
SMART, Mr. Philip David Noble, MSc ACA *1990;* 360 Scott Crossing, ROSWELL, GA 30076, UNITED STATES.
SMART, Mr. Philip James, BSc ACA *1999;* Ernst & Young Llp, 1 More London Place, LONDON, SE1 2AF.
SMART, Mr. Raymond Matthew, BSc ACA *1994;* Les Arbres Les Lohiers, St. Saviour, GUERNSEY, GY7 9FB.
SMART, Mr. Richard Anthony, FCA *1966;* 2 Fox Hollows, Maendy, COWBRIDGE, CF71 7TS. (Life Member)
SMART, Mr. Richard William Kaye, BA ACA *2002;* The Royal Bank of Scotland Plc, 8th Floor, 280 Bishopsgate, LONDON, EC2M 4RB.
SMART, Mr. Robert Christopher, MA FCA *1975;* Flat 1, 40 Wickham Avenue, BEXHILL-ON-SEA, EAST SUSSEX, TN39 3EN.
SMART, Mr. Robert Kevin, FCA *1988;* (Tax Fac), 41 Tilsworth Road, BEACONSFIELD, HP9 1TR.
SMART, Mr. Roger Bernard, FCA *1967;* Kenora Farm, Pilning Street, Pilning, BRISTOL, BS35 4HN. (Life Member)
•**SMART, Mr. Ronald Cyril, FCA** *1963;* Bridger Smart & Co., Unitek House, Churchfield Road, Chalfont St. Peter, GERRARDS CROSS, BUCKINGHAMSHIRE SL9 9EW.
SMART, Mr. Simon Sean, BSc FCA *1972;* Treslea House Cardinham, BODMIN, CORNWALL, PL30 4DL.
SMART, Mrs. Susan Merrifield May, MSc ACA *2004;* 5 Catley Grove, Long Ashton, BRISTOL, BS41 9NH.

•SMART, Mr. Tony James, FCA *1970;* Tony J Smart, 29 Lancaster Way, Glen Parva, LEICESTER, LE2 9UA.
SMART, Miss. Tracy Elena, BA(Hons) ACA MSI *2003;* 22 Old Palace Lane, RICHMOND, SURREY, TW9 1PG.
•SMART, Miss. Valerie Yvette, BA FCA *1987;* PO Box HM 3085, HAMILTON HMNX, BERMUDA.
•SMART, Mr. William, BCom ACA *2002;* WS Accountants Limited, 114 Park Avenue North, NORTHAMPTON, NN3 2JB.
SMARTT, Miss. Michelle, BA ACA *2006;* 19 Wellburn Lane, Lesmahagow, LANARK, ML11 0FP.
SMATHERS, Mrs. Wendy, BA(Hons) ACA *2001;* 1 St. Albans Close, Bracebridge Heath, LINCOLN, LN4 2TQ.
SMEATH, Mr. David John, BA ACA *2005;* 3 Malvern Priors, Malvern Place, CHELTENHAM, GLOUCESTERSHIRE, GL50 2JL.
SMEATON, Miss. Linda, BA ACA *1994;* 33 Kinnaird Avenue, LONDON, W4 3SH.
SMEATON, Mr. Richard Paul, BA(Hons) ACA *1999;* 20 Crossbeck Road, ILKLEY, WEST YORKSHIRE, LS29 9JN.
SMEDLEY, Mrs. Ann Dougal, FCA *1970;* 60 Huntly Road, Talbot Woods, BOURNEMOUTH, BH3 7HJ.
SMEDLEY, Mr. David Guy, BSc ARCS ACA *1995;* 145 King St W, TORONTO M5H 1V8, ON, CANADA.
SMEDLEY, Mr. Ian Frederick, FCA *1966;* The Barn Grange Farm, Wood End Lane, Fillongley, COVENTRY, CV7 8DB.
•SMEDLEY, Mr. James Douglas, ACA *2004;* with Dutton Moore, 6 Silver Street, HULL, HU1 1JA.
SMEDLEY, Mr. John Richard, BSc FCA *1973;* 40D Ridout Road, SINGAPORE 248440, SINGAPORE.
SMEDLEY, Mr. Mark Andrew, BSc ACA *1987;* 30 Laurel Crescent, WOKING, GU21 5SS.
•SMEDLEY, Mr. Richard John, FCA *1968;* (Tax Fac), 60 Huntly Road, Talbot Woods, BOURNEMOUTH, BH3 7HJ.
•SMEDLEY, Mr. Richard William, ACA *1991;* (Tax Fac), Richard Smedley Limited, Oakford House, 291 Low Lane, Horsforth, LEEDS, LS18 5NU. See also Flaxton Ventures LLP
•SMEDLEY, Mr. Robert Charles Boleyne, FCA *1973;* (Tax Fac), Willow Farm, Brokes, Hudswell, RICHMOND, NORTH YORKSHIRE, DL11 6DD.
SMEDLEY, Miss. Shona Ann, MMath ACA AMCT *2002;* Commonwealth Bank, Treasury Finance, Floor 25, 201 Sussex Street, SYDNEY, NSW 2000 AUSTRALIA.
SMEE, Mr. Anthony John, FCA *1955;* 38 Stafford Road, PETERSFIELD, HAMPSHIRE, GU32 2JG.
SMEE, Ms. Deborah Elizabeth, ACA *1991;* 50 Wood Lodge Lane, WEST WICKHAM, BR4 9NA.
SMEE, Mr. Philip James Brock Mcneill, FCA *1969;* 84 North Road, RICHMOND, SURREY, TW9 4HQ.
SMEE, Mr. Richard Anthony, ACA *1980;* Lance Levy Farmhouse Wildmoor Lane, Sherfield-on-Loddon, HOOK, RG27 0HB.
SMEE, Mr. Richard James, MSc ACA *2007;* 1 Briar Way, GUILDFORD, GU4 7JY.
SMEED, Mr. James Andrew Brian, ACA *2009;* 68 Hailwood Avenue, Douglas, ISLE OF MAN, IM2 7DH.
•SMEED, Mr. Nicholas Anthony, ACA *1984;* Carl Associates, 186 Wanstead Park Road, ILFORD, ESSEX, IG1 3TR.
SMEETH, Mr. Jeremy, BA ACA *1997;* National Theatre of Scotland Civic House, 26 Civic Street, GLASGOW, G4 9RH.
SMEETON, Mrs. Debra, ACA *1995;* October Cottage Lyndhurst Road, Landford, SALISBURY, SP5 2AJ.
SMEETON, The Revd. Nicholas Guy, MA(Cantab) BA ACA *1999;* 13 Brooklands Court, ROCHDALE, OL11 4EJ.
SMEETON, Mrs. Nicola Joy, BA ACA *1994;* with Parlane Purkis & Co, 177 London Road, SOUTHEND-ON-SEA, SS1 1PW.
•SMEETON, Mr. Nigel David, LLB FCA *1981;* Parlane Purkis & Co, 177 London Road, SOUTHEND-ON-SEA, SS1 1PW.
SMEETON, Mr. Nigel David, BSc ACA *1995;* P K F Accountants & Business Advisors Farringdon Place, 20 Farringdon Road, LONDON, EC1M 3AP.
SMEETON, Mr. Robert John, BSc ACA *1992;* October Cottage, Lyndhurst Road, Landford, SALISBURY, SP5 2AJ.
SMELLIE, Mr. Keith Graham, FCA *1961;* Old Orchards, Broad Campden, CHIPPING CAMPDEN, GLOUCESTERSHIRE, GL55 6UX. (Life Member)
SMELT, Mr. Paul Anthony, FCA *1961;* 39 Broad Lane, Upperthong, HOLMFIRTH, WEST YORKSHIRE, HD9 3XE.
SMERDON, Mr. Andrew Keith, BA ACA *2005;* HBOS plc, Commercial Street, HALIFAX, WEST YORKSHIRE, HX11BW.
SMERDON, Mr. Jason Cosmo, BA FCA *1994;* Abbots Chase, Moat Lane, Taynton, GLOUCESTER, GL19 3AR.
SMERDON, Mr. Stuart James, BA ACA *2005;* B A E Systems, Warton Aerodrome, Warton, PRESTON, PR4 1AX.
•SMETHAM, Mr. Clive Douglas Michael, BA FCA *1994;* Sagars LLP, Gresham House, 5-7 St. Pauls Street, LEEDS, LS1 2JG.
SMETHERS, Mr. John Charles, FCA *1947;* The White Cottage, Cooden Close, Cooden, BEXHILL-ON-SEA, TN39 4TQ. (Life Member)
SMETHERS, Mr. Mark, MEng ACA *2007;* with KPMG LLP, Two Financial Center, 60 South Street, BOSTON, MA 02111, UNITED STATES.
•SMETHERS, Mr. Nigel, MA FCA *1978;* Smethers & Co, 41 Albion Road, Pitstone, LEIGHTON BUZZARD, LU7 9AY.
SMETHERS, Mr. Robert Graham, FCA *1973;* 53 High Street, Coton, CAMBRIDGE, CB3 7PL.
SMETHERS, Mr. Thomas Michael, BSc ACA *1999;* 1a Wick Avenue, Wheathampstead, ST. ALBANS, HERTFORDSHIRE, AL4 8QD.
•①SMETHURST, Mr. Christopher Frederick, FCA *1981;* Circs Insolvency & Recovery, Dallam Court, Dallam Lane, WARRINGTON, CHESHIRE, WA2 7LT.
SMETHURST, Mr. David Howard, FCA *1969;* with Rushtons (NW) Limited, Shorrock House, 1 Faraday Court, Fulwood, PRESTON, PR2 9NB.
•SMETHURST, Mr. Ian Thomas, BSc FCA *1984;* (Tax Fac), CLB Coopers, Laurel House, 173 Chorley New Road, BOLTON, BL1 4QZ.
SMETHURST, Ms. Katharine, BSc ACA *2005;* 68 Kleine Wharf, 8-14 Orsman Road, LONDON, N1 5QJ.
•SMETHURST, Mr. Paul Duncan, BA FCA *1986;* Carter Backer Winter LLP, Enterprise House, 21 Buckle Street, LONDON, E1 8NN.
SMETHURST, Mr. Richard, BSc ACA *2011;* 6 Badgers Croft, Mobberley, KNUTSFORD, CHESHIRE, WA16 7GZ.
SMEULDERS, Mr. John Michael, BSc ACA *2005;* 28 Green Road, READING, RG6 7BS.
SMEULDERS, Mr. Paul Francis, BSc ACA *2001;* 40 Okebourne Park, Liden, SWINDON, SN3 6AH.
SMIDDY, Mr. Francis Paul, BA FCA *1978;* 4 Manor Lane Terrace, LONDON, SE13 5QL.
SMILES, Mr. George, BA ACA *1999;* with National Audit Office, 157-197 Buckingham Palace Road, Victoria, LONDON, SW1W 9SP.
SMILEY, Mr. Anthony Edward, BSc ACA *2003;* 107 Vivian Road, BIRMINGHAM, B17 0DN.
SMILEY, Mr. Patrick Josephh, FCA *1969;* 4 Ravenswood, BIRMINGHAM, B15 3LN.
SMINK, Mrs. Fiona, BA ACA ATII *1996;* 4, Heather Close, BISHOP'S STORTFORD, CM23 4LZ.
SMIRFITT, Mr. Richard Francis, BA ACA *1993;* 178 Windsor Road, MAIDENHEAD, BERKSHIRE, SL6 2DW.
SMIRNOV, Miss. Nataliya, BA ACA *2007;* Elm Shadows, Forest Road, East Horsley, LEATHERHEAD, SURREY, KT24 5BA.
•SMIT, Mr. Andries Bernard, ACA CA(SA) *2010;* Investment Quality Services Limited, Hacienda, Church Hill, Lawford, MANNINGTREE, ESSEX CO11 2JX.
•SMIT, Mr. Christopher Willem, BA ACA *2000;* CWS Accounting Limited, 50 Skylark Way, Shinfield, READING, RG2 9AJ.
SMIT, Miss. Madelein, ACA *2000;* Postbus 75371, 1070 AJ AMSTERDAM, NETHERLANDS.
•SMITH, Mr. Adam, BA FCA *1997;* Deloitte LLP, 4 Brindley Place, BIRMINGHAM, B1 2HZ. See also Deloitte & Touche LLP
SMITH, Mr. Adam Brant, BA FCA MAE QDR *1995;* with BDO LLP, 1 Bridgewater Place, Water Lane, LEEDS, LS11 5RU.
SMITH, Mr. Adam David, BSc ACA *2000;* 8 Branscombe Road, BRISTOL, BS9 1SN.
SMITH, Mr. Adam James, ACA *2011;* 34 Marcus Street, LONDON, SW18 2JT.
SMITH, Mr. Adrian Christopher, FCA *1975;* The Law Society Ipsley Court, Berrington Close, REDDITCH, WORCESTERSHIRE, B98 0TD.
•SMITH, Mr. Adrian Dagley, FCA *1988;* (Tax Fac), Lings, Provident House, 51 Wardwick, DERBY, DE1 1HN.
SMITH, Mr. Adrian Holmes, BSc FCA CF *1973;* 57 St Ives Park, Ashley Heath, RINGWOOD, BH24 2JX.
•SMITH, Mr. Adrian James, FCA *1974;* Taylor Viney & Marlow, 46-54 High Street, INGATESTONE, CM4 9DW.
SMITH, Mr. Adrian Stephen Lind, FCA *1970;* 12 Campion Road, Putney, LONDON, SW15 6NW.
SMITH, Mr. Adrian William, BMus FCA ARCM *1991;* with FTI Forensic Accounting Limited, 322 High Holborn, LONDON, WC1V 7PB.
SMITH, Mr. Aidan Christopher, BSc ACA *1986;* 50 Wavendon Avenue, LONDON, W4 4NS.
SMITH, Mr. Alan, ACA *1978;* 24 Albany Road, Stroud Green, LONDON, N4 4RJ.
SMITH, Mr. Alan, BSc ACA *1995;* Don Johns Farm, Earls Colne, COLCHESTER, CO6 2NP.
SMITH, Mr. Alan, BA FCA *1998;* R&R Ice Cream UK Ltd, Leeming Bar Ind Estate, Leeming Bar, NORTHALLERTON, NORTH YORKSHIRE, DL7 9UL.
SMITH, Mr. Alan, FCA *1959;* 33 Reddings, WELWYN GARDEN CITY, AL8 7LA. (Life Member)
SMITH, Mr. Alan, FCA *1965;* 11 Blaidwood Drive, St Oswalds Park, DURHAM, DH1 3TD.
SMITH, Mr. Alan, FCA *1966;* 16 Summers Way, MARKET HARBOROUGH, LE16 9QE.
SMITH, Mr. Alan, FCA *1970;* The Poplars, Edenfield Estate, Marlborough, HORNSEA, HU18 1UE. (Life Member)
SMITH, Mr. Alan, BSc ACA *1986;* 12 Coolangatta Avenue, ELANORA HEIGHTS, NSW 2101, AUSTRALIA.
SMITH, Mr. Alan David, MPhil BSc ACA *1986;* 1 Melrose Avenue, SALE, CHESHIRE, M33 3AZ.
SMITH, Mr. Alan Dixon, FCA *1958;* 2 Petuaria Close, BROUGH, HU15 1AR. (Life Member)
SMITH, Mr. Alan Edward, FCA FCMA *1968;* Orchard House, Halloughton Road, SOUTHWELL, NG25 0LR. (Life Member)
SMITH, Mr. Alan Frederick, FCA *1949;* 38 Trowell Grove, Long Eaton, NOTTINGHAM, NG10 4AZ. (Life Member)
SMITH, Mr. Alan Frederick, BSc FCA *1958;* 911 Ponderosa Way, WOODLAND PARK, CO 80863-9003, UNITED STATES. (Life Member)
•SMITH, Mr. Alan Gregson, BA FCA *1976;* (Tax Fac), Barlow Andrews LLP, Carlyle House, 78 Chorley New Road, BOLTON, BL1 4BY. See also Beech Business Services Limited
SMITH, Mr. Alan Howard, BSc ACA *1990;* 4 The Paddocks, Ramsbury, MARLBOROUGH, WILTSHIRE, SN8 2QF.
SMITH, Mr. Alan James, BSc ACA *1988;* 59 Maelduin, DUNSHAUGHLIN, COUNTY MEATH, IRELAND.
SMITH, Mr. Alan John, FCA *1972;* 15 Beach Street, Sandspit, RD 2, WARKWORTH 0982, NEW ZEALAND.
SMITH, Mr. Alan John, MA FCA *1975;* 6 Greenford Gardens, HULL, HU8 0RQ.
SMITH, Mr. Alan Ley, BSc ACA *1989;* 9 Crispin Close, Locks Heath, SOUTHAMPTON, SO31 6TD.
SMITH, Mr. Alan Louis Pottier, FCA *1951;* Colwood Park, Cross Colwood Lane, Bolney, HAYWARDS HEATH, RH17 5RY. (Life Member)
•SMITH, Mr. Alan Nigel, MBA FCA *1990;* 9 Harrow Fields Gardens, Harrow-on-the-Hill, HARROW, MIDDLESEX, HA1 3SN.
SMITH, Mr. Alan Simon Nicholas, MA FCA *1980;* Vine Court House, Ticehurst, WADHURST, EAST SUSSEX, TN5 7HT.
SMITH, Mr. Alan Victor, BA FCA *1977;* 3 Princess Cottages, Rookhope, BISHOP AUCKLAND, COUNTY DURHAM, DL13 2BP.
SMITH, Mr. Alan Wilson, FCA *1958;* Buzon T111, Calle Zragoza 29, Moraira Teulada, 03724 ALICANTE, SPAIN. (Life Member)
SMITH, Mr. Alaric Michael, MA ACA *1989;* Temple Retail Ltd, The Lodge, Coleshill Manor, COLESHILL, B46 1DP.
SMITH, Mr. Alasdair John, FCA *1990;* 4 Bridgelands, Barcombe, LEWES, EAST SUSSEX, BN8 5BW.
•SMITH, Mr. Alastair Gray, BA FCA DChA *1979;* Mazars LLP, The Lexicon, Mount Street, MANCHESTER, M2 5NT.
SMITH, Mr. Alastair James, BSc FCA *1990;* 138 Castelnau, LONDON, SW13 9ET.
•SMITH, Mr. Albert Malcolm, FCA *1957;* (Tax Fac), A.M. Smith, 5 Corns Grove, Wombourne, WOLVERHAMPTON, WV5 0BZ.
SMITH, Mr. Alex Michael, ACA *2011;* 29 Bowmore Road, BROMSGROVE, WORCESTERSHIRE, B60 2HH.
SMITH, Mr. Alexander Charles Willis, ACA *2009;* 17 The Strouds, Beenham, READING, RG7 5NW.
SMITH, Mr. Alexander David, BA ACA *1992;* The Knoll, Village Way, AMERSHAM, BUCKINGHAMSHIRE, HP7 9PU.
•SMITH, Mr. Alexander Emmott, BSc(Hons) ACA *2001;* My Tax Accountant Limited, 38 Bretonside, PLYMOUTH, PL4 0AU.
SMITH, Mrs. Alexandra Louise, ACA *2003;* with PricewaterhouseCoopers LLP, 31 Great George Street, BRISTOL, BS1 5QD.
SMITH, Mr. Alfred, FCA *1949;* Room 18, Nazareth House, 118 Harlestone Road, NORTHAMPTON, NN5 6AD. (Life Member)
SMITH, Mrs. Alison, BSc ACA *1992;* 3 Lovett Road, Napsbury Park, ST. ALBANS, HERTFORDSHIRE, AL2 1UE.
SMITH, Mrs. Alison Claire, BA ACA *1999;* 31 Adel Green, Adel, LEEDS, LS16 8JX.
SMITH, Mrs. Alison Doris Margaret, BA ACA *1993;* Uplands, Prayors Hill, Sible Hedingham, HALSTEAD, ESSEX, CO9 3LE.
SMITH, Mrs. Alison Fiona, BTech FCA *1986;* 18 Bramhall Drive, High Generals Wood, WASHINGTON, TYNE AND WEAR, NE38 9DB.
SMITH, Mrs. Alison Heather, BA ACA *1989;* (Tax Fac), with PricewaterhouseCoopers LLP, 1 Embankment Place, LONDON, WC2N 6RH.
SMITH, Mrs. Alison Jayne, BA ACA *1999;* A Coupland (Surfacing) Ltd, Pudding Lane, Pinchbeck, SPALDING, LINCOLNSHIRE, PE11 3TJ.
SMITH, Mrs. Alison Mary, BA ACA CTA DChA *1984;* York Council for Voluntary Service Priory Street Centre, 15 Priory Street, YORK, YO1 6ET.
SMITH, Mr. Alistair, ACA *2011;* Flat 4, 18-20 St. Pancras Way, LONDON, NW1 0QG.
SMITH, Mr. Alistair David, BA ACA *2006;* 24 Holly Bank Road, Lindley, HUDDERSFIELD, HD3 3LX.
•SMITH, Mr. Alistair Henry Ellis, BSc FCA *1982;* Ferguson Maidment & Co, Sardinia House, Sardinia Street, Lincolns Inn Fields, LONDON, WC2A 3LZ.
SMITH, Mr. Alistair Hugh, BSc FCA *1975;* Apartment 20, 1 Blackthorn Avenue, Arundel Square, LONDON, N7 8BD.
SMITH, Mr. Alister Wayne, ACA *2009;* Setters, 47 Chestnut Springs, Lydiard Millicent, SWINDON, SN5 3NB.
•SMITH, Mr. Allan Esler, BSc FCA *1990;* (Tax Fac), Allan Smith Accounting & Tax Ltd, 5 The Green, Codicote, HITCHIN, HERTFORDSHIRE, SG4 8UR.
SMITH, Ms. Allison, ACA CA(SA) *2011;* Flat 13, Hawker Court, Queens Road, KINGSTON UPON THAMES, SURREY, KT2 7SE.
SMITH, Mr. Alyn Douglas, BA ACA *1999;* 103 Fountains Crescent, LONDON, N14 6BD.
SMITH, Mr. Amahl, MA ACA *1996;* Royal Commission for the Exhibition of 1851, 453 Sherfield Building Imperial College, LONDON, SW7 2AZ.
•SMITH, Mrs. Amanda Anne, BA FCA *1992;* (Tax Fac), Whittocks End Accountancy Ltd, Whittocks End, Kempley, DYMOCK, GLOUCESTERSHIRE, GL18 2BS.
SMITH, Ms. Amanda Elizabeth, BA(Hons) ACA *1984;* (Tax Fac), 23 Wellsic Lane, Rothley, LEICESTER, LE7 7QB.
SMITH, Mrs. Amanda Helen, MA ACA *1992;* AIS Limited, Sheward House, Cranmore Avenue, Shirley, SOLIHULL, B90 4LF.
SMITH, Mrs. Amanda Jane, LLB ACA *2000;* Four Winds, 2 Halloughton Road, SUTTON COLDFIELD, WEST MIDLANDS, B74 2QG.
SMITH, Miss. Amanda Jane, BSc ACA *1992;* Woodside, Kirkley, NEWCASTLE UPON TYNE, NE20 0BD.
SMITH, Miss. Amanda Jane, BSc(Hons) ACA *2001;* 22 St. Aidans Road, CARLISLE, CA1 1LS.
SMITH, Miss. Amanda Jayne, ACA *2008;* P K F, 105 Carrow Road, NORWICH, NR1 1HP.
SMITH, Mrs. Amanda Lara, BA FCA *1999;* 26 Priory Field Drive, EDGWARE, MIDDLESEX, HA8 9PU.
SMITH, Mrs. Amanda Louise, ACA *1992;* 11 Hartley Close, BROMLEY, BR1 2TP.
SMITH, Miss. Amy, BA(Hons) ACA *2011;* 41 Chesson Road, LONDON, W14 9QR.
SMITH, Mr. Andrew, ACA *2009;* 79 Newlands, PERSHORE, WORCESTERSHIRE, WR10 1BP.
SMITH, Mr. Andrew, BA ACA *2008;* Flat 205 Montana Building, Deals Gateway, LONDON, SE13 7QF.
•SMITH, Mr. Andrew, MA FCA *1983;* AS Financial Services Ltd, 2 Russetts, Great Berry, BASILDON, ESSEX, SS16 6SH.
SMITH, Mr. Andrew, BCom ACA *1989;* 25 Sycamore Avenue, Wickersley, ROTHERHAM, SOUTH YORKSHIRE, S66 2NW.
SMITH, Mr. Andrew Arthur, BA(Hons) ACA *2000;* Associated British Foods Plc, 10 Grosvenor Street, LONDON, W1K 4QY.
SMITH, Mr. Andrew Broadhurst, ACA *1982;* March House, Old Vicarage Garden, Wellow, BATH, BA2 8QS.
SMITH, Mr. Andrew Charles Picton, ACA *1981;* 196 Gower Road, Sketty, SWANSEA, SA2 9HT.
SMITH, Mr. Andrew Christopher Melville, BCom ACA *1998;* The Old Bovey, Farm Lane, Shurdington, CHELTENHAM, GLOUCESTERSHIRE, GL51 4XJ.
SMITH, Mr. Andrew Crawford, LLB FCA *1975;* Allied Group, Depot Road, NEWMARKET, SUFFOLK, CB8 0AL.

SMITH, Mr. Andrew David, ACA *1985;* (Tax Fac), 17 Millfield Lane, TARPORLEY, CHESHIRE, CW6 0BF.
SMITH, Mr. Andrew George, BA FCA *1974;* 69 Hemnall Street, EPPING, ESSEX, CM16 4LZ.
SMITH, Mr. Andrew Howard, BCom ACA *1993;* 30 Hawthorne Road, Kings Norton, BIRMINGHAM, B30 1EE.
SMITH, Mr. Andrew Iain Blair, BA ACA *1986;* The Revvo Castor Co, Somerford Road, CHRISTCHURCH, DORSET, BH23 3PZ.
SMITH, Mr. Andrew James, BSc ACA *2009;* Flat 2, Brockway House, 257 Holloway Road, LONDON, N7 8HF.
SMITH, Dr. Andrew James, MSci ACA *2010;* Flat 3 Malins Court, Nightingale Lane, LONDON, SW12 8NU.
SMITH, Mr. Andrew James, BEng ACA *1993;* 1 Victoria Gardens, COLEFORD, GL16 8DX.
SMITH, Mr. Andrew James, BA ACA *2006;* with KPMG LLP, 1 The Embankment, Neville Street, LEEDS, LS1 4DW.
SMITH, Mr. Andrew John, BSc ACA *1991;* 6 Chatsworth Square, HOVE, BN3 1WD.
SMITH, Mr. Andrew John, BA ACA *2004;* 128 Longwood Gate, HUDDERSFIELD, HD3 4US.
SMITH, Mr. Andrew John, BA ACA *2006;* Matra Petroleum Plc, 120 Bridge Road, CHERTSEY, SURREY, KT16 8LA.
SMITH, Mr. Andrew John, BSocSc ACA *1992;* Pearson Shared Services Ltd, Edinburgh Gate, HARLOW, CM20 2JE.
SMITH, Mr. Andrew Jonathan, MA ACA *1978;* Nandana, Beacon Edge, PENRITH, CUMBRIA, CA11 8BN.
SMITH, Mr. Andrew Jonathan, FCA *1972;* Qenos PTY Ltd, 471 Koroit Road, ALTONA, VIC 3018, AUSTRALIA.
SMITH, Mr. Andrew Lawrence Tysoe, BSc ACA *1984;* Aslotel Ltd, Aslotel House, Pebble Close, TADWORTH, SURREY, KT20 7PA.
SMITH, Mr. Andrew Malcolm, FCA *1956;* 105-4074 Gellatly Road, WESTBANK V4T 2S8, BC, CANADA. (Life Member)
SMITH, Mr. Andrew Mark, BA ACA *1993;* 9 Leven Gardens, WETHERBY, WEST YORKSHIRE, LS22 7YH.
SMITH, Mr. Andrew Mark, BSc ACA AMCT *1992;* 77 Rosebery Road, Langley Vale Epsom Downs, EPSOM, KT18 6AB.
SMITH, Mr. Andrew Michael Anthony, BA FCA *1977;* 8 Leewood Way, Effingham, LEATHERHEAD, SURREY, KT24 5JN.
•**SMITH, Mr. Andrew Mowbray, BA FCA** *1994;* Salway & Wright, 32 The Crescent, SPALDING, LINCOLNSHIRE, PE11 1AF. See also Salway and Wright (Spalding) Limited
•**SMITH, Mr. Andrew Nathan, BA ACA** *1999;* (Tax Fac), PricewaterhouseCoopers LLP, 7 More London Riverside, LONDON, SE1 2RT. See also PricewaterhouseCoopers
SMITH, Mr. Andrew Neville Hawker, BSc ACA *1994;* 38A Glover Street, MOSMAN, NSW 2088, AUSTRALIA.
SMITH, Mr. Andrew Nicholas Michael, BSc ACA *1980;* Leigh Grove Abbots Leigh Road, Abbots Leigh, BRISTOL, BS8 3QG.
Ⓓ**SMITH, Mr. Andrew Norman Aird, BSc ACA** *1984;* with Grant Thornton UK LLP, Enterprise House, 115 Edmund Street, BIRMINGHAM, B3 2HJ.
SMITH, Mr. Andrew Parkin, BA ACA *1991;* Sunnydale, 4 Vale Wood Drive, Lower Bourne, FARNHAM, SURREY, GU10 3HW.
•**SMITH, Mr. Andrew Peter, BA FCA** *1983;* (Tax Fac), SATS Ltd, Milton House, Gatehouse Road, AYLESBURY, HP19 8EA.
SMITH, Mr. Andrew Peter, BSc ACA *1991;* 101 Pixmore Way, LETCHWORTH GARDEN CITY, HERTFORDSHIRE, SG6 3TR.
SMITH, Mr. Andrew Philip Richard, ACA *2009;* Holcombe House, Irthington, CARLISLE, CA6 4NJ.
SMITH, Mr. Andrew Ray, FCA *1970;* P O Box 16403, LYTTELTON, 0140, SOUTH AFRICA.
SMITH, Mr. Andrew Timothy, BSc FCA *1981;* 3 Garnet Field, YATELEY, HAMPSHIRE, GU46 6FN.
SMITH, Mr. Andrew Tyler, FCA *1968;* St Osyth, Station Road, Legbourne, LOUTH, LN11 8LL. (Life Member)
SMITH, Mr. Andrew William, BSc ACA *1984;* Smith & Sons (Bletchington) Ltd, Enslow, KIDLINGTON, OXFORDSHIRE, OX5 3AY.
SMITH, Mr. Andrew William, BA ACA *2006;* with Deloitte LLP, 1 City Square, LEEDS, WEST YORKSHIRE, LS1 2AL.
SMITH, Mr. Andrew William, MPhys ACA *2011;* 114 Marine Crescent, Wordsley, STOURBRIDGE, WEST MIDLANDS, DY8 4XR.
SMITH, Mr. Andrew James, ACA *2010;* 11 Ullswater Avenue, STOURPORT-ON-SEVERN, WORCESTERSHIRE, DY13 8QP.
SMITH, Miss. Angela, BA ACA *1989;* 3 Lydham Close, REDDITCH, WORCESTERSHIRE, B98 8GA.
•**SMITH, Mrs. Anita Janine Mary, FCA** *1978;* (Tax Fac), 9 Russet Way, North Holmwood, DORKING, SURREY, RH5 4TP.
SMITH, Miss. Ann Elizabeth, ACA *1993;* The Old Rectory, Bidbury Lane, HAVANT, HAMPSHIRE, PO9 3JG.
SMITH, Miss. Anna Louise, BSc ACA *2005;* 7 Warren Avenue, BIRMINGHAM, B13 8HE.
SMITH, Miss. Anna Margaret, ACA *2008;* Deloitte & Touche Financial Advisory Services, 6 Shenton Way #32-00 DBS Building Tower Two, SINGAPORE 068809, SINGAPORE.
SMITH, Mrs. Anne Helen Louise, BA ACA *1993;* Dun & Bradstreet Ltd Marlow International, Parkway, MARLOW, BUCKINGHAMSHIRE, SL7 1AJ.
SMITH, Mrs. Anne Linda, BSc ACA *1990;* 9 Lodge End, RADLETT, WD7 7EB.
SMITH, Mrs. Anne Marie, FCA *1964;* 8 College View, The Maples, CIRENCESTER, GL7 1WD. (Life Member)
SMITH, Mr. Anthony Arthur, BCom FCA *1998;* Appartment26, 29 Holtermann Street, CROWS NEST, NSW 2065, AUSTRALIA.
SMITH, Mr. Anthony Barnaby, BSc FCA *1975;* Rosemont, 15 High Road, Wilmington, DARTFORD, DA2 7EQ.
SMITH, Mr. Anthony Brian, FCA *1971;* 51 Keats Close, HORSHAM, RH12 5PL.
SMITH, Mr. Anthony Clive, FCA *1961;* 7 Avon Grove, BRISTOL, BS9 1PJ. (Life Member)
SMITH, Mr. Anthony Drake, FCA *1957;* Bear House, Bisley, STROUD, GL6 7BB. (Life Member)
SMITH, Mr. Anthony Duncan, BSc ACA *1998;* 38 Leather Lane, Gomshall, GUILDFORD, GU5 9NB.
SMITH, Mr. Anthony Gerald, BSc FCA *1975;* 10 Camellia Way, WOKINGHAM, RG41 3NB.
SMITH, Mr. Anthony Graham, FCA *1974;* 1 Abbey Lane, Lode, CAMBRIDGE, CB25 9EP.
•**SMITH, Mr. Anthony Granville, MA MEng FCA** *2000;* Humphrey & Co, 7-9 The Avenue, EASTBOURNE, EAST SUSSEX, BN21 3YA.
SMITH, Mr. Anthony Henry, FCA *1953;* F15, 71 Monkhams La, WOODFORD GREEN, IG8 0NN. (Life Member)
SMITH, Mr. Anthony Hugh, BSc ACA *1986;* 81 wyman st, WALTHAM, MA 02454, UNITED STATES.
SMITH, The Revd. Anthony James, BA FCA *1983;* Summit Skills Vega House Opal Court, Opal Drive Fox Milne, MILTON KEYNES, MK15 0DF.
SMITH, Mr. Anthony John, FCA *1967;* Old Mill House, Speltham Hill, Hambledon, WATERLOOVILLE, HAMPSHIRE, PO7 4SE.
SMITH, Mr. Anthony John, BA ACA *1993;* Hillside Lodge, Three Mile Lane, Whitmore, NEWCASTLE, STAFFORDSHIRE, ST5 5HW.
SMITH, Mr. Anthony Meville, FCA *1961;* 114 Charlton Lane, CHELTENHAM, GL53 9EA.
SMITH, Mr. Anthony Michael, BA ACA *2005;* Tanzanite 104, Tiara Residence, Palm Jumeirah, DUBAI, UNITED ARAB EMIRATES.
SMITH, Mr. Anthony Roger, FCA *1964;* 16 Bow Field, HOOK, RG27 9SA. (Life Member)
SMITH, Mr. Antony Paul, BSc ACA *1992;* 122 Mau Po, CLEARWATER BAY, HONG KONG SAR.
SMITH, Mr. Avi Jeremy, BSc ACA *2009;* UK Car Group, Nixon Street, ROCHDALE, LANCASHIRE, OL11 3JW.
SMITH, Miss. Barbara Anne, BSc ACA *1992;* 2 Hollymount Close, LONDON, SE10 8TH.
SMITH, Mr. Barrie Edwin, OBE JP FCA *1959;* Cliffe House, 4 Cavendish Road, SHEFFIELD, S11 9BH. (Life Member)
•**SMITH, Mr. Barrie Michael, FCA** *1963;* Barrie M. Smith, 10a Winchester Street, BASINGSTOKE, RG21 7DY.
SMITH, Mr. Barrie Richard, FCA *1959;* 354 Broad Lane, Bramley, LEEDS, LS13 2HF. (Life Member)
SMITH, Mr. Barry David, MBA FCA *1969;* 4 Thornhills Lane, Clifton, BRIGHOUSE, WEST YORKSHIRE, HD6 4JG.
SMITH, Mr. Barry Douglas, FCA *1972;* 1 Castle Hill Glade, HARROGATE, NORTH YORKSHIRE, HG2 9JG.
•**SMITH, Mr. Barry James, FCA** *1972;* ECL Howard Watson Smith LLP, E C L House, Lake Street, LEIGHTON BUZZARD, BEDFORDSHIRE, LU7 1RT.
•**SMITH, Mr. Barry Kevin, ACA** *1981;* PricewaterhouseCoopers LLP, Donington Court, Pegasus Business Park, Castle Donington, DERBY, DE74 2UZ. See also PricewaterhouseCoopers
SMITH, Miss. Becky, MA ACA *2006;* Ravensworth Digital Services Ltd, 2 Arcot Court Nelson Industrial Estate, CRAMLINGTON, NORTHUMBERLAND, NE23 1BB.
SMITH, Mr. Ben, BSc ACA *2006;* 9 Shearman Road, Blackheath, LONDON, SE3 9HY.
SMITH, Mr. Ben Russell, ACA *2010;* 4 Cooden Ledge, ST. LEONARDS-ON-SEA, EAST SUSSEX, TN38 8ET.
SMITH, Mr. Benedict James, BA ACA *1994;* Harrods Holdings Ltd, Knightsbridge, LONDON, SW1X 7XL.
SMITH, Mr. Benjamin Andrew, MEng ACA *2009;* 39 Mill View Lane, Horwich, BOLTON, BL6 6TL.
SMITH, Mr. Benjamin Charles, MA MA(Cantab) ACA *2009;* Rae Barn Weston Road, Bletchingdon, KIDLINGTON, OXFORDSHIRE, OX5 3DH.
•**SMITH, Mr. Benjamin Keenan, LLB ACA** *2003;* Ernst & Young LLP, 1 More London Place, LONDON, SE1 2AF. See also Ernst & Young Europe LLP
SMITH, Mr. Benjamin Thomas, ACA *2009;* Flat 19 Stafford House, 9 Scott Avenue, LONDON, SW15 3PA.
SMITH, Mr. Bernard Creese, FCA *1965;* Llanwecha House, Llandenny, USK, NP15 1DP.
SMITH, Mr. Bernard William, FCA *1973;* Tibco Software Ltd, Braywick Gate, Braywick Road, MAIDENHEAD, BERKSHIRE, SL6 1DA.
SMITH, Mr. Bert Eric, FCA *1967;* Tamarind, 7 Damask Close, TRING, HP23 5UA.
SMITH, Miss. Beryl Christina, BA ACA *1982;* The Old Vicarage, Hickleton, DONCASTER, DN5 7BA.
SMITH, Mrs. Beverley Ann, BA ACA *1985;* 2a Woodlands Avenue, WORCESTER PARK, SURREY, KT4 7AN.
SMITH, Mr. Beverley Bligh, FCA *1957;* 2 The Granary, Dawpool Farm, Station Road Thurstaston, WIRRAL, CH61 0HL. (Life Member)
SMITH, Mr. Beverley Kennett, FCA *1980;* 5 Hawthorn Terrace, Broomhill, SHEFFIELD, S10 1BT.
•**SMITH, Miss. Beverley Louise, BSc ACA CTA** *1998;* (Tax Fac), Ellaway-Smith, Frights Bridge Farm, Woodchurch, ASHFORD, KENT, TN26 3PR.
SMITH, Mr. Brendon, BA ACA *2001;* 58 Frances Road, WINDSOR, SL4 3AJ.
SMITH, Mr. Brian, FCA *1965;* 22 Carbis Close, Port Solent, PORTSMOUTH, PO6 4TW. (Life Member)
SMITH, Mr. Brian, FCA *1966;* Meal Hill House, Sheffield Road, Jackson Bridge, HOLMFIRTH, HD9 7HS.
SMITH, Mr. Brian Charles, BA ACA *1989;* 8 The Rowells, Cottenham, CAMBRIDGE, CB4 8XJ.
SMITH, Mr. Brian David, BSc FCA *1966;* 227 Ashley Gardens, LONDON, SW1P 1PA.
SMITH, Mr. Brian Duncan, FCA *1984;* with Grant Thornton UK LLP, Royal Liver Building, Pier Head, LIVERPOOL, L3 1PS.
SMITH, Mr. Brian Ernest, FCA FCT *1958;* The West Grange, Hunts Lane, Felmersham, BEDFORD, MK43 7JH. (Life Member)
SMITH, Mr. Brian James, BA ACA *1981;* Barclays Capital, 5 North Colonnade, Canary Wharf, LONDON, E14 4BB.
SMITH, Mr. Brian Stanley, FCA *1971;* North Downs Cottage, Kennedy Gardens, SEVENOAKS, TN13 3UG.
SMITH, Mr. Brian Stephen Pottier, FCA *1952;* 109 Shelvers Way, TADWORTH, KT20 5QQ. (Life Member)
SMITH, Mr. Bruce David, BA FCA *1991;* Firgrove Cottage, 18 Fernhill Lane, FARNHAM, GU9 0JJ.
SMITH, Mr. Bryan John, BSc FCA *1982;* with ICAEW, Metropolitan House, 321 Avebury Boulevard, MILTON KEYNES, MK9 2FZ.
SMITH, Mr. Bryan John, BSc FCA *1982;* The Channings, 21A Parkfield Road, Coleshill, BIRMINGHAM, B46 3LD.
SMITH, Mr. Campbell Jonathan Holdich, BSc ACA *1995;* 3 Maplespeen Court, NEWBURY, RG14 1NL.
•**SMITH, Mr. Carl Jonathan, BA FCA** *1991;* C J Smith Accountancy Limited, 92 Hamilton Road, TAUNTON, SOMERSET, TA1 2ES.
SMITH, Mrs. Carly Louise, BCom ACA *2005;* 32 Cross Road, WATFORD, WD19 4DJ.
SMITH, Mrs. Carol Frances, FCA *1972;* 11 Lambourn Close, SOUTH CROYDON, SURREY, CR2 6GP. (Life Member)
SMITH, Mrs. Carole Ann, BA ACA *1990;* 3 Douglas Grange, Hurst, READING, RG10 0TT.
SMITH, Miss. Caroline, LLB ACA *2003;* with Deloitte LLP, Hill House, 1 Little New Street, LONDON, EC4A 3TR.
SMITH, Mrs. Caroline Ann, BSc ACA *1997;* 11 Rylestone Grove, BRISTOL, BS9 3UT.
SMITH, Mrs. Caroline Elizabeth, ACA *2008;* 26 Highclere Way, Chandler's Ford, EASTLEIGH, HAMPSHIRE, SO53 3PQ.
SMITH, Mrs. Caroline Jane, BA ACA *1994;* 11 Dunster Road, West Bridgford, NOTTINGHAM, NG2 6JF.
SMITH, Mrs. Carolyn Jane, BSc ACA *1990;* 70 Springbank Gardens, LYMM, CHESHIRE, WA13 9GR.
SMITH, Ms. Catherine, BSc ACA *2006;* Shipka, Kingsdale Road, BERKHAMSTED, HERTFORDSHIRE, HP4 3BS.
SMITH, Miss. Catherine Anne, BSc ACA CTA *1998;* (Tax Fac), 58 Willow House, Lucas Court, LEAMINGTON SPA, CV32 5JL.
•**SMITH, Mrs. Catherine Elizabeth, ACA CTA** *2004;* Catherine Smith & Co, 3 Campsie View Drive, Blanefield, GLASGOW, G63 9JE.
SMITH, Mrs. Catherine Elizabeth, BA ACA *1990;* 8 Henslow Mews, CAMBRIDGE, CB2 8BX.
SMITH, Mrs. Catherine Mary, BSc ACA *1990;* 15 Creighton Avenue, Muswell Hill, LONDON, N10 1NX.
SMITH, Ms. Catherine Mary, BSc ACA *1991;* 6 North Park, Chalfont St. Peter, GERRARDS CROSS, SL9 8JW.
SMITH, Mrs. Catherine Susanna, BCom ACA *1991;* 30 Hawthorne Road, Kings Norton, BIRMINGHAM, B30 1EE.
SMITH, Ms. Catriona Macinnes, BSc ACA *1990;* Fern Cottage, Wallage Lane, Rowfant, CRAWLEY, RH10 4NG.
SMITH, Mr. Cecil Ronald Davey, FCA *1949;* 57 Harefield, Long Melford, SUDBURY, CO10 9DE. (Life Member)
SMITH, Mrs. Celia Bernadette, LLB ACA *1992;* Price Forbes & Partners Ltd, 2 Minster Court, LONDON, EC3R 7PD.
SMITH, Mrs. Celia Dorrice, FCA *1970;* 2 Healey Close, ABINGDON, OX14 5RL.
SMITH, Miss. Chantel Luana, BA ACA *2006;* 23 The Weavers, NORTHAMPTON, NN4 0PU.
•**SMITH, Mr. Charles Alan, ACA** *1978;* Charles Smith & Co, Hillside, Gills Hill Lane, RADLETT, HERTFORDSHIRE, WD7 8DB.
SMITH, Mr. Charles Andrew, BA FCA *1989;* Cow Flat Cottage, West Haddlesey, SELBY, NORTH YORKSHIRE, YO8 8QA.
•**SMITH, Mr. Charles Geoffrey Gregory, BA ACA** *1980;* Cinderhall Limited, Moor End, Silkstone Common, BARNSLEY, S75 7RA.
SMITH, Mr. Charles William, FCA *1959;* 2009 SE Oxton Drive, PORT ST LUCIE, FL 34952-6066, UNITED STATES. (Life Member)
SMITH, Mrs. Charlotte Elisabeth, BSc ACA *2000;* Rudsey Cottage, Bleasby, NOTTINGHAM, NG14 7FR.
SMITH, Mrs. Charlotte Elizabeth, ACA *2006;* 17 Littlemoor View, PUDSEY, WEST YORKSHIRE, LS28 9LX.
SMITH, Miss. Charlotte Marie, BSc ACA *2011;* 42 East Lane, Cuddington, NORTHWICH, CHESHIRE, CW8 2QQ.
SMITH, Mrs. Christine Mary, BA ACA *1985;* 1 Thorns Clough, Diggle, OLDHAM, OL3 5NF.
SMITH, Mrs. Christine Mary, MA ACA CTA *1981;* Derek J Stenner Ltd, The Mews, Hounds Road, Chipping Sodbury, BRISTOL, BS37 6EE.
SMITH, Mr. Christopher, BA ACA *1990;* 23 Belle Vue Avenue, Gosforth, NEWCASTLE UPON TYNE, NE3 1AH.
•**SMITH, Mr. Christopher, BA(Hons) ACA** *2001;* Grant Thornton UK LLP, Grant Thornton House, 22 Melton Street, Euston Square, LONDON, NW1 2EP. See also Grant Thornton LLP
SMITH, Mr. Christopher Darren, BA ACA *1999;* 67 Woodstock Road, LONDON, W4 1EE.
SMITH, Mr. Christopher Ian, BSc ACA *1999;* 60 Cambridge Road, Langford, BIGGLESWADE, BEDFORDSHIRE, SG18 9PS.
SMITH, Mr. Christopher Ian Charles, BSc ACA *1990;* A P I Group plc, Second Avenue, Poynton Industrial Estate, Poynton, STOCKPORT, CHESHIRE SK12 1ND.
SMITH, Mr. Christopher James, BA ACA *1998;* with PricewaterhouseCoopers LLP, 488 Almaden Boulevard, SAN JOSE, CA 95110, UNITED STATES.
SMITH, Mr. Christopher James, BCom FCA *1973;* 3116 Underhill Drive N.W., CALGARY T2N 4E6, AB, CANADA.
SMITH, Mr. Christopher James, MA ACA *1993;* with Deloitte LLP, One Trinity Gardens, Broad Chare, NEWCASTLE UPON TYNE, NE1 2HF.
SMITH, Mr. Christopher James, BSc ACA *2011;* 50 Rose Hill Park West, SUTTON, SURREY, SM1 3LB.
SMITH, Mr. Christopher John, ACA *1983;* Financial Ombudsman Service, 183 Marsh Wall, LONDON, E14 9SR.
SMITH, Mr. Christopher John, BSc ACA *1998;* The Cartwright Group, Head Office, Atlantic Street, Broadheath, ALTRINCHAM, CHESHIRE WA14 5EW.
•**SMITH, Mr. Christopher John, BSc FCA** *1998;* Granite Morgan Smith, 122 Feering Hill, Feering, COLCHESTER, CO5 9PY.
SMITH, Mr. Christopher John, BSc ACA *1994;* 15 Limeworth, Ballincollig, CORK, COUNTY CORK, IRELAND.

SMITH, Mr. Christopher John, LLM FCA *1974;* 3 Salisbury Street, Great Harwood, BLACKBURN, BB6 7SJ.

SMITH, Mr. Christopher John, BA ACA CTA *2001;* 10 Heavenside, East Leake, LOUGHBOROUGH, LEICESTERSHIRE, LE12 6RT.

SMITH, Mr. Christopher John Addison, BA FCA *1974;* 60 Roseneath Road, LONDON, SW11 6AQ.

SMITH, Mr. Christopher Michael, OBE MA ACA *1980;* Erich-Zeigner-Allee 43, 04229 LEIPZIG, GERMANY.

•**SMITH, Mr. Christopher Michael, FCA** *1974;* Smiths, P O Box 487, PORT MORESBY, PAPUA NEW GUINEA.

SMITH, Mr. Christopher Noel, BSc FCA *1996;* Flat 7, Gonville House, Manor Fields, Putney, LONDON, SW15 3NH.

SMITH, Mr. Christopher Paul, BSc(Hons) ACA *2001;* 36 Hazeldell, Watton-at-Stone, HERTFORD, SG14 3SN.

SMITH, Mr. Christopher Phillip, BSc ACA *2009;* 33 Finkle Lane, Gildersome Morley, LEEDS, LS27 7DX.

SMITH, Mr. Christopher Robert, BA ACA *1995;* 1643 6th Avenue, #302, SAN DIEGO, CA 92101, UNITED STATES.

SMITH, Mr. Christopher Stuart, BA ACA *2003;* Mercer Limited, Marsh Ltd, 1 Tower Place West, LONDON, EC3R 5BU.

SMITH, Mr. Christopher Winston, FCA *1967;* 7 The Avenue, Sneyd Park, BRISTOL, BS9 1PD.

SMITH, Mrs. Claire, BSc ACA *1990;* 14 Bardoo Avenue, NORTH BALGOWLAH, NSW 2093, AUSTRALIA.

•**SMITH, Mrs. Claire, BSc ACA** *1992;* Claire Smith ACA Accountancy Services, 77 Rosebery Road, Langley Vale, EPSOM, SURREY, KT18 6AB.

SMITH, Mrs. Claire-Victoria, BA ACA CTA *2005;* with PricewaterhouseCoopers LLP, Donington Court, Pegasus Business Park, Castle Donington, DERBY, DE74 2UZ.

SMITH, Mrs. Clare, BA ACA *2000;* 17 Rickleton Avenue, CHESTER LE STREET, COUNTY DURHAM, DH3 4AE.

SMITH, Miss. Clare Elizabeth, BSc ACA *2007;* 42 Dorien Road, LONDON, SW20 8EJ.

SMITH, Mr. Clifford Harry, FCA *1947;* 72 West Farm Close, ASHTEAD, KT21 2LJ. (Life Member)

SMITH, Mr. Clifford Vivian, BA ACA *1980;* 4 Poplar Drive, BANSTEAD, SM7 1LJ.

SMITH, Mr. Clive Edward, BA ACA *1979;* 25 Salisbury Road, CARSHALTON, SM5 3HA.

SMITH, Mr. Clive Kevin, BSc ACA *1987;* 25 Sketty Avenue, Sketty, SWANSEA, SA2 0TE.

SMITH, Mr. Clive Richard, BSc ACA *1985;* 14 Leamington Road, ILKLEY, LS29 8EN.

•**SMITH, Mr. Clive Richard, FCA** *1995;* MWS, Kingsridge House, 601 London Road, WESTCLIFF-ON-SEA, ESSEX, SS0 9PE.

SMITH, Mr. Colin Charles, BA ACA *1981;* 4 Yew Tree Close, Lapworth, SOLIHULL, B94 6NB.

•**SMITH, Mr. Colin David, BSc(Hons) FCA** *2001;* PricewaterhouseCoopers LLP, 7 More London Riverside, LONDON, SE1 2RT. See also PricewaterhouseCoopers

SMITH, Mr. Colin Deverell, OBE BCom FCA *1973;* Pyes, Penn Road, Knotty Green, BEACONSFIELD, HP9 2TS.

SMITH, Mr. Colin Dudley, BSc FCA *1975;* The Ridge, 15E Copse Hill, Wimbledon, LONDON, SW20 0NB.

SMITH, Mr. Colin Geoffrey, BA ACA *1998;* 71 Ravenwood Drive, Forrest Hill, AUCKLAND 0620, NEW ZEALAND.

•**SMITH, Mr. Colin Harold Pottier, FCA** *1960;* (Tax Fac), Colin H P Smith, Little Twitten, Mount Street, BATTLE, EAST SUSSEX, TN33 0EG.

SMITH, Colin North, Esq CBE FCA *1948;* Traverly, 29 Esher Park Avenue, ESHER, KT10 9NX. (Life Member)

SMITH, Mr. Colin Paul, FCA *1965;* 1 Sampson Gardens, Ponsanooth, TRURO, CORNWALL, TR3 7RS.

SMITH, Mr. Colin Richard, BA ACA *1983;* 15 The Avenue, BRENTWOOD, ESSEX, CM13 2AD.

SMITH, Mr. Cornelius Frederick, FCA *1974; (FCA Ireland 1943);* 90 Mount Albany, Newtownpark Avenue, BLACKROCK, COUNTY DUBLIN, IRELAND. (Life Member)

SMITH, Mr. Craig Robert, BSc FCA *1997;* Barratt Homes, Unit 6 Alpha Court, Monks Cross Drive Huntington, YORK, YO32 9WN.

SMITH, Mr. Damian, BSc ACA *2006;* 4 Notley Place, Hucclecote, GLOUCESTER, GL3 3PJ.

SMITH, Mr. Damien George, ACA *2006;* 194 Hurdsfield Road, MACCLESFIELD, CHESHIRE, SK10 2PX.

SMITH, Mr. Daniel, ACA *2010;* K P M G, 1 The Embankment, LEEDS, LS1 4DW.

SMITH, Mr. Daniel, ACA *2008;* Flat 115, The High, Streatham High Road, LONDON, SW16 1HA.

SMITH, Mr. Daniel Alan, BSc ACA *2008;* 26d Fontenoy Road, LONDON, SW12 9LU.

SMITH, Mr. Daniel Finlay, BA ACA *2005;* 55 Appleby Gardens, DUNSTABLE, BEDFORDSHIRE, LU6 3DB.

SMITH, Mr. Daniel Francis, BSc ACA *2009;* 24 Hampton Park, BRISTOL, BS6 6LH.

SMITH, Mr. Daniel James, BSc ACA *1998;* ISG Plc, Woodland Park, Bradford Road, Chain Bar, CLECKHEATON, WEST YORKSHIRE BD19 6BW.

SMITH, Mr. Daniel James Mark, BA ACA *1999;* with Deloitte LLP, PO Box 500, 2 Hardman Street, MANCHESTER, M60 2AT.

SMITH, Mr. Daniel James Robert, BA(Hons) ACA *2011;* 30 Carnation Crescent, Eden Village, SITTINGBOURNE, KENT, ME10 4RY.

SMITH, Mr. Daniel Peter, MEng ACA *1992;* Bijwater No. 4, 3317 DORDRECHT, NETHERLANDS.

•**SMITH, Mr. Daniel Robert Whiteley, BA FCA** *1987;* Grant Thornton UK LLP, 30 Finsbury Square, LONDON, EC2P 2YU. See also Grant Thornton LLP

SMITH, Mrs. Danielle Stephanie, BSc ACA *1992;* 5 Bedfordshire Down, Warfield, BRACKNELL, RG42 3UA.

SMITH, Mr. Darren Andrew, BSc ACA *2004;* 99 Arcadian Gardens, LONDON, N22 5AG.

SMITH, Mr. Darren Mark, BSc ACA *1992;* 25 Derwentwater Avenue, SANDY BAY, TAS 7005, AUSTRALIA.

•**SMITH, Mr. Darren Paul, BA ACA** *1993;* SW Accountants Limited, 51 Eaton Hill, Cookridge, LEEDS, LS16 6SE.

SMITH, Mr. Darren Stewart, BEng FCA *1997;* 297 Oldham Road, ROCHDALE, LANCASHIRE, OL16 5JG.

SMITH, Mr. Darryl Clifford, BA ACA *2010;* Fund Accountant, UBS Fund Services (Cayman) Ltd, UBS House 227 Elgin Avenue, P.O. Box 852 GT, GEORGE TOWN, GRAND CAYMAN CAYMAN ISLANDS.

SMITH, Ms. Daryl Ann, ACA *1985;* 12B Hoi Deen Court, 276 Gloucester Road, CAUSEWAY BAY, HONG KONG ISLAND, HONG KONG SAR.

SMITH, Mr. David, BA FCA FCT *1972;* Spear Fir, Daneshill, WOKING, GU22 7HQ.

•**SMITH, Mr. David, FCA** *1977;* Bolton Smith & Co Limited, 158 High Street, Wealdstone, HARROW, HA3 7AX.

•**SMITH, Mr. David, FCA** *1988;* Smith Mercia Accountancy Services, 4 Sudeley, Dosthill, TAMWORTH, B77 1JR.

SMITH, Mr. David Alexander, BA FCA *1985;* Grainger Plc Citygate, St. James Boulevard, NEWCASTLE UPON TYNE, NE1 4JE.

SMITH, Mr. David Andrew, BSc ACA *1999;* 377 Durham Road, GATESHEAD, TYNE AND WEAR, NE9 5AL.

SMITH, Mr. David Andrew, FCA *1975;* 5 Hunts Field Close, LYMM, CHESHIRE, WA13 0SS.

SMITH, Mr. David Anthony, BSc FCA *1975;* 9 Hale Court, Willow Tree Road, Hale, ALTRINCHAM, WA14 2EA.

•**SMITH, Mr. David Austin, BSc FCA** *1990;* (Tax Fac), Nash Harvey LLP, The Granary, Hermitage Court, Hermitage Lane, MAIDSTONE, KENT ME16 9NT. See also Nash Harvey Payroll Services Ltd and Nash Harvey Taxation Services Ltd

SMITH, Mr. David Charles, BA ACA *1981;* Cold Drawn Products Ltd, Park House Road, Low Moor, BRADFORD, WEST YORKSHIRE, BD12 0PX.

•**SMITH, Mr. David Charles, FCA** *1966;* (Tax Fac), David Smith & Co, 41 Welbeck Street, LONDON, W1G 8HH.

SMITH, Mr. David Christopher, BA ACA *1988;* 14 Honey Lane, Hurley, MAIDENHEAD, SL6 6RH.

SMITH, Mr. David Christopher, BA ACA *1984;* Pendle House, 20 Park Close, Sudbrooke, LINCOLN, LN2 2RE.

SMITH, Mr. David Edward, BSc FCA *1977;* Collards, HASLEMERE, GU27 2HX.

SMITH, Mr. David Edward, BSc ACA *1993;* Woodene Blounts Court Road, Peppard Common, HENLEY-ON-THAMES, OXFORDSHIRE, RG9 5EU.

SMITH, Mr. David Francis, FCA *1960;* Fair Leigh, Knoll Hill, Sneyd Park, BRISTOL, BS9 1QU. (Life Member)

SMITH, Mr. David Frederick, FCA *1974;* 24 Montreal House, Benmore Avenue, BIRMINGHAM, B5 7XR.

SMITH, Mr. David Garven, BEng ACA *2002;* 213 Maroondah Highway, HEALESVILLE, VIC 3777, AUSTRALIA.

•**SMITH, Mr. David George, FCA** *1971;* (Tax Fac), Darnells, Quay House, Quay Road, NEWTON ABBOT, TQ12 2BU.

SMITH, Mr. David Giles, BSc ACA *1994;* 64 Brook Lane, Warsash, SOUTHAMPTON, HAMPSHIRE, SO31 9FG.

SMITH, Mr. David Guy, BA ACA *1988;* 3 Mabbots, TADWORTH, SURREY, KT20 5TS.

SMITH, Mr. David Harold, BSc ACA *1980;* East Haugh, Carleton Road, PONTEFRACT, WEST YORKSHIRE, WF8 3RP.

SMITH, Mr. David Harrington, FCA *1965;* 2 Coppins Close, CHELMSFORD, CM2 6AY. (Life Member)

SMITH, Mr. David Henry, FCA *1964;* 15 West Lane, Sutton-In-Craven, KEIGHLEY, BD20 7NT. (Life Member)

SMITH, Mr. David Ian, BSc ACA *1997;* 19 Ashgrove Croft, Kippax, LEEDS, LS25 7RB.

SMITH, Mr. David James, BSc ACA *1999;* with Deloitte LLP, Athene Place, 66 Shoe Lane, LONDON, EC4A 3BQ.

SMITH, Mr. David James, BA ACA *1983;* 25 Woodhouse Gardens, BRIGHOUSE, HD6 3UH.

SMITH, Mr. David James, BA ACA *1982;* 8 Chancery Close, ST. ALBANS, AL4 9YF.

SMITH, Mr. David John, BSc ACA *1998;* 34 Battlefield Road, ST. ALBANS, HERTFORDSHIRE, AL1 4DD.

SMITH, Mr. David John, BA ACA *1990;* Red Hill House Holcot Road, Walgrave, NORTHAMPTON, NN6 9QP.

•**SMITH, Mr. David John, FCA** *1978;* (Tax Fac), Gauzebrook Limited, The Old Barton, Rodbourne Rail Centre, Rodbourne, Grange Lane, MALMESBURY WILTSHIRE SN16 0ES.

•**SMITH, Mr. David John, FCA** *1979;* (Tax Fac), D.J. Smith, 23 Welford Road, Kingsthorpe, NORTHAMPTON, NN2 8AQ.

SMITH, Mr. David John, FCA *1973;* 138 2723 - 37 Avenue NE, CALGARY T1Y 5R8, AB, CANADA.

SMITH, Mr. David John, FCA *1960;* 5 Cages Way, Melton, WOODBRIDGE, SUFFOLK, IP12 1TE. (Life Member)

SMITH, Mr. David John, FCA *1975;* 4 Arundel Close, Aston, STEVENAGE, SG2 7HW.

SMITH, Mr. David John, BA ACA *1993;* 87 N Hunters Crossing, SPRING, TX 77381, UNITED STATES.

SMITH, Mr. David John, BA ACA *1999;* The Shrubbery, 47 Postern Road, Tatenhill, BURTON-ON-TRENT, STAFFORDSHIRE, DE13 9SJ.

SMITH, Mr. David John, BSc ACA *1990;* Spring Lodge, 21 Wellington Avenue, FLEET, HAMPSHIRE, GU51 3BJ.

SMITH, Mr. David John, FCA *1959;* 5 Churchgate, Station Road, Sutterton, BOSTON, LINCOLNSHIRE, PE20 2NS. (Life Member)

SMITH, Mr. David John Timothy, ACA *2009;* 369 Oxhill Road, BIRMINGHAM, B21 8JT.

•**SMITH, Mr. David Joseph, FCA** *1991;* Maynard Heady LLP, Matrix House, 12-16 Lionel Road, CANVEY ISLAND, ESSEX, SS8 9DE. See also Maynard Heady

SMITH, Mr. David Kirkpatrick, BSc ACA *1987;* MR Engineering Group, 107 - 123 Bridge Street, BIRKENHEAD, MERSEYSIDE, CH41 1BD.

SMITH, Mr. David Leslie, FCA ATII *1954;* Heron Bank, Tang Road, High Birstwith, HARROGATE, HG3 2JU. (Life Member)

SMITH, Mr. David Mark, MBA BSc FCA *1996;* (Tax Fac), 6 Hampstead Lane, LONDON, N6 4SB.

SMITH, Mr. David Martin, BA FCA *1977;* 1st Floor Business House F, The Royal Bank of Scotland Plc, PO Box 1000, EDINBURGH, EH12 1HQ.

SMITH, Mr. David Martin, FCA *1972;* 3 Woodside, Stubbs Lane, Lower Kingswood, TADWORTH, KT20 7AW.

SMITH, Mr. David Michael, BSc FCA *1982;* 171 Gardner Road, Formby, LIVERPOOL, L37 8DG.

•**SMITH, Mr. David Michael John, FCA** *1978;* Winterwood, George Eyston Drive, WINCHESTER, HAMPSHIRE, SO22 4PE.

•**SMITH, Mr. David Micheal Ashley, MBA BA FCA** *1982;* with Grant Thornton UK LLP, Grant Thornton House, 22 Melton Street, Euston Square, LONDON, NW1 2EP.

SMITH, Mr. David Mowbray, FCA ATII *1961;* Cala Mayor, 29A High Street, SPALDING, PE11 1TX. (Life Member)

SMITH, Mr. David Nigel, BSc ACA *1980;* Composite Ltd Eastleigh House, Upper Market Street, EASTLEIGH, SO50 9RD.

•**SMITH, Mr. David Owen, ACA** *2000;* (Tax Fac), Cottons Accountants LLP, Regency House, 3 Albion Place, NORTHAMPTON, NN1 1UD.

SMITH, Mr. David Paul, BSc ACA *1990;* Brookfields, Station Road, Holme, PETERBOROUGH, CAMBRIDGESHIRE, PE7 3PH.

•**SMITH, Mr. David Peter Ansley, FCA** *1977;* Aims - David Smith, 3 Bank Buildings, 149 High Street, CRANLEIGH, SURREY, GU6 8BB. See also Cranfield Associates Ltd

SMITH, Mr. David Ralph, BCom FCA *1964;* Bradgate House, Wetherby Road, Bardsey, LEEDS, LS17 9BB.

SMITH, Mr. David Revell, FCA *1952;* 14 Florence Court Eastern, Esplanade Cliftonville, MARGATE, CT9 2JD. (Life Member)

SMITH, Mr. David Richard, FCA *1986;* Flat 211, Pierpoint, 16 Westferry Road, LONDON, E14 8NQ.

SMITH, Mr. David Richard, BA ACA *1990;* The Old Vicarage, Frensham, FARNHAM, SURREY, GU10 3DU.

SMITH, Mr. David Robert, BAcc ACA *1999;* Chessington World of Adventures, Leatherhead Road, CHESSINGTON, SURREY, KT9 2NE.

SMITH, Mr. David Robert, BA FCA *1996;* 7a Severus Avenue, YORK, YO24 4LX.

SMITH, Mr. David Ronald James, ACA ACCA *2008;* 24 Brougham Close, Ingleby Barwick, STOCKTON-ON-TEES, CLEVELAND, TS17 5GH.

SMITH, Mr. David Ross, BSc FCA *1993;* Church Lane House, Church Lane, Westley Waterless, NEWMARKET, SUFFOLK, CB8 0RL.

SMITH, Mr. David Ryder, BA ACA *1988;* 5 Acacia Avenue, Hale, ALTRINCHAM, WA15 8QX.

SMITH, Mr. David Terence, FCA *1964;* 16 Beaumont Green, Coleorton, COALVILLE, LE67 8FU.

SMITH, Mr. David Travers, FCA *1967;* 44 Sandrock Hill Road, Wrecclesham, FARNHAM, GU10 4RJ. (Life Member)

SMITH, Mr. David Tudor, BA ACA *1993;* Flat 229, Waterman Building, 14 Westferry Road, LONDON, E14 8NG.

SMITH, Mr. David Vincent, BA ACA *1986;* 3 Bennetts Way, CROYDON, CR0 8AE.

SMITH, Mr. David William, BSc FCA *1983;* 4 Emma Terrace, The Drive, LONDON, SW20 8QL.

SMITH, Mr. David William, MBA LLB FCA *1971;* 75 rue St Charles, 75015 PARIS, FRANCE.

SMITH, Mr. David William, BSc FCA *1974;* Vale House, Halstock, YEOVIL, SOMERSET, BA22 9SF.

SMITH, Mrs. Deborah Claire, BSc ACA *1988;* 17 Furzefield Crescent, REIGATE, RH2 7HQ.

SMITH, Ms. Deborah Louise, BA ACA *1992;* 2 Scot Grove, PINNER, HA5 4RT.

SMITH, Mr. Dennis Arthur, FCA *1965;* 12 Rectory Road, BURNHAM-ON-SEA, TA8 2BY.

SMITH, Mr. Dennis Leslie, FCA *1964;* 38 Larkhill Road, SHREWSBURY, SY3 8XA. (Life Member)

SMITH, Mr. Dennis Michael, BSc ACA *1979;* 15 Astor Close, KINGSTON UPON THAMES, KT2 7LT.

SMITH, Mr. Dennis Pritchard, FCA *1962;* 22 Chadfield Road, Duffield, BELPER, DE56 4DU. (Life Member)

SMITH, Mr. Derek Alan, ACA *1984;* 24 The Hythe, Two Mile Ash, MILTON KEYNES, MK8 8PB.

SMITH, Mr. Derek Arthur, FCA *1959;* 57 Barford Drive, WILMSLOW, CHESHIRE, SK9 2GB. (Life Member)

SMITH, Mr. Derek Arthur Hodgson, BA ACA *1991;* The Former Rectory, 152 Fletton Avenue, Old Fletton, PETERBOROUGH, PE2 8DF.

SMITH, Mr. Derek Charles, FCA *1956;* Womans Land, Dent, SEDBERGH, LA10 5RE. (Life Member)

SMITH, Colonel Derek Eward, FCA *1975;* 36 Dinorben Close, FLEET, GU52 7SL.

SMITH, Mr. Derek Graham, BA FCA *1973;* (Member of Council 2001 - 2004), The Damas Partnership, 12 Meeson Meadows, MALDON, ESSEX, CM9 6YS.

•**SMITH, Mr. Derek James, FCA** *1972;* 5 Hightree Drive, Henbury, MACCLESFIELD, SK11 9PD.

SMITH, Mr. Derek Leslie, FCA *1952;* 20 Hollies Drive, Edwalton, NOTTINGHAM, NG12 4BZ. (Life Member)

•**SMITH, Mr. Derek William, FCA** *1982;* with HW Group Services Limited, 11A Park House, Milton Park, ABINGDON, OX14 4RS.

•①**SMITH, Mr. Derrick Arthur, FCA** *1972;* Oury Clark, PO Box 150, Herschel House, 58 Herschel Street, SLOUGH, SL1 1HD.

SMITH, Mrs. Diane, BA ACA *1993;* 51 High Street, Buckden, ST NEOTS, CAMBRIDGESHIRE, PE19 5TA.

SMITH, Mrs. Diane, BA ACA *2000;* 10 North Nook, OLDHAM, OL4 3QR.

SMITH, Miss. Diane Joy, ACA *2007;* (Tax Fac), with Phoenix IT Group plc, Hunsbury Hill Avenue, NORTHAMPTON, NN4 8QS.

SMITH, Mr. Donald, FCA *1956;* Lyndon, 78 Hackney Road, MATLOCK, DE4 2PX. (Life Member)

SMITH, Mr. Donald, FCA *1959;* 26 Barnfield Avenue, SHEFFIELD, S10 5TA. (Life Member)

•**SMITH, Mr. Donald Barry, FCA CTA** *1971;* Rossiter Smith & Co, Bank House, 1 Burlington Road, BRISTOL, BS6 6TJ.

SMITH, Mr. Donald Earle, ACA *1983;* Aiekenya Aviation Ltd, PO Box 24103, NAIROBI, KENYA.

•SMITH, Mr. Donald Michael, FCA *1970;* Donald M. Smith, Hadleigh House, 5 Rivercourt Road, LONDON, W6 9LD.
SMITH, Mrs. Donna Louise, BSc ACA *1997;* 9 Arkendale Drive, Hardwicke, GLOUCESTER, GL2 4JA.
SMITH, Mr. Douglas, FCA *1952;* Shepherd's Cottage, 68 Tong Lane, Tong Village, BRADFORD, BD4 0RX. (Life Member)
SMITH, Dr. Douglas Gordon, BSc ACA *2002;* 1 Darvel Crescent, PAISLEY, RENFREWSHIRE, PA1 3EF.
SMITH, Mr. Duncan Alexander, MMath ACA *2010;* 7 Grosvenor Buildings, Crescent Road, HARROGATE, NORTH YORKSHIRE, HG1 2RT.
SMITH, Mr. Duncan Allan Edward, BA ACA *1985;* The Old School Church Lane, Boxted, COLCHESTER, CO4 5GW.
SMITH, Mr. Duncan Christopher, BA ACA *1990;* 61 rue Laach, L-6945 NIEDERANVEN, LUXEMBOURG.
SMITH, Mr. Duncan Ian, FCA *1994;* 28 Shoesmith Lane, Kings Hill, WEST MALLING, ME19 4FF.
SMITH, Mr. Duncan Paul, BSc ACA *1988;* 42 High View, PINNER, MIDDLESEX, HA5 3PB.
SMITH, Mr. Duncan Robert Embleton, BSc ACA *1997;* Bishops Court, Chase Lane, HASLEMERE, SURREY, GU27 3AG.
SMITH, Ms. Edel Mary, BSc ACA *1992;* 8 Voltaire, Ennerdale Road, RICHMOND, SURREY, TW9 3PQ.
SMITH, Mr. Edward Andrew, LLB ACA *1987;* Old Timbers Woodhill, Send, WOKING, GU23 7JW.
SMITH, Mr. Edward David, BEng ACA *2006;* 108 Harlow Terrace, HARROGATE, NORTH YORKSHIRE, HG2 0PP.
SMITH, Mr. Edward William Akeroyd, BSc ACA *2001;* 6 Barnswick View, LEEDS, LS16 7DP.
SMITH, Mr. Edwin David, MA ACA *1988;* 124 St. Georges Avenue, LONDON, N7 0AH.
SMITH, Mr. Edwin Ronald, FCA *1958;* 7 Hamilton Close, Byrons Wood, Powick, WORCESTER, WR2 4NH. (Life Member)
SMITH, Miss. Elaine Angela, BSc ACA *1982;* Touche Ross & Co., 1633 Broadway, NEW YORK, NY 10019, UNITED STATES.
SMITH, Ms. Elaine Louise, BA ACA *1989;* 26 Route Du Buisson, 78490 GROSROUVRE, FRANCE.
SMITH, Miss. Eleanor, MA FCA *1978;* 53 Kings Avenue, Lower Parkstone, POOLE, BH14 9QQ.
•SMITH, Mrs. Elizabeth, ACA FCCA *2009;* Davisons Ltd, Lime Court, Pathfields Business Park, SOUTH MOLTON, DEVON, EX36 3LH.
SMITH, Mrs. Elizabeth, BSc ACA *1988;* 7 Pilgrims Gate, WINCHESTER, HAMPSHIRE, SO22 6RQ.
SMITH, Miss. Elizabeth Ann, BSc ACA *1991;* 12 Severn Grange, Northwick Road, WORCESTER, WR3 7RE.
SMITH, Mrs. Elizabeth Anne, BA ACA *1985;* (Tax Fac), with CLB Coopers, Fleet House, New Road, LANCASTER, LA1 1EZ.
SMITH, Miss. Elizabeth Jane, BA ACA *1989;* 6 Langton Place, Southfields, Wimbledon, LONDON, SW18 5AZ.
SMITH, Miss. Elizabeth Laura, BA ACA *2005;* with Thomas Westcott, 26-28 Southernhay East, EXETER, DEVON, EX1 1NS.
SMITH, Mrs. Elizabeth Mary, BA ACA *1992;* with Thomas May & Co, Allen House, Newarke Street, LEICESTER, LE1 5SG.
SMITH, Miss. Elizabeth Victoria Lindley, BA ACA *1992;* 44 Culmington Road, Ealing, LONDON, W13 9NH.
SMITH, Miss. Ellen Rachel, BAcc ACA *2001;* 27 Grinsdale Avenue, Belle Vue, CARLISLE, CA2 7LX.
SMITH, Mrs. Emily, BA ACA *2005;* 14 Loxley Road, SUTTON COLDFIELD, WEST MIDLANDS, B75 5NY.
SMITH, Mrs. Emily, BA ACA *2006;* with Grant Thornton UK LLP, 4 Hardman Square, Spinningfields, MANCHESTER, M3 3EB.
SMITH, Miss. Emily Jane, BSc ACA *2004;* 136 Sandy Lane, MANCHESTER, M21 8TZ.
SMITH, Miss. Emma, BA(Hons) ACA *2002;* Icho House, La Grande Route de la Cote, ST CLEMENT, JE2 6FY.
SMITH, Miss. Emma Jane, BSc ACA *2011;* 2 Stonepit Drive, Cottingham, MARKET HARBOROUGH, LE16 8XY.
SMITH, Miss. Emma Jane, BSc ACA *2002;* 49 Heol y Cadno, Thornhill, CARDIFF, CF14 9EW.
SMITH, Mrs. Emma Louise, ACA *2002;* 2 Westfields Farm, Ogbourne St. George, MARLBOROUGH, SN8 1SX.
SMITH, Mrs. Emma Louise, ACA *2004;* Unit 1 Claydon Business Park, Great Blakenham, IPSWICH, IP6 0NL.
SMITH, Mr. Eric John, FCA *1956;* 8 Pegasus Court, 159 Brampton Way, Portishead, BRISTOL, BS20 6ZE. (Life Member)
SMITH, Mr. Eric Peter, FCA *1953;* 48 Marsden Road, Kingsway, BATH, BA2 2LL. (Life Member)
SMITH, Mr. Eric Tysoe, FCA *1963;* Domik, Epsom Lane South, TADWORTH, KT20 5SX. (Life Member)
SMITH, Mr. Ernest Edmund, FCA *1935;* 82 Linkside, Woodside Park, LONDON, N12 7LG. (Life Member)
SMITH, Mr. Ewart William, BSc ACA *1997;* 69 Oathall Road, HAYWARDS HEATH, RH16 3EL.
SMITH, Mrs. Fiona Margaret, BA FCA *1980;* Azalea Cottage, Warfield Street, BRACKNELL, RG42 6BG.
SMITH, Mrs. Fleur Helena, BA FCA *1988;* with Moore Stephens Services, L'EstorilBloc C, 31 Avenue Princesse Grace, MONTE CARLOMC 98000, MONACO.
SMITH, Miss. Frances, MA(Cantab) ACA *2011;* Flat 4, 29 Burton Road, MANCHESTER, M20 3GB.
SMITH, Mrs. Frances Jane, BSc ACA *1992;* The Mill House, Brook Road, Bassingbourn, ROYSTON, SG8 5NS.
SMITH, Mrs. Francesca Katharine, BA ACA *1997;* 61 Elm Grove Road, LONDON, SW13 0BX.
SMITH, Mrs. Francesca Maria, BA ACA *1993;* 136 Manchester Road, WILMSLOW, SK9 2JW.
SMITH, Mr. Frank Arthur, MA FCA CTA *1966;* Eastnor Garden House, 73 Tranquil Vale, LONDON, SE3 0BP.
SMITH, Mr. Fraser John Lyttleton, RD MA FCA *1997;* 66 Bolingbroke Grove, LONDON, SW11 6HE.
SMITH, Mr. Frederick Campbell, FCA *1953;* 52 Parkhurst Road, TORQUAY, TQ1 4EP. (Life Member)
SMITH, Mr. Frederick Sydney Reresby, FCA *1953;* Manor Cottage, Calton, Airton, SKIPTON, BD23 4AD. (Life Member)
SMITH, The Revd. Gareth Hugh St John, BA FCA *1969;* Hill View, Willetts Lane, Blackham, TUNBRIDGE WELLS, TN3 9TU. (Life Member)
SMITH, Mr. Garrie Stephen, BA ACA *1983;* 6 Santers Court, Gills Green, CRANBROOK, TN18 5EQ.
SMITH, Mr. Garry Duncan, FCA *1970;* PO Box 681, Avarua, RAROTONGA, COOK ISLANDS.
SMITH, Mr. Gary, ACA *2011;* 47 Columbine Way, ROMFORD, RM3 0XN.
SMITH, Mr. Gary John, BA ACA *1994;* 24 Offerton Road, LONDON, SW4 0DJ.
SMITH, Mr. Gary Thomas, BSc ACA *1994;* Blackpool Borough Council Progress House, Clifton Road, BLACKPOOL, FY4 4US.
SMITH, Mr. Gary William, BA ACA *1988;* 5 Moralee Close, Haydon Grange, Coach Lane Little Benton, NEWCASTLE UPON TYNE, NE7 7GE.
SMITH, Mr. Gavin David, MBA BA ACA *1988;* Robinson Healthcare Ltd Lawn Road, Carlton-in-Lindrick, WORKSOP, NOTTINGHAMSHIRE, S81 9LB.
•SMITH, Miss. Gayner Anne, FCA *1989;* Bird Luckin limited, Aquila House, Waterloo Lane, CHELMSFORD, CM1 1BN.
SMITH, Mrs. Gemma, BA(Hons) ACA *2002;* 9 Troutbeck Close, Twyford, READING, RG10 9DA.
SMITH, Miss. Gemma Kim Patricia, ACA *2010;* Flat G/04, The Beaux Arts, Building 10-18, Manor Gardens, LONDON, N7 6JT.
SMITH, Miss. Gemma Louise, BCom ACA *2004;* 35 Station Road, RADLETT, HERTFORDSHIRE, WD7 8JY.
•SMITH, Mr. Geoffrey, FCA *1979;* (Tax Fac), J.I. Winder & Co., 125 Ramsden Square, BARROW-IN-FURNESS, LA14 1XA.
•SMITH, Mr. Geoffrey Dennis, FCA *1977;* (Tax Fac), Larkings (S.E) LLP, Cornwallis House, Pudding Lane, MAIDSTONE, KENT, ME14 1NH. See also Larkings Ltd
SMITH, Mr. Geoffrey John, BA FCA *1974;* 71 Peel Crescent, Ashton, CHESTER, CH3 8DA.
SMITH, Mr. Geoffrey Paul, FCA *1977;* 14 Stanhope Road, ST. ALBANS, AL1 5BL.
SMITH, Mr. Geoffrey Thurstan, FCA *1975;* Kaye Presteigne Ltd, Harper Street, PRESTEIGNE, POWYS, LD8 2AL.
SMITH, Mr. Geoffrey Walter Alfred, FCA *1948;* 5 Allamanda Court, 15 Bergerac Rd, MARAVAL, TRINIDAD AND TOBAGO. (Life Member)
SMITH, Mr. George, BA FCA *1971;* Slade House, Tredington, SHIPSTON-ON-STOUR, CV36 4NJ.
SMITH, Mr. George Arthur, FCA *1972;* Tanks and Vessels Industries Ltd, Bankwood Lane Trading Estate, Bankwood Lane, Rossington, DONCASTER, SOUTH YORKSHIRE DN11 0PS.
SMITH, Mr. George Ronald, MBE MA LLB CA *1976; (CA Scotland 1965);* 5 Pembroke Gardens, WOKING, SURREY, GU22 7DR.
•ⓘSMITH, Mr. Gerald Clifford, BSc FCA *1978;* FRP Advisory LLP, 10 Furnival Street, LONDON, EC4A 1YH.
SMITH, Mr. Gerald Harry, FCA *1965;* PO Box 11774, CHINGOLA, ZAMBIA.
SMITH, Mr. Gerard Martin, BA ACA *2000;* 34 Westmere Crescent, AUCKLAND 1022, NEW ZEALAND.
SMITH, Mrs. Gillian, FCA *1972;* 1 Bourn Bridge Road, Little Abington, CAMBRIDGE, CB21 6BJ.
SMITH, Miss. Gillian, BA ACA *1987;* with Allen & Overy, One Bishops Square, LONDON, E1 6AD.
SMITH, Mrs. Gillian Erica, BSc FCA *1977;* (Tax Fac), 7 Napier Road, Killearn, GLASGOW, G63 9PB.
SMITH, Ms. Gillian Grieg, BSc ACA *1993;* Farthing Cottage, 24 High Street, WESTERHAM, TN16 1RG.
SMITH, Mrs. Gillian Kathleen, BCom ACA *1992;* 14 March Pines, EDINBURGH, EH4 3PF.
SMITH, Mrs. Gillian Lucy, BSc ACA *2011;* 10a Orrysdale Road, West Kirby, WIRRAL, MERSEYSIDE, CH48 5EN.
SMITH, Mrs. Gillian Mary, ACA *1983;* 19 North Quay, ABINGDON, OXFORDSHIRE, OX14 5RY.
•SMITH, Miss. Gillian Wendy, BSc FCA CTA *1989;* (Tax Fac), Moore Stephens LLP, 150 Aldersgate Street, LONDON, EC1A 4AB. See also Moore Stephens & Co
SMITH, Mrs. Gillian Yvonne, ACA *1990;* with Ryecroft Glenton, 32 Portland Terrace, Jesmond, NEWCASTLE UPON TYNE, NE2 1QP.
SMITH, Miss. Gina, ACA *2009;* 4 Green Lane, Whitwick, COALVILLE, LEICESTERSHIRE, LE67 5EB.
SMITH, Mr. Glen Scott Tracey, BA ACA *1983;* Arranmhor, Ardersier, INVERNESS, IV2 7QX.
•SMITH, Mr. Glen Warren, ACA CA(SA) *2009;* (Tax Fac), Income Made Smart LLP, 9-13 Fulham High Street, LONDON, SW6 3JH.
SMITH, Mr. Glenton Ian Arthur, MA ACA *1999;* 8 Maes y Castell, Ewloe, DEESIDE, FLINTSHIRE, CH5 3BT.
SMITH, Mr. Glyn Michael, MA FCA *1977;* 8 Upper Golf Links Road, BROADSTONE, DORSET, BH18 8BU.
SMITH, Mr. Godfrey Brian, FCA *1968;* 14 Oxbow Crescent, MARCH, CAMBRIDGESHIRE, PE15 9UJ.
•SMITH, Mr. Gordon Allen, FCA *1950;* Gordon A. Smith, The Gables, 14 Beech Road, Saltford, BRISTOL, BS31 3BE.
SMITH, Mr. Gordon Charles, FCA *1968;* 3 Thornton Way, LONDON, NW11 6RY.
SMITH, Mr. Graeme George, BSc FCA *1991;* 29 Raleigh Drive, Victoria Dock, HULL, HU9 1UN.
•SMITH, Mr. Graeme Jonathan, BEng ACA *2002;* Zolfo Cooper LLP, 10 Fleet Place, LONDON, EC4M 7RB.
SMITH, Mr. Graham, FCA *1964;* Downland Bedding Co Ltd, Blackstock street, LIVERPOOL, L3 6ER.
SMITH, Mr. Graham, BSc ACA *2009;* 12 Sherwood Place, Headington, OXFORD, OX3 9PR.
SMITH, Mr. Graham, FCA *1973;* The Old Granary Brabling Green, Framlingham, WOODBRIDGE, SUFFOLK, IP13 9JD.
SMITH, Mr. Graham, MSc ACA *2002;* Harsco House, 299 Kingston Road, LEATHERHEAD, KT22 7SG.
SMITH, Mr. Graham, BA FCA *1975;* Middleton Crag, 117 Curly Hill, ILKLEY, LS29 0DT.
SMITH, Mr. Graham Alan, FCA *1975;* 70 Ashpole Furlong, Loughton, MILTON KEYNES, MK5 8DX.
SMITH, Mr. Graham Alan, ACA *1987;* TFC Europe Ltd Hale House, Ghyll Industrial Estate, HEATHFIELD, EAST SUSSEX, TN21 8AW.
SMITH, Mr. Graham Allott, FCA *1975;* Campden House, Beech Close, STRATFORD-UPON-AVON, CV37 7EB.
SMITH, Mr. Graham Anthony, BCom FCA *1969;* 210-1 McGill Street, MONTREAL H2Y 4A3, QC, CANADA. (Life Member)
SMITH, Mr. Graham Bruce, BA(Hons) ACA *2000;* Flat 6, Wolsey Court, 1-3 Harben Road, LONDON, NW6 4RG.
SMITH, Mr. Graham Cottingham, MA FCA *1993;* 2 Ridgeside, North Close, Kirk Merrington, SPENNYMOOR, COUNTY DURHAM, DL16 7HG.
SMITH, Mr. Graham Frederick, BSc FCA *1977;* Vicolo Sport 15, 20029 Turbigo, MILAN, ITALY.
SMITH, Mr. Graham Frederick, FCA *1964;* Crabtrees, Nairdwood Lane, Prestwood, GREAT MISSENDEN, BUCKINGHAMSHIRE, HP16 0QH.
SMITH, Mr. Graham Hurndall, FCA *1958;* 69 Lightridge Road, Fixby, HUDDERSFIELD, HD2 2HF. (Life Member)
SMITH, Mr. Graham James, MA ACA *1991;* B D O Stoy Hayward, Kings Wharf, 20-30 Kings Road, READING, RG1 3EX.
SMITH, Mr. Graham John, FCA *1973;* 15308 Basswood Court, ROCKVILLE, MD 20853, UNITED STATES.
SMITH, Mr. Graham Michael, BA ACA *1982;* Cort Business Services UK Ltd, 28 Barwell Business Park, Leatherhead Road, CHESSINGTON, SURREY, KT9 2NY.
SMITH, Mr. Graham Michael, BSc ACA *1985;* 1 Thorns Clough, Diggle, OLDHAM, OL3 5NF.
SMITH, Mr. Graham Paul, BSc ACA *1986;* 5 Wheatfield Avenue, HARPENDEN, AL5 2NU.
SMITH, Mr. Graham Roger, BA FCA *1984;* IOMAFIM Ltd, Ioma House, Hope Street, Douglas, ISLE OF MAN, IM1 1AP.
SMITH, Mr. Graham Ronald, BSc ACA *1985;* PO Box 950, COOROY, QLD 4563, AUSTRALIA.
•SMITH, Mr. Grant Peter, ACA *2001;* Armstrong Watson, Bute House, Montgomery Way, Rosehill, CARLISLE, CA1 2RW.
SMITH, Mr. Greg Simon Bryan, BSc ACA *2004;* I P Group PLC, 24 Cornhill, LONDON, EC3V 3ND.
SMITH, Mr. Gregory Anthony, BSc ACA *1986;* Willow House, Bowling Alley, CRONDALL, SURREY, GU10 5RN.
SMITH, Mr. Gregory Charles, FCA *1972;* 9 Ffordd Meirion, FAIRBOURNE, LL38 2QY.
SMITH, Mr. Gregory Paul, BA ACA *2003;* Vision Express, Abbeyfield Road, Lenton, NOTTINGHAM, NG7 2SP.
SMITH, Mrs. Hannah Charlotte, ACA *2011;* 8 Thomas Street, LOUGHBOROUGH, LEICESTERSHIRE, LE11 1SH.
SMITH, Mrs. Hannah Elizabeth, BA(Hons) ACA *2009;* 26 St. Catherines Drive, Douglas, ISLE OF MAN, IM1 4BQ.
SMITH, Miss. Hannah Louise, ACA *2008;* Flat 9, 26-28 Belvedere Road, LONDON, SE19 2HW.
SMITH, Mrs. Hannah Michelle, MSc ACA *2004;* 21 Ambrose Avenue, Golders Green, LONDON, NW11 9AP.
SMITH, Mr. Harold John, FCA *1961;* 9 Western Avenue, Branksome Park, POOLE, DORSET, BH13 7AL.
SMITH, Mr. Harold Stanley, FCA *1965;* Greenbotham, Chinley New Road, Bridgemont, Whaley Bridge, HIGH PEAK, SK23 7EE. (Life Member)
SMITH, Mrs. Harriet Jane Bronwen, BSc ACA *1990;* 15 Chapel Lane, Halebarns, ALTRINCHAM, WA15 0HN.
SMITH, Mr. Harvey Guy, MA ACA *1997;* 10 North Nook, Austerlands, OLDHAM, OL4 3QR.
SMITH, Mr. Harwood Martin, FCA *1967;* 82 Kings Road, Wimbledon, LONDON, SW19 8QW.
SMITH, Miss. Hayley Elizabeth, ACA *2009;* Flat 3, 8 Evesham Road, CHELTENHAM, GLOUCESTERSHIRE, GL52 2AB.
SMITH, Mrs. Hayley Jayne, ACA *2009;* with S C Miller Ltd, Clock Offices, High Street, Bishops Waltham, SOUTHAMPTON, SO32 1AA.
SMITH, Mrs. Hazel, BA ACA *1998;* Clock Cottage Newsam Green Road, Woodlesford, LEEDS, LS26 8AG.
•SMITH, Miss. Hazel Marie, MSc BSc ACA CTA *2007;* (Tax Fac), Greaves West & Ayre, 1-3 Sandgate, BERWICK-UPON-TWEED, TD15 1EW.
SMITH, Mrs. Hazel Sharon, MSc ACA ATII *1998;* (Tax Fac), 3 Moriarty Close, BROMLEY, BR1 2FN.
SMITH, Miss. Heather, MA ACA *2011;* 17 Morningside Drive, East Didsbury, MANCHESTER, M20 5PQ.
SMITH, Mr. Hedley Lockhart, BSc FCA *1971;* The Rocks, Ashwick, CHIPPENHAM, WILTSHIRE, SN14 8AP.
SMITH, Miss. Helen, BSc ACA *2011;* Flat 3, 41 Lyford Road, LONDON, SW18 3LU.
SMITH, Miss. Helen Elizabeth, LLB ACA *2007;* 19 Lapwing View, Horbury, WAKEFIELD, WEST YORKSHIRE, WF4 5NZ.
SMITH, Mrs. Helen Louise, BSc ACA *2002;* 29 Rushwick Grove, Shirley, SOLIHULL, B90 4XL.
SMITH, Mrs. Helen Louise, BSc ACA *1990;* Chesterfield Lodge, 31 Merlin Drive, SANDY, BEDFORDSHIRE, SG19 2UN.
SMITH, Mrs. Helen Mary, BA ACA AMCT *1994;* 2 South Cottage Gardens, Chorleywood, RICKMANSWORTH, HERTFORDSHIRE, WD3 5EH.
SMITH, Mrs. Helena Carmel, BA ACA *1990;* Asset Finance H S B C Forward Trust House, 12 Calthorpe Road Edgbaston, BIRMINGHAM, B15 1QZ.
SMITH, Mr. Helier James Bennett, BA FCA *1995;* Jersey New Waterworks Co, JERSEY, JE1 1DG.
•SMITH, Mrs. Hellen, BA FCA *1994;* Hayvenhursts Limited, Fairway House, Links Business Park, St. Mellons, CARDIFF, CF3 0LT. See also Hayvenhursts

SMITH, Mr. Henry Alfred, FCA *1952;* 56 Townley Road, Dulwich, LONDON, SE22 8SX. (Life Member)
SMITH, Mr. Henry Neil, FCA *1969;* Rose Cottage, 206 Longmeanygate, Leyland, PRESTON, PR26 7TB.
SMITH, Mrs. Hilary Jane, BSc ACA *2001;* 3 Holland Gardens, EGHAM, SURREY, TW20 8TA.
SMITH, Mr. Howard Brian, FCA *1954;* 12a Glapthorn Road, Oundle, PETERBOROUGH, PE8 4JA. (Life Member)
SMITH, Mr. Howard Dobree, FCA *1975;* Finches, Wigginton Bottom, TRING, HERTFORDSHIRE, HP23 6HW.
SMITH, Mr. Howard Douglas, MA FCA *1970;* 10 Churchfield Road, PETERSFIELD, HAMPSHIRE, GU31 4BT.
SMITH, Mr. Howard Graham, BSc ACA *1983;* 2 Barkers Well Fold, LEEDS, LS12 5TR.
•SMITH, Mr. Hugh Martin, FCA *1967;* H.Martin Smith & Co, 40 Springfield Gardens, Hirwaun, ABERDARE, MID GLAMORGAN, CF44 9LY.
•SMITH, Mr. Huw Kingsbury, BA ACA *1990;* PricewaterhouseCoopers LLP, 1 Embankment Place, LONDON, WC2N 6RH. See also PricewaterhouseCoopers
SMITH, Mr. Iain David, BA FCA *1978;* Alderwey, Hopgarden Lane, SEVENOAKS, KENT, TN13 1PU.
SMITH, Mr. Iain Edward Cameron, BA ACA ATII *1997;* 18 Steyning Crescent, Glenfield, LEICESTER, LE3 8PJ.
SMITH, Mr. Iain Matthew, ACA *2008;* 254 Wilmot Street, LONDON, E2 0BY.
SMITH, Mr. Iain Michael, BA ACA *1997;* 15 Wellfield Lane, Westhead, ORMSKIRK, L40 6HH.
SMITH, Mr. Ian, FCA *1973;* Scotiabank, Audit Department, 44 King Street West, TORONTO M4H 1H1, ON, CANADA.
•SMITH, Mr. Ian, FCA *1977;* (Tax Fac), Ian Smith, 54 Cockshutts Lane, Oughtibridge, SHEFFIELD, S35 0FX.
SMITH, Mr. Ian, BA ACA *1988;* 3 Douglas Grange, Hurst, READING, RG10 0TT.
SMITH, Mr. Ian Charles, BA(Hons) FCA MCIM *1989;* Bradford Grammar School, Keighley Road, BRADFORD, BD9 4JP.
•SMITH, Mr. Ian Dalgleish Stirling, BSc(Eng) FCA *1975;* Ian Smith & Co, Lockram Villas, 7 Collingwood Road, WITHAM, CM8 2DY.
SMITH, Mr. Ian David, ACA *1981;* 17 Kensington Close, RUSHDEN, NN10 6RR.
SMITH, Mr. Ian David, BSc ACA *1983;* 95 Ruskin Avenue, Rogerstone, NEWPORT, NP10 0BD.
SMITH, Mr. Ian Davidson, FCA *1969;* 10 Rosegate, Aglionby, CARLISLE, CA4 8AJ.
SMITH, Mr. Ian Douglas, BSc ACA *1982;* The Knoll, 23 Top Lane, Copmanthorpe, YORK, YO23 3UH.
SMITH, Mr. Ian Douglas, LLB FCA *1987;* Airbus S.A.S., 1 Rond-Point Maurice Bellonte, 31707 BLAGNAC, FRANCE.
SMITH, Mr. Ian Fredrick, ACA *1991;* Vertex Pharmaceuticals, 130 Waverley Street, CAMBRIDGE, MA 02139, UNITED STATES.
SMITH, Mr. Ian Graham, BSc ACA *2006;* 17 Newton Park Road Newton, West Kirby, WIRRAL, CH48 9XE.
SMITH, Mr. Ian Hamilton, BA FCA *1997;* The Nook, 5 Archway Road, Old Clipstone, MANSFIELD, NOTTINGHAMSHIRE, NG21 9BU.
•SMITH, Mr. Ian James, BA ACA *1998;* Deloitte LLP, Global House, High Street, CRAWLEY, RH10 1DL. See also Deloitte & Touche LLP
•SMITH, Mr. Ian James Crockatt, BA FCA FCCA CTA *1984;* Rabjohns LLP, 1-3 College Yard, WORCESTER, WR1 2LB.
SMITH, Mr. Ian Kenneth, BA ACA *1983;* 38 Church Street, Great Shelford, CAMBRIDGE, CB22 5EL.
SMITH, Mr. Ian Marshall, FCA *1978;* PO Box 38054, RPO King Edward, VANCOUVER V5Z 4L9, BC, CANADA.
•SMITH, Mr. Ian Morgan, FCA *1991;* Ryecroft Glenton, 32 Portland Terrace, Jesmond, NEWCASTLE UPON TYNE, NE2 1QP.
•SMITH, Mr. Ian Peter, BSc FCA *1979;* Oak Tree Cottage, Auclum La, Burghfield Common, READING, RG7 3DA.
•SMITH, Mr. Ian Raymond, BSc FCA *1983;* PricewaterhouseCoopers LLP, The Atrium, 1 Harefield Road, UXBRIDGE, UB8 1EX. See also PricewaterhouseCoopers
SMITH, Mr. Ian Richard, FCA *1969;* 24a Glentrammon Road, Green Street Green, ORPINGTON, BR6 6DE.
SMITH, Mr. Ian Richard, BA ACA *1993;* 56 Wakefield Road, Hipperholme, HALIFAX, HX3 8AQ.
SMITH, Mr. Ian Robert, ACA *1989;* Orchard Cottage, Mill Street, Kineton, WARWICK, CV35 0LB.
SMITH, Mr. Ian Robert, FCA *1996;* Little Deans Hill Farm, Deans Hill, Bredgar, SITTINGBOURNE, KENT, ME9 8BB.
SMITH, Mr. Ian Stewart, BSc FCA *1990;* 173 Thames Side, Off Beechtree Lane, STAINES, MIDDLESEX, TW18 2JH.
•SMITH, Mr. Ian Stuart, MA ACA *1992;* Deloitte LLP, Athene Place, 66 Shoe Lane, LONDON, EC4A 3BQ. See also Deloitte & Touche LLP
SMITH, Mr. Ian Sydney, BSc ACA *1985;* 13 Main Street, Burrough on the Hill, MELTON MOWBRAY, LEICESTERSHIRE, LE14 2JQ.
•SMITH, Mr. Ian William, FCA CTA *1973;* (Tax Fac), Ian W. Smith, 6 The Hawthorns, Nettleham, LINCOLN, LN2 2GD.
SMITH, Mr. Ian William, BA FCA *1988;* 11 St. Leonards Drive, Timperley, ALTRINCHAM, CHESHIRE, WA15 7RS.
SMITH, Mr. Iwan Rhodri, ACA *2008;* Flat 9 Wallace Place, Granby Hill, BRISTOL, BS8 4LH.
SMITH, Mr. James, LLB FCA *1960;* Kingslea, Kingsdale Road, BERKHAMSTED, HP4 3BS. (Life Member)
SMITH, Mr. James, BA(Hons) ACA *2011;* 31 The Rookery, Orton Wistow, PETERBOROUGH, PE2 6YT.
SMITH, Mr. James, BEng ACA *2011;* Flat 3, The Firs, 99 College Road, EPSOM, SURREY, KT17 4HZ.
SMITH, Mr. James, ACA *2011;* Flat 3, 12 Smyrna Road, LONDON, NW6 4LY.
SMITH, Mr. James Ackland, BSc FCA *1989;* 31 Saville Row, Hayes, BROMLEY, BR2 7DX.
SMITH, Mr. James Alexander, BA ACA *2003;* 11 Oakwood Drive, BILLERICAY, CM12 0SA.
SMITH, Mr. James Arthur, LLB ACA *1997;* 2 Hollyhock Cottages, Guildford Road, CRANLEIGH, SURREY, GU6 8LT.
SMITH, Mr. James Arthur, MA CA FCA *1987;* with Ernst & Young, 18/F, Two International Finance Centre, 8 Finance Street, CENTRAL, HONG KONG ISLAND HONG KONG SAR.
SMITH, Mr. James Christopher, ACA FCCA *2009;* 37 Rayner Drive, Arborfield, READING, RG2 9FB.
SMITH, Mr. James Colin, FCA *1962;* 18 Minerva Close, HAVERHILL, CB9 0NF.
SMITH, Mr. James Daniel, ACA *2009;* (Member of Council 2008 - 2009), 111 Redland Road, BRISTOL, BS6 6QY.
SMITH, Mr. James Desmond, FCA *1952;* Dacre Point, 128 Button Hill, SHEFFIELD, S11 9HJ. (Life Member)
•SMITH, Mr. James Duncan, BA ACA *1986;* 3 Ainsworth Place, CAMBRIDGE, CB1 2PG.
•SMITH, Mr. James Edmund, BSc FCA *1999;* James Smith (Accountant) Ltd, 43 East St. Helen Street, ABINGDON, OXFORDSHIRE, OX14 5EE. See also James Smith
SMITH, Mr. James Edward, BA(Hons) ACA *2002;* 9 Troutbeck Close, Twyford, READING, RG10 9DA.
•SMITH, Mr. James Luke Gladstone, BSc ACA *2002;* Foxleigh Knight & Co Limited, PO BOX 162, Ground Floor, Anley House, 5 Anley Street, St. Helier JERSEY JE4 5NZ.
SMITH, Mr. James Nicholas Bourke, BA ACA *1993;* Delphinstrasse 10, 8008 ZURICH, SWITZERLAND.
SMITH, Mr. James Robert, BA ACA *1986;* 29 Artillery Mews, Tilehurst Road, READING, RG30 2JN.
•ⓘSMITH, Mr. James Robert Drummond, BA FCA *1986;* Flat 21, Elm Park Mansions, Park Walk, LONDON, SW10 0AN.
SMITH, Mr. James Thomas, BA FCA *1993;* 21 Rowe Street, ROSEVILLE CHASE, NSW 2069, AUSTRALIA.
SMITH, Miss. Jancy, BSc ACA *1993;* Fidelity Bank (Cayman) Ltd, PO Box 914, GEORGE TOWN, GRAND CAYMAN, KY1-1103, CAYMAN ISLANDS.
SMITH, Mrs. Jane Barbara, BA(Econ) ACA *1997;* 4 Willow Lea, Mollington, CHESTER, CH1 6LW.
SMITH, Mrs. Jane Elizabeth, BSc(Econ) ACA *1983;* 29 The Smithy, Devauden, CHEPSTOW, GWENT, NP16 6QA.
•SMITH, Mrs. Jane Emma, BAcc ACA *1996;* 5 Ringwood Close, ACCRINGTON, LANCASHIRE, BB5 5EU.
SMITH, Mrs. Jane Louise, BSc FCA *1992;* 40 Kerria Way, West End, WOKING, GU24 9XB.
•SMITH, Mrs. Jane Marie, BA ACA *1994;* Jane Smith, 8 Kingland Drive, LEAMINGTON SPA, WARWICKSHIRE, CV32 6BL.
SMITH, Ms. Jane Sarah, BA ACA *1991;* 24 Holmbush Road, LONDON, SW15 3LE.
SMITH, Miss. Jane Theresa, BA ACA *1990;* 1700 Newberry Lane, RACINE, WI 53402, UNITED STATES.
SMITH, Miss. Janet, FCA *1975;* 11 Alder Drive, PUDSEY, LS28 8RD.
SMITH, Mrs. Janet Mary, ACA *1986;* 7 Hanbury Gardens, Braunston, RUTLAND, LE15 8QN.
SMITH, Miss. Janice Lorraine, BSc ACA *2007;* 59b Woodhouse Road North, WOLVERHAMPTON, WV6 8JD.
SMITH, Ms. Janine Alison, BCom ACA *2004;* 24 Hirdemons Way, SOLIHULL, WEST MIDLANDS, B90 1SE.
SMITH, Mr. Jason Anthony, BA ACA *1997;* 4 Gwalior Road, LONDON, SW15 1NP.
SMITH, Mr. Jason David, BA ACA *1992;* Solstice House, 251 Midsummer Boulevard, MILTON KEYNES, MK9 1EQ.
SMITH, Mr. Jason James, ACA *2009;* 8b Darling Road, LONDON, SE4 1YQ.
SMITH, Mr. Jason Robert, BA(Hons) FCA DChA *1996;* Technolog Holdings Limited, Ravenstor Road, Wirksworth, MATLOCK, DERBYSHIRE, DE4 4FY.
SMITH, Dr. Jayne, EdD MSc BSc(Hons) FCA ILTM *1981;* Flat 54 Penkhull Court, Honeywall, STOKE-ON-TRENT, ST4 1PA. (Life Member)
SMITH, Mrs. Jeanette Clare, ACA *2001;* 30 Greenwood Place, Eccles, MANCHESTER, M30 9EX.
•SMITH, Mr. Jeffrey Bernard, BSc FCA CTA *1975;* Eacotts Limited, Grenville Court, Britwell Road, Burnham, SLOUGH, SL1 8DF. See also Eacotts
SMITH, Mrs. Jenna Eden, ACA *2008;* 3 Sepia Grove, Middleton, MANCHESTER, M24 5DP.
SMITH, Mrs. Jennifer, ACA *1985;* 27 Hightown Road, BANBURY, OXFORDSHIRE, OX16 9BT.
SMITH, Mrs. Jennifer, BSc ACA *1980;* Old Mill Leat, Vicarage Hill, WESTERHAM, TN16 1TJ.
SMITH, Miss. Jennifer Claire, ACA *2006;* 118 William Street, Petone, LOWER HUTT 5012, NEW ZEALAND.
•SMITH, Miss. Jennifer Gwendolyn, FCA *1972;* Tricor Caribbean Limited, Worthing Corporate Centre, Worthing, P.O. Box 169W, CHRISTCHURCH, BB15008 BARBADOS.
SMITH, Miss. Jennifer Mary, BA ACA *1993;* 24 Clarence Road, ST. ALBANS, HERTFORDSHIRE, AL1 4NE.
SMITH, Mr. Jeremy Alan, BA FCA *1986;* Fountain Cottage, Groombridge Hill, Groombridge, TUNBRIDGE WELLS, KENT, TN3 9NA.
SMITH, Mr. Jeremy Charles Allan, BSc FCA *1983;* (Tax Fac), 5 Turner Road, NEW MALDEN, KT3 5NL.
SMITH, Mr. Jeremy Roger, BA ACA MSI *1996;* 122 Hadham Road, BISHOP'S STORTFORD, HERTFORDSHIRE, CM23 2QF.
SMITH, Mrs. Joanna Jane, ACA *2005;* Flat 46, Priory Court, Roots Hall Drive, SOUTHEND-ON-SEA, SS2 6HL.
SMITH, Mrs. Joanne Claire, BA ACA *1998;* 54 Eastcombe Avenue, Charlton, LONDON, SE7 7JE.
SMITH, Miss. Joanne Elizabeth, BSc ACA *2001;* 40 Park Mount, HARPENDEN, HERTFORDSHIRE, AL5 3AR.
SMITH, Mrs. Joanne Mary, BSc ACA *1996;* 40 Throgmorton Road, YATELEY, HAMPSHIRE, GU46 6FA.
SMITH, Mr. Joel Dominic, LLB ACA *2004;* with PricewaterhouseCoopers LLP, Benson House, 33 Wellington Street, LEEDS, LS1 4JP.
SMITH, Mrs. Johanna Mary, BSc(Hons) ACA *2000;* 34 Rectory Close, NEWBURY, BERKSHIRE, RG14 6DD.
SMITH, Mr. John, FCA *1975;* 6337 Nimtz Road, LOVES PARK, IL 61111, UNITED STATES.
SMITH, Mr. John Allison, FCA *1961;* Hawkley, Lower Pennington Lane, LYMINGTON, SO41 8AN. (Life Member)
SMITH, Mr. John Angus, BSc ACA *1989;* Flat 6 Old Court, 19c Montpelier Road, LONDON, W5 2QT.
SMITH, John Anthony, Esq MBE BA ACA *1986;* Flat 3, 21 Dartmouth Row, LONDON, SE10 8AW.
•SMITH, Mr. John Arthur, FCA *1960;* with J S Accountants Ltd, 11 Upper Hollis, GREAT MISSENDEN, HP16 9HP.
SMITH, Mr. John Barnard, FCA *1969;* Pains Hill Corner, Chapel Road, Limpsfield Chart, OXTED, RH8 0RB. (Life Member)
•SMITH, Mr. John Barry, FCA *1972;* Adam & Co Financial Management LLP, First Floor, 1 Edmund Street, BRADFORD, WEST YORKSHIRE, BD5 0BH. See also Smith Munir Accountancy Limited
SMITH, Mr. John Cedric, FCA *1962;* 16 Tenterfield Close, Greenfield, OLDHAM, OL3 7FP.
SMITH, Mr. John Driskill, FCA JDipMA *1956;* 21 Rustington Court, 8 St Johns Road, EASTBOURNE, BN20 7HS. (Life Member)
SMITH, Mr. John Edward, FCA *1975;* Sandlow Green Farm Holmes Chapel Road, Holmes Chapel, CREWE, CW4 8AS.
SMITH, Mr. John Edward Kitson, BA FCA *1980;* Old Mill Leat, Vicarage Hill, WESTERHAM, TN16 1TJ.
SMITH, Mr. John Edwin, BA ACA *1993;* 14 Hodgson Fold, Addingham, ILKLEY, LS29 0HA.
SMITH, Mr. John Ernest, FCA *1971;* (Member of Council 1987 - 1993), C P Holdings, C P House, Otterspool Way, WATFORD, WD25 8JJ.
SMITH, Mr. John Ernest, FCA MAAT *1986;* Old Mill Group, Unit 4, Challymead Business Park, Bradford Road, MELKSHAM, WILTSHIRE SN12 8BU.
•SMITH, Mr. John George, FCA *1958;* J.G. Smith, 74 Knight Street, Pinchbeck, SPALDING, LINCOLNSHIRE, PE11 3RB.
•SMITH, Mr. John Hartley, FCA *1979;* Egeria Limited, 83 Lightfoot Lane, Fulwood, PRESTON, PR2 3LS.
•SMITH, Mr. John Henry, FCA *1975;* John H Smith, Little Acre, Perryfields Road, BROMSGROVE, B61 8QW.
SMITH, Mr. John Leslie, FCA *1964;* Willow Farm, Fangfoss, YORK, YO41 5QH. (Life Member)
•SMITH, Mr. John Marshall Galloway, FCA *1975;* Galloway Smith & Company, 9 Hope Street, Douglas, ISLE OF MAN, IM1 1AQ.
SMITH, Mr. John Michael, FCA *1965;* 102 Brookwood Drive, TRYON, NC 28782, UNITED STATES.
SMITH, Mr. John Michael, BSc FCA *1972;* 22 Ashton Road, Oundle, PETERBOROUGH, PE8 4HP.
SMITH, Mr. John Michael, FCA *1965;* 100 Shirehall Road, Hawley, DARTFORD, DA2 7SF. (Life Member)
SMITH, Mr. John Nicholas Wilkins, FCA *1960;* Arranmore, Coach Drive, Quarndon, DERBY, DE22 5JX. (Life Member)
•SMITH, Mr. John Nigel, ACA *1979;* (Tax Fac), Segrave & Partners, Turnpike House, 1208/1210 London Road, LEIGH-ON-SEA, SS9 2UA.
SMITH, Mr. John Patrick, BSc FCA *1978;* Bullen Court Broadway, ILMINSTER, SOMERSET, TA19 9QY.
SMITH, Mr. John Simon Bertie, BA ACA *1992;* (Tax Fac), Pearl Group Ltd, Juxon House, 100 St. Paul's Churchyard, LONDON, EC4M 8BU.
•SMITH, Mr. John Stephen Richard, MA FCA *1988;* Schofield Smith & Co Limited, 69 East Craigs Rigg, EDINBURGH, EH12 8JA.
SMITH, Mr. John Vincent, FCA *1962;* 9 Highfield Drive, Standish, WIGAN, WN6 0EJ.
SMITH, Mr. John Wallace, BSc FCA *1960;* 23 High Street, Sharnbrook, BEDFORD, MK44 1PG. (Life Member)
SMITH, Mr. John Walton, FCA *1952;* 47 Ashfield Road, Compton Road West, WOLVERHAMPTON, WV3 9DP. (Life Member)
SMITH, The Revd. John William, FCA *1954;* 76 Martins Lane, Hardingstone, NORTHAMPTON, NN4 6DJ. (Life Member)
SMITH, Mr. Jon, FCA *1974;* 39 Bedgebury Close, ROCHESTER, ME1 2UT.
•SMITH, Mr. Jonathan Francis, FCA *1971;* (Tax Fac), AIMS - Jon Smith, Mid Thatch, Boon Street, Eckington, PERSHORE, WORCESTERSHIRE WR10 3BL.
SMITH, Mr. Jonathan Frederick, BSc ACA *1993;* (Tax Fac), Marks & Spencer Plc Waterside House, 35 North Wharf Road, LONDON, W2 1NW.
SMITH, Mr. Jonathan George Thomas, ACA *2008;* 55 Old Dickens Heath Road, Shirley, SOLIHULL, WEST MIDLANDS, B90 1SR.
•SMITH, Mr. Jonathan Graeme, BA ACA *1988;* Sterling Corporate Finance LLP, 12 York Place, LEEDS, LS1 2DS.
SMITH, Mr. Jonathan Paul Kenneth, BSc ACA *1988;* 4 Hall Close, Glen Parva, LEICESTER, LE2 9HZ.
SMITH, Mr. Jonathan Peter, MA ACA *1989;* Foxwood, 7 Burstead Close, COBHAM, SURREY, KT11 2NL.
SMITH, Mr. Jonathan Ward, BA ACA *1990;* 9 Flint Street, Haddenham, AYLESBURY, HP17 8AL.
SMITH, Mr. Joseph, FCA *1953;* 5 Fytton Close, Gawsworth, MACCLESFIELD, CHESHIRE, SK11 9RB. (Life Member)
SMITH, Mr. Joseph William Read, BA(Hons) ACA *2002;* Financial Services Authority, 10th Floor, 25 North Colonnade, Canary Wharf, LONDON, E14 5HS.
SMITH, Mrs. Josephine Margaret, MSc BSc ACA *2003;* PO Box 140, PEMBERTON, WA 6260, AUSTRALIA.
•SMITH, Mrs. Judith Mary, BSc FCA *1976;* Abbey Mount Accountancy Services, 44 High House Drive, Lickey, BIRMINGHAM, B45 8ET. See also Smith Judith M.
•SMITH, Mrs. Julia Rosalie, FCA *1981;* Rigbey Harrison, 4 Church Green East, REDDITCH, B98 8BT.
SMITH, Mr. Julian, BA ACA *1999;* 11 Lewin Road, Streatham, LONDON, SW16 6JZ.

•SMITH, Mr. Julian Lawrence, BA ACA *1991;* PricewaterhouseCoopers LLP, 7 More London Riverside, LONDON, SE1 2RT. See also PricewaterhouseCoopers
SMITH, Mr. Julian Matthew, BA ACA *1991;* 52 Princes Gate, LONDON, SW7 2PG.
SMITH, Mr. Julian Nicholas, BSc ACA *1989;* Maris Interiors LLP, 13th Floor, The Tower Building, 11 York Road, LONDON, SE1 7NX.
SMITH, Mr. Julian Wilson, FCA *1974;* 14 Handen Road, Lee, LONDON, SE12 8NP.
SMITH, Mrs. Julie, BA ACA *1985;* 13 Main Street, Burrough on the Hill, MELTON MOWBRAY, LEICESTERSHIRE, LE14 2JQ.
•SMITH, Mrs. Julie Christine, BSc FCA *1997;* Smith McBride Limited, Copthall Bridge House, Station Bridge, HARROGATE, NORTH YORKSHIRE, HG1 1SP.
SMITH, Miss. Juliet Claire, ACA CTA *2002;* 10 Granary Close, Wheathampstead, ST. ALBANS, HERTFORDSHIRE, AL4 8BA.
SMITH, Mr. Justin, BA ACA *2007;* 26 The Plantation, ALDEBURGH, SUFFOLK, IP15 5QG.
•SMITH, Mr. Justin Charles, BSc(Hons) ACA *2002;* Justin C Smith, 5 The Crescent, LYMM, CHESHIRE, WA13 0JY.
SMITH, Mr. Justin Matthew, ACA CA(AUS) *2010;* 54 Wattis Road, SMETHWICK, B67 5BB.
SMITH, Mrs. Justine Imogen, BA ACA *1999;* Lawlor Property Management Ltd, 1 Liverpool Street, LONDON, EC2M 7QD.
SMITH, Mrs. Karen Elizabeth, BA ACA *1995;* 82 Buchanan Drive, Cambuslang, GLASGOW, G72 8BA.
SMITH, Mrs. Karen Elizabeth, BSc ACA *1987;* Bolton Barn Farm, Edge Lane, Turton, BOLTON, BL7 0NJ.
SMITH, Mrs. Karen Mary, ACA *1981;* 5 Sedgefield Drive, Thurnby, LEICESTER, LE7 9PT.
SMITH, Mr. Karl Anthony, ACA *2005;* Kent County Cricket Club, St. Lawrence Ground, Old Dover Road, CANTERBURY, KENT, CT1 3NZ.
SMITH, Mrs. Karla, BA(Hons) ACA *2001;* Ogilvyone Worldwide, 10 Cabot Square, LONDON, E14 4GB.
SMITH, Mrs. Karyn Jeane, ACA *1985;* 5 Wheatfield Avenue, HARPENDEN, HERTFORDSHIRE, AL5 2NU.
SMITH, Miss. Kate Elizabeth, BSc(Hons) ACA *2009;* 9a Ravenstone Street, LONDON, SW12 9ST.
SMITH, Mrs. Katharine Olivia Helen, BA ACA *1999;* KCOM Group PLC, Melbourne House, Brandy Carr Road, Wrenthorpe, WAKEFIELD, WEST YORKSHIRE WF2 0UG.
SMITH, Mrs. Katherine Ann, BA ACA *1989;* 180 Rosehall Drive, LAKE ZURICH, IL 60047, UNITED STATES.
SMITH, Mrs. Katherine Elizabeth, ACA *1990;* 9 Elmers Park, Bletchley, MILTON KEYNES, MK3 6DJ.
SMITH, Miss. Katherine Jane, BA(Hons) ACA *2010;* 364a Old York Road, LONDON, SW18 1SP.
SMITH, Mrs. Kathleen Mary, BSc FCA *1983;* RC Diocese of Hexham & Newcastle, St. Vincents Diocesan Offices, St. Cuthberts House, West Road, NEWCASTLE UPON TYNE, NE15 7PY.
SMITH, Mrs. Kathryn, MA ACA *1987;* Church Farm, Church Lane, Hampton Poyle, KIDLINGTON, OXFORDSHIRE, OX5 2QF.
SMITH, Miss. Kathryn, ACA *2011;* 7 Camden Street, MAIDSTONE, ME14 1UU.
•SMITH, Mrs. Kathryn Anne, BSc FCA CTA *1988;* (Tax Fac), Watts Gregory LLP, Elfed House, Oak Tree Court, Mulberry Drive, Cardiff Gate Business Park Pontprennau, CARDIFF CF23 8RS. See also Taxation Advice & Consultancy Ltd
SMITH, Mrs. Katy Victoria, ACA *1992;* Lower House Farm, Pantygelli, ABERGAVENNY, NP7 7HR.
SMITH, Mr. Keith Ashton, FCA *1957;* 1 Whitefield Rd, Dentons Green, ST. HELENS, MERSEYSIDE, WA10 6AT.
SMITH, Mr. Keith Edward, BSc ACA *1985;* Flat 2, 44 Falkland Road, LONDON, NW5 2XA.
•SMITH, Mr. Keith Richard, FCA *1969;* Witchert Associates Limited, 133 Sheerstock, Haddenham, AYLESBURY, BUCKINGHAMSHIRE, HP17 8EY.
SMITH, Mr. Keith Sidney, BSc ACA *1991;* 18 Allen Street, SOUTH PERTH, WA 6151, AUSTRALIA.
SMITH, Mr. Keith Walton, FCA *1971;* Sycamore House, Kidnappers Lane, Leckhampton, CHELTENHAM, GL53 0NT.
SMITH, Miss. Kelly Rebecca, BSc ACA *1992;* Flat 73, Medland House, 11 Branch Road, LONDON, E14 7JT.
SMITH, Mr. Kenneth, FCA *1950;* 84 Watling Street, ST. ALBANS, HERTFORDSHIRE, AL1 2QG. (Life Member)
SMITH, Mr. Kenneth, FCA *1973;* Valleyside, Greenway, Tatsfield, WESTERHAM, TN16 2BT.
SMITH, Mr. Kenneth John, FCA *1952;* 5 Romanhurst Gardens, BROMLEY, BR2 0PA. (Life Member)
•SMITH, Mr. Kenneth William, BSc FCA *1981;* 49 Greenfield Avenue, Balsall Common, COVENTRY, CV7 7UG.
SMITH, Miss. Kerrie, LLB ACA *2002;* 1st floor flat, 15 Kellett Road, LONDON, SW2 1DX.
•SMITH, Mrs. Kerry Ann, BA ACA *1998;* (Tax Fac), Harrison Smith Ltd, The Spinney, Bracken Park, Scarcroft, LEEDS, LS14 3HZ.
SMITH, Mrs. Kerry Joanne, BCom ACA *2004;* 7 Aldershaws, Shirley, SOLIHULL, WEST MIDLANDS, B90 1SQ.
•SMITH, Miss. Kerry Louise, ACA *2005;* with Integra Accounting Limited, 5 Station Road, HINCKLEY, LEICESTERSHIRE, LE10 1AW.
SMITH, Mr. Kevin, BSc ACA CTA *2002;* 6 Herbert Road, KINGSTON UPON THAMES, SURREY, KT1 2SP.
SMITH, Mr. Kevin John, BA FCA *1977;* 19 Millford, WOKING, GU21 3LH.
SMITH, Mr. Kevin John, BA ACA *1987;* 12 Bayswell Park, DUNBAR, EH42 1AE.
SMITH, Mrs. Kim Elizabeth, BSc ACA FCCA *1983;* 17 Milton Road, HAMPTON, TW12 2LL.
SMITH, Mr. Kimball Robyn Gordon, FCA *1962;* (Tax Fac), 7 Neville Drive, ROMSEY, HAMPSHIRE, SO51 7RP.
SMITH, Miss. Kirsty, MA ACA *2007;* Cargill Plc, Witham St. Hughs, LINCOLN, LN6 9TN.
•SMITH, Mrs. Kirsty Lian, BSc(Hons) ACA *2001;* Smith & Williamson Ltd, 25 Moorgate, LONDON, EC2R 6AY. See also Nexia Audit Limited
SMITH, Miss. Laura, BA ACA *2007;* Flat 10 Brigantine Court, 7 Spert Street, LONDON, E14 8EB.
SMITH, Mrs. Laura Jane, BSocSc ACA *2001;* 25 Aldren Road, LONDON, SW17 0JT.
SMITH, Miss. Laura Jayne, BA ACA *2009;* 16 Columbia Close, Kesgrave, IPSWICH, IP5 1EY.
SMITH, Mrs. Laura Rachel, ACA *2008;* 18 Monument Close, Portskewett, CALDICOT, MONMOUTHSHIRE, NP26 5UE.
SMITH, Mr. Lawrence George Andrew, FCA *1976;* Lynwood House, 353/355 Station Road, HARROW, MIDDLESEX, HA12AW.
SMITH, Mr. Lee Jason, BA ACA *1992;* 9 Arkendale Drive Hardwicke, GLOUCESTER, GL2 4JA.
SMITH, Mr. Lee Matthew, BSc ACA *1999;* MatlinPatterson, 520 Madison Avenue, 35th Floor, NEW YORK, NY 10022, UNITED STATES.
SMITH, Mr. Leo Alastair, ACA *2008;* 12 Willow Court, Corney Reach Way, Chiswick, LONDON, W4 2TW.
SMITH, Mr. Leon Andrew, BSc ACA *2006;* Flat 1 Conifer Court, Moor Green Lane, BIRMINGHAM, B13 8NB.
SMITH, Mrs. Leonie Dawn Ellis, BA ACA *2002;* 42 Ainsty Avenue, YORK, YO24 1HH.
SMITH, Miss. Lesley Ann, BA ACA *1994;* 25 Kingston Lane, Winford, BRISTOL, BS40 8DA.
SMITH, Mr. Leslie Clive, BA FCA *1974;* 4 Friends Close, Yelling, ST. NEOTS, PE19 6SF.
•SMITH, Mr. Leslie Frederick, LLB FCA *1984;* (Tax Fac), Clearline Business Consultants, 552-554 Bristol Road, Selly Oak, BIRMINGHAM, B29 6BD.
•SMITH, Mr. Leslie John, FCA *1968;* LJ Smith Accountants Limited, Orwell House, 50 High Street, HUNGERFORD, BERKSHIRE, RG17 0NE.
•SMITH, Mr. Leslie Terry John, FCA *1962;* L.T.J Smith, 3 Manor Farm Walk, Portesham, WEYMOUTH, DORSET, DT3 4PH.
SMITH, Mr. Liam James Edward, BSc ACA *1996;* 67 Clarence Mews, LONDON, SE16 5GD.
SMITH, Miss. Linda Mary, BA ACA *1990;* 33 Chatsworth Avenue, West Wimbledon, LONDON, SW20 8JZ.
SMITH, Miss. Lindsay Adele, BSc ACA *2006;* Terra Nova, 9 Trimingham Hill, PAGET PG05, BERMUDA.
SMITH, Mr. Lindsay Meredith, BA ACA *1978;* Cloisters Design Ltd, 271 St. Albans Road, HEMEL HEMPSTEAD, HERTFORDSHIRE, HP2 4RP.
SMITH, Mr. Lionel Michael Wheeler, FCA *1970;* Pound House, Hope-under-Dinmore, LEOMINSTER, HEREFORDSHIRE, HR6 0PR.
SMITH, Mrs. Lorna Claire, BSc ACA *1993;* (Tax Fac), with Grant Thornton UK LLP, Grant Thornton House, 22 Melton Street, Euston Square, LONDON, NW1 2EP.
SMITH, Mrs. Louise Nicola, BA ACA *1996;* 14 Gordon Walk, YATELEY, HAMPSHIRE, GU46 6AP.
SMITH, Mrs. Lucinda Mary, BA ACA *1994;* 7 Moberly Road, SALISBURY, SP1 3BZ.
SMITH, Mrs. Lucy Jane, BA ACA *1999;* 11 Lewin Road, Streatham, LONDON, SW16 6JZ.
SMITH, Mrs. Lucy Jane, ACA *2009;* Flat 19 Elizabeth House, Elizabeth Drive, BANSTEAD, SURREY, SM7 2FE.
SMITH, Mrs. Lyn Susan, BA ACA *2006;* with Grant Thornton UK LLP, Royal Liver Building, Pier Head, LIVERPOOL, L3 1PS.
SMITH, Miss. Lynne Dawn, BSc ACA *1987;* 32 Oak Tree Road, Milford, GODALMING, GU8 5JJ.
SMITH, Mr. Malcolm Anthony Richard, BA ACA *1984;* 7 Highland Avenue, Highcliffe, CHRISTCHURCH, DORSET, BH23 5LN.
•SMITH, Mr. Malcolm Colin, FCA *1975;* The Robins Wood, Cobham Road, Fetcham, LEATHERHEAD, KT22 9SJ.
SMITH, Mr. Malcolm John, FCA *1962;* George House, Church Street, Hay On Wye, HEREFORD, HR3 5DQ. (Life Member)
•SMITH, Mr. Malcolm John, BA FCA *1977;* Campagna-Smith, Fernleigh House, 10 Uttoxeter Road, Mickleover, DERBY, DE3 0DA.
SMITH, Mr. Malcolm Roger, FCA *1973;* Garden Cottage Wrigwell, Bickington, NEWTON ABBOT, DEVON, TQ12 6NX.
SMITH, Mr. Malcolm Stuart, BSc ACA *1980;* Osborne Clarke, 2 Temple Back East, BRISTOL, BS1 6EG.
SMITH, Mrs. Mandy Elizabeth, BA(Hons) ACA *2000;* Little Deans Hill Farm, Deans Hill, Bredgar, SITTINGBOURNE, KENT, ME9 8BB.
SMITH, Mr. Marcus George, LLB ACA *1993;* CB Richard Ellis Limited, St. Martins Court, 10 Paternoster Row, LONDON, EC4M 7HP.
SMITH, Mrs. Margaret Elizabeth, BSc ACA *1985;* Chateau De Cabrieres, 84220 CABRIERES D'AVIGNON, FRANCE.
SMITH, Miss. Margaret Rosemary, BA FCA *1975;* 24 Eversley Way, Shirley, CROYDON, CR0 8QR.
SMITH, Mrs. Maria, BSc ACA *1988;* 2 South View, Rotherfield Greys, HENLEY-ON-THAMES, RG9 4QD.
SMITH, Mrs. Maria Michelle, BSc ACA *1994;* 1 Victoria Gardens, COLEFORD, GLOUCESTERSHIRE, GL16 8DX.
SMITH, Miss. Maria Suzanne, BSc ACA *1991;* 3 Orchard Close, Welford on Avon, STRATFORD-UPON-AVON, CV37 8HA.
SMITH, Mrs. Marianne Hazel, BA ACA *1996;* 33 Windermere Close, EGHAM, SURREY, TW20 8JR.
SMITH, Miss. Marie, BA ACA *2009;* 16 Morton Close, Frimley, CAMBERLEY, GU16 9UY.
SMITH, Mr. Mark, BSc ACA *1997;* Old Change House, 128 Queen Victoria Street, LONDON, EC4V 4BJ.
SMITH, Mr. Mark, BSc ACA *2000;* 19/F Bowens Lookout, 13 Bowen Road, MID LEVELS, HONG KONG ISLAND, HONG KONG SAR.
SMITH, Mr. Mark Alastair, BA ACA *1992;* Unterster Zwerchweg 7, 60599 FRANKFURT AM MAIN, GERMANY.
SMITH, Mr. Mark Andrew, BA ACA *2000;* 53 Milden Road, Wadsley, SHEFFIELD, S6 4AT.
SMITH, Mr. Mark Andrew, MBA BA ACA *1995;* 2506 Shays Lane, BRENTWOOD, TN 37027, UNITED STATES.
SMITH, Mr. Mark Anthony, BA ACA *1995;* 62 Westwood Avenue, Heighington Village, NEWTON AYCLIFFE, COUNTY DURHAM, DL5 6SA.
SMITH, Mr. Mark Aynsley, FCA *1963;* Old Chestnut, 38 Meadway, ESHER, KT10 9HF.
SMITH, Mr. Mark Charles, MA ACA *1994;* 20 Pettiward Close, Putney, LONDON, SW15 6QL.
SMITH, Mr. Mark Colin, ACA *1995;* 24 Hibernia Court, North Star Boulevard, GREENHITHE, KENT, DA9 9UJ.
SMITH, Mr. Mark Funge, FCA *1971;* Lonesome Lodge West, Lonesome Lane, REIGATE, RH2 7QT.
SMITH, Mr. Mark Gregory, ACA *2009;* Flat 2, 21 Popham Street, LONDON, N1 8QW.
SMITH, Mr. Mark Ian Andrew, MA FCA *1984;* with Day Smith & Hunter, Globe House, Eclipse Park, Sittingbourne Road, MAIDSTONE, KENT ME14 3EN.
SMITH, Mr. Mark James, ACA *2011;* 24 Violet Way Yaxley, PETERBOROUGH, PE7 3WE.
•SMITH, Mr. Mark Jeffries, BA ACA *1987;* Deloitte LLP, PO Box 500, 2 Hardman Street, MANCHESTER, M60 2AT. See also Deloitte & Touche LLP
SMITH, Mr. Mark John, BA ACA *2004;* 9 Roebuck Lane, SALE, CHESHIRE, M33 7SY.
SMITH, Mr. Mark Jonathan, BSc FCA *1984;* 1 Home Farm Saunders Lane, Walkington, BEVERLEY, HU17 8TX.
SMITH, Mr. Mark Leyland, FCA ACIS CDir *1987;* The Learning Trust, 1 Reading Lane, LONDON, E8 1GQ.
•SMITH, Mr. Mark Lyndon, BA ACA *1989;* PricewaterhouseCoopers LLP, Cornwall Court, 19 Cornwall Street, BIRMINGHAM, B3 2DT. See also PricewaterhouseCoopers
•SMITH, Mr. Mark Peter, BA FCA *1994;* Logika Limited, 12 Romney Place, MAIDSTONE, KENT, ME15 6LE. See also Logika Solutions India Pvt Limited
SMITH, Mr. Mark Richard, MA FCA *1990;* Tomkins Plc, East Putney House, 84 Upper Richmond Road, LONDON, SW15 2ST.
SMITH, Mr. Mark Richard, BEng ACA *2003;* Room G80, Astrazeneca Alderley House, Alderley Park, MACCLESFIELD, CHESHIRE, SK10 4TF.
SMITH, Mr. Mark Robert, BSc ACA *1982;* Ignite Consulting Ltd., 18 New Concordia Wharf, Mill Street, LONDON, SE1 2BB.
•SMITH, Mr. Mark Robert, BSc ACA *1983;* (Tax Fac), Smiths, Unit 114, Boston House, Grove Technology Park, WANTAGE, OX12 9FF.
•SMITH, Mr. Mark Robert Gardner, BA FCA *1982;* Forrester Boyd, 26 South Saint Mary's Gate, GRIMSBY, NORTH LINCOLNSHIRE, DN31 1LW.
SMITH, Mr. Mark Rodney Weston, MA FCA *1981;* Walsal End House, Walsal End Lane, Hampton-in-Arden, SOLIHULL, B92 0HX.
SMITH, Mr. Mark Russell, BSc ACA *1987;* 1860 W Pelican Dr, CHANDLER, AZ 85286-5163, UNITED STATES.
SMITH, Mr. Mark Stephen, FCA *1961;* Cherry Grove, Cowbeech, HAILSHAM, EAST SUSSEX, BN27 4JD.
SMITH, Mr. Mark William, FCA *1978;* Overbrook, Farley Green, Albury, GUILDFORD, GU5 9DN.
SMITH, Mr. Mark William, FCA *1965;* 1 Rue Du Midi, 92200 NEUILLY-SUR-SEINE, FRANCE. (Life Member)
SMITH, Mr. Mark William, BSc ACA *1995;* 30 Complins, Holybourne, ALTON, GU34 4EJ.
SMITH, Mr. Martin, BSc FCA *1978;* Runshaw College, Langdale Road, LEYLAND, PR25 3DQ.
SMITH, Mr. Martin Alex, BA(Hons) ACA *2003;* 517 Darwen Road Bromley Cross, BOLTON, BL7 9BD.
•SMITH, Mr. Martin Anthony, FCA *1992;* (Tax Fac), Cunninghams, 61 Alexandra Road, LOWESTOFT, SUFFOLK, NR32 1PL.
•ⓘSMITH, Mr. Martin Frederick Peter, BSc FCA FABRP *1977;* Dains LLP, St. Johns Court, Wiltell Road, LICHFIELD, STAFFORDSHIRE, WS14 9DS.
SMITH, Mr. Martin Gordon, BA(Hons) ACA *2001;* Investec Bank, 2 Gresham Street, LONDON, EC2V 7QP.
SMITH, Mr. Martin Gordon Alfred, BA ACA *1979;* Holmrook, Lower Chaddesley, KIDDERMINSTER, WORCESTERSHIRE, DY10 4QN.
SMITH, Mr. Martin James, BSc ACA *2000;* 69 Norreys Road, DIDCOT, OX11 0AW.
•SMITH, Mr. Martin James, BSc ACA *1995;* Martin Smith, 17 Garbridge Court, APPLEBY-IN-WESTMORLAND, CUMBRIA, CA16 6JE.
SMITH, Mr. Martin James, BSc FCA *1974;* 34 Glenshiel Road, LONDON, SE9 1AQ.
SMITH, Mr. Martin John, BSc ACA *1992;* 36 Greenfield Crescent, Grange Moor, WAKEFIELD, WF4 4WA.
SMITH, Mr. Martin Lightoller, FCA *1960;* 15 Wheeler Avenue, Tylers Green, Penn, HIGH WYCOMBE, HP10 8EN. (Life Member)
SMITH, Mr. Martin Paul, FCA *1972;* The Old Coach House, Hillhampton, Great Witley, WORCESTER, WR6 6JU.
SMITH, Mr. Martin Peter, BSc FCA *1981;* J J Smith & Co Ltd, Moorgate Road, Knowsley Ind. Estate Kirkby, LIVERPOOL, L33 7DR.
SMITH, Mr. Martin Phillip, BSc ACA CTA *1998;* (Tax Fac), IMS Health HQ Ltd, 7 Harewood Avenue, LONDON, NW1 6JB.
SMITH, Mr. Martin Ronald, BSc FCA *1981;* Windmill House, Hadley Green, BARNET, HERTFORDSHIRE, EN5 4PT.
SMITH, Mr. Martin Shannon, BSc ACA *1992;* 67 Brudenell Road, LONDON, SW17 8DB.
SMITH, Mr. Martyn, BA(Hons) ACA *2011;* 10 Cress Gardens, ANDOVER, HAMPSHIRE, SP10 2NA.
SMITH, Mr. Martyn, BSc ACA *2011;* 4 Church Road, Brean, BURNHAM-ON-SEA, SOMERSET, TA8 2SF.
SMITH, Mr. Martyn Charles Patrick, FCA *1972;* Plum Views, 3 Orchard Close, St. Johns Road Wroxall, VENTNOR, ISLE OF WIGHT, PO38 3FH.
SMITH, Mr. Martyn Denis, BSc FCA *1978;* 47 The Willows, Little Harrowden, WELLINGBOROUGH, NN9 5BJ.
SMITH, Mr. Martyn Douglas, MA FCA *1985;* (Tax Fac), Butt House, Butt Green, Painswick, STROUD, GL6 6QS.
•SMITH, Mr. Martyn Robert, FCA *1976;* Stephenson & Co, Ground Floor Austin House, 43 Poole Road, Westbourne, BOURNEMOUTH, BH4 9DN.

•**SMITH, Mr. Martyn Stuart, FCA** *1989;* (Tax Fac), Phipps Henson McAllister, 22/24 Harborough Road, Kingsthorpe, NORTHAMPTON, NN2 7AZ.
SMITH, Mrs. Mary, BSc ACA *1991;* Bramshill, 33 Queens Drive West, Ramsey, ISLE OF MAN, IM8 2JD.
SMITH, Mrs. Mary Elizabeth, BA ACA *1994;* Greenwood Lee Farm, Widdop Road, Heptonstall, HEBDEN BRIDGE, WEST YORKSHIRE, HX7 7AZ.
SMITH, Mr. Matthew, BSc ACA *2006;* 1a Rowan Way, HARPENDEN, HERTFORDSHIRE, AL5 5TJ.
SMITH, Mr. Matthew, BSc(Hons) ACA *2011;* 29 The Gallery, 26 Blackfriars Street, SALFORD, M3 5JS.
•**SMITH, Mr. Matthew Brent, BSc ACA** *1998;* Barnes Roffe LLP, Leytonstone House, Leytonstone, LONDON, E11 1GA.
SMITH, Mr. Matthew Damian, MSc BA ACA *2002;* 506 Jupiter House, 2 Turner Street, LONDON, E16 1FH.
•①**SMITH, Mr. Matthew David, BA ACA** *1995;* Deloitte LLP, Athene Place, 66 Shoe Lane, LONDON, EC4A 3BQ. See also Deloitte & Touche LLP
SMITH, Mr. Matthew David Lawrence, BSc FCA *1989;* c/o Sterling Fluid Services Limited, 3 The Stables Howbery Park Crowmarsh Gifford, WALLINGFORD, OXFORDSHIRE, OX10 8BA.
SMITH, Mr. Matthew George, ACA *1995;* The Manor House, 47 High Street, Harpole, NORTHAMPTON, NN7 4BS.
•**SMITH, Mr. Matthew Hurndall, BSc FCA** *1992;* M.H. Smith Ltd, 3 Ambassador Drive, Halewood Village, LIVERPOOL, L26 6LT. See also AIMS - Matthew H Smith
SMITH, Mr. Matthew Nicholas, BA ACA *1996;* Tate & Lyle Ltd Sugar Quay, Lower Thames Street, LONDON, EC3R 6DQ.
SMITH, Mr. Matthew Paul, BA(Hons) ACA MBA BArch RIBA *2002;* 2 Holt Cottages, Noke Lane, ST. ALBANS, HERTFORDSHIRE, AL2 3NX.
SMITH, Mr. Matthew Robert, ACA *2011;* 37 Garfield Road, LONDON, SW11 5PL.
SMITH, Mr. Matthew Robert, BA ACA *2006;* Orchard Cottage Low Lane, Stainburn, OTLEY, LS21 2LL.
SMITH, Mr. Matthew Steven Lee, ACA *2005;* with Hurst & Company Accountants LLP, Lancashire Gate, 21 Tiviot Dale, STOCKPORT, CHESHIRE, SK1 1TD.
SMITH, Mr. Matthew William, ACA *1998;* 4 Post Office Lane, St. Ives, RINGWOOD, HAMPSHIRE, BH24 2PG.
SMITH, Mrs. Melanie Bernice, BA FCA *1988;* The Beeches, Beech Avenue, Effingham, LEATHERHEAD, SURREY, KT24 5PJ.
SMITH, Mr. Michael, BA ACA *2006;* Idle Acre, New Road, Wormley, GODALMING, SURREY, GU8 5SU.
SMITH, Mr. Michael, FCA *1966;* 18 Hightown Gardens, RINGWOOD, HAMPSHIRE, BH24 3EH. (Life Member)
SMITH, Mr. Michael, FCA *1977;* 3 The Kilns, Oxford Road, CALNE, WILTSHIRE, SN11 8HJ.
SMITH, Mr. Michael, BSc ACA *2011;* 19 Marsh End, BIRMINGHAM, B38 9BB.
•**SMITH, Mr. Michael Alan, BA FCA CF** *1984;* Tait Walker LLP, Bulman House, Regent Centre, Gosforth, NEWCASTLE UPON TYNE, NE3 3LS. See also Tait Walker Management Limited
SMITH, Mr. Michael Alan Kingsley, BA FCA *1971;* 12 Williams Way, RADLETT, HERTFORDSHIRE, WD7 7EZ. (Life Member)
SMITH, Mr. Michael Albert, FCA *1972;* The Haven, St Andrews Drive, Charmouth, BRIDPORT, DT6 6LN.
SMITH, Mr. Michael Andrew, BA FCA *1985;* 91 Hilltop Lane, Chaldon, CATERHAM, CR3 5BL.
SMITH, Mr. Michael Andrew, BA ACA *1982;* 13 Osborne House, Grosvenor Square, SOUTHAMPTON, SO15 2DA.
SMITH, Mr. Michael Andrew, FCA *1974;* 22 Colney Heath Lane, ST. ALBANS, AL4 0TU.
SMITH, Mr. Michael Anthony, FCA *1949;* 10 Derwent Gardens, Derwent Avenue, MATLOCK, DERBYSHIRE, DE4 3LX. (Life Member)
•**SMITH, Mr. Michael Anthony, BA FCA** *1994;* Broomwood, Newport Road, Machen, CAERPHILLY, MID GLAMORGAN, CF83 8RA.
SMITH, Mr. Michael Anthony, BA ACA *1997;* C/O Qatar Investment Authority, Legal Department, PO Box 23224, DOHA, QATAR.
SMITH, Mr. Michael Anthony, ACA *1998;* Long Acre, The Ridge, Redlynch, SALISBURY, SP5 2LN.
SMITH, Mr. Michael Anthony, MSc ACA *1995;* 5 The Meadows, CHURCH STRETTON, SHROPSHIRE, SY6 7EG.
SMITH, Mr. Michael Bernard, BSc ACA *1991;* 7 Chancellors Road, AYLESBURY, HP19 9SH.
SMITH, Mr. Michael Charles, MA FCA MCT *1987;* Tigerturf (UK) Limited, Unit 229, Ikon Industrial Estate, Droitwich Road, Hartlebury, KIDDERMINSTER WORCESTERSHIRE DY10 4EU.
SMITH, Mr. Michael David, BSc ACA *2010;* 14 Latimer Close, Guiseley, LEEDS, LS20 9PT.
•**SMITH, Mr. Michael David Edwin, BA FCA** *1984;* with Woolford & Co LLP, Hillbrow House, Hillbrow Road, ESHER, SURREY, KT10 9NW.
SMITH, Mr. Michael David Graham, BSc ACA *1995;* 35 Prusoms Island, 135 Wapping High Street, LONDON, E1W 3NH.
SMITH, Mr. Michael Dennis, BSc FCA *1982;* 16 Fitzwilliam Road, Bearsted, MAIDSTONE, ME14 4PY.
•**SMITH, Mr. Michael Derek Loxley, FCA** *1979;* Lovewell Blake LLP, 102 Prince of Wales Road, NORWICH, NORFOLK, NR1 1NY.
SMITH, Mr. Michael Frank Torble, FCA *1973;* (Tax Fac), 36 Belgravia Court, 33 Ebury Street, LONDON, SW1W 0NY.
SMITH, Mr. Michael Geoffrey Widman, FCA *1975;* C M S (Kidderminster) Ltd, Churchfields, KIDDERMINSTER, WORCESTERSHIRE, DY10 2JL.
SMITH, Mr. Michael Graham, BA FCA *1972;* 176 Dinnick Crescent, TORONTO M4N 1M3, ON, CANADA.
SMITH, Mr. Michael Hedley, BSc FCA FCT *1982;* 6 Grove Shaw, Kingswood, TADWORTH, SURREY, KT20 6QL.
SMITH, Mr. Michael James, BSc(Hons) ACA *2010;* Beacon View, Church Road, Swanmore, SOUTHAMPTON, SO32 2PA.
SMITH, Mr. Michael James, BA ACA *2000;* 3 Walnut Gardens, Claydon, BANBURY, OXFORDSHIRE, OX17 1NA.
SMITH, Mr. Michael James, ACA *2008;* 8 Mavis Avenue, LEEDS, LS16 7LJ.
SMITH, Mr. Michael James, FCA *1961;* Avenida 25 de Abril 42, 2 Dto, 2005-159 SANTAREM, PORTUGAL. (Life Member)
•**SMITH, Mr. Michael John, FCA** *1979;* 5 Granville Close, HAVANT, HAMPSHIRE, PO9 2TR.
•**SMITH, Mr. Michael John, FCA** *1958;* (Tax Fac), M J Smith & Co Ltd, Woodbury House, Green Lane, Exton, EXETER, EX3 0PW.
SMITH, Mr. Michael John, FCA *1965;* Shoe Zone Haramead Business Centre, Humberstone Road, LEICESTER, LE1 2LH.
SMITH, Mr. Michael John, MA ACA *1988;* Ederoyd, Silver Street, Whitley, GOOLE, DN14 0JQ.
SMITH, Mr. Michael John, BSc(Hons) ACA *2000;* 56 Elvington Park, Elvington, YORK, YO41 4DW.
SMITH, Mr. Michael John, BA ACA *1989;* Hamilton House, Bakeham Lane, Englefield Green, EGHAM, SURREY, TW20 9TU.
SMITH, Mr. Michael John, MA ACA *1984;* (Tax Fac), 17 Milton Road, HAMPTON, TW12 2LL.
SMITH, Mr. Michael John Campbell, FCA *1978;* 11 Killieser Avenue, LONDON, SW2 4NU.
SMITH, Mr. Michael Kendrick, FCA *1960;* Dells Cottage, Wheelers Lane, Brockham Green, BETCHWORTH, RH3 7LE. (Life Member)
SMITH, Mr. Michael Leslie, FCA *1974;* 15 Freefolk Priors, Freefolk, WHITCHURCH, HAMPSHIRE, RG28 7NJ.
SMITH, Mr. Michael Neil, BSc ACA *2003;* 3/ 24 Kensington Road, South Yarra, MELBOURNE, VIC 3141, AUSTRALIA.
SMITH, Mr. Michael Paul Niven, MA ACA *2000;* 16 Russell Close, BRACKNELL, BERKSHIRE, RG12 7FE.
SMITH, Mr. Michael Percy, FCA *1955;* Fraynes House, East Street, North Molton, SOUTH MOLTON, EX36 3HT. (Life Member)
SMITH, Mr. Michael Ralph, BSc ACA *1992;* 14 Tangway, Chineham, BASINGSTOKE, RG24 8SU.
SMITH, Mr. Michael Richard, FCA *1968;* 3 Highcroft Court, Bookham, LEATHERHEAD, KT23 3QU.
SMITH, Mr. Michael Seddon, FCA *1969;* The Old School House, Slindon, STAFFORD, ST21 6LX. (Life Member)
SMITH, Mr. Michael William, BA ACA *1985;* 14 Binden Road, LONDON, W12 9RJ.
SMITH, Dr. Michael William George, FCA *1966;* 19A St. Mary's Road, KLOOF, KWAZULU NATAL, 3610, SOUTH AFRICA. (Life Member)
SMITH, Ms. Michelle Anne, ACA *1994;* 6F Cranmer Square, CHRISTCHURCH 8013, NEW ZEALAND.
SMITH, Miss. Michelle Louise, BSc ACA *2010;* Flat 49 Collinson Court, Great Suffolk Street, LONDON, SE1 1PA.
SMITH, Mrs. Michelle Louise, BA ACA *1997;* B U P A Bridge House, Outwood Lane Horsforth, LEEDS, LS18 4UP.
SMITH, Miss. Michelle Rosanne, BSc ACA *1993;* Jane Norman Ltd, 3 Tenterden Street, Hanover Square, LONDON, W1S 1TD.
SMITH, Miss. Natalie Emma, MChem ACA *2003;* 15 Blenheim Road, NEWBURY, BERKSHIRE, RG14 5LB.
SMITH, Mrs. Natalie Jayne, MSc ACA *2001;* 3 Defkaliona Iakovidi Street, Ayia Fyla, 3117 LIMASSOL, CYPRUS.
SMITH, Mr. Nathan Michael, BSc ACA *1999;* 7 Park Rise, HARPENDEN, HERTFORDSHIRE, AL5 3AH.
SMITH, Mr. Neale David, BA FCA *1988;* Flat 12 South Beach Apartments, Greve D'Azette, St Clement, JERSEY, JE2 6PX.
SMITH, Mr. Neil Andrew, ACA *1997;* 338 Langer Lane, Wingerworth, CHESTERFIELD, S42 6TX.
SMITH, Mr. Neil Anthony, BSc ACA DChA *1990;* Homestead, The Green, Hook Norton, BANBURY, OXFORDSHIRE, OX15 5LE.
SMITH, Mr. Neil Anthony, BA ACA *1997;* Kaliaco Court no 57, Kolonaciou Street, Office 101, 1st floor, Linopetra, 4308 LIMASSOL CYPRUS.
SMITH, Mr. Neil Campbell, BA ACA *1994;* 31 Ashburnham Grove, LONDON, SE10 8UL.
•**SMITH, Mr. Neil Cedric, BSc FCA** *1992;* Folkes Worton LLP, 15-17 Church Street, STOURBRIDGE, WEST MIDLANDS, DY8 1LU.
SMITH, Mr. Neil Christian, MA BA ACA *1987;* 45 Pine Road, MANCHESTER, M20 6UZ.
SMITH, Mr. Neil Christopher, BA FCA MCMI *1982;* 21 Dukes Way, NORTHWICH, CHESHIRE, CW9 8WA.
SMITH, Mr. Neil Colin, BCom ACA *1993;* BT Group Plc, The Jays, 108 High Street, Horsell, WOKING, SURREY GU21 4ST.
SMITH, Mr. Neil David, BEng ACA *1993;* (Tax Fac), Furstenwall 11, D40219 DUSSELDORF, GERMANY.
SMITH, Mr. Neil Douglas, BSc ACA *1990;* Selsey, Herbert Road, Wimbledon, LONDON, SW19 3SH.
SMITH, Mr. Neil Ingrey, BA ACA *2006;* with Ernst & Young LLP, 1 More London Place, LONDON, SE1 2AF.
SMITH, Mr. Neil James, BA ACA *2006;* 133 Manor Lane, SUNBURY-ON-THAMES, MIDDLESEX, TW16 6JE.
SMITH, Mr. Neil Martin, BSc ACA *1987;* 73 Germander Place, Conniburrow, MILTON KEYNES, MK14 7DW.
SMITH, Mr. Neil Martin, ACA *1997;* Ark Syndicate Management Ltd, St. Helens, 1 Undershaft, LONDON, EC3A 8EE.
SMITH, Mr. Neil Peter, BA ACA ACIM MBA DipM *1995;* 25 Greatfield Drive, Charlton Kings, CHELTENHAM, GLOUCESTERSHIRE, GL53 9BT.
SMITH, Mr. Neil Reynolds, BSc ACA *1991;* Enterprise Inns Plc, 3 Monkspath Hall Road Shirley, SOLIHULL, B90 4SJ.
SMITH, Mr. Nicholas, MA ACA *2001;* 46 Crossfield Park, Felling, GATESHEAD, TYNE AND WEAR, NE10 9SA.
SMITH, Mr. Nicholas Alexander, BSc ACA *1987;* Grange House The Grange, Hartford, NORTHWICH, CHESHIRE, CW8 1QH.
•**SMITH, Mr. Nicholas Andrew, BA ACA** *1993;* PricewaterhouseCoopers LLP, Savannah House, 3 Ocean Way, Ocean Village, SOUTHAMPTON, SO14 3TJ. See also PricewaterhouseCoopers
SMITH, Mr. Nicholas James, ACA *2010;* with Ernst & Young LLP, 1 More London Place, LONDON, SE1 2AF.
•**SMITH, Mr. Nicholas John, BA ACA** *1990;* Smith Austin Limited, 50 Hoyland Road, Hoyland Common, BARNSLEY, S74 OPB.
•**SMITH, Mr. Nicholas Mark, ACA CTA** *1990;* Villars Hayward LLP, Boston House, 2a Boston Road, HENLEY-ON-THAMES, OXFORDSHIRE, RG9 1DY.
SMITH, Mr. Nicholas Michael Norman, FCA *1975;* Hunters Acre, Burdenshot Hill, Worplesdon, GUILDFORD, GU3 3RL.
SMITH, Mr. Nicholas Paul, FCA *1963;* Scrag Oak, WADHURST, TN5 6NP. (Life Member)
•**SMITH, Mr. Nicholas Peter, FCA** *1972;* N.P. Smith & Co, 10 Tudman Close, Walmley, SUTTON COLDFIELD, WEST MIDLANDS, B76 1GP. See also N P Smith & Co Limited
•**SMITH, Mr. Nicholas Peter, BA ACA** *1996;* Eades Limited, 2b Haddo Street, Greenwich, LONDON, SE10 9RN. See also Smith & Eades
SMITH, Mr. Nicholas Ralph, MA ACA *1988;* The Astors, 48 Aylesbury Road, Aston Clinton, AYLESBURY, BUCKINGHAMSHIRE, HP22 5AH.
SMITH, Mr. Nicholas Spensley, BSc FCA *1974;* Hazelside, 9 Chantry Road, BISHOP'S STORTFORD, CM23 2SB.
SMITH, Ms. Nicola Charlotte, BA ACA *1998;* Little Thatch, Pennymead Drive, East Horsley, LEATHERHEAD, SURREY, KT24 5AH.
SMITH, Miss. Nicola Elizabeth, BSc ACA *2004;* The University of Manchester, John Owens Building, Oxford Road, MANCHESTER, M13 9PL.
SMITH, Miss. Nicola Jane, MA ACA *2000;* Flat 11 The Old Fire Station, 99 Rose Road Harborne, BIRMINGHAM, B17 9LW.
SMITH, Miss. Nicola Joanne, ACA MAAT *2011;* 6 Cayley Close, Rawcliffe, YORK, YO30 5PT.
SMITH, Mrs. Nicola Mary-Anne, BSc ACA *1997;* 64 Brook Lane, Warsash, SOUTHAMPTON, SO31 9FG.
•**SMITH, Mrs. Nicola Susan, BSc FCA** *1992;* Davies Mayers Barnett LLP, Pillar House, 113-115 Bath Road, CHELTENHAM, GLOUCESTERSHIRE, GL53 7LS. See also Barnett DM Limited
•**SMITH, Mr. Nicolas Scott, BA ACA** *2000;* KPMG LLP, 15 Canada Square, LONDON, E14 5GL. See also KPMG Europe LLP
•**SMITH, Mr. Nigel David, FCA** *1982;* (Tax Fac), Hall Farm Accountancy Services, 2 Hall Farm Cottage, Main Street, Netherseal, SWADLINCOTE, DERBYSHIRE DE12 8BZ.
SMITH, Mr. Nigel Hugh Hamilton, MA FCA *1973;* White House Farm, Debenham Road, Kenton, STOWMARKET, IP14 6JH.
SMITH, Mr. Nigel Jonathan, BSc ACA *1992;* Homes & Communities Agency St. Georges House, Kingsway Team Valley Trading Estate, GATESHEAD, TYNE AND WEAR, NE11 0NA.
SMITH, Mr. Nigel Kevan, BSc FCA *1983;* 19 Highbury Way, Great Cornard, SUDBURY, CO10 0HE.
SMITH, Mr. Nigel Leslie, FCA *1971;* 6 The Chestnuts, Shiplake, HENLEY-ON-THAMES, OXFORDSHIRE, RG9 3JZ.
SMITH, Mr. Nigel Peter, BA ACA *1995;* Graham Tiso Limited, 41 Commercial Street, Leith, EDINBURGH, EH6 6JD.
SMITH, Mr. Nigel Robert, BSc FCA *1978;* 14 Blackthorn Close, West Kingsdown, SEVENOAKS, TN15 6UF.
•**SMITH, Mr. Nigel Roderick, FCA** *1971;* Nigel Smith, The Old Church, Shelton New Road, STOKE-ON-TRENT, ST4 6DP.
SMITH, Mr. Nigel Stephen, BSc ACA ATII *1985;* Santander UK Plc, 2-3 Triton Square, LONDON, NW1 3AN.
SMITH, Mr. Nigel Victor, FCA *1975;* The Miles Partnership, Rotherwick House, 19-21 Old Bond Street, LONDON, W1S 4PX.
SMITH, Mr. Nigel William, FCA *1968;* Hermitage Dairy Farm, Whitwell, VENTNOR, ISLE OF WIGHT, PO38 2PD.
SMITH, Mrs. Nina Catherine, BA ACA *2006;* with KPMG LLP, 15 Canada Square, LONDON, E14 5GL.
SMITH, Mr. Noel Edmund Torrance, BSc ACA *1991;* The Old Coach House, 8 Copse Road, VERWOOD, DORSET, BH31 6HB.
SMITH, Norman Arthur, Esq MBE TD FCA *1939;* Dalnagairn, Highfields, East Horsley, LEATHERHEAD, KT24 5AA. (Life Member)
SMITH, Mr. Norman Edward, FCA *1946;* 10 Cordova Court, Sandgate Road, FOLKESTONE, CT20 2HQ. (Life Member)
SMITH, Mr. Norman Robert, FCA *1949;* 1 The Drive, Long Ashes Park, Threshfield, SKIPTON, BD23 5RX. (Life Member)
SMITH, Mr. Olayinka Olabode, BSc ACA *2010;* Flat 2, 57 Streatham High Road, LONDON, SW16 1PN.
SMITH, Mr. Oliver, BA(Hons) ACA *2006;* 18th Floor, Co-operative Insurance Society Ltd, Miller Street, MANCHESTER, M60 0AL.
SMITH, Mr. Oliver Samuel, BSc(Hons) ACA *2011;* (Tax Fac), 33 Bridges View, GATESHEAD, TYNE AND WEAR, NE8 1NZ.
SMITH, Mr. Patrick Dale, BSc ACA *1995;* 1 Weavers Grange, Guiseley, LEEDS, LS20 9PG.
SMITH, Mr. Patrick John, BSc ACA *1991;* Terminus House, 52 Grosvenor Gardens, LONDON, SW1W 0AU.
•**SMITH, Mr. Patrick Joseph, BA FCA** *1979;* DNG Dove Naish, Eagle House, 28 Billing Road, NORTHAMPTON, NN1 5AJ.
SMITH, Mr. Patrick Matthew, BSc ACA *1991;* Whittocks End, Kempley, DYMOCK, GL18 2BS.
SMITH, Mr. Patrick Owen, BSc ACA *1987;* 15 Chipchase Court, Woodstone Village, HOUGHTON-LE-SPRING, DH4 6TT.
SMITH, Mr. Patrick Vincent Carroll, ACA CA(SA) *2010;* Pines House, Pines Road, FLEET, HAMPSHIRE, GU51 4NL.
SMITH, Mr. Paul, BSc ACA *2003;* 35 South Parade, West Kirby, WIRRAL, MERSEYSIDE, CH48 0QG.
SMITH, Mr. Paul Adrian, Mchem ACA *2003;* 13 Mafeking Street, HARROGATE, NORTH YORKSHIRE, HG1 4BZ.
SMITH, Mr. Paul Andrew, BA ACA CTA *1988;* Building 29, Royal School of Military Engineering Brompton Barracks, Dock Road, CHATHAM, ME4 4UG.
SMITH, Mr. Paul Andrew, ACA *2009;* 10 Meriton Road Handforth, WILMSLOW, CHESHIRE, SK9 3HB.

SMITH, Mr. Paul Andrew, BA ACA *1988;* 29 Gwendoline Way, Walsall Wood, WALSALL, WS9 9RG.
SMITH, Mr. Paul Anthony, BA ACA *1985;* Robin Hill Farm, Littleham, BIDEFORD, DEVON, EX39 5EG.
SMITH, Mr. Paul Anthony, MA ACA *2001;* Beech Cottage, 60 Beech Lane, MACCLESFIELD, CHESHIRE, SK10 2DS.
SMITH, Mr. Paul Barton, BA ACA *1999;* Ivy House Moor Lane, Murton, YORK, YO19 5UH.
SMITH, Mr. Paul Bernard, BSc FCA *1981;* (Tax Fac), 18 Admirals Walk, ST. ALBANS, HERTFORDSHIRE, AL1 5RX.
•SMITH, Mr. Paul Brendan, LLB ACA MBA TEP *2002;* 11 Kermode Road, Eyreton Lea, Crosby, ISLE OF MAN, IM4 4BZ.
•SMITH, Mr. Paul Byron, MBA BSc FCA CTA *1991;* PricewaterhouseCoopers LLP, 101 Barbirolli Square, Lower Mosley Street, MANCHESTER, M2 3PW. See also PricewaterhouseCoopers
SMITH, Mr. Paul Charles Robert, BSc ACA *1985;* 35 Grange Estate, ILKLEY, LS29 8NW.
SMITH, Mr. Paul Daniel, ACA *2010;* 62 Highfield Close, STOCKPORT, CHESHIRE, SK3 8UB.
SMITH, Mr. Paul Duncan Sawyer, BSc FCA *1978;* Equity, Guild House, Upper St. Martin's Lane, LONDON, WC2H 9EG.
SMITH, Mr. Paul Edward, ACA *1978;* 220 Ombersley Road, WORCESTER, WR3 7HA.
•SMITH, Mr. Paul Edward Hill, BSc FCA *1977;* BDO LLP, 2 City Place, Beehive Ring Road, GATWICK, WEST SUSSEX, RH6 0PA. See also BDO Stoy Hayward LLP
SMITH, Mr. Paul Gareth, BSc ACA *2002;* 15 Buxton Road, Whaley Bridge, HIGH PEAK, DERBYSHIRE, SK23 7HT.
•SMITH, Mr. Paul Gerard, BA FCA *1976;* Reconta Ernst & Young, Via Della Chiusa 2, 20123 MILAN, ITALY. See also Ernst & Young Europe LLP
SMITH, Mr. Paul Gerard, BA ACA *1995;* 28 Burdon Walk, Castle Eden, HARTLEPOOL, CLEVELAND, TS27 4FD.
SMITH, Mr. Paul Henry, MA FCA CFA *1984;* Flat 3A Wyndham Mansion, 30-32 Wyndham Street, CENTRAL, HONG KONG ISLAND, HONG KONG SAR.
SMITH, Mr. Paul Hugh, FCA *1962;* 101 Shrubbery Road, Drakes Broughton, WORCESTER, WR10 2BE.
SMITH, Mr. Paul James, ACA *2008;* 12 Chester Close, NEWBURY, BERKSHIRE, RG14 7RR.
SMITH, Mr. Paul John, BSc ACA *1993;* Green Acre Bayswater Road, Headington, OXFORD, OX3 9RZ.
SMITH, Mr. Paul Joseph, BSc(Hons) ACA *2004;* 126 Kenilworth Road, Balsall Common, COVENTRY, CV7 7EX.
SMITH, Mr. Paul Kevin, BA ACA *1978;* Vicarsmead Hayes Lane, East Budleigh, BUDLEIGH SALTERTON, DEVON, EX9 7DA.
•SMITH, Mr. Paul Lester, FCA *1977;* Lancaster Clements Limited, Stanley House, 27 Wellington Road, BILSTON, WV14 6AH.
•SMITH, Mr. Paul Martin, BSc FCA *1992;* (Tax Fac), Williams & Co, 8-10 South Street, EPSOM, KT18 7PF.
SMITH, Mr. Paul Matthew, BA ACA *2001;* 43a, Wiltshire Avenue, CROWTHORNE, BERKSHIRE, RG45 6NH.
SMITH, Mr. Paul Mervyn, BA FCA *1984;* Capita Business Travel Ltd, Meridian Court 18 Stanier Way, DERBY, DE21 6BF.
SMITH, Mr. Paul Michael, BSc ACA *1989;* Intertek Labtest UK Ltd, Centre Court Meridian North Meridian Business Park, LEICESTER, LE19 1WD.
SMITH, Mr. Paul Richard Mark, BSc ACA *1995;* 6 St. Matthews Avenue, SURBITON, SURREY, KT6 6JJ.
SMITH, Mr. Paul Robert, MA FCA *1980;* All England Netball Association Ltd, 9 Paynes Park, HITCHIN, HERTFORDSHIRE, SG5 1EH.
SMITH, Mr. Paul Robert, FCA *1974;* 27 Beech Avenue, Sandiacre, NOTTINGHAM, NG10 5EH.
SMITH, Mr. Paul Robin Monrad, BSc FCA CF *1981;* Summerhill House, 5 Fort Road, GUILDFORD, SURREY, GU1 3TB.
SMITH, Mr. Paul Stephen, BA ACA *1990;* 5 Penates, Littleworth Common Road, ESHER, KT10 9UH.
SMITH, Mrs. Paula Justine, BA(Hons) ACA *2001;* 24 Crackthorne Drive, RUGBY, CV23 0GL.
SMITH, Mrs. Paula Lynn, BA ACA *1984;* Bella Vista, New Mills, NEWTOWN, SY16 3NH.
SMITH, Miss. Paula Mary, BCom ACA *1991;* 7 Campden House Terrace, Kensington Church Street, LONDON, W8 4BQ.
•SMITH, Mrs. Pauline Amanda, BSc ACA *2007;* with Celtic Associates Limited, The Red House, One The Parade, Castletown, ISLE OF MAN, IM9 1LG.
SMITH, Mrs. Penelope Jayne, BA FCA *1984;* (Tax Fac), 2 Barkers Well Fold, LEEDS, LS12 5TR.
SMITH, Mr. Peter, BA ACA *1989;* (Tax Fac), 5 Applegarth, WYMONDHAM, NORFOLK, NR18 0BZ.
SMITH, Mr. Peter, FCA *1978;* Glebe House, Vicarage Lane, Hawkshead, AMBLESIDE, CUMBRIA, LA22 0PD. (Life Member)
•SMITH, Mr. Peter, BA FCA DChA *1989;* Chittenden Horley Limited, 456 Chester Road, Old Trafford, MANCHESTER, M16 9HD.
•SMITH, Mr. Peter, FCA *1965;* (Tax Fac), Peter Smith & Co, 12 Bonneycroft Lane, Easingwold, YORK, YO61 3AR.
SMITH, Mr. Peter Alan, BSc FCA *1970;* (Member of Council 1997 - 2003), The Old Vicarage, Hughenden Park, Hughenden, HIGH WYCOMBE, HP14 4LA.
•SMITH, Mr. Peter Andrew, BSc FCA *1991;* Constantin, 25 Hosier Lane, LONDON, EC1A 9LQ.
SMITH, Mr. Peter Antony, BA ACA *1989;* Ross Auto Engineering Ltd, 2-3 Westfield Road, WALLASEY, MERSEYSIDE, CH44 7HX.
SMITH, Mr. Peter Baden, FCA CTA *1963;* 215 Greenmount Lane, Heaton, BOLTON, BL1 5JB.
SMITH, Mr. Peter Bryan, BSc ACA *2000;* PO Box 140, PEMBERTON, WA 6260, AUSTRALIA.
SMITH, Mr. Peter Charles, BSc ACA PGCE *2010;* 131 Riversdale Road, LONDON, N5 2SU.
SMITH, Mr. Peter Donald, FCA *1961;* 35 Pedmore Lane, Pedmore, STOURBRIDGE, WEST MIDLANDS, DY9 0SY.
•SMITH, Mr. Peter Franklin, FCA *1974;* London Journals Limited, 26 Loftus Road, LONDON, W12 7EN.
SMITH, Mr. Peter James, BA FCA *1966;* 10 Beatty Avenue, GUILDFORD, GU1 2PD. (Life Member)
SMITH, Mr. Peter James, BSc ACA *1983;* Peer Group Plc, The Hop Exchange, 24 Southwark Street, LONDON, SE1 1TY.
SMITH, Mr. Peter James, BSc(Econ) ACA *1983;* Falcon Group Plc, 41-44 Triangle West, BRISTOL, BS8 1ER.
SMITH, Mr. Peter James Walker, FCA *1968;* 56 Rylett Crescent, LONDON, W12 9RH.
SMITH, Mr. Peter Jeffrey, ACA *1980;* 4 Linden Square, Riverhead, SEVENOAKS, TN13 2DF.
SMITH, Mr. Peter John, FCA *1960;* Kertonwood, Clink Road, FROME, BA11 2EQ. (Life Member)
SMITH, Mr. Peter John, FCA *1964;* Flat 2, Monterey Court, Varndean Drive, BRIGHTON, BN1 6TE.
•SMITH, Mr. Peter John, FCA *1958;* Peter Smith, Rose Cottage, Brill Road, Horton-Cum-Studley, OXFORD, OX33 1BN.
SMITH, Mr. Peter John, BA ACA *1984;* Hall O'Coole, Heatley Lane, Broomhall, NANTWICH, CHESHIRE, CW5 8BA.
SMITH, Mr. Peter John, MBA FCA *1978;* 17 The Clovers, Northfleet, GRAVESEND, DA11 8TD.
SMITH, Mr. Peter John, BSc ACA *1989;* with Ernst & Young LLP, 1 More London Place, LONDON, SE1 2AF.
SMITH, Mr. Peter Leslie, BSc ACA *1987;* The Riggs Main Street, Felton, MORPETH, NORTHUMBERLAND, NE65 9PN.
SMITH, Mr. Peter Lonsdale, MA FCA *1977;* King's House, Choice Hill Road, Over Norton, CHIPPING NORTON, OX7 5PP.
SMITH, Mr. Peter Malcolm, FCA *1980;* 23 Badingham Drive, Fetcham, LEATHERHEAD, SURREY, KT22 9EU.
SMITH, Mr. Peter Matthew, BA ACA *2003;* 5 Calver Mill, Calver, HOPE VALLEY, S32 3YU.
•SMITH, Mr. Peter Maurice, BSc FCA *1992;* Quantis Limited, 13 Newgate Street, MORPETH, NORTHUMBERLAND, NE61 1AL.
•SMITH, Mr. Peter Ralph William, FCA *1975;* Powdrill & Smith, 120 Bull Head Street, Wigston Magna, WIGSTON, LE18 1PB. See also Glenoaks Accounting Services Ltd
•SMITH, Mr. Peter Richard, FCA *1973;* Farrar Smith Limited, 2 Woodside Mews, Clayton Wood Close, LEEDS, LS16 6QE.
SMITH, Mr. Peter Thomas, BA ACA *1986;* 86 B Clyde Road, Ilam, CHRISTCHURCH 8041, NEW ZEALAND.
SMITH, Mr. Peter William, FCA *1952;* 29 Poltimore Road, GUILDFORD, GU2 7PR. (Life Member)
SMITH, Mr. Peter William, FCA *1953;* 32A Satanita Road, WESTCLIFF-ON-SEA, SS0 8DE. (Life Member)
SMITH, Mr. Peter William, ACA *1987;* 3 Highbury Gate, Elswick, PRESTON, PR4 3ZG.
SMITH, Mr. Philip, BSc ACA *1999;* 11 Rylestone Grove, BRISTOL, BS9 3UT.
SMITH, Mr. Philip Antony, BSc ACA AMCT *1998;* Adfirmo Group Limited, 24 Greville Street, LONDON, EC1N 8SS.
SMITH, Mr. Philip Graham, FCA *1972;* Hackleton House, Pell Lane, RYDE, ISLE OF WIGHT, PO33 3LT.
SMITH, Mr. Philip James, ACA *2008;* 28 Dunkeld Close, GATESHEAD, TYNE AND WEAR, NE10 8WH.
•SMITH, Mr. Philip James Walker, BA(Hons) ACA *1989;* Finance and Management Consulting, 32 Belle Vue Avenue, Gosforth, NEWCASTLE UPON TYNE, NE3 1AH.
SMITH, Mr. Philip John, BSc FCA *1989;* Villa Cervino, Botley Road, Horton Heath, EASTLEIGH, HAMPSHIRE, SO50 7DT.
SMITH, Mr. Philip John, FCA *1963;* 36A Draycott Park, SINGAPORE 259389, SINGAPORE.
SMITH, Mr. Philip John, BSocSc ACA *1997;* 2 Bramcote Rise, SUTTON COLDFIELD, B75 6ED.
SMITH, Mr. Philip John Bagnell, MA ACA *1995;* Flat H, 1 Groveway, LONDON, SW9 0AH.
SMITH, Mr. Philip Kenneth, LLB FCA *1990;* 4 The Bank, Marcliff, Bidford-on-Avon, ALCESTER, B50 4NT.
SMITH, Mr. Philip Mark, MA ACA *1985;* 77 Rees Avenue, COORPAROO, QLD 4151, AUSTRALIA.
SMITH, Mr. Philip Mark Christopher, BSc ACA *2003;* 105 Tolmers Road, Cuffley, POTTERS BAR, HERTFORDSHIRE, EN6 4JL.
SMITH, Mr. Philip Martin, BSc ACA *1997;* 8 Nutfields, Ightham, SEVENOAKS, TN15 9EA.
SMITH, Mr. Philip Mckelvie, FCA *1970;* (Tax Fac), Nant Lonydd, 21 Penaber, CRICCIETH, GWYNEDD, LL52 0ES.
SMITH, Dr. Philip Michael Forster, DBA *1974;* MEMBER OF COUNCIL, 19 Bowers Way, HARPENDEN, HERTFORDSHIRE, AL5 4EP.
SMITH, Mr. Philip Nigel, BSc FCA *1977;* 1022 Golden Way, LOS ALTOS, CA 94024, UNITED STATES.
SMITH, Mr. Philip Raoul, BA(Hons) ACA *2001;* 2 High Street, Braunston, OAKHAM, LEICESTERSHIRE, LE15 8QU.
SMITH, Mr. Philip Robin, ACA *1981;* 4 Bridgeman Road, TEDDINGTON, TW11 9AH.
SMITH, Mr. Philip Wallace, BA ACA *1993;* 24/27F One Island East, 18 Westlands Road, Island East, QUARRY BAY, HONG KONG ISLAND, HONG KONG SAR.
SMITH, Miss. Philippa Claire, ACA *2008;* 57 Desswood Place, ABERDEEN, AB25 2EF.
SMITH, Mrs. Philippa Jane, BSc ACA *1994;* 9 Farm Close, Ickford, AYLESBURY, BUCKINGHAMSHIRE, HP18 9LY.
SMITH, Mr. Phillip, ACA *2010;* 5 Kyle Close, Renishaw, SHEFFIELD, S21 3WW.
SMITH, Mr. Phillip Scott, ACA *2009;* 61 Ferry Street, LONDON, E14 3DT.
SMITH, Miss. Rachael Catherine, BSc(Hons) ACA *2010;* Flat 3, 3 Almorah Crescent, Lower Kings Cliff St. Helier, JERSEY, JE2 3GU.
SMITH, Mr. Ralph Jerome, FCA *1949;* 59 Naseby Road, SOLIHULL, WEST MIDLANDS, B91 2DR. (Life Member)
SMITH, Mr. Ramon Harold Kingsbury, FCA *1956;* 25c Adelaide Road, SURBITON, SURREY, KT6 4TA. (Life Member)
SMITH, Mr. Raymond, FCA *1968;* 20 Westlands Grove, Stockton Lane, YORK, YO31 1EF.
SMITH, Mr. Raymond, FCA *1971;* 22 Queens Drive, Windle, ST.HELENS, MERSEYSIDE, WA10 6HF.
SMITH, Mr. Raymond, FCA *1975;* La Radieuse, 24 Boulevard D'Italie, MONTE CARLO, MC98000, MONACO.
SMITH, Mr. Raymond, BSc ACA *1996;* 674 Blueridge Ave, NORTH VANCOUVER V7R 2J3, BC, CANADA.
SMITH, Mr. Raymond Arthur, FCA *1959;* 11 Winterdale Close, NEWARK, NOTTINGHAMSHIRE, NG24 2LZ. (Life Member)
SMITH, Mr. Raymond Frederick, BA ACA *1990;* 7 Carron Close, Linslade, LEIGHTON BUZZARD, LU7 2XB.
SMITH, Mr. Raymond Gerald, FCA *1975;* Amberwood Hollybush Ride Finchampstead, WOKINGHAM, BERKSHIRE, RG40 3QR.
•SMITH, Mr. Raymond Michael, FCA *1966;* New Zealand House, 9th Floor, 80 Haymarket, LONDON, SW1Y 4TQ.
SMITH, Mrs. Rebecca, BA ACA *1996;* 14 St. Michaels Way, Burley in Wharfedale, ILKLEY, WEST YORKSHIRE, LS29 7PP.
SMITH, Mrs. Rebecca Louise, ACA *2008;* 37a Bedale Road, Aiskew, BEDALE, NORTH YORKSHIRE, DL8 1BL.
SMITH, Ms. Rebecca Louise, MA MPhil ACA *2003;* 79 Blakemore Drive, SUTTON COLDFIELD, B75 7RW.
SMITH, Miss. Rebecca Victoria, ACA *2009;* 20 Waller Court, Caversham, READING, RG4 6DB.
SMITH, Mr. Reginald Trevor, FCA *1954;* with JWPCreers, 20-24 Park Street, SELBY, NORTH YORKSHIRE, YO8 4PW. (Life Member)
SMITH, Mr. Reuben Maxwell, ACA *2009;* 16 Vicars Hall Lane, Worsley, MANCHESTER, M28 1HS.
SMITH, Mr. Richard, ACA *2009;* 19 Leathwaite Road, LONDON, SW11 1XG.
SMITH, Mr. Richard, BA ACA *2007;* 26 Woodfield Crescent, LONDON, W5 1PD.
SMITH, Mr. Richard Alexander Buchan, MA FCA *1996;* 13 Crown Lane, Benson, WALLINGFORD, OXFORDSHIRE, OX10 6LP.
•SMITH, Mr. Richard Anthony, BSc ACA *1979;* Smith Partnership, 5 Sedgefield Drive, Thurnby, LEICESTER, LE7 9PT.
SMITH, Mr. Richard Barnsley, FCA *1946;* 53 Plas Derwen View, Monmouth Road, ABERGAVENNY, NP7 9SX. (Life Member)
SMITH, Mr. Richard Charles, BSc ACA *1993;* 46 Cameron Close, HAILSHAM, BN27 3WF.
SMITH, Mr. Richard Clive, BSc FCA AMCT *1989;* 19 Gable Thorne, Wavendon Gate, MILTON KEYNES, MK7 7RT.
SMITH, Mr. Richard David, BSc FCA *1981;* East Coombe, Chagford, NEWTON ABBOT, DEVON, TQ13 8DX.
SMITH, Mr. Richard David James, MEng ACA *2011;* Flat 23, Gemini Court, 852 Brighton Road, PURLEY, SURREY, CR8 2FD.
SMITH, Mr. Richard George, BA FCA *1983;* (Tax Fac), Forest Gate, Bere Heath, WAREHAM, BH20 7NS.
SMITH, Mr. Richard Henry, ACA *1997;* Advanced Medical Solutions Unit A, 33 Road One Winsford Industrial Estate, WINSFORD, CHESHIRE, CW7 3RT.
•SMITH, Mr. Richard Ian, ACA *1979;* Mark Smith & Co., Rear of, 8 The Shubberies, George Lane South Woodford, LONDON, E18 1BD.
SMITH, Mr. Richard Ian, BA ACA *1998;* L N T Automotive Unit 2 47 Helios, 1 Isabella Road Garforth, LEEDS, LS25 2DY.
SMITH, Mr. Richard Ian, BSc ACA *1991;* Sunny Bank, 53 Stanbury, KEIGHLEY, WEST YORKSHIRE, BD22 0HA.
SMITH, Mr. Richard James, BSc ACA *2006;* Flat 6, 77 Albemarle Road, BECKENHAM, BR3 5HW.
SMITH, Mr. Richard James, FCA *1970;* Tudor Croft, 11 Waterford Road, Henleaze, BRISTOL, BS9 4BT.
SMITH, Mr. Richard James Baden, BSc ACA *1999;* 20 Thirsk Road, LONDON, SW11 5SX.
SMITH, Mr. Richard Jeffrey, MA MSc FCA *1972;* The White House Farm, Billesdon Road, Ingarsby, LEICESTER, LE7 9JD. (Life Member)
SMITH, Mr. Richard John, FCA *1951;* 60 Wood Glen, 105 Karalta Road, ERINA, NSW 2250, AUSTRALIA. (Life Member)
SMITH, Mr. Richard John, BSc(Hons) ACA *2001;* 2 Kelmscott Place, ASHTEAD, KT21 2HD.
•SMITH, Mr. Richard John, FCA *1975;* Bates Weston Audit Limited, The Mill, Canal Street, DERBY, DE1 2RJ. See also BW Business Services Limited
•SMITH, Mr. Richard Marfell, FCA *1973;* (Tax Fac), The Lawford Company, Lawford House, Leacroft, STAINES, TW18 4NN.
•SMITH, Mr. Richard Martin, BA ACA *1994;* The Ollis Partnership Limited, 2 Hamilton Terrace, Holly Walk, LEAMINGTON SPA, WARWICKSHIRE, CV32 4LY.
SMITH, Mr. Richard Michael, BA ACA *1983;* N R International Ltd, Park House, Bradbourne Lane, AYLESFORD, KENT, ME20 6SN.
SMITH, Mr. Richard Neil, BA ACA *1995;* Old Hall Cottage, 41 West Street, Gargrave, SKIPTON, BD23 3RJ.
SMITH, Mr. Richard William, BSc ACA *1988;* Pearl Group, 1 Wythall Green Way Wythall, BIRMINGHAM, B47 6WG.
SMITH, Mr. Richard William, BA ACA *1984;* Cleckheaton Holdings, PO Box 24, Clemo, Bradford Road, CLECKHEATON, BD19 3LN.
SMITH, Mr. Robert Alestair, BSc(Hons) ACA *2000;* Summerfield Developments S W Ltd Tauntfield, South Road, TAUNTON, SOMERSET, TA1 3ND.
•SMITH, Mr. Robert Alexander, BSc ACA *2003;* RNS, 50-54 Oswald Road, SCUNTHORPE, NORTH LINCOLNSHIRE, DN15 7PQ.
•SMITH, Mr. Robert Allan Charles, BA ACA *1997;* PricewaterhouseCoopers LLP, Hays Galleria, 1 Hays Lane, LONDON, SE1 2RD. See also PricewaterhouseCoopers
SMITH, Mr. Robert Andrew Craig, BSc ACA *1998;* Office 429, Regus Victoria House, 101-105 Victoria Road, CHELMSFORD, CM1 1JR.
SMITH, Mr. Robert Andrew Ross, BSc ACA *1996;* Wolseley Plc Parkview, 1220 Arlington Business Park Theale, READING, RG7 4GA.

SMITH - SMITH Members - Alphabetical

•**SMITH, Mr. Robert Charles, FCA** *1957;* R.C Smith, 1 Tower Close, ORPINGTON, BR6 0SP.
SMITH, Mr. Robert David, BSc FCA *1986;* 35 Cavendish Road, Eccles, MANCHESTER, M30 9EE.
SMITH, Mr. Robert David, BSc(Hons) ACA *2002;* 33 St. Marys Road, TONBRIDGE, KENT, TN9 2LD.
SMITH, Mr. Robert Edward, FCA *1972;* 17 Pit Farm Road, GUILDFORD, GU1 2JL. (Life Member)
SMITH, Mr. Robert Graham, ACA *1992;* Petrofac Engineering Ltd Brook House, 88-100 Chertsey Road, WOKING, GU21 5BJ.
SMITH, Mr. Robert Henry, FCA *1976;* 10 Ridgemere Close, Syston, LEICESTER, LE7 2ZR.
SMITH, Mr. Robert Iain, BSc ACA *2006;* Flat 6, 114 St Georges Road, BRISTOL, BS1 5TU.
•**SMITH, Mr. Robert James, FCA** *1968;* Robert J Smith, 17 Meadow Close, Hinchley Wood, ESHER, SURREY, KT10 0AY.
SMITH, Mr. Robert James Cort, FCA *1969;* Oakdale, 23 Cockshot Road, MALVERN, WORCESTERSHIRE, WR14 2TT. (Life Member)
SMITH, Mr. Robert John, FCA *1973;* Fairfield, Layton Road, Horsforth, LEEDS, LS18 5ET.
SMITH, Mr. Robert John, MBA BA FCA FRSA *1983;* 113 Molesey Park Road, EAST MOLESEY, KT8 0JX.
•**SMITH, Mr. Robert Mark, ACA** *2008;* PGU Accounting Ltd, St. Oswald House, St. Oswald Street, CASTLEFORD, WEST YORKSHIRE, WF10 1DH.
SMITH, Mr. Robert Marshall, MA ACA *1998;* Fidelity Investments Ltd Beech Gate, Millfield Lane Lower Kingswood, TADWORTH, SURREY, KT20 6RP.
SMITH, Mr. Robert Scotson, FCA *1964;* 33 Iveston Grove, BILLINGHAM, CLEVELAND, TS22 5EA.
SMITH, Mr. Robert Simon, BSc(Econ) ACA *2002;* Willifield Hedgerow, Chalfont St. Peter, GERRARDS CROSS, BUCKINGHAMSHIRE, SL9 0HD.
SMITH, Mr. Robert William, MA FCA *1978;* Apartment E/4, House 19 (new), Plot CEN (A) 17, Road 96, Gulshan-2, DHAKA 1212 BANGLADESH.
SMITH, Mr. Robin, BA FCA *1965;* 63 Station Road, Foxton, CAMBRIDGE, CB22 6SD.
•**SMITH, Mr. Robin, FCA** *1985;* Paul Crowdy Partnership Limited, Redmayne House, 4 Whiteladies Road, Clifton, BRISTOL, BS8 1PD. See also Paul Crowdy Partnership
SMITH, Mr. Robin Alastair Kirkpatrick, BSc ACA *2008;* Symphony Management Ltd, Astwood Dickinson Building (2nd & 3rd Floors), 83-85 Front Street, HAMILTON HM 12, BERMUDA.
SMITH, Mr. Robin Alec, BSc FCA *1978;* 44 High House Drive, Rednal, BIRMINGHAM, B45 8ET.
SMITH, Mr. Robin Anthony Cowin, FCA *1971;* 7875 English Street, MANASSAS, VA 20112, UNITED STATES.
SMITH, Mr. Robin James, BSc FCA *1983;* Oaklands House, 3b Broad Walk, Winchmore Hill, LONDON, N21 3DA.
SMITH, Mr. Robin Oliver, BA ACA *1986;* 31 Howes Drive, Marston Moretaine, BEDFORD, MK43 0FD.
SMITH, Mr. Roderick James Anthony, FCA *1974;* (Tax Fac), Stemcor Holdings Ltd, Level 27, City Point, 1 Ropemaker Street, LONDON, EC2Y 9ST.
•**SMITH, Mr. Roger, MA FCA** *1973;* with KPMG LLP, 15 Canada Square, LONDON, E14 5GL.
SMITH, Mr. Roger, FCA *1969;* 79 Quebec Road, BLACKBURN, BB2 7DE. (Life Member)
SMITH, Mr. Roger Ackworth, BA FCA *1970;* Beechcroft The Street, Bramerton, NORWICH, NR14 7DW.
SMITH, Mr. Roger Anthony Frederick, FCA *1967;* 12 Three Springs Road, PERSHORE, WORCESTERSHIRE, WR10 1HH.
SMITH, Mr. Roger Charles, FCA *1967;* 6 Beaufort Close, MARLOW, BUCKINGHAMSHIRE, SL7 1EN. (Life Member)
SMITH, Mr. Roger David, FCA *1968;* The Gables, Boulevard Road, West Runton, CROMER, NORFOLK, NR27 9QL.
SMITH, Mr. Roger David, BSc ACA *1991;* 5 Weringa Avenue, CAMMERAY, NSW 2062, AUSTRALIA.
SMITH, Mr. Roger Guy, FCA *1968;* 1474 54th Street, Tsawwassen, DELTA V4M 3H5, BC, CANADA.
•**SMITH, Mr. Roger John, FCA** *1976;* (Tax Fac), Milne Eldridge & Co, The Little House, 88A West Street, FARNHAM, SURREY, GU9 7EN.
SMITH, Mr. Roger Ling, BSc FCA *1976;* 9 Wedgewood Court, Parkhill Road, BEXLEY, DA5 1HL.
SMITH, Mr. Roger Michael, FCA *1966;* Latchetts, 3 Homestead Close, Cossington, LEICESTER, LEICESTERSHIRE, LE7 4UN.
•**SMITH, Mr. Roger Michael, BCom(Acc) FCA** *1983;* Fairhurst, Douglas Bank House, Wigan Lane, WIGAN, WN1 2TB.
SMITH, Mr. Roger Neil, BA FCA *1982;* Investindustrial Advisors Ltd, 1 Duchess Street, LONDON, W1W 6AN.
SMITH, Mr. Roger Philip, FCA *1977;* The Old Constabulary, 21 Manchester Road, Tideswell, BUXTON, SK17 8LL.
SMITH, Mr. Roger Philip, BA ACA *1985;* 17 Ave L'ammonciade B 3.4, 98000 MONACO, MONACO.
SMITH, Mr. Roger Stephen, BA FCA *1962;* 8 Philip Avenue, SWANLEY, BR8 8HG.
SMITH, Miss. Rona Kathleen, BSc ACA *1980;* 101 Copse Avenue, WEST WICKHAM, BR4 9NW.
SMITH, Mr. Ronald Arthur, FCA *1951;* 197 Whitehall Road, WOODFORD GREEN, IG8 0RG. (Life Member)
•**SMITH, Mr. Ronald Charles Peter, FCA** *1976;* (Tax Fac), Wilkins Kennedy, Bridge House, London Bridge, LONDON, SE1 9QR.
SMITH, Mr. Ronald George Stanley, BSc(Econ) FCA *1965;* 7 Charteris Rd, WOODFORD GREEN, IG8 0AP. (Life Member)
SMITH, Mr. Ronald Stuart, FCA *1973;* John Barritt & Son Ltd, P.O. Box HM 174, HAMILTON, BERMUDA.
SMITH, Mr. Ross Raymond, ACA CA(AUS) *2009;* 1407/3 Kings Cross Road, RUSHCUTTERS BAY, NSW, AUSTRALIA.
SMITH, Mr. Roy Thomas, BSc(Econ) FCA *1972;* Woodleigh, Ockham Road North, East Horsley, LEATHERHEAD, KT24 6NU. (Life Member)
SMITH, Mr. Rupert Christopher, ACA *2010;* Top Flat, Circularising Ltd, 6 Landor Road, LONDON, SW9 9PP.
•**SMITH, Mr. Russell, FCA** *1987;* JWP Creers, Foss Place, Foss Islands Road, YORK, YO31 7UJ. See also JWPCreers LLP
•**SMITH, Mr. Russell Paul Hanson, BA ACA** *2002;* Russell Smith Tax & Accountancy Services Limited, G3 Round Foundry, Media Centre, Foundry Street, LEEDS, LS11 5QP.
SMITH, Miss. Ruth, ACA *2010;* 3 Glen Avenue, Holbrook, BELPER, DERBYSHIRE, DE56 0UE.
SMITH, Mrs. Ruth Maxine, ACA MAAT *1999;* MGTS, Gulson Road, COVENTRY, CV1 2JG.
SMITH, Mrs. Sally, BSc(Hons) ACA *2010;* 39 Mill View Lane, Horwich, BOLTON, BL6 6TL.
SMITH, Mr. Sam Roy, BSc ACA *2010;* 44c, Powis Square, LONDON, W11 2AX.
SMITH, Mrs. Samantha, BA(Hons) ACA *2003;* with Sam Rogoff & Co Limited, 2nd Floor, 167-169 Great Portland Street, LONDON, W1W 5PF.
SMITH, Miss. Samantha Jane, BSc ACA *1999;* Finncap Ltd, 60 New Broad Street, LONDON, EC2M 1JJ.
SMITH, Mr. Samuel Dale, FCA *1971;* 54 Woodfield Road, Cheadle Hulme, CHEADLE, CHESHIRE, SK8 7JS.
SMITH, Mr. Samuel Graham, FCA *1972;* 5833 Nebraska Ave. NW, WASHINGTON, DC 20015, UNITED STATES.
SMITH, Mrs. Sandra, BA FCA CTA *1986;* 12 Benenden Way, ASHBY-DE-LA-ZOUCH, LE65 2QS.
SMITH, Miss. Sandra Jane, BA ACA *1980;* Flat 1, Flat 3 Balmoral Terrace, Le Mont de la Trinite St. Helier, JERSEY, JE2 4NJ.
SMITH, Mrs. Sandra Lynn, BA ACA *1992;* 33 Rimbury Way, CHRISTCHURCH, BH23 2RQ.
SMITH, Mrs. Sara Joanne, MA FCA *1985;* 25 Woodhouse Gardens, BRIGHOUSE, HD6 3UH.
SMITH, Mrs. Sara Lucy Claire, BA(Hons) FCA *2000;* KPMG Forensic, K P M G, 1 The Embankment, LEEDS, LS1 4DW.
SMITH, Mrs. Sarah, BA ACA *2003;* 70 Middle Meadow, Shireoaks, WORKSOP, NOTTINGHAMSHIRE, S81 8PX.
SMITH, Mrs. Sarah Ai-Ling, BA(Hons) ACA *2001;* 6 Barnswick View, LEEDS, LS16 7DP.
SMITH, Mrs. Sarah Ann, BSc ACA *2004;* Priory Group, Northern Office, Park Hall, Middleton St George Hospital, DARLINGTON, COUNTY DURHAM DL2 1TS.
SMITH, Mrs. Sarah Anne, BA ACA *1991;* 6 Swadelands Close, Lenham, MAIDSTONE, ME17 2AF.
SMITH, Ms. Sarah Elisabeth Gibson, ACA *1983;* Goldman Sachs, 200 West Street, 24th Floor, NEW YORK, NY 10282, UNITED STATES.
SMITH, Mrs. Sarah Jane, BSc ACA *1992;* 9 Ashworth Close, NEWARK, NOTTINGHAMSHIRE, NG24 2LJ.
•**SMITH, Mrs. Sarah Jean, BA ACA** *2008;* Rowett Bookkeeping Services, 5 Franklin Street, EXETER, EX2 4HF.
SMITH, Miss. Sarah Karen, ACA *1988;* Ty Bryn, 2 Inglewood Lane, PAGET PG06, BERMUDA.
SMITH, Mrs. Sarah Kathrin, BSc ACA *2003;* 54 London Road, ROYSTON, HERTFORDSHIRE, SG8 9EL.
SMITH, Mrs. Sarah Louise, BA ACA *1998;* 17 Manor Road, Cheadle Hulme, CHEADLE, CHESHIRE, SK8 7DQ.
SMITH, Mrs. Sarah Louise, BSc ACA *2001;* National Grid Plc National Grid House, Warwick Technology Park Gallows Hill, WARWICK, CV34 6DA.
SMITH, Miss. Sarah Louise, BSc ACA *2004;* The Garden Flat, 12 Frederick Place, BRISTOL, BS8 1AS.
•**SMITH, Miss. Sarah Louise, BA FCA** *1984;* S.L. Smith & Co, Barbican House, 26-34 Old Street, LONDON, EC1V 9QR.
SMITH, Mr. Scott, ACA CA(AUS) *2008;* 22 West Street, Oundle, PETERBOROUGH, PE8 4EG.
SMITH, Mr. Scott, MBA BSc FCA *1992;* 89 Washington Place, Apartment 2J, NEW YORK, NY 10011, UNITED STATES.
SMITH, Mr. Sean Harvey, BSc ACA *1995;* 21 Wren Way, MANCHESTER, M11 3NH.
SMITH, Mr. Sean Leonard, BA FCA *1991;* 61 Mirlaw Road, Whitelea Chase, CRAMLINGTON, NE23 6UD.
•**SMITH, Mr. Sean Russell, FCA** *1992;* (Tax Fac), Thomas Westcott, Petitor House, Nicholson Road, TORQUAY, TQ2 7TD.
SMITH, Mrs. Sharon Lisa, BSc ACA *1996;* The Old Vicarage, Bush End, Takeley, BISHOP'S STORTFORD, CM22 6NF.
SMITH, Mrs. Sharon Louise, ACA *2004;* 15 Teal Close, Quedgeley, GLOUCESTER, GL2 4GR.
SMITH, Mrs. Sheila, FCA *1959;* Caldcleugh, Cake Street, Old Buckenham, ATTLEBOROUGH, NR17 1RU. (Life Member)
SMITH, Mrs. Shelagh Katherine, BA ACA *1995;* Old Hall Cottage, 41 West Street, Gargrave, SKIPTON, BD23 3RJ.
SMITH, Miss. Shirley Anne Elizabeth, BSc FCA *1987;* 142 Rotton Park Road, Edgbaston, BIRMINGHAM, B16 0LH.
SMITH, Mr. Simon Alexander, BA ACA *1994;* 9 Fontenoy Road, Balham, LONDON, SW12 9LZ.
SMITH, Mr. Simon Andrew, BSc ACA *1992;* 35 Gainsborough Avenue Eaton Ford, ST NEOTS, CAMBRIDGESHIRE, PE19 7RJ.
SMITH, Mr. Simon Antony, BA(Hons) ACA *2001;* 82 Tottenham Lane, LONDON, N8 7EE.
SMITH, Mr. Simon Christopher, BSc FCA *1979;* Fairdene, Harnham Lane, Withington, CHELTENHAM, GLOUCESTERSHIRE, GL54 4DD. (Life Member)
SMITH, Mr. Simon Christopher, BA ACA *1993;* 136 Manchester Road, WILMSLOW, SK9 2JW.
SMITH, Mr. Simon Frederick, BA ACA *1985;* 24 Beech Lane, Kislingbury, NORTHAMPTON, NN7 4AL.
SMITH, Mr. Simon Kenneth, BA ACA *1984;* Seaspray, 1 Purbeck Avenue, POOLE, DORSET, BH15 4DN.
SMITH, Mr. Simon Lawrence, BA ACA *1985;* 10 Beechwood Dale, Low Ackworth, PONTEFRACT, WF7 7NP.
SMITH, Mr. Simon Lindsay, BA FCA *1979;* Rowallan International Ltd, Rowallan House, 1 Rowallan Drive, BEDFORD, MK41 8AW.
SMITH, Mr. Simon Michael Longfellow, BSc ACA *1985;* 5 SWORD STREET, ASCOT, QLD 4007, AUSTRALIA.
SMITH, Mr. Simon Paul, BA ACA *1999;* 30 Bracken Park, Scarcroft, LEEDS, LS14 3HZ.
SMITH, Mr. Simon Paul, BA ACA *1991;* Bridgeworks, Bridge Road, SUNNINGHILL, BERKSHIRE, SL5 9NL.
•**SMITH, Mr. Simon Richard, ACA FCCA** *2005;* Rigel Wolf Limited, Orion House, 28a Spital Terrace, GAINSBOROUGH, LINCOLNSHIRE, DN21 2HQ.
SMITH, Mr. Stanley, FCA *1960;* 45 Liverpool Road, Formby, LIVERPOOL, L37 6BT. (Life Member)
SMITH, Mrs. Stefanie Claire, ACA DChA *2004;* with Lovewell Blake LLP, Sixty Six, North Quay, GREAT YARMOUTH, NORFOLK, NR30 1HE.
SMITH, Mrs. Stella Jane, ACA *2008;* 352 Platt Lane, Fallowfield, MANCHESTER, M14 7FA.
SMITH, Mrs. Stephanie, BSc ACA *1991;* Market Link, 30 St. Georges Square, WORCESTER, WR1 1HX.
SMITH, Mr. Stephen, BA FCA *1985;* 45 Campion Park, Up Hatherley, CHELTENHAM, GLOUCESTERSHIRE, GL51 3WA.
SMITH, Mr. Stephen, BSc ACA *1993;* 19 Smirrells Road, BIRMINGHAM, B28 0LA.
SMITH, Mr. Stephen, BSc ACA *2011;* 96 Sydney Road, LONDON, SW20 8EF.
SMITH, Mr. Stephen Alan, BA ACA *1989;* Dunedin House, Yew Tree Way, Prestbury, MACCLESFIELD, CHESHIRE, SK10 4EX.
SMITH, Mr. Stephen Allan, FCA *1984;* 47A Cornhill Road, Urmston, MANCHESTER, M41 5TD.
SMITH, Mr. Stephen Andrew, BSc FCA *1985;* 21 The Finches, HERTFORD, SG13 7TB.
SMITH, Mr. Stephen Andrew, BA ACA *1991;* 105-7 Rosehill Drive, BURPENGARY, QLD 4505, AUSTRALIA.
SMITH, Mr. Stephen Andrew, BSc ACA *2003;* Chaucer Insurance Ltd, Prospect House, Chaucer Business Park, Thanet Way, WHITSTABLE, KENT CT5 3FD.
•**SMITH, Mr. Stephen Andrew, BSc(Econ) ACA** *1996;* (Tax Fac), PricewaterhouseCoopers, Waterfront Plaza, 8 Laganbank Road, BELFAST, COUNTY ANTRIM, BT1 3LR. See also PricewaterhouseCoopers LLP
SMITH, Mr. Stephen Anthony, BA FCA *1975;* Tudor House, Week St. Mary, HOLSWORTHY, DEVON, EX22 6UL.
SMITH, Mr. Stephen Benedict, BSc ACA *2001;* 5 St Leonards Road, HARROGATE, HG2 8NX.
SMITH, Mr. Stephen Christopher, BSc ACA *1995;* JS Investment Consultancy FZE, PO Box 22735, DUBAI, UNITED ARAB EMIRATES.
SMITH, Mr. Stephen David, BA(Hons) ACA *2002;* 29 Rushwick Grove, Shirley, SOLIHULL, B90 4XL.
SMITH, Mr. Stephen Dudley, BA ACA *1996;* Millswood Old Neighbouring, Chalford, STROUD, GL6 8AA.
SMITH, Mr. Stephen Edward, MA FCA FIIA *1981;* Bank of Cyprus (London) Ltd, PO Box 17484, LONDON, N14 5WH.
SMITH, Mr. Stephen Elliot, LLB ACA *2001;* Super Group Plc, Unit 60, The Runnings, CHELTENHAM, GLOUCESTERSHIRE, GL51 9NW.
•**SMITH, Mr. Stephen Gardiner, BA FCA** *1985;* KPMG LLP, 15 Canada Square, LONDON, E14 5GL. See also KPMG Europe LLP
SMITH, Mr. Stephen Gary, ACA *1983;* 27 Dunnock Avenue, Clayton Heights, BRADFORD, BD6 3XH.
SMITH, Mr. Stephen Gerard, BSc FCA *1982;* P.O. Box 2763, RANDBURG, GAUTENG, 2125, SOUTH AFRICA.
SMITH, Mr. Stephen Hugh, BA ACA *1983;* 13 Downs Way, TADWORTH, KT20 5DH.
SMITH, Mr. Stephen Ian, BCom ACA *1983;* Old Stable, Clifton Hampden, ABINGDON, OXFORDSHIRE, OX14 3DF.
SMITH, Mr. Stephen James, BSc ACA *2009;* 34 Allington Road, ORPINGTON, BR6 8BA.
SMITH, Mr. Stephen James, BSc ACA *2007;* Flat 5, 57 Cleveland Road, South Woodford, LONDON, E18 2AE.
•**SMITH, Mr. Stephen James, BA FCA** *1993;* KS Accountancy, 32 Wilderness Heights, West End, SOUTHAMPTON, SO18 3PS.
SMITH, Mr. Stephen James Harrison, BA ACA *1995;* RT 01 RW 06, Wirun Mojolaban, SUKOHARJO, JAVA, 57554, INDONESIA.
SMITH, Mr. Stephen John, BA ACA *2005;* 24 Pretoria Avenue, MIDHURST, GU29 9PP.
SMITH, Mr. Stephen John, FCA *1989;* 20 Colleen Avenue, Kings Norton, BIRMINGHAM, B30 3NN.
SMITH, Mr. Stephen John, BSc ACA *1981;* White House, High Lane, Maltby, MIDDLESBROUGH, CLEVELAND, TS8 0BG.
SMITH, Mr. Stephen John, BA ACA *1989;* 103 Discovery Drive, Kings Hill, WEST MALLING, ME19 4DS.
SMITH, Mr. Stephen John, MA ACA AMCT *2001;* 4 Broadway Road, Bishopston, BRISTOL, BS7 8ES.
•**SMITH, Mr. Stephen Michael, BA ACA** *1996;* S M Smith Ltd, 7 Slingsby Close, Apperley Bridge, BRADFORD, WEST YORKSHIRE, BD10 0UJ.
•**SMITH, Mr. Stephen Paul, FCA** *1982;* (Tax Fac), Steve Smith FCA, 38 Timbertree Road, CRADLEY HEATH, WEST MIDLANDS, B64 7LE.
SMITH, Mr. Stephen Paul, BSc ACA *1993;* 54, Frederick Road, SUTTON COLDFIELD, B73 5QN.
SMITH, Mr. Stephen Robert, BSc ACA *1985;* 2 Arden Grove, ORPINGTON, BR6 7WD.
•**SMITH, Mr. Stephen Roger, FCA** *1982;* (Tax Fac), Murphy Salisbury, 15 Warwick Road, STRATFORD-UPON-AVON, CV37 6YW.
SMITH, Mr. Steven George, BSc ACA *2006;* 7 De Bawdrip Road, Pengam Green, CARDIFF, CF24 2TN.
SMITH, Mr. Steven James, BA ACA *1986;* 1 Ember Lane, ESHER, KT10 8DZ.
•①**SMITH, Mr. Steven Leslie, FCA** *1978;* Mercer & Hole, Gloucester House, 72 London Road, ST. ALBANS, HERTFORDSHIRE, AL1 1NS.
SMITH, Mr. Steven Miles, BCom ACA CTA *1983;* Hawkesbury, Braye Du Valle, St. Sampson, GUERNSEY, GY2 4RB.

SMITH, Mr. Steven Philip Thomas, BA ACA *1994;* UBS AG, 100 Liverpool Street, LONDON, EC2M 2RH.

SMITH, Mr. Steven Richard, BSc ACA *2002;* Brookfield Farm, London Road, DAVENTRY, NORTHAMPTONSHIRE, NN11 4NQ.

SMITH, Mr. Stuart, MA(Hons) ACA *2003;* Citrus House, Caton Road, LANCASTER, LA1 3UA.

•**SMITH, Mr. Stuart Graham, BSc FCA** *1978;* ZAO Deloitte CIS, Lesnaya Street 5 Building B, 125047 MOSCOW, RUSSIAN FEDERATION.

SMITH, Mr. Stuart Martin, BSc FCA CF *1981;* Wolferlow House, Wolferlow, BROMYARD, HEREFORDSHIRE, HR7 4QA.

SMITH, Mr. Stuart Peter James, BSc ACA *1999;* The Old Bakery, 10 Bearley Road, Aston Cantlow, HENLEY-IN-ARDEN, B95 6HS.

SMITH, Mr. Stuart William, BSc ACA *2002;* 43 Barrett Road, LONDON, E17 9ES.

SMITH, Mrs. Susan, FCA *1983;* 59 Mill Park Avenue, HORNCHURCH, ESSEX, RM12 6HD.

SMITH, Mrs. Susan Ann, BA ACA *1993;* 1 Birchley View, Moss Bank, ST.HELENS, WA11 7NT.

SMITH, Mrs. Susan Ann, BA FCA *1989;* White Lodge, 10 Fitzroy Road, FLEET, HAMPSHIRE, GU51 4JH.

•**SMITH, Mrs. Susan Anne, ACA** *2000;* Hunter Smith, Allens Wall, Black Hill, Lindfield, HAYWARDS HEATH, WEST SUSSEX RH16 2HE.

SMITH, Mrs. Susan Caroline, LLB ACA *1990;* The Old Vicarage, 15 Severn Bank, SHREWSBURY, SY1 2JD.

SMITH, Miss. Susan Mary, BSc ACA *1983;* 5c Church Street, DEVONPORT 0624, NEW ZEALAND.

SMITH, Mrs. Susan Wendy, ACA *1990;* 17 Dents Road, LONDON, SW11 6JA.

SMITH, Mrs. Suzanne, ACA *2009;* 4imprint Broadway House, Trafford Wharf Road Trafford Park, MANCHESTER, M17 1DD.

SMITH, Mrs. Suzanne Claire, BSc ACA *1992;* 7 Saxilby Road, East Morton, KEIGHLEY, WEST YORKSHIRE, BD20 5WB.

SMITH, Mr. Terence, FCA *1972;* Sandhill House, Sandhill Lane, Sutton on Derwent, YORK, YO41 4BX.

•**SMITH, Mr. Terence Albert, FCA** *1965;* (Tax Fac), Accounting and Business Development Limited, Unit 6, Cooksoe Farm, Chicheley, NEWPORT PAGNELL, BUCKINGHAMSHIRE MK16 9JP.

SMITH, Miss. Teresa Geraldine, BSc FCA *1977;* 40 Oliver Close, Thames Road, Strand on the Green, LONDON, W4 3RL. (Life Member)

SMITH, Mr. Terrence Kevin, FCA *1979;* 46 Springfield Close, Burton-on-the-Wolds, LOUGHBOROUGH, LE12 5AN.

SMITH, Mrs. Terri Jocelyn, ACA *2009;* 30 St Catherines Road, CHELMSFORD, ESSEX, CM1 2SP.

SMITH, Mr. Thomas, MSci BA ACA *2005;* 4 Warberry Road, Wood Green, LONDON, N22 7TQ.

SMITH, Mr. Thomas Adam, BSc ACA *2005;* 395 Duffield Road, Allestree, DERBY, DE22 2DN.

SMITH, Mr. Thomas Alan, BCom FCA *1955;* Broad Oaks, 38 Broad Oaks Road, SOLIHULL, B91 1JB. (Life Member)

SMITH, Mr. Thomas Bertram, MA FCA *1939;* Brookside, Church Hill, Earls Colne, COLCHESTER, CO6 2RG. (Life Member)

SMITH, Mr. Thomas Charles Milner, MA ACA *1997;* Charles Russell Business Services, 5 Fleet Place, LONDON, EC4M 7RD.

•**SMITH, Mr. Thomas Edward James, MA FCA** *1981;* (Tax Fac), Brebners, The Quadrangle, 180 Wardour Street, LONDON, W1F 8LB.

•**SMITH, Mr. Thomas Howard, BSc FCA** *1974;* Little Stone Edge Farm, Gisburn Road, Blacko, NELSON, BB9 6LS.

SMITH, Mr. Thomas Ian James, BSc ACA *2002;* 26 William Sim Wood, Winkfield Row, BRACKNELL, BERKSHIRE, RG42 6PW.

SMITH, Mr. Thomas James, BA(Hons) ACA *2004;* (Tax Fac), 8 Verlands, Congresbury, BRISTOL, BS49 5BL.

SMITH, Mr. Thomas Martyn, FCA *1962;* 3 Winston Drive, Isham, KETTERING, NN14 1HS.

SMITH, Mr. Thomas Oliver, BA ACA *2005;* 6 Crofton Avenue, BEXLEY, DA5 3AR.

•**SMITH, Mr. Timothy David, FCA** *1981;* PKF (UK) LLP, 8th Floor, Helmont House, Churchill Way, CARDIFF, CF10 2HE.

SMITH, Mr. Timothy David, FCA *1990;* 2 The Fairway, Alsager, STOKE-ON-TRENT, ST7 2AZ.

•**SMITH, Mr. Timothy Guy Knowles, BSocSc ACA** *1996;* (Tax Fac), AIMS - Guy Smith ACA, 5 Oakwood Park, LEEDS, LS8 2PJ.

•**SMITH, Mr. Timothy John, MA FCA CTA** *1972;* (Member of Council 1992 - 1994), (Tax Fac), Nevill Hovey & Co Limited, Southgate Close, LAUNCESTON, CORNWALL, PL15 9DU. See also Williams H.M.

•**SMITH, Mr. Timothy Richard, FCA** *1966;* Tim Smith, 14 Newton Park, Newton Solney, BURTON-ON-TRENT, DE15 0SX.

SMITH, Mr. Tom, FCA *1961;* Hall Cottage, Lumby, South Milford, LEEDS, LS25 5JA.

SMITH, Mr. Tom David Ian, ACA *2008;* 46 Oakdene Road, SEVENOAKS, TN13 3HL.

SMITH, Mr. Tom Edward Oliver, ACA *2010;* 287b Lee High Road, LONDON, SE12 8RU.

SMITH, Mrs. Tracy Jane, BA ACA *1987;* 153 Kingsway, Chandler's Ford, EASTLEIGH, HAMPSHIRE, SO53 5BY.

•①**SMITH, Mr. Trevor, FCA** *1974;* Smithaston, The Royal, 25 Bank Plain, NORWICH, NR2 4SF.

•**SMITH, Mr. Trevor Alan, BSc(Hons) ACA** *2002;* with PricewaterhouseCoopers LLP, Savannah House, 3 Ocean Way, Ocean Village, SOUTHAMPTON, SO14 3TJ.

SMITH, Mr. Trevor David, FCA *1985;* with ICAEW, Metropolitan House, 321 Avebury Boulevard, MILTON KEYNES, MK9 2FZ.

SMITH, Mr. Trevor Edward, FCA *1962;* 1305 w island club square, VERO BEACH, FL 32963, UNITED STATES.

•**SMITH, Mr. Trevor James, FCA** *1983;* Price Bailey Private Client LLP, Richmond House, Broad Street, ELY, CAMBRIDGESHIRE, CB7 4AH. See also Price Bailey LLP

SMITH, Mr. Trevor John, FCA *1970;* (Tax Fac), 2 Forest View Road, LOUGHTON, IG10 4DX.

SMITH, Mrs. Valerie, BSc ACA *1996;* 18 Danesbury Park, North Ride, WELWYN, AL6 9SA.

SMITH, Miss. Valerie Jane, BA FCA *1978;* 20 Elsworthy, THAMES DITTON, KT7 0YP.

SMITH, Mrs. Vicky Samantha, BA FCA *1998;* with ICAEW, Metropolitan House, 321 Avebury Boulevard, MILTON KEYNES, MK9 2FZ.

SMITH, Mr. Victor, FCA *1960;* Flat 9 Bentley Lodge, 182 High Road, Bushey Heath, BUSHEY, WD23 1NS.

SMITH, Mr. Victor Douglas, FCA *1960;* 59 Southall Drive, Hartlebury, KIDDERMINSTER, WORCESTERSHIRE, DY11 7LD. (Life Member)

SMITH, Miss. Victoria, BSc ACA *2000;* 43 Mullaloo Drive, MULLALOO, WA 6027, AUSTRALIA.

SMITH, Miss. Victoria, LLB ACA *2007;* 70 Merevale Way, YEOVIL, SOMERSET, BA21 3UW.

SMITH, Miss. Victoria, BSc ACA *2011;* 20 St. Davids Avenue, DINAS POWYS, SOUTH GLAMORGAN, CF64 4JP.

SMITH, Mrs. Victoria Elizabeth, BA ACA *1992;* Quantis Ltd, 13 Newgate Street, MORPETH, NORTHUMBERLAND, NE61 1AL.

SMITH, Mrs. Victoria Jane, BA(Hons) ACA *2002;* Barclays Capital, 5 North Colonnade, Canary Wharf, LONDON, E14 4BB.

SMITH, Mrs. Victoria Mary, BSc ACA *2004;* Corin Group Plc, The Corinium Centre, Love Lane Industrial Estate, CIRENCESTER, GLOUCESTERSHIRE, GL7 1YJ.

SMITH, Mr. Vincent Robert, BA ACA *1985;* 13 Rothamsted Avenue, HARPENDEN, AL5 2DD.

SMITH, Mrs. Vivien Jean, BSc ACA *1995;* 4 Tythe Barn Lane, Shirley, SOLIHULL, B90 1RW.

•**SMITH, Mr. Wayne Philip, ACA CTA** *2003;* (Tax Fac), J S Bethell & Co, 70 Clarkehouse Road, SHEFFIELD, S10 2LJ.

•**SMITH, Miss. Wendy Anita, BA(Hons) ACA** *2004;* Year End Solutions Limited, 26 Stockham Close, Cricklade, SWINDON, SN6 6EF.

SMITH, Mr. Wilfrid, FCA *1953;* 6 South Lodge Close, Tankerton, WHITSTABLE, CT5 2AD. (Life Member)

SMITH, Mr. William Charles, FCA *1965;* Heath House, 36 Bulkington Lane, NUNEATON, CV11 4SA.

SMITH, Mr. William David, FCA *1977;* 8 Woods Loke East, LOWESTOFT, SUFFOLK, NR32 3DR.

SMITH, Mr. William George David, FCA *1975;* 55 Bettws-Y-Coed Road, Cyncoed, CARDIFF, CF23 6PJ.

SMITH, Mr. William Henry, BSc FCA *1969;* Steddles, Church Lane, Northney, HAYLING ISLAND, PO11 0SB. (Life Member)

SMITH, Mr. William James, FCA *1963;* Flat 4, 19 Shore Road, Ainsdale, SOUTHPORT, PR8 2PX. (Life Member)

SMITH, Mr. William James, MSc BSc FCA *1983;* 33 Binns Lane, HOLMFIRTH, HD9 3BL.

SMITH, Mr. William John Akeroyd, FCA *1959;* Washburn Cottage, Leathley Lane, Leathley, OTLEY, WEST YORKSHIRE, LS21 2JY.

•**SMITH, Mr. William Richard, MA ACA** *2001;* Deloitte LLP, PO Box 500, 2 Hardman Street, MANCHESTER, M60 2AT. See also Deloitte & Touche LLP

•**SMITH, Mr. William Thomas, BSc ACA** *1996;* KPMG LLP, Dukes Keep, Marsh Lane, SOUTHAMPTON, HAMPSHIRE, SO14 3EX.

SMITH, Mr. William Tom James, FCA *1971;* Barnfield Farm, Lower Road, Erlestoke, DEVIZES, SN10 5UE.

SMITH, Mr. William Winfield, FCA *1956;* 3 St. Oswalds Close, Oswaldkirk, YORK, YO62 5YH. (Life Member)

SMITH, Mr. William James, ACA *2011;* Ground Floor Flat, 15 York Place, Clifton, BRISTOL, BS8 1AH.

SMITH-BECKER, Mr. Russell Austin, MA ACA *1999;* with Berg Kaprow Lewis LLP, 35 Ballards Lane, LONDON, N3 1XW.

SMITH-BOSANQUET, Mr. Samuel George Daniel Christian, BSc ACA *2008;* 9 Warbeck Road, LONDON, W12 8NS.

SMITH-COX, Mr. Peter, FCA *1971;* 11 Orion Road, Kirstenhof, CAPE TOWN, 7945, SOUTH AFRICA.

•**SMITH-DAYE, Mr. John Martin, FCA** *1982;* Lambert Chapman, West House, West Square, MALDON, ESSEX, CM9 6HA. See also Lambert Chapman LLP

SMITH WRIGHT, Mr. Richard Dayrell, FCA *1958;* Povey's Barns, Stoney Heath, Ramsdell, TADLEY, RG26 5SN. (Life Member)

SMITHAM, Mr. Phillip Llewellyn Lawrence, FCA *1975;* The Woodlands, 107 Old Woking Rd, West Byfleet, WEST BYFLEET, KT14 6HY.

SMITHAM, Mrs. Shirin Sarah, BA ACA *1999;* (Tax Fac), 17 Phillip Street, #05-02 Grand Building, SINGAPORE 048695, SINGAPORE.

SMITHARD, Mr. Brett Lewis, ACA CA(SA) *2010;* Flat 1, Barrington Lodge, Princes Road, WEYBRIDGE, SURREY, KT13 9DB.

SMITHEMAN, Miss. Laura Elizabeth, BSc ACA *2010;* 15 Stonebow Avenue, SOLIHULL, B91 3UP.

SMITHERMAN, Miss. Claudia, BA(Hons) ACA *2000;* 67 Mexfield Road, LONDON, SW15 2RG.

SMITHERS, Ms. Nicola Jane, MA BSc ACA *1990;* 107 Fallsworth Drive, CARY, NC 27513, UNITED STATES.

SMITHIE, Mr. Nicholas Dearden, MA ACA *1993;* C/O UBS, 1285 Avenue of the Americas, NEW YORK, NY 10019, UNITED STATES.

SMITHIES, Mr. Christopher, ACA *2007;* 203/34 Wentworth Street, GLEBE, NSW 2037, AUSTRALIA.

SMITHIES, Mr. James Charles King, MA MPhil ACA *2007;* 31 Woodlands Road, SURBITON, KT6 6PR.

SMITHIES, Mr. John Andrew, BA ACA *1999;* 11 Deanbrook Close, Shirley, SOLIHULL, WEST MIDLANDS, B90 4XS.

•**SMITHIES, Mr. John Morton, FCA** *1972;* Morton Smithies Consultancy Limited, The Studio, Lower Lodge, Weetwood Lane, LEEDS, LS16 5PH.

•**SMITHIES, Miss. Julia Mary, BA ACA** *1985;* PricewaterhouseCoopers LLP, 1 Embankment Place, LONDON, WC2N 6RH.

SMITHIES, Mr. Maurice, FCA *1960;* 40 Hall Bank Drive, BINGLEY, WEST YORKSHIRE, BD16 4BZ.

SMITHSON, Mr. Andrew Kinnear, BSc ACA *1995;* 95 Lime Avenue, LEAMINGTON SPA, CV32 7DG.

•**SMITHSON, Mr. Anthony John Michael, FCA** *1976;* (Tax Fac), Anthony Smithson Limited, 20 Larch Close, TAUNTON, SOMERSET, TA1 2SF.

SMITHSON, Mr. Antony Mark, BSc ACA *1998;* M A S T A Ltd Moorfield Road Estate, Yeadon, LEEDS, LS19 7BN.

SMITHSON, Mr. Christopher John, FCA *1967;* Kenneth Easby Llp, Hanover House, 13 Victoria Road, DARLINGTON, COUNTY DURHAM, DL1 5SF.

•**SMITHSON, Mr. David, ACA** *1988;* Mazars LLP, Mazars House, Gelderd Road, Gildersome, LEEDS, LS27 7JN.

SMITHSON, Mrs. Jo-Anne Cathryn, BA ACA *1990;* Sterling House, 175 High Street, RICKMANSWORTH, WD3 1AY.

SMITHSON, Mrs. Judith Elaine, ACA *1980;* Micklefield, Beck Lane, BINGLEY, WEST YORKSHIRE, BD16 4DN.

SMITHSON, Mr. Keith Victor, BCom ACA *1987;* Spinney House, Warwick Road, Leek Wootton, WARWICK, CV35 7RD.

SMITHSON, Mr. Peter, BA ACA *2002;* 38 Beulah Road, TUNBRIDGE WELLS, TN1 2NR.

SMITHSON, Mr. Peter Donald, BA FCA *1986;* 76 Sycamore Road, Croxley Green, RICKMANSWORTH, HERTFORDSHIRE, WD3 3TF.

SMITHSON, Miss. Prudence Joanna, ACA *2008;* 537A Old York Road, LONDON, SW18 1TG.

•**SMITHSON, Mr. Robert Erald, FCA** *1974;* R.E. Smithson, 14 Lister Avenue, HITCHIN, SG4 9ES.

SMITHWICK, Mrs. Jenifer Linda, ACA *2008;* 3/77 Belgrave St, CREMORNE, NSW 2090, AUSTRALIA.

SMITHWICK, Mrs. Nicola Jane, BA(Hons) ACA *2001;* 19 Oakwood Way, Hamble, SOUTHAMPTON, SO31 4HJ.

SMOCZYNSKI, Mr. Joseph, MA ACA *1985;* MEMBER OF COUNCIL, Baker Tilly Poland, Hrubieszowska 2, 01 209 WARSAW, POLAND. See also Baker Tilly Smoczynski & Partners Sp. z o. o.

SMOKER, Mrs. Joanne Stella, BSc ACA *1983;* Lovely Hall Broadhead Road, Turton, BOLTON, BL7 0BG.

SMOLAREK, Miss. Magdalena, MSc ACA *2010;* Flat 1 Branden Lodge, 37 Burlington Road, LONDON, W4 4BE.

SMOLEY, Mr. David Marcus, BA FCA *1991;* 29 Chancellors, ARLESEY, BEDFORDSHIRE, SG15 6YB.

SMOLINSKI, Mr. Paul, BA ACA *1990;* Thomsons Online Benefits Gordon House, 10 Greencoat Place, LONDON, SW1P 1PH.

SMOLIY, Mr. Pavlo, ACA *2011;* 173 Buckhurst Way, BUCKHURST HILL, IG9 6JA.

SMOLLETT, Mrs. Susan Caroline, BA ACA *1986;* 20 Gresham Street, LONDON, EC2V 7JE.

SMOUHA, Mr. Brian Andrew, MA FCA *1964;* 97 West Eaton Place Mews, LONDON, SW1X 8LY.

SMOUT, Mr. Geoffrey John, BA ACA *1991;* 66 Mayfield Road, SUTTON, SM2 5DT.

SMOUT, Mrs. Karen Denise, BA ACA *1995;* 5 The Gardens, Raydon, IPSWICH, IP7 5LU.

SMULAND, Mr. John Martinon, BSc FCA *1978;* 107a Colebrook Street, WINCHESTER, HAMPSHIRE, SO23 9LH.

SMULLEN, Miss. May, FCA *1956;* 15 The Meads, Northchurch, BERKHAMSTED, HP4 3QX. (Life Member)

•**SMULOVITCH, Mrs. Judith, FCA CTA** *1974;* Gerald Kreditor & Co, Hallswelle House, 1 Hallswelle Road, LONDON, NW11 0DH.

•**SMULOVITCH, Dr. Peter Phillip, PhD FCA CTA** *1975;* Gerald Kreditor & Co, Hallswelle House, 1 Hallswelle Road, LONDON, NW11 0DH.

SMURTHWAITE, Mr. John, FCA *1955;* 4 Beeches Walk, Tiddington, STRATFORD-UPON-AVON, WARWICKSHIRE, CV37 7AT. (Life Member)

SMURTHWAITE, Mr. Jonathan, BA ACA *2005;* 136 St. Johns Road, KETTERING, NORTHAMPTONSHIRE, NN15 5AT.

SMY, Mr. David Charles, FCA *1975;* Beaufort Rise, London Road, BATH, BA1 6PZ.

•**SMY, Mr. Michael David, BA FCA** *1975;* (Tax Fac), Michael Smy, 12 Woodditton Road, NEWMARKET, Suffolk, CB8 9BQ.

•**SMY, Mr. Nicholas, BSc ACA** *1991;* Thomas Westcott, Timberly, South Street, AXMINSTER, DEVON, EX13 5AD.

SMYE-RUMSBY, Mr. Gregory Peter, MMath ACA *2010;* 71 Baizdon Road, LONDON, SE3 0UN.

SMYK, Mrs. Catherine, BSc ACA ATII *1992;* (Tax Fac), 22 Redland Court Road, Redland, BRISTOL, BS6 7EQ.

SMYLLIE, Mr. Alastair James, ACA *2008;* (Tax Fac), 18 Penny Close, Longlevens, GLOUCESTER, GL2 0NP.

SMYRNIOU, Miss. Oriana, BA ACA *1989;* PO Box 27373, NICOSIA, CYPRUS.

SMYTH, Mr. Alastair Tudor, BSc FCA *1974;* 24 Brewster Lane, Wainfleet, SKEGNESS, PE24 4QJ.

SMYTH, Mrs. Alison Sarah, BA ACA *2005;* 4 High Street, Langford, BIGGLESWADE, BEDFORDSHIRE, SG18 9RR.

•**SMYTH, Mr. Andrew David, BA ACA** *1994;* Ernst & Young LLP, 1 More London Place, LONDON, SE1 2AF. See also Ernst & Young Europe LLP

SMYTH, Mr. Benjamin Noel, BA ACA *2006;* Flat 10, Bowyer House, 14 Slievemore Close, LONDON, SW4 6BZ.

SMYTH, Mr. David Anthony, BSc FCA *1975;* 68 Webster Gardens, Ealing, LONDON, W5 5NH.

•**SMYTH, Mr. David Hugh, FCA** *1977;* WKH, 22/24 Kneesworth Street, ROYSTON, SG8 5AA. See also Virtual Business Source Limited

SMYTH, Mr. David Michael, FCA *1972;* 118 Brownhill Road, Chandler's Ford, EASTLEIGH, HAMPSHIRE, SO53 2FL.

SMYTH, Mr. Edward Joseph, BSc ACA *1999;* Norbrook Laboratories Ltd, Carnbane Industrial Estate, NEWRY, COUNTY DOWN, BT35 6QQ.

SMYTH, Miss. Elaine Mary, BA ACA *1992;* 9 Holmwood Road, Didsbury, MANCHESTER, M20 3JY.

SMYTH, Mr. Gerard Evelyn Raymond, FCA *1959;* Thorns Cottage, Down Road, North Wraxall, CHIPPENHAM, SN14 7AP. (Life Member)
•**SMYTH, Mr. Gregory David, BA ACA** *2005;* Smyth & Co Limited, 4 High Street, Langford, BIGGLESWADE, BEDFORDSHIRE, SG18 9RR.
SMYTH, Mr. Harvey John, BSc ACA *1994;* Staithe House, Chiswick Mall, Chiswick, LONDON, W4 2PR.
SMYTH, Mrs. Helen Jane, BA ACA *1996;* 77 Killane Road, LIMAVADY, COUNTY LONDONDERRY, BT49 0DL.
•**SMYTH, Mr. Hugh Francis, FCA** *1967;* 7 Grange Lane, FORMBY, L37 7BR.
SMYTH, Mr. James Francis, MSc ACA *1989;* 35 Willifield Way, LONDON, NW11 7XU.
SMYTH, Mrs. Jenny Louise, MMath ACA *2007;* 12 Hofstrasse, 8032 ZURICH, SWITZERLAND.
SMYTH, Mr. Jonathan Alexander, ACA *2011;* Flat 29 Q2, Watlington Street, READING, RG1 4AY.
SMYTH, Miss. Lucy Joanne, BA(Hons) ACA *2001;* Newcastle City Council, Baras Bridge, NEWCASTLE UPON TYNE, NE99 1RD.
SMYTH, Mr. Mark Howard Lee, BSc ACA *1993;* 4 Keswick Mews, LONDON, W5 5PG.
SMYTH, Mr. Michael James, FCA *1952;* 6 The Priory, GODSTONE, SURREY, RH9 8NL. (Life Member)
SMYTH, Miss. Millicent Emma Janet, MEng ACA *2003;* 8 Wychwood Crescent, Earley, READING, RG6 5RA.
SMYTH, Mr. Nicholas Robin, LLB ACA *1998;* Hill House La Rue Au Moestre, St. Brelade, JERSEY, JE3 8AE.
•**SMYTH, Mr. Oliver Richard, FCA** *1991;* Harris Carr Ltd, Cheriton, Farnham Lane, HASLEMERE, SURREY, GU27 1HD.
SMYTH, Mr. Oliver Thomas, ACA *2008;* Frimanns gate 24b, 0165 OSLO, NORWAY.
SMYTH, Mr. Robert Franklin, BSc ACA FIoD FRSA MBA CDir *2008;* 3 Tangier Road, GUILDFORD, SURREY, GU1 2DE.
SMYTH, Mr. Timothy Wallace, BSc FCA *1973;* 8 St Matthew Avenue, SURBITON, KT6 6JJ. (Life Member)
SMYTH, Mrs. Wendy, ACA *1980;* Holly House, Burtonhole Lane, Mill Hill, LONDON, NW7 1AZ.
SMYTH, Mr. William Arthur, BA FCA *1963;* 6 Oxford Street, HEREFORD, HR4 0DP.
SMYTH-OSBOURNE, Mrs. Annabel Claire, BA ACA *1997;* Bullington Manor, Sutton Scotney, WINCHESTER, HAMPSHIRE, SO21 3RD.
SMYTH-OSBOURNE, Mr. Michael Alexander, BSc ACA *1993;* Mallett Plc, 141 New Bond Street, LONDON, W1S 2BS.
SMYTHE, Mr. Anthony Kenneth, BA FCA *1990;* Interserve Plc, Interserve House, Ruscombe Park, Ruscombe, READING, RG10 9JU.
SMYTHE, Mrs. Carol-Anne, BA ACA *1990;* Haseley Cottage, Five Ways, Haseley, WARWICK, CV35 7HD.
SMYTHE, Mrs. Julianne Kathryn, BA ACA *1992;* Maple, Dibden Hill, CHALFONT ST. GILES, BUCKINGHAMSHIRE, HP8 4RD.
SMYTHE, Mr. Paul Francis, FCA *1970;* Gate Cottage, Uffington, FARINGDON, SN7 7SG.
SMYTHE, Mr. Stewart, BSc ACA *2000;* Warwick Lodge Soldridge Road, Medstead, ALTON, HAMPSHIRE, GU34 5JF.
SNADDON, Mr. Colin Douglas, ACA CA(SA) *2009;* Flat H/21 Du Cane Court, Balham High Road, LONDON, SW17 7JS.
SNAILHAM, Mr. Christopher Charles, BSc ACA *2004;* Deutsche Bank, Winchester House, 1 Great Winchester Street, LONDON, EC2N 2DB.
•**SNAITH, Mr. Christopher John, FCA** *1975;* (Tax Fac), Christopher J. Snaith, Tarn House, 55 The Meadows, Leven, BEVERLEY, HU17 5LX.
•**SNAITH, Mr. Malcolm, FCA** *1976;* Northfield Accountancy Services, Unit 2, St Catherines Court, Sunderland Enterprise Park, SUNDERLAND, TYNE AND WEAR SR5 3XJ.
SNAITH, Mr. Michael Jonathan, BA FCA *1980;* Industrial & Financial Systems UK Ltd Artisan, Hillbottom Road Sands Industrial Estate, HIGH WYCOMBE, BUCKINGHAMSHIRE, HP12 4HJ.
SNAITH, Mrs. Sarah Dawn, BA(Hons) ACA *2001;* 58 Park Mount, HARPENDEN, HERTFORDSHIRE, AL5 3AR.
SNAITH, Mr. Steven James, LLB FCA *1990;* PricewaterhouseCoopers, White Square Office Center, 10 Butyrsky Val, 125047 MOSCOW, RUSSIAN FEDERATION.
SNAPE, Mrs. Andrea Carole, BSc ACA *1998;* 5 Anthea Road, PAIGNTON, DEVON, TQ3 1JY.
SNAPE, Mr. Antony Paul Alfred, BCom ACA *1980;* Wilkinson Corporation LTD, Shield Drive, Wardley Industrial Estate, Worsley, MANCHESTER, M28 2WD.
SNAPE, Ms. Caroline, BA ACA *2006;* 2 Crosby Road, BOLTON, BL1 4EL.
SNAPE, Mr. Charles Neil, FCA *1966;* 18 Burrows Vale, Brixworth, NORTHAMPTON, NORTHAMPTONSHIRE, NN6 9US.
SNAPE, Mr. David Brereton, FCA *1953;* 9 Bollin Grove, Prestbury, MACCLESFIELD, CHESHIRE, SK10 4JJ. (Life Member)
•**SNAPE, Mr. George, FCA** *1972;* (Tax Fac), George Snape, 214 High Street, WINSFORD, CW7 2AU.
•**SNAPE, Mr. Gerald Paul, FCA** *1976;* GPS Accounting Services, 172 Croston Road, Farington Moss Leyland, PRESTON, PR26 6PQ.
SNAPE, Mr. Ian Leslie, BSc FCA *1977;* The Coach House, West Common Road, KESTON, KENT, BR2 6AJ.
SNAPE, Miss. Jeanette, BA(Hons) ACA *2001;* 90 Sandalwood, Westhoughton, BOLTON, BL5 2RQ.
SNAPE, Mrs. Keiko, BSc ACA *1981;* The Coach House, West Common Road, KESTON, KENT, BR2 6AJ.
SNAPE, Mr. Nigel Ruskin, BA ACA *1988;* The Paddocks, Colchester Road, Chappel, COLCHESTER, CO6 2DQ.
SNAPE, Mr. Paul, BA ACA *1997;* with KPMG LLP, 15 Canada Square, LONDON, E14 5GL.
SNAPE, Mr. Roy, FCA *1956;* 55 Vere Road, Kirkmuirhill, LANARK, ML11 9RP. (Life Member)
SNAREY, Mrs. Rebecca, BSc ACA *2004;* Fidelity, Kingswood Fields, Millfield Lane, Lower Kingswood, TADWORTH, SURREY KT20 6RP.
SNARY, Mr. Jonathan, MA(Oxon) ACA FCCA *1997;* B P P Bristol Ltd B P P House, Grove Avenue, BRISTOL, BS1 4QY.
SNEAD, Mr. Stephen Michael, BA ACA *1997;* 40 Quarry Lane, Red Lake, TELFORD, TF1 5EB.
SNEATH, Miss. Anna Jane, BSc ACA *2010;* Flat 47, Templar House, Shoot up Hill, LONDON, NW2 3TD.
SNEATH, Mr. Christopher George, FCA *1957;* Ascot House, Paradise Drive, EASTBOURNE, EAST SUSSEX, BN20 7SX. (Life Member)
SNEDDEN, Mrs. Donna Lea, BSc ACA *2007;* 14 Adelaide Close, LEICESTER, LE4 2NZ.
SNEDDEN, Mr. Ian Francis, ACA CA(NZ) *2009;* Flat 3, 61 Warwick Road, LONDON, SW5 9HB.
SNEDDON, Mr. Alexander, FCA *1966;* 30 Hepscott Drive, WHITLEY BAY, NE25 9XJ.
•**SNEDDON CHOW, Mrs. Selina Yuen Yi, ACA** *2006;* Ho Sneddon Chow CPA Ltd, Unit 1202 Mirror Tower, 61 Mody Road, TSIM SHA TSUI, HONG KONG SAR. See also Ho Sneddon Chow
•**SNEDKER, Mr. Neil Douglas, BA ACA** *1986;* Snedkers Accountants Ltd, Angel House, Hardwick, WITNEY, OXFORDSHIRE, OX29 7QE.
SNELGAR, Mrs. Alison Margaret, LLB ACA CTA *2001;* (Tax Fac), 22 Lower St Helens Road, SOUTHAMPTON, HAMPSHIRE, SO30 0LW.
SNELGAR, Mr. Eric Frank, FCA *1947;* Livery Hill Farmhouse, Livery Road, Winterslow, SALISBURY, SP5 1RJ. (Life Member)
SNELL, Mrs. Amy, ACA *2007;* 2 Epsom Crescent, NEWBURY, RG14 7TR.
SNELL, Mr. Andrew David, BSc FCA *1989;* 23 THe Holloway, Compton, WOLVERHAMPTON, WV6 8LH.
SNELL, Mr. Andrew Peter, MA(Oxon) ACA *2006;* CRA International, 1155 Avenue of the Americas, 18th Floor, NEW YORK, NY 10036, UNITED STATES.
•**SNELL, Mr. David Alan, BSc ACA** *1989;* PricewaterhouseCoopers LLP, 1 Embankment Place, LONDON, WC2N 6RH. See also PricewaterhouseCoopers
SNELL, Mr. David Christopher, MPA BSc ACA *1990;* The Treasury, PO Box 3724, WELLINGTON 6140, NEW ZEALAND.
SNELL, Mr. David John, FCA *1968;* Orchard Cottage, Alcester Road, Wootton Wawen, HENLEY-IN-ARDEN, WEST MIDLANDS, B95 6BQ.
SNELL, Mr. John William, FCA *1960;* Hazelwood House, Merlin Coppice, Apley, TELFORD, SHROPSHIRE, TF1 6TB. (Life Member)
SNELL, Miss. Julia, BA ACA *2003;* 85 Albert Road, LONDON, N22 7AG.
SNELL, Mr. Mark James, BA ACA *2004;* 14 Hogarth Road, HOVE, EAST SUSSEX, BN3 5RG.
•**SNELL, Mr. Martin John, FCA** *1980;* John Snell Ltd, 302 Hursley Road, Chandlers Ford, EASTLEIGH, SO53 5PF.
SNELL, Mr. Michael Clive, FCA *1970;* Living Streets Universal House, 88-94 Wentworth Street, LONDON, E1 7SA.
SNELL, Mr. Peter, FCA *1968;* Old Quinings, Old Quinings Down Street, West Ashling, CHICHESTER, WEST SUSSEX, PO18 8DS.
SNELL, Mr. Roger Harley, FCA *1956;* 10 Conference Place, LYMINGTON, SO41 3TQ. (Life Member)
SNELL, Mrs. Victoria, ACA *2010;* Privolnaya ul. d.61 k.1 kv. 198, 109431 MOSCOW, RUSSIAN FEDERATION.
SNELLGROVE, Mr. Clive, BSc ACA *2003;* Ashley House, Kirtleton Avenue, WEYMOUTH, DORSET, DT4 7JL.
SNELLING, Mr. Andrew Edward, BA ACA *1987;* Sheffield International Venues, Don Valley Stadium, Worksop Road, SHEFFIELD, S9 3TL.
SNELLING, Mr. Christopher Anthony Peter, FCA *1972;* 118 Pixmore Way, LETCHWORTH GARDEN CITY, SG6 3TR.
•**SNELLING, Mr. Gordon Ronald Lindsey, ACA** *1982;* Charter Trust Company Ltd, PO Box 134, Town Mills, Trinity Square, St Peter Port, GUERNSEY GY1 3HN.
•**SNELLING, Mr. Jean-Philippe Albion, ACA** *2000;* (Tax Fac), Nihonbo, PO Box 497, GODALMING, GU8 5WB. See also Nihonbo Ltd
SNELLING, Miss. Marie-Louise Hella, MA ACA *2000;* J Sainsbury Plc, 33 Holborn, LONDON, EC1N 2HT.
SNELLING, Mr. Nicholas Paul, BA ACA *1992;* 13 Bostock Hill East, PAGET PG 02, BERMUDA.
SNELLING, Miss. Olwen Margaret, FCA *1974;* 89 High Street, Hadleigh, IPSWICH, IP7 5EA.
•**SNELLING, Mr. Richard Hugh, FCA** *1970;* Richard H. Snelling, 9 West Hill, Sanderstead, SOUTH CROYDON, Surrey, CR2 0SB.
SNELLING, Mr. Richard Neil James, BA ACA DChA *1989;* with Menzies LLP, Heathrow Business Centre, 65 High Street, EGHAM, SURREY, TW20 9EY.
SNELLING, Mr. Robin Christopher, ACA *1980;* 46 Chirnside Drive, CHIRNSIDE PARK, VIC 3116, AUSTRALIA.
SNELLING, Mr. Stephen John, BA ACA *1996;* 17 Thornfield Road, BISHOP'S STORTFORD, HERTFORDSHIRE, CM23 2RB.
SNELLING-NASH, Mrs. Christine Anne, BSc ACA *1993;* 33 Church Lane, Kimpton, HITCHIN, SG4 8RR.
SNELSON, Mrs. Helen Louise, BA ACA *2000;* Quarter Moon Cottage, 1 Long Hedge Lane, Worthington, ASHBY-DE-LA-ZOUCH, LEICESTERSHIRE, LE65 1RL.
•**SNELSON, Mrs. Kathleen, FCA CTA** *1975;* Snelson & Co, 26 Denholme, Upholland, SKELMERSDALE, WN8 0AU.
SNELSON, Mr. Michael, BCom ACA *2006;* 14 St. Helena Road, BRISTOL, BS6 7NR.
SNELSON, Mrs. Shelley, BSc ACA *2006;* 14 St. Helena Road, BRISTOL, BS6 7NR.
SNELSON, Mr. Thomas Robert, MA(Hons) ACA *2010;* 10 Holloway, BATH, BA2 4PT.
•**SNELUS, Mr. Richard Mark, MA FCA** *1973;* Monahans, Clarks Mill, Stallard Street, TROWBRIDGE, BA14 8HH.
SNG, Mr. Eng Juay, FCA *1972;* 8 Webb Street, MITTAGONG, NSW 2575, AUSTRALIA.
SNG, Mrs. Hup Suan, FCA *1966;* 88 Siglap Drive, SINGAPORE 456187, SINGAPORE.
SNG, Mr. Ngiap Koon, ACA *1980;* 6 Jalan Sri Hartamas 12, Sri Hartamas, 50480 KUALA LUMPUR, FEDERAL TERRITORY, MALAYSIA.
SNIDVONGSE, Mrs. Phenkae, BA FCA *1958;* 16 Sukhumuit 31, BANGKOK 10110, THAILAND. (Life Member)
SNIPE, Mr. Daniel, ACA *2009;* 40a, Beatrice Road, LONDON, N4 4PD.
SNITTER, Mr. Anthony John Godfrey, FCA *1949;* 76 Brookmead, Hildenborough, TONBRIDGE, TN11 9EZ. (Life Member)
SNOAD, Mr. Jeremy Paul, MA ACA *1987;* 37 Watten Heights, SINGAPORE 287469, SINGAPORE.
SNODGRASS, Mrs. Heather Lynn, BCom ACA *2002;* 17 Hereford Close, EPSOM, KT18 5DZ.
•**SNODGRASS, Mr. Norman Henry, FCA** *1975;* Mayes Business Partnership Ltd, 22-28 Willow Street, ACCRINGTON, LANCASHIRE, BB5 1LP.
SNOOK, Mr. Alan, FCA *1977;* (Tax Fac), with Reeves & Co LLP, 37 St. Margarets Street, CANTERBURY, KENT, CT1 2TU.
SNOOK, Mr. Alexander Paul, BSc ACA *2007;* 30 Rose Avenue, Horsforth, LEEDS, LS18 4QE.
•**SNOOK, Mrs. Alison Jane, FCA** *1986;* with Target Consulting Limited, Bloxam Court, Corporation Street, RUGBY, WARWICKSHIRE, CV21 2DU.
SNOOK, Mr. Andrew, MSci ACA *2009;* R & J Snook, Westover Farm, Wootton Fitzpaine, BRIDPORT, DORSET, DT6 6NE.
SNOOK, Mr. Andrew Michael, BA ACA *1991;* 2 Harrier Close, Worsley, MANCHESTER, M28 7AH.
SNOOK, Mrs. Catherine Anne, BSc ACA *1990;* 2 Harrier Close, Worsley, MANCHESTER, M28 7AH.
SNOOK, Mr. Duncan Cyril, ACA *1991;* 12 Welland Close, Long Lawford, RUGBY, CV23 9SX.
SNOOK, Mr. George Frank William, FCA FCMA *1954;* 3 Robert Smith Cottages, London Street, Brancaster, KING'S LYNN, PE31 8AS. (Life Member)
SNOOK, Mr. John Thomas, MA ACA *1979;* The Oaks, Tag Lane, Hare Hatch Wargrave, READING, RG10 9ST.
SNOOK, Mrs. Julie Alexandra, BSc ACA *1992;* Bradford Chamber of Commerce Devere House, Vicar Lane, BRADFORD, WEST YORKSHIRE, BD1 5AH.
SNOOK, Mrs. Laura, MA ACA *1991;* 26 The Crescent, SOLIHULL, B91 1JR.
SNOOK, Mr. Peter Kenneth, BSc ACA *1986;* 138 Radnor Avenue, WELLING, DA16 2BY.
•**SNOOK, Mr. Richard George, FCA** *1968;* W.Y.Thomson & Co, 7 Telgarth Road, Ferring, WORTHING, WEST SUSSEX, BN12 5PX.
•**SNOOK, Mr. Stephen Richard, BSc ACA** *1991;* PricewaterhouseCoopers LLP, Cornwall Court, 19 Cornwall Street, BIRMINGHAM, B3 2DT.
SNOOKS, Mr. Ian Temple, FCA *1969;* 7 Waterloo Road, Edgmond, NEWPORT, SHROPSHIRE, TF10 8EW.
SNOW, Miss. Anna Margaret, BA ACA *1982;* 8 Meredyth Road, Barnes, LONDON, SW13 0DY.
SNOW, Mr. Benjamin George, ACA *2009;* 10a Barmouth Road, LONDON, SW18 2DN.
SNOW, Mr. Benjamin Richard, MA BA ACA *2002;* 61 Upper South Wraxall, BRADFORD-ON-AVON, WILTSHIRE, BA15 2SE.
SNOW, Miss. Emma Josephine, MChem ACA DChA *2005;* 46 Reverdy Road, LONDON, SE1 5QD.
SNOW, Mr. Ernest James, FCA *1977;* 21 Hayes Garden, BROMLEY, BR2 7DQ.
SNOW, Mr. Geoffrey Bernard, FCA *1961;* Archways, Stanley Moss Lane, Stockton Brook, STOKE-ON-TRENT, ST9 9LH. (Life Member)
SNOW, Mrs. Helen Mary, FCA *1982;* 2 Broxfield Close, Oadby, LEICESTER, LE2 5WJ.
SNOW, Mr. Ian, BSc ACA *1998;* 468 Fulwood Road, SHEFFIELD, S10 3GH.
SNOW, Mr. James Richard Anthony, BSocSc ACA *1992;* 6 2nd Street, BROOKLYN, NY 11231, UNITED STATES.
SNOW, Miss. Joanne Marie, BSc ACA *1996;* 1 Poulton Crescent, Woolston, WARRINGTON, WA1 4QW.
SNOW, Mr. Jonathan Paul, BSc ACA *1995;* 13 Sea View Estate, Netley Abbey, SOUTHAMPTON, SO31 5BP.
SNOW, Mr. Matthew Richard, BA ACA *2003;* 29 Station Road, Menston, ILKLEY, LS29 6JH.
SNOW, Mr. Michael Stephen, BA ACA *1978;* 2 Broxfield Close, Oadby, LEICESTER, LE2 5WJ.
SNOW, Mr. Reginald John, FCA *1955;* Stoneybridge House, Martley, WORCESTER, WR6 6QB. (Life Member)
SNOW, Mr. Richard Charles, MA ACA *1991;* 11 Ashington Road, LONDON, SW6 3QJ.
SNOW, Mr. Thomas George, BA ACA *1981;* Walnut House, 6A Brandy Hole Lane, CHICHESTER, WEST SUSSEX, PO19 5RJ.
SNOW, Mr. William Henry Robert Esdaile, BA ACA *1983;* Ibthorp, Kings Road, BERKHAMSTED, HERTFORDSHIRE, HP4 3BP.
SNOWBALL, Mr. David Matthew, ACA *2008;* 37 White Clover Square, LYMM, CHESHIRE, WA13 0RX.
SNOWBALL, Mr. John, BSc FCA *1986;* 27 St Oswalds Court, NEWTON AYCLIFFE, DL5 4DD.
SNOWBALL, Mr. John Edward, FCA *1964;* Roseberry, 3 Netherby Rise, DARLINGTON, COUNTY DURHAM, DL3 8SE.
SNOWBALL, Mr. Joseph, FCA *1968;* 33 Meek Road, NEWENT, GL18 1UA.
SNOWBALL, Mr. Thomas Edward James, BSc ACA *2010;* Flat 26 Pimlico Appartments, 60 Vauxhall Bridge Road, LONDON, SW1V 2RD.
SNOWDEN, Miss. Amanda Louise, BA ACA *1997;* 50 Brock Hill, Runwell, WICKFORD, ESSEX, SS11 7NR.
SNOWDEN, Mr. Andrew James, BSc ACA *1989;* 12 Waterfront House, 20 Lombard Road, LONDON, SW11 3RU.
SNOWDEN, Mr. David James, FCA *1961;* 317 Bishopville Loop, THE VILLAGES, FL 32162, UNITED STATES.
SNOWDEN, Mr. Geoffrey John, BSc ACA *2005;* Downlands, Salcombe Hill, SIDMOUTH, DEVON, EX10 0NX.
SNOWDEN, Mr. John Barry, FCA *1963;* 10 Sycamore Avenue, HATFIELD, AL10 8LZ.
•**SNOWDEN, Mr. John Frederick Hugh, BA FCA** *1981;* (Tax Fac), Snowden & Co, Dial House, High Street, Hook Norton, BANBURY, OXFORDSHIRE OX15 5NQ.

SNOWDEN, Mr. Kenneth George, FCA *1951;* 6 The Avenue, Ingol, PRESTON, PR2 7AX. (Life Member)
SNOWDEN, Mr. Richard, ACA *2009;* 3 Caldervale Road, LONDON, SW4 9LY.
SNOWDEN, Mr. Richard Frank, FCA *1950;* 17 Hall Close, Kibworth Harcourt, LEICESTER, LE8 0ND. (Life Member)
SNOWDEN, Mr. Thomas Edward, MEng ACA *2001;* Zenith Vehicle Contracts Ltd Anglia House, 1-3 Holly Park Mills Woodhall Road Calverley, PUDSEY, LS28 5QS.
SNOWDEN, Mr. Trevor David, FCA *1960;* Keynsham Cottage, Woolaston, LYDNEY, GL15 6PY.
SNOWDON, Mr. Clive John, BA FCA *1977;* New End Barn, Spernal Lane, Great Alne, ALCESTER, B49 6JD.
SNOWDON, Mr. David John, BSc FCA *1970;* 24 South Approach, Moor Park, NORTHWOOD, HA6 2ET.
SNOWDON, Mr. Derek Rochester, FCA *1959;* 5 Riverdale Court, KENDAL, CUMBRIA, LA9 7LQ. (Life Member)
SNOWDON, Mrs. Donna Mary, BSc ACA *2002;* 1a Russetts Drive, FLEET, HAMPSHIRE, GU51 3XE.
①SNOWDON, Mr. James Alexander, BA ACA *2000;* 76 Park Road, BECKENHAM, KENT, BR3 1QH.
SNOWLING, Mr. Malcolm Charles, ACA *1985;* 24 Booker Close, CROWBOROUGH, EAST SUSSEX, TN6 2XT.
SNOWLING, Mr. Martin James, ACA MAAT *2001;* (Tax Fac), July House Lower Farm Road, Ringshall, STOWMARKET, SUFFOLK, IP14 2JE.
•SNOXALL, Mr. Richard John, BSc FCA *1978;* Rowland Hall, 44-54 Orsett Road, GRAYS, RM17 5ED.
SNOXHILL, Mr. Douglas James, FCA *1948;* Highbanks, South Park, SEVENOAKS, TN13 1EL. (Life Member)
SNUDDEN, Mrs. Janet Diane, ACA *1986;* Readers Trading Limited, 79 Place Road, COWES, ISLE OF WIGHT, PO31 7AF.
SNYDER, Mr. Heath Lee, BA ACA *1995;* Deloitte & Touche Financial Advisory, 6 Shenton Way #32-00, DBS Building Tower Two, SINGAPORE 068809, SINGAPORE.
•SNYDER, Sir Michael John, FCA *1973;* (Tax Fac), Kingston Smith LLP, Devonshire House, 60 Goswell Road, LONDON, EC1M 7AD. See also Kingston Smith Limited Liability Partnership, Devonshire Corporate Services LLP, Kingston Smith Consulting LLP, Kingston Smith Services Limited and Devonshire Corporate Finance Limited
SNYMAN, Mr. Hendrik Johannes, ACA CA(SA) *2009;* 1st Floor, Atlantic House, 4 - 8 Circular Road, Douglas, ISLE OF MAN, IM1 1AG.
SO, Mr. Chi Fai Anka, ACA *2008;* Flat F 44/F Robinson Place Tower 2, 70 Robinson Road, MID LEVELS, HONG KONG ISLAND, HONG KONG SAR.
SO, Mr. Clarence, ACA *2011;* 11 Trevelyan, BRACKNELL, BERKSHIRE, RG12 8YD.
SO, Miss. Gerry, BSc ACA *2004;* 12 Lovell Place, Ropemaker Road, LONDON, SE16 6QQ.
SO, Miss. Ivy Yu Wai, BSc ACA *2009;* B Z W, 10 South Colonnade, LONDON, E14 4PU.
SO, Mr. Kai Tong Stanley, ACA *2008;* Stanley So & Co, 1405 Cosco Tower, 183 Queens Road, CENTRAL, HONG KONG ISLAND, HONG KONG SAR.
SO, Mr. Kang Wong, ACA *2008;* Flat A, 16/F, Jade Mansion, 28-32 Fort Street, NORTH POINT, HONG KONG ISLAND HONG KONG SAR.
SO, Mr. Kin Hing, ACA *2005;* Flat E 18/F, Block 2 Waterside Plaza, 38 Wing Shun Street, TSUEN WAN, NEW TERRITORIES, HONG KONG SAR.
SO, Ms. Kit Yee Anita, ACA *2005;* Ernst & Young Transactions Limited, 62/F One Island East, 18 Westlands Road, Island East, QUARRY BAY, HONG KONG ISLAND HONG KONG SAR.
SO, Mr. Kui, ACA *2008;* 2nd Floor, 25 Luk Ming Street, TO KWA WAN, KOWLOON, HONG KONG SAR.
SO, Mr. Kwok Keung Keith, ACA *2008;* East Asia Sentinel Ltd, 22nd Floor, Tai Yau Building, 181 Johnston Road, WAN CHAI, HONG KONG SAR.
SO, Mr. Kwong Man, ACA *2006;* KMS CPA Limited, Suite 1912, 19th Floor, Tower 1 The Gateway, 25 Canton Road, TSIM SHA TSUI KOWLOON HONG KONG SAR.
SO, Dr. Peter Kwok Kin, ACA ACMA *2010;* 4th Floor Flat C, Block 1 Elegant Terrace, 36 Conduit Road, MID LEVELS, HONG KONG ISLAND, HONG KONG SAR.
SO, Mr. Sinclair Tat Peng, BSc ACA *2010;* with Stewart & Co, Knoll House, Knoll Road, CAMBERLEY, GU15 3SY.
SO, Mr. Stephen, MA ACA *1995;* 81 Chadwick Place, SURBITON, SURREY, KT6 5RG.
SO, Ms. Sylvia, ACA *2006;* Flat 1006 10/F, Block M, Kornhill, QUARRY BAY, HONG KONG ISLAND, HONG KONG SAR.
SO, Mr. Tung Cheong, ACA *2007;* Rm. 1609 Nan Fung Tower 173 Des Voeux Road Central, CENTRAL, HONG KONG SAR.
SO, Mr. Wai Bon, ACA *1986;* KPMG, 8th Floor Princes Building, Charter Road, CENTRAL, HONG KONG ISLAND, HONG KONG SAR.
SO, Mr. Yuen Hon Michael, ACA *2005;* Flat D 18/F. Block 1 Cascades, 93 Chung Hau Street, HO MAN TIN, KOWLOON, HONG KONG SAR.
SOAKELL, Mr. Peter, BA ACA *1989;* Barker And Stonehouse Ltd, Marsh Street, Cannon Park, MIDDLESBROUGH, TS1 5JH.
SOAMES, Mr. Michael, MSc ACA *2004;* 8 Townley Mill, Townley Street, MACCLESFIELD, CHESHIRE, SK11 6HY.
SOAN, Mr. Christopher Ian, BA(Hons) ACA *2002;* Room 2.12 2nd floor Armstrong Building, University of Newcastle upon Tyne, Claremont Road, NEWCASTLE UPON TYNE, NE1 7RU.
SOANE, Mr. Andrew Patrick, BSc ACA *1990;* Opus Dei Charitable Trust, 6 Orme Court, Bayswater, LONDON, W2 4RL.
SOANE, Mr. Paul Emile, FCA *1957;* 8795 E Iliff Drive, DENVER, CO 80231-3812, UNITED STATES. (Life Member)
SOANES, Mr. Christopher Michael, BSc FCA *1993;* Kewill Bramley House The Guildway, Old Portsmouth Road Artington, GUILDFORD, GU3 1LR.
SOANES, Mr. David Charles James, FCA *1962;* 2 The Watercourse, NEWMARKET, SUFFOLK, CB8 8LW. (Life Member)
SOANES, Mr. Ian Derek, BSc ACA *1993;* Hazel Barton, Chedington, BEAMINSTER, DORSET, DT8 3HY.
SOAR, Mr. Brian Francis, FCA *1961;* Flat 4, Woolbury House, High Street, STOCKBRIDGE, HAMPSHIRE, SO20 6HB.
•SOAR, Mr. Jeff, BSc(Hons) ACA *2001;* Ernst & Young LLP, 1 More London Place, LONDON, SE1 2AF. See also Ernst & Young Europe LLP
SOAR, Mr. Jeffrey, BA(Hons) ACA *2002;* 37 Chalsey Road, LONDON, SE4 1YN.
SOAR, Mr. Jonathan Charles, FCA *1969;* Paradise Farm, Burton Road, Needwood, BURTON-ON-TRENT, DE13 9PB. (Life Member)
SOAR, Ms. Lucy Jane, BA ACA *1997;* 9a Millers Road, BRIGHTON, BN1 5NP.
SOAR, Mr. Manjeet Singh, BA ACA *1991;* Haringvlietstraat 3 HG 1, 1078JX AMSTERDAM, NETHERLANDS.
SOAR, Mr. Martin Thomas, FCA *1977;* 113 St. Anthonys Avenue, WOODFORD GREEN, IG8 7EN.
SOAR, Mr. Peter, FCA *1977;* Osborne & Little Ltd, Riverside House, 26 Osiers Road, LONDON, SW18 1NH.
SOARDS, Mr. Christopher John, BEng ACA *1999;* 7 Barnard Close, Gorleston, GREAT YARMOUTH, NORFOLK, NR31 7RN.
SOARE, Mr. Vernon, ACA *2009;* with ICAEW, Chartered Accountants' Hall, Moorgate Place, LONDON, EC2P 2BJ.
•SOARES, Mr. Athanasio Luis Santana, FCA *1975;* Soares & Co., 1A Colin Parade, Edgware Road Colindale, LONDON, NW9 6SG.
SOAVE, Mr. Antonio Caspere, BA ACA *1998;* 43 Church Crescent, LONDON, N20 0JR.
•SOBELL, Mr. Melvyn Barry, FCA MAE FPC *1972;* Sobell Rhodes LLP, Monument House, 215 Marsh Road, PINNER, MIDDLESEX, HA5 5NE.
•SOBER, Mr. Anthony Lionel, BSc FCA FCIArb *1966;* (Tax Fac), Lubbock Fine, Russell Bedford House, City Forum, 250 City Road, LONDON, EC1V 2QQ. See also Russell Bedford Ltd
SOBER, Miss. Belinda Clare, BSc ACA *1988;* The Sycamores, 2B Dorset Road, Merton Park, LONDON, SW19 3HA.
SOBER, Mr. Phillip, FCA *1953;* 67b Clarendon Road, LONDON, W11 4JE. (Life Member)
SOBERG, Mr. Christian, MSci ACA *2005;* RBS Global Banking and Markets, RBS Tower, 88 Phillip Street, SYDNEY, NSW 2000, AUSTRALIA.
SOBHAN, Mr. Mohammad Gholam, FCA *1965;* 19 K.M. Das Lane, Tikatuly, DHAKA 1203, BANGLADESH. (Life Member)
SOBKE, Mr. Bodo, MSc ACA *1998;* Black & Decker Ltd, 210 Bath Road, SLOUGH, SL1 3YD.
SOBOWALE, Miss. Bukki, ACA *2008;* 91 Louisville Road, LONDON, SW17 8RN.
SOBRATEE, Miss. Leanne, BSc ACA *2010;* 28 Murray Drive, LEEDS, LS10 4GE.
SOBRATEE, Miss. Mumtaz Begum Yahya, BA ACA *2006;* 570 Tyburn Road, BIRMINGHAM, B24 9RS.
SOBTI, Mr. Parminder Pal, ACA *2005;* Aurobindo Pharma Ltd, Ares, Odyssey Business Park, West End Road, RUISLIP, MIDDLESEX HA4 6QD.
•SOCCI, Mr. James Francis, FCA *1981;* J.F. Socci & Co Limited, 83 Blackwood Road, Streetly, SUTTON COLDFIELD, WEST MIDLANDS, B74 3PW. See also Carroll Business Consulting Ltd
•SOCHALL, Mr. Brian Donald, BCom FCA *1972;* Sochalls, 9 Wimpole Street, LONDON, W1G 9SR. See also Auia
•SOCHIERA, Mrs. Juliet Elizabeth, BA FCA *1995;* Muhlbachweg 2, 69469 WEINHEIM, GERMANY.
SOCKER, Mr. Marc Nathan, BCom ACA *2003;* Invesco UK Ltd, 43-45 Portman Square, LONDON, W1H 6LY.
SOCKETT, Mr. Greville William Talbot, MA FCA *1963;* Pipits, 26 Meadow View Close, Haylands, RYDE, ISLE OF WIGHT, PO33 3EY. (Life Member)
SOCKETT, Mr. Martin John, BSc ACA *2002;* Office Depot, Hoods Close, LEICESTER, LE4 2BN.
SOCRATOUS, Mr. Christoforos, BA ACA *2007;* PO Box 60363, 8102 PAFOS, CYPRUS.
SOCRATOUS, Mr. Socratis Evagora, BSc FCA *1992;* SIS, 38 Karaiskaki Street, KANIKA Alexander Center, Block 1, Office 113 C/D, PC 3032 LIMASSOL CYPRUS.
SODAWALA, Mr. Hatimali Taherali, FCA *1963;* 7 Ascot Mews, WALLINGTON, SM6 9PQ.
SODAWALA, Mr. Zakiyuddin Taherali, FCA *1973;* 23 Lynton Road, CHESHAM, HP5 2BU. (Life Member)
SODEN, Mr. Adrian Carl, BA ACA *1993;* 7 Turners Drive, Totteridge Road, HIGH WYCOMBE, HP13 7PA.
SODEN, Miss. Christine Helen, BSc ACA *1981;* 8 Ridge Way, VIRGINIA WATER, GU25 4TE.
SODEN, Mr. David Philip, BSc ACA *2006;* with Deloitte LLP, Athene Place, 66 Shoe Lane, LONDON, EC4A 3BQ.
SODEN, Mr. John Francis, BSc FCA *1979;* 98 Alleyn Road, LONDON, SE21 8AH.
SODEN, Mr. Matthew James, BSc(Hons) ACA *2004;* (Tax Fac), 15 Thorold Road, FARNHAM, GU9 7JY.
•SODEN, Miss. Melanie Sue, ACA *1988;* Woodlands, Copse Lane, Walberton, ARUNDEL, WEST SUSSEX, BN18 0QH.
SODERSTROM, Mr. Rolf-Kristian Berndtson, BA ACA *1993;* Chalks, Manor Lane, West Hendred, WANTAGE, OXFORDSHIRE, OX12 8RX.
•SODHA, Mr. Ashok Maganlal, FCA *1979;* Ashmans, Zone G, Salamander Quay West, Park Lane, Harefield, UXBRIDGE MIDDLESEX UB9 6NZ.
•SODHA, Mr. Kamal, BA FCA *1982;* (Tax Fac), KAS & Co (UK) Limited, 95 Vivian Road, BIRMINGHAM, B17 0DR.
•SODHA, Mr. Kishorkumar Ratilal, FCA *1977;* Harrison Reeds, 59 Kynance Gardens, STANMORE, HA7 2QJ.
SODHA, Mr. Paresh Kumar Amratlal, ACA *1985;* UBS Global Asset Management, Pelikanstrass 6/8, 8098 ZURICH, SWITZERLAND.
SODHA, Mr. Sunil, BSc ACA CFA *2002;* 1a Barham Road, SOUTH CROYDON, SURREY, CR2 6LD.
•SODHI, Mr. Anup Singh, BSc ACA *1999;* with Ernst & Young LLP, 1 More London Place, LONDON, SE1 2AF.
SODHI, Miss. Priya, ACA *2010;* Flat A 809 Nav Nirman, CGHS Plot No 6A, Sector 2, Dwarka Sub City, NEW DELHI 75, INDIA.
SOERAKOESOEMAH, Dr. Moehamad, FCA *1964;* Jl. Golf Barat XII/13, Arcamanik, BANDUNG, 40293, INDONESIA. (Life Member)
•SOETING, Mr. Michiel, ACA *2011;* KPMG Europe LLP, 15 Canada Square, LONDON, E14 5GL.
SOFAT, Mr. Janardan, BSc FCA *1983;* 47 Pilgrims Road, North Halling, ROCHESTER, ME2 1HN.
SOFER, Mr. Yousef Arther Moshi Dawood, FCA *1968;* 12 St. Johns Wood Park, LONDON, NW8 6QP.
•SOFIANOS, Mr. Nicolaos, BSc FCA *1981;* Deloitte Hadjipavlou Sofianos & Cambanis S.A, 3a Fragoklissias & Granikou Str, Maroussi, 15125 ATHENS, GREECE.
SOFOCLEOUS, Mr. Alexander, ACA *2008;* 23 Psaron Street, Agios Tychonas, 4521 LIMASSOL, CYPRUS.
SOFOCLEOUS, Ms. Aloe, BSc ACA *2003;* PricewaterhouseCoopers Limited City House 6 Karaiskakis Street, CY-3032 LIMASSOL, CYPRUS.
SOFOCLEOUS, Ms. Eleni, BSc ACA *2003;* 13A Tasou Isaak, Mesa Yitonia, 4004 LIMASSOL, CYPRUS.
•SOFOCLEOUS, Mr. Sofoclis, BA FCA *1990;* KPMG, 2 Sotiras Street, P O Box 33200, 5280 PARALIMNI, CYPRUS. See also KPMG Metaxas Loizides Syrimis
SOFOKLEOUS, Miss. Maria, BSc ACA *2010;* Eleftherias 4, Yeri, NICOSIA, CYPRUS.
SOGA, Mr. Shingo, MEng ACA *2010;* 14a Westow Street, LONDON, SE19 3AH.
SOGBETUN, Mrs. Temidire, ACA *2008;* 66 Boxley Street, LONDON, E16 2AN.
SOH, Miss. Cheng Lin, FCA *1975;* 99 Tai Hwan Heights, SINGAPORE 555444, SINGAPORE.
SOH, Mr. Daniel Po-Chuan, ACA *2008;* 113 Jalan Pelatok, Singapore 488452, SINGAPORE 488452, SINGAPORE.
SOH, Mr. Kam Giap, BA ACA *1983;* 50 Medway Drive, SINGAPORE 556550, SINGAPORE.
SOH, Mr. Ken Zsu, ACA *2011;* Flat 5, 1 Hithe Grove, LONDON, SE16 2XS.
SOH, Mr. Kiang Ming, FCA *1977;* 47 Jalan Sri Hartamas, 17 Sri Hartamas, 50480 KUALA LUMPUR, FEDERAL TERRITORY, MALAYSIA.
•SOH, Mrs. Lorraine Esther, BCom ACA *1998;* 31 Cranhams Lane, CIRENCESTER, GLOUCESTERSHIRE, GL7 1TZ.
SOH, Ms. Pick Har, BSc ACA ACMA ATII *1980;* 3 University Walk, SINGAPORE 297797, SINGAPORE.
SOH, Mr. Stanley, LLB ACA CFA *2004;* 113 Jalan Pelatok, SINGAPORE 488452, SINGAPORE.
SOH, Miss. Yee Tyng, ACA *2008;* 28 Jalan 20/144A, Taman Bukit Cheras, 56000 KUALA LUMPUR, FEDERAL TERRITORY, MALAYSIA.
SOHAIL, Mr. Muhammad Nadeem, ACA *2009;* 10 Amberwood Close, WALLINGTON, SURREY, SM6 8QH.
SOHAIL, Miss. Sabrina, BA ACA *2010;* 3 Woodpecker Close, BUSHEY, WD23 1AW.
SOHAL, Miss. Aanjli Kaur, MSc BCom ACA *2005;* 13 Garland Crescent, HALESOWEN, B62 9NJ.
SOHAL, Mr. Awtar Singh, FCA *1965;* Anglebury, Kingsway Avenue, WOKING, SURREY, GU21 6NX.
SOHAL, Mr. Balkar, BSc ACA *2000;* 5 North Park, Berry Hill, MANSFIELD, NG18 4PA.
SOHAL, Miss. Jagdish Kaur, BSc ACA *2003;* 522 Railway Avenue, APT 395, CAMPBELL, CA 95008, UNITED STATES.
SOHAL, Mr. Jaswinder Singh, BEng ACA *1993;* 74 Banquo Approach, Warwick Gates, WARWICK, CV34 6GB.
SOHAL, Miss. Namneet Kaur, BSc ACA *2010;* 26 Kendrick Road, SLOUGH, SL3 7PQ.
SOHAL, Mr. Rakesh Kumar, BSc ACA *2006;* 3 Broomhurst, Edgbaston, BIRMINGHAM, B15 3NL.
SOHI, Mr. Jujhar Singh, ACA *2008;* Flat 26, Sir John Lyon House, 8 High Timber Street, LONDON, EC4V 3PA.
SOHI, Mr. Kashmir, MSc BSc FCA *1995;* 18 Eaton Rise, LONDON, W5 2ER.
SOHODELE, Mr. Madan, ACA *1993;* 8 Wellington Road, LONDON, E11 2AU.
•SOHOR, Mr. Michael Eugene, FCA *1979;* (Tax Fac), Michael Sohor & Co Ltd, 74 St. Georges Road, BOLTON, BL1 2DD.
SOKHAL, Mr. Gurcharn Singh, ACA *2009;* 26 Faircross Avenue, BARKING, ESSEX, IG11 8RD.
•SOKHAL, Mr. Jagdish Paul Roy, BSc FCA *1991;* (Tax Fac), The Roy Sokhal Group, Suite 235, 2nd Floor, Island Business Centre, 18-36 Wellington Street, Woolwich LONDON SE18 6PF.
SOKHI, Mrs. Sukhpreet, ACA *2011;* 134b Rosemary Hill Road, SUTTON COLDFIELD, B74 4HN.
SOKIRI, Mrs. Larraine Alys, BSc ACA *2004;* London Television Centre, 58-72 Upper Ground, LONDON, SE1 9LT.
SOKOLOVA, Ms. Daria, BA ACA *2008;* Flat 42, 28 Metohiou Street, 1101 NICOSIA, CYPRUS.
SOKOLOWSKI, Mr. Eric, ACA *2008;* The Royal Bank of Scotland Plc, 280 Bishopsgate, LONDON, EC2M 4RB.
•SOKOTA, Mr. George, FCA *1974;* Deloitte & Touche, Kafue House, 1 Nairobi Place, P O Box 30030, LUSAKA, ZAMBIA.
SOKOTA, Miss. Kaela, ACA *2009;* Hornsey Lane, Highgate, 13 Ridgeway Gardens, LONDON, N6 5XR.
SOLA, Mrs. Hannah Desanka, ACA *2009;* 4 Upper Rawreth Walk, LONDON, N1 8TW.
SOLAN, Mr. Glenn Michael, BSc ACA *1997;* with Grant Thornton UK LLP, 1 Whitehall Riverside, Whitehall Road, LEEDS, WEST YORKSHIRE, LS1 4BN.
SOLANKI, Mrs. Ambika, BA ACA *2007;* 70 Finchfield Road West, WOLVERHAMPTON, WV3 8BA.
SOLANKI, Mr. Ashwin Damji, FCA *1976;* (Tax Fac), 34a Little Bushey Lane, BUSHEY, WD23 4JU.
SOLANKI, Mr. Bepin, BSc ACA *2011;* 23 Scarle Road, WEMBLEY, MIDDLESEX, HA0 4SR.
SOLANKI, Miss. Kiran, ACA *2009;* 94 Carlyle Avenue, SOUTHALL, MIDDLESEX, UB1 2BJ.

•**SOLANKI, Mr. Kishor Gopal, ACA** *1980;* K.G. Solanki & Co, Hamilton House, 315 St.Saviours Road, LEICESTER, LE5 4HG.
SOLANKI, Mr. Milan Ashwin, ACA *2008;* with Ernst & Young Europe LLP, 1 More London Place, LONDON, SE1 2AF.
SOLANKI, Mr. Vijay, BA FCA *1995;* (Tax Fac), 180 Dorset House, Gloucester Place, LONDON, NW1 5AH.
SOLARSKI, Mr. Phillip James, ACA *2008;* Seef Palms Apartments, No.406, Building 274, Road 2804, Al Seef District, MANAMA BAHRAIN.
SOLAZZO, Mr. Antonio Mario, BA FCA *1997;* 16 Lanthorn Close, BROXBOURNE, EN10 7NR.
•**SOLAZZO, Mr. Salvatore, FCA** *1983;* (Tax Fac), Solazzo & Co Ltd, Woodlands, 27 Ferney Road, Cheshunt, WALTHAM CROSS, EN7 6XQ.
SOLDI, Mrs. Sarah Jayne Maylin Meikle, BSc ACA *2005;* with H W, Sterling House, 5 Buckingham Place, Bellfield Rd West, HIGH WYCOMBE, HP13 5HQ.
SOLE, Mrs. Amy Elizabeth, ACA *2009;* 40 St. Michaels Way, Roche, ST. AUSTELL, CORNWALL, PL26 8FG.
SOLE, Mr. James, ACA *2011;* K P M G Llp, 15 Canada Square, LONDON, E14 5GL.
SOLE, Mr. Leonard Paul, ACA *2006;* Whitakers Bryndon House, 5-7 Berry Road, NEWQUAY, CORNWALL, TR7 1AD.
SOLE, Mr. Tony Charles, BSc FCA *1981;* Palm Utilities LLC, P.O.Box 215122, DUBAI, 215122, UNITED ARAB EMIRATES.
SOLEIMAN, Mr. Shlomo, BA FCA *1985;* 12 Carriage Road, Great Neck, NEW YORK, NY 11024, UNITED STATES.
SOLES, Mrs. Gillian Hazel, BSc ACA *2002;* 78 Starring Way, LITTLEBOROUGH, LANCASHIRE, OL15 8NT.
SOLEY, Mr. James Andrew, BA ACA *1992;* 136 Vicarage Road, Wollaston, STOURBRIDGE, WEST MIDLANDS, DY8 4QT.
SOLIMANI, Mr. Siamak, BSc ACA *1997;* 85 Ash Grove, LONDON, N13 5AW.
SOLL, Mr. Elliot Stephen, BA(Hons) ACA *2001;* 52 Linden Crescent, ST. ALBANS, HERTFORDSHIRE, AL1 5DD.
SOLLEN, Mr. Ian, FCA *1971;* Bowden Bridle Lane, Loudwater, RICKMANSWORTH, WD3 4JQ.
SOLLIS, Mrs. Deborah Jane, ACA *1990;* MGI Richard Keen LLP, 7 Nelson Street, SOUTHEND-ON-SEA, ESSEX, SS1 1EH.
SOLLY, Mr. Geoffrey Raymond, FCA *1972;* Kimberley Lodge, High Broom Road, CROWBOROUGH, TN6 3SL.
SOLLY, Mr. John Douglas, FCA CIOT *1968;* JADE, PO Box 561, Suite 6/456, 1/5 Irish Town, GIBRALTAR, GIBRALTAR.
SOLLY, Mrs. Linda Jane, ACA *2002;* 168 Livingstone Road, GRAVESEND, DA12 5DY.
SOLLY, Mr. Mark William, FCA *1968;* 35 Malew Street, Castletown, ISLE OF MAN, IM9 1AE.
SOLLY, Miss. Melissa, BSc ACA *2010;* Freemasons Arms, 81-82 Long Acre, LONDON, WC2E 9NG.
SOLOMAN, Mr. Gareth Richard, FCA *1974;* 7 West Town Grove, BRISTOL, BS4 5EQ.
SOLOMIDES, Mr. Christopher, ACA *2008;* with PricewaterhouseCoopers LLP, 1 Embankment Place, LONDON, WC2N 6RH.
SOLOMON, Miss. Alison Elizabeth Ann, BSc ACA *1987;* (Tax Fac), 17 High Street, Manton, MARLBOROUGH, SN8 4HH.
SOLOMON, Mr. Antony James, BSc(Hons) ACA *2003;* Ridge End, The Avenue, RADLETT, HERTFORDSHIRE, WD7 7DQ.
•**SOLOMON, Mr. Edward Samuel Elizer, FCA** *1964;* E.S.Solomon FCA, Le Chalet, Long Lane, Bovingdon, HEMEL HEMPSTEAD, HP3 0NE.
SOLOMON, Mr. Henry Maurice, FCA *1964;* 16 Riverside Gardens, Finchley, LONDON, N3 3GR. (Life Member)
SOLOMON, Mr. Mark Vivian, BSc(Eng) ACA *1992;* 15 Mount View, ENFIELD, MIDDLESEX, EN2 8LF.
•**SOLOMON, Mr. Michael Brodie, FCA** *1957;* Forshaws, Railex Business Centre, Crossens Way, Marine Drive, SOUTHPORT, MERSEYSIDE PR9 9LY.
SOLOMON, Miss. Nicola Shelley, BSc ACA *1992;* 31 Braithwaite Gardens, STANMORE, HA7 2QG.
•**SOLOMON, Mr. Richard Grahame, MA FCA** *1995;* 32 Paines Lane, PINNER, MIDDLESEX, HA5 3BD.
SOLOMON, Mr. Richard Sydney Clive, FCA *1962;* 60 Summerland Lane, Caswell, SWANSEA, SA3 4RS. (Life Member)
SOLOMON, Mr. Robert Barry, FCA *1975;* 12 Driftway Road, HOOK, HAMPSHIRE, RG27 9SB.
•**SOLOMON, Mr. Sefton Alexander, BA FCA FCCA ATII** *1963;* (Tax Fac), Sefton Solomon, Peterden House, 1a Leighton Road, West Ealing, LONDON, W13 9EL.
SOLOMONIDES, Mrs. Angela, FCA *1982;* 16 Kyriacou Matsi Avenue, Agioi Omologites, 1082 NICOSIA, CYPRUS.
SOLOMONIDES, Miss. Eftychia Charalambous, BA ACA *2011;* 25 28th October Street, Delta Court Flat 44, Acropolis, 2012 NICOSIA, CYPRUS.
•**SOLOMONS, Mr. Alan Jeffrey, BSc FCA** *1973;* Alan Solomons & Co., 2 Gayton Road, HARROW, MIDDLESEX, HA1 2XU. See also Exit Strategy Ltd, and Accounts Department (The)
SOLOMONS, Mrs. Alice Olivia, ACA *2009;* 37 Drayton Road, BOREHAMWOOD, HERTFORDSHIRE, WD6 2DA.
SOLOMONS, Mr. Anthony Nathan, FCA *1953;* 10 Constable Close, LONDON, NW11 6TY. (Life Member)
•**SOLOMONS, Mr. Eric Philip, BA FCA** *1988;* BDO LLP, 6th Floor, 3 Hardman Street, Spinningfields, MANCHESTER, M3 3AT. See also BDO Stoy Hayward LLP
SOLOMONS, Mr. Jonathan Ernest, FCA *1973;* More House, 514 Finchley Road, LONDON, NW11 8DD.
SOLOMONS, Mr. Jonathan Mark, BA ACA *1998;* Global Crossing, 10 Fleet Place, LONDON, EC4M 7RB.
•**SOLOMONS, Mr. Kenneth Sidney, FCA** *1961;* (Tax Fac), K.S. Solomons & Co, 6 Raleigh Close, Hendon, LONDON, NW4 2TA.
SOLOMONS, Miss. Laura Martine Sarah, BSc ACA *2009;* 9 Meads Close, INGATESTONE, CM4 0AF.
SOLOMONS, Mr. Richard Leslie, BA ACA *1986;* 8 Abbey View, RADLETT, WD7 8LT.
SOLOMOU, Mr. Antonakis Michael, BSc ACA *1980;* 41 ave Hector Otto, MC98000 MONACO, MONACO.
SOLOMOU, Mr. Nicolas, MBA MEng BEng ACA *1992;* 11 Park Road, Regent's Park, LONDON, NW1 6XN.
SOLOMOU, Mrs. Phani, MBA BSc ACA *1993;* 11 Park Road, LONDON, NW1 6XN.
•**SOLT, Mr. Nicholas John, BSc FCA** *1999;* Moore Stephens, P O Box 236, First Island House, Peter Street, St. Helier, JERSEY JE4 8SG.
SOLTANOVSKAYA, Mrs. Irina Georgievna, BSc ACA *2010;* Solomou 40, 15344 GERAKAS, ATHENS, GREECE.
•**SOLWAY, Mrs. Amanda Jane, BSc ACA** *1998;* A J Solway Limited, 37 Bosvean Road, Shortlanesend, TRURO, CORNWALL, TR4 9DX.
SOLWAY, Ms. Kate, BA ACA *2007;* 5 Doyle Clos, Route Militaire, St. Sampson, GUERNSEY, GY2 4FD.
•**SOLYOM, Mr. Robert Michael, BA FCA ATII** *1985;* Brown Butler, Leigh House, 28-32 St Paul's Street, LEEDS, LS1 2JT.
SOLYOM, Mrs. Susan Anne, BA ACA *1986;* The Brambles, 30 Creskeld Lane, Bramhope, LEEDS, LS16 9EX.
SOM, Mr. Mihir Kumar, FCA *1972;* 6Route de Founex, 1296 COPPET, SWITZERLAND.
SOMAIA, Mrs. Jocelyn Fay Heath, MA ACA *1995;* 26 Midland Road, Bramhall, STOCKPORT, SK7 3DR.
SOMAIA, Mr. Sharad Kumar Karsandas Bhimji, FCA *1972;* P.O. Box 255, KISUMU, KENYA.
SOMAIYA, Mr. Rameshchandra Hemraj, FCA *1974;* 70 Bishops Road, Trumpington, CAMBRIDGE, CB2 9NH.
SOMAIYA, Mr. Ravindra, FCA *1972;* Tower F, Flat 052, Raheja Atlantis, Sector 31, GURGAON 122001, HARYANA INDIA.
SOMAIYA, Mr. Vinaykant, FCA *1967;* P.O.Box 284, DAR ES SALAAM, TANZANIA.
SOMAIYA, Mr. Vipulkumar, ACA *2011;* 101 Lichfield Grove, LONDON, N3 2JL.
SOMAL, Mr. Amarpal Singh, ACA *1979;* 3 Brompton Close, HOUNSLOW, TW4 5HP.
SOMALYA, Mr. Seifudin Abdultayab, ACA *1980;* Binzagr Co, PO BOX 54, JEDDAH, 21411, SAUDI ARABIA.
SOMANATHAN, Dr. Trikkur Vaidyanathan, ACA *2010;* Soma Lakshmi, No. 4 8th Cross Street, Shastri Nagar, Adyar, CHENNAI 60020, TAMIL NADU INDIA.
SOMANI, Miss. Rupal, BSc ACA *2002;* Deutsche Bank, 1 Appold Street, LONDON, EC2A 2UU.
SOMASUNDARAM, Mr. Thanneermalai, ACA *1980;* PricewaterhouseCoopers, P.O.Box 10192, Level 10 1 Sentral, Jalan Travers, 50470 KUALA LUMPUR, FEDERAL TERRITORY MALAYSIA.
SOMCHAND, Mr. Rajan Pramodray, BSc ACA *2002;* 86 Southover, LONDON, N12 7HD.
SOMECH, Mr. Peter David, FCA *1967;* Villa C-12, DORADO, 00646, PUERTO RICO. (Life Member)
SOMERFIELD, Mrs. Adrienne B, BA(Econ) FCA *1976;* (Tax Fac), Kensington, 6 Brackenwood Drive, Bruntwood, CHEADLE, SK8 1JX.
SOMERFIELD, Ms. Jill Lisbeth, FCA *1992;* with PricewaterhouseCoopers, Private Bag 92162, AUCKLAND 1142, NEW ZEALAND.
SOMERS, Mrs. Alison Olive, BA(Hons) ACA *2002;* Beggars Roost, Smallridge, AXMINSTER, DEVON, EX13 7JH.
SOMERS, Mrs. Janet, BSc FCA *1983;* with ICAEW, Metropolitan House, 321 Avebury Boulevard, MILTON KEYNES, MK9 2FZ.
SOMERS, Mr. John Patrick, ACA ACMA *2007;* Vorden Lodge Slay Pit Lane, Thorpe Salvin, WORKSOP, NOTTINGHAMSHIRE, S80 3JW.
SOMERS, Miss. Melissa, ACA *2011;* Top Flat, 27 Marjorie Grove, LONDON, SW11 5SH.
•**SOMERS, Mr. Michael Ian, FCA** *1968;* M Somers & Co, 60 Croham Valley Road, SOUTH CROYDON, SURREY, CR2 7NB.
SOMERS, Mr. Michael John, FCA *1970;* Links Cottage Perry Green, Bradwell, BRAINTREE, CM77 8DS.
SOMERS, Mr. Michael Kevin, FCA *1970;* 1 Stanford Close, HOVE, EAST SUSSEX, BN3 6PU.
SOMERS, Mr. Peter Leonard, BSc FCA *1983;* Greenhill, Crowborough Hill, CROWBOROUGH, TN6 2DD.
•**SOMERS, Mr. Richard, FCA** *1970;* R Somers - Accountancy, Grafton, Waterlane, Oakridge, STROUD, GLOUCESTERSHIRE GL6 7PL. See also R Somers -Accountancy
SOMERS, Mr. Robert Louis, FCA *1963;* 29 Morrison Avenue, Tottenham, LONDON, N17 6TU.
SOMERS, Mrs. Sarah, BSc FCA *1993;* Moore Stephens, 1 Church Street, Kirkbymoorside, YORK, YO62 6AZ.
SOMERS, Miss. Sian Marie, BSc ACA *1994;* 184 Fishpool Street, ST. ALBANS, HERTFORDSHIRE, AL3 4SB.
•**SOMERS, Mr. Timothy Gervase, BA FCA** *1988;* The Trevor Jones Partnership LLP, Springfield House, 99-101 Crossbrook Street, Cheshunt, WALTHAM CROSS, HERTFORDSHIRE EN8 8JR. See also Colesgrove Trustees Ltd, Springfield Tax Services Ltd and Crossbrook Property Services Limited
SOMERSET, Mr. Ian James, BA ACA *2006;* 2 Thomas Close, Alsager, STOKE-ON-TRENT, ST1 2YR.
•**SOMERSTON, Mr. Malcolm Steven, FCA** *1983;* (Tax Fac), Carter Backer Winter LLP, Enterprise House, 21 Buckle Street, LONDON, E1 8NN. See also Gordon Leighton Limited
SOMERTON, Mr. Hubert Graham, FCA *1946;* 153 Gibson Hill, LONDON, SW16 3EX. (Life Member)
SOMERVELL, Mr. John Matthew, BA FCA *1982;* Morgan Law Partners LLP, 4th Floor Clareville House, 26-27 Oxendon Street, LONDON, SW1Y 4EL.
SOMERVILLE, Mr. Andrew Forbes, BSc ACA *1984;* Robin Hill, London Road, CHALFONT ST. GILES, HP8 4NQ.
•**SOMERVILLE, Mr. Arthur Colin, FCA** *1975;* Arthur Somerville, 108 Vineyard Hill Road, Wimbledon, LONDON, SW19 7JJ.
SOMERVILLE, Mr. Bruce Patrick, BSc ACA *1995;* 60 Parklands Manor, Tuke Grove, WAKEFIELD, WF1 4AF.
SOMERVILLE, Mr. Howard Neil, BSc FCA *1973;* Fernside, Heather Drive, ASCOT, BERKSHIRE, SL5 0HR.
SOMERVILLE, Mr. Hugh, BSc FCA *1974;* 111 St Albans Rd, EDINBURGH, EH9 2PQ.
SOMERVILLE, Mr. Ian Christopher, BSc FCA *1973;* (Tax Fac), Flowers Green, Golden Acre, East Preston, LITTLEHAMPTON, BN16 1QP. (Life Member)
SOMERVILLE, Mr. Michael John, BSc ACA *1991;* 6 Rochford Close, Whitefield, MANCHESTER, M45 7QR.
SOMERVILLE, Mr. Michael John Branscombe, FCA *1963;* 4624 Eagle Crescent, WINDSOR N9G 2N5, ON, CANADA. (Life Member)
SOMERVILLE, Miss. Rebecca Emmeline, ACA *2007;* 10 Cleves Court, Firs Avenue, WINDSOR, BERKSHIRE, SL4 4EF.
•**SOMERVILLE-WOODWARD, Mrs. Lynn Patricia, BSc FCA** *1987;* (Tax Fac), Simpkins Edwards LLP, Michael House, Castle Street, EXETER, EX4 3LQ.
•**SOMJI, Mr. Akberali Fazel, FCA** *1975;* (Tax Fac), Akber & Co, 451 Moseley Road, BIRMINGHAM, B12 9BX.
SOMJI, Mr. Aminmohamed, ACA *1981;* 84 Green Lane, WORCESTER PARK, KT4 8AR.
SOMJI, Mr. Muhsin, BSc ACA *1991;* 96 Village Way, PINNER, HA5 5AZ.
SOMMERS, Miss. Catherine Louise, BSc ACA *2000;* (Tax Fac), Flawith Grange Flawith Alne, YORK, YO61 1SF.
SOMMERS, Mrs. Judy Winifred, BA ACA *1981;* 1 Prestwick Road, Biddenham, BEDFORD, MK40 4FH.
SOMMERS, Mr. Mark Richard, BA(Hons) ACA *2006;* 2 Shadow Walk, Elborough, WESTON-SUPER-MARE, AVON, BS24 8PH.
SOMMERS, Mrs. Robyn Lindsey, ACA *2009;* 2 Shadow Walk, Elborough, WESTON-SUPER-MARE, AVON, BS24 8PH.
SOMMERVILLE, Mr. Andrew John Conyers, FCA *1961;* Ash House, Ampney Crucis, CIRENCESTER, GLOUCESTERSHIRE, GL7 5RY. (Life Member)
SOMOGYI, Mr. Levente, ACA *2002;* 129 Staunton Road, Headington, OXFORD, OX3 7TN.
SOMRAH, Mr. Jaswinder Singh, BA ACA *1992;* 27 Ashford Avenue, HAYES, UB4 0LY.
SONABEND, Mr. Paul Simon David, BSc ACA *1982;* 31 Platts Lane, LONDON, NW3 7NN.
SONAIKE, Mr. Kayode Biodun, FCA *1975;* Kayode Sonaike & Co, 20 Bombay Crescent, Apapa, PO Box 8430, LAGOS, NIGERIA.
•**SONDHELM, Mr. Martin David, BSc FCA** *1989;* 11 Faber Gardens, Hendon, LONDON, NW4 4NP.
SONECHA, Mr. Krushant, BA ACA *1994;* 53 Ten Shilling Drive, COVENTRY, CV4 8GZ.
SONEJI, Mr. Jay-Kumar Dhirajlal, BA ACA *1995;* 55 The Avenue, West Ealing, LONDON, W13 8JR.
SONES, Mr. John Stafford, FCA *1960;* 1 Laurel Drive, Willaston, NESTON, CH64 1TN. (Life Member)
SONG, Mrs. Yae-Lee, BSc(Hons) ACA *2001;* Wiesenau 2, 61476 KRONBERG, GERMANY.
SONGHURST, Mr. Andrew John, BA ACA *1991;* 15 Roslyn Road, HARROGATE, NORTH YORKSHIRE, HG2 7SB.
SONGI, Mr. Mark Philip, MA ACA *1987;* Orchards, Summerhill Lane, HAYWARDS HEATH, WEST SUSSEX, RH16 1RN.
SONGO, Mrs. Thembi, MSc BBA ACA *2006;* 26 Mere Drive, MANCHESTER, LANCASHIRE, M27 8SD.
SONI, Mr. Jogesh Kumar, ACA *1984;* 175a Uxbridge Road, Harrow Weald, HARROW, HA3 6TP.
•**SONI, Mrs. Prem Lata, FCA** *1975;* Bradley Soni & Co, 365 South Coast Road, Telscombe Cliffs, PEACEHAVEN, EAST SUSSEX, BN10 7HA.
SONI, Mr. Rishi, BSc ACA *2005;* 23 Sussex Court, Eaton Road, HOVE, EAST SUSSEX, BN3 3AS.
SONI, Miss. Sadhna, ACA *1991;* 33 Alderney Avenue, HOUNSLOW, TW5 0QN.
•**SONIA, Mrs. Emma Jane, BSc(Hons) ACA** *2001;* Emma J Sonia BSc(Hons) ACA, 13 Tarn Hows Walk, Ackworth, PONTEFRACT, WEST YORKSHIRE, WF7 7QS.
•**SONN, Mr. Michael Anthony, FCA** *1971;* (Tax Fac), Michael Sonn & Company, 140 Hall Lane, UPMINSTER, RM14 1AL.
•**SONNEBORN, Mr. Peter Michael, FCA** *1963;* (Tax Fac), Sonneborn & Co, High Holborn House, 52-54 High Holborn, LONDON, WC1V 6RL.
SONPAR, Miss. Mona, BSc FCA *1990;* 14 Brookfield Road, LONDON, W4 1DQ.
•**SONUGA, Mr. Adeyemi Olaseni, FCA** *1985;* 340 Summerside Cove SW, EDMONTON T6X 1B3, AB, CANADA.
SOO, Mr. Alan Wei Kwang, BSc ACA *2001;* Flat 41 The Westbourne, 1 Artesian Road, LONDON, W2 5DL.
•**SOO, Mr. James Weng Fatt, ACA** *1992;* James Soo & Co, 65 Jalan Lanjut, SINGAPORE 577708, SINGAPORE.
SOO, Miss. Joanne Wei Lin, BSc ACA *2004;* Flat 41 The Westbourne, 1 Artesian Road, LONDON, W2 5DL.
SOO, Mr. Tuck Choong, BCom ACA *1985;* HPH-EBIS, 2/F Tower 2 Terminal 4, Container Port Road South, KWAI CHUNG, HONG KONG SAR.
SOO THO, Mr. Him Yip, FCA *1976;* 14 Jalan SS 22A/3, Damansara Jaya, 47400 PETALING JAYA, SELANGOR, MALAYSIA.
SOOD, Mr. Aman, BSc(Hons) ACA ATT *2010;* 46 Cymbeline Way, WARWICK, CV34 6FQ.
SOOD, Mr. Anmol Kumar, ACA *2008;* Mulralto, Pine Glade, ORPINGTON, KENT, BR6 8NT.
SOOD, Mr. Mohinder Pal Roshanlal, FCA *1964;* 12 Lansdowne Road, Seven Kings, ILFORD, IG3 8NE. (Life Member)
SOOD, Mrs. Monica, ACA *2008;* 5 Cavalry Gardens, LONDON, SW15 2QQ.
SOOD, Miss. Pameta Lindley, BSc ACA *1992;* 25 Totley Hall Croft, SHEFFIELD, S17 4BE.
SOOD, Mrs. Pooja, ACA *2003;* 12 West Close, WEMBLEY, MIDDLESEX, HA9 9PJ.
SOOD, Mr. Rahul, ACA *1995;* PricewaterhouseCoopers LLP, One North Wacker Drive, CHICAGO, IL 60606, UNITED STATES.
SOOD, Mr. Rajesh Kumar, BSc ACA *1999;* 19 New Farm Avenue, BROMLEY, BR2 0TX.
SOOD, Mr. Rajinder Kumar, LLB ACA ACCA *2002;* M D A Ltd, Gillingham House, 38-44 Gillingham Street, LONDON, SW1V 1HU.

SOOD, Mr. Raman, BSc ACA CFA *1996;* Flat 19E, Panorama Garden, 103 Robinson Road, MID LEVELS, HONG KONG ISLAND, HONG KONG SAR.
•SOOD, Mr. Sanjeev, FCA *1989;* (Tax Fac), Sansons, 35 Beaufort Court, Admirals Way, South Quay Waterside, LONDON, E14 9XL.
SOOD, Mrs. Sarita, BSc ACA *1997;* Takeda Pharmaceuticals Europe Ltd, 61 Aldwych, LONDON, WC2B 4AE.
SOOD, Mr. Satchiv, ACA *2009;* Heathside Food Store, 636 Hanworth Road, HOUNSLOW, TW4 5NP.
SOOD, Mrs. Shalni, BSc ACA *1997;* 35 Cunningham Hill Road, ST. ALBANS, HERTFORDSHIRE, AL1 5BX.
SOOD BAJAJ, Miss. Reena, ACA *2009;* with PricewaterhouseCoopers LLP, Donington Court, Pegasus Business Park, Castle Donington, DERBY, DE74 2UZ.
SOODEEN, Ms. Nicole, ACA *2005;* 28 Talbot Drive, Euxton, CHORLEY, LANCASHIRE, PR7 6PD.
SOOKE, Mr. Thomas Peter, MA FCA *1971;* 45 Faroe Road, Brook Green, LONDON, W14 0EL.
SOOKIA, Mr. Adam Joel, BSc ACA *2010;* 20 Silver Cross Way, LEEDS, LS20 8FG.
SOOKIA, Mr. Mikail Farouk, BCom ACA *2002;* 1/133-137 Sydney Street, NORTH WILLOUGHBY, NSW 2068, AUSTRALIA.
SOOLEEHALL, Mr. Chandraduth, ACA FCCA *2010;* 52 Cypress Grove, ILFORD, ESSEX, IG6 3AT.
SOOLIA, Mr. Rajen, BSc ACA *1984;* 239 Liverpool Road, LONDON, N1 1LX.
SOOMAL, Mr. Jatinder, ACA *2009;* Flat B, 88 Woodside, LONDON, SW19 7BA.
SOON, Mr. David Lim Hun, BA ACA *1982;* with KPMG, Level 10, KPMG Tower, 8 First Avenue, Bandar Utama, 47800 PETALING JAYA MALAYSIA.
SOON, Mr. Julian Sien Yik, MEng ACA *2010;* 192a Ferme Park Road, LONDON, N8 9BN.
SOON, Ms. Mei Fong, ACA *2011;* F-13A-05, Metropolitan Square, Jalan PTU 8/1, Damansara Perdana, 47820 PETALING JAYA, MALAYSIA.
SOON, Mr. Po Seng, BSc FCA *1984;* Soon & Associates, 8 Jalan Edgecumbe, 10250 PENANG, MALAYSIA.
SOON, Miss. Siew Eng, FCA *1974;* General Post Office, P.O.Box 7550, CENTRAL, HONG KONG ISLAND, HONG KONG SAR.
SOON, Mr. Su Long, BSc ACA *1993;* Unit D15-6 Kelana D'Putera, Condo 19 Jalan SS7/26, Taman Kelana IndahKelana Jaya, 47301 PETALING JAYASelangor, MALAYSIA.
SOONG, Miss. Mei Jean, ACA *2009;* Flat, 167 Draycott Avenue, LONDON, SW3 3AJ.
SOOR, Mr. Baldeep Singh, BSc ACA *2010;* 33 Courtlands Avenue, SLOUGH, SL3 7LD.
SOORKIA, Mr. Vishal, ACA *2007;* 46 Saviour's Place, Pleasant Street St. Helier, JERSEY, JE2 4FB.
SOPER, Mr. Brendon Ward, FCA *1967;* 10 Heathfield Close, Bovey Tracey, NEWTON ABBOT, DEVON, TQ13 9DZ.
SOPER, Mr. John Stephen, BSc ACA *1990;* 2 Pentervin, Minsterley, SHREWSBURY, SY5 0EZ.
SOPER, Mr. William Robert, FCA *1978;* 80 Westbrook Avenue, WAHROONGA, NSW 2076, AUSTRALIA.
•SOPHER, Mr. Daniel Richard Murad, LLB ACA *2002;* Sopher + Traqs International Taxation Limited, 38 Berkeley Square, LONDON, W1J 5AL.
SOPHER, Mr. Henry, BSc ACA *1987;* 37 Ferris Drive, WEST ORANGE, NJ 07052, UNITED STATES.
•SOPHER, Mr. Ivan, FCA *1973;* Sopher + Co, 5 Elstree Gate, Elstree Way, BOREHAMWOOD, WD6 1JD. See also Sopher + Traqs International Taxation Limited
SOPHER, Mr. Jon Andrew Victor, BA ACA *1993;* Smerrill Barns, Nr Kemble, CIRENCESTER, GL7 6BW.
SOPHER, Mr. Richard Moshe, MA FCA *1984;* 3 Upper Belgrave Street, LONDON, SW1X 8BD.
SOPHER, Mr. Victor, FCA *1955;* (Tax Fac), 10 Winscombe Way, STANMORE, MIDDLESEX, HA7 3AU. (Life Member)
SOPHIANOS, Mr. Yiannis, BSc ACA *2003;* Flat 101, 12 Ellados Street, Strovolos, 2003 NICOSIA, CYPRUS.
SOPHOCLEOUS, Mr. Andreas, BA FCA *1991;* 8 Ayios Iosif Street, Archangelos, 2055 NICOSIA, CYPRUS.
SOPHOCLEOUS, Miss. Marianna, ACA *2007;* 12 Kassos Street, Theta 61, Agioi Omologites, 1086 NICOSIA, CYPRUS.
SOPP, Mrs. Rachel Elizabeth, MA FCA FCT *1983;* Maryvale Associates Ltd, 16 Maryvale, GODALMING, SURREY, GU7 1SW.
SOPPITT, Miss. Janet Elizabeth, FCA *1963;* 3 Farquhar Road, Wimbledon Park, LONDON, SW19 8DA.
SOPPITT, Mr. Paul, ACA *2011;* 4 Lyham Road, LONDON, SW2 5QA.
SORABJI, Mr. Pervez, FCA *1980;* with ICAEW, Metropolitan House, 321 Avebury Boulevard, MILTON KEYNES, MK9 2FZ.
SORAFF, Mr. Allen John, FCA *1972;* Chasedene, Millfield Lane, Bury Green, Little Hadham, WARE, HERTFORDSHIRE SG11 2ED. (Life Member)
SORBIE, Mr. Dennis, ACA *2011;* 23 Lime Road, Normanby, MIDDLESBROUGH, CLEVELAND, TS6 0DL.
SORBY, Mr. Ryan Thomas, ACA *2006;* 26 Charnock Grove, Gleadless, SHEFFIELD, S12 3HE.
SORENSEN, Mr. Andrew Wallace, FCA *1949;* 36 Park Avenue, Roker, SUNDERLAND, SR6 9DJ. (Life Member)
SORKIN, Mr. Alexander Michael, BA FCA *1967;* New Court, 19 St. Swithin's Lane, LONDON, EC4N 8AD.
SORLEY, Mr. Peter Gruer, BA FCA *1957;* 18 White Lion Gate, COBHAM, SURREY, KT11 1AQ. (Life Member)
SOROHAN, Mr. Peter Anthony, BSc ACA *1983;* with PricewaterhouseCoopers LLP, The Atrium, 1 Harefield Road, UXBRIDGE, UB8 1EX.
SORRELL, Miss. Barbara Ann, BSc ACA *1994;* 43 Grove Park, TRING, HERTFORDSHIRE, HP23 5JS.
SORRELL, Mrs. Caroline Anne, BA ACA *2002;* 23 Wedgewood Drive, SPALDING, LINCOLNSHIRE, PE11 3FJ.
SORRELL, Mr. David Walter, FCA *1975;* 16 Keswick Drive, Cherry Tree, BLACKBURN, BB2 5HH. (Life Member)
•SORRELL, Mrs. Janet Susan, ACA *1984;* Sorrell Ltd, Glaven Farm Barn, Thornage Road, Letheringsett, HOLT, NORFOLK NR25 7JE.
SORRELL, Mr. John Patrick, BA FCA ACIS *1985;* 4 Birch Close, Little Melton, NORWICH, NR9 3QX.
SORRELL, Mr. Roderick John, ACA *1970;* 68 Poethlyn Drive, Costessey, NORWICH, NR8 5ET.
SORRELL, Miss. Susan Margaret, ACA *1991;* 6 Topfield, Popes Lane, COLCHESTER, CO3 3JR.
SORSBIE, Mr. Richard Graham, BA ACA *1988;* 7 Park View, Shawford, WINCHESTER, SO21 2BS.
•SORSKY, Mr. Harold John, FCA *1967;* SPW (UK) LLP, Gable House, 239 Regents Park Road, LONDON, N3 3LF.
SORTWELL, Miss. Karen Ruth, CA ACA *2010;* 74 London Road, Wollaston, WELLINGBOROUGH, NORTHAMPTONSHIRE, NN29 7QP.
SOSAH, Mrs. Velda, BA ACA *1991;* 10 Pickwick Place, HARROW, HA1 3BG.
•SOSEILOS, Mr. Philip, ACA *1992;* PricewaterhouseCoopers Limited, Julia House, 3 Themistocles Dervis Street, CY-1066 NICOSIA, CYPRUS.
SOSHINA, Ms. Elena, ACA *2008;* PricewaterhouseCoopers Sp. z o.o., Al. Armii Ludowej 14, 00-638 WARSAW, POLAND.
SOTERI, Miss. Androulla, BSc ACA *2006;* 75 Longmore Avenue, BARNET, HERTFORDSHIRE, EN5 1JZ.
•SOTERI, Mr. Philippos Kalli, BSc FCA *1974;* (Tax Fac), Philips, 1160 High Rd, LONDON, N20 0RA.
SOTERIOU, Mr. Adonis, BA ACA *1997;* 40 Ethnikis Antistaseos Street, 3026 LIMASSOL, CYPRUS.
SOTERIOU, Ms. Helen, BA ACA *1992;* Argo Capital Management Ltd, 80 New Bond Street, LONDON, W1S 1SB.
•SOTERIOU, Mr. Panicos, BA FCA *1991;* (Tax Fac), Soteriou Christou Ltd, 6a Dickenson's Place, LONDON, SE25 5HL. See also Soteriou Christou
•SOTERIOU, Mr. Piero Theodore, FCA *1980;* Soteriou Banerji, 253 Grays Inn Road, LONDON, WC1X 8QT. See also The Accounts Dept. Limited
•SOTERIOU, Mr. Robert, FCA *1978;* (Tax Fac), Soteriou Banerji, 253 Grays Inn Road, LONDON, WC1X 8QT. See also The Accounts Dept. Limited
SOTINWA, Prince George Adetola, FCA *1968;* P.O Box 52505, Falomo, Ikoy, LAGOS, NIGERIA.
•SOTINWA, Mr. Kolawole Adetola, BA ACA *2004;* Sotinwa Business Services, 51 Elm Park, READING, RG30 2HT.
•SOTIRIOU, Mr. Achilleas, BSc FCA *2000;* (Tax Fac), API Partnership Limited, 75 Westow Hill, Crystal Palace, LONDON, SE19 1TX.
SOTIRIS, Miss. Katie Anne, ACA *2010;* Flat 1, Garlinge House, Gosling Way, LONDON, SW9 6LU.
SOTIRIS, Mr. Ronald Leslie, FCA *1964;* 65 Trevor Drive, Allington Park, MAIDSTONE, ME16 0QW.
SOTOODEH, Mr. Navid, ACA *2009;* 87 Sherrards Way, BARNET, HERTFORDSHIRE, EN5 2BP.
•SOUGHTON, Mr. John Edward, FCA *1961;* Hill Wooldridge & Co Limited, 107 Hindes Road, HARROW, MIDDLESEX, HA1 1RU.
SOULSBY, Mrs. Erica Clare, MA ACA *2000;* 3 Lyndhurst Avenue, CHESTER-LE-STREET, DH3 4AR.
•SOULSBY, Mrs. Heidi Jean Renee, BSc FCA *1991;* Norman House, PO Box 142, GUERNSEY, GY1 3HT.
SOULSBY, Mr. Nicholas John, BSc FCA *1992;* L C H.Clearnet Ltd Aldgate House, 33 Aldgate High Street, LONDON, EC3N 1EA.
SOULSBY, Mr. Paul Gerard, BA ACA *1986;* AIDA Cruises, Am Strande 3D, 18055 ROSTOCK, GERMANY.
SOULSBY, Mr. Philip Dominic, BSc ACA *1991;* The Ferrers1 Milton Gardens, La Rue CauchezSt. Martin, GUERNSEY, GY4 6NU.
SOUMAKI, Ms. Maria, ACA *2010;* 17 Bouboulinas Street, Athienou, 7600 LARNACA, CYPRUS.
SOUSA, Miss. Silvia, ACA CA(AUS) *2008;* 9a Rodmarton Street, LONDON, W1U 8BH.
•SOUSTER, Mr. Nigel York, PhD BSc FCA *1974;* CFO Solutions Limited, 47 Maplehurst Road, CHICHESTER, WEST SUSSEX, PO19 6QL.
SOUSTER, Mr. Peter John Robertson, MA FCA *1970;* Orchard House, 5 Clifford Manor Road, GUILDFORD, GU4 8AG. (Life Member)
•SOUTAR, Mr. James, FCA *1972;* (Tax Fac), James Soutar & Co, Firland, High Street, Othery, BRIDGWATER, TA7 0QA.
SOUTER, Mr. Andrew Neil, BSc ACA *1982;* 22 Beach Road East, Portishead, BRISTOL, BS20 7ES.
SOUTER, Ms. Gwen Henderson, BCom ACA *1987;* (Tax Fac), 20 Cockburn Avenue, DUNBLANE, PERTHSHIRE, FK15 0FP.
SOUTER, Mrs. Jinny Susan, FCA *1974;* Secretariat Of HH The Aga Khan, Aiglemont, 60270 GOUVIEUX, FRANCE.
SOUTER, Mr. John Charles Mcdonald, BSc FCA *1974;* La Vieille Maison, 1 Rue de Senlis, Vineuil-St-Firmin, 60500 CHANTILLY, FRANCE.
SOUTH, Mr. Alistair Robert Lumley, BA ACA *2007;* The Old Dairy, Foley Estate, LIPHOOK, GU30 7JF.
SOUTH, Mr. Frank Rayner, FCA *1956;* 3245 Point Nepean Road, SORRENTO, VIC 3943, AUSTRALIA. (Life Member)
•SOUTH, Mr. Neil Frank, BA FCA *1991;* Clayton & Brewill, Cawley House, 149-155 Canal Street, NOTTINGHAM, NG1 7HR.
SOUTH, Mr. Richard Dawson, FCA *1969;* Millbank 2, Cornmill Lane, Bardsey, LEEDS, LS17 9EQ.
•SOUTH, Mr. Stephen Michael, FCA *1994;* Wise & Co, Wey Court West, Union Road, FARNHAM, SURREY, GU9 7PT. See also Firmvalue Payrolls Ltd
SOUTH, Mr. Timothy John, ACA *1984;* Deep Sea Electronics Plc, Highfield House, Hunmanby Industrial Estate, Hunmanby, FILEY, NORTH YORKSHIRE YO14 0PH.
•SOUTHALL, Mr. David, FCA *1974;* Heywood Shepherd, 1 Park Street, MACCLESFIELD, CHESHIRE, SK11 6SR.
SOUTHALL, Mr. Gregory John, BSc FCA *1984;* 28 Coldharbour Lane, Hildenborough, TONBRIDGE, TN11 9JT.
SOUTHALL, Mr. Ivan James, FCA *1970;* 12 Sandy Ridge, CHISLEHURST, BR7 5DR.
SOUTHALL, Mr. Jeffrey Malcolm, FCA *1965;* 30 Wightwick Hall Road, Wightwick, WOLVERHAMPTON, WV6 8BZ.
SOUTHALL, Mr. Peter Robert, BSc ACA *1991;* 13 Vicarage Drive, BECKENHAM, BR3 1JW.
SOUTHALL, Mr. Philip Edward, BSc ACA *1990;* 8 Ockenden Way, HASSOCKS, BN6 8HS.
SOUTHALL, Mr. Philip James, BSc FCA *1999;* PO Box 13165, SUTTON COLDFIELD, B73 5RJ.
SOUTHAM, Mr. Andrew, BA ACA *2004;* 38 Sandy Lane, SUTTON, SURREY, SM2 7PQ.
SOUTHAM, Mr. Christopher David, FCA *1989;* 1 Marina Boulevard, #22-01 OMB, SINGAPORE 018989, SINGAPORE.
SOUTHAM, Mr. Joseph Russell, FCA *1971;* P.O. Box 45521, ABU DHABI, UNITED ARAB EMIRATES.
•SOUTHAM, Mr. Kenneth Hubert, FCA *1955;* Southam & Co, 23 Penshurst Road, POTTERS BAR, HERTFORDSHIRE, EN6 5JR.
SOUTHBY, Mr. Peter John, MA FCA *1998;* Ener G Combined Power Ener G House, Daniel Adamson Road, SALFORD, M50 1DT.
SOUTHBY, Mr. Richard Henry Alexander, MA FCA *1967;* The Red House, Overbury, TEWKESBURY, GL20 7PB.
SOUTHCOMBE, Mr. James, BA(Hons) ACA AKC *2011;* 91 Tillingbourne Road, Shalford, GUILDFORD, GU4 8ET.
SOUTHCOTE, Mrs. Laura Rachel, ACA *2009;* 19 Knox Street, LEEDS, LS13 1LZ.
SOUTHCOTE, Mr. Liam David, ACA *2009;* 19 Knox Street, LEEDS, LS13 1LZ.
SOUTHCOTT, Mr. Andrew James, ACA *2009;* 114 South End Close, Hampstead, LONDON, NW3 2RE.
•SOUTHCOTT, Mr. Peter Martin, FCA *1989;* Carters Accountants Llp, 58 Bonnygate, CUPAR, FIFE, KY15 4LD.
SOUTHCOTT, Mr. Philip John, BSc ACA *1985;* PO Box 501, WAUCHOPE, NSW 2446, AUSTRALIA.
•SOUTHERINGTON, Mr. Nigel James, FCA *1985;* (Tax Fac), Southeringtons Limited, 71 Church Street, Langham, OAKHAM, LEICESTERSHIRE, LE15 7JE.
SOUTHERN, Mr. Andrew George, BSc ACA *1994;* 51, Parkfield Avenue, BOOTLE, L30 1PG.
SOUTHERN, Mr. Collingwood, FCA *1954;* Cherry Brook, Guildford Road, Pirbright, WOKING, SURREY, GU24 0LW. (Life Member)
•SOUTHERN, Mr. David Anthony, LLB FCA *1991;* 20 Campbell Gardens, Arnold, NOTTINGHAM, NG5 8RY.
SOUTHERN, Mr. Jonathan Alexander, FCA *1968;* 4 Devas Road, LONDON, SW20 8PD. (Life Member)
SOUTHERN, Mr. Jonathan Paul, BA FCA *1973;* Woodside, 51 Bracebridge Road, SUTTON COLDFIELD, B74 2SL.
SOUTHERN, Mrs. Julie Helen, BA ACA *1989;* Virgin Atlantic Airways Ltd The Office, Manor Royal, CRAWLEY, WEST SUSSEX, RH10 9NU.
SOUTHERN, Miss. Kerry Jane, ACA *2004;* Woodlea Farm, Station Approach, Medstead, ALTON, HAMPSHIRE, GU34 5EN.
SOUTHERN, Mr. Martin, ACA *1983;* The Old Pottery, Larkins Lane, Old Headington, OXFORD, OX3 9DW.
SOUTHERN, Mr. Martin John, BA(Hons) FCA *2000;* with Morris Crocker, Station House, 50 North Street, HAVANT, PO9 1QU.
SOUTHERN, Mr. Neil Victor, BSc(Hons) ACA *2002;* 5 Blackthorn Avenue, TUNBRIDGE WELLS, KENT, TN4 9YA.
SOUTHERN, Mr. Peter Cyril Bygate, FCA *1959;* 53 Oldfield Carr Lane, POULTON-LE-FYLDE, LANCASHIRE, FY6 8EN. (Life Member)
SOUTHERN, Mr. Robert Charles, BSc ACA *1998;* L E K Consulting Llp, 40 Grosvenor Place, LONDON, SW1X 7JL.
SOUTHERN, Ms. Susan Kay, MA ACA *1994;* UNICEF Lao PDR, KM3 Thadeua Road, PO Box 1080, VIENTIANE, LAO PEOPLE'S DEMOCRATIC REPUBLIC.
SOUTHERTON, Miss. Karen, BSc ACA *1994;* 37 Chapman Square, LONDON, SW19 5QT.
SOUTHEY, Mr. James David, BA ACA *2000;* Majesty House Ltd; Majesty House Building, Skyline 120, BRAINTREE, CM77 7AA.
SOUTHEY, Mrs. Maria Elizabeth, BSc ACA *1998;* The Knowle, Corry Road, Beacon Hill, HINDHEAD, GU26 6PB.
•SOUTHEY, Mr. Robert John, BA FCA *1989;* Wilkins Kennedy, Mount Manor House, 16 The Mount, GUILDFORD, SURREY, GU2 4HN.
SOUTHGATE, Mr. Crispin John, MA ACA *1981;* 55 Calton Avenue, Dulwich, LONDON, SE21 7DF.
SOUTHGATE, Mr. David Charles, BA ACA *1989;* 51 Woodmere Drive, Old Whittington, CHESTERFIELD, DERBYSHIRE, S41 9TE.
SOUTHGATE, Mr. Ian, FCA *1969;* 23 Raylton Avenue, Marton, MIDDLESBROUGH, CLEVELAND, TS7 8EF. (Life Member)
•SOUTHGATE, Mr. James Stephen, BA ACA *1992;* PricewaterhouseCoopers LLP, 1 Embankment Place, LONDON, WC2N 6RH. See also PricewaterhouseCoopers
•SOUTHGATE, Mr. Robert James, BA FCA CTA *1997;* (Tax Fac), Integrity Tax and Accounting Solutions, May Cottage, Ashfield Road, Norton, BURY ST. EDMUNDS, SUFFOLK IP31 3NF. See also Trilogic Family Office Limited
SOUTHGATE, Mrs. Sarah Jane, BSc ACA *2002;* The New House, Blundells Road, TIVERTON, DEVON, EX16 4NA.
SOUTHGATE, Mr. Stephen Robert, MA FCA FCCA CTA *1979;* 2424 Mark Lane, LAKE CHARLES, LA 70611, UNITED STATES.
SOUTHGATE, Mrs. Victoria Louise, BSc ACA *2009;* Crown Mortgage Management Ltd Crown House, Crown Street, IPSWICH, IP1 3HS.
SOUTHON, Mr. Mark Andrew, MA ACA *2000;* 38 Wycombe Road, MARLOW, BUCKINGHAMSHIRE, SL7 3HX.

•**SOUTHWARD, Mr. Eric James, FCA** *1974;* (Tax Fac), Saint & Co., 12-13 Church Street, WHITEHAVEN, CA28 7AY.
SOUTHWARD, Mr. Ian Douglas, FCA *1970;* Ian D. Southward, 40 Wingate Road, LONDON, W6 0UR.
SOUTHWELL, Mr. Alfred Mark, BEng ACA *1998;* 70 Eversleigh Road, Clapham, LONDON, SW11 5XA.
SOUTHWELL, Mrs. Annette Marie, FCA *1970;* 32 Park Crescent, EMSWORTH, HAMPSHIRE, PO10 7NT.
SOUTHWELL, Mr. Christopher John, BA ACA *1987;* Dodges House, 44 Fore Street, Bradninch, EXETER, EX5 4NN.
SOUTHWELL, Miss. Emma Catherine, BA ACA *1995;* 8a Darwin Road, LONDON, W5 4BD.
•**SOUTHWELL, Miss. Joanna Lesley, BSc ACA** *1992;* Mayfield Accounting Ltd, 36 Chiswick Green Studios, 1 Evershed Walk, LONDON, W4 5BW.
SOUTHWELL, Mr. Paul Graham, BSc FCA *1986;* West Heath House, Lower Wokingham Road, CROWTHORNE, BERKSHIRE, RG45 6BX.
SOUTHWELL, Mr. Philip Hugh, BA ACA *1993;* Blisland House, Fireball Hill, ASCOT, SL5 9PJ.
•**SOUTHWICK, Mr. Eric, BA(Hons) FCA FCIE DChA** *1989;* Eric Southwick & Co, 51 The Avenue, SEAHAM, COUNTY DURHAM, SR7 8NS.
SOUTHWICK, Mrs. Nicola Helen, BSc ACA *2005;* 50 Saffron Way, BOURNEMOUTH, BH11 8TJ.
SOUTHWOOD, Mr. Brian William, FCA *1960;* 121 Albert Road West, Heaton, BOLTON, BL1 5ED. (Life Member)
SOUTHWOOD, Mr. Chris, LLB ACA *2007;* 41 Woodlands Grange, Forest Hall, NEWCASTLE UPON TYNE, NE12 9DG.
SOUTHWOOD, Mr. David, FCA *1971;* 15 Northorpe Lane, Thurlby, BOURNE, PE10 0HE.
SOUTHWOOD, Mr. David Howell, BSc FCA *1976;* 74 Park Street, BRIDGEND, MID GLAMORGAN, CF31 4BB.
SOUTHWOOD, Mr. Mark Andrew, BSc(Hons) ACA *2002;* 28 Sandwath Drive, Church Fenton, TADCASTER, NORTH YORKSHIRE, LS24 9US.
•**SOUTHWOOD, Mr. Wayne Edward, ACA** *2003;* KPMG LLP, 15 Canada Square, LONDON, E14 5GL. See also KPMG Europe LLP
SOUTHWORTH, Mr. Alan James, MA FCA *1973;* 7 Manor Road, Marple, STOCKPORT, SK6 6PW.
•**SOUTHWORTH, Mr. Ian Gerard, BSc FCA** *1982;* (Tax Fac), Southworth & Co, Unit 3 Investment House, 28 Queens Road, WEYBRIDGE, SURREY, KT13 9UT.
SOUTHWORTH, Miss. Jane, BSc(Hons) ACA *2004;* Unit 5, 11-13 Alfreda Street, COOGEE, NSW 2034, AUSTRALIA.
SOUTHWORTH, Mr. John Ashurst, BA FCA *1975;* Peterhill, 49 Monument Lane, Chalfont St. Peter, GERRARDS CROSS, BUCKINGHAMSHIRE, SL9 0HY.
•**SOUTHWORTH, Mr. John Peter, FCA** *1970;* Southworth & Co Ltd, Woodlea, Four Elms, EDENBRIDGE, TN8 6NE.
SOUTHWORTH, Mr. Jonathan, BSc ACA *2009;* 15 Dukes Road, TUNBRIDGE WELLS, TN1 2PA.
SOUTHWORTH, Mrs. Michaela Jayne, BA(Hons) ACA *2001;* 36 Capstan Square, Docklands, LONDON, E14 3EU.
SOUTHWORTH, Mr. Paul Anthony, BA ACA *1998;* 20 Goodwood Close, MIDHURST, WEST SUSSEX, GU29 9JG.
SOUTHWORTH, Mr. Peter David, FCA *1968;* Rivendell, 11a Grange Road, Duxford, CAMBRIDGE, CB22 4QE.
SOUTHWORTH, Mr. Roger Walter Geoffrey, BCom FCA *1974;* Johnson & Johnson Consumer Zug, Landis & Gyr Strasse, 6304 ZUG, SWITZERLAND.
SOUTHWORTH, Mrs. Ruth Emma, BA ACA *1987;* 47 Cambridge Road, Abington, CAMBRIDGE, CAMBRIDGESHIRE, CB21 6BL.
SOUTHWORTH, Miss. Sarah Elaine, BSc ACA *2002;* 8 Woodland Road, ULVERSTON, CUMBRIA, LA12 0DX.
SOUTHWORTH, Ms. Sarah Jane Louise, BSc ACA *1996;* 6 Standring Avenue, BURY, BL8 2DT.
SOUTHWORTH, Mrs. Zoe Jane, BSc ACA *2003;* 27 St. Marks Avenue, HARROGATE, NORTH YORKSHIRE, HG2 8AF.
SOUTTER, Mr. David George Michael, BA FCA *1981;* Dryden, Baunton Lane, Stratton, CIRENCESTER, GL7 2LL.
SOUTTER, Mr. David John Mark, FCA *1982;* Heron House, Durford Road, PETERSFIELD, GU31 4EW.
SOUTTER, Mrs. Julie Ann, BSc FCA *1984;* North Star House, Technology Strategy Board North Star House, North Star Avenue Hawksworth Trading Estate, SWINDON, SN2 1JF.
SOUTZOS, Mr. Nicholas Aristotle, BA(Hons) ACA *2000;* 96 Claxton Grove, Hammersmith, LONDON, W6 8HE.
SOUZOU, Mr. Marios, BA(Econ) ACA *1998;* LIMASSOL AVE 5, PO BOX 26758, 1647 NICOSIA, CYPRUS.
SOVMIZ, Miss. Bella, ACA *2009;* 126 Amathountos Avenue, Alania Complex, Block 3 Flat 41, Ag. Tychonas, 4532 LIMASSOL, CYPRUS.
SOWDEN, Mr. Daniel John, BEng ACA *2004;* 48 Rythergate, Cawood, SELBY, NORTH YORKSHIRE, YO8 3TP.
SOWDEN, Mr. David Richard, BA FCA *1989;* 31 West End Drive, CLECKHEATON, BD19 6JD.
SOWDEN, Mrs. Joanna Sarah, BSc ACA *2005;* 76 Talbot Road, RICKMANSWORTH, HERTFORDSHIRE, WD3 1HE.
•**SOWDEN, Mrs. Leah Janice, FCA DChA** *1984;* Saffery Champness, Fox House, 26 Temple End, HIGH WYCOMBE, HP13 5DR.
SOWDEN, Mr. Philip, FCA *1975;* Oxford Brookes University, Kennet House, London Road, OXFORD, OXFORDSHIRE, OX3 7PE.
•**SOWERBUTTS, Ms. Liesl Glennie, BA ACA** *1999;* Sowerbutts & Co Ltd, Fiscal House, 367 London Road, CAMBERLEY, GU15 3HQ.
SOWERBUTTS, Mr. Richard, BA FCA *1973;* 2 North Square, Hampstead Garden Suburb, LONDON, NW11 7AA.
SOWERBY, Mrs. Clare Elizabeth, ACA *2006;* Ellendale, Oughterside, WIGTON, CUMBRIA, CA7 2PY.
SOWERBY, Mr. David Richard, BA FCA *1969;* Little Beeches, Holsome Lane, Diptford, TOTNES, DEVON, TQ9 7NU.
SOWERBY, Miss. Emma Louise, BA ACA *2010;* with PricewaterhouseCoopers LLP, The Atrium, 1 Harefield Road, UXBRIDGE, UB8 1EX.
•**SOWERBY, Mr. John, FCA** *1968;* John Sowerby, 9 Dyson Drive, KETTERING, NN16 9HR.
SOWERBY, Mr. John, BSc FCA *1989;* 1 Beechwood Drive, BISHOP AUCKLAND, DL14 6XS.
SOWERBY, Mr. John Alexander, FCA *1955;* Holm Hurst, Dedswell Drive, West Clandon, GUILDFORD, SURREY, GU4 7TQ. (Life Member)
SOWERBY, Mr. John Keith, FCA *1957;* 99 Freshfield Road, Formby, LIVERPOOL, L37 7BJ. (Life Member)
SOWERBY, Miss. Lauren, ACA *2011;* 26 Charnley Drive, LEEDS, LS7 4ST.
•**SOWERBY, Mrs. Lynnette, BSc ACA** *1995;* Buchanan Lodge, Scorton, RICHMOND, NORTH YORKSHIRE, DL10 6EW.
SOWERBY, Mr. Mark Andrew, BSc ACA *1996;* Buchanan Lodge, Scorton, RICHMOND, NORTH YORKSHIRE, DL10 6EW.
SOWERBY, Miss. Rachael Rose, BSc ACA *2009;* 11 Marine Parade, SALTBURN-BY-THE-SEA, CLEVELAND, TS12 1DP.
SOWERBY, Mr. Richard Anthony, BA ACA *1993;* 49a Carr Hill Road, Upper Cumberworth, HUDDERSFIELD, HD8 8XN.
SOWERBY, Mr. Richard Thomas, FCA *1971;* Wentworth House, Week St. Mary, HOLSWORTHY, EX22 6UL. (Life Member)
SOWERBY, Mr. Stephen Michael, ACA *2010;* 585 Didsbury Road, STOCKPORT, CHESHIRE, SK4 3AS.
•**SOWMAN, Mr. Christopher Stephen, FCA** *1979;* Kenneth Law Sowman & Co, 3 Leicester Road, Oadby, LEICESTER, LE2 5BD.
SOWMAN, Mr. Ian Michael, BSc ACA *2004;* 9 Marlpit Rise, SUTTON COLDFIELD, B75 5LU.
SOWMAN, Mr. William, FCA *1950;* 2 The Albany, 240 London Road, LEICESTER, LE2 1RH. (Life Member)
SOWRY, Miss. Heather Madeleine, ACA *2007;* 3 First Avenue, WALTON-ON-THAMES, SURREY, KT12 2HL.
SOWTER, Miss. Rachel Ann, BSc ACA *2004;* Meadow Farm, Park Lane, Kirkby-in-Ashfield, NOTTINGHAM, NG17 9LE.
SOWTER, Mr. Timothy James, BA ACA *2000;* (Tax Fac), 76 South Vale, HARROW, MIDDLESEX, HA1 3PH.
SOWTON, Mr. Matthew, BSc(Hons) ACA *2004;* Flat 218 Berglen Court, 7 Branch Road, LONDON, E14 7JZ.
SOYE, Mr. Andrew, BSc ACA *1998;* 12 Evelyn Road, Wimbledon, LONDON, SW19 8NU.
SOYEGE, Miss. Oluwakemi Titilayo, BA ACA *1993;* 86 Sirdar Road, LONDON, W11 4EG.
SOYFOO, Mr. Fazeel, ACA *2008;* Citigroup Centre, 33 Canada Square, LONDON, E14 5LB.
SOZOU, Mr. George, BSc FCA *1993;* Aristo Developers Ltd, Aristo Centre, 8 April 1st Street, P.O. Box 60269, PAPHOS, 8101 CYPRUS.
SOZOU, Mr. Panicos, BA ACA *2001;* Deloitte & Touche LLP, Brookfield Place, 181 Bay Street, Suite 1400, TORONTO M5J 2V1, ON CANADA.
SPACEY, Mrs. Katherine Jane, BSc(Hons) ACA *2004;* 9 Bodiam Close, Ingleby Barwick, STOCKTON-ON-TEES, CLEVELAND, TS17 5GQ.
SPACKMAN, Mrs. Anne-Marie Dilini, BSc ACA *1993;* 71 Highlands Road, LEATHERHEAD, KT22 8NW.
SPACKMAN, Mr. Simon Christopher, BSc ACA *1995;* British American Tobacco, Globe House, 4 Temple Place, LONDON, WC2R 2PG.
SPAIN, Mr. Alexander Jerome, BCom ACA *1975; (ACA Ireland 1958);* 24 Mount Merrion Avenue, Blackrock, DUBLIN, COUNTY DUBLIN, IRELAND. (Life Member)
SPAIN, Mr. Robert David, ACA *2008;* Flat 4, 91 Sunny Gardens Road, LONDON, NW4 1SH.
SPAIN, Mr. William Graeme, FCA *1961;* Crestacre House Bruton Road, Evercreech, SHEPTON MALLET, SOMERSET, BA4 6HN. (Life Member)
SPALDIN, Mr. Terence Anthony, BA ACA *1982;* 21 Relton Way, The Woodlands, HARTLEPOOL, TS26 0BB.
SPALDING, Ms. Amanda Elizabeth, BA ACA FCMI *1983;* 17 Egan Place, BEACON HILL, NSW 2100, AUSTRALIA.
SPALDING, Mr. Nigel Joseph Crichton, BSc ACA *1990;* 46 Princes Court, LONDON, SE16 7TD.
SPALDING, Mr. Richard Lionel, FCA *1963;* 9 Britannia Square, WORCESTER, WR1 3DG.
SPALDING, Mr. Stuart Oliver, FCA *1972;* 85 Main Road, Harlaston, TAMWORTH, B79 9HG.
•**SPALL, Mr. Christopher John, BA FCA** *1993;* KPMG LLP, 15 Canada Square, LONDON, E14 5GL. See also KPMG Europe LLP
SPALL, Miss. Nina-Beth, ACA *2010;* 33 Burn Road, HUDDERSFIELD, HD3 3BT.
SPALTER, Mr. Jonathan Andrew, LLB ACA *2001;* 75 Sunnyfield, Mill Hill, LONDON, NW7 4RE.
SPALTON, Mr. Andrew John, BA ACA *2001;* 9a Macklin Street, LONDON, WC2B 5NE.
SPALTON, Miss. Eileen Kirsten, ACA *2009;* 12 Francis Street, READING, RG1 2QB.
•**SPALTON, Mr. John Arthur, FCA** *1976;* James Worley & Sons, 9 Bridle Close, Surbiton Road, KINGSTON UPON THAMES, SURREY, KT1 2JW.
•**SPALTON, Mrs. Natalie Sara, FCA** *2000;* Dickinsons, Enterprise House, Beesons Yard, Bury Lane, RICKMANSWORTH, HERTFORDSHIRE WD3 1DS.
SPANKIE, Mr. Edward Ellison, BA ACA *1981;* 5 Longfield, Manorbier, TENBY, SA70 7TN.
SPANKIE, Mr. Gordon Robert, BA FCA *1985;* Queens College, High Street, OXFORD, OX1 4AW.
SPANN, Mr. Neil, BSc ACA *1999;* 61 White Rocks Grove, Whitburn, SUNDERLAND, SR6 7LL.
SPANNER, Mr. Trevor William, BA ACA *1986;* Broadgate West, The Depository Trust & Clearing Corporation, 1 Snowden Street, LONDON, EC2A 2DQ.
•**SPANO, Mr. Marco, BSc ACA** *1992;* (Tax Fac), Roccia LLP, 19 Crown Passage, St James, LONDON, SW1Y 6PP.
SPANOS, Mr. Ioannis, BSc ACA *2010;* Flat 204, 17 Achilleos Street, Engomi, 2413 NICOSIA, CYPRUS.
SPANOU, Miss. Katerina, BSc ACA *2010;* 6 Makedenias St., Aglantzia, 2107 NICOSIA, CYPRUS.
SPANOUDAKIS, Mr. Christopher John, BSc ACA *1990;* Equita Corporate Finance, Bury Court, Little Linford Lane, Little Linford, MILTON KEYNES, MK19 7EB.
SPANTON, Mr. Christopher Michael, BSc ACA *1989;* 783 Loburn Whiterock Road, RD2, RANGIORA 7472, NEW ZEALAND.
SPARE, Miss. Amy Joy, BA(Hons) ACA *2010;* 43 Halton Road, LONDON, N1 2EN.
SPARGO, Mr. Kenvyn, FCA *1954;* 21 Mountbatten Close, Roath Park, CARDIFF, CF23 5QG. (Life Member)
SPARGO, Mr. Nicholas Edward, FCA MAAT *1998;* 24 Swale Road, SUTTON COLDFIELD, B76 2BH.
SPARHAM-SOUTER, Mr. Ian James, BSc ACA *1993;* 15 Clocktower Mews, Islington, LONDON, N1 7BB.
SPARK, Mr. Alexander James, BA ACA *1998;* 44a Culverden Down, TUNBRIDGE WELLS, KENT, TN4 9SG.
SPARK, Miss. Frances Rebecca, BSc ACA *1987;* 890 Winter Street, Suite 200, WALTHAM, MA 02451, UNITED STATES.
•**SPARK, Mrs. Kirsty Joanne, BSc ACA** *2003;* 3 Fieldhead Drive, Guiseley, LEEDS, LS20 8DX.
SPARKE, Ms. Caroline Emma, BSc ACA *1995;* West Aish Farm, Morchard Bishop, CREDITON, DEVON, EX17 6RX.
SPARKE, Mrs. Joanne, BSc ACA ATII *1994;* 12 Glastonbury Avenue, Upton, CHESTER, CH2 1NG.
•**SPARKE, Mr. Michael, FCA** *1978;* (Tax Fac), Jones Avens Limited, Piper House, 4 Dukes Court, Bognor Road, CHICHESTER, PO19 8FX.
SPARKE, Mr. Richard John, BSc FCA *1977;* 3 White Lion Way, YATELEY, GU46 7TA.
SPARKE, Ms. Sarah Elizabeth, BSc(Hons) ACA *2004;* 42 The Wynd, NORTH SHIELDS, TYNE AND WEAR, NE30 2TE.
SPARKES, Mrs. Gemma Victoria, BSocSc ACA *2002;* 119 Oak Farm Road, BIRMINGHAM, B30 1ET.
•**SPARKES, Mr. John, FCA** *1970;* 48 Browning Avenue, Boscombe, BOURNEMOUTH, BH5 1NW.
SPARKES, Mr. John Leslie, MBE FCA *1961;* High House, Lamarsh, BURES, CO8 5EP.
SPARKES, Mr. Jonathan Andrew, BSc ACA *2000;* with PricewaterhouseCoopers LLP, Princess Court, 23 Princess Street, PLYMOUTH, PL1 2EX.
SPARKES, Mr. Paul Trevor, MSc ACA *2002;* Nutwood Arbour Lane, Wickham Bishops, WITHAM, CM8 3NT.
SPARKES, Mr. Peter Leonard Hargreave, FCA *1967;* Cherrycroft, Knowle, BRAUNTON, DEVON, EX33 2LW.
•**SPARKES, Mr. Ralph Edward, FCA** *1967;* Sparkes & Co, Tarquin, Brinsea Road, Congresbury, BRISTOL, BS49 5JF.
•**SPARKES, Mr. Richard William, ACA** *1986;* (Tax Fac), Richard Sparkes, Garden Cottage, Barking, IPSWICH, IP6 8HJ.
SPARKES, Mr. Stuart David, BSc(Econ) ACA *2001;* 8 Bertram Cottages, Wimbledon, LONDON, SW19 1LQ.
SPARKES, Miss. Susan Jane, BSc ACA *1987;* Tyrrell and Company, Suite D, South Cambridgeshire Business Park, Babraham Road, Sawston, CAMBRIDGE CB22 3JH.
SPARKS, Mr. David Hilary, BA ACA *1998;* 7/ 230 Coogee Bay Road, COOGEE, NSW 2034, AUSTRALIA.
SPARKS, Mr. Denis Colin Reginald, FCA *1969;* 12 Denton Court, 1a Avenue Road, ISLEWORTH, MIDDLESEX, TW7 4RS. (Life Member)
•**SPARKS, Mr. Justin, BSc ACA** *1995;* Springboard Corporate Finance Limited, Baskerville House, Centenary Square, BIRMINGHAM, B1 2ND.
SPARKS, Mrs. Laura Catherine, ACA *2005;* 17 Nunnery Walk, South Cave, BROUGH, NORTH HUMBERSIDE, HU15 2JA.
SPARKS, Mr. Nigel, ACA *2002;* Synpac Ltd Saxon Way, Priory Park, HESSLE, NORTH HUMBERSIDE, HU13 9PB.
•**SPARKS, Mr. Paul Antony, ACA FCCA** *2009;* Cheney & Co, 310 Wellingborough Road, NORTHAMPTON, NN1 4EP.
SPARKS, Mr. Philip Nigel, MEng FCA *1992;* 90 Queens Road, Wimbledon, LONDON, SW19 8LS.
SPARKS, Mr. Robert John, BSc ACA *1997;* The Long House, Church Lane, Chearsley, AYLESBURY, BUCKINGHAMSHIRE, HP18 0DH.
SPARKS, Mr. Russell George, BSc ACA *1996;* Bracken Cottage, 45 Silver Street, Nailsea, BRISTOL, BS48 2AA.
SPARKS, Miss. Tina Louise, BSc ACA *2005;* 67 Station Road, Castlethorpe, MILTON KEYNES, MK19 7HF.
SPARROW, Mrs. Caroline, BA ACA *2011;* 73 Ryeworth Road, Charlton Kings, CHELTENHAM, GLOUCESTERSHIRE, GL52 6LS.
SPARROW, Mr. Charles Edward, MA FCA *1988;* 18 Church Road, RICHMOND, TW9 1UA.
SPARROW, Mr. Christopher John Ward, BSc ACA *1991;* Cross Commons, Sweethaws Lane, CROWBOROUGH, EAST SUSSEX, TN6 3SS.
SPARROW, Mr. Christopher Simon, BSc FCIB FCA MCT MSI CISA *1990;* 20 Cliff Way, Claremont, PERTH, WA 6010, AUSTRALIA.
SPARROW, Mr. Douglas William, ACA *2008;* 73 Ryeworth Road, Charlton Kings, CHELTENHAM, GLOUCESTERSHIRE, GL52 6LS.
SPARROW, Mrs. Heather, BSc FCA *1992;* (Tax Fac), 20 Cliff Way, CLAREMONT, WA 6010, AUSTRALIA.
SPARROW, Miss. Helen Jane, BSc ACA *1993;* 37 Elborough Street, LONDON, SW18 5DP.
SPARROW, Mr. James Edward, BA ACA *1995;* RBS 135 Bishopsgate, LONDON, EC2M 3UR.
SPARROW, Mr. Mark Edward, BSc ACA *2010;* 1601 West MacArthur Boulevard, Apt 1C, SANTA ANA, CA 92704, UNITED STATES.

SPARROW, Mr. Richard Charles, LLB FCA *1982;* 25 Glen Road, LEIGH-ON-SEA, ESSEX, SS9 1EU.
SPARROW, Mr. Stephen Roy, BA ACA *1983;* 19 South Drive, SUTTON, SM2 7PH.
SPARROW, Mr. Thomas Marc, ACA *2008;* Actis Capital Llp, Eighth Floor, 2 More London Riverside, LONDON, SE1 2JT.
SPARROW, Mrs. Vanessa Jayne, ACA MAAT *2004;* One Capital Place PO Box 847, GEORGE TOWN, KY1-1103, CAYMAN ISLANDS.
SPARSHATT, Ms. Alison Gail, BSc FCA *1985;* Tyisha, Llangorse, BRECON, POWYS, LD3 7UA.
SPARSHOTT, Mr. Graham Neal, BA ACA *1992;* 112 Edge Hill, Ponteland, NEWCASTLE UPON TYNE, NE20 9JQ.
•**SPARSHOTT, Mr. Ian Robert, BSc ACA** *1998;* Deloitte LLP, Athene Place, 66 Shoe Lane, LONDON, EC4A 3BQ. See also Deloitte & Touche LLP
SPARY, Mr. Charles, MSc BEng ACA *1999;* Cartref Lodge La Rue Du Froid Vent, St. Saviour, JERSEY, JE2 7LJ.
SPASH, Mrs. Susan, BSc ACA CTA *1990;* (Tax Fac), 88 Cambridge Street, Pimlico, LONDON, SW1V 4QG.
•**SPASHETT, Mr. Mark Geoffrey, BSc FCA** *1990;* Guilfoyle Sage Gloucester, 58 Eastgate Street, GLOUCESTER, GL1 1QN.
SPATER, Miss. Mariana, FCA *1980;* Fountain Television Ltd, 128 Wembley Park Drive, WEMBLEY, MIDDLESEX, HA9 8HQ.
SPATH, Mr. Christopher Antony, ACA *2009;* 63 Old Newtown Road, NEWBURY, RG14 7DE.
SPAUGHTON, Mr. Bernard, FCA *1950;* 18 The Avenue, Cheam, SUTTON, SM2 7QB. (Life Member)
•**SPAUL, Mrs. Gillian Frances Mary, MA ACA** *1993;* 34 Thornton Hill, EXETER, EX4 4NS.
SPAUL, Dr. Sophie Anne, ACA *2008;* 3 Thwaite Hall Barns, Bungay Road Thwaite, BUNGAY, SUFFOLK, NR35 2EF.
•**SPAULS, Mrs. Helen Jayne, ACA CTA** *2007;* (Tax Fac), with Smethurst & Buckton Ltd, 12 Abbey Road, GRIMSBY, SOUTH HUMBERSIDE, DN32 0HL.
SPAVEN, Mr. Richard Alexander, ACA *2011;* 31 Park Road, Southville, BRISTOL, BS3 1PU.
SPAVENTA, Mr. Lee, BEng ACA *2001;* 30 Drovers Way, BISHOP'S STORTFORD, HERTFORDSHIRE, CM23 4GF.
SPAVINS, Mr. John Chamberlain, FCA *1965;* 2 Macandrew Road, POOLE, DORSET, BH13 7JQ. (Life Member)
SPAWFORTH, Mrs. Sara Anne, MA ACA *1990;* The Croft, Reeds School, Sandy Lane, COBHAM, SURREY, KT11 2ES.
SPEAIGHT, Mr. Crispin John, FCA *1969;* 75 St. Georges Avenue, LONDON, N7 0AJ. (Life Member)
SPEAK, Mr. Andrew Aitchison, BA ACA *1982;* 19 Sandown Road, ESHER, KT10 9TT.
SPEAK, Mr. Peter James, BA ACA *1987;* 152 Harestone Valley Road, CATERHAM, CR3 6HJ.
SPEAK, Mr. William Gary, ACA *1992;* 48 Pendle Drive, Calderstones Park, Whalley, CLITHEROE, LANCASHIRE, BB7 9JT.
SPEAKE, Mr. Michael James, FCA *1974;* 504 Montroyal Place, NORTH VANCOUVER V7N 3E4, BC, CANADA.
•**SPEAKMAN, Mr. Allan John, BA FCA** *1994;* Beever and Struthers, St George's House, 215-219 Chester Road, MANCHESTER, M15 4JE.
SPEAKMAN, Mr. David, ACA *1995;* Meadow View, Swan Bank, Madeley Heath, CREWE, CW3 9LE.
SPEAKMAN, Mr. David William Henry, FCA *1972;* 9 Maldon Road, Ashfield Park, Standish, WIGAN, LANCASHIRE, WN6 0EX.
SPEAKMAN, Mr. Kenneth Ian, FCA *1972;* 1 Croesmere Drive, Great Sutton, ELLESMERE PORT, CH66 2WQ. (Life Member)
SPEAKMAN, Mr. Nicholas, BA(Hons) ACA *2002;* Rookery Barn, Station Road, Madeley, CREWE, CW3 9PW.
SPEAKMAN, Mr. Paul Jonathan, BSc ACA *1998;* 7 Barncroft Drive, Horwich, BOLTON, BL6 6NZ.
SPEAKMAN, Mrs. Samantha Claire, BA ACA *2000;* Rookery Barn, Station Road, Madeley, CREWE, CW3 9PW.
SPEAR, Mr. Alistair Giles, BSc ACA *1989;* 7 Thornton Mews, Cambridge Road, CROWTHORNE, RG45 7EF.
SPEAR, Mrs. Debra Jane, BA ACA *1989;* Applicable Ltd Great Western Court, Hunts Ground Road Stoke Gifford, BRISTOL, BS34 8HP.
SPEARE, Mr. David Frederick, FCA *1957;* 11 Locking Stumps Lane, Birchwood, WARRINGTON, WA3 7LZ. (Life Member)
SPEARING, Mr. Christopher John, FCA *1977;* 47 Field Gardens, Steventon, ABINGDON, OX13 6TF.
SPEARING, Mr. Christopher Philip, ACA *2009;* Flat 3, Richbourne Court, 9 Harrowby Street, LONDON, W1H 5PT.
SPEARING, Mrs. Michelle Louise, BA FCA *1996;* The Sycamores Shoreham Road, Small Dole, HENFIELD, BN5 9YG.
SPEARING, Mr. Roger Edward, FCA *1968;* Tee Financial Plc, 47 Dane Street, BISHOP'S STORTFORD, HERTFORDSHIRE, CM23 3BT.
SPEARINK, Mr. James Robert, BSc(Hons) ACA *2006;* Sussex Finance Consultancy Ltd Silverdale, Lower Road, FOREST ROW, EAST SUSSEX, RH18 5HE.
SPEARMAN, Ms. Jessica Ann, BA(Hons) ACA *2002;* 34b Gainsborough Road, LONDON, N12 8AG.
SPEARS, Mrs. Jacqueline Helen, BSocSc ACA *1996;* 31 Lodge Hill Road, Lower Bourne, FARNHAM, GU10 3QW.
•**SPECK, Mr. Graham, ACA** *2000;* Clarkson Hyde LLP, 3rd Floor, Chancery House, St. Nicholas Way, SUTTON, SURREY SM1 1JB.
•**SPECTERMAN, Mr. Darren, BA FCA** *1991;* (Tax Fac), Glazers, 843 Finchley Road, LONDON, NW11 8NA. See also Glazers Ltd
•**SPECTERMAN, Mr. David Barry, FCA MBA** *1976;* (Tax Fac), DBS Accounting Services Limited, Parade House, 135 The Parade, WATFORD, WD17 1NA. See also DBS Accountinh Services Limited
SPECTERMAN, Mr. Leonard Paul, FCA DChA *1970;* 10 Heather Walk, EDGWARE, MIDDLESEX, HA8 9TS.
SPECTOR, Mr. Ivor, BSc FCA *1975;* Endways, 10 Copthall Close, Chalfont St. Peter, GERRARDS CROSS, SL9 0DH.
SPECTOR, Mr. Simon Francis, FCA *1974;* 63 Sutton Crescent, BARNET, HERTFORDSHIRE, EN5 2SW.
SPEDDING, Mrs. Amanda Jane, BA ACA *1983;* Hazel Croft Rise, 27 Congleton Road, ALDERLEY EDGE, SK9 7AE.
SPEDDING, Mr. David Newman, BA FCA *1973;* (Tax Fac), 32 Hobart Road, DEWSBURY, WEST YORKSHIRE, WF12 7LS.
SPEDDING, Mr. Nigel Keith, MA ACA *1985;* The Police House, Hatton Green, Hatton, WARWICK, CV35 7LA.
•**SPEDDING, Mr. Robert Wynne, LLB FCA** *1980;* KPMG LLP, 15 Canada Square, LONDON, E14 5GL. See also KPMG Europe LLP
•**SPEDDING, Mr. Roger Philip, FCA** *1977;* Elliott & Partners, 1 Sudley Terrace, High Street, BOGNOR REGIS, WEST SUSSEX, PO21 1EY.
SPEDDY, Mr. Roger, MSc ACA *1979;* c/o Booker Tate Limited, Masters Court, Church Road, THAME, OX9 3FA.
SPEECHLEY, Mr. Clifford, FCA *1953;* Rosebank, 17 Givendale Road, SCARBOROUGH, YO12 6LE. (Life Member)
SPEECHLEY, Mr. James Andrew, BA ACA *2008;* 46 Haworth Avenue, ROSSENDALE, LANCASHIRE, BB4 8SS.
SPEED, Mr. Jeremy Edward Martin, FCA *1964;* Overdale, Wallow Green, Horsley, STROUD, GLOUCESTERSHIRE, GL6 0PD.
SPEED, Mrs. Joanne, BA ACA *1994;* visyon Ltd, Congleton Borough Council Municipal Offices, Market Square, CONGLETON, CHESHIRE, CW12 1EX.
•**SPEED, Mr. John Anthony Bradley, BSc FCA** *1992;* JS2 Limited, 1 Crown Square, Church Street East, WOKING, SURREY, GU21 6HR.
SPEED, Mr. Mark James, BSc ACA *1992;* 6 Bronte Avenue, Stotfold, HITCHIN, HERTFORDSHIRE, SG5 4FB.
SPEED, Mrs. Sara Elizabeth, BA(Hons) ACA *2002;* 7a rue de Mondorf, L-5670 ALTWIES, LUXEMBOURG.
SPEED, Mr. Trevor John, FCA *1974;* 18 Rutland Road, Wanstead, LONDON, E11 2DY.
SPEED-ANDREWS, Mr. John Charles Langford, BSc ACA *1985;* 73 Waterfall Avenue, CRAIGHALL, 2196, SOUTH AFRICA.
•**SPEEDIE, Mr. Hugh Ian, FCA** *1972;* 86 Grange Close, Horam, HEATHFIELD, EAST SUSSEX, TN21 0EG.
SPEER, Mr. Michael Patrick, FCA *1963;* 83a Thoroughfare, WOODBRIDGE, SUFFOLK, IP12 1AH.
SPEER, Mr. Sidney Edward, FCA *1953;* 22 Greenhill Road, Otford, SEVENOAKS, KENT, TN14 5RS. (Life Member)
SPEIGHT, Mr. Charles Edmund, FCA *1951;* Flat 2 Osborne House, 73 Alderley Road, WILMSLOW, CHESHIRE, SK9 1PA. (Life Member)
SPEIGHT, Mrs. Deborah Elizabeth, BSc ACA *1990;* Fidelity International, PO Box HM 670, HAMILTON HN CX, BERMUDA.
SPEIGHT, Miss. Dorcas Rebecca, BA(Hons) ACA *2000;* 103 Moat Way, Swavesey, CAMBRIDGE, CAMBRIDGESHIRE, CB4 5GQ.
SPEIGHT, Mr. Humphrey John Westby, FCA *1967;* 5 Birchitt Close, SHEFFIELD, S17 4QJ.
SPEIGHT, Mr. Michael Robert, BSc ACA *2007;* 15 Lickless Gardens Horsforth, LEEDS, LS18 5QU.
SPEIGHT, Mr. Neil, BSc ACA *1989;* P O Box 932, HAMILTON HM DX, BERMUDA.
SPEIGHT, Mr. Neil Geoffrey, LLB ACA *2004;* with KPMG LLP, 15 Canada Square, LONDON, E14 5GL.
SPEIR, Mr. James, BSc(Hons) ACA CTA *2004;* 37 Tall Cedars, IRVINE, CA 92620, UNITED STATES.
SPEIRS, Mr. Allan Bernard, FCA *1958;* The Old Vicarage, Church Lane, West Pennard, GLASTONBURY, BA6 8NT. (Life Member)
•**SPEIRS, Mr. Geoffrey Paul, BSc FCA** *1978;* RSM Tenon Audit Limited, Third Floor Howard House, Queens Avenue, Clifton, BRISTOL, BS8 1QT.
SPEIRS, Mr. Ian Lambie, MEng ACA *1998;* 17 Evelyn Road, LONDON, SW19 8NU.
SPEIRS, Mr. John Frederick, ACA *2009;* 34 Balcombe Street, LONDON, NW1 6ND.
SPEKE, Mr. Jeffrey Peter Hanning, BSc FCA *1988;* Rapps Farm, Ashill, ILMINSTER, TA19 9LG.
SPEKSNYDER, Mr. Gary, FCA *1979;* Somerfield, 1 Manor Drive, SUTTON COLDFIELD, WEST MIDLANDS, B73 6ER.
SPELLER, Mr. Adam Mark, ACA *1987;* 7 Vineyard Mews, Preston Place, RICHMOND, SURREY, TW10 6DD.
SPELLER, Mr. Andrew, BA ACA *2007;* Apartment 12, 8 Dog Kennel Hill, LONDON, SE22 8AA.
•**SPELLER, Mr. Christopher Kenneth, BA FCA** *1976;* (Tax Fac), C K Speller, 2 Claremont Court, Rose Hill, DORKING, SURREY, RH4 2EE. See also Speller
•**SPELLER, Mr. Derek Charles, FCA** *1972;* Churchmill House Ltd, Churchmill House, Ockford Road, GODALMING, SURREY, GU7 1QY.
•**SPELLER, Mr. John Stanley, FCA** *1970;* (Tax Fac), Butler & Speller, 1436 London Road, LEIGH-ON-SEA, ESSEX, SS9 2UL. See also Butler Speller & Stapleton and Taxwrite.co.uk Limited
•**SPELLER, Mr. Leonard Frank, FCA** *1971;* Redwood, Elmstead Road, West Byfleet, WEST BYFLEET, KT14 6JB.
•**SPELLER, Mr. Mark Kirby, MA ACA** *1982;* PricewaterhouseCoopers, Emirates Towers Offices, PO Box 11987, Level 40, Sheikh Zayed Road, PO Box 11987 DUBAI UNITED ARAB EMIRATES.
SPELLER, Mr. Ronald William, FCA *1957;* 529 Johnstone Road Unit 9, PARKSVILLE V9P 2K1, BC, CANADA. (Life Member)
•**SPELLER, Mr. Simon John, ACA** *2003;* Simon Speller Limited, 64 Clarendon Road, WATFORD, WD17 1DA.
SPELLER, Miss. Vicki Lorraine, BA ACA *1997;* with Monahans, 38-42 Newport Street, SWINDON, SN1 3DR.
SPELLISSY, Mr. Peter Turlough, FCA *1969;* 4 Hillcrest Road, Nailsea, BRISTOL, BS48 2JB.
SPELLMAN, Mr. John Ashley, BA FCA *1977;* Applewood, Watling Lane, Thaxted, DUNMOW, ESSEX, CM6 2RA.
•**SPELLMAN, Mr. Stephen Gerard, BA ACA** *1993;* KPMG LLP, 15 Canada Square, LONDON, E14 5GL. See also KPMG Europe LLP
SPENCE, Mr. Adam Max, ACA *2009;* Ingenious Media Plc, 15 Golden Square, LONDON, W1F 9JG.
SPENCE, Mr. Alastair James, BSc ACA *1993;* Chief Financial Officer, Direct Energy, 2225 Sheppard Avenue East, TORONTO M2J 5C2, ON, CANADA.
•**SPENCE, Mr. Andrew, BSc FCA ATII** *1993;* Ernst & Young LLP, Citygate, St James' Boulevard, NEWCASTLE UPON TYNE, NE1 4JD. See also Ernst & Young Europe LLP
SPENCE, Mr. Andrew Martin, BA ACA *1996;* 1635 Kilmer Road, NORTH VANCOUVER V7K 1R6, BC, CANADA.
SPENCE, Miss. Barbara Elizabeth, BA ACA *1986;* 42 Parliament Hill, LONDON, NW3 2TN.
SPENCE, Ms. Barbara Jane, MSc ACA *1980;* 217 Hoylake Crescent, Ickenham, UXBRIDGE, UB10 8JN.
•**SPENCE, Mr. Brian Walter Frederick, MA FCA** *1977;* Montpelier Audit Limited, Montpelier House, 62-66 Deansgate, MANCHESTER, M3 2EN. See also Montpelier Professional (Manchester) Limited, Montpelier Professional (Borders) Limited, Montpelier Professional (Fylde) Limited and Montpelier Professional (Sheffield) Limited
SPENCE, Mr. Darren, BSc ACA *1998;* N M Rothschild & Sons Ltd, PO Box 185, LONDON, EC4P 4DU.
SPENCE, Mrs. Dawn, BSc ACA *2006;* 7 Portgate Close, LIVERPOOL, L12 0SF.
SPENCE, Miss. Deborah Jacqueline, BA ACA *1994;* 3 Lonsdale House, Lonsdale Road, BIRMINGHAM, B17 9QY.
SPENCE, Mr. Iain Mark, BSc FCA *1991;* 2 Bath Street, ILKLEY, LS29 8EL.
SPENCE, Mr. Ian Stuart, BA ACA *1987;* 4653 Newell Drive, MARIETTA, GA 30062, UNITED STATES.
SPENCE, Mr. James Barclay, MA ACA *1990;* Flat 1, 29 Craven Hill Gardens, LONDON, W2 3EA.
SPENCE, Mr. James Sinton, MBE BSc ACA *1980;* P O Box 6861, BOROKO, NATIONAL CAPITAL DISTRICT, 111, PAPUA NEW GUINEA.
SPENCE, Mrs. Kathryn Ann, BA ACA *1979;* Henderson Global Investors, 201 Bishopsgate, LONDON, EC2M 3AE.
SPENCE, Mr. Magnus Andrew Eric, BA FCA *1991;* Wardsbrook House, Wardsbrook Road, Ticehurst, WADHURST, TN5 7DR.
•**SPENCE, Mr. Maxwell Stanley, FCA** *1997;* (Tax Fac), Bennett Jones & Co, 94 Fore Street, BODMIN, PL31 2HR.
SPENCE, Mr. Neil William David, BA FCA *1979;* Greenways, 2 Amersham Road, Chesham Bois, AMERSHAM, HP6 5PE.
SPENCE, Miss. Nicola Clair, BSc ACA *2010;* Flat 18 Hornby House, Clayton Street, LONDON, SE11 5DA.
•**SPENCE, Mr. Nigel Anthony, FCA** *1985;* Nigel Spence & Co, Tan House, 15 South End, Bassingbourn, ROYSTON, HERTFORDSHIRE SG8 5NJ.
•**SPENCE, Mrs. Pamela Helen, BSc ACA** *1995;* Ernst & Young LLP, 1 More London Place, LONDON, SE1 2AF. See also Ernst & Young Europe LLP
SPENCE, Mr. Paul Anthony, MCMI FCA CPA(K) *1962;* P.O. Box 20112, NAIROBI, 00200, KENYA. (Life Member)
SPENCE, Mr. Paul David, BA ACA *2010;* Flat 23 Cumberland Mansions, West End Lane, LONDON, NW6 1LL.
SPENCE, Mr. Robert Gordon, CA ACA *1981;* 41 Beanhill Road, Ducklington, WITNEY, OXFORDSHIRE, OX29 7XZ.
SPENCE, Mr. Robert Jeffrey, BSc ACA *1992;* 24 The Park, Potterhanworth, LINCOLN, LN4 2EB.
SPENCE, Mr. Robert Thomas, ACA *2009;* 17/37 St Georges Terrace, PERTH, WA 6000, AUSTRALIA.
SPENCE, Mrs. Sarah Bethan, ACA *2009;* 29 Glendower Approach, Heathcote, WARWICK, CV34 6ET.
SPENCE, Mr. Sean Michael, BA ACA *1990;* 29 Yester Road, CHISLEHURST, KENT, BR7 5HN.
SPENCE, Miss. Shona Jean Margaret, BSc FCA *1986;* 23 Roland Gardens, LONDON, SW7 3PF.
SPENCE, Mr. Timothy James, BA ACA *2000;* 8 Crofton Avenue, ORPINGTON, BR6 8DU.
SPENCE, Mr. Timothy William, BA(Econ) FCA *1995;* Willow Tree Cottage, Stoney Lane, Ashmore Green, THATCHAM, BERKSHIRE, RG18 9HE.
•**SPENCE CLARKE, Mr. Alistair Marino Archibald, FCA** *1975;* (Tax Fac), Spence Clarke & Co, Edificio Los Pinos L-1, Calle Jacinto Benavente 32, 29600 MARBELLA, SPAIN.
SPENCELAYH, Mr. Robert, ACA *1983;* 14 Millston Close, HARTLEPOOL, CLEVELAND, TS26 0PX.
SPENCELEY, Miss. Carolyn Deborah, BA ACA *1989;* 9 Willow Way, Ponteland, NEWCASTLE UPON TYNE, NE20 9RJ.
SPENCELEY, Mr. Graeme Peter, BSc ACA *1990;* Headlands Hotel, 53 Milnthorpe Road, KENDAL, CUMBRIA, LA9 5QG.
•**SPENCELEY, Mr. John, FCA** *1975;* Clough Tomblin & Co, Nat.Westminster Bank Chmbrs, The Grove, ILKLEY, LS29 9LS.
SPENCER, Mr. Andrew David, BSc ACA *1993;* 63 Percheron Drive, Knaphill, WOKING, GU21 2QY.
SPENCER, Mr. Andrew John, BA ACA *2006;* 78 Hillfield Avenue, LONDON, N8 7DN.
SPENCER, Mr. Anthony, FCA *1967;* 11 Dollis Avenue, Finchley, LONDON, N3 1UD. (Life Member)
SPENCER, Mr. Anthony Edward Tully, BSc FCA *1985;* (Tax Fac), with Hillier Hopkins LLP, Charter Court, Midland Road, HEMEL HEMPSTEAD, HERTFORDSHIRE, HP2 5GE.
SPENCER, Mr. Arthur Matthew, FCA *1952;* 11 Shrewsbury Close, Church GreenLittle Benton, NEWCASTLE UPON TYNE, NE7 7YS. (Life Member)
SPENCER, Mrs. Caroline, BSc ACA *2002;* 26 St. Andrews, Amington, TAMWORTH, STAFFORDSHIRE, B77 4RA.
SPENCER, Mrs. Caroline Diana, BA ACA *1981;* 2 Braeside, HALIFAX, HX2 0AQ.
SPENCER, Mrs. Carolyn Mary, FCA *1972;* (Tax Fac), Brambles, 37a Highfield Close, AMERSHAM, HP6 6HQ.
•**SPENCER, Miss. Christa Andrea Elizabeth, BSc FCA CTA** *1993;* (Tax Fac), CW Fellowes Limited, Templars House, Lulworth Close, Chandlers Ford, EASTLEIGH, SO53 3TL.
SPENCER, Mr. Christopher Maurice, FCA *1951;* 122 Copse Hill, Wimbledon, LONDON, SW20 0NL. (Life Member)

SPENCER, Mr. Christopher Neil, BA ACA *1990;* 26 Avenue Alphonse de Neuville, 92380 GARCHES, FRANCE.
SPENCER, Mr. Christopher Paul, FCA *1975;* Whitewings, Les Camps Du Moulin, St. Martin, GUERNSEY, GY4 6DZ.
SPENCER, Mr. Christopher William, BA ACA *1985;* Green Shires Group Ltd, 160-164 Barkby Road, LEICESTER, LE4 9LF.
SPENCER, Mrs. Claire Ann, BA ACA *2000;* Nene Bridge House, Mill Road, Oundle, PETERBOROUGH, PE8 4BW.
SPENCER, Miss. Claire Emma, BA ACA *2006;* Newbury Racecourse Plc, Newbury Racecourse, NEWBURY, BERKSHIRE, RG14 7NZ.
SPENCER, Miss. Clare, BSc ACA *2011;* 83 Hut Farm Place, Chandler's Ford, EASTLEIGH, HAMPSHIRE, SO53 3LQ.
SPENCER, Mr. Clement Rodney, FCA *1953;* Gorse Green Barn, Gorse Green Lane, Belbroughton, STOURBRIDGE, WEST MIDLANDS, DY9 9UH. (Life Member)
SPENCER, Mr. Clive, BEng ACA *1994;* 79 Plymouth Road, PENARTH, CF64 3DE.
SPENCER, Mr. David Ernest, BA FCA *1996;* 5 Queen Marys Close, Upper Saxondale, Radcliffe-on-Trent, NOTTINGHAM, NG12 2NR.
SPENCER, Mr. David Ingram, FCA *1966;* Birchetts Green Farm, Birchetts Green, WADHURST, TN5 6HS.
SPENCER, Mr. David Neil, BA ACA *1990;* Bartle Bogle Hegarty Limited, 60 Kingly Street, LONDON, W1B 5DS.
SPENCER, Mr. David Stephen, LLB ACA *2006;* 63 Butlers & Colonial Wharf, LONDON, SE1 2PY.
SPENCER, Mr. Derek, FCA *1953;* 5 Saxon Court, Tettenhall, WOLVERHAMPTON, WV6 8SA. (Life Member)
•**SPENCER, Mrs. Eleftheria, BA ACA** *1982;* with Ernst & Young LLP, Apex Plaza, Forbury Road, READING, RG1 1YE.
SPENCER, Mrs. Elizabeth Jane, BSc FCA *1978;* Butts Close Cottage, Stockbridge Road, WINCHESTER, SO22 5JA.
SPENCER, Mrs. Elizabeth Nicola, MSc ACA *2001;* Wildfowl & Wetlands Trust, Slimbridge, GLOUCESTER, GL2 7BT.
SPENCER, Mr. Elliott Louis, ACA *1991;* 4038 Newhaven Circle NE, ATLANTA, GA 30319-1880, UNITED STATES.
SPENCER, Mr. Eric Bryan, MC FCA *1951;* Bay House, 15 Queens Valley, Ramsey, ISLE OF MAN, IM8 1NG. (Life Member)
SPENCER, Miss. Gemma Louise, BSc ACA *2008;* 32 Fortinbras Way, CHELMSFORD, CM2 9PA.
•**SPENCER, Mr. Geoffrey Michael, FCA** *1973;* Geoffrey M. Spencer, The Wincombe Centre, Wincombe Business Park, SHAFTESBURY, DORSET, SP7 9QJ.
SPENCER, Mr. Gordon James, BA FCA *1967;* 1 Emmets Park, Binfield, BRACKNELL, RG42 4HQ. (Life Member)
•**SPENCER, Mr. Gordon Thomas, FCA** *1968;* Gordon Spencer, 70A Victoria Road, WORTHING, BN11 1UN.
SPENCER, Miss. Hayley Louise, ACA *2007;* 53 Beaumont Road, Flitwick, BEDFORD, MK45 1AL.
SPENCER, Miss. Helen, ACA *2009;* 9 Toller Road, LEICESTER, LE2 3HP.
SPENCER, Mr. Henry James, BA ACA *1996;* Garden Flat, 70 Santos Road, Wandsworth, LONDON, SW18 1NS.
•**SPENCER, Mr. Howard Peter, FCA** *1974;* UHY Hacker Young LLP, Quadrant House, 4 Thomas More Square, LONDON, E1W 1YW.
SPENCER, Mrs. Jacqueline Ann, BSc ACA *1995;* 146 Alexandra Gardens, Knaphill, WOKING, SURREY, GU21 2DL.
SPENCER, Mrs. Janice, ACA *1982;* 2 Hanger Way, PETERSFIELD, GU31 4QE.
SPENCER, Mrs. Jean, BA ACA *1984;* Anglian Water Services Ltd Anglian House, Ambury Road South, HUNTINGDON, PE29 3NZ.
SPENCER, Mr. John Herbert, FCA *1959;* 3 Wychford Drive, SAWBRIDGEWORTH, CM21 0HA. (Life Member)
•**SPENCER, Mr. John Leslie, FCA** *1980;* Connor Spencer & Co, Unit 5, Waterside, Station Road, HARPENDEN, HERTFORDSHIRE AL5 4US.
•**SPENCER, Mr. Jonathan Francis, ACA** *1982;* Broomfield & Alexander Limited, Ty Derw, Lime Tree Court, Cardiff Gate Business Park, CARDIFF, CF23 8AB.
SPENCER, Mr. Joseph Jonathan Stephen, ACA *2010;* 73 Johnson Place, 65 Walsworth Road, HITCHIN, HERTFORDSHIRE, SG4 9FJ.
SPENCER, Mrs. Julia Claire, BSc ACA *1993;* 7 Upper Roman Road, CHELMSFORD, CM2 0EX.
SPENCER, Mr. Julian John, BA FCA *1982;* 19 Windmill Lane, EAST GRINSTEAD, RH19 2DT.
SPENCER, Mrs. Katharine Claire, BSc ACA *1996;* 21 Webster Gardens, LONDON, W5 5NA.
SPENCER, Mrs. Kathleen Ann, MRes BSc ACA PGCE *1993;* 10 Royal Avenue, Chorlton, MANCHESTER, M21 9EU.
SPENCER, Mr. Keith, BA FCA *1973;* 2 The Paddock, Manchester Road, Greenfield, OLDHAM, OL3 7PU.
•**SPENCER, Mr. Keith Terence, FCA** *1984;* (Tax Fac), First Call Accounting Ltd, 2nd Floor, Chantrey House, 8-10 High Street, BILLERICAY, ESSEX CM12 9BQ.
SPENCER, Mrs. Lesley, BA ACA *1995;* 5 Queen Marys Close, Radcliffe-on-Trent, NOTTINGHAM, NG12 2NR.
SPENCER, Mrs. Lucy Ellen, BA ACA *2008;* 42 Ouse Road, ST. IVES, CAMBRIDGESHIRE, PE27 3FT.
SPENCER, Mr. Malcolm Geoffrey Harris, FCA ATII *1953;* 7 Lord Austin Drive, Marlbrook, BROMSGROVE, WORCESTERSHIRE, B60 1RB. (Life Member)
SPENCER, Mr. Martin John, FCA *1956;* Bracken Cottage, Cherry Tree Lane, Fulmer, SLOUGH, SL3 6JE. (Life Member)
•**SPENCER, Mr. Martin Russell William, FCA** *1978;* (Tax Fac), CBHC LLP, Riverside House, 1-5 Como Street, ROMFORD, RM7 7DN.
SPENCER, Mr. Martin Steven, BSc ACA *1982;* Q V C, Customer Operations Centre, LIVERPOOL, L70 2QA.
SPENCER, Mr. Maurice Daniel William, BA ACA *1992;* Watercatch East, 3 Frithcote Lane, WARWICK WK 09, BERMUDA.
SPENCER, Mr. Michael George, BCom FCA *1964;* 96 Meols Drive, West Kirby, WIRRAL, MERSEYSIDE, CH48 5DB.
SPENCER, Mr. Nicholas Courtenay Carvosso, FCA *1975;* Hill House, Hollington Cross, Highclere, NEWBURY, RG20 9SE.
SPENCER, Mr. Nicholas David Howard, BA ACA *1987;* 24 Quinton Street, Earlsfield, LONDON, SW18 3QS.
SPENCER, Mr. Nigel Guy, LLB ACA *1989;* Manor Farm House, Main Street, Bilbrough, YORK, YO23 3PH.
SPENCER, Mr. Norman George, FCA *1973;* Redbourne Properties, Suite 700, 1555 Peel Street, MONTREAL H3A 3L8, QUE, CANADA.
SPENCER, Mr. Patrick, BSc ACA *1994;* 11 Sandy Close, HERTFORD, SG14 2BB.
SPENCER, Mr. Paul Michael, BSc ACA *1995;* 3 Hopkins Field, Bowdon, ALTRINCHAM, CHESHIRE, WA14 3AL.
SPENCER, Mr. Peter Thomas, ACA *2008;* 4 Longs Drive, Yate, BRISTOL, BS37 5XN.
•**SPENCER, Mr. Philip, BSc(Econ) FCA** *1976;* (Tax Fac), BDO LLP, 55 Baker Street, LONDON, W1U 7EU. See also BDO Stoy Hayward LLP
SPENCER, Mr. Philip, FCA *1950;* Grenell, Carmel, HOLYWELL, CLWYD, CH8 8QT. (Life Member)
SPENCER, Mr. Philip Leon, BSc ACA *1993;* 7 Ware Road, NORTH BERWICK, EAST LOTHIAN, EH39 4BN.
SPENCER, Miss. Rachel Louisa, BA(Hons) ACA *2003;* Sentinel House, 37/43 Surrey Street, NORWICH, NORFOLK, NR1 3PG.
SPENCER, Mr. Raymond, BA FCA *1979;* 20 Fairway, Kibworth Beauchamp, LEICESTER, LE8 0LB.
•**SPENCER, Mr. Raymond John, BSc ACA** *1980;* 77 West Drive, Highfields Caldecote, CAMBRIDGE, CB23 7RY.
SPENCER, Mr. Richard Allan, BA ACA *1987;* 25 Fitzjohns Road, LEWES, EAST SUSSEX, BN7 1PP.
SPENCER, Mr. Richard Glover, FCA *1961;* Newlands Cottage, Mealsgate, WIGTON, CA7 1AB.
•**SPENCER, Mr. Richard John, BA ACA** *1997;* Buckler Spencer Limited, Old Police Station, Church Street, SWADLINCOTE, DERBYSHIRE, DE11 8LN.
SPENCER, Mr. Robert Bernard, BA FCA *1963;* 8 Rue de la Vallee, 60300 COURTEUIL, FRANCE. (Life Member)
•**SPENCER, Mr. Robert Mcpherson, FCA** *1970;* Robert M Spencer FCA, Heritage House, 6 Wragby Road, Sudbrooke, LINCOLN, LN2 2QU.
SPENCER, Mr. Ronald Ernest, FCA *1937;* 6 Elizabeth Street, CHEGUTU, ZIMBABWE. (Life Member)
SPENCER, Mrs. Rosalind Louise, BSc ACA *1990;* 26 Avenue Alphonse de Neuville, 92380 GARCHES, FRANCE.
SPENCER, Miss. Sally Helen, MChem ACA *2006;* Griffin Marine Travel Ltd, 20-21 Angel Gate, LONDON, EC1V 2PT.
SPENCER, Mr. Simon, FCA *1953;* 3 Barnett Homesteads, Erskine Hill, Hamptead Garden Suburb, LONDON, NW11 6HS. (Life Member)
SPENCER, Mr. Simon Mark, BA ACA *1993;* 37 Andover Road, CHELTENHAM, GL50 2TH.
SPENCER, Mr. Simon Paul, BSc ACA *1989;* Flat 18, 130 Wapping High Street, LONDON, E1W 2NH.
SPENCER, Mr. Stephen John, MSci ACA *2008;* 11 Century Way, HALESOWEN, B63 2TQ.
SPENCER, Mr. Stephen Parr, ACA *1979;* 111 Cheapside, WORKSOP, NOTTINGHAMSHIRE, S80 2JD.
SPENCER, Mr. Steven Lewis, BEng ACA *2000;* 116 Fulwell Road, TEDDINGTON, MIDDLESEX, TW11 0RQ.
SPENCER, Mr. Stuart Peter, BSc FCA *1985;* Redwalls, 36 Beech Hill, Hadley Wood, BARNET, EN4 0JP.
•**SPENCER, Mrs. Tamara Susan, BSc ACA** *1993;* Network 4M Limited, Suite 1, Park Farm Barn, Brabourne, ASHFORD, KENT TN25 6RG.
•**SPENCER, Mr. Terence John, FCA** *1966;* Buckler Spencer Limited, Old Police Station, Church Street, SWADLINCOTE, DERBYSHIRE, DE11 8LN.
SPENCER, Mrs. Theresa Erica, BSc ACA *1995;* Fellowes, Yorkshire Way, Westmoor Park, DONCASTER, DN3 3FB.
SPENCER, Mr. Thomas Anthony John, BSc *2001;* Bishopgate Corporate Finance Ltd, St Peter's Callis, 13 All Saints Street, STAMFORD, LINCOLNSHIRE, PE9 2PA.
SPENCER, Mr. Thomas James, BA ACA *2007;* Newton 609, Nottingham Trent University, Burton Street, NOTTINGHAM, NG1 4BU.
•**SPENCER, Mr. Tim David, BSc ACA** *2002;* Whitten Spencer Limited, 29 High Street, Bridge, CANTERBURY, KENT, CT4 5JZ.
SPENCER, Mr. Timothy Jonathan, BSc ACA *1992;* Flat 18 Riverside Mill House, 20 Church Street, ISLEWORTH, MIDDLESEX, TW7 6XB.
SPENCER, Mr. Tudor George, MBA BA FCA FCIPD *1976;* 2 Stanley Road, East Finchley, LONDON, N2 0NB.
SPENCER, Mrs. Victoria Louise, ACA *2000;* 150 Grove Park, KNUTSFORD, CHESHIRE, WA16 8QD.
SPENCER, Mr. William James Graham, FCA *1956;* 26 Firs Road, Edwalton, NOTTINGHAM, NG12 4BX. (Life Member)
SPENCER-CROW, Mr. David Brian, FCA *1964;* Shere Cottage, 36 Curley Hill Road, LIGHTWATER, GU18 5YH.
SPENCER-GREGSON, Miss. Judith Mary, BCom FCA DChA *1978;* 43 Bardsley Close, Park Hill, CROYDON, CR0 5PT.
•**SPENCER-SMITH, Mr. Thomas Peter, MA FCA** *1973;* Spencer-Smith & Co, The Old Rectory, Llanvetherine, ABERGAVENNY, GWENT, NP7 8RG. See also Orco Services
SPENS-BLACK, Miss. Hannah, BA ACA *2007;* Westgates, Hurst, MARTOCK, SOMERSET, TA12 6JU.
SPENSER, Mr. John Laurence, FCA *1977;* 85 EARLY STREET, MORRISTOWN, NJ 07960, UNITED STATES.
SPENSLEY, Mrs. Angela Rose, ACA *1987;* with Francis Clark, Francis Clark LLP, Sigma House, Oak View Close, Edginswell Park, TORQUAY TQ2 7FF.
SPENSLEY, Mr. Michael Charles, ACA *1993;* 7 Reade Close, Milton-under-Wychwood, CHIPPING NORTON, OXFORDSHIRE, OX7 6LY.
SPENSLEY, Mrs. Sally Sharon Bird, MA ACA MCT *1984;* J Walter Thompson Group Ltd, 1 Knightsbridge Green, LONDON, SW1X 7NW.
SPENSLEY, Mr. Stuart Metcalfe, FCA *1969;* Almonds, Pudding Pie Nook Lane, Goosnargh, PRESTON, PR3 2JL.
•**SPERLING, Mr. Peter John, ACA** *1982;* 1 Bishop House North, Hitcham Road, Taplow, MAIDENHEAD, BERKSHIRE, SL6 0LZ.
SPERO, Mr. Nick Joseph, BA(Hons) ACA *2002;* with BDO LLP, 55 Baker Street, LONDON, W1U 7EU.
SPERRY, Mr. Ian Nicholas, BSc ACA *1995;* Eat Ltd Unit 32-34, Fourth Way, WEMBLEY, MIDDLESEX, HA9 0LH.
SPERRY, Mr. Roy Edward, FCA *1959;* 126 Davenport Road, Evington, LEICESTER, LE5 6SB. (Life Member)
SPERRYN JONES, Mrs. Arline Audrey, BA ACA *2005;* Fedway Petworth Road, Wormley, GODALMING, SURREY, GU8 5TR.
SPERRYN-JONES, Mr. Simon, BA ACA *2006;* Fedway, Petworth Road, Wormley, GODALMING, SURREY, GU8 5TR.
SPETCH, Mr. John Gregory, MA FCA *1992;* 10 Home Farm Mews, Grape Lane Croston, LEYLAND, PR26 9JT.
•**SPEVACK, Mr. Simon Alexander, FCA** *1981;* Wellden Turnbull LLP, 78 Portsmouth Road, COBHAM, SURREY, KT11 1PP. See also WT Accountants Ltd
SPEYER, Mr. David Paul, ACA *1985;* 22 Burke Road, MALVERN EAST, VIC 3145, AUSTRALIA.
SPEYER, Mr. Nicholas John, BSc ACA *1987;* 9 St. Johns Court, AXBRIDGE, SOMERSET, BS26 2AY.
SPEYER, Mr. Richard James Kaye, MA FCA *1965;* Ground Floor Flat, 24 Marlborough Buildings, BATH, BA1 2LY. (Life Member)
SPEZIALI, Miss. Diana Anita, BSc ACA *1997;* 50 Haw Lane, Bledlow Ridge, HIGH WYCOMBE, BUCKINGHAMSHIRE, HP14 4JJ.
SPIBEY, Miss. Suzanne Patricia, FCA *1975;* 180A Rocking Horse Road, Southshore, CHRISTCHURCH 8062, NEW ZEALAND.
SPIBY, Mr. Geoffrey Edward, FCA *1961;* 126 Mottram Old Road, STALYBRIDGE, CHESHIRE, SK15 2SZ. (Life Member)
SPIBY, Mr. Paul Francis, BA ACA *1999;* 16 Sandy Croft, Kings Heath, BIRMINGHAM, B13 0EP.
SPICE, Ms. Helen, BSc ACA *1989;* 33 Balmoral Avenue, TORONTO M4V 1J5, ON, CANADA.
SPICER, Mr. Alan Philip, BA FCA *1974;* 9 Autumn Crescent, Horsforth, LEEDS, LS18 4HT.
SPICER, Mr. Anthony, BSc(Hons) ACA *2002;* 3 Lansdowne Close, TWICKENHAM, TW1 4JB.
•①**SPICER, Mr. Anthony Cliff, BSc ACA** *1988;* Smith & Williamson Ltd, 25 Moorgate, LONDON, EC2R 6AY.
SPICER, Mr. Ashley Nicholas, BA ACA *1995;* 535 Dean St, Apt 805, BROOKLYN, NY 11217, UNITED STATES.
•**SPICER, Mr. Barry Leslie, FCA** *1968;* (Tax Fac), B.L. Spicer FCA, 3 Inwood Kilns, The Street, Binsted, ALTON, GU34 4PB.
SPICER, Mr. Colin, ACA *2008;* 30 Beechers Road, Portslade, BRIGHTON, BN41 2RG.
SPICER, Mr. Darren Alan, BA ACA *1998;* 62 Ash Grove, CLEVEDON, AVON, BS21 7JZ.
SPICER, Ms. Gail Suzanne, BA ACA *1989;* 3 Shorehill Court, Kemsing, SEVENOAKS, TN15 6BF.
SPICER, Mr. Hugh Westcott, FCA *1973;* 28 Lodge Lane, CHALFONT ST.GILES, HP8 4AF.
SPICER, Miss. Lucinda, MA ACA *1984;* Convinth Steading, Kiltarlity, BEAULY, INVERNESS-SHIRE, IV4 7HT.
SPICER, Mr. Mark Edward, BA(Hons) ACA *2001;* 3 curtin crescent, MAROUBRA, NSW 2035, AUSTRALIA.
•**SPICER, Mrs. Michelle, BA ACA** *1990;* (Tax Fac), Swan Accountancy Solutions Limited, 21 Leacroft Close, STAINES, MIDDLESEX, TW18 4NP.
SPICER, Mr. Nigel Brian, BSc ACA *1990;* The Gables, Wrenbury Road, Wrenbury, NANTWICH, CHESHIRE, CW5 8HA.
•**SPICER, Mr. Patrick John, FCA** *1968;* P.J.Spicer, 43 Turners Hill, Cheshunt, WALTHAM CROSS, EN8 8NJ.
SPICER, Mr. Paul, BSc(Econ) ACA *1999;* Imago Publishing, Albury Court, Albury, THAME, OXFORDSHIRE, OX9 2LP.
SPICER, Mr. Paul Brian, BSc FCA *1984;* 10 McNaughton Close, Southwood, FARNBOROUGH, HAMPSHIRE, GU14 0PX.
•**SPICER, Mr. Paul Frederick, BA ACA** *1988;* (Tax Fac), KPMG LLP, 100 Temple Street, BRISTOL, BS1 6AG. See also KPMG Europe LLP
SPICER, Mr. Richard Alan, BSc ACA *1979;* Project Office Bldg P05, Merville Barracks Post Room, Circular Road South, COLCHESTER, CO2 7UT.
SPICER, Mr. Robert Patrick, FCA *1968;* 16 Hayse Hill, WINDSOR, BERKSHIRE, SL4 5SZ.
•**SPICER, Mr. Russell, ACA** *1985;* (Tax Fac), Bristow Burrell, 4 Riverview, Walnut Tree Close, GUILDFORD, GU1 4UX.
•**SPICER, Mrs. Suzanne, BA FCA MMus** *1997;* Suzanne Spicer, 7 Keswick Close, DUNSTABLE, LU6 3AW.
SPICER, Mr. Thomas Edward, ACA *2008;* Flat 21, 22 Peel Street, KIRRIBILLI, NSW 2061, AUSTRALIA.
•**SPIEGEL, Mr. Ronald Raphael, FCA** *1973;* R.R. Spiegel, 5 Ledway Drive, WEMBLEY, HA9 9TH.
SPIEKMAN, Miss. Marlies Marrieke Elisabeth, BA ACA *1994;* 8 Chiswick Quay, LONDON, W4 3UR.
SPIELER, Mr. Anthony, FCA *1960;* Apartment 7 Amurlee, 70 Upper Park Road, SALFORD, M7 4JA. (Life Member)
SPIELMAN, Mrs. Amanda Mary Victoria, MA ACA *1986;* 27 Gauden Road, LONDON, SW4 6LR.
SPIER, Mr. Alan Philip, FCA *1965;* 12 Weetwood Drive, SHEFFIELD, S11 9QL.
SPIER, Mr. Robert Fitzhardinge Jenner, BCom FCA *1962;* The Barn, High Street North, Stewkley, LEIGHTON BUZZARD, LU7 0EZ. (Life Member)
SPIERING, Mr. Jan Jaap, FCA *1978;* Somerhill, 11 Pokiok Crescent, SMITHS FL05, BERMUDA.
SPIERS, Mr. Adam Matheson, BA ACA *1993;* Michael Spiers(Jewellers)Ltd, 54 Cornwall Street, PLYMOUTH, PL1 1LR.

SPIERS, Mrs. Fiona Mahala, BSc ACA *1992;* 18A Fern Hill Road, Moorhead, SHIPLEY, BD18 4SL.
SPIERS, Mr. Huw David, BSc FCA *1988;* 17a Ailesbury Grove, DUNDRUM 16, COUNTY DUBLIN, IRELAND.
•SPIERS, Mr. Martin Harold, FCA *1977;* Wychwood, Royston Grove, PINNER, MIDDLESEX, HA5 4HF.
•SPIERS, Mr. Michael John, MBA BA(Hons) FCA *1983;* Mike Spiers Associates, 2 Crouch Farm Cottages, Bloxham Road, BANBURY, OXFORDSHIRE, OX16 9UN.
SPIERS, Mr. Richard Duncan, ACA *2008;* K P M G Arlington Business Park, Theale, READING, RG7 4SD.
SPIERS, Mr. Robert John, ACA *1980;* Flat 9, Westhorpe Hall, Westhorpe, SOUTHWELL, NG25 0NG.
SPIERS, Mrs. Samantha Jay, BA ACA *2006;* 13 Gordon Road, SEVENOAKS, TN13 1HE.
SPIGHT, Mr. Jonathan Paul William, MBA BSc ACA *1994;* 4 Romsey Drive, Farnham Common, SLOUGH, SL2 3RE.
SPIKING, Mr. Ronald Thomas, FCA *1963;* Prospect Lodge, 14 Prospect Road, HYTHE, KENT, CT21 5NL.
SPILIOTIS, Mr. Stelios, BA ACA *2005;* Karatheodoti 8a, Omonoia, 3011 LIMASSOL, CYPRUS.
SPILL, Mr. Stephen Brian, MA FCA *1982;* Dittrichova 4/346, PRAGUE, CZECH REPUBLIC.
SPILLANE, Miss. Amy Catherine, BSc ACA *2001;* 43 Stanway Road, CHELTENHAM, GLOUCESTERSHIRE, GL51 6BU.
SPILLANE, Mr. Colum Joseph, BBS ACA *1997;* Sanne Trust Company Ltd, 13 Castle Street, St Helier, JERSEY, JE4 5UT.
SPILLANE, Mr. Philip Mark Dalton, BSc ACA *1990;* 77 Nightingale Avenue, OXFORD, OX4 7GD.
SPILLER, Mr. Andrew Kenneth, BSc ACA *1980;* Walon Ltd, Boundary Way, Lufton Trading Estate, Lufton, YEOVIL, SOMERSET BA22 8HZ.
SPILLER, Mr. Jonathan Mansell, BSc FCA CPA *1976;* 509 Ponte Vedra Boulevard, PONTE VEDRA BEACH, FL 32082, UNITED STATES.
SPILLER, Mrs. Julie, BSc ACA *1992;* 14 Alexandra Crescent, ILKLEY, WEST YORKSHIRE, LS29 9ER.
SPILLER, Mr. Martin Richard, BSc ACA *2001;* Flat 17, Oast Lodge, Corney Reach Way, Chiswick, LONDON, W4 2TN.
SPILLETT, Mr. David George, FCA *1975;* 45 Upper Glen Road, ST. LEONARDS-ON-SEA, EAST SUSSEX, TN37 7AX.
SPILLMAN, Mr. Harvey, FCA *1982;* Worshipful Company of Saddlers, Saddlers Hall, 40 Gutter Lane, LONDON, EC2V 6BR.
SPILMAN, Mr. Gary, BSc FCA *1982;* Motability, Warwick House, Roydon Road, HARLOW, ESSEX, CM19 5PX.
SPILSBURY, Mr. Richard, BA FCA *1997;* Future Publishing Ltd, Beauford Court, 30 Monmouth Street, BATH, SOMERSET, BA1 2BW.
SPILSBURY, Mr. Richard Charles, MSc BSc FCA *1980;* 142 Hill Hook Road, SUTTON COLDFIELD, B74 4XA.
•SPILSBURY, Mr. Richard John, BSc ACA *1995;* PricewaterhouseCoopers LLP, 1 Embankment Place, LONDON, WC2N 6RH. See also PricewaterhouseCoopers
SPINAGE, Miss. Rosalind, ACA *2001;* 21 Okus Road, SWINDON, SN1 4LE.
SPINK, Mr. Alex, BSc ACA *2011;* 33 Prairie Street, LONDON, SW8 3PL.
SPINK, Mr. Geoffrey, FCA *1970;* Fiddlers Green Clandon Road West Clandon, GUILDFORD, SURREY, GU4 7TL.
SPINK, Mrs. Helen, BSc ACA *2001;* Glaxo Smithkline Plc, G S K House, 980 Great West Road, BRENTFORD, MIDDLESEX, TW8 9GS.
SPINK, Mr. John Clarkson, FCA *1967;* Tulip Tree House, Hollow Lane, Wilton, MARLBOROUGH, WILTSHIRE, SN8 3SR.
SPINK, Mrs. Lucy Mary, BSc ACA DChA *1993;* Cumnor House School London Road, Danehill, HAYWARDS HEATH, WEST SUSSEX, RH17 7HT.
SPINK, Mr. Martin David, BSc ACA *1999;* 75 Pine Road, Hiltingbury, Chandler's Ford, EASTLEIGH, HAMPSHIRE, SO53 1JU.
SPINK, Mr. Stuart Colin, FCA *1977;* Orchard House, 25 Dry Drayton Road, Oakington, CAMBRIDGE, CB24 3BD.
SPINKS, Mr. Anthony George, LLB FCA *1974;* Matcon Ltd, Matcon House, London Road, MORETON-IN-MARSH, GLOUCESTERSHIRE, GL56 0HJ.
SPINKS, Miss. Catherine, ACA *2009;* with PricewaterhouseCoopers LLP, Savannah House, 3 Ocean Way, Ocean Village, SOUTHAMPTON, SO14 3TJ.
SPINKS, Mr. Christopher James William, FCA *1974;* Apartment 7, Plaisance House, Royal Garden, St. Peter Port, GUERNSEY, GY1 2JE.
SPINKS, Miss. Clare Rebecca, ACA *2008;* 115a Nine Mile Ride, Finchampstead, WOKINGHAM, BERKSHIRE, RG40 4HY.
•SPINKS, Mr. Gordon, BSc ACA *1987;* (Tax Fac), Dixon Wilson, 22 Chancery Lane, LONDON, WC2A 1LS.
SPINKS, Mr. Graeme Charles, BSc ACA *1990;* 9-13 Kean Street, LONDON, WC2B 4AY.
SPINKS, Mr. Jeffrey Thomas, FCA *1974;* 9 Villefranche, 5 Huguenot Road, FRANSCHHOEK, WESTERN CAPE PROVINCE, 7690, SOUTH AFRICA.
SPINKS, Mr. Jonathan Mark, BA(Hons) ACA *2002;* 6 Prickwillow Road, ELY, CAMBRIDGESHIRE, CB7 4QP.
SPINKS, Mr. Joseph Edward, BA ACA *2006;* 7 Green Lane Avenue Hersham, WALTON-ON-THAMES, SURREY, KT12 5HL.
SPINKS, Mr. Paul William, FCA *1974;* 5 Silverdale Avenue, LEEDS, LS17 8SZ.
SPINKS, Mr. Philip Graham, BSc ACA AMCT *1996;* Oxford Advanced Surfaces Begbroke Business & Science Park, Sandy Lane Yarnton, KIDLINGTON, OXFORDSHIRE, OX5 1PF.
SPINKS, Mr. Philip John Harold, BSc FCA CISA *1986;* 1534 High Road, Whetstone, LONDON, N20 9PT.
SPINNER, Miss. Francesca, BA FCA *1974;* 206 Wilson Park Drive, Tarrytown, NEW YORK, NY 10591, UNITED STATES.
SPINNER, Dr. Sonja Grace, BSc ACA *2002;* Flat 113 Building 22, Cadogan Road, LONDON, SE18 6YU.
SPINNLER, Ms. Rosamund, MA ACA *2011;* 49 Green Bank, Brockworth, GLOUCESTER, GL3 4NF.
SPIRA, Prof. Laura Frances, PhD BA(Econ) FCA *1973;* 5 Cummings Close, Headington, OXFORD, OX3 8ND.
SPIRES, Mr. Adam Christopher, ACA *2009;* 8 Stag Drive, Hedge End, SOUTHAMPTON, SO30 2QN.
SPIRES, Mrs. Angela Kathleen, BA ACA *2004;* Alliance Medical Ltd Iceni Centre, Warwick Technology Park Gallows Hill, WARWICK, CV34 6DA.
•SPIRES, Mr. Jason, BSc FCA DChA *2000;* robinson+co, Oxford Chambers, New Oxford Street, WORKINGTON, CA14 2LR. See also Robinson J.F.W. & Co
•SPIRES, Mr. Paul Edward, BSc FCA CF *2000;* 5 Cofton Lake Road, Rednal, BIRMINGHAM, B45 8PL.
•SPIRES, Mr. Robert Andrew, BA ACA *1982;* R.A. Spires & Co, 97 Stonald Road, Whittlesey, PETERBOROUGH, PE7 1QP.
SPIRI, Mrs. Catherine Lucy, BA ACA *1998;* 26 The Deerings, HARPENDEN, HERTFORDSHIRE, AL5 2PE.
SPIRI, Mr. Dominic, MEng BA ACA CTA *2000;* Terra Firma Capital Partners, 2 More London Riverside, LONDON, SE1 2AP.
SPIRING, Miss. Louise Margaret Joanna, BA ACA *2008;* BusinessHeads, 23 Old Steine, BRIGHTON, BN1 1EL.
SPIRING, Mr. Philip Jonathan, BSc ACA *1994;* Spiring Enterprises Ltd, Unit8e Gillmans, Natts Lane, BILLINGSHURST, WEST SUSSEX, RH14 9EZ.
SPIRITOSANTO, Mrs. Elinor Ruth, BA ACA *1994;* 22 Beltana Street, DENISTONE EAST, NSW 2112, AUSTRALIA.
SPIRO, Mr. Leon, FCA *1961;* 26 Woburn Close, BUSHEY, WD23 4XA. (Life Member)
SPIRO, Mr. Robin Myer, MA MPhil FCA *1956;* 82 St Johns Wood Court, St Johns Wood Road, LONDON, MIDDLESEX, NW8 8QR. (Life Member)
SPITERI, Mr. Bertrand, ACA *1994;* Ground Floor Flat, 18 Harbledown Road, LONDON, SW6 5TP.
SPITERI, Mr. George, LLM BSc ACA *2007;* 81 Lampton Road, Long Ashton, BRISTOL, BS41 9AQ.
SPITERI, Mrs. Kelly, BSc ACA *2007;* 81 Lampton Road, Long Ashton, BRISTOL, BS41 9AQ.
SPITERI, Mr. Norman Alfred, FCA *1964;* 'Il-Kirxa', 18 St Julians Hil, Balluta, ST JULIANS STJ 1341, MALTA. (Life Member)
•SPITTLE, Mr. Martin Henry Peter, FCA *1971;* (Tax Fac), Colston Bush, Lacemaker House, 5-7 Chapel Street, MARLOW, BUCKINGHAMSHIRE, SL7 3HN.
SPITTLE, Mrs. Sarah Ann, BA ACA *1996;* 1 Chivenor Place, ST. ALBANS, HERTFORDSHIRE, AL4 0AD.
SPITTLE, Mr. Timothy David, FCA *1975;* 24 Rose Walk, WEST WICKHAM, BR4 0SD.
SPITZ, Mr. David Richard, ACA *2009;* 33 Broadway, CHEADLE, CHESHIRE, SK8 1LB.
SPITZ, Mr. Roger Brett, MSc FCA *1996;* Flat 30A Wetherby Mansions, Earl's Court Square, LONDON, SW5 9DJ.
SPIVEY, Miss. Claire, ACA *2009;* 46 Gladsmuir Road, LONDON, N19 3JU.
SPIVEY, Mrs. Hilary, BSc ACA *1982;* Carters House, 52 Friars Street, SUDBURY, CO10 2AG.
SPIVEY, Mr. Ralph, FCA *1958;* 34 Woodpond Avenue, HOCKLEY, SS5 4PX. (Life Member)
•SPOFFORTH, Mr. Alexander James, BA FCA *1987;* Spofforths LLP, One Jubilee Street, BRIGHTON, BN1 1GE.
•SPOFFORTH, Mr. David Mark, BSc FCA CTA FRSA *1982;* DEPUTY-PRESIDENT MEMBER OF COUNCIL, (Tax Fac), Spofforths LLP, 9 Donnington Park, 85 Birdham Road, CHICHESTER, WEST SUSSEX, PO20 7AJ.
SPOFFORTH, Mr. Ian James Richard, FCA *1962;* 842 Bayport Way, Longboat Key, SARASOTA, FL, UNITED STATES. (Life Member)
SPOFFORTH, Mr. Jeremy David, JP FCA *1958;* Flat 33, 5 Sloane Court East, LONDON, SW3 4TQ. (Life Member)
•SPOFFORTH, Mr. Richard Charles Patrick Piers, BSc FCA *1995;* Spofforths LLP, 2nd Floor, Comewell House, North Street, HORSHAM, WEST SUSSEX RH12 1RD.
•SPOKES, Mr. Andrew Paul, BA FCA *1981;* Williamson West, 10 Langdale Gate, WITNEY, OX28 6EX.
SPOKES, Mr. Benedict, ACA *2011;* Barnfield, Penshurst Road, Speldhurst, TUNBRIDGE WELLS, KENT, TN3 0PH.
SPOKES, Mr. Christopher Daniel, BSc(Econ) FCA NDA FInstCPD *1976;* MEMBER OF COUNCIL, (Tax Fac), Bidwells, Trumpington Road, CAMBRIDGE, CB2 2LD.
•SPOONER, Mr. Andrew Charles, BA ACA *1993;* (Tax Fac), Tax Accounting Consultancy Service, 31 Ullswater Road, LONDON, SW13 9PL.
•SPOONER, Mr. Andrew James, BA(Hons) ACA *2000;* Deloitte LLP, 2 New Street Square, LONDON, EC4A 3BZ. See also Deloitte & Touche LLP
SPOONER, Mrs. Anna, ACA MBA *1999;* 20 Kings Road, SALISBURY, SP1 3AD.
SPOONER, Mr. Charles William Casswell, BA FCA *1973;* Flat 15, Palliser Court, Palliser Road, LONDON, W14 9ED.
SPOONER, Mr. Christopher David, FCA *1974;* HSBC Holdings plc, L41 GHQ Tax, 8 Canada Square, LONDON, E14 5HQ.
•SPOONER, Mr. Darren, ACA FCCA *2011;* P J Hamson & Co Limited, 99 Wilsthorpe Road, Long Eaton, NOTTINGHAM, NG10 3LE.
SPOONER, Mr. David John, BSc ACA *1991;* 41 Temples Court, Helpston, PETERBOROUGH, PE6 7EU.
SPOONER, Miss. Elizabeth, ACA *2005;* The Old Dairy Feoffee Farm, Fancott Toddington, DUNSTABLE, BEDFORDSHIRE, LU5 6HT.
SPOONER, Mrs. Helen Clare Ruth, BA ACA *1993;* Taylor Roberts Chartered Accountants Unit 9b, Wingbury Courtyard Business Village Wingrave, AYLESBURY, BUCKINGHAMSHIRE, HP22 4LW.
SPOONER, Mr. Ian George, FCA *1961;* Maracas Herons Lea, Copthorne, CRAWLEY, WEST SUSSEX, RH10 3HE.
SPOONER, Mr. John Arthur, FCA *1977;* Glebe Farm, Great Rissington, CHELTENHAM, GLOUCESTERSHIRE, GL54 2LH.
SPOONER, Mr. John William, BSc ACA *1979;* Thomson Reuters Thomson Reuters Building, 30 South Colonnade, LONDON, E14 5EP.
SPOONER, Mr. Jonathan Mark, BSc ACA *1995;* with PricewaterhouseCoopers LLP, Benson House, 33 Wellington Street, LEEDS, LS1 4JP.
SPOONER, Mrs. Katy Helen, BSc ACA *1991;* PricewaterhouseCoopers, Prince's Building, 22/F, 10 Chater Road, CENTRAL, HONG KONG ISLAND HONG KONG SAR.
•SPOONER, Mr. Richard Hamilton, BA ACA *1980;* Baker Tilly Tax and Advisory Services LLP, 25 Farringdon Street, LONDON, EC4A 4AB.
•SPOONER, Mr. Richard Michael, BA FCA *1991;* Spooner & Co, Mulberry, Shrubbs Hill Lane, Sunningdale, ASCOT, SL5 0LD. See also Spooner & Co Ltd
SPOONER, Mr. Roy, FCA *1952;* 28 Melrose Crescent, Hale, ALTRINCHAM, WA15 8NL. (Life Member)
SPOONER, Mr. Terence Martin, MA ACA *1982;* 183 Chipstead Way, Woodmansterne, BANSTEAD, SM7 3JL.
SPOONER, Mr. Timothy Charles, LLB ACA *2005;* with KPMG, 10 Shelley Street, SYDNEY, NSW 2000, AUSTRALIA.
SPOONER, Mr. Timothy John, FCA *1982;* MGI Perth, GPO Box 2570, PERTH, WA 6001, AUSTRALIA.
•SPOOR, Mr. Jonathan Brian, BSc ACA *2006;* Argents, 15 Palace Street, NORWICH, NR3 1RT.
SPOOR, Roger Charlton, Esq OBE FCA *1955;* 5 Graham Park Road, Gosforth, NEWCASTLE UPON TYNE, NE3 4BH. (Life Member)
SPOORS, Mr. Mark, BA ACA *1997;* 82 Broadmoor Lane, Weston, BATH, BA1 4LB.
SPORBORG, Mr. William Henry, BA ACA *1990;* Somerville Rooms, Queensberry Road, NEWMARKET, SUFFOLK, CB8 9AU.
SPORE, Mr. Geoffrey Charles, BSc ACA *1983;* R N L I, West Quay Road, POOLE, DORSET, BH15 1HZ.
SPORLE, Miss. Clare Diane, BA ACA *2000;* with Ernst & Young, The Ernst & Young Building, 680 George Street, SYDNEY, NSW 2000, AUSTRALIA.
•SPOTTISWOOD, Mr. James Arthur, FCA *1959;* with Livesey Spottiswood Limited, 17 George Street, ST.HELENS, WA10 1DB.
SPOTTISWOODE, Miss. Claire Elizabeth, BA ACA *2009;* Computershare Services Plc, The Pavilions, Bridgwater Road, BRISTOL, BS13 8AE.
SPOTTISWOODE, Mr. David Martin, FCA *1975;* (Tax Fac), 19 Reedley Road, Westbury-on-Trym, BRISTOL, BS9 3SR.
SPOUSE, Mr. William Reynolds, FCA *1964;* 58 Archibald Road, ROMFORD, RM3 0RH. (Life Member)
•SPOWART, Mr. John Henry, FCA *1987;* The Alnwick Accountants Ltd, 16 Bondgate Without, ALNWICK, NORTHUMBERLAND, NE66 1PP.
SPRACKLING, Mr. Anthony George, FCA *1963;* Crossways, Binton Lane, Seale, FARNHAM, SURREY, GU10 1LG. (Life Member)
SPRACKLING, Mr. John Hayball, FCA *1955;* Bridge View, Ewyas Harold, HEREFORD, HR2 0ES.
SPRACKMAN, Mr. Andrew William, FCA *1974;* Principality Holdings Ltd, 7 Park Street, BRISTOL, BS1 5NF.
SPRAGG, Miss. Andrea Juliet, BSc(Hons) ACA *2009;* Ground Floor Flat, 30 Hampton Park, BRISTOL, BS6 6LH.
•SPRAGG, Mrs. Patricia Mary, BSc ACA *1989;* P S Accounting, 41 Sycamore Drive, Hollywood, BIRMINGHAM, B47 5QX.
SPRAGGE, Mr. Peter Mark Ferguson Statter, FCA *1966;* 29 Ash Grove, Wheathampstead, ST.ALBANS, AL4 8DF.
SPRAGGETT, Mrs. Helen Clare, BSc ACA *1992;* 56 rue Jean-Baptiste Broussin, 78160 MARLY LE ROI, FRANCE.
SPRAGGON, Mr. Ewan John, BA(Hons) CA *2011;* Scotland 2001); Baker Tilly Channel Islands Limited, PO Box 437, 13 Castle Street, St Helier, JERSEY, JE4 0ZE.
•SPRAGUE, Miss. Carole Evette, BSc FCA *1999;* (Tax Fac), Dunelm, The Chase, Flempton Road, Risby, BURY ST. EDMUNDS, SUFFOLK IP28 6QJ.
SPRAGUE, Mr. Patrick Steains, FCA *1970;* Tickners East, Slip Mill Road, Hawkhurst, CRANBROOK, TN18 4JT.
SPRAGUE, Mr. Philip Arthur, ACA *1989;* Telesoft Technologies Ltd Observatory House, Stour Park Blandford St. Mary, BLANDFORD FORUM, DT11 9LQ.
SPRANKLING, Mr. Nicholas James, BA ACA *1998;* 11 Chapel Road, LONDON, W13 9AE.
SPRATLEY, Mr. Derek John, MA FCA *1962;* 9 Larksmead Way, NEWTON ABBOT, TQ12 6BT.
SPRATT, Mr. Antony John, BA ACA *2001;* 10 Rathborne Close, Earlswood, Ashtown, DUBLIN 15, COUNTY DUBLIN, IRELAND.
SPRATT, Mr. Craig, ACA *2011;* 8 Lynstede, BASILDON, ESSEX, SS14 1TU.
SPRATT, Mr. Edward Robin, FCA *1971;* 1 Longthorpe House, Longthorpe, PETERBOROUGH, PE3 6NU.
SPRATT, Mr. Harold Anthony, FCA *1955;* 793 Ridgebury Road, RIDGEFIELD, CT 06877, UNITED STATES. (Life Member)
•①SPRATT, Mr. Jeremy Simon, BA FCA *1983;* KPMG LLP, 15 Canada Square, LONDON, E14 5GL. See also KPMG Europe LLP
SPRATT, Mr. Nicholas Anthony, FCA *1973;* The Long House, The Wilderness, Lindfield, HAYWARDS HEATH, RH16 2JD.
SPRATT, Mr. Peter Frank, FCA *1964;* The Croft, Foxhill Avenue, Weetwood, LEEDS, LS16 5PB.
•①SPRATT, Mr. Peter Norman, ACA *1982;* Pricewaterhousecoopers, 12 Plumtree Court, LONDON, EC4A 4HT. See also PricewaterhouseCoopers LLP
SPRAWSON, Mr. Peter, FCA *1947;* 5 Elizabeth Court, Myton Crescent, WARWICK, CV34 6QB. (Life Member)
SPRAWSON, Mr. Robert Timothy, BA FCA *1996;* Swan House, 11 Taylors Lane, Swavesey, CAMBRIDGE, CB24 4QN.
SPRAY, Mr. David Robert, BA FCA *1958;* (Member of Council 1981 - 1987), 18 Harberton Mead, Headington, OXFORD, OX3 0DB. (Life Member)
SPREADBURY, Mr. Andrew David, MA ACA *1992;* 3 Lower Farm Barns High Street Barley, ROYSTON, HERTFORDSHIRE, SG8 8HR.
SPREADBURY, Miss. Beth Alexandra Hansford, BSc(Hons) ACA *2004;* Flat 6 Beechcroft, 35 Wellington Road, BOURNEMOUTH, BH8 8JH.
SPREADBURY, Mr. Christopher John, BA ACA *1996;* 14 Shearling Drive, Lower Cambourne, CAMBRIDGE, CB23 6BZ.
SPREADBURY, Mr. James Mark, BA(Hons) ACA *2009;* 19 Wetherby Gardens, FARNBOROUGH, GU14 6BW.

SPREADBURY, Mrs. Joanna, BA ACA *2004;* 68 Lambton Road, LONDON, SW20 0LP.

SPREADBURY, Mr. Martin Joseph, BSc ACA *2004;* Commerzbank, 30 Gresham Street, LONDON, EC2V 7PG.

SPREADBURY, Mr. Neil Andrew, ACA *2008;* 2 Curlew Close, FERNDOWN, DORSET, BH22 9TN.

SPREADBURY, Mr. Sean Michael, BA ACA *2005;* 68 Lambton Road, LONDON, SW20 0LP.

SPRECKLEY, Mr. Caleb, ACA CA(AUS) *2010;* with Deloitte LLP, Stonecutter Court, 1 Stonecutter Street, LONDON, EC4A 4TR.

•**SPRENGER, Mr. Magnus, ACA** *2007;* with PricewaterhouseCoopers GmbH, Olof-Palme-Strasse 35, 60439 FRANKFURT AM MAIN, GERMANY.

SPREULL, Mrs. Daphne Patricia, BA FCA *1978;* 19 Rossall Drive, Bramhall, STOCKPORT, CHESHIRE, SK7 2ES.

SPRIDDELL, Mr. David Henry, BSc ACA *1986;* Oast Farmhouse, Felcourt Lane, Felcourt, EAST GRINSTEAD, RH19 2LQ.

SPRIDDLE, Mrs. Karen Dawn, BSc ACA *2007;* 3 Auden Close, NEWPORT PAGNELL, BUCKINGHAMSHIRE, MK16 8TA.

SPRIGG, Mrs. Belinda Jane, BA FCA *1976;* Apartment 42 Double Reynolds Warehouse, The Docks, GLOUCESTER, GL1 2EN.

SPRIGGS, Mr. Alan, FCA *1970;* The Old Vicarage, Belmore Lane, LYMINGTON, SO41 3NN.

SPRIGGS, Mr. Andrew John, BA ACA *1991;* 147 Waldegrave Road, TEDDINGTON, TW11 8LU.

SPRIGGS, Mr. Christopher Alan, FCA *1967;* 78 Barnett Road, BARDON, QLD 4065, AUSTRALIA.

•**SPRIGGS, Mr. David Anthony, FCA** *1978;* Sproull & Co, 31-33 College Road, HARROW, MIDDLESEX, HA1 1EJ.

SPRIGGS, Miss. Frances Louise, BA ACA *1995;* 2 Brookfield House, Wilmslow Road, CHEADLE, SK8 1HJ.

•**SPRIGGS, Mr. Harvey John William, FCA** *1962;* (Tax Fac), Harvey Spriggs, Dovecote House, 11 Malvern Close, KETTERING, NORTHAMPTONSHIRE, NN16 9JP.

SPRIGGS, Mr. Kenneth Raymond, LLB FCA *1974;* 31 Harrow View Road, LONDON, W5 1NA.

SPRING, Mr. Andrew John, BSc ACA *1996;* 1 Woolton Lodge Gardens, Woolton Hill, NEWBURY, BERKSHIRE, RG20 9SU.

•**SPRING, Mr. Ian David, FCA** *1968;* (Tax Fac), The Farm House, 28 Briton Hill Road, Sanderstead, SOUTH CROYDON, SURREY, CR2 0JL.

SPRING, Mr. Jeremy Simon, FCA *1975;* Po Box 259, St Helier, JERSEY, JE4 8TZ.

SPRING, Mr. Spencer Leon, FCA *1965;* 841A Christchurch Road, BOURNEMOUTH, BH7 6AR.

SPRINGALL, Mr. Keith John, BSc ACA *1984;* 4 Leigh Villas, Cedar Road, COBHAM, SURREY, KT11 2AE.

SPRINGALL, Mr. Ronald, BSc FCA *1957;* Flat 33, Elizabeth House, Elizabeth Drive, BANSTEAD, SURREY, SM7 2FE. (Life Member)

SPRINGATE, Mrs. Amanda Jane, ACA *1989;* Flat 5 The Elms, Dymchurch Road, NEW ROMNEY, KENT, TN28 8BA.

SPRINGBETT, Mr. Adam Charles William, BA ACA *1983;* 30 Rushworth Road, REIGATE, RH2 0PE.

•**SPRINGBETT, Ms. Jill Louise, BA FCA CTA TEP** *1984;* (Tax Fac), 30 Rushworth Road, REIGATE, RH2 0PE. See also Weston Kay

•**SPRINGER, Mr. Nicholas Sidney, FCA FCCA** *1971;* Westbury, 145/157 St John Street, LONDON, EC1V 4PY.

•**SPRINGER, Mr. Nigel Frank, FCA FCCA** *1975;* (Tax Fac), Thornton Springer LLP, 67 Westow Street, Upper Norwood, LONDON, SE19 3RW. See also Chelepis Watson Limited

SPRINGER, Mr. Paul, BA ACA *1989;* 17 Fitzjames Avenue, CROYDON, CR0 5DL.

SPRINGETT, Mr. Andrew Peter, MA FCA *1988;* Amlin PLC, St Helens, 1 Undershaft, LONDON, EC3A 8ND.

SPRINGETT, Mr. Ian, BA FCA *1983;* 37 Prospect Lane, HARPENDEN, HERTFORDSHIRE, AL5 2PL.

SPRINGETT, Mr. Ian Michael, BA ACA *1994;* 2 Prews Farm Cottages, Tannery Lane, Send, WOKING, SURREY, GU23 7EQ.

SPRINGETT, Mr. Neil Gordon, BA(Hons) ACA *2003;* King Sturge Llp, 30 Warwick Street, LONDON, W1B 5NH.

SPRINGFIELD, Mr. Paul, BSc ACA *2003;* 12 Humber Drive, UPMINSTER, ESSEX, RM14 1PU.

•**SPRINGFIELD, Mrs. Rosemary Jane, FCA** *1980;* R J Springfield, Kelani, 32 Teign View Road, Bishopsteignton, TEIGNMOUTH, TQ14 9SZ.

SPRINGHALL, Mr. Timothy David William, BSc ACA *1998;* Lazard Asset Management, 50 Stratton Street, LONDON, W1J 8LL.

SPRINGHAM, Miss. Christine Louise, BA ACA *1993;* 68 Stoke Fields, GUILDFORD, GU1 4LT.

SPRINGHAM, Mrs. Denise Esther Margaret, FCA *1972;* 88 Crockfords Road, NEWMARKET, Suffolk, CB8 9BG.

SPRINGHAM, Mrs. Mary Grace, PhD FCA *1978;* 5 Linden Crescent, WOODFORD GREEN, ESSEX, IG8 0DG.

SPRINGHAM, Mr. Michael John, BSc ACA *1991;* 8 Brecon Avenue, WORCESTER, WR4 0RJ.

SPRINGLE, Mr. Richard, BSc(Hons) ACA CTA *2003;* 22 Bewlay Street, YORK, YO23 1JT.

SPRINGSGUTH, Mr. Ceri Thomas, BSc ACA AMCT *1988;* May Cottage, 4 Manor Walk, WEYBRIDGE, KT13 8SD.

SPRINGSGUTH, Mrs. Farhana Alia, LLB ACA *2000;* with PricewaterhouseCoopers LLP, 1 Embankment Place, LONDON, WC2N 6RH.

SPRINGTHORPE, Mr. David John, BSc FCA *1983;* Cheriton House, Roman Road, Chilworth, SOUTHAMPTON, SO16 7HE.

SPROCK, Mrs. Wendy Marie, BA FCA *1990;* Bellmannstrasse 1, 22607 HAMBURG, GERMANY.

SPROT, Mrs. Katherine, ACA *2009;* Hart Shaw Sheffield Airport Business Park, Europa Link, SHEFFIELD, S9 1XU.

SPROT, Mr. Michael, BA ACA *2005;* 72 Blake Street, SHEFFIELD, S6 3JR.

•**SPROUL, Mr. David, FCA** *1983;* Deloitte LLP, 2 New Street Square, LONDON, EC4A 3BZ. See also Deloitte & Touche LLP

SPROUL, Mr. Louden Allen, MA FCA *1991;* C/- DHL, CyberTower, Cybercity, EBENE, MAURITIUS.

SPROUL, Mr. Peter James, BSc(Hons) ACA *2002;* with PricewaterhouseCoopers LLP, 125 High Street, BOSTON, MA 02110, UNITED STATES.

SPROWELL, Miss. Suzanne Clare, BSc(Hons) ACA *2000;* Nymphenburgerstrasse 150, 80634 MUNICH, BAVARIA, GERMANY.

SPRUNT, Mr. Ernest, FCA *1962;* 11 Station Road, BILLERICAY, CM12 9DP. (Life Member)

SPRUNT, Mr. Norman William, FCA *1960;* Orchard House, Church Green, Totternhoe, DUNSTABLE, LU6 1RF. (Life Member)

SPRUZEN, Mr. David Andrew, BSc FCA *1992;* Homewood, The Avenue, Farnham Common, SLOUGH, SL2 3JY.

SPRUZEN, Mrs. Sarah-Lynn, BSc ACA *1994;* Homewood, The Avenue, Farnham Common, SLOUGH, SL2 3JY.

SPRY, Mr. Andrew, BEng ACA *2001;* Darind, Pound Lane, Knockholt, SEVENOAKS, TN14 7NA.

•**SPRY, Mr. John Walter, FCA** *1968;* J W Spry FCA, 21 Hildenfields, TONBRIDGE, KENT, TN10 3DQ. See also Hendraws Limited

SPRY, Mr. Jonathan, BSc(Hons) ACA *2009;* 38 Penderyn Crescent, Ingleby Barwick, STOCKTON-ON-TEES, CLEVELAND, TS17 5DD.

SPRY, Mr. Matthew William Roland, BSc(Hons) ACA *2003;* 7 Lawrence Grove, BRISTOL, BS9 4EL.

SPUNTARELLI, Mrs. Paola, ACA *1998;* via Trionfale 8263, 00135 ROME, ITALY.

•**SPURDEN, Mr. Peter, FCA** *1977;* Oaklea Accounting Limited, Oaklea, Cowards Lane, Codicote, HITCHIN, HERTFORDSHIRE SG4 8UN.

SPURDLE, Mr. Michael William Farrell, FCA ACMA *1959;* 11 Roseacre Close, Emerson Park, HORNCHURCH, RM11 3NJ. (Life Member)

•**SPURGEON, Mr. Christopher Nigel, BA FCA** *1980;* Media Finance Ltd, Riverside Studios, Crisp Road, LONDON, W6 9RL.

SPURGEON, Mr. David, ACA *2011;* 3 Hall Cottages, Caistor Lane, Caistor St. Edmund, NORWICH, NR14 8QT.

SPURGEON, Ms. Lisa Marie, BMus ACA *2005;* 2 Drayton Terrace, Drayton, Belbroughton, STOURBRIDGE, WEST MIDLANDS, DY9 0BW.

SPURGEON, Mr. Thomas Arthur, MA ACA *1995;* Monitise International Ltd, Warnford Court, 29 Throgmorton Street, LONDON, EC2N 2AT.

SPURLING, Mr. Paul, ACA *2009;* 12 Dalby Road, LONDON, SW18 1AW.

•**SPURLING, Mr. Roger David, FCA** *1967;* Spurling & Co, 18 Marlborough Drive, WEYBRIDGE, SURREY, KT13 8PA. See also Ardiesse Consultants Limited

SPURR, Mr. Alasdair George, BSc ACA *2003;* 13a Windsor Road, LONDON, W5 3UL.

SPURR, Mr. Craig Edward, ACA *2001;* 53 Bromedale Avenue, Mulbarton, NORWICH, NR14 8GG.

SPURR, Mrs. Gemma, BEng ACA *1999;* 25 Field Rise, SWINDON, SN1 4HP.

•**SPURR, Mr. Geoffrey Stuart, BSc ACA** *1979;* (Tax Fac), Geoff Spurr & Co Limited, 41 Fore Hill, ELY, CB7 4AA.

SPURR, Mr. John Duncan, FCA CF *1983;* 27 Linden Way, Ponteland, NEWCASTLE UPON TYNE, NE20 9DP.

SPURR, Mr. Matthew, ACA *2009;* 33 Eltham Road, LONDON, SE12 8ES.

SPURR, Mr. Michael George, BA ACA *1989;* 173 Hundred Acre Road, SUTTON COLDFIELD, B74 2BH.

SPURRIER, Mr. Edward John Marston, BA ACA *1992;* Manor Farm House, Clarkes Lane, Tangley, ANDOVER, HAMPSHIRE, SP11 0SH.

•**SPURRIER, Mr. Lance Edward, BSc FCA** *1983;* Moore Stephens, P O Box 25, 26-28 Athol Street, Douglas, ISLE OF MAN, IM99 1BD. See also Moore Stephens Limited

SPURRS, Mr. Peter Anthony, BA ACA *1980;* Chemin Maula 35, 1680 ROMONT, SWITZERLAND.

SPURWAY, Mr. Eustace John, FCA *1951;* PO Box 73089, Fairland, JOHANNESBURG, GAUTENG, 2030, SOUTH AFRICA. (Life Member)

SPURWAY, Mr. Peter John Oliver, FCA *1975;* PO Box MG-7226, MARIGOT, SAINT LUCIA.

SPYCHALSKI, Mr. Richard Bruno Andrew, MA ACA *1991;* Mamas & Papas Ltd, Colne Bridge Road, HUDDERSFIELD, HD5 0RH.

SPYKER, Mr. Luc Zwier, ACA *1986;* Timber Ridge, Farnham Lane, HASLEMERE, SURREY, GU27 1EU.

SPYRIDES, Mr. Spyros, BA FCA *1990;* Homer Street 30, Strovolos, NICOSIA, CYPRUS.

SPYROU, Miss. Alexandra, BSc ACA *2010;* 8 A. Krouaze Str, LIMASSOL, CYPRUS.

SPYROU, Miss. Chryso Andrea, ACA *1998;* Stavrouli & Nicolaou, P.O. Box 33586, 5315 PARALIMNI, CYPRUS.

SPYROU, Mr. David Nicholas, FCA *1975;* 60 Pettman Close, HERNE BAY, CT6 5TL.

SPYROU, Miss. Marina, BA ACA *2010;* 17 Galileou Street, Ayios Ioannis, LIMASSOL, CYPRUS.

SPYROU, Mr. Pericles, BSc ACA *2006;* 16 Tricoupi st, 2113 NICOSIA, CYPRUS.

SPYROU, Mr. Spiros, ACA *1999;* 22 Dimitri Pyrka, 2679 MAMMARI, CYPRUS.

•**SPYROU, Mr. Spyros Panayiotis, BSc ACA ACCA** *1997;* S P Spyrou & Co, Unit 2, Old Court Mews, 311a Chase Road, Southgate, LONDON N14 6JS. See also Phillips Spyrou LLP

SQUIER, Mr. Martin, ACA CA(AUS) *2008;* with PricewaterhouseCoopers LLP, 1 Embankment Place, LONDON, WC2N 6RH.

SQUIRE, Mrs. Christine Cynthia, FCA *1969;* 15 Cloister Crofts, LEAMINGTON SPA, CV32 6QG. (Life Member)

•**SQUIRE, Mr. Colin John, FCA** *1980;* McCranors Limited, Clifford House, 38-44 Binley Road, COVENTRY, CV3 1JA. See also McCranor Kirby Smale Limited

SQUIRE, Mr. David Michael, MA FCA *1973;* Normanby Gateway, Lysaghts Way, SCUNTHORPE, SOUTH HUMBERSIDE, DN15 9YG.

SQUIRE, Ms. Helen Margaret, BA ACA *2002;* with Experian plc, Landmark House, Experian Way, NOTTINGHAM, NG80 1ZZ.

SQUIRE, Mr. Ian David, FCA *1965;* 15 Cloister Crofts, LEAMINGTON SPA, CV32 6QG. (Life Member)

•**SQUIRE, Mr. John David, FCA** *1977;* Graham Paul Limited, 10-12 Dunraven Place, BRIDGEND, MID GLAMORGAN, CF31 1JD.

•**SQUIRE, Mr. Peter, FCA** *1988;* AGS Accountants and Business Advisors Ltd, Castle Court 2, Castlegate Way, DUDLEY, WEST MIDLANDS, DY1 4RH.

SQUIRE, Mr. Peter John, FCA *1962;* Horrowmore, Dunsford, EXETER, EX6 7BG.

SQUIRE, Mr. Philip Stuart, BA(Hons) ACA *2001;* 10 Manor Crescent, EPSOM, SURREY, KT19 7EF.

SQUIRE, Mr. Robin Clifford, FCA *1966;* Robin Squire, Flat 3, 63 Millbank, LONDON, SW1P 4RW.

SQUIRES, Mr. David, ACA *2010;* 6a Radbourne Avenue, LONDON, W5 4XD.

SQUIRES, Mr. Eric Geoffrey, FCA *1951;* 444 New Bedford Road, LUTON, LU3 2BA. (Life Member)

•**SQUIRES, Mr. Gary Peter, BSc FCA FIPA** *1987;* with Zolfo Cooper Ltd, 10 Fleet Place, LONDON, EC4M 7RB.

SQUIRES, Mr. Gordon Albert Upton, FCA *1963;* The Yews, 54 Stoughton Lane, Stoughton, LEICESTER, LE2 2FH. (Life Member)

SQUIRES, Mrs. Joanna Kerry, BA ACA *1992;* 11 Delmar Road, KNUTSFORD, WA16 8BG.

SQUIRES, Mr. John Robert, FCA *1972;* Coeplare Limited, 1 Derby Buildings, Wavertree Road, LIVERPOOL, L7 3ES.

SQUIRES, Mr. Keith Brian, MBA FCA *1956;* 43 Kingsley Crescent, Long Eaton, NOTTINGHAM, NG10 3DA. (Life Member)

SQUIRES, Mr. Michael Bernard, FCA FCCA FTII ATT *1976;* 18 Augustus Road, BIRMINGHAM, B15 3NJ. (Life Member)

SQUIRES, Mr. Paul Martin, BSc ACA *1987;* The Old Stables, Hall Farm Barns, Oxborough, KING'S LYNN, NORFOLK, PE33 9PS.

SQUIRES, Mr. Peter John, FCA *1959;* Flat 3, 92 Wilton Road, LONDON, SW1V 1DW.

SQUIRES, Mr. Peter William, FCA *1980;* Holbeck, Back Lane, Burnham Market, KING'S LYNN, NORFOLK, PE31 8EY.

•**SQUIRES, Mr. Reginald George, FCA** *1969;* Blythe Squires Wilson, 1-2 Vernon Street, DERBY, DE1 1FR.

SQUIRES, Mr. Richard Anthony, FCA *1957;* Wayside House, 191 Station Lane, Lapworth, SOLIHULL, B94 6JG. (Life Member)

SQUIRES, Mr. Robert Freeland, FCA *1964;* York House, 5 Phoebes Orchard, Stoke Hammond, MILTON KEYNES, MK17 9LW.

SQUIRES, Mrs. Sandra Ann, MCom FCA *1970;* 18 Augustus Road, BIRMINGHAM, B15 3NJ.

SQUIRES, Miss. Sarah Marie, BEng ACA *2010;* 59 Warburton Road, TWICKENHAM, TW2 6EW.

SQUIRES, Mrs. Sarah Ruth, BSc ACA *2002;* 11 St. James Road, HARPENDEN, HERTFORDSHIRE, AL5 4NX.

SQUIRES, Mr. Simon Gregory, BA ACA *1991;* The Patch, Browns Lane, Storrington, PULBOROUGH, RH20 4LQ.

SQUIRES-EVANS, Mrs. Tracey Michelle, BSc ACA *2003;* Adagio, 78 Riverside Drive, Hambleton, POULTON-LE-FYLDE, LANCASHIRE, FY6 9EB.

SQUIRRELL, Mr. James Andrew, BA ACA *1997;* 11/27 Morton Street, WOLLSTONECRAFT, NSW 2065, AUSTRALIA.

SRAM, Mrs. Vivian Carol Maitland, MA ACA *1982;* Vivian Sram Ltd, Portland Tower, Portland Street, MANCHESTER, M1 3LF.

SREEVALSAN, Mr. Nicky, BSc ACA *2001;* Decathlon UK, Ikea Retail Park, Nottingham Road East, Giltbrook, NOTTINGHAM, NG16 2RP.

•**SRI RAGAVAN, Mrs. Gowry, ACA FCCA ACMA CTA** *2007;* Sri & Co Accountants Ltd, 36 Brent House, 214 Kenton Road, HARROW, MIDDLESEX, HA3 8BT.

•**SRI RAGAVAN, Mr. Maheswaran, ACA FCCA ACMA** *2008;* Sri & Co Accountants Ltd, 36 Brent House, 214 Kenton Road, HARROW, MIDDLESEX, HA3 8BT.

SRIHIRAN-BROWN, Mr. Toby, BA(Hons) FCA MBA *1999;* ALICO, 119 Kifissias Ave., 15124 ATHENS, GREECE.

SRIKANDAN, Miss. Tanya Darani, BSc ACA *2004;* Nyetimber, Broughton House 6-8 Sackville Street, LONDON, W1S 3DG.

SRIKANTHAN, Mr. Branavan, BSc ACA *2008;* 59 Summit Drive, WOODFORD GREEN, ESSEX, IG8 8QW.

SRINIVASAN, Miss. Divia, BA ACA *2007;* c/o Abraaj Capital, Gate Village 8 Floor 3, PO BOX 504905, DUBAI, UNITED ARAB EMIRATES.

SRINIVASAN, Mr. Dwarkanath, FCA *1973;* c/o Arab Consulting Group, DUBAI, POB 450101, UNITED ARAB EMIRATES.

SRINIVASAN, Mr. Rahul, BSc ACA *2002;* Flat 8, Yew House, 2 Woodland Crescent, LONDON, SE16 6YH.

SRIPURAM, Mr. Bharath Kumar, BA ACA *2011;* 95 Parnell Road, LONDON, E3 2RT.

SRIRANJAN, Mr. Rasiah Ramakrishna, BSc ACA *1993;* 86 Wattleton Road, BEACONSFIELD, BUCKINGHAMSHIRE, HP9 1RY.

•**SRISKANDAN, Mr. Ranjan, MA ACA** *1986;* PricewaterhouseCoopers LLP, 1 Embankment Place, LONDON, WC2N 6RH. See also PricewaterhouseCoopers

SRISKANTHARAJAH, Miss. Ramani, BA(Hons) ACA *2002;* Shell International Petroleum Co Ltd Shell Centre, York Road, LONDON, SE1 7NA.

SRIVASTAVA, Mr. Aditya, ACA *1983;* PO Box 23073, DUBAI, UNITED ARAB EMIRATES.

SRIVASTAVA, Mr. Dhruv, FCA *1972;* 2 Richmond Close, FARNBOROUGH, Hampshire, GU14 0RH.

SRIVASTAVA, Mrs. Helen Genevieve, BA ACA *1986;* PO Box 23073, DUBAI, UNITED ARAB EMIRATES.

SRIVASTAVA, Mr. Vijay Krishna, FCA *1971;* Villa Vikuniya, Mehrauli-Gurgaon Road, P.O. Mehrauli Sultanpur, NEW DELHI 110 031, INDIA.

SRIVASTAVA, Mr. Vivek, FCA *1970;* Ferguson A F Associates, 6H Hansalaya, 15 Barakhamba Road, NEW DELHI 110 001, INDIA.

SRIVICHIT, Mr. Thienchai, FCA *1959;* SVOA Public Co Ltd, 900/29 Rama 3 Road, Yannawa, BANGKOK 10120, THAILAND.

SROKOSZ, Mr. Jeremy, BSc ACA *2007;* 57 Stackpool Road, BRISTOL, BS3 1NL.

SROKOSZ, Mrs. Lynne, BA ACA *2006;* 57 Stackpool Road, BRISTOL, BS3 1NL.
ST CLAIR-GEORGE, Mr. Michael Anthony, FCA *1969;* Farthingfield, Udimore, RYE, EAST SUSSEX, TN31 6AE. (Life Member)
ST GEORGE, Mr. Julian, ACA *1982;* 54 Downage, Hendon, LONDON, NW4 1AH.
ST HELENE, Mrs. Alison Jane, MA ACA *1989;* 7 Hillside Avenue, LONDON, N11 3DE.
•ST JOHN, Mr. Iain Spencer, BA ACA *1993;* 81 Eastwood Road, Bramley, GUILDFORD, GU5 0DX.
ST JOHN COOPER, Mr. Harry, BSc(Econ) FCA *1986;* 70 Jermyn Street, LONDON, SW1Y 6NY.
ST JOHN GLEW, Mr. Bernard, BSc FCA *1976;* 14 Wensley Close, HARPENDEN, AL5 1RZ.
ST JOHN-HART, Miss. Rachael Louise, BA ACA *2002;* 3 Hanover Park, Burleigh Road, ASCOT, BERKSHIRE, SL5 7HZ.
ST LEGER, Mr. Patrick Anthony, FCA *1963;* Doneraile, 4 David Evans Court, LETCHWORTH GARDEN CITY, HERTFORDSHIRE, SG6 4WA. (Life Member)
ST PIER, Mrs. Amanda Jane, BSc ACA *1992;* Les Quartier Farm, Route Des Quartiers, St. Sampsons, GUERNSEY, GY2 4GB.
ST PIER, Mr. Gavin Anthony, LLB FCA *1992;* Les Quartier Farm Les Quartiers, St. Sampson, GUERNSEY, GY2 4GB.
•STABBINS, Mr. Derek Henry, FCA *1974;* (Tax Fac), Butterworth Jones, Tallford House, 38 Walliscote Road, WESTON-SUPER-MARE, SOMERSET, BS23 1LP. See also Chedzoy Butterworth Limited
STABLER, Mr. Alan, FCA *1950;* 43 Longleat Court, Park Road, FROME, BA11 1ED. (Life Member)
STABLER, Mr. John Spedding, FCA *1953;* 61 Manor Farm Avenue, SHEPPERTON, TW17 9AG. (Life Member)
STABLER, Mr. Roy, FCA *1972;* Mooshed, 3 Laker Hall, Newton, STOCKSFIELD, NORTHUMBERLAND, NE43 7UZ.
STABLES, Mr. Andrew Angelo, BEng ACA *1990;* Omnibus Systems Ltd Stanford House, Main Street Stanford on Soar, LOUGHBOROUGH, LE12 5PY.
STABLES, Ms. Carol Ann, BA ACA *1990;* Amp Centre, Level 27, 50 Bridge Street, SYDNEY, NSW 2000, AUSTRALIA.
•STABLES, Mr. John, BA FCA *1982;* Openfield Group Ltd, Honey Pot Lane, Colsterworth, GRANTHAM, LINCOLNSHIRE, NG33 5LY.
•STABLES, Miss. June Christine, FCA *1962;* (Tax Fac), Haviland & Co, 11 Biddulph Road, LONDON, W9 1JA.
STABLES, Miss. Patricia Anne, BSc ACA *1985;* 6 Bucklers Mead, Yetminster, SHERBORNE, DORSET, DT9 6LA.
•STABLES, Mr. Peter, FCA *1973;* (Tax Fac), Peter Stables, 77 Smith House Lane, BRIGHOUSE, WEST YORKSHIRE, HD6 2LF.
STABLES, Mr. Richard Mark, BSc ACA *1990;* with Lazard, 50 Stratton Street, LONDON, W1J 8LL.
STABLES, Mr. Stuart, BSc FCA *1989;* 39 St Francis Avenue, SOLIHULL, B91 1EB.
STABLES, Mr. Thomas Findlay, BA ACA *1998;* Arminger House Parkers Lane, Kington Langley, CHIPPENHAM, SN15 5PH.
STACEY, Mrs. Anne Louise, BSc ACA *1993;* 2 Lion Gate Mews, Southfields, LONDON, SW18 5EN.
STACEY, Mr. Anthony Edward, FCA *1968;* Appletree Cottage Manchester Road, Sway, LYMINGTON, SO41 6AS.
STACEY, Mr. Christopher Mark William, BSc ACA *1992;* 25 Keel Street, BIRKDALE, QLD 4159, AUSTRALIA.
•STACEY, Mr. Colin James, BSc FCA *1990;* Colin Stacey Associates, 39 Silk Mill Road, Redbourn, ST. ALBANS, HERTFORDSHIRE, AL3 7GE.
STACEY, Mr. David William Lewis, ACA *2010;* 11 Nottingham Road, ISLEWORTH, MIDDLESEX, TW7 6PB.
STACEY, Mr. Edward John, BA ACA *1983;* Appledore, Harestone Hill, CATERHAM, CR3 6BG.
STACEY, Ms. Fiona Clare, LLB ACA *1992;* 33B Seahorse Lane, Discovery Bay, LANTAU ISLAND, NEW TERRITORIES, HONG KONG SAR.
STACEY, Mr. Graeme Duncan, LLB FCA *1992;* 32 Belgrave Crescent, BATH, BA1 5JU.
•STACEY, Mr. Ian, FCA *1993;* (Tax Fac), Stacey & Co Limited, Prime House, 14 Porters Wood, ST. ALBANS, HERTFORDSHIRE, AL3 6PQ.
STACEY, Mr. John William, FCA *1959;* 51A Hardwick Lane, BURY ST.EDMUNDS, IP33 2RB. (Life Member)
•STACEY, Mr. Jonathan Huw, BA FCA *1994;* Riley, 51 North Hill, PLYMOUTH, PL4 8HZ.
STACEY, Mrs. Juliette Natasha, BA ACA *1998;* Woodland Cottage, Highmoor, HENLEY-ON-THAMES, OXFORDSHIRE, RG9 5DH.
STACEY, Miss. Kylie, ACA *2010;* Afren Plc Kinnaird House, 1 Pall Mall East, LONDON, SW1Y 5AU.
STACEY, Mr. Mark Everett, BA FCA CISA *1995;* C/ Josep Pla no.2, Torres Diagonal Litoral, Edificio B2 - 6 planta, 08019 BARCELONA, SPAIN.
STACEY, Mr. Michael Andrew, BA ACA *1989;* Popely's Piece, Bishops Drive, SOUTHWELL, NOTTINGHAMSHIRE, NG25 0JP.
STACEY, Mr. Michael John, FCA *1959;* 19 Arleston Drive, Wollaton, NOTTINGHAM, NG8 2FR. (Life Member)
STACEY, Mr. Michael Richard, ACA *2008;* Carling House, Coors Brewers Ltd, 137 High Street, BURTON-ON-TRENT, STAFFORDSHIRE, DE14 1JZ.
STACEY, Mr. Paul Alexander, FCA *1993;* 8/ 169 Horsley Road, PANANIA, NSW 2213, AUSTRALIA.
•STACEY, Mr. Paul Derek Gilbert, BA FCA *1996;* IQ Business Consulting Ltd, The Old Police House, Damerham, FORDINGBRIDGE, HAMPSHIRE, SP6 3HB.
STACEY, Mrs. Philippa Jane, ACA *2009;* with PricewaterhouseCoopers LLP, Pricewaterhousecoopers, 12 Plumtree Court, LONDON, EC4A 4HT.
STACEY, Miss. Rebecca Jane, MMath ACA *2005;* 30 Stanley Road, NEWMARKET, SUFFOLK, CB8 8AF.
STACEY, Mr. Richard John, ACA *1989;* 15 Crimicar Lane, Fulwood, SHEFFIELD, S10 4FA.
STACEY, Mr. Simon Nicholas, BSc FCA *1990;* The Coach House, 24 Church Street, Bathford, BATH, BA1 7RS.
STACEY, Mr. Steven Anthony, BA ACA *2008;* 12 Baxter Mews, SHEFFIELD, S6 1LW.
STACEY, Mr. Thomas Robert, BA FCA *1992;* 119 Lansdowne Road, LONDON, W11 2LF.
STACEY, Mr. Timothy Brian, BSc ACA *1992;* 75 Minster Way, BATH, BA2 6RL.
STACEY-CONNOR, Miss. Claire, ACA *2010;* 56 Trent Road, HINCKLEY, LEICESTERSHIRE, LE10 0XX.
STACEY-HIBBERT, Mr. Christopher John, BA ACA *1990;* Flat 14 98 Belgrave Road, LONDON, SW1V 2BJ.
STACEY-SALMON, Mr. Peter Lynton, FCA *1966;* 2511 11 Avenue N.W., CALGARY T2N 1H6, AB, CANADA.
STACK, Mr. Keith Sidney, FCA *1960;* PO Box 333824, DUBAI, UNITED ARAB EMIRATES. (Life Member)
STACK, Ms. Susan Patricia, BSc ACA *1995;* Route de St-Cergue 14, 1260 NYON, SWITZERLAND.
STACKABLE, Mr. Steve Joseph, BSc ACA *1996;* 2a Kingston Drive, SALE, CHESHIRE, M33 2FS.
STACKHOUSE, Mr. Andrew, LLB ACA *2002;* (Tax Fac), Dale View Bilsborrow Lane, Bilsborrow, PRESTON, PR3 0RN.
•STACKPOOLE, Mr. Michael James Thomas, FCA *1975;* Midicorp Corporate Finance Ltd, New Bond House, 124 New Bond Street, LONDON, W1S 1DX.
STACY, Mr. Arthur Robert, FCA *1936;* 114 Bromley Road, BECKENHAM, KENT, BR3 5NU. (Life Member)
STACY, Graham Henry, Esq CBE FCA *1955;* 31 Fordington Road, Highgate, LONDON, N6 4TD. (Life Member)
STACY, Mr. Peter Jeremy, BSc(Hons) ACA *2003;* 9 Peppard Close, Redbourn, ST. ALBANS, HERTFORDSHIRE, AL3 7EB.
STADDON, Mr. David Colin, BEng FCA *1990;* 81 The Birches, Bramhope, LEEDS, LS16 9DP.
STADDON, Mr. John Nigel, FCA *1952;* 125 Kimbolton Road, BEDFORD, MK41 8DT. (Life Member)
STADDON, Mr. Keith Anthony, BA ACA *1991;* 6012 Kestrel Point Avenue, LITHIA, FL 33547, UNITED STATES.
•STADDON, Mr. Mark Thomas, BA ACA *1982;* Graham Smith, 11 Green Lane, REDRUTH, TR15 1JY.
STADDON, Mr. Simon Richard, ACA ATII *1995;* Norwyn, 27 School Road, Bethersden, ASHFORD, KENT, TN26 3AH.
STADEN, Mr. Paul Sidney, BA FCA *1983;* Marlborough Properities Ltd, 14 White Lion Walk, BANBURY, OXFORDSHIRE, OX16 5UD.
•STADIUS, Mrs. Judith Margaret, BA FCA CTA *1984;* (Tax Fac), Mole Valley Accountants Limited, Windrush, 25 Riverside Drive, ESHER, SURREY, KT10 8PG.
STAFF, Miss. Heather Lucy, BA(Hons) ACA *2010;* 10 Hazelhurst Fold, Worsley, MANCHESTER, M28 2JU.
STAFF, Mr. Michael Ernest, FCA *1972;* 27 Lincoln Gardens, Claydon, IPSWICH, IP6 0BH.
STAFFORD, Miss. Alyson Jane, MA ACA CPFA *1992;* 2 Loanend Park, Dolphinton, WEST LINTON, PEEBLESSHIRE, EH46 7HZ.
STAFFORD, Mrs. Amanda Alice, ACA *2008;* Ground Floor, 11 Ilminster Gardens, LONDON, SW11 1PJ.
STAFFORD, Mr. Andrew Paul, BA FCA *1979;* 16 College Close, Great Casterton, STAMFORD, LINCOLNSHIRE, PE9 4AW.
STAFFORD, Mr. Brian John, BA FCA *1963;* 3 Furness Close, Holmes Chapel, CREWE, CW4 7LG.
STAFFORD, Mr. Christopher Charles Harvey, BA ACA *2007;* Twemlow Edge, Twemlow Green, Holmes Chapel, CREWE, CW4 8BG.
STAFFORD, Mr. Christopher Roy, BA ACA *1999;* 268 Rutland Road, West Bridgford, NOTTINGHAM, NG2 5EB.
•STAFFORD, Mr. Craig James, BA ACA *1997;* with PricewaterhouseCoopers LLP, Hays Galleria, 1 Hays Lane, LONDON, SE1 2RD.
STAFFORD, Mrs. Frances Elizabeth Anne, FCA *1966;* Celestina, 110 Boyes Drive, ST JAMES, C.P., 7945, SOUTH AFRICA.
STAFFORD, Mr. Frank, FCA *1955;* 20 St. Martins Road, Marple, STOCKPORT, SK6 7BY. (Life Member)
STAFFORD, Miss. Helen, BA ACA *2005;* Wensum Tailoring Ltd K1, Southwell Road Horsham St. Faith, NORWICH, NR10 3JU.
STAFFORD, Mrs. Helen Joanne, BA ACA *1991;* 9 Pipers Lane, WIRRAL, CH60 9HS.
STAFFORD, Ms. Helen Patricia, BSc(Econ) ACA AMCT *1996;* Lyndhurst, 32 High Street, Sherston, MALMESBURY, WILTSHIRE, SN16 0LQ.
STAFFORD, Mr. Herbert Roderick Paul, FCA *1970;* 4 Alington House, Alington Road, POOLE, BH14 8LY.
STAFFORD, Mr. Ian Neil, BA FCA *1990;* 10 Harwood Close, Sandal, WAKEFIELD, WF2 6QY.
STAFFORD, Mrs. Jennifer, BSc(Hons) ACA *2001;* Willow Farm House, Norwich Road, South Burlingham, NORWICH, NR13 4EZ.
•STAFFORD, Mr. Jonathan, BCom ACA *2001;* JSE Accountants Limited, 167 Quinton Lane, BIRMINGHAM, B32 2TY.
STAFFORD, Mr. Jonathan Simon, BSc ACA *2004;* 5 Hardman Road, LONDON, SE7 7QX.
•STAFFORD, Mr. Julian Robert, LLB FCA *1982;* (Tax Fac), Staffords Cambridge LLP, CPC1, Capital Park, Fulbourn, CAMBRIDGE, CB21 5XE.
•STAFFORD, Mr. Kenneth James, FCA *1975;* (Tax Fac), SCCA Ltd, 2nd Floor, Nelson Mill, Gaskell Street, BOLTON, BL1 2QE.
STAFFORD, Mr. Martin David, MA ACA *1982;* with PricewaterhouseCoopers LLP, Abacus House, Castle Park, CAMBRIDGE, CB3 0AN.
•STAFFORD, Mr. Michael, FCA *1980;* (Tax Fac), Killicks Ltd, 35/37 Kingsway, Kirkby-in-Ashfield, NOTTINGHAM, NG17 7DR.
STAFFORD, Mr. Nicholas James, BA ACA *1999;* 2425 L ST NW, Apt 502, WASHINGTON, DC 20037, UNITED STATES.
STAFFORD, Mr. Paul David, BSc ACA *2001;* 2 Eyam Close, Bramcote, NOTTINGHAM, NG9 3GQ.
•STAFFORD, Mr. Paul Martyn, FCA *1981;* P M Stafford, 22 Foyle Street, SUNDERLAND, SR1 1LE.
STAFFORD, Mr. Peter Moore, FCA *1965;* Twemlow Edge, Twemlow Green, Holmes Chapel, CREWE, CW4 8BG.
STAFFORD, Mr. Peter Nigel Jeremy, FCA *1977;* 86 Rue Menard, 30000 NIMES, FRANCE.
•STAFFORD, Mr. Robert James, BA(Hons) ACA *2004;* SCCA Ltd, 2nd Floor, Nelson Mill, Gaskell Street, BOLTON, BL1 2QE.
STAFFORD, Mrs. Roberta Frances, LLB ACA *2001;* Apartment 2 Cavendish House, Park Terrace, NOTTINGHAM, NG1 5AY.
STAFFORD, Mr. Rodney Frank John, FCA *1966;* 8a The Glade, Fetcham, LEATHERHEAD, KT22 9TH. (Life Member)
•STAFFORD, Mr. Roger Thomas, BA ACA *1989;* (Tax Fac), Stafford Thursz, Cavendish House, Clarke Street, POULTON-LE-FYLDE, LANCASHIRE, FY6 8JW.
STAFFORD, Mr. Scott John, BSc(Hons) ACA *2009;* (Tax Fac), Flat 5 Beaufort House, 4 Andre Street, LONDON, E8 2FN.
STAFFORD, Mr. Simon Matthew James, BSc FCA *1996;* 23 Pepper Place, Kesgrave, IPSWICH, SUFFOLK, IP5 2DB.
STAFFORD, Mr. Stephen Alexander, ACA FCCA *2011;* Flat 30, Fairland House, Masons Hill, BROMLEY, BR2 9JJ.
STAFFORD ALLEN, Mr. Nigel Garth, FCA *1972;* Tudor Lodgings Castle Acre, KING'S LYNN, NORFOLK, PE32 2AN. (Life Member)
STAFFORD ALLEN, Mr. Samuel, ACA *2011;* Tudor Lodgings, Castle Acre, KING'S LYNN, NORFOLK, PE32 2AN.
STAFFORD-HILL, Miss. Lisa Carol, BSc ACA *1993;* 74 Birdhurst Road, SOUTH CROYDON, SURREY, CR2 7EB.
STAGG, Mrs. Carole Ann, BA FCA *1987;* International Baccalaureate Organization, Peterson House, Malthouse Avenue, Cardiff Gate, CARDIFF CF23 8GL.
STAGG, Mrs. Catherine Anne, BSc ACA *1994;* J D Williams & Co Ltd, Griffin House, 40 Lever Street, MANCHESTER, M60 6ES.
STAGG, Miss. Claire Alexandra, ACA *2008;* Flat 20 Oldfield House, West Drive, LONDON, SW16 1RT.
STAGG, Mr. Denis, FCA *1959;* 39 Southlands Grove, SCARBOROUGH, NORTH YORKSHIRE, YO12 5PQ. (Life Member)
STAGG, Miss. Hannah Frances, BSc ACA *2010;* 3 Curgenven Close, Byfield, DAVENTRY, NORTHAMPTONSHIRE, NN11 3HP.
STAGG, Mr. Nicholas Simon, BSc FCA *1985;* 43 Sutherland Place, LONDON, W2 5BY.
STAGG, Mr. Paul Michael, BA ACA *2009;* 3 Cote Lea Park, Westbury on Trym, BRISTOL, BS9 4AQ.
STAGG, Mr. Timothy Venn, BA ACA *1992;* 94 Albert Road, Caversham, READING, RG4 7PL.
STAGGS, Mr. Cyril Richard, FCA *1956;* Caerhuan, Church Street, CARDIGAN, SA43 1DJ. (Life Member)
STAHEL, Mr. Robert John, BSc ACA *1999;* 17 The Dairy, HENLOW, BEDFORDSHIRE, SG16 6JD.
STAHEYEFF, Mr. Michael Peter, ACA *1986;* 1 HarbourFront Avenue, Keppel Bay Tower #14-05, SINGAPORE 098632, SINGAPORE.
STAHEYEFF, Mr. Nicholas Peter, BA ACA *1982;* Sonnenbergrain 4, CH-3013 BERNE, SWITZERLAND.
STAIG, Mrs. Jacqueline Ann, BA FCA CTA *1997;* Wolseley Plc, Parkview, 1220 Arlington Business Park, Theale, READING, RG7 4GA.
STAIGHT, Mr. Matthew, ACA *2008;* 10 Fitzalan Place, Maidenbower, CRAWLEY, WEST SUSSEX, RH10 7XZ.
STAIN, Miss. Sara Melanie, BA ACA *1989;* 27 Clairvaux Road, Vaucluse, SYDNEY, NSW 2030, AUSTRALIA.
STAINER, Mrs. Catrin Mary Copeland, BA ACA *1987;* 19 Chatsworth Road, Chiswick, LONDON, W4 3HY.
STAINER, Mr. David-Lloyd John, BCom FCA *1991;* Piazza Giacomo Matteotti 13, 41121 MODENA, MO, ITALY.
STAINER, Mr. Robin, MA FCA *1974;* Radcot House, Radcot, BAMPTON, OXFORDSHIRE, OX18 2SX. (Life Member)
STAINES, Mr. Andrew Henry, BA(Hons) ACA *2003;* 22 Old Palace Lane, RICHMOND, SURREY, TW9 1PG.
STAINES, Mr. Christopher Michael Adrian, BSc FCA *1987;* 2 Arum Avenue, Kommetjie, CAPE TOWN, C.P., 7975, SOUTH AFRICA.
STAINES, Miss. Leanne, BA(Hons) ACA *2011;* 52 Lullington Garth, LONDON, N12 7BY.
STAINES, Mr. Leonard Henry, BA FCA *1972;* Newlands, 21 Waxwing Close, AYLESBURY, BUCKINGHAMSHIRE, HP19 0WT.
•STAINES, Mrs. Lorelie Marion, BA ACA *1986;* Lorelie Staines, 2 Garrick Close, WALTON-ON-THAMES, KT12 5NY.
STAINES, Mr. Philip John, BA FCA *1974;* Conseil National De La Compatabilite, 3 Boulevard Diderot, 75572 PARIS, FRANCE.
STAINES, Mr. Simeon Howard, BSc(Hons) ACA *2002;* The Bungalow, Studham Nursery Clements End Road, Studham, DUNSTABLE, BEDFORDSHIRE, LU6 2NG.
STAINES, Mrs. Stacey Anne, BSc ACA *2006;* 11 Close Toalt, Ballawattleworth Estate Peel, ISLE OF MAN, IM5 1XB.
STAINFORTH, Mr. Alan John, ACA *1984;* 31a Church Street, Braunston, OAKHAM, LEICESTERSHIRE, LE15 8QT.
STAINFORTH, Mr. Brian, FCA *1969;* PO Box 432, Fourways, JOHANNESBURG, GAUTENG, 2055, SOUTH AFRICA. (Life Member)
STAINFORTH, Mr. Christopher Graham, FCA *1976;* 77 Holland Park, LONDON, W11 3SQ.
STAINFORTH, Mr. Christopher John, BA ACA *1990;* 31 Hercules Drive, Newark, NEWARK, NOTTINGHAMSHIRE, NG24 1RA.
STAINFORTH, Mr. Nigel David Moxon, FCA *1964;* PO Box 871, CRAMERVIEW, GAUTENG, 2060, SOUTH AFRICA. (Life Member)
STAINFORTH, Mr. Roger, FCA *1967;* P.O.Box 1399, SEDGEFIELD, WESTERN CAPE PROVINCE, 6573, SOUTH AFRICA. (Life Member)
STAINFORTH, Mrs. Susan Jennifer, ACA *1992;* 31 Hercules Drive, NEWARK, NOTTINGHAMSHIRE, NG24 1RA.
STAINROD, Mr. Darren, BA ACA *1992;* 316 Patricks Avenue, 31253 Seven Mile Beach, PROSPECT, GRAND CAYMAN, KY1 1206, CAYMAN ISLANDS.
•STAINTON, Mrs. Helen, MA ACA CTA *1992;* (Tax Fac), Tax Training Solutions, 19 Vale Coppice, Ramsbottom, BURY, LANCASHIRE, BL0 9FJ.
STAINTON, Mr. Lee, ACA *2003;* 44 Greenbriar Close, BLACKPOOL, FY3 7SA.

STAINTON, Mr. Michael John, BA *1988;* 10 Tempsford Close, ENFIELD, MIDDLESEX, EN2 7EP.
STAINTON, Ms. Valerie Ruth, BA ACA *1991;* 20 Ulundi Road, Blackheath, LONDON, SE3 7UG.
STAIRMAND, Mr. Robert James, BA FCA *1993;* PO Box 7308, General Post Office, CENTRAL, HONG KONG SAR.
STAIRS, Dr. Anthony John, BA MBChB ACA CF *1996;* Barnside House, Kimbolton Road, Lower Dean, HUNTINGDON, CAMBRIDGESHIRE, PE28 0LJ.
STAIRS, Mr. Brian Terence Leslie, FCA *1961;* The Grange, 38B Newbury Lane, Silsoe, BEDFORD, MK45 4ET. (Life Member)
STAIT, Mrs. Alison Jane, BA ACA *1992;* Pound Cottage, Brampford Speke, EXETER, EX5 5DU.
STAIT, Miss. Beatrice Emily Ann, BA ACA *1998;* Fujitsu Observatory House, Windsor Road, SLOUGH, SL1 2EY.
STAIT, Mr. Geraint Wynn, BA ACA *1992;* Pound Cottage, Brampford Speke, EXETER, EX5 5DU.
STAIT, Mr. Philip Gordon, ACA *1987;* (Tax Fac), 5 Heron Close, Great Glen, LEICESTER, LE8 9DZ.
STAITE, Mr. Adam Daniel, ACA *2011;* 12/20 Cromwell Road, SOUTH YARRA, VIC 3141, AUSTRALIA.
STAITE, Mr. John Frederick, FCA *1972;* 30 Byfords Close, Huntley, GLOUCESTER, GL19 3SA.
STAKES, Mrs. Jayne, BA(Econ) ACA *2000;* 126 Stockport Road, Timperley, ALTRINCHAM, WA15 7SR.
STAKES, Mrs. Tracey, BSc ACA DChA *1990;* 25 Jessop Way, Haslington, CREWE, CW1 5FU.
STALBOW, Mr. Michael Robert, BCom FCA *1969;* 38 St. Mary's Avenue, NORTHWOOD, HA6 3AZ. (Life Member)
STALEY, Mrs. Catherine Sara, BA FCA *1994;* West View High Street, Marchington, UTTOXETER, STAFFORDSHIRE, ST14 8LD.
STALEY, Mr. Graham David, BCom FCA *1979;* Anheuser - Busch InBev, 2nd Floor, 250 Park Avenue, NEW YORK, NY 10177, UNITED STATES.
STALEY, Mr. Lance, BEng ACA *1995;* 72 Walmer Road, Woodley, READING, RG5 4PN.
STALEY, Miss. Miriam Louise, BSc ACA *1994;* 8 Claremont Road, BROMLEY, BR1 2JL.
STALKER, Mrs. Catherine Jane, MA ACA *2001;* 124 Ashdon Road, SAFFRON WALDEN, CB10 2AL.
STALKER, Mr. Christopher David, BA ACA *1982;* 3-4 Popes Lane, Cookham, MAIDENHEAD, SL6 9NY.
STALKER, Mrs. Hayley, LLB ACA *2006;* with PricewaterhouseCoopers LLP, 89 Sandyford Road, NEWCASTLE UPON TYNE, NE1 8HW.
•STALKER, Mr. John Lawson, BSc FCA *1977;* Crowe Clark Whitehill LLP, Aquis House, 49-51 Blagrave Street, READING, RG1 1PL. See also Horwath Clark Whitehill LLP and Crowe Clark Whitehill
STALKER, Mrs. Justine Ann, BA ACA *2003;* 13 Green Way, HARROGATE, NORTH YORKSHIRE, HG2 9LR.
STALKER, Mr. Matthew, ACA *2009;* ServiceMagic UK, Zoopla Ltd, 182-194 Union Street, LONDON, SE1 0LH.
STALKER, Mr. Stuart Carl, ACA *2004;* 66 Martello Gardens, NEWCASTLE UPON TYNE, NE7 7LE.
STALLABRASS, Mr. David Lawrence, FCA *1950;* 5 Peter Hill Close, Chalfont St. Peter, GERRARDS CROSS, SL9 0HZ. (Life Member)
STALLABRASS, Mr. John Lawrence, BSc FCA *1983;* 23 Austenway, Chalfont St. Peter, GERRARDS CROSS, BUCKINGHAMSHIRE, SL9 8NN.
•STALLABRASS, Mr. Matthew Christopher, MA ACA *2003;* Crowe Clark Whitehill LLP, St Bride's House, 10 Salisbury Square, LONDON, EC4Y 8EH. See also Horwath Clark Whitehill LLP
STALLARD, Miss. Angela, BSc ACA *2004;* Flat A, 14 Hamilton Road, LONDON, SW19 1JF.
STALLARD, Mr. Guy William, BSc ACA *1991;* 5 Bramble Close, Chalfont St. Peter, GERRARDS CROSS, BUCKINGHAMSHIRE, SL9 0JP.
STALLARD, Ms. Jane Michal, MA ACA *1994;* 5 Bramble Close, Chalfont St. Peter, GERRARDS CROSS, SL9 0JP.
STALLARD, Mr. Michael James, BSc ACA *2007;* 48 Willow Way, MANCHESTER, M20 6JS.
STALLARD, Mr. Nigel David, BSc ACA *1988;* Kings College London, James Clerk Maxwell Building, 57 Waterloo Road, LONDON, SE1 8WA.
•STALLARD, Mr. Philip Adrian, BSc FCA *1991;* (Tax Fac), Lentells Limited, Ash House, Cook Way, Bindon Road, TAUNTON, SOMERSET TA2 6BJ.
STALLEY, Mr. Jonathan Marcus, BSc ACA *1992;* 9 Agoho Street, North Forbes Park, MAKATI CITY 1219 Manil, PHILIPPINES.
STALLEY, Mr. Michael, FCA *1995;* Fiscal Reps Ltd, The Stables, Seale, FARNHAM, SURREY, GU10 1HL.
STALLEY, Mr. Ronald Charles, FCA *1959;* Oaks, Brays Green Lane, Hyde Heath, AMERSHAM, HP6 5RL. (Life Member)
STALMANIS, Mr. John Andrew, MA ACA *1991;* 22 Connaught Gardens, Muswell Hill, LONDON, N10 3LB.
STALS, Mr. Peter, BSc ACA *2006;* Flat 2, 7 Balham Grove, LONDON, SW12 8AZ.
STAMFORD, Mrs. Elizabeth Jane, BMus FCA *1989;* with PricewaterhouseCoopers LLP, 300 Madison Avenue, NEW YORK, NY 10017, UNITED STATES.
STAMMERS, Mr. Ashley Thomas, FCA *1992;* with Baker Chapman & Bussey, Magnet House, 3 North Hill, COLCHESTER, CO1 1DZ.
STAMMERS, Mr. Darren Anthony, BSc ACA *1996;* 4 McCubbin Street, Kew East, MELBOURNE, VIC 3102, AUSTRALIA.
STAMMERS, Mr. Dominic Mark James, BSc(Hons) ACA *2004;* with BDO LLP, 55 Baker Street, LONDON, W1U 7EU.
STAMMERS, Mr. Douglas William, BA FCA *1984;* 6 Camp Field, Winchester Road, Kings Somborne, STOCKBRIDGE, HAMPSHIRE, SO20 6QB.
STAMMERS, Mr. Jeremy James Gordon, BA ACA *2001;* British Petroleum Co Plc, 1 St. James's Square, LONDON, SW1Y 4PD.
STAMMERS, Mrs. Kristina Louise, BSc(Hons) ACA *2004;* 10 Linfields, AMERSHAM, BUCKINGHAMSHIRE, HP7 9QH.
STAMMERS, Mr. Robert Ashley, ACA *1984;* Julianalaan 91, 1483 VH DE RIJP, NETHERLANDS.
•STAMP, Mr. Andrew Charles Morrell, MSc BBS FCA *1974;* Farm Cottage Widworthy Court, Wilmington, HONITON, DEVON, EX14 9JN.
STAMP, Mr. Ewen George Morrell, TD FCA *1964;* The Gables, Lower Street, Stutton, IPSWICH, IP9 2SQ.
•STAMP, Mr. James Robert, MA MEng ACA *2000;* KPMG LLP, 15 Canada Square, LONDON, E14 5GL. See also KPMG Europe LLP
STAMP, Mr. Kenneth Edward, FCA *1945;* 9 Burnham Drive, REIGATE, SURREY, RH2 9HD. (Life Member)
STAMP, Mr. Matthew Rupert Franklyn, BSc(Hons) ACA *2001;* with Deloitte LLP, 3 Victoria Square, Victoria Street, ST. ALBANS, HERTFORDSHIRE, AL1 3TF.
STAMP, Miss. Penny Caroline, MSc BA ACA AMCT *1984;* PCS Services Ltd, 45 Elephant Lane, LONDON, SE16 4JD.
STAMP, Mr. Stephen Anthony, BA ACA *1988;* Suite 112, 2 Lansdowne Row, Berkeley Square, LONDON, W1J 6HL.
STAMP, Mr. Thomas Andrew, BSc FCA *1978;* 22 Cumberland Close, AYLESBURY, BUCKINGHAMSHIRE, HP21 7HH.
STAMP, Mr. William, BA(Hons) ACA *2009;* Flat 2, 32 Avonmore Road, LONDON, W14 8RS.
STAMPER, Mr. Christopher Ian, LLB ACA *2000;* Sandbanks, Knowle Grove, VIRGINIA WATER, SURREY, GU25 4JB.
•STAMPS, Mr. Barry Kenneth, FCA *1971;* Algonquin Trust S.A., Cour du Moulin, 5-9 Route de L'Etat, 1380 LASNE, BELGIUM.
STAMPS, Miss. Emma, BA ACA *1993;* Transys Projects Limited, 2 Priestley Wharf, Aston Science Park, Holt Street, BIRMINGHAM, B7 4BN.
STANBRA, Mr. Graham Michael, BSc(Hons) ACA CTA *1990;* (Tax Fac), 12 Martin Rise, BEXLEYHEATH, KENT, DA6 8NB.
STANBRIDGE, Mr. Alan Frank, BSc FCA *1976;* 159 The Street, Rustington, LITTLEHAMPTON, WEST SUSSEX, BN16 3DP.
•STANBROOK, Mr. Toby Jonathan, BBA ACA *2004;* Mazars LLP, The Pinnacle, 160 Midsummer Boulevard, MILTON KEYNES, MK9 1FF.
STANBURY, Mr. Colin Douglas, FCA *1969;* 7 Claremont Gardens, WHITLEY BAY, NE26 3SF.
•STANBURY, Mr. David John, BA ACA *1995;* Wellers, Stuart House, 55 Catherine Place, LONDON, SW1E 6DY.
STANBURY, Ms. Deborah, BEng ACA *1994;* 84 Frenchay Road, OXFORD, OX2 6TF.
•STANBURY, Mr. James Humphrey Flavell, MA FCA *1991;* RGL LLP, 8th Floor, Dashwood, 69 Old Broad Street, LONDON, EC2M 1QS.
STANBURY, Mr. Nicholas Henry, FCA FCII *1972;* 17 Woodbury Park Road, TUNBRIDGE WELLS, TN4 9NQ.
STANBURY, Mr. Philip William, MA ACA *1981;* Ashridge Business School, Ashridge, BERKHAMSTED, HERTFORDSHIRE, HP4 1NS.
STANBURY, Mr. Timothy Jason, BA ACA *1995;* 84 Frenchay Road, OXFORD, OX2 6TF.
STANCEY, Miss. Sarah, BA ACA *1992;* Cairn Energy Plc Clydesdale Bank Plaza, 50 Lothian Road, EDINBURGH, EH3 9BY.
STANCIULESCU, Mr. Cosmin, ACA *2009;* Flat 4, 51 Hertslet Road, LONDON, N7 6PH.
STANCLIFFE, Mr. Geoffrey Walter, FCA *1958;* 4 Ullswater Rise, Linton Park, WETHERBY, LS22 6YP. (Life Member)
STANCLIFFE, Mr. Nigel James, BA ACA *1984;* 30, Canning Road, CROYDON, CR0 6QD.
STANCOMBE, Mr. Christopher John, MA FCA *1989;* 8 Wellington Gardens, Southend Bradfield, READING, RG7 6EJ.
STANCOMBE, Mrs. Fiona Eliza, BA ACA *1997;* 6 Wilton Crescent, LONDON, SW19 3QZ.
STAND, Mr. Robert Roy, FCA *1963;* 185 Ravenhurst Road, Harborne, BIRMINGHAM, B17 9HU.
STANDEN, Mr. Barry Michael, BA ACA *2005;* Brevan Howard Asset Management, 55 Baker Street, LONDON, W1U 8EW.
STANDEN, Mr. Brian Malcolm John, MBA BSc FCA *1979;* Branxholme, Gills Hill Lane, RADLETT, HERTFORDSHIRE, WD7 8DD.
STANDEN, Miss. Caragh Margaret, MA ACA *2001;* Sherborne School, Abbey Road, SHERBORNE, DORSET, DT9 3AP.
STANDEN, Mr. Howard, BSc ACA *1995;* 2 Loveclough Place, ROSSENDALE, BB4 8QU.
STANDEN, Mrs. Karen Belinda, FCA *1990;* 42 Kings Drive, Littleover, DERBY, DE23 6EY.
STANDEN, Mr. Matthew Eric, BSc ACA *2005;* Hill View Farm, Chestnut Lane, Kneesworth, ROYSTON, SG8 5JH.
•STANDEN, Mr. Nicholas Charles, BA ACA *1986;* KPMG LLP, 1 Forest Gate, Brighton Road, CRAWLEY, WEST SUSSEX, RH11 9PT. See also KPMG Europe LLP
STANDEN, Mrs. Susan Jane, BSc ACA *1988;* Upper Sent, Oakwood Hill, DORKING, SURREY, RH5 5PT.
STANDEVEN, Mr. Allen, FCA *1966;* 35 Leicester Drive, GLOSSOP, DERBYSHIRE, SK13 8SH.
•STANDEVEN, Mr. Nicholas Robert Crossley, ACA *1985;* Crossley & Co, Royal Mews, St. Georges Place, CHELTENHAM, GLOUCESTERSHIRE, GL50 3PQ.
STANDFIELD, Mr. Paul John, MEng ACA *2007;* 270, Pickhurst Lane, BROMLEY, BR40HR.
STANDING, Mr. David Joseph, BSc ACA *2002;* 23 Main Road, Old Dalby, MELTON MOWBRAY, LEICESTERSHIRE, LE14 3LR.
STANDING, Mrs. Hannah Louise, MA ACA *2004;* BSS GROUP PLC, Fleet House, Lee Circle, LEICESTER, LE1 3QQ.
•STANDING, Mr. John Edward, FCA DChA *1983;* James Todd & Co, Greenbank House, 141 Adelphi Street, PRESTON, PR1 7BH.
STANDING, Miss. Lucy, BSc(Hons) ACA *2010;* 6 Elms Close, SOLIHULL, B91 2ND.
STANDING, Mr. Neil, FCA *1963;* 2A Tower Lane, Fulwood, PRESTON, PR2 9HP. (Life Member)
STANDING, Mr. Paul Hollerton, BSc ACA *1990;* 54 Aberdeen Road, LANCASTER, LA1 3DA.
STANDING, Mr. Philip, BSc ACA *2006;* with Ernst & Young LLP, 1 More London Place, LONDON, SE1 2AF.
STANDING, Mr. Richard Neil, BSc ACA *1986;* with Deloitte & Touche, 6 Shenton Way, 32-00, DBS Building Tower Two, SINGAPORE 068809, SINGAPORE.
STANDING, Miss. Sarah Elizabeth Anne, BSc ACA *1989;* 45 Hartismere Road, LONDON, SW6 7UB.
STANDING, Mr. Timothy Mark, ACA *1982;* Kew (Electrical Distributors) Ltd, 2 Chapel Road Portslade, BRIGHTON, BN41 1PF.
•STANDISH, Mr. Martin John, BEd FCA *1983;* Baker Tilly Tax & Advisory Services LLP, 2 Humber Quays, Wellington Street West, HULL, HU1 2BN. See also Baker Tilly UK Audit LLP
STANDISH, Mr. Peter John, FCA *1966;* 49a The Gateway, WOKING, GU21 5SL.
STANDRING, Mr. Geoffrey Nigel, BSc ACA *1986;* 16 Llys Nercwys, MOLD, FLINTSHIRE, CH7 1HR.
STANDRING, Mr. John Paul, BA ACA *1991;* 567 Nod Hill Road, WILTON, CT 06897, UNITED STATES.
STANDRING, Miss. Lauren Alexis, ACA *2008;* Santander, 298 Deansgate, MANCHESTER, M3 4HH.
STANDRING, Mrs. Suzanna Clare, BA ACA *1992;* 37820 N. 97th Place, SCOTTSDALE, AZ 85262, UNITED STATES.
STANFIELD, Mr. Eugene David, BSc ACA *1997;* 2 Bracondale, ESHER, SURREY, KT10 9EN.
STANFIELD, Mrs. Helen, BSc ACA *1992;* 17 Holm Oaks, Cowfold, HORSHAM, RH13 8AQ.
STANFIELD, Mr. Neil Anthony, BSc FCA *1993;* London Chamber of Commerce & Industry Swan House, 33 Queen Street, LONDON, EC4R 1AP.
STANFIELD, Mr. Nicholas Simon, BA(Hons) ACA *2011;* 99 Route des Grands Champs, 74370 METZ TESSY, FRANCE.
STANFIELD, Mrs. Philippa Claire Louise, BSocSc ACA *2000;* 2 Bracondale, ESHER, SURREY, KT10 9EN.
STANFORD, Mr. Alexander James, MEng ACA *2006;* 11 McConnell Street, KENSINGTON, VIC 3031, AUSTRALIA.
STANFORD, Mr. Clive David, MA FCA ATII *1978;* Orchard Farm, Chalk Lane, East Horsley, LEATHERHEAD, SURREY, KT24 6TH.
STANFORD, Mr. David Andrew, FCA *1974;* 92 Mill on the Mole Residential Park, SOUTH MOLTON, DEVON, EX36 3QG.
STANFORD, Mr. Henry Julian Aglionby, MA ACA *1992;* Albion Ventures LLP, 1 Kings Arms Yard, LONDON, EC2R 7AF.
STANFORD, Miss. Joelle Louise, BA ACA *1998;* 11 Fen Meadow, Ightham, SEVENOAKS, KENT, TN15 9HT.
•STANFORD, Mr. Paul, FCA CTA *1982;* (Tax Fac), Harben Barker Limited, Drayton Court, Drayton Road, SOLIHULL, WEST MIDLANDS, B90 4NG.
STANFORD, Mr. Stanley Colin, FCA CTA *1954;* 40 Harewood Avenue, Littledown, BOURNEMOUTH, DORSET, BH7 6NH. (Life Member)
STANFORD, Mr. Thomas James Francis, PhD MA MLitt BA FCA *1964;* 41 Brandling Place South, NEWCASTLE UPON TYNE, NE2 4RU.
STANGENBERG-HAVERKAMP, Mr. Johannes, BA ACA *2007;* Dieburger Str. 235, 64287 DARMSTADT, HESSEN, GERMANY.
STANGER, Mr. David John, FCA *1968;* 6 Cottingwood Lane, MORPETH, NE61 1EA. (Life Member)
STANGER, Mrs. Margaret, BSc ACA *1983;* 33 London Road South, Merstham, REDHILL, RH1 3AX.
•STANGER, Mr. Mark John, FCA *1990;* Gibbons, Lakeland Office, 2 Europe Way, COCKERMOUTH, CUMBRIA, CA13 0RJ. See also Gibbons & Company
STANGER, Mr. Michael James, BSc ACA *1985;* 33 London Road South, Merstham, REDHILL, RH1 3AX.
STANGER, Ms. Samantha Penelope, MMath ACA CTA *2004;* Adviva Media Ltd, 26-30 Strutton Ground, LONDON, SW1P 2HR.
STANIER, Mr. Peter Andrew, BSc ACA *1986;* Unit 5, Athena Court, Athena Drive, Tachbrook Park, WARWICK, CV34 6RT.
STANIEWSKI, Mr. Tomasz, ACA *2007;* 42 Hellyer Way, BOURNE END, BUCKINGHAMSHIRE, SL8 5XN.
•STANIFORTH, Mr. Adrian Charles Dominic, BEng FCA *1992;* (Tax Fac), Barber Harrison & Platt, 57/59 Saltergate, CHESTERFIELD, S40 1UL.
STANIFORTH, Mr. Adrian Martyn Christopher, BA FCA *1960;* (Member of Council 1973 - 1980), Park Hall, Walton Back Lane, Walton, CHESTERFIELD, S42 7LT. (Life Member)
STANIFORTH, Mrs. Elaine Ruth, MA ACA *1997;* 65 Appledore Drive, COVENTRY, CV5 7PH.
•STANIFORTH, Mr. John William, BSc(Hons) ACA *2000;* Kingston Smith LLP, Devonshire House, 60 Goswell Road, LONDON, EC1M 7AD. See also Kingston Smith Limited Liability Partnership, Devonshire Corporate Services LLP, Kingston Smith Consulting LLP and Kingston Smith(Bangladesh) Limited
•STANIFORTH, Mr. Leslie Gordon, BSc FCA *1978;* Duncan Sheard Glass, Castle Chambers, 43 Castle St, LIVERPOOL, L2 9TL. See also DSG Accountancy and Taxation Services Limited
STANIFORTH, Mrs. Louise Joanne, MEng ACA *1999;* 81a Palmerston Road, BUCKHURST HILL, ESSEX, IG9 5NS.
STANIFORTH, Mr. Martin Paul, ACA *2009;* Flat B, 124 Branksome Road, LONDON, SW2 5JA.
•STANIFORTH, Mr. Philip Guy, FCA *1995;* (Tax Fac), Page Kirk LLP, Sherwood House, 7 Gregory Boulevard, NOTTINGHAM, NG7 6LB.
STANIFORTH, Mr. Richard William, BSc ACA *1995;* Barcode Warehouse Ltd, Telford Drive, NEWARK, NOTTINGHAMSHIRE, NG24 2DX.
STANILAND, Mrs. Emma, BA ACA *1999;* 8 Herdings Court, Gleadless, SHEFFIELD, S12 2LT.
•STANILAND, Mr. James Bryce, MA ACA *1983;* Doncaster Deaf Trust, Doncaster College & School for the Deaf, Leger Way, DONCASTER, SOUTH YORKSHIRE, DN2 6AY.

•STANILAND, Mr. John Joseph, FCA *1961;* J.J. Staniland, 28 Peveril Drive, Riddings, ALFRETON, DE55 4AP.
STANILAND, Mr. Mark, ACA *1995;* 8 Herdings Court, SHEFFIELD, S12 2LT.
STANILAND, Mr. Paul John, BSc FCA *1980;* 25 High Street, Needingworth, ST.IVES, CAMBRIDGESHIRE, PE27 4SA.
•STANISZEWSKI, Mr. Alexander Adam Donald, BSc ACA *1990;* Staniszewski & Richter Sp. z.o.o., ul.Lwowska 10/21, 00-658 WARSAW, POLAND.
•STANKIEWICZ, Mr. Paul Mark, BSc FCA *1991;* Paul Marks & Co, Flat 1, 3 Lansdowne Road, Wimbledon, LONDON, SW20 8AP. See also Paul Stankiewicz & Co
STANLAKE, Mr. Howard John, FCA *1971;* 12 Deacon Drive, SALTASH, PL12 4SL.
STANLAKE, Mr. Ian John, BA(Hons) ACA *2001;* Ground Floor, 6 Castellain Road, LONDON, W9 1EZ.
STANLEY, Mr. Andrew David, FCA DChA *1980;* 29 School House Lane, TEDDINGTON, TW11 9DP.
STANLEY, Mr. Andrew James, BSc(Hons) ACA *2004;* Mercedes-Benz UK Limited, Delaware Drive, MILTON KEYNES, BUCKINGHAMSHIRE, MK15 8BA.
STANLEY, Mr. Brian Robert, FCA *1958;* Zlatorog, Bryants Bottom Road, GREAT MISSENDEN, HP16 0JU. (Life Member)
STANLEY, Mr. David Alan, BSc ACA *1992;* 26 The Queensway, Chalfont St. Peter, GERRARDS CROSS, BUCKINGHAMSHIRE, SL9 8NB.
•STANLEY, Mr. David Norman Charles, BSc FCA *1990;* Alwyns LLP, Crown House, 151 High Road, LOUGHTON, ESSEX, IG10 4LG.
•STANLEY, Mr. David Powell, ACA *1983;* David P Stanley, Floridian Palace, 21 Boulevard du Larvotto, MONTE CARLO, 98000, MONACO.
STANLEY, Mrs. Diane Julie, BA ACA *1988;* Clarendon House, 7 The Gables, Fenstanton, HUNTINGDON, CAMBRIDGESHIRE, PE28 9QP.
STANLEY, Mr. Donald Eric, MA ACA *1999;* 94 Short Street, BALMAIN, NSW 2041, AUSTRALIA.
STANLEY, Miss. Elizabeth, BA ACA *1992;* Audit Commission Millbank Tower, 21-24 Millbank, LONDON, SW1P 4HQ.
STANLEY, Mr. Graham Barry, MA ACA MCT *1993;* 31 Brite Avenue, SCARSDALE, NY 10583, UNITED STATES.
STANLEY, Mrs. Helen, BA ACA ATII *1995;* 16 Clive Avenue, HASTINGS, EAST SUSSEX, TN35 5LW.
STANLEY, Miss. Jane Elizabeth, BA ACA *1989;* 7 Woodbury Close, CROYDON, CR0 5PR.
•STANLEY, Mr. Jeffrey Alan, BSc(Econ) FCA *1981;* The Mudd Partnership, Lakeview House, 4 Woodbrook Crescent, BILLERICAY, ESSEX, CM12 0EQ.
STANLEY, Mr. John Charles, DBA MSc FCA ATII FRSA *1954;* 23 Crown Lane, CHISLEHURST, BR7 5PL. (Life Member)
STANLEY, Mr. John Michael, FCA *1955;* 12 Willow Way, Ponteland, NEWCASTLE UPON TYNE, NE20 9RJ. (Life Member)
STANLEY, Mr. Jonathan Michael Bryce, ACA *1991;* Enstar (EU) Ltd, Avaya House 2 Cathedral Hill, GUILDFORD, GU2 7TL.
STANLEY, Mr. Jonathan Paul, BA ACA *1992;* 2 Meadway, Cringleford, NORWICH, NR4 6XS.
STANLEY, Mr. Jonathan Richard Sherwood, BSc ACA *1993;* Fairmead Ashampstead Road, Upper Basildon, READING, RG8 8NS.
STANLEY, Mrs. Karen Elizabeth, BSc ACA *1992;* John Lewis of Hungerford Plc Grove Technology Park, Downsview Road, WANTAGE, OXFORDSHIRE, OX12 9FA.
STANLEY, Mrs. Karen Lesley, BA ACA *1993;* 12 Gladstone Grove, Heaton Moor, STOCKPORT, SK4 4DA.
STANLEY, Miss. Kate Ann, BSc ACA DChA *1989;* Affinity Sutton Group Ltd, 6 More London Place, LONDON, SE1 2DA.
STANLEY, Mr. Larry Alexander Leonidas, BA ACA *1993;* 75 St. John Street, Creetown, NEWTON STEWART, WIGTOWNSHIRE, DG8 7JB.
STANLEY, Mr. Mark, BSc ACA *1988;* 81 Devonshire Road, Dore, SHEFFIELD, S17 3NU.
STANLEY, Mr. Matthew Joseph, BSc ACA *2007;* 25 Beamont Walk, Brockworth, GLOUCESTER, GL3 4BL.
STANLEY, Miss. Melissa Rachel, BA ACA *2009;* 80 Providence Way, Waterbeach, CAMBRIDGE, CB25 9QJ.
STANLEY, Mr. Michael, FCA *1972;* St Malo, Gryffe Road, KILMACOLM, PA13 4AZ. (Life Member)
STANLEY, Mr. Michael Patrick, FCA *1964;* Ferncliff, Potters Hill, Crockerton, WARMINSTER, BA12 8AD. (Life Member)
STANLEY, Mr. Norman Frederick, FCA *1956;* 164 Norsey Road, BILLERICAY, CM11 1BU. (Life Member)
•ⒾSTANLEY, Mr. Paul, BSc FCA *1987;* Begbies Traynor (Central) LLP, 340 Deansgate, MANCHESTER, M3 4LY. See also Begbies Traynor Limited
STANLEY, Mr. Paul, MEng ACA *1992;* Nether Crutches Copse Lane, Jordans, BEACONSFIELD, BUCKINGHAMSHIRE, HP9 2TA.
•STANLEY, Mr. Paul, FCA *1986;* Bryn Teg, Drury Lane, BUCKLEY, CH7 3JD.
STANLEY, Mr. Paul Michael, BA ACA *1992;* Waverley, The Avenue, Collingham, WETHERBY, LS22 5BU.
STANLEY, Mr. Philip David Shaw, BSc ACA *1995;* 4317 Blenheim Circle, MINNETONKA, MN 55345, UNITED STATES.
STANLEY, Mr. Richard, BA ACA *1989;* with PricewaterhouseCoopers GmbH, Elsenheimerstrasse 31-33, D-80687 MUNICH, GERMANY.
STANLEY, Mr. Richard John, BSc ACA *1979;* 15 Nettle Gap Close, Wootton, NORTHAMPTON, NN4 6AH.
•STANLEY, Mr. Roger Clayton Holbrook, FCA *1970;* (Tax Fac), R.C.H. Stanley, Hoth Farm House, Danegate, Eridge Green, TUNBRIDGE WELLS, TN3 9HU.
STANLEY, Mr. Roger Mark, BSc ACA *1987;* Springhill Farm, Alkington, WHITCHURCH, SHROPSHIRE, SY13 3NJ.
STANLEY, Mr. Rupert Mark, BSc ACA *1993;* 26 Harwood Close, Tewin, WELWYN, AL6 0LF.
STANLEY, Mrs. Sharon Loveday, BA ACA *1994;* 157 Reeds Lane, Moreton, WIRRAL, MERSEYSIDE, CH46 1ST.
STANLEY, Mrs. Susan Janet, BSc ACA *1991;* 1 Glebe Close, ALDERSHOT, HAMPSHIRE, GU11 3FN.
STANLEY, Mr. Terence Frank, FCA *1963;* Flat 1, 37 Beach Road, WESTON-SUPER-MARE, AVON, BS23 1BG.
•STANLEY, Mr. Terence John, BSc FCA *1983;* (Tax Fac), Cornaby & Stanley, 18 Bath Rd, Old Town, SWINDON, SN1 4BA.
•STANLEY, Mr. Timothy Alan, FCA *1969;* 5 The Orchard, Holcombe, DAWLISH, DEVON, EX7 0JD.
STANLEY, Mr. Timothy John, BA FCA *1971;* The Laurels, Sleepers Hill, WINCHESTER, SO22 4NA.
STANLEY-CRITCHLOW, Mr. John, FCA *1972;* PO Box 279, SPIT JUNCTION, NSW 2088, AUSTRALIA.
STANLEY-JONES, Ms. Charlotte Suzanne, ACA *1993;* Oak Ridge, Hook Heath Road, WOKING, SURREY, GU22 0LF.
STANLEY-WARD, Miss. Hannah, ACA *2009;* 14 Tower Point, Godinton Road, ASHFORD, TN23 1AH.
STANNARD, Mrs. Amanda, ACA *1993;* 64 First Avenue, NEWHAVEN, EAST SUSSEX, BN9 9HX.
STANNARD, Miss. Andrea, BA ACA *1988;* 5 Old Garden Court, ST. ALBANS, HERTFORDSHIRE, AL3 4RQ.
STANNARD, Mr. John Marcus, ACA *1990;* Garden Flat, 1d Hill Road, LONDON, NW8 9QE.
STANNARD, Mr. Kenneth, BA(Hons) FCA *1973;* 108 Heavygate Road, SHEFFIELD, S10 1PF.
STANNARD, Mr. Michael Noel, BSc FCA *1977;* 11 Seafield Road, CHRISTCHURCH, DORSET, BH23 4ET.
STANNARD, Miss. Nicola Jane, BA(Hons) ACA *2002;* 13 Simmental Crescent, Somerville, Howick, MANUKAU CITY 2014, AUCKLAND, NEW ZEALAND.
STANNARD, Mr. Timothy Charles, BA ACA *1983;* Investec Bank (UK) Ltd, 2 Gresham Street, LONDON, EC2V 7QP.
•STANNARD, Mr. Wayne, FCA *1987;* (Tax Fac), RS Partnership LLP, Riverside House, 14 Prospect Place, WELWYN, HERTFORDSHIRE, AL6 9EN.
•STANNETT, Mr. Duncan, BA FCA *1995;* Barnes Roffe LLP, 16-19 Copperfields, Spital Street, DARTFORD, DA1 2DE.
STANNETT, Mr. Philip John, BA ACA *1992;* Shefford House, Lower Wokingham Road, CROWTHORNE, BERKSHIRE, RG45 6DB.
STANNETT, Mr. Robert William, BA ACA *1993;* 6 Northfield, Shalford, GUILDFORD, GU4 8JN.
STANNING, Mr. Kenneth Duncan, BSc ACA *1979;* PO Box 201374, DURBAN NORTH, KWAZULU NATAL, 4016, SOUTH AFRICA.
STANOTKINA, Miss. Maria, ACA *2010;* Lyapidevskogo str 2-1-9, 125581 MOSCOW, RUSSIAN FEDERATION.
STANSBY, Mr. Jonathan, BA ACA *1980;* API Group plc, Second Avenue Poynton Industrial Estate Poynton, STOCKPORT, CHESHIRE, SK12 1ND.
STANSFELD, Mr. Edward John Buxton, BSc FCA CISA *1997;* Audit Scotland, 18 George Street, EDINBURGH, EH2 2QU.
STANSFELD, Mr. Robert George Wilmot, BSc FCA *1992;* 4 York Road, EDINBURGH, EH5 3EH.
•STANSFIELD, Mr. Andrew, BSc FCA DChA *1987;* Stansfield & Co, Suite 303, Queens Dock Business Centre, Norfolk Street, LIVERPOOL, L1 0BG.
STANSFIELD, Mrs. Angela, BA ACA *1989;* 8 Calverley Avenue, Burnage, MANCHESTER, M19 2JR.
STANSFIELD, Mr. David John, FCA *1972;* 31 Wood Lane, Heskin, CHORLEY, PR7 5NU. (Life Member)
STANSFIELD, Mr. James Philip, BSc FCA *1977;* The Downings, Church Lane, South Cerney, CIRENCESTER, GL7 5TT.
STANSFIELD, Mr. John Philip, FCA *1958;* Lowbank House, Pinfold Lane, Romiley, STOCKPORT, SK6 4NR. (Life Member)
STANSFIELD, Mr. Jonathan Richard, BSc ACA *2002;* 23 Cooks Meadow, Edlesborough, DUNSTABLE, BEDFORDSHIRE, LU6 2RP.
•STANSFIELD, Mr. Kevin Edward, ACA *1992;* Action House, 1 Coopers Close, East Wellow, ROMSEY, SO51 6AZ.
STANSFIELD, Mr. Mark, BA ACA *1989;* Audit Commission, Aspinall Close, Middlebrook, Horwich, BOLTON, BL6 6QQ.
STANSFIELD, Mr. Mark, BA ACA *1992;* The Acorns, 9 Gilmores Lane, Balderton, NEWARK, NOTTINGHAMSHIRE, NG24 3GX.
STANSFIELD, Mr. Mark Philip, BA FCA *1984;* Brow Top Farm May Lane, Claughton-on-Brock, PRESTON, PR3 0PE.
STANSFIELD, Mr. Norman, FCA *1961;* Lindra, 11 Wainscot Close, Wadsworth, HEBDEN BRIDGE, HX7 8TA. (Life Member)
•STANSFIELD, Mr. Paul, FCA *1987;* Cowgill Holloway LLP, Regency House, 45-51 Chorley New Road, BOLTON, BL1 4QR. See also Multisolo Limited and Cowgill Holloway & Co
STANSFIELD, Miss. Rachelle Victoria, ACA MAAT *2009;* 9 Chaucer Avenue, Stanley, WAKEFIELD, WF3 4QE.
STANSFIELD, Mr. Richard, BA ACA *1981;* 15 Grosvenor Court, Lime Tree Avenue, WOLVERHAMPTON, WV6 8HB.
•STANSFIELD, Mrs. Sarah Margaret, BA ACA *1983;* Stansfield & Co, 2 Fountain Place, Barbourne, WORCESTER, WR1 3HW.
STANSIL, Mr. Frank, FCA *1958;* Roselea, 10 Dulwich Village, LONDON, SE21 7AL. (Life Member)
•STANT, Mr. Andrew Warren, FCA *1980;* (Tax Fac), Johnson Murkett & Hurst, Rawdon House, Rawdon Terrace, ASHBY-DE-LA-ZOUCH, LE65 2GN. See also Johnson, Murkett & Hurst (Computer Services) Ltd
•STANT, Mr. Mark John, BA FCA *1989;* BellGranger Limited, Copperfield, Grey Road, ALTRINCHAM, CHESHIRE, WA14 4BT.
•STANTON, Mr. Adam Hugh, FCA *1975;* Upper Shelderton House, Clungunford, CRAVEN ARMS, SHROPSHIRE, SY7 0PE.
STANTON, Miss. Carolyn Jean, BSc ACA *1992;* 89 Bulwer Road, LONDON, E11 1BY.
STANTON, Mrs. Celeste, ACA ACMA *2010;* 65 Overton Hill, Overton, BASINGSTOKE, HAMPSHIRE, RG25 3PE.
STANTON, Mr. Christopher George, FCA *1955;* 10 Park View Road, Ealing, LONDON, W5 2JB. (Life Member)
STANTON, Mr. Christopher Paul, BA FCA *1992;* Shoosmiths, 5 The Lakes, NORTHAMPTON, NN4 7SH.
STANTON, Mr. David, FCA *1982;* 28 Avenue Rise, BUSHEY, WD23 3AS.
STANTON, Mr. David Mark, BA ACA *1995;* 2nd Floor, 8 Cavendish Square, LONDON, W1G 0ER.
•STANTON, Mrs. Elizabeth, BSc ACA *1979;* (Member of Council 2009 - 2011), Ernst & Young LLP, 1 More London Place, LONDON, SE1 2AF. See also Ernst & Young Europe LLP
STANTON, Mr. Francis, FCA *1954;* 27 Regent Drive, PRESTON, PR2 3JB. (Life Member)
STANTON, Mr. Gary Jonathan, BA ACA *1996;* PO Box 396, GILLITTS, KWAZULU NATAL, 3603, SOUTH AFRICA.
STANTON, Miss. Jane Mary, BA ACA *1989;* B5 42 Stanley Village Road, STANLEY, HONG KONG SAR.
STANTON, Mr. Jeffrey, FCA *1971;* 9 Brownswood Road, BEACONSFIELD, HP9 2NU.
STANTON, Miss. Jennifer Kim, ACA *2009;* 31 Homewood Road, ST. ALBANS, HERTFORDSHIRE, AL1 4BG.
STANTON, Ms. Jo Anne Elizabeth, BA ACA *1989;* Bushy Park Cottage, 13 Somerset Road, SANDYS MA 03, BERMUDA.
STANTON, Mr. John, BA ACA *1979;* (Tax Fac), Harlequin House, 7 high Street, TEDDINGTON, MIDDLESEX, TW11 8EE.
STANTON, Mr. Jonathan Adam, BSc ACA *1992;* 27 Dollarbeg Park, DOLLAR, CLACKMANNANSHIRE, FK14 7LJ.
STANTON, Mrs. Kathleen, BA ACA *1992;* The Elms, Kinsbourne Green Lane, Kinsbourne Green, HARPENDEN, AL5 3PF.
STANTON, Mr. Kenneth John, FCA *1970;* 34a Ridgmount Gardens, Bloomsbury, LONDON, WC1E 7AS. (Life Member)
STANTON, Mr. Lewis Harris, BSc FCA CPA *1979;* Stanton Associates, 3682 Berry Drive, STUDIO CITY, CA 91604, UNITED STATES.
STANTON, Mrs. Lorraine, BA ACA *1997;* 51 Oak Tree Drive, Cutnall Green, DROITWICH, WR9 0QY.
STANTON, Mr. Louis, FCA *1953;* Flat 27, Birnbeck Court, 850 Finchley Road, LONDON, NW11 6BB. (Life Member)
STANTON, Mrs. Mandy Harriet, BA ACA *1989;* 163 Hill Village Road, Four Oaks, SUTTON COLDFIELD, WEST MIDLANDS, B75 5JQ.
STANTON, Mr. Marcus John, BA ACA *1979;* Grove Hill House, Norton, Sutton Scotney, WINCHESTER, SO21 3ND.
•STANTON, Mrs. Marion Janet, BA FCA *1982;* (Tax Fac), Stanton Partnership, 55 Lynwood Drive, WORCESTER PARK, KT4 7AE.
STANTON, Mr. Matthew Pierre, BA ACA *2001;* Balfour Beatty Capital, 350 Euston Road, Regents Place, LONDON, NW1 3AX.
STANTON, Mr. Michael Philip, BA ACA *1983;* West Haddon Lodge, Northampton Road, West Haddon, NORTHAMPTON, NN6 7AS.
•STANTON, Mr. Neville Thomas, FCA *1965;* Neville T. Stanton, 3 Buckingham Road West, Heaton Moor, STOCKPORT, SK4 4AZ.
STANTON, Mr. Paul, FCA *1969;* 15 Moorside Terrace, Drighlington, BRADFORD, BD11 1HX.
•STANTON, Mr. Robert John, MBA FCA *1974;* (Tax Fac), R J Stanton & Co, Mill Hill, Chop Gate, Stokesley, MIDDLESBROUGH, TS9 7HY.
STANTON, Mr. Roger Francis Gordon, BA FCA *1993;* Genesys Europe, Genesys House, Frimley Business Park, Frimley, CAMBERLEY, SURREY GU16 7SG.
•STANTON, Mr. Stuart David, FCA *1975;* Stanton Partners, Warren House, Carrington Close, Arkley, BARNET, HERTFORDSHIRE EN5 3NA.
STANTON, Mr. Thomas Edward Ide, MSc BSc ACA *2009;* 48 Islington Road, BRISTOL, BS3 1QB.
•STANTON, Mr. Victor Raymond, FCA *1974;* Victor Stanton Associates, Steden, Reenglass Road, STANMORE, MIDDLESEX, HA7 4NT. See also Privilege Accounts Limited
STANTON, Mr. Walter, FCA *1952;* 65 Heddon Court Avenue, Cockfosters, BARNET, EN4 9NG.
STANWAY, Mr. Ian Robert, FCA MSI *1977;* 100 Waterside Heights, Waterside Shirley, SOLIHULL, B90 1UD.
STANWAY, Mr. Mark Thomas, BA ACA CF *1998;* 57 Lordswood Road, BIRMINGHAM, B17 9QT.
STANWAY, Mrs. Thea, BSc ACA *1988;* Weathercock Hill House, Chevington, BURY ST.EDMUNDS, IP29 5RG.
STANWELL, Mr. David Michael, FCA *1972;* L'Ancien Presbytere, Le Bourg, 16190 SAINT AMAND DE MONTMOREAU, FRANCE.
STANWELL, Mr. Trevor John, FCA *1966;* 22/31 Soi Naya, Moo 1, Tambon Rawai Amphur Muang, PHUKET 83100, THAILAND.
•STANWIX, Mr. David, BA FCA *1985;* Allen Sykes Limited, 5 Henson Close, South Church Enterprise Park, BISHOP AUCKLAND, COUNTY DURHAM, DL14 6WA.
STANWIX, Mr. Paul Stuart, BSc ACA *1995;* Level 21, 50 Bridge Street, SYDNEY, NSW 2000, AUSTRALIA.
STANWORTH, Mr. Albert Denis, MA FCA *1960;* 14 Calumet, Reynolds Road, BEACONSFIELD, BUCKINGHAMSHIRE, HP9 2LZ. (Life Member)
STANWORTH, Mrs. Alison Jane, BA ACA *1994;* Reed Business Information Ltd, Quadrant House, The Quadrant, Brighton Road, SUTTON, SM2 5AS.
STANWORTH, Miss. Claire Anne, BSc ACA *1992;* 22 Eliot Place, LONDON, SE3 0QL.
STANWORTH, Mr. Mark, BSc ACA *1990;* 45 Park Avenue, Shelley, HUDDERSFIELD, HD8 8JY.
STANWORTH, Miss. Tanya Maria, BSc ACA *2007;* (Tax Fac), 13 Hallgate, COTTINGHAM, NORTH HUMBERSIDE, HU16 4DN.
STANYARD, Mr. Miles Anthony, BA ACA CTA *1984;* Beck Farmhouse, Marton Cum Grafton, YORK, YO51 9QJ.
STANYARD, Mr. Robert James, FCA *1966;* The Shambles, Shadows Lane, Congerstone, NUNEATON, WARWICKSHIRE, CV13 6NF.

STANYARD, Mr. Stuart Richard, BA ACA *1992;* Stuart Stanyard, General Manager Finance & Admin, HONG KONG SAR Aero Engine Services Limited, 70 Chun Choi Street, Tseung Kwan O Industrial Estate, MONG KOK KOWLOON HONG KONG SAR.
STANYER, Mr. Adam Tobias, BA ACA *1992;* Zehdenicker, Str 19, 10119, BERLIN, GERMANY.
STANYER, Mr. David, FCA *1972;* 261 Knighton Church Road, LEICESTER, LE2 3JQ.
STANYER, Mr. Peter Jeremy, FCA *1963;* 27 Woodcock Close, Impington, CAMBRIDGE, CB24 9LD.
STANYER, Mr. Philip Allen, FCA *1974;* 4 The Old School Close, Tideswell, BUXTON, DERBYSHIRE, SK17 8NG.
STAPLEHURST, Mr. John Clive, FCA *1972;* Swiss RE Properties Ltd, 30 St. Mary Axe, LONDON, EC3A 8EP.
STAPLEHURST, Mr. John Martyn, FCA *1981;* 6 The Gorses, BEXHILL-ON-SEA, TN39 3BE.
•STAPLEHURST, Mr. Trevor, FCA *1976;* (Tax Fac), T. Staplehurst, April Cottage, Sturt's Lane, TADWORTH, KT20 7RQ.
•STAPLES, Mr. Alan Edward James, BSc FCA CTA *1980;* Manningtons, 8 High Street, HEATHFIELD, EAST SUSSEX, TN21 8LS.
STAPLES, Mr. Alexander William, BA(Hons) ACA *2002;* 77 Uxbridge Road, RICKMANSWORTH, HERTFORDSHIRE, WD3 7DQ.
STAPLES, Mr. Andrew James, BSc ACA *1995;* Redgates Farm, Willshaw Bottom, Hollinsclough, BUXTON, DERBYSHIRE, SK17 0RE.
STAPLES, Mr. Anthony John, MA FCA *1974;* Park Cottage, Frittenden, CRANBROOK, TN17 2AU. (Life Member)
STAPLES, Mr. David Payne, BSc FCA CTA *1982;* La Colline, Guelles Road, St. Peter Port, GUERNSEY, GY1 2DP.
STAPLES, Mrs. Elizabeth Jane, MA ACA MCT *1992;* 8 Burghley Road, LONDON, SW19 5BH.
•STAPLES, Mr. Jonathan, BSc FCA DChA *1991;* Horsfield-Smith Limited, Tower House, 269 Walmersley Road, BURY, LANCASHIRE, BL9 6NX.
STAPLES, Mr. Paul Andrew, BSc ACA *2007;* 95 Denmark Road, CARSHALTON, SURREY, SM5 2JE.
STAPLES, Mr. Paul Jonathan Kensit, MA ACA *1992;* 8 Burghley Road, LONDON, SW19 5BH.
STAPLES, Mr. Roderick Hubert Collingwood, MA ACA AMCT *1990;* Carreg House, Silver Street, Brixworth, NORTHAMPTON, NN6 9BY.
STAPLETON, Mrs. Annette, BSc ACA *2000;* Affane, CAPPOQUIN, COUNTY WATERFORD, IRELAND.
•STAPLETON, Mr. Benjamin John, BA ACA *1999;* 2 Tintern Close, HARPENDEN, HERTFORDSHIRE, AL5 3NZ.
STAPLETON, Mr. Brian Laurence, MSc FCA *1960;* Jublilee House, 11a Mell Road, Tollesbury, MALDON, ESSEX, CM9 8SW. (Life Member)
STAPLETON, Mr. Colin Gardner, FCA *1966;* Oak Cottage, Holywell, ST. IVES, CAMBRIDGESHIRE, PE27 4TG. (Life Member)
STAPLETON, Mr. Gary Michael, BA FCA *1989;* 5 Point Road, NORTHWOOD, NSW 2066, AUSTRALIA.
•STAPLETON, Mr. Graham Martin, BSc ACA *1979;* (Tax Fac), Howard & Stapleton, 1st Floor Offices, Natwest Bank, Market Square, ROCHFORD, SS4 1AJ. See also Howard & Stapleton Ltd
•STAPLETON, Mrs. Lucy Elizabeth, BA ACA *1997;* PricewaterhouseCoopers LLP, 7 More London Riverside, LONDON, SE1 2RT. See also PricewaterhouseCoopers
STAPLETON, Mr. Mark, BA ACA *2004;* Flat 37 Bombay House, 59 Whitworth Street, MANCHESTER, M1 3AB.
STAPLETON, Mr. Martin Gordon Robert, BSc ACA *1995;* 33 Earl's Court Square, LONDON, SW5 9BY.
STAPLETON, Mr. Maurice Henry, FCA *1954;* The Gig House, Castle Barns, Coplowe Lane, Bletsoe, BEDFORD, MK44 1TL. (Life Member)
STAPLETON, Prof. Pamela, MSc BSc FCA *1980;* Lyndhurst, 94 Hall Lane, Aspull, WIGAN, WN2 2SF.
•STAPLETON, Mr. Paul David, FCA *1981;* (Tax Fac), Parkhurst Hill Limited, Torrington Chambers, 58 North Road East, PLYMOUTH, DEVON, PL4 6AJ. See also Parkhurst Hill
STAPLETON, Mr. Peter, FCA *1968;* The Timbers, 14 Westcliff Gardens, SCUNTHORPE, DN17 1DT.
•STAPLETON, Mr. Peter Brian, FCA *1976;* P&A Associates, 30 Offham Slope, Woodside Park, LONDON, N12 7BZ.
STAPLETON, Mrs. Philippa Jean, BA ACA *1999;* 2 Tintern Close, HARPENDEN, HERTFORDSHIRE, AL5 3NZ.
STAPLEY, Mr. Andrew, BA ACA *1979;* 85 Whitefield Road, Stockton Heath, WARRINGTON, WA4 6NB.
STAPLEY, Mr. Brian Frederick George, MA FCA *1962;* Aptdo 201, Santa Ponsa, 07180 CALVIA, MALLORCA, SPAIN.
STAPLEY, Mr. Greg, BA(Hons) ACA *2004;* Thomson Cooper, 3 Carnegie Campus, Castle Court, DUNFERMLINE, FIFE, KY11 8PB.
STAPLEY, Mrs. Jacqueline Anne, MA ACA *1992;* American International Underwriters, American International Building 2-8 Altyre Road, CROYDON, CR9 2LG.
STAPLEY, Mr. Marc Andrew, BSc ACA *1994;* 8 Rockridge Court, BASKING RIDGE, NJ 07920, UNITED STATES.
STAPLEY, Mrs. Michelle, BEng ACA *2002;* Flat 37, Merchants House, Collington Street, LONDON, SE10 9LX.
•STAPLEY, Mr. Richard James, BSc ACA *1992;* Richard Stapley Limited, PO Box 349, Maison de Haut, La Grande Rue, St Saviours, GUERNSEY GY1 3UZ.
•STARBUCK, Mr. David Charles, FCA *1982;* David Starbuck Limited, 609 Delta Office Park, Welton Road, SWINDON, SN5 7XF.
STARBUCK, Mr. Gary, FCA *1961;* The Oast House, Gate Street, Bramley, GUILDFORD, GU5 0LR.
STARBUCK, Mr. Mark Patrick, BSc ACA *1990;* U B S Group Compliance, 21 Lombard Street, LONDON, EC3V 9AH.
STARES, Mr. John Bertram, BSc FCA *1977;* Highfield, La Route de Sausmarez, St. Martin, GUERNSEY, GY4 6SE.
STARES, Mr. Martin, FCA *1963;* 25 Regent Drive, BILLERICAY, ESSEX, CM12 0GD.
STARK, Mr. Andrew Marshall, BSc ACA *1992;* 25 Huntsmead Close, Thornhill, CARDIFF, CF14 9HY.
STARK, Mr. David Alun, BEng ACA *1992;* Thorneybrow, Low Westwood, NEWCASTLE UPON TYNE, NE17 7PR.
STARK, Mr. David John, FCA *1956;* 7 Manadon Drive, PLYMOUTH, PL5 3DH.
•STARK, Mr. David Nigel Croll, BSc ACA *1997;* with Deloitte Corporate Finance Ltd, The Gate Precinct Building 3, Dubai Int'al Financial Centre, DUBAI, 282056, UNITED ARAB EMIRATES.
STARK, Mrs. Gail Charlotte, BA ACA *2006;* 72 Columbus Drive, Sarisbury Green, SOUTHAMPTON, SO31 7LW.
STARK, Mr. Graham David, BSc ACA *1992;* 2 Porters Lane, Easton on the Hill, STAMFORD, LINCOLNSHIRE, PE9 3NF.
STARK, Mr. Graham Dugald Croll, MA ACA *1988;* 3 Red Oak Close, Bromham, BEDFORD, BEDFORDSHIRE, MK43 8GP.
STARK, Mr. Ian William, BSc ACA *2007;* Quarry Cottage, Loves Lane, Ashwell, BALDOCK, SG7 5HZ.
STARK, Mr. Jason Alexander, BSc ACA *1990;* 36 Grove Lane, KINGSTON-UPON-THAMES, KT1 2ST.
STARK, Ms. Leigh Ann, BEng ACA *2002;* 5 Selwyn Street, PYMBLE, NSW 2073, AUSTRALIA.
STARK, Mrs. Lorna Claire, BA(Hons) ACA *2004;* 93 Pevensey Way, Frimley, CAMBERLEY, SURREY, GU16 9UU.
STARK, Mr. Matthew James, BA ACA *2004;* 10 Causton Gardens, EASTLEIGH, HAMPSHIRE, SO50 9PJ.
STARK, Mrs. Pamela Margaret, FCA *1960;* Tara, 15 Copsem Drive, ESHER, KT10 9HD. (Life Member)
•STARK, Mr. Paul Graeme, BSc FCA *1993;* (Tax Fac), PGS Accountancy Ltd, 54 Ridgestone Avenue, Bilton Kingston-Upon-Hull, HULL, HU11 4AJ.
STARK, Mr. Raymond, BA FCA *1978;* 8 Rectory Park Avenue, SUTTON COLDFIELD, WEST MIDLANDS, B75 7BN.
STARK, Mrs. Rebecca Jane, BSc ACA CTA *1996;* 7 High Street, Donington, SPALDING, LINCOLNSHIRE, PE11 4TA.
STARK, Mr. Richard, BA ACA *2011;* Apartment 7, Block 3 Larke Rise, off Mersey Road, Didsbury, MANCHESTER, M20 2UL.
STARK, Mr. Roger Law, FCA *1953;* Tweedsmuir, 22 Sedbergh Park, ILKLEY, LS29 8SZ. (Life Member)
STARK DUCE, Mrs. Jennifer Vivienne, ACA ACCA *2007;* Sidley Austin Brown & Wood, Woolgate Exchange, 25 Basinghall Street, LONDON, EC2V 5HA.
STARKE, Mr. Andrew Lars, ACA *2009;* 82 Liberty Street, LONDON, SW9 0EF.
STARKE, Mr. Christopher Charles, BSc ACA *1988;* 35 Byng Road, TUNBRIDGE WELLS, TN4 8EG.
STARKE, Mr. Donald Brackley, FCA *1947;* 64 Windsor Avenue, Radyr, CARDIFF, CF15 8BY. (Life Member)
STARKEY, Mrs. Caroline Jane, BA ACA *1987;* 124 Browns Lane, Knowle, SOLIHULL, WEST MIDLANDS, B93 9BD.
STARKEY, Mrs. Caroline Margaret, BSc ACA *1993;* 69 Barkham Road, WOKINGHAM, RG41 2RG.
STARKEY, Mr. Charles Stuart, FCA *1951;* 4 Hamilton Road, ST. ALBANS, HERTFORDSHIRE, AL1 4PZ. (Life Member)
•STARKEY, Mr. David Richard, BA FCA *1973;* Starkey Saunders, 4 Clare Road, HALIFAX, HX1 2HX.
•STARKEY, Mr. Ian Marshall, BSc ACA *1986;* KPMG LLP, One Snowhill, Snow Hill Queensway, BIRMINGHAM, B4 6GN. See also KPMG Europe LLP
STARKEY, Miss. Karen Emma Louise, BA ACA *2007;* 224 Highfields Park Drive, Broadway, DERBY, DE22 1JY.
STARKEY, Mr. Mark Richard, BSc ACA *1999;* Glenwye, Windsor Lane, Wooburn Green, HIGH WYCOMBE, BUCKINGHAMSHIRE, HP10 0EG.
STARKEY, Mr. Richard Justin, BA ACA *1988;* 124 Browns Lane, Knowle, SOLIHULL, WEST MIDLANDS, B93 9BD.
STARKEY, Mrs. Sophie Anne, BSc ACA *1995;* (Tax Fac), with KPMG LLP, 15 Canada Square, LONDON, E14 5GL.
STARKEY, Mr. Torben Andrew Victor, BEng ACA *1998;* Willows, Culross Avenue, HAYWARDS HEATH, WEST SUSSEX, RH16 1JF.
STARKIE, Mr. David Eric, BA ACA *1992;* 4420 Wordsworth Drive, Plano, DALLAS, TX 75093, UNITED STATES.
STARKIE, Miss. Elizabeth, MA BA(Hons) ACA *2011;* Maple Hayes, Twemlow Green, Holmes Chapel, CREWE, CW4 8BQ.
STARKIE, Mr. Francis William Michael, MA FCA *1974;* 99 Mildmay Road, LONDON, N1 4PU.
STARKIE, Mrs. Katrina, BCom ACA *1992;* 4420 Wordsworth Drive, Plano, DALLAS, TX 75093, UNITED STATES.
•STARKIE, Mr. Thomas Oliver Matthew, FCA ATII *1968;* (Tax Fac), Willow House, 77 Main Road, Hackleton, NORTHAMPTON, NN7 2AD.
STARKINS, Mr. Robert Neil, LLB ACA *2009;* Chantrey Vellacott D F K, Russell Square House, 10-12 Russell Square, LONDON, WC1B 5LF.
•STARLEY, Mr. John Keith, FCA *1979;* (Tax Fac), AIMS - John Starley FCA, Moonrakers, Back Lane, Birdingbury, RUGBY, WARWICKSHIRE CV23 8EN.
•STARLING, Mrs. Bridget Mary, MA ACA CTA DChA *1992;* Wright Vigar Limited, 15 Newland, LINCOLN, LN1 1XG.
STARLING, Mr. Gareth Julian Adam, ACA *2009;* Flat 58 Artesian House, 96 Alscot Road, LONDON, SE1 3GG.
STARLING, Mrs. Hannah, MA ACA *1998;* 21 Malkin Way, WATFORD, WD18 7AT.
STARLING, Miss. Heather, ACA *1997;* Meadowcroft, 71 Phoenix Drive, Wateringbury, MAIDSTONE, KENT, ME18 5RS.
STARLING, Mr. John Anthony, FCA *1969;* Seymour House, 4 Kingsman Lane, SHAFTESBURY, SP7 8HD.
STARLING, Mr. Keith Andrew, BSc FCA *1988;* 14 Holden Way, UPMINSTER, RM14 1BP.
STARLING, Mr. Ross Daniel, BSc(Econ) ACA *2010;* 109 Kings Road, HASLEMERE, SURREY, GU27 2QQ.
STARR, Miss. Alison Jane, BSc(Hons) ACA *2001;* 1 Sheralds Croft Lane, Thriplow, ROYSTON, CAMBRIDGESHIRE, SG8 7RB.
STARR, Mrs. Camilla Anne, BSc ACA *2007;* with PricewaterhouseCoopers CI LLP, PO Box 321, Royal Bank Place, 1 Glategny Esplanade, St Peter Port, GUERNSEY GY1 4ND.
STARR, Mr. Christopher, BA ACA *1979;* (Tax Fac), 23 Chipping Cross, CLEVEDON, BS21 5JG.
STARR, Mr. Christopher John, FCA *1967;* 8 Braymeadow Lane, Little Melton, NORWICH, NR9 3NQ. (Life Member)
•STARR, Mr. David Jack, FCA *1974;* P3 Learning Limited, 30 Brudenell Drive, Stoke Mandeville, AYLESBURY, BUCKINGHAMSHIRE, HP22 5UR.
STARR, Mr. David Kellow, FCA *1960;* Santa Barbara Screen & Shade Co., 2930 Delavina Street, SANTA BARBARA, CA 93105, UNITED STATES. (Life Member)
STARR, Dr. John Edward Owen, CEng FCA CITP MBCS MRI *1975;* 22 The Loning, LONDON, NW9 6DR.
•STARR, Mr. Lionel, FCA *1976;* (Tax Fac), Starr & Co, 76 Wellington Road South, STOCKPORT, SK1 3SU.
STARR, Mrs. Mary Margaret, FCA *1994;* with Grant Thornton UK LLP, Grant Thornton House, 22 Melton Street, Euston Square, LONDON, NW1 2EP.
STARR, Mr. Richard Stuart, BA ACA *2010;* 106a Mill Lane, LONDON, NW6 1NF.
STARR, Mrs. Samantha Anne, BCom ACA *2003;* 20 Highfield Close, Snitterfield, STRATFORD-UPON-AVON, CV37 0JJ.
STARR, Miss. Sarah Jane, BSc ACA *2005;* 541 Garratt Lane, LONDON, SW18 4SR.
•STARR, Mr. Stephen Goddard, FCA *1971;* Stephen Starr Limited, 12 Aldenham Avenue, RADLETT, HERTFORDSHIRE, WD7 8HX.
•STARR, Mr. Warren Spencer, FCA MAE QDR *1975;* WSS Forensic Accounting, 25 Manchester Square, LONDON, W1U 3PY.
STARRETT, Miss. Hayley Marie, ACA *2009;* 24 Ledbury Drive, Calcot, READING, RG31 7EE.
START, Mrs. Emma Louise, BSc(Hons) ACA MAAT *2003;* 57 Churchfields Drive, Bovey Tracey, NEWTON ABBOT, TQ13 9QU.
STARTE, Mr. Michael Anthony William, FCA *1957;* Monte Do Magarreiro, 7250-201 ALANDROAL, PORTUGAL. (Life Member)
STARTIN, Mr. David Paul, BCom ACA *1986;* 166 Woodcock Lane, Northfield, BIRMINGHAM, B31 1DD.
•STARTIN, Mr. Frank David, LLB FCA *1991;* (Tax Fac), The Chartwell Practice, Chartwell House, 4 St. Pauls Square, BURTON-ON-TRENT, STAFFORDSHIRE, DE14 2EF. See also The PayCompany Ltd
STARTIN, Mr. Richard John, FCA *1973;* 94 Oakley Lane, Oakley, BASINGSTOKE, RG23 7JX.
•STARTUP, Mr. Martyn John, BA FCA *1985;* M.J. Startup & Co Ltd, 4 New Cottages, Furzedown Lane, Amport, ANDOVER, SP11 8BQ.
•STARTUP, Mr. Michael John, FCA *1982;* Day Smith & Hunter, Globe House, Eclipse Park, Sittingbourne Road, MAIDSTONE, KENT ME14 3EN.
STAS, Mr. Peter Nicholas, BA FCA *1971;* 23 Malvern Drive, WOODFORD GREEN, IG8 0JR.
STASOPOULOS, Mr. Phivos Michael, BA ACA *1994;* PO Box 28679, NICOSIA, CYPRUS.
STASSOPOULOS, Mr. Anastasios, MA ACA *1996;* Flat 256, Lauderdale Mansions, Lauderdale Road, LONDON, W9 1NQ.
STASZEWSKI, Mr. Michael Walter, FCA *1987;* 61 Cranbourne Gardens, LONDON, NW11 0JB.
STASZEWSKI, Mr. Paul Abraham, BA FCA *1977;* Chaim Bejayo Street 1/10, 93145 JERUSALEM, ISRAEL.
STASZKIEWICZ, Mr. Ryszard Paul, BA ACA *1986;* 34 Almond Walk, Gedling, NOTTINGHAM, NG4 4AH.
STATHAM, Mr. Gordon, BSc FCA *1977;* Hademore Farmhouse, Fisherwick Road, LICHFIELD, STAFFORDSHIRE, WS14 9JL.
STATHAM, Mr. James, MA MEng ACA *2000;* 4 Achilles Road, LONDON, NW6 1EA.
STATHAM, Mr. James Edward Anthony, FCA *1966;* Highlands, Helford Passage, FALMOUTH, TR11 5LA.
STATHAM, Mr. John, FCA *1939;* 30 Bucklers Court, Anchorage Way, LYMINGTON, HAMPSHIRE, SO41 8JN. (Life Member)
•STATHAM, Mrs. Laurel Yvonne, FCA *1976;* Paterson Brodie, Cliveden Chambers, Cliveden Place, Longton, STOKE-ON-TRENT, ST3 4JB. See also P B Support Services Limited
STATHAM, Miss. Sara Margaret, BSc FCA *1978;* Alverstoke, Brockwell Lane, Wootton Courtenay, MINEHEAD, TA24 8RN.
STATHER, Mr. Cyril, FCA *1960;* 30 Clarke Hall Road, Stanley, WAKEFIELD, WF3 4ND. (Life Member)
STATHOPOULOS, Mr. Dimitri Gregory, BEng ACA *1993;* Taylor Cocks, 3 Acorn Business Centre Northarbour Road, PORTSMOUTH, PO6 3TH.
STATON, Mr. Andrew, BA ACA *2006;* 3 Woodhill Crescent, LEEDS, LS16 7BX.
STATON, Mr. Michael Alexander, FCA *1969;* Endon House, Kerridge, MACCLESFIELD, SK10 5AR.
•STATTON, Mr. Reginald Leslie, FCA *1975;* R.L. Statton, 1st Floor, Regency Arcade, Molesworth Street, WADEBRIDGE, PL27 7DH.
•STAUB, Mr. Frederick Ian, FCA *1975;* Staub & Co, 5 Mansfield Avenue, Denton, MANCHESTER, M34 3NS.
STAUNTON, Mr. Gary Brendan, BSc(Hons) ACA *2001;* with Haines Watts, New Derwent House, 69-73 Theobalds Road, LONDON, WC1X 8TA.
STAUNTON, Mr. Henry Eric, BA FCA *1974;* Fairfield, Nursery Road, Walton-On-The-Hill, TADWORTH, KT20 7TZ.
•STAUNTON, Mr. Ian Bernard, FCA CF *1979;* Chantrey Vellacott DFK LLP, Russell Square House, 10-12 Russell Square, LONDON, WC1B 5LF.
STAUNTON, Miss. Launa, BSc(Hons) ACA *2001;* 16 Thorverton Road, Cricklewood, LONDON, NW2 1RE.
STAUNTON, Miss. Laura, BSc(Hons) ACA *2004;* Hazards, Fairfield Road, Shawford, WINCHESTER, HAMPSHIRE, SO21 2DA.

•①STAUNTON, Mrs. Susan Rosemary, MA ACA *1988;* James Cowper LLP, Willow Court, 7 West Way, Botley, OXFORD, OX2 0JB. See also JC Payroll Services Ltd
STAVELEY, Mr. Charles Andrew Rover, BSc ACA *1988;* 17 Riverdale Gardens, TWICKENHAM, TW1 2BX.
STAVELEY, Mr. Christopher Nigel, BSc FCA *1984;* 20 Hadzor Road, OLDBURY, B68 9LA.
STAVELEY, Mrs. Natalie Anne, BA ACA *2005;* Charterhouse, 23 London Road, ASCOT, SL5 7EN.
STAVELEY, Mr. Norman Stuart, FCA *1953;* (Member of Council 1974 - 1983), 23 Anlaby Park Road North, HULL, HU4 6XN. (Life Member)
STAVRIDES, Mr. Michael Stavrou, BSc ACA *2003;* 4 DROSINI STREET, CY-2023 NICOSIA, CYPRUS.
STAVRINIDES, Mr. Christos, BSc ACA *2010;* 4 Rigainas Street, 2049 NICOSIA, CYPRUS.
•STAVRINIDES, Mr. Nicolaos, BSc ACA *1999;* (Tax Fac), with PKF Savvides & Co Ltd, Meliza Court, 4th & 7th Floor, 229 Arch Makorious III Avenue, 3105 LIMASSOL, CYPRUS.
STAVRINIDIS, Mr. Hector Solon, BSc ACA *1989;* 35 Granville Park, LONDON, SE13 7DY.
STAVROU, Mr. Andreas Panayiotis, BSc(Econ) ACA *1999;* Strofiliou 71, Nea Erithrea, 14671 ATHENS, GREECE.
STAVROU, Miss. Androula, MA ACA *2001;* Atreos 3, Halandri, 152 38 ATHENS, GREECE.
STAVROU, Mr. Charalambos, BEng ACA *2004;* 37 Kimonos Street, 3095 LIMASSOL, CYPRUS.
STAVROU, Mr. Iacovos, BSc ACA *1997;* 5 Tarsos, Nicosia, 2035 STROVOLOS, CYPRUS.
STAVROU, Mr. Nicos, BSc(Econ) ACA *2003;* 1 El Venizelos Street, Makedonitissa, 2414 NICOSIA, CYPRUS.
STAVROU, Mr. Panayiotis, ACA *2009;* Vasili Michailidi 6 Flat 301, Lakatamia, 2314 NICOSIA, CYPRUS.
STAVROU, Mr. Panayiotis, BSc FCA *1969;* 91 A. Avraamides Str., Dassoupolis, NICOSIA, CYPRUS. (Life Member)
STAVROU, Miss. Savvia, BSc ACA *2011;* PO BOX 28172, 2091 STROVOLOS NICOSIA, CYPRUS, 2091 NICOSIA, CYPRUS.
•STAVROU, Mr. Stavros, BA FCA *1987;* PKF Savvides & Co Ltd, Meliza Court, 4th & 7th Floor, 229 Arch Makorious III Avenue, 3105 LIMASSOL, CYPRUS.
STAVROU, Mr. Stavros Andreou, BA FCA *1986;* L'Estoril Block B, 31 Avenue Princesses Grace, 98000 MONTE CARLO, MONACO.
STAVROU, Mr. Stelios, BSc ACA *2009;* P.O Box 28172 2091 Strovolos, 2091 NICOSIA, CYPRUS.
STAVROU, Mr. Theocharis, MA FCA *1975;* 8 Ilia Kokkoni Str., 171 24 Nea Smyrni, ATHENS, GREECE.
STAY, Mr. Simon John, BA ACA *1982;* 42 route du Soulor, 65400 ARRENS-MARSOUS, FRANCE.
STAZIKER, Dr. David James, BSc ACA *1999;* Finance Wales, 3rd Floor, Oakleigh House, 14-16 Park Place, CARDIFF, CF10 3DQ.
STAZIKER, Miss. Gillian Mary, BSc ACA *1999;* 10 Park Road, BECKENHAM, BR3 1QD.
STEAD, Mr. Adrian George Curry, BEng ACA *1995;* The Old Rectory, School Road, Bursledon, SOUTHAMPTON, SO31 8BW.
STEAD, Mr. Alan George, FCA *1972;* (Tax Fac), Flat 7 Dunbar Wharf, 108-124 Narrow Street, Limehouse, LONDON, E14 8BB.
•STEAD, Mrs. Amanda Jane, BA ACA *1999;* Amanda Stead Limited, Weavers Cottage, Holt Lane, Brindle, CHORLEY, LANCASHIRE PR6 8NE.
STEAD, Mr. Andrew John, BA ACA *1990;* 49 Fernhurst Road, Fulham, LONDON, SW6 7JN.
STEAD, Mr. Andrew John, FCA FCCA *1976;* 3 Cockley Meadows, Kirkheaton, HUDDERSFIELD, HD5 0LA.
STEAD, Mr. Arthur, FCA *1955;* 201 Whitechapel Road, CLECKHEATON, BD19 6HN. (Life Member)
STEAD, Mr. Brian Charles, FCA *1950;* 1 West Court, Hollins Hall, Lund Lane, Hampsthwaite, HARROGATE, NORTH YORKSHIRE HG3 2WY. (Life Member)
STEAD, Mr. Carl, BSc ACA *1988;* 19 Barshaw Gardens, Appleton, WARRINGTON, WA4 5FA.
STEAD, Mr. Carl, BA ACA CTA *2003;* 14 Applecroft, Northchurch, BERKHAMSTED, HERTFORDSHIRE, HP4 3RX.
STEAD, Mr. Christopher Alan, ACA *1992;* 33 Howard Avenue, EPSOM, SURREY, KT17 2QJ.
•STEAD, Mr. David Andrew, BSc FCA CTA *1989;* Money Talks Training Ltd, 52 Horsley Court, Montaigne Close, LONDON, SW1P 4BF.
STEAD, Mr. David Anthony, BA ACA *1985;* Dunelm Group Plc, Fosse Way, Syston, LEICESTER, LE7 1NF.
STEAD, Mr. David Richard, BSc ACA *1996;* Christies, 8 King Street, LONDON, SW1Y 6QT.
STEAD, Mr. Dennis, FCA *1952;* 238 Burncross Road, Chapeltown, SHEFFIELD, S35 1SG. (Life Member)
STEAD, Mr. Ian Leslie, BA ACA *1984;* Sirdar Spinning Limited, Flanshaw Lane Alverthorpe, WAKEFIELD, WF2 9ND.
STEAD, Mr. John Gordon Anderson, FCA *1973;* 15 Rowan Road, Hammersmith, LONDON, W6 7DT.
STEAD, Mr. John Rustrick, BSc ACA *1996;* 39 Owlstone Road, CAMBRIDGE, CB3 9JH.
STEAD, Mr. Michael Neville, MBA FCA *1963;* 2 Greville Close, Boughton, NORTHAMPTON, NN2 8RZ.
•STEAD, Mr. Nicholas Paul Clayton, BSc FCA CTA *1981;* Windle & Bowker Limited, Duke House, Duke Street, SKIPTON, NORTH YORKSHIRE, BD23 2HQ.
STEAD, Mr. Nigel David, BSc FCA *1979;* 31 Club Street #03-01 Emerald Garden, SINGAPORE 069468, SINGAPORE.
STEAD, Mr. Peter Vernon, FCA *1961;* The Stuart House, Woolley, WAKEFIELD, WF4 2JL.
STEAD, Mr. Richard, FCA *1966;* Sandholme, Green Lane East, Sowerby, THIRSK, YO7 1NA.
•STEAD, Mr. Stuart Peter, BA FCA *1998;* Cowgill Holloway LLP, Regency House, 45-51 Chorley New Road, BOLTON, BL1 4QR. See also Cowgill Holloway Care 1 Limited
STEAD, Mr. Terence Keith Parsons, BSc FCA *1975;* Derry Aire, 1 The Derry, Ashton Keynes, SWINDON, SN6 6PW.
STEAD, Mr. Tony, BSc ACA *1999;* 46 Westville Road, THAMES DITTON, SURREY, KT7 0UJ.
•STEADMAN, Mrs. Catherine Louise, BSc FCA *1991;* Limelight Accountancy Limited, 60 Midhurst Road, LIPHOOK, GU30 7DY.
STEADMAN, Mr. David, FCA *1969;* 9 Hunters Park, BERKHAMSTED, HERTFORDSHIRE, HP4 2PT.
STEADMAN, Mrs. Lisa Joanne, BSc ACA CTA *2001;* with PricewaterhouseCoopers, Darling Park Tower 2, 201 Sussex Street, GPO Box 2650, SYDNEY, NSW 1171 AUSTRALIA.
•STEADMAN, Mr. Luke, BA FCA *1995;* Sunways, 118c Moulsham Street, CHELMSFORD, CM2 0JW.
STEADMAN, Mr. Paul James, BA ACA *1992;* 7 The Glades, HEMEL HEMPSTEAD, HERTFORDSHIRE, HP1 2TH.
STEADMAN, Mr. Paul John, FCA *1974;* Brook Farm, Tedburn St. Mary, EXETER, EX6 6DS.
STEADMAN, Mrs. Rachel, BSc ACA *1988;* 35 Ravenstone Drive, SALE, M33 2WD.
•STEAN, Mr. Michael Frank, MA ACA *1986;* (Tax Fac), Baker Tilly Tax and Advisory Services LLP, 25 Farringdon Street, LONDON, EC4A 4AB.
STEAN, Mr. Ronald Norman, FCA *1967;* Autocost Options Ltd, 14 Blacketts Wood Drive, Chorleywood, RICKMANSWORTH, HERTFORDSHIRE, WD3 5QH.
STEANE, Mr. Jeremy John, BSc ACA *1996;* FSI Capital, PO Box 23035, Naema Ali Abu Amim Building, Suite 114, Al Dhiyafah Road, DUBAI UNITED ARAB EMIRATES.
STEANE, Miss. Katherine Louise, BSc ACA *1993;* 126 Cat Rock Road, COS COB, CT 06807, UNITED STATES.
STEANS, Mr. Barry, BSc FCA *1979;* Hillsdowne, School Lane, Bradnop, LEEK, ST13 7LZ.
STEARE, Mr. John Crossley, FCA *1953;* 83 Hayes Lane, BROMLEY, BR2 9EF. (Life Member)
STEARMAN, Mr. Steven John, FCA *1977;* with PKF (UK) LLP, New Guild House, 45 Great Charles Street, BIRMINGHAM, B3 2LX.
STEARN, Miss. Amanda Carolyn, BSc ACA *1991;* 9 Huron Road, LONDON, SW17 8RE.
STEARN, Mr. Andrew Charles, MPhil MSc ACA *2002;* 4 Bishop Court, MAIDENHEAD, BERKSHIRE, SL6 4EX.
STEARN, Mr. Darren Antony Kerr, BSc ACA *1998;* 2 Delapre Drive, BANBURY, OXFORDSHIRE, OX16 3WP.
STEARN, Mrs. Jennifer Patricia, MA ACA *2001;* 13 Searle Road, FARNHAM, GU9 8LJ.
STEARN, Mr. Richard James, BSc ACA *1995;* 13 Searle Road, FARNHAM, GU9 8LJ.
STEARS, Mr. David, BSc ACA *2006;* D202 Carmine Wharf, 30 Copenhagen Place, LONDON, E14 7FE.
STEBBENS, Mr. Toby James, MAppFin(A) BSc FCA *1989;* PO Box 8028, CAMBERWELL, VIC 3124, AUSTRALIA.
•STEBBING, Mr. Christopher George, FCA *1980;* Simmons Gainsford LLP, 52 New Town, UCKFIELD, EAST SUSSEX, TN22 5DE.
STEBBING, Mrs. Clare Frances, BA(Hons) ACA *2002;* 110 Ramsay Road, LONDON, E7 9ER.
•STEBBING, Mr. Gavin Frederick Mark, MA ACA ATII *1986;* WSM Partners LLP, Pinnacle House, 17/25 Hartfield Road, Wimbledon, LONDON, SW19 3SE. See also Windsor Stebbing Marsh
STEBBINGS, Mr. Adam Drysdale Lincolne, BA ACA *1983;* 23 Radnor Road, TWICKENHAM, TW1 4NH.
•STEBBINGS, Mr. Alan John, BA FCA *1975;* (Tax Fac), Nicholson Blythe Limited, Claremont House, 223 Branston Road, BURTON-ON-TRENT, STAFFORDSHIRE, DE14 3BT.
•STEBBINGS, Mr. Dudley James, FCA *1975;* (Tax Fac), U H Y Hacker Young, 4 Thomas More Square, LONDON, E1W 1YW.
STEBBINGS, Mr. Peter Graham, FCA *1974;* Down Mill Corporate Services Ltd, The Old Forge, Church Road, Hedenham, BUNGAY, SUFFOLK NR35 2LF.
•STEBBINGS, Mr. Robert John, FCA *1975;* Finch Lynton Limited, 2/4 Ash Lane, Rustington, LITTLEHAMPTON, WEST SUSSEX, BN16 3BZ. See also Finch Lynton
STEBBINGS, Mr. Robert Thomas, BA FCA *1999;* 20 Merlin Road North, WELLING, KENT, DA16 2JF.
•STEBBINGS, Mr. Thomas Raymond, FCA *1971;* T.R. Stebbings & Co., Onega House, 112 Main Road, SIDCUP, KENT, DA14 6NE.
•STECHLER, Mr. Alain Leon, BA ACA *1989;* (Tax Fac), Grunberg & Co., 10-14 Accommodation Road, Golders Green, LONDON, NW11 8ED. See also Grunberg & Co Limited
STECHMAN, Mr. Robert Clive, LLB ACA *1996;* 66c Wilberforce Road, LONDON, N4 2SR.
STECKEL, Miss. Colette Donna, BSc ACA *1999;* Olicana, Thame Road, Piddington, BICESTER, OXFORDSHIRE, OX25 1PY.
STEDMAN, Mr. Brian Peter, BA FCA *1973;* 4 Tranmere Drive, Handforth, WILMSLOW, SK9 3BW.
STEDMAN, Mr. David Julian, BSc ACA *1992;* Initial Medical Services Garland Ct, Garland Rd, EAST GRINSTEAD, WEST SUSSEX, RH19 1DN.
STEDMAN, Mr. Jonathan Robert, FCA *1964;* Popinjay, Valley Road, Harmans Cross, SWANAGE, BH19 3DX.
•STEDMAN, Mr. Julian Frank, FCA *1969;* Stedman & Co, Cassel, 33 Foley Road, Claygate, ESHER, SURREY KT10 0LU.
STEDMAN, Miss. Philippa Ann, BSc ACA *1980;* (Tax Fac), 176 Astonville Street, LONDON, SW18 5AG.
STEDMAN, Mr. Simon Christoffer, BA ACA *1993;* Francis Wilks Jones, 6 Coldbath Square, LONDON, EC1R 5HL.
•STEED, Mr. Anthony Jos, FCA *1960;* (Tax Fac), A.J. Steed, 75 Bell Hill, PETERSFIELD, GU32 2EA.
STEED, Mr. Jonathan Milner, BEng ACA *1992;* with Grant Thornton UK LLP, 1 Whitehall Riverside, Whitehall Road, LEEDS, WEST YORKSHIRE, LS1 4BN.
STEED, Mr. Mark Wickham, ACA MCIM MSI *1980;* Keepers Cottage, The Shaw, Leckhampstead, BUCKINGHAM, MK18 5PA.
STEED, Mr. Michael Northam, FCA *1952;* 9 Uplowman Road, TIVERTON, EX16 4LU. (Life Member)
•STEED, Mr. Nicholas, ACA *1999;* COG Accountancy Limited, 4 Heol Tre Forys, PENARTH, SOUTH GLAMORGAN, CF64 3RE.
STEEDEN, Miss. Emma Rachael, BA(Hons) ACA *2003;* Bauer Media Endeavour House, 189 Shaftesbury Avenue, LONDON, WC2H 8JG.
STEEDEN, Mr. Graham Anthony, BSc ACA *1979;* 79 Kings Road, KINGSTON-UPON-THAMES, KT2 5JB.
STEEDEN, Mr. Nigel Jeremy, FCA *1981;* Music Box Leisure Ltd, Unit 9, Lancashire Enterprise Business Park, LEYLAND, PR26 6TZ.
STEEDMAN, Ms. Ruth, BEng ACA CTA *1992;* with Deloitte LLP, 2 New Street Square, LONDON, EC4A 3BZ.
•STEEDS, Mr. David William Howitt, MA FCA *1974;* Steeds & Co, 1 Littleworth Avenue, ESHER, KT10 9PB.
STEEL, Mr. Alexander Mark, BA ACA *2003;* Störklingasse 44, 4125 RIEHEN, SWITZERLAND.
STEEL, Mr. Andrew John, BSc ACA *1990;* 9 Mourne View, Peel, ISLE OF MAN, IM5 1UJ.
STEEL, Mr. Angus Kennedy, BA ACA *1991;* 83 Pomswick Road, CHELTENHAM, GLOUCESTERSHIRE, GL50 2EX.
STEEL, Mr. David Christopher, MEng ACA *2006;* British Petroleum Co Plc, Chertsey Road, SUNBURY-ON-THAMES, MIDDLESEX, TW16 7LN.
STEEL, Mr. David Michael, BA ACA *1987;* Danescroft, 37 Kingsway, Chalfont St. Peter, GERRARDS CROSS, SL9 8NX.
STEEL, Mr. David Roy Burnett, BA FCA *1952;* 15 Maldon Close, LONDON, SE5 8DD. (Life Member)
STEEL, Mr. Donald Matthew, FCA *1964;* Yew Tree House, Snitterfield Street, Hampton Lucy, WARWICK, CV35 8AX.
STEEL, Mrs. Donna Zylpha, BA(Hons) ACA *2003;* with Grant Thornton UK LLP, Unit 2, Broadfield Court, SHEFFIELD, S8 0XF.
STEEL, Mr. Gavin Robert, BSc ACA *1992;* Pricewaterhouse Coopers, PO 11987, DUBAI, UNITED ARAB EMIRATES.
STEEL, Mr. Ian Simon, BA ACA *1996;* Iggesund Paperboard (Workington) Ltd, Siddick, WORKINGTON, CUMBRIA, CA14 1JX.
STEEL, Mr. James Benedict Wyatt, BSc ACA *1991;* C A F O D Romero House, 55 Westminster Bridge Road, LONDON, SE1 7JB.
STEEL, Mr. James Ian, FCA *1967;* Flint Cottages, High Rougham, BURY ST.EDMUNDS, IP30 9LN.
STEEL, Mr. John Harry, FCA *1971;* Orchard View, Banady Lane, Stoke Orchard, CHELTENHAM, GLOUCESTERSHIRE, GL52 7SJ.
•STEEL, Mr. John William Anthony, MA ACA *1998;* Werner von Siemens Strasse 67, 91052 ERLANGEN, GERMANY.
STEEL, Mr. Jonathan Robin, FCA *1974;* 202 Linden Avenue, ITHACA, NY 14850, UNITED STATES.
STEEL, Mrs. Julie Ann, ACA ATII *1996;* Greenways, Wenham Lane, Great Wenham, COLCHESTER, CO7 6PJ.
•STEEL, Mr. Lindesay David, FCA *1975;* Gilchrist Tash, Cleveland Bldgs., Queen's Square, MIDDLESBROUGH, TS2 1PA.
STEEL, Miss. Lynda Jane, BSc ACA *2005;* Hillview, Austell Gardens, Mill Hill, LONDON, NW7 4NS.
STEEL, Mr. Mark, BSc ACA *2005;* Energetix Group plc - Unit 1, Capenhurst Technology Park, CHESTER, CHESHIRE, CH1 6EH.
STEEL, Mr. Martin John, BSc FCA *1982;* 115 Radley Road, ABINGDON, OX14 3RP.
STEEL, Mr. Michael Leonard, FCA *1974;* Highcroft, 11 Minster Road, GODALMING, GU7 1SP.
STEEL, Mr. Peter Thomas, BA ACA *2000;* Evolution Securities Limited, 1 King Street, LEEDS, LS1 2HH.
STEEL, Mr. Roger James, BSc FCA *1977;* 3 White Holme Drive, Pool In Wharfedale, OTLEY, LS21 1TX.
•STEEL, Mr. Timothy Deane, BA ACA *1991;* Deloitte LLP, 2 New Street Square, LONDON, EC4A 3BZ. See also Deloitte & Touche LLP
•STEEL, Dr. Timothy James, BSc ACA *2000;* Ernst & Young LLP, 1 More London Place, LONDON, SE1 2AF. See also Ernst & Young Europe LLP
STEELE, Miss. Abbie Carol, ACA *2010;* 163 Rochford Road, SOUTHEND-ON-SEA, SS2 6SS.
STEELE, Mr. Alan, FCA *1964;* 3 Ladypool Close, HALESOWEN, B62 8SY.
•STEELE, Mr. Andrew Mark, ACA FCCA *2008;* 360 Accountants Limited, Melton Court, Gibson Lane, Melton, HULL, HU14 3HH. See also 5 Four Payroll Bureau Limited
STEELE, Mr. Anthony Arthur, MA FCA *1977;* 42 Heathcote Road, TWICKENHAM, TW1 1RX.
STEELE, Miss. Barbara, BSc FCA *1977;* Richlin, Manor Way, Oxshott, LEATHERHEAD, KT22 0HS.
STEELE, Mr. Christopher, BA ACA *2005;* with Deloitte & Touche, P.O.Box HM 1556, Corner House, Church & Parliament Streets, HAMILTON HM FX, BERMUDA.
STEELE, Mr. David Roger, FCA *1964;* 25 Detillens Lane, Limpsfield, OXTED, RH8 0DH.
STEELE, Mr. Dennis Arthur, FCA *1962;* 9 Fox Holes Lane, Calverley, PUDSEY, LS28 5NS.
STEELE, Mr. Gary David, MSc ACA *1999;* 2 Sparrow Close, Watermead, AYLESBURY, BUCKINGHAMSHIRE, HP19 0UJ.
STEELE, Mr. Gavin William, BA ACA *1987;* Corporation Of Lloyd's, 1 Lime Street, LONDON, EC3M 7HA.
•STEELE, Mr. Geoffrey Frederick, FCA *1956;* 59 Ramsgate Road, MARGATE, KENT, CT9 5SA.
STEELE, Ms. Gillian Eva, BA FCA *1978;* 100 Summerfield Street, DANVILLE, CA 94506, UNITED STATES.
STEELE, Mrs. Hilary Ann, BSc ACA *1994;* 8 Haywards Field, Longthorpe, PETERBOROUGH, PE3 6FB.
STEELE, Mr. Jerrold Turner, FCA *1954;* P.O.Box 244, Wits, JOHANNESBURG, GAUTENG, 2050, SOUTH AFRICA. (Life Member)
•STEELE, Mr. John, BA FCA *1979;* Wilson Insurance Broking Group Ltd, 1/3 Waverley Street, NOTTINGHAM, NG7 4HG.

STEELE, Mr. Jonathan, BSc ACA *2000;* 20 Woodford Road, Poynton, STOCKPORT, CHESHIRE, SK12 1DY.
STEELE, Mr. Jonathan Richard, BSc ACA *1992;* 3 Rodmell Avenue, Saltdean, BRIGHTON, BN2 8LT.
STEELE, Miss. Katherine Mary, BA ACA *1982;* Frith Accountants Ltd Moorgate House, 7b Station Road West, OXTED, RH8 9EE.
•STEELE, Mr. Keith Anthony, BA ACA *2002;* 8 Station Close, HENLOW, BEDFORDSHIRE, SG16 6FL.
STEELE, Mrs. Laura Anne, BA ACA *1993;* 2 Richhill Crescent, BELFAST, BT5 6HF.
STEELE, Miss. Lynda Joy, BSc ACA *1984;* 2 / 4 Ash Lane, RUSTINGTON, WEST SUSSEX, BN16 3BU.
STEELE, Mrs. Margaret Anne, FCA *1977;* 36 Elmhurst Road, West Moors, FERNDOWN, BH22 0DH.
STEELE, Mr. Matthew James, ACA *2009;* 11 Warlters Road, LONDON, N7 0RZ.
STEELE, Mr. Michael Anthony, ACA *1981;* 28 Mill Lane, Upholland, SKELMERSDALE, WN8 0HJ.
STEELE, Mr. Michael David, BSc FCA *1974;* Benquhat, 25 Park Avenue, WOODFORD GREEN, IG8 0EU.
STEELE, Mr. Nicholas John, MA BA ACA *1987;* Keythorpe Lodge Cottage, Hallaton Road, Tugby, LEICESTER, LE7 9WB.
STEELE, Miss. Nicola Josephine, LLB ACA *2001;* Flat 2, 33 Earlsfield Road, LONDON, SW18 3DB.
STEELE, Mr. Nigel Peter, BA FCA *1981;* (Tax Fac), 1 Hadlow Park, Hadlow, TONBRIDGE, KENT, TN11 0HY.
STEELE, Mrs. Odette, LLB ACA *2000;* 20 Woodford Road, Poynton, STOCKPORT, CHESHIRE, SK12 1DY.
•STEELE, Mr. Paul Christopher, FCA *1983;* Paul Steele Limited, 18 Newport Street, TIVERTON, DEVON, EX16 6NL.
STEELE, Mr. Paul Edward, BSc FCA *1978;* The Coach House Norton Lane, Norton, CHICHESTER, PO20 3NH.
STEELE, Mr. Philip Anthony, FCA *1974;* Willow Cottage, 12 Orchard Close, CROOK, DL15 8QU. (Life Member)
STEELE, Mr. Richard John, BCom FCA *1979;* 10 Newton Park, Newton Solney, BURTON-ON-TRENT, DE15 0SX.
•STEELE, Mr. Robert Jackson, MA FCA *1979;* Steeles Support Services, c/o Stoneleigh, 6 Carlton Gardens, Stanwix, CARLISLE, CA3 9NP.
STEELE, Mr. Robert Malcolm, FCA *1970;* Wildsmith House, Marton, Sinnington, YORK, YO62 6RD. (Life Member)
STEELE, Miss. Sarah, ACA *2011;* 8 Newlands Park, Dearham, MARYPORT, CUMBRIA, CA15 7ED.
STEELE, Dr. Simon Andrew, BSc ACA *1998;* 2 Cambridge Road, Fowlmere, ROYSTON, SG8 7QN.
STEELE, Mr. Simon Naunton, BEng ACA *1999;* 18 Atbara Road, TEDDINGTON, MIDDLESEX, TW11 9PD.
STEELE, Mr. Timothy, ACA *2007;* 35 Brunswick Quay, LONDON, SE16 7PU.
STEELE, Mr. Toby Andrew Murray, BA(Hons) ACA *2002;* C T C Aviation Services Building 130, Nursling Industrial Estate Mauretania Road Nursling, SOUTHAMPTON, SO16 0YS.
STEELE, Mrs. Vanessa, BA(Hons) ACA *2001;* 20 Clifton St, BLACKBURN, VIC 3130, AUSTRALIA.
STEELE, Miss. Victoria, BSc ACA *1999;* Glazemount, Glazebrook Lane, Glazebrook, WARRINGTON, WA3 5BL.
STEELE-MORTIMER, Mr. Frank Patrick Odell, BSc ACA *1991;* Golden Grove House, Golden Grove, Llanasa, HOLYWELL, CLWYD, CH8 9NA.
STEELE-PERKINS, Mr. James Anthony, BSc ACA *2002;* Pricewaterhousecoopers Llp, 1 Hays Lane, LONDON, SE1 2RD.
STEELL, Mr. David Graham, FCA *1971;* 403 129th Avenue SE, CALGARY T2J 5H5, AB, CANADA.
STEEMSON, Mr. Brian, MA FCA *1981;* 37 Dickson Drive, HEXHAM, NORTHUMBERLAND, NE46 2RB.
STEEN, Mr. Anthony Francis, BA ACA *1991;* Parcelvej 97, Virum, 2830 COPENHAGEN, DENMARK.
•STEEN, Mr. Colin, BA FCA *1976;* (Tax Fac), Colin Steen, 19 Polwarth Drive, Brunton Park, NEWCASTLE UPON TYNE, NE3 5NH.
STEEN, Mr. David, ACA *2002;* 44 King Street West, Scotia Capital, 65th Floor, TORONTO M5H 1H1, ON, CANADA.
STEEN, Dr. Preston Stourton Thomas, MA FCA *1996;* 2 Harmsworth Mews, LONDON, SE11 4SQ.
STEENBERG, Mr. Axel Werner Francis, BSc ACA *1993;* Steenbergs, 6 Hallikeld Close Melmerby, RIPON, NORTH YORKSHIRE, HG4 5GZ.
STEENKAMP, Mr. Daniel, FCA *2010;* 43 Greenwood Way, Summerwood Estate, DURBANVILLE, 7550, SOUTH AFRICA.
STEEPER, Mrs. Carolyn Gaye, BA ACA ACILA *1982;* 33 Owlthorpe Avenue, Mosborough, SHEFFIELD, S20 5JS.
STEEPLES, Mr. Paul Michael, BSc ACA *1994;* Dormer House Hollies Drive Edwalton, NOTTINGHAM, NG12 4BZ.
STEER, Mr. Allan Christopher, FCA *1969;* 17 Rose Road, Harborne, BIRMINGHAM, B17 9LL.
STEER, Mr. Christopher Charles David, MA FCA *1967;* 24 Vine Farm Close, Talbot Village, POOLE, BH12 5EJ.
STEER, Mrs. Deirdre Anne, BA ACA *1989;* 46 Surrey Road, SEAFORD, BN25 2NR.
STEER, Mrs. Jill Margaret, BA ACA *1998;* The Jesmond Trust, Jesmond Parish Church, Eskdale Terrace, NEWCASTLE UPON TYNE, NE2 4DJ.
•STEER, Mr. Keith, FCA *1969;* 6 Sylvan Avenue, EXETER, EX4 6ES.
STEER, Mr. Kevin John, BSc ACA *1992;* 46 Surrey Road, SEAFORD, BN25 2NR.
STEER, Miss. Louise Ann, BA ACA *2000;* 15 Hallam Grange Road, SHEFFIELD, S10 4BH.
STEER, Mr. Mark, ACA *1985;* National Federation of Builders Limited B&CE Building, Manor Royal, CRAWLEY, WEST SUSSEX, RH10 9QP.
STEER, Mr. Mark Dudley, FCA *1961;* Many Waters, Neadon Lane, Bridford, EXETER, EX6 7JE. (Life Member)
STEER, Mr. Michael James, ACA *1991;* 32 Coniston Avenue, UPMINSTER, ESSEX, RM14 3XP.
STEER, Mr. Nicholas John, BA ACA *1986;* 4th Floor St Clare House, 30-33 Minories, LONDON, EC3N 1DD.
STEER, Mrs. Sarah Jane, ACA *1979;* 21 The Triangle, Longlevens, GLOUCESTER, GL2 0NF.
•STEER-FOWLER, Mrs. Victoria, BSc FCA *1999;* Fowler & Co, 1st Floor Norton House, 41 Arbory Street, Castletown, ISLE OF MAN, IM9 1LL.
STEERE, Mr. Colin James, FCA *1960;* 5 The Courtyard, Sheffield Park, UCKFIELD, EAST SUSSEX, TN22 3QW. (Life Member)
STEERE, Mr. Ian Robert, MA FCA *1974;* 15 Ralliwood Road, ASHTEAD, KT21 1DD.
STEERE, Mr. Leslie Anthony, FCA *1949;* La Cachette, Prince Albert Road, St. Peter Port, GUERNSEY, GY1 1EZ.
STEERS, Mr. John Stuart Young, BA ACA *1992;* Elderbury House, 49a Howards Thicket, GERRARDS CROSS, SL9 7NU.
STEERS, Mr. Jonathan Richard, BSc ACA *1997;* 4 Gardnor Road, LONDON, NW3 1HA.
STEERS, Mrs. Patricia Catherine, BA ACA *1986;* with Grant Thornton UK LLP, 3140 Rowan Place, John Smith Drive, Oxford Business Park South, OXFORD, OX4 2WB.
STEFANI, Ms. Eleni, BA ACA *2002;* 23 Tamasou Street, Synikismos Athalassas, 2115 NICOSIA, CYPRUS.
STEFANYSZYN, Mr. Paul Simon, BA ACA *1986;* 10 The Garthlands, STAFFORD, ST17 9ZP.
STEFF, Mr. Darryl Richard, BA(Hons) ACA *1999;* 6 Comport Street, BEAUMARIS, VIC 3193, AUSTRALIA.
STEGENWALNER, Mr. Steven John, ACA *1995;* Somerston Holdings Limited, PO Box 525, 45 Esplanade, St Helier, JERSEY, JE4 0WZ.
STEGER-LEWIS, Mrs. Catherine Nicola, ACA *1993;* Cobham plc, Flight Refuelling Ltd, Brook Road, WIMBORNE, BH21 2BJ.
STEGGALL, Mr. Brian Richard, BA FCA *1976;* 88 Shurland Avenue, BARNET, HERTFORDSHIRE, EN4 8DD.
STEGGALS, Mr. Martin Frank, FCA *1966;* 111 Carshalton Park Road, CARSHALTON, SM5 3SJ. (Life Member)
STEGGALS, Mr. Roger John, FCA *1966;* Abstrakt Services Ltd, 58 Chester Street, Aston Waterlinks, BIRMINGHAM, WEST MIDLANDS, B6 4LW.
•STEGGLES, Mr. Anthony, FCA *1976;* Steggles & Co, 2a Peel Street, Farnworth, BOLTON, BL4 8AA.
STEGGLES, Mrs. Caroline Anne, BA ACA *2007;* Fielding Cottage, Anchor Corner, Little Ellingham, ATTLEBOROUGH, NORFOLK, NR17 1JX.
STEIGER, Mr. Christopher Dominic, BSc ACA *1998;* 273 Buxton Road, MACCLESFIELD, CHESHIRE, SK11 7ET.
STEIGER, Mr. John Giles, BSc ACA ATII *1997;* Rietbrunnen 20, 8808 PFAFFIKON, SWITZERLAND.
•STEIN, Mr. Adam Paul, BSc FCA *1974;* Critchleys LLP, Greyfriars Court, Paradise Square, OXFORD, OX1 1BE.
STEIN, Mr. Anthony Karl, BA ACA *1993;* Rectory Court, Old Rectory Lane, Alvechurch, BIRMINGHAM, B48 7SX.
STEIN, Mr. David Julian, ACA *1981;* 3 Old Turnpike Cottages, Tibberton, DROITWICH, WORCESTERSHIRE, WR9 7NR.
STEIN, Mrs. Deborah, BA ACA *1988;* Unit 5 Coopies Field, Coopies Lane Industrial Estate, MORPETH, NORTHUMBERLAND, NE61 6JT.
STEIN, Mr. Iain, BA ACA *1985;* Principal House, 5 Back Grove Avenue, NEWCASTLE UPON TYNE, TYNE AND WEAR, NE3 1NT.
STEIN, Mr. Neil David, FCA *1953;* 6 Densham Drive, PURLEY, CR8 2XG. (Life Member)
STEIN, Mr. Nicholas Martin, ACA *1983;* Flat 2, 98 Ellison Road, LONDON, SW16 5DD.
STEIN, Mr. Richard Jonathan Beaver, MA FCA *1963;* 57 Deansway, East Finchley, LONDON, N2 0HX. (Life Member)
STEIN, Mr. Warren Lester, BSc ACA *1989;* 16016 Woodvale Road, ENCINO, CA 91436, UNITED STATES.
STEINBACH, Mrs. Nicola Jane, BA FCA *1988;* The Dairy 5 The Woodlands Tatenhill, BURTON-ON-TRENT, STAFFORDSHIRE, DE13 9QZ.
STEINBARTH, Mr. Michael Kurt, ACA *1999;* 66 Rectory Lane, Long Ditton, SURBITON, KT6 5HW.
•STEINBERG, Mr. Allan Melvyn, FCA *1970;* Allan Steinberg & Co, 25A York Road, ILFORD, IG1 3AD.
STEINBERG, Mr. Gerald, FCA FFA CTA *1968;* Primrose Lodge, 1 Lodge End, RADLETT, HERTFORDSHIRE, WD7 7EB.
•STEINBERG, Mr. Ian Beverley, BCom FCA *1985;* (Tax Fac), Ian B. Steinberg, 40 Woodford Avenue, Gants Hill, ILFORD, IG2 6XQ.
STEINBERG, Mr. Jason Lee, BA ACA CTA *1997;* 31 Beverley Crescent, WOODFORD GREEN, ESSEX, IG8 9DD.
STEINBERG, Mr. Jerrold, FCA *1975;* 17 Parkway, LONDON, NW11 0EX.
STEINBERG, Mr. Jonathan Ashley, BA FCA *1993;* 20 Sixteen, 13 Clifton Avenue, LONDON, N3 1BN.
•STEINBERG, Mr. Nathan Anthony, FCA CF *1978;* MEMBER OF COUNCIL, (Tax Fac), Munslows, 2nd Floor, Manfield House, 1 Southampton Street, LONDON, WC2R 0LR.
STEINBERG, Mr. Spencer Mitchell, BA ACA *1995;* Primrose Lodge, 1 Lodge End, RADLETT, WD7 7EB.
STEINEPREIS, Mr. David Christian, ACA CA(AUS) *2009;* 96 Roseneath Road, LONDON, SW11 6AQ.
•STEINER, Mr. Anthony Nicholas, BA FCA *1990;* with RSM Tenon Limited, Clive House, Clive Street, BOLTON, BL1 1ET.
•STEINER, Mrs. Elsa Sau-Wai, MBA BSc FCA *1994;* Finance Associates Limited, 65 London Wall, LONDON, EC2M 5TU.
STEINER, Mr. Nick, ACA *2011;* 673 Brannan Street, Unit 105, SAN FRANCISCO, CA 94107, UNITED STATES.
STEINER, Mr. Paul Anthony, BA FCA *1983;* Harris Watson Holdings Plc Unit 3, Ashted Lock Way, BIRMINGHAM, B7 4AZ.
•STEINER, Mr. Timothy Alexander, ACA *1980;* Alexander Maitland Limited, 50 Cowick Street, St Thomas, EXETER, EX4 1AP. See also Steiner & Co
STEINGOLD, Mr. Lawrence Gerald, BSc FCA *1976;* Action Coach, Saddlers House, 4-6 South Parade, Bawtry, DONCASTER, SOUTH YORKSHIRE DN10 6JH.
•STEINHAUS, Mr. Simcha Yehuda, FCA *1973;* Hager Stenhouse & Co, 206 High Road, LONDON, N15 4NP.
STEINLE, Mrs. Louise Joanne, BSc ACA *1999;* Bridge Bungalow High Street, Ufford, WOODBRIDGE, SUFFOLK, IP13 6EQ.
STEINSBERG, Mr. Graham Lawrence, BA ACA *1982;* Bakers Close, 104 Lower Radley, ABINGDON, OX14 3BA.
STEINSON, Miss. Nicola Jane, ACA *2007;* Glenesk, Holbrook, IPSWICH, IP9 2PZ.
•STEINSON, Mrs. Rosemary Jane, FCA *1975;* (Tax Fac), Rosemary J. Steinson, Glenesk, Holbrook, IPSWICH, IP9 2PZ.
•STEINTHAL, Mr. Anthony Paul Richard, BA FCA DChA *1982;* (Tax Fac), Chantrey Vellacott DFK LLP, Russell Square House, 10-12 Russell Square, LONDON, WC1B 5LF.
STEINTHAL, Mr. Peter John, MA FCA *1970;* 2 Albany Park Road, KINGSTON UPON THAMES, SURREY, KT2 5SW. (Life Member)
STEINWENDER, Mr. Peter, BSc FCA *1978;* Postfach 1414, 82004 UNTERHACHING, GERMANY.
STEKEL, Mr. Ronald, FCA *1964;* Gad Tadeski 7/25, 93786 JERUSALEM, ISRAEL.
•STELFOX, Mr. Eric Richard, FCA *1975;* 53 Leegate Road, STOCKPORT, CHESHIRE, SK4 4AX. See also KPMG
•STELFOX, Miss. Susan, BSc FCA *1988;* Susan Stelfox, 46 The Keep, Blackheath, LONDON, SE3 0AF.
STELL, Mrs. Julia Michelle, BSc ACA *2005;* 26 Mornington Avenue, IPSWICH, IP1 4LA.
STELL, Mrs. Phillipa Kate, BSc ACA *1997;* 9 Arden Grove, HARPENDEN, HERTFORDSHIRE, AL5 4SJ.
STELLAKIS, Mr. Nicholas John, FCA *1978;* Mavromichali 43, Filothei, 152 37 ATHENS, GREECE.
STELZER, Miss. Rebecca Janine, BA ACA *2009;* Basement, 11 Friars Stile Road, RICHMOND, TW10 6NH.
STEMBRIDGE, Mr. Douglas Edward, BA ACA *1981;* Oxford House, 1 High Street, Evercreech, SHEPTON MALLET, BA4 6HZ.
•STEMMER, Mr. Robert Anthony, BSc FCA *1993;* Maddocks & Gamble Limited, 1a Warrington Road, Ashton-in-Makerfield, WIGAN, LANCASHIRE, WN4 9PL.
STEMP, Miss. Kelly, BA(Hons) ACA CTA *2003;* (Tax Fac), with TWP Accounting LLP, The Old Rectory, Church Street, WEYBRIDGE, SURREY, KT13 8DE.
STENDALL, Mr. Giles Timothy, BSc(Hons) ACA *2002;* with PKF (UK) LLP, New Guild House, 45 Great Charles Street, BIRMINGHAM, B3 2LX.
STENHAM, Mr. Jeremy, BA ACA *1984;* 43 Flower Lane, LONDON, NW7 2JN.
STENHOUSE, Mr. Robert Bruce, BSc FCA ATII *1989;* Deloitte & Touche, 2 New Street Square, LONDON, EC4A 3BZ.
•STENNER, Mr. Derek James, BA ACA *1985;* Derek J. Stenner Ltd, The Mews, Hounds Road, Chipping Sodbury, BRISTOL, BS37 6EE.
STENNER, Mrs. Maureen Elizabeth, BSc ACA *1991;* The Mews, Hounds Road, Chipping Sodbury, BRISTOL, BS37 6EE.
STENNETT, Mr. Mark Harwood, BSc ACA *1982;* 81 Warren Road, LEIGH-ON-SEA, SS9 3TT.
STENNING, Mr. Daniel Raymond, LLB ACA *2004;* 4 Blacksmith Close, Corfe Mullen, WIMBORNE, DORSET, BH21 3QW.
•STENNING, Mrs. Kim Joyce, BA FCA CTA *1994;* 7 Longwater, Orton Longueville, PETERBOROUGH, PE2 7JS.
STENNING, Mr. Paul Sydney Arthur, BA ACA *1979;* 5 Elderslie Road, Eltham, LONDON, SE9 1UD.
STENNING, Mr. Vernon Charles, BSc ACA *1986;* 58 Griffiths Road, Wimbledon, LONDON, SW19 1ST.
STENNING, Mr. William Nicholas, BEng ACA *1995;* Rockhurst, Danes Hill, WOKING, SURREY, GU22 7HQ.
STENSON, Mr. Christopher, ACA *2011;* Apartment 38a, 5 Quay, 232 Ordsall Lane, SALFORD, M5 3NB.
•STENSON, Miss. Mary Teresa, BSc FCA *1985;* Littlejohn LLP, 1 Westferry Circus, Canary Wharf, LONDON, E14 4HD.
•STENT, Mr. Christopher Peter, ACA *1989;* 51 Kilmarnock Street, Riccarton, CHRISTCHURCH 8011, NEW ZEALAND.
STENT, Mr. Graham George, BSc(Hons) ACA *2001;* 9 Woodavon Gardens, THATCHAM, BERKSHIRE, RG18 4DN.
•STENT, Mr. John Henry, FCA *1968;* (Tax Fac), John Stent, 30 Elizabeth Drive, Hartford, HUNTINGDON, CAMBRIDGESHIRE, PE29 1WA.
STENT, Mr. John Julian, BSc FCA *1979;* Melrose House, 33 Ganghill, GUILDFORD, GU1 1XF.
STENT, Mrs. Katherine, BSc ACA *1998;* 9 Woodavon Gardens, THATCHAM, BERKSHIRE, RG18 4DN.
STENT, Mr. Peter Jervis, FCA *1969;* Bredon, Oxford Road, GERRARDS CROSS, SL9 7DL.
STENTON, Mr. Joseph Edward, FCA *1954;* 27 Mowson Crescent, Worrall, SHEFFIELD, S35 0AG. (Life Member)
STENTON, Mr. Raymond, BSc ACA *1997;* 20 Broadoak Road, Worsley, MANCHESTER, M28 2TG.
STENZEL, Mr. Christopher, BSc ACA *1993;* 235 North Bloomfield Road, CANANDAIGUA, NY 14424, UNITED STATES.
STENZEL, Mrs. Jennifer, MA ACA *1994;* 59 Mahogany Run, PITTSFORD, NY 14534, UNITED STATES.
STEPANOVA, Miss. Yaroslavna, ACA *2010;* 5-68 Stroitelnaya Str, 143400 KRASNOGORSK, RUSSIAN FEDERATION.
•STEPHAN, Mr. John Arthur, MA ACA *1988;* BDO LLP, 125 Colmore Row, BIRMINGHAM, B3 3SD. See also BDO Stoy Hayward LLP
STEPHAN, Mr. Matthew Paul, ACA *2009;* 2/11 Croydon Street, TOOWONG, QLD 4066, AUSTRALIA.
STEPHANI, Mr. Christakis Costas, BCom FCA *1951;* P.Nirvana Street 7, 1080 NICOSIA, CYPRUS. (Life Member)
STEPHANIDES, Mr. Andreas, BSc FCA *1980;* 28 Dionisou Avenue, Drosia, 14572 ATHENS, GREECE.
STEPHANIDES, Mr. Stephanos, BSc ACA *2001;* 18 Aristagora Street, Halandri, 15238 ATHENS, GREECE.
•STEPHANIDES, Mr. Stephos, BSc FCA *1981;* PricewaterhouseCoopers Limited, Julia House, 3 Themistocles Dervis Street, CY-1066 NICOSIA, CYPRUS.

STEPHANOU, Miss. Maria, BSc ACA *2006;* 4 Alexi Minoti, Potamos Germasouias, 4103 LIMASSOL, CYPRUS.
STEPHANOU, Mr. Michalis, BSc ACA *2009;* 28 Kato Varosion, Lakatamia, 2324 NICOSIA, CYPRUS.
STEPHANOU, Mr. Stylianos, BSc ACA *1990;* 48B Pefkon Str, 14562 KIFISIA, ATTICA, GREECE.
STEPHANY, Mr. John David, MA FCA *1973;* L D I C Group Ltd, 9 Bentinck Street, LONDON, W1U 2EL.
STEPHEN, Miss. Ceri Louise, ACA *2003;* 19 Gleneagles, Waltham, GRIMSBY, DN37 0XD.
STEPHEN, Mr. Robert James, BSc ACA *1995;* Oliver Wright EAME LLP, The Steadings Business Centre, Maisemore Court, Maisemore, GLOUCESTER, GL2 8EY.
•**STEPHEN, Mr. Thomas Mark, BSc ACA** *1985;* PricewaterhouseCoopers LLP, Hays Galleria, 1 Hays Lane, LONDON, SE1 2RD. See also PricewaterhouseCoopers
•**STEPHEN-HAYNES, Mr. Christopher Mayo, MA FCA FCIE** *1991;* Bloomer Heaven Limited, Rutland House, 148 Edmund Street, BIRMINGHAM, B3 2FD. See also Midland Accountancy Group Limited and Christopher M. Stephen-Haynes
STEPHEN-MARTIN, Miss. Kelly, ACA *2009;* Venture Finance Plc, Sheencroft House, 10-12 Church Road, HAYWARDS HEATH, WEST SUSSEX, RH16 3SN.
•①**STEPHENS, Dr. Adam Henry, BA(Hons) ACA** *2002;* with Re10 (UK) Plc, Albemarle House, 1 Albemarle Street, LONDON, W1S 4HA.
STEPHENS, Mr. Adam Peter, MEng ACA *2010;* 71 Beakes Road, SMETHWICK, WEST MIDLANDS, B67 5RS.
STEPHENS, Mr. Alan David, MA BA ACA *2007;* with Cole Marie Partners Ltd, Priory House, 45-51 High Street, REIGATE, SURREY, RH2 9AE.
STEPHENS, Mr. Alexander Edward, BA(Hons) ACA *2002;* 2 Burlington Road, ALTRINCHAM, WA14 1HR.
STEPHENS, Mr. Alexander Geoffrey, FCA *1980;* 74 Skipper Way, Little Paxton, ST. NEOTS, CAMBRIDGESHIRE, PE19 6LQ.
STEPHENS, Mrs. Alison Jean, BA ACA *1993;* 17 Harcourt Close, HENLEY-ON-THAMES, RG9 1UZ.
STEPHENS, Mr. Andrew Paul, BSc(Hons) ACA DIS MIoD *1995;* Valtech Ltd, 120 Aldersgate Street, LONDON, EC1A 4JQ.
STEPHENS, Mr. Aylwin Kersey, FCA *1969;* Warwick House, 21 South Park, GERRARDS CROSS, BUCKINGHAMSHIRE, SL9 8HQ.
STEPHENS, Miss. Beulah Vijayanthi, ACA *1980;* PO Box 389, DONCASTER, VIC 3108, AUSTRALIA.
STEPHENS, Mrs. Caroline Patricia Anne, BA(Hons) FCA *2000;* with Grant Thornton UK LLP, Hartwell House, 55-61 Victoria Street, BRISTOL, BS1 6FT.
•**STEPHENS, Mrs. Christine Alice, BSc FCA** *1983;* Mayhills Cottage, Froxfield, PETERSFIELD, GU32 1DX.
STEPHENS, Mr. Christopher, BA ACA *1998;* 7 Newmarket Gardens, ST.HELENS, MERSEYSIDE, WA9 5FR.
STEPHENS, Miss. Clare Elizabeth, BSc(Hons) ACA *2001;* 1 School Lane, Castle Combe, CHIPPENHAM, SN14 7HJ.
STEPHENS, Mr. Daniel Weatherill, BA(Hons) ACA *2001;* UNIT 3304 151 George Street, BRISBANE, QLD 4000, AUSTRALIA.
STEPHENS, Mr. David, MA ACA *1985;* MDA Ltd, Gillingham House, 38-44 Gillingham Street, LONDON, SW1V 1HU.
STEPHENS, Mr. David Anthony Stuart, MA ACA *1996;* 2 Latton Close, ESHER, SURREY, KT10 8PX.
STEPHENS, Mr. David Charles, FCA *1974;* Chinham House, Chinham Road, Bartley, SOUTHAMPTON, SO40 2LF.
•**STEPHENS, Mr. David Geoffrey, FCA** *1983;* (Tax Fac), Anthony Williams & Co Ltd, 14 North Parade, PENZANCE, TR18 4SL.
STEPHENS, Mr. David William, FCA *1967;* (Tax Fac), 9 Kidder Bank, WELLS, SOMERSET, BA5 3JT.
STEPHENS, Mrs. Elizabeth, BSc ACA *1979;* Townsend Mill, Rectory Road, Steppingley, BEDFORD, MK45 5AT.
STEPHENS, Miss. Emma Louise, BA(Hons) ACA *2003;* Alstom Power Plants Ltd Booths Hall, Chelford Road, KNUTSFORD, CHESHIRE, WA16 8GE.
STEPHENS, Mr. Gareth George, BA ACA *1981;* 92 Epsom Road, GUILDFORD, SURREY, GU1 2LB.
•**STEPHENS, Mr. Geoffrey Francis, FCA** *1983;* Markamber Ltd, 2 Haydock Close, Cheadle, STOKE-ON-TRENT, ST10 1UE. See also Stephens Geoffrey
STEPHENS, Mr. Geoffrey Ralph, FCA *1957;* Windrush, 22 Rosewarne Gardens, CAMBORNE, TR14 8TH. (Life Member)
STEPHENS, Mr. George John, BSc ACA *2004;* 109 Dorset Road, 05-01 Vogx, SINGAPORE 219498, SINGAPORE.
STEPHENS, Mrs. Helene Claire, BA ACA *1991;* 52 Bassett Crescent West Bassett, SOUTHAMPTON, SO16 7DX.
STEPHENS, Mr. Ian Gordon Hugh, ACA CA(SA) *2010;* Willow Tree House, Noke, OXFORD, OX3 9TT.
STEPHENS, Mr. Ian Richard, FCA CTA MCT *1982;* (Tax Fac), 8 Wildcroft Drive, WOKINGHAM, RG40 3HY.
STEPHENS, Mr. James, BEng ACA *2004;* with Ernst & Young LLP, 1 Colmore Square, BIRMINGHAM, B4 6HQ.
STEPHENS, Miss. Janice, BA ACA MBA *1991;* 18 Coleridge Court, Milton Road, HARPENDEN, AL5 5LD.
STEPHENS, Miss. Joanne Louise, BA(Hons) ACA *2010;* 9 Kimble Close, NORTHAMPTON, NN4 0RF.
STEPHENS, Mrs. Joanne Marie, BA ACA *1998;* 212 St Johns Road, TUNBRIDGE WELLS, KENT, TN4 9XD.
STEPHENS, Mr. John Arthur, FCA *1967;* 42 Creek Road, HAYLING ISLAND, HAMPSHIRE, PO11 9RD. (Life Member)
STEPHENS, Mr. John Stuart, FCA *1967;* Shelleys, 11 High Drive, Oxshott, LEATHERHEAD, KT22 0NG.
STEPHENS, Mr. Jonathan David, BA ACA *1994;* 88 Coventry Road, MARKET HARBOROUGH, LE16 9DA.
STEPHENS, Mrs. Judith, BA(Hons) ACA *2001;* 2 Burlington Road, ALTRINCHAM, CHESHIRE, WA14 1HR.
STEPHENS, Mrs. Julie Anne, BSc(Hons) ACA *2001;* 18 Aldermore Drive, SUTTON COLDFIELD, WEST MIDLANDS, B75 7HW.
•**STEPHENS, Mr. Leon Trevor, BA ACA** *2001;* LTS Consulting Limited, New Media House, Davidson Road, LICHFIELD, STAFFORDSHIRE, WS14 9DU.
STEPHENS, Mrs. Ling, BA ACA *1995;* Tresanton, 7 Gledhow Wood, Kingswood, TADWORTH, KT20 6JQ.
STEPHENS, Mr. Marc John, BSc ACA *2002;* 10 Lyme Regis Road, BANSTEAD, SURREY, SM7 2EZ.
STEPHENS, Mr. Mark Richard, BA ACA *1987;* 13 Mount Pleasant, ST. ALBANS, AL3 4QH.
STEPHENS, Mr. Martin Peter, BSc ACA *2010;* 88 Polwarth Terrace, EDINBURGH, EH11 1NN.
STEPHENS, Mr. Marvin Charles, FCA *1971;* Flat 7 Keythorpe, 27 Manor Road, BOURNEMOUTH, BH1 3ER.
STEPHENS, Mr. Michael, MSc BTech ACA *1980;* Virgin Media, PO Box 1001, BRADFORD, WEST YORKSHIRE, BD4 8YD.
STEPHENS, Mrs. Nancy, BSc ACA *1999;* 31 Riversdale Road, THAMES DITTON, SURREY, KT7 0QN.
STEPHENS, Mr. Nigel John, BSc ACA *2000;* with Ernst & Young LLP, 1 Colmore Square, BIRMINGHAM, B4 6HQ.
STEPHENS, Mr. Nigel Michael Colin, FCA *1950;* 33 Vincent Road, Stoke D'Abernon, COBHAM, KT11 3JA. (Life Member)
STEPHENS, Mr. Noel Melville, MA FCA *1966;* Little Hadlow Bagshot Road, Worplesdon Hill, WOKING, SURREY, GU22 0QY. (Life Member)
STEPHENS, Mr. Paul Christopher, BSc ACA *1988;* 17 The Broadway, COWBRIDGE, SOUTH GLAMORGAN, CF71 7ER.
STEPHENS, Mr. Philip Norman, BSc ACA *1991;* 8 Marie Close, Penrhyn Madoc, Penrhyn Bay, LLANDUDNO, GWYNEDD, LL30 3LF.
STEPHENS, Mr. Robert Alan, FCA *1969;* PO Box 197, SOUTHDOWNS ESTATE, 0123, SOUTH AFRICA.
STEPHENS, Mr. Roy Edward, FCA *1960;* 6 Clockwood Gardens, YARM, TS15 9RW. (Life Member)
STEPHENS, Miss. Sandra Lee, FCA *1975;* Pear Tree Cottage, Stanton, BROADWAY, WR12 7NE.
STEPHENS, Mrs. Sarah Caroline, BA ACA *1998;* Royal Bank of Scotland, 3rd Floor, 3 Temple Back East, BRISTOL, BS1 6DZ.
STEPHENS, Mrs. Sarah Louise, ACA *2006;* 32 Bull Drive, Kesgrave, IPSWICH, IP5 2BS.
•**STEPHENS, Mr. Simon James, LLB ACA** *2001;* Deloitte LLP, Hill House, 1 Little New Street, LONDON, EC4A 3TR. See also Deloitte & Touche LLP
STEPHENS, Mrs. Sonya, ACA CA(SA) *2010;* Brambling, Green Lane East, Normandy, GUILDFORD, SURREY, GU3 2JL.
STEPHENS, Ms. Tanya, BSc ACA *2007;* Apartment 39, 18 Church Street, MANCHESTER, M4 1PN.
STEPHENS, Mr. Tim Peter, BEng ACA *2002;* Cambridge Water Co Ltd, 90 Fulbourn Road, CAMBRIDGE, CB1 9JN.
STEPHENS, Mr. Toby John, BA ACA *1988;* Pricewaterhousecoopers, 161 Marsh Wall, LONDON, E14 9SQ.
STEPHENS, Mrs. Victoria Helen, BSc(Hons) ACA *2001;* 72 Cicada Road, LONDON, SW18 2NZ.
STEPHENS, Mr. William John, BA(Hons) ACA *2010;* Flat 3 The Carriage House, 9a Grassington Road, EASTBOURNE, EAST SUSSEX, BN20 7FB.
STEPHENS, Mr. William Robert, BSc ACA *1997;* 11 Oriel Hill, CAMBERLEY, GU15 2JW.
STEPHENSON, Mrs. Alison Jane, BA ACA *1992;* 18 Parrys Grove, Stoke Bishop, BRISTOL, BS9 1TT.
STEPHENSON, Mrs. Amanda Louise, BSc ACA *1991;* Oaksdown, Forest Edge Road, Crowhill, RINGWOOD, BH24 3DF.
STEPHENSON, Mr. Andrew James, BA ACA *1989;* Grampian Country Foods, 14 Freebournes Road, WITHAM, CM8 3DG.
STEPHENSON, Mr. Andrew Jarlath, MA ACA *1987;* A3 Trochettia House, Ylang Ylang, QUATRE-BORNES, MAURITIUS.
•**STEPHENSON, Miss. Anne May, BSc ACA** *1982;* PricewaterhouseCoopers LLP, 1 Embankment Place, LONDON, WC2N 6RH. See also PricewaterhouseCoopers
STEPHENSON, Miss. Antonia Jane, BA(Hons) ACA *2004;* 6 Falkland Grove, LEEDS, LS17 6JF.
STEPHENSON, Mr. Barry, FCA *1972;* 1 Brierydale Lane, Stainburn, WORKINGTON, CA14 4UH.
STEPHENSON, Mr. Brian, FCA *1959;* MERRYWEATHER, Lower Brook Meadow, Sidford, SIDMOUTH, DEVON, EX10 9PS. (Life Member)
STEPHENSON, Mrs. Catherine Anne, BSc ACA *1997;* 242 Brooklands Road, MANCHESTER, M23 9HD.
STEPHENSON, Mrs. Catherine Jane, BSc ACA *1987;* 59 Highbury, Jesmond, NEWCASTLE UPON TYNE, NE2 3LN.
STEPHENSON, Mrs. Christine, ACA *2008;* 16 Vandyck Avenue, BURNLEY, LANCASHIRE, BB11 5HQ.
STEPHENSON, Mr. Christopher, BA ACA *1994;* Apartment 3700, 34 Woodfield Road, ALTRINCHAM, CHESHIRE, WA14 4RR.
STEPHENSON, Mr. Christopher Alan, BSc ACA *1989;* 16 Dakara Drive, FRENCHS FOREST, NSW 2086, AUSTRALIA.
STEPHENSON, Miss. Claire, BSc FCA *1996;* 3 Popes Road, ABBOTS LANGLEY, WD5 0EY.
STEPHENSON, Mr. Colin George, BSc FCA *1977;* 1 Rushmoor Avenue, Hazlemere, HIGH WYCOMBE, BUCKINGHAMSHIRE, HP15 7NT.
STEPHENSON, Mr. David Andrew, BA FCA *1987;* Ernst & Young L L P, 1 More London Place, LONDON, SE1 2AF.
STEPHENSON, Mr. David Andrew, BSc ACA *1988;* 3 Ingleby Close Dronfield Woodhouse, DRONFIELD, DERBYSHIRE, S18 8RB.
STEPHENSON, Mr. David Hilary, FCA *1959;* 37 Ingham Way, BIRMINGHAM, B17 8SW. (Life Member)
STEPHENSON, Mr. David James, BSc(Hons) ACA *2001;* Flat 32 Wood Court, 205 Brooklands Road, SALE, CHESHIRE, M33 3PY.
•**STEPHENSON, Mr. David John, FCA CTA** *1968;* (Tax Fac), with Cansdales, Bourbon Court, Nightingales Corner, Little Chalfont, AMERSHAM, HP7 9QS.
STEPHENSON, Mr. Duncan, BA FCA *1986;* 9 Stanley Drive, Roundhay, LEEDS, LS8 2EZ.
STEPHENSON, Miss. Gemma, BSc ACA *2009;* Flat 3, 362 Cowbridge Road East, CARDIFF, CF5 1HE.
STEPHENSON, Mr. Harry Douglas, FCA *1956;* 3 Highmoor, Kirkhill, MORPETH, NE61 2AL. (Life Member)
STEPHENSON, Mrs. Helen Ann, BSc ACA *2000;* 13 Hollies Drive, Edwalton, NOTTINGHAM, NG12 4BZ.
•①**STEPHENSON, Miss. Jacqueline Barbara, BA ACA** *1979;* J B Stephenson, Third Floor, 3 Field Court, Grays Inn, LONDON, WC1R 5EF.
STEPHENSON, Mr. James, ACA *2011;* 137 Lavender Sweep, LONDON, SW11 1EA.
STEPHENSON, Miss. Jane Simone Elizabeth, BA ACA *1991;* The Laurels, 282 The Common, Holt, TROWBRIDGE, BA14 6QJ.
STEPHENSON, Mrs. Jill, BA(Hons) ACA *2003;* 260 Catherwoods Road, RD1, RANGIORA 7471, NEW ZEALAND.
STEPHENSON, Mr. John Alfred, FCA *1967;* Farnley Hill, CORBRIDGE, NE45 5RP.
STEPHENSON, Mr. John Nelson, FCA *1958;* Brackley, Belmont Road, Hale, ALTRINCHAM, WA15 9PU. (Life Member)
STEPHENSON, Mr. John Paul Ashley, BA(Hons) ACA *2003;* 63 Wenlock Drive, West Bridgford, NOTTINGHAM, NG2 6UB.
STEPHENSON, Mr. John Samuel, BSc FCA *1982;* 18 Springfield Road, LEIGHTON BUZZARD, LU7 2QS.
STEPHENSON, Mr. John Trevor, FCA *1955;* 54 Fairfield Road, STOCKTON-ON-TEES, TS19 7BY.
•**STEPHENSON, Mr. John Wilson, MA BSc FCA** *1982;* (Tax Fac), John Stephenson, 3 Bank Cottages, Teeton, NORTHAMPTON, NN6 8LL. See also Stephenson J.W.
STEPHENSON, Mrs. Kaetrin Barbara, BSc FCA *1992;* 228 Belmont Road, Pauatahanui, PORIRUA 5381, NEW ZEALAND.
STEPHENSON, Mr. Keith Caville, BA ACA *1980;* 36 West Coast Road #05-30, Varsity Park Condominiums, SINGAPORE 127343, SINGAPORE.
STEPHENSON, Mr. Kevin Leslie, BA ACA *1999;* The White House, 31 Couchmore Avenue, ESHER, KT10 9AS.
STEPHENSON, Ms. Leah Jane, ACA *2009;* Flat 5, 3 Kendrick Road, READING, RG1 5DU.
•**STEPHENSON, Mr. Mark, MA ACA** *1997;* Deloitte LLP, PO Box 500, 2 Hardman Street, MANCHESTER, M60 2AT. See also Deloitte & Touche LLP
STEPHENSON, Mr. Martin Clive, BA ACA *1991;* Brooklands, 20b Hilton Road, Fenstanton, HUNTINGDON, CAMBRIDGESHIRE, PE28 9LJ.
STEPHENSON, Miss. Michelle Lesley, BA(Hons) FCA *2000;* 7 Partridge Road, HAMPTON, MIDDLESEX, TW12 3SB.
STEPHENSON, Mr. Neil, BSc ACA *1987;* Searle Manufacturing Co, 20 Davis Way, FAREHAM, PO14 1AR.
•**STEPHENSON, Mr. Neil, BSc ACA** *1999;* with PricewaterhouseCoopers LLP, Donington Court, Pegasus Business Park, Castle Donington, DERBY, DE74 2UZ.
STEPHENSON, Mr. Neil Ian Mackenzie, BA FCA *1971;* 37 Bidborough Ridge, Bidborough, TUNBRIDGE WELLS, KENT, TN4 0UT.
STEPHENSON, Mr. Oliver, ACA *2011;* 16 Queenswood Gardens, LEEDS, LS6 3ED.
•**STEPHENSON, Mr. Paul, BA FCA** *1992;* Holeys, Stuart House, 15/17 North Park Road, HARROGATE, HG1 5PD. See also Holeys Limited
STEPHENSON, Mr. Paul, BSc FCA *1991;* 228 Belmont Rd, Pauatahanui, PORIRUA 5381, NEW ZEALAND.
•**STEPHENSON, Mr. Paul, FCA** *1974;* Payne Walker Limited, Suite 2, 10 High Street, MELTON MOWBRAY, LEICESTERSHIRE, LE13 0TR.
STEPHENSON, Mr. Paul Alexander, BSc ACA *2003;* Dene Leazes Farm, Hesleden, HARTLEPOOL, CLEVELAND, TS27 4PD.
STEPHENSON, Mr. Paul George, BSc ACA *1991;* 18 Parrys Grove, Stoke Bishop, BRISTOL, BS9 1TT.
•**STEPHENSON, Mr. Paul Robert, BA FCA** *1993;* Deloitte LLP, Hill House, 1 Little New Street, LONDON, EC4A 3TR. See also Deloitte & Touche LLP
STEPHENSON, Mr. Paul William Berry, BA ACA *1980;* 818 Hidden Meadow Trail, EAGAN, MN 55123, UNITED STATES.
STEPHENSON, Mr. Percy, FCA *1962;* Flat 33, Nuneham Estate, 23 Garrads Road, LONDON, SW16 1JY. (Life Member)
STEPHENSON, Mr. Philip, ACA *1993;* 5 Grayling Close, Abbeymead, GLOUCESTER, GL4 5ED.
STEPHENSON, Mr. Philip William, BSc(Hons) ACA *2000;* Pasture House, Rye Hill Farm, Slaley, HEXHAM, NORTHUMBERLAND, NE47 0AH.
STEPHENSON, Mr. Rodney, FCA *1965;* 40 Henge Way, Portslade, BRIGHTON, BN41 2EP.
STEPHENSON, Mr. Roger Anthony, BSc ACA *1981;* (Tax Fac), Rush Hollow, 25 Stourton Crescent, STOURBRIDGE, WEST MIDLANDS, DY7 6RR.
STEPHENSON, Mr. Roger John, FCA *1969;* 5295 Greystone Way, BIRMINGHAM, AL 35242, UNITED STATES. (Life Member)
STEPHENSON, Mr. Rowland Ernest, FCA *1955;* 46A East Avenue, Talbot Woods, BOURNEMOUTH, BH3 7DA.
STEPHENSON, Mrs. Sally, BSc ACA CTA *2005;* 27 Bryan Street, Farsley, PUDSEY, LS28 5JP.
STEPHENSON, Mrs. Simone, ACA *2006;* 11 McQuade Place, BARRY, SOUTH GLAMORGAN, CF62 5UR.
STEPHENSON, Miss. Susan Lesley, MSc ACA *1984;* Forest Oak Milton Road, WOKINGHAM, RG40 1DD.
STEPHENSON, Mr. Timothy Andrew, MA FCA *1987;* Aarhus Karlsham UK Ltd, King George Dock, HULL, HU9 5PX.
STEPHENSON, Mr. Timothy David, BA ACA *1983;* Prior Pursglove College, Church Walk, GUISBOROUGH, TS14 6BU.
STEPHENSON, Mr. Timothy Richard, BA ACA *1992;* Huidevettersstraat 38, Bus 404, 2000 ANTWERP, BELGIUM.
•**STEPHENSON, Mr. Tobias Robert, BA ACA** *1993;* PKF (UK) LLP, New Guild House, 45 Great Charles Street, BIRMINGHAM, B3 2LX.

STEPNEY, Mr. Robert Adam, BA(Hons) ACA *2002;* (Tax Fac), Synarbor Plc, Sir Wilfrid Newton House, Thorncliffe Park Estate, Newton Chambers Road, Chapeltown, SHEFFIELD S35 2PH.
•STEPPLER, Mrs. Carolyn Sarah, DPhil ACA *1990;* Ernst & Young LLP, 1 More London Place, LONDON, SE1 2AF. See also Ernst & Young Europe LLP
STEPTO, Mr. Jon Morgan, BSc ACA *1988;* Drinkmaster Ltd, Plymouth Road, LISKEARD, CORNWALL, PL14 3PG.
STEPTOE, Mr. Reginald Peter, FCA *1966;* 59 Chevening Road, Upper Norwood, LONDON, SE19 3TD. (Life Member)
STERBOUL, Ms. Isabelle, BA ACA *2004;* 4 Hall Farm Close, STANMORE, HA7 4JT.
STERLAND, Mr. John Hardwick, FCA *1950;* 76 Foxhollow, Bar Hill, CAMBRIDGE, CB23 8ES. (Life Member)
STERLING, Miss. Frances Elizabeth, ACA *1991;* 19 Redgrave Road, Putney, LONDON, SW15 1PX.
STERLING, Miss. Harriet Adele, BSc ACA *2002;* 98 Milton Park, LONDON, N6 5PZ.
STERLING, Mr. John David, BA ACA *1980;* 93 Catalonia Apartments, Metropolitan Station Approach, WATFORD, WD18 7BN.
•STERLING, Mr. Peter Robert, LLB ACA *1987;* Cooper Parry LLP, 3 Centro Place, Pride Park, DERBY, DE24 8RF.
STERLING, Miss. Susan Aline, BSc ACA *1987;* 2 Headley Court, 76 Worple RoadWimbledon, LONDON, SW19 4HY.
STERLING, Mr. William Robert, FCA *1954;* 15 St. Georges Close, Allestree, DERBY, DE22 1JH. (Life Member)
STERN, Mr. Adrian Lionel, FCA *1976;* Flat 3, 10 Rubin Street, JERUSALEM, 97730, ISRAEL.
STERN, Mr. Charles, BSc ACA *2004;* 19 Marine Approach, Burton Waters, LINCOLN, LN1 2WW.
STERN, Mrs. Chitra, ACA MBA BEng(Hons) *1997;* Martinhal Resort, Apt 54, 8650-908 SAGRES, PORTUGAL.
STERN, Mr. Daniel, BA ACA *2006;* 62B Trinity Church Square, LONDON, SE1 4HT.
•STERN, Mr. David Alan, FCA MAE MCIArb *1986;* Stone Turn LLP, 85 Fleet Street, LONDON, EC4Y 1AE.
•STERN, Mr. George Gabor, BSc FCA *1979;* Stern & Company Limited, 12-15 Hanger Green, Ealing, LONDON, W5 3AY. See also Stern & Co, HGR Secretaries Limited
•STERN, Mr. Graham Stewart, FCA *1980;* Blinkhorns, 27 Mortimer Street, LONDON, W1T 3BL.
STERN, Mr. Harry, FCA *1965;* (Member of Council 2002 - 2005), Flat 36 South Grove House, South Grove, LONDON, N6 6LR. (Life Member)
STERN, Mr. Iain James, BSc ACA ATII *1992;* (Tax Fac), with Grant Thornton UK LLP, Grant Thornton House, 202 Silbury Boulevard, MILTON KEYNES, BUCKINGHAMSHIRE, MK9 1LW.
STERN, Miss. Katharine Jessica, BA ACA *2004;* Flat 5, 81 Shepherds Hill, LONDON, N6 5RG.
•STERN, Mr. Michael Charles, FCA *1964;* (Tax Fac), Michael Stern & Co, 61 Shalimar Gardens, Acton, LONDON, W3 9JG.
STERN, Mr. Neil Richard, ACA *2010;* 7 Brookside Close, BARNET, HERTFORDSHIRE, EN5 2PT.
•STERN, Mrs. Sarah Louise, BSc ACA *2005;* Mazuma (North London) Limited, 344-354 Gray's Inn Road, LONDON, WC1X 8BP.
•STERN, Mr. Simon Dan, BSc ACA *1988;* (Tax Fac), Stern Associates, 2 Helenslea Avenue, LONDON, NW11 8ND.
STERN-GILLET, Mrs. Sameera, ACA *2009;* 12 Highfield Drive, Eccles, MANCHESTER, M30 9PZ.
STERNBACH, Mr. Moni, MA ACA *2002;* 31 Kingswood Avenue, LONDON, NW6 6LR.
STERNBERG, Mr. Andrew Peter, BA ACA *2005;* Stemcor Ltd, Citypoint, 1 Ropemaker Street, LONDON, EC2Y 9ST.
•STERNLICHT, Mr. Asher, FCA *1979;* (Tax Fac), Cohen Arnold, New Burlington House, 1075 Finchley Road, Temple Fortune, LONDON, NW11 0PU. See also Cohen Arnold & Co
STERRETT, Mr. Alan Laurence, BSc(Hons) ACA *2003;* Keepax, Coalway Road, Coalway, COLEFORD, GLOUCESTERSHIRE, GL16 7HL.
STERRY, Miss. Gemma, ACA *2010;* Westbrook House, The Village, WESTBURY-ON-SEVERN, GLOUCESTERSHIRE, GL14 1LN.
STERRY, Mr. John Alfred, FCA *1964;* 22 Shelley Avenue, Tiptree, COLCHESTER, CO5 0SF.
STEUART, Mr. Michael John, BA ACA *1988;* 20 Northbourne Road, LONDON, SW4 7DJ.
STEUP, Miss. Vivienne Claudia, BA(Hons) ACA *2001;* 6 Parklawn Avenue, EPSOM, KT18 7SQ.
STEVART, Mr. John Edward Douglas, FCA *1966;* (Tax Fac), 37 Bridge Avenue, UPMINSTER, ESSEX, RM14 2LX.
STEVEN, Mr. Chris, BSc ACA *2006;* 9d Cranwich Road, LONDON, N16 5HZ.
STEVEN, Mr. John Alexander, FCA *1963;* Havencroft, Sevenoaks Way, St Paul's Cray, ORPINGTON, KENT, BR5 3JE.
STEVEN, Mr. Kevin Michael, BA ACA *2011;* 33 Thorncliffe View, Chapeltown, SHEFFIELD, S35 3XU.
STEVEN, Mr. William Frederick Dennis, FCA *1967;* 84 Great Tattenhams, Epsom Downs, EPSOM, KT18 5SE. (Life Member)
STEVENI, Mrs. Alison Clare, MA ACA *1988;* 77A Hereford Road, LONDON, W2 5BB.
•STEVENI, Mr. John Kristian, MA ACA ATII *1988;* PricewaterhouseCoopers LLP, 1 Embankment Place, LONDON, WC2N 6RH. See also PricewaterhouseCoopers
STEVENS, Mr. Adam, MA ACA *2011;* Flat 46, Joules House, 6 Christchurch Avenue, LONDON, NW6 7QW.
STEVENS, Mr. Adrian, BSc ACA *1984;* Fujitsu Observatory House, Windsor Road, SLOUGH, SL1 2EY.
STEVENS, Mr. Alexander, BSc ACA *2010;* Tapycers, High Street, NEWPORT, ESSEX, CB11 3PQ.
•STEVENS, Mrs. Alison Mary, BSc FCA ATII *1990;* (Tax Fac), Alison Stevens & Co, 1 Churchfield, Appledore, BIDEFORD, DEVON, EX39 1RL.
STEVENS, Mr. Alistair David John, BA ACA *1995;* 115 Grandison Road, LONDON, SW11 6LT.
STEVENS, Miss. Amy, BSc ACA *2010;* Flat 4, 17 Broad Street, BANBURY, OXFORDSHIRE, OX16 5BN.
STEVENS, Mr. Andrew Guy Melville, BCom ACA *1990;* Nationwide Autocentres, 7-9 Richmond Road, Olton, SOLIHULL, WEST MIDLANDS, B92 7RN.
•STEVENS, Mr. Andrew Lewes, FCA *1980;* Moore Stephens (South) LLP, The French Quarter, 114 High Street, SOUTHAMPTON, HAMPSHIRE, SO14 2AA. See also Moore Secretaries Limited
STEVENS, Mrs. Anne Maria, ACA *1985;* 15 St. Johns Road, LOUGHTON, ESSEX, IG10 1RZ.
•STEVENS, Mr. Anthony Charles, BSc(Hons) FCA *1994;* CFW, 1 Sterling Court, Loddington, KETTERING, NN14 1RZ.
STEVENS, Mr. Anthony Michael, BA FCA *1982;* 138 Victoria Rise, LONDON, SW4 0NW.
STEVENS, Mr. Ashley, MA ACA *1997;* Axa, 7 Newgate Street, LONDON, EC1A 7NX.
STEVENS, Mrs. Barbara Elizabeth, FCA *1957;* 1 Furners Cottages, Furners Mead, HENFIELD, WEST SUSSEX, BN5 9HL. (Life Member)
STEVENS, Mr. Bernard John, FCA FCMA *1972;* Ardenholme, 47 London Road, GUILDFORD, GU1 1XB.
STEVENS, Mrs. Bridget Dawn, BA ACA *1992;* 12 Lime Tree Road, NORWICH, NR2 2NQ.
•STEVENS, Mr. Bryan Martin, FCA *1986;* Churchills, Lindens House, 16 Copse Wood Way, NORTHWOOD, MIDDLESEX, HA6 2UE.
•STEVENS, Mr. Bryan Russell, ACA *1983;* Armida Limited, Bell Walk House, High Street, UCKFIELD, TN22 5DQ. See also Armida Business Recovery LLP
STEVENS, Mrs. Carol Anne, FCA *1976;* with Shipleys LLP, 3 Godalming Business Centre, Woolsack Way, GODALMING, SURREY, GU7 1XW.
STEVENS, Mrs. Carol Patricia, BA ACA *1996;* Willis Management (Iom) Ltd Tower House, Loch Promenade Douglas, ISLE OF MAN, IM1 2LZ.
STEVENS, Mr. Christian Roger, BSc ACA *1999;* 35 Cirencester Close, BROMSGROVE, WORCESTERSHIRE, B60 2RE.
STEVENS, Mr. Christopher Alexander Simitch, FCA *1972;* Lumirova 21 / 105, 12800 PRAGUE, CZECH REPUBLIC.
STEVENS, Mr. Christopher Brian Murray, BSc ACA *1992;* 34 Argyle Street, PENSHURST, VIC 2222, AUSTRALIA.
STEVENS, Mr. Christopher John Russell, BEng ACA *1993;* 21 Sidegate, HADDINGTON, EAST LOTHIAN, EH41 4BZ.
STEVENS, Miss. Clare Helen, BSc ACA *1996;* 2 Uplands, Llanrhidian, SWANSEA, SA3 1EQ.
•STEVENS, Mr. Clive Robert, FCA *1980;* (Tax Fac), Reeves & Co LLP, Montague Place, Quayside, Chatham Maritime, CHATHAM, KENT ME4 4QU.
•STEVENS, Mr. Colin Roland, FCA *1969;* (Tax Fac), C.R. Stevens, 57 Station Road, TRING, HP23 5NW.
•STEVENS, Mr. Danny, ACA MAAT *2009;* 20 Wren Gardens, Portishead, BRISTOL, BS20 7PQ.
STEVENS, Mr. David, FCA *1964;* 16 Mildmay Court, Odiham, HOOK, RG29 1AX. (Life Member)
STEVENS, Mr. David, FCA *1980;* Fallowfield, Plains Road, Wetheral, CARLISLE, CUMBRIA, CA4 8LE.
STEVENS, Mr. David, FCA *1967;* Bracken End, Combe, Malborough, KINGSBRIDGE, TQ7 3DN. (Life Member)
•STEVENS, Mr. David Anthony, BA ACA *2000;* with BDO LLP, 125 Colmore Row, BIRMINGHAM, B3 3SD.
STEVENS, Mr. David Ernest, FCA *1957;* 32 Island View Avenue, Friars Cliff, CHRISTCHURCH, BH23 4DS. (Life Member)
STEVENS, Mr. David James, LLB ACA *2007;* 1 King George Crescent, Stony Stratford, MILTON KEYNES, MK11 1EF.
•STEVENS, Mr. David John, ACA *1989;* (Tax Fac), Taylor Viney & Marlow, 46-54 High Street, INGATESTONE, CM4 9DW.
STEVENS, Mr. David John, BSc ACA *1988;* C N A Insurance Co Ltd, 2 Minster Court, LONDON, EC3R 7BB.
STEVENS, Mr. David John, BA FCA *1992;* 10 Wyvern Close, WILLENHALL, WEST MIDLANDS, WV12 5UF.
•STEVENS, Mr. David Lee, MBA BA FCA CF *1986;* 2 Murton Street, NEWCASTLE UPON TYNE, TYNE AND WEAR, NE13 9AF.
STEVENS, Miss. Deborah Anne, BSc ACA *1989;* Haydn House, Terrace Lane, RICHMOND, SURREY, TW10 6NF.
STEVENS, Mr. Dennis, FCA *1971;* 22 Brocks Mount, Stoke-Sub-Hamdon, TAUNTON, TA14 6PJ.
STEVENS, Mr. Derek Maurice, BSc FCA *1964;* 62 Dukes Avenue, LONDON, W4 2AF.
STEVENS, Miss. Elizabeth Ann, BSc ACA *1993;* 5/15-21 Dudley Street, COOGEE, NSW 2034, AUSTRALIA.
STEVENS, Mr. Eric, FCA *1954;* High Corner, 28 Merlins Avenue, Merlins Bridge, HAVERFORDWEST, SA61 1JS. (Life Member)
STEVENS, Mr. Gary Charles, BA ACA *1985;* Alfa Laval Ltd, 7 Doman Road, CAMBERLEY, GU15 3DN.
STEVENS, Mr. Geoffrey Robert, BSc FCA *1980;* Beech House, 3 Millhouse Court, SHEFFIELD, S11 9HZ.
•STEVENS, Mr. Geoffrey Wade, BSc FCA *1977;* Wade Stevens, 7a The Broadway, Cheam, SUTTON, SURREY, SM3 8BH.
STEVENS, Mrs. Gim Hoon, BA ACA *1990;* Leag House, 26 Oldborough Drive, Loxley, WARWICK, CV35 9HQ.
STEVENS, Ms. Grace Elanor, BA ACA CTA *2001;* (Tax Fac), Flat 10 Tarranbrae, Willesden Lane, LONDON, NW6 7PL.
STEVENS, Mr. Graham Anthony, FCA *1968;* 27 North Road, Highgate Village, LONDON, N6 4BE.
STEVENS, Mr. Graham George, BA ACA *1981;* 270 Abbeydale Road South, Totley Rise, SHEFFIELD, S17 3LN.
STEVENS, Mr. Gregory Patrick, BA ACA *1987;* Daiwa Capital Markets Europe Ltd, 5 King William Street, LONDON, EC4N 7DA.
STEVENS, Mr. Guy, BSc ACA *1991;* SDMC Consulting Ltd, 27 Westville Road, THAMES DITTON, SURREY, KT7 0UH.
STEVENS, Mr. Guy Julian, BA ACA *1994;* Aslanbucak Mah., 255 Sok No. 2, KEMER, ANTALYA PROVINCE, TURKEY.
STEVENS, Mrs. Helen, BA(Hons) ACA *2001;* W.E.Stevens Haulage, Contractors Limited, 312 Hednesford Road, Norton Canes, CANNOCK, STAFFORDSHIRE WS11 9SA.
STEVENS, Ms. Helen Carolyn, BSc ACA MBA *1990;* 76 Belsize Park Gardens, Hampstead, LONDON, NW3 4NG.
STEVENS, Mrs. Helen Rachael, BA ACA *1994;* 51 Albany Park Drive, Winnersh, WOKINGHAM, RG41 5HZ.
STEVENS, Mr. Hugh Charles, FCA *1973;* Normanton House, Butt Lane, Normanton On Soar, LOUGHBOROUGH, LE12 5EE.
STEVENS, Mr. Ian Douglas, BSc ACA *1992;* 28 The Flats, BROMSGROVE, B61 8LE.
STEVENS, Mr. Ian Herbert, MA ACA *1995;* Bendameer House, BURNTISLAND, FIFE, KY3 0AG.
STEVENS, Mr. Ian James, FCA *1971;* P O Box 24257, Karen, NAIROBI, 00502, KENYA.
•STEVENS, Mr. Ivan Hardy, FCA *1968;* (Tax Fac), I.H. Stevens & Co, 14 Westover Farm, Goodworth Clatford, ANDOVER, HAMPSHIRE, SP11 7LF.
STEVENS, Mr. James William Wade, MA(Cantab) ACA *2010;* 74a Tachbrook Street, LONDON, SW1V 2NA.
STEVENS, Mrs. Jane Hunter, BSocSc ACA *1993;* 12 Tor Avenue, Greenmount, BURY, BL8 4HG.
STEVENS, Miss. Jane Lesley, BSc ACA *1985;* 3 Broadoaks, North Road Leigh Woods, BRISTOL, BS8 3PN.
STEVENS, Mr. Jeremy Grenville, BA ACA *1993;* Concorde Logistics Ltd Unit 4, International Trading Estate Trident Way, SOUTHALL, UB2 5LF.
•STEVENS, Ms. Joanne, BA ACA *1997;* DB Strategies LLP, Unit 1a, Little Braxted Hall, Little Braxted, ESSEX, CM8 3EU. See also Dolphin Business Strategies Ltd
STEVENS, Mr. John Frederick, FCA *1954;* Chestnut Cottage, 1 Blenheim Court, George Hill, ROBERTSBRIDGE, EAST SUSSEX, TN32 5BQ. (Life Member)
STEVENS, Mr. John Frederick, BSc FCA *1974;* (Tax Fac), Crichel Bank, Fore Street, West Camel, YEOVIL, SOMERSET, BA22 7QW.
STEVENS, Mr. John Oliver, FCA *1952;* 21 Derwent Road, Kinsbourne Green, HARPENDEN, AL5 3PA. (Life Member)
STEVENS, Mrs. Joy Melissa, LLB ACA *2002;* 21 Blackett Street, LONDON, SW15 1QG.
STEVENS, Mrs. Karen, ACA *2009;* Camm's House, 64 Church Street, Eckington, SHEFFIELD, S21 4BH.
STEVENS, Mrs. Karen Louise, ACA *2002;* May Gurney Ltd, Trowse, NORWICH, NR14 8SZ.
STEVENS, Mrs. Karen Marie, BA ACA *1987;* 12 Fairwater Close, EVESHAM, WR11 1GF.
STEVENS, Mrs. Katherine Frances Granger, BA ACA *1992;* Redcliffe School, 47 Redcliffe Gardens, LONDON, SW10 9JH.
STEVENS, Mrs. Kathryn Jane, BA(Hons) ACA *2001;* Ashley House Bracknell Lane, Hartley Wintney, HOOK, RG27 8QQ.
STEVENS, Mr. Kevin Michael, BSc ACA *2005;* Kwik-Fit Divisional Office, 216 East Main Street, BROXBURN, WEST LOTHIAN, EH52 5AS.
•STEVENS, Mrs. Lee Sara, BA ACA *1988;* Lee Stevens, Tyelands, Parsonage Lane, Margaretting, INGATESTONE, ESSEX CM4 9JL.
STEVENS, Miss. Leonora Rebecca, ACA *2008;* Flat 109, Ormonde Court, Upper Richmond Road, LONDON, SW15 6TR.
STEVENS, Mr. Leslie Ronald, BA ACA *1986;* Larkspur Cottage, The Plantation, Curdridge, SOUTHAMPTON, SO32 2DT.
STEVENS, Mrs. Linda Mary, ACA *1979;* 5 Sona Merg Close, Hea CornerHeamoor, PENZANCE, TR18 3QL.
STEVENS, Mrs. Lindsey Emma, ACA MAAT *2002;* 1 Mannock Way, Woodley, READING, RG5 4XW.
STEVENS, Mr. Mark Alexander, BSc ACA *1984;* 1 Park Farm Cottages, 32 Leonard Ave, Otford, SEVENOAKS, TN14 5RB.
STEVENS, Mr. Mark David Andrew, BA ACA *1987;* 85 Beatty Avenue, High West Jesmond, NEWCASTLE UPON TYNE, NE2 3QS.
•STEVENS, Mr. Mark Frederick, FCA *1982;* Chantrey Vellacott DFK LLP, 73-75 High Street, STEVENAGE, HERTFORDSHIRE, SG1 3HR.
STEVENS, Mr. Mark Nathan, BA ACA *2003;* Murco Petroleum Ltd, 4 Beaconsfield Road, ST. ALBANS, HERTFORDSHIRE, AL1 3RH.
STEVENS, Mr. Mark Richard, BA FCA *1986;* 7 Emmett Close, Shenley, RADLETT, HERTFORDSHIRE, WD7 9LG.
STEVENS, Mr. Martin John Pemble, FCA *1965;* 38 Deanway, CHALFONT ST. GILES, BUCKINGHAMSHIRE, HP8 4JR. (Life Member)
STEVENS, Mr. Martin Walter, BA FCA CIA *1981;* Konsernrevisjonen, Gjensidige Forsikring, Postboks276, 1326 LYSAKER, NORWAY.
STEVENS, Mr. Matthew, BEng ACA *1996;* Park House, 27 South Avenue, NORWICH, NR7 0EZ.
STEVENS, Mr. Maurice Trevor, FCA *1975;* 44 The Lindens, LOUGHTON, IG10 3HS.
STEVENS, Mr. Michael, ACA *2011;* Flat A, 21 Oldridge Road, LONDON, SW12 8PL.
STEVENS, Mr. Michael Cecil, FCA *1966;* London + Associated Properties plc, 22a St James's Square, LONDON, SW1Y 4JH.
STEVENS, Mr. Michael John, FCA *1973;* 44 Maple Way, COULSDON, SURREY, CR5 3RN.
STEVENS, Mr. Michael John, LVO FCA *1982;* Buckingham Palace, LONDON, SW1A 1AA.
STEVENS, Mr. Michael Joseph Kingaby, FCA *1958;* 64 Hapil Close, Sandford Station, Sandford, WINSCOMBE, AVON, BS25 5AA. (Life Member)
STEVENS, Mr. Michael Kelvin Grist, MA FCA *1975;* Rystwood House, FOREST ROW, RH18 5NA. (Life Member)
•STEVENS, Mr. Michel Hunter, FCA CTA *1974;* Hunter Stevens Limited, 5-6 Maiden Lane, STAMFORD, LINCOLNSHIRE, PE9 2AZ.
STEVENS, Mrs. Nadine Rebecca, BSc ACA *1991;* 27 Westville Road, THAMES DITTON, SURREY, KT7 0UH.
STEVENS, Mr. Nicholas John, BA ACA *2006;* Holy Trinity Brompton, Brompton Road, LONDON, SW7 1JA.
STEVENS, Mr. Nicholas John, BSc ACA *1991;* 16 Royal Belgrave House, Hugh Street, LONDON, SW1V 1RR.

•**STEVENS, Mr. Nicholas Leonard, BA ACA** *2005;* KPMG Channel Islands Limited, 5 St. Andrew's Place, Charing Cross, St. Helier, JERSEY, JE4 8WQ.
STEVENS, Mr. Nicholas Martin, BA ACA *1999;* Ashley House, Bracknell Lane, Hartley Wintney, HOOK, HAMPSHIRE, RG27 8QQ.
•**STEVENS, Mr. Nicholas William, FCA** *1982;* Beever and Struthers, 3rd Floor, Alperton House, Bridgewater Road, WEMBLEY, MIDDLESEX HA0 1EH.
STEVENS, Mr. Nigel Brent, BA ACA *1983;* (Tax Fac), Merrill Lynch Financial Centre, 2 King Edward Street, LONDON, EC1A 1HQ.
STEVENS, Mrs. Panayiota, MA(Oxon) ACA *2000;* 15 Sayes Court, ADDLESTONE, KT15 1LZ.
STEVENS, Mr. Patrick Richard, FCA *1961;* Staddle Stones, Brickyard Lane, Farnsfield, NEWARK, NOTTINGHAMSHIRE, NG22 8JS. (Life Member)
•**STEVENS, Mr. Patrick Tom, FCA** *1972;* (Tax Fac), Ernst & Young LLP, 1 More London Place, LONDON, SE1 2AF. See also Ernst & Young Limited, Ernst & Young Europe LLP
STEVENS, Mr. Paul Richard, BA ACA AMCT *1991;* 38 Silchester Road, GLENAGEARY, COUNTY DUBLIN, IRELAND.
STEVENS, Mr. Peter Douglas, FCA *1974;* 8 Chaucer House, Upper Edgeborough Road, GUILDFORD, GU1 2BD.
STEVENS, Mr. Peter Graham, BA(Hons) ACA *2003;* Sayers Butterworth Llp, 12 Gough Square, LONDON, EC4A 3DW.
•**STEVENS, Mr. Peter John, FCA** *1974;* Carless Stebbings & Co, 31 Westminster Palace Gardens, Artillery Row, LONDON, SW1P 1RR.
STEVENS, Mr. Peter Michael, FCA *1952;* Hurley, 24 The Chilterns, HITCHIN, SG4 9PP. (Life Member)
STEVENS, Mr. Peter William Squire, ACA *1979;* 42 Sutton Court Road, Chiswick, LONDON, W4 4NJ.
STEVENS, Mr. Philip Martin, MSc ACA *1992;* The Forge House, Maiden Street, Weston, HITCHIN, SG4 7AA.
•**STEVENS, Mr. Richard Austin, FCA** *1980;* Reeves & Co LLP, Third Floor, 24 Chiswell Street, LONDON, EC1Y 4YX. See also F W Stephens Taxation Limited
STEVENS, Mr. Richard Bruce, MA FCA *1977;* 15 Deemount Road, ABERDEEN, AB11 7TY.
•**STEVENS, Mr. Richard David, BSc FCA** *1978;* PricewaterhouseCoopers LLP, 1 Embankment Place, LONDON, WC2N 6RH. See also PricewaterhouseCoopers
STEVENS, Mr. Richard David, FCA *1977;* Foxbank, Linden Chase Road, SEVENOAKS, TN13 3JU.
STEVENS, Mr. Robert, BSc FCA *1977;* Spanair, 602 Kingston Road, LONDON, SW20 8DN.
STEVENS, Mr. Robert Brian, BA ACA *1987;* Garden Cottage, Nettleden Road, Little Gaddesden, BERKHAMSTED, HP4 1PN.
•**STEVENS, Mr. Robin, BA FCA** *1980;* Crowe Clark Whitehill LLP, St Bride's House, 10 Salisbury Square, LONDON, EC4Y 8EH. See also Horwath Clark Whitehill LLP
STEVENS, Miss. Rosalind Gayle, BSc ACA *2003;* 68 Tremaine Road, LONDON, SE20 7TZ.
STEVENS, Mrs. Rosemary Ann, BA ACA *1983;* Les Plichons, Courtil De Bas, St. Sampson, GUERNSEY, GY2 4XJ.
•**STEVENS, Mr. Roy, BA(Hons) FCA FCCA** *1977;* Barbel Consulting Limited, Bridge House, Restmor Way, WALLINGTON, SURREY, SM6 7AH.
STEVENS, Mr. Roy, FCA *1955;* 191 Forest Drive, South Park, LYTHAM ST.ANNES, FY8 4QG. (Life Member)
STEVENS, Mrs. Ruth Elizabeth, BA ACA *1995;* 50 Granville St, WILSTON, QLD 4051, AUSTRALIA.
•**STEVENS, Mrs. Sally Elizabeth, BA ACA** *1995;* Applewood LLP, Sycamore House, Church Street, Bentworth, ALTON, HAMPSHIRE GU34 5RB.
STEVENS, Miss. Sarah Jane, BSc ACA *1990;* 69 Pine Road, Chandler's Ford, EASTLEIGH, HAMPSHIRE, SO53 1JU.
STEVENS, Dr. Sheila Jane, PhD BSc ACA *1991;* 9 Aysgarth Close, NUNEATON, CV11 6WA.
STEVENS, Mr. Simon Mark Anthony, BSc ACA *1991;* Leag House 26 Oldborough Drive Loxley, WARWICK, CV35 9HQ.
•**STEVENS, Mrs. Stacey Dawn, ACA** *2001;* Stacey D Charleston ACA, 7 Tug Wilson Close, Northway, TEWKESBURY, GLOUCESTERSHIRE, GL20 8RJ.
STEVENS, Mrs. Stephanie, BSc(Hons) ACA *2002;* 21 Wheatfield, STALYBRIDGE, CHESHIRE, SK15 2TZ.
STEVENS, Mrs. Susan Jane, BSc(Hons) ACA *2004;* Iceland Foods Group Limited, Second Avenue, Deeside Industrial Park, DEESIDE, CLWYD, CH5 2NW.
STEVENS, Miss. Susan Joan, BSc ACA *1988;* 45 Harrow Road, Wollaton, NOTTINGHAM, NG8 1FG.
STEVENS, Mr. Timothy Charles, FCA *1974;* Saul Ewing LLP, Centre Square West, 1500 Market Street, 38th Floor, PHILADELPHIA, PA 19102 UNITED STATES.
STEVENS, Mr. Timothy Dominic Kenneth, BSc(Hons) ACA *2010;* 20 Westmoreland Place, Ealing, LONDON, W5 1QE.
STEVENS, Mr. Trevor Alan, BA FCA *1980;* 22 Park Road, Smallfield, HORLEY, RH6 9RZ.
STEVENS, Miss. Valierie Ann Hedley, FCA MBA *1982;* 21 Holyhead Close, HAILSHAM, BN27 3WD.
•**STEVENS, Mrs. Virginia Jane, BSc FCA** *1987;* KPMG LLP, 3 Assembly Square, Britannia Quay, CARDIFF, CF10 4AX. See also KPMG Europe LLP
STEVENS, Mr. William Paul, FCA *1966;* 11 The Ridge, Blunsdon, SWINDON, SN26 7AD.
STEVENSON, Mr. Adrian John, FCA *1989;* 1 Degens Way, Hugglescote, COALVILLE, LE67 2XD.
•**STEVENSON, Mr. Alan Leonard, BSc FCA** *1979;* (Tax Fac), Stevensons, 6 Sylvan Gardens, SURBITON, SURREY, KT6 6PP.
STEVENSON, Mr. Andrew Mark, MA(Hons) ACA *2001;* 11 Eton Grove, LONDON, SE13 5BY.
STEVENSON, Mr. Anthony, ACA *2009;* Flat 3 Nexus Court, 79 Holywell Hill, ST. ALBANS, HERTFORDSHIRE, AL1 1HF.
•**STEVENSON, Mr. Barr Alexander Peter, BSc(Hons) ACA** *2002;* J&S Accountants Limited, 6 Northlands Road, SOUTHAMPTON, HAMPSHIRE, SO15 2FL.
STEVENSON, Mrs. Beverley Jane, ACA *1986;* The Quoin Stoney Lane Ashmore Green, THATCHAM, BERKSHIRE, RG18 9HE.
STEVENSON, Mr. Christopher Burnett, FCA *1964;* 16 Evelyn Gardens, RICHMOND, SURREY, TW9 2PL.
STEVENSON, Miss. Claire, ACA *2010;* 19 Rowanhill Way, Port Seton, PRESTONPANS, EAST LOTHIAN, EH32 0SZ.
STEVENSON, Mr. Colin Andrew, BA ACA *1989;* 29 Greenways, Hinchley Wood, ESHER, KT10 0QH.
STEVENSON, Mr. Damian Jon, BSc ACA *1995;* Longbenton Foods Ltd, Benton Lane, Londbenton, NEWCASTLE UPON TYNE, NE12 8EF.
STEVENSON, Mr. Darran Mark, BA ACA *1999;* 65 Williams Grove, Long Ditton, SURBITON, SURREY, KT6 5RP.
STEVENSON, Mr. David James, BA ACA *1996;* DEUTSCHE BANK, One Raffles Quay, South Tower, 12th Floor, SINGAPORE 048583, SINGAPORE.
STEVENSON, Mr. David John, BSc FCA *1974;* 36 Salisbury Avenue, WIRRAL, MERSEYSIDE, CH48 0QP.
STEVENSON, Miss. Deborah, FCA *1989;* Rozel Forge, Stapleford Lane, Durley, SOUTHAMPTON, SO32 2BU.
STEVENSON, Miss. Elizabeth, ACA *2010;* 21 Comyn Road, LONDON, SW11 1QB.
•**STEVENSON, Miss. Elizabeth Anne, BA FCA** *1985;* Elizabeth Stevenson, Mullion, Westfield Road, Oakley, BEDFORD, MK43 7SU.
STEVENSON, Miss. Fiona Margaret, BA ACA *1992;* Garth House, Sandy Bank, RIDING MILL, NORTHUMBERLAND, NE44 6HT.
STEVENSON, Mr. Gareth James, BSc ACA *2005;* 18th Floor, CIS Tower, Miller Street, MANCHESTER, M60 0AL.
STEVENSON, Mr. Gavin James, BA ACA *2000;* 36 St Andrew Square, The Royal Bank of Scotland Plc, PO Box 51, EDINBURGH, EH2 2YB.
STEVENSON, Mr. Geoffrey William Hope, BA FCA *1965;* 3 Portinscale Road, LONDON, SW15 2HR. (Life Member)
STEVENSON, Mr. Gordon, BSc ACA *2004;* with RSM Tenon Limited, Salisbury House, 31 Finsbury Circus, LONDON, EC2M 5SQ.
•**STEVENSON, Mr. Gregory Nicholas Christopher Dominic, BA FCA** *1992;* Knox Cropper, 8-9 Well Court, LONDON, EC4M 9DN.
STEVENSON, Miss. Helen, BSc ACA *2010;* 114 Norfolk Street, CAMBRIDGE, CB1 2LF.
STEVENSON, Mrs. Helen Louise, BA ACA *1993;* 1a Ellendale Grange, Worsley, MANCHESTER, M28 7UX.
STEVENSON, Mrs. Jacqueline Denise, BA ACA *1998;* 65 Williams Grove, Long Ditton, SURBITON, KT6 5RP.
•**STEVENSON, Mrs. Janet Mary, BSc FCA** *1975;* (Tax Fac), Henderson Loggie, 34 Melville Street, EDINBURGH, EH3 7HA.
STEVENSON, Mrs. Jean Margaret, MA ACA *1979;* 32 Clapham Common South Side, LONDON, SW4 9BS.
STEVENSON, Mr. Jeremy, ACA *2011;* 14 Florence Close, WATFORD, WD25 0AS.
STEVENSON, Mr. John Anthony, BSc ACA *1998;* The Nook, Wicker Lane, Halebarns, ALTRINCHAM, WA15 0HG.
STEVENSON, Mr. John Christopher, BSc ACA *1989;* 3 Fitzalan Road, Claygate, ESHER, SURREY, KT10 0LX.
STEVENSON, Mr. John Keith, FCA *1975;* 10 Wintringham Crescent, Woodthorpe, NOTTINGHAM, NG5 4PE.
STEVENSON, Mr. John Peter, MBA FCA *1968;* Croft Farm, Whixley, YORK, YO26 8AS.
STEVENSON, Ms. Kathleen Graham Scott, MA ACA *1986;* 36 Graemeslea View, Aberuthven, AUCHTERARDER, PH3 1FG.
STEVENSON, Mr. Kenneth Anthony Patrick, FCA *1973;* 13a Magajin Rumfa Road, PO Box 1021, KANO, NIGERIA.
•**STEVENSON, Miss. Margaret Heather, BA ACA** *1989;* KPMG LLP, 15 Canada Square, LONDON, E14 5GL. See also KPMG Europe LLP
STEVENSON, Mr. Mark, BSc ACA *2000;* K P M G Salisbury Square House, 8 Salisbury Square, LONDON, EC4Y 8BB.
STEVENSON, Mr. Mark Damian, MA ACA *1990;* AAE Ahaus Alstaetter, Neuhofstrasse 4, 6341 BAAR, SWITZERLAND.
•①**STEVENSON, Mr. Michael Francis, BEng FCA** *1990;* Fairleigh, Burgate Cross, FORDINGBRIDGE, HAMPSHIRE, SP6 1LY.
STEVENSON, Mr. Michael James, FCA *1974;* 42 Wilmington Avenue, LONDON, W4 3HA.
STEVENSON, Mr. Michael John, CA *1988;* Scotland 1991); Flat 28 Leicester Court, 24 Clevedon Road, TWICKENHAM, TW1 2TB.
•**STEVENSON, Mr. Nicholas Paul, BA ACA** *1998;* PricewaterhouseCoopers LLP, 1 Embankment Place, LONDON, WC2N 6RH. See also PricewaterhouseCoopers
•**STEVENSON, Mr. Nicholas Raymond, BSc FCA** *1995;* (Tax Fac), Moore and Smalley LLP, Broad House, 8 Regan Way, Chetwynd Business Park, Chilwell, NOTTINGHAM NG9 6RZ.
•**STEVENSON, Mr. Paul, FCA** *1975;* Miller & Co., 86 Princess Street, LUTON, LU1 5AT. See also M & CCA Limited
STEVENSON, Mr. Paul, BA ACA *1983;* Wienerberger Ltd Wienerberger House, Brooks Drive, CHEADLE, CHESHIRE, SK8 3SA.
STEVENSON, Mr. Paul Gregory, BSc ACA *2004;* 2 Bank View, Birkenshaw, BRADFORD, WEST YORKSHIRE, BD11 2AG.
STEVENSON, Mr. Paul Harry, FCA *1964;* The Academy, Gainsborough Road, Winthorpe, NEWARK, NG24 2NR.
STEVENSON, Mr. Paul Montagu, BA ACA *1989;* 2 Mere View Gardens, Appleton, WARRINGTON, WA4 5GA.
•**STEVENSON, Mr. Peter James, MA FCA** *1972;* Peter J Stevenson, 8 Harbord Road, OXFORD, OX2 8LJ.
•**STEVENSON, Mr. Peter John Michael, FCA** *1985;* Hodgsons, 12 Southgate Street, LAUNCESTON, PL15 9DP.
STEVENSON, Mr. Peter Martin, LLB FCA *1974;* 52 Windermere Avenue, LONDON, N3 3RA.
STEVENSON, Mr. Peter Thomas Baxendale, ACA *1981;* 15 Queens Road, SALE, M33 6QA.
STEVENSON, Miss. Rachel, MSc BA ACA *2006;* Warner Brothers Entertainment UK, 98 Theobalds Road, LONDON, WC1X 8WB.
STEVENSON, Mr. Ralph John, BA ACA *1986;* 53 West Avenue South, Chellaston, DERBY, DE73 5SH.
•**STEVENSON, Mr. Robert Andrew, BA FCA ATII** *1985;* with KPMG LLP, Arlington Business Park, Theale, READING, RG7 4SD.
STEVENSON, Mr. Robert Mannington, MA FCA FCII *1979;* Stevenson Consulting Associates Ltd, The Corner Cottage, Devonshire Road, WEYBRIDGE, SURREY, KT13 8HB.
STEVENSON, Mr. Robert Mark, BSc ACA *1999;* 2 The Close, Bladon Houses Newton Solney, BURTON-ON-TRENT, STAFFORDSHIRE, DE15 0SZ.
STEVENSON, Mr. Roy Blandford, FCA *1968;* 14 Woodland Way, PURLEY, CR8 2HU.
STEVENSON, Ms. Terri Louise, BA(Hons) ACA *2009;* Fredericks Foundation, GDLF, PO Box 1086, CHELTENHAM, GLOUCESTERSHIRE, GL50 9LF.
STEVENSON, Mr. Thomas, BSc ACA *1991;* 46 Broadcroft Road, Petts Wood, ORPINGTON, BR5 1EU.
STEVENSON, Mr. William Ronald, MA BA ACA *1991;* Flat 8 Cypress Place, 83 Albemarle Road, BECKENHAM, BR3 5NY.
STEVENSON, Miss. Zowie, BA ACA *2006;* with BDO LLP, 55 Baker Street, LONDON, W1U 7EU.
STEVENSON-HAMILTON, Mr. James Robert Hamish, BSc ACA *1988;* Hayfield House, Park Wall Lane, Upper Basildon, READING, RG8 8NE.
STEVENTON, Mr. David, BA ACA *2004;* 16 Charnwood Drive, Pontprennau, CARDIFF, CF23 8NN.
STEVENTON, Ms. Dianne Michelle, ACA *2002;* 3 Arundel Street, BAYSWATER, WA 6053, AUSTRALIA.
•**STEVENTON, Mr. Michael Alan, BA ACA** *1990;* KPMG LLP, One Snowhill, Snow Hill Queensway, BIRMINGHAM, B4 6GN. See also KPMG Europe LLP
STEWARD, Mr. Andrew, BSc ACA *1996;* 8 Carrion View, Gateford Meadows, WORKSOP, S81 8YZ.
STEWARD, Mr. Andrew James King, BSc FCA *1982;* Furzefield, West End Lane, HASLEMERE, GU27 2EN.
•**STEWARD, Mr. Clive James, BA FCA** *1981;* (Tax Fac), Clive Steward Limited, 7 Spoonbill Road, BRIDGWATER, SOMERSET, TA6 5QZ.
STEWARD, Mrs. Hazel Marie, BSc ACA *1994;* The Warren, High Street, Pidley, HUNTINGDON, PE28 3BX.
STEWARD, Mr. Herbert David Carr, FCA *1965;* The Old Vicarage, Main Street, Askham Richard, YORK, YO23 3PT.
STEWARD, Mr. Ian Keith, BSc FCA *1990;* with BDO LLP, 55 Baker Street, LONDON, W1U 7EU.
STEWARD, Mr. Jack Kenneth, FCA *1953;* 10 Ewhurst Close, SUTTON, SM2 7LN. (Life Member)
STEWARD, Miss. Jane Mary, BSc ACA *1995;* Tower Cottage, Ockham Road South, East Horsley, LEATHERHEAD, SURREY, KT24 6RL.
STEWARD, Mr. Jason, BSc ACA *1995;* 2 West Farm Close, South Luffenham, OAKHAM, LE15 8FE.
•**STEWARD, Mr. John Andrew, MA FCA** *1971;* (Tax Fac), Steward & Co, 5 East Lane, LONDON, SE16 4UD.
STEWARD, Mr. Jonathan Mark, BSc ACA *2007;* Flat 20, 205 Balham High Road, LONDON, SW17 7AD.
STEWARD, Mrs. Kirsty Helen, BA(Hons) ACA *2002;* Atrium Underwriters Ltd, Room 790, Lloyds Building, 1 Lime Street, LONDON, EC3M 7DQ.
STEWARD, Mr. Leslie Charles, FCA *1957;* Papillons, 3 Thomson Close, BRIDPORT, DT6 5EU. (Life Member)
STEWARD, Mrs. Mandy Jayne, BSc FCA *1990;* 2 Meadow Bank, GUILDFORD, GU1 1FD.
•**STEWARD, Mrs. Valerie Elizabeth, BSc ACA FCCA** *1986;* VS Consultancy Limited, Greenfield Farm, 23 West Street, Hibaldstow, BRIGG, SOUTH HUMBERSIDE DN20 9NY.
STEWARD, Mr. William Robert, BEng ACA *2002;* U B S AG, 100 Liverpool Street, LONDON, EC2M 2RH.
STEWARDSON, Mr. Christopher David, BSc ACA *2010;* 31 Station Street, Hazel Grove, STOCKPORT, CHESHIRE, SK7 4EX.
STEWART, Mrs. Abigail Alexandra, BSc ACA *2002;* with KPMG LLP, St. James's Square, MANCHESTER, M2 6DS.
STEWART, Mr. Alan Trevor, BA ACA *1986;* 1 Norwich Road, Stoke Holy Cross, NORWICH, NR14 8AB.
STEWART, Mr. Alasdair Bruce, MA FCA *1983;* Ernst & Young, Wanderers Office Park, 52 Corlett Drive, ILLOVO, SOUTH AFRICA.
STEWART, Mr. Alastair, BSc ACA *2011;* 10 Swift Road, STRATFORD-UPON-AVON, CV37 6TS.
•**STEWART, Mr. Alastair James, FCA** *1969;* (Tax Fac), with Plummer Parsons, 18 Hyde Gardens, EASTBOURNE, BN21 4PT.
STEWART, Mr. Alaster Neil Macdonald, BA ACA *1999;* 116C Horatio Place, 116 Kingston Road, Wimbledon, LONDON, SW19 1LY.
STEWART, Mr. Alistair Grahame, FCA *1973;* Newhouse of Jackton, East Kilbride, GLASGOW, G75 8RR.
•**STEWART, Ms. Alysoun Freya Elisabeth, BA ACA** *1987;* 5 St Lawrence Road, South Hinksey, OXFORD, OX1 5AZ.
STEWART, Mrs. Amanda, BSc ACA CTA MCT *1993;* 11 Hillersdon Avenue, Barnes, LONDON, SW13 0EG.
STEWART, Mr. Andrew Dominic, BSc ACA *2006;* Butlers Cottage, Tichborne, ALRESFORD, SO24 0NA.
STEWART, Mr. Andrew Martin Douglas, ACA *2009;* 49 Meols Drive, Hoylake, WIRRAL, MERSEYSIDE, CH47 4AF.
STEWART, Mrs. Angela, BA ACA *1991;* Hollyberry House, Village Street, Offchurch, LEAMINGTON SPA, WARWICKSHIRE, CV33 9AP.
STEWART, Miss. Angeline, BA(Hons) ACA *2010;* 17 Hurn Walk, Thornaby, STOCKTON-ON-TEES, CLEVELAND, TS17 9EF.
STEWART, Miss. Anna, BSc ACA *1993;* 38 Gosforth Lane, DRONFIELD, DERBYSHIRE, S18 1PR.
STEWART, Miss. Anna, BSc ACA *2011;* 35 Spring Lane Colden Common, WINCHESTER, SO21 1SB.
STEWART, Mrs. Annette Jeanette, ACA *2008;* 24 Sutterton Drove, Amber Hill, BOSTON, LINCOLNSHIRE, PE20 3RQ.

STEWART, Mr. Archibald Ian Thomas, FCA *1970;* W C F Fuels Ltd, Craw Hall, BRAMPTON, CA8 1TN.
STEWART, Miss. Barbara Ann, BA ACA *1984;* 17 Chapel Lane, Letty Green, HERTFORD, SG14 2PA.
•STEWART, Mr. Barry John, LLB ACA *1999;* Wilson Andrews Limited, 145 St. Vincent Street, GLASGOW, G2 5JF. See also Wilson Andrews
STEWART, Mr. Barry Sinclair, FCA *1960;* Flat 3, Kingsland Court, 16 Ravine Road, Canford Cliffs, POOLE, DORSET BH13 7HX. (Life Member)
•STEWART, Mr. Calum William, ACA *1982;* PKF (UK) LLP, Farringdon Place, 20 Farringdon Road, LONDON, EC1M 3AP.
•STEWART, Mrs. Caroline Elizabeth, BSc FCA CTA *1989;* Professional Accountancy & Business Services Limited, 5 Plainview Close, Aldridge, WALSALL, WS9 0YY.
STEWART, Mr. Charles James, FCA *1967;* Clyvers, Toys Hill, WESTERHAM, TN16 1QE. (Life Member)
STEWART, The Revd. Charles Michael, MA BA FCA AKC *1976;* Rickstones, Punchbowl Lane, DORKING, RH5 4BN.
STEWART, Mr. Charles Robert, BA ACA *1983;* Melrose Sunny Bank, Widmer End, HIGH WYCOMBE, BUCKINGHAMSHIRE, HP15 6PA.
STEWART, Mrs. Cherry, BSc ACA *2006;* Flat 19 Smeaton Court, Cornmill View Horsforth, LEEDS, LS18 5NG.
STEWART, Mrs. Christina Marie, BSc ACA CTA *2001;* 12 Cambrian Drive, Marshfield, CARDIFF, CF3 2TE.
STEWART, Mr. Christopher James Edward, FCA *1966;* 30 Maple Walk, Pucklechurch, BRISTOL, BS16 9RJ.
•STEWART, Mr. Christopher John, FCA *1970;* (Tax Fac), Stewart & Co LLP, Ebenezer House, 5a Poole Road, BOURNEMOUTH, BH2 5QJ.
STEWART, Mr. Christopher Joseph, ACA *1995;* 8 Tayberry Grove, Up Hatherley, CHELTENHAM, GLOUCESTERSHIRE, GL51 3WF.
•STEWART, Mr. Christopher Norman, BA FCA *1988;* (Tax Fac), Stewarts Accountants Limited, 271 High Street, BERKHAMSTED, HERTFORDSHIRE, HP4 1AA.
STEWART, Miss. Claire Elizabeth, BSc ACA *2005;* with KPMG LLP, 15 Canada Square, LONDON, E14 5GL.
STEWART, Mr. Colin Leonard, ACA *1988;* 29 Beech Avenue, BIGGLESWADE, SG18 0EG.
STEWART, Mr. Craig Andrew, MA ACA *1997;* R & H Fund Services (Jersey) Ltd, Ordnance House, 31 Pier Road, St Helier, JERSEY, JE4 8PW.
•STEWART, Ms. Danielle Caroline, FCA FCCA FRSA *1985;* Baker Tilly UK Audit LLP, The Clock House, 140 London Road, GUILDFORD, SURREY, GU1 1UW. See also Baker Tilly Tax and Advisory Services LLP
•STEWART, Mr. David, BSc FCA *1986;* Rowland Hall, 44-54 Orsett Road, GRAYS, RM17 5ED.
STEWART, Mr. David, BA ACA *1991;* Hollyberry House, Village Street, Offchurch, LEAMINGTON SPA, WARWICKSHIRE, CV33 9AP.
STEWART, Mr. David Andrew, BSc ACA *1992;* 1 Hilltop Road, Cults, ABERDEEN, AB15 9RN.
STEWART, Mr. David Ian, BSc ACIB FCA *1979;* Rushall House, Earls Lane, Deddington, BANBURY, OX15 0TH.
STEWART, Mr. David Purcell, FCA *1963;* Flat 21, St. Michaels, Wolfs Row, Limpsfield, OXTED, SURREY RH8 0QL. (Life Member)
STEWART, Miss. Diane, BCom ACA *1992;* Buchanan Communications, 45 Moorfields, LONDON, EC2Y 9AE.
STEWART, Mrs. Eleanor, ACA *2007;* Flat 10, 8 East Pilton Farm Crescent, EDINBURGH, EH5 2GH.
STEWART, Miss. Emma Helen Hamilton, MA ACA *2002;* Newlands Manor House Bournemouth Road, Charlton Marshall, BLANDFORD FORUM, DORSET, DT11 9NE.
STEWART, Mr. Frank Arthur, FCA *1934;* 4 Sheriffs Close, Boley Park, LICHFIELD, WS14 9RZ. (Life Member)
STEWART, Mr. Giles Alexander Jamie, MA(Hons) ACA *2000;* 215 Richmond Road, TWICKENHAM, TW1 2NJ.
STEWART, Mr. Gordon, BSc ACA *1982;* BAE Systems Finance, FSS Pavillions, Portway, PRESTON, PR2 2YQ.
STEWART, Mr. Graeme Rodger, BSc ACA *2002;* 2/56 St Georges Bay Road, Parnell, AUCKLAND 1052, NEW ZEALAND.
STEWART, Mr. Hamish John, BSc FCA *1983;* Postfach 18 24, 53828 TROISDORF, GERMANY.
STEWART, Mrs. Hilary, BSc ACA *1988;* 22 Lindisfarne Road, LONDON, SW20 0NW.
•STEWART, Mr. Iain Elliott, BA ACA *1980;* (Tax Fac), 35 Cambridge Road, BROMLEY, BR1 4EB. See also Elliott Stewart & Co
STEWART, Mr. Iain James, BA ACA *2001;* 77 Grosvenor Street, LONDON, W1K 3JR.
STEWART, Mr. Ian Christopher, BA ACA *1984;* with Ernst & Young LLP, 1 More London Place, LONDON, SE1 2AF.
STEWART, Mr. Ian Gordon, BA ACA *1986;* 1 Chevet Croft, Sandal, WAKEFIELD, WF2 6QR.
•STEWART, Mr. Ian Peter, FCA *1976;* (Tax Fac), Independent Auditors LLP, Emstrey House, Sitka Drive, Shrewsbury Business Park, SHREWSBURY, SY2 6LG. See also Contractor Taxation Services Limited
STEWART, Mr. Ian Philip, BA ACA *1982;* 214 Wellmeadow Road, Catford, LONDON, SE6 1HS.
•STEWART, Mr. James Alexander Hugh, FCA *1968;* James Stewart & Co., 72 Church Road, WINSCOMBE, BS25 1BJ.
•STEWART, Mr. James Bishop, FCA *1969;* James Stewart & Co, St Marys, Forches Cross, Bovey Road, NEWTON ABBOT, TQ12 6PU.
STEWART, Mr. James Henry, BA ACA *2002;* 9 Zenobia Mansions, Queens Club Gardens, LONDON, W14 9TD.
STEWART, Dr. Jamie Douglas, PhD BSc ACA *2005;* Provident Financial PLC Business Risk, No.1 Godwin Street, BRADFORD, BD1 2SU.
STEWART, Mrs. Jane Victoria, BA ACA *1987;* 43 Homewood Road, ST. ALBANS, HERTFORDSHIRE, AL1 4BG.
STEWART, Mrs. Janice Elizabeth, BSc ACA *1988;* 2a Beacon Drive, WIRRAL, MERSEYSIDE, CH48 7ED.
•STEWART, Mr. Jeremy David, FCA *1980;* (Tax Fac), Jeremy Stewart, Basepoint Centre, 70 The Havens, IPSWICH, IP3 9BF. See also J D Stewart
STEWART, Mrs. Jill Dianne, BEng ACA *1990;* 20 Lady Place, Sutton Courtenay, ABINGDON, OX14 4FB.
•STEWART, Mr. John Alexander, FCA *1969;* SASPI, Via della Moscova 3, 20121 MILAN, MI, ITALY.
STEWART, Mr. John Ashley, BA ACA *1995;* U B S, 1 Broadgate, LONDON, EC2M 2BS.
•STEWART, Mr. John Francis, MA FCA *1974;* Tuschgenweg 89, 8041 ZURICH, SWITZERLAND.
STEWART, Mr. John Hamish Watson, ACA *2010;* 16b Beauchamp Road, Clapham, LONDON, SW11 1PQ.
STEWART, Mr. John Hugh, BSc ACA *1988;* 18 Welbeck Street, Whitwell, WORKSOP, S80 4TW.
STEWART, Mr. John Hugh Shipley, FCA *1966;* 78 Southampton Road, FAREHAM, PO16 7EA.
•STEWART, Mr. John Purves, FCA *1958;* J.P. Stewart, Devenish Cottage, Devenish Road, Sunningdale, ASCOT, SL5 9QP.
STEWART, Mr. John Sanderson, MA MSc FCA *1977;* (Tax Fac), Amberlea, College Avenue, MAIDSTONE, ME15 6YJ.
STEWART, Mr. John Wyllie, BA FCA *1961;* 6 Kingsbury Drive, WILMSLOW, CHESHIRE, SK9 2GU. (Life Member)
•STEWART, Miss. Kathrine Gay, ACA *1995;* Kathrine Stewart, Fieldview, La Rue de Samares, St. Clement, JERSEY, JE2 6LZ.
STEWART, Miss. Katrina Louise, BSc(Hons) ACA *2001;* 11 Silure Way, Langstone, NEWPORT, GWENT, NP18 2NU.
STEWART, Miss. Lauren Louise, LLB ACA *1989;* (Tax Fac), Idea Group Ltd, Station House, 2-6 Station Approach, HARPENDEN, HERTFORDSHIRE, AL5 4SS.
STEWART, Miss. Lucy, MA ACA *2007;* 7 Kenilworth Gate, Wellgate Drive Bridge of Allan, STIRLING, FK9 4RG.
STEWART, Mr. Malcolm De Mowbray Adam, FCA *1959;* Turnberry Consulting Ltd, 41-43 Maddox Street, LONDON, W1S 2PD. (Life Member)
STEWART, Mr. Martin David, BA ACA *1991;* 109 Castelnau, Barnes, LONDON, SW13 9EL.
STEWART, Mr. Martin Richard, BA FCA *1986;* Park Group Plc, Valley Road, BIRKENHEAD, MERSEYSIDE, CH41 7ED.
STEWART, Mrs. Mary Helen, BSc ACA *1979;* Brilley Green Farm, Brilley, Whitney-on-Wye, HEREFORD, HR3 6JB.
STEWART, Mr. Matthew Hartley, BSc ACA *2004;* P Z Cussons (UK) Ltd, 3500 Aviator Way, MANCHESTER, M22 5TG.
•STEWART, Mr. Michael Alasdair, BEng FCA *1999;* Mazars LLP, Clifton Down House, Beaufort Buildings, Clifton Down, Clifton, BRISTOL BS8 4AN.
STEWART, Mr. Michael Anthony, FCA *1967;* 395 Cordell Drive, DANVILLE, CA 94526, UNITED STATES.
•STEWART, Mr. Michael George, FCA *1962;* (Tax Fac), with Chavereys, Mall House, The Mall, FAVERSHAM, KENT, ME13 8JL.
STEWART, Mr. Michael Guy, BA FCA *1989;* Round Lodge, Reigate Road, Buckland, BETCHWORTH, SURREY, RH3 7BQ.
STEWART, Mr. Michael Henley, BA FCA *1974;* Oak Cottage Cheapside Lane, Denham, UXBRIDGE, UB9 5AD.
STEWART, Mr. Michael John, BSc ACA *1995;* 5 Charleston Court, Forestfield, CRAWLEY, WEST SUSSEX, RH10 6PT.
STEWART, Mr. Michael John, FCA *1956;* Coin of the Realm Ltd, P O Box N.4845, NASSAU, BAHAMAS. (Life Member)
STEWART, Mr. Michael Richard, BA ACA *1991;* 105 Hemper Lane, Greenhill, SHEFFIELD, S8 7FB.
STEWART, Miss. Natalie Emma, BSc ACA *2004;* 30 Allergill Park, Upperthong, HOLMFIRTH, HD9 3XH.
STEWART, Mr. Nicholas, BA FCA *1991;* I D S Ltd, 10 Didcot Way Boldon Business Park, BOLDON COLLIERY, TYNE AND WEAR, NE35 9PD.
•STEWART, Mr. Nicholas David, ACA FCCA *1983;* Dental Business Solutions, Network House, Station Yard, THAME, OXFORDSHIRE, OX9 3UH.
STEWART, Mr. Nick James, LLB ACA *2005;* Barclays Capital, 5 North Colonnade, LONDON, E14 4BB.
STEWART, Mrs. Nina, BSc ACA CTA *2002;* Acergy, 200 Hammersmith Road, LONDON, W6 7DL.
STEWART, Mr. Patrick Robert Nesbitt, MC TD FCA *1947;* Middle Point, Castle Drive, FALMOUTH, TR11 4NQ. (Life Member)
STEWART, Mr. Patrick Rupert Cooper, FCA *1982;* 137 West End Lane, LONDON, NW6 2PH.
STEWART, Mr. Paul Douglas, BA ACA *1985;* Shell UK, Rowlandsway House, Rowlandsway, Wythensuawe, MANCHESTER, M22 5SB.
•STEWART, Mr. Peter, FCA *1976;* Gregory Priestley & Stewart, Lyndhurst, 1 Cranmer Street, Long Eaton, NOTTINGHAM, NG10 1NJ. See also Good Payroll Services Ltd
•STEWART, Mr. Peter Denis, BSc FCA *1982;* Moore Stephens LLP, 150 Aldersgate Street, LONDON, EC1A 4AB. See also Moore Stephens & Co
•STEWART, Mr. Peter Geoffrey, ACA *1979;* Peter G Stewart, 41 Warren Road, BANSTEAD, SM7 1LG.
STEWART, Mr. Peter Norman, BSc ACA *1997;* 19 Mount Pleasant Road, LONDON, W5 1SG.
STEWART, Mr. Philip, BA ACA *1982;* 29 The Maltings Staithe Road, BUNGAY, SUFFOLK, NR35 1EJ.
STEWART, Mr. Philip James, BSc ACA *2004;* 19 Rupert Neve Close, Melbourn, ROYSTON, HERTFORDSHIRE, SG8 6FB.
STEWART, Mr. Quentin Richard, BA ACA *1994;* Flat 62, Anchor Brewhouse, 50 Shad Thames, LONDON, SE1 2LY.
STEWART, Mr. Richard, LLB ACA *2006;* 12 Orchard Green, ALDERLEY EDGE, CHESHIRE, SK9 7DT.
•STEWART, Mr. Richard Charles, FCA *2000;* (Tax Fac), Burgess Hodgson, Camburgh House, 27 New Dover Road, CANTERBURY, CT1 3DN.
STEWART, Mr. Richard Matthew, LLB ACA *2003;* Bramdean Asset Management Llp, 6 Derby Street, LONDON, W1J 7AD.
STEWART, Mr. Robert George, BSc ACA *2009;* 6c South Terrace, SURBITON, KT6 6HT.
STEWART, Mr. Robin Graham, FCA *1971;* suite 7, Belgrave Mansions, Belgrave Gardens, LONDON, NW8 0RA. (Life Member)
STEWART, Mr. Robin Hinton, MA FCA *1957;* The Corn House, Mottram Hall Farm, Wilmslow Road, Mottram St. Andrew, MACCLESFIELD, CHESHIRE SK10 4QT. (Life Member)
STEWART, Mr. Ronald, BA(Hons) ACA *1998;* 60 Dalton Way, HOLLAND, PA 18966, UNITED STATES.
STEWART, Miss. Rosemary Elizabeth, BSc ACA *2007;* GECC (Funding) Limited The Ark, 201 Talgarth Road, LONDON, W6 8BJ.
STEWART, Mrs. Ruth Mary, FCA *1953;* Farm Cottage, Trevorrick, St Merryn, PADSTOW, PL28 8PP. (Life Member)
STEWART, Miss. Sally Ann, BA(Hons) ACA *2011;* 3 Warwick House, Warwick Road, BEACONSFIELD, HP9 2PE.
STEWART, Mr. Samuel Stephen, BSc ACA FSI *1994;* 43 Effra Road, LONDON, SW2 1BZ.
STEWART, Miss. Sarah Lindsey, BSc ACA CTA *1995;* I Hennig & Co Ltd, 27 Ely Place, LONDON, EC1N 6TD.
STEWART, Miss. Sophie, BSc ACA *2011;* Flat 33, North Contemporis, 20 Merchants Road, Clifton, BRISTOL, BS8 4HH.
STEWART, Mrs. Susan Linda, BSc ACA *1987;* 109 Castelnau, LONDON, SW13 9EL.
STEWART, Mr. Terence Martyn, FCA *1964;* 257 Avenue des Alpes, 01220 DIVONNE-LES-BAINS, FRANCE. (Life Member)
STEWART, Mr. Terry Turner, ACA *2010;* 76 Butlers Close, BRISTOL, BS5 8AX.
STEWART, Mr. Timothy Paul, LLM ACA *2001;* RBS Plc, RBS Tower, 88 Philip Street, SYDNEY, NSW 2000, AUSTRALIA.
STEWART, Mrs. Victoria Anne, BSc(Hons) ACA *2001;* Millgrove, 1 Chailey Rise, Clutton, CHESTER, CH3 9SL.
STEWART, Mrs. Victoria Elaine, BCom ACA *2005;* 12 Orchard Green, ALDERLEY EDGE, CHESHIRE, SK9 7DT.
STEWART-ROBERTS, Mr. Daniel James Bamfield, MA ACA *1984;* CEOC Limited, 33 St. James's Square, LONDON, SW1Y 4JS.
STEWART-SANDEMAN, Mr. Nairnee, FCA *1951;* Ronda De Toledo 36 4D, 28005 MADRID, SPAIN. (Life Member)
STEYER, Miss. Hanna Wyn, ACA *2008;* 21 Tai ar y Bryn, BUILTH WELLS, POWYS, LD2 3US.
STEYN, Mr. Leon, ACA CA(SA) *2009;* 10 Close Des Fontaines, Rue Croutes, St Marten, GUERNSEY, GY4 6RF.
STEYN, Mrs. Sarita, ACA CA(SA) *2011;* 10 Clos Des Fountaines, Rue Des Croutes, St Martin, GUERNSEY, GY4 6RF.
STHANKIYA, Mr. Pratish Ramesh, BA ACA *2000;* 1550 W Cornelia Avenue, Unit 305, CHICAGO, IL 60657, UNITED STATES.
STIBBARD KINSEY, Mrs. Joanne Clare, BSc ACA *1993;* 1 Oxendown, Meonstoke, SOUTHAMPTON, SO32 3AE.
STIBBS, Mr. Christopher John, MA ACA MCT *1990;* 1 Noah's Court Gardens, Mangrove Road, HERTFORD, HERTFORDSHIRE, SG13 8FD.
STIBBS, Mr. Paul William, ACA *1979;* 6 Highfield Gr, STAFFORD, ST17 9RA.
STICKELLS, Mr. Richard John, FCA *1972;* Triscombe, Stormore, Dilton Marsh, WESTBURY, BA13 4BH. (Life Member)
STICKINGS, Mr. Robert Anthony, FCA *1967;* Tebmar LTD, 77 Harrowden Road, WELLINGBOROUGH, NORTHAMPTONSHIRE, NN8 5BD.
STICKLAND, Mr. Alfred Francis, FCA *1956;* Hillcrest, Beach Road, Carlyon Bay, ST AUSTELL, CORNWALL, PL25 3PQ. (Life Member)
•STICKLAND, Mr. Andrew John, BA FCA *1987;* BDO LLP, Emerald House, East Street, EPSOM, SURREY, KT17 1HS. See also BDO Stoy Hayward LLP
STICKLAND, Mrs. Annabel Kate, BA ACA *1999;* Jonathans Thatch, Ramsdell Road, Monk Sherborne, TADLEY, HAMPSHIRE, RG26 5HS.
STICKLAND, Mr. David George, BSc FCA MBA CDir *1997;* Leaseplan UK Ltd, 165 Bath Road, SLOUGH, SL1 4AA.
STICKLER, Mr. Michael Macdonald, BA FCA *1970;* Park House, 8 Somerville Gardens, TUNBRIDGE WELLS, TN4 8EP. (Life Member)
STICKLEY, Miss. Claire Marie, BSc(Hons) AMIMA ACA *2009;* Flat 12, Carlton House, 1-6 Western Parade, SOUTHSEA, HAMPSHIRE, PO5 3ED.
STICKLEY, Mrs. Sakiko, MA ACA *2003;* 806 Compartment Tokyo-Chuo, 3-24-1, Hachobori, Chuo-ku, TOKYO, JAPAN.
STIDWELL, Mr. Raymond Henry, BSc FCA *1979;* Vine Tree House Back Street, Wendover, AYLESBURY, BUCKINGHAMSHIRE, HP22 6EB.
STIEBER, Mr. Anthony David Simeon, BSc FCA *1962;* 154 Route de Suisse, 1290 VERSOIX, SWITZERLAND. (Life Member)
STIER, Mr. John Robert, BA FCA *1992;* 23 Coppins Close, BERKHAMSTED, HP4 3NZ.
STIFF, Mr. David Charles, FCA *1972;* 27 Corringway, LONDON, W5 3AB.
STIFF, Mr. Geoffrey William, BA ACA *1995;* Black Pond FarmHouse, Fleming Road, Woodnesborough, SANDWICH, KENT, CT13 0PX.
STIFF, Mr. Graeme Robert George, BA ACA *1986;* Parkdene, Park Avenue, Farnborough Park, ORPINGTON, BR6 8LH.
STIHL, Miss. Selina, MSc BA ACA *2006;* Hollandische Reihe 11, 22765 HAMBURG, GERMANY.
STILES, Miss. Alison Clare, MA ACA *1997;* Willow Tree Cottage, Stoney Lane, Ashmore Green, THATCHAM, RG18 9HE.
STILES, Miss. Deborah, BA ACA *1992;* 74 Wilford Road, Ruddington, NOTTINGHAM, NG11 6EY.
STILES, Mrs. Gillian Ann Elizabeth, BSc FCA *1978;* 22 Fairford Close, HAYWARDS HEATH, WEST SUSSEX, RH16 3EF.
STILES, Mrs. Holly, BA(Hons) ACA *2002;* Grant Thornton, Level 1, 10 Kings Park Road, WEST PERTH, WA 6005, AUSTRALIA.
STILES, Mrs. Janet, FCA *1982;* 16 New Road, Aston Clinton, AYLESBURY, HP22 5JD.

STILES, Miss. Janice Susan, BSc ACA CTA TEP *1992;* Cleaver Croxford LLP, Riding School House, Bulls Lane, Wishaw, SUTTON COLDFIELD, WEST MIDLANDS B76 9QW.
STILES, Mrs. Kathryn Mary, BSc(Hons) ACA CTA *1994;* Kings House, 12 - 42 Wood Street, KINGSTON UPON THAMES, SURREY, KT1 1TG.
STILES, Mr. Neil Jonathan, BA FCA *1976;* 15 Greyfriars Crescent, Redwood, Tawa, WELLINGTON 5028, NEW ZEALAND.
STILES, Mr. Neville Cutcliffe, FCA *1962;* 67 Butcher Road, Roleystone, PERTH, WA 6111, AUSTRALIA. (Life Member)
STILGOE, Mr. Charles Robin John, FCA *1964;* 4A Eliot Place, LONDON, SE3 0QL. (Life Member)
STILGOE, Miss. Rachael Emily, BSc(Hons) ACA *2002;* Grounds Farm, Oxford Road, Adderbury, BANBURY, OX17 3HQ.
STILING, Miss. Dianne Margaret, BA FCA *1973;* Flat 111, Lily Close, St. Pauls Court, LONDON, W14 9YB.
STILL, Mr. Anthony William, FCA *1965;* 10 Abbey Water, ROMSEY, SO51 8EJ. (Life Member)
STILL, Mrs. Barbara, BA ACA *1978;* Newstead Mill, Main Street, Newstead, MELROSE, ROXBURGHSHIRE, TD6 9RR.
•STILL, Mr. David Roy, FCA *1979;* Bristow Still, 39 Sackville Road, HOVE, BN3 3WD.
STILL, Mrs. Marie Irene Jane, BSc FCA *1978;* Greencoat House, 15 Francis Street, LONDON, SW1P 1DH.
STILL, Mr. Richard Dudley, BA FCA *1966;* 9 Royal Chase, TUNBRIDGE WELLS, TN4 8AX.
STILL, Mr. Richard Matthew, ACA *1989;* Danoptra Ltd, Low Lane, Horsforth, LEEDS, LS18 4ER.
STILL, Mr. Simon Anthony, BA ACA *1999;* 29 Winterwell Road, LONDON, SW2 5JB.
STILL, Mr. Simon Raymond, BSc ACA *2001;* 7 Avenue Road, BRENTFORD, MIDDLESEX, TW8 9NS.
STILLERMAN, Mr. Barry Ian, FCA *1974;* Hazelmere Lodge, 34 Canons Drive, EDGWARE, MIDDLESEX, HA8 7QT.
STILLIT, Mr. Gerald Barry, FCA *1960;* 11 Hyde Park Street, LONDON, W2 2JW. (Life Member)
STILLWELL, Mr. Geoffrey Stanton, BSc ACA *1995;* Greenways, Church Fields, Hurstpierpoint, HASSOCKS, WEST SUSSEX, BN6 9TU.
STILLWELL, Mr. Michael Ian, FCA *1962;* Snarlton Farm, Wingfield, TROWBRIDGE, BA14 9LH.
•STILWELL, Ms. Margaret Ann, BCom ACA *1995;* Ernst & Young LLP, 1 More London Place, LONDON, SE1 2AF. See also Ernst & Young Europe LLP
STILWELL, Mr. Michael James, BSc(Hons) ACA *2001;* 59 Rumbush Lane, Dickens Heath, Shirley, SOLIHULL, B90 1TJ.
STILWELL, Mr. Russell Erich Norman, BSc ACA *1994;* 7 Kingsbury Avenue, ST. ALBANS, AL3 4TA.
STIMPSON, Mr. Andrew David, BA ACA *1989;* Warmup Plc Unit 702, Tudor Estate Abbey Road, LONDON, NW10 7UW.
STIMPSON, Mr. Anthony Gwilym, BSc ACA *1986;* The Garden House, 18 Heathway, Blackheath, LONDON, SE3 7AN.
STIMPSON, Mr. Jeremy Guy, ACA *1990;* Crown Closures UK Plc, Lake Road, POOLE, DORSET, BH15 4LJ.
STIMPSON, Mrs. Joanne Elizabeth, LLB ACA *1986;* South East Water Ltd, Rocfort Road, SNODLAND, KENT, ME6 5AH.
STIMPSON, Mr. John Mercer, FCA *1958;* White Ladies, 27 Chacombe Road, Middleton Cheney, BANBURY, OX17 2QU. (Life Member)
•STIMPSON, Mr. John Robert, FCA *1982;* (Tax Fac), Hand in Hand Business Solutions Ltd, 1 & 2 Hillbrow House, Linden Drive, LISS, HAMPSHIRE, GU33 7RJ. See also Howard Smith & Co Limited and Hand in Hand Buisness Solutions Ltd
•STIMPSON, Mrs. Linda Gwyneth, BA ACA *1981;* 29 Mill Close, Fishbourne, CHICHESTER, WEST SUSSEX, PO19 3JW.
STIMPSON, Mr. Michael Harborne, FCA *1955;* 3 Orchard Close, Grove Lane, HOLT, NR25 6AT. (Life Member)
STIMPSON, Mr. Peter Richard, BA ACA *1987;* Converteam UK Ltd, Alstom Power Conversion Ltd, Boughton Road, RUGBY, CV21 1BU.
STIMSON, Mr. John Brian, FCA *1968;* 61 Voyagers Drive, BANKSIA BEACH, QLD 4507, AUSTRALIA.
STIMSON, Mr. Philip Edward Maxwell, BSc(Econ) ACA *1999;* Thurston House Danes Road, Awbridge, ROMSEY, HAMPSHIRE, SO51 0HL.
STIMSON, Mrs. Rachel, BSc ACA *2007;* Camera Dynamics Ltd, Western Way, BURY ST. EDMUNDS, SUFFOLK, IP33 3TB.
STINCHCOMBE, Mr. David William, BA ACA *1992;* 4 Darlington Close, CARSELDINE, QLD 4034, AUSTRALIA.
STINCHCOMBE, Mr. Mark Andrew, BSc ACA *1983;* 14 Gossmore Walk, MARLOW, SL7 1QZ.
STINSON, Mr. Gregory John, ACA *2008;* 3 Roseberry View, Newton under Roseberry, MIDDLESBROUGH, CLEVELAND, TS9 6QT.
STINSON, Miss. Julie, BSc ACA *2004;* Mountain Warehouse, 3 Eccleston Street, LONDON, SW1W 9LX.
STIPIC, Mrs. Samantha Jane, BSc ACA *2002;* Estee Lauder Unit 3, Kites Croft Business Park, FAREHAM, HAMPSHIRE, PO14 4FL.
STIRK, Mr. Craig, BA ACA *1996;* The Oaks, The Ridge, Cold Ash, THATCHAM, BERKSHIRE, RG18 9HX.
STIRK, Mr. Denzil James, BSc FCA *1983;* 1 Brockhurst Cottages, Salisbury Lane, Over Wallop, STOCKBRIDGE, HAMPSHIRE, SO20 8JH.
STIRK, Mrs. Monique, BA ACA *1994;* 8 Swift Way, Sandal, WAKEFIELD, WF2 6SQ.
STIRK, Mr. Robert David, LLB ACA *2001;* 6 Meadowgate Vale, Lofthouse, WAKEFIELD, WEST YORKSHIRE, WF3 3SP.
STIRLAND, Mr. David, FCA *1974;* 21 Dursley Court, Auckley, DONCASTER, DN9 3QG.
STIRLAND, Miss. Victoria, MMath ACA *2010;* 21 Wike Ridge Mount, LEEDS, LS17 9NP.
STIRLING, Miss. Adriana Victoria, BSc ACA *2003;* Pricewaterhousecoopers, 12 Plumtree Court, LONDON, EC4A 4HT.
STIRLING, Mr. Alfred Patrick, FCA *1961;* 3 Spital Yard, Spital Square, LONDON, E1 6AQ.
STIRLING, Mrs. Amy, BA ACA *1995;* 56 Belsize Avenue, LONDON, NW3 4AA.
•STIRLING, Mr. Archibald Christopher, MA FCA *1986;* KPMG LLP, 15 Canada Square, LONDON, E14 5GL. See also KPMG Europe LLP
STIRLING, Mrs. Blanka, BA ACA *2005;* 26 Matthews Chase, Binfield, BRACKNELL, BERKSHIRE, RG42 4UR.
STIRLING, Mr. Colin Robert, MA ACA *1991;* Oakfield, Oak Road, Cowthorpe, WETHERBY, LS22 5EY.
STIRLING, Mr. Graham David Hugh, ACA *1980;* 6 Lyneham Road, CROWTHORNE, RG45 6NJ.
STIRLING, Mr. James Edward, MA(Hons) ACA *2001;* 48 Holmbush Road, LONDON, SW15 3LE.
STIRLING, Mr. John, BSc ACA *1993;* 423 Wakefield Road, Denby Dale, HUDDERSFIELD, HD8 8QD.
•STIRLING, Mrs. Judith Ann, MA FCA *1981;* (Tax Fac), Judy Stirling, Holly Lodge, 28 Norwich Road, Hethersett, NORWICH, NR9 3DD.
STIRLING, Mr. Malcolm Douglas, FCA *1957;* Exhall Court, Exhall, ALCESTER, B49 6EA. (Life Member)
STIRLING, Mr. Mark Charles, BA ACA *1981;* 15 Millrace View, Aldermill Grange Sheepy Rd., ATHERSTONE, CV9 3AR.
STIRLING, Mr. Nicholas Charles, FCA *1974;* Dipton Cottage, Corbridge, HEXHAM, NORTHUMBERLAND, NE45 5RY.
STIRLING, Mr. Patrick Charles Ternent, FCA *1962;* PO Box 781627, SANDTON, GAUTENG, 2146, SOUTH AFRICA.
STIRLING, Mr. Robert Benjamin, BA ACA *1992;* Aviva Investors, 1 Poultry, LONDON, EC2R 8EJ.
STIRLING, Mr. Robert Findlay, ACA *2008;* Flat 7, Alphington Flats Roseville Street, St. Helier, JERSEY, JE2 4PL.
STIRRAT, Mrs. Amy Margaret, BA ACA *2003;* with KPMG LLP, Aquis Court, 31 Fishpool Street, ST. ALBANS, HERTFORDSHIRE, AL3 4RF.
STIRRUP, Mr. Adrian John, BSc ACA *1979;* Ground Floor New Uberior House, Bank of Scotland, 11 Earl Grey Street, EDINBURGH, EH3 9BN.
STIRRUP, Mrs. Alison Louise, BSc ACA *2000;* 68 Red Spruce Ln, Rochester, MONROE, NY 14616, UNITED STATES.
•STIRRUP, Mr. John Richard, FCA *1969;* James Todd & Co, Greenbank House, 141 Adelphi Street, PRESTON, PR1 7BH.
STIRRUP, Mrs. Nicola, BSc ACA *1982;* Maranatha, Gryffe Road, KILMACOLM, PA13 4AZ.
STIRTON, Mr. Neil, BSc ACA *2009;* 9 Grovelands, Lower Bourne, FARNHAM, GU10 3RQ.
STITCH, Mr. David John, BA ACA *2001;* 1 Gough Place, CHEDDAR, SOMERSET, BS27 3DJ.
STITCHER, Mr. Robert Anthony, BA ACA *1995;* Dryveres, Hillview Road, LONDON, NW7 1AJ.
STITCHMAN, Mr. John Adam, BSc ACA *2000;* Bannister House Chesterfield Road, Two Dales, MATLOCK, DERBYSHIRE, DE4 2EZ.
STITFALL, Mr. Bernard, BSc FCA *1978;* Apartment 17 Bron y Glyn House, 18 Bridgeman Road, PENARTH, SOUTH GLAMORGAN, CF64 3AW.
STITSON, Mr. John David, FCA *1956;* 32 Southwell Road, Widey Court, PLYMOUTH, PL6 5BG. (Life Member)
•STITT, Mr. Anthony Vincent Portman, FCA *1972;* (Tax Fac), Tony Stitt, 257 Goldhurst Terrace, LONDON, NW6 3EP.
STITT, Mr. Iain Paul Anderson, MSc FRIN FCA FTII *1970;* 2 Hereford Road, HARROGATE, HG1 2NP. (Life Member)
STITT, Mr. Paul Benedict Anderson, BSc ACA *1991;* (Tax Fac), with PricewaterhouseCoopers, 15th Floor, Bangkok City Tower, 179/74-80 South Sathorn Road, BANGKOK 10120, THAILAND.
•STOAKES, Mrs. Christina, ACA *2008;* Union Partners Limited, 38 South Molton Street, Mayfair, LONDON, W1K 5RL.
STOAKES, Mr. Harry, BSc ACA *2007;* 27a Woodstock Road, LONDON, N4 3ET.
STOAKES, Mr. Simon John, BA(Hons) ACA *2002;* 13 rte de Florissant, PO Box 518, 1211 GENEVA, SWITZERLAND.
STOBART, Mr. Anthony Joseph, BA ACA CTA *1999;* with Deloitte LLP, Athene Place, 66 Shoe Lane, LONDON, EC4A 3BQ.
STOBART, Mr. Eric St Clair, MSc FCA *1970;* Dormy Cottage, 2 Alan Road, Wimbledon Village, LONDON, SW19 7PT.
STOBART, Mrs. Helen, BA ACA *1991;* Rose Mount, Leeds Road, Hipperholme, HALIFAX, HX3 8NH.
STOBART, Mr. Paul Lancelot, BA ACA *1984;* The Old Mill, Dalton, NEWCASTLE UPON TYNE, NE18 0AX.
STOBART, Mr. Philip Christopher, ACA *1988;* Rose Mount, Leeds Road, Hipperholme, HALIFAX, HX3 8NH.
STOBART, Mr. Robert Alexander Guy, MA ACA *1992;* 3 Alfred Place, EDINBURGH, EH9 1RX.
STOBAUGH, Mrs. Patricia Kay, MA ACA *1990;* Cititrust Switzerland Limited, 9-11 Reitergasse, P.O. Box 131, 8027 ZURICH, SWITZERLAND.
STOBBART, Mr. Arun George, ACA *1990;* Mentor IMC Ltd, Exchange Tower, Suite 9.05, 1 Harbour Exchange Square, LONDON, E14 9GE.
STOBBART, Mr. John William, BSc FCA *1970;* 7 Residence des Orangers, Targa, MARRAKECH, 40120, MOROCCO.
STOBBS, Miss. Christine, LLB ACA *1999;* 7 Martello Gardens, Cochrane Park, NEWCASTLE UPON TYNE, NE7 7LD.
STOBBS, Ms. Eileen Lesley, MA FCA *1985;* 4 Malton Road, STOCKPORT, CHESHIRE, SK4 4DE.
STOBBS, Mr. Geoffrey Nicholas, FCA *1964;* South Lodge, Bank Street, Conon Bridge, DINGWALL, ROSS-SHIRE, IV7 8HF. (Life Member)
STOBBS, Mr. Paul Robert, BSc ACA *1982;* 14 Bernborough Place, GOONDIWINDI, QLD 4390, AUSTRALIA.
STOBBS, Mr. Paul Robert, BSc ACA *1995;* 1 Summer Hollow, Broadmore Green Rushwick, WORCESTER, WR2 5TE.
STOBBS, Mr. Ralph Anthony Cunningham, FCA *1964;* 93 Holliers Crescent, Middle Barton, CHIPPING NORTON, OX7 7HW.
STOBO, Mrs. Christina Eva, BSc ACA *1995;* 41 Elm Walk, RADLETT, WD7 8DP.
STOBO, Mr. James Philip, BSc ACA *1996;* 41 Elm Walk, RADLETT, WD7 8DP.
STOCK, Mr. Andrew Francis, ACA *1982;* 37 Hudson Close, Chipping Sodbury, BRISTOL, BS37 4NP.
STOCK, Mr. Anthony John, ACA *1980;* Innisfree Rectory Lane, Guarlford, MALVERN, WORCESTERSHIRE, WR13 6NT.
STOCK, Mrs. Barbara Ann, BA FCA *1986;* 14 Bylands, WOKING, SURREY, GU22 7LA.
STOCK, Mr. Bryan, BSc FCA *1977;* The Coach House, 10 Shepley Road, Barnt Green, BIRMINGHAM, B45 8JW.
STOCK, Mr. John Patrick, FCA *1972;* Belton, 3A Highlands Road, Heath End, FARNHAM, GU9 0LX.
STOCK, Miss. Keeley, ACA *2008;* 249 Boundary Road, LONDON, E17 8NE.
•STOCK, Mr. Lynton Robert, BA FCA *1982;* (Tax Fac), Shelley Stock Hutter LLP, 7-10 Chandos Street, LONDON, W1G 9DQ.
STOCK, Mr. Mark Lievesley, BSc ACA *1989;* 12 Rothsay Gardens, BEDFORD, MK40 3QB.
STOCK, Mr. Michael John, BA ACA *1989;* Foredraught House Foredraught Lane, Tibberton, DROITWICH, WORCESTERSHIRE, wr9 7nh.
STOCK, Mr. Neil Edward, BA ACA *1994;* Isitabee in Sitges SL, Apartado Correos No151, 08810 SANT PERE DE RIBES, CATALONIA, SPAIN.
STOCK, Mr. Nicholas Anthony Janson, BSc FCA *1987;* Diversey Inc., PO Box 902, Mailstation 726, 8310 16th Street, STURTEVANT, WI 53177 UNITED STATES.
STOCK, Miss. Rachel Clare, ACA *2010;* 62 Tadorne Road, TADWORTH, SURREY, KT20 5TF.
STOCK, Mr. Simon John, FCA *1977;* 62 Tadorne Road, TADWORTH, SURREY, KT20 5TF.
STOCK, Miss. Sophie Amanda, BA(Hons) ACA *2000;* 15 Chearsley Road, Long Crendon, AYLESBURY, BUCKINGHAMSHIRE, HP18 9BS.
STOCK, Mr. Stephen James De Carteret, ACA *2008;* Flat 2, 94a Belsize Lane, LONDON, NW3 5BE.
STOCK, Mr. Thomas William, BSc ACA *2005;* Flat 17 Silvers, 59-61 Palmerston Road, BUCKHURST HILL, IG9 5NX.
STOCKBRIDGE, Mr. Nicolas Hedley, FCA *1975;* Highley Pens Ltd, Highley, BRIDGNORTH, SHROPSHIRE, WV16 6NN.
STOCKBRIDGE, Mr. Simon John, BA ACA *1988;* HiFi Industrial Film, Stevenage Business Park, Wedgewood Way, STEVENAGE, SG1 4SX.
•STOCKDALE, Mr. Anthony Leonard Clark, ACA *1978;* with RSM Tenon Limited, 1 Hollinswood Court, Stafford Park 1, TELFORD, SHROPSHIRE, TF3 3DE.
STOCKDALE, Mr. Ben Robert, BSc ACA *1999;* 7 Lawnhurst Close, Cheadle Hulme, STOCKPORT, CHESHIRE, SK86RH.
STOCKDALE, Mrs. Catherine Holly, ACA *2009;* 1/1 Coolac Court, LINDISFARNE, TAS 7015, AUSTRALIA.
STOCKDALE, Mr. Harry Tevis Minshull, BA ACA *2004;* 47 Basuto Road, LONDON, SW6 4BL.
STOCKDALE, Mr. Ivor David, BA ACA *1998;* Frazer Nash Consultancy Stonebridge, The Dorking Business Park Station Road, DORKING, RH4 1HJ.
STOCKDALE, Mr. Kevin Anthony, BSc ACA *1990;* 35 Shrubland, BANSTEAD, SM7 2ES.
STOCKDALE, Mr. Nicholas James, BA BSc FCA *1998;* 362 Fulham Palace Road, Fulham, LONDON, SW6 6HT.
STOCKDALE, Mr. Paul Leslie, MA ACA *2000;* 27 Elmway, CHESTER LE STREET, COUNTY DURHAM, DH2 2LE.
STOCKDALE, Mr. Richard Michael, FCA *1969;* 62 Spofforth Hill, WETHERBY, LS22 6SE. (Life Member)
STOCKER, Miss. Anna, BSc ACA *2010;* 58 Idlecombe Road, LONDON, SW17 9TB.
STOCKER, Mr. David Andrew, BA ACA *1999;* 93 Montague Road, Clarendon Park, LEICESTER, LE2 1TJ.
STOCKER, Mr. Gerald Julian, FCA *1951;* The Covers, Lower Road, East Farleigh, MAIDSTONE, ME15 0JW. (Life Member)
•STOCKER, Mr. Jon Westbury, BA ACA *1991;* Milsted Langdon, Winchester House, Deane Gate Avenue, TAUNTON, SOMERSET, TA1 2UH. See also Milsted Langdon LLP
STOCKER, Mr. Paul, ACA *1983;* Woodbre, Station Road, Wakes Colne, COLCHESTER, CO6 2DS.
STOCKER, Mr. Philip Keith, BSc ACA *1992;* Kitsons Solicitors, Minerva House Edginswell Park, TORQUAY, DEVON, TQ2 7FA.
•STOCKER, Mr. Russell Victor, FCA *1984;* (Tax Fac), Alan Cooper Saunders Angel, Kenton House, 666 Kenton Road, HARROW, HA3 9QN.
•STOCKER, Mr. Terence David, FCA *1971;* Rothman Pantall LLP, 10 Landport Terrace, PORTSMOUTH, PO1 2RG.
STOCKFORD, Mr. Peter Jack, FCA *1974;* 89 Dulsie Road, BOURNEMOUTH, BH3 7DZ.
STOCKFORD, Mr. Ronald Warwick, FCA *1961;* NefynHeol Spencer, Coity BRIDGEND, Mid Glamorgan, CF35 6AT. (Life Member)
STOCKFORD, Mrs. Rosemary Heather, FCA *1974;* (Tax Fac), 89 Dulsie Road, BOURNEMOUTH, BH3 7DZ.
STOCKHAM, Mrs. Pamela Anne, MA ACA *1995;* Oakdene, Stone Cross Road, MAYFIELD, EAST SUSSEX, TN20 6EJ.
•STOCKHAUSEN, Mrs. Claire Louise, BSc ACA *1998;* with PricewaterhouseCoopers LLP, 7 More London Riverside, LONDON, SE1 2RT.
•STOCKILL, Mr. Geoffrey Martin, BA ACA *1991;* Integri-FD Limited, The Old Toll House, Hill Top, Barlby, SELBY, NORTH YORKSHIRE YO8 5JQ.
STOCKLEY, Mr. Dean, BSc ACA *2007;* with PricewaterhouseCoopers LLP, 1 Embankment Place, LONDON, WC2N 6RH.
STOCKLEY, Mrs. Susan, BA FCA *1993;* Fir Trees, 38 Spofforth Hill, WETHERBY, WEST YORKSHIRE, LS22 6SE.
•STOCKLEY, Mr. Timothy Robert, FCA *1974;* (Tax Fac), Joy Lane & Co, 4 South Terrace, South Street, DORCHESTER, DT1 1DE.

STOCKMAN, Mr. Adrian Paul, BSc ACA *1990;* 68 Madan Road, WESTERHAM, KENT, TN16 1DX.

STOCKMANN, Mrs. Caroline Anne, BA FCA DChA *1994;* Save the Children Cambridge House, 100 Cambridge Grove, LONDON, W6 0LE.

STOCKS, Mrs. Alison Ruth, ACA *2008;* 125 Eastfield Road, Westbury-on-Trym, BRISTOL, BS9 4AN.

STOCKS, Mr. Benjamin Thomas, ACA *2008;* 125 Eastfield Road, Westbury-on-Trym, BRISTOL, BS9 4AN.

STOCKS, Mr. David, BA ACA *2009;* 14 Micklebring Lane, Braithwell, ROTHERHAM, SOUTH YORKSHIRE, S66 7AS.

STOCKS, Mr. David Page, FCA *1970;* Great Hay, Wambrook, CHARD, SOMERSET, TA20 3DF.

STOCKS, Mr. Francis William Richard, FCA *1964;* Cherry's, St. George's Avenue, WEYBRIDGE, KT13 0BS.

STOCKS, Mr. Henry Martyn, FCA *1967;* 24 Ospringe Place, FAVERSHAM, KENT, ME13 8TB. (Life Member)

STOCKS, Mr. John, BSc ACA *1998;* RBS Securities Inc., 600 Washington Blvd, STAMFORD, CT 06901, UNITED STATES.

STOCKS, Mr. Nigel Robert, BSc ACA *1995;* 2 Ivy Lane, Stewkley, LEIGHTON BUZZARD, BEDFORDSHIRE, LU7 0EN.

STOCKS, Mr. Paul, BSc ACA *1997;* 27 Sandwath Drive, Church Fenton, TADCASTER, NORTH YORKSHIRE, LS24 9US.

STOCKS, Mr. Rodger Andrew Martin, FCA *1973;* Tivernon, 8 Imber Road, WARMINSTER, BA12 9DB.

STOCKS, Mr. Rupert Anthony, BSc FCA *1966;* 21 Church Road, DARTMOUTH, DEVON, TQ6 9HQ.

STOCKS, Mr. Simon John, BSc FCA *1978;* 2 The Gables Nightingale Lane, Storrington, PULBOROUGH, RH20 4TB.

STOCKS, Mr. Timothy John, BSc ACA *1989;* 5 Pightle Close, ROYSTON, SG8 5AZ.

STOCKTING, Mr. Martin Paul, ACA *1989;* Monahans, Clarks Mill Stallard Street, TROWBRIDGE, BA14 8HH.

STOCKTON, Ms. Deborah Louise, BSc ACA *1992;* Flat 149 The Circle, Queen Elizabeth Street, LONDON, SE1 2JL.

STOCKTON, Mr. Geoffrey, FCA *1957;* 19 Kingtree Avenue, COTTINGHAM, HU16 4DS. (Life Member)

STOCKTON, Mr. John, BA ACA *1986;* 8 Hectors Way, Blandford St. Mary, BLANDFORD FORUM, DORSET, DT11 9QP.

STOCKTON, Mr. John William Blaze, FCA *1964;* 16 Clarence Gardens, BISHOP AUCKLAND, COUNTY DURHAM, DL14 7RB.

STOCKTON, Mr. Jonathan, BSc ACA *2010;* 38 Canada Road, Rawdon, LEEDS, LS19 6LR.

STOCKTON, Mr. Mark, BSc ACA *1991;* Aldgate House, I S G Interior Exterior Aldgate House, 33 Aldgate High Street, LONDON, EC3N 1AG.

•STOCKTON, Mr. Nicholas Charles, BA FCA *1990;* Cassons, St Crispin House, St. Crispin Way, Haslingden, ROSSENDALE, LANCASHIRE BB4 4PW. See also Cassons & Associates

•STOCKTON, Mr. Paul Richard, FCA *1983;* Moore Stephens LLP, 150 Aldersgate Street, LONDON, EC1A 4AB. See also Moore Stephens & Co

STOCKTON, Mrs. Paula Jane, BSc ACA *1991;* 32 Freshland Road, MAIDSTONE, KENT, ME16 0WJ.

STOCKTON, Mr. Richard, BA ACA *1991;* 60 Tenford Lane, Tean, STOKE-ON-TRENT, ST10 4EN.

STOCKTON, Mr. Robert Paul, BSc ACA *1992;* Rathbone Brothers plc, 159 New Bond Street, LONDON, W1S 2UD.

STOCKWELL, Mr. Adam, BA ACA *2005;* Buzzacott & Co, 12 New Fetter Lane, LONDON, EC4A 1AG.

STOCKWELL, Mr. Christopher Edmund Vigurs, MA ACA *1981;* 2200 South Ocean Lane, Apt 2607, FORT LAUDERDALE, FL 33316, UNITED STATES.

STOCKWELL, Mr. Christopher Mark, BSc ACA *1993;* 20 Denbank Crescent, Crosspool, SHEFFIELD, S10 5PD.

•STOCKWELL, Miss. Claire Josephine, BSc ACA *2003;* Apple Tree Cottage, Water End Lane, Beeston, KING'S LYNN, PE32 2NL.

STOCKWELL, Mrs. Diane Heather, ACA *1995;* Mirabelle, 62 Le Clos Orange, La Route Orange, St. Brelade, JERSEY, JE3 8GU.

STOCKWELL, Mr. Mark John, FCA MSI TEP *1994;* Mirabelle, 62 Le Clos Orange, La Route Orange, St. Brelade, JERSEY, JE3 8GU.

•STOCKWELL, Mr. Mark John, ACA *1985;* Berry Kearsley Stockwell Limited, Sterling House, 31/32 High Street, WELLINGBOROUGH, NN8 4HL.

•STOCKWELL, Mr. Ralph Alan Owen, BA FCA *1967;* with Rawlinson & Hunter, Eighth Floor, 6 New Street Square, New Fetter Lane, LONDON, EC4A 3AQ.

STOCKWELL, Mrs. Victoria, BSc ACA *1995;* 54 Elwill Way, BECKENHAM, KENT, BR3 6RZ.

STODDARD, Mr. Derek, FCA *1969;* Douglas Quay Group, 32 High Street, Old Whittington, CHESTERFIELD, DERBYSHIRE, S41 9JT.

STODDARD, Mr. Edward John, FCA *1958;* 6 Ivy Place, Vincent Heights, EAST LONDON, 5247, SOUTH AFRICA.

STODDARD, Mr. Michael, BA ACA *1983;* Walnut Cottage, Main Street, Hanwell, BANBURY, OX17 1HN.

•STODDARD, Mr. Michael James, FCA *1974;* with RSM Tenon Audit Limited, 5 Ridge House, Ridge House Drive, Festival Park, STOKE-ON-TRENT, ST1 5SJ.

STODDART, Mrs. Anne, BA ACA *1982;* 5 Kingswood Avenue, High West Jesmond, NEWCASTLE UPON TYNE, NE2 3NS.

•STODDART, Mr. Gavin Devereux, MA ACA *1992;* 150 Aldersgate Street, LONDON, EC1A 4AB.

STODDART, Mr. Mark Alan, BSc ACA *1989;* Orchard House 43 Wallingford Road Cholsey, WALLINGFORD, OXFORDSHIRE, OX10 9LG.

•STODDART, Mr. Peter, FCA *1969;* (Tax Fac), Peter Stoddart FCA, 226 Chester Road, SUNDERLAND, SR4 7HR.

STODDART, Mr. Wilfrid Hamish, MA ACA *1990;* The Leaden Porch House, New Street, Deddington, BANBURY, OX15 0SP.

STODHART, Mr. Andrew James, BA ACA *1983;* 1 Kingsdown Road, EPSOM, SURREY, KT17 3PU.

STOESSER, Mr. Nils Ian, MEng ACA *1999;* 11-12 Charles II Street, LONDON, SW1Y 4QU.

STOFFELL, Mr. Nicholas Raymond, ACA MAAT *2009;* 19 Dawlish Drive, LEIGH-ON-SEA, SS9 1QX.

STOGDALE, Mrs. Beverly Ann, BA ACA *1989;* 46 Knightons Way, Brixworth, NORTHAMPTON, NN6 9UE.

STOIMENOVA, Dr. Lara, PhD BSc ACA *2003;* Fieldgate Oak End Way, Woodham, ADDLESTONE, KT15 3DU.

STOJANOSKI, Mr. Goran, ACA CA(AUS) *2011;* Flat 2, 4 Bentinck Mews, LONDON, W1U 2AJ.

STOK, Mrs. Suzannah Helen, BA ACA *2005;* 32 Melrose Gardens, NEW MALDEN, SURREY, KT3 3HQ.

STOKER, Mr. Alistair John, BA FCA *1975;* 31 Dryburgh Road, Putney, LONDON, SW15 1BN.

•STOKER, Mr. Douglas Brian, FCA *1974;* D. Stoker & Co, Abacus House, 367 Blandford Road, BECKENHAM, BR3 4NW.

STOKER, Mr. Jonathan, BSc ACA *1992;* Stokers Ltd, 277 Wennington Road, SOUTHPORT, MERSEYSIDE, PR9 7TW.

STOKER, Miss. Karen Jane, BA ACA *2002;* 22 Rolling Mill, CONSETT, COUNTY DURHAM, DH8 6NH.

•STOKER, Mr. Peter Jeffrey, FCA *1981;* (Tax Fac), Freedman Frankl & Taylor, Reedham House, 31 King Street West, MANCHESTER, M3 2PJ.

STOKER, Miss. Sarah, BA ACA *2000;* with PricewaterhouseCoopers LLP, 1 Embankment Place, LONDON, WC2N 6RH.

•STOKES, Mr. Aidan Thomas, BA FCA *1993;* Ernst & Young LLP, 1 More London Place, LONDON, SE1 2AF. See also Ernst & Young Europe LLP

STOKES, Miss. Alison Jane, BSc FCA *1995;* 19 Shenley Road, Shenley Church End, MILTON KEYNES, MK5 6AB.

STOKES, Mr. Alistair, BA ACA *2006;* 3 Conference Grove, Crowle, WORCESTER, WR7 4SF.

STOKES, Mr. Andrew James, ACA *2010;* 8 Lindley Avenue, WARRINGTON, WA4 1QB.

•STOKES, Mr. Anthony Michael, FCA *1975;* M. Wasley Chapman & Co, 3 Victoria Square, WHITBY, NORTH YORKSHIRE, YO21 1EA.

STOKES, Mr. Barry Howard, FCA *1967;* c/o International Brewries Plc, PMB 5104, ILESA, OSUN STATE, NIGERIA.

STOKES, Miss. Candida Lucy, ACA *2008;* with Ernst & Young LLP, The Paragon, Counterslip, BRISTOL, BS1 6BX.

STOKES, Miss. Caroline Janet Diane, FCA *1968;* 29 Carpenters, BILLINGSHURST, WEST SUSSEX, RH14 9RA.

•STOKES, Mrs. Carrie Louise, ACA *2003;* Carrie Stokes Limited, 2 Mountbatten Close, SHIFNAL, SHROPSHIRE, TF11 8TU.

STOKES, Mr. David Andrew, BSc ACA *2002;* 43 Charlton Road, SOUTHAMPTON, SO15 5FL.

STOKES, Miss. Deborah Anne, BSc ACA ATII *1991;* (Tax Fac), 98 Roseneath Road, Clapham Common Westside, LONDON, SW11 6AQ.

STOKES, Mr. Dominik, ACA *2009;* R Twining & Co Ltd, South Way, ANDOVER, SP10 5AQ.

•STOKES, Mr. Donald Clifford, FCA *1974;* (Tax Fac), Donald Stokes, 33 Mossy Bank Close, Queensbury, BRADFORD, BD13 1PX.

STOKES, Mr. Edward John, FCA *1945;* 10 Harness Close, Colehill, WIMBORNE, BH21 2UF. (Life Member)

STOKES, Mr. Edward Philip, FCA *1946;* Avenida Dom Vasco Da Gama, 50-3 Esq., 1400, 1400128 LISBON, PORTUGAL. (Life Member)

STOKES, Miss. Emma Helen, BSc ACA *1993;* 3 Crown Heights, Alresford Road, WINCHESTER, SO23 0JX.

•STOKES, Mr. Gareth Anthony, ACA *1992;* Hunt Johnston Stokes Ltd, 12-14 Carlton Place, SOUTHAMPTON, SO15 2EA.

•STOKES, Mr. Graham Richard, FCA *1966;* Stokes Accountants, 1 Bentley Way, Coton Green, TAMWORTH, STAFFORDSHIRE, B79 8LJ. See also Graham Stokes

STOKES, Mr. Harold Nelson, FCA *1955;* Trenos, Killerton Road, BUDE, EX23 8EN.

STOKES, Mr. Henry Armstrong Allen, MA ACA *2001;* 1 Bective Road, LONDON, SW15 2QA.

•STOKES, Mr. Ian, BSc ACA *1988;* I. Stokes & Co, Oxenleaze Farm, 88 Keevil, TROWBRIDGE, WILTSHIRE, BA14 6NH.

STOKES, Mrs. Jane Eidden, BA ACA *1978;* 37 Lavington Road, St George, BRISTOL, BS5 8SQ.

STOKES, Miss. Jayne Elizabeth, MChem ACA *2011;* Currency House, Building 1, Level 5, DIFC Dubai International Finance Centre, PO Box 282056, DUBAI UNITED ARAB EMIRATES.

•STOKES, Mr. John, FCA *1978;* McDade Roberts Accountants Limited, 316 Blackpool Road, Fulwood, PRESTON, PR2 3AE.

STOKES, Mr. Jonathan James, BA ACA *1986;* Grain Bulk Handlers Ltd, P.O Box 80569-80100, MOMBASA, KENYA.

STOKES, Mr. Jonathan Paul, ACA MAAT *2008;* Top Flat, 961 Oldham Road, MANCHESTER, M40 2FF.

STOKES, Mrs. Julia Marie, ACA *2006;* Spring Villa Bunts Lane, Stockton Brook, STOKE-ON-TRENT, ST9 9PR.

•STOKES, Mr. Keith Albert, FCA *1970;* K.A. Stokes, 52 Liverpool Road, STOKE-ON-TRENT, ST4 1AZ.

STOKES, Mr. Lee Antony, BSc ACA *2003;* with Buzzacott LLP, 130 Wood Street, LONDON, EC2V 6DL.

STOKES, Mr. Mark Bryan, BA FCA *1990;* Montague L. Meyer Limited, Unit 5 Bromford Gate Bromford Lane, BIRMINGHAM, B24 8DW.

STOKES, Mr. Martin Howard, FCA *1971;* 1 Hazel Grove, WINCHESTER, SO22 4PQ.

STOKES, Mr. Michael Albert, FCA *1971;* 43 Knighton Road Four Oaks, SUTTON COLDFIELD, B74 4NX. (Life Member)

STOKES, Mr. Michael Peter, BA ACA *1995;* PO Box 17295, Hewlett-Packard (Middle East) FZ LLC, DUBAI, UNITED ARAB EMIRATES.

STOKES, Mr. Paul Michael, BEng ACA *2005;* 20 Beaufort Crescent, Stoke Gifford, BRISTOL, BS34 8QX.

STOKES, Mr. Peter John, FCA *1977;* P O Box N-9901, NASSAU, BAHAMAS.

STOKES, Mr. Peter Montague, FCA *1962;* 9 Dean Court Road, Rottingdean, BRIGHTON, BN2 7DE. (Life Member)

STOKES, Mr. Peter Roger, FCA *1974;* Hall for Cornwall Trust, Back Quay, TRURO, CORNWALL, TR1 2LL.

STOKES, Mr. Philip John, BA FCA *1982;* 1 Platt Meadow, Merrow Park, GUILDFORD, GU4 7EF.

•STOKES, Mr. Philip John Anthony, BA ACA *1994;* PricewaterhouseCoopers LLP, 1 Embankment Place, LONDON, WC2N 6RH. See also PricewaterhouseCoopers

•STOKES, Mr. Richard Allen, FCA *1972;* The Dairy Cottage, Corton, WARMINSTER, BA12 0SZ.

STOKES, Mr. Richard Edward, BSc(Hons) FCA *1978;* 3 Kiamala Crescent, KILLARA, NSW 2071, AUSTRALIA.

STOKES, Mr. Robert Michael, ACA *2009;* 16 Victoria Road, Stirchley, BIRMINGHAM, B30 2LS.

STOKES, Mr. Roger Henry, FCA *1960;* 80 Whyteleafe Road, CATERHAM, CR3 5EF. (Life Member)

STOKES, Mr. Toby Jaspar Lawson, BSc ACA *1999;* 46 Durham Road, LONDON, N2 9DT.

•STOKOE, Ms. Anna Marie, BA(Hons) FCA *1992;* (Tax Fac), Stokoe Loughlin, 1 The Parade, CHESTER LE STREET, COUNTY DURHAM, DH3 3LR.

STOKOE, Mr. Christopher Arton, FCA *1967;* Dale Fold Cottage, Dale House Fold, Poynton, STOCKPORT, SK12 1DG. (Life Member)

•STOKOE, Mr. David Edward, FCA *1988;* Stokoe Rodger, 15 Bankside, The Watermark, GATESHEAD, TYNE AND WEAR, NE11 9SY.

STOKOE, Miss. Helen Katherine, BSc ACA *2006;* 55 Venus Street, Congresbury, BRISTOL, BS49 5HA.

•①STOKOE, Mr. Ian David, BSc FCA *1981;* with PricewaterhouseCoopers, Strathvale House, PO Box 258, GEORGE TOWN, GRAND CAYMAN, KY1-1104 CAYMAN ISLANDS.

STOKOE, Mr. John Edward, FCA *1960;* Stonecroft, 3 Manor Park, RIDING MILL, NE44 6BU. (Life Member)

STOKOE, Mr. Peter William, ACA *1980;* 11 Dean Terrace, RYTON, TYNE AND WEAR, NE40 3HQ.

STOKOE, Mr. Roger Simon, ACA *1982;* 77 High Street, Market Deeping, PETERBOROUGH, PE6 8ED.

STOKSTAD, Ms. Madeleine, MA ACA *2003;* 42a Blandford Avenue, OXFORD, OX2 8DZ.

STOLERMAN, Mr. Jonathan Philip, BA ACA *1983;* Pensions First, 90 Long Acre, LONDON, WC2E 9RA.

STOLERMAN, Mr. Peter Ian, BSc FCA *1980;* 224-232 St. John Street, LONDON, EC1V 4QR.

STOLLIDAY, Mr. Stephen Paul, BSc ACA *1989;* 7 Al Farabi Ave Nurly Tau Off 14, ALMATY 050059, KAZAKHSTAN.

STOLTZ, Mr. David Albert, ACA CA(SA) *2011;* (Tax Fac), Studio 104, 17 Piries Place, HORSHAM, WEST SUSSEX, RH12 1BF.

STOLWOOD, Mr. Peter John, FCA *1968;* 7 Broom Hill Coppice, Cabus, PRESTON, PR3 1LX. (Life Member)

STOLZI, Mr. Graziano, ACA *2008;* via di Villa Ada 24, 00199 ROME, ITALY.

STONARD, Mr. Nicholas Brent, MA ACA *1981;* 4 Dukes Close, FARNHAM, GU9 0DR.

•STONE, Mr. Adrian John, BSc ACA *1988;* KPMG LLP, 1 The Embankment, Neville Street, LEEDS, LS1 4DW. See also KPMG Europe LLP

STONE, Mr. Barry Christopher, BSc ACA *1984;* 3a College Avenue, MAIDENHEAD, BERKSHIRE, SL6 6AR.

STONE, Mr. Benjamin James, BSc ACA *2010;* 14 Woodbridge Road, BIRMINGHAM, B13 8EJ.

STONE, Mr. Brian Charles, BSc FCA *1976;* Hall House Cottage, Great Hormead, BUNTINGFORD, SG9 0NT. (Life Member)

STONE, Mr. Brian John, FCA *1957;* Windlesham House, Cornwallis Road, Milford-on-Sea, LYMINGTON, SO41 0NF. (Life Member)

STONE, Miss. Caroline Sarah, BSc ACA *1997;* 35 Edward Road, West Bridgford, NOTTINGHAM, NG2 5GE.

STONE, Mrs. Catherine Anne, BSc ACA *1990;* I E Design Consultancy Ltd Aquinas House, 63 Warstone Lane, BIRMINGHAM, B18 6NG.

•STONE, Mr. Christopher Charles, FCA *1975;* Christopher C. Stone, 3 Tormead, 27 Dene Road, NORTHWOOD, MIDDLESEX, HA6 2BX.

STONE, Dr. Claire, PhD MSc BA ACA *2004;* 37 Lavengro Road, LONDON, SE27 9EQ.

STONE, Mrs. Claire, BSc(Hons) ACA *2002;* The Wickets, 51 Rayneham Road, ILKESTON, DERBYSHIRE, DE7 8RJ.

STONE, Mrs. Claire Ellen, BSc ACA *1996;* 50 Rue du Rhone, CH 1204 GENEVA, SWITZERLAND.

STONE, Mr. Clifford, FCA *1948;* 11 Vicarage Road, Urmston, MANCHESTER, M41 5TP. (Life Member)

STONE, Mr. Colin Edward, BSc ACA *1985;* 91 Great Gardens Road, HORNCHURCH, ESSEX, RM11 2BA.

STONE, Mr. Daniel, FCA *1984;* 9 Oaklands Park, Grasscroft, Saddleworth, OLDHAM, OL4 4JY. (Life Member)

STONE, Dr. Darren Ashley, PhD MSc ACA *2011;* 14 Fir Tree Green, Alwoodley, LEEDS, LS17 7ER.

STONE, Mr. Darren Howard, ACA *2009;* with AlixPartners Ltd, 20 North Audley Street, LONDON, W1K 6WE.

•STONE, David, Esq OBE FCA *1980;* (Tax Fac), David Stone, 16 Goldhurst Terrace, LONDON, NW6 3HU.

STONE, Mr. David Ian, BA ACA *2005;* 1/174 Brook Street, COOGEE, NSW 2034, AUSTRALIA.

STONE, Mr. David James, BSc ACA *1992;* with Baker Tillly Tax & Advisory Services LLP, St Philips Point, Temple Row, BIRMINGHAM, B2 5AF.

•STONE, Mr. David Michael, FCA ACMA *1981;* The Paddocks, 147 Gillway Lane, TAMWORTH, B79 8PN.

STONE, Mr. Dennis Walmsley, BA FCA *1956;* Deneside, Brookdene, Ashwell, OAKHAM, LE15 7LQ. (Life Member)
STONE, Mr. Derek, BA FCA *1958;* 4 Wimpole Mews, LONDON, W1G 8PE. (Life Member)
STONE, Miss. Elaine Alexandra, BSc ACA *2001;* with ICAEW, Metropolitan House, 321 Avebury Boulevard, MILTON KEYNES, MK9 2FZ.
STONE, Miss. Elizabeth Angela, BA ACA *1990;* 16 Cleveden Road, Kelvinside, GLASGOW, G12 0PG.
•**STONE, Mr. Gary Ralph, BSc FCA** *1985;* G R Stone Limited, 1 Union Street, FAREHAM, HAMPSHIRE, PO16 7XX.
STONE, Mr. Geoffrey Alan, FCA *1957;* F15, 22 Woodland Way, WOODFORD GREEN, IG8 0QG. (Life Member)
•**STONE, Mr. Geoffrey George, FCA** *1970;* (Tax Fac), Stephenson Sheppard & Co Limited, Albany House, 5 New Street, SALISBURY, SP1 2PH.
STONE, Mr. Gwyn Rees, BA FCA *1961;* 40A Heol y Bryn, Rhiwbina, CARDIFF, CF14 6HY. (Life Member)
STONE, Miss. Hannah Elizabeth, ACA *2008;* 63 Wheatlands Road, PAIGNTON, DEVON, TQ4 5HX.
STONE, Mr. Harold Ivor, FCA *1957;* 33 Lodge Close, EDGWARE, MIDDLESEX, HA8 7RL.
STONE, Mrs. Helen Lucy, BCom ACA *2001;* 1 Papworth Drive, BROMSGROVE, WORCESTERSHIRE, B61 0BD.
STONE, Mr. Henry, FCA *1954;* 12 Anthus Mews, NORTHWOOD, MIDDLESEX, HA6 2GX. (Life Member)
STONE, Mr. Hubert, FCA *1952;* East Torr, Chapel Road, Yealmpton, PLYMOUTH, PL8 2LZ.
•**STONE, Mr. Ian Michael, BA ACA** *1993;* Deloitte LLP, 3 Rivergate, Temple Quay, BRISTOL, BS1 6GD. See also Deloitte & Touche LLP
STONE, Miss. Jacqueline Ann, BCom ACA *1993;* Biddenden Farm, Station Road, Rotherfield, CROWBOROUGH, EAST SUSSEX, TN6 3HP.
STONE, Ms. Jacqueline Carol, BA ACA *1990;* 14 Oaklands, CIRENCESTER, GLOUCESTERSHIRE, GL7 1FA.
STONE, Mrs. Jane, BCom ACA *1984;* 3a College Avenue, MAIDENHEAD, SL6 6AR.
•**STONE, Mrs. Janet, BSc FCA** *1977;* Stone & Partners, 571 Fishponds Road, Fishponds, BRISTOL, BS16 3AF.
•**STONE, Miss. Jennifer Anne, ACA MAAT** *2001;* (Tax Fac), Ramsay Brown and Partners, Ramsay House, 18 Vera Avenue, Grange Park, LONDON, N21 1RA.
•**STONE, Mr. Jeremy David, FCA** *1973;* Abacus Accounting and Business Solutions Limited, Harbridge, Hardimead, Lamerton, TAVISTOCK, DEVON PL19 8SE. See also Abacus Business and Accounting Solutions
•**STONE, Mr. Jeremy Graham Tempest, MA FCA** *1965;* Jeremy G. Stone, 197 Bristol Point, LONGWOOD, FL 32779, UNITED STATES.
STONE, Mrs. Joanne Marie, BSc ACA *1991;* 31 Sturges Road, WOKINGHAM, RG40 2HG.
•**STONE, Mr. John Clifford, BA FCA** *1976;* John Stone, Hillcrest, Main Street, Elton, MATLOCK, DE4 2BU.
STONE, Mr. John Gordon, FCA *1959;* Downsbridge House, 5 Downs Bridge Road, BECKENHAM, BR3 5HX. (Life Member)
•**STONE, Mr. John Kenneth, FCA** *1984;* Thompson Jones LLP, 2 Heap Bridge, BURY, LANCASHIRE, BL9 7HR. See also Thompson Jones Business Solutions Limited
STONE, Mr. Jonathan Andrew, MA ACA *1993;* 19 Gipsy Lane, LIVERPOOL, L18 3HL.
STONE, Mr. Jonathan Graham, ACA *2008;* 44 St. Helens Grove, Monkston, MILTON KEYNES, MK10 9FG.
STONE, Mr. Jonathan Peter, BSc ACA *1999;* 20 Grove Avenue, Finchley, LONDON, N3 1QP.
STONE, Mr. Jonathan Peter, BA ACA *1991;* 7 Alleyn Road, LONDON, SE21 8AB.
STONE, Ms. Kayoko Doreen, BSc ACA *1998;* 27022 SE 9th Way, SAMMAMISH, WA 98075-7987, UNITED STATES.
STONE, Mr. Kenneth Benjamin, FCA *1953;* 7 Siddon Drive, Almondbury, HUDDERSFIELD, WEST YORKSHIRE, HD5 8UG. (Life Member)
STONE, Mr. Leon Robert, BSc ACA *1993;* 65 Queen Street, BEACONSFIELD, NSW 2015, AUSTRALIA.
STONE, Mrs. Lindsey Ann, BSc ACA *2007;* 27 Cuckmere Drive, Stone Cross, PEVENSEY, EAST SUSSEX, BN24 5PT.
STONE, Ms. Lisa, BA ACA *1995;* (Tax Fac), Belron International Ltd, Milton Park, Stroude Road, EGHAM, TW20 9EL.
STONE, Mrs. Lucie Hannah, BA ACA *2006;* 209-215, Blackfriars Road, LONDON, SE1 8NL.
STONE, Miss. Lynne Avis, BA ACA *1979;* 40 Harolds Way, Hanham, BRISTOL, BS15 8HW.
STONE, Miss. Marie-Clare, BA ACA *1985;* 3 Coln Manor, Coln St. Aldwyns, CIRENCESTER, GLOUCESTERSHIRE, GL7 5AD.
STONE, Mr. Martin Howard, FCA *1973;* Jemstone Financial Ltd, Cooper House, 316 Regents Park Road, LONDON, N3 2JX.
STONE, Mr. Matthew Martin, BCom ACA *1986;* 23 Alton Road, CROYDON, CR0 4LZ.
STONE, Mr. Maurice, MA FCA *1976;* 53 Spencer Close, LONDON, N3 3TY.
•**STONE, Mr. Michael, FCA CF** *1980;* Downlands, Sheeps Pond Lane, Droxford, SOUTHAMPTON, SO32 3QZ.
•**STONE, Mr. Michael Ralph, MA ACA** *1991;* (Tax Fac), Jamieson Stone, Windsor House, 40-41 Great Castle Street, LONDON, W1W 8LU.
STONE, Mr. Nicholas, BSc ACA *1994;* Two Hoots, Yester Park, CHISLEHURST, KENT, BR7 5DG.
STONE, Mr. Nicholas Henry, BSc ACA *1992;* 21 Earlsthorpe Road, LONDON, SE26 4PD.
STONE, Mr. Nick Philip, BSc ACA *1990;* KBC Advanced Technologies plc, 42-50 Hersham Road, WALTON-ON-THAMES, KT12 1RZ.
STONE, Mr. Owain Rhys, BSc ACA *1988;* KordaMentha Pty Ltd, Level 24, 333 Collins Street, MELBOURNE, VIC 3000, AUSTRALIA.
•**STONE, Mr. Paul Alan, FCA** *1995;* Ayres Bright Vickers, Bishopstone, 36 Crescent Road, WORTHING, BN11 1RL.
STONE, Mr. Paul Allan, FCA *1973;* 1 Kensington Way, NORTHWICH, CHESHIRE, CW9 8GG.
STONE, Mrs. Pauline Margaret, ACA *1985;* Millstream Associates, 9 Station Road, Cippenham, SLOUGH, SL1 6JJ.
STONE, Mr. Peter Benedict, FCA FCCA *1975;* Intrust Ltd, 33 Wigmore Street, LONDON, W1U 1AU.
STONE, Mr. Peter Christopher, FCA *1961;* Pine Paddock, Whitchurch Hill, READING, RG8 7PB.
STONE, Mr. Peter Denis, FCA *1959;* 8 Norton Ride, Lychpit, BASINGSTOKE, RG24 8SF. (Life Member)
•**STONE, Mr. Peter Graham, FCA** *1969;* Stone Osmond Limited, 75 Bournemouth Road, Chandlers Ford, EASTLEIGH, SO53 3AP.
STONE, Mr. Peter William, MA ACA *1999;* 5 Pickenfield, THAME, OXFORDSHIRE, OX9 3HG.
STONE, Dr. Philip Andrew, MA ACA *1996;* 273 Jalan Kampong Chantek, Binjai Crest, SINGAPORE 587944, SINGAPORE.
STONE, Mr. Philip David, ACA *1981;* Stone & Associates, 40 Beaulieu Drive, PINNER, HA5 1NG.
STONE, Mr. Philip Norrish, FCA *1953;* 6 Grove Mews, TOTNES, DEVON, TQ9 5GT. (Life Member)
STONE, Mr. Rex, FCA *1961;* Chevin Mount, Farnah Green, BELPER, DE56 2UP. (Life Member)
•**STONE, Mr. Richard Andrew, FCA** *1990;* (Tax Fac), Innisfree 2000 Limited, Charnwood House, Marsh Road, Ashton, BRISTOL, BS3 2NA.
STONE, Mr. Richard Anthony, MA FCA *1969;* Flat 9, 3 Onslow Gardens, LONDON, SW7 3LX.
STONE, Mr. Richard Charles, BSc ACA *1990;* 9 Stockton View, Gainsborough Road, WARRINGTON, WA4 6BJ.
STONE, Mr. Richard William, BA ACA *1999;* Lamplight House, 47 High Street, Milton, ABINGDON, OXFORDSHIRE, OX14 4EJ.
STONE, Mr. Robert Charles, BA(Hons) FCA *2000;* Q B E, 88 Leadenhall Street, LONDON, EC3A 3BP.
•①**STONE, Mr. Robert Duncan, FCA** *1981;* Stone R. Duncan & Co, Sunrise House, Newdigate Road, Beare Green, DORKING, RH5 4QD.
•**STONE, Mr. Robert Edwin, BA FCA** *1979;* (Tax Fac), Robert Stone Accountancy Limited, Old Magistrates Court, East Street, ILMINSTER, SOMERSET, TA19 9AJ. See also Stone Robert & Co
STONE, Mr. Roger, BA FCA *1989;* Endress & Hauser Ltd, Floats Road, Roundthorn Industrial Estate, MANCHESTER, M23 9NF.
•**STONE, Mr. Roger William, FCA** *1969;* 28 Riverside Mead, PETERBOROUGH, PE2 8JN.
STONE, Mrs. Sharron, BSc ACA *1991;* Holme Garth, 38 Ranmoor Cliffe Road, Ranmoor, SHEFFIELD, S10 3HB.
STONE, Mrs. Shirley Anne, BA ACA *2000;* Rivendale, Canal Lane, Alderbury, SALISBURY, SP5 3NY.
•**STONE, Mr. Stephen Courtney, FCA** *1975;* (Tax Fac), Stephen C Stone & Co, 32 Green Lane, LONDON, NW4 2NG.
STONE, Mr. Stephen John, BSc ACA *1995;* Punch Taverns Ltd Jubilee House, Second Avenue Centrum One Hundred, BURTON-ON-TRENT, STAFFORDSHIRE, DE14 2WF.
STONE, Mr. Stuart Alexander, ACA *2010;* 63 Beatty Avenue, NEWCASTLE UPON TYNE, NE2 3QS.
•**STONE, Mrs. Susan Bernadette, BSc ACA** *1992;* Sue Stone Bookkeeping Services, Longfield, Boraston Lane, TENBURY WELLS, WORCESTERSHIRE, WR15 8RB.
STONE, Mr. Terence John, FCA *1959;* Brushford, Hervines Road, AMERSHAM, BUCKINGHAMSHIRE, HP6 5HS.
STONE, Mr. Timothy Arthur, BA ACA *1979;* 304 Duffield Road, DERBY, DE22 1EQ.
STONE, Mr. Timothy John, BA ACA *1982;* All Adds Up (Hildenborough), 17 Hill View Road, Hildenborough, TONBRIDGE, TN11 9DB.
•**STONEBRIDGE, Mrs. Elizabeth, ACA CTA** *1980;* Liz Stonebridge, 38 Manners Road, Balderton, NEWARK, NOTTINGHAMSHIRE, NG24 3HW.
STONEBRIDGE, Mr. Michael Peter, FCA *1969;* Morrisons Solicitors LLP, Clarendon House, Clarendon Road, REDHILL, RH1 1FB.
STONEBRIDGE, Mr. Paul William, BA ACA *1989;* Paramount Building, 206-212 St John Street, LONDON, EC1V 4JY.
•**STONEFIELD, Mr. David Anthony, BA FCA** *1981;* (Tax Fac), David Stonefield & Company Limited, 70 Grasmere Road, Gatley, CHEADLE, CHESHIRE, SK8 4RS.
STONEHAM, Mr. Desmond John Russell, FCA *1967;* 32 Avenue De La Bourdonnais, 75007 PARIS, FRANCE.
STONEHAM, Dr. Eleanor Mary, FCA *1977;* Finmere, 4 Parklands, Icehouse Wood, OXTED, SURREY, RH8 9DP. (Life Member)
STONEHEWER-SMITH, Mr. Robert Christopher William, BA ACA ACII *1992;* Ash Street Farm, Ash Street Semer, Hadleigh, IPSWICH, IP7 6QZ.
STONEHOUSE, Mr. Christopher Brian, BSc ACA *2005;* 68 Woodbine Road, NEWCASTLE UPON TYNE, NE3 1DE.
STONEHOUSE, Mr. David Coulson, BA FCA *1980;* Technology Services Group Limited, 1 Gosforth Park Way, Gosforth Business Park, NEWCASTLE UPON TYNE, NE12 8ET.
•**STONEHOUSE, Mr. Jolyon Roger Geoffrey, BA ACA CF** *1992;* Old Mill, The Old Mill, Park Road, SHEPTON MALLET, SOMERSET, BA4 5BS. See also Old Mill Accountancy LLP and Old Mill Audit LLP
STONEHOUSE, Mrs. Julia Anne, ACA *2007;* 11 Bradgate Drive, SUTTON COLDFIELD, B74 4XG.
STONEHOUSE, Mrs. Tara Kirsty, BA ACA *2004;* 68 Woodbine Road, Gosforth, NEWCASTLE UPON TYNE, NE3 1DE.
STONELAKE, Mr. Colin Robert, BSc FCA *1991;* Carrington House, The Balk, Pocklington, YORK, YO42 2NZ.
•**STONELEY, Mr. Anthony William, FCA** *1971;* 79 Churchgate, SOUTHPORT, PR9 7JF.
STONELEY, Mr. Paul, BCom FCA *1975;* 18 Stonewood Grove, Sandygate, SHEFFIELD, S10 5SS.
•**STONEMAN, Mr. Andrew Gordon, BSc ACA** *1992;* MCR, 43-45 Portman Square, LONDON, W1H 6LY.
STONEMAN, Mr. Christopher James, BA(Hons) ACA *2001;* 6 Partridge Lane, Bromham, BEDFORD, MK43 8PQ.
STONEMAN, Mrs. Sarah Jane, BEng ACA *1992;* 22 Mulberry Lane, PORTSMOUTH, PO6 2QU.
•**STONER, Mr. David John, FCA** *1963;* Stoner Cottingham, 42 London Rd, HORSHAM, RH12 1AY.
STONER, Miss. Fern Karen, BA ACA *1998;* 21a Danbury Street, Islington, LONDON, N1 8LE.
•**STONER, Mr. Gavin Robert, BA(Hons) ACA** *2002;* PricewaterhouseCoopers LLP, 7 More London Riverside, LONDON, SE1 2RT. See also PricewaterhouseCoopers
STONER, Mr. Gregory Neil, BSc FCA *1981;* University of Glasgow, Central Mail Room, University Avenue, GLASGOW, G12 8QQ.
STONER, Mr. Ian Martin, FCA *1970;* York House, 22 Lynch Road, FARNHAM, GU9 8BZ.
STONES, Mr. Andrew William, BA ACA *1982;* Wellingtonia, 6 Dovaston Court, West Felton, OSWESTRY, SY11 4EQ.
STONES, Mrs. Claire Joanne, BA ACA *1995;* 10 Lady Acre Close, LYMM, CHESHIRE, WA13 0SR.
STONES, Mr. Jak Richard, BSc ACA *1995;* Seafield Lodge Victoria Avenue, St. Helier, JERSEY, JE2 3TB.
•**STONES, Mr. James Edward, BA ACA** *1997;* Park Place Corporate Finance LLP, 19 Park Place, LEEDS, LS1 2SJ.
STONES, Mrs. Mairi Alison, BA ACA *1990;* Inverlochan, Benderloch, OBAN, ARGYLL, PA37 1SA.
STONES, Mr. Mark, BA ACA *2007;* 3/190 Hastings Parade, NORTH BONDI, NSW 2026, AUSTRALIA.
STONES, Miss. Rebecca Frances, BA ACA *1992;* Credit Suisse, 1-5 Cabot Square, LONDON, E14 4QJ.
•**STONES, Mr. William Marcus, FCA** *1951;* 46 Queens Road, WATERLOOVILLE, HAMPSHIRE, PO7 5SB.
•**STONEY, Mrs. Pamela, BSc FCA** *1979;* Pamela Stoney, 61 Earith Road, Willingham, CAMBRIDGE, CB24 5LS.
•①**STONHAM, Mr. Eric John, MA FCA FABRP** *1977;* Stonham.Co, 1 Market Avenue, CHICHESTER, WEST SUSSEX, PO19 1JU.
•**STONIER, Mr. Christopher, FCA** *1971;* (Tax Fac), Rice & Co, Harance House, Rumer Hill Business Estate, Rumer Hill Road, CANNOCK, STAFFORDSHIRE WS11 0ET.
•**STONIER, Mr. Richard Neil, BSc(Econ) FCA** *2000;* Dean Statham, Bank Passage, STAFFORD, ST16 2JS.
STOODLEY, Mr. Andrew, ACA *1991;* Streamside Bledlow Road Saunderton, PRINCES RISBOROUGH, BUCKINGHAMSHIRE, HP27 9NG.
STOOKE, Mrs. Amanda Jane, BA ACA *1986;* 21 College Road, Dulwich, LONDON, SE21 7BG.
•**STOOKE, Mr. Christopher Macdonald, BA FCA** *1981;* 21 College Road, Dulwich, LONDON, SE21 7BG.
STOOKS, Mr. Timothy David, BCom ACA *2000;* 53 Cliffe Way, WARWICK, CV34 5JG.
STOPA, Mr. Christopher Paul Michael, LLB FCA *1972;* 2 King's Bench Walk, Temple, LONDON, EC4Y 7DE.
•**STOPFORD, Mrs. Anne Louise, MA FCA** *1989;* (Tax Fac), Grant Thornton UK LLP, 30 Finsbury Square, LONDON, EC2P 2YU. See also Grant Thornton LLP
•**STOPFORD, Mr. Brian John, ACA** *1981;* (Tax Fac), Stopford Associates Limited, Synergy House, 7 Acorn Business Park, Commercial Gate, MANSFIELD, NOTTINGHAMSHIRE NG18 1EX.
STOPFORD, Mr. Nicholas John, BSc(Hons) ACA *2002;* Compass Group UK Ltd Rivermead, Oxford Road Denham, UXBRIDGE, MIDDLESEX, UB9 4BF.
STOPFORD, Mrs. Patricia Anne, ACA *1987;* Stopford Associates Ltd, 7 Acorn Business Park Commercial Gate, MANSFIELD, NOTTINGHAMSHIRE, NG18 1EX.
•**STOPFORD, Mrs. Prudence Jane Louise, FCA** *1976;* (Tax Fac), Pilgrim Cottage, Polson Hill, Morchard Bishop, CREDITON, DEVON, EX17 6SD.
STOPFORD SACKVILLE, Mr. Lionel Geoffrey, FCA *1959;* Drayton Estate Office, Lowick, KETTERING, NN14 3BG. (Life Member)
STOPFORTH, Mr. Andrew, BA LLB ACA *2004;* 23 Bristow Close, Great Sankey, WARRINGTON, WA5 8EU.
STOPHER, Miss. Kelly, ACA *2010;* Flat 6 Servalan Court, 34 Vernon Close, EPSOM, KT19 9AL.
STOPNIKOV, Mr. Igor Borisovich, ACA *1995;* 5A-55 3 PROYEZD PEROVA POLYA, 111141 MOSCOW, RUSSIAN FEDERATION.
STOPP, Mr. Matthew Peter, BSc ACA *2007;* 93c Frant Road, TUNBRIDGE WELLS, TN2 5LP.
STOPPARD, Mr. Richard Frederick, FCA *1973;* (Tax Fac), 9 Bullock Road, Terrington St. Clement, KING'S LYNN, PE34 4PP.
STOPPARD, Mrs. Susan Jean, FCA *1975;* 9 Bullock Road, Terrington St Clement, KING'S LYNN, PE34 4PP.
STOPPIELLO, Mr. Giovanni, BA ACA *1998;* Flat 3, 80 Fitzjohns Avenue, LONDON, NW3 5LS.
•**STOPPS, Mr. Kevin Peter, BA ACA** *1988;* (Tax Fac), Smith & Williamson Ltd, 25 Moorgate, LONDON, EC2R 6AY.
•**STOPYRA, Mrs. Jacqueline Elizabeth, BA ACA** *1987;* (Tax Fac), Davies & Crane, 80 Lytham Road, Fulwood, PRESTON, PR2 3AQ. See also Davies & Crane Accounting Services Ltd
STORAH, Mr. John Duncan, BEng ACA *1994;* 25 Bentworth Crescent, OTTAWA K2G3X1, ON, CANADA.
STORAH, Mr. Richard, MChem ACA *2003;* Manchester Evening News, 1 Scott Place, 164 Deansgate, MANCHESTER, M3 3RN.
•**STORAN, Mr. Kieran Michael, FCA** *1989;* BDO LLP, Prospect Place, 85 Great North Road, HATFIELD, HERTFORDSHIRE, AL9 5BS. See also BDO Stoy Hayward LLP
•**STORAN, Mrs. Tracy Frances, ACA** *1990;* Tracy Storan, Highlands, 72 Stevenage Road, KNEBWORTH, HERTFORDSHIRE, SG3 6NN.
•**STORER, Mr. Anthony Frank, BSc FCA** *1975;* Isles Storer & Emsden, 129 High Street, Needham Market, IPSWICH, IP6 8DH. See also Isles & Storer and Isles & Storer Ltd

STORER, Mr. James Martin, BA FCA *1981;* 5 Arden Close, Overstrand, CROMER, NORFOLK, NR27 0PH.
STORER, Mr. John Campbell, BCom FCA *1956;* 11 The Wynd, NORTH SHIELDS, TYNE AND WEAR, NE30 2TD. (Life Member)
STORER, Mr. Paul Anthony Brownlee, FCA CF *1975;* with Price Bailey LLP, Causeway House, 1 Dane Street, BISHOP'S STORTFORD, HERTFORDSHIRE, CM23 3BT.
•**STORER, Mr. Philip Charles, BA ACA** *1996;* BDO LLP, 6th Floor, 3 Hardman Street, Spinningfields, MANCHESTER, M3 3AT. See also BDO Stoy Hayward LLP
STORER, Mr. Richard Eric, FCA *1955;* 1a The Promenade, Scratby, GREAT YARMOUTH, NR29 3PA. (Life Member)
•**STOREY, Mr. Andrew Robert William, BSc FCA** *1991;* Cotterell Partnership Limited, The Curve, 83 Tempest Street, WOLVERHAMPTON, WV2 1AA.
STOREY, Mr. Christopher Mark, BSc ACA *1992;* Braeside, Hare Lane, Little Kingshill, GREAT MISSENDEN, BUCKINGHAMSHIRE, HP16 0EF.
STOREY, Mr. Christopher Michael, BA(Hons) ACA *2000;* Level 2, 650 Lorimer Street, PORT MELBOURNE, VIC 3207, AUSTRALIA.
STOREY, Mr. Craig Michael, BA ACA *1986;* 137 The Broadway, Tynemouth, NORTH SHIELDS, NE30 3TA.
STOREY, Mr. David Ian, BSc ACA *1980;* 10 Pinfold Lane, MIRFIELD, WF14 9HZ.
•**STOREY, Mrs. Elisabeth Ann, BA(Hons) ACA** *2001;* with Moore Stephens (Guildford) LLP, Priory House, Pilgrims Court, Sydenham Road, GUILDFORD, SURREY GU1 3RX.
STOREY, Mr. Ernest Robert, FCA *1962;* 21 Clacton Road, Walthamstow, LONDON, E17 8AP. (Life Member)
•**STOREY, Mr. Giles Henry Christian, BSc FCA** *1981;* Christian Douglass LLP, 2 Jordan Street, Knott Mill, MANCHESTER, M15 4PY.
STOREY, Miss. Helen Natalie, BA(Hons) ACA *2000;* 34 Bloomfield Road, HARPENDEN, HERTFORDSHIRE, AL5 4DB.
STOREY, Mr. Iain Kenneth, BA FCA *1999;* 39 Priory Court, Apton Road, BISHOP'S STORTFORD, CM23 3SF.
STOREY, Mr. Jake Colin, BA FCA *1990;* 21 Crown Walk, Apsley Lock, HEMEL HEMPSTEAD, HERTFORDSHIRE, HP3 9WS.
STOREY, Mr. James Michael, BA ACA *1999;* Electronic Data Processing Plc Beauchief Hall, Beauchief, SHEFFIELD, S8 7BA.
STOREY, Miss. Jill Frances, BA ACA MBA *1993;* 26 Moor Road North, NEWCASTLE UPON TYNE, NE3 1AD.
STOREY, Miss. Joanna Katharine, LLB ACA *2005;* Flat 2 The Ridings, Riddings Road, ILKLEY, LS29 9LU.
STOREY, Mr. John, MA ACA *1982;* Springfield, 35, St Marys Road, Portishead, BRISTOL, BS20 6QP.
STOREY, Mr. John Colin, FCA *1965;* 47 St. Michaels Avenue, Bramhall, STOCKPORT, SK7 2PL. (Life Member)
•**STOREY, Mrs. Julia, BSc ACA** *1989;* (Tax Fac), Ainsworths Limited, Charter House, Stansfield Street, NELSON, LANCASHIRE, BB9 9XY.
STOREY, Miss. Kay, MA ACA *1988;* Flint Cottage, 1 Millfield Mews, Caddington, LUTON, LU1 4DZ.
STOREY, Mrs. Kerry Sarah, BSc ACA *2005;* 11 Lowcroft, Woodthorpe, NOTTINGHAM, NG5 4JR.
STOREY, Mr. Liam James, BSc ACA *1979;* 2 Santa Lucia Court, 40 Yarmouth Road, NORWICH, NORFOLK, NR7 0EQ.
STOREY, Mr. Malcolm Ian, BTech FCA *1978;* Whaddon Lodge, Whaddon Drive, CHESTER, CH4 7ND.
STOREY, Mrs. Margaret Anne, MA ACA *1982;* Springfield, 35 St. Marys Road, Portishead, BRISTOL, BS20 6QP.
STOREY, Mrs. Maria Gabrielle, BA FCA *1990;* Gorstage Hall, Weaverham Road, Gorstage, NORTHWICH, CHESHIRE, CW8 2SG.
STOREY, Mr. Mark Nicholas, BA ACA *1999;* 1 Park Road, TRING, HERTFORDSHIRE, HP23 6AT.
STOREY, Mr. Michael Charles, FCA *1970;* (Tax Fac), Oxleaze Barn, Hawling, CHELTENHAM, GLOUCESTERSHIRE, GL54 5TB.
STOREY, Mr. Neil John Magnus, BSc ACA *1994;* 75 Radwinter Road, SAFFRON WALDEN, CB11 3HY.
STOREY, Mr. Neil Thexton, FCA *1954;* 18 Sefton Drive, ILKLEY, LS29 8SH. (Life Member)
•**STOREY, Mr. Patrick Desmond, BSc FCA** *1984;* Grant Thornton UK LLP, 30 Finsbury Square, LONDON, EC2P 2YU. See also Grant Thornton LLP
STOREY, Mr. Philip Frank, ACA *2007;* 885 NE Mulberry Drive, BOCA RATON, FL 33487, UNITED STATES.
STOREY, Mr. Richard Lionel, BSc FCA *1979;* Long Reach Rue de Putron, St. Peter Port, GUERNSEY, GY1 2TE.
STOREY, Mr. Ryan Marc, BSc ACA *2010;* 58 Morley Drive, ELY, CAMBRIDGESHIRE, CB6 3FQ.
STOREY, Mrs. Sarah, BA ACA *2005;* 77 Northen Grove, Didsbury, MANCHESTER, M20 2JL.
STOREY, Mrs. Sarah Louise, BA ACA *1998;* 6 Foxglove Close, Abbeyfields, Douglas, ISLE OF MAN, IM2 7EG.
STOREY, Mr. Terence Edwin, BSc FCA *1978;* 15a West Street, Brant Broughton, LINCOLN, LN5 0SF.
STOREY, Mr. Thomas Michael, FCA *1967;* Newells Farmhouse, Newells Lane, Lower Beeding, HORSHAM, WEST SUSSEX, RH13 6LN. (Life Member)
STORFER, Mr. Michael, FCA *1974;* 55 Downage, Hendon, LONDON, NW4 1HR.
STORIE, Mr. Brian Jonathan, MBA LLB FCA *1992;* Struan Park, Westfield Road, CUPAR, FIFE, KY15 5DS.
STORK, Mr. Nicholas, BEng ACA *1998;* H S B C, 97 Bute Street, CARDIFF, CF10 5NA.
STORKEY, Mrs. Gillian Anne, BA ACA *1988;* Pippins South View Road, Sparrows Green, WADHURST, EAST SUSSEX, TN5 6TW.
STORM, Mr. Kevin John, ACA *1989;* 5 Rye Croft, Conisbrough, DONCASTER, SOUTH YORKSHIRE, DN12 2BD.
STORMER, Mr. Andrew John, BSc ACA *1999;* 18 Acacia Avenue, RUISLIP, MIDDLESEX, HA4 8RG.
STORMER, Mrs. Frances Amanda, BA ACA *1987;* 67 Rodenhurst Road, LONDON, SW4 8AE.
STORMER, Mr. Simon John, BA ACA *1988;* 67 Rodenhurst Road, LONDON, SW4 8AE.
STOROR, Mr. Richard James, BEng FCA *1992;* 60 Whitchurch Lane, Shirley, SOLIHULL, WEST MIDLANDS, B90 1PB.
STORR, Mrs. Andrea, ACA *2001;* Commerzbank, Corporates & Markets, Mainzer Landstrasse 153, DLZ 2, 60327 FRANKFURT AM MAIN, GERMANY.
STORR, Mr. Jonathan Graeme, MSc ACA *1985;* 72 Moorside South, Fenham, NEWCASTLE UPON TYNE, NE4 9BB.
STORR, Mr. Leonard Glenn, FCA *1969;* 854 Lantana Avenue, CLEARWATER BEACH, FL 33767, UNITED STATES.
STORRAR, Mr. Colin, MSc BA ACA *1998;* Beechroyd, Clifford Road, Boston Spa, WETHERBY, WEST YORKSHIRE, LS23 6DB.
STORRIE, Mr. Adrian Alexander, FCA *1981;* with Grant Thornton UK LLP, Earl Grey House, 75-85 Grey Street, NEWCASTLE UPON TYNE, NE1 6EF.
STORRS, Mr. Jeremy Simon John, BA FCA *1993;* The Royal Bank of Scotland Plc, 280 Bishopsgate, LONDON, EC2M 4RB.
STORRS, Mrs. Laura Elizabeth, BSc ACA *1999;* 4 Windmill Close, Mountsorrel, LOUGHBOROUGH, LE12 7HR.
•**STORVIK, Mr. Simon, BA FCA** *1983;* Simon Storvik & Company Limited, 7 Rockleaze Avenue, BRISTOL, BS9 1NG.
STORY, Miss. Charlotte Jane, BA ACA *2002;* BDO LLP, 85 Great North Road, HATFIELD, HERTFORDSHIRE, AL9 5BS.
STORY, Mr. Christopher John, BSc ACA *2006;* RBS Gogarburn, 175 Glasgow Road, EDINBURGH, EH12 9BH.
•**STORY, Mrs. Debora Jane, BSc FCA** *1997;* Sleigh & Story Limited, 46b Bradford Road, BRIGHOUSE, WEST YORKSHIRE, HD6 1RY.
STORY, Mr. Derek Alfred, FCA *1954;* Haons, Castletons Oak Road, Biddenden, ASHFORD, TN27 8DJ. (Life Member)
STORY, Mr. Gary, BSc ACA *1992;* 12 Cherrywood Close, Thornhill, CARDIFF, CF14 9DH.
STORY, Miss. Rebecca, BSc ACA *2003;* 11 Oaklands Avenue, LEEDS, LS13 1LH.
STORY, Mr. Sam Oliver, BSc(Hons) ACA *2009;* KPMG, P.O. Box 493, Century Yard Cricket Square, GEORGETOWN, GRAND CAYMAN, KY1-1106 CAYMAN ISLANDS.
STORY, Mr. Thomas Christopher, BA ACA *2001;* 31 Sun Lane, GRAVESEND, KENT, DA12 5HQ.
STOTEN, Mrs. Pamela Joan, BSc FCA *1983;* 13 Codrington Street, SANDRINGHAM, VIC 3191, AUSTRALIA.
STOTEN, Mr. Simon Austin, ACA *1992;* Greene King Plc, Abbot House, Westgate Street, BURY ST. EDMUNDS, SUFFOLK, IP33 1QT.
STOTHARD, Mr. Edward, BSc ACA *1983;* 40 Sharps Lane, RUISLIP, HA4 7JQ.
•**STOTHARD, Mr. Mark Lee, BA(Hons) ACA** *2003;* HW, 117-119 Cleethorpe Road, GRIMSBY, LINCOLNSHIRE, DN31 3ET.
STOTHARD, Mr. Neil Andrew, MA FCA *1984;* Vp Plc, Central House, Beckwith Knowle, Otley Road, HARROGATE, NORTH YORKSHIRE HG3 VD.
STOTHARD, Mr. Paul Robert, BA FCA *1982;* Manor Barn, 68 Church Street, Helmdon, BRACKLEY, NORTHAMPTONSHIRE, NN13 5QJ.
STOTHART, Mr. Stephen, BSc ACA *1988;* 40 Heathfield, LEEDS, LS16 7AB.
STOTHART, Mr. Tom Edgar, BA ACA *2008;* 8 Hollingwood Park, ILKLEY, WEST YORKSHIRE, LS29 9NZ.
STOTHART, Mr. William Scott, BA FCA *1982;* Wirral Metropolitan College, Carlett Park Campus, Eastham, WIRRAL, MERSEYSIDE, CH62 0AY.
STOTT, Mr. Alexander James Herbert, LLB ACA *1989;* 3 Lambert Road, PORT ALFRED, 6170, SOUTH AFRICA.
STOTT, Mr. Anthony David, BA ACA *1992;* 5 Edstone Close, Dorridge, SOLIHULL, B93 8DP.
STOTT, Mr. Carl Raymond, BSc FCA *1973;* 12 Martingale Road, BILLERICAY, CM11 1SG.
STOTT, Mrs. Catherine Mary, BSc FCA *1977;* 43 Apperley Road, STOCKSFIELD, NE43 7PQ.
STOTT, Mr. Christopher Anthony Peter, MA FCA *1963;* Cobbolds Mill, Monks Eleigh, IPSWICH, IP7 7JB. (Life Member)
STOTT, Mr. Christopher Ian, BA ACA *1987;* 5 Grange Park, St. Arvans, CHEPSTOW, NP16 6EA.
•**STOTT, Mr. Christopher James, BSc ACA** *1998;* KPMG LLP, Quayside House, 110 Quayside, NEWCASTLE UPON TYNE, NE1 3DX.
STOTT, Mr. Christopher John, BSc ACA *1992;* Edelweiss, 11 The Acres, Barrow, CLITHEROE, BB7 9BH.
STOTT, Mr. Daniel Paul, BSc ACA *2000;* Chestnut Croft, High Street, Carlton, GOOLE, NORTH HUMBERSIDE, DN14 9LY.
STOTT, Miss. Deborah Lynne, ACA *2009;* Langley Holmes Farm, Barnsley Road, Flockton, WAKEFIELD, WEST YORKSHIRE, WF4 4AT.
STOTT, Mr. Edward James, MBA FCA *1970;* Tophouse, Woodcote Green, BROMSGROVE, WORCESTERSHIRE, B61 9EF.
STOTT, Mrs. Elisa Jane, BA(Hons) ACA *2000;* with James Cowper LLP, Mill House, Overbridge Square, Hambridge Lane, NEWBURY, BERKSHIRE RG14 5UX.
STOTT, Mr. Gavin Cyril, FCA *1960;* Kurnalpi, P.O. Box 14, UMTENTWENI, KWAZULU NATAL, 4235, SOUTH AFRICA. (Life Member)
STOTT, Mr. James Alexander, FCA *1961;* The Old Stables, Knowsley Road, Ainsworth, BOLTON, BL2 5QB.
STOTT, Mr. Jeffrey Alan, FCA *1977;* 12 Oakfield Close, Bramhall, STOCKPORT, SK7 1JE.
STOTT, Mr. Jonathan Michael, BSc ACA *2004;* 10 Kings Ride, DINAS POWYS, SOUTH GLAMORGAN, CF64 4BA.
STOTT, Miss. Katherine, ACA *2007;* Flybe Limited, Jack Walker House, Exeter International Airport, EXETER, EX5 2HL.
STOTT, Mr. Kenneth Entwistle, FCA *1952;* Wilderley, Guilsfield, WELSHPOOL, SY21 9BX. (Life Member)
•**STOTT, Miss. Lisa Joanne, BSc ACA** *1991;* Deloitte LLP, Abbots House, Abbey Street, READING, RG1 3BD. See also Deloitte & Touche LLP
STOTT, Mr. Malcolm, BSc ACA *1992;* 9050 Hammock Lake Court, CORAL GABLES, FL 33156, UNITED STATES.
STOTT, Mr. Mark Anthony, FCA *1968;* 279 Newbridge Road, BATH, BA1 3HL.
STOTT, Mr. Mark David, BA ACA *1992;* Coppermead, 20 Amersham Road, Chesham Bois, AMERSHAM, BUCKINGHAMSHIRE, HP6 5PE.
STOTT, Mr. Martin, FCA *1982;* 175 Wright Road, Redvale 4, ALBANY 0794, NEW ZEALAND.
STOTT, Mr. Michael Moreton, BA(Hons) ACA *2001;* (Tax Fac), 55 Moorside Avenue, Parkgate, NESTON, CH64 6QS.
STOTT, Mr. Michael Norman, BSc FCA *1976;* 22 Wensley Gardens, EMSWORTH, PO10 7RA.
STOTT, Mr. Myles Tweedale, MA FCA *1967;* Myles T. Stott, 12 Chemin du Hameau, 1255 VEYRIER, SWITZERLAND.
STOTT, Miss. Patricia Anne, BSc FCA DChA *1984;* with Baker Tilly UK Audit LLP, St Philips Point, Temple Row, BIRMINGHAM, B2 5AF.
STOTT, Mr. Paul Douglas, ACA *2008;* with Deloitte LLP, PO Box 500, 2 Hardman Street, MANCHESTER, M60 2AT.
STOTT, Mr. Paul Garfield, BSc ACA *1994;* with PricewaterhouseCoopers, Darling Park Tower 2, 201 Sussex Street, GPO Box 2650, SYDNEY, NSW 1171 AUSTRALIA.
STOTT, Mr. Paul Richard, BSc ACA *1990;* RCi Financial Services Limited, Egale House, 78 St. Albans Road, WATFORD, WD17 1AF.
STOTT, Mr. Roger John, BSc ACA *1990;* Calverley House, Lawshare Ltd, 55 Calverley Road, TUNBRIDGE WELLS, TN1 2TU.
STOTT, Mr. Roland Frederick, FCA *1952;* 61 Haglane Copse, Pennington, LYMINGTON, SO41 8DQ. (Life Member)
STOTT, Ms. Ruth, BSc ACA *1990;* 27 Silver Leigh, Aigburth, LIVERPOOL, L17 5BL.
STOTT, Mr. St John, BA ACA *1989;* 17 Uplands Chase, Fulwood, PRESTON, PR2 7AW.
•**STOTT, Miss. Susan Carol, FCA** *1978;* Susan C. Stott, 34 Tom Lane, Crosland Moor, HUDDERSFIELD, HD4 5PS.
STOTT, Mrs. Susan Glenys, BSc ACA *1998;* 162 Darras Road, Ponteland, NEWCASTLE UPON TYNE, NE20 9AF.
STOTT, Mr. William David, MPhys ACA *2009;* 16 Clifton Road, WOKINGHAM, RG41 1NB.
STOUT, Mr. Christopher, FCA *1962;* 12 Cedar Drive, Thornton, MIDDLESBROUGH, CLEVELAND, TS8 9BY.
STOUT, Mr. John Steven Turley, FCA *1976;* PO Box HM 905, HAMILTON HMDX, BERMUDA.
STOUT, Mr. John William Priestner, BA FCA *1980;* 16 Queen Annes Gate, Caversham, READING, RG4 5DU.
•①**STOUT, Mr. Keith Barry, FCA** *1976;* with KSA Business Recovery LLP, 2 Nelson Street, SOUTHEND-ON-SEA, SS1 1EF.
STOUT, Mr. Paul, BSc ACA *2003;* 10 Oughtrington Lane, LYMM, CHESHIRE, WA13 0RD.
STOUT, Mr. Paul Martin, BSc ACA CF *2000;* with Grant Thornton UK LLP, 1 Dorset Street, SOUTHAMPTON, SO15 2DP.
STOUT, Mr. Thomas Francis, MA FCA *1967;* Kingston House, Moresby, WHITEHAVEN, CA28 8UW.
STOVEL, Mr. Richard Campbell, BA FCA *1974;* 6 Gardiner Close, ABINGDON, OX14 3YA. (Life Member)
STOVELL, Mrs. Amanda Louise, ACA *1995;* 63 Leicester Road, Quorn, LOUGHBOROUGH, LEICESTERSHIRE, LE12 8BA.
STOVOLD, Mr. Brian Sidney Charles, FCA *1964;* 64 The Orchards, EPPING, ESSEX, CM16 7AT.
STOVOLD, Ms. Karen Vanessa, BSc ACA *1993;* 11 Ravensbourne Gardens, Ealing, LONDON, W13 8EW.
•**STOVOLD, Mr. Timothy Frederick John, BA(Hons) ACA CTA** *2002;* Kingston Smith & Partners LLP, Devonshire House, 60 Goswell Road, LONDON, EC1M 7AD. See also Kingston Smith Limited Liability Partnership, Kingston Smith LLP, Devonshire Corporate Services LLP, Kingston Smith Consulting LLP and Kingston Smith(Bangladesh) Limited
STOW, Mrs. Clare, BSc(Hons) ACA *2007;* Northfield House, 1a The Glen, Kirk Ella, HULL, HU10 7TN.
•**STOW, Miss. Rosalind Mary, MA FCA** *1987;* Financial Forensics LLP, The Brighton Forum, 95 Ditchling Road, BRIGHTON, BN1 4ST.
STOW, Mr. Stephen, BA(Hons) ACA *2009;* 76 Holland House Road, Walton-le-Dale, PRESTON, PR5 4JG.
STOWELL, Ms. Katharine Susan, BSc ACA *1990;* Dairy Crest Ltd, Frome Pre-Pack, Manor Road, Marston Trading Estate, FROME, BA11 4BN.
•**STOWER, Mr. Matthew Thomas, BA FCA** *1992;* Clarke & Co, Acorn House, 33 Churchfield Road, Acton, LONDON, W3 6AY. See also Datacount Limited
STOWER, Mr. Ronald Michael, FCA *1974;* Janome UK Ltd, Janome Centre, Southside, Bredbury, STOCKPORT, CHESHIRE SK6 2SP.
STOYTCHKOVA, Miss. Simona, BA ACA *2005;* Flat 429, Anchor House, Smugglers Way, LONDON, SW18 1EX.
STRACEY, Mr. David Sydney, FCA *1951;* 7 Maypole Road, EAST GRINSTEAD, RH19 1HL. (Life Member)
STRACEY, Mr. Michael John Louis, FCA *1954;* Highfield, The Green, Saxtead, WOODBRIDGE, SUFFOLK, IP13 9QB. (Life Member)
STRACHAN, Mr. Adam James, BEng ACA *1994;* St Ronans, 8 The Oval, HARROGATE, NORTH YORKSHIRE, HG2 9BA.
STRACHAN, Mr. Andrew Crichton, BSc FCA *1975;* 17a Blackroot Road, SUTTON COLDFIELD, WEST MIDLANDS, B74 2QJ.
STRACHAN, Miss. Angela Margaret, BA(Hons) ACA *2002;* Snowhill Cottage, Okewood Hill, DORKING, SURREY, RH5 5NB.
STRACHAN, Mr. Anthony George, FCA *1969;* Golant Farmhouse, Fore Street, Golant, FOWEY, CORNWALL, PL23 1LN.
STRACHAN, Mr. Anthony William, FCA *1976;* Orchard Cottage, Clock House Lane, Bramley, GUILDFORD, GU5 0AP.

STRACHAN, Mr. Campbell Neil, LLB ACA *2003;* Ripley Lodge, 70a Acacia Grove, NEW MALDEN, SURREY, KT3 3BU.
•**STRACHAN, Mr. David Alistair, BA ACA** *1990;* Strachan & Co, Summerhill Cottage, 9 Summerhill Road, DARTFORD, KENT, DA1 2LP.
STRACHAN, Mr. David William, ACA *2011;* Curlew Cottage, Moor Road, Strathblane, GLASGOW, G63 9EU.
STRACHAN, Mr. Iain John, BA ACA *1999;* 36 Watling Street, ST. ALBANS, HERTFORDSHIRE, AL1 2QB.
STRACHAN, Mr. Keith, BSc ACA *1993;* 3 Walnut Close, CARSHALTON, SURREY, SM5 3RT.
STRACHAN, Mr. Leigh Melvin, FCA *1970;* 5 White Oaks, The Rutts, Bushey Heath, BUSHEY, WD23 1LH.
STRACHAN, Mr. Malcolm Maxwell, FCA *1952;* Rylestone, 2 Southfield, HESSLE, HU13 0EX. (Life Member)
STRACHAN, Mr. Nigel Gleave, BA ACA *2002;* Oak View Clos Des Arbres, La Grande Route de Faldouet St. Martin, JERSEY, JE3 6UG.
STRACHAN, Mrs. Ruth Elizabeth, BSc ACA *1999;* 36 Watling Street, ST. ALBANS, HERTFORDSHIRE, AL1 2QB.
STRADLING, Mr. Ceri Richard, BA FCA *1983;* Ty Celyn, 12 Maes Celyn, Llanbedr D.C., RUTHIN, LL15 1YR.
STRADLING, Mr. Robert James, BA FCA *1989;* Rowheath Pavilion, Heath Road, BIRMINGHAM, B30 1HH.
STRADLING, Mr. Stuart Rhys, FCA *1968;* 68 Howards Lane, LONDON, SW15 6QD.
STRAFFORD, Mr. Guy Philip Cyril, BA FCA *1998;* 134 Ebury Street, LONDON, SW1W 9QQ.
STRAFFORD, Mrs. Marian Nora, ACA MAAT *2002;* 12A BURNS AVENUE, TAKAPUNA 0622, NEW ZEALAND.
STRAIN, Mrs. Helen Verina, BA ACA *2002;* Northwold, Woodacre Crescent, Bardsey, LEEDS, LS17 9DQ.
STRAIN, Mr. Terence, BSc ACA *1988;* AB Mauri Group, Sugar Way, PETERBOROUGH, PE2 9AY.
STRAIN, Mr. Trevor John, BSc ACA *2002;* Northwold Woodacre Crescent, Bardsey, LEEDS, LS17 9DQ.
STRAKER, Mr. Allan, BSc ACA *1991;* Maison Fleur, La Route Des Delisles, Castel, GUERNSEY, GY5 7JW.
STRAKER, Mr. George William, FCA *1975;* with Ryecroft Glenton, 189 Park View, WHITLEY BAY, NE26 3RD.
STRAKER, Miss. Kate Abigail, BSc ACA *2007;* Man Investments Limited, Sugar Quay, Lower Thames Street, LONDON, EC3R 6DU.
STRAKER, Mr. Michael, BMus ACA *2007;* PSE Finance Operations, Sony Business Europe Viables Industrial Estate, Jays Close, BASINGSTOKE, HAMPSHIRE, RG22 4SB.
STRAKOSCH, Mr. Christopher Frederick, FCA *1976;* Wilhelm-Meister-Strasse 6, D-61348 BAD HOMBURG, GERMANY.
STRAND, Mr. Andrew Paul, BA ACA *1989;* 120 Broadway, PETERBOROUGH, PE1 4DG.
STRANG, Mr. David Nicholas, MA FCA *1975;* 38 Pleasant Road, HAWTHORN EAST, VIC 3123, AUSTRALIA.
STRANG, Mr. Malcolm James, BA ACA *1986;* Brittoncot, Holly Bank Road, Hook Heath, WOKING, SURREY, GU22 0JN.
STRANG, Mr. Richard William, BA FCA *1975;* 18 Lansdowne Walk, LONDON, W11 3AH.
STRANG, Mrs. Susan Elizabeth, BSc ACA *1989;* 4 The Cleeve, CORSHAM, WILTSHIRE, SN13 9JG.
STRANGE, Mr. David Hilary, BSc ACA *1989;* GN Netcom (UK) Limited, Tamesis The Glanty, EGHAM, TW20 9AW.
STRANGE, Mr. Edward Arthur, FCA *1961;* 34 Montacute Way, Merley, WIMBORNE, BH21 1TZ.
STRANGE, Miss. Emma, BA(Hons) ACA *2011;* 34 Bryniau Road, LLANDUDNO, GWYNEDD, LL30 2EZ.
STRANGE, Mr. Graham Mark, BA ACA *1993;* 4 The Grove, Roundhay, LEEDS, LS8 2QQ.
STRANGE, Mr. Ian Michael, BA FCA *1979;* (Tax Fac), ICAEW, Chartered Accountants Hall, Moorgate Place, LONDON, EC2P 2BJ.
STRANGE, Mr. John Francis, FCA *1973;* The Vicarage, Eddington Road, SEAVIEW, ISLE OF WIGHT, PO34 5EF.
STRANGE, Miss. Laura, ACA *2011;* Mazars LLP, The Pinnacle, 160 Midsummer Boulevard, MILTON KEYNES, MK9 1FF.
STRANGE, Mr. Nicholas John, BSc FCA *1984;* 4 Brockwell Park Row, LONDON, SW2 2YH.
STRANGE, Mrs. Patricia Heather, BSc FCA *1977;* 40 Lucas Road, HIGH WYCOMBE, HP13 6HP.
STRANGE, Mr. Philip, BSc ACA *1986;* 4 Dairy Cottages Siddington, CIRENCESTER, GL7 6ET.
STRANGWOOD, Miss. Ann, BA FCA *1978;* Allington, New Street, LEDBURY, HR8 2EL.
STRANKS, Mr. Andrew, BSc ACA *1993;* 84 The Lawns, Rolleston-on-Dove, BURTON-ON-TRENT, STAFFORDSHIRE, DE13 9DE.
STRANKS, Mr. Harold Moreton, FCA *1963;* The Old Bakery, High Street, Bloxham, BANBURY, OX15 4LU. (Life Member)
STRANNER, Miss. Charlotte Alexandra, ACA *2008;* Finncap, 60 New Broad Street, LONDON, EC2M 1JJ.
STRASSER, Mrs. Katja Daniela, BA ACA *1991;* Hoehenweg 72, 6314 UNTERAEGERI, SWITZERLAND.
•**STRATFORD, Mr. Craig Matthew, ACA** *2007;* Simpson Wood, Bank Chambers, Market Street, HUDDERSFIELD, HD1 2EW.
•**STRATFORD, Mr. Duncan, BSc ACA** *2000;* with PricewaterhouseCoopers LLP, 31 Great George Street, BRISTOL, BS1 5QD.
STRATFORD, Mrs. Fiona Margaret, FCA *1987;* 23 Emperor Close, BERKHAMSTED, HP4 1TD.
STRATFORD, Mr. Frederick Anthony, BSc FCA *1989;* L P M Group 4 Crayside, Five Arches Business Estate Maidstone Road, SIDCUP, DA14 5AG.
STRATFORD, Mr. George Richard, FCA *1974;* Woodsmoke, Silkmore Lane, West Horsley, LEATHERHEAD, KT24 6JQ.
STRATFORD, Mr. Jonathan Richard, BA ACA *1997;* Stoniss, 7 Midway, WALTON-ON-THAMES, SURREY, KT12 3HY.
•**STRATFORD, Mr. Rowland Charles, FCA** *1963;* Rowland Stratford & Co, 53 The Mews, Newton Croft, SUDBURY, CO10 2RW.
STRATFORD, Miss. Sarah Jane, ACA *2004;* 12 Cumnor Road, SUTTON, SM2 5DW.
STRATFORD-HALL, Mr. Barton, ACA *2008;* Ashbrook, Les Quartiers, St. Sampson, GUERNSEY, GY2 4GB.
•**STRATHDEE, Mr. Neil John, BAcc ACA** *1999;* Ernst & Young LLP, 1 More London Place, LONDON, SE1 2AF. See also Ernst & Young Europe LLP
STRATHEARN, Mr. Daniel, BSc ACA *2001;* 29 Isis Street, LONDON, SW18 3QL.
STRATHEARN, Mr. Derek John, BA FCA *1976;* 4th Floor, 96-98 Baker Street, LONDON, W1U 6TJ.
STRATTON, Mrs. Adele, BA(Hons) ACA *2004;* 6 Crossland Avenue, ELLENBROOK, WA 6069, AUSTRALIA.
STRATTON, Mr. Barney Martin, BA ACA *1991;* 42 Great Bottom, Stockton, WARMINSTER, BA12 0SJ.
•**STRATTON, Mr. Christopher Frederick, FCA** *1971;* MacIntyre Hudson LLP, Euro House, 1394 High Road, Whetstone, LONDON, N20 9YZ.
STRATTON, Mr. Colin, BSc ACA *1992;* St Austell Brewery Co Ltd, 63 Trevarthian Road, ST AUSTELL, CORNWALL, PL25 4BY.
STRATTON, Mr. David John, BSc ACA *1989;* 6 Malmesbury Close, BRISTOL, BS6 7TR.
STRATTON, Mrs. Ellie Jacqueline, BSc ACA *2006;* 71a Trowley Rise, ABBOTS LANGLEY, HERTFORDSHIRE, WD5 0LN.
STRATTON, Mr. Henry Robert, BSc ACA *2006;* Manor Farm, Kingston Deverill, WARMINSTER, BA12 7MB.
STRATTON, Mr. James Edward, ACA *1998;* Basement Flat, 200 Sheen Road, RICHMOND, SURREY, TW10 5AL.
STRATTON, Mrs. Janice Hazel, BA ACA *1990;* Naturetrek Ltd, Cheriton Mill, Cheriton, ALRESFORD, HAMPSHIRE, SO24 0NG.
STRATTON, Mr. Maurice, BSc ACA *1987;* The Willows, Wickham Heath, NEWBURY, BERKSHIRE, RG20 8PH.
STRATTON, Mr. Paul Graham, BSc ACA *1987;* Arqiva Ltd Crawley Court, Crawley, WINCHESTER, SO21 2QA.
STRATTON, Mr. Peter, BA ACA *1994;* 52 Handen Road, Lee, LONDON, SE12 8NR.
•**STRATTON, Mr. Philip Richard, BA FCA** *1974;* P.R. Stratton, 2 Butlers Yard, 7 Main Road, EMSWORTH, PO10 8AP.
STRATTON, Mrs. Sarah Caroline, BA ACA *1993;* The Willows, Wickham Heath, NEWBURY, RG20 8PH.
STRATTON-BROWN, Mrs. Helen Celia, BSc ACA CTA *1993;* (Tax Fac), 2026 Regency Drive, WYOMISSING, PA 19610, UNITED STATES.
STRATTON-BROWN, Mr. Henry, BA ACA *1989;* 2026 Regency Drive, WYOMISSING, PA 19610, UNITED STATES.
•**STRAUGHAN, Mr. Brian Jonathan, FCA** *1982;* (Tax Fac), B J Straughan & Partners, Epworth House, 7 Lucy Street, CHESTER LE STREET, DH3 3UP.
STRAUGHAN, Mr. Charles Frank, FCA *1971;* 12A South Park Rd, LONDON, SW19 8SU.
•**STRAUGHAN, Mr. Jonathan Nicholson, FCA** *1952;* B J Straughan & Partners, Epworth House, 7 Lucy Street, CHESTER LE STREET, DH3 3UP. See also Alderdice John & Son
STRAUGHAN, Mr. Timothy David, BChD ACA *1991;* HSCIC, 1 Trevelyan Square, Boar Lane, LEEDS, LS1 6AE.
STRAUS, Mr. Aaron, FCA *1957;* 27 Shirehall Park, LONDON, NW4 2QN. (Life Member)
•**STRAUSS, Mr. Bradley Malcolm, BSc FCA** *1989;* Strauss Phillips & Co, PO Box 585, EDGWARE, MIDDLESEX, HA8 4DU.
STRAUSS, Miss. Colleen Dianne, BA ACA *1997;* 5 Thurleigh Road, LONDON, SW12 8UB.
STRAUSS, Mr. Johannes Muller, ACA CA(SA) *2008;* 13 Brighton Street, Midstream Estate, MIDRAND, GAUTENG, SOUTH AFRICA.
•**STRAUSS, Mr. Steven Michael, BSc FCA** *1985;* (Tax Fac), Simmons Gainsford LLP, 5th Floor, 7-10 Chandos Street, Cavendish Square, LONDON, W1G 9DQ.
STRAUSS, Mr. Warren, ACA *2005;* PO Box 785156, Sandton City, JOHANNESBURG, 2146, SOUTH AFRICA.
STRAUTHER, Mr. Kevin, BA ACA *2006;* 61 Pigeon Bridge Way, SHEFFIELD, SOUTH YORKSHIRE, S26 2GX.
STRAW, Mr. Anthony Robert James, MA ACA *2000;* (Tax Fac), The Coach House La Vassalerie St. Andrew, GUERNSEY, GY6 8XL.
STRAW, Mrs. Chris Lesley, BA ACA *1991;* Academy of Medical Sciences, 10 Carlton House Terrace, LONDON, SW1Y 5AH.
STRAW, Mr. David John, BSc ACA *1989;* Mouchel, Knights House, 2 Parade, SUTTON COLDFIELD, WEST MIDLANDS, B72 1PH.
STRAW, Mr. John Sorby, FCA *1955;* 34 Bath Road, EMSWORTH, PO10 7ER.
STRAW, Mr. Robert Martin, MSc ACA *2003;* Tidal Generation, University Gate East, Park Row, BRISTOL, BS1 5UB.
•**STRAW, Mr. Timothy John, BA FCA** *1991;* Arnold Hill & Co LLP, Craven House, 16 Northumberland Avenue, LONDON, WC2N 5AP. See also Arnold Hill & Co
STRAWBRIDGE, Mrs. Lesley Mary, BSc ACA *1990;* Royal Bank of Scotland, 10th Floor, 280 Bishopsgate, LONDON, EC2M 4RB.
STRAWSON, Mr. Andrew Frederick Hugh, MA FCA *1980;* Court House, 4 Abbots Way, GUILDFORD, GU1 2XP.
•**STRAWSON, Mrs. Kay Vanessa, BA FCA CTA** *1984;* (Tax Fac), Kay V. Strawson & Co Limited, Red Cottage, Moor Road, Walesby, MARKET RASEN, LINCOLNSHIRE LN8 3UR.
•**STREATFEILD, Mr. Michael John Champion, BA ACA** *1989;* Shongwe, 7 Cole Mead, BRUTON, SOMERSET, BA10 0DL.
STREATFEILD, Mr. Timothy James, MA FCA *1974;* The Old Vic, Cook Lane, North Stoke, WALLINGFORD, OXFORDSHIRE, OX10 6BG.
STREATFIELD, Mr. Paul Richard, BA ACA *1979;* 45 Castle Lane, Chandler's Ford, EASTLEIGH, HAMPSHIRE, SO53 4AH.
•**STREDDER, Miss. Diane, BA ACA** *1988;* Stredder & Co, Rose Cottage, Manley Road, Alvanley, FRODSHAM, WA6 9DE.
STREET, Mr. Andrew John, BSc(Hons) ACA *2001;* 553 N Marion Street, OAK PARK, IL 60302-1679, UNITED STATES.
•**STREET, Mrs. Catriona Margaret, ACA ATT** *2009;* with LeonSchiller, 100 High Ash Drive, LEEDS, LS17 8RE.
STREET, Mr. Christopher, BSc(Hons) ACA *2003;* 27 Goldsmith Street, ELWOOD, VIC 3184, AUSTRALIA.
STREET, Mr. Guy Benedict, BA ACA *1992;* Alt Schuerkesfeld 22, 40670 MEERBUSCH, GERMANY.
STREET, Mrs. Helen Ann, BA ACA *1994;* 20 Willow Way, RADLETT, WD7 8DX.
STREET, Mr. John William, FCA *1959;* The Knoll, Crifty Craft Lane, Churchdown, GLOUCESTER, GL3 2LJ. (Life Member)
STREET, Mrs. Karen Elaine, BSocSc ACA CTA *1996;* 11 Fairmead Rise, Kings Norton, BIRMINGHAM, B38 8BS.
STREET, Mr. Kevin Patrick, MA ACA *1998;* Darwin Private Equity LLP, 15 Bedford Street, LONDON, WC2E9HE.
STREET, Mr. Paul Raymond, BA ACA *1987;* 32 Cranleigh Gardens, KINGSTON-UPON-THAMES, KT2 5TX.
STREET, Miss. Rachel Jennifer, BSc(Hons) ACA *2004;* with Grant Thornton UK LLP, Grant Thornton House, 22 Melton Street, Euston Square, LONDON, NW1 2EP.
STREET, Mr. Robert David, BEng ACA *2003;* St. Dominic's School, Off Hosur Road Attibele, BANGALORE 562107, INDIA.
STREET, Mr. Robert Derek, BSc ACA *1993;* 11 Ford Street, Braughing, WARE, HERTFORDSHIRE, SG11 2PW.
STREET, Miss. Theresa Anne, BA FCA *1978;* (Tax Fac), 31 Chesterwood Road, Kings Heath, BIRMINGHAM, B13 0QG.
STREET, Mr. William John, BA(Econ) ACA *1979;* 53 Mucklow Hill, HALESOWEN, WEST MIDLANDS, B62 8BS.
STREET, Mr. William Michael, MA MBA ACA *1991;* Rexam Plc, 4 Millbank, LONDON, SW1P 3XR.
STREETEN, Mr. Robert Douglas Renwick, BA ACA *2008;* Paramount Pictures International Building 5 Chiswick Park, 566 Chiswick High Road, LONDON, W4 5YF.
STREETER, Mr. Andrew Martin, BA ACA *1991;* 1 Weller Close, Worth, CRAWLEY, RH10 7QE.
STREETER, Mrs. Jacqueline Roberta, BSc FCA *1987;* Telford College of Arts & Technology, Haybridge Road, Wellington, TELFORD, SHROPSHIRE, TF1 2NP.
STREETER, Mr. Luke, ACA *2011;* 57 Commonwealth Drive, CRAWLEY, WEST SUSSEX, RH10 1AE.
STREETER, Mr. Patrick Thomas, FCA *1972;* Waterman's End Cottage, Matching Green, HARLOW, CM17 0RQ.
STREETER, Mrs. Pauline Josephine, FCA *1977;* Holy Trinity School, Addison Road, GUILDFORD, SURREY, GU1 3QF.
STREETER, Mr. Richard James, BA ACA *2000;* 44 Chestnut Grove, SOUTH CROYDON, CR2 7LH.
STREETS, Mr. Matthew, BA(Hons) ACA *2011;* Wentwood House, Carr Lane, HEBDEN BRIDGE, WEST YORKSHIRE, HX7 8NR.
STRETCH, Mr. Andrew Philip, BSc ACA *2005;* Pilkington Technology & Management Ltd, Pilkington Technology Centre Hall Lane Lathom, ORMSKIRK, L40 5UF.
STRETCH, Mr. David, BA ACA *1993;* 24 Leather Lane, Gomshall, GUILDFORD, SURREY, GU5 9NB.
•**STRETCH, Mr. David Gordon, ACA** *1979;* 3 St Margarets Court, Kineton Green Road, SOLIHULL, B92 7DZ.
STRETCH, Mr. Graham John, BA ACA *1989;* 5 The Street, North Stoke, WALLINGFORD, OX10 6BL.
STRETCH, Mr. James Lionel, FCA *1960;* Clibbons, 87 Bramfield Road, Datchworth, KNEBWORTH, SG3 6SA. (Life Member)
STRETTEN, Mr. Ian William, FCA *1973;* 9 South Grove, FLEET, HAMPSHIRE, GU51 2TU.
STRETTLE, Mr. Geoffrey William, FCA *1974;* 3 Barrington Drive, Ainsdale, SOUTHPORT, PR8 2PR.
STRETTLE, Miss. Helena, MA(Cantab) ACA *2010;* Smallburn East, North Road, Smallburn, NEWCASTLE UPON TYNE, NE20 0AD.
STRETTON, Mrs. Johannah Jane, BA ACA *1989;* The Barn, Broadstones Farm Mill Brow, Marple, STOCKPORT, SK6 5DG.
•**STRETTON, Mrs. Lisa Marie, BSc ACA** *1999;* Lisa M Stretton, 9 Felstead Close, Dosthill, TAMWORTH, STAFFORDSHIRE, B77 1QD.
STREVENS, Mr. Andrew Charles, BA ACA *1995;* 59 Hatherley Road, WINCHESTER, HAMPSHIRE, SO22 6RR.
STREVENS, Mrs. Carol Ann, ACA *1984;* BPTW Partnership, Hilton Wharf, 30 Norman Road, Greenwich, LONDON, SE10 9QX.
STREVENS, Mr. Nigel Jeremy, BSc ACA *1997;* Ford & Slater Ltd, Hazel Drive, LEICESTER, LE3 2JG.
STREVENS, Mr. Peter Jeffrey, FCA *1968;* 9 Hither Bush, Lyde, HEREFORD, HR4 8EF. (Life Member)
STRHAN, Mr. Lou, FCA *1980;* 18 Grove Gardens, TEDDINGTON, MIDDLESEX, TW11 8AP.
STRIBLING, Mr. David Michael, FCA *1959;* 23 Church Street, Modbury, IVYBRIDGE, DEVON, PL21 0QR. (Life Member)
STRICKER, Mrs. Maria, MPhil(Cantab) ACA *2010;* 31 Wimpole Street, LONDON, W1G 8GS.
STRICKLAND, Mr. Andrew James, ACA *2009;* Flat 4 Ollerton Court, 175 Manchester Road, MANCHESTER, M16 0ED.
STRICKLAND, Mr. Andrew John, BSc FCA *1982;* 12 Exeter Close, Cheadle Hulme, CHEADLE, SK8 6JE.
•**STRICKLAND, Mr. Andrew Paul, MA FCA** *1976;* Scrutton Bland, 820 The Crescent, Colchester Business Park, COLCHESTER, CO4 9YQ.
STRICKLAND, Miss. Anna Louise Helen, ACA *2009;* 56 Clarendon Road, LYTHAM ST. ANNES, LANCASHIRE, FY8 3HX.
STRICKLAND, Mr. Anthony William Bryen, FCA *1963;* 18 Sheppard Way, Minchinhampton, STROUD, GL6 9BZ. (Life Member)
STRICKLAND, Mr. Benjamin Vincent Michael, MA FCA *1967;* 23 Juer Street, LONDON, SW11 4RE.
STRICKLAND, Mr. Brian, FCA *1965;* 15 Bramley Lane, Handsworth, SHEFFIELD, S13 8TY.
STRICKLAND, Mr. David Peter, BA ACA *2001;* Stour Vista Skates Hill, Glemsford, SUDBURY, SUFFOLK, CO10 7SH.
•**STRICKLAND, Mrs. Emma Jane, BA(Hons) ACA** *2001;* Kingsley, 25 Kingsley Drive, Cheadle Hulme, CHEADLE, CHESHIRE, SK8 5LZ.

STRICKLAND, Mr. George Cameron Lamb, ACA *2010;* 25 St. Michaels Church Road, LIVERPOOL, L17 7BD.

•STRICKLAND, Mrs. Gillian Judith, FCA *1984;* Higson & Co, White House, Wollaton St, NOTTINGHAM, NG1 5GF.

STRICKLAND, Mrs. Paula, BA ACA *2005;* 29 Spartan Way, CRAWLEY, WEST SUSSEX, RH11 7GH.

•STRICKLAND, Mr. Thomas Beck, BA ACA *1984;* Hawes Strickland, Federation House, 36/38 Rockingham Road, KETTERING, NORTHAMPTONSHIRE, NN16 8JS.

STRICKLAND, Mr. Thomas Graham, MA FCA *1984;* 6 Templecombe Road, Bishopstoke, EASTLEIGH, HAMPSHIRE, SO50 8QL.

STRICKLAND, Mr. William James, BSc(Hons) ACA *2001;* 25 Kingsley Drive, Cheadle Hulme, CHEADLE, CHESHIRE, SK8 5LZ.

STRICKLAND, Mr. William John, BSc FCA *1974;* 1 Mill Street, Prestbury, CHELTENHAM, GL52 3BE.

STRIDE, Miss. Elaine Anne, BA ACA *1999;* Invista Real Estate Investment Management Limited, 107 Cheapside, LONDON, EC2V 6DN.

STRIDE, Mr. Ronald William, FCA *1967;* PO Box 453, SOUTH YARRA, VIC 3141, AUSTRALIA.

•STRIKE, Mr. Duncan John, ACA FCCA *1990;* (Tax Fac), Bright Star Accounting Limited, 3 Branksome Park House, Branksome Business Park, Bourne Valley Road, POOLE, DORSET BH12 1ED. See also Cameron Cavey LLP

STRIKE, Miss. Lucy, BA(Hons) ACA *2006;* 193 Thunder Lane, NORWICH, NR7 0JF.

STRINGER, Mr. Andrew John, BSc FCA *1987;* Entaco Ltd Unit 90, The Washford Industrial Estate Heming Road, REDDITCH, WORCESTERSHIRE, B98 0EA.

STRINGER, Mr. Andrew Paul, ACA *1992;* 14 Longtye Drive, Chestfield, WHITSTABLE, CT5 3NG.

•STRINGER, Mr. Anthony Charles, FCA *1977;* (Tax Fac), PKF (UK) LLP, 2nd Floor, 1 Redcliff Street, BRISTOL, BS1 6NP.

STRINGER, Mr. Arthur John, BSc ACA *1989;* 7 Highfields, ASHTEAD, SURREY, KT21 2NL.

STRINGER, Mrs. Cathryn Michelle, BA ACA *2006;* 9 The Spinney, KNARESBOROUGH, NORTH YORKSHIRE, HG5 0TD.

•STRINGER, Mr. Charles Geoffrey George, FCA *1976;* Charles Stringer, 17 Frith Way, HINCKLEY, LE10 0JE.

STRINGER, Mr. David, BSc FCA *1977;* Crystalclear Consulting LTD, 29 Crescent Gardens, BATH, BA1 2NB.

•①STRINGER, Mr. David John, FCA *1976;* Stringer & Co, 5 Bassett Wood Drive, SOUTHAMPTON, SO16 3PT.

STRINGER, Mr. George, FCA *1958;* 42 Sherford Road, Elburton, PLYMOUTH, PL9 8BS. (Life Member)

STRINGER, Mr. George Michael, FCA *1973;* Fold End, Town End Road, HOLMFIRTH, WEST YORKSHIRE, HD9 1XT.

STRINGER, Mrs. Kimberley Louise, BA ACA *1997;* HSBC Bank Middle East Limited, Emaar Square Building No.5 Level 2, P.O. Box 502601, DUBAI, UNITED ARAB EMIRATES.

STRINGER, Mrs. Louise Anne, FCA *1991;* Oakwood, Whitewayhead Lane, Knowbury, LUDLOW, SHROPSHIRE, SY8 3LE.

STRINGER, Mr. Martin James, BEng ACA *2009;* TMF Management (UK) Limited, 400 Capability Green, LUTON, LU1 3AE.

STRINGER, Mr. Michael Geoffrey, BSc ACA *1982;* The Stables Austerson Hall, Austerson, NANTWICH, CHESHIRE, CW5 8AT.

STRINGER, Mr. Nigel John Leslie, FCA *1978;* Yarlet Hall Preparatory School Yarlet, STAFFORD, ST18 9SU.

•STRINGER, Mr. Paul William, BA ACA *1995;* Cowgill Holloway LLP, 4th Floor, 49 Peter Street, MANCHESTER, M2 3NG. See also Cowgill Holloway Care 1 Limited

STRINGER, Mr. Simon Jeremy, BSc ACA *2000;* 10 Chariot Road, Wootton, NORTHAMPTON, NN4 6JP.

STRINGER, Mr. Simon Michael Donald Charles, BSc ACA *2009;* Flat 3, 1 Westbourne Road, LONDON, N7 8AR.

STRINGER, Mr. Thomas Vivian Stewart, BSc ACA *1986;* KEB Zentrum, CH-4438 KILCHZIMMER, SWITZERLAND.

STRINGER, Mr. William Paton, ACA ATII CTA ACIS *1982;* 15 Manor Links, BISHOP'S STORTFORD, CM23 5RA.

STRINGFELLOW, Mr. Jonathan Charles, BSc ACA *1991;* 118 Chirnside Street, Kingsville, MELBOURNE, VIC 3012, AUSTRALIA.

STRINGFELLOW, Mr. Kenneth Copeland, FCA *1958;* 56 Highcliffe Drive, SHEFFIELD, S11 7LU. (Life Member)

STRINGFELLOW, Ms. Linda Carol, BA ACA *1987;* 5 Baily Gardens, Wray Common Road, REIGATE, SURREY, RH2 0GY.

STRINGFELLOW, Mr. Tor, ACA *2009;* 63 Collingwood Way, Westhoughton, BOLTON, BL5 3TS.

STRIVENS, Mr. Andrew James, MA ACA *1989;* 11 Rawlinson Road, OXFORD, OX2 6UE.

STROBRIDGE, Miss. Alison Jane, ACA *2009;* Cay-Os New Road, St. Sampson, GUERNSEY, GY2 4QB.

STROBRIDGE, Mrs. Jennifer Jessie, BSc ACA *1980;* Cay-os, New Road, St Sampsons, GUERNSEY, GY2 4QB.

STROBRIDGE, Mr. John Frederick, BSc ACA *1980;* Cay-os, New Road, St Sampsons, GUERNSEY, GY2 4QB.

STRODE, Mr. Philip Horsley, FCA *1950;* Broyle Farmhouse, Pook Lane, East Lavant, CHICHESTER, PO18 0AX. (Life Member)

STRODE, Mr. Richard John, BA ACA *1998;* Summerfields, West End Lane, Frensham, FARNHAM, SURREY, GU10 3BE.

STROEBELE, Mrs. Suzanne Farouk, BA ACA *1998;* Goldbergstrasse 6, 86650 WEMDING, BAVARIA, GERMANY.

•STROH, Dr. Matthew John, PhD BA(Hons) ACA *2004;* with Grant Thornton UK LLP, 1 Whitehall Riverside, Whitehall Road, LEEDS, WEST YORKSHIRE, LS1 4BN.

•STRONACH, Mr. Adam James, FCA MAE MEWI *1994;* (Tax Fac), Harwood Hutton Limited, 22 Wycombe End, BEACONSFIELD, BUCKINGHAMSHIRE, HP9 1NB. See also Harwood Hutton Tax Advisory LLP

•STRONACH, Mr. Andrew Malcolm, MA FCA *1979;* 6 Orchard Close, North Petherton, BRIDGWATER, SOMERSET, TA6 6TW.

STRONACH, Mr. James Barker Robertson, BCom ACA *1982;* Flat 4 The Leather House, 76-78 St. Georges Street, NORWICH, NR3 1AB.

STRONACH, Mr. John Dixon, FCA *1973;* Beaconside, Ivegill, CARLISLE, CA4 0PJ.

STRONACH, Mrs. Judith Helen, LLB ACA *1981;* 12 Laxton Drive, Oundle, PETERBOROUGH, PE8 5TW.

STRONACH, Mr. William James, BSc(Econ) ACA *1995;* 26 Grange Road, SEVENOAKS, TN13 2PQ.

STRONELL, Mrs. Annette Gail, ACA *1987;* 33 Raisins Hill, PINNER, HA5 2BU.

STRONELL, Mr. Brian Peter, FCA *1977;* 51 Emlyn Road, HORLEY, RH6 8RX.

STRONG, Mr. Andrew Neil, BSc ACA *1998;* 8 Alexandra Road, BATH, BA2 4PW.

STRONG, Mr. Andrew William, BSc(Econ) ACA *1996;* 23 Whitcliffe Drive, PENARTH, CF64 5RY.

STRONG, Mr. Christopher Noel, BA FCA *1984;* 40 Larkhall Rise, Clapham, LONDON, SW4 6JX.

STRONG, Miss. Clare Marie, BSc ACA *2010;* 18 Whist Avenue, WICKFORD, ESSEX, SS11 8LN.

STRONG, Mr. Douglas Gordon, BSc FCA *1982;* The New House The Street, Stisted, BRAINTREE, CM77 8AW.

STRONG, Mr. Michael John Francis, BSc FCA *1999;* Saffery Champness, Beaufort House, 2 Beaufort Road, Clifton, BRISTOL, BS8 2AE.

STRONG, Mrs. Momke, MA ACA *2002;* 7 Church View Close, Llandough, PENARTH, SOUTH GLAMORGAN, CF64 2NN.

STRONG, Mr. Neil William, ACA MAAT *2003;* (Tax Fac), 51 Buchanan Drive, Cambuslang, GLASGOW, G72 8BB.

STRONG, Mr. Nicholas George, MA FCA *1973;* Nicholas Strong Consulting Ltd, 43 The Village, Green Road, NEWBRIDGE, COUNTY KILDARE, IRELAND.

STRONG, Mr. Noel Richard Whitley, FCA *1972;* Treperran, Trebetherick, WADEBRIDGE, CORNWALL, PL27 6SB.

•STRONG, Mr. Norman, FCA *1973;* BSG Valentine, Lynton House, 7/12 Tavistock Square, LONDON, WC1H 9BQ.

STRONG, Miss. Pippa, MA(Hons) ACA *2003;* 52 Cloudesdale Road, LONDON, SW17 8EU.

STRONG, Mr. Robert William Jack, BSc ACA *1994;* 68 Orange Grove Drive, Highlands, HARARE, ZIMBABWE.

STRONG, Mrs. Sally Pauline, MA ACA *1986;* 28 The Avenue, Bengeo, HERTFORD, SG14 3DS.

STRONG, Mr. Simon Robert, BSc FCA *1992;* 7 Church View Close, Llandough, PENARTH, SOUTH GLAMORGAN, CF64 2NN.

STRONG, Mr. Timothy David Luke, BSc ACA *1999;* Farm Cott Clanville Lodge, Clanville, ANDOVER, SP11 9HL.

STRONG, Mr. Wayne Martin, BSc ACA *1989;* 50 Purcell Road, PENARTH, SOUTH GLAMORGAN, CF64 3QN.

STRONGE, Mr. Abel Clifford, LLB ACA *1999;* 2 Dahlia Close, Cheshunt, WALTHAM CROSS, HERTFORDSHIRE, EN7 6NW.

STRONGE, Mr. Christopher James, MA FCA *1960;* 12 Tudor Close, CHICHESTER, WEST SUSSEX, PO19 5QZ. (Life Member)

STROTHER, Mr. Ian Greenfield, FCA *1966;* 158 Queen Alexandra Road, SUNDERLAND, SR3 1XL. (Life Member)

STROTHERS, Mr. Russell, ACA *2010;* 3 Bellevue, BRISTOL, BS8 1DA.

STROUD, Miss. Catherine Margaret, MA ACA *1985;* Flat 5, 40 Anson Road, LONDON, N7 0AB.

STROUD, Mr. David Alan, LLB ACA *2002;* 2 Langton Place, LONDON, SW18 5AZ.

STROUD, Mr. David Richard, BA ACA *2001;* 342 Riddell Road, GLENDOWIE 1071, NEW ZEALAND.

STROUD, Mrs. Elaine Rachel, BA(Hons) ACA *2001;* 342 Riddell Road, Glendowie, AUCKLAND 1071, NEW ZEALAND.

STROUD, Mr. Hedley Stuart, BA ACA *1980;* Bourne Services Group, Cherry Holt Road, BOURNE, LINCOLNSHIRE, PE10 9LA.

STROUD, Mrs. Helen, FCA *1973;* 2 Ryde Avenue, South Knighton, LEICESTER, LE2 3RD.

STROUD, Miss. Helen Louise, ACA *2009;* 117 Ferndale Road, LONDON, SW4 7RL.

STROUD, Mr. John Kerbey, FCA *1970;* Langley Abbey Langley Green, Langley, NORWICH, NR14 6DG.

STROUD, Mr. Mark, BA ACA *2004;* Bridgepoint Capital Ltd, 30 Warwick Street, LONDON, W1B 5AL.

STROUD, Mr. Nicholas Lawson, BSc FCA CTA *1988;* The Serious Fraud Office, Elm House, 10-16 Elm Street, LONDON, WC1X 0BJ.

STROUD, Mr. Robert Adam, BSc ACA *1997;* Civica UK Ltd, 2 Burston Road, Putney, LONDON, SW15 6AR.

STROUD, Mr. Robert Sinclair, FCA ACMA *1973;* Royal Mail, Wheatstone House, Wheatstone Road, SWINDON, SN3 5JN.

STROUD, Miss. Ruth Julia, JP LLB ACA *1987;* (Tax Fac), 7 Windermere Road, West End, SOUTHAMPTON, SO18 3PB.

STROUD, Ms. Sara, ACA *2008;* 16 Pevensey Road, LONDON, SW17 0HW.

STROUD, Mrs. Susan Margaret, BSc ACA *1986;* 1 Exon Street, HAMPTON, VIC 3188, AUSTRALIA.

STROUD, Mrs. Tracey Dianne, ACA *2009;* 4 Sherbourne Court, Ludlow Road, MAIDENHEAD, BERKSHIRE, SL6 2RS.

STROUTS, Mr. Henry Murton, BEng ACA *2001;* 31 Alacross Road, LONDON, W5 4HT.

STROVER, Mr. Antony Miles, FCA *1966;* Kuwait Projects Co, PO Box 23982, SAFAT, 13100, KUWAIT.

STROVER, Mrs. Claire Elizabeth, BA ACA *1999;* Call Credit Information Group, 1 Park Lane, LEEDS, LS3 1EP.

STROVER, Mr. John Yates Richard, FCA *1964;* Ashdeane, 13 Cricket Green, MITCHAM, SURREY, CR4 4LB.

STROVER, Mr. Richard Guy, FCA *1965;* (Member of Council 1993 - 1995), Perry Farm House, Bear Street, Nayland, COLCHESTER, CO6 4HX.

•STROVOLIDES, Mr. Georghios Andrea, BSc FCA *1982;* George A. Strovolides, Hermes Building Office 501, 31 Chr Sozos Street, PO Box 22104, 1517 NICOSIA, CYPRUS.

STROWBRIDGE, Ms. Maria Elena, BA ACA *1987;* Glenridding House, Station Road, BRAMPTON, CUMBRIA, CA8 1EX.

STROWGER, Mr. Clive, FCA *1964;* High Veld, The Ridge, Woldingham, CATERHAM, CR3 7AX.

STROWGER, Mr. John Benjamin, BSc ACA *2009;* 68 Ormiston Grove, LONDON, W12 0JS.

STRUBE, Mr. Conrad Reginald Percival, FCA *1976;* 4 Albany Villas, HOVE, BN3 2RU.

STRUDWICK, Mr. Andrew, BSc ACA *2000;* 27 Shenley Hill, RADLETT, HERTFORDSHIRE, WD7 7AU.

STRUDWICK, Miss. Hazel Jennifer, BSc ACA *1992;* 14 Midley Close, Allington, MAIDSTONE, ME16 0TY.

•STRUDWICK, Mr. Howard Bernard, FCA *1972;* Heywards, 6th Floor, Remo House, 310-312 Regent Street, LONDON, W1B 3BS.

STRUDWICK, Mrs. Jennifer Clare, BSc FCA DChA *1986;* 18 Essenden Road, SOUTH CROYDON, SURREY, CR2 0BU.

STRUDWICK, Miss. Lisa Jayne, ACA *2011;* 19 Glynde Avenue, EASTBOURNE, EAST SUSSEX, BN22 9QE.

STRUDWICK, Mr. Paul David, FCA *1968;* 59 High View Road, South Woodford, LONDON, E18 2HL.

STRUDWICK, Mr. Rupert Joseph, MA ACA *1997;* 48, Woodgrange Road, LONDON, E7 0QH.

STRUDWICK, Mrs. Victoria Pamela, BSc ACA *2007;* 1 Fair View Cottages, High Road, Cookham, MAIDENHEAD, BERKSHIRE, SL6 9JE.

STRUDWICKE, Mr. Brian Dennis, FCA *1963;* The Stables, Nortoft, Guilsborough, NORTHAMPTON, NN6 8QB. (Life Member)

STRUEL, Mr. Simon Daniel, ACA *1988;* 14 Craig Yr Haul Drive, Castleton, CARDIFF, CF3 2SA.

•STRUGGLES, Mr. Richard, FCA *1970;* KWG Ltd, Millstream House, 39a East Street, WIMBORNE, DORSET, BH21 1DX.

STRUNKS, Miss. Christina Susan, BSc ACA *1992;* Rowtree Cottage, Low Road, North Tuddenham, DEREHAM, NORFOLK, NR20 3DQ.

STRUTHERS, Mr. Angus, BSc FCA *1981;* 5 The Medlars, Woodlands, MAIDSTONE, ME14 5RZ.

STRUTHERS, Mrs. Harriet Elizabeth Charnock, BSc ACA *1999;* 30 The Hill Avenue, Battenhall, WORCESTER, WR5 2AW.

STRUTHERS, Mr. James Gavin, ACA *1987;* 73275 Pinyon Street, PALM DESERT, CA 92260, UNITED STATES.

STRUTT, Dr. Alison Jane, BSc ACA *2000;* Building 3 3T121, Glaxo Group Research Ltd, PO Box 97, STEVENAGE, HERTFORDSHIRE, SG1 2NY.

STRUTT, Mrs. Helen Sandra Louise, MEng ACA DChA *2006;* 40 St Johns Road, THATCHAM, RG19 3SY.

STRUTT, Mr. Henry Clavering Tollemache, BA ACA *1979;* Stutton Hall, Stutton, IPSWICH, IP9 2TQ.

STRUTT, Mr. Jonathan Andrew, ACA *2009;* 8 Newton Park Road, BENFLEET, SS7 3SD.

STRUTT, Mr. Raymond Arthur, FCA *1958;* 53 Barnfield Avenue, Shirley, CROYDON, CR0 8SF. (Life Member)

STRUTTON, Mrs. Sarah Louise, BSc ACA *2002;* 73 Malden Road, SUTTON, SM3 8QU.

•STRUYVEN, Dr. Geert Jean Paul Emile, ACA MBA *1999;* Crowe Clark Whitehill, Jaeger House, 5 Clanricarde Gardens, TUNBRIDGE WELLS, KENT, TN1 1PE. See also Horwath Clark Whitehill LLP

STUART, Mrs. Amanda Jane, BSc(Hons) ACA *2001;* Morgan Stanley International, 25 Cabot Square, LONDON, E14 4QA.

•STUART, Mr. Andrew Louis, ACA *1990;* A L Stuart ACA, Longcroft House, 2-8 Victoria Avenue, LONDON, EC2M 4NS. See also Logicum

STUART, Mrs. Carey, ACA *2009;* 13 Matlock Avenue, MANCHESTER, M20 1JS.

STUART, Mr. Christopher Gregory Harold, MA FCA *1991;* K B C (Kingston) Ltd Kingsgate Business Centre 12-50, Kingsgate Road, KINGSTON UPON THAMES, KT2 5AA.

STUART, Mr. Colin Charles, BSc ACA *1992;* 3 Dorchester Gardens, West Bridgford, NOTTINGHAM, NG2 7AW.

STUART, Mr. David Lewis, MA FCA *1977;* The Orchards, Houghton Green Lane, Playden, RYE, EAST SUSSEX, TN31 7PJ.

STUART, Mr. Gordon Mckenzie, BSc FCA *1987;* Alexander Mann Solutions, 3 Waterhouse Square 138-142 Holborn, LONDON, EC1N 2SW.

STUART, Mr. Graham Neil, ACA *1981;* Wychwood, Bole Hill, Wingerworth, CHESTERFIELD, S42 6RF.

•STUART, Mr. James Macdonald, BA ACA *1996;* with Ernst & Young LLP, 1 More London Place, LONDON, SE1 2AF.

STUART, Dr. Jamie Alistair, PhD BSc ACA *2001;* 29 Lilac Way, East Goscote, LEICESTER, LE7 4XU.

STUART, Mr. John Morris, FCA *1954;* Cromdale, 26 Foxglove Avenue, Roundhay, LEEDS, LS8 2QR. (Life Member)

STUART, Mr. Mark David, FCA *1991;* 3 Walnut Close, Thornbury, BRISTOL, BS35 2LS.

STUART, Mr. Neil, BA FCA *1983;* 6 Belmont Road, REIGATE, SURREY, RH2 7EE.

STUART, Mr. Paul Edward, BA FCA *1995;* 17 St. Edyths Road, BRISTOL, BS9 2EP.

STUART, Mrs. Rachel Elizabeth, BSocSc ACA *1995;* 3 Dorchester Gardens, West Bridgford, NOTTINGHAM, NG2 7AW.

STUART, Mrs. Sarah Jane, BA(Hons) ACA *2004;* 106 Marsh Lane, Shepley, HUDDERSFIELD, HD8 8AS.

•STUART, Mr. Stephen, FCA FCCA CF *1981;* Brabners Stuart LLP, Horton House, Exchange Flags, LIVERPOOL, L2 3YL.

STUART, Miss. Susan Catherine, ACA *1982;* Thrive, Park Yard, Battersea Park, LONDON, SW11 4NJ.

STUART, Mr. Timothy Ian, BSc ACA *2000;* 18 Jay Close, Lower Earley, READING, RG6 4HE.

STUART DAVIES, Mr. Neale Owen, BA ACA *1986;* 12 Hamilton Court Maitland Drive, HIGH WYCOMBE, BUCKINGHAMSHIRE, HP13 5BN.

•STUART-HARRIS, Mr. Graham Leslie, FCA *1969;* with Barber Harrison & Platt, 2 Rutland Park, SHEFFIELD, S10 2PD.

STUART-MILLS, Mr. James Euan, BSc ACA *1995;* Mill House, North Stainley, RIPON, NORTH YORKSHIRE, HG4 3HT.

STUART-MILLS, Mrs. Lucinda Jane, BSc ACA *1995;* Mill House, North Stainley, RIPON, NORTH YORKSHIRE, HG4 3HT.

STUART-SMITH, Mr. Jonathan Miles, BA FCA *1992;* with Deloitte Touche Tohmatsu, 35/F One Pacific Place, 88 Queensway, CENTRAL, HONG KONG ISLAND, HONG KONG SAR.

STUART-SMITH, Mr. Mark Nigel, BA ACA *1990;* Somerset House Trust Somerset House, Strand, LONDON, WC2R 1LA.
STUBBERFIELD, Mr. Andrew James Frederick, FCA *1975;* 129 Haslemere Road, LIPHOOK, GU30 7BX.
STUBBERFIELD, Mr. Matthew John, BA ACA *1999;* 58a Davigdor Road, HOVE, EAST SUSSEX, BN3 1RB.
STUBBINGS, Mr. Howard Bayley, BA FCA *1975;* 22 Ashdene Road, Heaton Mersey, STOCKPORT, SK4 3AD.
STUBBINGS, Mr. Jonathan Andrew, MA ACA *2006;* 227b Devonshire Road, LONDON, SE23 3NJ.
STUBBINGTON, Mr. Kenneth Arthur, FCA *1951;* Walnut Tree Cottage, Green Lane, Woodcote, READING, RG8 0RT. (Life Member)
STUBBINGTON, Mr. Toby Peter, BA(Hons) ACA *2001;* 1 Lower Paddock Road, WATFORD, WD19 4DU.
STUBBINS, Mr. Christopher John, ACA *2008;* M & A Partners, 7 The Close, NORWICH, NR1 4DJ.
STUBBINS, Mr. David Riley, MA FCA *1978;* Brome, Green Lane, Flookburgh, GRANGE-OVER-SANDS, CUMBRIA, LA11 7JT.
STUBBINS, Mrs. Lesley Elizabeth, BSc ACA *1979;* GEM Associates Ltd, Hersham Place, Molesey Road, Hersham, WALTON-ON-THAMES, SURREY KT12 4RS.
STUBBINS, Mr. Richard Malcolm, BCom ACA *1982;* Sanofi Aventis M S D Ltd, Mallards Reach, Bridge Avenue, MAIDENHEAD, SL6 1QP.
STUBBLES, Miss. Hannah Jane, LLB ACA CTA *2002;* with Francis Clark, North Quay House, Sutton Harbour, PLYMOUTH, PL4 0RA.
STUBBS, Mr. Adam, BA ACA *1999;* Lyndhurst, 33 Darrs Lane, Northchurch, BERKHAMSTED, HERTFORDSHIRE, HP4 3RJ.
STUBBS, Ms. Anne, ACA FCCA *2009;* McEwan Wallace, 68 Argyle Street, BIRKENHEAD, MERSEYSIDE, CH41 6AF.
STUBBS, Mr. Anthony Paul, BSc ACA *1987;* 55 Woodhill Road, Portishead, BRISTOL, BS20 7EY.
STUBBS, Mr. Barrie, FCA *1971;* 16 Aston Way, EPSOM, KT18 5LZ. (Life Member)
STUBBS, Mr. Christopher John, BSc ACA *1987;* 29 Alton Road, WILMSLOW, SK9 5DY.
STUBBS, Mr. Colin Anthony, BCom FCA *1964;* 230 Headstone Lane, HARROW, MIDDLESEX, HA2 6LY. (Life Member)
STUBBS, Mr. David Earl, FCA *1975;* Kerjezequel, Sizun, 29450 SIZUN, BRETAGNE, FRANCE.
STUBBS, Mr. Gary, FCA *1969;* (Tax Fac), with Sutcliffe & Co, 3 Branch Road, BATLEY, WEST YORKSHIRE, WF17 5RY.
STUBBS, Mrs. Helen, BA ACA *2005;* with Dyke Yaxley Limited, 1 Brassey Road, Old Potts Way, SHREWSBURY, SY3 7FA.
•STUBBS, Mr. Ian David, FCA *1977;* Websters, Baker Street Chambers, 136 Baker Street, LONDON, W1U 6UD.
STUBBS, Mr. Jason Mark, ACA *2003;* with Baker Tilly (BVI) Limited, P.O. Box 650, Tropic Isle Building, Nibbs Street, Road Town, TORTOLA VIRGIN ISLANDS (BRITISH).
•STUBBS, Mr. John Michael, FCA *1969;* Howarth Corporate Finance Limited, 64 Wellington Street, LEEDS, LS1 2EE.
STUBBS, Mrs. Lavinia Angela, BSc ACA *1994;* 40 Clarendon Drive, LONDON, SW15 1AE.
STUBBS, Miss. Mai-Ling, BA ACA *2006;* 84 Beaconsfield Road, SURBITON, KT5 9AP.
•STUBBS, Mr. Noel James, LLB FCA *1979;* Stubbs & Co, 21 Bridle Lane, Streetly, SUTTON COLDFIELD, B74 3QE.
STUBBS, Mr. Paul, BSc FCA *1985;* 3 Beresford Road, HARROW, HA1 4QP.
STUBBS, Mr. Philip Downes, ACA *2009;* 28 Southwood Lawn Road, LONDON, N6 5SF.
STUBBS, Mr. Richard Graham, BA ACA *1986;* 26 Arundel Road, KINGSTON UPON THAMES, KT1 3RZ.
•STUBBS, Mr. Robert, BA(Econ) FCA MIoD *1977;* Robert Stubbs, Briarmead, St. Johns Park, Menston, ILKLEY, LS29 6ES.
STUBBS, Mr. Robert John, BA ACA *1979;* Enerflex Systems Ltd, PO Box, 48294, ABU DHABI, UNITED ARAB EMIRATES.
STUBBS, Mr. Roger Gordon, FCA *1974;* Beech House, 36-38 Parkgate Road, NESTON, CH64 6QG.
STUBBS, Mr. Toby Alexander, BA ACA *2003;* with Grant Thornton UK LLP, Grant Thornton House, 22 Melton Street, Euston Square, LONDON, NW1 2EP.
STUBER, Mr. Jeremy Robert, MA MEng FCA *2000;* Newton Investment Management, Mellon Financial Centre, 160 Queen Victoria Street, LONDON, EC4V 4LA.
STUBLEY, Mr. Andrew, BA(Hons) ACA *2011;* 26 Parkway, ST. IVES, CAMBRIDGESHIRE, PE27 5NS.
STUBLEY, Mr. Ian Alan, BSc(Hons) ACA *2001;* 542 The Heart, WALTON-ON-THAMES, KT12 1GF.
STUBLEY, Mr. Noel James, BSc ACA *1994;* Lloyds Bank Corporate Markets, 8th Floor 40 Spring Gardens, MANCHESTER, M2 1EN.
STUBLEY, Mr. Peter, ACA *2007;* 6 Monarchs Road, Sutterton, BOSTON, LINCOLNSHIRE, PE20 2HJ.
•STUBLEY, Mr. Richard Anthony, MA ACA *1992;* FAIR Audit GmbH & Co. KG, Niedernstr. 10, 20095, HAMBURG, GERMANY.
STUBLEY, Mr. Roderick Ian, BA FCA *1986;* 23 Royal Oak Place, WEST PENNANT HILLS, NSW 2125, AUSTRALIA.
•STUBLEY, Mr. Rodney, FCA *1971;* Winburn Glass Norfolk, Convention House, St. Mary's Street, LEEDS, LS9 7DP.
STUCKEY, Mrs. Helen Margaret, MA ACA *1983;* Westfield House, Tytherton Lucas, CHIPPENHAM, WILTSHIRE, SN15 3RL.
•STUCKEY, Mr. John Graham Hart, BSc FCA *1967;* Stuckeys, 19 Highfield Road, Edgbaston, BIRMINGHAM, B15 3BH.
•STUDD, Mr. Michael Richard, FCA *1972;* Quantum Accountancy Ltd, 4 Forest Court, Oaklands Park, WOKINGHAM, BERKSHIRE, RG41 2FD.
STUDD, Mr. Philip Alastair Fairfax, FCA *1987;* Stewarts Law Llp, 5 New Street Square, LONDON, EC4A 3BF.
STUDD, Mr. Richard Andrew, BA(Hons) ACA *2001;* 16 Ferry Road, FELIXSTOWE, IP11 9LY.
•STUDHAM, Mr. Michael David, FCA FCCA *1974;* (Tax Fac), Spurling Cannon Limited, 424 Margate Road, Westwood, RAMSGATE, KENT, CT12 6SR.
STUDHOLME, Sir Henry William, Bt MA FCA ATII *1983;* Perridge House, Perridge Lane, Longdown, EXETER, EX6 7RU.
STUDHOLME, Miss. Joanne, ACA *2007;* H S S Hire Service Group Ltd, 25 Willow Lane, MITCHAM, CR4 4TS.
STUDHOLME, Mr. Jonathan Shields, BA ACA *2005;* with PricewaterhouseCoopers LLP, 101 Barbirolli Square, Lower Mosley Street, MANCHESTER, M2 3PW.
STUKAN, Mrs. Yetty, BA ACA *1988;* PO Box 3250, SOUTH PASADENA, CA 91031, UNITED STATES.
STUMBKE, Mr. Thomas, ACA *2008;* The Bank of England, Threadneedle Street, LONDON, EC2R 8AH.
STUMP, Mr. Christopher Jeremy, FCA *1974;* Armstrong World Industries Inc., PO Box 3001, LANCASTER, PA 17603, UNITED STATES.
STUMP, Miss. Janet Anne, BSc ACA *1989;* 33 Gatcombe, Great Holm, MILTON KEYNES, MK8 9EA.
STUNT, Mr. Jeremy Richard William Handley, BA ACA *1990;* E2 Unicorn Gardens, 11 Shouson Hill Road East, SHOUSON HILL, HONG KONG ISLAND, HONG KONG SAR.
•STUPACK, Mr. Colin Lloyd, FCA *1979;* Felton Associates, 112 Wembley Park Drive, WEMBLEY, MIDDLESEX, HA9 8HS. See also Felton Associates Limited
STUPART, Mr. Ross Ian, LLB ACA CTA *2003;* 20 Roman Park, DALKEITH, MIDLOTHIAN, EH22 2QX.
STURDEE, Mr. Christopher Rodney Piers, MA ACA MCT *1982;* Comptons Barn, 108 Frog Grove Lane, Wood Street Village, GUILDFORD, GU3 3HA.
STURDY, Mr. John Leonard, MA ACA *1988;* Jones & Partners, 5th Flr Julco House, 26-28 Great Portland Street, LONDON, W1W 8AS.
•STURE, Mr. Timothy John, BSc(Econ) FCA *1989;* Scisco Forensic, First Floor 9 Stocks Street, MANCHESTER, M8 8GW.
STURGE, Mr. Alexander James, BSc(Econ) ACA *2000;* 9 Firth Close, SANDBACH, CHESHIRE, CW11 1JH.
STURGE, Mr. Anthony Michael, MEng ACA *2009;* 27 Hobgate, YORK, YO24 4HE.
STURGE, Miss. Deborah Alice, BCom FCA *1974;* 36 Milford Road, BIRMINGHAM, B17 9RL.
STURGE, Mr. Michael Wilson, BSc FCA *1973;* 27 Hobgate, Acomb, YORK, YO24 4HE.
STURGE, Mr. Richard James, BA ACA *1987;* 30 Arden Close, Bradley Stoke, BRISTOL, BS32 8AX.
STURGE, Mr. Simon Harold, FCA *1964;* Lyndhurst, Woodhouse Lane, Holmbury St. Mary, DORKING, RH5 6NN. (Life Member)
•STURGEON, Mr. Andrew John Scott, BA ACA *1993;* Brebners, Tubs Hill House, London Road, SEVENOAKS, KENT, TN13 1BL.
STURGEON, Mr. Colin, MA FCA *1970;* 109 Parkgate Road, NESTON, CHESHIRE, CH64 6QF.
STURGEON, Mr. David Andrew, MA ACA *1993;* 52 Charles Street, LONDON, W1J 5EU.
STURGEON, Mr. David John, BSc FCA *1978;* 438 Station Road, Dorridge, SOLIHULL, B93 8EU.
STURGEON, Mr. Edwin D'Arcy, FCA *1961;* P.O. Box 657, BARBERTON, 1300, SOUTH AFRICA. (Life Member)
STURGEON, Mrs. Julie Alice, BSc ACA *1992;* Garlands Farmhouse, Birch, COLCHESTER, CO2 0NS.
STURGEON, Mr. Paul Stuart, BA ACA *1992;* Garlands Farmhouse, Birch, COLCHESTER, CO2 0NS.
STURGEON, Mr. Peter Fraser, ACA *2011;* 6 Adams Drive, FLEET, HAMPSHIRE, GU51 3DZ.
STURGES, Mr. Edward James Mansfield, BA ACA *1986;* with KPMG LLP, 15 Canada Square, LONDON, E14 5GL.
STURGES, Mr. Hugh Francis Dering, BA ACA *1982;* Medway Long Cross Hill, Headley, BORDON, GU35 8BS.
STURGES, Miss. Isabel Edith, BSc ACA *2002;* 17 Park Street, Long Eaton, NOTTINGHAM, NG10 4NA.
STURGES, Mr. Jonathan Lee, BA ACA *2007;* 56 Beatrice Road, KETTERING, NORTHAMPTONSHIRE, NN16 9QS.
STURGESS, Mr. Andrew Charles, BA FCA *1981;* 27 Dalkeith Avenue, Dumbreck, GLASGOW, G41 5LF.
STURGESS, Mr. Bruce Eric, FCA *1958;* Thrashers, Old Lane, COBHAM, KT11 1NA. (Life Member)
STURGESS, Ms. Catherine Ruth, BA FCA *1990;* 178 Thunder Lane, Thorpe St Andrew, NORWICH, NR7 0AB.
STURGESS, Mr. Christopher Julian, BCom FCA *1986;* Larges House, Lower Village, Blunsdon, SWINDON, SN26 7BJ.
STURGESS, Mr. Daniel, MPhil BA ACA *2002;* 409 - 2768 Cranberry Drive, VANCOUVER V6K 4V1, BC, CANADA.
STURGESS, Mr. David Antony, FCA *1953;* Via Vinicio Cortese 180, 00128 ROME, ITALY. (Life Member)
STURGESS, Mr. Geoffrey, FCA *1969;* 57 Whitcliffe Drive, RIPON, HG4 2JX. (Life Member)
STURGESS, Mr. Henry James Higgerty, ACA *2009;* Duplex Home Pinheiros, Rua Alves Guimarães 150, Apto. 2111, SAO PAULO, 05412-001, BRAZIL.
STURGESS, Mr. Martin William, BA ACA *2000;* Westlands, 32 Main Street, Hartshorne, SWADLINCOTE, DERBYSHIRE, DE11 7ES.
•STURGESS, Mr. Michael James, BSc FCA FCCA *1980;* (Member of Council 2009 - 2011), Swat UK Limited, Tor View House, Darklake View, Estover, PLYMOUTH, PL6 7TL.
STURGESS, Mr. Michael John, BA ACA *1985;* 5, Furber Court, NORTHAMPTON, NN3 3RW.
STURGESS, Mr. Michael Raymond, BTech FCA *1975;* 9 Marshall Drive, PICKERING, YO18 7JT.
STURGESS, Mr. Philip John, MBA BSc FCA CA(SA) *1980;* Postnet Suite 214, Private Bag X2600, HOUGHTON, GAUTENG, 2041, SOUTH AFRICA.
STURGESS, Mrs. Sheridan Jane, MA FCA *1980;* Holywell, Pengover Road, LISKEARD, CORNWALL, PL14 3NW.
STURGIS, Mr. Simon Roy Owen, FCA *1954;* Le Vey, 14700 VILLY-LEZ-FALAISE, FRANCE. (Life Member)
STURLEY, Mr. Trefor Douglas, BSc ACA *1988;* 40 Skomer Drive, MILFORD HAVEN, DYFED, SA73 2RF.
•STURMAN, Mr. Bramwell Ashley, BA FCA *1978;* Sturmans, The Seedbed Centre, Langston Road, LOUGHTON, ESSEX, IG10 3TQ.
STURMAN, Ms. Helen, ACA *2010;* 3 Lime Kiln Mews, NORWICH, NR3 2ET.
STURMAN, Mr. Keith, FCA *1964;* 49 Battenhall Rise, WORCESTER, WR5 2DE.
STURMAN, Mrs. Marcella Convey Mineo, ACA *1992;* 24A Acol Road, West Hampstead, LONDON, NW6 3AG.
STURMAN, Mr. Richard Leslie, FCA *1971;* 12A Nailcote Avenue, Tile Hill Village, COVENTRY, CV4 9GL.
STURMAN, Mr. Robert, MA FCA *1973;* Rangers, Pembley Green, Copthorne, CRAWLEY, RH10 3LF.
STURMEY, Mr. Christopher John, FCA *1966;* Rolleston House, Spinney Nook Main Street, Tugby, LEICESTER, LE7 9EY.
•STURMEY, Mr. Neil John, MA FCA *1988;* (Tax Fac), Grant Thornton UK LLP, Royal Liver Building, Pier Head, LIVERPOOL, L3 1PS. See also Grant Thornton LLP
STURMY, Mr. Trevor, BSc ACA *1992;* 65 Sotheby Road, LONDON, N5 2UP.
STURNIOLO, Mrs. Pamela Linda, BSc ACA *2006;* 3 Orchard Gardens, CHESSINGTON, SURREY, KT9 1AG.
•STURROCK, Ms. Laura-Ann, BSc FCA CTA *1980;* (Tax Fac), Laura Sturrock Ltd, 39 Church Street, Nether Heyford, NORTHAMPTON, NN7 3LH.
STURT, Mr. Brian, FCA *1957;* 12 Turmore Dale, WELWYN GARDEN CITY, AL8 6HS. (Life Member)
STURT, Mr. David Roy, BA FCA *1975;* 198 Beech Road, ST. ALBANS, AL3 5AX.
•STURT, Mrs. Jennifer Mary, BSc ACA *1989;* Jennifer Sturt, 16 North Street, Rothersthorpe, NORTHAMPTON, NN7 3JB.
•STURT, Miss. Sarah Louise, MA ACA *1997;* Deloitte LLP, 3 Rivergate, Temple Quay, BRISTOL, BS1 6GD. See also Deloitte & Touche LLP
STURTIVANT, Mr. Brian Frederick, FCA *1959;* Malham, Hough Lane, Norley, FRODSHAM, WA6 8JZ. (Life Member)
STURTRIDGE, Mr. Gerald Arthur, LLD BSc FCA *1969;* The Lugger, Globe Ley, Globefield, Topsham, EXETER, EX3 0DL.
STURZAKER, Mr. Andrew James, BA(Econ) ACA *2001;* 37 Lindale Avenue, Grimsargh, PRESTON, PR2 5LL.
STUTELY, Miss. Jade Helen, ACA *2002;* 23 Lansdowne Road, Frimley, CAMBERLEY, SURREY, GU16 9UW.
STUTT, Miss. Elizabeth Anne Victoria, ACA *2008;* NB Vita Nova II, Macclesfield Canal Centre Ltd, Brook Street, MACCLESFIELD, CHESHIRE, SK11 7AW.
STUTT, Mr. Ian Hamilton, BSc FCA *1981;* 10 Church Path, Merton Park, LONDON, SW19 3HJ.
STUTTARD, Mr. Derek, FCA *1951;* 1 Meadowcroft, Formby, LIVERPOOL, L37 4HT. (Life Member)
STUTTARD, John Boothman, Kt MA FCA *1970;* West End House, 56 Totteridge Common, LONDON, N20 8LZ.
STUTTARD, Mrs. Louise Ann, BA ACA *2001;* C S First: Credit Suisse Financial Produ, 1 Cabot Square, LONDON, E14 4QJ.
STUTTARD, Mr. Thomas Henry Boothman, MA ACA *2001;* 5b The Avenue, HERTFORD, SG14 3DG.
STUTTLE, Mr. Colin Henry Robert, FCA *1969;* PO Box 584, PARAPARAUMU 5254, NEW ZEALAND.
STUTTLE, Mr. Paul Charles, FCA *1975;* 3 Far Croft, Breaston, DERBY, DE72 3HL.
STYAN, Mr. Andrew John, BSc ACA *1999;* The Willows, Southwell Road West, Rainworth, MANSFIELD, NOTTINGHAMSHIRE, NG21 0HJ.
•STYANT, Ms. Sarah Louise, BA ACA *1998;* with KPMG LLP, 15 Canada Square, LONDON, E14 5GL.
•STYBURSKI, Mr. George Francis, FCA *1962;* Dauman & Co Limited, 9 Station Parade, Uxbridge Road Ealing Common, LONDON, W5 3LD.
•STYLE, Mr. Alan Chaim, FCA *1959;* Style Accountants Limited, Bank House, Southwick Square, Southwick, BRIGHTON, BN42 4FN.
•STYLE, Mr. Rodney Hill, ACA *1981;* HW, Sterling House, 19-23 High Street, KIDLINGTON, OXFORDSHIRE, OX5 2DH. See also HW Corporate Finance LLP and Haines Watts
STYLE, Mr. Simon Anthony, BA ACA *1987;* Ammerhurst Ltd Colton House, Princes Avenue, LONDON, N3 2DB.
STYLES, Ms. Caroline Jane, ACA *1991;* Conocophillips Ltd Humber Refinery, Eastfield Road South Killingholme, IMMINGHAM, SOUTH HUMBERSIDE, DN40 3DW.
STYLES, Mr. Daniel, ACA *2008;* J A Fell & Co, 40 Hoghton Street, SOUTHPORT, MERSEYSIDE, PR9 0PQ.
STYLES, Mr. David James, BEng ACA *1996;* 149 Darras Road, Ponteland, NEWCASTLE UPON TYNE, NE20 9PQ.
•STYLES, Mr. David Michael, FCA *1980;* Trading Skills Limited, 3 Rushmere Close, Adlington, MACCLESFIELD, CHESHIRE, SK10 5SR.
STYLES, Mrs. Gillian Mary, BA ACA *1992;* 67 Hinckley Road, Sapcote, LEICESTER, LE9 4LG.
STYLES, Mr. Jeremy Wilson, MA FCA *1983;* Marchettigasse 2-6/7, A-1060, VIENNA, AUSTRIA.
•STYLES, Mr. Leslie, BSc ACA *1978;* (Tax Fac), Styles & Co Accountants Limited, Heather House, 473 Warrington Road, Culcheth, WARRINGTON, WA3 5QU.
STYLIANAKIS, Mr. Stelios Michael, MSc BA ACA *2000;* 2 Stasinou Street, Strvolos, 2014 NICOSIA, CYPRUS.
STYLIANIDES, Mr. Christoforos Vassos, BSc ACA *1995;* 8 Finea Street, Strovolos, 2036 NICOSIA, CYPRUS.
STYLIANIDES, Mr. Christos John, BSc ACA *1988;* Marfin Popular Bank Public Co Ltd, 152 Limassol Avenue, PO Box 2032, CY-1598 NICOSIA, CYPRUS.

•**STYLIANIDES, Mr. George Eugene, MSc FCA** *1989;* PricewaterhouseCoopers LLP, Hays Galleria, 1 Hays Lane, LONDON, SE1 2RD.

STYLIANIDES, Mrs. Julie Caroline, BSc ACA *1992;* 38 Roundwood Park, HARPENDEN, HERTFORDSHIRE, AL5 3AF.

STYLIANIDES, Mr. Stelios, BSc ACA *2006;* 60 Platonos Street, Ayios, 4001 LIMASSOL, CYPRUS.

STYLIANOU, Miss. Anastasia, BSc ACA *2011;* Panikou Charaki, 97 Panthea, Mesa Geitonia, 4007 LIMASSOL, CYPRUS.

•**STYLIANOU, Mr. Andreas Christofi, ACA FCCA** *1980;* Kounnis and Partners Ltd, Sterling House, Fulbourne Road, Walthamstow, LONDON, E17 4EE. See also Kounnis and Partner Plc

STYLIANOU, Mr. Andreas Costa, BSc ACA MBA *1997;* 25 Pegasou Street, 2057 Strovolos, NICOSIA, CYPRUS.

STYLIANOU, Mr. Angelos, BA ACA *2002;* PO Box 59670, 4011 LIMASSOL, CYPRUS.

STYLIANOU, Mr. Aristides Stelios, MSc BA ACA *2002;* P.O.BOX 66022, Polis Chrysohous, 8830 PAPHOS, CYPRUS.

STYLIANOU, Mr. Aristos Anastasiou, MSc BSc ACA *1985;* PO Box 24382, 1703 NICOSIA, CYPRUS.

STYLIANOU, Mr. Byron, FCA *1972;* PO Box 22470, 1522 NICOSIA, CYPRUS. (Life Member)

•**STYLIANOU, Mr. Charalambos, BSc ACA** *1993;* Ernst & Young Cyprus Limited, Nicosia Tower Centre, 36 Byron Avenue, P.O Box 21656, 1511 NICOSIA, CYPRUS.

STYLIANOU, Mr. Constantinos, MA BSc ACA *1981;* Flat 3, Rita Court 16, Kivellis Street 16-18, 138 NICOSIA, CYPRUS.

STYLIANOU, Mr. Demetrios Antoniou, FCA *1970;* c/o Mrs D P Woodman, Agelef Shipping co (london), Manning House, 22 Carlisle Place, LONDON, SW1P 1JA.

STYLIANOU, Mr. George, ACA *2008;* 32 Iakovos Christodoulides, PAPHOS, CYPRUS.

STYLIANOU, Miss. Mary Efterpi, MBA BA ACA *1984;* Route de Chene 40, 1208 GENEVA, SWITZERLAND.

STYLIANOU, Mr. Michael, ACA *1982;* Romanou 15, Latsia, 2237 NICOSIA, CYPRUS.

STYLIANOU, Mr. Theodoros, BA ACA *2001;* AYIAS PARASKEVIS 72, 4044 YERMASOYIA, CYPRUS.

STYMAN, Mr. Nicholas Vincent, BA ACA *1991;* 48 King Edwards Grove, TEDDINGTON, TW11 9LX.

STYNES, Mrs. Catherine, MA BSc FCA *1979;* 3 Playle Chase, Great Totham, MALDON, CM9 8UT.

STYRING, Mr. Robert Alan, BSc ACA *1998;* Applegarth, Oakridge Lane, WINSCOMBE, AVON, BS25 1LZ.

STYRING, Mr. William Robert, FCA *1969;* Marland, Marland Cross, Yealmpton, PLYMOUTH, PL8 2ER. (Life Member)

SU, Mr. Pui Kwan, ACA *2008;* Flat L, 9th Floor Southern Building, 273 Kings Road, NORTH POINT, HONG KONG ISLAND, HONG KONG SAR.

SU, Ms. Suat Mei, BA(Hons) ACA *2001;* Ernst & Young, Level 16, Tower E3, Oriental Plaza, No 1 East Chang Avenue, Dong Cheng Street BEIJING CHINA.

SUAREZ, Mr. Carlos Robert, FCA *1968;* 13 Ferrers Road, Weston, STAFFORD, ST18 0JN.

SUAREZ, Mr. Glen Patrick, BA FCA *1989;* Villa Hollandia, 22 Rue Bellevue, MC 98000 MONACO, MONACO.

SUAREZ, Mr. Trevor Lloyd, BSc ACA *1996;* 61 Sutton Lane South, LONDON, W4 3JT.

SUAREZ-PEREZ, Ms. Penelope Mary, BSc FCA *1975;* 25 Herrison Cottages, Charminster, DORCHESTER, DT2 9RJ.

SUAZNABAR, Mrs. Rachel Anne, BSc ACA *2004;* 2 The Byways, Skinners Lane, ASHTEAD, SURREY, KT21 2NR.

SUBBIAH, Mrs. Sharmila, BSc ACA *2001;* Blue Pearl, 8 Old Manor Way, CHISLEHURST, BR7 5XS.

SUBEDI, Mr. Sanjeeb, ACA *2010;* Flat 20, 5B Bear Lane, LONDON, SE1 0UH.

SUBENDRANATHAN, Miss. Lukshmi Abirami, BSc ACA *1995;* 1751 Vermont Court, ALLEN, TX 75013, UNITED STATES.

SUBERAMAMIAM, Mr. Paragash C R, FCA *1982;* C/o Magna Segmen SDN BHD, Unit 607 Block C, Pusat Phileo Damansara 1, No 9 Jalan 16/11, 46350 PETALING JAYA, SELANGOR MALAYSIA.

SUBERBERE, Mrs. Marie-Mathilde, ACA *1992;* Apartment 21, 3 Blackthorn avenue, LONDON, N7 8AW.

•**SUBERT, Mr. Michael John, FCA** *1972;* The Granary Loft 12 Foremans Walk, High Street Headcorn, ASHFORD, TN27 9NE.

SUBJALLY, Mr. Habib, BSc ACA *1990;* 30 The Terrace, Barnes, LONDON, SW13 0NR.

•**SUBRAMANIAM, Mr. Andrew, BSc FCA** *1997;* H W Fisher & Company Limited, Acre House, 11/15 William Road, LONDON, NW1 3ER. See also FisherEase Limited, H.W. Fisher & Company

SUBRAMANIAM, Mr. Natarajan, FCA *1970;* 245 Orchard Boulevard, Apt 12-03 Orchard Bel Air, SINGAPORE 2486 48, SINGAPORE.

SUBRAMANIAM, Mr. Ramarao, ACA *1995;* 125 Lorong Setiabistari 1, Bukit Damansara, 50490 KUALA LUMPUR, FEDERAL TERRITORY, MALAYSIA.

SUBRAMANIAM, Mr. Sivarajah, ACA *1981;* Sivash Holdings Berhad, A-1-5 Megan Avenue 1, Jalan Tun Razak, 50400 KUALA LUMPUR, FEDERAL TERRITORY, MALAYSIA.

SUBRAMANIAN, Mr. Ramanan, MSc ACA ACCA *2007;* with CPAA - CPA Australia, Level 20, 28 Freshwater Place, SOUTHBANK, VIC 3006, AUSTRALIA.

SUBRAMANIUM, Mrs. Emma Louise, BSc ACA *1997;* 104 Sackville St, KEW, VIC 3101, AUSTRALIA.

SUBRAMANIYAN, Mr. Jaya, PhD FCA *1992;* 31 Brim Hill, LONDON, N2 0HD.

SUBZWARI, Miss. Sana, ACA *2008;* Newlyns, Cwmgelli, BLACKWOOD, GWENT, NP12 1BR.

SUCH, Mr. Herbert William, FCA *1952;* 386 Whirlowdale Road, SHEFFIELD, S11 9NJ. (Life Member)

•**SUCHAK, Mr. Anant, FCA** *1983;* (Tax Fac), KPMG LLP, 15 Canada Square, LONDON, E14 5GL. See also KPMG Europe LLP

SUCHAK, Miss. Rayna, BSc ACA *2010;* 50 Knoll Crescent, NORTHWOOD, MIDDLESEX, HA6 1HJ.

•**SUCHAK, Mr. Shailesh Manilal, FCA** *1972;* (Tax Fac), Ableman Shaw & Co, Mercury House, 1 Heather Park Drive, WEMBLEY, HA0 1SX. See also Castle Ryce

SUCHER, Dr. Patricia Helen, MSc ACA *1982;* 7 Marlborough Road, LONDON, W5 5NY.

SUCHLAND, Mrs. Emma Kate, BA ACA *2001;* with BDO LLP, 6th Floor, 3 Hardman Street, Spinningfields, MANCHESTER, M3 3AT.

SUCHOCKI, Mrs. Mandy Elizabeth, BA ACA *1990;* 21 Haughley Drive, Rushmere St Andrew, IPSWICH, SUFFOLK, IP4 5QU.

SUCHOPAREK, Mr. Paul Anton, BSc ACA *1987;* 15 Sherbrooke Close, SALE, M33 5SZ.

•**SUCHOPAREK, Mrs. Susan Elizabeth, BA FCA** *1986;* with KPMG LLP, 15 Canada Square, LONDON, E14 5GL.

SUCKLING, Mr. Adrian William, BSc ACA *2003;* 33 Corbets Avenue, UPMINSTER, RM14 2EG.

SUCKLING, Mr. Andrew, BA ACA *1995;* 9 Adam Drive, SINGAPORE 289969, SINGAPORE.

SUCKLING, Mr. Clive Roy, MA FCA *1978;* with PricewaterhouseCoopers LLP, 1 Embankment Place, LONDON, WC2N 6RH.

SUCKLING, Mr. David John, BA FCA *1998;* 3 Cranbrook Road, Redland, BRISTOL, BS6 7BJ.

•**SUCKLING, Mr. David John, FCA** *1989;* (Tax Fac), DSCO Limited, The Old Boardroom, Collett Road, WARE, HERTFORDSHIRE, SG12 7LR.

•**SUCKLING, Mr. Paul William, FCA** *1973;* Paul Suckling & Co, Mousetraps, Hall Green, Little Yeldham, HALSTEAD, CO9 4LF.

•**SUD, Miss. Raka, ACA** *1983;* Doctors Surgery, 134 Bath Road, HOUNSLOW, TW3 3ET.

SUDBURY, Mrs. Cindy Anne, BSc ACA *1997;* North Eastling Farmhouse, Eastling, FAVERSHAM, ME13 0AE.

SUDBURY, Mr. Nicholas Harry Edward, FCA *1991;* 6 St. Johns Road, CHELMSFORD, CM2 9PE.

SUDDABY, Mr. Gilbert Peter, FCA *1955;* Camerton Croft, 72 Main Street, Bubwith, SELBY, YO8 6LX. (Life Member)

SUDDABY, Mr. Mark Keith, MA ACA *1987;* 35 Uplands Road, Saltford, BRISTOL, BS31 3JQ.

SUDDABY, Mr. Paul, BA FCA *1987;* PricewaterhouseCoopers, Emirates Towers Offices, PO Box 11987, Level 40, Sheikh Zayed Road, PO Box 11987 DUBAI UNITED ARAB EMIRATES.

SUDELL, Mr. Walter Francis, FCA *1953;* 29 Woodlands Avenue, Ribbleton, PRESTON, PR2 6DT. (Life Member)

SUDHAKAR, Mrs. Neha, BSc ACA *2003;* 35 Culver Grove, STANMORE, MIDDLESEX, HA7 2NJ.

SUDLOW, Mr. Christopher Wray, FCA *1968;* 5 Solent Drive, BASINGSTOKE, RG22 4XS.

SUDLOW, Mr. Michael, ACA *2008;* 79a Millbrook Road, LONDON, SW9 7JD.

SUDRA, Mrs. Rajni, ACA *1982;* 32 Wensley Avenue, WOODFORD GREEN, ESSEX, IG8 9HE.

SUDWARTS, Mr. Israel Alexander, FCA *1969;* 6 Elm Park Gardens, LONDON, NW4 2PJ.

•**SUDWORTH, Mr. John, BA ACA** *1981;* (Tax Fac), John Sudworth, 5 The Street, Molash, CANTERBURY, KENT, CT4 8HH.

SUE, Mrs. Sally Katherine, BA ACA *2010;* 30 Totland Road, BRIGHTON, BN2 3EN.

SUEKE, Mr. Daniel, BA ACA *2007;* Shai agnon 15/ 2, 93589 JERUSALEM, ISRAEL.

SUEN, Mr. David Kin-Man, ACA CA(AUS) *2009;* 4A 8/F Broadway, Stage 1, MEI FOO SUN CHUEN, KOWLOON, HONG KONG SAR.

SUEN, Mr. Dennis Kin Yan, BSc ACA *1992;* Sanmina-SCI (China) Limited, 5/F Kader Industrial Building, 22 Kai Cheung Road, KOWLOON BAY, KOWLOON, HONG KONG SAR.

SUEN, Miss. Kwai Har, BA ACA CPA CICPA *1990;* 22 Wycombe Gardens, LONDON, NW11 8AL.

SUEN, Ms. Lok Ting Hanna, ACA *2008;* Rm 110 Block F, Kam Fung Court, Ma On Shan, SHA TIN, NEW TERRITORIES, HONG KONG SAR.

SUEN, Ms. Yuen Fun, ACA *2007;* Flat E 11/F, Block 1 Aria, 51 Fung Shing Street, NGAU CHI WAN, KOWLOON, HONG KONG SAR.

SUFFOLK, Mr. Rodney James, ACA CA(AUS) *2009;* Flat 5, 50 Pear Tree Street, LONDON, EC1V 3SB.

SUFI, Mr. Parvez Hussain, FCA *1976;* Pharmagen Limited, 5/A Zafar Ali Road, Gulberg-V, LAHORE 54660, PAKISTAN.

•**SUFRAZ, Mr. Hassam, ACA** *1983;* (Tax Fac), Sufraz & Co, 13 Newton Road, Canford Cliffs, POOLE, BH13 7EX.

SUFRIN, Mr. Michael Maurice, BSc FCA *1975;* (Tax Fac), Marsh Croft, Shaw Lane, LICHFIELD, WS13 7AG.

SUGAR, Mr. Malcolm Ivor, FCA *1957;* 30 Links Drive, RADLETT, HERTFORDSHIRE, WD7 8BE. (Life Member)

•**SUGARMAN, Mr. Clive Jonathan, FCA** *1977;* (Tax Fac), Lewis Alexander & Connaughton, Second Floor, Boulton House, 17-21 Chorlton Street, MANCHESTER, M1 3HY. See also Lewis Alexander & Collins

•**SUGARMAN, Mr. Ivan Phineas, FCA** *1953;* Leigh Carr, 72 New Cavendish Street, LONDON, W1G 8AU.

•**SUGARMAN, Mr. Jack, FCA** *1958;* (Tax Fac), King & King, Roxburghe House, 273-287 Regent Street, LONDON, W1B 2HA.

SUGARMAN, Mr. Marc Louis, BA ACA *1998;* Blue Lizzard, 34 Jamestown Road, LONDON, NW1 7BY.

•**SUGARMAN, Mr. Montague Aaron, FCA** *1960;* Willowdyke, Quarry Lane, HARROGATE, NORTH YORKSHIRE, HG1 3HR.

SUGARS, Mr. Paul Mervyn, MA ACA *1991;* Ivy Dene Cottage, 9 Church Lane, Netherton, WAKEFIELD, WF4 4HE.

•**SUGARWHITE, Mr. Jeffrey, FCA** *1961;* (Tax Fac), Sugarwhite Associates, 5 Windus Road, LONDON, N16 6UT.

SUGDEN, Mr. Andrew, BA FCA *1985;* Nielsen Book Services 3rd Floor, Midas, 62 Goldsworth Road, WOKING, GU21 6LQ.

SUGDEN, Mr. Andrew James, BSc ACA *2010;* 4 Westdale Gardens, MANCHESTER, M19 1JD.

•**SUGDEN, Mr. Anthony Brendan, FCA** *1974;* (Tax Fac), Sudgens LLP, Unit 20, Zenith Park, Whaley Road, BARNSLEY, SOUTH YORKSHIRE S75 1HT.

SUGDEN, Miss. Araminta Constance, BSc ACA *2003;* with PKF (UK) LLP, Farringdon Place, 20 Farringdon Road, LONDON, EC1M 3AP.

SUGDEN, Mr. Bernard Brian, FCA *1974;* Beck House, Beck Lane, BINGLEY, WEST YORKSHIRE, BD16 4DD. (Life Member)

SUGDEN, Mr. David Arnold, BSc FCA CCMI *1977;* Wantsley Barn, Broadwindsor, BEAMINSTER, DORSET, DT8 3PT.

SUGDEN, Mr. Elwyn James, FCA *1969;* 51 Withy Park, Bishopston, SWANSEA, SA3 3EY. (Life Member)

SUGDEN, Mr. James Arthur, MA FCA *1999;* The Old Forge, Buxhall, STOWMARKET, SUFFOLK, IP14 3DJ.

SUGDEN, Mr. John Philip, MSc FCA *1972;* Scaw Ghyll, Town Head, Grassington, SKIPTON, BD23 5BL. (Life Member)

SUGDEN, Mr. John Robert, FCA *1965;* 17 Foxglove Road, HUDDERSFIELD, HD5 8LW. (Life Member)

SUGDEN, Mr. Keith Francis, MPhil BA FCA *1974;* 83 Fir Road, Bramhall, STOCKPORT, SK7 2JF.

SUGDEN, Mr. Martin Leslie, BSc ACA *1983;* Damales House Borough Court Road, Hartley Wintney, HOOK, HAMPSHIRE, RG27 8JA.

SUGG, Mr. Christopher Charles, BA ACA *1985;* Grey Walls, Hook Heath Road, WOKING, SURREY, GU22 0QD.

SUGG, Mr. James Michael St John, BSc ACA *1999;* Upper Northend House, Northend, Batheaston, BATH, BA1 8ES.

SUGGETT, Mr. Adam, ACA *2008;* Flat 3 Belvedere Court 1 Paulin Drive, LONDON, N21 1AZ.

•**SUGGETT, Mr. Alan Moore, BSc FCA** *1980;* UNW LLP, Citygate, St. James Boulevard, NEWCASTLE UPON TYNE, NE1 4JE.

SUGGETT, Mr. Gavin Robert, MA MSc FCA *1971;* Mill of Forneth, BLAIRGOWRIE, PH10 6SP.

SUGGETT, Mrs. Kirsty Ann, ACA *2008;* 3 Belvedere Court, 1 Paulin Drive, LONDON, N21 1AZ.

SUGGITT, Mr. Peter Francis, ACA *1991;* Osprey Ltd, Dunslow Road, Eastfield, SCARBOROUGH, YO11 3UT.

SUGIARTO, Miss. Amelia, ACA *2010;* with PricewaterhouseCoopers LLP, 1 Embankment Place, LONDON, WC2N 6RH.

SUGIYAMA, Miss. Emi, BA ACA *1999;* 1-21-2-803 Ebisu, Shibuya-ku, TOKYO, 150-0013 JAPAN.

SUGIYAMA, Miss. Noelle, ACA *2008;* 2-9-1-801, Kanda Jimbocho, Chiyoda-ku, TOKYO, 101-0051 JAPAN.

SUGRUE, Miss. Claire, BA(Hons) ACA *2004;* 61e, Third Floor Flat, Highbury Park, LONDON, N5 1TH.

SUGUNASINGHA, Mr. Milinda De Alwis, BA FCA *1991;* 7 Woodbury Drive, SUTTON, SURREY, SM2 5RA.

•**SUHAIL, Mr. Nazmil, BA(Econ) ACA** *2002;* (Tax Fac), 27 Abergeldie Road, LONDON, SE12 8BH.

SUI TIT TONG, Mr. Andrew, ACA *2011;* 4 Daffodil Close, CROYDON, CR0 8XQ.

SUI TIT TONG, Mr. Wan Kong, ACA *1979;* 4 Daffodil Close, Shirley Oaks, CROYDON, CR0 8XQ.

SUIDAN, Mr. Jad Anis, FCA *1976;* Suidan & Co, P.O. Box 16-5708, BEIRUT, LEBANON.

SUJAUDDAWLA, Mr. Suji, ACA *1978;* 77 Chestnut Crescent, TORONTO M1L 1Y6, ON, CANADA.

SUKARNO, Ms. Sherissa, MEng ACA *2011;* 35 Porchester Square, LONDON, W2 6AW.

SUKHIJA, Miss. Saira Jane, BSc ACA *2001;* 30 Alwyne Road, Wimbledon, LONDON, SW19 7AB.

SULAIMAN, Mr. Nik Shahrizal, BA(Hons) ACA *2003;* 8 JALAN TITIAN U8/42D, BUKIT JELUTONG, 40150 SHAH ALAM, MALAYSIA.

•**SULAIMAN, Mr. Shazali, BA FCA** *1987;* KPMG, Unit 402-403A, Wisma Jaya, Jalan Pemanca, BANDAR SERI BEGAWAN, BS8811 BRUNEI DARUSSALAM.

SULAT, Mrs. Susanna Kay Christine, BCom ACA *1981;* The Pickaquoy Centre Trust, Muddisdale Road, KIRKWALL, ORKNEY, KW15 1LR.

•**SULEMAN, Mr. Abdul Kayoom, MBA MSc FCA** *1983;* (Tax Fac), A.K. Suleman, 11 Clovelly Road, Hornsey, LONDON, N8 7RL.

•**SULEMAN, Mr. Ebrahim, ACA** *1983;* (Tax Fac), Forrest Burlinson, 20 Owl Lane, DEWSBURY, WEST YORKSHIRE, WF12 7RQ. See also Accounting Management Services Ltd

SULEMAN, Mr. Mahboob Hussain, BEng ACA *1992;* 86 Burford Gardens, LONDON, N13 4LP.

SULEMAN, Mr. Salim, BA ACA *2004;* Flat 47 Hannah Buildings, 56 Watney Street, LONDON, E1 2QU.

SULEMAN, Mr. Sharjeel, MPHIL BSc ACA *2004;* ITV, 88-100 Quay Street, MANCHESTER, M3 4PR.

SULERI-JOHNSON, Mr. Chris Steven, ACA *2010;* 41 Streetly Crescent, SUTTON COLDFIELD, WEST MIDLANDS, B74 4PZ.

SULKIN, Mr. Ronald, FCA *1955;* 25 Brockley Avenue, STANMORE, MIDDLESEX, HA7 4LT. (Life Member)

SULLAM, Mr. Guido, ACA *2004;* 40 Primrose Close, LUTON, LU3 1EU.

SULLINGE, Mr. Rynton Haydon, FCA *1962;* The Paddock, Randalls Green, Chalford Hill, STROUD, GLOUCESTERSHIRE, GL6 8LG. (Life Member)

SULLIVAN, Mr. Adrian, BA(Hons) ACA *2010;* 124 Stancliffe Road, MANCHESTER, M22 4PR.

SULLIVAN, Mrs. Adrienne Mary, BSc ACA *1992;* Bowden Farmhouse, 16 Bowden Hill, Lacock, CHIPPENHAM, SN15 2PW.

SULLIVAN, Mr. Andrew George James, BSc ACA *1994;* Outspan, Guildford Road, Loxwood, BILLINGSHURST, WEST SUSSEX, RH14 0SE.

SULLIVAN, Mr. Andrew Graham, BA ACA *2001;* 258 Dacre Park, LONDON, SE13 5DD.

SULLIVAN, Mr. Andrew John, FCA *1981;* 16 Willoughby Way, Piddington, NORTHAMPTON, NN7 2EH.

SULLIVAN, Mr. Anthony John, BSc ACA *1998;* 9 Cadet Way, Church Crookham, FLEET, HAMPSHIRE, GU52 8UG.

SULLIVAN, Mr. Anthony Nicholas John, FCA *1955;* 10 Dukes Orchard, BEXLEY, KENT, DA5 2DU. (Life Member)
SULLIVAN, Mr. Brian Charles, BA FCA *1987;* 10 Jury Street, WARWICK, CV34 4EW.
SULLIVAN, Mr. Carl Antony, BA ACA *1991;* 27 Lynton Road, SOUTHEND-ON-SEA, SS1 3BE.
SULLIVAN, Mrs. Caroline, BSc FCA *1976;* P.O.Box 1099, MBABANE, SWAZILAND.
SULLIVAN, Mrs. Carys Jane, ACA *2011;* 124 Stancliffe Road, MANCHESTER, M22 4PR.
SULLIVAN, Mrs. Catherine Margaret, MMath ACA DChA *2007;* 5 Marneys Close, EPSOM, KT18 7HR.
•SULLIVAN, Mr. Christopher Robin, FCA *1965;* (Tax Fac), 48 Bonners Close, MALMESBURY, WILTSHIRE, SN16 9UF.
SULLIVAN, Mr. David Dimitri, FCA ATII *1965;* 123 Burges Road, Thorpe Bay, SOUTHEND-ON-SEA, SS1 3JL.
SULLIVAN, Mr. David John, MBA MCMI FCA CTA *1981;* (Tax Fac), with ICAEW, Metropolitan House, 321 Avebury Boulevard, MILTON KEYNES, MK9 2FZ.
•SULLIVAN, Mr. David Mark, BSc ACA *1985;* (Tax Fac), 5 Maes-y-Deri Graigwen, PONTYPRIDD, MID GLAMORGAN, CF37 2JA.
SULLIVAN, Mr. David Wallace-Jones, BSc ACA *1993;* Fordlands Farm, Crowhurst Road, Catsfield, BATTLE, EAST SUSSEX, TN33 9BT.
SULLIVAN, Mrs. Deborah Anne, LLB ACA *1988;* Tees Valley Community Foundation, Wallace House, Falcon Court, Preston Farm, STOCKTON-ON-TEES, TS18 3TX.
SULLIVAN, Mr. Derek Maurice, FCA *1960;* Green End Orchard, Radnage, HIGH WYCOMBE, HP14 4BZ. (Life Member)
SULLIVAN, Mr. Dominic, BSc ACA *1991;* Lomax Carpark Corporation Ltd, Curnock Estate Car Park 38-40, Pratt Street, LONDON, NW1 0LY.
SULLIVAN, Mrs. Emma, BAcc ACA *2000;* Crawley Borough Council Town Hall, The Boulevard, CRAWLEY, WEST SUSSEX, RH10 1UZ.
SULLIVAN, Mr. Eugene Peter, FCA *1967;* 30A Waldemar Avenue, Ealing, LONDON, W13 9PY.
SULLIVAN, Ms. Helen Clare, BA ACA *1994;* 8 Top Manor Close, Ockbrook, DERBY, DE72 3TN.
SULLIVAN, Miss. Helen Lesley, MA BA ACA *1992;* Hurworth Cotttage, 7 Croft Road, Hurworth, DARLINGTON, COUNTY DURHAM, DL2 2HD.
SULLIVAN, Mrs. Jane Margaret Emilie, BA(Hons) ACA *2004;* Level 4, Lloyds TSB Bank Plc, 25 Gresham Street, LONDON, EC2V 7HN.
SULLIVAN, Miss. Joanne Lesley, BSc ACA *1989;* 3 Park Edge, Hathersage, HOPE VALLEY, DERBYSHIRE, S32 1BS.
SULLIVAN, Mr. John, BA ACA *1990;* Bowden Farmhouse, Bowden Hill, Lacock, CHIPPENHAM, WILTSHIRE, SN15 2PW.
SULLIVAN, Mr. John Guy Michael, FCA *1966;* Ellinge Cottage, Alkham, DOVER, KENT, CT15 7EG.
SULLIVAN, Mr. Joseph William, ACA *2009;* 31 Gordon Road, Eccles, MANCHESTER, M30 9QB.
SULLIVAN, Mrs. Julie Ann, ACA *1996;* 4 Oakdale Manor, HARROGATE, NORTH YORKSHIRE, HG1 2NA.
SULLIVAN, Ms. Kate, MSc BSc ACA *2009;* PricewaterhouseCoopers, Av. Francisco Matarazzo 1400, Torrino Torre, SAO PAULO, 05001-903, BRAZIL.
SULLIVAN, Mr. Kevin John Patrick, BA FCA *1987;* 22 Webster Road, LONDON, SE16 4DF.
SULLIVAN, Miss. Louise Victoria Margaret, BA ACA *2007;* Ground Floor Flat, 20 Chesson Road, LONDON, W14 9QX.
•SULLIVAN, Mr. Martyn David, BSc ACA *1996;* Deloitte LLP, Athene Place, 66 Shoe Lane, LONDON, EC4A 3BQ. See also Deloitte & Touche LLP
SULLIVAN, Mr. Matthew Thomas, MA ACA *1990;* SNV, Edificio Gallery, Av. La Coruna E12-148, Esq Valledoid, Floresta, QUITO ECUADOR.
SULLIVAN, Miss. Melanie, MSc ACA *1996;* Magpie Cottage, Coulsdon Lane, Chipstead, COULSDON, CR5 3QH.
SULLIVAN, Mr. Michael William, FCA *1971;* 64 Common Lane, Hemingford Abbots, HUNTINGDON, CAMBRIDGESHIRE, PE28 9AW.
SULLIVAN, Mr. Niall Joseph Anthony, ACA *2008; (ACA Ireland* Sullivan & Co, 7 Newry Park, CHESTER, CH2 2AR.
SULLIVAN, Miss. Nicola Anne, MSc ACA *2002;* with Ernst & Young LLP, 1 More London Place, LONDON, SE1 2AF.
SULLIVAN, Ms. Patricia Julie, BA ACA *1988;* 7 The Cloisters, Bishops Cleeve, CHELTENHAM, GL52 8YW.
SULLIVAN, Mr. Paul Andrew, ACA *2004;* 1/6a Sunnynook Road, NORTH SHORE 0620, AUCKLAND, NEW ZEALAND.
SULLIVAN, Mr. Peter, FCA *1972;* Welsh Harp, Newsells Village, Barkway, ROYSTON, SG8 8DE.
SULLIVAN, Mr. Philip Graham, BA ACA *1995;* 89 Addison Road, MANLY, NSW 2095, AUSTRALIA.
•SULLIVAN, Mr. Richard, FCA *1984;* Barnard Sampson LLP, 3a Quay View Business Park, Barnards Way, LOWESTOFT, SUFFOLK, NR32 2HD.
•SULLIVAN, Mr. Russell Anthony, LLB FCA *1988;* Censis, Exchange Building, 66 Church Street, HARTLEPOOL, TS24 7DN.
SULLIVAN, Mr. Sandy, BSc ACA *2007;* 3 Sherwood Court High Road Leavesden, WATFORD, WD25 7PA.
SULLIVAN, Mr. Steven John, BSc ACA *1989;* Little Foxes, Rycroft Lane, Bayleys Hill, SEVENOAKS, KENT, TN14 6HT.
SULLIVAN, Mrs. Susan, BSc ACA *1991;* 26 Waterside Park, HEBBURN, NE31 1RS.
•SULLIVAN, Miss. Susan Ann, FCA *1981;* (Tax Fac), Rothman Pantall LLP, 10 St. Ann Street, SALISBURY, SP1 2DN.
•SULLIVAN, Mr. Timothy Andrew, FCA *1995;* Martin Greene Ravden LLP, 55 Loudoun Road, St John's Wood, LONDON, NW8 0DL.
SULLIVAN, Mr. William Thomas, BA(Hons) ACA *2010;* Flat 21 Whiston House, Bingham Court Halton Road, LONDON, N1 2DH.
SULLY, Mr. John Melbourne, BA FCA *1964;* 19 Kingfishers, Orton Wistow, PETERBOROUGH, PE2 6YH.
SULLY, Miss. Juliet Marion, BSc FCA *1977;* 40 Danesboro Road, BRIDGWATER, SOMERSET, TA6 7LT.
SULOLA, Mr. Lanre, ACA *2010;* 149 Windsor Road, LONDON, E7 0RA.
•SULTAN, Mr. Anthony Albert, BA FCA *1995;* Sultan Business Management Limited, Elm Point, East End Way, PINNER, MIDDLESEX, HA5 3BS.
SULTAN, Mr. Muhammad Hafeez, ACA *2009;* Flat 24 Hewetts Quay, 26-32 Abbey Road, BARKING, ESSEX, IG11 7BX.
SULTAN, Mr. Sami Mohamed Ibrahim, BCom FCA *1962;* 4 Ezeldin St, Apt 6, Kobesy - Eldaher, CAIRO, EGYPT. (Life Member)
SULTAN, Mr. Sikander, ACA *2010;* Flat 36 Loxley House, Hirst Crescent, WEMBLEY, MIDDLESEX, HA9 7HL.
SULTAN ALI, Mr. Yousaf, MSc BSc ACA *2003;* Abu Dhabi Investment Authority, Fixed Income & Treasury Department, 211 Corniche Street, PO Box 3600, ABU DHABI, UNITED ARAB EMIRATES.
SULTAN MYDIN, Miss. Nabihah, BSc(Hons) ACA *2010;* Apartment 76, Burford Wharf Apartments, 3 Cam Road, LONDON, E15 2SL.
SULTANA, Miss. Jafrin, BA(Hons) ACA *2006;* 15 Ridley Close, BARKING, IG11 9PJ.
SULZBACHER, Mr. Max, FCA *1958;* Bayit Balev, 35 Ben-Zwi Blvd, 96260 JERUSALEM, ISRAEL. (Life Member)
SUM, Mrs. Alison Jane, BSc ACA *1995;* 3 Cecil Street, BRIGHTON EAST, VIC 3187, AUSTRALIA.
SUM, Mr. Ka Ho Stanley, ACA *2009;* Room 7 16/F Block 35, Heng Fa Chuen, 100 Shing Tai Road, CHAI WAN, HONG KONG SAR.
SUM, Ms. Pui Kwan Linda, ACA *2007;* 27D Blessing Garden, Phase 1, 95 Robinson Road, MID LEVELS, HONG KONG SAR.
SUM, Mr. Pui Ying, ACA *2007;* Flat C 2/F Tower 3, Flora Garden, 7 Chun Fai Road, JARDINE'S LOOKOUT, HONG KONG ISLAND, HONG KONG SAR.
SUM, Mr. Raymond, BSc(Hons) ACA *2003;* 18 The Croft, Meriden, COVENTRY, CV7 7NQ.
SUMAL, Mr. Amardeep, ACA *2011;* 14 Ermington Road, WOLVERHAMPTON, WV4 5DZ.
SUMAR, Mr. Krish, BA ACA *1984;* 36 Beechwood Avenue, South Harrow, HARROW, HA2 8BY.
•SUMAR, Mr. Sajjad, FCA *1993;* Brindleys Limited, 2 Wheeleys Road, Edgbaston, BIRMINGHAM, B15 2LD.
SUMAR, Mr. Zaki, ACA *2008;* PO Box 1750, Ernst & Young Building, 112 MUSCAT, OMAN.
SUMARA, Mr. Robert Alexander, ACA *2010;* 30 Cromwell Road, Stretford, MANCHESTER, M32 8QX.
•SUMARIA-SHAH, Mr. Surendra Kumar Devshi, FCA *1979;* (Tax Fac), Ardners, 18 Hand Court, LONDON, WC1V 6JF.
SUMM, Mr. William Henry, FCA *1970;* Home Farm, Church Street, Donisthorpe, SWADLINCOTE, DE12 7PY.
SUMMER, Mr. Friedrich Georg, BA FCA *1981;* 5 West Cliff, Southgate, SWANSEA, SA3 2AN.
SUMMER, Dr. Keith Godfrey, PhD BSc FCA *1976;* 54 Forestdale, LONDON, N14 7DX.
•SUMMER, Mr. Neil, BSc FCA *1976;* Gerald Edelman, Edelman House, 1238 High Road, Whetstone, LONDON, N20 0LH. See also Neil Summer LLP
SUMMERBEE, Mrs. Janette Sophia, BSc ACA *1987;* 36 Mariners Drive, Sneyd Park, BRISTOL, BS9 1QG.
SUMMERBEE, Mr. Stephen John, BSc ACA *1984;* 36 Mariners Drive, Sneyd Park, BRISTOL, BS9 1QG.
SUMMERBELL, Mr. Mark, BA ACA *1994;* 29 Burnhill Road, BECKENHAM, BR3 3LA.
•SUMMERFIELD, Mr. Christian Paul, BEng ACA DipCII *2001;* BDO Limited, PO Box 1200, Montagu Pavilion, 8-10 Queensway, GIBRALTAR, GIBRALTAR. See also BDO Fidecs
SUMMERFIELD, Mr. Christopher James, MSc ACA *2002;* ACIL Tasman, Level 4, 114 William Street, MELBOURNE, VIC 3000, AUSTRALIA.
SUMMERFIELD, Mr. Hamish Albert, BSc ACA *1999;* Flat 42 Edison Building 20, Westferry Road, LONDON, E14 8LU.
•SUMMERFIELD, Mr. Hugh John Edward, BA(Hons) FCA *1979;* Wilkins Kennedy FKC Limited, Stourside Place, 35-41 Station Road, ASHFORD, KENT, TN23 1PP. See also W K Finn-Kelcey & Chapman Limited
SUMMERFIELD, Mr. Jeremy Paul, BA ACA *2004;* 109 Victoria Road, LONDON, N22 7XG.
SUMMERFIELD, Mrs. Judith Ann, BA FCA *1989;* (Tax Fac), 5 Bowyers Close, Copmanthorpe, YORK, YO23 3XW.
SUMMERFIELD, Mrs. Juliette Marie-Anne, BA ACA *1996;* Volumatic Ltd, Taurus House, Endemere Road, COVENTRY, CV6 5PY.
SUMMERFIELD, Miss. Katy Jayne, ACA *2008;* 15 Reins Avenue, Baildon, SHIPLEY, WEST YORKSHIRE, BD17 7NT.
SUMMERFIELD, Miss. Lorna Kathryn, BSc(Hons) ACA *2000;* Garban-Intercapital Plc, 2 Broadgate, LONDON, EC2M 7UR.
SUMMERFIELD, Mr. Mark, BSc ACA *1987;* 10208 Castlewood Lane, OAKTON, VA 22124, UNITED STATES.
•SUMMERFIELD, Mr. Mark, BSc FCA *1992;* KPMG LLP, 15 Canada Square, LONDON, E14 5GL. See also KPMG Europe LLP
SUMMERFIELD, Mr. Richard Thomas, FCA *1962;* 1 Willow Crescent, Milton, CAMBRIDGE, CB24 6BY. (Life Member)
SUMMERFIELD, Mr. Roger William, FCA *1971;* 2 Gordon Road, Chandler's Ford, EASTLEIGH, SO53 5AN.
•SUMMERFIELD, Mr. Timothy Hugh, BA ACA *1995;* Canterbury House, 117 Main Street, Higham-on-the-Hill, NUNEATON, WARWICKSHIRE, CV13 6AJ.
SUMMERFORD, Mrs. Heidi Louise, BSc ACA *1997;* with PricewaterhouseCoopers LLP, 1 Embankment Place, LONDON, WC2N 6RH.
SUMMERFORD, Mr. Luke, ACA *2010;* 1 Anguilla Close, EASTBOURNE, EAST SUSSEX, BN23 5TS.
SUMMERHAYES, Mrs. Rachel Kay, MA ACA *1999;* Dungeon Farm, Croscombe, WELLS, SOMERSET, BA5 3RP.
SUMMERHAYES, Mr. William John, ACA *1994;* Dungeon Farm, Croscombe, WELLS, SOMERSET, BA5 3RP.
SUMMERHILL, Mr. Laurence Gordon, FCA *1968;* 2 The Charters, Church End, DUNMOW, ESSEX, CM6 2SJ. (Life Member)
SUMMERILL, Miss. Lois Jane, ACA *2009;* 12 Kelston Grove, BRISTOL, BS15 9NL.
SUMMERLIN, Mr. John Michael, BA FCA *1976;* The Rectory, Harvest Hill, BOURNE END, SL8 5JJ.
•SUMMERS, Mr. Alistair Gerald, MSc BSc FCA *1991;* (Tax Fac), Summers & Co., 6 Jacobs Well Mews, LONDON, W1U 3DY.
•SUMMERS, Mr. Anthony Richard, BA ACA *1996;* Baker Tilly UK Audit LLP, 12 Gleneagles Court, Brighton Road, CRAWLEY, WEST SUSSEX, RH10 6AD. See also Baker Tilly Tax and Advisory Services LLP
•SUMMERS, Mr. David, FCA *1970;* (Tax Fac), H and S Accountants Ltd, Argo House, Kilburn Park Road, LONDON, NW6 5LF. See also David Summers & Co Limited
SUMMERS, Mr. Gary Joseph, BSc FCA *1991;* Malco Holdings Ltd, Office 6, Willow Farm, Allwood Green, Rickinghall, DISS NORFOLK IP22 1LQ.
SUMMERS, Mr. George Richard Cameron, BSc ACA *1992;* 31/2 Drumsheugh Gardens, EDINBURGH, EH3 7RN.
SUMMERS, Mr. Graeme, BA FCA FSI *1992;* Brewin Dolphin, Time Central, 32 Gallowgate, NEWCASTLE UPON TYNE, NE1 4SR.
•SUMMERS, Mrs. Heekhoy, FCA *1974;* H Summers Ltd, 26 Lake View, EDGWARE, MIDDLESEX, HA8 7RU.
•SUMMERS, Mr. James George, BA FCA *1980;* INTO Newcastle University, 6 Kensington Terrace, NEWCASTLE UPON TYNE, NE1 7RU.
SUMMERS, Miss. Jenny Louise, BSc ACA ACIS FSI *1997;* Finance Dept Royal Bank of Canada (CI) Ltd., 19-21 Broad Street, St Helier, JERSEY, JE1 8PB.
SUMMERS, Mr. John Patrick, FCA *1963;* The Old Laundry, Little Easton, DUNMOW, ESSEX, CM6 2JW.
SUMMERS, Mrs. Karen, BSc FCA *1977;* 7 Clifford Manor Road, GUILDFORD, GU4 8AG.
SUMMERS, Mrs. Kathleen Mary, BA FCA ATII *1983;* Newtown Grange, Newtown Common, NEWBURY, RG20 9DB.
SUMMERS, Mr. Marc, BAcc ACA FSI *1999;* with KPMG LLP, St. James's Square, MANCHESTER, M2 6DS.
•SUMMERS, Mr. Marc William, BSc(Hons) FCA *2000;* with Grant Thornton UK LLP, Grant Thornton House, 22 Melton Street, Euston Square, LONDON, NW1 2EP.
SUMMERS, Miss. Nicola, BA ACA *2005;* 9 The Grove, Ratton, EASTBOURNE, EAST SUSSEX, BN20 9DA.
SUMMERS, Mr. Philip John, FCA *1951;* Flat 59, Madeira Court, Knightstone Road, WESTON-SUPER-MARE, BS23 2BH. (Life Member)
SUMMERS, Mr. Richard John, FCA *1970;* Quantum Care Ltd, 4 Silver Court, Watchmead, WELWYN GARDEN CITY, HERTFORDSHIRE, AL7 1TS.
SUMMERS, Mr. Robert Michael, FCA *1962;* 6 Woodtree Close, Hendon, LONDON, NW4 1HQ.
•SUMMERS, Mr. Robin, FCA *1963;* (Tax Fac), Summers & Co., 6 Jacobs Well Mews, LONDON, W1U 3DY.
SUMMERS, Mr. Timothy Edward, BSc ACA *1991;* WJ Aldiss Ltd, Old Lane, FAKENHAM, NR21 8AF.
SUMMERS, Mr. Tony, FCA *1966;* 2 Lime Grove, Alveston, BRISTOL, BS35 3PN.
SUMMERSALL, Mr. Kevin David, BSc ACA *1989;* 6 Midhurst Road, NEWCASTLE UPON TYNE, NE12 9NU.
SUMMERSCALE, Mr. Gideon Zachary, BA ACA *1997;* Whitmoor Hatch Whitmoor Common, Worplesdon, GUILDFORD, SURREY, GU3 3RP.
SUMMERSON, Mr. Mark, ACA *2009;* 28 Turnpike Walk, Sedgefield, STOCKTON-ON-TEES, CLEVELAND, TS21 3NP.
SUMMERTON, Mr. Ian Roger, FCA *1979;* Holly House, Main Street, Morton, SOUTHWELL, NOTTINGHAMSHIRE, NG25 0UT.
SUMMERTON, Mr. Phillip Alan, BSc ACA *1982;* Group 4 Securicor, The Manor, Manor Royal, CRAWLEY, WEST SUSSEX, RH10 9UN.
SUMNER, Mr. Adam, LLB ACA *2007;* 40 Bouverie Road, LONDON, N16 0AJ.
SUMNER, Mr. Adam Ian James, BSocSc ACA *2003;* with KPMG LLP, 15 Canada Square, LONDON, E14 5GL.
SUMNER, Mr. Adam Winston, BA FCA *1996;* 174 Dobbin Hill, SHEFFIELD, S11 7JG.
SUMNER, Mr. Andrew John, BA ACA *1995;* 10 Shetland Way, Radcliffe, MANCHESTER, M26 4UH.
SUMNER, Mr. Andrew Neil, BA FCA *1991;* Turner House, Ivydene, Betley, CREWE, CW3 9BQ.
SUMNER, Mr. Christopher, ACA *2011;* 34 Hunters Lane, Tattershall, LINCOLN, LN4 4PB.
SUMNER, Mr. Dale Mcdonald, FCA *1957;* Manuel Montilla 4, 28016 MADRID, SPAIN. (Life Member)
SUMNER, Mr. David Michael Edward, MA(Oxon) FCA *1997;* Gabriels Lodge, Mill Hill, EDENBRIDGE, KENT, TN8 5PL.
SUMNER, Mr. Donald Hugh, FCA *1967;* 67 Milton Avenue, Eaton Ford, ST. NEOTS, PE19 7LH.
SUMNER, Mr. Francis Wilfrid, FCA *1959;* 26 Penfold Lane, Great Billing, NORTHAMPTON, NN3 9EF. (Life Member)
SUMNER, Mr. Jonathan, BSc ACA *2009;* 17 Beach Street, Fitzroy, NEW PLYMOUTH, NEW ZEALAND.
•SUMNER, Mr. Jonathan Rowan, FCA *1976;* SB&P LLP, Oriel House, 2-8 Oriel Road, BOOTLE, MERSEYSIDE, L20 7EP. See also Satterthwaite Brooks & Pomfret LLP and SB&P Corporate Finance Ltd
SUMNER, Miss. Louise Frances, ACA *2008;* 46 De Montfort Road, LONDON, SW16 1LZ.
SUMNER, Mr. Mark James, BCom ACA *2009;* 26 Kidmore End Road, Emmer Green, READING, RG4 8SE.
SUMNER, Mr. Matthew James, BA FCA AMCT *1996;* Pfizer Ltd, Ramsgate Road, SANDWICH, KENT, CT13 9NJ.
SUMNER, Mr. Neil Dudley, BSc ACA *2003;* 28 Regent Road, Harborne, BIRMINGHAM, B17 9JU.
SUMNER, Mr. Peter Gerard, BA ACA *1990;* 21 Gladstone Terrace, Bulk Road, LANCASTER, LANCASHIRE, LA1 1DW.

SUMNER, Mr. Philip Alan, BSc ACA *1998;* 7 Greylag Crescent, Ellenbrook, Worsley, MANCHESTER, M28 7AB.
SUMNER, Mrs. Rachael, BSc(Hons) ACA *2002;* 28 Regent Road, Harborne, BIRMINGHAM, B17 9JU.
SUMNER, Mr. Richard, LLB ACA *2006;* KPMG Phoomchai Business Advisory Ltd., 48th Floor Empire Tower, 195 South Sathorn Road, BANGKOK 10120, THAILAND.
SUMNER, Mr. Richard, BA ACA *2001;* 15 Swaffield Road, LONDON, SW18 3AH.
SUMNER, Mr. Richard James, BA ACA *1993;* with PricewaterhouseCoopers LLP, 1 Embankment Place, LONDON, WC2N 6RH.
SUMNER, Mr. Richard John, BSc ACA *1992;* Lane End Littlewick Common, Knaphill, WOKING, SURREY, GU21 2JZ.
SUMNER, Mr. William Bruce, BA ACA *1999;* 16 The Crossways, GUILDFORD, SURREY, GU2 7QQ.
SUMPSTER, Miss. Alice Jane, BA ACA *2004;* Flat 12 Ashburnham Mansions, Ashburnham Road, LONDON, SW10 0PA.
SUMPSTER, Mr. Matthew, ACA *2009;* Flat 4, 3 Madeira Park, TUNBRIDGE WELLS, TN2 5SU.
SUMPTER, Mr. John Dennis, FCA *1952;* 98 Derby Road, Swanwick, ALFRETON, DERBYSHIRE, DE55 1AD. (Life Member)
SUMPTER, Mr. Martin Andrew, BA FCA *1977;* Moore College, 1 King Street, NEWTOWN, NSW 2042, AUSTRALIA.
•**SUMPTER, Mr. Paul Derrick, MBA FCA AIMC** *1973;* HWEA Ltd, 8 Hopper Way, Diss Business Park, DISS, NORFOLK, IP22 4GT. See also Haines Watts, Haines Watts, Haines Watts, Haines Watts Colchester Ltd
SUMPTON, Mrs. Lisa Yvonne, BSc ACA *1998;* 23 Kingfisher Reach, Collingham, WETHERBY, LS22 5LX.
SUMPUTH, Mr. Kevin, BSc ACA *2002;* 33 Boundary Lane, Shirley, SOLIHULL, B90 1TX.
SUMRA, Mr. Gurinder Singh, BSc ACA *1992;* 50 Langley Road, SLOUGH, SL3 7AD.
SUN, Miss. Beishan, ACA *2008;* Flat 71 Abady House, Page Street, LONDON, SW1P 4EP.
SUN, Mr. Foo Kwei, ACA *1980;* 1 Hillgate Place, Castle Hill, SYDNEY, NSW 2154, AUSTRALIA.
SUN, Mr. Xiaokang, MSc ACA *2010;* 139 Montreal House, Surrey Quays Road, LONDON, SE16 7AQ.
SUNDAR, Mr. Kartik, BSc ACA *2005;* UBS AG, 677 Washington Boulevard, STAMFORD, CT 06901-3707, UNITED STATES.
SUNDAR, Mr. Shiv Charan Dass, BA ACA *1993;* 5 Barker Drive, Bromham, BEDFORD, MK43 8TJ.
SUNDERJI, Mr. Hasanain Sultanali Mohamedali Amersi, BSc ACA *1989;* Mombasa Commercial & Industrial Enterprises Ltd, P.O. Box 81124, MOMBASA, 80100, KENYA.
SUNDERJI, Mr. Mansoor Abdulrasul Walji, FCA *1974;* 120 Collins Street, COLLINGWOOD L9Y 2K2, ON, CANADA.
SUNDERJI, Mr. Mohamed Iqbal Sultanali Mohamedali, FCA *1976;* Jethabham Enterprises Ltd, P.O. Box 81124, MOMBASA, 80100, KENYA.
SUNDERLAND, Mr. Amos Patrick, FCA *1973;* Flat 9, Watersedge, Sandside, MILNTHORPE, LA7 7HN.
•**SUNDERLAND, Mr. Ben, BA ACA** *2008;* The Internet Retailer Limited, 12 Riverview Business Park, Station Road, FOREST ROW, EAST SUSSEX, RH18 5DW.
SUNDERLAND, Mr. David, FCA *1971;* Butterfield Signs Ltd, 174 Sunbridge Road, BRADFORD, WEST YORKSHIRE, BD1 2RZ.
•**SUNDERLAND, Mr. David Grahame, FCA** *1967;* (Tax Fac), Dagas Limited, 1 Gate Lodge Way, Laindon, BASILDON, ESSEX, SS15 4AR.
SUNDERLAND, Ms. Jane Susan, BA FCA *1988;* Leslie Ward & Drew Kingston House, Pierrepont Street, BATH, BA1 1LA.
SUNDERLAND, Mr. John Victor, FCA *1951;* 22 The Ash Grove, Carstens Road Kamma Ridge, PORT ELIZABETH, E C 6070, SOUTH AFRICA. (Life Member)
SUNDERLAND, Mr. Kevin, FCA *1970;* 37 Crownest Road, BINGLEY, BD16 4PS. (Life Member)
SUNDERLAND, Mr. Michael, BA ACA *2011;* 28 Firs Close, Hazlemere, HIGH WYCOMBE, BUCKINGHAMSHIRE, HP15 7TF.
SUNDERLAND, Mr. Michael John, FCA FSI *1969;* Walker Crips Group Plc, Finsbury Tower, 103-105 Bunhill Row, LONDON, EC1Y 8LZ.
SUNDERLAND, Mr. Robert, FCA *1980;* 76 Elmwood Drive, Blythe Bridge, STOKE-ON-TRENT, ST11 9NY.
•**SUNDERLAND, Mr. Roy, FCA** *1958;* Crossways, 2 Westwood Crescent, Grange Park, BINGLEY, BD16 1NN. (Life Member)
SUNDERLAND, Mr. Trevor Dudley Ardern, FCA *1962;* Box SS 6290, NASSAU, BAHAMAS.
SUNDIN, Mrs. Sarah Anne, ACA *2000;* 11 Turnberry Court, NORMANTON, WEST YORKSHIRE, WF6 1UH.
SUNDT, Mr. Robin Charles, FCA *1973;* 45 Somerset Road, REDHILL, RH1 6LT.
SUNEJA, Mr. Vishal, ACA *1992;* E-34, Saket, Avenue One, NEW DELHI 110017, INDIA.
SUNER, Mr. Omer Cevdet, FCA *1975;* 8c Akmerkez Residence, Ulus, Etiler, ISTANBUL 34340, TURKEY. (Life Member)
SUNG, Mr. Chi Sin, BA ACA *2006;* 15 Carlett Boulevard, Eastham, WIRRAL, CH62 8BZ.
SUNG, Mr. James Kam Ho, MSc ACA *1992;* Flat I 14th Floor, 46 Nassau Street, MEI FOO SUN CHUEN, KOWLOON, HONG KONG SAR.
SUNG, Mr. Nee, ACA *2007;* A Ho Sung & Co CPA, Room 908, 9/F, 248 Queen's Road, CENTRAL, HONG KONG ISLAND HONG KONG SAR.
SUNG, Mr. Wing Sum, ACA *2007;* Flat 1, 24/F, Kay Yue House, On Kay Court, NGAU TAU KOK, KOWLOON HONG KONG SAR.
SUNG, Miss. Yerk-Kwan Muriel, BSc FCA *1991;* 119 Lychee North Road, Fairview Park, YUEN LONG, NEW TERRITORIES, HONG KONG SAR.
SUNG, Miss. Yuk Lan, ACA *1982;* 4 Mears Close, BIRMINGHAM, B23 5YJ.
SUNLEY, Miss. Lydia Rachel, ACA *2009;* Flat 9, 15 Tarves Way, GREENWICH, SE10 9JP.
SUNLEY, Mrs. Mairead, BA ACA *2007;* Cleveland Potash Ltd, Boulby Mine, Loftus, SALTBURN-BY-THE-SEA, CLEVELAND, TS13 4UZ.
SUNNER, Mr. Gurinder, ACA *2009;* 92a Hampton Lane, SOLIHULL, WEST MIDLANDS, B91 2RS.
SUNNUCKS, Mr. William D'urban, MA MBA ACA *1981;* East Gores Farm, Salmons Lane, Coggeshall, COLCHESTER, CO6 1RY.
SUNTER, Mr. Mark Oliver, ACA *2008;* Ainsworths Ltd Charter House, Stansfield Street, NELSON, BB9 9XY.
SUNTER, Mr. Michael Calvert, FCA *1954;* 4 Beeston Hall Mews, Beeston, TARPORLEY, CHESHIRE, CW6 9TZ. (Life Member)
SUNTER, Mr. Stephen Charles, LLB ACA *1991;* 5990 E. Naples Plaza Apt #8, LONG BEACH, CA 90803, UNITED STATES.
SUNTOOK, Mr. Zarir Rustom, FCA *1968;* 37 Ashbourne Road, Ealing, LONDON, W5 3EH.
SUPEDA, Mr. Vinesh Naran, BSc ACA *1995;* 8 Carisbrooke Park, LEICESTER, LE2 3PQ.
SUPIAT, Mr. Zafian, BSc(Econ) ACA *2001;* MMC Corp Berhad, Leve II, Kompleks Antarabangsa, Jln Sultan Ismail, 50250 KUALA LUMPUR, FEDERAL TERRITORY MALAYSIA.
SUPRAN, Mr. Jonathan Michael, FCA *1966;* 10 Cattley Close, BARNET, HERTFORDSHIRE, EN5 4SN.
SUR, Mr. Julian Girindra, BA ACA *1983;* 2120 Inverness Lane, BERWYN, PA 19312, UNITED STATES.
SURACE, Mr. Francesco, BA ACA *2011;* 7 Rays Close, Bletchley, MILTON KEYNES, MK2 3FG.
SURANA, Mr. Shashi Prakash, ACA *2009;* 8 Franklin Drive, Weavering, MAIDSTONE, KENT, ME14 5SY.
SURANA, Mr. Veenit, ACA *2008;* Flat 8, 114 Christchurch Road, LONDON, SW19 2PE.
SURBUTS, Mr. David Michael, BSc ACA *1999;* 66 Ottways Lane, ASHTEAD, SURREY, KT21 2PJ.
SURCH, Mr. Christopher, BCom ACA *1987;* 2 Newmans Place, Sunningdale, ASCOT, SL5 0HN.
•**SURCOUF, Mr. Robert Philip, BSocSc FCA FCCA** *1994;* Caversham, Elizabeth House, 9 Castle Street, St Helier, JERSEY, JE4 2QP. See also Lubbock Fine
SURENDRA, Mr. Visvalingam, FCA *1973;* 22/16-20 Henley Road, HOMEBUSH WEST, NSW 2140, AUSTRALIA.
SURFLEET, Mr. Robert John, FCA *1970;* (Tax Fac), 71 Slayleigh Lane, SHEFFIELD, S10 3RG.
•**SURGETT, Miss. Caroline, BA ACA** *1998;* Ascent Accounting Ltd, 33 Dover Road, BRIGHTON, BN1 6LP.
SURGUY, Mr. Martyn Russell, BA ACA *1990;* Dove Tree House, Grassy Lane, SEVENOAKS, TN13 1PL.
SURI, Mr. Irvindjit Singh, MEng ACA *1995;* 141A Slough Road, Datchet, SLOUGH, SL3 9AE.
SURI, Mrs. Swati, MA(Hons) ACA *2000;* 20 King Henry Road, FLEET, HAMPSHIRE, GU51 1JH.
SURINGAR, Mr. William Humphrey, FCA *1972;* 1 Chapel Street, Belmont, BOLTON, BL7 8AU.
SURKOVIC, Mr. Anthony, MA MBA ACA *1989;* Tower Bridge Court, 226 Tower Bridge Road, LONDON, SE1 2UP.
•**SURMAN, Mr. Robert Neil, FCA** *1974;* Kingston Smith LLP, Orbital House, 20 Eastern Road, ROMFORD, RM1 3PJ. See also Kingston Smith Limited Liability Partnership, Devonshire Corporate Services LLP and Kingston Smith Consulting LLP
SURPLICE, Mr. John Michael Edward, MA ACA *1996;* Russetts, Schoolfields, Shiplake Cross, HENLEY-ON-THAMES, RG9 4DH.
SURRALL, Mr. Peter Howard, BSc ACA *1984;* (Tax Fac), 104 Cowleigh Road, MALVERN, WR14 1QW.
SURRELL, Mr. Andrew James, ACA *2011;* 15 Ashburn Place, DIDCOT, OXFORDSHIRE, OX11 7FN.
•**SURREY, Mr. John Peter, FCA** *1969;* Barber & Co LLP, Level 5, City Tower, 40 Basinghall Street, LONDON, EC2V 5DE. See also Surrey J.P.
SURREY, Mr. Malcolm Robert, BA FCA *1977;* Murray General Steels Group Limited, Brightgate House Cobra Court Brightgate Way, MANCHESTER, M32 0TB.
•**SURREY, Mr. Samuel Michael James, BA ACA** *1998;* with BDO Corporate Finance (Middle East) LLP, DIFC, Al Fattan Currency Tower, Floor 33 East, PO Box 506802, DUBAI UNITED ARAB EMIRATES.
SURRIDGE, Miss. Alison Mary, BA ACA *1994;* (Tax Fac), Clarins (UK) Ltd, 10 Cavendish Place, LONDON, W1G 9DN.
SURRIDGE, Mr. Christopher, FCA *1975;* Systematic Business Solutions Limited, Bulse Grange, Wendens Ambo, SAFFRON WALDEN, ESSEX, CB11 4JT.
SURRIDGE, Mr. Ian, BSc FCA *1988;* 14 Heath Road, Downend, BRISTOL, BS16 6HA.
SURRIDGE, Miss. Ranja, BSc ACA *2007;* 43 Hadrians Way, Abbeymead, GLOUCESTER, GL4 5DD.
SURRIDGE, Mrs. Sangita, MA ACA *2005;* Trent & Dove Housing Ltd, Trinity Square, BURTON-ON-TRENT, STAFFORDSHIRE, DE14 1BL.
•**SURRIDGE, Mr. Timothy Donal North, BSc ACA** *1996;* KPMG LLP, 15 Canada Square, LONDON, E14 5GL. See also KPMG Europe LLP
SURRY, Mr. Andrew James, BSc ACA *1992;* Two Peachtree Point, 1555 Peachtree Street NE, ATLANTA, GA 30309, UNITED STATES.
SURRY, Mrs. Chabala Beverley, BA ACA *2011;* Flat 20, Skyline Court, 9 Grange Yard, LONDON, SE1 3AN.
•**SURRY, Mr. Keith Raymond Stewart, FCA** *1982;* (Tax Fac), Pearson May, 67/68 St. Mary Street, CHIPPENHAM, SN15 3JF.
SURTEES, Mrs. Caroline Margaret, BA ACA *1992;* Wearside, 188 Park Road, HARTLEPOOL, TS26 9LW.
SURTEES, Mr. David William, BSc ACA *1994;* 66 Canford Road, LONDON, SW11 6PD.
SURTEES, Mrs. Gemma Susan, MMath ACA *2010;* 59 Sanderson Villas, GATESHEAD, TYNE AND WEAR, NE8 3BU.
SURTEES, Mr. Henry John Conyers, BSc ACA *1997;* Caspian Ltd, Plot 77 Nyerere Road, PO Box 409 54, DAR ES SALAAM, TANZANIA.
SURTEES, Mrs. Sarah Louise, BSc ACA *1994;* 66 Canford Road, LONDON, SW11 6PD.
SURTEES, Mr. Simon Matthew, BA ACA *1992;* 41 Hillcrest Road, LOUGHTON, ESSEX, IG10 4QH.
SURTI, Mr. Adi Maneck, FCA CPA *1975;* 305 Dover Way Court, ELLISVILLE, MO 63021-2004, UNITED STATES.
SUSGAARD-VIGON, Mr. Marc James, BA ACA *2006;* (Tax Fac), with KPMG LLP, 15 Canada Square, LONDON, E14 5GL.
SUSHAMS, Mr. Keith Alan, BA FCA *1980;* 1 Healey's Row, Main Street, Normanby By Spital, MARKET RASEN, LN8 2HE.
•**SUSSMAN, Mr. Ian Anthony, FCA** *1966;* (Tax Fac), 9 Parkside drive, EDGWARE, HA8 8JU.
SUSSMAN, Mr. Keith Andrew, BA FCA *1997;* (Tax Fac), Cohen Arnold & Co, 1075 Finchley Road, LONDON, NW11 0PU.
SUSSMAN, Mr. Steven Anthony, BA ACA *1982;* (Tax Fac), Tilty Hill Farmhouse, Cherry Street, Duton Hill, DUNMOW, CM6 2EE.
SUSSMANN, Mr. Adrian Edward, BSc ACA *1994;* GP Sports Management, 885 Arapahoe Avenue, BOULDER, CO 80302, UNITED STATES.
•**SUTARIA, Mr. Nalin Kumar, FCA** *1973;* N.K. Sutaria & Co, Unison, Epping Road, Roydon, HARLOW, CM19 5HN.
SUTARIA, Mr. Prashant Prakash, BA FCA *1994;* 16 Victor Grove, WEMBLEY, HA0 4JJ.
SUTARIA, Mr. Sunil, BSc FCA *1996;* 3 Hill House Close, Turners Hill, CRAWLEY, WEST SUSSEX, RH10 4YY.
SUTCH, Mr. James Francis, BSc ACA *2010;* N M Rothschild & Sons, New Court, St Swithin's Lane, LONDON, EC4P 4DU.
SUTCLIFF, Mrs. Johanna Louise, BA ACA *1999;* 35 Elfindale Road, LONDON, SE24 9NN.
SUTCLIFFE, Mr. Adam James, BA ACA *2001;* Allotts Old Grammar School, 11 Moorgate Road, ROTHERHAM, SOUTH YORKSHIRE, S60 2EN.
SUTCLIFFE, Mr. Alan, FCA *1947;* PO Box 140, East Kew, MELBOURNE, VIC 3102, AUSTRALIA. (Life Member)
SUTCLIFFE, Miss. Alison Jayne, BA ACA *1988;* 118 Earl Place, TORONTO M4Y 3B9, ON, CANADA.
SUTCLIFFE, Mr. Andrew Charles, BA ACA *1984;* 10 Hollows Farm Ave, Shawclough, ROCHDALE, OL12 6LY.
SUTCLIFFE, Mr. Anthony James, BCom ACA *2003;* Interface Europe Ltd, Shelf Mills, HALIFAX, WEST YORKSHIRE, HX3 7PA.
SUTCLIFFE, Miss. Brigid Ann, MA ACA *1983;* 6 Holmbush Road, LONDON, SW15 3LE.
SUTCLIFFE, Mr. Charles Edmund Taylor, BSc ARCS FCA *1973;* HCWA Limited, c/o Sagars, Gresham House, 5-7 St. Pauls Street, LEEDS, LS1 2JG.
SUTCLIFFE, Mr. David Kay, BA FCA *1975;* 6 Fitzgerald Avenue, Mortlake, LONDON, SW14 8SZ.
SUTCLIFFE, Mr. David Phillip, BA ACA *1981;* Les Petites Capelles, La Rue de la Mare Ballam, St. John, JERSEY, JE3 4EJ.
•**SUTCLIFFE, Mr. David Stewart, FCA** *1972;* David S. Sutcliffe & Co, 14 First Avenue, Church, ACCRINGTON, BB5 5EH.
SUTCLIFFE, Mr. Edward Michael, BA ACA *2006;* 72 Bishop Street, St Albans, CHRISTCHURCH 8014, NEW ZEALAND.
•**SUTCLIFFE, Mrs. Emma Caroline, BA(Hons) ACA** *2002;* Emma Sutcliffe, 9 Low Mill, Caton, LANCASTER, LA2 9HY.
SUTCLIFFE, Miss. Emma Jane, BA ACA *1998;* 13 Parkgate Mews, LONDON, N6 5NB.
SUTCLIFFE, Mr. Frank, FCA *1950;* Four Oaks, Egypt Lane, Farnham Common, SLOUGH, SL2 3LF. (Life Member)
•**SUTCLIFFE, Mr. Ian Timothy, BA FCA** *1988;* KPMG AG, Badenerstrasse 172, CH 8004 ZURICH, SWITZERLAND. See also KPMG Ltd
SUTCLIFFE, Mr. James Alistair, ACA *2009;* Grant Thornton, L5 Grant Thornton House, Cathedral Square, CHRISTCHURCH 8140, NEW ZEALAND.
SUTCLIFFE, Mr. James Holden, BSc ACA *1992;* Meadowcroft House, 2 Priors Close, Histon, CAMBRIDGE, CB24 9HX.
SUTCLIFFE, Mr. John, BSc FCA *1971;* Flat 58 Ashworth Mansions, Grantully Road, LONDON, W9 1LW.
SUTCLIFFE, Mr. John Michael, BA FCA *1974;* Theatre for a Change, PO Box 31739, Capital City, LILONGWE, MALAWI.
•**SUTCLIFFE, Mr. John Richard Mark, FCA** *1981;* Bennett Verby LLP, 7 St Petersgate, STOCKPORT, CHESHIRE, SK1 1EB. See also De La Wyche Baker Limited
SUTCLIFFE, Mr. John Stanley, FCA *1936;* 36 Brueton Avenue, SOLIHULL, WEST MIDLANDS, B91 3EN. (Life Member)
SUTCLIFFE, Mr. John Trevor, BA ACA *1985;* Berry Brow House, 6 Stanningden Rise, Ripponden, HALIFAX, WEST YORKSHIRE, HX6 4FE.
•**SUTCLIFFE, Mr. Jonathan, BSc FCA** *1995;* Kingston Smith LLP, Devonshire House, 60 Goswell Road, LONDON, EC1M 7AD. See also Kingston Smith Limited Liability Partnership, Devonshire Corporate Services LLP and Kingston Smith Consulting LLP
SUTCLIFFE, Mr. Julian Alexander, BA ACA *1990;* Mardon Plc, 10 Fenton Street, LANCASTER, LA1 1TE.
SUTCLIFFE, Mrs. Katherine Elizabeth, BSc ACA *2004;* Flat 717 Maurer Court, John Harrison Way, LONDON, SE10 0SX.
SUTCLIFFE, Mr. Martyn, ACA *1989;* 78 Mitton Road, Whalley, CLITHEROE, BB7 9JN.
SUTCLIFFE, Mr. Matthew Christian, BA ACA *2002;* 63 George Street, SHIPLEY, WEST YORKSHIRE, BD18 4PL.
•**SUTCLIFFE, Mr. Michael Anthony, MBE FCA** *1966;* M.A. Sutcliffe, 213 Castle Hill Road, Totternhoe, DUNSTABLE, LU6 2DA.
SUTCLIFFE, Mr. Neil Raymond, BSc FCA *1982;* 10 Park Lane, Penwortham, PRESTON, PR1 9JB.
SUTCLIFFE, Mrs. Nicola, BSc ACA *2005;* 25-27 Hillfoot Road, DOLLAR, CLACKMANNANSHIRE, FK14 7BD.
SUTCLIFFE, Mrs. Nicola Claire, ACA *2002;* 61 Coleman Road, Fleckney, LEICESTER, LE8 8BH.
SUTCLIFFE, Mr. Nigel Paul, BA ACA *2001;* E W S, Carolina Way, DONCASTER, SOUTH YORKSHIRE, DN4 5PN.
SUTCLIFFE, Mr. Paul, BA ACA *1996;* Ernst & Young LLP, Condominio Sao Luiz, Torre 1-5 andar, Av Pres. Juscelino Kubitschek 1830, SAO PAULO, 04543-900 BRAZIL.
SUTCLIFFE, Mr. Paul John, BSc ACA *1984;* 4 Waterpath, Westford, WELLINGTON, SOMERSET, TA21 0DS.

SUTCLIFFE, Mr. Paul Nicholas Anthony, BSc ACA *2005;* with BPP Learning Media, Aldine House, 142-144 Uxbridge Road, LONDON, W12 8AW.
SUTCLIFFE, Mr. Richard John, ACA *1998;* 34 Moorland Rise, Haslingden, ROSSENDALE, BB4 6UA.
SUTCLIFFE, Mr. Richard Thomas, ACA *2009;* 199 Highbury Hill, LONDON, N5 1TB.
SUTCLIFFE, Mr. Robert Crozier, FCA *1963;* BD Smith & Co, 25 Bonegate Road, BRIGHOUSE, WEST YORKSHIRE, HD6 1TQ.
SUTCLIFFE, Mr. Robert Keith, FCA *1972;* Woodlands, 40 Beechwood Avenue, Little Chalfont, AMERSHAM, HP6 6PN.
SUTCLIFFE, Mr. Roger Stephen, FCA *1970;* 6 College Lane, Rawtenstall, ROSSENDALE, LANCASHIRE, BB4 7LA.
SUTCLIFFE, Mr. Samuel Andrew, FCA *1963;* Lane Ends Farm, 1 Lane Ends, Luddendenfoot, HALIFAX, HX2 6TU.
SUTCLIFFE, Mrs. Sarah Jane, BSc ACA ATII *1990;* Schwyzerstrasse 48, 8805 RICHTERSWIL, SWITZERLAND.
•SUTCLIFFE, Mr. Stephen George, FCA *1973;* Sutcliffe & Co, 3 Branch Road, BATLEY, WEST YORKSHIRE, WF17 5RY. See also Walker Sutcliffe & Cooper
SUTCLIFFE, Mr. Steven Gary, FCA *1978;* 6 Nook Green, Tingley, WAKEFIELD, WF3 1ER.
SUTCLIFFE, Mr. Steven Roger, BSc FCA *1978;* Datong PLC 1 Low Hall Business Park, 1 Low Hall Road, Horsforth, LEEDS, LS18 4EG.
SUTCLIFFE, Mrs. Susan Ann, BSc ACA *2005;* with RSM Tenon Limited, Sumner House, St Thomas's Rd, CHORLEY, PR7 1HP.
•SUTCLIFFE, Mrs. Susanna Mary, BSc ACA *1995;* Marshals Accounting, 26 Chandlers Road, Marshalswick, ST. ALBANS, HERTFORDSHIRE, AL4 9RS.
SUTCLIFFE, Mrs. Tracey Heather, BSc ACA *1993;* Wey Estates Ltd, 3 Tannery House, Tannery Lane, Send, WOKING, SURREY GU23 7EF.
•SUTER, Ms. Diane Elizabeth, FCA *1988;* Thompson Taraz LLP, 35 Grosvenor Street, Mayfair, LONDON, W1K 4QX.
SUTER, Mr. Paul David, BA FCA *1982;* Bramble Cottage, 96 Rose Green Road, Rose Green, BOGNOR REGIS, WEST SUSSEX, PO21 3EQ.
SUTER, Mr. Philip Charles Anthony, BSc(Hons) ACA *2010;* 45 High Street, Wing, LEIGHTON BUZZARD, BEDFORDSHIRE, LU7 0NS.
SUTERWALLA, Mrs. Aina, BA ACA *2000;* 19 Ashbourne Road, Ealing, LONDON, W5 3ED.
SUTERWALLA, Mr. Riyaz, BSc ACA *2000;* PO Box 111956, DUBAI, UNITED ARAB EMIRATES.
SUTHAR, Miss. Seema, BSc ACA *2006;* 141 Heath Road, HOUNSLOW, TW3 2NR.
SUTHERLAND, Mr. Alexander, BA(Hons) ACA *2009;* with Garbutt & Elliott LLP, Arabesque House, Monks Cross Drive, Huntington, YORK, YO32 9GW.
SUTHERLAND, Mr. Alexander Campbell, MA FCA *1999;* 21 The Crosspath, RADLETT, HERTFORDSHIRE, WD7 8HR.
SUTHERLAND, Miss. Alexandra, ACA *2008;* Flat 15 Mowbray Court, Mowbray Road, LONDON, SE19 2RL.
•SUTHERLAND, Mr. Andrew, BA FCA *1978;* KPMG, Pobrezni 1a, 186 00 PRAGUE, CZECH REPUBLIC.
SUTHERLAND, Mr. Andrew Charles, BSc FCA *1981;* Monstermob Group Plc, 76 Church Street, LANCASTER, LA1 1ET.
SUTHERLAND, Mr. Brian George, FCA *1960;* 12 Goldrings Road, Oxshott, LEATHERHEAD, SURREY, KT22 0QR. (Life Member)
•SUTHERLAND, Bruce Wilson, Esq CBE FCA *1951;* (Tax Fac), Bruce Sutherland & Co, Moreton House, MORETON-IN-MARSH, GL56 0LH.
SUTHERLAND, Mr. Christopher James, BA ACA *2004;* Level 24, RBS Tower, 88 Phillip Street, SYDNEY, NSW 2000, AUSTRALIA.
•SUTHERLAND, Miss. Claire, BA ACA *2001;* Baker Tilly Tax & Advisory Services LLP, Abbotsgate House, Hollow Road, BURY ST. EDMUNDS, SUFFOLK, IP32 7FA. See also Baker Tilly UK Audit LLP
SUTHERLAND, Mr. Dennis Alfred, FCA *1954;* Chartwell, Newton Road, Sturminster Marshall, WIMBORNE, DORSET, BH21 4BT. (Life Member)
SUTHERLAND, Mr. Donald Alexander, FCA *1956;* 14 Harrop Road, Hale, ALTRINCHAM, CHESHIRE, WA15 9BX. (Life Member)
SUTHERLAND, Mr. Euan Oman, LLB ACA *2006;* 13 Meteor Street, LONDON, SW11 5NZ.
•SUTHERLAND, Mr. Graham John, BSc ACA *1984;* 6 Land Lane, WILMSLOW, CHESHIRE, SK9 1DG.
SUTHERLAND, Mr. Graham John, BA ACA *1984;* Westwood, Towers Road, Poynton, STOCKPORT, SK12 1DD.
SUTHERLAND, Mrs. Helen Catherine, BA ACA *2004;* 40 Breezehill, Wootton, NORTHAMPTON, NN4 6AG.
SUTHERLAND, Mr. Hugh, MA ACA *1992;* 41 Merrivale Square, OXFORD, OX2 6QX.
SUTHERLAND, Mr. Ian James, MSc FCA *1970;* Wheelwrights, Mill Lane, SAFFRON WALDEN, CB10 2AS.
SUTHERLAND, Dr. Jacqueline Anderson, PhD BSc ACA ATII *1997;* 8 Newton Grove, LONDON, W4 1LB.
SUTHERLAND, Mr. John Alexander, BCom FCA *1973;* 55a Parson Street, LONDON, NW4 1QT.
SUTHERLAND, Mr. Kenneth, MA FCA *1989;* Pine Lodge, Pinewood Hill, FLEET, HAMPSHIRE, GU51 3AW.
SUTHERLAND, Mr. Luke, BSc ACA *2011;* 33 Bristol Road, NORWICH, NR5 0UL.
SUTHERLAND, Mr. Mark Justin, BA ACA *1994;* Lipowa 8H, Bielawa, 05 520 KONSTANCIN-JEZIORNA, POLAND.
SUTHERLAND, Mr. Neil Colin Allan, FCA *1969;* 30 Downsview Drive, Wivelsfield Green, HAYWARDS HEATH, RH17 7RW. (Life Member)
SUTHERLAND, Mr. Neil Robert, ACA *1981;* 10 Moselle Close, FARNBOROUGH, HAMPSHIRE, GU14 9YB.
SUTHERLAND, Mr. Robert, MA(Hons) ACA *2004;* 40 Breezehill, Wootton, NORTHAMPTON, NN4 6AG.
SUTHERLAND, Mr. Robert Wilson, FCA *1973;* 20 Lord Napier Place, LONDON, W6 9UB.
SUTHERLAND, Mrs. Roslyn Anne, BA ACA *1991;* Fairfield House, Wittington Green, Henley Road, Medmenham, MARLOW, BUCKINGHAMSHIRE SL7 2ES.
SUTHERLAND, Mrs. Ruby Maria, BSc ACA CTA *1995;* 45 Alfreton Close, Wimbledon, LONDON, SW19 5NS.
SUTHERLAND, Mrs. Sally, ACA *1989;* 92 The Common, Earlswood, SOLIHULL, B94 5SJ.
SUTHERLAND, Mr. Simon Jack, BSc(Hons) ACA *1996;* 45 Alfreton Close, LONDON, SW19 5NS.
SUTHERLAND-THOMAS, Mrs. Natalie, BSc ACA *2006;* 19 Meadway, BARNET, EN5 5LG.
SUTHERS, Mr. Andrew, BA ACA *1988;* 27 School Street, PUDSEY, LS28 8PN.
SUTHERS, Mrs. Elizabeth Caroline, BSc(Hons) ACA *2001;* with PricewaterhouseCoopers LLP, 1 Embankment Place, LONDON, WC2N 6RH.
SUTHERS, Mr. Gordon, FCA *1958;* twin pines cottage, Pine Close, Halton, LANCASTER, LANCASHIRE, LA2 6PL. (Life Member)
SUTHERST, Mr. Christopher John, FCA *1971;* The Old Grange, Blackwell, SHIPSTON-ON-STOUR, CV36 4PE.
SUTHON, Mrs. Claire Denise, BA ACA *1992;* 51 Priest Hill, Caversham, READING, RG4 7RY.
SUTTER, Mr. Michael John, ACA *1982;* Moorfield, Cotherstone, BARNARD CASTLE, COUNTY DURHAM, DL12 9PJ.
SUTTERS, Mr. Charles Alexander, BA ACA *2005;* 19 Corney Reach Way, LONDON, W4 2TZ.
SUTTERS, Mrs. Clem Jane, BA ACA *2005;* 19 Corney Reach Way, LONDON, W4 2TZ.
SUTTIE, Miss. Amy Jayne, BSc ACA *2010;* Apartment 99 Liberty Place, 26-38 Sheepcote Street, BIRMINGHAM, B16 8JT.
SUTTILL, Mr. Ronald, FCA *1957;* Aviva Petroleum Inc, 10290 Monroe Drive #102, DALLAS, TX 75229, UNITED STATES.
SUTTON, Mr. Adam Timothy Owen, MSc(Econ) ACA *1999;* 11 Whittingstall Road, LONDON, SW6 4EA.
SUTTON, Mr. Aidan James, MA(Oxon) ACA *1999;* with PricewaterhouseCoopers LLP, 1 Embankment Place, LONDON, WC2N 6RH.
•SUTTON, Mr. Alain Peter, FCA *1976;* Griffin Sutton & Partners, 207/215 High Street, ORPINGTON, BR6 0PF.
SUTTON, Mr. Alan George, FCA *1967;* 2 Frog Lane, Felton, BRISTOL, BS40 9UN.
SUTTON, Mr. Andrew, MA FCA *1971;* West Walls, Cotmandene, DORKING, SURREY, RH4 2BL.
SUTTON, Mr. Andrew, BSc ACA *1991;* Citigroup Centre, 33 Canada Square, LONDON, E14 5LB.
SUTTON, Mrs. Anna-Maria, BA ACA *1995;* 30 Park Square West, LEEDS, LS1 2PF.
SUTTON, Mr. Antony Nigel, BA ACA *2000;* Hull FC, Kingston Communications Stadium, HULL, HU3 6JU.
SUTTON, Mr. Barry, ACA *1980;* Concord Filing Products Ltd, Stretton Way, LIVERPOOL, L36 6JF.
•SUTTON, Mr. Barry Read, FCA *1972;* (Tax Fac), B R & S Sutton Limited, 1a Fernville Avenue, Sunniside, Whickham, NEWCASTLE UPON TYNE, NE16 5PE.
SUTTON, Mrs. Beverley Ann, BSc ACA *1982;* 339 Charlestown Road, MANCHESTER, M9 7BS.
•SUTTON, Mr. Brian, FCA CTA *1960;* Mabe Allen LLP, 29 St. Mary Street, ILKESTON, DERBYSHIRE, DE7 8AB.
SUTTON, Mr. Brian Francis, FCA *1953;* 11 Crabtree Close, BEACONSFIELD, HP9 1UQ. (Life Member)
SUTTON, Mrs. Cathryn Anne, BA ACA *2005;* 1 Bridge Down, Bridge, CANTERBURY, KENT, CT4 5AZ.
SUTTON, Mr. Christopher Miles Bridges, MA FCA *1989;* 2 Eastlands Farm Cottages, Maidstone Road Paddock Wood, TONBRIDGE, TN12 6BU.
•SUTTON, Mr. Christopher Nigel, FCA *1982;* MacIntyre Hudson LLP, New Bridge Street House, 30-34 New Bridge Street, LONDON, EC4V 6BJ.
SUTTON, Mrs. Clare Louise, BA ACA *1993;* The Sixth Form College Solihull, Widney Manor Road, SOLIHULL, B91 3WR.
SUTTON, Mr. David, ACA *2010;* 28 Waterside, SALE, CHESHIRE, M33 7LQ.
•SUTTON, Mr. David Ian, BA FCA *1993;* Sutton McGrath Ltd, 5 Westbrook Court, Sharrow Vale Road, SHEFFIELD, S11 8YZ.
SUTTON, Mr. Dominic Stephen Paul, BSc(Hons) ACA *2002;* 39 Buttercup Way, Drighlington, BRADFORD, WEST YORKSHIRE, BD11 1EE.
SUTTON, Mr. Edwin Frederick Lawrence, FCA *1950;* 2 Cordova Court, Sandgate Road, FOLKESTONE, CT20 2HQ. (Life Member)
SUTTON, Mr. Gary, BA ACA *1992;* 8 Swallowdale, Walsall Wood, WALSALL, WS9 9RE.
•SUTTON, Mr. Geoffrey Robert, BA ACA CTA *1991;* M R Salvage Limited, 7-8 Eghams Court, Boston Drive, BOURNE END, BUCKINGHAMSHIRE, SL8 5YS.
SUTTON, Mr. Graham, BSocSc ACA *1988;* 38 Tamworth Road, Dosthill, TAMWORTH, B77 1LB.
SUTTON, Mr. Graham Keith, FCA *1970;* 108 Grove Road, TRING, HERTFORDSHIRE, HP23 5PA.
SUTTON, Mr. Howard, FCA *1974;* High Hedges, Elms Cross, BRADFORD-ON-AVON, BA15 2AD.
SUTTON, Mr. Ian Nicholas, BA FCA *1983;* 1 Peakes Place, Granville Road, ST. ALBANS, HERTFORDSHIRE, AL1 5AY.
•SUTTON, Mr. Ian Raymond, FCA *1982;* Sutton Dipple Limited, 8 Wheelwright's Corner, Old Market, Nailsworth, STROUD, GL6 0DB.
•SUTTON, Mr. James Francis, BA(Hons) FCA *2001;* HW (Leeds) LLP, Sterling House, 1 Sheepscar Court, Meanwood Road, LEEDS, WEST YORKSHIRE LS7 2BB.
•SUTTON, Mr. John Edward, FCA *1972;* (Tax Fac), Goldwells, Heaton House, 4 Gordon Street, NAIRN, IV12 4DQ. See also John Sutton & Co
SUTTON, Mr. John Nigel, FCA *1967;* 5 Oak Tree Grove, Shaldon, TEIGNMOUTH, DEVON, TQ14 0BU.
SUTTON, Mr. Jonathan Guy, BSc ACA *2000;* 29 Tormead Road, GUILDFORD, GU1 2JA.
•SUTTON, Mr. Jonathan Lawrence, BSc ACA *1997;* Dixon Wilson, 22 Chancery Lane, LONDON, WC2A 1LS.
SUTTON, Mrs. Julia Anne, ACA *2008;* 1 Tranby Park Meadows, HESSLE, NORTH HUMBERSIDE, HU13 0TF.
SUTTON, Mrs. Julie, ACA *1995;* 15 Queens Road, RAYLEIGH, SS6 8JY.
SUTTON, Ms. Kaye, BSc ACA *1986;* Judges House, Winforton, HEREFORD, HR3 6EA.
SUTTON, Miss. Kelly Ann, BA ACA *2006;* Deloitte & Touche Llp Horton House, Exchange Flags, LIVERPOOL, L2 3PG.
SUTTON, Mr. Kenneth, FCA *1962;* Highfield House, Bristol Road, RADSTOCK, BA3 3EE.
SUTTON, Mr. Kenneth William, BSc FCA *1988;* 20 Middleton Road, Hackney, LONDON, E8 4BL.
SUTTON, Mrs. Kerry Anne, ACA MAAT *2003;* 73 Norfolk Road, Wangford, BECCLES, SUFFOLK, NR34 8RE.
SUTTON, Mrs. Kirsty Jayne, BSc(Hons) ACA *2004;* 8 The Beeches Pool in Wharfedale, OTLEY, WEST YORKSHIRE, LS21 1TL.
SUTTON, Mrs. Lesley Ann, MSc BA FCA *1991;* with Ernst & Young LLP, 1 Colmore Square, BIRMINGHAM, B4 6HQ.
SUTTON, Miss. Lesley Jane, ACA *1994;* (Tax Fac), Revell Ward Llp, 30 Market Street, HUDDERSFIELD, HD1 2HG.
SUTTON, Mr. Leslie Mark, FCA MBCS *1960;* Sun Villa, The Leas, Kingsdown, DEAL, CT14 8ER. (Life Member)
•SUTTON, Mr. Lewis George, FCA *1968;* Dawes & Sutton, Springfield House, 4 Millicent Road, West Bridgford, NOTTINGHAM, NG2 7LD.
SUTTON, Mrs. Louisa Charlotte, BA ACA *2004;* 3 The Gattons, BURGESS HILL, WEST SUSSEX, RH15 9SW.
SUTTON, Mr. Mark Arnold Joseph, MSc BA ACA *1995;* 28 Lee Park, LONDON, SE3 9HU.
SUTTON, Mr. Martin Paul, BSc ACA *1986;* 20 Larkspur Close, WOKINGHAM, BERKSHIRE, RG41 3NA.
•SUTTON, Mr. Matthew Paul, BSc ACA *2007;* Burgess Hodgson, Camburgh House, 27 New Dover Road, CANTERBURY, CT1 3DN.
SUTTON, Mr. Michael Alan, BA FCA *1975;* 25a Westbourne Road, SOUTHPORT, MERSEYSIDE, PR8 2HZ.
SUTTON, Mr. Neil Robert, BSc(Hons) ACA *1999;* 201 Copeland Road East, BEECROFT, NSW 2119, AUSTRALIA.
SUTTON, Mr. Nicholas Nelson, BA ACA *1995;* Imperial Property Company Limited, 11 Gough Square, LONDON, EC4A 3DE.
•SUTTON, Mr. Peter James, FCA *1972;* (Tax Fac), Haines Watts Kent LLP, 4-5 Kings Row, Armstrong Road, MAIDSTONE, KENT, ME15 6AQ.
•SUTTON, Mr. Peter John, MA FCA *1968;* 2 West Hill Road, Foxton, CAMBRIDGE, CB22 6SZ.
SUTTON, Mr. Peter John, BA ACA *1992;* Abbey, 2 Triton Square, LONDON, NW1 3AN.
•SUTTON, Mr. Peter Michael, BA FCA *1984;* Matthews Sutton & Co Ltd, 48-52 Penny Lane, LIVERPOOL, L18 1DG. See also The Company Specialists (Accounting Services) Ltd
SUTTON, Mrs. Rachel, BSc ACA *1997;* 36a Cholmeley Park, LONDON, N6 5ER.
SUTTON, Mrs. Rebecca Jane, BA ACA *1999;* 1 Downsedge Terrace Epsom Road, GUILDFORD, GU1 2SS.
SUTTON, Mr. Richard Alan, FCA *1958;* 4 Pinewood Court, South Downs Road, Hale, ALTRINCHAM, WA14 3HY. (Life Member)
SUTTON, Mr. Richard Alan, FCA *1976;* Spring Lodge, 32 Uppingham Road, Houghton-On-The-Hill, LEICESTER, LE7 9HH.
•SUTTON, Mr. Richard Derek, BSc ACA *1987;* Taylor Brooker Accountancy Limited, Barham Court, Teston, MAIDSTONE, KENT, ME18 5BZ.
SUTTON, Mr. Richard Frederick, ACA FRSA *1979;* Charles Green & Son Ltd, 37-42 Tenby Street, BIRMINGHAM, B1 3EF.
SUTTON, Mr. Richard Ian, MA ACA *2000;* 59 Casimir Road, LONDON, E5 9NU.
SUTTON, Mr. Richard John, BA ACA *1980;* The Limes, 9 Welham Road, Great Bowden, MARKET HARBOROUGH, LEICESTERSHIRE, LE16 7HS.
SUTTON, Mr. Richard John, FCA *1975;* 44 Kilgour Road, Honor Oak Park, LONDON, SE23 1PQ.
SUTTON, Mr. Robert Alan, MA ACA *1988;* Irininskaya 5/24, 01034 KIEV, UKRAINE.
•SUTTON, Mr. Robert David, ACA *1988;* (Tax Fac), R.D. Sutton & Company, 544 Leeds Road, Thackley, BRADFORD, BD10 8JH.
SUTTON, Mr. Robert Gabert, FCA *1970;* Legh Cottage, Wrenshot Lane, High Legh, KNUTSFORD, WA16 6PF.
SUTTON, Mr. Robin Ashley, BA FCA *1985;* Fianium Ltd 20 Compass Point, Ensign Way Hamble, SOUTHAMPTON, SO31 4RA.
•SUTTON, Mr. Rodney Maginess, BA ACA FCCA CA(SA) *2001;* (Tax Fac), Reeves & Co LLP, Montague Place, Quayside, Chatham Maritime, CHATHAM, KENT ME4 4QU.
•SUTTON, Mr. Roger William, FCA *1973;* (Tax Fac), Roger Sutton & Co. Limited, 79 High Street, TEDDINGTON, MIDDLESEX, TW11 8HG.
SUTTON, Mr. Russell Stephen, FCA *1979;* 15 Clynden Avenue, Malvern East, MELBOURNE, VIC 3145, AUSTRALIA.
SUTTON, Mrs. Stephanie, BSc ACA *2003;* with RSM Tenon Limited, Lowgate House, HULL, HU1 1EL.
•SUTTON, Mr. Steven Maxwell, BA FCA *1977;* (Tax Fac), Burgess Hodgson, Camburgh House, 27 New Dover Road, CANTERBURY, CT1 3DN.
SUTTON, Miss. Susan, ACA *2011;* 27 Medway Drive, Kearsley, BOLTON, BL4 8PQ.
SUTTON, Mr. Timothy James, ACA *1988;* Constantine Ltd, 20-26 Sandgate Street, LONDON, SE15 1LE.
SUTTON, Mr. Timothy Martin, BA FCA *1996;* CAMELOT GROUP PLC, TOLPITS LANE, WATFORD, WD18 9RN.
SUTTON, Mr. William George, FCA *1975;* Trepibau, Sarnau, LLANDYSUL, SA44 6QA.
SUTTON, Mr. William John Seagrave, BA FCA *1984;* La Ravenelle, La Rue Des Raisies, St. Martin, JERSEY, JE3 6AT.
SUTTON, Mr. William Michael, FCA *1974;* 26 Amesbury Road, Moseley, BIRMINGHAM, B13 8LE.
•SUTTON, Mr. William Neil, BSc ACA *1986;* PricewaterhouseCoopers LLP, 7 More London Riverside, LONDON, SE1 2RT. See also PricewaterhouseCoopers

SUTTON-TUOHY, Mr. Denis Thomas Patrick, BSc ACA 1982; 2nd Floor Cap House, 9-12 Long Lane, LONDON, EC1A 9HA.
SVASTI-SALEE, Prof. Joy Elisabeth, FCA CTA 1981; with Ernst & Young LLP, 1 More London Place, LONDON, SE1 2AF.
SVENSSON, Ms. Johanna Maria Theresia, ACA 2009; Mourant Services Ltd, 22 Grenville Street, St Helier, JERSEY, JE4 8PX.
SVIDERSKIY, Mr. Anton, ACA 2009; Gerasimou Markora street Constantia Court ap. 202, CY-3085 LIMASSOL, CYPRUS.
SVOBODA, Mr. Julian James, BA(Hons) ACA 2003; 164 Parsonage Lane, ENFIELD, MIDDLESEX, EN2 0AA.
SWABEY, Mr. Richard Patrick, FCA 1972; 11 The Greenacre, Clifton, ASHBOURNE, DE6 2DW.
SWABY, Mr. Glenn, BSc ACA 1983; 18 Gypsy Lane, WARE, SG12 9RN.
SWABY, Mr. Mark William, BSc ACA 1984; Linden Lodge Offchurch Road, Hunningham, LEAMINGTON SPA, WARWICKSHIRE, CV33 9DR.
SWABY, Mr. Paul Everton, MBA BA ACA 1993; 40 Sutton Square, Urswick Road, LONDON, E9 6EQ.
SWABY, Mr. Richard Matthew, BSc ACA 2006; 28/166 Wickham Terrace, Spring Hill, BRISBANE, QLD 4000, AUSTRALIA.
•**SWADDLE, Mr. William Anthony, BSc FCA** 1978; Prontax Ltd, 25 Briardene Drive, South Wardley, GATESHEAD, NE10 8AN.
SWADEN, Mr. David, BCom FCA 1978; 52 Delamer Road, Bowdon, ALTRINCHAM, WA14 2LP.
SWAFFIELD, Miss. Amanda Clare, MA ACA 2001; with Deloitte LLP, 2 New Street Square, LONDON, EC4A 3BZ.
SWAFFIELD, Mrs. Claire Elena, BA ACA 1998; 28 Premier Street, MARRICKVILLE, NSW 2204, AUSTRALIA.
SWAFFIELD, Dr. Claire Helen, PhD BSc ACA 2002; 8 Chantry Close, Swavesey, CAMBRIDGE, CB4 5GJ.
SWAFFIELD, Mr. Ian Nicholas, BSc ACA 1999; 16 Channel Street, DULWICH HILL, NSW 2203, AUSTRALIA.
SWAFFIELD, Mr. Paul Anthony, FCA 1966; 2 Pye Lane, Burnt Yates, HARROGATE, HG3 3EH.
•**SWAFFIELD, Mr. Roger, FCA** 1972; (Tax Fac), Evans Weir Limited, The Victoria, 25 St. Pancras, CHICHESTER, WEST SUSSEX, PO19 7LT.
SWAFFIELD, Mr. Roger Leslie, FCA 1969; ISLAND COTTAGE, WEST MILLS, NEWBURY, RG14 5HT.
SWAFFIELD, Mr. Stephen Richard, BSc FCA 1975; The Haven, Back Lane, West Lutton, MALTON, YO17 8TA.
SWAGE, Mr. Sayed Hashim, BA FCA 1961; 4 Tiverton Road, HOUNSLOW, TW3 4JF. (Life Member)
SWAIN, Mrs. Aileen Patricia, FCA 1982; Rushbrook Farmhouse, Rushbrook Lane, Tanworth-in-Arden, SOLIHULL, WEST MIDLANDS, B94 5HW.
•**SWAIN, Mr. Brian Geoffrey, FCA** 1972; BGS Accountancy & Taxation Services, 127 Dale Street, Milnrow, ROCHDALE, LANCASHIRE, OL16 3NW.
SWAIN, Mr. Charles de Pina Beauchamp, BA FCA 1986; 226 Seal Road, SEVENOAKS, TN15 0AA.
SWAIN, Mr. David Alan, FCA 1973; Delfim House, Back Lane South, Middleton, PICKERING, NORTH YORKSHIRE, YO18 8NU.
•**SWAIN, Mr. Frank Colin, FCA** 1980; (Tax Fac), Harris Lacey and Swain, 8 Waterside Business Park, Livingstone Road, HESSLE, NORTH HUMBERSIDE, HU13 0EN.
SWAIN, Mr. Gareth Nigel, BA ACA 1992; The History Press Ltd The Mill, Brimscombe Hill Brimscombe, STROUD, GLOUCESTERSHIRE, GL5 2QG.
SWAIN, Mr. Ian, BA ACA 1992; 22 Westminster Drive, Kings Heath, BIRMINGHAM, B14 6BG.
SWAIN, Miss. Imogen, ACA 2009; R G L Forensics Dashwood House, 69 Old Broad Street, LONDON, EC2M 1QS.
SWAIN, Mr. John Kenneth, FCA 1970; 2 Kingslake Rise, Mudbank Lane, EXMOUTH, EX8 3EL.
SWAIN, Mr. John Richard, MA FCA 1980; 38 Fernwood Rise, BRIGHTON, BN1 5EP.
•**SWAIN, Mr. Kim, MA ACA** 1981; Swain & Company (Accountants) Limited, 73 High Street, ALDERSHOT, HAMPSHIRE, GU11 1BY. See also Swain & Co
SWAIN, Miss. Linda Jane, BA(Hons) ACA 2003; 3116 13th St NW, Unit 2, WASHINGTON, DC 20010, UNITED STATES.
SWAIN, Mrs. Louisa Jade, BSc ACA 2006; with Murphy Salisbury, 15 Warwick Road, STRATFORD-UPON-AVON, CV37 6YW.
SWAIN, Mr. Michael Anthony, ACA 1987; PO Box HM 3044, HAMILTON HM NX, BERMUDA.
SWAIN, Mr. Paul Anthony, BA FCA 1981; with Ernst & Young LLP, 1 More London Place, LONDON, SE1 2AF.
SWAIN, Mr. Richard Allan, FCA 1960; 8 Tramar Drive, Sutton, ELY, CB6 2QP. (Life Member)
SWAIN, Mr. Samuel Edward, BA(Hons) ACA 2005; Flat 12 Princess Court Gordon Road, HAYWARDS HEATH, WEST SUSSEX, RH16 1EF.
SWAIN, Mrs. Sandra Esther, BSocSc ACA 1996; Wesleyan Assurance Society, Colmore Circus Queensway, BIRMINGHAM, B4 6AR.
SWAINE, Mr. David, MA ACA 2010; Dixon Wilson, 22 Chancery Lane, LONDON, WC2A 1LS.
SWAINE, Mr. Gordon Trevor, FCA 1952; 8 Montagu Court, Marlborough Drive, DARLINGTON, COUNTY DURHAM, DL1 5YF. (Life Member)
SWAINE, Mrs. Heather, ACA 1983; (Tax Fac), M Wasley Chapman & Co, 3-5 Victoria Square, WHITBY, NORTH YORKSHIRE, YO21 1EA.
SWAINE, Mrs. Melissa Jane, BSc(Hons) ACA 2002; 33 Donegal Road, SUTTON COLDFIELD, B74 2AA.
SWAINSON, Mr. Hugh Jeromy, BA ACA 2007; 3 Haydon Park Road, LONDON, SW19 8JQ.
SWAINSON, Mr. John Frederick, FCA 1976; Royal Parks, Old Police House, HYDE PARK, W2 2UH.
SWAINSON, Mr. Nicholas James, BA ACA 2001; A4 the Terrace, Grantham Street, LINCOLN, LN2 1BD.
SWAINSTON, Mr. Andrew Nicholas, BSc(Hons) ACA 2001; 43 St Cuthbert's Avenue, Marton, MIDDLESBROUGH, TS7 8RG.
SWAINSTON, Mr. Anthony Henry, FCA 1970; The Beacon Beacon Road, Kingswear, DARTMOUTH, DEVON, TQ6 0BS.
SWAINSTON, Mr. John Bell, FCA 1965; Pembroke Lodge, Beamsley, Bolton Abbey, SKIPTON, BD23 6HZ.
SWAITE, Mr. John Peter, BA(Hons) ACA 2002; AdEPT Telecom, 77 Mount Ephraim, TUNBRIDGE WELLS, TN4 8BS.
SWALES, Mr. David Rowell, BSc ACA 1989; 67 Sebert Road, BURY ST.EDMUNDS, IP32 7EH.
SWALES, Mr. Geoffrey John, BSc FCA 1986; Apartment 15, Admirals Place, 24-27 The Leas, WESTCLIFF-ON-SEA, SS0 7BF.
SWALES, Miss. Imogen Ruth, LLB ACA 1998; 27 Ravenstone Street, Balham, LONDON, SW12 9ST.
•**SWALES, Mr. John William, FCA** 1971; (Tax Fac), J.W.Swales & Co, The Grange, Yatton Keynell, CHIPPENHAM, SN14 7BA.
SWALES, Miss. Lara Claire, BA ACA 2004; 49 New Park Vale, Farsley, LEEDS, LS28 5TY.
•**SWALES, Mr. Marcus James, BSc ACA** 1996; Grant Thornton UK LLP, 30 Finsbury Square, LONDON, EC2P 2YU. See also Grant Thornton LLP
•**SWALES, Mr. Matthew Haydn, BA ACA** 2006; 1 Oak Cottages, High Street, Leigh, TONBRIDGE, TN11 8RW.
SWALES, Mr. Michael Christopher, BA(Hons) ACA 2002; D L A Piper Rudnick Gray Cary UK St. Pauls Place, 121 Norfolk Street, SHEFFIELD, S1 2JX.
SWALES, Mr. Nick, BA(Hons) ACA 2008; 7 Harewood Avenue, Ainsdale, SOUTHPORT, PR8 2PH.
SWALES, Mr. Patrick Nigel Quentin, FCA 1961; Aysgarth, Ground Floor, 3 East Budleigh Road, BUDLEIGH SALTERTON, DEVON, EX9 6HF. (Life Member)
SWALES, Mr. Sean, ACA 2009; Rotolok Group Ltd Unit 1, Millennium Place Tiverton Business Park, TIVERTON, DEVON, EX16 6SB.
SWALES, Mr. Timothy, BA ACA 2004; Barclays Private Equity, Condor House, St Pauls Churchyard, LONDON, EC4M 8AL.
SWALES, Mr. Warren, BA ACA 1997; 80 Coningsby House, Sandygate Grove, SHEFFIELD, S10 5TG.
•**SWALLOW, Mr. Christopher John, BSc FCA** 1991; Howard Worth, Drake House, Gadbrook Park, NORTHWICH, CHESHIRE, CW9 7RA.
•**SWALLOW, Mr. David Addison, FCA** 1973; Swallow & Co, Commercial House, 10 Bridge Road, Stokesley, MIDDLESBROUGH, TS9 5AA.
•**SWALLOW, Mr. Jake Brangwyn Sheridan, MA FCA** 1974; Sheridan Swallow, Brickhill House, North Oakley, TADLEY, HAMPSHIRE, RG26 5TT.
•**SWALLOW, Mr. James Malcolm, FCA** 1980; Abell Morliss International Limited, 18 Clarendon Road, S Woodford, LONDON, E18 2AW. See also Abell Morliss Limited
SWALLOW, Miss. Katherine Elisabeth, BSc(Eng) ACA 1996; 2nd FloorPrama House, 267 Banbury Road, OXFORD, OXFORDSHIRE, OX2 7HT.
SWALLOW, Mr. Keith Eugene, BSc ACA 1992; 43 Grove Road, Halton, LEEDS, LS15 0LH.
SWALLOW, Mr. Mark Francis, BA ACA 1995; Hickoringill, Thirlby, THIRSK, NORTH YORKSHIRE, YO7 2DJ.
SWALLOW, Mr. Robert Henry, FCA 1975; 78A Causeway Side, Linthwaite, HUDDERSFIELD, HD7 5NW.
SWALLOW, Miss. Rowena Gay, MA ACA 2000; 3 Fitzgerald Road, LONDON, SW14 8HA.
SWALWELL, Mr. Stephen George, FCA 1983; Cedar Cottage, High Street, Spofforth, HARROGATE, HG3 1BQ.
SWAN, Mr. Andrew Conrad Henry Joseph, BSc ACA 1993; 10th Floor, Morgan Stanley, 20 Bank Street, LONDON, E14 4AD.
SWAN, Ms. Caroline Margaret, MA ACA 1997; Suite 1/1, 79 West Regent Street, GLASGOW, G2 2AW.
SWAN, Mr. David, FCA ACA CA(AUS) 2011; White Rose Farm, Hextalls Lane, Bletchingley, REDHILL, RH1 4QT.
SWAN, Mr. Douglas William Fraser, MA FCA 1976; Berry Barn Donafuil, Keltneyburn, ABERFELDY, PERTHSHIRE, PH15 2LE.
SWAN, Mrs. Elizabeth Anne, BSc ACA 2006; 16 Carnoustie Close, CONSETT, COUNTY DURHAM, DH8 5XQ.
•①**SWAN, Mrs. Julie Ann, LLB ACA** 1989; Pitman Cohen Recoveries LLP, Great Central House, Great Central Avenue, RUISLIP, MIDDLESEX, HA4 6TS.
•**SWAN, Mrs. Lisa Joanne, BSc ACA CFA** 1996; Parkes & Swan Limited, White Rose Farm, Hextalls Lane, Bletchingley, REDHILL, RH1 4QT.
SWAN, Mrs. Melanie Jane, BSc ACA 2009; 89-91 Jesmond Road, NEWCASTLE UPON TYNE, NE2 1NH.
•**SWAN, Mr. Michael David, BA(Hons) FCA CTA** 1992; Wilkins Kennedy FKC Limited, Stourside Place, 35-41 Station Road, ASHFORD, KENT, TN23 1PP. See also W K Finn-Kelcey & Chapman Limited
SWAN, Mrs. Natasha, ACA 2006; 19 Avon Green, Chandler's Ford, EASTLEIGH, HAMPSHIRE, SO53 2NL.
SWAN, Miss. Nikki, ACA 2009; 40 Hambalt Road, LONDON, SW4 9EG.
SWAN, Mr. Peter Thomas, OBE FCA 1957; West Lodge, 2 Priorygate Court, CASTLE CARY, BA7 7HT. (Life Member)
•**SWAN, Mr. Philip Arthur, BA FCA** 1984; Hazlewoods LLP, Staverton Court, Staverton, CHELTENHAM, GLOUCESTERSHIRE, GL51 0UX.
SWAN, Miss. Susan Carol, ACA 2007; Jeesal Cawston Park, Aylsham Road, Cawston, NORWICH, NR10 4JD.
•**SWANE, Mrs. Genevieve Samantha, BA FCA** 1992; 23 Chevington Road, Chedburgh, BURY ST. EDMUNDS, SUFFOLK, IP29 4UL.
SWANE, Mr. Jeremy Richard, BSc ACA 1992; BPP Cambridge, 3rd Floor, Lion House, Lion Yard, CAMBRIDGE, CB2 3NA.
SWANIKER, Ms. Carole Gladys, BSc FCA CPA 1992; 561 9th Avenue, MENLO PARK, CA 94025, UNITED STATES.
SWANN, Mr. Allen Harry Kevin, BA ACA 2007; 85 Devonshire Mews, Devonshire Road, CAMBRIDGE, CB1 2BB.
SWANN, Mr. Andrew David, BA ACA 1993; James Hallam Ltd, Meridien House, 69-71 Clarendon Road, WATFORD, WD17 1DS.
SWANN, Miss. Carol Jane, BA ACA 1984; 18 Enterprise Lane, Campbell Park, MILTON KEYNES, MK9 4AP.
•**SWANN, Mr. Darren Andrew, ACA FCCA** 2010; Leonherman, 7 Christie Way, Christie Fields, MANCHESTER, M21 7QY.
SWANN, Mr. Derek Kenneth, FCA 1960; Mailpoint, Buzon 31, 41 Av.Maria del Mar Rodriguez, Algorfa, 03169 ALICANTE, SPAIN. (Life Member)
SWANN, Mr. Francis Edwin William, FCA 1953; 5 Manvers Grove, Radcliffe-on-Trent, NOTTINGHAM, NG12 2FT. (Life Member)
SWANN, Mr. Hugo Oliver Holland, BA ACA 2005; 18 Eland Road, LONDON, SW11 5JY.
•**SWANN, Mrs. Jane Louise, BA FCA** 1992; dhjh LLP, Springhill House, 94-98 Kidderminster Road, BEWDLEY, WORCESTERSHIRE, DY12 1DQ.
SWANN, Mr. Jonathan Graham, BA ACA 1996; P O Box 213255, DUBAI, UNITED ARAB EMIRATES.
SWANN, Mrs. Julie Ann, BCom ACA 1995; with Deloitte LLP, 4 Brindley Place, BIRMINGHAM, B1 2HZ.
SWANN, Mr. Mark Christopher, BA ACA 1988; 25 Gorse Avenue, THORNTON-CLEVELEYS, LANCASHIRE, FY5 2PH.
SWANN, Mr. Martin Jonathan, BSc ACA 1989; 136 Walton Road, Walton, CHESTERFIELD, S40 3BU.
SWANN, Mr. Michael Andrew, BCom ACA 1991; 16 Sydney Road, SMETHWICK, WEST MIDLANDS, B67 5QQ.
SWANN, Mr. Paul Albert Ronald, FCA 1952; 13 Cross Road, UXBRIDGE, UB8 2UQ. (Life Member)
SWANN, Mr. Peter William James, BSc ACA 1998; 82 Penland Road, HAYWARDS HEATH, WEST SUSSEX, RH16 1PH.
SWANN, Mr. Philip Reginald, BSc FCA 1955; 1 Tithe Close, WITHAM, CM8 2HN. (Life Member)
SWANN, Mr. Robert Grimshaw, FCA 1950; 10 Arden Court, Bramhall Park Road, Bramhall, STOCKPORT, SK7 3NG. (Life Member)
SWANN, Mr. Ryan, BA ACA 2010; 24 Forum Court, BURY ST. EDMUNDS, SUFFOLK, IP32 6BP.
SWANN, Ms. Sally Louise, BSc ACA 1992; 16 Hatley Drive, Burwell, CAMBRIDGE, CB25 0AY.
SWANN, Mr. Simon Michael, BSc ACA 1982; Affolternstrasse 56, CH 8050 ZURICH, SWITZERLAND.
SWANN, Mr. Steven Patrick, BA ACA 1992; Kaplan Financial, 10-14 White Lion Street, LONDON, N1 9PD.
SWANN, Mrs. Vivien Marie, ACA 1983; 26 Knotts Avenue, WORCESTER, WR4 0HZ.
SWANN, Mr. William Charles, BSc FCA 1974; Greenleaves, Finchfield Gardens, WOLVERHAMPTON, WV3 9LT.
•**SWANN-JONES, Mrs. Paula Tracy, FCA** 2000; The Rowleys Partnership Limited, 6 Dominus Way, Meridian Business Park, LEICESTER, LE19 1RP. See also Rowleys Partnership LLP
SWANNELL, Mrs. Barbara, BSc ACA CTA 1984; (Tax Fac), 59 Shepperton Close, Appleton, WARRINGTON, WA4 5JZ.
SWANNELL, Mr. Robert William Ashburnham, FCA 1973; 40 Ashley Gardens, Ambrosden Avenue, LONDON, SW1P 1QE.
SWANNEY, Mr. Richard, ACA 2008; Apartment 1, 16 Honeysuckle Court, Huncoat, ACCRINGTON, LANCASHIRE, BB5 6NU.
SWANNICK, Mr. Paul Harvey, FCA 1965; 6 Foster Place, Kempston, BEDFORD, MK42 8BX. (Life Member)
•**SWANSBOROUGH, Mr. John, ACA FCCA** 2011; The Leaman Partnership LLP, 51 Queen Anne Street, LONDON, W1G 9HS. See also Leaman Partnership LLP
SWANSBURY, Mr. Carl, ACA 2007; with RSM Tenon Limited, The Poynt Building, 45 Wollaton Street, NOTTINGHAM, NG1 5FW.
•**SWANSBURY, Mr. Mark, BSc ACA** 1992; Hindsight Tax Partners LLP, 12 The Riverside Studios, Amethyst Road, NEWCASTLE UPON TYNE, NE4 7YL.
SWANSON, Miss. Alison, BA ACA PGCE 1992; 12 Linton Avenue, Silsden, KEIGHLEY, BD20 9LE.
SWANSON, Mrs. Carol Elspeth, FCA 1980; (Tax Fac), H L Barnes & Sons Barclays Bank Chambers, Bridge Street, STRATFORD-UPON-AVON, CV37 6AH.
SWANSON, Mrs. Vicki, BA ACA 1994; 1705 Pemberton Road, RICHMOND, VA 23238, UNITED STATES.
•**SWANSTON, Ms. Heather, BSc ACA** 1992; PricewaterhouseCoopers LLP, Pricewaterhousecoopers, 12 Plumtree Court, LONDON, EC4A 4HT. See also PricewaterhouseCoopers
SWANTON, Mr. James Edward, MEng ACA 2004; with PricewaterhouseCoopers LLP, Hays Galleria, 1 Hays Lane, LONDON, SE1 2RD.
SWANTON, Mr. Mark Thomas, BEng ACA 2003; 1 Church Crescent, LONDON, E9 7DH.
SWANWICK, Mrs. Josephine Ruth, FCA 1968; 43 Hormare Crescent, Storrington, PULBOROUGH, RH20 4QX.
•**SWARBRECK, Mr. Guy Richard Beaumont, BCom ACA** 2005; with UHY Hacker Young LLP, Quadrant House, 4 Thomas More Square, LONDON, E1W 1YW.
•**SWARBRICK, Mr. Andrew Thomas, BA FCA** 1978; Deloitte LLP, City House, 126-130 Hills Road, CAMBRIDGE, CB2 1RY. See also Deloitte & Touche LLP
•①**SWARBRICK, Dr. Angela, BSc ACA** 1993; Ernst & Young LLP, 1 More London Place, LONDON, SE1 2AF. See also Ernst & Young Europe LLP
SWARBRICK, Mr. Benjamin John, BSc ACA 2006; Flat B4, Kenilworth Court Hagley Road, BIRMINGHAM, B16 9NS.
SWARBRICK, Mr. David Ian, BA ACA 1994; Suite 3 Ground Floor, Progress House, 17 Cecil Road Hale, ALTRINCHAM, CHESHIRE, WA15 9NZ.
SWARBRICK, Mr. John Frederick, BA ACA 1984; Lloyds Development Capital, 1 City Square, LEEDS, LS1 2ES.
SWARBRICK, Mr. John Richard, MA FCA 1981; Nationwide Bldg Soc, Nationwide House, Pipers Way, SWINDON, SN38 1NW.

SWARBRICK, Mrs. Kathryn Emma, BSc ACA *2006;* 1 Sartoris Close, Warsash, SOUTHAMPTON, SO31 9EW.
SWARBRICK, Mr. Michael Anthony John, BSc FCA *1982;* 12 Bonville Chase, ALTRINCHAM, WA14 4QA.
SWARBRICK, Mr. Nicholas Andrew, BA FCA *1993;* 26 Nursery Avenue, Hale, ALTRINCHAM, WA15 0JP.
•SWARBRICK, Mr. Peter, BSc ACA *1985;* (Tax Fac), Crossley & Davis, 348-350 Lytham Road, BLACKPOOL, FY4 1DW. See also Campbell Crossley & Davis
SWARC, Mr. Alan, FCA *1962;* 32 Loveday Road, Ealing, LONDON, W13 9JS.
SWARUP, Mr. Arun Kumar, FCA *1960;* 22 St. Paul's Hill, WINCHESTER, SO22 5AB. (Life Member)
•SWARUP, Mr. Girish Kumar, FCA *1967;* G.K.Swarup & Co, Shyam Kutir, 12/11 Station Road, Teen Batti, JAMNAGAR 361001, INDIA.
SWASH, Mr. Anthony Howard, FCA *1970;* Iles Green, Far Oakridge, STROUD, GL6 7PD. (Life Member)
•SWASH, Mrs. Karen, BSc ACA *2001;* Karen Swash, Hillside, Woolstone, FARINGDON, OXFORDSHIRE, SN7 7QL.
SWASH, Mr. Peter Charles, FCA *1978;* (Tax Fac), 14 Mellor Chase, COLCHESTER, CO3 9BN.
SWASH, Mr. Thomas Jago James, BA(Hons) ACA *2002;* Hillside, Woolstone, FARINGDON, OXFORDSHIRE, SN7 7QL.
•SWATMAN, Mr. Derek James, FCA *1961;* (Tax Fac), D.J. Swatman, 24 Wilkinson Way, NORTH WALSHAM, NR28 9BB.
SWATMAN, Mr. Philip Hilary, BA FCA *1974;* Cardinal House, George Road, KINGSTON-UPON-THAMES, KT2 7NU.
SWATTRIDGE, Mr. Peter John, BSc FCA *1998;* 19 Norfolk House Road, Streatham, LONDON, SW16 1JJ.
SWAYLES, Mr. William Henry, BA ACA *1986;* 4 Astrey Close, Harlington, DUNSTABLE, BEDFORDSHIRE, LU5 6ND.
SWAYNE, Mr. Anthony William John, BSc FCA *1975;* The Old Vicarage, East Meon, PETERSFIELD, GU32 1PG.
SWAYNE, Mr. Bruce Empson, FCA *1978;* Middleton Maintenance Services Ltd, 224-232 High Street, Erdington, BIRMINGHAM, B23 6SJ.
SWAYNE, Mr. David Foard, FCA *1975;* Southernhay, The Byeway, West Wittering, CHICHESTER, PO20 8LJ.
SWAYNE, Mr. David John, FCA *1965;* 48 Upper Way, FARNHAM, GU9 8RF. (Life Member)
SWAYNE, Mr. Jonathan Paul, ACA *1991;* 22 Hanson Road, ABINGDON, OX14 1YL.
SWAYNE, Mr. Julian Timothy, BA ACA *1985;* 3 Gardenia Way, WOODFORD GREEN, IG8 0BL.
SWAYSLAND, Mr. Edward Lawrence Cresswell, FCA *1954;* White Wicketts, Wilderness Road, OXTED, RH8 9HS. (Life Member)
SWEATMAN, Mr. Chris, ACA *2002;* Renewable Energy Systems Ltd, Faraday House, Station Road, KINGS LANGLEY, HERTFORDSHIRE, WD4 8LH.
SWEENEY, Mr. Andrew, ACA *1992;* Veolia Environmental Services Grimaldi Park House, 154a Pentonville Road, LONDON, N1 9PE.
SWEENEY, Mr. Andrew Christopher, BCom ACA MBA *1981;* Hampton Park, Bridgnorth Road, Stourton, STOURBRIDGE, WEST MIDLANDS, DY7 5BJ.
SWEENEY, Miss. Angela, BA ACA *2004;* 35 Beverley Road, Low Fell, GATESHEAD, TYNE AND WEAR, NE9 5UJ.
SWEENEY, Mrs. Carol Diane, BA(Hons) ACA *2001;* 4B Blaxland Road, Killara, SYDNEY, NSW 2071, AUSTRALIA.
SWEENEY, Mr. Charles Terence, BCom FCA *1973;* 259 Sutton Park, Sutton, DUBLIN 13, COUNTY DUBLIN, IRELAND. (Life Member)
SWEENEY, Mr. Christopher John, BA ACA AMCT *1999;* 6th Floor Cardinal Place, 100 Victoria Street, LONDON, SW1E 7JL.
SWEENEY, Mrs. Elaine, BSc FCA *1993;* 17 Crosby Road, Birkdale, SOUTHPORT, PR8 4SU.
SWEENEY, Mr. Fabian Malachy, FCA *1975;* The Bank of New York, 43rd Floor, One Canada Square, LONDON, E14 5AL.
SWEENEY, Mr. Francis Joseph, FCA *1960;* 22 Tollerton Road, LIVERPOOL, L12 7HQ. (Life Member)
SWEENEY, Mrs. Hazel Claire, BA FCA CTA *1993;* 54 Ton-yr-Ywen Avenue, CARDIFF, CF14 4PB.
•SWEENEY, Mr. James William, BSc FCA *1980;* Packhams, Station Road, Rotherfield, CROWBOROUGH, EAST SUSSEX, TN6 3HP.
SWEENEY, Mrs. Kaye, BA ACA *1995;* (Tax Fac), Marstons Plc Marstons House, Brewery Road, WOLVERHAMPTON, WV1 4JT.
SWEENEY, Mr. Malcolm, BSc FCA *1974;* 27 Freemans Close Stoke Poges, SLOUGH, SL2 4ER.
SWEENEY, Mr. Michael George, BSc ACA *2007;* 22 Hambalt Road, LONDON, SW4 9EF.
SWEENEY, Mr. Neil William, BSc ACA *1991;* 29 Gordon Road, Claygate, ESHER, SURREY, KT10 0PJ.
SWEENEY, Mr. Niall Aidan, BSc FCA *1976;* M S M Media Ltd, Thames House, 18 Park Street, LONDON, SE1 9ER.
SWEENEY, Miss. Pamela Jane, ACA *1992;* Rock Cottage Fryern Park, Fryern Road Storrington, PULBOROUGH, WEST SUSSEX, RH20 4FF.
SWEENEY, Miss. Sian Margaret, MA FCA *1993;* 25 Camphill Avenue, WORCESTER, WORCESTERSHIRE, WR5 2HQ.
SWEENEY, Miss. Siobhan Catriona Ann, ACA *1998;* 18 Queen Annes Grove, Bedford Park Chiswick, LONDON, W4 1HN.
SWEENEY, Mr. Terence James, MA ACA *1989;* Harrington Brooks Ltd, Sale Point, 126-150 Washway Road, SALE, CHESHIRE, M33 6AG.
SWEENEY, Mr. Terence John, BSc ACA *1992;* Willfred Brown Building Room A013, Brunel University, Kingston Lane, UXBRIDGE, MIDDLESEX, UB8 3PH.
SWEENEY, Mrs. Tessa Clare, LLB ACA *1991;* 29 Gordon Road, Claygate, ESHER, SURREY, KT10 0PJ.
SWEENEY, Ms. Wang Hui, BA ACA *1999;* 2 Long Meadow, Riverhead, SEVENOAKS, KENT, TN13 2QY.
SWEENEY-MAY, Mrs. Jasmin Amanda, BSc ACA *1999;* 30 Vancouver Road, LONDON, SE23 2AF.
SWEENY, Mr. John Trevor, BA FCA *1986;* 56 Buccaneer Court, Kestrel Road, FARNBOROUGH, GU14 7GP.
SWEERTS, Mr. Michael Franciscus Lambertus, LLB ACA *2002;* 8 Rue des Jardins, L-5762 HASSEL, LUXEMBOURG.
SWEET, Mr. Antony Charles Samuel, BA ACA *1981;* Willow Bank, Easthampstead Road, WOKINGHAM, BERKSHIRE, RG40 3BW.
SWEET, Mr. David James, BA ACA *1994;* 155 High Street, AMERSHAM, BUCKINGHAMSHIRE, HP7 0EB.
SWEET, Mr. David John, FCA *1960;* 6 Gardens Road, CLEVEDON, BS21 7QG. (Life Member)
SWEET, Mr. Edward John, BA FCA *1975;* Chestnut Cottage, Walford, ROSS-ON-WYE, HR9 5QS.
SWEET, Mr. Geoffrey Eustace, FCA *1964;* 10 Sambrook Crescent, MARKET DRAYTON, SHROPSHIRE, TF9 1NG. (Life Member)
•SWEET, Mr. John Godfrey, BSc ACA *1989;* AJM Grant Services, Q E D Centre, Main Avenue, Treforest Industrial Estate, PONTYPRIDD, MID GLAMORGAN CF37 5YR. See also AJM Grant Services Limited
SWEET, Mrs. Margaret Craine, FCA *1961;* 12 Fenwicks Lane, Fulford, YORK, YO10 4PL.
SWEET, Mr. Richard Hugh Mcmurdo, MA FCA *1966;* 10 Cotteswold Road, TEWKESBURY, GL20 5DL.
SWEET, Mr. Robert Andrew Inglis, BA ACA *1992;* 7 Berkeley Court, London Road, GUILDFORD, GU1 1SN.
SWEET, Mrs. Sandra Maria, LLB ACA *1985;* Willow Bank, Easthampstead Road, WOKINGHAM, RG40 3BW.
SWEET, Mr. Stephen Graham, BA ACA *2006;* Deloitte & Touche, 2 New Street Square, LONDON, EC4A 3BZ.
SWEETEN, Mr. Frank Christopher, FCA *1965;* Le Village, 11420 VILLAUTOU, FRANCE. (Life Member)
SWEETING, Mrs. Amanda Jane, MA BA ACA *1992;* The Lilacs, 117 Hall Lane, Horsforth, LEEDS, LS18 5LZ.
SWEETING, Mr. James Ian, BSc ACA *2000;* Investcorp Bank BSC, Diplomatic Area, MANAMA, PO 5340, BAHRAIN.
SWEETING, Mr. Mark, BA(Hons) ACA *2002;* 2 Laws Cottages, Sundridge Road Ide Hill, SEVENOAKS, KENT, TN14 6JP.
SWEETING, Mr. Mark Jackson, ACA *2010;* with PricewaterhouseCoopers LLP, 1 Embankment Place, LONDON, WC2N 6RH.
•SWEETING, Mr. Richard Charles Anthony, FCA *1971;* Sweeting & Co, 22 Willowbrook Close, Broughton Astley, LEICESTER, LE9 6HF.
SWEETING, Prof. Robert Charles, PhD BSc FCA *1976;* The Business School, Manchester Metropolitan, Aytoun Building, Aytoun Street, MANCHESTER, M1 3GH.
SWEETLAND, Mr. Christopher Paul, BSc ACA *1981;* 32 Herondale Avenue, LONDON, SW18 3JL.
SWEETLAND, Mr. Darren, BA(Hons) ACA *2010;* Wayside, Lime Grove, LONDON, N20 8PX.
SWEETLAND, Mr. Duncan Barrington John, BSc FCA *1990;* 2 Hemsley Court, Stoughton Road, GUILDFORD, GU2 9PW.
SWEETLAND, Mr. Richard, BA(Hons) ACA *2011;* 34 Clarence Road, Wimbledon, LONDON, SW19 8QE.
SWEETMAN, Mr. Andrew David, BSc ACA *1997;* 75 Farm Close, EAST GRINSTEAD, RH19 3QQ.
SWEETMAN, Mr. Anthony, BSc ACA *1987;* Basement, 5 Beaconsfield Road, GLASGOW, G12 0PJ.
SWEETMAN, Mr. Jonathan Michael, BSc FCA *1976;* Knole House, Shaw Green Lane, Prestbury, CHELTENHAM, GLOUCESTERSHIRE, GL52 3BP.
SWEETMAN, Mr. Nigel Anthony, FCA *1955;* Little Beck House, Rectory Garth, Wensley, LEYBURN, DL8 4HS. (Life Member)
SWEETMAN, Mr. Paul, ACA *2006;* 763 Prestwick Circle S.E, CALGARY T2Z 4Y7, AB, CANADA.
SWEETMAN, Mrs. Pauline, BSc ACA *1990;* 2 Witham Close, Chandlers Ford, EASTLEIGH, SO53 4TJ.
•SWEETMAN, Mr. Richard John, BSc FCA *1973;* Strathbraid Limited, 22 Braid Farm Road, EDINBURGH, EH10 6LF.
SWEETMAN, Mr. Ronald Andrew, FCA *1957;* 20 Osborne Street, OTTAWA K1S 4Z9, ON, CANADA. (Life Member)
SWEETMAN, Mr. Thomas Edward, FCA *1951;* Belmings, Middle Street, Nazeing, WALTHAM ABBEY, EN9 2LH. (Life Member)
•SWEETMAN-HICKS, Mrs. Karen Amanda, ACA *1991;* 45 Marlowe Road, WORTHING, BN14 8EY.
SWEISS, Mr. Nadeem Suheil, BA HND ACA JIEB *1998;* with KPMG LLP, 15 Canada Square, LONDON, E14 5GL.
SWEMMER, Mr. Anton, BA(Hons) ACA *2002;* Asl Financial and Commercial Services Ltd Asl House, 12-14 David Place St. Helier, JERSEY, JE2 4TD.
•SWERDLOW, Mr. Ian Matthew, FCA *1979;* Alexander Myerson & Co, Alexander House, 61 Rodney Street, LIVERPOOL, L1 9ER.
SWETE, Mr. Peter Gerald, FCA *1970;* Tinkers Green Farm, Cornish Hall end, BRAINTREE, ESSEX, CM7 4HP. (Life Member)
SWETE, Mr. Trevor John, FCA *1969;* Upper House Farm Harpsden Bottom Harpsden, HENLEY-ON-THAMES, OXFORDSHIRE, RG9 4HY. (Life Member)
SWETENHAM, Mr. Stephen Oliver, FCA *1953;* 24 Morda Close, OSWESTRY, SY11 2BA. (Life Member)
•SWETTENHAM, Mr. Ian Robert, LLB FCA *1988;* 1 Westminster Avenue, CHESTER, CH4 8JB.
SWETTENHAM, Mr. Malcolm Keith, BA ACA *1991;* with Grant Thornton UK LLP, 30 Finsbury Square, LONDON, EC2P 2YU.
SWIFT, Mr. Allen James, BSc ACA *1984;* 22 Grasmere Road, Sandbanks, POOLE, BH13 7RH.
SWIFT, Mr. Anthony Alec, FCA *1965;* 7 Roughley Farm Road, SUTTON COLDFIELD, B75 5TY.
•SWIFT, Mr. Anthony Hugh, BSc ACA *1985;* 9 Millbank, Mill Road, MARLOW, BUCKINGHAMSHIRE, SL7 1UA.
SWIFT, Mr. Aston George William, BA ACA AMCT *1995;* Iptehaj, Beechwood Avenue, WEYBRIDGE, SURREY, KT13 9TT.
SWIFT, Mr. Christopher Bradley, MA ACA *2002;* 70 Quarryfield Lane, COVENTRY, CV1 2UJ.
SWIFT, Mr. David John, FCA *1963;* 6 Le Marchant Avenue, Lindley, HUDDERSFIELD, HD3 3DF. (Life Member)
SWIFT, Mrs. Diane, ACA *2002;* 6 Orchid Grove, Netherton, HUDDERSFIELD, HD4 7HR.
•SWIFT, Mr. Duncan Kenric, MSc BSc(Hons) ACA FABRP *1987;* Newlands, Chapel Lane, Redlynch, SALISBURY, WILTSHIRE, SP5 2HN.
SWIFT, Mr. Edward James, BSc ACA *1996;* Glendene, Glendene Avenue, East Horsley, LEATHERHEAD, SURREY, KT24 5AY.
•SWIFT, Mr. George Michael, FCA MAE QDR MCIArb *1972;* Swift Resolutions Limited, 84 Brimstage Road, Heswall, WIRRAL, MERSEYSIDE, CH60 1XQ. See also Bennett Brooks & Co Ltd
SWIFT, Mrs. Helen Clare, BA ACA *1997;* 7 Harewood, Mottram Road, Broadbottom, HYDE, CHESHIRE, SK14 6BB.
SWIFT, Mr. Ian Rodney Allan, BSc FCA *1970;* Coppywood, Ben Rhydding Drive, ILKLEY, WEST YORKSHIRE, LS29 8BD.
SWIFT, Miss. Jessica Jane, BA ACA *1992;* Alacer Software Ltd, L20, South Fens Business Centre, Fenton Way, CHATTERIS, CAMBRIDGESHIRE PE16 6TT.
SWIFT, Mr. John Barry, BCom FCA *1962;* 16 Crabtree Lane, SHEFFIELD, S5 7AY. (Life Member)
SWIFT, Mr. John Richard, BEng ACA *1992;* 40 McLoughlin Way, Kiveton Park, SHEFFIELD, S26 6QJ.
SWIFT, Mr. Jonathan Truscott, BSc ACA *1980;* The Royal Agricultural College, Stroud Road, CIRENCESTER, GLOUCESTERSHIRE, GL7 6JS.
•SWIFT, Mr. Joseph John, FCA FCCA ATII TEP *1986;* (Tax Fac), 57 The Woodlands, Lostock, BOLTON, BL6 4JD.
SWIFT, Mrs. Lorraine Angela, FCA *1987;* Shipley College, Exhibition Road, Saltaire, SHIPLEY, WEST YORKSHIRE, BD18 3JW.
SWIFT, Dr. Michael Joseph Robert, BSc ACA CTA *1993;* (Tax Fac), Primary Group Services, 78 Pall Mall, LONDON, SW1Y 5ES.
SWIFT, Mr. Neil Harvey, BSc ACA MBA *1992;* 27, Holywell Row, LONDON, EC2A4JB.
SWIFT, Mr. Nicholas, BSc ACA *1989;* 34 The Grove, Brookmans Park, HATFIELD, AL9 7RN.
SWIFT, Mr. Nigel John, ACA *1993;* The Barn, Salletts Green, Nr Great Dunmow, DUNMOW, CM6 1ND.
SWIFT, Mrs. Orlaith Mary, BA ACA *1990;* 20 Rock House Close, Tibshelf, ALFRETON, DE55 5LE.
•SWIFT, Mr. Peter James, BTech ACA *1985;* Peter J Swift ACA FCCA Accounting Services, 23 Parkland View, BARNSLEY, S71 5LG.
SWIFT, Mr. Peter James, ACA *2008;* Flat 8, 1 Prescot Street, LONDON, E1 8RJ.
SWIFT, Mr. Peter Nicholas, BSc ACA *1983;* Peninsula Business Services Ltd The Peninsula, 2 Cheetham Hill Road, MANCHESTER, M4 4FB.
SWIFT, Mr. Peter Raymond, BA FCA *1999;* Great Northern Tower, Block C 15-2, 1 Watson Street, MANCHESTER, M3 4EF.
SWIFT, Mr. Richard Brett Allan, BCom ACA *2002;* Flat 33 Groveside Court, 4 Lombard Road, LONDON, SW11 3RQ.
•SWIFT, Mr. Roger Alistair, BSc ACA *1992;* R A Swift Financial Consulting Limited, 221 Station Road, Knowle, SOLIHULL, WEST MIDLANDS, B93 0PU.
SWIFT, Mr. Roy Bernard, MA FCA *1967;* Rodborough, 819 Liverpool Road, SOUTHPORT, PR8 3NU. (Life Member)
•SWIFT, Mrs. Susan Winifred, MA ACA *1989;* (Tax Fac), Saffery Champness, Kintail House, Beechwood Park, INVERNESS, IV2 3BW.
SWIMER, Mr. Warren Sydney, BSc ACA *2001;* Bellville Rodair International Ltd, 27a Shad Thames, LONDON, SE1 2XZ.
•SWINBANK, Mr. Stuart Martin Abram, BSc FCA *1982;* Sanders Swinbank Limited, 7 Victoria Road, DARLINGTON, DL1 5SN.
SWINBURN, Miss. Kirsty Suzanne, BA ACA *1995;* 84 Arnold Avenue, Charnock, SHEFFIELD, S12 3JE.
SWINBURNE, Mr. Alan Philip, MA FCA *1983;* 19 Caesars Way, BROADSTONE, BH18 9DP.
SWINBURNE, Mr. Ernest, FCA *1940;* 7 Sanford Court, Ashbrooke, SUNDERLAND, SR2 7AU. (Life Member)
SWINBURNE, Mr. Geoffrey Brown, FCA *1964;* 20 Melton Road, NORTH FERRIBY, HU14 3ET.
SWINBURNE, Mr. John Paul, BSc ACA *1995;* Mitchells & Butlers, Fleet Street, BIRMINGHAM, B3 1JP.
SWINBURNE, Mr. Michael Francis, BA FCA *1987;* Cambridge Manufacturing Stafford House, Brakey Road, CORBY, NORTHAMPTONSHIRE, NN17 5LU.
SWINBURNE, Mr. Michael Robert, LLB FCA FCCA *1971;* Practice Growth, Lauren Court, Wharf Road, Sale, MANCHESTER, M33 2AF.
SWINBURNE, Mrs. Sarah Elizabeth, BA ACA *1982;* 24 Littleton Close, KENILWORTH, CV8 2WA.
SWINBURNE-JOHNSON, Mr. Anthony Richard, FCA *1970;* Brownings Farm, Southerton, OTTERY ST. MARY, EX11 1SF.
SWINDALE, Mr. David, FCA *1968;* Manderlay, Park Lane, LLANDRINDOD WELLS, POWYS, LD1 5NN.
SWINDELL, Mr. Christopher, BA ACA *2010;* 2 Glenlea Drive, MANCHESTER, M20 5QJ.
SWINDELL, Mr. John Frank, FCA *1948;* 56 Elmdon Lane, Marston Green, BIRMINGHAM, B37 7EQ. (Life Member)
SWINDELL, Mr. Timothy Andrew, BSc FCA *1987;* 91 New Road, WARE, SG12 7BY.
SWINDELLS, Mr. Nicholas, ACA *2008;* Carcraft of Rochdale Ltd, Nixon Street, ROCHDALE, OL11 3JW.
SWINDELLS, Mr. Paul Andrew, ACA *2009;* 20 Beech Street, Summerseat, BURY, LANCASHIRE, BL9 5PR.
SWINDIN, Mr. Timothy James Ashley, ACA *1992;* 9 Stratton Park, Swanland, NORTH FERRIBY, NORTH HUMBERSIDE, HU14 3NN.
SWINDLE, Mr. Gregory David, BA ACA *2000;* 145 West 58th Street, Apt 14A, NEW YORK, NY 10019, UNITED STATES.

•**SWINDLEHURST, Mr. David, FCA** *1971;* D. Swindlehurst, Flat 2, 67 Stockport Road, Timperley, ALTRINCHAM, WA15 7LH.
SWINDLEHURST, Mr. Philip, FCA *1967;* Flat 12 Seville Court, Clifton Drive, LYTHAM ST. ANNES, FY8 5RG. (Life Member)
SWINDLES, Mrs. Sophie Louise, ACA *2010;* 57 Como Road, LONDON, SE23 2JL.
SWINERD, Mr. Lee John, BSc ACA *1998;* 155 Newtown Turnpike, WESTPORT, CT 06880, UNITED STATES.
SWINERD, Mr. Mark Frank, BSc ACA *1995;* 19 Blenheim Avenue, FAVERSHAM, ME13 8NW.
SWINGLEHURST, Mr. Alan John, BA FCA *1973;* (Tax Fac), Richard Falkner & Co, Lowfield House, 222 Wellington Road South, STOCKPORT, CHESHIRE, SK2 6RS.
SWINNERTON, Mr. Peter Richard, FCA *1961;* 202 Foresters Drive, WALLINGTON, SURREY, SM6 9LE. (Life Member)
SWINNERTON, Mr. Raymond Frank, FCA *1980;* Starmount Villa Residental Care Home, Browns Road Bradley Fold, BOLTON, BL2 6RG.
SWINNEY, Mr. Jonathan Anthony Robert, BSc ACA *1992;* Petrofac Energy Developments Rex House, 4-12 Regent Street, LONDON, SW1Y 4PE.
•**SWINSON, Mr. Christopher, OBE MA FCA** *1974;* (President 1998 - 1999) (Member of Council 1985 - 2001), Chris Swinson, Roseheath Wood, Bullbeggars Lane, BERKHAMSTED, HERTFORDSHIRE, HP4 2RS.
•**SWINSON, Mrs. Margaret Anne, MA ACA CTA** *1982;* MA Swinson, 46 Glenmore Avenue, LIVERPOOL, L18 4QF.
SWINSON, Miss. Rachel Anne, BSc ACA *1996;* 116 Everton Road, Potton, SANDY, BEDFORDSHIRE, SG19 2PD.
SWINTON, Mr. Aaron David, ACA MAAT *2009;* 38 Abbots Close, MACCLESFIELD, CHESHIRE, SK10 3PB.
SWINYARD, Mr. Richard Mark William, BSc FCA *2000;* 5 High Ridge, GODALMING, SURREY, GU7 1YE.
SWIRE, Mr. Ian, BSc ACA *1988;* Amalgamated Construction Co Ltd, Whaley Road, BARNSLEY, SOUTH YORKSHIRE, S75 1HT.
SWIRE, Mr. Mark Stephen, BA ACA *1998;* 1 Spadger Lane, West Stafford, DORCHESTER, DORSET, DT2 8UB.
SWIRE, Mr. Rhoderick Martin, BSc FCA *1975;* Aldenham Park, Morville, BRIDGNORTH, WV16 4RN.
SWIRE, Mr. Robert, BA ACA *1986;* 59 Waterloo Road, SOUTHPORT, PR8 2ND.
SWIRSKI, Mr. George Zygmunt, BSc ACA *1983;* 35 London Road, GUILDFORD, GU1 1SW.
SWITHENBANK, Miss. Natalie, BCom ACA *2005;* 921 Le Prieure, 111 rue Emile Zola, 33400 TALENCE, FRANCE.
SWORD, Mr. Charles Anthony, BA ACA *1997;* 78 St Josephs Vale, LONDON, SE3 0XG.
SWORDY, Mr. Christopher Alan, ACA *1983;* 15 Roundhill Grove, Southdown, BATH, BA2 1JT.
SWORN, Mr. Christopher Howard, PhD MA FCA *1975;* Hazel Farm, Main Street, Preston, OAKHAM, LE15 9NJ. (Life Member)
•**SWYCHER, Mr. Ian Irvin, BA ACA** *1984;* Accounting Help Ltd, 2 Orange Street, LONDON, WC2H 7DF. See also IS Associates Ltd
SWYNNERTON, Mr. John Ralph, BA FCA *1970;* 30 Bents Road, SHEFFIELD, S11 9RJ. (Life Member)
SWYNY, Miss. Karen Ann, BA FCA CTA *1991;* 22 Nightingale Lane, BURGESS HILL, WEST SUSSEX, RH15 9JJ.
SYAL, Mr. Vivek, MA ACA *1998;* 34 Antill Road, LONDON, E3 5BP.
SYAN, Mr. Inderdip, LLB ACA *2003;* 34 Craven Avenue, LONDON, W5 2SX.
•**SYCAMORE, Miss. Linda Marie, BSc FCA** *1990;* Accountancy Plus Plus Limited, 9 Parkfield View, POTTERS BAR, EN6 1US.
•**SYDDALL, Mr. Peter Brocklehurst, FCA** *1973;* P.B. Syddall & Co, Grafton House, 81 Chorley Old Road, BOLTON, BL1 3AJ.
•**SYDDALL, Mr. Simon Nicholas, FCA** *1982;* Duncan & Toplis, 18 Northgate, SLEAFORD, LINCOLNSHIRE, NG34 7BJ.
SYDEE, Miss. Louise Claire, BSc ACA *1998;* 10 Combe View, HUNGERFORD, RG17 0BZ.
SYDENHAM, Mr. Richard Wyndham, FCA *1966;* 10 St. Gregory Close, EASTBOURNE, EAST SUSSEX, BN20 7JL.
SYDENHAM, Mr. Timothy Roger, BA ACA *1997;* Unit 7/107 Wentworth Street, RANDWICK, NSW 2031, AUSTRALIA.
SYDNEY-SMITH, Mr. Nicholas, BA ACA *2011;* Flat 1208, 20 Palace Street, LONDON, SW1E 5BB.
SYDNEY-SMITH, Mr. Peter Edward, MA FCA *1979;* Old Bakery, Old Bakery The Street, Rotherwick, HOOK, RG27 9BG.
SYDONIE, Mr. Aldo Nicholas, BSc ACA *2009;* 19 St. Olaf's Road, LONDON, SW6 7DL.
SYDOR, Miss. Helena Elizabeth, BSc(Hons) ACA *2010;* 9 Plover Mills, Lindley, HUDDERSFIELD, HD3 3ZF.
SYED, Mr. Ali Abbas, ACA *2006;* 4 Lulworth Close, HARROW, MIDDLESEX, HA2 9NR.
SYED, Mr. Jamil Raza, ACA *1997;* 6 Shenton Way, DBS Building Tower 2, SINGAPORE 068809, SINGAPORE.
SYED, Mr. John Richard Handforth, MA ACA *1996;* 21 Withyholt Park, Charlton Kings, CHELTENHAM, GLOUCESTERSHIRE, GL53 9BP.
SYED, Mr. Mahmood Amjad, FCA *1969;* 5 The Lincolns, Mill Hill, LONDON, NW7 4PD. (Life Member)
SYED, Mr. Mohammad, BSc ACA *2011;* 174 Twickenham Road, LONDON, E11 4BH.
SYED, Mr. Mohammad Ziyad Akhtar, BA FCA *1988;* 12-A/1 Central Avenue, Phase II, Defence Housing Authority, KARACHI 75500, PAKISTAN.
SYED, Mr. Mozammil, LLB ACA *2000;* Merrill Lynch Kingdom of Saudi Arabia, Level 22 Kingdom Tower, King Fahad Road, Riyadh 11623, P.O. Box 90534, RIYADH SAUDI ARABIA.
SYED, Mr. Raheel, ACA *2010;* John Hancock Financial, 147 Clarendon Street, Mailstop C-04-06, BOSTON, MA 02446, UNITED STATES.
SYED, Miss. Rebecca, LLB ACA *2007;* 98 Leathermarket Court, LONDON, SE1 3HT.
SYED, Mr. Sohail Anjum, BSc FCA MCT *1983;* 15 St. Marys Avenue, NORTHWOOD, MIDDLESEX, HA6 3AY.
SYED, Ms. Zarina Tasnim, BA ACA *2004;* 5 The Lincolns, Marsh Lane, LONDON, NW7 4PD.
SYEDA, Ms. Moniza, BSc(Econ) ACA *1998;* 22 Lansdowne Road, LUTON, LU3 1EE.
SYEDA, Miss. Yasmin Ahmed, BSc ACA *2002;* 95 Woodcote Grove Road, COULSDON, SURREY, CR5 2AN.
SYER, Mr. Gerald Francis Vivian, FCA *1969;* 71 Jessopp Avenue, BRIDPORT, DORSET, DT6 4AT.
•**SYERS, Mr. Colin David, BSc ACA** *1990;* Kenneth Easby LLP, Hanover House, 13 Victoria Road, DARLINGTON, COUNTY DURHAM, DL1 5SF.
SYERS, Mr. Duncan Sinclair, BMus ACA *1984;* Paddocks, Harewood Road, Collingham, WETHERBY, LS22 5BY.
SYKAS, Mr. Yiannis, MBA BEng ACA *2006;* 19 M.Paride street, 3091 LIMASSOL, CYPRUS.
SYKES, Mr. Adam James, BA ACA *1995;* Grand Mill Quay, Barrow Street, DUBLIN 4, COUNTY DUBLIN, IRELAND.
SYKES, Mr. Alan Richard, FCA *1971;* 79 Green Pastures, STOCKPORT, SK4 3RB.
SYKES, Mr. Allister, MSci ACA *2011;* 87a Melbourne Grove, LONDON, SE22 8RR.
•**SYKES, Mr. Anthony James, BSc ACA** *1984;* KPMG LLP, 15 Canada Square, LONDON, E14 5GL. See also KPMG Europe LLP
SYKES, Miss. Carey Anne, BA ACA *1980;* Andrassy Utca 68, Flat A23, H-1062 BUDAPEST, HUNGARY.
SYKES, Mrs. Caroline Louise, BSc ACA *1989;* Route de la Claie aux Moines 90, 1090 LA CROIX SUR LUTRY, VAUD, SWITZERLAND.
SYKES, Mr. Christopher Andrew De Lavis, BSc ACA *1980;* The Beeches, Showell, CHIPPENHAM, SN15 2NU.
SYKES, Mr. Christopher Francis, BSc ACA *1982;* Wellers Auctions, 70-70a Guildford Street, CHERTSEY, KT16 9BB.
•**SYKES, Mr. Christopher John, BSc ACA** *1983;* (Tax Fac), Chris Sykes, 22 Hollin Lane, Weetwood, LEEDS, LS16 5LZ.
SYKES, Mr. Christopher John Gaskell, MA ACA *1979;* Home Cottage, Donhead St Mary, SHAFTESBURY, SP7 9DL.
SYKES, Mr. Christopher Vernon, BSc ACA *1994;* 25 Camel Grove, KINGSTON UPON THAMES, KT2 5GR.
SYKES, Mrs. Claire Simone, ACA CTA TEP *1992;* Loxley House, East Markham, NEWARK, NG22 0QW.
SYKES, Ms. Claudia Claire, BA ACA *1998;* 26 Marine Crescent, WHITSTABLE, KENT, CT5 2QL.
SYKES, Mr. Colin, FCA *1976;* 4 Craig Wen, Rhos on Sea, COLWYN BAY, CLWYD, LL28 4TS.
SYKES, Mr. Colin James, ACA CA(SA) *2010;* 10 Lansdown Road, ABERGAVENNY, GWENT, NP7 6AN.
SYKES, Mr. David, FCA *1970;* 9 Wainwright Road, ALTRINCHAM, WA14 4BW.
SYKES, Mr. David Andrew, BSc ACA ACII *1988;* SRS (Bermuda) Ltd, The Pearman Building, HAMILTON HM 08, BERMUDA.
SYKES, Mr. David Christopher, BSc ACA *1985;* Cullaford, Lower Coombe, BUCKFASTLEIGH, TQ11 0HT.
SYKES, Mrs. Eleanor, BA(Hons) ACA *2003;* 27 St. Georges Walk, HARROGATE, NORTH YORKSHIRE, HG2 9DX.
•**SYKES, Mr. Eric, FCA** *1942;* (Tax Fac), Eric Sykes, 62 Higher Lane, LYMM, WA13 0BG.
•**SYKES, Mrs. Fiona Margaret Langford, MSc FCA** *1989;* Langford Sykes Ltd, Cullaford House, Lower Coombe, BUCKFASTLEIGH, TQ11 0HT.
SYKES, Mr. Geoffrey Howarth, BA FCA *1970;* (Tax Fac), Stonethwaite, Elterwater, AMBLESIDE, CUMBRIA, LA22 9HW.
SYKES, Mr. Gerard William, FCA *1966;* Pine Dale, Lodge Road, Hollesley, WOODBRIDGE, SUFFOLK, IP12 3RR. (Life Member)
SYKES, Ms. Gillian Elizabeth, BA ACA *1986;* Chartered Accountants Hall, Moorgate Place, LONDON, EC2R 6EA.
SYKES, Mrs. Helen Marina, BA ACA *1991;* The Coach House, 37 Easby Drive, ILKLEY, WEST YORKSHIRE, LS29 9AZ. (Life Member)
SYKES, Mr. Henry John Leigh, FCA *1959;* Sligachan, 23 Bankwell Drive, Etherley, BISHOP AUCKLAND, DL14 0HG. (Life Member)
SYKES, Mr. James Michael, MA FCA *1957;* 97 Oakdale Drive, Heald Green, CHEADLE, SK8 3SN. (Life Member)
SYKES, Miss. Jemma Tracy, BA ACA *2006;* 87 Meadowhall Road, ROTHERHAM, SOUTH YORKSHIRE, S61 2JD.
SYKES, Mr. John, FCA *1975;* 120 Alan Avenue, Failsworth, MANCHESTER, M35 0PU.
SYKES, Mr. John Anthony, FCA *1963;* Larks House Farm, Meal Hill Lane, Jackson Bridge, HOLMFIRTH, HD9 7HS.
•**SYKES, Mr. John Buchanan, ACA** *1988;* (Tax Fac), Into University Partnerships, 102 Middlesex Street, LONDON, E1 7EZ.
•**SYKES, Mr. John George, BA ACA CF** *1989;* Skye Corporate Finance Limited, 307 High Road, Chilwell, Beeston, NOTTINGHAM, NG9 5DL.
SYKES, Mr. John Robert Charles, FCA *1966;* The Coppice, 13 Falconwood, East Horsley, LEATHERHEAD, SURREY, KT24 5EG. (Life Member)
•**SYKES, Mr. Jonathan James, BA ACA** *1991;* Saffery Champness, Lion House, Red Lion Street, LONDON, WC1R 4GB.
SYKES, Mr. Jonathan Raynor, BA ACA *1989;* 17 Pirton Close, ST. ALBANS, AL4 9YJ.
SYKES, Miss. Kate Sarah, BSc ACA *2007;* 4 Ashfield Park, LEEDS, LS6 2QT.
SYKES, Mr. Keith Anthony Mallalieu, LLB FCA *1964;* Knipe Wood, CONISTON, LA21 8AB.
SYKES, Mr. Kevin Richard, FCA *1968;* Langton Cottages, 19/20 Lime Street, Port St. Mary, ISLE OF MAN, IM9 5EF.
SYKES, Mr. Laurent Charles, MA ACA *2000;* 29 Empire Square East, Empire Square, LONDON, SE1 4NB.
SYKES, Mr. Leslie Joseph, BA ACA *2006;* (Tax Fac), 25 Curtis Road, STOCKPORT, CHESHIRE, SK4 3JU.
SYKES, Mrs. Margaret Jean, FCA *1966;* Raptor Ridge, Turnberry, Heads Nook, BRAMPTON, CA8 9DN. (Life Member)
•**SYKES, Mr. Mark, BA ACA** *1999;* PKF (UK) LLP, 5 Temple Square, Temple Street, LIVERPOOL, L2 5RH.
SYKES, Mr. Michael Anton, FCA *1952;* The Old Tap, Back Lane, WARWICK, CV34 4BZ. (Life Member)
SYKES, Mr. Michael Charles, FCA *1971;* The Red House, 31 Gillham Wood Road, Cooden, BEXHILL-ON-SEA, TN39 3BN.
SYKES, Mr. Michael Charles, BA FCA *1969;* 3 New Road, READING, RG1 5JD.
SYKES, Miss. Nicola Clare, LLB ACA *2004;* with BDO LLP, 6th Floor, 3 Hardman Street, Spinningfields, MANCHESTER, M3 3AT.
SYKES, Mr. Norman Edward, BSc FCA *1972;* 9 Wyncroft Grove, Bramhope, LEEDS, LS16 9DG.
SYKES, Mr. Oliver, ACA *2011;* 37 Kingsland Drive, Dorridge, SOLIHULL, B93 8SP.
SYKES, Mr. Paul, BSc ACA *1990;* 22 Woodbine Street, ROWAYTON, CT 06853, UNITED STATES.
•**SYKES, Mr. Philip, FCA** *1974;* 28 Bell Davies Road, LITTLEHAMPTON, BN17 6DU.
•**SYKES, Mr. Philip Peter, BA FCA** *1992;* Fisher Phillips, Summit House, 170 Finchley Road, LONDON, NW3 6BP. See also Fisher Phillips 2010 Ltd
•①**SYKES, Mr. Phillip Rodney, MA ACA FABRP** *1986;* Moore Stephens LLP, 150 Aldersgate Street, LONDON, EC1A 4AB. See also Moore Stephens & Co
SYKES, Mr. Richard Anthony, FCA *1973;* Top Barn, Warrington Road, Mickle Trafford, CHESTER, CH2 4EA.
SYKES, Mr. Richard Antony, BA FCA *1985;* 108 Cleveland Road, Ealing, LONDON, W13 0EL.
•**SYKES, Mr. Richard James, BSc FCA** *1980;* PricewaterhouseCoopers LLP, 1 Embankment Place, LONDON, WC2N 6RH. See also PricewaterhouseCoopers
SYKES, Mr. Richard Mark, BA ACA *1989;* Loxley House, East Markham, NEWARK, NG22 0QW.
SYKES, Mr. Richard Mark, BA ACA *1989;* News International, 1 Virginia Street, LONDON, E98 1XY.
SYKES, Mr. Richard Paul, BA ACA *2007;* 55 Park Terrace, Stump Cross, HALIFAX, WEST YORKSHIRE, HX3 7AF.
SYKES, Mr. Robert Eric, FCA *1965;* Tish Toms Cottage, Reeth, RICHMOND, NORTH YORKSHIRE, DL11 6TY. (Life Member)
SYKES, Mr. Rupert Stell, BSc FCA *1990;* Lime Tree Cottage, Gunville Road, Winterslow, SALISBURY, SP5 1PP.
SYKES, Mrs. Sarah Louise, FCA *1998;* The Fleetings, 19 Main Street, Sand Hutton, YORK, YO41 1LB.
SYKES, Ms. Suzanne Louise, BA ACA *1991;* (Tax Fac), Nomura International Plc, 1 Angel Lane, LONDON, EC4R 3AB.
SYKES, Mr. Timothy David, ACA *2010;* 8 Northwood Avenue, NEWTON-LE-WILLOWS, MERSEYSIDE, WA12 0DE.
SYKES, Mr. Timothy James, BSc FCA *1995;* The Fleetings, 19 Sand Hutton, YORK, YO41 1LB.
SYKES, Mr. William Richard, FCA *1973;* Lote 23, Quintinhas, Vila Moura, 8125-406 QUARTEIRA, ALGARVE, PORTUGAL.
•**SYKOPETRITIS, Mr. Evangelos Evripidou, BSc FCA** *1993;* SIS, 38 Karaiskaki Street, KANIKA Alexander Center, Block 1, Office 113 C/D, PC 3032 LIMASSOL CYPRUS.
SYLVA, Mr. Paul John, MBA ACA *2003;* Appuru, 43 Moreton Street, LONDON, SW1V 2NY.
SYLVESTER, Mrs. Celia, BA ACA *2007;* Dykes Farm Dykes Lane, Yealand Conyers, CARNFORTH, LA5 9SN.
SYLVESTER, Miss. Fiona, MSc BA ACA *2007;* 44 Lowfield Drive, Thornhill, CARDIFF, CF14 9HT.
SYLVESTER, Mrs. Helen Elizabeth, BA ACA *1992;* 26 Temple Road, WINDSOR, SL4 1HW.
SYLVESTER, Mr. Nicholas Michael, BA ACA *2001;* 86 Redlands Road, PENARTH, SOUTH GLAMORGAN, CF64 2WL.
SYLVESTER, Mr. Timothy John, BA ACA *1992;* Le Moulin de Maurissoux, 19390 St. Augustin, CORREZE, FRANCE.
•**SYLVESTER, Mr. Timothy Oliver, BA FCA** *1975;* T O SYLVESTER, 87 Winsley Hill, Limpley Stoke, BATH, WILTSHIRE, BA2 7FA.
SYLVESTER, Mrs. Vicky Maxine, BA ACA *1993;* 9 Kew Drive, DUDLEY, WEST MIDLANDS, DY1 2QX.
SYME, Mr. James Weller, BSc ACA AMCT *1994;* 7 Foxhollow Close, WALTON-ON-THAMES, KT12 3BG.
SYMEONIDIS, Mrs. Michelle Karen, ACA *1995;* 6 Edwin Court, CLARINDA, VIC 3169, AUSTRALIA.
SYMEONIDOU, Miss. Nicoletta, BEng ACA *2001;* Y & P Fresca, Imports-Exports Ltd, P.O Box 27867, CY-2433, CY-2433 NICOSIA, CYPRUS.
SYMERS, Mr. Alastair Kennedy, FCA *1972;* 11 allée Ronsard, 33200 BORDEAUX, FRANCE.
SYMES, Mr. Austin Charles, BA FCA *1970;* 63 Half Moon Lane, LONDON, SE24 9JX. (Life Member)
SYMES, Mr. David Mark, BA *1987;* 30 Helenslea Avenue, LONDON, NW11 8ND.
SYMES, Ms. Helen Margaret, ACA *2007;* Tenon, Highfield Court, Tollgate, Chandler's Ford, EASTLEIGH, HAMPSHIRE SO53 3TY.
SYMES, Mr. Peter Sigourney, FCA *1973;* (Tax Fac), Forest Way, Groombridge, TUNBRIDGE WELLS, TN3 9NG.
SYMES, Mr. Philip Leslie, BSc ACA *1988;* 7 Bedford Road, LONDON, W4 1JD.
SYMES, Mr. Roger James, FCA *1965;* Stores Cottage, Brightwell Street, Brightwell-Cum-Sotwell, WALLINGFORD, OX10 0RT.
SYMES, Mrs. Susan Melanie, BSc ACA *1995;* 17 Newbury Street, Kintbury, HUNGERFORD, BERKSHIRE, RG17 9UX.
SYMINGTON, Mr. Richard Andrew, BSc FCA *1980;* 30 Charles II Street, LONDON, SW1Y 4AE.
SYMMONDS, Mr. Andrew Bryant, BSc ACA *1996;* 21 Harrow Way, Sindlesham, WOKINGHAM, RG41 5GJ.
SYMMONDS, Mrs. Marie-Jeanne, ACA *1992;* 5 Grandview Heights, Shop Hill, ST. THOMAS, BARBADOS.
SYMMONDS, Miss. Ria, BSc ACA *2007;* 59 Grasmere Way, LEIGHTON BUZZARD, BEDFORDSHIRE, LU7 2QL.
SYMMONS, Mr. Garry Edward, BA ACA *1984;* 9 Tower Place, WARLINGHAM, CR6 9PW.
SYMMONS, Mr. James Michael, BA ACA *1996;* 5 The Coppice, MIRFIELD, WEST YORKSHIRE, WF14 0PG.
•**SYMMS, Mr. Robert John, FCA** *1974;* R J Symms Financial Services, 5 Coniston Road, Gatley, CHEADLE, CHESHIRE, SK8 4AP.
SYMON, Mr. Craig Andrew, MA ACA *2004;* Astra Zeneca Site Office, Derwent Avenue, MANCHESTER, M21 7QS.

SYMON, Mr. John Alexander, MA ACA *1987;* 6 Pitcullen Terrace, PERTH, PH2 7EQ.
SYMONDS, Mr. Brian Anthony, BSc FCA *1975;* Fortey Green, Hanley Swan, WORCESTER, WR8 0DR.
•SYMONDS, Mr. David, FCA *1978;* UHY Hacker Young Manchester LLP, St. James Buildings, 79 Oxford Street, MANCHESTER, M1 6HT.
SYMONDS, Mr. Edward Lewis, FCA *1954;* Kellaton Norrels Drive, East Horsley, LEATHERHEAD, KT24 5DL. (Life Member)
SYMONDS, Mr. Emlyn Joseph Hylton, ACA *2008;* 27 Florence Road, LONDON, SW19 8TH.
SYMONDS, Mr. Jonathan Richard, BA FCA *1983;* Novartis International AG, PO Box, Forum 1.2.05, 4002 BASEL, SWITZERLAND.
SYMONDS, Mr. Philip Gerard, BSc FCA *1977;* Boundary Cottage, Fen Pond Road, Ightham, SEVENOAKS, TN15 9JF.
SYMONDS, Mr. Richard Andrew, BA ACA MCT *1988;* Hill Cottage, Windsor Lane, Little Kingshill, GREAT MISSENDEN, BUCKINGHAMSHIRE, HP16 0DZ.
•SYMONDS, Mr. Richard Lloyd, ACA *2007;* Symonds & Co, Sunny Nook, Barhatch Road, CRANLEIGH, SURREY, GU6 7DJ.
SYMONDS, Mr. Robert, BA ACA *1999;* 4 The Croft, Thornholme Road, SUNDERLAND, SR2 7NR.
SYMONDS, Mr. Thomas William Edward, MA ACA *1983;* PT Energizer Indonesia, Jalan Raya Jakarta Bogor km 29.3, Cimang, CIBINONG, WEST JAVA, 16952 INDONESIA.
SYMONDS, Mr. William Reginald Flower, FCA *1950;* Flat 26, Churchfield Court, Roebuck Close, Bancroft Road, REIGATE, SURREY RH2 7RS. (Life Member)
SYMONS, Mr. David John, FCA *1973;* Milton Keynes Council, Saxon Court, 502 Avebury Boulevard, MILTON KEYNES, MK9 3HS.
SYMONS, Mr. Edward John, FCA *1951;* 8 Solent Avenue, LYMINGTON, HAMPSHIRE, SO41 3SD. (Life Member)
SYMONS, Mr. Edward William Frederick, BSc ACA *2011;* 16 Watts Avenue, ROCHESTER, KENT, ME1 1RX.
•SYMONS, Mrs. Karen Dawn, FCA *1986;* Symons, Willow Corner, 7 Ackrells Mead, SANDHURST, BERKSHIRE, GU47 8JJ.
SYMONS, Miss. Lynette Kathryn, BSc ACA *1996;* Kaplan Financial 5th Floor Finsbury Tower, 103-105 Bunhill Row, LONDON, EC1Y 8LR.
SYMONS, Mr. Michael John, MA FCA *1972;* The Limes, 129 High Street, Cheveley, NEWMARKET, SUFFOLK, CB8 9DG.
SYMONS, Mr. Nicholas Charles Peter, BSc FCA *1977;* 15 Werter Road, LONDON, SW15 2LL.
•SYMONS, Mr. Paul, FCA *1984;* (Tax Fac), Symons, Willow Corner, 7 Ackrells Mead, SANDHURST, BERKSHIRE, GU47 8JJ.
SYMONS, Mr. Raymond Anthony, FCA *1982;* Cable & Wireless Global, 114 Great Suffolk Street, LONDON, SE1 0SL.
SYMONS, Mr. Royston, FCA *1953;* 6 Hobart Close, NEWPORT, NP20 3QR. (Life Member)
SYMONS, Mr. Timothy Martin, BA ACA *1992;* Braeside Pangbourne Hill Pangbourne, READING, RG8 7AX.
SYMONS, Mr. William Patrick Mcneil, MA FCA *1975;* 2 Coppice Mews, 231 Forest Road, TUNBRIDGE WELLS, TN2 5HT.
SYNETT, Mr. Jacob Julian, FCA *1972;* Interphone Security Group Limited, 12-22 Herga Road, Wealdstone, HARROW, MIDDLESEX, HA3 5AS.
SYNGE, Mr. Timothy Peter, BA FCA *1989;* 118 Reedley Road, Stoke Bishop, BRISTOL, AVON, BS9 1BE.
SYNGHAL, Mr. Manoj Kumar, ACA *2000;* (Tax Fac), Norton Lewis & Co, 246-248 Great Portland Street, LONDON, W1W 5JL.
SYRADD, Mrs. Karen Anne, BSc ACA *1997;* Carval Investors UK Ltd, Knowle Hill Park, Fairmile Lane, COBHAM, SURREY, KT11 2PD.
SYRATT, Mr. Frank Lindsey, FCA *1977;* The New Internationalist, 55 Rectory Road, OXFORD, OX4 1BW.
•SYRATT, Dr. Richard William, BSc DIC ACA *1997;* Deloitte LLP, 2 New Street Square, LONDON, EC4A 3BZ. See also Deloitte & Touche LLP
SYRED, Ms. Kate Victoria, BSc ACA *1997;* 22 Shirley Church Road, CROYDON, CR0 5EE.
•SYREE, Mr. James Edward, BSc ACA *2008;* Ballard Dale Syree Watson LLP, Oakmoore Court, Kingswood Road, Hampton Lovett, DROITWICH, WORCESTERSHIRE WR9 0QH.
•SYREE, Mr. Jeremy Anton, FCA *1975;* (Tax Fac), Ballard Dale Syree Watson LLP, Oakmoore Court, Kingswood Road, Hampton Lovett, DROITWICH, WORCESTERSHIRE WR9 0QH.
SYRIMIS, Mr. George, ACA *2009;* Flat 602 Arethousa Building, 38 Rigas Fereos Street, 1087 NICOSIA, CYPRUS.
•SYRIMIS, Mr. Nicolas, FCA *1975;* (Member of Council 2004 - 2010), KPMG, 14 Esperidon Street, 1087 NICOSIA, CYPRUS. See also KPMG Metaxas Loizides Syrimis
•SYROCKI, Mr. Anton Kazimierz, BA FCA *1982;* Chantrey Vellacott DFK LLP, Russell Square House, 10-12 Russell Square, LONDON, WC1B 5LF.
•SYRON, Mr. Derek Vincent, MA ACA *1980;* (Tax Fac), Syron & Company, 7 Bell Villas, Ponteland, NEWCASTLE UPON TYNE, NE20 9BD.
SYSON, Mr. Antony Victor, BSc ACA *2006;* Mitsubishi U F J Securities International Plc, Ropemaker Place 25 Ropemaker Street, LONDON, EC2Y 9AJ.
SYSON, Mrs. Rachel Jane, BA ACA *1997;* 1 Beeches Walk, Tiddington, STRATFORD-UPON-AVON, WARWICKSHIRE, CV37 7AT.
SYSON, Mr. Russell Nigel, BSc FCA *1986;* (Tax Fac), 5 Summerfield Drive, Wootton, BEDFORD, MK43 9FE.
SYTHES, Mrs. Jamila Clare Dabbagh, BA(Hons) ACA *2002;* 109 Ravensbury Road, LONDON, SW18 4RY.
SYVRET, Mr. Andrew Thomas, MA ACA CF *2001;* Willow House, Norlands Drive, Otterbourne, WINCHESTER, HAMPSHIRE, SO21 2DT.
SYVRET, Mrs. Joanna Louise, BA(Econ) ACA *2001;* with Ernst & Young LLP, Wessex House, 19 Threefield Lane, SOUTHAMPTON, SO14 3QB.
SZABO, Mrs. Janice Elizabeth, BSc ACA *1994;* Krøyersvej 23, 2930 KLAMPENBORG, DENMARK.
SZACH, Miss. Claudia Andrea, ACA *2002;* Ludwig-Duerr-Strasse 6, 48147 MUNSTER, GERMANY.
•SZALANCZI, Ms. Andrea Michele, BA ACA *1979;* Andrea Szalanczi, 3 Brooksville Avenue, LONDON, NW6 6TH.
SZCZECHOWSKI, Mr. Jan, BA ACA *1985;* 11 Westcroft Road, Sedgley, DUDLEY, DY3 3QP.
SZCZEPANSKI, Mrs. Christine Ann, BSc ACA *1981;* 16 Durkar Rise, Crigglestone, WAKEFIELD, WF4 3QB.
•SZCZEPANSKI, Mr. Jan, MBA LLB DipPFS ACA *1981;* (Tax Fac), Sanders Geeson Limited, Raines Business Centre, Raines House, Denby Dale Road, WAKEFIELD, WEST YORKSHIRE WF1 1HR.
•SZCZESNIAK, Mr. Marek Tadeusz, FCA *1974;* Marek & Co, Kensington House, 7 Roe Lane, Hesketh Park, SOUTHPORT, PR9 9DT.
SZE, Ms. Chin Pei Pacita, ACA *2008;* Flat 2D, Blk 17, Provident Centre, 53 Wharf Road, NORTH POINT, HONG KONG ISLAND HONG KONG SAR.
SZE, Mr. Ching Po Tommy, ACA *2005;* Tommy C.P. Sze & Company, Flat 2003, 20/F, Wellborne Commercial Centre, 8 Java Road, NORTH POINT HONG KONG SAR.
SZE, Mr. Gary Yan, MSc FCA *1993;* 2A House 40, Villa Castell, 20 Yau King Lane, TAI PO, NEW TERRITORIES, HONG KONG SAR.
•SZE, Mr. Hua Ming, MA MSc FCA *1984;* (Tax Fac), Simmons Gainsford LLP, 5th Floor, 7-10 Chandos Street, Cavendish Square, LONDON, W1G 9DQ.
SZE, Ms. Mei Hang, ACA *2008;* Room 610 Hong Fu House Cheung Hong Estate, TSING YI, NEW TERRITORIES, HONG KONG SAR.
•SZE, Mr. Michael Tsai Ping, FCA *1973;* Flat A, 10/F 26 Magazine Gap Road, VICTORIA PEAK, Hong Kong Island, HONG KONG SAR.
•SZE, Mr. Robert Tsai To, FCA *1967;* 6/F Catalina Mansion, 100 MacDonnell Road, VICTORIA PEAK, Hong Kong Island, HONG KONG SAR.
SZE, Ms. Si Si Florence, ACA *2008;* 12C, Albron Court, 99 Caine Road, MID LEVELS, HONG KONG SAR.
SZENTESI, Mr. Gary Bela, BSc ACA *1993;* 52 Chase Farm Close, Waltham Chase, SOUTHAMPTON, SO32 2UD.
SZETO, Mr. Simon Ping Fai, ACA *1983;* 11th Floor, LaiSun Commercial Building, 680 Cheung Sha Wan Road, MEI FOO SUN CHUEN, KOWLOON, HONG KONG SAR.
SZILAGYI, Miss. Marisa Christine, MA ACA *2010;* Flat 111 The Belvedere, Homerton Street, CAMBRIDGE, CB2 0NU.
SZLEZINGER, Mr. Leon, BA FCA *1991;* 3 Patriots Farm Court, Armonk, NEW YORK, NY 10504, UNITED STATES.
SZMIGIN, Mr. Christopher Richard, FCA *1981;* (Tax Fac), The Davis Service Group Plc, 4-5 Grosvenor Place, LONDON, SW1X 7DL.
•SZOLIN-JONES, Mrs. Monica Jandira, FCA *1988;* Hobsons, Alexandra House, 43 Alexandra Street, NOTTINGHAM, NG5 1AY.
SZPARA, Mrs. Fiona Jane, BSc ACA CTA *1988;* Marstons Plc, Marstons House, Brewery Road, WOLVERHAMPTON, WV1 4JT.
SZREIDER, Mrs. Laura, MA ACA *2008;* 54 Coppice Drive, NORTHAMPTON, NN3 6NE.
SZULC, Miss. Alison Susan, BSc FCA *1977;* Bickton House, Bickton, FORDINGBRIDGE, SP6 2HA.
SZULEJEWSKI, Mr. Jan, MBA BA FCA *1983;* Siemens Sp Z o o, Ul Zupnicza 11, 03-821 WARSAW, POLAND.
SZULEJEWSKI, Mr. Marek, MSc ACA *2003;* KPMG Tax M.Michna sp.k., NIP: 527 25 63 257, ul. Chlodna 51, 00-867 WARSAW, POLAND.
•SZULIST, Mrs. Diane Victoria, ACA *1990;* Crowe Clark Whitehill LLP, Arkwright House, Parsonage Gardens, MANCHESTER, M3 2HP. See also Horwath Clark Whitehill LLP and Crowe Clark Whitehill
SZYMANSKA, Ms. Chantal Marie Julia, BSc ACA *1981;* Alba Marlbank Road, Welland, MALVERN, WORCESTERSHIRE, WR13 6NE.
SZYMANSKI, Mr. Jan Paul Benson, MA ACA *1980;* Alba, Marlbank Road, Welland, MALVERN, WORCESTERSHIRE, WR13 6NE.
TAAFFE, Miss. Lindsay Joanne, BSc ACA *2010;* 4 Rafborn Avenue, HUDDERSFIELD, HD3 3UJ.
•TAAFFE, Mr. Peter Heaward, MA BCom FCA ATII DChA *1983;* BW Macfarlane LLP, 3 Temple Square, LIVERPOOL, L2 5BA.
•TABASSUM, Mr. Naeem, ACA FCCA *2011;* 21 Leamington Crescent, HARROW, MIDDLESEX, HA2 9HH.
TABBAL, Miss. Antoinette, ACA *1986;* 92 The Vale, Golders Green, LONDON, NW11 8SJ.
TABBERNER, Mr. Robert James, FCA *1980;* Lickey End Farm House, 71 Alcester Road, Lickey End, BROMSGROVE, B60 1JT.
TABER, Mr. Jeremy Neil Fenton, BSc FCA *1982;* Roseberry Topping, Manor Orchard Main Street, Bishampton, PERSHORE, WORCESTERSHIRE, WR10 2LX.
TABER, Mrs. Noeleen Mary, BSc ACA *1981;* Roseberry Topping, Manor Orchard, Main Street, Bishampton, PERSHORE, WR10 2LX.
TABERER, Mr. Jonathan, BA ACA *2011;* 19 Freesland Rise, NUNEATON, WARWICKSHIRE, CV10 9QE.
•TABERNACLE, Mr. Andrew John, BA ACA *1991;* Bishop & Partners Ltd, Phoenix Park, Blakewater Road, BLACKBURN, BB1 5BG.
TABERNER, Mr. Benjamin Robert, BA ACA *1998;* 2 Greenway, WILMSLOW, CHESHIRE, SK9 1LU.
•TABERNER, Mr. Ian John, BA FCA *1986;* Turnbull & Co Accountants Limited, Pilgrim House, Oxford Place, PLYMOUTH, PL1 5AJ.
TABERNER, Mr. Neil, MA FCA *1969;* 43 Fife Road, LONDON, SW14 8BJ.
TABERNER, Mr. Robert John, BSc ACA *1983;* (Tax Fac), 30 Ridgeway Road, ISLEWORTH, TW7 5LA.
TABIBI, Mr. Siavash, BA FCA *1978;* 7a Galley Lane, Arkley, BARNET, EN5 4AR.
TABOIS, Mr. Christopher Andre, BSc ACA *2006;* 12 Rosewood Court, HEMEL HEMPSTEAD, HERTFORDSHIRE, HP1 2TQ.
TABOR, Mr. John Douglas, FCA *1955;* 61 Knighton Drive, WOODFORD GREEN, ESSEX, IG8 0NZ. (Life Member)
•TABOR, Ms. Myra, MBA FCA *1981;* 81 Woodwarde Road, LONDON, SE22 8UL.
TABOR, Mr. Peter Kenneth, FCA *1969;* 7 Sandy Close, Trimley St. Martin, FELIXSTOWE, IP11 0UJ.
TABOR, Mr. Robert Mark, BA ACA *1989;* (Tax Fac), Lantra House, Stoneleigh Park, KENILWORTH, WARWICKSHIRE, CV8 2LG.
TABRAH, Mr. Thomas, BA(Hons) ACA *2002;* 19 Eastview Road, Wargrave, READING, RG10 8BH.
TACCONE, Mr. Antony Mark, BA ACA *1994;* 14 Murrayfield Drive, EDINBURGH, EH12 6EB.
•TACCONI, Mr. Henry, FCA *1980;* (Tax Fac), Tacconi Green & Co. Ltd, 32a East Street, ST.IVES, PE27 5PD. See also Tacconi Green & Co Ltd
TACEY-GREEN, Mr. Bryan Anthony, BSc FCA *1983;* 12 Eaves Close, ADDLESTONE, SURREY, KT15 2BF.
TACEY-GREEN, Mrs. Jenny Yvette, ACA *2009;* 1 Cleveland Close, MAIDENHEAD, SL6 1XE.
TACEY-GREEN, Mrs. Pamela Margaret, BSc ACA *1981;* 12 Eaves Close, ADDLESTONE, SURREY, KT15 2BF.
•TACK, Mr. Harjinder Singh, BSc(Econ) FCA *1997;* My Accounts Centre Limited, 89 Shaggy Calf Lane, SLOUGH, SL2 5HP.
TACK, Mrs. Lois Ann, LLB ACA *2005;* 30 Hatherton Avenue, Cullercoats, NORTH SHIELDS, TYNE AND WEAR, NE30 3LG.
TACKLEY, Mrs. Kathryn Elizabeth, BSc ACA *2003;* 39 Butlers Court Road, BEACONSFIELD, BUCKINGHAMSHIRE, HP9 1SQ.
TACON, Mr. Andrew, FCA *1982;* with Grant Thornton UK LLP, 3140 Rowan Place, John Smith Drive, Oxford Business Park South, OXFORD, OX4 2WB.
TACON, Ms. Judith, MA MPhil ACA *2004;* with Deloitte LLP, Hill House, 1 Little New Street, LONDON, EC4A 3TR.
TACON, Mr. Peter Malcolm, FCA *1975;* Boston 323 Cromwell Lane, Burton Green, KENILWORTH, CV8 1PG.
•ⓓTACON, Mr. William Richard, BA FCA *1977;* Zolfo Cooper (BVI) Limited, 2nd Floor, Palm Grove House, Wickhams Cay, PO Box 4571, TORTOLA VIRGIN ISLANDS (BRITISH).
TADD, Mrs. Sarah Elizabeth, BA FCA *1994;* 39 Higher Brimley Road, TEIGNMOUTH, DEVON, TQ14 8JU.
TADDEI, Mr. Mark Anthony Paul, MA FCA *1995;* with Jeffrey Crawford & Co, 25 Castle Terrace, EDINBURGH, EH1 2ER.
•TADMAN, Mr. Moray Roger, BA FCA *1970;* (Tax Fac), Tadmans, Blandford House, Church Walk, Combe, WITNEY, OX29 8NQ.
TADROS, Miss. Nevine, BA BSc ACA *1998;* 8 Whitegale Close, HITCHIN, SG4 9LP.
•TAFFS, Mr. Andrew Bruce, FCA *1989;* Giess Wallis Crisp LLP, 10-12 Mulberry Green, HARLOW, ESSEX, CM17 0ET. See also Taffs Andrew
TAFFS, Mr. Roger Miles, MBA BSc FCA *1975;* 1/B Pomona Street, PENNANT HILLS, NSW 2120, AUSTRALIA.
•TAFSIRULLAH, Mr. Nur Mohammad, FCA *1974;* Winston Fox Nur & Co, Crown House, 2A Ashfield Parade, Southgate, LONDON, N14 5EJ.
TAGENT, Mr. Michael Edward, FCA *1966;* Challaborough Cottage, Ringmore, KINGSBRIDGE, TQ7 4HW. (Life Member)
•TAGG, Mr. David Allen, FCA *1977;* The Lodge, Berrier Road, Greystoke, PENRITH, CUMBRIA, CA11 0UE.
TAGG, Mr. Michael, BA ACA *2007;* 27 Low Gosforth Court, NEWCASTLE UPON TYNE, NE3 5QU.
•TAGG, Mr. Peter, FCA *1974;* Hobsons, Alexandra House, 43 Alexandra Street, NOTTINGHAM, NG5 1AY.
TAGG, Mr. Roger James Gilroy, BSc ACA *1989;* 2045 Balsam Drive, BOULDER, CO 80304, UNITED STATES.
TAGGART, Mr. Freddy, BA(Hons) ACA *2001;* The Brook, Old Alresford, ALRESFORD, HAMPSHIRE, SO24 9DH.
•TAGGART, Mr. Gary John, BSc FCA CTA TEP *1985;* G J Taggart Ltd, Fach Uchaf, Cwmllinau, MACHYNLLETH, POWYS, SY20 9PF.
•TAGGART, Mr. John Michael, MCom FCA *1960;* (Tax Fac), J.M. Taggart, 64 Eshe Road North, Blundellsands, LIVERPOOL, L23 8UF.
TAGGART, Mr. Kenneth, BSc FCA *1992;* 33 Highbury Crescent, Highbury, WELLINGTON 6012, NEW ZEALAND.
TAGGART, Mrs. Leigh Nicholi, BA ACA MCT *1992;* 33 Highbury Crescent, Highbury, WELLINGTON 6012, NEW ZEALAND.
TAGIA, Miss. Simoni, ACA *2010;* Papaflessa 18, Aigaleo, 12244 ATHENS, GREECE.
TAGLIAFERRO, Mr. Anton, BA ACA *1984;* 23 Noble Street, MOSMAN, NSW 2088, AUSTRALIA.
TAGNEY, Mrs. Kerry, BA ACA *2005;* Thomson Reuters Ltd, Aldgate House, 33 Aldgate High Street, LONDON, EC3N 1DL.
TAH, Mr. Davinder Vijay, BSc ACA *1980;* 66 Church Drive, HARROW, MIDDLESEX, HA2 7NS.
TAHER, Mr. Ehsan Mohamud Swadeck, FCA CF *1992;* Ligne Berthaud, FLOREAL, MAURITIUS.
TAHER, Mr. Robin, BSc(Hons) ACA AMSB *2009;* GECC (Funding) Limited, The Ark, 201 Talgarth Road, LONDON, W6 8BJ.
TAHIR, Miss. Norazilla, BA ACA *1992;* 7 Jln SS17/2L, 47500 SUBANG, SELANGOR, MALAYSIA.
TAHMASEBI, Mr. Khosrow, FCA *1976;* Coppice Alupack Limited, Isfryn Industrial Estate, Blackmill, Mid Glamorgan, BRIDGEND, CF35 6EQ.
TAHSEEN, Mr. Malik Mohammad, FCA *1967;* Plot 111 Flat 74, Azad Apartment, I P Extension, NEW DELHI 110092, INDIA.
TAHSIN, Mr. Ender, ACA *2009;* 4 Novus House, 181 Hatfield Road, ST. ALBANS, HERTFORDSHIRE, AL1 4LG.
TAI, Mr. Anthony Wilson, BSc ACA *1992;* Flat B 13/F, Valley View Terrace, 68 Blue Pool Road, HAPPY VALLEY, HONG KONG ISLAND, HONG KONG SAR.
TAI, Miss. Ching, ACA *2007;* Flat G 28/F, Fu Dat Court, Fortress Garden, Fortress Hill Road, NORTH POINT, HONG KONG SAR.
TAI, Mr. Dominic Kiun Ngee, BA ACA *1988;* Dominic K. N. Tai & Company, 16E Neich Tower, 128 Gloucester Road, WAN CHAI, HONG KONG ISLAND, HONG KONG SAR.

TAI - TAM Members - Alphabetical

TAI, Miss. Felicia Siew Lin, BSc ACA *1990;* 16 Westbere Road, LONDON, NW2 3SR.
TAI, Mr. Henry Hon Leung, BSc ACA *1986;* 26D Amber Garden, 70 Kennedy Road, MID LEVELS, HONG KONG ISLAND, HONG KONG SAR.
TAI, Mr. Jeffery, BA ACA *1993;* Igroup Ltd Building 4, Hatters Lane, WATFORD, WD18 8YF.
TAI, Mr. Kim Hong, FCA *1975;* 27 Jalan Melayu, 50100 KUALA LUMPUR, FEDERAL TERRITORY, MALAYSIA.
TAI, Mr. King Foon, ACA *2005;* Flat B40/F, Tower 6, The Belcher's, 89 Pokfulam Road, POK FU LAM, HONG KONG ISLAND HONG KONG SAR.
TAI, Mr. Man Hin Tony, ACA *2008;* Flat 9b, Kenville Building, 32 Kennedy Road, THE PEAK, HONG KONG ISLAND, HONG KONG SAR.
TAIABJEE, Mr. Asgerali Abbasbhai, BSc FCA *1961;* 7 Emcarr Drive, SCARBOROUGH M1E 4Z9, ON, CANADA. (Life Member)
•TAIANO, Mr. Paul George, BA FCA *1981;* Nyman Libson Paul, Regina House, 124 Finchley Road, LONDON, NW3 5JS.
TAIB, Miss. Marina, BA ACA *1999;* 6 Lorong 14/37D, 46100 PETALING JAYA, Selangor, MALAYSIA.
TAIBEL, Mr. Deon Gidon, ACA *1998;* 5 Park View Road, LONDON, NW10 1AD.
TAILBY, Mr. Douglas John, BSc ACA *2009;* Flat 4 Walton House, Grove Road, SURBITON, KT6 4DB.
TAILBY, Mr. Matthew Michael, BSc(Hons) ACA *2002;* Beckenhofstrasse 10, 8006 ZURICH, SWITZERLAND.
TAILOR, Mr. Ajay Ramesh, ACA *2009;* 26 Dinsmore Road, LONDON, SW12 9PS.
TAILOR, Mr. Bhasker, BA FCA *1983;* (Tax Fac), Tailor & Co, 157 Colin Crescent, LONDON, NW9 6ET.
TAILOR, Mr. Chhaganlal Jinabhai Naran, FCA *1968;* 1 Armstrong Close, PINNER, MIDDLESEX, HA5 2LA.
TAILOR, Mr. Hitesh, BA FCA *1983;* 7 Upper Montagu Street, LONDON, W1H 2PG.
TAILOR, Miss. Leena Jayantilal, BSc ACA *2009;* 632 Dunstable Road, LUTON, LU4 8SE.
TAILOR, Mr. Paresh, MSc ACA *2000;* (Tax Fac), 10 Brantwood Close, Westcroft, MILTON KEYNES, MK4 4FP.
TAILOR, Miss. Priya, Bsc BSc(Hons) ACA *2011;* 40 Morley Crescent West, STANMORE, MIDDLESEX, HA7 2LW.
TAILOR, Mrs. Vanita Bhupendra, FCA *1995;* (Tax Fac), 2 Silver Close, HARROW, MIDDLESEX, HA3 6JT.
TAIT, Mr. Alistair Ian, BCom ACA *1984;* Marchbankwood House, Beattock, MOFFAT, DUMFRIESSHIRE, DG10 9RG.
TAIT, Mr. Allan Hugh, FCA *1977;* J & J Baigent Manor Farm, East Worldham, ALTON, GU34 3AY.
TAIT, Mr. Allan Stewart, BSocSc ACA *1984;* 3 Murray Street, YARRAVILLE, VIC 3013, AUSTRALIA.
TAIT, Mr. Andrew John Sinclair, BSc ACA *1997;* 2E Etage 35 Nieuwe Uitleg, 2514 BR DEN HAAG, NETHERLANDS.
TAIT, Mr. Christopher Ian, BSocSc ACA *2003;* Merrill Corporation Ltd, 101 Finsbury Pavement, LONDON, EC2A 1ER.
TAIT, Mr. Christopher John, BSc ACA *1992;* 60 Hanby Street, BRIGHTON, VIC 3186, AUSTRALIA.
TAIT, Mr. Christopher Simon, ACA *1995;* 3 Sunningdale Gardens, LIVERPOOL, L37 3RL.
TAIT, Mrs. Ciara, ACA *2009;* 1 Haute Vue, La Rue Du Carrefour Trinity, JERSEY, JE3 5JH.
TAIT, Miss. Fiona Elisabeth, BA ACA *1997;* with Clifford Chance LLP, 10 Upper Bank Street, LONDON, E14 5JJ.
TAIT, Miss. Gillian Ann, BA ACA *2005;* J Sainsbury Plc, 33 Holborn, LONDON, EC1N 2HT.
TAIT, Mr. Grant Petrie, FCA *1971;* 20 rue des Acacias, 78600 LE MESNIL LE ROI, FRANCE.
TAIT, Mrs. Hazel Margaret, BSc FCA CTA *1990;* (Tax Fac), Sheen Stickland LLP, 4 High Street, ALTON, HAMPSHIRE, GU34 1BU.
TAIT, Mrs. Helen, MA ACA *1999;* 5 Kellaway Avenue, Westbury Park, BRISTOL, BS6 7XP.
TAIT, Mrs. Helen Elizabeth, BSc ACA *1996;* 3 Sunningdale Gardens, Formby, LIVERPOOL, L37 3RL.
TAIT, Mr. Ian Keith Benjamin, BA ACA *2009;* Haute Vue, La Rue Du Carrefour, Trinity, JERSEY, JE3 5JH.
TAIT, Mr. James Archibald Linton, MA ACA *1995;* 17 Jonagold Drive, Great Horkesley, COLCHESTER, CO6 4ED.
TAIT, Mr. Jonathan Douglas, FCA *1962;* 15 Barham Close, WEYBRIDGE, KT13 9PR.
TAIT, Mrs. Katy Emma, BA ACA ATII *2002;* 11 Victoria Road, Stockton Heath, WARRINGTON, WA4 2AL.
•TAIT, Mr. Michael John Hewson, FCA *1976;* (Tax Fac), Straughans Limited, Hadrian House, Front Street, CHESTER LE STREET, COUNTY DURHAM, DH3 3DB.
TAIT, Mr. Nicholas Alexander James, BSc ACA *1998;* 133 Birdwood Road, CAMBRIDGE, CB1 3TB.
•TAIT, Mr. Nicholas Sebastian Charles, MA BA ACA *2001;* (Tax Fac), Charles Tait Accounting, 124 Sharps Lane, RUISLIP, MIDDLESEX, HA4 7JB.
TAIT, Mr. Simon John, BA ACA *1995;* with PricewaterhouseCoopers LLP, 1201 Louisiana, Suite 2900, HOUSTON, TX 77002, UNITED STATES.
TAIT, Mr. Steven Alan, MA(Hons) MSc ACA *2004;* 34 Albert Street, ST. ALBANS, HERTFORDSHIRE, AL1 1RU.
TAIT, Miss. Victoria Jane, MA BA FCA *2000;* (Member of Council 2004 - 2008), 58 Meadow Croft, PENRITH, CUMBRIA, CA11 8EH.
TAIT, Mr. Walter, FCA *1961;* 26 Dunster Road, Hillside, SOUTHPORT, PR8 3AQ.
TAIT, Mr. William Gillon, FCA *1960;* Edendale, Royal Drive, Onchan, ISLE OF MAN, IM3 1HG. (Life Member)
TAITT, Mrs. Helen Elizabeth, BSc ACA *2003;* Yew Tree Farm, Broad Lane, Grappenhall, WARRINGTON, WA4 3HT.
TAJASQUE, Mr. Paul Julian, BA ACA *1985;* Applegate, 6 Crutchfield Lane, WALTON-ON-THAMES, KT12 2QZ.
•TAJDEEN, Mr. Ahmed Rostom, ACA *2006;* Ernst & Young, Ring Road, Zone #10A, Rama Tower, P O Box 20, Kattameya CAIRO EGYPT.
TAJUDIN, Ms. Dina, ACA *2011;* Apartment 19, Fitzharris House, James Joyce Street, DUBLIN 1, COUNTY DUBLIN, IRELAND.
TAKAGI, Mrs. Miyuki, BA FCA *1993;* 2-16-7-2907 Konan, Minato-ku, TOKYO, 108-0075 JAPAN.
TAKAGI, Mr. Yoichi, ACA *2010;* Flat 6, 424 Clapham Road, LONDON, SW9 9DA.
•TAKAHASHI, Mrs. Fiona Helen, BSc FCA *1997;* (Tax Fac), F H Takahashi, 2/2 287 Wilton Street, GLASGOW, G20 6DD.
TAKAHASHI, Mr. Seiya, BSc ACA *1987;* KPMG AZSA LLC, Tokyo Sankei Building, 172 Otemachi, Chiyoda-Ku, TOKYO, 100-8172 JAPAN.
TAKAI, Ms. Chikako Michelle, MA ACA *1999;* Rue du Clocher 27, 1040 BRUSSELS, BELGIUM.
TAKANO, Mr. Makoto Andrew, BA ACA *1999;* 35 Ridgway Place, Wimbledon, LONDON, SW19 4EW.
TAKESHITA, Ms. Akiko, ACA *2000;* Glorio Oji-Kamiya 701, 5-20-3 Oji, KITA-KU, 114-0002 JAPAN.
•TAKHAR, Miss. Anita, ACA FCCA *2010;* 6 Rosemary Drive, Redbridge, ILFORD, ESSEX, IG4 5JD.
TAKHAR, Mr. Kamaldeep Singh, BSc FCA *1996;* 7 Riverview Gardens, LONDON, SW13 8QY.
TAKHAR, Mrs. Kamaljit Kaur, BSc ACA *1999;* (Tax Fac), 30 Scholars Close, BIRMINGHAM, B21 0UB.
TAKHAR, Mr. Sukhraj, BSc ACA *2005;* 205 Wrotham Road, GRAVESEND, DA11 7LE.
TAKHAR, Mr. Sundeep Singh, BSc(Econ) ACA *1997;* 6 Rosemary Drive, ILFORD, IG4 5JD.
TAKKAS, Mr. Costas Michael, BSc ACA *1982;* 2642 Collins Avenue, Apt 305, MIAMI, FL 33140, UNITED STATES.
TAKODARA, Mrs. Jayshree, BA ACA *1992;* 9 Kenton Park Avenue, Kenton, HARROW, HA3 8DX.
TAKOOR, Mr. Santosh Kumar, BEng ACA *1994;* 17 Regency Park, Ingleby Barwick, STOCKTON-ON-TEES, TS17 0QR.
TAKOS, Mr. Konstantinos, ACA *2008;* Flat 37 Hereford House, Fulham Road, LONDON, SW10 9UY.
TAKYAR, Mr. Amit, ACA *2008;* 17 Whytecroft, HOUNSLOW, TW5 9HH.
•TALATI, Mr. Shahrukh Godrej, FCA *1973;* S.G. Talati, 17 St Georges Road, SOUTHSEA, PO4 9PL.
TALATI, Miss. Sheherazad Asad, BSc ACA *1993;* 2318 Devon Road, OAKVILLE L6J 5R4, ON, CANADA.
•TALAVERA, Mr. Christopher John, FCA *1977;* Ballaoates, Glen Road, Colby, ISLE OF MAN, IM9 4HW.
•TALBERT, Mrs. Alison Clare, BSc ACA *1994;* (Tax Fac), ACTA Services Limited, The Pound, Nell Hill, Hannington, SWINDON, SN6 7RT.
•TALBOT, Mr. Adrian Michael, BA ACA *1989;* House B, 66 Sheung Sze Wan, CLEARWATER BAY, NEW TERRITORIES, HONG KONG SAR.
TALBOT, Mr. Adrian Robert, BSc ACA *1992;* College Hill Associates The Registry, 3 Royal Mint Court, LONDON, EC3N 4QN.
TALBOT, Mr. Andrew James, BSc ACA *1989;* 292 Laird Drive, EAST YORK M4G 3X5, ON, CANADA.
TALBOT, Mr. Colin Howard Travis, BA FCA *1971;* 23 Bradgreen Road, Eccles, MANCHESTER, M30 8BZ. (Life Member)
•TALBOT, Mr. Damian Mark, FCA CTA *1999;* Warrener Stewart Limited, Harwood House, 43 Harwood Road, LONDON, SW6 4QP.
TALBOT, Mr. David, BSc ACA *1990;* 7 Kimberley Way, Western Downs, STAFFORD, ST17 9QU.
TALBOT, Mr. David Christopher, BSc ACA *1993;* Northgate Information Solutions Peoplebuilding Estate, Maylands Avenue Hemel Hempstead Industrial Estate, HEMEL HEMPSTEAD, HERTFORDSHIRE, HP2 4NW.
•TALBOT, Mr. David Graham, BA FCA *1999;* with RSM Tenon Audit Limited, 66 Chiltern Street, LONDON, W1U 4JT.
TALBOT, Mr. David Weston, ACA *1989;* with MA Partners LLP, 7 The Close, NORWICH, NORFOLK, NR1 4DJ.
TALBOT, Mrs. Elizabeth Sarah, ACA *1998;* 3 Parrys Close, BRISTOL, BS9 1AW.
TALBOT, Mrs. Esme Gillian, JP BA FCA *1975;* Daggers House, Market Place, Hope, HOPE VALLEY, S33 6RH.
TALBOT, Mrs. Fiona Margaret, BA ACA *1994;* (Tax Fac), Flat 319 Ben Jonson House, Barbican, LONDON, EC2Y 8NQ.
TALBOT, Miss. Gemma Elise, BSc ACA *2009;* 18 Turnstone Close, Winnersh, WOKINGHAM, BERKSHIRE, RG41 5LQ.
TALBOT, Mrs. Helen Jill, BA ACA *1990;* 1 St. Ronans Terrace, EDINBURGH, EH10 5NG.
•TALBOT, Mr. Ian Martin, FCA *1987;* Wilkins Kennedy, Parmenter House, 57 Tower Street, WINCHESTER, HAMPSHIRE, SO23 8TD.
TALBOT, Mr. James Keith, MSc ACA *1995;* Nomura International Plc, 25 Bank Street, LONDON, E14 5LS.
TALBOT, Miss. Jane Linda, BA ACA *1990;* Skyways House, Littlewoods Organisation Ltd, 2 Estuary Banks Speke, LIVERPOOL, L24 8RB.
TALBOT, Mr. John Andrew, FCA *1971;* Johnson Service Group plc, Sheraton House, Castle Park, CAMBRIDGE, CB3 0AX.
•TALBOT, Mr. John Guy, MA FCA *1981;* (Tax Fac), Francis Clark LLP, Ridge Grove, Russell Street, TAVISTOCK, DEVON, PL19 8BE.
TALBOT, Mr. John Philip, BSc(Hons) ACA *2003;* with BDO LLP, Fourth Floor, One Victoria Street, BRISTOL, BS1 6AA.
•TALBOT, Mr. Jonathan Michael, BA FCA *1998;* Smith & Williamson Ltd, Portwall Place, Portwall Lane, BRISTOL, BS1 6NA. See also Nexia Audit Limited
TALBOT, Mrs. Katherine Claire Shakespear, BSc ACA *2003;* The Old Estate Yard, Newton St. Loe, BATH, BA2 9BR.
TALBOT, Mr. Kimball Philip, FCA *1969;* Ivy Cottage, 60 Long Ashton Road, Long Ashton, BRISTOL, BS41 9LE. (Life Member)
TALBOT, Miss. Liza, ACA *2009;* 15 Lyttelton Road, LIVERPOOL, L17 0AS.
TALBOT, Mr. Mark Stephen, ACA *1992;* P. O. Box 33541, Takapuna, AUCKLAND 1332, NEW ZEALAND.
TALBOT, Mr. Mark Stowell, FCA *1970;* Long Sutton Stores, The Green, Long Sutton, LANGPORT, TA10 9HT.
TALBOT, Miss. Michaela Dawn, BSc ACA *1992;* Unit 3.1, York Central, 70 York Way, LONDON, N1 9AG.
•TALBOT, Mr. Nicholas John Alexander, FCA *1978;* 175 Woodstock Road, OXFORD, OX2 7NB.
TALBOT, Miss. Patricia Jane, BSc ACA *2003;* Credit Suisse, 1 Cabot Square, LONDON, E14 4QJ.
TALBOT, Mr. Philip, BSc ACA *1991;* 1 St. Ronans Terrace, EDINBURGH, EH10 5NG.
TALBOT, Mr. Philip John, BSS ACA *1991;* Sevacare(UK) Ltd, Unit 9, Pendeford Place, Pendeford Business Park, WOLVERHAMPTON, WV9 5HD.
TALBOT, Mr. Richard Charles, ACA *2009;* Falconhurst, Cowden Pound Road, Mark Beech, EDENBRIDGE, KENT, TN8 5NR.
TALBOT, Mrs. Ruth Elizabeth, BA ACA *1986;* St Abbs, Lawson Lane, Chilton, DIDCOT, OX11 0RX.
TALBOT, Mrs. Samantha Jayne, ACA *2003;* 5 Lambecroft, BARNSLEY, SOUTH YORKSHIRE, S71 3FH.
TALBOT, Mrs. Sarah Victoria, BA ACA *1992;* Amberley, Lees Hill, South Warnborough, HOOK, HAMPSHIRE, RG29 1RG.
•TALBOT, Mr. Stephen, BSc FCA *1994;* (Tax Fac), Langtons, The Plaza, 100 Old Hall Street, LIVERPOOL, L3 9QJ.
TALBOT-MARTIN, Mrs. Karen Lesley, BSc ACA CTA *1989;* Norwich Union, 2 Rougier Street, YORK, YO90 1UU.
TALBOTT, Mr. Richard John, BA ACA *1981;* (Tax Fac), Brookside Cottage, Moor Lane, Walton-In-Gordano, CLEVEDON, BS21 7AH.
TALFOURD-COOK, Mr. Brian, FCA *1960;* Covertside, Rotherfield Greys, HENLEY-ON-THAMES, OXFORDSHIRE, RG9 4QJ.
•TALFOURD-COOK, Mr. James Andrew Brian, BA *1993;* Berkeley Tax Consultants (UK) Limited, Berkeley Square House, Berkeley Square, LONDON, W1J 6BD.
TALHA, Mr. Ahmad Tifli Mohd, ACA *1989;* NO.9 JALAN PUALAM TIGA 7/32C, 40000 SHAH ALAM, MALAYSIA.
TALIADOROS, Mr. Costas, ACA *2004;* 16 Idipodos Street, Strovolos, 2063 NICOSIA, CYPRUS.
TALIB, Mr. Hamed Bin Omar, FCA *1973;* 66 Bursaria Crescent, GLENMORE PARK, NSW 2745, AUSTRALIA.
TALIJANCIC, Mrs. Stephanie Jane, LLB ACA *2001;* Catlin, 20 Gracechurch Street, LONDON, EC3V 0BG.
TALINTYRE, Miss. April Carolyn, BSc ACA *1992;* flat b4, 28 Guildhouse Street, LONDON, SW1V 1JJ.
TALIOTI, Miss. Christina, BSc ACA *2006;* 46 Avenue Cbc, Aglantzia, 2122 NICOSIA, CYPRUS.
•TALIOTIS, Mr. Antonis Fidia, BA ACA *1992;* P.O. Box 57219, 3313 LIMASSOL, CYPRUS.
TALJAARD, Mr. Desmond Louis Mildmay, BSc ACA *1985;* 59 Crescent West, Hadley Wood, BARNET, EN4 0EQ.
TALL, Mr. Andrew Brian Orme, BSc(Hons) ACA CTA *2001;* (Tax Fac), with Mazars LLP, Tower Bridge House, St. Katharines Way, LONDON, E1W 1DD.
•TALL, Mrs. Carina Ellen, BSc ACA *1986;* Ganymede Business Services Limited, Long Field House, Station Road, Bratton Fleming, BARNSTAPLE, DEVON EX31 4TZ.
TALLANTIRE, Mr. John Hugh Drummond, FCA *1965;* 17 St. Lukes Grove, YORK, YO30 6DD. (Life Member)
TALLENT, Mr. Michael Stephen, BA ACA *1996;* Alvarez & Marsal, 1 Finsbury Circus, LONDON, EC2M 7EB.
TALLENTIRE, Mrs. Katherine, ACA *2009;* 27 Kent Drive, Endon, STOKE-ON-TRENT, ST9 9EH.
TALLENTIRE, Mr. Robert Graham, ACA *1982;* 1 Pinfold Lane, Shelford, NOTTINGHAM, NG12 1EH.
TALLENTS, Mr. Craig Stephen, TD BA FCA *1991;* St. Davids, Oaklands Lane, Smallford, ST. ALBANS, HERTFORDSHIRE, AL4 0HT.
TALLING, Mr. Kenneth Neil, ACA *1990;* Nine Lives, Tom Cat Lane, Bickerton, WETHERBY, LS22 5ES.
TALLON, Mr. David Seymour, FCA *1964;* (Tax Fac), 26a Cunningham Hill Road, ST. ALBANS, HERTFORDSHIRE, AL1 5BY.
TALLON, Mr. John Mark, FCA *1970;* (Tax Fac), Pump Court Tax Chambers, 16 Bedford Row, LONDON, WC1R 4EF.
TALLON, Mr. Paul William, BA(Hons) ACA *2002;* with BDO LLP, 125 Colmore Row, BIRMINGHAM, B3 3SD.
•TALLON, Ms. Paula Christina, BBS FCA *1999;* (Tax Fac), Tallon Tax, 33 Cavendish Square, LONDON, W1G 0PW.
TALLON, Mr. Toby Mark Brodrick, BA ACA *2006;* Flat 1, 355 Clapham Road, LONDON, SW9 9BT.
TALLOWIN, Mrs. Elizabeth Emma, ACA *2001;* Manor Farm, Stubb Road Hickling, NORWICH, NORFOLK, NR12 0BS.
TALMA, Mrs. Deborah Gale, BSc ACA *1997;* 87 Plover Court, Chancery Lane, CHRISTCHURCH, BARBADOS.
TALREJA, Mr. Prakash Shrikrishin, FCA *1971;* Prakash S. Talreja, 1149 Brattleboro Arch, VIRGINIA BEACH, VA 23464, UNITED STATES.
TALTY, Mr. Matthew, BMus ACA *2007;* Sagana, The Hatches, FARNHAM, GU9 8UE.
•TALUKDAR, Mr. Muhammad Noorul Huda, ACA *1979;* (Tax Fac), Talukdar & Co, 158 Whitworth Road, ROCHDALE, OL12 0JG.
TALWAR, Mr. Gurdeep Singh, BSc ACA ACT *1999;* 213 Bedok South Avenue 1, Casafina #02-03, SINGAPORE, SINGAPORE.
TALWAR, Mr. Pravir, FCA *1979;* 56 Russell Road, Moor Park, NORTHWOOD, HA6 2LR.
TALWAR, Mr. Rajeev Chander, ACA *2007;* Deutsche Bank Winchester House, 1 Great Winchester Street, LONDON, EC2N 2DB.
TALWAR, Dr. Sanjiv, ACA *1984;* 14 West Heath Close, Hampstead, LONDON, NW3 7NJ.
TALWAR, Mr. Sudesh Chander, ACA *1980;* 8 Dover Park, CALCUTTA 700 019, INDIA.
TALYARKHAN, Mr. Darab Rustom, FCA *1971;* Talyarkhan & Co, Lyndewode House, Bomanji Petit Road, Cumballa Hill, MUMBAI 400036, MAHARASHTRA INDIA.
•TALYARKHAN, Mr. Faredoon Rustom, FCA *1972;* Al Kauther United Establishment, PO Box 1750, Ruwi PC112 MUSCAT, OMAN.
TAM, Mr. Benson Bing Chung, MSc ACA *1989;* Apt 3400, Pacific Place Apartments, 88 Queensway, CENTRAL, HONG KONG ISLAND, HONG KONG SAR.

TAM, Miss. Catherine Wing Yee, BSc ACA *1989;* 8G Block 2, Academic Terrace, 101 Pokfulam Road, POK FU LAM, HONG KONG ISLAND, HONG KONG SAR.

•TAM, Mr. Chi Ming, FCA *1976;* Tam Chi Ming, Room 1805 18th Floor, Wellborne Commercial Centre, 8 Java Road, NORTH POINT, HONG KONG ISLAND HONG KONG SAR. See also Tam C.M. & Co

TAM, Mr. Chi Kwan Michael, ACA *2004;* TLC CPA Limited, Room 1203, 12/F Wing on Centre, 111 Connaught Road, CENTRAL, HONG KONG SAR.

TAM, Miss. Chiew Lin, FCA *1975;* Jerneh Asia BHD, Wisma Jerneh 16th Floor, 38 Jln Sultan Ismail, 50250 KUALA LUMPUR, FEDERAL TERRITORY, MALAYSIA.

TAM, Ms. Ching Wah, ACA *2005;* Flat G 16/F Block 10, Laguna City, LAM TIN, KOWLOON, HONG KONG SAR.

TAM, Mr. Chiu Yin, ACA *2006;* Tsang Tam & Company, Room 704, 7/F Kai Wong Commercial Building, 222-226 Queens Road, CENTRAL, HONG KONG ISLAND HONG KONG SAR.

TAM, Mr. Chu Fai, ACA *2007;* 6/F, Block 47, Baguio Villa, 550 Victoria Road, POK FU LAM, HONG KONG ISLAND HONG KONG SAR.

TAM, Mr. Chun Pong Stephen, BSc ACA MBA *2002;* 3B Monmouth Place, 9L Kennedy Road, MID LEVELS, HONG KONG ISLAND, HONG KONG SAR.

TAM, Mr. Chun Wan, ACA *2007;* C W Leung & Co, Room 403, Wing on House, 71 Des Voeux Road, CENTRAL, HONG KONG ISLAND HONG KONG SAR.

TAM, Ms. Fung Chee, ACA *2007;* Tam Au & Co, Unit B, 22/F Tak Lee Commercial Building, 113 Wan Chai Road, WAN CHAI, HONG KONG ISLAND HONG KONG SAR.

TAM, Miss. Haley Ann, MA(Hons) ACA CFA *2000;* Citi Investment Research, Citigroup Centre, Canada Square, Canary Whare, LONDON, E14 5LB.

TAM, Ms. Ho Ting, ACA *2008;* Flat A, 9/F, Block 8, Bauhinia Garden, 11 Tong Chun Street, TSEUNG KWAN O HONG KONG SAR.

TAM, Mr. Hok Wah Simon, ACA *2007;* Flat B 5th Floor Tower 2, Neptune Terrace, CHAI WAN, HONG KONG SAR.

TAM, Mr. Hon Bun Edwin, ACA *2007;* 63th Floor, Two IFC, CENTRAL, HONG KONG SAR.

TAM, Mr. James Man Kit, BA ACA *1994;* with PricewaterhouseCoopers, 33/F Cheung Kong Center, 2 Queen's Road, CENTRAL, HONG KONG ISLAND, HONG KONG SAR.

TAM, Mr. Joseph Shun Tai, ACA *2004;* C/- JST Tam, Shun Tak Holdings Ltd, 39/F Shun Tak Centre, West Tower, 200 Connaught Road, CENTRAL HONG KONG ISLAND HONG KONG SAR.

TAM, Mr. Kam Biu, ACA *2007;* K.B.Tam & Co, Rooms C-F, 5th Floor, Shing Lee Commercial Building, 6-12 Wing Kut Street, CENTRAL HONG KONG ISLAND HONG KONG SAR.

TAM, Mr. Kam Shing, ACA *2006;* 45th Floor Raffles City, 268 Xizang Zhong Road, Huangpu District, SHANGHAI 200001, CHINA.

TAM, Mr. Kim Wah, ACA *2005;* 12C Block 2, Ronsdale Garden, 25 Tai Hang Drive, JARDINE'S LOOKOUT, HONG KONG ISLAND, HONG KONG SAR.

TAM, Mr. King Tong, ACA *2005;* 12/F Pico Tower, 66 Gloucester Road, WAN CHAI, HONG KONG ISLAND, HONG KONG SAR.

TAM, Mr. Kuang Wei, BA(Hons) ACA *2009;* Flat 11, Lancaster Court, 36-38 Newman Street, LONDON, W1T 1QH.

TAM, Mr. Kwok Fai Paul, ACA *2007;* with W S Wong & Co, 16th Floor, Jonsim Place, 228 Queen's Road East, WAN CHAI, HONG KONG ISLAND HONG KONG SAR.

TAM, Mr. Lup Kwan Dennis, ACA *2006;* 36G Tower 3, Nob Hill, LAI CHI KOK, KOWLOON, HONG KONG SAR.

TAM, Ms. Man Kuen, ACA *2005;* Rooms 1001-1003 10/F. Manulife Provident Funds Place, 345 Nathan Road, YAU MA TEI, KOWLOON, HONG KONG SAR.

TAM, Ms. Pei Ching, BSc ACA *2003;* 61 Jalan Indah 1/22, Taman Universiti Indah, Seri Kembangan, 43300 SERI KEMBANGAN, SELANGOR, MALAYSIA.

TAM, Mr. Raymond, ACA *2004;* Hutchison Whampoa Properties Ltd, 3/F One Harbourfront, 18 Tak Fung Street, HUNG HOM, KOWLOON, HONG KONG SAR.

TAM, Mr. Raymond Tak Kei, BA ACA *1990;* 12A King Tien Mansion, Taikoo shing, QUARRY BAY, HONG KONG ISLAND, HONG KONG SAR.

TAM, Ms. Shui Ying, ACA *2007;* Flat D 7/F, Tak Tung House, 155 Des Voeux Road West, SAI YING POON, HONG KONG ISLAND, HONG KONG SAR.

TAM, Ms. Shuk Wah Carrie, ACA *2007;* Flat 2, 11/F, Ka Sing House, Ka Lung Court, Kellett Bay, POK FU LAM HONG KONG ISLAND HONG KONG SAR.

TAM, Miss. Su Mey, BA ACA CF *1997;* 5 Jalan Camar 4/25, Villa Damansara, 47810 PETALING JAYA, MALAYSIA.

TAM, Mr. Thomas Kwan Ming, ACA *2007;* Flat B4/F, Tower 4, Park Belvedere, Ma On Shan, SHA TIN, NEW TERRITORIES HONG KONG SAR.

TAM, Mr. Tsz Kan, ACA *2008;* Flat 2216 Wai Man House, Oi Man Estate, HO MAN TIN, KOWLOON, HONG KONG SAR.

TAM, Mr. Woon Cheong, ACA *2008;* IMS International Limited, 2804A Cable TV Tower, 9 Hoi Shing Road, TSUEN WAN, NEW TERRITORIES, HONG KONG SAR.

TAM, Dr. Yat Kung, ACA *2005;* 35/F Dah Sing Financial Centre, 108 Gloucester Road, WAN CHAI, HONG KONG ISLAND, HONG KONG SAR.

TAM, Mr. Yiu Kei, ACA *2008;* Flat B, 20/F, Markfield Building, 8 Smithfield, KENNEDY TOWN, HONG KONG SAR.

TAM, Ms. Yuen Ying, ACA *2008;* Flat 2 6/F Block B, Y. Y. Mansions, 96 Pokfulam Road, POK FU LAM, HONG KONG ISLAND, HONG KONG SAR.

TAM, Mr. Yui Kin, ACA CPA CISA CIA *2005;* 35/F One Pacific Place, 88 Queensway, CENTRAL, HONG KONG ISLAND, HONG KONG SAR.

TAMAMOUNA, Miss. Marilena, BSc ACA MBA *2004;* 6 Apollonos Street, 6016 LARNACA, CYPRUS.

TAMANA, Ms. Andrea, ACA *2009;* 11 Gaudion Road, EAST DONCASTER, VIC 3105, AUSTRALIA.

•TAMANI-PHELLA, Mrs. Aegli, BA ACA *2003;* InterTaxAudit, Kyreania House, 5 Skra Street, Agios Andreas, 1100 NICOSIA, CYPRUS. See also Ledra Audit Services Limited

TAMAYO, Mr. Richard James, MBA BSc FCA *1991;* 84 Westwood Drive, AMERSHAM, BUCKINGHAMSHIRE, HP6 6RW.

TAMBACOPOULO, Mrs. Patricia Mary, BEng FCA *1986;* with Baker Tilly UK Audit LLP, Lancaster House, 7 Elmfield Road, BROMLEY, BR1 1LT.

•TAMBAYAH, Mr. Navaratnam Prasad, BSc FCA *1968;* Tambayah & Co, 7 Norland Square, Holland Park, LONDON, W11 4PX.

TAMBIAH, Mr. Vidhi, BSc(Econ) ACA MBA CFA *1997;* 10 Rue des Chaudronniers, CH 1204 GENEVA, SWITZERLAND.

TAMBLYN, Mr. Joseph Andrew, BSc(Hons) ACA *2011;* 11 Lower Elms, Tredrizzick, St. Minver, WADEBRIDGE, CORNWALL, PL27 6QB.

TAMBLYN, Mr. Nicholas John, BSc FCA *1982;* 3 Broadway, Broad Street, BIRMINGHAM, B15 1BQ.

•TAMBLYN, Mrs. Susan Elizabeth, BSc ACA *1983;* Tamblyn & Co Limited, Kinnersley House, Kinnersley, Nr Severn Stoke, WORCESTER, WR8 9JR.

TAMBLYN, Mr. Timothy Guy, BA FCA *1978;* 54 Church Road, Alphington, EXETER, EX2 8TA.

TAME, Mr. John Townsend, MSc FCA MCIE *1962;* 30 Rushbearers Walk, Almondbury, HUDDERSFIELD, HD5 8DG.

TAME, Mr. Richard John, BSc(Hons) ACA CTA *2001;* 2 Raglan Court, 14 Raglan Road, Ballsbridge, DUBLIN 4, COUNTY DUBLIN, IRELAND.

TAME, Mr. William, BA ACA *1982;* The Riddings, Long Preston, SKIPTON, BD23 4QN.

TAME, Mrs. Zoe Maria, ACA *2002;* 54 Pelican Road, Pamber Heath, TADLEY, HAMPSHIRE, RG26 3EL.

TAMLYN, Miss. Alison Clare, ACA *2008;* 12 Lydden Grove, LONDON, SW18 4LL.

TAMLYN, Mr. Neil David, BSc ACA *1985;* 269b Valley Road, Streatham, LONDON, SW16 2AB. (Life Member)

TAMPLIN, Mrs. Ami, BA(Hons) ACA *2011;* Apartment 78, Sandling Park, Sandling Lane, MAIDSTONE, KENT, ME14 2NY.

TAMPLIN, Mr. Nigel Vernon, FCA *1977;* Tithe Barn, 35 Lambley Road, Lowdham, NOTTINGHAM, NG14 7AZ.

•TAMS, Mrs. Daphne, FCA *1960;* Mrs D Tams, 4 Conway Court, Stirling Close, NEW MILTON, BH25 6AR. See also D Tams

TAMS, Miss. Emma-Jayne, MChem ACA *2004;* Braemar Group Plc Suite 2 Richmond House, 1a Heath Road Hale, ALTRINCHAM, CHESHIRE, WA14 2XP.

TAMS, Mr. Julian David, BSc ACA *1995;* Lang House Hardwick Close, Oxshott, LEATHERHEAD, SURREY, KT22 0HZ.

TAMSETT, Mr. John Stewart, BA FCA *1976;* Lazard & Co Ltd, 50 Stratton Street, LONDON, W1J 8LL.

TAMSETT, Mrs. Judith Mary, FCA *1969;* 249 Belmont Road, RR2 Newport, HANTS COUNTY B0N 2A0, NS, CANADA.

TAMSONS, Mrs. Joanne Kirsty, BA ACA *1997;* The Old Barn, 2 Havelock Square, Thornton, BRADFORD, BD13 3EZ.

TAMTEKIN, Mrs. Nalan, ACA *1993;* Markgravelei 132, 2018 ANTWERP, BELGIUM.

•TAMURI, Mr. Shamim Uddin, FCA *1969;* (Tax Fac), S.U. Tamuri, 1 Forrest Gardens, LONDON, SW16 4LP.

TAMWORTH, Viscount Robert William Saswalo Shirley, FCA *1976;* Ruffer LLP, 80 Victoria Street, LONDON, SW1E 5JL.

TAN, Mr. Ah Lai, ACA *1985;* 9 Persiaran Greentown 7, Greentown Busness Centre, 30450 IPOH, PERAK, MALAYSIA.

TAN, Mr. Allan Teck Beng, BCom ACA *1988;* Terrace Unit 2, 100 Bowen Terrace, New Farm, BRISBANE, QLD 4005, AUSTRALIA.

TAN, Mr. Allen Shou Wei, BA ACA *1984;* Tan Choon Chye & Co., 6001 Beach Road, 12-10, Golden Mile Tower, SINGAPORE 199589, SINGAPORE.

TAN, Mr. Andre, BSc ACA *2006;* 20 Woodville Gardens, Ealing, LONDON, W5 2LQ.

TAN, Miss. Annie Wan Pheng, MA ACA *1992;* 11 Gerbang Midlands, 10250 PENANG, MALAYSIA.

TAN, Mr. Anthony Kim Seong, FCA *1977;* 2065 West 14Th Avenue, VANCOUVER V6J 2K3, BC, CANADA.

TAN, Mr. Beng Hai, FCA *1977;* 1 Belmont Road, 09-00 The Belmont, SINGAPORE 269852, SINGAPORE.

TAN, Mr. Benjamin Chee Keong, ACA *1993;* 125 Paremoremo Road, Lucas Heights, NORTH SHORE CITY 0632, NEW ZEALAND.

TAN, Mr. Bian Hong, MBA FCA *1975;* 3 Merrywood, Fortyfoot Road, LEATHERHEAD, SURREY, KT22 8RN.

TAN, Mr. Bien-Chuan, BSc ACA *1985;* 50 Goldhill Avenue, 01-07 Mount Rosie Garden, SINGAPORE 309031, SINGAPORE.

TAN, Mr. Boon Ching, ACA *2009;* 100 Jalan Burung Balam, Taman Bukit Maluri, 52100 KUALA LUMPUR, FEDERAL TERRITORY, MALAYSIA.

TAN, Mr. Braden Choon Thong, ACA *2008;* 4 Homer Drive, LONDON, E14 3UB.

TAN, Ms. Chee Peng, ACA *2010;* with BDO, 12th Floor Menara Uni. Asia, Jalan sultan Ismail, 50250 KUALA LUMPUR, FEDERAL TERRITORY, MALAYSIA.

TAN, Mr. Cheong Kang, FCA *1975;* 20 East 61st Ave, VANCOUVER V5X 2B4, BC, CANADA.

TAN, Ms. Cheryl Pei Ee, ACA *2008;* 12 Caldecott Close, SINGAPORE 299121, SINGAPORE.

TAN, Mr. Chi Kin, ACA *2004;* with PricewaterhouseCoopers, 26/F Office Tower A, Beijing Fortune Plaza, 23 Dongsanhuan North Road, Chaoyang District, BEIJING 100020 CHINA.

TAN, Mr. Chih Wen, BA ACA *1998;* Search Investment Group, 57th Floor, Cheung Kong Centre, 2 Queens Road, CENTRAL, HONG KONG ISLAND HONG KONG SAR.

TAN, Mr. Chin Guan, FCA *1974;* 15 West 40th Avenue, VANCOUVER V5Y 2P9, BC, CANADA.

TAN, Mr. Chin Kok, BSc ACA ATII *1996;* with Deloitte Touche Tohmatsu, 30th Floor, Bund Centre, 222 Yan An Road East, SHANGHAI 20002, CHINA.

TAN, Mr. Chin Leong, ACA *1990;* 5 Leighton Way, EPSOM, SURREY, KT18 7QZ.

TAN, Mr. Chong Hoe, BAcc ACA *2006;* 60 Bridport Avenue, SINGAPORE 559350, SINGAPORE.

TAN, Mr. Chong Yeang, BA FCA *1983;* 25/305 Evans Bay Parade, Hataitai, WELLINGTON 6021, NEW ZEALAND.

TAN, Mr. Choong Himm, ACA *1980;* 75 Prospector Loop, BASSENDEAN, WA 6054, AUSTRALIA.

TAN, Mr. Chuan Chong, ACA *2011;* 74, Lebuh Pulau Pinang 3, Kaw 18, Off Jalan Meru, 41050 KLANG, SELANGOR MALAYSIA.

•TAN, Mr. David Tiong Teet, BA FCA *1985;* Richardson Watson & Co, Mint House, 6 Stanley Park Road, WALLINGTON, SM6 0HA.

TAN, Miss. Dawn Kirsten, MSc ACA *2005;* Flat 1010 New Providence Wharf, 1 Fairmont Avenue, LONDON, E14 9PB.

TAN, Miss. E Hun, ACA *2009;* (Tax Fac), First floor flat, 37 Priory Road, LONDON, NW6 4NN.

TAN, Mr. Edmund Seng Oon, BA FCA *1981;* Cedar Lodge, London Road, Prestbury, MACCLESFIELD, CHESHIRE, SK10 4EA.

TAN, Mr. Edwin An Tar, ACA *1984;* 155 Victoria Street, SAN FRANCISCO, CA 94132, UNITED STATES.

TAN, Miss. Elizabeth Mee Loo, BSc FCA *1980;* Shelvin, 1 Cuffs Mead, Forton, CHARD, TA20 2NQ.

TAN, Mr. Eng Cheong, FCA *1989;* Tower 2, Emerald Park, 2 Indus Road Apt. 12-07, SINGAPORE 169586, SINGAPORE.

TAN, Mr. Eng Lay, FCA *1993;* 6 Hougang Street 92, Regentville, Tower 5 #09-02, SINGAPORE 538 685, SINGAPORE.

TAN, Mr. Eng Kwee, ACA *2010;* Flat 42, Toronto House, Surrey Quays Road, LONDON, SE16 7AJ.

TAN, Ms. Esther Choon Hwa, FCA *1977;* GEP Associates, 25-3 Jalan PJU 1/42A, Dataran Prima, 47301 PETALING JAYA, Selangor, MALAYSIA.

TAN, Mr. Fei Meng, ACA *1980;* 56 JALAN USJ 4/4C, 47600 SUBANG, SELANGOR, MALAYSIA.

TAN, Mr. Frank Stuart, MA ACA *1995;* 3 Moreton Close, STRATFORD-UPON-AVON, WARWICKSHIRE, CV37 7HB.

TAN, Miss. Gaik Ann, BSc ACA *2002;* 73 Jln Athinahapan 2, Taman Tun Dr Ismail, 60000 KUALA LUMPUR, FEDERAL TERRITORY, MALAYSIA.

TAN, Mr. Gerald Yew Meng, BA ACA *2003;* 195 St. Davids Square, LONDON, E14 3WE.

TAN, Mr. Gerard Wee Seng, ACA *1982;* PricewaterhouseCoopers LLP, 17-00 PWC Building, 8 Cross Street, SINGAPORE 048424, SINGAPORE.

•TAN, Mr. Ghee Kiat, FCA *1974;* (Tax Fac), Sekhar & Tan, Suite 16-8 Level 16, Wisma UOA II, 21 Jalan Pinang, 50450 KUALA LUMPUR, FEDERAL TERRITORY MALAYSIA.

TAN, Mr. Gim Soo, FCA *1969;* G.S.Tan & Co, 116 Middle Road, #06-01 ICB Enterprise House, SINGAPORE 188972, SINGAPORE.

•TAN, Miss. Gok Hui, FCA *1978;* G. Tan & Co, 88 Ventnor Drive, LONDON, N20 8BS.

TAN, Mr. Hien Leng, BA FCA *1978;* 1778 West 37th Avenue, VANCOUVER V6M 1N1, BC, CANADA.

TAN, Mr. Hock Leong, BA ACA *1988;* 38 Lindley Road, WALTON-ON-THAMES, SURREY, KT12 3HA.

TAN, Mr. Hock Seng, ACA *1978;* 1262 Sweetbirch Ct., MISSISSAUGA L5C 3R3, ON, CANADA.

TAN, Mr. Hoon San, BSc ACA *1991;* 156-0-12 Villa Flora Condominium, Jalan burhanuddin Helmi, Taman Tun Dr Ismail, 60000 KUALA LUMPUR, FEDERAL TERRITORY, MALAYSIA.

TAN, Mr. Hun Seng, FCA *1983;* Raffles Beijing Hotel, 33 East Chang An Avenue, BEIJING 100004, CHINA.

TAN, Miss. Irene Ai Leng, BSc ACA *2003;* Kaitovayla 23 C17, 90570 OULU, FINLAND.

TAN, Miss. Irene Ai Lin, ACA *1994;* Flat 9 Southside Quarter, 38 Burns Road, LONDON, SW11 5GY.

TAN, Miss. Jean Mei Mei, ACA *1989;* 9 Broadwater Down, TUNBRIDGE WELLS, TN2 5NJ.

TAN, Miss. Jennifer, BSc ACA *1993;* 4304 43/F, China Resources Building, 26 Harbour Road, WAN CHAI, HONG KONG ISLAND, HONG KONG SAR.

TAN, Ms. Jennifer Yuen Chun, ACA *2007;* Hutchison Telecommunications (HK) Ltd, 19/F, Hutchison Telecom Tower, 99 Cheung Fai Road, TSING YI, HONG KONG SAR.

TAN, Miss. Jie, MSc ACA *2009;* Flat 14 Aurora Building, 164 Blackwall Way, LONDON, E14 9NZ.

TAN, Mr. Jing Kuan, BA ACA *1996;* No 17 Jalan Damar sd 15/4a, Bandar Sri Damansara, 52200 KUALA LUMPUR, FEDERAL TERRITORY, MALAYSIA.

TAN, Mr. Jing Yong, BA ACA ATII *1999;* 4 Flora Road, Azalea Park 0902, SINGAPORE 509726, SINGAPORE.

TAN, Mr. Jonathan, ACA *2008;* 38, Belgrave Road, SALE, CHESHIRE, m33 7ua.

TAN, Mr. Joon Yew, FCA *1983;* Ottostrasse 3-5, Apartment 67, 80333 MUNICH, GERMANY.

TAN, Miss. Josephine, LLB ACA *2007;* 20 Malvern Close, Woodley, READING, RG5 4HL.

TAN, Mr. Ju Thai, MSc FCA *1975;* 25 Maple Avenue, SINGAPORE 277581, SINGAPORE.

TAN, Miss. Jun Li, ACA *2009;* 20 Jalan Birai U8/68, Bukit Jelutong, 40150 SHAH ALAM, MALAYSIA.

TAN, Ms. June Beng Siew, BSc ACA *1992;* 7a Mount Rosie Road, SINGAPORE 308058, SINGAPORE.

TAN, Mr. Justin Edward, BSc ACA *2010;* 69 Belvedere Avenue, ILFORD, IG5 0UH.

TAN, Miss. Kai Yeh, ACA *2008;* 17 Jalan Cahaya 6, Salak South Garden, 57100 KUALA LUMPUR, FEDERAL TERRITORY, MALAYSIA.

TAN, Mr. Kang Fun, ACA *1986;* Blk 22 Simei Street 1 #09-04 Melville Park, SINGAPORE 529945, SINGAPORE.

TAN, Mr. Kang Hong, ACA *1983;* 740 Arthurs Creek Road, ARTHURS CREEK, VIC 3099, AUSTRALIA.

TAN - TANG

Members - Alphabetical

TAN, Miss. Karen Hui Keen, BSc ACA *2004;* #49-15 Block 1B, Cantonment Road, SINGAPORE 085201, SINGAPORE.
TAN, Miss. Karen Siok Ling, BSc ACA *1991;* Flat 15, Beechcroft House, 47-49 Park View Road, Ealing, LONDON, W5 2JF.
TAN, Mr. Kelvin Say Liang, BSc ACA *2007;* Flat 3/A Welles Court, 4 Premiere Place, LONDON, E14 8SE.
TAN, Miss. Keng Lin, BSc ACA *1991;* 24 Jalan 2/3, Taman Tun Abdul Razak, 68000 AMPANG, Selangor, MALAYSIA.
•**TAN, Mr. Keng Nam, ACA** *1987;* (Tax Fac), K N TAN, 54 Weald Lane, HARROW, MIDDLESEX, HA3 5EX.
TAN, Mr. Kenneth Kean Leng, BSc FCA *1989;* 50 Pymers Mead, West Dulwich, LONDON, SE21 8NH.
TAN, Mr. Kenneth Kok-Oon, FCA *1965;* 4304 43/F, China Resources Building, 26 Harbour Road, WAN CHAI, 4304, HONG KONG SAR. (Life Member)
TAN, Mr. Kenneth Tze Ping, BAcc ACA CPA *2000;* 86 Braemar Drive, Serangoon Garden Estate, SINGAPORE 559489, SINGAPORE.
TAN, Mr. Khee Yang Justin, ACA *2009;* Apartment 106 West Block, Forum Magnum Square, LONDON, SE1 7GL.
TAN, Mr. Kheng Cheng, ACA *1993;* 29 Apt 01-07, Jalan Sempadan, SINGAPORE 457402, SINGAPORE.
TAN, Mr. Kian Seng, ACA *1980;* 22 Taman Ayer Rajah, 10350 PENANG, MALAYSIA.
•①**TAN, Mr. Kian Seng, FCA FABRP** *1980;* K.S. Tan & Co, 1st Floor, 10/12 New College Parade, Finchley Road, LONDON, NW3 5EP.
TAN, Mr. Kit Heng, ACA *1981;* 6 Sunrise Way, SINGAPORE 806152, SINGAPORE.
TAN, Mr. Koon Wah, FCA *1978;* 8 High Garth, ESHER, KT10 9DN.
TAN, Mr. Kwang Heng, FCA *1975;* 8/36 Willis Street, Kingsford, SYDNEY, NSW 2032, AUSTRALIA.
TAN, Miss. Lay Ching, FCA *1987;* Mutiara Oriental Conominium, D-16-01, Jalan BM1/8, Taman Bukit Mayang Emas, 47301 PETALING JAYA, SELANGOR MALAYSIA.
TAN, Mrs. Lay Choo, FCA *1977;* 8 High Garth, ESHER, SURREY, KT10 9DN.
•**TAN, Miss. Lay Koon, BSc ACA** *1990;* 34 Limerston Street, LONDON, SW10 0HH.
TAN, Ms. Lay Lee, BSc(Hons) ACA *2003;* 6 JALAN SS 2/99, 47300 PETALING JAYA, MALAYSIA.
TAN, Miss. Lay Suan, BSc ACA *1995;* 15 Willow Drive, BURY, BL9 8NT.
TAN, Mr. Leng Cheo, FCA *1977;* 257 Arcadia Road, Apt 06-05, SINGAPORE 289849, SINGAPORE.
TAN, Mr. Lenny Kah Wan, BA FCA CFA *1998;* 9 Harper Close, Chafford Hundred, GRAYS, ESSEX, RM16 6DA.
TAN, Mr. Leong Hin, BSc ACA *1992;* Kah Bintang Auto Sdn Bhd, Wisma Kah Motor, No 566 Batu 3 1/2 Jalan Ipoh, 51200 KUALA LUMPUR, FEDERAL TERRITORY, MALAYSIA.
TAN, Miss. Li-Ann, BA ACA *2009;* Flat 55, Bedford Court Mansions, Bedford Avenue, LONDON, WC1B 3AD.
TAN, Mr. Li-Ren, BSc ACA *2004;* UNIT G 15 FLOOR, TUNG SHING TERRACE, 39 BRIDGES STREET, CENTRAL, HONG KONG SAR.
TAN, Miss. Li-shien, ACA *2009;* 11 Magistrate's Walk, EAST MELBOURNE, VIC 3002, AUSTRALIA.
TAN, Miss. Mary Anne Siew Gek, ACA *1981;* 68 Bayshore Road, #23-06 Costa del Sol, SINGAPORE 469986, SINGAPORE.
TAN, Miss. Mavis Wee Gene, BSc ACA *2003;* 2C House 1, Aqua 33, 33 Consort Rise, POK FU LAM, HONG KONG ISLAND, HONG KONG SAR.
TAN, Mr. Meng Tze, MSc ACA *2005;* 34 Warriner Gardens, LONDON, SW11 4EB.
TAN, Mr. Meng Kiat, ACA *2008;* 50 Geylang Lorong 40, #04-50, SINGAPORE 398074, SINGAPORE.
TAN, Miss. Michelle Hwa Imm, BSc ACA *1993;* 23 Jalan Tebu, Ukay Heights, 68000 AMPANG, Selangor, MALAYSIA.
TAN, Mr. Nicholas Tsung Yuan, BEng ACA *1992;* with Deloitte & Touche, 35/F One Pacific Place, 88 Queensway, CENTRAL, HONG KONG ISLAND, HONG KONG SAR.
TAN, Mr. Peter Beng Teck, BA ACA *2010;* 197 Rotherhithe Street, LONDON, SE16 5QY.
TAN, Miss. Pey Jean, BSc ACA *2008;* Flat 20, 50 Kensington Gardens Square, LONDON, W2 4BA.
•**TAN, Miss. Phaik Leng, PhD BA FCA** *1989;* P.L. Tan, 80 Druid Stoke Avenue, Stoke Bishop, BRISTOL, BS9 1DQ.
TAN, Ms. Phaik-Lee, MSc ACA *1993;* 635 Kathleen Place, Westbury, NEW YORK, NY, 11590, UNITED STATES.
•**TAN, Mr. Phillip Eng Seong, FCA** *1974;* 25 Merryn Road, SINGAPORE S298473, SINGAPORE.
TAN, Mr. Poh Hock, ACA *1981;* No. 30 SS5B/5, Taman Seaport, 47301 PETALING JAYA, SELANGOR, MALAYSIA.
TAN, Mr. Poh Oon, ACA *1978;* Wan & Company, 16-2 Jalan 1/76D, Desa Pandan, 55100 KUALA LUMPUR, FEDERAL TERRITORY, MALAYSIA.
TAN, Miss. Pwee-Tjeng, ACA *1981;* 9 Brookfield Road, LONDON, W4 1DE.
TAN, Miss. Reina Chui-Lin, LLB ACA *2002;* Shepherds Building Central, Endermol Entertainment The Shepherds Building, Charecroft Way, LONDON, W14 0EE.
TAN, Mr. Richard Hiang-Tuck, BSc ACA *1993;* 20 Fordwich Hill, HERTFORD, SG14 2BQ.
TAN, Miss. Sarah Chia Ling, ACA *2008;* 1a Kingshill Avenue, ST. ALBANS, HERTFORDSHIRE, AL4 9QE.
TAN, Mr. Seng Choon, ACA *1996;* 6A Lincoln Road, #21-14 Park Infinia at Wee Nam, SINGAPORE 308366, SINGAPORE.
TAN, Mr. Seng Ngee, ACA *1980;* 2127 Dellesta Drive, BELLINGHAM, WA 98226, UNITED STATES.
TAN, Mr. Seng Teck, FCA *1976;* 16195 Promontory Rd, CHINO HILLS, CA 91709, UNITED STATES.
TAN, Miss. Seok Eng, FCA *1982;* 19 Carmen Street, SINGAPORE 459747, SINGAPORE.
TAN, Miss. Seok Eng Farahnaz, LLM ACA *1998;* 84 Three Colt Street, LONDON, E14 8AP.
TAN, Ms. Sharyn Peik Mun, BSc ACA *2005;* Winchester House, 1 Great Winchester Street, LONDON, EC2N 2DB.
TAN, Miss. Sheau Peng, BA ACA *2001;* 56 West Coast Crescent, #02-09 Westbay Condominium, SINGAPORE 128038, SINGAPORE.
TAN, Miss. Sheau Yen, FCA *1977;* 239 Arcadia Rd, #02-04, SINGAPORE 289845, SINGAPORE. (Life Member)
TAN, Miss. Shereen Suet Lin, BSc(Hons) ACA *2002;* 50 Jalan 1/149G, Taman Sri Endah, Bandar Baru, 57000 SRI PETALING, MALAYSIA.
TAN, Mr. Shian, BSc ACA *2009;* Ying Chuan East Hanningfield Road, Sandon, CHELMSFORD, CM2 7TQ.
TAN, Miss. Shir Ley, ACA *2010;* No. 10, Pengkalan Tiara 5, Taman Pengkalan Tiara, 31650 IPOH, MALAYSIA.
TAN, Miss. Shulin, ACA *2008;* 30 TAI HWAN HEIGHTS, SINGAPORE 555377, SINGAPORE.
TAN, Mr. Siang King, BSc ACA *2002;* 26A JALAN 19/144A, Taman Bukit Cheras, Cheras, 56000 KUALA LUMPUR, FEDERAL TERRITORY, MALAYSIA.
TAN, Miss. Siew Boi, BA ACA *1983;* 26H Shouson Hill Road, WONG CHUK HANG, HONG KONG ISLAND, HONG KONG SAR.
TAN, Mr. Siew Hiong, BSc ACA *1993;* B5-22 Menara Megah, Jalan Kolam Air, 51200 KUALA LUMPUR, FEDERAL TERRITORY, MALAYSIA.
TAN, Miss. Siew Tian, BSc ACA *1979;* 28 Norland Square, LONDON, W11 4PU.
TAN, Miss. Siong Cheng, BSc ACA *1982;* 32 Bampfylde Road, KUCHING, SARAWAK, MALAYSIA.
TAN, Ms. Song Ping, BSc ACA *1983;* Flat F10/F Pearl Gardens, 7 Conduit Road MID LEVELS, Hong Kong Island, HONG KONG SAR.
TAN, Mr. Soo Leong, ACA *1981;* 201 Tanjong Rhu Road, Apt 08-06 Parkshore, SINGAPORE 436917, SINGAPORE.
TAN, Mr. Soon Hoe, MSc BSc ACA *2006;* Suite 1308, 13F Two Pacific Place, 88 Queensway, ADMIRALTY, HONG KONG ISLAND, HONG KONG SAR.
TAN, Mr. Steven Chee Chuan, FCA CPA *1961;* Steven Tan Russell Bedford PAC, 25 International Business Park, #04 - 22/26 German Centre, SINGAPORE 609916, SINGAPORE. See also Steven Tan Pac
TAN, Miss. Suat Hwee, BA ACA *2000;* 18A Rosyth Road, SINGAPORE 546160, SINGAPORE.
TAN, Ms. Suet Lee, BSc ACA *1992;* 15 Jalan Ketumbit, SINGAPORE 808867, SINGAPORE.
TAN, Mr. Swan Jeng, FCA *1965;* 100 Ming Teck Park, SINGAPORE 277467, SINGAPORE.
TAN, Mr. Teck Lun, BEng ACA *2007;* One Raffles Quay, North Tower, #10-02, SINGAPORE 048583, SINGAPORE.
TAN, Miss. Tien Tien, ACA *2011;* Flat 11, Queens Mansions, Watford Way, LONDON, NW4 3AN.
TAN, Ms. Tin Hsien, BA FCA *1998;* c/o Goldman Sachs (Asia) LLC, 68/F Cheung Kong Centre, 2 Queens Road, CENTRAL, HONG KONG ISLAND, HONG KONG SAR.
TAN, Mr. Vincent Poh Hin, BA FCA *1983;* C/- Qatar Shell GTL Ltd, PO Box 3747, DOHA, QATAR.
TAN, Mrs. Viruna, BSc FCA *1992;* 5 Burntwood Road, SEVENOAKS, TN13 1PS.
TAN, Mr. Wah Yeow, FCA *1987;* KPMG LLP, 16 Raffles Quay, # 22-00, Hong Leong Building, SINGAPORE 048581, SINGAPORE.
TAN, Mr. Wai Kee, BSc FCA *1974;* 11 Bijou Hamlet, DISCOVERY BAY, NEW TERRITORIES, HONG KONG SAR. (Life Member)
TAN, Mr. Wee Khim, FCA *1979;* Tecity Group, 9 Battery Road, 09-01 Straits Trading Building, SINGAPORE 019910, SINGAPORE.
TAN, Miss. Wei Tze, BSc FCA *1999;* Flat E, 10/F Tower 2, 1 Austin Road, KOWLOON CITY, KOWLOON, HONG KONG SAR.
TAN, Miss. Wendy Khoon Pheng, BA ACA *1992;* Unit 9, 20 Ocean Avenue, Double Bay, SYDNEY, NSW 2028, AUSTRALIA.
TAN, Mr. Whye Seng Wilson, BA ACA *1992;* 1 SIGLAP GARDENS, SINGAPORE 456107, SINGAPORE.
TAN, Mr. Wooi Meng, FCA *1974;* 11 Jalan USJ 17/7B, 47630 SUBANG, SELANGOR, MALAYSIA.
TAN, Miss. Yan Ling, ACA *1993;* 93A Jalan Dedap Batik, Sierramas, 47000 SUNGAI BULOH, SELANGOR, MALAYSIA.
TAN, Mr. Yee Sing, ACA *1982;* 57 Burgundy Drive, SINGAPORE 658846, SINGAPORE.
TAN, Ms. Yi Ying, ACA *2009;* 217 Jalan Kiara Payong, Sierramas, 47000 SUNGAI BULOH, SELANGOR, MALAYSIA.
TAN, Miss. Yii Ting, BSc ACA *2000;* 1 Jalan SS2/38, 47300 PETALING JAYA, SELANGOR, MALAYSIA.
TAN-JONES, Miss. Li Yen, BA(Hons) ACA *2011;* 104 Times Square, LONDON, E1 8GE.
TANAKA, Miss. Mai, BSc(Econ) ACA *2001;* Flat 3, 94 Stapleton Hall Road, LONDON, N4 4QA.
TANAKOOR BHOGUN, Ms. Veerha, ACA ACCA *2004;* 1Deakin Place, WEST PENNANT HILLS, NSW 2125, AUSTRALIA.
TANCOCK, Mr. Colin David, BSc ACA *2005;* 17 Mora Street, LONDON, EC1V 8BT.
•①**TANCOCK, Mr. Stephen John, BA FCA** *1989;* Reeves & Co LLP, Montague Place, Quayside, Chatham Maritime, CHATHAM, KENT ME4 4QU.
TANDON, Mr. Manu, FCA *1970;* 16 Solitaire, 4 Samadhi Rd, Off Nagar Rd, PUNE 411006, MAHARASHTRA, INDIA.
TANDON, Mr. Rajat, BSc ACA *1993;* Deutsche Bank AG Singapore, One Raffles Quay 12th Floor, South Tower, SINGAPORE 048583, SINGAPORE.
TANDON, Miss. Sangeeta, BSc ACA *1997;* One Coleman Street, LONDON, EC2R 5AA.
TANDY, Mrs. Elizabeth Hilary, LLB ACA *1985;* Pathways, Crosemere Crescent, Crosemere, Cockshutt, ELLESMERE, SHROPSHIRE SY12 0JW.
TANDY, Mr. Michael John, FCA *1964;* The Hollows Farmhouse, Downton on the Rock, LUDLOW, SY8 2LJ.
TANDY, Mr. Nicholas Anthony James, MA ACA MCT *2000;* HSBC Global Markets, Level 18, HSBC Main Building, 1 Queens Road Central, CENTRAL, HONG KONG SAR.
TANEJA, Mr. Rajiv, ACA *1980;* I.J. Parkash Ltd, Pentex House, 30 Brunswick Street, MANCHESTER, M13 9TQ.
TANFIELD, Mr. Geoffrey, FCA *1970;* 15 Airedale Avenue, Tickhill, DONCASTER, SOUTH YORKSHIRE, DN11 9UD.
TANFIELD, Mrs. Gillian Christine, BA(Hons) ACA *2003;* 16 Dairy Lane, REDDITCH, WORCESTERSHIRE, B97 6TR.
TANFIELD, Mr. Graeme, BSc(Hons) ACA *2000;* Flat 4, 155 Endlesham Road, LONDON, SW12 8JN.
TANFIELD, Mr. Lawrence John Bryce, FCA *1970;* Clock House, Birchall Green, Sinton Green Hallow, WORCESTER, WR2 6NT.
TANFIELD, Mr. Stuart Richard, BA(Hons) ACA *2003;* 16 Dairy Lane, Brockhill, REDDITCH, WORCESTERSHIRE, B97 6TR.
TANG, Mr. Anthony Hoy Hoong, FCA *1975;* 56 Winton Crescent, Murarrie, BRISBANE, QLD 4172, AUSTRALIA.
TANG, Mr. Chee Kin, MBA MCMI ACA ACMA FRSA CPA MIBC *2006;* 10657 Pine Haven Terrace, ROCKVILLE, MD 20852, UNITED STATES.
TANG, Mr. Chi Fai, ACA *2005;* 24/F One Pacific Place, 88 Queensway, ADMIRALTY, HONG KONG ISLAND, HONG KONG SAR.
TANG, Mr. Chi Wai, ACA *2008;* Flat A 6/F Block 6, Villa Concerto, Symphony Bay, 530 Sai Sha Road, SAI KUNG, NEW TERRITORIES HONG KONG SAR.
TANG, Mr. Chin Wun, BSc ACA *1992;* (Tax Fac), The Taihon, 24 Ludlow Avenue, LUTON, LU1 3RW.
TANG, Mr. Chung Ping, BA ACA *1980;* 1A Wah Shing Ind Building, 18 Cheung Shun Street, CHEUNG SHA WAN, KOWLOON, HONG KONG SAR.
•**TANG, Mr. Chung Wah, MSc FCA** *1985;* 43/F The Lee Gardens, 33 Hysan Avenue, CAUSEWAY BAY, HONG KONG SAR.
TANG, Mr. Daniel Kong Hong, FCA *1974;* 14 Ownstead Gardens, Sanderstead, SOUTH CROYDON, SURREY, CR2 0HH.
TANG, Mr. Edmund Chee Yuen, BA ACA *1998;* 2 Compton Close, Cricklewood, LONDON, NW11 8SX.
TANG, Mr. Edmund Koon Kay, BSc FCA *1992;* 125 Arthur Road Apt 10-02, Arthur Mansions, SINGAPORE 439829, SINGAPORE.
TANG, Mr. Fook Weng, ACA *1979;* 60 / 37 Slobodian Avenue, EIGHT MILE PLAINS, QLD 4113, AUSTRALIA.
TANG, Mr. Gabriel Tuong Hock, ACA *1981;* 26c Lorong Crookshank 2A, Jalan Crookshank, 93000 KUCHING, SARAWAK, MALAYSIA.
TANG, Mr. George King Hung, ACA *1981;* PO Box 7908, GPO, CENTRAL, HONG KONG ISLAND, HONG KONG SAR.
TANG, Miss. Hei Ting Hilda, ACA *2011;* Block 418/FFlat A, City Garden, Electric Road, NORTH POINT, HONG KONG ISLAND, HONG KONG SAR.
TANG, Miss. Hoi Lin Helen, BA ACA CPA *1990;* Moore Stephens, 905 Silvercord, Tower 2, 30 Canton Road, TSIM SHA TSUI, KOWLOON HONG KONG SAR.
TANG, Miss. Hoi Yan Jennifer, BA ACA *2005;* Flat 110 Ability Place, 37 Millharbour, LONDON, E14 9HW.
TANG, Miss. Hong-Ling, BSc(Hons) ACA *2010;* Flat A 10/F Block 12, Villa Rhapsody, Symphony Bay, Sai Sha Road, Ma On Shan, SHA TIN NEW TERRITORIES HONG KONG SAR.
TANG, Mr. James Hing Bun, BA ACA *1988;* 21/F Manhattan Place, 23 Wang Tai Road, KOWLOON BAY, KOWLOON, HONG KONG SAR.
TANG, Miss. Jen Nee, BSc ACA *1999;* 1080 Boranda Avenue, MOUNTAIN VIEW, CA 94040, UNITED STATES.
TANG, Ms. Jenny Ching Lai, ACA *2006;* Flat A, 11/F Tower 1, The Regalia, 33 King's Park Rise, HO MAN TIN, KOWLOON HONG KONG SAR.
TANG, Mr. Jiunn-Man Matthew, BA ACA *2004;* Head Office Wetherspoons, Wetherspoon House Reeds Crescent, WATFORD, WD24 4QL.
TANG, Mr. Ka Siu Johnny, ACA *2007;* B1 8th Floor, Wisdom Court, 5 Hattan Road, MID LEVELS, HONG KONG ISLAND, HONG KONG SAR.
TANG, Mr. Kai Bond, ACA *2009;* 63 Armytage Road, Heston, HOUNSLOW, TW5 9JL.
TANG, Mr. Kim Ming, ACA *2007;* Room 3 28/F Block B, Sun Kwail Hing Garden, 163 Tai Wo Hau Road, KWAI CHUNG, KOWLOON, HONG KONG SAR.
TANG, Mr. Kin Wa Randolph, ACA *2008;* Flat A11/F, Block 7, Provident Centre, Wharf Road, NORTH POINT, HONG KONG ISLAND HONG KONG SAR.
TANG, Mr. Kok Kwai, BCom ACA *1980;* 70 Palmer Road, #02-03 Palmer House, SINGAPORE 079427, SINGAPORE.
TANG, Mr. Koon Chiu Framton, ACA *2007;* Flat 3 22/F Block B, Kin Kwun Mansion, 395 King's Road, NORTH POINT, HONG KONG SAR.
TANG, Ms. Kwan Lai, ACA *2008;* 13/F Flat 16, Block E, Kam Fung Court, Ma On Shan, SHA TIN, NEW TERRITORIES HONG KONG SAR.
TANG, Ms. Lai Yee, ACA *2007;* Flat D 33rd floor Tower 2, Grand Promenade, 38 Tai Hong Street, SAI WAN HO, HONG KONG ISLAND, HONG KONG SAR.
•**TANG, Mr. Long-Sing Raymond, BSc ACA** *1990;* (Tax Fac), Tang & Co, Flat D 5th Floor Block 13, Pristine Villa 18 Pak Lok Path, Tai Wai, SHA TIN, NEW TERRITORIES HONG KONG SAR.
TANG, Miss. Loren Gertrud Yuen Yee, MSc ACA *1997;* KPMG, 8/F Prince's Building, 10 Chater Road, CENTRAL, HONG KONG ISLAND, HONG KONG SAR.
TANG, Miss. Louisa Wing Hung, BSc ACA *2008;* Flat 9A Block 14 Braemar Hill Mansions 41 Braemar Hill Road, NORTH POINT, HONG KONG SAR.
TANG, Mr. Man Chung John, ACA *2008;* Room 9-11, 16/F Tai Yau Building, WAN CHAI, HONG KONG ISLAND, HONG KONG SAR.
TANG, Ms. Man Yi, ACA *2008;* Flat H 3/F, Block 4 Lok Hin Terrace, 350 Chai Wan Road, CHAI WAN, HONG KONG SAR.
TANG, Mr. Michael Sek Leong, MBA BA FCA *1982;* Deutsche Bank, Winchester House, 1 Great Winchester Street, LONDON, EC2N 2DB.

TANG, Mr. Nelson Ka Ming, ACA *2006;* Flat A, 11/F Tower 1, The Regalia, 33 King's Park Rise, HO MAN TIN, KOWLOON HONG KONG SAR.
TANG, Mr. Piu Hung, ACA *2008;* P H Tang & Co, 3rd Floor, Rammon House, 101 Sai Yeung Choi Street South, MONG KOK, KOWLOON HONG KONG SAR.
TANG, Mr. Po Yuen, BSc ACA *1988;* Flat 78 Edge Hill Court, Edge Hill, Wimbledon, LONDON, SW19 4LW.
TANG, Mr. Raymond, ACA *2007;* c/o Atico International (HK) Ltd, G/F - 2/F, Hung Hom Bay Centre, 22 - 24 Hung Hom Wan Street, HUNG HOM, KOWLOON HONG KONG SAR.
TANG, Mr. Raymond Suk Ngao, BSc ACA *1991;* Flat 906 Block A, Peninsula Heights, 63 Broadcast Drive, KOWLOON TONG, KOWLOON, HONG KONG SAR.
•TANG, Mr. Renold Lee On, BSc FCA *1984;* (Tax Fac), TBW, E3 The Premier Centre, Abbey Park, ROMSEY, SO51 9DG.
TANG, Miss. Rosalind Lo Lin, BSc ACA *1991;* 20 Westport Road, WILTON, CT 06897, UNITED STATES.
TANG, Dr. See Wah, PhD ACA *2010;* 6 Horace Road, LONDON, E7 0JG.
TANG, Mr. Seng Choon, ACA *2010;* with BDO, 12th Floor Menara Uni. Asia, Jalan sultan Ismail, 50250 KUALA LUMPUR, FEDERAL TERRITORY, MALAYSIA.
TANG, Mr. Shu Lun, ACA *2005;* Unit 1005 10/F, Tower B, Hunghom Commercial Centre, 37 Ma Tau Wai Road, HUNG HOM, KOWLOON HONG KONG SAR.
TANG, Mr. Siaw Hung, FCA *1970;* 2596 Westhill Way, WEST VANCOUVER V7S 3E4, BC, CANADA.
TANG, Mr. Simon Chee Wai, BSc(Econ) ACA *2009;* Apartment 21, New Gothic Lodge, 1 Old Devonshire Road, LONDON, SW12 9RE.
TANG, Ms. Siu Ping, ACA *2007;* Unit F 31 Floor Tower 1, Ocean Shores, Tiu Keng Leng, TSEUNG KWAN O, KOWLOON, HONG KONG SAR.
TANG, Ms. So Sen Susan, BSc ACA *1997;* 59 St Lawrence Road, UPMINSTER, RM14 2UN.
TANG, Mrs. Sonali, ACA *1993;* 121 Sunset Way, #05-01, Clementi Park, SINGAPORE 597153, SINGAPORE.
TANG, Miss. Stephanie Yen Chin, BSc ACA *1992;* 111 West 16th St Apt. 4A, NEW YORK, NY 10011, UNITED STATES.
TANG, Mr. Sui Pan Ivan, ACA *2009;* Flat 86 Ionian Building, 45 Narrow Street, LONDON, E14 8DW.
TANG, Mr. Tay Boon, BA ACA *1988;* 12 Jln Bagan 39, Taman Bagan, 13400 BUTTERWORTH, MALAYSIA.
•TANG, Mr. Thomas Wing Yung, BSc ACA *1981;* Sino Land Company Limited, 12/F Tsim Saa Tsui Centre, Salisbury Road, TSIM SHA TSUI, KOWLOON, HONG KONG SAR.
TANG, Mr. Tze-Hong, MA ACA *1993;* Flat A 11/F Tower 1, Grand Pacific Views, Palatial Coast, Castle Peak Road, TUEN MUN, NEW TERRITORIES HONG KONG SAR.
TANG, Ms. Vanessa San Yuit, BSc ACA *1984;* KHL Printing Co PTE Ltd, 57 Loyang Drive, SINGAPORE 508968, SINGAPORE.
TANG, Miss. Wai Ha, BEd ACA *1992;* Flat E 23rd Floor, Greenery Court, Discovery Bay, LANTAU ISLAND, NEW TERRITORIES, HONG KONG SAR.
TANG, Miss. Wai Yue Winnie, BA FCA *1980;* 10 Stewart Terrace, 87 Peak Road, THE PEAK, Hong Kong Island, HONG KONG SAR.
TANG, Ms. Wai Yan Shirley, ACA *2008;* Flat B 1/F Tower 2, Ocean Shores, 88 O King Road, TSEUNG KWAN O, KOWLOON, HONG KONG SAR.
TANG, Mr. Wallace Sui Hei, ACA *2009;* 5B Tower 2 Aquamarine, LAI CHI KOK, HONG KONG SAR.
TANG, Mr. William, BSc ACA *1993;* One Beacon Hill, Tower 9 Flat 1C, 1 Beacon Hill Road, KOWLOON TONG, KOWLOON, HONG KONG SAR.
TANG, Mr. Wing Fai, ACA BEng(Hons) *2010;* 77 G/F Ma Mei Ha Village, FANLING, NEW TERRITORIES, HONG KONG SAR.
TANG, Mrs. Xue Mei, ACA CPA *2010;* Room 2708, Building No. 55, Hu Bin Bei Road, XIAMEN 361000, FUJIAN PROVINCE, CHINA.
TANG, Mr. Yau Sing Gareth, ACA *2005;* Suites 31-35, 24F sun Hung Kai Centre, 30 Harbour Road, WAN CHAI, HONG KONG SAR.
TANG, Mr. Yu Ping, ACA *2008;* Flat 5A, 33 Broadcast Drive, KOWLOON TONG, KOWLOON, HONG KONG SAR.
TANG, Mrs. Yuen Man Ginda, BA FCA *1987;* Flat 11 Clarendon Court, 20 Eastbury Avenue, NORTHWOOD, MIDDLESEX, HA6 3LN.
TANG, Mr. Yuen Shun, ACA *2005;* c/o Cree Asia Pacific Limited, Unit 301, 3/F, Photonics Centre, 2 Science Park East Avenue, HONG KONG SAR Science Park SHA TIN HONG KONG SAR. See also Tang Yuen Shun
TANG KOON CHEONG, Mr. King Tat, FCA *1979;* Kong Ltd, 47 Royal Road, MAHEBOURG, MAURITIUS.
TANGRI, Mr. Abhishek, BSc ACA *2005;* 37 Gunnersbury Way, Nuthall, NOTTINGHAM, NG16 1QD.
TANGRI, Mr. Kumar, BSc ACA *1995;* Financial Services Authority, 25 North Colonnade, LONDON, E14 5HS.
TANIGUCHI, Miss. Hiromi, ACA *1993;* 9 Hanover Avenue, Britannia Village, Royal Victoria Docks, LONDON, E16 1SD.
TANJANIKA, Miss. Helmy, BAcc ACA *2004;* 203c Compassvale, RD No. 03-31, SINGAPORE 543203, SINGAPORE.
TANKARIA, Mr. Rajesh, BA ACA *1998;* A S R Estates, 100 College Road, HARROW, MIDDLESEX, HA1 1BQ.
TANKEL, Mrs. Michele Alison, ACA *1982;* 69 College Cross, Islington, LONDON, N1 1PT.
TANN, Mr. Alan Kenneth George, BSc FCA *1977;* Fox Farm, Raydon, IPSWICH, IP7 5QL.
TANN, Mrs. Hilary Jane, FCA *1977;* Vincent House, Brough, Bradwell, HOPE VALLEY, S33 9HG.
TANN, Mr. Kenneth Edward, FCA *1957;* 75 Love Lane, RAYLEIGH, SS6 7DX. (Life Member)
TANN, Mr. Richard Walter, BA FCA *1964;* 83 Gunterstone Road, LONDON, W14 9BT. (Life Member)
TANNA, Mr. Anil, FCA *1973;* 149 Albury Drive, PINNER, HA5 3RH.
TANNA, Mr. Bhavanesh Chhaganlal, FCA *1980;* 7 Lynde Court, WHITBY L1N 3H6, ON, CANADA.
TANNA, Mr. Biharilal Keshavji, FCA *1965;* PO Box 948, DAR ES SALAAM, TANZANIA.
TANNA, Mr. Davendra Prabhudas, BA ACA *1998;* 41 Richmond Drive, WATFORD, WD17 3BQ.
•TANNA, Mr. Dilip Pranjivanbhai, FCA *1980;* Tanna & Co., 6 Ravenscroft Avenue, WEMBLEY, MIDDLESEX, HA9 9TL.
•TANNA, Miss. Dipika Chandulal, BSc FCA *1986;* D. Tanna & Co, 32 Berry Hill, STANMORE, MIDDLESEX, HA7 4XS.
TANNA, Mr. Hasmukh G, ACA *1981;* Sheldon House, 1 Lunsford Road, LEICESTER, LEICESTERSHIRE, LE5 0HH.
•TANNA, Mr. Kirtikumar Bhagwanji, FCA *1978;* D'Auria Quick & Tanna, Antonia House, 262 Holloway Road, LONDON, N7 6NG.
TANNA, Mr. Mitesh, BSc(Hons) ACA *2002;* 149 Shenley Road, Bletchley, MILTON KEYNES, MK3 7AR.
TANNA, Miss. Niladevi Velji, FCA *1975;* 9 White Craig Close, PINNER, MIDDLESEX, HA5 4AQ.
•TANNA, Mr. Piyush Jayantilal, BSc FCA *1990;* (Tax Fac), Magus, 140 Buckingham Palace Road, LONDON, SW1W 9SA.
TANNA, Mr. Prakash, BSc ACA *1982;* 66 Yorkminster Road, TORONTO M2P 1M3, ON, CANADA.
•TANNA, Mr. Pratap, ACA *1980;* Tanna & Co., 13 Sheaveshill Parade, Sheaveshill Avenue, LONDON, NW9 6RS.
TANNA, Mr. Shashikant Jamnadas, BSc FCA *1975;* 16 Southfield Way, ST. ALBANS, AL4 9JJ.
•TANNA, Mr. Sudhir Amratlal, ACA *1981;* Burleys (Midlands) LLP, Unit 9 St Matthew's Business Centre, Gower Street, LEICESTER, LEICESTERSHIRE, LE1 3LJ.
TANNA, Mr. Sunil, BSc ACA *2001;* (Tax Fac), 2 Covington Gardens, LONDON, SW16 3SE.
TANNA, Mr. Sunil Chandulal, BSc ACA *2009;* with PricewaterhouseCoopers LLP, Hays Galleria, 1 Hays Lane, LONDON, SE1 2RD.
TANNA, Mr. Sureshchandra Velji, BSc FCA *1977;* Nakasero Soapworks, P O Box 218, KAMPALA, UGANDA.
•TANNA, Mr. Vikash, BSc ACA *1996;* Knights & Company (Hampton) Limited, 280 Cooden Drive, BEXHILL-ON-SEA, EAST SUSSEX, TN39 3AB.
TANNA, Mr. Vinaykant Gordhandas, BSocSc FCA *1986;* 51 Thornhill Road, Ickenham, UXBRIDGE, UB10 8SQ.
TANNAHILL, Mr. Richard Quentin Philip, ACA *1980;* 11 Hawkewood Road, SUNBURY-ON-THAMES, MIDDLESEX, TW16 6HL.
TANNAHILL, Mr. William Boyd, BAcc ACA *2007;* 10 The Chequers, Hale, ALTRINCHAM, CHESHIRE, WA15 8ZL.
TANNEN, Mr. Hyman, BA FCA *1965;* Flat 9 Harcourt, 15 Derby Road, BOURNEMOUTH, DORSET, BH1 3PZ. (Life Member)
TANNER, Mr. Alexander John, BSc FCA *1977;* 11 Burses Way, Hutton, BRENTWOOD, Essex, CM13 2PL.
TANNER, Mr. Alistair James, BA ACA *1999;* 48 Westwood Avenue, Timperley, ALTRINCHAM, WA15 6QF.
TANNER, Mr. Brian Charles, FCA *1965;* The Gate House, Corston, BATH, BA2 9AN. (Life Member)
TANNER, Mr. Christopher James, BA ACA *1999;* 22 Aden Grove, LONDON, N16 9NJ.
•TANNER, Mr. Christopher John, BSc FCA *1973;* C.J. Tanner, 6 Rose Hill, DORKING, SURREY, RH4 2EG.
TANNER, Mr. David Anthony, FCA *1986;* 17 Windsor Road, DOVER, MA 02030, UNITED STATES.
TANNER, Mrs. Dawn, BSc ACA *1991;* 16 Beadon Road, BROMLEY, BR2 9AT.
TANNER, Mr. Dudley John Raymond, BSc FCA *1979;* CP394A Mealhas, 8150 SAO BRAS DE ALPORTEL, ALGARVE, PORTUGAL.
TANNER, Mr. Edward Ismar, FCA *1959;* 22 Cumberland Terrace, Regents Park, LONDON, NW1 4HP. (Life Member)
TANNER, Mr. Gareth John, LLB ACA CTA *2000;* Deloitte Tax LLP, 111 S Wacker Drive, CHICAGO, IL 60606, UNITED STATES.
TANNER, Mr. Graham John, MChem ACA *2005;* 13 Admiral Place, LONDON, SE16 5NY.
TANNER, Mr. Harvey Lewis, BA ACA CTA *2003;* linear park, avon street, BRISTOL, bs2 0ps.
•TANNER, Mr. Henry John, FCA *1983;* (Tax Fac), Streets, The Railway Station, Green Road, NEWMARKET, SUFFOLK, CB8 9WT. See also Streets Whitmarsh Sterland
TANNER, Mr. Hugh Philip, ACA *2008;* 1 Spring Gardens, WEST MOLESEY, KT8 2JA.
TANNER, Mr. Joseph, BA ACA *2007;* General Motors, Griffin House, Osborne Road, LUTON, LU1 3YT.
•TANNER, Mr. Kevin Peter, ACA *1985;* K P Tanner Limited, 3-4 Westbourne Grove, HOVE, EAST SUSSEX, BN3 5PL. See also Westbournes Limited
•TANNER, Mr. Laurence John, BSc ACA *1981;* Laurence Tanner, 9 Grove Way, ESHER, KT10 8HH.
TANNER, Mr. Matthew Colenso, ACA *2010;* Flat 3 Whitehouse Court, 38b Foxgrove Road, BECKENHAM, BR3 5BD.
TANNER, Mr. Michael Leslie John, FCA *1958;* Flat 33, Fairburn Court, St. John's Avenue, LONDON, SW15 2AU. (Life Member)
TANNER, Mrs. Paula, LLB ACA *1998;* 48 Westwood Avenue, Timperley, ALTRINCHAM, CHESHIRE, WA15 6QF.
TANNER, Mr. Phillip John, FCA *1975;* Shilling House, High Street, West Lydford, SOMERTON, SOMERSET, TA11 7DB.
TANNER, Mr. Richard Curnow, MA ACA *1989;* 26 Cassiobury Park Avenue, WATFORD, WD18 7LB.
TANNER, Mr. Richard Howard John, BA FCA *1991;* with Lathe Investments LLP, The Brewery, Bells Yew Green, TUNBRIDGE WELLS, KENT, TN3 9BD.
•TANNER, Mr. Stephen Paul, BSc(Econ) FCA *1987;* (Tax Fac), Reeves & Co LLP, Third Floor, 24 Chiswell Street, LONDON, EC1Y 4YX.
TANNER, Mr. William Charles, FCA *1971;* Stubbings, Tremeer Lane, St. Tudy, BODMIN, PL30 3NF. (Life Member)
TANNETT, Mr. William Morton, FCA *1968;* 49 Little Gaddesden, BERKHAMSTED, HP4 1PL.
TANNEY, Miss. Clare, BA ACA *1998;* 377 Durham Road, GATESHEAD, TYNE AND WEAR, NE9 5AL.
TANNIAN, Mr. Adrian, MPhil BA ACA *1991;* 55 Wolfpit Avenue, NORWALK, CT 06851, UNITED STATES.
TANSELL, Mrs. Elizabeth, BSc ACA *1989;* Third Floor Exchange House, 54-62 Athol Street, Douglas, ISLE OF MAN, IM1 1JD.
TANSEY, Mr. Glenn, BSc ACA *1993;* 60 Netherwood Road, LONDON, W14 0BG.
TANSEY, Mr. Philip, BSc FCA *1985;* B G C, 1 Churchill Place, LONDON, E14 5RD.
•TANSLEY, Mr. David Shelton, FCA *1976;* Sinnett & Tansley Limited, 3 Richfield Place, Richfield Avenue, READING, RG1 8EQ.
TANSLEY, Ms. Emma Jane, BSc ACA *1998;* 50 Cecil Road, LONDON, N10 2BU.
TANSLEY, Mr. Graham, FCA *1974;* National Construction College, Bircham Newton, KING'S LYNN, NORFOLK, PE31 6RH.
TANSLEY, Mr. Jonathan Joseph, ACA *2008;* The Carphone Warehouse, 1 Portal Way, LONDON, W3 6RS.
TANT, Mr. Oliver Reginald, CA *2009;* Scotland 1986); KPMG LLP, 15 Canada Square, LONDON, E14 5GL. See also KPMG Europe LLP, KPMG Audit plc
TANT, Mr. Paul James, BA ACA DChA *1991;* London Rebuilding Society Floor 1, 9 Bonhill Street, LONDON, EC2A 4PE.
TANTER, Mr. John Bruce, MA ACA CTA *1999;* 59 Greenend Road, LONDON, W4 1AH.
TANWIR, Mr. Zulfiqar, BSc ACA *2002;* 5 Fitzwilliam Avenue, RICHMOND, TW9 2DQ.
TAO, Miss. Connie, BSc ACA *2011;* 2 Brasted Close, Belmont, SUTTON, SURREY, SM2 5BE.
TAO, Mr. Lei, ACA *2008;* PricewaterhouseCoopers LLP, 8 Cross Street #17-00, PwC Building, SINGAPORE 048424, SINGAPORE.
TAO, Miss. Meng, ACA *2008;* Flat 45, 17 Fawe Street, LONDON, E14 6FD.
TAO, Mr. Sam, ACA *2009;* 2 Brasted Close, SUTTON, SURREY, SM2 5BE.
TAO, Mr. Yiran, ACA *2011;* 6 Bridge House Quay, LONDON, E14 9QW.
TAPARIA, Mr. Mihir, FCA *1979;* PT Trans-Pacific Petrochemical, Indotama, Midplaza 2 Bldg Flr 21, Jl Jend Sudirman Kav 10-11, JAKARTA, 10220 INDONESIA.
•TAPARIA, Mr. Sudhir, FCA *1987;* Taparia Consultants Limited, Taparia House, 1096 Uxbridge Road, HAYES, MIDDLESEX, UB4 8QH.
TAPLEY, Mr. Nicholas Rex, BA FCA *1991;* Brook Cottage La Vallee, Alderney, GUERNSEY, GY9 3XA.
TAPLEY, Miss. Pia, ACA *2010;* Top Floor Apartment, 6 Maiden Lane, LONDON, WC2E 7ND.
TAPLEY, Mr. William Richard, FCA *1968;* Greystones, 323 Chartridge Lane, CHESHAM, HP5 2SQ.
TAPLIN, Mr. Andrew Jeremy, MA FCA *1978;* 1 Ter rue du Faubourg Saint Jean, 42600 MONTBRISON, FRANCE.
TAPLIN, Mrs. Clare Louise, BSc(Econ) ACA *2000;* 2 Kirkstone Walk, NUNEATON, WARWICKSHIRE, CV11 6EZ.
TAPLIN, Mr. Ian Richard, BSc FCA *1990;* 67 Chantry Road, Moseley, BIRMINGHAM, B13 8DN.
•TAPLIN, Mr. Ian William Charles, MA LLB ACA *1982;* Rosevine, Wellgreen Lane, Kingston, LEWES, EAST SUSSEX, BN7 3NS.
TAPLIN, Mr. James Arthur, BA(Hons) ACA *2000;* 2 Kirkstone Walk, NUNEATON, CV11 6EZ.
•TAPNACK, Mr. David Ian, BSc ACA *2002;* PricewaterhouseCoopers LLP, 7 More London Riverside, LONDON, SE1 2RT. See also PricewaterhouseCoopers
•TAPP, Mr. Alexander Charles David, BA ACA *1997;* BDO LLP, 55 Baker Street, LONDON, W1U 7EU. See also BDO Stoy Hayward LLP
TAPP, Mrs. Katharine Anne, BA(Hons) ACA *2001;* R S M Tenon Davidson House, The Forbury, READING, RG1 3EU.
TAPP, Mr. Paul William James, BSc ARCS ACA *1993;* 3 Cheriswood Close, EXMOUTH, DEVON, EX8 4DZ.
TAPP, Miss. Vanessa Clare, MA(Hons) ACA *2009;* Pricewaterhousecoopers, 1 Embankment Place, LONDON, WC2N 6RH.
TAPPENDEN, Mr. Benjamin, BA(Hons) ACA *2010;* 50 Weller Avenue, ROCHESTER, KENT, ME1 2LG.
TAPPER, Mr. James Edward, BSc ACA *1993;* 6 Tall Trees, Baunton Lane, CIRENCESTER, GLOUCESTERSHIRE, GL7 2AF.
TAPPER, The Revd. John A'court, FCA *1965;* Mill Cottage, Mill Lane, Sissinghurst, CRANBROOK, KENT, TN17 2HX.
TAPPER, Mr. Paul James, BSc ACA *1990;* Egret Management LLP, S G House, 41 Tower Hill, LONDON, EC3N 4SG.
TAPPERN, Mrs. Nicola Susan, BA(Hons) ACA *2001;* 4 Ffosyceilog, Llannon, LLANELLI, DYFED, SA14 6AB.
•TAPPIN, Mr. Andrew Brice, FCA *1967;* (Tax Fac), Andrew B Tappin, 18 East Sheen Avenue, LONDON, SW14 8AS.
TAPPIN, Christopher John, Esq CBE FCA *1959;* Wagers Court, Charlton Kings, CHELTENHAM, GL53 8QG. (Life Member)
TAPPIN, Miss. Sara, BSc ACA *2009;* with Begbies Traynor, Glendevon House, Hawthorn Park, Coal Road, LEEDS, LS14 1PQ.
TAPPING, Mrs. Adele, BSc ACA *1988;* Fairycroft, Rose Lane, Great Chesterford, SAFFRON WALDEN, CB10 1PN.
•TAPPING, Mr. Guy Mark, BSc ACA *1987;* GT Management Consultancy Limited, 19 Cheriton Avenue, BOURNEMOUTH, BH7 6SD.
TAPPING, Mr. Steven Donald Murray, MA ACA *1985;* Fairy Croft, Rose Lane, Great Chesterford, SAFFRON WALDEN, CB10 1PN.
TAPSON, Mr. Andrew Michael Ebsworthy, BSc ACA *1984;* 7 Ashdown Road, EPSOM, KT17 3PL.
TARA, Mr. Ravi Singh, BSc ACA *2006;* 118 Harrowgate Drive, Birstall, LEICESTER, LE4 3GP.

TARACHAND, Mrs. Lilawattee, ACA FCMA *2009;* with BDO De Chazal du Mee, P.O. Box 799, 10 Frere Felix, De Valois Street, PORT LOUIS, MAURITIUS.
TARAKANOV, Mr. Evgeny, ACA *2009;* 16 Makedonitissis Street flat 104, Strovolos, 2058 NICOSIA, CYPRUS.
•**TARAMIDES, Mr. Agis, MSc ACA** *2002;* Cor Limited, 1 Lampousas Street, 1095 NICOSIA, CYPRUS.
•**TARAZ, Mr. Afshin, MSc BA FCA** *1976;* (Tax Fac), Thompson Taraz LLP, 35 Grosvenor Street, Mayfair, LONDON, W1K 4QX.
•**TARBARD, Mr. Christopher John, FCA** *1974;* (Tax Fac), AIMS - Chris Tarbard, 5 Huxley Close, MACCLESFIELD, SK10 3DG.
TARBATT, Mr. Richard John, BA ACA *1994;* Ashover Business Centre Matlock Road, Kelstedge Ashover, CHESTERFIELD, DERBYSHIRE, S45 0DX.
TARBIT, Mr. Andrew James, ACA *2010;* Flat 8, Baring Court, Baring Street, LONDON, N1 3DR.
TARBIT, Miss. Pamela, BSc(Hons) ACA *2010;* 33 Harborough Road, LONDON, SW16 2XP.
TARBOTTON, Mr. Robert, FCA *1980;* Pine View, 1 Greenways, NORTH FERRIBY, NORTH HUMBERSIDE, HU14 3JN.
TARBUCK, Mrs. Donna Rachel, BA ACA *1993;* Black Horse Cottage, The Street, Swannington, NORWICH, NR9 5NW.
TARBUCK, Mr. Shaun Roger, ACA *1987;* 12 Rivershill Gardens, Halebarns, ALTRINCHAM, WA15 0AZ.
•**TARBUN, Mr. Philip James, ACA** *2008;* Tarbun & Company Limited, 10 Bishopdale Close, MORECAMBE, LANCASHIRE, LA3 3SU.
TAREEN, Mr. Tayyab Ahmad, ACA *1994;* Abraaj Capital Limited, 3rd floor, Gate Village 8, DIFC, DUBAI, 504905 UNITED ARAB EMIRATES.
TAREV, Mr. Alexei, BSc ACA *2011;* ZAO KPMG, Naberezhnaya Tower Complex, Block C, 10 Presnenskaya Naberezhnaya, 123317 MOSCOW, RUSSIAN FEDERATION.
TARGETT, Mr. Colin Paul, BEng ACA *1997;* Standard Bank Offshore, PO Box 583, JERSEY, JE4 8XR.
TARGETT, Mr. Neil John, MSci FCA *2000;* 23 Northcote Road, TWICKENHAM, TW1 1PB.
TARGETT, Mrs. Rachel Louise, BA ACA *1998;* 23 Northcote Road, St Margarets, TWICKENHAM, TW1 1PB.
TARIMO, Mr. David Timothy, LLB FCA ATII *1990;* PricewaterhouseCoopers, International House, Garden Avenue, PO Box 45, DAR ES SALAAM, TANZANIA.
TARIMO, Mr. Philip William, BSc ACA CF *1997;* 67 Swann Lane, Cheadle Hulme, CHEADLE, CHESHIRE, SK8 7HU.
TARIN, Mr. Jalil-Ur-Rehman, FCA *1975;* 87/II Khayaban-E-Shujjat, DHA VI, KARACHI, PAKISTAN. (Life Member)
TARIQ, Mr. Ali, BA ACA *2000;* Unilever Asia Pte Ltd, 20 Pasir Panjang Road, #06-22 Mapletree Business City, SINGAPORE 117439, SINGAPORE.
TARKANYI, Mr. John Leslie, BSc ACA *1984;* 42 Oakleigh Close, Backwell, BRISTOL, BS48 3JU.
TARLETON, Miss. Lucy Constance, BA ACA *2005;* 103a Oakhill Road, Putney, LONDON, SW15 2QL.
TARLING, Mrs. Jacqueline Claire, ACA *2001;* Corbis UK Ltd, 111 Salusbury Road, LONDON, NW6 6RG.
TARLING, Mr. Richard Ian, BSc ACA *1998;* Thomson Reuters Ltd Aldgate House, 33 Aldgate High Street, LONDON, EC3N 1DL.
TARLING, Mr. Stephen Carl, MA ACA *2002;* 143 Grovely Terrace, BRISBANE, QLD 4053, AUSTRALIA.
TARLTON, Ms. Polly, BA ACA *2003;* 81 Mallinson Road, Battersea, LONDON, SW11 1BW.
TARN, Mr. Nicholas James, BSc ACA *1990;* 64 Park Hill, Carshalton Beeches, CARSHALTON, SM5 3RZ.
•**TARN, Mr. Robert, FCA** *1981;* Addison & Co (Teesdale) Limited, Ebor House, 91 Galgate, BARNARD CASTLE, COUNTY DURHAM, DL12 8ES.
TARN, Mr. Stephen Ian, FCA *1958;* The Covey Chattisham Road, Washbrook, IPSWICH, IP8 3HB. (Life Member)
TARN, Mrs. Tara, ACA *2002;* Sunnycrest, High Lands, Cockfield, BISHOP AUCKLAND, COUNTY DURHAM, DL13 5AR.
TARPLEE, Mrs. Marion Eileen, BSc ACA *1988;* Rosenhuset, 4 Livingstone Close, CRANLEIGH, SURREY, GU6 7NX.
TARR, Miss. Elizabeth Ann, ACA *2010;* 3 Seymour Road, KINGSTON UPON THAMES, KT1 4HN.
TARR, Mr. Gareth Duncan, BSc ACA *1984;* 23 Jersey Close, CHERTSEY, KT16 9PA.
•**TARR, Mr. Geoffrey Henry, FCA** *1972;* Griffin Chapman, Blackburn House, 32a Crouch Street, COLCHESTER, CO3 3HH.
TARR, Mrs. Heather Catherine, BA ACA *1989;* 39 Woodville Drive, PORTSMOUTH, PO1 2TQ.
TARR, Mr. Henry, BA ACA *2005;* 59 Hambalt Road, LONDON, SW4 9EQ.
TARR, Mrs. Natalie Ann, BSc ACA *2007;* with PricewaterhouseCoopers LLP, 31 Great George Street, BRISTOL, BS1 5QD.
•**TARR, Mr. Richard Laurence, FCA** *1976;* Richard Tarr & Co, Wood Park, East Down, BARNSTAPLE, EX31 4LZ.
TARR, Mr. Simon Charles Vaughan, BA ACA *1996;* People 1st, Second Floor, Armstrong House, 38 Market Square, UXBRIDGE, MIDDLESEX UB8 1LH.
TARR, Mr. Steven John, BSc ACA *2000;* 14 Blaisedell View, BRISTOL, BS10 7XB.
TARR, Mrs. Susan Jane, BSc ACA *1986;* 67 Ellis Peters Drive, TELFORD, SHROPSHIRE, TF3 1AW.
•**TARRAGANO, Mr. Morris, BSocSc ACA** *1992;* Link Kaplan Limited, 166 Upper Richmond Road, LONDON, SW15 2SH.
TARRAN, Mr. John, FCA *1953;* 119 The Chantry, HARLOW, ESSEX, CM20 2NA. (Life Member)
TARRAN, Mr. Michael John, BA ACA *1999;* 100 Pottersville Road, Apt 3 Caretakers Cottage, CHESTER, NJ 07930, UNITED STATES.
TARRAN, Mr. Paul James, BSc FCA *1980;* 54 Chapel Hill, STANSTED, ESSEX, CM24 8AQ.
TARRANT, Mrs. Charlotte Kate, BA ACA *1995;* Modern Plant Hire Ltd, 6 Somers Road, RUGBY, WARWICKSHIRE, CV22 7DE.
TARRANT, Mr. Christopher Gerard, BA ACA *1990;* 12 Repton Ave, Denton, MANCHESTER, M34 2LD.
TARRANT, Mr. David Desmond, FCA *1966;* 246/2 Tonglor 8, Sukhumvit Soi 55, BANGKOK, 10110, THAILAND. (Life Member)
TARRANT, Mr. Edmund John, BSc ACA *1996;* with Whyatt Pakeman Partners, Colkin House, 16 Oakfield Rd, Clifton, BRISTOL, BS8 2AP.
TARRANT, Miss. Emma Louise, BSc ACA *2010;* Flat 6, 74 Branston Street, BIRMINGHAM, B18 6BP.
TARRANT, Mr. Jeremy Bertram Gordon, BSc FCA *1981;* 58 Glasslyn Road, LONDON, N8 8RH.
TARRANT, Mr. John Michael, BSc ACA *1995;* Modern Plant Hire, 6 Somers Road, RUGBY, WARWICKSHIRE, CV22 7DE.
TARRANT, Mr. Lindsay Esmond, MA FCA *1991;* with RSM Tenon Audit Limited, 2 Wellington Place, LEEDS, LS1 4AP.
•**TARRANT, Mr. Michael Francis, FCA** *1966;* Michael Tarrant, 22 Updown Hill, HAYWARDS HEATH, WEST SUSSEX, RH16 4GD.
TARRANT, Mr. Michael Hastings, MA ACA *1982;* Cradle House Farm, Wigginton, BANBURY, OX15 4LF.
TARRANT, Mr. Nicholas, ACA *1986;* Ball Baker Leake LLC, 122 East 42nd Street #810, NEW YORK, NY 10168, UNITED STATES.
TARRANT, Mrs. Oonagh, BA ACA *1991;* 58 Glasslyn Road, Crouch End, LONDON, N8 8RH.
TARRANT, Mr. Robert Frank, BA FCA *1979;* 23 Tangmere, Harrison St, LONDON, WC1H 8JJ.
TARRANT, Mr. Robert George, BCom FCA *1988;* Meadow Hill, 90 Lower Street, Salhouse, NORWICH, NR13 6AD.
TARRANT, Mr. Stuart Stanley, FCA *1965;* Appletree Cottage, Winkfield Row, BRACKNELL, RG42 6NA. (Life Member)
TARRATT, Mr. George David Nicholas, MSc ACA *2002;* Snowhill Cottage, Okewood Hill, DORKING, SURREY, RH5 5NB.
TARRATT, Mr. Nicholas Joyl, FCA *1976;* Bianca & Alena, Textile House, Cline Road, LONDON, N11 2LX.
•**TARREN, Mr. Peter, FCCA** *1981;* (Tax Fac), Eura Audit UK, 87 South Parade, NORTHALLERTON, NORTH YORKSHIRE, DL7 8SJ. See also Lishman Sidwell Campbell & Price LLP
TARRY, Mr. Charles Anthony, BSc ACA *1979;* Honeypound, Croom, LIMERICK, COUNTY LIMERICK, IRELAND.
TARRY, Mr. James Robson Edwin, MA(Oxon) ACA *2001;* 51 Madeira Park, TUNBRIDGE WELLS, TN2 5SY.
TARRY, Mr. Robert Brian, BSc FCA *1990;* 57 Low Road, Grimston, KING'S LYNN, NORFOLK, PE32 1AF.
TARSHIS, Mrs. Sondra Michelle, FCA *1992;* 12 Cole Park Gardens, TWICKENHAM, TW1 1JB.
TARSKY, Mrs. Susan Evelyn, ACA *1995;* with Francis Clark, North Quay House, Sutton Harbour, PLYMOUTH, PL4 0RA.
TARVER, Mr. Allan Leigh, GM FCA *1980;* 1 The Spain, PETERSFIELD, HAMPSHIRE, GU32 3JZ.
TASCH, Mrs. Catherine Mary, BSocSc ACA *1996;* 26 Pendarves Road, LONDON, SW20 8TS.
TASCH, Mr. Jonathan, BSc ACA *1994;* 58 West Hill Avenue, EPSOM, KT19 8JU.
TASEER, Mr. Salmaan, FCA *1968;* First Capital Securites Corporation Limited, 103-c/2 Gulberg, LAHORE, PUNJAB, PAKISTAN.
•**TASH, Mr. Brian David, BSc FCA** *1976;* PKF (UK) LLP, Farringdon Place, 20 Farringdon Road, LONDON, EC1M 3AP.
TASIOULAS, Mr. Achilleas, MSc ACA *2005;* Danaos Shipping Co. Ltd., 14 Akti Kondyli Str., 18545 PIRAEUS, GREECE.
TASKER, Mr. Alan Michael Edric, BSc ACA *1980;* Global Aerospace, Underwriting Managers Ltd, Fitzwilliam House, 10 St Mary Axe, LONDON, EC3A 8EQ.
TASKER, Mr. Andrew, BCom ACA *1998;* 6 Atterbury Way, Great Houghton, NORTHAMPTON, NN4 7AU.
TASKER, Mr. Brian Thomas, MBA FCA *1969;* 6 Roopers, Speldhurst, TUNBRIDGE WELLS, TN3 0QL.
•**TASKER, Mrs. Caroline Jayne, BA ACA** *1992;* Tasker Accounting Services Limited, 14 Sunnybank Crescent, Yeadon, LEEDS, LS19 7TE.
TASKER, Miss. Cristina Emma, ACA *2006;* Argos Ltd, 489-499 Avebury Boulevard, MILTON KEYNES, MK9 2NW.
TASKER, Mr. Dennis, FCA *1953;* 7 Parkland Close, Southlands, MANSFIELD, NG18 4PP. (Life Member)
TASKER, Mr. Dereck Arthur, BSc ACA *1980;* 22 Sorbus Way, Lepton, HUDDERSFIELD, HD8 0EY.
TASKER, Mrs. Gillian Maxine, LLB FCA ATII TEP *1987;* (Tax Fac), 54 Sandringham Drive, Brinscall, CHORLEY, PR6 8SU.
TASKER, Mr. Huw John, ACA *2010;* 2a Roman Road, Wheatley, OXFORD, OX33 1UU.
TASKER, Mr. Jeffrey James, FCA *1989;* K P M G LLP, 1 Canada Square, LONDON, E14 5AG.
TASKER, Mrs. Karen Anne, BA ACA *2001;* 6 Atterbury Way, Great Houghton, NORTHAMPTON, NN4 7AU.
TASKER, Mrs. Marie Alexandra, ACA *2008;* 80 Lake View, PONTEFRACT, WEST YORKSHIRE, WF8 1JJ.
TASKER, Mr. Robert Vincent, BA ACA *1988;* 65 Main Street, Stanbury, KEIGHLEY, BD22 0HA.
TASKER, Mr. Simon Harry, BSc ACA *1993;* Five Ways House, Tennysons Lane, HASLEMERE, SURREY, GU27 3BA.
•**TASKER, Mr. Thomas William, FCA** *1980;* T.W. Tasker, 52a Station Rd, ASHINGTON, NE63 9UJ.
TASNEY, Mr. Ian George, FCA *1976;* Hope Cottage, The Street, Lodsworth, PETWORTH, WEST SUSSEX, GU28 9BZ.
TASNIM, Mr. Naveed Amman, ACA *2009;* 83 Derwen Fawr Road, Sketty, SWANSEA, SA2 8DR.
TASOREN, Mrs. Heather Flora Jean, ACA *1989;* 124 West Coast Rise, SINGAPORE 127532, SINGAPORE.
TASOU, Mr. Peter, BSc ACA *2007;* 1 Compton Terrace, Hoppers Road, LONDON, N21 3NR.
TASSELL, Mr. Martin Andrew, FCA *1975;* 18 Burvill Street, LYNTON, DEVON, EX35 6HA. (Life Member)
TAT, Miss. Tammy Sze Mei, BSc ACA *2007;* Flat D 2/F, Tower 8, Laguna Verde, HUNG HOM, KOWLOON, HONG KONG SAR.
TATA, Miss. Shirin Phiroze, BSc ACA *1979;* 38 Myddelton Square, LONDON, EC1R 1YB.
TATA, Mr. Yezi Homi, FCA *1952;* 1 Arti Building, 1 Ratilal Thakkar Marg, Winter Road Flat, Malabar Hill, MUMBAI 400006, INDIA.
TATAR, Mr. Ersin Rustem, MA FCA *1986;* Tatar & Co, 11 Hasene Ilgaz Str, P.O. Box 768, LEFKOSA MERSIN 10, TURKEY.
•**TATAR, Mr. Munir, ACA FCCA MCIM** *2009;* Munir Tatar & Associates, 32 Willoughby Road, Hornsey, LONDON, N8 0JG.
TATAR, Mr. Roustem Zihni, BA FCA *1955;* Tatar & Co, 11 Hasene Ilgaz Str, P.O. Box 768, LEFKOSA MERSIN 10, TURKEY.
TATAR, Mr. Zihni Erhan Rustem, BSc ARCS ACA *1990;* RBS Gogarburn House F Floor 2, The Royal Bank of Scotland Plc, PO Box 1000, EDINBURGH, EH12 1HQ. See also Tatar & Co
TATCHELL, Mr. Ian Spencer, BA ACA *1991;* 30 Kimmerghame Drive, EDINBURGH, EH4 2GJ.
TATE, Mr. Adrian John Anthony, MA ACA *1984;* (Tax Fac), The Penthouse, Flat 7 Combe Down, Shawford, WINCHESTER, SO21 2AA.
TATE, Mr. Andrew Wayne, BA ACA *1990;* Grenaby Farm, Grenaby, Castletown, ISLE OF MAN, IM9 3BD.
TATE, Miss. Beverley, ACA MAAT *2010;* 30 Carleton View, PONTEFRACT, WF8 2SD.
TATE, Mr. Christopher, BA ACA *2007;* 18 Tadburn Close, Chandler's Ford, EASTLEIGH, HAMPSHIRE, SO53 2NF.
•**TATE, Mr. Christopher Allan, BA FCA** *1980;* 352 Filey Road, SCARBOROUGH, YO11 3JQ.
TATE, Mr. Christopher Ian, BA ACA *1991;* Jaywing, 212-214 Kirkgate, WAKEFIELD, WEST YORKSHIRE, WF1 1UF.
TATE, Mr. Christopher James, BA(Econ) ACA *2003;* 92 North Cray Road, BEXLEY, DA5 3NA.
TATE, Mr. David Ian, BSc ACA *1989;* 29 Reeves Road, MANCHESTER, M21 8BU.
TATE, Mr. David James, BA ACA *1993;* 76 Handen Road, LONDON, SE12 8NR.
TATE, Mr. David Read, MA MSc FCA *1980;* Silverwood, 9 Lodge Road, BROMLEY, BR1 3ND.
TATE, Ms. Emily Sarah, BA(Hons) ACA *2001;* 60 St. Cross Road, WINCHESTER, HAMPSHIRE, SO23 9PS.
TATE, Mrs. Gabrielle Frances, ACA *1978;* Le Chalet, Rue De Longis, Alderney, GUERNSEY, GY9 3YB.
TATE, Mr. Graeme David Stewart, BA ACA *2006;* 49 Southwoods, YEOVIL, SOMERSET, BA20 2QQ.
TATE, Mr. Graham John, FCA *1969;* 16 Tiree Place, CRIEFF, PERTHSHIRE, PH7 3BF. (Life Member)
•**TATE, Mr. Gregory Alistair, BA FCA** *1990;* Abraxas Corporate Finance Limited, 4 Croft Gardens, Grappenhall Heys, WARRINGTON, WA4 3LH.
•**TATE, Mr. Harold Bryan Keith, FCA** *1976;* (Tax Fac), Tate & Co., 11 Bridge Wharf Road, ISLEWORTH, MIDDLESEX, TW7 6BS.
TATE, Ms. Helen Elizabeth, BSc ACA *1988;* The Royal Bank of Scotland plc, 135 Bishopsgate, LONDON, EC2M 3UR.
TATE, Mr. Jason Rodney, BA(Hons) ACA *2003;* Deverose House, Waste Lane, Kelsall, TARPORLEY, CHESHIRE, CW6 0PE.
TATE, Mr. Jeffrey Norman, BA ACA *1988;* Longcroft Cottage, 52 Hall Carr Lane, Walmer Bridle, PRESTON, PR4 5JJ.
TATE, Mr. Jonathan, BA ACA *2004;* 2 Avenue Approach, KINGS LANGLEY, HERTFORDSHIRE, WD4 8DN.
•**TATE, Mr. Jonathan Colin, BA FCA** *1993;* The Oaks, 3 Fosters Booth Road, Pattishall, TOWCESTER, NORTHAMPTONSHIRE, NN12 8JU.
TATE, Mr. Jonathan Robert, BA ACA *1989;* Coyne Butterworth & Chalmers, Lupins Business Centre, 1-3 Greenhill, WEYMOUTH, DORSET, DT4 7SP.
TATE, Mr. Mark Peter, ACA MAAT *1999;* 39 Plantation Gardens, Alwoodley, LEEDS, LS17 8SX.
TATE, Mr. Maurice Stanley, FCA *1962;* Byways, Dartnell Avenue, WEST BYFLEET, KT14 6PJ. (Life Member)
TATE, Ms. Maxine, BSc ACA *1994;* 201 Old Shoreham Road, Southwick, BRIGHTON, BN42 4LS.
•**TATE, Mr. Nicholas Laurence, MA ACA** *1981;* N Tate & Co Limited, 42 St. Andrews Road, RAMSGATE, KENT, CT11 7EQ.
•**TATE, Mr. Paul Michael, BSc FCA** *1981;* Paul M Tate, 3 Hanwell Court, Hanwell, BANBURY, OX17 1HF.
TATE, Mrs. Rachael, BA ACA CTA *1995;* 62 Bailielands, LINLITHGOW, WEST LOTHIAN, EH49 7TF.
TATE, Dr. Rebecca Helen, ACA *2003;* Deverose House Waste Lane, Kelsall, TARPORLEY, CHESHIRE, CW6 0PE.
TATE, Mr. Sam James, ACA *2009;* 14 Windsor Avenue, SKIPTON, NORTH YORKSHIRE, BD23 1HS.
TATE, Mrs. Tracy Joanne, BA ACA *1991;* 27 Sandhill Drive, Alwoodley, LEEDS, LS17 8DU.
TATE, Miss. Victoria Ann Christina, BSc ACA *2006;* 4 Blossom Court, Forge Close Sturry, CANTERBURY, CT2 0BQ.
TATE, Mr. William Stanley, FCA *1954;* 21 Louisville, North Road, Ponteland, NEWCASTLE UPON TYNE, NE20 9SH. (Life Member)
TATHAM, Mr. Alexander Charles Heathcote, BSc ACA *1992;* 24 Kirkstall Road, LONDON, SW2 4HF.
TATHAM, Mr. Benjamin David, BA ACA *2003;* 2 Clavering Avenue, Barnes, LONDON, SW13 8DY.
TATHAM, Mr. Christopher Harle, BA ACA *1993;* 5 The Avenue, Scholes, LEEDS, LS15 4AS.
TATHAM, Mr. Harding William, FCA *1950;* Fairlands, P. Bag 13001 Cambridge, 5206, EAST LONDON, C.P., SOUTH AFRICA. (Life Member)
TATHAM, Mr. Jeremy Paul, BSc ACA *1998;* 11 Vicarage Avenue, EGHAM, TW20 8NW.
TATHAM, Mr. John Gordon, BCom ACA *1995;* 200 Broadway, DERBY, DE22 1BP.
TATIANOS, Mr. Michael, ACA *1982;* Residence La Boheme, 15 Rue Des Forains, 1533 LUXEMBOURG, LUXEMBOURG.

TATLOCK, Mr. David Norman, MA FCA *1980;* The Leas, Dartford Road, Horton Kirby, DARTFORD, DA4 9JE.
•**TATLOCK, Mr. Stephen, FCA** *1982;* Northline Business Consultants Ltd, 2nd Floor, Clarendon Centre, 38 Clarendon Road, Monton, Eccles MANCHESTER M30 9ES.
TATON, Mr. Simon William, ACA *2011;* Flat 3, 10 Crossland Road, REDHILL, SURREY, RH1 4AN.
TATTAM, Mr. David Eric, ACA *1987;* PO Box Q1688, Queen Victoria Building, SYDNEY, NSW 1230, AUSTRALIA.
TATTAR, Mr. Balbinder Singh, BA ACA *1993;* 15 Grosvenor Street, LONDON, W1K 4QZ.
TATTERSALL, Mrs. Anna Charlotte Louise, BA ACA *1990;* 34 Chemin Perdu, 06620 LE BAR SUR LOUP, FRANCE.
•**TATTERSALL, Mr. Christopher David, BSc(Econ) FCA** *1999;* Ernst & Young, Bleicherweg 21, P.O. Box 5272, CH-8022 ZURICH, SWITZERLAND. See also Ernst & Young Europe LLP
TATTERSALL, Mr. David Nowell, FCA *1956;* 31 Bollin Grove, Prestbury, MACCLESFIELD, CHESHIRE, SK10 4JJ. (Life Member)
•**TATTERSALL, Mr. John Anthony, FCA** *1972;* Tattersalls Accountancy Services Limited, Concept House, 3 Dene Street, DORKING, SURREY, RH4 2DR.
TATTERSALL, Mr. John Hartley, MA FCA *1978;* 3 St.Ann's Villas, LONDON, W11 4RU.
TATTERSALL, Mr. John Neville, FCA *1964;* 1 Charles Avenue, Southowram, HALIFAX, WEST YORKSHIRE, HX3 9RZ.
TATTERSALL, Mr. John Richard, FCA *1952;* 51 Cobden Hill, RADLETT, WD7 7JL. (Life Member)
TATTERSALL, Miss. Julie, BA FCA *1992;* 11 Corve Dale Walk, West Bridgford, NOTTINGHAM, NG2 6TY.
TATTERSALL, Mrs. Kathryn, BSc ACA *1980;* Ty Newydd Burton Road, Rossett, WREXHAM, CLWYD, LL12 0HU.
•**TATTERSALL, Mr. Luke Ben, BSc(Hons) ACA** *2005;* John Belford & Co Ltd, 14a Main Street, COCKERMOUTH, CUMBRIA, CA13 9LQ.
TATTERSALL, Mr. Michael David, BA ACA *2000;* Cazenove Group PLC, 20 Moorgate, LONDON, EC2R 6DA.
TATTERSALL, Mr. Michael George, FCA *1966;* Redvale, Old Hall Clough, Lostock, BOLTON, BL6 4LB.
TATTERSALL, Mr. Simon Gaire, BA ACA *1986;* 34 Chemin Perdu, 06620 BAR SUR LOUP, PROVENCE, FRANCE.
•**TATTERSALL, Mr. Stephen Martin, FCA** *1973;* Lacy Watson, Carlyle House, 107 Wellington Road South, STOCKPORT, SK1 3TL. See also Powell & Powell Limited
TATTERSALL, Mrs. Susan Elisabeth, FCA *1959;* 31 Bollin Grove, Prestbury, MACCLESFIELD, CHESHIRE, SK10 4JJ. (Life Member)
TATTERSFIELD, Mr. Keith, FCA *1965;* 25 Bridge Road Ickford, AYLESBURY, BUCKINGHAMSHIRE, HP18 9HU.
TATTERSHALL, Miss. Alison Elizabeth, BA ACA *2007;* Anglo American Plc Anglo American House, 20 Carlton House Terrace, LONDON, SW1Y 5AN.
TATTERSHALL, Mr. Richard Philip, ACA *2008;* 6 Braeside Avenue, Wimbledon, LONDON, SW19 3PT.
TATTERSHAW, Mrs. Julie Margaret, FCA *1963;* 24 Lewis Street, GORE, NEW ZEALAND.
TATTERSHAW, Mr. Robert, FCA *1960;* 24 Lewis Street, GORE, NEW ZEALAND. (Life Member)
TATTON, Mr. Alastair Graham, MA ACA *2000;* 35 Edmunds Walk, East Finchley, LONDON, N2 0HU.
TATTON, Mr. James Andrew, LLB ACA *2003;* 208 Walmley Road, SUTTON COLDFIELD, WEST MIDLANDS, B76 2PY.
•**TATTON, Mr. Malcolm, BSc FCA** *1977;* (Tax Fac), Walletts, 2-6 Adventure Place, Hanley, STOKE-ON-TRENT, ST1 3AF.
TATTON, Miss. Melissa Joanne, BA(Hons) ACA *2001;* 4/11-13 Martins Avenue, BONDI, NSW 2026, AUSTRALIA.
TATTON, Mr. Peter Graham, BCom FCA *1976;* 44 Castle Gardens, Castle Boulevard, NOTTINGHAM, NG7 1HH.
TATTUM, Mrs. Susan Ruth, BSc ACA *1995;* (Tax Fac), Ty Gwyn, Llys Gwyddfid, Ffordd Y Gilrhos, Treuddyn, MOLD, CH7 4NW.
•**TATUM, Mr. Paul Nigel, BSc FCA** *1982;* (Tax Fac), Whiting & Partners, Garland House, Garland Street, BURY ST. EDMUNDS, SUFFOLK, IP33 1EZ.
TATUM-HORSFIELD, Mrs. Vicki, BSc ACA *1996;* Old Station Works, Station Road, Shepreth, ROYSTON, HERTFORDSHIRE, SG8 6PZ.
•**TAUB, Mr. Alan Grahame, FCA** *1978;* 77 Michleham Down, Woodside Park, LONDON, N12 7JL.
•**TAUB, Mr. Leonard Keith, FCA** *1977;* 4 Rees Drive, STANMORE, HA7 4YN.
•**TAUB, Mr. Michael Bernard, BA FCA** *1982;* 9 Adamson Road, LONDON, NW3 3HX.
TAUBMAN, Mr. Stephen John, BSc ACA CMC *1987;* Big Sky House, 21a The Crescent, Henleaze, BRISTOL, BS9 4RP.
TAUBMAN, Mr. Timothy Richard, BEng ACA *1996;* 11 Kelmscott Road, LONDON, SW11 6QX.
TAUKOORDASS, Mr. Udaysingh, BSocSc ACA *1995;* 7 Ramji Patel Street, BEAU BASSIN, MAURITIUS.
TAULBUT, Mr. Shaun Mark, MA ACA MCT *1986;* 190 Reading Road, WOKINGHAM, BERKSHIRE, RG41 1LH.
TAUNT, Mr. Nigel David Wynne, BSc FCA *1977;* Impax Asset Management Pegasus House, 37-43 Sackville Street, LONDON, W1S 3EH.
•**TAUNTON, Mr. Francis Basil Trafford, FCA** *1966;* 90 Babbacombe Road, BROMLEY, BR1 3LS.
•**TAURAE, Mr. Paolo, ACA CA(NZ)** *2011;* PricewaterhouseCoopers, 7 More London Riverside, LONDON, SE1 2RT. See also PricewaterhouseCoopers LLP
TAUSIG, Mr. Benjamin Daniel, BA ACA *2006;* with Deloitte LLP, Hill House, 1 Little New Street, LONDON, EC4A 3TR.
TAUTSCHER, Mrs. Amanda Jane, ACA *1994;* Jardin De Haut, Route De L'Eclet, St Pierre Du Bois, GUERNSEY, GY7 9PA.
TAUTSCHER, Mr. Andreas Josef, BSc ACA *1994;* Deutsche Bank International, PO Box 424, GUERNSEY, GY1 3WT.
•**TAUWHARE, Mr. John Michael, BA FCA** *1984;* 25 Edis Way, Foxton, CAMBRIDGE, CB22 6RW.
TAVAKOLI, Mr. Farhad, BSc ACA *1982;* Samco Capital S.A., PO Box 5443, 4 Place de Neuve, 1211 GENEVA, SWITZERLAND.
TAVANA, Mr. Joseph, BSc FCA *1971;* 1110 Sheppard Avenue East, Suite 408, TORONTO M2K 2W2, ON, CANADA.
•**TAVARES, Mr. George Felix Joseph, FCA** *1984;* George Tavares, 55 Purtell Street, EAST BENTLEIGH, VIC 3165, AUSTRALIA.
TAVASOLI, Miss. Mariam, BA(Hons) ACA *2009;* 11b Cedar Road, SUTTON, SURREY, SM2 5DA.
TAVELIS, Mr. Christos, BSc(Econ) ACA *2000;* 15 Vatilis Street, Kato Lakatamia, 2323 NICOSIA, CYPRUS.
TAVENER, Mr. Mark Wrenford, MA ACA *1998;* 28 Pegasus Place, ST. ALBANS, AL3 5QT.
TAVENER, Mr. Peter Mark, BEng ACA *1998;* 4 St. Katherines, Winterbourne Bassett, SWINDON, SN4 9QG.
TAVENER, Mr. Richard Mark, BSc FCA *1987;* The Willows, 17 Donnington Park, Donnington, NEWBURY, BERKSHIRE, RG14 2DZ.
TAVERNER, Mrs. Amanda Jane, BA(Hons) ACA *2000;* Birkby The Avenue, Collingham, WETHERBY, WEST YORKSHIRE, LS22 5BU.
TAVERNER, Mr. Colin, BSc ACA *2000;* Birkby, The Avenue, Collingham, WETHERBY, WEST YORKSHIRE, LS22 5BU.
TAVERNER, Mr. John Ernest, FCA *1961;* Ivy House, Hanley Swan, WORCESTER, WR8 0DR. (Life Member)
•**TAVITIAN, Mr. Aram, BSc ACA** *1994;* PricewaterhouseCoopers Limited, Julia House, 3 Themistocles Dervis Street, CY-1066 NICOSIA, CYPRUS.
TAVITIAN, Mr. Nareg, BSc(Hons) ACA *2000;* 5 Nikis Str, Strovolos, 2045 NICOSIA, CYPRUS.
TAVROS, Mr. Marios, BA ACA *1996;* PO Box 64009, 8071 PAPHOS, CYPRUS.
TAVROS, Mr. Odysseus, BSc ACA *1992;* c/o TAVROS HOTEL APTS, P O BOX 66199, 8831 PAPHOS, CYPRUS.
TAWNEY, Mr. Christopher, MA FCA *1983;* The White House, Easton Royal, PEWSEY, SN9 5LY.
TAWTON, Mr. Gerald John, BA ACA *1983;* 216 Sleaford Road, BOSTON, LINCOLNSHIRE, PE21 7PG.
TAXITARIS, Mr. Demetris, ACA *2001;* Frank Court 39, Flat 302, 12 Dositheou Street, Strovolos, 2028 NICOSIA, CYPRUS.
TAY, Mr. Ah Kee, FCA *1969;* 25 Greenleaf Avenue, SINGAPORE 279606, SINGAPORE.
TAY, Ms. Ai Huey, BSc ACA *2003;* 87Jalan 29, Desa Jaya, Kepong, KUALA LUMPUR, FEDERAL TERRITORY, MALAYSIA.
TAY, Miss. Beng Keong, FCA *1977;* 55 Sommerville Road, SINGAPORE 358286, SINGAPORE.
TAY, Mr. Charlie Choon Leng, FCA *1975;* 88 Weston Drive, STANMORE, HA7 2EN.
TAY, Mr. Chong Chim, FCA *1972;* 78 Jalan Bangkung, Bukit Bandaraya, 59100 KUALA LUMPUR, FEDERAL TERRITORY, MALAYSIA.
TAY, Miss. Hui Ling, BSc(Econ) ACA *2002;* Flat 42 Marlow Court, 221 Willesden Lane, LONDON, NW6 7PS.
TAY, Miss. Joanne Siok Wan, BA ACA *1983;* 54 Hume Avenue #02-03, SINGAPORE 596231, SINGAPORE.
TAY, Mrs. Kristy Siew Hwa, MSc ACA *1999;* 31 Lorong Setiabistari, Damansara Heights, 50490 KUALA LUMPUR, FEDERAL TERRITORY, MALAYSIA.
TAY, Mr. Kuan Ming, BSc ACA *1992;* 40 Bridport Avenue, SINGAPORE 559330, SINGAPORE.
TAY, Miss. Lee Foon, BSc ACA *1983;* 20 Elmcroft Crescent, North Harrow, HARROW, MIDDLESEX, HA2 6HN.
TAY, Miss. Lian Pheck, FCA *1971;* 2 Peach Garden, #15-04 Meyer Road, SINGAPORE 437603, SINGAPORE.
TAY, Ms. Lynda Adjoyoo Dzigbodi, MSc(Econ) ACA *2001;* 117 Hanover Road, LONDON, NW10 3DN.
TAY, Mr. Melvin, Bsc ACA *2010;* Room 302 Unit 3 Block 2 Da Tong Cheng Fu Gong Guan Apartment, No. Jia 42San Cai Tang Hai Dian District, BEIJING 100190, CHINA.
TAY, Mr. Paul Guan Hoe, MBA FCA *1982;* Paul Tay & Co, 63 Stead Street, MELBOURNE, VIC 3205, AUSTRALIA.
TAY, Miss. Shan Li, BSc ACA *2001;* 68 Jalan Denai Selatan 5, Southlake Terraces, Desa Parkcity, 52200 KUALA LUMPUR, FEDERAL TERRITORY, MALAYSIA.
TAY, Miss. Sok Kian, BSc FCA *1982;* c/o Office of Resource Planning, National University of Singapore University Hall #03-02, 21 Lower Kent Ridge Road, SINGAPORE 119077, SINGAPORE.
TAY, Ms. Valerie Kok Keow, BA ACA *1988;* 21 West Avenue, Finchley, LONDON, N3 1AU.
TAY, Miss. Yng Hwei Serene, BSc ACA *2004;* Flat B 28/F South Tower 2, Residence Bel-Air, 38 Bel-Air Avenue, POK FU LAM, HONG KONG SAR.
•**TAYABALI, Mr. Imran Zafar, BSc ACA** *2003;* TT&W Limited, 5 High Green, Great Shelford, CAMBRIDGE, CB22 5EG.
TAYAL, Mr. Anurag Kumar, BSc ACA *2004;* Periwinkle Cottage Perry Hill, Worplesdon, GUILDFORD, GU3 3RG.
TAYAL, Mrs. Shailly, ACA *2009;* 25-A Ashok Marg, Uttar Pradesh, LUCKNOW 226001, INDIA.
•**TAYAL, Mr. Vijay, BA ACA** *1989;* 60 Heath Street, RICHMOND HILL L4B 2BB, ON, CANADA.
TAYAR, Mr. Clifford George, FCA *1960;* 1 Ridge Crescent, Meir Heath, STOKE-ON-TRENT, STAFFORDSHIRE, ST3 7LG. (Life Member)
TAYLAUR, Mr. Mervyn Clive, FCA *1965;* P.O. Box 70303, Victoria Island, LAGOS, NIGERIA. (Life Member)
TAYLER, Mr. Colin Richard, BEng ACA *1995;* 1 Arthur Road, CHRISTCHURCH, BH23 1PU.
TAYLER, Mr. David Robert, FCA *1966;* 16 Ridge Langley, SOUTH CROYDON, Surrey, CR2 0AR. (Life Member)
•**TAYLER, Mr. Hugh Edgar, BSc FCA** *1979;* (Tax Fac), Chalmers & Co, 6 Linen Yard, South Street, CREWKERNE, SOMERSET, TA18 8AB. See also Chalmers & Co (SW) Limtied
TAYLER, Mr. Ian John Charles, BSc ACA *2003;* 4 Melrose Street, MOSMAN, NSW 2088, AUSTRALIA.
TAYLOR, Mrs. Abigail Sarah, LLB ACA *2006;* 15 Windmill Hill, Fring Road, Great Bircham, KING'S LYNN, PE31 6RE.
TAYLOR, Mr. Adam Jan, MA ACA *2003;* 1st Floor 3000b, Zurich Insurance Co The Zurich Centre, 3000 Parkway Whiteley, FAREHAM, HAMPSHIRE, PO15 7JZ.
TAYLOR, Mr. Adrian Anthony, BA FCA *1972;* Suntrap, Enstone Road, Charlbury, CHIPPING NORTON, OXFORDSHIRE, OX7 3QR.
TAYLOR, Mr. Adrian Richard Colin, BA ACA *1990;* 26 Abinger Road, Chiswick, LONDON, W4 1EL.
•**TAYLOR, Mr. Aidan Maurus, LLB FCA** *1981;* Armstrong Watson, 15 Victoria Place, CARLISLE, CA1 1EW.
TAYLOR, Mr. Alan, FCA *1952;* 701 Leeds Road, Shaw Cross, DEWSBURY, WF12 7HP. (Life Member)
•**TAYLOR, Mr. Alan, FCA** *1973;* 49 Broadfields Avenue, EDGWARE, MIDDLESEX, HA8 8PF.
TAYLOR, Mr. Alan Bennett, MA FCA *1979;* 30 Cholmeley Park, LONDON, N6 5EU.
•**TAYLOR, Mr. Alan George, FCA** *1972;* 267 Rue de la Poste, 62990 BEAURAINVILLE, FRANCE.
TAYLOR, Mr. Alan Guy, FCA *1951;* 15 Oak Tree Road, KENDAL, CUMBRIA, LA9 6AN. (Life Member)
TAYLOR, Mr. Alan John, BTech FCA *1972;* Mount Cottage, Off Redcliff Drive, Wombourne, WOLVERHAMPTON, WV5 0JE.
TAYLOR, Mr. Alan Michael, FCA *1974;* 87 Maple Street, LINCOLN, LN5 8QS.
•**TAYLOR, Mr. Alan Thomas, MA DPhil FCA** *1979;* Alan Taylor, 28 Aldrich Drive, Willen, MILTON KEYNES, MK15 9LU.
TAYLOR, Mr. Alastair, BSc ACA *2011;* 47 Venn Street, LONDON, SW4 0AZ.
•**TAYLOR, Mr. Alastair James, BSc FCA FPC** *2000;* (Tax Fac), Chicksand Gordon Avis Limited, 12 Northfields Prospect, Putney Bridge Road, LONDON, SW18 1PE.
TAYLOR, Mr. Alex, ACA *2009;* 94 Ingelow Road, LONDON, SW8 3PF.
TAYLOR, Mr. Alexander, BSc ACA *2005;* with RSM Tenon Limited, International House, 66 Chiltern Street, LONDON, W1U 4JT.
TAYLOR, Mr. Alexander Bruce Keightley, FCA *1966;* 7 Arbory Road, Castletown, ISLE OF MAN, IM9 1NA.
TAYLOR, Mrs. Alison, BA ACA *2004;* 66 Lesbourne Road, REIGATE, RH2 7JX.
TAYLOR, Miss. Alison Jane, MA BSc ACA *2000;* National Australian Bank, 33 Gracechurch Street, LONDON, EC3V 0BT.
TAYLOR, Mrs. Alison Mary, ACA *1982;* Architecture PLB Ltd, 1 St. Thomas Mews, St. Thomas Street, WINCHESTER, HAMPSHIRE, SO23 9HD.
TAYLOR, Mr. Allan Watson, PhD ACA *1991;* 129 Desswood Place, ABERDEEN, AB15 4DP.
TAYLOR, Miss. Amanda Jayne, BSc ACA *1998;* Flat 30 Alexander House, Royal Quarter Seven Kings Way, KINGSTON UPON THAMES, SURREY, KT2 5BY.
•**TAYLOR, Mrs. Amanda Joyce, ACA** *1980;* Taylors, 51 High Street, Stokesley, MIDDLESBROUGH, CLEVELAND, TS9 5AD.
TAYLOR, Mrs. Amanda Leeann, BSc ACA *2001;* 7 Heardman Close, THATCHAM, BERKSHIRE, RG19 4FB.
TAYLOR, Mr. Amit Peter, BSc ACA *1998;* HSBC Securities (Guernsey) Ltd, PO Box 208, GUERNSEY, GY1 3NF.
TAYLOR, Mrs. Amy Elizabeth Vautier, BA ACA *2006;* 60 Le Vier Mont, St. Helier, JERSEY, JE2 4NG.
TAYLOR, Mrs. Amy May, BSc(Hons) ACA *2005;* 8 Wardlow Road, ILKESTON, DERBYSHIRE, DE7 8US.
TAYLOR, Mr. Andrew, BA ACA *1998;* 3 Woodville Road, Harborne, BIRMINGHAM, B17 9AS.
TAYLOR, Mr. Andrew, BA ACA *1995;* 2 Hilton Mews, Bramhope, LEEDS, LS16 9LF.
TAYLOR, Mr. Andrew, ACA *2009;* The Hoseasons Group, Spring Mill Earby, BARNOLDSWICK, BB94 0AA.
•**TAYLOR, Mr. Andrew Charles, FCA** *1982;* Baker Chapman & Bussey, Magnet House, 3 North Hill, COLCHESTER, CO1 1DZ.
TAYLOR, Mr. Andrew Clifford, FCA CTA *1979;* 2 Kingfisher Way, Kelvedon, COLCHESTER, CO5 9NS.
TAYLOR, Mr. Andrew David, BSc ACA *1984;* 73 Windmill Lane, Reddish, STOCKPORT, CHESHIRE, SK5 6SU.
TAYLOR, Mr. Andrew Herbert Ian, BA ACA *1988;* 10 Aldwycks Close, Shenley Church End, MILTON KEYNES, MK5 6HZ.
TAYLOR, Mr. Andrew James, BSc ACA *2000;* 11 Richmond Grove, Handsworth, SHEFFIELD, S13 8UH.
TAYLOR, Mr. Andrew James, ACA *2009;* 2 Highfields, Main Street Polebrook, PETERBOROUGH, PE8 5LN.
•**TAYLOR, Mr. Andrew James, BSc ACA** *2007;* Andrew Taylor & Co, Thames Court, 1 Victoria Street, WINDSOR, BERKSHIRE, SL4 1YB.
TAYLOR, Mr. Andrew John, BA ACA *1990;* University Hospital, Clifford Bridge Road, COVENTRY, CV2 2DX.
•**TAYLOR, Mr. Andrew John, BA FCA** *1976;* Phanton Music Management Ltd, Bridle House, 36 Bridle Lane, LONDON, W1F 9BZ.
TAYLOR, Mr. Andrew John, BSc ACA *1997;* Thomas Miller & Co Ltd, 90 Fenchurch Street, LONDON, EC3M 4ST.
TAYLOR, Mr. Andrew Joseph Jackson, BA ACA *1986;* Sonic Solutions Ltd, 15 Riverside Way, Ravensthorpe Industrial Estate, DEWSBURY, WEST YORKSHIRE, WF13 3LG.
•**TAYLOR, Mr. Andrew Kemp, FCA** *1972;* Kemp Taylor LLP, The Oval, 14 West Walk, LEICESTER, LE1 7NA. See also Williams Resource Management Ltd
TAYLOR, Mr. Andrew Lyn, BA ACA *2004;* 5317 Coveview Court, GREENSBORO, NC 27407, UNITED STATES.
TAYLOR, Mr. Andrew Mark, BA ACA *1999;* 6 Edwardian Way, Miskin, PONTYCLUN, MID GLAMORGAN, CF72 8SJ.
TAYLOR, Mr. Andrew Peter, FCA *1980;* Vollmer UK Ltd, Unit 2, Orchard Park Industrial Estate, Town Street, Sandiacre, NOTTINGHAM NG10 5BP.
TAYLOR, Mr. Andrew Richard Geoffrey, ACA *2010;* 167 Overstone Court, CARDIFF, SOUTH GLAMORGAN, CF10 5NT.
TAYLOR, Mr. Andrew Stephen, BA ACA *1992;* 11 The Avenue, SALE, CHESHIRE, M33 4PD.

TAYLOR, Mr. Andrew William, BSc ACA *1995;* 13 Pretoria Road, CAMBRIDGE, CB4 1HD.
TAYLOR, Mrs. Angela, BA FCA *1993;* 44 St. Leonards Road, HARROGATE, NORTH YORKSHIRE, HG2 8NS.
•TAYLOR, Mrs. Angela June, ACA MAAT *2000;* Ivy Villa, Cirencester Road, FAIRFORD, GLOUCESTERSHIRE, GL7 4BS.
•TAYLOR, Mrs. Anju, BSc ACA *1990;* The Old Drill Hall, Atkinson Evans & Co, 10 Arnot Hill Road Arnold, NOTTINGHAM, NG5 6LJ.
TAYLOR, Miss. Anne, BSc ACA *1984;* Abingdon, 15 Saffrons Road, EASTBOURNE, EAST SUSSEX, BN21 1DT.
TAYLOR, Miss. Anne Elizabeth, BA FCA *1994;* Davington, School Road, Messing, COLCHESTER, CO5 9TL.
TAYLOR, Ms. Anne Martina, BA ACA *1985;* Assystem Ltd Club Street, Bamber Bridge, PRESTON, PR5 6FN.
TAYLOR, Miss. Annie, ACA *2011;* Durrows, Quarry Lane, Kelsall, TARPORLEY, CHESHIRE, CW6 0PD.
TAYLOR, Miss. Anthea Jane, BA ACA *1995;* (Tax Fac), 56 Strawberry Mead, Fair Oak, EASTLEIGH, SO50 8RG.
•TAYLOR, Mr. Anthony Charles, MBA BSc FCA FRSA *1978;* Anthony Taylor & Co., 25 Lordswood Road, Harborne, BIRMINGHAM, B17 9RP.
TAYLOR, Mr. Anthony Charles, FCA *1966;* 16 Sidmouth Road, CHELMSFORD, CM1 6LR.
TAYLOR, Mr. Anthony Christopher, FCA *1968;* Wynfrith, 8 Church Avenue, Penwortham, PRESTON, PR1 0AH.
TAYLOR, Mr. Anthony David, FCA *1958;* Linford Hill, Hangersley, RINGWOOD, BH24 3JU. (Life Member)
TAYLOR, Mr. Anthony James, BA ACA *1992;* Little Castlemans Bath Road, Knowl Hill, READING, RG10 9UT.
•TAYLOR, Mr. Anthony John, FCA *1971;* with DTE Business Advisory Services Limited, DTE House, Hollins Mount, Hollins Lane, BURY, BL9 8AT.
TAYLOR, Mr. Anthony Julian, MA FCA *1965;* 1 Forge Lane, RICHMOND, SURREY, TW10 7BF. (Life Member)
TAYLOR, Mr. Antony Thomas, FCA *1960;* P.O Box 109, MOUNT MARTHA, VIC 3934, AUSTRALIA. (Life Member)
TAYLOR, Mr. Arran James, BA ACA *2005;* 39 Wedderburn Road, HARROGATE, NORTH YORKSHIRE, HG2 7QH.
TAYLOR, Mr. Ashley Paul, ACA *2008;* Flat 6 Reigate Court, Reigate Road, WORTHING, WEST SUSSEX, BN11 5LD.
TAYLOR, Ms. Barbara Janet, ACA CA(SA) *2010;* 1a Chandos Avenue, LONDON, W5 4EP.
TAYLOR, Mr. Barrie, FCA *1967;* 33 Mill Brow, Chadderton, OLDHAM, OL1 2RT.
TAYLOR, Mr. Barry Benjamin, BA ACA *2006;* 25 Kingsley Road, ILFORD, ESSEX, IG6 2LL.
TAYLOR, Mr. Basil George, BA FCA *1973;* 118 Church Road, Moseley, BIRMINGHAM, B13 9AA.
TAYLOR, Mr. Basil John, FCA *1974;* Tellings Golden Miller Group Plc, Building 16300 MT2, Electra Avenue, London Heathrow Airport, HOUNSLOW, TW6 2DN.
TAYLOR, Mr. Benjamin Heywood, BA(Hons) ACA *2004;* 65 Ormeley Road, LONDON, SW12 9QF.
TAYLOR, Mr. Benjamin Paul, BA(Hons) ACA *2000;* 11932 Diamond Springs Drive, JACKSONVILLE, FL 32246, UNITED STATES.
TAYLOR, Mr. Bhaven Ashok, BSc ACA *2007;* with PricewaterhouseCoopers LLP, 1 Embankment Place, LONDON, WC2N 6RH.
•TAYLOR, Mr. Brian, FCA *1962;* Brian Taylor FCA, 4 Lee Lane, Lumbutts, TODMORDEN, OL14 6HS.
TAYLOR, Mr. Brian, FCA *1955;* Blairlea, 30 St Christopher's Way, Bare, MORECAMBE, LA4 6EE. (Life Member)
TAYLOR, Mr. Brian Alan, BA ACA *1984;* BTA Consulting, Level A Close House, 84 Crouch Lane, Borough Green, SEVENOAKS, TN15 8LU.
TAYLOR, Mr. Brian Arthur, MSc FCA *1963;* 16 Greenway, Woodmancote, CHELTENHAM, GLOUCESTERSHIRE, GL52 9HU. (Life Member)
•TAYLOR, Mr. Brian Charles, BSc FCA *1974;* (Tax Fac), B.C Taylor, The Bungalow, The Avenue, Rowington, WARWICK, CV35 7BX.
TAYLOR, Mr. Brian Colston, FCA *1956;* 7222 East Fifth Street, NORTH VANCOUVER V7L 1L7, BC, CANADA. (Life Member)
TAYLOR, Mr. Brian David, FCA FInstD *1973;* (Tax Fac), 39 St. Johns Road, DRIFFIELD, NORTH HUMBERSIDE, YO25 6RS.
•TAYLOR, Mr. Brian Holmes, FCA *1974;* Titus Thorp & Ainsworth Limited, 132 Highfield Road, BLACKPOOL, FY4 2HH.
TAYLOR, Mr. Brian John, FCA *1966;* 5 Hale Green Farm, Hale, MILNTHORPE, LA7 7BJ. (Life Member)
TAYLOR, Mr. Brian Ward, BA FCA *1961;* Svedala, Sugar Lane, Adlington, MACCLESFIELD, SK10 5SQ.
TAYLOR, Mr. Bruce Havelock, BA ACA *1993;* Bay Tree Cottage, 85 Culverden Down, TUNBRIDGE WELLS, KENT, TN4 9SL.
TAYLOR, Mr. Bryan John, FCA *1973;* The Corner House, 4 Grocott Close, Penkridge, STAFFORD, ST19 5SN.
TAYLOR, Mr. Carl, MBA MEng ACA *1991;* 10 Waterside Avenue, BECKENHAM, BR3 3GJ.
TAYLOR, Mr. Carl Preston, BSc ACA *1987;* Uplands Cottage, Four Ashes Road, Cryers Hill, HIGH WYCOMBE, HP15 6LG.
TAYLOR, Mrs. Carole Ann, BA ACA *1986;* BAE Systems Australia Ltd, Taranaki Road, Edinburgh Parks, Edinburgh, ADELAIDE, SA 5111 AUSTRALIA.
TAYLOR, Mrs. Caroline Susan, BSc FCA DChA *1986;* Toybox PO Box 5967, Bletchley, MILTON KEYNES, MK3 6WD.
TAYLOR, Mrs. Catherine Elizabeth, BA(Hons) ACA *2001;* La Frontchiethe, La Rue de Cambrai, Trinity, JERSEY, JE3 5AL.
TAYLOR, Miss. Catherine Jane, BA ACA *1995;* 6 Langham Place, LONDON, W4 2QL.
TAYLOR, Mr. Charles David, BSc ACA *1994;* Aviva UK, Yorkshire House, 2 Rougier Street, YORK, YO90 1UU.
TAYLOR, Mr. Charles Edward MacDougall, ACA *2009;* PricewaterhouseCoopers, 26/F Office Tower A, Beijing Fortune Plaza, 7 Dongsanhuan Zhong Road Chaoyang District, BEIJING 100020, CHINA.
•TAYLOR, Mr. Charles Nigel Patrick, MBA BA ACA *1982;* c/o Taylor Brothers Bristol Ltd, 13-25 Wilder Street, BRISTOL, BS2 8PY.
TAYLOR, Dr. Charlotte, ACA *2011;* 7 Henley Street, OXFORD, OX4 1ER.
TAYLOR, Miss. Charlotte Emma Lucea, BA ACA *2003;* Aquamarine Power Elder House, 24 Elder Street, EDINBURGH, EH1 3DX.
•TAYLOR, Mr. Chilton Richard Vernon, MA *1978;* Baker Tilly Tax and Advisory Services LLP, 25 Farringdon Street, LONDON, EC4A 4AB. See also Baker Tilly Corporate Finance LLP
TAYLOR, Mrs. Christine Angela, BSc ACA *1988;* 58 Florence Road, NEDLANDS, WA 6009, AUSTRALIA.
TAYLOR, Mrs. Christine Lesley, BA FCA *1979;* 28 Aldrich Drive, Willen, MILTON KEYNES, MK15 9LU.
•TAYLOR, Mr. Christopher, BSocSc FCA *1996;* Adler Shine LLP, Aston House, Cornwall Avenue, LONDON, N3 1LF.
•TAYLOR, Mr. Christopher Howard, BSc FCA *1984;* PricewaterhouseCoopers LLP, 1 Embankment Place, LONDON, WC2N 6RH. See also PricewaterhouseCoopers
TAYLOR, Mr. Christopher Huw, BSc ACA *1999;* Abu Dhabi Finance, 14th Floor, ADCB HO, Al Salam Street, ABU DHABI, 107616 UNITED ARAB EMIRATES.
TAYLOR, Mr. Christopher John, BA ACA *1981;* UNEP/GEF, P.O Box 47074, NAIROBI, KENYA.
•TAYLOR, Mr. Christopher John, FCA *1982;* Taylor Viney & Marlow, 1422-4 London Road, LEIGH-ON-SEA, SS9 2UL.
TAYLOR, Mr. Christopher John, BSc ACA *1991;* Staddles, Bath Road, STURMINSTER NEWTON, DT10 1ED.
•TAYLOR, Mr. Christopher John, BSc FCA *1986;* Duncan Boxwell & Company Limited, Montrose House, Clayhill Industrial Park, NESTON, CH64 3RU.
TAYLOR, Mr. Christopher Neil, BSc ACA *1993;* Tudor Lodge, Mellersh Hill Road, Wonersh, GUILDFORD, SURREY, GU5 0QJ.
TAYLOR, Mr. Christopher St John, ACA *2009;* Flat 3, Clifton Wood Court, Clifton Wood Road, BRISTOL, BS8 4UL.
TAYLOR, Mr. Christopher William, MSci ACA *2006;* with PricewaterhouseCoopers LLP, 9 Greyfriars Road, READING, RG1 1JG.
TAYLOR, Mrs. Claire, ACA *2002;* 14 Welton Wold View, Swanland, NORTH FERRIBY, NORTH HUMBERSIDE, HU14 3PX.
TAYLOR, Miss. Claire Elaine, BA ACA *2005;* Flat 3, 45 Ridge Road, LONDON, N8 9LJ.
TAYLOR, Mrs. Claire Elizabeth, MA ACA *2000;* 36 Ringford Road, LONDON, SW18 1RR.
TAYLOR, Miss. Claire Zoe, BSc(Hons) ACA *2006;* with RSM Tenon Limited, The Poynt Building, 45 Wollaton Street, NOTTINGHAM, NG1 5FW.
TAYLOR, Miss. Claire-Louise, BA FCA *1992;* L'Abaille, 11 Rue Edgard Moulineau, 17240 CHAMPAGNOLLES, FRANCE.
•TAYLOR, Mr. Colin, FCA *1976;* 5 Ashford Close, BURY, LANCASHIRE, BL8 2XE.
TAYLOR, Mr. Colin Bernard, FCA *1970;* 3 Priory Way, Chalfont St. Peter, GERRARDS CROSS, SL9 8SD. (Life Member)
TAYLOR, The Revd. Colin Edward, FCA MCIM CTA *1959;* 177 Masefield Road, WARMINSTER, WILTSHIRE, BA12 8HY. (Life Member)
TAYLOR, Mr. Colin Harwood, FCA *1970;* Petrofac House, Al Khan, SHARJAH, 23467 shj, UNITED ARAB EMIRATES.
•TAYLOR, Mr. Colin Heatley, BA FCA *1974;* Rosscot Limited, Thomas Edge House, Tunnell Street, St Helier, JERSEY, JE2 4LU. See also Le Rossigmol, Scott Warren and Partners
•TAYLOR, Mr. Colin Jeffrey, FCA *1970;* (Tax Fac), Donald Jacobs & Partners, Suite 2 1st Floor, Fountain House, 1a Elm Park, STANMORE, HA7 4AU.
TAYLOR, Mr. Colin Mark, BA ACA *1988;* Pepper's End, 10 Hungershall Park, TUNBRIDGE WELLS, TN4 8NE.
•TAYLOR, Mr. Colin Richard Newton, FCA *1982;* Taylors, 203 London Road, Hadleigh, BENFLEET, SS7 2RD.
TAYLOR, Mr. Craig, BSc ACA *1999;* 2a Back Lane West, Royston, BARNSLEY, SOUTH YORKSHIRE, S71 4SB.
TAYLOR, Mr. Craig John Donald, BSc ACA *2004;* 84 Stone Row, Malinslee, TELFORD, TF3 2HJ.
•TAYLOR, Mr. Dale Christopher, FCA *1976;* Baker Tilly UK Audit LLP, 25 Farringdon Street, LONDON, EC4A 4AB.
TAYLOR, Mr. Damian Peter, BSc ACA *1997;* (Tax Fac), 11 Warwick Drive, BEVERLEY, HU17 9TB.
TAYLOR, Mr. Daniel Adam, ACA *2008;* P K F Regent House, Clinton Avenue, NOTTINGHAM, NG5 1AZ.
TAYLOR, Mr. Daniel Barlow, BA FCA *1968;* 11 Priory Road, Chalfont St. Peter, GERRARDS CROSS, BUCKINGHAMSHIRE, SL9 8SB.
TAYLOR, Mr. Daniel James Frederick, ACA *2011;* 23 Park Lane, Hartford, NORTHWICH, CHESHIRE, CW8 1PZ.
TAYLOR, Mr. Daniel James Robert, BSc ACA *2000;* with Rawlinson & Hunter, Lower Mill, Kingston Road, Ewell, EPSOM, KT17 2AE.
TAYLOR, Mr. Daniel John, BEng ACA *2007;* 32 Trebellan Drive, HEMEL HEMPSTEAD, HERTFORDSHIRE, HP2 5EL.
•TAYLOR, Mr. Daniel Michael, BA(Hons) ACA *2001;* BDO LLP, 55 Baker Street, LONDON, W1U 7EU. See also BDO Stoy Hayward LLP
•TAYLOR, Mr. Daniel Stuart, MA BA(Hons) ACA *2001;* Grant Thornton UK LLP, Pinnacle Building, 20 Tudor Road, READING, RG1 1NH. See also Grant Thornton LLP
TAYLOR, Mrs. Daphne Gillian, BSc FCA *1981;* 13 St. Peters Grove, YORK, YO30 6AQ.
TAYLOR, Mr. Darren, ACA *1999;* 4 St. Georges Court, Willerby, HULL, HU10 6FN.
TAYLOR, Mr. Darren Mark, BA ACA *1992;* 16 Heather Court, Ty Canol, CWMBRAN, GWENT, NP44 6JQ.
•TAYLOR, Mr. David, BA FCA *1988;* Taylor & Co Accountancy Services Ltd, 64 Lewin Street, MIDDLEWICH, CHESHIRE, CW10 9AS.
TAYLOR, Mr. David, FCA *1960;* 2 Pond Farm Drive, Hove Edge, BRIGHOUSE, HD6 2RT. (Life Member)
TAYLOR, Mr. David, FCA *1962;* 4 Portmellon Park, Mevagissey, ST AUSTELL, CORNWALL, PL26 6XD. (Life Member)
TAYLOR, Mr. David, BA(Hons) FCA *1979;* 5 Frant Court, Frant, TUNBRIDGE WELLS, KENT, TN3 9DW.
TAYLOR, Mr. David, BSc FCA *1976;* 26 Cleveland Crescent, DARTMOUTH B3A 2L6, NS, CANADA.
TAYLOR, Mr. David, BA ACA *1983;* Scarth Nick House Redmire, LEYBURN, NORTH YORKSHIRE, DL8 4NL.
•TAYLOR, Mr. David Alan, BA FCA *1978;* Stubbs Parkin Taylor & Co, 18a London Street, SOUTHPORT, MERSEYSIDE, PR9 0UE. See also Stubbs Parkin Taylor & Co Limited
TAYLOR, Dr. David Alan, MA DMS ACA ATII *1997;* (Tax Fac), The Haven, 42 Cambridge Road, Impington, CAMBRIDGE, CB24 9NU.
•TAYLOR, Mr. David Albert, BA FCA *1984;* (Tax Fac), David A Taylor, The Old Rectory, Boltongate, WIGTON, CUMBRIA, CA7 1DA.
•TAYLOR, Mr. David Alexander John, FCA *1987;* Harts LLP, Westminster House, 10 Westminster Road, MACCLESFIELD, CHESHIRE, SK10 1BX. See also Hart Shaw Macclesfield LLP
•TAYLOR, Mr. David Anthony, BA ACA *1982;* David Taylor, 15 Hill Rise, WOODSTOCK, OXFORDSHIRE, OX20 1AA.
•TAYLOR, Mr. David Arthur, FCA *1966;* Taylor Croft & Winder, 16 Bond Street, WAKEFIELD, WF1 2QP.
TAYLOR, Mr. David Brian, FCA *1987;* Ross Aldridge Solicitors Eagle Tower, Montpellier Drive, CHELTENHAM, GLOUCESTERSHIRE, GL50 1TA.
TAYLOR, Mr. David Bryan, FCA *1969;* Cornerways, Pilcorn Street, WEDMORE, SOMERSET, BS28 4AW.
TAYLOR, Mr. David George, FCA *1968;* P.O. Box 203, CONSTANTIA, C.P., 7848, SOUTH AFRICA. (Life Member)
TAYLOR, Mr. David Hugh, FCA *1974;* 2 Windermere Road, BACUP, OL13 9DN.
TAYLOR, Mr. David John, FCA *1967;* 31 Sion Hill, BATH, BA1 2UW.
TAYLOR, Mr. David John, BSc ACA *1987;* 35 Williams Grove, SURBITON, KT6 5RW.
TAYLOR, Mr. David John, MA ACA *1990;* 28 St Oswalds Road, BRISTOL, BS6 7HT.
TAYLOR, Mr. David John, MSc ACA *1982;* 4b Castle Road, North Finchley, LONDON, N12 9ED.
TAYLOR, Mr. David John Simon, BCom ACA *1984;* 23 Park Lane, Hartford, NORTHWICH, CW8 1PZ.
•TAYLOR, Mr. David Jonathan, BSc ACA *1992;* PricewaterhouseCoopers LLP, Hays Galleria, 1 Hays Lane, LONDON, SE1 2RD. See also PricewaterhouseCoopers
TAYLOR, Mr. David Kirk, MA FCA *1979;* 10 Eascote Road, AYLESBURY, BUCKINGHAMSHIRE, HP21 9XL.
TAYLOR, Mr. David Lee, BSc FCA *1975;* (Tax Fac), Oil Spill Response Ltd, Lower William Street, SOUTHAMPTON, SO14 5QE.
TAYLOR, Mr. David Michael, BEng ACA *1998;* Holsworthy, 95 Fullers Hill, CHESHAM, BUCKINGHAMSHIRE, HP5 1LS.
TAYLOR, Mr. David Michael, MA FCA *1979;* 103 Moorhead Lane, SHIPLEY, BD18 4LH.
TAYLOR, Mr. David Mills, FCA *1958;* 2 Beechwood Drive, COBHAM, KT11 2DX.
TAYLOR, Mr. David Richard, FCA *1983;* 34 Spruce Avenue, LOUGHBOROUGH, LEICESTERSHIRE, LE11 2QW.
•TAYLOR, Mr. David Robert, FCA *1974;* 34 Cross Lane, Stocksmoor, HUDDERSFIELD, HD4 6XH.
TAYLOR, Mr. David Robert John, LLB ACA *2004;* 67 Regent Road North, Gosforth, NEWCASTLE UPON TYNE, NE3 1EH.
TAYLOR, Mr. David Ross, FCA *1974;* 85 Bassaleg Road, NEWPORT, GWENT, NP20 3NA.
TAYLOR, Mr. David Stuart, BSc ACA *1991;* Auchenlarich, Gartocharn, ALEXANDRIA, G83 8RR.
TAYLOR, Mr. David Vernon, BSc FCA *1973;* 37713 S Golf Course Dr, TUCSON, AZ 85739-3055, UNITED STATES.
TAYLOR, Mr. Dean Paul, BSc ACA *2006;* 6 Llys y Berllan, RUTHIN, CLWYD, LL15 1PJ.
TAYLOR, Mrs. Deborah, BSc ACA *1990;* 15 Barshaw Gardens, Appleton, WARRINGTON, WA4 5FA.
TAYLOR, Miss. Deborah, MSc ACA *2005;* 10 Radnor Road, LONDON, NW6 6TT.
TAYLOR, Mrs. Deborah, BA ACA *1985;* 177 Gatton Park Road, REIGATE, SURREY, RH2 0SU.
TAYLOR, Mr. Denis Brook, FCA *1951;* Flat 88, Lord's View, St John's Wood Road, LONDON, NW8 7HG. (Life Member)
TAYLOR, Mr. Dennis, FCA *1957;* D Taylor, 18 Kelvon Close, Glenfield, LEICESTER, LE3 8AT. (Life Member)
TAYLOR, Mr. Denzil Jon, MA ACA *2001;* 22 Hartlebury Way, Charlton Kings, CHELTENHAM, GLOUCESTERSHIRE, GL52 6YB.
TAYLOR, Mr. Derek Edward, FCA *1969;* with Dutton Moore, 6 Silver Street, HULL, HU1 1JA.
TAYLOR, Mr. Derek John, FCA *1960;* 6 Court House Road, Llanvair Discoed, CHEPSTOW, NP16 6LW. (Life Member)
TAYLOR, Mr. Derrick Radcliffe Hanson, FCA *1960;* Snowdowne, 12 Derby Road, HASLEMERE, GU27 1BP.
•TAYLOR, Mr. Donald Thomas, FCA *1977;* (Tax Fac), Rowlands, Gladstone House, Gladstone Street, CROOK, DL15 9ED. See also Rowlands Limited
TAYLOR, Mrs. Dorothy Margaret, BA FCA CTA *1982;* 5 Carrs Meadow, Escrick, YORK, YO19 6JZ.
TAYLOR, Mrs. Dorothy Ruth, BA FCA *1977;* (Tax Fac), Lafarge (UK) Services Ltd, Regent House, Station Approach, DORKING, SURREY, RH4 1TH.
TAYLOR, Mr. Duncan Andrew, BA ACA *1996;* (Tax Fac), 25 Crawley Close, Slip End, LUTON, LU1 4BT.
TAYLOR, Mr. Duncan Cameron, BA ACA *1989;* 5 Kenwood Drive, SHREWSBURY, SY3 8SZ.
TAYLOR, Mr. Duncan Sidney, BA ACA *1981;* 4 Westleigh Park, Hengrove, BRISTOL, BS14 9TH.
TAYLOR, Mr. Edward, ACA *2003;* 13 Howell Avenue, Surrey Hills, MELBOURNE, VIC 3127, AUSTRALIA.

TAYLOR, Mr. Edward Allen, FCA *1953;* Apartment 51, Deercote Court, Glen Luce, Cheshunt, WALTHAM CROSS, HERTFORDSHIRE EN8 8NW. (Life Member)
TAYLOR, Mr. Edward John, FCA *1965;* 4 Holloway Lane, Chesham Bois, AMERSHAM, BUCKINGHAMSHIRE, HP6 6DJ. (Life Member)
TAYLOR, Mr. Edward Michael, BEng ACA *1994;* Fromentine, Curridge Road, Curridge, THATCHAM, BERKSHIRE, RG18 9DH.
TAYLOR, Mr. Edward Miles, FCA *1973;* 11 Queens Gate Place, LONDON, SW7 5NX.
TAYLOR, Mr. Edward Nicholas, BSc ACA *1997;* 2 Gilbert Road, Hale, ALTRINCHAM, CHESHIRE, WA15 9NR.
TAYLOR, Mr. Edwin, FCA *1964;* 27 Irwell Road, WARRINGTON, WA4 6BA. (Life Member)
TAYLOR, Miss. Eleanor, MEng ACA *2006;* 16 Annscroft, BIRMINGHAM, B38 8YU.
TAYLOR, Ms. Eleanor Victoria, LLB ACA CTA AKC *2004;* with Deloitte LLP, Hill House, 1 Little New Street, LONDON, EC4A 3TR.
TAYLOR, Mrs. Elizabeth, BA(Hons) ACA *2002;* 4 Franklin Way, Cherry Willingham, LINCOLN, LN3 4GL.
TAYLOR, Mrs. Elizabeth Clare, BSc ACA *1997;* 35 Dama Road, Fazeley, TAMWORTH, STAFFORDSHIRE, B78 3SU.
TAYLOR, Miss. Emily Ruth, BSc ACA *2007;* Flat B, 52 Elspeth Road, LONDON, SW11 1DS.
TAYLOR, Mrs. Emma, BA ACA *1996;* 2 Gilbert Road, Hale, ALTRINCHAM, CHESHIRE, WA15 9NR.
TAYLOR, Miss. Emma Jayne, BA ACA *2006;* 119 Albury Road, Merstham, REDHILL, RH1 3LW.
TAYLOR, Miss. Emma Louise, MA(Hons) ACA *2003;* 10a Morningside Place, EDINBURGH, EH10 5ER.
TAYLOR, Miss. Emma Victoria, BA ACA *2007;* K P M G, 1 The Embankment, LEEDS, LS1 4DW.
•TAYLOR, Mr. Eric, BSc FCA *1986;* Gibbons, Carleton House, 136 Gray Street, WORKINGTON, CUMBRIA, CA14 2LU. See also Gibbons & Company
TAYLOR, Mr. Eric Suresh Sivapragasam, BSc ACA *1993;* Springfield, The Street, North Warnborough, HOOK, RG29 1BE.
TAYLOR, Mr. Eric William, FCA *1961;* 1 Orchard Close, Appleton Roebuck, YORK, YO23 7DB. (Life Member)
TAYLOR, Mrs. Erica Jane, BA ACA *1995;* 49 Holmlea Road, Goring, READING, RG8 9EX.
•TAYLOR, Mr. Ernest Brian, FCA *1964;* E. B. Taylor Limited, Haven Lea, Canterbury Road, Chilham, CANTERBURY, KENT CT4 8AE.
TAYLOR, Mrs. Eun Young, BA ACA *2003;* 76 Maple Avenue, LITTLE SILVER, NJ 07739, UNITED STATES.
TAYLOR, Miss. Fiona Caroline, BSc ACA *2010;* Flat 23 Gemini Court, 852 Brighton Road, PURLEY, CR8 2FD.
•①TAYLOR, Miss. Fiona Livingstone, BSc ACA *1993;* with Ernst & Young LLP, G1, 5 George Square, GLASGOW, G2 1DY.
TAYLOR, Miss. Frances, BA ACA *2006;* 59 Edward Road, BARNET, HERTFORDSHIRE, EN4 8AZ.
TAYLOR, Miss. Frances Mary, BSc ACA *2006;* 25 Forton Road, NEWPORT, SHROPSHIRE, TF10 7JR.
TAYLOR, Mr. Frederick, FCA *1969;* Tanners Cottage, Highmoor Cross, HENLEY-ON-THAMES, RG9 5DR.
TAYLOR, Mr. Frederick Mackford, FCA *1949;* Oakland, Egypt Hill, COWES, PO31 8BP. (Life Member)
TAYLOR, Miss. Gabrielle, BSc ACA *2005;* Riedtlistrasse 19, 8006 ZURICH, SWITZERLAND.
TAYLOR, Mr. Gareth Henry John, BSc ACA *1990;* Threadneedle Asset Management Ltd St. Mary Axe House, 60 St. Mary Axe, LONDON, EC3A 8JQ.
TAYLOR, Mr. Gareth John Spencer, BA(Hons) ACA *2002;* 9 Nightingale Lane, BROMLEY, BR1 2QH.
TAYLOR, Mr. Garic Jefferson, BSc ACA *1995;* Granary House Main Street, Newton Kyme, TADCASTER, NORTH YORKSHIRE, LS24 9LS.
TAYLOR, Mr. Gary, BSc FCA *1998;* 18 Primula Drive, DARWEN, BB3 0SW.
TAYLOR, Mr. Gary David, BA ACA *1992;* Liberum Capital, 1 City Square, LEEDS, LS1 2ES.
TAYLOR, Mr. Gary David, ACA *2010;* 18 Manor Gardens, GATESHEAD, TYNE AND WEAR, NE10 8UZ.
TAYLOR, Mr. Gary Douglas, BA FCA *1989;* 4 Elmfield Gardens, NEWCASTLE UPON TYNE, NE3 4XB.
•TAYLOR, Mr. Gary Lee, ACA *1985;* G.L. Taylor & Co, 10 Tudor Close, Cheam, SUTTON, SM3 8QS. See also G L Taylor & Co(Accountants) Limited
•TAYLOR, Mr. Gavin John, BCom ACA *1997;* Mayes Business Partnership Ltd, 22-28 Willow Street, ACCRINGTON, LANCASHIRE, BB5 1LP.
•TAYLOR, Mrs. Gaye Louise, BA ACA *1999;* 58 Brimmers Hill, Widmer End, HIGH WYCOMBE, BUCKINGHAMSHIRE, HP15 6NP.
TAYLOR, Mrs. Gemma Helen, BSc ACA *2003;* Pine Court, Beacon Road West, CROWBOROUGH, TN6 1QL.
TAYLOR, Mr. Geoffrey, MA FCA *1979;* Larks Hill, Linton Lane, Linton, WETHERBY, WEST YORKSHIRE, LS22 4HH.
TAYLOR, Mr. George Brian, FCA *1957;* Uplands, Warley Wood Lane, Luddendenfoot, HALIFAX, HX2 6BL. (Life Member)
TAYLOR, Mr. George William, FCA *1964;* El Retiro, Meadow View, Little Mountain Road, BUCKLEY, CH7 3BX.
TAYLOR, Mrs. Georgina Jane, BSc ACA *2003;* New Look New Look House, Mercery Road, WEYMOUTH, DORSET, DT3 5HJ.
TAYLOR, Ms. Georgina Margaret, BA ACA *2000;* with Ernst & Young LLP, 1 More London Place, LONDON, SE1 2AF.
TAYLOR, Miss. Georgina Michelle, BA ACA *2005;* 28 Ember Gardens, THAMES DITTON, KT7 0LN.
TAYLOR, Mr. Gerald Brian, FCA *1966;* 39 Oakridge Avenue, RADLETT, HERTFORDSHIRE, WD7 8EW.
TAYLOR, Mr. Gethin James, ACA *1993;* Chancery Trust Company Ltd First Floor East Wing, Shearwater House Nunnery Mills Old Castletown Road Dougla, ISLE OF MAN, IM2 1QA.
TAYLOR, Mr. Giles Benjamin Francis, BA ACA *1999;* K P M G, 1 The Embankment, LEEDS, LS1 4DW.
TAYLOR, Mr. Giles Stephen Frederick, MA MSc ACA *1986;* 65 Dresden Road, LONDON, N19 3BG.
•TAYLOR, Mrs. Gillian, FCA *1978;* Gillian Taylor, 49 Creighton Avenue, Muswell Hill, LONDON, N10 1NR.
TAYLOR, Mrs. Glynis Ann, FCA *1974;* P.O Box 625, CHRISTCHURCH 8140, NEW ZEALAND.
TAYLOR, Mr. Godfrey Lionel Fozard, MA FCA CTA *1974;* Frogs Leap, Fulshaw Park, WILMSLOW, SK9 1QQ.
TAYLOR, Mr. Graeme Stewart, BA ACA *1986;* 152 Dover Park, Masterton, DUNFERMLINE, KY11 8HX.
•TAYLOR, Mr. Graham E, ACA FCCA *2007;* Langdowns DFK Limited, Fleming Court, Leigh Road, EASTLEIGH, HAMPSHIRE, SO50 9PD.
•TAYLOR, Mr. Graham John, FCA *1972;* Barnett Hill & Co, 1 Hazelbury Crescent, LUTON, LU1 1DS. See also Taylor G.J.
TAYLOR, Mr. Grant Stephen Victor, BA FCA *1995;* 2 The Old Coalyard, Styles Lane Puddletown, DORCHESTER, DORSET, DT2 8SJ.
TAYLOR, Mr. Gregory Robert, BSc FCA MCT *1984;* 37 Clifford Road, New Barnet, BARNET, EN5 5PD.
TAYLOR, Mr. Greig Robert, BA ACA *2003;* 76 Maple Avenue, LITTLE SILVER, NJ 07739, UNITED STATES.
TAYLOR, Mr. Guy James, BA ACA *2004;* with Yorkshire Bank PLC, Manchester Financial Solutions Centre, The Chancery, 58 Spring Gardens, MANCHESTER, M2 1YB.
TAYLOR, Miss. Hazel Veronica, DPh FCA *1980;* 32 Axtaine Road, ORPINGTON, BR5 4HX.
TAYLOR, Miss. Heather Loyce Scott, BA FCA *1979;* with PricewaterhouseCoopers, 63 rue de Villiers, 92208 NEUILLY SUR SEINE CEDEX, FRANCE.
TAYLOR, Mrs. Helen Beryl, BSc ACA *1992;* 9 Church Close, Longcot, FARINGDON, SN7 7TN.
TAYLOR, Miss. Helen Mary, BA ACA *1992;* 194 Donlea Drive, TORONTO M4G 2M8, ON, CANADA.
TAYLOR, Mrs. Helen Rachel, BSc ACA *1995;* Giggleswick School, Giggleswick, SETTLE, NORTH YORKSHIRE, BD24 0DE.
TAYLOR, Miss. Helen Ruth, BSc ACA *1993;* 18 Minot Close, MALMESBURY, WILTSHIRE, SN16 9JG.
TAYLOR, Miss. Helga Clare, BA ACA *1993;* 5 Gladwyn Road, LONDON, SW15 1JY.
•TAYLOR, Mr. Henry John Corbett, MA FCA *1973;* John Taylor, 11 Jacobean Lane, Copt Heath, SOLIHULL, B93 9LP.
TAYLOR, Mr. Hereward Charles, BA ACA *1995;* 32 Clifford Manor Road, GUILDFORD, SURREY, GU4 8AQ.
TAYLOR, Mrs. Hilary, BA ACA *1996;* 2 Impasse de Maisons, 73700 SEEZ, SAVOIE, FRANCE.
TAYLOR, Mrs. Hilary Claire, MSc FCA *1986;* 19 Kestrel Way, Woosehill, WOKINGHAM, RG41 3HA.
TAYLOR, Mr. Howard Alan Bernard, ACA CA(SA) *2008;* 208 Old Barn Lane, CHAPEL HILL, NC, UNITED STATES.
TAYLOR, Mr. Howard Iain Paul, BSc(Hons) ACA *2010;* Flat 5, 100 Drayton Park, LONDON, N5 1NF.
TAYLOR, Mr. Howard John, BA FCA MBA *1991;* 10 Garnett Hall, DUNBOYNE, COUNTY MEATH, IRELAND.
TAYLOR, Mr. Hugh Andrew Raymond, ACA *1980;* Old Kingsham Farm Cooks Pond Road, Milland, LIPHOOK, GU30 7JY.
TAYLOR, Mr. Hugh Edward, FCA *1966;* 1 Orchard Lea, Hildenborough, TONBRIDGE, TN11 9BZ.
TAYLOR, Mr. Iain George, MA CA *1988; (CA Scotland 1979);* 2 Woodfield Way, ST. ALBANS, AL4 9RX. (Life Member)
•TAYLOR, Mr. Ian, FCA *1973;* Mulberry House, Wilkin Hill, Barlow, DRONFIELD, S18 7TE.
TAYLOR, Mr. Ian Ashbourne, FCA *1975;* 33 South Lodge, 142 Nelson Road, TWICKENHAM, TW2 7BX.
TAYLOR, Mr. Ian Clifford, FCA *1966;* Callejon de la Baranca 3, Ciudad Santo Domingo, Algete, 28120 MADRID, SPAIN. (Life Member)
TAYLOR, Mr. Ian David, FCA *1966;* (Tax Fac), 58 Apollo Avenue, BURY, BL9 8HG. (Life Member)
TAYLOR, Mr. Ian Duncan, BA ACA *2006;* 18/ 24 Fairlight Street, FAIRLIGHT, NSW 2094, AUSTRALIA.
TAYLOR, Mr. Ian Gerald, ACA *1981;* Blue Fin Building, 110 Southwark Street, LONDON, SE1 0TA.
TAYLOR, Mr. Ian Quinney, BSc FCA *1980;* 22 Grune Point Close, Skinburness, WIGTON, CUMBRIA, CA7 4QX.
TAYLOR, Mr. Ian Richard, MA FCA *1990;* (Tax Fac), with KPMG LLP, 15 Canada Square, LONDON, E14 5GL.
•TAYLOR, Mrs. Imogen Clare, MA FCA DChA *1984;* Imogen Taylor, Hilldene, Paddock Lane, Audlem, CREWE, CW3 0DP.
TAYLOR, Miss. Isla Kathryn, ACA *2007;* 41 Cowleigh Bank, MALVERN, WORCESTERSHIRE, WR14 1QP.
TAYLOR, Mr. Jacob Edmund, BA ACA *2006;* 59 Edward Road, BARNET, HERTFORDSHIRE, EN4 8AZ.
TAYLOR, Mrs. Jacqueline Anne, BSc FCA *1988;* Holly Tree Lodge, Hockley Lane, Stoke Poges, SLOUGH, SL2 4QE.
TAYLOR, Mr. James Alexander, BA ACA *2000;* JP Morgan Cazenove Limited, 20 Moorgate, LONDON, EC2R 6DA.
TAYLOR, Mr. James Andrew, LLB ACA *2004;* with Ernst & Young LLP, 1 More London Place, LONDON, SE1 2AF.
TAYLOR, Mr. James Mark, BSc ACA *2005;* 14 Mere Hey, Eccleston, ST. HELENS, WA10 5AJ.
TAYLOR, Mr. James Moorhouse, FCA *1961;* Calle Curro Claros 7, Edf. Dovysa 4oD, Los Boliches, Feungirola, 29640 MALAGA, SPAIN.
TAYLOR, Mr. James Richard, BSc ACA *2002;* 17 Laurel Crescent, Smalley Village, DERBY, DE7 6EJ.
TAYLOR, Mr. James William Matthew, BA(Hons) ACA *2001;* GHD, Bridgewater Place, Water Lane, LEEDS, LS11 5BZ.
TAYLOR, Mr. Jamie Lewis, BSc(Hons) ACA *2010;* 16 Rendlesham Avenue, RADLETT, HERTFORDSHIRE, WD7 8PF.
TAYLOR, Mrs. Jane, BA ACA *1993;* Hollybank, Church Street, Ainsworth, BOLTON, BL2 5RU.
TAYLOR, Miss. Jane Elizabeth, BSc ACA *2002;* 9 Blackheath Close, WASHINGTON, NE37 2LU.
TAYLOR, Mrs. Jane Elizabeth, BA FCA *1986;* Wyndways, Rosehill Road, Stoke Heath, MARKET DRAYTON, SHROPSHIRE, TF9 2LF.
TAYLOR, Miss. Jane Hilary, FCA *1976;* 3 Stace Close, Beacon Oak Road, TENTERDEN, TN30 6RP.
TAYLOR, Mrs. Jane Susan, BSc ACA *1993;* Runcton Mill, Mill Lane, Runcton, CHICHESTER, WEST SUSSEX, PO20 1PR.
TAYLOR, Mrs. Janet Margaret, ACA *1992;* victoria villa, 26 Victoria Road, KINGSTON UPON THAMES, KT1 3DW.
TAYLOR, Mr. Jason Michael, MA ACA *1995;* C/Joaquin Ibarra 2, Casa 6, 28042 MADRID, SPAIN.
TAYLOR, Mr. Jeffrey, FCA *1977;* Redmayne Bentley, 10 Victoria Avenue, HARROGATE, NORTH YORKSHIRE, HG1 1ED.
TAYLOR, Mrs. Jemma Lucy, BSocSc ACA *1996;* 9 Bangalore Street, LONDON, SW15 1QD.
TAYLOR, Miss. Jennifer, MA ACA CTA *1989;* 107 Houldsworth Mill Waterhouse Way, Reddish, STOCKPORT, SK5 6DD.
TAYLOR, Miss. Jennifer Kim, BSc ACA *2010;* 170 Forbes Street, WOOLLOOMOOLOO, NSW 2011, AUSTRALIA.
TAYLOR, Mr. Jeremy Nicolas, BSc ACA *1991;* Rua Inocencio Nogueira 115, Casa 21, Cidade Jardim, SAO PAULO, 05676-030, BRAZIL.
TAYLOR, Miss. Jessica Anne, BA ACA *2010;* 94 Finsbury Park Avenue, LONDON, N4 1DS.
TAYLOR, Miss. Jillian Margaret, BSc ACA *1985;* City College, Fordrough Lane, Bordesley Green, BIRMINGHAM, B9 5NA.
TAYLOR, Mrs. Joanna Claire, MA FCA *1983;* Balnageine, FORRES, MORAYSHIRE, IV36 2RR.
TAYLOR, Miss. Joanna Shan, BMus ACA *1993;* 14 The Drive, Hartley, PLYMOUTH, PL3 5SU.
TAYLOR, Ms. Joanne Elizabeth, LLB ACA CTA *2003;* (Tax Fac), K P M G, St. James's Square, MANCHESTER, M2 6DS.
TAYLOR, Dr. Joanne Elizabeth, BSc ACA *2000;* Amey Colas Church Road, Stoke Gifford, BRISTOL, BS34 8QA.
TAYLOR, Miss. Joanne Lesley, BA ACA *1990;* Central Finance 3rd Floor East, Unipart Group of Companies Unipart House, Garsington Road Cowley, OXFORD, OX4 2PG.
TAYLOR, Mr. John Alfred, FCA *1963;* 14 Turner Court, High Street, BERKHAMSTED, HERTFORDSHIRE, HP4 3ZE. (Life Member)
TAYLOR, Mr. John Arthur, FCA *1972;* Jatco Energy, 1 Thornbill Rise, Albany, AUCKLAND 0632, NEW ZEALAND.
•TAYLOR, Mr. John Christopher, BA ACA CF *1988;* Smith Cooper, 2 Lace Market Square, NOTTINGHAM, NG1 1PB. See also F B 40 Limited
TAYLOR, Mr. John David, BSc FCA *1981;* with PricewaterhouseCoopers LLP, 1 Embankment Place, LONDON, WC2N 6RH.
TAYLOR, Mr. John David, BA CA FCA *1984;* (Tax Fac), 56 56 Coogan Close, CARLISLE, CA2 5SG.
TAYLOR, Mr. John Edward, FCA *1956;* Lindisfarne, 9 Southcote Orchard, TOTNES, TQ9 5PA. (Life Member)
TAYLOR, Mr. John Fallows, FCA *1943;* Manorfield, Butterwick, Weaverthorpe, MALTON, YO17 8HF. (Life Member)
TAYLOR, Mr. John Frederick, FCA *1960;* 2 Tarn Brow, ORMSKIRK, L39 4SS. (Life Member)
TAYLOR, Mr. John Guy, FCA *1976;* 2330 Kearney Street, DENVER, CO 80207, UNITED STATES.
TAYLOR, Mr. John Harvey, FCA *1964;* 21443 Lakefront Drive, LAGO VISTA, TX 78645, UNITED STATES. (Life Member)
TAYLOR, Mr. John Henry, FCA *1953;* 3 Amelia Court, Shore Road, East Wittering, CHICHESTER, WEST SUSSEX, PO20 8BG. (Life Member)
TAYLOR, Mr. John Howard, MA FCA *1977;* D L A Design Group of Companies Ltd, Wakefield 41 Business Park, WAKEFIELD, WEST YORKSHIRE, WF2 0XJ.
TAYLOR, Mr. John Keith, BCom FCA *1981;* 12 Newholme Close, Croxteth Park, LIVERPOOL, L12 0JG.
TAYLOR, Mr. John Massey, BA FCA *1977;* Alfonso Esparza Oteo 144 int 505-507, Colonia Guadalupe Inn, 01020 MEXICO CITY, FEDERAL DISTRICT, MEXICO.
•TAYLOR, Mr. John Michael, ACA *1982;* JT Financial Services, 163 Lily Hill Street, Whitefield, MANCHESTER, M45 7SP.
•TAYLOR, Mr. John Murray, BSc FCA ATII *1987;* M R Salvage Limited, 7-8 Eghams Court, Boston Drive, BOURNE END, BUCKINGHAMSHIRE, SL8 5YS.
TAYLOR, Mr. John Patrick Enfield, FCA *1972;* Pitthouse Farm, Ashford Hill, THATCHAM, RG19 8BN.
•TAYLOR, Mr. John Paul, BA FCA *1990;* Taylor Dawson Plumb Limited, 2 King Street, NOTTINGHAM, NG1 2AS.
TAYLOR, Mr. John Paul, FCA *1970;* 14 Rue Claude Debussy, Domaine De La Bataille, 78370 PLAISIR, FRANCE. (Life Member)
TAYLOR, Mr. John Richard, FCA *1975;* c/o Lindsey Dunbar, HQ SSAFA Forces Help, Episkopi, 53 BFPO, CYPRUS.
TAYLOR, Mr. John Richard Frederick, BA ACA *1989;* 1 Sunningdale Avenue, Perton, WOLVERHAMPTON, WV6 7YR.
•TAYLOR, Mr. John Robert, ACA *1993;* with RSM Tenon Limited, Vantage, Victoria Street, BASINGSTOKE, RG21 3BT.
TAYLOR, Mr. John Robert, BA FCA *1974;* Cheshire & Wirral Partnership NHS Trust, 40 Mill Lane, WALLASEY, MERSEYSIDE, CH44 5UG.
TAYLOR, Mr. John Stanley, BCom ACA *1984;* 2 Daimler Close, STAFFORD, STAFFORDSHIRE, ST17 4XX.
TAYLOR, Mr. John Tudor, BSc FCA *1977;* 48 Dovers Park, Bathford, BATH, BA1 7UD.
TAYLOR, Mr. Jonathan, BSc FCA *1997;* 3 Dawson Avenue, Simonstone, BURNLEY, LANCASHIRE, BB12 7JF.

TAYLOR, Mr. Jonathan Burder, MA ACA *1992;* 78 Palace Road, LONDON, SW2 3JX.
TAYLOR, Mr. Jonathan Edwin, ACA *1982;* 22 Kayemoor Road, SUTTON, SM2 5HT.
TAYLOR, Mr. Jonathan Michael, BSc ACA *1998;* Chartwell 21a Stoke Hill, BRISTOL, BS9 1JN.
TAYLOR, Mr. Jonathon James, BSc ACA *1997;* 12 St. Edeyrns Road, CARDIFF, CF23 6TB.
TAYLOR, Mr. Joseph, MA FCA *1974;* 13 Elmstead Close, Totteridge, LONDON, N20 8ER. (Life Member)
TAYLOR, Mr. Joseph John, ACA *2008;* 11 Tanfield Road, MANCHESTER, M20 5GE.
TAYLOR, Mr. Josh, BSc ACA *2010;* The Red Wine House, Brick House Road, Tolleshunt Major, MALDON, ESSEX, CM9 8JX.
TAYLOR, Mrs. Judith Ann, BA ACA *1993;* 2 Mayfield Road, Ashton-on-Ribble, PRESTON, PR2 1EX.
TAYLOR, Mrs. Julia Margaret Olive, BSc ACA *1985;* 28 Hyperion Rd, Stourton, STOURBRIDGE, DY7 6SB.
TAYLOR, Dr. Julian Matthew Corfield, ACA *1991;* 4 Kenilworth Terrace, Worcester Road, Cheam, SUTTON, SURREY, SM2 6JQ.
TAYLOR, Mrs. Julie, BSc ACA *1992;* 79 Woodfield Road, Oadby, LEICESTER, LE2 4HQ.
TAYLOR, Mrs. Julie Ann, BA ACA *1989;* 25 Crawley Close, Slip End, LUTON, LU1 4BT.
TAYLOR, Dr. Justin, PhD BA ACA *2007;* with Deloitte LLP, 3 Rivergate, Temple Quay, BRISTOL, BS1 6GD.
•**TAYLOR, Mrs. Karen, BSc ACA** *1995;* Taylored Accountancy Services, Northfield, Low Street, Carlton, GOOLE, NORTH HUMBERSIDE DN14 9PN.
TAYLOR, Mrs. Karen, BA FCA *1992;* with Baines Jewitt, Barrington House, 41-45 Yarm Lane, STOCKTON-ON-TEES, CLEVELAND, TS18 3EA.
TAYLOR, Mrs. Karen Denise, BSc ACA *2004;* 25 Chichester Close, GRANTHAM, LINCOLNSHIRE, NG31 8AS.
TAYLOR, Mrs. Karen Elisabeth, ACA ACMA *2011;* 5 Pembroke Road, Hatherley, CHELTENHAM, GLOUCESTERSHIRE, GL51 3JX.
TAYLOR, Mrs. Karen Rosemary, FCA *1977;* 5 The Coppice, Middleton, ILKLEY, WEST YORKSHIRE, LS29 0EZ.
TAYLOR, Miss. Kate, ACA *2011;* 106 Pepper Lane, Standish, WIGAN, LANCASHIRE, WN6 0PW.
TAYLOR, Mrs. Katherine, ACA *2000;* Peasemore House, Peasemore, NEWBURY, BERKSHIRE, RG20 7JH.
TAYLOR, Miss. Katherine Beverley, BA(Hons) ACA *2002;* 33 Rustat Road, CAMBRIDGE, CB1 3QR.
TAYLOR, Mrs. Kathryn Jane, BSc ACA *2007;* 49 Wheatfield Drive, Tickhill, DONCASTER, SOUTH YORKSHIRE, DN11 9US.
TAYLOR, Miss. Kathryn Sheena, ACA *1993;* 15 Murdoch Road, WOKINGHAM, BERKSHIRE, RG40 2DG.
•**TAYLOR, Mr. Keith, FCA** *1976;* Freedman Frankl & Taylor, Reedham House, 31 King Street West, MANCHESTER, M3 2PJ.
TAYLOR, Mr. Keith Bernard, FCA *1973;* 28 Berkeley Road, Westbury Park, BRISTOL, BS6 7PJ.
•**TAYLOR, Mr. Keith Gardner, FCA** *1985;* Keith G Taylor FCA, 22 Western Way, WHITLEY BAY, TYNE AND WEAR, NE26 1JE.
TAYLOR, Mr. Keith Leonard, BCom FCA *1976;* 14 Natalie Place, TORONTO M4M 3P7, ON, CANADA.
TAYLOR, Mr. Keith Rodney, FCA *1968;* 3 The Springs, Chalgrove, OXFORD, OX44 7QN.
TAYLOR, Mr. Keith William, BSc ACA *1982;* 27 Maes Cadwgan, Creigiau, CARDIFF, CF15 9TQ.
TAYLOR, Mr. Keith William, BSc FCA *1976;* 11 Gagewell Lane, Horbury, WAKEFIELD, WEST YORKSHIRE, WF4 6BQ.
TAYLOR, Mr. Kenneth, MA FCA *1969;* Mission Aviation Fellowship Operations Centre, Henwood, ASHFORD, TN24 8DH.
TAYLOR, Mr. Kenneth, BSc FCA *1977;* 12 D'Aincourt Park, Branston, LINCOLN, LN4 1NL.
TAYLOR, Mr. Kenneth, FCA *1970;* 22a Rope Lane, Wistaston, CREWE, CW2 6RD.
TAYLOR, Mr. Kenneth, FCA *1969;* Four Winds, 8 Whittam Road, Whalley, CLITHEROE, BB7 9SB.
TAYLOR, Mr. Kenneth Hartland, FCA *1960;* Highlands, Milwr, HOLYWELL, CH8 7SE. (Life Member)
TAYLOR, Mr. Kenneth Ian, FCA *1974;* 20 Avondale Road, WIRRAL, MERSEYSIDE, CH47 3AS.
TAYLOR, Mr. Kenneth James, FCA *1949;* 33 Rhewl Lane, Gobowen, OSWESTRY, SY10 7XA. (Life Member)
TAYLOR, Mr. Kenneth John, FCA *1962;* 33 Walsingham, St Johns Wood Park, LONDON, NW8 6RJ. (Life Member)
TAYLOR, Mr. Kenneth Mervyn, BSc FCA *1967;* 24 Nightingale Court, HERTFORD, SG14 1PD.
TAYLOR, Mr. Kenneth Ronald, ACA *1982;* 3 Musket Copse, Old Basing, BASINGSTOKE, HAMPSHIRE, RG24 7NQ.
TAYLOR, Mr. Kevan, FCA *1980;* 11 Meadowbrook Close, Lostock, BOLTON, BL6 4HX.
TAYLOR, Mr. Kevin, BSc ACA *1992;* 65 Bretby Lane, Bretby, BURTON-ON-TRENT, DE15 0QW.
TAYLOR, Mr. Kim Michael, MA FCA *1982;* BEACON HOUSE, LONG ACRE, BIRMINGHAM, B7 5JJ.
TAYLOR, Mrs. Laura, ACA *1990;* (Tax Fac), 17 Vancouver Close, ORPINGTON, BR6 9XQ.
TAYLOR, Mrs. Laura Anne-Marie, BA(Hons) ACA *2002;* The Gables Carmel Street, Great Chesterford, SAFFRON WALDEN, CB10 1PH.
TAYLOR, Miss. Laura Mary, BSc ACA *2003;* Abcam plc, Unit 330 Science Park Milton Road, CAMBRIDGE, CB4 0FL.
TAYLOR, Mr. Laurence, BA FCA *1980;* 33 Scugdale Close, YARM, CLEVELAND, TS15 9UG.
•**TAYLOR, Mr. Laurence, BSc FCA** *1961;* Laurence Taylor, 9 Handel Close, EDGWARE, HA8 7QZ.
TAYLOR, Mr. Lawrence Russell, FCA *1975;* 30 Fawcett Crescent, ST ALBERT T8N 1W3, AB, CANADA.
TAYLOR, Miss. Leanne, BA(Hons) ACA *2010;* 213 Alston Crescent, SUNDERLAND, SR6 8NG.
TAYLOR, Mr. Lee, BA ACA *1999;* 201 Ernest Street, CAMMERAY, NSW 2062, AUSTRALIA.
TAYLOR, Mr. Lee, MSc ACA *2000;* Flat 110, West City One, 6 Naoroji Street, LONDON, WC1X 0GD.
TAYLOR, Mrs. Lesley, ACA FMAAT *1998;* Fagus Lodge, Brearton, HARROGATE, HG3 3BX.
TAYLOR, Mr. Leslie, FCA *1953;* 6 Penny Croft, HARPENDEN, AL5 2PB. (Life Member)
TAYLOR, Mrs. Linda Joan, BA ACA *1990;* 5 Pinetum Close, DEVIZES, SN10 5EW.
TAYLOR, Mrs. Linsey Ruth, LLB ACA *1993;* 8 Pusey Way, Lane End, HIGH WYCOMBE, HP14 3LG.
TAYLOR, Miss. Lisa, BA(Hons) ACA ACIL *2000;* 16 Argyll Road, GLOUCESTER, GL2 0QR.
TAYLOR, Mrs. Lisa Ann, ACA MAAT *1998;* 8 Catherines Hill, Coddenham, IPSWICH, IP6 9QG.
•**TAYLOR, Mrs. Lisa Jayne, BCom ACA** *2002;* LJT Financial Management Limited, 31 Lloyd Road, Handsworth Wood, BIRMINGHAM, B20 2ND.
TAYLOR, Miss. Lorna Susan, BA ACA *1996;* 8 Ashington Road, LONDON, SW6 3QJ.
TAYLOR, Mrs. Lorraine Allison, ACA *1986;* 7 Spencer Close, The Straits Sedgley, DUDLEY, DY3 3BL.
•**TAYLOR, Mr. Louis Philip Chetwynd, FCA** *1974;* Pont Marquet Farm, La Rue Du Pont Marquet, St. Brelade, JERSEY, JE3 8DS.
TAYLOR, Miss. Louise, ACA *2011;* 6a Church Studios, Camden Park Road, LONDON, NW1 9AY.
TAYLOR, Miss. Louise Irene, BA(Hons) ACA *2004;* 327 Cavendish Road, LONDON, SW12 0PQ.
TAYLOR, Miss. Lucy, ACA *2008;* 48 West Street, WALLSEND, TYNE AND WEAR, NE28 8LD.
TAYLOR, Mrs. Lucy Hannah, ACA *2008;* with Bishop Fleming, Stratus House, Emperor Way, Exeter Business Park, EXETER, EX1 3QS.
TAYLOR, Ms. Lucy Jane, BSc ACA *2002;* with HSBC, 8-14 Canada Square, LONDON, E14 5HQ.
TAYLOR, Miss. Lynn Carol, BSc FCA *1996;* Chi-Nowydh, Trevarren, ST COLUMB, CORNWALL, TR9 6PJ.
TAYLOR, Miss. Mandie Dawn, BA ACA *1995;* Camelot Group Plc, Tolpits Lane, WATFORD, WD18 9RN.
TAYLOR, Mr. Marc Jeffrey, ACA *1990;* Heathlock, Canterbury Road, Challock, ASHFORD, KENT, TN25 4DW.
TAYLOR, Mr. Marc Robert John, BSc ACA *1998;* West Lodge, 204 Amersham Road, Hazlemere, HIGH WYCOMBE, BUCKINGHAMSHIRE, HP15 7QT.
•**TAYLOR, Mrs. Marina Amy, BSc(Hons) ACA** *1998;* Amy Taylor Accountancy, 10 Blackbird Street, Potton, SANDY, BEDFORDSHIRE, SG19 2LT.
TAYLOR, Mr. Mark, BSc ACA *1999;* H J Phillips & Sons Ltd, Bynea Garage, Yspitty Road, LLANELLI, DYFED, SA14 9TD.
TAYLOR, Mr. Mark, FCA *1982;* 19 Doran Close, HALESOWEN, B63 1JZ.
TAYLOR, Mr. Mark, ACA *1990;* 57 Craigengar Avenue, Uphall, BROXBURN, WEST LOTHIAN, EH52 5SQ.
•**TAYLOR, Mr. Mark Adrian, BCom ACA** *1987;* Grant Thornton UK LLP, Enterprise House, 115 Edmund Street, BIRMINGHAM, B3 2HJ. See also Grant Thornton LLP
TAYLOR, Mr. Mark Andrew, BA FCA *1994;* Yewhurst, 10 Court Hill, Chipstead, COULSDON, SURREY, CR5 3NQ.
•**TAYLOR, Mr. Mark Barri, BA FCA CPA** *1990;* GPO Box 7467, CENTRAL, HONG KONG ISLAND, HONG KONG SAR.
TAYLOR, Mr. Mark Christopher, BSc ACA *1992;* Electrocomponents PLC, 8050 Oxford Business Park North, OXFORD, OX4 2HW.
TAYLOR, Mr. Mark Douglas, BA ACA *1984;* 1 Nursery Drive, Formby, LIVERPOOL, L37 6HD.
TAYLOR, Mr. Mark James, BSc ACA *1993;* Unit 3, 42 Julia Street, WAVELL HEIGHTS, QLD 4012, AUSTRALIA.
•**TAYLOR, Mr. Mark Jason, BA ACA** *1998;* KPMG LLP, 6 Lower Brook Street, IPSWICH, IP4 1AP.
•**TAYLOR, Mr. Mark Jeremy, BA FCA** *1993;* Venthams Limited, 51 Lincolns Inn Fields, LONDON, WC2A 3NA.
TAYLOR, Mr. Mark John, MA ACA *1991;* 14 Higher Dean, BUCKFASTLEIGH, TQ11 0LX.
TAYLOR, Mr. Mark Jonathan, BA ACA *1992;* Wollzeile 20/11, 1010 VIENNA, AUSTRIA.
•**TAYLOR, Mr. Mark Owen, BSc FCA** *1986;* (Tax Fac), Taylor Roberts, Unit 9B, Wingbury Business Village, Upper Wingbury Farm, AYLESBURY, HP22 4LW.
TAYLOR, Mr. Mark Patrick Graham, BA ACA *1998;* with Charles Stanley, 25 Luke Street, LONDON, EC2A 4AR.
TAYLOR, Mr. Mark Peter, BA ACA *1998;* 83 Pentney Road, LONDON, SW12 0PA.
•**TAYLOR, Mr. Mark Philip Jonathan, BEng FCA** *1994;* Mazars LLP, Tower Bridge House, St. Katharines Way, LONDON, E1W 1DD.
TAYLOR, Mr. Mark Reginald, BA ACA *1987;* Westbury Research Ltd, 31 Harley Street, LONDON, W1G 9QS.
TAYLOR, Mr. Mark Stephen, MSc ACA *1988;* 9 Sandale Close, Gamston, NOTTINGHAM, NG2 6QG.
TAYLOR, Mr. Mark Steven, BSc ACA *1986;* 1 Cunningham CLose, Brotton, SALTBURN-BY-THE-SEA, TS12 2FH.
TAYLOR, Mr. Mark Steven, MA ACA *1999;* with Deloitte LLP, 3 Rivergate, Temple Quay, BRISTOL, BS1 6GD.
TAYLOR, Mr. Martin, BA ACA *1990;* 30 Hillfield Road, Chalfont St. Peter, GERRARDS CROSS, BUCKINGHAMSHIRE, SL9 0DX.
•**TAYLOR, Mr. Martin Anthony, FCA** *1976;* (Tax Fac), H W Fisher & Company, Acre House, 11-15 William Road, LONDON, NW1 3ER. See also H W Fisher & Company Limited
TAYLOR, Mr. Martin Gibbeson, CBE MA FCA *1961;* 28 Ormond Avenue, HAMPTON, TW12 2RU. (Life Member)
TAYLOR, Mr. Martin Harvey, MBA FCA *1965;* Lower Farmhouse, Byford, HEREFORD, HR4 7LD.
TAYLOR, Mr. Martin Leslie, MA FCA *1978;* 4 Cambridge Terrace Mews, LONDON, NW1 4JJ.
TAYLOR, Mr. Martin Peter, BA ACA *2002;* Flat 4, Frances Court, 3 Gandhi Close, LONDON, E17 8LW.
TAYLOR, Mr. Martin Philip, ACA *1985;* Thornbury House, Thorp, Royton, OLDHAM, OL2 5TH.
TAYLOR, Mr. Martyn, BSc ACA *1985;* Ardenode, Broom Way, WEYBRIDGE, SURREY, KT13 9TQ.
TAYLOR, Mr. Martyn Graeme, MA FCA *1963;* 7 Waters Green Court, BROCKENHURST, HAMPSHIRE, SO42 7QR. (Life Member)
TAYLOR, Miss. Mary Clare, MA ACA *1996;* 86 Marshals Drive, ST. ALBANS, HERTFORDSHIRE, AL1 4RE.
TAYLOR, Mr. Matthew, BA ACA *1997;* Battersea Power Station, 188 Kirtling Street, LONDON, SW8 5BN.
•**TAYLOR, Mr. Matthew Herbert, MA FCA** *1984;* Ernst & Young LLP, 1 More London Place, LONDON, SE1 2AF. See also Ernst & Young Europe LLP
TAYLOR, Mr. Matthew Ian, LLB ACA *2001;* 45 Dartmouth Hill, Greenwich, LONDON, SE10 8AJ.
TAYLOR, Mr. Matthew James, BEng ACA *2007;* 54 Hardwicke Road, LONDON, N13 4SG.
TAYLOR, Mr. Melvyn James, FCA *1969;* 22 Apsley Grove, Dorridge, SOLIHULL, B93 8QP.
TAYLOR, Mr. Melvyn Paul, BSc ACA *1990;* Platform Home Loans Ltd, 2 Harbour Exchange Square, LONDON, E14 9FR.
TAYLOR, Mr. Michael, FCA *1974;* 1 Grange Park, St. Arvans, CHEPSTOW, GWENT, NP16 6EA.
TAYLOR, Mr. Michael Barry, FCA *1980;* 22 Linden Lea, Hampstead Garden Suburb, LONDON, N2 0RG.
TAYLOR, Mr. Michael Colin, BA ACA *1979;* (Tax Fac), Flat 9 Copyground Court, Copyground Lane, HIGH WYCOMBE, BUCKINGHAMSHIRE, HP12 3HG.
TAYLOR, Mr. Michael David, BSc FCA *1971;* 8 Gleneagles Avenue, Hopwood, HEYWOOD, OL10 2BZ. (Life Member)
•**TAYLOR, Mr. Michael Denis, FCA ATII TEP** *1973;* (Tax Fac), Pearson May, 5 Wicker Hill, TROWBRIDGE, BA14 8JS.
TAYLOR, Mr. Michael Donald John, BA FCA *1980;* 49 Leckhampton Road, CHELTENHAM, GLOUCESTERSHIRE, GL53 0BJ.
•**TAYLOR, Mr. Michael Eric Charles, BA FCA** *1973;* Michael E C Taylor, 3 Sandalwood, GUILDFORD, SURREY, GU2 7NZ.
TAYLOR, Mr. Michael George, BA FCA *1986;* Huntsman Surface Sciences, Everslaan 45, B-3078 EVERBERG, BELGIUM.
TAYLOR, Mr. Michael George, FCA *1967;* 24 Woodside Way, SOLIHULL, B91 1HB.
TAYLOR, Mr. Michael Ian, MA ACA CTA *1984;* with Deloitte LLP, Athene Place, 66 Shoe Lane, LONDON, EC4A 3BQ.
TAYLOR, Mr. Michael John, BA FCA *1967;* 6 Garratts Lane, BANSTEAD, SM7 2DZ. (Life Member)
•**TAYLOR, Mr. Michael John, BA(Hons) ACA** *2002;* Taylored Business Solutions Ltd, 15 Junction Gardens, PLYMOUTH, PL4 9AR.
TAYLOR, Mr. Michael John, ACA *1986;* with Humphrey & Co, 7-9 The Avenue, EASTBOURNE, EAST SUSSEX, BN21 3YA.
•**TAYLOR, Mr. Michael John Graham, FCA** *1961;* Michael J.G. Taylor, Hunters End, Uvedale Road, OXTED, RH8 0EN.
TAYLOR, Mr. Michael John Kirkham, BSc FCA *1982;* Zurich Financial Services, Mythenquai 2, 8002 ZURICH, SWITZERLAND.
TAYLOR, Mr. Michael Joseph, BA ACA *1992;* 88 Mona Road, West Bridgford, NOTTINGHAM, NG2 5BT.
TAYLOR, Mr. Michael Joseph, BA ACA *2007;* 6 Asland Gardens, SOUTHPORT, MERSEYSIDE, PR9 8PT.
TAYLOR, Mr. Michael Richard, BSc ACA *1998;* 3 Dairy Court, Holyport, MAIDENHEAD, SL6 2US.
TAYLOR, Mr. Michael Ronald, FCA *1953;* Y Goedwig, The Woodlands, Llanerchydol Park, WELSHPOOL, SY21 9QE. (Life Member)
TAYLOR, Mrs. Michelle Amber, BA(Hons) ACA *2000;* 21 Winchester Avenue, LINDFIELD, NSW 2070, AUSTRALIA.
TAYLOR, Ms. Michelle Antonia, BA ACA *1994;* P O Box 31125, SEVEN MILE BEACH, GRAND CAYMAN, CAYMAN ISLANDS.
TAYLOR, Miss. Michelle Claire, ACA *2009;* Flat 81 Meyrick Court, 17 St. Anthonys Road, BOURNEMOUTH, BH2 6PB.
TAYLOR, Miss. Michelle Clare, BSc(Hons) ACA CTA *2001;* 57A Clap Gate Lane, WIGAN, LANCASHIRE, WN3 6RW.
TAYLOR, Mrs. Michelle Lesley Jean, BSc ACA *2005;* Critchleys, Avalon House, Marcham Road, ABINGDON, OXFORDSHIRE, OX14 1UD.
TAYLOR, Mrs. Natalie, BA ACA *2006;* Mercia Corporate Finance, The Mews, 278 Eccleshall Road, SHEFFIELD, S11 8PE.
TAYLOR, Mr. Neil, BSc ACA *1993;* J P Morgan Chase, 10 Aldermanbury, LONDON, EC2V 7RF.
•**TAYLOR, Mr. Neil, ACA** *1984;* M. Wasley Chapman & Co, 3 Victoria Square, WHITBY, NORTH YORKSHIRE, YO21 1EA.
TAYLOR, Mr. Neil, ACA *2010;* 14 Vernon Court, London Road, ASCOT, SL5 8DS.
TAYLOR, Mr. Neil David, BA ACA *1992;* 141 Boughton, CHESTER, CH3 5BH.
TAYLOR, Mr. Neil Edwin, FCA *1965;* 8 Milton Court, Paddockhall Road, HAYWARDS HEATH, WEST SUSSEX, RH16 1EY.
TAYLOR, Mr. Neil Gregory, BA ACA *1983;* 216 Clinton Avenue, OAK PARK, IL 60302, UNITED STATES.
TAYLOR, Mr. Neil Howard, BA ACA *1984;* 6 Coleman Close, Crick, NORTHAMPTON, NN6 7GB.
•**TAYLOR, Mr. Neil James, BA FCA** *1992;* Edwards, Harmony House, 34 High Street, Aldridge, WALSALL, WS9 8LZ.
TAYLOR, Mr. Neville, FCA *1958;* 43 Birchitt Road, Bradway, SHEFFIELD, S17 4QN. (Life Member)
TAYLOR, Mr. Neville Keith, FCA *1977;* 34 Mayfield Road, Eastrea Whittlesey, PETERBOROUGH, PE7 2AY. (Life Member)
TAYLOR, Mr. Neville Kenneth John, BA ACA *1986;* (Tax Fac), Standard Chartered Bank, 1 Basinghall Avenue, LONDON, EC2V 5DD.
TAYLOR, Mr. Nicholas Anthony, BSc(Hons) ACA *2003;* 55 Newman Road, DEVIZES, SN10 5LE.
•**TAYLOR, Mr. Nicholas Charles, FCA** *1969;* N C Taylor Limited, Temple Chambers, 4 Abbey Road, GRIMSBY, DN32 0HF.

•**TAYLOR, Mr. Nicholas Charles Duncan, FCA** *1989;* Patro Limited, Holly House, Burnsall, SKIPTON, NORTH YORKSHIRE, BD23 6BN.
TAYLOR, Mr. Nicholas Charles Fraser, BA(Hons) ACA *2001;* 15 Longbeach Road, LONDON, SW11 5SS.
TAYLOR, Mr. Nicholas David, BSc ACA *1984;* Loves House, New Road, Sutton, WITNEY, OX29 5RT.
TAYLOR, Mr. Nicholas David, BA ACA *2002;* 10 Sutherland Gardens, LONDON, SW14 8DB.
TAYLOR, Mr. Nicholas Edward, BSc ACA *2004;* 149 Clonmore Street, Southfields, LONDON, SW18 5HD.
•**TAYLOR, Mr. Nicholas Edwin, BSc FCA** *1993;* (Tax Fac), Taylor Rushby Limited, 32 Crouch Street, COLCHESTER, CO3 3HH.
TAYLOR, Mr. Nicholas Esmond Johnson, FCA *1971;* 142 Collis Street, STOURBRIDGE, WEST MIDLANDS, DY8 4EE.
TAYLOR, Mr. Nicholas Harris, BSc ACA *2007;* Glebe Farm House, Exeter Close, Trumpington, CAMBRIDGE, CB2 2NG.
TAYLOR, Mr. Nicholas James, BSc FCA *1984;* Ivy Well, La Route Des Issues, St John, JERSEY, JE3 4FA.
TAYLOR, Mr. Nicholas James Anthony Vye, FCA *1970;* 50 HAMSTEAD MARSHALL, NEWBURY, RG20 0JG.
•**TAYLOR, Mr. Nicholas John, BSc ACA** *1982;* BDO LLP, 2 City Place, Beehive Ring Road, GATWICK, WEST SUSSEX, RH6 0PA. See also BDO Stoy Hayward LLP
TAYLOR, Mr. Nicholas John Mardon, FCA *1973;* 6 Millers Court, Chiswick Mall, LONDON, W4 2PF.
TAYLOR, Mr. Nicholas Peter, ACA *2010;* 31 Spareleaze Hill, LOUGHTON, ESSEX, IG10 1BS.
•**TAYLOR, Mr. Nicholas Roy, FCA** *1970;* (Tax Fac), Nicholas Taylor, 57 Willows Road, BOURNE END, BUCKINGHAMSHIRE, SL8 5HG.
TAYLOR, Mr. Nigel Anthony William, BSc FCA *1975;* 46 Fortismere Avenue, Muswell Hill, LONDON, N10 3BL.
TAYLOR, Mr. Nigel Charles, BA FCA *1991;* 26 Amberley Road, Downend, BRISTOL, BS16 2RP.
•**TAYLOR, Mr. Nigel Francis Glanvill, FCA** *1972;* AIMS - Nigel Taylor, Lower Farm, Green Lane, Ellisfield, BASINGSTOKE, RG25 2QL.
TAYLOR, Mr. Nigel Holden, FCA *1974;* Ivanhoe, Enfield Road, Ash Vale, ALDERSHOT, HAMPSHIRE, GU12 5EJ.
TAYLOR, Mr. Nigel Robert John, MA ACA *1982;* Nigel R J Taylor M.A A.C.A, 7 St. Martins Lane, BECKENHAM, BR3 3XT.
TAYLOR, Mr. Norman, FCA *1959;* Unit 18, 14 Ross Street, WAVERTON, NSW 2060, AUSTRALIA. (Life Member)
•**TAYLOR, Mr. Norman, FCA** *1975;* 42 Tenterden Drive, LONDON, NW4 1ED.
TAYLOR, Mr. Norman Dennis, FCA *1949;* 299 Ringinglow Road, SHEFFIELD, S11 7PZ. (Life Member)
TAYLOR, Miss. Olivia Frances, MA ACA *2005;* Kirker Holidays Unit 4 Waterloo Court, 10 Theed Street, LONDON, SE1 8ST.
TAYLOR, Mrs. Pamela Ann, BSc FCA *1977;* Farnham Hall, Farnham, KNARESBOROUGH, NORTH YORKSHIRE, HG5 9JE.
TAYLOR, Miss. Pamela Wendy Lucille, BA ACA *2005;* 36 My Base, 130 Webber Street, LONDON, SE1 0JN.
•**TAYLOR, Mrs. Patricia Jane, FCA** *1968;* Mrs P.J.Taylor, 3 Ninnings Road, Chalfont St Peter, GERRARDS CROSS, SL9 0EF.
TAYLOR, Mr. Paul, ACA *2009;* N R Barton & Co, 19-21 Bridgeman Terrace, WIGAN, WN1 1TD.
TAYLOR, Mr. Paul, BA ACA *1995;* Paragon Publishing Ltd, 4 Queen Street, BATH, BA1 1HE.
•**TAYLOR, Mr. Paul Anthony, BSc FCA** *1981;* (Tax Fac), The Kings Mill Partnership, 75 Park Lane, CROYDON, CR9 1XS. See also Kingsmill Ltd
TAYLOR, Mr. Paul Anthony, BSc ACA PGDipED *1983;* City College, 50 Swanswell Street, COVENTRY, CV1 5DG.
TAYLOR, Mr. Paul Anthony, MA BSc FCA *1975;* 7 Portland Street, LANCASTER, LA1 1SZ.
TAYLOR, Mr. Paul Anthony, FCA *1974;* 17 Falmouth Road, TRURO, CORNWALL, TR1 2BL.
TAYLOR, Mr. Paul Antony, BSc(Hons) ACA *2001;* 28 Jedburgh Street, Clapham, LONDON, SW11 5QB.
TAYLOR, Mr. Paul Christopher, BSc FCA *1983;* 3 West End Close, Horsforth, LEEDS, LS18 5JN.
TAYLOR, Mr. Paul David, ACA *2008;* 34 Larkspur Drive, Chandler's Ford, EASTLEIGH, HAMPSHIRE, SO53 4HU.
TAYLOR, Mr. Paul Duncan, FCA *1959;* Oakwood House, Upper Batley, BATLEY, WF17 0AL. (Life Member)
•**TAYLOR, Mr. Paul Edwin, FCA FCCA** *1993;* (Tax Fac), Taylor Long 2008 Limited, 22 Middleton Street, WYMONDHAM, NORFOLK, NR18 0AD. See also Paul Taylor
TAYLOR, Mr. Paul Gayton, FCA *1975;* with The Rowleys Partnership LLP, 6 Dominus Way, Meridian Business Park, LEICESTER, LE19 1RP.
TAYLOR, Mr. Paul Jonathon, BA ACA *1989;* 58 Florence Road, NEDLANDS, WA 6009, AUSTRALIA.
TAYLOR, Mr. Paul Joseph, BSc ACA CTA *2005;* with Deloitte LLP, Hill House, 1 Little New Street, LONDON, EC4A 3TR.
TAYLOR, Mr. Paul Kingston, BSc FCA *1979;* Mellor House, 9 Ickford Road, Shabbington, AYLESBURY, BUCKINGHAMSHIRE, HP18 9HN.
•**TAYLOR, Mr. Paul Norman, ACA ATII** *1993;* (Tax Fac), TCP Holdings Ltd, 3 Acorn Business Centre, Northarbour Road, PORTSMOUTH, PO6 3TH. See also The Taylor Cocks Partnership Limited
TAYLOR, Mr. Paul William, BA ACA *1986;* 36 Annbrook Road, IPSWICH, IP2 9JN.
TAYLOR, Mr. Paul William, BA FCA *1983;* Hepworth Building Products Ltd, Hepworth Plumbing Products Edlington Lane, Edlington, DONCASTER, SOUTH YORKSHIRE, DN12 1BY.
TAYLOR, Mrs. Paula, MA BSc ACA *2010;* 20 Hartdames, Shenley Brook End, MILTON KEYNES, MK5 7HP.
TAYLOR, Mrs. Paula Fay, LLB ACA *1986;* Ethitec, 37 Millstone Lane, LEICESTER, LE1 5JN.
TAYLOR, Mr. Peter, BA FCA *1978;* 1A Brook Crescent, Wall Heath, KINGSWINFORD, WEST MIDLANDS, DY6 9AT.
TAYLOR, Mr. Peter, MA ACA *1984;* 79 Crimple Meadows, HARROGATE, NORTH YORKSHIRE, HG3 1EL.
•**TAYLOR, Mr. Peter Alan, FCA** *1974;* (Tax Fac), Richard Anthony & Company, 13 Station Road, Finchley, LONDON, N3 2SB. See also RA Payroll Services Ltd
TAYLOR, Mr. Peter Anthony, MBA FCA *1975;* 9 Warren House Lane, HUDDERSFIELD, HD3 3RS.
TAYLOR, Mr. Peter Charles, JP FCA *1974;* 5 Stonelands Park, RYDE, ISLE OF WIGHT, PO33 3BD.
TAYLOR, Mr. Peter Christopher, FCA *1969;* 252 Turney Road, Dulwich, LONDON, SE21 7JP.
TAYLOR, Mr. Peter Damien, BA ACA *1994;* 37 Comfrey, Coulby Newham, MIDDLESBROUGH, CLEVELAND, TS8 0XT.
TAYLOR, Mr. Peter David, FCA *1964;* Av Del Vinyet, No 3 C3-3, Sitges, 08870 BARCELONA, SPAIN. (Life Member)
TAYLOR, The Revd. Peter David, FCA *1960;* 33 Aspendale Close, Longton, PRESTON, PR4 5LJ. (Life Member)
TAYLOR, Mr. Peter Duncan, FCA *1951;* 2 Barnbrook Road, Knowle, SOLIHULL, WEST MIDLANDS, B93 9PW. (Life Member)
TAYLOR, Mr. Peter Frank Graham, BSc ACA *1979;* 27 Ferndale Avenue, CHERTSEY, KT16 9RB.
•**TAYLOR, Mr. Peter Geoffrey, FCA** *1977;* (Tax Fac), Crombies Accountants Limited, 34 Waterloo Road, WOLVERHAMPTON, WV1 4DG.
TAYLOR, Mr. Peter George, BCom FCA *1967;* The Grange, Earthcott, Alveston, BRISTOL, BS35 3TA.
•**TAYLOR, Mr. Peter Graham, FCA** *1975;* Harding Higgins, 36 Church Street, UTTOXETER, STAFFORDSHIRE, ST14 8AD.
TAYLOR, Mr. Peter Howard, BSc FCA *1978;* 22 Chemin de La Source, 1296 COPPET, VAUD, SWITZERLAND.
TAYLOR, Mr. Peter James, ACA *2004;* 14 Welton Wold View, Swanland, NORTH FERRIBY, NORTH HUMBERSIDE, HU14 3PX.
TAYLOR, Mr. Peter James, FCA *1976;* 3 Sadler Close, Adel, LEEDS, LS16 8NN.
•**TAYLOR, Mr. Peter Matthew, FCA** *1969;* W. Rowland Waller & Co., 6 Trinity Rd, SHEERNESS, ME12 2PJ.
TAYLOR, Mr. Peter Michael Miles, FCA *1966;* Harestock Cottage, 47 Harestock Road, WINCHESTER, SO22 6NT. (Life Member)
TAYLOR, Mr. Peter Richard, BSc ACA *1996;* 26 Brighton Road, LONDON, N16 8EG.
TAYLOR, Mr. Peter Roger, BA ACA *2005;* AB Foods & Beverages (Thailand) Ltd, 11th Floor 2535 Sukhumvit Rd Kwaeng Bangchack Khet Prakhanong, BANGKOK 10250, THAILAND.
TAYLOR, Mr. Philip Arthur, BCom ACA *1979;* The Grange, 34 Oldfield Road, Heswall, WIRRAL, CH60 6SF.
•**TAYLOR, Mr. Philip Charles, FCA** *1973;* (Tax Fac), with Barringtons Limited, 570-572 Etruria Road, NEWCASTLE, ST5 0SU.
•**TAYLOR, Mr. Philip Harry, FCA** *1974;* (Tax Fac), Bakers, Arbor House, Broadway North, WALSALL, WS1 2AN. See also Baker (Midlands) Limited
TAYLOR, Mr. Philip Ivor, BSc ACA *1990;* Blenheim Barn, Meer End Road, Honiley, KENILWORTH, WARWICKSHIRE, CV8 1PW.
•**TAYLOR, Mr. Philip John, BA FCA** *1980;* Pitt Godden & Taylor, Brunel House, George Street, GLOUCESTER, GL1 1BZ.
TAYLOR, Mr. Philip John, BSc FCA *1977;* 17 Ethan Allen Drive, ACTON, MA 01720, UNITED STATES.
TAYLOR, Mr. Philip Keats, FCA *1962;* The Lodge Follifoot Hall, Pannal Road, Follifoot, HARROGATE, HG3 1DP.
TAYLOR, Mr. Philip Michael, BA FCA *1959;* 36 Medalist Road, Willowdale, NORTH YORK M2P 1Y5, ON, CANADA. (Life Member)
TAYLOR, Mr. Philip Robert, FCA *1966;* 825 La Mirada Street, LAGUNA BEACH, CA 92651, UNITED STATES. (Life Member)
TAYLOR, Miss. Rachel, ACA *2009;* Foresters, Winsor Road, Winsor, SOUTHAMPTON, SO40 2HR.
TAYLOR, Mrs. Rachel, ACA MAAT *2007;* with Knill James, One Bell Lane, LEWES, EAST SUSSEX, BN7 1JU.
TAYLOR, Mrs. Rachel Anne Elliott, BA ACA *2002;* 126 St. Dunstans Road, LONDON, W6 8RA.
TAYLOR, Mrs. Rachel Elizabeth, BSc ACA *1993;* G4S plc, The Manor, Manor Royal, CRAWLEY, WEST SUSSEX, RH10 9UN.
TAYLOR, Mrs. Rachel Mary, BA ACA *1998;* Cbus Property Pty Ltd, Level 7, 550 Bourke Street, MELBOURNE, VIC 3000, AUSTRALIA.
TAYLOR, Ms. Rachel Mary, BA ACA *1999;* 12 Mount Pleasant Crescent, 8-20 Mount Pleasant Crescent, LONDON, N4 4HP.
TAYLOR, Mrs. Rachel Mary, BA(Hons) ACA *2001;* 12 High View Close, MARLOW, BUCKINGHAMSHIRE, SL7 3QN.
TAYLOR, Mrs. Rebecca, BSc ACA *2002;* 20 Rochester Grove, FLEET, GU51 3LU.
TAYLOR, Mrs. Rebecca Clare, BA ACA *2009;* The Global Travel Group Plc Glendale House Glendale Park, Glendale Avenue Sandycroft Industrial Estate Sandycroft, DEESIDE, CLWYD, CH5 2DL.
TAYLOR, Miss. Rebecca Louise, ACA *2008;* Flat 3, 90 Ditton Road, SURBITON, SURREY, KT6 6RH.
•**TAYLOR, Mrs. Rebecca Louise, ACA** *1993;* Rebecca Taylor, 11 Sea View Road, SKEGNESS, LINCOLNSHIRE, PE25 1BW.
TAYLOR, Miss. Rebecca Margarete, ACA *2008;* 19 Withering Road, SWINDON, SN1 4GU.
TAYLOR, Miss. Rebecca Susan, BA FCA *1989;* 56 Dales Lane, Whitefield, MANCHESTER, M45 7NN.
TAYLOR, Mr. Reginald, FCA *1957;* Little Ayotte Cottage, Ayot Green, WELWYN, AL6 9AB. (Life Member)
TAYLOR, Mr. Reginald Valentine, MA FCA *1957;* 9 Friars Furlong, Long Crendon, AYLESBURY, BUCKINGHAMSHIRE, HP18 9DQ. (Life Member)
TAYLOR, Mr. Reubin Derek, FCA *1951;* Flat 3 Bentley Lodge, 182 High Road, Bushey Heath, BUSHEY, WD23 1NS. (Life Member)
TAYLOR, Mr. Richard, BA ACA *1999;* 1 Lyndon Cottages, York Road, Burton Salmon, LEEDS, LS25 5JW.
TAYLOR, Mr. Richard, ACA *1985;* unit 205, 141-157 Acre Lane, LONDON, SW2 5UA.
TAYLOR, Mr. Richard Beaumont, FCA *1957;* Chaddlewood, Hurstclough Lane, Bamford, HOPE VALLEY, S33 0BW. (Life Member)
•**TAYLOR, Mr. Richard Cecil Charlton, FCA** *1969;* (Tax Fac), Richard Taylor & Co, Orchard Chambers, 4 Rocky Lane, Heswall, WIRRAL, CH60 0BY.
TAYLOR, Mr. Richard Charles, FCA CTA *1967;* 3 Locks Green, Yarwell, PETERBOROUGH, PE8 6PY. (Life Member)
•**TAYLOR, Mr. Richard Charles, FCA** *1975;* R.C. Taylor, Brailsford Green, Church Lane, Brailsford, ASHBOURNE, DE6 3BX.
TAYLOR, Mr. Richard Colin, BA ACA *2002;* 119 Ruthven Street, BONDI JUNCTION, NSW 2022, AUSTRALIA.
TAYLOR, Mr. Richard George, MA FCA *1971;* 13807 Silven Avenue NE, BAINBRIDGE ISLAND, WA 98110, UNITED STATES.
TAYLOR, Mr. Richard Gerard Anthony, BSc ACA *1981;* 14080 Goodall Road, LAKE OSWEGO, OR 97034, UNITED STATES.
TAYLOR, Mr. Richard Hewitt, BA ACA *1986;* VT Support Services, 1 Enterprise Way, Bournemouth Airport, CHRISTCHURCH, DORSET, BH23 6BS.
TAYLOR, Mr. Richard Ian, BSc FCA *1989;* 12 Belvedere View, LEEDS, LS17 8BR.
•**TAYLOR, Mr. Richard Ian, BSc FCA** *1989;* DTE Business Advisory Services Limited, DTE House, Hollins Mount, Hollins Lane, BURY, BL9 8AT.
TAYLOR, Mr. Richard James, MPhil BA ACA *1998;* 62 Castle Lodge Avenue, Rothwell, LEEDS, LS26 0ZD.
TAYLOR, Mr. Richard James, BSc ACA *1988;* Syngenta Crop Protection AG, WRO 1008.2.12, Schwarzwaldallee 215, CH 4002 BASEL, SWITZERLAND.
TAYLOR, Mr. Richard John, BSc ACA *1997;* 9 Beaumont Avenue, ST. ALBANS, HERTFORDSHIRE, AL1 4TH.
TAYLOR, Mr. Richard John, MBA BA FCA *1984;* PRUDENTIAL CORPORATION ASIA, 13F ONE INTERNATIONAL FINANCE CENTRE, 1 HARBOUR VIEW STREET, CENTRAL, HONG KONG SAR.
•**TAYLOR, Mr. Richard John, BSc FCA** *1977;* (Tax Fac), Pool Bank Park Road OULTON, TARPORLEY, CHESHIRE, CW6 9BH.
TAYLOR, Mr. Richard John, BSc ACA *1999;* T.Bailey Asset Management Ltd, 64 St. James's Street, NOTTINGHAM, NG1 6FJ.
•**TAYLOR, Mr. Richard John, FCA** *1986;* R.J. Taylor Limited, Unit A2, Imex Business Park, Flaxley Road, Stechford, BIRMINGHAM B33 9AL. See also Rolyat Limited
TAYLOR, Mr. Richard John, BA ACA *1987;* 149 Bilborough Road, NOTTINGHAM, NG8 4DS.
TAYLOR, Mr. Richard John Hall, FCA *1972;* Inscape Design Services Ltd, The Bridewell, Dockacre Road, LAUNCESTON, CORNWALL, PL15 8YY.
TAYLOR, Mr. Richard Mark, BA ACA *1984;* Cetlas, Farm Road, NORTHWOOD, HA6 2NZ.
TAYLOR, Mr. Richard Mark, BSc ACA *1991;* Commenden Manor, Camden Hill, Sissinghurst, CRANBROOK, KENT, TN17 2AS.
TAYLOR, Mr. Richard McKechnie, BA ACA *2000;* 21 Winchester Avenue, LINDFIELD, NSW 2070, AUSTRALIA.
TAYLOR, Mr. Richard Michael, BA ACA *2008;* 66 Bexley Street, WINDSOR, SL4 5BX.
TAYLOR, Mr. Richard Neil, FCA *1973;* 68 Heath Lane, Blackfordby, SWADLINCOTE, DERBYSHIRE, DE11 8AA.
TAYLOR, Mr. Richard Philip Mark, BA(Hons) ACA *2010;* Nieuwevaart 126, 1018ZM AMSTERDAM, NETHERLANDS.
TAYLOR, Mr. Richard Samuel, BA ACA *1999;* S C Johnson Ltd Frimley Green Road, Frimley, CAMBERLEY, GU16 7AJ.
TAYLOR, Mr. Richard Scott, BA ACA *1986;* Field House, Back Lane, East Langton, MARKET HARBOROUGH, LEICESTERSHIRE, LE16 7TB.
TAYLOR, Mr. Richard Stuart, BA ACA *2005;* Flat 50, 100 Drayton Park, LONDON, N5 1NF.
TAYLOR, Mr. Richard Thomas, BA(Hons) ACA *2002;* 26 Fremlin Close, Rusthall, TUNBRIDGE WELLS, KENT, TN4 8SF.
TAYLOR, Mr. Ricky Roy, BSc(Hons) ACA *2010;* Brighton House, Kirkbride, WIGTON, CUMBRIA, CA7 5JH.
TAYLOR, Mr. Robert Alan, FCA *1973;* 71 Laidon Avenue, Berkeley Park, Wistaston, CREWE, CW2 6RU.
•**TAYLOR, Mr. Robert Anthony Steven, FCA** *1979;* (Tax Fac), RTA Limited, PO Box 851, 2nd Floor, 24-26 Broad Street, JERSEY, JE4 0XE.
•**TAYLOR, Mr. Robert Derrick, BSc FCA DChA** *1983;* Y Drydedd Ddraig Cyf, RFOZ, Orbit Business Centre, Rhydycar Business Park, MERTHYR TYDFIL, MID GLAMORGAN CF48 1DL. See also BTP Associates
TAYLOR, Mr. Robert Digby, BSc FCA *1975;* Dreams 6 Nairn Road, POOLE, DORSET, BH13 7NG.
TAYLOR, Mr. Robert George, BSc ACA *1979;* 17 Hunters Park, BERKHAMSTED, HP4 2PT.
TAYLOR, Mr. Robert James, BSocSc ACA *2001;* 33 Fresher Mews, Three Score, NORWICH, NR5 9HF.
TAYLOR, Mr. Robert Mark, BSc FCA *1977;* 30 West Street, Apt 33G, NEW YORK, NY 10004, UNITED STATES.
TAYLOR, Mr. Robert Mark, BSc FCA *1975;* 65 Botley Road, CHESHAM, BUCKINGHAMSHIRE, HP5 1XG.
TAYLOR, Mr. Robert Simon, FCA *1973;* Acktif Group, PO Box 65, SANDRINGHAM, VIC 3191, AUSTRALIA.
TAYLOR, Mr. Robert Wesley James, BSc ACA *2006;* Flat 32 Bush House, Berber Parade, LONDON, SE18 4GB.
TAYLOR, Mr. Robert William, BA FCA *1981;* with Barber Harrison & Platt, 57/59 Saltergate, CHESTERFIELD, S40 1UL.
TAYLOR, Mr. Robert William, BSc(Hons) ACA *2004;* 66 Lesbourne Road, REIGATE, SURREY, RH2 7JX.
•**TAYLOR, Mrs. Roberta Jayne, BSc ACA** *1992;* R J Taylor, 26 Midholm, Hampstead Garden Suburb, LONDON, NW11 6LN.
TAYLOR, Mr. Robin Arden, FCA *1951;* 30 Green Lane, Chesham Bois, AMERSHAM, HP6 5LQ. (Life Member)

TAYLOR, Mr. Robin Julian, MA ACA *1995;* 353 Brookdale Avenue, TORONTO M5M 1P9, ON, CANADA.
•**TAYLOR, Mr. Rodney Basil, MA FCA** *1979;* Rodney Taylor Ltd, 119 Norman Road, Barton-le-Clay, BEDFORD, MK45 4QG.
TAYLOR, Mr. Rodney Stuart, BA ACA *1993;* 20 Gipsy Lane, Balsall Common, COVENTRY, CV7 7FW.
TAYLOR, Mr. Roger Clive, FCA *1972;* 96a Gladeside, Shirley, CROYDON, CR0 7RH.
TAYLOR, Mr. Roger David, BA ACA *1999;* Wild Acre, South Munstead Lane, GODALMING, GU8 4AG.
TAYLOR, Mr. Roger King, FCA *1954;* Southdown, Hollymead Lane, Stoke Bishop, BRISTOL, BS9 1LN. (Life Member)
TAYLOR, Mr. Roger William, FCA *1973;* 23 Derwen Fawr, CRICKHOWELL, POWYS, NP8 1DQ.
TAYLOR, Mr. Roger William, ACA *1988;* Apple Trees, 2 Beechwood Road, BEACONSFIELD, HP9 1HP.
TAYLOR, Mr. Ronald, FCA *1966;* Manor Mews, Cleeve Prior, EVESHAM, WORCESTERSHIRE, WR11 8LQ.
•**TAYLOR, Mr. Ronald Anthony, FCA** *1976;* with Roddis Taylor Robinson, Unit 6, Acorn Business Park, Woodseats Close, SHEFFIELD, S8 0TB.
•**TAYLOR, Mr. Ronald George, FCA** *1964;* Goorney & Taylor, 14 Abingdon Street, BLACKPOOL, FY1 1PY.
TAYLOR, Miss. Rosemary, FCA *1989;* Top House Farm Lincoln Road, Doddington, LINCOLN, LN6 4RS.
TAYLOR, Mrs. Rosemary Helen, FCA *1963;* 87 Rue du Montluisant, 78630 ORGEVAL, FRANCE. (Life Member)
TAYLOR, Mr. Ross Howard, BA ACA *1993;* 12 College Parade, KEW, VIC 3101, AUSTRALIA.
TAYLOR, Mr. Roy Benbow, ACA *1985;* Hospitality Advisors Ltd, Larkwood, 12 St Boltophs Road, SEVENOAKS, KENT, TN13 3AQ.
TAYLOR, Mr. Russell David, BA(Hons) ACA *2001;* 18 Highbank, BRIGHTON, BN1 5GB.
TAYLOR, Mr. Russell James, BA ACA *1997;* with Pricewaterhousecoopers, King Faisal Foundation Building, PO Box 8282, RIYADH, 11482, SAUDI ARABIA.
TAYLOR, Mr. Russell William, BA ACA *1984;* I T E Group Plc, 105 Salusbury Road, LONDON, NW6 6RG.
TAYLOR, Mr. Ryan, ACA *2010;* 18 Baryntyne Crescent, Hoo, ROCHESTER, KENT, ME3 9GE.
TAYLOR, Miss. Sally, BA ACA *2003;* Hayleigh, 328 Sandyhurst Lane, ASHFORD, TN25 4PE.
TAYLOR, Mrs. Sally Ann, FCA *1977;* 17 South Road, HAYLING ISLAND, HAMPSHIRE, PO11 9AE.
TAYLOR, Mrs. Sally Ann Elizabeth, BSc FCA *1984;* St Lukes Hospice, Stamford Road, Turnchapel, PLYMOUTH, PL9 9XA.
TAYLOR, Miss. Sally Anne, BSc ACA *2003;* J P Morgan Chase, 10 Aldermanbury, LONDON, EC2V 7RF.
TAYLOR, Miss. Sally Jane, BA(Hons) ACA *2003;* The International Institute for Strategic Studies, 13-15 Arundel Street, LONDON, WC2R 3DX.
TAYLOR, Miss. Sally Jane, BSc ACA *2007;* 6 Pemberton Way, SHREWSBURY, SY3 7AY.
•**TAYLOR, Mr. Sam Jeremy, BSc(Hons) ACA** *2000;* with PricewaterhouseCoopers, 1 Embankment Place, LONDON, WC2N 6RH.
TAYLOR, Miss. Samantha Jane, LLB FCA *1999;* 18 Winchester Close, WALTHAM ABBEY, ESSEX, EN9 1BB.
TAYLOR, Mrs. Samantha Jayne, BSc ACA *2009;* 12 St. Edeyrns Road, CARDIFF, CF23 6TB.
•**TAYLOR, Mrs. Samantha Leigh, BSc(Econ) ACA** *2002;* Samantha Taylor ACA, 72 Mid Street, South Nutfield, REDHILL, SURREY, RH1 4JX.
TAYLOR, Mrs. Samantha Louise, BSc ACA *1999;* 11 Mussons Close, Corby Glen, GRANTHAM, LINCOLNSHIRE, NG33 4NY.
TAYLOR, Mr. Samuel John, BA ACA *2005;* A G N Shipleys, 10 Orange Street, LONDON, WC2H 7DQ.
TAYLOR, Mrs. Sarah Jane, MA ACA *2004;* 46 Stanwell Road, PENARTH, SOUTH GLAMORGAN, CF64 2EY.
TAYLOR, Mrs. Sarah Katherine, BSc ACA *1992;* Blenheim Barn, Meer End Road, Honiley, KENILWORTH, CV8 1PW.
TAYLOR, Mrs. Sarah Louise, FCA *1975;* 27 Hawthorn Way, SHIPSTON-ON-STOUR, CV36 4FD.
TAYLOR, Miss. Sarah Louise, BSc ACA *1998;* C/O Derren Sanders, HSBC, PO Box 242, ABU DHABI, UNITED ARAB EMIRATES.
TAYLOR, Mrs. Sarah Louise Susan, LLB ACA *2002;* 69 Gipsy Lane, WOKINGHAM, BERKSHIRE, RG40 2BW.
TAYLOR, Mrs. Sarah Scott, LLB ACA CTA *2000;* Taxation Department, Floor 5, Al Mamoura A Building, Mubadala Development Company PJSC, PO Box 45005, ABU DHABI UNITED ARAB EMIRATES.
TAYLOR, Mrs. Sarah Virginia, BSocSc ACA *1997;* with PricewaterhouseCoopers, Cornwall Court, 19 Cornwall Street, BIRMINGHAM, B3 2DT.
TAYLOR, Mr. Saul, MA ACA *1999;* with PricewaterhouseCoopers LLP, 1 Embankment Place, LONDON, WC2N 6RH.
TAYLOR, Ms. Sharon Dawn, MSc BSc ACA CPA *1990;* Department of Psychology, University of York, Heslington, YORK, YO10 5DD.
TAYLOR, Mr. Shaun, BA ACA *1996;* 18 Grove Park, Misterton, DONCASTER, DN10 4HF.
TAYLOR, Mr. Shaun John, BSc ACA *1997;* 28 Leonie Hill, 12-28 Leonie Towers, SINGAPORE 239227, SINGAPORE.
TAYLOR, Mr. Shawn Karl, BSc FCA *1991;* Little Wishanger Wishanger Lane, Churt, FARNHAM, GU10 2QJ.
TAYLOR, Mrs. Shona Patricia, BA ACA *1995;* Lowe Alpine (UK) Ltd, Ann Street, KENDAL, CUMBRIA, LA9 6AA.
TAYLOR, Mr. Simon, ACA *2009;* 21 Delamere Close, BLACKBURN, BB2 2QJ.
TAYLOR, Mr. Simon, ACA *2010;* 35 Longacre Rise, Chineham, BASINGSTOKE, RG24 8BD.
TAYLOR, Mr. Simon David, LLB ACA *1999;* with KPMG, KPMG Centre, 18 Viaduct Harbour Avenue, P.O. Box 1584, AUCKLAND 1140, NEW ZEALAND.
TAYLOR, Mr. Simon Guy, MBA ACA *1988;* 34 Tinwell Road, STAMFORD, PE9 2SD.
TAYLOR, Mr. Simon James, BA ACA *2000;* 41 Lucerne Close, Huntington, CHESTER, CHESHIRE, CH3 6DL.
TAYLOR, Mr. Simon Jon, BSc ACA *2007;* Strickland Tracks Limited, Heath Park, B4084 near Cropthorne, PERSHORE, WORCESTERSHIRE, WR10 3NE.
TAYLOR, Mr. Simon Nicholas, BSc ACA FSI *1992;* with Swiss Re, 30 St. Mary Axe, LONDON, EC3A 8EP.
TAYLOR, Mr. Simon Richard, BSc ACA *1999;* 67d Wallwood Road, LONDON, E11 1AY.
TAYLOR, Mr. Solomon James, ACA *2008;* 28 Hawthorne Road, Stapleford, CAMBRIDGE, CB22 5DU.
TAYLOR, Miss. Stephanie Frances, ACA *2008;* Level 3 Business Recovery Services, Pricewaterhousecoopers, 12 Plumtree Court, LONDON, EC4A 4HT.
TAYLOR, Mr. Stephen, BA ACA *1982;* Deloitte Touche Tohmatsu, 35/F One Pacific Place, 88 Queensway, CENTRAL, HONG KONG ISLAND, HONG KONG SAR.
TAYLOR, Mr. Stephen Charles, BSocSc ACA *1997;* 1 Sentry Way, SUTTON COLDFIELD, B75 7HZ.
TAYLOR, Mr. Stephen Charles, MA ACA *1985;* Uppingham School, The Bursary, High Street West, Uppingham, RUTLAND, LE15 9QE.
TAYLOR, Mr. Stephen Donald, BA ACA *1979;* 2 Fairway, WARE, HERTFORDSHIRE, SG12 9JP.
TAYLOR, Mr. Stephen John, FCA *1970;* 33 The Fairway, HERNE BAY, CT6 7TW.
TAYLOR, Mr. Stephen John Fenwick, MA FCA *1973;* Foxglade, 66c Cleeve Hill, Downend, BRISTOL, BS16 6HQ.
•ⓘ**TAYLOR, Mr. Stephen Jonathan, BMus FCA** *1982;* Alix Partners Ltd, 20 North Audley Street, LONDON, W1K 6WE. See also AlixPartners UK LLP
TAYLOR, Mr. Stephen Joseph, BSc FCA *1986;* GE Healthcare, White Lion Road, AMERSHAM, HP7 9LL.
TAYLOR, Mr. Stephen Richard Kent, MA FCA *1971;* 1 Beeches Close, Ixworth, BURY ST. EDMUNDS, SUFFOLK, IP31 2EW.
TAYLOR, Mr. Stephen Rigby, MA FCA *1958;* Pilgrims Lodge, 11 Monks Walk, REIGATE, RH2 0SS. (Life Member)
TAYLOR, Mr. Stephen Robert, MEng ACA *2000;* T A C S Partnership Graylaw House, Mersey Square, STOCKPORT, CHESHIRE, SK1 1AL.
•**TAYLOR, Mr. Steven Cristopher, BSc ARCS FCA** *1992;* Ernst & Young LLP, 1 More London Place, LONDON, SE1 2AF. See also Ernst & Young Europe LLP
TAYLOR, Mr. Steven David, BSc ACA *2003;* Arcelormittal Distribution Solutions UK Ltd Highfield Road, Little Hulton, MANCHESTER, M38 9ST.
TAYLOR, Mr. Steven George Anthony, BA ACA *1992;* T337 Alderley House, Astrazeneca Pharmaceutical Division, Mereside Alderley Park, MACCLESFIELD, CHESHIRE, SK10 4TG.
TAYLOR, Mr. Stewart Ian, BA ACA *1998;* 44a Parr Terrace, MILFORD 0620, NEW ZEALAND.
TAYLOR, Mr. Stuart, ACA *2011;* 16a Greenwich South Street, LONDON, SE10 8TY.
TAYLOR, Mr. Stuart Hayden, BA ACA *1998;* Ground Floor Flat, 217 Elgin Avenue, Maida Vale, LONDON, W9 1NH.
•**TAYLOR, Mrs. Susan, ACA FCCA** *2009;* Brays Ltd, 23 Market Place, WETHERBY, WEST YORKSHIRE, LS22 6LQ.
TAYLOR, Miss. Susan Constance, BA FCA *1981;* Little Meadows Stockcroft Road, Balcombe, HAYWARDS HEATH, WEST SUSSEX, RH17 6LL.
TAYLOR, Mrs. Susan Fiona, BSc ACA *1987;* 1 Middlefield Lane, Hagley, STOURBRIDGE, WEST MIDLANDS, DY9 0PY.
TAYLOR, Mrs. Susan Jane, ACA *1986;* 71 Hospital Road, BURY ST.EDMUNDS, IP33 3JY.
•**TAYLOR, Mrs. Susan Mary, ACA** *2006;* 25 Jersey Way, Barwell, LEICESTER, LE9 8HR.
TAYLOR, Miss. Susannah Natalie, BSc ACA *2001;* 18 Lowndes Avenue, CHESHAM, BUCKINGHAMSHIRE, HP5 2HH.
TAYLOR, Miss. Suzanne Elizabeth, BA ACA *2002;* (Tax Fac), 24 Minniedale, SURBITON, KT5 8DH.
TAYLOR, Mrs. Suzanne Lesley, BSc ACA *1998;* Home Farm Harewood House Estate, Harewood, LEEDS, LS17 9LF.
TAYLOR, Mr. Sydney Alan, FCA *1966;* 9 Disserth View, Howey, LLANDRINDOD WELLS, POWYS, LD1 5PJ.
TAYLOR, Miss. Tania, ACA *2011;* 37 Aylesford Street, LONDON, SW1V 3RY.
TAYLOR, Mrs. Tanya Michele, BSc ACA *1998;* Albis (UK) Ltd, Parkgate Industrial Estate, KNUTSFORD, CHESHIRE, WA16 8XW.
TAYLOR, Mr. Terence Robin, FCA *1968;* 106 Victoria Avenue, RAYLEIGH, ESSEX, SS6 9DB. (Life Member)
TAYLOR, Mr. Thomas Michael, BSc ACA *1983;* Central Route Charges Office, EUROCONTROL, Rue de la Fusée 96, B-1130 BRUSSELS, BELGIUM.
•**TAYLOR, Mr. Tim Mark, BSc FCA** *1990;* Tim Taylor & Co Ltd, 24 Brynfield Road, Langland, SWANSEA, SA3 4SX.
TAYLOR, Mr. Timothy, MA FCA *1972;* 5 The Coppice, Middleton, ILKLEY, WEST YORKSHIRE, LS29 0EZ.
TAYLOR, Mr. Timothy John, BA(Hons) ACA *2011;* 35 Cygnet Drive, TELFORD, SHROPSHIRE, TF3 1NP.
TAYLOR, Mr. Timothy John, BSc ACA *1991;* (Tax Fac), 10 Drummond Way, MACCLESFIELD, CHESHIRE, SK10 4XJ.
TAYLOR, Mr. Timothy Macdonald, ACA *2008;* Scrutton Bland Sanderson House, 17-19 Museum Street, IPSWICH, IP1 1HE.
TAYLOR, Mr. Timothy Rupert, BSc ACA *1997;* 15 Montfort Close, Horsforth, LEEDS, LS18 5SX.
TAYLOR, Mrs. Tina Jane, BA ACA *1989;* 224 Old Cider Mill Road, SOUTHINGTON, CT 06489, UNITED STATES.
TAYLOR, Mrs. Tracy Ann, BSc(Hons) ACA *2003;* 423 Port Hills Road, CHRISTCHURCH 8022, NEW ZEALAND.
TAYLOR, Mrs. Tracy Elaine, BSc ACA *2002;* DW Stadium, Loire Drive, WIGAN, WN5 0UH.
TAYLOR, Mr. Trevor, BSc ACA *2006;* 49 Wheatfield Drive, Tickhill, DONCASTER, SOUTH YORKSHIRE, DN11 9US.
TAYLOR, Miss. Tsara Jayne, BSc ACA *2005;* 28 Sarek Park, NORTHAMPTON, NN4 9YA.
TAYLOR, Mrs. Vanessa Wellings, MA ACA ATII *1992;* (Tax Fac), 1 Semaphore Road, GUILDFORD, SURREY, GU1 3PS.
TAYLOR, Mr. Victor David, FCA *1966;* The Malthouse West Steadings, West Street, Gayles, RICHMOND, NORTH YORKSHIRE, DL11 7FD.
TAYLOR, Mrs. Victoria Jane, BSc ACA *1996;* 165 Eastgate, LOUTH, LINCOLNSHIRE, LN11 8DB.
TAYLOR, Mr. Walter, FCA *1955;* Hill House, Drakewell Road, Bow Brickhill, MILTON KEYNES, MK17 9LF. (Life Member)
TAYLOR, Mr. Wayne John Kennedy, ACA *1990;* 33, Wigmore Street, LONDON, W1U 1BZ.
•**TAYLOR, Mr. Will, MA BA(Hons) ACA** *2002;* Lucraft Hodgson & Dawes, Ground Floor, 19 New Road, BRIGHTON, BN1 1UF.
TAYLOR, Mr. William, BA ACA *1980;* 25 Camberwell Grove, LONDON, SE5 8JA.
TAYLOR, Mr. William, ACA *2008;* 2 Chiswick Road, Didsbury, MANCHESTER, M20 6RZ.
TAYLOR, Mr. William, FCA *1965;* 3 Chiltenhurst, EDENBRIDGE, KENT, TN8 5PJ. (Life Member)
TAYLOR, Mr. William Brian, MSc FCA *1964;* 9 Uppleby, Easingwold, YORK, YO61 3BQ. (Life Member)
TAYLOR, Mr. William George, BA FCA *1989;* Rockedge, 6 St Roberts Gardens, KNARESBOROUGH, HG5 8EH.
TAYLOR, Mr. William John, BCom ACA *1982;* 7 Osgood Avenue, ORPINGTON, BR6 6JT.
TAYLOR, Mrs. Zoe Carolyn, BCom ACA *1990;* Jacks Corner, 11 Hazelcombe, Waltham Road, Overton, BASINGSTOKE, HAMPSHIRE RG25 3NX.
TAYLOR-CHEATER, Mrs. Jane Ann, BSc ACA *1987;* 54 Munnion Road, Ardingly, HAYWARDS HEATH, RH17 6RP.
TAYLOR-CLAGUE, Mr. Stephen James, BA ACA *1987;* 72 Shinfield Road, READING, RG2 7DA.
TAYLOR-FIRTH, Mr. Christopher Alan, BSc ACA *1991;* 1 Windsor Crescent, Folly Hill, FARNHAM, GU9 0DH.
TAYLOR-GOOBY, Mr. James Stephen, BSc ACA *2000;* 83 John Archer Way, LONDON, SW18 2TT.
TAYLOR-GREGG, Mr. Alexander Fergus, BA ACA *1992;* 4 Park View, 87 Park Road Chiswick, LONDON, W4 3ER.
TAYLOR-MOORE, Miss. Kim, MA BSc FCA *1986;* Radclive Hall, Radclive, BUCKINGHAM, MK18 4AB.
•**TAYLOR REA, Mr. David Gordon, FCA** *1977;* (Tax Fac), Oury Clark, PO Box 150, Herschel House, 58 Herschel Street, SLOUGH, SL1 1HD.
TAYLOR REA, Mr. Rupert, BSc ACA *2004;* 52 Cecil Road, LONDON, SW19 1JP.
TAYLOR-SMITH, Mr. Kim David Spencer, FCA *1982;* 52 Sydney Street, LONDON, SW3 6PS.
TAYLOR-THOMAS, Mr. Mark, FCA *1967;* 35 The Orchard, LONDON, W4 1JZ. (Life Member)
TAYLORSON, Mr. Brian Geoffrey, MA ACA *1982;* Elementis Plc, 10 Albemarle Street, LONDON, W1S 4HH.
TAYLORSON, Mr. Nigel David, FCA *1975;* Little Egypt, Hamptons, Shipbourne, TONBRIDGE, TN11 9SR.
TAYUB, Mr. Abdul Aziz, ACA *1982;* (Tax Fac), 111 Trevino Drive, Rushey Mead, LEICESTER, LE4 7PH.
TAZIKER, Miss. Helen Rachel, BA(Econ) ACA *1998;* 110 Bloomsbury Lane, Timperley, ALTRINCHAM, CHESHIRE, WA15 6NT.
TCHOUKOV, Mrs. Michelle Moetu, ACA CA(NZ) *2009;* 19 Landseer Close, LONDON, SW19 2UT.
TE, Ms. Yuk Wai Elisa, ACA *2008;* 2001 Kam Yung House, Kam Fung Court, Ma On Shan, SHA TIN, NEW TERRITORIES, HONG KONG SAR.
TEACHER, Mr. Kenneth John, BCom FCA *1956;* 7 Gurney Drive, LONDON, N2 0DF. (Life Member)
TEACHER, Mr. Michael John, MSc FCA *1969;* hillsdown house, Hillsdown Holdings, 32 Hampstead High Street, LONDON, NW3 1QD.
•**TEAGER, Mr. David Anthony, BSc(Hons) ACA** *2002;* with PricewaterhouseCoopers LLP, Donington Court, Pegasus Business Park, Castle Donington, DERBY, DE74 2UZ.
TEAGLE, Mr. Nicholas Paul, ACA *2004;* Leighton House, Station Road, CHEDDAR, SOMERSET, BS27 3AH.
TEAGUE, Mr. Cecil John, BSc FCA *1973;* 10 Radyr Avenue, Mayals, SWANSEA, SA3 5DT. (Life Member)
TEAGUE, Mrs. Claire Helen, BSc ACA *1992;* The Cottage, Malvern Road, Staunton, GLOUCESTER, GL19 3NT.
TEAGUE, Mr. David Robert, FCA *1975;* Velcourt Group plc, The Veldt House, Much Marcle, LEDBURY, HR8 2LJ.
TEAGUE, Mrs. Frances Louise, BA ACA *1995;* 11 Carmel Gardens, TAVISTOCK, PL19 8RG.
TEAGUE, Mr. Ian Roger, ACA *1992;* The Cottage, Malvern Road, Staunton, GLOUCESTER, GLOUCESTERSHIRE, GL19 3NT.
TEAGUE, Miss. Kim, BA(Hons) ACA *2010;* 4 Ashbourne Grove, OMAGH, COUNTY TYRONE, BT78 1HG.
TEAGUE, Mr. Matthew Stephen, BSc ACA *1999;* Landmark Information Group Ltd, Unit 5-7, Abbey Court, Eagle Way, Sowton Industrial Estate, EXETER EX2 7HY.
TEAGUE, Mr. Peter Roy, BSc ACA *1980;* Heath Wood House, Turville Heath, HENLEY-ON-THAMES, OXFORDSHIRE, RG9 6JS.
TEAGUE, Mr. Robert, MA FCA *1976;* Beachfame Pty Limited, 229 Eastern Road, Wahroonga, SYDNEY, NSW 2076, AUSTRALIA.
TEAGUE, Mr. Stephen Richard, BA FCA *1984;* 10 Whiteway Road, Kingsteignton, NEWTON ABBOT, TQ12 3HL.
TEAGUE, Mr. Steven, MA ACA *1999;* 11 Finchley Way, LONDON, N3 1AG.
TEAL, Mr. Edward Stuart, FCA *1971;* Flat 23-F, Residencial Terracalpe, La VallesaCalpe, 03710 ALICANTE, SPAIN.
TEAL, Miss. Katie, BSc ACA *2005;* 6 St. Johns Road, Clifton, BRISTOL, BS8 2EX.
•**TEAL, Mr. Kelvin John, FCA** *1978;* Tomkinson Teal LLP, Hanover Court, 5 Queen Street, LICHFIELD, STAFFORDSHIRE, WS13 6QD.

Members - Alphabetical TEALE - TEMPLE

TEALE, Mr. Alan David, BSc FCA *1978;* 27 Haworth Crescent, ROTHERHAM, S60 3BW.
TEALE, Mr. Clifford Norman, FCA *1959;* 2996 East Prospect Road, YORK, PA 17402, UNITED STATES.
TEALE, Mr. Mark Andrew, BCom ACA *1986;* 7 Beaurevoir Way, WARWICK, CV34 4NY.
TEALE, Mr. Peter Andrew, BCom ACA *1985;* 45 Thanstead Copse, Loudwater, HIGH WYCOMBE, HP10 9YH.
TEALE, Mrs. Sarah Kate, BA ACA *1999;* 57 Rydens Avenue, WALTON-ON-THAMES, KT12 3JE.
TEALE, Mr. Shaun Douglas, LLB ACA *1990;* 6 Easby Close, ILKLEY, LS29 9DJ.
TEAR, Mr. Brian Jefferson, BSc ACA *1994;* Oakfield Cottage Stratford Road, Wootton Wawen, HENLEY-IN-ARDEN, B95 6DF.
TEAR, Mr. Denis William, FCA *1958;* 8 Wymondley Road, HITCHIN, HERTFORDSHIRE, SG4 9PH. (Life Member)
TEAR, Mr. Mark David, BA ACA *1992;* 427 Monteray Avenue, NORTH VANCOUVER V7H 3EN, BC, CANADA.
•TEARE, Mr. Alastair Guy Beaumont, BSc ACA *1993;* Dozsa Gyorgy ut 84/C, 1068 BUDAPEST, HUNGARY. See also Deloitte & Touche
TEARE, Mr. John Anthony, FCA *1962;* 3 Delavor Close, Heswall, WIRRAL, MERSEYSIDE, CH60 4SX.
TEARE, Mr. Jonathan Andrew Holland, BA ACA *1997;* Little Munden House, Dane End, WARE, HERTFORDSHIRE, SG12 0NT.
TEARE, Mr. Richard Geoffrey, FCA *1970;* Southgate College, High Street, LONDON, N14 6BS.
TEARE, Mr. Richard Maxwell, BSc FCA *1971;* 83 Kneeton Road, East Bridgford, NOTTINGHAM, NG13 8PH.
TEARE, Mr. Robert John, ACA *2011;* 5 Wareham Close, West Bridgford, NOTTINGHAM, NG2 7UD.
TEARE, Mr. Robert Lewis, FCA *1949;* 35 Giles Court, Rectory Road, West Bridgford, NOTTINGHAM, NG2 6BL. (Life Member)
TEARE, Mr. Robin James Mylroie, MA BSc ACA *2010;* Flat 14, Maple Court, St. Leonards Road, WINDSOR, BERKSHIRE, SL4 3EE.
TEARLE, Mr. David John, BCom ACA *1985;* 11 Tunis, Laguna Niguel, CALI, CA 92677, UNITED STATES.
TEARLE, Mr. Duncan Patrick Jonathan, BA ACA *1984;* 264 Reservoir Road, Selly Oak, BIRMINGHAM, B29 6TE.
TEARLE, Mr. John George, FCA *1958;* The Gables, Main Street, Padbury, BUCKINGHAM, MK18 2AY. (Life Member)
TEARLE, Mr. Michael John, BA ACA *1986;* I T W Industry, Threemilestone, TRURO, CORNWALL, TR4 9LD.
TEASDALE, Mrs. Alison, BSc ACA *2003;* 88 Bolton Road, Silsden, KEIGHLEY, WEST YORKSHIRE, BD20 0JT.
TEASDALE, Mrs. Gail Louise, BCom ACA *1993;* Aire Valley Homes Leeds Ltd, 8 George Mann Road, Hunslet, LEEDS, LS10 1DJ.
TEASDALE, Mr. Graham, BSc FCA *1990;* (PwC St Petersburg) c/o Sharon Pain Pricewater House Coopers, 1 Embankment Place, LONDON, WC2N 6NN.
TEASDALE, Mr. Hadrian Peter, BA ACA *1985;* Ilsestr. 23, 12051 BERLIN, GERMANY.
TEASDALE, Mr. Ian Stanley, BA ACA *1998;* 18 Claremont Avenue, WOKING, GU22 7SG.
TEASDALE, Miss. Lynne Joyce, BA ACA *1988;* Sykes Cottages Ltd, Lime Tree House, Hoole Lane, CHESTER, CH2 3EG.
TEASDALE, Mrs. Marion, FCA *1974;* 5 Annandale Grove, Scalby, SCARBOROUGH, YO13 0PL.
TEASDALE, Mr. Nicholas John, BSc FCA *1976;* Lime Trees, Church Road, Cookham, MAIDENHEAD, SL6 9PG.
•TEASDALE, Mr. Paul Anthony, BA DipLaw FCA FRSA MAE *1983;* Accent Capital LLP, 1 Dane Road Industrial Estate, Dane Road, SALE, CHESHIRE, M33 7BP. See also Inter Forensics Ltd
TEASDALE, Mr. Paul Raymond, FCA *1972;* (Tax Fac), Stonecroft Associates, Clifton Road, Deddington, BANBURY, OXFORDSHIRE, OX15 0TP.
TEASDALE, Mr. Peter James, BSc FCA *1978;* The Three Horseshoes, 34 Main Street, Wymondham, MELTON MOWBRAY, LE14 2AG.
TEASDALE, Mrs. Sarah Elizabeth, BSc ACA *1995;* Auburn, 47 Ottways Lane, ASHTEAD, SURREY, KT21 2PS.
TEASDALE, Mrs. Sarah Jane, MSc ACA *2004;* with Hardcastle France, 30 Yorkersgate, MALTON, YO17 7AW.
TEASDALE, Mr. William Moore, FCA *1965;* Lindisfarne, Gubeon Wood, Tranwell Woods, MORPETH, NE61 6BH.
TEASDALE, Mr. William Robert, FCA *1973;* 17 Brompton Drive, MAIDENHEAD, SL6 6SP.
TEATHER, Mrs. Janet Barbara, ACA *1982;* 5 Nether Court, Farnsfield, NEWARK, NG22 8JU.
•TEATHER, Mr. Keith Michael, BA FCA *1991;* Teather & Co Limited, Tile Oak, Old Slade Lane, Richings Park, IVER, SL0 9DR.
TEATHER, Mr. Richard Paul, BA ACA *1997;* (Tax Fac), The Old Mill, Doddings, WAREHAM, BH20 7NJ.
TEATHER, Mr. Stephen Colin, BSc ACA *1994;* 3 Moselle Road Biggin Hill, WESTERHAM, KENT, TN16 3HS.
TEBBENHAM, Miss. Clare Madeline, MEng ACA *2007;* 53 Mount Harry Road, SEVENOAKS, TN13 3JN.
TEBBETT, Mr. Jeremy Richard, BSc FCA *1980;* 31 Telford Close, MACCLESFIELD, CHESHIRE, SK10 2QH.
•TEBBETT, Mr. Keith Andrew, ACA *1980;* Keith Tebbett, 357 Coppice Road, Arnold, NOTTINGHAM, NG5 7HH.
TEBBETT, Mr. Simon Edward, FCA *1980;* Ardquin Cottage, Hazel Grove, HINDHEAD, GU26 6BJ.
TEBBUTT, The Revd. Christopher Michael, BA ACA ATII *1980;* The Vicarage, Canford Magna, WIMBORNE, BH21 3AF.
TEBBUTT, Mr. Jeremy Martin, BSc ACA *1994;* 21 Bellevue Road, LONDON, SW13 0BJ.
TEBBUTT, Mr. Nicholas, BA ACA *2011;* 20 Andover Road, LONDON, N7 7RA.
TEBBUTT, Mr. Oliver, BA ACA *2005;* with Deloitte LLP, PO Box 500, 2 Hardman Street, MANCHESTER, M60 2AT.
TECKHAM, Mrs. Pauline, BA ACA *1992;* with Ernst & Young, 9th Floor, Tower 1, NextTeracom, Cybercity, EBENE MAURITIUS.
•TECKOE, Mr. David Alfred, FCA CTA *1970;* (Tax Fac), HW, Sterling House, 19-23 High Street, KIDLINGTON, OXFORDSHIRE, OX5 2DH. See also Haines Watts
•TECWYN, Mr. Deian, BA FCA *1981;* PricewaterhouseCoopers LLP, 1 Embankment Place, LONDON, WC2N 6RH. See also PricewaterhouseCoopers
TEDCASTLE, Mr. Oliver Jon, ACA *2007;* Perceptive Informatics, Lady Bay House, Meadow Grove, NOTTINGHAM, NG2 3HF.
TEDDER, Mr. John Arthur, FCA *1960;* 103 Shelvers Way, TADWORTH, KT20 5QQ. (Life Member)
TEDDER, Mr. Julian Lester, BA FCA *1996;* 2 Swaynes Lane, GUILDFORD, SURREY, GU1 2XX.
TEDDER, Ms. Kirsten Jill, BA ACA *1998;* Christies, 8 King Street, LONDON, SW1Y 6QT.
•TEDDER, Mrs. Sarah, BA ACA *1993;* 2 Hardwick Close, Great Notley, BRAINTREE, CM77 7FQ.
TEDESCO, Mr. Diego Fernando, ACA *2009;* 18 Turnstone Close, Winnersh, WOKINGHAM, BERKSHIRE, RG41 5LQ.
TEDESCO, Mr. Donato, BSc ACA *1992;* 32 Lansdowne Gardens, Llantarnam, CWMBRAN, GWENT, NP44 3GB.
TEDSTONE, Mr. Gavin Martin, BA ACA *1999;* 15 Engine Mews, Hampton-in-Arden, SOLIHULL, B92 0AZ.
TEE, Miss. Anna Clare, BA(Hons) ACA *2001;* 3 Grove Lane, KINGSTON UPON THAMES, KT1 2SU.
TEE, Mr. Brian Nicholas, FCA *1976;* The Parsonage, Shipton Oliffe, CHELTENHAM, GL54 4HH. (Life Member)
TEE, Mr. James Anthony Haselden, FCA *1970;* Drivers, Tibberton, GLOUCESTER, GL2 8EB. (Life Member)
TEE, Miss. May Ying, BSc ACA *2009;* 29 Kewferry Road, NORTHWOOD, MIDDLESEX, HA6 2PE.
•TEE, Mr. Simon Robert, BA FCA *1992;* Kilsby & Williams LLP, Cedar House, Hazell Drive, NEWPORT, GWENT, NP10 8FY. See also Simon Tee Business Services Limited
TEE, Mr. Tong Lam, ACA *1980;* Oak Tree Corner, 29 Kewferry Road, NORTHWOOD, HA6 2PE.
TEECE, Mr. Bryan Charles, FCA *1954;* (Member of Council 1985 - 1995), 28 Queen Elizabeth Lodge, Laleham Gardens, Cliftonville, MARGATE, KENT, CT9 3PR. (Life Member)
TEECE, Mrs. Emma Louise, BSc ACA *2004;* 18 Millfield Crescent, PONTEFRACT, WEST YORKSHIRE, WF8 4LU.
•TEECE, Mr. John Leslie, BSc FCA *1981;* Montpelier Professional (Lancashire) Limited, Charter House, Pittman Way, Fulwood, PRESTON, PR2 9ZD.
TEECE, Mr. Paul, BA ACA *1996;* 20 Westwind Drive, METHUEN, MA 01844-1960, UNITED STATES.
TEESDALE, Mr. Paul John Stanton, BA ACA *1982;* 11 Oaklands Road, LONDON, SW14 8NJ.
TEESDALE, Mr. Peter, FCA *1962;* 58 Broad Road, BRAINTREE, CM7 9RT. (Life Member)
•TEGG, Mr. Malcolm Frederick, FCA *1971;* (Tax Fac), Malcolm F. Tegg, The Old Gun House, Sedlescombe, BATTLE, TN33 0QJ.
TEH, Mr. Ah Kiam Kenneth, FCA *1975;* 83A Jalan Setiabistari, Bukit Damansara, 50490 KUALA LUMPUR, FEDERAL TERRITORY, MALAYSIA.
TEH, Mr. Cheng Hock, BA ACA *1996;* 20 Jalan SS1/26, Kg Tunku, PETALING JAYA, SELANGOR, 47300, MALAYSIA.
TEH, Mr. Cheng Kiang, FCA *1980;* 2 Erlestoke Place, CASTLE HILL, NSW 2154, AUSTRALIA.
TEH, Mr. Choon Meng, FCA *1974;* 10 Solok Gurney Satu, 10250 PENANG, MALAYSIA.
TEH, Miss. Colene Siew Mei, BSc ACA *1996;* Flat 3 7/F Block A, Wisdom Court, 5 Hatton Road, MID LEVELS, HONG KONG ISLAND, HONG KONG SAR.
TEH, Miss. Lay Yong, FCA *1977;* 5 Jalan Batai Laut 10, Taman Bukit Camerlang, 41300 KLANG, Selangor, MALAYSIA.
TEH, Miss. Michelle Chee Ying, BSc ACA *1996;* 36 Ewell Downs Road, EPSOM, SURREY, KT17 3BW.
•TEH, Ms. Poh Kim, FCA *1986;* E-Accountants Limited, 36 Bardolph Road, RICHMOND, SURREY, TW9 2LH.
TEHAN, Mrs. Elizabeth Jayne, BSc ACA *2000;* 39 The Hawnelands, HALESOWEN, B63 3RT.
TEHRANCHIAN, Ms. Tiraneh, BSc ACA *1992;* 68 Hornsey Lane, LONDON, N6 5LU.
TEIGH, Mr. Carl Andrew, BA ACA *2003;* 4 Oddys Fold, LEEDS, LS6 4ND.
TEJA, Mr. Nizar Ali, FCA *1969;* Digital Print Leicester Ltd, 9 Abbey Business Park, Friday Street, LEICESTER, LE1 3BW.
TEJANI, Mr. Amirali Sharif, ACA *1981;* 14 Manor Road Extention, Oadby, LEICESTER, LE2 2LL.
•TEJI, Mr. Tarlok, BSc FCA MBA *1985;* Glen Cairn, 32 Park Avenue, HARROGATE, HG2 9BG.
TEJPAR, Mr. Zavhar Kassamali, CA FCA CFP *1975;* Suite 840 Sun Life Place, 10123-99 Street, EDMONTON T5J 3H1, AB, CANADA. See also Gardiner Karbani Audy & Partners
TEJWANI, Mr. Roger Brian, LLB ACA FSI *2000;* C/o SBG Securities, 4th Floor, 2 Exchange Square, 85 Maude Street, SANDTON, GAUTENG 2146 SOUTH AFRICA.
TEKLOS, Mr. Lambros, BA ACA *2007;* 2 Sina Street Tsirio Area, 3077 LIMASSOL, CYPRUS.
TEKLOU, Miss. Maria, BA(Econ) ACA *2002;* 36 Charalambou Evagorou Street, Agios Athanasios, 4107 LIMASSOL, CYPRUS.
TELFER, Mr. Andrew James William, BSc(Eng) ACA *1995;* Lingfield House, East Grinstead Road, LINGFIELD, RH7 6ES.
TELFER, Miss. Laura, ACA *2011;* 48 Baltic Quay, Mill Road, GATESHEAD, TYNE AND WEAR, NE8 3QW.
•TELFER, Mr. Martin Russell, BSc FCA *1982;* Martin Telfer, 5 Brookfields, Pavenham, BEDFORD, MK43 7QA.
TELFER, Mrs. Miranda Lauraine, BSc ACA *1994;* Old Mutual Asset Managers, Old Mutual Place, 2 Lambeth Hill, LONDON, EC4V 4GG.
TELFORD, Mr. Brian William, MBA BA FCA *1980;* 34 York Street, CARDIFF, CF5 1NE.
TELFORD, Mr. David Andrew, ACA *2011;* Ground Floor Flat, 36 Poplar Grove, LONDON, W6 7RE.
TELFORD, Ms. Deborah Mary, BSc ACA *2002;* 38B Rambler Crescent, Beach Haven, NORTH SHORE 0626, NEW ZEALAND.
•TELFORD, Mr. Gary Alan, BA FCA CTA *1983;* (Tax Fac), PricewaterhouseCoopers LLP, Cornwall Court, 19 Cornwall Street, BIRMINGHAM, B3 2DT. See also PricewaterhouseCoopers
TELFORD, Mrs. Gillian, BSc ACA *1990;* Corner House, Monk Ing Road, Dacre, HARROGATE, HG3 4EX.
TELFORD, Miss. Juliet Sarah, BSc FCA CFA *1991;* Apex Credit Management Ltd, 27 Arden Street, STRATFORD-UPON-AVON, CV37 6NW.
TELFORD, Mr. Peter Thomas, BSc ACA *1990;* Corner House, Monk Ing Road, Dacre, HARROGATE, HG3 4EX.
TELFORD, Mr. Robert Mark, BA ACA *1995;* The Mount, Barrow Hill, Sellindge, ASHFORD, KENT, TN25 6JQ.
TELFORD, Mrs. Rosalind Margaret, BSc ACA *1990;* The Knoll, Stockcroft Road, Balcombe, HAYWARDS HEATH, RH17 6LG.
TELFORD, Mr. Thomas Henry, ACA *2010;* 21 Brooker Street, HOVE, EAST SUSSEX, BN3 3YX.
TELFORD, Mr. Thomas Noel Andrew, MA FCA FCT *1978;* Lyoth House, Lewes Road, HAYWARDS HEATH, RH17 7SY.
TELFORD, Mr. William, BA FCA *1975;* (Member of Council 2005 - 2009), Telford Financial Training, 2 Paygate Cottages, New Road, Ringmer, LEWES, EAST SUSSEX BN8 5HA.
TELI, Mr. Ashraf, ACA *1984;* 37/1 Commercial Avenue, Phase IV, Defence Housing Authority, KARACHI, SINDH, PAKISTAN.
TELL, Miss. Sara Helena, ACA *2009;* Howarth Clark Whitehill & Co St. Brides House, 10 Salisbury Square, LONDON, EC4Y 8EH.
TELLALIAN, Mr. Vicken, BSc ACA *2009;* 22 Ypilanti Str, Platy, NICOSIA, CYPRUS.
•TELLER, Mr. Jonathan Moses, FCA MBA *1983;* MEMBER OF COUNCIL, JTAnalytics, 4 Leadale Road, LONDON, N16 6DA.
TELLING, Mr. Jeremy David, BA ACA *1991;* 27 Renshaw Road, Greystones, SHEFFIELD, S11 7PD.
TELLING, Mr. John Alfred, ACA *1985;* 74 Ellerby Street, LONDON, SW6 6EZ.
TELLING, Mr. Martin, ACA *1991;* 4 Meadow Way, Farnborough Park, ORPINGTON, KENT, BR6 8LW.
•TELLING, Mr. Richard Christopher, FCA *1961;* Telling R.C., Warecott, Old Worcester Road, Hartlebury, KIDDERMINSTER, DY11 7XL.
TELLIS, Mr. Ronald Ivor Salvadore, FCA *1961;* Flat 12A, Rest House Apartments, Rest House Road, BANGALORE 560 001, INDIA.
TELYTSKA, Miss. Tetiana, MSc BSc ACA *2005;* 256 Franklin Road, BIRMINGHAM, B30 2EJ.
TEMERLIES, Mr. Marc Stephen, BSc ACA *1996;* 6 Sirkin Street, 43374 RA'ANANA, ISRAEL.
•TEMLETT, Mr. John Christopher, FCA *1970;* (Tax Fac), Garners Limited, Bermuda House, 45 High Street, Hampton Wick, KINGSTON UPON THAMES, SURREY KT1 4EH.
TEMPERLEY, Miss. Alison Lynn, MA BA ACA *1989;* 1 The Paddocks, Blackmore Way, Wheathampstead, ST. ALBANS, AL4 8HE.
TEMPERLEY, Mr. Peter John, MA ACA *1987;* A O N Ltd, 8 Devonshire Square, LONDON, EC2M 4PL.
TEMPEST, Mr. Andrew John, MA ACA *1989;* 4 Crane Close, Little Cransley, KETTERING, NORTHAMPTONSHIRE, NN14 1QN.
•TEMPEST, Mr. David Barry, FCA *1971;* Bostocks, Empire House, 15 Mulcture Hall Road, HALIFAX, HX1 1SP. See also Bostocks, Boyce Welch
TEMPEST, Ms. Kylie May, ACA CA(AUS) *2011;* (Tax Fac), Ground Floor, 22 Racton Road, LONDON, SW6 1LP.
TEMPEST, Mr. Michael Richard, BCom FCA *1977;* 73 Green Road, SOUTHSEA, HAMPSHIRE, PO5 4DX.
TEMPLAR, Mr. Robert David, BSc ACA *1989;* 18 Oakburn Road, ILKLEY, LS29 9NN.
TEMPLE, Mr. Alan Duncan, FCA *1962;* Crayford House, 46 Fleet Road, Holbeach, SPALDING, LINCOLNSHIRE, PE12 8LA. (Life Member)
TEMPLE, Miss. Angela Joanna, BA(Hons) ACA *2003;* 19a Collingham Place, LONDON, SW5 0QF.
•TEMPLE, Mr. Christopher John, BA(Hons) ACA *2000;* PricewaterhouseCoopers LLP, 7 More London Riverside, LONDON, SE1 2RT. See also PricewaterhouseCoopers
TEMPLE, Mr. Dominic John, BA ACA *1998;* Rodalvej 8, 8340 MALLING, DENMARK.
TEMPLE, Mr. Gary Paul, BSc ACA *1992;* 94a Ermine Street, Caxton, CAMBRIDGE, CB23 3PQ.
TEMPLE, Mr. George Barry, FCA *1960;* 41 Kirkwood Drive, Cookridge, LEEDS, LS16 7DY. (Life Member)
TEMPLE, Mr. Ian Richard, BSc ACA *1992;* Hydrogen Group Plc, Pountney Hill House, 6 Laurence Pountney Hill, LONDON, EC4R 0BL.
TEMPLE, Mr. John George Stuart, LLB FCA *1957;* 14 Castle Rise, Belmesthorpe, STAMFORD, PE9 4JL. (Life Member)
TEMPLE, Mr. Jonathan Paul Edward, BA ACA *1999;* Pret A Manger, 1 Hudson's Place, LONDON, SW1V 1PZ.
TEMPLE, Mr. Kevin Paul, BSc ACA *2005;* Close Asset Finance Ltd Tolworth Tower, Ewell Road, SURBITON, KT6 7EL.
TEMPLE, Mr. Martin Andrew, BSocSc ACA *2002;* Grey Garth, 60 Francis Street, MIRFIELD, WEST YORKSHIRE, WF14 9BB.
•TEMPLE, Mr. Michael Barry, FCA *1965;* Michael B Temple, 56 Allandale Crescent, POTTERS BAR, HERTFORDSHIRE, EN6 2JZ.
TEMPLE, Mr. Michael Nicholas Fraser, BSc FCA *1974;* Missenden, Danes Hill, WOKING, GU22 7HQ.
TEMPLE, Mr. Neil William, BSc(Econ) ACA *2001;* 27 Station Road, Histon, CAMBRIDGE, CB24 9LQ.
TEMPLE, Mr. Ralph, FCA *1956;* 2 Culverlands Close, Green Lane, STANMORE, HA7 3AG. (Life Member)
TEMPLE, Mr. Stephen David Miles, BA ACA *1986;* Ashbrook, Church Lane, Appleton Roebuck, YORK, YO23 7DF.
TEMPLE, Mr. Stephen Paul, BSc ACA *1996;* 18 Langdale Avenue, HARPENDEN, HERTFORDSHIRE, AL5 5QU.

TEMPLE-COLE, Mr. John Paul, BSc CA FCA *1999;* Level 5 Chifley Tower, 2 Chifley Square, SYDNEY, NSW 2000, AUSTRALIA.
TEMPLEMAN, Ms. Clare Elisabeth, BSc FCA *1991;* (Tax Fac), I N G Bank, 60 London Wall, LONDON, EC2M 5TQ.
TEMPLEMAN, Mr. Daniel John Felix, BSc FCA *1992;* Erlenhalde 20, 8832 WOLLERAU, SWITZERLAND.
TEMPLEMAN, Mr. David George, BSc ACA *1988;* Coopers Church Lane, Laughton, LEWES, EAST SUSSEX, BN8 6AH.
TEMPLEMAN, Mr. Jonathan, MA ACA *1989;* 46 Harewelle Way, Harrold, BEDFORD, BEDFORDSHIRE, MK43 7DY.
TEMPLEMAN, Mr. Robert, LLB FCA *1974;* Balnakeil, Bryants Bottom, GREAT MISSENDEN, HP16 9RN.
TEMPLER, Mr. Marc, LLB ACA *1993;* 107 Guilford Street, LONDON, WC1N 1DP.
TEMPLER, Mr. Michael, FCA *1967;* Chemin de Fillieux 6, CH-2073 ENGES, SWITZERLAND.
TEMPLETON, Mr. Gary Iain, BA(Hons) ACA *2001;* 12 Wellesley Court, Dukes Ride, CROWTHORNE, RG45 6DG.
TEMPLETON, Mr. Kenneth Nelson, FCA *1963;* Orchard Grange, The Street, Brightwell-Cum-Sotwell, WALLINGFORD, OX10 0RT. (Life Member)
•**TEMPLETON, Mr. Mark David, BSc FCA** *1992;* Kirk Newsholme Ltd, 4315 Park Approach, Thorpe Park, LEEDS, LS15 8GB.
TEMPLETON, Mr. Peter, BSc ACA *2006;* Manchester Airport Plc, 6th Floor Olympic House, Manchester Airport, MANCHESTER, M90 1QX.
•**TEMPLETON, Mr. Robert Ian, BA FCA ACA** *1966;* Acorn Capital Partners Limited, Metropolitan House, Station Road, Cheadle Hulme, CHEADLE, CHESHIRE SK8 7AZ.
TEMPLING, Mr. Jonathan David, BSc(Hons) ACA *2001;* Save The Children, 54 Wilton Avenue, NORWALK, CT 06851-4534, UNITED STATES.
•**TEN, Miss. Petrina Fui Ling, ACA FCCA** *2009;* Anderson Ross LLP, Waltham Forest Business Centre, 5 Blackhorse Lane, LONDON, E17 6DS. See also Interbusiness Services Ltd
TEN BROEKE, Mr. Felix William, BA ACA *2006;* 32 Aphelion Way, Shinfield, READING, RG2 9FR.
TENDELL, Mr. Donald Ian, FCA *1969;* Redcourt, Beaconsfield Road, Farnham Royal, SLOUGH, SL2 3BY.
TENDLE, Miss. Anuradha Ashok, BA(Hons) ACA *2001;* 307 Vicente Street, SAN FRANCISCO, CA 94127, UNITED STATES.
•**TENDLER, Mrs. Gail Paulette, MA ACA** *1984;* Tendler & Co, 7 Frithwood Avenue, NORTHWOOD, HA6 3LY.
•**TENDLER, Mr. Marc Jeremy, BSc FCA** *1984;* Tendler & Co, 7 Frithwood Avenue, NORTHWOOD, HA6 3LY.
•**TENG, Mrs. Priscilla Mee Hung, ACA FCCA** *2010;* Sullivans Associates Limited, 14 Gelliwastad Road, PONTYPRIDD, MID GLAMORGAN, CF37 2BW.
TENG HIN VOON, Miss. Laura Astrid, ACA *2009;* 85 Ylang Ylang, QUATRE-BORNES, MAURITIUS.
TENG HIN VOON, Mrs. Yuen Kiow, BSc ACA *1987;* BDO De Chazal du Mee, P.O. Box 799, 10 Frere Felix, De Valois Street, PORT LOUIS, MAURITIUS.
TENGERIS, Mr. Nicholas, BSc ACA *2004;* Kerkyras 17 Anayia, 2640 NICOSIA, CYPRUS.
•**TENGRA, Mr. Perozshah Byramji, ACA** *1982;* Mehta & Tengra, 24 Bedford Row, LONDON, WC1R 4TQ.
TENISON-COLLINS, Mr. Anthony Edward, FCA *1952;* 37 Chester Road, NORTHWOOD, HA6 1BG. (Life Member)
TENNANT, Mr. Alan David, BA FCA *1980;* 16 rue de la mairie, 78450 CHAVENAY, FRANCE.
•**TENNANT, Mr. Alexander Simon, FCA** *1984;* LKT Limited, Ravenshill Cottage, Yewleigh Lane, Upton-upon-Severn, WORCESTER, WR8 0QW. See also LKT
TENNANT, Mr. Alistair George, MSc ACA *1995;* 29 Birch Green, HERTFORD, SG14 2LR.
TENNANT, Mr. Christopher John, BA ACA *1985;* 6 Lonsdale Square, LONDON, N1 1EN.
TENNANT, Mr. Duncan, ACA *2009;* Generation Investment Management LLP, 1 Vine Street, LONDON, W1J 0AH.
TENNANT, Mr. Nicholas John, BSc ACA *1982;* 34 Alma Hill, Kimberley, NOTTINGHAM, NG16 2JF.
•**TENNANT, Mr. Ralph, FCA** *1976;* R. Tennant & Co, Mellowbrook House, 1A Stratford Lane, Hilton, BRIDGNORTH, SHROPSHIRE WV15 5PF.
TENNANT, Mr. Richard William, FCA *1975;* Uplyme, Baildon Close, Oundle DriveWollaton Park, NOTTINGHAM, NG8 1BS.
TENNANT, Mr. Timothy Spence, BA FCA *1981;* Woodlands Farmhouse, Holford, BRIDGWATER, TA5 1SE.
TENNANT, Mr. Victor William, FCA *1951;* 9 Westmore Court, Westmoreland Road, BROMLEY, KENT, BR2 0RZ. (Life Member)
TENNENT, Mrs. Angela Louise, BSc FCA *1987;* Barnfield, Mark Way, GODALMING, SURREY, GU7 2BD.
TENNENT, Miss. Harriet Sophie, MEng ACA *2010;* 66 Granville Park, LONDON, SE13 7DX.
TENNENT, Mr. John Charles Roger, ACA *1988;* Barnfield, Mark Way, GODALMING, SURREY, GU7 2BD.
TENNER, Mr. Brian Thomas, LLB ACA *1995;* Renold Plc Renold House, Styal Road, MANCHESTER, M22 5WL.
•**TENNER, Mr. Colin Isaac, MA FCA** *1992;* 6 Strathearn Lane, BELFAST, BT4 2BT.
TENNER, Mrs. Lucia Jane, BSc ACA *1993;* 7 Gilwern Close, CHESTER, CH1 4AP.
TENNYSON, Mr. John Gordon Allan, FCA *1959;* Palazzo Litta, Via Luisa Brielli 3, 28921 VERBANIA INTRA, ITALY. (Life Member)
TENTORI, Mr. Mark Ian, BA FCA *1991;* Holly Hedges, Tingrith Road, Eversholt, MILTON KEYNES, MK17 9EF.
•**TENZER, Mr. Mark Stuart, FCA** *1982;* Jeffreys Henry LLP, Finsgate, 5-7 Cranwood Street, LONDON, EC1V 9EE.
•**TENZER, Mr. Russell Paul, FCA** *1979;* (Tax Fac), Hazlems Fenton LLP, Palladium House, 1-4 Argyll Street, LONDON, W1F 7LD. See also Argyll Street Management Services Ltd
TEO, Mr. Chiang Lim, ACA *1979;* 6 Jalan SS22/27A, 47400 PETALING JAYA, MALAYSIA.
TEO, Mr. Donald Cheng Tuan, FCA *1971;* 235 Arcadia Road #10-04, SINGAPORE 289843, SINGAPORE. (Life Member)
TEO, Mr. George Eng Kim, FCA *1970;* Khattar Capital International Pte Ltd, 80 Ruffles Place, 14-01 UOB Plaza 1, SINGAPORE 048624, SINGAPORE.
TEO, Mr. John Cheng Lok, FCA *1974;* 130 Tanjong Rhu Road, #09-10 Pebble Bay, SINGAPORE 436918, SINGAPORE. (Life Member)
TEO, Mr. Kok Chye, ACA *1983;* 06-232 Block 168A, Queensway, SINGAPORE 140168, SINGAPORE.
TEO, Ms. Pei Jean, BA ACA *2002;* No 2 Jalan SS 3/41, 47300 PETALING JAYA, MALAYSIA.
TEO, Mr. Pek Hui, MA BSc ACA *2011;* Flat 104, Basque Court, Garter Way, LONDON, SE16 6XE.
TEO, Mr. Robert Keng Tuan, FCA *1973;* RSM Robert Teo Kuan & Co, Penthouse Wisma RKT Block A No2, Jalan Raja Abdullah, Off Jalan Sultan Ismail, 50300 KUALA LUMPUR, FEDERAL TERRITORY MALAYSIA.
TEO, Mrs. Siew May, BSc(Hons) ACA *2003;* 34 Tanah Merah Kechil Road, 5th Fl. Unit 32, Tower 2A, SINGAPORE 465560, SINGAPORE.
TEO, Mr. Tian Rong, ACA *2011;* 18 Jalan SS21/3 Damansara Utama, 47400 PETALING JAYA, SELANGOR, MALAYSIA.
TEO, Miss. Yian Ping, BSc(Econ) ACA *1999;* 47 Hindhede Walk, #10-08, SINGAPORE 587977, SINGAPORE.
TEOH, Mr. Choon Beng, LLB ACA *2011;* 37 Gurdon Road, LONDON, SE7 7RP.
TEOH, Mr. Chun Ming Nelson, ACA *2005;* Flat D 18/F, Blk 6 Verbena Heights, 8 Mau Tai Road, Tseung Kwan O, SAI KUNG, NEW TERRITORIES HONG KONG SAR.
TEOH, Mr. Danny Leong Kay, ACA *1981;* 15 Namly Hill, SINGAPORE 267278, SINGAPORE.
TEOH, Mr. Hock Eng, FCA *1979;* 63M Solok York, 10450 PENANG, MALAYSIA.
TEOH, Mr. Hock Seng, ACA *1983;* Kuok Brothers Sdn Bhd, 18th Fl. Wisma Jerneh, 38 Jalan Sultan Ismail, 50250 KUALA LUMPUR, FEDERAL TERRITORY, MALAYSIA.
TEOH, Mr. Hwai Chong, BSc ACA *2002;* C3-3-5 Ara Hill, Jalan PJU1A/31, Ara Damansara, 47301 Petaling Jaya, Selangor, PETALING JAYA MALAYSIA.
TEOH, Mr. James Beng Hooi, FCA *1994;* 16 Jalan Taman Senangin, Taman Senangin, Kelang Lama, 09000 KULIM, KEDAH, MALAYSIA.
TEOH, Ms. Joon Leng, BSc(Econ) ACA *2000;* 94 Jalan Wawasan 4/6, Pusat Bandar, 47100 PUCHONG, SELANGOR, MALAYSIA.
TEOH, Miss. Leng Lan, FCA *1974;* 30 Jalan Mambu, Bukit Bandar Raya, 59100 KUALA LUMPUR, FEDERAL TERRITORY, MALAYSIA.
TEOH, Mr. Nicky Hui Leng, BA ACA *2003;* 4 DUNN ROAD, 10350 PENANG, MALAYSIA.
TEOH, Miss. Su Yen, BSc ACA *2010;* ABBOTTS CHAMBERS, Flat 3, 202 Bishopsgate, LONDON, EC2M 4NR.
TEOH, Mr. Teik Kee, BSc ACA *1986;* 2D Bishopsgate, SINGAPORE 249968, SINGAPORE.
TEOH, Miss. Tit Eng, FCA *1975;* Lim Teoh & Co, 503-A Jalan Pintu Sepuluh, 05100 ALOR STAR, KEDAH, MALAYSIA.
TEOH, Miss. Yin Meng, BSc ACA *1994;* 25 Jalan 5/3, 46000 PETALING JAYA, MALAYSIA.
TEPER, Mr. Daniel, ACA *2008;* Unit 12, 39-41 Denham Street, BONDI BEACH, NSW 2026, AUSTRALIA.
TERAOKA, Mr. Jeremy Nicholas Wilfrid, BA FCA *1982;* Novelix Pharmaceuticals Inc, 8008 Girard Avenue, Suite 330, LA JOLLA, CA 92037, UNITED STATES.
TERAOKA, Tokuji Wilfrid Michael, Esq MBE BCom FCA *1952;* 23 Wentworth Court, Beech Grove, HARROGATE, HG1 0EL. (Life Member)
TERBLANS, Mr. Steven Hermanus, ACA CA(SA) *2008;* 127 Donnithorne Avenue, NUNEATON, WARWICKSHIRE, CV11 4QL.
TEREZAKIS, Mr. Andreas, BSc FCA MBA *1997;* KRINIS 27, VOULA, 16673 ATHENS, GREECE.
TERHOVEN, Mr. Alan, ACA CA(SA) *2008;* 2 Dalston End, MILTON KEYNES, BUCKINGHAMSHIRE, MK10 9QB.
TERIACA, Mr. Piero Clifford Paul, BSc ACA *1991;* Flat 1, 28 Baron Street, LONDON, N1 9ES.
TERMINIELLO, Mr. Piermarco, BSc ACA *2004;* 20 More Road, GODALMING, SURREY, GU7 3PU.
TERNOUTH, Mr. Mark James, MA ACA *1993;* 27 Avenue Gardens, LONDON, SW14 8BP.
TERRAS, Mr. Antony Michael, BA FCA *1958;* 9 Green Courts, Green Walk, Bowdon, ALTRINCHAM, CHESHIRE, WA14 2SR. (Life Member)
TERRAS, Mr. Christopher Richard, MA FCA *1962;* 21 St. Hilarys Park, ALDERLEY EDGE, CHESHIRE, SK9 7DA. (Life Member)
TERRELL, Mr. Jonathan Raymond, BA FCA *1988;* KCIC LLC, Suite 650 East, 1100 New York Avenue NW, WASHINGTON, DC 20005, UNITED STATES.
TERRELL, Mr. Robin James, BSc ACA *1994;* 7 Lord Reith Place, BEACONSFIELD, BUCKINGHAMSHIRE, HP9 2GE.
TERRETT, Mr. Benjamin John, BA ACA *1998;* U I A (Insurance) Ltd Kings Court, London Road, STEVENAGE, HERTFORDSHIRE, SG1 2TP.
TERREY, Mr. John Leslie, FCA *1974;* Wheelgate Cottage, Longbyre, Greenhead, BRAMPTON, CUMBRIA, CA8 7HR.
TERRILL, Mr. John Middleton, BSc ACA *1989;* Gilbeck House, Barningham, RICHMOND, NORTH YORKSHIRE, DL11 7DU.
TERRIS, Mr. Stuart Robert, BA ACA *1997;* Meachers Global Logisitics, Unit 19, Nursling Industrial Estate, Mauretania Road, Nursling, SOUTHAMPTON SO16 0YS.
•**TERRONI, Miss. Andrea Jane, BSc FCA** *1995;* Andrea Terroni, 28 Beechdale, Winchmore Hill, LONDON, N21 3QG.
TERRY, Miss. Alison Jane, BA(Hons) ACA *2001;* with National Audit Office, 157-197 Buckingham Palace Road, Victoria, LONDON, SW1W 9SP.
•**TERRY, Mr. Christopher, ACA ATII** *1979;* (Tax Fac), C. Terry & Co., The Birches, Todds Green, STEVENAGE, SG1 2JE.
TERRY, Mr. Christopher John, ACA *1994;* 54 Asgard Drive, BEDFORD, BEDFORDSHIRE, MK41 0US.
TERRY, The Revd. Christopher Laurence, FCA *1975;* The Rectory, Town Wall Rd, GREAT YARMOUTH, NORFOLK, NR301DJ.
TERRY, Mr. Christopher Malcolm, BSc ACA *1989;* 12a The Park, Mayfield, ASHBOURNE, DERBYSHIRE, DE6 2HT.
TERRY, Mr. Colin David, BA FCA *1989;* Jardine OneSolution, 19/F Tower One, Millennium City 1, 388 Kwun Tong Road, KWUN TONG, KOWLOON HONG KONG SAR.
•**TERRY, Mr. David, FCA** *1979;* Ramon Lee & Partners, Kemp House, 152-160 City Road, LONDON, EC1V 2DW. See also RLP Accounting Limited
TERRY, Mr. David Robins, FCA *1968;* Tapenhall House, Porters Mill, DROITWICH, WR9 0AN.
TERRY, Mr. Douglas William, BSc ACA *1990;* RPS Group plc, Centurion Court, 85 Milton Park, ABINGDON, OXFORDSHIRE, OX14 6RY.
TERRY, Mr. Geoffrey George, FCA *1952;* Maes Canol, Llanaber Road, BARMOUTH, LL42 1YS. (Life Member)
TERRY, Ms. Helen Mary, BSc ACA *1987;* 7 Orchard Chase, Hurst, READING, RG10 0SW.
•**TERRY, Mr. James Richard, BSc ACA** *1985;* (Tax Fac), James Terry, Flat 29, Holly Lodge, 90 Wimbledon Hill Road, LONDON, SW19 7PB. See also Lingfield Partners LLP and Beechcroft Associates Limited
TERRY, Mrs. Joanne Margaret, BSc ACA *1996;* 167 Old Woosehill Lane, WOKINGHAM, RG41 3HR.
TERRY, Mr. Jonathan, BA(Hons) ACA *2011;* 1 Chellow Gardens, Deanwood Crescent Allerton, BRADFORD, BD15 9BZ.
•**TERRY, Mr. Jonathan Mark, BA FCA** *1993;* Blackman Terry LLP, Bolney Place, Cowfold Road, Bolney, HAYWARDS HEATH, WEST SUSSEX RH17 5QT.
•**TERRY, Mr. Jonathan Paul, BSc ACA CTA** *1991;* PricewaterhouseCoopers LLP, Pricewaterhousecoopers, 12 Plumtree Court, LONDON, EC4A 4HT. See also PricewaterhouseCoopers
TERRY, Mr. Joseph Anthony, FCA *1954;* 15 Hapil Close, Sandford, WINSCOMBE, BS25 5AA. (Life Member)
TERRY, Mrs. Lucy Caroline, BA ACA *1999;* 6 Regent Close, Otterbourne, WINCHESTER, SO21 2DN.
TERRY, Mr. Mark James, BSc(Hons) ACA *2003;* 19 Kneller Road, TWICKENHAM, TW2 7DF.
TERRY, Mr. Mark Stuart, BA FCA *1994;* Cedar Cottage, La Rue de L'Etocquet, St. John, JERSEY, JE3 4AS.
•**TERRY, Mr. Michael Charles William, FCA** *1968;* (Tax Fac), Merwald House, Walmer Castle Road, Walmer, DEAL, KENT, CT14 7NG.
TERRY, Mr. Michael David, FCA *1962;* 50 The Leavens, Apperley Bridge, BRADFORD, BD10 0UW.
TERRY, Mr. Michael Eaton, BA FCA *1974;* 26 Pinewood Avenue, BOURNEMOUTH, BH10 6BT.
TERRY, Mr. Michael John, BSc ACA *1993;* 206/56 Spit Road, Mosman, SYDNEY, NSW 2088, AUSTRALIA.
TERRY, Mr. Neil, BSc ACA *2011;* 77 Cromwell Avenue, BILLERICAY, ESSEX, CM12 0AG.
TERRY, Mr. Nicholas, BSc ACA *2003;* Kritonos 24, Agios Athanasios, 4106 LIMASSOL, CYPRUS.
TERRY, Mr. Nicholas Frank, BEng ACA *2000;* 29 Sebastopol Street, CAULFIELD NORTH, VIC 3161, AUSTRALIA.
TERRY, Mrs. Nicola Ruth, BSc ACA *1994;* with Harris Carr Ltd, Cheriton, Farnham Lane, HASLEMERE, SURREY, GU27 1HD.
•**TERRY, Mr. Nigel Joseph Douty, BSc ACA** *1996;* PricewaterhouseCoopers LLP, Hays Galleria, 1 Hays Lane, LONDON, SE1 2RD. See also PricewaterhouseCoopers
TERRY, Mrs. Paula Ann, BSc ACA *1992;* 1 Greystoke Avenue, SALE, CHESHIRE, M33 3NT.
•**TERRY, Mr. Peter, BSc ACA CF MSI** *1994;* Mazars LLP, The Lexicon, Mount Street, MANCHESTER, M2 5NT.
•①**TERRY, Mr. Peter, BSc FCA** *1979;* The Croft, Cowpe Road, Waterfoot, ROSSENDALE, BB4 7DQ.
TERRY, Mr. Steven Paul, BSc ACA *1989;* 42 Maryland Drive, MAIDSTONE, ME16 9EA.
•**TERRY, Mrs. Wendy Jane, ACA** *1991;* Pawley & Malyon, Pishiobury House, Pishiobury Drive, SAWBRIDGEWORTH, HERTFORDSHIRE, CM21 0AF.
TERRY, Mrs. Yvonne Julia, FCA *1975;* 2 Cheviot Close, Kings Acre, HEREFORD, HR4 0TF.
TERZIAN, Mr. Onik, ACA *2011;* 39 Haileybury Road, ORPINGTON, BR6 9EZ.
TESCHKE, Mr. Robert, BA ACA *1999;* Alstom, Haus56 Technologie Park, Friedrich Ebert Str, 51429 BERGISCH GLADBACH, GERMANY.
•**TESCIUBA, Mr. Anthony Jeffrey, FCA FCIArb CTA** *1982;* Tesciuba Limited, The Chambers, 13 Police Street, MANCHESTER, M2 7LQ.
TESFAJOHANNES, Mrs. Taddeset, BSc FCA *1977;* 41-43 Meadow Garth, LONDON, NW10 3BN.
TESFAY, Mr. Thomas, ACA *2011;* 4 Goddards Way, ILFORD, ESSEX, IG1 4BF.
TESH, Miss. Jo-Anna, BSc ACA *2003;* 6 Commonside, STOURPORT-ON-SEVERN, WORCESTERSHIRE, DY13 0RB.
TESHOME, Ms. Sarah, BA ACA *1994;* (Tax Fac), Arrandale House, The Nook, Haigh Moor, Tingley, WAKEFIELD, WF3 1EB.
•**TESLER, Mr. Simon, FCA** *1974;* Simon Tesler And Associates, 149 Albion Road, LONDON, N16 9JU.
•**TESTA, Mr. William John, BA ACA** *1994;* with Ernst & Young LLP, 1 More London Place, LONDON, SE1 2AF.
TESTER, Mr. Jack Leslie James, FCA *1950;* 6A Long Acres Close, Coombe Dingle, BRISTOL, BS9 2RF. (Life Member)
TETHER, Mr. Donald John, MA ACA *1983;* 4 Kemble Court, Downhead Park, MILTON KEYNES, MK15 9AX.

TETLEY, Mr. Alexander, LLB ACA *2002;* with A.C. Mole & Sons, Stafford House, Blackbrook Park Avenue, TAUNTON, SOMERSET, TA1 2PX.
TETLEY, Miss. Alison Jane, BA FCA *1987;* 14 Fenton Street, Burley-in-Wharfedale, ILKLEY, LS29 7EX.
TETLEY, Mr. Brian, FCA *1961;* Manor Farm House, Manor Road, Farnley Tyas, HUDDERSFIELD, HD4 6UL.
TETLEY, The Revd. Brian, FCA *1962;* 23 Cripley Road, OXFORD, OX2 0AH. (Life Member)
•TETLEY, Mrs. Christine Mary, BSc FCA *1981;* (Tax Fac), Christine Tetley, 195 Bramhall Lane, STOCKPORT, SK2 6JA.
TETLEY, Mr. Garry Francis Derek, BSc ACA *2001;* with Deloitte LLP, Saltire Court, 20 Castle Terrace, EDINBURGH, EH1 2DB.
TETLEY, Mr. James Colin, BA ACA *2006;* Brewin Dolphin Time Central, 32 Gallowgate, NEWCASTLE UPON TYNE, NE1 4SR.
TETLEY, Mr. James Robert, ACA *2007;* (Tax Fac), 8 Barley Hill, Dunbridge, ROMSEY, SO51 0LF.
TETLEY, Mr. John Charles Norman, FCA *1963;* Les Dindons, Baccas, 24250 CENAC ET ST JULIEN, FRANCE.
•TETLEY, Mr. Robert Paul, FCA *1979;* Lavant Corner, Mid Lavant, CHICHESTER, PO18 0BW.
TETLOW, Miss. Clare Ellen, BSc ACA *2007;* Black Rock, 33 King William Street, LONDON, EC4R 9AS.
TETLOW, Mrs. Helen Elizabeth, BCom ACA *1989;* 22 Rossmith Avenue, BEAUMARIS, VIC 3193, AUSTRALIA.
TETLOW, Miss. Sarah Julia, BSc ACA *1998;* Macquarie Group Limited, 1 Martin Place, SYDNEY, NSW 2000, AUSTRALIA.
TETRADIS, Mrs. Angela, BA ACA *1992;* 8 Draycott Close, The Glebe Estate, Norton, STOCKTON-ON-TEES, TS20 1ST.
TETT, Mr. Colin Christopher, FCA *1970;* Wormstall, Wickham, NEWBURY, BERKSHIRE, RG20 8HB. (Life Member)
TETT, Mrs. Joanna Louise, BSc(Hons) ACA *2000;* 24 Ashley Down Road, BRISTOL, BS7 9JW.
TETTAMANZI, Ms. Francesca Grazia Anna, BA ACA *1999;* 38 avenue de la Faiencerie, LUXEMBOURG, LUXEMBOURG.
TETZLAFF, Mr. John Stefan Ashby, MA ACA *1990;* PO Box 1564, ROZELLE, NSW 2039, AUSTRALIA.
TETZLAFF, Mr. Michael Alex Witold, MEng ACA *2000;* Flat C-f Mowbray Grange, 2 Mowbray Road, LONDON, SE19 2RN.
TEUNON, Mr. Nicholas John, MA ACA *1991;* 11 Groveside, Bookham, LEATHERHEAD, SURREY, KT23 4LD.
TEUTEN, Mr. Paul Theodore, BA FCA *1988;* Duff & Phelps Ltd, 40 Bank Street, LONDON, E14 5NR.
TEVERSON, Miss. Lisa Helen, MA ACA *1992;* (Tax Fac), Kapellenstrasse 3, 4052 BASEL, SWITZERLAND.
TEVIOTDALE, Miss. Wilma Wallace, BA FCA CTA FHEA *1979;* 34 Cleveland Road, Edgerton, HUDDERSFIELD, HD1 4PW.
TEVLIN, Mrs. Jennifer Louise, ACA *2008;* Deloitte & Touche, PO Box 500, MANCHESTER, M60 2AT.
TEW, Ms. Beverley Jane, BA FCA *1992;* 30 Flanchford Road, LONDON, W12 9ND.
•TEW, Mr. Colin Charles, FCA CTA *1964;* Beaumont Tew & Co, Forsythia Cottage, 4 Sefton Paddock, Stoke Poges, SLOUGH, SL2 4PT.
TEW, Mr. Darren Roy, ACA *1996;* 16a Summers Mead, Brimsham Park, Yate, BRISTOL, BS37 7RB.
TEW, Mr. Frank Arthur, FCA *1975;* Gerald McDonald & Co, Cranes Farm Road, BASILDON, ESSEX, SS14 3GT.
TEW, Mrs. Karen Patricia, ACA *1987;* The Earls House Mill Green, Edwardstone, SUDBURY, SUFFOLK, CO10 5PX.
•TEW, Mr. Paul Frank, FCA *1985;* Gibbons, Carleton House, 136 Gray Street, WORKINGTON, CUMBRIA, CA14 2LU. See also Gibbons & Company
•TEW, Mr. Philip George, MA FCA *1982;* PricewaterhouseCoopers LLP, 1 Embankment Place, LONDON, WC2N 6RH. See also PricewaterhouseCoopers
TEW, Mr. Russell Barry, MMath ACA *2005;* The Royal of Scotland plc, 135 Bishopsgate, LONDON, EC2M 4UR.
TEW, Miss. Serena Elizabeth, BA ACA CTA *1985;* (Tax Fac), RTL Group Support Services Ltd, 1 Stephen Street, LONDON, W1T 1AL.
TEWOLDE, Miss. Sara, ACA *2011;* 8 Barlow Terrace, Meadowside, LONDON, SE9 6BX.
TEY, Miss. Amy, BSc(Hons) ACA *2002;* 54 Jalan Setia Jaya, Bukit Damansara, 50490 KUALA LUMPUR, FEDERAL TERRITORY, MALAYSIA.
TEY, Mr. Chin-Ann, BSc ACA *2006;* Royal Bank of Canada, PO Box 611, LONDON, EC4V 4DE.
TEY, Mr. Chun Kee, ACA *2009;* Flat 33 Constable House, Cassilis Road, LONDON, E14 9LH.
TEYMOURIAN, Mrs. Mahnaz, BSc ACA *2003;* Flat 6 Windermere House, 9a Warwick Road, BARNET, HERTFORDSHIRE, EN5 5DX.
•THACKABERRY, Mrs. Claire Anne, BA(Hons) ACA CTA *2000;* (Tax Fac), Clockwork Tax & Accountancy, 15 Ormonds Close, LICHFIELD, STAFFORDSHIRE, WS13 8EG.
THACKABERRY, Mr. Timothy Stuart, BA ACA *2004;* with RSM Tenon Audit Limited, Charterhouse, Legge Street, BIRMINGHAM, B4 7EU.
THACKER, Mrs. Alison Jane, ACA *1995;* 34 Burford Close, CHRISTCHURCH, DORSET, BH23 2QF.
THACKER, Mr. David Stephen, ACA *2009;* 20 Windsor Park, DEREHAM, NORFOLK, NR19 2SU.
THACKER, Mr. Dennis, FCA *1956;* 327 Mac Donald Road, OAKVILLE L6J 2A8, ON, CANADA. (Life Member)
THACKER, Mr. Gregory Douglas, FCA *1969;* 11 Selbourne Road, WESTON-SUPER-MARE, AVON, BS23 4LU. (Life Member)
THACKER, Mrs. Linda, BA ACA *1988;* Lavender House, 11 Pasture Way, Wistow, SELBY, YO8 3UQ.
THACKER, Mr. Mark Patrick Jason, FCA *1995;* Shell International Petroleum Co Ltd, Shell Centre, York Road, LONDON, SE1 7NA.
THACKER, Mr. Muskan, BSc ACA *1995;* Caam Saudi Fransi, P.O Box 23454, RIYADH, 11426, SAUDI ARABIA.
•THACKER, Mr. Peter John, BSc FCA DChA *1983;* Clark Brownscombe Limited, 8 The Drive, HOVE, EAST SUSSEX, BN3 3JT.
•THACKER, Mr. Richard Stephen, BA FCA *1987;* Beavis Morgan Audit Limited, 82 St. John Street, LONDON, EC1M 4JN. See also Beavis Morgan LLP
THACKER, Mr. Timothy John, BSc ACA *1996;* 32 Efflinch Lane, Barton under Needwood, BURTON-ON-TRENT, STAFFORDSHIRE, DE13 8ET.
THACKERAY, Mrs. Rachel Jane, BA ACA *2010;* 25 The Elms, Clayton-le-Woods, CHORLEY, LANCASHIRE, PR6 7TU.
•THACKERAY, Miss. Vivien Amanda, BA FCA *1983;* (Tax Fac), The Sinden Thackeray Partnership, 23 Star Hill, ROCHESTER, KENT, ME1 1XF.
THACKERAY, Miss. Zoe Claire, BSc ACA *1994;* 12 Yewdale, 196 Harborne Park Road, Harborne, BIRMINGHAM, B17 0BP.
THACKERY, Mr. Mathew Richard, BSc ACA *2006;* 80 Henry Doulton Drive, LONDON, SW17 6DD.
THACKSTONE, Mrs. Jane, BA ACA ATII *1998;* 15 Mallow Crescent, Burpham, GUILDFORD, GU4 7BU.
THACKWRAY, Mr. Ian Stuart, MA FCA *1982;* Holcim Group Support Ltd, Hagenholzstrasse 85, 8050 ZURICH, SWITZERLAND.
THACKWRAY, Mr. Stephen, BSc ACA *2003;* 54 Holly Farm Close, Caddington, LUTON, BEDFORDSHIRE, LU1 4ET.
•THACOOR, Mr. Yuvraj, FCA *1983;* Grant Thornton, 2nd Floor, Fairfax House, 21 Mgr Gonin Street, PORT LOUIS, MAURITIUS.
THADANI, Mr. Suresh Jethmal, FCA *1974;* 172A Jolly Maker Apts No 1, Cuffe Parade, MUMBAI 400 005, MAHARASHTRA, INDIA.
THADHANI, Mr. Suresh Hotechand, FCA *1965;* 29 Renfrew Avenue, MONTREAL H3Y 2X3, QUE, CANADA.
THAI, Miss. Tina Mei-Ming, ACA *1992;* 118 Coronation Road West, SINGAPORE 269342, SINGAPORE.
•THAIN, Mr. Christopher Anthony, ACA *1981;* Thain Osborne & Co., 1st Floor, 94A High Street, SEVENOAKS, KENT, TN13 1LP.
THAIRANI, Miss. Pooja, ACA *2011;* 4011 Kirby Drive, Apt 423, DALLAS, TX 76155, UNITED STATES.
THAKARAR, Mr. Rakesh Madhukant, BA ACA *1999;* Lahallsvagen 17, 18356 TABY, SWEDEN.
THAKARIA, Mr. Dhiren, BSc(Hons) ACA *2002;* 52 Western Way, BARNET, HERTFORDSHIRE, EN5 2BT.
THAKARIYA, Mr. Rahul, ACA *2009;* 178 Cavendish Road, LONDON, SW12 0DA.
THAKE, Mr. Alan Roy, BSc FCA *1993;* 35 Jackson Street, BALGOWLAH, NSW 2093, AUSTRALIA.
THAKE, Miss. Gemma Elizabeth, ACA *2011;* 69 Little Walden Road, SAFFRON WALDEN, ESSEX, CB10 2DL.
THAKE, Mrs. Julie Anne, BSc ACA *1995;* S C Johnson Ltd Frimley Green Road, Frimley, CAMBERLEY, SURREY, GU16 7AJ.
•THAKE, Mr. Philip Arthur, FCA *1977;* HPH, 54 Bootham, YORK, YO30 7XZ.
•THAKER, Mr. Beepinchandra Jashvantrai, FCA *1981;* Thaker & Co., 31 Southwood Gardens, Gants Hill, ILFORD, ESSEX, IG2 6YF.
•THAKER, Mr. Navinchandra Jaswantrai, FCA *1975;* H W Fisher & Company, Acre House, 11-15 William Road, LONDON, NW1 3ER. See also FisherEase Limited, and H W Fisher & Company Limited
THAKER, Mr. Rajiv, BA(Hons) ACA *2011;* 27 Anthus Mews, NORTHWOOD, MIDDLESEX, HA6 2GX.
THAKERAR, Mr. Dipak, BSc ACA *1993;* 43a Postern Green, ENFIELD, MIDDLESEX, EN2 7DE.
•THAKERAR, Mr. Rajiv Chhotalal, BSc FCA *1998;* Simmons Gainsford LLP, 5th Floor, 7-10 Chandos Street, Cavendish Square, LONDON, W1G 9DQ.
THAKKAR, Mr. Aneesh, MPhys(Hons) ACA *2010;* 118 Church Lane, Meanwood, LEEDS, LS6 4NR.
THAKKAR, Mr. Ashok Keshavji, FCA *1975;* 160 Blue Sky Drive, MARIETTA, GA 30068, UNITED STATES.
THAKKAR, Miss. Bhavika, BSc ACA *2004;* 517 Lady Margaret Road, SOUTHALL, MIDDLESEX, UB1 2QD.
•THAKKAR, Mr. Haren Kunjabihari Chhotalal, BSc FCA *1979;* Forshaws, Railex Business Centre, Crossens Way, Marine Drive, SOUTHPORT, MERSEYSIDE PR9 9LY.
THAKKAR, Mr. Kamal Narendra, BSc(Econ) ACA *2004;* 12 Parkinson Avenue, SOUTH TURRAMURRA, 2074, AUSTRALIA.
THAKKAR, Miss. Lena, BSc ACA *2007;* Flat 3604 Landmark East Tower, 24 Marsh Wall, LONDON, E14 9EG.
•THAKKAR, Mr. Mayur Chinubhai, FCA *1978;* (Tax Fac), MCT Partnership, 1 Warner House, Harrovian Business Village, Bessborough Road, HARROW, HA1 3EX. See also Harrovian Business Services Limited
•THAKKAR, Mr. Narendrakumar Ambalal, FCA *1965;* A.H. Thakkar & Sons, P.O.Box 2903, KAMPALA, UGANDA.
THAKKAR, Mrs. Neha, ACA *2009;* Clovelly, The Chase, PINNER, MIDDLESEX, HA5 5QP.
•THAKKAR, Mr. Sanjay, BSc ACA *1996;* KPMG LLP, 15 Canada Square, LONDON, E14 5GL. See also KPMG Europe LLP
THAKKAR, Mr. Uday Jayantilal, BSc MCMI FCA CMC *1984;* 36 Ingersoll Road, LONDON, W12 7BD.
THAKKER, Mr. Bharat Girdharlal, MSc FCA *1976;* 152 Albury Drive, PINNER, HA5 3RG.
•THAKKER, Mr. Bhupendra Vallabhdas Kalidas, FCA *1979;* Unit 1, 59 Brooklyn Road, BROOKLYN, NSW 2083, AUSTRALIA.
•THAKKER, Mr. Naresh Jayantilal, FCA *1978;* ST-Partnership, Mandeville House, 45-47 Tudor Road, HARROW, HA3 5PQ.
THAKORE, Mr. Suhrid Madhukant, ACA *1980;* Mann Frankfort Stein & Lipp, 12 Greenway Plaza, Suite 800, HOUSTON, TX 77016-8810, UNITED STATES.
•THAKRAR, Mr. Ajit Kalidas, FCA *1982;* (Tax Fac), TG Associates Limited, Monument House, 215 Marsh Road, PINNER, HA5 5NE.
THAKRAR, Mr. Amit, ACA *1983;* 46 Westbury Road, NORTHWOOD, HA6 3BX.
•THAKRAR, Mr. Atul Devji, BSc ACA *1992;* DMA Business Improvement Services, Business Box, Oswin Road, LEICESTER, LE3 1HR.
•THAKRAR, Mr. Bhupendra Ratilal, FCA *1974;* Landau Morley LLP, Lanmor House, 370-386 High Road, WEMBLEY, MIDDLESEX, HA9 6AX.
THAKRAR, Mrs. Chandrabala Dilipkumar, FCA *1977;* Flat 1 Bluesprings, Off Woodridge Way, 10a Sandy Lodge Way, NORTHWOOD, MIDDLESEX, HA6 2AH.
THAKRAR, Mr. Dhiren Dayalji, BA ACA *1991;* 8 Treetops Close, LEICESTER, LE5 2FJ.
•THAKRAR, Mr. Dineshchandra Narshidas, FCA *1977;* Harris Kafton, Ground Floor, Elizabeth House, 54-58 High Street, EDGWARE, HA8 7EJ.
THAKRAR, Mrs. Dipti, BA(Hons) ACA CTA *2002;* 8 The Meadway, Syston, LEICESTER, LE7 2BD.
•THAKRAR, Mr. Harish Mathuradas, BA FCA *1984;* (Tax Fac), Harish Thakrar Limited, 29 - 31 Finedon Road, WELLINGBOROUGH, NORTHAMPTONSHIRE, NN8 4AS.
THAKRAR, Mr. Jayantilal Purshottam, FCA *1965;* 3852 Arbourview Terrace, MISSISSAUGA L5M 7B6, ON, CANADA.
THAKRAR, Mr. Jayantilal Vrajlal, FCA *1970;* 2309-330 Rathburn Road West, MISSISSAUGA L5B 3Y1, ON, CANADA.
•THAKRAR, Mr. Jaysukh Amritlal, FCA *1983;* (Tax Fac), Dub & Co, 7 Torriano Mews, LONDON, NW5 2RZ.
•THAKRAR, Mr. Jentilal Prabhudas, ACA *1979;* (Tax Fac), 42 Christchurch Avenue, Kenton, HARROW, MIDDLESEX, HA3 8NJ.
THAKRAR, Miss. Nisha Jaysukh, ACA *2011;* 205/2 Albert Road, SOUTH MELBOURNE, VIC 3205, AUSTRALIA.
THAKRAR, Mrs. Parul Bharat, ACA *1998;* 4 Cumberland Road, HARROW, HA1 4PJ.
•THAKRAR, Mr. Pradeep Girdharlal, ACA *1982;* (Tax Fac), Hamptans Limited, Compton House, 20(a) Selsdon Road, SOUTH CROYDON, SURREY, CR2 6PA.
THAKRAR, Mrs. Rachana, BA ACA *1992;* 1 Dennis Lane, STANMORE, MIDDLESEX, HA7 4JR.
THAKRAR, Mr. Rajan, BA(Hons) ACA *2001;* 79 Belmont Lane, STANMORE, MIDDLESEX, HA7 2QA.
THAKRAR, Mr. Rajiv Rasiklal, BSc(Hons) ACA *2000;* 5 Grove Farm Park, NORTHWOOD, MIDDLESEX, HA6 2BQ.
•THAKRAR, Mr. Rajni Gordhandas, FCA *1976;* (Tax Fac), AT & RT Consultants Ltd, 7 Michleham Down, LONDON, N12 7JJ.
THAKRAR, Mr. Sanjay Kantilal, BA BSc CA ACA *1992;* 410 - 123 Eglinton Avenue East, TORONTO M4P1J2, ON, CANADA.
THAKRAR, Mr. Shailen, BSc ACA *1998;* 62 Lake View, EDGWARE, HA8 7RU.
THAKRAR, Miss. Shreenal, BA(Hons) ACA *2011;* 26 Park Drive, LONDON, N21 2LR.
•THAKRAR, Mr. Subhash Vithaldas, BCom FCA *1982;* (Tax Fac), Blackstone Franks LLP, Barbican House, 26-34 Old Street, LONDON, EC1V 9QR.
•THAKRAR, Mr. Vijay Champaklal, BSc FCA *1986;* Deloitte LLP, 1 Woodborough Road, NOTTINGHAM, NG1 3FG. See also Deloitte & Touche LLP
•THAKRAR, Mr. Vinodrai Shantilal, ACA *1980;* Thakrar & Co, 48 Dean Road, LEICESTER, LE4 6GN.
THAKRAR, Mr. Vishal, ACA *2008;* 10 Iona Road, Syston, LEICESTER, LE7 1QP.
THAKUR, Mr. Robin, BA ACA CFA *1993;* City Learning Ltd, 4 Chiswell Street, LONDON, EC1Y 4UP.
•THALMESSINGER, Mr. Ian Frederick, FCA *1977;* Consultus Care & Nursing Agency Ltd, 17-19 London Road, TONBRIDGE, KENT, TN10 3AB.
THAM, Mr. Colin Nigel, MSc BEng ACA *1998;* 58 Elmcroft Avenue, Wanstead, LONDON, E11 2BL.
THAM, Miss. Hsueh Yun, BA ACA *2000;* with BDO, 12th Floor Menara Uni. Asia, Jalan sultan Ismail, 50250 KUALA LUMPUR, FEDERAL TERRITORY, MALAYSIA.
THAM, Mr. Kok Yin, FCA *1976;* 44 Mariam Way, SINGAPORE 508563, SINGAPORE.
THAM, Miss. Pooi Fong, BSc ACA *1982;* 24 CANTEX COURT, RICHMOND HILL L4S 1B1, ON, CANADA.
THAM, Mr. Ronald Seng-Yum, MEng ACA CPA *1995;* Flat F Block 4, Tam Gardens, 25 Sha Wan Drive, POK FU LAM, HONG KONG ISLAND, HONG KONG SAR.
THAM, Mr. Sai-Choy, BA FCA *1984;* KPMG LLP, 16 Raffles Quay, # 22-00, Hong Leong Building, SINGAPORE 048581, SINGAPORE.
THAM, Mr. Tony Yoke Meng, FCA *1979;* 27 Caledonian Ave, WINSTON HILLS, NSW 2153, AUSTRALIA.
THAM, Miss. Yee-King Carol, BCom ACA *1987;* 21 West Acres, AMERSHAM, BUCKINGHAMSHIRE, HP7 9BY.
THAM, Miss. Yok Mui, BSc ACA *1980;* Suite B1916 Harbourfront Horizon, 8 Hung Luen Road, HUNG HOM, KOWLOON, HONG KONG SAR.
•THAME, Mr. John Richard Stuchfield, BSc ACA *1995;* Ellacotts LLP, Countrywide House, 23 West Bar Street, BANBURY, OXFORDSHIRE, OX16 9SA.
THAMFALD, Mrs. Elizabeth, ACA *1989;* Geschwister Scholl 7, 66994 DAHN, GERMANY.
•THAMMANNA, Mr. Subbash Chandra, MEng ACA *2004;* (Tax Fac), 30 Lloyd Villas Lewisham Way, LONDON, SE4 1US.
THAMOTHERAM, Mr. Nandakumar Nirmal, ACA *1980;* 878/7 Narasiri Village, Soi 20 Srinakarin Road, SUAN LUANG 10250, THAILAND.
•THANAWALA, Mr. Atul Maneklal, FCA *1977;* (Tax Fac), Atkins & Partners, 3rd Floor Brent House, 214 Kenton Road, HARROW, HA3 8BT. See also Atlas Euro Limited
THANAWALA, Mr. Hemant Maneklal, FCA *1982;* Sherbourne House, 3 St. Martins, NORTHWOOD, MIDDLESEX, HA6 2BP.
THANDI, Mr. Perminder Singh, BSc ACA *1992;* The Royal Bank of Scotland, 42 Islington High Street, LONDON, N1 8XL.
THANDI, Mrs. Renu, BA ACA *1991;* 2 Westbury Grove, Finchley, LONDON, N12 7PE.
THANDI, Miss. Rumel, MEng ACA *2006;* 62a Harmondsworth Lane, Harmondsworth, Sipson, WEST DRAYTON, MIDDLESEX, UB7 0AA.

THANKEY, Mr. Bharat Lalji, BCom FCA *1992;* 24 Laundon Way, Whetstone, LEICESTER, LE8 6ZL.
THANKI, Mr. Harshad Tansukhlal, BEng ACA *1994;* 9 Napier Avenue, LONDON, E14 3QB.
•**THANKI, Mr. Narendrakumar Dayaram, ACA** *1985;* Thanki Associates Limited, 16 Wembley Park Drive, WEMBLEY, MIDDLESEX, HA9 8HA.
•**THANTREY, Mr. Shabir-Ud-Deen, FCA** *1977;* (Tax Fac), UHY Hacker Young (S.E) Ltd, 168 Church Road, HOVE, EAST SUSSEX, BN3 2DL. See also UHY Hacker Young
THAPA, Mrs. Natalie Ann, BSc ACA *2000;* 17 Dinorben Avenue, FLEET, HAMPSHIRE, GU52 7SQ.
THAPAR, Mr. Rajinder, BSc ACA *1993;* Oxford House, 101 Bath Road, SWINDON, SN1 4AX.
THAPAR, Mr. Vijay Kumar, FCA *1974;* apt. no. 2603, the links east tower, the greens, DUBAI, 119888, UNITED ARAB EMIRATES.
THAPTHIMTHONG, Mr. Akani, BA FCA *1976;* 10 Sukumvit 7, BANGKOK, 10110, THAILAND.
THARAN, Mrs. Shanti, BA ACA *1996;* with PricewaterhouseCoopers LLP, 7 More London Riverside, LONDON, SE1 2RT.
THARANI, Mrs. Archna, BSc ACA *2001;* Flat 2, 9-10 Downleaze Stoke Bishop, BRISTOL, BS9 1NA.
THARANI, Mr. Azim Gulamhussein, FCA *1977;* Goldstar Insurance Co. Ltd, P. O. Box 7781, KAMPALA, UGANDA.
•**THARANI, Mr. Salim Aziz, BA ACA** *2001;* KPMG LLP, 100 Temple Street, BRISTOL, BS1 6AG. See also KPMG Europe LLP
•**THARBY, Mr. Shane Leigh, BA(Hons) FCA** *2001;* Streets, Charter House, 62-64 Hills Road, CAMBRIDGE, CB2 1LA. See also Streets Whitmarsh Sterland
THARMALINGAM, Mr. Kandiah, FCA *1963;* Bodiam, St Fillans Road, Catford, LONDON, SE6 1DG. (Life Member)
THARMARATNAM, Ms. Nandhini, MA ACA *1995;* (Tax Fac), The Old Meeting House, Shirenewton, CHEPSTOW, NP16 6AQ.
THATCHER, Miss. Celeste Mary, BEng ACA *2003;* 48 Bryony Close, Killamarsh, SHEFFIELD, S21 1TF.
•**THATCHER, Mrs. Hannah Claire, LLB ACA** *2007;* Time Business Services, 250 Harbour Way, SHOREHAM-BY-SEA, WEST SUSSEX, BN43 5HZ.
THATCHER, Miss. Lindsay Jane, BSc ACA *1988;* 29 Campbell Road, Walthamstow, LONDON, E17 6RR.
•**THATCHER, Mr. Paul John Hotston Brinton, BSc FCA** *1990;* 25 Hayling Rise, High Salvington, WORTHING, WEST SUSSEX, BN13 3AL.
THATCHER, Mr. Peter Stephen, BSc FCA *1984;* 3 Blacksmiths End, Bluntisham, HUNTINGDON, CAMBRIDGESHIRE, PE28 3JH.
•**THAUOOS, Mr. Omar Farook, FCA** *1972;* Thauoos & Co, 201 High Street, Penge, LONDON, SE20 7PF.
•**THAVAKUMARAN, Mr. Thiagarajah, BBA ACA** *2009;* Accma Limited, 359a Hanworth Road, HOUNSLOW, TW3 3SQ.
THAVAPALAN, Mr. Mayuresh Sanjeev, BSc(Hons) ACA *2001;* Flat 28 Tamarind Court, 18 Gainsford Street, LONDON, SE1 2NE.
THE PRINCE OF WALES, His Royal Highness FCA(Honorary) Clarence House, St. James's, LONDON, SW1A 1BA.
THEAKER, Mr. George Malcolm Barnshaw, FCA *1965;* 15 Mount Field, FAVERSHAM, ME13 8SZ. (Life Member)
THEAKER, Mr. Paul Alan, BA FCA *1981;* Middle House, The Hatch, Burghfield Village, READING, RG30 3TH.
•**THEAKER, Mr. Stephen Michael, FCA** *1989;* (Tax Fac), Peacheys CA Limited, Lanyon House, Mission Court, NEWPORT, GWENT, NP20 2DW.
THEAKSTON, Mr. Melvyn John, FCA *1970;* Flat 3 Riverhead Court, Riverhead, DRIFFIELD, NORTH HUMBERSIDE, YO25 6NW.
THEAKSTONE, Mr. Antony, BA ACA *1984;* 24 The Poplars, Ashtree Drive, Leconfield, BEVERLEY, HU17 7NB.
THEAN, Mr. Stephen Chee Beng, ACA *1983;* 26-28, Hammersmith Grove, LONDON, W8 7BA.
THEARIA, Mr. Sanjeev, BSc ACA *1994;* 2 Busbys Piece, Monks Kirby, RUGBY, CV23 0RQ.
•**THEBRIDGE, Mr. David Lawrence, BSc FCA** *1981;* (Tax Fac), Bissell & Brown Ltd, Charter House, 56 High Street, SUTTON COLDFIELD, WEST MIDLANDS, B72 1UJ. See also Bissell & Brown Birmingham Ltd
•**THECKSTON, Mr. Robert William, FCA** *1966;* Tom Carroll Associates Ltd, 166 Prescot Road, ST. HELENS, MERSEYSIDE, WA10 3TS.
THEI, Mr. John Anthony, FCA *1971;* 59 Oakington Avenue, WEMBLEY, HA9 8HX.
THEIN, Mr. Kim Mon, CA FCA *1982;* A16-05 ANGKASA IMPIAN 2 CONDOMINIUM, JALAN SAHABAT, 50200 KUALA LUMPUR, FEDERAL TERRITORY, MALAYSIA.
THEIN, Mr. Maung Maung, FCA *1964;* 9 Garden Way, LOUGHTON, ESSEX, IG10 2SF. (Life Member)
THEIN, Mr. Reggie Myint, FCA *1963;* 16A Lady Hill Road, SINGAPORE 258682, SINGAPORE.
THEIS, Mr. John, ACA *2011;* KPMG, 147 Collins Street, MELBOURNE, VIC 3000, AUSTRALIA.
THEIVENTHIRAMPILLAI, Mr. Kapilan, ACA *2009;* 208 Bilton Road, Perivale, GREENFORD, MIDDLESEX, UB6 7HL.
THEJOPAL, Miss. Reshma, MEng ACA *2007;* 159 Buckswood Drive, CRAWLEY, WEST SUSSEX, RH11 8JD.
THELWALL-JONES, Mrs. Nicola, BA ACA *1991;* The Hayloft, Mulsford Lane, Sarn, MALPAS, CHESHIRE, SY14 7LW.
•**THELWALL-JONES, Mr. Simon, BSc ACA CF** *1994;* Platinum Capital Partners LLP, The Hayloft, Mulsford Lane, Sarn, MALPAS, CHESHIRE SY14 7LW.
THELWELL, Mr. Eric Coulter, FCA MBA *1970;* The Old School House, Alvediston, SALISBURY, SP5 5JY.
•**THEMISTOCLEOUS, Mr. Chris, BSc FCA** *1984;* PricewaterhouseCoopers Limited, Artemidos Tower, 7th & 8th Floors, 3 Artemidos Avenue, 6020 LARNACA, CYPRUS.
•**THEMISTOCLEOUS, Miss. Elena, BA(Econ) ACA** *1999;* with PricewaterhouseCoopers, 268-270 Kifissias Avenue, Halandri, 15232 ATHENS, GREECE.
THEMISTOCLEOUS, Mr. Evripides, ACA *2009;* Petraki Kyprianoy 12A, Agios Georgios, Hauouzas, 3080 LIMASSOL, CYPRUS.
•**THEMISTOCLEOUS, Mr. Themis, BA FCA** *1983;* Themistocleous Themis, 20a Mouson Street, Egkomi, 2412 NICOSIA, CYPRUS.
THEMISTOCLI, Mr. Nicolas, BSc FCA CFA *1986;* Dorincourt, 5 Cedar Close, LONDON, SW15 3SD.
•**THEMISTOCLI, Mr. Themis, BSc FCA** *1979;* (Tax Fac), Themis & Co., 80 Lyonsdown Road, BARNET, EN5 1JL.
THEOBALD, Mr. Brian John, BSc ACA *1992;* Basingstoke College of Technology, Worting Road, BASINGSTOKE, RG21 8TN.
THEOBALD, Mrs. Catherine Emma, BSc ACA *2000;* 10 Hunters Close, Medomsley, CONSETT, DH8 6SP.
THEOBALD, Mr. Christopher James, LLB ACA *2010;* 3 Chestnut Walk, WATFORD, WD24 6NS.
THEOBALD, Mr. Damian John, BA(Hons) ACA *2010;* Acorn Cottage, Lye Green, CROWBOROUGH, EAST SUSSEX, TN6 1UU.
THEOBALD, Mrs. Juliet Eve, BA ACA *1993;* 71 Meadway, HARPENDEN, HERTFORDSHIRE, AL5 1JH.
THEOBALD, Mr. Michael Francis, PhD MA BSc FCA FSIP *1972;* Accounting & Finance Group, Birmingham Business School, University of Birmingham, University House, Edgbaston, BIRMINGHAM B15 2TT.
THEOBALD, Mr. Paul Michael, BSc ACA *1993;* 7 Contra Costa P1, HENDERSON, NV 89052, UNITED STATES.
THEOBALD, Mr. Richard Gordon, FCA *1955;* Prospect House, 7 Cliff Road, FOLKESTONE, KENT, CT20 2JD. (Life Member)
THEOBALD, Miss. Sarah, ACA *2008;* 18 Packmore Street, WARWICK, CV34 5BX.
THEOBALD, Mr. Timothy Paul, BSc ACA *1993;* 5 St. Helier Road, Sandridge, ST. ALBANS, HERTFORDSHIRE, AL4 9LG.
THEOCHARIDES, Mr. Adonis, BSc ACA *2007;* 36 Parthenonos streetEgomi apt. 101, 2413 NICOSIA, CYPRUS.
THEOCHARIDES, Mr. Phivos, ACA *2008;* 25 Epias Street, Engomi, 2411 NICOSIA, CYPRUS.
THEOCHAROUS, Miss. Helena, ACA *2009;* 117 Wardo Avenue, LONDON, SW6 6RB.
THEOCHAROUS, Ms. Irene, FCA ACA *2009;* 176 Strovolos Ave, Flat 401, Strovolos, 2048 NICOSIA, CYPRUS.
THEOCLI, Mr. Chrysostomos, FCA *1969;* P O Box 12632, CY 2251 NICOSIA, CYPRUS.
THEODORESON, Mr. Duncan Ian, FCA *1981;* Church House, Great Smith Street, LONDON, SW1P 3AZ.
THEODORIDES, Mr. Andreas, BA ACA *1995;* 8 Gregoriou Louvia, Dasoupolis, 2015 NICOSIA, CYPRUS.
THEODOROPOULOS, Mr. Pantelis, ACA CA(AUS) *2010;* 93 Hatherley Court, Hatherley Grove, LONDON, W2 5RF.
THEODOROU, Mr. Christodoulakis, FCA *1979;* 5 Eletherias Street, Aglandija, 2102 NICOSIA, CYPRUS.
•**THEODOROU, Mr. Elias, BSc FCA** *1990;* City House, 6 Karaiskakis Street, CY 3032 LIMASSOL, CYPRUS. See also PricewaterhouseCoopers Limited
THEODOROU, Miss. Georgia, ACA *2011;* PO Box 42338, 6533 LARNACA, CYPRUS.
•**THEODOROU, Mr. Soteris Georgiou, FCA** *1979;* S Theodorou Accountants Limited, 14 Souliou, Aglantzia, 2102 NICOSIA, CYPRUS.
THEODOSIADOU, Ms. Joanna, BSc ACA *1993;* 36 Lyndhurst Gardens, LONDON, N3 1TD.
THEODOSIOU, Miss. Apostolena, BSc ACA *2003;* Parthenanos 28, 2335, Lakatamia, 2335 NICOSIA, CYPRUS.
THEODOSIOU, Mr. Christoforos, ACA *2011;* Kanari 3, Flat 4, Germasogeia, 4044 LIMASSOL, CYPRUS.
THEODOSIOU, Mr. Constantinos, ACA *2009;* 9 Anexartisias Street, Aglantzia, 2108 NICOSIA, CYPRUS.
THEODOSIOU, Mr. Marcos Soteriou, MSc ACA *2001;* 7 Henley House, Friern Park, LONDON, N12 9UE.
THEODOSIOU, Mr. Marios Andreas, BSc(Econ) ACA CF *1999;* 77 Kyprou Street, Glyfada, 16674 ATHENS, GREECE.
THEODOTOU, Miss. Antigoni, ACA *2009;* P G Economides & Co Ltd, 30 GR Xenopoulou Str, 3030 LIMASSOL, CYPRUS.
THEODOTOU, Mr. Louis, ACA *2009;* 61 Alecou Constandinou, 2024 STROVOLOS, CYPRUS.
THEODOTOU, Miss. Xanthippi, ACA *2005;* 20 Demokratias Ave, Agios Dometios, 2370 NICOSIA, CYPRUS.
THEODOULOU, Mr. Christakis, BSc ACA *2010;* Syrou 22A, Anthoupolis, NICOSIA, CYPRUS.
•**THEODOULOU, Mr. Nicolaos Andreas, MA FCA** *1992;* PricewaterhouseCoopers Limited, Julia House, 3 Themistocles Dervis Street, CY-1066 NICOSIA, CYPRUS.
THEODOULOU, Mr. Theo, BA ACA *1985;* 30 Willowcourt Avenue, HARROW, HA3 8ES.
THEOFILOU, Mr. George, BSc ACA *2010;* Alexandrou Douma 8, Floor 101, Lakatamia, NICOSIA, CYPRUS.
•**THEOKLITOU, Mr. Yiannakis, BA FCA** *1984;* Ernst & Young Cyprus Limited, Nicosia Tower Centre, 36 Byron Avenue, P.O Box 21656, 1511 NICOSIA, CYPRUS. See also Ernst & Young Europe LLP
THEOLOGITIS, Mr. Ioannis, MSc BSc ACA *2010;* 24 Marathonos Street, Panorama Voulas, 16673 ATHENS, GREECE.
THEOPHANOUS, Mr. Andreas, MSc BSc ACA *2005;* 6 Kentavrou Street, Makedonitissa, 2414 NICOSIA, CYPRUS.
THEOPHILOU, Mr. Christos, ACA *2008;* Kaissarianis 11. Tseri, P.C, 2480 NICOSIA, CYPRUS.
THEOPHILOU, Mr. Loizos, BA ACA *2004;* 64 Heroon str., Syn. Agiou Eleftheriou, Latsia, 2222 NICOSIA, CYPRUS.
THEOPHILOU, Mr. Theophilos Artemi, BSc FCA *1967;* 6 Solonos Street, Strovolos, 2063 NICOSIA, CYPRUS.
THEOPHILUS, Mr. John Angus, FCA *1969;* Southern Properties & Management Ltd, 5 Borelli Yard, FARNHAM, GU9 7NU.
THERON, Mr. Daniel Sebastian, ACA CA(SA) *2010;* 42 Old Hertford Road, HATFIELD, HERTFORDSHIRE, AL9 5EY.
THERON, Mr. Frederik Johannes, ACA CA(SA) *2010;* 9 Wardown Crescent, LUTON, LU2 7JS.
THERON, Mr. Thomas Arnoldus, ACA CA(SA) *2010;* 42 Old Hertford Road, HATFIELD, HERTFORDSHIRE, AL9 5EY.
THESIGER, Mr. Michael Eric, FCA *1961;* Wrays Cottage, Crutchfield Lane, Hookwood, HORLEY, RH6 0HT.
THETHI, Mr. Harseerit Singh, BSc ACA *2004;* 7 Cleveland Close, MAIDENHEAD, BERKSHIRE, SL6 1XE.
THEUNISSEN, Miss. Emma, MA ACA *2004;* Flat 6 Sarum House, 55 Portobello Road, LONDON, W11 3DF.
THEVENAU, Mr. Jean Francois Robert, FCA *1977;* Food & Allied Ind Ltd, Gentilly, MOKA, MAURITIUS.
THEW, Mr. Stephen, BSc ACA *2010;* Flat 21 Hermitage House, Gerrard Road, LONDON, N1 8AT.
THEWLIS, Mr. Andrew Mark, BA ACA *1989;* Landmark Wholesale Ltd, 7 Davy Avenue Knowlhill, MILTON KEYNES, MK5 8HJ.
THEWLIS, Mr. Clive Roger, BA FCA *1976;* Witts End, 8 Harolds Close, Leafield, WITNEY, OXFORDSHIRE, OX29 9PU.
THEWLIS, Miss. Nicole, BA ACA *2007;* Oakmere Pickmere Lane, Wincham, NORTHWICH, CHESHIRE, CW9 6EB.
THEXTON, Mr. Christopher William, BA ACA *1988;* Pendragon Plc, Centre House, Village Way, Trafford Park, MANCHESTER, M17 1QG.
•**THEXTON, Mr. Michael John, MA FCA CTA** *1983;* (Tax Fac), with Thexton Training Limited, 45 Leyborne Park, RICHMOND, SURREY, TW9 3HB.
THIAGARAJAH, Mrs. Soundharie, BA ACA *1997;* 300 Cambridge Drive, MARS, PA 16046, UNITED STATES.
THIANG, Mr. Kai Goh, FCA *1974;* Thiang & Co, 10 Lebuh Gopeng, 41400 KLANG, SELANGOR, MALAYSIA.
THIARYA, Mrs. Nirmala, BA ACA *1997;* Foley Lodge, 15 Foley Road East, Streetly, SUTTON COLDFIELD, B74 3HN.
•**THIARYA, Mr. Surinder Singh, ACA CTA** *1995;* with PricewaterhouseCoopers LLP, Cornwall Court, 19 Cornwall Street, BIRMINGHAM, B3 2DT.
THIBAUT, Mr. Neale Frederick, BA ACA *1995;* Flat 1, 33a Brunswick Square, HOVE, EAST SUSSEX, BN3 1ED.
THICKETT, Ms. Helen Lesley, BA ACA *1992;* 15 Dealtry Road, LONDON, SW15 6NL.
THICKPENNY, Mr. Roger John, FCA CTA *1980;* (Tax Fac), 5 Hermitage Court, Oakwood, DERBY, DE21 2LG.
THIEL, Mr. Geoffrey William, BA FCA FCIPD *1975;* 17 Browning Road, HARPENDEN, AL5 4TS.
THIEL, Mr. Julian Anthony, FCA *1968;* RLH Developments Ltd, 3 Coombe Avenue, CROYDON, SURREY, CR0 5SD.
THILAGARAJ, Mrs. Kohila Vani, BA ACA *1985;* Fairview House, Lambourne Road, CHIGWELL, ESSEX, IG7 6HX.
THILLAIRAJAH, Mr. Sabapathy, BCom FCA *1957;* 10008 Holmhurst Road, BETHESDA, MD 20817, UNITED STATES. (Life Member)
THIMAYA, Mr. Kongandra Ayapa, MA ACA *1984;* 7 Overhills, OLNEY, MK46 5PP.
THIMBLEBY, Mrs. Mary, BA ACA *1991;* 7 Birchwood Grove, GREENHITHE 0632, NEW ZEALAND.
THIMONT, Ms. Ann Mary, BA ACA *1984;* (Tax Fac), 1 Hunter Road, West Wimbledon, LONDON, SW20 8NZ.
THIMONT, Mr. Paul Andrew, BA FCA *1978;* 54 New Concordia Wharf, Mill Street, LONDON, SE1 2BB.
•**THIND, Mr. Jitender Singh, BA FCA ATII** *1989;* (Tax Fac), SRN Sonico, 60 Wensleydale Road, HAMPTON, MIDDLESEX, TW12 2LX. See also Harper Cavendish (International) Ltd
THIO, Miss. Caroline Puan Ling, BSc ACA *1994;* 17110 Santa Suzanne Street, FOUNTAIN VALLEY, CA 92708, UNITED STATES.
THION, Miss. Helene, ACA *2011;* Flat 6, 227 St. John's Hill, LONDON, SW11 1TH.
THIRKELL, Mr. Martin Neal, ACA MAAT *2004;* 31 Tudor Drive, BOSTON, LINCOLNSHIRE, PE21 9PB.
THIRKETTLE, Mr. James, BSc FCA *1981;* Stephensons Solicitors LLP, 24 Lord Street, LEIGH, LANCASHIRE, WN7 1AB.
•**THIRKETTLE, Mr. Roger, FCA CTA** *1978;* (Tax Fac), Adams Lee Clark, Adam House, 71 Bell Street, HENLEY-ON-THAMES, RG9 2BD. See also Thirkettle R.
THIRLBY, Mr. Peter John, BA ACA *2008;* Katanga Mining, KOLWEZI, CONGO Democratic Republic of.
THIRLWALL, Mr. Jamie, ACA *2011;* 233 High Road, BROXBOURNE, HERTFORDSHIRE, EN10 6PZ.
•**THIRLWALL, Mrs. Nicola Jane, ACA** *2003;* (Tax Fac), Dyer & Co Audit Services Ltd, Onega House, 112 Main Road, SIDCUP, KENT, DA14 6NE. See also Dyer & Co Accountants Limited
THIRLWELL, Mr. David, ACA *2003;* with Deloitte LLP, Hill House, 1 Little New Street, LONDON, EC4A 3TR.
THIRSK, Mr. Bryan Edward, FCA *1962;* #116 1744 128th Street, SURREY V4A 3V4, BC, CANADA. (Life Member)
THIRTLE, Mrs. Lindsay Anne, BA(Hons) ACA *2000;* 7 Rushington Avenue, MAIDENHEAD, SL6 1BY.
THIRTLE, Mr. Paul Nigel, DPhil BSc ACA *2002;* 7 Rushington Avenue, MAIDENHEAD, BERKSHIRE, SL6 1BY.
THIRUCHELVARAJAH, Mr. Rajivan, ACA *2008;* 17 Conifer Crest, NEWBURY, BERKSHIRE, RG14 6RS.
•**THIRUKAILAYANATHAN, Mr. Jegan, ACA** *2008;* Clearscope, 63 Lanercost Road, CRAWLEY, WEST SUSSEX, RH11 8YA.
THIRUMOORTHY, Mr. Ramana, BSc ACA *2011;* Flat 908 Cascades Tower, 4 Westferry Road, LONDON, E14 8JN.
•**THIRUVASAGAM, Mr. Maniccavasagan, ACA** *2006;* (Tax Fac), M Thiruvasagam, SVS House, Oliver Grove, LONDON, SE25 6EJ. See also Accountancy Group
THISELTON-DYER, Mr. Martin John, BSc ACA *1996;* with PricewaterhouseCoopers LLP, Three Embarcadero Center, SAN FRANCISCO, CA 94111, UNITED STATES.
•**THISTLE, Mr. Richard Henry, FCA** *1977;* HJF (Personal Tax) Limited, First Floor, 74 Chancery Lane, LONDON, WC2A 1AD.

THISTLETHWAITE, Mr. John, FCA *1966;* Hunters Moon, Bow Bridge, Embsay, SKIPTON, NORTH YORKSHIRE, BD23 6QS.
THISTLETHWAITE, Miss. Susan, BSc ACA *1998;* 26b St. Stephens Gardens, TWICKENHAM, TW1 2LS.
THISTLEWOOD, Mr. Anthony William, FCA *1965;* 3C/10 Hilltop Crescent, FAIRLIGHT, NSW 2094, AUSTRALIA. (Life Member)
THISTLEWOOD, Mrs. Joanna Mary, BA ACA CPFA *1994;* Craiglea, Victoria Road, FRESHWATER, ISLE OF WIGHT, PO40 9PP.
THISTLEWOOD, Ms. Lucinda Mary, MA(Hons) MSc ACA *2001;* 19 Broom Road, Hale, ALTRINCHAM, CHESHIRE, WA15 9AR.
•**THIXTON, Mr. Malcolm Barry, FCA** *1982;* BDO LLP, Arcadia House, Maritime Walk, Ocean Village, SOUTHAMPTON, SO14 3TL. See also BDO Stoy Hayward LLP
THOBANI, Mr. Masood Madatali, BSc FCA *1977;* 12 Evergreen Lane SW, CALGARY T2Y 3T8, AB, CANADA.
THOBANI, Miss. Salina, BSc ACA *2005;* 21 Avondale Drive, HAYES, UB3 3PZ.
THOBANI, Mr. Shokatali Pyarali, FCA *1974;* Via Palmieri 36, 10138 TORINO, ITALY. (Life Member)
•**THOBURN, Mrs. Fiona Jane, ACA** *1990;* (Tax Fac), Thoburn & Chapman Limited, 14 Barrington Street, SOUTH SHIELDS, TYNE AND WEAR, NE33 1AJ. See also Wealthy Creations LLP
•**THOBURN, Mr. Ralph Wood, BA FCA** *1988;* Thoburn & Chapman Limited, 14 Barrington Street, SOUTH SHIELDS, TYNE AND WEAR, NE33 1AJ. See also Wealthy Creations LLP
THOBURN, Mr. William John, FCA *1956;* Park Fell House, Park Lane, ALSTON, CA9 3AB. (Life Member)
THODAY, Mr. Francis David Fraser, MA ACA *1980;* 1 Cronk Cullyn, Colby, ISLE OF MAN, IM9 4NQ.
THODY, Mr. Roy Shepherd, MSc FCA *1958;* 5 Portsdown Road, LEICESTER, LE2 3RB. (Life Member)
THOLE, Mr. Martin David, BCom ACA *1995;* Shaw Healthcare (Group) Ltd, 1 Links Court, Links Business Park, St. Mellons, CARDIFF, CF3 0LT.
THOLSTRUP, Mr. Christopher Erik, MA(Hons) ACA *2002;* Flat 8, Fairacres, Roehampton Lane, LONDON, SW15 5LX.
•**THOM, Mr. Adam Stewart Bagnall, BA FCA** *1992;* Beever and Struther, Central Buildings, Richmond Terrace, BLACKBURN, BB1 7AP.
THOM, Mr. Denis, FCA *1962;* 3 Nairdwood Way, Prestwood, GREAT MISSENDEN, HP16 0QW.
THOM, Mr. Gordon Lindsay, FCA *1969;* Horton Grange, Cockering Road, Chartham, CANTERBURY, CT4 7LG. (Life Member)
THOM, Mr. James Demmink, FCA *1969;* Tollgate Cottage, Turners Hill Road, Crawley Down, CRAWLEY, RH10 4HG.
THOM, Mr. Paul Ritchie, FCA *1962;* The Gwythers, Lee, ILFRACOMBE, EX34 8LR. (Life Member)
THOM, Mr. Richard Denholm, BA(Hons) FCA *1976;* Royal Academy of Dance, 36 Battersea Square, LONDON, SW11 3RA.
THOM, Mr. Robert Graeme, FCA *1967;* 39/1 Orchard Brae Avenue, EDINBURGH, EH4 2UP. (Life Member)
THOM, Mr. Stephen Andrew, ACA *2009;* 10 Jasmine Way, CARLUKE, LANARKSHIRE, ML8 5AU.
THOM, Mr. Stuart David, ACA *2010;* 65 West Carr Road, RETFORD, NOTTINGHAMSHIRE, DN22 7NW.
THOM, Mr. Timothy Ritchie, FCA *1964;* Woodclose, Woodlands Road, Portishead, BRISTOL, BS20 7HE. (Life Member)
THOMA, Mr. Lenas, BSc ACA *2006;* 6a Costakis Pantelides, 3020 LIMASSOL, CYPRUS.
THOMAS, Mr. Aaron John, BA(Econ) ACA *1999;* Dell Cottage, Ffordd Pentre Bach, Nercwys, MOLD, CLWYD, CH7 4EG.
THOMAS, Mr. Abraham Idaseril, FCA *1959;* Idaseril Kunnam Estate, Olayambady P.O, (via) Mathamangalam Bazar, Kannur, KANNUR 670306, KERALA INDIA. (Life Member)
THOMAS, Mr. Adam Bradley, BSc ACA *2010;* Flat 509, Dakota Building, Deals Gateway, LONDON, SE13 7QE.
THOMAS, Mr. Adrian Anthony Michael, MA ACA *1986;* (Tax Fac), 23 Oxford Gardens, LONDON, N20 9AG.
THOMAS, Mr. Adrian Peter James, MA ACA *2001;* B P P Holdings Plc Aldine House, 142-144 Uxbridge Road, LONDON, W12 8AA.
THOMAS, Mr. Adrian Victor Austin, FCA *1970;* 10 Mavis Bank, Newburgh, ELLON, AB41 6FB.
THOMAS, Mr. Aidan David Henry, FCA *1960;* 79 Oakington Avenue, AMERSHAM, HP6 6ST. (Life Member)
THOMAS, Mr. Alan Ernest, BSc FCA *1972;* Ivy Hall Farm, Bowes, BARNARD CASTLE, COUNTY DURHAM, DL12 9LL.
THOMAS, Mr. Alan Michael, BA ACA *1988;* The Farmhouse Lodge Farm, Catts Hill Mark Cross, CROWBOROUGH, EAST SUSSEX, TN6 3NH.
THOMAS, Mr. Alan Philip, BA ACA *1999;* 17 Walkers Close, Bottesford, NOTTINGHAM, NG13 0FF.
THOMAS, Mr. Alan Richard Havelock, FCA *1971;* Corner Hoppit, Guildford Road, Runfold, FARNHAM, GU10 1PG.
THOMAS, Mr. Alan Robert, FCA *1958;* 12 The Pyghtle, OLNEY, MK46 5PS. (Life Member)
THOMAS, Mr. Alastair Richard Stuart, BA ACA *1992;* Hatchers Farm Carters Clay, Lockerley, ROMSEY, SO51 0GN.
THOMAS, Mr. Alastair Wake Macmeikan, MA ACA *1992;* Bower Farm, The Vale, CHESHAM, BUCKINGHAMSHIRE, HP5 3NS.
THOMAS, Mr. Alexander Michael, BA ACA *1999;* Chestnut Lodge Squires Mount, LONDON, NW3 1EG.
THOMAS, Mr. Alfred Brian, FCA *1951;* 3 Old Rectory Close, Mulbarton, NORWICH, NR14 8LX. (Life Member)
THOMAS, Mrs. Alison, BA ACA *2007;* Rue des Pâquis 59, 1201 GENEVA, SWITZERLAND.
THOMAS, Mr. Allen Lloyd, ACA *2009;* Flat 604, 20 Palace Street, LONDON, SW1E 5BA.
THOMAS, Mr. Alun, BA FCA *1965;* Meadowside Lodge, Pen-y-Turnpike Road, DINAS POWYS, SOUTH GLAMORGAN, CF64 4HG.
THOMAS, Mr. Alun Christopher, BA ACA *1995;* 6 Anlaby Road, TEDDINGTON, TW11 0PU.
THOMAS, Mr. Alun Christopher Nicholas, FCA *1975;* The Environment Agency Aqua House, East Station Road, PETERBOROUGH, PE2 8AG.
•**THOMAS, Mr. Alwyn, MA ACA** *1982;* Alwyn Thomas, Glenaub House, Old School Road, PORTHCAWL, MID GLAMORGAN, CF36 3AW.
THOMAS, Miss. Amanda Rachel, BSc ACA *2002;* with Wise & Co, Wey Court West, Union Road, FARNHAM, SURREY, GU9 7PT.
THOMAS, Miss. Amy Bethan, MA ACA *2009;* Yew Tree Cottage, Lingen, BUCKNELL, SHROPSHIRE, SY7 0DX.
THOMAS, Ms. Andrea Clare, BSc ACA *1994;* with KPMG LLP, 8 Princes Parade, LIVERPOOL, L3 1QH.
THOMAS, Mrs. Andrea Margaret, BA FCA *1978;* Oakview, The Green, Croxley Green, RICKMANSWORTH, WD3 3HN.
THOMAS, Mr. Andrew Crawford, FCA *1971;* 4 Bendrick Drive, Southgate, SWANSEA, SA3 2AL.
THOMAS, Mr. Andrew Dennis, BSc FCA *1992;* 95 Woodlands Park Drive, NEATH, WEST GLAMORGAN, SA10 8AW.
THOMAS, Mr. Andrew Edward, BSc FCA *1982;* Norwood, Arbory Road, Castleton, ISLE OF MAN, IM9 1ND.
•**THOMAS, Mr. Andrew Gerald, FCA** *1964;* Moors Andrew Thomas & Co LLP, 94 Wilderspool Causeway, WARRINGTON, WA4 6PU. See also Moors Andrew Thomas (Private Clients) Limited
THOMAS, Mr. Andrew James, BA ACA *2009;* 19 Robin Hill, MAIDENHEAD, SL6 2GZ.
•**THOMAS, Mr. Andrew James, BSc ACA ACIS** *1998;* AJH Resourcing Limited, Trinity House, Bath Street, St. Helier, JERSEY, JE2 4ST.
THOMAS, Mr. Andrew James, BA ACA *2007;* 43 Dove Park, Chorleywood, RICKMANSWORTH, WD3 5NY.
THOMAS, Mr. Andrew John, BSc ACA *1988;* 1 Ash Drive, St. Ippolyts, HITCHIN, SG4 7SJ.
THOMAS, Mr. Andrew Philip, BSc(Hons) ACA *2000;* 4 Deanway, WILMSLOW, CHESHIRE, SK9 2JT.
THOMAS, Mr. Andrew Richard, BA(Hons) ACA *2004;* 41 Larkfield Court, BRIGHOUSE, WEST YORKSHIRE, HD6 1AW.
THOMAS, Mr. Andrew Richard, BA ACA *1997;* Hillarys Blinds Ltd Unit 2, Private Road 2 Colwick Industrial Estate, NOTTINGHAM, NG4 2JR.
THOMAS, Mr. Andrew Russell, ACA *1978;* Rail tech Group Railway & Signal Engineering Ltd, 91 Dales Road, IPSWICH, IP1 4JR.
THOMAS, Mr. Andrew Simon, MA ACA *2002;* 36 Greenway, HORSHAM, WEST SUSSEX, RH12 2JS.
THOMAS, Mrs. Angela Lesley, MA ACA *2001;* S S L International Plc, 4th Floor, Venus, 1 Old Park Lane, Urmston, MANCHESTER M41 7HA.
THOMAS, Mrs. Ann Elizabeth Walwyn, BSc FCA *1976;* The Bartons, Station Road, Bramley, GUILDFORD, SURREY, GU5 0AY.
THOMAS, Miss. Anna Louise, BSc ACA *2009;* 33 Edyvean Close, RUGBY, CV22 6LD.
THOMAS, Mrs. Anne Elizabeth, ACA *1983;* The Crown Estate, 16 New Burlington Place, LONDON, W1S 2HX.
THOMAS, Mr. Anthony, FCA *1959;* 22 Tudor Court, 59 Hatherley Crescent, SIDCUP, DA14 4HY. (Life Member)
THOMAS, Mr. Anthony Duncan, BSc ACA *2010;* 150 Whitchurch Road, SHREWSBURY, SY1 4EJ.
THOMAS, Mr. Anthony Edward, BA FCA *1974;* 8 Henley Grove, Henleaze, BRISTOL, BS9 4EG.
•**THOMAS, Mr. Anthony Haydn, FCA** *1972;* (Tax Fac), UHY Hacker Young, First Floor, Pembroke House, Ellice Way, Wrexham Technology Park, WREXHAM CLWYD LL13 7YT.
•**THOMAS, Mr. Antony Robert, FCA** *1970;* A.R. Thomas, Glanton House, 19 Wyatts Lane, WAREHAM, BH20 4NH.
THOMAS, Mr. Arthur Robert, FCA *1966;* Callen House, 37 Fairfield, Penperlleni, PONTYPOOL, NP4 0AQ.
THOMAS, Mrs. Barbara Anne, BSc ACA *1992;* Broome Perrow House Old Road, Buckland, BETCHWORTH, RH3 7DY.
THOMAS, Mrs. Belinda Liza Marie, BA(Hons) ACA *2001;* Garden Flat 26a Lime Grove, LONDON, W12 8EA.
THOMAS, Mrs. Beverley Ann Herbert, BA ACA *1994;* 32 Ffordd Derwen, Margam, PORT TALBOT, WEST GLAMORGAN, SA13 2TX.
THOMAS, Mr. Brendan, BSc ACA *2000;* Po Box 2, BOROKO, NATIONAL CAPITAL DISTRICT, PAPUA NEW GUINEA.
THOMAS, Mr. Brian, FCA *1959;* The Spinney, Foulden, BERWICK-UPON-TWEED, TD15 1UH. (Life Member)
THOMAS, Mr. Brian, ACA CA(SA) *2009;* 102 Priory Lane, LONDON, SW15 5SL.
THOMAS, Mr. Bryan Peter, FCA *1961;* 21 Ashleigh Road, SOLIHULL, B91 1AE.
THOMAS, Mr. Bryn Richard, BA FCA MBA *1992;* 25 Weaver Avenue, SUTTON COLDFIELD, B76 2BG.
THOMAS, Mrs. Carol Ann, BA FCA *1975;* 111 North Road, Parkstone, POOLE, DORSET, BH14 0LU.
THOMAS, Mrs. Carol Mary, BSc ACA *1984;* SOG Limited, The Heath Business & Technical Park, RUNCORN, CHESHIRE, WA7 4QF.
THOMAS, Mrs. Caroline Louise, ACA *2008;* 86 Brocklebank Road, LONDON, SW18 3AX.
•**THOMAS, Mrs. Caroline Sally, BSc ACA MAE QDR** *2004;* Haines Watts LLP, 3 Southernhay West, EXETER, DEVON, EX1 1JG.
THOMAS, Miss. Catherine, BA(Hons) ACA *2010;* 35 Huron Road, LONDON, SW17 8RE.
THOMAS, Mrs. Catherine, BSc FCA *1991;* with Ernst & Young LLP, 1 More London Place, LONDON, SE1 2AF.
•**THOMAS, Mrs. Catherine Helen, BSc FCA ATII DChA** *1982;* (Tax Fac), Dyke Yaxley Limited, 1 Brassey Road, Old Potts Way, SHREWSBURY, SY3 7FA.
THOMAS, Miss. Catrin Sian, ACA *2009;* 36 Landor Avenue, Killay, SWANSEA, SA2 7BP.
THOMAS, Mr. Cennydd Llwyd, BSc ACA *2009;* 21 Bruce Street, CARDIFF, CF24 4PJ.
•**THOMAS, Mr. Charles Glyn, FCA** *1977;* Thomas & Young LLP, 240-244 Stratford Road, Shirley, SOLIHULL, WEST MIDLANDS, B90 3AE. See also Thomas & Young
THOMAS, Mr. Charles Roger, FCA *1974;* Greenwoods, Llanfach Road, Abercarn, NEWPORT, GWENT, NP11 5LA. (Life Member)
THOMAS, Mrs. Charlotte Claire, BA ACA *2000;* Chestnut Lodge Squires Mount, LONDON, NW3 1EG.
THOMAS, Mrs. Cheryl, BSc ACA CTA *2003;* 88 Hatfield Road, POTTERS BAR, HERTFORDSHIRE, EN6 1HT.
THOMAS, Mr. Christian, MSc BSc ACA *2003;* Mesogeion Avenue 400B, Agia Paraskevi 153 42, ATHENS, GREECE.
THOMAS, Mr. Christian David, BA ACA *2000;* 13 Winsu Avenue, PAIGNTON, TQ3 1QG.
THOMAS, Ms. Christina Rachel, BA ACA *1992;* 6 Weavers Field, Girton, CAMBRIDGE, CB3 0XB.
THOMAS, Mrs. Christine Mary, FCA *1966;* 39 Medina Close, Alvaston, DERBY, DE24 0UD.
THOMAS, Mrs. Christine Mary, BSc(Hons) ACA *2001;* 71 Scholars Road, LONDON, SW12 0PF.
THOMAS, Mr. Christopher, FCA *1966;* 10 Laithwaite Close, COCKERMOUTH, CA13 0AQ.
THOMAS, Mr. Christopher, FCA *1965;* The Grange, Manely St. Veep, LOSTWITHIEL, PL22 0NS. (Life Member)
THOMAS, Mr. Christopher, BSc ACA *1990;* 16 Richmond Road, SUTTON COLDFIELD, B73 6BJ.
THOMAS, Mr. Christopher, BSc(Hons) ACA *2001;* 4 Maple Gardens, Dunchurch Road, RUGBY, WARWICKSHIRE, CV22 6DZ.
THOMAS, Mr. Christopher Andrew, BSc ACA *2000;* 15 Bradwell Avenue, West Didsbury, MANCHESTER, M20 1JX.
THOMAS, Mr. Christopher Charles Arnold, BA ACA *1989;* 38 Perrymead Street, LONDON, SW6 3SP.
THOMAS, Mr. Christopher David, BA ACA *1989;* Flat 18, Watson House, Elmgrove Road, HARROW, MIDDLESEX, HA1 2QQ.
THOMAS, Mr. Christopher Henry, FCA *1970;* Quarries, Parkfield, SEVENOAKS, TN15 0HX.
THOMAS, Mr. Christopher Henry, FCA *1974;* 18 Hogarth Court, Rembrandt GroveSpringfield, CHELMSFORD, CM1 6GE.
THOMAS, Mr. Christopher John, BA FCA *1990;* Wycombe Wanderers Football Club Ltd Adams Park, Hillbottom Road Sands Industrial Estate, HIGH WYCOMBE, BUCKINGHAMSHIRE, HP12 4HJ.
THOMAS, Mr. Christopher Owen, FCA *1970;* 22 Woodlands Road, LONDON, SW13 0JZ.
•**THOMAS, Mr. Christopher Paul, BSc FCA** *1992;* Horner Downey & Company Limited, 30 Bromborough Village Road, Bromborough, WIRRAL, MERSEYSIDE, CH62 7ES. See also Cornerstone Accountancy & Taxation Solutions Limited
•**THOMAS, Mr. Christopher Rowland, BA FCA** *1980;* Thomas Harris Limited, The 1929 Building, 18 Watermill Way, LONDON, SW19 2RD.
•**THOMAS, Mr. Christopher Tamlyn, BSc ACA** *2001;* Deloitte LLP, 2 New Street Square, LONDON, EC4A 3BZ. See also Deloitte & Touche LLP
THOMAS, Mrs. Claire Louise, BA ACA *1999;* 106 Risca Road, Rogerstone, NEWPORT, GWENT, NP10 9FZ.
THOMAS, Mrs. Claire Louise, ACA *2007;* 1C/16 Market Place, CBD, AUCKLAND 1010, NEW ZEALAND.
THOMAS, Mrs. Claire Michele, FCA *1986;* Richmond, Thinholme Lane, Westwoodside, DONCASTER, DN9 2DY.
•**THOMAS, Mr. Clive Raymond, BA ACA** *1990;* Clive Thomas, 16 Quat Goose Lane, Swindon Village, CHELTENHAM, GLOUCESTERSHIRE, GL51 9RX. See also Interim Business Management Ltd
THOMAS, Mr. Colin David, FCA *1956;* (Member of Council 1979 - 1985), 8 Wheeler Avenue, OXTED, RH8 9LE. (Life Member)
THOMAS, Mr. Colin Joseph, BSc ACA *1991;* 1 Heol-Yr-Haul, Groesfaen, PONTYCLUN, CF72 8RS.
THOMAS, Mr. Colin Patrick, FCA *1961;* 16 Penyfai Lane, Furnace, LLANELLI, DYFED, SA15 4EN.
•**THOMAS, Mr. Colin Roger, FCA** *1982;* Thomas & Company, 261 Hatherley Road, CHELTENHAM, GL51 6HF.
THOMAS, Mr. Daniel, BSc ACA *2003;* 8 Canada Square, H S B C, 8-16 Canada Square, LONDON, E14 5HQ.
THOMAS, Mr. Daniel Edwin George, BSc FCA *1977;* Elysian, Manor Close, Tylers Green, HIGH WYCOMBE, HP10 8HZ.
THOMAS, Mrs. Daphne Helen, BSc ACA *1993;* 39 Bourton Road, BUCKINGHAM, MK18 1BG.
THOMAS, Mr. Darren James, BSc ACA *2010;* Flat 4, 3 Queens Parade, CHELTENHAM, GLOUCESTERSHIRE, GL50 3BB.
THOMAS, Mr. Daryl Lee, BSc ACA *1995;* Syngenta Seeds, Forsterstrasse 30, 8044 ZURICH, SWITZERLAND.
THOMAS, Mr. David, BA ACA *2010;* Flat 2, Saxoncroft House, 2 Fisher's Close, LONDON, SW16 1JN.
THOMAS, Mr. David Alan, FCA *1975;* Castle Villa, Millers Lane, Outwood, REDHILL, RH1 5QB.
•**THOMAS, Mr. David Arthur, ACA** *1980;* (Tax Fac), David A. Thomas & Co, Garden Reach, 5 Hurn Close, Ashley, RINGWOOD, BH24 2AD.
THOMAS, Mr. David Brian, BA ACA *2000;* 11 Castlemead Walk, NORTHWICH, CW9 8GP.
•**THOMAS, Mr. David Charles, BA FCA** *1981;* 11 Tirionfa, Rhuddlan, RHYL, CLWYD, LL18 6LT.
•**THOMAS, Mr. David Ernest, FCA** *1979;* J Llywelyn Hughes & Co, Ty'r Bont, LLANRWST, LL26 0EY.
THOMAS, Mr. David Fraser, BA ACA *1989;* Woodlands, Farm Drive, PURLEY, CR8 3LP.
THOMAS, Mr. David Gareth, FCA *1972;* 27 Lower Way, Great Brickhill, MILTON KEYNES, MK17 9AG.

THOMAS, Mr. Penry Wyn Richards, BSc FCA *1989;* Dinefwr, 61 Butleigh Avenue, CARDIFF, CF5 1BY.
THOMAS, Mr. Peter Crawford, FCA *1966;* 10 Lon-y-Rhyd, Rhiwbina, CARDIFF, CF14 6JS.
THOMAS, Mr. Peter George Adrian, FCA *1957;* 1 The Glebe, Thorverton, EXETER, EX5 5LS. (Life Member)
THOMAS, Mr. Peter Glyn, FCA *1980;* 8 Heol-Y-Felin, Rhiwbina, CARDIFF, CF14 6NB.
•THOMAS, Mr. Peter Gordon, FCA *1970;* Plas Newydd, Llansadwrn, MENAI BRIDGE, LL59 5SL.
THOMAS, Mr. Peter Hugh Clifton, FCA *1974;* 77 South Hill, GODALMING, GU7 1JU.
THOMAS, Mr. Peter James, BA(Hons) ACA *2010;* Flat 8, 75 Leigham Court Road, LONDON, SW16 2NR.
THOMAS, Mr. Peter John Rutland, FCA *1969;* Wychwood House, Old Minster Lovell, Minster Lovell, WITNEY, OXFORDSHIRE, OX29 0RN.
THOMAS, Mr. Peter Leonard, FCA *1970;* 4 Barnes Street Oasts, Three Elm Lane, Golden Green, TONBRIDGE, KENT, TN11 0LD. (Life Member)
THOMAS, Mr. Peter Murray Scott, BSc ACA *2008;* 6 Burns Close, HITCHIN, HERTFORDSHIRE, SG4 0RB.
THOMAS, Mr. Peter Neil, BSc FCA *1988;* 47 Elm Grove Road, LONDON, SW13 0BU.
THOMAS, Mr. Peter Russell, BA FCA *1982;* Monitor Company Europe, Michelin House, 81 Fulham Road, LONDON, SW3 6RD.
THOMAS, Mr. Peter Stuart, FCA *1967;* 11 Kingston Quay, Sovereign Harbour, EASTBOURNE, EAST SUSSEX, BN23 5UP. (Life Member)
THOMAS, Mr. Philip, FCA *1967;* Ridgeway, Coach Road, Ivy Hatch, SEVENOAKS, KENT, TN15 0PF.
THOMAS, Mr. Philip, BSc FCA *1984;* Stolt Nielsen Ltd, 65 Kingsway, LONDON, WC2B 6TD.
THOMAS, Mr. Philip Anthony, FCA *1965;* 34 Cable Street, Formby, LIVERPOOL, L37 3LX.
•THOMAS, Mr. Philip John Gordon, ACA *1985;* Thomas and Company, 2a Lord Street, Douglas, ISLE OF MAN, IM1 2BD.
THOMAS, Mr. Philip Kenyon, FCA *1964;* The Rydings, 4 Hill Grove, Salendine Nook, HUDDERSFIELD, HD3 3TL.
THOMAS, Mr. Philip Simon Jeremy, BSc ACA *1990;* 81A Kintail Road, APPLECROSS, WA 6153, AUSTRALIA.
•THOMAS, Mr. Philip Stuart George, FCA *1974;* Phil Thomas FCA, 18 Home Close, Middleton Cheney, BANBURY, OXFORDSHIRE, OX17 2LD.
THOMAS, Miss. Rachel, BA ACA *1996;* 14 Boswell Road, Kingstanding, BIRMINGHAM, B44 8EJ.
THOMAS, Miss. Rachel Claire, BSc ACA *2007;* 10 Partington Street, BOLTON, BL3 3LE.
THOMAS, Miss. Rachel Suzanne, BA ACA *1997;* 74 North Street, LONDON, SW4 0HE.
THOMAS, Mr. Ramon, BSc ACA *1992;* Countess Of Chester Hospital, The Countess Of Chester, Health Park, Liverpool Road, CHESTER, CH2 1UL.
THOMAS, Mr. Raymond David, FCA ATII *1969;* The Choristers, Old Roman Road, Langstone, NEWPORT, NP18 2JW. (Life Member)
THOMAS, Mr. Raymond Vernon, FCA *1951;* 3 Fforest Road, Fforest, Pontarddulais, SWANSEA, SA4 0TN. (Life Member)
THOMAS, Mr. Rees Samuel, FCA *1960;* Green Lane House, Caerwent, CALDICOT, NP26 5NZ.
THOMAS, Ms. Rhian Lynfa, BA(Hons) ACA *2001;* Williams Ross Limited, 4 Ynys Bridge Court, Gwaelod Y Garth, CARDIFF, CF15 9SS.
THOMAS, Miss. Rhiannon, ACA *2010;* Courtil Pierre, Rue Des Buttes, St. Andrew, GUERNSEY, GY6 8XS.
THOMAS, Mr. Rhys Gifford, BSc FCA *1968;* 3470 Poinciana Avenue, Coconut Grove, MIAMI, FL 33133, UNITED STATES.
THOMAS, Mr. Richard, MSc BA ACA *2000;* Room 3E/07, H M Revenue & Customs, 100 Parliament Street, LONDON, SW1A 2BQ.
THOMAS, Mr. Richard, BSc ACA *1992;* 12 Grasmere Road, Dronfield Woodhouse, DRONFIELD, S18 8PS.
•THOMAS, Mr. Richard Alun, FCA *1975;* (Tax Fac), J Llywelyn Hughes & Co, Ty'r Bont, LLANRWST, LL26 0EY.
THOMAS, Mr. Richard Arnold, FCA *1951;* Church House, Slindon, ARUNDEL, BN18 0RB. (Life Member)
•THOMAS, Mr. Richard Brian, FCA *1975;* (Tax Fac), Thomas Westcott, 26-28 Southernhay East, EXETER, DEVON, EX1 1NS.
THOMAS, Mr. Richard Charles, BSc ACA *2006;* 27 Roebuck Road, BIRMINGHAM, B16 0QG.
THOMAS, Mr. Richard David, BSc ACA *2004;* Enterprise Plc, Lancaster House, Centurion Way, Leyland, PRESTON, PR26 6TX.
THOMAS, Mr. Richard David Marshall, ACA MAAT *2006;* 8 Trent Avenue, Garforth, LEEDS, LS25 2AY.
THOMAS, Mr. Richard Davis, ACA *2011;* 42 Marina Way, ABINGDON, OXFORDSHIRE, OX14 5TN.
•THOMAS, Mr. Richard Emlyn Rhys, BA FCA CTA *1984;* Tynllwyn, Foel, WELSHPOOL, POWYS, SY21 0NR.
THOMAS, Mr. Richard Forbes, FCA *1969;* 51 Bloomfield Road, HARPENDEN, AL5 4DD.
THOMAS, Mr. Richard John, FCA *1953;* Midwaye, Bournebridge Lane, Stapleford Abbotts, ROMFORD, RM4 1LT. (Life Member)
THOMAS, Mr. Richard Lloyd, BSc(Hons) ACA *2001;* Flat 10, Clyde House, Samuel Gray Gardens, KINGSTON UPON THAMES, SURREY, KT2 5UZ.
THOMAS, Mr. Richard Michael, BA ACA *2000;* Upper Silkstead Barn Silkstead Lane, Hursley, WINCHESTER, SO21 2LG.
THOMAS, Mr. Richard Michael, BA ACA *1989;* Level 13, Woodside Building, 240 St George's Terrace, PERTH, WA 6000, AUSTRALIA.
THOMAS, Mr. Richard Peter, BA ACA *1989;* 86 Bond Road, SURBITON, SURREY, KT6 7SG.
THOMAS, Mr. Robert David, BSc(Hons) ACA *2000;* 26 Albany Gardens, Hampton Lane, SOLIHULL, B91 2PT.
•THOMAS, Mr. Robert Dudley, FCA *1968;* Harold D. Pritchard & Co, Old Oak House, 49-51 Lammas Street, CARMARTHEN, DYFED, SA31 3AL.
THOMAS, Mr. Robert Edward James, MA ACA *2000;* European Commission, Directorate-General for Competition, Office J 70 5/86, B-1049 BRUSSELS, BELGIUM.
•THOMAS, Mr. Robert Eric, BSc FCA *1982;* RH Jeffs & Rowe Ltd, 27-28 Gelliwastad Road, PONTYPRIDD, MID GLAMORGAN, CF37 2BW.
THOMAS, Dr. Robert Hugh, FCA *1990;* Chevalier House, Woodnesborough, SANDWICH, CT13 0EH.
THOMAS, Mr. Robert Huw, MA ACA *2001;* The Hound House Grove Farm, Ivinghoe Aston, LEIGHTON BUZZARD, BEDFORDSHIRE, LU7 9DF.
THOMAS, Mr. Robert John, BSc ACA *2005;* 85 Kingsfield Drive, MANCHESTER, M20 6HX.
•THOMAS, Mr. Robert Keith, FCA *1966;* R K Thomas, Pools Close House, Pools Close, Chapel Street, Welford on Avon, STRATFORD-UPON-AVON WARWICKSHIRE CV37 8QB.
THOMAS, Mr. Robert William Bleddyn, BSc ACA *1987;* Norah's Cottage, 48 Main Road, East Hagbourne, DIDCOT, OXFORDSHIRE, OX11 9LR.
THOMAS, Mr. Robin Grenville, MA FCA *1973;* (Tax Fac), Dixon Wilson, 22 Chancery Lane, LONDON, WC2A 1LS.
THOMAS, Mr. Rodney Maxwell, BSc FCA *1978;* Axis Property Investment, Gemini Business Centre 136-140, Old Shoreham Road, HOVE, EAST SUSSEX, BN3 7BD.
•THOMAS, Mr. Roger, FCA *1976;* PricewaterhouseCoopers LLP, 1 Embankment Place, LONDON, WC2N 6RH. See also PricewaterhouseCoopers
THOMAS, Mr. Roger Ewart, BSc ACA *1979;* 86 Mallards Reach, Marshfield, CARDIFF, CF3 2PR.
THOMAS, Mr. Roger Francis, BSc FCA *1986;* 33 Over Nidd, HARROGATE, NORTH YORKSHIRE, HG1 3DB.
THOMAS, Mr. Roger Gwynne, MA FCA *1968;* rue du Lac 4, 1095 LUTRY, SWITZERLAND. (Life Member)
THOMAS, Mr. Roger Haslam, BA FCA *1977;* 85 Bluehouse Lane, Limpsfield, OXTED, RH8 0AP.
•THOMAS, Mr. Roger Nigel, FCA *1964;* R.N. Thomas & Co, 31 Silver Street, BRADFORD-ON-AVON, BA15 1JX.
THOMAS, Mrs. Rosalind Ann, BSc ACA ATII *1991;* 71 Wordsworth Avenue, NEWPORT PAGNELL, BUCKINGHAMSHIRE, MK16 8DY.
THOMAS, Mrs. Rosemary Elizabeth, LLB ACA *1989;* Clarence House, St. James's, LONDON, SW1A 1BA.
THOMAS, Mr. Roy Granville David, FCA *1973;* 44 St. Helens Road, SWANSEA, SA1 4BB.
THOMAS, Mr. Roy Henwood, FCA *1966;* Clark's College Ltd, Southdown House, High Street, Brasted, WESTERHAM, TN16 1JE.
THOMAS, Mr. Royston Edward, FCA *1959;* Wayseal Properties Ltd, Lancaster House, Barrack Lane, WINDSOR, SL4 1HD. (Life Member)
•THOMAS, Mr. Russell Leslie, FCA *1975;* (Tax Fac), AIM - Russell Thomas FCA, 9 Bullfinch Lane, SEVENOAKS, KENT, TN13 2DY.
THOMAS, Miss. Sally Victoria, ACA *2010;* 14a Northumberland Avenue, BLACKPOOL, FY2 9SB.
THOMAS, Mrs. Sally-Ann, ACA *1988;* (Tax Fac), 2 Littondale Avenue, KNARESBOROUGH, HG5 0BQ.
THOMAS, Mr. Sam, BA ACA *2011;* Flat 3, 4 Rainbow Quay, LONDON, SE16 7UF.
THOMAS, Miss. Sara Michelle, BSc ACA *1992;* 63 Baileys Barn, BRADFORD-ON-AVON, WILTSHIRE, BA15 1BW.
THOMAS, Mrs. Sarah, BA ACA *1998;* 228 Marsland Road, SALE, CHESHIRE, M33 3NA.
THOMAS, Miss. Sarah, BSc ACA *2011;* 133 Redland Road, BRISTOL, BS6 6XX.
THOMAS, Ms. Sarah Catherine, BA ACA *1992;* Longcause Cross Cottage, Dartington, TOTNES, DEVON, TQ9 6DQ.
THOMAS, Miss. Sarah Doreen, BA ACA *2000;* 6 Long Wood Meadows, Cheswick, BRISTOL, BS16 1GB.
THOMAS, Mrs. Sarah Jane, BSc ACA *1991;* Burnside, Broadwath Road, Great Corby, CARLISLE, CA4 8ND.
THOMAS, Mrs. Sarah Louise, BSc(Hons) ACA *2003;* Flat 2 Palliser Court, 41 Palliser Road, LONDON, W14 9ED.
THOMAS, Mrs. Sarah Margaret, BSc ACA *1999;* 73 Crimple Meadows Pannal, HARROGATE, NORTH YORKSHIRE, HG3 1EL.
THOMAS, Miss. Sarah Michelle, ACA *2010;* Deloitte AG, General Guisan-Quai 38, 8022, ZURICH, SWITZERLAND.
THOMAS, Miss. Sarah Victoria, BA ACA *2002;* 20 Langham Court, Mersey Road, MANCHESTER, M20 2PX.
THOMAS, Miss. Selina Kathryn, ACA *2010;* 2 Rock Road, PENZANCE, CORNWALL, TR18 4PJ.
THOMAS, Mrs. Serena Elizabeth, BSc ACA *1993;* 38 Perrymead Street, LONDON, SW6 3SP.
THOMAS, Mr. Shaun Hamilton, BA ACA *1991;* 3 West Street, Weedon, NORTHAMPTON, NN7 4QU.
•THOMAS, Miss. Sian-Kathryn, BA ACA *1991;* 44 Brookside Avenue, Waterloo Park, LIVERPOOL, L22 3YD.
THOMAS, Mr. Simon, ACA *2011;* 46 Birling Avenue, Bearsted, MAIDSTONE, KENT, ME14 4LN.
THOMAS, Mr. Simon George, BSc ACA *1990;* Broome Perrow House Old Road, Buckland, BETCHWORTH, RH3 7DY.
•THOMAS, Mr. Simon Reginald, FCA *1976;* (Tax Fac), Thomas & Co, Coolibah House, Polhorman Lane, Mullion, HELSTON, CORNWALL TR12 7JD.
THOMAS, Mr. Simon Robert, BSc ACA *2005;* with Deloitte LLP, Athene Place, 66 Shoe Lane, LONDON, EC4A 3BQ.
•①THOMAS, Mr. Simon Robert, ACA *1991;* Moorfields Corporate Recovery LLP, 88 Wood Street, LONDON, EC2V 7QR. See also Moorfields Corporate Finance LLP
THOMAS, Mrs. Simone Sherena, BA ACA *1999;* 17 Walkers Close, Bottesford, NOTTINGHAM, NG13 0FF.
THOMAS, Mr. Stanley Alfred Gunter, FCA *1958;* 3 Queen Anne's Gate, White House Walk, FARNHAM, SURREY, GU9 9AN. (Life Member)
THOMAS, Mrs. Stephanie Jane, BA ACA *1992;* 256 Edgerstoune Road, PRINCETON, NJ 08540, UNITED STATES.
•THOMAS, Mr. Stephen, FCA *1972;* Stephen Thomas, Greenlands, Parkside Drive South, Whittle-Le Woods, CHORLEY, PR6 7PH.
THOMAS, Mr. Stephen, MSc ACA *2009;* 4 Beverley Avenue, Urmston, MANCHESTER, M41 0RY.
THOMAS, Mr. Stephen Alan, ACA *2009;* 14 Trouville Road, LONDON, SW4 8QL.
THOMAS, Mr. Stephen Andrew Rhys, ACA *2001;* 7 Brunswick Road, Ealing, LONDON, W5 1BB.
THOMAS, Mr. Stephen Christopher, ACA *2009;* with Coller Capital Limited, 33 Cavendish Square, LONDON, W1G 0TT.
THOMAS, Mr. Stephen John, BA ACA *1991;* 83 Heathfield North, TWICKENHAM, TW2 7QN.
THOMAS, Mr. Stephen Mark, ACA *2008;* 407/23 Shelley Street, King Street Wharf, SYDNEY, NSW 2000, AUSTRALIA.
THOMAS, Mr. Stephen Paul, BSc ACA *1998;* 2 Celyn Grove, CARDIFF, CF23 6SH.
THOMAS, Mr. Stephen Paul, BA ACA *1981;* 16 Marefield, Lower Earley, READING, RG6 3DZ.
•THOMAS, Mr. Stephen Richard, FCA *1969;* Stephen R Thomas, Hawthorn House, Tunnel Lane, North Warnborough, HOOK, HAMPSHIRE RG29 1JT.
THOMAS, Mr. Steven John, BSc ACA *1993;* 69 Heatherwood Crescent, UNIONVILLE L3R 8V6, ON, CANADA.
THOMAS, Mr. Steven Michael, BSc ACA *2001;* 10 Palmer Close, Storrington, PULBOROUGH, WEST SUSSEX, RH20 3HN.
•THOMAS, Mr. Steven Richard, MA FCA *1986;* Flat 34 Aegean Apartments, 19 Western Gateway, LONDON, E16 1AR.
•THOMAS, Mr. Steven Vaughan, BA ACA *1982;* Milne Thomas & Co, 27 Seller Street, CHESTER, CH1 3NA.
THOMAS, Mr. Stuart Gerald, ACA *1984;* 3rd Floor Matrix House, Matrix Business Park, SWANSEA, WEST GLAMORGAN, SA6 8RE.
THOMAS, Mr. Stuart Richard, BA ACA *1994;* Norfolk House, Bamfords Lane, Turvey, BEDFORD, MK43 8DT.
THOMAS, Mr. Sunil, ACA CA(AUS) *2009;* Capco, Broadgate West, 9 Appold Street, LONDON, EC2A 2AP.
THOMAS, Mrs. Susan Avril, BA ACA *1987;* 14 Burnt Close Grantchester, CAMBRIDGE, CB3 9NJ.
THOMAS, Mrs. Susan Teresa, FCA CTA *1984;* (Tax Fac), 68 Sutherland Avenue, Petts Wood, ORPINGTON, BR5 1RB.
THOMAS, Mr. Timothy Charles Fedden, MA ACA *1998;* 2 Langley Grove, NEW MALDEN, SURREY, KT3 3AL.
THOMAS, Mr. Timothy Huw, BSc ACA *1987;* Western Cork Ltd, Penarth Road, CARDIFF, CF11 8YN.
•THOMAS, Mr. Timothy Mervyn, FCA *1968;* Church Cottage, The Street, Halvergate, NORWICH, NORFOLK, NR13 3PL.
THOMAS, Mr. Timothy Roger Holt, BSc FCA *1974;* Crantock, High Street, Coddenham, IPSWICH, IP6 9PN. (Life Member)
THOMAS, Mrs. Tina Elizabeth, MBChB ACA *1993;* Robin Hill, Welsh St Donats, COWBRIDGE, CF71 7SS.
THOMAS, Ms. Tracey Samantha, BSc ACA *2000;* 22 Allen Avenue, Quorn, LOUGHBOROUGH, LEICESTERSHIRE, LE12 8TR.
•THOMAS, Mr. Trevor Robert Mitchell, BA FCA *1974;* 115 Anchor Lane, HEMEL HEMPSTEAD, HERTFORDSHIRE, HP1 1NS.
THOMAS, Mrs. Valerie Helena, BA FCA *1982;* Sholand, Woodhill Road, Sandon, CHELMSFORD, CM2 7SE.
•THOMAS, Mrs. Vivien Nicola, MA FCA *1982;* 31 Oswin Street, LONDON, SE11 4TF.
THOMAS, Mr. Warren, MA ACA *1992;* 54 Casewick Lane, Uffington, STAMFORD, LINCOLNSHIRE, PE9 4SX.
•THOMAS, Mr. Wayne Douglas, ACA *1998;* (Tax Fac), Bates Weston Audit Limited, The Mill, Canal Street, DERBY, DE1 2RJ. See also BW Business Services Limited
THOMAS, Mr. Wayne Leslie, BA ACA *1996;* 99 Cuerdale Lane, Walton-le-Dale, PRESTON, PR5 4EP.
THOMAS, Mr. William Arnold, FCA *1956;* 14 Oakhill Drive, WELWYN, AL6 9NW. (Life Member)
THOMAS, Mr. William Brian, BA(Econ) FCA FCCA *1969;* HW Lee Associates, New Derwent House, 69-73 Theobalds Road, LONDON, WC1X 8TA.
•THOMAS, Mr. William Edward Lloyd, FCA *1960;* (Tax Fac), Bill Thomas & Co, 58 France Street, Westhoughton, BOLTON, BL5 2HP.
THOMAS, Mr. William Ernest Arnold, FCA *1958;* 20 Webb Court, Drury Lane, STOURBRIDGE, WEST MIDLANDS, DY8 1BN. (Life Member)
THOMAS, Mr. William Guy, BSc ACA *1984;* Beech House, Wolverhampton Road, SHIFNAL, TF11 9HA.
THOMAS, Mr. William Keith, MA ACA *1984;* 64 Fishmarket Road, RYE, EAST SUSSEX, TN31 7LP.
THOMAS, Mr. William Stuart, FCA *1959;* The Old Barn, Bryhampton Lane, Little Hereford, LUDLOW, SY8 4LN. (Life Member)
THOMAS, Mrs. Yvonne, LLB ACA *1986;* 101 Cyncoed Road, CARDIFF, CF23 6AE.
THOMAS, Mrs. Yvonne Kathleen, FCA *1980;* 19 Lime Tree Way, Wellington, TELFORD, SHROPSHIRE, TF1 3PJ.
THOMAS, Miss. Zoe Anne, FCA *1990;* 219 Whitworth Road, SWINDON, SN25 3BX.
THOMAS ADDERSON, Mr. David, ACA *2008;* with PricewaterhouseCoopers LLP, 7 More London Riverside, LONDON, SE1 2RT.
THOMAS-FERRAND, Mr. William, BA ACA *2004;* Flat 15, 64/65 Ix Xatt The Strand, SLIEMA SLM1022, MALTA.
THOMAS-WIDGER, Mr. Graham, BA ACA *1992;* 79 Broadmoor Lane, Kelston Chase, Weston, BATH, BA1 4LD.
THOMASON, Mr. Darren, BSc ACA *1994;* 2 Pond Gardens, POULTON-LE-FYLDE, FY6 7FH.
•THOMASON, Mr. David Victor, FCA *1972;* Leggatt Bell, 14 Railway Street, CHELMSFORD, CM1 1QS.
THOMASSEN, Mrs. Jane Alexandra, BSocSc ACA *1989;* 34 Hapua Street, Hataitai, WELLINGTON 6021, NEW ZEALAND.
THOMLINSON, Mrs. Joanne, BSc ACA *2011;* The Rowans, Manse Row, Blennerhasset, WIGTON, CUMBRIA, CA7 3RE.

THOMOPULOS, Mr. Anthimos, MSc ACA *1991;* 13 Pleiadon Street, K.Kifisia, 14561 ATHENS, GREECE.
THOMPKINS, Miss. Claire Ellen, ACA *2006;* 5 Lindsay Road, New Haw, ADDLESTONE, KT15 3BD.
THOMPSETT, Mr. Maurice Edward, FCA *1957;* 4 Park View, Seal Hollow Road, SEVENOAKS, KENT, TN13 3BU. (Life Member)
THOMPSON, Mr. Adam Euan, MPhil BA ACA *2002;* Calor Gas Ltd Athena House, Athena Drive Tachbrook Park, WARWICK, CV34 6RL.
THOMPSON, Mr. Adam Robert Lindsay, ACA *2008;* 14 Oundle Drive, Moulton, NORTHAMPTON, NN3 7DB.
THOMPSON, Mr. Adrian Ferguson, ACA *1983;* with Whitehead & Aldrich, 5 Ribblesdale Place, PRESTON, PR1 8BZ.
THOMPSON, Mr. Adrian James, FCA *1968;* Lamp Cottage, The Street, East Clandon, GUILDFORD, SURREY, GU4 7RY. (Life Member)
THOMPSON, Mr. Alan Martin, BA(Econ) ACA *1997;* 16 Hall Orchard Lane, Frisby on the Wreake, MELTON MOWBRAY, LEICESTERSHIRE, LE14 2NH.
•①**THOMPSON, Mr. Alan Roderick, BA LLB FCA ACIArb ATII MAE MABRP** *1963;* Alan Thompson, Brockhampton House, Brockhampton Park, Bringsty, WORCESTER, WR6 5TB.
THOMPSON, Mr. Alastair James, BA ACA *2003;* 2 Woodside Gardens, Cayton Low Road Eastfield, SCARBOROUGH, NORTH YORKSHIRE, YO11 3DB.
THOMPSON, Mr. Alexander, BA FCA *1991;* Guido Van Dethlaan 26, 1187 TT AMSTELVEEN, NETHERLANDS.
THOMPSON, Mr. Alexander Patrick, ACA *2010;* with Deloitte Touche Tohmatsu, 30/F Bund Center, 222 Yan An Road East, SHANGHAI 200002, CHINA.
THOMPSON, Miss. Alexandra Louise, BA(Hons) ACA *2005;* Istithmar World, PO Box 17000, DUBAI, UNITED ARAB EMIRATES.
•**THOMPSON, Mr. Alfred Charlton, FCA** *1960;* Lonsdale & Marsh, Orleans House, Edmund Street, LIVERPOOL, L3 9NG.
THOMPSON, Miss. Alice, ACA *2011;* Media Centre MC2A4, British Broadcasting Corporation Media Centre, 201 Wood Lane, LONDON, W12 7TQ.
THOMPSON, Mrs. Alison Jane, BA FCA *1994;* 29 Monkseaton Drive, WHITLEY BAY, NE26 1SY.
THOMPSON, Mr. Alistair Donald Vaughan, BA ACA *2001;* 53 Benthal Road, LONDON, N16 7AR.
THOMPSON, Mrs. Amy, BA ACA *2001;* 34 Strait Lane, Stainton, MIDDLESBROUGH, CLEVELAND, TS8 9BB.
THOMPSON, Miss. Amy Louise, BSc(Hons) ACA *2002;* Flat 43, 41 Provost Street, LONDON, N1 7NB.
THOMPSON, Mr. Andrew, LLB ACA *2002;* (Tax Fac), 20 The Mews, NEWCASTLE UPON TYNE, NE1 4DA.
THOMPSON, Mr. Andrew, BA ACA *2011;* Flat C, 33 Grosvenor Avenue, LONDON, N5 2NP.
THOMPSON, Mr. Andrew Barry, BA FCA *1978;* Ivy Cottage, 97 Maplewell Road, Woodhouse Eaves, LOUGHBOROUGH, LE12 8QY.
THOMPSON, Mr. Andrew John, BSc FCA *1982;* 23 Churchill Drive, TEIGNMOUTH, DEVON, TQ14 8QD.
THOMPSON, Mr. Andrew John, MA ACA *1981;* Age Concern Hammersmith & Fulham, 105 Greyhound Road, LONDON, W6 8NJ.
THOMPSON, Mr. Andrew Michael, BTech ACA *1986;* Highlands, 69 Kings Road, BERKHAMSTED, HERTFORDSHIRE, HP4 3BP.
•**THOMPSON, Mr. Andrew Patrick George, BSc ACA** *1991;* Shortlands Ltd, Shortlands, Frimley Road, Ash Vale, ALDERSHOT, HAMPSHIRE GU12 5PP. See also Shortlands Administrative Services
THOMPSON, Mr. Andrew Paul, ACA *2009;* Flat 21 Lockyer House, The Platt, LONDON, SW15 1EE.
THOMPSON, Mr. Andrew Paul, LLB ACA *2001;* 9 Buchanans Wharf South, Ferry Street, BRISTOL, BS1 6HJ.
THOMPSON, Mr. Andrew Robert, BA ACA *1985;* Blaenafon, Efailwen, Clunderwen, NARBERTH, SA66 7UT.
THOMPSON, Mr. Andrew Timothy, FCA *1995;* with KPMG, 10 Shelley Street, SYDNEY, NSW 2000, AUSTRALIA.
•**THOMPSON, Mr. Andrew William, FCA** *1977;* Kenilworth Associates Limited, 2 Kenilworth Road, Blundellsands, LIVERPOOL, L23 3AD.
THOMPSON, Mrs. Ann Helen, BSc ACA *1991;* 19 Hall Walk, COTTINGHAM, HU16 4RL.
•**THOMPSON, Mrs. Ann Margaret, BA ACA** *1979;* (Tax Fac), Chan Lodge, Whams Lane, Bay Horse, LANCASTER, LA2 9BY.
THOMPSON, Miss. Anna Marie, ACA *2009;* 5 Magnolia Close, DRIFFIELD, NORTH HUMBERSIDE, YO25 6QU.
THOMPSON, Mrs. Anne Fiona, PhD MSc BA ACA *1987;* Flat 51, 48 Wells Street, LONDON, W1T 3PW.
THOMPSON, Mr. Anthony, BA ACA *1982;* 36 Saxon Way, Melton, WOODBRIDGE, SUFFOLK, IP12 1LG.
THOMPSON, Ms. Barbara Zofia, BA ACA *1982;* 6 Melrose Avenue, LONDON, NW2 4JS.
THOMPSON, Mr. Benjamin, BSc ACA *2011;* Top Floor Flat, 5 Ferndale Road, LONDON, SW4 7RJ.
THOMPSON, Brian, Esq OBE BSc FCA *1971;* 79 Darras Road, Darras Hall, Ponteland, NEWCASTLE UPON TYNE, NE20 9PQ. (Life Member)
THOMPSON, Mr. Brian Parker, FCA *1964;* 3 Standing Stones, Gt Billing, NORTHAMPTON, NN3 9HA. (Life Member)
THOMPSON, Mr. Carl Anthony, ACA *1987;* 1 Oaklands Drive, ASCOT, SL5 7NE.
•**THOMPSON, Mrs. Carol Annette, BCom(ACC) ACA** *1993;* Carol A Thompson, 137 Brays Road, Sheldon, BIRMINGHAM, B26 2UL.
THOMPSON, Miss. Carol Elizabeth, BA FCA *1983;* Mistal Barn, Lower Castle Hill, Almondbury, HUDDERSFIELD, HD4 6TA.
THOMPSON, Mrs. Catherine Patricia, BA ACA *1998;* 56 Woodcote Road, Timperley, ALTRINCHAM, WA14 5PN.
THOMPSON, Mr. Charles Mark Hill, BSc ACA *1986;* Bredon Coast Hill, Westcott, DORKING, SURREY, RH4 3LH.
•**THOMPSON, Mr. Charles Martin, BA FCA DChA** *1982;* 9 Shelley Road, HIGH WYCOMBE, BUCKINGHAMSHIRE, HP11 2UP.
THOMPSON, Miss. Charlotte, BSc ACA *2011;* Flat 39 Heritage Court, 15 Warstone Lane, BIRMINGHAM, B18 6HP.
THOMPSON, Mr. Christopher David, BSc ACA *1987;* 31 Chetwynd Drive, Bassett, SOUTHAMPTON, SO16 3HY.
THOMPSON, Mr. Christopher Edward Bellairs, MA FCA *1950;* 31 Ipswich Road, WOODBRIDGE, SUFFOLK, IP12 4BT. (Life Member)
THOMPSON, Mr. Christopher Howard Gould, BA FCA *1981;* The University of Nottingham, Kings Meadow Campus, Lenton Lane, NOTTINGHAM, NG7 2NR.
•**THOMPSON, Mr. Christopher John, BA FCA** *1980;* Power Thompson, 199 Clarendon Park Road, LEICESTER, LE2 3AN.
•**THOMPSON, Mr. Christopher John, FCA** *1968;* Thorpe Thompson, 1st Floor Lincoln Lodge, 2 Tettenhall Road, WOLVERHAMPTON, WV1 4SA.
THOMPSON, Mr. Christopher John, BSc(Econ) ACA *1986;* with MacIntyre Hudson LLP, Euro House, 1394 High Road, Whetstone, LONDON, N20 9YZ.
THOMPSON, Mr. Christopher Martin, FCA *1968;* Croft House, Great Salkeld, PENRITH, CA11 9NB. (Life Member)
THOMPSON, Mr. Christopher Robert, BA ACA *2009;* H S B C, 62-76 Park Street, LONDON, SE1 9DZ.
THOMPSON, Mr. Christopher William, BSc ACA *1993;* British Salt Ltd, Cledford Lane, MIDDLEWICH, CHESHIRE, CW10 0JP.
THOMPSON, Mrs. Claire Patricia, FCA *1980;* 1 Manor Farm Place, Great Smeaton, NORTHALLERTON, DL6 2HP.
•**THOMPSON, Mrs. Claire Suzanne, BSc ACA** *2004;* Thompsons Accountancy Limited, 7 Kingsway, HAYLING ISLAND, HAMPSHIRE, PO11 0LZ.
•**THOMPSON, Mrs. Clare Eleanor, BA FCA** *1979;* PricewaterhouseCoopers LLP, Hays Galleria, 1 Hays Lane, LONDON, SE1 2RD. See also PricewaterhouseCoopers
THOMPSON, Mr. Colin Graeme, FCA *1953;* 62 Manor Way, BECKENHAM, BR3 3LJ. (Life Member)
THOMPSON, Mr. Daniel, LLB ACA *2001;* Rinching Maidstone Road, Seal, SEVENOAKS, TN15 0EH.
THOMPSON, Mr. Daniel Robert, BA(Hons) ACA *2002;* 34 Beacon House, Burrells Wharf Square, LONDON, E14 3TJ.
THOMPSON, Mr. Daniel Thor, BA ACA *1996;* 29 Oak Road, Hale, ALTRINCHAM, WA15 9JA.
THOMPSON, Mr. Darren, BA FCA *1996;* 9 Eastgate, Hallaton, MARKET HARBOROUGH, LEICESTERSHIRE, LE16 8UB.
THOMPSON, Mr. David, BSc ACA *2004;* 112 Cavendish Road, LONDON, SW12 0DF.
•**THOMPSON, Mr. David, FCA** *1969;* Stone Lea, Badsworth Court, Badsworth, PONTEFRACT, WF9 1NW.
THOMPSON, Mr. David Alan, LLB FCA *1979;* Vergo Retail, 4 Renshaw Street, LIVERPOOL, L1 4AD.
THOMPSON, Mr. David Alexander Edwin, FCA *1977;* Rectory Barn, School Road, Brisley, DEREHAM, NORFOLK, NR20 5LH.
•**THOMPSON, Mr. David Andrew, FCA** *1973;* (Tax Fac), R.A. & D.A. Thompson, 30 High Street, LEIGHTON BUZZARD, BEDFORDSHIRE, LU7 1EA.
THOMPSON, Mr. David Andrew, BSc ACA *1987;* 249 Upton Road South, BEXLEY, DA5 1QU.
•**THOMPSON, Mr. David Andrew, BSc FCA** *1997;* Littlejohn LLP, 1 Westferry Circus, Canary Wharf, LONDON, E14 4HD.
THOMPSON, Mr. David Anthony, FCA *1969;* P O Box 130839, BRYANSTON, GAUTENG, 2074, SOUTH AFRICA.
THOMPSON, Mr. David Anthony Roland, FCA *1964;* The Court, Main Street, Cropwell Butler, NOTTINGHAM, NG12 3AB.
•**THOMPSON, Mr. David D'arcy, FCA** *1973;* (Tax Fac), Thompsons, 19 East Parade, HARROGATE, NORTH YORKSHIRE, HG1 5LF.
•**THOMPSON, Mr. David Elliott, ACA** *1979;* (Tax Fac), 8 Holborn Drive, ORMSKIRK, LANCASHIRE, L39 3QL.
THOMPSON, Mr. David Frederick, FCA *1973;* 33 Russell Road, NORTHWOOD, HA6 2LP.
THOMPSON, Mr. David Gareth, BA(Hons) ACA *2001;* Investec Bank (UK) Ltd, 2 Gresham Street, LONDON, EC2V 7QP.
THOMPSON, Mr. David James, BA ACA *1994;* 3 Micklethwaite Road, LONDON, SW6 1QD.
•**THOMPSON, Mr. David John, FCA** *1972;* RHK Business Advisers LLP, Coburg House, 1 Coburg Street, GATESHEAD, TYNE AND WEAR, NE8 1NS. See also RHK Corporate Finance LLP
THOMPSON, Mr. David John, FCA *1975;* 2 Chiltern Avenue, BEDFORD, MK41 9EQ.
THOMPSON, Mr. David Keith, FCA *1970;* Northfield House, 4 Melford Road, SUDBURY, SUFFOLK, CO10 1LS.
THOMPSON, Mr. David Lawrence, BA ACA *1979;* 45 Stanmore Crescent, LEEDS, LS4 2RY.
THOMPSON, Mr. David Philip, BA ACA *1990;* OVUM Ventures Management Limited, Gleissentalstr. 5a, 82041 DEISENHOFEN, GERMANY.
THOMPSON, Mr. David Robert, BSc ACA *1998;* Unit B 5 Gables Lane, DEVONSHIRE DV 07, BERMUDA.
THOMPSON, Mr. David William, BSc ACA *1984;* 70 Broadway, Earlsdon, COVENTRY, CV5 6NU.
•**THOMPSON, Mr. David William Moffat, MA FCA** *1975;* KPMG Hungaria Kft, Vaci ut 99, H 1139 BUDAPEST, HUNGARY.
THOMPSON, Mrs. Deborah Ann, BA ACA *1995;* 24 Handel Avenue, WORONGARY, QLD 4213, AUSTRALIA.
•**THOMPSON, Ms. Delma Lynne, FCA ACA** *1987;* D.L. Thompson, c/- P O Box 294, CIVIC SQUARE, ACT 2608, AUSTRALIA.
THOMPSON, Miss. Diane Catherine, ACA *2000;* B D O Stoy Hayward, 1 Bridgewater Place, Water Lane, LEEDS, LS11 5RU.
THOMPSON, Mr. Donald Oswald, FCA *1950;* Greenboughs, 9 Orchard Close, Bromham, BEDFORD, MK43 8HN. (Life Member)
•**THOMPSON, Mr. Douglas Malcolm, FCA** *1964;* LloydThompson & Carl, 41 Eastwood Road, The Mount, SHREWSBURY, SY3 8YJ.
THOMPSON, Mr. Dudley Stuart, FCA FCT *1965;* Cobwebs, 3 The Beeches, Fetcham, LEATHERHEAD, SURREY, KT22 9DT. (Life Member)
•**THOMPSON, Mr. Edward Guy Matthew, BA ACA** *1997;* Lancaster & Co, Granville House, 2 Tettenhall Rd, WOLVERHAMPTON, WV1 4SB. See also Lancaster Haskins LLP
THOMPSON, Mr. Edward Lyon James, BSc(Hons) ACA *2001;* 91 Western Beach, 36 Hanover Avenue, LONDON, E16 1DZ.
THOMPSON, Miss. Eleanor Jane, BSc(Hons) ACA *2002;* 17 Statham Place, Oldbrook, MILTON KEYNES, MK6 2HB.
THOMPSON, Ms. Emma Jane, BSc(Hons) ACA *2002;* 20 Linden Court, Rothwell, LEEDS, LS26 0GF.
•**THOMPSON, Miss. Eudora Lucretia, ACA** *1981;* 7 North Block, Chicheley Street, LONDON, SE1 7PJ.
THOMPSON, Mrs. Fiona Ann, BA ACA *2008;* 1 Clintz Road, EGREMONT, CUMBRIA, CA22 2QU.
THOMPSON, Miss. Francesca, ACA *2008;* The Vardy Group, Venture House Aykley Heads, DURHAM, DH1 5TS.
THOMPSON, Mr. Francis John Perronet, MA MBA FCA *1972;* Green Holly, Back Lane, CHALFONT ST. GILES, BUCKINGHAMSHIRE, HP8 4PB. (Life Member)
THOMPSON, Mr. Frank, FCA *1961;* The Barn, Thursby, CARLISLE, CA5 6PJ.
THOMPSON, Mr. Gary Howard, BA ACA *1998;* Provident Financial PLC, 1 godwin Street, BRADFORD, BD1 2SU.
THOMPSON, Mr. Gary Mark, BSc ACA *1993;* 14 High Street, Chalfont St. Peter, GERRARDS CROSS, BUCKINGHAMSHIRE, SL9 9QA.
THOMPSON, Mr. Geoffrey Alan, BA FCA *1977;* Overbrook House, Over Wallop, STOCKBRIDGE, SO20 8HT.
THOMPSON, Mr. Geoffrey Barrington, FCA *1963;* 115 Seaforth Gardens, Stoneleigh, EPSOM, KT19 0LW. (Life Member)
THOMPSON, Mr. George Anthony, FCA *1969;* 2nd floor Viking House, Nelson Street, Douglas, ISLE OF MAN, IM99 2LJ.
THOMPSON, Mr. George Hungerford, BSc ACA *2011;* 19 Portsmouth Road, THAMES DITTON, KT7 0SY.
THOMPSON, Mrs. Georgina, BA ACA *2003;* BOS Finance Bunzl Disposables Ltd Epsom Chase 1 Hook Road, EPSOM, SURREY, KT19 8TY.
THOMPSON, Mr. Gerald Vincent Bodenham, MA FCA *1978;* Easton Partners LLP, 1 Cornhill, LONDON, EC3V 3ND.
THOMPSON, Mrs. Geraldine, BSc ACA *2007;* 20 Denzil Road, GUILDFORD, SURREY, GU2 7NQ.
THOMPSON, Mr. Giles Mansell, MA ACA *1996;* 20 Lansdowne Road, ST KILDA EAST, VIC 3183, AUSTRALIA.
THOMPSON, Mrs. Gillian Lesley, FCA *1977;* 29 Sedgefield Close, Worth, CRAWLEY, RH10 7XG.
THOMPSON, Mrs. Glynis Patricia, FCA *1973;* 19 Ringwood Road, LUTON, LU2 7BG.
THOMPSON, Mr. Graeme Mark, BA ACA *1995;* Wellmont House Truggist Lane, Berkswell, COVENTRY, CV7 7BW.
THOMPSON, Mr. Graham, FCA *1959;* 40 Church Lane, Weddington, NUNEATON, CV10 0EX. (Life Member)
THOMPSON, Mr. Graham, BSc FCA *1977;* 18 St Francis Avenue, Olton, SOLIHULL, B91 1EB.
THOMPSON, Mr. Graham Mark, BA ACA *1984;* J P Morgan Fleming Asset Management Finsbury Dials, 20 Finsbury Street, LONDON, EC2Y 9AQ.
•**THOMPSON, Mr. Graham Philip, FCA** *1971;* (Tax Fac), Graham P Thompson, Beaufoys, Firle Road, SEAFORD, BN25 2HU.
•**THOMPSON, Mr. Graham William, FCA** *1983;* (Tax Fac), Benson Wood Limited, 10 Yarm Road, STOCKTON-ON-TEES, CLEVELAND, TS18 3NA. See also Benson Wood & Co Limited and Benson Wood Bureau Services Limited
THOMPSON, Mr. Harold, FCA *1953;* Hawthorne Bungalow, Copster Green, BLACKBURN, BB1 9EP. (Life Member)
THOMPSON, Mr. Harold Gregor, FCA *1961;* 4 Tuscany Villas, 11 Elizabeth Rd, BEDFORDVIEW, GAUTENG, 2007, SOUTH AFRICA.
THOMPSON, Miss. Helen, ACA *2009;* 62 Falstone Drive, CHESTER LE STREET, COUNTY DURHAM, DH2 3ST.
THOMPSON, Mrs. Helen, BA ACA *1997;* Timpson Shoe Repairs Ltd, Timpson House, Claverton Road, Roundthorn Industrial Estate, MANCHESTER, M23 9TT.
THOMPSON, Mrs. Helen Clare, BA(Hons) ACA *2002;* 135 Lambley Lane, Burton Joyce, NOTTINGHAM, NG14 5BN.
THOMPSON, Miss. Helen Marie, BSc(Hons) ACA *2001;* 20 Wesley Place, SILSDEN, BD20 0PH.
THOMPSON, Mrs. Helen Patricia, BSc ACA *1987;* Halfpenny Barn, Cranes Lane, Lathom, ORMSKIRK, LANCASHIRE, L40 5UJ.
THOMPSON, Miss. Helen Rowan, BSc ACA *2001;* with PKF (UK) LLP, Farringdon Place, 20 Farringdon Road, LONDON, EC1M 3AP.
THOMPSON, Mrs. Henrietta Jane, BSc ACA *1987;* 39 Blackthorn Close, Wistaston, CREWE, CW2 6PQ.
THOMPSON, Mr. Howard Julian, MA ACA *2001;* Flat 2, 52 Lavender Gardens, Battersea, LONDON, SW11 1DN.
THOMPSON, Mr. Hubert William Eccles, FCA *1955;* The Old Coaching House, The Courtyard, Swettenham, CONGLETON, CW12 2JZ. (Life Member)
THOMPSON, Mr. Hugh Crighton, FCA *1959;* Gwillen, Trenance, Mawgan Porth, NEWQUAY, TR8 4BZ. (Life Member)
THOMPSON, Mr. Hugh Reginald Patrick, FCA *1958;* with Target Consulting Limited, Bloxam Court, Corporation Street, RUGBY, WARWICKSHIRE, CV21 2DU. (Life Member)
•**THOMPSON, Mr. Ian, FCA** *1967;* (Tax Fac), I. Thompson & Co, The Arcade, Belsay, NEWCASTLE UPON TYNE, NE20 0DY.
THOMPSON, Mr. Ian, ACA *1984;* i6 Building, 6-8 Charlotte Square, NEWCASTLE UPON TYNE, TYNE AND WEAR, NE1 4XF.

•**THOMPSON, Mr. Ian, BA FCA** *1995;* Saint & Co., The Old Police Station, Church Street, AMBLESIDE, LA22 0BT.
THOMPSON, Mr. Ian, ACA *1989;* 6 Arthur Street, High Handenhold, CHESTER LE STREET, DH2 1QE.
•**THOMPSON, Mr. Ian Barry, BSc FCA** *1984;* (Tax Fac), Ian B Thompson Limited, Blades Enterprise Centre, John Street, SHEFFIELD, S2 4SU.
THOMPSON, Mr. Ian James Aird, MA ACA *2003;* with FTI Forensic Accounting Limited, 322 High Holborn, LONDON, WC1V 7PB.
THOMPSON, Mr. Ian John, BSc ACA *1979;* 12 Overdale Grange, SKIPTON, BD23 6AG.
THOMPSON, Mr. Ian Michael, BSc ACA *1983;* 81 Woodrow Crescent, Knowle, SOLIHULL, B93 9EQ.
THOMPSON, Mr. Ian Michael, BSc ACA *1994;* 23 Rosaville Road, LONDON, SW6 7BN.
THOMPSON, Mr. Ian Morris, FCA *1956;* 43 Canada Drive, Rawdon, LEEDS, LS19 6LU. (Life Member)
THOMPSON, Mr. Ian Nicholas, FCA *1981;* 4 Abingdon Road, Dorchester-On-Thames, WALLINGFORD, OX10 7JY.
THOMPSON, Mr. Ian Peter, BSc ACA *1991;* Fibrelite Composites Ltd Unit 2, Snaygill Industrial Estate Keighley Road, SKIPTON, NORTH YORKSHIRE, BD23 2QR.
THOMPSON, Mr. Ian William, BA ACA *1995;* 9 Rufford Close, WATFORD, WD17 4UU.
THOMPSON, Mr. James Christopher, MA ACA *1988;* 61 Stradella Road, LONDON, SE24 9HL.
•**THOMPSON, Mr. James Cyril, FCA** *1976;* Dudley & Co., 33 New Street, CARNFORTH, LA5 9BX. See also Thompson & Co
THOMPSON, Mr. James Richard, ACA *1996;* 536 Kenilworth Road, Balsall Common, COVENTRY, CV7 7DQ.
THOMPSON, Miss. Janine, LLB ACA *2001;* 5 / 29 Belmont Avenue, SYDNEY, NSW 2065, AUSTRALIA.
THOMPSON, Miss. Jean, MSc BSc FCA *1975;* 2 Newenden Road, Whitley, WIGAN, WN1 2PX.
THOMPSON, Mr. Jeremy David, BA ACA *1988;* Old Lodge East, High Street, Taplow, MAIDENHEAD, SL6 0EX.
THOMPSON, Mr. Jeremy Miles Allan, BCom FCA *1976;* 20 Hampstead Lane, Highgate, LONDON, N6 4SB.
THOMPSON, Mr. Jeremy Sinclair, MA ACA *1981;* Milton Manor, Milton Abbas, BLANDFORD FORUM, DT11 0AZ.
THOMPSON, Mrs. Jessica Sophia, MSci ACA *2006;* 4 Trelawney, Rydens Road, WALTON-ON-THAMES, SURREY, KT12 3AR.
THOMPSON, Mrs. Joan Evelyn, FCA *1974;* 56 The Green Barton under Needwood, BURTON-ON-TRENT, STAFFORDSHIRE, DE13 8JD.
THOMPSON, Miss. Joanna Claire, BSc ACA *2005;* 318 Milton Road, CAMBRIDGE, CB4 1LH.
THOMPSON, Mrs. Joanna Louise, BA ACA *1998;* 2 Hazel Drive, Burn Bridge, HARROGATE, NORTH YORKSHIRE, HG3 1NY.
THOMPSON, Mrs. Joanne Elizabeth, ACA *2008;* 5b Brookside, Burbage, HINCKLEY, LEICESTERSHIRE, LE10 2TG.
THOMPSON, Mr. John, FCA *1959;* 211 Manchester Road, ACCRINGTON, BB5 2PF. (Life Member)
THOMPSON, Mr. John, BA ACA *1992;* 28/8 Pattanawej Soi 12, Sukhumuit Soi 71, BANGKOK, 10110, THAILAND.
•**THOMPSON, Mr. John Alan, BA FCA** *1989;* J S Bethell & Co, 70 Clarkehouse Road, SHEFFIELD, S10 2LJ.
THOMPSON, Mr. John Alan, BSc ACA *1988;* 12 Chapel Street, Woburn Sands, MILTON KEYNES, MK17 8PG.
THOMPSON, Mr. John Andrew, FCA *1978;* 7 Burlington Close, Breaston, DERBY, DE72 3UB. (Life Member)
THOMPSON, Mr. John Andrew, BSc FCA *1981;* Finance Department, Nissan Motor Manufacturing (UK) Ltd, Washington Road, SUNDERLAND, SR5 3NS.
THOMPSON, Mr. John Andrew, BSc ACA *1988;* 18 Hollytree Road, Woolton, LIVERPOOL, L25 5PA.
THOMPSON, Mr. John Barton de Courcy, FCA *1964;* Gaveston, Bishops Down Park Road, TUNBRIDGE WELLS, TN4 8XR. (Life Member)
•**THOMPSON, Mr. John Flynn, BA FCA** *1993;* 28 St. Swithin Way, ANDOVER, HAMPSHIRE, SP10 4NU.
•**THOMPSON, Mr. John Henry, FCA** *1979;* J.H. Thompson & Co, 5 Burns Close, Long Crendon, AYLESBURY, BUCKINGHAMSHIRE, HP18 9BX.
THOMPSON, Mr. John Martin Perronet, BA ACA *2007;* 40a Bassett Road, LONDON, W10 6JL.
THOMPSON, Mr. John Michael, FCA *1966;* Flat 408, The Butlers Wharf Building, 36 Shad Thames, LONDON, SE1 2YE.
THOMPSON, Mr. John Richard, BSc ACA *2004;* Renaissance House, 8-20 East Broadway, HAMILTON HM 19, BERMUDA.
THOMPSON, Mrs. Jolene, ACA CA(SA) *2010;* 71 Mortimer Crescent, WORCESTER PARK, KT4 7QN.
•**THOMPSON, Mr. Jonathan Hugo Eccles, BSc ACA** *1986;* KPMG LLP, 15 Canada Square, LONDON, E14 5GL. See also KPMG Europe LLP
THOMPSON, Mr. Jonathan Roger, BSc FCA *1978;* 1 Manor Farm Place, Great Smeaton, NORTHALLERTON, NORTH YORKSHIRE, DL6 2HP.
THOMPSON, Mr. Joseph Henry, FCA *1953;* 12 Berwick Drive, Fulwood, PRESTON, PR2 3JS. (Life Member)
THOMPSON, Mrs. Josephine Mary, BSc ACA *1989;* The Bar Convent Museum, 17-19 Blossom Street, YORK, YO24 1AQ.
THOMPSON, Mrs. Julia Lindsey, ACA *1996;* Ant Hire Limited, Queen Street, Stourton, LEEDS, LS10 1SL.
THOMPSON, Mrs. Julie Caren, BA ACA *1984;* 16 Langtree Avenue, SOLIHULL, WEST MIDLANDS, B91 3YJ.
THOMPSON, Miss. Julie May, ACA *2006;* 8 Mercer Close, Larkfield, AYLESFORD, KENT, ME20 6QY.
THOMPSON, Mrs. Juliet, BSc ACA *1993;* Nomura Code Securities, 1 Carey Lane, LONDON, EC2V 8AE.
•**THOMPSON, Mrs. Juliet Anne, BA ACA** *1992;* Thompsons MK Limited, 1 Hathaway Court, Crownhill, MILTON KEYNES, MK8 0LG. See also Thompson MK Bookkeeping Services Limited
THOMPSON, Mr. Juliet Lorna Guestina, BA ACA *1985;* 9 Lichfield Road, Kew, RICHMOND, SURREY, TW9 3JR.
•**THOMPSON, Ms. Karen Jane, MA FCA** *1996;* PKF (UK) LLP, Farringdon Place, 20 Farringdon Road, LONDON, EC1M 3AP.
THOMPSON, Mrs. Katharine, LLB ACA *1992;* Sloelands Farm, Ashley Green Road, CHESHAM, HP5 3PF.
•**THOMPSON, Mrs. Katharine Emma, ACA** *2004;* Stubbs Parkin Taylor & Co, 18a London Street, SOUTHPORT, MERSEYSIDE, PR9 0UE. See also Stubbs Parkin Taylor & Co Limited
THOMPSON, Mrs. Katharine Jane, BSc ACA *1990;* Eaton House, 4 High Street, South Anston, SHEFFIELD, S25 5AY.
THOMPSON, Mrs. Katharine Mary, BSc(Econ) ACA *1997;* Britannia Building Society, Cheadle Road, LEEK, STAFFORDSHIRE, ST13 5RG.
THOMPSON, Miss. Katherine Elizabeth, BEng ACA *1998;* 78 Ormeley Road, LONDON, SW12 9QG.
THOMPSON, Mrs. Katherine Elizabeth, BA ACA *2004;* 44 Langdale Crescent, GRANTHAM, LINCOLNSHIRE, NG31 8DF.
THOMPSON, Mrs. Kathryn Martha Elizabeth, BSc ACA *1993;* 3 Goodwood Close, Battenhall, WORCESTER, WR5 2HS.
THOMPSON, Mr. Kenneth Attu Kwamina Busumptwi, BSc ACA *1993;* PMB 268, Cantonments, ACCRA, GHANA.
THOMPSON, Mr. Kenneth Muir, FCA *1960;* Malcoff, Woodside, Duxbury Park, CHORLEY, PR7 4AE. (Life Member)
THOMPSON, Mr. Kenneth Philip, BA FCA *1977;* 6 The Russets, Chestfield, WHITSTABLE, KENT, CT5 3QG.
•**THOMPSON, Mr. Kevin, BA ACA** *2000;* with Deloitte LLP, 2 New Street Square, LONDON, EC4A 3BZ.
THOMPSON, Mr. Kevin John, BSc FCA *1984;* Halma plc, Misbourne Court, Rectory Way, AMERSHAM, HP7 0DE.
THOMPSON, Miss. Kimberley Dawn, BA ACA *2010;* 57 Haddon Drive, EASTLEIGH, SO50 4PF.
THOMPSON, Mrs. Kirsten, BSc ACA ATII *1998;* 126 Howard Road, Westbury Park, BRISTOL, BS6 7XA.
THOMPSON, Miss. Laura Jayne, BSc ACA *2010;* Apartment 211 Skyline, 165 Granville Street, BIRMINGHAM, B1 1JY.
THOMPSON, Miss. Lavell Mary Leeson, MA ACA *1992;* 13 Vanderbilt Road, WEST HARTFORD, CT 06119, UNITED STATES.
THOMPSON, Mr. Lawrence Henry, FCA *1954;* 5a College Close, WILMSLOW, CHESHIRE, SK9 5PY. (Life Member)
THOMPSON, Mr. Lee, BSc ACA *1996;* 141 Parsonage Road, Castlehill, SYDNEY, NSW 2154, AUSTRALIA.
•**THOMPSON, Mr. Leonard Frederick, ACA** *1983;* Thompson Accountancy Limited, 2 Gloucester Way, Heath Hayes, CANNOCK, STAFFORDSHIRE, WS11 7YN.
THOMPSON, Mrs. Lesley Margaret, MA ACA *1988;* Lucy Cavendish College, CAMBRIDGE, CB3 0BU.
THOMPSON, Miss. Lindsey Sarah, BSc ACA *2002;* 38 St. Pauls Road, LONDON, N1 2QW.
THOMPSON, Mrs. Lisa Sian, BA ACA *2004;* 41 Constance Road, TWICKENHAM, TW2 7HT.
THOMPSON, Mrs. Louise Andrea, MA ACA *2002;* 401 Red Lees Road, Cliviger, BURNLEY, LANCASHIRE, BB10 4TF.
THOMPSON, Miss. Lucy Frances, BMus ACA *2008;* 23B Manor Drive, Rolleston, CHRISTCHURCH 7614, NEW ZEALAND.
THOMPSON, Miss. Lucy Joanna, BSc ACA *1984;* Apt. 12M, 420 E 55th Street, NEW YORK, NY 10022, UNITED STATES.
THOMPSON, Mrs. Madeleine Jane, BSc ACA *1997;* 11 Weston Road, THAMES DITTON, SURREY, KT7 0HN.
THOMPSON, Mr. Malcolm, FCA *1954;* 78 Kingston Road, Willerby, HULL, HU10 6BH. (Life Member)
THOMPSON, Mr. Marcus Patrick, BSc ACA *1988;* Gundelhardtstrasse 78, 65779 KELKHEIM, GERMANY.
THOMPSON, Mrs. Margaret Ruth, BA ACA *1989;* Les Rouvets, Rouvets Road, Vale, GUERNSEY, GY6 8NQ.
THOMPSON, Mr. Mark, MA FCA *1997;* Serious Fraud Office, Elm House, 10-16 Elm Street, LONDON, WC1X 0BJ.
•**THOMPSON, Mr. Mark Andrew, BSc ACA** *1991;* Mark Thompson Ltd, 12 Beech Road, Stockton Heath, WARRINGTON, WA4 6LT.
THOMPSON, Mr. Mark Andrew, BSc ACA *1997;* 72 Fairfield Road, TADCASTER, LS24 9SN.
THOMPSON, Mr. Mark David, ACA CTA *1986;* 154 Boundaries Road, LONDON, SW12 8HG.
THOMPSON, Mr. Mark David, BA ACA *1996;* with PricewaterhouseCoopers LLP, Donington Court, Pegasus Business Park, Castle Donington, DERBY, DE74 2UZ.
THOMPSON, Mr. Mark Nicholas, BSc ACA *1987;* Apartment 1205, Eclipse Hotel Apartments, PO Box 113499, ABU DHABI, UNITED ARAB EMIRATES.
•**THOMPSON, Mr. Mark Robert, BA FCA** *1988;* KPMG Channel Islands Limited, 20 New Street, St Peter Port, GUERNSEY, GY1 4AN.
THOMPSON, Mrs. Mary Loretta Ann, BSc ACA *1982;* 5 Yeates Close, THAME, OX9 3AR.
THOMPSON, Mr. Matthew James Robert, BA ACA *1991;* 5 Manor Park, TEWKESBURY, GLOUCESTERSHIRE, GL20 8BQ.
THOMPSON, Mr. Michael, ACA *2010;* 58 Wansdyke, MORPETH, NORTHUMBERLAND, NE61 3RA.
•**THOMPSON, Mr. Michael Andrew, FCA** *1955;* Michael Thompson & Co, 10 Auckland Terrace, Parliament Street, Ramsey, ISLE OF MAN, IM8 1AF.
THOMPSON, Mr. Michael Geoffrey, FCA *1971;* 101 Blacketts Wood Drive, Chorleywood, RICKMANSWORTH, WD3 5PS.
THOMPSON, Mr. Michael James, ACA *1982;* 5 Yeates Close, THAME, OX9 3AR.
•**THOMPSON, Mr. Michael James, BSc ACA FCCA** *1984;* Thompson Elphick Limited, The Corner House, 2 High Street, AYLESFORD, KENT, ME20 7BG.
•**THOMPSON, Mr. Michael John, BSc FCA** *1982;* with Gardiner Fosh Limited, 31 St. Johns, WORCESTER, WR2 5AG.
•**THOMPSON, Mr. Michael John, MA ACA** *1983;* (Tax Fac), Michael Thompson Accountants Ltd, 32 Surrey Street, NORWICH, NR1 3NY.
THOMPSON, Mr. Michael John, BA ACA *1998;* Metdist Trading Limited, 80 Cannon Street, LONDON, EC4N 6EJ.
THOMPSON, Mr. Michael Peter, BA ACA *2007;* 14 Old Watling Street, CANTERBURY, CT1 2DX.
THOMPSON, Mr. Michael Robert, FCA *1977;* 20 Park Road, Alrewas, BURTON-ON-TRENT, DE13 7AG.
•**THOMPSON, Mr. Michael Roger, BA ACA** *1987;* KPMG LLP, Quayside House, 110 Quayside, NEWCASTLE UPON TYNE, NE1 3DX. See also KPMG Europe LLP
THOMPSON, Miss. Michelle, BA ACA *1989;* 14 Brompton Way, West Bridgford, NOTTINGHAM, NG2 7SU.
•**THOMPSON, Mrs. Michelle, BA ACA** *1994;* Batterbee Thompson & Co Limited, Units 7&8, Cargo Workspace, 41 - 43 George Place, PLYMOUTH, PL1 3DX. See also Thinking Book-keeping Ltd
THOMPSON, Miss. Michelle Louise, BA ACA *2007;* Farthings, Ashampstead, READING, RG8 8RR.
•**THOMPSON, Mr. Myles Heywood, BEng ACA** *1989;* KPMG LLP, 15 Canada Square, LONDON, E14 5GL. See also KPMG Europe LLP
THOMPSON, Mrs. Natacha Jayne, ACA *2003;* Charnwood, 26 Lakeside Road, LYMM, CHESHIRE, WA13 0QE.
THOMPSON, Mr. Neil Philip, BSc ACA CTA *1996;* Ash Cottage, 8 Bankhall Lane, Hale, ALTRINCHAM, CHESHIRE, WA15 0JZ.
THOMPSON, Mrs. Nichola Anne, BSc ACA *1993;* 15 Waldegrave Gardens, TWICKENHAM, TW1 4PQ.
THOMPSON, Mr. Nicholas Raymond, BA FCA *1983;* Nick Thompson Consulting Ltd, 4 Eynella Road, Dulwich, LONDON, SE22 8XF.
THOMPSON, Ms. Nicola Frances, BA ACA *1997;* Charter House The Lane, Gate Helmsley, YORK, YO41 1JT.
THOMPSON, Mr. Patrick, BA(Hons) ACA CF *2001;* Red Roof, Beech Road, Tokers Green, READING, RG4 9EB.
THOMPSON, Mr. Paul, BA ACA *2001;* Yell - One Reading Central, Yell, 23 Forbury Road, READING, RG1 3YL.
THOMPSON, Mr. Paul, BSc ACA *1991;* International Federation of Accountants, 545 Fifth Avenue, 14th Floor, NEW YORK, NY 10017, UNITED STATES.
THOMPSON, Mr. Paul, BSc FCA *1976;* 41 Moorgate Road, ROTHERHAM, SOUTH YORKSHIRE, S60 2AD.
THOMPSON, Mr. Paul, MBA FCA *1970;* Prosper Capital LLP, 4 Quarry Court, Lime Quarry Mews, GUILDFORD, SURREY, GU1 2RD.
THOMPSON, Mr. Paul, BA ACA *2011;* 7 Avocet Wharf, NOTTINGHAM, NG7 1TH.
THOMPSON, Mr. Paul Adrian, BSc ACA *1985;* 5 Lon y Fro, Pentyrch, CARDIFF, CF15 9TE.
THOMPSON, Mr. Paul Craig, BA(Hons) ACA *2010;* Flat 407, Naylor Building West, 1 Assam Street, LONDON, E1 7QL.
•**THOMPSON, Mr. Paul Martin, BA ACA** *1992;* Deloitte LLP, 1 City Square, LEEDS, WEST YORKSHIRE, LS1 2AL. See also Deloitte & Touche LLP
THOMPSON, Mr. Paul Matthew, ACA *1993;* Wash House, Casewick, STAMFORD, LINCOLNSHIRE, PE9 4RX.
THOMPSON, Mr. Paul Simon, BEng ACA CF *1997;* The Granary, Farley Farm Barns, Farley Corner, Great Haywood, STAFFORD, ST18 0UD.
THOMPSON, Mr. Paul Stephen, MEng ACA *1992;* 3 Bull Hill, FOWEY, CORNWALL, PL23 1BZ.
THOMPSON, Mr. Paul William, ACA *2003;* 60 Cherry Tree Way, WITNEY, OXFORDSHIRE, OX28 1AJ.
THOMPSON, Mrs. Pepper Norah, BSc ACA *1990;* 84 Moorside North, Fenham, NEWCASTLE UPON TYNE, NE4 9DU.
THOMPSON, Mr. Peter Barrie, FCA *1974;* 5 Walters Cottages, WADHURST, TN5 6BG.
THOMPSON, Mr. Peter Brian, BCom FCA *1976;* 11 Lancaster Way, Scalby, SCARBOROUGH, YO13 0QH.
THOMPSON, Mr. Peter Geoffrey, BSc ACA *1982;* 9 Jameson Street, LONDON, W8 7SH.
THOMPSON, Mr. Peter Harold Leslie, FCA *1967;* 14 The Wynd, NORTH SHIELDS, TYNE AND WEAR, NE30 2TE. (Life Member)
THOMPSON, Mr. Peter John, ACA *2009;* 672 Chatsworth Road, CHESTERFIELD, DERBYSHIRE, S40 3NU.
•**THOMPSON, Mr. Peter John, BA FCA** *1975;* Peter J. Thompson, 3 Streatley Farm Cottages, Wallingford Road, Streatley, READING, RG8 9PX.
THOMPSON, Mr. Peter Lane, MA FCA *1972;* Klaguni, Mill Fields, NEWTOWN, POWYS, SY16 3JP.
THOMPSON, Mr. Peter Richard, FCA *1971;* 36 Grosvenor Road, Frampton, BOSTON, PE20 1DB.
THOMPSON, Mr. Peter Thomas, FCA *1970;* 39 Claremont Road, Highgate, LONDON, N6 5DA.
THOMPSON, Mr. Philip Anthony, BSc FCA *1979;* with PricewaterhouseCoopers LLP, Benson House, 33 Wellington Street, LEEDS, LS1 4JP.
THOMPSON, Mr. Philip Anthony, FCA *1974;* 18 Maesmelyn, ABERDARE, MID GLAMORGAN, CF44 8RF.
•**THOMPSON, Mr. Philip David, FCA CTA** *1992;* Thompsons MK Limited, 1 Hathaway Court, Crownhill, MILTON KEYNES, MK8 0LG. See also Thompson MK Bookkeeping Services Limited
•**THOMPSON, Mr. Philip Geoffrey, FCA** *1971;* (Tax Fac), P.G. Thompson & Co, 239B High Street, ALDERSHOT, HAMPSHIRE, GU11 1TJ.
THOMPSON, Mr. Philip Gordon, FCA *1950;* 26 Norbury Court, Purton, SWINDON, WILTSHIRE, SN5 4BF. (Life Member)
THOMPSON, Mr. Philip Walker, FCA *1978;* Pinfold Lodge, Main Street, Carsington, MATLOCK, DERBYSHIRE, DE4 4DE.
THOMPSON, Miss. Philippa Claude, MA ACA *2000;* with Deloitte LLP, 2 New Street Square, LONDON, EC4A 3BZ.

THOMPSON, Mr. Phillip Barry, FCA *1970;* 169 Blagdon Road, NEW MALDEN, KT3 4AN.
THOMPSON, Mrs. Rachel Rebecca Rosannette, MA ACA *1997;* The Seasons Mole Hill Green, Felsted, DUNMOW, ESSEX, CM6 3JP.
•THOMPSON, Mr. Richard, BA(Hons) FCA MLIA(Dip) *1986;* (Tax Fac), Wellway Accountants Limited, Borough Hall, Wellway, MORPETH, NORTHUMBERLAND, NE61 1BN. See also Richard Thompson Accountants Limited
•THOMPSON, Mr. Richard, FCA *1975;* R. Thompson & Co, 6 Worthington Crescent, POOLE, DORSET, BH14 8BW.
•THOMPSON, Mr. Richard Charles Woodbridge, BA ACA *1988;* PricewaterhouseCoopers LLP, 7 More London Riverside, LONDON, SE1 2RT. See also PricewaterhouseCoopers
THOMPSON, Mr. Richard Henry, LLB ACA *1983;* 9 Harvey Road, GUILDFORD, GU1 3SG.
THOMPSON, Mr. Richard James, BSc ACA *1988;* 19 Fairfields Drive, Ravenshead, NOTTINGHAM, NG15 9HR.
•THOMPSON, Mr. Richard Lawrence, BA FCA *1994;* Westwood, Knutsford Road, WILMSLOW, CHESHIRE, SK9 6JB. See also Thompson Wright Limited
THOMPSON, Mr. Richard Lee, BA ACA *1998;* 3 Middlethorne Close, LEEDS, LS17 8SD.
THOMPSON, Mr. Richard William, MEng ACA *2000;* 5 Homestead Garth, Ingleby Barwick, STOCKTON-ON-TEES, CLEVELAND, TS17 5FD.
•THOMPSON, Mr. Richard William, BA FCA *1972;* (Tax Fac), Anthony Mundy & Co Ltd, 14 High Street, EAST GRINSTEAD, WEST SUSSEX, RH19 3AW.
•THOMPSON, Mr. Richard William Graham, FCA *1970;* (Tax Fac), Richard Thompson & Company, 15 Swanswell Road, Olton, SOLIHULL, B92 7ET.
THOMPSON, Mr. Robert Charles, LLB *2000;* 9th floor, The Royal Bank of Scotland Plc, 135 Bishopsgate, LONDON, EC2M 3TP.
THOMPSON, Mr. Robert David, BA FCA *1979;* The International School of Kuala Lumpur, PO Box 12645, 50784 KUALA LUMPUR, FEDERAL TERRITORY, MALAYSIA.
THOMPSON, Mr. Robert Graham, BA FCA *1975;* 5 Barcheston Road, Knowle, SOLIHULL, WEST MIDLANDS, B93 9JR.
THOMPSON, Mr. Robert Gregory, BSc ACA CTA *1998;* 1 Rowton Bridge Road, Christleton, CHESTER, CH3 7BD.
THOMPSON, Mr. Robert Jan, BSc ACA *2002;* 24 Edzell Crescent, Westcroft, MILTON KEYNES, MK4 4EW.
THOMPSON, Mr. Robert Malcolm, BSc FCA *1975;* Moorfield School, 11 Ben Rhydding Road, ILKLEY, WEST YORKSHIRE, LS29 8RL.
THOMPSON, Mr. Robert Michael, BA FCA *1983;* D W Group Holdings Ltd, Netherfield Lane, Stanstead Abbotts, WARE, HERTFORDSHIRE, SG12 8HE.
THOMPSON, Mr. Robert Michael Alan, BSc ACA *1998;* 3 Lansdowne Road, TUNBRIDGE WELLS, KENT, TN1 2NG.
THOMPSON, Mr. Robert Nigel, BA ACA *1984;* 354 Woodend Road, WOLVERHAMPTON, WV11 1YD.
THOMPSON, Mr. Robin Mark Eccles, MA ACA MBA *1984;* IBM UK Ltd, 76 Upper Ground, LONDON, SE1 9PZ.
•THOMPSON, Mr. Roger Herbert, FCA *1986;* Clough Taxation Solutions LLP, New Chartford House, Centurion Way, CLECKHEATON, WEST YORKSHIRE, BD19 3QB. See also Clough & Company LLP
THOMPSON, Mr. Roger Martin James, BA ACA *1993;* J P Morgan Fleming Asset Management Finsbury Dials, 20 Finsbury Street, LONDON, EC2Y 9AQ.
THOMPSON, Miss. Roseanne, ACA *2008;* 35 Huron Road, LONDON, SW17 8RE.
•THOMPSON, Mr. Roy Laurence, FCA *1972;* Jasmine Cottage, Highlands Avenue, Ridgewood, UCKFIELD, EAST SUSSEX, TN22 5TD.
•THOMPSON, Mr. Russell Graham, BA ACA CTA FPC *1988;* Thompson & Co, Sterling Offices, 60 Midland Road, WELLINGBOROUGH, NN8 1LU. See also R Thompson & Co Ltd
THOMPSON, Miss. Sally Joanne, MA BSc ACA *2004;* Traidcraft Exchange, Kingsway, GATESHEAD, TYNE AND WEAR, NE11 0NE.
•THOMPSON, Mrs. Samantha Jane, ACA *1997;* Samantha Thompson, Westside, 1 Halliford Drive, Barnham, BOGNOR REGIS, WEST SUSSEX PO22 0AB.
•THOMPSON, Mrs. Sandra June, BA FCA *1990;* PricewaterhouseCoopers LLP, 1 Embankment Place, LONDON, WC2N 6RH. See also PricewaterhouseCoopers
•THOMPSON, Miss. Sara Louise, BA FCA CF *1985;* Smith & Williamson (Bristol) LLP, Portwall Place, Portwall Lane, BRISTOL, BS1 6NA. See also Smith & Williamson Ltd
THOMPSON, Mrs. Sarah, BSc ACA *2001;* The Beeches, Chesham Road, BERKHAMSTED, HERTFORDSHIRE, HP4 2SZ.
THOMPSON, Mrs. Sarah Alison Hilary, BSc ACA *2003;* Alterra House, PO Box HM2565, HAMILTON HMKX, BERMUDA.
THOMPSON, Mrs. Sarah Ann, BA ACA *2000;* Bromley House Bromley Lane, Wellpond Green Standon, WARE, HERTFORDSHIRE, SG11 1NW.
THOMPSON, Miss. Sarah Elizabeth, BA ACA *2005;* The Gateshead Housing Co, Keelmans House, Fifth Avenue, Team Valley Trading Estate, GATESHEAD, TYNE AND WEAR NE11 0XA.
THOMPSON, Mrs. Sarah Janette, BSc ACA AMCT *2002;* 27 Clyde Road, LONDON, N22 7AD.
THOMPSON, Miss. Sarah Louise, BSc ACA *2001;* 36 Manland Avenue, HARPENDEN, HERTFORDSHIRE, AL5 4RF.
THOMPSON, Mr. Simeon John, MEng ACA *2004;* Berendsen Sourcing, Exportgatan 26, Hisings Backa, 42246 GOTHENBURG, SWEDEN.
THOMPSON, Mr. Simon, MEng ACA *2011;* 36 Aland Court, Finland Street, LONDON, SE16 7LA.
•THOMPSON, Mr. Simon Andrew, BA(Hons) FCA *2000;* KPMG Deutsche Treuhand-Gesellschaft, Wirtschaftsprüfungsgesellschaft, Ganghoferstrasse 29, 80339 MUNICH, GERMANY.
THOMPSON, Mr. Simon Christopher, BA ACA *1999;* Queen Camel Cottage High Street, Queen Camel, YEOVIL, SOMERSET, BA22 7NG.
THOMPSON, Mr. Simon John, BSc ACA *1995;* Dods Group Plc, 21 Dartmouth Street, LONDON, SW1H 9BP.
THOMPSON, Mr. Simon Marshall, BA ACA *2001;* 7 Pretoria Road, LONDON, SW16 6RR.
THOMPSON, Mr. Stanley, FCA *1958;* 1 Grey Towers Drive, Nunthorpe, MIDDLESBROUGH, CLEVELAND, TS7 0LS. (Life Member)
•THOMPSON, Mr. Stephen Anthony, BA ACA *1994;* Accounts4business, 20 Moscow Lane, Shepshed, LOUGHBOROUGH, LEICESTERSHIRE, LE12 9EX.
THOMPSON, Mr. Stephen Charles, BA(Hons) ACA *2003;* Sir Joseph Isherwood Ltd Centre for Advanced Industry, Coble Dene, NORTH SHIELDS, TYNE AND WEAR, NE29 6DE.
•THOMPSON, Mr. Stephen Grant, BSc ACA *1989;* with KPMG LLP, One Snowhill, Snow Hill Queensway, BIRMINGHAM, B4 6GN.
THOMPSON, Mr. Stephen Raymond, BA FCA *1983;* 6 Woodhall Park Crescent West, Stanningley, PUDSEY, LS28 7EZ.
THOMPSON, Mr. Stuart, BSc(Hons) ACA *2001;* 8 Fredericks Avenue, CHIPPENHAM, WILTSHIRE, SN14 0UQ.
THOMPSON, Mrs. Susan, BA ACA *1992;* Grey Walls, Boat Lane, Sprotbrough, DONCASTER, DN5 7LU.
THOMPSON, Mrs. Susan Hilary, BA ACA *1985;* with Ernst & Young LLP, 1 Bridgewater Place, Water Lane, LEEDS, LS11 5QR.
THOMPSON, Mrs. Suzanne Nicole, BSc ACA *1992;* 7 Dalebury Road, LONDON, SW17 7HQ.
THOMPSON, Mrs. Theresa Suzanne, BSc ACA *1988;* The Old Lodge East, High Street, Taplow, MAIDENHEAD, SL6 0EX.
THOMPSON, Mr. Timothy Bonar Oldaker, BA ACA *1983;* 9 Cole Close, Witchford, ELY, CB6 2JX.
THOMPSON, Mr. Timothy Clement Bewick, FCA *1972;* Village Farm, Frog Lane, Chilmark, SALISBURY, SP3 5BB.
THOMPSON, Mr. Timothy John, FCA *1970;* 16 Manor Road, ROMFORD, RM1 2RA.
THOMPSON, Mr. Timothy Richard, BA FCA *1978;* 5 Squirrel Chase, Fields End, HEMEL HEMPSTEAD, HP1 2TL.
•ⒹTHOMPSON, Mr. Tony James, FCA *1981;* Piper Thompson, Mulberry House, 53 Church Street, WEYBRIDGE, KT13 8DJ.
THOMPSON, Mrs. Victoria, BSc(Hons) ACA *2008;* Garden Flat, 27 Clarendon Road, BRISTOL, BS6 7EX.
THOMPSON, Miss. Victoria, BA ACA *2011;* 33 Burr Close, LONDON, E1W 1NB.
THOMPSON, Mrs. Victoria Louise, BSc ACA *1999;* Queen Camel Cottage, High Street, Queen Camel, YEOVIL, SOMERSET, BA22 7NG.
THOMPSON, Mr. Vincent Leslie, FCA *1958;* 24 Cadman Road, BRIDLINGTON, NORTH HUMBERSIDE, YO16 6YZ. (Life Member)
THOMPSON, Mr. William Bryan, BA ACA *1996;* 19 Tangmere Grove, KINGSTON UPON THAMES, SURREY, KT2 5GT.
THOMPSON, Mr. William Cummings, BSc(Econ) FCA *1976;* 61 Norman Road, WEST MALLING, ME19 6RN.
•THOMPSON, Mr. William Leslie, FCA *1966;* William L. Thompson & Co, Arbeia Business Centre, 8 Stanhope Parade, SOUTH SHIELDS, TYNE AND WEAR, NE33 4BA.
THOMPSON, Mr. William Murray Howard, LLB ACA *1983;* Webber Wentzel, 10 Fricker Road, Illovo Boulevard, JOHANNESBURG, GAUTENG, 2196 SOUTH AFRICA.
THOMPSON, Mr. William Stuart, FCA *1974;* P O Box HM 967, HAMILTON HM DX, BERMUDA.
THOMPSON, Mrs. Yvonne Christine, BSc ACA *1984;* Lynbury House, Blackdown Avenue, WOKING, GU22 8QG.
THOMPSON-ARNOLD, Mrs. Zoe, LLB ACA *2004;* 27 Homefield Way Earls Colne, COLCHESTER, CO6 2SL.
THOMPSON-CLARKE, Mr. Liam John, ACA *2009;* 102 Bonneville Gardens, LONDON, SW4 9LE.
THOMPSON DIXON, Mrs. Vicki, BA ACA *2001;* 5 Hipsburn Steadings, Hipsburn, Lesbury, ALNWICK, NORTHUMBERLAND, NE66 3QP.
THOMPSON SMITH, Mrs. Amanda Jane, BSc ACA *1994;* Plum Tree House, Thornaby, STOCKTON-ON-TEES, CLEVELAND, TS17 9LF.
THOMPSTONE, Mr. Jason, LLB ACA *2004;* 87 Moss Lane, Timperley, ALTRINCHAM, CHESHIRE, WA15 6JU.
THOMPSTONE, Mrs. Suzanne, BSc(Hons) ACA *2003;* 87 Moss Lane, Timperley, ALTRINCHAM, CHESHIRE, WA15 6JU.
THOMS, Mr. Andrew, BSc ACA *2007;* 9/25 Warringah Road, MOSMAN, NSW 2088, AUSTRALIA.
THOMS, Mr. Mark Ashley, BSc ACA *1994;* 72 The Boulevard, WORTHING, WEST SUSSEX, BN13 1LA.
THOMS, Mr. Peter Young, FCA *1969;* Thoms International Ltd, Suite 1908, St George's Building, Ice House Street, CENTRAL, HONG KONG SAR.
THOMSEN, Mr. Richard, ACA CA(SA) *2008;* Sapphire House, Formula One Management Ltd Sapphire House Churchill Way, Biggin Hill Airport Biggin Hill, WESTERHAM, TN16 3BN.
THOMSETT, Mr. Joe, ACA *2010;* 27 Woodlands Road, SITTINGBOURNE, KENT, ME10 4SP.
THOMSON, Mr. Alan Alexander, BSc ACA DChA *1983;* (Tax Fac), Chantrey Vellacott, Russell Square House, 10-12 Russell Square, LONDON, WC1B 5LF.
•THOMSON, Mr. Alan Stormont, MSc BSc ACA *1990;* Sandison Easson & Co, Rex Buildings, Alderley Road, WILMSLOW, CHESHIRE, SK9 1HY.
THOMSON, Mr. Alasdair Charles Kruger, BSc ACA *1984;* 1 Littledown Avenue, BOURNEMOUTH, DORSET, BH7 7AT.
THOMSON, Mr. Alastair Ogilvie, BA ACA *1979;* 41 Williams Grove, Long Ditton, SURBITON, SURREY, KT6 5RW.
THOMSON, Mr. Alexander James, ACA *2000;* 33 Cranwells Park, BATH, BA1 2YE.
•THOMSON, Mr. Alexander John, FCA *1970;* (Tax Fac), Manningtons, 7-9 Wellington Square, HASTINGS, EAST SUSSEX, TN34 1PD.
THOMSON, Mr. Alexander Steven, ACA *2008;* Flat 4 Elm Court, Royal Oak Yard, LONDON, SE1 3TP.
THOMSON, Mr. Andrew David, MA CA CF *1989; (CA Scotland 1987);* Hurst Morrison Thomson Corporate Finance LLP, The Hub, 14 Station Road, HENLEY-ON-THAMES, OXFORDSHIRE, RG9 1AY. See also Hurst Morrison Thomson
THOMSON, Mr. Andrew James, MMath ACA *2005;* 8 Sandfield Road, ST. ALBANS, HERTFORDSHIRE, AL1 4LA.
THOMSON, Mr. Andrew James, MSc ACA *1999;* Lloyds Banking Group, Floor 4 phase 2, Lovell Park Road, LEEDS, LS1 1NS.
THOMSON, Mr. Andrew James Edward, BSc ACA *1996;* 42 Collett Close, Hedge End, SOUTHAMPTON, HAMPSHIRE, SO30 2RR.
THOMSON, Mr. Andrew James Murray, BA ACA *1986;* 17 Swains Road, BUDLEIGH SALTERTON, EX9 6HT.
THOMSON, Mr. Andrew John, BA FCA *1983;* Bindman & Partners, 275 Gray's Inn Road, LONDON, WC1X 8QB.
THOMSON, Miss. Anne Lesley, FCA *1987;* 19 Berenbel Place, Westleigh, SYDNEY, NSW 2120, AUSTRALIA.
THOMSON, Mr. Brent Antony, ACA CA(NZ) *2009;* 49 Edgar Street, EAST BRISBANE, QLD 4169, AUSTRALIA.
THOMSON, Mr. Brian, FCA *1957;* 16 Clarendon Park, LYMINGTON, HAMPSHIRE, SO41 8AX. (Life Member)
•THOMSON, Mr. Calum MacKenzie, BA FCA *1985;* Deloitte LLP, Hill House, 1 Little New Street, LONDON, EC4A 3TR. See also Deloitte & Touche LLP
THOMSON, Mrs. Carol Emma, BSc(Hons) ACA *2000;* 55 Lincoln Road, LONDON, SE25 4HG.
•THOMSON, Ms. Catherine Jane, MA ACA *1997;* 54 Stewart Street, Paddington, SYDNEY, NSW 2021, AUSTRALIA.
•THOMSON, Mr. Charles Peter, BSc FCA *1983;* Bishop Fleming, Cobourg House, Mayflower Street, PLYMOUTH, PL1 1LG.
THOMSON, Mr. Christopher Frank, FCA *1972;* 4 Wimbledon Road, LONDON, SW17 0UQ.
•THOMSON, Mr. Christopher John, FCA *1968;* Voisey & Co., 8 Winmarleigh Street, WARRINGTON, WA1 1JW.
THOMSON, Mrs. Claire Louise, BA ACA *2001;* 24 Hartington Road, Bramhall, STOCKPORT, CHESHIRE, SK7 2DZ.
THOMSON, Mrs. Claire Therese, BA ACA *1996;* Thorn Lighting Ltd House of Light, Butchers Race, SPENNYMOOR, COUNTY DURHAM, DL16 6HL.
THOMSON, Miss. Clare Elizabeth, BSc ACA *1991;* Oracle Corporation Australia Pty Limited, Tower 5A, 4 Julius Avenue, NORTH RYDE, NSW 2113, AUSTRALIA.
THOMSON, Miss. Clare Josephine, BA FCA ATII *1980;* 4 Horstmann Close, BATH, BA1 3NX.
THOMSON, Mr. Colin Lee, BA ACA *1994;* 24 Hermiston, WHITLEY BAY, TYNE AND WEAR, NE25 9AN.
THOMSON, Mr. Colin Newman, FCA *1973;* 16 Rutland Gardens, SANDY, BEDFORDSHIRE, SG19 1JG.
THOMSON, Mr. Craig Fergus, BSc ACA *1992;* 17 Kings Avenue, LONDON, W5 2SJ.
•THOMSON, Mr. David Bruce, FCA *1967;* Ivensco Limited, 50 Regent Street, RUGBY, WARWICKSHIRE, CV21 2PU.
THOMSON, Mr. David George, BSc ACA *2007;* with PKF (UK) LLP, 4th Floor, 3 Hardman Street, MANCHESTER, M3 3HF.
THOMSON, Mr. David Richmond, MA FCA *1962;* Coppice House, 3 Manor Lane, Glaston, OAKHAM, LE15 9BT. (Life Member)
THOMSON, Mr. Donald Macbeth, BA FCA *1977;* 8 West Chapelton Avenue, Bearsden, GLASGOW, G61 2DG. (Life Member)
THOMSON, Mrs. Ekaterina, ACA *1997;* 17 Kings Avenue, LONDON, W5 2SJ.
THOMSON, Miss. Emma Jane Margaret, BA(hons) ACA *2009;* 8 Old Dairy Mews, LONDON, SW12 8EL.
THOMSON, Miss. Fiona, LLB ACA CTA *2003;* with Ernst & Young LLP, 1 More London Place, LONDON, SE1 2AF.
THOMSON, Mrs. Frith, BSc ACA *2005;* 8 Sandfield Road, ST. ALBANS, HERTFORDSHIRE, AL1 4LA.
THOMSON, Mr. Geoffrey Alexander, FCA *1950;* Chiltern, Homend Crescent, LEDBURY, HR8 1AQ. (Life Member)
THOMSON, Mr. George Ian Collier, FCA *1973;* 1 Pednor Cottages, Pednor, CHESHAM, BUCKINGHAMSHIRE, HP5 2SX.
THOMSON, Mr. Graeme Paul, MA FCA MInstD *1982;* 197 Kings Hall Road, BECKENHAM, BR3 1LL.
THOMSON, Mr. Graham Arnold, BSc ACA *1990;* 8 Caplaw Way, PENICUIK, EH26 9JE.
THOMSON, Mr. Graham Ronald, ACA *2007;* 19 Stoneacre Avenue, Ingleby Barwick, STOCKTON-ON-TEES, CLEVELAND, TS17 0XE.
THOMSON, Mr. Gregor Currie, LLB ACA *1999;* 24 Chipstead Street, LONDON, SW6 3SS.
THOMSON, Mr. Hamish Blyth, BA ACA CPA *1986;* Office of the Attorney General State of New Mexico, 111 Lomas Blvd. NW Suite 300, ALBUQUERQUE, NM 87102, UNITED STATES.
THOMSON, Mr. Iain Kenneth Cameron, MA FCA *1964;* Worcester Cottage, Mews Lane, WINCHESTER, HAMPSHIRE, SO22 4PS.
THOMSON, Mr. Ian Stewart, BSc ACA *1988;* Brooklaines Farm, Staverton, CHELTENHAM, GLOUCESTERSHIRE, GL51 0TW.
THOMSON, Mr. Ian Stuart, BSc ACA CTA *1986;* 42 Whistler Street, Highbury, LONDON, N5 1NH.
THOMSON, Mr. James, ACA *2011;* Flat 44 Ionian Building, 45 Narrow Street, LONDON, E14 8DW.
THOMSON, Mr. James Alexander, LLB ACA *2000;* 96 Waverley Road, ST. ALBANS, HERTFORDSHIRE, AL3 5TQ.
THOMSON, Mr. James David, ACA *2010;* 94 Commodore House, Juniper Drive, LONDON, SW18 1TZ.
THOMSON, Mr. James Michael Douglas, MA ACA *1992;* DTZ Holdings Plc, 125 Old London Street, LONDON, EC2N 2BQ.
THOMSON, Mr. Jeremy Duncan, BSc ACA *1991;* 21 Moss Drive, SUTTON COLDFIELD, B72 1JQ.

•**THOMSON, Miss. Joanna Clare, BA ACA** *1992;* Cirrus Accounting & Bookkeeping Ltd, 39 Linden Road, Westbury Park, BRISTOL, BS6 7RN.
THOMSON, Mrs. Joanna Mary, BA ACA *1995;* 42 Ewell Downs Road, EPSOM, SURREY, KT17 3BW.
THOMSON, Mr. John Thacker, FCA *1948;* 25 Heath Road, WEYBRIDGE, SURREY, KT13 8TJ. (Life Member)
THOMSON, Mr. John Wells, MA FCA *1964;* 16 Royal York Crescent, Clifton, BRISTOL, BS8 4JY.
•**THOMSON, Mr. John Wilson, FCA** *1974;* Ghyseland 93, 3161 VH RHOON, NETHERLANDS.
THOMSON, Mr. Jonathan David, MA ACA *2000;* Rua Afonso Braz 747, Apto 201C, Vila Nova Conceicao, SAO PAULO, 04511-011, BRAZIL.
THOMSON, Mr. Jonathan David, BSc ACA *1983;* 288A Reef Road, FAIRFIELD, CT 06824, UNITED STATES.
THOMSON, Mr. Jonathan Paul, BSc ACA *2006;* Flat 11 Kingfisher Court, 8 Swan Street, LONDON, SE1 1BF.
THOMSON, Miss. Kathryn Ann, BSc ACA DChA *2001;* with Kingston Smith LLP, Devonshire House, 60 Goswell Road, LONDON, EC1M 7AD.
THOMSON, Miss. Kathryn Elizabeth, BA(Hons) ACA *2000;* 10 Avenue Road, KINGSTON UPON THAMES, SURREY, KT1 2RB.
THOMSON, Mr. Keith, BCom ACA *1981;* 6 High Street, Great Baddow, CHELMSFORD, CM2 7HQ.
•**THOMSON, Mr. Kevin Michael, BA FCA** *1989;* Laverick Walton & Co, Unit A1 Marquis Court, Team Valley, GATESHEAD, TYNE AND WEAR, NE11 0RU.
THOMSON, Miss. Lauren, ACA *2006;* Flat D, 51 Milner Square, LONDON, N1 1TX.
•**THOMSON, Mrs. Lesley Rowena, LLB(Hons) FCA** *1983;* Ivensco Limited, 50 Regent Street, RUGBY, WARWICKSHIRE, CV21 2PU. See also Novatax Limited
THOMSON, Mrs. Lucy, BA ACA *1992;* Linhay Barn, Tuell, Milton Abbot, TAVISTOCK, DEVON, PL19 8PY.
THOMSON, Mrs. Margaret Ann, MA FCA *1977;* Millbrook House, High Street, Tattenhall, CHESTER, CH3 9PX.
•**THOMSON, Miss. Margaret Jane, BSc FCA** *1976;* (Tax Fac), Margaret Thomson, 6 Broadpark, Brampford Speke, EXETER, EX5 5HP.
THOMSON, Mrs. Melanie, BSc ACA *2003;* 3 Helvellyn Rise, The Beeches, CARLISLE, CA2 6QL.
THOMSON, Mr. Michael Robert, BSc ACA *1987;* Delta Partnership, Mezzanine Floor, Berkeley Court, Glentworth Street, LONDON, NW1 5PG.
THOMSON, Mr. Neil Hamilton, BA ACA *1996;* Yum! Restaurants (India) Pvt. Ltd, 12th FloorTower D, Global Business Park, DELHI, CAPITAL TERRITORY OF DELHI, INDIA.
THOMSON, Mr. Neil John Macaulay, MA ACA *1992;* Rue du President 58, 1050 BRUSSELS, BELGIUM.
•**THOMSON, Mr. Paul Jonathan, BA ACA** *1995;* Deloitte LLP, 1 City Square, LEEDS, WEST YORKSHIRE, LS1 2AL. See also Deloitte & Touche LLP
THOMSON, Mr. Paul Ryan, BA FCA *1981;* 4400 Biscayne Blvd., Suite 900, MIAMI, FL 33137, UNITED STATES.
THOMSON, Mr. Peter, BA ACA *1982;* 87 Candle Tce. SW, CALGARY T2W 6G7, AB, CANADA.
THOMSON, Mr. Peter Charles, FCA CTA TEP *1982;* Fiduciary Management Ltd, Portland House, Glacis Road, GIBRALTAR, GIBRALTAR.
THOMSON, Mr. Peter James, BA(Hons) ACA *2001;* Mabe, Carr Federal 51 km.110, Poblado Ojo Seco, 38158 CELAYA, MEXICO.
THOMSON, Mrs. Polly Louise, MA ACA *1991;* Burchanan Cottage, Drymen, GLASGOW, G63 0BG.
THOMSON, Mr. Richard, BSc ACA *2002;* 13 Alfriston Road, LONDON, SW11 6NS.
THOMSON, Mr. Richard, BA ACA *2011;* 23a Seaford Road, Ealing, LONDON, W13 9HP.
THOMSON, Mr. Richard Stewart, BSc(Hons) ACA *2003;* Husco International Ltd, 6 Rivington Road Whitehouse Industrial Estate, RUNCORN, CHESHIRE, WA7 3DT.
•**THOMSON, Mr. Robert Brian, BA FCA** *1970;* (Tax Fac), Thomson & Co, 2 Oakfield Lane, KESTON, BR2 6BY. See also Electronic Tax Limited
THOMSON, Mr. Robert David, MA ACA *1992;* Newhouse Farm, Low Street, Oakley, DISS, IP21 4AP.
THOMSON, Mr. Robert George, BSc(Econ) FCA *1965;* Flat 7, 8 Arkwright Road, LONDON, NW3 6AE. (Life Member)
THOMSON, Mr. Robert Hugh Gordon, MA FCA *1974;* Low Murrah, Berrier, PENRITH, CA11 0XD. (Life Member)
THOMSON, Mr. Robert Keith, BSc FCA *1969;* Yew Trees, 4 New Road, ESHER, KT10 9PG. (Life Member)
THOMSON, Mr. Roger Philip Alexander, FCA *1964;* Ingleboro, Villocq Lane, Castel, GUERNSEY, GY5 7SB. (Life Member)
THOMSON, Miss. Ruth, BSc ACA *1992;* 48 Hamilton Road, TWICKENHAM, TW2 6SN.
•**THOMSON, Mrs. Sarah Margaret Elaine, BA ACA** *1999;* with KPMG LLP, 6 Lower Brook Street, IPSWICH, IP4 1AP.
THOMSON, Ms. Shona, BA ACA *1993;* 9 Crosby Road, West Bridgford, NOTTINGHAM, NG2 5GG.
THOMSON, Mr. Simon Christopher, BA ACA *1996;* #01-15 Gold Coast Condo, 360 Pasir Panjang Road, SINGAPORE 118699, SINGAPORE.
THOMSON, Miss. Sonya Le'Anne, ACA *2008;* 15 Torlesse Street, NELSON 7011, NEW ZEALAND.
•**THOMSON, Mr. Stephen, BSc ACA** *1988;* Liberty Financial Solutions Group Ltd, Cranfield Innovation Centre, University Way, Cranfield Technology Park, Cranfield, BEDFORD MK43 0BT.
THOMSON, Mr. Stephen Ian, BEng ACA *1994;* The Old Mill, The Green, Coleford, RADSTOCK, BA3 5LY.
THOMSON, Mr. Stuart Nicholas, LLB ACA *1993;* 17 Kings Orchard, Brightwell-cum-Sotwell, WALLINGFORD, OXFORDSHIRE, OX10 0QY.
THOMSON, Mr. William Arthur Ian, MA ACA *1979;* 856 W Buckingham, Unit 2W, CHICAGO, IL 60657, UNITED STATES.
THOMSON, Mr. William Graham, BSS FCA *1972;* P.O. Box 7, Wallan, MELBOURNE, VIC 3756, AUSTRALIA.
THOMSON, Mr. William Robert, BA FCA *1989;* 8 Turnberry Lane Collingtree, NORTHAMPTON, NN4 0PA.
THONG, Mr. Harry Wan Seang, MSc ACA FCCA *2007;* 17 Station Close, LONDON, N3 2SE.
THONG, Mr. Hou Loo, BA ACA *1981;* Lot 23 3 floor Block C Damai Plaza, Phase IV Luyang, 88300 KOTA KINABALU, SABAH, MALAYSIA.
THONG, Mr. John How Ley, ACA *1981;* 315 Telok Kurau Road, SINGAPORE 423863, SINGAPORE.
THONG, Miss. Lau Theng, BSc ACA *1990;* 17 Cantonment Drive, 10350 PENANG, MALAYSIA.
THONG, Miss. Mei Hui, BA ACA *2010;* 22 Newmarket Way, FLEMINGTON, VIC 3031, AUSTRALIA.
THONG, Mr. Peng Hoong, FCA *1975;* Unit 11, 1088 Heidelberg Road, IVANHOE, VIC 3079, AUSTRALIA.
THONG, Mr. Ricky Yew Fook, FCA *1979;* 330 Sikamat Gardens, 70400 SEREMBAN, MALAYSIA.
THONG, Ms. Siew Quen, ACA *2007;* 6B Block 1, Villa Rhapsody, Symphony Bay, SHA TIN, NEW TERRITORIES, HONG KONG SAR.
THOOFER, Ms. Rajkamal Kaur, BCom FCA *2001;* 4 Park Lane, Langley, SLOUGH, SL3 7PF.
THOONG, Ms. Cai Lay, BSc ACA *2007;* 60 Broomfield Street, Poplar, LONDON, E14 6BQ.
THORBURN, Miss. Felicity, ACA *2011;* 15 Stonehill Road, Headley Down, BORDON, HAMPSHIRE, GU35 8JJ.
THORBURN, Mr. Ian Gordon, MA FCA *1966;* 6 Alan Road, LONDON, SW19 7PT.
THORBURN, Mr. John Alexander, BSc FCA *1993;* Danbro Accounting Limited, Unit 15 Thompson Road Whitehills Business Park, BLACKPOOL, FY4 5PN.
•**THORBURN, Mr. Paul James, ACA** *1980;* Baker Tilly Tax & Advisory Services LLP, 1210 Centre Park Square, WARRINGTON, WA1 1RU.
THORLEY, Mr. Andrew Mark, BSc ACA *1994;* Littlewoods Shop Direct Home Shopping Ltd Skyways House, Speke Road Speke, LIVERPOOL, L70 1AB.
THORLEY, Miss. Carolyn Elizabeth, MA ACA *2001;* 84 Clarence Road, WINDSOR, BERKSHIRE, SL4 5AT.
THORLEY, Mr. Malcolm David, FCA *1958;* Flat 2B, 12 Rutland Road, HARROGATE, HG1 2PY. (Life Member)
THORLEY, Miss. Michelle Amanda, BA ACA *2005;* 12 Broadmead, FARNBOROUGH, HAMPSHIRE, GU14 0RJ.
THORLEY, Mrs. Naomi, BA ACA *2001;* 20 Pickets Street, LONDON, SW12 8QB.
THORLEY, Mr. Richard Stephen, BSc ACA *1985;* 1 The Lawns, Westbury, SHERBORNE, DORSET, DT9 3EL.
THORMAN, Mr. Colin Patrick, BSc ACA *1998;* 4 Riddings Road, Hale, ALTRINCHAM, CHESHIRE, WA15 9DS.
THORN, Mr. Brian Stephen, BSc ACA *1978;* 21 Penn Hill Avenue, Lower Parkstone, POOLE, BH14 9LU.
THORN, Mr. David Andrew, BA ACA *1990;* The Tanzania Cigarette Company, 20 Nyerere Road, P.O Box 40114, DAR ES SALAAM, TANZANIA.
•**THORN, Mrs. Deborah Louise, FCA** *1991;* Champion Accountants LLP, 54 Caunce Street, BLACKPOOL, FY1 3LJ. See also Champion Howarth Moore Limited
THORN, Mr. Denis James, BA ACA *1979;* with Ernst & Young, Ernst & Young Building, 8 Exhibition Street, MELBOURNE, VIC 3000, AUSTRALIA.
THORN, Mr. Dennis Harold, FCA *1955;* 45 Lankers Drive, North Harrow, HARROW, HA2 7PA. (Life Member)
•**THORN, Mr. Ernest Joseph, FCA** *1969;* Ernie Thorn, 47 Buttermere Drive, Onchan, ISLE OF MAN, IM3 2EB.
THORN, Mr. Maurice Leslie, FCA *1971;* 3 Cefn Morfa, LLANDRINDOD WELLS, POWYS, LD1 5NP.
•**THORN, Mr. Peter, FCA CTA** *1980;* (Tax Fac), Peter Thorn, 38 Greenways, CHELMSFORD, CM1 4EF.
THORN, Mr. Peter John, FCA *1968;* The Taft, Wolseley Bridge, STAFFORD, ST17 0XL. (Life Member)
THORN, Miss. Rebecca Julie, ACA *2008;* 107 Claremont, ALLOA, CLACKMANNANSHIRE, FK10 2DN.
THORN, Mr. Rex Stuart, FCA *1959;* White Horses, 2 Tanners Dean, LEATHERHEAD, KT22 8RU.
THORN, Mr. Tony William Albert, FCA *1957;* 24 Moffats Lane, Brookmans Park, HATFIELD, AL9 7RU. (Life Member)
THORNBER, Mr. Andrew John, LLB ACA *1992;* 16 Tufters Fold, Bailiff Bridge, BRIGHOUSE, WEST YORKSHIRE, HD6 4EY.
THORNBER, Mr. Mark, BSc ACA *1990;* ch. des Voirons 18, CH-1296 COPPET, SWITZERLAND.
THORNBERRY, Mr. Mark, BSc(Hons) ACA *2003;* 38 Pole Lane, DARWEN, LANCASHIRE, BB3 3LD.
THORNBORROW, Mr. Michael David, BCom ACA *2000;* 1 Brookhouse Place, BISHOP'S STORTFORD, HERTFORDSHIRE, CM23 2GA.
THORNBURY, Mr. Anthony, BSc FCA *1978;* Courtney House, Riverside, Newland, SELBY, NORTH YORKSHIRE, YO8 8PS.
THORNDIKE, Mr. Cyril William, FCA *1951;* 16 Bryn y Bia Road, LLANDUDNO, GWYNEDD, LL30 3AS. (Life Member)
THORNDYKE, Mrs. Helen Louise, BA ACA *1999;* 9a Pinecroft Road, WOKINGHAM, BERKSHIRE, RG41 4AL.
THORNDYKE, Mr. James Anthony, BSc ACA *1999;* 9a Pinecroft Road, WOKINGHAM, BERKSHIRE, RG41 4AL.
THORNE, Miss. Alana Kim Marie, ACA *2008;* 45c St. Johns Park, LONDON, SE3 7JW.
THORNE, Mrs. Alison Claire, BA ACA *1996;* Lane End Cottage, Brimpton Lane, Brimpton, READING, RG7 4RF.
THORNE, Mr. Andrew Derek, BA FCA *1993;* 2 Letcombe Place, Horndean, WATERLOOVILLE, HAMPSHIRE, PO8 0DE.
THORNE, Mr. Ben, ACA *2011;* 16 Julian Street, PLYMOUTH, PL4 0PR.
THORNE, Mr. Christopher Derek, MSc BEng ACA *1998;* Garden Flat, 55 Avonmore Road, LONDON, W14 8RT.
THORNE, Mr. Colin Charles, ACA *1981;* 12 Gelli Crescent Risca, NEWPORT, GWENT, NP11 6QG.
THORNE, Mr. David Charles, BSc ACA *1980;* British Petroleum Co Plc, 3rd Floor, 1 St. James's Square, LONDON, SW1Y 4PD.
•**THORNE, Mr. David John, BSc FCA** *1983;* Charles Taylor Insurance Services Ltd, Lloyds Chambers, 1 Portsoken Street, LONDON, E1 8BT.
THORNE, Mrs. Elizabeth Jane, BA ACA *1997;* 7 Little Woodfalls Drive, Woodfalls, SALISBURY, SP5 2NN.
THORNE, Mr. George Alan, FCA *1973;* 62 The Crescent, Tingley, WAKEFIELD, WEST YORKSHIRE, WF3 1SA.
THORNE, Mr. Gerald Anthony, FCA *1964;* 34 Gorham Avenue, Rottingdean, BRIGHTON, BN2 7DP. (Life Member)
THORNE, Mr. Graham Peter, BA ACA *1986;* Hitachi Solutions Europe Ltd, Hillgate House 26 Old Bailey, LONDON, EC4M 7HW.
THORNE, Mr. James Maurice, BSc ACA *2010;* 27 Radbourne Road, LONDON, SW12 0EA.
THORNE, Mr. Jason Mark, ACA *1998;* Deloitte Touche Tohmatsu, Grosvenor Place, 225 George Street, P.O. Box No 250, SYDNEY, NSW 2000 AUSTRALIA.
THORNE, Mr. John Graham, FCA *1965;* Copplestone, Bridge Street, Great Kimble, AYLESBURY, HP17 9TW.
•**THORNE, Mr. John Trevor, ACA FCCA** *2009;* TTR Barnes Limited, 3-5 Grange Terrace, Stockton Road, SUNDERLAND, SR2 7DG. See also TTR Barnes Financial Services Limited
•**THORNE, Mr. Jonathan Townsend, MA FCA CTA DChA** *1984;* Financial Reporting Council, Aldwych House, 71-91 Aldwych, LONDON, WC2B 4HN.
THORNE, Mr. Julian Robert, FCA *1991;* 3 Old Town Mews, 26 Market Close, POOLE, DORSET, BH15 1NE.
THORNE, Mrs. Karen Julia, BSc ACA *1993;* C J T Thorne & Co Ltd, Union Point, Eastbourne Road, Ridgewood, UCKFIELD, TN22 5SS.
THORNE, Mr. Kenneth Frank, FCA *1965;* The Bungalow, 22 Homestead Gardens, Frenchay, BRISTOL, BS16 1PH.
THORNE, Mr. Mark, BSc(Hons) ACA *2004;* 49 Cobbold Road, LONDON, W12 9LA.
THORNE, Mr. Matthew James, MSci ACA *2001;* 3 Paradise Walk, LONDON, SW3 4JL.
THORNE, Mr. Matthew Wadman John, MA FCA *1978;* The Mount, Bannerdown Road, BATH, BA1 8EG.
•**THORNE, Mr. Michael, BSc ACA** *1999;* Deloitte LLP, Abbots House, Abbey Street, READING, RG1 3BD. See also Deloitte & Touche LLP
THORNE, Mrs. Nicola Louise, BA ACA *2000;* Flat 2, 141 Redland Road, Redland, BRISTOL, BS6 6XX.
THORNE, Mr. Nigel John, FCA *1975;* 219 Exeter Road, HARROW, HA2 9PF.
THORNE, Ms. Philippa Marie, BSc(Hons) ACA *2003;* Basement Flat, 36 Belmont Road St. Andrews, BRISTOL, BS6 5AS.
THORNE, Mr. Raymond, FCA *1966;* Peckwater, Eddystone Road, Thurlestone, KINGSBRIDGE, TQ7 3NU.
THORNE, Mr. Robert James, BA ACA *1991;* 62 Littlebrook Gardens, Cheshunt, WALTHAM CROSS, HERTFORDSHIRE, EN8 8QH.
THORNE, Mr. Simon, BSc FCA *1984;* 20 Woodend Park, COBHAM, KT11 3BX.
THORNELL, Miss. Stephanie Mary, BA ACA *2004;* 29/6-12 Pacific Street, MANLY, NSW 2095, AUSTRALIA.
THORNELOE, Mr. Simon Darius, BSc ACA *2010;* 84 Iverson Road, LONDON, NW6 2HH.
THORNES, Mr. Frederick Colin, FCA *1961;* 4 Wendron Way, Idle, BRADFORD, BD10 8TW.
THORNETT, Mr. Dennis William Eric, FCA *1972;* 8 Leighton Street, Woburn Sands, MILTON KEYNES, MK17 9PJ.
THORNEWELL, Mr. Andrew Gordon, ACA *1988;* PO Box 124, MKONDENI, 3204, SOUTH AFRICA.
THORNEYCROFT, Mrs. Amanda Cecile, MA ACA *1987;* 18 Great Groves, St James Hamlet, WALTHAM CROSS, EN7 6SX.
•**THORNEYCROFT, Mr. Gary Martin, FCA** *1987;* Charcroft Baker, 5 West Court, Enterprise Road, MAIDSTONE, KENT, ME15 6JD. See also Real Time Accounting Limited
THORNEYCROFT, Mr. Martin, BCom ACA *1987;* 18 Great Groves, Goffs Oak, WALTHAM CROSS, EN7 6SX.
THORNEYCROFT, Mr. Neville Clifford, FCA *1959;* 16 Cestreham Crescent, CHESHAM, HP5 3DB. (Life Member)
THORNHILL, Miss. Amanda Mary, BSc ACA *1997;* 9 Highfield Road, DERBY, DE22 1GX.
THORNHILL, Mr. Andrew James, BA ACA *2004;* 5/4 Fairlight Crescent, Fairlight, SYDNEY, NSW 2094, AUSTRALIA.
THORNHILL, Miss. Deborah Jane, BSc FCA *1980;* Allys Mill, Derby Road, KINGSBRIDGE, DEVON, TQ7 1JL.
THORNHILL, Miss. Emma, ACA AMAT *2011;* 46 Woodnook Drive, LEEDS, LS16 6PF.
THORNHILL, Mr. Howard, FCA *1976;* 126 Osmaston Road, LEICESTER, LE5 5JG.
THORNHILL, Mr. Martin James, BA(Hons) ACA *2000;* 109 Langley Grove, Sandridge, ST. ALBANS, HERTFORDSHIRE, AL4 9DZ.
THORNHILL, Mr. Michael Jack McCoan, FCA *1970;* Hillbrow Bungalow, Pitt Lane, Hurstpierpoint, HASSOCKS, BN6 9QA.
THORNHILL, Mr. Paul, BA ACA *1997;* Barclaycard, 1234 Pavilion Drive, NORTHAMPTON, NN4 7SG.
THORNHILL, Mr. Richard, BSc ACA *1999;* 121 Salcott Road, LONDON, SW11 6DG.
THORNHILL, Mr. Russell, BA(Hons) FCA *1989;* 9 Keswick Road, TWICKENHAM, TW2 7HL.
THORNHILL, Mr. Stephen Paul, ACA *1988;* 66 Allport Road, CANNOCK, STAFFORDSHIRE, WS11 1DY.
THORNILEY, Mr. Owen Richard, FCA *1956;* Sunnydale, 10 Stoke Road, Leavenheath, COLCHESTER, CO6 4PP. (Life Member)

THORNLEY, Mr. Colin, FCA *1959;* Apartment B12/1D, Vila Sol, Morgadinhos, 8125-307 VILAMOURA, ALGARVE PORTUGAL. (Life Member)
THORNLEY, Mr. Dennis Anthony, FCA *1947;* 115 Willifield Way, LONDON, NW11 6YE. (Life Member)
THORNLEY, Mrs. Helen, ACA *1992;* Vickers Laboratories Ltd Richardshaw Road Grangefield Industrial Estate, PUDSEY, WEST YORKSHIRE, LS28 6QW.
THORNLEY, Miss. Helen Annette, MA ACA *2006;* The Flat, Carleton Hill, Carleton, PENRITH, CUMBRIA, CA11 8TZ.
•THORNLEY, Mr. James, BSocSc ACA *1995;* KPMG d.o.o. Beograd, Kraljice Natalije 11, 11000 BELGRADE, SERBIA.
•THORNLEY, Mr. Mark Stephen, BSc ACA *1988;* Mark Thornley Associates, 3 Wain Close, Little Heath, POTTERS BAR, EN6 1NF.
THORNLEY, Mr. Richard William, BSc ACA *1983;* Beech Cottage Oakmere Avenue, Withnell, CHORLEY, LANCASHIRE, PR6 8AX.
THORNLEY, Miss. Sarah Judith, ACA *2010;* 21 Primrose Drive, Yaxley, PETERBOROUGH, PE7 3WD.
•THORNTON, Mr. Alan Frederick, FCA *1982;* Morgan Cameron Limited, Wittas House, Two Rivers, Station Lane, WITNEY, OXFORDSHIRE OX28 4BH.
THORNTON, Mrs. Allison Jane, BA ACA *1990;* 2 Riversmeade, Bromley Cross, BOLTON, BL7 9YJ.
THORNTON, Mr. Alvin Richard, FCA *1958;* 22 Jalan Datuk, Sulaiman 3, 60000 KUALA LUMPUR, FEDERAL TERRITORY, MALAYSIA. (Life Member)
•THORNTON, Mrs. Amanda Louise, BSc ACA *1995;* Amanda Thornton, Saltwood, Onslow Crescent, WOKING, SURREY, GU22 7AU.
THORNTON, Mrs. Ann Margaret, BSc FCA *1973;* 2179 Chesapeake Harbour, Drive E, ANNAPOLIS, MD 21403, UNITED STATES.
THORNTON, Mr. Anthony Gerard, BSc ACA *1982;* The Communication Group Plc, 19 Buckingham Gate, LONDON, SW1E 6LB.
THORNTON, Mr. Bernard, FCA *1973;* Cranehurst, High Street, CRANBROOK, TN17 3DT.
THORNTON, Mrs. Catrin Elisabeth, BSc ACA *1987;* 28 Alwyn Avenue, Chiswick, LONDON, W4 4PB.
THORNTON, Mr. Charles Gerard, BSc ACA *1990;* 22 Park Drive East, MIRFIELD, WF14 9NH.
THORNTON, Mr. Christopher Ronald, BSc ACA *1990;* Dairy Crest Ltd, 14-40 Victoria Road, ALDERSHOT, GU11 1TH.
THORNTON, Mr. Christopher William, ACA *2005;* 28 Mast Close, Carlton Colville, LOWESTOFT, SUFFOLK, NR33 8GU.
THORNTON, Mrs. Claire Patricia, ACA *2008;* 62 Shawdene Road, MANCHESTER, M22 4AL.
THORNTON, Mr. Clifford, FCA *1969;* 17 Springfield, Ovington, PRUDHOE, NE42 6EQ.
THORNTON, Mr. Craig Russell, LLB ACA *2003;* Kingsmead, 2 Abingdon Close, WORCESTER PARK, SURREY, KT4 8UL.
•THORNTON, Mr. David, ACA *1979;* High Fold, Keighley Road, Cowling, KEIGHLEY, BD22 0LA.
THORNTON, Mr. David Anthony, BSc FCA *1998;* 14 Heathside Park, CAMBERLEY, SURREY, GU15 1PT.
THORNTON, Mr. David Charles, BA ACA *1990;* 80 Melaleuca Drive, PALM BEACH, QLD 4221, AUSTRALIA.
THORNTON, Mr. David Ian, FCA *1961;* Wren House, 27 Manor Road, Bishopsteignton, TEIGNMOUTH, DEVON, TQ14 9SU.
THORNTON, Mr. David John, FCA *1965;* 16 Nichols Way, WETHERBY, WEST YORKSHIRE, LS22 6AD.
THORNTON, Mr. David Leslie, FCA *1968;* 4 Cricketers Close, Ackworth, PONTEFRACT, WF7 7PW. (Life Member)
THORNTON, Mr. David Stephen, BSc FCA *1980;* Suite 601 Wing On House, 71 Des Voeux Road, CENTRAL, HONG KONG ISLAND, HONG KONG SAR.
•THORNTON, Mrs. Denise, FCA *1970;* Apartment 502, Valley Mill, Park Road, ELLAND, WEST YORKSHIRE, HX5 9GZ.
THORNTON, Mr. Desmond James, FCA *1977;* 4 Ailesbury Way, Ailesbury Road, Ballsbridge, DUBLIN 4, COUNTY DUBLIN, IRELAND.
THORNTON, Mr. Dominic, ACA *2009;* 22 Nottingham Road, Nuthall, NOTTINGHAM, NG16 1DP.
THORNTON, Mr. Edward Damian Charles, MA ACA *1988;* 128 Court Lane, Dulwich, LONDON, SE21 7EA.
THORNTON, Ms. Elisabeth Anne, BSc ACA *2003;* 142 Topsham Road, LONDON, SW17 8SP.
THORNTON, Mr. Francis Philip, BA FCA *1979;* Failand, 7 The Ridge, WALTON ON THE NAZE, CO14 8RF.
THORNTON, Mr. Gary John, MA FCA *1993;* 15 Ewart Road, Forest Hill, LONDON, SE23 1AY.
THORNTON, Mr. George, FCA *1960;* Taree, 3 Brecklands Green, North Pickenham, SWAFFHAM, PE37 8LG. (Life Member)
THORNTON, Mr. George Mark, BSc ACA *1993;* 22 Leonie Hill Road, 08-02 Leonie Parc View, SINGAPORE 239195, SINGAPORE.
THORNTON, Miss. Gillian, BA(Hons) ACA *2009;* 17 Kings Park, LEIGH, WN7 1UE.
THORNTON, Mr. Graham, BSocSc ACA *1998;* (Tax Fac), 14 Moor Lane, Sherburn-In-Elmet, LEEDS, LS25 6DN.
THORNTON, Mr. Graham Francis, FCA *1959;* 19 Glenroy Road, HAWTHORN, VIC 3122, AUSTRALIA. (Life Member)
THORNTON, Mr. Henry Forster, LLB FCA *1965;* 9 Whinfell Road, Darras Hall, NEWCASTLE UPON TYNE, NE20 9EP.
THORNTON, Mr. James, BSc ACA *1981;* 17 Hunter Close, EAST BOLDON, NE36 0TB.
THORNTON, Mr. James Fitzgerald, MA MBA ACA *1983;* Strand Partners Ltd, 26-28 Mount Row, LONDON, W1K 3SQ.
•THORNTON, Mr. James Paul, FCA *1972;* (Tax Fac), J.P. Thornton & Co, The Old Dairy, Adstockfields, Adstock, BUCKINGHAM, MK18 2JE.
THORNTON, Mr. James Stephen, BA ACA *1991;* 2 Riversmeade, Bromley Cross, BOLTON, BL7 9YJ.
•THORNTON, Mr. John Geoffrey, FCA *1955;* J.G. Thornton, Elfrey, 157 Holly Lane, Erdington, BIRMINGHAM, B24 9LA.
•THORNTON, Mr. John Richard, FCA *1978;* (Tax Fac), Thorntons, 2 Tuffnells Way, HARPENDEN, AL5 3HH.
THORNTON, Mr. John Timothy, FCA *1969;* 5 Gayhurst Court Mews, Clares Cottage, Gayhurst, NEWPORT PAGNELL, BUCKINGHAMSHIRE, MK16 8LG.
THORNTON, Mr. Jonathan Douglas, BSc ACA *1995;* 5 Southwood Lawn Road, Highgate, LONDON, N6 5SD.
THORNTON, Mr. Jonathan George Trevelyan, MA FCA *1971;* 79 Woodland Gardens, LONDON, N10 3UD.
THORNTON, Mr. Jonathan Henry, BA ACA *1984;* 1 Woodsome Lees, Kirkburton, HUDDERSFIELD, HD8 0PJ.
THORNTON, Miss. Juliet Margaret Claire, ACA *1992;* South Barn, Chestlion Lane, Bourton Road, Clanfield, BAMPTON, OXFORDSHIRE OX18 2PA.
THORNTON, Mr. Justin Charles David, BA ACA *2000;* 3 The Paddocks, SOUTHWELL, NOTTINGHAMSHIRE, NG25 0NR.
THORNTON, Mrs. Louise Jane, BSc ACA *2002;* with PricewaterhouseCoopers LLP, 101 Barbirolli Square, Lower Mosley Street, MANCHESTER, M2 3PW.
THORNTON, Mrs. Lynnette Marie, BA ACA *1999;* 6 Rockingham Court, Towton, TADCASTER, NORTH YORKSHIRE, LS24 9TL.
•THORNTON, Mrs. Margaret Rosemary, FCA *1981;* (Tax Fac), Morgan Cameron Limited, Wittas House, Two Rivers, Station Lane, WITNEY, OXFORDSHIRE OX28 4BH.
THORNTON, Mrs. Marion, FCA *1968;* 41 Long Meadow Lane, Natland, KENDAL, CUMBRIA, LA9 7QZ.
THORNTON, Mr. Mark Robert, BSc ACA *2004;* with BDO LLP, 1 Bridgewater Place, Water Lane, LEEDS, LS11 5RU.
•THORNTON, Mr. Martin Stephen Richard, BSc FCA *1991;* Calthorn & Co, Headwell House, Headwell, Curry Mallet, TAUNTON, TA3 6SX.
THORNTON, Mr. Michael, FCA *1962;* 11 Valley View, Burnopfield, NEWCASTLE UPON TYNE, NE16 6JD. (Life Member)
THORNTON, Mr. Michael John, FCA *1975;* 14 Fielding Road, Bedford Park, LONDON, W4 1HL.
•THORNTON, Mr. Michael Jonathan, BSc ACA CF *1987;* Grant Thornton UK LLP, 30 Finsbury Square, LONDON, EC2P 2YU. See also Grant Thornton LLP
•THORNTON, Mr. Michael Robert, BEng ACA *2001;* with PricewaterhouseCoopers LLP, 2 Humber Quays, Wellington Street West, HULL, HU1 2BN.
THORNTON, Mr. Michael Royston, ACA *2008;* 1 The Spinney, BROXBOURNE, HERTFORDSHIRE, EN10 7LR.
•THORNTON, Miss. Naomi Jane, MA ACA *1997;* Completion Accounts Ltd, 19 St. Margarets Road, LONDON, SE4 1YL.
THORNTON, Mr. Neil, BEng ACA *1993;* 24 St Stephens Avenue, ASHTEAD, KT21 1PL.
THORNTON, Mr. Oliver Philip, MEng ACA *2007;* 62 Shawdene Road, MANCHESTER, M22 4AL.
•THORNTON, Mr. Reginald Bruce, BA ACA *1983;* 11 Kent Road, NOTTINGHAM, NG3 6BE.
THORNTON, Mr. Richard Francis, BSc ACA *1980;* 33 Castellain Mansions, Castellain Road, Maida Vale, LONDON, W9 1HE.
THORNTON, Mr. Richard James, BA FCA *1975;* The Old Farm, Nant Alyn Road, Rhydymwyn, MOLD, CH7 5HQ.
THORNTON, Mr. Robert, FCA *1969;* 142 Baslow Road, SHEFFIELD, S17 4DR.
THORNTON, Mr. Robert Walter, BA ACA *1996;* Royal Free Hospital, Pond Street, LONDON, NW3 2QG.
•THORNTON, Mr. Robert William, FCA *1973;* Williamson Morton Thornton LLP, 47 Holywell Hill, ST. ALBANS, HERTFORDSHIRE, AL1 1HD.
THORNTON, Mr. Robin Miles, BA ACA *1983;* Kirklees Leisure Ltd, Stadium Way, HUDDERSFIELD, HD1 6PG.
THORNTON, Mrs. Rosemary Anna, MA ACA *1996;* 8 Wimbish Road, Papworth Everard, CAMBRIDGE, CB23 3XJ.
THORNTON, Mrs. Sarah Frances Elizabeth, BSc ACA *2009;* 7 Eastfield Close, Cockett, SWANSEA, SA1 6SG.
THORNTON, Mrs. Sarah Jayne, BA ACA *2001;* 18 Chestnut Green Monk Fryston, LEEDS, LS25 5PN.
THORNTON, Mr. Scott, ACA *2008;* 58 Lady Ediths Park, SCARBOROUGH, NORTH YORKSHIRE, YO12 5PD.
•THORNTON, Dr. Simon John, PhD BA ACA *1996;* PKF (Channel Islands) Ltd, PO Box 296, Sarnia House, Le Truchot, St Peter Port, GUERNSEY GY1 4NA. See also PKF Guernsey Ltd
THORNTON, Mr. Stuart, BSc ACA *1988;* Prospect Hospice, Moormead Road, Wroughton, SWINDON, SN4 9BY.
THORNTON, Mrs. Sunita, BSc ACA ATII ACT *1995;* 7 Islington Park Mews, LONDON, N1 1QL.
THORNTON, Mr. Terrence Michael, BSc FCA *1989;* 25 Quarrendon Road, AMERSHAM, HP7 9EF.
THORNTON, Mr. Thomas Noel, MA FCA *1969;* Dunelm, Main Street, Stoke Dry, RUTLAND, LE15 9JG.
THORNTON, Mr. Timothy Edward, BA(Hons) ACA *2009;* Flat 402 Castlegate, 2 Chester Road, MANCHESTER, M15 4QG.
THORNTON, Mr. Timothy John, BSc(Hons) ACA CFA *2001;* 97 Luscinia View, Napier Road, READING, RG1 8AE.
THORNTON, Mrs. Tracey Anne, BA ACA *2002;* Walton Lodge Laundry Ltd, 374 Coldharbour Lane, LONDON, SW9 8PL.
THORNTON, Mrs. Victoria, BSc ACA *2007;* with PricewaterhouseCoopers LLP, 1 Embankment Place, LONDON, WC2N 6RH.
THORNTON, Mrs. Victoria Jane, BSc ACA *2005;* 97 Luscinia View, Napier Road, READING, RG1 8AE.
THORNTON, Miss. Zoe Kristine, BA ACA *2000;* 9 Vine Road, GREAT SUTTON, CHESHIRE, CH66 2XX.
THORNTON-BRYAR, Mr. Mark Alister, BA FCA *1997;* 1 Bakers End, LONDON, SW20 9ER.
THORNTON-BRYAR, Ms. Sara Louise, BSc ACA *1998;* 60 Leigh Road, COBHAM, KT11 2LD.
THOROGOOD, Mr. Frank Arnold, FCA *1961;* 4 Rue Du Chemin Noir, 78711 MANTES LA VILLE, FRANCE. (Life Member)
•THOROGOOD, Mr. Kingsley Marcus, FCA *1965;* Calpe Lodge, 31/6 Governor's Parade, PO Box 889, GIBRALTAR, GIBRALTAR.
THOROGOOD, Mr. Neil Grant, BA FCA *1984;* Care First Management Services Ltd, Unit 3 Great Barr Business Park, BIRMINGHAM, B42 1DY.
THOROGOOD, Mr. Robert, ACA *2007;* B D O Stoy Hayward Llp 2 City Place, Beehive Ring Road London Gatwick Airport, GATWICK, WEST SUSSEX, RH6 0PA.
THOROUGHGOOD, Mr. Ian, ACA *2010;* 44 Collingwood Fields, East Bergholt, COLCHESTER, CO7 6QN.
•THORP, Mrs. Barbara Elizabeth, BSc ACA *1981;* FM Associates, 49 Newall Terrace, DUMFRIES, DG1 1LN.
THORP, Mr. David Allan, BA FCA *1970;* Southlands Farm, Dunkeswell, HONITON, DEVON, EX14 4SH.
THORP, Mr. Mark Stuart, BSc FCA ATII *1987;* Byways, 105 Lache Lane, CHESTER, CH4 7LT.
THORP, Mr. Paul Michael, FCA *1980;* 76 Downlands, ROYSTON, SG8 5BY.
THORP, Mr. Richard Simon, BSc FCA *1989;* 26 Murray Mews, LONDON, NW1 9RJ.
THORP, Mr. Simon Peter John, BA ACA *1998;* 9 St. Georges Terrace, Jesmond, NEWCASTLE UPON TYNE, NE2 2SU.
THORP, Mr. Timothy Geoffrey, BA ACA *1992;* 3 St. Georges Road, SEVENOAKS, KENT, TN13 3ND.
THORP, Mr. William Peter Thompson, BA(Hons) ACA *2002;* 17 Park Road, STOCKPORT, CHESHIRE, SK4 4PY.
THORP-HINCKS, Miss. Amanda Jane, FCA *1976;* 24 Palamos Road, LONDON, E10 7JF.
THORPE, Mr. Adam Patrick, BA ACA *1998;* 41 Rue Emile Roux, 94120 FONTENAY SOUS BOIS, FRANCE.
THORPE, Mr. Alan John, BCom FCA *1968;* Coetir, 7c Wrecclesham Hill, FARNHAM, SURREY, GU10 4JN.
THORPE, Mrs. Amrat, BSc ACA *2000;* 59 Woodland Drive, WATFORD, WD17 3BY.
THORPE, Mr. Andrew, FCA *1986;* 3 Stead Mews, Eckington, SHEFFIELD, S21 4YF.
THORPE, Mr. Andrew John, BA ACA *2005;* Flat 3 Brooklands, Park Crescent, Roundhay, LEEDS, LS8 1HX.
THORPE, Mr. Andrew Julian, BSc ACA *1992;* 52 Priory Road, LOUGHBOROUGH, LE11 3PP.
THORPE, Mrs. Angela Maria Adele, BA ACA *2004;* DE & S Site, Room113 F Block Ensleigh, Granville Road, BATH, BA1 9BE.
THORPE, Mrs. Carole Elizabeth, ACA *1988;* (Tax Fac), Church View, 7a Strumpshaw Road, Brundall, NORWICH, NR13 5PA.
THORPE, Miss. Catherine Jane, BA ACA *2002;* with Deloitte LLP, Hill House, 1 Little New Street, LONDON, EC4A 3TR.
THORPE, Mr. Christopher James, MEng ACA *2004;* with KPMG LLP, 15 Canada Square, LONDON, E14 5GL.
THORPE, Mr. Christopher Peter, BA ACA *1991;* 6912 Howard Lane, EDEN PRAIRIE, MN 55346, UNITED STATES.
•THORPE, Mr. Dale Antony, BSc FCA DChA *1990;* Baker Tilly Tax & Advisory Services LLP, 3 Hardman Street, MANCHESTER, M3 3HF. See also Baker Tilly Corporate Finance LLP
THORPE, Mr. David Michael, BSc ACA *1989;* 29 Cairn Avenue, Guiseley, LEEDS, LS20 8QQ.
THORPE, Mr. David Peter Baxter, BSc ACA *2006;* 63g Lewisham Hill, Lewisham, LONDON, SE13 7PL.
THORPE, Mr. David Rodney, FCA *1959;* 9 Oakwell Crescent, ILKESTON, DE7 5GX. (Life Member)
THORPE, Mr. Derek, BSc ACA *1993;* 77 Mead Way, COULSDON, SURREY, CR5 1PQ.
THORPE, Mr. Godfrey Clifford, FCA *1973;* 12 Walnut Drive, Wendover, AYLESBURY, HP22 6RT.
THORPE, Mr. Hereward, FCA *1955;* 13 Duffield Road, Irlams O'th Height, SALFORD, LANCASHIRE, M6 7RE. (Life Member)
THORPE, Mr. Hugh Mansfield, LLB ACA *2002;* 52 Hawkins Crescent, Bradley Stoke, BRISTOL, BS32 8EH.
•THORPE, Mr. John Albert, FCA *1974;* Penlee Consulting Ltd, 32 Chiltern Road, Wendover, AYLESBURY, BUCKINGHAMSHIRE, HP22 6DA.
THORPE, Miss. Katie Elizabeth, BA ACA *2006;* Spencer House, 27 St James's Place, LONDON, SW1A 1NR.
THORPE, Ms. Lynne, BA ACA *1985;* 40 Mulberry Close, Goldthorpe, ROTHERHAM, SOUTH YORKSHIRE, S63 9LB.
THORPE, Mr. Michael, BSc ACA *1988;* Liverpool & Victoria Insurance, 80 Cheapside, LONDON, EC2V 6EE.
•THORPE, Mr. Michael Christopher, ACA *1994;* 12 Highfield Court, Wombwell, BARNSLEY, SOUTH YORKSHIRE, S73 8JJ.
THORPE, Mr. Michael Edwin, BSc(Econ) ACA *1987;* Group Finance Old Bank Building, The Co-operative Group (C W S) Ltd New Century House, Corporation Street, MANCHESTER, M60 4ES.
THORPE, Mr. Nicholas Andrew, FCA *1986;* (Tax Fac), Thomas Cook Ltd, Unit 15-30, The Thomas Cook Business Park, Coningsby Road, Bretton, PETERBOROUGH PE3 8SB.
THORPE, Mr. Nicholas Bruce Hugh, FCA *1964;* Calle Angel Urzaiz 16, El Puerto de Santa Maria, 11500 CADIZ, SPAIN.
•THORPE, Mr. Paul, BA(Hons) ACA *2002;* Thorpes Limited, Moorgate Crofts Business Centre, South Grove, ROTHERHAM, SOUTH YORKSHIRE, S60 2DH.
THORPE, Mr. Peter John, BSc ACA *1999;* 19B Woodland Road, LONDON, SE19 1NS.
THORPE, Mr. Peter John, FCA *1971;* Whitethorn Lodge, Harrington Road, Brinkhill, LOUTH, LN11 8QY.
•THORPE, Mr. Phillip Arthur, ACA FCCA *1989;* (Tax Fac), Church View, Strumpshaw Road Brundall, NORWICH, NORFOLK, NR13 5PA.
THORPE, Mr. Richard John, BA FCA *1982;* 3 Nelson Road, NEW MALDEN, KT3 5EA.
THORPE, Mr. Simon Anthony, BA FCA AMCT *1993;* c/o Compliance Section, Investment Services Department, ADIA, PO Box 3600, ABU DHABI, UNITED ARAB EMIRATES.
THORPE, Mr. Simon Charles, BA ACA *1986;* Southbank, 13 Avenue Road, BISHOP'S STORTFORD, CM23 5NS.

THORPE, Mr. Simon Peter, CEng FCA JDipMA *1972;* Harlesford Cottage, Stoke Talmage Road, Tetsworth, THAME, OXFORDSHIRE, OX9 7BU. (Life Member)
THORPE, Mr. Stuart Kenneth, BA(Hons) FCA *2000;* (Tax Fac), Arnold Clark Automobiles Ltd, 134 Nithsdale Drive, GLASGOW, G41 2PP.
THORPE, Mr. Terence, BSc ACA *1987;* 2 The Lock Cottages, Springwell Lane, RICKMANSWORTH, HERTFORDSHIRE, WD3 8UF.
THORPE, Mr. William Bloice, FCA *1970;* 3 Wedgwood Way, Beulah Hill, LONDON, SE19 3ES.
•**THORPE-MANLEY, Mrs. Claire Simone, BA(Hons) ACA** *2002;* Langdowns DFK Limited, Fleming Court, Leigh Road, EASTLEIGH, HAMPSHIRE, SO50 9PD.
THOULASS, Mrs. Emma, FCA *2001;* (Tax Fac), with Miller & Co., 86 Princess Street, LUTON, LU1 5AT.
THOY, Miss. Samantha Suzanne, BSc(Hons) ACA *2002;* 11 Brookfield Avenue Nettleham, LINCOLN, LN2 2TF.
THOYTS, Mr. Robert David William, FCA *1964;* 25 Carlton Road, Porchester, FAREHAM, HAMPSHIRE, PO16 8JN.
THRALL, Mr. Andrew John, FCA *1970;* Lansdowne, Church View, Stowmarket Road, Wetherden, STOWMARKET, SUFFOLK IP14 3JP.
THRASHER, Mr. Mark Adrian, BA ACA *1991;* Pump Cottage Taylors Lane, Oakhanger, CREWE, CW1 5XB.
THRASHER, Mrs. Maxine, BA ACA *1994;* Bussey Stool Farm, Tarrant Gunville, BLANDFORD FORUM, DORSET, DT11 8JS.
THRASYVOULOU, Miss. Dena, BA ACA *2005;* 174A Eirinis Str, Megaron Petrides, 1st floor Flat 12, Katholiki, 3022 LIMASSOL, CYPRUS.
THRASYVOULOU, Mr. Spyros, BA ACA *2008;* 13 Emmanouel Xantou, Makedonitissa, 2415 NICOSIA, CYPRUS.
THRASYVOULOU, Mr. Stelios, MEng BA ACA *2002;* Al Habtoor - Specon LLC, PO Box 320, DUBAI, UNITED ARAB EMIRATES.
THRAVES, Mr. Alan, FCA *1964;* 17 Red Scar Lane, Newby, SCARBOROUGH, YO12 5RH.
THRAVES, Mr. Jonathan Mark, BA ACA *1994;* 42 Northumberland Road, BRISTOL, BS6 7BD.
THREADGOLD, Ms. Sarah Jennifer, BEng ACA *1994;* 20 Nugent Road, LISBURN, COUNTY ANTRIM, BT28 3NB.
THRELFALL, Mr. Christopher Richard, BSc FCA *1981;* with KPMG LLP, 15 Canada Square, LONDON, E14 5GL.
THRELFALL, Mr. John Peter, FCA *1959;* Wynyates, The Drive, Hook Heath, WOKING, GU22 0JS. (Life Member)
THRELFALL, Mr. Nicholas David, BSc ARCS ACA *1996;* Polygon Investment Partners Llp, 4 Sloane Terrace, LONDON, SW1X 9DQ.
THRELFALL, Mrs. Rachael Anne, BSc ACA CTA *1995;* Nationwide Bldg Soc, Kings Park Road, Moulton Park, NORTHAMPTON, NN3 6NW.
THRELFALL, Mr. Thomas Roger Bracewell, FCA *1953;* P.O. Box 633, MOUNT ELIZA, VIC 3290, AUSTRALIA. (Life Member)
•**THRELKELD, Mr. David John, ACA CTA** *2001;* Armstrong Watson, First Floor East, Bridge Mills, Stramongate, KENDAL, CUMBRIA LA9 4UB.
①**THRESH, Mr. Charles Richard, BSc ACA** *1993;* KPMG, Crown House, 4 Par-la-Ville Road, HAMILTON HM 08, BERMUDA.
THRESH, Mr. John Harold, ACA *1983;* Aspen House, 10 Highfield Grove, Kew, MELBOURNE, VIC 3101, AUSTRALIA.
THRESH, Mr. Richard John, BSc ACA *1985;* 48 Chevington Drive, Heaton Mersey, STOCKPORT, CHESHIRE, SK4 3RG.
THRESHER, Mr. Warwick Richard, MEng ACA *2001;* 7 Coombe Lane, BRISTOL, BS9 2AB.
THRIFT, Mr. David John, FCA *1950;* 5 The Bramblings, Rustington, LITTLEHAMPTON, WEST SUSSEX, BN16 2DA. (Life Member)
THRIFT, Miss. Robin Louise, BA ACA *1990;* Crag House Farm, Low Snowdon, OTLEY, WEST YORKSHIRE, LS21 2NH.
•**THRING, Mr. Christopher Charles, BA ACA** *1991;* Longhill Accounting, 1 Longhill Lodge, Ditcheat, SHEPTON MALLET, SOMERSET, BA4 6QR. See also Chris Thring
THRING, Mr. Clifford Guy, MA FCA ACA *1977;* TBG Limited, Level 8 Penthouse, Bay Street Complex, St. George's Bay, ST JULIANS STJ 3311, MALTA.
THRING, Mr. Peter Streatfeild, TD MA FCA *1960;* Old School House, Cheverells Green, Markyate, ST. ALBANS, AL3 8AB. (Life Member)
•**THROSSELL, Mr. Andrew, FCA** *1983;* (Tax Fac), Hebblethwaites, Westbrook Court, Sharrow Vale Road, SHEFFIELD, S11 8YZ.
THROSSELL, Mr. Colin Paul, BA ACA *2003;* 30 The Street Old Basing, BASINGSTOKE, HAMPSHIRE, RG24 7BX.
THROUP, Mr. Jonathan Mark, BA(Hons) ACA *2003;* 36 Oldacre Close, SUTTON COLDFIELD, B76 1WF.
THROUP, Mrs. Zoe Melissa, BSc ACA *2003;* 36 Oldacre Close, SUTTON COLDFIELD, B76 1WF.
THROWER, Mr. John James, BA ACA *1988;* 222/18 Soi 34, Piman Chon 2, KHON KAEN 40000, THAILAND.
THROWER, Mr. Richard David, BA ACA *2009;* 50 Pullman Lane, GODALMING, GU7 1XY.
THRUSH, Ms. Emma Jane, BSc ACA *1996;* 23 Adelaide Street, Balgowlah Heights, SYDNEY, NSW 2093, AUSTRALIA.
•**THRUSH, Mr. Giles Anthony, BSc FCA CTA** *1990;* (Tax Fac), Richardson Jones Limited, Mercury House, 19/21 Chapel Street, MARLOW, BUCKINGHAMSHIRE, SL7 3HN.
THRUSH, Mrs. Kristina Trudy, BSc ACA *1991;* 9 St. Nicholas Road, HEXHAM, NORTHUMBERLAND, NE46 2EZ.
THRUSSELL, Mr. David, BA ACA *2002;* Wytelow Cottage School Lane, Bunbury, TARPORLEY, CHESHIRE, CW6 9NR.
THRUSSELL, Mrs. Florence Joan, BA ACA *1981;* 2 Wentworth Court, Station Road Harlington, DUNSTABLE, LU5 6HZ.
THRUSTLE, Mr. Ian, BSc ACA *1998;* 1d Fairmile, HENLEY-ON-THAMES, OXFORDSHIRE, RG9 2JR.
•**THUBRON, Mr. Christopher Robert Stanley, FCA** *1971;* Moore Stephens FS, Blue Tower, Avenue Louise 326, Box 30, B 1050 BRUSSELS, BELGIUM. See also Thubron C.R.S.
THULBOURN, Mrs. Deborah Elizabeth, BA ACA *1991;* 49 Falcon Drive, Hartford, HUNTINGDON, PE29 1LP.
•**THUM, Mr. Wai Kar, BA FCA** *1994;* 36 Wood Lane, CATERHAM, SURREY, CR3 5RT.
THUMBI, Mr. John Gichuha, ACA *1995;* Kenya Airports Authority, Jomo Kenyatta Int Airport, PO Box 19001, NAIROBI, 00501, KENYA.
THUMPSTON, Mr. Mark Charles, BSc ACA *2009;* 39 Woodfield Road, SOLIHULL, B91 2DN.
THURAISINGAM, Miss. Sian, BA ACA *2003;* 56 Kingston Road, COVENTRY, CV5 6LR.
THURAISINGHAM, Mr. Amirtharatnam, ACA *1983;* 27 Cassia Drive, SINGAPORE 289720, SINGAPORE.
•**THURBIN, Mr. Jeremy David, MA ACA** *1997;* Ernst & Young S R L, 41 Rue Ybry, 92200 NEUILLY-SUR-SEINE, FRANCE. See also Ernst & Young Europe LLP
•**THURBURN, Mr. Andrew James, FCA** *1977;* Andrew Thurburn & Co, 38 Tamworth Road, CROYDON, CR0 1XU.
THURGOOD, Mr. Christopher John, FCA *1970;* 1520 - 1100 Melville Street, VANCOUVER V6E4A6, BC, CANADA.
•**THURGOOD, Mr. David Robert, FCA** *1983;* with Grant Thornton UK LLP, 30 Finsbury Square, LONDON, EC2P 2YU.
THURGOOD, Mr. Henry Ian, FCA *1972;* The Business Explorer Ltd, Rozel House, 9 High Ridge Crescent, NEW MILTON, HAMPSHIRE, BH25 5BT.
THURGOOD, Mr. Mark, MA ACA *2002;* 10 Taman Warna, Chip Bee Garden, Holland Village, SINGAPORE, SINGAPORE.
THURGOOD, Mr. Simon John, BA FCA *1976;* The Old Coach House, 10 Cotman Road, Thorpe, NORWICH, NR1 4AF.
•**THURKETTLE, Mr. David Malcolm, ACA** *1984;* PricewaterhouseCoopers LLP, 1 East Parade, SHEFFIELD, S1 2ET.
•**THURLBECK, Mr. Ernest Brian, FCA** *1974;* Brian Thurlbeck, Beechmount, 33 Beechwood Terrace, SUNDERLAND, SR2 7LY.
THURLOW, Mr. Alan Christopher, BSc FCA *1980;* with IBM, 76 Upper Ground, South Bank, LONDON, SE1 9PZ.
THURLOW, Mr. David John, FCA *1961;* 5024 Hunting Hills Square, ROANOKE, VA 24018, UNITED STATES. (Life Member)
THURLOW, Mrs. Jane Alice, BA ACA *1999;* 1 Highland Drive, FLEET, GU51 2TH.
THURMAN, Mrs. Deborah Anne, BSc ACA *2005;* Autumn Cottage, 17 High Street, Lois Weeden, TOWCESTER, NORTHAMPTONSHIRE, NN12 8PL.
THURMAN, Mr. James Andrew, BA ACA *2005;* HR Pillar Ref A17.G, Barclaycard, 1234 Pavilion Drive, NORTHAMPTON, NN4 7SG.
THURMAN, Mrs. Sally Elizabeth, BCom ACA *1996;* 8 Church Lane, LONDON, SW19 3PD.
THURMAN, Mrs. Sarah-Jane, ACA *2008;* 11 Railway Terrace, Storforth Lane Hasland, CHESTERFIELD, DERBYSHIRE, S41 0RF.
THURSBY-PELHAM, Mr. Vaughan Brian George, FCA *1955;* 2 Woodlands Avenue, NEW MALDEN, KT3 3UN. (Life Member)
•**THURSFIELD, Mr. David John, BSc FCA DChA** *1981;* (Tax Fac), J W Hinks, 19 Highfield Road, Edgbaston, BIRMINGHAM, B15 3BH.
THURSFIELD, Mr. Ian Charles, ACA *1994;* with KPMG, KPMG Centre, 18 Viaduct Harbour Avenue, P.O. Box 1584, AUCKLAND 1140, NEW ZEALAND.
THURSFIELD, Mr. Paul Anthony, FCA *1976;* 1 Portmans Way, Tasley, BRIDGNORTH, WV16 5AT.
•**THURSFIELD, Mr. Peter, BA FCA** *1989;* Plummer Parsons Accountants Limited, 5 North Street, HAILSHAM, BN27 1DQ. See also Plummer Parsons
THURSTAN, Mr. Matthew James, MSc BSc ACA *2005;* 24 Woodlands Avenue, HARROGATE, NORTH YORKSHIRE, HG2 7SJ.
THURSTANS, Mr. Kenneth John, FCA *1958;* 6 Halatte Gardens, Great Shelford, CAMBRIDGE, CB22 5LE. (Life Member)
THURSTANS, Mr. Stanley Harry, FCA *1950;* 41 Binghams Road, Crossways, DORCHESTER, DT2 8BW. (Life Member)
THURSTON, Mr. Christopher Luke, BA(Hons) ACA *2010;* 235 Aylestone Road, LEICESTER, LE2 7QJ.
THURSTON, Mr. David, BSc ACA *1994;* 89 Chase Side, ENFIELD, MIDDLESEX, EN2 6NL.
THURSTON, Mr. Ernest Albert, FCA *1951;* 10 Cranbrook Drive, ROMFORD, RM2 6AP. (Life Member)
•**THURSTON, Miss. Ivy Elizabeth, FCA** *1955;* Honeywell, High Street, Horam, HEATHFIELD, EAST SUSSEX, TN21 0HA. (Life Member)
THURSTON, Mr. Mark Stuart, BSc ACA *1990;* The Garth, High Lane, HASLEMERE, SURREY, GU27 1BD.
THURSTON, Mrs. Penelope Annette, MA ACA *1979;* 10 Sir Alfreds Way, SUTTON COLDFIELD, B76 1ES.
THURSTON, Mr. Peter, BSc ACA *1990;* 36 Jacey Road, Shirley, SOLIHULL, WEST MIDLANDS, B90 3LJ.
THURSTON, Mr. Peter Leonard, BA FCA *1983;* 20 Guildown Road, GUILDFORD, GU2 4EN.
THWAITES, Mr. George Bernard, BEng ACA *1992;* 144 Cardigan Street, Stanmore, SYDNEY, NSW 2048, AUSTRALIA.
THWAITES, Mr. John Conrad, MSc ACA *1990;* 67 Exley Lane, ELLAND, HX5 0SW.
THWAITES, Mr. Joseph Brian, FCA *1966;* Bayhills, Old Road, Crosby, MARYPORT, CUMBRIA, CA15 6TA. (Life Member)
THWAITES, Mr. Peter, ACA *2011;* K P M G Llp, 15 Canada Square, LONDON, E14 5GL.
•**THWAITES, Mr. Russell John, FCA** *1998;* Gibbons, Lakeland Office, 2 Europe Way, COCKERMOUTH, CUMBRIA, CA13 0RJ. See also Gibbons & Company
THWAITES, Mr. Stuart John, BSc(Hons) ACA *2000;* 1 The Lawns, Bowdon, ALTRINCHAM, CHESHIRE, WA14 2YA.
THYNE, Mr. Peter Lindsay, FCA *1975;* 2 Beekman Place Apt # 3F, NEW YORK, NY 10022, UNITED STATES.
THYNNE, Mr. Adam Charles, MA ACA *1984;* Glenhurst, Linden Gardens, LEATHERHEAD, SURREY, KT22 7HB.
THYNNE, Mrs. Lindsey Patricia, BSc ACA *1985;* Glenhurst, Linden Gardens, LEATHERHEAD, SURREY, KT22 7HB.
THYRA, Mr. Jeetender Singh, BCom ACA *1996;* 25 Stonebridge Road, Brewood, STAFFORD, ST19 9HB.
TIAN, Miss. Kuanrong, MSc BSc ACA *2011;* 13 Undine Road, LONDON, E14 9UW.
TIAN, Miss. Lin Jie, BSc ACA *2008;* 19 Alresford Road, SALFORD, M6 7RF.
•**TIANO, Mr. Martin, FCA** *1986;* Martin Tiano & Co, 2nd Floor, Highview House, 165-167 Station Road, EDGWARE, MIDDLESEX HA8 7JU.
TIBBATTS, Mrs. Christine Anne, BA(Hons) ACA *2004;* 16 Brook Lane, Coton, CAMBRIDGE, CB23 7PY.
TIBBELLS, Mr. John Terence, FCA *1955;* Clarence House, Bryniau, Dyserth, RHYL, LL18 6BY. (Life Member)
TIBBERT, Mr. Mark Richard, BSc ACA *2003;* with Hazlewoods LLP, Windsor House, Bayshill Road, CHELTENHAM, GLOUCESTERSHIRE, GL50 3AT.
TIBBETTS, Mr. Christopher, ACA *1997;* 62 Hunnington Crescent, HALESOWEN, WEST MIDLANDS, B63 3DJ.
TIBBETTS, Mrs. Lindsay Anne, MBA BA ACA *1989;* 3 Baillieswells Terrace, Bieldside, ABERDEEN, AB15 9AR.
TIBBETTS, Mr. Terence Ernest Joseph, FCA *1965;* 5 Bow Bank, Longworth, ABINGDON, OXFORDSHIRE, OX13 5ER. (Life Member)
TIBBITS, Mr. Robert Charles David, BSc ACA *1990;* Second Avenue, Rockley New Road, CHRISTCHURCH, BB 15126, BARBADOS.
TIBBITTS, Mr. Giles St John, ACA *2009;* Deloitte, 80 Queen Street, Private Bag 115-033, AUCKLAND 1140, NEW ZEALAND.
TIBBITTS, Mrs. Victoria Caroline, ACA *2008;* Deloitte Centre, Private Bag 115-033, AUCKLAND 1010, NEW ZEALAND.
TIBBLE, Mr. Timothy Howard, BA FCA *1974;* 326 Madison Avenue, SOUDERTON, PA 18964, UNITED STATES.
TIBELL, Mrs. Zoe Evette, ACA MAAT *1995;* Bounty Group Ltd, 29 Broadwater Road, WELWYN GARDEN CITY, HERTFORDSHIRE, AL7 3BQ.
TIBREWAL, Mrs. Priyanka, ACA *2010;* 59 Elmstead Lane, CHISLEHURST, KENT, BR7 5EQ.
TIBREWAL, Mr. Ratiraj, FCA ACA *2011;* Tibrewal Chand & Co, Chartered Accountants, 1st Floor KK-5, Civil Township, ROURKELA 769004, ORISSA INDIA.
•**TICE, Mr. Colin, FCA** *1986;* (Tax Fac), Cassons, St Crispin House, St. Crispin Way, Haslingden, ROSSENDALE, LANCASHIRE BB4 4PW. See also Cassons & Associates
TICE, Mr. Geoffrey Malcolm, FCA *1970;* 14 Western Road, Branksome Park, POOLE, BH13 7BW.
TICE, Mr. Stephen Graham, ACA *2008;* 5 Trusley Brook, Hilton, DERBY, DE65 5LA.
TICEHURST, Mr. Philip Charles, FCA *1970;* 20 Sadlers Way, Ringmer, LEWES, BN8 5HG.
TICHBAND, Mr. Benjamin Peter, ACA *2008;* 14 Heather Drive, THATCHAM, BERKSHIRE, RG18 4BU.
TICHIAS, Mr. Charles Alan, FCA *1963;* 22 The Wolds, COTTINGHAM, NORTH HUMBERSIDE, HU16 5LF.
TICHIAS, Mr. Ian Alan, BSc ACA *1997;* 16 Priory Road, NEWBURY, RG14 7QN.
•**TICKEL, Mrs. Amanda Judith, LLB ACA** *1999;* (Tax Fac), KPMG LLP, 15 Canada Square, LONDON, E14 5GL. See also KPMG Europe LLP
•**TICKEL, Mr. Mark William, BA FCA** *1991;* with Hilton Sharp & Clarke, 30 New Road, BRIGHTON, BN1 1BN.
TICKELL, Mr. James Richard, BSc FCA *1987;* 21 Southdown Road, Horndean, WATERLOOVILLE, HAMPSHIRE, PO8 0ET.
TICKELL, Mr. Lawson John, ACA *1992;* Sunset Cottage, Old Portreath Road, Sparnon Gate, REDRUTH, TR16 4JA.
•**TICKELL, Mr. Robert Michael, MA FCA** *1987;* LCA Services Ltd, 13 Silver Street, BARNSTAPLE, DEVON, EX32 8HR. See also Devon Finance Director LLP
•**TICKETT, Mr. John, FCA** *1961;* Tickett & Co, 97 Wilmot Way, BANSTEAD, SURREY, SM7 2QA.
TICKLE, Mr. Alan, BSc FCA *1975;* 12 Inglewood, BARROW-IN-FURNESS, LA13 9UN.
TICKLE, Miss. Helen Virginia, MA ACA *2004;* 24 Daisy Hill Close, SALE, CHESHIRE, M33 2HW.
TICKLE, Mr. Mark Simon, BSc FCA *1990;* 57 Seymour Avenue, EPSOM, SURREY, KT17 2RS.
TICKLE, Mr. Paul Jonathan, BSc ACA *1988;* 12 Cunningham Road, BANSTEAD, SM7 3HG.
TICKNER, Mr. Bryan, FCA *1983;* Tejas, 4 The Copse, Turton, BOLTON, BL7 0DP.
TICKNER, Mr. Harry Albert, FCA *1957;* Prospect House, 42A Littlemoor Road, PUDSEY, LS28 9JD. (Life Member)
TICKNER, Mr. William Keith, FCA *1954;* 1 Ebor Close, West Parley, FERNDOWN, BH22 8LZ. (Life Member)
TICKRIDGE, Mr. Malcolm John Graham, FCA *1973;* 22 Stringers Avenue, Jacob's Well, GUILDFORD, SURREY, GU4 7NW.
TIDBALL, Mr. Christopher Nelson, BA ACA *1984;* Europa Partners Limited, 33 St. James's Square, LONDON, SW1Y 4JS.
•**TIDBURY, Mr. Gary, FCA** *1983;* Maynard Heady LLP, 40-42 High Street, MALDON, ESSEX, CM9 5PN. See also Maynard Heady
TIDBURY, Mr. Hugh Anthony Charles, MA ACA *1985;* Hartley Mauditt House, Hartley Mauditt, ALTON, GU34 3BL.
•**TIDBURY, Mr. Nigel Oliver, FCA** *1979;* (Tax Fac), Tiffin Green, 11 Queens Road, BRENTWOOD, ESSEX, CM14 4HE. See also Tiffin Green Accounting Limited
•**TIDBURY, Mr. Raymond Clive, PhD BSc FCA** *1988;* Mazars LLP, Tower Bridge House, St. Katharines Way, LONDON, E1W 1DD.
TIDBY, Mr. Hugh Robert, FCA *1970;* 74 Park Drive, ROTHESAY E2H 2S9, NB, CANADA.
TIDBY, Mr. Martin Lee, BA FCA *1997;* 33 Harvey Crescent, Warsash, SOUTHAMPTON, SO31 9TA.
TIDD, Mr. Benjamin James, MA ACA *2001;* Henderson Global Investors, 201 Bishopsgate, LONDON, EC2M 3AE.
TIDD, Mr. Howard George, FCA *1967;* 1 The Firs, Ongar Road, BRENTWOOD, Essex, CM15 9JF.

TIDDY, Mrs. Kathryn Jane, BSc ACA *1994;* with PricewaterhouseCoopers LLP, 1 Embankment Place, LONDON, WC2N 6RH.
TIDEY, Mr. Andrew Ian, BA(Hons) ACA *2002;* 61 Balham Park Road, LONDON, SW12 8DZ.
TIDMAN, Mr. Duncan, FCA *1965;* 9 Ringley Park Road, REIGATE, RH2 7BJ. (Life Member)
TIDMAN, Miss. Natasha, BSc ACA *2004;* Genesis Housing Group Ltd, Capital House, 25 Chapel Street, LONDON, NW1 5DT.
TIDMARSH, Mr. Alan, BSc FCA *1977;* 10 Whins Avenue, Sabden, CLITHEROE, LANCASHIRE, BB7 9DY.
TIDMARSH, Mr. Anthony Clive Bickerton, FCA *1962;* The White House, Dunley, STOURPORT-ON-SEVERN, DY13 0UF. (Life Member)
TIDMARSH, Mr. John Stephen, FCA *1976;* Gisela Graham Ltd, 12 Colworth Grove, 5 BROWNING STREET, LONDON, SE17 1LR.
•TIDMARSH, Mr. Richard John Studley, ACA *1979;* (Tax Fac), Tidmarsh & Co., Wallace House, 45 Portland Road, HOVE, BN3 5DQ.
TIDSALL, Mr. Peter Eugene, BCom FCA *1954;* Cornerways, 11 Church Lane, Breadsall, DERBY, DE21 5LD. (Life Member)
TIDY, Mr. Alan John, BA FCA *1972;* 55 Le Marchant Road, CAMBERLEY, GU15 1HZ.
TIDY, Mr. Philip David, FCA *1974;* Hinton Cottage, Broad Layings, Woolton Hill, NEWBURY, RG20 9TU.
TIDY, Mr. Thomas Peter, BSc FCA *1973;* Abbots Wootton Cottage, Wootton Fitzpaine, BRIDPORT, DORSET, DT6 6NL.
TIEN, Miss. Van Thi, BSc ACA *2006;* Flat 15, Lockview Court, 67 Narrow Street, LONDON, E14 8EN.
TIERNAN, Miss. Amice Catherine Coyney, BSc(Hons) ACA *2001;* 76 Tennyson Street, LONDON, SW8 3SX.
TIERNAN, Mr. Christopher Cruz, BA ACA *2009;* 254B Lavender Hill, LONDON, SW11 1LJ.
TIERNAN, Mr. Patrick Colm, BBLS ACA *2001;* Dunbar Bank, 33 Jermyn Street, LONDON, SW1Y 6AD.
•TIERNAN, Mr. Sean Michael, ACA *1984;* KPMG LLP, 15 Canada Square, LONDON, E14 5GL. See also KPMG Europe LLP
•TIERNAY, Mr. John Peter Benedict, FCA *1972;* MEMBER OF COUNCIL, TiernayFedrick, 19 Trinity Square, LLANDUDNO, GWYNEDD, LL30 2RD.
•TIERNAY, Mrs. Nicola Ferris, FCA *1972;* (Tax Fac), TiernayFedrick, 19 Trinity Square, LLANDUDNO, GWYNEDD, LL30 2RD.
TIERNEY, Mr. David, BSc ACA *1990;* 136 Old Chester Road Higher Walton, WARRINGTON, WA4 6TG.
TIERNEY, Mrs. Mary Ann, BSc ACA *1991;* (Tax Fac), Mazars The Lexicon, 10-12 Mount Street, MANCHESTER, M2 5NT.
•TIERNEY, Ms. Rose Marie, BA FCA CTA AITI *1994;* Tierney Tax Consultancy, Kilcorran House, Kilcorran, SMITHBORO, COUNTY MONAGHAN, IRELAND. See also Tierney Tax Consultants
TIERNEY, Mr. Wayne, BA ACA *1988;* 5 Old Oak Close, Bradley Fold, BOLTON, BL2 6SF.
TIETJEN, Mr. Clive Richard, BSc ACA *1992;* 1 Manor Barns Lane, FINCHAMPSTEAD, BERKSHIRE, RG40 3TQ.
TIFF, Mr. Nigel, ACA *1986;* National Grid Transco, N G T House, Warwick Technology Park, WARWICK, CV34 6DA.
TIFFEN, Mrs. Jane, BSc ACA *1988;* Finance, Nissan Motor Manufacturing (UK) Ltd, Washington Road, SUNDERLAND, SR5 3NS.
TIFFEN, Mr. John Ronald, FCA *1959;* 85 Riverside Drive, SOLIHULL, B91 3HR. (Life Member)
TIFFIN, Mr. Christopher Donald, ACA CA(SA) *2008;* Mr C Tiffin, P.O.Box 2445, Lonehill, JOHANNESBURG, 2062, SOUTH AFRICA.
•TIFFIN, Mr. Colin Michael, FCA *1967;* Colin Tiffin FCA, Oak Lodge, Livermere Road, Great Barton, BURY ST. EDMUNDS, SUFFOLK IP31 2RZ.
•TIFFIN, Mr. Ralph Cleland, BSc FCA *1976;* McLachlan & Tiffin, Clifton House, Craigard Road, CRIEFF, PH7 4BN.
TIFFIN, Mr. Roy Robert, BA FCA *1967;* P.O. Box 12-111, Thorndon, WELLINGTON, NEW ZEALAND.
TIFFIN, Mr. Steven Neil, MEng ACA *2005;* 10 Campus Martius, Heddon-on-the-Wall, NEWCASTLE UPON TYNE, NE15 0BP.
•TIFFNEY, Mrs. Helen Louise, BA ACA *1990;* South Wing Guildhall, Worcester City Council, Guildhall, WORCESTER, WR1 2EY.
TIGG, Mr. Justin Edward, BSc ACA CTA *2003;* 17 Vale Road, EXMOUTH, DEVON, EX8 2LZ.
TIGHE, Mr. Alan Francis, FCA *1960;* 3 Greenwood Close, Farnsfield, NEWARK, NG22 8DJ. (Life Member)
TIGHE, Miss. Fionnuala Maria, BSc ACA *1998;* 7 Whitmoor Road, BAGSHOT, SURREY, GU19 5QE.
•TIGHE, Miss. Grainne Mary, BE ACA *1989;* 28 Kidmore Road, Caversham, READING, RG4 7LU.
•TIGWELL, Mr. Patrick Jonathan, BSc FCA *1995;* Haines Watts Exeter LLP, 3 Southernhay West, EXETER, EX1 1JG.
TIJANI, Miss. Omolara, BA ACA *2011;* 11 Jamestown Way, LONDON, E14 2DE.
TIKKAS, Mr. Pantelis, PhD MA ACA *1985;* 47 Th. Sofouli Street, Nea Smyrni, 171 22 ATHENS, GREECE.
TIKKIS, Mr. Kyriakos, BSc ACA *2004;* K.N.D.M Purple Property Consultants Ltd, 2 Ammochostou, Dherynia, P.O.Box 36080, 5380 FAMAGUSTA, CYPRUS.
TIKKOO, Mr. Kushan, ACA *2009;* 23 Lime Road, Southville, BRISTOL, BS3 1LS.
TIKKU, Mr. Kaushal, FCA *1975;* Hutchison Whampoa Limited, 22/F Hutchison House, 10 Harcourt Road, CENTRAL, HONG KONG ISLAND, HONG KONG SAR.
•TILBROOK, Mr. Andrew Charles, BA ACA *1982;* AIMS - Andrew Tilbrook, 47 Scraptoft Lane, LEICESTER, LE5 2FD.
TILBROOK, Mr. Christopher John, BA ACA *1995;* 20 Gombards, ST. ALBANS, AL3 5NW.
TILBROOK, Mr. John Jeremy, FCA *1964;* 87 Newmarket Road, NORWICH, NR2 2HP.
•TILBROOK, Mr. Philip Michael, BA FCA *1984;* Tilbrook & Co Ltd, The Lawn, 9 Cross Road, TADWORTH, KT20 5SP.
•TILBROOK, Mr. Roger Gordon, FCA *1973;* Hutchison 3 G UK Ltd Star House, 20 Grenfell Road, MAIDENHEAD, BERKSHIRE, SL6 1EH.
TILBROOK, Mrs. Ruth Elizabeth, BA ACA *1996;* Vinci Plc, Astral House, Imperial Way, WATFORD, WD24 4WW.
TILBROOK, Mrs. Sarah Elizabeth, BA ACA *1996;* 20 Gombards, ST. ALBANS, AL3 5NW.
TILBURY, Mr. Douglas Keith, FCA *1961;* 49 Glenville Road, Rustington, LITTLEHAMPTON, BN16 2EA. (Life Member)
TILBY, Mr. Richard Paul, FCA *1972;* 12 Mill Lane, off The BankScholar Green, STOKE-ON-TRENT, ST7 3LD.
•TILDESLEY, Mr. John Michael, FCA *1959;* J.M. Tildesley, 5 Pednandrea, St. Just, PENZANCE, TR19 7UA.
TILDESLEY, Mr. Thomas Richard William, BA ACA *2001;* 7 Medallion Place, MAIDENHEAD, BERKSHIRE, SL6 1TF.
TILDSLEY, Miss. Genna, BA ACA *2008;* 10a Radbourne Road, LONDON, SW12 0DZ.
•TILE, Mr. Jonathon Warden, ACA *1981;* Tile & Co, Warden House, 37 Manor Road, COLCHESTER, CO3 3LX.
•TILEY, Mrs. Angela, BSc FCA *1983;* Tiley & Co, Parkway Cottage, Andover Road, Highclere, NEWBURY, RG20 9QU.
•TILEY, Mr. John Sheridan, FCA *1966;* J.S. Tiley, Spignalls, Woodlands Road, BROMLEY, BR1 2AE.
•TILEY, Mr. Mark Stephen, BSc FCA *1982;* (Tax Fac), Tiley & Co, Parkway Cottage, Andover Road, Highclere, NEWBURY, RG20 9QU.
TILEY, Mr. Michael Edward Thornhill, MA FCA *1972;* 30 Devonshire Road, Ealing, LONDON, W5 4TP.
TILEY, Mr. Nicholas John, MA ACA *1991;* 149 Coleridge Road, CAMBRIDGE, CB1 3PN.
TILEY-HILL, Ms. Michele Ruth, BSc ACA *1998;* 9 Pages Hill, LONDON, N10 1PX.
TILL, Mr. David John, BA *1992;* 3 Cadogan Gate, LONDON, SW1X 0AS.
•TILL, Mr. Gary Redmond, BA FCA *1987;* Abbots, Printing House, 66 Lower Road, HARROW, MIDDLESEX, HA2 0DH. See also Abbots Chartered Certified Accountants
TILL, Mr. Mark Andre, BA ACA *1982;* 3 Ronbury Close, Barrowford, NELSON, BB9 6SD.
TILL, Mr. Michael Andrew Simon, BA ACA *1994;* Avendia Libertador 2695, Piso 12, BUENOS AIRES, 1425, ARGENTINA.
TILL, Mr. Thomas Laurence, FRICS ACA FAAV *1979;* Powis Castle Estate Office, WELSHPOOL, SY21 8RG.
TILLER, Mr. Frank Barry, FCA *1977;* 44 Bracken Drive, CHIGWELL, IG7 5RF.
•TILLER, Mr. John Alexander, MA FCA DChA *1977;* John Tiller Associates Limited, Glenthorne, Elmstead Road, WEST BYFLEET, SURREY, KT14 6JB.
TILLER, Mr. Matthew John, BSc ACA *1992;* 313 High Street, EASTLEIGH, SO50 5NE.
TILLETT, Mr. David Rupert, FCA *1963;* 2 The Drive, Fordington Road, LONDON, N6 4TD.
TILLETT, Mr. Matthew Russell, BA ACA *1994;* Bank Point Cottage, 62 Jacksons Lane, LONDON, N6 5SX.
TILLETT, Mr. Paul William, BSc ACA *1989;* 6 Nutter Lane, Wanstead, LONDON, E11 2HZ.
TILLEY, Mr. Alan Reginald, BA FCA *1968;* Bryan Mansell & Tilley LLP, 23 Austin Friars, LONDON, EC2N 2QP.
TILLEY, Mrs. Amanda Louise, BSc ACA *1998;* The Old Stall Church Farm, Sunningwell, ABINGDON, OXFORDSHIRE, OX13 6RH.
TILLEY, Mr. Anthony Paul, FCA *1971;* Eversholt Rail (UK) Limited, 210 Pentonville Road, LONDON, N1P 2AR.
TILLEY, Mr. Bruce Anthony Michell, BA ACA *1998;* Little Partridges, Partridge Lane, WADHURST, EAST SUSSEX, TN5 6LA.
TILLEY, Mr. Charles Basil, FCA *1974;* 58 Brodrick Road, LONDON, SW17 7DY.
TILLEY, Mr. Christopher Mark, BSc ACA *1990;* QBE Limited, 88 Leadenhall Street, LONDON, EC3A 3BP.
TILLEY, Mr. Christopher Michael, BSc ACA *2006;* with PricewaterhouseCoopers LLP, 31 Great George Street, BRISTOL, BS1 5QD.
TILLEY, Mr. Christopher Stuart, BSc(Hons) ACA *2001;* Spring Technology, Hazlitt House, 4 Bouverie Street, LONDON, EC4Y 8AX.
TILLEY, Miss. Deborah, BA ACA *2005;* 2a Topsfield Parade, Tottenham Lane, LONDON, N8 8PR.
TILLEY, Mr. Edward John, BSc ACA *1999;* The Old Stall Church Farm, Sunningwell, ABINGDON, OXFORDSHIRE, OX13 6RH.
TILLEY, Mr. James Hugh, MSc FCA *1982;* 50 Dalmeny Road, LONDON, N7 0DY.
TILLEY, Mr. James Stephen, BA ACA *2000;* 2b Tower Street, HERTFORD, SG14 3HD.
TILLEY, Miss. Johanna Ruth, BA ACA *1999;* 90 Nelson Road, LONDON, N8 9RT.
TILLEY, Mr. John Kenneth, ACA *2008;* 15 Mowbray Court, Mowbray Road, LONDON, SE19 2RL.
TILLEY, Miss. Lisa Jane, ACA *1994;* 45 Miles Avenue, Sandford, WAREHAM, DORSET, BH20 7AS.
TILLEY, Mrs. Lucy, BA ACA *2001;* 2 Springbank Court, Sanctuary Lakes, POINT COOK, VIC 3030, AUSTRALIA.
TILLEY, Mrs. Lucy Claire, BSc ACA *1997;* Little Partridges, Partridge Lane, WADHURST, EAST SUSSEX, TN5 6LA.
TILLEY, Mr. Matthew David, BA ACA *2011;* Owen Webb House, 4 Gresham Place, CAMBRIDGE, CAMBRIDGESHIRE, CB1 2EB.
TILLEY, Mrs. Nicola, BA(Hons) ACA *2010;* The Brew House, Talbots End, Cromhall, WOTTON-UNDER-EDGE, GLOUCESTERSHIRE, GL12 8AJ.
TILLEY, Mr. Patrick Anthony, BSc ACA *1992;* Oldfield, 55 Lewes Road, HAYWARDS HEATH, WEST SUSSEX, RH17 7TA.
TILLEY, Mr. Paul, ACA *2004;* Tyco Healthcare, Ashwood, Crockford Lane, Chineham Business Park, Chineham, BASINGSTOKE HAMPSHIRE RG24 8EH.
TILLEY, Mr. Peter Charles, BA ACA *1996;* Rui Visconde de Pirajá, 250 / 7 Andar, Ipanema, RIO DE JANEIRO, 22410-000, BRAZIL.
TILLEY, Mr. Robert Alfred, BA FCA *1965;* Bockhill House, Royal Albert Place, Albert Road North, MALVERN, WORCESTERSHIRE, WR14 2TL. (Life Member)
TILLEY, Mr. Roy William, BA ACA *1989;* 36 Hedgerow Close Rownhams, SOUTHAMPTON, SO16 8JU.
TILLEY, Miss. Suzanne, ACA *2009;* 8 Flacks Mews, Station Road, EPPING, CM16 4HS.
TILLIER, Mr. Daniel George, BSc ACA *2007;* 15 Mallard Row, READING, RG1 6QA.
TILLIN, Mr. Anthony Michael, FCA *1968;* Las Paomas de Son Roig, Apartado de Correos 10, 07184 CALVIA, MALLORCA, SPAIN. (Life Member)
TILLMAN, Mr. Edward Albert, FCA *1961;* Burgstrasse 236, 8706 MEILEN, SWITZERLAND. (Life Member)
TILLMAN, Mr. Michael John, BA ACA *1983;* 2 Church Cottages, Shirwell, BARNSTAPLE, EX31 4JU.
TILLOTSON, Mr. David Malcolm, BA ACA *1981;* Heathfield House, Hollowmoor Heath, Great Barrow, CHESTER, CH3 7LF.
TILLOTSON, Mr. Geoffrey Ronald, MSc FCA *1969;* 104 Gunnersbury Avenue, Ealing, LONDON, W5 4HB. (Life Member)
TILLOTSON, Mr. James Robert, BSc ACA *2007;* with Brebners, The Quadrangle, 180 Wardour Street, LONDON, W1F 8LB.
TILLOTSON, Mr. John Gavin, BSc ACA *1997;* Greetlands, Thornfield Avenue, Waterfoot, ROSSENDALE, LANCASHIRE, BB4 9AP.
TILLOTSON, Mr. Kevin, MSc BA ACA *2007;* 24 Edgell Road, STAINES, MIDDLESEX, TW18 2ES.
TILLS, Ms. Victoria, ACA *2011;* 11 Fairmount Road, Brixton, LONDON, SW2 2BJ.
TILLY, Mr. Andrew Jeremy, BCom ACA *1988;* Apartment 184 Liberty Place, 26-38 Sheepcote Street, BIRMINGHAM, B16 8JZ.
TILLY, Mr. Jervis Alexander, ACA *1995;* 43a Prince Street, MOSMAN, NSW 2088, AUSTRALIA.
TILLYER, Mr. David John, BA ACA *1999;* 44 Mill Pond Close, LONDON, SW8 4SL.
TILMAN, Mrs. Anne, LLB FCA *1982;* Fairmead, Woodland Drive, East Horsley, LEATHERHEAD, KT24 5AN.
TILMAN, Mr. David Ward, BSc ACA *1978;* Fairmead, Woodland Drive, East Horsley, LEATHERHEAD, KT24 5AN.
•TILMAN, Miss. Joan Ann, MA FCA *1982;* (Tax Fac), Tilman & Co, 15 Searle Way, Eight Ash Green, COLCHESTER, CO6 3QS.
TILMOUTH, Mr. Graeme Croft, ACA *1984;* Chedworth, 123 Easthampstead Road, WOKINGHAM, RG40 2HU.
TILNEY, Mr. Michael William Deane, BCom ACA *2009;* 25 Arthur Road, FARNHAM, GU9 8PD.
•TILNEY, Mr. Robin Stenhouse, FCA *1964;* RS Tilney & Co, PO Box 1882, GABORONE, BOTSWANA.
TILSLEY, Mr. Alfred Roy, FCA *1968;* The Cottage, Acton, NEWCASTLE, ST5 4EF.
TILSLEY, Mr. Rhodri Llywelyn, BSc ACA *2003;* 24 Fisher Hill Way Radyr, CARDIFF, CF15 8DR.
TILSON, Mr. Alexander Charles Philip, LLB ACA *2004;* 7 Minshull Place, Park Road, BECKENHAM, BR3 1QF.
TILSON, Miss. Deborah Elizabeth, ACA *1997;* with PricewaterhouseCoopers LLP, 80 Strand, LONDON, WC2R 0AF.
TILSON, Ms. Hannah Lindsay, ACA CTA *2003;* (Tax Fac), Meryka, Darenth Drive, GRAVESEND, DA12 4TA.
•TILSON, Mr. Keith, MA FCA *1980;* PricewaterhouseCoopers LLP, 1 Embankment Place, LONDON, WC2N 6RH. See also PricewaterhouseCoopers
TILSON, Mr. Kevin, BA(Hons) ACA *2003;* Meryka, Darenth Drive, GRAVESEND, DA12 4TA.
TILSTON, Mrs. Claire Marie, BA ACA *1982;* The Orchard, 1 Hare Lane, Claygate, ESHER, KT10 9BT.
TILSTON, Mr. David Frank, BSc FCA FCT *1982;* Mouchel Export House, Cawsey Way, WOKING, GU21 6QX.
TILSTON, Mr. Philip Andrew, BSc ACA *1986;* Hop Cottage Sadlers Hill, Goodnestone, CANTERBURY, CT3 1PF.
TILT, Mr. Jonathan Richard, MA ACA *1995;* 10 Lidgett Way, Royston, BARNSLEY, SOUTH YORKSHIRE, S71 4FD.
TILTMAN, Mr. Edwin Peter, FCA *1955;* 2 Tree Tops, Wombourne, WOLVERHAMPTON, WV5 8DY. (Life Member)
TILTON, Mr. Stephen James, MA FCA *1992;* Apax Partners Ltd, 33 Jermyn Street, LONDON, SW1Y 6DN.
TILY, Miss. Helen Margaret, ACA *1991;* 18 Broad Lane, Upper Bucklebury, READING, RG7 6QJ.
TIMBERLAKE, Mr. Anthony Keith, MA FCA *1966;* 162 Park Hill Road, Harborne, BIRMINGHAM, B17 9HD.
TIMBERS, Mr. Colin Richard, FCA *1975;* 24 Oak Avenue, South Wootton, KING'S LYNN, PE30 3JQ.
•TIMBERS, Mr. Dennis Charles, FCA *1971;* Thickbroom Coventry, 147a High Street, WALTHAM CROSS, EN8 7AP.
TIMBRELL, Ms. Christine Jennifer, FCA *1969;* Flat 6 Eton Court, Vesey Close, SUTTON COLDFIELD, B74 4QN.
•TIMBRELL, Mr. John Darrell, BSc ACA *1993;* Timbrell & Co Ltd, Chiltern House Business Centre, 45 Station Road, HENLEY-ON-THAMES, OXFORDSHIRE, RG9 1AT.
•TIMBRELL, Mrs. Sarah Elizabeth, BSc ACA *1999;* (Tax Fac), Timbrell & Co Ltd, Chiltern House Business Centre, 45 Station Road, HENLEY-ON-THAMES, OXFORDSHIRE, RG9 1AT.
•TIMINIS, Mr. Loizos, BSc ACA *1990;* Sofouli 40 Office 309, 1096 NICOSIA, CYPRUS.
•TIMMERMANS, Mr. Xavier Jean-Pierre Benoit, BA ACA *1987;* with KPMG LLP, One Snowhill, Snow Hill Queensway, BIRMINGHAM, B4 6GN.
•TIMMINS, Mrs. Claire Sarah, ACA FCCA *2011;* 70 St. Peters Road, STOURBRIDGE, DY9 0TU.
TIMMINS, Mr. David John, BA FCA *1983;* Morgan Stanley, 25 Cabot Square, Canary Wharf, LONDON, E14 4QA.
TIMMINS, Mr. David Peter, BA FCA *1977;* HTSPE Ltd, Thamesfield House, Boundary Way, Hemel Hempstead Industrial Estate, HEMEL HEMPSTEAD, HERTFORDSHIRE HP2 7SR.
TIMMINS, Mr. Francis, MA BSc FCA *1975;* Grant Thornton, Private Bag X28, BENMORE, GAUTENG, 2010, SOUTH AFRICA.
TIMMINS, Mrs. Gail, BSc ACA ATII *1990;* (Tax Fac), 4 Oldean Close, Tilehurst, READING, RG31 5QA.
TIMMINS, Mrs. Karen Michelle, BA ACA *1998;* 23 Daintree Way, Hemingford Grey, HUNTINGDON, PE28 9DZ.

TIMMINS, Mr. Norman Edward, FCA *1952;* Sonrisa, Woodstock View, ENNIS, COUNTY CLARE, IRELAND. (Life Member)
TIMMINS, Ms. Wendy Jane, BSc ACA *1991;* St. Germain, The Warren, East Horsley, LEATHERHEAD, SURREY, KT24 5RH.
•TIMMIS, Mr. John Whittome, FCA *1969;* John W Timmis Ltd, Beggars Roost, Whitegates Lane, WADHURST, EAST SUSSEX, TN5 6QG.
TIMMIS, Mr. Michael James Guy, FCA *1959;* 45 Meddins Lane, Kinver, STOURBRIDGE, WEST MIDLANDS, DY7 6BZ.
TIMMS, Miss. Alison Mary, BA ACA *1990;* 27 Kings Ride, Tylers Green, HIGH WYCOMBE, BUCKINGHAMSHIRE, HP10 8BJ.
•TIMMS, Mr. Andrew Henry, BA ACA *2000;* Cooper Parry LLP, 1 Colton Square, LEICESTER, LE1 1QH.
TIMMS, Mrs. Ann, FCA *1974;* Hilton House, 512 Manchester Road, Paddington, WARRINGTON, WA1 3TZ.
TIMMS, Mr. Anthony Arthur, FCA *1972;* 4058 Saanich Road, VICTORIA V8X 1Z5, BC, CANADA.
TIMMS, Mr. Christopher George, BA FCA *1970;* 5 Warwick Dene, Ealing, LONDON, W5 3JG.
TIMMS, Mr. Christopher John, FCA *1975;* Farmborough House, 26 Providence Lane, Long Ashton, BRISTOL, BS41 9DJ.
•TIMMS, Mr. Christopher Michael, BSc FCA *1980;* Easterbrook Eaton Limited, Cosmopolitan House, Old Fore Street, SIDMOUTH, DEVON, EX10 8LS.
TIMMS, Mr. Clive, BSc FCA *1971;* 12 Forest Drive, LONDON, E12 5DF.
TIMMS, Mr. Michael David, BSc(Econ) ACA *2001;* 29 Trefoil Close, WOKINGHAM, RG40 5YQ.
TIMMS, Mr. Michael Jonathan, BSc FCA *1974;* 28 Buckingham Avenue, WEST MOLESEY, KT8 1SY.
TIMMS, Mr. Michael Richard, FCA *1971;* 122 Hazelhurst Road, Kings Heath, BIRMINGHAM, B14 6AG.
•TIMMS, Mr. Peter John, FCA *1968;* (Tax Fac), Kingston Smith LLP, Devonshire House, 60 Goswell Road, LONDON, EC1M 7AD. See also Kingston Smith Limited Liability Partnership, Devonshire Corporate Services LLP and Kingston Smith Consulting LLP
TIMMS, Miss. Rebecca, BSc ACA *2010;* Flat 4 Hillfield Mansions, Haverstock Hill, LONDON, NW3 4QR.
TIMMS, Mr. Roger Edward, FCA *1963;* Acorns, 7 Poplar Row, Theydon Bois, EPPING, ESSEX, CM16 7NB.
TIMMS, Mr. Simon Stuart, FCA *1968;* Rochford House, Church Road, Froxfield, MARLBOROUGH, SN8 3JY. (Life Member)
TIMMS, Mr. Steven Martin, MA FCA *1974;* 44a Jalan Arnap, SINGAPORE 249351, SINGAPORE.
TIMOSHENKO, Mr. Andrey, ACA *2009;* 38 Emlyn Road, LONDON, W12 9TD.
TIMPANY, Ms. Dene, ACA CA(SA) *2009;* B D O Novus Ltd, PO Box 180, GUERNSEY, GY1 3LL.
TIMPERLAKE, Mr. John Edwin, FCA *1956;* 17 Cranmere Avenue, The Wergs, WOLVERHAMPTON, WV6 8TR. (Life Member)
•①TIMPERLEY, Miss. Alison, LLB(Hons) ACA *2001;* with Cooper Parry LLP, 1 Colton Square, LEICESTER, LE1 1QH.
TIMPERLEY, Mrs. Andrea Jane, BSc ACA *1994;* 20 Bishopdale Drive, Collingham, WETHERBY, LS22 5LP.
TIMPERLEY, Mr. Anthony John, MA ACA *1987;* Blythestone, 5 Diddington Lane, Hampton-In-Arden, SOLIHULL, B92 0BY.
TIMPERLEY, Mrs. Louise Helen, BSc ACA *1990;* 19 Meadway, BURY, BL9 9TY.
TIMPERLEY, Mr. Richard Neil, BA ACA *1981;* Countrywide Estate Agents Lombard House, 2 Carrs Road, CHEADLE, CHESHIRE, SK8 2HR.
TIMPSON, Mrs. Julia Helen, BA ACA *2002;* The Dial House, Tirley Lane, Kelsall, TARPORLEY, CHESHIRE, CW6 0PF.
TIMS, Mr. Adam John, BCom ACA *1998;* Steria Ltd, Three Cherry Trees Lane, HEMEL HEMPSTEAD, HERTFORDSHIRE, HP2 7AH.
TIMS, Mr. Ian James, ACA *1992;* 15 Cambridgeshire Close, Warfield, BRACKNELL, RG42 3XW.
TIMS, Mr. Jonathan Paul, BA FCA *1982;* Myrtle Cottage, 182 Castle Street, Portchester, FAREHAM, PO16 9QH.
TIMSON, Mr. Oliver Daniel, BA(Hons) FCA *2001;* Pear Tree House, Attleborough Road, Rockland All Saints, ATTLEBOROUGH, NORFOLK, NR17 1UG.
TIMSON, Mrs. Sara Catreona, FCA *1998;* 72 Arden Way, MARKET HARBOROUGH, LEICESTERSHIRE, LE16 7DD.
TIN, Mr. Chung Fat, ACA *2008;* No 5 Lorraine Place, Oatlands, SYDNEY, NSW 2117, AUSTRALIA.
TIN, Mr. William, ACA *2005;* 4C Tower One, Grandview Garden, 18 Bridges Street, MID LEVELS, HONG KONG ISLAND, HONG KONG SAR.
TIN YAN, Mr. Lim Min Koon Qee Fong, ACA *1986;* 16 Candlelight Drive, RICHMOND HILL L4E 5E4, ON, CANADA.
TINCKLER, Mr. Robert William, FCA *1974;* YR Ltd, 44 Trevelyan, BRACKNELL, RG12 8YD.
TINCKNELL, Miss. Karen Clare, BA(Hons) ACA *2003;* 1 Bywell Court, Kingsmead, MILTON KEYNES, MK4 4HE.
TINCKNELL, Mr. Richard John Charles, BSc FCA *1988;* 4 Lamtarra Way, NEWBURY, BERKSHIRE, RG14 7WB.
•TINDAL, Mrs. Sian Alison, MA ACA *1991;* Sian Tindal, The Brew House, School Lane, Cookham, MAIDENHEAD, BERKSHIRE SL6 9QN.
TINDAL-ROBERTSON, Mr. James Timothy, MSci ACA *2002;* 33 Rudloe Road, LONDON, SW12 0DR.
TINDALE, Mr. Oliver, BSc ACA *2010;* 50 Woodstock Road North, ST. ALBANS, HERTFORDSHIRE, AL1 4QF.
TINDALE, Mr. Patrick Arthur, ACA *1988;* 4energy Ltd, Block B Phase 2, Debdale Lane Industrial Estate, Keyworth, NOTTINGHAM, NG12 5HN.
TINDALE, Ms. Samantha Jayne, BSc ACA *1992;* Dinmore, 10 Woodville Road, Hartshorne, SWADLINCOTE, DERBYSHIRE, DE11 7ET.
TINDALE, Ms. Sandra Elsie, BSc ACA *1995;* 86 Pannal Ash Road, HARROGATE, NORTH YORKSHIRE, HG2 9AB.
TINDALL, Mr. David Graham, BA(Hons) ACA *2000;* 3 Yorkshire Close, BUCKSHAW VILLAGE, LANCASHIRE, PR7 7BS.
TINDALL, Mrs. Janet Dorothy, BA ACA *1980;* F E Metcalfe & Co, 40a Market Place South, RIPON, NORTH YORKSHIRE, HG4 1BZ.
TINDALL, Mr. Jonathan Emerson, BA(Hons) ACA CTA *2002;* Malmar West Apartment, 12 Ocean Lane, PEMBROKE HM13, BERMUDA.
•TINDALL, Mrs. Marguerite Jane, BSc FCA *1976;* Winburn Glass Norfolk, Convention House, St. Mary's Street, LEEDS, LS9 7DP.
TINDALL, Ms. Sarah Jane, BSc ACA *1993;* Knowles View, Knowl Hill, READING, RG10 9UR.
TINDALL, Mr. Thomas James, MEng MSc ACA *2006;* 43 Audley Way, ASCOT, BERKSHIRE, SL5 8EE.
TINDALL-DOMAN, Mrs. Zoe, BSc(Econ) ACA *1998;* Higher Farm Barn, Portbury Lane, Portbury, BRISTOL, BS20 7SN.
TINDLE, Mr. Chris, BSc ACA *2009;* 5 Earlsmeadow, Earsdon View, Shiremoor, NEWCASTLE UPON TYNE, NE27 0GB.
TINDLE, Mrs. Deborah Jayne, BA ACA *1999;* 10 Blenkinsopp Mews, NEWCASTLE UPON TYNE, NE3 5RN.
TINDLE, Miss. Helen Mary, BA(Hons) ACA *2005;* JPMorgan Asset Management Real Assets (Asia) Limited, 19/F Chater House, 8 Connaught Road, CENTRAL, HONG KONG ISLAND, HONG KONG SAR.
•TINDLE, Mr. Malcolm, FCA *1972;* Bell Tindle Williamson LLP, The Old Post Office, 63 Saville Street, NORTH SHIELDS, TYNE AND WEAR, NE30 1AY. See also BTW LLP and Bell Tindle Williamson Services Limited
•TINDLE, Mr. Robert Ralph, BA FCA *1988;* (Tax Fac), Tindles LLP, Scotswood House, Teesdale South, STOCKTON-ON-TEES, CLEVELAND, TS17 6SB.
TINEGATE, Mr. Stephen Bruce, BSc FCA *1984;* 16 Maegan Way, CLEETHORPES, DN35 8EW.
TINER, Mr. John Ivan, CBE FCA *1980;* 23 Savile Row, LONDON, W1S 2ET.
•TING, Mrs. Christina Kiik Ing, FCA *1977;* (Tax Fac), Jacob Ting & Co, 40 Homer Street, LONDON, W1H 4NL.
TING, Miss. Ei Leen, LLM LLB BCom ACA *2008;* (Tax Fac), 36 Strahan Road, LONDON, E3 5DB.
TING, Mr. Leung Huel Stephen, ACA *2006;* Ting Ho Kwan & Chan, 9th Floor Tung Ning Bldg, 249-253 Des Voeux Road C, CENTRAL, HONG KONG ISLAND, HONG KONG SAR.
TING, Ms. Shuk Kam Cindy, ACA *2006;* Ting Ho Kwan & Chan, 9th Floor Tung Ning Bldg, 249-253 Des Voeux Road C, CENTRAL, HONG KONG ISLAND, HONG KONG SAR.
TING, Mr. Siew Chai, FCA *1984;* 9706 Carmel Ct, Bethesda, MARYLAND, MD 20817, UNITED STATES.
TING, Mr. Sii Tien, ACA *1980;* 17 Lorong Kismis, Apt. 03-02 Kismis View, SINGAPORE 598010, SINGAPORE.
TING, Miss. Susie Chin Kee, LLB ACA *1994;* 148 Simei St 1, No. 06-117, SINGAPORE 520148, SINGAPORE.
TING, Mr. Tiong-Pong, BA FCA *1983;* 8 Howitt Drive, LOWER TEMPLESTOWE, VIC 3107, AUSTRALIA.
TING, Mr. Yick Man Edmund, ACA *2006;* Flat C 6/F, Block 3 Majestic Park, 11 Farm Road, TO KWA WAN, KOWLOON, HONG KONG SAR.
TING, Mr. Yiu Sing, ACA *2007;* Room 2001, The Metropolis Tower, 10 Metropolis Drive, HUNG HOM, HONG KONG SAR.
TING, Ms. Yuen Mei, ACA *2005;* Flat G 20/F Tower 2, Ocean Shores, TSEUNG KWAN O, NEW TERRITORIES, HONG KONG SAR.
TINGER, Mr. Stuart Alan, FCA *1970;* 28 Countisbury Drive, Childwall, LIVERPOOL, L16 0JJ.
TINGLE, Mr. Arthur John, FCA *1962;* Flat 3, 18 Wood Lane, Headingley, LEEDS, LS6 2AE. (Life Member)
TINGLE, Mr. Kenneth Ernest, FCA *1961;* 52 Magpie Way, Winslow, BUCKINGHAM, MK18 3PZ. (Life Member)
•TINGLE, Mr. Kevan Alec, FCA *1977;* Tingle Ashmore Ltd, Enterprise House, Broadfield Court, SHEFFIELD, S8 0XF.
TINGLE, Mrs. Theresa, BA ACA *1999;* 74 Dringthorpe Road, YORK, YO24 1LG.
•TINHAM, Mr. Alan Clement John, FCA *1970;* Reeves & Co LLP, 37 St. Margarets Street, CANTERBURY, KENT, CT1 2TU.
•TINKER, Mr. Anthony, BSc FCA *1977;* PM+M Solutions for Business LLP, Greenbank Technology Park, Challenge Way, BLACKBURN, BB1 5QB. See also PM & M Corporate Finance Limited
TINKER, Mr. Benjamin Stuart, BA ACA *2003;* 17 Coombe Road, Nailsea, BRISTOL, BS48 2HH.
TINKER, Mr. David Graham, FCA *1977;* HSBC Bank Plc, Level 31, 8 Canada Square, LONDON, E14 5HQ.
TINKER, Mr. David Timothy, BA FCA *1980;* 44 Missenden Acres, Hedge End, SOUTHAMPTON, SO30 2RE.
TINKER, Mr. George Barron, FCA *1961;* 3 Cedar Covert, WETHERBY, LS22 7XW.
TINKER, Mr. Ian Grieve, LLB FCA *1977;* 47 Heather Lea Avenue, Dore, SHEFFIELD, S17 3DL.
TINKER, Mr. Kevin John, FCA *1968;* 15 View Point, Baywater Drive, TWIN WATERS, QLD 4564, AUSTRALIA.
TINKER, Mr. Mark Duerden, BA ACA *2002;* 15 Addison Place, LONDON, W11 4RJ.
•TINKER, Mr. Nicholas John, BA FCA *1995;* Zolfo Cooper LLP, Toronto Square, Toronto Street, LEEDS, LS1 2HJ.
TINKER, Mr. Philip Ingram, FCA *1973;* Oak End Farm, Taxal, Whaley Bridge, HIGH PEAK, SK23 7EA.
TINKLER, Mr. Jonathan James, BA ACA *2006;* 67 The Spinney, BEACONSFIELD, BUCKINGHAMSHIRE, HP9 1SA.
TINKLER, Mr. Steven, BSc ACA *2007;* with BDO LLP, Emerald House, East Street, EPSOM, SURREY, KT17 1HS.
TINKLER, Mr. Tony Neville, FCA *1958;* Branscombe, 44 Nursery Lane, South Wootton, KING'S LYNN, PE30 3LR. (Life Member)
•TINKLER, Mrs. Yvonne Karen, ACA *1985;* (Tax Fac), A Plus Accountants Limited, 10 Canberra House, Corby Gate Business Park, CORBY, NORTHAMPTONSHIRE, NN17 5JG.
TINMOUTH, Mr. John, FCA *1966;* 23 Tynedale Road, SOUTH SHIELDS, NE34 6EX.
TINNER, Mr. Richard, FCA *1980;* (Tax Fac), Vtesse Networks John Tate Road, Foxholes Business Park, HERTFORD, SG13 7DT.
•TINNEY, Mr. Andrew James, BSc ACA *1992;* Barclays Bank Plc, 1 Churchill Place, LONDON, E14 5HP.
TINNEY, Mrs. Clair Louise, BSc ACA *1995;* Field End, Kelmscott Road, LECHLADE, GLOUCESTERSHIRE, GL7 3HB.
TINNISWOOD, Mrs. Nicola Jane, BA ACA *1998;* with Deloitte LLP, Abbots House, Abbey Street, READING, RG1 3BD.
TINNISWOOD, Mr. Toby George, BSc ACA *2001;* 12 Beech Hill Road, Spencers Wood, READING, RG7 1HL.
TINOFIREI, Miss. Wadzie, ACA *2011;* 2 Chalk Hill, CHESHAM, BUCKINGHAMSHIRE, HP5 2DN.
TINSLEY, Mr. Adam David Luke, BA(Hons) ACA *2004;* C/Barranc no 11 A-2, Cascat, 07181 CALVIA, MALLORCA, SPAIN.
TINSLEY, Miss. Alison, ACA *2008;* 127 Bushey Lane, Rainford, ST. HELENS, MERSEYSIDE, WA11 7LN.
TINSLEY, Mr. Anthony John, FCA *1969;* 19 Hawsley Road, HARPENDEN, AL5 2BL.
TINSLEY, Mr. David John, BA ACA *2002;* D H L, Ocean House, The Ring, BRACKNELL, BERKSHIRE, RG12 1AX.
TINSLEY, Mr. Denis Knowles, MA FCA *1973;* 6 Edwardes Square, LONDON, W8 6HE.
TINSLEY, Mr. Derek Charles Alexander, BA(Hons) ACA *2001;* Davies Arnold Cooper, 6-8 Bouverie Street, LONDON, EC4Y 8DD.
TINSLEY, Mr. Gerald Hubert, FCA *1956;* 12 St Marys Close, SHOREHAM-BY-SEA, BN43 5ZB. (Life Member)
TINSLEY, Mr. Peter Antony, MA FCA *1963;* 119 The Avenue, LEEDS, LS17 7PA.
TINSLEY, Mrs. Tamsin, BSc ACA *1993;* with PricewaterhouseCoopers LLP, 1 Embankment Place, LONDON, WC2N 6RH.
TINSON, Mrs. Barbara Elizabeth, BSc FCA *1985;* 34 Harwood Rise, Woolton Hill, NEWBURY, RG20 9XW.
•TINTON, Mr. Stephen Christopher Ben, MA FCA *1973;* Cherryridge, 37 Ewell Downs Road, EPSOM, KT17 3BT.
TIONG, Mr. Heng Liong, ACA *2010;* Blk 752 Woodlands Circle #06-528, SINGAPORE 730752, SINGAPORE.
•TIPLADY, Mr. Andrew David Ross, BSc FCA CTA TEP *1978;* 28 Turnpike Way, MARKFIELD, LEICESTERSHIRE, LE67 9QT.
TIPLADY, Mr. Duncan Anthony, LLB ACA *2002;* Prologue Capital 6th Floor, 20 Balderton Street, LONDON, W1K 6TL.
TIPLADY, Mr. Sean Patrick, BA ACA *1997;* 2 Willerby Court, Willerby Low Road, Willerby, HULL, HU10 6EF.
TIPLADY, Mr. Simon John, BA ACA *1994;* with Deloitte LLP, Saltire Court, 20 Castle Terrace, EDINBURGH, EH1 2DB.
TIPLIN, Mr. Thomas, ACA *2011;* with Moore Stephens LLP, 150 Aldersgate Street, LONDON, EC1A 4AB.
•①TIPPEN, Mr. Roderick George, ACA *1984;* with PricewaterhouseCoopers LLP, 7 More London Riverside, LONDON, SE1 2RT.
TIPPER, Mr. Adrian Lee, ACA *2010;* 153 Green Lanes, Wylde Green, SUTTON COLDFIELD, WEST MIDLANDS, B73 5LT.
TIPPER, Mr. Andrew Walter, FCA *1969;* 63 Gaia Lane, LICHFIELD, WS13 7LR.
TIPPER, Mr. Christopher Stuart, MSc BA FCA *1978;* 1 Red Lion Lane, Newbold Vernon, LEICESTER, LE9 9LS.
TIPPER, Mr. Gary William, BA ACA *1989;* Zeus Private Equity Llp Lowry House, 17 Marble Street, MANCHESTER, M2 3AW.
TIPPER, Mr. Jonothan Craig, BSc FCA *1990;* 7 Imperial Way, HEMEL HEMPSTEAD, HERTFORDSHIRE, HP3 9FJ.
TIPPER, Mrs. Karen Lenore, BA ACA *2003;* 384 Marine Parade, South Brighton, CHRISTCHURCH, NEW ZEALAND.
TIPPER, Mr. Luke Alexander, ACA *2008;* 31 Cranbury Road, READING, RG30 2XE.
TIPPET, Mr. Charles Lowther, FCA *1972;* Little London Farm, Brill Road, Oakley, AYLESBURY, HP18 9QH.
TIPPET, Ms. Rebecca, BSc ACA *2006;* Silver Birch, Sheepwood Road, BRISTOL, BS10 7BP.
TIPPETT, Mr. Gareth John, BA ACA *2004;* 19 Pen-Y-Cae, Ystrad Mynach, HENGOED, CF82 7FA.
•TIPPETT, Mr. Jonathan Charles Morley, BSc FCA TEP *1985;* (Tax Fac), Morley Tippett, White Park Barn, Loseley Park, GUILDFORD, SURREY, GU3 1HS.
TIPPETT, Miss. Louisa Clare, BSc ACA *1984;* Whittle & Co, 15 High Street West Mersea, COLCHESTER, CO5 8QA.
TIPPETT, Mr. Nicholas Paul, BSc ACA *2010;* 4 Thornyville Drive, PLYMOUTH, PL9 7LF.
•TIPPING, Mr. Andrew, BSc ACA ATII *1997;* (Tax Fac), Tippings Accountants Limited, 115 Chapel Lane, Longton, PRESTON, PR4 5NA.
TIPPING, Mr. Barry Peter, BA ACA *1987;* Orbital Marketing Services Group, The Boulevard, Orbital Park, ASHFORD, KENT, TN24 0GA.
TIPPING, Mr. David Keith, BA FCA *1973;* Fairview New Homes Ltd, 50 Lancaster Road, ENFIELD, MIDDLESEX, EN2 0BY.
TIPPING, Miss. Elizabeth Claire, ACA *2006;* 188 Kings Road, HARROGATE, NORTH YORKSHIRE, HG1 5JG.
TIPPING, Mrs. Jillian Elaine, MA MSc CA ACA CTA *1996;* 3700 Gilmore Way, BURNABY V5G 4M1, BC, CANADA.
•TIPPING, Mr. John Alfred, BSc FCA *1980;* (Tax Fac), J.K. Research Ltd, 6-8 The Wash, HERTFORD, SG14 1PX.
TIPPING, Mr. Kenneth John James, FCA *1967;* 5 Amesbury Avenue, ST.IVES 2075, NSW 2075, AUSTRALIA.
TIPPING, Mr. Paul Richard, FCA *1970;* (Tax Fac), 8 Pickwick Way, CHISLEHURST, BR7 6RZ.
TIPPINS, Miss. Nicola Jean, BA ACA *1995;* 22 Saugatuck River Road, WESTON, CT 06883, UNITED STATES.
TIPPLE, Ms. Heather, BA ACA *1995;* 6 Pembury Road, Wollaton, NOTTINGHAM, NG8 2DA.
TIPPLE, Mr. Michael Roger, FCA *1973;* 50 Elizabeth Road, Moseley, BIRMINGHAM, B13 8QJ. (Life Member)
TIPPLES, Mr. Sidney Tobias, BA ACA *1997;* 63 Thurleigh Road, LONDON, SW12 8TZ.

TIPPLESTON, Mr. Charles Edward, BA ACA CTA *1998;* Alliance Healthcare, 43 Cox Lane, CHESSINGTON, KT9 1SN.
•**TIPTAFT, Mr. David Howard Palmer, CBE FCA** *1962;* Tiptaft Smith & Co, Montagu Chambers, Montagu Square, MEXBOROUGH, S64 9AJ. See also Tiptaft Smith & Co Secretarial Services
TIPTON, Mrs. Claire Amanda, ACA *2002;* 910 New Hey Road, HUDDERSFIELD, HD3 3FE.
TIPTON, Mr. David Charles, BA ACA *1993;* Corner House, 1 The Farthingales, MAIDENHEAD, BERKSHIRE, SL6 1TE.
TIRKIDES, Mr. Ioannis, MA ACA *1991;* Manglis Group of Companies, 136 Elaionon Str, 2060 Strovolos, NICOSIA, CYPRUS.
•**TISCOE, Mr. Anthony Malcolm, MBE FCA** *1960;* Anthony Tiscoe & Co, Brentmead House, Britannia Road, LONDON, N12 9RU.
TISDALE, Mr. Robert Nicholas George, BSc ACA *1996;* 4 Quarry Cottages, Woodcote Lane, Leek Wootton, WARWICK, CV35 7QH.
TISDALL, Mr. Leslie Alan, BSc ACA *1981;* 66 Lower Guildford Road, Knaphill, WOKING, GU21 2EN.
TISH, Mr. Darren Paul, BA(Hons) ACA *2000;* 6 Hazel Lane, ILFORD, IG6 2AG.
•**TISH, Mr. Harvey Lester, FCA** *1968;* (Tax Fac), Harvey Tish, Whispers, Dog Kennel Lane, Chorleywood, RICKMANSWORTH, HERTFORDSHIRE WD3 5EE. See also Casey Lester
TISI, Mr. Julian Peter, BA ACA *1999;* Centrica Plc, Millstream, Maidenhead Road, WINDSOR, BERKSHIRE, SL4 5GD.
TISSEVERASINGHE, Mr. Trevor, BEng ACA *2000;* River Point Tower #1612 1-11-6 Tuskuda Chuo-ku, TOKYO, JAPAN.
TISSIER, Mr. Omid Paul, BSc ACA *2006;* Flat 31 Wendela Court, Sudbury Hill, HARROW, MIDDLESEX, HA1 3NB.
TITCHEN, Mr. Andrew, FCA *1995;* 25 Queens Court, Alderham Close, SOLIHULL, WEST MIDLANDS, B91 2PR.
TITCHENER, Mrs. Jane Lucy, BA(Hons) ACA *2001;* Appletree House, 7 St. Nicholas Road, WALLINGFORD, OX10 8HU.
TITCHENER, Mr. Nicholas Simon Charles, BA(Hons) ACA *2003;* Waterloo House Pye Corner, Ulcombe, MAIDSTONE, KENT, ME17 1EH.
TITCHENER, Mr. Paul, MA ACA *1989;* The Old Farmhouse, Stoodleigh, TIVERTON, DEVON, EX16 9PQ.
TITCHMARSH, Miss. S. Emily, ACA *2011;* 13 Rodney Road, LONDON, E11 2DE.
TITCOMB, Mr. Jeremy Norman Charles, BSc FCA *1983;* Wayfield House, Wayfield, Snitterfield, STRATFORD-UPON-AVON, WARWICKSHIRE, CV37 0JB.
TITCOMB, Mrs. Joanna Claire, MA ACA *1994;* 5 The Cedars, Milford, GODALMING, GU8 5DH.
TITCOMB, Miss. Lesley Jane, MA ACA *1990;* Hadham Lodge, Hadham Cross, MUCH HADHAM, SG10 6AP.
TITCOMB, Mr. Paul Andrew, MA FCA AMCT PgDip *1993;* Atkins Plc Woodcote Grove, Ashley Road, EPSOM, KT18 5BW.
TITCOMBE, Mr. Colin Michael, FCA *1975;* 10 Trinity Village Close, La Rue de la Boucterie, Trinity, JERSEY, JE3 5HQ.
TITCOMBE, Mrs. Paula Catherine, BSc ACA *1995;* 4 Brandon Close, Chafford Hundred, GRAYS, ESSEX, RM16 6QX.
TITE, Mr. Malcolm George, ACA *1985;* 2 Hale View, Glen Road, Beacon Hill, HINDHEAD, GU26 6QE.
TITE, Mr. Robert John, ACA *2006;* Flat 33, 5 Freehold Street, NORTHAMPTON, NN2 6BF.
TITFORD, Mr. Austen Jeffrey, BSc ACA *1989;* Meadhurst Lynx Hill, East Horsley, LEATHERHEAD, KT24 5AX.
TITFORD, Mr. Derek Swinden, FCA *1962;* Ivy Cottage, Shurlock Road, Waltham St Lawrence, READING, RG10 0HN. (Life Member)
TITHECOTT, Mr. Stephen John, ACA *1988;* Flat 2, 9 Richmond Hill, Clifton, BRISTOL, BS8 1AT.
TITHER, Miss. Keri Louise, BSc ACA *2006;* 16 Portland Grove, STOCKPORT, CHESHIRE, SK4 4AA.
TITHERADGE, Mr. David Edward Hettrel, FCA *1959;* Hunters Lodge, Mallard Way, Hutton Mount, BRENTWOOD, CM13 2NF.
TITHERIDGE, Mr. James, ACA CTA MAAT *2001;* 10 Horseshoe Road, Pangbourne, READING, RG8 7JQ.
TITHERIDGE, Mr. Rob, ACA *2009;* Pricewaterhousecoopers, 1 Embankment Place, LONDON, WC2N 6RH.
•①**TITLEY, Mr. John Malcolm, BSc ACA** *1984;* Leonard Curtis, D T E House, Hollins Mount, BURY, LANCASHIRE, BL9 8AT. See also DTE Leonard Curtis Limited and Leonard Curtis Limited
TITLEY, Mr. Joseph Cunningham, FCA *1966;* Orchard House, Station Road, Cotes Heath, STAFFORD, ST21 6RT. (Life Member)
TITLEY, Mr. Mitchell Cunningham, BEng ACA *2001;* 5 Austrey Close, Knowle, SOLIHULL, WEST MIDLANDS, B93 9JE.
TITLEY, Mr. Sean Barra, BA(Hons) ACA *2001;* with National Audit Office, 157-197 Buckingham Palace Road, Victoria, LONDON, SW1W 9SP.
TITLEY, Mr. William Albert, FCA *1969;* 52 Church Aston, NEWPORT, SHROPSHIRE, TF10 9JN.
TITMAS, Mr. John Richard Graeme, ACA *1979;* Flat 1, 70 Carlton Hill, St Johns Wood, LONDON, NW8 0ET.
TITMUS, Mr. Adam, BSc ACA *2007;* 14 Nightingale Way, Stotfold, HITCHIN, HERTFORDSHIRE, SG5 4FN.
TITMUS, Mr. Peter, BSc FCA *1991;* 15 Woodland Avenue, HOVE, BN3 6BH.
TITMUSS, Mr. James, MA ACA *2000;* Isis Equity Partners, 2nd Floor, The Exchange, 3 New York Street, MANCHESTER, M1 4HN.
TITMUSS, Mr. John Austin, FCA *1971;* 21 Compton Avenue, Leagrave, LUTON, LU4 9AX.
TITMUSS, Mr. John Yarwood, FCA *1954;* 14 Goddens Close, Northiam, RYE, TN31 6QH. (Life Member)
TITMUSS, Mrs. Rachael Elizabeth, BA ACA *2001;* Wilsford House, Ashcombe Place, BOLTON, LANCASHIRE, BL7 0QN.
TITMUSS, Miss. Rachel, BSc ACA ATII *1998;* (Tax Fac), Jardine Lloyd Thompson Ltd, Jardine House, 6 Crutched Friars, LONDON, EC3N 2PH.
TITT, Mr. Nigel John, BSc FCA *1994;* 77 COUGAR RIDGE VIEW SW, CALGARY T3H 4X3, AB, CANADA.
•**TITTENSOR, Mr. Hew Victor, FCA** *1969;* Tittensor & Co LLP, Fourwinds, Wengeo Lane, WARE, HERTFORDSHIRE, SG12 0EH.
TITTLE, Mr. Ian Sidney, FCA *1969;* 72 Mount Douglas Point, CALGARY T2Z 3J9, AB, CANADA.
TITTLE, Mr. Richard John, BSc FCA *1978;* Kings College London James Clerk Maxwell Building, 57 Waterloo Road, LONDON, SE1 8WA.
TIUM, Mr. Beng Teck Jimmy, ACA *2008;* No 8 Jalan Wawasan 4/6, Pusat Bandar Puchong, 47100 PUCHONG, SELANGOR, MALAYSIA.
TIVERTON BROWN, Mr. Jonathan, BCom ACA *2001;* 123 Eskdale Avenue, CHESHAM, BUCKINGHAMSHIRE, HP5 3BE.
•**TIVEY, Mr. Andrew David, BA FCA** *1982;* Ernst & Young LLP, 1 More London Place, LONDON, SE1 2AF. See also Ernst & Young Europe LLP
•**TIVEY, Mr. Paul, ACA FCCA** *2007;* Pinfields Limited, Meryll House, 57 Worcester Road, BROMSGROVE, WORCESTERSHIRE, B61 7DN.
TIVNAN, Mr. Seamus, ACA *1989;* PO Box 1159, GEORGE TOWN, GRAND CAYMAN, KY1 1102, CAYMAN ISLANDS.
TIVNAN, Mr. Stephen Edward, BSc ACA *2000;* 25 Wood Green Drive, THORNTON-CLEVELEYS, FY5 3DH.
TIWANA, Mrs. Gurpreet Kaur, BA ACA *1991;* c/o Simon James STI Pvt Ltd., RMZ Centennial Campus B, 8B Kundanahalli Main Road, BANGALORE 560048, KARNATAKA, INDIA.
TIWARI, Ms. Manjari, ACA *2005;* 90 Abbotsbury Gardens, PINNER, MIDDLESEX, HA5 1SU.
TIWARI, Mr. Pradeep, ACA *2010;* BLK-291D COMPASSVALE STREET, #03-272, SINGAPORE 544291, SINGAPORE.
•**TIWARI, Mr. Sudarshan Simon, FCA** *1981;* Tiwari & Co, 25 Knighton Close, New Duston, NORTHAMPTON, NN5 6NE.
TIZARD, Mr. Geoffrey Nigel, FCA *1974;* 28 Owen Road, WINDLESHAM, GU20 6JG.
TIZARD, Mrs. Jean, BSc FCA *1978;* 28 Owen Road, WINDLESHAM, GU20 6JG.
•**TIZARD, Mr. Michael Robert, FCA** *1982;* (Tax Fac), Wilkins Kennedy, 3-4 Eastwood Court, Broadwater Road, ROMSEY, HAMPSHIRE, SO51 8JJ.
TIZARD, Miss. Suzanne Marie, BSc BSc(HONS) ACA *2011;* Flat 83 Aubert Court, Avenell Road, LONDON, N5 1BL.
TIZICK, Mr. Robert, FCA *1971;* 11 Brampton Place, Gansiebos Street, Weltevreden Park 1709, Northcliffe, PO Box 1489, JOHANNESBURG 2115 SOUTH AFRICA.
TIZZARD, Mr. Bryan Ralph, FCA *1961;* Cornerways, 4a Ipswich Road, Westbourne, BOURNEMOUTH, BH4 9HZ. (Life Member)
•**TJEN-A-LOOI, Mr. Rudy, FCA** *1972;* 4 Little Common, STANMORE, MIDDLESEX, HA7 3BZ.
TJENDANA, Mr. Wira, BA ACA *1989;* Taman Alfa Indah, Blok B20 No 9, JAKARTA, 11640, INDONESIA.
TJIU, Mr. Cheung Yung, ACA *2008;* Flat 21 Horse Shoe Court, 11 Brewhouse Yard, LONDON, EC1V 4JU.
TO, Mr. Alex Pak Lam, ACA *2005;* G. P. O. Box 1800, CENTRAL, HONG KONG SAR.
TO, Miss. Anh Thuy, BCom ACA *1993;* 2/F Etown2 Building, 364 Cong Hoa St., Tan Binh District, HO CHI MINH CITY, VIETNAM.
TO, Mr. Cuong, MA BA(Hons) ACA *2003;* 9 Downsedge Terrace Epsom Road, GUILDFORD, GU1 2SS.
TO, Miss. Elizabeth, BSc ACA *2002;* 69 Ha Wong Yi Au Village, Yung Yi Road, TAI PO, NEW TERRITORIES, HONG KONG SAR.
TO, Mr. James Yue-Shing, BSc ACA *1982;* Home Farm House, Barton Hartshorn, BUCKINGHAM, MK18 4JX.
TO, Ms. Ka Yan Alvina, ACA *2010;* RM 2 5/F Blk E, Wo Hang House, Cheung Wo Crt, KWUN TONG, KOWLOON, HONG KONG SAR.
TO, Mr. Kok Wing, BSc ACA CFA *1994;* Flat A 12/F Block 5, One Beacon Hill, 1 Beacon Hill Road, KOWLOON TONG, KOWLOON, HONG KONG SAR.
TO, Miss. Oiwah, BA ACA *2006;* 82 Guinness Square, Pages Walk, LONDON, SE1 4HP.
TO, Mr. Peter Lai-Him, FCA *1976;* 3 Barker Avenue, WHITE PLAINS, NY 10601, UNITED STATES.
TO, Mr. Sai Kong, BSc ACA *1999;* 23 Blairderry Road, Streatham Hill, LONDON, SW2 4SD.
TO, Ms. Siu Ha, ACA *2005;* Rm 802 Wo Kwan House, Cheung Wo Court, KWUN TONG, KOWLOON, HONG KONG SAR.
TO, Mr. Tai Loy, ACA *2007;* 601 Block 23, 88 Songle Road, Songjiang, SHANGHAI 201600, CHINA.
TO, Mr. Truc Ngoc, BSc FCA *1992;* KPMG LLP, Suite 2000, 303 Peachtree Street N.E., ATLANTA, GA, 30308 UNITED STATES.
TO, Miss. Wai Kum, ACA *2005;* To Wai Kum, 1711 North Tower, Concordia Plaza, 1 Science Museum Road, TSIM SHA TSUI, KOWLOON HONG KONG SAR.
TO, Mr. Wing Keung, ACA *2005;* 3/F Antonia House, 8 Broom Road, HAPPY VALLEY, HONG KONG ISLAND, HONG KONG SAR.
TO, Mr. Wing Tsan Alex, ACA *2005;* Flat C 9/F Yick Wah Building 319-321 Hennessy Road, WAN CHAI, HONG KONG SAR.
TO, Mr. Yan Kuen Ronny, BSc ACA *1985;* 103 Ho Chung Road, Ho Chung, SAI KUNG, NEW TERRITORIES, HONG KONG SAR.
TOAL, Mr. Michael, BA ACA *2007;* 7 Kestrel Way, ROYSTON, HERTFORDSHIRE, SG8 7XW.
TOAN, Mrs. Roslyn Sarah, BA ACA *2006;* 62 Circular Drive, CHESTER, CH4 8LX.
TOBIAS, Mr. Adam Marshall, BA FCA *1978;* 71 Avenue Road, Winslow, BUCKINGHAM, MK18 3DF.
TOBIAS, Mrs. Geraldine, BA ACA *1999;* 4 Savernake Court, Old Church Lane, STANMORE, HA7 2RJ.
TOBIN, Mrs. Carolyn Jane, BSc ACA *1981;* 63 Ravenscourt Road, LONDON, W6 0UJ.
TOBIN, Mr. Daniel John, BA(Hons) ACA *2000;* 35 Broadwell Court, Castledene, Gosforth, NEWCASTLE UPON TYNE, NE3 1YS.
TOBIN, Mr. David Llewellyn, ACA CA(SA) *2010;* Black Swan Manor, Crooks Court Lane, West Hougham, DOVER, KENT, CT15 7BN.
TOBIN, Mr. Hugh John, BA ACA *2004;* Top floor flat, 60 Roxborough Park, HARROW, MIDDLESEX, HA1 3AY.
TOBIN, Mr. Iain John, FCA *1995;* Monks Cottage, 22 Upper Rose Hill, DORKING, RH4 2EB.
TOBIN, Mrs. Janet Alison, BSc FCA *1987;* 51 Sandham Grove, Barnston Heswall, WIRRAL, CH60 1XN.
TOBIN, Mr. John, BSc FCA *1983;* Freizland House, High Hoyland Lane, Cawthorne, BARNSLEY, SOUTH YORKSHIRE, S75 4AX.
•**TOBIN, Mrs. Maria Angela, FCA** *1974;* (Tax Fac), M.A. Tobin, 17 Wilbury Avenue, Cheam, SUTTON, SM2 7DU.
TOBIN, Mrs. Tracy, BSc ACA *1990;* 95 Glen Road, West Cross, SWANSEA, SA3 5QJ.
TOBUTT, Mr. Scott Douglas, BA ACA *1999;* 43/48A Consul Rd, BROOKVALE, NSW 2100, AUSTRALIA.
TOBY, Mr. Jack Hugh, FCA *1975;* 31C Richmond St, North Perth, PERTH, WA 6006, AUSTRALIA.
TOCK, Mr. Christopher Paul, BSc ACA *2002;* 8 Longburgh Close, Hoole, CHESTER, CH2 3TA.
TOCKNELL, Mr. Brian David, FCA *1970;* Tree Tops, Ashmead Green, DURSLEY, GL11 5EW.
TOD, Mrs. Pauline June, FCA *1965;* 10 Brookfield Road, LYMM, CHESHIRE, WA13 0QJ. (Life Member)
TODD, Mr. Alan Michael, FCA *1972;* Flat 320, 1 Coprolite Street, IPSWICH, IP3 0BL.
TODD, Miss. Alison Jean, BA ACA *1994;* 57 Woodlands Drive, HARROGATE, NORTH YORKSHIRE, HG2 7AX.
TODD, Mr. Alistair Mark, BA ACA *2003;* 3 Parkfield Way, Topsham, EXETER, EX3 0DP.
•**TODD, Mr. Andrew George, BA ACA** *1998;* Deloitte LLP, 1 City Square, LEEDS, WEST YORKSHIRE, LS1 2AL. See also Deloitte & Touche LLP
•**TODD, Mr. Andrew William, BSc FCA** *1978;* (Tax Fac), Andrew Todd, Highcroft, Deadmans Ash Lane, Sarratt, RICKMANSWORTH, WD3 6AL.
TODD, Mrs. Anne Catherine, BCom ACA *1993;* 32 Ashford Drive, Appleton, WARRINGTON, WA4 5GG.
TODD, Mr. Benjamin John, ACA MAAT *2004;* 100 Main Street, Kirby Muxloe, LEICESTER, LE9 2AP.
TODD, Mrs. Carol Joanna, BSc ACA *1994;* 5 Rue Du General Lambert, 75007 PARIS, FRANCE.
TODD, Mr. Charles Louis, BA ACA *1978;* Apt 402, 199 Knightsbridge, LONDON, SW7 1RH.
TODD, Miss. Christina Grace, BSc ACA *1998;* C.P. No.29, V. Petrarca No.2, Perantonio, 06015 PERUGIA, ITALY.
TODD, Mr. Christopher John, ACA *2011;* 10 Keighley Close, BURY, BL8 2JY.
TODD, Mr. Christopher Michael, BA ACA *1994;* 15 Gisborne Crescent, DERBY, DE22 2FJ.
•**TODD, Mr. Colin Michael William, FCA CTA** *1991;* (Tax Fac), Compliance Financial, 36 Tor Bryan, INGATESTONE, CM4 9JZ.
•**TODD, Mr. David Andrew Thompson, BSc FCA** *1991;* KPMG LLP, 15 Canada Square, LONDON, E14 5GL. See also KPMG Europe LLP
TODD, Mr. David Robert, BA ACA *2002;* Invesco Asset Management, 30 Finsbury Square, LONDON, EC2A 1AG.
TODD, Miss. Debra Elizabeth, BA ACA *1983;* British Petroleum Co Plc, 20 Canada Square, LONDON, E14 5NJ.
TODD, Mr. Derek, MA FCA DChA *1985;* St. Albans School, Abbey Gateway, ST. ALBANS, HERTFORDSHIRE, AL3 4HB.
TODD, Mr. Dirk Robertson, LLB ACA DChA *1988;* 135 Rusthall Avenue, Chiswick, LONDON, W4 1BL.
TODD, Mr. Donald John, FCA *1953;* 36/144 Dorville Road, CARSELDINE, QLD 4034, AUSTRALIA. (Life Member)
TODD, Mr. Edward McLean, BA ACA *1999;* 29b Edith Road, LONDON, W14 0SU.
TODD, Miss. Emma Jane, ACA *1993;* Hazelridge, Cummings Cross, Liverton, NEWTON ABBOT, DEVON, TQ12 6HJ.
TODD, Mr. Geoffrey Richard, BA FCA *1972;* Field View, Homestead Road, Medstead, ALTON, GU34 5NA.
TODD, Mrs. Gillian, BSc ACA FABRP *1983;* Ernst & Young Llp, 1 More London Place, LONDON, SE1 2AF.
TODD, Mr. Gordon Douglas Stuart, FCA *1969;* Apartado 3403, Figueiral, 8135-905 ALMANCIL, ALGARVE, PORTUGAL.
TODD, Mr. Henry, BSc ACA *2005;* 27 Colwell Road, LONDON, SE22 8QP.
•**TODD, Mr. Ian David Edward, FCA** *1974;* Ian Todd & Co, Holdford Road, Witton, BIRMINGHAM, B6 7EP.
TODD, Mr. Ivan, BSc ACA *1992;* 28 Southlands, High Heaton, NEWCASTLE UPON TYNE, NE7 7YJ.
TODD, Mr. Jeffrey Stuart, BSc(Econ) FCA *1981;* PricewaterhouseCoopers, 9th Floor, East Tower, Abu Dhabi Trade Centre, PO Box 45263, ABU DHABI UNITED ARAB EMIRATES.
•**TODD, Miss. Jennifer, BA ACA** *1993;* Jennifer Todd, Fairgreen Cottage, Clamhunger Lane, Mere, KNUTSFORD, WA16 6QG.
TODD, Mr. Jeremy Fergus Benedict, BSc FCA *1993;* Knoleway, West Street, MAYFIELD, EAST SUSSEX, TN20 6DS.
TODD, Mr. John Paul, BA FCA *1976;* with KPMG LLP, One Snowhill, Snow Hill Queensway, BIRMINGHAM, B4 6GN.
•**TODD, Mrs. Julia Mary, BSc FCA** *1975;* Mrs Julia Todd FCA, 22 Mayfair Avenue, WORCESTER PARK, KT4 7SL.
•**TODD, Mr. Julian, MA FCA** *1971;* Julian Todd, Rue De France 36, B4800 VERVIERS, BELGIUM.
TODD, Mr. Kenneth Stanley, FCA *1953;* Treetops, Higher Lane, Dalton, WIGAN, WN8 7TW. (Life Member)
TODD, Mr. Kristoffer, BA ACA *2005;* 2 Skendleby Drive, NEWCASTLE UPON TYNE, NE3 3GJ.
TODD, Mrs. Laura Jill, BSc ACA *2007;* 57 Beach Croft Avenue, NORTH SHIELDS, TYNE AND WEAR, NE30 3SR.
TODD, Miss. Lindsey, BA(Hons) ACA *2011;* 4b Barnes Close, WINCHESTER, SO23 9QX.
TODD, Mrs. Lisa Clare, MMath ACA *2003;* 26 Fletcher Gardens, Binfield, BRACKNELL, BERKSHIRE, RG42 1FJ.

TODD - TOMLIN **Members - Alphabetical**

TODD, Mrs. Louise Jane, BA ACA *1999;* 4 Lake Cottages, Witley Park Thursley, GODALMING, GU8 6NG.

•**TODD, Mr. Martyn Walter, MBA BA ACA** *1990;* (Tax Fac), Bradley Cave Limited, 18 Jordan Close, KENILWORTH, WARWICKSHIRE, CV8 2AE. See also Bradley Cave

TODD, Mr. Michael Anthony, BCom ACA *1985;* 26 Avenue Road, SWINDON, SN1 4BZ.

•**TODD, Mr. Michael Arthur, FCA** *1971;* Kemp & Co, Room 2-02, The Cotton Exchange Building, Old Hall Street, LIVERPOOL, L3 9LQ.

•**TODD, Mr. Michael Kenneth, FCA** *1980;* The cba Partnership, 72 Lairgate, BEVERLEY, HU17 8EU.

TODD, Mr. Neil James, BSc ACA *1990;* 134B Hillview Avenue, 09-03 Hilltop Grove, SINGAPORE 669621, SINGAPORE.

TODD, Mr. Nicholas Douglas Mclaren, FCA *1974;* 25 Dovedale Road, LEICESTER, LE2 2DN. (Life Member)

TODD, Mrs. Nicola Jane, BSc ACA *1988;* Bruettenerstrasse 6B, 8309 OBERWIL, SWITZERLAND.

TODD, Mr. Nigel Phillip, FCA *1975;* 15 Gipsy Lane, Balsall Common, COVENTRY, CV7 7FW.

•**TODD, Mrs. Noreen, FCA** *1973;* Noreen Todd FCA, Wheal Betty, Trevenen Bal, HELSTON, CORNWALL, tr13 0pr.

TODD, Mr. Philip Arthur, BSc FCA *1980;* Acorn Lodge 142 Barkham Ride Finchampstead, WOKINGHAM, BERKSHIRE, RG40 4EL.

TODD, Mr. Richard Laurence, BA FCA *1973;* 5 Neville Avenue, NEW MALDEN, KT3 4SN.

TODD, Mr. Robert Brian, FCA *1967;* Prince's Cottage, 16 The Paragon, Clifton, BRISTOL, BS8 4LA.

TODD, Mr. Ronald Edward, BSc FCA *1973;* 22 Mayfair Avenue, WORCESTER PARK, KT4 7SL.

TODD, Mr. Sam, ACA *2011;* Flat 13, Ellerton, 30 Mill Lane, LONDON, NW6 1LX.

TODD, Mrs. Samantha Jane, BSc ACA *1993;* with Bradley Cave Limited, 18 Jordan Close, KENILWORTH, WARWICKSHIRE, CV8 2AE.

TODD, Mr. Simon William, ACA *2010;* Nampara, Kenwyn Church Road, TRURO, CORNWALL, TR1 3DR.

TODD, Mr. Stephen Charles, BA ACA *1997;* The Old Forge, The Square, Nether Wallop, STOCKBRIDGE, HAMPSHIRE, SO20 8EX.

TODD, Mr. Stephen Colin, BA ACA *1984;* 19 Willow Wood Close, ASHTON-UNDER-LYNE, OL6 6RA.

•**TODD, Mr. Stephen Graham, FCA** *1970;* S G Todd Limited, Little Mount, 9b Southfield Road, PAIGNTON, TQ3 2SW.

TODD, Mr. Steven Philip, FCA *1981;* PO Box 5014, Wellesley St, AUCKLAND, NEW ZEALAND.

TODD, Mrs. Susan, BEng ACA *1999;* 15 Gisborne Crescent, Allestree, DERBY, DE22 2FJ.

TODD, Mrs. Susanna Louisa, MA ACA *1986;* 54 Queens Road, BECKENHAM, BR3 4JL.

TODD, Mr. Thomas Richard, BSc ACA *2000;* 558 Grandview Road, Pullenvale, BRISBANE, QLD 4069, AUSTRALIA.

TODD, Miss. Victoria Kay, ACA *2010;* Williams Giles, 12 Conqueror Court, SITTINGBOURNE, ME10 5BH.

TODD, Mr. William Philip, FCA *1949;* Hawksmoor, 55 Park Road, BECKENHAM, BR3 1QG. (Life Member)

TODD-DUNNING, Mr. Christopher John, ACA *2008;* Flat G, 105 Honor Oak Park, LONDON, SE23 3LB.

TODE, Mrs. Swee Leng, BSc ACA *1990;* c/o Hyder Consulting ME Ltd, PO Box 52750, Dubai, United Arab Emirates, DUBAI, UNITED ARAB EMIRATES.

•**TODESCO, Mr. Giovanni Antonio, BEng ACA** *1995;* Court Park Financial Services Limited, 11 Court Drive, HILLINGDON, MIDDLESEX, UB10 0BL.

TODHUNTER, Mr. Frank, FCA *1950;* 134 Chaucer Road, WORKINGTON, CA14 4HP. (Life Member)

TODMAN, Mr. Paul, BA ACA *2002;* 71 Welford Road, Shirley, SOLIHULL, WEST MIDLANDS, B90 3HU.

TODMAN, Mrs. Tracy Lee, BA FCA *1992;* 14 Audley Road, SAFFRON WALDEN, ESSEX, CB11 3HW.

TOFARIDES, Mr. Giannis, ACA *2007;* 20 Androkleous St., Apt. 402, 1061 NICOSIA, CYPRUS.

TOFARIDOU, Miss. Niki, BSc ACA *2011;* 3 Posidonos Street, Lakatamia, 2311 NICOSIA, CYPRUS.

TOFFOLO, Mr. Daniel Warren, BSc FCA *1992;* 18 Peterborough Road, SHEFFIELD, S10 4JE.

TOFFOLO, Mr. Stefano, MBA BA ACA *1989;* The Moat House, Perrywood Lane, Watton-at-Stone, HERTFORD, SG14 3RB.

TOFFOLO, Mrs. Susan, BA ACA ATII *1990;* The Moat House, Perrywood Lane, Watton-at-Stone, HERTFORD, SG14 3RB.

TOFIA, Ms. Maria, BSc ACA *2010;* 6 Lesvou, Latsia, NICOSIA, CYPRUS.

TOFIELD, Mr. John Francis, FCA *1975;* Merrie Leas, Eaton Hill, Baslow, BAKEWELL, DE45 1SB.

TOFT, Mr. Simon David, BSc FCA *1983;* Little White Alice, Carnmenellis, REDRUTH, CORNWALL, TR16 6PL.

•**TOGHILL, Mr. Malcolm Stewart, FCA** *1976;* (Tax Fac), Advanta Business Services Limited, 29 Gildredge Road, EASTBOURNE, EAST SUSSEX, BN21 4RU.

TOGHILL, Mr. Stephen Timothy, ACA *1991;* 1 Hartington Drive, Standish, WIGAN, WN6 0UA.

TOGNARELLI, Mr. Thomas Gerard, ACA *2009;* 11 Eccles Bridge Road, Marple, STOCKPORT, CHESHIRE, SK6 7PF.

TOGUNLOJU, Miss. Adeola, BSc ACA *2002;* 19831 BIG CANYON DRIVE, KATY, TX 77450, UNITED STATES.

TOH, Mr. Chun Wah, BSc FCA *1983;* 30/15 Abel Smith Crescent, MOUNT OMMANEY, QLD 4074, AUSTRALIA.

TOH, Mr. Michael Gym, FCA *1973;* Lytton House, Strachey Close, Tidmarsh, READING, RG8 8EP.

TOH, Mr. Yee Seng, BCom ACA *1985;* 67 Victoria Street East, PO Box 10089, ALLISTON L9R 0B7, ON, CANADA.

TOI, Mr. Tee Jian, ACA *2009;* 55 Jalan SS21/3, Damansara Utama, 47400 PETALING JAYA, MALAYSIA.

TOINKO, Mr. Dan, BSc ACA *2004;* 6 Poppy Close, LUTON, LU3 1EX.

•**TOINTON, Mr. Stephen Leslie, FCA** *1984;* (Tax Fac), Saul Fairholm, 12 Tentercroft Street, LINCOLN, LN5 7DB. See also Atkinson Saul Fairholm Limited

TOLAINI, Mr. Simon Joseph, BSc ACA *1994;* 11 Hillhouse Close, BILLERICAY, CM12 0BB.

•**TOLAN, Mr. John Peter, FCA** *1974;* (Tax Fac), Santa Maria, 133 Hanging Hill Lane, Hutton Shenfield, BRENTWOOD, ESSEX, CM13 2HE.

TOLAND, Mr. John, BA ACA *1998;* Direct Group Limited, Direct House, White Rose Way, DONCASTER, SOUTH YORKSHIRE, DN4 5NU.

TOLAT, Mr. Suresh, BA FCA *1982;* (Tax Fac), Cranbrook, 12 Cottenham Park Road, Wimbledon, LONDON, SW20 0RZ.

TOLCHER, Mr. Robin John, BSc ACA *1995;* 101 Hillview Crescent, Pont Faen Estate, NEWPORT, NP19 4NU.

TOLE, Mr. Oscar Malcolm Goodridge, FCA *1970;* 1101 Mews Lane, WEST CHESTER, PA 19382, UNITED STATES. (Life Member)

TOLE, Mr. Richard Edward, BSc(Hons) ACA *2002;* 3 Stonynge Place, LICHFIELD, STAFFORDSHIRE, WS13 8FQ.

TOLEY, Miss. Nicola, BA ACA *2004;* 4 Queens Gardens, LONDON, W5 1SF.

•**TOLFREE, Mr. William Norman, FCA** *1970;* W.N. Tolfree, 6 Ledsgrove, Ipplepen, NEWTON ABBOT, TQ12 5QY.

TOLHURST, Mr. David James, ACA *2008;* 11 Lilley Walk, HONITON, DEVON, EX14 2EA.

TOLHURST, Mr. Peter Frederick, FCA *1974;* 3 Ockenden Lane, Cuckfield, HAYWARDS HEATH, RH17 5LD.

TOLL, Mr. John Edmund, BSc(Econ) FCA *1962;* 31 Aston Court, Broomhill Road, WOODFORD GREEN, ESSEX, IG8 9EY. (Life Member)

TOLL, Mr. Jonathan Richard Francis, BA ACA *1980;* 120 Boardwalk Drive, TORONTO M4L 3X4, ON, CANADA.

TOLLAN, Mr. Miles, BA ACA *2001;* 71 Morgan Street, Petersham, SYDNEY, NSW 2049, AUSTRALIA.

TOLLEMACHE, Miss. Stephanie, BA ACA *2011;* 41 Lochaline Street, LONDON, W6 9SJ.

TOLLER, Mr. Hugh Sandbach, BA ACA *1979;* 22 Breer Street, LONDON, SW6 3HD.

TOLLER, Mr. Mark Geoffrey Charles, ACA *1986;* Hall Farm, Walden Road, Radwinter, SAFFRON WALDEN, CB10 2SW.

TOLLER, Mr. Simon Christopher, BSc ACA *2002;* 21 Laitwood Road, LONDON, SW12 9QN.

TOLLERTON, Mr. Roger, FCA *1966;* Ayletts, Mill End Green, Great Easton, DUNMOW, CM6 2DN.

TOLLERTON, Mrs. Sara Louise, BSc ACA *1999;* Roseberry House, Station Road, Newport, SAFFRON WALDEN, ESSEX, CB11 3PL.

TOLLERTON, Mr. William Norris, BSc(Hons) ACA *2002;* Deutsche Bank, Winchester House, 1 Great Winchester Street, LONDON, EC2N 2DB.

TOLLET, Mr. William Ernest, FCA *1958;* 28 Firwood Grove, Ashton-In-Makerfield, WIGAN, WN4 9ND.

TOLLEY, Mrs. Claire Helen, BSc ACA *1993;* (Tax Fac), 17 Wyndham Grove, Priorslee, TELFORD, SHROPSHIRE, TF2 9GL.

•**TOLLEY, Mr. Mark David Rex, BA ACA** *1999;* with Deloitte LLP, 2 New Street Square, LONDON, EC4A 3BZ.

TOLLEY, Mr. Richard David, BA ACA *1992;* The Prudential Assurance Co Ltd, 121 Kings Road, READING, RG1 3ES.

TOLLMAN, Mr. David Kenneth, ACA *2008;* Apartment 76, Globe View, 10 High Timber Street, LONDON, EC4V 3PQ.

•**TOLLOW, Miss. Joanne Louise, BA(Hons) ACA** *2001;* 37 Recreation Road, GUILDFORD, SURREY, GU1 1HP.

•**TOLMIE, Mrs. Jennifer Lynne, ACA** *2000;* Griffin Stone Moscrop & Co., 41 Welbeck Street, LONDON, W1G 8EA.

TOLMIE, Mr. Michael James, MA ACA *1992;* Volunteer Reading Help Unit 14-15 Perseverance Works, 38 Kingsland Road, LONDON, E2 8DD.

TOLSMA, Mrs. Brigitte Claire, MA ACA *1991;* Cedar Cottage, Vallei 2, 4851-EG ULVENHOUT, NETHERLANDS.

TOLSON, Mr. Michael, FCA *1963;* Ryefield Cottage, 20 Upperthong Lane, Holmfirth, HUDDERSFIELD, HD9 3BE.

TOLSON, Mr. Neville, FCA *1961;* Heatherlea, 111 Chain House Lane, Whitestake, PRESTON, PR4 4LB.

TOMALIN, Mr. Mark Ian, BA FCA *1994;* Bilton Hall Barn, Bilton Hall Farm, Bilton Hall Drive, HARROGATE, NORTH YORKSHIRE, HG1 4DW.

TOMASELLI, Mrs. Madhulika, ACA *1983;* 6a Links Road, EPSOM, KT17 3PS.

TOMASIEWICZ, Miss. Patrycja, ACA MBA *1997;* Flat 18 Brunswick Court, 1 Darlaston Road, LONDON, SW19 4LF.

TOMASSEN, Mr. Fred, ACA *1994;* Windy Nook, Belle Vue Lane, Guilden Sutton, CHESTER, CH3 7EJ.

•**TOMASZEWSKI, Mr. Christopher Ryszard Gregory, FCA** *1980;* (Tax Fac), Alexanders, Redhill Chambers, High Street, REDHILL, RH1 1RJ. See also Alexanders Strategic Planning Ltd and Alexanders Professional Services Ltd

TOMASZEWSKI, Mr. Ireneusz Zygmunt Eligiusz, ACA *1981;* 6 Ghyll Crescent, HORSHAM, RH13 6BG.

•**TOMBLESON, Mr. Paul John, BCom FCA** *1993;* KPMG Europe LLP, 15 Canada Square, LONDON, E14 5GL. See also KPMG LLP

TOMBLESON, Mrs. Sarah Jane, BA ACA *1990;* Lismore, 2 West Road, GUILDFORD, SURREY, GU1 2AU.

TOMBLIN, Mrs. Denise Lynne, BSc ACA *1988;* HMV Group plc, Shelley House, 2-4 York Road, MAIDENHEAD, SL6 1SR.

TOMBS, Mr. Brian John, FCA *1958;* 28 Warren Avenue, Cheam, SUTTON, SM2 7QN.

TOMBS, Mr. David Martin, BA ACA *1989;* 102 Coutts Drive, BUSHLAND BEACH, QLD 4818, AUSTRALIA.

TOMBS, Mr. Derek Michael, FCA *1965;* 61 Eversden Road, Harlton, CAMBRIDGE, CB23 1ET. (Life Member)

TOMBS, Mr. Frederick George, FCA *1951;* Hawthorns, 90 Hoe Lane, Abridge, ROMFORD, RM4 1AU. (Life Member)

TOMBS, Mr. Guy Scott, BA ACA *1993;* 174 Rochester Drive, BEXLEY, DA5 1QG.

•**TOMBS, Mrs. Helen Margaret, BA ACA** *1992;* Helen Tombs, 50 Wellfield Road, Culcheth, WARRINGTON, WA3 4JT.

•**TOMBS, Mrs. Joyce, BSc FCA** *1979;* Moore and Smalley LLP, Priory Close, St Mary's Gate, LANCASTER, LA1 1XB.

TOMBS, Mr. Lee Michael, LLB ACA *2002;* Protocol National, Castle Marina Road, Castle Marina Park, NOTTINGHAM, NG7 1TN.

TOMBS, Mr. Matthew John, BSc ACA *2001;* Pricewaterhousecoopers Donington Court Herald Way, East Midlands Airport Castle Donington, DERBY, DE74 2UZ.

TOMBS, Mr. Robin John, BSc ACA *1997;* Butlers Main Road, Broomfield, CHELMSFORD, CM1 7AW.

•**TOMBS, Mr. William Edward Rupert, BA(Hons) ACA** *2001;* Key Accountancy Services Limited, 92 Whitton View, Rothbury, MORPETH, NORTHUMBERLAND, NE65 7QN.

TOMEI, Mrs. Leigh, BSc ACA *2002;* with PricewaterhouseCoopers, Level 21, PWC Tower, 188 Quay Street, Private Bag 92162, AUCKLAND 1142 NEW ZEALAND.

•**TOMES, Mr. Clive Philip Le Brun, FCA CFE** *1984;* Clive Tomes & Co, PO Box 771, Ground Floor, Colomberie Close, St. Helier, JERSEY JE4 0RX.

TOMINEY, Mr. Bernard Christopher, FCA *1975;* 1 Heybrigge Close, Redbourn, ST. ALBANS, HERTFORDSHIRE, AL3 7DT.

TOMINEY, Miss. Louise Elizabeth Bernadette, BCom ACA *2001;* 4 Shakespeare Road, HARPENDEN, HERTFORDSHIRE, AL5 5ND.

TOMKINS, Mr. Andrew Neville, BSc ACA *1984;* Hallsford Farm, Hethersgill, CARLISLE, CUMBRIA, CA6 6JD.

TOMKINS, Mrs. Ann, FCA *1985;* Grant Thornton House, Grant Thornton, 202 Silbury Boulevard, MILTON KEYNES, MK9 1LW.

TOMKINS, Mr. Anthony Bernard, FCA *1952;* Apple Trees, 1 Windsor Hill, PRINCES RISBOROUGH, BUCKINGHAMSHIRE, HP27 9HZ. (Life Member)

TOMKINS, Mr. Anthony Charles, FCA *1960;* 52 Winchester Drive, MABLETHORPE, LN12 2AY. (Life Member)

TOMKINS, Mr. Brett Edward, BA ACA *1995;* 6 Bryant Place, Glendowie, AUCKLAND 1071, NEW ZEALAND.

TOMKINS, Mr. Charles Edward Graham, BEng FCA CTA AMCT *1996;* CT Compliance Ltd, Mayfair House, 14 Heddon Street, LONDON, W1B 4DA.

TOMKINS, Mr. Daniel Andrew, BA ACA *2003;* KPMG LLP, Edward VII Quay, Navigation Way, Ashton-on-Ribble, PRESTON, PR2 2YF.

TOMKINS, Mr. Derek Charles, BSc ACA *1983;* 169 Severn Drive, UPMINSTER, RM14 1PN.

TOMKINS, Miss. Jessica, BA(Hons) ACA *2009;* Flat 3 Blue Boar House, 177 Victoria Avenue, SOUTHEND-ON-SEA, SS2 6EQ.

TOMKINS, Mr. Michael Allan, BSc ACA *1986;* 78 Bury Road, HEMEL HEMPSTEAD, HERTFORDSHIRE, HP1 1HW.

TOMKINS, Mr. Neil, BSc(Econ) ACA *1995;* Oxford University Press, Great Clarendon Street, OXFORD, OX2 6DP.

TOMKINS, Mr. Nicholas Graeme, BSc FCA *1988;* (Tax Fac), Hlb International, 21 Ebury Street, LONDON, SW1W 0LD.

TOMKINS, Mr. Peter Gerard Linton, FCA *1958;* Stoneacre, Corfe, TAUNTON, TA3 7BU. (Life Member)

TOMKINS, Mr. Simon Charles, BA ACA *1989;* Rivendell, Nicker Hill, Keyworth, NOTTINGHAM, NOTTINGHAMSHIRE, NG12 5EA.

TOMKINS, Miss. Sophie, MA BA ACA *1995;* The Paddocks, 25 Charlwood Drive, Oxshott, LEATHERHEAD, SURREY, KT22 0HB.

TOMKINS, Mrs. Susan Angela, BA ACA *1982;* Bantons Cottage, 12 Bantons Lane, Ticknall, DERBY, DE73 7NZ.

TOMKINS, Mrs. Tracy Suzanne, BA ACA *1992;* Rivendell, Nicker Hill, Keyworth, NOTTINGHAM, NG12 5EA.

TOMKINSON, Mr. Adrian Shaun, BSc ACA *1989;* Certex Ltd Unit C/1 Harworth Industrial Estate, Bryans Close Harworth, DONCASTER, SOUTH YORKSHIRE, DN11 8RY.

TOMKINSON, Mr. Andrew Robert, BA ACA *2005;* with PricewaterhouseCoopers LLP, 101 Barbirolli Square, Lower Mosley Street, MANCHESTER, M2 3PW.

TOMKINSON, Mr. Christopher David, MEng ACA *2002;* Belbins Dene, Sandy Lane, ROMSEY, SO51 0PD.

TOMKINSON, Mr. Craig Ashley, ACA *2006;* 2nd Floor 9 Colmore Row, Colmore Row, BIRMINGHAM, B3 2BJ.

•**TOMKINSON, Mr. Derek William, FCA** *1973;* (Tax Fac), Tomkinson Teal LLP, Hanover Court, 5 Queen Street, LICHFIELD, STAFFORDSHIRE, WS13 6QD.

TOMKINSON, Mr. Geoffrey, BSc FCA *1974;* Sandy & Co (Contractors) Limited, Grey Friars Place, STAFFORD, ST16 2SD.

TOMKINSON, Mr. Robert Charles, MA FCA FCT *1966;* Home Farm, Wappenham, TOWCESTER, NN12 8SJ. (Life Member)

TOMLEY, Ms. Mary Patricia, BA ACA *1983;* 78 Priors Way, Braywick, MAIDENHEAD, SL6 2EN.

TOMLIN, Mr. Alan Colin, BA ACA *1985;* Park House Twineham Lane, Twineham, HAYWARDS HEATH, WEST SUSSEX, RH17 5NP.

TOMLIN, Mr. Gary Lee, BA(Hons) ACA *2001;* 4 Sandringham Road, LONDON, E10 6HJ.

TOMLIN, Mr. Jake, BSc ACA *2010;* 197/3403 Castlereagh Street, SYDNEY, NSW 2000, AUSTRALIA.

TOMLIN, Mr. Jamie Alexander, BA ACA *1991;* 57 Lytton Avenue, LETCHWORTH GARDEN CITY, SG6 3HY.

TOMLIN, Mrs. Janet Ruth, FCA *1959;* 1 The Oval, Brookfield, MIDDLESBROUGH, TS5 8ET.

TOMLIN, Mr. Julian Spencer, BSc ACA *1990;* 53 Park Hall Road, East Finchley, LONDON, N2 9PY.

TOMLIN, Mrs. Karen, BA ACA *1991;* 57 Lytton Avenue, LETCHWORTH GARDEN CITY, SG6 3HY.

TOMLIN, Mrs. Mary, BSc FCA *1975;* with Cocke Vellacott & Hill, Unit 3, Dock Offices, Surrey Quays Road, Surrey Quays, LONDON SE16 2XU.

TOMLIN, Mrs. Rebecca Catherine, BA ACA ATII *1993;* (Tax Fac), 53 Park Hall Road, East Finchley, LONDON, N2 9PY.

TOMLINS, Mr. Alan Christopher, BA ACA *1983;* 17 Belton Drive, West Bridgford, NOTTINGHAM, NG2 7SJ.
TOMLINS, Mr. James Richard, BSc ACA *2005;* First Floor, Zurich Financial Services UK Life Centre, Station Road, SWINDON, SN1 1EL.
TOMLINSON, Mr. Alan, MA ACA *1980;* Bijogi 2-1-5, TODA, SAITAMA PREFECTURE, 335 0031 JAPAN.
•TOMLINSON, Mr. Alan Howard, BA FCA *1981;* Begbies Traynor (Central) LLP, 340 Deansgate, MANCHESTER, M3 4LY.
TOMLINSON, Mr. Alan John, BA ACA *1995;* 1 Homage Place, Coven, WOLVERHAMPTON, WV9 5BT.
TOMLINSON, Mrs. Alison Margaret, BA ACA *2000;* 19 Broadway, Finchfield, WOLVERHAMPTON, WV3 9HG.
TOMLINSON, Mr. Andrew James, BA FCA *1998;* Flat 55 Follingham Court, Drysdale Place, LONDON, N1 6LZ.
TOMLINSON, Mr. Andrew Peter, BSc ACA *1984;* Guide Security Services, 3 Arkwright Court, Blackburn Interchange, DARWEN, LANCASHIRE, BB3 0FG.
TOMLINSON, Mr. Anthony Peter, FCA *1958;* 27 Peplins Way, Brookmans Park, HATFIELD, AL9 7UR. (Life Member)
TOMLINSON, Mr. Barry, FCA *1977;* 14 Derwent Road, TWICKENHAM, TW2 7HQ.
TOMLINSON, Mr. Christopher John, FCA *1969;* 6 Glebe Avenue, Flitwick, BEDFORD, MK45 1HS. (Life Member)
TOMLINSON, Mr. Colin, BSc ACA *1985;* 62 Main Street, Gunthorpe, NOTTINGHAM, NG14 7EU.
TOMLINSON, Mr. Colin Howard, MA ACA *1986;* High Gable, 62 Banks Road, Pound Hill, CRAWLEY, RH10 7BP.
TOMLINSON, Mr. David, BA ACA *2010;* Flat 59, The High, Streatham High Road, LONDON, SW16 1EY.
TOMLINSON, Mrs. Elizabeth Ann, MA ACA *1983;* River House, 9 Aldgate, Ketton, STAMFORD, PE9 3TD.
TOMLINSON, Mr. Eric, BSc(Hons) ACA *1993;* 2 Granton Green, Northlake, PERTH, WA 6163, AUSTRALIA.
TOMLINSON, Mr. Garry John, FCA *1972;* Oak Ridge, Theobalds, Hawkhurst, CRANBROOK, TN18 4AJ.
•TOMLINSON, Mr. Gary Martin, BA ACA *2003;* Its Purely Financial Limited, Laurel Cottage, The Batch, Butcombe, BRISTOL, BS40 7UY.
TOMLINSON, Mrs. Gillian Margaret, BSc ACA *2005;* 59 Kewstoke Road, BRISTOL, BS9 1HF.
TOMLINSON, Ms. Gillian Mary, BA FCA *1987;* 26 Clover Court, Calverley, PUDSEY, LS28 5SY.
TOMLINSON, Mr. Graham, ACA *2009;* 42 Emlyn Road, REDHILL, RH1 6EW.
•TOMLINSON, Mr. Ian Edward, LLB FCA *1963;* (Tax Fac), Ian E. Tomlinson, 11 Hitherwood, CRANLEIGH, GU6 8BW.
TOMLINSON, Mr. James Russell, FCA *1974;* 68 Sandford View, NEWTON ABBOT, DEVON, TQ12 2TH.
TOMLINSON, Miss. Jane Ellen, BA ACA *1992;* 35 Clough Grove, Oughtibridge, SHEFFIELD, S35 0JU.
TOMLINSON, Mrs. Jenifer Chi Mei, BSc ACA ATII *1994;* 59 Westgate Tranmere Park, Guiseley, LEEDS, LS20 8HH.
TOMLINSON, Mr. Jeremy Richard, MA FCA *1986;* 9 Mayfield, OAKHAM, LEICESTERSHIRE, LE15 6PT.
TOMLINSON, Ms. Joanne Elizabeth, BSc ACA *1995;* 1 Mawsley Lodge, Mawsley, KETTERING, NORTHAMPTONSHIRE, NN14 1SW.
TOMLINSON, Miss. Joanne Marguerite, ACA *2008;* (Tax Fac), 19 Corderoy Place, CHERTSEY, SURREY, KT16 9NE.
TOMLINSON, Mr. John, FCA *1964;* Skiddaw, Whiteshoot, Redlynch, SALISBURY, SP5 2PR.
TOMLINSON, Mr. John Anthony, FCA *1967;* 6 Endcliffe Edge, SHEFFIELD, S10 3EH.
TOMLINSON, Mr. John Carl, BA ACA *1995;* Brasenose Farmhouse, Oxford Road, Steeple Aston, BICESTER, OXFORDSHIRE, OX25 5QG.
TOMLINSON, Mr. John Richard, MA LLB ACA *1984;* County Hall, Fishergate, PRESTON, PR1 0LD.
TOMLINSON, Mr. John Stuart Thomas, MA ACA *1981;* River House, 9 Aldgate, Ketton, STAMFORD, PE9 3TD.
TOMLINSON, Miss. Katie, BSc ACA *2010;* 18 Macefin Avenue, MANCHESTER, M21 7QQ.
TOMLINSON, Miss. Katy, BA(Hons) ACA *2002;* 106e Kyverdale Road, LONDON, N16 6PL.
TOMLINSON, Mrs. Kulvinder, BA ACA *1991;* The Limes, 110a London Road, Holybourne, ALTON, HAMPSHIRE, GU34 4EW.
TOMLINSON, Mr. Mark William, BSc ACA *1994;* 27 Chaffinch Road, Four Marks, ALTON, GU34 5FG.
TOMLINSON, Mrs. Mary, FCA *1974;* 19 Long Meadows, Burley-in-Wharfedale, ILKLEY, LS29 7RX.
TOMLINSON, Mr. Matthew James, BEng BCom ACA *2007;* 4 Larkway, BEDFORD, MK41 7JW.
TOMLINSON, Mrs. Mhairi Elizabeth, BA ACA *1999;* 25 Beverley Rise, ILKLEY, WEST YORKSHIRE, LS29 9DB.
•TOMLINSON, Mr. Michael, FCA *1973;* Churchills, 1st Floor, Shenstone Station, Station Road, Shenstone, LICHFIELD STAFFORDSHIRE WS14 0NW.
•TOMLINSON, Mr. Michael David, BSc ACA *1994;* Peter Durbin & Company Limited, Holiday House, Valley Road, ILKLEY, LS29 8PA.
TOMLINSON, Mrs. Natasha Louise, BSc ACA *2003;* 10 Willingham Way, Kirk Ella, HULL, HU10 7NL.
TOMLINSON, Mr. Nevil Edwin, BA FCA *1977;* 21 Orford Gardens, TWICKENHAM, TW1 4PL.
TOMLINSON, Mr. Norman Edward, FCA *1951;* 28 Hillrise, WALTON-ON-THAMES, SURREY, KT12 2PE. (Life Member)
•TOMLINSON, Mrs. Paula Jane, BSc FCA CTA *1991;* On The Spot Tax Limited, 3 Springfield Close, Bolney, HAYWARDS HEATH, WEST SUSSEX, RH17 5PQ.
TOMLINSON, Mr. Peter, FCA *1967;* Miramonte Pauls Lane, Hambleton, POULTON-LE-FYLDE, FY6 9AE.
TOMLINSON, Mr. Peter Colin, MSc BSc FCA *1978;* International Training Centre of the ILO, Viale Maestri del Lavoro 10, 10127 TURIN, ITALY.
TOMLINSON, Mr. Philip George, BA FCA *1974;* Gamache, route de Riscle, 32110 URGOSSE, FRANCE. (Life Member)
TOMLINSON, Mr. Robert Sykes, BA FCA *1962;* Conifers, Rectory Drive, Bidborough, TUNBRIDGE WELLS, KENT, TN3 0UN.
•TOMLINSON, Ms. Rosemary Olive, BSc FCA CTA TEP *1989;* (Tax Fac), Rosemary Tomlinson, 2 Bank Farm Cottages, Bran Mill Lane, Paxford, CHIPPING CAMPDEN, GL55 6XJ. See also Tomlinson R O
TOMLINSON, Mr. Rudolph Leslie, ACA CA(NZ) *2010;* 140 Old Woolwich Road, Greenwich, LONDON, SE10 9PR.
•TOMLINSON, Mr. Samuel Paul, BA(Hons) ACA *2003;* with PricewaterhouseCoopers LLP, 1 Embankment Place, LONDON, WC2N 6RH.
TOMLINSON, Mr. Simon, BA ACA *1995;* 10 Castlerow Close, Bradway, SHEFFIELD, S17 4RA.
TOMLINSON, Mr. Simon Andrew, BA ACA *1993;* 3060 Carrick Road, CUMMING, GA 30040, UNITED STATES.
TOMLINSON, Mr. Simon James, BSc ACA *1992;* Errigal Investments Limited, 4 Lockside Office Park Cockside Road Riversway, PRESTON, PR2 2YS.
TOMLINSON, Mr. Simon John Lloyd, LLB ACA *1995;* 19 Ashfurlong Close, Dore, SHEFFIELD, S17 3NN.
•TOMLINSON, Mr. William Harris, BCom FCA *1976;* Kelvin Burke & Co Ltd, 81a Stanley Road, WAKEFIELD, WF1 4LH. See also Financial Consulting Services Ltd
TOMLINSON, Mr. William Leonard, BA ACA *1982;* A F Blakemore and Son Limited, Longacre Trading Estate, Rose Hill, WILLENHALL, WV13 2JP.
TOMOS, Mrs. Jill, BA ACA *1982;* Galilea, 14 Cae Coedmore, Cwmann, LAMPETER, DYFED, SA48 8EH.
TOMPKINS, Mr. Andrew, BA ACA *1997;* 38 Peregrine Crescent, COOMERA, QLD 4209, AUSTRALIA.
TOMPKINS, Mr. Mark Edward, BA FCA *1998;* with Smith & Nephew plc, 15 Adam Street, LONDON, WC2N 6LA.
TOMPKINS, Mr. Michael George, FCA *1972;* 11 Beaumont Park, Danbury, CHELMSFORD, CM3 4DE.
TOMPKINS, Mr. Nigel William Alan, BA ACA *1987;* 57 Grena Road, RICHMOND, TW9 1XS.
TOMPKINS, Mr. Richard John, FCA *1969;* 30 La Montagne, Bakkerskloof Road, SOMERSET WEST, C.P., 7130, SOUTH AFRICA. (Life Member)
TOMPKINS, Mr. Richard Laurence, ACA *2009;* 39 Winders Road, LONDON, SW11 3HE.
TOMPKINS, Mr. Simon Peter, BSc ACA *1991;* 18 Green Oak Road, SHEFFIELD, S17 4FP.
•TOMPSETT, Mr. Clifford Peter, MA ACA *1985;* PricewaterhouseCoopers LLP, 1 Embankment Place, LONDON, WC2N 6RH. See also PricewaterhouseCoopers
TOMPSETT, Miss. Daisy, ACA *2010;* 49 Wilbury Road, HOVE, EAST SUSSEX, BN3 3PB.
TOMPSETT, Miss. Fiona Margaret, BSc ACA *1985;* Crowe Clark Whitehill llp, 49-51 Blagrave Street, READING, Rg1 1PL.
•TOMPSETT, Mr. Michael Frederick, BSc FCA *1973;* (Tax Fac), Fletcher & Partners, Crown Chambers, Bridge Street, SALISBURY, SP1 2LZ.
TOMS, Mr. Alan Adrian, FCA *1971;* Original Additions (Beauty Products)) Ltd, Ventura House, Bullsbrook Road, HAYES, MIDDLESEX, UB4 0UJ.
TOMS, Mrs. Alexandra Lucy Swinburn, BA ACA *2006;* 64 Capelands, New Ash Green, LONGFIELD, KENT, DA3 8LQ.
TOMS, Mr. David, BSc FCA *1960;* 39 Berkeley Waye, Heston, HOUNSLOW, TW5 9HJ. (Life Member)
TOMS, Miss. Deborah Carol, ACA *2010;* 15 Black Bank Road, Little Downham, ELY, CAMBRIDGESHIRE, CB6 2UA.
TOMS, Prof. John Steven, MA ACA *1987;* The York Management School, Freboys Lane, YORK, YO10 5GD.
TOMS, Mrs. Katy Emma, ACA *2008;* 62 Lagoon View, West Yelland, BARNSTAPLE, DEVON, EX31 3LE.
TOMS, Mr. Keith James-Ray, BA(Hons) ACA *2000;* 13/2-4 Trafalgar Street, CROWS NEST, NSW 2065, AUSTRALIA.
TOMSETT, Alan Jeffrey, Esq OBE BCom FCA JDipMA *1952;* (Tax Fac), 14 Colts Bay, Craigwell on Sea, BOGNOR REGIS, WEST SUSSEX, PO21 4EH. (Life Member)
TOMSETT, Mrs. Cecilia, MSc BA(Hons) ACA *2000;* Avda de la Vega 10 portal IV 4 Dcha, Alcobendas, 28108 MADRID, SPAIN.
•TOMSETT, Mr. Eric George, BA FCA *1974;* (Tax Fac), 113 Fellows Road, LONDON, NW3 3JS.
•TOMSETT, Mr. Julian, FCA *1997;* Derek J Read Limited, 107 North Street, MARTOCK, SOMERSET, TA12 6EJ.
TOMSETT, Mr. Richard John, BSc ACA *1999;* Avenida de la Vega 10 portal IV 4 Dcha, 28108 MADRID, SPAIN.
TOMSETT, Mrs. Sarah Rachel, BA ACA *2001;* 198 Trowell Road, NOTTINGHAM, NG8 2DP.
TOMSKI, Mr. Robert Maurice Ernst, BSc FCA *1984;* 10 Victoria Terrace, HARROW, HA1 3EW.
TON, Ms. Ke-Huong, ACA *2008;* 3 The Crest, LONDON, N13 5JT.
TON NU, Ms. Phuong Lien Lynnette, BA ACA *1992;* 38 Grove Drive, SINGAPORE 279078, SINGAPORE.
TONDELLI, Mr. Modesto Manfredo Francesco, FCA *1974;* 18 Greenway, Old Southgate, LONDON, N14 6NN.
•TONER, Mr. David Charles, BA ACA *1999;* A C Grace & Company Limited, Brook Lane House, 1a Rossett Business Village, Rossett, WREXHAM, CLWYD LL12 0AY.
TONER, Mr. Francis Gerard Malachy, BCom ACA *1979;* 38 Selkirk Road, Curzon Park, CHESTER, CH4 8AH.
TONER, Mr. Gary Gerard, LLB ACA *1994;* 63 Pine Gardens, Berrylands, SURBITON, KT5 8LJ.
TONER, Miss. Katherine Mary, ACA *2009;* 41 Oakdene Road, HEMEL HEMPSTEAD, HERTFORDSHIRE, HP3 9TS.
•TONER, Mr. Robert Anthony, BCom FCA *1987;* Compelling Solutions Consulting, 29 Lamb Close, WATFORD, WD25 0TB.
TONG, Mr. Alec Chi Chiu, MSc ACA CPA *1990;* The Dairy Farm Group, 7/F Devon House, Taikoo Place, 979 King's Road, QUARRY BAY, HONG KONG ISLAND HONG KONG SAR.
TONG, Mr. Alexander William, BA ACA *2009;* 3 Kings Court, Market Weighton, YORK, YO43 3FN.
TONG, Mr. Carl Ka Wing, ACA *1980;* Excel Master Limited Flat D 3/F. Yeung Yiu Chung (No.8) Ind. Bldg. No. 20 Wang Hoi Road, KOWLOON BAY, KOWLOON, HONG KONG SAR.
•TONG, Mr. Carlson, FCA *1979;* Room 1502 15 F, Waga Commercial Centre, 99 Wellington Street, CENTRAL, HONG KONG SAR.
TONG, Mrs. Catherine Louise, BA ACA *2001;* 5 Dawes Lane, Wheathampstead, ST. ALBANS, HERTFORDSHIRE, AL4 8FF.
TONG, Miss. Charlotte, BSc(Econ) ACA *2011;* 7 Caswall Close, Binfield, BRACKNELL, BERKSHIRE, RG42 4EF.
TONG, Mr. Eric, BA FCA *1990;* Deloitte Touche Tohmatsu, 35/F One Pacific Place, 88 Queensway, CENTRAL, HONG KONG ISLAND, HONG KONG SAR.
TONG, Mr. James Edward, MA MEng ACA *1999;* (Tax Fac), 64 Ancastle Green, HENLEY-ON-THAMES, OXFORDSHIRE, RG9 1TS.
TONG, Miss. Karen, ACA *2008;* 414 West Carriage House, Royal Carriage Mews, LONDON, SE18 6GB.
TONG, Mr. King Hang, ACA *2005;* Flat H 5/F Tower 9, Park Central, 9 Tong Tak Street, TSEUNG KWAN O, NEW TERRITORIES, HONG KONG SAR.
TONG, Mr. Lap Hong, ACA *2006;* KTC Partners CPA Limited, Unit 501502 &508, 5/F, Mirror Tower, 61 Mody Road, TSIM SHA TSUI KOWLOON HONG KONG SAR. See also Tong, Lap Hong and KTC CPA Limited
TONG, Ms. Mei Kuen Tommei, ACA *2007;* House M6, Floral Villas, 18 Tso Wo Road, SAI KUNG, NEW TERRITORIES, HONG KONG SAR.
TONG, Mr. Raphael Tai-Wai, BSc ACA *1991;* 145 Connaught Road West, SAI YING POON, HONG KONG ISLAND, HONG KONG SAR.
TONG, Mr. Wilson Chakwai, ACA *2006;* Flat B 13/F Regal Crest, 9 Robinson Road, MID LEVELS, HONG KONG ISLAND, HONG KONG SAR.
TONG, Mr. Wing Kin, ACA *2007;* Flat J9/F Block One, Smithfield Court, 43 Smithfield Road, KENNEDY TOWN, HONG KONG ISLAND, HONG KONG SAR.
TONG, Mr. Yu Keung, ACA *2008;* 28G Block 8, Beverly Garden, 1 Tong Ming Road, TSEUNG KWAN O, HONG KONG SAR.
TONG, Ms. Yuen Han, ACA *2005;* 38F Block 3, Estoril Court, 55 Garden Road, MID LEVELS, HONG KONG ISLAND, HONG KONG SAR.
TONG, Miss. Yuk Ying Angel, BSc FCA *1989;* House No. 5, Marigold Path, Palm Springs, YUEN LONG, NEW TERRITORIES, HONG KONG SAR.
•TONG SAM, Mr. Mike Jimmy, BSc FCA *1994;* Mayfair Trust SARL, BP 2634, L-1026 LUXEMBOURG, LUXEMBOURG.
TONGE, Mr. Alexander, ACA *2010;* 39 Loosen Drive, MAIDENHEAD, BERKSHIRE, SL6 3UT.
TONGE, Mrs. Alyson, BSc ACA *1980;* 8 Meadow Court, Scruton, NORTHALLERTON, NORTH YORKSHIRE, DL7 0QU.
TONGE, Mr. David, BA ACA *1987;* 54 George Harvey Road, RD1, Upper Moutere, NELSON 7173, NEW ZEALAND.
TONGE, Mrs. Jacqueline, BSc(Hons) ACA CTA *2002;* J J B Sports Plc, Challenge Way, Martland Mill Industrial Estate, WIGAN, LANCASHIRE, WN5 0LD.
TONGE, Miss. Jennifer Anne, BSc ACA *2002;* Stagecoach Manchester, Daw Bank, STOCKPORT, CHESHIRE, SK3 0DU.
TONGE, Mr. Jeremy Michael, BA ACA *1989;* Luminar House, Deltic Avenue Rooksley, MILTON KEYNES, MK13 8LW.
TONGE, The Revd. Malcolm, BA FCA *1978;* 8 Meadow Court, Scruton, NORTHALLERTON, NORTH YORKSHIRE, DL7 0QU.
TONGE, Mr. Robert Christopher, FCA *1960;* 5 Old Hall Drive, Whaley Bridge, HIGH PEAK, SK23 7HF.
•TONGUE, Mr. Graham Derek, BSc ACA *1995;* Delta Tax Services Limited, 6 Fair Field, Waltham on the Wolds, MELTON MOWBRAY, LEICESTERSHIRE, LE14 4AX.
•TONGUE, Mr. Ian Richard, BSc(Hons) ACA *2001;* Sandison Easson & Co, Rex Buildings, Alderley Road, WILMSLOW, CHESHIRE, SK9 1HY.
TONGUE, Mrs. Rachel Frances, BSc ACA CTA *1996;* 6 Fair Field, Waltham On The Wolds, MELTON MOWBRAY, LEICESTERSHIRE, LE14 4AX.
TONKIN, Mr. Andrew John, BSc FCA *1993;* Tor Homes, Tor House, St. Peters Quay, TOTNES, TQ9 5SH.
•TONKIN, Ms. Claire Alexandra, BSc ACA *1995;* Bishop Fleming, Cobourg House, Mayflower Street, PLYMOUTH, PL1 1LG. See also CAT Accounting Services
TONKIN, Dr. David John, PhD MA FCA *1975;* Company Reporting, 11 Johns Place, EDINBURGH, EH6 7EL.
•TONKIN, Mr. Keith Michael, BA ACA *1985;* Clement House, Weydown Road Industrial Estate, HASLEMERE, GU27 1HR.
TONKIN, Mr. Laurence James, MA ACA *2010;* 6 Oakbury Drive, WEYMOUTH, DORSET, DT3 6JB.
TONKIN, Miss. Rachael Lisa, BSc ACA *1994;* 13 Constable Close, Keynsham, BRISTOL, BS31 2UN.
TONKIN, Miss. Saphia Teresa, ACA *2008;* 2 Garden View 5 Paget Drive, PAGET PG 04, BERMUDA.
TONKINSON, Mr. David Harry, FCA *1951;* Flat 11, Edward House, 43 New Church Road, HOVE, EAST SUSSEX, BN3 4BH. (Life Member)
TONKINSON, Mr. Nicholas David, FCA *1973;* c/o Wallem Group Ltd, 12/F Warwick House East, TaiKoo Place, 979 King's Road, QUARRY BAY, HONG KONG ISLAND HONG KONG SAR.
TONKS, Mrs. Carla Barbara, ACA *2009;* with PricewaterhouseCoopers LLP, 31 Great George Street, BRISTOL, BS1 5QD.
TONKS, Mr. David John, FCA *1975;* 4 Goldfinch Gardens, GUILDFORD, SURREY, GU4 7DN.

TONKS, Mr. George Howard, BSc FCA *1978;* (Tax Fac), 47 York Avenue, Finchfield, WOLVERHAMPTON, WV3 9BX.
TONKS, Mr. Ian Daniel, BA ACA *1997;* 13 Knowsley Road, Hazel Grove, STOCKPORT, CHESHIRE, SK7 6BW.
TONKS, Mr. Mark Howard, BA ACA *1982;* Sunrise, Church Road, North Leigh, WITNEY, OX29 6TX.
TONKS, Mr. Michael Louis, ACA *1994;* with Hawsons, Pegasus House, 463a Glossop Road, SHEFFIELD, S10 2QD.
TONKS, Mr. Paul David, BSc ACA *1989;* Randstad C P E Ltd Forum, 4 Parkway Whiteley, FAREHAM, PO15 7AD.
•TONKS, Mr. Paul John, BSc(Econ) ACA *2004;* 11 Ferndale Road, Essington, WOLVERHAMPTON, WV11 2JG.
TONKS, Mr. Paul Jonathan, BSc ACA *1989;* Magnolia House, Upper Main Street, Upper Benefield, Nr Oundle, PETERBOROUGH, PE8 5AN.
TONROE, Mr. Michael John, BSc ACA *1993;* Australian Synchrotron, 800 Blackburn Road, CLAYTON, VIC 3168, AUSTRALIA.
TONTHAT, Mr. Richard, ACA *2008;* Flat 2, 90 Ballater Road, LONDON, SW2 5QP.
TONUCCI, Mr. Paolo Roberto, MA ACA *1994;* 16 St. Marks Crescent, Primrose Hill, LONDON, NW1 7TS.
•TOOGOOD, Mr. Alan Frederick, FCA *1970;* 11 Hazel Road, Cheadle Hulme, CHEADLE, CHESHIRE, SK8 7BN.
TOOGOOD, Mr. Dennis Victor, FCA *1963;* 74 The Pastures, Lower Westwood, BRADFORD-ON-AVON, BA15 2BH. (Life Member)
TOOGOOD, Mr. Edward George, BSc ACA *2007;* 153 Oswald Road, Chorlton cum Hardy, MANCHESTER, M21 9AZ.
TOOGOOD, Mr. John Barry, BA FCA *1977;* 147 Manor Green Road, EPSOM, KT19 8LL.
TOOGOOD, Mr. Mark Lee, BSc ACA *1991;* 5th Floor, 151 Wardour Street, LONDON, W1F 8WE.
TOOGOOD, Mrs. Rosemary, BSc ACA *1992;* Amsel str 3, 14195 BERLIN, GERMANY.
TOOHER, Miss. Bridie Clare, ACA *2009;* 47 22-28 Penkivil Street, BONDI, NSW 2026, AUSTRALIA.
•TOOK, Mr. Chay Justin, BSc(Econ) FCA *2000;* Spofforths LLP, A2 Yeoman Gate, Yeoman Way, WORTHING, WEST SUSSEX, BN13 3QZ.
TOOKE, Mr. Peter Michael, FCA *1974;* 126 High Street, Bildeston, IPSWICH, IP7 7ED.
TOOKE-KIRBY, Mrs. Ann Daphne, BSc FCA *1980;* Mulberry House, Chelmsford Road, High Ongar, ONGAR, CM5 9NL.
TOOKER, Mr. Alan John, BA FCA *1974;* PO Box 10250, Grand Pavilion Commercial Centre, Suite # 7, GEORGE TOWN, GRAND CAYMAN, KY1-1003 CAYMAN ISLANDS.
TOOKER, Mr. Steven Paul, ACA *2001;* with Ernst & Young, 155 N Wacker Drive, CHICAGO, IL 60606, UNITED STATES.
TOOKEY, Mr. Keith Alan Stanley, BSc ACA *1983;* Wassell Hill, Hoarstone Lane, Trimpley, BEWDLEY, WORCESTERSHIRE, DY12 1NQ.
TOOKEY, Mr. Timothy James William, BSc FCA *1989;* The Coach House, 2 Elwill Way, Park Langley, BECKENHAM, KENT, BR3 3AD.
TOOLAN, Miss. Angela Catherine, BA ACA *1990;* 26 Foxbank Close, WIDNES, CHESHIRE, WA8 9DP.
TOOLE, Mr. Pat Edward, FCA *1956;* 77 Foxholes Road, Great Baddow, CHELMSFORD, CM2 7HS. (Life Member)
TOOLE, Mr. Patrick John, FCA *1957;* Mundays, Frog Lane, Kingsdon, SOMERTON, SOMERSET, TA11 7LL. (Life Member)
TOOLE, Mr. Stephen Derrick, BA FCA CF *1988;* Barton Willmore Beansheaf Farm House, Bourne Close Calcot, READING, RG31 7BW.
•TOOLEY, Mr. David Alan, FCA *1973;* David Tooley, 68 Westbury Road, NORTHWOOD, HA6 3BY.
TOOLEY, Mr. Jonathan Andrew, BSc FCA *1990;* Rua do Duque da Terceira 358, 4000 - 534 PORTO, PORTUGAL.
•TOOLEY, Mrs. Lesley Ann, LLB FCA CTA *1984;* (Tax Fac), Page Kirk LLP, Sherwood House, 7 Gregory Boulevard, NOTTINGHAM, NG7 6LB.
•TOOLEY, Mr. Robert Graham, FCA *1968;* Robert Tooley, 38 Farm Way, NORTHWOOD, HA6 3EF.
TOOMBS, Miss. Claire Louise, ACA *1993;* 79a Lynmouth Crescent, Furzton, MILTON KEYNES, MK4 1JP.
TOOMEY, Mr. Stephen Andrew, BA ACA *1984;* Castle Lodge, Castle Gate, LEWES, BN7 1YS.
TOOMS, Miss. Melanie Jane, BA ACA *1996;* 93a Fairfield Road, MARKET HARBOROUGH, LEICESTERSHIRE, LE16 9QH.
TOON, Mrs. Alice Harriet Clarissa, ACA *2008;* with Mazars LLP, Tower Bridge House, St. Katharines Way, LONDON, E1W 1DD.
TOON, Mr. Andrew John, BA ACA *1983;* Walnut Tree Cottage, Old Bawtry Road, Finningley, DONCASTER, DN9 3BU.
TOON, Mr. Angus James Stuart, ACA *2009;* 1235 S. Prairie Avenue, Apt 3601, CHICAGO, IL 60605, UNITED STATES.
TOON, Mr. Christopher James, BA ACA *2008;* 3 Lower Paxton Road, ST. ALBANS, HERTFORDSHIRE, AL1 1PG.
TOON, Mr. David Mark, BA(Hons) ACA *2001;* Flat 17 Viewpoint, Lee Park, LONDON, SE3 9TN.
TOON, Mr. John Andrew, ACA *2007;* Montpelier Professional Charter House, Pittman Way Fulwood, PRESTON, PR2 9ZD.
TOON, Mrs. Linda, BSc ACA *1982;* G A Mell (Builders) Ltd, 2 The Courtyard, Bawtry, DONCASTER, SOUTH YORKSHIRE, DN10 6JG.
•TOON, Mr. Nicholas Shaun, FCA *1992;* Cross & Fairhead Business Consultants Limited, 5 Queen Street, GREAT YARMOUTH, NORFOLK, NR30 2QP.
TOON, Miss. Rebecca Louise, BA(Hons) ACA *2001;* 74 Coombe Bridge Avenue, Stoke Bishop, BRISTOL, BS9 2LS.
TOON, Miss. Sally, BSc ACA *2003;* 41 Omapere Street, Whitby, WELLINGTON 5024, NEW ZEALAND.
TOON, Mrs. Sarah, BA ACA *2004;* 43 Vale Drive, Hampton Vale, PETERBOROUGH, PE7 8EP.
TOONE, Mr. David Richard, BSc FCA *1980;* 4219 Doncaster Way, VANCOUVER V6S 1W1, BC, CANADA.
TOONE, Mrs. Helen Susan, ACA *1990;* Little Mullions, 3 Gatton Road, REIGATE, RH2 0EX.
•TOONE, Mr. Jeremy Martin, BA ACA *1997;* Grant Thornton UK LLP, 30 Finsbury Square, LONDON, EC2P 2YU. See also Grant Thornton LLP
TOONE, Mr. John Ralph, BSc FCA *1982;* 15 Tenbury Road, Cleobury Mortimer, KIDDERMINSTER, DY14 8RB.
•①TOONE, Mr. Richard Howard, BSc ACA *1992;* Chantrey Vellacott DFK LLP, Russell Square House, 10-12 Russell Square, LONDON, WC1B 5LF.
TOOP, Mr. Christopher Yates, BSc ACA *1981;* 10 Marksbury Avenue, Kew Gardens, RICHMOND, TW9 4JF.
TOOP, Mr. Geoffrey Herbert, FCA *1969;* Primrose Cottage, 60 Little Gaddesden, BERKHAMSTED, HP4 1PL. (Life Member)
TOOP, Mr. John Frank, FCA *1966;* 11 Randiddles Close, Hurstpierpoint, HASSOCKS, BN6 9BG.
TOOR, Miss. Baljit Kaur, BA ACA *2002;* 73 Mount Drive, HARROW, MIDDLESEX, HA2 7RW.
TOOR, Mr. Bhupinder Singh, ACA *2008;* 6 Melrose Road, SOUTHAMPTON, SO15 7PA.
TOOR, Ms. Diljit Kaur, BSc ACA *1998;* 1401 Ferncrest Road, Oakville, ONTARIO L6H 7W2, ON, CANADA.
TOOR, Mr. Hardeep Singh, BSc ACA *2002;* 73 Kingsway, Chandler's Ford, EASTLEIGH, HAMPSHIRE, SO53 1FH.
TOOR, Mr. Jaswinder Singh, MSc BSc ACA *2004;* U B S Investment Bank, 100 Liverpool Street, LONDON, EC2M 2RH.
TOOR, Mr. Najem Ud Din, FCA *1975;* Najem D Toor, 37-A PCSIR Housing Society, Canal Bank, LAHORE, PAKISTAN.
TOOR, Mr. Sarvjit Singh, BSc ACA *1990;* Hillview, 303 Old Bedford Road, LUTON, LU2 7BW.
TOOR, Miss. Satwinder Kaur, BA ACA *2005;* Apartment 111 King Edwards Wharf, 25 Sheepcote Street, BIRMINGHAM, B16 8AB.
TOOR, Mr. Surinder Singh, MA ACA *1997;* J P Morgan Asset Management Infrastructure Investments Group, Finsbury Dials, 20 Finsbury Street, LONDON, EC2Y 9AQ.
TOORA, Miss. Karen, ACA *2009;* 16 Raglan Road, SMETHWICK, WEST MIDLANDS, B66 3NE.
TOORAWA, Ms. Rubina Anver, BSc FCA *1991;* International Financial Services Limited, IFS Court, TwentyEight, Cybercity, Ebene, REDUIT MAURITIUS. See also Interantional Financial Services
TOOSEY, Miss. Nicola Rachel, BSc ACA *1990;* c/o Express Printing Services, PO Box 10263, DUBAI, UNITED ARAB EMIRATES.
TOOTELL, Mr. Barry, BA FCA *1986;* 59 Heybridge Lane, Prestbury, MACCLESFIELD, CHESHIRE, SK10 4ER.
TOOTH, Mrs. Christine Joy, BSc ACA *1985;* Blossom View, 37 Orchard Place, Harvington, EVESHAM, WORCESTERSHIRE, WR11 8NF.
TOOTH, Mr. David Henshall, FCA *1975;* 27 Stafford Avenue, Clayton, NEWCASTLE, ST5 3BN.
TOOTH, Mr. Mark Colin, BEng ACA *2001;* 43 New Road Wonersh, GUILDFORD, SURREY, GU5 0SF.
TOOTH, Mr. Matthew Edmund Frederick, BSocSc ACA *1997;* 5 Courthope Villas, Wimbledon, LONDON, SW19 4EH.
TOOTH, Mr. Shaun David, BSc(Econ) ACA *1999;* 106 West Street, North Creake, FAKENHAM, NORFOLK, NR21 9LH.
TOOTHE, Mrs. Lucia Andrea, MSc BSc ACA *2006;* Flat 6, 52 Lullingstone Lane, Heather Green, LONDON, SE13 6UH.
TOOTHILL, Mr. David Arthur, FCA *1956;* Yew Tree Cottage, Silkmore Lane, West Horsley, LEATHERHEAD, SURREY, KT24 6JQ. (Life Member)
TOOTLE, Mr. Leon, ACA *2011;* 18 Lydford Road, LIVERPOOL, MERSEYSIDE, L12 5HF.
TOOVEY, Mr. Richard, BA FCA *1990;* (Tax Fac), Toovey Eaton & Macdonald Ltd, P.O. Box 44, WELLINGTON, NEW ZEALAND.
TOOZE, Mr. Martin Lee James, BA ACA *2010;* 32 Wherretts Well Lane, SOLIHULL, B91 2SD.
TOOZE, Mr. Michael Frederick, FCA *1974;* 38 Manor Road, Bramhall, STOCKPORT, SK7 3LY.
TOPHAM, Mr. Barrie, FCA *1970;* Ivy Bank Cottage, The Green, Clayton, NEWCASTLE, ST5 4AA.
TOPHAM, Mr. Brandon Rodney, ACA CA(SA) *2008;* Box 2887, Montana Park, PRETORIA, GAUTENG, 0159, SOUTH AFRICA.
TOPHAM, Mr. Joel Richard, ACA *2008;* 44 Cross Road, Idle, BRADFORD, WEST YORKSHIRE, BD10 9RU.
TOPHAM, Mr. John Christopher, ACA *1979;* Greythorne, Grays Road, Westerham Hill, WESTERHAM, TN16 2HX.
TOPHAM, Mr. Matthew Edward Currer, FCA *1983;* Court Yard House, Chapel-en-le-Frith, HIGH PEAK, DERBYSHIRE, SK23 9UE.
TOPHAM, Mr. Michael Robert Mason, BA ACA *1999;* Biffa Waste Services Ltd Accuray House, Coronation Road Cressex Business Park, HIGH WYCOMBE, BUCKINGHAMSHIRE, HP12 3TZ.
TOPHAM, Mr. Nigel John, BA ACA *1983;* Unit 7, Eterniti Steels Ltd 7 Langthwaite Road, Langthwaite Grange Ind Estate South Kirkby, PONTEFRACT, WEST YORKSHIRE, WF9 3AP.
TOPHAM, Mrs. Ruth Patricia, ACA *1999;* The Castle, Staleen Road, Donore, DROGHEDA, COUNTY MEATH, IRELAND.
TOPIA, Mr. Mohammed, BSc(Hons) ACA *2011;* 76 Blenheim Road, GLOUCESTER, GL1 4ER.
TOPLAS, Mr. David Hugh Sheridan, MA MSc ACA *1981;* Hillcrest, 25 Guildown Road, GUILDFORD, GU2 4EU.
TOPLASS, Mr. Gerard Andrew Lindley, ACA *1993;* Rosemount, Jenny Brough Lane, HESSLE, NORTH HUMBERSIDE, HU13 0JX.
TOPLEY, Mr. Alan, FCA *1966;* 4 Jubilee Court, Bridewell Lane, TENTERDEN, KENT, TN30 6EY.
TOPLEY, Mrs. Gillian Mary, FCA *1965;* 4 Jubilee Court, Bridewell Lane, TENTERDEN, KENT, TN30 6EY.
•TOPLEY, Mr. Robert John, BSc ACA AMCT *1997;* Deloitte LLP, Saltire Court, 20 Castle Terrace, EDINBURGH, EH1 2DB. See also Deloitte & Touche LLP
TOPLIFF, Miss. Melanie Jane, BA ACA *1989;* Trevorrick Farm, St. Issey, WADEBRIDGE, PL27 7QH.
TOPLIS, Mr. Howard Mark, BSc ACA ACT *1990;* Tor Homes Tor House, St. Peters Quay, TOTNES, TQ9 5SH.
TOPLISS, Mr. John Martin, MSc FCA *1969;* Executive Insight Meathe House, 1 Brooklands Farm Close Fordcombe, TUNBRIDGE WELLS, TN3 0SF.
TOPLISS, Mr. Simon Paul, BA ACA *2007;* 37 Studfield Road, Wisewood, SHEFFIELD, S6 4ST.
•TOPOL, Mr. Geoffrey Ian, ACA CA(SA) *2009;* Global Payroll Services Ltd, 102 Selby Road, West Bridgford, NOTTINGHAM, NG2 7BA.
TOPP, Mr. John Gabriel Patchett, BA FCA *1967;* Taigh A'Ghaoul, Bulwark, Maud, ABERDEEN, ABERDEENSHIRE, AB42 5PX. (Life Member)
•TOPPER, Mr. Alan, FCA *1969;* (Tax Fac), 55 Newberries Avenue, RADLETT, HERTFORDSHIRE, WD7 7EL.
•TOPPERMAN, Mr. Simon, LLB FCA *1975;* (Tax Fac), Alexander & Co, 17 St Ann's Square, MANCHESTER, M2 7PW.
•TOPPIN, Mr. John Eric, MA FCA *1986;* Nomizon Associates, The Old Rectory, Sutton Road, Langley, MAIDSTONE, KENT ME17 3LY.
•TOPPING, Mr. Alistair John, BEng ACA *1999;* A J Topping LLP, 6 High Lea, Marsden, HUDDERSFIELD, HD7 6DZ.
•TOPPING, Mr. David John, ACA *1996;* Topping & Van Gerwen Limited, 1 Long Street, TETBURY, GLOUCESTERSHIRE, GL8 8AA. See also Premier Payroll Limited
TOPPING, Ms. Diane Gail, BA ACA *1989;* with Seligman Percy, Hilton House, Lord Street, STOCKPORT, SK1 3NA.
TOPPING, Mrs. Jane, LLB ACA *1992;* Littlebeck House, 7 Clark Beck Close, HARROGATE, NORTH YORKSHIRE, HG3 1RS.
•TOPPING, Mrs. Janet, BA FCA *1985;* (Tax Fac), Topping Consultancy Limited, 209 Liverpool Road, SOUTHPORT, MERSEYSIDE, PR8 4PH.
TOPPING, Mr. John, BSc ACA *1990;* 25 Swanside Avenue, LIVERPOOL, L14 7NP.
TOPPING, Mr. John Robert, BSc ACA *1989;* Marshalls Plc Landscape House, Premier Way Lowfields Business Park, ELLAND, WEST YORKSHIRE, HX5 9HT.
•TOPPING, Mr. Michael, FCA *1975;* Topping Partnership, 9th Floor, 8 Exchange Quay, SALFORD, M5 3EJ. See also Topping Partnership Limited
TOPPING, Miss. Sarah Louise, BA ACA *2007;* 19 Rutland Road, HOVE, EAST SUSSEX, BN3 5FF.
TOPPLE, Mr. Barry Stanley, FCA *1963;* Beck Ford, 680 Gums Lane, YASS, NSW 2582, AUSTRALIA.
TOPSOM, Mr. Alexander David, ACA *2008;* 19 Water View, Riverside, CAMBRIDGE, CB5 8JQ.
•TOPSY, Mr. Alen Keswachand, MBA FCA *1980;* DGT Associates, Sodnac Business Centre, 24 Avenue des Hirondelles, Sodnac, QUATRE-BORNES, MAURITIUS.
TORBE, Mr. Christopher Doylah Sigmund, BEng FCA *1977;* W. Wing Yip PLC, 375 Nechells Park Road, BIRMINGHAM, B7 5NT.
•TORBITT, Mr. Geoffrey Colin, FCA *1969;* (Tax Fac), Torbitt & Co Ltd, 27 Durham Road, Birtley, CHESTER LE STREET, COUNTY DURHAM, DH3 2QG.
TORDOFF, Mr. Philip James, BA ACA *2005;* 32 Snowdonia Way, HUNTINGDON, CAMBRIDGESHIRE, PE29 6XP.
TOREVELL, Mrs. Marianna Helen, ACA *2010;* 387 Astley Street, DUKINFIELD, CHESHIRE, SK16 4QW.
TOREVELL, Mr. Martyn Philip, BA ACA *1992;* 10 Darley Avenue, West Didsbury, MANCHESTER, M20 2XF.
TOREVELL, Mrs. Valerie Jane, BA ACA *1998;* 10 Darley Avenue, West Didsbury, MANCHESTER, M20 2XF.
•TORGERSEN, Mr. Stephen John, BSc FCA *1972;* UHY Torgersens, Somerford Buildings, Norfolk Street, SUNDERLAND, SR1 1EE. See also UHY Torgersens Limited
TORGOV, Mr. Konstantin, ACA *1995;* Flat 14 Halcyon Wharf, 5 Wapping High Street, LONDON, E1W 1LH.
•TORINO, Mr. Peter Antony, BSc ACA *1980;* Peter Torino BSc ACA - AIMS Accountants for Business, 25 Leith Mansions, Grantully Road, LONDON, W9 1LQ.
TORJUSSEN, Mrs. Deborah Jane, BA ACA *2006;* 28 Talbot Way, NANTWICH, CHESHIRE, CW5 7RQ.
TORKINGTON, Mr. Andrew, BSc ACA *2006;* 10 Merlin Close, Offerton, STOCKPORT, SK2 5UH.
TORKINGTON, Mr. Christian Roy, MA ACA *1988;* Scottish Widows, 69 Morrison Street, EDINBURGH, EH3 8YF.
TORKINGTON, Mr. David, BA FCA *1974;* 385 Isla Dorada Boulevard, MIAMI, FL 33143, UNITED STATES.
TORKINGTON, Mr. John Stephen, MA FCA *1971;* Yew Tree Cottage, Rostherne Lane, Rostherne, KNUTSFORD, CHESHIRE, WA16 6SB.
TORKINGTON, Miss. Laura Anne, BA ACA *2003;* 13 Mitchell Way, South Woodham Ferrers, CHELMSFORD, CM3 5PJ.
TORLESSE, Mr. Charles David, FCA *1960;* Treverbyn, High Street, Stillington, YORK, YO61 1LG.
TORLEY, Mr. John Joseph, MA ACA *1989;* 29 Victoria Park Gardens South, GLASGOW, G11 7BX.
TORN, Mr. Simon, MSci ACA *2005;* 9 Shepherds Way, HORSHAM, WEST SUSSEX, RH12 4LT.
TORNERO, Mr. Luke Benedict Martin, BSc FCA *1995;* Del Hotel Colon 1 C. al Sur Media C. arriba contiguo a la Funeraria Don Bosco Casa 68, MANAGUA, NICARAGUA.
TORODE, Mr. Matt, BSc(Hons) ACA *2009;* 89 Chelsham Road, SOUTH CROYDON, CR2 6HZ.
TOROK, Mr. Oliver, BA ACA *2002;* 91 Powney Road, MAIDENHEAD, BERKSHIRE, SL6 6EG.
TOROND, Mr. James Leonard, FCA *1962;* Flat 19, Farringdon House, 12 Strand Drive, Kew, RICHMOND, SURREY TW9 4EU. (Life Member)
TORPY, Mr. Max, MSci ACA *2007;* with PricewaterhouseCoopers LLP, 1 Embankment Place, LONDON, WC2N 6RH.

TORR, Mrs. Nina Jane, BSc ARCS ACA *1990;* 51 West Common Lane, SCUNTHORPE, SOUTH HUMBERSIDE, DN17 1DR.
TORR, Mr. Roger Mark, BSc FCA *1993;* Parkinson Matthews Llp, Cedar House, 35 Ashbourne Road, DERBY, DE22 3FS.
•TORRANCE, Mr. Gregory Lee, ACA *2009;* Torrance Accountancy Services, 6 Hillcrest, RYE, EAST SUSSEX, TN31 7HP.
TORRENS, Mr. Richard Peter, BA(Hons) ACA *2004;* 24 Woollards Lane, Great Shelford, CAMBRIDGE, CB22 5LZ.
TORRIJOS, Miss. Manuela, MPhil BA ACA *2005;* 33 Banning Street, LONDON, SE10 9PH.
TORRY, Mr. Nicholas Jeffrey, BSc ACA *2007;* 3 Furze Lane, PURLEY, CR8 3EJ.
TORY, Mr. Peter Martin, FCA *1974;* 48 Crown Road, MARLOW, BUCKINGHAMSHIRE, SL7 2QG.
•TORY, Mr. Robert Michael Annesley, FCA *1971;* Annesley Tory & Co, Clock House, Tandridge Lane, OXTED, RH8 9NJ.
TORY, Mr. Simon Edward, BA ACA *1983;* 148 Kristiansand Way, LETCHWORTH GARDEN CITY, HERTFORDSHIRE, SG6 1TY.
TOSE, Mr. Michael Bernard Leigh, BA FCA *2000;* Dorland House, 20 Regent Street, LONDON, SW1Y 4PH.
TOSELAND, Mr. Anthony John, BSc ACA *1983;* 39 Back Lane, Hardingstone, NORTHAMPTON, NN4 6BY.
TOSELAND, Mrs. Susan Mary, BA ACA *1983;* Harland Accountants 1a Berkeley Court, Berkeley Vale, FALMOUTH, CORNWALL, TR11 3PB.
TOSEN, Mr. Graeme, CA ACA CFA FRM *2005;* Flat 67 China Court, Asher Way, LONDON, E1W 2JF.
TOSEY, Mr. Daniel Dante, BSc FCA *1957;* Mansard, 43 Aultone Way, SUTTON, SM1 3LD. (Life Member)
•TOSH, Mr. Peter McLaren, FCA *1963;* (Tax Fac), Tosh & Co, 105B High Str, HONITON, EX14 1PE.
TOSSELL, Mrs. Bharati Priyadarshini, ACA *1985;* 8 Frobisher Close, KENLEY, CR8 5HF.
TOSSELL, Mr. Christopher John, ACA *1980;* 40 Boroughbridge Road, KNARESBOROUGH, HG5 0NJ.
•TOSSELL, Mr. David Ralph, ACA FCCA ACMA *2008;* David Lindon & Co, Avaland House, 110 London Road, Apsley, HEMEL HEMPSTEAD, HP3 9SD.
TOSSELL, Mr. Maurice Richard Nathaniel, BA ACA *1989;* 2 Hillthorpe Close, PURLEY, CR8 2JZ.
TOSSELL, Mr. Nicholas George Anthony, BSc ACA *1991;* Corner House, The Street, Farley, SALISBURY, SP5 1AB.
TOSSWILL, Mr. Simon Richard, FCA *1960;* Chilfrome Farmhouse, Chilfrome, DORCHESTER, DT2 0HA. (Life Member)
•TOSTEVIN, Mr. Philip James, BA FCA CTA *1981;* (Tax Fac), Hardcastle Burton (Newmarket) Limited, 90 High Street, NEWMARKET, SUFFOLK, CB8 8FE.
TOTH, Miss. Gabriella, ACA *2011;* 338a Kennington Road, LONDON, SE11 4LD.
•TOTHAM, Mr. Anthony Nigel, BSc FCA *1986;* Hayes & Co, St Andrews House, 11 Dalton Court, Commercial Road, Blackburn Interchange, DARWEN LANCASHIRE BB3 0DG.
•TOTHAM, Mr. Nicholas, BA ACA *1986;* Bennington Finance Limited, 30 Church Street, Long Bennington, NEWARK, NOTTINGHAMSHIRE, NG23 5EN. See also AIMS - Nick Totham
TOTHILL, Mr. Mark Jonathon, MA ACA *1991;* Rock Cottage Harbour Way, Cockwood, EXETER, EX6 8SG.
TOTHILL SCOTT, Miss. Hilary, FCA *1972;* CO4A Du Cane Court, LONDON, SW17 7JF.
TOTT, Mr. Ashley James, BSc ACA *1999;* Storgatan 6, 2 Trappor, 852 30 SUNDSVALL, SWEDEN.
TOTTEN, Miss. Jane Louise, BA ACA *1999;* with Deloitte LLP, Hill House, 1 Little New Street, LONDON, EC4A 3TR.
TOTTERDELL, Mr. Giles Alexander, BA(Hons) ACA *2000;* Room 4500, British Broadcasting Corporation White City, 201 Wood Lane, LONDON, W12 7TS.
TOTTERDILL, Mr. Paul Rupert, ACA CFA *1999;* C/-Adia, PO Box 3600, ABU DHABI, UNITED ARAB EMIRATES.
TOTTMAN, Mr. James David, BA ACA *2001;* 34a Keildon Road, LONDON, SW11 1XH.
TOTTON, Mr. Andrew John, BSc(Hons) ACA *2004;* 97 Foxhill, OLNEY, BUCKINGHAMSHIRE, MK46 5HE.
TOTTY, Mrs. Susan Rosemary, FCA *1972;* Bertram Burrows & Co, 10 Grange Road West Kirby, WIRRAL, MERSEYSIDE, CH48 4HA.
TOUCHE, Sir Anthony George, Bt FCA *1951;* Stane House, Stane Street, Ockley, DORKING, RH5 5TQ. (Life Member)
•TOUCHE, Mr. William George, BA ACA *1989;* Deloitte LLP, 2 New Street Square, LONDON, EC4A 3BZ. See also Deloitte & Touche LLP
TOUGH, Mr. Graeme Lawrence, MA ACA *2006;* 36/6 Roseburn Terrace, EDINBURGH, EH12 6AN.
TOUGH, Mr. Peter Grant, FCA *1973;* April Cottage, 26 Chalfont Road, Seer Green, BEACONSFIELD, HP9 2YG.
TOUGH, Mr. Robert James, BSc(Hons) ACA *2010;* 31 Culm Grove, EXETER, EX2 7QX.
TOUGH, Mr. Stephen Guy, MA(Oxon) ACA *1993;* 43 Coronation Drive, Donhead St. Mary, SHAFTESBURY, DORSET, SP7 9NA.
TOULL, Mr. Michael John, BSc FCA *1971;* 25 Orlando Crescent, VOYAGER POINT, NSW 2172, AUSTRALIA. (Life Member)
TOULSON, Mrs. Emma Louise Walton, BA ACA *1999;* Strawberry Hill, Church Hill, Shamley Green, GUILDFORD, SURREY, GU5 0UD.
TOULSON, Miss. Heather Maria, BA ACA *2001;* Pass the Post (612), Locked Bag 1, KEPERRA, QLD 4054, AUSTRALIA.
•TOULSON, Mrs. Jennifer Ann, ACA *1989;* HW, 117-119 Cleethorpe Road, GRIMSBY, LINCOLNSHIRE, DN31 3ET.
TOULSON, Mr. Sam Matthew, BSc ACA *1998;* Strawberry Hill Church Hill, Shamley Green, GUILDFORD, GU5 0UD.
•TOULSON, Mr. Stephen Reginald, FCA *1976;* (Tax Fac), Deeks Evans, 36 Cambridge Road, HASTINGS, TN34 1DU. See also Deeks Evans Audit Services Limited
•TOUMADJ, Mr. Saeed, BSc FCA *1981;* Ingram Consluting Limited, 9 Milton Close, LONDON, N2 0QH.
TOUMAZI, Miss. Eleonora, BSc ACA *2006;* 7 Thessalonikis Avenue, 6035 LARNACA, CYPRUS.
TOUMAZI, Miss. Kate Janice, BSc ACA *2004;* Flat 116, Ionian Building, 45 Narrow Street, LONDON, E14 8DX.
TOUMAZIS, Mr. Kyriacos Char, MA(Cantab) ACA *1990;* P O Box 51708, 3508 LIMASSOL, CYPRUS.
•TOUMBAS, Mr. Panayiotis Georgiou, BA FCA *1989;* Toumbas & Co, 5 Long Road, CANVEY ISLAND, SS8 0JA.
TOURICK, Mr. Colin Peter, MSc FCA *1979;* Colin Tourick & Associates Ltd, 47 Park Crescent, Elstree, BOREHAMWOOD, HERTFORDSHIRE, WD6 3PT.
TOUT, Miss. Chloe Josephine, BSc(Hons) ACA *2004;* with Grant Thornton UK LLP, 1 Dorset Street, SOUTHAMPTON, SO15 2DP.
TOUT, Mr. Daniel John, ACA *2009;* Flat 3 Sherway House, 9 Kingsbridge Road, POOLE, DORSET, BH14 8TL.
•TOUT, Mr. Derrick Hugh, BSc FCA *1972;* Littlejohn LLP, 1 Westferry Circus, Canary Wharf, LONDON, E14 4HD.
TOUT, Ms. Karen Suzanne, BSc ACA *1996;* Ann Summers Ltd, Gold Group House, Godstone Road, WHYTELEAFE, SURREY, CR3 0GG.
TOVELL, Mr. Andrew William, BA ACA *1994;* New Court, St Swithin's Lane, LONDON, EC4P 4DU.
TOVELL, Mr. Anthony John, BSc FCA *1978;* I G E Energy Systems, 2 The Arena Downshire Way, BRACKNELL, RG12 1PU.
•TOVELL, Mr. Lee Malcolm, FCA *1968;* Lower Chilland Cottage, Martyr Worthy, WINCHESTER, SO21 1EB.
TOVELL, Mrs. Melissa Alice, BA ACA *1993;* 4 Stokes Mews, Cambridge Crescent, TEDDINGTON, MIDDLESEX, TW11 8GR.
TOVEY, Mrs. Emma Elizabeth, BSc ACA *1999;* Schroder Plc, 31 Gresham Street, LONDON, EC2V 7QA.
TOVEY, Mr. Gordon Stanley, FCA *1974;* 7 Birch Lane, PENARTH, CF64 5BY. (Life Member)
TOVEY, Mr. Humphrey Paul, FCA *1960;* Mouzel, Llandevaud, NEWPORT, NP18 2AG. (Life Member)
TOVEY, Mr. James Francis, MA ACA *1997;* 21 Netherbury Road, LONDON, W5 4SP.
TOVEY, Mr. James Frederick Paul, MA ACA *1997;* 1 Broadlands Court, Vinegar Hill, Undy Magor, CALDICOT, NP26 3FA.
TOVEY, Miss. Jillian Mary, MA ACA *1984;* The Vicarage, 66 St. Michaels Avenue, Bramhall, STOCKPORT, CHESHIRE, SK7 2PG.
TOVEY, Mrs. Joanne Patricia, BA ACA *1998;* 7 Taunton Road, West Bridgford, NOTTINGHAM, NG2 6EW.
TOVEY, Mr. John Arthur Humphrey, BSc ACA *1993;* 2 Royal York Mews, Royal York Crescent, BRISTOL, BS8 4LF.
TOVEY, Mr. John Roger, FCA *1953;* Marraways, Binfield Heath, HENLEY-ON-THAMES, RG9 4LE. (Life Member)
TOVEY, Mr. Malcolm Jillard, FCA *1973;* 43 The Grove, Biggin Hill, WESTERHAM, TN16 3TA.
•TOVEY, Mr. Michael John, FCA *1976;* Chantrey Vellacott DFK LLP, Russell Square House, 10-12 Russell Square, LONDON, WC1B 5LF.
TOVEY, Mr. Norman, BA ACA *1992;* 6 Evelyn Road, BATH, BA1 3QF.
TOVEY, Ms. Paula Suzanne, FCA *1992;* 34 Glenbare Court, BATHGATE, EH48 1DR.
TOVEY, Mr. Robert Stephen John, ACA *2009;* 89 Geraldine Road, LONDON, SW18 2NS.
•TOVEY, Mr. Roger William, FCA *1968;* Roger W. Tovey, 30 Maidenhall, Highnam, GLOUCESTER, GL2 8DL.
TOVEY, Mr. Ryan Neil, BSc ACA *2001;* 6 St Peters Drive, Libanus Fields, Pontllanfraith, BLACKWOOD, NP12 2ER.
TOVEY, Mr. Simon George Houghton, MA FCA *1974;* 16 St. Germans Place, Blackheath, LONDON, SE3 0NN.
TOVEY, Mr. Vincent Antony, ACA CA(AUS) *2011;* 19 Southmill Road, BISHOP'S STORTFORD, HERTFORDSHIRE, CM23 3DH.
TOW, Miss. Christine Lee Cheng, BA ACA *1982;* 46A Draycott Park, SINGAPORE 259394, SINGAPORE.
TOWELL, Mrs. Larissa, MA(Hons) ACA *2002;* 208A Watling Street, Park Street, ST. ALBANS, HERTFORDSHIRE, AL2 2PA.
TOWELL, Mr. Robert John, FCA *1959;* 102 Haygarth Road, KLOOF, KWAZULU NATAL, 3610, SOUTH AFRICA. (Life Member)
TOWERS, Miss. Abigail, BSc ACA *2011;* 51 Albion Place, Campbell Park, MILTON KEYNES, MK9 4AJ.
TOWERS, Mr. Adrian Anthony, BA FCA *1982;* 31 Huntsmill, Fulbourn, CAMBRIDGE, CB21 5RH.
TOWERS, Mr. Alan Victor, FCA *1967;* 6 Talbot Road, Highgate, LONDON, N6 4QR.
TOWERS, Mr. Anthony Domonic Peter, BSc FCA *1991;* with Mazars LLP, 37 Frederick Place, BRIGHTON, BN1 4EA.
TOWERS, Mr. Basil Clifford, FCA *1956;* West Lodge Cottage, Grange Lane, Pitsford, NORTHAMPTON, NN6 9AN. (Life Member)
TOWERS, Mr. Bernard, FCA *1961;* 4 Arthington Lawns, Pool in Wharfedale, OTLEY, WEST YORKSHIRE, LS21 1QN. (Life Member)
TOWERS, Mr. Christopher James, BSc(Hons) ACA *2002;* Coniston 2, United Utilities Lingley Green Avenue, Lingley Mere Business Park Great Sankey, WARRINGTON, WA5 3LP.
TOWERS, Mr. David John, BSc FCA *1977;* 31 Lucknow Drive, Mapperley Park, NOTTINGHAM, NG3 5EU.
TOWERS, Mr. David Thomas, BA ACA *1980;* 20 Tiger Maple Drive, TIMBERLEA B3T 1G7, NS, CANADA.
TOWERS, Mrs. Emma Ruth, BSc(Hons) FCA *2001;* The Arches Chevin End, Menston, ILKLEY, LS29 6BN.
TOWERS, Mr. Gary, BSc ACA *1995;* 35 Gadwell Road, Walton Cardiff, TEWKESBURY, GL20 7RT.
•TOWERS, Mrs. Julie Ann, FCA CTA AIIT *1989;* (Tax Fac), Francis Clark LLP, Vantage Point, Woodwater Park, Pynes Hill, EXETER, EX2 5FD.
•TOWERS, Mrs. Keilah, BSS FCA *1978;* Accounting for Charities Ltd, Arena, Holyrood Close, POOLE, DORSET, BH17 7BA.
TOWERS, Mr. Keith, FCA *1976;* Greensleeves, 65 Harestone Lane, CATERHAM, SURREY, CR3 6AL.
TOWERS, Miss. Louise Clare, BSc ACA *2002;* 2 Shirley Close, Milton, CAMBRIDGE, CB24 6BG.
TOWERS, Ms. Margaret Elizabeth, ACA *1982;* 13 Robinson Street, CHATSWOOD, NSW 2067, AUSTRALIA.
TOWERS, Mrs. Maria Teresa, BA ACA *1985;* 10 Enniskerry Demesne, Enniskerry, WICKLOW, COUNTY WICKLOW, IRELAND.
TOWERS, Mr. Martin George, BA FCA *1977;* The ArchesIntake Farm, Chevin End, Menston, ILKLEY, WEST YORKSHIRE, LS29 6BP.
•TOWERS, Mr. Neil Campbell, BA FCA *1969;* N Towers & Co Limited, 63 Spring Meadow, Clayton-le-Woods, LEYLAND, PR25 5UR.
TOWERS, Mr. Neil William, MA FCA *1975;* (Tax Fac), 33 Shearman Road, Blackheath, LONDON, SE3 9HY.
TOWERS, Mr. Nicholas, BSc ACA *1987;* Yew Cottage Mill Road, Whitfield, BRACKLEY, NORTHAMPTONSHIRE, NN13 5TQ.
TOWERS, Miss. Nicola Carol, ACA *2008;* 2250 Broadway, Apt 5E, NEW YORK, NY 10024, UNITED STATES.
TOWERS, Mr. Paul Francis, BA ACA *1986;* 9 St. Hughs Close, CRAWLEY, WEST SUSSEX, RH10 3HH.
TOWERS, Mr. Richard John, BEng ACA *1991;* Swanline Print, Whitebridge Park, STONE, STAFFORDSHIRE, ST15 8LQ.
•TOWERS, Mr. Simon George Clifford, BSc FCA *1987;* Clifford Towers (Accountants) Limited, 1st Floor Suites, Units 8-9, Webb Ellis Business Park, RUGBY, CV21 2NP.
TOWERS-CLARK, Mrs. Jane, ACA *1992;* Oxford Brookes University, Wheatley Campus, Wheatley, OXFORD, OX33 1HX.
TOWERS-CLARK, Mr. Richard James, BSc ACA *1992;* Greatworth Court, Brackley Road, Greatworth, BANBURY, OXFORDSHIRE, OX17 2DX.
TOWHILL, Mr. Brian Lindsay, BA FCA *1980;* Le Clos Vigny, 4 Rue du Point Du Jour, 78250 GAILLON-SUR-MONTCIENT, FRANCE.
TOWILL, Mr. Robert Stephen, FCA *1969;* Bumblebees, Duntisbourne Abbots, CIRENCESTER, GLOUCESTERSHIRE, GL7 7JW.
TOWLE, Mr. Andrew John, BA ACA *1994;* 7 Seymour Road, ST. ALBANS, HERTFORDSHIRE, AL3 5HL.
TOWLER, Mr. Ashton, BSc(Hons) ACA *1995;* 12 Kimi Road, Karen, NAIROBI, 1202-00502, KENYA.
TOWLER, Mr. Ralph Thorsby, FCA *1960;* 24 Chatsworth Drive, Spofforth Hill, WETHERBY, LS22 6XY. (Life Member)
TOWLER, Mr. Roy Sydney, FCA *1959;* 3 Home Farm, Blakeney Rd, Letheringsett, HOLT, NR25 7JL. (Life Member)
TOWLSON, Mr. Malcolm Richard, BSc ACA *1989;* (Tax Fac), Elavon Financial Services Ltd, Block E, Cherrywood Business Park, LOUGHLINSTOWN, COUNTY DUBLIN, IRELAND.
TOWN, Mr. Graham Victor, FCA *1961;* 32 Newbury Road, Rastrick, BRIGHOUSE, HD6 3PG.
TOWN, Mr. John Richard, BA FCA CTA *1965;* 95 Lord Street, BLACKPOOL, FY1 2DJ.
TOWN, Mr. Mark, BA(Hons) ACA *2003;* 1 33 Arthur Street, FAIRLIGHT, NSW 2094, AUSTRALIA.
TOWN, Mr. Michael Allan, FCA *1970;* 4 Elmstead Park Road, West Wittering, CHICHESTER, WEST SUSSEX, PO20 8NQ. (Life Member)
TOWN, Mr. Philip James, BA ACA *2000;* 98 Mays Lane, BARNET, HERTFORDSHIRE, EN5 2LL.
TOWNDROW, Miss. Angela Katharine, BA ACA *1995;* 209 - 2425 West 4th Avenue, VANCOUVER V6K 1P4, BC, CANADA.
•TOWNE, Mr. Stephen David, BSc FCA *1990;* Towne & Co, Norbreck House, Landmere Lane, Edwalton, NOTTINGHAM, NG12 4DG.
TOWNELL, Mr. Alexander James, BSc ACA *2007;* Barclays Wealth, QVH1, Queen Victoria House, Victoria Street, Douglas, ISLE OF MAN IM99 1DS.
TOWNEND, Mr. Andrew, BA ACA *1999;* Industri Kapital Ltd, Brettenham House, 5 Lancaster Place, LONDON, WC2E 7EN.
TOWNEND, Mr. Andrew James, BSc FCA *1987;* BBC World Service Trust, Pariska 7, BELGRADE, SERBIA.
TOWNEND, Mr. Charles Russell Balme, MA FCA *1951;* 8 Lincoln Street, Chelsea, LONDON, SW3 2TS. (Life Member)
•TOWNEND, Mr. David James, FCA *1963;* David J. Townend, 17 Stoneleigh Road, SOLIHULL, WEST MIDLANDS, B91 1DG.
•TOWNEND, Mr. Frank Dyson, FCA *1975;* Townend English, 80 Market Street, Pocklington, YORK, YO42 2AB. See also Townend English Ltd
TOWNEND, Mr. John Ernest, FCA *1957;* J Townend & Sons (Hull) Ltd, Red Duster House, 101 York Street, HULL, HU2 0QX.
TOWNEND, Mr. John Robert, FCA *1968;* 6 Peace Grove, WELWYN, AL6 0RS.
TOWNEND, Mr. Jonathan Kurt, LLB ACA *1998;* BMW Group France, Jonathan Townend (V1-FR-F), 78886 SAINT-QUENTIN-EN-YVELINES CEDEX, FRANCE.
TOWNEND, Mr. Nicholas Adam, BA ACA *1993;* Acresfield, 48 Brooklands Drive, Goostrey, CREWE, CW4 8JD.
TOWNEND, Mr. Nicholas John, BA ACA *1985;* The Coppice, 24 Devonshire Park Road, Davenport Park, STOCKPORT, SK2 6JW.
TOWNEND, Mr. Peter, FCA *1962;* 232 The Point, 61 Noosa Springs Drive, NOOSA HEADS, QLD 4567, AUSTRALIA. (Life Member)
TOWNEND, Mr. Peter William, FCA *1951;* Carandon, Victoria Road, ELLAND, WEST YORKSHIRE, HX5 0QF.
TOWNEND, Mr. Simon James Shad, BA FCA CF *1994;* with KPMG, Montague Sterling Centre, East Bay Street, PO Box N123, NASSAU, BAHAMAS.
TOWNER, Mrs. Anna Louise, BSc ACA *2005;* 8a Tilford Road, FARNHAM, GU9 8DL.
TOWNER, Mr. Christopher John Nicholas, FCA *1974;* St James House, Second Street, ST. JAMES, BARBADOS.
TOWNER, Mr. James Edward, BSc ACA *1993;* MUJV Limited Aspire Business Centre, Ordnance Road, TIDWORTH, WILTSHIRE, SP9 7QD.

TOWNER, Ms. Katherine Anne, BA(Hons) ACA *2003;* PO Box 003, Institute of Psychiatry, 16 De Crespigny Park, LONDON, SE5 8AF.
TOWNLEY, Mr. David, BA ACA *1986;* 79 Waresley Park, Hartlebury, KIDDERMINSTER, WORCESTERSHIRE, DY11 7XF.
TOWNLEY, Mr. John Heneage, BA ACA *1992;* 62 Lancaster Avenue, LONDON, SE27 9EB.
TOWNLEY, Mr. John Michael, BA ACA *1992;* Woodlands Kiln Road, Prestwood, GREAT MISSENDEN, BUCKINGHAMSHIRE, HP16 9DG.
TOWNLEY, Mr. Mark Geoffrey, BA ACA *1999;* Wadsley Park Village, 14 Queenswood Gate, SHEFFIELD, S6 1RL.
TOWNLEY, Mr. Paul John, FCA DChA *1980;* 20 Norwood Road, Cheshunt, WALTHAM CROSS, EN8 9RW.
TOWNLEY, Mr. Simon, BA ACA *1986;* 11 Rothwell Court, Leyland, PRESTON, PR25 2NU.
TOWNLEY-JONES, Mr. Paul, BSc ACA *2000;* 33 Chestnut Grove, FLEET, GU51 3LN.
TOWNSEND, Mr. Arthur Vincent, FCA *1967;* Dowry House, Brandlesholme Road, Greenmount, BURY, BL8 4DZ.
TOWNSEND, Mr. Benjamin Piers, BSc FCA *1970;* The Haig, Crown Hill, Ropsley, GRANTHAM, LINCOLNSHIRE, NG33 4BH.
TOWNSEND, Mrs. Catherine Grania, BA ACA *1988;* 4 Erin Close, Port Erin, ISLE OF MAN, IM9 6FH.
TOWNSEND, Miss. Christine Rowena, FCA *1992;* 18 Cobbles Crescent, CRAWLEY, RH10 8HA.
TOWNSEND, Mr. Damien Scott, ACA *2009;* 49 Frobisher Road, NEWTON ABBOT, DEVON, TQ12 4HT.
TOWNSEND, Mr. David Arthur, FCA *1962;* 11 Janmead, Hutton, BRENTWOOD, CM13 2PU. (Life Member)
TOWNSEND, Mr. David Henry, BSc ACA *1992;* 34 Cardigan Close, Callands, WARRINGTON, WA5 9RE.
•TOWNSEND, Mr. David John, ACA *1985;* Townsend & Co Accountants Ltd, Office 3, The Kings Head Centre, 38 High Street, MALDON, ESSEX CM9 5PN.
TOWNSEND, Mrs. Deepti Leeanne, BSc FCA *1991;* Wildwood, 8 Bird in Hand Lane, Bickley, BROMLEY, BR1 2NB.
TOWNSEND, Mr. Derek Albert, MA ACA *1979;* 956 Glenwood Avenue SE, ATLANTA, GA 30316, UNITED STATES.
TOWNSEND, Mr. Edward Charles, FCA *1966;* Llwyn Celyn, Llansoar, Caerleon, NEWPORT, NP18 1LS.
TOWNSEND, Miss. Emma, ACA *2009;* 7 Pond Farm Estate, Millfields Road, LONDON, E5 0AA.
TOWNSEND, Miss. Emma Diana, ACA *2008;* G E Healthcare, Pollards Wood, Nightingales Lane, CHALFONT ST. GILES, BUCKINGHAMSHIRE, HP8 4SP.
TOWNSEND, Mr. Frederick Lee, BCom FCA *1975;* Casa Leo, Urbanizacion La Alqueria Buzon 55, Avda Agata s/n, 29650 MIJAS, MALAGA, SPAIN.
TOWNSEND, Mr. Gary, FCA *1981;* JACARANDA, ERIDGE ROAD, CROWBOROUGH, EAST SUSSEX, TN6 2SR.
TOWNSEND, Mr. Geoffrey Robert, MA FCA *1973;* Frunzenskaya Nabareshnaya 50/90, 119270 MOSCOW, RUSSIAN FEDERATION.
TOWNSEND, Mr. George Bernard, FCA *1960;* Flat 23, Harnleigh Green, Harnham Road, SALISBURY, SP2 8JN. (Life Member)
TOWNSEND, Miss. Georgina Jayne, ACA *2008;* Homelands, Upper Dunsforth, YORK, YO26 9RU.
TOWNSEND, Mrs. Helen Louise, BA ACA *2000;* 40 Myamblah Crescent, MEREWETHER, NSW 2291, AUSTRALIA.
TOWNSEND, Mr. Ian, FCA *1977;* Homelands, Upper Dunsforth, YORK, YO26 9RU.
TOWNSEND, Mr. Ian Gregory, BA ACA *1989;* 4 Erin Close, Port Erin, ISLE OF MAN, IM9 6FH.
TOWNSEND, Mr. James Pendrill Charles, BSc ACA *2003;* Standard Chartered, 1 Basinghall Avenue, LONDON, EC2V 5DD.
TOWNSEND, Mrs. Jenifer Ann, ACA *1984;* Higher Wotton Cottage, Yeoford, CREDITON, EX17 5EX.
TOWNSEND, Miss. Jennifer, BA ACA *1996;* 139 Elm Road, NEW MALDEN, SURREY, KT3 3HP.
TOWNSEND, Mrs. Jennifer Anne, MBA BSc ACA *1992;* Coombe Barn, Coombe Lane, Naphill, HIGH WYCOMBE, BUCKINGHAMSHIRE, HP14 4QR.
TOWNSEND, Mrs. Jenny, BSc ACA *2003;* 23 Netherside Drive, Chellaston, DERBY, DE73 6QU.
TOWNSEND, Mr. Jeremy Charles Douglas, BSc FCA *1989;* 8 Bird in Hand Lane, BROMLEY, BR1 2NB.
TOWNSEND, Mr. John George, BA ACA *1992;* 3 Fold Cottages, Woods Lane Dobcross, OLDHAM, OL3 5AU.
TOWNSEND, Mr. John Raymond, BA ACA *1988;* Vodafone, 1 Kingdom Street, LONDON, W2 6BY.
TOWNSEND, Mr. Jonathan, FCA *1967;* Jelka, Victoria Road, Wargrave, READING, RG10 8AD.
TOWNSEND, Mrs. Julia Anne, BA ACA *1990;* 54 Haydon Park Road, Wimbledon, LONDON, SW19 8JY.
TOWNSEND, Mr. Julian, ACA FCCA *2009;* with Dains LLP, Unit 306, Third Floor, Fort Dunlop, Fort Parkway, BIRMINGHAM B24 9FD.
TOWNSEND, Mr. Julian Benedict Christopher, MA ACA *1986;* Flat 5, Aston House, Church Hill, TOTLAND BAY, ISLE OF WIGHT, PO39 0EU. (Life Member)
TOWNSEND, Mr. Kenneth Mayne, FCA *1948;* Newcote, 3 Combe Gate, Combe, WITNEY, OX29 8NY. (Life Member)
TOWNSEND, Mr. Kevin, MA ACA *2004;* 47 Chaseside Avenue, Twyford, READING, RG10 9BT.
TOWNSEND, Mr. Martin, BEng FCA *1997;* A F Ltd, Bassington Industrial Estate, CRAMLINGTON, NORTHUMBERLAND, NE23 8AF.
TOWNSEND, Mr. Martin Roger, BSc ACA *1991;* 2526 Kilpatrick Court, SAN RAMON, CA 94583, UNITED STATES.
•TOWNSEND, Mr. Matthew, BSc ACA *2002;* 25 Altenburg Gardens, LONDON, SW11 1JH.
TOWNSEND, Mr. Michael, MA FCA *1967;* Hawthorns, Oakley Road, Battledown, CHELTENHAM, GL52 6NZ.
TOWNSEND, Mr. Michael John Bligh, BSc FCA *1994;* 9 Greenacres Drive, Ringmer, LEWES, BN8 5LZ.
TOWNSEND, Mr. Nicholas Edward, ACA *2008;* Centrica Energy Upstream, Kings Close 62 Huntly Street, ABERDEEN, AB10 1RS.
TOWNSEND, Mr. Patrick John Charles, BA ACA *1993;* c/o Instrata Capital, PO Box 26300, MANAMA, BAHRAIN.
TOWNSEND, Mr. Paul Andrew, BSc ACA *1996;* Mando Corporation Ltd, 27 Faraday Road, Rabans Lane Industrial Area, AYLESBURY, BUCKINGHAMSHIRE, HP19 8TY.
TOWNSEND, Miss. Paula Jane, BSc ACA *1981;* The Old Forge, Shere Road, Ewhurst, CRANLEIGH, GU6 7PJ.
TOWNSEND, Mr. Peter Herbert, FCA JDipMA CPA *1961;* 1648 South 310th Street, Suite 6, FEDERAL WAY, WA 98003, UNITED STATES. (Life Member)
•TOWNSEND, Mr. Peter Sandham, FCA *1973;* Duncan & Toplis, 3 Castlegate, GRANTHAM, LINCOLNSHIRE, NG31 6SF.
TOWNSEND, Mrs. Rebecca Dawn, ACA *2009;* Duncan & Toplis, 3 Castlegate, GRANTHAM, LINCOLNSHIRE, NG31 6SF.
TOWNSEND, Mrs. Rebecca Louise, BSc ACA *1990;* The Old School, School Lane, East Keswick, LEEDS, LS17 9DA.
TOWNSEND, Mr. Robert William, BSc ACA *1979;* 135 Kingsway, Petts Wood, ORPINGTON, BR5 1PP.
TOWNSEND, Miss. Sally, BA(Econ) ACA *1996;* Ground Floor Flat, 14 Ingersoll Road, LONDON, W12 7BD.
TOWNSEND, Mrs. Susan Marie, ACA *2007;* 31 Birchwood Grove, HAMPTON, MIDDLESEX, TW12 3DU.
TOWNSEND, Miss. Victoria Sarah Hoare, ACA *2009;* Llwyn Celyn, Llansoar, Caerleon, NEWPORT, GWENT, NP18 1LS.
TOWNSEND-JOHNSON, Mr. Tom Frederick, FCA *1974;* Old Post House 2 Bladen Valley Briantspuddle, DORCHESTER, DORSET, DT2 7HP.
TOWNSHEND, Mr. Roberto Ugo Patrizio, BA ACA *1990;* Via Bixio 32, 00185, ROME, ITALY.
TOWNSHEND, Miss. Victoria Lynne, MSci ACA *2010;* FAO Stephen Sowerby, ITA 3rd Floor, K P M G, St. James's Square, MANCHESTER, M2 6DS.
TOWNSLEY, Miss. Sarah, BA ACA *2003;* G A M (UK) Ltd, 12 St. James's Place, LONDON, SW1A 1NX.
TOWNSON, Mrs. Alexandra Margarita, BSc ACA *2006;* Finance, Npower Ltd Oak House, Bridgwater Road, WORCESTER, WR4 9FP.
TOWNSON, Miss. Heather, BSc(Hons) ACA *2009;* Ground Floor, 75 Laitwood Road, LONDON, SW12 9QH.
TOWNSON, Mr. Neil David, BA ACA *1985;* 53 Havering Drive, ROMFORD, RM1 4BH.
TOWSE, Mr. Clifford Scott, FCA *1968;* Redwood, Plantation Road, LEIGHTON BUZZARD, LU7 7HU.
TOWSE, Mr. Dan, MEng ACA *2009;* Deloitte & Touche Llp, 3 Rivergate, BRISTOL, BS1 6GD.
TOWSE, Mr. George Roger, BA FCA *1965;* 36 Leeward Gardens, Wimbledon, LONDON, SW19 7QR. (Life Member)
TOWSE, Mr. Mark Nicholas, BSc ACA *1996;* 32 Newick Avenue, SUTTON COLDFIELD, B74 3DA.
TOWSE, Mr. Michael Ian, ACA *1984;* Level 39 AMP Centre, 50 Bridge Street, SYDNEY, NSW 2000, AUSTRALIA.
TOWSEY, Mr. Matthew Simon, BA ACA *2006;* Flat 51 Lock House, 35 Oval Road, LONDON, NW1 7BF.
TOY, Mr. Geoffrey Norman, FCA *1973;* 40 Collins Road, Brunswick Estate, WEDNESBURY, WS10 0RX.
TOY, Mr. John Berkeley, ACA *1980;* 25 Hillcrest Park, EXETER, EX4 4SH. (Life Member)
TOY, Mrs. Margaret Elizabeth, BSc FCA ATII *1977;* 29 Farley Copse, BRACKNELL, BERKSHIRE, RG42 1PF.
TOY, Mrs. Natasha, ACA *2008;* 3 Radlet Drive, Timperley, ALTRINCHAM, CHESHIRE, WA15 6DE.
TOYE, Mrs. Catherine Hannah, MA ACA *1998;* c/o Clyde & Co, PO Box 31645, Sheikh Zayed Road, DUBAI, UNITED ARAB EMIRATES.
TOYE, Miss. Emma Claire, MA ACA *2009;* 53 Quickswood, LONDON, NW3 3SA.
•TOYE, Mr. Nicholas Matthew, MEng FCA *2000;* BPU Limited, Radnor House, Greenwood Close, Cardiff Gate Business Park, CARDIFF, CF23 8AA.
TOYE, Mr. Philip David, BSocSc ACA *1996;* C/o Clyde & Co, PO Box 31645, City Tower 2, Sheikh Zayed Road, DUBAI, UNITED ARAB EMIRATES.
TOYE, Mr. Roger William Curzon, MBA FCA *1966;* 53 Quickswood, LONDON, NW3 3SA.
TOYER, Mr. Daniel Kevin, BSc ACA *2000;* 88 Rose Street, Coburg, MELBOURNE, VIC 3058, AUSTRALIA.
TOYN, Mr. Charles Clifford, BSc ACA *1992;* 47 Langmuir Avenue, IRVINE, KA11 2DS.
TOYN, Mrs. Ruth, BA(Hons) ACA *2003;* 18 Seagrave Drive, Hasland, CHESTERFIELD, S41 0YE.
TOYNTON, Mr. Gregory Giles, BSc ACA *2008;* Hakluyt & Co Ltd, 34 Upper Brook Street, LONDON, W1K 7QS.
TOYNTON, Mr. Peter Anthony, FCA *1970;* Twytten House The Street, Wilmington, POLEGATE, EAST SUSSEX, BN26 5SN.
TOZE, Mr. Reginald Antony, FCA *1961;* 54 Azalea Crescent, FITZGIBBON, QLD 4018, AUSTRALIA.
TOZER, Miss. Avril Marion, BA(Hons) ACA *2001;* with Condy Mathias, 6 Houndiscombe Road, PLYMOUTH, PL4 6HH.
TOZER, Mr. David Lawrence, MA FCA *1964;* 10 Fairwater House, Twickenham Road, TEDDINGTON, TW11 8AY. (Life Member)
TOZER, Mrs. Debbie, BA ACA *1994;* 81 Grove Park, TRING, HERTFORDSHIRE, HP23 5JR.
TOZER, Mr. John Michael, BA(Hons) ACA *2011;* Brogues Wood, High Drive, Woldingham, CATERHAM, SURREY, CR3 7ED.
TOZER, Mr. Paul Henry, FCA *1966;* Hedgerow, Perrymead, BATH, BA2 5AY.
•TOZER, Mr. Richard, FCA FCIS *1971;* (Tax Fac), Richard Tozer LLP, Tricor Suite, 7th Floor, 52-54 Gracechurch Street, LONDON, EC3V 0EH. See also Richard Tozer
TOZER, Mr. Richard Edward, MA FCA *1969;* Lodge Farm, Elmdon, SAFFRON WALDEN, CB11 4LU. (Life Member)
TOZER, Mr. Robert Stanley, FCA *1953;* 39 High Road East, FELIXSTOWE, IP11 9JS. (Life Member)
TOZER, Mr. Robin Gerald, FCA *1968;* Brogues Wood High Drive, Woldingham, CATERHAM, CR3 7ED.
TOZER, Miss. Rowena Jane, ACA *2008;* Hedgerow House, Church Lane, Elvington, YORK, YO41 4AD.
TRAAVIK, Mr. Jarle Valgard, ACA CISA CIA MIB *1996;* Kirkeveien 78A, 0364 OSLO, NORWAY.
TRACE, Mr. Anthony Patrick, FCA *1973;* Anthony Trace Consulting, (PTY) Ltd, P.O. Box 224, HONEYDEW, GAUTENG, 2040 SOUTH AFRICA.
TRACE, Mr. David John Arthur, FCA *1968;* 88 Burbage Road, LONDON, SE24 9HE.
TRACE, Miss. Emily Frances, BA ACA *2006;* C H Trace & Son Gortleigh Farm, Sheepwash, BEAWORTHY, DEVON, EX21 5HU.
TRACE, Mr. Harold Griffith, BA FCA *1955;* 101 Parkland Grove, ASHFORD, Middlesex, TW15 2JF. (Life Member)
TRACE, Mr. Maurice William, FCA *1965;* 58 Buttermere Drive, Onchan, ISLE OF MAN, IM3 2EA.
TRACE, Miss. Nicola Louise, BA ACA *2007;* Top floor flat, 151 Dalling Road, LONDON, W6 0ET.
TRACE, Mr. Peter Timothy, FCA *1970;* P O Box 7533, GOLD COAST, QLD 9726, AUSTRALIA.
TRACEY, Mr. David James, BA ACA *1995;* Smedjevägen 3, 16 732 STOCKHOLM, SWEDEN.
TRACEY, Mr. Eric Frank, FCA *1982;* 6 De Beauvoir Square, LONDON, N1 4LG.
TRACEY, Miss. Laura Marie, BA ACA *2007;* 66a Sidney Road, TWICKENHAM, MIDDLESEX, TW1 1JR.
TRACEY, Mrs. Margaret Anne, ACA *1982;* 51 Carlton St, Hillsborough, AUCKLAND 1042, NEW ZEALAND.
TRACEY, Miss. Victoria Emma, ACA *2005;* 3 Weavers Orchard, ARLESEY, BEDFORDSHIRE, SG15 6PD.
TRACEY, Mrs. Wendy Jane, BSc ACA *1989;* The Old Manor House, Snitterton, MATLOCK, DE4 2JG.
TRACHONITIS, Mr. Andreas, ACA *2008;* 5 Str Apostolou Louka, Chrisopolitissa, 6012 LARNACA, CYPRUS.
•TRACHONITIS, Mr. George, BSc FCA *1986;* Abacus Limited, P O Box 25549, CY-1310 NICOSIA, CYPRUS.
TRACY, Mr. Oliver, ACA *2011;* First Floor Flat, 26 Marius Road, LONDON, SW17 7QQ.
TRACY, Mr. William Miles DeLap, MA ACA *1989;* 34 Vant Road, LONDON, SW17 8TJ.
TRADEWELL, Mrs. Caroline Michelle, BSc ACA *2004;* 12 Noel Avenue, OAKHAM, LE15 6SQ.
TRADGETT, Mrs. Ghislaine Elizabeth, BEng ACA *2002;* with Buzzacott LLP, 130 Wood Street, LONDON, EC2V 6DL.
TRAFFORD, Mr. Christopher, BSc ACA *2009;* 19 Northfold Road, LEICESTER, LE2 3YG.
TRAFFORD, Mr. Jeremy, ACA *1981;* 93 Station Lane, Scraptoft, LEICESTER, LE7 9UG.
TRAFFORD, Mr. Kenneth Cyril Ronald, FCA *1950;* 12 Rochester Place, Charlbury, CHIPPING NORTON, OXFORDSHIRE, OX7 3SF. (Life Member)
TRAFFORD, Mr. Philip Grenville, BA ACA *1995;* DV Estates Ltd, Mount Farm, Shirley, ASHBOURNE, DERBYSHIRE, DE6 3AR.
•TRAFFORD, Mrs. Sophie Clare, BSc ACA *1992;* Sophie Trafford, Church Lodge, Station Road, Wrington, BRISTOL, BS40 5LG.
TRAGEN, Mr. Martin Lawrence, BSc ACA *1983;* 13 The Spinney, CHEADLE, CHESHIRE, SK8 1JA.
TRAGEN, Mr. Robert, LLB ACA *2007;* 7 Gleneagles Close, Harold Wood, ROMFORD, ESSEX, RM3 0RU.
TRAGETT, Miss. Veronique Rebecca Agnes, BA ACA *2001;* 6 Grovemont Court, DECATUR, GA 30030, UNITED STATES.
TRAHEARN, Mr. James William Henry, BA FCA *1979;* 22 Arlington Drive, NOTTINGHAM, NG3 5EN.
TRAICE, Miss. Joanne Paula, BA(Hons) ACA *2002;* DP World -Head Office, PO Box 1700, DUBAI, UNITED ARAB EMIRATES.
TRAILL, Mr. George Adam, FCA *1980;* Barn Court Maidford Road, Farthingstone, TOWCESTER, NN12 8HE.
TRAILL, Mr. James Robin Gilbert, FCA *1976;* Kelvedon, Langham Road, ROBERTSBRIDGE, EAST SUSSEX, TN32 5DX.
TRAILL, Ms. Patricia Eileen Macleod, MA ACA *1985;* 25 Wedderburn Road, DUNBLANE, PERTHSHIRE, FK15 0FN.
TRAILL, Miss. Sarah Ellen, BSc ACA ATII *2002;* with PricewaterhouseCoopers, 1 East Parade, SHEFFIELD, S1 2ET.
•TRAIN, Mr. Gordon Stewart Campbell, BSc ACA *1987;* Train Consulting Limited, 42 Ryecroft Road, LONDON, SW16 3EQ.
TRAIN, Mr. Peter Brian, FCA *1956;* 105 Bricknell Avenue, HULL, HU5 4EU. (Life Member)
TRAIN, Mr. Robert, ACA *2009;* 73 MacMillan Way, LONDON, SW17 6AS.
TRAINER, Mr. Martin John, BSc ACA FRSA *1989;* 125 Wood Street, LONDON, EC2V 7AN.
•TRAINER, Mr. Tom Michael, BSc ACA *1992;* Business Experts, 40 Womersley Road, LONDON, N8 9AN.
•TRAMONTINI, Mr. Clive, PhD BSc FCA *1983;* (Tax Fac), Clive Tramontini & Co, Bruce House, 15 The Street, Hatfield Peverel, CHELMSFORD, CM3 2DP. See also C & M Tramontini Limited
TRAMOUNTANELLIS, Mr. Kyriakos, BSc ACA *2008;* 56 E ARCHIBSHOP MAKARIOS STREET AGLANTZIA NICOSIA CYPRUS, 2107 NICOSIA, CYPRUS.
TRAN, Mr. Hung Quoc, BSc FCA *1996;* Mars Chocolate UK Ltd, PO Box 4, SLOUGH, SL1 4JX.
TRAN, Ms. Lesley, ACA CA(AUS) *2010;* 87c Ladbroke Grove, Nottinghill, LONDON, W11 2HD.
TRAN, Mr. Michael, ACA *2011;* 10 Preston Gardens, ILFORD, ESSEX, IG1 3QG.

TRAN, Mr. Sean, ACA CA(AUS) *2009;* HSBC, Level 20, 8 Canada Square, LONDON, E14 5HQ.
TRAN, Miss. Susan, BA(Hons) ACA *2003;* 21 Bernay Gardens, Bolbeck Park, MILTON KEYNES, MK15 8QD.
TRAN, Ms. Thanh Nhu, ACA CA(AUS) *2006;* with Ernst & Young LLP, 1 More London Place, LONDON, SE1 2AF.
TRAN, Mr. William, ACA *2008;* (Tax Fac), Flat 708 Wharfside Point South, 4 Prestons Road, LONDON, E14 9EL.
TRANFIELD, Mrs. Carolyn Elizabeth, BSc ACA *1988;* Fernwood, 85a Mill Road, Lisvane, CARDIFF, CF14 0UG.
TRANFIELD, Mr. Daniel, BSc ACA *1988;* Fernwood 85a Mill Road Lisvane, CARDIFF, CF14 0UG.
TRANGMAR, Mr. David John, BEng ACA *1997;* Macro 4 Plc The Orangery, Turners Hill Road Worth, CRAWLEY, WEST SUSSEX, RH10 4SS.
TRANMER, Mrs. Judith, BSc ACA *2003;* Adult and Community Services Project Team, Worcestershire County Council, County Hall, Spetchley Road, WORCESTER, WR5 2NP.
•TRANTER, Mr. Alan Anthony, BSc FCA *1977;* Baker Tilly Tax & Advisory Services LLP, 1210 Centre Park Square, WARRINGTON, WA1 1RU. See also Baker Tilly UK Audit LLP
•TRANTER, Mrs. Angela Elizabeth, BSc FCA *1991;* (Tax Fac), Rushtons (NW) Limited, Shorrock House, 1 Faraday Court, Fulwood, PRESTON, PR2 9NB.
TRANTER, Mr. Christopher Winsley, BSc ACA *1985;* 50 Prestwood Road West, Wednesfield, WOLVERHAMPTON, WV11 1HL.
TRANTER, Mr. Dean, LLB ACA *2003;* 6 Court Way, TWICKENHAM, TW2 7SN.
TRANTER, Miss. Helen Rasmussen, MSc BA ACA *2011;* 6 Buckingham Grove, KINGSWINFORD, WEST MIDLANDS, DY6 9ED.
TRANTER, Miss. Ingrid, MEng ACA *1991;* 20 Copt Oak Road, Narborough, LEICESTER, LE19 3EF.
•TRANTER, Mr. Jim, BSc FCA *1969;* (Tax Fac), Tranter Lowe (Oakengates) Ltd, International House, 6 Market Street, Oakengates, TELFORD, SHROPSHIRE TF2 6EF.
TRANTER, Mr. John, BSc FCA *1989;* 11 Dickins Way, HORSHAM, RH13 6BQ.
TRANTER, Miss. Nicola, ACA *2008;* 21 Norfolk Avenue, HEYWOOD, OL10 4RN.
•TRANTER, Mr. Paul Alistair, BSc FCA *1974;* (Tax Fac), Paul Tranter & Company, 31 High Street, STOKESLEY, NORTH YORKSHIRE, TS9 5AD.
TRANTER, Mr. Paul Anthony, BCom FCA *1967;* 16 Dewsbury Drive, WOLVERHAMPTON, WV4 5RQ.
•TRANTER, Mr. Stephen Ernest William, FCA *1977;* (Tax Fac), Wilkes Tranter & Co Limited, Brook House, Moss Grove, KINGSWINFORD, WEST MIDLANDS, DY6 9HS.
TRANTHAM, Mr. Christopher James, MA ACA *2010;* 1 Maypole Close, Clutton, BRISTOL, BS39 5PP.
TRANTUM, Mr. Neil Antony, BSc ACA *1988;* 1 Matching Lane, BISHOP'S STORTFORD, CM23 2PP.
TRAPANI, Mr. Antonino, FCA *1971;* 26 Prince Consort Drive, ASCOT, SL5 8AW.
TRAPANI, Mr. Girolamo, ACA FCCA *2011;* 6 Marl Road, DUDLEY, WEST MIDLANDS, DY2 0HR.
TRAPNELL, Mr. David Neil, ACA *1988;* 96 Alderbury Street, Floreat, PERTH, WA 6014, AUSTRALIA.
TRAPNELL, Mr. Hugh Andrew, FCA *1974;* Sparex Limited, Exeter Airport, EXETER, EX5 2LJ.
TRAPNELL, Mr. Michael John, FCA *1964;* Little Orchard, 7 Northview Road, BUDLEIGH SALTERTON, EX9 6BZ. (Life Member)
TRAPP, Mr. John Frazer, FCA *1974;* Templegreen Property Services Ltd, Mountbatten House, Fairacres, WINDSOR, SL4 4LE. (Life Member)
TRAPP, Mr. John Timothy, FCA *1968;* Associated Liver, Launderettes Ltd., 104 Prescot Road, LIVERPOOL, L7 0JA.
TRAPPE, Mrs. Amy, ACA *2010;* 7 Oak Avenue, STOCKPORT, CHESHIRE, SK4 4EU.
TRASK, Mr. Ben Peter Allan, BSc ACA *2005;* with Deloitte LLP, Abbots House, Abbey Street, READING, RG1 3BD.
TRASK, Mr. Christopher James, BA ACA *2000;* 3 Willow Bank, Cheadle Hulme, CHEADLE, CHESHIRE, SK8 7NR.
TRASK, Mr. Michael Geoffrey, BSc ACA *1990;* 10 Portwey Close, Brixworth, NORTHAMPTON, NN6 9XE.
•TRATALOS, Ms. Nicola Frances, BSc FCA ATII *1988;* Deloitte LLP, 4 Brindley Place, BIRMINGHAM, B1 2HZ. See also Deloitte & Touche LLP
•TRAVERS, Mr. Anthony Howard, FCA *1971;* (Tax Fac), Henry R. Davis & Co, 33 Chester Road West, Queensferry, DEESIDE, CH5 1SA.
TRAVERS, Mr. Brendan Patrick, FCA *1965;* 14 Castlelawn, Tulla Road, ENNIS, COUNTY CLARE, IRELAND.
TRAVERS, Mr. Glen, ACA CA(AUS) *2008;* PO Box 239, COBHAM, SURREY, KT11 1WF.
TRAVERS, Mr. Harry Thomas, BSc FCA *1977;* Eastern Lodge, Old North Road, Kempsey, WORCESTER, WR5 3JZ.
TRAVERS, Mr. John Paul, MA ACA *1984;* Cyrus Audio Limited, 4/5 Spitfire Close, Ermine Business Park, HUNTINGDON, CAMBRIDGESHIRE, PE29 6XY.
TRAVERS, Mr. Lewis, FCA *1939;* 6 Sandringham House, Windsor Way, Brook Green, LONDON, W14 0UD. (Life Member)
•TRAVERS, Mr. Peter Michael, FCA *1968;* Peter Travers & Co., 28 Manor Road Extension, Oadby, LEICESTER, LE2 4FF.
TRAVERS, Mr. Steven David, BEng ACA *2001;* 1 Charnwood, Station Road, ASCOT, SL5 0QU.
TRAVERS CLARKE, Mr. John, MA FCA *1952;* 6 Ashley Gardens, LONDON, SW1P 1QD. (Life Member)
TRAVIS, Mr. Alexander Daniel, BEng ACA *1992;* 5 Bankside Road, MANCHESTER, M20 5QE.
TRAVIS, Mrs. Anne-Marie, BA(Econ) FCA *1966;* Manor Farmhouse, Glandford, HOLT, NR25 7JP.
TRAVIS, Mr. Anthony William, FCA *1971;* Roosstrasse 10A, CH-8832 WOLLERAU, SWITZERLAND.
TRAVIS, Mr. Benjamin William Norman, BA(Hons) ACA *2001;* 50 Hillier Road, LONDON, SW11 6AU.
•TRAVIS, Mr. David Joseph, FCA *1986;* CLB Coopers, Ship Canal House, 98 King Street, MANCHESTER, M2 4WU.
TRAVIS, Mrs. Frances Sheilagh, MA ACA *1991;* 18 Park Parade, CAMBRIDGE, CB5 8AL.
TRAVIS, Mr. Gilbert Wilson, MA FCA *1962;* 36 Beech Avenue, Chartham, CANTERBURY, CT4 7TA.
TRAVIS, Mr. Gordon, MA FCA *1976;* 31 Haggate Crescent, Royton, OLDHAM, LANCASHIRE, OL2 5NF.
•TRAVIS, Mr. Graham Charles Fotheringham, FCA *1981;* Clarke Nicklin LLP, Clarke Nicklin House, Brooks Drive, Cheadle Royal Business Park, CHEADLE, CHESHIRE SK8 3TD.
TRAVIS, Mr. Nicolas Bingley, BSc ACA *1993;* 21 Monckton Rise, North Newbald, YORK, YO43 4RX.
•TRAVIS, Mr. Philip John, FCA CF *1991;* TMG Corporate Finance LLP, 16 Oxford Court, MANCHESTER, M2 3WQ.
TRAVIS, Mr. Rupert Alan, MA FCA *1966;* Manor Farmhouse, Glandford, HOLT, NR25 7JP.
TRAVIS, Mr. Warren Anthony, BEng ACA *1992;* New Farm House, Crostwight, NORTH WALSHAM, NORFOLK, NR28 9PA.
•TRAVISS, Mr. Malcolm John, FCA *1974;* Traviss & Co, Newtown House, Newtown Road, LIPHOOK, HAMPSHIRE, GU30 7DX.
TRAVLOS, Ms. Olga Marilyn, ACA CA(SA) *2010;* Unit 3 Clive Court, Bartholomew's Walk, ELY, CAMBRIDGESHIRE, CB7 4EH.
TRAWFORD, Miss. Candase Helen, BA(Hons) ACA *2002;* Siemens Sir William Siemens Square, Frimley, CAMBERLEY, GU16 8QD.
•TRAWNY, Mr. Peter David, BA FCA ATII *1992;* Dhl Worldwide Network Sa/nv, 1 De Kleetlaan, 1831 DIEGEM, BELGIUM.
TRAYLEN, Mr. Geoffrey Francis, BSc FCA *1974;* (Tax Fac), 15 Holmbush Road, Putney, LONDON, SW15 3LE.
TRAYLEN, Miss. Jane, BSc ACA *2010;* 139 Sabine Road, LONDON, SW11 5LU.
TRAYNOR, Ms. Anne Geraldine, MBA BA ACA *1984;* 150 Burbage Road, Dulwich, LONDON, SE21 7AG.
TRAYNOR, Mr. Darrell Martin, BSc ACA *1996;* Ernst & Young, Level 11 Al Ghaith Tower, PO Box 136, Hamdan Street, ABU DHABI, UNITED ARAB EMIRATES.
•TRAYNOR, Mr. John Thomas, BCom FCA *1975;* (Tax Fac), John Traynor & Co, 35 Stockdale Drive, Whittle Hall, WARRINGTON, WA5 3RU.
TRAYNOR, Mr. John William, BTech ACA *1983;* Newdigate Place, Dukes Road, Newdigate, DORKING, SURREY, RH5 5BP.
TRAYNOR, Mr. Joseph, FCA *1961;* 15 Stoneleigh Avenue, SALE, M33 5FF. (Life Member)
TRAYNOR, Mr. Joseph George, BA ACA *1999;* 145 St. Elmo Road, LONDON, W12 9DY.
•ⓘTRAYNOR, Mr. Richard William, BCom ACA *1985;* Begbies Traynor, 340 Deansgate, MANCHESTER, M3 4LY. See also Begbies Traynor(Central) LLP and Begbies Traynor Limited
TRAYNOR, Mrs. Sarah Jane, BSc ACA *1991;* 63 Old Mt Coot-tha Road, TOOWONG, QLD 4066, AUSTRALIA.
TREACY, Miss. Fiona, BA ACA *2000;* Cloughmartin, Thurles, TIPPERARY, COUNTY TIPPERARY, IRELAND.
TREACY, Mr. Ian Kinsman, BA FCA *1970;* Dry Sandford Old School, 195 Cothill Road, Dry Sandford, ABINGDON, OX13 6JW. (Life Member)
TREACY, Miss. Zoe Danae, MA ACA *2003;* 300 boulevard Gambetta, 59200 TOURCOING, FRANCE.
TREADAWAY, Mr. Jonathan Andrew, BA ACA *2001;* Flat 1 Hill House, 24 Grove Hill Road, LONDON, SE5 8DG.
•TREADGOLD, Mr. Peter William, BSc FCA *1989;* (Tax Fac), Nexia Smith & Williamson Audit Limited, Old Library Chambers, 21 Chipper Lane, SALISBURY, SP1 1BG. See also Smith & Williamson Ltd and Nexia Audit Limited
TREADGOLD, Sydney William, Esq CBE FCA *1960;* 23 Sturges Road, WOKINGHAM, RG40 2HG. (Life Member)
TREADWAY, Mr. Gordon Thomas, FCA *1976;* 9A Oxford Gardens, LONDON, W4 3BN.
•TREADWELL, Mr. James Stewart, BSc ACA *1999;* Moore and Smalley LLP, Richard House, 9 Winckley Square, PRESTON, PR1 3HP.
TREANOR, Mrs. Jennifer Caroline, ACA *2001;* CB Richard Ellis Limited, St. Martins Court, 10 Paternoster Row, LONDON, EC4M 7HP.
TREANOR, Mr. John Charles, FCA *1965;* 90 Flume Avenue, MARSTONS MILLS, MA 02648, UNITED STATES. (Life Member)
TREANOR, Mr. John Derek Seymour, MA FCA *1958;* Craven Cottage, Heronsgate, RICKMANSWORTH, WD3 5DN. (Life Member)
TREANOR, Ms. Nadia, ACA *2004;* Flat E203, 12 Hertsmere Road, LONDON, E14 4AE.
TREASURE, Mr. Geoffrey Dean, BSc FCA *1995;* 26 Coryton Crescent, Whitchurch, CARDIFF, CF14 7EP.
TREASURE, Miss. Tabitha Laura, BSc ACA *2007;* 25 Clouds Hill Avenue, BRISTOL, BS5 7JD.
TREBBLE, Mr. Arthur Stephen, BSc FCA *1980;* 20 Griffiths Drive, SOUTHPORT, PR9 7DP.
TREBILCOCK, Mr. Christopher Gordon, BSc FCA *1983;* St Richards House, 110 Eversholt Street, LONDON, NW1 1BS.
TREBILCOCK, Mrs. Jill Rosalind, BSc FCA *1981;* 58 Holmwood Road, Cheam, SUTTON, SM2 7JP.
TREBINSKI, Mrs. Sandra Denise, BSc ACA *1981;* Watergate House, 99a Straight Road, WINDSOR, SL4 2SE.
TREBLE, Mr. Alan John, FCA *1957;* 1 Pinfold Lane, Ainsdale, SOUTHPORT, PR8 3QH. (Life Member)
TREBLE, Mrs. Ann, ACA *2002;* 52 Manesty Rise, Low Moresby, WHITEHAVEN, CUMBRIA, CA28 6RY.
TREBLE, Mr. David Michael, FCA *1969;* G M Treble Ltd New Street, Parkfields, WOLVERHAMPTON, WV4 6AN.
TREBY, Miss. Lauren Marie Therese, BA ACA *2006;* with Moore Stephens LLP, 150 Aldersgate Street, LONDON, EC1A 4AB.
•TREBY, Mr. Paul Geoffrey, FCA *1974;* Old Mill Accountancy LLP, The Old Mill, Park Road, SHEPTON MALLET, SOMERSET, BA4 5BS. See also Old Mill Audit LLP
•TRECO, Mrs. Alison Jane, ACA *1984;* One Montague Place, East Bay St, PO Box N3932, NASSAU, BAHAMAS.
TREDGETT, Mrs. Emma Louise, BSc ACA *1998;* Croft House, Oak End Way, GERRARDS CROSS, BUCKINGHAMSHIRE, SL9 8DB.
TREDWELL, Mr. Robert, BSc FCA *1975;* Barlach Strasse 16, 69226 NUSSLOCH, GERMANY.
TREDWIN, Mr. Richard Nicholas, BA ACA *1995;* Churngold Contruction Holding Ltd, St. Andrews House, St. Andrews Road, Avonmouth, BRISTOL, BS11 9DQ.
•TREE, Mr. Norman, FCA *1961;* N. Tree, Flat 17, Gun Wharf, 124 Wapping High Street, LONDON, E1W 2NJ.
TREECE-BIRCH, Miss. Rehana, BSc ACA *2004;* 63 Saffron Drive, Oakwood, DERBY, DE21 2SW.
TREEN, Mrs. Donna Marie, ACA *1995;* Forge Cottage, Solesbridge Lane, Chorleywood, RICKMANSWORTH, WD3 5SN.
TREEN, Mr. Richard James, FCA *1962;* Fairlands, Storrington Road, Thakeham, PULBOROUGH, RH20 3ED. (Life Member)
TREGAR, Mr. David Paul, BA FCA *1977;* 4 Icklingham Road, COBHAM, KT11 2NL.
TREGASKES, Mr. Charles Richard, MA FCA *1972;* Edificio 'El Malecon 1', Apto No 1503, Rambla Claudio Williman, s/n La Mansa, Parada 1, Punta Del Este MALDONADO CP 20000 URUGUAY. (Life Member)
TREGASKES, Mr. Geoffrey William, FCA *1966;* 12 Leelands, Pennington, LYMINGTON, HAMPSHIRE, SO41 8EY. (Life Member)
TREGASKES, Mr. Leon Paul, BSc ACA *1986;* 15 Poplar Close, Aller Park, NEWTON ABBOT, TQ12 4PG.
TREGASKES, Mrs. Polly Kerenza, BEng ACA *2005;* Robinson Reed Layton Peat House, Newham Road, TRURO, CORNWALL, TR1 2DP.
TREGENZA-HALL, Mr. Sydney Alisdair, FCA FCCA *1974;* 6 Grovehill Drive, FALMOUTH, TR11 3HS.
TREGONING, Mr. Andrew Frederick, BA ACA *1991;* CityPoint, 1 Ropemaker Street, LONDON, MIDDLESEX, EC2Y 9NY.
TREGONING, Mr. James, BA ACA *2003;* 4 Arthur Villas, Windmill Lane, EPSOM, KT17 3AH.
TREGURTHA, Mr. Edward, BSc ACA *2010;* 3 Larkhall Rise, LONDON, SW4 6JB.
TREGURTHA, Mrs. Helen, BSocSc ACA *2004;* PO Box 167, NOORDHOEK, WESTERN CAPE PROVINCE, 7979, SOUTH AFRICA.
TREHAN, Mr. Amit, BSc ACA *2005;* Flat 3, Hardy Court, 1 Makepeace Road, LONDON, E11 1UP.
TREHAN, Mr. Naveen Kumar, ACA *1978;* 213 Chappaqua Road, BRIARCLIFF MANOR, NY 10510, UNITED STATES.
TREHAN, Miss. Nidhi, ACA *2008;* 62 Carrwood, Hale Barns, ALTRINCHAM, CHESHIRE, WA15 0EP.
•TREHARNE, Miss. Clare Louise, LLB ACA *2002;* BDO Alto Limited, Windward House, La Route de la Liberation, St Helier, JERSEY, JE1 1BG.
TREHARNE, Mrs. Kerry, BA ACA *2005;* 32 Black Swan Crescent, Hampton Hargate, PETERBOROUGH, PE7 8HF.
TREHARNE, Mr. Myles Gregory Dale, MA ACA CTA *2007;* (Tax Fac), Barclays Capital, 5 North Colonnade, Canary Wharf, LONDON, E14 4BB.
•ⓘTREHARNE, Mr. Stephen, FCA *1984;* with KPMG LLP, 1 Forest Gate, Brighton Road, CRAWLEY, WEST SUSSEX, RH11 9PT.
TREHERNE, Mr. Andrew John, BA ACA *1980;* Fulwood House, 5 Old Fulwood Road, SHEFFIELD, SOUTH YORKSHIRE, S10 3TG.
TREHERNE, Mr. Mark James, BA FCA ATII *1996;* 2 Millers Point, Mayfield Road, WEYBRIDGE, KT13 8XD.
TREITEL, Mr. Henry Marcus, BA ACA *1989;* 5 Mortimer Lodge, 34 Albert Drive, LONDON, SW19 6JZ.
TREITEL, Mrs. Rene, FCA *1954;* 14 Dunstan Road, LONDON, NW11 8AA. (Life Member)
TREITEL, Mr. Richard Julius, ACA *1982;* 252 West 85th Street, Apt 1D, NEW YORK, NY 10024, UNITED STATES.
TRELEAVEN, Mr. Christopher Perry, BA ACA *1995;* Skanska Integrated Projects, Maple Cross House, Denham Way, Maple Cross, RICKMANSWORTH, HERTFORDSHIRE WD3 9SW.
TRELEAVEN, Mr. Timothy James, BSc ACA *2003;* Synovate sp. z o.o., ul. Ciszewskiego 15, 02-777 Warszawa, WARSAW, POLAND.
TRELOAR, Mr. Stephen, BA ACA *1996;* Greatlee Wood Burnhams Road, Bookham, LEATHERHEAD, KT23 3AX.
TREMAIN, Mrs. Xanthe, ACA *2006;* 177 Main Road, Sutton at Hone, DARTFORD, DA4 9HW.
TREMAYNE, Mr. Edward Charles, BA ACA *2003;* Flat 4, Hurlingham Court, Ranelagh Gardens, LONDON, SW6 3SH.
•TREMAYNE, Mr. Paul Michael, FCA *1970;* Bissell & Brown Ltd, Charter House, 56 High Street, SUTTON COLDFIELD, WEST MIDLANDS, B72 1UJ.
TREMBATH, Mr. David John, FCA *1972;* Cherry Cottage, Botus Fleming, SALTASH, PL12 6NJ.
TREMBATH, Mr. Ernest, FCA *1955;* 36 Kennet Drive, CONGLETON, CW12 3RH. (Life Member)
TREMBATH, Mr. William Ernest, BSc(Hons) ACA *2001;* Calle Jaime Marquet 17, 28200 SAN LORENZO DE EL ESCORIAL, SPAIN.
TREMBERTH, Mr. John William, MA FCA *1969;* 59 Avenue de la Ferme, Des Hezards, 778112 FOURQUEUX, FRANCE.
TREMBETH, Mr. Anthony Broderick, MA FCA *1969;* 32 Plantation Lane, Bearsted, MAIDSTONE, KENT, ME14 4BJ. (Life Member)
TREMBLE, Mr. Kerry, BA ACA *1987;* 16 Oakcroft Road, LONDON, SE13 7ED.
•TREMBLING, Mr. Mark Philip, FCA *1980;* (Tax Fac), Fowler & Trembling, 24 Forge End, ST. ALBANS, AL2 3EQ.
TREMEER, Mrs. Claire Mary-Louise, ACA *1981;* Penthouse 3, Bickenhall Mansions, Bickenhall Street, LONDON, W1U 6BS.
TREMEER, Miss. Tamsyn Charlotte, BA ACA *2006;* Flat 5, 1 Grove Park Road, LONDON, SE9 4NP.

TREMELLEN, Mr. Andrew Richard, BA ACA *1995;* 6 Mount Pleasant, WEYBRIDGE, KT13 8EP.
TREMLETT, Mr. Brian Ronald, FCA *1967;* 9 Alyngton Road, SpringwoodNorthchurch, BERKHAMSTED, HERTFORDSHIRE, HP4 3XP.
TREMLETT, Mr. Terence Ronald, MSc FCA *1970;* 127 Downer Road South, BENFLEET, SS7 1HX.
TREN, Mr. Nicholas Stephen Rudolph, BSc ACA *1994;* Glaxo Smithkline Plc G S K House, 980 Great West Road, BRENTFORD, MIDDLESEX, TW8 9GS.
TRENCH, Mr. Michael, BSc ACA *2007;* Flat 2, 50 Atherley Road, SOUTHAMPTON, SO15 5DS.
TRENCH, Miss. Michelle, ACA *2011;* 40 Water Tower Way, BASINGSTOKE, HAMPSHIRE, RG24 9RF.
TRENCHARD, Mrs. Anne Valerie, FCA *1960;* Roxton Dene, 46 South Road, Chorleywood, RICKMANSWORTH, WD3 5AR. (Life Member)
TRENCHARD, Mr. Brian Morris, BA FCA *1957;* 43 Birch Court, Latteys Close, CARDIFF, CF14 4PZ. (Life Member)
TRENCHARD, Mr. Jeremy Paul, BSc ACA *1991;* 37 Siskin Close, Bishops Waltham, SOUTHAMPTON, SO32 1RP.
TRENCHARD, Mr. Kenneth John, FCA *1948;* 93 Sidford Road, SIDMOUTH, DEVON, EX10 9NR. (Life Member)
TRENDELL, Mr. Derek, FCA *1967;* Greystone House, Brackley Avenue, Hartley Wintney, HOOK, RG27 8QX.
TRENDLE, Mr. David Charles, BSc FCA *1997;* Redhill Lodge, 4 Pendleton Road, ST Johns, REDHILL, SURREY, RH1 6QJ.
TRENFIELD, Mr. Dennis Walter Stuart, BSc FCA *1952;* (Tax Fac), 8 Thornhurst, BURGESS HILL, WEST SUSSEX, RH15 0BF. (Life Member)
•TRENT, Mr. Bernard, FCA *1953;* Sherman Bass Trent & Co, 1 Ormonde Court, 70 Parson Street, LONDON, NW4 1RE.
TRENT, Mr. Brian Frank, FCA *1964;* Gorse Bank Lane, Baslow, BAKEWELL, DE45 1SG. (Life Member)
•TRENT, Mr. Jeremy Steven, BSc FCA *1984;* (Tax Fac), H W Fisher & Company Limited, Acre House, 11/15 William Road, LONDON, NW1 3ER. See also H.W. Fisher & Company
TRENT, Mr. William Edward James, BA ACA *1982;* 57 Rosslyn Hill, Hampstead, LONDON, NW3 5UQ.
TRENTER, Mr. Kevin John, FCA *1994;* 30 Church Lane, Henley, IPSWICH, IP6 0RQ.
TREON, Mr. Amar, BEng ACA *1993;* Virgin Media, 10-14 Bartley Wood Business Park Bartley Way, HOOK, RG27 9UP.
TREON, Mr. Anoup, BSc ACA *1981;* 28 Welbeck Street, LONDON, W1G 8EW.
TREON, Mr. Sham, BSc ACA *1993;* 38 Main Avenue, NORTHWOOD, MIDDLESEX, HA6 2LQ.
TREPTE, Mr. Paul Norman, FCA *1959;* Beech House, 12A Yewbarrow Road, ULVERSTON, CUMBRIA, LA12 9JS. (Life Member)
TRESADERN, Mr. William, FCA *1958;* 15 Cecil Road, Cheam, SUTTON, SM1 2DL. (Life Member)
TRESEDER-GRIFFIN, Mr. Robert Ian, FCA *1968;* Baredown Mead, Scures Hill, Nately Scures, HOOK, RG27 9JS. (Life Member)
TRESIDDER, Mr. Hereward Tolmie, LLB ACA *1981;* Morningside, 33 Belle Vue Road, ASHBOURNE, DERBYSHIRE, DE6 1AT.
TRESIGNE, Mrs. Victoria Mary, BSc ACA *1992;* 117 Richmond Park Road, LONDON, SW14 8JY.
TRESISE, Mr. Michael Charles, BSc FCA *1989;* 28 Evesham Walk, Owlsmoor, SANDHURST, GU47 0YU.
•TRESISE, Mrs. Wendy Anne, ACA *1989;* Tresise & Company, Brockhurst, 28 Evesham Walk, Sandhurst, SANDHURST, GU47 0YU.
TRESS, Mr. Thomas Gregory James, BA FCA *1973;* The Red House, 29 Palace Road, EAST MOLESEY, KT8 9DJ.
TRESTAIN, Mr. David Peter, BCom FCA *1970;* Le Rocher de Haut Route de Pleinmont, Torteval, GUERNSEY, GY8 0PG.
TRESTON, Mr. Nicholas Richard, ACA *1997;* 6 Tarragon Way, Burghfield Common, READING, BERKSHIRE, RG7 3YU.
TRETT, Mr. Thomas Sydney, FCA *1974;* 11 Keswick Road, Cringleford, NORWICH, NR4 6UH.
TREVAN-HAWKE, Mr. Herbert Edgar, FCA *1940;* 2 Richmond Court, White Lodge Close, SEVENOAKS, KENT, TN13 3BF. (Life Member)
TREVELLYAN, Mr. Lance John Philip, BSc ACA *1979;* Greenhills House, Greenhills Est Tilford Rd, Tilford, FARNHAM, GU10 2DZ.
TREVELYAN, Ms. Anne-Marie Belinda, BSc ACA *1994;* Netherwitton Hall, Netherwitton, MORPETH, NORTHUMBERLAND, NE61 4NW.
TREVELYAN, Mr. Edward Calverley Thornton, FCA *1962;* 14 South Side, Stamfordham, NEWCASTLE UPON TYNE, NE18 0PB.
TREVELYAN, Mr. Julian Blackett Thornton, BSc ACA *1989;* 9 Holmwood Gardens, LONDON, N3 3NS.
TREVELYAN, Mr. Nigel David, BA ACA *1991;* (Tax Fac), Berwin Leighton Paisner LLP, Adelaide House, London Bridge, LONDON, EC4R 9HA.
TREVELYAN-CLARK, Mr. Peter Alexander, LLB *1987;* 100 Cannon Street, LONDON, EC4N 6EU.
TREVENA, Mr. Paul John, BA ACA *2000;* 18 Pine Grove, #14-04 Cavendish Park, SINGAPORE 597597, SINGAPORE.
TREVERTON, Mr. Paul Benjamin, FCA *1969;* 540 S.Webster St, NAPERVILLE, IL 60540, UNITED STATES.
TREVETHICK, Mr. Jeremy Richard, FCA *1972;* 23 Beauchamp Road, EAST MOLESEY, KT8 0PA.
TREVETT, Mr. James, ACA *2009;* 66 Trident Close, Erdington, BIRMINGHAM, B23 5TB.
TREVETT, Mr. Simon Lawrence Ralph, BSc ACA *1985;* P.O Box R1755, ROYAL EXCHANGE, NSW 1225, AUSTRALIA.
•TREVOR, Mr. Christopher John, BA ACA CTA *1998;* (Tax Fac), Stoten Gillam Limited, Alban House, Stoten Gillam, 99 High Street South, DUNSTABLE, BEDFORDSHIRE LU6 3SF.
TREW, Mr. Gordon Alexander, FCA *1960;* 33 Bruce Close, HAYWARDS HEATH, RH16 4QE. (Life Member)
TREW, Mrs. Karen Jacqueline, BSc ACA *1986;* White Stubbs White Stubbs Lane, BROXBOURNE, HERTFORDSHIRE, EN10 7QA.
TREW, Mr. Richard John, FCA *1967;* 1 Wisborough Lodge, Billingshurst Road, Wisborough Green, BILLINGSHURST, WEST SUSSEX, RH14 0DZ.
TREW, Mr. Robert Scott, BSocSc ACA *1988;* 16 Weald Rise, Tilehurst, READING, RG30 6UY.
TREW, Miss. Sarah Ann, BSc(Hons) ACA *2002;* Flat 6, 68 Stainton Road, LONDON, SE6 1AR.
TREWEEK, Mr. Roger James, BSc ACA *1987;* High Tor, Cliff Road, TEIGNMOUTH, TQ14 8TW.
TREWIN, Miss. Emily, BSc ACA *2007;* 17 Bluecoat Close, NOTTINGHAM, NG1 4DP.
TREWIN, Ms. Parizan Vistasp, BSc(Hons) FCA *2001;* 8 Dalton Close, ORPINGTON, BR6 9QY.
TREZISE, Miss. Alexa Jayne, ACA *2004;* Vebra Solutions Ltd Pocklington Industrial Estate, Pocklington, YORK, YO42 1NP.
TRIANCE, Mr. Theo, BSc FCA *1976;* Napa House, The Green, Church Lane, Brailsford, ASHBOURNE, DERBYSHIRE DE6 3BX.
TRIANTAFYLLIDES, Mr. Kyriacos Ioannou, BSc ACA *1984;* 63 Egerton Gardens, LONDON, SW3 2DA.
TRIANTAFYLLIDES, Mr. Solon Antoniou, FCA *1956;* PO Box 21012, 1500 NICOSIA, CYPRUS. (Life Member)
TRIANTAFYLLIDIS, Mr. Paris-Panagiotis, ACA FCCA *2010;* 36 Omirou Street, Kifissia, 145-62 ATHENS, GREECE.
TRIBE, Mr. Andrew John, BA ACA ACMA *2002;* Ministry of Justice, 102 Petty France, LONDON, SW1H 9AJ.
•TRIBE, Mrs. Karen Elizabeth, BA ACA *1999;* Brite Accounting Limited, 26 St. Nicholas Road, Copmanthorpe, YORK, YO23 3UX.
TRIBE, Mr. Raymond John, FCA *1962;* Greenways, Church Lane, Chearsley, AYLESBURY, BUCKINGHAMSHIRE, HP18 0DF.
•TRIBE, Mr. Trevor David, FCA *1988;* G P Financial Management Limited, 8-9 The Old Yard, Lodge Farm Business Centre, Wolverton Road, Castlethorpe, MILTON KEYNES MK19 7ES.
TRICK, Mrs. Sarah, BA ACA *2009;* Holy Trinity Vicarage, Fairway, PORT TALBOT, WEST GLAMORGAN, SA12 7HG.
•TRICKER, Mr. Jonathan Matthew, MA ACA *2005;* Deloitte Limited, PO Box 758, Merchant House, 22-24 John Mackintosh Square, GIBRALTAR, GIBRALTAR.
TRICKETT, Mr. Alexander Toby Michael, BA ACA *2005;* Flat 3 Penrhyn, 37 Knyveton Road, BOURNEMOUTH, BH1 3QJ.
TRICKETT, Mr. Ian David, BA FCA *1962;* Granville House, Tyning Road, Combe Down, BATH, BA2 5ER.
•TRICKETT, Mr. Paul Russell, BCom ACA CF *1993;* Deloitte LLP, 1 City Square, LEEDS, WEST YORKSHIRE, LS1 2AL. See also Deloitte & Touche LLP
TRICKLE, Mrs. Anne Marie, ACA *1984;* 166 Barnett Wood Lane, ASHTEAD, KT21 2LW.
TRICKSEY, Mrs. Rosamond Teresa, LLB ACA *2004;* 12 Hepburn Avenue, GLADESVILLE, NSW 2111, AUSTRALIA.
TRICOT, Mrs. Annette Ruth Julia, BA(Hons) ACA *2002;* 24 Spencer Drive, LONDON, N2 0QX.
TRIEFUS, Mr. Graham Peter, FCA *1977;* Aristotle Holdings Ltd, 51 Chalcot Road, Primrose Hill, LONDON, NW1 8LY.
TRIFFITT, Miss. Melanie, BA ACA *2007;* Deloitte & Touche, PO Box N250, Grosvenor Place, 1217, SYDNEY, NSW 2000 AUSTRALIA.
•TRIFFITT, Mr. Philip Brian, BSc FCA *1974;* The Barker Partnership, Bank Chambers, 17 Central Buildings, Market Place, THIRSK, YO7 1HD. See also The Barker Partnership Limited
TRIFILETTI, Mr. Roberto Giuseppe, BSc ACA *1997;* 20 Garth Road, SEVENOAKS, TN13 1RT.
TRIGER, Miss. Sara, BA ACA *2006;* 8 Bentley Mount, LEEDS, LS6 4AU.
TRIGG, Mr. Andrew John, BA ACA *1996;* Broadlands, Northwood Green, WESTBURY-ON-SEVERN, GLOUCESTERSHIRE, GL14 1NB.
•TRIGG, Mr. Andrew Kenneth, FCA *1971;* Thompsons Accountants and Advisors Limited, 1 Grove Place, BEDFORD, MK40 3JJ. See also Thompsons Corporate Services Ltd
TRIGG, Mr. Christopher Michael, BSc ACA *1991;* 1 Croft Gardens, Sully, PENARTH, CF64 5GB.
TRIGG, Mr. Christopher Michael, BSc ACA *2000;* 8e West Mill Road, EDINBURGH, EH13 0NX.
TRIGG, Mr. Giles Roderick Leslie, BA ACA *1996;* CP Foods UK Ltd, Avon House, Hartlebury Trading Estate, Hartlebury, KIDDERMINSTER, WORCESTERSHIRE DY10 4JB.
•TRIGG, Mr. Mark Anthony, BSc ACA *1986;* Trigg Management Limited, 117 Layhams Road, WEST WICKHAM, KENT, BR4 9HE.
•TRIGG, Mr. Michael Jonathan, FCA *1975;* (Member of Council 2000 - 2009), (Tax Fac), Michael Trigg Accounting Limited, 19 Old Exeter Street, Chudleigh, NEWTON ABBOT, DEVON, TQ13 0LD.
TRIGG, Mr. Michael Steven, BSc ACA *2010;* 66 Hookstone Drive, HARROGATE, NORTH YORKSHIRE, HG2 8PF.
TRIGG, Mrs. Nichola Elinor, BSc ACA *1993;* Birch Cottage, Brake Lane, Hagley, STOURBRIDGE, DY8 2XW.
TRIGG, Mr. Nicholas Mark Fitzgerald, BSc FCA *1991;* 35 St Vincent Drive, ST. ALBANS, AL1 5SL.
TRIGG, Mr. Steven, BSc FCA ATII *1981;* 66 Hookstone Drive, HARROGATE, HG2 8PF.
•TRIGG, Mr. Timothy Jon, FCA *1968;* Trigg & Co, 1 Merton Mansions, Bushey Road, LONDON, SW20 8DQ.
TRIGGER, Mr. Jeremy Neil Michael, BA ACA *2002;* 19 Scaife Road, BROMSGROVE, WORCESTERSHIRE, B60 3SE.
TRIGGER, Mrs. Karen Ann, FCA *1974;* Challacombe Bungalow, Manor Road, Landkey, BARNSTAPLE, DEVON, EX32 0JJ.
•TRIGGER, Mr. Roy, FCA *1972;* (Member of Council 1978 - 1985), Roy Trigger & Associates, 22 Brickfield Avenue, HEMEL HEMPSTEAD, HERTFORDSHIRE, HP3 8NP.
TRIGGS, Miss. Patricia Winifred, FCA *1963;* 2 Borrowdale Gardens, CAMBERLEY, GU15 1QZ.
TRIGGS, Mr. Peter Henry, BA FCA ATII TEP *1982;* Moulin De La Grenouille, Serres Et Montguyard, 24500 EYMET, FRANCE.
TRIGGS, Mrs. Rebecca Katharine, MA ACA *1993;* 19 Becket Wood, Newdigate, DORKING, SURREY, RH5 5AQ.
TRIKOUPIS, Mr. Constantinos, BSc ACA *1991;* 6 Electra Street, Engomi, CY 2400 NICOSIA, CYPRUS.
•TRILL, Mr. David John, FCA *1967;* (Tax Fac), David J. Trill, Thorley Houses Farm, Thorley Lane West, BISHOP'S STORTFORD, HERTFORDSHIRE, CM23 4BN.
TRILL, Mr. Peter John, FCA *1964;* Belvedere, Woodlands Road, Sonning Common, READING, RG4 9TE.
TRILL, Miss. Susan, BA FCA DChA *1988;* Oasis Academy Bristol, Petherton Road, BRISTOL, BS14 9BU.
TRILLO, Mr. David John, BA FCA *1969;* 45 Ellington Street, Islington, LONDON, N7 8PN.
TRIM, Mrs. Jennifer Jean, BSc ACA *1988;* 14 Somerton Gardens, Earley, READING, RG6 5XG.
TRIMBLE, Mr. John David, BA FCA *1980;* 63 Thackeray Drive, Vicars Cross, CHESTER, CH3 5LP.
TRIMBLE, Mrs. Julie Ann, BA ACA *2000;* Whitehouse Barn Broad Lane, Grappenhall, WARRINGTON, WA4 3HU.
TRIMBLE, Mr. Melville Fitzgibbon, BSc ACA *1981;* 22 Rylett Rd, LONDON, W12 9SS.
TRIMBLE, Mr. Michael Patton, BSc ACA *2000;* Axminster Power Tool Centre Ltd, Weycroft Avenue, Millwey Rise Industrial Estate, AXMINSTER, DEVON, EX13 5PH.
TRIMBLE, Mr. Timothy Wilson, BSc ACA *1987;* The Council for World Mission, 32-34 Great Peter Street, LONDON, SW1P 2DB.
TRIMBY, Mrs. Clare Joanne, ACA *2003;* Future Publishing Ltd, 30 Monmouth Street, BATH, BA1 2BW.
TRIMBY, Mr. David George, TD BA FCA *1962;* 21 St Georges Court, Semington, TROWBRIDGE, BA14 6GA. (Life Member)
•TRIMBY, Mr. James Edward, ACA CTA *1991;* (Tax Fac), James Trimby, Woodruffs, Wingfield, TROWBRIDGE, WILTSHIRE, BA14 9LE.
TRIMINDIS, Mr. Aristides, ACA *2005;* 63 Protis Apriliou Street, Kato Lakatamia, 2310 NICOSIA, CYPRUS.
TRIMM, Mr. Michael James, BSc ACA *1994;* (Tax Fac), Deutsche Post AG, Headquarters, 53250 BONN, GERMANY.
TRIMMINGS, Mr. Adrian David, MEng ACA *2006;* Timbers Edge Long House Lane, Warninglid, HAYWARDS HEATH, WEST SUSSEX, RH17 5TE.
•TRINDER, Mr. Alan Frederick, MBA FCA *1969;* Alan F. Trinder, 22 Laburnham Gardens, UPMINSTER, ESSEX, RM14 1HU.
TRINDER, Mr. Andrew Ian Michael, BA(Hons) ACA *2001;* GLE, 10-12 Queen Elizabeth Street, LONDON, Se1 2JN.
TRINDER, Mr. Christopher Michael, PhD BSc ACA *1994;* 92 The Hurst, Kings Heath, BIRMINGHAM, B13 0DD.
TRINDER, Mr. Ian Jens, BSc ACA *2000;* 3 Acuba Road, Earlsfield, LONDON, SW18 4RR.
TRINDER, Mrs. Joan Margaret, BSc ACA *1980;* 8 Castleton Close, NEWCASTLE UPON TYNE, NE2 2HF.
TRINDER, Miss. Kirsten Jane, MSc BCom ACA *2011;* 3 Madeleine Terrace, 5a Bushey Hill Road, LONDON, SE5 8QF.
TRINDER, Mr. Paul Simon, BSc ACA *1987;* Ul. Konwaliowa 3, Osiedle Sloneczne, 05-805 KANIE, POLAND.
TRINDER, Mr. Paul William, BSc ACA *1992;* 13 Firstbrook Close, Penylan, CARDIFF, CF23 9ER.
TRINDER, Mrs. Tamsin Jane, BA ACA *2006;* Egerton House Torr Lane, Torr Yealmpton, PLYMOUTH, PL8 2HW.
TRINGHAM, Mr. Roger Martin, BSc FCA *1973;* Beckside, Ainstable, CARLISLE, CA4 9QN.
•TRINHAM, Mr. John Dennis, FCA *1967;* (Tax Fac), Price Pearson Ltd, Finch House, 28-30 Wolverhampton Street, DUDLEY, DY1 1DB. See also Trinham J.D.
•TRINHAM, Mr. Peter Joseph, FCA *1974;* Worton Rock Limited, Churchfield House, 36 Vicar Street, DUDLEY, WEST MIDLANDS, DY2 8RG. See also Worth LLP
TRINIMAN, Mr. Clifford Paul, BSc ACA *1985;* Kings Barrow, Grange Road, WAREHAM, DORSET, BH20 5AJ.
TRINKOFF, Mr. Lloyd Jay, FCA *1979;* 3a Spring Back Way, Uppingham, OAKHAM, LE15 9TT.
TRIPP, Mr. Ian Charles, ACA *1990;* Lista de Correos, 11320 SAN PABLO DE BUCEITE, SPAIN. (Life Member)
•TRIPP, Mr. Mark Barry, BA FCA ATII *1990;* Tripp Accountancy Ltd, The Old Brewery, Newtown, BRADFORD-ON-AVON, WILTSHIRE, BA15 1NF.
•TRIPP, Mr. Michael Leslie, ACA *1978;* Michael L Tripp & Co Limited, 29 Nutter Road, THORNTON-CLEVELEYS, LANCASHIRE, FY5 1BQ.
TRIPPAS, Mr. Geoffrey Ronald, FCA *1968;* 13 Shirehall Plain, HOLT, NR25 6HT.
•TRIPPETT, Mr. James, FCA *1965;* James Trippett, 12 Bluebells, WELWYN, AL6 0XD.
TRIPPICK, Mr. Ben, BSc(Econ) ACA *2003;* KPMG Azsa & Co Marunouchi Trust Tower North 10F, 8-1 Marunouchi 1-Chome, Chiyoda-Ku, TOKYO, 100 8250 JAPAN.
TRISK-GROVE, Mr. Ian Michael, BEng ACA *2004;* Finance, Camelot Group Plc Unit 2, Wolsey Business Park Tolpits Lane, WATFORD, WD18 9RN.
TRISTANO, Ms. Meldy, ACA *2009;* Deloitte & Touche Abbots House, Abbey Street, READING, RG1 3BD.
•TRISTEM, Mr. Nigel John, BCom FCA *1985;* Baker Tilly Tax and Advisory Services LLP, 25 Farringdon Street, LONDON, EC4A 4AB. See also Baker Tilly Corporate Finance LLP, Baker Tilly Tax and Accounting Limited and Baker Tilly & Co Limited
TRITTON, Mr. Charles William George, MA FCA *1990;* 37 Abinger Road, Chiswick, LONDON, W4 1EU.
TRITTON, Mrs. Gillian Mary, BA ACA *1991;* 37 Abinger Road, Chiswick, LONDON, W4 1EU.
TRIVEDI, Mr. Amit, BA(Hons) ACA *2002;* 57 Roseneath Avenue, Rushey Mead, LEICESTER, LE4 7GU.
TRIVEDI, Miss. Arti, BSc ACA *2004;* with Deloitte LLP, 4 Brindley Place, BIRMINGHAM, B1 2HZ.
TRIVEDI, Miss. Asha, BSc(Econ) ACA *1996;* 3 Copperfield Mews, Bethnal Green, LONDON, E2 6DE.

TRIVEDI, Mr. Hetal, BSc ACA *2004;* Flat 3 Wooburn Court, 2a Winchmore Hill Road, LONDON, N14 6PT.
TRIVEDI, Mr. Rajesh, BSc ACA *1998;* 155 Covington Way, Norbury, LONDON, SW16 3AQ.
TRIVETT, Mr. Mark Harold, BA ACA *1996;* 66 Rosebery Road, Muswell Hill, LONDON, N10 2LA.
TRKULJA-AMJARV, Miss. Riina, MSc ACA *2007;* Flat 3, Deansgate House, 151 Coombe Road, CROYDON, CR0 5SQ.
TROBIA, Mr. Alessandro, ACA *2009;* (Tax Fac), Flat 7 Pickering Court, Granville Road, LONDON, N22 5LZ.
•TROBRIDGE, Mr. Simon John, BA FCA *1995;* The Business Services Office, 57 Moorview Way, SKIPTON, NORTH YORKSHIRE, BD23 2JW.
•TROCKI, Miss. Krystyna Irena, BA FCA *1987;* GRA Enterprises Ltd, 15 Perry Road, Sherwood, NOTTINGHAM, NG5 3AD.
TRODDEN, Mr. David, MSc BSc ACA *1980;* London Metropolitan University, 84 Moorgate, LONDON, EC2M 6SQ.
•TRODDEN, Mr. Paul John, FCA *1978;* Paul Trodden & Co, 30 St Mary's Row, Moseley, BIRMINGHAM, B13 8JG.
TROISE, Mr. Christopher Joseph James, ACA *1988;* (Tax Fac), 34 Caistor Lane, Caistor St. Edmund, NORWICH, NR14 8RB.
TROKKOU, Mrs. Olga, BSc ACA *2008;* 3 Themistocles Dervis Street, CY-1066 NICOSIA, CYPRUS.
•TROKOUDES, Mr. Anthoulis Michael, FCA *1971;* P.O.Box 23957, 1687 NICOSIA, CYPRUS.
TROKOUDES, Mr. Michael, BA ACA *2007;* Flat 5 Bishops Court, 76 Bishops Bridge Road, LONDON, W2 6BE.
TROLLOPE, Mr. David Alastair, BA FCA *1984;* Smith & Nephew PLC, 15 Adam Street, LONDON, W.
TROLLOPE, Mrs. Linden Anne, BSc ACA *1987;* The Cottages, 22-24 Lemsford Village, Lemsford, WELWYN GARDEN CITY, HERTFORDSHIRE, AL8 7TN.
TROLLOPE, Mr. Philip Bryan, FCA *1957;* 44 Nant Talwg Way, BARRY, CF62 6LZ. (Life Member)
•TROMANS, Mr. David Brian, BA FCA *1979;* (Tax Fac), Parkhurst Hill Limited, Torrington Chambers, 58 North Road East, PLYMOUTH, DEVON, PL4 6AJ. See also Parkhurst Hill
TROMANS, Mrs. Lucy Margaret, BSc(Hons) ACA *2005;* with Mason Law LLP, 9 Frederick Road, Edgbaston, BIRMINGHAM, B15 1TW.
TROOD, Mr. Jeremy Neil, MA ACA *1988;* St. Crispins, Leather Lane, Great Yeldham, HALSTEAD, ESSEX, CO9 4HX.
TROOP, Mrs. Melanie Ann, BA ACA *1992;* 31 Byfeld Gardens, Barnes, LONDON, SW13 9HP.
TROPIS, Mr. Angelos, BA(Econ) ACA *2000;* Ayiou Eudokimou 16A, 2055 Strovolos, NICOSIA, CYPRUS.
•TROPP, Mr. David, BA FCA *1988;* with FSPG, 21 Bedford Square, LONDON, WC1B 3HH.
TROTMAN, Mr. Alan Gloucester, BA ACA *1994;* 48 Speer Road, THAMES DITTON, KT7 0PW.
TROTMAN, Mr. Brian Martin, FCA *1975;* High Tilt, Old Road, Wheatley, OXFORD, OX33 1NX.
•TROTMAN, Mr. Daniel Paul, BSc ACA *2000;* Ernst & Young LLP, 1 More London Place, LONDON, SE1 2AF. See also Ernst & Young Europe LLP
TROTMAN, Miss. Emily Teresa, BSc ACA *2003;* 14 Kings Ride, CAMBERLEY, SURREY, GU15 4HX.
•TROTMAN, Mr. Geoffrey Robert, ACA *1978;* Trotman & Co, Queensborough House, 2 Claremont Road, SURBITON, KT6 4QU.
TROTMAN, Miss. Heather, ACA *2011;* Flat 36, Crystal Wharf, 36 Graham Street, Islington, LONDON, N1 8GH.
TROTMAN, Mr. John Richard, BA(Hons) ACA *2002;* 16c Agate Road, Hammersmith, LONDON, W6 0AH.
TROTMAN, Mr. Mark David, BA ACA *1986;* 7 Matthew Way, WEST PENNANT HILLS, NSW 2125, AUSTRALIA.
TROTMAN, Mr. Paul Stanley, FCA *1964;* Goose Green, Southington, Overton, BASINGSTOKE, RG25 3DA.
TROTT, Mr. Benjamin Clement, BA ACA *2003;* Lany na Dulku 116, 53002 PARDUBICE, CZECH REPUBLIC.
TROTT, Mr. Eric Hav, ACA *1989;* PO Box FL161, FLATTS FLBX, BERMUDA.
TROTT, Mr. Nicholas Mark, BEng ACA *1990;* The Arthouse, 141 Station Road, BEACONSFIELD, BUCKINGHAMSHIRE, HP9 1LG.
TROTT, Mr. Peter Michael, FCA *1965;* 1 The Ridings, Maisemore, GLOUCESTER, GL2 8JD.
TROTTER, Mr. Christopher Robert, BA FCA *1990;* N C Y P E, St. Piers Lane, LINGFIELD, SURREY, RH7 6PW.
TROTTER, Miss. Faye, BSc ACA *2007;* 3 The Walk, HORNCHURCH, ESSEX, RM11 3TL.
•TROTTER, Mrs. Gillian Pamela, BSc FCA *1983;* Cook Trotter Ltd, 3 Sceptre House, Hornbeam Square North, Hornbeam Park, HARROGATE, NORTH YORKSHIRE HG2 8PB.
TROTTER, Mr. John Keith, BA FCA *1965;* High Winds, Cragg Drive, Off Ben Rhydding Drive, ILKLEY, LS29 8BE.
TROTTER, Mr. Michael Gerald, MA ACA *1987;* Merrydown, Humbly Grove, South Warnborough, HOOK, RG29 1RX.
TROTTER, Sir Neville Guthrie, BCom FCA *1955;* 1 Kingsland, Jesmond, NEWCASTLE UPON TYNE, NE2 3AL. (Life Member)
TROTTER, Mr. Owen, BA ACA *1996;* Key Capital Partners, 43 Temple Row, BIRMINGHAM, B2 5LS.
TROTTER, Miss. Tilly, ACA *2009;* Flat C, 52 Caversham Road, LONDON, NW5 2DS.
•TROUBRIDGE, Mr. Thomas Richard, BSc FCA *1980;* PricewaterhouseCoopers LLP, 1 Embankment Place, LONDON, WC2N 6RH. See also PricewaterhouseCoopers
•TROUGHTON, Mr. Roger, FCA *1983;* (Tax Fac), robinson+co, Oxford Chambers, New Oxford Street, WORKINGTON, CA14 2LR. See also Robinson J.F.W. & Co
TROULLIS, Mr. Michael Peter, BA ACA *1980;* 5208 Newstead Manor Lane, RALEIGH, NC 27606, UNITED STATES.
TROUNCE, Mr. Timothy Michael, BSc ACA *1987;* Redlands, 43 Poplar Road, Shalford, GUILDFORD, GU4 8DH.
TROUP, Mr. Alistair Charles Westray, BEng ACA *1989;* Duke Street Capital Ltd, Almack House, 28 King Street, LONDON, SW1Y 6XA.
TROUP, Mrs. Gillian Elizabeth, BAcc ACA *1996;* D C Thomson Limited, Finance Department, Courier Buildings, Albert Square, DUNDEE, DD1 9QJ.
TROUP, Mr. Kevin James, MA ACA *1993;* 58a Gamekeeper's Road, EDINBURGH, EH4 6LS.
TROUP, Mr. Robin William, FCA *1971;* P.O. Box 30160-00200, NAIROBI, KENYA.
TROUSDALE, Miss. Lesley, BSc ACA CTA *2011;* 61 Addenbrookes Road, NEWPORT PAGNELL, BUCKINGHAMSHIRE, MK16 9FD.
TROUSE, Mr. Martin John, BSc FCA *1960;* H10, 32 Leyfield, WORCESTER PARK, KT4 7LR. (Life Member)
•TROUT, Mr. David Harold, FCA *1975;* (Tax Fac), Simpkins Edwards, 12 The Square, HOLSWORTHY, DEVON, EX22 6DL.
TROW, Mr. David John, BSc FCA *1993;* PwC Romania, Lakeview, Barbu Vacarescu 301-311, 020276 BUCHAREST, ROMANIA.
•TROWBRIDGE, Mr. Andrew Derek, FCA *1975;* DBH, 16 Dorcan Business Village, Murdock RoadDorcan, SWINDON, SN3 5HY.
TROWBRIDGE, Mr. Paul Norman, BMus ACA *2004;* 1 Cordale Road, BASINGSTOKE, HAMPSHIRE, RG21 3LU.
TROWBRIDGE, Mr. Stephen Neil, BA FCA *1998;* Elm Tops Longhurst Road, East Horsley, LEATHERHEAD, KT24 6AG.
TROWELL, Mr. Peter Gordon, BA FCA *1963;* 34 Fore Street, HATFIELD, HERTFORDSHIRE, AL9 5AH. (Life Member)
TROWLER, Mr. Philip, BSc ACA *2002;* 810 1/2 Woodlawn Avenue, VENICE, CA 90291, UNITED STATES.
TROY, Miss. Esther Mary, MA(Hons) ACA *2002;* Cisco Systems Ltd, 10 New Square Park, Bedfront Lanes, FELTHAM, MIDDLESEX, TW14 8HA.
TROY, Miss. Katrina, BA(Hons) ACA *2002;* 85 Riverview Grove, LONDON, W4 3QP.
TROY, Mr. Samuel Josiah, BMus(Hons) ACA *2011;* 262 London Road, WOKINGHAM, RG40 1QY.
TROYNA, Mr. Lawrence Joseph, BCom FCA *1968;* 114 Lambourne Road, CHIGWELL, ESSEX, IG7 6EF. (Life Member)
TRUBEE, Mr. Richard John, BSc ACA *1988;* 2 Hawthorne Road, Caversham, READING, RG4 6LY.
TRUBODY, Mr. Derek James, BSc FCA DChA *1977;* 5a Toll Down Way, Burton, CHIPPENHAM, SN14 7PD.
TRUBY, Mr. William George, BA FCA ATII *1964;* 9 Woodland Way, Failand, BRISTOL, BS8 3UD.
TRUDGEON, Mr. Eric John, FCA *1952;* 16 Bridge View, WADEBRIDGE, PL27 6BZ. (Life Member)
TRUDGEON, Mr. Paul, BSc ACA *1994;* The Hadley Shipping Co Ltd Office 6, Telfords Yard, LONDON, E1W 2BS.
TRUDGETT, Miss. Rebecca Jane, BSc ACA *2007;* Alliotts Friary Court, 13-21 High Street, GUILDFORD, SURREY, GU1 3DL.
TRUDGETT, Mrs. Stephanie Jane, BSc FCA CTA *1993;* 343 The Rowans, Milton, CAMBRIDGE, CB24 6ZR.
TRUE, Mrs. Tracy Maria, BSc ACA *1989;* Stafford House Training Centre, 91 Keymer Road, HASSOCKS, BN6 8QJ.
•TRUELOVE, Mr. Charles Richard, FCA *1971;* (Tax Fac), Sykes Dalby & Truelove, 63 High Street, Hurstpierpoint, HASSOCKS, WEST SUSSEX, BN6 9RE.
TRUELOVE, Mr. Joseph Michael, MA ACA *2000;* Kleinwort Benson (Guernsey) Ltd, PO Box 44, GUERNSEY, GY1 3BG.
TRUELOVE, Ms. Kathleen Anna, BA ACA *1989;* Godshill Park Farm House, Godshill, VENTNOR, ISLE OF WIGHT, PO38 3JF.
TRUELOVE, Mr. Michael John, FCA *1975;* 2 Swanland Drive, TONBRIDGE, TN9 2RA.
TRUEMAN, Mr. Ian, FCA *1976;* 44 Clarehaven, Stapleford, NOTTINGHAM, NG9 7JF.
TRUEMAN, Mrs. Jean Margaret, FCA *1974;* Cooper Parry LLP, 14 Park Row, NOTTINGHAM, NG1 6GR.
TRUEMAN, Mr. John Nigel, BSc ACA *1982;* Dunhelm, 2 The Avenue, MAIDENHEAD, SL6 8HG.
TRUEMAN, Mr. Paul Roland, BSc FCA *1983;* 71 Park Road, BRENTWOOD, Essex, CM14 4TU.
TRUEMAN, Mr. Peter Douglas, BA ACA *1979;* 8 Dunstall Rd, LONDON, SW20 0HR.
•TRUEMAN, Mr. Richard John, FCA *1975;* (Tax Fac), MCABA Limited, 91-97 Saltergate, CHESTERFIELD, DERBYSHIRE, S40 1LA. See also Mitchells
TRUEMAN, Mr. Richard Michael, BA ACA *1993;* 15 Lapwing Drive, Hampton-In-Arden, SOLIHULL, B92 0BF.
TRUEMAN, Miss. Sheena Louise, BA ACA *1989;* 13 West Field, Abington, CAMBRIDGE, CB21 6BE.
TRUEMAN, Mrs. Susan, BSc ACA *1987;* S M E Invoice Finance Ltd, Chertsey Court, 56-58 Chertsey Street, GUILDFORD, SURREY, GU1 4HL.
TRUEMAN, Mr. Thomas, ACA MAAT *2009;* 9 Eagles Court, WREXHAM, CLWYD, LL13 8DJ.
TRUEMAN, Mrs. Vanessa Ann, BSc ACA *1991;* Jumar Solutions Europe Ltd Jumar House Pinewood Court, Coleshill Road Marston Green, BIRMINGHAM, B37 7HG.
TRUESDALE, Mr. Nevin John, MA ACA *1999;* 27 Mizen Close, COBHAM, KT11 2RJ.
TRUESDELL, Mr. Alan Peter, BSc FCA *1980;* 36 Firs Road, Hethersett, NORWICH, NR9 3EH.
TRUGLIA, Miss. Jessica Ann, ACA *2010;* Flat B2, #36 St 302, Boeung Keng Kong, PHNOM PENN, CAMBODIA.
•TRUIN, Mr. William James, BSc ACA CTA *1985;* with is4 Housing & Regeneration Ltd, 69 Buchanan Street, GLASGOW, G1 3HL.
TRUJILLO HERNANDEZ, Mr. Gonzalo Alonso, BEng ACA *1998;* The Coach House, Martcombe Road, Easton-In-Gordano, BRISTOL, BS20 0QD.
TRUMAN, Mr. David Albert, BSc ACA *1984;* PO BOX 507, MORNINGSIDE, QLD 4170, AUSTRALIA.
TRUMAN, Mr. David Michael, BSc ACA *1987;* 11 Maple Gardens Forest Road, TUNBRIDGE WELLS, KENT, TN2 5JL.
•TRUMAN, Miss. Elizabeth, BSc FCA *1990;* (Tax Fac), Rimmer & May, 19 Murray Street, LLANELLI, DYFED, SA15 1AQ.
TRUMAN, Mr. Leslie Samuel Alfred, FCA *1955;* (Tax Fac), 5 Rectory Lawn, BURNHAM-ON-SEA, TA8 2DP.
TRUMAN, Mr. Matthew Arthur, BSc ACA *2004;* 21 Corsellis Square, TWICKENHAM, TW1 1QT.
TRUMAN, Miss. Stephanie Evelyn, BSc(Hons) ACA *2009;* with Michael J Dodden & Co, 34 & 38 North Street, BRIDGWATER, TA6 3YD.
TRUMAN, Mr. Stephen Jeffrey, LLB FCA *1986;* 6 Phillips Court, Whitchurch Lane, EDGWARE, HA8 6QD.
TRUMAN, Mr. William John, BA(Hons) ACA *2002;* 63 Wollaton Vale, NOTTINGHAM, NG8 2PD.
•TRUMFIELD, Miss. Diane Elaine, ACA *1984;* (Tax Fac), Northcott Trumfield, Devonshire Villa, 52 Stuart Road, Stoke, PLYMOUTH, PL3 4EE.
TRUMP, Mr. Matthew, BSc ACA *2007;* 4 Somerset Road, Erdington, BIRMINGHAM, B23 6NG.
TRUMPER, Mr. Ian Carl, BSc ACA *1992;* Neville House, 301-309 Marsh Road, LUTON, LU3 2RZ.
•TRUMPER, Mr. Ian Francis Scobie, FCA *1973;* Torii Pines, Firs Road, KENLEY, CR8 5LH.
TRUMPER, Mr. James Ronald, BSc FCA *1987;* Hall House, The Street, Crudwell, MALMESBURY, SN16 9ET.
•TRUNCHION, Mr. Robert William, MSc FCA *1985;* (Tax Fac), MacIntyre Hudson LLP, Equipoise House, Grove Place, BEDFORD, MK40 3LE.
TRUNDLE, Mr. James Michael, BA(Hons) ACA *2004;* C/o Alanna Grace, PO Box 1363, GEORGE TOWN, GRAND CAYMAN, KY1-1108, CAYMAN ISLANDS.
TRUNDLE, Miss. Samantha Jane, BSc ACA *1994;* Santander UK Plc, 2 Triton Square, LONDON, NW1 3AN.
TRUONG, Miss. Anh Lac, BA(Hons) ACA *2003;* 198 Fratton Road, PORTSMOUTH, PO1 5HD.
TRUP, Mr. Neal Howard, BA FCA *1991;* 51 Grenville Place, LONDON, NW7 3SF.
TRURAN, Mr. Michael Cyril, BA ACA *1982;* The Old Farmhouse, 7 Church Street, Ducklington, WITNEY, OX29 7UA.
•TRURAN, Mrs. Sanjana, ACA FCCA *2008;* Bush & Co, 2 Barnfield Crescent, EXETER, EX1 1QT. See also Westcountry Payroll Ltd
•TRURAN, Mr. Terry, FCA *1981;* 7 Ryedale Close, Woodshires Park, YARM, TS15 9UN.
TRUSCH, Miss. Victoria, BA ACA *2010;* 6 Penlands Walk, Colton, LEEDS, WEST YORKSHIRE, LS15 9DL.
TRUSCOTT, Mr. Andrew Thomas, BSc ACA *1992;* (Tax Fac), 6 Royal Oak Road, Sketty, SWANSEA, SA2 8ES.
•TRUSCOTT, Mr. Colin Robert Elvin, BSc ACA *1987;* Lang Bennetts, The Old Carriage Works, Moresk Road, TRURO, CORNWALL, TR1 1DG.
TRUSCOTT, Mr. Geoffrey John, BA FCA *1976;* Soil Association, South Plaza, Marlborough Street, BRISTOL, BS1 3NX.
•TRUSCOTT, Mr. Harold Roy, LLB ACA *1983;* Backtobusiness Limited, 5 Wheatfield, Leybourne, WEST MALLING, KENT, ME19 5QB.
TRUSCOTT, Mr. James Clifton, FCA *1967;* Bourne Martyn, 58 Marshal's Drive, ST. ALBANS, AL1 4RG. (Life Member)
TRUSDALE, Mr. Andrew Robert, BSc ACA *2007;* with PricewaterhouseCoopers LLP, Benson House, 33 Wellington Street, LEEDS, LS1 4JP.
TRUSLER, Mr. George Martin, BSc ACA *1987;* 44 Hamilton Road, East Finchley, LONDON, N2 0SW.
TRUSLER, Mr. Peter Michael Anthony, BSc ACA *1978;* Columbyne House, Clandon Road, West Clandon, GUILDFORD, SURREY, GU4 7TL.
TRUSLOVE, Mr. David Peter, BA ACA *1987;* 1 Macnaughton Woods, CAMBERLEY, GU15 3RD.
TRUSSELL, Mrs. Anita Claire, BA ACA *1994;* 30 Northumberland Road, BRISTOL, BS6 7BB.
TRUSSELL, Mr. Antony, BA ACA *1991;* 30 Northumberland Road, Redland, BRISTOL, BS6 7BB.
•TRUSSELL, Miss. Mary Helen, LLB ACA *1990;* with KPMG LLP, 15 Canada Square, LONDON, E14 5GL.
•TRY, Mr. Christopher Colin, BA FCA *1981;* (Tax Fac), Try Lunn & Co, Roland House, Princes Dock Street, HULL, HU1 2LD.
TRYE, Mr. Christopher Peter, MA MSc FCA *1974;* 59 Northumberland Road, LEAMINGTON SPA, WARWICKSHIRE, CV32 6HF.
•TRYHORN, Mr. Nicholas Adrian, FCA *1966;* Tryhorn and Hall, 153 Stafford Road, WALLINGTON, SM6 9BN. See also Tryhorn & Lloyd
TRZCINSKI, Mr. Phillip Mark, BSc ACA *1994;* 266 Hillbury Road, WARLINGHAM, CR6 9TP.
TSAI, Ms. Hung Mei, ACA *2007;* Room C, 6th Floor, Tower 1 The Astoria, 198 Argyle Street, MONG KOK, KOWLOON HONG KONG SAR.
TSAI, Mr. Philip Wing Chung, ACA *2007;* (Tax Fac), Deloitte & Touche, 35/F One Pacific Place, 88 Queensway, CENTRAL, HONG KONG ISLAND, HONG KONG SAR.
TSAI, Miss. Xinyi, ACA *2010;* Blk 170 Yishun Avenue 7, Apt 10-875, SINGAPORE 760170, SINGAPORE.
TSAI, Mr. Zachary David, MEng ACA *2010;* 37 Panyers Gardens, DAGENHAM, ESSEX, RM10 7FG.
TSALIKI, Miss. Maria, ACA *2011;* 55 Sistou Str, Nikea, 18450 PIRAEUS, GREECE.
•TSALIKIS, Mr. Aristides, FCA *1982;* Tsalikis & Co, 30 Carrwood Avenue, Bramhall, STOCKPORT, CHESHIRE, SK7 2PY.
TSANG, Mr. Anthony, BSc ACA *1990;* 98 Roseneath Road, LONDON, SW11 6AQ.
TSANG, Ms. Chee Ping Catherine, ACA *2007;* 20B Braemar Hill Mansions, 19 Braemar Hill Road, NORTH POINT, HONG KONG ISLAND, HONG KONG SAR.
TSANG, Mr. Cheong Wai, ACA *2006;* PricewaterhouseCoopers, 33/F Cheung Kong Center, 2 Queen's Road, CENTRAL, HONG KONG ISLAND, HONG KONG SAR.

TSANG, Ms. Cheuk Man Eve, ACA *2008;* Suite 16F Splendid Place, 39 Taikoo Shing Road, QUARRY BAY, HONG KONG ISLAND, HONG KONG SAR.
TSANG, Mr. Cheung Wong, FCA *1978;* Flat C Block 12, 21/F City One Shatin, SHA TIN, New Territories, HONG KONG SAR.
TSANG, Ms. Chiu Woon, ACA *2007;* Rm 3306, Block G, Allway Garden, TSUEN WAN, NEW TERRITORIES, HONG KONG SAR.
TSANG, Ms. Chiu Ki Kaylina, ACA *2008;* 70 La Salle Road, Ground Floor, KOWLOON TONG, KOWLOON, HONG KONG SAR.
TSANG, Miss. Chiu Kit Letitia, BCom(ACC) FCA *1992;* Flat A 2/F Block 5, Villa Oceania 8 On Chun St, Ma On Shan, SHA TIN, NEW TERRITORIES, HONG KONG SAR.
•**TSANG, Mr. Cho Tai, ACA** *1981;* Tsang Cho Tai, Unit 1411, 14/F Lippo Sun Plaza, 28 Canton Road, TSIM SHA TSUI, KOWLOON HONG KONG SAR.
TSANG, Miss. Choi, BSc ACA *2009;* 59 Rutland Drive, BIRMINGHAM, B26 1UB.
TSANG, Mr. Chun Hung, BSc ACA *1993;* 4 Harlech Green, SHEFFIELD, S10 4NR.
TSANG, Mr. Chun Yiu, ACA *2005;* Room 3004 Kwong Yin House, Kwong Ming Court, TSEUNG KWAN O, NEW TERRITORIES, HONG KONG SAR.
TSANG, Mr. David, BA ACA *2003;* 184 Kent Avenue, Apt D513, BROOKLYN, NY 11211, UNITED STATES.
TSANG, Mr. Ernest Kwong Wing, BSc ACA *1992;* Flat 7 13th Floor, 39a Waterloo Road, KOWLOON TONG, KOWLOON, HONG KONG SAR.
TSANG, Mr. Garrison Hon Yiu, MA ACA *2007;* Flat 23 Ionian Building, 45 Narrow Street, LONDON, E14 8DW.
TSANG, Mr. Heung Yip, ACA *2008;* Flat 12 1/F, Block M, Kornhill, QUARRY BAY, HONG KONG SAR.
TSANG, Mr. Hin Fai, ACA *2007;* 10/F, Flat 1002, Tim Man House, Ho Man Tin Estate, HO MAN TIN, KOWLOON HONG KONG SAR.
•**TSANG, Mr. Hin Kwong Alan, MBA BSc(Hons) ACA** *2007;* Leftley Rowe & Co, The Heights, 59-65 Lowlands Road, HARROW, MIDDLESEX, HA1 3AW.
TSANG, Mr. Hing Hung, ACA CF *2004;* Ka Wah International Holdings Limited, 29/F Ka Wah Centre, 191 Java Road, NORTH POINT, HONG KONG SAR.
TSANG, Mr. Hung Kei, ACA *2007;* Flat B 25/F Block 6, Phase 4, Tai Po Centre, 8 On Pong Road, TAI PO, NEW TERRITORIES HONG KONG SAR.
TSANG, Ms. Jenny, BA ACA *1996;* 31 St. John's Avenue, LONDON, SW15 6AL.
TSANG, Miss. Kaitlin Cho Young, BA ACA *2009;* Apt 4, 33 Dunscombe road, WARWICK WK10, BERMUDA.
TSANG, Miss. Karen Yukmui, BA ACA *1997;* Block A1, 6/F Sheffield Garden, 1 College Road, KOWLOON CITY, KOWLOON, HONG KONG SAR.
TSANG, Mr. Ki Lo, ACA *2007;* G/F, 71 Hung Uk, Mang Kung Uk, CLEARWATER BAY, KOWLOON, HONG KONG SAR.
TSANG, Ms. Kwai Ping, ACA *2009;* Room 3309, Ming Wik House, Kin Ming Estate, TSEUNG KWAN O, NEW TERRITORIES, HONG KONG SAR.
TSANG, Mr. Kwon Yau, BA ACA *2010;* Apartment 189 Westgate Apartments, 14 Western Gateway, LONDON, E16 1BP.
TSANG, Miss. Lina, ACA *2008;* Flat 39 Toronto House, Surrey Quays Road, LONDON, SE16 7AJ.
TSANG, Miss. Min-Li, BSc ACA *2008;* St. Catherines Place St. Catherines Road, Frimley, CAMBERLEY, SURREY, GU16 9NN.
TSANG, Mr. Philip Fan-Sui, FCA *1984;* 8 Maghera Drive, HOWICK 1705, AUCKLAND, NEW ZEALAND.
TSANG, Ms. Pui Yan Judy, ACA *2007;* Flat D 11/F Block 8, Laguna City, KWUN TONG, KOWLOON, HONG KONG SAR.
•**TSANG, Mr. Robert, LLM ACA** *1994;* with Deloitte & Touche, 6 Shenton Way, 32-00, DBS Building Tower Two, SINGAPORE 068809, SINGAPORE.
TSANG, Mr. Sai Lung, ACA *2008;* Flat C, 21/F, Tower 1, Caribbean Coast, 2 Kin Tung Road, Tung Chung LANTAU ISLAND NEW TERRITORIES HONG KONG SAR.
TSANG, Ms. Sau Lai Stella, ACA *2010;* Flat C 16/F Block 3, Granville Gon, 18 Pik Tin St, TAI WAI, NT, HONG KONG SAR.
TSANG, Mr. Siu For Thomas, ACA *2009;* LTC & Associates, 1 Raffles Place, 20-02 OUB Centre, SINGAPORE 048616, SINGAPORE.
TSANG, Mr. Siu Ki, ACA *2008;* Flat A, 11/F, Block 4, Cheerful Garden, Siu Sai Wan, CHAI WAN HONG KONG SAR.
TSANG, Mr. Steven Tuck-Jeng, ACA CA(AUS) *2009;* Flat 33 Tideway Court, 238 Rotherhithe Street, LONDON, SE16 5QS.
TSANG, Mr. Thomas Hin Shun, ACA *2004;* Unit 2802 28/F, Admirality Centre Tower One, 18 Harcourt Road, WAN CHAI, HONG KONG SAR.
TSANG, Mr. Tin For, MA ACA MCT *1989;* MTR Corporation Ltd, 18/F MTR Heardquarters Building Telford Plaza, KOWLOON BAY, KOWLOON, HONG KONG SAR.
TSANG, Mr. Tony Shei Man, ACA *2007;* Ernst & Young, 18/F, Two International Finance Centre, 8 Finance Street, CENTRAL, HONG KONG ISLAND HONG KONG SAR.
TSANG, Miss. Wai Yee, BSc ACA *2005;* Flat 42, Gaumont Tower, Dalston Square, LONDON, E8 3BQ.
TSANG, Ms. Wai Lui, ACA *2011;* (Tax Fac), 136 Spectrum Apartments, Central Promenade, Douglas, ISLE OF MAN, IM2 4JL.
TSANG, Mr. Wai Ming, ACA *2007;* K.F. Leung & Co., Room 1003, 10/F, Yue Shing Commercial Bldg, 15-16 Queen Victoria Street, CENTRAL HONG KONG SAR.
TSANG, Ms. Wai Yi Alexandra, ACA *2005;* Room 1103 11/F Block 12, Heng Fa Chuen, CHAI WAN, HONG KONG ISLAND, HONG KONG SAR.
TSANG, Mr. Wai Yip Patrick, ACA *2007;* 12/F Austin Tower, 22-26A Austin Road, TSIM SHA TSUI, KOWLOON, HONG KONG SAR.
•**TSANG, Miss. Wan Man, BSc FCA** *1988;* 2303-4 Wing On Centre, 111 Connaught Road, CENTRAL, HONG KONG ISLAND, HONG KONG SAR. See also Wan Man Tsang
TSANG, Mr. Wing Hung, BA ACA *1993;* 2W3007 Clifford Estates, Panyu, GUANGZHOU 511495, GUANGDONG PROVINCE, CHINA.
TSANG, Ms. Wing Kiu, ACA *2008;* Flat A 9/F Kwong Fai Mansion, 13 Kwong Wa Street, MONG KOK, HONG KONG SAR.
TSANG, Mr. Yu Hei, ACA *2007;* 6/F Long Mansion, 24A Caine Road, CENTRAL, HONG KONG ISLAND, HONG KONG SAR.
TSANG CHIU WING, Mr. Andrew, ACA *1987;* Flat H 21/F Block 2, Tanner garden, 18 Tanner Road, NORTH POINT, HONG KONG ISLAND, HONG KONG SAR.
TSANG KWONG HONG, Mr. Derek Hsien Pin, BA ACA *1998;* Office of the Auditor General for WA, 4th Floor Dumas House, 2 Havelock Street, WEST PERTH, WA 6005, AUSTRALIA.
TSANGARI, Mr. George, BSc ACA *1998;* Pinewood, Heddon Court Avenue, BARNET, HERTFORDSHIRE, EN4 9NE.
TSANGARIDES, Miss. Fanoula, BSc(Hons) ACA *2003;* 25 Drayton Gardens, LONDON, N21 2NR.
TSANGARIDES, Mr. George, ACA *2010;* 38 Demokratias, Lakatamia, 2331 NICOSIA, CYPRUS.
TSANGARIS, Mr. Georgios, ACA *2011;* 30 Ploutarchou Street, 3060 LIMASSOL, CYPRUS.
TSANGARIS, Mr. Michalis, ACA *2002;* Nicosia General Hospital, 215 Nicosia Limassol Old Road, Strovolos, 2029 NICOSIA, CYPRUS.
TSANTEKIDI, Miss. Eirini, ACA *2009;* Flat 68 Lancaster Close, 13-15 St. Petersburgh Place, LONDON, W2 4JZ.
TSAOUSI, Ms. Alexia, ACA *2009;* 33 EVGENIOU VOULGARI STREET, KATO POLEMIDIA, 4153 LIMASSOL, CYPRUS.
TSE, Mr. Barry, BEng ACA *2002;* 2F 144 Caine Road, MID LEVELS, HONG KONG ISLAND, HONG KONG SAR.
TSE, Mr. Chiang Kwok Nassar, ACA *2007;* C W Leung & Co, Room 403, Wing on House, 71 Des Voeux Road, CENTRAL, HONG KONG ISLAND HONG KONG SAR.
TSE, Ms. Ching Wah, ACA *2010;* Flat G 40F Block 6, Banyan Garden, 863 Lai Chi Kok Road, CHEUNG SHA WAN, KOWLOON, HONG KONG SAR.
TSE, Miss. Emily Wei-Ling, ACA *2009;* 221a Broomwood Road, LONDON, SW11 6JX.
TSE, Mr. Gabriel Chi Wai, ACA *2006;* Gabriel Tse, Unit 1601, 16/F Malaysia Building, 50 Gloucester Road, WAN CHAI, HONG KONG ISLAND HONG KONG SAR.
TSE, Mr. Hau Yin Aloysius, FCA *1974;* Dianaville Holdings Limited, 17/F Sang Woo Building, 227-228 Gloucester Road, WAN CHAI, HONG KONG ISLAND, HONG KONG SAR.
TSE, Miss. Judith Wing See, BSc ACA *2001;* 39 Rabournmead Drive, NORTHOLT, MIDDLESEX, UB5 6YH.
TSE, Dr. Ka Lun, MSc FCA *1986;* Unit C 7th Floor Block 7, 28 Tsing Fat Street, SIU LAM, HONG KONG SAR.
TSE, Mr. Kai Chi, BSc ACA *1989;* Flat E 3/F, Eastbourne Court, 7 Eastbourne Road, KOWLOON TONG, KOWLOON, HONG KONG SAR.
TSE, Mr. King Sing, ACA *2007;* Flat D 35/F, Tower 11, Metro City Phase II, 8 Yan King Road, TSEUNG KWAN O, NEW TERRITORIES HONG KONG SAR.
TSE, Ms. Lai Kiu Edith, ACA *2008;* Parkson & Company, Unit 1301, 13/F Lemmi Centre, 50 Hoi Yuen Road, KWUN TONG, KOWLOON HONG KONG SAR.
TSE, Mr. Man Chun, BSc ACA *2003;* 33 Tymawr, Caversham, READING, RG4 7XR.
TSE, Miss. Ming Yee, FCA MBA *1994;* with PricewaterhouseCoopers, Prince's Building, 22/F, 10 Chater Road, CENTRAL, HONG KONG ISLAND HONG KONG SAR.
TSE, Ms. Oi Nei Annie, ACA *2007;* with Deloitte Touche Tohmatsu, 8-F Tower W2, The Towers, Oriental Plaza, 1 East Chang An Avenue, BEIJING 100738 CHINA.
TSE, Mr. Peter Pak Wing, MSc FCA *1977;* CLP Holdings Limited, 147 Argyle Street, MONG KOK, KOWLOON, HONG KONG SAR.
TSE, Mr. Ping Shing, ACA *2004;* Miramar Hotel and Investment Limited, Internal Audit Dept, 15/F Miramar Tower, 132 Nathan Road, TSIM SHA TSUI, KOWLOON HONG KONG SAR.
TSE, Mr. Pui Hong, ACA *2007;* 27E Tower 1, Aegean Coast, 2 Kwun Tsing Road, TUEN MUN, NEW TERRITORIES, HONG KONG SAR.
TSE, Mr. Rennike, MEng ACA *2011;* 21 Canterbury Avenue, ILFORD, ESSEX, IG1 3NA.
TSE, Mr. Robert Cheung Long, ACA *2006;* Tse & Lam, Unit A, 5F China Overseas Building, 139 Hennessy Road, WAN CHAI, HONG KONG ISLAND HONG KONG SAR. See also Tse, Robert
TSE, Mr. See Man Andrew, ACA *2007;* Andrew Tse & Company, Suite 610, 6th Floor Tower1, Silvercord, 30 Canton Road, TSIM SHA TSUI KOWLOON HONG KONG SAR.
TSE, Mr. Stephen Dat-Yin, BSc ACA *2001;* WestLB AG, 7 World Trade Center, 250 Greenwich Street, NEW YORK, NY 10007, UNITED STATES.
TSE, Ms. Suk Yee, ACA *2008;* Flat D, 31/F Bayshore Apartments, 244 Aberdeen Main Road, ABERDEEN, HONG KONG ISLAND, HONG KONG SAR.
TSE, Mr. Sung Yiu, ACA *2010;* Flat C, 8/F Block 6, Pokfulam Gardens, POK FU LAM, HONG KONG ISLAND, HONG KONG SAR.
TSE, Mrs. Sylvia Sau-Bing, BA FCA *1997;* (Tax Fac), with Wilkins Kennedy, Gladstone House, 77-79 High Street, EGHAM, TW20 9HY.
TSE, Mr. Tam Kam Collins, ACA *2008;* Flat B, 17/F Block 10, Park Island, MA WAN, NEW TERRITORIES, HONG KONG SAR.
TSE, Mr. Wai Hing Derek, FCA FCPA(Practising) FCIS *1989;* Unit G 47/F Tower 9, Island Resort, 28 Siu Sai Wan Road, CHAI WAN, HONG KONG ISLAND, HONG KONG SAR.
TSE, Mr. Wing Ho Charles, ACA *2008;* Flat A, 10/F Asia Mansion, 390 King's Road, NORTH POINT, HONG KONG SAR.
TSE, Ms. Wun Ying, ACA *2007;* Flat F 27th floor Block 1 Phase 1, Belvedere Garden, 530 Castle Peak Road, TSUEN WAN, NEW TERRITORIES, HONG KONG SAR.
TSE, Mr. Yiu Tak Anthony, ACA *2007;* Anthony Y.T.Tse & Co, Room 711, Argyle Centre, 7th Floor, 688 Nathan Road, MONG KOK KOWLOON HONG KONG SAR.
TSE, Ms. Yuk Lin, ACA *2008;* Deloitte Touche Tohmatsu, 35/F One Pacific Place, 88 Queensway, CENTRAL, HONG KONG ISLAND, HONG KONG SAR.
TSE SHEUNG CHEONG, Mr. Tse Took Chong, MEc DipEd FCA MBA *1975;* 3 Nanbarree Road, RYDE, NSW 2112, AUSTRALIA.
TSE SIM, Mrs. Jean Hui Hsien, BA ACA *1997;* Flat 6, 6 Floor Tower 16, Yee Tsui Court, South Horizons, AP LEI CHAU, HONG KONG ISLAND HONG KONG SAR.
•**TSE YOUNG SUN, Mr. Joseph, FCA** *1975;* (Tax Fac), Joseph Tseyoungsun, Tempo House, 15 Falcon Road, LONDON, SW11 2PH.
TSEN, Mr. Keng Yam, FCA *1976;* 23 Lorong Istana, Taman Istana, 30000 IPOH, PERAK, MALAYSIA.
TSEN, Mr. Vui Chung, ACA CA(NZ) *2009;* PO Box 62370, 91033 TAWAU, SABAH, MALAYSIA.
TSENG, Mr. Wai Yeung Francis, BSc ACA *1989;* Flat 8 5/FBlock K, Kornhill QUARRY BAY, Hong Kong Island, HONG KONG SAR.
TSENG-LIU, Mr. Collin Chern Yang, BSc(Hons) ACA *2001;* Allen & Gledhill LLP, One Marina Boulevard 28-00, SINGAPORE 018989, SINGAPORE.
TSENTAS, Miss. Anastasia, BSc ACA *2007;* 10 Kallikratous Street, Geri, 2200 NICOSIA, CYPRUS.
•**TSERKEZOS, Mr. Demos Vasiliou, MA ACA** *1994;* Tserkezos Savvides Associates Limited, PO Box 23452, 1683 NICOSIA, CYPRUS.
TSIAKKAS, Mr. Agathoclis, MSc FCA CF *1994;* P.O. Box 57407, CY-3315 LIMASSOL, CYPRUS.
TSIAKKAS, Mr. Nicos, BSc ACA *1996;* 7 Argonafton Street, 4156 LIMASSOL, CYPRUS.
TSIAKLIDES, Mr. Constantinos, BSc(Econ) ACA *2010;* Polymnias 34, Aglandjia, 2102 NICOSIA, CYPRUS.
TSIAKOURIS, Miss. Evangelia, ACA *2009;* 7 Isidorou Street, Strovolos, 2029 NICOSIA, CYPRUS.
TSIAMPIS, Miss. Andrea George, ACA *2009;* 7 Uvedale Road, ENFIELD, MIDDLESEX, EN2 6HA.
TSIANTIS, Mr. Nikolaos, ACA *2011;* Ioannou Theologou 9, Zografou, 5773 ATHENS, GREECE.
TSIARTAS, Mr. Elias Andrea, BA ACA *1984;* GALATAS 5, AYIOS ATHANASIOS, 4106 LIMASSOL, CYPRUS.
TSIARTAS, Miss. Stavrina, BSc ACA *2004;* 24 Kritonos Street Ayios Athanasios, 4106 LIMASSOL, CYPRUS.
TSIELEPIS, Mr. Alexis Constantine, BSc(Econ) ACA *2003;* with Costas Tsielepis & Co Limited, 205, 28th October Avenue, Louloupis Court, 1st Floor, PO Box 51631 3507 LIMASSOL CYPRUS.
•**TSIELEPIS, Mr. Costas George, FCA** *1968;* 12 Aisopou Street, Agios Tychonas, 4521 LIMASSOL, CYPRUS.
•**TSIELEPIS, Mr. George Costas, BSc FCA** *1999;* Costas Tsielepis & Co Limited, 205, 28th October Avenue, Louloupis Court, 1st Floor, PO Box 51631 3507 LIMASSOL CYPRUS.
TSIELEPIS, Mr. Kyriacos Costas, BA(Hons) ACA *2001;* P.O.Box 51631, 3507 LIMASSOL, CYPRUS.
•**TSIELEPIS, Mr. Manolakis Georghiou, BA FCA** *1972;* Chelepis Watson Limited, 67 Westow Street, Upper Norwood, LONDON, SE19 3RW. See also Thornton Springer LLP
TSIKOURIS, Mr. Christos, BSc ACA *2006;* 131 Athalassas Avenue, Dasoupoli, 2024 NICOSIA, CYPRUS.
TSIM, Mr. Paul Ambrose Tak-Po, BSc ACA *1982;* PO Box 5146, CENTRAL, HONG KONG ISLAND, HONG KONG SAR.
TSIM, Ms. Sin Ling Ruth, ACA *2007;* Flat A, 8/F Dragon View Court, 5 Kotewall Road, MID LEVELS, HONG KONG ISLAND, HONG KONG SAR.
TSIM, Mr. Wing Kit, ACA *2008;* c/o Group Finance Department, SUNeVision Holdings Ltd, 32/F Mega-iAdvantage, 399 Chai Wan Road, CHAI WAN, HONG KONG SAR.
TSINGIS, Mr. Demetrios Andreas, MBA BSc ACA *2004;* Flat 101 Prosol 1 Mouson 1 Chryseleousa Strovolos, 2060 NICOSIA, CYPRUS.
TSIOLAKKIS, Mr. Constantinos, ACA *1980;* Constantinos Tsiolakkis, Agion Ioxkim 10, Archangelos, STROVOLOS, CYPRUS.
TSIOLAS, Mr. Theodosis, BA ACA *2001;* Agiou Georgiou Avion 21, 5510 Avgorou, 5510 FAMAGUSTA, CYPRUS.
TSIRIKOS, Mr. Alexandros, MSc ACA *2005;* Top Ships Building, 1 Vas. Sofias & Meg. Alexandrou Street, Maroussi, 15124 ATHENS, GREECE.
TSIVILIKAS, Mr. Ioannis, MSc BA ACA *2006;* 6 Vernardaki Street, Maroussi, 151 26 ATHENS, GREECE.
TSO, Mr. Kwai Ping George, ACA *2005;* George Tso & Co, 807 Fortress Tower, 250 King's Road, NORTH POINT, HONG KONG ISLAND, HONG KONG SAR.
TSOI, Mr. Chee Kin Norman, BCom FCA *1992;* Flat D Floor 43, Island Lodge, 180 Java Road, NORTH POINT, HONG KONG SAR.
TSOI, Mr. Hung, ACA *2004;* 7/F Hong Kong Trade Centre, 161-167 Des Voeux Road Central, CENTRAL, HONG KONG ISLAND, HONG KONG SAR.
TSOI, Mr. Ka Ho, ACA *2007;* Flat H 10th Floor, Golden Dragon Garden, 77 Kung Lok Road, KWUN TONG, KOWLOON, HONG KONG SAR.
TSOI, Mr. Michael, ACA *2007;* Michael Tsoi and Company, Unit 101, 1st Floor Silicon Tower, 88 Larch Street, MONG KOK, KOWLOON HONG KONG SAR.
TSOI, Mr. Tai Wai David, ACA *2005;* Alliott Tsoi CPA Limited, 22nd Floor, Hing Yip Commercial Centre, 280 Des Voeux Road, CENTRAL, HONG KONG ISLAND HONG KONG SAR.
•**TSOLAKIS, Mr. Christos, BCom ACA** *1993;* PricewaterhouseCoopers Limited, Julia House, 3 Themistocles Dervis Street, CY-1066 NICOSIA, CYPRUS.
TSOLAKIS, Mr. Kyriacos, BA FCA *1992;* Flat 2, 12 Minoos Str., 6030 LARNACA, CYPRUS.

TSOUKKA, Miss. Zena, BSc ACA *2010;* 9A Kozanis Street, Agios Gerogios Chavouzas, 3070 LIMASSOL, CYPRUS.
TSU, Miss. Soo-Wen, FCA *1977;* H M Customs & Excise PO Box 134, Patchway, BRISTOL, BS34 5QL.
TSUI, Mr. Alex Hoi Lik, ACA *2009;* 1a Dornden Drive, Langton Green, TUNBRIDGE WELLS, KENT, TN3 0AA.
TSUI, Mr. Chun Leung, ACA *2007;* Flat C 16/F, Blk 6, CARADO GARDEN, SHA TIN, NEW TERRITORIES, HONG KONG SAR.
TSUI, Mr. Cyril Kwan Lit, BA ACA *1991;* Flat C 11/F Swiss Towers, 113 Tai Hang Road, CAUSEWAY BAY, HONG KONG SAR.
•**TSUI, Mr. Edward, BA FCA** *1988;* (Tax Fac), Carter Backer Winter LLP, Enterprise House, 21 Buckle Street, LONDON, E1 8NN.
TSUI, Ms. Fung Wah April, ACA *2005;* Flat D 14/F, Block 3 Jubilant Place, 33 Ma Tau Kok Road, TO KWA WAN, KOWLOON, HONG KONG SAR.
TSUI, Mr. Hanson, BSc FCA CISA CIA *1995;* 11A Bella Vista, 3 Ying Fai Terrace, MID LEVELS, HONG KONG ISLAND, HONG KONG SAR.
TSUI, Ms. Ho Yan, ACA *2011;* 4b Craven Hill, LONDON, W2 3DS.
TSUI, Mr. Hon Man, ACA *2007;* Flat 8, 8/F Block 39, Heng Fa Chuen, CHAI WAN, HONG KONG ISLAND, HONG KONG SAR.
TSUI, Mr. Hong Ping Michael, ACA *2008;* Flat 23H Block 27, South Horizons, 18a South Horizon Drive, AP LEI CHAU, HONG KONG ISLAND, HONG KONG SAR.
TSUI, Mr. Ka Yiu Dickson, ACA *2007;* 3115 Lung Yat House, WONG TAI SIN, KOWLOON, HONG KONG SAR.
TSUI, Mr. Ka Yiu, ACA *2009;* Flat J 31/F. Tower 5, Harbour Place, 8 Oi King Street, HUNG HOM, HONG KONG SAR.
TSUI, Miss. Marina Lok Si, MSci ACA *2007;* 43 Summit Avenue, Kingsbury, LONDON, NW9 0TH.
TSUI, Ms. Pui Ling, ACA *2007;* Flat B, 21/F, Block 20, Laguna City, KWUN TONG, KOWLOON HONG KONG SAR.
TSUI, Miss. Sue May, ACA *2008;* Flat 47 Dunbar Wharf, 108-124 Narrow Street, LONDON, E14 8BB.
TSUI, Mr. Yik To, ACA *2008;* 331 W.Live Oak Ave, ARCADIA, CA 91007, UNITED STATES.
TSUI, Mr. Yip Kin Henry, ACA *2007;* Prime Virtue CPA & Co, Unit 1603, 16/F, Omega Plaza, 32 Dundas Street, MONG KOK KOWLOON HONG KONG SAR.
TSUI, Mr. Yun Cheung Steve, BSc ACA *1993;* 68 Ferndale Road, Leytonstone, LONDON, E11 3DN.
TSUN, Mr. Alexander Yat Pang, BSc FCA *1995;* c/o GELEC (HK) Limited, Units 905B-908, Manulife Financial Centre, 223 Wai Yip Street, KWUN TONG, KOWLOON HONG KONG SAR.
TSUNODA, Ms. Ritsuko, ACA *1997;* Merrill Lynch Japan Securities Ltd, Nihonbashi 1-chome Building, 1-4-1 Nihonbashi, Chuo-Ku, TOKYO, 103-8230 JAPAN.
TU, Miss. Fangrong, ACA *2010;* Flat 37 Gainsborough House, Cassilis Road, LONDON, E14 9LQ.
TU, Ms. Ya Ching, ACA *2008;* Flat C 24/F Block 1, La Cite Noble, 1 Ngan O Road, TSEUNG KWAN O, NEW TERRITORIES, HONG KONG SAR.
TUACH, Mrs. Lynne Mary, BSc ACA *1991;* Stroud Slad Farm, The Vatch, STROUD, GL6 7LE.
TUBB, Mr. Andrew Ernest John, FCA *1969;* 102 Claremont, NEWPORT, NP20 6PN.
•**TUBB, Mr. Sebastian Mark, BSc ACA** *1995;* Mazars LLP, The Pinnacle, 160 Midsummer Boulevard, MILTON KEYNES, MK9 1FF.
TUBBS, Mr. Christopher Stafford, FCA *1971;* Stretchline UK Ltd, Sherston Mill, Sherston, MALMESBURY, WILTSHIRE, SN16 0NG.
TUBBS, Mr. Daniel Stuart, BA(Hons) ACA *2001;* 11 Florence Street, LONDON, N1 2DX.
TUBBY, Mr. Colin David, ACA *1983;* 17B Serene Court, 8 Kotewell Road, MID LEVELS, Hong Kong Island, HONG KONG SAR.
TUBBY, Mr. Dennis Albert, FCA *1953;* 63 St Clements Court, Broadway West, LEIGH-ON-SEA, SS9 2BP. (Life Member)
TUBBY, Mr. James Robert, BA(Hons) ACA *2002;* with PricewaterhouseCoopers LLP, 1 Embankment Place, LONDON, WC2N 6RH.
•**TUBBY, Mr. Kevin Eric, FCA** *1982;* (Tax Fac), K E Tubby Limited, Showell, New Road, Greenham, NEWBURY, RG14 7RY. See also K E Tubby
TUBBY, Mr. Malcolm Dennis, BA ACA *1986;* P.O.Box 32 381, Devonport, AUCKLAND, NEW ZEALAND.
TUBMAN, Mr. Derek Hedley, FCA *1968;* 3 Hickmore Heys, Guilden Sutton, CHESTER, CH3 7SN.
TUBRIDY, Mr. Andrew, BA ACA *1992;* 24 Thorncote Road, Northill, BIGGLESWADE, BEDFORDSHIRE, SG18 9AQ.
TUCCI, Mr. Paolo Camillo, BSc ACA *1989;* 180 Rue Leone de Joinville, 01170 GEX, FRANCE.
TUCH, Mr. David Paul, LLB FCA *1984;* Hewitt Associates, 6 More London Place, LONDON, SE1 2DA.
TUCH, Mr. Peter Ellis, LLB ACA *1987;* Hall House, Broad Oak End, Off Bramfield Road, HERTFORD, SG14 2JA.
•**TUCHBAND, Mr. Norman Leslie, FCA** *1967;* Tuchbands, 925 Finchley Road, LONDON, NW11 7PE. See also Tuchband N L
TUCHWEBER, Mr. Sergey, MSc ACA *2009;* Napolniy proyezd bld. 12 5, MOSCOW, RUSSIAN FEDERATION.
•**TUCK, Mr. Andrew Mark, FCA** *1984;* AMT Consulting Limited, 26 Kings Hill Avenue, Kings Hill, WEST MALLING, KENT, ME19 4AE.
•**TUCK, Mr. Brian Peter, FCA** *1973;* 5 Wellsfield, RAYLEIGH, SS6 8DW.
TUCK, Mr. David, BA ACA *2009;* Flat C, 208 Bravington Road, LONDON, W9 3AP.
•**TUCK, Mr. David Hudson, FCA** *1982;* DH Tuck & Co Ltd, 167 Park Street, CLEETHORPES, SOUTH HUMBERSIDE, DN35 7LX.
TUCK, Mr. Gareth, BA(Hons) ACA *2003;* B B C Trust, 180 Great Portland Street, LONDON, W1W 5QZ.
TUCK, Mr. Graham Matthew, BA(Hons) ACA *2003;* Beaufort Underwriting Agency Ltd, 1 Minster Court, LONDON, EC3R 7AA.
TUCK, Mr. John Beaumont, FCA *1949;* 1 Zetland Court, Zetland Road, MALVERN, WORCESTERSHIRE, WR14 2JQ. (Life Member)
TUCK, Mr. Neville Andrew William, BSc FCA *1986;* Terberg Matec UK Ltd, Leacroft Road, Birchwood, WARRINGTON, WA3 6PJ.
TUCK, Mr. Paul Edward John, BSc FCA *1981;* The University of Buckingham, Hunter Street, BUCKINGHAM, MK18 1EG.
TUCK, Dr. Penelope Ann Louise, PhD BSc FCA CTA *1984;* (Tax Fac), Charlton Hill Farmhouse, 8 Winslow Road, Swanbourne, MILTON KEYNES, MK17 0SW.
TUCKER, Mr. Adrian Nicholas Brian, BSc FCA CTA *1987;* 23 Crescent Road, SHEPPERTON, TW17 8BL.
•**TUCKER, Mr. Alan Clive, FCA** *1990;* A C Tucker & Co Limited, Manor Cottage, 18a Waxwell Lane, PINNER, MIDDLESEX, HA5 3EN.
•**TUCKER, Mr. Alan William, BA(Hons) FCA** *1977;* (Tax Fac), EQ Accountants LLP, Westby, 64 West High Street, FORFAR, ANGUS, DD8 1BJ.
TUCKER, Mr. Allan Thomas, FCA *1975;* 7 Goodman Grove, Kesgrave, IPSWICH, IP5 2DZ.
TUCKER, Mrs. Amy Louise, ACA *2009;* 16 Eldergrove, FARNBOROUGH, HAMPSHIRE, GU14 6LY.
TUCKER, Mrs. Andrea Nicola, BA ACA *1991;* with BDO LLP, Fourth Floor, One Victoria Street, BRISTOL, BS1 6AA.
TUCKER, Mr. Andrew Cephas, BSc ACA *1994;* Savills (L&P) Ltd, 132-134 Hills Road, CAMBRIDGE, CB2 8PA.
TUCKER, Mr. Anthony Laurence, BA *1978;* ComFin Limited, 50 Woodcote Road, Caversham, READING, RG4 7BB.
TUCKER, Mr. Brian George, FCA *1974;* Rolling Hills, Pendomer, YEOVIL, BA22 9PA. (Life Member)
TUCKER, Miss. Cassandra, ACA *2011;* Flat 10, Tangerine House, 119 Weston Street, LONDON, SE1 4XE.
TUCKER, Mr. Charles Edward Michael, MA FCA *1969;* Hindringham Hall, Hindringham, FAKENHAM, NR21 0QA. (Life Member)
•**TUCKER, Mrs. Charlotte Rebecca Lucy, LLB ACA** *2001;* Charlotte Tucker, 92 Craiglea Drive, EDINBURGH, EH10 5PH.
TUCKER, Mr. David Allon, FCA *1962;* Suite 3 The Old School House, Bell Street, SHAFTESBURY, DORSET, SP7 8BP.
•**TUCKER, Mr. David Andrew, BSc ACA CF** *1994;* Jasper CF Limited, 80 Caroline Street, BIRMINGHAM, B3 1UP.
TUCKER, Mr. David Arthur, FCA *1958;* Tanyard, Calver Road, Baslow, BAKEWELL, DERBYSHIRE, DE45 1RR. (Life Member)
TUCKER, Mr. David John, BSc ACA *1991;* 505 Concord Drive, MENLO PARK, CA 94025, UNITED STATES.
•**TUCKER, Mr. David Lambert, FCA** *1962;* Weir Cottage, Moorhall Road, Harefield, UXBRIDGE, MIDDLESEX, UB9 6PB.
TUCKER, Miss. Elizabeth Dawn, ACA *2009;* 10/6 Stafford Street, DOUBLE BAY, NSW 2028, AUSTRALIA.
TUCKER, Mrs. Emily Marian, BSc ACA *2005;* 7a Schubert Road, LONDON, SW15 2QT.
TUCKER, Mrs. Fiona Margaret, BSc ACA *1988;* 52 London Road, Harston, CAMBRIDGE, CB22 7QJ.
TUCKER, Mr. Frederick James, FCA *1962;* Cliffside, 2 Marine Parade, Shaldon, TEIGNMOUTH, TQ14 0DP. (Life Member)
•**TUCKER, Miss. Gail Louise, BSc FCA** *1989;* PricewaterhouseCoopers LLP, 1 Embankment Place, LONDON, WC2N 6RH. See also PricewaterhouseCoopers
TUCKER, Mr. Gareth Neil, BSc(Hons) ACA *2001;* K P M G Plym House, 3 Longbridge Road, PLYMOUTH, PL6 8LT.
TUCKER, Mr. Gerald Louis, MA ACA *1983;* 11 Burleigh Gardens, Southgate, LONDON, N14 5AH.
TUCKER, Mr. Graham Peter, BSc ACA *1982;* Byways, Newton St. Cyres, EXETER, EX5 5AG.
TUCKER, Mr. Hadrian Amador, MSc ACA *1979;* State Bank Of India, US Operations, 460 Park Avenue, NEW YORK, NY 10022, UNITED STATES.
TUCKER, Mrs. Hazel Joy, ACA *2010;* The Auld Ridge, Bampton, TIVERTON, DEVON, EX16 9AB.
TUCKER, Mr. Huw Martin, BSc ACA *1986;* Jefferies International Ltd Vintners Place, 68 Upper Thames Street, LONDON, EC4V 3BJ.
TUCKER, Mr. James Robert, ACA *2001;* Brookbank House, Kings Mead, Pebmarsh, HALSTEAD, ESSEX, CO9 2NA.
•①**TUCKER, Mr. James Robert, BSc ACA** *1991;* KPMG LLP, 15 Canada Square, LONDON, E14 5GL. See also KPMG Europe LLP
TUCKER, Miss. Jane Renee, BSc ACA *2001;* 18 Priolo Road, Charlton, LONDON, SE7 7PT.
TUCKER, Mr. Jason Courtney, MSc BA ACA *1999;* with PKF (UK) LLP, 5 Temple Square, Temple Street, LIVERPOOL, L2 5RH.
TUCKER, Mr. Jay Steven, BSc ACA *1996;* 12 Tennyson Road, Hutton, BRENTWOOD, ESSEX, CM13 2SJ.
TUCKER, Mr. John Barry Michael, FCA *1968;* 6 Benson Avenue, East Ham, LONDON, E6 3ED.
TUCKER, Mr. Jonathan Lucien, BSc ACA *1993;* British American Tobacco Japan Ltd, 22/F Atago Mori Tower, 2-5-1 Atago Minato-Ku, TOKYO, JAPAN.
TUCKER, Mr. Julian Andrew, BSc ACA *1998;* 11 Tynings Way Lower Westwood, BRADFORD-ON-AVON, WILTSHIRE, BA15 2BT.
TUCKER, Mrs. Katherine Victoria, BSc(Econ) ACA *1996;* Rowberry House, Donhead St. Andrew, SHAFTESBURY, DORSET, SP7 0ET.
TUCKER, Ms. Lesley Anne, BSc ACA CPFA *1980;* Byways, Langford, Newton St. Cyres, EXETER, EX5 5AG.
TUCKER, Mr. Louis George De Normanville, BSc(Hons) ACA *2002;* Flat A, 95 St. Georges Drive, LONDON, SW1V 4DB.
TUCKER, Miss. Lynsey Marie, BA ACA *2000;* Unit 30, St. Johns Innovation Centre St. Johns Innovation Park, Cowley Road, CAMBRIDGE, CB4 0WS.
TUCKER, Mr. Mark Edward, BA ACA *1985;* 35/F AIA Central, No. 1 Connaught Road, CENTRAL, HONG KONG ISLAND, HONG KONG SAR.
TUCKER, Mr. Mark James, BSc ACA *2004;* 24 Sapphire Close, CAVES BEACH, NSW 2281, AUSTRALIA.
TUCKER, Mr. Nicholas William, BA ACA *1987;* 701 Columbia St, Apt 706, VANCOUVER, WA 98660-3473, UNITED STATES.
TUCKER, Mr. Paul Duncan, BSc ACA *2005;* 62 Stortford Hall Park, BISHOP'S STORTFORD, HERTFORDSHIRE, CM23 5AN.
•**TUCKER, Mr. Peter David, FCA** *1980;* MEMBER OF COUNCIL, (Tax Fac), Dickinsons, Enterprise House, Beesons Yard, Bury Lane, RICKMANSWORTH, HERTFORDSHIRE WD3 1DS.
•**TUCKER, Mr. Philip Martin, BA ACA** *1987;* Philip M Tucker, 58 Park Grange Croft, SHEFFIELD, S2 3QL.
TUCKER, Mrs. Rebekah Alexi, BSc ACA *2000;* 24 Oulder Hill Drive, ROCHDALE, OL11 5LB.
TUCKER, Mr. Richard Lawford Duncan, FCA *1972;* Kiondroughad, 7 Balladoyne Estate, St. Johns, ISLE OF MAN, IM4 3LX.
TUCKER, Mr. Robert John, BA FCA *1973;* (Tax Fac), 4 Limmerhill Road, WOKINGHAM, BERKSHIRE, RG41 4BU.
TUCKER, Mr. Roy Clifford, FCA *1964;* Nettlestead Place, Maidstone Road, Nettlestead, MAIDSTONE, ME18 5HA.
TUCKER, Mr. Russell, MEng ACA *2011;* Hewell Dairy, The Drive, Hewell Grange, REDDITCH, WORCESTERSHIRE, B97 6QE.
TUCKER, Mr. Samuel, BA(Hons) ACA *2011;* Flat 205 Compass House, Smugglers Way, LONDON, SW18 1DQ.
TUCKER, Mr. Santhosh, MA ACA *1992;* Wilhelm Waldeyer Str. 16, 50937 KOLN, GERMANY.
TUCKER, Miss. Sarah May, ACA *2008;* Apartment 28 28 Maxim, 21 Lionel Street, BIRMINGHAM, B3 1AT.
TUCKER, Mr. Simon Patrick, BA ACA *1986;* 30 Cumberland Street, WOODBRIDGE, SUFFOLK, IP12 4AD.
TUCKER, Miss. Susan Jayne, BA ACA *1995;* with KPMG LLP, 1 Forest Gate, Brighton Road, CRAWLEY, WEST SUSSEX, RH11 9PT.
TUCKER, Miss. Teresa Yvonne, BSc(Hons) ACA *2002;* 10 St. Leonards Road, WINCHESTER, HAMPSHIRE, SO23 0QD.
TUCKER, Miss. Terri June Lesley, BA ACA *1990;* KST Ltd, Fountain House, 130 Fenchurch Street, LONDON, EC3M 5DJ.
TUCKER, Dr. Toby Terence, MA DPhil BA(Hons) ACA MSI *2001;* 92 Craiglea Drive, EDINBURGH, EH10 5PH.
TUCKER, Mr. Troy Mitchell, BSc(Hons) ACA *2000;* 34 Stirling Road, SUTTON COLDFIELD, WEST MIDLANDS, B73 6PS.
TUCKER, Mr. Warren Gordon, BSc ACA *1988;* Cobham Plc, Brook Road, WIMBORNE, DORSET, BH21 2BJ.
TUCKER, Miss. Yema Louise, BSc ACA *1989;* Flat 3 Building 47, Marlborough Road, LONDON, SE18 6RU.
TUCKETT, Mr. Andrew John, BA ACA *1998;* 18 Richmond Hill, Irvington, NEW YORK, NY 10533, UNITED STATES.
TUCKETT, Mr. Andrew Richard Lawson, BSc ACA MRICS *1989;* WTC Schiphol Airport, Tower F 6th Floor, Schiphol Boulevard 115, 1118 BG SCHIPHOL, NETHERLANDS.
TUCKETT, Miss. Katherine Mary, BA ACA *2003;* J Sainsbury Plc, 33 Holborn, LONDON, EC1N 2HT.
•**TUCKETT, Mrs. Pamela Wendy Anne, FCA DChA** *1988;* Bishop Fleming, Stratus House, Emperor Way, Exeter Business Park, EXETER, EX1 3QS.
TUCKETT, Miss. Sabine Mary, BSc ACA *2002;* with Thomas Westcott, 26-28 Southernhay East, EXETER, DEVON, EX1 1NS.
TUCKEY, Mr. Daniel Thomas James, BA ACA *1991;* 12 Myers Close, Swanmore, SOUTHAMPTON, SO32 2RN.
•**TUCKEY, Mr. Herbert William, FCA** *1954;* Herbert W Tuckey FCA, 17 Avonside, Mill Lane, STRATFORD-UPON-AVON, CV37 6BJ. See also Herbert W Tuckey
TUCKEY, Miss. Lorraine Helen, MA ACA *2004;* with Ernst & Young LLP, 1 More London Place, LONDON, SE1 2AF.
TUCKEY, Mr. Mark Alexander, BSc ACA *1987;* 8 Beech Close, VERWOOD, DORSET, BH31 6XB.
•**TUCKEY, Mr. Michael Anthony, FCA FCMA** *1969;* (Tax Fac), Michael Tuckey, The Dutch House, 24 The Downsway, SUTTON, SURREY, SM2 5RN.
TUCKEY, Miss. Rose Helen, BA ACA *2007;* 95 Elgin Crescent, LONDON, W11 2JF.
TUCKFIELD, Mr. Sean William, BA ACA *1992;* with PricewaterhouseCoopers, Prince's Building, 22/F, 10 Chater Road, CENTRAL, HONG KONG ISLAND HONG KONG SAR.
TUCKLEY, Mr. Jason Edward, MA(Oxon) FCA *1997;* 113 Williamson Court, RICHMOND, VA 23229, UNITED STATES.
TUCKLEY, Mr. Steven Antony, BSc FCA *1992;* Beringea, 39 Earlham Street, LONDON, WC2H 9LT.
TUCKMAN, Mr. Stanley, FCA *1953;* 11 Northwick Circle, HARROW, HA3 0EJ. (Life Member)
TUCKNOTT, Mr. Mark Richard, BSc ACA *2007;* 51 Priory Ridge, Crofton, WAKEFIELD, WEST YORKSHIRE, WF4 1TF.
TUCKWELL, Mr. Keith John, BCom FCA *1975;* 358 Redditch Road, Kings Norton, BIRMINGHAM, B38 8PS.
TUCZKA, Mrs. Sylvia, ACA *2002;* 4/5 Richterqasse, 1070 VIENNA, AUSTRIA.
TUDAWE, Mr. Ajith Erandan, ACA *2007;* 175/2 Havelock Road, Havelock Town, 5 COLOMBO, SRI LANKA.
TUDBALL, Mr. Ian Gordon, FCA *1962;* 9 Almond Way, HARROW, HA2 6NU. (Life Member)
TUDDENHAM, Mrs. Helen, BSc ACA *1998;* with PricewaterhouseCoopers LLP, 1 Embankment Place, LONDON, WC2N 6RH.
TUDDENHAM, Mrs. Sandra, BA ACA *1990;* Hillview, 9 March Pines, EDINBURGH, EH4 3PF.
TUDGE, Mr. Stephen John, BSc ACA *1990;* Woodlands, Croft Lane, KNUTSFORD, CHESHIRE, WA16 8QH.
•**TUDOR, Mrs. Ann Hancock, FCA** *1981;* A H Tudor Limited, 20 St. Johns Hill, SHREWSBURY, SY1 1JJ.
TUDOR, Mrs. Elaine Alison, BSc ACA *1992;* Goldwel Lodge, Church Road, Brightlingsea, COLCHESTER, CO7 0QU.
TUDOR, Miss. Helen Elizabeth, BA ACA *1996;* Woodfield, 73 Park Street, BRIDGEND, MID GLAMORGAN, CF31 4AZ.
TUDOR, Mr. Hugo Richard, BA ACA *1988;* 6 Granville Road, SEVENOAKS, TN13 1ER.

TUDOR, Mrs. Jennifer Anne, BA ACA *1990;* 6 Granville Road, SEVENOAKS, TN13 1ER.
TUDOR, Mr. John Michael, BA ACA *1993;* Barkston, Bath Old Road, RADSTOCK, BA3 3HF.
TUDOR, Mr. Keith John Patrick, BA ACA *1988;* 56 Heather Road, Binley Woods, COVENTRY, CV3 2DD.
•TUDOR, Mr. Robert Graham, FCA *1968;* Robert G Tudor Limited, 21 Heycroft, Gibbet Hill, COVENTRY, CV4 7HE.
•TUDOR, Mr. Ross Laurence, BA ACA *2004;* with KPMG LLP, 15 Canada Square, LONDON, E14 5GL.
TUDOR, Dr. Ruth Susan Elizabeth, ACA CTA *1991;* 28 Lancaster Road, ST. ALBANS, HERTFORDSHIRE, AL1 4ET.
TUDOR, Mr. Simon Rodney, BSc ACA *1985;* Langdale House, 43 Worcester Lane, Pedmore, STOURBRIDGE, DY8 2PA.
TUDOR-EVANS, Mr. Edward Simonn, MA FCA *1966;* The Grange, North Rode, CONGLETON, CW12 2NY.
•TUDOR PRICE, Mr. Simon Hywel, ACA *1985;* (Tax Fac), I 4 Business Limited, 4 The Close, Leckhampstead Road, Akeley, BUCKINGHAM, MK18 5HD. See also 1st Option Consulting Services Limited
TUDOR WILLIAMS, Mr. David, FCA *1957;* 7 Chestnuts, Hutton, BRENTWOOD, CM13 2PA. (Life Member)
TUDSBERY, Mr. Julian Farnsworth, BSc ACA *1985;* Townsend Farmhouse, Whelford, FAIRFORD, GL7 4DY.
•TUER, Mr. Brian, FCA *1982;* 11 Petteril Street, CARLISLE, CA1 2AJ.
TUESLEY, Mrs. Deborah Jane, BSc ACA *1992;* 54 Valebridge Road, BURGESS HILL, WEST SUSSEX, RH15 0QY.
TUFF, Mr. Anthony Eric, LLB FCA *1967;* 201 Chessington Road, Ewell, EPSOM, SURREY, KT19 9XE. (Life Member)
TUFF, Mrs. Lyn Caroline, ACA *1991;* (Tax Fac), Wayside, St Georges Road, REDHILL, SURREY, RH1 5RD.
TUFFILL, Mr. Richard James, BSc ACA *1997;* 5210 Valiant Court Gloucester Business Park, Delta Way, GLOUCESTER, GL3 4FE.
TUFFIN, Mr. Christopher George Allon, ACA *2008;* 118 East 60th Street, Apartment 9B, NEW YORK, NY 10022, UNITED STATES.
TUFFIN, Mr. James Charles Richard, MBA BSc ACA *1982;* Heath Cottage, Main Road, Brighstone, NEWPORT, ISLE OF WIGHT, PO30 4AQ.
TUFFIN, Mr. James Wilfred, BSc ACA *2009;* 350W 42nd Street, Apartment 21K, NEW YORK, NY 10036, UNITED STATES.
•TUFFIN, Mr. Peter Jonathan, FCA *1989;* (Tax Fac), John A Tuffin & Co LLP, 12-13 Ship Street, BRIGHTON, BN1 1AD.
•TUFFIN, Mr. Roger Quentin Allon, ACA *2006;* (Tax Fac), John A Tuffin & Co LLP, 12-13 Ship Street, BRIGHTON, BN1 1AD.
TUFFREY, Mr. Michael William, BA ACA *1984;* 50 Lynette Avenue, LONDON, SW4 9HD.
TUFFY, Mr. William Patrick, MBA ACA FCCA *2008;* Rosecroft, 144 East Lane, West Horsley, LEATHERHEAD, SURREY, KT24 6NY.
TUFNELL, Mr. Mark Henry, MA ACA CTA *1991;* (Tax Fac), Calmsden Manor, CIRENCESTER, GLOUCESTERSHIRE, GL7 5ET.
•TUFNELL, Mr. Richard Godfrey, FCA *1993;* Walters and Tufnell Limited, 122 New London Road, CHELMSFORD, CM2 0RG.
•TUFTON, Mr. Matthew John, ACA MAAT *2004;* MJT Accountancy Services, 9 Elmleigh, YEOVIL, SOMERSET, BA21 3UJ.
TUFTS, Mrs. Claire Louise, BCom FCA *1993;* Centrica Storage Ltd Venture House, 42-54 London Road, STAINES, MIDDLESEX, TW18 4HF.
TUFTS, Mr. Dean Stuart, BSc ACA *1985;* A2dominion Group Capital House, 25 Chapel Street, LONDON, NW1 5WX.
TUGNAIT, Mr. Kamaljit, MA ACA *1989;* 22 Ickenham Road, RUISLIP, MIDDLESEX, HA4 7BX.
TUGNAIT, Mrs. Mira, BA ACA *1997;* Green Tiles, Thornton Grove, PINNER, MIDDLESEX, HA5 4HG.
TUGWELL, Miss. Jane Elizabeth, LLB FCA *1992;* Lilacs, 129 Mill Road, BURGESS HILL, RH15 8AY.
TUHAMI, Mrs. Sally, BSc ACA *2007;* 33 Holborn, Sainsburys Supermarkets Ltd, 33 Holborn, LONDON, EC1N 2HT.
TUHME, Mrs. Claire Louise, BA(Hons) ACA *2004;* 31 Pennyfields Boulevard, Long Eaton, NOTTINGHAM, NG10 3QJ.
TUKE, Mr. Graham David, BSc FCA *1977;* 68 Clipstone Road West, Forest Town, MANSFIELD, NG19 0BU.
TUKE, Mr. John Ernest, FCA *1961;* Denniker Cottage, Fletching, UCKFIELD, EAST SUSSEX, TN22 3SH. (Life Member)
TUKKER, Mr. Michiel, ACA *2011;* Flat 44, Gainsborough House, Erasmus Street, LONDON, SW1P 4HX.
TULETT, Mr. Greg, BA ACA *2004;* Ground Floor Flat, 62 Nansen Road, LONDON, SW11 5NT.
TULEY, Mr. Richard James, FCA *1966;* Anchorage, 1 Arun Close, WORTHING, BN13 3HT. (Life Member)
TULEY, Mr. Simon, BSc ACA *1992;* 9 Woodfields, Simonstone, BURNLEY, BB12 7SB.
TULIP, Mr. Danny, FCA *1972;* 10974 Setchell Road, NORTH SAANICH V8L 5P2, BC, CANADA.
TULIP, Mr. Michael, ACA *1990;* James Sharp & Co, Exchange House, 39 Knowsley Street, BURY, BL9 0ST.
TULIP, Miss. Pauline, BA ACA *1992;* 2 Reeceton Gardens, BOLTON, BL1 5BG.
TULL, Mr. Andrew, BA(Econ) ACA *1998;* 59 Louisville Road, LONDON, SW17 8RL.
TULL, Mr. David, ACA *2010;* 237 Perry Street, BILLERICAY, ESSEX, CM12 0QN.
TULL, Mr. Robert Geoffrey, BA ACA *1998;* Henderson Gartmore Japan Limited, Hibiya Marine Building, 1-5-1 Yurakucho, Chiyoda-Ku, TOKYO, 100-0006 JAPAN.
TULL, Mr. Steven Derek, ACA *2008;* 8 Elim Estate, Weston Street, LONDON, SE1 4BY.
TULLETT, Mrs. Debra Jayne, LLB FCA *1988;* Mercer Limited, 5 Bedford Park, CROYDON, CR0 2AQ.
TULLETT, Mr. Keith Martin, BA FCA *1982;* 5/105 Victoria Street Potts Point, SYDNEY, NSW 2011, AUSTRALIA.
•TULLETT, Mr. Mark Dexter, BA FCA *1991;* Civvals Ltd, 50 Seymour Street, LONDON, W1H 7JG. See also Civvals Ellam Ltd
TULLETT, Mr. Peter John, BSc ACA *1987;* (Tax Fac), 1 Downsview Road, SEVENOAKS, KENT, TN13 2JT.
•TULLETT, Mr. Timothy William, MBA BA FCA *1983;* Corner House, 1a Castlegate, KNARESBOROUGH, NORTH YORKSHIRE, HG5 8AR.
TULLEY, Dr. Matthew James Christopher, BA ACA *1998;* New Hospitals Programme Director, Barts & London N H S Trust, 9 Prescot Street, LONDON, E1 8PR.
TULLIS, Mr. Neil Donald, BSc ACA *1979;* Chimneys, 59 Greenways, BECKENHAM, BR3 3NQ.
TULLOCH, Miss. Ann-Marie, BSc ACA *2004;* with Dodd & Co., Clint Mill, Cornmarket, PENRITH, CA11 7HW.
TULLOCH, Mrs. Caroline Louise, BA ACA *1989;* 20 Lancaster Drive, EAST GRINSTEAD, WEST SUSSEX, RH19 3XF.
TULLOCH, Mr. Clive William, FCA CTA *1971;* (Tax Fac), Lamorna, Sleepers Hill, WINCHESTER, HAMPSHIRE, SO22 4NB.
TULLOCH, Mr. Donald Coryn Dickon, MChem ACA *2006;* Viale Ezio 5, 20149 MILAN, ITALY.
TULLOCH, Miss. Elizabeth Anne, BA ACA *1992;* Flat 2, 52 Castle Hill Avenue, FOLKESTONE, CT20 2RE.
•TULLOCH, Mr. Jonathan Christopher, BSc ACA *2006;* Hardcastle Burton LLP, Lake House, Market Hill, ROYSTON, HERTFORDSHIRE, SG8 9JN.
TULLOCH, Miss. Louise Claire, BA ACA *2005;* Apartment 8 Block 1, Larke Rise Off Mersey Road, MANCHESTER, LANCASHIRE, M20 2UL.
•TULLOCH, Mr. Roger, BA ACA *1999;* with Deloitte LLP, Athene Place, 66 Shoe Lane, LONDON, EC4A 3BQ.
TULLY, Mr. Andrew John Howard, MA ACA *1994;* 75 Station Road, HARPENDEN, HERTFORDSHIRE, AL5 4RL.
TULLY, Miss. Donna Louise, BA ACA *2001;* 5 St Peter's Court, 27 Henrietta Street, LONDON, WC2E 8NA.
•TULLY, Mr. Edward Christopher, FCA *1979;* (Tax Fac), Edwards, 15 Station Road, ST. IVES, CAMBRIDGESHIRE, PE27 5BH.
TULLY, Mr. John, ACA *2010;* 207 Windle Hall Drive, ST. HELENS, MERSEYSIDE, WA10 6PY.
TULLY, Mr. Jonathan, BSc ACA *2010;* Apartment 217 Liberty Place, 26-38 Sheepcote Street, BIRMINGHAM, B16 8JZ.
TULLY, Mr. Raymond Paul, BSc ACA *1993;* Flat 74 Cinnabar Wharf East 28, Wapping High Street, Wapping, LONDON, E1W 1NG.
TULLY, Mr. Robert Thomas, BSc ACA *1986;* 151 Hooe Rd, Plymstock, PLYMOUTH, PL9 9NL.
TULLY, Miss. Sian Frances, MEng ACA *2009;* 45 St. Davids Way, WICKFORD, ESSEX, SS11 8EX.
TULLY, Mr. William Samuel Nicholson, MA ACA *1993;* Seymour Pierce Ltd, 20 Old Bailey, LONDON, EC4M 7EN.
TULP, Mr. Richard, BSc ACA *1980;* 26 Foxcote Way, Walton, CHESTERFIELD, S42 7NP.
•TULSIDAS, Mr. Sunjay Kumar Ram, BCom FCA *1995;* Financial Angels Ltd, 7 Plaza Parade, Maida Vale, LONDON, NW6 5RP.
TUMBRIDGE, Mr. James William, FCA *1955;* 23 Percy Road, Winchmore Hill, LONDON, N21 2JA.
•TUMBRIDGE, Miss. Michelle, BSc FCA DChA *1992;* M Tumbridge & Co, 20 Anderson Close, LONDON, N21 1TH.
TUMILTY, Ms. Alison, BA ACA *1990;* 27 Woodale Close, Whittlehall, WARRINGTON, WA5 3GL.
TUMMEY, Miss. Rebecca Jane, BA(Hons) ACA *2007;* 81 Ruskin, Henley Road, Caversham, READING, RG4 6LF.
TUN, Mr. Maurice Myo Aye, ACA *2007;* 12 Woodleigh Cl, 03-13 Blossoms at Woodleigh, SINGAPORE 357907, SINGAPORE.
TUNCER, Miss. Dia Duygu, BSc BSc(Hons) ACA *2011;* 202 Risley Avenue, LONDON, N17 7EP.
TUNE, Mr. Christopher James, BA ACA *2002;* 44C Fairlawn Park, Sydenham, LONDON, SE26 5RY.
TUNE, Mr. John Charles, FCA *1965;* 4 Smythe Close, Southbough, TUNBRIDGE WELLS, TN4 0TY.
TUNE, Miss. Katherine, ACA *2009;* 20 Ashacre Lane, WORTHING, WEST SUSSEX, BN13 2DA.
TUNE, Mr. Nicholas James, BSc ACA *2005;* Winsel, Manor Road, WOKING, GU21 4RY.
TUNG, Mr. Min Eric, MSc ACA *1989;* 39 Quaggy Walk, LONDON, SE3 9EJ.
TUNG, Mr. Shiu Bun Albert, ACA *2007;* Flat H Floor 24, Block 1 Tanner Garden, 18 Tanner Road, NORTH POINT, HONG KONG SAR.
TUNG, Miss. Yoke Chan, FCA *1977;* 21-05-07 Indah Damamsara, 21 Jalan Endah Damansara, 50490 KUALA LUMPUR, FEDERAL TERRITORY, MALAYSIA.
•TUNG SING, Mr. Cheong Mou Yuen, FCA *1973;* (Tax Fac), Tung Sing & Co Limited, 26 Oakleigh Park South, LONDON, N20 9JU.
TUNKEL, Mr. Benjamin Samuel, BA ACA *2008;* 8 Fairway, Prestwich, MANCHESTER, M25 0JH.
TUNLEY, Miss. Louise Victoria, ACA DChA *2007;* Camden Jobtrain, 301-305 Kentish Town Road, LONDON, NW5 2TJ.
TUNLEY, Mr. Nicholas Philip, LLB ACA *2002;* with Deloitte LLP, 2 New Street Square, LONDON, EC4A 3BZ.
TUNNADINE, Mrs. Clare Caroline, BA ACA *1999;* 2 Jaras Drive, Baschurch, SHREWSBURY, SY4 2DH.
TUNNARD, Mr. Conolly Finnur, FCA *1977;* Grove House, Shadey Bower, SALISBURY, SP1 3RH.
•TUNNARD, Mr. Nicholas Charles, BSc ACA *1983;* AVN Arena Limited, 42 Chapel Street, KING'S LYNN, NORFOLK, PE30 1EF. See also Arena Business Solutions LLP
TUNNELL, Mr. Jonathan Frederick, BSc ACA *1982;* Sucden Financial Ltd Plantation Place South 3rd Floor, 60 Great Tower Street, LONDON, EC3R 5AZ.
TUNNELL, Mr. Neil Barry, BSc ACA *1999;* 15 Friesian Place, HAMILTON, NEW ZEALAND.
TUNNEY, Mr. Mark Joseph, BSc ACA *1995;* 269 Beacon Road, LOUGHBOROUGH, LE11 2RA.
TUNNICLIFF, Mr. Andrew, BSc ACA *1988;* Oracle Corporation (UK) Ltd, Oracle Parkway, READING, RG6 1RA.
TUNNICLIFF, Mr. Andrew Philip, BSc ACA *1979;* 6/37 Barry Street, NEUTRAL BAY, NSW 2089, AUSTRALIA.
TUNNICLIFF, Mr. Paul, BSc ACA MAAT *2011;* H W Fisher & Co, Acre House, 11-15 William Road, LONDON, NW1 3ER.
•TUNNICLIFFE, Mr. Richard Dale, BA ACA *2004;* Rily Accountancy and Business Solutions Ltd, Rily House, 55 Stryd Hywel Harris, HENGOED, MID GLAMORGAN, CF82 7DN.
TUNNICLIFFE, Miss. Yvonne, BD ACA *1995;* 22 Dixon Street, ROTHERHAM, S65 1EY.
TUNSTALL, Mr. David James, MA FCA *1984;* 48 Greenbank Crescent, EDINBURGH, EH10 5SQ.
TUNSTALL, Mr. Graham, FCA *1972;* 24 Ormskirk Road, Rainford, ST.HELENS, MERSEYSIDE, WA11 8BT.
TUNSTALL, Mr. Martin Cuthbert, OBE FCA FFA *1969;* Residence les Bizontines, Batiment B, Appartement 316, Avenue des Devises, 14390 CABOURG, FRANCE.
TUNSTALL, Mr. Neil Alexander, FCA *1969;* Cowside Cottage, Langcliffe, SETTLE, NORTH YORKSHIRE, BD24 9PZ.
TUPHOLME, Mr. Andrew Ian, BA ACA *1995;* 1 Whirlow Grange Avenue, Whirlow, SHEFFIELD, S11 9RW.
TUPHOLME, Mrs. Joanna Lucy, BSc ACA *1996;* 1 Whirlow Grange Avenue, Whirlow, SHEFFIELD, S11 9RW.
TUPLIN, Miss. Joanna Elise, BSc ACA *2002;* 133 Ravensbury Road, LONDON, SW18 4RY.
TUPLING, Mr. Michael Charles, BSc ACA *1986;* with Baker Tilly Tax & Advisory Services LLP, 2 Humber Quays, Wellington Street West, HULL, HU1 2BN.
TUPMAN, Mr. Jonathan, ACA *2008;* Willow Cottage The Green, Charney Bassett, WANTAGE, OXFORDSHIRE, OX12 0EU.
TUPMAN, Mr. Robert Ivan, FCA *1975;* with Higgisons, Higgison House, 381/383 City Road, LONDON, EC1V 1NW.
TUPPEN, Mr. Graham Edward, CBE FCA *1974;* Enterprise Inns Plc, 3 Monkspath Hall Road, Shirley, SOLIHULL, WEST MIDLANDS, B90 4SJ.
TUPPEN, Ms. Harriet Jane, BA(Hons) ACA *2001;* 98 Ferrier Avenue, TORONTO M4K 3H4, ON, CANADA.
TUPPENNEY, Mr. Steven Peter, BSc ACA *1992;* 1405 Grand Diamond Condo, 888 Petchburi Road, Pratunam, BANGKOK 10400, THAILAND.
TUPPER, Mr. Robin Charles, ACA *1982;* (Tax Fac), Ventura Yachts.S.L., Casa B Local 12, Puerto Banus, Marbella, 29660 MALAGA, SPAIN.
TUPPIN, Mr. Dudley Michael, FCA *1973;* Hollydene, Half Moon Hill, HASLEMERE, GU27 2JW.
TUQAN, Mr. Usama Jamaal, FCA *1971;* 3 Brompton Square, LONDON, SW3 2AA. (Life Member)
TURAEVA, Miss. Nodira, ACA *2009;* Flat 44 Derwent House, Southern Grove, LONDON, E3 4PU.
TURAY, Miss. Hawa, BA(Hons) ACA *2009;* Flat 40 Dexter House, 3 Kale Road, ERITH, DA18 4BD.
TURBERVILLE-SMITH, Mr. Andrew, BA ACA *1992;* South Lodge, Haselbech Hill, Haselbech, NORTHAMPTON, NN6 9LL.
TURBITT, Miss. Alison, BSc ACA *2008;* 8 Lynton Drive, KEIGHLEY, WEST YORKSHIRE, BD20 5BA.
•TURFORD, Mr. Andrew John, BSc(Econ) ACA *1979;* (Tax Fac), Andrew Turford & Co Limited, 33 Stow Park Avenue, NEWPORT, NP20 4FN.
TURGOOSE, Mr. George Keith, BSc FCA *1955;* Briars Mead, 26 Rockery Close, Dibden, SOUTHAMPTON, SO45 5HE. (Life Member)
TURGUT, Mr. Yashar, MSc FCA *1983;* 46 Oulderhill Drive, Bamford, ROCHDALE, OL11 5LB.
•TURIGEL, Mrs. Tracy Anita, ACA *2004;* Maytree Accountancy, 148 Neale Avenue, KETTERING, NORTHAMPTONSHIRE, NN16 9HD.
TURK, Mr. Andrew Mark, BSc FCA *1984;* Roystone Lodge, Chesterfield Road, Matlock Moor, MATLOCK, DERBYSHIRE, DE4 5LZ.
TURK, Mr. Arthur Cyril, FCA *1971;* 3 Lynton Close, EAST GRINSTEAD, RH19 3XE.
•TURK, Mr. Darrell John, FCA *1975;* (Tax Fac), Kingscott Dix Limited, 60 Kings Walk, GLOUCESTER, GL1 1LA.
TURK, Mr. Nigel John, FCA *1967;* Birch Tree Cottage, The Common, Whiteparish, SALISBURY, SP5 2RD.
TURK, Mr. Rodney Jack, FCA *1949;* 2 The Hatch, Godden Green, SEVENOAKS, TN15 0JR. (Life Member)
TURK, Mrs. Sarah Elizabeth, BA ACA *1992;* 5 Huia Road, Days Bay, LOWER HUTT 5013, NEW ZEALAND.
TURK, Mr. Stephen Richard Lloyd, MA FCA *1980;* 6367 W 80th St, LOS ANGELES, CA 90045, UNITED STATES.
TURKINGTON, Mr. John, FCA *1968;* Briar House, 16 Drews Park, Knotty Green, BEACONSFIELD, HP9 2TT.
TURKINGTON, Miss. Sarah Louise, ACA *2008;* Flat 60, Jackman House, Watts Street, LONDON, E1W 2PU.
TURKSON, Mr. George Kofi Ofosuhene, FCA *1957;* PO Box 5571, Accra North, ACCRA, GHANA. (Life Member)
•TURLAND, Mr. Alan John, BA FCA *1975;* (Tax Fac), Johnson Murkett & Hurst, Rawdon House, Rawdon Terrace, ASHBY-DE-LA-ZOUCH, LE65 2GN. See also Johnson, Murkett & Hurst (Computer Services) Ltd
TURLAND, Mr. Christopher Harry, BSc FCA *2000;* 4 Beech Grove, TRING, HERTFORDSHIRE, HP23 5NU.
TURLAND, Mr. Kevin John, BA ACA ATII *1995;* (Tax Fac), 15 Paget Close, CAMBERLEY, SURREY, GU15 1PZ.
TURLEY, Mr. Allan, FCA *1978;* 2 Newby Farm Close, Newby, SCARBOROUGH, YO12 6UH.
•TURLEY, Mr. Gary Peter, BSc FCA *1991;* 24 Clarry Drive, Four Oaks, SUTTON COLDFIELD, B74 2QT.
TURLEY, Mr. Gerard Perry, FCA *1972;* Eastdene, 7 Brynview Close, Reynoldston, SWANSEA, SA3 1AG.
•TURLEY, Mrs. Janet Valerie, BSc FCA *1979;* (Tax Fac), Janet Turley FCA, Manor Barn, 4 The Rickyard, Newton Blossomville, BEDFORD, MK43 8AF.

TURLEY, Mr. Raymond Cornelius, FCA *1961;* Yulans, Heavegate Road, CROWBOROUGH, TN6 1UA. (Life Member)
TURLEY, Mr. Richard Lyndon, LLB ACA *2004;* 1/15 Carlisle Street, TAMARAMA, NSW 2026, AUSTRALIA.
TURLEY, Miss. Ruth Melanie, BA ACA *1989;* 24 Glenlyon Road, Eltham, LONDON, SE9 1AJ.
TURLEY, Mr. Seamus George, BCom ACA *1984;* Law Society of Ireland, Blackhall Place, DUBLIN, COUNTY DUBLIN, IRELAND.
•**TURLEY, Mr. William Jonathan, FCA** *1979;* (Tax Fac), Freeman Rich Ltd, 284 Clifton Drive South, LYTHAM ST. ANNES, LANCASHIRE, FY8 1LH. See also Freeman Rich
TURNAGE, Mr. Anthony Philip, FCA *1967;* 3 Deacon Place, CATERHAM, SURREY, CR3 5FN.
TURNBULL, Mrs. Alison Jane, BA ACA ATII *1990;* (Tax Fac), Silver Gable, Forest Road, Pyrford, WOKING, GU22 8LU.
TURNBULL, Mr. Alister Mark, BSc ACA *1996;* 3 Skippon Terrace, Thorner, LEEDS, LS14 3HA.
TURNBULL, Miss. Amy, ACA *2010;* 258 Honeysuckle Road, SOUTHAMPTON, HAMPSHIRE, SO16 3BP.
TURNBULL, Mr. Andrew John, ACA *1981;* 14A Wilfield Avenue, Vaucluse, SYDNEY, NSW 2030, AUSTRALIA.
TURNBULL, Mr. Anthony, BSc FCA *1990;* 10a Victoria Gardens, SAFFRON WALDEN, CB11 3AF.
TURNBULL, Mr. Benedict Bedford, BSc(Hons) FCA *2000;* 50 Priory Street, COLCHESTER, CO1 2QB.
TURNBULL, Mr. Brian George, FCA FCIS *1969;* Bridale Manor, Thornton Le Dale, PICKERING, YO18 7SF.
TURNBULL, Mr. Brian Phipps, MA FCA *1968;* Hayes, Church Road, Colaton Raleigh, SIDMOUTH, EX10 0LH. (Life Member)
TURNBULL, Ms. Carol, BSc ACA *1983;* 3 Elliver Street, SMITHFIELD, QLD 4878, AUSTRALIA.
TURNBULL, Mr. Charles Robert, BSc ACA *1999;* 9 High Street, SHAFTESBURY, DORSET, SP7 8HZ.
TURNBULL, Mr. Colin, BA BSc ACA *2007;* 11 Tithing Road, FLEET, HAMPSHIRE, GU51 1GG.
TURNBULL, Mr. Colin George, BA(Hons) ACA *2004;* with PKF (UK) LLP, Farringdon Place, 20 Farringdon Road, LONDON, EC1M 3AP.
TURNBULL, Mr. Craig Beatty, FCA *1972;* 28 Wayfield Avenue, HOVE, BN3 7LW. (Life Member)
TURNBULL, Mr. David Knight Thomas, BSc FCA *1975;* Halfway Grange, Chantry View Road, GUILDFORD, GU1 3YZ.
TURNBULL, Miss. Deborah, BSc ACA *2007;* 22 Aldwych Street, SOUTH SHIELDS, TYNE AND WEAR, NE33 3BZ.
TURNBULL, Mr. Francis Malcolm, FCA *1976;* 86 Polwarth Road, Brunton Park, Gosforth, NEWCASTLE UPON TYNE, NE3 5NE.
TURNBULL, Mr. Gavin James, BAcc ACA *1998;* 21 Homemead Road, Bickley, BROMLEY, BR2 8BB.
TURNBULL, Mrs. Georgina Martin, ACA *1998;* 50 Priory Street, COLCHESTER, CO1 2QB.
TURNBULL, Mr. Gordon, FCA *1974;* 26 Sandstone Ave, Walton, CHESTERFIELD, S42 7NS.
TURNBULL, Miss. Helen Mary, BA ACA DChA *2002;* with PricewaterhouseCoopers LLP, Hays Galleria, 1 Hays Lane, LONDON, SE1 2RD.
TURNBULL, Mr. Ian, BSc ACA *2005;* 11 Mowbray Villas, SOUTH SHIELDS, TYNE AND WEAR, NE33 3GA.
TURNBULL, Mr. James Michael, FCA *1975;* 6248 Paso Los Cerritos, SAN JOSE, CA 95120, UNITED STATES.
TURNBULL, Mr. James Nicholson, FCA *1968;* Woodhill, Medburn, Ponteland, NEWCASTLE UPON TYNE, NE20 0JE.
TURNBULL, Mr. Jeremy Scott, BSc FCA *1991;* with RSM Tenon Limited, International House, 66 Chiltern Street, LONDON, W1U 4JT.
TURNBULL, Mr. Jonathan James, BA ACA *1987;* 9 Alexander Place, LONDON, SW7 2SG.
TURNBULL, Mr. Jonathan Richard, BA ACA *1989;* 1 Rothsay Gardens, BEDFORD, MK40 3QA.
TURNBULL, Mrs. Julie, BA FCA ACA *1998;* 125 Missenden Acres, Hedge End, SOUTHAMPTON, HAMPSHIRE, SO30 2RD.
TURNBULL, Mrs. Louise, BA ACA *1985;* 69 Fiddens Wharf Road, KILLARA, NSW 2070, AUSTRALIA.
TURNBULL, Mr. Michael James, BA ACA *1989;* 151 Leeds Road, HARROGATE, HG2 8EZ.
•**TURNBULL, Mr. Michael Roy, BSc ACA** *1984;* (Tax Fac), Turnbull & Co Accountants Limited, Pilgrim House, Oxford Place, PLYMOUTH, PL1 5AJ.
TURNBULL, Mr. Nigel Victor, CVO BSc FCA FCT *1966;* (Member of Council 2000 - 2003), The Old Vicarage, Church Way, East Claydon, BUCKINGHAM, MK18 2ND.
TURNBULL, Mrs. Patricia Anne, BSc ACA *1979;* 22 Blackthorn Close, Hasland, CHESTERFIELD, S41 0DY.
TURNBULL, Mr. Paul Raymond, BA ACA *1994;* Romulus Construction Ltd Sandford House, 10 Maynard Close, LONDON, SW6 2DB.
TURNBULL, Miss. Peta Laurinne, BA FCA *1982;* Mermaid Cottage, 119 Chiswell, PORTLAND, DORSET, DT5 1AP.
TURNBULL, Mr. Peter Reginald, FCA *1973;* 49A West Street, FARNHAM, SURREY, GU9 7DX.
TURNBULL, Mr. Reginald Edward, FCA *1948;* 30 Greenwich Drive, Lytham, LYTHAM ST.ANNES, FY8 4QT. (Life Member)
TURNBULL, Mr. Richard Michael, BEng ACA *2006;* 1 The Old School, Church Road Southborough, TUNBRIDGE WELLS, TN4 0RU.
TURNBULL, Mr. Roger Alder Brinkler, FCA *1968;* 6 Hammond Close, Pampisford, CAMBRIDGE, CB22 3EP.
TURNBULL, Mr. Ronald, ACA *1980;* Sundial House, Wear Street, Chilton Moor, HOUGHTON LE SPRING, TYNE AND WEAR, DH4 6LZ.
TURNBULL, Mrs. Rosemarie, BA ACA *1992;* 151 Leeds Road, HARROGATE, HG2 8EZ.
TURNBULL, Miss. Sarah Lee, MA BSc ACA *2006;* Earls Court & Olympia Ltd, Exhibition Centre, Warwick Road, LONDON, SW5 9TA.
TURNBULL-HALL, Mrs. Caroline Sarah, BSc FCA *1990;* (Tax Fac), with PricewaterhouseCoopers LLP, Pricewaterhousecoopers, 12 Plumtree Court, LONDON, EC4A 4HT.
TURNELL, Mrs. Christine, BCom ACA *1995;* 5 Heritage Court, Boley Park, LICHFIELD, STAFFORDSHIRE, WS14 9ST.
TURNER, Mr. Adam Mark, BA(Hons) ACA *2003;* Apartment 66 Centenary Plaza, 18 Holliday Street, BIRMINGHAM, B1 1TB.
TURNER, Mr. Adrian Lee, MMath ACA *2007;* 29 West Square, LONDON, SE11 4SP.
TURNER, Mr. Alan, BA ACA *1981;* 5 Paddock Walk, WARLINGHAM, CR6 9HW.
TURNER, Mr. Alan, FCA *1949;* 47 Cornwall Drive, Bayston Hill, SHREWSBURY, SY3 0EP. (Life Member)
TURNER, Mr. Alan Charles, LLB FCA *1966;* Little Graces, Park Gate, Elham, CANTERBURY, KENT, CT4 6NF. (Life Member)
TURNER, Mr. Alan John, BA ACA *1993;* Enstar (Eu) Ltd Avaya House, Cathedral Hill, GUILDFORD, GU2 7YL.
TURNER, Mr. Alan Michael, PhD BSc ACA *1980;* Woodmancot, Foxmoor Lane, Ebley, STROUD, GL5 4PN.
TURNER, Mrs. Aline, BA ACA *1995;* Pearle Cottage, Howe Green, Howe, NORWICH, NR15 1HD.
TURNER, Mrs. Alison, BA ACA *1992;* 1 Woodbine Cottages, Pipe Bridge, ROWLANDS GILL, NE39 1PQ.
TURNER, Mr. Allister Paul, BSc ACA *1998;* 2 Acre Lane, Holmbridge, HOLMFIRTH, HD9 2PN.
TURNER, Mrs. Andrea Joanne, BSc ACA *1991;* Fellstone Cottage, Mill Lane, Black Bourton, BAMPTON, OXFORDSHIRE, OX18 2PJ.
TURNER, Mr. Andrew Charles, MA FCA *1980;* The Old Rectory, 15 High Street, Graveley, ST. NEOTS, CAMBRIDGESHIRE, PE19 6PL.
TURNER, Mr. Andrew Evan Paul, BA ACA MAAT *1997;* 5 Vicarage Court, Church Lane, Shinfield, READING, RG2 9HJ.
TURNER, Mr. Andrew John, ACA *2008;* 5 Bramblewood Drive, Finchfield, WOLVERHAMPTON, WEST MIDLANDS, WV3 9DB.
TURNER, Mr. Andrew Richard, BA ACA *1985;* Wilshire House, Dawns Lane, Aslockton, NOTTINGHAM, NG13 9AD.
•**TURNER, Mr. Andrew Robert, ACA FMAAT** *2003;* Mark J Rees, Granville Hall, Granville Road, LEICESTER, LE1 7RU.
TURNER, Mr. Andrew Simon, BSc(Hons) ACA *2002;* 1 Milton Close, POOLE, DORSET, BH14 9QE.
TURNER, Mr. Andrew Simon Gough, MA ACA *2002;* 26 Langham Road, Knowle, BRISTOL, BS4 2LJ.
TURNER, Mr. Andrew Stewart, MA FCA *1968;* Brynkelhowe, York Road, THIRSK, NORTH YORKSHIRE, YO7 3AA.
TURNER, Mr. Andrew Walford, FCA *1969;* The Old Pack House, GODSTONE, RH9 8BL. (Life Member)
•**TURNER, Mr. Andrew William, BA FCA** *1992;* 26 Azalea Close, London Colney, ST. ALBANS, HERTFORDSHIRE, AL2 1UA.
TURNER, Mrs. Anna, BSc ACA *2009;* 46 Ravenswood Road, LONDON, SW12 9PJ.
TURNER, Mrs. Anne Sandra, BA ACA *1985;* 27 Gordon Drive, CHERTSEY, KT16 9PP.
•**TURNER, Mr. Anthony Barry, BSc ACA** *2004;* Goodier Smith and Watts Limited, Devonshire House, Manor Way, BOREHAMWOOD, HERTFORDSHIRE, WD6 1QQ.
TURNER, Mr. Anthony William, MSc ACA *1988;* 62 Cowslip Bank, Lychpit, BASINGSTOKE, RG24 8RR.
TURNER, The Venerable Antony Hubert Michael, FCA *1952;* 15 Avenue Road, HAYLING ISLAND, PO11 0LX. (Life Member)
TURNER, Mr. Barry, FCA *1974;* 5 Brackendale, LEEK, STAFFORDSHIRE, ST13 8PD.
TURNER, Mr. Barry, FCA *1974;* with Nicholsons, Newland House, The Point, Weaver Road, LINCOLN, LN6 3QN.
TURNER, Mr. Ben David, BA(Hons) ACA *2011;* 90 Wallington Avenue, NORTH SHIELDS, TYNE AND WEAR, NE30 3QB.
•**TURNER, Mrs. Beverley Elizabeth, BA FCA CTA ACIS** *1982;* Lamburn & Turner, Riverside House, 1 Place Farm, Place Farm, Wheathampstead, ST. ALBANS AL4 8SB. See also The Accounts Factory Ltd
TURNER, Mr. Brian Arthur, FCA *1975;* Old Farm, Farm Lane East End Lane, Ditchling, HASSOCKS, BN6 8UN.
TURNER, Mr. Brian Richard, BSc ACA *1982;* 2 Goldfinch Place, FLAGSTAFF HILL, SA 5159, AUSTRALIA.
TURNER, Mr. Bruce Wilson, BEng ACA *1992;* 8 Grindstone Handle Corner, Knaphill, WOKING, GU21 2SD.
TURNER, Ms. Carole-Ann, BA ACA *1996;* Goldbacherstrasse 56, CH8700 KUESNACHT, SWITZERLAND.
TURNER, Mrs. Caroline Jane, BSc ACA *1990;* M J Metalcraft Ltd, 33-34 Sampson Road North, BIRMINGHAM, B11 1BL.
TURNER, Mrs. Carolyn Jane, BA ACA *1997;* 17 Pilgrims Way, GUILDFORD, SURREY, GU4 8AD.
•**TURNER, Mrs. Cassandra Louise, ACA** *2008;* G&T Accountancy Services Ltd, Denby Dale Business Park, Wakefield Road, Denby Dale, HUDDERSFIELD, HD8 8QH.
TURNER, Mrs. Catherine Jane, BSc ACA *2004;* 12 Edward Road, POOLE, DORSET, BH14 9ES.
TURNER, Mrs. Cathryn Jane, BA ACA *1991;* Caterpillar (UK) Ltd, The Phoenix, Central Boulevard, Blythe Valley Park, Shirley, SOLIHULL WEST MIDLANDS B90 8BG.
TURNER, Mrs. Chloe Isobel, BA ACA *2002;* 3 The Nook, Symn Lane, WOTTON-UNDER-EDGE, GL12 7BG.
TURNER, Miss. Christine, BA ACA *2003;* International Paints Ltd, Stoneygate Lane, GATESHEAD, TYNE AND WEAR, NE10 0JY.
TURNER, Mrs. Christine Janet, BSc ACA *1991;* (Tax Fac), 3 Oaklands Close, Collingham, NEWARK, NOTTINGHAMSHIRE, NG23 7RQ.
•**TURNER, Mrs. Christine Marie, BA FCA** *1999;* (Tax Fac), Turner & Co, 4 Bridle Ways, East Bridgford, NOTTINGHAM, NG13 8PT.
TURNER, Mr. Christopher Charles, FCA *1970;* 8A Warwick Drive, Hale, ALTRINCHAM, WA15 9EA.
TURNER, Mr. Christopher David, BCom ACA *2004;* 8 Green Lane, Hazel Grove, STOCKPORT, CHESHIRE, SK7 4DZ.
•**TURNER, Mr. Christopher John, FCA** *1977;* Turners Accounting & Business Solutions Ltd, Suite 170, Lomeshaye Business Village, Turner Road, NELSON, LANCASHIRE BB9 7DR.
TURNER, Mr. Christopher John, BA ACA *1998;* 33 Littlebrook Gardens, CHESHUNT, HERTFORDSHIRE, EN8 8QQ.
TURNER, Mr. Christopher John Gentry, FCA *1963;* Spring Grove, Goudhurst Road, Marden, TONBRIDGE, TN12 9NW.
TURNER, Mr. Christopher John Howarth, BA ACA *1985;* 6 Cranleigh Gardens, Grange Park, LONDON, N21 1DS.
TURNER, Mr. Christopher Michael, BSc ACA *1981;* (Tax Fac), Holly Cottage, Pheasants Hill, Hambleden, HENLEY-ON-THAMES, OXFORDSHIRE, RG9 6SN.
TURNER, Mr. Christopher Raymond William, BSc(Hons) ACA *2002;* with Group Finance Lloyd's Register, 71 Fenchurch Street, LONDON, EC3M 4BS.
•**TURNER, Mr. Christopher Robert, BA ACA** *1979;* C.R. Turner & Co., 15 Marroway, Weston Turville, AYLESBURY, HP22 5TQ.
TURNER, Mr. Christopher William, BCom FCA *1964;* 36 Lee Lane East, Horsforth, LEEDS, LS18 5RE. (Life Member)
TURNER, Mr. Christopher William, FCA *1972;* Blue Dawn Riverside Quarter Moorings, c/o Milliners House Eastfields Avenue, LONDON, SW18 1LP.
TURNER, Miss. Claire Elizabeth, BSc ACA *2006;* with PricewaterhouseCoopers LLP, 31 Great George Street, BRISTOL, BS1 5QD.
TURNER, Miss. Claire Elizabeth, BA ACA *2003;* 6 Palm Court, 11-13 Fellows Road, LONDON, NW3 3LT.
TURNER, Mrs. Claire Louise, BSc ACA *1993;* 3 Tanna Hill Court, BALDWIN PLACE, NY 10505, UNITED STATES.
TURNER, Miss. Clare Susan Grove, BSc ACA *1989;* 6 Gladwyn Road, Putney, LONDON, SW15 1JY.
TURNER, Mr. Clarence William, FCA *1974;* 4 Langmead Drive, Bushey Heath, BUSHEY, WD23 4GD.
TURNER, Mr. Colin Trevor Pellatt, FCA *1971;* 97 Elwill Way, BECKENHAM, BR3 6RX.
•**TURNER, Mr. Colin William, FCA** *1967;* C W Turner, 28 Wilman Road, TUNBRIDGE WELLS, TN4 9AP.
TURNER, Mr. Dan Eric, BSc(Hons) ACA *2007;* with BDO LLP, 6th Floor, 3 Hardman Street, Spinningfields, MANCHESTER, M3 3AT.
TURNER, Mr. Daniel David, BSc FCA *1998;* with Larking Gowen, 43 Bull Street, HOLT, NR25 6HP.
•**TURNER, Mr. Darren Keith, BSc FCA** *1991;* KPMG LLP, One Snowhill, Snow Hill Queensway, BIRMINGHAM, B4 6GN. See also KPMG Europe LLP
TURNER, Mr. David, FCA *1968;* 29 Penwood Heights, Penwood Highclere, NEWBURY, BERKSHIRE, RG20 9EY.
•**TURNER, Mr. David Charles, MA FCA** *1985;* Turner Barratt Corporate Finance Limited, 15 Market Place, NEWBURY, BERKSHIRE, RG14 5AA.
•**TURNER, Mr. David Christopher, BSc ACA** *1991;* AIMS - David Turner, 38 Caxton House, Northampton Science Park, Kings Park Road, Moulton Park, NORTHAMPTON NN3 6LG.
•**TURNER, Mr. David Daniel, FCA** *1962;* (Tax Fac), 63 Brookmans Avenue, Brookmans Park, HATFIELD, AL9 7QG.
TURNER, Mr. David Harold William, BSc ACA *1986;* Thomson Reuters Building, Three Times Square, 22nd Floor, NEW YORK, NY 10036, UNITED STATES.
TURNER, Mr. David Howard, LLB ACA *1988;* Wedge Group Plc, Wedge House, White Hart Lane, Tottenham, LONDON, N17 8HJ.
TURNER, Mr. David James, ACA *2009;* 24 Fairfax Court, BECCLES, SUFFOLK, NR34 9XG.
TURNER, Mr. David John, FCA *1969;* 38 The Grove, MOSMAN, NSW 2088, AUSTRALIA.
TURNER, Mr. David John, ACA *2008;* 26 Grand Drive, LEIGH-ON-SEA, SS9 1BG.
TURNER, Mr. David Kingsley, FCA *1962;* 11 Hantone Hill, Bathampton, BATH, BA2 6XD.
•**TURNER, Mr. David Michael, BSc FCA** *1980;* Johnsons Financial Management Limited, 2nd Floor, 109 Uxbridge Road, LONDON, W5 5TL.
•**TURNER, Mr. David Robert Bett, BSc FCA** *1986;* David Turner & Co, Studio 701, 17 Princess Street, HULL, HU2 8BJ. See also David Turner Associates
TURNER, Mr. David Scott, FCA *1969;* 123 Broadwood Avenue, RUISLIP, HA4 7XU.
TURNER, Mr. David William, ACA *1979;* 2188 Acadia Road, VANCOUVER V6T 1R5, BC, CANADA.
TURNER, Mr. David William, BSc ACA *2001;* 52 Waveney Road, HARPENDEN, HERTFORDSHIRE, AL5 4QY.
•**TURNER, Mr. Dean Peter, FCA** *1989;* Turner Beaumont & Co Limited, Thorncliffe Mews, Thorncliffe Park Estate, Newton Chambers Road, Chapeltown, SHEFFIELD S35 2PH.
TURNER, Mr. Denis William, FCA *1950;* Waverley House, Edgeworth, STROUD, GL6 7JE. (Life Member)
TURNER, Mr. Derek, FCA *1968;* 52 Creighton Avenue, Muswell Hill, LONDON, N10 1NT.
TURNER, Mr. Derek Clifford, BCom FCA *1965;* Clavella, Grassy Lane, SEVENOAKS, TN13 1PW. (Life Member)
TURNER, Mr. Duncan Philip, BA ACA *2001;* Pricewaterhousecoopers, 12 Plumtree Court, LONDON, EC4A 4HT.
•**TURNER, Mr. Edward Elwyn, ACA** *1998;* Turner Peachey, Column House, London Road, SHREWSBURY, SY2 6NN.
TURNER, Mr. Edward Michael, FCA *1967;* Coton Villa Farm, Milwich, STAFFORD, ST18 0ET.
TURNER, Mr. Edward Morton, FCA *1962;* Downs, Grand View Road, Hope Cove, KINGSBRIDGE, TQ7 3HE. (Life Member)
TURNER, Mr. Edward Thomas, BA ACA *1993;* Grant Thornton House, 22 Melton Street Euston Square, LONDON, NW1 2EP.
TURNER, Miss. Elizabeth, BSc(Hons) FCA *2000;* Deloitte & Touche Llp, 3 Rivergate, BRISTOL, BS1 6GD.
TURNER, Miss. Emma Louise, LLB ACA *2005;* 41 Brattswood Drive, Church Lawton, STOKE-ON-TRENT, ST7 3EJ.

TURNER, Mrs. Estelle, ACA *1981;* Baldwin Cox Accountants, 15-17 Foster Avenue, Beeston, NOTTINGHAM, NG9 1AE.
TURNER, Mr. Frederick Charles, FCA *1954;* 12 Pellan Crescent, Kanata, OTTAWA K2K 1J5, ON, CANADA. (Life Member)
TURNER, Mr. Gavin Neil Surtees, ACA *1981;* 4 Ditchburn Road, South Charlton, ALNWICK, NORTHUMBERLAND, NE66 2JU.
TURNER, Mr. Geoffrey Leonard, FCA *1951;* 60 St. Davids Road, TAVISTOCK, DEVON, PL19 9BT. (Life Member)
TURNER, Mr. George Mark, MA BA ACA *1990;* 38 Church Street, Thriplow, ROYSTON, HERTFORDSHIRE, SG8 7RE.
TURNER, Mr. Gerald John, BA(Hons) FCA *1969;* 19 Park Road, WALLINGTON, SM6 8AA.
TURNER, Miss. Gillian Mary, BA ACA *2001;* 52 Windhill, BISHOP'S STORTFORD, HERTFORDSHIRE, CM23 2NH.
TURNER, Mrs. Gillian Patricia, BA ACA *1984;* 33 New Road, BRADFORD-ON-AVON, BA15 1AR.
TURNER, Mr. Gordon Hedley, FCA *1963;* 29 Rockcliffe Avenue, BACUP, LANCASHIRE, OL13 8JH. (Life Member)
TURNER, Mr. Graham, BA ACA *1984;* 8 Stourhead Close, ANDOVER, SP10 3UP.
TURNER, Mr. Graham, BSc ACA *1988;* 38 Chalcot Square, LONDON, NW1 8YP.
TURNER, Mr. Graham Neil, BA ACA *1992;* 17 Longfield, Upton-on-Severn, WORCESTER, WR8 0NR.
TURNER, Mr. Grahame Howard Jonathan, LLM BSc FCA CTA *1978;* (Tax Fac), Estseon, Pilgrims Way, Westhumble, DORKING, RH5 6AP.
TURNER, Mr. Guy Peter, BSc ACA *1996;* Parkview Withy Lane, Hemyock, CULLOMPTON, DEVON, EX15 3UD.
TURNER, Mrs. Helen Clare, BA FCA DChA *1987;* 128 Southwark Street, LONDON, SE1 0SW.
TURNER, Miss. Helen Elizabeth, BA ACA *1992;* 175 Blossom Street, Apt 1306, BOSTON, MA 02114, UNITED STATES.
TURNER, Miss. Helen Jane, BSc FCA *1979;* TC214d, Thames Valley University, St. Marys Road, LONDON, W5 5RF.
TURNER, Mrs. Helen Mary, BSc ACA *2000;* 6 Marshall Howard Close, Cawston, NORWICH, NR10 4TB.
•**TURNER, Mr. Hugh David, BSc FCA** *1975;* (Tax Fac), Hugh D Turner, Kirk Syke, High Street, Gargrave, SKIPTON, BD23 3RA.
TURNER, Mr. Ian Andrew, FCA *1982;* (Tax Fac), 43 Thorpe Bay Gardens, SOUTHEND-ON-SEA, SS1 3NR.
•**TURNER, Mr. Ian Christopher, FCA** *1978;* Leonard Wilson & Co, Colinton House, Leicester Road, BEDWORTH, WARWICKSHIRE, CV12 8AB.
TURNER, Mr. Ian Geoffrey, BA ACA *1985;* 97 Longwood Gardens, Clayhall, ILFORD, IG5 0EE.
•**TURNER, Mr. Ian Michael, BSc ACA** *1988;* Cleddon Consulting, Rose Cottage, Cleddon, MONMOUTH, NP25 4PN.
•**TURNER, Mr. Ian Richard, BA ACA** *1989;* 6 Water Street, Thornton, Crosby, LIVERPOOL, L23 1TD.
TURNER, Mr. Ian Rutherford, FCA *1961;* Woodville, Woodside Villas, HEXHAM, NE46 1HX. (Life Member)
TURNER, Mrs. Jaime Louise Christine, BSc ACA *2009;* with Hilton Sharp & Clarke, Atlantic House, Jengers Mead, BILLINGSHURST, WEST SUSSEX, RH14 9PB.
TURNER, Mr. James, MA FCA *1985;* (Tax Fac), McKinsey & Co, 1 Jermyn Street, LONDON, SW1Y 4UH.
TURNER, Mr. James Nicholas, BEng ACA *2000;* 22 Althorp Road, LONDON, SW17 7ED.
TURNER, Mr. James Phillip, BSc ACA *1993;* 36O PRIVATE TRAVEL FLOOR 28, 30 ST MARY AXE, LONDON, EC3A 8BF.
TURNER, Mr. James Richard, BEng ACA *2009;* 46 Ravenswood Road, LONDON, SW12 9PJ.
TURNER, Mr. James Robert, BSc ACA *1992;* 3 Tanna Hill Court, BALDWIN PLACE, NY 10505, UNITED STATES.
•**TURNER, Mrs. Jane Margaret, BSc ACA** *1988;* 13 Thorn Park, PLYMOUTH, PL3 4TG. See also Turner Accounting Assistance
TURNER, Miss. Janet, BCom ACA *1985;* Lloyds TSB Bank Plc, 2nd Floor, Shaftesbury Avenue, LONDON, WC2H 8AD.
TURNER, Mr. Jason Christopher Godsell, BSc ACA *1997;* Avis Management Services Avis House, Park Road, BRACKNELL, RG12 2EW.
TURNER, Miss. Jennifer Helen, ACA *2009;* Lionsgate UK Ltd, 60 Charlotte Street, LONDON, W1T 2NU.
TURNER, Miss. Jessica, ACA *2011;* 96 Shelgate Road, LONDON, SW11 1BQ.
TURNER, Miss. Jill Marie, BA ACA *2006;* with Crowe Clark Whitehill LLP, Black Country House, Rounds Green Road, OLDBURY, WEST MIDLANDS, B69 2DG.
TURNER, Miss. Joanna Louise, BSc ACA *2005;* 14 Pawson Street, Morley, LEEDS, LS27 0QA.
TURNER, Miss. Joanne, ACA *1995;* 73 Sandringham Road, Bredbury, STOCKPORT, SK6 2EJ.
TURNER, Miss. Joanne, BA ACA *1995;* Overwater House, High Street, Wilden, BEDFORD, MK44 2PB.
TURNER, Miss. Jocelyn Dawn, BNurs ACA *2007;* 3 Wingmore Road, LONDON, SE24 0AS.
TURNER, Miss. Jodie, BSc ACA *2006;* 6 Trimdon, Plender Street Camden Town, LONDON, NW1 0HA.
TURNER, Mrs. Johanna, BSc ACA *2001;* 56 Lupin Ride, CROWTHORNE, BERKSHIRE, RG45 6UR.
TURNER, Mr. John, BSc ACA PGCE *2004;* Aiglon College, Avenue Centrale, 1885 CHESIERES, SWITZERLAND.
•**TURNER, Mr. John, FCA** *1970;* Oakwood, 104 Penistone Road, Kirkburton, HUDDERSFIELD, HD8 0TA.
TURNER, Mr. John Deacon, FCA *1968;* 15 Bracken Park, Scarcroft, LEEDS, LS14 3HZ.
•**TURNER, Mr. John Duncan, FCA** *1964;* with B M Howarth Limited, West House, Kings Cross Road, HALIFAX, WEST YORKSHIRE, HX1 1EB.
TURNER, Mr. John Graham, MA ACA *1985;* 32 Wingate Road, LONDON, W6 0UR.
•**TURNER, Mr. John James, BA FCA** *1989;* John Turner FCA, Berkshire House, 252/256 Kings Road, READING, RG1 4HP.
•**TURNER, Mr. John Michael, BA(Hons) FCA** *2000;* Zolfo Cooper LLP, 10 Fleet Place, LONDON, EC4M 7RB.
TURNER, Mr. John Powell, BSc FCA *1972;* 1 Chiswick Mall, LONDON, W4 2QH. (Life Member)
TURNER, Mr. John Richard, FCA *1954;* 18 Woodlands Crescent, Barton, PRESTON, PR3 5HB.
TURNER, Mr. John Richard, BA FCA *1980;* 43 Military Road, Heddon-on-the-Wall, NEWCASTLE UPON TYNE, NE15 0HA.
TURNER, Mr. John Robert, FCA *1956;* Flat 2, 27 Westbourne Street, HOVE, BN3 5PE. (Life Member)
TURNER, Mr. Jonathan Mark, BA ACA *2001;* 141 Morningside Drive, EDINBURGH, EH10 5NR.
TURNER, Mr. Jonathan Nicholas, BA(Hons) ACA *2001;* Swiss Reinsurance Company Ltd, Canadian Branch, 150 King Street West, Suite 2200, TORONTO M5H 1J9, ON CANADA.
TURNER, Mr. Jonathan Paul, BA(Hons) ACA *2004;* 3 The Nook, Symn Lane, WOTTON-UNDER-EDGE, GL12 7BG.
TURNER, Mrs. Joy Saint, LLB ACA *1986;* with BDO LLP, 55 Baker Street, LONDON, W1U 7EU.
TURNER, Miss. Judith, BA ACA *2006;* 2 Wyrescourt Road, LIVERPOOL, L12 9EP.
TURNER, Mr. Julian Alan, MA ACA CTA *1991;* Xchanging Lilly House, 13 Hanover Square, LONDON, W1S 1HN.
TURNER, Mr. Julian Howard, BSc(Hons) FCA *2001;* 51 The Oaks, WEST BYFLEET, SURREY, KT14 6RN.
TURNER, Mr. Julian Philip Charles, BA ACA *1992;* 14 South Side, Stamfordham, NEWCASTLE UPON TYNE, NE18 0PB.
TURNER, Mr. Justin, MA FCA *1959;* 29 The Dell, ST. ALBANS, HERTFORDSHIRE, AL1 4HE. (Life Member)
TURNER, Mrs. Justine Erica, BSc ACA *1995;* 8 Cherry Tree Close, St. Leonards, RINGWOOD, HAMPSHIRE, BH24 2QN.
TURNER, Miss. Kara Jane, BA ACA *2006;* 122 Talke Road, Alsager, STOKE-ON-TRENT, ST7 2PP.
•**TURNER, Mrs. Karen Anita, FCA FCCA** *1997;* (Tax Fac), Price Pearson Ltd, Finch House, 28-30 Wolverhampton Street, DUDLEY, DY1 1DB. See also Finch House Properties Limited
TURNER, Mrs. Karen Elizabeth, BA ACA *1992;* Food Processing Faraday Partnership Ltd Unit 2 Brook Park, Gaddesby Lane Rearsby, LEICESTER, LE7 4ZB.
TURNER, Mr. Karl Stephen, MMan BSc ACA *1995;* Comonwealth Bank Of Australia, Level 8, 201 Sussex Street, SYDNEY, NSW 2000, AUSTRALIA.
TURNER, Ms. Kathryn Elizabeth, BA ACA *2005;* 76 Gateway Gardens, ELY, CAMBRIDGESHIRE, CB6 3DE.
TURNER, Mr. Kevin John, BA ACA *1987;* 10 Topaz Business Park, Topaz Way, BROMSGROVE, WORCESTERSHIRE, B61 0GD.
•**TURNER, Mr. Kevin William, FCA** *1984;* (Tax Fac), White Hart House, Silwood Road, ASCOT, BERKSHIRE, SL5 0PY.
TURNER, Mrs. Kimberley, ACA *2009;* 15 Front Street, Sherburn Village, DURHAM, DH6 1HA.
•**TURNER, Miss. Kirsten Louise, BSc ACA** *1999;* PricewaterhouseCoopers LLP, 1 Embankment Place, LONDON, WC2N 6RH. See also PricewaterhouseCoopers
TURNER, Miss. Laura Elizabeth, BSc ACA *2005;* Apartment 9 Darwin House 53 Wake Green Road, BIRMINGHAM, B13 9HW.
TURNER, Mrs. Laura Lesley, BA(Hons) ACA *2009;* 2 Chapel Cottages, Chapel Lane Newbold on Stour, STRATFORD-UPON-AVON, CV37 8TY.
TURNER, Mr. Lee Geoffrey, BSc(Hons) ACA *2001;* States of Jersey Police, PO Box 789, St. Helier, JERSEY, JE4 8ZD.
TURNER, Mr. Leslie James, FCA *1980;* Whyatt Pakeman Partners Colkin House, 16 Oakfield Road, Clifton, BRISTOL, BS8 2AP.
TURNER, Miss. Lisa Marie, ACA *2009;* 55 Cranleigh Drive, Brooklands, SALE, CHESHIRE, M33 3PN.
TURNER, Mrs. Loretta Margaret Ann, BSc ACA *1989;* 21 Steeres Hill, Rusper, HORSHAM, RH12 4PT.
TURNER, Mrs. Louisa Jane, MA ACA *1999;* Halifax Plc, Trinity Road, HALIFAX, WEST YORKSHIRE, HX1 2RG.
TURNER, Mrs. Lynne Moira, BA ACA *1988;* Millstream West, Maidenhead Road, WINDSOR, BERKSHIRE, SL4 5GD.
TURNER, Mr. Malcolm John, FCA *1973;* 73 Lonsdale Road, Harborne, BIRMINGHAM, B17 9QX. (Life Member)
•**TURNER, Mrs. Margaret, FCA** *1984;* Mitchells, The Old Stables, Fox Hole Lane, WADHURST, EAST SUSSEX, TN5 6NB.
•**TURNER, Mrs. Margaret, FCA** *1981;* Turner & Co, 10A White Hart Parade, London Road, Blackwater, CAMBERLEY, SURREY GU17 9AD.
•**TURNER, Mr. Mark, FCA** *1984;* Champion Accountants LLP, 1 Worsley Court, High Street, Worsley, MANCHESTER, M28 3NJ.
TURNER, Mr. Mark, BA ACA *1990;* 4 Finsbury Drive, Priorslee, TELFORD, TF2 9GU.
TURNER, Mr. Mark David, BA(Hons) ACA *2003;* with Ernst & Young LLP, 1 Bridgewater Place, Water Lane, LEEDS, LS11 5QR.
TURNER, Mr. Mark Grenville, MA FCA *1979;* Green Acres, New Road, Shiplake, HENLEY-ON-THAMES, OXFORDSHIRE, RG9 3LA.
•**TURNER, Mr. Mark Julian, FCA** *1995;* Lubbock Fine, Russell Bedford House, City Forum, 250 City Road, LONDON, EC1V 2QQ.
TURNER, Mr. Mark Richard, BSc ACA *1992;* A O N Ltd, 8 Devonshire Square, LONDON, EC2M 4PL.
TURNER, Mr. Mark Richard Charles, BSc ACA *1993;* (Tax Fac), Unit 1, Amphire International Ltd Unit 1 Stokenchurch Business Par, Ibstone Road Stokenchurch, HIGH WYCOMBE, BUCKINGHAMSHIRE, HP14 3FE.
TURNER, Mr. Mark Robert James, BSc ACA *1997;* with ISIS EP LLP, 100 Wood Street, LONDON, EC2V 7AN.
TURNER, Mr. Mark Simon Kenneth, BSc ARCS ACA *1999;* Ruxley Cottage, Common Lane, Claygate, ESHER, SURREY, KT10 0HY.
TURNER, Miss. Martha Lawrence, BSc ACA *2005;* L2B 833 Collins Street, MELBOURNE, VIC 3008, AUSTRALIA.
TURNER, Mr. Martin Bruce, BSc ACA *1995;* 7 Oakcroft Road, LONDON, SE13 7ED.
TURNER, Mr. Martin Jeffery Shenton, FCA *1977;* Cheetham Salt Pty Ltd, Level 4, 565 Bourke Street, MELBOURNE, VIC 3000, AUSTRALIA.
TURNER, Mr. Martin Robert, BSc FCA *1982;* Little Frith, Frithsden Copse, Potten End, BERKHAMSTED, HERTFORDSHIRE, HP4 2RQ.
•**TURNER, Mr. Matthew Lloyd, BEng FCA CF** *1991;* 115 Headlands, KETTERING, NN15 6AB.
TURNER, Mr. Matthew Philip, MEng ACA ACGI *1999;* 6 Carlton Gardens, LONDON, SW1Y 5AD.
TURNER, Mr. Michael Alan, BSc FCA *1985;* Actis, PO Box 43233-00100, NAIROBI, KENYA.
•**TURNER, Mr. Michael Anthony, ACA FCCA** *2008;* Bentleys, Hazlemere, 70 Chorley New Road, BOLTON, BL1 4BY.
•**TURNER, Mr. Michael Bryan, BA FCA** *1978;* Michael Turner & Co, 17 Hope Street, Douglas, ISLE OF MAN, IM1 1AQ.
TURNER, Mr. Michael Charles, FCA *1980;* Audit Commission, Mill House, Brayford Wharf North, LINCOLN, LN1 1YX.
TURNER, Mr. Michael Edward, BSc ACA *1999;* 91 Featherstone Grove, Melbury, Gosforth, NEWCASTLE UPON TYNE, NE3 5RF.
TURNER, Mr. Michael Ignatius, BA ACA *1995;* 30 Lawson Avenue, Gatley, CHEADLE, SK8 4PL.
TURNER, Mr. Michael John, FCA *1972;* Miyabi, 92 Burwood Road, WALTON-ON-THAMES, KT12 4AP.
TURNER, Mr. Michael John, BSc ACA *1993;* 5 Meadow Close, HOVE, BN3 6QQ.
TURNER, Mr. Michael John, FCA *1974;* Fuller Smith & Turner, Griffin Brewery, Chiswick, LONDON, W4 2QB.
•**TURNER, Mr. Michael Richard, BSc ACA** *1988;* (Tax Fac), Turner & Turner (Preston) Ltd, Bank House, 9 Victoria Road, Fulwood, PRESTON, PR2 8ND.
TURNER, Mrs. Michele, BA ACA *1995;* 6 Kestrel Close, HOVE, EAST SUSSEX, BN3 6NS.
TURNER, Mrs. Monica, BSc FCA *1993;* 314 Fulford Road, YORK, YO10 4PE.
•**TURNER, Mr. Neil Kenneth, BA ACA** *1992;* TT Turner Limited, 21 Greenbank Road, Marple Bridge, STOCKPORT, SK6 5ED.
TURNER, Mr. Neil Martyn, FCA *1994;* 4 Bridle Ways, East Bridgford, NOTTINGHAM, NG13 8PT.
TURNER, Mr. Nicholas Fyers, FCA *1975;* (Tax Fac), The Old Farm House, 5 Kennel Lane, Steventon, ABINGDON, OX13 6SB.
TURNER, Mr. Nigel, MBA FCA *1989;* 7 Silvermere, Langdon Hills, BASILDON, SS16 6RA.
TURNER, Mr. Nigel Charteris, FCA *1981;* 5 South Crescent, HARTLEPOOL, CLEVELAND, TS24 0QH.
TURNER, Mr. Nigel John, BA ACA *1998;* Decision Support 3rd Floor, Green Flag, Cote Lane, PUDSEY, WEST YORKSHIRE, LS28 5GF.
TURNER, Mr. Nigel Paul, BSc FCA *1998;* 5 Le Clos de la Chasse, La Rue de la Guilleaumerie, St. Saviour, JERSEY, JE2 7RY.
•**TURNER, Mr. Nigel William, BA FCA** *1982;* Brooks Mayfield, 12 Bridgford Road, West Bridgford, NOTTINGHAM, NG2 6AB. See also Brooks Mayfield Audit Limited
TURNER, Mr. Noel Charles William, FCA *1949;* 58 Vandenboschstraat, 1652 ALSEMBERG, BELGIUM. (Life Member)
TURNER, Mr. Paul Andrew, BA ACA MBA *1993;* Wheal Bush Cottage, Cox Hill, Chacewater, TRURO, CORNWALL, TR4 8LY.
•**TURNER, Mr. Paul Anthony, BA ACA** *1988;* Charmes Limited, 14a Farlands Road, Oldswinford, STOURBRIDGE, WEST MIDLANDS, DY8 2DD.
•**TURNER, Mr. Paul Anthony Edward, BA ACA** *1989;* Sound Accounting, Wingfield House, 13 Thorn Park, Mannamead, PLYMOUTH, PL3 4TG. See also Turner Accounting Assistance
TURNER, Mr. Paul Damian, FCA MBA *1978;* Poole Hospital, Poole Hospital NHS Trust, Longfleet Road, POOLE, BH15 2JB.
TURNER, Mr. Paul Gary, BSc ACA *1992;* 7 Link Road, Stoneygate, LEICESTER, LE2 3RA.
TURNER, Mr. Paul Gregory, BSc ACA *2007;* 64 Mellor Brow, Mellor, BLACKBURN, BB2 7EX.
TURNER, Mr. Paul Robert, BSc ACA *1984;* 10 Bowman Avenue, Belair, ADELAIDE, SA 5052, AUSTRALIA.
TURNER, Mr. Paul St John, BSS FCA *1975;* Cades Peak, Old St. Johns Road, St. Helier, JERSEY, JE2 3LG.
TURNER, Miss. Paula Anne, BEng ACA *1995;* 2 Rowley, Cam, DURSLEY, GL11 5NT.
TURNER, Miss. Penelope Anne, BSc ACA *1998;* Apsley Ridge, Hurstbourne Priors, WHITCHURCH, HAMPSHIRE, RG28 7SD.
TURNER, Mr. Peter Andrew, BA FCA *1996;* 17 Pilgrims Way, GUILDFORD, SURREY, GU4 8AD.
TURNER, Mr. Peter George Alexander, FCA *1958;* Apple Cottage, 8 Allee du Chateau, 27300 VALAILLES, FRANCE. (Life Member)
TURNER, Mr. Peter Henry, FCA *1966;* 13 Monsal Drive, South Normanton, ALFRETON, DERBYSHIRE, DE55 2BG.
TURNER, Mr. Peter Jeremy, BSc ACA *1979;* Company Enterprises Ltd, 3 Railway Bridge Cottages Long Itchington Road, Offchurch, LEAMINGTON SPA, WARWICKSHIRE, CV33 9AU.
TURNER, Mr. Peter John, FCA *1965;* Lane Head, COCKERMOUTH, CA13 0DL. (Life Member)
TURNER, Mr. Peter Michael, FCA TEP *1964;* High Rising, Queens Drive, ILKLEY, LS29 9QW.
TURNER, Mr. Peter Michael Fisher, BSc ACA *1986;* TCS John Huxley Europe Limited, Salamanca Square 9G Albert Embankment, LONDON, SE1 7SP.
TURNER, Mr. Peter Vincent, FCA *1962;* 5 Mounthaven Close, WIRRAL, CH49 6NX.
TURNER, Mr. Philip Haydn, BSc FCA *1988;* 3 Wedderburn Road, LONDON, NW3 5QS.
TURNER, Mr. Philip John, ACA *1989;* 32 Lane Green Road, Codsall, WOLVERHAMPTON, WV8 2JU.

•**TURNER, Mr. Raymond Charles, FCA** *1976;* (Tax Fac), R.C. Turner, Almond House, Grange Street, Clifton, SHEFFORD, BEDFORDSHIRE SG17 5EW.
TURNER, Mr. Raymond Thomas, FCA *1960;* Punchetts, West Riding, Tewin Wood, WELWYN, HERTFORDSHIRE, AL6 0PD. (Life Member)
TURNER, Mrs. Rebecca Edith Joan, BA(Hons) ACA *2002;* The Fresh Produce Centre, Transfesa Road, Paddock Wood, TONBRIDGE, KENT, TN12 6UT.
•**TURNER, Mrs. Rebecca Jane, BA ACA** *2001;* with Ernst & Young LLP, 1 More London Place, LONDON, SE1 2AF.
TURNER, Mrs. Rhian Mair, MA BA ACA *1996;* 24 Bracewood Gardens, CROYDON, SURREY, CR0 5JL.
TURNER, Mr. Richard David, BSc ACA *1998;* (Tax Fac), White Eves, Longparish, Wherwell, ANDOVER, HAMPSHIRE, SP11 7AW.
TURNER, Mr. Richard Edward, FCA *1975;* 69 Clementine Avenue, SEAFORD, BN25 2UU.
TURNER, Mr. Richard John, BSc ACA *1999;* Rectory Cottage, Checkendon, READING, RG8 0SR.
TURNER, Mr. Richard Mark Julian, LLB ACA *1993;* 13 Palfreyman Lane, Oadby, LEICESTER, LE2 4UR.
TURNER, Mr. Richard Patrick, MSc BA FCA *1972;* The Stewardry Sydenham, Lewdown, OKEHAMPTON, DEVON, EX20 4PR.
TURNER, Mr. Robert Bryan, BA ACA *1985;* 33 Parkfield Crescent, Kimpton, HITCHIN, SG4 8EQ.
TURNER, Mr. Robert Edward, BA ACA *1991;* 2 Highfield, Blackden Holmes Chapel, CREWE, CW4 8DQ.
TURNER, Mr. Robert Ian, FCA *1965;* Weston Mark, Upton Grey, BASINGSTOKE, RG25 2RJ. (Life Member)
•**TURNER, Mr. Robert Ian MacLachlan, BA FCA** *1984;* 34 Harvey Street, TAURANGA 3010, NEW ZEALAND.
TURNER, Mr. Roger John Langdon, BSc FCA *1972;* 45 Hurdles Way, Duxford, CAMBRIDGE, CB22 4PA. (Life Member)
TURNER, Mr. Ronald Frederick, FCA *1972;* Taney's Dell, Heath Park Rd, LEIGHTON BUZZARD, LU7 3BB. (Life Member)
TURNER, Mrs. Ruth Isabel, BA ACA *1992;* 22 Sackville Close, BEVERLEY, NORTH HUMBERSIDE, HU17 8XF.
TURNER, Mrs. Sarah Elizabeth, BA ACA *1998;* Grove End, Pearson Road, Sonning-on-Thames, READING, RG4 6UH.
TURNER, Ms. Sarah Elizabeth, BA ACA CTA *2000;* 2 Castleton Court, Surbiton Hill Park, SURBITON, SURREY, KT5 8EG.
TURNER, Mrs. Sarah Frances, BSc(Hons) ACA CTA *2000;* with Ernst & Young LLP, 1 More London Place, LONDON, SE1 2AF.
TURNER, Mrs. Sarah Jane, BSc ACA *2001;* Home Group Ltd, 2 Gosforth Park Way Salters Lane, NEWCASTLE UPON TYNE, NE12 8ET.
TURNER, Mr. Shane Anthony, ACA *1995;* 4 St. Michaels Mount, Swanland, NORTH FERRIBY, NORTH HUMBERSIDE, HU14 3NR.
TURNER, Miss. Sharon, ACA *2011;* 9 Thorncliffe Road, BARROW-IN-FURNESS, CUMBRIA, LA14 5PZ.
•**TURNER, Mrs. Sian, BA ACA** *1992;* Accounting Solutions, 28 Brackley Drive, SHREWSBURY, SY3 8BX.
TURNER, Mr. Simon, BCom ACA *1992;* 85 Holt Avenue, MOSMAN, NSW 2088, AUSTRALIA.
TURNER, Mr. Simon Jeffrey, BSc ACA *2005;* South Staffordshire Water Plc, Green Lane, WALSALL, WS2 7PD.
•**TURNER, Mr. Simon Justin, BA(Hons) HND FCA** *2000;* ST Hampden Limited, 57 London Road, HIGH WYCOMBE, BUCKINGHAMSHIRE, HP11 1BS. See also Seymour Taylor Audit Ltd
TURNER, Mr. Simon Lawson, FCA *1980;* 7 Summerhouse Lane, Round Bush Aldenham, WATFORD, WD25 8DL.
TURNER, Mr. Simon William, MEng ACA *1996;* 94C, Milton Park, ABINGDON, OXFORDSHIRE, OX14 4RY.
TURNER, Mr. Spenser Clifford, BCom FCA *1968;* 1 Holly Court, Endcliffe Vale Road, SHEFFIELD, S10 3DS.
TURNER, Mr. Stanley David, FCA *1965;* 5 Cricklewood Drive, HALESOWEN, WEST MIDLANDS, B62 8SN.
TURNER, Mr. Stanley Richard, FCA *1961;* Greenalees, 21 Hertford Road, STEVENAGE, SG2 8RZ.
TURNER, Mr. Stephen Anthony, BA ACA *1991;* 4 Long Meadow, CHESHAM, BUCKINGHAMSHIRE, HP5 2BN.
•**TURNER, Mr. Stephen John, BA FCA** *1993;* SMP Accounting and Tax Limited, PO Box 227, Clinch's House, Lord Street, Douglas, ISLE OF MAN IM99 1RZ.
TURNER, Mr. Stephen John, ACA *2009;* 92A, 92 Hambalt Road, LONDON, SW4 9EJ.
TURNER, Mr. Stephen John, BA ACA *2008;* The Fairways, Rowan Close, SANDBACH, CW11 1XN.
•**TURNER, Mr. Stephen Paul, BSc(Hons) ACA** *1998;* STAS Ltd, 11 Marguerites Way, St Fagans, CARDIFF, CF5 4QW.
TURNER, Mr. Stephen Paul, BSc ACA *1996;* (Tax Fac), 42 The Wills Building, Wills Oval, NEWCASTLE UPON TYNE, NE7 7RW.
•**TURNER, Mr. Stephen Roger, ACA** *1978;* Insite Corporate Management Limited, DeVirgo House, Valepits Road, Garretts Green, BIRMINGHAM, B33 0TD.
TURNER, Mr. Steven Bruce, BA FCA *1995;* 161 Hammerman Drive, ABERDEEN, AB24 4SF.
TURNER, Mr. Steven Paul, BSc ACA *1995;* 8 Cherry Tree Close, St. Leonards, RINGWOOD, HAMPSHIRE, BH24 2QN.
TURNER, Mr. Stuart Carl, BSc ACA *1988;* 10 Appletree Close, LIVERPOOL, L18 9XN.
TURNER, Mr. Stuart James, BA ACA *1993;* Prudential PLC, 12 Arthur Street, LONDON, EC4R 9AQ.
TURNER, Mrs. Susan Caroline, BSocSc ACA *1999;* Ruxley Cottage, Common Lane, Claygate, ESHER, SURREY, KT10 0HY.
TURNER, Mrs. Susan Natalie, BSc FCA ATT CTA *1984;* (Tax Fac), 71 Maidenhead Road, STRATFORD-UPON-AVON, CV37 6XY.
TURNER, Mrs. Suzanna Christina, BEng ACA *1994;* Wheal Bush Cottage, Cox Hill, Chacewater, TRURO, CORNWALL, TR4 8LY.
TURNER, Mr. Sydney Roy, FCA *1951;* 1 Kensington Court, Lodge Moor, SHEFFIELD, S10 4NL. (Life Member)
TURNER, Mr. Terrance, ACA *2011;* Flat 4, Chipping Lodge, 87 Western Road, ROMFORD, RM1 3LW.
TURNER, Mr. Thomas Joseph, BA ACA *1992;* 12 rue Clérisseau, 57070 METZ, FRANCE.
TURNER, Dr. Thomas Stephen, BSc ACA *1998;* (Tax Fac), B Z W, 10 South Colonnade, LONDON, E14 4PU.
TURNER, Mr. Timothy William, BSc FCA *1989;* P O Box 157, SUITE 9.3.1.A, EUROPORT, GIBRALTAR, GIBRALTAR.
•**TURNER, Mrs. Treena Joan, FCA** *1998;* Wise & Co, Wey Court West, Union Road, FARNHAM, SURREY, GU9 7PT.
TURNER, Mrs. Valerie Anne, MA ACA *1982;* Turner Barratt Corporate Finance Ltd, 200 Brook Drive, Green Park, READING, BERKSHIRE, RG2 6UB.
TURNER, Mrs. Vicki Louise, ACA *2008;* Provident Financial, 1 Godwin Street, BRADFORD, BD1 2SU.
TURNER, Mr. William Herbert, FCA *1952;* 178 Bants Lane, Dallington, NORTHAMPTON, NN5 6AH. (Life Member)
•ⓘ**TURNER, Mr. William John, BSc ACA** *1993;* with BDO LLP, Prospect Place, 85 Great North Road, HATFIELD, HERTFORDSHIRE, AL9 5BS.
TURNER, Mrs. Zoe Fleur, BSc ACA *1995;* Greenleaves Green End Road, Radnage, HIGH WYCOMBE, BUCKINGHAMSHIRE, HP14 4DB.
TURNEY, Mr. Jonathan Matthew, MA(Oxon) BA ACA *2005;* 38 Upham Park Road, LONDON, W4 1PG.
TURNEY, Mr. Julian Stephen, MEng ACA *1992;* Park Hall House, Heathencote, TOWCESTER, NORTHAMPTONSHIRE, NN12 7LD.
TURNEY, Miss. Katharine Rebecca, ACA *2009;* Deloitte LLP, Bin Ghanem Tower, Hamdan Street, ABU DHABI, PO Box 990, UNITED ARAB EMIRATES.
TURNEY, Mr. Michael John, BA ACA *1998;* Shaws Cottage, 2 Green Lane, Ashley, MARKET HARBOROUGH, LEICESTERSHIRE, LE16 8HD.
TURNHAM, Mrs. Sally Jane, BA ACA *1990;* 9 Crest View, GREENHITHE, KENT, DA9 9QY.
TURNOCK, Mrs. Jane Elizabeth, BSc ACA *1989;* 8 Millwood Close, Withnell Fold, CHORLEY, LANCASHIRE, PR6 8AR.
TURNOCK, Mr. Matthew John, ACA *1993;* Fountains LTD, Blenheim Court, George Street, BANBURY, OX16 5BH.
•**TURNOCK, Miss. Rachel, BA ACA** *2006;* RKT Business Solutions, 28 Fairfield Road, TADCASTER, NORTH YORKSHIRE, LS24 9SN.
TURNOCK, Mr. Stephen Barry, BSc ACA *1987;* 8 Millwood Close, Withnell, CHORLEY, LANCASHIRE, PR6 8AR.
TURNOR, Mrs. Jane Sarah, BA ACA *2000;* with Ernst & Young LLP, Apex Plaza, Forbury Road, READING, RG1 1YE.
TURNOR, Mr. Matthew Keith, BSc ACA *1998;* 11 Moor Place, WINDLESHAM, GU20 6JS.
TURNSEK, Ms. Alenka, BA ACA *1999;* 8 Polkerris Way, Church Crookham, FLEET, HAMPSHIRE, GU52 8UJ.
•**TURPIN, Mr. Alan Robert, MA FCA** *1973;* Nether Barowe, Chancel Close, Berrow, MALVERN, WORCESTERSHIRE, WR13 6AX.
TURPIN, Mr. Andrew Neil, FCA *1966;* Jenkinsons Farm, Sollom, Tarleton, PRESTON, PR4 6HR.
TURPIN, Mr. Daniel, ACA *2011;* Flat 16, 63 Dalston Lane, LONDON, E8 2AB.
•**TURPIN, Mr. Graham John, BSc FCA** *1997;* Creaseys LLP, 12 Lonsdale Gardens, TUNBRIDGE WELLS, KENT, TN1 1PA.
TURPIN, Mr. Harry, FCA *1955;* Stonygarth, 286 Tadcaster Road, YORK, YO24 1ET. (Life Member)
TURPIN, Mr. Ian Johnstone, MSc FCA *1969;* LBJ Asset Management Partners Ltd, 114 W 7th Street, Ste 900, AUSTIN, TX 78701, UNITED STATES.
TURPIN, Miss. Jacqueline Lesley, MA ACA *1986;* The Joseph Rowntree Charitable Trust, The Garden House, Water End, YORK, YO30 6WQ.
TURPIN, Mr. Laurence Geoffrey, BSc ACA *1992;* Haddon House, Vicarage Road, Finchingfield, BRAINTREE, ESSEX, CM7 4LD.
TURPIN, Mr. Michael Benjamin, FCA *1957;* c/o Le Petit Chateau, 50200, 50200 NICORPS, FRANCE. (Life Member)
TURPIN, Mr. Paul Hill, FCA *1970;* 24 Harts Grove, WOODFORD GREEN, ESSEX, IG8 0BN.
TURPIN, Mr. Philip Lawrence, BA(Hons) ACA *2001;* La Crespinerie La Rue de la Piece Mauger, Trinity, JERSEY, JE3 5HW.
TURPIN, Miss. Susan Marie Anstee, BA ACA *1998;* La Crespinerie La Rue de la Piece Mauger, Trinity, JERSEY, JE3 5HW.
TURRALL, Mr. Graham Michael, MSc ACA *2003;* Research Machines Plc, New Mill House, 183 Milton Park, ABINGDON, OXFORDSHIRE, OX14 4SE.
•**TURRELL, Mr. Adam William, BA FCA** *1992;* Maxwells, 4 King Square, BRIDGWATER, SOMERSET, TA6 3YF.
TURRELL, Mr. Alistair Michael, BSc ACA *1985;* 78 Brentwood, LEYBURN, NORTH YORKSHIRE, DL8 5HT.
TURRELL, Mr. Atholl Denis, ACA *1985;* Arbuthnot Banking Group Plc, Arbuthnot House, 20 Ropemaker Street, LONDON, EC2Y 9AR.
TURRELL, Miss. Rachel, BSc ACA *2011;* Flat 17 Woodbridge House, 145 Mornington Road, LONDON, E11 3DZ.
•**TURTINGTON, Miss. Cara Jayne, BA ACA DChA** *2003;* Saffery Champness, Lion House, Red Lion Street, LONDON, WC1R 4GB.
TURTLE, Mr. Stephen Roger, BEng ACA *1992;* 14 Newmeadow Copse, Peatmoor, SWINDON, SN5 5AQ.
TURTLE, Miss. Tracy, BSc ACA *2002;* Flat 10 Wesley House, 5 Little Britain, LONDON, EC1A 7BX.
•**TURTON, Mrs. Angela Clare, BD ACA** *1992;* (Tax Fac), ACT, 104 High Street, CROWTHORNE, BERKSHIRE, RG45 7AX. See also ACT Accounting Services
TURTON, Mrs. Helen Olga, BSc ACA *2002;* IBCS Limited, 46 Catley Road, Darnal, SHEFFIELD, S9 5JF.
TURTON, Mrs. Hester Antonia, MA ACA *1994;* Sous La Borne, 1864 VERS-L'EGLISE, SWITZERLAND.
TURTON, Mr. Jonathan Michael, BSc(Hons) ACA *2002;* with KPMG LLP, 1 The Embankment, Neville Street, LEEDS, LS1 4DW.
TURTON, Mr. Kevin, MA ACA *1988;* Galleries Two, 23 Church Street Cawthorne, BARNSLEY, SOUTH YORKSHIRE, S75 4HL.
TURTON, Mr. Robert Peter, FCA *1981;* 58 Mount Road, Penn, WOLVERHAMPTON, WV4 5SW.
TURTON, Mr. Stephen, FCA *1982;* Fradswell Cottage, Fradswell, STAFFORD, ST18 0EX.
TURTON, Mr. William John, FCA *1960;* 121 Kimberley Road, Nuthall, NOTTINGHAM, NG16 1DD.
TURVEY, Miss. Alison, BSc ACA *2002;* 9 The Albany, Gloucester Square, SOUTHAMPTON, SO14 2GH.
•**TURVEY, Mr. Andrew Rowan, MEng ACA** *2003;* Andrew Turvey Solutions Limited, 23 Cartwright Way, Beeston, NOTTINGHAM, NG9 1RL.
TURVEY, Miss. Joanne Marie, BA ACA *2005;* B D O Stoy Hayward, 1 Bridgewater Place Water Lane, LEEDS, LS11 5RU.
TURVEY, Miss. Leanne, BSc ACA *2005;* 24a Longton Grove, LONDON, SE26 6QE.
TURVEY ROE, Ms. Cathryn Ruth, ACA *2008;* Flat B, 43 Tytherton Road, LONDON, N19 4PZ.
TURVIL, Mrs. Gillian, BCom ACA *2004;* 29 Chaucer Way, COLCHESTER, ESSEX, CO3 4HA.
TURVIL, Mr. James Alexander, BSc(Hons) ACA *2002;* 29 Chaucer Way, COLCHESTER, CO3 4HA.
TUSHINGHAM, Mr. Christopher James, BA ACA *1981;* Soalt y Cottier, The Dhoor, Lezayre, ISLE OF MAN, IM7 4ED.
TUSON, Mr. Paul Adam Edward, BSc ACA *1993;* 512 Wokingham Road, Earley, READING, RG6 7HY.
TUSON, Mr. Stephen David, BA ACA *2000;* 306 Watford Road, ST. ALBANS, HERTFORDSHIRE, AL2 3DW.
TUSSAUD, Mr. Michael John, FCA *1968;* Gordon Dadds Solicitors, 80 Brook Street, Mayfair, LONDON, W1K 5DD.
•**TUSSIE, Mr. Rafael David, FCA** *1987;* Tussies Limited, 31 Wilmslow Road, Cheadle Hulme, CHEADLE, SK8 1DR.
TUSTIAN, Mr. James Edward, BA ACA *2003;* The Gables West End, Kingham, CHIPPING NORTON, OXFORDSHIRE, OX7 6YL.
•**TUSTIAN, Mr. Neil Richard, BSc ACA** *1998;* with BDO LLP, Kings Wharf, 20-30 Kings Road, READING, RG1 3EX.
TUSTIN, Mrs. Elizabeth Helen, BA ACA *1983;* Route De Soldome 14, 1271 GIVRINS, SWITZERLAND.
•**TUTIN, Mr. Brian John, FCA** *1976;* B.J. Tutin & Co, 141 Ashwood Road, POTTERS BAR, EN6 2QD.
•**TUTIN, Mr. Paul Frederick, BA FCA** *1988;* Streets, Building 15, Gateway1000, A1 (M) Junction 7, STEVENAGE, HERTFORDSHIRE SG1 2FP. See also Streets Audit LLP, Streets Whitmarsh Sterland and SMS Corporate Partner Unlimited
TUTIN, Mrs. Renitha Thomas, BSc ACA *1999;* 84 Oaktree Crescent, Bradley Stoke, BRISTOL, BS32 9AD.
TUTIN, Mr. Richard Philip, BSc ACA *1999;* (Tax Fac), 84 Oaktree Crescent, Bradley Stoke, BRISTOL, BS32 9AD.
TUTON, Mr. Alan, FCA *1965;* 1 Royal Garth, Queensgate, BEVERLEY, HU17 8NL.
•**TUTT, Mrs. Anne Catherine, BSc FCA** *1978;* Anne Tutt, Jasmine Cottage, The Green, Hook Norton, BANBURY, OXFORDSHIRE OX15 5LE.
•**TUTT, Mr. Antony Timothy David, FCA** *1988;* (Tax Fac), Magee Gammon Corporate Limited, Henwood House, Henwood, ASHFORD, KENT, TN24 8DH. See also Magee Gammon Partnership LLP
TUTT, Mr. Nigel Charles, BA ACA *1979;* Via Villoresi 5, 20143 MILAN, ITALY.
TUTT, Mr. Simon Paul, BA ACA *2000;* Well Cottage, Well Lane, Welton, DAVENTRY, NORTHAMPTONSHIRE, NN11 2JU.
TUTT, Mr. Stephen Brian Reginald, BSc FCA *1993;* 23 Connaught Road, HARPENDEN, HERTFORDSHIRE, AL5 4TW.
TUTTE, Mrs. Alice, ACA *2010;* 17 Hawthorn Road, Horndean, WATERLOOVILLE, PO8 0EG.
TUTTELL, Mr. Ian, BSc ACA *1989;* 43 Brookdale Avenue, TORONTO M5M 1P2, ON, CANADA.
TUTTLE, Mr. Philip Geoffrey, BSc ACA *2011;* 72 Fenwick Place, LONDON, SW9 9NW.
TUTTON, Miss. Alyson Lesley, BSc ACA *1985;* Apartment 39, Historic Royal Palaces, Hampton Court Palace, EAST MOLESEY, KT8 9AU.
TUTTON, Mr. Richard John, BSc FCA *1983;* Oil Spill Response Ltd, Lower William Street, SOUTHAMPTON, SO14 5QE.
•**TUVEY, Mrs. Sarah Jayne Elizabeth, BA ACA** *1991;* S.J.E Tuvey, The Old Farmhouse, Chapel Lane, Shotteswell, BANBURY, OX17 1JB.
TUZIO, Mrs. Jane Elizabeth, BSc ACA *1991;* 18 Park Avenue, Timperley, ALTRINCHAM, WA14 5AX.
•**TWADDLE, Mr. Andrew Bryan, BA FCA** *1985;* (Tax Fac), CTC, 13 Portland Terrace, Jesmond, NEWCASTLE UPON TYNE, NE2 1SN. See also Rowlands Newcastle
TWADDLE, Mr. Ian Michael, BA ACA *1989;* 39 Southway, Guiseley, LEEDS, LS20 8JB.
TWADDLE, Mr. William Simon, FCA *1956;* 14 Wilson Gardens, NEWCASTLE UPON TYNE, NE3 4JA. (Life Member)
•**TWAMLEY, Mr. Alan, FCA FCCA** *1976;* Twamley and Co, Enterprise House, 7 Coventry Road, COLESHILL, WARWICKSHIRE, B46 3BB. See also Alcon Limited
TWAMLEY, Mr. Paul James, FCA *1970;* Parkmount, 4 Bridgeman Road, PENARTH, SOUTH GLAMORGAN, CF64 3AW.
TWEDDLE, Mr. Allan Joseph James, BA(Hons) ACA *2002;* 101 Crofton Avenue, ORPINGTON, KENT, BR6 8DY.
TWEDDLE, Mr. Andrew John, LLB ACA *1989;* 15 Repton Gardens, Gidea Park, ROMFORD, RM2 5LS.
TWEDDLE, Mr. James Scott, ACA *2009;* with PricewaterhouseCoopers LLP, Benson House, 33 Wellington Street, LEEDS, LS1 4JP.
TWEDDLE, Mr. William Geoffrey, BSc(Hons) ACA *2001;* 149III POSTJESKADE, 1058 DN AMSTERDAM, NETHERLANDS.
TWEED, Miss. Elizabeth, ACA *2009;* 10 Lyndhurst Close, CROYDON, CR0 5LU.

TWEED, Mr. Jonathon Michael, BA ACA *2004;* Societe Generale S G House, 41 Tower Hill, LONDON, EC3N 4SG.
TWEED, Mr. Mark Allan, BSc(Hons) ACA *2003;* The Old Ox Barn Llantwit Road, Wick, COWBRIDGE, SOUTH GLAMORGAN, CF71 7QD.
TWEED, Mr. Michael, ACA *2011;* 9 Franklin Drive, Weavering, MAIDSTONE, KENT, ME14 5SY.
TWEED, Mr. Richard Charles Newton, FCA *1974;* 10 Lyndhurst Close, Park Hill, CROYDON, CR0 5LU.
•**TWEEDALE, Mr. Charles Edward Walter, FCA CTA** *1977;* Charles Tweedale, Dangerous Corner, PO Box 605, Brookledge Lane, Adlington, MACCLESFIELD CHESHIRE SK10 4JX.
TWEEDALE, Mr. Roger Thomas, BSc FCA *1990;* 85 Lyncombe Hill, BATH, BA2 4PJ.
TWEEDALE, Mr. Ross, ACA *2008;* Baker Tilly St. Philips Point, Temple Row, BIRMINGHAM, B2 5AF.
TWEEDIE, Mr. Alexander Hugh Carmichael, MA FCA *1968;* West Hill House, 74 Bristol Street, MALMESBURY, WILTSHIRE, SN16 0AX.
TWEEDIE, Sir David Philip, PhD BCom CA *1982; (CA Scotland 1972);* (Member of Council 1989 - 1991), International Accounting Standards Board, 30 Cannon Street, LONDON, EC4M 6XH.
TWEEDIE, Mr. Matthew Stuart, BA FCA *1999;* (Tax Fac), 5 St. Thomas Place Wheathampstead, ST. ALBANS, HERTFORDSHIRE, AL4 8BG.
TWEEDIE, Mr. Peter John, FCA *1974;* Flat 54 Putney Wharf Tower, Brewhouse Lane, LONDON, SW15 2JQ.
TWEEDIE, Mrs. Susan Jane, BSc ACA DChA *1994;* 2 Westbury Drive, Pandy, WREXHAM, LL12 8PZ.
TWEEDIE-WAGGOTT, Mr. Stanley Charles, FCA *1954;* 46 Thornton Court, Girton, CAMBRIDGE, CB3 0NS.
TWEEN, Mr. Neil Andrew, ACA *2009;* 1 Saberton Close, Waterbeach, CAMBRIDGE, CB25 9QW.
TWEINI, Mr. Bassam, ACA *1980;* An-Nahar Building, Hamra Street, BEIRUT, LEBANON.
TWELLS, Mr. Mark Andrew, BSc ACA *1999;* Unit 5, 23 Dudley Street, COOGEE, NSW 2034, AUSTRALIA.
TWELVES, Mrs. Helen Michelle, BSc ACA *1996;* 26 Orchard Dene, ROWLANDS GILL, NE39 1DW.
TWELVES, Mr. Jonathan Ian, BA ACA *1997;* 26 Orchard Dene, ROWLANDS GILL, NE39 1DW.
TWELVETREE, Mr. David Stephen, BSc FCA *1988;* Finance Dept., Sellafield Limited, Banna Court, Ingwell Drive, Westlakes Science & Technology Park, MOOR ROW CUMBRIA CA24 3HW.
TWEMLOW, Miss. Clare Gillian, BSc(Hons) ACA *2004;* 11 Newmarket Road, Cheveley, NEWMARKET, SUFFOLK, CB8 9EQ.
TWEMLOW, Mr. Mark David, BSc ACA *1997;* 12 Hilbre Road, West Kirby, WIRRAL, CH48 3HD.
TWEMLOW, Ms. Masha Lucy, MA ACA *1996;* 1 Ladysden Cottages, Winchet Hill Goudhurst, CRANBROOK, TN17 1JX.
TWENA, Mr. Albert Ezra, FCA *1968;* 30 Cumberland Gardens, Holders Hill Road Hendon, LONDON, NW4 1LD.
TWENA, Mr. Ernest Nissim, FCA *1961;* 151 Wentworth Road, LONDON, NW11 0RJ.
TWENA, Mr. Solomon Ferris, FCA *1954;* 16 Clil HaHoresh, PO BOX 471, 84965 OMER, ISRAEL. (Life Member)
TWENEBOAH, Mr. Alfred Bio Boakye, ACA *2009;* 96 Fortescue Road, EDGWARE, MIDDLESEX, HA8 0HN.
TWENTYMAN, Mr. Alexander, BA FCA *1966;* 10 Burnaby Gardens, Chiswick, LONDON, W4 3DT.
TWENTYMAN, Mr. Christian Henry Richard, BA(Hons) ACA *2003;* Lloyds TSB Bank Plc Canons House, Canons Way, BRISTOL, BS1 5LL.
TWENTYMAN, Mrs. Judith, BA ACA *1991;* 22 Hollycroft Avenue, LONDON, NW3 7QL.
TWENTYMAN, Mr. Philip, FCA *1970;* 8 Ampney St. Peter, CIRENCESTER, GL7 5SH. (Life Member)
TWI-YEBOAH, Mr. Justice Kwabena, BA ACA *1983;* 74 Valetta Grove, LONDON, E13 0JR.
TWIDALE, Mrs. Sarah Elizabeth, ACA *2008;* Lote F Encosta Das Oliveiras, Vale Da Ribeira, 122 Arao, Mexilhoeira Grande, 8500 PORTIMAO, ALGARVE PORTUGAL.
•**TWIDDLE, Mr. Michael John Robert, FCA** *1980;* Mike J R Twiddle & Co Limited, 5 Iona Close, Langsett Road, Sutton, HULL, HU8 9XU.
TWIDDY, Mrs. Anita Kerry, BCom ACA *1992;* 38 Hollow Way Lane, AMERSHAM, BUCKINGHAMSHIRE, HP6 6DP.
TWIGG, Mrs. Janet Mary, MSc ACA *1988;* Dawford Cottage, 81 Limekiln Lane, Lilleshall, NEWPORT, SHROPSHIRE, TF10 9EU.
TWIGG, Mr. John Sidney, FCA *1968;* 1378 Brenner Park Drive, VENICE, FL 34292, UNITED STATES. (Life Member)
TWIGG, Mr. Mark James, BSc ACA *2010;* 17 Wesley Apartments, 202 Wandsworth Road, LONDON, SW8 2JU.
TWIGG, Miss. Penny Linda, BSc ACA *2004;* Deloitte, 66-67 Athol Street, Douglas, ISLE OF MAN, IM1 1JE.
TWIGG, Mr. Richard John, BSc ACA *1989;* 1 Whiddon Croft, Menston, ILKLEY, LS29 6QQ.
TWIGG, Mr. Trevor Joseph, LLB FCA *1962;* 10 Galmington Drive, Stychevale, COVENTRY, CV3 6PZ.
TWIGGER, Mr. David Isaiah, FCA *1960;* 27 Oakside Crescent, Evington, LEICESTER, LE5 6SL. (Life Member)
TWIGGER, Mr. David Michael, BSc ACA *1993;* Ulborough, 3 Old Totnes Road, NEWTON ABBOT, TQ12 1LR.
TWIGGER, Mrs. Harriet Teresa, BA ACA *1995;* 156 Piccotts End, HEMEL HEMPSTEAD, HERTFORDSHIRE, HP1 3AU.
TWIGGER, Mr. James, BSc(Hons) *2010;* 32 Leeward Lane, TORQUAY, TQ2 7GB.
•**TWIGGER, Mr. Steven Allen, ACA FCCA** *2009;* Luckmans Duckett Parker Limited, 44-45 Queens Road, COVENTRY, CV1 3EH.
TWIGGER, Mr. Terence, BSc FCA *1975;* The Walled Garden, Holly Hill Lane, Sarisbury Green, SOUTHAMPTON, SO31 7AH.
TWIGGER-ROSS, Mr. Malcolm, BA FCA *1989;* The Cardinal Hume Centre, 3-7 Arneway Street, LONDON, SW1P 2BG.
TWINBERROW, Mr. Stuart Eric, BSc ACA *2005;* 16 Little London Court, Mill Street, LONDON, SE1 2BF.
TWINEY, Mr. Tom, BSc ACA *2009;* 162 Bridgewater Street, SALE, CHESHIRE, M33 7HB.
TWINN, Mr. David Charles, BA FCA *1973;* 32 East Street, LITTLEHAMPTON, BN17 6AW.
TWINN, Mr. Eric Robin, BA FCA ATII *1971;* Wayside, Chitts Hill, COLCHESTER, CO3 9SY.
TWINNING, Mr. Mark William, ACA *2008;* 72 New Copper Moss, ALTRINCHAM, CHESHIRE, WA15 8EG.
TWINNING, Mr. Michael Andrew, BCom FCA *1987;* Porthkerry, 16 Camp Road, GERRARDS CROSS, BUCKINGHAMSHIRE, SL9 7PE.
TWISELTON, Mr. George Alfred, FCA *1966;* 3302 High Ridge Court, GREENSBORO, NC 27410-2127, UNITED STATES. (Life Member)
•**TWISSELL, Mr. Michael John, FCA** *1970;* (Tax Fac), Twissell Neilson Budd & Co Limited, Belgravia House, High Street, Hartley Wintney, HOOK, RG27 8NS. See also Twissell Neilson Budd & Co
TWIST, Mr. Anthony Sidney, FCA *1973;* Twytech Ltd, 29 Cotton Close, Alrewas, BURTON-ON-TRENT, STAFFORDSHIRE, DE13 7BF.
TWIST, Miss. Jennifer Clare, BA ACA *2006;* 8a Larkhill Road, LEEDS, LS8 1RE.
TWIST, The Revd. John Dominic, FCA *1962;* Stonyhurst College, CLITHEROE, LANCASHIRE, BB7 9PZ. (Life Member)
TWIST, Mr. Martin Declan, BA ACA *2001;* 32 Albert Road, Beeston, NOTTINGHAM, NG9 2GU.
TWIST, Mr. Neil Nicholas, MA FCA *1968;* 2 The Garth, COBHAM, KT11 2DZ.
TWIST, Mr. Nicholas Charles, FCA *1978;* Picketts Heath Farmhouse, Boars Hill, OXFORD, OX1 5HD.
•**TWIST, Mr. Robert James, BA FCA** *1965;* Robert J. Twist, 42 Rue de Bassano, 75008 PARIS, FRANCE.
TWIST, Mrs. Sarah Louise, ACA *2010;* 14 Juniper Road, TAUNTON, SOMERSET, TA1 2QD.
TWIST, Miss. Victoria Jane, MA ACA *1991;* Blauwkarper 17, 2318 NM LEIDEN, NETHERLANDS.
TWITCHEN, Mr. Brian Frank Gerald, FCA *1960;* 45 Harvest Road, Denmead, WATERLOOVILLE, PO7 6LL. (Life Member)
TWITCHETT, Miss. Camilla, BSc(Hons) ACA *2011;* Cranbourne, Fleetwood Road, Greenhalgh, PRESTON, LANCASHIRE, PR4 3ZA.
TWITE, Miss. Catherine Joanne, BSc ACA *2001;* 12 John Archer Way, Wandsworth, LONDON, SW18 2TQ.
TWITE, Mr. Mark Roger, BSc ACA *1998;* PO Box DV08, Devonshire DVBX, Bermuda, DEVONSHIRE DVBX, BERMUDA.
•①**TWIZELL, Mr. John Hedley, BSc FCA** *1982;* Geoffrey Martin & Co, 4th Floor, St Andrew House, 119-121 The Head Row, LEEDS, LS1 5JW.
TWOGOOD, Mr. Neil Gordon, BA ACA *1983;* 1 Poultry, LONDON, EC2R 8JR.
TWOHIG, Mr. Raymond John, BA ACA *1981;* Broadmeadow The Lea, Bishopsteignton, TEIGNMOUTH, TQ14 9PH.
TWOMEY, Mr. Dennis Gordon Patrick, BA ACA *1997;* Eastbeare Farm, Merton, OKEHAMPTON, DEVON, EX20 3DJ.
TWOMEY, Miss. Marie, ACA *2011;* Flat 79, Penshurst, Queens Crescent, LONDON, NW5 3QJ.
TWOMLOW, Mr. David John, ACA *1982;* 44 Manor Rise, LICHFIELD, WS14 9RF.
TWORT, Mrs. Elizabeth Jean, BA ACA *1999;* 3 The Willows, Burton-on-the-Wolds, LOUGHBOROUGH, LEICESTERSHIRE, LE12 5AP.
TWOSE, Mr. Paul, BCom FCA *1991;* 100 Raddlebarn Farm Drive, Bournville, BIRMINGHAM, B29 6UW.
•**TWUM-AMPOFO, Mr. Mark, ACA** *2000;* Kingston Smith LLP, Devonshire House, 60 Goswell Road, LONDON, EC1M 7AD. See also Kingston Smith Limited Liability Partnership, Devonshire Corporate Services LLP and Kingston Smith Consulting LLP
TWYDELL, Mr. Paul James, ACA *2009;* Flat 3a, 54 Grange Park, Ealing, LONDON, W5 3PR.
TWYDELL, Mr. Richard William, FCA *1974;* Drug Delivery Solutions Ltd, Leatherhead Enterprise Centre, Randalls Road, LEATHERHEAD, SURREY, KT22 7RY.
•**TWYDLE, Mr. Robert Michael, FCA** *1981;* (Tax Fac), Lavender Cottage, 54 Whielden Street, AMERSHAM, HP7 0HU.
TWYMAN, Mr. Brian Charles, FCA *1958;* Frobishers, Coolham Road, West Chiltington, PULBOROUGH, RH20 2LJ. (Life Member)
TWYMAN, Ms. Kerry, MA ACA MBA *2002;* Scottish Government Victoria Quay, Leith Docks, EDINBURGH, EH6 6QQ.
TWYMAN, Mr. Patrick Austin, BA ACA *1990;* 300 South Adams Street, TALLAHASSEE, FL 32301, UNITED STATES.
TWYNAM, Mr. Andrew Thomas, MSc BEng ACA *2003;* 9 Castle Mead, HEMEL HEMPSTEAD, HERTFORDSHIRE, HP1 1PR.
TWYNHAM, Miss. Lisa, BSc ACA *1991;* Home Farm, Water Street, East Harptree, BRISTOL, BS40 6AD.
TWYNHOLM, Miss. Julie, ACA *2010;* c/o 10 Portland Road, RUGBY, WARWICKSHIRE, CV21 3RU.
•**TWYNING, Miss. Katy Elizabeth, BSc ACA** *2000;* Green Square Partners LLP, 33 Cavendish Square, LONDON, W1G 0PW.
TYACK, Mrs. Katherine Susan, BSc ACA PGCE *2004;* 3 Copper Beech Close, Dunnington, YORK, YO19 5PY.
•**TYACKE, Ms. Sara Louise, BSS ACA** *1994;* (Tax Fac), M C S Build Ltd, Station Road, Claverdon, WARWICK, CV35 8PE.
•**TYAS, Mr. Stephen Richard, FCA** *1977;* (Tax Fac), Tyas & Company, 5 East Park, CRAWLEY, RH10 6AN.
TYBINKOWSKI, Mr. Lee Andrew, BA ACA *2000;* 7 Saracen Close, LYMINGTON, HAMPSHIRE, SO41 8AT.
TYCE, Mrs. Victoria Margaret, BSc ACA *2003;* 17 St. Michaels Avenue, Aylsham, NORWICH, NR11 6YA.
TYDEMAN, Mr. Justin Antony James, BA ACA *1996;* Hinterbergstrasse 20, 6330 CHAM, SWITZERLAND.
TYDEMAN, Mrs. Kirsty, BA ACA *2004;* 25 Chalkenden Avenue, GILLINGHAM, KENT, ME8 6AQ.
•**TYDEMAN, Mr. Robert Kenneth, FCA** *1971;* (Tax Fac), Robert Tydeman & Co, 58 Gipsy Hill, Upper Norwood, LONDON, SE19 1PD.
TYE, Miss. Alexandra, BA ACA *2003;* 52 Elmfield Road, STOCKPORT, CHESHIRE, SK3 8SE.
TYE, Ms. Alice Louisa Jolliffe, BSc FCA *1999;* Flat 5, Elm Court, 138-144 Cranworth Gardens, LONDON, SW9 0NX.
TYE, Mrs. Amy Ling Yee, BSc ACA *1995;* Flat 6C, United Mansion, 7 Shiu Fai Terrace, HAPPY VALLEY, HONG KONG ISLAND, HONG KONG SAR.
TYE, Mrs. Caroline Rachel, BA ACA *1999;* The Crown House, 27 High Street, Wheathampstead, ST. ALBANS, HERTFORDSHIRE, AL4 8BB.
TYE, Mr. Christopher Nathan, BA ACA *1999;* 13 Hammarsfield Close, Standon, WARE, HERTFORDSHIRE, SG11 1PG.
TYE, Mr. Craig Kuan Ming, BSc(Hons) ACA *2004;* with Deloitte LLP, Athene Place, 66 Shoe Lane, LONDON, EC4A 3BQ.
TYE, Mr. Graham Robert, LLB ACA *2002;* 14 Fairmead, BROMLEY, BR1 2JU.
TYE, Mr. Graham Stuart, BSc ACA *1989;* Moorcroft Group Plc, Moorcroft House, PO Box 17, 2 Spring Gardens, STOCKPORT, CHESHIRE SK1 4AJ.
TYE, Mr. Jeffrey Charles Joseph, FCA *1964;* Portree, Abbeystead Road, Dolphinholme, LANCASTER, LA2 9AY.
TYE, Mrs. Joanne Elizabeth, BA ACA *1999;* 7 Searston Avenue, Holmewood, CHESTERFIELD, S42 5QZ.
TYE, Mr. Jonathan Andrew, BSc(Hons) ACA *2001;* 7 Mistletoe Close, CROYDON, CR0 8YE.
TYE, Mrs. Julia Elizabeth, BSc ACA *2002;* 13 Hammarsfield Close, Standon, WARE, HERTFORDSHIRE, SG11 1PG.
TYE, Mr. Martin Anders Bjorn, BSc ACA *1991;* G E C Anderson Ltd, Oakengrove, Hastoe, TRING, HP23 6LY.
TYE, Mr. Philip Andrew, BSc ACA *1992;* Flat 6C, United Mansion, 7 Shiu Fai Terrace, HAPPY VALLEY, HONG KONG ISLAND, HONG KONG SAR.
TYE, Ms. Sheryl Anne, BSc FCA ATII *1982;* 47 Sherrardspark Road, WELWYN GARDEN CITY, AL8 7LD.
TYE, Mr. Simon, BA FCA *1991;* Gigatronix Ltd Zullard House, 4 Downley Road, HAVANT, PO9 2NJ.
TYERMAN, Mrs. Abigail Jane, BA ACA *2002;* 14 Tameside, Stokesley, MIDDLESBROUGH, CLEVELAND, TS9 5PE.
TYERMAN, Mr. Daniel Richard, BSc ACA *2002;* The Shireburn Effingham Common Road, Effingham, LEATHERHEAD, KT24 5JG.
•**TYERMAN, Mrs. Gillian Caroline, BSc ACA CTA** *2002;* Gillian Tyerman & Co, 2-3 Robinson Terrace, WASHINGTON, TYNE AND WEAR, NE38 7BD.
TYERMAN, Mr. Stephen Charles, MPhil BSc ACA *1999;* The Valley, Willingham Road, Hainton, MARKET RASEN, LINCOLNSHIRE, LN8 6LN.
TYERS, Mr. Robin James, BCom FCA *1961;* 24 The Close, HARPENDEN, HERTFORDSHIRE, AL5 3NB.
TYGHE, Mrs. Claire, ACA *2006;* 34 Linnets Park, RUNCORN, WA7 1LS.
TYLDESLEY, Mr. Stephen James, BSc ACA *1992;* 16 Yarrennan Avenue, WEST PYMBLE, NSW 2073, AUSTRALIA.
TYLDSLEY, Mr. Marcus, BSc ACA *2005;* 15 Suffield Road, Gildersome Morley, LEEDS, LS27 7WA.
TYLECOTE, Mrs. Fiona Jane, BSc ACA *1998;* 4 Meadowfield, OAKHAM, LEICESTERSHIRE, LE15 6PU.
TYLER, Mr. Andrew Frank, BA ACA *1991;* 15 Ringford Road, LONDON, SW18 1RP.
TYLER, Mr. Andrew John, FCA *1986;* 5 Beathwaite Drive, Bramhall, STOCKPORT, CHESHIRE, SK7 3NY.
TYLER, Mr. Andrew Peter, BA ACA *1992;* Pricewaterhouse Coopers, White Square office, Centre Butyrsky, Vale 10, 125047 MOSCOW, RUSSIAN FEDERATION.
TYLER, Mrs. Angela Lee, BSc ACA *1999;* 10 Far Lane, Normanton on Soar, LOUGHBOROUGH, LEICESTERSHIRE, LE12 5HA.
TYLER, Mr. Bernard John Croxon, BA FCA *1976;* 2 Southdean Gardens, LONDON, SW19 6NU.
TYLER, Mr. Christopher Patric, BSc FCA *1987;* Porvair Plc, 7 Regis Place North Lynn Industrial Estate, KING'S LYNN, NORFOLK, PE30 2JN.
•**TYLER, Mr. Christopher Robert, FCA DChA** *1987;* with Clark Brownscombe Limited, 8 The Drive, HOVE, EAST SUSSEX, BN3 3JT.
TYLER, Mr. Colin James, BSc ACA MCT *1985;* 7 Green Park, Prestwood, GREAT MISSENDEN, HP16 0PZ.
TYLER, Mr. Colin Raymond, FCA *1975;* 13 Godre'r Mynydd, Gwernymynydd, MOLD, CLWYD, CH7 4AD. (Life Member)
TYLER, Mrs. Corinne, BSc ACA *2006;* 57 Marshall Square, SOUTHAMPTON, SO15 2PB.
TYLER, Mr. David, BSc ACA *2002;* Wiltshire Wholesale Electrical Co Ltd, Unit 5 Kennet Way, Canal Road Industrial Estate, TROWBRIDGE, WILTSHIRE, BA14 8RN.
TYLER, The Revd. David Stuart, BSc ACA ODM *1995;* The Rectory, Swan Lane, Long Hanborough, WITNEY, OXFORDSHIRE, OX29 8BT.
TYLER, Mrs. Dawn Louisa, MA ACA *2004;* with Ernst & Young LLP, 100 Barbirolli Square, MANCHESTER, M2 3EY.
TYLER, Miss. Deborah, BSc ACA *1986;* 86 Court Way, TWICKENHAM, TW2 7SW.
TYLER, Mr. Denis, FCA *1971;* 18 Deptford Avenue, Kings Langley, SYDNEY, NSW 2147, AUSTRALIA.
TYLER, Mr. Derek Richard, BA ACA *1986;* 18 Dorin Court, Landscape Road, WARLINGHAM, CR6 9JT.
TYLER, Mr. Duncan Edward, BSc ACA *1998;* Molins PLC, Rockingham Drive, MILTON KEYNES, MK14 6LY.
TYLER, Miss. Fiona Jayne, BSc ACA *1986;* Santander Uk Plc, Abbey National Plc Abbey House, 201 Grafton Gate East, MILTON KEYNES, MK9 1AN.
•**TYLER, Mr. Frank William, FCA** *1965;* F.W. Tyler, 9 Colby Drive, Thurmaston, LEICESTER, LE4 8LD.

TYLER, Miss. Georgia, ACA *2011;* 9 Bramling Avenue, YATELEY, HAMPSHIRE, GU46 6NX.
TYLER, Mr. Gerard Peter, BA FCA *1986;* School House Forest Road, WOKINGHAM, BERKSHIRE, RG40 5SD.
TYLER, Mr. Gordon Gerard, BA(Hons) ACA *2000;* 32 Lonsdale Road, BIRMINGHAM, B17 9RA.
•TYLER, Mr. Graham Arthur, ACA *1984;* Kingston Smith LLP, 141 Wardour Street, LONDON, W1F 0UT. See also Kingston Smith Limited Liability Partnership, Devonshire Corporate Services LLP and Kingston Smith Consulting LLP
TYLER, Mr. Henry Peters, FCA *1955;* 55 Spylaw Bank Road, EDINBURGH, EH13 0JB. (Life Member)
TYLER, Mr. Ian Paul, BCom ACA *1985;* Moorlands Lunghurst Road, Woldingham, CATERHAM, CR3 7EJ.
•TYLER, Mr. Jeffrey Steven, FCA *1973;* Tyler & Co, 3 Home Farm Way, Easter Compton, BRISTOL, BS35 5SE.
TYLER, Mrs. Joanne Elizabeth, BSc ACA *1988;* 47 Valley Road, Bramhall, STOCKPORT, SK7 2NJ.
TYLER, Ms. Karen Margaret, BSc ACA *2000;* PCAOB, 901 Mariner's Island Blvd, Suite 400, SAN MATEO, CA 94404, UNITED STATES.
TYLER, Mrs. Lindsey, ACA *2008;* 66 The Briars, HERTFORD, SG13 7TR.
TYLER, Miss. Marilyn Anne, BA FCA *1975;* 729 D Timber Ridge Trail SW, VERO BEACH, FL 32962, UNITED STATES.
TYLER, Mr. Mark Stuart, BA FCA *1996;* 23 Havenwood Drive, Thornhill, CARDIFF, CF14 9HX.
TYLER, Mr. Martin Keith, BA(Hons) ACA *2002;* Bluefin Advisory Services Ltd, 4-6 Ripon Road, HARROGATE, NORTH YORKSHIRE, HG1 2HH.
TYLER, Mr. Matthew, ACA *2009;* 11/14 Leichhardt Street, GLEBE, NSW 2037, AUSTRALIA.
TYLER, Mr. Matthew, BSc ACA *2006;* 57 Marshall Square, SOUTHAMPTON, SO15 2PB.
TYLER, Mr. Michael, BSc FCA *1978;* 8 Green Road, Birchington On Sea, BIRCHINGTON, CT7 9JZ.
•TYLER, Mr. Michael, FCA *1990;* Peyton Tyler Mears, Middleborough House, 16 Middleborough, COLCHESTER, CO1 1QT.
TYLER, Mr. Michael Edward, FCA *1967;* 58 Cleaver Square, LONDON, SE11 4EA.
TYLER, Mr. Neil Christopher, MA ACA *1999;* The Priest House Rotten End, Wethersfield, BRAINTREE, ESSEX, CM7 4AL.
TYLER, Mr. Neil John, MA FCA *2001;* 46 Newton Avenue, LONDON, N10 2NB.
TYLER, Mr. Neil Leslie, BA FCA *1991;* First Floor Flat, 137 Muswell Avenue, LONDON, N10 2EN.
TYLER, Mr. Nicholas Richard, BSc ACA *1988;* Wellhampton House, Upper Green Road, Shipbourne, TONBRIDGE, TN11 9PN.
TYLER, Mr. Nicholas Shaw, BSc FCA *1972;* Chartis Inc, 175 Water Street, Floor 24, NEW YORK, NY 10038, UNITED STATES.
TYLER, Mr. Nigel Barlow, FCA *1975;* Glen Rosa, 3 Tannersfield, Shalford, GUILDFORD, GU4 8JW.
TYLER, Mr. Paul Barry, BSc FCA *1977;* P O BOX 2397, CLAREINCH, 7740, SOUTH AFRICA.
TYLER, Mr. Paul Edward, BA ACA *2005;* 2 Beardsley Gardens, Barton Seagrave, KETTERING, NORTHAMPTONSHIRE, NN15 5UB.
TYLER, Mr. Peter Stanley, FCA *1965;* Hopwoods House, Walden Road, Sewards End, SAFFRON WALDEN, CB10 2LE. (Life Member)
•TYLER, Mr. Philip Geoffrey, BSocSc FCA CTA *1988;* (Tax Fac), Tyler Redmore Limited, 157 Redland Road, BRISTOL, BS6 6YE.
TYLER, Mr. Richard John, FCA *1968;* 8 Barton Close, Witchford, ELY, CAMBRIDGESHIRE, CB6 2HS.
TYLER, Mr. Ronald Geoffrey, FCA *1968;* Black Howe, Keld, RICHMOND, NORTH YORKSHIRE, DL11 6LP.
TYLER, Mr. Simon, LLB ACA *2007;* 67 Eton Rise, Eton College Road, LONDON, NW3 2DA.
TYLER, Mr. Thomas William, BA ACA *2006;* Pricewaterhousecoopers, 101 Barbirolli Square, MANCHESTER, M2 3PW.
•TYLER-WADDINGTON, Mrs. Clair Maria, FCA CTA *1992;* Tyler-Waddington Ltd, 15 Old Watling Street, Flamstead, ST. ALBANS, HERTFORDSHIRE, AL3 8HL.
•TYLER-WADDINGTON, Mr. Eliot Archer Grant, BA ACA *1990;* Tyler Waddington, The Gables, 15 Old Watling Street, Flamstead, ST. ALBANS, HERTFORDSHIRE AL3 8HL.
TYLEY, Ms. Clare Lilian, MA ACA *1995;* 12 Prospect Road, ST. ALBANS, HERTFORDSHIRE, AL1 2AX.
TYLEY, Mr. Gwynfor Paul, MA ACA *1995;* 12 Prospect Road, ST. ALBANS, AL1 2AX.
TYLKA, Miss. Stacey, ACA *2008;* 801 Travis Street, Suite 1500, HOUSTON, TX 77002, UNITED STATES.
TYM, Mrs. Rebecca Jane, BA(Hons) ACA *2002;* Westerlea, Rockfield Road, OXTED, SURREY, RH8 0HA.
TYMIENIECKA, Miss. Karolina, MA(Cantab) ACA *2006;* Ground Floor Flat, 10 Hafer Road, LONDON, SW11 1HF.
TYMMS, Mr. Paul, BA ACA *2002;* 24 Bedford Road, ST. ALBANS, HERTFORDSHIRE, AL1 3BQ.
•TYMMS, Mr. Peter Paul, BA ACA *1989;* F.W. Berringer & Co, Lygon House, 50 London Road, BROMLEY, BR1 3RA.
TYMMS, Mrs. Sharon Jane, ACA *1990;* 95 Upper North Street, BRIGHTON, BN1 3FJ.
TYMOSHYSHYN, Mr. Peter William, ACA *2011;* Arundale & Co Stowe House, 1688 High Street Knowle, SOLIHULL, B93 0LY.
TYMVIOS, Mr. Sofocles, BA(Econ) ACA *1996;* 37 Dorieon Street Flat 01, 1101 NICOSIA, CYPRUS.
TYNAN, Mrs. Gillian, BA ACA *1996;* 3 Yetlington Drive, NEWCASTLE UPON TYNE, NE3 4YX.
TYNDALL, Mrs. Janette, BA ACA *2002;* Capita Financial Group Ltd 2 The Boulevard, City West One Office Park Gelderd Road, LEEDS, LS12 6NT.
TYNE, Mr. David Trevor North, FCA *1955;* 10 The Mews, Fulford Chase, Fulford Road, YORK, YO10 4QN. (Life Member)
TYRER, Miss. Catherine Anne Amelia, BSc ACA *2010;* Langdale House, Lower Dukes Road, Douglas, ISLE OF MAN, IM2 4BQ.
TYRER, Miss. Elizabeth Henderson, BSc ACA *1988;* 14 New Campden Court, Holly Bush Vale, Hampstead, LONDON, NW3 6TY.
TYRER, Mr. Ian Richard, BSc ACA *1990;* Woodbine Cottage, Tockington Green, Tockington, BRISTOL, BS32 4LG.
•TYRER, Mr. James Barry, FCA *1975;* Cherry Lodge, Alder Road, LIVERPOOL, L12 2BA.
TYRER, Mr. James Edward, BA(Hons) ACA *2007;* 12 Alder Road, LIVERPOOL, L12 2AY.
TYRER, Mr. Michael Richard, FCA *1967;* Hillcrest, Farnham Beeches, Langton Green, TUNBRIDGE WELLS, TN3 0HX. (Life Member)
TYRER, Mrs. Miranda, ACA *1993;* Badgers Copse, Blackhorse Lane, Shedfield, SOUTHAMPTON, SO32 2HT.
TYRER, Mr. Peter Gerald, FCA *1961;* Solesbridge House, Solesbridge Lane, Chorleywood, RICKMANSWORTH, WD3 5SR.
TYRER, Miss. Philippa Diane, BEng ACA *1998;* 15 Keane Close, Blidworth, MANSFIELD, NOTTINGHAMSHIRE, NG21 0QY.
TYRER, Mr. Richard Thomas, BSc(Hons) ACA *2003;* 17 Wooldridge Ave, MILLSWOOD, SA 5034, AUSTRALIA.
TYRIMOU, Miss. Christiana, BSc ACA *2003;* 8/45-49 Gladstone Street, KOGARAH, NSW 2217, AUSTRALIA.
TYRLS, Mr. Michael, FCA *1961;* M22, 8 Birch Glade, Finchfield, WOLVERHAMPTON, WV3 9ES.
TYRRELL, Mr. Adam David, BSc ACA *1995;* The Old Rectory, The Street, West Clandon, GUILDFORD, SURREY, GU4 7RG.
TYRRELL, Mr. Andrew Graham, BSc(Hons) ACA *2001;* 57 New Lane, YORK, YO24 4NU.
TYRRELL, Mr. Christopher Patrick, BA ACA *1990;* 135 Kings Parade Holland-on-Sea, CLACTON-ON-SEA, ESSEX, CO15 5JL.
TYRRELL, Mr. David John, BA(Hons) ACA *2002;* 5 Comeragh Road, LONDON, W14 9HP.
•TYRRELL, Mr. Derek Frank, FCA *1973;* Tyrrells Limited, 69 Princess Victoria Street, Clifton, BRISTOL, BS8 4DD.
TYRRELL, Miss. Fionnuala Catherine, BA ACA *2000;* with Ernst & Young LLP, 1 More London Place, LONDON, SE1 2AF.
TYRRELL, Mrs. Glynis, MA ACA *1985;* Belmont, 21 Woodlane, FALMOUTH, TR11 4RD.
TYRRELL, Mr. James Michael, MA FCA *1966;* Tree Tops, Aldworth Road, Upper Basildon, READING, RG8 8NH.
•TYRRELL, Mr. Jeremy John, BA(Hons) FCA *1996;* Keens Shay Keens Limited, Christchurch House, Upper George Street, LUTON, LU1 2RS.
TYRRELL, Miss. Josephine Melanie, BSc ACA *1992;* 1 Portland Square, Hill Brow Road, LISS, GU33 7LD.
TYRRELL, Mr. Roydon Alfred, FCA *1949;* Merton House, 11 Barrack Street, BRIDPORT, DT6 3LX. (Life Member)
TYRRELL-EVANS, Mr. Nicholas John Tyrrell, MA FCA *1962;* 15 The Croft, Elstead, GODALMING, GU8 6JL.
TYRWHITT, Mr. John Edward Charles, MA FCA *1979;* 36 Melrose Road, LONDON, SW18 1NE.
TYSOE, Miss. Katherine Louise, BA ACA *2010;* Flat 2, Romanby Court, 31 Mill Street, REDHILL, RH1 6PA.
TYSOE, Mr. Peter, FCA *1956;* 32 Werneth Road, Woodley, STOCKPORT, SK6 1HP. (Life Member)
•TYSOE, Mr. Stephen Roy, BA FCA *1984;* F B 40 Limited, 2 Lace Market Square, NOTTINGHAM, NG1 1PB. See also Smith Cooper LLP and Smith Cooper
TYSON, Mr. Andrew John Baird, BA ACA *1985;* P.O. Box 847, GEORGE TOWN, GRAND CAYMAN, KY1-1103, CAYMAN ISLANDS.
TYSON, Miss. Carrie Leanne, BSc ACA *2002;* 32 Alma Street, Woodlesford, LEEDS, LS26 8PN.
TYSON, Mr. Charles Henry Edward, MA FCA *1967;* Ashurst, Abberton Field, Hurstpierpoint, HASSOCKS, BN6 9QD. (Life Member)
TYSON, Mr. David Richard, FCA *1961;* Baycliff House, 7 The Knoll, Daltongate, ULVERSTON, CUMBRIA, LA12 7TN.
TYSON, Mr. Edward Addison, FCA *1954;* 7 Marsh Garth, KIRKBY-IN-FURNESS, LA17 7UU. (Life Member)
TYSON, Mr. Iain George, BSc ACA *2006;* Flat 3, 21 Fog Lane, Didsbury, MANCHESTER, M20 6AR.
•TYSON, Mr. Kenneth Frank, FCA *1971;* Via Rasori 15, 20145 MILAN, ITALY.
•TYSON, Mr. Matthew Ronald, FCA CTA *1992;* (Tax Fac), Richard Place Dobson Services Limited, Ground Floor, 1-7 Station Road, CRAWLEY, WEST SUSSEX, RH10 1HT. See also Richard Place Dobson LLP
TYSON, Miss. Melanie Jacqueline, BSc(Hons) ACA MCSI *2001;* 34 Silkstone Way, LEEDS, LS15 8TN.
TYSON, Mr. Rob Macdonald, BSc ACA *2003;* 11 Dove Park, Chorleywood, RICKMANSWORTH, HERTFORDSHIRE, WD3 5NY.
TYSON, Mrs. Shelley Louise, LLB ACA *2001;* 12 Carr Road, Calverley, PUDSEY, WEST YORKSHIRE, LS28 5RH.
TYSON, Mrs. Simone Samantha, BSc ACA *2003;* 11 Dove Park, Chorleywood, RICKMANSWORTH, HERTFORDSHIRE, WD3 5NY.
TYSON, Miss. Sophie Elspeth Charlotte, BAcc ACA DChA *2007;* 6 Montreal Street, CARLISLE, CA2 4EE.
TYSZEWICZ, Miss. Julita Ann, BCom ACA *1986;* 30th Floor South Tower, Royal Bank Plaza, 200 Bay Street, TORONTO M5J 2J5, ON, CANADA.
TYTE, Ms. Elizabeth Doreen, BSc FCA *1983;* 43 Wellington Road, LONDON, W5 4UJ.
TYTE, Mrs. Katy Ann, BSc ACA *2005;* 99 Woodfield Avenue, EDINBURGH, EH13 0QR.
TYTHERIDGE, Mr. Geoffrey John, FCA *1961;* 3 Highland Court, Church Road, HAYWARDS HEATH, RH16 3NZ.
TYTHERLEIGH, Mr. Colin, FCA *1958;* 129 Ashley Gardens, Thirleby Road, LONDON, SW1P 1HL. (Life Member)
TYTLER, Mr. Richard Morton, BA FCA *1961;* 16 Scotlands Close, HASLEMERE, SURREY, GU27 3AE. (Life Member)
TYZACK, Mr. Jonathan David, BSc ACA *2003;* Clifford House North Street, Hundon, SUDBURY, SUFFOLK, CO10 8ED.
•TYZZER, Mr. Andrew Thomas, BA ACA *1984;* (Tax Fac), AIMS - AndrewTyzzer, 3 Foden Close, Shenstone, LICHFIELD, STAFFORDSHIRE, WS14 0LE.
TZIAKOURI, Ms. Irene, ACA *2010;* 21st Ayiasmaton Latsia, NICOSIA, CYPRUS.
TZIONIS, Mr. Xenios, BSc ACA *2007;* P.O.BOX 53168, 3301 LIMASSOL, CYPRUS.
TZORTZI, Miss. Maria, BA ACA *2007;* 7 Onisilou Street, Naafi, 3075 LIMASSOL, CYPRUS.
•TZOULIOU, Mr. Tzoulios Andreas, ACA *1992;* (Tax Fac), TAT Accounting Limited, 26 Hillfield Park, LONDON, N21 3QH.
TZOUROS, Mr. Theodoros, BSc ACA *2006;* 13 Ypsilantou Steet, Dionisos, 14576 ATHENS, GREECE.
U, Mr. Chin Wei, FCA *1977;* 41 Jalan SetiaBistari, Bukit Damansara, 50490 KUALA LUMPUR, FEDERAL TERRITORY, MALAYSIA.
UBEROI, Mr. Ameet, BSc ACA *1993;* Flat 12 Admirals Court, Eastbury Avenue, NORTHWOOD, HA6 3JP.
UBEROI, Mr. Bobby, BSc(Econ) ACA *1998;* 27 Elers Road, LONDON, W13 9QB.
UBEROI, Ms. Shivani, ACA *2008;* 44 Harte Road, HOUNSLOW, TW3 4LD.
UCAR, Mrs. Emine, ACA *2008;* 84 Cheyne Walk, Grange Park, LONDON, N21 1DE.
UD DIN, Mr. Ahsan, FCA *1969;* 302 Upper Mall, LAHORE, PAKISTAN.
UD-DIN, Mr. Waheed, FCA *1971;* CORE MANAGEMENT CONSULTANTS, 65 Z DHA, LAHORE, PAKISTAN.
UDA, Mr. Raja Arshad, FCA *1971;* Payong, 16 Jalan 12, Taman Tun Abdul Razak, 68000 AMPANG, SELANGOR, MALAYSIA.
•UDAL, Mr. Nicholas Andrew, BSc ACA *1986;* BDO LLP, 55 Baker Street, LONDON, W1U 7EU. See also BDO Stoy Hayward LLP
UDALE, Mr. Andrew, BSc ACA *1989;* A O N Hewitt Ltd, 10 Devonshire Square, LONDON, EC2M 4YP.
•UDALE, Mr. Robinson, BA ACA CTA *1988;* Robinson Udale Limited, The Old Bank, 41 King Street, PENRITH, CUMBRIA, CA11 7AY.
UDALL, Mrs. Claire Louise, BA ACA CFE *1999;* Ruxley Cottage, Rectory Road, North Fambridge, CHELMSFORD, CM3 6NG.
UDALL, Mr. David Charles, BSc FCA *1987;* 12 Hebble Close, BOLTON, BL2 3FS.
•UDALL, Mr. David Victor, FCA *1963;* D.V. Udall & Co, Dukes Edge, Lunghurst Road, Woldingham, CATERHAM, CR3 7HE.
•UDALL, Mrs. Stephanie Pamela, BSc FCA ATII *1989;* (Tax Fac), PricewaterhouseCoopers LLP, Savannah House, 3 Ocean Way, Ocean Village, SOUTHAMPTON, SO14 3TJ. See also PricewaterhouseCoopers
UDALL, Mr. William Horace Trevor, FCA *1958;* Sherford House, Organford Road, Organford, Holton Heath, POOLE, DORSET BH16 6LA. (Life Member)
•UDANI, Mr. Paresh, BSc ACA *1984;* (Tax Fac), AccountPro Services Limited, Premier House, 112 Station Road, EDGWARE, HA8 7BJ.
UDDIN, Mr. Abul Fazal Mohammad Nasir, FCA *1971;* 81 Devon Road, Cheam, SUTTON, SM2 7PE.
UDDIN, Mr. Fakir Syed Aijaz, OBE FCA *1965;* R-134, Defence Housing Association, LAHORE 54792, PAKISTAN. (Life Member)
UDDIN, Mr. Fawwad, BSc(Hons) ACA *2009;* Flat 12, 18 Addiscombe Grove, CROYDON, CR0 5LL.
UDDIN, Mr. Jamal, ACA *2008;* Flat 14, Trendell House, Dod Street, LONDON, E14 7EA.
•UDDIN, Mr. Mohammad Rukn, FCA *1973;* Uddin & Co, 12 Fairlawns, SUNBURY-ON-THAMES, TW16 6QR.
UDDIN, Mr. Mohammed Mosleh, FCA *1963;* KPMG - RRH, 102 Agrabad Commercial Area, CHITTAGONG, BANGLADESH.
UDDIN, Mr. Moin, ACA *2009;* 27 Norman Avenue, BRADFORD, BD2 2LY.
UDDIN, Miss. Nazmeen, ACA *2009;* 59 Falmouth Gardens, ILFORD, IG4 5JQ.
UDDIN, Miss. Nilufa, LLB ACA *2010;* 67 Perry Hill Road, OLDBURY, WEST MIDLANDS, B68 0AW.
UDDIN, Mr. Rashed, BSc(Hons) FCA *2000;* 20 Cranbrook Road, BARNET, HERTFORDSHIRE, EN4 8UN.
•UDDIN, Mr. Shalim, BA(Econ) FCA CertPFS *2000;* SKN, SKN Business Centre, 1 Guildford Street, BIRMINGHAM, B19 2HN. See also SKN Services Ltd
UDELL, Mr. Brian Arthur, FCA *1967;* 9 Canons Hill, COULSDON, SURREY, CR5 1HB. (Life Member)
UDY, Miss. Rachel Kate, ACA *2007;* 12 Glebe Aalin, Station Road Ballaugh, ISLE OF MAN, IM7 5BW.
UFLAND, Mr. Edward, BA ACA *1992;* 17 Cavendish Avenue, LONDON, N3 3QP.
•UFLAND, Mr. Stephen Michael, FCA *1980;* Beechams LLP, 3rd Floor, 167 Fleet Street, LONDON, EC4A 2EA.
UGLOW, Mr. Peter Frederick, FCA *1970;* Unit 12, The Gate Centre, Bredbury Park Way, STOCKPORT, CHESHIRE, SK6 2SN.
UGONO, Mr. Uvie, BSc ACA *2003;* Dark Pines, Crab Hill, BECKENHAM, KENT, BR3 5HH.
UGRADAR, Mrs. Rehana, ACA *2003;* 26 Nightingale Close, BLACKBURN, BB1 2RE.
UGUR, Mr. Ahmet Agah, BSc ACA *1987;* Borusan Holding AS, 103 Meclisi Mebusan Cad, Salipazan, ISTANBUL, TURKEY.
UGWUNZE, Mrs. Ijeoma Doreen Pauline, BSc ACA *2003;* 2 Linden Close, STANMORE, MIDDLESEX, HA7 3NW.
UL-HAQ, Mr. Aziz, BA ACA CF *1999;* 4 Spring Bank Lane, ROCHDALE, OL11 5SF.
UL-HAQ, Mr. Ikram, MSc BA(Hons) ACA *2002;* 79/56 Bansmandi, KANPUR 208 001, INDIA.
UL-HASSAN, Mr. Muhammad Siddiq, ACA *2010;* 46 Lorenzo House, Medici Close, ILFORD, IG3 8FF.
ULBRICK, Mr. Victor Charles, FCA *1951;* 10 Athol Place, CARLINGFORD, NSW 2118, AUSTRALIA. (Life Member)
ULHAQ, Mr. Mahmud, FCA *1975;* 41 Glenwood Road, LONDON, N15 3JS.
ULLAH, Mr. Mohammed Rizvan, BSc ACA *1995;* 55 Grange Park Crescent, LEEDS, LS8 3BD.

ULLAH, Mr. Nadim Ahmed, BA ACA *1998;* Morgan Stanley, International Commerce Centre, 1 Austin Road West, Kowloon, TSIM SHA TSUI, KOWLOON HONG KONG SAR.
ULLATHORNE, Mrs. Anne Elizabeth, BA FCA *1975;* Birmingham Business School, University of Birmingham, Edgbaston, BIRMINGHAM, B15 2TT.
ULLATHORNE, Mr. Peter John, LLB FCA *1973;* 1 Ramsden Close, BIRMINGHAM, B29 4JX.
ULLATHORNE, Mr. William Royston, BSc ACA *1978;* Intex Hawkshaw Ltd, 3 Croich Green, Hawkshaw, BURY, LANCASHIRE, BL8 4PH.
ULLMANN, Miss. Anna-Marie, ACA *2002;* Kleinwort Benson Asia Pte Ltd, 14-04 71 Robinson Road, SINGAPORE 068895, SINGAPORE.
ULLMANN, Mr. Herman, ACA *1982;* (Tax Fac), Haffner Hoff & Co, 86 Princess Street, MANCHESTER, M1 6NP.
ULLMANN, Mr. Phillip Lionel, MA FCA *1993;* 36 Highfield Gardens, LONDON, NW11 9HB.
ULLMER, Mr. Michael James, BSc FCA *1975;* PO Box 8012, ARMADALE, VIC 3143, AUSTRALIA.
•ULLYOTT, Mrs. Samantha Jane, FCA *1995;* (Tax Fac), Ullyott Limited, 6 George Street, DRIFFIELD, NORTH HUMBERSIDE, YO25 6RA.
ULREY, Mrs. Susan, BA FCA *1988;* 13129 Brooks Landing Place, CARMEL, IN 46033, UNITED STATES.
•ULRICH, Mr. Michael Philip, ACA *1981;* (Tax Fac), M Ulrich, 24 Highfield Road, Tolworth, SURBITON, KT5 9LP.
ULYATT, Miss. Rachelle Maria, BSc ACA *1995;* Dane Court Copt Hill, Danbury, CHELMSFORD, CM3 4NW.
ULYETT, Mr. John Anthony Patrick, BA ACA *1989;* 18 Southlands Drive, LEEDS, LS17 5NZ.
UMANEE, Mr. Akesh, ACA *2005;* Plot 15 Morc Bellouguet, Brown Sequard Street, CUREPIPE, MAURITIUS.
UMBERS, Mr. Douglas Patrick William, BA ACA *1991;* Tyrrel House, Tyrrel Road, Chandlers Ford, EASTLEIGH, SO53 1GG.
•UMBERS, Mr. Richard Anthony Edward, FCA *1983;* Gibson Booth, New Court, Abbey Road North, Shepley, HUDDERSFIELD, HD8 8BJ.
•UMBLEJA, Mr. Evan Peter, FCA *1980;* (Tax Fac), BPU Limited, Radnor House, Greenwood Close, Cardiff Gate Business Park, CARDIFF, CF23 8AA.
UMER, Mr. Badaa-Saheb, BSc ACA *2006;* RasGas Company Limited, Finance Department, PO Box 24200, DOHA, QATAR.
UMNEY, Mr. Reginald Claude, FCA *1937;* 4/ 42 Frederick Street, GOSFORD, NSW 2250, AUSTRALIA. (Life Member)
UMNEY, Mr. Stuart Edward, MSc ACA *1997;* 8 Blyton Road, Papworth Everard, CAMBRIDGE, CB3 8XY.
UMPELBY, Mr. Stephen Alan, BA ACA *1993;* 20 Links Green Way, COBHAM, SURREY, KT11 2QH.
•UMPLEBY, Mr. Christopher, FCA *1975;* C. Umpleby & Co, Westbourne House, 60 Bagley Lane, Farsley, PUDSEY, WEST YORKSHIRE LS28 5LY.
UNADKAT, Mr. Mitul, BA ACA *2008;* 35 Grove Farm Park, NORTHWOOD, HA6 2BQ.
•UNADKAT, Mr. Narendrakumar Rangdas, ACA *1981;* Naren Unadkat & Co, 50 Wychwood Avenue, EDGWARE, HA8 6TH.
•UNADKAT, Mr. Nitin Rameshchandra, FCA *1982;* Unadkat & Co Limited, 12 The Wharf, Bridge Street, BIRMINGHAM, B1 2JS.
UNADKAT, Mr. Sachin Shyam, BSc ACA *2010;* 112 Gordon Avenue, STANMORE, MIDDLESEX, HA7 3QU.
UNALKAT, Miss. Roshni, ACA *2009;* 7 Stoneyfields Lane, EDGWARE, MIDDLESEX, HA8 9SH.
UNAOGU, Miss. Adaugo Chinagorom, BSc ACA *2010;* 2 Wards Wharf Approach, LONDON, E16 2EY.
UNDERDOWN, Mrs. Joanna Elizabeth, MA(Cantab) ACA *2005;* with BDO LLP, 55 Baker Street, LONDON, W1U 7EU.
UNDERHAY, Mrs. Abigail Helen Rhodes, BA ACA *2007;* 211 Shurland Avenue, BARNET, HERTFORDSHIRE, EN4 8DG.
UNDERHILL, Mr. Alan, BA FCA *1967;* (Tax Fac), Robert Hitchins Ltd The Manor, Boddington Lane Boddington, CHELTENHAM, GLOUCESTERSHIRE, GL51 0TJ.
UNDERHILL, Miss. Caroline Elizabeth, BSc ACA *2009;* Flat 1 Saffron Court, Saffron Close Earley, READING, RG6 7AB.
UNDERHILL, Mr. Henry John, FCA *1966;* 5 Gore Farm Close, East Dean, EASTBOURNE, EAST SUSSEX, BN20 0BD. (Life Member)
•UNDERHILL, Mr. John Lewis Laird, MA FCA *1972;* (Tax Fac), Collingbourne Consultants, Glebe View House, Collingbourne Kingston, MARLBOROUGH, WILTSHIRE, SN8 3SE.
UNDERHILL, The Hon. Robert, BSc FCA *1973;* The Hay Loft, Old Hall Farm, Puddington Village, Puddington, NESTON, CH64 5SP.
UNDERHILL, Mr. Roger John, FCA *1962;* 1 Dragons Hill Gardens, Keynsham, BRISTOL, BS31 1LN.
UNDERHILL, Mr. Stephen, BCom FCA *1984;* White House Farm, Village Road, Northop Hall, MOLD, CH7 6HT.
•UNDERHILL, Mrs. Virginia Julie, BSc FCA *1983;* Price Firman, Prince Consort House, Albert Embankment, LONDON, SE1 7TJ.
UNDERWOOD, Miss. Amy Elizabeth, BSc ACA *2006;* 18/24 Fairlight Street, FAIRLIGHT, NSW 2094, AUSTRALIA.
UNDERWOOD, Miss. Amy Louise, BSc ACA *2006;* 4 Sibley House, 328 Brixton Road, LONDON, SW9 7AD.
UNDERWOOD, Mr. Brian Reid, FCA *1951;* Abington, 14 Jeffreys Way, TAUNTON, TA1 5JJ. (Life Member)
UNDERWOOD, Mr. Christopher Gordon, FCA *1975;* 8 Partridge Down, Olivers Battery, WINCHESTER, SO22 4HL.
UNDERWOOD, Mrs. Claire Ann Dannyelle, BA ACA *1998;* The Gables, Hatches Lane, Great Kingshill, HIGH WYCOMBE, BUCKINGHAMSHIRE, HP15 6DS.
UNDERWOOD, Mrs. Claire Anne, BA ACA *2000;* Tower View, Lumb Carr Road, Holcombe, BURY, LANCASHIRE, BL8 4NN.
UNDERWOOD, Miss. Claire Elizabeth, BA(Hons) ACA *2000;* International Power Plc, Senator House, 85 Queen Victoria St, LONDON, EC4V 4DP.
UNDERWOOD, Miss. Clare Jane, ACA *1992;* 4 Silver Close, Minety, MALMESBURY, WILTSHIRE, SN16 9QT.
UNDERWOOD, Mrs. Clare Patricia, BSc ACA *1999;* 3 Padbrook Close, OXTED, SURREY, RH8 0DQ.
UNDERWOOD, Mr. Daniel, MEng ACA *2010;* All Saints Lodge, Pointout Road, SOUTHAMPTON, SO16 7DL.
UNDERWOOD, Mr. Gary, BA ACA *1992;* 43F Yuchengco Tower RCBC Plaza, Ayala Avenue cor Gil Puyat Avenue, MAKATI CITY 1200, METRO MANILA, PHILIPPINES.
•UNDERWOOD, Mr. Gary, BSc FCA *1997;* (Tax Fac), Franklin Underwood, 1 Pinnacle Way, Pride Park, DERBY, DE24 8ZS.
UNDERWOOD, Mrs. Helen Louise, BSc(Hons) ACA *2003;* Church Cottage Church Lane, Arborfield, READING, RG2 9JA.
UNDERWOOD, Mr. Keith Nigel, FCA *1969;* The White House, Chinnor Road, Bledlow Ridge, HIGH WYCOMBE, HP14 4AA.
UNDERWOOD, Mr. Keith Robert, BA(Econ) ACA *2002;* 133 Duke Road, LONDON, W4 2BX.
UNDERWOOD, Mrs. Louise Sarah, ACA *2005;* Cullum Capital Ventures Ltd, 2 County Gate Staceys Street, MAIDSTONE, ME14 1ST.
•UNDERWOOD, Mr. Mark, BCom ACA *1984;* M Underwood Accountancy Services, 2 Oakhurst Road, Wylde Green, SUTTON COLDFIELD, B72 1EJ.
UNDERWOOD, Mr. Mark David, BSc FCA *1993;* 14 Greaves Fold, Holywell Green, HALIFAX, WEST YORKSHIRE, HX4 9DY.
UNDERWOOD, Mr. Michael John Elphinstone, BSc ACA *2003;* 9 Common Lane, HARPENDEN, HERTFORDSHIRE, AL5 5BU.
UNDERWOOD, Mr. Michael Roy, FCA *1966;* 168 Westley Road, BURY ST. EDMUNDS, SUFFOLK, IP33 3SE.
UNDERWOOD, Mrs. Nicola Helen, BSc ACA *1994;* Unit 14, Riverside Business Centre Foundry Lane, Milford, BELPER, DERBYSHIRE, DE56 0RN.
UNDERWOOD, Mr. Nigel David, BA ACA *1999;* Whittan Group Limited, Link House Halesfield 6, TELFORD, SHROPSHIRE, TF7 4LN.
UNDERWOOD, Mr. Patrick, FCA *1960;* 36 Balsam Park, WINCANTON, SOMERSET, BA9 9HB. (Life Member)
UNDERWOOD, Mr. Paul David, BSc ACA *1992;* 157 El Camino Real, BERKELEY, CA 94705, UNITED STATES.
UNDERWOOD, Mr. Paul David, BSc ACA *2001;* 37 Rotton Row, Raunds, WELLINGBOROUGH, NORTHAMPTONSHIRE, NN9 6HU.
UNDERWOOD, Mr. Paul Kenneth, BCom FCA ACIM MBA MCMI *1998;* 7 Bretby Close, Bentley Heath, SOLIHULL, WEST MIDLANDS, B93 9BY.
UNDERWOOD, Mr. Paul Laurence, BA FCA *1979;* 24-26 Vincent Avenue, Crownhill, MILTON KEYNES, MK8 0AB.
UNDERWOOD, Ms. Sally Ann, BA ACA *1996;* 37 Collins Street, Essendon, MELBOURNE, VIC 3040, AUSTRALIA.
UNDERWOOD, Mr. Steven Graham, FCA *1972;* Brandenburg, 28-29 Navigation Drive Hurst Business Park, BRIERLEY HILL, DY5 1UT.
UNDERWOOD, Mr. Steven Keith, BSc ACA *1999;* Peel Holdings Ltd The Dome, The Trafford Centre, MANCHESTER, M17 8PL.
UNDERWOOD, Ms. Susan, BSc ACA *1983;* 71 Winnipeg Quay, Grain Wharf Salford Quays, SALFORD, M50 3TY.
UNDERWOOD, Mr. Wilfrid John, BSc ARCS ACA *1980;* 36 Mitchell Avenue, VENTNOR, PO38 1DP.
UNDERWOOD, Mr. William Greaves, FCA *1960;* Temple House, Temple Street, Brill, AYLESBURY, HP18 9SX. (Life Member)
UNDRILL, Miss. Louise Jane, BA ACA *1999;* B P P Financial Education, 3 London Wall Buildings, LONDON, EC2M 5PD.
UNERMAN, Prof. Jeffrey David, PhD MSc BA ACA *1989;* School of Management, Royal Holloway University of London, Egham Hill, EGHAM, TW20 0EX.
UNETT, Mr. Anthony Leonard, BSc ACA *1986;* 4 Oldroyd Way, DEWSBURY, WF13 2JJ.
UNGER, Mr. Glen Edmund Stanislaw, MA ACA *1995;* 3 St. Mary's Road, LONDON, SW19 7DF.
UNGKU AHMAD, Miss. Ungku Safiah, BA(Hons) ACA FCCA *2003;* 24 Sir John Newsom Way, WELWYN GARDEN CITY, HERTFORDSHIRE, AL7 4FL.
UNITE, Mr. Roger William, MA ACA *1981;* 19 Bolton Gardens, TEDDINGTON, TW11 9AX.
UNITT, Mr. Andrew Neil, ACA *2008;* 9 Alexander Court, Lovelace Road, SURBITON, SURREY, KT6 6PQ.
UNITT, Mr. Clive Martin, FCA *1981;* Silverwood, 56 Dibbinsdale Road, WIRRAL, MERSEYSIDE, CH63 0HJ.
UNSWORTH, Mrs. Alison Mary, LLB ACA *1993;* N R Barton & Co, 19-21 Bridgeman Terrace, WIGAN, WN1 1TD.
•UNSWORTH, Mr. Anthony Richard, FCA *1972;* A.R. Unsworth, 23 Royal Gardens, Davenham, NORTHWICH, CW9 8HB.
UNSWORTH, Mr. Derek, FCA *1967;* 4 Heol Coed Cae, CARDIFF, CF14 1HL. (Life Member)
UNSWORTH, Mr. John Warburton, BA FCA *1978;* 2 The Stables, Little Horwood Manor Little Horwood, MILTON KEYNES, MK17 0PU.
UNSWORTH, Mr. Justin Roland Martin, BA(Hons) ACA *1995;* Bidvest International Limited, Murdoch Chambers, South Quay, Douglas, ISLE OF MAN, IM1 5AS.
UNSWORTH, Mr. Martin John, BA(Hons) ACA *2001;* 2 Eanleywood Farm Close, Norton Cross, RUNCORN, CHESHIRE, WA7 6RY.
UNSWORTH, Mr. Neil David, BSc ACA *1994;* 123 Claremont Road, SALFORD, M6 8NL.
UNSWORTH, Mr. Paul James, BSc(Econ) ACA *1981;* Plum Tree Cottage, The Row, Lyth Valley, KENDAL, LA8 8DD.
UNSWORTH, Mr. Peter, BA ACA *1990;* 26 Southwood Avenue, BOURNEMOUTH, BH6 3QB.
•UNSWORTH, Mr. Peter Maurice, BCom FCA *1964;* (Tax Fac), Copplestone Unsworth & Co, 9 Abbey Square, CHESTER, CH1 2HU.
UNSWORTH, Mr. Robert Marshall, BA FCA *1978;* 81 Irnham Road, SUTTON COLDFIELD, B74 2TG.
UNSWORTH, Mr. Robert Nicholls, BSc ACA *2002;* Aimia Foods Limited, Penny Lane, Haydock, ST. HELENS, MERSEYSIDE, WA11 0QZ.
UNSWORTH, Mrs. Stella Jane, BA ACA *1989;* 26 Southwood Avenue, BOURNEMOUTH, BH6 3QB.
UNSWORTH, Mr. Stephen William, FCA *1973;* 27a Park Road, TRING, HP23 6BN.
UNSWORTH, Miss. Susan Rhian, BEng ACA *2000;* Corin Group PLC, Corinium Centre, CIRENCESTER, GLOUCESTERSHIRE, GL7 1YJ.
•UNTHANK, Mr. John Arthur Salusbury, BSc ACA *1984;* Unthank & Co, 4 Coniston Close, FELIXSTOWE, IP11 9SW.
UNTHANK, Miss. Lisa Marie, BSc ACA *2006;* 40 Summer Road, EAST MOLESEY, KT8 9LS.
•UNTHANK, Mrs. Rosemary Anne, ACA *1989;* (Tax Fac), Rosemary Unthank, 15 Thornley Road, FELIXSTOWE, IP11 7LA.
•UNUIGBE, Mr. Samuel Uaboi, FCA *1974;* Unuigbe Akintola & Co., Marble House (2nd Floor), 1 Kingsway Road, P.O. Ikoyi, LAGOS, NIGERIA.
UNWAY, Mr. William Peter, BA ACA *1981;* CSL Behring GmbH, Postfach 1230, 35002 MARBURG, GERMANY.
UNWIN, Miss. Andrea Cecelia, BA ACA *1999;* 39 Albacore Way, Maraetai, AUCKLAND, NEW ZEALAND.
UNWIN, Mr. Charles James, BSc ACA *1980;* Romanian Intl Business Advisors, Strada Aurel Vlaicu Nr 87, Apt 4, 020093 BUCHAREST, ROMANIA.
UNWIN, Miss. Chloe Davinia, BA ACA *2005;* Flat 13 Beaufort House, 2a Lower Downs Road, LONDON, SW20 8QB.
•UNWIN, Mr. David Charles William, MA ACA *1982;* Baker Tilly Tax & Advisory Services LLP, Abbotsgate House, Hollow Road, BURY ST. EDMUNDS, SUFFOLK, IP32 7FA.
UNWIN, Miss. Diane Amanda, BA ACA *1987;* 12 Box Ridge Avenue, PURLEY, CR8 3AP.
UNWIN, Mr. James, BA FCA *1980;* 59 Jickell Street, PALMERSTON NORTH, NEW ZEALAND.
UNWIN, Mr. Nigel James, BSc ACA *1996;* The Core, 40 St Thomas Street, BRISTOL, BS1 6JX.
UNWIN, Mr. Thomas James, FCA *1959;* 39B West Street, TADLEY, HAMPSHIRE, RG26 3ST. (Life Member)
UPADHYAY, Miss. Dipti Rhianon, BSc(Hons) ACA *2010;* 26 Halfpenny Walk, Wilford, NOTTINGHAM, NG11 7GX.
UPCOTT, Mr. Simon Christopher, BA FCA *1983;* (Tax Fac), with Cookson Group plc, 165 Fleet Street, LONDON, EC4A 2AE.
UPCRAFT, Mrs. Karen Anne, BA ACA *1992;* The Elms, Rectory Lane, Itchen Abbas, WINCHESTER, HAMPSHIRE, SO21 1BN.
UPCRAFT, Mr. Stuart John, BSc ACA *1992;* The Elms, Rectory Lane, Itchen Abbas, WINCHESTER, HAMPSHIRE, SO21 1BN.
•UPEX, Mr. Mark Andrew, BA ACA *1989;* PGU Accounting Ltd, St. Oswald House, St. Oswald Street, CASTLEFORD, WEST YORKSHIRE, WF10 1DH.
UPFOLD, Mr. Charles Arthur, FCA *1956;* 7 Foxdale Drive, Angmering Village, LITTLEHAMPTON, BN16 4HF. (Life Member)
UPHILL, Mr. Terence Edwin, FCA *1962;* Cherry Orchard, 68 Hazlemere Road, Penn, HIGH WYCOMBE, HP10 8AG.
UPPAL, Mrs. Aliena, BA(Hons) ACA *2002;* 13 Tulip Tree Drive Framingham Earl, NORWICH, NORFOLK, NR14 7UL.
•UPPAL, Mr. Balbir Singh, BCom ACA *1991;* (Tax Fac), B.S. Uppal & Co, 31 Oak Avenue, Ickenham, UXBRIDGE, UB10 8LR.
•UPPAL, Mr. Iftikar Hussein, ACA *1982;* Uppal & Warr, 452 Manchester Road, Heaton Chapel, STOCKPORT, SK4 5DL.
•UPPAL, Mrs. Lukhvinder, BSc(Econ) ACA *2001;* 13 Grange Close, Ingrave, BRENTWOOD, ESSEX, CM13 3QP.
UPPAL, Miss. Monica, BSc ACA *1993;* 29 West Hatch Manor, RUISLIP, MIDDLESEX, HA4 8QU.
UPPAL, Mr. Rajan, ACA *1987;* Bybrook House, 1 Cross Bank, Great Easton, MARKET HARBOROUGH, LE16 8SR.
UPPAL, Mr. Sandeep, LLM ACA *2000;* Acteon Group Ltd, Ferry Road, NORWICH, NR1 1SW.
•UPPARD, Mr. Malcolm, FCA *1974;* E.J. Williams & Co, 31 Lonsdale Street, CARLISLE, CA1 1BJ.
UPPERTON, Mr. Peter William, BSocSc FCA *1971;* 12th Floor, Vanissa Building, 29 Soi Chidlom, Pathumwan, BANGKOK 10330, THAILAND. (Life Member)
•UPSDELL, Mr. Keith Edward, FCA *1974;* Gorrie Whitson Limited, 18 Hand Court, LONDON, WC1V 6JF.
UPSHALL, Mrs. Jolene, BSc ACA *2002;* 1 Brays Close, Hyde Heath, AMERSHAM, BUCKINGHAMSHIRE, HP6 5RZ.
UPSHAW, Mr. Eric Lewis, FCA *1953;* 65 Neville Road, Heacham, KING'S LYNN, NORFOLK, PE31 7HD. (Life Member)
UPSHER, Mr. John Joseph, FCA *1980;* 18 Fairmead Avenue, WESTCLIFF-ON-SEA, SS0 9RX.
UPSON, Mr. Anthony Peter, BSc FCA *1977;* P K F Accountants & Business Advisors Farringdon Place, 20 Farringdon Road, LONDON, EC1M 3AP.
UPSON, Mr. George Michael, FCA *1973;* Rectory Accounts, Rectory Barn, Boylestone, ASHBOURNE, DERBYSHIRE, DE6 5AD.
•UPSON, Mr. Julien Keith, BA FCA *1982;* Hartley Fowler LLP, 4th Floor, Tuition House, 27-37 St. Georges Road, Wimbledon, LONDON SW19 4EU.
•UPSTONE, Mr. David Robert, FCA *1973;* (Tax Fac), David Upstone, 9 Market Place, BRACKLEY, NORTHAMPTONSHIRE, NN13 7AB.
UPSTONE, Ms. Emma Louise, BSc ACA *1996;* Close Bros Group Plc, 10 Crown Place, LONDON, EC2A 4FT.
UPSTONE, Mr. Haydn David, BSc FCA *1994;* 26 The Rex, High Street, BERKHAMSTED, HERTFORDSHIRE, HP4 2BT.
UPSTONE, Mr. Simon Benedict, BSc ACA *1998;* Doosan Babcock Energy Ltd Doosan House, Crawley Business Quarter Manor Royal, CRAWLEY, WEST SUSSEX, RH10 9AD.

UPTON, Mr. Alex Paul, BSc ACA *2011;* Flat 5, Grayling Court, De Montfort Road, READING, RG1 8DL.
UPTON, Miss. Catherine Frances, BA ACA *2005;* 72b St. James Road, SURBITON, SURREY, KT6 4QN.
UPTON, Mr. Christopher George, FCA *1974;* C U Associates Limited, Little Heath, Kent hatch Road, Limpsfield Chart, OXTED, SURREY RH8 0SZ.
UPTON, Mr. David Christopher, MEng ACA *2000;* Lantern Cottage The Street, Wilmington, POLEGATE, EAST SUSSEX, BN26 5SL.
UPTON, Mr. David James, ACA *2003;* 22 Bridge Down, Bridge, CANTERBURY, CT4 5AZ.
UPTON, Mr. David John, FCA *1969;* Corporate Health Ltd, The Buckingham Centre, Bradford Road, SLOUGH, SL1 4PG.
•UPTON, Mr. Dean Vearncombe, ACA *1990;* (Tax Fac), Upton Neenan Lees, 6a Croydon Road, CATERHAM, SURREY, CR3 6QB.
UPTON, Miss. Fiona Elizabeth, ACA *2004;* 33 Foredrift Close, Southcrest, REDDITCH, B98 7NP.
•UPTON, Mr. Frank, MA FCA *1978;* Friend LLP, Eleven Brindley Place, 2 Brunswick Square, BIRMINGHAM, B1 2LP.
UPTON, Mr. George Robert, FCA *1960;* 21 Old Farmhouse Drive, Oxshott, LEATHERHEAD, KT22 0EY. (Life Member)
UPTON, Miss. Gillian Margaret, BSc FCA *1974;* 12 Teviotdale Place, EDINBURGH, EH3 5HY.
UPTON, Mr. Gregory Philip, BSc ACA *1991;* 3 Baxter Green, Doxey, STAFFORD, ST16 2ER.
UPTON, Mr. Jonathan James, BA(Hons) ACA *2003;* 50 Manor Lane, SUNBURY-ON-THAMES, MIDDLESEX, TW16 5EG.
UPTON, Mr. Jonathan Mark, BA ACA *2003;* 7 Perry Court, 1 Maritime Quay, Napier Avenue, Docklands, LONDON, E14 3QF.
•UPTON, Mrs. Kim Tracey, BSc FCA *1989;* Paul A Hill & Co, 3 Bull Lane, ST. IVES, CAMBRIDGESHIRE, PE27 5AX. See also Paul A Hill & Co Limited
UPTON, Mr. Lawrence Edwin, BSc FCA *1981;* IBM Singapore Pte Ltd, 7 Changi Business Park Central 1, SINGAPORE 486072, SINGAPORE.
UPTON, Mrs. Lucinda Caroline, ACA *2008;* Pilmoor Growers, Broomhill, Whitemoor, Holt, WIMBORNE, DORSET BH21 7DA.
•ⒹUPTON, Mr. Mark Stephen, BA ACA *1990;* with Ensors, Cardinal House, 46 St Nicholas Street, IPSWICH, IP1 1TT.
UPTON, Mr. Matthew David Grosvenor, BA ACA *1997;* Unique Solutions for Pharma Ltd Endeavour House, Coopers End Road London Stansted Airport, STANSTED, CM24 1SJ.
UPTON, Mr. Neville, BSc ACA *1990;* Waterford, The Drive, CHICHESTER, WEST SUSSEX, PO19 5QA.
•UPTON, Mr. Nicholas Peter, BSc FCA *1980;* Anderson Barrowcliff LLP, Waterloo House, Thornaby Place, Thornaby on Tees, STOCKTON-ON-TEES, CLEVELAND TS17 6SA. See also Anderson Barrowcliff
•UPTON, Mrs. Nova, BA(Hons) ACA *2000;* Elliott Upton Limited, 30 St. Annes Crescent, LEWES, EAST SUSSEX, BN7 1SB.
UPTON, Mr. Patrick Francis, BSc FCA *1973;* East Lodge, Little Linford, MILTON KEYNES, MK19 7EB.
UPTON, Mrs. Pauline Ann, FCA *1961;* 21 Old Farmhouse Drive, Oxshott, LEATHERHEAD, KT22 0EY.
•UPTON, Mr. Peter John Henry, FCA ATII *1971;* (Member of Council 1991 - 1997), Peter Upton Limited, The Counting House, 7 Bridge Street, MAIDENHEAD, BERKSHIRE, SL6 8PA. See also WP Audit Limited
UPTON, Mr. Philip David Mainwaring, BSc FCA *1991;* with PricewaterhouseCoopers LLP, 300 Madison Avenue, NEW YORK, NY 10017, UNITED STATES.
UPTON, Mr. Philip Peter Ferguson, FCA *1983;* 27 Reid Park Road, Jesmond, NEWCASTLE UPON TYNE, NE2 2ER.
UPTON, Mr. Robert Gordon, MSc BA ACA *1978;* Capper & Co Ltd, Lanelay Road Industrial Estate, Talbot Green, PONTYCLUN, MID GLAMORGAN, CF72 8XX.
UPTON, Mr. Robin, ACA *2007;* 6 Nursery Court, Carrington Road, HIGH WYCOMBE, BUCKINGHAMSHIRE, HP12 3HS.
•UPTON, Mr. Robin Andrew, FCA FCCA MABRP *1970;* Robin Upton Insolvency, 284 Clifton Drive South, St Annes, LYTHAM ST. ANNES, FY8 1LH.
•UPTON, Mrs. Rosalind Eileen, LLB FCA *1983;* Ernst & Young LLP, 1 More London Place, LONDON, SE1 2AF. See also Ernst & Young Europe LLP
UPWARD, Mr. David Graham, BA FCA *1973;* 3 Clay Hall Place, Acton, SUDBURY, SUFFOLK, CO10 0BT.
URANG, Miss. Rebecca, MSc BSc ACA *2006;* 7 Amberley Grove, LONDON, SE26 6DG.
•URANIC, Mr. Janez, FCA *1992;* Ernst & Young Revizija posiovno svetovanje d.o.o, Dunajska Cesta 111, 1000 LJUBLJANA, SLOVENIA. See also Ernst & Young Europe LLP
URASA, Mr. Godfrey Shiletikwa, FCA *1970;* P O Box 485, DAR ES SALAAM, TANZANIA.
•URBAN, Ms. Helena Claire, MA DPhil FCA *2000;* (Tax Fac), Urban Accountancy, 20 Alverton Avenue, POOLE, DORSET, BH15 2QG.
URBANOWICZ, Miss. Anna, BA ACA *1992;* Pensbury, Cotherstone, BARNARD CASTLE, COUNTY DURHAM, DL12 9PQ.
URBAS, Mr. Jan Jerzy, FCA *1975;* Rue De Louveigne 66, 4052 BEAUFAYS, BELGIUM.
URDING, Mr. Rian, BSc(Hons) FCA *2000;* Charnwood Buildings, Holywell Park, Ashby Road, LOUGHBOROUGH, LEICESTERSHIRE, LE11 3GR.
URE, Mr. Christopher David, BA ACA *1989;* 7 Cottage Road, Headingley, LEEDS, LS6 4DD.
UREN, Mr. David Bruce, BSc ACA *1981;* 19 Manor Close, Shrivenham, SWINDON, SN6 8AE.
UREN, Mr. Edward John, BCom FCA *1973;* The Barn, Hambledon Park, Hambledon, GODALMING, GU8 4ER.
UREN, Mr. Ian Stanley, BSc ACA *1990;* 23 Scholars Green Lane, LYMM, WA13 0QA.
URMSON, Mr. Daniel Edward, BSc(Hons) ACA *2000;* 10 Brookfield, Oxspring, SHEFFIELD, S36 8WG.
URMSTON, Mr. Eric, FCA *1962;* 29 Millbrook Close, Glazebury, WARRINGTON, WA3 5LT. (Life Member)
URMSTON, Mr. Gary Martin, BSc ACA *1992;* 64 Middle Meadow, Shireoaks, WORKSOP, NOTTINGHAMSHIRE, S81 8PX.
•URMSTON, Mr. Philip, BSc FCA *1989;* (Tax Fac), Voisey & Co., 8 Winmarleigh Street, WARRINGTON, WA1 1JW.
•URQUHART, Mr. Adrian Clive, FCA *1986;* Moore Stephens, Oakley House, Headway Business Park, 3 Saxon Way West, CORBY, NORTHAMPTONSHIRE NN18 9EZ.
URQUHART, Mr. Andrew Vidal, FCA *1963;* El Desierto 175, La Planicie, La Molina, LIMA, 12, PERU.
URQUHART, Mr. Ian Gawthorp, BSc FCA *1978;* 11 Sycamore Avenue, EVESHAM, WORCESTERSHIRE, WR11 1YE.
URQUHART, Mr. John Andrew, BEng ACA *1996;* The Shepherds Building, Rockley Road, LONDON, W14 0DA.
URQUHART, Mr. Martin Paul, ACA *1995;* 7200 The Quorum, Oxford Business Park North, OXFORD, OXFORDSHIRE, OX4 2JZ.
URQUHART, Mrs. Nicola, BSc FCA *1998;* The Granary, 2 Hall Barn, Olney Road, Weston Underwood, OLNEY, BUCKINGHAMSHIRE MK46 5JZ.
URQUHART, Mr. Paul, ACA *2004;* 11 Morley Street, PORT MELBOURNE, VIC 3207, AUSTRALIA.
URQUHART, Mrs. Sheridon Lee, BA FCA *1978;* 8 Ashton Way, SUNDERLAND, SR3 3RX.
URRESTARAZU, Miss. Victoria, MEng ACA *2011;* 47 Carlton Avenue East, WEMBLEY, MIDDLESEX, HA9 8LZ.
URRY, Mr. Jason Peter, BA ACA *1995;* 37 Amity Grove, LONDON, SW20 0LQ.
URRY, Mr. Stephen John, BA FCA *1994;* New Cottage, Maxstoke Close, Maxstoke Lane, COVENTRY, CV7 7NB.
URRY, Mr. Stewart Wallace, LLB FCA *1971;* Hursey House, Hursey, BEAMINSTER, DORSET, DT8 3LN.
URWIN, Miss. Claire Elizabeth, ACA *2009;* 52 Buttermere Way, LOWESTOFT, NR33 8FN.
URWIN, Mr. Jonathan, MA(Hons) ACA *2011;* 7 Tomlinson Close, LONDON, E2 7LJ.
URWIN, Mr. Mark Robson, BA ACA *1983;* Flat 1 Belvoir Lodge, 59 Underhill Road, LONDON, SE22 0QX.
URWIN, Mr. Peter Muggeridge, FCA *1952;* 86 Cantley Lane, Bessacarr, DONCASTER, DN4 6NH. (Life Member)
USHER, Mr. Antony Edward, BA FCA *1993;* Brit Insurance, 55 Bishopsgate, LONDON, EC2N 3AS.
USHER, Mr. Daniel Philip, BA ACA *2000;* Clock Cottage, Church Road, Offham, WEST MALLING, KENT, ME19 5NX.
USHER, Mr. Derek George, ACA *1989;* Everest Farm, Church Road, Weald, SEVENOAKS, KENT, TN14 6LU.
USHER, Mr. Howard James Warwick, ACA *2000;* 16 Shandwick Close, Arnold, NOTTINGHAM, NG5 8AZ.
USHER, Miss. Joan Beatrice, MA ACA *1992;* (Tax Fac), with Grant Thornton UK LLP, 1 Whitehall Riverside, Whitehall Road, LEEDS, WEST YORKSHIRE, LS1 4BN.
•USHER, Mr. Keith, FCA *1972;* Keith Usher, High View, 81a Main Street, Greetham, OAKHAM, RUTLAND LE15 7NJ.
USHER, Mrs. Kim, BA ACA *1992;* Everest Farm, Church Road, Weald, SEVENOAKS, KENT, TN14 6LU.
USHER, Mr. Leonard Anthony, FCA *1964;* 7 Penwood End, Hook Heath, WOKING, GU22 0JU.
USHER, Mr. Liam, BSc(Econ) ACA *2010;* 5 Towle Close, Borrowash, DERBY, DE72 3FJ.
•USHER, Mr. Neil Robert, BA(Hons) ACA *2002;* Thorne Lancaster Parker, 8th Floor, Aldwych House, 81 Aldwych, LONDON, WC2B 4HN.
USHER, Mr. Paul William, FCA *1972;* 21 Holmesdale Park, Coopers Hill Road, Nutfield, REDHILL, RH1 4NW. (Life Member)
USHER, Mr. Peter, FCA *1965;* 7 Colebrooke, Birtley, CHESTER-LE-STREET, DH3 2LF.
USHER, Mr. Peter John, BA ACA *1992;* 10 Oaks Lane, Kirkbampton, CARLISLE, CA5 6HY.
USHER, Mr. Robert Francis, FCA *1963;* Usher & Roberts PTY Ltd, PO Box 745, CROWS NEST, NSW 1585, AUSTRALIA.
USHER, Mr. Stuart, FCA *1962;* Oakwood House Farm, Cliffe Cum Lund, SELBY, YO8 6PD.
USHER, Mr. William Ernest Broadbent, MA FCA *1964;* Hollow Way, 15 The Square, Aynho, BANBURY, OX17 3BL. (Life Member)
•USHER-SOMERS, Mr. Robert John, FCA ATII TEP *1983;* (Tax Fac), Arnold Hill & Co LLP, Craven House, 16 Northumberland Avenue, LONDON, WC2N 5AP. See also Arnold Hill & Co
USHERWOOD, Mr. David Nicholas Daniell, MSc BA ACA *1981;* Coheris Infocat Ltd Riverside House, 27-29 Vauxhall Grove, LONDON, SW8 1SY.
USMAN, Mr. Ahmed, BSc(Hons) ACA AIT *2003;* 241 Harefield Road, UXBRIDGE, MIDDLESEX, UB8 1PS.
•USMAN, Mr. Amer, BA ACA *2005;* Usman Accountancy, Communications House, 26 York Street, LONDON, W1U 6PZ.
USMAN, Mr. Hassan Tanimu, BA ACA *1994;* 19 Amazon Street, Ministers Hill, Maitama, ABUJA, NIGERIA.
USMANI, Mr. Akbar Husain, FCA *1978;* F-17/I Block IV, Clifton, KARACHI, PAKISTAN.
USMANI, Ms. Seema, BA ACA *1993;* 15 Birchlea, ALTRINCHAM, CHESHIRE, WA15 8WF.
USTEL, Mr. Paul, ACA *2011;* 172 Nightingale Road, Edmonton, LONDON, N9 8PT.
USTUN, Miss. Sarah, ACA *2011;* 23 Reservoir Road, STOCKPORT, CHESHIRE, SK3 9QJ.
USZKO, Mr. Pawel Jan, ACA *2008;* Apartment 29 Theatro Tower, Creek Road, LONDON, SE8 3FD.
UTAMSINGH, Mr. Vikram, ACA *1990;* KPMG India Private Limited, Lodha Excelus 3rd Floor, Apollo Mills Compound, N.M. Joshi Marg, Mahalaxmi, MUMBAI 400 011 INDIA.
UTHAMAKUNAN, Mr. Lavan, ACA *2008;* 10 Sylvan Avenue, Chadwell Heath, ROMFORD, RM6 6BE.
UTHAMAKUNAN, Miss. Vani, ACA *2008;* 10 Sylvan Avenue, Chadwell Heath, ROMFORD, RM6 6BE.
UTLEY, Ms. Catherine Julia, BA ACA *1988;* 108 Priory Gardens, Highgate, LONDON, N6 5QT.
UTLEY, Mr. Charles Edward, BSc ACA *1998;* 40 East 9th Street, Apartment 1F, NEW YORK, NY 10003, UNITED STATES.
UTLEY, Mrs. Narmali Shivonne, BSc ACA *1996;* Larkins Farm, 199 Nine Ashes Road, Nine Ashes, INGATESTONE, ESSEX, CM4 0JY.
UTTAMCHANDANI, Miss. Natasha, ACA *2009;* Flat 7, Hollin Court, Hollin Lane, LEEDS, LS16 5LZ.
UTTAMOT, Mr. Vivat, FCA *1961;* 134 Nakorn Sawan Road, BANGKOK, THAILAND. (Life Member)
UTTING, Mr. Frederick Charles, FCA *1959;* 4 Hill Crescent, HONITON, EX14 2HY. (Life Member)
•UTTING, Miss. Helen Louise, BSc FCA *1996;* (Tax Fac), Armstrong Watson, Bute House, Montgomery Way, Rosehill, CARLISLE, CA1 2RW.
UTTING, Mr. John Michael, MA FCA *1987;* KPMG Huazhen, 8th Floor Tower E2 Oriental Plaza, 1 East Chang An Avenue, BEIJING 100738, CHINA.
UTTING, Mr. Kevin James, BSc ACA *1992;* 33 Oakfield Road, Southgate, LONDON, N14 6LT.
UTTING, Mr. Steven Victor, BSc ACA *1986;* Flat 109, South Block, 1b Belvedere Road, LONDON, SE1 7GD.
UTTLEY, Mr. Andrew Peter, BA ACA *1989;* 82 Malthouse Lane, KENILWORTH, WARWICKSHIRE, CV8 1AD.
•UTTLEY, Mr. Anthony John, BA CA ACA *1991;* Level 2 100 Molesworth Street, Thorndon, PO Box 3928, WELLINGTON 6140, NEW ZEALAND.
UTTLEY, Mr. Carl, BA ACA *2000;* 10 Hall Drive, LIVERSEDGE, WF15 7AH.
•UTTLEY, Mr. Robert David, FCA *1956;* R.D. Uttley Limited, Shaw Cottage, Shaw Wood Road, Langfield, TODMORDEN, OL14 6HP. See also Uttley R.D.
UTTLEY, Mr. Stephen Michael, BA ACA *1986;* 1 Pinehurst, SEVENOAKS, KENT, TN14 5AQ.
UTTLEY, Mr. Steven David, BSc(Hons) ACA *2001;* 16 Field Park Grange, Gildersome, Morley, LEEDS, LS27 7WQ.
UWINS, Miss. Alison Jane Rashleigh, BCom ACA *1983;* 2a Kenilworth Avenue, LONDON, SW19 7LW.
UZ, Mr. Reha Ismail, FCA *1977;* Yeni Ulus Sitesi A - 11/10, Ilgin sokak Nisbetiye mah., Besiktas, ISTANBUL 34340, TURKEY.
UZEL, Mr. Radek, ACA *1998;* Cariad, Knoll Road, GODALMING, GU7 2EL.
UZIELLI, Mr. Michael Robin, MA ACA *1996;* Dunstable Cottage, 49 The Mount, GUILDFORD, GU2 4JA.
VACALOPOULOS, Mr. Alexander Paul, BSc ACA *2005;* 4 Litchfield Way, GUILDFORD, SURREY, GU2 7QL.
VACAS, Miss. Pilar, BSc ACA *2011;* 9 Longfield, LOUGHTON, IG10 4EE.
VACCARO, Mr. Filippo, ACA *1984;* Brockway Carpets Ltd Kidderminster Industrial Estate, Spennells Valley Road, KIDDERMINSTER, WORCESTERSHIRE, DY10 1XS.
VACHELL, Mr. Andrew, BSc ACA *1999;* 110 Tilt Road, COBHAM, KT11 3HQ.
VACHELL, Mr. John Annesley, FCA *1967;* Flat 2, 122 Wakefield Road, Lightcliffe, HALIFAX, HX3 8TH.
VACHER, Mr. Davinder, FCA *1966;* Davinder Vacher, 2 A Kirpa Narain Marg, Civil Lines, NEW DELHI 110054, INDIA. (Life Member)
•VACHHA, Mr. Kersi Homy, FCA *1977;* PricewaterhouseCoopers Ltd, 252 Veer Savarkar Marg, Shivaji Park Dadr, MUMBAI 400028, MAHARASHTRA, INDIA. See also Choksey Bhargava & Co
VACHHANI, Miss. Mayuri Kantilal, BSc ACA *1995;* Flat 6, Abercorn Mansions, 17 Abercorn Place, LONDON, NW8 9DY.
VADAKETH, Mr. Tom George, ACA *1986;* 1727 Jockeys Way, YARDLEY, PA 19067, UNITED STATES.
VADAS, Miss. Alison Claire, BSc ACA *1993;* with British Sky Broadcasting Group Plc, 7 Centaurs Business Centre, Grant Way, ISLEWORTH, MIDDLESEX, TW7 5QD.
VADASZ, Mr. Anthony Michael, MA ACA *1989;* Pinehaven Cottage Long Hill Seale, FARNHAM, SURREY, GU10 1NQ.
VADEHRA, Mr. Tarun, FCA *1972;* D-40 Defence Colony, NEW DELHI 110024, CAPITAL TERRITORY OF DELHI, INDIA.
VADERA, Mr. Ricky, BSc(Hons) ACA *2010;* 131 Canon Street, LEICESTER, LE4 6NJ.
VADGAMA, Mr. Mahesh, FCA *1988;* 57 Ormesby Way, HARROW, HA3 9SE.
VADGAMA, Miss. Noopur Rameshchandra, BA ACA *2010;* 47a Woodville Road, THORNTON HEATH, SURREY, CR7 8LN.
VADUKUL, Miss. Geeta, BA ACA *2004;* 59 Plover Close, ROCHDALE, OL11 5PU.
VAFEAS, Mrs. Caroline Noel, BA ACA *1991;* 25 Glen Drive, Stoke Bishop, BRISTOL, BS9 1SA.
VAGHADIA, Mr. Vinod Pragji Gordhan, ACA *1981;* 6 Ormonde Road, NORTHWOOD, HA6 2EL.
VAGHELA, Mr. Vijay, BSc ACA *1992;* Trinity Mirror PLC, 1 Canada Square, LONDON, E14 5AP.
•VAHORA, Mr. Zakir Hussain Moosa, ACA *2001;* (Tax Fac), ZHM Consultants, 53 De Vere Gardens, ILFORD, ESSEX, IG1 3EB.
VAID, Mr. Chandan, ACA *2007;* 19 Halleys Walk, ADDLESTONE, SURREY, KT15 2DH.
VAID, Mr. Kamal, ACA *2008;* 22 The Ridgeway, Kenton, HARROW, MIDDLESEX, HA3 0LL.
VAIDYA, Mr. Anil Vinayak, BA ACA *2000;* 23 Hurst Road, BUCKHURST HILL, ESSEX, IG9 6AB.
VAIDYA, Mr. Deepak Calian, FCA *1971;* Suraj, 3rd Floor-251, Walkeshwar Road, MUMBAI 400006, MAHARASHTRA, INDIA.
VAIDYA, Mrs. Elizabeth, BSc ACA *1999;* 23 Hurst Road, BUCKHURST HILL, IG9 6AB.
VAIGHT, Miss. Diane Elizabeth, BSc ACA *1990;* 27 Kylemore Drive, Heswall, WIRRAL, CH61 6UG.
VAILE, Mr. Ian Lawrence Berkeley, FCA *1962;* Bramleys, 12 Fountain Hill, BUDLEIGH SALTERTON, DEVON, EX9 6BX. (Life Member)
VAILE, Mrs. Sarah Anne, BCom ACA *1992;* 87 Northgate Street, UNLEY PARK, SA 5061, AUSTRALIA.
VAINES, Mr. Gordon William Harry, BSc ACA *2006;* 39 St. Margarets Grove, TWICKENHAM, TW1 1JF.
•VAINES, Mr. Peter Stephen, FCA *1972;* (Tax Fac), Bakers Close, Long Crendon, AYLESBURY, BUCKINGHAMSHIRE, HP18 9BP.

•**VAINKER, Mr. Nicholas Marcel, MA MSc FCA** *1984;* (Tax Fac), Vainker & Associates Sarl, 17bd Royal, L-2449 LUXEMBOURG, LUXEMBOURG.
VAISEY, Mr. Nicholas Harry, FCA *1964;* 20 Brantwood Road, Herne Hill, LONDON, SE24 0DJ. (Life Member)
VAITHIANATHAR, Miss. Geetha, BSc ACA *1994;* 26, Oakview Gardens, LONDON, N2 0NJ.
VAIZEY, Mr. George Arthur, BEng ACA *2011;* Flat A, 85 Felsham Road, LONDON, SW15 1BA.
VAIZEY, Mr. John Russell, MA FCA *1977;* The Dyers Co, Dyers Hall, 10 Dowgate Hill, LONDON, EC4R 2ST.
VAJA, Mr. Ajai, BSc(Hons) ACA *2010;* 34 Wenford, Broughton, MILTON KEYNES, MK10 7AL.
VAJA, Mr. Ashwin Dahyalal, BSc ACA *1979;* 587 Eaglewood Drive, HAMILTON L8W 3J8, ON, CANADA.
VAJPEYI, Mr. Alok, BSc ACA *1989;* Dawnay Day AV Financial Services Private Limited, B Wing, Marathon Innova, Ganpatrao Kadam Marg, Lower Parel (W), MUMBAI 400013 INDIA.
VAJPEYI, Mrs. Tina, BSc ACA *1991;* The Akanksha Foundation, Voltas C, T B Kadam Marg, Chinchpokli, MUMBAI 400033, MAHARASHTRA INDIA.
VAKIL, Mr. Imtyaz Mohmed, BA ACA *1996;* 102 Balfour Road, ILFORD, IG1 4JE.
VAKIL, Miss. Mona Madhu, BSc ACA *1999;* 17C Sylvan Road, Snaresbrook, LONDON, E11 1QL.
•**VAKIS, Mr. Christos, BA FCA** *1984;* PO Box 20446, Aglandjia, 2152 NICOSIA, CYPRUS.
•**VAKIS, Mr. Demetris Stavrou, BSc FCA CF** *1987;* KPMG Limited, P O Box 21121, 1502 NICOSIA, CYPRUS. See also KPMG Metaxas Loizides Syrimis
VAKIS, Mr. Phivos, BSc ACA *1988;* Columbia Shipmanagment Ltd, Columbia House, Dodekanlson Street, POBox 1624 LIMASSOL, CYPRUS.
VALANIDOU, Miss. Ourania Demetriou, BA FCA *1986;* 10 Ypsilantis, Aglantzia, 2113 NICOSIA, CYPRUS.
VALANJU, Mrs. Nina, BSc ACA *1998;* 10 Uphill Grove, LONDON, NW7 4NJ.
VALBERG, Ms. Florence Susannah, BA ACA *2000;* B P P Professional Education, 137 Stamford Street, LONDON, SE1 9NN.
VALE, Mr. Anthony John, MA FCA *1982;* 6 Valiant Close, Bowerhill, MELKSHAM, SN12 6SW.
•**VALE, Mr. Christopher John, BA ACA** *1991;* (Tax Fac), Oaks Financial Ltd, Race Course Farm, Mary Lane, Bescaby, MELTON MOWBRAY, LEICESTERSHIRE LE14 4AU.
VALE, Mr. Donald Winston, MA FCA FCMA *1966;* 802 Palm Grove, The Oasis, CENTURY CITY, WESTERN CAPE PROVINCE, 7441, SOUTH AFRICA.
VALE, Miss. Janice Karen, LLB ACA *1983;* 6 Cathedral Lodge, Aldersgate Street, LONDON, EC1A 4JE.
VALE, Mr. John, FCA *1959;* 7 Highfield Road, DERBY, DE22 1GX. (Life Member)
VALE, Miss. Julie, ACA *2008;* with PricewaterhouseCoopers LLP, The Atrium, St. Georges Street, NORWICH, NR3 1AG.
VALE, Mrs. Laura McKendrick, BSc ACA *1998;* 11 Glasseys Lane, RAYLEIGH, ESSEX, SS6 7SN.
VALE, Ms. Louise Elizabeth, MA ACA *1987;* Whitestones, 46 Tadworth Street, TADWORTH, KT20 5RF.
VALEINIS, Miss. Indra Klara, BA(Hons) ACA *2004;* 3 Wensley Crescent, LEEDS, LS7 3QT.
•**VALEMBOIS, Mr. Alan, BA ACA** *1999;* VIVA Accounting Limited, 115 Whitby Road, IPSWICH, IP4 4AG.
VALENTE, Mrs. Kelly, BSc ACA *2005;* 55 Bartley Drive, Northfield, BIRMINGHAM, B31 1AR.
VALENTI, Miss. Catherine Assunta, BSc ACA *1987;* 2 Cornwallis Close, CATERHAM, CR3 5BX.
VALENTIN, Mr. Mark Andrew, MA(Hons) ACA *2002;* with Deloitte LLP, 2 New Street Square, LONDON, EC4A 3BZ.
VALENTINE, Mrs. Aileen, FCA *1975;* 53 Smithills Croft Road, BOLTON, BL1 6LN.
VALENTINE, Miss. Amanda Jayne, MA ACA *1992;* 147 Bradshaw Road, Bradshaw, BOLTON, BL2 3EN.
VALENTINE, Mrs. Corinna Dorothee, ACA *1998;* Fidelity Investment Managers, Millfield Lane, Lower Kingswood, TADWORTH, KT20 6RB.
•**VALENTINE, Mr. Daniel Martin, BSc ACA** *1993;* Begbies Chettle Agar, Epworth House, 25 City Road, LONDON, EC1Y 1AR. See also Begbies Everett Chettle
VALENTINE, Mr. Ian David, ACA *1979;* 2 Gadbrook Grove, Atherton, MANCHESTER, M46 0GZ.
VALENTINE, Mrs. Jane Louise, BA(Hons) ACA *2004;* Ravenair Business Aviation Centre, Viscount Drive, Liverpool John Lennon Airport, Hale Village, LIVERPOOL L24 5GA.
VALENTINE, Mr. Jonathan Dinesh Andrew, MEng ACA *2006;* Flat 2, 32 Hemstal Road, LONDON, NW6 2AL.
VALENTINE, Ms. Kathryn Claire, BSc ACA *1997;* 2 Fromelles Avenue, SEAFORTH, NSW 2092, AUSTRALIA.
VALENTINE, Mr. Kenneth Harry, BA ACA *1991;* 203 Cardamom Building, 31 Shad Thames, LONDON, SE1 2YR.
VALENTINE, Mr. Michael John, BSc ACA *2001;* 5 Pepys Road, #04-01 Westpoint Condo, SINGAPORE 118443, SINGAPORE.
VALENTINE, Mr. Paul, BA FCA *1977;* Gebhardiweg 5, 21339 LUENEBURG, GERMANY.
VALENTINE, Mr. Peter John, FCA *1966;* Rust en Vreugdlaan 14, 2243 AS WASSENAAR, NETHERLANDS. (Life Member)
•**VALENTINE, Mr. Robert Henriques, FCA** *1970;* 3 Kirkstall House, The Ridgeway, Mill Hill, LONDON, NW7 4EH.
VALENTINE, Miss. Shireen, BA ACA *2006;* Flat 1, 22 Craven Hill, LONDON, W2 3DS.
•**VALENTINE, Mr. Stephen William, FCA** *1983;* Cameron Valentine Ltd, Unit 2, Ferry Road Office Park, Ferry Road, Riversway, PRESTON PR2 2YH. See also C. V. Book Keeping
VALENTINE, Mr. Stuart Andrew, MMath ACA *2006;* 23 Grasgarth Close, LONDON, W3 9HS.
VALENTINE, Mr. Timothy, BA(Hons) ACA *2001;* 17b Petworth Street, LONDON, SW11 4QR.
VALENTINE-GALE, Mrs. Lisa-Anne, BA ACA *1998;* 14 Desford Road, Kirby Muxloe, LEICESTER, LE9 2BB.
VALENY, Mr. Rony, BSc(Econ) ACA *2000;* Currency House, Building 1 5th Floor DIFC, Dubai International Financial Centre, P O Box 282056, DUBAI, UNITED ARAB EMIRATES.
•**VALENZIA, Mr. David Aidan, ACA** *1989;* PricewaterhouseCoopers, 167 Merchants Street, VALLETTA VLT 1174, MALTA.
•**VALENZIA, Mr. Kevin John, FIA FCA CPA** *1979;* PricewaterhouseCoopers, 167 Merchants Street, VALLETTA VLT 1174, MALTA.
•**VALERA, Mr. Ashok Kumar Harilal, BA ACA** *1988;* A.K. Valera, 343 High Road, ILFORD, IG1 1TE.
VALERA, Mr. Ashraf Mahomed-Hussein, BSc ACA *1993;* 359 Humberstone Road, LEICESTER, LE5 3DF.
VALERO, Miss. Anna, MSc BSc ACA *2006;* 31b Altenburg Gardens, LONDON, SW11 1JH.
VALIYI, Mr. Mark Mazyar, BSc ACA *1986;* 1 Courtland Avenue, Ilford, ESSEX, IG1 3DN.
•**VALJI, Mr. Nazir Mohamed Hussein, FCA** *1974;* (Tax Fac), Steele Robertson Goddard, 26-28 Ely Place, LONDON, EC1N 6AA.
VALKENBURG, Mrs. Inge, ACA *2003;* 89 Gibraltar Crescent, West Ewell, EPSOM, SURREY, KT19 9BU.
VALKS, Mr. David Allan, BA ACA *1991;* 122 The Mount, YORK, NORTH YORKSHIRE, YO241AS.
VALKS, Miss. Jacqueline, ACA *2011;* 13 Bertie Road, NORWICH, NR3 2HA.
VALKS, Mr. Richard Peter, BSc FCA *1979;* 14 Crow Tree Street, Great Gransden, SANDY, BEDFORDSHIRE, SG19 3AZ.
VALLANCE, Mr. Alan Keith, BA FCA FAICD *1990;* Phoenix Lodge, 86 Highfield Lane, Tyttenhanger, ST. ALBANS, HERTFORDSHIRE, AL4 0RL.
VALLANCE, Mrs. Ann Patricia, ACA *1992;* 3 Caldwell Close, Stapeley, NANTWICH, CHESHIRE, CW5 7JD.
VALLANCE, Mr. Daniel, ACA *2008;* National Audit Office, 157-197 Buckingham Palace Road, LONDON, SW1W 9SP.
VALLANCE, Mr. Ian, BSc ACA *1993;* 23 Stradbroke Grove, BUCKHURST HILL, ESSEX, IG9 5PD.
VALLANCE, Mr. James Michael Alexander, BSc ACA *1992;* 10 Austenway, Chalfont St. Peter, GERRARDS CROSS, SL9 8NW.
VALLANCE, Mrs. Leslie Helen, BSc ACA *1992;* The Chalfonts Community College Narcot Lane, Chalfont St. Peter, GERRARDS CROSS, BUCKINGHAMSHIRE, SL9 8TP.
VALLANCE, Mrs. Susan, BSc ACA *1996;* 23 Stradbroke Grove, BUCKHURST HILL, ESSEX, IG9 5PD.
•**VALLANCE, Mr. Thomas Henry, BSc ACA** *2004;* 4 South View, Hett, DURHAM, DH6 5LT.
VALLAT, Mr. David Arthur Richard, MA FCA *1975;* PO Box 408, 9001-956 FUNCHAL, Madeira, PORTUGAL. (Life Member)
VALLAT, Miss. Georgia Alison, BSc ACA *2004;* with Deloitte LLP, 3 Victoria Square, Victoria Street, ST. ALBANS, HERTFORDSHIRE, AL1 3TF.
VALLELY, Mr. Anthony William, BA ACA *1992;* 30 Hulme Hall Avenue, Cheadle Hulme, CHEADLE, SK8 6LN.
•**VALLENDER, Mr. Ian, FCA** *1986;* Harbour Crest, 3 rue Louis Aureglia, MC98000 MONACO, MONACO.
VALLI, Miss. Sobayha, BSc ACA *2010;* 7 Albert Road, BOLTON, BL1 5HE.
VALLI, Mrs. Zainul Iqbal, BCom ACA *1989;* P O Box 99403, MOMBASA, 80100, KENYA.
VALLIANI, Mr. Turhan, FCA *1975;* 86 Centre Avenue, NORTH YORK M2M 2L6, ON, CANADA.
VALLIS, Mr. Andrew Colin, BA FCA *1986;* Standard Chartered Bank, 22 Billiter Street, LONDON, EC3M 2RY.
VALLIS, Mrs. Anna, BSc ACA *2002;* 30 Dellands, Overton, BASINGSTOKE, HAMPSHIRE, RG25 3LB.
VALLIS, Mr. Roger Frederick, FCA *1959;* La Bastidiole, 830 Chemin de Bressan, 13760 SAINT CANNAT, FRANCE. (Life Member)
VALT, Mrs. Alyson Juliet, MA ACA *1994;* 4 Regency Terrace, LONDON, SW7 3QW.
VAN, Miss. Le Thuy, BCom ACA *1999;* 74 Courtfield Cres., MARKHAM L6C2R9, ON, CANADA.
VAN, Mr. Rodney, BSc ACA *1993;* 21 Kentchurch Bend, Woburn Park, THE VINES, WA 6069, AUSTRALIA.
VAN AERT, Mrs. Miranda Mary, BA(Hons) ACA *2001;* 15 Damson Crescent, Fair Oak, EASTLEIGH, HAMPSHIRE, SO50 8RD.
VAN ALPHEN, Mr. Rainer Adriaan, FCA *1995;* PricewaterhouseCoopers AG, St Jakobs-Strasse 25, Postfach 4152, 4052 BASEL, SWITZERLAND.
VAN BREDA, Mrs. Karen, BSc ACA *1994;* Robins Croft, 55 Linersh Wood Road, Bramley, GUILDFORD, GU5 0EF.
VAN BUUREN, Mr. Allan, ACA *2010;* 3 Ferngrove Close, Fetcham, LEATHERHEAD, SURREY, KT22 9EQ.
VAN COLLE, Mr. Irwin, FCA *1970;* 1 Greenhill Way, WEMBLEY, HA9 9HL.
VAN DAM, Mr. Hein, ACA CF CA(SA) *2004;* with Deloitte Consultanta SRL, 4-8 Nicolae Titulescu Road, East Wing Entrance, 3rd Floor, Sector 1, 011141 BUCHAREST ROMANIA.
VAN DE WATER, Mr. Michael Neil, ACA *2006;* Unit 68, 1045 Morrison Drive, OTTAWA K2H 7L6, ON, CANADA.
VAN DE WEGHE, Mr. Antoon Jean Willem, MA ACA *1990;* The Berries, Briff Lane, Turners Green, Upper Bucklebury, READING, RG7 6RD.
VAN DEN AARDWEG, Mr. Douglas, ACA CA(SA) *2009;* Fernwood, Herons Croft, WEYBRIDGE, SURREY, KT13 0PL.
•**VAN DEN AREND, Mr. Charles Edward Frederik, BA ACA** *1998;* PricewaterhouseCoopers LLP, The Atrium, 1 Harefield Road, UXBRIDGE, UB8 1EX. See also PricewaterhouseCoopers
VAN DEN BERG, Ms. Madeleine, ACA CA(SA) *2010;* The Chartis Building, 2-8 Altyre Road, CROYDON, CR9 2LG.
VAN DEN BERGH, Mr. Richard John Andrew, MA FCA *1972;* Ditton Park Cottage, Ditton Park Road, Datchet, SLOUGH, SL3 7JB.
VAN DEN BERGH, Miss. Sonja Patricia Maria, LLB ACA *2003;* 88 Cowper Road, HARPENDEN, HERTFORDSHIRE, AL5 5NH.
VAN DEN BROEK, Mr. Adriaan, BSc ACA *1992;* Glenwood, 126 Liberty Lane, ADDLESTONE, KT15 1NL.
VAN DEN DOEL, Ms. Alexandra Christina Elizabeth, BSc ACA *1996;* Kerkstraat 178, Hoogkerk, NL-9745 CN GRONINGEN, NETHERLANDS.
VAN DER BORGH, Mr. Jonathan, FCA *1958;* Bulls Farm, Sedgwick Lane, HORSHAM, RH13 6QE. (Life Member)
VAN DER FLIER, Mr. Eamon Rudolf, BBS FCA *1992;* Western House, 141 High Street, Odiham, HOOK, HAMPSHIRE, RG29 1NW.
VAN DER GRAAF, Mr. John Thomas, FCA *1972;* 4 Priory Road, NEWCASTLE, ST5 2EW. (Life Member)
VAN DER HELM, Mrs. Dolly, BCom FCA *1984;* 24 Chemin de La Lecherette, 1233 GENEVA, SWITZERLAND.
VAN DER HOEK, Mr. Brendan, ACA CA(AUS) *2008;* Lloyds TSB Bank Plc, 25 Gresham Street, LONDON, EC2V 7HN.
VAN DER KLUGT, Mr. Humphrey, BSc FCA *1980;* 5 South Pallant, CHICHESTER, WEST SUSSEX, PO19 1SY.
VAN DER LINDE, Mr. Nils Elmar, MSc ACA *1999;* 7 Alderston Gardens, HADDINGTON, EAST LOTHIAN, EH41 3RY.
VAN DER LINDEN, Mr. Anthony Christiaan, BA FCA *1971;* P.O Box 1268, NOOSAVILLE, QLD 4566, AUSTRALIA.
VAN DER MEULEN, Mrs. Katherine Alexandra, BA ACA *1997;* Honingerdijk 34, 3062 NW ROTTERDAM, NETHERLANDS.
VAN DER PANT, Mr. Gavin Lawrence, BEng ACA *1991;* Halma Plc, Misbourne Court Rectory Way, AMERSHAM, HP7 0DE.
VAN DER SLUIS, Mrs. Beverley Joanne, BA ACA *1992;* 8 Fergus Road, LONDON, N5 1JS.
VAN DER SPUY, Mr. Andre Jacques, ACA *1998;* 84 Park Road, KINGSTON UPON THAMES, SURREY, KT2 5JZ.
VAN DER VELDE, Mr. Jan Cornelis, BEng ACA *1992;* Kit For Kids Ltd, The Clock House, 3-4 Blighs Road, SEVENOAKS, KENT, TN13 1DA.
•**VAN DER VLIET, Miss. Linda Mary, ACA FCCA** *2009;* with Rosscot Limited, Thomas Edge House, Tunnell Street, St Helier, JERSEY, JE2 4LU.
VAN DER VORD, Mr. Andrew David, BA ACA *1990;* J P Morgan, 383 Madison Avenue, NEW YORK, NY 10172, UNITED STATES.
VAN DER WALT, Mrs. Caoilfhionn, MA ACA *2003;* Sasol Group Services (Pty) Limited, PO Box 5486, JOHANNESBURG, 2000, SOUTH AFRICA.
VAN DER WALT, Mr. Paul, MEng ACA MBA *1997;* 11 Marshalls Way, Wheathampstead, ST. ALBANS, HERTFORDSHIRE, AL4 8HZ.
VAN DER WALT, Mrs. Sanet, ACA CA(SA) *2009;* PO Box 1337, WILGEHEUWEL, GAUTENG, 1736, SOUTH AFRICA.
VAN DER WALT, Mr. Stephanus Petrus, ACA CA(SA) *2009;* PO Box 1337, Wilgeheuwer, ROODEPOORT, GAUTENG, 1736, SOUTH AFRICA.
VAN DER WELLE, Mr. Charles Ward, BSc ACA MCT *1986;* 12b Townsend Drive, ST. ALBANS, AL3 5RQ.
VAN DER WELLE, Mr. John Alexander, BSc ACA *1983;* Northlands, 22 Sandpit Lane, ST. ALBANS, HERTFORDSHIRE, AL1 4HL.
VAN DEVENTER, Mr. Michael, ACA CA(SA) *2009;* 5 Dunstable Road, Dagnall, BERKHAMSTED, HERTFORDSHIRE, HP4 1RG.
•**VAN-DOREN, Mr. Kevin Johannes, FCA** *1981;* K.J. Van-Doren, The Northdown, Cranbrook Road, Goudhurst, CRANBROOK, TN17 1DP.
VAN DYK, Mr. Stephen James, MEng ACA *2003;* 13 Clydesdale Gardens, RICHMOND, TW10 5EG.
VAN EGERAAT, Mrs. Kathleen Durnoo, FCA *1952;* Unit 265 Azalea Court, Hopetoun Village, CASTLE HILL, NSW 2154, AUSTRALIA. (Life Member)
•**VAN EMDEN, Mr. Lewis, BSc ACA** *1991;* The AOB Group Limited, Highdale House, 7 Centre Court, Main Avenue, Treforest Industrial Estate, PONTYPRIDD MID GLAMORGAN CF37 5YR.
VAN EUPEN, Mr. Barry, BA FCA *1975;* Meritin Management Ltd, Little Timbers, 8 Pond Chase, COLCHESTER, CO3 4RD.
VAN EYKEN, Mr. John Francis, MSc BA ACA *1981;* Weyside Tunbridge Lane, Bramshott, LIPHOOK, GU30 7SP.
VAN EYKENHOF, Mrs. Elisabeth Claire, BSc ACA *1991;* 10 Sydney Road, GUILDFORD, GU1 3LJ.
VAN GELDER, Mr. Stanley Malcolmm, FCA *1954;* Flat 3a Kingston House South, Ennismore Gardens, LONDON, SW7 1NF. (Life Member)
VAN GURP, Mrs. Clare Mary, ACA *1998;* Sunnyside Cottage The Green, Old Buckenham, ATTLEBOROUGH, NORFOLK, NR17 1RG.
VAN HAAZEL, Mrs. Sarah Lyn, BSc(Hons) ACA MSI *2000;* High Moor View, 173 Lane Head Road, HUDDERSFIELD, WEST YORKSHIRE, HD8 8BL.
VAN HEYNINGEN, Mrs. Jane Lindsey Bourne, BSocSc ACA *2002;* 34 Fernlea Road, LONDON, SW12 9RN.
VAN HIEN, Miss. Indriatti, BA(Hons) ACA *2011;* 22 Cedar Drive, ASCOT, BERKSHIRE, SL5 0UA.
VAN HIEN, Mr. Leonard David Gordon, FCA *1972;* Wisma Bharata, Jalan Surya Kencana No 72. RT 001/05, Pamulang Barat, Tangerang Selatan, JAKARTA, 15417 INDONESIA.
VAN HOUPLINES, Mr. Lee, ACA *2008;* 4 Esher Drive, SALE, CHESHIRE, M33 3PE.
VAN HOUTEN, Mr. Stephen Robert, MA ACA *2002;* Department of Education Rathgael House, 43 Balloo Road, BANGOR, COUNTY DOWN, BT19 7PR.
VAN HOVE, Mrs. Lucy Alexandra, MA ACA *2002;* 90 Balham Park Road, LONDON, SW12 8EA.
VAN INGEN, Mr. John James, FCA *1965;* 131 Ember La, ESHER, KT10 8EH.
VAN KROONENBURG, Miss. Andrea Christine, BA(Hons) ACA *2002;* Michael Page International, 5 Aldermanbury Square, LONDON, EC2V 7HR.
VAN LAMSWEERDE, Mr. Thomas, MRes BSc ACA *2011;* 5 Haigh Side, Rothwell, LEEDS, LS26 0UF.
VAN MESSEL, Mr. Michael Laurent, BSc FCA *1991;* 25 Highcroft Gardens, LONDON, NW11 0LY.

•**VAN NIEKERK, Mrs. Yolande, ACA** *2006;* VN Tax & Accounts, Mashbury Hall, Mashbury, CHELMSFORD, ESSEX, CM1 4TF.
VAN ONSELEN, Mr. Leon, ACA *2009;* Flat 2, 18 Claremont Road, SURBITON, SURREY, KT6 4QU.
VAN PELT, Mr. Christopher Gerard Stephen, FCA *1971;* Wild Acres Forest Drive, Kingswood, TADWORTH, KT20 6LP.
VAN POORTVLIET, Mr. Roger John, BSc ACA *1998;* 134 Bridge Street, Whaddon, ROYSTON, HERTFORDSHIRE, SG8 5SN.
VAN PRAAGH, Mr. Michael, BA ACA *1992;* 40 Sefton Avenue, Mill Hill, LONDON, NW7 3QD.
VAN RAALTE, Mr. Steven Philip, ACA *2006;* 23 Cyprus Street, NORWICH, NR1 3AX.
VAN RANDWYCK, Baron Carel Eduard, FCA *1986;* UBS Investment Bank, 100 Liverpool Street, LONDON, EC2M 2RH.
VAN REENEN, Mr. Michael Roger Geoffrey, FCA *1966;* 4 Rivermead Gardens, CHRISTCHURCH, BH23 2EQ.
VAN ROOTSELAAR, Mr. Wouter, MSc ACA *2011;* Apartment 106, 45 Holloway Road, LONDON, N7 8JW.
VAN RYNEVELD, Mr. Ewan Michael, FCA *1995;* 7 Elmgrove Road, Redland, BRISTOL, BS6 6AH.
VAN SPALL, Mr. Oscar Anthony, FCA *1962;* 66 Sherwood Park Road, SUTTON, SURREY, SM1 2SG. (Life Member)
VAN STAVEREN, Mr. Abel-Thomas, BBA FCA MBA *2001;* Jebsen Asset Management, 4.obergeschoss, Brandschenkestrasse 6, CH8001 ZURICH, SWITZERLAND.
VAN TIJN, Mr. Occo Vincentt, BSc FCA *1976;* 9500 Grasshopper Park Road, RR #1, BOWMANVILLE L1C 3K2, ON, CANADA.
•**VAN VEEN, Mr. Christopher Willem, FCA MBA** *1975;* (Tax Fac), AIMS - Christopher van Veen, 420 Outwood Common Road, BILLERICAY, CM11 1ET.
VAN VELP FERNAND, Mr. Richard, BA ACA *2000;* 102 Bedford Road, LONDON, N2 9DA.
VAN VLIET, Mr. Chris, BA(Hons) ACA *2010;* Kingfisher, Blanches Pierres Lane, St. Martin, GUERNSEY, GY4 6SA.
VAN VLIET, Mr. Richard Christopher, ACA CA(SA) *2011;* (Tax Fac), Kingfisher, Blanches Pierres Lane, St. Martin, GUERNSEY, GY4 6SA.
VAN WIJNGAARDEN, Mr. Justin James, BSc FCA *1994;* 24 Spareleaze Hill, LOUGHTON, IG10 1BT.
VAN ZWANENBERG, Mr. Guy Christopher, FCA *1977;* V Z Limited, Mole End, Crowsley Road, Shiplake, HENLEY-ON-THAMES, OXFORDSHIRE RG9 3LD.
•**VANAGS, Mrs. Samantha Joanne, BA ACA ATII** *1995;* (Tax Fac), Grant Thornton UK LLP, 3140 Rowan Place, John Smith Drive, Oxford Business Park South, OXFORD, OX4 2WB. See also Grant Thornton LLP
VANCE, Mrs. Laura Grace, BA ACA *2007;* International Personal Finance, 3 Leeds City Office Park, Holbeck, LEEDS, LS11 5BD.
VANCE, Mrs. Marion, ACA CA(AUS) *2008;* Rosemount, 60 Portland Villas, HOVE, EAST SUSSEX, BN3 5SB.
VANDAMME, Mr. Tom David, MMath ACA *2007;* Group Audit, Zurich Financial Services The Tri Centre, New Bridge Square, SWINDON, SN1 1HN.
VANDENABEELE, Mr. Cedric Benoit Louis, BA(Hons) ACA *2002;* with Deloitte & Touche, 35/F One Pacific Place, 88 Queensway, CENTRAL, HONG KONG ISLAND, HONG KONG SAR.
VANDERPUIJE, Mrs. Antoinette, BA ACA *2007;* (Tax Fac), 137 Claremont Road, LONDON, NW2 1AH.
VANDERPUMP, Mr. Charles Peter Arthur, BSc FCA *1973;* 1 Bradda Glen Close, Port Erin, ISLE OF MAN, IM9 6PG.
VANDERPUMP, Mr. Robert James, BA FCA *1975;* Hammerden, Stonegate, WADHURST, TN5 7ER.
VANDERPUMP, Mr. William James, BA ACA *2004;* 8 Lovelace Road, LONDON, SE21 8JX.
VANDERSTEEN, Mr. Martin Hugh, FCA *1957;* 2 Bristol Gardens, Putney Heath, LONDON, SW15 3TG. (Life Member)
VANDERVELDE, Mr. Peter Richard Alexander, BSc ACA *1991;* with RSM Tenon Limited, Highfield Court, Tollgate, Chandler's Ford, EASTLEIGH, HAMPSHIRE SO53 3TY.
VANDOME, Mr. Michael John, FCA *1964;* Muninga, Fir Tree Lane, Little Baddow, CHELMSFORD, CM3 4SS.
VANDRILL, Mr. Paul, BA ACA *1990;* 46 Melbourne Avenue, Dronfield Woodhouse, DRONFIELD, S18 8YW.
VANE, Mr. Alexander Chandos Tempest, BSc ACA *1999;* Farnham Springs, Blackpond Lane, Farnham Common, SLOUGH, SL2 3EG.
VANE, Mrs. Bridgeite Elise Demeritt, BSc ACA *2004;* 37 Mona Street, Beeston, NOTTINGHAM, NG9 2BY.
•**VANE, Mr. Christopher James Tempest, FCA** *1973;* Summers Cottage, Dinton, AYLESBURY, HP17 8UG.
VANEZIS, Mr. Christopher Pieris, BSc ACA *1992;* 305 Streetsbrook Road, SOLIHULL, B91 1RS.
VANEZIS, Mr. Pangratios, BA ACA *2006;* 18 Ayiou Dometiou, Archangelos, 2334 NICOSIA, CYPRUS.
•**VANGELATOS, Mrs. Emma, BSc(Hons) ACA** *2004;* Rumford & Co, Conex House, 148 Field End Road, Eastcote, PINNER, MIDDLESEX HA5 1RJ.
VANN, Mr. Geoffrey Douglas, BSc ACA *1979;* 6 South View, Rothwell, LEEDS, LS26 0NT.
VANN, Mrs. Kathryn Michelle, BA ACA *2002;* 40 St. Stephens Avenue, ASHTEAD, SURREY, KT21 1PL.
•**VANN SMITH, Mrs. Joanna, ACA** *1985;* (Tax Fac), C & M Scott Ltd, Unit 1, Leylands Farm Business Park, Colden Common, WINCHESTER, HAMPSHIRE SO21 1TH.
VANNAN, Miss. Emma Louise Eleanor, BA(Hons) ACA MAAT *2010;* 35 Fairoaks Drive, Raunds, WELLINGBOROUGH, NORTHAMPTONSHIRE, NN9 6HJ.
VANNER, Mr. David Reginald, BA FCA *1962;* 104 Stanwell Road, PENARTH, CF64 3LP.
VANNIEKERK, Mr. Jacobus Oostenwald, ACA CA(SA) *2009;* 60 Ann Moss Way, Rotherhithe, LONDON, SE16 2TL.
•**VANNINEN, Miss. Paula Helena, MA ACA** *1996;* Paula Vanninen, Flat 3, 50 Eardley Crescent, LONDON, SW5 9JZ.
VANNOZZI, Mr. Paul, FCA *1975;* (Tax Fac), 12 Ormond Crescent, HAMPTON, MIDDLESEX, TW12 2TH. (Life Member)
VANPERCY, Mr. Paarock Asuman, BA FCA *1993;* P.O. Box 328, Achimota, ACCRA, GHANA.
•**VANSTON, Mrs. Julia Anne, BSc FCA** *1979;* J.A. Cound & Co., Caple Mead, How Caple, HEREFORD, HR1 4TA.
VANSTONE, Mr. David Paul, FCA *1974;* Sutton Park House, Sutton Place, GUILDFORD, GU4 7QL.
VANSTONE, Mr. Paul David, MA ACA *2002;* Catalyst Corporate Finance LLP, 5th Floor, 12-18 Grosvenor Gardens, LONDON, SW1W 0DH.
VANSTONE, Mrs. Rebecca, BSc ACA *2003;* 14 Birchfield Close, Tonteg, PONTYPRIDD, CF38 1NS.
•**VANZA, Mr. Bharat Amratlal, ACA FCCA** *2010;* Sterling, 505 Pinner Road, HARROW, MIDDLESEX, HA2 6EH.
VARA, Mr. Metesh, BSc ACA *2008;* 14 Gloster House, 49 Rouge Bouillon St. Helier, JERSEY, JE2 3ZA.
VARACHIA, Mrs. Claire, BA ACA *2002;* Tennyson House, 5 Rockingham Close, Dorridge, SOLIHULL, B93 8EH.
VARAH, Mr. David John Raphael, FCA *1972;* 12 Lounts Crescent, Great Easton, MARKET HARBOROUGH, LE16 8SX.
VARAH, Miss. Gayle Suzanne, BA ACA *2002;* 12 St. Kentigerns Way, Aspatria, WIGTON, CUMBRIA, CA7 3BY.
VARATHARAJAH, Mr. Sinnathamby, FCA *1970;* Faculty of Business & Law, Multimedia University, Jalan Ayer Keroh Lama, Bukit Beruang, 75450 MALACCA, MELACCA STATE MALAYSIA.
VARCOE, Mr. Brian Richard, FCA *1959;* Walford House, 3 Riverside, Combwich, BRIDGWATER, SOMERSET, TA5 2QX. (Life Member)
VARCOE, Mr. Myles Grosvenor, FCA *1956;* Perlees Meadow, St. Breock, WADEBRIDGE, PL27 7HU. (Life Member)
VARCOE, Mrs. Pamela Elizabeth, LLB ACA *1990;* 105 Thingwall Park, Fishponds, BRISTOL, BS16 2AR.
VARCOE, Dr. Richard Antony Bruce, ACA *1992;* 105 Thingwall Park, BRISTOL, BS16 2AR.
VARDIGANS, Mr. Simon Geoffrey, BSc ACA *1986;* 19 Mayfield Avenue, Chiswick, LONDON, W4 1PN.
VARDON, Mr. James Lewes, BA FCA *1966;* Holman's Place, Butleigh, GLASTONBURY, BA6 8SZ. (Life Member)
VARDON, Mrs. Sarah, ACA MAAT *2003;* Slieve Gallion, La Rue D'Elysee, St. Peter, JERSEY, JE3 7DT.
VARDON, Mr. Simon Michael, ACA *2003;* Slieve Gallion La Rue D'Elysee, St. Peter, JERSEY, JE3 7DT.
VARDY, Mr. James, BA ACA *2004;* with Mazars LLP, Tower Bridge House, St. Katharines Way, LONDON, E1W 1DD.
VARE, Mr. William Anthony Normanton, BCom FCA *1975;* The Old Rectory Dumbs Lane, Hainford, NORWICH, NR10 3BH.
VARELLA, Miss. Chrysanthi, BA ACA *2011;* 6 Nikis Street, Carisa Nafsica Court, Flat 203, Mesa Yitoma, 4003 LIMASSOL, CYPRUS.
VARIA, Mr. Dipesh Yogendra, BA(Hons) ACA *2003;* 91 St. Ethelbert Avenue, LUTON, LU3 1QJ.
VARIAN, Mr. David Ian Alfred, BBS ACA *1992;* Varian Financial Services, 11 Foxrock Manor, Leopardstown Road, Foxrock, DUBLIN 18, COUNTY DUBLIN IRELAND.
VARIANOS, Mr. Christopher, BSc ACA *1993;* C.Varianos Co Ltd, P.O.Box 23397, 1682 NICOSIA, CYPRUS.
•**VARLEY, Mr. Cameron Joseph, BEng ACA** *2000;* BlueSky Corporate Finance Ltd, Milestone Farm, 56-58 Westgate, North Cave, BROUGH, NORTH HUMBERSIDE HU15 2NJ.
•**VARLEY, Mr. Christopher Keith, BSc FCA** *1984;* Cedar Solutions (Management) Ltd, Prospect House, 2 Sinderland Road, Broadheath, ALTRINCHAM, CHESHIRE WA14 5ET. See also HLM Secretaries Limited
VARLEY, Mr. Christopher Raymond, BSc FCA *1983;* 9 Island View Avenue, Friars Cliff, CHRISTCHURCH, BH23 4DS.
VARLEY, Mr. David Harry, FCA *1973;* Magrini Limited, Unit 5, Maybrook Ind Estate, Brownhills, WALSALL, WS8 7DG.
VARLEY, Ms. Dawn, BSc ACA *1995;* Route d'Hermance 332C, Anieres, 1247 GENEVA, SWITZERLAND.
VARLEY, Mr. Gary David, BSc ACA *1998;* Eredene Capital, Level 19 Waterfront Place, 1 Eagle St, BRISBANE, QLD 4000, AUSTRALIA.
•**VARLEY, Mrs. Heather Marion, BSc ACA** *2001;* with PricewaterhouseCoopers LLP, 101 Barbirolli Square, Lower Mosley Street, MANCHESTER, M2 3PW.
VARLEY, Miss. Helen, FCA *1994;* 37 Holmfield Avenue, Stoneygate, LEICESTER, LE2 2BG.
VARLEY, Mrs. Helen Frances, FCA *1977;* Hathaway, 90 The Street, West Horsley, LEATHERHEAD, KT24 6BE.
•**VARLEY, Mr. James Andrew, BSc ACA DChA** *1989;* Deane Consulting Limited, 42 Deane Croft Road, PINNER, MIDDLESEX, HA5 1SR.
VARLEY, Mr. James Gilbert, FCA *1973;* Eyton Old Hall, Eyton, LEOMINSTER, HR6 0AQ.
VARLEY, Mr. John Edward Thomas, BSc ACA *1992;* 12 Ivy Lane, Boston Spa, WETHERBY, LS23 6PP.
VARLEY, Mrs. Katherine Dorcas, BSc ACA *1992;* 12 Ivy Lane, Boston Spa, WETHERBY, WEST YORKSHIRE, LS23 6PP.
•**VARLEY, Mr. Kenneth Roger, BCom FCA** *1967;* Rawse Varley & Co, Lloyds Bank Chambers, Hustlergate, BRADFORD, BD1 1UQ.
VARLEY, Mr. Michael, FCA *1971;* 6 Copper Beech Court, Walton, WAKEFIELD, WF2 6TD.
VARLEY, Mr. Nigel Richard, BCom ACA MSI *2000;* with Deloitte LLP, 4 Brindley Place, BIRMINGHAM, B1 2HZ.
•**VARLEY, Mr. Peter, BA ACA CF** *1989;* Crowe Clark Whitehill LLP, St Bride's House, 10 Salisbury Square, LONDON, EC4Y 8EH. See also Horwath Clark Whitehill LLP and Crowe Clark Whitehill
VARLEY, Mr. Philip Graham, MBA FCA *1983;* 1 Mountain Cedar Lane, LITTLETON, CO 80127, UNITED STATES.
•**VARLEY, Mr. Philip Michael, BA FCA** *1975;* Rawse Varley & Co, Lloyds Bank Chambers, Hustlergate, BRADFORD, BD1 1UQ.
VARLEY, Mr. Robert George, FCA *1963;* 1 The Old Court House, Maiden Street, Stratton, BUDE, EX23 9DQ.
VARLEY, Mr. Rodney Richard, FCA *1970;* 99 Knightlow Road, Harborne, BIRMINGHAM, B17 8PX.
VARLEY, Mr. William Robin, FCA *1970;* 43 Calico Drive, SHERWOOD PARK T8A 5P2, AB, CANADA.
VARMA, Mr. Abhay, BA ACA *1998;* 3 Valencia Road, STANMORE, MIDDLESEX, HA7 4JL.
VARMA, Miss. Aikta, ACA *2010;* Apartment 218, City Gate 3, 5 Blantyre Street, MANCHESTER, M15 4JJ.
VARMA, Miss. Anshu, LLB ACA *2003;* Flat 31 Aura House, 39 Melliss Avenue, RICHMOND, TW9 4BX.
•**VARMA, Mr. Ashok, FCA** *1980;* Avar & Company Limited, Avar Suite 2.8, Central House, 1 Ballards Lane, LONDON, N3 1LQ. See also Avar Consulting Ltd and Statutory Auditors LLP
VARMA, Mr. Danesh Kumar, FCA *1974;* Brook Corporate Finance, Painters Hall Chambers, 8 Little Trinity Lane, LONDON, EC4V 2AP.
VARMA, Mr. Dilip Raja Moshe, BSc ACA *1983;* Financial Reporting Council Aldwych House, 71-91 Aldwych, LONDON, WC2B 4HN.
VARMA, Mr. Jagdish Chander, FCA *1957;* 1-5 Rowland Road, CALCUTTA 700 020, INDIA. (Life Member)
VARMA, Mr. Nishant, ACA *2011;* 32 Hillwood Grove, Hutton, BRENTWOOD, ESSEX, CM13 2PD.
VARMA, Mr. Rajan, BCom ACA *1981;* 95 Sundernagar, NEW DELHI 110003, INDIA.
VARMA, Mr. Sohan Lal, FCA *1965;* 3025 Cedar Ave, MONTREAL H3Y 1Y8, QUE, CANADA.
VARMEN, Mr. Richard John David, FCA *1973;* Ivy Farm, Common Farm Lane, Snelson, MACCLESFIELD, CHESHIRE, SK11 9BJ.
VARNAVA, Mr. Paul Andrew, BSc ACA *1994;* Flat 23 Pied Bull Court, Galen Place, LONDON, WC1A 2JR.
VARNEY, Mr. Adrian Simon, BSc ACA *1994;* (Tax Fac), L I F F E, Cannon Bridge House, 1 Cousin Lane, LONDON, EC4R 3XX.
VARNEY, Mr. Andrew Jonathan, BSc ACA *1989;* Biernfels Old Odiham Road, ALTON, GU34 4BW.
VARNEY, Mrs. Anne Felicity, BSc ACA *1986;* Biernfels Old Odiham Road, ALTON, GU34 4BW.
VARNEY, Mr. Craig, ACA CA(SA) *2009;* 80 Hamilton Road, Wimbledon, LONDON, SW19 1JF.
VARNEY, Mr. Henry, BA ACA *1999;* 2 Saw Mill Lane, Addingham, ILKLEY, WEST YORKSHIRE, LS29 0ST.
•**VARNEY, Mr. Keith Bernard, FCA** *1966;* (Tax Fac), Varney & Co, 46 Mile End Road, Highweek, NEWTON ABBOT, TQ12 1RW.
VARNEY, Mr. Nicholas, LLB ACA *1987;* Holly House, Spencers Lane, Berkswell, COVENTRY, CV7 7BZ.
VARNEY, Mr. Paul, FCA *1969;* The Cottage, Leamington Hastings, RUGBY, CV23 8DZ. (Life Member)
VARNEY, Mr. Richard Norman, BA FCA *1975;* Linton House North Moor Easingwold, YORK, NORTH YORKSHIRE, YO61 3NB.
VARNHAM, Mr. Jonathan, ACA *2010;* 6/1A Brisbane Street, LAUNCESTON, TAS 7250, AUSTRALIA.
VARRO, Mrs. Claire Marie, ACA *2002;* 68 Rosedale Road, GLEN IRIS, VIC 3146, AUSTRALIA.
VARSANI, Mr. Jay, ACA *2009;* 169 Camrose Avenue, EDGWARE, MIDDLESEX, HA8 6DG.
VARSANI, Mr. Manohar Premji, BA ACA *1989;* 49 Elliot Road, Hendon, LONDON, NW4 3DN.
VARSANI, Mr. Rajesh, BSc(Hons) ACA *2000;* 38 Colvin Gardens, Wanstead, LONDON, E11 2DD.
VARSHANI, Mr. Sandeep Kunvarji Shivji, BA ACA *1993;* THE MOORINGS, 6 Lytton Road, PINNER, HA5 4RH.
VARTHOLOMIS, Mr. Vartholomeos Panayiotis, BA ACA *1991;* 14 Kenwood Avenue, LONDON, N14 4SR.
•**VARTY, Mr. Paul Andrew, BA ACA** *1986;* (Tax Fac), Paul Varty, 24 St Cuthberts Way, DARLINGTON, DL1 1GB.
VARU, Mr. Jayesh, MA BSc(Hons) ACA *2001;* 27 Heathley Park Drive, LEICESTER, LE3 9EQ.
VARU, Mr. Manoj Kantilal, BA ACA CTA *1992;* Dalmeny, 2a Monahan Avenue, PURLEY, SURREY, CR8 3BA.
VARZINA, Ms. Ksenia, BA ACA *2011;* 26 Archimidous Street, App. 102, Ayios Dhometios, 2365 NICOSIA, CYPRUS.
VAS, Mr. Vincent Anthony, BSc ACA *1984;* 1/4 Crowther Avn, Greenwich, SYDNEY, NSW 2065, AUSTRALIA.
VASANJI, Mr. Nasirdin Noormohamed, ACA *1979;* 768 Hill Rise Lane, Cordova Bay, VICTORIA V8Y 3K2, BC, CANADA.
•**VASDEV, Mr. Hari Om, MEng ACA** *2004;* Sibbalds Ltd, Oakhurst House, 57 Ashbourne Road, DERBY, DE22 3FS.
VASDEV, Mr. Yogeshwar Chander, BSc ACA *1979;* 10 Wheeler Avenue, Tylers GreenPenn, HIGH WYCOMBE, HP10 8EN.
VASEY, Mr. Andrew David, ACA *2008;* 14 Mill Vale, NEWCASTLE UPON TYNE, NE15 8HF.
•**VASEY, Mr. Charles Harold, LLB FCA FTII** *1982;* (Tax Fac), Charles Vasey & Co, 75 Richmond Park Road, East Sheen, LONDON, SW14 8JY. See also Vasey Charles
VASEY, Mr. George Andrew, FCA *1971;* 14 Bluebell Close, DARLINGTON, DL3 0YU.
VASEY, Mr. Gilbert Thomas, MSc ACA *1994;* 4 Moatlands, Wickersley, ROTHERHAM, S66 1DQ.
VASEY, Mr. Nigel, BA ACA *1992;* 2 Jacombe Close, WARWICK, WARWICKSHIRE, CV34 6JN.
VASEY, Mr. Stephen Gavin, FCA *1972;* 78 Brookfield Crescent, Hampsthwaite, HARROGATE, NORTH YORKSHIRE, HG3 2EE.
VASHISHT, Mr. Arvind, BSc ACA *1990;* Flat 17 Mandeville Court, Finchley Road, LONDON, NW3 6HB.
VASI, Mr. Hooseini Haider, FCA *1966;* Petrochem Middle East, P.O. Box 23910, DUBAI, UNITED ARAB EMIRATES.
VASI, Miss. Tasneem, ACA *1992;* 47 Chuan Drive, Chuan Vista, SINGAPORE 554848, SINGAPORE.

VASILIOU, Mr. Andreas, ACA *2008;* 50 Tetney Road, Humberston, GRIMSBY, SOUTH HUMBERSIDE, DN36 4JF.
•**VASILIOU, Mr. Christos, BA FCA CF** *1994;* KPMG, 14 Esperidon Street, 1087 NICOSIA, CYPRUS. See also KPMG Metaxas Loizides Syrimis
VASILIOU, Mr. Michalis, BSc ACA *2011;* 59 Dimitriou Hamatsou, Dali, 2540 NICOSIA, CYPRUS.
VASLET, Mrs. Jane Elizabeth, BSc ACA *1988;* 4 Coniston Crescent, Redmarshall, STOCKTON-ON-TEES, TS21 1HT.
VASOU, Miss. Terpsoula, BA ACA *2007;* Kanari 4, Timi, 8507 PAPHOS, CYPRUS.
VASS, Miss. Rebecca Louise, BSc(Hons) ACA *2003;* with PricewaterhouseCoopers, Royal Trust Tower, Suite 3000 TD Centre, Box 82, 77 King Street West, TORONTO M5K 1G8 ON CANADA.
•**VASS, Mr. Richard Leslie, BA ACA** *1992;* Price Bailey Private Client LLP, 7th Floor Dashwood House, 69 Old Broad Street, LONDON, EC2M 1QS. See also Price Bailey LLP
VASS, Mr. Steven Roland, BA ACA *1991;* 21 Rayleigh Road, Coombe Dingle, BRISTOL, BS9 2AU.
VASSALLO, Mr. Michael, BA ACA *2002;* Brewin Dolphin Time Central, 32 Gallowgate, NEWCASTLE UPON TYNE, NE1 4SR.
VASSAR, Mr. Stephen Peter, ACA *2008;* 45 Tyne Road, AYLESBURY, BUCKINGHAMSHIRE, HP21 9JS.
VASSIB, Prince Osman Selaheddin, FCA *1965;* 7 Kingfisher Close, ABINGDON, OX14 5NP. (Life Member)
•**VASSILIADES, Mr. Aristos Nicolaou, BSc(Econ) ACA FCCA** *2009;* Nicos A. Vassiliades & Sons Limited, PO Box 60112, 8100 PAPHOS, CYPRUS.
VASSILIADES, Mr. Panayiotis, BSc ACA *2008;* Kritonos 8, Agios Athanasios, CY-4106 LIMASSOL, CYPRUS.
•**VASSILIADES, Mr. Thrasos, FCA** *1982;* EA (UK) LLP, 869 High Road, LONDON, N12 8QA. See also EA Associates
•**VASSILIOU, Mr. Demetrakis, FCA** *1982;* Shipleys LLP, 10 Orange Street, Haymarket, LONDON, WC2H 7DQ.
VASSILIOU, Miss. Despo, ACA *2011;* 41A Ayiou Pavlou Archangelos, 2334 NICOSIA, CYPRUS.
VASSILIOU, Mr. Diomedes Efthymiou, BSc ACA *1997;* 6 Piliou Street, Dionysos, 145 76 ATHENS, ATTIKI, GREECE.
VASSILIOU, Mr. Leontios, ACA *2008;* PO Box 53298, 3301 LIMASSOL, CYPRUS.
VASSILIOU, Mr. Michalis, MSc ACA *2011;* 16 Christou Mantika, 4154 LIMASSOL, CYPRUS.
VASSILIOU, Mr. Michalis, MSc BA ACA *2011;* Flat 301, 4 Karaiskaki Street, Acropolis, NICOSIA, CYPRUS.
VASSILIOU, Mr. Stelios, BSc ACA *2006;* VASHIOTIS LOUKAS COURT, FLAT 402, 7 MANOLI KALOMIRI STREET, CY-3030 LIMASSOL, CYPRUS.
VASSILIOU, Miss. Vassiliki, BSc ACA *2007;* 5 Othonos street, Flat 301, Engomi, 2414 NICOSIA, CYPRUS.
•**VASSILOUNIS, Mr. Nicholas Antony, BA FCA** *1993;* Mitchell Gordon LLP, 43 Coniscliffe Road, DARLINGTON, COUNTY DURHAM, DL3 7EH.
•**VASWANI, Mr. Mahesh, BA FCA** *1991;* (Tax Fac), Vaswani & Co, 29a Hendon Avenue, Finchley Central, LONDON, N3 1UJ.
VASWANI, Miss. Sunita, BA ACA *2011;* 49 Dowsefield Lane, LIVERPOOL, L18 3JG.
VAUDREY, John Randle, Esq MBE FCA *1946;* Warren Lodge, Warren Lane, Finchampstead, WOKINGHAM, BERKSHIRE, RG40 4HR. (Life Member)
•**VAUDREY, Mr. Thomas Henry, BSc ACA** *1983;* Keith Vaudrey & Co, First Floor, 15 Young Street, LONDON, W8 5EH.
•**VAUGHAN, Mr. Alan John, FCA** *1967;* (Tax Fac), 13 Rockwell Avenue, Kingsweston, BRISTOL, BS11 0UF.
VAUGHAN, Mrs. Alexandra Fern, MA ACA *2001;* 18 Swains Lane, Flackwell Heath, HIGH WYCOMBE, BUCKINGHAMSHIRE, HP10 9BU.
VAUGHAN, Mrs. Alison Elizabeth, BSc ACA *1984;* 43 Calton Avenue, LONDON, SE21 7DF.
VAUGHAN, Mrs. Amanda Jayne, BSc ACA *2006;* 17 Coppice Lane, Hammerwich, BURNTWOOD, STAFFORDSHIRE, WS7 0JX.
VAUGHAN, Miss. Catherine Maria, BAcc ACA *2000;* 449 Orwell Park Green, Templeogue, DUBLIN 6, COUNTY DUBLIN, IRELAND.
•**VAUGHAN, Mr. Christopher, BA FCA** *1975;* Reeves & Co, Argyle commercial Centre, Argyle Street, SWINDON, SN2 6AR.
VAUGHAN, Mr. David Andrew, BSc FCA *1980;* 5 Castle Close, Flax Bourton, BRISTOL, BS48 3RG.
•**VAUGHAN, Mr. David Barry, BA ACA** *1986;* Vaughan & Company, Telford House, 1 Claremont Bank, SHREWSBURY, SY1 1RW.
VAUGHAN, Mr. David Bertram, FCA *1958;* 5 Wilton Street, LONDON, SW1X 7AF. (Life Member)
VAUGHAN, Mr. David John, BSocSc ACA *1987;* 23 Waverley Place, Off Adolphus Road, Finsbury Park, LONDON, N4 2BU.
VAUGHAN, Mr. David Keith, FCA CTA *1982;* Mace Limited, Atelier House, 64 Pratt Street, LONDON, NW1 0LF.
•**VAUGHAN, Mr. David Lewis, BSc ACA** *1981;* Ernst & Young LLP, 1 More London Place, LONDON, SE1 2AF. See also Ernst & Young Europe LLP
•**VAUGHAN, Mr. David Robin, BSc FCA FCCA** *1993;* (Tax Fac), Ashmole & Co, Abertawe House, Ystrad Road, Fforestfach, SWANSEA, SA5 4JB.
VAUGHAN, Mr. Douglas James, FCA *1957;* 2 The Crescent, Felpham, BOGNOR REGIS, WEST SUSSEX, PO22 7HB. (Life Member)
VAUGHAN, Mr. Edgar Keith, FCA *1956;* 45 Oakridge Avenue, RADLETT, HERTFORDSHIRE, WD7 8EW. (Life Member)
VAUGHAN, Mrs. Emily Elizabeth, BSc ACA *2003;* V I Distribution Ltd Unit 7-8, Springvale Business Centre Millbuck Way, SANDBACH, CHESHIRE, CW11 3HY.
VAUGHAN, Mr. George Philip, ACA *2009;* Flat 3 Clayton House, 50 Trinity Church Road, LONDON, SW13 8EL.
VAUGHAN, Mrs. Jane Margaret, BSc ACA *1992;* The Old Rectory, Ridlington, RUTLAND, LEICESTERSHIRE, LE15 9AU.
•**VAUGHAN, Mr. Jeremy, BSc ACA** *1997;* Ernst & Young LLP, 1 More London Place, LONDON, SE1 2AF. See also Ernst & Young Europe LLP
VAUGHAN, Mr. Jeremy John, FCA *1975;* 75 Coombe Vale, Saltdean, BRIGHTON, BN2 8HN. (Life Member)
VAUGHAN, Mr. John Martin, FCA *1973;* Iko Industries Ltd., Suite 602, 1 Yorkdale Rd., TORONTO M6A 3A1, ON, CANADA.
VAUGHAN, Mr. Laurence Edward William, BA ACA *1990;* Opus Ventures LLP, The Giraffe House, Burrough Court, Burrough on the Hill, MELTON MOWBRAY, LEICESTERSHIRE LE14 2QS.
VAUGHAN, Miss. Margaret Helen, BA FCA *1991;* Court Lodge, Vanity Lane, Linton, MAIDSTONE, KENT, ME17 4BP.
•**VAUGHAN, Mrs. Mary, BA ACA** *2001;* (Tax Fac), byte size accounting, 70 Pilley Crescent, CHELTENHAM, GLOUCESTERSHIRE, GL53 9ET.
VAUGHAN, Mr. Mathew Gareth, MA ACA *2003;* British Salt Ltd, Cledford Lane, MIDDLEWICH, CHESHIRE, CW10 0JP.
VAUGHAN, Mr. Maxwell Lucas, BEng ACA MBA AMCT *1997;* Windrush, 9 The Common, Quarndon, DERBY, DE22 5JY.
VAUGHAN, Mr. Michael, ACA *2011;* 23 Quinn Way, LETCHWORTH GARDEN CITY, HERTFORDSHIRE, SG6 2TX.
VAUGHAN, Mr. Michael Anthony, BSc ACA *2002;* 23 Harebell Close, Huntington, CHESTER, CH3 6RT.
VAUGHAN, Mr. Oliver, BA ACA *2009;* The Cottage, The Square, Hanmer, WHITCHURCH, SHROPSHIRE, SY13 3DE.
•**VAUGHAN, Mr. Peter Thomas, FCA** *1964;* P.T. Vaughan, 31 Temples Court, Helpston, PETERBOROUGH, PE6 7EU.
VAUGHAN, Mr. Richard Charles, FCA *1966;* Richard Vaughan & Co, The Newstead, Main Street, Tugby, LEICESTER, LE7 9WD.
VAUGHAN, Mr. Richard David Crofts, FCA *1977;* 134 Lots Road, LONDON, SW10 0RJ.
VAUGHAN, Mr. Richard Ifor, BA ACA *1989;* 21 Chingford Road, LONDON, E17 4PW.
•**VAUGHAN, Mr. Richard Leslie, FCA MBCS** *1960;* (Tax Fac), R.L. Vaughan & Co, Mortimer House, 40 Chatsworth Parade, Queensway, Petts Wood, ORPINGTON KENT BR5 1DE.
•**VAUGHAN, Mr. Roger Albert, FCA** *1973;* (Tax Fac), Cassonbeckman.co.uk Limited, Rose Villa, Reading Road, Mattingley, HOOK, HAMPSHIRE RG27 8JZ.
VAUGHAN, Mr. Seth, BA ACA *2007;* Clydesdale Bank Plc, Corporate and Structure Finance, 4 Victoria Place, Holbeck, LEEDS, LS11 5AE.
VAUGHAN, Mr. Timothy John Maurice, MA FCA *1985;* 1 Monkhams Farm Barns, Monkhams, WALTHAM ABBEY, EN9 2EP.
VAUGHAN-JACKSON, Mr. Colin James, FCA *1974;* Milden Cottage, Charlton Horethorne, SHERBORNE, DT9 4PB.
VAUGHAN-OWEN, Mr. Andrew, MSc ACA *2000;* 18 Pant y Sais, Jersey Marine, NEATH, WEST GLAMORGAN, SA10 6JS.
VAUGHAN-WILLIAMS, Mrs. Anne May, BSc ACA *1992;* 41 Saxon Way, Bradley Stoke, BRISTOL, BS32 9AR.
VAUGHAN-WILLIAMS, Mr. Jonathan, BSc ACA *1992;* 41 Saxon Way, Bradley Stoke North, BRISTOL, BS32 9AR.
VAUGHTON, Mr. Gary, ACA *2008;* 8 Barden Drive, BARNSLEY, SOUTH YORKSHIRE, S75 2QT.
VAUGHTON, Mr. Philip Nicholas, FCA *1970;* Kingswood, 5 Loudwater Ridge, Loudwater, RICKMANSWORTH, WD3 4AR. (Life Member)
VAULKS, Mr. Christopher, ACA *2011;* K P M G Quayside House, 110 Quayside, NEWCASTLE UPON TYNE, NE1 3DX.
•**VAUSE, Mr. Alan Charles, FCA** *1954;* Alan Vause, Wood End, High Cotts Lane, West Clandon, GUILDFORD, GU4 7XA.
•**VAUSE, Mr. Andrew Nigel, BSc FCA** *1984;* Godfrey Holland Limited, Venture House, 341 Palatine Road, Northenden, MANCHESTER, M22 4FY.
VAUSE, Mr. Arthur Halliday, MA BA FCA *1966;* 2 Links Road, Kennington, OXFORD, OX1 5RX.
VAUTIER, Mrs. Lynda Jayne, BSc FCA *1989;* FML Trust & Corporate Services, Mielles House, La Rue Des Mielles, St. Helier, JERSEY, JE2 3QD.
VAUTIER, Mr. Stephen John, BSc ACA *2001;* Lubborn Cheese Ltd, Manor Farm, Cricket St. Thomas, CHARD, SOMERSET, TA20 4BZ.
VAUX, Mr. Benedict, BA(Hons) ACA *2011;* 16 Hillbank View, HARROGATE, NORTH YORKSHIRE, HG1 4DR.
VAUX, Mr. Kevin John, BA ACA *1984;* UK Greetings Limited, Mill Street East, DEWSBURY, WF12 9AW.
VAUX, Mr. Martin, BSc ACA *1984;* 171 Foxon Lane, CATERHAM, CR3 5SH.
VAUX, Mrs. Sandra, BA ACA *1993;* Eurodirect Ltd, 1 Park Lane, LEEDS, LS3 1EP.
VAWDA, Ms. Sarah Bibi, BA ACA *1992;* 21 Paines Lane, PINNER, MIDDLESEX, HA5 3DF.
VAYIANOS, Mr. Demetrios, BA(Hons) ACA *2011;* 91 Phaneromenis Street, 6031 LARNACA, CYPRUS.
VAZ, Mr. Derek Alan, BSc FCA *1992;* Lloyds TSB Bank plc, Staten Bolwerk, 2011 Mk Haarlem, PO Box 2092, HAARLEM, NOORD HOLLAND NETHERLANDS.
VAZE, Mr. Sunil Madhukar, BSc ACA *1993;* D102 West End Village, Bhusari Colony, Paude Road, PUNE 411 030, MAHARASHTRA, INDIA.
VAZIRANI, Mr. Avinash, ACA *1987;* 4 Gloucester Square, LONDON, W2 2TJ.
VAZIRANI, Mrs. Priya, BSc ACA *1991;* 4 Gloucester Square, LONDON, W2 2TJ.
•**VEAL, Mr. Alan, FCA** *1979;* 4 Blakeney Close, Bearsted, MAIDSTONE, ME14 4QF.
VEAL, Mr. Edward, MChem ACA *2007;* Flat D 35/F Moon Tower (2A), The Arch, 1 Austin Road West, TSIM SHA TSUI, KOWLOON, HONG KONG SAR.
VEAL, Mrs. Jane Anne, BSc *1983;* 4 Blakeney Close, Bearsted, MAIDSTONE, ME14 4QF.
VEAL, Mr. Matthew John, BA ACA *1992;* 5 Kildare Avenue, Glendowie, AUCKLAND, NEW ZEALAND.
VEAL, Mr. Peter James, FCA *1963;* 1 Pembroke Mansions, Oakfield Road, BRISTOL, BS8 2AH.
VEAL, Mr. Robert Alan, FCA *1967;* 9 Heron Way, HORSHAM, RH13 6DP. (Life Member)
VEALE, Mrs. Alison Mary, FCA *1971;* 4 Plough Close, Cranfield, BEDFORD, MK43 0DN.
VEALE, Mr. Denis Robert, FCA *1961;* 15 Burleigh Manor, Torr Lane Hartley, PLYMOUTH, PL3 5NT. (Life Member)
VEALE, Mr. Gordon James, FCA *1972;* 100 Hartley Down, PURLEY, CR8 4EB.
•**VEALE, Mr. Michael Alan, FCA** *1971;* 4 Plough Close, Cranfield, BEDFORD, MK43 0DN.
VEALE, Mr. Michael John, BSocSc ACA *2000;* Wells Fargo Bank Plantation Place, 30 Fenchurch Street, LONDON, EC3M 3BD.
•**VEALL, Mr. Malcolm Peter, LLB ACA** *1988;* (Tax Fac), Malcolm Veall & Co Ltd, 60 Howard Road, LEICESTER, LE2 1XH.
VEALL, Mrs. Nicola Jane, MA ACA *1987;* 1a Hawthorne Drive, LEICESTER, LE5 6DL.
VEAR, Miss. Deborah Catherine, BA ACA *2005;* 44 Churchill Way, PLYMOUTH, PL3 4PS.
VEAR, Mr. Harold Arthur Julian, MA FCA *1962;* PO Box 529, FRANKSTON, VIC 3199, AUSTRALIA. (Life Member)
VEARES, Mr. Howard Richard, LLB ACA *1998;* (Tax Fac), Apartment 19, Belvoir House, 181 Vauxhall Bridge Road, LONDON, SW1V 1ER.
VEARY, Mr. Howard Wagner, BA FCA *1976;* Herons Landing, Hollybush Ride, Finchampstead, WOKINGHAM, RG40 3QR.
VEASEY, Mr. Allan Arthur, FCA *1949;* Meadow View, Main Street, Foxton, MARKET HARBOROUGH, LE16 7RB. (Life Member)
VEASEY, Mr. Graham Robert, BA ACA *1990;* 7 Melba Place, THORNLIE, WA 6147, AUSTRALIA.
VEASEY, Mrs. Lisa Jeanette, BSc ACA *1996;* Hotzenmattstrasse 8, 8915 HAUSEN AM ALBIS, SWITZERLAND.
VEASEY, Mr. Sherard Jeremy, BSc ACA *1992;* 7 Polstead Road, OXFORD, OX2 6TW.
VEASEY, Mr. Simon John, BA ACA *2004;* 136 East Hill, LONDON, SW18 2HF.
VECK, Miss. Julie Ann, ACA *1988;* 7 Woodland Walk, Ovingdean, BRIGHTON, BN2 7AR.
VED, Mr. Carlos Prakash Kanakshi, BSc ACA *1989;* Rua Do Sacramento A Lapa 47, Bloco A1 Esq, 1200-793 LISBON, PORTUGAL.
•**VED, Mr. Jayendra Janardan, FCA** *1989;* (Tax Fac), Sterling Associates, 5 Theobald Court, Theobald Street, Elstree, BOREHAMWOOD, HERTFORDSHIRE WD6 4RN. See also A U Chauhan Limited
VEDHERA, Mr. Deven, BA(Hons) ACA *2011;* 24 Redewater Road, NEWCASTLE UPON TYNE, NE4 9UD.
VEDI, Mr. Anu Kiran, CBE ACA *1981;* Silver Springs Over the Misbourne Road, Denham, UXBRIDGE, UB9 5DR.
•**VEDI, Mr. Vishal, MA ACA** *1998;* Deloitte LLP, Hill House, 1 Little New Street, LONDON, EC4A 3TR. See also Deloitte & Touche LLP
•**VEEDER, Mr. Terence, FCA** *1969;* Edwards Veeder LLP, Alex House, 260-268 Chapel Street, SALFORD, M3 5JZ.
•**VEELENTURF, Mrs. Emma Lydia, BSc(Hons) ACA** *1992;* Emma Veelenturf BSc ACA, 51 Victoria Road, OXFORD, OX2 7QF.
VEENHUIS, Mr. Darren, ACA CA(SA) *2010;* Deutsche Bank, Winchester House, 1 Great Winchester Street, LONDON, EC2N 2DB.
VEERAPPAN, Mr. Barathan, BSc ACA *1985;* 33 Fairway, CARSHALTON, SM5 4HR.
VEERASAMY, Mrs. Soo Lee, ACA *1984;* 12 Craven Gardens, Wimbledon, LONDON, SW19 8LU.
VEERASINGHAM, Miss. Beatrice Roshnie, BA ACA *1997;* 98 Tutsham Way, Paddock Wood, TONBRIDGE, TN12 6UB.
VEERMAN, Mr. Robert Arnold, BSc ACA *1984;* Pentaren Cottage, Mansfield Road, Heath, CHESTERFIELD, S44 5SE.
•**VEGA-LOZANO, Miss. Helena, BA ACA** *1999;* Deloitte LLP, Stonecutter Court, 1 Stonecutter Street, LONDON, EC4A 4TR. See also Deloitte & Touche LLP
•**VEGLIO, Mr. Howard Martin, MA FCA** *1975;* with Chantrey Vellacott DFK LLP, Russell Square House, 10-12 Russell Square, LONDON, WC1B 5LF.
VEILLARD, Mr. Antony Robert, BSc FCA *2000;* Saffery Champness, La Tonnelle House, Les Banques, St Sampson, GUERNSEY, GY1 3HS.
VEILLARD, Mr. Brian Eugene, FCA *1956;* Aigle Houmtel Lane, Vale, GUERNSEY, GY3 5LQ.
VEITCH, Mr. George Colin, FCA *1957;* 25 Emsworth Drive, Eaglescliffe, STOCKTON-ON-TEES, TS16 0NR. (Life Member)
VEITCH, Mr. John Andrew, BA ACA *1998;* 251 Raglan Street, Mosman, SYDNEY, NSW 2088, AUSTRALIA.
VEITCH, Mr. Peter Francis, FCA *1969;* Sabre Holdings (UK) Ltd, Golf Road, Hale, ALTRINCHAM, CHESHIRE, WA15 8AH.
VEITCH, Mrs. Sally Jane, MA ACA *1998;* 44 Tuffnells Way, HARPENDEN, HERTFORDSHIRE, AL5 3HG.
VEITH, Mr. Philip Dennis, FCA *1975;* 51 Grevillea Avenue, ST. IVES, NSW 2075, AUSTRALIA.
VEKARIA, Miss. Jyoti, BSc ARCS ACA *2010;* 109 Malvern Gardens, HARROW, MIDDLESEX, HA3 9PQ.
VEKARIA, Mr. Manish, BA ACA *1993;* 6 Harmsworth Way, LONDON, N20 8JU.
•**VEKARIA, Mr. Mansukh Mawji, BSc ACA** *1995;* M.M. Vekaria & Co, 36 St. Andrews Drive, STANMORE, MIDDLESEX, HA7 2NB. See also Parkwell Business Solutions Limited
VEKARIA, Mr. Pradeep, BSc(Econ) ACA *1998;* 52 Lyon Meade, STANMORE, MIDDLESEX, HA7 1JA.
VEKARIA, Mr. Rashik Samji, BSc(Hons) ARCS ACA *2010;* 144 Turner Road, EDGWARE, MIDDLESEX, HA8 6AR.
VELA, Mr. Robin Tendai, BSc ACA MSI *1998;* Lonsa Capital PTY Limited, PO BOX 783302, SANDTON, 2146, SOUTH AFRICA.
VELANI, Mr. Mitesh, ACA *2008;* 78 Brackendale, POTTERS BAR, HERTFORDSHIRE, EN6 2LX.
VELANI, Mrs. Roohi Mavji, ACA *2008;* 205 23 on Arthurs, Arthurs Road, Seapoint, CAPE TOWN, WESTERN CAPE PROVINCE, 8005 SOUTH AFRICA.
VELAUTHAM, Mr. Arun, BSc(Hons) ACA *2001;* 46 Albert Road, NEW MALDEN, KT3 6BS.
VELAUTHAPILLAI, Mr. Muttiah, BSc FCA *1966;* Rajes, 24 Bickney Way, Fetcham, LEATHERHEAD, KT22 9QQ. (Life Member)
VELDMAN, Miss. Caroline Anne, MA(Hons) ACA *2009;* 26 Verran Road, LONDON, SW12 8BA.

VELICKOVIC, Mrs. Margaret Mary, BSc ACA *1988;* 144 Upper Road, Kennington, OXFORD, OX1 5LW.

•**VELIDA, Mr. Don Robert William, FCA** *1989;* D. Velida & Co, Centurion House, Central Way, Walworth Business Park, ANDOVER, SP10 5AN.

VELJI, Mr. Shabir, ACA *1981;* Shabir Velji, 260 Hollingham Rd, UNIONVILLE LR3 8J6, ON, CANADA.

VELLA, Miss. Charlmaine, BSc FCA *1996;* 2 Aubin Les Vanniers, La Route de St. Aubin, St. Helier, JERSEY, JE2 3AA.

VELLA, Mr. Claude, BA(Hons) ACA *2002;* 13 Fawcett Road, CROYDON, CR0 1SP.

VELLA, Mr. Noel, BA FCA *1993;* 214 Kingston Road, EPSOM, KT19 0SQ.

VELLA, Mr. Sebastian Benedict Ethelwald, BSc ACA *2005;* Flat 2 Aldersgate Court, 30 Bartholomew Close, LONDON, EC1A 7ES.

VELLACOTT, Mr. Philip, MEng ACA *2007;* with PricewaterhouseCoopers LLP, 1 Embankment Place, LONDON, WC2N 6RH.

VELLACOTT, Mr. Richard John, BSc ACA *2002;* with Deloitte LLP, City House, 126-130 Hills Road, CAMBRIDGE, CB2 1RY.

VELLANI, Mr. Mehboob ShamshudeenAbdulrasul, FCA *1975;* 787 Ponce De Leon Terrace, ATLANTA, GA 30306, UNITED STATES.

VELOSO, Dr. Ignacio, BSc ACA *2004;* with Deloitte LLP, 4 Brindley Place, BIRMINGHAM, B1 2HZ.

VELTMAN, Mrs. Denise Anne, FCA CTA *1973;* H S B C, Level 36, 8 Canada Square, Canary Wharf, LONDON, E14 5HQ.

VELUPILLAI, Mr. Seevaratnam, FCA *1953;* 23 Chestnut Close, Southgate, LONDON, N14 4SG. (Life Member)

VENABLE, Mr. Paul St John Lloyd, BA FCA *1990;* 23 Edgerton Drive, TADCASTER, NORTH YORKSHIRE, LS24 9QW.

VENABLES, Mrs. Carla, ACA *2006;* Lower Flat, 20 Angerstein Road, PORTSMOUTH, PO2 8HL.

VENABLES, Mr. Graham Ralph, ACA MAAT *1999;* 250 Long Lane, Finchley, LONDON, N3 2RN.

VENABLES, Mrs. Hazel Margaret, BA ACA *1988;* The Boathouse, Bolney Road, Lower Shiplake, HENLEY-ON-THAMES, OXFORDSHIRE, RG9 3NR.

VENABLES, Mrs. Judith Mary, BSc ACA *1992;* A B L Aluminium Components Ltd Premier House, Garretts Green Trading Estate Valepits Road, BIRMINGHAM, B33 0TD.

VENABLES, Mr. Paul, BA ACA *1987;* Hicks Farmhouse, Roke, WALLINGFORD, OXFORDSHIRE, OX10 6JD.

VENABLES, Mr. Peter Robert Charles, ACA *2009;* Garden Flat, 5 Bellevue, BRISTOL, BS8 1DA.

VENABLES, Mr. Peter Turrill, FCA *1963;* 31 Mill Street, KIDLINGTON, OXFORDSHIRE, OX5 2EE.

VENABLES, Miss. Rosalind Louise, BSc ACA *2011;* 20 Meadow Place, LONDON, SW8 1XZ.

VENABLES, Mr. Simon, BA(Hons) ACA *2004;* 4 Broadlake, Willaston, WIRRAL, CH64 2XB.

VENABLES, Mr. Tobias Arthur, ACA *2009;* Maison Clairval, La Rue de St. Mannelier, St. Saviour, JERSEY, JE2 7HJ.

VENCHARD, Mr. Eendren, BSc ACA *1992;* Bowen Square, Dr Ferriere Street, PORT LOUIS, MAURITIUS.

VENESS, Mr. David Frank, MA FCA *1981;* The Firs, Main Street, Forest Hill, OXFORD, OX33 1EF.

VENESS, Miss. Jacqueline Susan, BA ACA *1986;* 22 Murrin Road, MAIDENHEAD, SL6 5EQ.

VENET, Mr. Harry, FCA *1965;* 72 Buckstone Oval, LEEDS, LS17 5HH.

VENEY, Miss. Katie, BA(Hons) ACA *2009;* 36 Heathfield Close, Formby, LIVERPOOL, L37 7HP.

•**VENGADASALAM, Mr. Radha Krishnan, CA ACA** *1994;* NO 17 Jalan 45 / 70A, Desa Sri Hartamas, 50480 KUALA LUMPUR, FEDERAL TERRITORY, MALAYSIA.

•**VENITT, Mr. Malcolm Alan, ACA** *1983;* (Tax Fac), Venitt and Greaves, 115 Craven Park Road, LONDON, N15 6BL.

VENKATARANGA, Mr. Setlur Srinath, LLB ACA *1992;* 13/2 5 d main I Block Koramangala Layout, BANGALORE 560034, INDIA.

VENKATASAWMY, Mr. Soorianarain, ACA *1994;* Blue Penny Inc., 1314 Bohler Court, ATLANTA, GA 30327, UNITED STATES.

VENN, Mr. Daniel, MEng ACA *2009;* Flat B, 14 Barnsbury Park, LONDON, N1 1HQ.

VENN, Mrs. Enid Jean, MA ACA *1981;* Cambridge Microfab Ltd Broadway Barn, Broadway Bourn, CAMBRIDGE, CB23 2TA.

•**VENN, Mr. Paul Brealey, MA FCA** *1976;* Paul Venn Accountants, 40 Woodborough Road, WINSCOMBE, SOMERSET, BS25 1AG. See also Paul Venn MA FCA

VENN, Mr. Peter William, MBA BA FCA *1985;* AigB Consulting, 60 Hedley Hill Terrace, Waterhouses, DURHAM, DH7 9AZ.

VENNER, Mr. Andrew James, BSc ACA *2001;* 28 Fitzharding Road, Pill, BRISTOL, BS20 0EH.

VENNER, Mr. Edward Stephen Squires, BA FCA *1999;* Kirklea, The Green, Peters Green, LUTON, LU2 9QL.

VENNER, Mrs. Lindsey Elizabeth Anne, BSc ACA *1996;* 29 Hillside Road, HARPENDEN, AL5 4BS.

VENNER, Mr. Michael Ross, FCA *1978;* 5 Huxley Street, WEST RYDE, NSW 2114, AUSTRALIA.

VENNER, Miss. Nicola Melanie, ACA *2001;* 11 Scotch Horn Close, Nailsea, BRISTOL, BS48 1TF.

•**VENNEY, Mr. Brian, BSc FCA** *1986;* Bondeastleigh Limited, 59B Leigh Road, EASTLEIGH, HAMPSHIRE, SO50 9DF.

VENNING, Mr. Bernard Bruce, FCA *1955;* PO Box 624, FRANSCHHOEK, 7690, SOUTH AFRICA. (Life Member)

VENNING, Miss. Jasmine Bryony, ACA *2008;* Dun & Bradstreet Ltd Marlow International, Parkway, MARLOW, BUCKINGHAMSHIRE, SL7 1AJ.

VENNING, Mr. John Robert, FCA *1957;* May House, 21 Church Street, Sherston, MALMESBURY, WILTSHIRE, SN16 0LR. (Life Member)

•**VENNING, Mr. Martin John Wentworth, FCA** *1965;* Martin JW Venning, The Alma, School Lane, Baslow, BAKEWELL, DERBYSHIRE DE45 1RZ. See also Marven Consultants

VENNING, Mrs. Victoria Carol, BSc(Hons) ACA *2002;* with Deloitte LLP, 4 Brindley Place, BIRMINGHAM, B1 2HZ.

VENPIN, Mr. Eric Alain Koo Khen Heong, FCA *1991;* 58 Dr Lesur Street, BEAU BASSIN, MAURITIUS.

VENTER, Mr. Izack Hendrik, ACA CA(SA) *2008;* International Accounting Standards Board, 30 Cannon Street, LONDON, EC4M 6XH.

•**VENTER, Mr. Philippus Lodewyk, ACA CA(SA)** *2009;* Naylor Wintersgill Ltd, Carlton House, Grammar School Street, BRADFORD, WEST YORKSHIRE, BD1 4NS.

•**VENTHAM, Mr. Michael John, FCA** *1973;* MJV & Co Ltd, Unit 22A, West Station Yard, Spital Road, MALDON, ESSEX CM9 6TS. See also Michael J. Ventham

•**VENTHAM, Mr. Paul Anthony, FCA** *1971;* George Hay & Company, 83 Cambridge Street, Pimlico, LONDON, SW1V 4PS.

•**VENTOUR, Mr. Leon, BA(Hons) ACA** *2004;* Ventour & Co, 18 Oldfield Lane South, GREENFORD, MIDDLESEX, UB6 9LD.

VENTRE, Mr. Neil Jeremy, ACA *1986;* Pipers Wrights Green Lane, Wrights Green, Little Hallingbury, BISHOP'S STORTFORD, CM22 7RE.

VENTRESS, Mrs. Nicola Suzanne, BA ACA *1997;* 1 Lichfield Road, PARNELL 1052, NEW ZEALAND.

VENTRESS, Mrs. Vanessa Celia, BA ACA *1997;* Heather Bank, 16 Dry Hill Park Road, TONBRIDGE, KENT, TN10 3BN.

VENTURA, Mr. Michael William James Roy, ACA *1988;* Amberfield Cottage, Peasley Lane, GOUDHURST, KENT, TN17 1HP.

VENUGOPALAN, Ms. Shujoya Shenaiya, BA ACA *2006;* 130 St. Dunstans Road, LONDON, W6 8RA.

•**VERBER, Mr. Stephen, BA FCA** *1980;* Alexander & Co, 17 St Ann's Square, MANCHESTER, M2 7PW.

VERBRUGGEN, Ms. Reinielde Lydia, BBS ACA *1993;* The Thorny Field, Kilmullen Lane, NEWTOWN MOUNT KENNEDY, COUNTY WICKLOW, IRELAND.

VERCOE, Mr. Peter Nicolas, FCA *1960;* The Orchard, Backsideans, Wargrave, READING, RG10 8JP. (Life Member)

VERDIER, Mr. James Russell, BSc(Econ) FCA *2000;* Little Dawyck, Woodhurst Lane, OXTED, RH8 9HD.

VERDIN, Mr. Christopher Peter, MA ACA *1993;* 16 Coates Avenue, LONDON, SW18 2TH.

VERDUYN, Mrs. Anna Louise, BA ACA *1991;* EON UK, Westwood Way, Westwood Park, COVENTRY, CV4 8LG.

VERE-HODGE, Mr. Nicholas Miles, FCA *1967;* Westcott House, Upton, TAUNTON, SOMERSET, TA4 2JJ.

VERE NICOLL, Mr. Kenneth Charles, FCA *1966;* 28 Wallingford Avenue, LONDON, W10 6PX.

VERGHIS, Mr. Viju George, MBA FCA *1982;* 7 West Lane, SUMMIT, NJ 07901, UNITED STATES.

VERGOPOULOS, Mr. John David, BSocSc ACA *1993;* 6 Chatsworth Road, Chiswick, LONDON, W4 3HY.

•**VERINDER, Mr. Alan Lovell, FCA** *1970;* Verinder & Associates, 1-3 Crosby Road South, LIVERPOOL, L22 1RG.

VERINDER, Mr. Mark, LLB ACA *2007;* Flat 84, Dundee Wharf, 100 Three Colt Street, LONDON, E14 8AY.

VERITY, Miss. Alison, BSc ACA *1991;* 1 The Barn, Cage End, Hatfield Broad Oak, BISHOP'S STORTFORD, CM22 7HZ.

VERITY, Mr. Gordon Justin, FCA *1966;* Fleetwood, Cow Lane, Kimpton, ANDOVER, HAMPSHIRE, SP11 8NY.

•**VERITY, Mr. Philip Andrew, BA FCA** *1990;* Mazars LLP, The Pinnacle, 160 Midsummer Boulevard, MILTON KEYNES, MK9 1FF.

VERITY, Mr. Richard John, BSc ACA *2007;* Long Ridge Arkesden Road, Clavering, SAFFRON WALDEN, ESSEX, CB11 4QU.

VERITY, Mr. Robert Andrew, BA ACA *1986;* HSBC, Level 25, HSBC Main Building, 1 Queens Road, CENTRAL, HONG KONG ISLAND HONG KONG SAR.

VERITY, Mr. Roger Michael, BCom FCA *1968;* 58 Bramley Lane, Lightcliffe, HALIFAX, HX3 8NS.

VERITY, Ms. Sarah Ruth Elizabeth, BA ACA *2005;* Cinven Services Ltd Warwick Court, 5 Paternoster Square, LONDON, EC4M 7AG.

•**VERJEE, Mr. Kassamali RehemtullaKassam Suleman, FCA** *1976;* Spanish Oak, 3 Coolarne Rise, CAMBERLEY, SURREY, GU15 1NA.

VERJUS, Miss. Nathalie, MA ACA *2007;* 118 RUE FALGUIERE, 75015 PARIS, FRANCE.

VERKADE-CAVE, Mrs. Rebecca Ann, BSc FCA *1990;* (Tax Fac), with Taxwriter Ltd, 81 Pattison Lane, Woolstone, MILTON KEYNES, MK15 0AY.

VERKHOVSKAYE, Mrs. Maria, ACA *2006;* 67 Manor Road, CHIGWELL, ESSEX, IG7 5PH.

VERLANDER, Mr. David Arthur, FCA *1969;* Holme View, Deer Croft Avenue, HUDDERSFIELD, HD3 3SH.

•**VERMA, Mr. Alok, FCA** *1983;* SRLV, 89 New Bond Street, LONDON, W1S 1DA.

VERMA, Mr. Atul Kumar, ACA *2010;* B-33 Nico Middle East, Oil Field Supply Centre, PO Box261005, Jafza, DUBAI, UNITED ARAB EMIRATES.

VERMA, Mr. Mohinder Paul, FCA *1974;* 823 Sector 21A, Faridabad, HARYANA 121001, INDIA. (Life Member)

VERMA, Ms. Radhika, ACA *1988;* 63 Parliament Hill, LONDON, NW3 2TB.

VERMA, Mr. Ravi Kant, BSc(Hons) ACA AMCT *2000;* 148 Uxbridge Road, SOUTHALL, MIDDLESEX, UB1 3DP.

VERMA, Mr. Sandeep, BSc ACA CFA *1993;* 1615 GREEN LEAF OAKS DRIVE, SUGARLAND, TX 77479, UNITED STATES.

VERMA, Mr. Sanjeev, BCom ACA *1998;* 91 Weston Drive, STANMORE, HA7 2EW.

VERMA, Mrs. Seema, BSc ACA *2001;* 9 Parkwood Avenue, Roundhay, LEEDS, LS8 1JW.

VERMA, Dr. Shraddha, BSc ACA *1991;* 21 Hartington Road, Millhouses, SHEFFIELD, S7 2LE.

VERMA, Mr. Shwetank, ACA *2008;* C/O Mr. Lov Verma, C II/82, Motibagh 1, NEW DELHI 110021, INDIA.

VERMA, Mr. Vijay Kumar, ACA *1979;* 61 Marine Parade, ELWOOD, VIC 3184, AUSTRALIA.

VERMES, Mrs. Pamela, BSc ACA *1980;* 54 Langley Park Road, SUTTON, SM2 5HG.

•**VERMEULEN, Mr. Nicholas John, BSc FCA** *1998;* with PricewaterhouseCoopers CI LLP, PO Box 321, Royal Bank Place, 1 Glategny Esplanade, St Peter Port, GUERNSEY GY1 4ND.

VERMEULEN, Mr. Peter John, BA(Hons) ACA *2009;* P.O. Box 8, SEDGEFIELD, WESTERN CAPE PROVINCE, 6573, SOUTH AFRICA.

VERMEULEN, Mr. Peter Jules Maria, BSc ACA *2003;* 28 Danbury Way, WOODFORD GREEN, ESSEX, IG8 7EZ.

VERNALLS, Mr. David Michael, BA FCA *1996;* Wards Solicitors, 52 Broad Street, BRISTOL, BS1 2EP.

VERNASCHI, Mr. Remo Giacomo Vittorio, BSc FCA *1983;* Orangebox Ltd 3 East Road, Penallta Industrial Estate Penallta, HENGOED, MID GLAMORGAN, CF82 7SU.

VERNAZZA, Mr. Matthew James, BA ACA *2005;* 4 Oriel Court, Heath Street, LONDON, NW3 6TG.

VERNEDE, Mr. Charles Arthur, FCA *1969;* Nightingale Cottage, Conghurst Lane, Hawkhurst, CRANBROOK, TN18 4RH.

VERNEDE, Mr. John Michael, BSc ACA *2002;* Garden Flat, 12 Sisters Avenue, LONDON, SW11 5SG.

VERNER, Mr. Rory Neil, BA ACA *1997;* 13 Saxon Road, Worth, CRAWLEY, WEST SUSSEX, RH10 7SA.

•**VERNEY, Mr. David John, BSc FCA** *1985;* David Verney Limited, 83 Curtis Way, Kesgrave, IPSWICH, IP5 2FF. See also Conway Fielden Gough Limited

•**VERNEY, Mr. Frederick Charles, FCA** *1971;* (Tax Fac), Townends, Carlisle Chambers, Carlisle Street, GOOLE, DN14 5DX. See also Townends Accountants Limited

VERNEY, Mr. Harry Ulick Dennis, FCA *1965;* Pension & Investment Services, The Garden House, Cheriton, ALRESFORD, SO24 0QQ.

VERNEY, Ms. Helen Phyllis, BA ACA *1997;* 76 Woodwarde Road, LONDON, SE22 8UL.

VERNEY, Miss. Jean Margaret, BA ACA *1992;* 40 School Lane, Toft, CAMBRIDGE, CB23 2RE.

VERNEY, Mr. Stuart Peter, BSc ACA *1998;* Northgate House Mill Lane, Fenny Compton, SOUTHAM, CV47 2YF.

VERNEY, Mrs. Tina Mary, BA ACA *1993;* 21A St Andrews Road, HAYLING ISLAND, PO11 9JN.

VERNIER, Mr. Cyril, ACA *2008;* 131 rue d'Avron, 75020 PARIS, FRANCE.

•**VERNON, Mrs. Amanda Jane, ACA** *1994;* AJV Consultancy Limited, 4 The Ridings, WILMSLOW, CHESHIRE, SK9 6ES.

VERNON, Mrs. Christine Margaret, ACA *1981;* 3 Station Parade, Cherry Tree Rise, BUCKHURST HILL, ESSEX, IG9 6EU.

•**VERNON, Mr. Darren, ACA** *2009;* DVernon Accounting Services, 30 High Mount, Station Road, LONDON, NW4 3SS.

VERNON, Mr. Gordon, BA(Hons) ACA *2001;* 12 Clementine Close, HERNE BAY, KENT, CT6 6SN.

VERNON, Sir James William, Bt FCA *1973;* The Hall, Lygan-y-Wern, Pentre Halkyn, HOLYWELL, CH8 8BD.

VERNON, Mr. Jeremy Gwynne, BA(Hons) ACA *2001;* 3 Martree Court, Elworth, SANDBACH, CHESHIRE, CW11 3BN.

VERNON, Mrs. Karen Jane, BSc ACA *1997;* 25 Haslingden Close, HARPENDEN, HERTFORDSHIRE, AL5 3EW.

VERNON, Mr. Matthew, ACA *2011;* 62 Brewers Square, BIRMINGHAM, B16 0PN.

VERNON, Mr. Michael David Lang, ACA *1980;* 19 Harts Grove, WOODFORD GREEN, IG8 0BN.

VERNON, Mr. Richard John, BSc ACA *1997;* 25 Haslingden Close, HARPENDEN, HERTFORDSHIRE, AL5 3EW.

•**VERNON, Mr. Roderick William Pomeroy, MA FCA** *1964;* Vernon & Company, Fairfields, Pennypot Lane, Chobham, WOKING, GU24 8DJ.

VERNON, Mrs. Ruth Louise, BSc(Hons) ACA *2004;* Rotheham Doncaster & South Humber Mental Health NHS Foundation Trust, Internal Audit, Brincliffe House, 90 Osborne Road, SHEFFIELD, S11 9BD.

VERNON, Mrs. Sally, BA ACA *2000;* 10, Peregrine Close, Great Hadham Road, BISHOP'S STORTFORD, CM23 4LT.

VERNON, Miss. Sally Anne, BA ACA *1991;* 48 Upper Ashley Street, HALESOWEN, B62 8HJ.

VERNON, Mr. Scott, BSc ACA *2001;* 1st Floor Flat, 12 Oxford Gardens, LONDON, W4 3BW.

VERNON-PARRY, Mr. Christopher John Gareth, BSc ACA *1996;* National Grid, 1 Metro Tech Center, Brooklyn, NEW YORK, NY 11201, UNITED STATES.

VERNON-PARRY, Dr. Julie Ann, PhD BSc FCA *1997;* National Grid Plc Grand Buildings, 1-3 Strand, LONDON, WC2N 5EH.

VERNON-SMITH, Mr. Martyn, FCA *1968;* Hamewith, Birch Grove, Horsted Keynes, HAYWARDS HEATH, RH17 7BT. (Life Member)

VERO, Mr. Geoffrey Osborne, FCA *1970;* Vero Consultancy, The Old Vicarage, Bagshot Road, Chobham, WOKING, SURREY GU24 8DA.

VERON, Mr. Andrew Jonathon, BA ACA *1992;* P O Box 368, Helvetia Court, South Esplanade St Peter Port, GUERNSEY, GY1 3YJ.

VERRALL, Mr. Bernard Peter, FCA *1967;* (Tax Fac), 34 Beaufort Close, LEE-ON-THE-SOLENT, HAMPSHIRE, PO13 8FN.

VERRALL, Mr. Martin, ACA *2011;* 75 School Lane, Lower Halstow, SITTINGBOURNE, KENT, ME9 7ES.

VERRECCHIA, Mr. Nicholas Joseph Anthony, BSc ACA *1994;* DHL Global Forwarding Canada Inc, 6200 Edwards Bouvelard, MISSISSAUGA L5T 2V7, ON, CANADA.

VERRIER, Mr. Jonathan Simon, BA ACA *1995;* Barron & Barron, Bathurst House, 86 Micklegate, YORK, YO1 6LQ.

VERRIER, Mrs. Julie Ann, BA ACA *1998;* 4 East End, Garton-on-the-Wolds, DRIFFIELD, YO25 3EP.

VERRILL, Miss. Jennifer, BSc ACA *2011;* 46 Constable Road, ST. IVES, CAMBRIDGESHIRE, PE27 3EQ.

VERRINDER, Mr. Andrew James, BSc ACA RA *1985;* 2 Baskenridge Drive, MIDDLETOWN, NJ 07748 2539, UNITED STATES.

VERRION, Mr. Robert Edward, BSc FCA *1977;* 4th Floor, Berkeley Square House, Berkeley Square, LONDON, W1J 6BD.

VERSI, Mr. Azim Akbar, FCA *1978;* 240 - 4th. Avenue SW, CALGARY T2P 4H4, AB, CANADA.

VERSLUYS, Mr. Roger Louis, BA ACA *1994;* Byron, Park Lane, BROXBOURNE, HERTFORDSHIRE, EN10 7PJ.
VERSO, Ms. Bridget Debra, BA(Hons) ACA *2000;* 50 Birdbrook Road, Kidbrooke, LONDON, SE3 9QA.
VERWER, Mr. Daniel Federico, BSc FCA *1988;* Zone Vision, 105-109 Salusbury Road, LONDON, NW6 6RG.
VERWEY, Mr. Mark Henry, BSc(Hons) ACA *2002;* 7 Kenmore Close, RICHMOND, SURREY, TW9 3JG.
•**VERZHBITSKAYA, Mrs. Philippa Helen, BSc ARCS ACA** *1996;* Philippa Verzhbitskaya, 33A Hitchin Lane, Clifton, SHEFFORD, BEDFORDSHIRE, SG17 5RS.
VESEY, Mr. Richard Andrew, BA FCA *1978;* 11 Wealden Way, HAYWARDS HEATH, RH16 4AF.
VESEY, Mr. Thomas Francis, FCA FCMA *1973;* (Tax Fac), Winckworth Sherwood, Minerva House 5 Montague Close, LONDON, SE1 9BB.
•**VESSEY, Mrs. Claire Louise, ACA** *2002;* ACL, 5 Augustus Walk, Caistor, Market Rasen, LINCOLNSHIRE, ln7 6gh.
VESSEY, Mr. James, BA ACA *2001;* with Audit Inspection Unit, Financial Reporting Council, 5th Floor, Aldwych House, 71-91 Aldwych, LONDON WC2B 4HN.
VESSEY, Mr. John Frederick, FCA *1960;* 64 Sandall Park Drive, Wheatley Hills, DONCASTER, DN2 5RA. (Life Member)
VEST, Mr. Nicholas John, BA ACA *2000;* Les Champs Blancs 88, 1279 CHAVANNES-DE-BOGIS, SWITZERLAND.
VESTBIRK, Mrs. Georgina Mary, BSc ACA *1995;* Alward House Shute End, Alderbury, SALISBURY, SP5 3DJ.
VESTEY, Mrs. Nicola Jane, BA FCA *1978;* The Old School House, Bunloit, By Drumnadrochit, INVERNESS, IV63 6XG.
VESTY, Mr. John Edwin, FCA *1958;* Clifflands, 536 Loughborough Road, Birstall, LEICESTER, LE4 3EG. (Life Member)
VETCH, Mr. Robert Sean, MEng FCA *2000;* W R Berkley Syndicate Limited, 40 Lime Street, LONDON, EC3M 7AW.
VEVERS, Mr. Meyrick Raoul, BEng FCA *1986;* The Woodlands, Cavendish Road, WEYBRIDGE, SURREY, KT13 0JY.
VEVERS, Mr. Rawdon Quentin, BA ACA ACT *1982;* The Green Man, Arkesden, SAFFRON WALDEN, CB11 4EX.
VEVERS, Mr. Wilfred Peter, FCA *1964;* Pen Selwood, South Street, HINTON ST. GEORGE, TA17 8SW.
VEYS, Mr. Christopher Charles, BA ACA *1983;* 55 Bulstrode Way, GERRARDS CROSS, BUCKINGHAMSHIRE, SL9 7QT.
VEYS, Mrs. Deborah Frances, BCom ACA *1986;* Harewood Lodge, 55 Bulstrode Way, GERRARDS CROSS, SL9 7QT.
VEYSEY, Mrs. Rebecca Constance, BA ACA *1999;* 597 Second Street, BROOKLYN, NY 11215, UNITED STATES.
•**VEYSEY, Mr. Richard James, BSc FCA** *1996;* PricewaterhouseCoopers LLP, 300 Madison Avenue, NEW YORK, NY 10017, UNITED STATES. See also PricewaterhouseCoopers
•**VIALS, Mr. Andrew, LLB FCA** *1976;* KPMG LLP, 15 Canada Square, LONDON, E14 5GL. See also KPMG Europe LLP
VIANA, Mr. David Anthony, BSc FCA *1988;* 163 Montagu Mansions, LONDON, W1U 6LQ.
VIBERT, Mr. Colin David, FCA *1975;* Pinnacle Trustees Ltd, 14 Britannia Place Bath Street, St. Helier, JERSEY, JE2 4SU.
VICARS, Miss. Helen Claire, MA ACA *1997;* 5 Dalmahoy Road, Ratho, NEWBRIDGE, MIDLOTHIAN, EH28 8RE.
VICARY, Mr. Gary Kevin, BA ACA *1984;* Dunstan Wood Dunstan Lane, Burton, NESTON, CH64 8TG.
VICARY, Mrs. Laura Jane, ACA *2009;* 22 Princes Street, OXFORD, OX4 1DD.
•**VICCAJEE, Mr. Rutton Behram, FCA CTA** *1979;* (Tax Fac), Rutton B Viccajee Limited, Red Lion House, London Road, Bentley, FARNHAM, SURREY GU10 5HY.
•**VICE, Mr. David Patrick, FCA** *1969;* (Tax Fac), Mark J Rees, Granville Hall, Granville Road, LEICESTER, LE1 7RU.
VICE, Mr. Matthew David, ACA *2007;* 21 Montague Road, Clarendon Park, LEICESTER, LE2 1TG.
VICK, Mrs. Alexandria Christine, BA ACA *1998;* Audatex UK Limited, The Forum, Station Road, Theale, READING, RG7 4RA.
VICK, Mr. Andrew Richardson, BSc ACA *2001;* Morgan Stanley International 25 Cabot Square, LONDON, E14 4QA.
VICK, Mrs. Nicola Jane, BA ACA *1999;* 90 Clonmore Street, Southfields, LONDON, SW18 5HB.
VICK, Mr. Peter John William, BSc ACA *1995;* Top Flat, 258 Kew Road, Kew, RICHMOND, TW9 3EG.
VICKERMAN, Mr. John Stafford, BSc FCA *1975;* Sandford, 2 Clifford Manor Road, GUILDFORD, SURREY, GU4 8AG.
•**VICKERMAN, Mr. Peter Ian, FCA** *1975;* 87 Brighton Road, GODALMING, SURREY, GU7 1NX.
VICKERS, Mr. Adrian David, BSc ACA *1993;* Kingswood, 15 Belle Vue, Stone, AYLESBURY, BUCKINGHAMSHIRE, HP17 8PJ.
•**VICKERS, Mr. Alastair Noel, FCA** *1973;* Ayres Bright Vickers, Bishopstone, 36 Crescent Road, WORTHING, BN11 1RL.
VICKERS, Mr. Alexander, MEng ACA *2010;* 6 Halcyon House, Private Road, ENFIELD, MIDDLESEX, EN1 2EJ.
•**VICKERS, Miss. Alison, ACA** *1991;* Bevan & Buckland, Langdon House, Langdon Road, SA1 Swansea Waterfront, SWANSEA, SA1 8QY. See also Alison Vickers
VICKERS, Mrs. Amanda Louise, BA ACA *2001;* STF51, Shell International Trading & Shipping Co Ltd, Shell Mex House, 80 Strand, LONDON, WC2R 0ZA.
VICKERS, Miss. Anya, ACA *2009;* Victoria Hall, 11 Victoria Street, HAMILTON HM11, BERMUDA.
VICKERS, Miss. Caroline Nathalie, BA ACA *2010;* 229 Leaside Way, SOUTHAMPTON, SO16 3EQ.
VICKERS, Mrs. Cheryl, BSc FCA *1990;* Marley Ltd, 1 Suffolk Way, SEVENOAKS, KENT, TN13 1SD.
VICKERS, Mr. Christopher John, MA ACA *1993;* R P S Energy, Goldsworth House, Denton Way, The Goldsworth Park Centre, WOKING, SURREY GU21 3LG.
•**VICKERS, Mr. Colin Ian, BA ACA FCCA MIPA** *1989;* FRP Advisory LLP, Southfield House, 11 Liverpool Gardens, WORTHING, WEST SUSSEX, BN11 1RY.
VICKERS, Mr. Darren James, BSc ACA *2005;* Charles Stanley Co Ltd, 131 Finsbury Pavement, LONDON, EC2A 1NT.
VICKERS, Miss. Eleni, BSc ACA *2003;* 16 Jeanne D'Arc Street, 3071 LIMASSOL, CYPRUS.
VICKERS, Miss. Fiona, BA ACA *1992;* with Ernst & Young LLP, 1 More London Place, LONDON, SE1 2AF.
VICKERS, Mr. Frank, FCA FIMC *1958;* Woodside Cottage, Heath House Road, Worplesdon Hill, WOKING, GU22 0RD. (Life Member)
VICKERS, Mr. Graham Martin, BSc FCA *1977;* 21 Kewferry Drive, NORTHWOOD, MIDDLESEX, HA6 2NT.
VICKERS, Dr. Ian Paul, PhD BSc ACA *1997;* 31 Village Farm, Bonvilston, CARDIFF, CF5 6TY.
VICKERS, Mr. James Edward, BSc ACA *2008;* CPP Group PLC, Holgate Park, Holgate Road, YORK, YO26 4GA.
VICKERS, Mr. Jeremy Philip Hilton, BSc ACA *1983;* (Tax Fac), 4 Wilton Crescent, WINDSOR, BERKSHIRE, SL4 4YJ.
VICKERS, Mr. John Alan, BA ACA *2005;* Flat 3 Conifer Court, 5 Corkran Road, SURBITON, KT6 6PL.
VICKERS, Mr. Jonathan Glyn, BSc ACA *1987;* Longmead House, Hollow Street, Great Somerford, CHIPPENHAM, WILTSHIRE, SN15 5JD.
•**VICKERS, Mr. Keith Michael, FCA** *1966;* K.M. Vickers & Co Ltd, Avon Court, 82-84 Hotwell Road, Hotwells, BRISTOL, BS8 4UB.
VICKERS, Mrs. Lisa Katherine, BA ACA *2000;* 106 Marsh Lane, Crosspool, SHEFFIELD, S10 5NP.
VICKERS, Mr. Mark, MEng ACA *1997;* 7th Floor Albert Bridge House, 1 Bridge Street, MANCHESTER, M60 9AF.
•**VICKERS, Mr. Mark Spencer, FCA** *1974;* Mark Vickers FCA, Hyfrydle, Station Road, Valley Anglesey, HOLYHEAD, GWYNEDD LL65 3EB.
VICKERS, Mr. Matthew, DPhil MChem ACA *2010;* 70 Rowland Hill Court, Osney Lane, OXFORD, OX1 1LF.
VICKERS, Mr. Matthew Adam, BA ACA *2003;* BP Plc, 20 Canada Square, LONDON, E14 5NJ.
VICKERS, Mr. Michael Graham, FCA *1970;* 23 Roseberry Street, Kirkby-in-Ashfield, NOTTINGHAM, NG17 7DZ. (Life Member)
•**VICKERS, Mr. Michael John, FCA** *1977;* Angarrack Farmhouse, 12 Grist Lane, Angarrack, HAYLE, CORNWALL, TR27 5HZ.
VICKERS, Mr. Peter, BSc ACA *2003;* Great Yarmouth Borough Council, Trafalgar House, Hall Plain, GREAT YARMOUTH, NR30 2QG.
•**VICKERS, Dr. Peter Anthony, PhD BSc FCA** *1978;* Dr P A Vickers, Loydons, 17 Hitchin Road, LETCHWORTH GARDEN CITY, HERTFORDSHIRE, SG6 3LX.
VICKERS, Mrs. Philippa Hjordis, BA ACA *2005;* with Deloitte LLP, Hill House, 1 Little New Street, LONDON, EC4A 3TR.
VICKERS, Mr. Simon John, BSc ACA *1986;* 7 Bowmans Close, STEYNING, WEST SUSSEX, BN44 3SR.
•**VICKERS, Mr. Stephen, BA(Hons) ACA FCCA CTA** *2007;* (Tax Fac), Hart Shaw LLP, Europa Link, Sheffield Business Park, SHEFFIELD, S9 1XU.
VICKERS, Mr. Stephen Patrick, BA ACA *1983;* 6 Bonaly Steading, EDINBURGH, EH13 0HA.
VICKERS, Mr. William Arthur, FCA *1975;* 61 Little Sutton Lane, Four Oaks, SUTTON COLDFIELD, B75 6SJ.
VICKERSTAFF, Mr. Andrew James, BSc FCA *1972;* 5 Aldermoor Avenue, Storrington, PULBOROUGH, WEST SUSSEX, RH20 4PT.
VICKERSTAFF, Mrs. Beverly Jane, BSc FCA FHEA *1979;* Kilby Lodge, 8 Furnival Close, Fleckney, LEICESTER, LE8 8DZ.
VICKERTON, Mrs. Ursula Mary, BSc FCA *1981;* 6 Queen Street, BARTON-UPON-HUMBER, SOUTH HUMBERSIDE, DN18 5QP.
VICKERY, Mr. Andrew Mark, BSc ACA *2008;* 2 Beats Close, Awliscombe, HONITON, DEVON, EX14 3PZ.
VICKERY, Mrs. Anna Louise, ACA *2008;* Francis Clark Vantage Point, Pynes Hill, EXETER, EX2 5FD.
•**VICKERY, Mr. Anthony Jackson, BSc FCA** *1982;* Corporate Finance and Strategy LLP, Cherwell, St. Aldhelms Road, POOLE, DORSET, BH13 6BS.
VICKERY, Mr. Arthur Patrick, BSc FCA *1962;* 2 Sheepdown Road, Poundbury, DORCHESTER, DORSET, DT1 3RY. (Life Member)
•**VICKERY, Miss. Caroline Agnes, FCA** *1986;* Caroline A. Vickery FCA, Wealden Farm, Parrock Lane, Upper Hartfield, HARTFIELD, EAST SUSSEX TN7 4AT.
VICKERY, Miss. Claudine, BSc FCA *1992;* 42 Rookwood Park, HORSHAM, WEST SUSSEX, RH12 1UB.
VICKERY, Mr. Craig McKenzie, MA(Hons) ACA *2001;* 11 Alwyne Square, LONDON, N1 2JX.
VICKERY, Miss. Emma Louise, BSc ACA *2002;* Open GI Limited, Buckholt Drive, WORCESTER, WR4 9SR.
•**VICKERY, Mr. Jonathan Neil, BA FCA** *1997;* J.N.Vickery, 39 Green Lane, Blackwater, CAMBERLEY, SURREY, GU17 9DG.
•**VICKERY, Mr. Michael Paul, BSc FCA** *1995;* with PricewaterhouseCoopers LLP, 7 More London Riverside, LONDON, SE1 2RT.
VICKERY, Mr. Paul David James, BSc ACA *1992;* 22 Hatfield Heights, Hatfields Beach, OREWA 0931, NEW ZEALAND.
VICKERY, Mr. Richard James, BSc ACA *2006;* 1 The Gate House, INGATESTONE, ESSEX, CM4 0BL.
VICKERY, Mr. Roger Joseph, FCA *1969;* Little Boyton, Boyton Court Road, Sutton Valence, MAIDSTONE, KENT, ME17 3EG. (Life Member)
VICKERY, Mrs. Sarah Jane, MA ACA *1989;* Bauer, Mappin House, 4 Winsley Street, LONDON, W1W 8HF.
VICKERY, Miss. Sarah Lynn, BA ACA *1996;* 34 Kingsdown Way, BROMLEY, BR2 7PT.
VICTORY, Mrs. Stella Barbara, BCom FCA *1971;* (Tax Fac), 17 Brecon Road, BRISTOL, BS9 4DS.
VIDAMOUR, Dr. Jeanette, BSc FCA *1999;* H S B C Private Bank (C.I.) Ltd Park Place, Park Street St. Peter Port, GUERNSEY, GY1 1EE.
VIDELO, Mrs. Stephanie Ruth, BSc ACA *1992;* S A B Miller, S A B Miller House, Church Street West, WOKING, SURREY, GU21 6HS.
VIDLER, Edwin Norman, Esq MBE FCA *1955;* (Tax Fac), 22 Newnham Close, Spring Grove, LOUGHTON, IG10 4JG. (Life Member)
VIDLER, Mr. John Mark, ACA *1990;* 43 Waynflete Avenue, BRACKLEY, NN13 6AG.
VIDLER, Mr. Paul Stephen, BA ACA CTA *1985;* BG Group, 100 Thames Valley Park Drive, READING, RG6 1PT.
VIDYARTHI, Mr. Sanjay Kumar, BA ACA *2000;* with Dresdner Kleinwort Wasserstein, 30 Gresham Street, PO Box 52715, LONDON, EC2P 2XY.
VIEGAS, Mr. Marshall Anthony Firmin, BA(Hons) ACA *2010;* 105 Grifon Road, Chafford Hundred, GRAYS, ESSEX, RM16 6RL.
VIEIRA RIBEIRO, Mr. John Alexander, FCA *1971;* Casa Alvorada, CX Postal 113B, Telheiro, Sta Barbara De Nexe, 8005-532 FARO, PORTUGAL. (Life Member)
•**VIGAR, Miss. Amanda Adele, FCA CTA** *1993;* (Tax Fac), V & A Vigar & Co LLP, Stoneygate House, 2 Greenfield Road, HOLMFIRTH, HD9 2JT. See also Vigar & Associates Limited
•**VIGAR, Mr. Richard Leonard James, BBS FCA DChA** *1974;* (Tax Fac), Wright Vigar Limited, 15 Newland, LINCOLN, LN1 1XG. See also Camamile Limited and Camamile Associates Ltd
VIGGARS, Mr. Julian George, BSc ACA *1995;* Enterprise Ventures Ltd, Preston Technology Centre, Marsh Lane, PRESTON, PR1 8UQ.
VIGGERS, Mr. Gordon David, ACA *1978;* 74 Woodstock Road, SITTINGBOURNE, ME10 4HN.
VIGNESWAREN, Mr. Aaron, BSc ACA *2010;* 67 Westmeston Avenue, Saltdean, BRIGHTON, BN2 8AL.
VIGOR, Mr. David Alan, FCA *1960;* PO BOX 214, PEAPACK, NJ 07977-0214, UNITED STATES. (Life Member)
VIGOR, Mr. Norman John, FCA *1959;* 11 Bankside, SOUTH CROYDON, SURREY, CR2 7BL. (Life Member)
VIGORS, Mr. Patrick Mervyn Doyne, BSc FCA DChA *1982;* (Tax Fac), 79d Nightingale Lane, LONDON, SW12 8LY.
•**VIGUS, Miss. Samantha Juliette, FCA** *1994;* Mitchells, St Johns House, Castle Street, TAUNTON, SOMERSET, TA1 4AY.
VIJ, Mr. Arvind Kumar, ACA *1994;* 100F Stuart Court, 100 Richmond Hill, RICHMOND, TW10 6RJ.
VIJ, Mr. Shallu, BSc ACA *1999;* 24 Mill Street, Ashton-in-Makerfield, WIGAN, LANCASHIRE, WN4 9HP.
VIJAY, Mr. Anant, MA ACA *1980;* WHO, 20 Avenue Appia, 1211 Geneva 27, Switzerland, CH 1211 GENEVA, SWITZERLAND.
VIJAYAKUMARAN, Mr. Kathirkamathasan, ACA *1991;* 20 Highgate Street, AUBURN, NSW 2144, AUSTRALIA.
VIJAYARAJAH, Mr. Kirishanthan, MA ACA CFA *1998;* 51 Murray Road, NORTHWOOD, HA6 2YP.
VIJAYARATNAM, Miss. Shivani, FCA *1995;* 1192 Jalan Rasah, 70300 SEREMBAN, NEGERI SEMBILAN, MALAYSIA.
VIJENDRA, Ms. Lavanya, LLB ACA *2003;* 10 Havelock Road, BRIGHTON, BN1 6GF.
VIJEYARATNAM, Mr. Thamotharam Pillay, FCA *1976;* 17 Jalan Terasek Lapan, Bangsar Baru, 59100 KUALA LUMPUR, FEDERAL TERRITORY, MALAYSIA.
•**VIJH, Mr. Deepak, FCA** *1985;* (Tax Fac), Robinson Sterling, 551 Green Lane, ILFORD, ESSEX, IG3 9RJ.
•**VIJH, Mrs. Lynda Margaret Louise, BA ACA** *1986;* Lynda Vijh, 11 Everett Close, Cheshunt, WALTHAM CROSS, HERTFORDSHIRE, EN7 6XD.
VIJH, Mr. Rajeev, BSc ACA *1992;* 28 Franklin Avenue, North York, TORONTO M2N 1B6, ON, CANADA.
VILAR, Mrs. Caroline Margaret, MA ACA *2002;* 16 Hyrons Close, AMERSHAM, BUCKINGHAMSHIRE, HP6 6NH.
VILATHGAMUWA, Mr. Don Denzil Augustus, BSc FCA *1970;* 164 Draycott Avenue, Kenton, HARROW, HA3 0BZ.
VILCASSIM, Mrs. Parveen, ACA *2010;* 15 Burrell Close, EDGWARE, MIDDLESEX, HA8 8FH.
VILE, Mr. Karl Hayden, BSc ACA *1997;* 18 Rews Park Drive, EXETER, EX1 3QL.
VILES, Mr. Christopher Graeme, BA ACA *1998;* 6 Headingley Mews, WAKEFIELD, WEST YORKSHIRE, WF1 3AB.
•**VILES, Mr. David Paul, BSc ACA** *1992;* British Petroleum Co Plc, 1 St. James's Square, LONDON, SW1Y 4PD.
VILES, Mr. Paul John, BSc ACA *1992;* 30 Jerrard Drive, SUTTON COLDFIELD, B75 7TJ.
VILJOEN, Miss. Hayley, BSc(Hons) ACA *2009;* 22 Oakdene, ASCOT, BERKSHIRE, SL5 0BU.
VILJOEN, Mr. Paul, ACA *2004;* 6 Ridgway, Mount Ararat Road, RICHMOND, TW10 6PR.
VILLA, Mr. Charles Peter Wolferstan, FCA *1964;* Apollo Aviation Advisory Limited, 24 Cecil Pashley Way, Shoreham Airport, SHOREHAM-BY-SEA, WEST SUSSEX, BN43 5FF.
•**VILLA, Mr. Peter Edwin, FCA** *1968;* 11 Toucan Way, BASILDON, SS16 5ER.
VILLAGE, Mr. Anthony Noel, MA FCA *1976;* Noel Village (Steel Founder) Ltd, Carr Hill, Balby, DONCASTER, DN4 8DE.
VILLAR, Mr. Charles Alexander, MA ACA *1997;* 79 Elm Grove Road, LONDON, SW13 0BX.
VILLARS, Mr. Bryan Roy, FCA *1963;* Chiltern View, 8 Cook Lane, North Stoke, WALLINGFORD, OX10 6BG.
VILLIERS, Mr. Charles Nigel, MA FCA *1966;* 8 Sutherland Street, LONDON, SW1V 4LB. (Life Member)
•**VILLIS, Mrs. Deborah Anne, BA FCA CTA** *1999;* (Tax Fac), Maxwells, 4 King Square, BRIDGWATER, SOMERSET, TA6 3YF.
•**VILLIS, Mr. Michael Sidney John, ACA FCCA** *2008;* Maxwells, 4 King Square, BRIDGWATER, SOMERSET, TA6 3YF.
VIMALANATHAN, Miss. Nicola, ACA *2008;* 42a Sutton Lane, BANSTEAD, SURREY, SM7 3RB.
VIMPANY, Mr. Piers David Maurice, BSc FCA DChA *1994;* Marine Society and Sea Cadets, 202 Lambeth Road, LONDON, SE1 7JW.

VIMPANY, Mr. Richard John, BA ACA *1993;* Reydon Sports Plc Unit 17, Easter Park Lenton Lane, NOTTINGHAM, NG7 2PX.
VINALL, Mr. Trevor Gordon, MA BSc(Hons) FCA *1987;* 60 Reservoir Road, Southgate, LONDON, N14 4AX.
•VINAYAK, Mrs. Pramila, BA ACA CTA *1986;* Eton Orchard, 9 Agars Place, Datchet, SLOUGH, BERKSHIRE, SL3 9AH.
•VINCE, Mr. Andrew John, FCA *1982;* Moore Stephens, 30 Gay Street, BATH, BA1 2PA.
VINCE, Mrs. Jacqueline, ACA *1994;* Grinterley Ltd, 2 Lancer House, Hussar Court, Westside View, WATERLOOVILLE, HAMPSHIRE PO7 7SE.
VINCE, Mr. John Frederick William, BSc FCA *1977;* 14 Cornfield Avenue, Stoke Heath, BROMSGROVE, B60 3QU.
VINCE, Mr. Peter George, FCA *1954;* Holly Hyde, Frogham, FORDINGBRIDGE, SP6 2HS. (Life Member)
•VINCENT, Mrs. Ann Nalini, BSc ACA *1992;* Avassets Limited, Uplands, Mythe Road, TEWKESBURY, GLOUCESTERSHIRE, GL20 6EA.
•VINCENT, Mr. Anthony Richard, BSc FCA *1980;* Deloitte LLP, Hill House, 1 Little New Street, LONDON, EC4A 3TR. See also Anthony R Vincent BSc FCA FCIE
VINCENT, Miss. Bekki, ACA *2005;* 20 Kirk Place, CHELMSFORD, CM2 6TN.
VINCENT, Mr. Charlie, ACA *2008;* Rose Cottage, 38 Charlton, ANDOVER, SP10 4AP.
VINCENT, Miss. Claire Emma, ACA *2010;* 24a Broomfield, LEEDS, LS16 6AF.
VINCENT, Mr. David Glynn, FCA *1976;* 12 Hunter Court, Huntercombe Lane NorthBurnham, SLOUGH, SL1 6DS.
VINCENT, Mrs. Elizabeth Anne, BSc ACA *1990;* 8 Mostyn Street, STALYBRIDGE, SK15 1TX.
VINCENT, Mr. Geoffrey Charles, FCA *1969;* 182 Kirkway, Middleton, MANCHESTER, M24 1LN.
VINCENT, Miss. Georgina, ACA *2008;* 45 The Drive, Adel, LEEDS, LS16 6BQ.
VINCENT, Mrs. Helen, BA ACA *1999;* 4 Fairlawn Close, Claygate, ESHER, KT10 0EN.
VINCENT, Miss. Helen Joanna, BA ACA *1998;* 19 St. Marys Terrace, Barmoor Lane, RYTON, NE40 3AL.
VINCENT, Mr. Ian Keith, BSocSc ACA *1988;* 33 Station Road, Sturminster Marshall, WIMBORNE, DORSET, BH21 4BZ.
VINCENT, Mrs. Janet, BA ACA *2000;* 63 Hauraki Road, Palm Beach, WAIHEKE ISLAND 1240, NEW ZEALAND.
VINCENT, Mr. Jeffrey David, LLB FCA *1999;* Kuranda, 8 Gas Lane, St. Peter Port, GUERNSEY, GY1 2BD.
VINCENT, Mr. John Antony, MA FCA *1963;* The Croft, 97 Pinfold Lane, Ainsdale, SOUTHPORT, PR8 3QL.
VINCENT, Mr. John Charles, BA FCA *1953;* The Hawthorns, King Ina Road, SOMERTON, TA11 6JX. (Life Member)
VINCENT, Mr. John Philip, LLB ACA *1989;* CP Foods (UK) Ltd, Avon House, Hartlebury Trading Estate, Hartlebury, KIDDERMINSTER, WORCESTERSHIRE DY10 4JB.
•VINCENT, Mr. John Stephen, FCA FMAAT MCIArb *1968;* (Member of Council 1985 - 1997), (Tax Fac), Keens Shay Keens Limited, Christchurch House, Upper George Street, LUTON, LU1 2RS.
VINCENT, Mrs. Julia Clare, BSc ACA *2002;* The Grange, Temple Grange, Navenby, LINCOLN, LN5 0AU.
•VINCENT, Mr. Keith Henry David, FCA *1965;* Keith Vincent Limited, Y Felin, Fforest, Pontardulais, SWANSEA, SA4 0YJ.
VINCENT, Mrs. Kirsty, BSc(Hons) ACA *2002;* 119 Burland Avenue, Claregate, WOLVERHAMPTON, WV6 9JF.
VINCENT, Miss. Laura Louise, BA ACA *2007;* Flat 1 Marie Stopes Court, Jessie Blythe Lane, LONDON, N19 3YE.
VINCENT, Mr. Leo, MPhys ACA *2011;* 25 The Gastons, BRISTOL, BS11 0QZ.
VINCENT, Mr. Marc Thomas Raymond, BSc ACA *1997;* 1 Newstone Cottages, East Street, Turners Hill, CRAWLEY, WEST SUSSEX, RH10 4PX.
•VINCENT, Mr. Mark Andrew, ACA *1992;* with RSM Tenon Audit Limited, Charterhouse, Legge Street, BIRMINGHAM, B4 7EU.
VINCENT, Mr. Mark Peter, ACA *2007;* Flat 53, Belvedere Court, 372-374 Upper Richmond Road, LONDON, SW15 6HZ.
•VINCENT, Mr. Martin Russell, BA FCA *1988;* Vincent Ventures Limited, 2 Karen Drive, Backwell, BRISTOL, BS48 3JT.
VINCENT, Mr. Michael, MA ACA *1981;* 23 St. Aubyns Avenue, LONDON, SW19 7BL.
VINCENT, Mrs. Michelle Jane, BCom ACA *1985;* 13 The Old Dairy Farm, Hazelbury Bryan, STURMINSTER NEWTON, DT10 2ES.
VINCENT, Mr. Nicholas, MA FCA *1966;* Turnpike Cottage, Portsmouth Road, Milford, GODALMING, GU8 5HL.
VINCENT, Mrs. Nicola Diane, BA FCA *2000;* 38 Reayrt Carnane, Douglas, ISLE OF MAN, IM2 5LJ.
VINCENT, Mr. Paul John, BSS ACA *1991;* Field House, Hockering Road, The Hockering, WOKING, GU22 7HJ.
•VINCENT, Mr. Paul Malcolm John, FCA *1975;* (Tax Fac), Hemming Vincent LLP, 31 Abbey Road, GRIMSBY, SOUTH HUMBERSIDE, DN32 0HQ.
VINCENT, Mr. Paul Stephen, FCA *1970;* Sunway, Beech Drive, Kingswood, TADWORTH, KT20 6PS. (Life Member)
VINCENT, Mr. Peter John Clarke, MA FCA *1957;* 9 St. Pauls Mews, DORKING, SURREY, RH4 2HP. (Life Member)
VINCENT, Mr. Philip James, BSc ACA *1993;* 4 Fairlawn Close, Claygate, ESHER, KT10 0EN.
•VINCENT, Mr. Richard John, MA FCA *1976;* 33 Illingworth, St Leonards Hill, WINDSOR, BERKSHIRE, SL4 4UP.
VINCENT, Mr. Robert William, FCA *1975;* All Hallows, The Green, Ardeley, STEVENAGE, SG2 7AQ.
VINCENT, Mr. Stephen Derek, BSc ACA *1981;* PO Box 13024, AUCKLAND 1643, NEW ZEALAND.
VINCENT, Miss. Tracey, BA(Hons) ACA *2002;* CPG Finance 6th Floor Fry, Home Office, 2 Marsham Street, LONDON, SW1P 4DF.
VINCETT, Mr. Luke John, BA ACA *2000;* 12 Chattenden Court, Penenden Heath, MAIDSTONE, ME14 2AW.
VINCINI, Mr. Salvo, BSc FCA *1988;* 95 Chelmsford Road, Southgate, LONDON, N14 5PY.
VINE, Miss. Clare Marie, BA ACA CTA *2001;* (Tax Fac), 88 Southdown Crescent, HARROW, HA2 0QS.
VINE, Mr. Cleveland Francis Jack, FCA *1966;* 51 Sandhurst Road, CROWTHORNE, BERKSHIRE, RG45 7HY.
VINE, Miss. Emily Sarah, BSc ACA *2011;* Brolonydd, Reynoldston, Gower, SWANSEA, SA3 1AA.
•VINE, Mr. Geoffrey, ACA *1983;* Vine & Co, Beyond The Pond, 1 Bicester Road, Marsh Gibbon, BICESTER, OXFORDSHIRE OX27 0EU.
VINE, Mr. Jonathan, BSc ACA CTA *2004;* 2 Mortimer House Cottages, Mortimer Lane Mortimer, READING, RG7 3PR.
•VINE, Mr. Paul Simon, MA(Oxon) FCA CTA *1988;* (Tax Fac), Cresswells Accountants LLP, Barclays Bank Chambers, 12 Market Street, HEBDEN BRIDGE, WEST YORKSHIRE, HX7 6AA.
VINE, Mr. Robert Harding, BSc FCA *1980;* Brolonydd, Reynoldston, SWANSEA, SA3 1AA.
•VINE, Mr. Stuart Malcolm, FCA FCCA *1969;* Innerview Limited, Station House, 2 Station Road, RADLETT, WD7 8JX.
VINE, Mr. William Howard, FCA *1961;* 33 Greenfield Avenue, Balsall Common, COVENTRY, CV7 7UG.
VINE-CHATTERTON, Mr. Laurence, BA FCA *1975;* Im Flurchen 24, 66399 MANDELBACHTAL, GERMANY.
VINEBERG, Mr. Gerald, FCA *1975;* The Cottage, East Coldcoats, Ponteland, NEWCASTLE UPON TYNE, NE20 0AE.
•VINER, Mr. Andrew Saul, BSc FCA *1995;* BDO LLP, 55 Baker Street, LONDON, W1U 7EU. See also BDO Stoy Hayward LLP
VINER, Mr. Gordon, FCA *1963;* 5 Nield Court, Upton, CHESTER, CH2 1DN.
VINER, Mrs. Helen Elizabeth, BA(Hons) ACA *2002;* 89 Buckthorn Row, CORSHAM, SN13 9WE.
VINER, Mr. Jonathan Kirk, BSc(Hons) ACA *2000;* 1725 North Benson Road, LAWRENCEVILLE, GA 30043, UNITED STATES.
•VINER, Miss. Melanie Deborah, BSc FCA *1988;* Goodband Viner Taylor, Ellin House, 42 Kingfield Road, SHEFFIELD, S11 9AS.
VINER, Mr. Paul Lewis, BA(Hons) FCA *1995;* 24 Deansway, LONDON, N2 0JF.
VINER, Mr. Richard Frank, BA FCA *1990;* 15 Cheriton Avenue, Hayesford Park, BROMLEY, BR2 9DL.
•VINER, Mr. Robin Alexander Beckwith, BCom FCA *1968;* R.A.B. Viner & Co, Systems House, 42 Broad Street, KIDDERMINSTER, WORCESTERSHIRE, DY10 2LY.
VINER, Miss. Rosalind Caroline, BA ACA *1999;* 16 The Stewponey, Stourton, STOURBRIDGE, WEST MIDLANDS, DY7 6RL.
VINER, Mr. Simon Keith, BSc ACA *1998;* (Tax Fac), with PricewaterhouseCoopers LLP, 101 Barbirolli Square, Lower Mosley Street, MANCHESTER, M2 3PW.
VINES, Miss. Catherine Ann, BSc ACA *2005;* Pfizer, Dorking Road, TADWORTH, KT20 7NS.
VINES, Mrs. Christine Anne, BEng ACA AMCT *1994;* 2 Canadian Crescent, Selsey, CHICHESTER, WEST SUSSEX, PO20 0UQ.
VINES, Mr. Geoffrey William, FCA *1972;* 41 King William Street, GREENWICH, NSW 2065, AUSTRALIA.
VINES, Mr. Godfrey Edward, FCA *1956;* Apartment 13, Richmond Village, Stroud Road, Painswick, STROUD, GLOUCESTERSHIRE GL6 6UH. (Life Member)
•VINES, Mr. Jonathan Edwin, BA ACA ATII *1990;* (Tax Fac), KPMG LLP, 15 Canada Square, LONDON, E14 5GL. See also KPMG Europe LLP
VINES, Ms. Rachel, BSc ACA *2007;* Flat 10 Annecy Court, Queens Place, CHELTENHAM, GLOUCESTERSHIRE, GL51 7NZ.
VINES, Mr. Robert Andrew, FCA *1969;* Heath Dene, Brighton Road, Mannings Heath, HORSHAM, RH13 6HY.
VINEY, Mr. Benjamin James, BA ACA *2002;* 9 Lionel Road, LONDON, SE9 6DQ.
VINEY, Mr. David Victor Stephen, BSc ACA *1996;* 18 Montgomery Avenue, ESHER, KT10 9BB.
VINEY, Miss. Helen, BSc(Hons) ACA *2011;* 109 Welbeck Avenue, Highfield, SOUTHAMPTON, SO17 1SP.
•VINEY, Mr. Malcolm David, FCA *1978;* BKAS, 45 Deerstone Ridge, WETHERBY, WEST YORKSHIRE, LS22 7XN.
VINEY, Mr. Michael Edward, BA ACA *1994;* Beech Cottage, Withington, CHELTENHAM, GL54 4BE.
VINEY, Mr. Paul, ACA *1980;* PO BOX HM 2558, HAMILTON HM KX, BERMUDA.
VINEY, Mr. Peter Alan, FCA *1967;* with Taylor Viney & Marlow, 46-54 High Street, INGATESTONE, CM4 9DW.
VINEY, Miss. Victoria Sophie, BSc ACA *2002;* with PricewaterhouseCoopers, 1 Embankment Place, LONDON, WC2N 6RH.
VINGOE, Mr. Geoffrey Charles, BSc ACA *1992;* with Walker Moyle, 3 Chapel Street, REDRUTH, TR15 2BY.
VINING, Mr. Brian Thomas John, FCA *1974;* #6 - 1027 Belmont Avenue, VICTORIA V8S 3T4, BC, CANADA.
VINJIMOOR, Mr. Sanjay Thirumalai, ACA *2002;* 32 Bowmont Water, DIDCOT, OXFORDSHIRE, OX11 7GF.
VINK, Mr. Craig David, BSc(Econ) ACA *2004;* 42 Buxton Avenue, Caversham, READING, RG4 7BU.
VINKE, Ms. Jeannette, BA(Hons) ACA MBA *2001;* American University of Sharjah, School of Business and Management, Department of Accounting and Finance, PO Box 26666, SHARJAH, UNITED ARAB EMIRATES.
VINOCOURT, Mr. Amior, FCA *1962;* 4 Pasternak Street, TEL AVIV, 69205, ISRAEL. (Life Member)
VINSON, Mr. Daniel Paul Andrew, ACA *2009;* Flat 59 Dewsbury Court, 44-66 Chiswick Road, LONDON, W4 5RA.
VINSON, Mr. Richard Marcus, MA FCA *1974;* 758 rue des Plaisses, 45160 OLIVET, FRANCE.
VINSON, Mr. Simon Geoffrey, FCA *1982;* (Tax Fac), 9 Finch St, Malvern East, MELBOURNE, VIC 3145, AUSTRALIA.
VINTER, Mr. Andrew Hugh Cammack, BA FCA *1974;* 34 Airedale Avenue, LONDON, W4 2NW.
VINTER, Mr. Brian Mark, MSc FCA *1966;* 13 Paultons Square, LONDON, SW3 5AP.
VINTER, Mr. Simon Roy, MA ACA *1992;* Perot Systems Europe Ltd, 1 Oakwood Court, Little Oak Drive, Annesley, NOTTINGHAM, NG15 0DR.
VINTERS, Mrs. Emily Clare, BSc(Hons) ACA *2004;* 8 Nightingale Drive, Cringleford, NORWICH, NR4 7LR.
VINTINER, Mr. Richard Charles, FCA *1967;* 16 Orchard Close, Bushey Heath, BUSHEY, WD23 1LW.
VINTON, Mr. Alan William, BSc FCA *1972;* Spratton Grange Lodge, Spratton, NORTHAMPTON, NN6 8LA.
VINTON, Mr. Michael Craig, BA ACA *1999;* Thorn House, Manor Court, Bubwith, SELBY, YO8 6DU.
VIOLET, Miss. Julie Margaret, PhD BSc ACA *2001;* Unit 1A Horton Road, WEST DRAYTON, UB7 8JJ.
VIPOND, Miss. Dawn Nicola, BA(Hons) ACA *2004;* Deutsche Bank, 175 Bishopsgate, LONDON, EC2N 4DA.
•VIPOND, Mr. Philip Andrew, ACA *2002;* Rees Pollock, 35 New Bridge Street, LONDON, EC4V 6BW.
VIRANI, Mr. Shirazali Issa Rajan, FCA *1973;* Suite 304 Admiral Court, 3451 Springfield Drive, RICHMOND V7E 1Z2, BC, CANADA.
VIRANI, Mr. Viral Atul, BSc ACA *1992;* Applegarth, Green Lane, STANMORE, MIDDLESEX, HA7 3AA.
VIRDEE, Mr. Amritpal Singh, BA FCA *1993;* 114 Somerset Road, SOUTHALL, UB1 2TU.
VIRDEE, Mr. Gurvinder Paul Singh, BA ACA *1993;* 59 Marston Gardens, LUTON, LU2 7DX.
VIRDEE, Mr. Jagjit Singh, MA MSc FCA *1979;* 33 Atkins Road, LONDON, SW12 0AA.
VIRDEE, Mr. Kiran, BA ACA *1990;* 7 Riverway, STAINES, SURREY, TW18 2SJ.
VIRDEE, Mr. Rajvinderjeet Singh, BSc ACA *2004;* Flat 6 Rothesay Court, Harleyford Street, LONDON, SE11 5SU.
VIRDI, Miss. Gursharan Kaur, BSc ACA *1994;* Rajvilas, Kewferry Drive, NORTHWOOD, MIDDLESEX, HA6 2NT.
VIRDI, Mr. Ravinder Singh, BSc ACA *1995;* 27 West Drive, HARROW, MIDDLESEX, HA3 6TX.
•VIRGO, Mr. Timothy Peter James, ACA FCCA *2010;* Mitten Clarke Limited, Festival Way, Festival Park, STOKE-ON-TRENT, ST1 5TQ.
VIRGO, Mrs. Tracy Joan, BA ACA *1993;* 13 Millfield Road, Whickham, NEWCASTLE UPON TYNE, NE16 4QA.
•VIRJI, Mr. Abdul Rasul, BSc(Econ) FCA *1982;* Fairman Davis, Crown House, 72 Hammersmith Road, LONDON, W14 8TH.
VIRJI, Mr. Alnoor Nurali, ACA *1979;* #201 10559 - 172 Street, EDMONTON T5S 1P1, AB, CANADA.
VIRJI, Mrs. Nashila, FCA *1977;* 8 Prominence View SW, CALGARY T3H 3M8, AB, CANADA.
•VIRK, Mr. Riaz Naseer, FCA *1974;* R.N. Virk & Co, 25 Anley Road, West Kensington, LONDON, W14 0BZ.
VIRLEY, Mr. Christopher Athelstan, FCA *1973;* Mandwa House, 30 West Drive, Sonning, READING, RG4 6GD.
VIRLEY, Mrs. Yvonne Thomas, FCA *1975;* Mandwa House, 30 West Drive, Sonning, READING, RG4 6GD.
VIRMANI, Mr. Harish, FCA *1970;* S-71 Greater Kailash, Part One, NEW DELHI 110048, INDIA.
VIRMANI, Mr. Karan, BA ACA *2006;* S-71 Greater Kailash Part One, NEW DELHI 110048, INDIA.
VIRMANI, Mr. Raman, FCA *1974;* 4B/2 Ganga Ram Hospital, Marg, NEW DELHI 110060, INDIA.
VIRMANI, Mr. Sandeep, BSc ACA *1999;* 12 Harvest Fields Way, SUTTON COLDFIELD, B75 5RB.
VIRMANI, Mr. Tushar, BA(Hons) ACA MSI *2004;* 1435 Bedford Street, Apt 11M, STAMFORD, CT 06905, UNITED STATES.
VIRR, Mrs. Lesley Geraldine, BEng FCA *1992;* Craven Arms, St. James Court, Market Hill, SOUTHAM, CV47 0FL.
VIS, Ms. Elizabeth Anne, BSc ACA *1989;* 2 Lower Paddock Road, WATFORD, WD19 4DS.
•VISAGIE, Mr. Gerhard, ACA CA(SA) *2008;* Exceed UK Limited, Bank House, 81 St Judes Road, Englefield Green, EGHAM, SURREY TW20 0DF.
•VISANA, Mr. Raj Jethabhai, FCA *1977;* Visana, 43 Parade House, 135 The Parade, High Street, WATFORD, WD17 1NS. See also Visana Limited
VISANA, Mr. Sundeep, ACA *2008;* 24 Daymer Gardens, PINNER, MIDDLESEX, HA5 2HP.
VISANA, Mr. Vimal Jethabhai, FCA *1973;* 90 Elstree Road, Woodhall Farm, HEMEL HEMPSTEAD, HP2 7QP.
VISHNUBHOTLA, Mr. Krishnakumar, ACA *2000;* C M S Cameron McKenna Mitre House, 160 Aldersgate Street, LONDON, EC1A 4DD.
VISICK, Mr. Richard Martin, BSc ACA *1983;* 1 Treetops, Woodside, Chilworth, SOUTHAMPTON, SO16 7LB.
•VISRAM, Mr. Aniz, BSc FCA *1983;* (Tax Fac), Aniz Visram Accountancy Services Limited, Pinfold lodge, 32a Hampton Lane, SOLIHULL, WEST MIDLANDS, B91 2PY. See also Aniz Visram & Co
VISSER, Mr. James Peter, BA ACA AMCT *1997;* Upper Flat, 2 Brussels Road, LONDON, SW11 2AF.
VISY, Miss. Monika, ACA *2011;* Flat 31, Marshall Court, 10 Anerley Park, LONDON, SE20 8FH.
VITAI, Mr. Attila, OBE BA FCA MBA *1979;* Earley House, Earleydene, ASCOT, SL5 9JY.
•VITEZ, Mr. Charles Oscar, FCA *1972;* (Tax Fac), Charles Vitez & Co, 37 Preston Road, WEMBLEY, HA9 8JZ.
VITHALDAS, Ms. Jane Elizabeth, BA ACA *1993;* 6 The Chase, Great Amwell, WARE, SG12 9TN.
VITHALDAS, Mr. Vimal, LLB ACA *1993;* 6 The Chase, Great Amwell, WARE, HERTFORDSHIRE, SG12 9TN.
VITHLANI, Mr. Anilkumar Keshavji, FCA *1962;* 588 Cummer Avenue, WILLOWDALE M2K 2M6, ON, CANADA.
VITHLANI, Mr. Harish Keshavji, FCA *1980;* 20 Crofton Grove, LONDON, E4 6NY.

VITORIA, Mr. Jerome Patrick, BSc FCA *1979;* with BDO LLP, Emerald House, East Street, EPSOM, SURREY, KT17 1HS.
VITTLE, Mr. John Dawson, FCA CA(SA) *1960;* PO Box 720, FOURWAYS, GAUTENG, 2055, SOUTH AFRICA. (Life Member)
VITTLE, Mrs. Sarah, BSc ACA *2005;* 4 Wilde Court, Radyr, CARDIFF, CF15 8BF.
VITTY, Mr. Martyn John, BA(Hons) ACA *2001;* Cable Management Products Ltd, Station Road, Coleshill, BIRMINGHAM, B46 1HT.
VITTY, Mrs. Mary-Anne, MA(Hons) ACA *2002;* Ardenlaw, Ardens Grafton, ALCESTER, WARWICKSHIRE, B49 6DT.
•**VIVE, Mr. Rosh, FCA PIIA** *1981;* Vive & Co, The Isles, 203 Reading Road, WOKINGHAM, BERKSHIRE, RG41 1LJ.
VIVEKANANDA, Miss. Shanti, ACA *1987;* 14 Jalan Menerung 3, Taman Sato Amoy, Damansara Heights, 59000 KUALA LUMPUR, FEDERAL TERRITORY, MALAYSIA.
•**VIVEKANANDA, Mr. Uthaya Kumar, FCA CF** *1980;* PricewaterhouseCoopers, P.O.Box 10192, Level 10 1 Sentral, Jalan Travers, 50470 KUALA LUMPUR, FEDERAL TERRITORY MALAYSIA.
VIVEKANANDAN, Miss. Maya, BSc ACA *2002;* Hill House, Mount Park Road, HARROW, MIDDLESEX, HA1 3JY.
VIVIAN, Mrs. Alice Camilla, LLB ACA *1986;* 11 Dagmar Road, DORCHESTER, DORSET, DT1 2NA.
VIVIAN, Mr. Andrew David, BSc ACA *1990;* 68 Upton Way, BROADSTONE, BH18 9LZ.
VIVIAN, Mr. George Trevor, FCA *1959;* Spinney End., Bury Road, Cockfield, BURY ST.EDMUNDS, IP30 0JW. (Life Member)
VIZARD, Mr. Kenneth, FCA *1957;* 38 Craighill Road, LEICESTER, LE2 3FB. (Life Member)
VIZARD, Mr. Ronald Charles Harold, FCA *1969;* Field Fare, Pigeon Green, Snitterfield, STRATFORD-UPON-AVON, CV37 0LP.
VIZE, Mr. John Clifford, FCA *1958;* Carina, 1 Monks Hollow, MARLOW, SL7 3SY. (Life Member)
VLACHAKOU, Miss. Maria-Eleni, ACA *2009;* Kotopouli 1, Androutsou Str, 17455 ALIMOSHO, GREECE.
VLACHOS, Mr. Kyriakos, BA ACA *2008;* KORONIAS 13, POTAMOS YERMASOYIAS, 4042 LIMASSOL, CYPRUS.
VLASSOPOULOS, Mr. Thomas, MSc ACA *2004;* Freiherr vom Stein Str. 3, 60323 FRANKFURT AM MAIN, GERMANY.
VLEMMIKS, Ms. Kirsty, MEng ACA *2000;* 3 Holly Close, Walmley, SUTTON COLDFIELD, WEST MIDLANDS, B76 2PD.
VLOTOMAS, Mr. George, BA ACA *2002;* 13 Amfissis Street, LIMASSOL, CYPRUS.
VO, Mr. Hien, ACA *2011;* Flat 209, Peregrine House, Hall Street, LONDON, EC1V 7PS.
VOADEN, Mr. Noel Charles, FCA *1967;* Fernbank, Parsonage Road, BLACKBURN, BB1 4AG. (Life Member)
VOBES, Mr. Derek Gordon, FCA *1960;* 17 Meadow Drive, BEMBRIDGE, ISLE OF WIGHT, PO35 5XZ. (Life Member)
VODANOVICH, Mrs. Amanda Julie, BA ACA *1994;* 448 Riddell Road, Glendowie, AUCKLAND 1071, NEW ZEALAND.
VODDEN, Mr. Paul Andrew, BSc ACA *1990;* 13 Rue Marguerite, 78600 MAISONS LAFFITTE, FRANCE.
•**VOGAN, Mr. Ian, FCA** *1980;* (Tax Fac), Dix Vogan Limited, 2 Chancery Lane, WAKEFIELD, WEST YORKSHIRE, WF1 2SS.
VOGEL, Mr. Guy Gordon, FCA *1976;* 13 Raeburn Way, College Town, SANDHURST, GU47 0FH.
VOGEL, Mr. Isaac, FCA *1962;* Heshel Street 8/ 13, 32446 HAIFA, ISRAEL.
VOGEL, Mr. Norman David, BSc FCA *1980;* 21 Orchard Drive, EDGWARE, MIDDLESEX, HA8 7SE.
VOGEL, Mr. Raoul Werner Walter, ACA *2002;* Kornhauselgasse 9/8/13, A-1200 WIEN, AUSTRIA.
•**VOGEL, Mr. Timothy John, JP BSc FCA MEWI** *1996;* The Chamber of Experts, 48 The Street, Sporle, KING'S LYNN, PE32 2DR.
VOGELS, Mrs. Woan Theng, ACA CA(AUS) *2009;* Valeriusstraat 42 BVN, 1071 MK AMSTERDAM, NETHERLANDS.
VOGL, Mr. Alan Frank, FCA *1964;* Hauburgsteinweg 31, D 61476 KRONBERG, GERMANY. (Life Member)
VOGT, Mr. Klaus-Dieter, FCA *1976;* 54 Moss Lane, PINNER, HA5 3AX.
VOGWELL, Mr. Nicholas Peter, BA(Hons) ACA *2009;* 1 Ashley Terrace, Lower Weston, BATH, BA1 3DP.
VOHORA, Mr. Ashni Kumar, FCA *1972;* P O Box 159, ARUSHA, TANZANIA.
VOHORA, Mr. Praveen Kumar, FCA *1973;* Vohora & Company, Suite 309A, 15252 - 32nd Avenue, SURREY V3S 0R7, BC, CANADA.
•**VOHRA, Mr. Mushtaq Ahmed, FCA** *1968;* Mushtaq & Co, 407 Commerce Centre, Hasrat Mohani Road, KARACHI 74200, PAKISTAN.
VOHRA, Mr. Najeeb Mushtaq, BSc ACA *2000;* 19-B Block G, Gulberg 3, LAHORE, PAKISTAN.
VOHRA, Mr. Nasir Mushtaq, FCA *1989;* with Ernst & Young, Al Faisaliah Office Tower, Level 14, PO Box 2732, RIYADH, 11461 SAUDI ARABIA.
VOHRA, Mr. Sameet, BA ACA *1999;* Wentworth House, 3A Wraylands Drive, REIGATE, RH2 0LG.
VOHRA, Mr. Sandeep, BSc ACA *1999;* 197 Hale Lane, EDGWARE, HA8 9QN.
VOHRA, Mr. Sandeep, BSc ACA *1997;* 8 Edgar Close, Worth, CRAWLEY, WEST SUSSEX, RH10 7RF.
VOHRA, Mrs. Sukhjit, BA ACA *2008;* Flat 4, 21 Epsom Road, CROYDON, CR0 4NB.
•**VOICE, Mr. Hugh Alistair, BSc ACA** *1981;* (Tax Fac), Voice & Co Accountancy Services Limited, 14 Jessops Riverside, 800 Brightside Lane, SHEFFIELD, S9 2RX. See also Voice & Co Limited
VOICE, Mr. Mark Geoffrey, BEng ACA *1994;* West Wind, The Barrows, CHEDDAR, SOMERSET, BS27 3BG.
VOICE, Mr. Michael Aubrey, ACA *1995;* TV Guide, 6922 Hollywood Blvd, LOS ANGELES, CA 90028, UNITED STATES.
①**VOICE, Mr. Richard John, BA FCA** *1987;* with KPMG LLP, One Snowhill, Snow Hill Queensway, BIRMINGHAM, B4 6GN.
•**VOIGTS, Mr. Allen Keith, FCA** *1958;* (Tax Fac), A.K. Voigts, 14 Elm Grove, Thorpe Bay, SOUTHEND-ON-SEA, SS1 3EZ.
VOISEY, Mr. Christopher Nicholas, BSc ACA *2002;* 19 Priory Road, KENILWORTH, CV8 1LL.
•**VOISEY, Mr. Howard Gwyn, MSc ACA** *1979;* (Tax Fac), PKF (UK) LLP, New Guild House, 45 Great Charles Street, BIRMINGHAM, B3 2LX.
VOKES, Miss. Fiona Mary, BA ACA *1997;* 33 Warren Road, REIGATE, SURREY, RH2 0BN.
VOKES, Mr. Harold Michael, FCA *1963;* 119 Polwell Lane, Barton Seagrave, KETTERING, NN15 6TD. (Life Member)
VOKES, Miss. Rachel, ACA *2008;* 3 Fairway, WOODFORD GREEN, IG8 7RB.
VOKINS, Mr. Trevor William Derek, FCA *1958;* 56 Hove Park Road, HOVE, BN3 6LN. (Life Member)
VOLANTHEN, Mrs. Annabelle Lucy, BSc ACA *1996;* Consort House, Lloyds TSB Bank Plc, PO Box 359, BRISTOL, BS99 2EN.
VOLERICH, Mr. Martin Bernard, BA FCA *1985;* 198 Elm Street, TENAFLY, NJ 07670, UNITED STATES.
VOLLER, Mr. Kevin Nicholas, BSc ACA *1980;* (Tax Fac), 827 Madison Court, PALM BEACH GARDENS, FL 33410, UNITED STATES.
VOLLER, Mr. Scott, LLB ACA *2002;* U.B.S. AG, PO Box 350, JERSEY, JE4 8UJ.
VOLLERS, Mr. Hendrik Andrew, BA ACA *1979;* Calendar Club Ltd, Water Lane, Haven Banks, EXETER, EX2 8BY.
VOLSCHENK, Mr. Jan, ACA CA(SA) *2011;* 62 Hawkesworth Drive, BAGSHOT, SURREY, GU19 5QZ.
VON BERGEN, Mrs. Deborah Jane, BA ACA *1984;* Capel Lodge, Capel, DORKING, RH5 4PQ.
•**VON BERGEN, Mr. Hugh Robert, MA FCA** *1984;* (Tax Fac), KPMG LLP, 15 Canada Square, LONDON, E14 5GL. See also KPMG Europe LLP
VON BERGEN, Mr. Mark Thomas, FCA *1974;* Grant Thornton UK Llp Grant Thornton House, 22 Melton Street, LONDON, NW1 2EP.
VON BERTELE, Mr. Maurice, BSc ACA *2000;* (Tax Fac), 64 South Park Road, Wimbledon, LONDON, SW19 8SZ.
VON DER HEYDE, Mr. Paul Heinrich Sigisnund, FCA *1976;* Newton Brae, 9 The Street, West Horsley, LEATHERHEAD, SURREY, KT24 6AY.
VON FURER-HAIMENDORF, Mr. Nicholas Cristoph, FCA FInstD FCIArb *1974;* (Tax Fac), Forden Services Ltd, 16 Woodstock Road, LONDON, W4 1UE.
•**VON GEBSATTEL, Mrs. Antonia, FCA** *1960;* A. von Gebsattel, S. Polo 2733, 30125 VENICE, ITALY.
VON PALESKE, Mrs. Sophie Jane, BSc(Hons) ACA *2004;* 13 Hamilton Terrace, LONDON, NW8 9RE.
VON SCHMIDT, Mr. Johan Robin Charles, BA ACA *1997;* 58 Church Street, CHESHAM, HP5 1HY.
VON SEIDEL, Mr. Cronwright, FCA *1949;* 56 Simonstown Road, FISH HOEK, 7975, SOUTH AFRICA. (Life Member)
VON SEIDEL, Mr. Robert Cron, ACA *1994;* 5 Peter Cloete Avenue, Constantia, CAPE TOWN, 7806, SOUTH AFRICA.
VON SEMBACH, Mrs. Gail Emma, BEng ACA *2002;* 66 Bramfield Road, LONDON, SW11 6PY.
VON STRUENSEE, Mr. Christian Arthur, FCA *1965;* Ridge House, Lower Basildon, READING, RG8 9NX. (Life Member)
VON UNGERN-STERNBERG, Mr. Alexander Otto Andreas, MA FCA *1974;* Euro - IB Ltd, 1 Crown Court, LONDON, EC2V 6LR.
VONDY, Mr. James Neil, ACA *1993;* Manx Gas Ltd, Murdock House, South Quay, Douglas, ISLE OF MAN, IM1 5PA.
VONG, Miss. Samantha Jieng Mien, BA(Oxon) ACA *2010;* Flat 10, Thanet Lodge, 10 Mapesbury Road, LONDON, NW2 4JA.
VONGVIVATHCHAI, Miss. Piyathida, BSc ACA *2010;* 64/47 Flora House, Ekamai 10/4, Sukumvit 63, BANGKOK 10110, THAILAND.
VOO, Mr. Vivian, FCA *1973;* 29-2-2 Sri York Condominium, 29 Halaman York, 10450 PENANG, MALAYSIA.
VOO, Miss. Yen May, BA ACA *2003;* 121 East 23rd Street #8D, NEW YORK, NY 10010, UNITED STATES.
•**VOOGD, Mr. Christopher Jules, BA FCA** *1991;* Ernst & Young LLP, 1 Colmore Square, BIRMINGHAM, B4 6HQ. See also Ernst & Young Europe LLP
•①**VOOGHT, Mr. Nigel John, ACA** *1981;* PricewaterhouseCoopers LLP, Hays Galleria, 1 Hays Lane, LONDON, SE1 2RD. See also PricewaterhouseCoopers
•**VOOGHT, Mr. Paul David, FCA** *1979;* W R Frost & Co Limited, Riversdale, Ashburton Road, TOTNES, DEVON, TQ9 5JU.
VOON, Mr. Vincent Chee Leong, MSc BSc(Econ) FCA *1993;* Flat 5, 46 Queens Gardens, LONDON, W2 3AA.
VOONG, Miss. Cam Lay, BA ACA *2008;* 213 Coppermill Lane, Walthamstow, LONDON, E17 7HG.
VOONG, Mr. Che Yee, BSc ACA *1983;* PT HM Sampoerna, One Pacific Place Building, 16th Floor JL Jenderal Sudirman, KAV 52-53, JAKARTA, 12190 INDONESIA.
VORA, Mr. Ketan Kantilal, BSc ACA *2006;* P.O. Box 85234, MOMBASA, COAST PROVINCE, KENYA.
VORA, Mr. Keval Nalin, BSc ACA *1996;* P.O. Box 43975, NAIROBI, 00100, KENYA.
VORA, Mr. Krunal, ACA *2008;* 55 Ormesby Way, Kenton, HARROW, MIDDLESEX, HA3 9SE.
•**VORA, Mr. Narendra Navalchand, FCA** *1978;* Vora & Co, 30 Pasture Field Road, Peel Hall, MANCHESTER, M22 5JU.
VORA, Mrs. Paloma Irene Marina, BA ACA *1991;* Chemin du Panorama 1, Arzier, 1273 VAUD, SWITZERLAND.
•**VORA, Mr. Prakash Shantilal, ACA** *1981;* P.S. Vora & Co, 32 Doeshill Drive, WICKFORD, ESSEX, SS12 9RD.
•**VORA, Mr. Rajendra Shivalal, ACA** *1982;* (Tax Fac), R Vora & Co Limited, 6 Carlton Road, ROMFORD, ESSEX, RM2 5AA.
VORA, Miss. Reena, BA ACA *2006;* 93 Courtland Avenue, ILFORD, IG1 3DR.
VORA, Mr. Sujay Nalin, BSc ACA *1999;* c/o UTI, PO Box 43975, NAIROBI, GPO-00100, KENYA.
VORA, Mr. Sunil, BSc ACA *1992;* Chemin du Panorama 1, Arzier, 1273 VAUD, SWITZERLAND.
VORAJEE, Mr. Ismail, BA ACA *2007;* 12 Kingsbarn Close, Fulwood, PRESTON, PR2 9LZ.
•**VORALIA, Mr. Sunilkumar Ratilal, ACA** *1984;* Distinctive Accountancy Limited, First Floor, Allied Sainif House, 412 Greenford Road, GREENFORD, UB6 9AH. See also BRAAMS LLP
VORLEY, Mr. Rodney William, ACA *1983;* P.O.Box 30552, NAIROBI, 00100, KENYA.
VOS, Mr. Peter Benjamin, MA FCA *1975;* 17 Vicarage Lane, East Preston, LITTLEHAMPTON, BN16 2SP.
VOSE, Mr. George Graham, FCA *1950;* The Borie, 5 Balcarras Road, Charlton Kings, CHELTENHAM, GL53 8QG. (Life Member)
VOSE, Mr. Richard Anthony, FCA *1991;* 22 Campbell Road, Woodley, READING, RG5 3NA.
•**VOSKARIDES, Mr. Nicos Christoforou, FCA** *1978;* Nicos Voskarides, P O Box 25081, 1306 NICOSIA, CYPRUS.
VOSPER, Mr. Iain, BSc ACA *2002;* South West Water Plc Peninsula House, Rydon Lane, EXETER, EX2 7HR.
VOSPER, Mr. John Mark, BSc ACA *1989;* 43 The Copse, NEWTON-LE-WILLOWS, WA12 9YF.
VOSPER, Mr. Peter Graham, FCA *1968;* 1 Discovery Wharf, 15 North Quay, PLYMOUTH, PL4 0RB.
VOSS, Mr. Andrew James, BA ACA *2001;* 77/1 Foy Street Balmain, SYDNEY, NSW 2041, AUSTRALIA.
VOSS, Mrs. Emma Elizabeth, BSc(Hons) ACA *2001;* 104 Sternhold Avenue, LONDON, SW2 4PP.
VOSS, Mr. Graeme Clive, BCom ACA *1996;* Brickwalls Farm House Gilberts End, Hanley Castle, WORCESTER, WR8 0AS.
VOSS, Mr. Martin Leon, FCA *1966;* Spring House, Stokes Court, Swanmore, SOUTHAMPTON, SO32 2ET.
VOSSER, Mr. Richard Brooke, MA MSci ACA *2005;* 51 Fawe Park Road, LONDON, SW15 2EE.
VOUAL, Mr. Prithpal Singh, BSc ACA *2007;* 26 Crantock Drive, Almondsbury, BRISTOL, BS32 4HG.
VOUILLOZ, Mr. Simon, ACA *1990;* 1 Montacute Road, LEWES, EAST SUSSEX, BN7 1EN.
•**VOULTERS, Mr. Marc, BSc FCA** *1983;* SRLV, 89 New Bond Street, LONDON, W1S 1DA.
•**VOUSDEN, Mr. Michael Edwin, BSc FCA** *1993;* Thomas & Young LLP, 240-244 Stratford Road, Shirley, SOLIHULL, WEST MIDLANDS, B90 3AE. See also Thomas & Young
VOUT, Mrs. Sarah, LLB ACA *2006;* with Grant Thornton UK LLP, Enterprise House, 115 Edmund Street, BIRMINGHAM, B3 2HJ.
VOUT, Mr. William, BSc ACA *2004;* 51 Elmwood Road, SUTTON COLDFIELD, B74 2DD.
VOVOS, Mr. Ioannis, MSc BSc ACA *2007;* with PricewaterhouseCoopers, 268-270 Kifissias Avenue, Halandri, 15232 ATHENS, GREECE.
VOWELS, Mr. Robert Charles, BSc ACA *2004;* RWE Trading, Trigonos, Windmill Hill Business Park, Whitehill Way, SWINDON, SN5 6PB.
VOWLES, Miss. Angharad Kate, MSci ACA *2009;* Pricewaterhousecoopers Llp Marlborough Court, 10 Bricket Road, ST. ALBANS, HERTFORDSHIRE, AL1 3JX.
•**VOWLES, Mrs. Hilary Frances, LLB FCA CTA** *1981;* (Tax Fac), 62 Chelsham Road, LONDON, SW4 6NP.
VOWLES, Mr. John, BA FCA MCT *1978;* 62 Chelsham Road, LONDON, SW4 6NP.
•**VOWLES, Mr. Jonathan Cavill, BA FCA CTA DChA** *1991;* Jonathan Vowles, 114 High Street, Cranfield, BEDFORD, MK43 0DG. See also Jonathan Vowles Payroll Services Ltd
VOWLES, Mrs. Rachel, BSc ACA *2007;* 85 Trinity Road, LONDON, SW19 8QZ.
•**VOWLES, Mr. Richard Anthony, FCA** *1968;* (Tax Fac), R.A. Vowles & Co, 148 Commercial Road, Totton, SOUTHAMPTON, SO40 3AA.
VOYCE, Mrs. Sophie Claire, MA(Hons) ACA *2002;* Trespassers Will, Tidenham Chase, High Woolaston, LYDNEY, GLOUCESTERSHIRE, GL15 6PT.
VOYLE, Mr. William Brian, BSc ACA *1986;* Sunnymeade, CLARBESTON ROAD, SA63 4SL.
VOYSEY, Miss. Carole Jane, BA ACA *1986;* Netherwood House, 3 The Brow Church Road, Combe Down, BATH, BA2 5JL.
VRAALSEN, Ms. Stine, BCom ACA *2006;* 826 W. 54th Terrace, KANSAS CITY, MO 64112, UNITED STATES.
•**VRACHIMIS, Mr. Vassilios George, BA(Hons) ACA CFA** *2001;* with PricewaterhouseCoopers LLP, 7 More London Riverside, LONDON, SE1 2RT.
•**VRAHIMIS, Mr. Antonios, FCA** *1974;* Antonios Vrahimis, P O Box 21936, 1515 NICOSIA, CYPRUS.
VRANCKEN, Mr. David Charles, BSc ACA *1994;* C/o Qatar Telecom Q.S.C, PO Box 217, DOHA, QATAR. (Life Member)
VROLIJK, Mr. Arie, FCA *1971;* PO Box 244, VICTORIA PARK, WA 6979, AUSTRALIA.
VRONINKS, Mr. Jean-Philip, MA ACA *2004;* Jachthuislaan 31, 3210 LINDEN, BELGIUM.
VRONTAMITIS, Mr. Leon Nicholas, BSc ACA *1998;* 4 Keith Street, Lindfield, SYDNEY, NSW 2070, AUSTRALIA.
VRONTISSIS, Mr. Alexander, BSc(Hons) FCA *2000;* 8 Seymour Gardens, SURBITON, KT5 8QE.
VU, Ms. Phuong Anh, BSc(Hons) ACA *2011;* 4B, The Old Fire Station, 244 Shepherds Bush Road, LONDON, W6 7NN.
VUJACIC, Mr. Steven, BSc ACA *1985;* Apartado de Correos 128, 29680 ESTEPONA, MALAGA, SPAIN.
VUKOMANOVIC, Mrs. Anne, BA(Hons) ACA *2002;* 49 Tolverne Road, Raynes Park, LONDON, SW20 8RA.
VUN, Mr. Richard Foh Onn, ACA *1979;* 2 Lefroy Close, Westlake, BRISBANE, QLD 4074, AUSTRALIA.
VURDIEN, Mr. Predanen, ACA *1992;* Apartment 261, 41 Millharbour, LONDON, E14 9NE.
VUSIK, Miss. Yuliya, BSc ACA *2008;* with PricewaterhouseCoopers Limited, Julia House, 3 Themistocles Dervis Street, CY-1066 NICOSIA, CYPRUS.
VYAS, Miss. Arunima, BSc ACA *2006;* 253 West 72nd Street, 1405, NEW YORK, NY 10023, UNITED STATES.

•**VYAS, Mr. Bipinchandra Chandrakant, FCA** *1973;* Rawi & Co LLP, 128 Ebury Street, LONDON, SW1W 9QQ. See also Bipin Vyas & Co
VYAS, Mr. Dipak, BA ACA *1995;* 9 White Meadow Road, HILLSBOROUGH, NJ 08844, UNITED STATES.
VYAS, Mr. Dipesh, ACA *2009;* 95 Piedmont Road, LONDON, SE18 1TB.
VYAS, Mr. Guniraj Balkrishna Pokhardas, FCA *1974;* 15 Lockington Crescent, DUNSTABLE, LU5 4ST.
VYAS, Mr. Hitesh, LLB ACA *2007;* 66 Homeway Road, Evington, LEICESTER, LE5 5RG.
VYAS, Mr. Pravinchandra Dahyalal, FCA *1973;* 31 Sylvan Avenue, LONDON, NW7 2JH.
VYAS, Miss. Pujah, BA(Hons) ACA *2011;* 6 Evington Valley Road, LEICESTER, LE5 5LJ.
VYAS, Mr. Sanjay, BSc ACA *1998;* Unit 408 Anlaby House, 37 Boundary Street, LONDON, E2 7JQ.
VYAS, Mr. Sharadchandra Kanaiyalal, FCA *1970;* 4 Carrick Drive, Barkingside, ILFORD, ESSEX, IG6 2LX.
VYAS, Mrs. Sheetal, BSc ACA *2001;* 64 Carolina Road, THORNTON HEATH, CR7 8DL.
VYDRA, Miss. Anouschka, LLB ACA *2000;* Apt 12, 35 Place de la Gare, Residence de l'univers, 74400 CHAMONIX, FRANCE.
VYE, Mr. Andrew John, BA ACA *1993;* RasGas Company Limited, 26th Floor RasGas Tower, PO Box 24200, DOHA, QATAR.
VYE, Mrs. Anuradha, BA ACA *1993;* c/o Mr Andrew J Vye, RasGas Company Limited - Finance Dept., PO Box 24200, 26th Floor RasGas Tower, DOHA, QATAR.
VYSHEGORODTSEVA, Miss. Tatiana, ACA *2010;* Lesnaya Street 5B, 125047 MOSCOW, RUSSIAN FEDERATION.
WABY, Miss. Valerie Ann, BA FCA *1996;* 26 Deepdale Lane, Nettleham, LINCOLN, LN2 2LT.
WACHER, Mr. Thomas Blake, MEng ACA *2003;* with Reeves & Co LLP, 37 St. Margarets Street, CANTERBURY, KENT, CT1 2TU.
WACHMAN, Mr. Nigel David, MSc FCA *1982;* 71 Brodrick Road, LONDON, SW17 7DX.
WACHUKA, Miss. Mary, ACA *1998;* Suite 360, 12 Church Street, HAMILTON HM11, BERMUDA.
WACKERLE, Mr. Stephen, ACA CFA CA(SA) *2008;* 73 Lakes Lane, BEACONSFIELD, BUCKINGHAMSHIRE, HP9 2JZ.
WACKETT, Mr. Charles, FCA *1965;* 31 Cannon Crescent, EASTERN PASSAGE B3G 1E9, NS, CANADA. (Life Member)
•**WACKETT, Mr. Jonathon Rex, FCA** *1977;* The Victoria Cottage Oxford Road, Frilford Heath, ABINGDON, OXFORDSHIRE, OX13 5NW.
WACKETT, Mr. Martin John Sibley, BA ACA *1994;* GKP Chartered Accountants, 1st Floor, 5 Doolittle Yard, Froghall Road, Ampthill, BEDFORD BEDFORDSHIRE MK45 2NW.
•**WACKS, Mr. Anthony Charles, FCA** *1971;* (Tax Fac), Crawfords Accountants LLP, Stanton House, 41 Blackfriars Road, SALFORD, M3 7DB. See also Anthony Wacks Ltd
WACZKOW, Mrs. Zabetz Enge, ACA CA(SA) *2010;* (Tax Fac), 25 Links Green Way, COBHAM, KT11 2QH.
WADA, Mr. Christopher James, BA(Hons) ACA *2001;* 37 Kingswood Road, LONDON, SW19 3ND.
WADA, Mr. David Christopher George, FCA *1970;* 48 Hawkhurst Way, WEST WICKHAM, BR4 9PF.
WADA, Mrs. Helen, MSc BSc(Econ) ACA *2001;* 37 Kingswood Road, LONDON, SW19 3ND.
WADD, Ms. Clare Helen, BSc ACA *2001;* Sohonet Ltd, 60 Poland Street, LONDON, W1F 7NT.
WADDELL, Miss. Emma Louise, BSc ACA *2004;* 7 Stradey Hill, LLANELLI, DYFED, SA15 4AB.
WADDELL, Mrs. Gayle Christine, BSc ACA *2002;* (Tax Fac), H M Revenue & Customs Special Investigations, Trinity Bridge House 2 Dearmans Place, SALFORD, M3 5AQ.
WADDELL, Mr. Ian Alexander, BSc(Hons) ACA *2004;* 3 Headington Drive, WOKINGHAM, RG40 1XB.
WADDELL, Mr. John Everard Falconer, FCA *1973;* Waddells, P.O. Box 140, PORT OF SPAIN, TRINIDAD AND TOBAGO.
•**WADDELL, Mr. Philip Andrew, BSc FCA ATII** *1981;* The Gables, Stonebridge Fields, Shalford, GUILDFORD, SURREY, GU4 8EE.
WADDELOW, Mrs. Deborah Claire, BA ACA *2009;* with PricewaterhouseCoopers LLP, 1 Embankment Place, LONDON, WC2N 6RH.
•**WADDINGHAM, Mrs. Anne-Marie, BSc ACA** *1995;* Anne-Marie Waddingham, 4 Spruce Close, Fulwood, PRESTON, PR2 9WB.
WADDINGHAM, Mr. Bernard Joseph, BA FCA *1971;* Keyston House, 61 Putnoe Lane, BEDFORD, MK41 9AE.
WADDINGHAM, Miss. Elizabeth Mary Joan, MSc ACA *2006;* 21 Stanbridge Road, LONDON, SW15 1DX.
WADDINGHAM, Mrs. Fiona Helen, ACA *2008;* 2 Kingswear Road, RUISLIP, MIDDLESEX, HA4 6AT.
WADDINGHAM, Mr. Ian Gerard, BSc(Econ) ACA *2004;* 16 Birchwood Drive, Fulwood, PRESTON, PR2 9UJ.
WADDINGTON, Mr. Alan, MBA FCA *1970;* St Georges Farm, Mickley Lane, Totley, SHEFFIELD, S17 4HE.
WADDINGTON, Mr. Andrew John, BA FCA *1993;* 18b Hill Road, FAREHAM, HAMPSHIRE, PO16 8LA.
WADDINGTON, Mr. Andrew Russell, BEng ACA *1992;* 21 North Park Avenue, Barrowford, NELSON, LANCASHIRE, BB9 6DW.
WADDINGTON, Mr. Brian, FCA *1958;* 11 Dukes Wharf, Terry Avenue, YORK, YO23 1JE. (Life Member)
WADDINGTON, Mr. Carl Anthony, BSc ACA *2003;* The Agricultural Cottage, Everingham, YORK, YO42 4JF.
WADDINGTON, Miss. Carla, MA(Hons) ACA *2004;* 4 Top Lane, Copmanthorpe, YORK, YO23 3UJ.
WADDINGTON, Mr. Charles Anthony, BCom FCA *1975;* Thorney Croft, Arkholme, CARNFORTH, LANCASHIRE, LA6 1AZ.
WADDINGTON, Mr. Clifford Derek, FCA *1958;* Cokes Cottage, Cokes Farm Lane, CHALFONT ST.GILES, HP8 4TU. (Life Member)
•**WADDINGTON, Mr. David, BA ACA** *1994;* (Tax Fac), Waddington Tax Consultancy Ltd, Cragside, Delph Lane, Daresbury, WARRINGTON, WA4 4AN.
WADDINGTON, Mr. David Warren, FCA *1966;* 3 Musgrave Crescent, LONDON, SW6 4PT.
WADDINGTON, Mr. Ian Macpherson, BA ACA *1979;* Redwood, Nursery Lane, Sheldwich Lees, FAVERSHAM, ME13 0NG.
WADDINGTON, Mr. John Philip, MA FCA *1964;* 47 Caroline House, Bayswater Road, LONDON, W2 4RQ. (Life Member)
WADDINGTON, Mr. Roy, FCA *1959;* 9 Roundwood Avenue, Reedley, BURNLEY, BB10 2LH. (Life Member)
WADDINGTON, Ms. Sarah Esme, MA ACA *2002;* 31 Denholme Road, LONDON, W9 3HT.
WADDINGTON, Mr. Simon Charles, BSc ACA *1988;* Steart Farmhouse, Stoodleigh, TIVERTON, EX16 9QA.
WADDINGTON, Mr. William James Percy, BSc(Econ) ACA *1997;* 66 Wakeman Road, LONDON, NW10 5DH.
•**WADE, Mr. Alan, ACA** *1983;* Wakefield House, 32 High Street, PINNER, HA5 5PW.
•**WADE, Ms. Amanda, ACA** *1992;* with Grant Thornton UK LLP, 30 Finsbury Square, LONDON, EC2P 2YU.
WADE, Mrs. Anne Marie, ACA *1990;* Eric Bowes & Co Solicitors, 139 Stratford Road Shirley, SOLIHULL, B90 3AY.
WADE, Miss. Bryony Diana, ACA *2010;* 18 Rockley Road, LONDON, W14 0DA.
WADE, Mrs. Caroline Francis, BA ACA *1986;* 64 Downs Wood, EPSOM, KT18 5UL.
WADE, Mr. Christopher Nigel, BSc FCA *1997;* 28 Dale Way, Fernwood, NEWARK, NOTTINGHAMSHIRE, NG24 3GH.
WADE, Mr. David John, ACA *1995;* 27 Brian Avenue, Sanderstead, SOUTH CROYDON, SURREY, CR2 9NG.
WADE, Mrs. Deborah Louise, BSc ACA *1993;* BBC (White City), Room 1522, 201 Wood Lane, LONDON, W12 7TS.
WADE, Mr. Dominic Simon Francis, BSc ACA *1999;* 2 Avenue Place, Avenue Road, BISHOP'S STORTFORD, HERTFORDSHIRE, CM23 5GN.
•**WADE, Mrs. Donna Louise, BA ACA** *1995;* WadeX Limited, 11 Richmond Road, SUTTON COLDFIELD, WEST MIDLANDS, B73 6BJ.
WADE, Miss. Eleanor Charlotte, BA ACA *2011;* Thomson Reuters Ltd Aldgate House, 33 Aldgate High Street, LONDON, EC3N 1DL.
WADE, Mr. Graham Martin, MA(Cantab) ACA *2001;* 70 Morris Lane, SCARSDALE, NY 10583, UNITED STATES.
•**WADE, Mr. Grant, BA ACA** *1991;* Wells Richardson, Cannon House, Rutland Road, SHEFFIELD, S3 8DP.
WADE, Miss. Joanne Ruth, BA ACA *2007;* Flat 6, 15-19 Bedford Hill, LONDON, SW12 9DS.
WADE, Mr. John David, ACA *1980;* 24 Cottonwood, HOUGHTON LE SPRING, TYNE AND WEAR, DH4 7TA.
WADE, Mr. John Kenneth, BCom ACA *1980;* 10 Surrendale Place, LONDON, W9 2QW.
WADE, Mr. Jonathan Randal, MA ACA *1996;* Flat 2, 4 Lancaster Grove, LONDON, NW3 4NX.
WADE, Mrs. Katharine Anne, BSc FCA *1999;* Aspen RE Plantation Place, 30 Fenchurch Street, LONDON, EC3M 3BD.
WADE, Mr. Lawrence Edward, BEng ACA *1999;* 9 Lord Rosebery Mews, NORWICH, NR7 0GX.
WADE, Mrs. Louise, MPhys ACA *2011;* 68 Cobb Close, Datchet, SLOUGH, SL3 9QZ.
WADE, Mr. Matthew, MA BA ACA *2010;* 68 Cobb Close, Datchet, SLOUGH, SL3 9QZ.
WADE, Mr. Michael John, FCA *1967;* 12 Hullett Drive, HEBDEN BRIDGE, HX7 5QR.
WADE, Mr. Michael Musgrave, FCA CTA *1978;* (Tax Fac), Management Consulting Group Plc, 10 Fleet Place, LONDON, EC4M 7RB.
WADE, Mrs. Natalie Louise, ACA MAAT *2008;* 30 Hoylake Drive, Farcet, PETERBOROUGH, PE7 3BD.
WADE, Mr. Nicholas James, MSc ACA *2004;* 39 Aston Road, LONDON, SW20 8BG.
WADE, Miss. Nicola Jane, BEng FCA *1996;* Military Fitness Ltd Unit 7b-7c, 3-9 Imperial Road, LONDON, SW6 2AG.
WADE, Mr. Nigel Clement, FCA *1971;* 23 Coltsfoot Drive, GUILDFORD, SURREY, GU1 1YH. (Life Member)
WADE, Mr. Peter, BA ACA *1991;* Media Com, 124 Theobalds Road, LONDON, WC1X 8RX.
WADE, Mr. Philip Anthony, FCA *1960;* 8 Mill Lane Duxford, CAMBRIDGE, CB22 4PT. (Life Member)
WADE, Mr. Philip William, BSc ACA *1984;* (Tax Fac), Field House, New Road, Eckington, PERSHORE, WR10 3AZ.
WADE, Mr. Richard Alan, BD FCA *1973;* Amberlee House, Main Street, Countesthorpe, LEICESTER, LE8 5QX.
•**WADE, Mr. Robert John, MA FCA** *1983;* Flat 23, 66 Shepherds Hill, Highgate, LONDON, N6 5RN.
WADE, Mr. Robert Ludley, FCA *1959;* with Anderson Barrowcliff, Waterloo House, Teesdale South, Thornaby Place, STOCKTON-ON-TEES, TS17 6SA.
WADE, Mr. Roland John, BA FCA *1955;* Kilaguni, Rosemount Drive, BROMLEY, BR1 2LQ. (Life Member)
WADE, Mr. Ronan Jeffrey, MA ACA *2010;* 21 Elm Close, Elsenham, BISHOP'S STORTFORD, HERTFORDSHIRE, CM22 6LE.
WADE, Mr. Rory David, BSc ACA CF *1994;* with BTG Financial Consulting LLP, 9th Floor, Bond Court, LEEDS, LS1 2JZ.
WADE, Mr. Russell, FCA *1976;* 88 Mornington Road, STOKE-ON-TRENT, ST1 6EL.
WADE, Mr. Stephen Andrew, BSc ACA *1992;* (Member of Council 1995 - 2000), 24 Wentworth Drive, Oundle, PETERBOROUGH, PE8 4QF.
WADE, Mr. Terence James Alexander, BA FCA *1986;* 64 Downs Wood, EPSOM, KT18 5UL.
WADE, Mr. Thomas David, BEng ACA *1999;* Mill House, 146 Preston Old Road, Freckleton, PRESTON, PR4 1HD.
WADE, Mrs. Wendy Elizabeth, LLB ACA *1984;* 147 Collins Street, MELBOURNE, VIC 3000, AUSTRALIA.
•**WADE-JONES, Mrs. Amanda Jayne, BSc(Hons) FCA CTA** *2000;* (Tax Fac), A Wade Tax Consultancy, 2 Plough Cottages, Great Munden, WARE, HERTFORDSHIRE, SG11 1HS.
WADEL, Dr. Fabian Michael, DPhil ACA ATII *1992;* 17 Denton Hill, Cuddesdon, OXFORD, OX44 9HZ.
WADELIN, Mrs. Catherine Anne, LLB ACA *1987;* 26 Kings Coughton Lane, Kings Coughton, ALCESTER, B49 5QE.
WADELIN, Mr. Mark Thomas, BSc FCA *1986;* 26 Kings Coughton Lane, Kings Coughton, ALCESTER, B49 5QE.
WADEMAN, Mr. Chris Andrew, ACA *2010;* 2 Westfield Avenue, RYTON, TYNE AND WEAR, NE40 4DR.
WADEMAN, Mr. Stephen Paul, BSc ACA *2009;* 3 Grangeway Road, WIGSTON, LE18 1JE.
WADESON, Mr. Anthony Hugh, FCA *1968;* Low Wood Stile Barn, Foxfield, BROUGHTON-IN-FURNESS, CUMBRIA, LA20 6BT.
WADEY, Miss. Ashleigh Kim, ACA *2004;* Box Hill School London Road, Mickleham, DORKING, RH5 6EA.
WADEY, Ms. Claire Frances, BA(Hons) ACA CTA *1993;* (Tax Fac), 7d Varndean Road, BRIGHTON, BN1 6RL.
WADEY, Mr. Neil Arthur, MA ACA AMCT *1989;* British American Tobacco Plc, Globe House, 4 Temple Place, LONDON, WC2R 2PG.
WADGE, Miss. Teresa Jane, BSc ACA *1996;* 250 East 63rd Street, Apt. 18D, NEW YORK, NY 10065, UNITED STATES.
WADHAM, Mr. David John Kenneth, FCA *1970;* 3 Ewald Road, LONDON, SW6 3NA.
WADHAM, Miss. Jennifer Susan, LLB ACA *2001;* (Tax Fac), 1 Loveridge Way, EASTLEIGH, HAMPSHIRE, SO50 9PN.
WADHAM, Mr. Stephen, BSc ACA *2010;* 6 Western Lea, CREDITON, DEVON, EX17 3JQ.
WADHERA, Mr. Arvind, FCA *1988;* Avenue de Foestraets 5, B 1180 BRUSSELS, BELGIUM.
•**WADHWA, Mr. Mohindra, BA(Hons) ACA** *1997;* Accounting Services (London) Limited, 74 South Hill Avenue, HARROW, MIDDLESEX, HA2 0NL.
•**WADHWANI, Mr. Deepak, BSc ACA** *1993;* Cameron & Associates Ltd, 35-37 Lowlands Road, HARROW, MIDDLESEX, HA1 3AW.
WADHWANI, Mr. Prem Jean-Pierre, BCom ACA *1993;* 10A Betclick Limited, Belmont Street, LONDON, NW1 8HH.
WADHWANI, Mr. Sanjay, BSc FCA CTA *1998;* The Coach House, 5 Ellerdale Road, LONDON, NW3 6BA.
WADIA, Mr. Darayus, BA ACA *1980;* New House, Pishiobury Drive, SAWBRIDGEWORTH, HERTFORDSHIRE, CM21 0AF.
WADIE, Mr. Antony Hugh Charles, BSc ACA *1992;* Chemin de Mourat 20, 1095 LUTRY, SWITZERLAND.
WADIE, Mr. Graham, BSc(Hons) ACA *2011;* 18 Raymond Crescent, GUILDFORD, SURREY, GU2 7SX.
WADIE, Mrs. Judith Margaret, BSc ACA *1990;* 18 Insignia Close, Wootton, NORTHAMPTON, NN4 6RS.
•**WADKIN, Mr. Douglas John, FCA** *1969;* (Tax Fac), Douglas Wadkin Limited, 11 Amwell Street, LONDON, EC1R 1UL. See also Wadkin Douglas
WADLEY, Mr. Adam Simon, BSc ACA *2005;* 24 Rooks Hill, WELWYN GARDEN CITY, HERTFORDSHIRE, AL8 6ET.
WADLEY, Mr. Steven Mark, BSc ACA *2006;* with KPMG LLP, 15 Canada Square, LONDON, E14 5GL.
WADLOW, Mr. Scott Darin, BSc ACA *1995;* Barclays Capital, 5 North Colonnade, LONDON, E14 4BB.
WADMAN, Mr. Richard Andrew, BA ACA *1993;* 9 Bolenna Lane, PERRANPORTH, TR6 0LB.
WADSWORTH, Mr. Adrian Phillip, BA FCA *1974;* 33 South Dene, BRISTOL, BS9 2BN.
WADSWORTH, Mr. Brian Douglas, FCA *1961;* Park Lodge, 32 Manor Park Way, Lepton, HUDDERSFIELD, HD8 0AJ.
WADSWORTH, Mrs. Clare Elizabeth, ACA *1983;* Media House, Lynch Wood, PETERBOROUGH, PE2 6EA.
WADSWORTH, Mr. David, BA FCA *1975;* PFP Group LLP, 3 Windsor Court, Clarence Drive, HARROGATE, NORTH YORKSHIRE, HG1 2PE.
•**WADSWORTH, Mr. David Jeffrey, MA FCA** *1976;* David Wadsworth & Co, 47 Merthyr Terrace, Barnes, LONDON, SW13 8DL.
WADSWORTH, Mrs. Emma V, BA ACA *2005;* 55 Croft Way, MARKET DRAYTON, SHROPSHIRE, TF9 3UB.
•**WADSWORTH, Mr. Howard Peter, BSc ACA** *1979;* (Tax Fac), H P Wadsworth, 9 Hey Cliff Road, HOLMFIRTH, HD9 1XD.
WADSWORTH, Mrs. Jacqueline Mary, FCA *1993;* 93 Huddersfield Road, Skelmanthorpe, HUDDERSFIELD, HD8 9AR.
WADSWORTH, Mr. James Graham Hilton, FCA *1975;* Dower Cottage, 5 High Street, Chew Magna, BRISTOL, BS40 8PR.
•**WADSWORTH, Mr. John Richard, BSc FCA** *1981;* 93 Huddersfield Road, Skelmanthorpe, HUDDERSFIELD, HD8 9AR.
WADSWORTH, Mr. Kenneth Edwin, FCA *1951;* Skys'L, 6 Bonfire Hill, SALCOMBE, TQ8 8EE. (Life Member)
WADSWORTH, Mr. Linton Alec, BA ACA *2011;* 1 Blackthorn Close, Earley, READING, RG6 1DH.
WADSWORTH, Mr. Martin Geoffrey, MA(Hons) ACA *2001;* 30 Camac Road, TWICKENHAM, TW2 6NY.
WADSWORTH, Mr. Ralph, FCA *1957;* 701 King Farm Blvd, ROCKVILLE, MD 20850, UNITED STATES. (Life Member)
WADSWORTH, Mr. Saul Alexander, ACA *2009;* 36 Lime Grove, CHEADLE, CHESHIRE, SK8 1PF.
WADWELL, Mr. David Martin, MSc FCA FSI *1971;* 7 Hippodrome Mews, LONDON, W11 4NN. (Life Member)
WADWELL, Mr. George Richard, FCA *1967;* 7 Barkhart Drive, WOKINGHAM, RG40 1TW.
WAGADIA, Mr. Samir, ACA *2008;* 106 Wilton Road, SOUTHAMPTON, SO15 5JP.
WAGENAAR, Mr. Marcel Louis Francois, BSc ACA *1991;* 24 Newtown Glen, TRAMORE, COUNTY WATERFORD, IRELAND.
WAGENER, Mr. Edward Thomas Frank, MEng ACA *2005;* Flat A, 190 Bedford Hill, LONDON, SW12 9HL.

WAGER, Mr. Adrian Robert James, FCA *1975;* Willow Cottage, Blacksmith Lane, Prestbury, CHELTENHAM, GL52 5JA. (Life Member)
•**WAGER, Mr. Edwin John, BSc FCA** *1977;* (Tax Fac), Stacey & Partners, 88 High Street, NEWMARKET, SUFFOLK, CB8 8JX. See also Stacey & Partners Limited
•**WAGER, Mr. James, FCA** *1976;* 19 Station Road, PRINCES RISBOROUGH, HP27 9DE.
WAGG, Miss. Rachel Susannah, ACA *2008;* Deloitte & Touche, 2 New Street Square, LONDON, EC4A 3BZ.
WAGGETT, Mrs. Natasha Louise, MA ACA *1995;* Harrington, 32 Woodway Road, TEIGNMOUTH, DEVON, TQ14 8PZ.
WAGGETT, Mrs. Suzanne Elizabeth, BA ACA *1997;* 22 Edgar Road, WINCHESTER, HAMPSHIRE, SO23 9TW.
WAGGOTT, Mrs. Kim, BSc ACA *1994;* Mulberry Park Hill, Potter Row, GREAT MISSENDEN, BUCKINGHAMSHIRE, HP16 9LT.
WAGGOTT, Mr. Terence John, MSc FCA JDipMA *1967;* 31 Keable Road, Marks Tey, COLCHESTER, ESSEX, CO6 1XB. (Life Member)
WAGGOTT, Mr. William Harrison, BSc ACA *1990;* T U I UK Wigmore House, Wigmore Place Wigmore Lane, LUTON, LU2 9TN.
WAGHE, Mr. Navin, BSc(Hons) ACA *2003;* Flat 2, 3-5 Islington High Street, LONDON, N1 9LQ.
WAGHORN, Miss. Amy Sarah, BSc ACA *2005;* with Lindeyer Francis Ferguson, North House, 198 High Street, TONBRIDGE, TN9 1BE.
WAGHORN, Mr. Brian James, FCA *1959;* Smalls Farm, Park Corner Road, Groton, SUDBURY, CO10 5EG. (Life Member)
WAGHORN, Mrs. Margaret Elizabeth, FCA *1961;* Beechmead, Yarm Way, LEATHERHEAD, SURREY, KT22 8RQ. (Life Member)
WAGHORN, Mr. Richard Seymour, BA ACA *1986;* 2 High Garth, ESHER, SURREY, KT10 9DN.
•**WAGLE, Mr. Likhit Madhav, BA ACA** *1988;* 15 Hood Avenue, LONDON, SW14 7LH.
WAGMAN, Mr. Colin Barry, FCA *1970;* Delancey, 6th Floor Lansdowne House Berkeley Square, LONDON, W1J 6ER.
WAGMAN, Miss. Ruth Elizabeth, BSc(Hons) ACA *2004;* Alpha House, 4 Greek Street, STOCKPORT, CHESHIRE, SK3 8AB.
•**WAGMAN, Mr. Simon, BA FCA** *1993;* Blick Rothenberg, 12 York Gate, Regent's Park, LONDON, NW1 4QS.
WAGNER, Mr. Adam Richard, BSc ACA *1989;* The Elms, 27 Rex Close, Tile Hill Village, COVENTRY, CV4 9JB.
•**WAGNER, Mr. Leo Simon, BAcc FCA** *1992;* Proactive Tax Ltd, 9 Hopetoun Drive, Bridge of Allan, STIRLING, FK9 4QQ. See also Tax and Accounting Support Limited
WAGNER, Mrs. Liza Jane, BSc ACA *2005;* 4 Sheraton House, Chairmakers Close, PRINCES RISBOROUGH, BUCKINGHAMSHIRE, HP27 9BX.
WAGNER, Mr. Mark Anthony, MA ACA *1986;* 1 Durrington Avenue, LONDON, SW20 8NT.
WAGNER, Mr. Sidney, FCA *1957;* 37 Wykeham Road, Hendon, LONDON, NW4 2SS.
•**WAGNER, Mr. Simon David, ACA** *1994;* The Pines Woollards Road, Ash Vale, ALDERSHOT, GU12 5DS.
WAGNER, Mr. Steve, MsC BSc(Hons) ACA *2010;* 2 Portland Croft, PONTEFRACT, WEST YORKSHIRE, WF8 4SN.
WAGNER, Mrs. Svetlana, ACA *2010;* Monitise International Ltd Warnford Court, 29 Throgmorton Street, LONDON, EC2N 2AT.
WAGNER IMIG, Mrs. Silke, ACA *1999;* Sudetenring 46, 35510 BUTZBACH, GERMANY.
WAGON, Miss. Chantel, BA ACA *2007;* 100 Deforest Avenue, EAST HANOVER, NJ 07936, UNITED STATES.
WAGSTAFF, Mr. Allan, FCA *1958;* 120 Nottingham Road, Ravenshead, NOTTINGHAM, NG15 9HL. (Life Member)
WAGSTAFF, Mr. Andre Rex, FCA *1970;* The Gate House, Church Path, Abbotskerswell, NEWTON ABBOT, DEVON, TQ12 5NY. (Life Member)
WAGSTAFF, Mr. Christopher David, BA ACA *1992;* Royal Bank of Canada, PO Box 611, LONDON, EC4V 4DE.
WAGSTAFF, Mr. Craig Andrew, BA FCA *1984;* The English Golf Union Ltd, The National Golf Centre, The Broadway, WOODHALL SPA, LINCOLNSHIRE, LN10 6PU.
WAGSTAFF, Mr. Dale Roland, BSc ACA *1991;* 15 Walk House Close, Cranfield, BEDFORD, MK43 0HY.
•**WAGSTAFF, Mr. David, FCA** *1980;* 2 Netley Mansions, 29 South Parade, SOUTHSEA, PO4 0SH.
WAGSTAFF, Mr. David Christopher, MA ACA *1984;* (Tax Fac), 4 Seymour Road, SOUTHAMPTON, SO16 6RH.
•**WAGSTAFF, Mr. David John, BSc ACA** *1995;* ABC Accountants (Midlands) Limited, 85 Fairham Road, Stretton, BURTON-ON-TRENT, STAFFORDSHIRE, DE13 0BS. See also Burton Accountancy Services Limited
WAGSTAFF, Mr. Jack Norman, FCA *1948;* 18 Regents Walk, Leicester Forest East, LEICESTER, LE3 3PB. (Life Member)
WAGSTAFF, Mr. John Ivan, FCA *1968;* The Laurels, 4 Norton Close, Bath Road, WORCESTER, WR5 3EY. (Life Member)
•**WAGSTAFF, Mr. Paul Frederick, FCA FCMI** *1974;* MEMBER OF COUNCIL, Dickinsons, 4 Enterprise Cort, Downmill Road, BRACKNELL, BERKSHIRE, RG12 1QS. See also Rouse Partners LLP
WAGSTAFF, Mrs. Philippa Karen, FCA *1985;* 20 Boulevard de Suisse, 98000 MONACO, MONACO.
WAGSTAFF, Mr. Richard Paul, BSc ACA *1994;* The Old Rickyard, 1 Top Farm Lane, Great Doddington, WELLINGBOROUGH, NORTHAMPTONSHIRE, NN29 7UU.
WAGSTAFF, Mr. Ronald Ernest, FCA *1938;* 2 Forest Close, Lickey End, BROMSGROVE, B60 1JU. (Life Member)
WAGSTAFF, Mr. Stephen Alan, BSc(Econ) FCA *1975;* Wildbriar, Solefields Road, SEVENOAKS, KENT, TN13 1PJ.
WAGSTAFFE, Miss. Louise, BSc ACA *2011;* 41 Rosebury Drive, Longbenton, NEWCASTLE UPON TYNE, NE12 8RG.
WAGSTAFFE, Mr. Mark Clive, BA FCA *1997;* 20 Henleaze Gardens, BRISTOL, BS9 4HJ.
WAHAB, Miss. Yasmin Lailah, BSc ACA *1988;* 25 Bamburgh Circle, Apartment 2042, SCARBOROUGH M1W 3W2, ON, CANADA.
WAHEED, Mr. Amjad, FCA *1972;* 46A Main Gulberg, LAHORE 54660, PAKISTAN.
WAHEED, Mr. Junaid, BA ACA *1982;* 2464 RIDEAU DRIVE, OAKVILLE L6H 7R1, ON, CANADA.
WAHI, Mr. Abhishek, ACA *2008;* 35 Arlington Square, LONDON, N1 7DP.
WAHID, Miss. Nasreen, BSc FCA ATII *1987;* (Tax Fac), 3 Merton Hall Road, Wimbledon, LONDON, SW19 3PP.
•**WAHID, Mr. Shamsher, BSc ACA** *2005;* Aero Accountancy Services Ltd, 38 William Street, Totterdown, BRISTOL, BS3 4TT. See also SW Accountancy Services Ltd
WAHLE, The Revd. Francis Anton Alfred Paul, BSc FCA *1954;* 17 Chiltern Court, Baker Street, LONDON, NW1 5TD. (Life Member)
•**WAHNON, Mr. Joshua, FCA** *1970;* (Tax Fac), Kl Tob, 125 Wolmer Garden, EDGWARE, HA8 8QF.
WAI, Mr. Alex Hak Man, ACA *2007;* 18 Mockingbird Drive, RICHMOND HILL L4E 4L8, ON, CANADA.
WAI, Mr. Cliff Yiu Tong, ACA *2007;* Flat D 9th Floor, Wilton Place, 18 Park Road, CENTRAL, HONG KONG SAR.
WAI, Mr. Japhet Siu Hoi, BA ACA *1987;* Flat B 5/F, 4 Mount Davis Road, POK FU LAM, Hong Kong Island, HONG KONG SAR.
WAI, Mr. King Fai Francis, ACA *2007;* 15C, Skyscraper, 136 Tin Hau Temple Road, TIN HAU, HONG KONG SAR.
WAI, Mr. Lung Shing, ACA *2006;* 20/F Crocodile Centre, 79 Hoi Yuen Road, KWUN TONG, HONG KONG SAR.
WAI, Ms. Ming Hei, ACA *2008;* C K Lam & Co, Unit 704, Fourseas Building, 208-212 Nathan Road, KOWLOON CITY, KOWLOON HONG KONG SAR.
WAI, Mr. Ryan, BSc ACA *2011;* 1 Tudor Road, Crosby, LIVERPOOL, L23 3DH.
WAI, Mr. Yiu Leung, ACA *2007;* 19/F Flat 1 Block 47, Heng Fa Chuen, 100 Shing Tai Road, CHAI WAN, HONG KONG ISLAND, HONG KONG SAR.
•**WAIGHT, Mr. Peter Charles Staward, FCA** *1968;* (Tax Fac), Waight & Co Limited, 8 Lonsdale Gardens, TUNBRIDGE WELLS, KENT, TN1 1NU.
WAILES, Mr. Richard Franklyn, FCA *1990;* Flat 7, Lorne Court, 51 Putney Hill, LONDON, SW15 6RX.
WAILES, Mr. Simon Christian, MA ACA *2006;* Deloitte & Touche, 2 New Street Square, LONDON, EC4A 3BZ.
WAILING, Mr. John Malcolm, BSocSc FCA *1976;* 20 Ashburnham Grove, Greenwich, LONDON, SE10 8UH.
WAILING, Mr. Michael David, FCA *1968;* Little Orchard House, Atch Lench, EVESHAM, WORCESTERSHIRE, Wr11 4SW. (Life Member)
WAIN, Mr. Andrew Robert, BA ACA *1991;* 2 EQUESTRIAN LN, WESTFORD, MA 01886-4232, UNITED STATES.
•**WAIN, Mr. Anthony Charles, FCA** *1960;* A.C. Wain & Company, 3 Highlands Close, Chalfont St Peter, GERRARDS CROSS, SL9 0DR.
WAIN, Ms. Claire, BA(Hons) ACA *2004;* 16 Blackstone Road, LONDON, NW2 6BY.
•**WAIN, Mr. Colin Peter, BSc FCA ATII** *1990;* Begbies Chettle Agar, Epworth House, 25 City Road, LONDON, EC1Y 1AR. See also Begbies Everett Chettle and Begbies Chettle Agar Ltd
WAIN, Mr. Daniel Stephen, BSc ACA *2006;* 20 Hollyguest Road, BRISTOL, BS15 9NW.
WAIN, Mr. Denis Walter, FCA *1957;* 62 Main Street, Woodthorpe, LOUGHBOROUGH, LE12 8UG. (Life Member)
•**WAIN, Mr. Graham Frederick, FCA** *1971;* Cox Jerome, Churchill House, 59 Lichfield Street, WALSALL, WS4 2BX.
•**WAIN, Miss. Johanna Elizabeth, BA FCA** *1995;* Copplestone Unsworth & Co, 9 Abbey Square, CHESTER, CH1 2HU.
WAIN, Mr. John Anthony, FCA *1962;* 49 Palace Avenue, PAIGNTON, DEVON, TQ3 3EN.
WAIN, Mr. Nicholas Paul, BA ACA *1998;* 9 Howcombe Gardens, Napton, SOUTHAM, CV47 8PD.
WAIN, Mr. Peter Michael, FCA *1975;* Volkerfitzpatrick Ltd, Hertford Road, HODDESDON, HERTFORDSHIRE, EN11 9BX.
WAIN, Mr. Stephen Gerrard, BSc ACA *1982;* 35 Main Street, Norton Juxta Twycross, ATHERSTONE, WARWICKSHIRE, CV9 3QA.
WAIN, Mrs. Tracy Louise, BSc ACA *1998;* 9 Howcombe Gardens, Napton-on-the-Hill, SOUTHAM, WARWICKSHIRE, CV47 8PD.
WAINAINA, Mr. Allan, ACA *1995;* PO Box 52944-00200, NAIROBI, KENYA.
WAINE, Mr. Benjamin James, BA(Hons) ACA *2001;* (Tax Fac), 8 Martell Drive, Kempston (Rural), BEDFORD, MK42 7FJ.
WAINE, Mr. Nigel Jeremy, BA ACA ATII *1987;* (Tax Fac), 14 Rumsey Close, HAMPTON, TW12 3XY.
WAINE, Mr. Paul, MA FCA *1979;* 54 St. Winifreds Road, TEDDINGTON, MIDDLESEX, TW11 9JR.
WAINE, Mr. Philip Martin, FCA *1990;* 20 Brooklyn Court, 388 Wilmslow Road, Withington, MANCHESTER, M20 3NB.
WAINING, Mr. David Leslie, ACA *2008;* 345 Hollinsend Road, SHEFFIELD, S12 2NN.
•**WAINING, Mr. John Peter, ACA** *2008;* Waining Accountancy Limited, 6 Bramlyn Close, Clowne, CHESTERFIELD, DERBYSHIRE, S43 4QP.
WAINMAN, Mr. Edward Jack, BA ACA MBA *1996;* Cadogan Consulting Ltd, 35 Brompton Road, LONDON, SW3 1DE.
•**WAINMAN, Mr. Nigel Appleyard, FCA** *1973;* Hillside, Rigton Hill, Wetherby Road, Bardsey, LEEDS, LS17 9BR.
WAINMAN, Mr. Paul Russell, BA ACA *1990;* P O Box 786, KENNEBUNKPORT, ME 04046, UNITED STATES.
WAINNER, Mrs. Hayley, ACA *1995;* Bramble Orchard, Amber Lane, Chart Sutton, MAIDSTONE, ME17 3SE.
•**WAINWRIGHT, Mr. Brian Frank, FCA** *1961;* B. Wainwright & Co., 1st Floor, Harveys Depot, Daveys Lane, LEWES, EAST SUSSEX BN7 2BQ.
WAINWRIGHT, Mr. Brian Walter, FCA *1962;* 132 Trelawney Road, Peverell, PLYMOUTH, PL3 4JZ.
WAINWRIGHT, Miss. Brona Grice, BA ACA *2004;* Charles Topham Group Ltd, 1 Merchant's Place, River Street, BOLTON, BL2 1BX.
WAINWRIGHT, Mr. Christopher JohnFrancis, BA ACA *1987;* 76 Shrewsbury Road, OXTON, CHESHIRE, CH43 2HY.
WAINWRIGHT, Mr. David, FCA *1974;* 11a Medway Road, Worsley, MANCHESTER, M28 7UH.
WAINWRIGHT, Mrs. Emma Louise, BA ACA *2004;* Audit Commission Westward House, Lime Kiln Close Stoke Gifford, BRISTOL, BS34 8SR.
WAINWRIGHT, Mr. Glen Stephen, BA ACA *1997;* 7 Cranmere Drive, SALE, CHESHIRE, M33 4LB.
WAINWRIGHT, Mrs. Helen Clare, BA ACA *2006;* with KPMG LLP, 1 The Embankment, Neville Street, LEEDS, LS1 4DW.
WAINWRIGHT, Mr. Ian Alexander, BA FCA *1989;* Redbreast Gove, 111-115 High Street, Birstall, BATLEY, WF17 9HW.
WAINWRIGHT, Mr. John Christopher, MA ACA *1988;* 24 Colehill Lane, Fulham, LONDON, SW6 5EG.
WAINWRIGHT, Dr. Judith Clare, PhD BSc(Hons) ACA *2002;* 4 Anning Fold, Garforth, LEEDS, LS25 2PQ.
WAINWRIGHT, Mrs. Karen Elizabeth, ACA MAAT *2000;* 15 Kingsford Drive, CHELMSFORD, CM2 6YR.
WAINWRIGHT, Mrs. Kuldeep Kaur, BSc ACA *2003;* 7 Briarwood Mews, Rugeley Road, Armitage, RUGELEY, STAFFORDSHIRE, WS15 4BG.
WAINWRIGHT, Mr. Mark Russell, BSc ACA *2004;* 32 The Circuit, WILMSLOW, CHESHIRE, SK9 6DB.
WAINWRIGHT, Mr. Michael John, BA ACA *1984;* Goodchilds Hill, Stratfield Saye, READING, RG7 2DR.
WAINWRIGHT, Mr. Michael Richard, FCA *1982;* 37 Brookhill Way, Rushmere St. Andrew, IPSWICH, IP4 5UL.
•**WAINWRIGHT, Mr. Paul Nigel, FCA** *1983;* Mitchell Charlesworth, 5 Temple Square, Temple Street, LIVERPOOL, L2 5RH.
WAINWRIGHT, Mr. Philip, BEng ACA *1991;* (Tax Fac), 3 Palladian Circus, Ingress Park, GREENHITHE, KENT, DA9 9FS.
WAINWRIGHT, Mr. Robert Ian, BSc FCA *1995;* with KPMG LLP, 1 Forest Gate, Brighton Road, CRAWLEY, WEST SUSSEX, RH11 9PT.
WAINWRIGHT, Mr. Stephen, BA FCA *1989;* Knowle House, Meltham, HOLMFIRTH, HD9 4DT.
WAINWRIGHT, Mr. Stephen Barris, BCom FCA *1983;* 5 The Broadway, Gustard Wood, Wheathampstead, ST. ALBANS, HERTFORDSHIRE, AL4 8LW.
•**WAINWRIGHT, Mr. Steven Robert, BSc FCA** *1989;* Steven Wainwright FCA, 11 Sandling Avenue, Horfield, BRISTOL, BS7 0HS.
WAIS, Mr. Julian Dominic, BA FCA *1990;* Cobham plc, Brook Road, WIMBORNE, DORSET, BH21 2BJ.
WAIT, Mr. Matthew James Alan, BA ACA *1999;* 11 Fitzroy Mews, LONDON, W1T 6DN.
WAIT, Mr. Richard Peter, BSc ACA *2003;* 4 Brackenbury Road, LONDON, N2 0ST.
WAITE, Mr. Andrew John, BSc ACA *2004;* Morgan Crucible The Quadrant, 55-57 High Street, WINDSOR, BERKSHIRE, SL4 1LP.
WAITE, Miss. Antonia, BSc ACA *2011;* Flat 9, Sans Souci, 48 Leigh Park Road, LEIGH-ON-SEA, ESSEX, SS9 2DU.
WAITE, Mr. Antony Mark, BA ACA *1989;* Tamor House, Boyne Hill, Chapelthorpe, WAKEFIELD, WF4 3JH.
WAITE, Mr. Charles Francis Simon, BSc ACA *1992;* 2 Cricketers View, Shadwell, LEEDS, LS17 8WD.
WAITE, Mr. Danny, FCA *1966;* 1 Hillview Cottages, London Road, CROWBOROUGH, EAST SUSSEX, TN6 2TU.
WAITE, Mr. David Gerard, BA ACA ATII *1984;* 5 Woodlea Boston Spa, WETHERBY, WEST YORKSHIRE, LS23 6SB.
WAITE, Mrs. Gemma Elaine, BSc ACA *2010;* 20 Corner Brake, PLYMOUTH, PL6 7QP.
WAITE, Mr. Iain Richard, BSc ACA *1991;* University of Lincoln, Campus Way, LINCOLN, LN6 7TS.
WAITE, Mr. James Arthur, BA ACA *1992;* A D Architects Ltd, 63-65 Fore Street, HERTFORD, SG14 1AL.
WAITE, Miss. Julia, BA(Hons) ACA *2001;* with PricewaterhouseCoopers LLP, Donington Court, Pegasus Business Park, Castle Donington, DERBY, DE74 2UZ.
WAITE, Miss. Nicola, BA ACA *2011;* 12 Bronte Crescent, HEMEL HEMPSTEAD, HERTFORDSHIRE, HP2 7NT.
•**WAITE, Mr. Paul David, BSc FCA FCCA** *1985;* (Tax Fac), Aspen-Waite, Rubis House, 15 Friarn Street, BRIDGWATER, SOMERSET, TA6 3LH. See also Aspen Waite Limited
WAITE, Mr. Peter, FCA *1961;* 46 West End, Queensbury, BRADFORD, BD13 2ER. (Life Member)
WAITE, Mr. Phillip Martin, BSc ACA *1998;* 90 Brampton Road, ST. ALBANS, AL1 4PX.
WAITE, Mr. Stephen Bryan John, FCA *1973;* 10 Asquith Close, CHRISTCHURCH, DORSET, BH23 3DX.
WAITE, Mrs. Susan Jane, BA ACA *1999;* 90 Brampton Road, ST. ALBANS, AL1 4PX.
WAITE, Mrs. Susan Jane, MA ACA *1995;* Calla New Road Littleton, WINCHESTER, HAMPSHIRE, SO22 6QR.
•**WAITE, Mr. Terence Henry Richard, FCA** *1966;* KWK Limited, 11 Weston Road, SOUTHEND-ON-SEA, SS1 1AS. See also Kyles & Co
WAITE, Mrs. Tracy Jane, BSc ACA *1993;* 2 Cricketers View, Shadwell, LEEDS, LS17 8WD.
•**WAITE, Mr. William Andrew, BCom FCA** *1971;* 22 Heywood Court, Northowram, HALIFAX, WEST YORKSHIRE, HX3 7BQ.
WAITES, Mr. Arthur, FCA *1951;* 8 Grangeside, DARLINGTON, DL3 8QJ. (Life Member)
WAITES, Mrs. Jacqueline Anne, ACA MAAT *2003;* West Devon Borough Council, Kilworthy Park, TAVISTOCK, DEVON, PL19 0BZ.
WAITES, Mr. John Nigel Michael, BSc(Econ) FCA *1984;* The Old House, Water End, HEMEL HEMPSTEAD, HP1 3BH.
•**WAITES, Mr. Nicholas Stuart, BSc FCA** *1987;* (Tax Fac), C P Waites, 24 St Cuthberts Way, DARLINGTON, DL1 1GB.
WAITES, Mrs. Sharon Colette, BA ACA *1996;* 2 Spa Meadow Close, Greenham, THATCHAM, RG19 8ST.
•**WAJIH, Mr. Akbar Mahmoud, FCA** *1968;* A.M. Wajih FCA, 44 Clabon Mews, LONDON, SW1X 0EH.

WAKATSUKI, Ms. Asuka, BSc ACA *2006;* 35 Crescent Way, Cholsey, WALLINGFORD, OXFORDSHIRE, OX10 9NG.
WAKE, Mr. Derek Michael, BA ACA *1984;* Northern Rock plc, Northern Rock House, Gosforth, NEWCASTLE UPON TYNE, NE3 4PL.
WAKE, Mr. Gregor Malcolm, MA ACA *2003;* Burn Stewart Distillers Plc, 2-16 Milton Road East Kilbride, GLASGOW, G74 5BU.
•WAKE, Mrs. Jill Susan, BSc ACA ATII *1984;* 29 Clover Drive, Pickmere, KNUTSFORD, CHESHIRE, WA16 0WF.
WAKE, Mrs. Lorna, BSc ACA *2004;* Quadriga Worldwide Ltd, Forum 1, Station Road, Theale, READING, RG7 4RA.
WAKE, Mr. Nigel Lloyd, FCA *1980;* 5 Renown Way, Sorrento, PERTH, WA 6020, AUSTRALIA.
WAKE, Mr. Nigel Stanley, FCA FPC *1966;* 54 London Road, WORCESTER, WR5 2DS.
WAKE, Mr. Peter, BA FCA *1978;* 67 Empress Avenue, WOODFORD GREEN, IG8 9DZ.
WAKEFIELD, Mr. Andrew James Ben, BEng ACA *2001;* 28 Woodlands Road, ORPINGTON, BR6 6EB.
WAKEFIELD, Mr. David John, FCA *1963;* 65 Griffiths Close, Lower Station, SWINDON, SN3 4NP.
•WAKEFIELD, Mrs. Deborah Jane, ACA ACCA CTA *2009;* Edmund Carr LLP, 146 New London Road, CHELMSFORD, CM2 0AW. See also EC (Management Services) Ltd
WAKEFIELD, Mr. James Michael, FCA *1964;* Little Nettacott, Upton Pyne, EXETER, EX5 5HX. (Life Member)
WAKEFIELD, Mr. James Robert, BSc ACA *2001;* Silverwood, Ganges Hill, Fivehead, TAUNTON, SOMERSET, TA3 6PF.
•WAKEFIELD, Mr. John David Christopher, BA FCA CTA *1988;* (Tax Fac), Bright Grahame Murray, 131 Edgware Road, LONDON, W2 2AP.
WAKEFIELD, Mrs. Lisa Jayne, BEng ACA *2005;* 29 Rectory Close, Sutton Bonington, LOUGHBOROUGH, LEICESTERSHIRE, LE12 5PJ.
WAKEFIELD, Mr. Mark Penfold, FCA *1974;* 5 Burr Crescent, UNIONVILLE L3R 9B8, ON, CANADA.
WAKEFIELD, Mr. Nicholas, BSc ACA *1989;* Shell International Petroleum Co Ltd Shell Centre, York Road, LONDON, SE1 7NA.
WAKEFIELD, Miss. Nicola, ACA *2011;* 197 Northstand Apartments, Highbury Stadium Square, LONDON, N5 1FN.
•WAKEFIELD, Mrs. Nicola Jane, BSc ACA DChA *1997;* Mazars LLP, Sixth Floor, Times House, Throwley Way, SUTTON, SURREY SM1 4JQ.
•WAKEFIELD, Mr. Paul, BSc FCA *1981;* Paul Wakefield, Myrtle Cottage, Lower End, Great Milton, OXFORD, OX44 7NJ.
•WAKEFIELD, Mr. Paul George, BSc FCA *1982;* CNH France Representative Office, 1 Akhangaranskoye Shosse, TASHKENT 700091, UZBEKISTAN.
WAKEFIELD, Mr. Richard John, BA(Hons) ACA *2010;* Flat 3, 1b Bruce Road, MITCHAM, SURREY, CR4 2AS.
WAKEFIELD, Mr. Richard John, FCA *1973;* 5 Ranmoor Chase, Riverdale Road, SHEFFIELD, S10 3FA.
WAKEFIELD, Mr. Ryan, ACA *2009;* 21 Connaught Avenue, GRIMSBY, SOUTH HUMBERSIDE, DN32 0BS.
WAKEFIELD, Mrs. Sarah Louise, BA ACA *2002;* 28 Woodlands Road, ORPINGTON, BR6 6EB.
•WAKEFIELD, Mr. Steven Joseph, BSc ACA *1999;* Dixon Wilson, 22 Chancery Lane, LONDON, WC2A 1LS.
•WAKEFIELD, Mr. Stewart James, FCA *1992;* Lanham and Company Limited, 9 Great Chesterford Court, London Road, Gt Chesterford, SAFFRON WALDEN, CB10 1PF.
WAKEFIELD, Mrs. Susan Louise, BSc ACA *1994;* (Tax Fac), Bartle Bogle Hegarty, 60 Kingly Street, LONDON, W1B 5DS.
WAKEFIELD, Mr. Timothy, BA ACA *1999;* 7 Lynwood Gardens, HOOK, HAMPSHIRE, RG27 9DT.
WAKEFORD, Mr. Alexander, ACA *2008;* 33A Grosvenor Avenue, HIGHBURY, N5 2NP.
WAKEFORD, Mr. Brian Hugh, FCA *1971;* 11 Mill Hill, SHOREHAM-BY-SEA, WEST SUSSEX, BN43 5TG.
•WAKEFORD, Mrs. Julie Carol, BSc ACA *1987;* (Tax Fac), Julie Wakeford, 7 The Lawns, Yatton, BRISTOL, BS49 4BG.
•WAKEFORD, Mr. Michael Ian, FCA *1987;* (Tax Fac), Moore Stephens (South) LLP, City Gates, 2-4 Southgate, CHICHESTER, WEST SUSSEX, PO19 8DJ. See also Moore Secretaries Limited
WAKEHAM, Mr. Alex, ACA *2007;* 56 Farm Fields, SOUTH CROYDON, CR2 0HP.
WAKEHAM, Mr. Christopher Michael Sleeman, FCA *1971;* PO Box 98978, SLOANE PARK, 2152, SOUTH AFRICA.
WAKEHAM, Mr. Guy Ian, BSc ACA *1993;* 18 Farriers Way, Warboys, HUNTINGDON, CAMBRIDGESHIRE, PE28 2LW.
WAKEHAM, Lord John, JP DL FCA *1955;* Pinglestone House, ALRESFORD, SO24 9TB. (Life Member)
WAKEHAM, Mr. Peter Terence, BSc ACA *1993;* Radio House Apple Industrial Estate, Whittle Avenue, FAREHAM, PO15 5SX.
WAKEHAM, Mr. Robert James, BA ACA *1996;* 22 Park Street, Charlton, MALMESBURY, SN16 9DF.
WAKEHAM, Mr. Simon George, ACA *1980;* 19 Billson Street, BRIGHTON EAST, VIC 3187, AUSTRALIA.
•WAKELAM, Mr. Jason Carl, BA ACA *1994;* PricewaterhouseCoopers LLP, 9 Greyfriars Road, READING, RG1 1JG. See also PricewaterhouseCoopers
WAKELAM, Mr. Michael Charles, BSc ACA *1988;* S.Ross & Co Ltd, Manor Mill Lane, LEEDS, LS11 8LQ.
WAKELAM, Ms. Sarah Jane, BSc ACA *1996;* 14 TAYLOR AVENUE, TURRAMURRA, NSW 2074, AUSTRALIA.
WAKELEY, Mr. David Peacefull, FCA *1981;* 166 Rosemary Hill Road, SUTTON COLDFIELD, B74 4HN.
WAKELIN, Mr. Gerald Norman, BA FCA ATII *1963;* Larkenshaw Cottage, Old Chertsey Road, Chobham, WOKING, GU24 8HF. (Life Member)
WAKELIN, Mr. Patrick Bernard Steven, BA ACA *1982;* Formula Communications Limited, 8 Sunningdale, Amington, TAMWORTH, B77 4NW.
WAKELING, Mr. Anthony, FCA *1955;* Darrawella, Stafford Lane, Colyford, COLYTON, DEVON, EX24 6HQ. (Life Member)
•WAKELING, Miss. Margaret Anne, ACA *1979;* (Tax Fac), M.A. Wakeling, Picketts Mead, High Street, Cowden, EDENBRIDGE, TN8 7JH.
•WAKELING, Mrs. Tina Susan, FCA *1980;* Tina Wakeling FCA, 25 Southcote Close, South Cave, BROUGH, NORTH HUMBERSIDE, HU15 2BQ.
WAKELING, Mr. Vivian William, FCA *1953;* 148 Wenallt Road, Rhiwbina, CARDIFF, CF14 6TQ. (Life Member)
WAKELING, Mr. William John, FCA *1956;* 21 Anthony Close, COLCHESTER, CO4 0LD. (Life Member)
WAKELY, Mr. Stephen Victor, BA ACA *1989;* 277 Dobcroft Road, SHEFFIELD, S11 9LG.
WAKEMAN, Mrs. Helen Margaret, BA ACA *1987;* 7 Emilia Close, MAIDENHEAD, SL6 7HU.
•WAKEMAN, Mr. Martyn Gordon David, BA FCA *1981;* Charlton Cottage, Old Forge Lane, Granby, NOTTINGHAM, NG13 9PS.
•WAKEMAN, Mrs. Susan Elizabeth, BA ACA *1981;* Charlton Cottage, Old Forge Lane, Granby, NOTTINGHAM, NG13 9PS.
WAKERLEY, Mrs. Christine Louise, BA ACA CTA *2000;* with Revelation Business Solutions Limited, Woodland House, Bowson Square, Bream, LYDNEY, GLOUCESTERSHIRE GL15 6LB.
•WAKERLEY, Mr. Matthew Christian, BA FCA *2000;* Revelation Business Solutions Limited, Woodland House, Bowson Square, Bream, LYDNEY, GLOUCESTERSHIRE GL15 6LB.
WAKERLY, Mr. Daniel Alexander, BSc(Econ) ACA *2001;* Morgan Stanley, 20 Bank Street, LONDON, E14 4AD.
WAKLEY, Mr. Christopher, ACA *2008;* Flat 6 Chiltern House, 54-56 High Street, HARROW, MIDDLESEX, HA1 3LL.
•WAKSMAN, Mrs. Jane Michele, MSc BSc FCA *1986;* Jane Waksman ACA, 1 Parkhill Road, Hale, ALTRINCHAM, CHESHIRE, WA15 9JX.
•WALA, Mrs. Gwyneth, BA ACA *2000;* (Tax Fac), Kingscott Dix (Cheltenham) Limited, Malvern View Business Park, Stella Way, Bishops Cleeve, CHELTENHAM, GLOUCESTERSHIRE GL52 7DQ.
WALBERTON, Mr. Michael Andrew, BA FCA *1983;* (Tax Fac), Grove House, 37 Lodge Hill Road, Lower Bourne, FARNHAM, SURREY, GU10 3RE.
WALBOURN, Mr. Richard Alexander, BA ACA *1992;* 8 Northfield Farm Mews, COBHAM, SURREY, KT11 1JZ.
WALBURN, Miss. Sarah, BSc(Hons) ACA *2011;* 138 Leathwaite Road, LONDON, SW11 6RP.
WALBURN, Mrs. Sarah Honey Padam, BSc ACA MAAT *2002;* 80 Forest View Road, Tuffley, GLOUCESTER, GL4 0BY.
•WALBY, Mr. Clive Dennis, FCA *1993;* The Mudd Partnership, Lakeview House, 4 Woodbrook Crescent, BILLERICAY, ESSEX, CM12 0EQ.
WALBY, Mr. Marc Jeffrey, BSc ACA *1997;* 1991 Broadway, Apartment 5C, NEW YORK, NY 10023, UNITED STATES.
WALBY, Mr. Michael David, BA FCA *1999;* Flat 3, 22 Gladys Road, LONDON, NW6 2PX.
WALBYOFF, Miss. Megan, ACA *2011;* 14 Shire Place, The Ridings Worth, CRAWLEY, WEST SUSSEX, RH10 7XS.
WALCOTT, Miss. Katie Amanda, BSc ACA *2010;* 17 Albert Road, MITCHAM, SURREY, CR4 4AL.
WALCZAK, Mr. Stanley Andrew, BSc ACA *1985;* Ellerman Investments Ltd, 20 St. James's Street, LONDON, SW1A 1ES.
WALDBAUER, Mrs. Gillian Granger, FCA *1983;* Dumbergweg 23, D44879 BOCHUM, GERMANY.
WALDEN, Mr. Andrew Neil, BSc ACA *2002;* 74 Cowper Crescent, HERTFORD, SG14 3EA.
WALDEN, Mr. Ben, ACA *2011;* Apartment 653, Canal Wharf, 20 Waterfront Walk, BIRMINGHAM, B1 1SZ.
WALDEN, Mrs. Carolyn, BSc ACA *2002;* Mace Ltd Atelier House, 64 Pratt Street, LONDON, NW1 0LF.
WALDEN, Ms. Catherine Suzanne, MPhil ACA *1992;* National Gallery Company, St. Vincent House, 30 Orange Street, LONDON, WC2H 7HH.
WALDEN, Mr. Daniel, BA(Hons) ACA *2010;* 8 Suffolk Street, LEAMINGTON SPA, CV32 5YG.
WALDEN, Mr. David Simon, MA FCA *1985;* (Tax Fac), 20 St. John's Hill Grove, Battersea, LONDON, SW11 2RG.
WALDEN, Mr. Derek Colin, MA ACA *1982;* 9870 Granite Slope Lane, SANDY, UT 84092 6004, UNITED STATES.
WALDEN, Mr. Graham Howard, BA ACA MCT *1986;* Flat 6 Christchurch Place, Christ Church Mount, EPSOM, KT19 8RS.
WALDEN, Mr. Jonathan Kim, BSc FCA *1978;* Hyatt Lodge, Long Walk, CHALFONT ST.GILES, HP8 4AW.
WALDEN, Mr. Keith, FCA *1956;* Keepers Cottage, Heighington Road, Canwick, LINCOLN, LN4 2RN. (Life Member)
WALDEN, Mr. Michael James, FCA *1960;* 9021 Holly Leaf Lane, BETHESDA, MD 20817, UNITED STATES. (Life Member)
WALDEN, Mr. Samuel, BA MSt ACA *1994;* 16 Middleton Road, LONDON, NW11 7NS.
WALDEN, Mr. Simon David, FCA *1971;* P O Box 241, Banglamung Post Office, Banglamung, CHON BURI 20150, THAILAND.
WALDER, Mr. James Nicholas Hampton, MA ACA *2003;* 16 Ilford Road, NEWCASTLE UPON TYNE, NE2 3NX.
WALDER, Mr. Stephen, BCom FCA *1984;* Micros Fidelio UK Ltd, 6-8 The Grove, SLOUGH, BERKSHIRE, SL1 1QP.
WALDIE, Mr. Andrew Crawford, BA FCA ACMA CMC *1983;* 7 Summer Court, Wheeler Street, MAIDSTONE, KENT, ME14 2UX.
WALDIE, Mrs. Sandra Denise, BA ACA *1985;* 92 Woodside Road, TONBRIDGE, KENT, TN9 2PB.
WALDING, Mr. Keith John, FCA *1972;* Kintail, Halldore Hill, Cookham, MAIDENHEAD, BERKSHIRE, SL6 9EX.
•WALDING, Mrs. Nicola Louise, ACA *2008;* Crowthers Accountants Limited, The Courtyard, 19 High Street, PERSHORE, WORCESTERSHIRE, WR10 1AA.
•WALDING, Mr. Philip Douglas, FCA *1978;* Moore Stephens, Oakley House, Headway Business Park, 3 Saxon Way West, CORBY, NORTHAMPTONSHIRE NN18 9EZ.
WALDMAN, Mr. Gedalia, BA ACA *2010;* 18 Second Avenue, LONDON, NW4 2RN.
WALDMAN, Mr. Stuart Alexander, MEng ACA *1995;* 33 Athenaeum Road, LONDON, N20 9AL.
WALDOCK, Mr. Gary Robert, BSc ACA *1996;* 3790 Cesar Chavez, SAN FRANCISCO, CA 94110, UNITED STATES.
WALDREN, Mr. Anthony Roger, FCA *1966;* Ruby Cottage, Alresford Drove, South Wonston, WINCHESTER, HAMPSHIRE, SO21 3HW. (Life Member)
WALDRON, Miss. Amy Victoria, BSc ACA *2009;* K P M G Salisbury Square House, 8 Salisbury Square, LONDON, EC4Y 8BB.
•WALDRON, Mr. Benjamin Jay, BSc(Hons) ACA *2002;* 243 Sternhold Avenue, Streatham, LONDON, SW2 4PG.
•WALDRON, Mr. Bernard William, FCA *1975;* (Tax Fac), with ASG Accountancy, 17 St Peters Terrace, Lower Bristol Road, BATH, BA2 3BT.
WALDRON, Mr. Craig John, BA ACA *1995;* Ugo Foods Group Ltd, Unit 1, Hertsmere Industrial Park, Warwick Road, BOREHAMWOOD, HERTFORDSHIRE WD6 1GT.
WALDRON, Mr. Jonathon, BA FCA *1983;* Flat 10 Downings House, 21 Southey Road, LONDON, SW19 1ND.
WALDRON, Mrs. Karen Jane, BA ACA *1992;* Executive Communication Centres Ltd Vienna House, International Square Starley Way, BIRMINGHAM, B37 7GN.
WALDRON, Miss. Lisa, BA ACA *2011;* 5 The Horsefair, HENLEY-IN-ARDEN, B95 5BE.
•WALDRON, Mr. Patrick, BA ACA *1988;* Deloitte LLP, Abbots House, Abbey Street, READING, RG1 3BD. See also Deloitte & Touche LLP
WALDRON, Mrs. Sarah Jayne, BSc ACA *1996;* 10 Stadium Road, Henleaze, BRISTOL, BS6 7YE.
WALDRON, Mr. Simeon Paul, BA ACA *2001;* 443 South Raymond Avenue, PASADENA, CA 91105, UNITED STATES.
WALDRON, Mr. Simon John, BA ACA *1993;* Lawton Tube Co Ltd, Torrington Avenue, COVENTRY, CV4 9AB.
WALDRON, Mr. Simon Nicholas Gerrard, MA ACA *1988;* 22 rue du Four, 75006 PARIS, FRANCE.
WALDRON, Mr. Stephen Christopher, ACA *1983;* Globalgrange Limited, 58 Rochester Row, LONDON, SW1P 1JU.
WALDUCK, Mr. Alexander Harold Edward Peter, BA ACA *1999;* (Tax Fac), The Imperial London Hotels Ltd, c/o Directors Office, Russell Square, LONDON, WC1B 5BB.
•WALE, Mr. Jonathan Malcolm Masters, BA ACA *1986;* 32 White Hart Wood, SEVENOAKS, KENT, TN13 1RS. See also J.M.M. Wale
WALE, Mrs. Judith Margaret, MA DPhil FCA *1980;* Orchard House, Banbury Lane, Culworth, BANBURY, OX17 2AX.
WALE, Mrs. Susan Carole, BA ACA *1984;* Tigh Geal, 50 Copperkins Lane, Chesham Bois, AMERSHAM, HP6 5QR.
WALES, Mr. Andy, MSc BSc ACA *2006;* Flat 3, 23 Lillington Road, LEAMINGTON SPA, CV32 5YS.
WALES, Mr. Christopher John, PhD MA ACA *1982;* (Tax Fac), FTI UK Holdings Limited, 322 High Holborn, LONDON, WC1V 7PU.
WALES, Mr. Gregory John, BSc FCA *1974;* PO Box 859, Water Mill, NEW YORK, NY 11976, UNITED STATES.
WALES, Mr. James Alan, ACA *2011;* 52 Woodlands Road, Bookham, LEATHERHEAD, SURREY, KT23 4HH.
WALES, Mr. Jonathan Robert Hamilton, FCA *1980;* (Tax Fac), 8 Monks Well, FARNHAM, GU10 1RH.
WALES, Mr. Michael John, FCA *1974;* Theodor-Heuss-Strasse 1, 63512 HAINBURG, GERMANY.
WALES, Miss. Nicola Margaret, ACA *2009;* K P M G, St. James's Square, MANCHESTER, M2 6DS.
•WALFISZ, Mr. Nigel Joseph, BA FCA *1991;* Martin Greene Ravden LLP, 55 Loudoun Road, St John's Wood, LONDON, NW8 0DL. See also MGR Audit Limited
WALFORD, Miss. Alison Mary, BSc ACA *1989;* Malvern College, College Road, MALVERN, WORCESTERSHIRE, WR14 3DF.
WALFORD, Mr. Andrew, MA ACA *2004;* Marwyn, 11 Buckingham Street, LONDON, WC2N 6DF.
WALFORD, Mr. Christopher Thomas, BSc ACA *2004;* with Target Consulting Limited, Lawrence House, Lower Bristol Road, BATH, BA2 9ET.
WALFORD, Miss. Clare Louise, BSc ACA ATII *2001;* 12 Gopshill Lane, Gretton, CHELTENHAM, GLOUCESTERSHIRE, GL54 5ET.
WALFORD, Mr. David De Guise, TD DL FCA *1948;* 47 The Green, Norton, STOCKTON-ON-TEES, TS20 1DU. (Life Member)
•WALFORD, Mr. David John, FCA *1985;* Davenport Hodgkiss, 1a Wilton Street, Manchester Road, Hollinwood, OLDHAM, OL9 7NZ.
WALFORD, Mrs. Jacqueline Mary, BSc ACA *1987;* 2 Diddies House, Diddies, BUDE, CORNWALL, EX23 9NE.
•WALFORD, Mr. Peter Alan, FCA *1974;* Imagine Insurance, Cedar Court, 2nd Floor, Wildey Business Park, ST MICHAEL, BARBADOS. See also Walford P.A.
WALFORD, Mr. Ronald Norman, FCA *1968;* 12 Gopshill Lane, Gretton, CHELTENHAM, GL54 5ET. (Life Member)
WALFORD-FITZGERALD, Mrs. Victoria Elizabeth, BEng ACA *2003;* 2 Link Way, HORNCHURCH, ESSEX, RM11 3RW.
WALIA, Mr. Ravinder Singh, BSc ACA *2001;* 57 Green Street, LONDON, W1K 6RH.
WALIA, Mr. Suneet, BCom ACA CPA *1993;* 15 Marco Polo Court, FRANKLIN PARK, NJ 08823, UNITED STATES.
WALICZEK, Mr. Robert Adam, BSc ACA *1992;* with PricewaterhouseCoopers Sp. z o.o., Al.Armii Ludowej 14, WARSAW, 00638, POLAND.
•WALJI, Ms. Kanize-Fatema, MSc ACA CTA *2004;* Penny Lane, Third Floor, Borough House, 78-80 Borough High Street, LONDON, SE1 1LL.
WALJI, Mr. Murtaza Akberali, FCA *1973;* 321 Rayners Lane, PINNER, MIDDLESEX, HA5 5EH.

•**WALJI, Mr. Shabbirali Mohamed Hussein, FCA** *1980;* Walji & Co (UK) LLP, Prospect House, 50 Leigh Road, EASTLEIGH, HAMPSHIRE, SO50 9DT. See also Walji & Co Private Clients Ltd

WALK, Mr. Jonathan, BA ACA *1995;* 55 MOORGATE, LONDON, EC2R 6PA.

WALKDEN, Ms. Ann Marie, BEng ACA *2002;* 72 Town Lane, Whittle-le-Woods, CHORLEY, PR6 7DH.

WALKDEN, Mr. Christopher Barry, BSc FCA *1970;* 48 Daisy Hill Drive, Adlington, CHORLEY, LANCASHIRE, PR6 9NE. (Life Member)

WALKDEN, Mr. George Roger, FCA *1962;* Lompas, Binton Road, Welford-on-Avon, STRATFORD-UPON-AVON, CV37 8PT.

•**WALKDEN, Mr. Ian James, ACA** *1979;* Walkden I.J., Lower Hill Farm, Tockholes, DARWEN, BB3 0NF.

WALKDEN, Miss. Rachel Jane, BSc ACA *2002;* 22 Eccles Road, LONDON, SW11 1LY.

WALKDEN, Mr. Simon Edward, BA ACA *1996;* 27 Durvale Court, SHEFFIELD, S17 3PT.

WALKE, Mr. Gavin, BSc ACA *1997;* 58 Northease Drive, HOVE, EAST SUSSEX, BN3 8PP.

WALKE, Mr. Neil David, BSc ACA *2001;* 6 Four Oaks, Highclere, NEWBURY, RG20 9PB.

WALKER, Mr. Adam, BSc ACA *1994;* Glaxo Smithkline UK Ltd, 1-3 Iron Bridge Road Stockley Park, UXBRIDGE, MIDDLESEX, UB11 1BT.

WALKER, Mr. Adam Christopher, BA ACA *1992;* Gubelstrasse 11, 6300 ZUG, SWITZERLAND.

WALKER, Mr. Adam Paul, ACA *2011;* 11 Badminton Close, BOREHAMWOOD, HERTFORDSHIRE, WD6 1UL.

•**WALKER, Mr. Adrian, FCA** *1975;* (Tax Fac), Frank Brown & Walford, 314 Linthorpe Road, MIDDLESBROUGH, TS1 3QX.

WALKER, Mr. Adrian John, MA(Cantab) ACA CTA *1991;* 1 Appletree Close, Catherine-de-Barnes, SOLIHULL, WEST MIDLANDS, B91 2TQ.

•**WALKER, Mr. Alan David, LLB BCL ACA** *1989;* 39 High Firs, Gills Hill, RADLETT, WD7 8BH.

WALKER, Mr. Alan John, FCA *1962;* Southview, Bowlers Green, Magdalen Laver, ONGAR, ESSEX, CM5 0ET. (Life Member)

WALKER, Mrs. Alison Jane, BA ACA *1989;* 31 Vale Road, Claygate, ESHER, SURREY, KT10 0NL.

•**WALKER, Mr. Alistair Adam, FCA** *1973;* Folkes Worton & Wood, 56-58A Warwick Road, KENILWORTH, WARWICKSHIRE, CV8 1HH. See also Folkes Worton & Wood ltd

WALKER, Miss. Amy Louise, ACA *2007;* 9 Silkstone Place, SHEFFIELD, S12 4RG.

•**WALKER, Mr. Andrew, FCA** *1979;* Walker & Co., Belgrave House, 15 Belgrave Crescent, SCARBOROUGH, NORTH YORKSHIRE, YO11 1UB. See also Burley (Whitby) Philip Limited

•**WALKER, Mr. Andrew, BA ACA** *1993;* (Tax Fac), White Kite, 8 Forest Farm Business Park, Fulford, YORK, YO19 4RH.

WALKER, Mr. Andrew, ACA FCCA *2009;* with Old Mill Accountancy LLP, The Old Rectory, South Walks Road, DORCHESTER, DORSET, DT1 1DT.

WALKER, Mr. Andrew Charles, BA ACA *1989;* 114 Bundock Street, COOGEE, NSW 2034, AUSTRALIA.

WALKER, Mr. Andrew Charles Graham, BSc ACA *1979;* 14 Parchimbeau, 23160 ST SEBASTIEN, FRANCE.

WALKER, Mr. Andrew David, MA ACA *1989;* Stovax Ltd Falcon Road, Sowton Industrial Estate, EXETER, EX2 7LF.

WALKER, Mr. Andrew David, BSocSc ACA *1996;* 8 Hydestile Cottages, Hambledon Road, Hambledon, GODALMING, SURREY, GU8 4DL.

WALKER, Mr. Andrew David, BA(Hons) ACA *2001;* 39 Dale End Road, Hilton, DERBY, DE65 5FW.

WALKER, Mr. Andrew David, BA(Hons) ACA *2001;* 8 Lyminton Lane, Treeton, ROTHERHAM, SOUTH YORKSHIRE, S60 5UG.

WALKER, Mr. Andrew Dudley, FCA *1954;* PO Box 718, VANDERBIJLPARK, 1900, SOUTH AFRICA. (Life Member)

WALKER, Mr. Andrew James, BSc ACA *2003;* BPB UKSC, Finance Building, East Leake, LOUGHBOROUGH, LEICESTERSHIRE, LE12 6JU.

WALKER, Mr. Andrew James, BSc ACA *1991;* United Utilities Lingley Green Avenue, Lingley Mere Business Park Great Sankey, WARRINGTON, WA5 3LP.

WALKER, Mr. Andrew James, BA ACA *1993;* 240 Padgbury Lane, CONGLETON, CW12 4HU.

•**WALKER, Mr. Andrew John, BSc FCA** *1993;* KPMG LLP, St. James's Square, MANCHESTER, M2 6DS. See also KPMG Europe LLP

WALKER, Mr. Andrew John, BA ACA *1993;* 8 Pemberley Close, West Ewell, EPSOM, SURREY, KT19 9LW.

•**WALKER, Mr. Andrew John, BA ACA** *1992;* Benson Walker & Co, 1 Bachelor Lane, Horsforth, LEEDS, LS18 5NA.

WALKER, Mr. Andrew Michael, BCom FCA *1985;* 2 Stocking Leys, Burbage, HINCKLEY, LEICESTERSHIRE, LE10 2FH.

WALKER, Mr. Andrew Richard, BA ACA *2007;* 14 Southwood Avenue, Honley, HOLMFIRTH, HD9 6QP.

WALKER, Mr. Andrew Robert, BA(Hons) ACA *2002;* Deutsche Bank 1st Floor, 1 Appold Street, LONDON, EC2A 2HE.

WALKER, Mr. Andrew Stephen James, BSc FCA *1994;* Jeffries, Hedsor Road, BOURNE END, BUCKINGHAMSHIRE, SL8 5DH.

WALKER, Mrs. Ann Lesley, FCA *1978;* 12 Salet Way, Hawthorne Rise Cowplain, WATERLOOVILLE, PO7 8QS.

WALKER, Mr. Anthony, FCA *1952;* 64 Smithbarn, HORSHAM, RH13 6DU. (Life Member)

WALKER, Mr. Anthony, ACA *2011;* Pricewaterhousecoopers, 1 Embankment Place, LONDON, WC2N 6RH.

WALKER, Mr. Anthony John, FCA *1967;* 157 Rivermead Court, Ranelagh Gardens, LONDON, SW6 3SF. (Life Member)

WALKER, Mr. Anthony Richard, FCA *1965;* Walkers Cay 31 Sandyport Drive P. O. Box CB-13931, NASSAU, BAHAMAS.

WALKER, Mr. Antony James, BA FCA *1993;* PCS LLC, 101 Federal Street, Suite 1900, BOSTON, MA 02210, UNITED STATES.

WALKER, Mr. Antony Philip James, BSc ACA *1992;* Planet Holdings Ltd, Unit 3, Bellbrook Enterprise Centre, Bell Lane, UCKFIELD, EAST SUSSEX TN22 1QZ.

•**WALKER, Mr. Arthur, FCA** *1976;* with Townends, Carlisle Chambers, Carlisle Street, GOOLE, DN14 5DX.

WALKER, Mr. Arthur Edward, FCA *1963;* (Tax Fac), 6 Water Street, SKIPTON, NORTH YORKSHIRE, BD23 1PB. (Life Member)

WALKER, Mr. Barry Antony Ashton, FCA *1954;* 17 Burcot Court 51 Four Oaks Road, SUTTON COLDFIELD, WEST MIDLANDS, B74 2XU. (Life Member)

WALKER, Mr. Ben, BA ACA *2006;* 39 Childwall Crescent, LIVERPOOL, L16 7PG.

WALKER, Mr. Benjamin Dampier, ACA *2008;* Easyhotel House, 80 Old Street, LONDON, EC1V 9AZ.

WALKER, The Revd. Brian Cecil, FCA *1951;* 1 Chaucer Road, Aston Fields, BROMSGROVE, B60 2EE. (Life Member)

WALKER, Mr. Brian John, BSc ACA *1993;* Oak Hatch, 102a Oak Hill Wood Street Village, GUILDFORD, SURREY, GU3 3ES.

WALKER, Mr. Bruce, BBS FCA *1975;* 14 Beachfield Manor, Screen, ENNISCORTHY, COUNTY WEXFORD, IRELAND.

WALKER, Mr. Bruce Thomas, BSc ACA *1990;* The White House, Alvanley Road, Helsby, FRODSHAM, WA6 9PS.

WALKER, Mrs. Carol Louise, BSc ACA *1997;* 2 Falcon Mews, Morley, LEEDS, LS27 8UP.

•**WALKER, Miss. Carole Ann, BA ACA** *1987;* Carole Walker, 47 Brookdale, New Longton, PRESTON, PR4 4XL.

•**WALKER, Mrs. Catherine Ann, BSc FCA** *1995;* Walker Accountancy Limited, 2 Biscay Court, Oakwood, DERBY, DE21 2SG.

WALKER, Mrs. Cecilia Anne, MA FCA DChA *1981;* Ashcroft, 322 Shenley Road, BOREHAMWOOD, WD6 1TT.

WALKER, Mr. Charles, ACA *2008;* 50 Ivy Road, Stirchley, BIRMINGHAM, B30 2NU.

WALKER, Mr. Charles Mackay, FCA *1971;* 28 Hambling Drive, BEVERLEY, HU17 7GD. (Life Member)

•**WALKER, Mr. Charles Mark Sykes, FCA** *1980;* HPH, 54 Bootham, YORK, YO30 7XZ.

WALKER, Mr. Charles Richard Burrows, BA ACA *2010;* 30 South Island Place, LONDON, SW9 0DX.

WALKER, Mrs. Charlotte Ann, MA ACA *2001;* 39 Hertford Avenue, LONDON, SW14 8EH.

WALKER, Miss. Charlotte Louise, BA(Hons) ACA *2000;* Zwarte Mees 6, 1423 NJ UITHOORN, NETHERLANDS.

WALKER, Mr. Chris, BSc ACA *2000;* 16 North Road, West Bridgford, NOTTINGHAM, NG2 7NH.

WALKER, Mr. Christopher, BCom FCA *1986;* 23 Vicarage Gardens, SCUNTHORPE, SOUTH HUMBERSIDE, DN15 7BA.

WALKER, Mr. Christopher Brook, BA ACA *1990;* 12 Connaught Road, FLEET, HAMPSHIRE, GU51 3RA.

WALKER, Mr. Christopher Douglass, BA ACA *1986;* 60 Rowfant Road, LONDON, SW17 7AS.

WALKER, Mr. Christopher John, BSc ACA *2001;* 68 Adelaide Road, LONDON, W13 9EB.

WALKER, Mr. Christopher Julian, ACA *1994;* 37 Lime Street, EVESHAM, WORCESTERSHIRE, WR11 3AH.

WALKER, Mr. Christopher Neil, BSc ACA *1996;* 14A London Road, Aston Clinton, AYLESBURY, HP22 5HQ.

•**WALKER, Mr. Christopher Richard, MA ACA** *1989;* C.R. Walker, 8 Longford Park, Longford, NEWPORT, SHROPSHIRE, TF10 8LW.

WALKER, Miss. Claire, BA ACA *2003;* University of Liverpool, Chatham Building, LIVERPOOL, L69 7ZH.

WALKER, Mrs. Claire Jane, BSc ACA *2006;* 6 Church Road, Great Cornard, SUDBURY, SUFFOLK, CO10 0EL.

WALKER, Mr. Clive, BSc FCA *1973;* Hulcott Lodge, 24 Hogfair Lane, Burnham, SLOUGH, SL1 8BS. (Life Member)

WALKER, Mr. Clive Philip, BA ACA *1989;* 47 The Hall Foxes Dale, Blackheath, LONDON, SE3 9BE.

WALKER, Mr. Colin, FCA *1962;* 15 Crystal Avenue, The Heath, CARDIFF, CF23 5QJ. (Life Member)

•**WALKER, Mr. Colin Peter, ACA CTA** *1985;* Powrie Appleby LLP, Queen Anne House, 4 6 & 8 New Street, LEICESTER, LE1 5NR. See also MacIntyre Hudson LLP

WALKER, Mr. Colin Richard, BSc FCA *1976;* Legal Trustees (Jersey) Ltd, PO Box 781, JERSEY, JE4 0SG.

WALKER, Mrs. Corrina Jane, BA ACA *1992;* 28 Copenhagen Gardens, LONDON, W4 5NN.

WALKER, Mr. Craig William, BSc ACA *2009;* 49 Northwold Avenue, West Bridgford, NOTTINGHAM, NG2 7LQ.

WALKER, Mr. Daniel James, BSc ACA CTA AMCT *1993;* 30 Harrow Road, Elvetham Heath, FLEET, HAMPSHIRE, GU51 1JD.

WALKER, Mr. David, FCA *1961;* P O Box 1685, MBABANE, SWAZILAND.

WALKER, Mr. David, BA(Hons) ACA *2003;* 35 Netherford Road, Clapham, LONDON, SW4 6AF.

WALKER, Mr. David, ACA CA(SA) *2008;* Flat 3, 89 Crescent Lane, LONDON, SW4 9AW.

WALKER, Mr. David, MBA BSc FCA *1983;* 4 Stable Field Way, Hemsby, GREAT YARMOUTH, NORFOLK, NR29 4TE.

•**WALKER, Mr. David Allan, FCA** *1968;* (Tax Fac), Walker Hubble, 5 Parsons Street, DUDLEY, DY1 1JJ.

•**WALKER, Mr. David Anthony, FCA** *1969;* Walker & Sutcliffe, 12 Greenhead Road, HUDDERSFIELD, HD1 4EN. See also Walker Sutcliffe & Cooper

WALKER, Mr. David Ernest John, ACA *2005;* (Tax Fac), South Asian Real Estate, 27 Hill Street, LONDON, W1J 5LP.

•**WALKER, Mr. David Gordon, ACA FMAAT** *1995;* MEMBER OF COUNCIL, (Tax Fac), Walker & Associates Ltd, 47 Orrin Close, Woodthorpe, YORK, YO24 2RA.

•**WALKER, Mr. David Irvin, FCA** *1968;* David Walker, Trebarwith, 91 Ashbourne Road, Cowers Lane, BELPER, DERBYSHIRE DE56 2LF.

WALKER, Mr. David James, BA ACA *1992;* MBNA Europe Bank Ltd, M B N A International Bank Ltd, Chester Business Park, CHESTER, CH4 9FB.

WALKER, Mr. David John, FCA *1973;* Advanced Business Solutions, 300 Pavilion Drive, NORTHAMPTON, NN4 7YE.

•**WALKER, Mr. David John, BSc FCA** *1985;* Johnsons Accountants Limited, 2 Hallgarth, PICKERING, NORTH YORKSHIRE, YO18 7AW.

WALKER, Mr. David John, FCA *1970;* 8 Valley Park Close, EXETER, EX4 5HJ.

①**WALKER, Mr. David Malcolm, FCA** *1974;* Broomfield House, Baldwin Lane, Clayton, BRADFORD, WEST YORKSHIRE, BD14 6PN.

WALKER, Mr. David Mark, BA ACA *1999;* The Cottage Whitmoor House, Whitmoor Lane, GUILDFORD, GU4 7QB.

WALKER, Mr. David Nigel, BA ACA *1983;* Sitexorbis Holdings Ltd, Beaufort House, Cricket Field Road, UXBRIDGE, MIDDLESEX, UB8 1QG.

WALKER, Mr. David Paul, LLB ACA *1994;* 1 Carnforth Avenue, Chadderton, OLDHAM, OL9 9DN.

WALKER, Mr. David Robert, MSc BSc FCA *1981;* 6 Weybridge Close, Appleton, WARRINGTON, WA4 5LZ.

•**WALKER, Mr. David William, FCA** *1981;* (Tax Fac), Manor Close Limited, 114-116 High Street, Gosforth, NEWCASTLE UPON TYNE, NE3 1HB.

WALKER, David William, Esq FCA *1962;* 7 Washington Close, REIGATE, RH2 9LT. (Life Member)

WALKER, Mrs. Dena, LLB ACA *2002;* 14 Burghfield Walk, BASINGSTOKE, HAMPSHIRE, RG22 5AT.

•**WALKER, Mr. Derek George, FCA** *1977;* 10 Willis Avenue, SUTTON, SM2 5HS.

WALKER, Mr. Derek Tait, FCA CTA *1963;* Waterside Cottage, CORBRIDGE, NORTHUMBERLAND, NE45 5QX. (Life Member)

•**WALKER, Mrs. Dianne Gillian Davies, BA ACA** *1990;* Dianne Walker & Co, The White House, Alvanley Road, Helsby, FRODSHAM, WA6 9PS.

WALKER, Mr. Duncan, BSc ACA *1996;* 42 Highworth Road, LONDON, N11 2SH.

WALKER, Mr. Duncan, PhD MSc MBChB ACA *1997;* 3 Maythorn Gardens, Codsall, WOLVERHAMPTON, WV8 1GQ.

WALKER, Mr. Edward Ian Charles, BA ACA *2000;* 62 Dean Road, Fair Oak, EASTLEIGH, HAMPSHIRE, SO50 7JE.

WALKER, Mr. Edward Peter, BCom FCA *1963;* 23 Lake Julia Drive South, PONTE VEDRA BEACH, FL 32082, UNITED STATES. (Life Member)

WALKER, Mr. Edward Stevens, BCom FCA *1953;* Little Firs, The Street, Walberton, ARUNDEL, BN18 0PY. (Life Member)

•**WALKER, Mrs. Elaine, FCA** *1982;* (Tax Fac), EW Accountancy Practice Limited, 28a Hardwick Street, BUXTON, DERBYSHIRE, SK17 6DH. See also Walker Elaine

WALKER, Miss. Elizabeth Ann, ACA *1986;* N A C R O Unit 4 Park Place, 10-12 Lawn Lane, LONDON, SW8 1UD.

WALKER, Mrs. Emily, MA ACA *1998;* with PricewaterhouseCoopers LLP, 1 Embankment Place, LONDON, WC2N 6RH.

WALKER, Mrs. Emily Rebecca Louise, MSci BSc(Hons) ACA *2002;* 5 Birchfield Avenue, Gildersome, Morley, LEEDS, LS27 7HU.

WALKER, Miss. Emma Jane, BA ACA *1999;* 4 Hibberts Meadow, Wooburn Green, HIGH WYCOMBE, BUCKINGHAMSHIRE, HP10 0AN.

WALKER, Ms. Fay Helen, MA ACA *1999;* 38 Frederick Square, LONDON, SE16 5XR.

WALKER, Mrs. Fiona Ailsa, BSc ACA *1992;* Bollands, Minerva Mill, Station Road, ALCESTER, B49 5ET.

•**WALKER, Miss. Fiona Jane, BA(Hons) ACA** *2002;* Deloitte LLP, Hill House, 1 Little New Street, LONDON, EC4A 3TR. See also Deloitte & Touche LLP

WALKER, Mrs. Frances, ACA MAAT *2010;* 20 Highley Park, Clifton, BRIGHOUSE, HD6 4LE.

WALKER, Mr. Frederick Ewart, FCA *1963;* The Forge, Gotton, Cheddon Fitzpaine, TAUNTON, TA2 8LL.

WALKER, Mr. Frederick Neil, MA ACA *1989;* Odyssey Arena, 2 Queens Quay, BELFAST, BT3 9QQ.

WALKER, Mr. George Michael Henderson, BA FCA *1954;* Westfield, The Common, Dunsfold, GODALMING, GU8 4LE. (Life Member)

WALKER, Mr. George Ronald, FCA *1962;* 1 Auckland Way, West Park, HARTLEPOOL, TS26 0AN. (Life Member)

WALKER, Mr. Gerald Donald, FCA *1956;* amora, 100 London Road, STANMORE, HA7 4PW. (Life Member)

WALKER, Mr. Gilbert Heriot, FCA *1973;* 54 Lightburn Road, ULVERSTON, LA12 0BX. (Life Member)

WALKER, Mr. Gordon, FCA *1966;* Morningside, 8 Furzehatt Way, Plymstock, PLYMOUTH, DEVON, PL9 8LT. (Life Member)

WALKER, Mr. Graeme, FCA *1988;* 21 Warkworth Woods, Great Park, Gosforth, NEWCASTLE UPON TYNE, NE3 5RA.

WALKER, Mr. Graeme Neill, MA ACA *1987;* (Tax Fac), Woodacre Rowallan Street, HELENSBURGH, G849PP.

WALKER, Mr. Graham, ACA CA(SA) *2008;* Anam Cara, 24 Ennis Road, Parkview, JOHANNESBURG, 2193, SOUTH AFRICA.

WALKER, Mr. Graham Andrew Mackenzie, MA ACA *2005;* 20 Trystings Close, Claygate, ESHER, KT10 0TF.

WALKER, Graham Arthur James, Esq LVO MA FCA *1974;* 15 Devonshire Road, SUTTON, SM2 5HQ. (Life Member)

•**WALKER, Mr. Graham Barry, FCA** *1970;* Graham B Walker Ltd, 1 Westfield Cottages, Newton on Derwent, YORK, YO41 4DG.

WALKER, Mr. Graham John McRae, MBA BA FCA *1989;* Graham Walker, 1 Beverley Court, Healing, GRIMSBY, SOUTH HUMBERSIDE, DN41 7SP.

WALKER, Mr. Graham Peter, BA FCA *1999;* Fortis Prime Fund Solutions (Curacao), 14 John B. Gorsiraweg, WILLEMSTAD, CURACAO, AN 000, NETHERLANDS ANTILLES.

WALKER, Mr. Graham Robert Latto, FCA *1974;* c/o Alcatel-Lucent, 3 avenue Octave Greard, 75007 PARIS, FRANCE.

•**WALKER, Mr. Gregory Laurence, FCA** *1971;* Aims - Gregory Walker FCA, Yew Tree Farmhouse, Linton Road, Hadstock, CAMBRIDGE, CB21 4NU.

WALKER, Mr. Guy Christian, BA ACA *1986;* 23-26 Hydes Place, LONDON, N1 2XE.
WALKER, Mr. Guy Frederick, LLB ACA *2010;* 19 Skys Wood Road, ST. ALBANS, HERTFORDSHIRE, AL4 9NY.
WALKER, Mrs. Hazel, BSc ACA *1988;* Swinton Group Ltd, Swinton House, 6 Great Marlborough Street, MANCHESTER, M1 5SW.
•WALKER, Mr. Heath Lee, BA ACA CF *1993;* 59 College Road, Syston, LEICESTER, LE7 2AQ.
WALKER, Miss. Helen, BA ACA *2005;* Flat 4 Morningside, 15 Highgate Road, ALTRINCHAM, CHESHIRE, WA14 4QZ.
WALKER, Miss. Helen Briege, ACA DChA *2008;* Crowe Clark Whitehill Llp St. Brides House, 10 Salisbury Square, LONDON, EC4Y 8EH.
WALKER, Mrs. Helen Lorraine, BA ACA *1992;* 84 Bradbourne Road, SEVENOAKS, TN13 3QB.
•WALKER, Mr. Henry Iain Stancliffe, BSc(Hons) ACA *2003;* (Tax Fac), Ellam Oxtoby & Peck LLP, Malthouse Farm, Brooke Road, Shotesham All Saints, NORWICH, NR15 1XL.
WALKER, Mr. Hereward Roderik, ACA *2008;* Flat 2, 3a Nevill Park, TUNBRIDGE WELLS, KENT, TN4 8NW.
WALKER, Mrs. Hilary Catherine Thornhill, BA ACA *1983;* 8425 Sam Hill Drive, OWINGS, MD 20736, UNITED STATES.
WALKER, Mr. Hugh Stacey, BSc FCA *1971;* 3 Boxgrove Avenue, GUILDFORD, SURREY, GU1 1XG.
•WALKER, Mr. Hugh William, BA FCA DChA *1985;* Mount Stuart, Shore Road, Blairmore, DUNOON, ARGYLL, PA23 8TJ.
WALKER, Mr. Iain, LLB ACA *2003;* 8 Somerville Road, COBHAM, SURREY, KT11 2QU.
WALKER, Mr. Ian, BA FCA *1989;* Byways, 18 Church Lane, Scholar Green, STOKE-ON-TRENT, CHESHIRE, ST7 3QQ.
WALKER, Mr. Ian, FCA *1975;* 6 Hall Lane, Chapelthorpe, WAKEFIELD, WEST YORKSHIRE, WF4 3JE.
WALKER, Mr. Ian Charles, BSc ACA *1994;* Yorkshire House, Aviva UK Insurance, 2 Rougier Street, YORK, YO90 1UU.
•WALKER, Mr. Ian David, ACA FCCA *2008;* Springboard Suite 122, The Ron Cooke Hub, University of York, Heslington, YORK, YO10 5GE. See also Ian Walker & Co
•ⒹWALKER, Mr. Ian Edward, BSc FCA *1978;* Begbies Traynor, Balliol House, Southernhay Gardens, EXETER, EX1 1NP. See also Begbies Traynor(Central) LLP and Begbies Traynor Limited
WALKER, Mr. Ian Stuart, BA FCA *1978;* 8 Emmer Green Court, Caversham, READING, RG4 6NQ.
WALKER, Mrs. Inessa, BA ACA *2003;* 7 Chelmsford Road, HARROGATE, HG1 5NA.
•WALKER, Mr. Ivan, FCA *1991;* Stephenson Smart & Co, Stephenson House, 15 Church Walk, PETERBOROUGH, PE1 2TP.
WALKER, Mr. James, BSc ACA *2011;* Cedarwood Cottage, Dean Wood Road, Jordans, BEACONSFIELD, BUCKINGHAMSHIRE, HP9 2UU.
WALKER, Mr. James Gordon, FCA *1970;* Cedarwood Cottage Dean Wood Road, Jordans, BEACONSFIELD, BUCKINGHAMSHIRE, HP9 2UU. (Life Member)
•WALKER, Mr. James John, BEng BCom ACA CTA *2001;* JJ Walker LLP, 16 Old Queen Street, LONDON, SW1H 9HP.
WALKER, Mr. Jamie Michael, ACA *2008;* The MAC Services Group Limited, Level 3 5-13 Rosebery Avenue, ROSEBERY, NSW 2018, AUSTRALIA.
WALKER, Mrs. Jane Elizabeth, BCom ACA *1987;* 47 Hestercombe Avenue, LONDON, SW6 5LL.
WALKER, Mrs. Jane Louise, BA ACA *2001;* 73 Sabine Road, LONDON, SW11 5LN.
WALKER, Ms. Janet Hilary, BSc ACA *1987;* 2/ 26 Somerset Street, MOSMAN, NSW 2088, AUSTRALIA.
WALKER, Miss. Janet Sheila, MA FCA *1980;* Babylon, Common Lane, Eton College, WINDSOR, BERKSHIRE, SL4 6DU.
WALKER, Mr. Jason Mark, BA ACA *1999;* 5 rue Pasteur, 78600 MAISONS LAFFITTE, FRANCE.
WALKER, Mr. Jeffrey Ian, MA FCA *1976;* The Old Barn, Whittingslow, CHURCH STRETTON, SHROPSHIRE, SY6 6PZ.
WALKER, Mr. Jeffrey Maxwell, FCA *1950;* 1 Norfolk Road, LONDON, NW8 6AX. (Life Member)
WALKER, Mrs. Jennifer Anne, PhD BSc ACA *1982;* 3 Springhaven Close, GUILDFORD, SURREY, GU1 2JP.
WALKER, Miss. Jennifer Caroline Mary, BSc ACA *2006;* Flat 10, 532 New South Head Road, DOUBLE BAY, NSW 2028, AUSTRALIA.
WALKER, Miss. Jennifer Frances, ACA *2008;* 197 Northstand Apartments, Highbury Stadium Square, LONDON, N5 1FN.
WALKER, Mr. Jeremy Harry Holroyd, ACA *1980;* 2 Druids Cottage, Druids Lodge, SALISBURY, SP3 4UN.
WALKER, Ms. Jerusha Candace, ACA *2009;* 4 Windrose Close, LONDON, SE16 6DU.
WALKER, Ms. Jill, BSc ACA *1999;* 97 Wakeman Road, Kensal Green, LONDON, NW10 5BH.
WALKER, Mrs. Jill Catherine, BA ACA *1984;* 7 Birkheads Road, REIGATE, RH2 0AR.
WALKER, Miss. Joanna Claire, MA FCA *1998;* 4 Tandridge Gardens, SOUTH CROYDON, SURREY, CR2 9HU.
WALKER, Mrs. Joanne, PhD MA(Hons) MLitt ACA CTA *2001;* Henderson Loggie, 34 Melville Street, EDINBURGH, EH3 7HA.
WALKER, Mrs. Joanne Elizabeth, MA FCA *1992;* with Deloitte LLP, 2 New Street Square, LONDON, EC4A 3BZ.
WALKER, Mr. John, FCA *1969;* 8 Valleyview Drive, Rushmere St. Andrew, IPSWICH, IP4 5UW.
WALKER, Mr. John, BSc ACA *2007;* 88 Cowdenbeath Path, LONDON, N1 0LG.
WALKER, Mr. John Albert, FCA *1956;* The Thatched House, Tunley, Nr Sapperton, CIRENCESTER, GL7 6LW. (Life Member)
WALKER, Mr. John Angus, FCA *1972;* The Square House, Regent Road, Hoby, MELTON MOWBRAY, LE14 3DU.
•WALKER, Mr. John Christopher, BSc ACA *1983;* John C Walker, 11 Allergill Park, Upperthong, HOLMFIRTH, West Yorkshire, HD9 3XH.
WALKER, Mr. John David Pearson, FCA *1951;* 120 Claremount Road, WALLASEY, CH45 3JQ. (Life Member)
WALKER, Mr. John Edward Marriott, FCA *1980;* National Floorcoverings Ltd, PO Box 7, LIVERSEDGE, WEST YORKSHIRE, WF15 7XA.
WALKER, Mr. John Keith, MA ACA *1980;* 322 Shenley Road, BOREHAMWOOD, WD6 1TT.
WALKER, Mr. John Ross Hewitson, BA FCA *1965;* 27 Broadlands Road, Highgate, LONDON, N6 4AE. (Life Member)
WALKER, Mr. John Stuart, BSc FCA *1971;* Corka Bridge House, Corka Lane, LYTHAM ST.ANNES, FY8 4LX.
WALKER, Mr. John Terence, MA MBA ARCS FCA *1975;* 4 Doune Terrace, EDINBURGH, EH3 6DY.
WALKER, Mr. John Willis, FCA *1970;* 12 St James's Square, LONDON, SW1Y 4LB.
WALKER, Mr. Jonathan James, BSc ACA *1983;* Haberfield, Old Moor Road, Wennington, LANCASTER, LA2 8PD.
WALKER, Mr. Jonathan James, BSc ACA *1995;* with Ernst & Young LLP, 1 More London Place, LONDON, SE1 2AF.
WALKER, Mrs. Judith Anne, FCA *1982;* 18 Royal Oak Drive, ALFORDS POINT, NSW 2234, AUSTRALIA.
WALKER, Mr. Julian Heywood, BA FCA *1979;* Stream Farm High Street, North Wootton, SHEPTON MALLET, SOMERSET, BA4 4AA.
WALKER, Mrs. Julie Karen, BSc(Hons) ACA *2001;* 41 Ladysmith Road, ASHTON-UNDER-LYNE, LANCASHIRE, OL6 9BZ.
WALKER, Ms. Juliet Amanda, BSc ACA *1984;* 3 Downland Farm Cottages, Snatts Road, UCKFIELD, EAST SUSSEX, TN22 2AP.
WALKER, Miss. Karen, MA(Oxon) ACA *2011;* 25 Earl Street, OXFORD, OX2 0JA.
WALKER, Mrs. Karen Elizabeth, BA ACA *1988;* The Old Bakehouse, 3 Farm Lane, Crawley, WITNEY, OX29 9TL.
WALKER, Mr. Keith Alan, FCA *1965;* 2 Heathleigh Drive, Langdon Hills, BASILDON, SS16 6AR. (Life Member)
•WALKER, Mr. Kevin, BSc FCA *1986;* Walker Begley Limited, 207 Knutsford Road, Grappenhall, WARRINGTON, WA4 2QL.
WALKER, Miss. Lauren, BSc(Hons) ACA *2006;* with Tesco Stores Limited, New Tesco House, Delamare Road, Cheshunt, WALTHAM CROSS, HERTFORDSHIRE EN8 9SL.
WALKER, Mrs. Lisa-Jayne, BA ACA *1999;* Cedar House, Ling Lane, Scarcroft, LEEDS, LS14 3HT.
WALKER, Ms. Louise Anne, BA ACA *1998;* 5 Adel Park Gardens, LEEDS, LS16 8BN.
WALKER, Mrs. Lucy, BA ACA *1999;* 276 Stockingstone Road, LUTON, LU2 7DD.
WALKER, Mr. Luke, BA ACA ACCA *2001;* 5 Leather Lane, Gomshall, GUILDFORD, GU5 9NB.
WALKER, Miss. Lynne Mary, BA ACA *1985;* 9 Obthorpe Lane, Thurlby, BOURNE, LINCOLNSHIRE, PE10 0ES.
WALKER, Mr. Malcolm, FCA *1960;* 4 Hammerstones Road, ELLAND, HX5 0QP. (Life Member)
WALKER, Mr. Malcolm George, FCA *1967;* 6 Outwood Lane, Chipstead, COULSDON, CR5 3NA.
•WALKER, Mr. Malcolm Vincent, BMus FCA ATII *1989;* Walker Broadbent Associates Limited, Westgate House, 25 Westgate, OTLEY, WEST YORKSHIRE, LS21 3AT.
WALKER, Mr. Mark Howard, MA ACA *1989;* Woodford Lodge, 123 Woodford Road, Bramhall, STOCKPORT, SK7 1QB.
WALKER, Mr. Martin, FCA *1980;* 2 Devonshire CourtDevonshire Rd, Dore, SHEFFIELD, S17 3NT.
•WALKER, Mr. Matthew, BSc(Hons) ACA *2001;* Atraxa Consulting Limited, Brooke's Mill, Armitage Bridge, HUDDERSFIELD, HD4 7NR.
WALKER, Mr. Matthew, BA ACA *2011;* Jeremys Acre The Street, Dennington, WOODBRIDGE, SUFFOLK, IP13 8JF.
WALKER, Mr. Matthew Charles, BSc(Econ) ACA *2001;* with KPMG, 8th Floor, Tower E2, Oriental Plaza, 1 East Chang An Avenue, BEIJING 100738 CHINA.
WALKER, Mr. Matthew James, BSc ACA *1990;* Bristow Helicopters Ltd, Redhill Aerodrome, Kings Mill Lane, REDHILL, RH1 5JZ.
WALKER, Mr. Matthew Tom, BSc ACA *1995;* 5 Magnolia Grove, Fair Oak, EASTLEIGH, HAMPSHIRE, SO50 7LH.
WALKER, Mr. Maurice Raymond, FCA *1956;* 32 Rockingham Road, KETTERING, NN16 8JS. (Life Member)
WALKER, Mr. Michael Anthony, JP MA FCA *1970;* Tyroler, Nyetimber Lane, West Chiltington, PULBOROUGH, RH20 2NA.
WALKER, Mr. Michael Frederick, FCA *1967;* 88 Westminster Way, North Hinksey, OXFORD, OX2 0LP. (Life Member)
WALKER, Mr. Michael George, BA FCA *1974;* S R S Rail Systems Ltd, 3 Riverside Way, Gateway Business Park, Bolsover, CHESTERFIELD, DERBYSHIRE S44 6GA.
WALKER, Mr. Michael Lawrence, BSc ACA *1983;* 1 Thameside Centre, Kew Bridge Road, BRENTFORD, MIDDLESEX, TW8 0HF.
WALKER, Mr. Michael Robert, BA ACA *1979;* 7 Birkheads Road, REIGATE, RH2 0AR.
WALKER, Ms. Misty-Jane, BSc ACA *2005;* Old Post Office Tedburn St. Mary, EXETER, EX6 6EB.
WALKER, Mrs. Naseem, BEng ACA *2001;* 20 Pine Grove, LONDON, SW19 7HE.
WALKER, Mr. Neil Douglas, BSc ACA *1991;* Rua Da Acacia 11(Lote 224), Quinta Do Peru, 2975 666 QUINTA DO CONDE, PORTUGAL.
WALKER, Mr. Neil James, ACA *2002;* 224a Bramhall Lane South, Bramhall, STOCKPORT, CHESHIRE, SK7 3AA.
WALKER, Mr. Neil Julian, BA ACA *1995;* 25 Killarney Street, MOSMAN, NSW 2088, AUSTRALIA.
•WALKER, Mr. Nicholas Forbes, FCA *1978;* HLB Jackson Fox Limited, PO Box 264, Union House, Union Street, JERSEY, JE4 8TQ. See also HLB Jackson Fox
•WALKER, Mr. Nicholas Timothy, BSc ACA DChA *2005;* Sloane Walker Ltd, 33 Rosedale Close, Hardwicke, GLOUCESTER, GL2 4JL.
WALKER, Mr. Nigel, BA ACA *1981;* Flat 7 Rowan Court, 19 The Avenue, BECKENHAM, BR3 5LH.
WALKER, Mr. Oliver Frederick, MA FCA *1975;* 9 Cole Park Gardens, TWICKENHAM, TW1 1JB. (Life Member)
WALKER, Mr. Owen, ACA *2008;* 25 Farringdon Street, LONDON, EC4A 4AB.
WALKER, Mrs. Pamela, BSc ACA *1986;* 19 Otley Old Road, Lawnswood, LEEDS, LS16 6HB.
WALKER, Mr. Paul Antony, BA ACA *1997;* D F S Furniture Co Ltd, 1 Rockingham Way, Redhouse Interchange, Adwick-le-Street, DONCASTER, SOUTH YORKSHIRE DN6 7NA.
WALKER, Mr. Paul Ashton, BA ACA *1989;* 5 Elmfield Park, Gosforth, NEWCASTLE UPON TYNE, NE3 4UX.
WALKER, Mr. Paul David, BSc ACA *1988;* House of Walker Ltd, PO Box 703, LUTON, LU1 9ZQ.
•WALKER, Mrs. Pauline, BSc ACA *1982;* Howard Walker, Ivy House, Goodmanham Road, Middleton on the Wolds, DRIFFIELD, NORTH HUMBERSIDE YO25 9DE.
WALKER, Mr. Peter, BSc ACA *1979;* 5 Chesterfield Close, Littler Cross, WINSFORD, CW7 2NS.
WALKER, Mr. Peter, FCA *1982;* Hedgehogs At Work Ltd, 5 Woodland Grange, Earls Barton, NORTHAMPTON, NN6 0RG.
•WALKER, Mr. Peter, FCA *1993;* MWM, 24 Oxford Street, WELLINGBOROUGH, NN8 4JE.
WALKER, Mr. Peter, BA ACA *1993;* PO Box 705, Butterfield House 68 Fort Street, GEORGETOWN, KY1 1107, CAYMAN ISLANDS.
•WALKER, Mr. Peter, FCA *1968;* Peter Walker, 6 Aspin Lane, KNARESBOROUGH, HG5 8ED.
WALKER, Mr. Peter, BA ACA *1994;* 24-10-8B Deuxpere Sunshine, Asahi Cho, TOCHIGI-SHI, 328 0035 JAPAN.
WALKER, Mr. Peter Arthur, BA FCA *1977;* D P World, 16 Palace Street, LONDON, SW1E 5JQ.
WALKER, Mr. Peter Charles, LLB ACA *1990;* Geaters Barn, Tunstall, WOODBRIDGE, SUFFOLK, IP12 2JX.
WALKER, Mr. Peter Colin, ACA *1980;* 54 Perch Close, Larkfield, AYLESFORD, ME20 6TN.
WALKER, Mr. Peter Ian, BA FCA *1996;* Cedar House, Ling Lane, Scarcroft, LEEDS, LS14 3HT.
WALKER, Mr. Peter Jeffrey, MA ACA *1993;* The Grange, West Harlsey, NORTHALLERTON, NORTH YORKSHIRE, DL6 2DR.
WALKER, Mr. Peter Jeremy, MA FCA FCMC *1979;* Saxons, 10 Beck Road, SAFFRON WALDEN, ESSEX, CB11 4EH.
WALKER, Mr. Peter John, FCA *1954;* Dencombe, Rickmansworth Road, Chorleywood, RICKMANSWORTH, WD3 5SD. (Life Member)
WALKER, Mr. Peter Llewellyn, BSc FCA FCT *1982;* 38 Downshire Hill, LONDON, NW3 1NU.
WALKER, Mr. Peter Neil, BSc ACA *1984;* Peterborough Regional College, Park Crescent, PETERBOROUGH, PE1 4DZ.
•WALKER, Mr. Philip, BA FCA *1977;* (Tax Fac), Beldon Brook Limited, Sanderson House, Jubilee Way, Grange Moor, WAKEFIELD, WEST YORKSHIRE WF4 4TD.
WALKER, Mr. Philip, BA(Econ) ACA *1984;* Higher Asker Hill, Grindleton, CLITHEROE, BB7 4QT.
WALKER, Mr. Philip Edwin, BSc ACA *2005;* 330 Connecticut Street, SAN FRANCISCO, CA 94107, UNITED STATES.
WALKER, Mr. Philip Henry, BA ACA *2006;* Barclays Corporate, Park House, Newbrick Road, Stoke Gifford, BRISTOL, BS34 8YU.
WALKER, Mr. Philip Ian, BSc ACA *1993;* 84 Bradbourne Road, SEVENOAKS, KENT, TN13 3QB.
WALKER, Mr. Philip James, LLB *1998;* Nomura Code Securities Ltd, 1 Carey Lane, LONDON, EC2V 8AE.
•WALKER, Mr. Philip Oscar, FCA *1966;* Philip Walker, Anthony's Well, Chew Stoke, BRISTOL, BS40 8XG.
WALKER, Mrs. Rachel Anne, ACA *1989;* 265 Berwick Street, EAST VICTORIA PARK, WA 6101, AUSTRALIA.
WALKER, Mr. Reginald Frederick, FCA *1969;* 39 Millennium Court, La Greve d'Azette, St. Clement, JERSEY, JE2 6GS. (Life Member)
WALKER, Mrs. Rhian Wynne, BA FCA *1988;* 108 Inderwick Road, LONDON, N8 9JY.
WALKER, Miss. Rhonda Ophelia, BSc ACA *1993;* 44 Taylor Close, ST. ALBANS, AL4 9YB.
WALKER, Mr. Richard, BSc ACA *2006;* First Floor, 68 Hubert Grove, LONDON, SW9 9PD.
WALKER, Mr. Richard Alan, BSc ACA *1997;* Jewson Ltd, Merchant House, Binley Business Park, Harry Weston Road, COVENTRY, CV3 2TT.
WALKER, Mr. Richard Byas, BA ACA *1992;* Neueneichweg 35, 4153 REINACH, SWITZERLAND.
WALKER, Mr. Richard Derek John, FCA *1977;* Boesmattweg 9, 5454 BELLIKON, SWITZERLAND.
WALKER, Mr. Richard James, ACA *2002;* 1 Munstead Way, Welton, BROUGH, NORTH HUMBERSIDE, HU15 1FN.
WALKER, Mr. Richard Leigh, BA FCA *1965;* Dunsford, 18 Cassiobury Park Avenue, WATFORD, WD18 7LB.
WALKER, Mr. Richard Mark, BSc ACA *1990;* 38 Denbury Avenue, Stockton Heath, WARRINGTON, WA4 2BW.
WALKER, Mr. Richard Peter, BSc ACA *1999;* 19 Dalby Road, LONDON, SW18 1AW.
WALKER, Mr. Richard Thornborough, ACA *1993;* Upper Bupton Farmhouse, Upper Bupton Farm, Broad Hinton, SWINDON, SN4 9NP.
•WALKER, Mr. Richard William James, BA FCA *1976;* Richard W.J. Walker, Bracken Hills, Surby Road, Port Erin, ISLE OF MAN, IM9 6TD.
WALKER, Mr. Robert, FCA *1954;* 54 Greenacres, Werrington, PETERBOROUGH, CAMBRIDGESHIRE, PE4 6LH. (Life Member)
WALKER, Mr. Robert, MA FCA *1974;* 2122-42 Exeter Road, AJAX L1S 2J9, ON, CANADA. (Life Member)
WALKER, Mr. Robert Anthony, MSc ACA *2003;* 8 Thornton Drive, COLCHESTER, CO4 5WB.
WALKER, Mr. Robert Bruce, ACA *1984;* 72 Mornington Road, Brooklyn, WELLINGTON, NEW ZEALAND.

•**WALLIS, Ms. Nadina Sheila, BA FCA** *1987;* Clipper Accounting Limited, PO Box 5503, 11 Derwent Street, Draycott, DERBY, DE72 3ZH.
WALLIS, Mr. Nicholas Charles, BA ACA *1983;* 35 Woodstock Road North, ST. ALBANS, HERTFORDSHIRE, AL1 4QD.
WALLIS, Mr. Nicholas Simon, FCA *1970;* 3 The Glebe, Hildersley, ROSS-ON-WYE, HEREFORDSHIRE, HR9 5BL. (Life Member)
WALLIS, Miss. Nicole Annette, LLB ACA *2011;* 31 Heythorp Street, LONDON, SW18 5BW.
WALLIS, Mr. Peter Ian, FCA *1975;* Hawthorns, Wilderness Avenue, SEVENOAKS, TN15 0EA.
WALLIS, Miss. Rachel Elizabeth Kirsty, BA(Hons) ACA *2000;* Much More Cottage, Front Street, East Garston, HUNGERFORD, RG17 7EU.
•**WALLIS, Mrs. Rachel Louise Ramsay, BSc FCA** *1985;* 5 Hogs Orchard, School Lane, SWANLEY, BR8 7WX.
WALLIS, Mr. Richard, BSc FCA *1972;* 43 Branwell Close, CHRISTCHURCH, DORSET, BH23 2NP.
WALLIS, Mr. Richard Frank, FCA *1974;* Masons, The Street, Grittleton, CHIPPENHAM, SN14 6AP. (Life Member)
WALLIS, Mr. Richard Frederick, FCA *1973;* ID Dynamics, Tump Hill, Arlington, Bibury, CIRENCESTER, GLOUCESTERSHIRE GL7 5ND.
WALLIS, Mr. Robert, BA ACA *1985;* Barron McCann Technology Ltd, Bermac House, Fifth Avenue, LETCHWORTH GARDEN CITY, HERTFORDSHIRE, SG6 2HF.
WALLIS, Mr. Robert Mathew, ACA *1982;* 26 Hogarth Hill, LONDON, NW11 6BA.
WALLIS, Miss. Sarah Louise, LLB ACA *2000;* 1 Kegworth Road, Kingston On Soar, NOTTINGHAM, NG11 0DB.
WALLIS, Mr. Simon Andrew, ACA *2011;* Old Church Barn, Hempstead, HOLT, NORFOLK, NR25 6TW.
WALLIS, Mr. Stuart Richard, BA ACA *2006;* 3 Fanners Green, Great Waltham, CHELMSFORD, CM3 1EA.
WALLIS, Mr. William John, BA FCA *1963;* 5 Harestone Drive, CATERHAM, CR3 6HX.
WALLIS-HOSKEN, Mr. Romilly St John, FCA *1964;* Apple Trees, Swan Lane, Goudhurst, CRANBROOK, TN17 1JL. (Life Member)
WALLS, Mr. Andrew, FCA *1981;* Deloitte, City House, 126-130 Hills Road, CAMBRIDGE, CB2 1RY.
•**WALLS, Mr. Andrew James, BSc(Hons) ACA** *2003;* Ethos Corporate Finance Ltd, 1 City Square, LEEDS, LS1 2ES.
WALLS, Mr. Bryan Leslie, FCA *1966;* Meadow Bank, Brent Eleigh Road, Monks Eleigh, IPSWICH, IP7 7JG.
WALLS, Mr. Christopher, ACA *2011;* Burfords, Lower Green, Galleywood, CHELMSFORD, CM2 8QS.
WALLS, Mrs. Hilary Carol, BSc ACA *1988;* 282 The Ridgeway, Botany Bay, ENFIELD, EN2 8AP.
WALLS, Mr. Jerome Stewart, BSc ACA *1987;* 7 Kingshall Street, Rougham, BURY ST. EDMUNDS, SUFFOLK, IP30 9LH.
WALLS, Mrs. Juliet Helen, BA ACA *1998;* Cosmos, Rectory Lane, Broughton, STOCKBRIDGE, HAMPSHIRE, SO20 8AB.
WALLS, Mr. Robin, ACA *2007;* 56 Upton Rocks Avenue, WIDNES, CHESHIRE, WA8 9DB.
WALLS, Mr. Roger James, MA LLB FCA *1964;* 262 Station Road, Balsall Common, COVENTRY, CV7 7EE. (Life Member)
WALLS, Mrs. Sarah Jayne, BSc ACA *1997;* 20 Hallam Avenue, LANE COVE WEST, NSW 2066, AUSTRALIA.
WALLS, Mr. Stephen Roderick, FCA *1969;* Amblehurst Manor, Petworth Road, Wisborough Green, BILLINGSHURST, WEST SUSSEX, RH14 0EP.
WALLS, Mr. Timothy Edward, BA ACA *1991;* 1 Plevna Road, HAMPTON, TW12 2BS.
•**WALLWORK, Mr. David Richard, BA ACA** *1992;* Higson & Co, White House, Wollaton St, NOTTINGHAM, NG1 5GF.
WALLWORK, Mr. Geoffrey James, FCA *1965;* Higher Town Farmhouse, 4 Warwick Close, KNUTSFORD, CHESHIRE, WA16 8NA. (Life Member)
WALLWORK, Mr. Paul Antony Hewitt, BA ACA *1989;* Spring Barn, Main Street, Yarwell, PETERBOROUGH, PE8 6PR.
WALLWORK, Mr. Philip Weston, BSc FCA *1971;* Lowcross House, Hutton Lowcross, GUISBOROUGH, TS14 8EW.
WALLWORK, Mr. Steven, ACA *1989;* Torbay Care Trust Bay House, Nicholson Road, TORQUAY, TQ2 7TD.
WALLWORK, Ms. Tamsin, ACA *2008;* National Audit Office, 157-197 Buckingham Palace Road, LONDON, SW1W 9SP.
•**WALLYN, Mr. Peter Lee, FCA** *1979;* Thornton Springer LLP, 67 Westow Street, Upper Norwood, LONDON, SE19 3RW. See also Chelepis Watson Limited
•**WALMSLEY, Mr. Alastair Stewart, BSc ACA** *1994;* Alastair Walmsley Consulting Limited, Rosehill, Chapel Fold, Wiswell, CLITHEROE, LANCASHIRE BB7 9DE.
•**WALMSLEY, Mr. Alexander Peter, BA FCA** *1975;* with Thompson Jenner LLP, 1 Colleton Crescent, EXETER, EX2 4DG.
WALMSLEY, Miss. Annette, ACA *2005;* 59 Park Road, CHORLEY, LANCASHIRE, PR7 1QZ.
WALMSLEY, Mr. Benjamin William, MEng ACA *1995;* 207 Queens Road, LONDON, SW19 8NX.
•**WALMSLEY, Mr. Bernard Thomas, BA FCA** *1972;* Walmsley & Co Accountants Ltd, 8 Eastway, SALE, CHESHIRE, M33 4DX.
WALMSLEY, Mr. Charles Peter Dewhurst, FCA *1949;* 44 Lark Hill, Moulton, NEWMARKET, Suffolk, CB8 8RT. (Life Member)
•**WALMSLEY, Mr. Damian John, BA ACA** *1991;* Moore and Smalley LLP, Richard House, 9 Winckley Square, PRESTON, PR1 3HP.
WALMSLEY, Mr. David Charles, BSc ACA *2004;* 52 Cromwell Grove, MANCHESTER, M19 3QN.
WALMSLEY, Mr. David James, BA ACA *1990;* 35 Bridle Road, MAIDENHEAD, BERKSHIRE, SL6 6DT.
•**WALMSLEY, Mr. David John, BA ACA** *1989;* Cross House Alt Road, Hightown, LIVERPOOL, L38 3RH.
WALMSLEY, Mr. Derek Kerr, BSc FCA *1973;* Walnut Barn High Street, Pavenham, BEDFORD, MK43 7NJ.
WALMSLEY, Mr. Desmond Cecil, FCA *1970;* 3 Freeland Road, LONDON, W5 3HR. (Life Member)
WALMSLEY, Miss. Diane, BSc ACA *2006;* with PricewaterhouseCoopers, Prince's Building, 22/F, 10 Chater Road, CENTRAL, HONG KONG ISLAND HONG KONG SAR.
WALMSLEY, Miss. Jay Grace, FCA FCMA *1960;* 36 Salmons Lane, WHYTELEAFE, CR3 0AN. (Life Member)
WALMSLEY, Mrs. Joanna Louise, BSc(Hons) ACA *2002;* 15 Rosslyn Court, Rosslyn Avenue, PERTH, PH2 0GY.
WALMSLEY, Mr. John Arthur, BA FCA *1973;* CEAG Ltd, Apartment 311, East Block, County Hall, Forum Magnum Square, LONDON SE1 7GN.
WALMSLEY, Mr. John Philip, FCA *1974;* Robin Cross, Long Causeway, Cliviger, BURNLEY, LANCASHIRE, BB10 4RP.
WALMSLEY, Miss. Lisa Susan, ACA *1999;* Conoco Phillips, Humber Refinery, Eastfield Road, South Killingholme, IMMINGHAM, SOUTH HUMBERSIDE DN40 3DW.
WALMSLEY, Mr. Marcus Clive, BSc ACA *2000;* Liverpool Airport Plc, Liverpool John Lennon Airport, LIVERPOOL, MERSEYSIDE, L24 1YD.
WALMSLEY, Mr. Mark Alain, MA ACA *1993;* 13201 Edmonton Drive, MIDLOTHIAN, VA 23113, UNITED STATES.
WALMSLEY, Mr. Myles Keith, BA FCA *1977;* 29 Lower Cribden Avenue, Rawtenstall, ROSSENDALE, BB4 6SW.
WALMSLEY, Mr. Percy John, FCA *1955;* 49 Ashdene Gardens, KENILWORTH, CV8 2TS. (Life Member)
WALMSLEY, Mr. Richard Dominic, BSc ACA ATII *1984;* 61 Baldock Road, LETCHWORTH GARDEN CITY, SG6 3JP.
•**WALMSLEY, Mr. Robert Mervyn, BSc FCA** *1983;* R.M. Walmsley, 21 Clinton Terrace, BUDLEIGH SALTERTON, DEVON, EX9 6RY.
WALMSLEY, Mr. Stephen David, BA FCA *1987;* 14 Grassingham End, Chalfont St. Peter, GERRARDS CROSS, BUCKINGHAMSHIRE, SL9 0BP.
WALMSLEY, Mr. Thomas, BSc ACA *1992;* Inglewood, 2 Menlo Avenue, WIRRAL, MERSEYSIDE, CH61 3UR.
WALMSLEY, Mr. Vincent, FCA *1954;* 8 Alder Grove, POULTON-LE-FYLDE, FY6 8EH. (Life Member)
WALMSLEY, Mr. William Geoffrey, BSc FCA *1986;* 18 Lea Cross Grove, Hough Green, WIDNES, WA8 4FG.
•**WALNE, Mr. Murray, FCA** *1973;* Murray Walne LLP, The Willows, 10a Vicarage Road, OAKHAM, LE15 6EG.
WALPOLE, Mr. Derek Stephen, FCA *1969;* Dale Grange, Askrigg, LEYBURN, NORTH YORKSHIRE, DL8 3BN.
WALPOLE, Mr. Gary Allen, BSc ACA *1993;* Reed Specialist Recruitment Charles House, 61-69 Derngate, NORTHAMPTON, NN1 1UE.
WALPOLE, Mrs. Tracy Jane, BSc FCA *1994;* (Tax Fac), The White Lodge, Crays Hill, BILLERICAY, CM11 2XP.
WALSH, Mr. Adrian Paul, BA ACA *1993;* Past Times Trading Limited, Windrush House, Windrush Park, WITNEY, OX29 7DX.
WALSH, Mr. Alan Martin, BCom ACA *2003;* Pricewaterhousecoopers Cornwall Court, 19 Cornwall Street, BIRMINGHAM, B3 2DT.
WALSH, Mr. Alex Lewis Millbank, BA ACA *2002;* with Rayner Essex LLP, Faulkner House, Victoria Street, ST. ALBANS, HERTFORDSHIRE, AL1 3SE.
WALSH, Mr. Alex Michael, BSc ACA *1995;* 56 Victoria Park, CAMBRIDGE, CB4 3EL.
WALSH, Mr. Alistair James, BSc ACA *1999;* 73 Berkeleys Mead, Bradley Stoke, BRISTOL, BS32 8AU.
•**WALSH, Mr. Andrew John, BSc ACA** *1997;* Instant Accounting Solutions Ltd, Suite 404, 324 Regents Street, LONDON, W11 3HH.
•**WALSH, Mr. Andrew Keith, BA(Hons) ACA** *2004;* Southerns Office Interiors Ltd, Unit 2/B, Interiors House, Cranfield Road, Lostock, BOLTON BL6 4SB.
WALSH, Mr. Andrew Selby Lister, FCA *1970;* 6 Welford Place, Wimbledon, LONDON, SW19 5AJ.
WALSH, Mr. Barry John, BA(Hons) ACA *2004;* 43 Liverpool Road, ST. ALBANS, HERTFORDSHIRE, AL1 3UN.
WALSH, Mr. Brian Sinclair, FCA *1963;* Inglewood, School Road, Barkham, WOKINGHAM, RG41 4TN. (Life Member)
WALSH, Mr. Carl, BA ACA *2004;* Dart Group Plc, Low Fare Finder House, White House Lane, Leeds Bradford Airport, Yeadon, LEEDS LS19 7TU.
WALSH, Mrs. Charis Louisa, BSc ACA *2003;* 39 Nile Grove, EDINBURGH, EH10 4RE.
WALSH, Mrs. Claire, BEng ACA *2001;* with Anthony Abbott Limited, 48 St. Marys Street, BUNGAY, SUFFOLK, NR35 1AX.
WALSH, Miss. Claire Ruth, BA ACA *1999;* Beech House, 52 Eagle Brow, LYMM, CHESHIRE, WA13 0LZ.
WALSH, Mr. Colm Patrick, BSc ACA *2005;* Flat D, 43 Highbury Hill, LONDON, N5 1SU.
WALSH, Mr. Damian, ACA CA(AUS) *2009;* 3 Ridgway Gardens, LONDON, SW19 4SZ.
WALSH, Mr. Daniel William, ACA *2008;* 1a Doddinghurst Road, BRENTWOOD, ESSEX, CM15 9EJ.
WALSH, Mr. David, BA ACA *1990;* 38 Montagu Road, Datchet, SLOUGH, SL3 9DW.
WALSH, Mr. David John, MA ACA *1999;* 78 Otley Road, HARROGATE, NORTH YORKSHIRE, HG2 0DP.
WALSH, Mr. David Martin, BA ACA *1993;* Financial Services Authority, 25 North Colonnade, Canary Wharf, LONDON, E14 5HS.
WALSH, Mr. David Richard, FCA *1974;* Boley Cottage, Boley Cottage Lane, LICHFIELD, STAFFORDSHIRE, WS14 9JA.
WALSH, Mr. Dean, ACA *2010;* 18 Fernleigh Drive, LEIGH-ON-SEA, SS9 1LQ.
•**WALSH, Miss. Deborah Karen, BA FCA** *1996;* (Tax Fac), Horne Brooke Shenton, 21 Caunce Street, BLACKPOOL, FY1 3LA.
WALSH, Mr. Dominic, BSc ACA *1992;* 4 The Chestnuts, Newark Road, Cotham, NEWARK, NG23 5JS.
WALSH, Mr. Edward Joseph, BEng ACA *2002;* with BDO LLP, 6th Floor, 3 Hardman Street, Spinningfields, MANCHESTER, M3 3AT.
•**WALSH, Mr. Francis, LLM FCA** *1958;* (Tax Fac), Carraroe, 1 Polefield Road, Blackley, MANCHESTER, M9 6FN.
WALSH, Mr. Francis Anthony, FCA *1952;* 15 Mumfords Lane, Meols, WIRRAL, CH47 6AZ. (Life Member)
•**WALSH, Mr. Gary Michael, FCA CTA ASFA CFP** *1985;* (Tax Fac), Walshtax Limited, 977 London Road, LEIGH-ON-SEA, ESSEX, SS9 3LB. See also Walsh & Co
WALSH, Mr. George William, FCA *1955;* PO Box 1240, MARYBOROUGH, QLD 4650, AUSTRALIA. (Life Member)
WALSH, The Revd. Gerard Francis George, BSc ACA *1987;* Saint Joseph's Presbytery, 87 West Hill, Portishead, BRISTOL, BS20 6LN.
WALSH, Mr. Graham Anthony, FCA *1969;* 19 Argarmeols Road, Freshfield, LIVERPOOL, L37 7BX. (Life Member)
WALSH, Miss. Helen, BSc ACA *1993;* 152 Wrose Road, Wrose, BRADFORD, BD2 1PU.
WALSH, Mrs. Helen, BSc ACA *2003;* H S B C, 8-14 Canada Square, LONDON, E14 5HQ.
WALSH, Mrs. Helen Yvonne, LLB ACA *2000;* 6 Tall Trees, Baunton Lane, CIRENCESTER, GL7 2AF.
•**WALSH, Mr. Ian James, ACA** *2001;* (Tax Fac), Walsh & Co, First Floor Offices, 59 Appletree Gardens, WHITLEY BAY, TYNE AND WEAR, NE25 8XD.
•**WALSH, Mr. Ian Roland, FCA** *1982;* (Tax Fac), RSM Tenon Audit Limited, 3 Hollinswood Court, Stafford Park, TELFORD, TF3 3BD.
WALSH, Mr. Jake Ritchie, ACA *2009;* 62 Hadley Highstone, BARNET, HERTFORDSHIRE, EN5 4PU.
WALSH, Mr. James Martin, LLB ACA *2005;* with Moore Stephens LLP, 150 Aldersgate Street, LONDON, EC1A 4AB.
•**WALSH, Mr. Jeffrey William, FCA** *1986;* J W Walsh Accountants Ltd, Albion House, 163-167 King Street, DUKINFIELD, CHESHIRE, SK16 4LF. See also On-Line Accountants Ltd
WALSH, Miss. Joanna, ACA *2006;* Strathmore Accountants Ltd, Ivy Mill, Crown Street, Failsworth, MANCHESTER, M35 9BG.
WALSH, Mr. John Anthony Meade, BCom ACA *1989;* 21 Hawthorn Lane, WILMSLOW, SK9 5DD.
WALSH, Mr. John Campbell, FCA *1963;* 4 Creswick Meadow, AYLESBURY, HP21 7PE. (Life Member)
WALSH, Mr. John Henry Harrison, MA ACA *1981;* 23 Bramber Close, Crooked Lane, SEAFORD, EAST SUSSEX, BN25 1QA.
WALSH, Mr. John Patrick, FCA *1977;* Royal Oak House, Stowood, Beckley, OXFORD, OX3 9TY.
WALSH, Mr. John Patrick, BSc FCA *1977;* 10 Church Lane, Merivale, CHRISTCHURCH 8014, NEW ZEALAND.
WALSH, Mr. Joseph, BSc ACA *2009;* Ernst & Young LLP, 560 Mission Street, SAN FRANCISCO, CA 94105, UNITED STATES.
WALSH, Mrs. Julia Stephanie, MA ACA *1989;* with Ernst & Young LLP, 1 More London Place, LONDON, SE1 2AF.
WALSH, Mr. Julian Peter, MA ACA *1983;* 2310 Dominion Centre, 43-59 Queen's Road East, WAN CHAI, HONG KONG ISLAND, HONG KONG SAR.
•**WALSH, Mrs. Julie Irene, FCA** *1981;* Kingston Smith LLP, Devonshire House, 60 Goswell Road, LONDON, EC1M 7AD. See also Kingston Smith Limited Liability Partnership, Devonshire Corporate Services LLP and Kingston Smith Consulting LLP
•**WALSH, Mr. Kenneth Nicholas, BA FCA** *1994;* PricewaterhouseCoopers LLP, 7 More London Riverside, LONDON, SE1 2RT. See also PricewaterhouseCoopers
WALSH, Mr. Kenton, FCA *1991;* Winter House, 83 Hedgerley Lane, BEACONSFIELD, BUCKINGHAMSHIRE, HP9 2JS.
WALSH, Mr. Kevin Joseph, BSc ACA *2008;* 29 Northfield Rd, AYLESBURY, HP201PD.
•**WALSH, Mr. Kevin Michael, ACA** *1982;* (Tax Fac), MCA Breslins Solihull Ltd, 8 The Courtyard, 707 Warwick Road, SOLIHULL, WEST MIDLANDS, B91 3DA.
WALSH, Mr. Kevin Noel, MA ACA *1994;* 25 Thornton Road, LONDON, SW19 4NG.
WALSH, Mr. Kevin Paul, FCA *1973;* 133 Cat Hill, BARNET, HERTFORDSHIRE, EN4 8HR.
WALSH, Miss. Kiri Suzanne, BA(Hons) ACA *2004;* Flat 2, Flat 1-3, 262 Lavender Hill, LONDON, SW11 1LJ.
WALSH, Mr. Kirk Sean, ACA *2008;* 7 Florence Road, BRISTOL, BS16 4SN.
WALSH, Miss. Laura Marie, ACA *2009;* 10 Oxford Street, COLNE, BB8 9JJ.
WALSH, Mr. Leslie, FCA *1961;* Stuhrer Landstr. 47, 28816 STUHR, GERMANY. (Life Member)
WALSH, Mrs. Louise Ann, BA ACA *1992;* U F I Ltd, 1 Young Street, SHEFFIELD, S1 4UP.
WALSH, Mrs. Madeline Elizabeth, BA ACA CTA *2006;* 13 Albert Road, TWICKENHAM, TW1 4HU.
WALSH, Mr. Martin Peters, FCA *1977;* Lyndale, 67 Ruff Lane, ORMSKIRK, L39 4UL.
WALSH, Mr. Michael, ACA *2011;* 88 Farmers Close, WITNEY, OXFORDSHIRE, OX28 1NR.
WALSH, Mr. Michael Bernard, BA ACA *1988;* The Chestnuts, 174 Lodge Lane, GRAYS, ESSEX, RM16 2TP.
WALSH, Miss. Natalie, BSc ACA *2011;* 2a Chaldon Road, LONDON, SW6 7NJ.
WALSH, Mr. Nicholas James, BA(Hons) ACA *2003;* 5 Woodthorne Close, Tilehurst, READING, RG31 6XU.
WALSH, Mr. Patrick Anthony, ACA *1991;* 73 Chermside Road, IPSWICH, QLD 4305, AUSTRALIA.
WALSH, Mr. Patrick John, FCA *1957;* 1601 Baxter Forest Ridge Court, CHESTERFIELD, MO 63005, UNITED STATES. (Life Member)
WALSH, Mr. Patrick Joseph, BA ACA *1982;* Linksdown, Rectory Road, Streatley, READING, RG8 9QA.
WALSH, Mr. Patrick Seymour, MA FCA *1971;* 17 Kelvin Close, HIGH WYCOMBE, HP13 5ST.
WALSH, Mr. Peter John, BSc FCA *1977;* 44d The Broad Walk, Imperial Square, CHELTENHAM, GLOUCESTERSHIRE, GL50 1QG.
•**WALSH, Mr. Peter Terence, FCA** *1963;* P.T.Walsh, 11 Griffiths Drive, SOUTHPORT, PR9 7DP.
WALSH, Mr. Philip James, FCA *1965;* 48 Prune Park Lane, Allerton, BRADFORD, BD15 9JA.
WALSH, Mr. Philip Martin, BSc ACA *2003;* Flat 3, 211 Putney Bridge Road, LONDON, SW15 2NY.

WALSH, Mr. Philip Trevor, LLB ACA *1981;* Fitch Ratings Ltd, Fimalac, 30 North Colonnade, LONDON, E14 5GN.
WALSH, Mrs. Rhian Elizabeth, ACA *2010;* 115 Crest Way, Portslade, BRIGHTON, BN41 2EY.
•WALSH, Mr. Richard William, FCA *1967;* Richard Walsh, Jonquils, Marlow Common, MARLOW, SL7 2JQ.
•WALSH, Mr. Robert Daniel, FCA *1990;* Clear Vision Accountancy Ltd, 1 Abacus House, Newlands Road, CORSHAM, WILTSHIRE, SN13 0BH.
WALSH, Mr. Robert James, BSc(Hons) ACA *2002;* 61 Drysdale Street, LONDON, N1 6ND.
WALSH, Mr. Robin Lawrence, BSc ACA *1982;* Flat 15 Aspen Lodge, 61 Wimbledon Hill Road, LONDON, SW19 7QP.
WALSH, Mr. Scott Alexander, BSc(Hons) ACA *2002;* PricewaterhouseCoopers (L14), 201 Sussex Street, SYDNEY, NSW 2000, AUSTRALIA.
•WALSH, Mr. Shaun Henry Richard, BA ACA *1988;* Insight to Impact Consulting Ltd, 7 King Edward's Court, NOTTINGHAM, NOTTINGHAMSHIRE, NG1 1EW. See also MSO Ltd
WALSH, Miss. Sheila Mary, BSc FCA *1978;* (Tax Fac), 5 Kiln Way, GRAYS, RM17 5JE.
WALSH, Mr. Simon Timothy, BSc ACA *1993;* 132 Auckland Road, Upper Norwood, LONDON, SE19 2RQ.
WALSH, Ms. Simone, ACA CA(AUS) *2008;* 10671 Emerald Chase Drive, Dr Phillips, ORLANDO, FL 32836, UNITED STATES.
WALSH, Miss. Siobhan Mary, BA ACA *1991;* 616 Essex Court, Fox Hall, Fox Chapel, PITTSBURGH, PA 15238, UNITED STATES.
WALSH, Mr. Stanley Thomas, FCA *1957;* Highlands, Horrabridge, YELVERTON, DEVON, PL20 7TX. (Life Member)
WALSH, Mr. Stephen Wilfrid, MA ACA *1985;* 15 Golf Road, BROMLEY, BR1 2JA.
•WALSH, Mr. Steven Barry, FCA *1992;* Hatch Partnership LLP, 29 Wood Street, STRATFORD-UPON-AVON, CV37 6JG.
WALSH, Mr. Thomas Patrick, LLB ACA CFA *2003;* 10 Campbell Road, EDINBURGH, EH12 6DT.
•ⓘWALSH, Mr. Timothy Gerard, BA FCA *1987;* with PricewaterhouseCoopers LLP, 8 Princes Parade, St Nicholas Place, LIVERPOOL, L3 1QJ.
WALSH, Mr. Vincent Colin, FCA *1965;* 21 Appleton Road, Heaton Chapel, STOCKPORT, SK4 5NA.
WALSH, Mr. Wayne Mark, BA ACA *1991;* 301 East 22nd Street, Apt 8K, NEW YORK, NY 10010, UNITED STATES.
WALSH, Mrs. Wendy, MA ACA *1991;* Whistler, Sarum Road, WINCHESTER, HAMPSHIRE, SO22 5QE.
WALSH-EBBATSON, Miss. Isis, MSc BSc ACA *2009;* Flat 4 205, Putney Bridge Road, LONDON, SW15 2PZ.
WALSHAM, Mr. Andrew Stuart, BSc ACA *1989;* 15 Elm Road, FARINGDON, SN7 7EJ.
WALSHAW, Mr. Keith Ashley, FCA *1953;* 42 Caedmon Crescent, DARLINGTON, COUNTY DURHAM, DL3 8LF. (Life Member)
WALSHAW, Miss. Susan Jane, BEd ACA *1991;* Brackenside, Oldfield Road, Honley, HOLMFIRTH, HD9 6NL.
WALSHE, Mr. Brian John, BA ACA *1993;* Homedics Group Ltd Somerhill Business Park, Five Oak Green Road, TONBRIDGE, TN11 0GP.
WALTER, Mr. Alan Ernest Stephen Hill, FCA *1951;* 21 Carisbrooke Avenue, LEICESTER, LE2 3PA. (Life Member)
WALTER, Ms. Amanda Jane, BSc ACA *1989;* 72 Wokingham Road, CROWTHORNE, RG45 7QA.
WALTER, Mrs. Catherine Elizabeth, BA ACA *1986;* 7 Elm Drive, HARROW, HA2 7BS.
WALTER, Mr. Christopher Peter, ACA *2003;* Aviva UK Central Services St. Helens, 1 Undershaft, LONDON, EC3P 3DQ.
WALTER, Mr. Clive Nicholas, MA ACA *1993;* Nogs Cottage, Burtons Lane, CHALFONT ST. GILES, BUCKINGHAMSHIRE, HP8 4BB.
WALTER, Mr. David Robert, BA FCA *1973;* Cotman's Ash Farmhouse, Cotman's Ash Lane, Kemsing, SEVENOAKS, TN15 6XD.
WALTER, Mrs. Denise Brenda, BA(Hons) ACA *2002;* 55 Milton Hill, WESTON-SUPER-MARE, AVON, BS22 9RE.
WALTER, Mr. Derek Edmund Piers, MA FCA *1975;* 19 Hazlewell Road, Putney, LONDON, SW15 6LT.
•WALTER, Mr. Ian Alan, BSc ACA *1979;* Ian Walter, 9 Holly Tree Close, Ley Hill, CHESHAM, HP5 3QT.
WALTER, Mr. Ian David, BA ACA *1997;* 32 River Park, Honley, HOLMFIRTH, HD9 6PS.
•WALTER, Mr. James Mallorie, FCA *1968;* with Walter Wright, 89 High Street, Hadleigh, IPSWICH, IP7 5EA.
WALTER, Mr. Julian Michael Sydney, MA MBA FCA *1970;* PO Box 675, GROSVENOR PLACE, NSW 1220, AUSTRALIA.
WALTER, Miss. Katharine Anne, BA ACA *2007;* 17 Cherrywood Drive, LONDON, SW15 6DS.
WALTER, Miss. Katherine, MMath ACA *2009;* 20 Milne Field, Hatch End, PINNER, MIDDLESEX, HA5 4DP.
WALTER, Mrs. Lorna Anne, LLB ACA *2000;* 2 Dyrham Close, Henleaze, BRISTOL, BS9 4TF.
WALTER, Mr. Mark Andrew, BA(Hons) ACA *2001;* 11 Queens Road, BERKHAMSTED, HERTFORDSHIRE, HP4 3HU.
WALTER, Mrs. Sharon Louise, BSc ACA *2004;* Catlin Holdings Ltd, 3 Minster Court, LONDON, EC3R 7DD.
•WALTER, Mr. Stephen Richard, BA FCA *1985;* Casson Beckman Business and Tax Advisers Limited, Murrills House, 48 East Street, Portchester, FAREHAM, HAMPSHIRE PO16 9XS.
WALTER, Mrs. Susannah Helen, MA ACA *1997;* Ridge End, Bayleys Hill, SEVENOAKS, KENT, TN14 6HS.
WALTER, Mr. Toby Jonathan, BSc ACA *1998;* Ridge End, Bayleys Hill, SEVENOAKS, KENT, TN14 6HS.
WALTERS, Mr. Adrian Jeremy, BSc ACA *1995;* with Experian plc, Landmark House, Experian Way, NOTTINGHAM, NG80 1ZZ.
WALTERS, Mr. Alexander Hamilton, BA FCA *1977;* Whitcombe Manor, Whitcombe, DORCHESTER, DT2 8NY.
•WALTERS, Mr. Alun John, BA FCA *1972;* (Tax Fac), Alun Walters & Co, Llanddewi Castle, Llanddewi, Reynoldston, SWANSEA, SA3 1AU.
WALTERS, Mr. Andrew David, BSc ACA *1994;* Rushteam Properties Ltd, 11-21 Beavor Lane, LONDON, W6 9AR.
WALTERS, Miss. Anna Lise, MSci ACA *2009;* 27 Lyvedon Way, Long Ashton, BRISTOL, BS41 9ND.
WALTERS, Mr. Antony John, BA FCA MBA *1992;* Ashley House Plc, The Priory, Stomp Road, Burnham, SLOUGH, SL1 7LW.
WALTERS, Mr. Benjamin John, BSc ACA *2000;* Compass Plc, Compass House, Guildford Street, CHERTSEY, SURREY, KT16 9BQ.
WALTERS, Mr. Brian Edward, FCA *1958;* Yallingup, 8 Yew Tree Close, Stoke Mandeville, AYLESBURY, HP22 5TU. (Life Member)
WALTERS, Mrs. Carole, BSc ACA *1987;* 1 Northease Cottages, Newhaven Road, Rodmell, LEWES, EAST SUSSEX, BN7 3EY.
WALTERS, Mr. Chris Mark, ACA *2009;* 22 Ravensdon Street, LONDON, SE11 4AR.
WALTERS, Mrs. Claire Louise, ACA *2008;* The Old School Church Street, Melbourne, DERBY, DE73 8EJ.
WALTERS, Mrs. Claire Marie, BA(Hons) ACA *2002;* 13 N Riding Drive, PENNINGTON, NJ 08534, UNITED STATES.
•WALTERS, Mr. Clive Anthony, FCA *1974;* (Tax Fac), Rayner Essex LLP, Faulkner House, Victoria Street, ST. ALBANS, HERTFORDSHIRE, AL1 3SE.
•WALTERS, Mr. Daniel Robert, BSc(Hons) ACA *2003;* Harris & Trotter LLP, 65 New Cavendish Street, LONDON, W1G 7LS.
•WALTERS, Mr. David Ian, BSc FCA *1988;* (Tax Fac), Walters Hawson Limited, 26 Percy Street, ROTHERHAM, S65 1ED.
WALTERS, Mr. David Michael, BSc ACA *1999;* Macob Holdings Ltd, Unit 2, Ynys Bridge Court, Gwaelod-y-Garth, CARDIFF, CF15 9SS.
WALTERS, Mr. David Rhys, BSc FCA *1986;* Astrazeneca, Alderley House, Alderley Park, MACCLESFIELD, CHESHIRE, SK10 4TF.
WALTERS, Mr. David Robert, MA FCA *1992;* 22 Dark Lane, Hollywood, BIRMINGHAM, B47 5BT.
•WALTERS, Mr. David Royston Webb, BSc FCA *1990;* PricewaterhouseCoopers LLP, The Atrium, 1 Harefield Road, UXBRIDGE, UB8 1EX. See also PricewaterhouseCoopers
WALTERS, Mrs. Emma Morag Dorothy, BSc ACA *1999;* 1 Sandling Way, St. Marys Island, CHATHAM, ME4 3AZ.
WALTERS, Mr. Gareth William, BSc ACA *2005;* KPMG, Crown House, Par-la-Ville Road, HAMILTON HM08, BERMUDA.
WALTERS, Mr. Geoffrey Paul, BA(Hons) ACA DipM *1979;* Flat 15, 25-27 Courtfield Road, LONDON, SW7 4DA.
WALTERS, Mr. Gordon Malcolm Leys, BSc FCA FRSA *1995;* The Old Rectory Farleigh Lane, MAIDSTONE, ME16 9LX.
WALTERS, Mr. Hadrian Christopher, BSc ACA *1993;* 17 Abbey Meadow, TEWKESBURY, GL20 5FF.
WALTERS, Miss. Helen Jane, BSc ACA *2004;* with RGL LLP, 8th Floor, Dashwood, 69 Old Broad Street, LONDON, EC2M 1QS.
WALTERS, Mr. Howard, BSc FCA *1973;* Milton Lloyd Ltd, 42-44 Norwood High Street, LONDON, SE27 9NR.
WALTERS, Miss. Imogen Claire Carr, BSc ACA *2001;* 11 Victor Road, WINDSOR, BERKSHIRE, SL4 3JS.
WALTERS, Mr. Ivor, FCA *1957;* 12 Convent Fields, SIDMOUTH, EX10 8QR. (Life Member)
WALTERS, Mrs. Jane, BA ACA *1989;* The Barn, Notton Park, Lacock, CHIPPENHAM, SN15 2NG.
WALTERS, Mrs. Jane Marilyn, BA FCA *1978;* 25 Somerton Gdns, Earley, READING, RG6 5XG.
WALTERS, Mr. John Latimer, QC MA FCA *1974;* Grays Inn Tax Chambers, Grays Inn, LONDON, WC1R 5JA.
WALTERS, Mr. John Nelson, FCA *1971;* 25 Somerton Gardens, Earley, READING, RG6 5XG.
•WALTERS, Mr. John Philip, BSc ACA *1996;* J P Walters & Co, 67 Duke Street, DARLINGTON, COUNTY DURHAM, DL3 7SD. See also J P Walters & Co Ltd
WALTERS, Mr. Jonathan David, BSc ACA *1999;* 2 Hill View, Spencers Wood, READING, RG7 1QB.
WALTERS, Mr. Jonathan Neil, BSc ACA *1991;* The Priory, Braxted Road, Tiptree, COLCHESTER, CO5 0QB.
WALTERS, Mr. Jonathan Robert, BEng FCA *1998;* with PricewaterhouseCoopers LLP, 1 Embankment Place, LONDON, WC2N 6RH.
•WALTERS, Miss. Julia, ACA *1995;* (Tax Fac), JA Walters Limited, The Dairy, Buckwell Lane, Clifton-Upon-Dunsmore, RUGBY, CV23 0BJ. See also Walters Julia
WALTERS, Mr. Mark Alan, BSc ACA *2004;* J P Morgan Fleming Asset Management, Finsbury Dials, 20 Finsbury Street, LONDON, EC2Y 9AQ.
WALTERS, Mr. Michael, ACA *1995;* (Tax Fac), 45 Norroy Road, LONDON, SW15 1PQ.
WALTERS, Mr. Michael Arthur Lewis, BA FCA *1993;* Floor 29, Barclays Bank Plc, 1 Churchill Place, LONDON, E14 5HP.
•WALTERS, Mr. Michael Godfrey, FCA *1968;* (Tax Fac), M G Walters & Co Ltd, 21 Drake Road, WESTCLIFF-ON-SEA, ESSEX, SS0 8LP.
WALTERS, Mr. Michael Philip, BSc ACA *2006;* 200 Kim Seng Road, The Cosmopolitan, #32-02, SINGAPORE 239471, SINGAPORE.
WALTERS, Mr. Michael Rhys, BA ACA *1990;* Comet Plc Comet House, Homestead Road, RICKMANSWORTH, HERTFORDSHIRE, WD3 1FX.
WALTERS, Mrs. Nicola Janet, BSc ACA *1999;* 15 Sandling Way, St Marys Island, CHATHAM, ME4 3AZ.
WALTERS, Mr. Patrick Neil, BSc(Hons) ACA CF *2000;* 6 Orchard Way, Cambourne, CAMBRIDGE, CB23 5BN.
WALTERS, Mr. Patrick William, BA ACA *1992;* Tucker Mill, Buckland Rings, Sway Road, LYMINGTON, HAMPSHIRE, SO41 8NN.
WALTERS, Mr. Paul John, BSc ACA *1994;* with PricewaterhouseCoopers, 33/F Cheung Kong Center, 2 Queen's Road, CENTRAL, HONG KONG ISLAND, HONG KONG SAR.
WALTERS, Mr. Paul John, BSc ACA AMCT *2002;* 30 Hampton Road, Knowle, SOLIHULL, B93 0NT.
WALTERS, Mr. Philip, BSc(Hons) ACA *2011;* 26 Cefn Coed Avenue, CARDIFF, CF23 6HG.
WALTERS, Mr. Philip Donald, BSc FCA *1976;* Hartley Place, Thackhams Lane, Hartley Wintney, HOOK, RG27 8HT.
•WALTERS, Mr. Richard, FCA *1977;* 7 Linnet Close, Kempshott, BASINGSTOKE, RG22 5PD.
WALTERS, Mr. Richard Charles De Lancey, FCA *1964;* Beech Cottage, Castle Street, BAKEWELL, DE45 1DU.
•WALTERS, Mr. Robert Michael, MA FCA *1962;* Robert M. Walters, 5 Glen Drive, Stoke Bishop, BRISTOL, BS9 1SA.
WALTERS, Mr. Robert Oakley, FCA *1970;* 14 Vincent Square, LONDON, SW1P 2NA.
WALTERS, Mr. Roger Graham, FCA *1970;* 55 Ennismore Gardens, Knightsbridge, LONDON, SW7 1AJ.
WALTERS, Mr. Ronald Martin, FCA *1973;* 6 Claverton Way, Rushmere Park, IPSWICH, IP4 5XE.
WALTERS, Mr. Russell Ian, MA ACA *1990;* 8 Madison Way, SEVENOAKS, TN13 3EF.
WALTERS, Mrs. Sally Jane, BA ACA *2007;* 2 Mill Fleam, Hilton, DERBY, DE65 5HE.
WALTERS, Mrs. Sarah Anne, ACA *2009;* 16 Princes Road, ROMFORD, RM1 2SR.
WALTERS, Mr. Scott, BA FCA *1996;* 19 Roseworth Avenue, Gosforth, NEWCASTLE UPON TYNE, NE3 1NB.
•WALTERS, Mr. Simon Howard, FCA *1987;* DFM Limited, 100 Fenchurch Street, LONDON, EC3M 5JD. See also F D Solutions
WALTERS, Mr. Steven Benjamin John, BA ACA *1996;* 26 Carter Walk, Penn, HIGH WYCOMBE, HP10 8ER.
WALTERS, Mr. Trevor, FCA *1973;* Finance Yorkshire Limited, 2nd Floor 1 Capitol Court Dodworth, BARNSLEY, SOUTH YORKSHIRE, S75 3TZ.
WALTERS, Mr. Trevor Haydn, BSc FCA *1978;* Silverue, Wych Hill Way, WOKING, GU22 0AE.
WALTERS, Miss. Victoria Helen, BCom ACA *2009;* Luscombe Grange, Lawnswood Drive, STOURBRIDGE, WEST MIDLANDS, DY7 5QW.
WALTERS, Mr. William Huw, FCA *1968;* 87 The Drive, RICKMANSWORTH, WD3 4DY.
WALTERS, Mrs. Xenia, BSocSc ACA *1995;* Abbey Business Centres Abbey House, Wellington Way, WEYBRIDGE, KT13 0TT.
WALTERS-GOATER, Mr. Walter Warwick, BA FCA *1976;* 128 via napoli, NAPLES, FL 34105, UNITED STATES.
WALTHAM, Mr. Philip Anthony, FCA *1955;* 108 Hook Road, GOOLE, NORTH HUMBERSIDE, DN14 5JY. (Life Member)
WALTHER, Mr. David James, FCA *1963;* M04, 1 Beckett Rd, WORCESTER, WR3 7NJ.
WALTHER, Mr. Simon Robert, BSc ACA *1993;* 1 Skylark Rise, WHITCHURCH, HAMPSHIRE, RG28 7SY.
•WALTHO, Mr. Paul Kenneth Stanley, FCA *1975;* (Tax Fac), Kirk Hughes Medlock, Willson House, 25-31 Derby Road, NOTTINGHAM, NG1 5AW.
WALTHOE, Dr. Jonathan Michael, BSc ACA *2007;* 30 Jennings Road, LONDON, SE22 9JU.
•WALTON, Mr. Adrian, BA FCA ATII *1991;* Smith & Williamson Ltd, 25 Moorgate, LONDON, EC2R 6AY.
•WALTON, Mr. Alan Victor, FCA *1985;* 2 Oakfields Avenue, KNEBWORTH, SG3 6NP.
WALTON, Mr. Alfred Richard, BCom FCA *1953;* The Aire & Ouse Farme Ltd, Quosquo Hall Estate, Camblesforth, SELBY, NORTH YORKSHIRE, YO8 8JB. (Life Member)
•WALTON, Mr. Andrew, BA ACA *1994;* Ernst & Young LLP, 1 More London Place, LONDON, SE1 2AF. See also Ernst & Young Europe LLP
WALTON, Mr. Andrew James, BSc ACA *2007;* 465 Street Lane, LEEDS, LS17 6RA.
•WALTON, Mr. Andrew John, BSc ACA *1995;* Oxford Accountant Ltd, March Cottage, The Green, Great Milton, OXFORD, OX44 7NS. See also Walton Andy
•WALTON, Mrs. Ann Carol, FCA *1983;* (Tax Fac), Ushers Limited, 76 Manchester Road, Denton, MANCHESTER, M34 3PS.
WALTON, Mrs. Anna Louise, BA ACA *2001;* 3 Pyalla Street, NORTHBRIDGE, NSW 2063, AUSTRALIA.
WALTON, Miss. Anna-Marie, BSc(Hons) ACA *2001;* (Tax Fac), 9012 Ina Court, COLUMBIA, MD 21045, UNITED STATES.
WALTON, Mr. Anthony Frederic, ACA *1981;* C/O 11 Hedon Road, HULL, HU9 1LH.
WALTON, Mr. Benjamin Luke, BEng ACA *2005;* 23 Beckets View, NORTHAMPTON, NN1 5NQ.
WALTON, Mr. Brian Stenson, FCA *1956;* 14 The Crescent, Davenport, STOCKPORT, SK3 8SN. (Life Member)
•WALTON, Mr. Christopher George, FCA *1966;* C.G. Walton, The Tynings, Ham Lane, Kingston Seymour, CLEVEDON, AVON BS21 6XE.
WALTON, Mr. Christopher Jerome, FCA *1971;* 28/5 Moo 9, Tambon Pong, BANG LAMUNG 20150, THAILAND. (Life Member)
WALTON, Miss. Claire Elizabeth, BSc ACA *2005;* Flat D, 1 Fieldway Crescent, LONDON, N5 1PU.
WALTON, Mr. Colin Ralph, FCA *1966;* 18 Rectory Road, Churchtown, SOUTHPORT, MERSEYSIDE, PR9 7PU. (Life Member)
WALTON, Mr. David Andrew, BSc ACA *1991;* Sand Hills London Road, Hartley Wintney, HOOK, RG27 8HY.
•WALTON, Mr. David Anthony, FCA *1970;* Walton & Co, The Chimes Bannister Green, Felsted, DUNMOW, ESSEX, CM6 3NL.
WALTON, Mr. David John, BSc ACA *1990;* 26 Pine Tree Avenue, PONTEFRACT, WEST YORKSHIRE, WF8 4LS.
WALTON, Mr. David Stewart, MA FCA *1977;* Shortacre, Park Road, WINCHESTER, SO23 7BE.
WALTON, Mrs. Dawn Catherine, ACA *2007;* (Tax Fac), 17 Abingdon Court, NEWCASTLE UPON TYNE, NE3 2YQ.
WALTON, Mr. Derrick, FCA *1956;* 19 Lancaster Drive, Vicar's Cross, CHESTER, CH3 5JW. (Life Member)
WALTON, Mr. Deryck Percival, FCA *1934;* Fairways, Foxton, ALNWICK, NE66 3BD. (Life Member)
WALTON, Mr. Donald Robert, BA ACA *1983;* Flat C, 58 London Road, BRENTWOOD, ESSEX, CM14 4NJ.

WALTON, Miss. Felicity, BSc(Hons) ACA *2011;* Flat 11, Binding House, Binding Close, Carrington Point, NOTTINGHAM, NG5 1RG.
WALTON, Miss. Helen Elizabeth, MA(Cantab) ACA *2010;* 10 Shadows Lane, Mossley, ASHTON-UNDER-LYNE, OL5 9BS.
WALTON, Mr. Iain Scot, BSc ACA *1987;* 34 The Village, Hawthorn Village, SEAHAM, SR7 8SG.
•WALTON, Mr. Ian, BA FCA *1986;* D.& I. Walton, 17 Lancaster Drive, Vicars Cross, CHESTER, CH3 5JW.
•①WALTON, Mr. Ian William, FCA ACA *1986;* Albert Goodman CBH Limited, The Lupins Business Centre, 1-3 Greenhill, WEYMOUTH, DORSET, DT4 7SP. See also Coyne Butterworth Hardwicke Limited
WALTON, Mr. James Martin, BSc ACA *2005;* 1 Defford Close, WOKINGHAM, BERKSHIRE, RG41 1HJ.
WALTON, Miss. Janet, BSc ACA *1990;* J P Morgan Chase, 125 London Wall, LONDON, EC2Y 5AJ.
•WALTON, Mr. Jeffrey Andrew, BSc FCA *1972;* (Tax Fac), Compass Accountants Ltd, Venture House, The Tanneries, East Street, Titchfield, FAREHAM HAMPSHIRE PO14 4AR.
WALTON, Miss. Jenna, ACA *2009;* 55 Birches Park Road, Codsall, WOLVERHAMPTON, WV8 2DT.
WALTON, Mr. Jeremy Mark, BSc ACA PGCE *1994;* Clematis Cottage Blind Lane, Barton St. David, SOMERTON, SOMERSET, TA11 6BW.
WALTON, Miss. Joanna Frances, ACA *2008;* PwC, Plumtree Court, LONDON, EC4A 4HT.
WALTON, Mr. John Allan, BA FCA *1978;* 22 Bolton Gardens, TEDDINGTON, MIDDLESEX, TW11 9AY.
WALTON, Mr. John Anthony, FCA *1974;* Frank Brown & Walford, 314 Linthorpe Road, MIDDLESBROUGH, CLEVELAND, TS1 3QX.
WALTON, Mr. John David Maxwell, FCA *1962;* Sunnymead, 1 Goodwood Avenue, Felpham, BOGNOR REGIS, PO22 8EE. (Life Member)
WALTON, Mr. John Edward, BSc ACA *1997;* 2 Niplands Cottages, Kiln Lane, Wooburn Green, HIGH WYCOMBE, HP10 0JQ.
WALTON, Mr. Jonathan Christian, BSc ACA *2002;* 67 Manchuria Road, LONDON, SW11 6AF.
•WALTON, Mr. Jonathan Mark, ACA ACCA *2007;* Whitley Stimpson LLP, Penrose House, 67 Hightown Road, BANBURY, OXFORDSHIRE, OX16 9BE.
WALTON, Mrs. Judith Shipley, BA ACA *1982;* 21 Chevin Avenue, Homestead Estate Menston, ILKLEY, WEST YORKSHIRE, LS29 6PE.
WALTON, Mrs. Katharine Anne, BA FCA *1986;* Cheltenham Borough Homes Cheltenham House, Clarence Street, CHELTENHAM, GL50 3JR.
WALTON, Mrs. Kelly, ACA *2002;* 5 Patmore Fields, Ugley, BISHOP'S STORTFORD, HERTFORDSHIRE, CM22 6JW.
WALTON, Miss. Laragh Antonia Blanche, BA ACA *2006;* Deloitte & Touche Stonecutter Court, 1 Stonecutter Street, LONDON, EC4A 4TR.
WALTON, Mr. Martin Andrew, BSc ACA *1989;* Rainbow Tree House, 3 Denbigh Close, CHISLEHURST, BR7 5EB.
WALTON, Mr. Martin Robert, BSc ACA *1990;* T Clarke PLC, 116-118 Walworth Road, LONDON, SE17 1JY.
WALTON, Mr. Michael Edward D'arcy, FCA *1966;* 39 Frewin Road, LONDON, SW18 3LR.
WALTON, Mr. Michael John, BSocSc ACA *1987;* 11 Desborough Drive, Tewin, WELWYN, HERTFORDSHIRE, AL6 0HQ.
•WALTON, Neil, Esq MBE FCA *1966;* (Tax Fac), Neil Walton Ltd, Bank Foot Farm, Ingleby Greenhow, Great Ayton, MIDDLESBROUGH, CLEVELAND TS9 6LP.
WALTON, Mr. Neil, ACA *1996;* Shakespeare Foundry Ltd, Shakespeare House, Salop Street, BOLTON, BL2 1DZ.
WALTON, Mr. Nicholas David, BSc ACA *1986;* 14 Shire Avenue, FLEET, GU51 2TB.
WALTON, Mr. Peter, BA ACA *1994;* 1640 Maple Avenue 1301, EVANSTON, IL 60201, UNITED STATES.
•WALTON, Mr. Peter, FCA *1975;* Peter Walton, 23 Castleknowe Gardens, Kirkton Park, CARLUKE, ML8 5UX.
WALTON, Mr. Peter Nicholas Jeremy, FCA *1975;* PAL Group Plc, Darlaston Road, WEDNESBURY, WEST MIDLANDS, WS10 7TN.
WALTON, Mr. Peter William, BCom FCA *1975;* Carnanton, Camden Park, TUNBRIDGE WELLS, TN2 5AE.
WALTON, Mr. Richard, BA ACA *2003;* 51 Northover Road, BRISTOL, BS9 3LN.
WALTON, Mr. Richard Alan, BSc ACA *1994;* 294 Lordship Lane, LONDON, SE22 8LY.
WALTON, Mr. Robert, FCA *1947;* Apartado de Correos 85, 29600 MARBELLA, SPAIN. (Life Member)
WALTON, Mr. Robert Eric, MA FCA *1953;* 20 Wetherdown, PETERSFIELD, GU31 4PN. (Life Member)
•WALTON, Mr. Roger, FCA *1970;* Walton Dodge Forensic Limited, Dencora Court, 2 Meridian Way, NORWICH, NR7 0TA.
WALTON, Mrs. Rosalind Ann, BA ACA *1996;* 101 Burbage Road, LONDON, SE24 9HD.
WALTON, Mr. Roy Maxwell, BA FCA MCIArb *1987;* Long Heath, Black Horse Road, WOKING, GU22 0QT.
WALTON, Miss. Sarah Jane, BA ACA *1998;* 144 West 18th Street PH-W, NEW YORK, NY 1011-5465, UNITED STATES.
•WALTON, Mrs. Sarah Jane, BA ACA *2003;* Walton Accounting Services, 11 Pargate Close, RIPLEY, DERBYSHIRE, DE5 8JU.
WALTON, Mrs. Sarah Kate, MSc BSc ACA *2007;* 4 Glevum Close, ST. ALBANS, HERTFORDSHIRE, AL3 4JN.
WALTON, Mrs. Sharyn Louise, ACA *2004;* 4 Lovage Gardens, West Totton, SOUTHAMPTON, SO40 8FR.
•WALTON, Mr. Simon Jeffrey, ACA *2002;* Riley & Co Limited, 52 St.Johns Lane, HALIFAX, HX1 2BW.
WALTON, Mr. Simon Robert MacFarlane, BSc FCA *1989;* 700 Anderson Hill Road (2/2), PURCHASE, NY 10577, UNITED STATES.
WALTON, Mr. Stephen James, BA FCA *1988;* 241 Marlow Bottom, MARLOW, BUCKINGHAMSHIRE, SL7 3PZ.
•WALTON, Mr. Stephen Mark, BA ACA *1981;* PricewaterhouseCoopers LLP, 1 Embankment Place, LONDON, WC2N 6RH. See also PricewaterhouseCoopers
WALTON, Mr. Stewart William, BA FCA *1986;* 76 Painswick Road, CHELTENHAM, GLOUCESTERSHIRE, GL50 2EU.
WALTON, Mr. Stuart Murray, BA ACA *1991;* Cleeve Cottage, 3 Main Road, Milford, STAFFORD, ST17 0UL.
WALTON, Mr. Thomas Joseph, BSc ACA *2007;* 72a Warwick Way, LONDON, SW1V 1RZ.
WALTON, Mr. Tom, FCA *1971;* 180 Coastal Road, Bolton-Le-Sands, CARNFORTH, LA5 8JW. (Life Member)
WALTON, Mr. Trevor David, BA ACA *1989;* 1 Winsford Street, Karrinyup, PERTH, WA 6018, AUSTRALIA.
WALTON, Miss. Vanessa, BSc ACA *2011;* Flat 22 Hunsaker, Alfred Street, READING, RG1 7AU.
WALTON, Miss. Vanessa Margaret, BA ACA *1992;* PO Box 32045 SMB, GEORGETOWN, KY 1-2008, CAYMAN ISLANDS.
WALTON, Mrs. Victoria Emmi Carola Ellen, BA ACA *2003;* 67 Manchuria Road, LONDON, SW11 6AF.
WALTON, Mrs. Wendy Susan, ACA *2007;* 3 Greyside Cottages, Newbrough, HEXHAM, NORTHUMBERLAND, NE47 5AY.
WALTON-GREEN, Mr. Andrew John Scott, BA ACA *1989;* The Car Finance Company, 85 Kingston Crescent, PORTSMOUTH, PO2 8AA.
WALWYN, Mrs. Christine Helen, BSc ACA *1992;* Jambart Villa, Rue De Jambart, St. Clement, JERSEY, JE2 6LA.
WALWYN-JAMES, Mr. Benjamin, MA(Hons) ACA *2009;* Oakland House, Moorfield, NEWCASTLE UPON TYNE, NE2 3NL.
WALZER, Mr. Adam James, BA(Hons) ACA *2003;* 23 Kenneth Crescent, Willesden Green, LONDON, NW2 4PP.
WALZER, Miss. Bernice Frances, BSc FCA *1974;* (Tax Fac), 5 Salisbury Court, Salisbury Avenue, LONDON, N3 3AH.
WAN, Miss. Adeline Yoke Gee, FCA *1973;* 43a Elizabeth Street, BENTLEIGH, VIC 3165, AUSTRALIA.
•WAN, Mrs. Athena Chi Kwan, BA FCA CertPFS *1993;* Athena & Company Accountancy Limited, Unit 1 Marble House, 20 Grosvenor Terrace, LONDON, SE5 0DD. See also Athena & Co
WAN, Miss. Catherine, ACA *2011;* Jimmys Fish Bar, 160 New Road, PORTSMOUTH, PO2 7RJ.
WAN, Mr. Chalk-Yin, ACA *2008;* Flat H 13 Floor Block 13, Richland Gardens, KOWLOON BAY, KOWLOON, HONG KONG SAR.
WAN, Mr. Chung Yin, ACA *2008;* Flat A 29/F, Tower 1, Residence Bel-Air, Island South, 28 Bel-Air Avenue, POK FU LAM HONG KONG SAR.
WAN, Mr. Damien Gary, BA ACA *1985;* 195 Route de la Croix, 06260 PUGET THENIERS, FRANCE.
WAN, Mr. Dennis Jit-Yin, BEng ACA *1999;* Credit Suisse, 11 Madison Avenue 11/F, NEW YORK, NY 10280, UNITED STATES.
WAN, Mr. Donny, ACA *2008;* 31 Station Street, RYDE, ISLE OF WIGHT, PO33 2QH.
WAN, Mr. Fook Keung, ACA *2008;* 3C Tower 2, Parc Oasis, YAU YAT TSUEN, KOWLOON, HONG KONG SAR.
WAN, Mr. Hing Pui, ACA *2004;* H. P. Wan & Company, 711A Ocean Centre, Canton Road, TSIM SHA TSIU, KOWLOON, HONG KONG SAR.
WAN, Ms. How Yee Jennifer, ACA *2008;* 8/F Prince's Building, Ice House Street, CENTRAL, HONG KONG ISLAND, HONG KONG SAR.
WAN, Mr. Joseph Sai Cheong, FCA *1978;* Harvey Nichols Group Ltd, 3rd Floor, 67 Brompton Road, LONDON, SW3 1DB.
WAN, Mr. Kenneth, ACA *2010;* 1 Excalibur Close, NORTHAMPTON, NN5 4BJ.
WAN, Mr. Kenneth Kam-Fai, BSc FCA *1983;* unit 1 128 Labouchere Road South Perth, PERTH, WA 6151, AUSTRALIA.
WAN, Mr. Kin Man Tony, ACA *2010;* Room 2308, 23/F Wing Pak House, LAM TIN, KOWLOON, HONG KONG SAR.
WAN, Mr. King Yee, MEng ACA *1997;* 35 Emanuel Road, Langdon Hills, BASILDON, ESSEX, SS16 6EX.
WAN, Mr. Kwok Wai, ACA *2004;* K. W. Wan & Company, Room 605, 6 Floor Kai Wong Commercial Building, 222-226 Queen's Road Central, CENTRAL, HONG KONG ISLAND HONG KONG SAR.
WAN, Ms. Lily Wai Yee, BCom ACA *1997;* 4 Cassandra Grove, WARWICK, CV34 6XD.
WAN, Mr. Mark Tat Leung, BEng ACA *1991;* MF Global, Level 23, 100 Queens Road, CENTRAL, HONG KONG ISLAND, HONG KONG SAR.
WAN, Mr. Oscar Hoyin, BEng ACA *1995;* Flat 66 9/F Tower 3 Middleton Towers 140 Pokfulam Road, POK FU LAM, HONG KONG ISLAND, HONG KONG SAR.
•WAN, Mr. Paul Tong Chee, FCA *1983;* Paul Wan & Co, 10 Anson Road, No. 35-08International Plaza, SINGAPORE 079903, SINGAPORE.
WAN, Ms. Pui Yee Polly, ACA *2008;* with Deloitte Touche Tohmatsu, 35/F One Pacific Place, 88 Queensway, CENTRAL, HONG KONG ISLAND, HONG KONG SAR.
WAN, Mr. Raymond, ACA *2010;* 63 Beech Road, SALE, CHESHIRE, M33 2FA.
WAN, Miss. Sandy Yuen San, BA ACA *1993;* 19 Winsfield Gardens, 38 Shan Kwong Road, HAPPY VALLEY, HONG KONG ISLAND, HONG KONG SAR.
WAN, Mr. Tat Ming, ACA *2007;* Flat D 45/F Block 10, Villa Esplanada, 8 Nga Ying Chau Street, TSING YI, NEW TERRITORIES, HONG KONG SAR.
WAN, Mr. Tin Yau Alvin, ACA *2005;* Flat J 16/F Block 7, Charming Garden, MONG KOK, KOWLOON, HONG KONG SAR.
WAN, Miss. Vivien Yuet Sim, FCA *1985;* 1/505 Glenferrie Road, Hawtorn, MELBOURNE, VIC 3122, AUSTRALIA.
WAN, Mr. Wai-Yip, BSc ACA *2010;* 174 Stockwell Park Road, LONDON, SW9 0TN.
•WAN, Mr. William, ACA FCCA *2009;* Elliotts Shah, 2nd Floor, York House, 23 Kingsway, LONDON, WC2B 6UJ.
WAN, Mr. Yan Yoong, BA FCA *1992;* 59 Jalan Pertiwi, Taman Maluri, Cheras, 55100 KUALA LUMPUR, FEDERAL TERRITORY, MALAYSIA.
WAN, Mr. Yim Keung Daniel, ACA *2007;* 16/F Bank of East Asia Building, 10 Des Voeux Road, CENTRAL, HONG KONG ISLAND, HONG KONG SAR.
WAN, Miss. Yuen Ling, BA ACA *1988;* Flat 16D, Kawing Lau Ka Wai Chuen, HUNG HOM, KOWLOON, HONG KONG SAR.
WAN ABDUL RAHMAN, Mr. Wan Anwar, BSc ACA *2001;* No 4 Jalan SS 3/88, Kelana Jaya, 47300 PETALING JAYA, SELANGOR, MALAYSIA.
WAN ABDUL RAHMAN, Ms. Wan Daneena Liza, BSc ACA *1999;* 39 Jalan P14A 1/1, Presint 14, 62050 PUTRAJAYA, WILAYAH PERSEKUTUAN, MALAYSIA.
WAN ABDUL RAHMAN, Miss. Wan Munirah, ACA *2011;* N0 4, J/n SS3/88, 47300 PETALING JAYA, SELANGOR, MALAYSIA.
WAN BOK NALE, Miss. Jill, ACA *2008;* Level 8 Tower 1 NeXTeracom Cyber City, EBENE, MAURITIUS.
WAN HOK CHEE, Miss. Valerie, BSc ACA *2005;* 30 Clarence Road, LONDON, SW19 8QE.
WAN-KEE-CHEUNG, Mr. Daniel, BSc FCA *1973;* 14 Greystone Gardens, HARROW, HA3 0EG. (Life Member)
WAN MIN KEE, Mr. Anthony, BA ACA *2010;* 61 Acfold Road, Handsworth Wood, BIRMINGHAM, B20 1HG.
WAN MIN KEE, Mrs. Ching Pien, FCA *1976;* 9271 Dolphin Avenue, RICHMOND V6Y 1C7, BC, CANADA.
WAN MIN KEE, Mr. Voon Yue Choon, ACA *1979;* 21 Volcy de la Faye St, BEAU BASSIN, MAURITIUS.
WAN MIN KEE, Mr. Yeve Qhume, FCA *1974;* 9271 Dolphin Avenue, RICHMOND V6Y 1C7, BC, CANADA.
WAN SALLEH, Mr. Mohamad, BSc(Econ) FCA *1974;* 28Jalan Kubah U8/52, Bukit Jelutong, 40150 SHAH ALAM, MALAYSIA.
WAND, Mr. Alan Philip, FCA *1967;* 38 Fortescue Chase, Thorpe Bay, SOUTHEND-ON-SEA, SS1 3SS.
WAND, Mr. Philip, FCA *1948;* 10 Stafford Terrace, LONDON, W8 7BH. (Life Member)
WANDERER, Mr. Denis Harold, FCA *1967;* (Tax Fac), 14 Danescroft Gardens, LONDON, NW4 2ND. (Life Member)
WANE, Mr. Anthony Patrick, FCA *1971;* 16 Dane Court, Pyrford, WOKING, GU22 8SX.
WANE, Mr. Christopher John, BA FCA *1999;* 109 Topstreet Way, HARPENDEN, HERTFORDSHIRE, AL5 5TY.
WANE, Mrs. Esther Mary, LLB ACA *1999;* 109 Topstreet Way, HARPENDEN, HERTFORDSHIRE, AL5 5TY.
WANG, Miss. Ai Qun, BA ACA *2011;* Flat 2, 28 St. Agnes Road, Moseley, BIRMINGHAM, B13 9PW.
WANG, Mr. Bin, ACA *2011;* 26 Asland Road, LONDON, E15 3LL.
WANG, Mr. Charles Chong Guang, BA ACA *1992;* Flat 28A Block One, Elegant Terrace, 36 Conduit Road, MID LEVELS, HONG KONG ISLAND, HONG KONG SAR.
WANG, Mrs. Esther Mei Mei, FCA *1982;* 48 Ming Teck Park, SINGAPORE 277415, SINGAPORE.
WANG, Mrs. Fan, ACA *2011;* Flat 24, Squires Court, Bedminster Parade, BRISTOL, BS3 4BX.
WANG, Miss. Honghua, MSc BA ACA *2010;* 9 Pelham Road, BECKENHAM, KENT, BR3 4SQ.
WANG, Miss. Jia, MSc ACA *2010;* with KPMG LLP, 15 Canada Square, LONDON, E14 5GL.
WANG, Miss. Jie, ACA *2008;* Room 402 Building 1, No 675 of Shui-Cheng Road, ChangNing Region, SHANGHAI 200336, CHINA.
WANG, Mr. Jun, ACA *2008;* 4a Jubilee Drive, RUISLIP, HA4 0PB.
WANG, Dr. Jun, FCA(Honorary) Ministry of Finance PRC, Sanlihe, Xicheng District, BEIJING 100820, CHINA.
WANG, Miss. Liang, MSc BA(Hons) ACA *2011;* Flat 9 Myles Court, 86 Neptune Street, LONDON, SE16 7JP.
WANG, Miss. Lin, MSc BSc ACA *2009;* No.6-6 Yibao Garden, 12 Fengcheng Er Road, XI'AN 710016, SHANXI PROVINCE, CHINA.
WANG, Miss. Lin, ACA *2011;* Room 906 Building 26 Xizhimen South Street Xicheng District, BEIJING 100035, CHINA.
WANG, Miss. Lin, ACA *2011;* Flat 281, Ability Place, 37 Millharbour, LONDON, E14 9DL.
WANG, Ms. Mei, ACA *2005;* Dural Irrigation Pty Ltd, 270 New Line Road, DURAL, NSW 2158, AUSTRALIA.
WANG, Miss. Mei Ling, BA(Hons) ACA *2004;* 1 Jalan 21/4, Sea Park, 46300 PETALING JAYA, SELANGOR, MALAYSIA.
WANG, Miss. Mimi, ACA *2010;* Flat 4, 3 Rainbow Quay, LONDON, SE16 7UF.
WANG, Mr. Ping Hau Felix, BA ACA *1993;* 18A Park Garden, 6 Tai Hang Drive, TAI HANG, HONG KONG ISLAND, HONG KONG SAR.
WANG, Ms. Samantha Shiow Shing, MEng ACA *2001;* #09-01, 1 Moulmein Rise, SINGAPORE 308143, SINGAPORE.
WANG, Miss. Shirley Shu Mei, BSc FCA *1990;* 17F Block 2 Le Sommet, 28 Fortress Hill Road, NORTH POINT, HONG KONG ISLAND, HONG KONG SAR.
WANG, Miss. Si, ACA *2011;* 30/F Bund Center, 222 Yan An Road East, SHANGHAI 200002, CHINA.
WANG, Miss. Snooky Audrey Evelyn, BSc(Hons) ACA *2001;* 151a Kennington Park Road, LONDON, SE11 4JJ.
WANG, Miss. Tianwei, BSc ACA *2005;* 21/F Citibank Tower, Garden Road, CENTRAL, HONG KONG ISLAND, HONG KONG SAR.
WANG, Miss. Tingting, ACA *2009;* Flat 13 Kilby Court, Child Lane, LONDON, SE10 0PZ.
WANG, Miss. Wei, ACA *2009;* Flat 8B Block 1, Florient Rise, 38 Cherry Street, TAI KOK TSUI, KOWLOON, HONG KONG SAR.
WANG, Miss. Xiaoting, ACA *2011;* Room 1803 No 27 Lane 88, Tianshan Road, SHANGHAI 200336, CHINA.
WANG, Miss. Xinyue, ACA *2011;* 3 Nelson Road, Caversham, READING, RG4 5AT.
WANG, Miss. Yaxin, ACA *2010;* 76 avenue Kléber, 75784 PARIS, FRANCE.
WANG, Mr. Yee Wai Edward, ACA *2008;* Flat 22G, Nam Fung Court, 1 Fook Yum Road, NORTH POINT, HONG KONG SAR.
WANG, Miss. Yi-Dan, BSc ACA *2000;* 28 Royal Road, SIDCUP, DA14 4RQ.
WANG, Miss. Yinghua, BA ACA *2009;* British Petroleum Co Plc, 20 Canada Square, LONDON, E14 5NJ.

WANG, Miss. Yong-Huei, ACA *2009;* Flat 4, 139 West End Lane, LONDON, NW6 2PH.
WANG, Miss. Yue, ACA *2011;* Room 301, Building 11 Block 6, Lane 1467, Caobao Road, SHANGHAI 201101, CHINA.
WANIA, Mr. Cyrus, BSc ACA *2004;* Flat 6 Lanta House, 183 Holders Hill Road, LONDON, NW7 1ND.
WANIGASEKERA, Mr. Stanley Vincent, BCom FCA *1956;* 5 Cambridge Terrace, 7 COLOMBO, SRI LANKA. (Life Member)
WANKLING, Mrs. Jane Rosamund, BA ACA *1994;* Touche Bouais, 35 Highlands Close, Maison St Louis, St. Saviour, JERSEY, JE2 7LX.
WANLESS, Mrs. Anita, ACA DChA *1998;* with Mazars LLP, The Pinnacle, 160 Midsummer Boulevard, MILTON KEYNES, MK9 1FF.
WANLESS, Mrs. Cindy Christine, BSc ACA *2000;* Jasmine, 4 Jardin Des Sablons, Grouville, JERSEY, JE3 9HS.
WANLESS, Mr. James Bowman, BSc FCA *1974;* Kingdom Bank Ltd Mere Way, Ruddington Fields Business Park Ruddington, NOTTINGHAM, NG11 6JS.
WANLESS, Mr. Kenneth Edward, BSc ACA *1993;* Quartzelec Ltd, Harrier Parkway, LUTTERWORTH, LEICESTERSHIRE, LE17 4XT.
WANLESS, Mr. Mark, BSc ACA *1999;* Jasmine, 4 Jardin Des Sablons, Grouville, JERSEY, JE3 9HS.
WANLESS, Mr. Nicholas Andrew, BA ACA *1997;* 11 Marriott Road, BARNET, HERTFORDSHIRE, EN5 4NJ.
WANLEY, Mr. William Geoffrey, FCA *1971;* 60 Stoneleigh Avenue, COVENTRY, CV5 6BZ.
•**WANSBURY, Mr. Michael Victor, FCA** *1978;* 16 Hayes Chase, WEST WICKHAM, BR4 0HZ.
WANSBURY, Mr. Nicholas, BSc ACA *2009;* K P M G Llp, 15 Canada Square, LONDON, E14 5GL.
WANSEL, Mr. Florian Fred, BA ACA *2009;* (Tax Fac), Flat 56 Victoria Wharf, 46 Narrow Street, LONDON, E14 8DD.
WANSLEBEN, Mr. Kaspar, ACA *2008;* LMDF c/o ADA, 2 rue Sainte Zithe, 2763 LUXEMBOURG, LUXEMBOURG.
WANSTALL, Mrs. Rebecca Rhee, ACA *2008;* (Tax Fac), with Reeves, 37 St. Margarets Street, CANTERBURY, KENT, CT1 2TU.
WANTLING, Mr. Andrew Syd, BSc ACA *1992;* 34 Barrington Avenue, The Reddings, CHELTENHAM, GL51 6TY.
WAPLE, Mrs. Alison Helen, BSc ACA *1984;* c/o Exxon (Al Khalij) Inc, P.O. Box 30686, ABU DHABI, UNITED ARAB EMIRATES.
WAPLE, Mr. Gary, MBA FCA *1983;* Acanchi Ltd, 32-34 Great Marlborough Street, LONDON, W1F 7JB.
WAPLE, Mr. Richard Leslie, BSc ACA *1980;* 5 Annisgarth Close, WINDERMERE, LA23 2HP.
•**WAPPAT, Mr. Arthur, FCA** *1964;* Arthur Wappat, The Old Granary, Dilston Steadings, CORBRIDGE, NE45 5RF.
WAQAS, Mr. Muhammad, ACA *2008;* LSG Sky Chefs, Osprey House, 1 Falcon Way, Central Way, FELTHAM, MIDDLESEX TW14 0UQ.
WARAICH, Mr. Muddassir Bashir, MA FCA *1980;* Alpha Associates, 76 Watling Street, LONDON, EC4M 9BJ.
WARAICH, Mr. Sajid Mustasam, BSc ACA *2007;* 1 Harrisons Green, BIRMINGHAM, B15 3LH.
•**WARAN, Mr. Rajaram, FCA** *1968;* Ramar Accounting Services Limited, 111 Aldwick Road, BOGNOR REGIS, WEST SUSSEX, PO21 2NY.
WARANS, Mr. Edward John, FCA *1974;* 3 Hitherwood Close, REIGATE, RH2 0JJ.
WARAT-HUGHES, Mrs. Jennifer, ACA *2005;* 4a/73 Yarranabbe Road, DARLING POINT, NSW 2027, AUSTRALIA.
WARBEY, Mrs. Alison, BA ACA CTA *2006;* 102a Redland Road, BRISTOL, BS6 6QU.
WARBEY, Mr. Edward John, FCA *1968;* 10 Pilgrim Mews, REIGATE, SURREY, RH2 8AH. (Life Member)
WARBEY, Mr. Victor George, FCA *1963;* P O Box 191, MOOROOLBARK, VIC 3138, AUSTRALIA. (Life Member)
•**WARBOYS, Mrs. Stephanie Jane, BA ACA DChA** *1989;* 50 Glendon Way, Dorridge, SOLIHULL, B93 8SY.
WARBRICK, Mr. Michael Brian, ACA *2008;* Ernst & Young, 100 Barbirolli Square, MANCHESTER, M2 3EY.
WARBURTON, Mr. Adrian Graham, ACA *1985;* World Wildlife Fund Weyside Park, Catteshall Lane, GODALMING, GU7 1XR.
WARBURTON, Mrs. Anita Susan, BSc FCA *1973;* (Tax Fac), 38 Norwood, Thornhill, CARDIFF, CF14 9DE.
•**WARBURTON, Mrs. Carol Susan, BSc(Econ) FCA** *1995;* KTS Owens Thomas Limited, The Counting House, Dunleavy Drive, CARDIFF, CF11 0SN.
WARBURTON, Mr. Darren Paul, MA ACA *1997;* Home Group Ltd, 2 Gosforth Park Way Salters Lane, NEWCASTLE UPON TYNE, NE12 8ET.
WARBURTON, Mrs. Elaine Harrington, BSc ACA *1992;* 9 Hartley Way, PURLEY, SURREY, CR8 4EJ.
WARBURTON, Mr. Francis, FCA *1968;* Flat 7 The Granges 44 Grange Avenue Levenshulme, MANCHESTER, M19 2DW. (Life Member)
WARBURTON, Mr. Harold, BA FCA *1961;* 7 Willow Grove, Goosnargh, PRESTON, PR3 2DE. (Life Member)
WARBURTON, Mr. Ian Geoffrey, FCA *1975;* 92 Ringinglow Road, SHEFFIELD, S11 7PQ.
•**WARBURTON, Mrs. Ingrid Louise, BA ACA** *2003;* 40 Buxton Road West, Disley, STOCKPORT, CHESHIRE, SK12 2LY.
WARBURTON, Mr. James Christopher, BSc(Hons) ACA *2003;* Ground Floor Flat, 90 Elgin Avenue, LONDON, W9 2HD.
WARBURTON, Mrs. Joanna Ruth, BA ACA *2007;* 50 Parkstone Avenue, POOLE, DORSET, BH14 9LS.
WARBURTON, Mr. John Keith, FCA *1964;* 60 Presland Way, Irthlingborough, WELLINGBOROUGH, NORTHAMPTONSHIRE, NN9 5UL.
WARBURTON, Mr. Keith, BSc ACA *1995;* PO Box 602, Collins Street West, MELBOURNE, VIC 8007, AUSTRALIA.
•**WARBURTON, Mr. Lee Marcus, BA FCA** *1992;* Voisey & Co., 8 Winmarleigh Street, WARRINGTON, WA1 1JW.
WARBURTON, Mr. Mark Justin, BSc ACA *1992;* Via Ungaretti 4, Bussero, 20060 MILAN, ITALY.
WARBURTON, Mr. Michael Bruce, BSc FCA MBA *1978;* The Old Rectory, Taynton, GLOUCESTER, GL19 3AN.
WARBURTON, Mr. Michael Robert, BA ACA *1996;* 59 Redhouse Lane, Bredbury, STOCKPORT, SK6 1BX.
WARBURTON, Mr. Nicholas Arthur, BSc ACA *1997;* 75 Blinco Grove, CAMBRIDGE, CAMBRIDGESHIRE, CB1 7TX.
•**WARBURTON, Mr. Nigel, FCA** *1989;* NW Accounts Audit Limited, 40 Buxton Road West, Disley, STOCKPORT, CHESHIRE, SK12 2LY. See also NW Accounts Limited
WARBURTON, Mrs. Paula Louise, BA(Hons) ACA *2000;* P H Warr Plc Queens Keep, 1-4 Cumberland Place, SOUTHAMPTON, SO15 2NP.
•**WARBURTON, Mr. Peter, FCA** *1969;* Peter Warburton & Co, Gwalia, Llangynhafal, DENBIGH, CLWYD, LL16 4LN.
•**WARBURTON, Mr. Philip George, FCA** *1969;* (Tax Fac), Venthams Limited, Millhouse, 32-38 East Street, ROCHFORD, SS4 1DB. See also Brannans
WARBURTON, Mr. Ralph Eric, ACA ACCA *2010;* Ernst & Young, 680 George Street, SYDNEY, NSW 2000, AUSTRALIA.
•**WARBURTON, Mr. Robert William, BSc FCA** *1973;* Morlands Cottage, Crouch, SEVENOAKS, TN15 8QA.
•**WARBURTON, Mr. Russel Neale, FCA** *1975;* 29 Cromwell Place, CRANLEIGH, SURREY, GU6 7LF.
•**WARBURTON, Mrs. Sheila Rosemary, ACA** *1979;* S.R. Warburton, 34 Cherry Tree Avenue, Kirby Muxloe, LEICESTER, LE9 2HN.
WARBURTON, Mr. Simon Martin, ACA *1990;* 19 Copsem Lane, ESHER, KT10 9HE.
WARBY, Miss. Sara Jane, BSc ACA *1984;* Pinewood, 28A Mayfield Road, WEYBRIDGE, KT13 8XB.
WARCHOL, Mr. Andrew Wladyslaw, BA ACA *1986;* 2 Ancaster Gardens, NOTTINGHAM, NG8 1FR.
WARD, Mr. Adam Simon, MA ACA *2000;* 20 Shepherds Gate Drive, Weavering, MAIDSTONE, ME14 5UU.
WARD, Mr. Aidan, BA ACA *1992;* 14 Little Heath, LONDON, SE7 8HU.
WARD, Mr. Alan James, FCA *1968;* 21 Worrin Road, Shenfield, BRENTWOOD, CM15 8DE.
WARD, Mr. Alan James, FCA *1982;* 119 Wheatsheaf Road, Tividale, OLDBURY, B69 1SJ.
WARD, Mrs. Alison Nelson, BMus FCA *1975;* 203 Cumberland Rd, Plaistow, LONDON, E13 8LU.
WARD, Miss. Alison Suzanne, BSc ACA *1995;* Internal Audit FHG, Liverpool Victoria Friendly Society Ltd, County Gates, BOURNEMOUTH, BH1 2NF.
WARD, Mrs. Amanda, BSc ACA *1995;* 5 Tretawn Park, Mill Hill, LONDON, NW7 4PS.
WARD, Mr. Andrew, BA ACA *2009;* 44 High Street, Stanion, KETTERING, NORTHAMPTONSHIRE, NN14 1DF.
WARD, Mr. Andrew, BSc(Hons) ACA *2011;* Pricewaterhousecoopers, 7 More London Riverside, LONDON, SE1 2RT.
•**WARD, Mr. Andrew David, BSc(Hons) ACA** *2000;* with PricewaterhouseCoopers LLP, 1 East Parade, SHEFFIELD, S1 2ET.
WARD, Mr. Andrew Gerard, MA ACA *1990;* 32 Lindisfarne Close, Jesmond, NEWCASTLE UPON TYNE, NE2 2HT.
WARD, Mr. Andrew Graham, BSc FCA *1975;* 12 Windsor Close, Cottingham, HULL, HU16 5AY.
WARD, Mr. Andrew Jonathan, BA ACA *1991;* Christies, 8 King Street, LONDON, SW1Y 6QT.
WARD, Mr. Andrew Philip, ACA *1996;* Chess Dynamics Limited Unit 7, North Heath Lane Industrial Estate, HORSHAM, WEST SUSSEX, RH12 5QE.
WARD, Mr. Andrew Timothy, BA ACA *1994;* 8 Redhouse Close, Bentley Heath, SOLIHULL, B93 8AR.
WARD, Mrs. Anna, BSc ACA *2006;* with National Audit Office, 157-197 Buckingham Palace Road, Victoria, LONDON, SW1W 9SP.
WARD, Ms. Anna Katherine, BSc ACA *2002;* 43 Queens Crescent, ST. ALBANS, HERTFORDSHIRE, AL4 9QQ.
•**WARD, Mr. Anthony, BCom ACA** *1989;* Ernst & Young LLP, 1 Colmore Square, BIRMINGHAM, B4 6HQ. See also Ernst & Young Europe LLP
WARD, Mr. Anthony, FCA *1972;* 10 Pine Terrace, HOWICK 2014, AUCKLAND, NEW ZEALAND.
•**WARD, Mr. Anthony, MBA FCA** *1975;* Ward Randall Limited, The Parade, LISKEARD, CORNWALL, PL14 6AF. See also Tax Processing Limited
WARD, Mr. Anthony George, FCA *1950;* Field House, Bathley Lane, Little Carlton, NEWARK, NG23 6BY. (Life Member)
WARD, Mr. Anthony Martin, BA ACA *1994;* 5 Tretawn Park, Mill Hill, LONDON, NW7 4PS.
•**WARD, Mr. Anthony Maurice, BSc FCA** *1978;* (Tax Fac), Ward & Co., Wallington Cottage, Drift Road, FAREHAM, PO16 8SY.
WARD, Mr. Anthony Phillip, BA ACA *1992;* 3 Green Lane Close, HARPENDEN, HERTFORDSHIRE, AL5 1NF.
WARD, Mr. Barry Charles Bernard, BSc ACA *1995;* 129 Corbets Tey Road, UPMINSTER, RM14 2AX.
•①**WARD, Mr. Barry John, FCA** *1968;* Ward Sheldrake Consultancy, Lower Barrow Kiln, Acton Mill Lane, Suckley, WORCESTER, WR6 5EJ.
WARD, Mr. Brian, FCA *1961;* 9 Blue Gum Avenue, GYMEA, NSW 2227, AUSTRALIA. (Life Member)
WARD, Mr. Brian Richard, FCA *1970;* 54 Romulus Court, BRENTFORD, Middlesex, TW8 8QW.
WARD, Mr. Bryan Keith, BSc(Econ) FCA *1959;* 167 Wynchgate, Winchmore Hill, LONDON, N21 1QT. (Life Member)
WARD, Mr. Carl Victor, BA FCA MBA *1986;* 110a High Street, Clophill, BEDFORD, MK45 4BJ.
WARD, Mrs. Caroline Claude, BEd ACA *2005;* Financial Services Authority, 25 North Colonnade, LONDON, E14 5HS.
WARD, Mrs. Caryn Jane, BA ACA *1986;* PO BOX 4884, GOLD COAST, QLD 9726, AUSTRALIA.
WARD, Mrs. Catherine Alison, BA ACA *1999;* (Tax Fac), 20 Out Lane Croston, LEYLAND, PR26 9HJ.
WARD, Miss. Catherine Elaine, ACA *2008;* 79 Gleneagles Drive, Fulwood, PRESTON, PR2 7EU.
WARD, Mrs. Catherine Elizabeth, BSc ACA *2002;* 42 High View Road, Douglas, ISLE OF MAN, IM2 5BJ.
WARD, Mrs. Catherine Elizabeth, BSc ACA *1984;* Esso Petroleum Co Ltd Exxonmobil House, Ermyn Way, LEATHERHEAD, KT22 8UX.
WARD, Miss. Catherine Elizabeth, BA ACA *1995;* 11 Warwick Drive, Molescroft, BEVERLEY, HU17 9TB.
WARD, Mr. Charles John Nicholas, FCA *1964;* Flat 12, 77 Warwick Square, LONDON, SW1V 2AR.
WARD, Mr. Charles Patrick, BSc FCA *1978;* Glebe House, Tidmarsh, READING, RG8 8ES.
•**WARD, Mr. Christopher, BSc CF** *1974;* (Member of Council 2004 - 2008), with Deloitte Middle East, Currency House, Building 1 Level 5, DIFC, PO Box 282056, DUBAI UNITED ARAB EMIRATES.
•**WARD, Mr. Christopher Andrew, BA FCA** *1973;* Millbrook, Park Lane, Sharnbrook, BEDFORD, MK44 1LX.
WARD, Mr. Christopher Anthony, BSc FCA *1984;* Ashcroft Fen Road, Fenstanton, HUNTINGDON, CAMBRIDGESHIRE, PE28 9JT.
WARD, Mr. Christopher Ian, LLB ACA CF *2003;* with PricewaterhouseCoopers LLP, Cornwall Court, 19 Cornwall Street, BIRMINGHAM, B3 2DT.
WARD, Mr. Christopher James, BA ACA *2000;* York Race Committee The Racecourse, Knavesmire Road, YORK, YO23 1EX.
WARD, Mr. Christopher Michael, FCA *1974;* Atkin Automation Ltd, 11 Howlett Way, THETFORD, NORFOLK, IP24 1HZ.
WARD, Mr. Christopher Peter Alan, MA ACA *1993;* 36 Bacons Drive, Cuffley, POTTERS BAR, EN6 4DU.
WARD, Mr. Christopher Stuart, MA BPhil FCA *1977;* The Vicarage Hennock, Bovey Tracey, NEWTON ABBOT, DEVON, TQ13 9QD.
WARD, Miss. Claire, MMath ACA *2011;* 2 Hough Terrace, LEEDS, LS13 3QT.
WARD, Mrs. Claire Cecilia, BA ACA *2000;* 4 Mansdale Road, Redbourn, ST. ALBANS, HERTFORDSHIRE, AL3 7DN.
WARD, Mrs. Clare, BSc ACA *2005;* Terence Butler Holdings Ltd, Court Lodge Park, Lower Road, West Farleigh, MAIDSTONE, KENT ME15 0PD.
WARD, Mrs. Clare Elaine, BSc FCA *1994;* Oakwood, 12 Pelling Hill, Old Windsor, WINDSOR, BERKSHIRE, SL4 2LL.
•**WARD, Mr. Clifford William John, FCA** *1970;* Ward & Co, First Floor, 15 Young Street, LONDON, W8 5EH.
•**WARD, Mr. Clive Richard, MA FCA** *1971;* Market Heath House, Brenchley Road Brenchley, TONBRIDGE, KENT, TN12 7PA.
WARD, Mr. Colin, BSc FCA *1965;* 1A Cuckoo Hill Drive, PINNER, HA5 3PG. (Life Member)
•**WARD, Mr. Darren Lee, BSc FCA** *1996;* The Orange Partnership Ltd, Suite 9, Warwick Corner, 42 Warwick Road, KENILWORTH, WARWICKSHIRE CV8 1HE.
WARD, Mr. David, BEng ACA *2005;* 60 Wingate Drive, Ampthill, BEDFORD, MK45 2XF.
WARD, Mr. David, BA FCA *1982;* West Lyme, 27 Bartons Road, FORDINGBRIDGE, SP6 1JD.
WARD, Mr. David Anthony, MSci ACA *2009;* 87 Rydons Way, REDHILL, RH1 6ES.
WARD, Mr. David Anthony, BA ACA *1982;* 1 Hampton Road, Town Moor, DONCASTER, DN2 5DG.
WARD, Mr. David Bruce, FCA *1963;* 23 Avenue Road, Dorridge, SOLIHULL, WEST MIDLANDS, B93 8LD. (Life Member)
WARD, Mr. David John, FCA *1961;* Wards Garth, Lower End, Layer-de-la-Haye, COLCHESTER, CO2 0LE. (Life Member)
WARD, Mr. David John, MSc BA FCA *1983;* 8 The Croft, Hanging Houghton, NORTHAMPTON, NN6 9HW.
WARD, Mr. David John, BSc FCA *1988;* 7 Frobisher Close, PINNER, MIDDLESEX, HA5 1NN.
WARD, Mr. David Jonathon, BSc ACA *1990;* Five Oaks Hermitage Lane, WINDSOR, SL4 4AZ.
WARD, Mr. David Joynson, FCA *1962;* 6 The Fairway, TADCASTER, LS24 9HN.
WARD, Mr. David Mathew, BA ACA *2001;* 48 Wellington Road, STEVENAGE, HERTFORDSHIRE, SG2 9HS.
WARD, Mr. David Matthew, BA FCA CTA *1996;* (Tax Fac), North Park Lodge, Brisco, CARLISLE, CA4 0RB.
WARD, Mr. David Neville, BSc ACA *1982;* 168 Albertus Avenue, TORONTO M4R 1J7, ON, CANADA.
WARD, Mr. David Roger, FCA *1970;* Brook House, Bardsea, ULVERSTON, LA12 9QU.
•**WARD, Mr. David Stuart, BA FCA** *1985;* David Ward, 2 Ingleton Close, Holmes Chapel, CREWE, CW4 7LF.
WARD, Miss. Debra Veronica, ACA *1986;* with Ernst & Young LLP, 1 More London Place, LONDON, SE1 2AF.
WARD, Mr. Denis Ross, FCA *1949;* 215 Abbey Lane, SHEFFIELD, S8 0BT. (Life Member)
•**WARD, Mr. Donald Brinsley, FCA** *1969;* PO Box W1270, ST JOHNS, ANTIGUA AND BARBUDA.
WARD, Mrs. Doreen Margaret, BSc FCA *1980;* Alne House, Mill Lane, Tanworth-In-Arden, SOLIHULL, B94 5BB.
WARD, Mr. Douglas John Richard, FCA *1956;* 2 Nightingale Park, Storrington, PULBOROUGH, RH20 4LY. (Life Member)
WARD, Mr. Edward, BA(Hons) ACA *2011;* 79 Foster Street, LINCOLN, LN5 7QE.
WARD, Mr. Edward Nicholas, MA FCA *1974;* Hookwood House, Puttenden Road, Shipbourne, TONBRIDGE, TN11 9RJ. (Life Member)
WARD, Miss. Eleanor, BSc ACA *1999;* PricewaterhouseCoopers, 113-119 The Terrace, PO Box 243, WELLINGTON, NEW ZEALAND.
WARD, Mrs. Elisabeth Frances, BA ACA *1999;* Grampian Country Pork (Suffolk) Ltd, Little Wratting, HAVERHILL, SUFFOLK, CB9 7TD.
WARD, Miss. Elizabeth Ann, MA MEng ACA *2002;* Diageo North America, 24440 W 143rd Street, PLAINFIELD, IL 60544, UNITED STATES.

WARD, Mrs. Elizabeth Josephine, BA ACA *1994;* 36 Bacons Drive, Cuffley, POTTERS BAR, EN6 4DU.
WARD, Ms. Elizabeth Katherine, BCom ACA ATII *1992;* Beechwood House, Chestnut Road, Sutton Benger, CHIPPENHAM, SN15 4RP.
WARD, Mr. Elliott, FCA *1959;* Locksley Cottage, East Wallhouses, NEWCASTLE UPON TYNE, NE18 0LL. (Life Member)
WARD, Mr. Elliott Allan, BSc ACA *1992;* Bankside 6, The Watermark, GATESHEAD, TYNE AND WEAR, NE11 9SY.
WARD, Mr. Ezekiel, LLM LLB LLB(Hons) ACA *2011;* Bygdøy Alle 37, N-0265 OSLO, NORWAY.
WARD, Mrs. Fiona Ruth, BSc ACA *1991;* 16 Nimrod Close, ST. ALBANS, AL4 9XY.
WARD, Mr. Gary, BEng ACA *1993;* 39 St Stephens Road, LONDON, W13 8HJ.
WARD, Mr. Geoffrey Lawrence, FCA *1953;* 11 Lakeview Court, 418 Wimbledon Park Road, LONDON, SW19 6PP. (Life Member)
WARD, Mr. George Henry Reginald, FCA *1959;* Grunwick Processing Labs Ltd, Stirling Way, BOREHAMWOOD, WD6 2AZ.
WARD, Mr. George Rodney, MA FCA *1969;* 22 Castle Park, LANCASTER, LA1 1YQ.
WARD, Mr. Glen, ACA CA(AUS) *2011;* National Australian Bank, Level 5, 33 Gracechurch Street, LONDON, EC3V 0BT.
WARD, Mr. Graham, BA ACA *1988;* Danns New Pond Hill, Cross in Hand, HEATHFIELD, EAST SUSSEX, TN21 0NB.
WARD, Mr. Graham Charles, BA FCA *1985;* Goodwins Cottage, Goodwins Court, Rolleston, NEWARK, NOTTINGHAMSHIRE, NG23 5SD.
WARD, Mr. Graham David, BA ACA *1987;* 1100 Peachtree Street, Suite 700, ATLANTA, GA 30309-4516, UNITED STATES.
WARD, Mr. Graham Eyre, ACA *2009;* 311 Clay Lane, BIRMINGHAM, B26 1ER.
•WARD, Mr. Graham Leslie, FCA *1976;* Carringtons, 14 Mill Street, BRADFORD, WEST YORKSHIRE, BD1 4AB.
WARD, Mr. Graham Norman Charles, CBE MA FCA *1977;* (President 2000 - 2001) (Member of Council 1991 - 2003), 4 Post Office Square, London Road, TUNBRIDGE WELLS, TN1 1BQ.
WARD, Mr. Gregory Artemas, BSc ACA *1998;* Ernst & Young LLP, Suite 1600, 560 Mission Street, SAN FRANCISCO, CA 94105, UNITED STATES.
•WARD, Mr. Guy Stephen, BA FCA *1983;* Barron & Barron, Bathurst House, 86 Micklegate, YORK, YO1 6LQ.
WARD, Miss. Gwyneth Helen, MBA BSc ACA *1989;* Hazelhurst Cottage Storrs, Stannington, SHEFFIELD, S6 6GY.
WARD, Mrs. Helen Elizabeth, MMath ACA *2004;* 23 Raglan Road, SALE, CHESHIRE, M33 4AN.
WARD, Mrs. Helen Margaret, BSc ACA *1994;* The University Of Hull, Cottingham Road, HULL, HU6 7RX.
WARD, Mrs. Helen Mary, LLM LLB ACA *1982;* 8 Station Road, St Columb Major, TRURO, CORNWALL, TR9 6RY.
WARD, Mr. Ian Miles, MBA BA FCA *1984;* 19 Lansdowne Road, LUTON, LU3 1EE.
WARD, Miss. Isabel Mary, BSc ACA *1983;* 61 Worcester Crescent, WOODFORD GREEN, ESSEX, IG8 0LX.
•WARD, Mr. Ivan John, FCA *1963;* 80 Links Way, Croxley Green, RICKMANSWORTH, HERTFORDSHIRE, WD3 3RJ.
WARD, Mrs. Jacqueline Claire, BCom FCA *1986;* 42 Creskeld Lane, Bramhope, LEEDS, LS16 9ES.
WARD, Ms. Jade, ACA *2008;* 2 Claydon Path, Stoke Mandeville, AYLESBURY, BUCKINGHAMSHIRE, HP21 9EF.
•WARD, Mr. James, BA(Hons) ACA ACIS *1998;* Whale Rock Professional Services Group, 4th Floor, 15 Basinghall Street, LONDON, EC2V 5BR. See also Whale Rock Limited
•WARD, Mr. James, BSc FCA *1989;* (Tax Fac), Jonesward Ltd, 6 St. Catherine Street, CARMARTHEN, DYFED, SA31 1RE.
WARD, Mr. James Dewick, FCA *1956;* 22 Windermere Road, Beeston, NOTTINGHAM, NG9 3AS. (Life Member)
WARD, Mr. James Howard, BSc ACA *1996;* Howard Ward Associates Brewery House, Walkers Yard Radcliffe-on-Trent, NOTTINGHAM, NG12 2FF.
WARD, Mr. James Stephen, BA ACA *2007;* 23 Chestnut Close, Streetly, SUTTON COLDFIELD, WEST MIDLANDS, B74 3EF.
WARD, Mr. James William, BSc FCA *1980;* Innisfree Ltd, 33 Gutter Lane, LONDON, EC2V 8AS.
WARD, Mr. Jason Mark, BA ACA *1999;* Boots the Chemists, Thane Road, NOTTINGHAM, NG90 1BS.
•WARD, Mr. Jeffrey, MSc FCA *1979;* with RSM Tenon Audit Limited, 66 Chiltern Street, LONDON, W1U 4JT.
WARD, Mr. Jeffrey Simon, BA ACA *1994;* 26 Albyfield, BROMLEY, BR1 2HZ.
WARD, Mr. John, BSc FCA *1978;* 3 Shenfield Gardens, Hutton, BRENTWOOD, CM13 1DT.
WARD, Mr. John, FCA *1970;* 22 Holt Park Road, LEEDS, LS16 7QS.
•WARD, Mr. John Charles, FCA *1983;* Davisons Ltd, Lime Court, Pathfields Business Park, SOUTH MOLTON, DEVON, EX36 3LH.
WARD, Mr. John Christopher, BA FCA *1987;* Great Hunts Place, Whaddon Lane, Owslebury, WINCHESTER, HAMPSHIRE, SO21 1JL.
•WARD, Mr. John David, BA FCA FITI *1977;* (Tax Fac), John Ward & Co, 10 Steelstown Road, LONDONDERRY, COUNTY LONDONDERRY, BT48 8EU.
WARD, Mr. John Joseph, FCA *1993;* 94 Avenue Road, NORWICH, NR2 3HP.
WARD, Mr. John Michael, BA ACA *1981;* 22 Harewell Close, Glasshouses, HARROGATE, HG3 5DY.
WARD, Mr. John Michael, FCA *1961;* 8 The Spinney, Swanland, NORTH FERRIBY, HU14 3RD. (Life Member)
WARD, Mr. John Richard, BA ACA *1982;* Ann Gills, Gallowgate Lane, Weeton, LEEDS, LS17 0AU.
WARD, Mr. John Thomas Smith, BSc FCA *1975;* Homelands, Wall Hill, FOREST ROW, EAST SUSSEX, RH18 5EG.
WARD, Mr. Jonathan Christopher, BSc ACA *2004;* Flat 1, The Cooperage, 6 Gainsford Street, LONDON, SE1 2NG.
WARD, Mr. Jonathan Edward Hedderley, BA ACA *1984;* 6 Main Road, Little Gransden, SANDY, BEDFORDSHIRE, SG19 3DN.
•WARD, Mr. Jonathan Nigel, BSc FCA *1996;* Booth Ainsworth LLP, Alpha House, 4 Greek Street, STOCKPORT, CHESHIRE, SK3 8AB.
WARD, Mr. Jonathan Paul, MA ACA *2004;* Olympus House, Olympus Close, IPSWICH, IP15LN.
•WARD, Mr. Joseph William, BSc ACA *1981;* Ward Patel & Co, The Gables, Haggatt Hall, St Michael, BRIDGETOWN, BARBADOS.
WARD, Mrs. Juliet Margaret Ann, BSc(Hons) ACA *2001;* with BDO LLP, 55 Baker Street, LONDON, W1U 7EU.
WARD, Mr. Justin Paul, BSc ACA *1994;* 10 Larpent Avenue, LONDON, SW15 6UP.
WARD, Miss. Karen Jane, FCA *1993;* Finance Department, Connexions Cheshire & Warrington Partnership 2 The Stables, Gadbrook Park Rudheath, NORTHWICH, CHESHIRE, CW9 7RJ.
WARD, Mrs. Katherine, MA ACA *1999;* 139 Cole Road, RD 6, PALMERSTON NORTH 4476, NEW ZEALAND.
WARD, Mrs. Katrina Jane, BA ACA *1984;* 1712 Hansen Road, LIVERMORE, CA 94550, UNITED STATES.
WARD, Mrs. Katy Jane, ACA *2005;* Juniper House Sleaford Road, Beckingham, LINCOLN, LN5 0RF.
WARD, Mrs. Kay, BSc ACA *1992;* 3 Green Lane Close, HARPENDEN, HERTFORDSHIRE, AL5 1NF.
WARD, Mr. Keith Graham, BSc FCA *1977;* 12 Rosedene Gardens, FLEET, GU51 4NQ.
•WARD, Mr. Keith Langton, BA ACA *1990;* with Baker Tilly Tax & Advisory Services LLP, 3 Hardman Street, MANCHESTER, M3 3HF.
•WARD, Mr. Keith Watson, FCA *1981;* UHY Calvert Smith, 31 St Saviourgate, YORK, YO1 8NQ.
WARD, Mr. Kenneth Anthony, FCA *1949;* Avalon Cottage, Willey Park, Alton Road, FARNHAM, GU10 5ER. (Life Member)
WARD, Mr. Kenneth Duncan, FCA *1970;* Old Orchard, North Barrow, YEOVIL, SOMERSET, BA22 7LZ.
WARD, Mr. Kenneth Edward, FCA *1961;* Springwood, Emery Down, LYNDHURST, SO43 7EA.
WARD, Mr. Kevin Richard, ACA *1985;* Goymour Properties Ltd, The Grove, Banham, NORWICH, NR16 2HE.
WARD, Mrs. Laura Kate, LLB ACA *2007;* Flat 19, Edward Nicholl Court, Waterloo Road, Penylan, CARDIFF, CF23 9BW.
WARD, Mr. Lee Edward James, BA ACA *1992;* V T Nuclear Services Olympus Plaza, Olympus Park Quedgeley, GLOUCESTER, GL2 4NF.
•WARD, Ms. Lesley Jane, BSc FCA *1991;* Lesley Jane Baldwyn, Pinewood, Crockford Lane, Chineham Business Park, Chineham, BASINGSTOKE HAMPSHIRE RG24 8AL. See also Baldwyn Ward
WARD, Mrs. Lesley Karen, BSc ACA *1983;* 3 Mulberry Close, WELLINGBOROUGH, NN8 3JU.
WARD, Mrs. Lindsey Jane, BSc ACA *1988;* Holmewood, Beech Hill Terrace, KENDAL, LA9 4PB.
WARD, Mrs. Louise Angela, BSc ACA *2004;* 2 Evendons Close, WOKINGHAM, BERKSHIRE, RG41 4AB.
WARD, Mr. Malcolm Peter, FCA *1969;* 78 Hidcote Road, Oadby, LEICESTER, LE2 5PF.
WARD, Mr. Malcolm Robert, FCA *1969;* 18 Wayside, LONDON, SW14 7LN.
•WARD, Mr. Malcolm Robert, FCA *1989;* Grant Thornton UK LLP, Grant Thornton House, 22 Melton Street, Euston Square, LONDON, NW1 2EP. See also Grant Thornton LLP
WARD, Mr. Marcus David, BA ACA *1998;* 41, Hazlebury Road, LONDON, SW6 2NA.
WARD, Mr. Mark, BSc ACA *2007;* 43 Midhurst Road, Fernhurst, HASLEMERE, GU27 3EW.
WARD, Mr. Mark Andrew, BSc ACA *1995;* 2 Old School Close, Thurlby, BOURNE, PE10 0QH.
•WARD, Mr. Mark Derek, MBA BSc FCA *1990;* Deloitte LLP, Hill House, 1 Little New Street, LONDON, EC4A 3TR. See also Deloitte & Touche LLP
WARD, Mr. Martin Christopher, FCA *1983;* Chalkstream, Winchester Road, Kings Somborne, STOCKBRIDGE, HAMPSHIRE, SO20 6NZ.
WARD, Mr. Martin Gerard, BSc ACA *1996;* 145 Rusthall Avenue, LONDON, W4 1BL.
WARD, Mr. Martin Richard, BA ACA *1992;* 8 Lawrence Close, Nr Thurcaston, LEICESTER, LE4 2SB.
•WARD, Mr. Martin Stuart, BA FCA *1986;* Dodd & Co., Fifteen Rosehill, Montgomery Way, Rosehill Estate, CARLISLE, CA1 2RW.
WARD, Mrs. Mary Gerardine, LLB ACA *1989;* Meadow Lodge, Red Lion Lane, Sarratt, RICKMANSWORTH, WD3 6BW.
WARD, Mr. Matthew, BSc ACA *1999;* 6a Highgate West Hill, LONDON, N6 6JR.
WARD, Mr. Matthew, BA ACA *2005;* 11th Floor - European SIT, Baring Investment Services Ltd, 155 Bishopsgate, LONDON, EC2M 3XY.
WARD, Mr. Matthew Anthony, BA ACA *2007;* 60 Roselands Gardens, SOUTHAMPTON, SO17 1QJ.
WARD, Mr. Matthew Charles, BSocSc ACA *1993;* Ernst & Young LLP The Paragon, Counterslip, BRISTOL, BS1 6BX.
WARD, Mr. Matthew James, ACA *2008;* 18 Cherry Park Brandon, DURHAM, DH7 8TN.
WARD, Mr. Matthew Julian, BSc ACA *1982;* 21 Helsall Court, Sorrento, PERTH, WA 6020, AUSTRALIA.
WARD, Mr. Michael, BSc ACA *1981;* 2 Glebe Lane, Gnosall, STAFFORD, ST20 0ER.
•WARD, Mr. Michael, FCA *1977;* (Tax Fac), Rowley Ward, Tower House, 4 Tower Street, YORK, YO1 9SB.
WARD, Mr. Michael Ashley, MBA FCA MCT *1980;* Alne House, Mill Lane, Tanworth-In-Arden, SOLIHULL, B94 5BB.
WARD, Mr. Michael Cary, BA(Econ) ACA *2003;* 23 Raglan Road, SALE, CHESHIRE, M33 4AN.
WARD, Mr. Michael Gordon, BEng ACA *1993;* 96 Aspin Lane, KNARESBOROUGH, NORTH YORKSHIRE, HG5 8EP.
•WARD, Mr. Michael James Vincent, FCA *1976;* M.W. Consultancy Services, 8 James Martin Close, Denham, UXBRIDGE, MIDDLESEX, UB9 5NN.
•WARD, Mr. Michael John, FCA *1966;* (Tax Fac), M.J. Ward & Co., 6 Chislehurst Place, West Park, LYTHAM ST. ANNES, LANCASHIRE, FY8 4RU.
WARD, Mr. Michael John, BSc ACA *2010;* 1 Millbrook Cottage, La Rue Du Galet, St. Lawrence, JERSEY, JE3 1LQ.
WARD, Mr. Michael John Collins, BA FCA *1969;* Dormy Corner, Manor Road, MAIDENHEAD, SL6 2QG.
WARD, Mr. Michael Martin Thexton, FCA *1975;* 16 Oakhall Drive, Dorridge, SOLIHULL, B93 8UA.
WARD, Mr. Michael Thomas, FCA *1964;* Almondsbury Accountancy Services Ltd, 26 Yewhurst Road, SOLIHULL, WEST MIDLANDS, B91 1PN.
WARD, Mrs. Michelle Sylvia, BEng ACA CF *1993;* Aspria, Hill Place House, 55A High Street, LONDON, SW19 5BA.
WARD, Miss. Natalie, BSc ACA *2004;* with Deloitte LLP, Athene Place, 66 Shoe Lane, LONDON, EC4A 3BQ.
WARD, Miss. Natalie Kate, ACA *2011;* 21 Park View Road, Chapeltown, SHEFFIELD, S35 1WL.
WARD, Mr. Nicholas Alexander, BA(Hons) ACA *2010;* 193 Saint Georges Island, 1 Kelso Place, MANCHESTER, M15 4LE.
WARD, Mr. Nicholas John, BSc ACA *1999;* 10 Shepherd Way, Taverham, NORWICH, NR8 6UD.
WARD, Mr. Nicholas Timothy, BA ACA *1994;* 20 Mayford Road, Lords Wood, CHATHAM, KENT, ME5 8SZ.
WARD, Miss. Nicola, BA(Hons) ACA *2006;* Flat 215 Pacific Wharf, 165 Rotherhithe Street, LONDON, SE16 5QF.
•WARD, Mr. Nigel Graham, ACA *1991;* (Tax Fac), 97 Waverley Road, SOUTHSEA, PO5 2PL.
WARD, Mr. Nigel James, BA ACA *1994;* The Old Vicarage Church Road, Harby, NEWARK, NOTTINGHAMSHIRE, NG23 7ED.
•WARD, Mr. Nigel Mark, BCom FCA *1986;* PricewaterhouseCoopers LLP, Benson House, 33 Wellington Street, LEEDS, LS1 4JP. See also PricewaterhouseCoopers
•WARD, Mr. Nigel Richard, FCA *1984;* (Tax Fac), Stephenson Smart, 22-26 King Street, KING'S LYNN, NORFOLK, PE30 1HJ.
•WARD, Mr. Norman Roy, FCA *1961;* N.R. Ward, 36 Brushwood Road, HORSHAM, RH12 4PE.
WARD, Mr. Norman Telford, FCA *1955;* The Hollies, Thorpe Road, Harthill, SHEFFIELD, S26 7YF. (Life Member)
•WARD, Mr. Paul, BSc(Hons) ACA MCT *2001;* with PricewaterhouseCoopers LLP, 1 Embankment Place, LONDON, WC2N 6RH.
WARD, Mr. Peter, BA ACA *2009;* Flat 5, Voltaire Buildings, 330 Garratt Lane, Earlsfield, LONDON, SW18 4FQ.
WARD, Mr. Peter Anthony, FCA *1972;* SVS Securities Plc, 21 Wilson Street, LONDON, EC2M 2SN.
WARD, Mr. Peter Arnold Reuben, FCA *1950;* 72 Kingwell Road, Worsbrough, BARNSLEY, S70 4HG. (Life Member)
WARD, Mr. Peter Clifford, FCA *1974;* 2 Claremont Road, WINDSOR, SL4 3AX.
WARD, Mr. Peter Douglas, BSc FCA *1975;* Willowdale, Burley Lane, Menston, ILKLEY, LS29 6EH.
WARD, Mr. Peter James, FCA *1972;* ACT Offshores Ltd, PO Box 1377, VICTORIA, SEYCHELLES.
WARD, Mr. Peter James, FCA *1960;* 25 Lower Tail, Carpenders Park, WATFORD, WD19 5DD. (Life Member)
WARD, Mr. Peter John, BA ACA *1982;* The Old Malt House, Marlow Road, Well End, BOURNE END, BUCKINGHAMSHIRE, SL8 5PL.
WARD, Mr. Peter John Ernleigh, FCA *1970;* 12 Hurst Road, BUCKHURST HILL, IG9 6AB.
WARD, Mr. Peter Jonathan, BA ACA *1990;* Tomphubil Lodge, PITLOCHRY, PERTHSHIRE, PH16 5NL.
WARD, Mr. Peter Kenneth, BA(Hons) ACA *2011;* Flat 24, Stamford House, Great Heathmead, HAYWARDS HEATH, WEST SUSSEX, RH16 1FH.
•WARD, Mr. Peter Murray, BA ACA *1995;* (Tax Fac), PWP Accounting Services, Bournemouth Indoor Bowls Club, Kings Park Drive, Kings Park, BOURNEMOUTH, BH7 6JD.
WARD, Mr. Philip, BA ACA *1984;* Middle Barn, The Orchard, Staverton, DAVENTRY, NN11 6JA.
WARD, Mr. Philip Brian, BA ACA *1999;* 8 Brook Court, Horton, NORTHAMPTON, NN7 2BL.
•WARD, Mr. Philip Robert, BEng FCA *1994;* Lowson Ward Limited, 292 Wake Green Road, BIRMINGHAM, B13 9QP.
WARD, Miss. Rachel Elizabeth, BA ACA *2006;* 130 Tilehurst Road, LONDON, SW18 3EY.
WARD, Mr. Raymond, FCA *1953;* 41 Bushey Wood Road, Dore, SHEFFIELD, S17 3QA. (Life Member)
WARD, Mr. Raymond Geoffrey, BSc FCA *1989;* Cargill Plc Knowle Hill Park, Fairmile Lane, COBHAM, KT11 2PD.
WARD, Miss. Rebecca Louise, BEng ACA *2002;* Flat 8 Lyndenhurst, 32 Lee Road, LONDON, SE3 9RY.
WARD, Mr. Richard, BSc ACA *2010;* 35 Buttermere Drive, Allestree, DERBY, DE22 2SP.
WARD, Dr. Richard, PhD MRes BSc ACA *2011;* Community Solutions for Primary Care Holdings Ltd, 10 Furnival Street, LONDON, EC4A 1AB.
WARD, Mr. Richard George, ACA *2009;* Unit 76, 163 Sydney Street, New Farm, BRISBANE, QLD 4005, AUSTRALIA.
WARD, Mr. Richard John, BSc FCA *1978;* NAB, Level 15, 500 Bourke St, MELBOURNE, VIC 3000, AUSTRALIA.
WARD, Mr. Richard John, BSc ACA *2004;* Shire Pharmaceuticals Group Plc, Lime Tree Way, Hampshire Int Business Park, Chineham, BASINGSTOKE, HAMPSHIRE RG24 8EP.
•WARD, Mr. Richard John, FCA *1983;* Streets Audit LLP, Tower House, Lucy Tower Street, LINCOLN, LN1 1XW. See also Streets Whitmarsh Sterland and SMS Corporate Partner Unlimited
•WARD, Mr. Richard Peter Clifford, BA FCA *1975;* Whittle & Partners LLP, Century House South, North Station Road, COLCHESTER, CO1 1RE.
•WARD, Mr. Robert, FCA *1975;* Fisher Phillips, Summit House, 170 Finchley Road, LONDON, NW3 6BP. See also Fisher Phillips 2010 Ltd

WARD, Mr. Robert Andrew, FCA *1969;* 3/2 Lonsdale Terrace, EDINBURGH, EH3 9HN.
WARD, Mr. Robert Dennis, FCA *1973;* 29 Myddelton Park, Whetstone, LONDON, N20 0JH.
•**WARD, Mr. Robert Dennis, FCA** *1972;* Ward Accountancy Services Limited, 7 Manns Way, Rayleigh, ESSEX, SS6 9QB.
WARD, Mr. Robert Eric, FCA *1971;* Grey Roofs, 30 Stanstead Road, CATERHAM, CR3 6AA.
•ⒹWARD, Mr. Robert Johnathan, BSc ACA *1990;* Ernst & Young LLP, 1 More London Place, LONDON, SE1 2AF. See also Ernst & Young Europe LLP
WARD, Mr. Robert Richard Craufurd, BSc BPhil ACA *1994;* Hill House Farmhouse, Sawley Road, Grindleton, CLITHEROE, LANCASHIRE, BB7 4QS.
WARD, Mr. Robin D'arcy, MA FCA *1978;* Apartment 6, 29 Laycock Street, LONDON, N1 1UR.
WARD, Mr. Roger John, FCA *1973;* 27 Highland Road, AMERSHAM, BUCKINGHAMSHIRE, HP7 9AX.
WARD, Mr. Roger Norman, FCA *1985;* 99 Manor Rise, BURNTWOOD, STAFFORDSHIRE, WS7 4TR.
•**WARD, Mr. Roger Paul, FCA** *1977;* Creaseys LLP, 12 Lonsdale Gardens, TUNBRIDGE WELLS, KENT, TN1 1PA.
WARD, Miss. Rosemary, BA ACA *1991;* 83 Devonshire Road, Westbury Park, BRISTOL, BS6 7NH.
WARD, Mr. Rupert James Allen, MA ACA CTA *1992;* 400 East Randolph Street, Unit 903, CHICAGO, IL 60601, UNITED STATES.
WARD, Mrs. Sally Victoria, ACA *2008;* Northside, 4 Beacon Road, Ditchling, HASSOCKS, WEST SUSSEX, BN6 8UL.
WARD, Mr. Sam, ACA *2008;* 12a Cambridge Street, OTLEY, WEST YORKSHIRE, LS21 1JT.
WARD, Mr. Sam, ACA *2011;* 144 Upper Eastern Green Lane, COVENTRY, CV5 7DN.
•**WARD, Mrs. Sharon Elizabeth, BSc FCA CF** *1989;* Roffe Swayne, Ashcombe Court, Woolsack Way, GODALMING, GU7 1LQ.
WARD, Mr. Simon Douglas John, BA ACA *1996;* 9 Four Oaks Road, SUTTON COLDFIELD, B74 2XP.
WARD, Mr. Simon John, FCA *1968;* 3 Gar Street, WINCHESTER, HAMPSHIRE, SO23 8GQ.
WARD, Mrs. Stephanie, BSc ACA *1987;* 8 Redhouse Close, Bentley Heath, SOLIHULL, WEST MIDLANDS, B93 8AR.
WARD, Mr. Stephen, FCA *1955;* 2 Queens Court, Victoria Road, SHEFFORD, BEDFORDSHIRE, SG17 5AL. (Life Member)
WARD, Mr. Stephen, ACA *2002;* 109 Baldoon Sands, Acklam, MIDDLESBROUGH, CLEVELAND, TS5 8UF.
•**WARD, Mr. Stephen Andrew, BA ACA** *1985;* Deloitte LLP, 2 New Street Square, LONDON, EC4A 3BZ. See also Deloitte & Touche LLP
WARD, Mr. Stephen Arthur, BSc FCA *1985;* SIMSL, Aquatical House, 39 Bell Lane, LONDON, E1 7LU.
•**WARD, Mr. Stephen Barrie, BA ACA** *2000;* BDO LLP, 125 Colmore Row, BIRMINGHAM, B3 3SD. See also BDO Stoy Hayward LLP
WARD, Mr. Stephen Francis, BA FCA *1980;* Court House, Buckland, FARINGDON, OXFORDSHIRE, SN7 8QR.
WARD, Mr. Stephen John, BA ACA *1983;* 10 Prossers, TADWORTH, KT20 5TY.
WARD, Mr. Stuart Philip, FCA *1972;* Sukhumvit City Resort 21st floor 48/123 Soi Sukhumvit 11 Sukhumvit Road Klong Toei Nua Wattana, BANGKOK 10110, THAILAND.
WARD, Mrs. Susan Janice, BA FCA *1991;* 1 Arden Glade, Kington Lane Claverdon, WARWICK, CV35 8PP.
WARD, Mr. Thomas, BSc(Hons) ACA *2003;* 53/4 Grosvenor Street, LONDON, W1K 3HU.
WARD, Mr. Thomas Richard, MA FCA *1980;* 4 Belgrave Crescent, EDINBURGH, EH4 3AQ.
•**WARD, Mr. Thomas Saul, BSc FCA** *1982;* Moore Stephens LLP, 150 Aldersgate Street, LONDON, EC1A 4AB. See also Moore Stephens & Co
WARD, Mr. Thorin Paul, BA FCA CF *1996;* with Baker Tilly Tax & Advisory Services LLP, 1st Floor, 46 Clarendon Road, WATFORD, WD17 1JJ.
WARD, Mr. Timothy Charles, BA ACA *1993;* Tudor House, 2 Aberford Road, Barwick in Elmet, LEEDS, LS15 4DZ.
WARD, Mr. Timothy Raines Dorrington, MA MBA FCA *1982;* The Quoted Companies Alliance Ltd, 6 Kinghorn Street, LONDON, EC1A 7HW.
WARD, Mr. Tom, BA(Hons) ACA *2011;* 30 Whitehall Park Road, LONDON, W4 3NE.
WARD, Mrs. Vicki Suzanne, BSc ACA *1997;* with Experian plc, Landmark House, Experian Way, NOTTINGHAM, NG80 1ZZ.
WARD, Mrs. Virginia Mary, MA FCA *1969;* 102 Old Park Ridings, Grange Park, LONDON, N21 2EP.
WARD, Mrs. Wendy Jane, BA(Hons) ACA *2000;* 41 Hazlebury Road, LONDON, SW6 2NA.
WARD, Mr. William David, BA FCA *1981;* 3750 Zanker Road, SAN JOSE, CA 95134, UNITED STATES.
WARD-CAMPBELL, Mr. Iain Gordon Leeds, MA FCA *1968;* 12 Rossett Green Lane, HARROGATE, NORTH YORKSHIRE, HG2 9LJ.
WARD HUNT, Mr. Nicholas Christopher, BA(Hons) FCA *2001;* PPD, Granta Park, Great Abington, CAMBRIDGE, CB21 6GQ.
WARD JONES, Mrs. Ann Jill, BA ACA *1981;* 24 South Park Gardens, BERKHAMSTED, HP4 1HZ.
WARD-JONES, Mr. Stephen Anthony, BSc ACA *1985;* Arcelor Commercial UK F C S E Ltd, Arcelor House, 4 Princes Way, SOLIHULL, WEST MIDLANDS, B91 3AL.
•**WARD-THOMPSON, Mr. Graham Lance, BA FCA** *1983;* PricewaterhouseCoopers LLP, Benson House, 33 Wellington Street, LEEDS, LS1 4JP. See also PricewaterhouseCoopers
WARDALE, Mr. Colin Charles, BCom ACA *1981;* Hill Dickinson Co Ltd, 1 St. Pauls Square, LIVERPOOL, L3 9SJ.
WARDALE, Mr. Robert James, BSc ACA *1991;* 73 Whalley Drive, Bletchley, MILTON KEYNES, MK3 6HX.
WARDE, Mr. David Andrew, BA ACA *2006;* Heimdalsgatan 6, 113-28, STOCKHOLM, SWEDEN.
WARDE, Mr. Henry, BSc ACA *2005;* Squerryes Estate Office, 2 Home Farm Granary, Squerryes, WESTERHAM, KENT, TN16 1SL.
•**WARDE, Mrs. Lydia Claire, BSc ACA** *2006;* Scodie Deyong LLP, 85 Frampton Street, LONDON, NW8 8NQ.
WARDELL, Mrs. Abigail Sara, MA(Hons) ACA *2001;* 9 Ty-Gwyn Avenue, CARDIFF, CF23 5JJ.
•**WARDELL, Mr. Alistair Gareth, MA ACA** *2002;* Grant Thornton UK LLP, 11-13 Penhill Road, CARDIFF, CF11 9UP. See also Grant Thornton LLP
WARDELL, Mrs. Celine Anouk, MBA LLB ACA *2007;* 239 Old Dover Road, CANTERBURY, KENT, CT1 3ES.
•**WARDELL, Mr. James, FCA** *1982;* Horwath Corporate Advisory Services Ltd, Room 1601-02, 16th Floor, One Hysan Avenue, CAUSEWAY BAY, HONG KONG ISLAND HONG KONG SAR.
•**WARDELL, Mrs. Jane, ACA** *1998;* Wardell Accounting Services, 10 Meadowgate Croft, Lofthouse, WAKEFIELD, WEST YORKSHIRE, WF3 3SS.
WARDELL, Mr. John Michael, FCA *1979;* Dalton Estate, The Estate Office, West End, South Dalton, BEVERLEY, HU17 7PN.
WARDELL, Mr. Mark, BSc ACA *2003;* Pricewaterhousecoopers, 1 Embankment Place, LONDON, WC2N 6RH.
WARDELL, Mr. Philip Neville, FCA *1981;* 348 Old Bath Rd, CHELTENHAM, GL53 9AF.
•**WARDELL, Mr. Stephen John, BA ACA** *1989;* KPMG LLP, 15 Canada Square, LONDON, E14 5GL. See also KPMG Europe LLP
WARDEN, Miss. Alison Lois, BSc ACA FSI *1991;* 9 Cumin Place, EDINBURGH, EH9 2JX.
WARDEN, Mr. Ashley Maxwell Grant, BTech FCA *1986;* The Shippen, Beardley Farm, Kittisford, WELLINGTON, SOMERSET, TA21 0RZ.
WARDEN, Mr. Daniel Christopher Ian, BSc ACA *2002;* Goodman Jones Chartered Accountants, 29-30 Fitzroy Square, LONDON, W1T 6LQ.
WARDEN, Mr. David Charles, FCA *1967;* 18A Essex Road, STEVENAGE, SG1 3EZ.
WARDEN, Mr. Douglas James, ACA *2009;* 119 Avenell Road, LONDON, N5 1BH.
WARDEN, Mr. John Henderson, BA ACA *1987;* Fairfield, Silverdale Crescent, SHEFFIELD, S11 9JH.
•**WARDEN, Mr. Nicholas James, BA ACA** *1992;* Hatch Partnership LLP, 29 Wood Street, STRATFORD-UPON-AVON, CV37 6JG.
WARDEN, Mr. Richard Peter, BA ACA *1986;* 40-1-159, VEYERNAYA STREET, 119501 MOSCOW, RUSSIAN FEDERATION.
WARDER, Mr. Charles-Emile Michael, BA(Hons) ACA *2004;* 61 Beresford Road, LONDON, N5 2HR.
WARDLE, Mr. Alan, FCA *1968;* Bateman Fold Barn, Crook, KENDAL, CUMBRIA, LA8 8LN.
•**WARDLE, Mr. Andrew James, ACA** *1993;* Hayes & Co, 6 Eckersley Precinct, Alma Street, Atherton, MANCHESTER, M46 0DR.
WARDLE, Mr. Andrew William, BSc ACA *1981;* 14 College Square, Stokesley, MIDDLESBROUGH, CLEVELAND, TS9 5DL.
WARDLE, Mr. Anthony, MMath ACA *2010;* 6 Mowbray Road, NORTH SHIELDS, TYNE AND WEAR, NE29 7NA.
WARDLE, Mr. Christopher Jonathan, BEng ACA *1999;* 16 Nursery Croft, Wirksworth, MATLOCK, DERBYSHIRE, DE4 4DG.
WARDLE, Ms. Diana Mary, BSc FCA *1984;* 43 Ryland Road, Edgbaston, BIRMINGHAM, B15 2BN.
WARDLE, Mr. Eric Adrian, FCA *1982;* (Tax Fac), 92 Ironwood Avenue, Desborough, KETTERING, NORTHAMPTONSHIRE, NN14 2JJ.
WARDLE, Mr. Graeme Robert, BA(Hons) ACA *2002;* 12 Castle Acre, Monkston, MILTON KEYNES, MK10 9HS.
WARDLE, Mr. Graham Clifford, FCA *1965;* 520 Bolton Road, BURY, BL8 2DU. (Life Member)
WARDLE, Mrs. Hayley Alexandra, BA ACA *2007;* Idylwild, Dipe Lane, EAST BOLDON, TYNE AND WEAR, NE36 0PH.
WARDLE, Mr. Ian Martin, BA(Hons) ACA *2003;* Level 6, 15 Blue Street, NORTH SYDNEY, NSW 2060, AUSTRALIA.
WARDLE, Mr. John David, BA ACA *1983;* 15 Warrington Close, SUTTON COLDFIELD, B76 2BL.
WARDLE, Mr. John Henry, BSc ACA *1993;* 14 Woodpecker Close, BISHOP'S STORTFORD, HERTFORDSHIRE, CM23 4QA.
•**WARDLE, Mr. Martin John, BSc FCA** *1994;* KPMG, 8/F Prince's Building, 10 Chater Road, CENTRAL, HONG KONG ISLAND, HONG KONG SAR.
WARDLE, Mr. Michael Frank, BSc FCA *1976;* 35 Whinberry Way, Mearside, OLDHAM, OL4 2NN.
WARDLE, Mr. Nicholas Darlington, FCA *1963;* P.O. Box N.3189, NASSAU, BAHAMAS. (Life Member)
•**WARDLE, Mr. Peter James, ACA** *1980;* 3 Main Street, Lowick, KETTERING, NORTHAMPTONSHIRE, NN14 3BH.
•**WARDLE, Mr. Robert, BA ACA CTA** *2000;* CLB Coopers, Ship Canal House, 98 King Street, MANCHESTER, M2 4WU.
WARDLE, Mr. Roger David George, FCA *1965;* 30 Coppice Avenue, Great Shelford, CAMBRIDGE, CB2 5AQ. (Life Member)
WARDLE, Mrs. Sally Irene, BA ACA *2001;* Coachwise Ltd Unit 2-3, Chelsea Close, LEEDS, LS12 4HP.
WARDLE, Mr. Simon John, BSc ACA *1988;* 2 Bilberry Gardens, The Street, Mortimer, READING, RG7 3WU.
WARDLEY, Mr. David, FCA *1966;* 12 Kingfisher Parade, TOOGOOM, QLD 4655, AUSTRALIA.
WARDLEY, Miss. Michelle Diane, BCom ACA *2001;* with Grant Thornton UK LLP, 1 Whitehall Riverside, Whitehall Road, LEEDS, WEST YORKSHIRE, LS1 4BN.
WARDLEY, Miss. Tamzin Alexandra, ACA *1993;* PO BOX 1249, BOROKO, PAPUA NEW GUINEA.
WARDMAN, Mr. Frederick Arthur, FCA *1966;* 8 Sedbergh Park, ILKLEY, WEST YORKSHIRE, LS29 8SZ. (Life Member)
WARDMAN-BROWNE, Mr. Stuart, ACA *1988;* CHAMP Ventures, L4 Customs House, 31 Alfred Street., SYDNEY, NSW 2000, AUSTRALIA.
WARDNER, Mrs. Jane Elisabeth, BSc ACA *1992;* 18 Beamish Close, Appleton, WARRINGTON, WA4 5RH.
WARDNER, Mr. Richard Craig, BA ACA *1991;* 18 Beamish Close, Appleton, WARRINGTON, WA4 5RH.
WARDROP, Mr. Mark Steven, BSc ACA *1998;* with BDO LLP, 6th Floor, 3 Hardman Street, Spinningfields, MANCHESTER, M3 3AT.
WARDROPE, Mr. Drew, BSc ACA *2007;* Barclays Capital, 10 The South Colonnade, LONDON, E14 4PU.
WARDROPE, Mrs. Natalie, LLB ACA *2006;* (Tax Fac), with Grant Thornton UK LLP, Grant Thornton House, 22 Melton Street, Euston Square, LONDON, NW1 2EP.
WARDROPPER, Mr. James Alan, BA FCA *1955;* 25 Swinhoe Road, Beadnell, CHATHILL, NE67 5AG. (Life Member)
WARDROPPER, Mr. Nicholas John, FCA *1976;* 3800 Decarie, Apt.17, MONTREAL H4A 3J7, QUE, CANADA.
WARE, Miss. Amanda Jane, BSc ACA *1995;* 7 Graham Street, BUNDEENA, NSW 2230, AUSTRALIA.
•**WARE, Mr. Andrew John Arthur, BSc ACA** *1988;* BDO LLP, 55 Baker Street, LONDON, W1U 7EU. See also BDO Stoy Hayward LLP
WARE, Mr. Christopher Tom, BSc ACA *1988;* 4 Edward Close, ROCHFORD, SS4 3HS.
WARE, Mr. Henry John, BSc ACA *1989;* 12430 Calico Falls Lane, HOUSTON, TX 77041, UNITED STATES.
•**WARE, Mr. John David, FCA** *1949;* J.D. Ware, 52 The Fairway, Burnham, SLOUGH, SL1 8DS.
WARE, Mr. John Derek, MSc BSc ACA *2007;* 18 Ashberry Avenue, Douglas, ISLE OF MAN, IM2 1PX.
WARE, Mr. John Egerton David, FCA *1957;* Crofty, Llanrhian Road, Croesgoch, HAVERFORDWEST, SA62 5JT. (Life Member)
WARE, Mr. John Michael, BA ACA *1987;* 24 The Farthings, KINGSTON UPON THAMES, KT2 7PT.
WARE, Mr. John Robin, FCA *1953;* 7 Olde Market Court, Fair Park Road, WADEBRIDGE, CORNWALL, PL27 7LY. (Life Member)
WARE, Mr. Julian, ACA *2009;* with American Express Services Europe Ltd, Sussex House, Civic Way, BURGESS HILL, WEST SUSSEX, RH15 9AQ.
WARE, Mr. Mark, BA ACA *1998;* Flat 2, Marriotts Wharf, West Street, GRAVESEND, KENT, DA11 0BG.
•**WARE, Mr. Martin Geoffrey, FCA** *1974;* MGW Consultants Ltd, 2 Norbury Avenue, WATFORD, WD24 4PJ.
WARE, Mr. Maylin Jeremy, MA ACA *1995;* Chorley Manor, Chorley, BRIDGNORTH, SHROPSHIRE, WV16 6PP.
•**WARE, Mr. Nigel Digby, FCA** *1970;* Baker Tilly Tax and Advisory Services LLP, 25 Farringdon Street, LONDON, EC4A 4AB. See also Baker Tilly UK Audit LLP
WARE, Miss. Rachel Anne, BSc ACA *2003;* 65a Newstead Road, LONDON, SE12 0TB.
•**WARE, Mr. Robert, MA FCA** *1972;* (Member of Council 1993 - 1997), Via Diodoro Crono 20, 00125 ROME, ITALY.
WARE, Mrs. Rosemary Elizabeth, BA(Hons) ACA *2003;* with Deloitte LLP, 2 New Street Square, LONDON, EC4A 3BZ.
WARE, Mrs. Susan Jane Barford, BSc ACA *1989;* 12430 Calico Falls Lane, HOUSTON, TX 77041, UNITED STATES.
WAREHAM, Mr. Christopher John, FCA *1961;* Breidden, Greenfield Cottages, Four Crosses, LLANYMYNECH, POWYS, SY22 6RF. (Life Member)
WAREHAM, Mr. Kendrick James Calvin, BA ACA *1991;* 32 Elms Close, Little Wymondley, HITCHIN, HERTFORDSHIRE, SG4 7HP.
WAREHAM, Mr. Martin Richard, ACA *2002;* B-2-501 Li Hao Yuan, 55 Da Shi Qiao Hutong, Jiu Gulou Dajie, BEIJING 100009, CHINA.
WAREING, Mr. Barry, MSc ACA *1985;* Braewing Limited, 11 Sycamore Court, Penners Gardens, SURBITON, SURREY, KT6 6LG.
WAREING, Mr. Benjamin, BSc(Hons) ACA *2001;* Ernst & Young, P.O. Box 140, MANAMA, BAHRAIN.
WAREING, Mr. David Roy, BCom FCA *1979;* 200 Meadow Glen Lane, READING, PA 19607, UNITED STATES.
WAREING, Mr. Michael Peter, FCA *1977;* with KPMG LLP, 15 Canada Square, LONDON, E14 5GL.
WAREING, Mrs. Nicola Julie, BSc(Hons) ACA *2003;* 3 Westcott Court Parsonage Lane Westcott, DORKING, SURREY, RH4 3NL.
WAREING, Miss. Ruth Alice, ACA *2010;* Flat 4, 22 Gambier Terrace, LIVERPOOL, L1 7BL.
WAREING, Miss. Ruth Mary, BSc ACA *1980;* 94 White Lion St, LONDON, N1 9PF.
WARFIELD, Mr. John Edward Andrew, FCA *1971;* PO Box 97001, PETERVALE, 2151, SOUTH AFRICA.
•**WARFIELD, Mr. William Michael, FCA** *1982;* WMW Consultants, Bedford Heights, Manton Lane, BEDFORD, MK41 7PH.
WARFORD, Mr. Peter Frederick, BSc CertFMM ACA AMCT *2000;* ICAP Plc, 2 Broadgate, LONDON, EC2M 7UR.
WARGENT, Mrs. Belinda Ann, BA ACA *2000;* 105 West Street, Coggeshall, COLCHESTER, CO6 1NT.
WARGENT, Mr. Peter Stewart, BA(Hons) ACA *2004;* Pass the Post (612), Locked Bag 1, KEPERRA, QLD 4054, AUSTRALIA.
WARHAM, Mr. David Harold, FCA *1966;* Setzplatz 10, 83676 JACHENAU, GERMANY.
WARHURST, Mr. Brian, FCA *1962;* Leah & Warhurst, Lowfield House, 222 Wellington Road South, STOCKPORT, CHESHIRE, SK2 6RS.
WARHURST, Mr. Charles Thomas Winston, BA(Hons) ACA *2009;* 27A Tremlett Grove, LONDON, N19 5JY.
WARHURST, Mr. Haakon Justin, BA FCA *1990;* Lane 4 Management Group Limited, St Marks House, Station Road, BOURNE END, BUCKINGHAMSHIRE, SL8 5QF.
WARHURST, Mr. Martin David, BA ACA *2000;* Cestria Community Housing Association 1 Dunns, Bowes Offices Lambton Park, CHESTER LE STREET, COUNTY DURHAM, DH3 4AN.
WARHURST, Mr. Philip John, FCA *1970;* 37 Brown Edge Road, BUXTON, DERBYSHIRE, SK17 7AG.

WARHURST, Mrs. Sally Karen, BSc ACA *1989;* Kaplan Financial, Broadcasting House, 10 Havelock Road, SOUTHAMPTON, SO14 7FY.
•**WARIN, Mr. Jeffrey, BSc ACA** *1987;* Hewitt Warin Ltd, Harlow Enterprise Hub, Edinburgh Way, HARLOW, ESSEX, CM20 2NQ.
WARINER, Mr. John Michael, FCA *1960;* Saulfland, Glendene Avenue, East Horsley, LEATHERHEAD, KT24 5AY. (Life Member)
WARING, Miss. Amanda Jane, LLB ACA *1985;* Hazeley, Quarry Lane, Christleton, CHESTER, CH3 7AY.
WARING, Mr. Christopher Thomas, FCA *1983;* (Tax Fac), Mazars Unit 7-8, 2 New Fields Business Park Stinsford Road, POOLE, DORSET, BH17 0NF.
WARING, Mr. Ian David, BSc ACA *1982;* L P C Pharmaceuticals Ltd, 30 Chaul End Lane, LUTON, LU4 8EZ.
WARING, Mrs. Jacqueline, ACA *2008;* 18 Lovatt Close, Tilehurst, READING, RG31 5HG.
WARING, Mr. James, ACA *1991;* 11 Risedale Drive, Longridge, PRESTON, PR3 3SA.
WARING, Mr. James Robert, BA ACA *2010;* 16 Hawkhirst, WASHINGTON, TYNE AND WEAR, NE38 8SQ.
WARING, Miss. Joanna Marjorie, BA ACA *2003;* 16 Belfry Way, Edwalton, NOTTINGHAM, NG12 4FA.
WARING, Mr. Nicholas, BA(Hons) ACA *2003;* 27a, Battersea Rise, LONDON, SW11 1HG.
WARING, Mr. Nicholas Charles, BA FCA DChA *1996;* RAF Benevolent Fund, 12 Park Crescent, LONDON, W1B 1PH.
WARING, Mr. Paul George, BEng FCA *1985;* 33 High Street, Norley, FRODSHAM, WA6 8JD.
WARING, Mr. Richard Denton, FCA *1959;* 13 Moorlands Road, Skelton, YORK, YO30 1XZ. (Life Member)
WARING, Mr. Robert Bertram Collubell, FCA *1955;* Old Hall House, 10A Kneeton Road, East Bridgford, NOTTINGHAM, NG13 8PG. (Life Member)
WARING, Mr. Stephen Roy, BSc ACA *1992;* 100 Warwick Park, TUNBRIDGE WELLS, KENT, TN2 5EN.
WARING-JONES, Mrs. Sarah, BA ACA *2005;* with Grant Thornton UK LLP, Royal Liver Building, Pier Head, LIVERPOOL, L3 1PS.
WARING-MUNDY, Mr. Laurence Charles, ACA *1995;* 5 Apsley Manor Farm, Shendish, HEMEL HEMPSTEAD, HP3 0AA.
WARIRAH, Miss. Gladys Njeri, FCA *2000;* 31 Wantage Close, Maidenbower, CRAWLEY, WEST SUSSEX, RH10 7NU.
WARLAND, Mr. Edward Patrick, FCA *1962;* 68 Waxwell Lane, PINNER, HA5 3EU. (Life Member)
WARLOW, Mr. David Gordon, BEng ACA *1992;* 24 Holly Road, UTTOXETER, STAFFORDSHIRE, ST14 7NY.
WARLOW, Mr. David John, MBA BA ACA *1994;* 1 Waters Court, The Ridgeway, Bloxham, BANBURY, OX15 4FE.
WARLOW, Mrs. Jenny Wai Yee, BA(Hons) ACA *2003;* 27 Davenport Road, LONDON, SE6 2AY.
WARLOW, Mrs. Natalie, BA ACA *1996;* 1 Waters Court, The Ridgeway, Bloxham, BANBURY, OXFORDSHIRE, OX15 4FE.
WARMAN, Mrs. Alison Jane, BSc FCA *1975;* Brynawelon, Pen-y-Lan, COWBRIDGE, CF71 7RY.
WARMAN, Mr. Barrie Adrian, FCA *1969;* Broadfield House, Broadfield Crescent, FOLKESTONE, CT20 2PH.
WARMAN, Mr. Derek Graham, BSc FCA *1992;* 2 Glade Close, Long Ditton, SURBITON, KT6 5EA.
WARMAN, Ms. Helen Jean, BA ACA *1990;* 38 Weydon Hill Road, FARNHAM, SURREY, GU9 8NX.
WARMAN, Mr. Kenneth John, BA FCA *1975;* 109 Nightingale Lane, BROMLEY, BR1 2SG.
•**WARMAN, Mr. Mark, ACA FCCA** *2009;* Pinfields Limited, Meryll House, 57 Worcester Road, BROMSGROVE, WORCESTERSHIRE, B61 7DN.
WARMAN, Mr. Michael Frederick, ACA *2008;* with Arram Berlyn Gardner, 30 City Road, LONDON, EC1Y 2AB.
WARMAN, Mr. Neil, BA ACA *1999;* 5 Hereford Road, HARROGATE, NORTH YORKSHIRE, HG1 2NP.
WARMAN, Mr. Peter Charles, FCA *1959;* The Old Cottage, Priory Lane, Frensham, FARNHAM, GU10 3DW. (Life Member)
•**WARMAN, Mr. Richard Donald, FCA** *1974;* Richard D. Warman, Silver Birches, Heronsgate, RICKMANSWORTH, WD3 5DN.
WARMINGTON, Mr. Brian Laurence, BSc(Econ) FCA *1957;* 33 Sherfield Avenue, RICKMANSWORTH, WD3 1NN. (Life Member)
•**WARMINGTON, Mr. Peter, FCA** *1965;* Warmingtons Inc, Suite 6, 21B Cascades Crescent, Chase Valley, PIETERMARITZBURG, 3201 SOUTH AFRICA.
WARMINGTON, Mr. Ronald John, FCA *1971;* White Post, 9 Hillwood Grove, Hutton, BRENTWOOD, CM13 2PF.
•**WARN, Mr. Paul Edgar, LLB ACA** *2000;* Ernst & Young LLP, 1 More London Place, LONDON, SE1 2AF. See also Ernst & Young Europe LLP
WARNE, Mr. Christopher John, FCA *1969;* Little Knowle, Horn Lane, Woodmaricote, HENFIELD, BN5 9SA.
WARNE, Mr. Ian Christopher, BSc FCA *1977;* Coign Cottage, Gittisham, HONITON, DEVON, EX14 3AB. (Life Member)
WARNE, Mr. John Brian, FCA *1969;* 5 Hillway, Tranmere Park, Guiseley, LEEDS, LS20 8HU.
•**WARNE, Mr. Nicholas Charles, FCA ATII** *1980;* Cottons Accountants LLP, Regency House, 3 Albion Place, NORTHAMPTON, NN1 1UD.
WARNE, Mrs. Pauline Clare, BSc ACA *1989;* 133 Nile Street, NELSON 7010, NEW ZEALAND.
WARNE, Mr. Peter Stuart, BSc ACA *1997;* Flat 4, 7 Hornton Street, LONDON, W8 7NP.
WARNE, Mr. Robin James, BSc ACA *2002;* 2207 Fox Boro Lane, NAPERVILLE, IL 60564, UNITED STATES.
WARNE, Mrs. Sarah, BSc(Hons) ACA *2002;* 2207 Foxboro Lane, NAPERVILLE, IL 60564, UNITED STATES.
•**WARNE, Mr. Simon, BCom ACA** *1991;* (Tax Fac), Crowe Clark Whitehill LLP, 10 Palace Avenue, MAIDSTONE, KENT, ME15 6NF. See also Horwath Clark Whitehill LLP and Crowe Clark Whitehill
•**WARNEFORD, Mr. Brian Richard, FCA** *1973;* (Tax Fac), Warneford Gibbs, College House, 17 King Edwards Road, RUISLIP, HA4 7AE. See also Chapel Grange Associates Ltd
WARNER, Mr. Alan Tristram Nicholas, MA ACA *1979;* Duncan Lawrie Ltd, 1 Hobart Place, LONDON, SW1W 0HU.
WARNER, Mr. Andrew, ACA *2009;* 18 Fairmeadows Way, LOUGHBOROUGH, LEICESTERSHIRE, LE11 2QT.
WARNER, Mr. Andrew Peter Adair, ACA *2009;* 3 Overwater Close, HUNTINGDON, CAMBRIDGESHIRE, PE29 6GW.
WARNER, Mr. Andrew Simon, BSc ACA *1992;* Mitchell Hall, Old Gifford Road, HADDINGTON, EH41 4LB.
•**WARNER, Mrs. Anita, BSc ACA** *1993;* (Tax Fac), AWM Accountancy & Taxation Limited, Old Chambers, 93-94 West Street, FARNHAM, SURREY, GU9 7EB. See also Lanacre Management Services Limited
•**WARNER, Mr. Barry David, FCA** *1981;* Warners, 12-14 Greenhill Crescent, Watford Business Park, WATFORD, WD18 8JA.
WARNER, Mr. Barry Stuart, FCA *1973;* 5 The Chase, Great Totham, MALDON, ESSEX, CM9 8UU.
WARNER, Mrs. Charlotte Louise, BSc ACA *2004;* 37 Hardy Way, Stotfold, HITCHIN, HERTFORDSHIRE, SG5 4GL.
WARNER, Mr. Clive Howard, BSc FCA *1976;* 5 Hankins Lane, Mill Hill, LONDON, NW7 3AA.
WARNER, Mr. Colin, BSc ACA *2000;* FIPRA International Limited, Tenter House, 45 Moorfields, LONDON, EC2Y 9AE.
WARNER, Mr. Daren Lee, BA ACA FSI AMCT *1993;* C/O Standard Chartered Bank, Dubai International Financial Centre, Building 1 DIFC Gate Precinct, PO Box 999, DUBAI, UNITED ARAB EMIRATES.
WARNER, Mrs. Eleanor Jane, BDS ACA *1993;* 10757 Corte Crisalida, SAN DIEGO, CA 92127, UNITED STATES.
WARNER, Miss. Fiona Elizabeth Christine, BSc ACA *2003;* 169 Riverside Road, ST. ALBANS, HERTFORDSHIRE, AL1 1RZ.
WARNER, Mr. Graeme Raymond, BSc FCA *1983;* 1 Drovers Way, SANDBACH, CW11 1EL.
WARNER, Mr. Graham, FCA *1975;* 50 Townsend Lane, HARPENDEN, HERTFORDSHIRE, AL5 2QS.
WARNER, Mr. Graham Robert, ACA *1986;* M D J Services Ltd, Map House, 34-36 St. Leonards Road, EASTBOURNE, EAST SUSSEX, BN21 3UT.
WARNER, Mr. Harry Gilliat, FCA *1953;* Three Roods, New Barns Road, Arnside, CARNFORTH, LANCASHIRE, LA5 0BB. (Life Member)
WARNER, Mr. Ian, BA ACA *1999;* 34 Victoria Crescent, Horsforth, LEEDS, LS18 4PR.
WARNER, Mr. Ian Christopher, BSc ACA MCT *1982;* Monksgrove, Pilgrims Way, Compton, GUILDFORD, SURREY, GU3 1DZ.
•**WARNER, Mr. Ian Robert, FCA** *1977;* 20 Limes Avenue, LONDON, N12 8QN.
WARNER, Mr. James, FCA *1971;* 12 Frampton Mews, The Reddings, CHELTENHAM, GLOUCESTERSHIRE, GL51 6UG.
WARNER, Mr. James Michael, FCA *1966;* 122 Hydes Road, WEDNESBURY, WEST MIDLANDS, WS10 0DH.
WARNER, Mrs. Jane Adele, BSc FCA *1989;* Baronsmead Consulting LTD, 19 Lime Grove, LONDON, W12 8EE.
•**WARNER, Mr. John, LLB FCA CF** *1980;* (Tax Fac), Barber Harrison & Platt, 2 Rutland Park, SHEFFIELD, S10 2PD.
•**WARNER, Mr. John Douglas, FCA** *1975;* Friend-James Ltd, 169 Preston Road, BRIGHTON, EAST SUSSEX, BN1 6AG.
WARNER, Mr. John Michael, BSc ACA *1979;* 12 Primula Close, Millwood Park, NORTHAMPTON, NN3 3QD.
WARNER, Mr. Jonathan Paul, ACA *2006;* Flat 5 Vine Tree Court, St. Peters Close Mill End, RICKMANSWORTH, HERTFORDSHIRE, WD3 8QY.
•**WARNER, Mrs. Linda Ann, FCA CTA** *1989;* (Tax Fac), Roffe Swayne, Ashcombe Court, Woolsack Way, GODALMING, GU7 1LQ.
WARNER, Mrs. Lisa Marie, BA ACA *1998;* Braemar Yerburgh Road Mellor, BLACKBURN, BB2 7JJ.
WARNER, Mr. Mark, BA ACA *1994;* PricewaterhouseCoopers, White Square Business Center, 125047 MOSCOW, RUSSIAN FEDERATION.
WARNER, Mr. Michael, BA ACA *1993;* Tennant Services Authority, 4th Floor, 1 Piccadilly Gardens, MANCHESTER, M1 1RG.
•**WARNER, Mr. Michael John Pelham, FCA** *1970;* Michael Warner & Company, 37 Southgate Street, WINCHESTER, HAMPSHIRE, SO23 9EH.
WARNER, Mr. Michael Martin James, BA FCA *1987;* Stable Cottage Whiteway Lane, Rodmell, LEWES, EAST SUSSEX, BN7 3EX.
WARNER, Mr. Neil William, BA FCA MCT *1977;* Spring Hill, Heath Rise, CAMBERLEY, SURREY, GU15 2ER.
WARNER, Mr. Nicholas, BSc ACA *2006;* Flat 36 The Pinnacle, Kings Road, READING, RG1 4LY.
•**WARNER, Mr. Nicholas Giles, BEng ACA** *1997;* Deloitte LLP, Stonecutter Court, 1 Stonecutter Street, LONDON, EC4A 4TR. See also Deloitte & Touche LLP
WARNER, Mr. Paul Thomas, MBA BA FCA *1983;* 23 Clovelly Way, Devon Park, BEDFORD, MK40 3BJ.
WARNER, Mr. Philip John, BSc ACA *1989;* 8 The Woodlands, CRADLEY HEATH, B64 7JY.
•**WARNER, Mr. Philip Samuel, FCA** *1976;* Warner & Co, Lowe House, 55 Townsend Street, CHELTENHAM, GL51 9HA.
WARNER, Mr. Robert Edward, ACA *1997;* 17 Cavalry Close, MELTON MOWBRAY, LEICESTERSHIRE, LE13 0SZ.
•**WARNER, Mr. Robert Henry, ACA** *1985;* Robert Warner, 14 Hanborough Business Park, Long Hanborough, WITNEY, OXFORDSHIRE, OX29 8LH.
WARNER, Mr. Robert James, BEng ACA *1993;* 4 Uplowman Road, TIVERTON, DEVON, EX16 4LU.
WARNER, Mr. Russell John, MBA BA FCA *1993;* Westend Farm, Grove Lane, Westend, STONEHOUSE, GLOUCESTERSHIRE, GL10 3SJ.
WARNER, Mr. Stephen Bernard, ACA *1980;* 21 Dysart Avenue, PORTSMOUTH, PO6 2LY.
WARNER, Mr. Stuart Hamilton, BSc ACA *1997;* 5 Dollis Park, LONDON, N3 1HJ.
•**WARNER, Mr. Stuart Thomas, MA ACA** *1981;* Preseli Management Accounting, Ranelagh, Precelly Crescent, GOODWICK, DYFED, SA64 0HF.
WARNER, Mr. Terence Peter, ACA *1979;* The Met Office, Fitzroy Road, EXETER, DEVON, EX1 3PB.
WARNER, Mr. Timothy John, ACA *1981;* Fawley, Mare Hill Common, PULBOROUGH, RH20 2DX.
WARNER, Mr. Timothy Laurence, BSc ACA *1996;* 58 Lime Grove, NEW MALDEN, KT3 3TR.
WARNER, Mr. Trevor Arthur, BA FCA *1991;* 46 Pepys Road, LONDON, SW20 8PF.
WARNER-SMITH, Mr. Anthony, FCA *1965;* 21 Water Street, STAMFORD, LINCOLNSHIRE, PE9 2NJ.
WARNES, Mr. Brian Charles John, MA FCA *1965;* Business Dynamics Ltd, The Coach House, 50A Blackheath Park, LONDON, SE3 9SJ.
WARNES, Miss. Caroline, BSocSc ACA *2002;* Aduchtstr. 7, 50668 COLOGNE, GERMANY.
WARNES, Miss. Elizabeth Jane, BSc ACA *1992;* White Lodge, Church Lane, Twyford, WINCHESTER, HAMPSHIRE, SO21 1NT.
WARNES, Mr. Garth Terence Jon, ACA *1992;* Bar Battu, 48 Gresham Street, LONDON, EC2V 7AY.
WARNES, Mr. Howard, BA FCA *1984;* 15 St. Stephens Avenue, ST. ALBANS, HERTFORDSHIRE, AL3 4AA.
•**WARNES, Mr. Michael Reginald, FCA** *1974;* Michael Warnes, 2a High Haden Road, CRADLEY HEATH, WEST MIDLANDS, B64 7PE.
WARNES, Mr. Norman, FCA *1949;* 5 Manor Road, Sutton, PETERBOROUGH, PE5 7XG. (Life Member)
WARNES, Mr. Peter Edward, ACA *2009;* 12 Orchard Way, Chellaston, DERBY, DE73 6RE.
WARNES, Mr. Robert John, FCA *1976;* 6 Manor Lane Terrace, Lee, LONDON, SE13 5QL.
WARNETT, Mr. John Irving, FCA *1975;* Longacre, Walton Park, Walton, WAKEFIELD, WF2 6PW.
WARNOCK, Mr. Anthony, BA FCA *1989;* County Offices, Lincolnshire County Council Education Department, County Offices Newland, LINCOLN, LN1 1YQ.
WARNOCK, Mr. William Alan Keith, BA LLB FCA *1971;* National University of Ireland, Vice President's Office, GALWAY, COUNTY GALWAY, IRELAND.
WARNOCK-HORN, Mr. Kerry William, BA ACA *1983;* 4 Woodland Cottages, Highsted VAlley, Rodmersham, SITTINGBOURNE, ME9 0AD.
WARNSBY, Mr. Grant Darren, BA(Hons) ACA *2002;* British Petroleum Co Plc, 20 Canada Square, LONDON, E14 5NJ.
WARNSBY, Ms. Sarah Jane, ACA *1995;* Browne Jacobson LLP, 44 Castle Gate, NOTTINGHAM, NG1 7BJ.
WARR, Mrs. Anne Rosemary, BA FCA ATII *1978;* 216 Whyke Road, CHICHESTER, PO19 7AQ.
WARR, Mrs. Carly Louise, BSc ACA *2007;* 21 Dane Road, LONDON, W13 9AQ.
WARR, Mr. David John, FCA *1977;* Fortis Reads Guernsey, PO Box 119, Martello Court, St Peter Port, GUERNSEY, GY1 3HB.
WARR, Mr. John William, FCA *1966;* 66 South Road, Erdington, BIRMINGHAM, B23 6EE. (Life Member)
WARR, Mr. Steven Mark, MA ACA *1987;* Allied Irish Bank (Gb), 4 Tenterden Street, LONDON, W1S 1TE.
•**WARR, Mr. Timothy Vaughan, BSc ACA** *1979;* (Tax Fac), Warr & Co, Mynshull House, 78 Churchgate, STOCKPORT, SK1 1YJ. See also Warr & Co Limited
•**WARRAN, Mr. Stephen John, BSc FCA** *1976;* Turner Warran Accounting Ltd, 101 Ferriby High Road, NORTH FERRIBY, NORTH HUMBERSIDE, HU14 3LA. See also Turner Warran (Scunthorpe) Limited
WARRAN-SMITH, Mr. Nicholas Edgar, BA FCA *1976;* Combe House, Wadhurst Park, WADHURST, TN5 6NT.
WARRELL, Mr. Dan, BSc ACA *2011;* 7 Clayhill Road, Burghfield Common, READING, RG7 3HD.
WARREN, Mr. Adrian John, FCA *1983;* Highridge, 46A Hillcrest Road, CAMBERLEY, GU15 1LG.
WARREN, Mr. Alan Trueman, FCA *1967;* 24 Park Lane, Sutton Bonington, LOUGHBOROUGH, LEICESTERSHIRE, LE12 5NH.
WARREN, Mr. Alex Matthew, BSc ACA *2006;* 23 Chard Road, CLEVEDON, BS21 6LW.
WARREN, Mr. Alexander Matthew, LLB ACA *2001;* 13 Jubilee Lane, Wrecclesham, FARNHAM, GU10 4SZ.
WARREN, Mrs. Alexandra, BA ACA *2003;* with Deloitte LLP, Abbots House, Abbey Street, READING, RG1 3BD.
•**WARREN, Mr. Andrew James, BSc FCA** *1992;* McBrides Accountants LLP, Nexus House, 2 Cray Road, SIDCUP, KENT, DA14 5DA. See also McBrides Corporate Finance Limited
WARREN, Mr. Andrew John, BA ACA *1991;* 21 Sherwood Close, Fetcham, LEATHERHEAD, SURREY, KT22 9QT.
•**WARREN, Mr. Andrew Michael, BCom FCA** *1992;* Marshall Keen Limited, Pinewood, Crockford Lane, Chineham, BASINGSTOKE, HAMPSHIRE RG24 8AL.
WARREN, Mr. Andrew Paul, BA ACA *2005;* Percy Westhead & Co, Gregs Buildings, 1 Booth Street, MANCHESTER, M2 4AD.
WARREN, Mr. Andrew Richard, FCA *1981;* 109 Bradenstoke, CHIPPENHAM, WILTSHIRE, SN15 4ES.
WARREN, Mrs. Angela Pui-Yee, BA ACA *2001;* 43 Argyle Road, SEVENOAKS, TN13 1HJ.
WARREN, Mrs. Annette, BA ACA *1984;* with James Cowper LLP, Mill House, Overbridge Square, Hambridge Lane, NEWBURY, BERKSHIRE RG14 5UX.
WARREN, Mr. Anthony, BA FCA *1977;* Flat 1 Larch Court, Balmore Park Caversham, READING, RG4 8PY.
•**WARREN, Mr. Anthony Brian, FCA ATT CTA** *1963;* (Tax Fac), Howell Wade, 55 Church Road, Wimbledon Village, LONDON, SW19 5DQ.

WARREN, Mr. Anthony John, BCom FCA *1996;* The Paragon Group Of Companies, St Catherines Court, Herbert Road, SOLIHULL, B91 3QE.
WARREN, Mr. Arthur Frederick, FCA *1945;* Eddystone, Carlidnack Road, Mawnan Smith, FALMOUTH, TR11 5HA. (Life Member)
WARREN, Mr. Barry Frank, FCA *1969;* Coombe International Ltd, 4th floor, A M P House, Dingwall Road, CROYDON, CR9 2AU.
•WARREN, Mr. Benjamin Jack, BA(Hons) ACA *2002;* (Tax Fac), Hilton Consulting Limited, 119 The Hub, 300 Kensal Road, LONDON, W10 5BE. See also Hilton Holdings (UK) Limited
WARREN, Mr. Brian Stuart, BEng ACA *1994;* 49 West Hill Road, RYDE, PO33 1LG.
•WARREN, Mrs. Carmel Elizabeth, BA ACA *1990;* Marshall Keen Limited, Pinewood, Crockford Lane, Chineham, BASINGSTOKE, HAMPSHIRE RG24 8AL.
WARREN, Mr. Christopher, ACA *2002;* 29 Ropers Avenue, LONDON, E4 9EG.
•WARREN, Mr. Christopher Neil, BA ACA *1990;* Deloitte LLP, Athene Place, 66 Shoe Lane, LONDON, EC4A 3BQ. See also Deloitte & Touche LLP
WARREN, Mrs. Claire Louise, BA ACA *1999;* 22 Woodlands Ride, ASCOT, SL5 9HN.
•WARREN, Mr. Colin, FCA *1971;* Colin Warren Accountants Limited, The Warren, 30 Tewkesbury Close, Poynton, STOCKPORT, CHESHIRE SK12 1QJ.
WARREN, Mr. Colin Peter, FCA *1978;* Tye House, The Tye, East Hanningfield, CHELMSFORD, CM3 8AE.
•WARREN, Mr. Colin Rex, FCA *1984;* Warren & Co (Partnership), Meadhaven, Church Lane, Flax Bourton, BRISTOL, BS48 3QF. See also Warren & Co Business Consultancy Ltd and Warren & Co
WARREN, Mr. David, BSc FCA *1974;* 1269 3rd Street, WEST VANCOUVER V7S 1H8, BC, CANADA.
WARREN, Mr. David Alisdair, BSc ACA *1984;* Padre Burgos Castle Resort, Tangkaan, PADRE BURGOS 6602, PHILIPPINES.
•WARREN, Mr. David Edgar, FCA *1966;* (Tax Fac), David Warren & Co Limited, 32 Phipps Hatch Lane, ENFIELD, MIDDLESEX, EN2 0HN.
•WARREN, Mr. David Keith, BA ACA *1996;* Watson Buckle LLP, York House, Cottingley Business Park, BRADFORD, BD16 1PE.
WARREN, Mr. David Pierce, FCA *1971;* 7 Blenheim Rd, ST. ALBANS, AL1 4NS.
WARREN, Mr. David William, BSc ACA *1995;* 11A Jalan Lateh, SINGAPORE 359161, SINGAPORE.
WARREN, Mr. Derek, ACA *2009;* 809 Bradshaw Road, Turton, BOLTON, BL7 0HR.
•WARREN, Mr. Derek, FCA *1970;* (Tax Fac), CWW Limited, 149-151 Mortimer Street, HERNE BAY, KENT, CT6 5HA. See also Michael Curd & Co Limited
WARREN, Mr. Deryck Hugh, FCA *1973;* 16 Sienna Bay SW, CALGARY T3H 2C8, AB, CANADA.
WARREN, Mr. Eric Anthony, BA FCA *1982;* Port of Liverpool Building, Rathbone Investment Management Port of Liverpool Building, Pier Head, LIVERPOOL, L3 1NW.
WARREN, Miss. Evelyn Lydia, ACA *2008;* Flat 20 Park Lodge, 74 Wimbledon Park Road, LONDON, SW18 5SH.
WARREN, Mr. Frank, FCA *1954;* 673 Devonshire Road, BLACKPOOL, FY2 0AE. (Life Member)
WARREN, Mr. Geoffrey, FCA *1961;* 340 Filey Road, SCARBOROUGH, NORTH YORKSHIRE, YO11 3JQ. (Life Member)
WARREN, Mr. George Francis, BA FCA *1973;* 78 High Street, KIDLINGTON, OX5 2DR. (Life Member)
WARREN, Mrs. Gillian Evelyn Florence, BSc FCA *1985;* (Tax Fac), 40 Backwell Hill Road, Backwell, BRISTOL, BS48 3PL.
WARREN, Mr. Ian Gareth, BSc(Hons) ACA *2002;* 4 Pemberton Place, LONDON, E8 3RF.
WARREN, Mr. Jack, ACA *2008;* 8 Methuen Park, LONDON, N10 2JS.
WARREN, Mr. James Michael, ACA *2008;* 87 Cromwell Avenue, BILLERICAY, ESSEX, CM12 0AG.
WARREN, Mr. Jeremy Paul, BA ACA *1990;* 5 Brookfield, Penistone Road, Kirkburton, HUDDERSFIELD, HD8 0PE.
WARREN, Ms. Jill Anne, BSc ACA DChA *2003;* 10b, 10 Horsell Road, LONDON, N5 1XR.
WARREN, Mr. John, FCA *1975;* Flat 9 Hadleigh Court, 245 Willesden Lane, LONDON, NW2 5RY.
WARREN, Mr. John Anthony, BSc FCA *1977;* 45 Waldegrave Park, Strawberry Hill, TWICKENHAM, TW1 4TJ.
WARREN, Mr. John Richard Edward, FCA *1962;* 4 North Way, PINNER, MIDDLESEX, HA5 3NY.
•WARREN, Mr. John Spencer, BSc FCA *1986;* Price Bailey LLP, Causeway House, 1 Dane Street, BISHOP'S STORTFORD, HERTFORDSHIRE, CM23 3BT. See also Price Bailey Private Client LLP
WARREN, Mr. John William, FCA *1966;* 148 Salmons Lane, CATERHAM, CR3 0HA.
WARREN, Ms. Katherine Emily, MA ACA *2007;* Sanna, Droghadfayle Park, Port Erin, ISLE OF MAN, IM9 6EP.
WARREN, Mr. Lee, ACA *2008;* 39 June Road, STOKE-ON-TRENT, ST4 3RL.
WARREN, Mrs. Lesley Jane, BSc ACA CTA *1991;* 4 Ivy Grove, Rolleston Road, Horninglow, BURTON-ON-TRENT, DE13 0JU.
WARREN, Mr. Leslie James Valentine, FCA *1959;* Rua Francisco Leal 149, Itanhanga Barra Da Tijuca, 22641-180 RIO DE JANEIRO, BRAZIL. (Life Member)
•WARREN, Mrs. Linda Janet, FCA CTA *1988;* Warren & Co (Partnership), Meadhaven, Church Lane, Flax Bourton, BRISTOL, BS48 3QF. See also Warren & Co Business Consultancy Ltd and Warren & Co
WARREN, Miss. Lisa Catherine, BA ACA *1997;* Flat 39 Holme Court 158 Twickenham Road, ISLEWORTH, MIDDLESEX, TW7 7DL.
WARREN, Mrs. Marguerite Jeanette, BSc ACA *1989;* with Ernst & Young LLP, 1 More London Place, LONDON, SE1 2AF.
WARREN, Mr. Mark Lyell, BA FCA *1969;* Divona Park II, Adonide, 268 Boulevard des Epinettes, 01220 DIVONNE-LES-BAINS, FRANCE.
WARREN, Mr. Martin, FCA *1968;* 69 Paines Lane, PINNER, HA5 3BX. (Life Member)
WARREN, Mr. Martin John, BSc FCA *1979;* 233 Lake Road West, Roath Park, CARDIFF, CF23 5QY.
•WARREN, Mr. Martyn Jeffrey Gomer, FCA *1971;* (Tax Fac), A.W.G.Warren & Son, 74 Wyndham Crescent, CARDIFF, CF11 9EF.
WARREN, Mr. Michael, BSc ACA *1990;* 42 Blunts Wood Road, HAYWARDS HEATH, WEST SUSSEX, RH16 1NB.
WARREN, Mr. Michael, ACA *2008;* 42 Isleham Road, Fordham, ELY, CAMBRIDGESHIRE, CB7 5NN.
WARREN, Mr. Neil, ACA *2008;* 105 Beecham Road, READING, RG30 2RB.
WARREN, Mr. Neil Andrew, BSc FCA *1985;* Trading Standards Institute 1 Sylvan Court, Sylvan Way Southfields Business Park, BASILDON, SS15 6TH.
WARREN, Mr. Nicholas, ACA *2010;* Lammtarra, 8a Eaton Park, COBHAM, KT11 2JE.
WARREN, Mr. Nicholas Paul, BSc FCA *1978;* P O BOX HM 3362, HAMILTON HM PX, BERMUDA.
•WARREN, Mr. Nigel Keith, BA FCA *1985;* Bishop Fleming, 50 The Terrace, TORQUAY, TQ1 1DD.
WARREN, Mr. Norman Henry, FCA *1950;* 44 St.Georges Road, FELIXSTOWE, IP11 9PN. (Life Member)
WARREN, Mr. Paul, BA ACA *1999;* Apex Corporate Finance, 29 Harley Street, LONDON, W1G 9QR.
•WARREN, Mr. Paul Andrew, FCA *1979;* Pierce C A Ltd, Mentor House, Ainsworth Street, BLACKBURN, BB1 6AY. See also Pierce Group Limited
WARREN, Mr. Paul Patrick, FCA *1987;* Lingfield Park Ltd, Racecourse Road, LINGFIELD, RH7 6PQ.
WARREN, The Revd. Peter, FCA *1965;* 5 Bridge Farm, Pollington, GOOLE, NORTH HUMBERSIDE, DN14 0BF.
•WARREN, Mr. Peter John, FCA *1971;* Moore Stephens (South) LLP, 9 St. Johns Place, NEWPORT, ISLE OF WIGHT, PO30 1LH. See also Peter Waren Consultancy Limited
WARREN, Mrs. Philippa Jane, BA ACA *1989;* Meadow House, Bone Mill Lane, Enbourne, NEWBURY, RG20 0EX.
•WARREN, Mrs. Philippa Jane, BA ACA *1989;* Pippa Warren, 7 Dane Close, Winsley, BRADFORD-ON-AVON, BA15 2NA.
WARREN, Mr. Rafe Anthony, LLB ACA *1985;* Rose Cottage Crossways Road, Grayshott, HINDHEAD, GU26 6HD.
WARREN, Mr. Richard Harold, FCA *1972;* 24 Thornbury Drive, Uphill, WESTON-SUPER-MARE, BS23 4YH.
WARREN, Mr. Richard John, BSc FCA AMCT *1992;* Lloyds TSB, 10 Gresham Street, LONDON, EC2V 7AE.
WARREN, Mr. Richard Julian, ACA *2009;* First Floor Flat, 195 Upper Richmond Road, LONDON, SW15 6SG.
WARREN, Mr. Richard Mark, BA(Hons) ACA *2004;* 22 Briar Edge, NEWCASTLE UPON TYNE, NE12 7JN.
WARREN, Mr. Roger Schofield, FCA *1968;* The Old Chapel, Skirmett, HENLEY-ON-THAMES, OXFORDSHIRE, RG9 6TD.
•WARREN, Mr. Roy Anthony, MA FCA *1970;* Warren Clare, 5-6 George Street, ST. ALBANS, HERTFORDSHIRE, AL3 4ER.
WARREN, Mr. Stephen John, MA FCA *1971;* Beaconleigh, 257 Elmers Green Lane, Dalton, WIGAN, LANCASHIRE, WN8 7SH.
WARREN, Mr. Stephen Roderick, ACA CPFA *2011;* Flat 5, Gallery House, Copers Cope Road, BECKENHAM, KENT, BR3 1DQ.
WARREN, Mrs. Susan Clare, BA ACA *1996;* Figtree, Back Lane, Beenham, READING, RG7 5NG.
•WARREN, Mrs. Susan Elizabeth, MA(Hons) ACA *2001;* Hall Warren, 23 Braehead Road, EDINBURGH, EH4 6BN.
WARREN, Miss. Tamsin Tracy Lyn, BSc ACA *2004;* 41 Sanderson Villas, GATESHEAD, TYNE AND WEAR, NE8 3BU.
•WARREN, Miss. Theresa-Anne, FCA *2000;* G P Financial Management Limited, 8-9 The Old Yard, Lodge Farm Business Centre, Wolverton Road, Castlethorpe, MILTON KEYNES MK19 7ES.
WARREN, Mr. Timothy, MSc BSc ACA CFA *2011;* Flat 10, 73 Garnet Street, LONDON, E1W 3QS.
WARREN, Mr. Timothy Mark, MBA BSc ACA *1994;* 5 Rue Crevaux, 75116 PARIS, FRANCE.
WARREN, Mr. Tony, FCA *1968;* The Warren, Tyshute Lane, Polgooth, ST AUSTELL, CORNWALL, PL26 7BX.
WARREN, Mr. Trevor Julian, BSc ACA *1982;* 57 Waterman Way, LONDON, E1W 2QW.
WARREN, Mrs. Victoria Louise, BA ACA *1993;* Pestalozzistrasse 34, 8032 ZURICH, SWITZERLAND.
WARRENDER, The Hon. Anthony Michael, MA FCA *1978;* Warrender Associates Inc, P.O.Box 1431, MIDDLEBURG, VA 20118, UNITED STATES.
WARRENDER, Mr. Robin, FCA *1969;* Woodlands, Fiery Lane, Uley, DURSLEY, GL11 5DA.
WARRENER, Mr. Adrian Michael, FCA *1966;* Tilney, Green Cross Lane, Churt, FARNHAM, GU10 2NE.
WARRENER, Mr. Peter William George, FCA *1980;* Flat 63, Highlands Heath, Portsmouth Road, LONDON, SW15 3TX.
WARRENER, Mr. Stephen George, BA ACA *1994;* 18 Royal Gardens, Davenham, NORTHWICH, CW9 8HB.
WARRIAH, Mr. Mahmoud Hamid, BSc ACA *1994;* 47 Faraday Road, LONDON, SW19 8PE.
WARRICK, Mr. Andrew, ACA *2000;* 1 Ridgeway Road, ISLEWORTH, MIDDLESEX, TW7 5LB.
WARRICK, Mr. Jonathan Richard Newell, ACA *2007;* Flat 9, 37 Lexham Gardens, LONDON, W8 5JR.
WARRICK, Mr. Peter Christopher, FCA ATII *1967;* Old Stables, Chapel Lane, Osmington, WEYMOUTH, DT3 6ET. (Life Member)
WARRICKER, Mr. Christopher Brian, FCA *1983;* Katjeslaan 2, 3090 OVERIJSE, BELGIUM.
•WARRILOW, Mr. Andrew Peter, FCA CF *1991;* Wychbury Greaves LLP, Towers Point, Towers Business Park, Wheelhouse Road, RUGELEY, STAFFORDSHIRE WS15 1UN.
WARRILOW, Mr. Colin William, FCA *1963;* 1 Bluebird Way, Bricket Wood, ST. ALBANS, HERTFORDSHIRE, AL2 3UH.
WARRILOW, Mr. David Andrew, BA ACA *1996;* Shell International Ltd, Shell Centre, LONDON, SE1 7NA.
WARRILOW, Mr. Matthew, BSc ACA *2005;* 19 Foxhill, WETHERBY, LS22 6PS.
WARRINER, Mr. Benjamin Charles George, BSc ACA *2005;* Flat 33, Avondale Court, Churchfields, LONDON, E18 2RD.
WARRINER, Mr. Dean, ACA *2007;* 92 Langham Drive, RAYLEIGH, SS6 9TA.
WARRINER, Mr. Geoffrey Allan, ACA *1981;* 20 Burne-Jones Drive, SANDHURST, BERKSHIRE, GU47 0FS.
WARRINER, Mr. Lawrence Edward, BA ACA *1986;* 5 Parkwood Way, Roundhay, LEEDS, LS8 1JP.
WARRINER, Mr. Martin Gordon, FCA *1965;* Far View, Far Lane, Hepworth, HUDDERSFIELD, HD9 1TL. (Life Member)
WARRINER, Mr. Paul Michael, FCA *1968;* The Old Vicarage, Little Ouseburn, YORK, YO26 9TD.
WARRINER, Mr. Robert John, FCA *1969;* Old Rectory, Down Hatherley, GLOUCESTER, GL2 9QB.
•WARRINER, Mr. Stuart Neil, MA ACA *1990;* PricewaterhouseCoopers LLP, Benson House, 33 Wellington Street, LEEDS, LS1 4JP. See also PricewaterhouseCoopers
•WARRINGTON, Mrs. Caroline Michelle, BA ACA *1990;* Pennywise Accounting Limited, Dickhurst House, Rodgate Lane, HASLEMERE, SURREY, GU27 2EW.
•WARRINGTON, Mr. Guy Rodney, FCA *1982;* KPMG LLP, 15 Canada Square, LONDON, E14 5GL. See also KPMG Europe LLP
WARRINGTON, Miss. Helen Jane, BSc ACA *2004;* 1/57 Beatrice Terrace, ASCOT, QLD 4007, AUSTRALIA.
WARRINGTON, Ms. Helena Anne, ACA *2009;* C6 101 Caledonian Road, St Albans, CHRISTCHURCH 8014, NEW ZEALAND.
•WARRINGTON, Miss. Katharine, BSocSc ACA *1999;* with PricewaterhouseCoopers LLP, Donington Court, Pegasus Business Park, Castle Donington, DERBY, DE74 2UZ.
WARRINGTON, Mr. Niki James, ACA *2008;* 33 Sunnyfield Rise, Bursledon, SOUTHAMPTON, SO31 8FA.
WARRINGTON, Mr. Peter Edward, FCA *1953;* 21 Kepstorn Road, LEEDS, LS16 5HT. (Life Member)
•WARRINGTON, Mr. Richard Garsed, MA FCA *1964;* Lane Head House, Shepley, HUDDERSFIELD, HD8 8BW.
WARRINGTON, Mr. Robert Matthew, BSc FCA *1996;* 12 Abbott Clough Avenue, Knuzden, BLACKBURN, LANCASHIRE, BB1 3LP.
•WARRINGTON, Mrs. Sharon Barbara, BSc ACA *1986;* with Harris Bassett Limited, 5 New Mill Court, Phoenix Way, Enterprise Park, SWANSEA, SA7 9FG.
WARRY, Mr. John Lyndell, BSc FCA *1968;* Le Petit Clos Du Rey, La Rue Du Champ Du Rey, St. Martin, JERSEY, JE3 6DE.
WARRY, Mr. Marcus Timothy George, BA(Hons) ACA *2011;* 62 Amesbury Avenue, Streatham Hill, LONDON, SW2 3AA.
WARSOP, Mr. David, FCA *1969;* 22 The Stables, LECHLADE, GLOUCESTERSHIRE, GL7 3FE. (Life Member)
•WARSOP, Mr. Jonathan Philip, ACA FCCA *2007;* (Tax Fac), UHY Hacker Young, 22 The Ropewalk, NOTTINGHAM, NG1 5DT. See also UHY Hacker Young LLP
•WARWICK, Mr. Alan Harold, BSc FCA *1977;* (Tax Fac), Warwick Durham & Co., Senator House, 2 Graham Road, Hendon Central, LONDON, NW4 3HJ.
•ⒹWARWICK, Mr. Daryl, BA FCA *1999;* Armstrong Watson, Fairview House, Victoria Place, CARLISLE, CA1 1HP.
WARWICK, Mr. Edward John Roger, MEng ACA *2002;* 9 Parkside, Marcham, ABINGDON, OXFORDSHIRE, OX13 6NN.
WARWICK, Mrs. Elizabeth France, FCA *1974;* Tanglyn, Gorse Way, Hartley, LONGFIELD, DA3 8AE.
WARWICK, Mrs. Elizabeth Mary, BSc ACA *1985;* Ranyard Memorial Charitable Trust, 2b Brandram Road, LONDON, SE13 5EA.
WARWICK, Mr. Ian Peter, BSc ACA *1980;* 29 Hallam Grange Rise, SHEFFIELD, S10 4BE.
•WARWICK, Mr. Ian Stanley, ACA FCCA *2010;* M J Bushell Ltd, 8 High Street, BRENTWOOD, ESSEX, CM14 4AB.
WARWICK, Mr. James Leander, BA ACA *1996;* 3 Long Acre, SHEPTON MALLET, SOMERSET, BA4 4DE.
•WARWICK, Miss. Jane-Marie, BSc ACA *2005;* Ellis Dennis Warwick LLP, 59 Berks Hill, Chorleywood, RICKMANSWORTH, HERTFORDSHIRE, WD3 5AJ.
WARWICK, Mrs. Janet Amanda, MA ACA *1991;* 1 Elrington Road, Monkhams Grove, WOODFORD GREEN, IG8 0BW.
•WARWICK, Mr. John Arthur, FCA *1965;* John Warwick & Co., Flat 308 Peninsula Apartments, 4 Praed Street, Paddington, LONDON, W2 1JE.
•WARWICK, Mr. John Frederick, FCA *1968;* 22 Cornwall Road, SUTTON, SM2 6DT.
WARWICK, Mr. John Stephen, ACA *1984;* 11 Chase Hill, Geddington, KETTERING, NN14 1AG.
WARWICK, Mr. Keir William, BA(Hons) ACA *2010;* 87 Four Chimneys Crescent, Hampton Vale, PETERBOROUGH, PE7 8JF.
WARWICK, Mrs. Melanie, ACA *2003;* 2 White House, Walton, BRAMPTON, CUMBRIA, CA8 2DJ.
•WARWICK, Mr. Michael Timothy, FCA CTA *1980;* Chaimel Limited, 55 Longford Road, Bradway, SHEFFIELD, S17 4LP.
•WARWICK, Mr. Richard Austen, FCA *1982;* Langdowns DFK Limited, Fleming Court, Leigh Road, EASTLEIGH, HAMPSHIRE, SO50 9PD.
WARWICK, Miss. Sarah Jane, BSc(Hons) ACA *2003;* The Lodge Bourton Hall, Bourton, RUGBY, CV23 9QZ.
WARWICK, Mr. Steven Richard, BSc ACA *1993;* 1 Elrington Road, WOODFORD GREEN, ESSEX, IG8 0BW.
WARWICK, Mrs. Tina Elizabeth, ACA *1980;* 55 Longford Road, Bradway, SHEFFIELD, S17 4LP.
WARWICK JAMES, Mr. Nicholas Ridley, BA FCA *1962;* PO Box 499, EDGECLIFF, NSW 2027, AUSTRALIA.
WASANI, Mr. Shailen Shirish, BSc ACA *1985;* William Hill Organisation Ltd, Greenside House, 50 Station Road, Wood Green, LONDON, N22 7TP.

WASDELL, Mr. Arthur John, FCA *1940;* 11 Cricket Field Court, Cricket Field Lane, BUDLEIGH SALTERTON, EX9 6JB. (Life Member)
WASDELL, Mr. Donald Charles, FCA *1958;* Rookery House, Rookery Lane, Ettington, STRATFORD-UPON-AVON, WARWICKSHIRE, CV37 7TN. (Life Member)
•**WASDEN, Mrs. Jane Anita, BSc FCA** *1985;* (Tax Fac), Jane Wasden Limited, 77a South Hill Road, Thorpe St Andrew, NORWICH, NR7 0LR.
WASDEN, Mr. Mark, BA ACA *1986;* Smurfit Sheetfeeding, Fishergate, NORWICH, NR3 1SJ.
WASEEM, Mr. Muhammad Harris, BSc ACA *2006;* 9 Bishops Close, HATFIELD, HERTFORDSHIRE, AL10 9PW.
WASH, Mrs. Carol Marion, BSc ACA *1993;* The Gables, 13 Western Road, TRING, HP23 4BE.
•**WASH, Mr. Colin Leonard, FCA** *1977;* Brightwell, The Green, Thorpe Morieux, BURY ST. EDMUNDS, SUFFOLK, IP30 0NZ.
WASH, Mr. Justin Andrew Spencer, BSc ACA *1993;* Ironshore International Ltd 2nd Floor South, 3 Minster Court, Mincing Lane, LONDON, EC3R 7RR.
WASHBOURNE, Mr. Darren John, BA ACA *1992;* 6 Auckland Close, Berkeley Heywood, WORCESTER, WR4 0SU.
•**WASHBOURNE, Mr. Ian Garth, FCA** *1979;* (Tax Fac), Graham Paul Limited, 10-12 Dunraven Place, BRIDGEND, MID GLAMORGAN, CF31 1JD.
WASHBROOK, Mr. David Thomas, BSc ACA *2007;* with KPMG, 10 Shelley Street, SYDNEY, NSW 2000, AUSTRALIA.
WASHER, Mr. Cyril John, FCA *1952;* Flat 7, Bramley Court, Orchard Grove, ORPINGTON, KENT, BR6 0AT. (Life Member)
WASHER, Mr. David John, BSc FCA *1989;* Ground Floor Mail Point 7, Churchill Insurance Co Ltd Churchill Court, Westmoreland Road, BROMLEY, BR1 1DP.
WASHER, Mrs. Karen Anne, BA(Hons) ACA *2000;* 11 Trafalgar Street, CROWS NEST, NSW 2065, AUSTRALIA.
WASHER, Mr. Mark Wyatt, BSc ACA *1991;* 7 The Heights, Foxgrove Road, BECKENHAM, BR3 5BY.
WASHINGTON, Mr. Colin Eric, FCA *1976;* 11a Marshall Street, MANLY, NSW 2095, AUSTRALIA.
WASHINGTON, Mrs. Gail Louise, ACA *1999;* 64 Coleman Road, Fleckney, LEICESTER, LE8 8BH.
•**WASHINGTON, Mrs. Janet Patricia, ACA** *1986;* with RSM Tenon Audit Limited, 5 Ridge House, Ridge House Drive, Festival Park, STOKE-ON-TRENT, ST1 5SJ.
WASHINGTON, Mr. Kendrick, FCA *1976;* 2 Hall Road, Rolleston-on-Dove, BURTON-ON-TRENT, DE13 9BY.
WASHINGTON, Mrs. Linda Lodan, BSc ACA *2000;* 4 Lambourne Close, Thruxton, ANDOVER, SP11 8LS.
WASHINGTON, Mr. Neil David, BA(Hons) ACA *2004;* The Mill at Worston, Worston Lane, Great Bridgeford, STAFFORD, ST18 9QA.
WASHINGTON, Dr. Polly Anne, PhD BSc(Hons) ACA *2010;* 16 Love Lane, NEWCASTLE UPON TYNE, NE1 3DW.
•**WASINSKI, Mr. Michael David, BSc FCA** *1977;* UHY Hacker Young Manchester LLP, St. James Buildings, 79 Oxford Street, MANCHESTER, M1 6HT.
WASLEY, Mr. David James, BA FCA *1979;* Flat 3, 5 Lymington Road, LONDON, NW6 1HX.
•**WASLEY, Mr. Steven James, BSc ACA** *2002;* Ernst & Young LLP, 1 Colmore Square, BIRMINGHAM, B4 6HQ. See also Ernst & Young Europe LLP
WASLIDGE, Mr. Brian Ernest, FCA *1964;* 19 Church View, Thrybergh, ROTHERHAM, S65 4BL. (Life Member)
•**WASLIN, Mr. Adrian Robert, FCA** *1984;* A.R. Waslin, 17 Rochfort Avenue, NEWMARKET, SUFFOLK, CB8 0DL.
WASON, Mr. Fraser Campbell, BAcc ACA *2004;* 29 Lennoxmill Lane, Lennoxtown, GLASGOW, G66 7GN.
WASON, Mr. Ian Eugene Romer, BSc ACA *2003;* 6th Floor, Wale Street Chambers, 33 Church Street, CAPE TOWN, WESTERN CAPE PROVINCE, 8001 SOUTH AFRICA.
WASON, Miss. Sumira, FCA *1988;* Broad House, 1 The Broadway, Old Hatfield, HATFIELD, HERTFORDSHIRE, AL9 5BG.
•**WASPE, Mrs. Lisa Jane, ACA CTA** *2002;* 161 Beacon Avenue, Kings Hill, WEST MALLING, ME19 4FX.
WASPE, Mr. Richard Mark, BA(Hons) ACA *2001;* 161 Beacon Avenue, Kings Hill, WEST MALLING, ME19 4FX.
WASS, Mr. Edward Aston, BA ACA *1998;* Longcroft House, 1 Main Street, Egleton, OAKHAM, LEICESTERSHIRE, LE15 8AF.
WASS, Mrs. Helen Louise, BSc ACA *1997;* 8 Abbey Close, Pyrford, WOKING, SURREY, GU22 8RY.
WASS, Mrs. Joanna Louise, ACA *2009;* 6a Lauds Road, Crick, NORTHAMPTON, NN6 7TJ.
WASSALL, Mr. Jonathan Wayne, BA ACA *1985;* 29 Theatre Street, WARWICK, CV34 4DP.
WASSE, Mr. Ian Nigel Macleod, FCA *1971;* 148 Old Station Road, Hampton In Arden, SOLIHULL, B92 0HF.
WASSELL, Mr. Elliot George, BA ACA *1997;* 15 Mallard Close, STRATFORD-UPON-AVON, WARWICKSHIRE, CV37 9EL.
WASSELL, Mr. Julian Howard, BA ACA *1987;* Apartment 13, Tapton Court, 4 Tapton House Road, SHEFFIELD, S10 5BY.
WASSELL, Mr. Martin, BSc ACA ATT AMCT *1995;* 7 Pool End Close, Knowle, SOLIHULL, B93 9QR.
WASTENEY, Mr. Luke, MSci ACA *2006;* 11 Park Road, Blaby, LEICESTER, LE8 4ED.
WASTIE, Mr. Martin Scott, LLB FCA *2000;* 69 Parkside, Vanbrugh Fields, LONDON, SE3 7QF.
WASTIE, Mr. Sean Gordon, BA ACA *1985;* 6 High Point, Northlands Wood, HAYWARDS HEATH, RH16 3RU.
•**WASTLING, Ms. Karen Jane, BSc ACA** *1990;* Karen Wastling BSc ACA, 4 Dale Rise, Burniston, SCARBOROUGH, NORTH YORKSHIRE, YO13 0EG.
•**WASU, Mr. Jasvinder Singh, FCA** *1981;* JSW Associates Limited, Talbot House, 204-226 Imperial Drive, HARROW, HA2 7HH.
•**WASU, Mr. Jatinder Singh, FCA** *1983;* MEMBER OF COUNCIL, (Tax Fac), Sterling Hay, PO Box 970, BROMLEY, BR1 9JF.
WAT, Mr. Chi Wai, ACA *2007;* Chan & Wat, Suite A, 19th Floor, Ritz Plaza, 122 Austin Road, TSIM SHA TSUI KOWLOON HONG KONG SAR.
WAT, Miss. Suzanne, BSc FCA *1992;* with PricewaterhouseCoopers, 21/F Edinburgh Tower, 15 Queen's Road Central, CENTRAL, HONG KONG ISLAND, HONG KONG SAR.
WATANANGURA, Mr. Jason Kiatichai Nicholas, BA ACA *1999;* 12 DAISY STREET, NORTH BALGOWLAH, NSW 2093, AUSTRALIA.
•**WATCHMAN, Mr. Andrew George Ronald, BSc ACA** *1990;* 44a Lawford Road, LONDON, N1 5BL.
WATCHMAN, Mr. Charles Michael, FCA *1966;* 29 Mardley Hill, WELWYN, HERTFORDSHIRE, AL6 0TT.
WATCHMAN, Mr. Paul James Alan, BA ACA *1992;* 51 Wentworth Street, RANDWICK, NSW 2031, AUSTRALIA.
•**WATCHORN, Mr. David George, BSc FCA** *1992;* 8 Colebrook Road, Timperley, ALTRINCHAM, WA15 6NP.
•**WATCHORN, Mr. David John, BSc FCA** *1990;* Elwell Watchorn & Saxton LLP, 109 Swan Street, Sileby, LOUGHBOROUGH, LE12 7NN.
WATCHORN, Mr. Hugh John, ACA *1989;* Bonhams 1793 Ltd, 101 New Bond Street, LONDON, W1S 1SR.
WATCHORN, Mr. Mark, ACA *2005;* PO Box 10479, GEORGETOWN, GRAND CAYMAN, KY1-1004, CAYMAN ISLANDS.
WATCHORN, Mrs. Pauline Ann, BSc FCA *1990;* 8 Colebrook Road, Timperley, ALTRINCHAM, WA15 6NP.
WATERFALL, Mr. Matthew Patrick, ACA *2011;* 29 Henson Close, Radcliffe-on-Trent, NOTTINGHAM, NG12 2JQ.
WATERFIELD, Mrs. Anna, BA ACA *1999;* The Old Cottage, 26 New Road East, Scholes, CLECKHEATON, BD19 6EW.
WATERFIELD, Mr. Christopher Neal, BSc ACA *2003;* 7 Trostrey Road, Kings Norton, BIRMINGHAM, B30 3NE.
WATERFIELD, Mr. Edward William Leslie, MEng FCA *2001;* 44 Grampian Road, Penfields, STOURBRIDGE, DY8 4UE.
WATERFIELD, Mr. Ian James, BA ACA *1999;* The Old Cottage, 26 New Road East, Scholes, CLECKHEATON, WEST YORKSHIRE, BD19 6EW.
WATERFIELD, Miss. Ingrid, BA ACA *1998;* 48 Woodland Court, Dyke Road Avenue, HOVE, EAST SUSSEX, BN3 6DQ.
WATERFIELD, Mr. James Thomas, MA ACA *1986;* The Dragon School, Bardwell Road, OXFORD, OX2 6SS.
WATERFIELD, Ms. Lynne Janet, BA ACA *1984;* Juniper Cottage, Mount Carmel Road, Palestine, ANDOVER, HAMPSHIRE, SP11 7ER.
•**WATERHOUSE, Mr. Alan, FCA** *1967;* Alan Waterhouse, 106 Mount Albany, Newtownpark Avenue, BLACKROCK, COUNTY DUBLIN, IRELAND.
•**WATERHOUSE, Mrs. Amanda Elizabeth, BSc ACA** *2000;* (Tax Fac), Baker Tilly Tax & Advisory Services LLP, 2 Whitehall Quay, LEEDS, LS1 4HG.
WATERHOUSE, Mr. Anthony Keith, FCA *1963;* Springmead, Wetherby Road, Rigton Hill Bardsey, LEEDS, LS17 9BR.
WATERHOUSE, Mr. Christopher James, BA(Hons) ACA *2003;* Bloom Business Solutions, 10 Winter Neb, Luddendenfoot, HALIFAX, WEST YORKSHIRE, HX2 6BP.
WATERHOUSE, Mr. David James, BSc ACA *1978;* Springwood, The Ridge, Linton, WETHERBY, WEST YORKSHIRE, LS22 4HJ. (Life Member)
WATERHOUSE, Mr. Frank David, ACA *1981;* 9417 Macon Road, RALEIGH, NC 27613, UNITED STATES.
WATERHOUSE, Dr. Peter, PhD ACA *2011;* 17 Pickmere Close, SALE, CHESHIRE, M33 2XG.
WATERHOUSE, Mr. Ronald Daniel, FCA *1955;* Apartment 1, Stoke Court, 1 West Parade, WORTHING, WEST SUSSEX, BN11 3QP. (Life Member)
WATERHOUSE, Mrs. Ruth Carol, MSc ACA *1987;* Glenside, Hillcrest, Collingham, WETHERBY, LS22 5DN.
WATERHOUSE, Mr. Steven Alexander, FCA *1977;* Lark Rise Chalk Lane, Hyde Heath, AMERSHAM, BUCKINGHAMSHIRE, HP6 5SA.
WATERHOUSE-BROWN, Mr. Nicholas Alexander, BSc ACA CTA *2001;* 27 Windermere Drive, KINGSWINFORD, WEST MIDLANDS, DY6 8AN.
WATERLOW, Mr. David George, FCA *1975;* 3 Standhill Close, HITCHIN, SG4 9BW. (Life Member)
WATERMAN, Mr. Alan Robert, FCA *1975;* 132 Wolsey Drive, KINGSTON UPON THAMES, KT2 5DW.
WATERMAN, Mr. Barry Jesse, FCA *1977;* Alandar Park Ltd, 1 Guillemot Place, Wood Green, LONDON, N22 6XG.
WATERMAN, Mr. Brian David Percy, BCom FCA *1963;* Coney House Barn, Hopton Wafers, Cleobury Mortimer, KIDDERMINSTER, DY14 0DL.
WATERMAN, Mr. Geoffrey Mark, ACA *1980;* 11 Newminster Road, MORDEN, SM4 6HJ.
WATERMAN, Mr. Ian, BSc ACA *2010;* 34 Mount Pleasant, CLECKHEATON, BD19 4AF.
WATERMAN, Miss. Lisa Claire, BSc(Hons) ACA *2004;* Eurosteel Products Limited 5th Floor, 24 Chiswell Street, LONDON, EC1Y 4TY.
•**WATERMAN, Mr. Marc, BA FCA** *1993;* UHY Hacker Young LLP, Quadrant House, 4 Thomas More Square, LONDON, E1W 1YW.
•**WATERMAN, Mr. Mark Vernon, MA FCA** *1984;* (Tax Fac), Dixon Wilson, 22 Chancery Lane, LONDON, WC2A 1LS.
WATERMAN, Mr. Matthew Thomas, BSc ACA *1989;* J C Rathbone Holdings Ltd, 12 St. James's Square, LONDON, SW1Y 4LB.
WATERMAN, Mrs. Philippa, ACA *2011;* Flat 7, 19 Cheshire Street, LONDON, E2 6ER.
WATERMAN, Mr. Robert Stanley, FCA *1966;* The Mount, 15 Fieldway, Ditchling, HASSOCKS, WEST SUSSEX, BN6 8UA. (Life Member)
WATERS, Mr. Alan Geoffrey, ACA *2008;* Flat 14 Banister Gate, 19 Archers Road, SOUTHAMPTON, SO15 2NR.
•**WATERS, Mr. Andrew Floyd, BSc ACA** *1990;* Andrew Waters & Associates Ltd, 16 Westfield Road, Westbury-On-Trym, BRISTOL, BS9 3HG.
WATERS, Mr. Andrew John, FCA *1968;* South Down House, Park Place, Bessels Green, SEVENOAKS, TN13 2QD.
WATERS, Mr. Anthony Floyd, FCA *1959;* 86 Coldharbour Road, Redland, BRISTOL, BS6 7SB. (Life Member)
WATERS, Mrs. Bethan Margaret, BSc(Hons) ACA *2000;* 23 Springfield Lane, Rhiwderin, NEWPORT, GWENT, NP10 8QZ.
WATERS, Mr. Brian Wallace, FCA FCMA *1960;* (Member of Council 1983 - 1987), The Chequers, Preston, HITCHIN, SG4 7TY.
•**WATERS, Mrs. Carol Ann, BA ACA** *1985;* Carol Waters, Trefoil, Boucher Close, Shottery, STRATFORD-UPON-AVON, CV37 9YX.
WATERS, Mr. Christopher Stephen, MSc BSc FCA *1975;* 5 Five Acres, KINGS LANGLEY, HERTFORDSHIRE, WD4 9JU.
WATERS, Mr. Christopher Stephen, MA ACA *2002;* 25 Patterson Road, LONDON, SE19 2LE.
WATERS, Mrs. Clare Elizabeth, BSc ACA *1992;* Chiltern Haven Pednor, CHESHAM, BUCKINGHAMSHIRE, HP5 2SX.
WATERS, Mr. Colin, BA ACA *2006;* Flat 7, 17 Lewin Road, LONDON, SW16 6JZ.
WATERS, Mr. David, ACA *2011;* Flat 8 Noel Coward House, 65 Vauxhall Bridge Road, LONDON, SW1V 2SW.
•**WATERS, Mr. David Anthony, BSc(Hons) ACA** *2003;* (Tax Fac), UKTS Audit Limited, 221 High Street, BLACKWOOD, GWENT, NP12 1AL.
WATERS, Mr. David Frobisher, FCA *1970;* Green Lanes, Le Pont Au Bre, St. Peter, JERSEY, JE3 7DL.
WATERS, Ms. Deborah Elizabeth, BSc ACA *1993;* Lloyds TSB Insurance, Finance Department, Tredegar Park, NEWPORT, GWENT, NP10 8SB.
WATERS, Mr. Geoffrey, FCA *1970;* 147 Fellows Road, Swiss Cottage, LONDON, NW3 3JJ.
WATERS, Mr. Glen, BAEcon(Hons) ACA *2003;* with PricewaterhouseCoopers LLP, 1 Embankment Place, LONDON, WC2N 6RH.
WATERS, Mrs. Helen, BA ACA *1991;* Athgarvan, 41 Stillorgan Park, Blackrock, DUBLIN, COUNTY DUBLIN, IRELAND.
WATERS, Mr. Ian Michael, ACA *1990;* Flat 14, 30 Streatham Place, LONDON, SW2 4QY.
WATERS, Mr. James, BSc ACA *2011;* 35 Weald Rise, Tilehurst, READING, RG30 6XB.
WATERS, Mr. Jason David, BSc ACA *2008;* 8 Charminster Road, WORCESTER PARK, KT4 8PS.
WATERS, Mr. John James, BSc FCA *1976;* Browns Distribution Services Ltd, Ravensdale, STOKE-ON-TRENT, ST6 4NU.
•**WATERS, Mr. John MacDonald, MA FCA** *1991;* PricewaterhouseCoopers LLP, 1 Embankment Place, LONDON, WC2N 6RH. See also PricewaterhouseCoopers
•**WATERS, Mr. John Weston, BA FCA** *1986;* West & Co, Old Hempstead House, 10 Queensway, HEMEL HEMPSTEAD, HERTFORDSHIRE, HP1 1LR.
•**WATERS, Mr. Jonathan Mark, BA FCA** *1993;* Dutton Moore, 6 Silver Street, HULL, HU1 1JA.
WATERS, Mr. Keith Stuart, BA FCA *1976;* The Cow Shed, Bard Hill, Salthouse, HOLT, NORFOLK, NR25 7XB.
WATERS, Miss. Kirsty Anne, ACA *2008;* 94a St. John's Hill, LONDON, SW11 1SH.
•**WATERS, Mr. Leslie Colin, FCA** *1974;* 1 Beaulieu Gardens, ST. LEONARDS-ON-SEA, EAST SUSSEX, TN37 7QE.
WATERS, Mr. Liam Ross, ACA *2010;* 65 Southstand Apartments, Highbury Stadium Square, LONDON, N5 1EY.
WATERS, Mrs. Linda Jayne, ACA MBA *1991;* Wychwood Cottage Wood Lane Hailey, WITNEY, OXFORDSHIRE, OX29 9XB.
WATERS, Mr. Marcus Damian Napier, MEng ACA *2002;* 10d Thorney Crescent, Morgans Walk, Battersea, LONDON, SW11 3TR.
•**WATERS, Mr. Mark Andrew, BSc ACA** *1993;* AW, 117 Beech Road, ST. ALBANS, HERTFORDSHIRE, AL3 5AW.
WATERS, Mr. Martin, ACA *1997;* Deutsche Bank Royal Liver Building Pier Head, The Strand, LIVERPOOL, L3 1NY.
WATERS, Mr. Nicholas Anthony John, BA ACA *1985;* GKN Plc, PO Box 55, Ipsley House, Ipsley Church Lane, REDDITCH, WORCESTERSHIRE B98 0TL.
WATERS, Mr. Nigel Alastair Francis, BSc ACA *1990;* 18 Church Grove, Hampton Wick, KINGSTON UPON THAMES, KT1 4AL.
WATERS, Mr. Paul Ewart, BA ACA *1990;* 3 Waldemar Road, Wimbledon, LONDON, SW19 7LJ.
•**WATERS, Mr. Philip John, ACA** *1985;* A Q Accounting, Tall Trees, 26 Tranby Lane, Anlaby, HULL, HU10 7DS.
WATERS, Mr. Robert, BSc ACA *2010;* Flat 1, Strata Court, 28 Solway Road, LONDON, SE22 9BG.
WATERS, Mr. Robert James, BA ACA *2010;* Flat 118 Voltaire Buildings, 330 Garratt Lane, LONDON, SW18 4FR.
WATERS, Mr. Robert Paul, FCA *1970;* 16 Queens Road, Wivenhoe, COLCHESTER, ESSEX, CO7 9JH.
WATERS, Mr. Samuel Jonathan, ACA *2010;* Flat, 10 Belsize Crescent, LONDON, NW3 5QU.
WATERS, Mr. Simon Anthony John, BA ACA *1996;* Waitrose Ltd, Doncastle Road, BRACKNELL, BERKSHIRE, RG12 8YA.
WATERS, Mr. Stephen Ian Timothy, MA ACA *1983;* InfoCat Riverside House, 27-29 Vauxhall Grove, LONDON, SW8 1SY.
WATERS, Mr. Steven, BA ACA *2007;* 19 Horne Road, THATCHAM, BERKSHIRE, RG19 4RG.
WATERS, Mr. Thomas Edward, ACA *2008;* 6 Symonds Road, HITCHIN, HERTFORDSHIRE, SG5 2JL.
WATERSON, Mr. Brian Douglas, FCA *1958;* 8 Rivington Road, Hale, ALTRINCHAM, WA15 9PH. (Life Member)
WATERSON, Mr. Ian George, BA FCA *1997;* 19 Desford Road, LIVERPOOL, L19 3RB.
WATERSON, Mrs. Margaret Anne, FCA *1979;* Fenay Cottage, Fenay Lane, Fenay Bridge, HUDDERSFIELD, HD8 0LJ.
•**WATERSON, Mr. Michael, FCA** *1973;* Michael Waterson, Fenay Cottage, Fenay Lane, Fenay Bridge, HUDDERSFIELD, HD8 0LJ.

WATERSTON, Mr. Christopher James, BA ACA *1981;* 174 Allerburn Lea, ALNWICK, NORTHUMBERLAND, NE66 2QR.
WATERTON, Mrs. Katharine Alison, BSc ACA *1990;* Capco, rue des Alpes, GENEVA, SWITZERLAND.
WATERWORTH, Mr. David, LLB ACA *2000;* Stramit Building Products, Level 11, Tower B Zenith Centre, 821 Pacific Highway, CHATSWOOD, NSW 2067 AUSTRALIA.
•WATERWORTH, Mr. Gareth John, BSc ACA *1987;* 17 Sandy Ridge, Borough Green, SEVENOAKS, KENT, TN15 8HP.
WATERWORTH, Mr. Graeme Anthony Richard, ACA *1997;* 40 Daniell Street, TRURO, TR1 2DN.
•WATERWORTH, Mr. Martin, BA FCA *1990;* (Tax Fac), Martin Waterworth Limited, Bronwylfa, Llangunnor Road, CARMARTHEN, SA31 2PB.
WATERWORTH, Mr. Michael, FCA *1959;* 67 Gabalfa Road, Sketty, SWANSEA, SA2 8NA. (Life Member)
WATES, Mrs. Alison Jane, BA ACA *1991;* The Copse, Chelford Road, KNUTSFORD, CHESHIRE, WA16 8LY.
WATES, Sir Christopher Stephen, Kt BA FCA *1965;* Tufton Place, Ewhurst Place, Northam, RYE, EAST SUSSEX, TN31 6HL. (Life Member)
WATES, Mr. Hugh Randall, FCA *1961;* Hillfield House, Horsepond Road, Gallowstree Common, READING, RG4 9BX.
WATES, Mr. Martyn James, BA ACA *1991;* Cooperative Group Ltd, P.O. Box 53 New Century House Corporation St, MANCHESTER, M60 4ES.
WATES, Mr. Richard Peter, FCA *1978;* 1 Paget Close, Great Houghton, NORTHAMPTON, NN4 7EF.
WATFORD, Mr. Andrew Martin, BA ACA *2006;* Flat 2, 40 Park Avenue, HARROGATE, NORTH YORKSHIRE, HG2 9BG.
WATFORD, Mr. Mark Ian, BSocSc ACA *1992;* Wound Management, Smith & Nephew Ltd, PO Box 81, HULL, HU3 2BN.
WATFORD, Mr. Peter Clive, BA FCA *1973;* St Nicholas, Station Road, Chobham, WOKING, GU24 8AL.
WATFORD, Mr. Stephen James, BA(Hons) ACA *2003;* 15 Strickmere, Stratford St. Mary, COLCHESTER, CO7 6NZ.
WATHERSTON, Mr. David, ACA *2011;* 23 Gardner Road, LONDON, E13 8LN.
WATHERSTON, The Revd. Peter David, BSc FCA *1965;* First Fruit, Latimer Hall, Cleves Road, LONDON, E6 1QF.
•WATKIN, Mr. Andrew Bedford, BA FCA *1982;* (Tax Fac), Baker Watkin, Middlesex House, Rutherford Close, STEVENAGE, SG1 2EF.
•WATKIN, Ms. Joanne Louise, BA(Hons) FCA *1998;* Purple Cat Accountancy Limited, 87 Highgate Road, WALSALL, WS1 3JA.
WATKIN, Mr. Philip John, FCA *1974;* 5 Robinson Close, Backwell, BRISTOL, BS48 3BT.
WATKIN, Miss. Shelley Dawn, BA(Hons) ACA *2001;* 9 Cameron Road, BROMLEY, BR2 9AY.
WATKIN, Mr. Simon Edward, BSc ACA *1998;* 58 Ascot Drive, Dosthill, TAMWORTH, STAFFORDSHIRE, B77 1QL.
•WATKINS, Mr. Alan James, FCA *1971;* (Tax Fac), Bowen-Jones Watkins & Partners, 17 Dan-Y-Graig Avenue, Newton, PORTHCAWL, MID GLAMORGAN, CF36 5AA.
WATKINS, Mr. Alan Peter, FCA *1962;* Beech Hill Cottage, Possingworth Park, Cross In Hand, HEATHFIELD, TN21 0TA.
WATKINS, Mr. Alexander John, ACA *2008;* K P M G Salisbury Square House, 8 Salisbury Square, LONDON, EC4Y 8BB.
WATKINS, Miss. Amanda Jane, BA ACA *1997;* 53 Hichisson Road, LONDON, SE15 3AN.
WATKINS, Mr. Andrew Graham, FCA *1972;* Watkins Odendaal, No. 300 Windsor Square, 1959 152nd Street, WHITE ROCK V4A 9E3, BC, CANADA.
WATKINS, Mrs. Anna Rachel, BSc ACA *1984;* Rowan House, 17 Mountain Ash, Weston Park, BATH, BA1 2UU.
WATKINS, Mr. Anthony Douglas, FCA *1972;* Greysmead, Stoke Row Road, Peppard Common, HENLEY-ON-THAMES, RG9 5JD.
WATKINS, Mr. Antony William, BA ACA FSI *1998;* Grant Thornton LLP, 30 Finsbury Square, LONDON, EC2P 2YU.
WATKINS, Mr. Brian John, FCA *1961;* 8 Ormonde Road, Moor Park, NORTHWOOD, HA6 2EL.
WATKINS, Mr. Christopher William, BSc ACA *1989;* 29 Longacre, Woodthorpe, NOTTINGHAM, NG5 4JS.
WATKINS, Miss. Claire Catherine Grayson, BA(Hons) ACA *2007;* with Buzzacott LLP, 130 Wood Street, LONDON, EC2V 6DL.
WATKINS, Mr. Daniel Owen, BSS ACA *1995;* 497 South Circular Road, Kilmainham, DUBLIN 8, COUNTY DUBLIN, IRELAND.
WATKINS, Mr. David, BA FCA *1968;* 636 Glen Road, GIBSONS V0N 1V9, BC, CANADA.
WATKINS, Mr. David Russell, BSc ACA *1984;* 3 Cowdery Heights, Old Basing, BASINGSTOKE, RG24 7AN.
•WATKINS, Mr. Desmond Ralph, FCA *1971;* Bridgen Watkins & Wainwright, 10 Dashwood Avenue, HIGH WYCOMBE, HP12 3DN.
WATKINS, Miss. Dolores Louise, BSc(Econ) ACA *2000;* 55 Turners Avenue, FLEET, GU51 1DU.
•WATKINS, Mr. Edward Wilfred, FCA *1977;* Edward Watkins & Co, Glenmoir, New Street, LEDBURY, HR8 2DX.
WATKINS, Mrs. Elizabeth Claire, ACA *1979;* United World College of the Atlantic Ltd, St. Donats Castle, St. Donat's, LLANTWIT MAJOR, SOUTH GLAMORGAN, CF61 1WF.
WATKINS, Miss. Emma Louise, BA(Hons) ACA *2010;* 13 Grasmere Road, LYMM, CHESHIRE, WA13 9PL.
WATKINS, Mr. Gary Lyn, BSc ACA *1997;* 10004 125th Avenue NE, KIRKLAND, WA 98033, UNITED STATES.
•WATKINS, Mr. Giles St John, BSc ACA *1995;* 10 Pomeroy Close, Richmond Lock, Richmond upon Thames, TWICKENHAM, TW1 1QB.
WATKINS, Miss. Hannah, BA(Hons) ACA *2002;* 8 Rue de Rossignols, 68220 HESINGUE, FRANCE.
WATKINS, Mr. Howard William, MBA BSocSc FCA *1983;* 34 Sillswood, OLNEY, MK46 5PL.
•WATKINS, Mr. Hugh Richard, BSc FCA *1977;* Trinity Corporate Services Romania SRL, 24 Paleologu Street, 3rd District, 030552 BUCHAREST, ROMANIA.
•WATKINS, Mr. James Angus Wellwood, BSc ACA *1983;* (Tax Fac), King Watkins Limited, The Island House, Midsomer Norton, RADSTOCK, BA3 2DZ.
WATKINS, Mr. James Percival, FCA *1960;* 70 Janes Lane, BURGESS HILL, WEST SUSSEX, RH15 0QR. (Life Member)
WATKINS, Ms. Jayne Belinda, BSc FCA *1985;* Beechcroft, Middlesex Farm, Dunton, BIGGLESWADE, SG18 8RL.
WATKINS, Mr. Jeremy David Thomas, BA ACA *2006;* 32 Quilters Drive, BILLERICAY, CM12 9YE.
•WATKINS, Mr. John, FCA *1968;* (Tax Fac), John Watkins, 67 Park Road, WOKING, GU22 7DH.
WATKINS, Mr. John Charles, BA FCA *1997; (CA Scotland* with PKF (UK) LLP, Farringdon Place, 20 Farringdon Road, LONDON, EC1M 3AP.
WATKINS, Mrs. Katherine Emma, BSc ACA *2003;* 50 Heol Ynys DDU, CAERPHILLY, CF83 1SD.
•WATKINS, Mr. Keith, FCA *1966;* Makinson & Co, 1 Hill Street, LYDNEY, GLOUCESTERSHIRE, GL15 5HB.
•WATKINS, Mr. Keith John, FCA *1974;* (Tax Fac), Barter Durgan, 10 Victoria Road South, SOUTHSEA, PO5 2DA.
WATKINS, Ms. Lesley Susan, BSc FCA *1983;* Calculus Capital Ltd, 104 Park Street, LONDON, W1K 6NF.
WATKINS, Miss. Louise, BA(Hons) ACA *2011;* 8 Brookside Close, Cilfynydd, PONTYPRIDD, MID GLAMORGAN, CF37 4HX.
WATKINS, Mr. Malcolm Peter, BA ACA *1978;* Reabrook Ltd Rawdon Road, Moira, SWADLINCOTE, DERBYSHIRE, DE12 6DA.
•WATKINS, Mr. Mark David, FCA CTA *1991;* (Tax Fac), Place Campbell, Wilmington House, High Street, EAST GRINSTEAD, RH19 3AU.
•WATKINS, Mr. Mark Gareth, MA FCA *1984;* H W, Sterling House, 5 Buckingham Place, Bellfield Rd West, HIGH WYCOMBE, HP13 5HQ. See also Haines Watts
WATKINS, Mr. Mark James, ACA *2008;* 31 Longbridge Road, Bramley, TADLEY, HAMPSHIRE, RG26 5AN.
WATKINS, Mr. Matthew James, LLB ACA *2001;* 84 Norroy Road, LONDON, SW15 1PG.
WATKINS, Mr. Matthew John, BA(Hons) ACA PGCE *2002;* 14 Kingsland Drive Dorridge, SOLIHULL, WEST MIDLANDS, B93 8SP.
WATKINS, Mr. Michael, MEng ACA *2003;* Ernst & Young, 2323 Victory Avenue Suite 2000, DALLAS, TX 75219, UNITED STATES.
WATKINS, Mr. Michael Edward Henry, FCA *1966;* 94 Deansfield, Cricklade, SWINDON, SN6 6BW. (Life Member)
WATKINS, Mr. Nicholas Edward, BA FCA *1976;* 23 Alfred Road, Hawley, DARTFORD, DA2 7SQ.
WATKINS, Miss. Nicola Kim, MA ACA *1999;* 27 Cedar Terrace, RICHMOND, TW9 2JE.
WATKINS, Mr. Owen Gwyn, BSc(Econ) ACA *1989;* 73 Dee Banks, Great Boughton, CHESTER, CH3 5UX.
WATKINS, Mr. Paul Anthony, BSc ACA *1995;* 1 Gerddi Glasfryn Gardens, LLANELLI, DYFED, SA15 3LL.
WATKINS, Mr. Peter Howard, FCA *1970;* Wogen Group Ltd, 4 The Sanctuary, LONDON, SW1P 3JS.
WATKINS, Mr. Peter John, FCA *1969;* 205 Peach Leaf Way, SACRAMENTO, CA 95838-1863, UNITED STATES.
WATKINS, Mr. Philip David, BSc ACA *1993;* 58 Arthur Road, WOKINGHAM, RG41 2SY.
WATKINS, Mr. Philip Ronald Dexter, MSc ACA *1999;* 32 Holroyd Road, Putney, LONDON, SW15 6LN.
WATKINS, Mr. Raymond John, BA FCA *1977;* BP Plc, Chertsey Road, SUNBURY-ON-THAMES, MIDDLESEX, TW16 7LN.
WATKINS, Miss. Rebecca, ACA *2008;* Global Aerospace Underwriting Managers Ltd Fitzwilliam Hous, 10 St. Mary Axe, LONDON, EC3A 8EQ.
WATKINS, Mr. Richard Francis, BSc ACA *2005;* 18 St. Quintins Close, Wentworth Way, HULL, HU9 2AW.
WATKINS, Mr. Richard Henry, ACA *1978;* Tempus Computers Ltd, 21-23 St. Pauls Square, BIRMINGHAM, B3 1RB.
•WATKINS, Mr. Robert Gareth Elliott, BA(Hons) ACA *2004;* Bessler Hendrie, Albury Mill, Mill Lane, Chilworth, GUILDFORD, SURREY GU4 8RU.
WATKINS, Mrs. Sandra Elizabeth, FCA *1964;* Offas Dene, Sutton St Nicholas, HEREFORD, HR1 3AY. (Life Member)
WATKINS, Mrs. Sarah-Jane, BA ACA *1998;* 16 Dunster Street, KARRINYUP, WA 6018, AUSTRALIA.
WATKINS, Mrs. Saran Lisa, BSc ACA *2000;* with Ernst & Young, Compass House, 80 Newmarket Road, CAMBRIDGE, CB5 8DZ.
WATKINS, Miss. Taralee, BA(Hons) ACA *2011;* Barn 3 Cwrt y Bettws, Llandarcy, NEATH, WEST GLAMORGAN, SA10 6JX.
WATKINS, Mr. Thomas John, FCA *1958;* Falkland Lodge, Selsley West, STROUD, GL5 5LJ. (Life Member)
WATKINS, Mr. Timothy John, BSc FCA *1997;* 126 Church Hill, Eggbuckland, PLYMOUTH, PL6 5RB.
•WATKINS, Mr. Timothy John, FCA *1986;* (Tax Fac), Randall & Payne LLP, Rodborough Court, Walkley Hill, STROUD, GLOUCESTERSHIRE, GL5 3LR.
•WATKINS, Mr. Trevor, FCA *1966;* 15 The Avenue, STOKE-ON-TRENT, ST4 6BL.
WATKINS, Mr. Trevor Albert George, FCA *1967;* 15 Nursery Avenue, BEXLEYHEATH, KENT, DA7 4JX.
WATKINS, Mr. Vincent Paul, ACA *1982;* Hansard Global Plc, PO Box 192, Douglas, ISLE OF MAN, IM99 1QL.
WATKINS-WRIGHT, Mr. Edward Richard Charles, BSc ACA *2008;* 166 Eswyn Road, LONDON, SW17 8TN.
WATKINSON, Mr. Andrew John, BA ACA *1992;* 4 Pinfold Garth, MALTON, NORTH YORKSHIRE, YO17 7XQ.
•WATKINSON, Mr. Barry Ian, BSc FCA *1975;* (Tax Fac), Barry Watkinson & Co Limited, 683 Galleywood Road, CHELMSFORD, CM2 8BT. See also Moulsham Audits Limited
WATKINSON, Mr. Christopher, FCA *1965;* 169 Algernon Road, LONDON, SE13 7AP.
•WATKINSON, Mr. David John, BA FCA *1976;* (Tax Fac), Watkinson Black, 1st Floor, 264 Manchester Road, WARRINGTON, WA1 3RB.
•WATKINSON, Mr. David Richard, FCA *1982;* 90 Kipling Drive, BLACKPOOL, FY3 9UB.
•WATKINSON, Mrs. Denise Barbara, FCA *1976;* Murray Smith LLP, Darland House, 44 Winnington Hill, NORTHWICH, CHESHIRE, CW8 1AU.
•WATKINSON, Mr. Douglas Bruce, BA ACA *1999;* Deloitte LLP, 3 Rivergate, Temple Quay, BRISTOL, BS1 6GD. See also Deloitte & Touche LLP
WATKINSON, Mr. Howard Edmund, FCA *1956;* 61 Briggate, KNARESBOROUGH, NORTH YORKSHIRE, HG5 8BQ. (Life Member)
•WATKINSON, Mrs. Janet Ann, ACA *1992;* (Tax Fac), Jan Watkinson & Co, 8 Mallinson Close, HORNCHURCH, RM12 5HA.
WATKINSON, Mr. John, FCA *1976;* Ulster Yarns Limited, Ravensthorpe Mills, Ravensthorpe, DEWSBURY, WF13 3NA.
WATKINSON, Mrs. Makeda, BA ACA *1999;* with Martin and Company, 25 St Thomas Street, WINCHESTER, SO23 9HJ.
WATKINSON, Mr. Paul Leslie, BA CA FCA *1981;* 31 Ferero Street, EDENGLEN, 1609, SOUTH AFRICA.
WATKINSON, Mrs. Wendy Jane, BSc ACA *2005;* 8 The Avenue, Banks, SOUTHPORT, MERSEYSIDE, PR9 8AZ.
•WATLER, Mr. Dale Edward, FCA *1972;* Lithgow Perkins LLP, Crown Chambers, Princes Street, HARROGATE, HG1 1NJ. See also Jaydee Secretarial Ltd
WATLING, Mr. Hadley Graham, BEng ACA *2003;* Apartment 311 Asquith House, 27 Monck Street, LONDON, SW1P 2AR.
•WATLING, Mr. Henry Richard McLaren, ACA *1981;* Mclaren Cornel Limited, Penhurst House, 352-356 Battersea Park Road, LONDON, SW11 3BY. See also Blunt McLaren & Co Limited
WATLING, Mr. John Martin Paul, MA FCA *1956;* Beach Cottage, Beach, Bitton, BRISTOL, BS30 6NP. (Life Member)
WATLING, Mr. John Rodwell, FCA *1949;* P.O. Box 64364, NAIROBI, KENYA. (Life Member)
WATLING, Mrs. Margaret, ACA *1987;* with Armstrong Watson, Bute House, Montgomery Way, Rosehill, CARLISLE, CA1 2RW.
•WATLING, Mr. Simon Colin Graham, BSc ACA *2001;* Watling & Co, Beach House, La Route de St. Aubin, St. Lawrence, JERSEY, JE3 1LP.
WATOLA, Mr. Antoni Jozef, ACA *1979;* BRFC, Memorial Stadium, Filton Avenue, BRISTOL, BS7 0BF.
WATSHAM, Mr. Timothy James, BA ACA *1999;* 24 Marsham Lane, GERRARDS CROSS, BUCKINGHAMSHIRE, SL9 8HD.
WATSON, Mrs. Abigail Isolde Elizabeth, BA ACA *1984;* 9 Larklands, Longthorpe, PETERBOROUGH, PE3 6LL.
WATSON, Mr. Adrian Martin, BA ACA *1988;* Hallam Sampford Road Radwinter, SAFFRON WALDEN, ESSEX, CB10 2TL.
WATSON, Mr. Alan, BSc ACA *1986;* 44 Eaton Avenue, NORMANHURST, NSW 2076, AUSTRALIA.
WATSON, Mr. Alan Frank, FCA *1952;* 15 Harecroft Road, OTLEY, WEST YORKSHIRE, LS21 2BG. (Life Member)
WATSON, Mr. Alasdair Barry, ACA *2009;* 648 Stapleton Road, BRISTOL, BS5 6TG.
WATSON, Mr. Alastair Charles, BSc ACA *1994;* Second Floor, Berkeley Square House, Berkeley Square, LONDON, W1J 6BD.
WATSON, Mr. Alastair James, MPhil ACA *2000;* PO Box 67914, 20 Triton Street, LONDON, NW1W 8SU.
WATSON, Mr. Alexander William, BA(Hons) ACA *2002;* (Tax Fac), 19 Lockview Court, 67 Narrow Street, LONDON, E14 8EN.
•WATSON, Miss. Alison Janet, BSc ACA *1989;* Watson and Darbyshire Audit Ltd, Nymrod House, 85 King Street, Whalley, CLITHEROE, LANCASHIRE BB7 9SW.
WATSON, Mrs. Alison Tessa, BA ACA *1992;* The Old Dairy, Lower Street, SALISBURY, SP2 8HB.
WATSON, Miss. Amanda Louise, BSc ACA *1999;* GE Money, 8 Tangihua Street, AUCKLAND 1010, NEW ZEALAND.
WATSON, Mr. Andrew, BSc ACA *2003;* 30 Columbine Road, ELY, CAMBRIDGESHIRE, CB6 3WN.
•WATSON, Mr. Andrew, BA ACA CTA *1997;* Andrew Watson Consulting Ltd, Lane Cottage, Pound Green, Arley, BEWDLEY, WORCESTERSHIRE DY12 3LF.
WATSON, Mr. Andrew Charles, BSc FCA *1987;* RSM Farrell Grant Sparks, Molyneux House, Bride Street, DUBLIN 8, COUNTY DUBLIN, IRELAND.
•WATSON, Mr. Andrew Fraser, FCA *1965;* Johnstone Howell & Co, Fairfield House, 104 Whitby Road, ELLESMERE PORT, CHESHIRE, CH65 0AB.
WATSON, Mr. Andrew John, BA ACA *1986;* with Brindley Millen Limited, 167 Turners Hill, Cheshunt, WALTHAM CROSS, HERTFORDSHIRE, EN8 9BH.
•WATSON, Mr. Andrew John, BA ACA *1993;* 18 Chinnor Road, THAME, OXFORDSHIRE, OX9 3LW.
WATSON, Mr. Andrew Michael, BSc ACA *1992;* 5 Woodthorpe Close, WAKEFIELD, WEST YORKSHIRE, WF2 6JA.
WATSON, Mr. Andrew Michael, BSc FCA FCPAPNG *1974;* P.O. Box 5441, BOROKO, PAPUA NEW GUINEA.
•WATSON, Mr. Andrew Muirhead, BSc FCA *1982;* (Tax Fac), Lloydbottoms Limited, 118 High Street, Staple Hill, BRISTOL, BS16 5HH.
WATSON, Mr. Andrew Victor, BSc ACA *2003;* 3rd Floor, Monopolis House, 9 South Street, LONDON, W1K 2XA.
WATSON, Mrs. Angela Mary, BA ACA *1986;* The Old Oast House, Westhide, HEREFORD, HR1 3RQ.
WATSON, Mr. Angus, BSc ACA *1987;* 65 Teddington Park, TEDDINGTON, TW11 8DE.
WATSON, Mrs. Anna Elizabeth, ACA *2007;* 43 Ormonde Road, WOKINGHAM, RG41 2RA.
WATSON, Miss. Anna Louise, BA ACA *1998;* 2984 Neal Avenue, SAN JOSE, CA 95128, UNITED STATES.
WATSON, Mrs. Anne Doryl, BA ACA *1987;* 22 Cranley Road, Hersham, WALTON-ON-THAMES, SURREY, KT12 5BP.

WATSON, Mrs. Anne-Marie, BSc ACA *1994;* Milburn Lodge Foxcombe Road, Boars Hill, OXFORD, OX1 5DQ.
WATSON, Miss. Anneka, ACA *2011;* 31 Brindlefield, WIGTON, CUMBRIA, CA7 9LY.
WATSON, Mrs. Annette Clare, PhD BSc ACA *2004;* 104 Haynes Road, WORTHING, WEST SUSSEX, BN14 7LA.
WATSON, Mr. Anothony Robert, MA FCA *1978;* (Tax Fac), 28 Wargrave Road, Twyford, READING, RG10 9PQ.
•WATSON, Mr. Barry, FCA ATII *1979;* (Tax Fac), James Cowper LLP, 3 Wesley Gate, Queens Road, READING, RG1 4AP.
•WATSON, Mr. Bernard Anthony, FCA DChA *1977;* haysmacintyre, Fairfax House, 15 Fulwood Place, LONDON, WC1V 6AY.
•WATSON, Mr. Brian David, FCA *1960;* (Tax Fac), Brian D. Watson, 1A Windsor Sq, EXMOUTH, EX8 1JU.
WATSON, Mr. Brian Innes Kermack, FCA *1970;* 79 Nantucket Road, P O Box 1591, CRYSTAL BEACH L0S 1B0, ON, CANADA.
WATSON, Mr. Brian Richard Stewart, MBA BSc ACA *1993;* Applecross Egg Lane, Claines, WORCESTER, WR3 7SB.
WATSON, Mr. Bryan, BSc FCA *1974;* 18 Tarnway, Lowton, WARRINGTON, WA3 2QJ.
WATSON, Miss. Caroline, BEng ACA *2007;* with Baker Tilly, The Clock House, 140 London Road, GUILDFORD, GU1 1UW.
WATSON, Miss. Caroline Anne, BA(Hons) ACA *2000;* 4 Maple Gardens, TUNBRIDGE WELLS, TN2 5JL.
WATSON, Mrs. Caroline Jane, MA BA ACA *1989;* Fernroyde, 17 Ben Rhydding Drive, Ben Rhydding, ILKLEY, LS29 8AY.
WATSON, Mrs. Carolyn Vezetque, BA ACA *1986;* Highridge, Kerves Lane, HORSHAM, WEST SUSSEX, RH13 6ES.
WATSON, Mr. Christopher David, BA ACA *1984;* 7 Crescent Grove, Clapham, LONDON, SW4 7AF.
WATSON, Mr. Christopher John, FCA *1977;* 127 Edgepark Way NW, CALGARY T3A 4P4, AB, CANADA.
WATSON, Mr. Christopher John, BA ACA *1991;* 16 Rainham Avenue, MINDARIE, WA 6030, AUSTRALIA.
WATSON, Mr. Christopher Michael, FCA *1991;* (Tax Fac), with Reeves & Co LLP, 37 St. Margarets Street, CANTERBURY, KENT, CT1 2TU.
WATSON, Mr. Christopher Trevor, BSc ACA *1998;* 57 Mount Taylor Drive, GLENDOWIE 1071, AUCKLAND, NEW ZEALAND.
•WATSON, Mrs. Claire, BSc ACA *2005;* SPL Associates, 2nd Floor, De Burgh House, Market Road, WICKFORD, ESSEX SS12 0BB.
WATSON, Miss. Claire Suzanne, BSc(Hons) ACA *2003;* Eden House, Ridley Mill, STOCKSFIELD, NORTHUMBERLAND, NE43 7QU.
WATSON, Mr. Clive Graeme, BCom ACA *1982;* Spectris Plc, 35-51 Station Road, EGHAM, SURREY, TW20 9NP.
WATSON, Mr. Clive Royston, BA ACA *1988;* West Hall Farm, Church Lane, Pirbright, WOKING, GU24 0JJ.
WATSON, Mr. Colin John, FCA *1975;* River Island Clothing Co Ltd, Chelsea House, West Gate, Ealing, LONDON, W5 1DR.
WATSON, Mr. Craig, ACA *2011;* 54 Hallam Way, West Hallam, ILKESTON, DERBYSHIRE, DE7 6LE.
WATSON, Mr. Daniel, ACA *2009;* Apartment 46 Skyline Plaza Building, 80 Commercial Road, LONDON, E1 1NY.
WATSON, Mr. David, ACA *1979;* 40 Charlton, CHICHESTER, PO18 0HU.
WATSON, Mr. David, BA FCA *1965;* Milburn Lodge, Foxcombe Road, Boars Hill, OXFORD, OX1 5DQ.
WATSON, Mr. David, LLB ACA *2006;* 25/85 Palmer Street, BALMAIN, NSW 2041, AUSTRALIA.
WATSON, Mr. David Alexander, FCA *1972;* 25 St. Marys Grove, Tudhoe Village, SPENNYMOOR, DL16 6LR.
WATSON, Mr. David Arthur, FCA *1962;* 7 Elmpark Way, Stockton Lane, YORK, YO31 1DX.
WATSON, Mr. David Ashley, BSc FCA *1978;* Yew Tree Farm Rode Lane, Carleton Rode, NORWICH, NR16 1NW.
•WATSON, Mr. David Charles, FCA *1973;* The Red Barn, Newton-in-the-Willows, Nr Geddington, KETTERING, NN14 1BW.
WATSON, Mr. David Charles Darsie, MA ACA *1986;* 4 National Terrace, Bermondsey Wall East, LONDON, SE16 4TZ.
WATSON, Mr. David Christopher, ACA *2007;* St. Gabriels, Bussage, STROUD, GLOUCESTERSHIRE, GL6 8AT.
WATSON, Mr. David Cyril Clifford, BA FCA *1958;* 1a Gables Close, Wendover, AYLESBURY, BUCKINGHAMSHIRE, HP22 6NH. (Life Member)
WATSON, Mr. David Frederick, FCA *1971;* 135 Seafield Road East, Clontarf, DUBLIN 3, COUNTY DUBLIN, IRELAND.
•WATSON, Mr. David Ian, FCA *1970;* David Watson, Knoll Farm, Aston Lane, Hope, HOPE VALLEY, DERBYSHIRE S33 6RA.
WATSON, Mr. David James, LLB ACA *2006;* 32 Marian Drive, GATESHEAD, TYNE AND WEAR, NE10 0TL.
WATSON, Mr. David John, BSc ACA *2006;* 47 Whernside Road, Woodthorpe, NOTTINGHAM, NG5 4LB.
WATSON, Mr. David Kenneth, BSc ACA *1984;* 3 The Meades, Old Avenue, WEYBRIDGE, KT13 0LS.
WATSON, Mr. David Lindsay, MA FCA *1977;* PO Box SP 60842, NASSAU, BAHAMAS.
WATSON, Mr. David Philip Richard, BA(Hons) ACA *2003;* Rosedale, 35 Hough Green, CHESTER, CH4 8JQ.
WATSON, Mr. David Taylor Urquhart, FCA *1960;* Crossways, Little Heath Lane, Potten End, BERKHAMSTED, HP4 2RY. (Life Member)
WATSON, Mr. David Twells, MA FCA *1964;* Heathfield, 6 Blakebrook, KIDDERMINSTER, DY11 6AP.
WATSON, Miss. Deborah, BSc(Hons) ACA *2003;* Grant Thornton Byron House, 2 Cambridge Business Park Cowley Road, CAMBRIDGE, CB4 0WZ.
WATSON, Mr. Derek Alan, BA ACA MBA *1996;* 100 North Martine Avenue, FANWOOD, NJ 07023, UNITED STATES.
WATSON, Mr. Derek Stephen, BA FCA *1977;* 2 Pattison Road, LONDON, NW2 2HH.
WATSON, Mr. Donald, FCA *1955;* Upfield, Leamington Road, Princethorpe, RUGBY, WARWICKSHIRE, CV23 9PU. (Life Member)
•WATSON, Mr. Edward, BSc FCA *1973;* Glen C Rodger Limited, Cragside House, Heaton Road, NEWCASTLE UPON TYNE, NE6 1SE.
WATSON, Mr. Edward David, BA ACA *2007;* 1 The Priory, La Grande Route de St. Clement St. Clement, JERSEY, JE2 6GU.
WATSON, Mr. Edward Ian, BA(Hons) ACA *2002;* 120 Marie Louise Lane, APTOS, CA 95003, UNITED STATES.
WATSON, Mrs. Elen Gwenllian, BSc ACA *2001;* 58 Thorp Arch Park, Thorp Arch, WETHERBY, WEST YORKSHIRE, LS23 7AN.
WATSON, Mrs. Elisabeth, BA ACA *1997;* Ideal Standard, The Bathroom Works, National Avenue, HULL, HU5 4HS.
WATSON, Miss. Elizabeth Lois, BSc ACA *1992;* Carriers Cottage, 13 Church Street, Boughton, NORTHAMPTON, NN2 8SF.
WATSON, Ms. Emma Jane, ACA *1992;* 12 Marie Avenue, HILLSBOROUGH, AUCKLAND, NEW ZEALAND.
WATSON, Miss. Esme, ACA *2010;* 77a North Road, St. Andrews, BRISTOL, BS6 5AQ.
WATSON, Miss. Fiona Anne, BA ACA *2005;* with Deloitte LLP, Athene Place, 66 Shoe Lane, LONDON, EC4A 3BQ.
WATSON, Mr. Ford William, BSc ACA *1995;* 229 Hartington Road, BRIGHTON, BN2 3PA.
WATSON, Mr. Francis David, BSc ACA *1980;* 20 Grange Way, IVER, SL0 9NU.
WATSON, Mr. Francis William, FCA *1968;* Colina Verde, 15 Serra e Mar, 8500-158 PORTIMAO, ALGARVE, PORTUGAL.
WATSON, Mr. Frank Nahapiet, FCA *1954;* 4 Haymeads Drive, ESHER, KT10 9EX. (Life Member)
WATSON, Mr. Frederick Alick, BA FCA *1963;* 24 Fountayne Road, Hunmanby, FILEY, NORTH YORKSHIRE, YO14 0LU. (Life Member)
WATSON, Mrs. Gail Mary, BA ACA *1992;* Calle Santiago de Compostela7, Residencial Amaya 24, Dona Pepa, 03170 ROJALES, ALICANTE, SPAIN.
WATSON, Mr. Gavin Stuart, BSc ACA *1995;* 520 Madison Avenue, 32nd Floor, NEW YORK, NY 10022 4213, UNITED STATES.
WATSON, Mr. Geoffrey, BSc ACA *1990;* Willow House, Station Road, Stonegate, WADHURST, TN5 7EP.
WATSON, Mr. Geoffrey David, MA MEng ACA *1996;* R P S Group Plc, Centurion Court, 85 Milton Park, ABINGDON, OXFORDSHIRE, OX14 4RY.
WATSON, Mr. Gerald Thompson, MA FCA *1958;* 40 Hall Drive, MIDDLESBROUGH, CLEVELAND, TS5 7ET. (Life Member)
WATSON, Mr. Giles Peter, BA ACA *1989;* 6th Floor, 21 Bryanston Street, LONDON, W1H 7PR.
WATSON, Mr. Giles Richard, BA ACA *2003;* Allandale House, Moor Road, Ashover, CHESTERFIELD, DERBYSHIRE, S45 0AE.
WATSON, Miss. Gillian McQuarrie, BA ACA *1998;* 8 Blackmead, Riverhead, SEVENOAKS, TN13 2QU.
WATSON, Miss. Gillian Michelle, BSc ACA *1997;* Bodycote Plc Springwood Court, Springwood Close Tytherington Business Park, MACCLESFIELD, CHESHIRE, SK10 2XF.
WATSON, Mr. Gordon Graham, FCA *1969;* 29 The Knowe, Willaston, NESTON, CH64 1TA. (Life Member)
WATSON, Mr. Graham, BSc ACA *1998;* Flat 4, 5a High Lane, MANCHESTER, M21 9DJ.
WATSON, Mr. Graham Rees, BA ACA *2005;* with PricewaterhouseCoopers LLP, 101 Barbirolli Square, Lower Mosley Street, MANCHESTER, M2 3PW.
WATSON, Mr. Gregory Hamilton, BA ACA *1990;* 11 Furber Street, Hammersmith, LONDON, W6 0HE.
WATSON, Mr. Hamish Murray, FCA *1969;* Riverside House, Axford, MARLBOROUGH, WILTSHIRE, SN8 2HA.
WATSON, Miss. Hazel Anne Marie, BComm FCA ACIS *1992;* (Tax Fac), 15 Eaton House, 38 Westferry Circus, Canary Riverside, LONDON, E14 8RN.
WATSON, Mrs. Helen Ann, MSc ACA *2003;* with PricewaterhouseCoopers LLP, 31 Great George Street, BRISTOL, BS1 5QD.
WATSON, Mrs. Helen Patricia, BA(Hons) ACA *2001;* 14 Whitethorn Lane, LETCHWORTH GARDEN CITY, SG6 2DN.
WATSON, Mr. Henry Stuart, FCA *1954;* Small Trees, 29 Norman Road, Hatfield, DONCASTER, DN7 6AF. (Life Member)
WATSON, Mr. Howard Thomas, FCA *1960;* Waites Barn, 1 Little Hame, Milton Keynes Village, MILTON KEYNES, MK10 9AN.
WATSON, Mr. Hugh Edward, BEng ACA *1999;* Rose Cottage Main Street, Thurning, PETERBOROUGH, PE8 5RB.
WATSON, Mr. Huw Spencer, BA FCA *1984;* Malvernspa Hotel, Grovewood Road, MALVERN, WORCESTERSHIRE, WR14 1GD.
WATSON, Mr. Ian, FCA *1965;* 20 Milestone Road, KNEBWORTH, HERTFORDSHIRE, SG3 6DA.
WATSON, Mr. Ian James, FCA *1966;* Thornfield, 2 Hudsons Croft, Newton-on-the-Moor, MORPETH, NORTHUMBERLAND, NE65 9JZ.
•WATSON, Mr. Ian Michael, BSc ACA *1989;* I Watson & Co, Cuckolds Green, Wrentham, BECCLES, SUFFOLK, NR34 7NB.
WATSON, Mr. Ian Roland, FCA *1964;* Langlands Farm, Ashill, CULLOMPTON, DEVON, EX15 3NA. (Life Member)
WATSON, Ms. Jacqueline Jane, MA ACA *1998;* Moorfield Road Estate, Yeadon, LEEDS, LS19 7BN.
WATSON, Mr. James, ACA *2011;* Mulberry Trees, 99 Fairmile Lane, COBHAM, SURREY, KT11 2DD.
WATSON, Mr. James David, BA(Hons) ACA *2009;* Flat 51 Bridge View Court, 19 Grange Road, LONDON, SE1 3BT.
WATSON, Mr. James Kenneth, FCA *1960;* Benton Potts, Hawridge, CHESHAM, BUCKINGHAMSHIRE, HP5 2UH. (Life Member)
WATSON, Mr. James Tinto, ACA *2008;* 48 Isis Street, LONDON, SW18 3QN.
WATSON, Mr. Jeremy Filmer, FCA *1966;* 16th floor Sithakarn Condominium, Soi Chidlom, Pratumwan, BANGKOK 10330, THAILAND.
WATSON, Mrs. Jill, BA ACA *1991;* 34 Townfield Lane, FRODSHAM, WA6 7RD.
•WATSON, Mrs. Jillian Mary, BA FCA *1983;* Simpkins Edwards LLP, 21 Boutport Street, BARNSTAPLE, DEVON, EX31 1RP.
WATSON, Mrs. Jo-Anne Katie, ACA *2010;* 25 Chilham Street, BOLTON, BL3 3QX.
WATSON, Mrs. Joanna, MA ACA *1992;* Pricewaterhousecoopers Cornwall Court, 19 Cornwall Street, BIRMINGHAM, B3 2DT.
WATSON, Mr. John, FCA *1968;* 8 Charnwood Way, Woodborough, NOTTINGHAM, NG14 6EW. (Life Member)
WATSON, Mr. John, BSc FCA *1981;* 9 College Fields, Clifton, BRISTOL, BS8 3HP.
WATSON, Mr. John, MA ACA APMI *1986;* Diageo Plc Lakeside Drive, Park Royal, LONDON, NW10 7HQ.
WATSON, Mr. John, BSc(Hons) ACA *2011;* 12 Woodmans Way, Whickham, NEWCASTLE UPON TYNE, NE16 5TR.
WATSON, Mr. John Alexander, BSc ACA *1985;* 52 - 54 Queen's Road, ABERDEEN, AB15 4YE.
WATSON, Mr. John David, FCA *1959;* (Tax Fac), 23 Priory Avenue, Ravenshead, NOTTINGHAM, NG15 9BT. (Life Member)
WATSON, Mr. John Hastings, FCA *1970;* Rockleyvale, 10 Lockerbie Road, DUMFRIES, DG1 3AT.
WATSON, Mr. John Paul, BA ACA *1987;* 132 Baginton Road, Styvechale, COVENTRY, CV3 6FS.
WATSON, Mr. John Tinto, BA FCA *1976;* 49 Trinity Road, Wimbledon, LONDON, SW19 8QS.
WATSON, Mr. John William, MA FCA *1979;* Northern Rock plc, Northern Rock House, Gosforth, NEWCASTLE UPON TYNE, NE3 4PL.
WATSON, Mr. Joseph Martin, FCA *1952;* Roxburgh, 21 Grange Road, BUSHEY, WD23 2LQ. (Life Member)
WATSON, Ms. Julie Isobel, MA ACA *1997;* Leonardstown Stud, Mullagh, KILCOCK, COUNTY KILDARE, IRELAND.
WATSON, Miss. Karen Lesley Frances, BA ACA *2000;* Lyncourt, 4 Clifton Road, LONDON, SW19 4QT.
WATSON, Miss. Katharine Jane, BCom ACA *2001;* Open Administration Systems Ltd, Ampney House, Falcon Close, Quedgeley, GLOUCESTER, GL2 4LS.
WATSON, Mrs. Katherine Anne, BSc ACA *1990;* Old Inn Cottage Main Road, Bredon, TEWKESBURY, GLOUCESTERSHIRE, GL20 7LX.
WATSON, Mrs. Katherine Anne, MSc ACA *2001;* 2 Iris Road, Bisley, WOKING, SURREY, GU24 9HG.
WATSON, Mr. Keith Graham, BSc ACA *2007;* 5 Bramley Chase, MAIDENHEAD, BERKSHIRE, SL6 4BG.
WATSON, Mr. Kevin John, BSc FCA *1990;* Littlebourne, Hazeley Road, Twyford, WINCHESTER, HAMPSHIRE, SO21 1PZ.
WATSON, Mrs. Kristin, BA FCA *1986;* Acre Wood House, 7 The Maples, Silsoe, BEDFORD, MK45 4DL.
•WATSON, Mr. Lee William, BSc ACA *2000;* Ernst & Young LLP, 1 More London Place, LONDON, SE1 2AF. See also Ernst & Young Europe LLP
WATSON, Miss. Leonie Clare, BSc ACA *2009;* 363 Lyham Road, LONDON, SW2 5NT.
WATSON, Miss. Lisa Ann, BA ACA *1999;* Deloitte SA, Avenue du Montchoisi 15, Case postale 460, 1001 LAUSANNE, SWITZERLAND.
WATSON, Mrs. Lisa Joanne, BA(Hons) ACA *2002;* Glendonwyn, 1 Belvedere Road, Anderton, CHORLEY, LANCASHIRE, PR6 9NT.
WATSON, Mrs. Lisa Siobhan, BSc ACA *1990;* Parsons Barn, Cowlinge, NEWMARKET, Suffolk, CB8 9QA.
•WATSON, Mrs. Lorna, MA ACA *1987;* (Tax Fac), Shaw Gibbs LLP, 264 Banbury Road, OXFORD, OX2 7DY.
WATSON, Miss. Louise Carole, MSc BA ACA *1999;* Royal Mail Group Ltd, 100 Victoria Embankment, LONDON, EC4Y 0HQ.
WATSON, Mrs. Louise Emily, BA ACA *2005;* 38 Oakes Lane, Brockholes, HOLMFIRTH, HD9 7AR.
•WATSON, Ms. Lucy, MA FCA CTA *1986;* Kilda Ltd, 80 Warwick Street, OXFORD, OX4 1SY. See also Lucy Goodwin
WATSON, Miss. Lucy Victoria, BSc(Hons) ACA *2004;* Argos Ltd, 489-499 Avebury Boulevard, MILTON KEYNES, MK9 2NW.
•WATSON, Mr. Lyn Frederick, FCA *1980;* Willow Tree Cottage, 11 Roman Bank, Gedney Dyke, SPALDING, LINCOLNSHIRE, PE12 0AR.
WATSON, Mr. Macer Philip, BCom ACA *1997;* 2 Elvington Lane, Hawkinge, FOLKESTONE, KENT, CT18 7AF.
WATSON, Mr. Malcolm James, BSc ACA *1992;* 8 Lynwood Gardens, HOOK, RG27 9DT.
WATSON, Mr. Malcolm Joseph, FCA *1958;* 13 Stowey Park, Yatton, BRISTOL, BS49 4JX. (Life Member)
WATSON, Mr. Malcolm Peter, MA ACA *1980;* 8 High Street, Turvey, BEDFORD, MK43 8DB.
WATSON, Mrs. Manjula, BSc ACA *1998;* 213 Lucas Lane, CHAPEL HILL, NC 27516, UNITED STATES.
•WATSON, Mr. Mark Andrew, ACA *2007;* Mark Watson, 37 Beacon Way, SKEGNESS, LINCOLNSHIRE, PE25 1HJ.
WATSON, Mr. Mark David, BSc ACA *2001;* Cherry Cottage, 69 Heath End Road, Flackwell Heath, HIGH WYCOMBE, BUCKINGHAMSHIRE, HP10 9EW.
•WATSON, Mr. Mark William, MA FCA *1987;* Mark W Watson, 4 Malus Close, MALVERN, WORCESTERSHIRE, WR14 2WD.
WATSON, Mr. Martin, ACA *2011;* Flat 7, 244 Royal College Street, LONDON, NW1 9QP.
WATSON, Mr. Martin John, FCA *1985;* 415 Lichfield Road, Four Oaks, SUTTON COLDFIELD, B74 4DJ.
WATSON, Mr. Martin Michael, BSc ACA *1993;* C/O LODH (BERMUDA) LIMITED, P.O. BOX 2271, HAMILTON HM JX, BERMUDA.
WATSON, Mr. Mathew Raymond, BA ACA *1997;* 7010 Mariann Drive, EDEN PRAIRIE, MN 55346, UNITED STATES.
•WATSON, Mr. Matthew Albert, BA ACA ATII *1995;* Ballard Dale Syree Watson LLP, Oakmoore Court, Kingswood Road, Hampton Lovett, DROITWICH, WORCESTERSHIRE WR9 0QH.
WATSON, Mr. Matthew Anthony, BSc ACA *2005;* 46 Clarke Crescent, Kennington, ASHFORD, KENT, TN24 9SA.
WATSON, Mrs. Melanie Sue, MA ACA *1999;* 90A Curtis Road, Willesborough, ASHFORD, KENT, TN24 0DB.

WATSON, Mr. Michael, BA ACA *1991;* Amethyst Client Services, Dallam Court Dallam Lane, WARRINGTON, CHESHIRE, WA2 7LT.
WATSON, Mr. Michael, BA(Hons) ACA *2001;* 01-06 Jervois Mansion, 19 Jervois Road, SINGAPORE 249002, SINGAPORE.
WATSON, Mr. Michael David, BA FCA *1984;* 27 Highacre, DORKING, RH4 3BF.
WATSON, Mr. Michael John Bucknell, FCA *1958;* Ridge Cottage, High Barn Road, Effingham, LEATHERHEAD, SURREY, KT24 5PX. (Life Member)
•WATSON, Mr. Michael Raymond, FCA *1964;* (Tax Fac), Alcock Watson Associates, 15 High Street, LYDNEY, GLOUCESTERSHIRE, GL15 5DP.
•WATSON, Mr. Michael Steven, BA ACA CTA *1990;* (Tax Fac), Allotts, Sidings Court, Lakeside, DONCASTER, SOUTH YORKSHIRE, DN4 5NU.
WATSON, Mr. Michael Wilfred, BA FCA *1974;* 4 Shelton Close, WEDNESBURY, WS10 0TZ.
WATSON, Mrs. Nathalie, BSc ACA *1996;* Broad Oak, Burchetts Green Lane, Burchetts Green, MAIDENHEAD, BERKSHIRE, SL6 3QW.
WATSON, Mr. Neil, BSc ACA *1996;* Eville & Jones Ltd Century House, 1275 Century Way Thorpe Park, LEEDS, LS15 8ZB.
WATSON, Mr. Neil Bailey, FCA *1964;* 34 Dornden Drive, Langton Green, TUNBRIDGE WELLS, KENT, TN3 0AB.
WATSON, Mr. Neil Dykes, BEng ACA *1997;* Willow Vale, Tradespark Road, NAIRN, IV12 5NF.
WATSON, Mr. Neil Martin, BA ACA *1992;* Thickwood Lodge, Baslow Road, Owler Bar, SHEFFIELD, S17 3BQ.
WATSON, Mr. Nicholas, BSc(Hons) ACA *2001;* 2 Iris Road, Bisley, WOKING, SURREY, GU24 9HG.
•WATSON, Mr. Nicholas David, BA FCA *1982;* NW Consultants Limited, 55 Crown Street, BRENTWOOD, ESSEX, CM14 4BD.
•WATSON, Mr. Nicholas James, BSc ACA *1999;* Grant Thornton UK LLP, 1-4 Atholl Crescent, EDINBURGH, EH3 8LQ. See also Grant Thornton LLP
WATSON, Mr. Nicholas Jay, LLB ACA ATII *1998;* 122 Walsall Road, SUTTON COLDFIELD, WEST MIDLANDS, B74 4RB.
WATSON, Mr. Nicholas John, BSc ACA *1988;* Old Inn Cottage, Main Road, Bredon, TEWKESBURY, GLOUCESTERSHIRE, GL20 7LX.
WATSON, Mr. Nicholas Mark, BA(Hons) ACA *2003;* 15 Downend Road, Horfield, BRISTOL, BS7 9PD.
WATSON, Mr. Oliver William Argyle, ACA *1981;* Darfield House, Tissington, ASHBOURNE, DERBYSHIRE, DE6 1RA.
WATSON, Mr. Patrick, ACA *2008;* Elm Tree Barn Church Lane, Lower Heyford, BICESTER, OXFORDSHIRE, OX25 5NZ.
WATSON, Mr. Patrick Simon, BA ACA *2007;* 12B Beatty Road, LONDON, N16 8EB.
•WATSON, Mr. Paul, BEng ACA *2007;* Passman Leonard Limited, Bentinck House, Bentinck Road, WEST DRAYTON, MIDDLESEX, UB7 7RQ.
WATSON, Mr. Paul Douglas, MA ACA *2002;* 2 The Alders, Alder Road Denham, UXBRIDGE, MIDDLESEX, UB9 4AY.
WATSON, Mr. Paul Douglas, BSc ACA *1984;* #22 Hamptons Lane, SOUTHAMPTON SN02, BERMUDA.
WATSON, Mr. Paul Francis Turner, FCA *1965;* Buffers, Riverside Walk, OLNEY, MK46 4BP. (Life Member)
•WATSON, Mr. Paul Graham, BSc FCA *1992;* P G & S A Watson Ltd, Denstone, 6 Park Road, Chandlers Ford, EASTLEIGH, SO53 2EU.
WATSON, Mr. Paul James, BA ACA *1996;* 98 Hill View, Henleaze, BRISTOL, BS9 4QG.
WATSON, Mr. Paul Richard John, BA ACA *2002;* Charles Stanley & Co Ltd, 25 Luke Street, LONDON, EC2A 4AR.
WATSON, Mr. Peter, FCA *1965;* 3 Hever Place, St Stephens, CANTERBURY, CT2 7QP.
WATSON, Mr. Peter, FCA *1969;* 24 Richmond Way, Croxley Green, RICKMANSWORTH, HERTFORDSHIRE, WD3 3SE.
WATSON, Mr. Peter Begbie, BSc ACA *1986;* 19 High Street, Rowledge, FARNHAM, GU10 4BT.
WATSON, Mr. Peter Gareth, FCA *1975;* Therfield, 23 Mile House Lane, ST. ALBANS, HERTFORDSHIRE, AL1 1TF.
WATSON, Mr. Peter George, MA ACA FSI *1985;* (Tax Fac), Mint House, 77 Mansell Street, LONDON, E1 8AF.
WATSON, Mr. Peter James, FCA *1963;* 80 Chemin des Vignes, 01600 SAINT BERNARD, FRANCE.
WATSON, Prof. Peter Lawrence, MSc FCA *1969;* Bleak Hall Farmhouse, Dadford Road, Silverstone, TOWCESTER, NN12 8TJ.
WATSON, Mr. Peter Nigel, FCA *1963;* Aosta, Parkgate Road, Newdigate, DORKING, RH5 5AH.
WATSON, Mr. Peter Richard, BSc ACA *1990;* Cowling Corporate Broking Ltd The Maltings, High Street Burwell, CAMBRIDGE, CB25 0HB.
WATSON, Mr. Philip Hamish, MA ACA *2003;* with KPMG LLP, 15 Canada Square, LONDON, E14 5GL.
WATSON, Ms. Rebecca Joyce, ACA *2006;* Streets Tower House, Lucy Tower Street, LINCOLN, LN1 1XW.
WATSON, Mrs. Rebecca Louise, BA(Hons) ACA *2001;* 88 Moore Road, Mapperley, NOTTINGHAM, NG3 6EJ.
•WATSON, Mr. Richard, BSc FCA *1968;* (Tax Fac), Tudor Lodge, 16 Lime Tree Walk, RICKMANSWORTH, WD3 4BX.
WATSON, Mr. Richard Harry John, MA ACA *2002;* 39 Thorpe Road, ST ALBANS, AL1 1RF.
•WATSON, Mr. Richard Michael, MA FCA *1976;* Armstrong Watson, Currer House, 34/36 Otley Street, SKIPTON, BD23 1EW.
WATSON, Mr. Richard Paul, BMus FCA *1989;* 114 Harwoods Road, WATFORD, WD18 7RE.
WATSON, Mr. Richard Stuart, ACA *2004;* 108 Burnham Road, LEIGH-ON-SEA, SS9 2JS.
WATSON, Mr. Robert, BSc ACA *2007;* with Deloitte LLP, 2 New Street Square, LONDON, EC4A 3BZ.
WATSON, Mr. Robert Alan, FCA *1966;* 32 Station Road, AMERSHAM, BUCKINGHAMSHIRE, HP7 0BE.
•WATSON, Mr. Robert Charles, FCA *1974;* Robert Watson, 71 Hayes Hill, Hayes, BROMLEY, KENT, BR2 7HN.
•WATSON, Mr. Robert Ian, BA(Hons) ACA *2002;* Gibson Booth, 12 Victoria Road, BARNSLEY, SOUTH YORKSHIRE, S70 2BB. See also Salary Solutions Limited
•WATSON, Mr. Robert Michael, FCA *1969;* (Tax Fac), Passman Leonard Limited, Bentinck House, Bentinck Road, WEST DRAYTON, MIDDLESEX, UB7 7RQ.
WATSON, Mrs. Robina Mary, MA FCA *1976;* Castletown Insurance Services, Compton House, Parliament Square, Castleton, ISLE OF MAN, IM9 1LA.
WATSON, Mr. Roderick John Alderson, FCA *1971;* 36 Ashburnham Place, Greenwich, LONDON, SE10 8TZ.
WATSON, Mr. Roy, FCA *1977;* 244 Newton Road, Lowton, WARRINGTON, WA3 2AD.
WATSON, Mr. Rupert Michael Colvin, FCA *1975;* Little Waltham Hall, Little Waltham, CHELMSFORD, CM3 3LJ.
WATSON, Mr. Russell John, BSc ACA *1993;* 87 Bennerley Road, Battersea, LONDON, SW11 6DT.
WATSON, Miss. Ruth, ACA *2011;* 15 Malden Road, LEEDS, LS6 4QT.
WATSON, Miss. Sally Elizabeth, BA ACA *1990;* Old Well Cottage, Mapleton Road, WESTERHAM, TN16 1PS.
WATSON, Miss. Sarah, BSc ACA *2009;* 418/46 Shoreline Drive, RHODES, NSW 2138, AUSTRALIA.
WATSON, Mrs. Sarah Ann, BA(Hons) ACA *2000;* Standerton House, Seymour Drive, PLYMOUTH, PL3 5BG.
WATSON, Mr. Sean, ACA *2011;* 65 Burnelli Building, Chelsea Bridge Wharf, 352 Queenstown Road, LONDON, SW8 4NG.
WATSON, Mr. Sebastian Lawrence, BA(Hons) ACA MMus *2011;* 69 Queens Road, THAMES DITTON, KT7 0QY.
WATSON, Miss. Serena Nancy, FCA *1975;* 3 Church Close, Steeton, KEIGHLEY, WEST YORKSHIRE, BD20 6SF.
WATSON, Mrs. Shirley, BSc ACA *1981;* 68 Games Road, BARNET, HERTFORDSHIRE, EN4 9HT.
WATSON, Mrs. Sian Elizabeth, BSc ACA *1991;* (Tax Fac), Willow House, Station Road, Stonegate, WADHURST, TN5 7EP.
•WATSON, Mr. Simon David, BA FCA *1986;* BDO LLP, Kings Wharf, 20-30 Kings Road, READING, RG1 3EX. See also BDO Stoy Hayward LLP
WATSON, Mrs. Sonia Jayne, BSc ACA *1990;* Littlebourne, Hazeley Road, Twyford, WINCHESTER, HAMPSHIRE, SO21 1PZ.
•WATSON, Mr. Spencer Forrester, FCA *1993;* Buckley Watson, 57a The Broadway, LEIGH-ON-SEA, SS9 1PE.
WATSON, Mr. Stephen Alan, FCA *1975;* 3a Hill Farm Road, SOUTHAMPTON, SO15 5SP.
•WATSON, Mr. Stephen Andrew, FCA *1983;* (Tax Fac), Moore Stephens, 12/13 Alma Square, SCARBOROUGH, YO11 1JU.
WATSON, Mr. Stephen David, BSc ACA *1979;* 15 Highfield Road, Hall Green, BIRMINGHAM, B28 0EL.
WATSON, Mr. Stephen Joseph, FCA *1975;* The Old Builders Arms, Chalford Hill, STROUD, GL6 8EF.
WATSON, Mr. Stephen Nicholas, BA FCA *1985;* 4 Nimrod Close, ST. ALBANS, AL4 9XY.
WATSON, Mr. Stephen Richard Hurst, BSc ACA *1989;* 151 Victoria Road, Wednesfield, WOLVERHAMPTON, WV11 1RL.
WATSON, Mr. Steven Michael, BSc ACA *2003;* 169 Riverside Road, ST. ALBANS, HERTFORDSHIRE, AL1 1RZ.
WATSON, Mr. Steven Michael, BSc ACA DChA *1986;* Shakespeare Globe Trust Ltd, 21 New Globe Walk, LONDON, SE1 9DT.
WATSON, Mr. Steven Paul, BSc ACA *1987;* Highridge, Kerves Lane, HORSHAM, RH13 6ES.
WATSON, Mr. Steven Robert, BA ACA *1985;* Hill Barn, East Marden, CHICHESTER, WEST SUSSEX, PO18 9JB.
WATSON, Mr. Stuart, BSc(Hons) ACA *2000;* Group Internal Audit SCB Level 13, 8 Marina Boulevard, Marina Bay Financial Centre Tower 1, SINGAPORE 018981, SINGAPORE.
WATSON, Mr. Stuart John, BSc ACA *1995;* 20 Milestone Road, KNEBWORTH, HERTFORDSHIRE, SG3 6DA.
WATSON, Mr. Stuart Maxwell, FCA *1975;* (Tax Fac), 44 Kirkburn, LAURENCEKIRK, ABERDEENSHIRE, AB30 1LG.
•WATSON, Mr. Stuart William, BA FCA *1986;* Ernst & Young LLP, 1 Bridgewater Place, Water Lane, LEEDS, LS11 5QR. See also Ernst & Young Europe LLP
•WATSON, Mrs. Susan Carol, MA FCA *1988;* (Tax Fac), Susan Watson Accountancy Services, 28 Oak Drive, HENLOW, SG16 6BX.
WATSON, Miss. Susan Lesley, MA ACA *1985;* 157 Auckland Road, Upper Norwood, LONDON, SE19 2RH.
WATSON, Mrs. Susan Margaret, BSc FCA *1978;* with Harris Watson Holdings Plc, Unit 3, First Floor, Dartmouth Middleway, Aston Science Park, BIRMINGHAM B7 4AZ.
WATSON, Mrs. Suzannah, BSc ACA *2004;* with Larking Gowen, King Street House, 15 Upper King Street, NORWICH, NR3 1RB.
WATSON, Mr. Thomas Ronald Fletcher, ACA *1981;* Boeing UK Training & Flight Services Boeing House, Crawley Business Quarter Manor Royal, CRAWLEY, WEST SUSSEX, RH10 9AD.
•WATSON, Mr. Timothy, FCA *1983;* (Tax Fac), Gillard Watson, 7 The Pagets, Newick, LEWES, EAST SUSSEX, BN8 4PW.
WATSON, Mr. Timothy Julian, FCA *1963;* 50 Somerville Rd, LEICESTER, LE3 2EU.
WATSON, Mr. Timothy Patrick, BSc ACA *1991;* Lynnhatch 31 High Street Lindfield, HAYWARDS HEATH, WEST SUSSEX, RH16 2HJ.
WATSON, Mr. Trevor, FCA *1964;* 4 Little Clover, Hull Bridge Road, BEVERLEY, HU17 9HQ.
•WATSON, Ms. Valerie Diane, BSc FCA CTA *1989;* (Tax Fac), Moore Stephens LLP, 150 Aldersgate Street, LONDON, EC1A 4AB. See also Moore Stephens & Co
WATSON, Miss. Victoria Helen Christine, ACA *2010;* Cleaveside Verriotts Lane, Morcombelake, BRIDPORT, DORSET, DT6 6DU.
WATSON, Mr. William Allan, ACA *2009;* 40 Barnes End, NEW MALDEN, SURREY, KT3 6PB.
WATSON, Mr. William John, BSc ACA *1999;* 9 Oakley Road, Caversham, READING, RG4 7RL.
WATSON, Mr. William Wilson, BA FCA *1964;* 18 Lyttelton Road, DROITWICH, WORCESTERSHIRE, WR9 7AA. (Life Member)
WATSON BROWN, Mr. Hugo, BA ACA *1989;* Brabourne Consulting Ltd, 8 Park Avenue, East Sheen, LONDON, SW14 8AT.
•WATSON JONES, Mr. Robert, FCA *1980;* Watson Jones Accounting Limited, 18 Hillside, Lilleshall, NEWPORT, SHROPSHIRE, TF10 9HG.
WATT, Dr. Alan William, FCA *1991;* 3 Haslemere Gardens, OXFORD, OX2 8EL.
WATT, Ms. Alison Leigh, ACA CA(AUS) *2011;* 31 Brangwyn Crescent, Wimbledon, LONDON, SW19 2UA.
WATT, Mr. Andrew David, BA ACA *2000;* 10 Toynbee Road, LONDON, SW20 8SS.
•WATT, Mr. Andrew Michael, ACA CA(AUS) *2009;* with Ernst & Young LLP, 1 More London Place, LONDON, SE1 2AF.
WATT, Mrs. Caroline Lucy, BA ACA *1993;* 18 Union Road, LEAMINGTON SPA, WARWICKSHIRE, CV32 5LT.
WATT, Mr. Charles Edward, BCom ACA *1993;* Cranstons Ltd, Ullswater Road, PENRITH, CUMBRIA, CA11 7EH.
WATT, Mrs. Cheryl Ann, FCA *1989;* (Tax Fac), 3 Haslemere Gardens, OXFORD, OX2 8EL.
WATT, Mr. Christopher John, BA ACA *1998;* with E C I Partners, Brettenham House, Lancaster Place, LONDON, WC2E 7EN.
WATT, Mr. David, BCom ACA *2003;* 47 Alderbrook Road, LONDON, SW12 8AD.
WATT, Mr. David Alexander, BSc CMath FCA MIMA *1977;* (Tax Fac), 17 Huntsmans Meadow, ASCOT, SL5 7PF.
WATT, Mrs. Elizabeth Kay, BSc ACA *1980;* Oak Tree Farm, Foston-on-the-Wolds, DRIFFIELD, NORTH HUMBERSIDE, YO25 8BJ.
WATT, Mrs. Fiona Stephanie, BA(Hons) ACA *2009;* 7 Graf Bernadotte Strasse, 33719 BIELEFELD, GERMANY.
WATT, Mr. Gordon George, BA FCA *1977;* Alderbury Holt, Southampton Road, Clarendon, SALISBURY, SP5 3DG.
WATT, Mr. Graeme Alistair, BSc ACA *1988;* Bell Microproducts Ltd Fountain Court, Cox Lane, CHESSINGTON, KT9 1SJ.
WATT, Mr. Ian Lorimer, MA ACA *1979;* 27 Wheat Close, Jersey Farm, ST. ALBANS, AL4 9NN.
•WATT, Mr. Ian Stewart, BSc FCA *1984;* (Tax Fac), Langdon West Williams plc, Curzon House, 24 High Street, BANSTEAD, SM7 2LJ.
WATT, Mrs. Jacqueline Sheila Stanley, BA ACA *1979;* 88 Townsend Lane, HARPENDEN, AL5 2RQ.
WATT, Mr. Keith Allen, BA ACA *2006;* 48 Allen Street, Leichhardt, SYDNEY, NSW 2040, AUSTRALIA.
WATT, Miss. Mary Jane, BSc ACA *1992;* The Spinney, 34 Roundwood Avenue, Hutton, BRENTWOOD, CM13 2LZ.
WATT, Mr. Ninian Aitken, CA *1974; (CA Scotland 1963);* Bardsey Lodge, Tithe Barn Lane, Bardsey, LEEDS, LS17 9DX.
WATT, Mr. Paul Charles, BSc ACA *1979;* 16 Hamilton Road, Ealing, LONDON, W5 2EH.
WATT, Mr. Richard George, FCA *1973;* Highfield, Vallum Place, Monkhill, CARLISLE, CA5 6DE.
WATT, Mrs. Sarah, MA LLM FCA FRSA *1966;* 163 Coldhams Lane, CAMBRIDGE, CB1 3HY. (Life Member)
WATT, Mrs. Sarah Louise, ACA *1996;* Sunrise Software Ltd, 50 Barwell Business Park, Leatherhead Road, CHESSINGTON, SURREY, KT9 2NY.
WATT, Mrs. Shirley, FCA *1977;* 15 Lovatt Close, Tilehurst, READING, RG31 5HG.
WATT, Mr. Stephen John, MA ACA *1989;* 15 Greenfield Crescent, BALERNO, MIDLOTHIAN, EH14 7HD.
•WATT, Mr. Stephen Michael, BSc FCA CTA *1976;* Steve Watt Bsc FCA CTA, 1 Connaught Road, FOLKESTONE, KENT, CT20 1DA.
WATT, Mr. Stephen Mitchell Archibald, BA ACA *1994;* 15 Foxon Lane, CATERHAM, CR3 5SG.
WATT, Miss. Susan Katherine, BSc ACA *1998;* 39 Station Road, Llanishen, CARDIFF, CF14 5UT.
WATT, Mr. Timothy, BA ACA *2007;* 34 Booth Avenue, SANDBACH, CHESHIRE, CW11 4JN.
WATT, Mrs. Victoria Anne, BA(Hons) ACA *2001;* 46 Church Road, Longlevens, GLOUCESTER, GL2 0AH.
WATT SMITH, Mr. Simon Jonathan, FCA *1975;* 10 Dee Road, Mickle Trafford, CHESTER, CH2 4DL.
WATTAM, Mr. Julian Philip, ACA *1995;* 39 Lovatt Drive, Bletchley, MILTON KEYNES, MK3 7BU.
WATTAM, Mr. Neil John, ACA *2008;* 17 Westoby Close, Shepshed, LOUGHBOROUGH, LE12 9SS.
WATTAM, Mr. Paul Robert, BA FCA *1970;* Chainings Limited, Newent Business Park, NEWENT, GLOUCESTERSHIRE, GL18 1DZ.
WATTERS, Mr. Gordon, FCA *1965;* The Dipping Well, Back Lane, Billingley, BARNSLEY, S72 0JF.
WATTERS, Mr. Peter Christopher, ACA *2005;* 2 Delaware Drive, ST. LEONARDS-ON-SEA, EAST SUSSEX, TN37 7TJ.
WATTERSON, Mr. Bruce, MSc ACA *2004;* Dixcart Trust Corporation Ltd, PO Box 161, GUERNSEY, GY1 4EZ.
WATTERSON, Miss. Cheryl Ann, BSc(Hons) ACA *2004;* 10 Winnipeg Quay, Salford Quays, SALFORD, M50 3TY.
WATTERSON, Mr. Ian George Walter, BA ACA *1995;* 5057 Vernon Oaks Drive, ATLANTA, GA 30338, UNITED STATES.
WATTERSON, Mr. Jack Edward, FCA *1948;* South Riding, Chettisham, ELY, CB6 1SB. (Life Member)
WATTERSON, Mrs. Joanne Vanessa, BSc(Hons) ACA CTA *2003;* Meadowbank, 8 Keeil Pharick, Glen Vine, ISLE OF MAN, IM4 4EW.
WATTERSON, Mr. Juan Paul, BA(Hons) ACA MHK *2005;* (Member of Council 2006 - 2007), Legislative Buildings, ISLE OF MAN, IM1 3PW.
WATTERSON, Mr. Paul Michael, BA(Hons) ACA *2002;* Continent 8 Technologies Plc, Continent 8 House, Pulrose Road, Douglas, ISLE OF MAN, IM2 1AL.

WATTERSON, Mr. Richard John, BA ACA *1996;* 27 Wesley Street, OSSETT, WF5 8EU.

WATTERSTON, Miss. Anastasia Mary Lillian, ACA MAAT *2009;* Drake International Ltd, 20 Regent Street, LONDON, SW1Y 4PH.

•**WATTERSTON, Mrs. Juliana Marilyn, MSc FCA FTII** *1973;* Käthchen-Paulus-Straße 18, 60486 FRANKFURT AM MAIN, GERMANY.

WATTIS, Mr. David John, FCA *1966;* 859 Shirley Road, Hall Green, BIRMINGHAM, B28 9JJ. (Life Member)

WATTON, Mrs. Catherine Ruth, BA ACA *2000;* 14 Highfield Road, ISLEWORTH, TW7 5LD.

WATTON, Mr. David James, FCA *1994;* 12A Takitimu Street, Orakei, AUCKLAND 1071, NEW ZEALAND.

•**WATTON, Mr. David Keith, FCA** *1980;* Princecroft Willis LLP, Towngate House, 2-8 Parkstone Road, POOLE, DORSET, BH15 2PW. See also PW Business Solutions

WATTON, Mr. Mark John, BA ACA *2000;* 10 Combe View, HUNGERFORD, RG17 0BZ.

WATTON, Mr. Victor Charles, MA FCA *1975;* Thrushel Down, Thrushell Down, Thorndon Cross, OKEHAMPTON, DEVON, EX20 4NG.

•**WATTRUS, Miss. Rowena, ACA CA(SA)** *2006;* Freeman and Partners Limited, 30 St James's Street, LONDON, SW1A 1HB.

•**WATTS, Mrs. Alison Jane, BSc FCA CF** *1987;* Armstrong Watson, Fairview House, Victoria Place, CARLISLE, CA1 1HP.

•**WATTS, Mr. Andrew James, BSc FCA** *1998;* with PricewaterhouseCoopers LLP, Cornwall Court, 19 Cornwall Street, BIRMINGHAM, B3 2DT.

WATTS, Mr. Andrew William, BA(Hons) ACA *2003;* Flat 9 Heath Mansions, Putney Heath Lane, LONDON, SW15 3JJ.

•**WATTS, Miss. Angela Jean, BSc FCA** *1983;* (Tax Fac), A.J.Watts, 54 Beldam Avenue, ROYSTON, SG8 9UW.

•**WATTS, Mrs. Angela Therese, BSc ACA** *1987;* Globe Accounting, 19 Isaacson Road, Burwell, CAMBRIDGE, CB25 0AF.

WATTS, Mr. Anthony, BA ACA *1978;* 29 London Road, REIGATE, RH2 9PY.

WATTS, Mr. Augustine Francis Patmore, MBE FCA *1953;* 11 Conyers Way, Great Barton, BURY ST. EDMUNDS, SUFFOLK, IP31 2RL. (Life Member)

WATTS, Miss. Catherine Frances, BSc(Hons) ACA *2004;* 142 Welsh House Farm Road, BIRMINGHAM, B32 2JG.

WATTS, Miss. Catherine Jane, MA ACA *2001;* with Deloitte LLP, Athene Place, 66 Shoe Lane, LONDON, EC4A 3BQ.

•**WATTS, Mr. Charles Michael, FCA** *1966;* (Tax Fac), Michael Watts, Raven Gill, Parkhead, Renwick, PENRITH, CA10 1JQ.

WATTS, Mr. Christopher John, FCA *1956;* 51 Furzehill Road, BOREHAMWOOD, WD6 2DJ. (Life Member)

WATTS, Mr. Christopher John, BSc ACA *1995;* Suite 440 South Bank House, Black Prince Road, LONDON, SE1 7SJ.

•**WATTS, Mr. Christopher John, BA FCA** *1972;* 14 Liphook Crescent, Forest Hill, LONDON, SE23 3BW.

WATTS, Mr. Christopher Philip, BA FCA *1986;* Shaw Energy & Chemicals Ltd, Witan Gate House 500 - 600 Witan Gate West, MILTON KEYNES, MK9 1BA.

WATTS, Mr. Colin Andrew, BA ACA *1985;* 145 Ware Road, HERTFORD, SG13 7EG.

•**WATTS, Mr. David James, BA FCA** *1986;* ARAMARK, 250 Fowler Avenue, FARNBOROUGH, GU14 7JP.

•**WATTS, Mr. David James, FCA** *1953;* (Tax Fac), David J. Watts, White Wheels, Aston Abbotts, AYLESBURY, BUCKINGHAMSHIRE, HP22 4LU.

•**WATTS, Mr. David Leonard, BA FCA** *1982;* Newton & Garner Limited, Building 2, 30 Friern Park, North Finchley, LONDON, N12 9DA.

WATTS, Mr. David Michael, BA ACA AMCT *1991;* Somerden Farmhouse, Tonbridge Road, Bough Beech, EDENBRIDGE, KENT, TN8 7AJ.

WATTS, Mr. David Robert, BA ACA *1995;* 7 Westlands Road, Moseley, BIRMINGHAM, B13 9RH.

WATTS, Mr. Denis Stanley, FCA *1967;* Cherry Lodge, 29 Burley Road, Oakham, RUTLAND, LEICESTERSHIRE, LE15 6DH. (Life Member)

WATTS, Mr. Derek, FCA *1956;* Little Bospen, Casterills Road, HELSTON, TR13 8BJ. (Life Member)

WATTS, Mr. Duncan Matthew, LLB ACA *1991;* The Enterprise, 35 Walton Street, LONDON, SW3 2HU.

WATTS, Mr. Edgar, FCA *1952;* The Lodge, 18 Pendene Road, Stoneygate, LEICESTER, LE2 3DQ. (Life Member)

WATTS, Miss. Fiona Louise, BSc ACA *1992;* 8 Whitehead Grove, Balsall Common, COVENTRY, CV7 7US.

WATTS, Mr. Garry, FCA *1982;* 18 Rutland Street, LONDON, SW7 1EF.

WATTS, Mr. Gary William, BSc ACA *1989;* 6 Berryfield Rise, Osbaston, MONMOUTH, GWENT, NP25 3DU.

WATTS, Mr. Gordon Vernon, LLB ACA *1983;* 6 Loxwood Road, WATERLOOVILLE, HAMPSHIRE, PO8 9TU.

•**WATTS, Mr. Graham James, FCA** *1974;* (Tax Fac), R.J.Dixon & Co, 6 Woodland Way, Marden Ash, ONGAR, CM5 9EP.

WATTS, Mr. Graham Peter, FCA *1974;* Midway, Tyndale Road, Slimbridge, GLOUCESTER, GL2 7DJ. (Life Member)

WATTS, Mr. Grahame John, FCA *1971;* Morley Grange, Eccups Lane, Morley Green, WILMSLOW, SK9 5NZ. (Life Member)

•**WATTS, Mr. Gregory Alexander, BEng FCA** *1993;* KPMG LLP, One Snowhill, Snow Hill Queensway, BIRMINGHAM, B4 6GN. See also KPMG Europe LLP

WATTS, Mrs. Heather Anne, BSc FCA *1976;* Jack Burn, Whitestone, HEREFORD, HR1 3RZ.

WATTS, Mrs. Helen Kay, BSc FCA *1988;* 46 Swallow Rise, Knaphill, WOKING, GU21 2LH.

WATTS, Mr. Huw Edgar, BA ACA *1995;* 117 The Hawthorns, Charvil, READING, RG10 9TT.

WATTS, Mrs. Jacqueline Anne, BSc FCA *1989;* 21 Holliday Avenue, BEROWRA HEIGHTS, NSW 2082, AUSTRALIA.

WATTS, Ms. Jane Rowena, BA ACA *1985;* Marie Cottage, Bickenhill Lane, Catherine-De-Barnes, SOLIHULL, B92 0DE.

•**WATTS, Mr. Jeremy James, FCA** *1969;* (Tax Fac), Feltons Limited, 12 Sheet Street, WINDSOR, BERKSHIRE, SL4 1BG. See also Pumphrey Dasalo Limited, LW Feltons Limited and Feltons

WATTS, Mrs. Joanna Charlotte, BSc ACA DChA *2002;* 8 Thoroughfare Yard, NORWICH, NORFOLK, NR3 1LF.

WATTS, Mr. John Arthur, MA FCA *1973;* The Hustings, 34 West Lane Close, Keeston, HAVERFORDWEST, SA62 6EW. (Life Member)

WATTS, Mr. John Cranston, ACA *2009;* 118 Comiston Drive, EDINBURGH, EH10 5QU.

•**WATTS, Mr. John Garratt, FCA** *1959;* (Tax Fac), 24 Chard Road, Drimpton, BEAMINSTER, DORSET, DT8 3RF.

WATTS, Mr. John Ronald, FCA *1974;* 20 Landra Gardens, Grange Park, LONDON, N21 1RT.

WATTS, Mr. Jonathan Mark, MSc BSc ACA *2007;* 7 Burnet Close, MELKSHAM, SN12 7SJ.

WATTS, Mr. Joshua, MA FCA *1950;* 41 Lucombe Way, New Earswick, YORK, YO32 4DS. (Life Member)

WATTS, Mrs. Julia, BA ACA *1982;* 57 Toms Lane, KINGS LANGLEY, WD4 8NA.

WATTS, Mr. Julyan, MA FCA *1969;* World Bank Country Office, Taras Shevchenko St, DUSHANBE, TAJIKISTAN.

WATTS, Miss. Kathryn Anne, FCA *1982;* (Tax Fac), 52 Bower Street, BEDFORD, MK40 3RE.

WATTS, Mr. Kevin Paul, BSc ACA *1986;* Hill Farm, Foscote, TOWCESTER, NORTHAMPTONSHIRE, NN12 8PB.

WATTS, Miss. Kirsty Emma, ACA *2001;* Lawrence Webb Limited, McCrone House 155a Leighton Road, LONDON, NW5 2RD.

•**WATTS, Mr. Lawrence James, BSc ACA** *1993;* PricewaterhouseCoopers LLP, 7 More London Riverside, LONDON, SE1 2RT. See also PricewaterhouseCoopers

WATTS, Miss. Leslie, BSc ACA *1983;* Chiltern Way, 19 Upper Icknield Way, Aston Clinton, AYLESBURY, HP22 5NF.

WATTS, Mr. Leslie Charles, BSc FCA *1971;* Ringlands House, 7 Wellesley Road, ANDOVER, HAMPSHIRE, SP10 2HF.

WATTS, Mrs. Linda Teresa, BSc ACA *1993;* 5 Damson Way, ST. ALBANS, HERTFORDSHIRE, AL4 9XU.

•**WATTS, Mrs. Louise, BA ACA** *1994;* with Venthams Limited, Millhouse, 32-38 East Street, ROCHFORD, SS4 1DB.

WATTS, Mr. Mark, BEng ACA *1998;* Realm Ltd, The Farmhouse, Farm Road, STREET, SOMERSET, BA16 0FB.

•**WATTS, Mr. Mark Sanderson, BSocSc ACA** *1992;* Dow Schofield Watts Corporate Finance Limited, 7700 Daresbury Park, Daresbury, WARRINGTON, CHESHIRE, WA4 5BS.

WATTS, Mr. Martin James, BA ACA *1986;* Honeywell Analytical Ltd, Hatchpond House, 4 Stinsford Road, POOLE, DORSET, BH17 0RZ.

WATTS, Mr. Matthew John, MSc BSc ACA *2005;* National Grid, 31 Homer Road, SOLIHULL, B91 3LT.

WATTS, Mr. Matthew Lawrence, MA ACA *2001;* with Smith & Williamson Ltd, 25 Moorgate, LONDON, EC2R 6AY.

WATTS, Mr. Michael Alan, LTCL FCA CTA *1961;* Sa Font Del Mul 50, Apartamento 3, Carretera Del Puerto, 07108 PUERTO DE SOLLER, MALLORCA, SPAIN. (Life Member)

•**WATTS, Mr. Michael David, FCA** *1967;* (Tax Fac), Michael Watts & Co, 1 Upper Maltings Place, BIRCHINGTON, KENT, CT7 9PW.

WATTS, Mr. Michael John Colin, MA FCA *1972;* The Round House, 41 Sheen Road, RICHMOND, TW9 1AJ.

WATTS, Mr. Michael Lloyd, ACA *2008;* 61 Grove Park Road, BRISTOL, BS4 4JH.

WATTS, Dr. Michael Robert, BEng ACA *2002;* Experian Ltd Riverleen House, Electric Avenue, NOTTINGHAM, NG80 1RH.

WATTS, Mrs. Michelle Louise, BSc ACA *2002;* 3 Hastings Hollow, Measham, SWADLINCOTE, DERBYSHIRE, DE12 7GY.

•**WATTS, Mr. Nigel Anthony, FCA** *1974;* Nigel Watts Consultancy Limited, Watch House, The Ridge, Winchelsea Beach, WINCHELSEA, EAST SUSSEX TN36 4LU.

WATTS, Mr. Nigel Dudley, FCA *1967;* Greentiles, 7 Salter Road, Sandbanks, POOLE, DORSET, BH13 7RQ. (Life Member)

WATTS, Mr. Nigel William Roland, BA ACA *1984;* 9 Furlong Road, LONDON, N7 8LS.

WATTS, Mrs. Pamela, MMath ACA *2005;* Flat 9, Heath Mansions, Putney Heath Lane, LONDON, SW15 3JJ.

WATTS, Mr. Paul David, BSc FCA *1993;* 13 St. Catherines Place, EDINBURGH, EH9 1NU.

•**WATTS, Mr. Paul John, FCA** *1982;* (Tax Fac), Gibson Appleby, 1-3 Ship Street, SHOREHAM-BY-SEA, WEST SUSSEX, BN43 5DH.

•**WATTS, Mr. Paul Richard, BA FCA CF** *1989;* Baker Tilly Corporate Finance LLP, 25 Farringdon Street, LONDON, EC4A 4AB. See also Baker Tilly Tax and Advisory Services LLP, Baker Tilly UK Audit LLP

WATTS, Mr. Paul Robert, FCA *1971;* Owl Cottage, 10 Sandleigh Road, LEIGH-ON-SEA, ESSEX, SS9 1JU.

•**WATTS, Mr. Paul Victor, BSc ACA CTA** *1992;* Artume Limited, 97 Burge Crescent, Cotford St. Luke, TAUNTON, SOMERSET, TA4 1NU.

WATTS, Mr. Peter, FCA *1971;* Rushworth House, 8 Enborne Lodge Lane, Enborne, NEWBURY, BERKSHIRE, RG14 6RH.

WATTS, Mr. Peter Gerard, BA ACA *1988;* 3 I Group, 16 Palace Street, LONDON, SW1E 5JD.

•**WATTS, Mr. Peter John, FCA** *1992;* Cooper Murray, Fifth Floor, Tennyson House, 159-165 Great Portland Street, LONDON, W1W 5PA.

•**WATTS, Mr. Peter John Maurice, FCA** *1965;* Bourner Bullock, Sovereign House, 212-224 Shaftesbury Avenue, LONDON, WC2H 8HQ.

•**WATTS, Mr. Peter Michael, FCA** *1966;* Peter Watts & Co, Berrylands, Hawthorne Lane, ROSS-ON-WYE, HEREFORDSHIRE, HR9 5BG.

WATTS, Mr. Peter Ronald Stuart, BSc ACA *1987;* 66 Deanburn Park, LINLITHGOW, WEST LOTHIAN, EH49 6HA.

WATTS, Mr. Phillip, ACA *2010;* 21 Pitmaston Close, BANBURY, OXFORDSHIRE, OX16 1AH.

WATTS, Mrs. Rachel, BA ACA *2001;* with Deloitte LLP, 2 New Street Square, LONDON, EC4A 3BZ.

WATTS, Mr. Richard, ACA *2011;* 6 Orchard Drive, LEIGHTON BUZZARD, BEDFORDSHIRE, LU7 2PL.

WATTS, Mr. Robert, BA FCA *1974;* 46 Loxley Road, LONDON, SW18 3LN.

WATTS, Mr. Robin Stewart, BSc(Hons) ACA *2001;* 15 Eastmearn Road, LONDON, SE21 8HA.

WATTS, Mr. Ronald Anthony, FCA *1964;* 6 Ross Close, Harrow Weald, HARROW, HA3 6SR.

WATTS, Mrs. Ruth Sarah, BA ACA *1989;* Oxford Brookes University, Wheatley Campus, Wheatley, OXFORD, OX33 1HX.

WATTS, Miss. Sarah Caroline, BA(Hons) ACA *2003;* 48 Tytherington Drive, MACCLESFIELD, CHESHIRE, SK10 2HJ.

WATTS, Mr. Sean Alexander, BSc FCA *1997;* (Tax Fac), Flat 2, Grove House, Cornwallis Grove, BRISTOL, AVON, BS8 4DE.

WATTS, Mr. Steven John, FCA *1966;* Trevek, Church Lane, Thurlaston, RUGBY, CV23 9JY.

WATTS, Mr. Stuart Peter, BA ACA *1981;* 237 Beverley Road, Kirk Ella, HULL, HU10 7AG.

WATTS, Mrs. Susan Elizabeth, BSc ACA *1986;* Morgan Stanley International, 25 Cabot Square, LONDON, E14 4QA.

WATTS, Miss. Suzanne, BA ACA *2003;* 141 Chesterfield Road, SHEFFIELD, S8 0RN.

WATTS, Mrs. Tania Elizabeth, BSc ACA *1998;* 9 Crystal Wood Road, CARDIFF, CF14 4HU.

•**WATTS, Mr. Terry Marcel, FCA** *1955;* T.M. Watts & Co, 42 Wentworth Gardens, Palmers Green, LONDON, N13 5SN.

WATTS, Mr. Thomas, ACA *2009;* 122 New Dover Road, CANTERBURY, CT1 3EH.

WATTS, Mr. Timothy William, BSc ACA *1982;* Gorse House, Knutsford Road, ALDERLEY EDGE, SK9 7SW.

•**WATTS, Mr. Trevor, FCA** *1972;* Trevor Watts, P O Box 2162, PULBOROUGH, RH20 2WZ.

WATTS, Mr. Vincent Challacombe, OBE MA MSc FCA *1966;* (Member of Council 1987 - 1989), Hill House, Hill House Road, Bramerton, NORWICH, NR14 7EG.

WATTS, Mrs. Wendy Elizabeth, BA ACA *1991;* 117 The Hawthorns, Charvil, READING, RG10 9TT.

WATTS-MORGAN, Mrs. Gillian Margaret Emily, BSc ACA *1990;* 46 Grosvenor Road, Chiswick, LONDON, W4 4EG.

WATTS-MORGAN, Mr. Nigel John, BSc ACA *1990;* Hotcourses Ltd, 150-152 King Street, Hammersmith, LONDON, W6 0QU.

WAUD, Mr. Christopher Graham, FCA *1966;* Financial Services Authority, 25 The North Colonnade, Canary Wharf, LONDON, E14 5HS.

WAUDBY, Mr. Andrew John, ACA *2008;* Clough & Co New Chartford House, Centurion Way, CLECKHEATON, WEST YORKSHIRE, BD19 3QB.

WAUDBY, Miss. Sarah Lesley, BEng ACA *1994;* Restore plc 603, M W B Business Exchange Plc Marble Arch Tower, 55 Bryanston Street, LONDON, W1H 7AA.

•**WAUGH, Mr. David Gary, FCA** *1984;* (Tax Fac), Rowlands, Rowlands House, Portobello Road, Birtley, CHESTER LE STREET, COUNTY DURHAM DH3 2RY.

WAUGH, Mrs. Deborah, FCA *1983;* 20 Stanhope Road, Bowdon, ALTRINCHAM, CHESHIRE, WA14 3JY.

•**WAUGH, Mr. Elwyn Peter George, BSc FCA** *1979;* Waugh & Co., Springs, Millhayes, Stockland, HONITON, DEVON EX14 9DB.

•**WAUGH, Mr. Jamie, FCA** *1990;* Johnston Carmichael, Bishops Court, 29 Albyn Place, ABERDEEN, AB10 1YL.

WAUGH, Mr. John Maxwell, BA ACA *1988;* 6 Cromwell Close, Aughton, ORMSKIRK, LANCASHIRE, L39 5ET.

WAUGH, Mrs. Kirstie Dawn, BSc ACA *2001;* Yorkshire Bldg Soc Yorkshire House, Yorkshire Drive, BRADFORD, WEST YORKSHIRE, BD5 8LJ.

WAUGH, Mr. Matthew John, BA ACA *1997;* Stockford Ltd, Buckingham House, West Street, NEWBURY, BERKSHIRE, RG14 1BE.

WAUMSLEY, Miss. Clare Elizabeth, ACA *2009;* 12 Hobson Drive, Spondon, DERBY, DE21 7TU.

WAUMSLEY, Mr. Richard, BSc(Hons) ACA *2011;* 33 Laund Nook, BELPER, DERBYSHIRE, DE56 1GY.

WAWRYK, Mr. Matthew, BA(Hons) ACA *2010;* Apartment 9, 1 Paperhouse Close, Naden Mill, Norden, ROCHDALE, LANCASHIRE OL11 5LQ.

WAWRYKA, Mr. Kristian, BSc ACA *2010;* 15 Anchor Close, LINCOLN, LN5 7PE.

WAWRZYNIAK, Mr. Andrew Stefan, ACA CA(AUS) *2008;* 5 Alder Close, ROMSEY, SO51 5SJ.

•**WAX, Mr. Simon, BSocSc ACA** *2002;* with Buzzacott LLP, 130 Wood Street, LONDON, EC2V 6DL.

WAXLER, Mr. Bradley Samuel, BA ACA *1993;* 1 Gable House Rokefield, Westcott Street Westcott, DORKING, RH4 3NZ.

WAXLEY, Mr. Simon Andrew, BSc ACA *1995;* 28 Hampstead Way, LONDON, NW11 7JL.

WAXMAN, Mr. Anthony, FCA *1958;* 12 Nachshon Street, JERUSALEM, 93548, ISRAEL. (Life Member)

•**WAXMAN, Mr. Frank Stephen, FCA** *1967;* (Tax Fac), Elliot Woolfe & Rose, Equity House, 128-136 High Street, EDGWARE, MIDDLESEX, HA8 7TT. See also Lentongate Ltd

•**WAXMAN, Mr. Philip Howard, BCom FCA** *1985;* Ridgetown LLP, 4 Fernacre, SALE, CHESHIRE, M33 2BA.

•**WAXMAN, Mr. Stephen Anthony, FCA** *1971;* (Tax Fac), Stephen Waxman & Company, Canada House, 29 Hampton Road, TWICKENHAM, TW2 5QE. See also Grencodrive Limited

WAY, Mr. Adrian, ACA *2010;* 7 Edgarton Road, POOLE, DORSET, BH17 9AY.

WAY, Mr. Adrian Bromley, BA ACA *1993;* R R Donnelley Unit 3-5, Tower Close, HUNTINGDON, CAMBRIDGESHIRE, PE29 7YD.

WAY, Mrs. Chloe Jane, BA(Hons) ACA *2004;* Knowlands Cottage Five Fields Lane, Four Elms, EDENBRIDGE, TN8 6NA.

WAY, Mr. Christopher James, BSc ACA *2002;* 17A Brunswick St, HAMILTON HM10, BERMUDA.

WAY, Mrs. Claire Julia, BA ACA *1996;* Rooks Nest House, 122 Rooks Nest Road, Outwood, WAKEFIELD, WF1 3EE.

•**WAY, Mrs. Elaine Frances, BCom FCA** *1982;* (Tax Fac), Roffe Swayne, Ashcombe Court, Woolsack Way, GODALMING, GU7 1LQ.

Members - Alphabetical WAY - WEBB

WAY, Mrs. Hilary, BA ACA *1999;* 25 Bryanston Drive, DOLLAR, CLACKMANNANSHIRE, FK14 7EF.
WAY, Mr. John Stanley, FCA *1969;* J S Way Limited, Passworth, School Lane, Ockham, WOKING, SURREY GU23 6PA.
WAY, Mr. Mark Jonathan, BA ACA *1997;* 17 Old Harpenden Road, ST. ALBANS, HERTFORDSHIRE, AL3 6AX.
WAY, Mr. Matthew John, ACA *1995;* 66 Windsor Drive, ORPINGTON, KENT, BR6 6HD.
WAY, Mr. Robert Anthony, BSc ACA *1999;* Vogel Veide Poolhead Lane, Tanworth-in-Arden, SOLIHULL, B94 5EH.
WAY, Mr. Ronald Alan, FCA *1969;* Moortown Farm, Northlew, OKEHAMPTON, EX20 3PP. (Life Member)
WAY, Miss. Ruth Margaret, BSc FCA *1985;* 24 Avondale Road, Wimbledon, LONDON, SW19 8JX.
WAY, Mr. Stephen James, BSc ACA *1999;* 1 Military Drive, Kennet Heath, THATCHAM, RG19 4RZ.
WAY, Mr. Stephen Paul, BSc ACA *1979;* ICEIMP Ltd, 28 Wind Street, SWANSEA, SA1 1DZ.
•WAYLAND, Mr. Andrew Michael, BSc ACA *1991;* The Vines, 5 Round Close, YATELEY, GU46 6AQ.
WAYLAND, Mrs. Daphne Elizabeth, BSc FCA *1988;* 117 Picketts Valley Road, PICKETTS VALLEY, NSW 2251, AUSTRALIA.
•WAYMAN, Mr. John Thomas, FCA *1979;* PricewaterhouseCoopers LLP, 1 Embankment Place, LONDON, WC2N 6RH. See also PricewaterhouseCoopers
WAYMAN, Mr. Richard James, BA ACA *2000;* The British Horse Racing Authority, 75 High Holborn, LONDON, WC1V 6LS.
WAYMARK, Mrs. Claire Louise, MA(Hons) ACA *2002;* Mossy House, 44 West Mill Road, EDINBURGH, EH13 0NZ.
WAYMARK, Mr. Matthew Edward James, BSc ACA *2001;* Mossy House, 44 West Mill Road, EDINBURGH, EH13 0NZ.
WAYMARK, Miss. Yvonne Elizabeth, BSc ACA *2004;* with PKF (UK) LLP, Cedar House, 105 Carrow Road, NORWICH, NORFOLK, NR1 1HP.
WAYMONT, Mrs. Jacqueline Yvonne, ACA DChA *2002;* (Tax Fac), 14 College Road, The Historic Dockyard, CHATHAM, ME4 4QW.
WAYMONT, Mrs. Nina Elizabeth, ACA *2007;* The Beeches, 32 Main Street, Gedney Dyke, SPALDING, LINCOLNSHIRE, PE12 0AJ.
WAYMOUTH, Mr. Roger, BSc FCA *1978;* Bretworth Woodlands Road, Portishead, BRISTOL, BS20 7HE.
WAYNE, Mr. Harold, FCA *1958;* 3 Rolfe Close, BARNET, EN4 9QU. (Life Member)
•WAYNE, Mr. Nigel Keith, FCA *1977;* Nigel K Wayne & Co Limited, 15a East Street, OKEHAMPTON, DEVON, EX20 1AS. See also AIMS - Nigel K Wayne
WAYNE, Mr. Peter Howard, FCA *1952;* Flat 8, 55 Holland Park, LONDON, W11 3RS. (Life Member)
WAYT, Mrs. Clare Joan, BA ACA *1996;* Trelleborg Sealing Solutions UK Ltd International Drive, Tewkesbury Business Park, TEWKESBURY, GLOUCESTERSHIRE, GL20 8UQ.
WAYTE, Dr. Kenneth, FCA *1966;* Whiteways, Blundells Lane, Rainhill, PRESCOT, L35 6NB.
WAYTE, Mrs. Naomi Jane, BA ACA *1990;* 28 Ascott Gardens, West Bridgford, NOTTINGHAM, NG2 7TH.
WAYWELL, Mr. Richard Brian, FCA *1964;* 49 Reading Drive, SALE, CHESHIRE, M33 5DJ.
WAZIR, Mrs. Nina Aisha, BSc(Econ) ACA *1997;* 4 Whitehill Avenue, LUTON, LU1 3SP.
•WEAKS, Mr. Alasdair George, ACA *1995;* Simpson Wreford & Partners, Suffolk House, George Street, CROYDON, CR0 0YN.
WEALL, Mr. Paul, BSc(Hons) ACA *2002;* 8 Broadacre, Standish, WIGAN, LANCASHIRE, WN6 0SN.
WEAR, Miss. Lindsay Louise, BSc ACA *2002;* Highbury House, Tintern, CHEPSTOW, GWENT, NP16 6TH.
WEAR, Mr. Peter Graeme, BSc(Econ) ACA *2004;* 40 Maybrook, Chineham, BASINGSTOKE, RG24 8ST.
WEAR, Mr. Peter Michael Alexander, BA ACA *1991;* Laurel Cottage, Ely Grange, Frant, TUNBRIDGE WELLS, TN3 9DZ.
WEARDEN, Mr. Peter Francis, FCA *1974;* (Tax Fac), Beech House, 25a The Rowans, BALDOCK, SG7 6HL.
WEARE, Mr. Clive Edward, FCA *1962;* 3 Selwood Crescent, FROME, BA11 2HX.
•WEARE, Mr. Howard John, FCA *1971;* Howard J Weare & Co Limited, 34 Llwyn y Pia Road, Lisvane, CARDIFF, CF14 0SY.
WEARE, Mr. Marcus George Dobree, MA BA ACA *2003;* 155 W 68th Street, Apt 1415, NEW YORK, NY 10023, UNITED STATES.
•WEARE, Mr. Robin Denys Michael, FCA *1968;* R. Weare & Co., Brook House, Llandevaud, NEWPORT, NP18 2AA.
WEARE, Mr. Robin Sydney, FCA *1966;* 7 Kingsdene, TADWORTH, SURREY, KT20 5EB. (Life Member)
WEARING, Mr. Adam Charles, BA(Hons) ACA *2002;* 7 Vale Avenue, LEEDS, LS8 2DF.
WEARING, Mrs. Laura Jane, ACA *2006;* 11 Cromwell Road, Bolsover, CHESTERFIELD, DERBYSHIRE, S44 6SP.
WEARING, Dr. Robert Thomas, FCA *1973;* 6 The Dale, Wivenhoe, COLCHESTER, CO7 9NL.
WEARING, Miss. Sarah Barbara, BSc ACA DChA *2003;* with HPH, 21 Victoria Avenue, HARROGATE, HG1 5RD.
WEARMOUTH, Mrs. Bethan Mary, BSc ACA *2003;* 34/4 -16 kingsway, DEE WHY, NSW 2099, AUSTRALIA.
WEARMOUTH, Mr. Gordon, FCA *1975;* The Coach House, 31 Norlinton Close, Orlington, KETTERING, NN14 1FD.
WEARN, Mrs. Illana, ACA *2009;* Sumitomo Corporation Europe Ltd Vintners Place, 68 Upper Thames Street, LONDON, EC4V 3BJ.
WEASTELL, Mr. Terry Elwyn, FCA *1977;* Gorselands, Gold Hill Loop Road, Swainby, NORTHALLERTON, DL6 3HR.
WEATHERALL, Mr. George Alexander, BL ACA *2006;* 10 Dean Road, Woodthorpe, NOTTINGHAM, NG5 4FJ.
WEATHERALL, Mrs. Jennifer Anne, BA ACA *1988;* Oakfields, Park Edge, Hathersage, HOPE VALLEY, S32 1BS.
WEATHERALL, Mr. Jeremy Richard, BA ACA *1989;* 43 Spoonhill Ave, MARLBOROUGH, MA 01752, UNITED STATES.
•WEATHERALL, Mr. Martyn John, BSc FCA *1983;* Hawsons, Pegasus House, 463a Glossop Road, SHEFFIELD, S10 2QD.
WEATHERALL, Mr. Robert David Wellesley, BA FCA *1988;* Burnside, Wood Road, Ashill, ILMINSTER, SOMERSET, TA19 9NR.
WEATHERBURN, Mr. Andrew John, MBA BSc FCA *1983;* 45 La Charroterie Mills, La Charroterie, St. Peter Port, GUERNSEY, GY1 1DR.
WEATHERBURN, Mr. John, ACA *2008;* Ernst & Young, 1 Bridgewater Place Water Lane, LEEDS, LS11 5QR.
WEATHERBURN, Mrs. Sian Louise, BSc ACA *1993;* King Sturge Llp, 30 Warwick Street, LONDON, W1B 5NH.
WEATHERBY, Mr. Stephen John, BA ACA *1990;* 7 Ascot Close, CONGLETON, CHESHIRE, CW12 1LL.
WEATHERHEAD, Miss. Tina Michelle, BA ACA *1998;* Glencoe, Hollins Lane, Hampsthwaite, HARROGATE, NORTH YORKSHIRE, HG3 2HL.
WEATHERHILL, Mr. Ian Herbert, FCA *1981;* with KPMG LLP, Saltire Court, 20 Castle Terrace, EDINBURGH, EH1 2EG.
WEATHERHOGG, Mr. William Paul, BSc FCA *1959;* 9 Riverleaze, Portishead, BRISTOL, BS20 8EA. (Life Member)
•WEATHERILL, Mr. Andrew James, BSc FCA *1992;* (Tax Fac), CBAC Limited, Hamelin, Bell Hill, Finedon, WELLINGBOROUGH, NORTHAMPTONSHIRE NN9 5ND.
WEATHERILL, Mrs. Emma Karen, BSc ACA *2004;* 35 Amethyst Drive, SITTINGBOURNE, KENT, ME10 5JR.
WEATHERILL, Mr. Henry Bruce, BA FCA *1979;* 105 Burbage Road, LONDON, SE24 9HD.
WEATHERILL, Mr. John Frederick, BSc FCA *1973;* with ICAEW, Metropolitan House, 321 Avebury Boulevard, MILTON KEYNES, MK9 2FZ.
WEATHERITT, Mr. Philip John, MA FCA *1977;* 19 Aston Way, EPSOM, KT18 5LZ.
WEATHERLEY, Mr. Mark Francis, FCA *1978;* 105 Brigadoon, POINTE CLAIRE H9R 1J2, QC, CANADA.
WEATHERLEY, Mr. Stuart Graham, BA ACA *1986;* 12 Adur Close, West End, SOUTHAMPTON, SO18 3NH.
WEATHERSEED, Mr. David Ian Cameron, FCA *1975;* Survey Sampling International LLC, 6 Research Drive, SHELTON, CT 06484, UNITED STATES.
•WEATHERSEED, Mr. Philip Robert Francis, FCA *1976;* PRW Financial Services Limited, 10 The Minnels, HASSOCKS, WEST SUSSEX, BN6 8QW.
WEATHERSEED, Mr. Stephen Peter Stuart, BA FCA *1983;* with Mazars CPA Limited, 42nd Floor, Central Plaza, 18 Harbour Road, WAN CHAI, HONG KONG ISLAND HONG KONG SAR.
WEATHERSTON, Mr. Ian Robert, FCA *1960;* 12 Chillis Wood Rd, HAYWARDS HEATH, RH16 1JT. (Life Member)
WEATHERSTONE, Mr. Andrew Paul, BSc FCA *1990;* A T H Resources Plc Aardvark House, Sidings Court, DONCASTER, SOUTH YORKSHIRE, DN4 5NU.
WEATHERSTONE, Mrs. Jacqueline Margaret, BSc ACA *1991;* 6 Spring Farm, Notton, WAKEFIELD, WEST YORKSHIRE, WF4 2PT.
WEATHERUP, Ms. Laura Mary, BA ACA *2001;* Threadneedle Asset Management Ltd St. Mary Axe House, 60 St. Mary Axe, LONDON, EC3A 8JQ.
WEAVER, Mr. Andrew John, BSc ACA *1994;* Wychwood Lodge, Fitzroy Road, FLEET, GU51 4JH.
WEAVER, Mr. Anthony Scott, ACA *2008;* Flat 2, 95 Priory Road, LONDON, NW6 3NL.
•WEAVER, Mr. Ashley, LLB ACA CertPFS *1992;* Lyon Griffiths Limited, 17 Alvaston Business Park, Middlewich Road, NANTWICH, CHESHIRE, CW5 6PF.
WEAVER, Mr. Ceri David, BSc(Hons) ACA *2002;* ALICO AIG Life - Middle East Africa & South Asia, Dubai International Financial Centre, The Gate Building 7th Floor West Wing, P O Box 211012, DUBAI, UNITED ARAB EMIRATES.
WEAVER, Miss. Christine Anne, LLB ACA *2001;* (Tax Fac), 10 Roe Deer Green, NEWPORT, SHROPSHIRE, TF10 7JQ.
WEAVER, Mr. Christopher Giles Herron, MSc FCA *1970;* Greywalls, GULLANE, EH31 2EG.
WEAVER, Mr. Christopher Guy, BA(Hons) ACA *2003;* with KPMG LLP, St. James's Square, MANCHESTER, M2 6DS.
WEAVER, Mrs. Claire Lorraine, ACA *2008;* Teasdale Accountants, 13 St. Johns Street, WHITCHURCH, SHROPSHIRE, SY13 1QT.
•WEAVER, Mr. David John, FCA *1964;* D.J. Weaver, 4 Amis Avenue, New Haw, ADDLESTONE, KT15 3ET.
WEAVER, Mr. Dennis George, FCA *1954;* 26 Longland Drive, Totteridge, LONDON, N20 8HJ. (Life Member)
WEAVER, Mr. Derek, FCA *1966;* 38 Wigshaw Lane, Culcheth, WARRINGTON, WA3 4NB.
WEAVER, Mr. Derek Graham, FCA *1968;* Limestones, 3 Scotland Street, Whitwell, WORKSOP, S80 4RG. (Life Member)
WEAVER, Mr. Geoffrey, FCA *1966;* 25 St. Cleres Way, Danbury, CHELMSFORD, CM3 4AF. (Life Member)
WEAVER, Mr. Geoffrey Paul, ACA *2008;* T U I UK Wigmore House, Wigmore Place Wigmore Lane, LUTON, LU2 9TN.
WEAVER, Mrs. Hilary Jane, BA ACA *1995;* Lloyds, 1 Lime Street, LONDON, EC3M 7HA.
WEAVER, Mr. Ian George, ACA *2009;* 10 Station Court, NEWPORT, SHROPSHIRE, TF10 7RZ.
WEAVER, Miss. Jenny, BA ACA *2005;* 74 Queens Road, TUNBRIDGE WELLS, TN4 9JU.
WEAVER, Mr. Jonathan James, BA(Hons) ACA *2001;* 278 Staines Road, TWICKENHAM, TW2 5AS.
WEAVER, Miss. Julie Ann, BSc FCA *1988;* 20 Mill Pit Furlong, Littleport, ELY, CB6 1HT.
WEAVER, Mr. Keith, BA ACA MIOD *1980;* Optima Business Development Ltd, 54 Hither Green Lane Abbey Park, REDDITCH, WORCESTERSHIRE, B98 9BW.
WEAVER, Mr. Keith David, BA ACA *1994;* 66 Green Lane, Wincham, NORTHWICH, CHESHIRE, CW9 6EH.
WEAVER, Mrs. Lisa Jane, BA ACA *1996;* Paddocks Barn, Alveston Leys, Alveston, STRATFORD-UPON-AVON, WARWICKSHIRE, CV37 7QN.
WEAVER, Mr. Michael Charles, BSc FCA *1965;* 2d Clarence Road, HARPENDEN, HERTFORDSHIRE, AL5 4AJ.
•WEAVER, Mr. Michael James, BSc FCA *2000;* 9 Mortlake Road, RICHMOND, SURREY, TW9 3JE.
WEAVER, Mr. Michael John, BA FCA *1974;* Rivendell, Great Elm, FROME, SOMERSET, BA11 3NZ. (Life Member)
WEAVER, Mr. Michael Robert, BSc ACA *1999;* 116 Lawn Road, Fishponds, BRISTOL, BS16 5BB.
•WEAVER, Mr. Richard Charles Gavin, MA ACA *1991;* PricewaterhouseCoopers LLP, 1 Embankment Place, LONDON, WC2N 6RH. See also PricewaterhouseCoopers
•WEAVER, Mr. Richard John, LLB ACA DChA *1999;* haysmacintyre, Fairfax House, 15 Fulwood Place, LONDON, WC1V 6AY.
WEAVER, Mr. Roderick William, BSc FCA *1976;* 23 Llandennis Avenue, Cyncoed, CARDIFF, CF23 6JE.
WEAVER, Mr. Roy Powell, FCA *1953;* 2 Regent Court, Sheet Street, WINDSOR, SL4 1BP. (Life Member)
WEAVER, Mr. Simon Charles, BSc ACA *1981;* Clos de Meunier 9, 1970 WEZEMBEEK-OPPEM, BELGIUM.
WEAVER, Mr. Simon Christopher, BSc ACA *2010;* 18 Chorleywood Bottom, Chorleywood, RICKMANSWORTH, HERTFORDSHIRE, WD3 5JD.
WEAVER, Mr. Stephen Charles, MA ACA *1989;* 216a Nine Mile Ride, Finchampstead, WOKINGHAM, BERKSHIRE, RG40 3QD.
WEAVER, Mr. Steven John, ACA *1993;* 94 Cowslip Hall, LETCHWORTH GARDEN CITY, SG6 4EX.
•WEAVER, Mr. Wayne Geoffrey, MA FCA ATII *1993;* (Tax Fac), Deloitte LLP, Hill House, 1 Little New Street, LONDON, EC4A 3TR. See also Deloitte & Touche LLP
WEAVERS, Mr. Colin John, FCA *1972;* 2950 Phyllis Street, Victoria, VANCOUVER ISLAND V8N 1Z1, BC, CANADA.
WEAVERS, Mrs. Debbie Louise, ACA *1997;* 11 Glaisdale Gardens, GRANTHAM, NG31 8PZ.
WEAVERS, Mr. Stewart Paton, FCA *1984;* The Old School House, School Road, Snitterfield, STRATFORD-UPON-AVON, WARWICKSHIRE, CV37 0JL.
WEAVING, Mrs. Diane Sheila, BSc ACA *1985;* 15 Breary Lane East, Bramhope, LEEDS, LS16 9BH.
WEAVING, Mr. John Martin, BA ACA *1985;* Barratts Priceless Ltd B P L House, 880 Harrogate Road, BRADFORD, BD10 0NW.
WEAVIS, Mr. Mark Gavin, BSc ACA *1984;* Two Hoots, 7 Bidborough Ridge, Bidborough, TUNBRIDGE WELLS, TN4 0UT.
WEBB, Mrs. Abigail, LLB ACA *2001;* 75 Burdon Lane, SUTTON, SM2 7BY.
WEBB, Mr. Alan David, FCA *1960;* Selborne Cottage, Bar Road, Baslow, BAKEWELL, DE45 1SF. (Life Member)
WEBB, Mr. Alan Hugh, BSc FCA *1986;* 15 Brabazon Rd, Merley, WIMBORNE, BH21 1XN.
•WEBB, Mr. Alan James, ACA *1982;* with RSM Tenon Audit Limited, Charterhouse, Legge Street, BIRMINGHAM, B4 7EU.
•WEBB, Mr. Alan Walter, BSc FCA *1977;* The Shepherd Partnership Limited, Albion House, Rope Walk, Otley Street, SKIPTON, NORTH YORKSHIRE BD23 1ED. See also Glencoe Accounting
WEBB, Miss. Alison Elizabeth, BA ACA *1984;* Apps Pond Cottage, Appspond Lane, Potters Crouch, ST. ALBANS, HERTFORDSHIRE, AL2 3NL.
WEBB, Miss. Alison Joanna, LLB ACA *2009;* 22 Adams House, Rustat Avenue, CAMBRIDGE, CB1 3RE.
WEBB, Mr. Alistair Barry, BSc ACA *1998;* House 28, 20 Egmont Street, SHERWOOD, QLD 4075, AUSTRALIA.
•WEBB, Mrs. Angela Mary, FCA *1989;* Angela Paull & Co Ltd, 1 New Barn, Manor Farm Courtyard, Southam, CHELTENHAM, GLOUCESTERSHIRE GL52 3PB.
WEBB, Mr. Anthony Clifford, FCA *1960;* 20 East Cliff, Pennard, SWANSEA, SA3 2AS. (Life Member)
WEBB, Mr. Anthony Thomas, FCA *1963;* Camden House, School Lane, Seal, SEVENOAKS, TN15 0BE.
•WEBB, Mr. Arthur Richard, FCA *1977;* (Tax Fac), Richard Webb FCA, 71 Osborne Parc, HELSTON, CORNWALL, TR13 8TZ.
WEBB, Ms. Barbara Christine, BA FCA *1977;* The Little Manor, Tytherington Lane, Bollington, MACCLESFIELD, CHESHIRE, SK10 2JS.
WEBB, Mr. Barry Richard, BSc ACA *1992;* Little Beeches, Kemnal Park, HASLEMERE, SURREY, GU27 2LF.
WEBB, Mr. Benjamin, LLB ACA *2006;* Flat B, 98 Hackford Road, LONDON, SW9 0QU.
WEBB, Mr. Benjamin Joshua, ACA *2010;* The Old Post, Post Office Road, Inkpen, HUNGERFORD, BERKSHIRE, RG17 9PY.
WEBB, Mr. Bryndon Mark, BSc ACA *1989;* 12 Yare Valley Rise, Brundall, NORWICH, NR13 5JW.
WEBB, Miss. Caroline, ACA *2011;* 499 West Dyke Road, REDCAR, CLEVELAND, TS10 4QL.
•WEBB, Mrs. Caroline Ann, FCA *1991;* (Tax Fac), Eden Currie Limited, Pegasus House, Solihull Business Park, SOLIHULL, WEST MIDLANDS, B90 4GT.
WEBB, Mr. Christopher, ACA *2008;* 11 Westminster Drive, WREXHAM, CLWYD, LL12 7AT.
WEBB, Mr. Christopher Fulton, BA ACA *1996;* 5a Manor Road, Milford on Sea, LYMINGTON, HAMPSHIRE, SO41 0RG.
WEBB, Miss. Claire, LLB ACA *2000;* Maplin Electronics Ltd Unit 1, Brookfields Way Manvers, ROTHERHAM, SOUTH YORKSHIRE, S63 5DL.
WEBB, Mr. Clive Allum, BSc ACA *1990;* 7 Palmers Yard Headcorn, ASHFORD, KENT, TN27 9SN.
•WEBB, Mr. Colin Thomas, FCA *1973;* (Tax Fac), Marsh Accountancy, Preston House, 51 East Street, WARMINSTER, WILTSHIRE, BA12 9BY.
WEBB, Mr. Damian, LLB ACA CF *2002;* with Baker Tilly Corporate Finance LLP, St Philips Point, Temple Row, BIRMINGHAM, B2 5AF.
•WEBB, Mr. Darrell Henry, FCA *1974;* Darrell H. Webb, 1st Floor, 88 Charles Street, KEW, VIC 3101, AUSTRALIA.
•WEBB, Mr. David, FCA *1977;* 8 Hollycroft, Ashford Hill, THATCHAM, BERKSHIRE, RG19 8BU.

•**WEBB, Mr. David Charles Patrick, FCA** *1985;* (Tax Fac), Edwards, Harmony House, 34 High Street, Aldridge, WALSALL, WS9 8LZ.
WEBB, Mr. David Howard, BA ACA *1992;* Howard de Walden Estates Ltd, 23 Queen Anne Street, LONDON, W1G 9DL.
WEBB, Mr. David Iain, BSc FCA *1987;* 34 Wiggett Grove, Binfield, BRACKNELL, RG42 4DY.
WEBB, Mr. David John, BA ACA *1991;* 6 Greenwell Drive, PRUDHOE, NORTHUMBERLAND, NE42 5QP.
WEBB, Mr. David Martin, MSc ACA *1996;* 23 Milton Road, HARPENDEN, HERTFORDSHIRE, AL5 5LA.
WEBB, Mr. David Paul, BA ACA *1999;* 4 Tennyson Road, HARPENDEN, HERTFORDSHIRE, AL5 4BB.
WEBB, Mr. David Robert Andrew, BSc ACA *1980;* 107 Wimborne Road, Colehill, WIMBORNE, DORSET, BH21 2QR.
•**WEBB, Mr. David Rodney, FCA** *1979;* (Tax Fac), Bulley Davey & Co, 6 North Street, Oundle, PETERBOROUGH, PE8 4AL. See also Bulley Davey
•**WEBB, Mr. David Zillwood, FCA** *1974;* Fino Limited, 29 Cleveleys Avenue, ROCHDALE, LANCASHIRE, OL16 4PD.
•**WEBB, Mrs. Dawn, ACA** *2009;* Dale Cottage, Orrisdale, Kirk Michael, ISLE OF MAN, IM6 2HN.
WEBB, Mr. Desmond Charles, BSc ACA *1991;* 79 Shanklin Road, Upper Shirley, SOUTHAMPTON, SO15 7RG.
WEBB, Mr. Douglas Russell, MA FCA *1986;* Blackberry Barn, 4 Lidcote, Dunton, BUCKINGHAM, MK18 3RY.
WEBB, Mr. Edward Lloyd, MA FCA *1977;* 1A Poynings Close, HARPENDEN, AL5 1JD.
WEBB, Miss. Elizabeth Louise, BSc ACA *2005;* 30 Thanet Road, BEXLEY, DA5 1AP.
WEBB, Mr. Forbes Waddington, BSc FCA *1981;* 7 Firle Grange, SEAFORD, EAST SUSSEX, BN25 2HD.
WEBB, Mr. Frank William, FCA CTA *1969;* (Tax Fac), 10 Moorfield Drive, HALESOWEN, WEST MIDLANDS, B63 3TG.
WEBB, Miss. Gemma Louise, ACA MAAT *2009;* 53 Pavilion Road, ALDERSHOT, HAMPSHIRE, GU11 3NX.
WEBB, Mr. Geoffrey Alan, FCA ACMA *1953;* Stone Cottage, Valley Road, Bournheath, BROMSGROVE, B61 9HZ. (Life Member)
WEBB, Mr. Gordon Brian, BSc ACA *1987;* 15 Holland Road, FRINTON-ON-SEA, ESSEX, CO13 9DH.
•**WEBB, Mr. Gordon Robert, ACA** *1979;* G.R. Webb, 107 Canterbury Road, MARGATE, KENT, CT9 5AX.
WEBB, Mr. Graham Keith, BA ACA *1996;* 10 Champion Grove, LONDON, SE5 8BW.
WEBB, Mr. Graham Thomas, FCA *1962;* Little Frome, Forest Drive, Kirby Muxloe, LEICESTER, LE9 2EA.
WEBB, Mr. Harry Wulstan, FCA *1961;* Longnor House, 13 Westbeech Road, Pattingham, WOLVERHAMPTON, WV6 7AQ. (Life Member)
WEBB, Miss. Helen Eira, BA ACA *1996;* Wilshire Associates, Suite 700, 1299 Ocean Avenue, SANTA MONICA, CA 90401, UNITED STATES.
WEBB, Mrs. Helen Louise, BA(Hons) ACA *2002;* Stone Hayne, Stone Street, Stanford, ASHFORD, KENT, TN25 6DN.
WEBB, Mr. Ian John, MSc BSocSc ACA *2000;* 31 Chiphouse Road, BRISTOL, BS15 4TR.
WEBB, Miss. Jacqueline Elizabeth Joanna, BSc ACA *2005;* with BDO LLP, 55 Baker Street, LONDON, W1U 7EU.
WEBB, Mr. James Maurice, FCA *1955;* Golwgmynydd, Franksbridge, LLANDRINDOD WELLS, LD1 5SA. (Life Member)
WEBB, Mr. James Richard, FCA *1979;* 54 Summerlands Park Avenue, ILMINSTER, TA19 9BT.
WEBB, Mr. James Stuart, MSc FCA *1984;* 149B Westharbour Drive, Westharbour, WAITAKERE 0618, NEW ZEALAND.
WEBB, Mr. Jamie Benjamin, BA(Hons) ACA *2001;* 13 Westfield Green, Tockwith, YORK, YO26 7RE.
WEBB, Mrs. Jane Elizabeth, BBS ACA *2005;* 98 Hackford Road, LONDON, SW9 0QU.
WEBB, Mrs. Janet Rosemarie, BSc ACA *1990;* Wivenhoe Croft, 4 Eaglesfield End, Leire, LUTTERWORTH, LE17 5FG.
WEBB, Mr. Jeremy Denis, FCA MBA *1963;* Newlands, Church Road, Cookham Dean, MAIDENHEAD, BERKSHIRE, SL6 9PD.
•①**WEBB, Mr. Jeremy Robert, BA ACA** *2000;* with PricewaterhouseCoopers LLP, Pricewaterhousecoopers, 12 Plumtree Court, LONDON, EC4A 4HT.
WEBB, Mrs. Jill, MA BSc ACA *1993;* 12 Ludolf Drive, shadwell, LEEDS, LS17 8LJ.
WEBB, Miss. Joanne Louise, ACA *2005;* with Hardcastle Burton LLP, Lake House, Market Hill, ROYSTON, SG8 9JN.
WEBB, Mr. John Anthony Joseph, BA ACA *1981;* Marshall Securities Ltd, 145-157 St. John Street, LONDON, EC1V 4RE.
WEBB, The Revd. John Christopher Richard, FCA *1963;* Lower Farm Cottage, Church Street, Podimore, YEOVIL, SOMERSET, BA22 8JE.
WEBB, Mr. John David, BSc ACA *2002;* 1 Ironstone Close, SWINDON, SN25 2EQ.
•**WEBB, Mr. John Derek, FCA** *1991;* Webb Accountancy Services Ltd, 19 Diamond Court, Opal Drive, Fox Milne, MILTON KEYNES, MK15 0DU.
WEBB, Mr. John Thomas, FCA *1966;* 15 Five Acres, KINGS LANGLEY, HERTFORDSHIRE, WD4 9JU.
WEBB, Mr. Jonathan Ivan William, BSc ACA *2000;* Street House Cottage, The Street, Bramley, TADLEY, HAMPSHIRE, RG26 5DE.
WEBB, Mrs. Justine Mavis, BA ACA *1995;* 9 Ethelbert Road, West Wimbledon, LONDON, SW20 8QD.
WEBB, Mrs. Katherine, BSc ACA *2005;* 21 Florence Park, BRISTOL, BS6 7LS.
WEBB, Mrs. Kathryn, BA ACA *2001;* 48 Swans Reach, FALMOUTH, CORNWALL, TR11 5GG.
WEBB, Mr. Kenneth Ashley, FCA *1953;* Copper Beech Cottage, Bagot Street, Abbots Bromley, RUGELEY, WS15 3DB. (Life Member)
WEBB, Miss. Leah, BA BA(Hons) ACA *2011;* Flat 2, 2 Hartford Street, NEWCASTLE UPON TYNE, NE6 5BX.
WEBB, Miss. Linda, BSc FCA *2000;* 209 West Drive, THORNTON-CLEVELEYS, FY5 2EH.
WEBB, Mrs. Louisa Elizabeth Jayne, BSc(Hons) ACA *2003;* with Chantrey Vellacott DFK LLP, Prospect House, 58 Queens Road, READING, BERKSHIRE, RG1 4RP.
WEBB, Miss. Lucy Caroline Gordon, ACA *2010;* 4a Westbourne Road, LONDON, N7 8AU.
WEBB, Mr. Malcolm, BSc FCA *1985;* 11 Ravelin Close, Elvetham Heath, FLEET, HAMPSHIRE, GU51 1JP.
WEBB, Mr. Malcolm Victor, FCA *1969;* Otters Pool, Kingsmill Lane, Painswick, STROUD, GLOUCESTERSHIRE, GL6 6RZ. (Life Member)
WEBB, Mr. Mark Cameron Ross, BSc ACA *1993;* HSBC Limited, Level 19, HSBC Main Building, 1 Queens Road, CENTRAL, HONG KONG SAR.
WEBB, Mr. Mark Lindsay, BA ACA *1985;* Rivendell, 26 Station Road, Lidlington, BEDFORD, MK43 0SE.
•**WEBB, Mr. Martin, FCA** *1983;* (Tax Fac), Webb House Limited, 11 Duncan Close, Moulton Park Industrial Estate, NORTHAMPTON, NN3 6WL.
WEBB, Mr. Martin, MBA BSc FCA *1970;* 11 Essex Hall Road, COLCHESTER, CO1 1ZP.
WEBB, Mr. Martin James, FCA *1965;* 322 West 57 Street, Apartment 44F, NEW YORK, NY 10019, UNITED STATES.
WEBB, Miss. Mary Lynne Susan, BA ACA *1996;* 3 The Cooperage, Gainsford Street, LONDON, SE1 2NG.
WEBB, Mr. Matthew, BA(Hons) ACA *2011;* Deloitte Llp One Trinity Gardens, Broad Chare, NEWCASTLE UPON TYNE, NE1 2HF.
WEBB, Mr. Matthew John, MEng ACA *2001;* Wolseley Plc Parkview, 1220 Arlington Business Park Theale, READING, RG7 4GA.
WEBB, Mr. Matthew Paul, BA ACA *1999;* with KPMG, 10 Shelley Street, SYDNEY, NSW 2000, AUSTRALIA.
WEBB, Mr. Maurice Francis, FCA *1963;* 3 Forest Close, Highcliffe, CHRISTCHURCH, BH23 4QF.
WEBB, Mr. Maxim Charles Wickham, BSc ACA *1989;* 5921 Avenida Chamnez, LA JOLLA, CA 92037, UNITED STATES.
WEBB, Mr. Michael, BA ACA *2011;* 18 North Down, Sanderstead, SOUTH CROYDON, SURREY, CR2 9PA.
WEBB, Mr. Michael Bernard, BA ACA *1991;* 10 Lismore Road, SOUTH CROYDON, SURREY, CR2 7QA.
WEBB, Mr. Michael Chesterton, FCA *1960;* 2 Sycamore Drive, THAME, OX9 2AT. (Life Member)
•**WEBB, Mr. Michael Frederick, FCA** *1968;* (Tax Fac), Webb & Co Limited, 1 New Street, WELLS, SOMERSET, BA5 2LA.
WEBB, Mr. Michael John, BSc ACA *1987;* Wellman Robey Ltd, Newfield Road, OLDBURY, B69 3ET.
WEBB, Mr. Michael John, FCA *1969;* 19 Naseby Drive, HALESOWEN, WEST MIDLANDS, B63 1HJ.
WEBB, Mr. Michael Robert, ACA *2005;* 381 Carterhatch Lane, ENFIELD, EN1 4AN.
•**WEBB, Miss. Michele, BSc FCA** *1983;* Michele Webb, Woodpecker, Fir Tree Close, St. Leonards, RINGWOOD, HAMPSHIRE BH24 2QW.
WEBB, Mrs. Naila, FCA *1974;* Littledown, Lower Sandy Down, Boldre, LYMINGTON, SO41 8PP.
•**WEBB, Mr. Nicholas, BCom FCA** *1988;* (Tax Fac), DHH, Wychbury Chambers, 78 Worcester Road, Hagley, STOURBRIDGE, DY9 0NJ.
WEBB, Mr. Nicholas Hugh, MA ACA *1983;* The Elms, Marton, RUGBY, CV23 9RT.
WEBB, Mr. Nicholas Patrick, FCA *1964;* 46 Sunningvale Avenue, Biggin Hill, WESTERHAM, TN16 3BX.
WEBB, Mr. Nicholas Paul, BA ACA *2007;* 80 Hessel Road, LONDON, W13 9ET.
WEBB, Mr. Nicholas Richard, BSocSc ACA *2004;* 14 Torrington Road, Claygate, ESHER, KT10 0SA.
WEBB, Mrs. Nicola Margaret, BA ACA *1985;* 111 Lynwood Drive, Merley, WIMBORNE, BH21 1UU.
WEBB, Mr. Nigel Richard, ACA *1980;* Strawinskylaan 3159, 1077ZX AMSTERDAM, NETHERLANDS.
WEBB, Dr. Olivia Josephine, DPhil ACA *2006;* 464 Russell Court, Woburn Place Bloomsbury, LONDON, WC1H OLW.
WEBB, Miss. Pamela, ACA *2008;* 48 Bradley Crescent, BRISTOL, BS11 9SN.
WEBB, Mr. Patrick John Ryall, FCA *1970;* 17 Tower Road, TADWORTH, SURREY, KT20 5QY.
WEBB, Mr. Paul Derry, BA ACA *1992;* 43 Bulkeley Avenue, WINDSOR, SL4 3NG.
WEBB, Mr. Paul Warren, MBA BSc ACA *1987;* Stonelea HouseFantley Lane, Silton GILLINGHAM, Dorset, SP8 5AJ.
WEBB, Mr. Peter, FCA *1957;* 9 Breary Court, Bramhope, LEEDS, LS16 9LB. (Life Member)
WEBB, Mr. Peter Graham, FCA *1958;* Romilly Cottage, 139 Binscombe Lane, GODALMING, GU7 3QL. (Life Member)
•**WEBB, Mr. Peter Martin, FCA** *1983;* with Thomas Westcott, 22 Queen Anne Terrace, PLYMOUTH, PL4 8EG.
•**WEBB, Mr. Peter Ronald, FCA** *1973;* West Wake Price & Co, Abacus House, Cranbrook Road, HAWKHURST, KENT, TN18 4AR.
WEBB, Mr. Philip Andrew, FCA *1971;* 3 Larchwood Road, Borras Park, WREXHAM, LL12 7SG.
WEBB, Mr. Quentin Craig, ACA CA(SA) *2009;* 10/ 19 Fontenoy Road, Macquarie Park, SYDNEY, NSW 2113, AUSTRALIA.
WEBB, Mrs. Rebecca Louise, BSc ACA *2002;* with National Audit Office, 157-197 Buckingham Palace Road, Victoria, LONDON, SW1W 9SP.
WEBB, Mr. Reginald Vallance, FCA FCMA *1997;* 270/6, 5522 ST. MARTIN AM TENNENGEBIRGE, AUSTRIA.
WEBB, Mr. Richard Allan, FCA *1967;* Grebe Lodge, Riversdale, BOURNE END, BUCKINGHAMSHIRE, SL8 5EB.
WEBB, Mr. Richard Anthony, BA(Hons) ACA *2000;* 1 Wyvern Close, Tangmere, CHICHESTER, WEST SUSSEX, PO20 2GQ.
WEBB, Mr. Richard August, FCA *1962;* 5 Hopkins Field, Bowdon, ALTRINCHAM, WA14 3AL. (Life Member)
WEBB, Mr. Richard David Robert, MA ACA *2004;* 44 Brayburne Avenue, LONDON, SW4 6AA.
WEBB, Mr. Richard John Samuel, BA ACA *2009;* 197 Upper Woodcote Road, Caversham, READING, RG4 7JP.
WEBB, Mr. Richard Neil, BSc(Econ) FCA ATII *1983;* (Tax Fac), 179 Lake Road West, Roath Park, CARDIFF, CF23 5PL.
WEBB, Mr. Richard Owen, BA ACA *2007;* 12 Chelsea Drive, Four Oaks, SUTTON COLDFIELD, B74 4UG.
WEBB, Mr. Robert Charles Mansell, BA FCA *1971;* (Member of Council 1999 - 2007), 9 Leathley Close, Menston, ILKLEY, LS29 6GB.
WEBB, Mr. Robert Malcolm, FCA *1974;* 5 Elmley House, Cardy Close, Batchley, REDDITCH, WORCESTERSHIRE, B97 6LS.
WEBB, Mr. Rodney Anson John, JP FCA *1965;* Shirrenden, Brenchley Road, Horsmonden, TONBRIDGE, KENT, TN12 8DN. (Life Member)
WEBB, Mr. Roger, FCA *1968;* 5 Edgemont Road, Weston Favell, NORTHAMPTON, NN3 3DF.
•**WEBB, Mr. Roger John, BCom FCA** *1967;* R.J. Webb & Co, 26 Ben Rhydding Road, ILKLEY, LS29 8RL.
WEBB, Mrs. Ruth Zita, BA ACA *1999;* 4 Tennyson Road, HARPENDEN, HERTFORDSHIRE, AL5 4BB.
WEBB, Mr. Samuel David, BSc ACA *2006;* 4 Vales Close, SUTTON COLDFIELD, B76 1LJ.
WEBB, Mr. Scott, MSc BA ACA *2003;* 40 Grovehill Road, REDHILL, SURREY, RH1 6DB.
•**WEBB, Miss. Sharron Elizabeth, ACA** *1986;* (Tax Fac), Willow Accountants, Rivers Lodge, West Common, HARPENDEN, HERTFORDSHIRE, AL5 2JD.
WEBB, Mr. Shaun, BSc ACA *1992;* De Poel Managed Services Ltd The Old Shippon, Moseley Hall Farm Chelford Road, KNUTSFORD, CHESHIRE, WA16 8RB.
WEBB, Mr. Simon, ACA *2011;* 1 Park View, Mill Lane Lower Slaughter, CHELTENHAM, GLOUCESTERSHIRE, GL54 2HX.
WEBB, Mr. Simon Arthur, BSc ACA *1989;* 23 Glenwood, Norton, RUNCORN, CHESHIRE, WA7 6UL.
WEBB, Mr. Simon Charles, BA ACA *1990;* 55 Hertford Avenue, LONDON, SW14 8EH.
WEBB, Mr. Simon James, ACA *2010;* 56 Bradenham Road, Grange Park, SWINDON, SN5 6EB.
WEBB, Mr. Simon John, ACA *2009;* Globeleq, 2 More London Riverside, LONDON, SE1 2JT.
WEBB, Mr. Stephen John, BA ACA *1980;* with Deloitte Touche Tohmatsu, 35/F One Pacific Place, 88 Queensway, CENTRAL, HONG KONG ISLAND, HONG KONG SAR.
WEBB, Mr. Stephen John, ACA *1982;* Polkacrest Ltd, Platt Industrial Estate, SEVENOAKS, KENT, TN15 8FD.
WEBB, Mr. Terence Dudley, FCA *1958;* 11 Wesley Grange, 7 Portarlington Road, BOURNEMOUTH, BH4 8BU. (Life Member)
WEBB, Mr. Thomas, BA ACA *1999;* 12 Ludolf Drive, LEEDS, LS17 8LJ.
WEBB, Mr. Thomas Gerald, FCA *1958;* 42 Wyndcliff Drive, Flixton, Urmston, MANCHESTER, M41 6LH. (Life Member)
WEBB, Mr. Thomas John, BSc ACA *1997;* 12 Ashburnham Grove, LONDON, SE10 8UH.
WEBB, Mrs. Tina, BSc ACA *2002;* 10 Caigers Green, Burridge, SOUTHAMPTON, SO31 1EE.
WEBB, Trevor Hugh, Esq OBE FCA *1953;* 8 Michaelmas Road, COVENTRY, CV3 6HG. (Life Member)
WEBB, Miss. Vanessa Jayne, BA ACA *1994;* Courtlands, Tidmarsh Road, Pangbourne, READING, RG8 7AY.
WEBB, Mr. Victor Robert, FCA *1957;* Moorings, 2 Castle Gardens, DORKING, RH4 1NY. (Life Member)
WEBB-HARVEY, Mrs. Julia Clare, BSc ACA *1994;* Old Beith House Fernhurst Road, Milland, LIPHOOK, HAMPSHIRE, GU30 7LU.
WEBB WARE, Mr. Timothy Gibbard, MA ACA *1979;* 35 Coniston Court, Kendal Street, LONDON, W2 2AN.
WEBBER, Mrs. Amanda Louise, BA ACA *1996;* 65 Merton Hall Road, Wimbledon, LONDON, SW19 3PX.
WEBBER, Mr. Andrew Brian, BA ACA *1992;* 320 Ohio River Blvd, PITTSBURGH, PA 15202, UNITED STATES.
WEBBER, Mr. Bernard Walter, FCA *1953;* 10 Orchard Avenue, DEAL, KENT, CT14 9RW. (Life Member)
WEBBER, Mrs. Beverly Jane, BSc ACA *1990;* 22 Montague Avenue, LEIGH-ON-SEA, SS9 3SL.
WEBBER, Miss. Caroline Anne, BSc FCA *1991;* 125 Church Farm Road, Emersons Green, BRISTOL, BS16 7BE.
WEBBER, Mr. Craig Timothy, BA ACA *1983;* 3 Morgan Row, Lower Hillmorton Road, RUGBY, WARWICKSHIRE, CV21 3UN.
WEBBER, Mr. Daniel John, BA(Hons) ACA *2002;* 1 Bywell Court, Kingsmead, MILTON KEYNES, BUCKINGHAMSHIRE, MK4 4HE.
WEBBER, Mr. David Paul, BSc ACA *1989;* New Buildings Farm, Bullington End, Hanslope, MILTON KEYNES, MK19 7BQ.
WEBBER, Mrs. Fiona Carol, BSc ACA *1988;* 51 Geales Crescent, ALTON, GU34 2NE.
WEBBER, Miss. Frances Mary, BSc ACA *1999;* Flat 6, 2 Battery Road Portishead, BRISTOL, BS20 7HP.
WEBBER, Mrs. Gail Anita, BA ACA *1993;* 27 Mount Way, CHEPSTOW, GWENT, NP16 5NF.
WEBBER, Mrs. Hannah, BA(Hons) ACA *2006;* 46 Weston Park, THAMES DITTON, KT7 0HL.
WEBBER, Mrs. Helen Mary, BSc ACA *1995;* 80 Canada Road, Gabalfa, CARDIFF, CF14 3BY.
WEBBER, Mr. Ian James, TD MA FCA *1983;* 30 Granville Road, OXTED, SURREY, RH8 0DA.
WEBBER, Mr. James, ACA *2009;* 3 Williams Grove, Long Ditton, SURBITON, KT6 5RN.
WEBBER, Mr. John David, LLB FCA *1972;* c/o Curry Popeck Solicitors, 87 Wimpole Street, LONDON, W1G 9RL.
WEBBER, Mr. Jonathan Charles, MSc BEng ACA *1999;* 33 Rumsam Gardens, Rumsam Road, BARNSTAPLE, EX32 9EY.
WEBBER, Miss. Laura Jayne, BSc(Hons) ACA *2009;* The Cuparius, 3 The Old Cooperage, Sivell Place, EXETER, EX2 5EU.
WEBBER, Mr. Leslie Colin, FCA *1957;* Inveroran, The Warren, ASHTEAD, KT21 2SG. (Life Member)
•**WEBBER, Mrs. Linda, LLB FCA** *1990;* Minerva Business Advisors, 123 Ellerton Road, SURBITON, SURREY, KT6 7UA.

WEBBER, Miss. Lisa Catherine, BSc(Hons) ACA *2004;* 63 Pleasant Valley, SAFFRON WALDEN, ESSEX, CB11 4AW.
WEBBER, Mrs. Lisa Marie, ACA *2009;* 12 High Street, BILLINGSHURST, WEST SUSSEX, RH14 9PH.
WEBBER, Mrs. Lynn-Jane, BCom CA *1989; (CA Scotland 1987);* Clarendon House, King Lane, Over Wallop, STOCKBRIDGE, SO20 8JQ.
•WEBBER, Mr. Malcolm, FCA *1974;* Harris & Trotter LLP, 65 New Cavendish Street, LONDON, W1G 7LS.
WEBBER, Mr. Mark Timothy, MA ACA *1984;* European Bank For Reconstruction, & Development, 1 Exchange Square, LONDON, EC2A 2JN.
WEBBER, Miss. Melanie, BSc(Econ) ACA *2003;* Glencore UK Ltd, 50 Berkeley Street, LONDON, W1J 8HD.
WEBBER, Mr. Michael, FCA *1969;* Yew Tree Cottage, Artists Lane, Nether Alderley, MACCLESFIELD, CHESHIRE, SK10 4UA.
WEBBER, Mr. Michael James, BSc ACA *2004;* 46 Weston Park, THAMES DITTON, KT7 0HL.
WEBBER, Mr. Nicholas, FCA *1966;* Brandon Steel, 799 London Road, GRAYS, ESSEX, RM20 3LH.
WEBBER, Mr. Nigel John, BSc ACA *1979;* HSBC Private Bank (Suisse), 1 Queens Road, CENTRAL, HONG KONG SAR.
WEBBER, Mr. Nigel John, BA ACA *1991;* 17 Walton Road, Milton Keynes Village, MILTON KEYNES, MK10 9AQ.
WEBBER, Mr. Richard Lewis, BSc ACA *2000;* 8 Lasgarn Place, Abersychan, PONTYPOOL, NP4 6TG.
WEBBER, Mr. Roger Alan, FCA *1958;* 6 Westridge Close, Chartridge Lane, CHESHAM, BUCKINGHAMSHIRE, HP5 2RF. (Life Member)
•WEBBER, Mr. Roman Hilary, BA ACA *1997;* Deloitte LLP, 2 New Street Square, LONDON, EC4A 3BZ. See also Deloitte & Touche LLP
WEBBER, Ms. Sally Anne, ACA *1991;* 5 Hillford Place, REDHILL, RH1 5AT.
WEBBER, Mrs. Sara Jane, BA FCA *1988;* Clifton House, The Street, Shotesham All Saints, NORWICH, NR15 1YW.
WEBBER, Mr. Simon John, ACA *1990;* (Tax Fac), Dormans, Charterhouse Road, GODALMING, GU7 2AW.
•WEBBER, Mr. Simon Luke, BA ACA *2006;* Spofforths LLP, 9 Donnington Park, 85 Birdham Road, CHICHESTER, WEST SUSSEX, PO20 7AJ.
WEBBER, Mr. Simon Ross, BSc ACA *1991;* 5816 Chambertin Drive, SAN JOSE, CA 95118, UNITED STATES.
WEBBER, Mr. Stanley Edward, FCA *1965;* Apt.3 Parkmore House, Dublin Road, LIMERICK, COUNTY LIMERICK, IRELAND.
WEBBER, Mrs. Stephanie Jane, MA ACA *1987;* Fishery Lodge The Fish Farm, Water End, HEMEL HEMPSTEAD, HERTFORDSHIRE, HP1 3BB.
WEBBER, Mr. Stephen, BSc ACA *1980;* RBS, PASSHEUVELWEG 25, AMSTERDAM, NETHERLANDS.
•WEBBER, Mr. Stuart James, MA BA ACA *1991;* Lewis Golden & Co, 40 Queen Anne Street, LONDON, W1G 9EL.
WEBBER, Mr. Terence Frank Lees, FCA *1957;* Frampton Court, Court Road, Frampton Cotterell, BRISTOL, BS36 2DW. (Life Member)
WEBBER, Mr. Timothy, LLB ACA *1989;* 4 Fairmile Heights, Fairmile Park Road, COBHAM, SURREY, KT11 2PP.
WEBBER, Mr. William John, FCA *1969;* Kafue, 33 Five Bells, WATCHET, TA23 0HY.
WEBBERLEY, Mr. Mark Andrew, BA ACA *1991;* Telent Technology Service Ltd Point, 3 Haywood Road, WARWICK, CV34 5AH.
•WEBER, Miss. Angela Louise, ACA *2002;* (Tax Fac), Ashcroft Anthony, Heydon Lodge, Flint Cross, Newmarket Road, Heydon, ROYSTON HERTFORDSHIRE SG8 7PN. See also Ashcroft Anthony Ltd
WEBER, Mr. David, ACA *2009;* 11 Magistrates Walk, MELBOURNE, VIC 3002, AUSTRALIA.
WEBER, Mr. David Michael James, FCA *1966;* 1 Kingscombe Cottages, Factory Road, Llanblethian, COWBRIDGE, SOUTH GLAMORGAN, CF71 7JD.
WEBER, Mr. James Reginald Craig, FCA *1940;* Cold Harbour, Hilden Way, Littleton, WINCHESTER, HAMPSHIRE, SO22 6QH. (Life Member)
WEBER, Mr. Jan George, BSc CA *1990; (CA Scotland 1981);* MEMBER OF COUNCIL, Flat 3, Dean Wace House, 7 Wine Office Court, LONDON, EC4A 3BY.
•WEBER, Mr. John Stuart, FCA *1971;* J.S. Weber & Co., 29 Woodvale Avenue, Cyncoed, CARDIFF, CF23 6SP.
WEBER, Mrs. Julie Alison, BSc ACA *1998;* Smith Cooper, Wilmot House, St. James Court, Friar Gate, DERBY, DE1 1BT.
WEBER, Mr. Peter Anthony, FCA *1966;* Shubette House, 2 Apsley Way, LONDON, NW2 7HF.
WEBER, Mr. Stanley Joseph, FCA *1948;* Flat 7, 1 St. Mildreds Gardens, WESTGATE-ON-SEA, CT8 8TP. (Life Member)
WEBER, Miss. Toni Sharon, ACA *1991;* The Met Condo unit 40F-D2, 123/86 South Sathorn Road, Thungmahamek Sathorn, BANGKOK 10120, THAILAND.
WEBLEY, Mr. John Philip, FCA *1970;* Ash Oast, School House Lane, Horsmonden, TONBRIDGE, KENT, TN12 8BJ.
WEBLEY, Mr. Malcolm Anthony Charles, FCA *1960;* PO Box 496, PACIFIC FAIR, QLD 4218, AUSTRALIA.
WEBLEY, Mr. Owen David, ACA *2009;* Flat 22 Worcester Court, Park View Close, ST. ALBANS, HERTFORDSHIRE, AL1 5TS.
WEBSPER, Mrs. Elizabeth Jane, BA(Hons) ACA *2003;* 29 Derwentwater Road, LONDON, W3 6DF.
WEBSTER, Mr. Adam Bjorn, MA ACA *1999;* Hobsons Plc 3rd Floor, Idt House, 44 Featherstone Street, LONDON, EC1Y 8RN.
WEBSTER, Mr. Alistair Keith, BSc ACA *2002;* Graylands Cottage, Egg Pie Lane, Hildenborough, TONBRIDGE, KENT, TN11 8PE.
WEBSTER, Mr. Allan Firth, BSc FCA *1975;* Business Employment Services Training Ltd, Warwick House, Wade Lane, LEEDS, LS2 8NL.
WEBSTER, Mrs. Andrea, BSc ACA *1992;* 82 Westgate, Guiseley, LEEDS, LS20 8HJ.
WEBSTER, Mr. Andrew Geoffrey, BSc ACA *1998;* Littlehurst, The Ridgeway, Chalfont St Peter, GERRARDS CROSS, BUCKINGHAMSHIRE, SL9 8NT.
•WEBSTER, Mr. Andrew Gilbert, FCA MIoD FRSA DChA *1975;* Andrew Webster Associates, 48 St. Martins Hill, CANTERBURY, KENT, CT1 1PP. See also Webster
WEBSTER, Mrs. Anne Elizabeth, ACA *1985;* The Brandon Trust, Kestrel Court, Waterwells Drive, Waterwells Business Park, Quedgeley, GLOUCESTER GL2 2AT.
WEBSTER, Mr. Anthony Peter, MA FCA *1977;* 579 5th Avenue, 17th Floor, NEW YORK, NY 10017, UNITED STATES.
WEBSTER, Mr. Barry William Brady, FCA *1952;* Beechmount, Weaponness Drive, SCARBOROUGH, YO11 2TZ. (Life Member)
•WEBSTER, Mrs. Caroline Sarah, BA FCA *1992;* with Critchleys LLP, Critchleys, Avalon House, Marcham Road, ABINGDON, OXFORDSHIRE OX14 1UD.
WEBSTER, Miss. Catherine, BSc ACA *1989;* London Business School, Sussex Place, Regents Park, LONDON, NW1 4SA.
WEBSTER, Mrs. Catherine Emma, BSc ACA *2000;* 29 Farley Crescent, Oakworth, KEIGHLEY, WEST YORKSHIRE, BD22 7SH.
•WEBSTER, Mr. Charles Neil, FCA *1967;* Sundown, Heversham, MILNTHORPE, LA7 7EQ.
WEBSTER, Miss. Charlotte Judith, BA(Hons) ACA *2003;* Thomson Reuters, Thomson Reuters Building, 30 South Colonnade, LONDON, E14 5EP.
WEBSTER, Mr. Clive Adrian, BA FCA *1976;* 2 St. Clements Drive, LEIGH-ON-SEA, SS9 3BJ.
WEBSTER, Mr. Colin Peter, MEng ACA *1998;* 17 Mayfield Road, SOUTH CROYDON, SURREY, CR2 0BG.
WEBSTER, Mr. Daniel James, BA ACA *2010;* 4 Grove Road, ST. ALBANS, HERTFORDSHIRE, AL1 1DQ.
WEBSTER, Mr. David Christopher, BSc FCA *1977;* The Beeches, Croft Lane, KNUTSFORD, CHESHIRE, WA16 8QH.
WEBSTER, Mr. David James, ACA *2009;* 54 Hedgerow Close, REDDITCH, WORCESTERSHIRE, B98 7QF.
WEBSTER, Mr. David Keith Thomas, FCA *1975;* ADP Associates Ltd White Doves 59 Millers Walk Pelsall, WALSALL, WS3 4QS.
WEBSTER, Mr. David Stephen, MA FCA *1992;* 25 Barton Road, WIRRAL, CH47 1HJ.
WEBSTER, Mrs. Deborah Louise, BA(Hons) ACA *2004;* 77 Walsingham Road, Woodthorpe, NOTTINGHAM, NG5 4NQ.
WEBSTER, Mr. Duncan, BA ACA *1986;* 83 Quentin Road, LONDON, SE13 5DG.
WEBSTER, Mr. Edgar John, FCA *1956;* Fulmere, 18 Dukes Kiln Drive, GERRARDS CROSS, BUCKINGHAMSHIRE, SL9 7HD. (Life Member)
WEBSTER, Miss. Elaine Margaret May, BA ACA *1986;* Porch Farm Cottage Village Road, Coleshill, AMERSHAM, BUCKINGHAMSHIRE, HP7 0LG.
WEBSTER, Miss. Elizabeth Helen, BA ACA *2005;* 27 Beech Close, WALTON-ON-THAMES, SURREY, KT12 5RQ.
WEBSTER, Mrs. Elizabeth Jane, BSc ACA CTA *1996;* 25 Barton Road, WIRRAL, CH47 1HJ.
WEBSTER, Mrs. Emma, MSc BA ACA *2004;* Old Coach House The Slade, Charlbury, CHIPPING NORTON, OXFORDSHIRE, OX7 3SJ.
WEBSTER, Mrs. Fiona Louise, BA FCA *1998;* 208 Tyler Avenue, SANTA CLARA, CA 95050, UNITED STATES.
WEBSTER, Mrs. Frances Janet, BSc FCA AMCT *1991;* RBC Wealth Management, RBC Trust Company (International) Limited, Le Gallias Chambers, 54 Bath Street, St Helier, JERSEY JE1 6PB.
WEBSTER, Mr. Giles Edmund, BA(Hons) ACA *2001;* Benenden Healthcare Society, Holgate Park Drive, YORK, YO26 4GG.
WEBSTER, Mr. Graham Stanley, MBA FCA *1969;* Edbrook Farm, Horn Hill, Cannington, BRIDGWATER, TA5 2QE.
•WEBSTER, Mrs. Heidi Elizabeth, BA ACA *1998;* HMW, 1 Stuarts Green, Pedmore, STOURBRIDGE, WEST MIDLANDS, DY9 0XR. See also Webster Heidi
WEBSTER, Miss. Helen, MSc ACA *2003;* 17 Swithens Street, Rothwell, LEEDS, LS26 0BU.
WEBSTER, Mr. Henry John, FCA *1951;* Heathers, Knowle Drive, SIDMOUTH, EX10 8HW. (Life Member)
WEBSTER, Mr. Ian Richard, BA ACA *1993;* Flat 4, 19 Upper Belgrave Road, BRISTOL, BS8 2XL.
•WEBSTER, Mr. Ian Stuart, FCA *1995;* (Tax Fac), Larking Gowen, Faiers House, Gilray Road, DISS, IP22 4WR.
WEBSTER, Mrs. Jacqueline Elaine, ACA *1995;* 19 Fairhope Avenue, MORECAMBE, LANCASHIRE, LA4 6LB.
WEBSTER, Mr. James Henrik, BA ACA *1995;* Carpenters Cottage, Payford, Redmarley, GLOUCESTER, GL19 3HY.
WEBSTER, Miss. Jane Allison, ACA *1981;* 108 Granville Way, SHERBORNE, DT9 4AT.
WEBSTER, Mrs. Jennifer Susan, BSc ACA *1995;* The Paddocks, Wetherby Road, Rufforth, YORK, YO23 3QB.
WEBSTER, Miss. Jenny, MPhys(Hons) ACA *2011;* 19 Epsom Croft, Anderton, CHORLEY, LANCASHIRE, PR6 9LL.
•WEBSTER, Mr. Jeremy, MA FCA *1957;* The White House, Beaumont-cum-Moze, CLACTON-ON-SEA, ESSEX, CO16 0AU.
WEBSTER, Mr. John, BA ACA *1980;* with PricewaterhouseCoopers Audit S.R.L, Lakeview Office, 301-311 Barbu Vacarescu Street, RO-020276 BUCHAREST, ROMANIA.
•WEBSTER, Mr. John Andrew, BA FCA *1994;* Webster & Co (York) Limited, The Paddocks, Wetherby Road, Rufforth, YORK, YO23 3QB.
WEBSTER, Mr. John Strachan, FCA *1964;* 1 Mill Mount House, Mill Mount, YORK, YO24 1BG.
WEBSTER, Mr. John Walter, BSc FCA *1961;* Woodmans Cottage, Bramley Road, Silchester, READING, RG7 2LT.
WEBSTER, Mr. Jonathan Mark Cook, BSc ACA *1993;* Okeford, Sutton Lane, Sutton, WITNEY, OX29 5RU.
•WEBSTER, Mr. Jonathan Paul, FCA *1973;* (Tax Fac), J P Webster Limited, 5 Nethergate Street, BUNGAY, SUFFOLK, NR35 1HE.
WEBSTER, Mr. Julian Mark Courtney, BSc ACA *1986;* House B5 Stanley Knoll, 42 Stanley Village Road, STANLEY, HONG KONG SAR.
WEBSTER, Mrs. Julie Catherine, BSc ACA *1994;* The Hollies, 1 Holly End, Naphill, HIGH WYCOMBE, HP14 4SJ.
WEBSTER, Miss. Kate, BA ACA *2005;* 9 Portland Place, SOUTH YARRA, VIC 3141, AUSTRALIA.
WEBSTER, Miss. Katharine Ann, BSc ACA *1992;* 53 Priests Lane, Shenfield, BRENTWOOD, CM15 8BX.
WEBSTER, Mrs. Katherine Mary, BSc ACA *2005;* 35 Tillingbourne Road, Shalford, GUILDFORD, GU4 8EY.
•WEBSTER, Mrs. Kathleen Winifred, BA FCA DChA *1979;* (Tax Fac), 23 St. Marys Road, KETTERING, NORTHAMPTONSHIRE, NN15 7BP.
WEBSTER, Miss. Kelly Barbara Sarah, ACA *2009;* Apartment 21, 24 Point Pleasant, LONDON, SW18 1GG.
WEBSTER, Miss. Laura, ACA *2010;* 15 Shamrock Street, LONDON, SW4 6HF.
•WEBSTER, Mr. Lawrence Andrew, BA ACA *1981;* (Tax Fac), Lawrence Webster Associates Limited, Eastlands Court, St Peters Road, RUGBY, WARWICKSHIRE, CV21 3QP. See also Webster Lawrence
•WEBSTER, Mr. Lee Barry, ACA FCCA *2008;* Jimalice Limited, Enterprise House, The Courtyard, Old Courtyard Road, Bromborough, WIRRAL MERSEYSIDE CH62 4UE.
WEBSTER, Miss. Leonie Jane, BA ACA *1999;* Deloitte & Touche Hill House, 1 Little New Street, LONDON, EC4A 3TR.
WEBSTER, Mrs. Lisa Eleanor, MA(Oxon) ACA *2009;* 85 Thicket Road, SUTTON, SURREY, SM1 4PX.
WEBSTER, Mr. Malcolm Ian, BA ACA *1986;* 22 Priory Avenue, Tollerton, NOTTINGHAM, NG12 4EE.
WEBSTER, Mr. Mark Edmund John, BSc ACA *1989;* 26 Bushey Way, Park Langley, BECKENHAM, BR3 6TB.
WEBSTER, Mr. Mark John, BA ACA *1998;* 1 Stuarts Green, Pedmore, STOURBRIDGE, WEST MIDLANDS, DY9 0XR.
WEBSTER, Mr. Mark M, MA ACA *1999;* Business Development Asia LLC, 16-02 The Center, 989 Changle Road, SHANGHAI 200031, CHINA.
•WEBSTER, Mr. Martin Edward, FCA *1968;* Childersleigh, Church Road, Southborough, TUNBRIDGE WELLS, TN4 0RT.
WEBSTER, Mr. Martin Guy, BSc FCA ACGI TEP *1979;* The Penthouse, 3 Les Arches, ST LAWRENCE, JE3 1JA.
WEBSTER, Mr. Martin James, BSc ACA *1992;* 7 Charles Street, SOUTH FREMANTLE, WA 6162, AUSTRALIA.
WEBSTER, Mr. Martin James, BA FCA *1985;* 82 Westgate, Guiseley, LEEDS, LS20 8HJ.
WEBSTER, Mr. Martin Richard, BA ACA *1980;* 9 Dukes Ride, GERRARDS CROSS, BUCKINGHAMSHIRE, SL9 7LD.
WEBSTER, Mr. Martyn, BSc ACA *1983;* (Tax Fac), St. Marys, West End, Waltham St. Lawrence, READING, RG10 0NT.
WEBSTER, Mr. Martyn John, BA FCA *1995;* 208 Tyler Avenue, SANTA CLARA, CA 95050, UNITED STATES.
WEBSTER, Mr. Martyn Robert, BSc FCA *1971;* Boundary House, 4 Sea Lane Close, East Preston, LITTLEHAMPTON, BN16 1NQ.
WEBSTER, Mr. Michael John, FCA *1975;* 60 Fore Street, HERTFORD, SG14 1BY.
•WEBSTER, Mr. Michael John Seymour, BSc FCA *1999;* Landin Wilcock & Co, Queen St Chmbrs, 68 Queen St, SHEFFIELD, S17 4BD.
WEBSTER, Mr. Miles Douglas, BA FCA *1982;* 6 Newman Lane, Drayton Village, ABINGDON, OXFORDSHIRE, OX14 4LP.
•WEBSTER, Mr. Neil, BA FCA *1986;* 30 Queensway, Rothwell, LEEDS, LS26 0NB.
WEBSTER, Mr. Neil Gordon, BA FCA *1992;* 15 Woolerton Park 01/12 Gallop Green, SINGAPORE 257535, SINGAPORE.
WEBSTER, Mr. Nicholas George, MMath ACA *2002;* Lloyds TSB Bank Plc Canons House, Canons Way, BRISTOL, BS1 5LL.
WEBSTER, Mr. Nicholas Gordon Cumyn, BSc(Hons) ACA *2004;* Flat 15, 32 Courtfield Gardens, LONDON, SW5 0PH.
•WEBSTER, Mr. Nicholas Mark, MA FCA *1986;* PricewaterhouseCoopers LLP, 89 Sandyford Road, NEWCASTLE UPON TYNE, NE1 8HW. See also PricewaterhouseCoopers
WEBSTER, Mr. Nicholas Peter Hamilton, BA FCA *1973;* Yew Tree Cottage, 39/40 Little Gaddesden, BERKHAMSTED, HP4 1PQ. (Life Member)
•WEBSTER, Mr. Nigel Buckley, FCA *1974;* (Tax Fac), Nigel Webster & Co Ltd, 129 North Hill, PLYMOUTH, PL4 8JY.
WEBSTER, Mr. Nigel David Burnby, FCA *1975;* 8 Worcester Close, Lodge Moor, SHEFFIELD, S10 4JF.
•WEBSTER, Mr. Paul, FCA *1966;* (Tax Fac), Paul Webster & Associates, 27 Cavendish Road, SUTTON, SURREY, SM2 5EY. See also Capel Cavendish & Co
WEBSTER, Mr. Paul Alan, BSc FCA CTA *1968;* (Tax Fac), Greenacres, Broadstreet Common, Nash, NEWPORT, NP18 2AZ.
WEBSTER, Mr. Paul David, BA ACA *1997;* Smith and Nephew Extruded Films Ltd, Gateway to Humberside Trading Estate, Gilberdyke, BROUGH, NORTH HUMBERSIDE, HU15 2TD.
•WEBSTER, Mr. Paul David, BA FCA CTA *1997;* Ingham & Co, George Stanley House, 2 West Parade Road, SCARBOROUGH, NORTH YORKSHIRE, YO12 5ED. See also Charles A Wood & Co Ltd
•WEBSTER, Mr. Paul Marsden, FCA *1963;* 3 Maple Garth, Melmerby, RIPON, HG4 5PA.
•WEBSTER, Mr. Paul Oliver, FCA *1975;* (Tax Fac), Mercer & Hole, Gloucester House, 72 London Road, ST. ALBANS, HERTFORDSHIRE, AL1 1NS.
•WEBSTER, Mr. Peter, FCA *1984;* (Tax Fac), Ascendant Accounting Limited, 44 Stamford Street, STALYBRIDGE, CHESHIRE, SK15 1LQ.
WEBSTER, Mr. Peter David, BA FCA *1965;* 34 West Common, HAYWARDS HEATH, RH16 2AH.
WEBSTER, Mr. Philip John, BSc ACA CISA *1985;* 92 Stanaway Street, Hillcrest, AUCKLAND 1310, NEW ZEALAND.
WEBSTER, Mr. Ranald Rory Henderson, BSc ACA *1991;* 21 Sudbourne Road, Brixton, LONDON, SW2 5AE.

WEBSTER, Mr. Richard Mark, BA ACA *1992;* 25 Megson Way, Walkington, BEVERLEY, HU17 8YA.
•**WEBSTER, Mr. Robert James, FCA** *1969;* (Tax Fac), Millweb, 49 Sheldon Road, Ickford, AYLESBURY, BUCKINGHAMSHIRE, HP18 9HY.
WEBSTER, Mr. Robert William Edward, ACA *1983;* 135 Bills Lane, Shirley, SOLIHULL, B90 2PQ.
WEBSTER, Mr. Robin William, MA ACA FCIBS *1982;* 2 Bank Cottages, Bank Lane, Wardle, ROCHDALE, LANCASHIRE, OL12 9ND.
WEBSTER, Mr. Roger, BA(Hons) ACA *2011;* St. Marys House, Sill Bridge Lane, Waltham St. Lawrence, READING, BERKSHIRE, RG10 0NT.
•**WEBSTER, Mr. Roger Barry, FCA** *1978;* Peters Elworthy & Moore, Salisbury House, Station Road, CAMBRIDGE, CB1 2LA. See also PEM VAT Services LLP, PEM Corporate Finance LLP
WEBSTER, Miss. Sarah Catherine, BSc(Hons) ACA *2006;* with PricewaterhouseCoopers, Dorchester House, 7 Church Street West, PO Box HM1171, HAMILTON HM EX, BERMUDA.
WEBSTER, Mrs. Sarah Jane Fletcher, ACA *2009;* My Time Active Linden House, 153-155 Masons Hill, BROMLEY, BR2 9HY.
WEBSTER, Miss. Sarah Ruth, BSc ACA *2002;* 17 Faircross Way, ST. ALBANS, HERTFORDSHIRE, AL1 4RT.
•**WEBSTER, Mr. Simon John, BCom ACA** *1986;* DPC Accountants Limited, Vernon Road, STOKE-ON-TRENT, ST4 2QY. See also The DPC Group Limited
WEBSTER, Mr. Simon Paul, BSc ACA *1986;* (Tax Fac), with PricewaterhouseCoopers LLP, Abacus Court, 6 Minshull Street, MANCHESTER, M1 3ED.
WEBSTER, Mr. Stephen, ACA MCT *1983;* with Qinetiq Limited, Cody Technology Park, Room 1022 Building A1, Ively Road, FARNBOROUGH, GU14 0LX.
WEBSTER, Mr. Stephen John, BSc FCA *1986;* 97 Lake Drive, POOLE, DORSET, BH15 4LR.
WEBSTER, Mr. Stephen John, BSc ACA *1993;* c/o S.Webster, 26 Spring Close, LUTTERWORTH, LEICESTERSHIRE, LE17 4DD.
WEBSTER, Mr. Stephen Mark Dale, BSc ACA *1998;* 10, Boundary Park, Parkgate, NESTON, CH64 6TN.
WEBSTER, Mr. Stephen Paul, FCA *1976;* 2 Melliss Avenue, Kew, RICHMOND, TW9 4BQ.
WEBSTER, Mr. Stephen William, BSc ACA *1989;* 7 Hildenbrook Farm, Riding Lane, TONBRIDGE, KENT, TN11 9JN.
WEBSTER, Miss. Susan Catherine, FCA *1977;* 11 Linnet Mews, LONDON, SW12 8JE.
WEBSTER, Mrs. Susan Jane, FCA *1983;* 14 West Acridge, BARTON-UPON-HUMBER, SOUTH HUMBERSIDE, DN18 5AN.
WEBSTER, Mrs. Suzanne Michelle, BA(Hons) ACA *2000;* G's Group Holdings Ltd, Barway Road, Barway, Soham, ELY, CAMBRIDGESHIRE CB7 5TZ.
•**WEBSTER, Mr. Timothy Martin, FCA** *1969;* (Tax Fac), T M Webster & Co, 6 Lanheverne Parc, St Keverne, HELSTON, TR12 6LX.
WEBSTER, Mrs. Tina, BSc ACA *1986;* 28 Manor Close, Brampton, HUNTINGDON, CAMBRIDGESHIRE, PE28 4UF.
WEBSTER, Mrs. Tina, ACA CTA *2004;* (Tax Fac), 2 Hampton Terrace, Burney Avenue, SURBITON, KT5 8DF.
WEBSTER, Mr. Tom James, BCom ACA *2004;* Commission for Social Care Inspection, 33 Greycoat Street, LONDON, SW1P 2QF.
WEBSTER, Mr. William Rutland, MA ACA *2004;* with Grant Thornton UK LLP, 30 Finsbury Square, LONDON, EC2P 2YU.
WECHSLER, Mr. John Anthony Magnus, BA FCA *1963;* 39 Ham Common, RICHMOND, SURREY, TW10 7JG. (Life Member)
•**WECHSLER, Mr. Michael, ACA** *1982;* M. Wechsler, 48 Brookside Road, LONDON, NW11 9NE.
WEDDERBURN, Mr. David Roland, BSc ACA *1984;* 71 Leicester Road, East Finchley, LONDON, N2 9DY.
•**WEDDERBURN, Miss. Mary-Louise, MA FCA FCCA** *1979;* Mary-Louise Wedderburn, 57 Beryl Road, LONDON, W6 8JS.
WEDEKIND, Mr. Frank Christian, ACA *2008;* 7 Ingle Mews, LONDON, EC1R 1XG.
WEDEKIND, Mrs. Helen Christina, MA FCA *1994;* E.ON Energie AG, Brienner Strasse 40, D-80333 MUNICH, GERMANY.
WEDEL, Mr. David Lloyd, FCA *1969;* Harthill House, Sandy Lane, Hewelsfield Common, LYDNEY, GL15 6XA. (Life Member)
WEDGBURY, Mrs. Catherine Anne, BSc ACA *1989;* 397 Johnson Avenue, ENGLEWOOD, NJ 07631, UNITED STATES.
WEDGBURY, Mr. Robert, FCA *1958;* 21 Oaklands Rise, WELWYN, AL6 0RN. (Life Member)
WEDGBURY, Mr. Simon Robert, BSc ACA *1989;* One New York Plaza, NEW YORK, NY 10004-1980, UNITED STATES.
WEDGE, Mr. Andrew Neil, BSc ACA *1995;* (Tax Fac), Idt House, 44 Featherstone Street, LONDON, EC1Y 8RN.
WEDGE, Mr. Bryan Kenneth, FCA *1959;* Flat 1, Brougham House, 32 St. James Road, MALVERN, WORCESTERSHIRE, WR14 2TS. (Life Member)
WEDGE, Mr. Michael Jonathan, ACA *2009;* 63 Hatfield Road, POTTERS BAR, HERTFORDSHIRE, EN6 1HS.
WEDGEWOOD, Mr. Matthew Robert, BA ACA AMCT *1998;* Tata Beverage Group, Parkview, 82 Oxford Road, UXBRIDGE, MIDDLESEX, UB8 1UX.
WEDGWOOD, Mr. Antony John, MA FCA *1969;* 10 Milner Place, LONDON, N1 1TN.
WEDGWOOD, Mr. Colin David, FCA *1958;* PO Box 630573, IRVING, TX 75063-0129, UNITED STATES. (Life Member)
WEDGWOOD, Mr. Stuart Thomas, BSc ACA *1992;* (Tax Fac), with PricewaterhouseCoopers LLP, Cornwall Court, 19 Cornwall Street, BIRMINGHAM, B3 2DT.
WEDLAKE, Mr. William John, BSc FCA *1982;* Furlongs Franksfield, Peaslake, GUILDFORD, GU5 9SR.
•**WEDMORE, Ms. Elizabeth Kenzie, MA ACA** *1984;* Hall Place, Bourne Road, BEXLEY, KENT, DA5 1PQ.
WEDMORE, Mr. Philip Thomas Martin Pole, MA ACA *1984;* 19 Burbage Road, LONDON, SE24 9HJ.
WEE, Miss. Anne Holk Eng, BSc ACA *1992;* 103 Beechcroft Road, Tooting, LONDON, SW17 7BP.
WEE, Mr. Bing Hok, ACA *1984;* 24 Lorong Taman Jaya 6, Jalan Pusara, 20400 KUALA TERENGGANU, MALAYSIA.
WEE, Mr. Choo Peng, FCA *1986;* 65 Jalan Jambu Ayer, SINGAPORE 2158, SINGAPORE.
WEE, Mr. Clinton Jeffrey Boon Hai, BSc(Econ) ACA *1997;* Block 164 Unit 10-268, Bishan Street 13, SINGAPORE 570164, SINGAPORE.
WEE, Mr. Hian Nam, FCA *1970;* Macs Pte Ltd, Unit H Lion City Hotel Complex, 15 Tanjong Katong Road, SINGAPORE 436950, SINGAPORE.
WEE, Mr. Hian Peng, FCA *1973;* 24 Thiam Siew Avenue, SINGAPORE 1543, SINGAPORE.
WEE, Mr. Hock Ho, FCA *1971;* 35 Amber Road #14-16, SINGAPORE 439945, SINGAPORE.
WEE, Miss. Swan Hui, ACA CTA *1988;* A-11-03 Kiara 1888 Condominium, No. 17 Jalan Kiara 3, Mont Kiara, 50480 KUALA LUMPUR, FEDERAL TERRITORY, MALAYSIA.
WEE, Mr. Teow Heng Albert, ACA *1980;* 94 Sunrise Avenue, SINGAPORE 806718, SINGAPORE.
•**WEEDEN, Mr. David William, BSc FCA** *1979;* (Tax Fac), Hamilton-Eddy & Co., 39 Tamworth Road, CROYDON, CR0 1XU.
•**WEEDEN, Mrs. Dawn, MA FCA** *1990;* (Tax Fac), Weeden Ltd, Orchard House, 15 Elizabeth Close, Scotter, GAINSBOROUGH, LINCOLNSHIRE DN21 3TA.
WEEDEN, Mr. Giles George, ACA *1995;* 20 Priory Grove, Ditton, AYLESFORD, KENT, ME20 6BA.
WEEDEN, Mr. Laurence Leonard, FCA *1949;* Goodfellows, Frensham, FARNHAM, GU10 3AB. (Life Member)
WEEDEN, Mr. Mark, BSc FCA *1981;* Citco (Luxembourg) SA, Carre Bonn, 20 Rue de la Poste, L2346 LUXEMBOURG, LUXEMBOURG.
•**WEEDEN, Mr. Nicholas Dennis, MA FCA** *1984;* Good Care Business Support Limited, 21 Orchard Avenue, Southgate, LONDON, N14 4NB.
WEEDEN, Mrs. Shelagh Mary, FCA *1967;* Cyprians Cot, 47 New Street, Chagford, NEWTON ABBOT, DEVON, TQ13 8BB.
•**WEEDEN, Mr. Simon Richard, FCA** *1970;* TSW International Taxation Consulting Limited, Lower Floor, 41 Forehill, ELY, CAMBRIDGESHIRE, CB7 4AA. See also TSW International Taxation Consulting
WEEDING, Mr. Kevin Anthony, BA ACA *1999;* 35 Linden Lea, Down Ampney, CIRENCESTER, GLOUCESTERSHIRE, GL7 5PF.
WEEDON, Mr. Clive Victor, BA ACA *1980;* Flat 15A, 151 Lockhart Road, WAN CHAI, HONG KONG SAR.
WEEKES, Mr. Brendan, ACA *2009;* 1 Cornwall Avenue, LONDON, N3 1LH.
WEEKES, Miss. Gillian, BSc ACA *2007;* with Goodman Jones LLP, 29-30 Fitzroy Square, LONDON, W1T 6LQ.
•**WEEKES, Mr. Ian, BA ACA** *1988;* Crowe Clark Whitehill LLP, 10 Palace Avenue, MAIDSTONE, KENT, ME15 6NF. See also Horwath Clark Whitehill LLP and Crowe Clark Whitehill
WEEKES, Mr. Ian David, BSocSc ACA *1992;* Vratislavova 31, 128 00 PRAGUE, CZECH REPUBLIC.
WEEKES, Mrs. Kristiina Anne, BSc ACA ATII *1994;* with Crowe Clark Whitehill LLP, 10 Palace Avenue, MAIDSTONE, KENT, ME15 6NF.
WEEKES, Mr. Philip Nathaniel, BA ACA *2001;* 87b Gauden Road, Clapham North, LONDON, SW4 6LJ.
WEEKES, Ms. Rachel Elaine, MA FCA *1993;* Flat 66c 66 Southwood Lane, LONDON, N6 5DY.
•**WEEKES, Mr. Stuart Richard, BA(Hons) FCA CTA** *2001;* Crowe Clark Whitehill LLP, Aquis House, 49-51 Blagrave Street, READING, RG1 1PL. See also Horwath Clark Whitehill LLP
WEEKS, Mr. Andrew Patrick Carl, BSc ACA *1994;* 48 Lyme Road, Hazel Grove, STOCKPORT, SK7 6LA.
WEEKS, Mrs. Clare Victoria, BA(Hons) ACA *2000;* Sheen Stickland Llp, 7 East Pallant, CHICHESTER, WEST SUSSEX, PO19 1TR.
•**WEEKS, Mr. Clive Anthony, FCA** *1969;* with BDO LLP, Emerald House, East Street, EPSOM, SURREY, KT17 1HS.
WEEKS, Mr. David Charles, MEng ACA *1993;* Longlands Barn, The Poplars, Eathorpe, LEAMINGTON SPA, WARWICKSHIRE, CV33 9DE.
WEEKS, Mr. Geraint John, BA ACA *1993;* 3 Liddell Close, Pontprennau, CARDIFF, CF23 8PF.
WEEKS, Mr. Gwilym Powell, FCA *1958;* 250 Ashford Close South, Croesyceiliog, CWMBRAN, NP44 2BH. (Life Member)
WEEKS, Miss. Heather, ACA *2009;* Monahans Ledbury Martin, 38-42 Newport Street, SWINDON, SN1 3DR.
WEEKS, Mr. James Daniel, BSc ACA *2003;* Netherfield, Church Road, WINDLESHAM, GU20 6BT.
WEEKS, Miss. Kathryn Heidi, BA ACA *2005;* 19 Plumtree Grove, Hempstead, GILLINGHAM, ME7 3RW.
WEEKS, Miss. Kathy, BA(Hons) ACA *2001;* Dolphin House, Ormond Road, RICHMOND, TW10 6TH.
•**WEEKS, Mr. Kenneth Hamilton, FCA** *1978;* Griffins Business Advisers LLP, Griffins, 24-32 London Road, NEWBURY, BERKSHIRE, RG14 1JX.
WEEKS, Mr. Laurence, BA ACA *1992;* 22 White Road, LONDON, E15 4HA.
•**WEEKS, Mr. Leonard Edward, FCA** *1969;* Ringwood Accounting Limited, 1 Folly Farm Lane, Ashley, RINGWOOD, HAMPSHIRE, BH24 2NN.
WEEKS, Mr. Michael Robert David, BSc FCA *1984;* Hollyberry Cottage, Downend, Chieveley, NEWBURY, RG20 8TS.
WEEKS, Mr. Nicholas John, BSc ACA *2006;* Northern Trust Management Services, 50 Bank Street, LONDON, E14 5NT.
WEEKS, Mr. Nicholas John Charles, BSc ACA *1992;* 49 Chichester Close, Witley, GODALMING, GU8 5PA.
WEEKS, Mr. Paul Eric, ACA *1986;* 1 Glovers Close, HERTFORD, SG13 8DT.
WEEKS, Mrs. Susan Margaret, BSc ACA *1988;* 96 Harmer Green Lane, WELWYN, HERTFORDSHIRE, AL6 0ES.
WEEKS, Mr. Thomas Andrew, BSc ACA *2010;* 37 Florence Road, NORWICH, NR1 4BJ.
WEEMS, Mr. Mark Andrew, BSc ACA *1999;* 15 Lamerton Way, WILMSLOW, CHESHIRE, SK9 3UN.
•**WEEMYS, Mr. Michael Geoffrey, FCA** *1973;* Finax Limited, 28 Church Lea, Whitchurch, TAVISTOCK, PL19 9PS.
WEERERATNE, Mr. Hiran, FCA *1984;* 20 Coombe Gardens, LONDON, SW20 0QU.
WEETCH, Mr. Michael John, FCA *1970;* The Flamboyants, Upton, ST MICHAEL, BB 11103, BARBADOS.
WEGE, Miss. Sarah Lindsay, MA ACA *1983;* 6 St James School, Georges Road, LONDON, N7 8HD.
WEI, Miss. Quatseng Sharon, BA ACA *1998;* B32 14/F, 101 Repulse Bay Road, REPULSE BAY, HONG KONG SAR.
WEI, Miss. Xian, ACA *2010;* 19 Altair Court, 204 Southgate Road, LONDON, N1 3HA.
WEIBELL, Mr. Roger Johnsen, MSc BA ACA *2007;* Vålandsbakken 22, 4010 STAVANGER, NORWAY.
WEIDENBAUM, Mr. Daniel, BSc ACA *1983;* Barnside, Hedsor Road, BOURNE END, SL8 5EE.
WEIGALL, Mr. Geoffrey Ley, MA FCA *1956;* Flat 6, 47 Hollycroft Ave., LONDON, NW3 7QJ. (Life Member)
WEIGERT, Mr. Eric Charles, FCA *1966;* 20 Ventnor Drive, LONDON, N20 8BP.
WEIGH, Mr. Peter Langford, FCA *1961;* 7 West Towers Mews, off Church Lane, Marple, STOCKPORT, CHESHIRE, SK6 7GR. (Life Member)
WEIGHELL, Mrs. Susan, FCA *1981;* 3 Wellgreen Close, Hale, ALTRINCHAM, WA15 8PT.
WEIGHT, Mr. Alastair Iain Reid, FCA *1971;* 5 Bishopsmead Close, East Horsley, LEATHERHEAD, KT24 6RY. (Life Member)
WEIGHT, Mr. Damien Archer, ACA *1993;* Rydale, Mead Road, Livermead, TORQUAY, TQ2 6TE.
WEIGHT, Mrs. Linda Diana, BSc ACA *1992;* 27 Westlands Way, OXTED, RH8 0NB.
WEIGHT, Mrs. Rebecca, PhD ACA *1992;* Lloyds Banking Group, Retail Finance - FACC CL3, Trinity Road CL3, HALIFAX, HX1 2RG.
WEIGHTMAN, Mr. Colin John, BSc FCA MCT *1983;* 49 Foxgrove Road, BECKENHAM, KENT, BR3 5AR.
WEIGHTMAN, Mrs. Elaine, BSc ACA *1993;* 4 Highclere Road, Quedgeley, GLOUCESTER, GL2 4HD.
WEIGHTMAN, Mr. Geoffrey Michael, FCA *1966;* Apartment 10, The Waldorf, 35 Esplanade, South Cliff, SCARBOROUGH, NORTH YORKSHIRE YO11 2AR. (Life Member)
•**WEIL, Mr. Mark Frederick John, FCA** *1979;* Moore Stephens (South) LLP, City Gates, 2-4 Southgate, CHICHESTER, WEST SUSSEX, PO19 8DJ. See also Moore Secretaries Limited
•**WEILER, Mr. Frank Harryman Dan, FCA FCMI** *1968;* Weiler & Co, 12 Marchmont Road, RICHMOND, SURREY, TW10 6HQ.
WEIMANN, Mr. Brett Alan, ACA CA(SA) *2009;* (Tax Fac), 41 Bridge Street, Whaddon, ROYSTON, HERTFORDSHIRE, SG8 5SG.
WEIN, Mr. David Mark, BSc ACA *2000;* 465 Columbus Avenue, Apt 3A, NEW YORK, NY 10024, UNITED STATES.
•**WEINBERG, Mr. Frank Murray, FCA** *1979;* Somers Baker Prince Kurz LLP, 45 Ealing Road, WEMBLEY, HA0 4BA.
•**WEINBERG, Mr. Graham, LLB FCA** *1973;* (Tax Fac), with MacIntyre Hudson LLP, New Bridge Street House, 30-34 New Bridge Street, LONDON, EC4V 6BJ.
•Ⓓ**WEINBERG, Mr. Philip, FCA** *1970;* Marks Bloom Limited, 60 Old London Road, KINGSTON UPON THAMES, SURREY, KT2 6QZ.
WEINEL, Mr. Alastair James, BSc ACA CF *1991;* 11 Bottrells Lane, CHALFONT ST.GILES, HP8 4EX.
WEINEL, Mrs. Alison Claire, MA ACA *1992;* Sijsjeslaan 7, 3078 EVERBERG, BELGIUM.
WEINER, Mr. Alan David, FCA *1967;* 27 Platts Lane, LONDON, NW3 7NP.
•**WEINER, Mr. Alan Leonard, FCA** *1980;* CW & G Partnership LLP, 68 Great Portland Street, LONDON, W1W 7NG.
WEINER, Mr. Jonathan Hyam, FCA *1977;* 1 Chippendayle Drive, Harrietsham, MAIDSTONE, ME17 1AD.
WEINER, Mr. Mark Justin, ACA *1984;* Kinnaird, Peters Lane, Whiteleaf, PRINCES RISBOROUGH, HP27 0LQ.
WEINGARD, Mr. Jeremy Laurence Franklin, BA ACA *1998;* 142 Northampton Road, KETTERING, NN15 7JY.
WEINSTEIN, Mr. Jonathan Robert, ACA *2007;* 69 Bridge Lane, LONDON, NW11 0EE.
•**WEINTROB, Mr. Howard Frank, FCA** *1974;* (Tax Fac), 2 The Drive, Brookmans Park, HATFIELD, HERTFORDSHIRE, AL9 7BD.
WEIR, Mr. Alex Philip, BA ACA *1999;* 9 Hawks Road, KINGSTON UPON THAMES, SURREY, KT1 3DS.
WEIR, Mr. Allister Vincent, BSocSc ACA *2003;* TUI Tavel PLC, Crawley Business Quarter, Fleming Way, CRAWLEY, WEST SUSSEX, RH10 9QL.
WEIR, Mr. Andrew Walter Bougourd Ross, MA FCA *1991;* KPMG, 8/F Prince's Building, 10 Chater Road, CENTRAL, HONG KONG ISLAND, HONG KONG SAR.
WEIR, Mr. Anthony John, BA FCA *1984;* Unitedhealth UK Ltd, 3 Sheldon Square, LONDON, W2 6HY.
WEIR, Mr. Bruce Allan, BA(Hons) FCA *2000;* 1 Waddling Lane, Wheathampstead, ST. ALBANS, HERTFORDSHIRE, AL4 8FD.
WEIR, Mr. Clive Frederick, FCA *1959;* Cavanmore, 32 Main Road, ST JAMES, C.P., 7945, SOUTH AFRICA.
WEIR, Mr. Colin, FCA *1975;* with KPMG, Interseccion de las Avs, FCO de Miranda y Libestador, Chacao CARACAS, 1060A, VENEZUELA.
WEIR, Mr. David Ronald, BSc ACA *1993;* Brae House, 2 Church Lane, Goadby, LEICESTER, LE7 9EX.
WEIR, Mr. David Thomas, FCA *1969;* 21 Longaford Way, Hutton, BRENTWOOD, CM13 2LT.

WEIR, Mr. Duncan Gilbert, FCA *1975;* 637 Fairfax Way, WILLIAMSBURG, VA 23185, UNITED STATES.
WEIR, Mr. Graeme David, BA ACA *1988;* Virgin Wind Online Ltd, 39 Roman Way Industrial Estate, Ribbleton, PRESTON, PR2 5BD.
WEIR, Mr. James, FCA *1974;* 338 Boardwalk Place, LONDON, E14 5SH.
WEIR, Mrs. Jennifer Jane Rosemary, ACA *1995;* Meggitt Aircraft Braking Systems, Holbrook Lane, COVENTRY, CV6 4AA.
WEIR, Mr. John, BSc FCA *1967;* 48 Chalklands, Howe GreenSandon, CHELMSFORD, CM2 7TH.
•ⓘ**WEIR, Mr. Malcolm Stewart, BA FCA** *1988;* 43 Hasted Close, GREENHITHE, KENT, DA9 9HS.
WEIR, Mr. Matthew Alan, BSc ACA *1996;* 10 Oldfield Mews, Highgate, LONDON, N6 5XA.
WEIR, Mr. Peter David, BA ACA *2006;* 43 St. Augustines Drive, BROXBOURNE, HERTFORDSHIRE, EN10 7NA.
WEIR, Mr. Richard Adam, BSc(Hons) ACA *2003;* 6 Greenbraes Road, Gourdon, MONTROSE, DD10 0NE.
WEIR, Mr. Robert John Stuart, BA FCA *1978;* 5 Dyke Close, HOVE, BN3 6DB.
WEIR, Mr. Rodney Houghton, FCA *1970;* 20 Stevens Street, PENNANT HILLS, NSW 2120, AUSTRALIA.
WEIRS, Mrs. Margaret Clare, BA ACA *1993;* 45 Hollowdene, Hetton-le-Hole, HOUGHTON LE SPRING, TYNE AND WEAR, DH5 9NG.
WEISFELD, Mr. Jamie Adam, ACA *2010;* 18 Blenheim Mews, Shenley, RADLETT, HERTFORDSHIRE, WD7 9LL.
WEISGARD, Mr. David Steven, ACA *2008;* 58 Chandos Road, BOREHAMWOOD, HERTFORDSHIRE, WD6 1UX.
•ⓘ**WEISGARD, Mr. Geoffrey Michael, BA FCA** *1970;* 18 Daylesford Crescent, CHEADLE, CHESHIRE, SK8 1LH.
WEISS, Mr. Edward Louis Samuel, FCA *1955;* Cumbria, School Lane, Seer Green, BEACONSFIELD, HP9 2QJ.
WEISS, Mr. Gerhard Adolf, BCom FCA *1947;* 163 The Quadrangle, Cambridge Square, LONDON, W2 2PL. (Life Member)
WEISS, Mr. Howard Anthony, FCA *1962;* 1 Bishops Avenue, Elstree, BOREHAMWOOD, WD6 3LZ.
WEISS, Mr. Michael Carl, BSc(Hons) ACA *2000;* 42 Brewster Gardens, LONDON, W10 6AJ.
•**WEISS, Mr. Peter Alfred Mervyn, MSc BSc FCA** *1979;* (Tax Fac), Leapman Weiss, Hillside House, 2-6 Friern Park, LONDON, N12 9BT.
•**WEISS, Mr. Warren Richard, BSc LLB FCA** *1991;* Defries Weiss (Accountants) Limited, 311 Ballards Lane, North Finchley, LONDON, N12 8LY.
WEISSBART, Mr. Jonathan, BSc(Econ) ACA *1995;* S Weissbart 2nd Floor 32-33, Hatton Garden, LONDON, EC1N 8DL.
WEISSBERG, Mr. Christopher Edmund John, MEng ACA *2006;* 4 Leigh Woods House, Church Road, Leigh Woods, BRISTOL, BS8 3PQ.
WEISSBRAUN, Mr. Alan Oshi, ACA *2004;* 6 Elms Avenue, LONDON, NW4 2PG.
•**WEISSBRAUN, Mr. Michael, FCA** *1976;* Michael Pasha & Co, 220 The Vale, LONDON, NW11 8SR. See also Muallah Weissbraun & Co
WEISSEN, Miss. Emma Jane, MSc BA ACA *2011;* Flat 38, Mapesbury Court, 59-61 Shoot Up Hill, LONDON, NW2 3PU.
WEIST, Mr. Derek Jonathan, BA FCA *1988;* (Tax Fac), BLME, Sherbourne House, 119 Cannon Street, LONDON, EC4N 5AT.
WEISZ, Miss. Danielle Louise, BSc ACA *2010;* 100 Eton Rise, Eton College Road, LONDON, NW3 2DB.
WEITZ, Mr. Quintin Darroll, ACA CA(SA) *2008;* 2224 34 Ave Sw, Unit C, CALGARY T2T 2C6, AB, CANADA.
WEITZMAN, Mr. Joel Marc, BA FCA *1993;* 17 Fernside Court, Holders Hill Road, LONDON, NW4 1JT.
•**WEITZMAN, Mr. Neville Ossip, BSocSc FCA** *1978;* 1A Rehov Shikun Asher, RA'ANANA, 43558, ISRAEL.
WEITZMANN, Mr. David Maurice, BA ACA *1992;* Flat 1 Bloomsbury Mansions, 101 Widmore Road, BROMLEY, BR1 3AD.
WELBERRY, Mrs. Tami Claire, BA ACA *1999;* Drayton House, Sutterton Drove, Amber Hill, BOSTON, LINCOLNSHIRE, PE20 3RF.
WELBOURN, Mr. Charles Joseph C, BA ACA *1990;* 4 Howgill Close, Bolton Low Houses, WIGTON, CUMBRIA, CA7 8PG.
WELBOURN, Mrs. Gillian Frances, BA ACA *1995;* 4 Howgill Close, Bolton Low Houses, WIGTON, CUMBRIA, CA7 8PG.
•**WELBOURNE, Mr. Michael Lance, ACA** *2000;* Coalraven, 127 Station Road, Hugglescote, COALVILLE, LEICESTERSHIRE, LE67 2GD.
WELBOURNE, Mrs. Rachel Annette, BSc ACA *1995;* 14 High Street, Whitwell, HITCHIN, SG4 8AG.
WELBURN, Mrs. Josie Rebecca, BSc ACA *1997;* Ancon Building Products, 9 President Way, SHEFFIELD, S4 7UR.
WELBURN, Mr. Stephen Richard, BSocSc ACA *1997;* 16 Wignall Avenue, Wickersley, ROTHERHAM, SOUTH YORKSHIRE, S66 2AX.
WELBY, Mrs. Camilla, BA ACA *1993;* 23 Cumnor Rise Road, OXFORD, OX2 9HD.
WELBY, Ms. Michaela Ann, BSc ACA *1990;* Unit 13/103A Stokes Street, PORT MELBOURNE, VIC 3207, AUSTRALIA.
•ⓘ**WELBY, Mr. Robert Paul, FCA** *1973;* SFP Forensic Ltd, Suite 9, Ensign House, Admirals Way, LONDON, E14 9XQ.
WELCH, Miss. Alexandra, BA(Hons) ACA *2011;* Flat 10, Vincent Square Mansions, Walcott Street, LONDON, SW1P 2NT.
•**WELCH, Mr. Anthony John, FCA** *1974;* A.J. Welch, 30 St George's Place, CANTERBURY, CT1 1UT.
WELCH, Mrs. Carol Ann, BA ACA *1990;* Isos Housing Limited, No 5, Gosforth Park Avenue, Gosforth Business Park, NEWCASTLE UPON TYNE, NE12 8EG.
WELCH, Mrs. Caroline Elizabeth, BA ACA *1993;* Old Laundry, Bradford Royal Infirmary, Duckworth Lane, BRADFORD, WEST YORKSHIRE, BD9 6RJ.
WELCH, Mrs. Carolyn Jane Clare, BA ACA *1994;* 5 The Chase, LOUGHTON, IG10 4RE.
WELCH, Mr. Christopher James, BEng ACA *1993;* Macquarie Infrastructure and Real Assets, Level 21, 1 Martin Place, SYDNEY, NSW 2000, AUSTRALIA.
WELCH, Mr. Christopher Michael, BA FCA *1980;* Palintest Ltd, Palintest House, Kingsway, Team Valley, Team Valley Trading Estate, GATESHEAD TYNE AND WEAR NE11 0NS.
WELCH, Mr. Colin Hughan, FCA *1954;* 8 Larkspur Close, Thornbury, BRISTOL, BS35 1UQ. (Life Member)
WELCH, Mr. David John, FCA *1963;* 7 Landseer Road, SOUTHWELL, NG25 0LX.
•**WELCH, Mr. David Reginald Stuart, FCA DChA** *1977;* David R S Welch, 3 Alvington Grove, Hazel Grove, STOCKPORT, SK7 5LS.
WELCH, Mr. Giles, BSc ACA *2010;* 92C Bromfelde Road, LONDON, SW4 6PS.
•**WELCH, Mr. James David, BEng ACA** *1993;* (Tax Fac), PKF (UK) LLP, Farringdon Place, 20 Farringdon Road, LONDON, EC1M 3AP.
WELCH, Mr. Jeremy David, MA FCA *2001;* 27 Balaclava Road, LONDON, SE1 5PX.
WELCH, Mr. John David, FCA *1964;* Willowdene, Green Lane, Moorgate, ROTHERHAM, SOUTH YORKSHIRE, S60 3AT.
WELCH, Mr. John Edward Frank, FCA *1966;* High Stile Limited, Rose Cottage, Iron Mills, Gobowen, OSWESTRY, SHROPSHIRE SY10 7BS.
WELCH, Mr. Mark Christopher, BA(Hons) ACA *2002;* Vacant Property Security Ltd Elstree Business Centre, Elstree Way, BOREHAMWOOD, HERTFORDSHIRE, WD6 1RX.
WELCH, Mr. Martin Brian, BSc ACA *1993;* (Tax Fac), 46 Heol Don, Whitchurch, CARDIFF, CF14 2AS.
•**WELCH, Mr. Nicky Rod, ACA** *2008;* NRW, 1480a London Road, LEIGH-ON-SEA, ESSEX, SS9 2UR.
WELCH, Mr. Paul David, BSc FCA *1978;* 36 Church End Lane, Tilehurst, READING, RG30 4UU.
WELCH, Mr. Peter Duncan, BSc ACA *1989;* 4 Normandy Gardens, HORSHAM, WEST SUSSEX, RH12 1AS.
WELCH, Mr. Peter John, FCA *1961;* 4 Malthouse Way, MARLOW, BUCKINGHAMSHIRE, SL7 2UE.
WELCH, Miss. Philippa Jonquil, BA(Hons) ACA *2003;* 86 rue Lafayette, 75009 PARIS, FRANCE.
WELCH, Mr. Richard Thompson, FCA *1969;* 3 Woodside Road, COBHAM, SURREY, KT11 2QR.
WELCH, Mr. Robert William Antony, BA FCA *1974;* 49 Woodstone Avenue, Stoneleigh, EPSOM, KT17 2JT.
•**WELCH, Mr. Roderick Brett, MA ACA** *1982;* Wellkept Financial Services, 10 Newent Road, Northfield, BIRMINGHAM, B31 2ED.
WELCH, Mr. Samuel Peter, ACA *2008;* 18 Chessington Way, WEST WICKHAM, BR4 9NZ.
WELCH, Miss. Sarah, ACA *2011;* Baker Tilly, St. Philips Point, Temple Row, BIRMINGHAM, B2 5AF.
WELCH, Miss. Sarah, BA(Hons) ACA *2011;* Flat 2, 124 Alderney Street, LONDON, SW1V 4HA.
WELCH, Mr. Stephen William, FCA *1974;* Long Acre, Howe Lane, Great Sampford, SAFFRON WALDEN, CB10 2NY.
WELCH, Mr. Stuart Paul, BSc ACA *1992;* 15 Wingfield Court, Off Priestthorpe Road, BINGLEY, BD16 4TE.
WELCH, Miss. Yvonne, ACA *1983;* 20 Woodlands, Preston Village, NORTH SHIELDS, TYNE AND WEAR, NE29 9JT.
WELCHMAN, Mr. Graham Robert, FCA *1972;* Steeple View, 3 Pollards Close, Barrowden, OAKHAM, LEICESTERSHIRE, LE15 8AQ.
WELD, Mr. Simon John, BA ACA *1991;* 15a Wood Ride, Petts Wood, ORPINGTON, KENT, BR5 1PZ.
WELDEN, Mr. Michael Anthony, FCA *1993;* Gelert Ltd, Gelert House, Penamser Road, PORTHMADOG, GWYNEDD, LL49 9NX.
WELDON, Ms. Celia Jane, BSc ACA *1990;* 26 Grange Avenue, STOCKTON-ON-TEES, TS18 4LU.
WELDON, Mr. Christopher James, MMath ACA *2004;* 31 Duke Street, OXFORD, OX2 0HX.
WELDON, Dr. John Phillips, MEc(ANU) BSc(Econ) FCA *1963;* 22 Hawkesbury Crescent, FARRER, ACT 2607, AUSTRALIA.
WELDON, Mr. Jonathan Graham Edward, BSc FCA *1992;* 183 Upper Woodcote Road, Caversham, READING, RG4 7JR.
•**WELDON, Mr. Peter, BA(Hons) ACA** *1986;* Peter Weldon & Co Ltd, 87 Station Road, ASHINGTON, NORTHUMBERLAND, NE63 8RS.
WELDON, Mr. Peter George Hazelwood, BSc FCA *1975;* Weldon Matthews Forensic Accountants Inc, 666 Burrard Street, Suite 600, VANCOUVER V6C 2X8, BC, CANADA.
WELFARE, Mr. Richard John, BSc ACA *2002;* Clover Cottage, Silchester Road, Bramley, TADLEY, RG26 5DQ.
WELHAM, Mr. Fraser Andrew Norton, BSc ACA *1991;* Element Power, 1st Floor 3 Sheldon Square, LONDON, W2 6HY.
WELHAM, Mr. Ian Rodger, BSc FCA *1987;* 555 Alden Ave, WESTFIELD, NJ 07090, UNITED STATES.
WELHAM, Mr. Jason, ACA *2011;* 3 Woodside Close, LEIGH-ON-SEA, ESSEX, SS9 4TE.
WELHAM, Mr. Lee Peter, BA(Hons) ACA *2006;* 7 Goldfinch Drive, Cottenham, CAMBRIDGE, CB24 8XY.
WELIKALA, Mr. Nihal Senanayake, FCA *1975;* National Development Bank Limited, No 40 Navam Mawatha, P O Box 1825, 2 COLOMBO, SRI LANKA.
WELIKALA, Miss. Terentia Mary Priyani, BSc ACA *1993;* Hadlaubstrasse 73, 8006, ZURICH, SWITZERLAND.
WELINKAR, Mr. Anil, BA ACA *1993;* PO Box 64909, Shuwaikh-B, KUWAIT CITY, 70460, KUWAIT.
WELLACOTT, Mr. John Howe Baber, FCA *1933;* 3 Berry Lane, DARIEN, CT 06820, UNITED STATES. (Life Member)
WELLAND, Mr. Grant James, BA(Econ) ACA *1998;* 2 Palmeira Avenue, WESTCLIFF-ON-SEA, SS0 7RP.
•**WELLAND, Mr. Ross Adrian, BA ACA CTA** *1986;* (Tax Fac), Haines Watts, Sterling House, 177-181 Farnham Road, SLOUGH, BERKSHIRE, SL1 4XP. See also Haines Watts London LLP, Haines Watts Slough LLP
WELLBURN, Mr. Richard, BA ACA *1997;* 27 Midholm, LONDON, NW11 6LL.
WELLBY, Mrs. Barbara Agnes, FCA *1972;* 50 Hurlingham Road, LONDON, SW6 3RQ.
WELLBY, Mr. Christopher Mark, MA FCA *1969;* 50 Hurlingham Road, LONDON, SW6 3RQ.
WELLENS, Mr. David Hugh, FCA *1965;* Axholme, Woodbourne Road, New Mills, HIGH PEAK, SK22 3JX.
WELLER, Mr. Antony Graham, FCA *1960;* Watermeadow, Smugglers Lane, Bosham, CHICHESTER, PO18 8QW. (Life Member)
WELLER, Ms. Carolyn Vanessa, MSc BSc ACA *1985;* 18 Arlington Drive, Woodsmoor, STOCKPORT, SK2 7EB.
WELLER, Mr. Christopher John, BA ACA *1991;* 5 Stubfield, HORSHAM, WEST SUSSEX, RH12 2AJ.
WELLER, Mr. Christopher Stewart, FCA *1967;* 9 Calverley Park, TUNBRIDGE WELLS, KENT, TN1 2SH. (Life Member)
WELLER, Mr. David John, MA MBA ACA *2001;* 64 Knightbridge Walk, BILLERICAY, ESSEX, CM12 0HL.
WELLER, Miss. Elizabeth, ACA *2007;* 11 Orchard Hill, Little Billing, NORTHAMPTON, NN3 9AG.
WELLER, Mrs. Elizabeth Caroline, ACA *1997;* Hillingdon Hospital, Pield Heath Road, UXBRIDGE, MIDDLESEX, UB8 3NN.
WELLER, Mr. Gerald Ben Avrom, LLB FCA *1997;* 11 St. Nicholas Drive, SHEPPERTON, MIDDLESEX, TW17 9LD.
WELLER, Mr. John Norris, FCA *1961;* 1 Cedar Drive, Fetcham, LEATHERHEAD, KT22 9ET.
WELLER, Mr. Mark Richard, BSc(Hons) ACA *2001;* Richwood, 3 Spring Lane, Ightham, SEVENOAKS, TN15 9DN.
WELLER, Mr. Nicholas James David, MA FCA *1990;* 12 North Ash, Hawthorn Close, HORSHAM, RH12 2BW.
WELLER, Mr. Paul Stanley, ACA *1983;* Beckett House, 6 Littlehampton Road, WORTHING, WEST SUSSEX, BN13 1QE.
WELLER, Mr. Timothy Peter, BSc FCA *1989;* Bracondale, 9 Spencer Road, EAST MOLESEY, KT8 0SP.
WELLESLEY, Mr. Derek Ransford Ansley, BA ACA *1988;* 17 Blandford Road, Ealing, LONDON, W5 5RL.
WELLESLEY, Mr. William Valerian, MA ACA *1992;* Salehurst Park Farm, Salehurst, ROBERTSBRIDGE, EAST SUSSEX, TN32 5NG.
WELLFAIR, Miss. Nicola Clare, BA(Hons) ACA *2001;* 160a North View Road, LONDON, N8 7NB.
WELLING, Mr. Ronald Peter, FCA *1961;* L'Enclos, La Rue Des Marettes, St. Martin, JERSEY, JE3 6DS.
WELLINGS, Mr. Alan Stanley, FCA *1954;* Flat 5 Viceroy Court, 26A Silverdale Road, Lower Meads, EASTBOURNE, BN20 7BB. (Life Member)
•**WELLINGS, Mr. Andrew Neeld, BA FCA** *1980;* Neeld Wellings, Rawlings Barn, Wambrook, CHARD, TA20 3DF. See also A.N. Wellings
WELLINGS, Mr. Donald David, FCA *1963;* 50 Millbrook Drive, Shenstone, LICHFIELD, WS14 0JL.
WELLINGS, Mr. Gareth Mahon, BA ACA *1996;* 189 New Church Road, HOVE, EAST SUSSEX, BN3 4DA.
WELLINGTON, Mr. David Simon, ACA *2008;* 62 Falstone Drive, CHESTER LE STREET, COUNTY DURHAM, DH2 3ST.
•**WELLINGTON, Mrs. Jacqueline Marie, ACA** *1984;* J.M. Wellington, 13 Lancing Road, ORPINGTON, BR6 0QS.
WELLOCK, Mrs. Diane Elizabeth, BSc ACA *2006;* Kirkby Beck Barn, Kirkby Malham, SKIPTON, NORTH YORKSHIRE, BD23 4BL.
WELLS, Mr. Adrian Peter, FCA *1976;* ConocoPhillips (UK) Ltd, Portman House, 2 Portman Street, LONDON, W1H 6DU.
WELLS, Mr. Alan Christopher, BA ACA *2004;* with Grant Thornton UK LLP, Enterprise House, 115 Edmund Street, BIRMINGHAM, B3 2HJ.
WELLS, Mr. Alan John, ACA *1987;* British Sugar Plc, Sugar Way, PETERBOROUGH, PE2 9AY.
•**WELLS, Mr. Allan Anthony, FCA ATII** *1958;* Anthony Wells & Co, 19 Norrice Lea, LONDON, N2 0RD.
WELLS, Mrs. Amanda Jane Elizabeth, BCom FCA *1978;* High Firs Crook Road, Brenchley, TONBRIDGE, KENT, TN12 7BL.
WELLS, Ms. Amy, MSc BA ACA *2005;* 65a Rosebery Road, LONDON, N10 2LE.
WELLS, Mr. Andrew David, BA ACA *1996;* Silvers, 25 Crooksbury Road, FARNHAM, SURREY, GU10 1QD.
WELLS, Mr. Andrew Irvine Lancaster, MA FCA *1972;* Springfield House, South Newington, BANBURY, OXFORDSHIRE, OX15 4JW. (Life Member)
WELLS, Mr. Andrew James Richard, MA ACA *2004;* 56 Alexandra Road, Hataitai, WELLINGTON, NEW ZEALAND.
WELLS, Mr. Andrew John, MA ACA *2007;* 2 Becton Cottages, Becton Lane Barton on Sea, NEW MILTON, BH25 7AD.
WELLS, Mrs. Anne Victoria, BSc ACA *1986;* 23 Warwick Road, Hale, ALTRINCHAM, WA15 9NP.
WELLS, Mr. Anthony Bernard, BA FCA *1971;* 28 Forest Rise, Oadby, LEICESTER, LE2 4FH.
WELLS, Mr. Anthony Laurence, BSc FCA *1973;* 21 Leaside Avenue, Muswell Hill, LONDON, N10 3BT. (Life Member)
WELLS, Mr. Antony Edmond, FCA *1973;* North Farm House, Great Durnford, SALISBURY, SP4 6AZ.
WELLS, Mr. Brian Bernard, BA ACA ACIM MBA DipM *1998;* Gategroup, Balsberg, Balz Zimmermannstrasse 7, PO Box QVF, Zurich Airport, CH-8058 ZURICH SWITZERLAND.
WELLS, Mrs. Carey Jane Patricia, BA ACA *1990;* Linden House, Penn Green, BEACONSFIELD, HP9 2RT.
WELLS, Mr. Christopher Ian, BSc FCA *1979;* Man Roland GB Ltd, 110-112 Morden Road, MITCHAM, SURREY, CR4 4XB.
•**WELLS, Mr. Christopher John, FCA** *1972;* C.J. Wells & Co, 84 Western Road, LEWES, EAST SUSSEX, BN7 1RP.
WELLS, Mr. Christopher John, BSc ACA *1997;* 4 Farmcombe Road, TUNBRIDGE WELLS, TN2 5DF.
WELLS, Mr. Clinton Ashley, BSc ACA *1998;* 14 Third Avenue, Kingsland, AUCKLAND 1021, NEW ZEALAND.
WELLS, Mr. Colin Nigel, BA ACA *1989;* 16 Tiffany Close, WOKINGHAM, BERKSHIRE, RG41 3BN.
WELLS, Mr. Daniel James, BSc ACA *2005;* 6 Lidiard Road, LONDON, SW18 3PL.

•**WELLS, Mr. David, FCA** *1977;* Griffin Stone Moscrop & Co., 41 Welbeck Street, LONDON, W1G 8EA.
WELLS, Mr. David Arthur, FCA *1963;* 22 Tipton Drive, CROYDON, CR0 5JY.
WELLS, Mr. David Francis, BA ACA *1993;* Ashley Farmhouse Ashley, Box, CORSHAM, SN13 8AJ.
WELLS, Mr. David George, BA FCA *1966;* 11 Parklands, OXTED, RH8 9DP.
•**WELLS, Mr. David John Richard, BA FCA** *1966;* David Wells FCA, 14 Dukes Court, 77 Mortlake High Street, LONDON, SW14 8HS.
WELLS, Mr. David Patrick Austin, BA FCA *1976;* 60 Bourne Street, LONDON, SW1W 8JD.
•**WELLS, Mr. David Richard, BSc FCA** *1976;* David Wells, 33 Purnells Way, Knowle, SOLIHULL, WEST MIDLANDS, B93 9JN.
WELLS, Mr. David Roy, FCA *1956;* 4 Dalby Avenue, Bushby, LEICESTER, LE7 9RD. (Life Member)
WELLS, Mr. Derek James, FCA *1952;* 48 Newton Lane, ROMSEY, HAMPSHIRE, SO51 8GX. (Life Member)
WELLS, Mrs. Dominique, BA MSt ACA *2005;* 10 Lakeswood Road, Petts Wood, ORPINGTON, KENT, BR5 1BJ.
WELLS, Mr. Donald George, FCA *1955;* 3 Oaklands, Kemnal Road, CHISLEHURST, KENT, BR7 6LZ. (Life Member)
WELLS, Miss. Emma Louise, ACA *2008;* 25 Aldgate Close, Potton, SANDY, BEDFORDSHIRE, SG19 2RU.
WELLS, Mrs. Emma Louise, BA ACA *1997;* 28 Tiffany Close, WOKINGHAM, RG41 3BN.
WELLS, Mr. Fergus, BA ACA *2006;* Fluorocarbon Co Ltd Fluorocarbon House, Caxton Hill, HERTFORD, SG13 7NH.
WELLS, Mr. Francis William, FCA *1971;* Satec Limited, Englefield Estate Office, Englefield Road, Theale, READING, RG7 5DU.
WELLS, Mr. Gareth David Hugh, BSc ACA *1988;* with KPMG LLP, 3 Assembly Square, Britannia Quay, CARDIFF, CF10 4AX.
WELLS, Mr. George, BA ACA *1997;* 30 Route Jean Jacques Rigaud, 1224 CHENE BOUGERIES, SWITZERLAND.
WELLS, Mrs. Georgina, ACA MAAT *1997;* 116 Fidelio Street, Opera Estate, SINGAPORE 458491, SINGAPORE.
WELLS, Mr. Gerald Mervyn, FCA *1974;* Bulldog Remoulds Ltd, Cherry Holt Road, BOURNE, LINCOLNSHIRE, PE10 9LA.
•**WELLS, Miss. Hazel Anne, BA FCA** *1997;* (Tax Fac), Balanced Accounting LLP, Unit Q, The Brewery, Bells Yew Green, TUNBRIDGE WELLS, KENT TN3 9BD.
WELLS, Miss. Heather, BSc ACA *1993;* 69 Church Drive, East Keswick, LEEDS, LS17 9EP.
WELLS, Miss. Jacqueline Yvonne, BSc ACA *1987;* 11 Admirals Walk, ST. ALBANS, AL1 5SF.
WELLS, Mr. James, ACA *2011;* 27 The Drive, Bardsey, LEEDS, LS17 9AE.
WELLS, Ms. Joanne Louise, BA ACA *1995;* 35 Milliners Way, BISHOP'S STORTFORD, HERTFORDSHIRE, CM23 4GG.
WELLS, Miss. Joanne Marie, BA ACA *1996;* 2a Kingston Drive, SALE, CHESHIRE, M33 2FS.
•**WELLS, Mr. John Bernard, FCA** *1972;* Mossgroves LLP, 3 The Deans, Bridge Road, BAGSHOT, SURREY, GU19 5AT.
WELLS, Mr. John David, FCA *1968;* 34 Canynge Square, Clifton, BRISTOL, BS8 3LB. (Life Member)
WELLS, Mr. John Kenneth, FCA *1969;* 15 Roedean Drive, Eaglescliffe, STOCKTON-ON-TEES, CLEVELAND, TS16 9HT.
WELLS, Mr. John Luther, FCA *1951;* 13 Hanover Close, Barton Seagrave, KETTERING, NN15 6GH. (Life Member)
WELLS, Mr. Jonathon Mark, BSc ACA *1992;* 31 George Lane, Walkington, BEVERLEY, HU17 8XX.
WELLS, Mrs. Karen Ann, BA FCA CTA *1999;* 33 Oak Avenue, South Wootton, KING'S LYNN, PE30 3JQ.
WELLS, Mr. Kenneth Henry, MA FCA *1978;* Toft Meadow, Toft, Dunchurch, RUGBY, WARWICKSHIRE, CV22 6NR. (Life Member)
•**WELLS, Mrs. Kirstie, BSc FCA** *2000;* Numis Limited, 1st Floor, Brook House, Mount Pleasant, CROWBOROUGH, EAST SUSSEX TN6 2NE.
WELLS, Mrs. Laura Catherine, MA ACA *2009;* with Deloitte LLP, 2 New Street Square, LONDON, EC4A 3BZ.
WELLS, Miss. Lois Margaret, BA ACA *1986;* 313 Leigh Hunt Drive, Southgate, LONDON, N14 6BZ.
WELLS, Mrs. Louise Margaret, BSc ACA PGCE *2000;* 41 Penwortham Road, LONDON, SW16 6RF.
WELLS, Mr. Malcolm Henry Weston, FCA *1951;* Willow Cottage, The Wad, West Wittering, CHICHESTER, PO20 8AH. (Life Member)
•**WELLS, Mr. Mark Gilbert, FCA** *1973;* Mark Wells Consulting Ltd, 84 Mill Street, Steventon, ABINGDON, OX13 6SP.
WELLS, Mr. Matthew Donald, BSc ACA *2005;* 15 Milverton Drive, Bramhall, STOCKPORT, SK7 1EY.
WELLS, Mr. Mervyn Robin, FCA *1967;* 44 Newbury Avenue, CALNE, WILTSHIRE, SN11 9UN. (Life Member)
WELLS, Mr. Michael Ian, BA FCA *1985;* Accenture Kingsley Hall 20 Bailey Lane Manchester Airport, MANCHESTER, M90 4AN.
WELLS, Mr. Michael James, BSc ACA *1996;* 49 Lyme Road, Hazel Grove, STOCKPORT, CHESHIRE, SK7 6LA.
WELLS, Mr. Michael James, ACA *2011;* 202 Station Road, Rolleston-on-Dove, BURTON-ON-TRENT, STAFFORDSHIRE, DE13 9AD.
WELLS, Mr. Michael John, BSc ACA *1980;* 7 Alliance Way, Paddock Wood, TONBRIDGE, TN12 6TY.
WELLS, Mr. Michael John, BCom ACA *1998;* 4/2 Cowper Street, Randwick, SYDNEY, NSW 2031, AUSTRALIA.
WELLS, Mrs. Michelle Marguerite, LLB ACA *2003;* Greenways, School Road, WOKINGHAM, NG414JN.
WELLS, Mr. Murray Roman, BA ACA *1982;* Braeside Castle Hill, Mottram St. Andrew, MACCLESFIELD, CHESHIRE, SK10 4AX.
WELLS, Mr. Neil David, BSc FCA *1985;* States of Jersey, Cyril Le Marquand House, The Parade, St Holier, JERSEY, JE4 8QT.
•**WELLS, Mr. Nicholas Richard, BA FCA** *1985;* Nicholas Wells, 7 Fenbrook Close, Hambrook, BRISTOL, BS16 1QJ.
WELLS, Mr. Nicholas Weston, MA ACA *1980;* Cenkos Securities Ltd, 6.7.8 Tokenhouse Yard, LONDON, EC2R 7AS.
WELLS, Mr. Paul Thomas, BA(Hons) ACA *2010;* Flat 1, 176 Merton Road, LONDON, SW19 1EG.
WELLS, Mr. Peter James, FCA *1960;* 24 Brambling Road, HORSHAM, RH13 6AY. (Life Member)
•**WELLS, Mr. Peter John, ACA** *1994;* Ernst & Young S R O, Karlovo Namesti 10, 12000 PRAGUE, CZECH REPUBLIC. See also Ernst & Young Europe LLP
WELLS, Mr. Philip George Henry, BSc ACA DChA *1985;* Wirral Autistic Society, 2 Grisedale Road, Old Hall Estate, Bromborough, WIRRAL, MERSEYSIDE CH62 3QA.
WELLS, Mr. Philip Laird, BSc ACA *1992;* Cluster Bayu Nirwana E 8, BNR, BOGOR, WE24, INDONESIA.
WELLS, Mr. Ralph Frederick, FCA *1943;* 4 Lucastes Road, HAYWARDS HEATH, RH16 1JL. (Life Member)
WELLS, Mr. Raymond Neil, LLB ACA *2003;* 32 Talbot Crescent, LEEDS, LS8 1AL.
WELLS, Mr. Raymond Peter, ACA *1982;* Wayside Steventon End, Ashdon, SAFFRON WALDEN, CB10 2JE.
WELLS, Mrs. Rhonda Carol Louise, BA ACA *1998;* Mecom Group PLC, 70 Jermyn Street, LONDON, SW1Y 6NY.
WELLS, Mr. Richard Charles, BSc FCA *1988;* 19 Church View, Northborough, PETERBOROUGH, PE6 9DQ.
•**WELLS, Mr. Richard John, FCA** *1968;* Thomas Edward Dixon & Company, 376 London Road, Hadleigh, BENFLEET, SS7 2DA.
WELLS, Mr. Richard Sinclair, FCA *1975;* Rilkeweg 9, 71032 BOEBLINGEN, GERMANY.
WELLS, Mr. Robert Simon, BSc ACA *1992;* 3 Stone Cross Oast, Ashurst Road, Ashurst, TUNBRIDGE WELLS, TN3 9SX.
WELLS, Ms. Rowena Jane, BA ACA *1987;* 45 Staunton Road, KINGSTON UPON THAMES, KT2 5TN.
•**WELLS, Miss. Samantha, BA FCA** *1994;* Lindeyer Francis Ferguson, North House, 198 High Street, TONBRIDGE, TN9 1BE.
WELLS, Mrs. Sharon Hazel, ACA *1997;* 80 Bramfield Road, Datchworth, KNEBWORTH, SG3 6RZ.
WELLS, Mr. Stephen, MA FCA *1978;* S&S Wells Consultants Ltd, 14 Tall Elms Close, BROMLEY, BR2 0TT.
WELLS, Mr. Stewart James, FCA *1976;* 2a Northampton Road, Blisworth, NORTHAMPTON, NN7 3DN.
•**WELLS, Mr. Timothy Adrian, BA FCA** *1985;* (Tax Fac), Wells & Co., Telford House, Hamilton Close, BASINGSTOKE, RG21 6YT.
WELLS, Mr. Timothy James, BAcc ACA *1997;* 20 Stirling Road, BRISTOL, BS4 3PD.
WELLS, Mr. Trevor Arthur, FCA *1966;* 31 Elizabeth Avenue, Laleham, STAINES, TW18 1JW.
WELLS, Mrs. Wendy Jayne, BA ACA *1985;* Lynnfield House, Church Street, ALTRINCHAM, CHESHIRE, WA144DZ.
WELLS, Mr. William Anthony, FCA *1963;* 15 Birch Court, The Gables Oxshott, LEATHERHEAD, KT22 0SD.
WELLS, Mrs. Yvonne Janet, BSc ACA *1997;* 4 High Meadows, Walton, WAKEFIELD, WEST YORKSHIRE, WF2 6TN.
•**WELLSBURY, Mr. Martin William, FCA** *1961;* The Integrity Partnership Ltd, 36 High Street, Madeley, TELFORD, SHROPSHIRE, TF7 5AS.
•**WELLSTOOD, Mr. Terry Robert, FCA** *1967;* Terry R. Wellstood & Co, Copse Lodge, Cogges Lane, Stanton Harcourt, WITNEY, OXFORDSHIRE OX29 5AJ.
WELPLY, Mr. Ian James, FCA *1969;* Residence Le Gallia Montfleury, 25 Bvd, Montfleury, 06400 CANNES, FRANCE.
WELSBY, Mr. David Alan, BA ACA *1987;* 25 Victoria Road, DORCHESTER, DORSET, DT1 1SB.
WELSBY, Mr. David Andrew, BA FCA *1980;* 2 Little Oxley, Leybourne, WEST MALLING, ME19 5QU.
WELSBY, Mr. Glyn Mikal, BA FCA *1994;* The Garth, Westfield Court, Copmanthorpe, YORK, YO23 3TA.
•**WELSBY, Mr. Gordon Robert John, MBA FCA** *1976;* Welsby Associates Limited, Sintra, Bethesda Street, Upper Basildon, READING, RG8 8NU.
WELSBY, Mr. Jack, ACA *2010;* 3c Somerset Road, LONDON, W13 9PD.
WELSBY, Mr. Philip Worthington, ACA *2007;* 5 Sandhill Terrace, WARRINGTON, WA4 1HU.
WELSBY, Mr. Richard Armstrong, ACA *1996;* The Bowes Museum, Newgate, BARNARD CASTLE, COUNTY DURHAM, DL12 8NP.
•**WELSBY, Mr. Roy, BA FCA** *1982;* Grant Thornton UK LLP, Grant Thornton House, 22 Melton Street, Euston Square, LONDON, NW1 2EP. See also Grant Thornton LLP
WELSFORD, Mr. Darren Mark, BA ACA *2006;* 6 Roebuck Lane, BUCKHURST HILL, IG9 5QR.
WELSFORD, Mr. John Harley, FCA *1975;* The Manor House, 2 Norton Lane, Gaulby, LEICESTER, LE7 9BU.
•**WELSFORD, Mr. Paul Simon, BSc(Econ) FCA** *1982;* Crossmount, Highlands House, 165 The Broadway, Wimbledon, LONDON, SW19 1NE.
WELSFORD, Mr. Peter Anthony, FCA *1952;* Flat 34 Hartslock Court, Shooters Hill, Pangbourne, READING, RG8 7BJ. (Life Member)
WELSH, Mr. Andrew, BA ACA *1999;* PricewaterhouseCoopers, GPO Box 1331L, MELBOURNE, VIC 3001, AUSTRALIA.
WELSH, Mr. Andrew Leslie, BSc FCA FSI *1980;* 43 Old Park View, ENFIELD, MIDDLESEX, EN2 7EG.
•**WELSH, Mr. Brian Frank, BA FCA ATII** *1987;* (Tax Fac), Robson Welsh Limited, 4 The Goose Green, WIRRAL, MERSEYSIDE, CH47 6BQ.
WELSH, Ms. Catherine Janice, BA ACA *1984;* 17-555 Raven Woods Drive, NORTH VANCOUVER V7g 0A4, BC, CANADA.
WELSH, Mrs. Charlotte, BA(Hons) ACA *2004;* Arval Ltd, Arval Centre, Windmill Hill, Whitehill Way, SWINDON, SN5 6PE.
WELSH, Mr. Edward Hedley Michael, MEng ACA *1999;* Church House, Church Street, Shoreham, SEVENOAKS, KENT, TN14 7SB.
WELSH, Mrs. Elaine Margaret, BA ACA *1993;* High Trees, Fairmile Park Road, COBHAM, SURREY, KT11 2PG.
WELSH, Mr. Ian William, MA FCA *1960;* White Cottage, Coronation Lane, Blakeney, HOLT, NORFOLK, NR25 7NS. (Life Member)
WELSH, Mrs. Joanne Marie, BA ACA *2002;* Witham Oil & Paint Ltd, Outer Circle Road, LINCOLN, LN2 4HL.
WELSH, Mr. John, FCA *1948;* 147 Victoria Road West, HEBBURN, TYNE AND WEAR, NE31 1UT. (Life Member)
WELSH, Mrs. Kerry Alison, LLB ACA *2004;* 81 Ashenground Road, HAYWARDS HEATH, WEST SUSSEX, RH16 4PY.
WELSH, Mr. Martin, ACA *2009;* 76 Holm Park, INVERNESS, IV2 4XU.
•**WELSH, Mr. Richard Michael, BA ACA** *1996;* Saul Fairholm, 12 Tentercroft Street, LINCOLN, LN5 7DB. See also Atkinson Saul Fairholm Limited
WELSH, Mr. Robert Iain, FCA *1965;* Box 12510, Die Boord, STELLENBOSCH, C.P., 7613, SOUTH AFRICA.
•**WELSH, Mr. Ronald Craig, BA ACA** *1992;* Ron Welsh (North West) Limited, Mannamead, Church Lane, NESTON, CH64 9US.
WELSH, Miss. Sally, BA ACA *2007;* Hornsdown Cottage The Row, Elham, CANTERBURY, CT4 6UP.
WELSH, Miss. Sarah Gay, BSc ACA *1985;* NCVO, National Council for Voluntary Organisations, 8 Regents Wharf All Saints Street, LONDON, N1 9RL.
•**WELSH, Mr. Simon Frederick, FCA** *1977;* (Tax Fac), Hall Livesey Brown, 68 High Street, TARPORLEY, CW6 0AT.
WELSH, Mr. Thomas, FCA *1958;* 168 Beechwood Avenue, TORONTO M2L 1K1, ON, CANADA. (Life Member)
•**WELSH, Mrs. Vered Barbara, ACA** *1997;* ITR Service Limited, 40 Plater Drive, OXFORD, OX2 6QU.
WELSMAN, Miss. Martine Claire, BSc ACA *1990;* Greenlodge, 45 Grosvenor Road, Wanstead, LONDON, E11 2EW.
WELSTEAD, Mr. Justin, MA LLB ACA *1998;* Eight Advisory, 40 rue de courcelles, 75008 PARIS, FRANCE.
WELTER, Miss. Manon, ACA *2008;* 1102/2 York Street, SYDNEY, NSW 2000, AUSTRALIA.
•**WELTMAN, Mr. Blake Laurence, BSc ACA** *1983;* Blake Weltman & Co, Sovereign House, 1 Albert Place, LONDON, N3 1QB.
•**WELTON, Mrs. Alison, BSc ACA** *2003;* with David Allen, Dalmar House, Barras Lane Estate, Dalston, CARLISLE, CA5 7NY.
WELTON, Mr. Andrew, MEng ACA *2009;* Flat 16, Cordwainer House, 43 Mare Street, LONDON, E8 4RX.
•**WELTON, Mr. Anthony, FCA CTA** *1963;* Warwick House, 2 Westminster Drive, BURY ST. EDMUNDS, IP33 2EZ.
•**WELTON, Mr. Christopher Frank, FCA** *1976;* LMW Limited, Riverside View, Basing Road, Basing, BASINGSTOKE, HAMPSHIRE RG24 7AL.
WELTON, Mr. Harold Ambrose, FCA *1963;* Flat 1, 30 Nairn Road, Canford Cliffs, POOLE, BH13 7NJ. (Life Member)
WELTON, Mrs. Jean Frances, FCA *1972;* Wynch House, Elmley Road, Ashton Under Hill, EVESHAM, WR11 6SW.
WELTON, Mrs. Jeannette Marie, BA ACA *1988;* 5 The Cornfields, Hatch Warren, BASINGSTOKE, HAMPSHIRE, RG22 4QB.
•**WEM, Mr. Alistair Ian, BSc FCA** *1980;* (Tax Fac), Wem & Co, Savoy House, Savoy Circus, LONDON, W3 7DA.
WEM, Mr. Douglas Stewart, BSc ACA MIAP MBCS *1983;* Mathews Green, Kingsley Close, CROWTHORNE, BERKSHIRE, RG45 7PH.
WEMYSS, Mrs. Leisha Jane, PhD BSc ACA *2003;* 29 Herongate Road, LONDON, E12 5EJ.
WEMYSS, Mrs. Linda Temple, BSc ACA *1986;* The Round House Deans Lane, Woodhouse Eaves, LOUGHBOROUGH, LEICESTERSHIRE, LE12 8TE.
WEMYSS, Mrs. Rebecca Wynn, BSc(Hons) ACA *2002;* 102 Park Rise, HARPENDEN, HERTFORDSHIRE, AL5 3AN.
WEN, Miss. Jing, MSc ACA *2009;* Flat 217 Ability Place, 37 Millharbour, LONDON, E14 9DF.
WENBAN, Mr. John Kenneth Peter, FCA *1961;* 45 Faulkland View, Peasedown St John, BATH, BA2 8TG.
WENBORN, Mr. Colin Michael, FCA *1955;* Fairways, Beech Avenue, Effingham, LEATHERHEAD, SURREY, KT24 5PJ. (Life Member)
WENBORN, Mr. David Richard, BSc FCA *1987;* 23 Thornbury, HARPENDEN, AL5 5SN.
WENBOURNE, Mr. Stewart James, ACA *1990;* CityPoint club, One Ropemaker Street, LONDON, EC2Y 9AW.
WENDEN, Mr. Geoffrey Alan, FCA *1972;* 2 Foxwarren, HAYWARDS HEATH, WEST SUSSEX, RH16 1EN.
WENDON, Mr. Michael Bryan, FCA *1963;* North End Cottage, Kestell Road, SIDMOUTH, EX10 8JJ. (Life Member)
WENG, Ms. Li Chien, ACA *2007;* Flat 3 22/F Block B, 395 King's Road, NORTH POINT, HONG KONG SAR.
•**WENHAM, Mr. David John, FCA** *1971;* David J. Wenham & Co, 7 Victoria Road, LONDON, E4 6BY.
WENHAM, Mr. Gerald John Charles, FCA *1951;* 27 Church Lane, Westbere, CANTERBURY, CT2 0HA. (Life Member)
•**WENHAM, Mr. Paul Thomas Cambage, FCA** *1981;* Paul T Wenham, GPO Box 2551, SYDNEY, NSW 2001, AUSTRALIA.
WENMAN, Mr. Barry, ACA *1982;* 26 Links View, Abbeyfields, HALESOWEN, B62 8SS.
WENMAN, Mr. Ian David, FCA *1982;* Stone Farm, Lidstone, CHIPPING NORTON, OXFORDSHIRE, OX7 4HL.
WENMAN, Mr. Peter William, FCA *1963;* 45 Lammas Way, LETCHWORTH GARDEN CITY, HERTFORDSHIRE, SG6 4LN. (Life Member)
WENMAN, Mr. Russell Elliot, BSc PgDL ACA *2001;* 3 Birkdale Close, Edwalton, NOTTINGHAM, NG12 4FB.
WENN, Mr. David Alan, BSc ACA *1980;* P.O. Box N - 10520, 15 Royal Palm Court, Seaview Drive, NASSAU, BAHAMAS.
WENNER, Mr. Ralph, ACA *2002;* Bayenwerft 14, 50678 COLOGNE, GERMANY.
WENNINGER, Mr. David William, FCA *1969;* 37 Cortworth Road, SHEFFIELD, S11 9LN. (Life Member)

WENNINGER, Mrs. Emma Jane, BSc ACA *2003;* A B S Industrial Resources, The Brickworks, Kilnhurst Road, Kilnhurst, MEXBOROUGH, SOUTH YORKSHIRE S64 5TE.
WENNINGER, Mr. James David, BA(Hons) ACA *2001;* 116 Millhouses Lane, SHEFFIELD, S7 2HB.
WENNINGER, Mr. John Richard, MA ACA *1987;* 7 Holland Road, ABINGDON, OXFORDSHIRE, OX14 1PH.
WENSLEY, Mr. Christopher, ACA *2011;* 11 Old Redstone Drive, REDHILL, RH1 4DA.
WENT, Mr. Clifford Sydney, BCom ACA *1990;* Deak Ferenc u. 53., 2458 KULCS, HUNGARY.
WENTWORTH, Mr. Brian, FCA *1972;* Dudley M.B.C., Directorate of Finance, The Council House, DUDLEY, DY1 1HF.
WENTWORTH, Mrs. Julie Anne, BSc ACA *1992;* Blenheim Cottage Primrose Lane, Waterbeach, CAMBRIDGE, CB25 9JZ.
WENTWORTH-JESSOP, Mr. Rupert Charles, BSc ACA *1996;* 97 Ravenscroft Road, BECKENHAM, KENT, BR3 4TP.
WENTWORTH-STANLEY, Mr. David Michael, FCA *1974;* JP Morgan Cazenove, 10 Aldermanbury, LONDON, EC2V 7RF.
WENTZEL, Mr. Jhean, ACA CA(SA) *2011;* Flat 1, 16 Dalebury Road, LONDON, SW17 7HH.
WENYON, Miss. Helen Louise, BA ACA *1994;* The Hollies, Frogham, FORDINGBRIDGE, HAMPSHIRE, SP6 2HN.
WENZERUL, Mr. Edward David, BSc ACA *1983;* Longacres, Bashley Common Road, NEW MILTON, HAMPSHIRE, BH25 5SF.
WENZERUL, Mr. Martyn, FCA *1957;* 51 Ornan Road, LONDON, NW3 4QD. (Life Member)
WERCHOLA, Mr. Daniel, MEng ACA *2007;* Flat 2, 107 Church Road, RICHMOND, TW10 6LS.
WERES, Miss. Halina, ACA *2009;* 4 Rushy Way, Emersons Green, BRISTOL, BS16 7BS.
WERNGREN CREASY, Mrs. Ulrika Helena, BA(Hons) ACA *2010;* Amiralsgatan 12, 211 55 MALMO, SWEDEN.
•WERNHAM, Mr. Frank, FCA *1973;* Wernham Wallace Skinner & Co, Summit House, 2A Highfield Road, DARTFORD, DA1 2JY.
WERNICK, Dr. Paul David, ACA *1978;* 2 Rockleigh, North Road, HERTFORD, SG14 1LS.
WERRETT, Mrs. Deborah, ACA *1994;* 3 Nolton Close, Great Barr, BIRMINGHAM, B43 5JY.
WERRY, Mr. David Geoffrey, MSc BSc ACA *1988;* Henry Chadwick Primary School, School Lane, Hill Ridware, RUGELEY, WS15 3QN.
WERTH, Mr. Gavin Lawrence, BSc ACA *2007;* (Tax Fac), 5 Saddlers Close, Arkley, BARNET, HERTFORDSHIRE, EN5 3LU.
WERTH, Mr. Richard Graham, BSc ACA *1985;* Heathbourne Cottage, Heathbourne Road, Bushey Heath, BUSHEY, WD23 1PA.
WERTHEIM, Mr. John Michael, BSc ACA *1981;* Marden House, 2 Woodside Road, SEVENOAKS, TN13 3HB.
WERTHEIMER, Mr. Christian, ACA *2009;* 3rd Floor, 175 Bishopsgate, LONDON, EC2A 2JN.
WERTHEIMER, Mr. Clive Roger, FCA *1973;* 23 The Glebe, Aynho, BANBURY, OXFORDSHIRE, OX17 3AZ.
WESBROOM, Mr. Paul Stuart, BCom ACA *2001;* Sav Credit Ltd, 11 Tower View, Kings Hill, WEST MALLING, KENT, ME19 4RL.
WESCOTT-SMITH, Mrs. Toni Victoria, ACA *2008;* 24 Beech Avenue, Thongsbridge, HOLMFIRTH, HD9 7SX.
WESKER, Mr. David Jonathan, BSc ACA *2003;* with Deloitte LLP, 1 Woodborough Road, NOTTINGHAM, NG1 3FG.
WESLEY, Miss. Carole Elizabeth, BSc ACA *1992;* Storage Design Ltd, Primrose Hill House, Primrose Hill, COWBRIDGE, SOUTH GLAMORGAN, CF71 7DU.
WESLEY, Mr. John Lee, BSc(Hons) ACA CTA *2002;* 509/5 Warayama Place, Rozelle, SYDNEY, NSW 2039, AUSTRALIA.
WESLEY, Mr. Matthew James, LLB(Hons) ACA *2010;* 40 Cobden Road, SEVENOAKS, TN13 3UB.
WESLEY, Mr. Michael Andrew, MMath ACA *2005;* with Wilkins Kennedy, Greytown House, 221-227 High Street, ORPINGTON, BR6 0NZ.
WESLEY, Mr. Michael David, ACA *1983;* 10 Higginson Close, Mossley, CONGLETON, CW12 3SU.
•WESLEY, Mr. Richard William, ACA *1986;* Wesley Wilson & Associates Ltd, Parker House, 44 Stafford Road, WALLINGTON, SURREY, SM6 9AA. See also Wesley Wilson LLP and Wesley Richard W. & Co
WESLEY, Mr. Stuart Ivor, BSc ACA *1988;* 9 Willmott Close, Four Oaks, SUTTON COLDFIELD, B75 5NP.
WESLEY-YATES, Mr. David Peter Christiern, BA FCA *1997;* Oak View Cottage, Trampers Lane, North Boarhunt, FAREHAM, HAMPSHIRE, PO17 6DQ.
WESOLOWSKI, Mr. Daniel Lee, ACA *2009;* 19 Oatlands Chase, READING, RG2 9FY.
•WESSON, Mr. Alan, FCA *1980;* 32 Ash Road, WEDNESBURY, WS10 9NN.
WESSON, Mr. Alan, ACA *1981;* 9 Mountain Ash Court, Naldrett Close, HORSHAM, RH12 4UQ.
•WESSON, Mr. Alistair John, BSc FCA *1987;* with RSM Tenon Audit Limited, The Poynt, 45 Wollaton Street, NOTTINGHAM, NG1 5FW.
WESSON, Mrs. Andrea Justine, BCom ACA MCT *1993;* 27 Crown Lane, SUTTON COLDFIELD, WEST MIDLANDS, B74 4SU.
WESSON, Mr. David Martin, ACA *1996;* The Garden Flat, 123 Parkway, LONDON, NW1 7PS.
WESSON, Mr. Michael James, BSc ACA *2011;* Apartment 40, 4 Sanctuary Street, LONDON, SE1 1EA.
WEST, Mr. Adam Brinkworth, ACA *1995;* 67 Hillside Road, ASHTEAD, SURREY, KT21 1SD.
WEST, Mr. Alan, FCA *1972;* 29 Oak Manor Drive, CHELTENHAM, GL52 6SZ.
WEST, Mr. Alex Edward, BA(Hons) ACA *2010;* 101 Ember Lane, ESHER, SURREY, KT10 8EQ.
•WEST, Mr. Alexander Matthew, ACA *2008;* with Somerbys Limited, 30 Nelson Street, LEICESTER, LE1 7BA.
WEST, Mr. Andrew, BSc ACA *1991;* Oakham School, Chapel Close Church Passage, OAKHAM, LE156DR.
WEST, Mr. Andrew Amery, BSc FCA *1995;* Cathay Pacific Airways Ltd, 7/F Cathay Pacific City, 8 Scenic Road, HongKong International Airport, LANTAU ISLAND, HONG KONG SAR.
•WEST, Mr. Andrew Richard, FCA *1977;* Somerbys Limited, 30 Nelson Street, LEICESTER, LE1 7BA.
•WEST, Mr. Angus, BA FCA *1990;* (Tax Fac), Swandec Limited, 550 Valley Road, Basford, NOTTINGHAM, NG5 1JJ. See also A West & Co
WEST, Mrs. Anne Caroline, MA ACA *1990;* 153 Stainburn Crescent, LEEDS, LS17 6NB.
WEST, Mr. Ayodeji Adesina Tolulope, BSc FCA *1991;* 50 Melrose Avenue, BOREHAMWOOD, HERTFORDSHIRE, WD6 2BJ.
•WEST, Mr. Brian William, FCA *1968;* (Tax Fac), B.W. West & Co, 150 Haydn Road, Sherwood, NOTTINGHAM, NG5 2LB.
WEST, Miss. Catherine, BA ACA *1995;* 6 / 83 Roscoe St, BONDI BEACH, NSW 2043, AUSTRALIA.
WEST, Mr. Christopher, BSc ACA *1987;* 30 Carr Road, Calverley, PUDSEY, WEST YORKSHIRE, LS28 5RH.
•WEST, Mr. Christopher, BA ACA *1992;* Mitchells (UK) Ltd, St Michaels Mews, 18-22 St. Michaels Road, LEEDS, LS6 3AW.
WEST, Mr. Christopher Gregory, BA ACA *1994;* with Deloitte LLP, Athene Place, 66 Shoe Lane, LONDON, EC4A 3BQ.
WEST, Mr. Christopher John, BA FCA *1986;* 10 Pope Court, Parkleys, RICHMOND, TW10 5LS.
WEST, Mr. Christopher Stephen, BA(Hons) ACA *2011;* 5 Martell Road, LONDON, SE21 8EA.
WEST, Mr. Colin Paul Nicholas, ACA *1990;* 18 Sevenoaks Drive, Spencers Wood, READING, RG7 1AZ.
WEST, Mr. Damian Richard, BSc ACA *2001;* 3 Glenville Road, KINGSTON UPON THAMES, SURREY, KT2 6DD.
WEST, Mr. Darren John, BA ACA *1990;* Quadra House, Quadra Foods Ltd Holland Road, Langage Business Park Plympton, PLYMOUTH, PL7 5HJ.
WEST, Mr. David, ACA *2011;* Flat 1, 35 Oberstein Road, LONDON, SW11 2AE.
WEST, Mr. David Frederick, BA FCA *1959;* 20 Fellside, Harwood, BOLTON, BL2 4HB. (Life Member)
•WEST, Mr. David James, MA FCA *1968;* David West, 24 The Woodlands, LONDON, N14 5RN.
WEST, Mr. David John, FCA *1993;* 135 Bedowan Meadows, Tretherras, NEWQUAY, CORNWALL, TR7 2TB.
WEST, Mr. David John, BSc ACA *2002;* 7 Ash Road, Lightpill, STROUD, GLOUCESTERSHIRE, GL5 3PF.
WEST, Mr. David William, FCA *1961;* Parkfield, Ashford-In-The-Water, BAKEWELL, DE45 1NJ.
WEST, Mr. Derek Robert, MA FCA *1987;* 46a Repton Road, Hartshorne, SWADLINCOTE, DE11 7AF.
WEST, Mr. Donald, FCA *1957;* 3 Glamis Drive, CHORLEY, PR7 1LX. (Life Member)
WEST, Mr. Edward Albert, FCA *1959;* 8 Webster Close, THAME, OX9 3TU. (Life Member)
WEST, Mrs. Elizabeth Susan, BSc ACA *1982;* Vine Farm, Hailey, WITNEY, OX29 9UB.
•WEST, Mrs. Gloria Heather, FCA *1970;* (Tax Fac), Matthams & Co, 41 Clarence Street, SOUTHEND-ON-SEA, SS1 1BH.
•WEST, Mr. Gordon Stuart, ACA *1984;* G.S. West & Company, 2 Inglewood, Kemnal Road, CHISLEHURST, KENT, BR7 6NF.
•WEST, Mr. Graham John, FCA *1970;* (Tax Fac), Rhodes & Rhodes, 42 Doughty Street, LONDON, WC1N 2LY.
WEST, Mr. Graham John, BSc ACA *1984;* with Grant Thornton UK LLP, The Explorer Building, Fleming Way, Manor Royal, CRAWLEY, WEST SUSSEX RH10 9GT.
WEST, Mr. Iain David, BA ACA *1995;* 12 Green Lane, LETCHWORTH GARDEN CITY, SG6 1EB.
WEST, Mr. Ian, BSc ACA *2001;* 100 Faraday Road, LONDON, SW19 8PB.
WEST, Mr. Ian Patrick, MA FCA *1996;* 7 Churchway, Stone, AYLESBURY, BUCKINGHAMSHIRE, HP17 8RG.
WEST, Mr. Ian Robert Kenneth, FCA *1975;* 15 Windover Close, Thornhill Park, SOUTHAMPTON, SO19 5JS.
WEST, Mr. James David, BA ACA *1993;* 22, Leaside Avenue, LONDON, N10 3BU.
WEST, Mr. James Glynn, FCA *1970;* Orchard House, Eastling, FAVERSHAM, ME13 0AZ.
WEST, Mrs. Jane Norma, BSc ACA *1993;* 26 Alderman Way, Weston Under Wetherley, LEAMINGTON SPA, CV33 9GB.
WEST, Miss. Janine, BSc ACA *2005;* 19 Dykes Way, BROMLEY, KENT, BR2 0SU.
WEST, Mr. Jason Matthieu, MA ACA *1999;* 45 Princes Gardens, Acton, LONDON, W3 0LP.
WEST, Mr. Jason Nicholas, BA ACA *1994;* 23 Bradmore Park Road, LONDON, W6 0DT.
WEST, Miss. Joanna, ACA *2009;* 2 Balmoral Road, HITCHIN, HERTFORDSHIRE, SG5 1XG.
WEST, Mrs. Joanne, BSc ACA *2002;* 22 Crystal Wood Drive, Miskin, PONTYCLUN, MID GLAMORGAN, CF72 8TH.
•WEST, Mr. John Anthony, BCom FCA *1981;* Williamson West, 10 Langdale Gate, WITNEY, OX28 6EX.
WEST, Mr. John Bernard, FCA *1973;* 44 rue du Montparnasse, 75014 PARIS, FRANCE.
WEST, Mr. John Charles, BA ACA *2000;* Walnut Tree Farmhouse, Main Road, Ashbocking, IPSWICH, IP6 9JX.
WEST, Mr. John Frederick Michael, FCA *1961;* Walnut Tree Farmhouse, The Green, Ashbocking, IPSWICH, SUFFOLK, IP6 9JX. (Life Member)
WEST, Mr. John Philip, MSc FCA *1972;* 5 Round Hill Close, Clayton Heights, BRADFORD, BD13 1HG.
WEST, Mr. John Vaughan Chanler, FCA *1966;* 63 Pasture Road, LETCHWORTH GARDEN CITY, HERTFORDSHIRE, SG6 3LS. (Life Member)
WEST, Mr. John William, FCA *1955;* Plantation Agencies Sdn Bhd, P.O.Box 706, Beach Street, 10790 PENANG, MALAYSIA.
WEST, Mr. Jonathan Andrew Templeton, BSc ACA *1990;* 19 Elmlea Avenue, Stoke Bishop, BRISTOL, BS9 3UU.
WEST, Mrs. Julia Anne, BSc ACA *1991;* 31507 BFPO 5357, Foreign & Commonwealth Office, West End Road, RUISLIP, MIDDLESEX, HA4 6EP.
WEST, Mrs. Karen Frances, BA ACA *1988;* 955 Peach Blossom Lane, ROCHESTER HILLS, MI 48306, UNITED STATES.
WEST, Miss. Karen Jane, BSc ACA *1993;* 13 Brunswick Road, KINGSTON UPON THAMES, KT2 6SB.
WEST, Mr. Laurie Peter, BSc ACA *1993;* Moorlands School Lane, Cookham, MAIDENHEAD, SL6 9QJ.
WEST, Mr. Lee Michael, BA(Hons) ACA *2003;* 9 Green Island, Ark Royal, Bilton, HULL, HU11 4EW.
WEST, Mr. Lee Robert, BA ACA *2000;* 207 Route des Bois, 74200 LYAUD, FRANCE.
•WEST, Mr. Leonard Francis, BA FCA *1978;* Sampson West, 34 Ely Place, LONDON, EC1N 6TD.
WEST, Mrs. Lindsey, BA ACA *1991;* 38 Bonaly Wester, EDINBURGH, EH13 0RQ.
WEST, Mrs. Lisa, BSc(Hons) ACA *2002;* 37 Boyslade Road, Burbage, HINCKLEY, LEICESTERSHIRE, LE10 2RF.
WEST, Mrs. Lisa Ann, ACA *1993;* 19 Leyside, Rayne, BRAINTREE, ESSEX, CM77 6DE.
WEST, Mr. Martin Alan, BSc ACA *2008;* 25 The Paddock, CANTERBURY, KENT, CT1 1SX.
WEST, Mr. Martin Graham, FCA *1962;* The Chaplains House, West Lane, High Legh, KNUTSFORD, CHESHIRE, WA16 6LR.
•WEST, Mr. Michael Sidney, FCA *1969;* with Golding West & Co Limited, 16 Station Road, CHESHAM, BUCKINGHAMSHIRE, HP5 1DH.
WEST, Mr. Michael Stuart, FCA *1967;* 480 Macclesfield Road, MACCLESFIELD, VIC 3782, AUSTRALIA.
WEST, Mr. Nicholas Antony, BSc ACA *1990;* Wyngates, Ivy Lane, Great Brickhill, MILTON KEYNES, MK17 9AH.
WEST, Mr. Nicholas Ashley James, BA FCA *1992;* 4 Swift Close, AYLESBURY, BUCKINGHAMSHIRE, HP19 0UR.
WEST, Mr. Nicholas James, ACA FCCA *2011;* 17/10-16 Melrose Parade, Clovelly, SYDNEY, NSW 2031, AUSTRALIA.
WEST, Mr. Nicholas Jonathan, BSc ACA *1993;* 1662 Sherwoood Drive, NANAIMO V9T 1H3, BC, CANADA.
WEST, Ms. Nicola, BA ACA *1992;* Lindens, Alton Drive, COLCHESTER, ESSEX, CO3 3ST.
•WEST, Mr. Nigel Frank, BA ACA *1980;* NFW Accounting Services Limited, 1 Bailey Close, Frimley, CAMBERLEY, SURREY, GU16 7EN.
•WEST, Mr. Nigel Robert Sands, MA FCA *1970;* Nigel West & Co, 18 Rother View, Burwash, ETCHINGHAM, TN19 7BN.
•WEST, Mr. Paul Kevan, BA ACA *1991;* PKW Accountancy Limited, Second Floor, 1 Church Square, LEIGHTON BUZZARD, BEDFORDSHIRE, LU7 1AE.
WEST, Mr. Paul Robert, BSc FCA *1982;* 10 Cranworth Road, WINCHESTER, SO22 6SD.
WEST, Mr. Peter Edgar James, FCA *1964;* 20 Anglesey Mead, CHIPPENHAM, SN15 3UB.
WEST, Mr. Peter Thomas, BSc ACA *1989;* 7 Deauville Court, Eleanor Close, LONDON, SE16 1PE.
WEST, Mr. Philip, ACA *2007;* Ernst & Young Llp, 1 More London Place, LONDON, SE1 2AF.
WEST, Mr. Philip John, BSc ACA *1998;* Brinkhurst, Central Avenue, Hullbridge, HOCKLEY, ESSEX, SS5 6AU.
WEST, Mr. Reginald Philip, FCA *1952;* 9 Grange Court Road, HARPENDEN, AL5 1BY. (Life Member)
WEST, Mr. Robert Harry, BA FCA *1968;* 19 Langthorn Close, Frampton Cotterell, BRISTOL, BS36 2JH.
WEST, Mr. Robert Kirby, FCA *1954;* 34 Branziert Road North, Killearn, GLASGOW, G63 9RF. (Life Member)
•WEST, Mr. Robin Nicholas, BA FCA *1987;* Blue Surf Consulting Ltd, Darvells Farm, Dunt Avenue, Hurst, READING, RG10 0SY.
WEST, Mr. Robin Simon, BA ACA *1992;* 67 Warwick Way, LONDON, SW1V 1QR.
•WEST, Mr. Roderick John, BA FCA *1975;* The Gables, 237B Birmingham Rd, Shenstone Wood End, LICHFIELD, STAFFORDSHIRE, WS14 0PD.
•WEST, Mrs. Rosemary Ada Christina, BA FCA *1987;* (Tax Fac), R.A.C. West & Co, 1 St. Peter Street, TIVERTON, DEVON, EX16 6NE.
WEST, Mrs. Sally Jane, BSc ACA *1990;* 55 Aveling Close, PURLEY, CR8 4DX.
WEST, Miss. Sarah Elizabeth Broughton, BA FCA *1998;* The Gable House Yattendon Road, Hermitage, THATCHAM, RG18 9RG.
WEST, Mrs. Sarah Jane, BA(Hons) ACA *2003;* with KPMG LLP, St. James's Square, MANCHESTER, M2 6DS.
WEST, Miss. Sheila Diane, BA FCA ACIL *1977;* 7 Eaton Court, Eaton Gardens, HOVE, EAST SUSSEX, BN3 3PL.
WEST, Mr. Simon Gordon Edward, BA FCA *1989;* 9 The Rhees East Street, Colne, HUNTINGDON, PE28 3NA.
WEST, Mr. Stephen, BA ACA *1995;* Windsor, Oldfield Avenue, DARWEN, BB3 1QY.
WEST, Mr. Stephen, BA ACA *1995;* 62 Windsor Road, RICHMOND, TW9 2EL.
WEST, Mr. Stephen Daniel, MSc BA FCA *1975;* World Ort Trust, 126 Albert Street, LONDON, NW1 7NE.
•WEST, Mr. Stephen John, FCA *1975;* West & Co, Old Hempstead House, 10 Queensway, HEMEL HEMPSTEAD, HERTFORDSHIRE, HP1 1LR.
WEST, Mr. Stephen John, BA ACA *1993;* 18 Acorn Way, BEDFORD, MK42 0QN.
WEST, Mr. Stephen Raymond, BSc FCA *1983;* 103 Kings Avenue, ELY, CAMBRIDGESHIRE, CB7 4QW.
WEST, Mr. Stephen Reginald, FCA FCMA *1964;* 3 Riverside Drive, CHIPPENHAM, WILTSHIRE, SN15 3NU.
WEST, Mr. Stephen Reginald, BA(Hons) ACA *1982;* 1 Burley Ave, CLEETHORPES, DN35 0TH.
WEST, Mr. Steven Roger, BSc ACA *2000;* 30 Repton Gardens, Hedge End, SOUTHAMPTON, SO30 2AE.
•WEST, Mrs. Susan, BSc ACA *1978;* West, Office 2 Greswolde House, 197b Station Road, Knowle, SOLIHULL, WEST MIDLANDS B93 0PU.
WEST, Mrs. Susan Jane, BEng ACA *1992;* 26 Windy Arbour, KENILWORTH, CV8 2AS.
WEST, Mr. Thomas Morton, MA ACA *2010;* Flat 5, 1 Parliament Court, LONDON, E1 7NA.
WEST, Mr. Thomas Philip, BSc ACA *2010;* Manhattan, Bay View Road, LOOE, CORNWALL, PL13 1JP.

•**WEST, Mr. Timothy, BSc ACA** *2001;* Moore Stephens LLP, 150 Aldersgate Street, LONDON, EC1A 4AB.
•**WEST, Mr. Timothy John Anthony, BSc FCA** *1993;* Ernst & Young LLP, 1 Bridgewater Place, Water Lane, LEEDS, LS11 5QR. See also Ernst & Young Europe LLP
WEST, Mr. Trevor William, FCA *1963;* White Hayes, Garden Close, Givons Grove, LEATHERHEAD, KT22 8LT.
WEST, Mr. William Frederick, FCA *1957;* 16 Bridle Close, EPSOM, SURREY, KT19 0JW. (Life Member)
WEST-EVANS, Mr. Errol Llewellyn, ACA CA(SA) *2011;* 52 Blind Lane, BOURNE END, BUCKINGHAMSHIRE, SL8 5JY.
•**WESTACOTT, Mr. Anthony James, MSc BA(Hons) ACA** *2000;* James Westacott ACA, 478 Hendrefoilan Road, Killay, SWANSEA, SA2 7NU.
WESTALL, Mr. Alan Jackson, FCA *1958;* (Member of Council 1975 - 1977), 76 Yealm Road, NEWTON FERRERS, PLYMOUTH, PL8 1BL. (Life Member)
WESTALL, Mr. Anthony Robert, BSc ACA *1979;* Kildale, 8 Highfield Road, Bickley, BROMLEY, BR1 2JW.
WESTALL, Mr. Derek Graham, FCA *1964;* 2 Parkgate Drive, Leyland, PRESTON, PR25 1BU.
WESTALL, Ms. Paula Susan, BSc FCA *2000;* with National Audit Office, 157-197 Buckingham Palace Road, Victoria, LONDON, SW1W 9SP.
WESTAWAY, Mr. Ben Ernest, BA ACA *2003;* 71 Hillcote Close, SHEFFIELD, S10 3PT.
WESTAWAY, Mr. Jonathan James, BA ACA *2000;* Purlieu Farm, Thornby Road, Naseby, NORTHAMPTON, NN6 6BY.
WESTAWAY, Mr. Peter Richard, ACA *2008;* Flat 10 Mercury Mansions, Dryburgh Road, LONDON, SW15 1BT.
WESTAWAY, Miss. Tamryn Jess, ACA *2011;* 45c Linden Gardens, LONDON, W2 4HQ.
WESTBROOK, Mr. Andrew, MChem ACA *2007;* Flat 5, 4 The Paragon, LONDON, SE3 0NX.
•**WESTBROOK, Mr. Andrew James, BA ACA CF** *1994;* Deloitte LLP, PO Box 500, 2 Hardman Street, MANCHESTER, M60 2AT. See also Deloitte & Touche LLP
WESTBROOK, Mrs. Caroline Mary, BSc ACA *2005;* BskyB Ground Floor, 2 Wellington Place, LEEDS, LS1 4AP.
WESTBROOK, Mr. Clive John, BSc FCA *1980;* 1 Cottesmore Gardens, Hale Barns, ALTRINCHAM, CHESHIRE, WA15 8TS.
WESTBROOK, Mr. Mark Andrew Michael, ACA *2009;* 23 Llanberis Road, Cheadle Hulme, CHEADLE, CHESHIRE, SK8 6BU.
WESTBROOK, Miss. Nicki Anne, BSc ACA *2008;* Goldwyns, Rutland House, 90-92 Baxter Avenue, SOUTHEND-ON-SEA, SS2 6HZ.
WESTBROOK, Mr. Paul Trevor, BA FCA *1995;* 27 Roman Road, HOVE, EAST SUSSEX, BN3 4LB.
WESTBROOK, Mr. Simon John, BSc ACA *2001;* with RSM Tenon Audit Limited, 2 Wellington Place, LEEDS, LS1 4AP.
WESTBROOK, Mr. Simon Pembruge, MA FCA *1973;* 10 Timber Ridge Lane, SCOTTS VALLEY, CA 95066, UNITED STATES.
WESTBROOK, Mrs. Suzanne Greig, BA ACA *1995;* 63 Revell Road, KINGSTON UPON THAMES, KT1 3SL.
WESTBROOKE, Mrs. Nicola Margaret, MA ACA *1997;* 13 Pinehurst, SEVENOAKS, TN14 5AQ.
•**WESTBURY, Mr. Clive Julian, FCA** *1982;* Harrop Marshall, Ashfield House, Ashfield Road, CHEADLE, CHESHIRE, SK8 1BB.
WESTBURY, Mr. Frank, FCA *1953;* Grant Grierson & Co, 129 Gerald Road, SALFORD, M6 6BL.
WESTBURY, Miss. Hazel Dawn, BA ACA *1993;* 31 Otterbourne Walk, Sherfield-on-Loddon, HOOK, HAMPSHIRE, RG27 0SE.
•**WESTBURY, Mrs. Sharon, ACA** *2004;* (Tax Fac), David Milnes Limited, Premier House, Bradford Road, CLECKHEATON, WEST YORKSHIRE, BD19 3TT.
WESTBY, Mr. Peter John, FCA *1970;* 41 Chequers Lane, Prestwood, GREAT MISSENDEN, HP16 9DR.
WESTCOTT, Mr. Christopher Leslie, FCA *1962;* 55 Bradbourne Street, LONDON, SW6 3TF.
WESTCOTT, Mrs. Clare Louise, BSc ACA *1996;* 27 The Paddocks, Freshfield, LIVERPOOL, L37 7HQ.
WESTCOTT, Miss. Emily Margaret Alice, BSc ACA *2010;* Shepherd Construction Ltd Frederick House, Fulford Road, YORK, YO10 4EA.
WESTCOTT, Mr. Frederick Michael, FCA *1965;* FMW Consulting Limited, 20 Thorneyholme Drive, KNUTSFORD, CHESHIRE, WA16 8BT.
WESTCOTT, Miss. Helen Margaret, FCA *1976;* (Tax Fac), 14 Collens Road, HARPENDEN, AL5 2AJ.
WESTCOTT, Mr. Jonathan Owen, FCA *1979;* Long Mynd, 35 Brendon Road, WATCHET, SOMERSET, TA23 0AX.
WESTCOTT, Mr. Myles St John, BSc ACA *1995;* W386, B A E Systems Warton Aerodrome, Warton, PRESTON, PR4 1AX.
WESTCOTT, Mr. Nicholas Toby, BSc ACA *2002;* 17 Denbridge Road, BROMLEY, BR1 2AG.
WESTCOTT, Mr. Richard Henry, FCA FTII *1970;* 118 Somerset Road, Wimbledon, LONDON, SW19 5LA.
WESTCOTT, Mr. Steven Blaire, MSc BA(Hons) ACA FCCA *2009;* 8 Fouracre Road, BRISTOL, BS16 6PE.
WESTCOTT, Mr. Timothy Mark, BSc FCA *1984;* 15 Stancombe Park, Westlea, SWINDON, SN5 7AP.
WESTCOTT-STEWART, Mrs. Kerry Siobhan, BA ACA *1999;* 9 The Pasture, Somersham, HUNTINGDON, CAMBRIDGESHIRE, PE28 3YX.
WESTCOUGH, Mrs. Anne Elizabeth, BSc ACA ATII *1988;* (Tax Fac), 48 Crothall Close, LONDON, N13 4BN.
WESTCOUGH, Mr. Steven, BSc ACA *1988;* 48 Crothall Cl, Palmers Green, LONDON, N13 4BN.
WESTELL, Mr. Keith George, FCA *1973;* Buckland House, Tarn Road, HINDHEAD, GU26 6TP.
WESTENBERGER, Mr. Andrew Thomas Karl, BSc ACA *1991;* Level 7, 100 Wood Street, LONDON, EC2V 7AN.
WESTERBEEK, Mr. Louis Henry Cornelis, BSc(Econ) FCA *1968;* 135 Broad Oak Lane, Penwortham, PRESTON, PR1 0XA.
WESTERBY, Mr. Roy Thomas, FCA *1971;* Tallents, 3 Middle Gate, NEWARK, NOTTINGHAMSHIRE, NG24 1AQ.
WESTERMAN, Mrs. Lisa Marie, BSc ACA CTA *1999;* 8c Elms Road, LEICESTER, LE2 3JF.
WESTERMAN, Mr. Max Samuel Henry, LLB ACA *2005;* with Ernst & Young LLP, 400 Capability Green, LUTON, LU1 3LU.
•**WESTERMAN, Mr. Philip Robert, BA ACA** *1999;* Grant Thornton UK LLP, 30 Finsbury Square, LONDON, EC2P 2YU. See also Grant Thornton LLP
WESTERMAN HOLT, Mrs. Lynn Marie, BA ACA *1998;* 8 Royal Crescent, HARROGATE, NORTH YORKSHIRE, HG2 8AB.
WESTERN, Mr. Andrew Barry, BEng ACA *2000;* 98 Villa Delle Rose, Taman Nakhoda, SINGAPORE 257792, SINGAPORE.
WESTERN, Mrs. Kay Louise, BSc(Econ) ACA *2002;* Flat 1, The Old Vicarage, Birley, HEREFORD, HR4 8ET.
WESTERN, Mr. Michael Ian, FCA *1958;* 32 The Dell, ST. ALBANS, HERTFORDSHIRE, AL1 4HE. (Life Member)
WESTERN, Mr. Peter James, BA FCA *1976;* D X Network Services Ltd D X House, The Ridgeway, IVER, BUCKINGHAMSHIRE, SL0 9JQ.
WESTERN, Miss. Sian Lesley Honor, BSc ACA *1986;* 58 Elizabeth Road, HENLEY-ON-THAMES, RG9 1RA.
WESTERN, Mr. Steven Roger, BSc ACA *1986;* Enstar (Eu) Ltd Avaya House, Cathedral Hill, GUILDFORD, GU2 7YL.
WESTERN, Miss. Victoria Elizabeth, BA ACA *1993;* Woodbury, Farnham Lane, HASLEMERE, GU27 1EZ.
WESTGARTH, Mr. John Rivers, FCA *1973;* Decoy Cottage, Broad Road, Ranworth, NORWICH, NORFOLK, NR13 6HS.
WESTGATE, Mr. Richard Charles, BSc ACA *1989;* 26 Chesterfield Road, LONDON, N3 1PR.
WESTHEAD, The Revd. David Robert, FCA *1966;* 26 Bleasdale Road, CREWE, CW1 4PZ.
WESTHEAD, Mr. Jeremy James, MA ACA *2003;* Burleigh House, 357 Strand, LONDON, WC2R 0HS.
WESTHEAD, Mr. John Simon, FCA CTA MABRP *1962;* (Member of Council 1977 - 1987), The White House, 37 Mellor Brow, Mellor, BLACKBURN, BB2 7EX.
WESTHEAD, Mr. Norman Alban, FCA *1956;* Hillcrest, 26 St Johns Road, Rowley Park, STAFFORD, ST17 9AS. (Life Member)
WESTHEAD, Mr. Rodney James, FCA *1969;* The Manor House, Monks Kirby, RUGBY, CV23 0RJ.
WESTHEAD, Mr. Stephen, MSc ACA *1999;* Cranswick Plc, Helsinki Road, HULL, HU7 0YW.
WESTINGHOUSE, Mr. Timothy Adrian, FCA *1971;* Miglio Co Ltd, 29a Market Street, CREWKERNE, SOMERSET, TA18 7JU.
WESTLAKE, Mr. Anthony John Treliving, MA FCA *1986;* The Grange, Bayleys Hill, SEVENOAKS, KENT, TN14 6HS.
WESTLAKE, Mr. Jeremy William, BA MSt ACA *1991;* Rolls-Royce Plc, PO Box 31, DERBY, DE24 8BJ.
WESTLAKE, Mr. Michael Frederick, FCA *1957;* Culzean, 46 Green Curve, BANSTEAD, SM7 1NY. (Life Member)
WESTLAKE, Mr. Peter, MA FCA *1995;* 9410 Carroll Park Drive, SAN DIEGO, CA 92121, UNITED STATES.
WESTLEY, Mrs. Carla Danielle Chantal, ACA *2001;* 23 Lister Close, St. Leonards, EXETER, DEVON, EX2 4SD.
WESTLEY, Miss. Corinna Jayne, BSc(Hons) ACA *2002;* 8 Hebden Grove, WILLENHALL, WV12 5FJ.
WESTLEY, Miss. Gemma Louise, BSc ACA *2011;* 6 Uplands Avenue, WOLVERHAMPTON, WV3 8AA.
•**WESTLEY, Mr. Jonathan Paul, BA ACA** *1996;* Thompson Jenner LLP, 1 Colleton Crescent, EXETER, EX2 4DG.
WESTLEY, Mr. Kevin Anthony, BA FCA *1973;* HSBC Ltd, L34 1 Queen's Road Central, CENTRAL, HONG KONG ISLAND, HONG KONG SAR.
WESTLEY, Mr. Mark James, BSc ACA *1998;* Societe Generale, Level 38, 3 Pacific Place, WAN CHAI, HONG KONG ISLAND, HONG KONG SAR.
WESTMACOTT, Mr. Paul Simon, BA ACA *1993;* Birchwood 76 Nantwich Road, MIDDLEWICH, CW10 9HG.
WESTMACOTT, Mr. Ruscombe Charles, MA FCA *1964;* 2 Hudnall Common, Little Gaddesden, BERKHAMSTED, HERTFORDSHIRE, HP4 1QL. (Life Member)
WESTMACOTT, Mr. Ryan, LLB ACA *2008;* 16a Ashcombe Crescent, BRISTOL, BS30 5NX.
•**WESTMACOTT, Mr. Simon Field, BSc FCA** *1973;* Alpha Advice, Greenacre, Meopham Green, GRAVESEND, DA13 0PY.
•**WESTMAN, Mr. Nigel Christopher, FCA** *1980;* (Tax Fac), Clough & Company LLP, 15/17 Devonshire Street, KEIGHLEY, BD21 2BH. See also Corporate Finance Services LLP, Clough Taxation Solutions LLP and Clough Management Services LLP
WESTMAN, Mr. Peter Mark Anders, FCA *1972;* Ernst B Westman Ltd, Wild Oak House, Wild Oak Lane, Trull, TAUNTON, SOMERSET TA3 7JR.
WESTMORE, Mr. Geoffrey David, FCA *1972;* Staple Inn Partnership, Staple Inn Buildings, LONDON, WC1V 7PZ.
WESTMORE, Miss. Kathryn May Clemett, MA(Hons) ACA *2010;* Flat 10 Cunningham Court, Maida Vale, LONDON, W9 1AE.
WESTMORE, Mrs. Lydia, MSc BSc ACA *2007;* Triodos Bank Brunel House, 11 The Promenade Clifton Down, BRISTOL, BS8 3NN.
WESTMORE, Mr. Peter Alan James, BSc ACA *2007;* Basement Flat, 38 Burghley Road, BRISTOL, BS6 5BN.
WESTMORELAND, Mrs. Hannah, BSc ACA *1997;* 28 Kennel Lane, Fetcham, LEATHERHEAD, SURREY, KT22 9PJ.
WESTMORELAND, Mr. Stephen, BSc ACA *1993;* 3 Gascoigne Way Bloxham, BANBURY, OXFORDSHIRE, OX15 4TJ.
WESTOBY, Mr. Stephen Charles, FCA *1975;* 156 Ridge Road, MOUNT DANDENONG, VIC 3767, AUSTRALIA.
WESTON, Mr. Alan Harry, FCA *1973;* St Albans Snooker Club, Unit 8, Vernlam Ind Est, London Road, ST. ALBANS, AL1 1PN.
WESTON, Mrs. Andrea Lynne, BSc ACA *1992;* 16 Augusta Road, PENARTH, SOUTH GLAMORGAN, CF64 5RH.
WESTON, Mr. Andrew Albert, FCA *1982;* 6 Tennyson Street, Narborough, LEICESTER, LE19 3FD.
WESTON, Miss. Anna Louise, BSc ACA *2009;* 8 Broadmead Crescent, Bishopston, SWANSEA, SA3 3BA.
WESTON, Mr. Anthony Peter, FCA *1956;* 62 Stratford Road, BROMSGROVE, B60 1AU. (Life Member)
WESTON, Mr. Caspar Tobin, BSc FCA *1982;* Courts Farm, Petworth Road, HASLEMERE, GU27 3AX.
WESTON, Mr. Christopher Mark, BSc FCA *1988;* ul Plycwianska 14, WARSAW, POLAND.
WESTON, Mr. Clifford Ronald, FCA *1954;* The Sheiling, Straight Half Mile, Maresfield, UCKFIELD, TN22 2HH. (Life Member)
WESTON, Mr. Clive, BSc FCA *1982;* Actant Ltd, 14-16 Dowgate Hill, LONDON, EC4R 2SU.
WESTON, Mr. David James, BA ACA *2000;* 8 Bramwell Drive, Bramcote, NOTTINGHAM, NG9 3ST.
•**WESTON, Mr. David John, FCA** *1966;* Weston & Co, 1 Arundel Close, Lynchborough Road, Passfield, LIPHOOK, GU30 7RW.
•**WESTON, Mrs. Deborah Jill, BA FCA** *1984;* with Ernst & Young LLP, 1 More London Place, LONDON, SE1 2AF.
WESTON, Mr. Douglas Malcolm, FCA *1962;* 28 Seaforth Gardens, Winchmore Hill, LONDON, N21 3BS. (Life Member)
WESTON, Mrs. Elizabeth Mary Sophia, BSc ACA *1985;* The Prudential Assurance Co Ltd, 121 Kings Road, READING, BERKSHIRE, RG1 3ES.
WESTON, Mrs. Emily Claire, BA ACA *2004;* 49 Grylls Park, Lanreath, LOOE, CORNWALL, PL13 2NG.
WESTON, Mr. James Neville, FCA *1961;* 17 Gardners Meadow, Severnside South, BEWDLEY, DY12 2DG.
•**WESTON, Mr. John Thomas, MSc FCA** *1960;* John Weston, Rhodenwood, 40 Hillcrest Road, CAMBERLEY, GU15 1LG.
•**WESTON, Mr. Joseph Harry Lawrence, FCA** *1979;* (Tax Fac), Weston Kay, 73/75 Mortimer Street, LONDON, W1W 7SQ.
WESTON, Mr. Julian Ralph, FCA *1970;* Glorieta Norte 46, Fracc. Club de Golf México, 14620 TLALPAN, MEXICO.
WESTON, Miss. Karen Marie, LLB ACA *2001;* 3460 Kingsboro Rd NE, ATLANTA, GA 30326, UNITED STATES.
•**WESTON, Mr. Keith Andrew, ACA** *1979;* (Tax Fac), YPO, The Granary, Haggs Farm Business Park, Haggs Road, HARROGATE, NORTH YORKSHIRE HG3 1EQ. See also YPOC
WESTON, Mr. Kevin, BA ACA *1997;* 15 Bolinas Ave, PO Box 1666, ROSS, CA 94957, UNITED STATES.
WESTON, Miss. Leonie Elizabeth, BA ACA *1998;* 1 The Limes, ST. ALBANS, HERTFORDSHIRE, AL1 4AT.
WESTON, Mrs. Louise Mary Patricia, BA ACA *1992;* Fircroft Engineering Services Ltd Trinity House, 114 Northenden Road, SALE, CHESHIRE, M33 3FZ.
WESTON, Mrs. Lucy Jane, BA(Hons) ACA *2002;* 1 Field House Drive, OXFORD, OX2 7NT.
•**WESTON, Mrs. Margaret Mary, BA ACA** *1983;* The Accounts Bureau Limited, 2nd Floor, 1 Warwick Row, LONDON, SW1E 5ER.
WESTON, Mr. Mark, BA FCA *1982;* Triton, 105 Piccadilly, LONDON, W1J 7NJ.
WESTON, Mr. Mark Daniel, BSc ACA *2002;* 26 Forfield Drive, Beggarwood, BASINGSTOKE, HAMPSHIRE, RG22 4FS.
WESTON, Mr. Michael Andrew, FCA *1986;* Maison de la Ville Bagot L'Amont de la Ville Bagot, St. Ouen, JERSEY, JE3 2DF.
WESTON, Mr. Michael Arthur, BSc ACA *1991;* (Tax Fac), Coopers Farm House, Bashurst Hill, Itchingfield, HORSHAM, RH13 0PE.
WESTON, Mr. Neil Alexander, ACA *1992;* The Tober, Frimley Road, Ash Vale, ALDERSHOT, GU12 5NT.
•**WESTON, Mr. Nicholas Hugo, FCA** *1980;* Baker Tilly Corporate Finance LLP, St Philips Point, Temple Row, BIRMINGHAM, B2 5AF. See also Baker Tilly Tax and Advisory Services LLP
WESTON, Mrs. Patricia Mary, BSc ACA *1997;* 10 Dunstall Road, LONDON, SW20 0HR.
WESTON, Mr. Paul David James, BA ACA *1991;* Lapley Hall, Lapley, STAFFORD, ST19 9JR.
WESTON, Mr. Philip Richard, BSc ACA *1991;* Kelso Place Asset Management, 110 St. Martin's Lane, LONDON, WC2N 4BA.
•**WESTON, Mr. Richard Harry, BA FCA** *1979;* (Tax Fac), Littlestone Martin Glenton, 73 Wimpole Street, LONDON, W1G 8AZ.
•**WESTON, Mr. Robert Charles, BSc LLB FCA** *1987;* Weston & Co, 10 Chendre Close, Hayfield, HIGH PEAK, SK22 2PH.
•①**WESTON, Mr. Roderick John, BEng FCA MBA** *1986;* Mazars LLP, Tower Bridge House, St. Katharines Way, LONDON, E1W 1DD.
WESTON, Mr. Roger David, BSc ACA *2006;* 7 Northdown Road, LONGFIELD, DA3 7QN.
WESTON, Mr. Russell, BA ACA *2007;* 16 Bowen Streeet, Prahran, PRAHRAN, VIC 3181, AUSTRALIA.
WESTON, Mr. Samuel James Holroyd, TD BA FCA *1959;* Melrose House, 777 Wollaton Road, Wollaton, NOTTINGHAM, NG8 2AN. (Life Member)
WESTON, Mr. Simon Dominic, BSc(Hons) ACA *2004;* Flat 14 Hill Court Wimbledon Hill Road, LONDON, SW19 7PD.
WESTON, Mr. Simon Zigmond, FCA *1954;* Flat 9, Hambleden Place, 32 Gills Hill, RADLETT, HERTFORDSHIRE, WD7 8BT. (Life Member)
WESTON, Mr. Stephen Alan, BA ACA *1984;* 16 Bellara Street, CARSELDINE, QLD 4034, AUSTRALIA.
•**WESTON, Mr. Stephen George, BCom ACA** *1993;* Deloitte LLP, Hill House, 1 Little New Street, LONDON, EC4A 3TR. See also Deloitte & Touche LLP
WESTON, Mrs. Susan, MA ACA *1993;* The Tober Frimley Road, Ash Vale, ALDERSHOT, HAMPSHIRE, GU12 5NT.
WESTON, Mr. Thomas Charles, FCA *1973;* 59 Croham Valley Road, SOUTH CROYDON, CR2 7JG.
WESTON PATEL, Ms. Sharon June, ACA *1991;* 2314 Briana Drive, BRANDON, FL 33511, UNITED STATES.

WESTON SMITH, Mr. Anthony Stafford, FCA *1965;* 132 Oakhill Road, SEVENOAKS, TN13 1NX. (Life Member)

WESTON SMITH, Mrs. Julie Anne, ACA *1982;* Walsal End House, Walsal End Lane, Hampton-in-Arden, SOLIHULL, B92 0HX.

WESTON SMITH, Mr. Michael, FCA *1950;* Lapworth Park, Bushwood Lane, Lapworth, SOLIHULL, B94 5PJ. (Life Member)

•WESTON UNDERWOOD, Mr. Charles, BA ACA *2003;* Weston Underwood, 63 Agar Road, Illogan Highway, REDRUTH, CORNWALL, TR15 3EJ.

WESTRAN, Mr. Ben, BSc ACA *2002;* Mole Cottage, 12 Ashmead Green, Ashmead Green, DURSLEY, GLOUCESTERSHIRE, GL11 5EW.

WESTREN, Mr. Colin, FCA *1967;* 190 Dales Road, IPSWICH, IP1 4JY.

WESTRIP, Mr. Edward Mark, BSc ACA *1991;* with Mazars LLP, Tower Bridge House, St. Katharines Way, LONDON, E1W 1DD.

WESTROPP, Mr. Richard Beverley, ACA *1979;* Little Barton, Chew Magna, BRISTOL, BS40 8RS.

WESTWATER, Mr. William Terence, FCA *1966;* Lark Rise, Norman Road, St. Margarets Bay, DOVER, CT15 6DA. (Life Member)

WESTWELL, Miss. Lisa, ACA *2011;* 43 Moorgate Street, BLACKBURN, LANCASHIRE, BB2 4PB.

WESTWICK, Mr. Christopher Alan, BSc FCA *1957;* 20 Brookway, LONDON, SE3 9BJ. (Life Member)

WESTWOOD, Mr. Adam Thomas, BSc ACA *2009;* Flat 2, 135 Petherton Road, LONDON, N5 2RS.

WESTWOOD, Mr. Andrew Oakley, FCA *1959;* 5 Ryefield Close, Hagley, STOURBRIDGE, WEST MIDLANDS, DY9 0JS.

WESTWOOD, Mr. Barry John, FCA *1954;* 22 Cromhamstone, Stone, AYLESBURY, HP17 8NH. (Life Member)

WESTWOOD, Mr. Benjamin Thomas, ACA *2009;* 56 Handside Lane, WELWYN GARDEN CITY, HERTFORDSHIRE, AL8 6SJ.

WESTWOOD, Mr. David Alfred, BA FCA *1963;* Suite 491, 48 Par-La-Ville Road, HAMILTON HM II, BERMUDA.

WESTWOOD, Mr. David John Morris, FCA *1958;* 1 St. James Court, Barton under Needwood, BURTON-ON-TRENT, STAFFORDSHIRE, DE13 8HN. (Life Member)

•WESTWOOD, Miss. Fiona Gillian, BEng ACA DChA *1998;* with PricewaterhouseCoopers LLP, 31 Great George Street, BRISTOL, BS1 5QD.

WESTWOOD, Mr. Geoffrey, FCA *1956;* 171 Leeds Road, HARROGATE, HG2 8HQ. (Life Member)

WESTWOOD, Mr. Gordon Christopher John, BA ACA *1994;* 13 Prior Park Road, BATH, BA2 4NG.

WESTWOOD, Mr. Graham Phillip, ACA *2010;* (Tax Fac), 6 Monkton Road, Borough Green, SEVENOAKS, KENT, TN15 8SD.

WESTWOOD, Mrs. Julie, BSc ACA *1982;* James Halstead Plc, Beechfield, Hollinhurst Road, Radcliffe, MANCHESTER, M26 1JN.

WESTWOOD, Miss. Laura Emily, BA(Hons) ACA *2011;* 8 Emma Close, The Broadway, BOURNEMOUTH, DORSET, bh10 7ab.

•WESTWOOD, Mr. Neil Adrian, FCA *1987;* (Tax Fac), Neil Westwood & Co, 101 Dixons Green Road, DUDLEY, DY2 7DJ.

WESTWOOD, Mrs. Nicola Joy, LLB ACA *1998;* 29 Fairway, Northfield, BIRMINGHAM, B31 5BB.

WESTWOOD, Lady Penelope, FCA *1968;* 23 Holly Avenue, Jesmond, NEWCASTLE UPON TYNE, NE2 2PU.

WESTWOOD, Mr. Peter Conway, FCA *1951;* Hamston Fawr, Dyffryn St.Nicholas, CARDIFF, CF5 6SU. (Life Member)

WESTWOOD, Mr. Stephen, BA FCA *1976;* 27 Cant Crescent, ST. ANDREWS, FIFE, KY16 8NF.

WESTWORTH, Mr. Christopher Napier, LLB FCA *1971;* 14 Valleyview Crescent, GREENWICH, NSW 2065, AUSTRALIA.

WETHERALD, Miss. Catherine Lucy, ACA *2007;* Peter Howard & Co, 1 Wharfe Mews Cliffe Terrace, WETHERBY, WEST YORKSHIRE, LS22 6LX.

WETHERALL, Miss. Christine, MA ACA *2010;* KPMG, Crown House, 4 Par-la-Ville Road, HAMILTON HM08, BERMUDA.

WETHERALL, Mr. Iain, BA ACA *1998;* 16 Quai du Cheval Blanc, Acacias, 1227, GENEVA, SWITZERLAND.

•WETHERALL, Mr. Jeremy, BA ACA *1993;* Queensgate Management (East Midlands) LLP, Unit 4, Henley Way, LINCOLN, LN6 3QR.

•WETHERALL, Mr. Stephen John, BA FCA FCCA *1977;* (Tax Fac), Shaw Gibbs LLP, 264 Banbury Road, OXFORD, OX2 7DY. See also Wetherall S.J.

WETHERALL, Mr. Stuart Anderson, BA ACA *1998;* 27 Beech Hill Road, ASCOT, SL5 0BW.

WETHERELL, Mr. Leslie, FCA *1961;* 95 Castlerigg Drive, BURNLEY, BB12 8AT. (Life Member)

WETHERELL, Mr. Simon Graham, BA ACA *2002;* 12 Redwald Drive, Guiseley, LEEDS, LS20 8QN.

WETHERELL, Mr. Terence Edgar, BA FCA *1973;* 8 Phillipa's Drive, HARROGATE, HG2 9BB.

WETHERHILL, Mr. Christopher, FCA *1971;* Baicliff, 1 Turtle Bay Crescent, SOUTHAMPTON SN01, BERMUDA.

WETHERLY, Mr. Stuart Andrew, BSc(Hons) ACA *2003;* 80 Sandbourne Avenue, LONDON, SW19 3EN.

WETHEY, Mr. Matthew John Julius, BSc ACA *1997;* PV Crystalox plc, 174 Milton Park, Milton, ABINGDON, OXFORDSHIRE, OX14 4SE.

WETTASINGHE, Mr. Dylan Christopher, ACA CA(AUS) *2009;* 8 Rochester Grove, CASTLE HILL, NSW 2154, AUSTRALIA.

WETTERN, Mrs. Anne Marie, BA ACA *1981;* 33 Bramley Way, ASHTEAD, KT21 1QZ.

WETTERN, Mrs. Clare Mary, LLB ACA *1984;* Ritherden, Toys Hill, WESTERHAM, TN16 1QE.

WETTERN, Mr. Thomas Hugh, BSc ACA *1980;* 3 Hatfield Road, ASHTEAD, SURREY, KT21 1BH.

WETTLER, Mr. Peter John, BA(Econ) ACA *2008;* 271 Birstall Road, Birstall, LEICESTER, LE4 4DJ.

WETTON, Mr. David Edward Llewellyn, BSc ACA *1989;* 16 Bridge Road, BROMSGROVE, WORCESTERSHIRE, B60 3GT.

•①WETTON, Mr. Edward Christopher, FCA MICM FABRP *1980;* Gibson Booth, 12 Victoria Road, BARNSLEY, SOUTH YORKSHIRE, S70 2BB.

WETTON, Mr. John Leslie, FCA *1972;* JOLO Farm, D 146, ROSETTA, KWAZULU NATAL, 3301, SOUTH AFRICA.

WETTON, Mr. Michael John Stewart, FCA *1969;* 5 Austens Orchard, Smallhythe Road, TENTERDEN, KENT, TN30 7LQ. (Life Member)

WETTON, Mr. Timothy James, FCA *1975;* 1 Priory Close, Lapworth, SOLIHULL, B94 6JL.

WETZ, Mr. Joseph Daniel, BSc ACA *2002;* 3 I Plc, 16 Palace Street, LONDON, SW1E 5JD.

•WEVILL, Mr. Michael John, FCA *1972;* (Tax Fac), Potter Baker, 20 Western Road, LAUNCESTON, PL15 7BA.

WEYER, Mr. Colin Albert, FCA *1973;* 3 Meriden, Foxcombe Road Boars Hill, OXFORD, OX1 5DG.

WEYMAN, Miss. Anne Judith, OBE BSc FCA *1968;* 8 College Cross, LONDON, N1 1PP.

WEYMAN, Mr. Jeremy Spencer, MSc BSc ACA *2007;* Laan van Meerweijde 19, 1713BM OBDAM, NOORD HOLLAND, NETHERLANDS.

•WHAITES, Miss. Anna Lorraine, ACA *2003;* Mitchams Accountants Limited, 1 Cornhill, ILMINSTER, SOMERSET, TA19 0AD.

WHALE, Mrs. Angela Judith, BA ACA *1991;* The Coach House, West Street, WIGTON, CUMBRIA, CA7 9PD.

WHALE, The Revd. Anthony, LLB FCA *1964;* The Priests House, The Marld, ASHTEAD, SURREY, KT21 1RS.

•WHALE, Mrs. Barbara Jean, FCA *1973;* (Tax Fac), WAC (Whale & Company) Limited, Holly Berry House, Rough Park, RUGELEY, STAFFORDSHIRE, WS15 3SQ.

WHALE, Mr. Brian James, FCA *1962;* 18 Roe Green Close, HATFIELD, HERTFORDSHIRE, AL10 9PE.

•WHALE, Mr. David Jonathan, ACA FCCA *2011;* Michael Dufty Partnership Limited, 61 Charlotte Street, St Paul's Square, BIRMINGHAM, B3 1PX.

WHALE, Mrs. Diane, BA ACA *1991;* 27 Mead Way, LEEDS, LS15 9JP.

WHALE, Mrs. Helen Sylvia, BSc ACA *1991;* Domaine de Douet, 4 Carteret Farm, La Rue de Grouville, Grouville, JERSEY, JE3 9HP.

WHALE, Mr. James Robert Benedict, BA ACA *1992;* Deutsche Bank, 1 Appold St, LONDON, EC2A 2HE.

WHALE, Mr. James William, BA ACA *2010;* 17 Badminton Road, LONDON, SW12 8BN.

WHALE, Mr. Michael, FCA *1969;* 37 Peaks Hill, PURLEY, CR8 3JJ.

WHALE, Mr. Roger Charles, FCA *1968;* 29 Holland Pines, Great Hollands, BRACKNELL, RG12 8UY.

•WHALE, Mr. Stephen, BA FCA *1992;* Caversham, Elizabeth House, 9 Castle Street, St Helier, JERSEY, JE4 2QP. See also Lubbock Fine

WHALEN, Mrs. Anna Margaret, BA ACA *1995;* International Paint Ltd, Stoneygate Lane, Felling, GATESHEAD, TYNE AND WEAR, NE10 0JH.

WHALEN, Mr. Thomas George, BA ACA *1993;* Bankside 2, 90-100 Southwark Street, LONDON, SE1 0SW.

WHALEY, Mrs. Celia Anne, BA ACA *1986;* 35A Alexander Street, COLLAROY, NSW 2097, AUSTRALIA.

•WHALEY, Mr. Geoffrey Alan, FCA *1968;* Geoffrey Alan Whaley, 23 Hillfield Road, Chalfont St Peter, GERRARDS CROSS, SL9 0DU.

WHALEY, Mr. Henry Thomas Sheffield, MA ACA *2001;* 43 East Craigs Wynd, EDINBURGH, EH12 8HJ.

WHALEY, Mr. Ian Douglas, BA FCA *1970;* 10 Oakdale, Harwood, BOLTON, BL2 3JX.

WHALEY, Mr. Martin James, BA(Hons) ACA *2003;* 38 Priory Road, Chiswick, LONDON, W4 5JA.

WHALEY, Mr. Philip James, BSc ACA CF *2002;* with Grant Thornton UK LLP, 30 Finsbury Square, LONDON, EC2P 2YU.

WHALEY, Mr. Scott David, BSc ACA *2009;* Flat 41 Falmouth House, Royal Quarter Seven Kings Way, KINGSTON UPON THAMES, KT2 5AH.

WHALL, Mr. Richard, FCA *1975;* 34 St. Davids Road, Hethersett, NORWICH, NR9 3DH.

•①WHALLEY, Mr. Alan Peter, BSc FCA CF *1983;* James Cowper LLP, 3 Wesley Gate, Queens Road, READING, RG1 4AP. See also JC Payroll Services Ltd

•WHALLEY, Miss. Alison Marjorie, BA FCA *1992;* Naylor Wintersgill Ltd, Carlton House, Grammar School Street, BRADFORD, WEST YORKSHIRE, BD1 4NS.

WHALLEY, Mr. Allan, FCA *1973;* Wheatley Cottage, Four Acre Lane, Thornley With Wheatley, Longridge, PRESTON, PR3 2TD.

WHALLEY, Mr. Anthony, FCA *1966;* Westcot Farm House, Westcot, WANTAGE, OXFORDSHIRE, OX12 9QA. (Life Member)

•WHALLEY, Mr. David Ian, FCA CTA *1975;* Whalley & Co., Whalley & Co, 29 Chester Road, Castle Bromwich, BIRMINGHAM, B36 9DA.

WHALLEY, Mr. David Johnson, BA FCA *1994;* (Tax Fac), Griffiths & Armour, Drury House, 19 Water Street, LIVERPOOL, L2 0RL.

WHALLEY, Mr. David Seymour, FCA *1971;* 53 Treguddock Drive, WADEBRIDGE, CORNWALL, PL27 6BQ.

WHALLEY, Mr. Gareth James, BSc ACA *2000;* MLC Centre, Level 45, 19 Martin Place, SYDNEY, NSW 2000, AUSTRALIA.

WHALLEY, Mr. George Benjamin, ACA *2009;* Apartment 18, Freshfield, Spindletree Avenue, MANCHESTER, M9 7HQ.

WHALLEY, Mr. Ian Michael, FCA *1966;* Smugglers, Sandy Lane, Rushmoor, FARNHAM, SURREY, GU10 2EX. (Life Member)

•WHALLEY, Mr. John Trevor, FCA *1972;* J.T. Whalley & Co, 41 Leywood Close, BRAINTREE, ESSEX, CM7 3NP.

•WHALLEY, Ms. Julie Heather, ACA *1995;* Howard Worth, Drake House, Gadbrook Park, NORTHWICH, CHESHIRE, CW9 7RA.

WHALLEY, Mr. Mark Christopher, ACA *2008;* 22 Meadowcroft, Euxton, CHORLEY, LANCASHIRE, PR7 6BU.

WHALLEY, Miss. Mary Jane, ACA *2011;* Station House Snape Bridge, Snape, SAXMUNDHAM, SUFFOLK, IP17 1ST.

WHALLEY, Mr. Neil Jeremy, MEng ACA *1993;* 2 Lime Trees, Staplehurst, TONBRIDGE, KENT, TN12 0SS.

•WHALLEY, Mr. Peter Anthony, BSc FCA *1993;* PricewaterhouseCoopers, 33/F Cheung Kong Center, 2 Queen's Road, CENTRAL, HONG KONG ISLAND, HONG KONG SAR.

WHALLEY, Mr. Peter James, FCA *1971;* (Tax Fac), Greystoke, Walker Lane, Fulwood, PRESTON, PR2 7AN.

WHALLEY, Miss. Rozalynne, ACA *2008;* 3 Holly Road, Woolmer Green, KNEBWORTH, HERTFORDSHIRE, SG3 6LL.

WHALLEY, Mr. Simon Graham, BA ACA *1999;* 55 Lydiate Park, Thornton, LIVERPOOL, L23 1XL.

WHALLEY, Mr. Stephen Bryan, ACA *1982;* 217 Long Lane, Aughton, ORMSKIRK, L39 5BU.

WHALLEY, Miss. Suzanne, LLB FCA CTA *1959;* 12 Coton Manor, Berwick Road, SHREWSBURY, SY1 2LT. (Life Member)

WHALLEY, Miss. Vicki Susan, ACA *1997;* Manor Farm, New Road, Anderton, NORTHWICH, CW9 6AE.

WHALLEY-HUNTER, Mrs. Caroline Mary, BCom ACA *1985;* 192 Moss Lane, Burscough, ORMSKIRK, L40 4AZ.

WHAPHAM, Miss. Gillian Ruth, BSc ACA *1992;* Jamaica Cottage, Watery Lane, Clifton Hampden, ABINGDON, OXFORDSHIRE, OX14 3EL.

WHAPPLES, Mr. Stuart James, BA(Hons) ACA *2001;* 74 Old Barber, HARROGATE, NORTH YORKSHIRE, HG1 3DF.

WHARAM, Mr. Martin William, BEng ACA *1995;* VBox 881580, SINGAPORE 919191, SINGAPORE.

•WHARIN, Mr. Martin, FCA *1984;* Hart Shaw LLP, Europa Link, Sheffield Business Park, SHEFFIELD, S9 1XU.

WHARMBY, Mrs. Helen, BMus ACA ATII *1997;* with Deloitte LLP, Stonecutter Court, 1 Stonecutter Street, LONDON, EC4A 4TR.

WHARMBY, Mr. Neil Christopher, BA ACA *1982;* 7 Knowle Green, SHEFFIELD, S17 3AP.

•WHARRIE, Mr. David Roy, FCA *1965;* David Wharrie & Co., Woodside House, Ashton, CHESTER, CH3 8AE.

WHARTON, Mr. Alan Thomas, FCA *1971;* 82 Gainsborough Avenue, LIVERPOOL, L31 7AZ.

WHARTON, Mr. Anthony, FCA *1965;* 1 Halsall Green, Poulton Lancelyn, WIRRAL, CH63 9NA.

•WHARTON, Mr. George Jacob Crookenden, BSc ACA *2008;* Cultra C T S, 102b Bangor Road, HOLYWOOD, COUNTY DOWN, BT18 0LR.

WHARTON, Miss. Harriet, BSc ACA *2010;* 33 Cherry Orchard Road, WEST MOLESEY, SURREY, KT8 1QZ.

WHARTON, Mr. Neil Charles, BA ACA *1992;* (Tax Fac), 9 Beaumont Avenue, RICHMOND, TW9 2HE.

WHARTON, Mr. Nicholas Barry Edward, ACA *1990;* Crumpsbank House Stakenbridge Lane, Churchill, KIDDERMINSTER, WORCESTERSHIRE, DY10 3LT.

•WHARTON, Mr. Nicholas Giles, BA FCA *1995;* BDO LLP, 1 Bridgewater Place, Water Lane, LEEDS, LS11 5RU. See also BDO Stoy Hayward LLP

WHARTON, Mr. Nicholas Scott, BA ACA *1989;* 5 Parcq Du Marais, La Route de la Haule, St. Lawrence, JERSEY, JE3 1BA.

WHARTON, Mrs. Nicola Jane Downer, BSc ACA *1992;* 20 New Road, Aston Clinton, AYLESBURY, BUCKINGHAMSHIRE, HP22 5JD.

•WHARTON, Mr. Nigel John, BSc FCA *1982;* M.J. Read & Co, 1 Cobden Road, SEVENOAKS, TN13 3UB.

WHARTON, Mr. Peter, BSc FCA *1991;* Wayfarer's Cottage, 37 Regent Street, STONEHOUSE, GL10 2AA.

•WHARTON, Mr. Robert Mark, BSc FCA MILM *2000;* Dodd & Co., Fifteen Rosehill, Montgomery Way, Rosehill Estate, CARLISLE, CA1 2RW.

WHARTON, Miss. Sarah, ACA *2009;* 65 Tilehouse Green Lane, Knowle, SOLIHULL, WEST MIDLANDS, B93 9EU.

•WHARTON, Mr. Stephen John, BSc ACA *1995;* Blinkhorns, 27 Mortimer Street, LONDON, W1T 3BL.

WHARTON, Mrs. Susan Elizabeth, BA ACA *1992;* 9 Beaumont Avenue, RICHMOND, SURREY, TW9 2HE.

WHARTON, Mrs. Swee Fong, BA ACA *1992;* 37 Regent Street, STONEHOUSE, GL10 2AA.

WHATCOTT, Miss. Jennifer Claire, BSc ACA *2010;* 32 Welbeck Road, LEEDS, LS9 9BY.

WHATELEY, Mr. Paul Richard, BSc ACA MBA *1995;* (Tax Fac), 17 Hartington Crescent, COVENTRY, CV5 6FU.

WHATFORD, Mrs. Cara Ann, BSc ACA *1997;* Reliance Mutual Insurance Society Ltd Reliance House, 6 Vale Avenue, TUNBRIDGE WELLS, TN1 1RG.

WHATLEY, Mr. Andrew Robert, BSc ACA *2001;* 32 Archway Street, LONDON, SW13 1AR.

WHATLEY, Mr. David Andrew, BSc ACA *1995;* Accident Exchange Group Plc, Alpha 1, Canton Lane, Hams Hall, BIRMINGHAM, B46 1GA.

•WHATLEY, Mr. Kevin Vincent, FCA *1975;* Kevin Whatley & Co, 16 Gellihaf Road, Fleur de Lis, BLACKWOOD, GWENT, NP12 3UY.

WHATLEY, Mr. Michael Chadwick, MA FCA *1954;* Graystones, Ling Lane, Scarcroft, LEEDS, LS14 3HX. (Life Member)

WHATLEY, Mr. Robert Southcott, FCA *1978;* 8819 Heather Circle, HOUSTON, TX 77055, UNITED STATES.

WHATLEY, Mrs. Sheree Denise, BSc ACA *1983;* Le Verdon A, 10 avenue du Domaine du Loup, 06800 CAGNES SUR MER, ALPES MARITIMES, FRANCE.

WHATLEY, Mr. William Richard, BA ACA *1989;* Interim Financial Resource Ltd, 3 The Burrows, Newbold on Stour, STRATFORD-UPON-AVON, WARWICKSHIRE, CV37 8UP.

WHATMAN, Mr. Alan Clement, FCA *1959;* 16 Shaftesbury Court, 47/51 Alexandra Road, FARNBOROUGH, HAMPSHIRE, GU14 6UT. (Life Member)

WHATMORE, Mr. Max, BSc FCA *1984;* 24 Argyll Road, LONDON, W8 7BG.

WHATMORE, Mr. Stephen Nicholas, FCA *1977;* 11 Woodstock Gardens, Appleton, WARRINGTON, WA4 5HN.

WHATMORE, Mrs. Zoe Victoria, BSc ACA *1996;* 102 Tuffnells Way, HARPENDEN, HERTFORDSHIRE, AL5 3HW.
WHATMOUGH, Mr. Michael John, MA FCA *1960;* 41 Kings Road, WINDSOR, SL4 2AD. (Life Member)
WHATNALL, Mr. Peter David, BA ACA *1987;* 7 Searle Road, FARNHAM, SURREY, GU9 8LJ.
WHATSON, Mr. Michael, MSc FCA *1971;* 26 Lindisfarne Drive, KENILWORTH, CV8 2PQ.
WHATSON, Mr. Peter James Clifford, FCA *1982;* PNC Business Credit Colmore Plaza, 20 Colmore Circus Queensway, BIRMINGHAM, B4 6AT.
WHATT, Mrs. Deborah Bernice, BA ACA *1992;* Eton College, WINDSOR, SL4 6DB.
WHATTON, Mrs. Susan Margaret, BSc ACA *1990;* Cleveland House, Forest Road, NORTHAMPTON, NN7 2HE.
WHAWELL, Mr. Benjamin Mark, LLB ACA *2000;* 14 Marine Terrace, LIVERPOOL, MERSEYSIDE, L22 5PR.
WHAYMAN, Mr. Stuart Mark, MA ACA *1998;* 122 Clayton Road, CHESSINGTON, SURREY, KT9 1NJ.
WHEADON, Mr. Anthony Cohu, FCA *1966;* 66 Naishcombe Hill, Wick, BRISTOL, BS30 5QS. (Life Member)
WHEADON, Mrs. Joanna Dawn, ACA *2009;* 6 Matthews Close, Earley, READING, RG6 7EQ.
WHEADON, Mr. Nicholas Charles, ACA *2009;* 6 Matthews Close, Earley, READING, RG6 7EQ.
WHEAL, Mr. David, BA ACA *1999;* Ashlea, 3 Ashwood Park, Fetcham, LEATHERHEAD, KT22 9NT.
WHEAL, Mr. Donovan, ACA *2011;* 59 Oak Hill, SURBITON, SURREY, KT6 6DY.
WHEALE, Mr. Peter Robert, PhD FCA *1968;* Flat 17, Village Apartments, 27 The Broadway, LONDON, N8 8DR. (Life Member)
WHEALS, Mr. Raymond Alvar, FCA *1963;* The Cottage, Rowner Road, BILLINGSHURST, WEST SUSSEX, RH14 9HT.
•WHEAT, Mr. Nicholas Raymond, MA BSc FCA FTII *1978;* Wheat & Butler, 19 Holbrook Lane, CHISLEHURST, BR7 6PE. See also Maratea Limited
WHEAT, Miss. Sara, BA ACA *2006;* Flat 10, Bowyer House, 14 Slievemore Close, LONDON, SW4 6BZ.
WHEATCROFT, Mr. Jonathan Harold Joseph, BSc ACA *2006;* Ground Floor Flat, 2 Radipole Road, LONDON, SW6 5DL.
WHEATCROFT, Mr. Martin David Ashcombe, MA FCA *1993;* National Grid USA, One Metrotech Center, BROOKLYN, NY 11201, UNITED STATES.
WHEATCROFT, Mr. Nigel Augustus, FCA *1949;* Westfield Farm, North Wheatley, RETFORD, DN22 9DU. (Life Member)
WHEATCROFT, Mr. Stephen John, BA ACA *1984;* 2 Meg Lane, MACCLESFIELD, CHESHIRE, SK10 3LB.
WHEATCROFT, Mr. Stephen Mark, BSc ACA *1989;* Room 4576 4th Floor, British Broadcasting Corporation White City Media Centre, 201 Wood Lane, LONDON, W12 7TQ.
WHEATCROFT, Miss. Wendy Jane, BSc ACA *1991;* 9 College Place, ST. ALBANS, HERTFORDSHIRE, AL3 4PU.
WHEATER, Mr. David Winston, FCA *1965;* Stratton, 30 Broom Lane, ROTHERHAM, S60 3EL.
•WHEATER, Dr. Richard Feather, ACA *1992;* 25 Caynham Avenue, PENARTH, SOUTH GLAMORGAN, CF64 5RR.
WHEATING, Mr. Justin Philip, FCA *1973;* 339 Hawk Pine Road, NORWICH, VT 05055, UNITED STATES.
WHEATLAND, Mr. David Michael, FCA *1969;* Cinders Cottage, Holmwood Park, South Holmwood, DORKING, RH5 4NU.
WHEATLEY, Mr. Alan Edward, FCA *1960;* 5 Plymouth Park, SEVENOAKS, KENT, TN13 3RR.
WHEATLEY, Mr. Andrew Paul, ACA *2007;* Unit 1208, 1 Kings Cross Road, Darlinghurst, SYDNEY, NSW 2010, AUSTRALIA.
WHEATLEY, Mr. Christopher James, FCA *1978;* Fabriweld Tubular Steel Products Ltd Harrimans Lane, Lenton Lane Industrial Estate, NOTTINGHAM, NG7 2SD.
•WHEATLEY, Mr. Christopher James, FCA *1977;* Duncan Sheard Glass, Unit 5, Evolution House, Lakeside Business Village, St Davids Park, Ewloe DEESIDE FLINTSHIRE CH5 3XP. See also DSG Accountancy and Taxation Services Limited
•WHEATLEY, Mr. Christopher Robert Kelvin, BA FCA *1975;* (Tax Fac), W Accountancy Limited, 369 Hertford Road, ENFIELD, MIDDLESEX, EN3 5JW.
WHEATLEY, Mr. Christopher Seaward, MA MBA ACA MCT *1995;* 77a Lower Sloane Street, LONDON, SW1W 8DA.
WHEATLEY, Mr. Clive Anthony, FCA *1981;* 12 Trinity Court, Baker Crescent, DARTFORD, DA1 2NH.
WHEATLEY, Mr. David John, FCA *1968;* Russets, Hopgarden Lane, SEVENOAKS, KENT, TN13 1PX.
•WHEATLEY, Mr. David John, BSc FCA *1991;* (Tax Fac), Wheatley, 5 Robin Close, Huntington, CANNOCK, STAFFORDSHIRE, WS12 4PQ.
WHEATLEY, Mrs. Donna, BSc ACA *1990;* 42 Cranesbill Drive, BICESTER, OX26 3WQ.
•WHEATLEY, Mr. Gregory Francis Marius, BA FCA *1988;* Buzzacott LLP, 130 Wood Street, LONDON, EC2V 6DL.
WHEATLEY, Mr. James Martyn, BA ACA *1987;* D B Broadcast Ltd Unit 18 Sedgeway Business Park, Common Road Witchford, ELY, CAMBRIDGESHIRE, CB6 2HY.
WHEATLEY, Mrs. Joanne, BSc(Hons) ACA *2002;* 15 North Road, Ponteland, NEWCASTLE UPON TYNE, NE20 9UH.
•WHEATLEY, Mr. John Stefan, FCA *1974;* Price Pearson Wheatley, Clarendon House, 14 St Andrews Street, DROITWICH, WR9 8DY. See also AFH Price Pearson Wheatley Limited
WHEATLEY, Mr. Jonathan Douglas Varley, BA(Hons) ACA *2003;* Royal Bank of Scotland, 90-100 Southwark Street, LONDON, SE1 0SW.
WHEATLEY, Mrs. Justine Elizabeth, MA BA ACA *1988;* 19 Avenue Road, ABERGAVENNY, NP7 7DA.
WHEATLEY, Mr. Leslie Alan, BSc FCA *1977;* 2 Little Gayton Farm, Gayton Farm Road, WIRRAL, MERSEYSIDE, CH60 8NN.
WHEATLEY, Mr. Mark Richard, FCA *1971;* Ch Du Chauchey 6, 1185 Mont Sur Rolle, VAUD, SWITZERLAND.
WHEATLEY, Mr. Martin, BCom ACA *2010;* 12a Oakleigh Road, STOURBRIDGE, WEST MIDLANDS, DY8 2JX.
WHEATLEY, Mr. Matthew Lewis, ACA *2008;* Flat 19 Cranemead Court, 43 Whitton Road, TWICKENHAM, TW1 1BL.
WHEATLEY, Mr. Neil, ACA *1985;* 42 Cranesbill Drive, BICESTER, OX26 3WQ.
WHEATLEY, Mr. Nicholas Anthony William, FCA *1965;* The Old Rectory, Stubbs Lane, Kington St Michael, CHIPPENHAM, SN14 6HY. (Life Member)
WHEATLEY, Mr. Owen James, BSc(Econ) FCA *2000;* 9 Oatlands Close, Botley, SOUTHAMPTON, SO32 2DF.
WHEATLEY, Mr. Peter, BSc ACA *1989;* 28 Maitland Terrace, SEACLIFF, SA 5049, AUSTRALIA.
WHEATLEY, Mr. Philip Andrew John, BA ACA *2000;* 8 Florence Terrace, BRAY, COUNTY WICKLOW, IRELAND.
WHEATON, Mrs. Anne, FCA *1961;* Warrenside, Woodlands Road East, VIRGINIA WATER, GU25 4PH.
WHEATON, Mr. Anthony Peter, BSc FCA *1979;* 12 Ashchurch Grove, LONDON, W12 9BT.
WHEATON, Mr. Benjamin Christopher, BA ACA *1998;* Carrer de Balboa 2-4 3-1, 08003 BARCELONA, SPAIN.
WHEATON, Mr. Benjamin Eric, BA FCA *1987;* Level 8, 118 Queen Street, MELBOURNE, VIC 3000, AUSTRALIA.
WHEATON, Mrs. Claire Louise, MSc ACA *1999;* Jean Davenport Accountants The Old Emporium, Bow Street, LANGPORT, SOMERSET, TA10 9PQ.
WHEATON, Mr. Daniel, BA ACA *2004;* 27 Regent Drive, BILLERICAY, ESSEX, CM12 0GD.
WHEATON, Mrs. Diane Ruth, BEng *1994;* Town Farm, Hitchin Road, Weston, HITCHIN, HERTFORDSHIRE, SG4 7DB.
WHEATON, Mrs. Jacqueline Anne, BSc FCA CTA *1990;* (Tax Fac), 17 Laurel Avenue, POTTERS BAR, EN6 2AF.
WHEATON, Mr. James Gordon, BSc ACA *1989;* 12 Highfield Mews, Compayne Gardens, LONDON, NW6 3GB.
WHEATON, Mr. Michael Henry, FCA *1954;* Warrenside, Woodlands Road East, VIRGINIA WATER, GU25 4PH. (Life Member)
WHEATON, Mr. Tom, BSc ACA *2009;* 23 Ashchurch Grove, LONDON, W12 9BT.
WHEELDON, Mr. Jonathan Mark, BA ACA *1990;* MacMillan Publishers Ltd MacMillan Building, 4 Crinan Street, LONDON, N1 9XW.
WHEELDON, Mrs. Julie Ann, BA ACA *2005;* 34 Ashdown Drive, CRAWLEY, WEST SUSSEX, RH10 5HB.
WHEELDON, Mr. Norman, FCA *1958;* Kelston, 110 Mains Lane, POULTON-LE-FYLDE, LANCASHIRE, FY6 7LD. (Life Member)
WHEELDON, Mrs. Sally Ann, MA ACA ATII *2002;* Hilton Lodge, Hilton, DERBY, DE65 5FP.
WHEELDON, Mr. Terence Roland, FCA *1958;* Flat 1, 2 Norfolk Road, HARROGATE, NORTH YORKSHIRE, HG2 8DA. (Life Member)
WHEELER, Mrs. Alison, FCA *1992;* Monahans, 38/42 Newport Street, SWINDON, SN1 3DR.
WHEELER, Mr. Andrew James, BEng ACA *1997;* K P M G Salisbury Square House, 8 Salisbury Square, LONDON, EC4Y 8BB.
WHEELER, Mr. Andrew James, BSc ACA *1992;* 29 Oriental Road, ASCOT, BERKSHIRE, SL5 7AZ.
WHEELER, Mrs. Carole Anne, BA ACA *2006;* 2 Willow Tree Gardens, Burley-in-Wharfedale, ILKLEY, LS29 7RL.
•WHEELER, Mrs. Caroline Jane, ACA MAAT *1998;* (Tax Fac), Bevan & Buckland, Castle Chambers, 6 Westgate Hill, PEMBROKE, SA71 4LB.
WHEELER, Mr. Christopher James, BEng FCA *1995;* Pinsent Masons Llp, 30 Crown Place, LONDON, EC2A 4ES.
WHEELER, Mr. Christopher John, FCA *1977;* Mediobanca, 33 Grosvenor Place, LONDON, SW1X 7HY.
WHEELER, Mr. Christopher Lempriere, BSc FCA *1987;* Tower 42, 25 Old Broad Street, LONDON, EC2N 1PB.
WHEELER, Mr. Christopher Marc, BA ACA *2007;* 19 The Ridgeway, Lympne, HYTHE, CT21 4PW.
WHEELER, Mr. Christopher Paul, BSc ACA *1980;* 8 Greenbank Lane, COCKERMOUTH, CA13 9EF.
WHEELER, Mr. Christopher Paul, BA FCA *1986;* Standard Chartered, 1 Basinghall Avenue, LONDON, EC2V 5DD.
WHEELER, Miss. Claire, ACA *2011;* 172 Casterton Road, STAMFORD, LINCOLNSHIRE, PE9 2XX.
WHEELER, Mrs. Claire Joanne, BA(Hons) ACA *2000;* 90 Ella Road, West Bridgford, NOTTINGHAM, NG2 5GU.
WHEELER, Mr. Daniel, BSc ACA *2010;* 5 Staithes Close, YORK, YO26 5PR.
WHEELER, Mr. David, ACA *2009;* 23 Russet Close, BEDFORD, MK41 7GB.
WHEELER, Mr. David, FCA *1965;* Priest Cottage, Meshaw, SOUTH MOLTON, EX36 4NG. (Life Member)
WHEELER, Mr. David Andrew, BSc FCA *1975;* 24 rue de Martignac, 75007 PARIS, FRANCE.
WHEELER, Mr. David Giles Cole, FCA *1965;* 2404 Ritz Tower B, 6745 Ayala Avenue, MAKATI CITY 1224, PHILIPPINES.
WHEELER, Mr. David Kenneth Anthony, FCA *1964;* Apt 3, Park Tower, 15 Bridgeman Road, PENARTH, CF64 3AW. (Life Member)
•WHEELER, Mr. David Roger, BSc FCA *1975;* Bradford House, Bradford on Tone, TAUNTON, SOMERSET, TA4 1EY.
WHEELER, Mr. Derek George, MA ACA *1985;* The Croft, Haultwick, WARE, SG11 1JQ.
WHEELER, Mr. Duncan John, BSc ACA *2005;* Rouse & Co International, 11th Floor, Exchange Tower, 1 Harbour Exchange Square, LONDON, E14 9GE.
WHEELER, Mr. Glyn John, BA FCA *1982;* Chestnuts, 14 Newstead Avenue, Bushby, LEICESTER, LE7 9QE.
WHEELER, Mr. Ian, BA FCA *1979;* 7 Clumber Close, ASHBOURNE, DERBYSHIRE, DE6 1JZ.
WHEELER, Mr. James Vashon, BA ACA *1989;* Bitterley Court Bitterley, LUDLOW, SHROPSHIRE, SY8 3HL.
WHEELER, Mr. John Arthur, FCA *1968;* 10 The Hoskins, Station Road West, OXTED, SURREY, RH8 9EB.
•WHEELER, Mr. John Edward, FCA *1977;* (Tax Fac), J.E. Wheeler, The Barn, Duck End, Offord Road, Graveley, ST. NEOTS CAMBRIDGESHIRE PE19 6PP.
•WHEELER, Mr. John Richard, FCA CTA *1982;* (Tax Fac), J.W.C.A Ltd, 1 Victoria Road, EXMOUTH, DEVON, EX8 1DL.
WHEELER, Mr. John Tregarthen, FCA *1974;* E Oppenheimer & Son (Luxembourg), Boite Postale 459., L-2014 LUXEMBOURG, LUXEMBOURG.
WHEELER, Mr. Jonathan, BA ACA *2006;* Duck End Farmhouse, Offord Road, Graveley, ST. NEOTS, CAMBRIDGESHIRE, PE19 6PP.
WHEELER, Miss. Kate, MA BA ACA *2011;* Flat 16 Cordwainer House, 43 Mare Street, LONDON, E8 4RX.
WHEELER, Mr. Keith John, FCA *1975;* 493 Caledonian Road, LONDON, N7 9RN.
•WHEELER, Mr. Kevin, FCA *1984;* Wheeler & Co, The Shrubbery, 14 Church Street, WHITCHURCH, Hampshire, RG28 7AB.
WHEELER, Mr. Kevin Thomas, ACA *2009;* 31 Blandford Avenue, BECKENHAM, KENT, BR3 4QP.
WHEELER, Miss. Lois Elaine, BA ACA *1986;* AB Mauri (UK) Ltd, Sugar Way, PETERBOROUGH, PE2 9AY.
WHEELER, Miss. Louise Jane, ACA *2008;* 17B Midland Court, 58-62 Caine Road, MID LEVELS, HONG KONG ISLAND, HONG KONG SAR.
WHEELER, Mr. Malcolm Graham, FCA *1961;* The Birks, White Rose Lane, WOKING, GU22 7LP. (Life Member)
WHEELER, Mr. Michael, BCom FCA *1977;* 4 Holtwood Road Oxshott, LEATHERHEAD, SURREY, KT22 0QJ.
WHEELER, Mr. Michael Edward John, MA FCA *1986;* Redmayne-Bentley LLP, Merton House 84 Albion Street, LEEDS, LS1 6AG.
•WHEELER, Mr. Michael John, FCA *1961;* Michael Wheeler, 8 Hall Drive, Sydenham, LONDON, SE26 6XB.
WHEELER, Mr. Nicholas Derek, BA FCA *1964;* 217 Upper Grosvenor Road, TUNBRIDGE WELLS, KENT, TN1 2EG. (Life Member)
WHEELER, Mr. Paul, ACA *2008;* Pricewaterhousecoopers, 1 Embankment Place, LONDON, WC2N 6RH.
WHEELER, Mr. Paul Clifford, BA ACA *1992;* 90 Ella Road, West Bridgford, NOTTINGHAM, NG2 5GU.
WHEELER, Mrs. Pauline Lesley, BSc ACA *1992;* Ty Jwbal, Bwlch-y-Cibau, LLANFYLLIN, POWYS, SY22 5LL.
•WHEELER, Mr. Peter John, MA FCA *1973;* (Tax Fac), Wheeler & Co CA Ltd, 24 Dukes Wood Avenue, GERRARDS CROSS, BUCKINGHAMSHIRE, SL9 7JT.
WHEELER, Mr. Peter Kenneth, FCA *1962;* 12 Fairfield Avenue, Kirk Ella, HULL, HU10 7UH.
WHEELER, Mr. Ralph, BA FCA *1985;* Pine Tops, 2 Newick Avenue, Little Aston, SUTTON COLDFIELD, B74 3DA.
WHEELER, Miss. Rebecca Jane, BSc ACA *2008;* Molsons Coors Brewing Company (UK) Ltd, Carling House, 137 High Street, BURTON-ON-TRENT, STAFFORDSHIRE, DE14 1JZ.
WHEELER, Mr. Richard, MBiochem ACA *2011;* (Tax Fac), Flat 90, Park West, Edgware Road, LONDON, W2 2QJ.
WHEELER, Mr. Richard David Herbert, BCom FCA *1969;* 23 Longmeadow Gardens, Birdham, CHICHESTER, WEST SUSSEX, PO20 7HP.
WHEELER, Mr. Richard Simon, BSc CMath ACA *1993;* Glentor, 46 Casterton Road, STAMFORD, PE9 2YL.
WHEELER, Mr. Richard Thomas, FCA *1958;* with Cocke Vellacott & Hill, Unit 3, Dock Offices, Surrey Quays Road, Surrey Quays, LONDON SE16 2XU. (Life Member)
WHEELER, Mr. Robin Patrick, BCom FCA *1975;* Elm Cottage, Birchill, AXMINSTER, DEVON, EX13 7LB.
WHEELER, Mr. Ronald Dennis, FCA *1975;* Buzon 5604, Calle Asuan 7, 03724 MORAIRA, ALICANTE, SPAIN. (Life Member)
WHEELER, Miss. Sarah Louise, BSc ACA *2003;* 4 Calendar Mews, Electric Parade, SURBITON, KT6 5NY.
WHEELER, Mrs. Sian, BA ACA *1999;* 18 Pant y Rhedyn, Margam, PORT TALBOT, WEST GLAMORGAN, SA13 2SZ.
WHEELER, Mr. Simon Charles, BSc ACA *1993;* Flat 26, St. James Mansions, West End Lane, LONDON, NW6 2AA.
•WHEELER, Mrs. Sophie Elisabeth, MA ACA *1999;* Sophie Wheeler, Church Farm, Podington, WELLINGBOROUGH, NORTHAMPTONSHIRE, NN29 7HS.
WHEELER, Mr. Steven David, BSc ACA *1993;* Caterpillar UK Ltd, Peckleton Lane, LEICESTER, LE9 9JT.
WHEELER, Mr. Steven Mark, BA ACA *1989;* HSBC Holdings plc, Level 40 8 Canada Square, LONDON, E14 5HQ.
WHEELER, Miss. Zoe, ACA *2011;* Inshallah, Weatherhill Close, HORLEY, SURREY, RH6 9LU.
WHEELER-CHERRY, Miss. Gemma Marie, ACA *2008;* with Hextall Meakin Limited, Beckett House, 4 Bridge Street, SALISBURY, SP1 2LX.
WHEELER-JONES, Mrs. Helen Laura, ACA *2009;* 57 St. Ives Road, WIGSTON, LEICESTERSHIRE, LE18 2JB.
•WHEELHOUSE, Mr. Grenville, FCA *1976;* Grenville Wheelhouse, 14 Rochdale Road, Milnrow, ROCHDALE, OL16 3LN.
•WHEELHOUSE, Miss. Heather Jane, BSc ACA *1990;* Baker Tilly UK Audit LLP, Hartwell House, 55-61 Victoria Street, BRISTOL, BS1 6AD. See also Baker Tilly Tax and Advisory Services LLP
WHEELHOUSE, Mrs. Victoria Margaret, MSc ACA *2000;* 43 Wychwood Avenue, Knowle, SOLIHULL, B93 9DL.
WHELAN, Mr. Andrew David, ACA *2006;* with KPMG LLP, 1 The Embankment, Neville Street, LEEDS, LS1 4DW.
•①WHELAN, Mr. Andrew John, BSc FCA *1990;* Marks Bloom Limited, 60 Old London Road, KINGSTON UPON THAMES, SURREY, KT2 6QZ.

WHELAN, Mr. Anthony, BSc ACA *2010;* 13 Vereker Drive, SUNBURY-ON-THAMES, MIDDLESEX, TW16 6HQ.
WHELAN, Mrs. Catherine Louise, BA ACA *1997;* 2 Oaklands Grove, LONDON, W12 0JA.
WHELAN, Mrs. Dionne Terese, BSc ACA *1997;* The Grange, 8 Worrelle Avenue, Middleton, MILTON KEYNES, MK10 9GW.
WHELAN, Mrs. Fiona Helen, BA ACA *1990;* Internal Audit Dept, Trust HQ, North Manchester General Hospital, Delaunays Road, Crumpsall, MANCHESTER M8 5RB.
•WHELAN, Mr. Gordon Frederick, BSc ACA FCCA *2011;* Gordon Whelan Associates Limited, 130 Bournemouth Road, Chandler's Ford, EASTLEIGH, HAMPSHIRE, SO53 3AL.
WHELAN, Mr. Gregory John Andrew, BSc ACA *1985;* 1 Glendale Road, BURGESS HILL, RH15 0EJ.
WHELAN, Mr. Ian Simon, BA ACA *1992;* 7 Rowan Green, WEYBRIDGE, KT13 9NF.
•WHELAN, Mr. John Patrick, BCom FCA *1992;* (Tax Fac), 26 Lynton Park Road, Cheadle Hulme, CHEADLE, CHESHIRE, SK8 6JA.
•WHELAN, Mrs. Julia Alison, BA FCA *1999;* (Tax Fac), Curo Professional Services Limited, Curo House, Greenbox, Westonhall Road, Stoke Prior, BROMSGROVE WORCESTERSHIRE B60 4AL.
WHELAN, Mrs. Louise, BSc(Hons) ACA *2002;* 66 The Grove, WEST WICKHAM, KENT, BR4 9JT.
WHELAN, Mrs. Marianna Barbara, LLB(Hons) ACA *2009;* Pricewaterhousecoopers, Abacus House, Castle Park, CAMBRIDGE, CB3 0AN.
WHELAN, Mr. Mark Anthony, BSc ACA *1988;* K P M G, 1-2 Dorset Rise, LONDON, EC4Y 8EN.
WHELAN, Mr. Martin, BA ACA *2005;* 54 Carpenter Street, Brighton, MELBOURNE, VIC 3186, AUSTRALIA.
•WHELAN, Mr. Michael John, FCA *1964;* M.J. Whelan, 85 Lime Walk, Moulsham Lodge, CHELMSFORD, CM2 9NJ.
WHELAN, Mr. Michael Paul, ACA *1982;* 305 Seventh Avenue, 7th Floor, NEW YORK, NY 10061, UNITED STATES.
WHELAN, The Revd. Patricia Jean, FCA *1955;* 81 Cogges Hill Road, WITNEY, OX28 3XU. (Life Member)
•WHELAN, Mr. Paul Christopher, BSc FCA *1980;* AIMS - Paul Whelan FCA, Ashby House, Bernard Lane, Green Hammerton, YORK, YO26 8BP.
•WHELAN, Mr. Paul Edward, FCA *1977;* 5 Longheadland, Ombersley, DROITWICH, WORCESTERSHIRE, WR9 0JB.
WHELAN, Mr. Peter John, BSc ACA *1991;* N M Rothschild & Sons Ltd, New Court, St Swithins Lane, LONDON, EC4P 4DU.
WHELAN, Mr. Philip Scott, BA ACA *2003;* 11b Earlsfield Road, Wandsworth, LONDON, SW18 3DB.
WHELAN, Mr. Roger Joseph Martin, FCA *1977;* 8 Forester Road, BATH, BA2 6QF. (Life Member)
WHELAN, Miss. Sharon Jayne, BSc ACA *1997;* 13 St. Matthews Road, LONDON, W5 3JT.
WHELAN, Mr. Thomas Peter, BSc ACA *2008;* 17 Verdale Avenue, LEICESTER, LE4 9TH.
WHELAN, Mr. Timothy James, BSc ACA *2000;* 134 Manor Road North, THAMES DITTON, SURREY, KT7 0BH.
WHELAN, Mr. Timothy James, MA(Oxon) BA ACA *2011;* 19 Colmore Avenue, Bebington, WIRRAL, MERSEYSIDE, CH63 9NL.
WHELDON, Mr. Paul Wilfred, MA ACA *1984;* 124 Edgwarebury Lane, EDGWARE, MIDDLESEX, HA8 8NB.
•WHELDON, Mrs. Rachel, MBA FCA CTA *1994;* TCP (GB) Audit LLP, 10 The Triangle, ng 2 Business Park, NOTTINGHAM, NG2 1AE.
WHELDON, Mrs. Ruth Mary, BA(Hons) ACA *2002;* Cummins Turbo Technologies, St. Andrews Road, HUDDERSFIELD, HD1 6RA.
WHELDON, Miss. Sarah Jane, BSc(Hons) ACA *2003;* Building 66UF, Ricardo UK Ltd Shoreham Technical Centre, Old Shoreham Road, SHOREHAM-BY-SEA, WEST SUSSEX, BN43 5FG.
WHELLER, Mrs. Diane Ruth, BSc FCA *1993;* Toul-an-Ouch Chapel Hill, Uffculme, CULLOMPTON, DEVON, EX15 3AD.
WHELLER, Mr. Douglas Stewart, BSc ACA *2003;* 16 Lion Road, TWICKENHAM, TW1 4JF.
WHELLER, Mr. Kevin John, ACA *1992;* Toul-an-Ouch Chapel Hill, Uffculme, CULLOMPTON, DEVON, EX15 3AD.
WHELTON, Mr. Steven John, BA ACA *1990;* 45 St. James Road, SUTTON, SURREY, SM1 2TP.
WHENT, Mr. Peter Lewis, BSc ACA *1981;* Tudor Briars, St. Johns Road, FARNHAM, GU9 8NT.
WHENT, Mr. Stuart, BSocSc ACA *2002;* 17 Chippendayle Drive, Harrietsham, MAIDSTONE, ME17 1AD.
WHERITY, Mr. Paul, ACA *2008;* Pricewaterhousecoopers, 9 Greyfriars Road, READING, RG1 1JG.
WHERRY, Miss. Emma Louise, BA ACA *2010;* 23 Sherwood Road, BUXTON, DERBYSHIRE, SK17 9ER.
•WHERRY, Mr. Ian Stuart, BA FCA CF *1989;* Baker Tilly Tax and Advisory Services LLP, Charter House, The Square, Lower Bristol Road, BATH, BA2 3BH. See also Baker Tilly Corporate Finance LLP
WHERTON, Mr. David Ivor John, BSc ACA *2005;* 12 Bumblehole Meadows, Wombourne, WOLVERHAMPTON, WV5 8BG.
•WHERTON, Mr. Richard Ivor John, ACA *1980;* Crowe Clark Whitehill LLP, Black Country House, Rounds Green Road, OLDBURY, WEST MIDLANDS, B69 2DG. See also Horwath Clark Whitehill LLP and Crowe Clark Whitehill
WHETHERLY, Mr. Antony Arthur, BSc ACA *1982;* 65a Ox Lane, HARPENDEN, AL5 4PH.
WHETNALL, Mr. Walter Jared Jarvis, RD FCA *1950;* 55 Ennismore Road, Crosby, LIVERPOOL, L23 7UQ. (Life Member)
WHETSTONE, Ms. Henrietta Patricia Eve, BSc ACA *1994;* Headmasters House, Malthouse Lane, Hurstpierpoint, HASSOCKS, WEST SUSSEX, BN6 9JX.
•WHETSTONE, Mrs. Pamela Dorothy, FCA *1980;* with Hardcastle France, 30 Yorkersgate, MALTON, YO17 7AW.
WHETSTONE, Mr. Stephen, FCA *1974;* The Grange, 7 Lakeside Gardens, Strensall, YORK, YO32 5WB.
WHETSTONE, Mr. William Keith, BSc ACA *1980;* 116 St. Martins Road, COVENTRY, CV3 6ER.
WHETTON, Mr. Barry Newton, BA FCA *1970;* The Stables, 179 Woodford Road, Woodford, STOCKPORT, SK7 1QE.
WHEWAY, Mr. Richard Charles, MA FCA *1957;* East Wing, Claxton House, Claxton, YORK, YO60 7SD. (Life Member)
WHEWELL, Miss. Anne Michelle, BSc ACA *2004;* 91 Turnberry Drive, WILMSLOW, CHESHIRE, SK9 2QW.
WHEWELL, Mr. Bernard James, FCA *1971;* Mill Cottage, Stainton, KENDAL, LA8 0LH.
WHEWELL, Mr. David Williams, BA ACA *2006;* 194 Abbey Road, LEEDS, LS5 3NG.
WHIBLEY, Mr. Ben Paul, BSc(Hons) ACA *2010;* Apartment 18 Ansty Court, 26 Mary St, BIRMINGHAM, B3 1UD.
WHICHELOW, Mr. Roger Alfred, FCA *1961;* 1 Rudd Hall Rise, CAMBERLEY, GU15 2JZ. (Life Member)
WHICKER, Mr. Simon Lovell Clayton, BSc FCA *1990;* KPMG, P O Box 493 Century Yard, Cricket Square, GEORGE TOWN, GRAND CAYMAN, KY1-1106 CAYMAN ISLANDS. See also KPMG (BVI) Limited
WHIDDETT, Mr. Michael Douglas, FCA *1969;* Ashdene, Morleys Road, Sevenoaks Weald, SEVENOAKS, TN14 6QY.
WHIDDETT, Mr. Oliver, BSc(Hons) ACA *2002;* 42 Kingsway, WOKING, SURREY, GU21 6NT.
WHIDDON, Mr. Christopher John, BSc ACA *1999;* 14 Elvedon Road, FELTHAM, MIDDLESEX, TW13 4RP.
WHIFFEN, Miss. Lisa, BA ACA *1991;* Bounds Oast, Bounds Lane, Staple Street, Hernhill, FAVERSHAM, KENT ME13 9TX.
WHIFFIN, Mr. Charles Henry, BSc ACA *1980;* 2 Yellowcress Drive, Bisley, WOKING, GU24 9HD.
WHIFFIN, Mr. Roger Michael, FCA *1969;* 8 Clandon Road, GUILDFORD, GU1 2DR. (Life Member)
WHIFFIN, Mr. Simon Toby, ACA *2009;* McCormick (UK) Plc Haddenham Business Park, Pegasus Way Haddenham, AYLESBURY, BUCKINGHAMSHIRE, HP17 8LB.
WHIGHAM, Mr. David Ronald, FCA *1969;* Discove, BRUTON, BA10 0NF.
WHIGHT, Mr. Peter Anthony, BA FCA *1974;* 105 North Road, Three Bridges, CRAWLEY, RH10 1SQ. (Life Member)
WHILE, Mr. Peter Graham, FCA *1955;* 4 Albany Close, Poulton, POULTON-LE-FYLDE, FY6 8DT. (Life Member)
WHILEMAN, Mr. David Alan, BSc ACA *1997;* 3 I Group, 16 Palace Street, LONDON, SW1E 5JD.
WHILEY, Mr. Steven John, ACA *1994;* PO Box 2586, LONEHILL, GAUTENG, 2062, SOUTH AFRICA.
WHILEY, Mrs. Vivienne Elizabeth, BA FCA *1983;* (Tax Fac), with PricewaterhouseCoopers LLP, Benson House, 33 Wellington Street, LEEDS, LS1 4JP.
WHILLANS, Mr. David Bowie, BSc ACA *1986;* The Old Vicarage, Church Lane, Ewshot, FARNHAM, GU10 5BD.
WHIMPENNY, Mr. Dominic James, BA(Hons) ACA *2010;* Palamon Capital Partner, Cleveland House, 33 King Street, LONDON, SW1Y 6RJ.
WHIMPERLEY-DIXON, Mrs. Elizabeth Ellen Rebecca, BSc ACA *2005;* 28 Lind Street, LONDON, SE8 4JE.
WHIMSTER, Mr. Angus James Lewis, FCA *1968;* 47 St. Nicholas Crescent, Pyrford, WOKING, SURREY, GU22 8TD.
WHIMSTER, Miss. Mary Isobel, ACA *1978;* Newlands Wycombe Road, Stokenchurch, HIGH WYCOMBE, BUCKINGHAMSHIRE, HP14 3RP.
WHINCUP, Mr. Brian, FCA *1971;* 214 Pilton Vale, Malpas, NEWPORT, GWENT, NP20 6LN.
WHINDER, Miss. Gemma, BA ACA *2005;* 307 Cavendish Road, LONDON, SW12 0PQ.
WHINES, Mr. Neil Andrew, BSc ACA *1981;* Springfield, Mountfield, ROBERTSBRIDGE, EAST SUSSEX, TN32 5LY.
WHINNEY, Mr. Anthony Mark Carnac, BEng ACA *1992;* 96 Balham Park Road, LONDON, SW12 8EA.
WHINNEY, Mr. Frederick John Golden, FCA *1960;* Shrublands, Butts Green Road, Sandon, CHELMSFORD, CM2 7RN. (Life Member)
WHINNEY, Mr. John Anthony Perrot, FCA *1956;* (Member of Council 1974 - 1987), 46 Homewood Road, ST. ALBANS, HERTFORDSHIRE, AL1 4BQ. (Life Member)
WHINNEY, Mrs. Karen Lesley, BA ACA AMCT *1996;* 22 Church Street, Great Gransden, SANDY, CAMBRIDGESHIRE, SG19 3AF.
WHINYATES, Mr. David Paul, FCA *1977;* 50 Elm Grove, Woburn Sands, MILTON KEYNES, MK17 8PS.
WHIPP, Mr. Colin Peter, FCA *1976;* Manor Barn, North Road, Chesham Bois, AMERSHAM, BUCKINGHAMSHIRE, HP6 5NA.
WHIPP, Mr. Edward Thomas, BSc ACA *2004;* Barony Trust Ltd, 7 Athol Street Douglas, ISLE OF MAN, IM1 1LD.
•WHIPP, Mr. Peter Thomas, BSc FCA *1975;* 7 Athol Street, Douglas, ISLE OF MAN, IM1 1LD.
WHIPP, Mr. Richard Anthony, BA FCA *1978;* Langdale, Lightowlers Lane, LITTLEBOROUGH, OL15 0LN.
WHIPP, Mr. Stephen John, BA ACA *1993;* 45 Teil Green, Fulwood, PRESTON, PR2 9PA.
WHIPP, Mr. Stuart Keith, MA ACA *1996;* 65 Littlewood Street, HAMPTON, VIC 3188, AUSTRALIA.
WHISKER, Mr. Jonathan Barclay, LLB ACA *1992;* 8 Shummard Close, Shiney Row, HOUGHTON LE SPRING, TYNE AND WEAR, DH4 7TP.
WHISTLER, Mr. Christopher Claude Lashmer, BA ACA *1983;* 16 King Edwards Grove, TEDDINGTON, TW11 9LU.
WHISTLER, Mr. David Geoffrey, BSc ACA *1983;* 4 Denver Road, Mickleover, DERBY, DE3 0PS.
WHISTLER, Mr. Harold Lawrence, BSc ACA *1995;* Champ Corboz, 1090 Route Bellevue, 01280 PREVESSIN MOENS, FRANCE.
WHISTON, Mrs. Carol Lorna, BSc ACA *1987;* 35 Tarragon Drive, Meir Park, STOKE-ON-TRENT, ST3 7YE.
WHISTON, Mr. Timothy Andrew, BSc ACA *1994;* Booths Hill Farm, Booths Lane, LYMM, WA13 0PF.
WHITAKER, Mr. Adrian Paul, BSc ACA *1995;* 3 Barcroft Flatt, BARNSLEY, S75 1HY.
WHITAKER, Miss. Anne, MA ACA *1983;* 36 St. Oswalds Place, LONDON, SE11 5JE.
WHITAKER, Mr. David Arthur, FCA *1973;* 133 Luscinia View, Napier Road, Reading, READING, RG1 8AF.
WHITAKER, Mr. David William, FCA *1969;* The Conifers, 14 Vine Close, Clifton, BRIGHOUSE, HD6 4JS.
WHITAKER, Miss. Emma, BSc ACA *2006;* 59 Avondale, Ash Vale, ALDERSHOT, HAMPSHIRE, GU12 5NE.
WHITAKER, Mr. Jack McDonald, FCA FCMA *1963;* 16 Broadmead Road, WOODFORD GREEN, IG8 0AY.
WHITAKER, Mrs. Jacqueline, BSc ACA *1993;* 19/4-8 Edgecumbe Avenue, COOGEE, NSW 2034, AUSTRALIA.
WHITAKER, Miss. Jill Suzanne, BA ACA *1999;* 7 Lindenfield, CHISLEHURST, KENT, BR7 5RG.
•WHITAKER, Mr. John Barry, BTech FCA *1972;* (Tax Fac), Long & Co, PO Box 109, BINGLEY, BD16 1ZQ.
WHITAKER, Sir John James Ingham, BSc FCA *1977;* Tiln Farms Ltd, Babworth Hall, RETFORD, DN22 8EP.
WHITAKER, Mrs. Kathryn Helen, BA ACA *1998;* Wyke Farm, Wyke, AXMINSTER, DEVON, EX13 8TN.
WHITAKER, Miss. Kerry, ACA *2011;* 1 Maltkiln Lane, Elsham, BRIGG, SOUTH HUMBERSIDE, DN20 0RL.
•WHITAKER, Mr. Nick Moule, MA FCA *1976;* PKF (UK) LLP, Farringdon Place, 20 Farringdon Road, LONDON, EC1M 3AP.
WHITAKER, Mrs. Patricia Rose, FCA *1954;* 23 Charnhill Brow, Mangotsfield, BRISTOL, BS16 9JW. (Life Member)
WHITAKER, Mr. Robert Geoffrey, BSc(Econ) ACA *1980;* Redgates, 10 Lower Radley, ABINGDON, OXFORDSHIRE, OX14 3AX.
WHITAKER, Mr. Robert Kidd, BSc(Hons) ACA *2001;* 6 Glebe Field Croft, WETHERBY, LS22 6WQ.
WHITAKER, Miss. Sarah, BSc ACA *2011;* 25 Aspenwood Drive, Chadderton, OLDHAM, OL9 9UP.
WHITAKER, Miss. Sheryl Diane, BSc ACA *1991;* 42 Standbridge Close, WAKEFIELD, WF2 7NU.
WHITAKER, Mr. Simon, BSc ACA *2002;* PO Box 54163, Adliya Post Office, MANAMA, 54163, BAHRAIN.
WHITAKER, Miss. Sophie Brigitte, BSc ACA *1995;* 12 Cynthia Road, BATH, BA2 3QH.
•WHITAKER, Mr. Stephen G, MEng CA ACA CTA *2008;* SGW & Co, Fairfields, 39 Main Street, Bunny, NOTTINGHAM, NG11 6QU.
WHITAKER, Mr. Steven, BA ACA *1995;* 74a Ember Lane, ESHER, KT10 8EN.
WHITAKER, Mrs. Tamsin Emma, BSc ACA *2003;* 18 Penyston Road, MAIDENHEAD, BERKSHIRE, SL6 6EH.
WHITAKER, Mr. Tara Lawrence, BA ACA *2007;* with KPMG LLP, 15 Canada Square, LONDON, E14 5GL.
•WHITBREAD, Mr. Francis Victor, ACA CTA *1980;* Edmund Carr LLP, 146 New London Road, CHELMSFORD, CM2 0AW. See also EC (Management Services) Ltd
WHITBREAD, Mr. Kevin Richard, BSc ACA *1979;* 32 Crowthorne Road, Sandhurst, SANDHURST, GU47 9EP.
WHITBREAD, Mr. Neville Anthony Leonard, FCA *1965;* Lower Huxley Hall Mill Lane, Hargrave, CHESTER, CH3 7RQ. (Life Member)
WHITBREAD, Mr. Roger Charles, FCA *1958;* 37 Harrington Drive, BEDFORD, MK41 8DB. (Life Member)
WHITBURN, Mrs. Louise, BSc ACA *1996;* (Tax Fac), 47 Route de Saint-Georges, 1213 PETIT LANCY, SWITZERLAND.
WHITBY, Mr. Daniel Stephen, BA ACA *2004;* Pear Tree Cottage, 25 Gibson Lane, Haddenham, AYLESBURY, BUCKINGHAMSHIRE, HP17 8AP.
WHITBY, Mr. David Victor, FCA *1970;* Rue de la Jonchaie 23, Bte 18, 1040 BRUSSELS, BELGIUM.
WHITBY, Mr. Dennis Victor, FCA *1951;* 32 Rackham Road, WORTHING, WEST SUSSEX, BN13 1LL. (Life Member)
WHITBY, Mr. James Robert, BSc ACA *2006;* Greenergy International Ltd, 198 High Holborn, LONDON, WC1V 7BD.
WHITBY, Mrs. Layla, BA ACA *2004;* Fuller Smith & Turner Plc Griffin Brewery, Chiswick Lane South, LONDON, W4 2QB.
•WHITBY, Mr. Paul William, FCA *1973;* 70 Windermere Cresent, Derriford, PLYMOUTH, PL6 5HX.
WHITBY, Mr. Peter Benjamin, BA FCA *1985;* 35 Brancaster Lane, PURLEY, CR8 1HJ.
WHITBY, Mr. Richard James, BSc ACA *2005;* D E Beers UK Ltd, 17 Charterhouse Street, LONDON, EC1N 6RA.
WHITBY, Mr. Stafford Paul, BSc ACA *1994;* 70 Kingswood Firs, Grayshott, HINDHEAD, GU26 6ER.
WHITBY, Miss. Victoria, BA ACA *2006;* Level 2, Darling Park Tower 1, 201 Sussex Street, SYDNEY, NSW 2000, AUSTRALIA.
WHITBY-SMITH, Mrs. Maryna, ACA *2003;* 16 The Close, SEVENOAKS, TN13 2HE.
WHITBY-SMITH, Mr. Robert James, BA ACA *2001;* 16 The Close, SEVENOAKS, TN13 2HE.
•WHITBY-SMITH, Mr. Scott John, BSc FCA *1975;* PRWS (Bristol) Limited, 53 High Street, Keynsham, BRISTOL, BS31 1DS. See also Richardson Whitby Smith Limited
WHITCHER, Mrs. Alexandra Laura, ACA *2007;* 77 Glebe Crescent, Broomfield, CHELMSFORD, CM1 7BH.
WHITCHER, Mr. Steven Andrew, BA ACA *1991;* Loreto, 28 Horley Row, HORLEY, SURREY, RH6 8NH.
WHITCHURCH, Mr. Christopher James, ACA ACIS *2004;* Apartment 12 Marina Court Glategny Esplanade St. Peter Port, GUERNSEY, GY1 1WP.
WHITCOMB, Mr. Brian John, FCA *1971;* 29 Seaforth Road, WESTCLIFF-ON-SEA, ESSEX, SS0 7SN.
WHITCOMB, Mr. John Michael, BSc FCA *1979;* C/O CLP Holdings Limited, Group Internal Audit Department, 3/F Shamshuipo Centre, 215 Fuk Wa Street, SHAM SHUI PO, KOWLOON HONG KONG SAR.
WHITCOMBE, Mr. Barry, FCA *1967;* 12 Vaughan Avenue, GRIMSBY, SOUTH HUMBERSIDE, DN32 8QE.

•ⓘ**WHITCOMBE, Miss. Clare Louise, ACA** *1996;* 24 Mimosa Drive, Shinfield, READING, RG2 9AQ.

WHITCOMBE, Mr. Paul Jeffrey, BSc ACA *1996;* (Tax Fac), Holly Cottage, 212 Everton Road, Hordle, LYMINGTON, HAMPSHIRE, SO41 0HE.

WHITE, Mr. Adrian, MA ACA CFA *1995;* Franklin Templeton Investments, 5 Morrison Street, EDINBURGH, EH3 8BH.

WHITE, Mr. Adrian Michael, FCA *1970;* 37 Ranelagh House, Elystan Place, LONDON, SW3 3LD.

WHITE, Mr. Adrian Philip, MA FCA *1973;* 51 Wincanton Road, LONDON, SW18 5TZ.

WHITE, Mr. Adrian Richard Dowding, ACA *1978;* 5 Weiss Road, Putney, LONDON, SW15 1DH.

WHITE, Mr. Adrian Tancred, FCA *1964;* Farnborough Downs Farm, Farnbourough, WANTAGE, OX12 8NW.

WHITE, Mr. Alan, LLB FCA *1979;* Whirley House Wrigley Lane, Over Alderley, MACCLESFIELD, CHESHIRE, SK10 4RP.

WHITE, Mr. Alan Mark, MA ACA *1995;* 6 Deerhurst Road, Streatham Wells, LONDON, SW16 2AN.

WHITE, Dr. Alastair Ian, PhD MA ACA *1981;* 71 Evans Road, Eynsham, WITNEY, OXFORDSHIRE, OX29 4QX.

•**WHITE, Mr. Alexander Charles, BA ACA** *1996;* BDO LLP, 55 Baker Street, LONDON, W1U 7EU. See also BDO Stoy Hayward LLP

•**WHITE, Mr. Alfred Andrew, MA FCA** *1978;* (Tax Fac), Carter Backer Winter LLP, Enterprise House, 21 Buckle Street, LONDON, E1 8NN.

•**WHITE, Mrs. Alison Barbara, BA FCA** *1993;* Alison White FCA, Combe Cottage, Stortford Road, Leaden Roding, DUNMOW, ESSEX CM6 1RB.

WHITE, Miss. Alison Bernadette, BSc FCA *1992;* Greensview Cottage, Prestwood Drive, Stourton, STOURBRIDGE, DY7 5QT.

WHITE, Miss. Alison May, ACA *2009;* 41 Brookfield Avenue, Timperley, ALTRINCHAM, CHESHIRE, WA15 6TH.

WHITE, Ms. Andrea Christine, ACA *1989;* Unit 34, First Avenue, Westfield Industrial Estate, Midsomer Norton, RADSTOCK, BA3 4BS.

WHITE, Mr. Andrew Brian, BA ACA *1995;* 116c Church Side, EPSOM, KT18 7SY.

WHITE, Mr. Andrew Douglas, FCA *1973;* Bridgwater Holdings Ltd Hamilton House, 39 Kings Road, HASLEMERE, GU27 2QA.

WHITE, Mr. Andrew Gerard, BSc ACA MABRP *1991;* with PricewaterhouseCoopers LLP, Pricewaterhousecoopers, 12 Plumtree Court, LONDON, EC4A 4HT.

WHITE, Mr. Andrew Gwynne Haydon, ACA *1986;* Solo Estates Ltd, Wormstall, Wickham, NEWBURY, BERKSHIRE, RG20 8HB.

WHITE, Mr. Andrew James, BA ACA *1995;* Virgin Mobile Ltd, Willow Grove House, White Horse Business Park, TROWBRIDGE, WILTSHIRE, BA14 0TQ.

WHITE, Mr. Andrew John, BSc ACA *2003;* 2 Aylmer Avenue, Gibraltar Road, SKEGNESS, LINCOLNSHIRE, PE24 4ST.

WHITE, Mr. Andrew John, BA ACA *2002;* K P M G, 100 Temple Street, BRISTOL, BS1 6AG.

WHITE, Mr. Andrew John, FCA MInstD *1970;* Jaegerstrasse 35, 10117 BERLIN, GERMANY.

WHITE, Mr. Andrew John Dean, BSc ACA *1990;* 39 Derwent Crescent, Titirangi, AUCKLAND, NEW ZEALAND.

WHITE, Mr. Andrew Mark, BA ACA *1994;* 17 Sandown Drive, SALE, CHESHIRE, M33 4PF.

WHITE, Mr. Andrew Morgan, BA ACA *1997;* 18 Damaskfield, WORCESTER, WR4 0HY.

WHITE, Dr. Anna Kathryn, PhD BA ACA *2001;* 23 Sutton Close, Milton, CAMBRIDGE, CB24 6DU.

WHITE, Mr. Anthony Alexander Harris, FCA *1964;* Windskip, Clappers Lane, Earnley, CHICHESTER, PO20 7JJ. (Life Member)

WHITE, Mr. Anthony Charles, ACA *1989;* Suite 2006, 20th floor, 340 Queen's Road, CENTRAL, HONG KONG ISLAND, HONG KONG SAR.

•**WHITE, Mr. Barry Howard, BSc FCA** *1970;* B H White & Co, 51 Fordington Road, Highgate, LONDON, N6 4TH.

WHITE, Mr. Barry Norris, FCA *1972;* 66 Cradle Bridge Drive, Willesborough, ASHFORD, Kent, TN24 0RF. (Life Member)

WHITE, Mr. Benjamin, BSc ACA *1999;* Anvil Cottage The Row, Redlynch, SALISBURY, SP5 2JT.

WHITE, Mr. Benjamin Michael, BA ACA *2005;* 19 Sandrock Hill Road, FARNHAM, SURREY, GU10 4NR.

•**WHITE, Mr. Benjamin Peter, ACA** *2008;* (Tax Fac), White & Company (UK) Limited, 6th Floor, Blackfriars House, Parsonage, MANCHESTER, M3 2JA.

WHITE, Mr. Bernard John, BA ACA *1988;* 6 Ledgers Meadow, Cuckfield, HAYWARDS HEATH, RH17 5EW.

WHITE, Mr. Bernard William, FCA *1971;* 40 Sanderstead Hill, Sanderstead, SOUTH CROYDON, SURREY, CR2 0HA.

WHITE, Mr. Brian, FCA *1951;* The Bungalow, Greenbank Farm, Grindleton, CLITHEROE, BB7 4QJ. (Life Member)

WHITE, Mr. Brian George, MA FCA JDipMA *1962;* 59 Saunders Way, Derwen Fawr, SWANSEA, SA2 8BA.

•**WHITE, Mr. Brian Harold, BSc ACA** *1991;* The Steading, Barkham, WOKINGHAM, RG41 4TL. See also Deloitte & Touche LLP

•**WHITE, Mr. Brian Jonathan, BA(Econ) FCA** *1988;* Deloitte LLP, PO Box 500, 2 Hardman Street, MANCHESTER, M60 2AT. See also Deloitte & Touche LLP

WHITE, Mr. Cameron Graham, BSc ACA *1992;* 12 Crossways, HINCKLEY, LE10 2HY.

•**WHITE, Mrs. Caroline, ACA** *2004;* Gatley Read, Prince of Wales House, 18/19 Salmon Fields Business Village, Royton, OLDHAM, OL2 6HT.

WHITE, Mrs. Caroline Louise Lewis, ACA *2002;* 40 Heol Erwin, Rhiwbina, CARDIFF, CF14 6QR.

•**WHITE, Mrs. Catherine Mary, BSc ACA** *1999;* Johnson White Accounting Ltd, 7 Highcliffe Close, Woodley, READING, BERKSHIRE, RG5 4RE.

WHITE, Miss. Catherine Mary, BSc ACA *1997;* 28 Titchfield Close, TADLEY, RG26 3UF.

WHITE, Mrs. Catherine Victoria Benedicte, MA ACA *2007;* 3 George Street, CAMBRIDGE, CB4 1AL.

WHITE, Mrs. Catriona Mary, BA ACA *1992;* Glenville, Ethorpe Close, GERRARDS CROSS, SL9 8PL.

WHITE, Mr. Charles Arthur Durham, FCA *1952;* 10a Canford Crescent, POOLE, DORSET, BH13 7ND. (Life Member)

WHITE, Mr. Chris, ACA *2009;* Cliffside, North Foreland Avenue, BROADSTAIRS, KENT, CT10 3QR.

WHITE, Mrs. Christina, ACA *1994;* 88 Dugdale Hill Lane, POTTERS BAR, HERTFORDSHIRE, EN6 2DL.

WHITE, Mrs. Christine, BA ACA *1996;* Institute of Grocery Distribution Grange Lane, Letchmore Heath, WATFORD, WD25 8GD.

WHITE, Mr. Christopher, BA FCA *1981;* 24 Greendale Road, ATHERSTONE, WARWICKSHIRE, CV9 1EG.

WHITE, Mr. Christopher, BSc(Hons) ACA *2011;* 57 Mallard Road, ABBOTS LANGLEY, HERTFORDSHIRE, WD5 0GF.

WHITE, Dr. Christopher Ben, BSc(Hons) ACA *2010;* Leafield, The Grove, ROWLANDS GILL, TYNE AND WEAR, NE39 1PN.

WHITE, Mr. Christopher Duncan, MBA BA ACA *1992;* 1 Copley Court, BRISTOL, BS15 3SH.

WHITE, Mr. Christopher James, MA ACA *1985;* 17 Cunningham Avenue, ST. ALBANS, HERTFORDSHIRE, AL1 1JJ.

WHITE, Mr. Christopher James, ACA *1993;* Woodside, Birchwood Lane, Chaldon, CATERHAM, SURREY, CR3 5DQ.

WHITE, Mr. Christopher John, ACA *2008;* 24 Prince of Wales Drive, LONDON, SW11 4SF.

WHITE, Mr. Christopher John Anthony, FCA *1970;* 2 Sunbeam Drive, Sunny Hills Subdivision, Talamban, CEBU CITY 6000, CEBU, PHILIPPINES.

•**WHITE, Mr. Christopher Michael, BSc ACA MABRP** *1999;* The P&A Partnership, 93 Queen Street, SHEFFIELD, S1 1WF.

WHITE, Mr. Christopher Peter Albert, BA FCA *1964;* c/o British High Commission, BANJUL, GAMBIA.

WHITE, Miss. Claire Joyce, BSc(Hons) ACA *2004;* No. 3 Maison de Derriere, Rue Des Friquettes, St. Saviour, JERSEY, JE2 7UF.

WHITE, Miss. Clare Alison, BSc ACA *2010;* 12 Radipole Road, LONDON, SW6 5DL.

WHITE, Mrs. Clare Anne, MA ACA *1990;* Knockbuckle House, BRIDGE OF WEIR, RENFREWSHIRE, PA11 3SJ.

WHITE, Ms. Clare Helen, ACA MSI *2001;* 13 Hazelhurst, BECKENHAM, KENT, BR3 5TL.

WHITE, Mrs. Clare Louise, BSc(Hons) ACA CTA *2000;* 10 Meaux Road, Wawne, HULL, HU7 5XD.

WHITE, Mr. Cliff Paul, BSc ACA *1996;* 32 Avenell Road, Highbury, LONDON, N5 1DP.

WHITE, Mr. Colin Andrew Holford, BA FCA *1968;* 89 Rue Basse, 1180 BRUSSELS, BELGIUM.

WHITE, Mr. Colin Meadows, BA ACA *1988;* 15 The Acres, Barrow, CLITHEROE, BB7 9BH.

WHITE, Mr. Colin Richard, BA ACA *1992;* 6 Honey Hill, Emberton, OLNEY, BUCKINGHAMSHIRE, MK46 5LT.

WHITE, Mr. Crispin Luke, BA ACA *1990;* Via Kennedy 3, 20090 RODANO, ITALY.

WHITE, Mr. Daniel, ACA *2009;* with Haines Watts, Sterling House, 177-181 Farnham Road, SLOUGH, BERKSHIRE, SL1 4XP.

WHITE, Mr. Daniel Benyon, TD MA ACA *2001;* 11 Baring Road, BEACONSFIELD, BUCKINGHAMSHIRE, HP9 2NB.

WHITE, Mr. Daniel Clifford, MPhys ACA *2008;* Ground Floor Flat, 6 Dynham Road, LONDON, NW6 2NR.

WHITE, Mr. Darryl Scott, BEng ACA *2010;* 31 Rushton Road, STOCKPORT, CHESHIRE, SK3 0UR.

WHITE, Mr. David, ACA *2008;* with Ernst & Young LLP, 400 Capability Green, LUTON, LU1 3LU.

WHITE, Mr. David, FCA *1973;* Thornymoor Mogador, Lower Kingswood, TADWORTH, SURREY, KT20 7HL.

WHITE, Mr. David, BA ACA *1984;* 8 Oaklands Road, SUTTON COLDFIELD, B74 2TB.

WHITE, Mr. David Allan, FCA *1952;* 17 Merchant Way, NORWICH, NR6 5HS. (Life Member)

WHITE, Mr. David Andrew, MA ACA *1998;* Aggreko Middle East Limited, JEBEL ALI, PO16875, UNITED ARAB EMIRATES.

•**WHITE, Mr. David Brandon, FCA** *1957;* David White & Co, Karen76 Dagoretti Road, P.O. Box 24911 NAIROBI, 00502, KENYA.

WHITE, Mr. David Douglas Percival, BSc ACA *1981;* 1 Dukes Wood Avenue, GERRARDS CROSS, BUCKINGHAMSHIRE, SL9 7JX.

WHITE, Mr. David Edward, BEng ACA *1999;* Activision, 3 Roundwood Avenue Stockley Park, UXBRIDGE, MIDDLESEX, UB11 1AF.

WHITE, Mr. David John, BSc ACA *2000;* Flat 2, 6 Barton Road, WIRRAL, MERSEYSIDE, CH47 1HH.

•**WHITE, Mr. David John, BA FCA** *1981;* with Xchange Group, Dairy House Farm, Bristol Road, WELLS, SOMERSET, BA5 3AA.

WHITE, Mr. David John, FCA *1963;* 17 Surrey Street, LOWESTOFT, SUFFOLK, NR32 1LW.

WHITE, Mr. David Julian, BSc ACA *1987;* 29 Avalon Road, Earley, READING, RG6 7NS.

•**WHITE, Mr. David Paul, BA FCA** *1992;* Grant Thornton UK LLP, Enterprise House, 115 Edmund Street, BIRMINGHAM, B3 2HJ. See also Grant Thornton LLP

WHITE, Mr. David Paul, MA FCA *2001;* with Ernst & Young LLP, 1 Bridgewater Place, Water Lane, LEEDS, LS11 5QR.

WHITE, Mr. David Richard, BSc ACA *2007;* Flat 18 Quennel House, Weir Road, LONDON, SW12 0NQ.

WHITE, Mr. David Robert, BA ACA *2003;* Unit 6 101A St Georges Crescent Drummoyne, SYDNEY, NSW 2047, AUSTRALIA.

WHITE, Mr. David York, FCA *1959;* 3 Priory Court, Fairmount Road, BEXHILL-ON-SEA, TN40 2HW.

WHITE, Mr. Dean James, BA(Hons) ACA *2002;* Bendalls Engineering Brunthill Road, Kingstown Industrial Estate, CARLISLE, CA3 0EH.

WHITE, Mrs. Debbie Jayne, MA ACA *1987;* Sodexo Inc, 9801 Washingtonian Boulevard, GAITHERSBURG, MD 20878, UNITED STATES.

WHITE, Mr. Duncan Alex, BSc ACA *1996;* 27 Oldfield Road, LONDON, N16 0RR.

WHITE, Mr. Edward, FCA *1965;* 3 College Street, BURY ST. EDMUNDS, SUFFOLK, IP33 1NH. (Life Member)

WHITE, Mr. Edward Christopher, BSc ACA *2002;* 1 Greenham Walk, WOKING, SURREY, GU21 3HB.

WHITE, Mr. Edward George, FCA *1953;* 13 Morris Lane, BATH, BA1 7PP. (Life Member)

WHITE, Mrs. Edwina Susan, ACA *1984;* 56 Downview Road, Yapton, ARUNDEL, BN18 0HJ.

WHITE, Miss. Elizabeth, BA ACA *2011;* 14b Eckstein Road, LONDON, SW11 1QF.

WHITE, Ms. Elizabeth Ann, BA(Hons) ACA *2004;* 2 Powell Gardens, REDHILL, RH1 1TQ.

WHITE, Miss. Emma Jane, BA(Hons) ACA *2010;* Flat 51, Lowry House, Cassilis Road, LONDON, E14 9LL.

•**WHITE, Mrs. Emma Louise, ACA MAAT** *2007;* with A4G Audit Limited, Kings Lodge, London Road, West Kingsdown, SEVENOAKS, TN15 6AR.

•**WHITE, Mrs. Emma Sarah, BA ACA** *2003;* White & Company (UK) Limited, 6th Floor, Blackfriars House, Parsonage, MANCHESTER, M3 2JA.

•**WHITE, Mrs. Esther Mary, ACA** *1996;* (Tax Fac), Pickled Parsnip Limited, 236 Henleaze Road, Henleaze, BRISTOL, BS9 4NG. See also Esther White

WHITE, Miss. Faye Elizabeth, ACA *2011;* Flat 4, 22 Comeragh Road, LONDON, W14 9HP.

WHITE, Mr. Fraser Charles, BSc ACA *1996;* Flat 2 St. Andrews House, Oakley Road, CHINNOR, OXFORDSHIRE, OX39 4ET.

WHITE, Mr. Fraser Ian Duncan, BSc FCA *1990;* Castle Keep Lodge Road, Sharnbrook, BEDFORD, MK44 1JP.

•**WHITE, Mr. Gareth Robin, FCA** *1977;* Deloitte Touche Tohmatsu, 30th Floor, Bund Centre, 222 Yan An Road East, SHANGHAI 20002, CHINA.

WHITE, Mr. Garry, BSc FCA *1970;* Garry White & Co, 24 James Street, EBBW VALE, GWENT, NP23 6JG.

WHITE, Mr. Garvin Alan, ACA *1992;* 80 Kinross Crescent, East Cosham, PORTSMOUTH, PO6 2NS.

WHITE, Mr. Gary Charles, BA ACA *1987;* Bauer Media, 189 Shaftesbury Avenue, LONDON, WC2H 8JR.

WHITE, Mr. Gavin Paul, MSc ACA *1997;* Birch Cottage Holt Road Little Horkesley, COLCHESTER, CO6 4DR.

•**WHITE, Mr. Geoff, FCA** *1969;* Ryecroft Glenton, 32 Portland Terrace, Jesmond, NEWCASTLE UPON TYNE, NE2 1QP.

WHITE, Mr. Geoff James, BA ACA *2007;* 7 Allestree Road, LONDON, SW6 6AD.

WHITE, Mr. Geoffrey Charles, FCA *1976;* Derwent Lodge, South Town, DARTMOUTH, DEVON, TQ6 9BU.

WHITE, Mr. Geoffrey David, FCA *1957;* 19 Lisburne Place, Lisburne Square, TORQUAY, TQ1 2PS. (Life Member)

WHITE, Mr. Geoffrey Ralph, FCA FCMA *1975;* 113 Main Street, Swithland, LOUGHBOROUGH, LEICESTERSHIRE, LE12 8TQ.

WHITE, Mr. George William Albert, DFC FCA *1959;* 54B Penny Street, PORTSMOUTH, PO1 2NL. (Life Member)

WHITE, Mr. George William Charles, FCA *1947;* 4 Hazlemere View, Hazlemere, HIGH WYCOMBE, BUCKINGHAMSHIRE, HP15 7BY. (Life Member)

•**WHITE, Mrs. Geraldine Patricia, BA ACA** *1990;* JFM Growing Business Solutions Limited, 38 Triscombe Drive, CARDIFF, SOUTH GLAMORGAN, CF5 2PN. See also Morris White Limited

WHITE, Mr. Graham Mcgillivray, FCA *1975;* (Tax Fac), 10 Belwood Road, Milton Bridge, PENICUIK, EH26 0QN.

WHITE, Mr. Graham Paul, BSc ACA MBA *1998;* with Allied Bakeries, 1 Kingsmill Place, Vanwall Road, MAIDENHEAD, BERKSHIRE, SL6 4UF.

WHITE, Mr. Graham Roger, BSc ACA *1991;* with Healthcare at Home Ltd, Fifth Avenue, Centrum 100, BURTON-ON-TRENT, STAFFORDSHIRE, DE14 2WS.

WHITE, Mr. Grenville Claude Hazeldene, FCA *1952;* 6 Wayland Avenue, EXETER, EX2 4PR. (Life Member)

WHITE, Mr. Guy Saxton, FCA *1978;* C C W Limited, 295-297 Church Street, BLACKPOOL, FY1 3PJ.

WHITE, Mr. Harold Edward, FCA *1974;* Hamar, Park Street, WORKSOP, S80 1HH.

•**WHITE, Mrs. Hazel, FCA** *1963;* (Tax Fac), Hazel White, 25 Ridge Hall Close, Caversham, READING, RG4 7EP.

WHITE, Miss. Helen Christina, BA(Hons) ACA *2000;* 1408 / 80 Clarendon Street, SOUTHBANK, VIC 3006, AUSTRALIA.

WHITE, Mrs. Helen Margaret, BA ACA *1981;* 6 Grange Park, Steeple Aston, BICESTER, OX25 4SR.

WHITE, Mrs. Helen Maria, ACA *1995;* 23 Huddersfield Road, Skelmanthorpe, HUDDERSFIELD, HD8 9AR.

•**WHITE, Mr. Howard Russell, BSc FCA** *1971;* 1st Floor Flat, Clarence House, 8 Clarence Terrace, Douglas, ISLE OF MAN, IM2 4LS.

WHITE, Mr. Iain Peter, BSc ACA *2000;* with Deloitte LLP, PO Box 500, 2 Hardman Street, MANCHESTER, M60 2AT.

•**WHITE, Mr. Ian Davison, LLB FCA** *1989;* with Deloitte LLP, PO Box 500, 2 Hardman Street, MANCHESTER, M60 2AT.

WHITE, Mr. Ian Howard, BSc ACA *1986;* Ineos Manufacturing Scotland Limited - Technical Building, PO Box 30 Bo'ness Road, GRANGEMOUTH, STIRLINGSHIRE, FK3 9XH.

WHITE, Mr. Ian James, BSc ACA *1993;* Wetherden Cottage, Wetherden Road, Haughley, STOWMARKET, SUFFOLK, IP14 3RE.

WHITE, Mr. Ian Trevor, BA ACA *2010;* with Mazars LLP, Sixth Floor, Times House, Throwley Way, SUTTON, SURREY SM1 4JQ.

WHITE, Ms. Jacqueline Anne, BSc ACA *1985;* Queen Victoria Hospital N H S Trust, Holtye Road, EAST GRINSTEAD, WEST SUSSEX, RH19 3DZ.

•**WHITE, Mrs. Jacqueline Sian, BEng ACA** *1995;* J White, 3 Wentworth Crescent, Mayals, SWANSEA, SA3 5HT.

•**WHITE, Mr. James, MSc BSc DIC AMIMA FCA** *1999;* (Tax Fac), Sable & Argent Limited, 2 Elvetham Crescent, FLEET, HAMPSHIRE, GU51 1BU.

WHITE, Mr. James Alexander, ACA *2011;* 15 Allerton Grange Crescent, LEEDS, LS176LN.

WHITE, Mr. James Alexander, ACA *2009;* 23 Church Lane, Meanwood, LEEDS, LS6 4NP.
WHITE, Mr. James Campbell, FCA *1965;* The Hill House, 98 Coombe Lane West, KINGSTON-UPON-THAMES, KT2 7DD. (Life Member)
•**WHITE, Mr. James Edward, BSocSc FCA ATII** *1994;* Baker Tilly Tax & Advisory Services LLP, Festival Way, Festival Park, STOKE-ON-TRENT, ST1 5BB.
WHITE, Mr. James Lyndon, ACA *1993;* with KPMG LLP, 15 Canada Square, LONDON, E14 5GL.
WHITE, Mr. James Michael, BSc ACA *2002;* with PKF Australia Ltd, Level 10, 1 Margaret Street, SYDNEY, NSW 2000, AUSTRALIA.
WHITE, Mr. James Paul, BA ACA *1994;* 22 St. Pauls Road, LONDON, N1 2QN.
•**WHITE, Mr. James Richard, MA ACA** *2005;* Brown Butler, Leigh House, 28-32 St Paul's Street, LEEDS, LS1 2JT.
WHITE, Mrs. Jane, BA ACA *1995;* 4 Rosebery Gardens, LONDON, W13 0HD.
WHITE, Mrs. Jane Susan, BSc ACA *1985;* 54 High Firs Crescent, HARPENDEN, AL5 1NA.
•**WHITE, Mrs. Janet Margaret, ACA** *1979;* (Tax Fac), Janet M. White ACA, 43 Sparch Hollow, May Bank, NEWCASTLE, STAFFORDSHIRE, ST5 9PE.
WHITE, Mrs. Janet Mary, BA FCA *1974;* Gullivers, 6 Abbotts Hill, Little Ann, ANDOVER, HAMPSHIRE, SP11 7PJ.
WHITE, Mr. Jason Stuart, BEng ACA CTA *1998;* 3 Wickham House, Longbourn, WINDSOR, BERKSHIRE, SL4 3TS.
WHITE, Mrs. Jayne Louise, BSc ACA *2002;* with Auker Rhodes Professional Services LLP, Sapphire House, Albion Road, Greengates, BRADFORD, WEST YORKSHIRE BD10 9TQ.
WHITE, Miss. Jennie, BA(Hons) ACA *2011;* 43 Woburn Drive, Hale, ALTRINCHAM, CHESHIRE, WA15 8NA.
WHITE, Mr. Jeremy Mark, BA ACA *1988;* Petrofac Ltd, PO Box 23467, SHARJAH, UNITED ARAB EMIRATES.
WHITE, Mr. Jeremy Mark, MA FCA *1977;* 52 Grange Road, Ealing, LONDON, W5 5BX.
WHITE, Mr. Jeremy Tobias, ACA *1987;* 19 West Beeches Road, CROWBOROUGH, EAST SUSSEX, TN6 2AN.
WHITE, Mr. Jeremy Wilmot Edward, FCA *1962;* Mole End, 5 Trews Weir Reach, EXETER, EX2 4EG. (Life Member)
WHITE, Miss. Jessica, ACA *2010;* 17 Goswick Avenue, NEWCASTLE UPON TYNE, NE7 7ER.
WHITE, Mrs. Joan Mary, BSc FCA *1978;* 16 Chapel Street, WARWICK, CV34 4HL.
WHITE, Mrs. Joanne Maddy, BA(Hons) ACA DChA *2003;* with Crowe Clark Whitehill LLP, Aquis House, 49-51 Blagrave Street, READING, RG1 1PL.
WHITE, Miss. Joanne Rebecca, ACA CTA MAAT *2007;* 5 Park Farm Close, HORSHAM, WEST SUSSEX, RH12 5EU.
WHITE, Mr. John, FCA *1957;* 25 Angel Lane, WOODBRIDGE, SUFFOLK, IP12 4NG. (Life Member)
WHITE, Mr. John, FCA *1971;* 15 Hyde Place, OXFORD, OX2 7JB.
WHITE, Mr. John Albert, BA FCA *1972;* 32 East Junipero Street, SANTA BARBARA, CA 93105, UNITED STATES.
WHITE, Mr. John Andrew, FCA *1970;* 23 Florence Avenue, MAIDENHEAD, SL6 8SJ.
WHITE, Mr. John Charles, FCA *1955;* 14 Stratton Road, PRINCES RISBOROUGH, HP27 9BH. (Life Member)
•**WHITE, Mr. John Leslie, FCA** *1967;* (Tax Fac), J. White & Co, 46 Engine Lane, Nailsea, BRISTOL, BS48 4RL.
•**WHITE, Mr. John Nigel, FCA** *1982;* (Tax Fac), Pelham, Pelham Business Centre, 16 Dudley Street, GRIMSBY, DN31 2AB. See also Johnson Hunt (UK) Ltd
•**WHITE, Mr. John Richard, MA FCA** *1981;* (Tax Fac), John White, 1 Egliston Road, LONDON, SW15 1AL.
WHITE, Mr. John Richard, FCA *1968;* 1 Mill Road, Swanland, NORTH FERRIBY, NORTH HUMBERSIDE, HU14 3PJ. (Life Member)
WHITE, Mr. John Rodney, FCA *1975;* The Drying House, 108 South Road, Oundle, PETERBOROUGH, PE8 4BP.
WHITE, Mr. John Stanley Meears, FCA *1963;* 4 Meare Close, TADWORTH, KT20 5RZ.
WHITE, Mr. Jonathan, BA ACA *2001;* Fountain Court, 21 Matham Road, EAST MOLESEY, KT8 0SX.
WHITE, Mr. Jonathan Barry, ACA *2008;* Flat 2, 104 Wake Green Road, BIRMINGHAM, B13 9PZ.
WHITE, Mr. Jonathan David, ACA *2010;* 54 Couthurst Road, LONDON, SE3 8TW.
WHITE, Mr. Jonathan David, BA ACA *2011;* Apartment 5, 10 Woodville Terrace, Douglas, ISLE OF MAN, IM2 4HB.
•**WHITE, Mr. Jonathan Francis, BSc ACA** *1988;* J F White Ltd, 36 Cotland Acres, Redhill Surrey, REDHILL, RH1 6JZ.
WHITE, Mr. Jonathan Mark, MA ACA *1987;* Beech House, 2 Gurney Close, BEACONSFIELD, HP9 1PX.
•**WHITE, Mr. Jonathan Robert Mark, BSc ACA** *1998;* KPMG LLP, 15 Canada Square, LONDON, E14 5GL. See also KPMG Europe LLP
•**WHITE, Mr. Joseph Nicolas, FCA** *1974;* Guard D'Oyly, 4 Mansell Street, STRATFORD-UPON-AVON, WARWICKSHIRE, CV37 6NR.
WHITE, Mrs. Julie Christine, BA ACA *1987;* Tenon The Poynt Building, 45 Wollaton Street, NOTTINGHAM, NG1 5FW.
WHITE, Mrs. Juliet Mary, BA(Hons) ACA *2002;* with Judge Institute of Management, Judge Business School, University of Cambridge, Trumpington Street, CAMBRIDGE, CB2 1AG.
WHITE, Miss. Katherine, ACA *2008;* Flat 3, 54 Ridgway, LONDON, SW19 4QR.
WHITE, Miss. Katherine Angela Jane, BA ACA *2004;* Flat 406 Spice Quay Heights, 32 Shad Thames, LONDON, SE1 2YL.
WHITE, Miss. Katherine Margaret, ACA *2009;* Buzzacott LLP, 130 Wood Street, LONDON, EC2V 6DL.
WHITE, Miss. Kathleen, BSc ACA *1979;* 25 Selworthy Green, LIVERPOOL, L16 9JJ.
WHITE, Ms. Kathryn, BA ACA *1998;* Live Nation, 3rd Floor, Regent Arcade House, 19-25 Argyll Street, LONDON, W1F 7TS.
•**WHITE, Miss. Katie Louise, BA ACA** *2004;* The Clifton Tax Practice LLP, The Pavilions, Eden Park, Ham Green, BRISTOL, BS20 0DD. See also CAM Holdings LLP
WHITE, Mrs. Kay Denise, BA ACA *1992;* 4 Redwing Road, Kempshott, BASINGSTOKE, RG22 5UJ.
WHITE, Mr. Keith, BSc ACA *2010;* 12 Pitchford Road, SHREWSBURY, SHROPSHIRE, SY1 3HS.
WHITE, Mr. Keith Alan, ACA *1981;* TWI Ltd, Granta Park, Great Abington, CAMBRIDGE, CB21 6AL.
WHITE, Mr. Keith Geoffrey, FCA *1965;* Old Timbers, Broad Lane, Wood End, SOLIHULL, WEST MIDLANDS, B94 5DY.
WHITE, Mrs. Kerry Elizabeth Williamson, BSc(Hons) ACA *2002;* 16 Lindale Close, Gamston, NOTTINGHAM, NG2 6PU.
WHITE, Mr. Kevin Robert, BA ACA *1993;* 22 Leyton Lea, Cuckfield, HAYWARDS HEATH, WEST SUSSEX, RH17 5AT.
•**WHITE, Mr. Kier Christian James, ACA** *1999;* with BDO LLP, Arcadia House, Maritime Walk, Ocean Village, SOUTHAMPTON, SO14 3TL.
WHITE, Miss. Laura Clare, BA(Econ) ACA *2006;* 11 Galleon Mews, GRAVESEND, KENT, DA11 9EE.
•**WHITE, Mrs. Lesley, BA FCA** *1996;* Lesley White FCA, Yew Tree Barn, Loads Road, Holymoorside, CHESTERFIELD, DERBYSHIRE S42 7EU.
WHITE, Mr. Letham Ian, ACA *1994;* 326 Lockington Road, Aongatete, RD2, KATIKATI 3178, BAY OF PLENTY, NEW ZEALAND.
WHITE, Mr. Lionel Charles, FCA *1953;* 7 Farm Close, Cockhill, TROWBRIDGE, WILTSHIRE, BA14 9AQ. (Life Member)
WHITE, Mrs. Louise Jayne, BSc ACA *2000;* 44 Bruce Grove, CHELMSFORD, ESSEX, CM2 9AY.
WHITE, Mrs. Louise Wendy, BSc ACA *1996;* Bromfold, Tuesley Lane, GODALMING, SURREY, GU7 1SJ.
WHITE, Mr. Malcolm George, LLB ACA *1999;* 2 Rue Maurice-Barraud, 1206 GENEVA, SWITZERLAND.
WHITE, Mr. Malcolm John, BA ACA *1983;* CLC Group Plc, Vincent Avenue, SOUTHAMPTON, SO16 6PQ.
WHITE, Mr. Mark, MA ACA *1983;* 9 Bowham Avenue, BRIDGEND, Mid Glamorgan, CF31 3PD.
WHITE, Mr. Mark Edward Furnival, BSc ACA *1992;* 900 Donner Ave, SONOMA, CA 95476, UNITED STATES.
WHITE, Mr. Mark Macdonald, BA ACA *1984;* PO Box 10066, GEORGE TOWN, GRAND CAYMAN, KY1-1001, CAYMAN ISLANDS.
WHITE, Mr. Mark William, BA ACA *1989;* Building B, British Petroleum Co Plc, Chertsey Road, SUNBURY-ON-THAMES, TW16 7LN.
WHITE, Mr. Martin James, BA ACA *2000;* Flat 12 Kent Court, Queens Drive, LONDON, W3 0HS.
WHITE, Mr. Matthew Alexander, BA ACA *1993;* Gig Cottage, 61 High Street, Sutton Courtenay, ABINGDON, OXFORDSHIRE, OX14 4AT.
WHITE, Mr. Matthew James, ACA *1990;* 14 Elm Grove Road, LONDON, W5 3JJ.
WHITE, Mr. Matthew Mair, BEng ACA *1994;* Barkers Cottage, School Lane, Stadhampton, OXFORD, OX44 7TR.
•**WHITE, Mr. Matthew Robert, BSc ACA** *1993;* BDO LLP, 55 Baker Street, LONDON, W1U 7EU. See also BDO Stoy Hayward LLP
WHITE, Miss. Megan, ACA *2011;* Basement Flat, 154 Old Woolwich Road, LONDON, SE10 9PR.
WHITE, Mrs. Melanie Jane Patricia, BSc ACA *1992;* Friarsfield, Priory Close, East Farleigh, MAIDSTONE, KENT, ME15 0EY.
WHITE, Mr. Melvyn Barrie, FCA *1968;* Hickmans Farm, Poundsbridge Hill Fordcombe, TUNBRIDGE WELLS, TN3 0RL.
WHITE, Mr. Michael, BA ACA *1991;* Stratton Street Capital Llp, 30 Charles II Street, LONDON, SW1Y 4AE.
•①**WHITE, Mr. Michael David, FCA MIPA FABRP** *1974;* R3 120 Aldersgate Street, LONDON, EC1A 4JQ.
WHITE, Mr. Michael David, BSc(Hons) ACA *2003;* 52 Elmfield Road, STOCKPORT, CHESHIRE, SK3 8SE.
WHITE, Mr. Michael Duncan, FCA *1969;* Woodlands, 160 St Helens Park Road, HASTINGS, EAST SUSSEX, TN34 2JN. (Life Member)
•**WHITE, Mr. Michael George, ACA MAAT** *2001;* M G White & Co, 48 Brook Lane Field, HARLOW, ESSEX, CM18 7AU.
WHITE, Mr. Michael Henry, FCA *1960;* 21 Fairview Road, HUNGERFORD, RG17 0BP. (Life Member)
WHITE, Mr. Michael James, BSc ACA *1995;* 24 Stourbridge Road, Fairfield, BROMSGROVE, B61 9LS.
WHITE, Mr. Michael John, FCA *1959;* 5 Abbeylands, Cobbetts Hill, WEYBRIDGE, KT13 0UB. (Life Member)
WHITE, Mr. Michael John Robert, BSc ACA *2007;* Ropemaker Place Level 11, 28 Ropemaker Street, LONDON, EC2Y 9HD.
•**WHITE, Mr. Michael John William, FCA** *1974;* Devon Square Partners Limited, 14 Torquay Road, NEWTON ABBOT, DEVON, TQ12 1AJ.
WHITE, Mr. Michael Robert, ACA *1979;* 29 Regency Gardens, BIRMINGHAM, B14 4JS.
WHITE, Mrs. Mollie, FCA *1976;* 4 Crowhill Road, NUNEATON, CV11 6PJ.
WHITE, Miss. Natalie Tara, BA ACA *2010;* 18 Campden Lawns, Alderminster, STRATFORD-UPON-AVON, CV37 8PA.
WHITE, Mr. Neil, FCA *1974;* 1 Barn Owl Cottage, Cromer Road, Sidestrand, CROMER, NORFOLK, NR27 0LT.
WHITE, Mr. Neil Antony, BSc ACA *1999;* 7 Highcliffe Close Woodley, READING, RG5 4RE.
•**WHITE, Mr. Neil Clifford, FCA** *1987;* Cliff White, Notre Coin, 31 Jardin De L'Epine, Collings Road, ST PETER PORT, GY11TX.
WHITE, Mr. Neil Gordon, BSc ACA *1997;* 1 Harborne Road, OLDBURY, B68 9JA.
•**WHITE, Mr. Neil John Alfred, BSc FCA** *1992;* Bennett Brooks & Co Ltd., St. Georges Court, Winnington Avenue, NORTHWICH, CHESHIRE, CW8 4EE.
WHITE, Mr. Neil Richard, BSc ACA *2005;* 383 Hurst Road, WEST MOLESEY, SURREY, KT8 1QW.
WHITE, Mr. Nicholas, BA ACA *1986;* Management Training Partnership, 15 Prebendal Court Oxford Road, AYLESBURY, BUCKINGHAMSHIRE, HP19 8EY.
•**WHITE, Mr. Nicholas, BA FCA** *1965;* (Tax Fac), N White & Co, 14 Abbey Walk, GREAT MISSENDEN, BUCKINGHAMSHIRE, HP16 0AY.
WHITE, Mr. Nicholas Charles Peter, FCA *1981;* 249 San Mateo Avenue, LOS GATOS, CA 95030, UNITED STATES.
•**WHITE, Mr. Nicholas John, BSc FCA MAE** *1987;* Stow Family Law LLP, The Old Court House Reglan Street, HARROGATE, NORTH YORKSHIRE, HG1 1LT.
WHITE, Mr. Nicholas Ralph Ingram, FCA *1972;* Crinan, Church Lane, Middleton, TAMWORTH, STAFFORDSHIRE, B78 2AN.
WHITE, Mr. Nicholas Warren, FCA *1976;* Flat A, 75 Portobello Road, LONDON, W11 2QB.
WHITE, Mrs. Nicola Jane, BA ACA *2004;* 57 Montrose Avenue, Whitton, TWICKENHAM, MIDDLESEX, TW2 6HG.
①**WHITE, Mrs. Nicola Jane, FCA MABRP** *1989;* 27 The Orchards, Pickmere, KNUTSFORD, WA16 0LS.
WHITE, Norman Hamflett, Esq OBE FCA *1966;* 6 Lakeside, Wingerworth, CHESTERFIELD, S42 6LP. (Life Member)
WHITE, Mr. Oliver Lewis, BA(Hons) ACA *2001;* 156 Nine Mile Ride, Finchampstead, WOKINGHAM, RG40 4JA.
WHITE, Mr. Owen Anthony, BA ACA *1992;* 7 Updown Hill, HAYWARDS HEATH, WEST SUSSEX, RH16 4GP.
WHITE, Mr. Paul, BSc ACA *1996;* Bromfold, Tuesley Lane, GODALMING, GU7 1SJ.
WHITE, Mr. Paul Anthony, FCA *1987;* 38 Court Street, Moretonhampstead, NEWTON ABBOT, DEVON, TQ13 8LG.
WHITE, Mr. Paul Matthew, BA ACA *1987;* 81 Speedwell Close, MELKSHAM, SN12 7TE.
WHITE, Mr. Paul Nicholas, MA FCA *1983;* Duncan Sheard Glass, 45 Hoghton Street, SOUTHPORT, PR9 0PG.
WHITE, Mr. Paul Richard, BSc ACA *1992;* Speedy Hire Unit 105-106, Golborne Enterprise Park Golborne, WARRINGTON, WA3 3GR.
WHITE, Mr. Peter, ACA *2009;* 19 Broad Lane Close, Bramley, LEEDS, LS13 2UD.
WHITE, Mr. Peter Ashby, BA ACA *1997;* 22 Observatory Road, LONDON, SW14 7QD.
WHITE, Mr. Peter David, BA ACA *1988;* 20 St Johns Villas, LONDON, N19 3EG.
WHITE, Mr. Peter Douglas, BSc ACA *2001;* 23 Manley Road, ILKLEY, WEST YORKSHIRE, LS29 8QP.
WHITE, Mr. Peter John, BA ACA *1992;* Russets, Roedean Road, TUNBRIDGE WELLS, TN2 5JX.
WHITE, Mr. Peter Mark, BSc ACA CF *1988;* Staffansvägen 16, 141 43 HUDDINGE, SWEDEN.
WHITE, Mr. Peter Martin, BSc ACA *2007;* Flat 5 St. Neras Court, 6 Parkland Mead, BROMLEY, BR1 2FQ.
•**WHITE, Mr. Peter Richard, BSc ACA** *2004;* (Tax Fac), Stewart Fletcher and Barrett, Manor Court Chambers, 126 Manor Court Road, NUNEATON, CV11 5HL. See also SFB Consultants Limited
WHITE, Mr. Philip Charles, MA FCA *1985;* Jacuzzi UK, Woodlands, Roydsdale Way, Euroway Industrial Estate, BRADFORD, WEST YORKSHIRE BD4 6SE.
WHITE, Mr. Philip Charles Anthony, MSc ACA *1995;* 20 St. Catherine Drive, Hartford, NORTHWICH, CHESHIRE, CW8 2FF.
WHITE, Mr. Philip Christopher, ACA *1982;* Architas Multi-Manager Limited, 5 Old Broad Street, LONDON, EC2N 1AD.
WHITE, Mr. Philip Graham, MA ACA *2006;* 95 Blackcurrant Drive, Long Ashton, BRISTOL, SOMERSET, BS41 9FP.
WHITE, Philip Michael, Esq CBE BCom FCA *1975;* Lookers Plc, 776 Chester Road, Stretford, MANCHESTER, M32 0QH.
WHITE, Mr. Philip Newton, BSc ACA *1979;* Newlyn Court, Merstone Close, BILSTON, WEST MIDLANDS, WV14 0LR.
WHITE, Mrs. Rebecca Louise, ACA *2008;* with Riches & Company, 34 Anyards Road, COBHAM, SURREY, KT11 2LA.
WHITE, Mr. Reginald, FCA *1960;* 66 St James Road, CARLISLE, CA2 5PD.
•**WHITE, Mr. Richard, FCA** *1975;* Baker Tilly Tax and Advisory Services LLP, 25 Farringdon Street, LONDON, EC4A 4AB. See also Baker Tilly Corporate Finance LLP
WHITE, Mr. Richard, BA ACA *2010;* with Davisons Ltd, Lime Court, Pathfields Business Park, SOUTH MOLTON, DEVON, EX36 3LH.
WHITE, Mr. Richard Andrew, ACA *2006;* 23 Hood Close, SLEAFORD, LINCOLNSHIRE, NG34 7WJ.
WHITE, Mr. Richard Frank, FCA *1975;* 19 St. Nicholas Cliff, SCARBOROUGH, NORTH YORKSHIRE, YO11 2ES.
•**WHITE, Mr. Richard Graham, BA ACA** *1989;* with Grant Thornton UK LLP, Grant Thornton House, 22 Melton Street, Euston Square, LONDON, NW1 2EP.
WHITE, Mr. Richard James, FCA *1968;* Peak House, Hall Lane, Witnesham, IPSWICH, IP6 9HN. (Life Member)
WHITE, Mr. Richard John, BA ACA *2003;* 70 Sheringham Road, POOLE, DORSET, BH12 1NS.
WHITE, Mr. Richard John, BA ACA *2003;* Wickhams cay 1, P.O. Box 3083, ROAD TOWN, TORTOLA ISLAND, VG1110, VIRGIN ISLANDS (BRITISH).
WHITE, Mr. Richard Stephen, BSc ACA *1994;* IFM Consulting (Beijing) Ltd, 22D Oriental Kenzo, No 48 Dungzhimenwai Av, Doncheng District, BEIJING 100027, CHINA.
WHITE, Mr. Robert Arthur, BSc FCA *1975;* 24 Kenwood Drive, BECKENHAM, BR3 6QX.
WHITE, Mr. Robert James, BSc ACA *1995;* Kembali, Back Lane, Rimington, CLITHEROE, LANCASHIRE, BB7 4EL.
WHITE, Mr. Robert Michael, MA BSc ACIB FCA ACMA *1974;* 21 Chesterfield Drive, SEVENOAKS, TN13 2EG.
WHITE, Mr. Robert Philip, BA ACA *1994;* I N G Barings Ltd, 60 London Wall, LONDON, EC2M 5TQ.
WHITE, Mr. Robert Shaun, BSc ACA AMCT *1993;* High Cedars, Firfields, Cobbetts Hill, WEYBRIDGE, SURREY, KT13 0UD.
WHITE, Mr. Robin Matthew, BSc ACA *1990;* 49 Lancaster Avenue, LONDON, SE27 9EL.
WHITE, Mr. Robin Nicholas, MA ACA *1983;* Sanofi-Adventis, 174 Avenue De France, Cedex 13, 75635 PARIS, FRANCE.
WHITE, Mr. Roger Alfred, FCA *1969;* The Old Bakery, Lovington, CASTLE CARY, BA7 7PX.
WHITE, Mr. Roger John Graham, FCA *1962;* (Member of Council 1979 - 1985), Courtlands, 20 Grange Court, WALTON-ON-THAMES, SURREY, KT12 1JD. (Life Member)

•**WHITE, Mr. Roger Martin, BA ACA** *1992;* Saul Fairholm, 12 Tentercroft Street, LINCOLN, LN5 7DB. See also Atkinson Saul Fairholm Limited
WHITE, Mr. Ronald Walter, FCA *1960;* Claywater, 4 Willowmere, ESHER, SURREY, KT10 9TY. (Life Member)
WHITE, Miss. Rosalind Mary, BA ACA *1985;* 23 Maidenhead Court Park, MAIDENHEAD, BERKSHIRE, SL6 8HN.
WHITE, Mrs. Rosemary Lynne, ACA *2008;* 10 Bluebell Lane, MACCLESFIELD, CHESHIRE, SK10 2JL.
WHITE, Mrs. Ruth, ACA *2011;* Flat 19, Lynden Mews, Dale Road, READING, RG2 0AT.
•**WHITE, Miss. Samantha Louise, FCA CTA** *1993;* Bostock White Limited, Unit 1, Cabourn House, Station Street, Bingham, NOTTINGHAM NG13 8AQ.
WHITE, Miss. Sarah, BSc(Hons) ACA *2006;* Flat 6 Cavell Court, 862 Garratt Lane, LONDON, SW17 0NB.
WHITE, Mrs. Sarah Emily, LLB ACA *1995;* The Meeting House, Lewins Mead, BRISTOL, BS1 2NN.
WHITE, Miss. Sarah Louise, BSc ACA *2005;* Westbrooke, High street, Alconbury Weston, HUNTINGDON, PE28 4JP.
WHITE, Miss. Sarah Louise, BSc(Hons) ACA *2004;* 26 Northpoint Square, LONDON, NW1 9AW.
WHITE, Mr. Selwyn, FCA *1965;* Hunters Lodge, 1 Hunters Way, Aston Abbotts, AYLESBURY, BUCKINGHAMSHIRE, HP22 4EQ.
WHITE, Mrs. Sharon Julie, BA ACA *1993;* 11b Vicarage Road, Marsworth, TRING, HP23 4LT.
WHITE, Mr. Simon Craig, ACA ATII *2000;* 6 Alders Reach, Rolleston-on-Dove, BURTON-ON-TRENT, STAFFORDSHIRE, DE13 9BB.
WHITE, Mr. Simon Douglas, BSc ACA *1992;* 4K The Manhattan, 33 Tai Tam Road, TAI TAM, HONG KONG SAR.
WHITE, Mr. Simon James, BSc ACA *2004;* 35 Station Lane, Lapworth, SOLIHULL, WEST MIDLANDS, B94 6LW.
WHITE, Mr. Simon John, BA ACA *1989;* 16 Genoa Avenue, LONDON, SW15 6BS.
•**WHITE, Mr. Simon John, BSc(Hons) ACA** *2002;* with PricewaterhouseCoopers LLP, 1 Embankment Place, LONDON, WC2N 6RH.
WHITE, Mr. Simon Meredith, BSc ACA *1981;* Schlumberger, Schlumberger House, Buckingham Gate, London Gatwick Airport, GATWICK, WEST SUSSEX RH6 0NZ.
WHITE, Mr. Simon Peter, FCA *1983;* 83 Burbage Road, LONDON, SE24 9HB.
WHITE, Mr. Simon Peter Robin, BSc ACA *1991;* 137 Heol-Y-Deri, Rhiwbina, CARDIFF, CF14 6UH.
•**WHITE, Mr. Simon Robert Franklin, BA(Hons) ACA** *2002;* (Tax Fac), TT&W Limited, 5 High Green, Great Shelford, CAMBRIDGE, CB22 5EG.
WHITE, Mrs. Stephanie Faye, LLB ACA *2001;* GN35, Department for Work & Pensions Quarry House, Quarry Hill, LEEDS, LS2 7UA.
WHITE, Mr. Stephen, ACA *2011;* 6 Prospect Place, Llangynwyd, MAESTEG, MID GLAMORGAN, CF34 9SR.
WHITE, Mr. Stephen Frank, BA ACA *1981;* 5 Halsey Street, LONDON, SW3 2QH.
WHITE, Mr. Stephen James, BSc ACA *1998;* 157 More Close, LONDON, W14 9BW.
WHITE, Mr. Stephen John, BA ACA *1992;* with Grant Thornton UK LLP, Grant Thornton House, 202 Silbury Boulevard, MILTON KEYNES, BUCKINGHAMSHIRE, MK9 1LW.
WHITE, Mr. Steven Martin, BA ACA *1990;* with PricewaterhouseCoopers LLP, Benson House, 33 Wellington Street, LEEDS, LS1 4JP.
WHITE, Mrs. Susan Clare Frances, BA ACA *1991;* Suite 203 Portsmouth Technopole, Kingston Crescent, PORTSMOUTH, PO2 8FA.
WHITE, Mr. Terence, BA ACA *1988;* 140 Richmond Hill Road, Sumner, CHRISTCHURCH 8081, NEW ZEALAND.
WHITE, Mr. Terence Stuart, FCA *1974;* PO Box 245, BERWICK, VIC 3806, AUSTRALIA. (Life Member)
WHITE, Mr. Thomas, BSc ACA *2010;* 50 Nicholas Drive, Cliffsend, RAMSGATE, KENT, CT12 5JS.
WHITE, Mr. Timothy James, ACA CA(AUS) *2008;* Abbey National Treasury TS1C01, Ground Floor, 2-3 Triton Square, LONDON, NW1 3AN.
•**WHITE, Mr. Timothy John, BSc FCA** *1989;* Paul Crowdy Partnership Limited, Redmayne House, 4 Whiteladies Road, Clifton, BRISTOL, BS8 1PD. See also Paul Crowdy Partnership
WHITE, Mr. Timothy Leigh, BA ACA ATII *1979;* (Tax Fac), Towcester Bld'ng Supplies Ltd., Hackwood Road, DAVENTRY, NN11 4ES.
WHITE, Miss. Vanessa, LLB ACA *1991;* 16 Croft Court, Honley, HOLMFIRTH, WEST YORKSHIRE, HD9 6HB.
WHITE, Miss. Vanessa Jane, BA ACA *1997;* 12 McDonald Street, NAPIER, NEW ZEALAND.
WHITE, Miss. Victoria Jane, BSocSc ACA *1998;* 75 Percy Road, LONDON, W12 9PX.
WHITE, Mrs. Victoria Lorraine, BA ACA *2001;* 11 Ebborn Square, Lower Earley, READING, BERKSHIRE, RG6 4JT.
WHITE, Mr. William James, BCom(ACC) FCA *1987;* 24 Bearcroft Avenue, Great Meadow, WORCESTER, WR4 0DR.
WHITE, Mr. William John, BA(Hons) ACA *2009;* 30 Imperial Square, LONDON, SW6 2AE.
WHITE, Mr. William Jonathan, LLB ACA *2004;* Barclays Bank, 1 Churchill Place, LONDON, E14 5HP.
WHITE, Mr. William Matthew Galbraith, BA(Hons) ACA MSI *1999;* 37 Marney Road, LONDON, SW11 5EW.
•**WHITE-ADAMS, Mr. Colin John, FCA** *1980;* (Tax Fac), White Adams & Co, 1 Famona House, Bridgwater Road, WINSCOMBE, SOMERSET, BS25 1NA.
WHITE JONES, Mr. David, BA FCA *1966;* Pitmilly, Upton Road, Upton, AYLESBURY, HP17 8UF. (Life Member)
WHITEAR, Mr. Mark Anthony, BA ACA *1998;* (Tax Fac), with Reeves & Co LLP, 37 St. Margarets Street, CANTERBURY, KENT, CT1 2TU.
WHITECOURT, Mr. Ian Bronson, FCA *1969;* Fiduciaire Whitecourt Korerup, 27 rue de Neuhaeusgen, Schuttrange, L-5368 LUXEMBOURG, LUXEMBOURG.
•**WHITECROSS, Mr. Duncan John, BSc BEng ACA** *1989;* Ernst & Young LLP, 1 More London Place, LONDON, SE1 2AF. See also Ernst & Young Europe LLP
WHITECROSS, Mr. Philip James, BSc ACA *1989;* Lower Dean Farm, Dean Road, Stewkley, LEIGHTON BUZZARD, LU7 0EU.
•**WHITEFIELD, Mr. Daniel, BSc FCA** *1992;* Daniel Whitefield Ltd, New Arch House, 57b Catherine Place, LONDON, SW1E 6DY.
WHITEFIELD, Mr. David, BSc(Econ) ACA *2002;* (Tax Fac), PO Box 105, 45825 AZRIEL, ISRAEL.
•**WHITEFOOT, Mr. George Brian, BSc FCA** *1979;* Pine Tree Cottage, Brookledge Lane, Adlington, MACCLESFIELD, CHESHIRE, SK10 4JU.
WHITEFOOT, Mr. Ian Ralph, ACA *2009;* 25 Lincoln Court, SOUTHAMPTON, SO15 7PY.
WHITEFOOT, Mr. Robert Graham, ACA *2003;* 150 Manor Road, Newton St. Faith, NORWICH, NR10 3LG.
WHITEHAIR, Mr. Colin Roy Keith, BSc ACA *1980;* 12 The Causeway, SUTTON, SM2 5RS.
WHITEHAIR, Mr. Richard James Russell, FCA *1978;* The Old Vicarage, Capel Road, Bentley, IPSWICH, IP9 2BL.
WHITEHALL, Mrs. Kirsten, BSc ACA *2008;* 34 Westwood Road, NEWCASTLE UPON TYNE, NE3 5NN.
•**WHITEHEAD, Mr. Allan Graham, FCA** *1974;* (Tax Fac), Whitehead Accountants Limited, 40 Lord Street, STOCKPORT, CHESHIRE, SK1 3NA.
WHITEHEAD, Mrs. Andrea Faye, ACA *2010;* 8 South View, Rawcliffe Bridge, GOOLE, NORTH HUMBERSIDE, DN14 8NY.
WHITEHEAD, Mr. Andrew John, BSc FCA *1978;* Merok, Camp Road, GERRARDS CROSS, SL9 7PD.
WHITEHEAD, Mr. Andrew Peter, BA ACA *1989;* 34 Illingworth Way, ENFIELD, EN1 2PA.
WHITEHEAD, Mr. Angus Joseph, MSc ACA *1992;* House of Townend, Wyke Way, MELTON, HU14 3HH.
WHITEHEAD, Miss. Anna Marie Rachel, BA ACA *2010;* 21 Hayes Grove, East Dulwich, LONDON, SE22 8DF.
•**WHITEHEAD, Mr. Anwyl Richard, BCom FCA** *1989;* (Tax Fac), TWJ Partnership LLP, The Moorings, Dane Road Industrial Estate, SALE, CHESHIRE, M33 7BP.
•**WHITEHEAD, Mr. Bevan, MA ACA** *1996;* Deloitte LLP, 2 New Street Square, LONDON, EC4A 3BZ. See also Deloitte & Touche LLP
WHITEHEAD, Mrs. Biliana, ACA *2005;* with Deloitte LLP, Athene Place, 66 Shoe Lane, LONDON, EC4A 3BQ.
WHITEHEAD, Miss. Carla, BA ACA *2007;* 47 Aysgarth Avenue, LIVERPOOL, L12 8QS.
WHITEHEAD, Mr. Christopher Glen, BA FCA *1974;* Birch Cottage, Pheasants Hill, Hambleden, HENLEY-ON-THAMES, RG9 6SN. (Life Member)
WHITEHEAD, Mr. Christopher Ralph, BSc ACA *2006;* Hope & Anchor Hotel, 11 Market Street Flookburgh, GRANGE-OVER-SANDS, CUMBRIA, LA11 7JU.
WHITEHEAD, Mr. Colin, FCA *1984;* Forest Chapel Ltd, Chapel House Farm, Forest Chapel, Macclesfield Forest, MACCLESFIELD, CHESHIRE SK11 0AR.
WHITEHEAD, Mr. Colin David, ACA *2006;* Naylor Wintersgill Carlton House, Grammar School Street, BRADFORD, BD1 4NS.
WHITEHEAD, Mr. Darryl Michael, BSc FCA *1973;* 113 St Georges Road, CHELTENHAM, GL50 3ED. (Life Member)
WHITEHEAD, Mr. David Christopher, BA ACA *1989;* 31 Capel Road, Oxhey, WATFORD, HERTFORDSHIRE, WD19 4FE.
WHITEHEAD, Mr. David Gordon Christopher, FCA *1975;* Otterbourne Lodge, St Marks Close, 255 Winchester Road, Chandler's Ford, EASTLEIGH, HAMPSHIRE SO53 2DX.
•ⓘ**WHITEHEAD, Mr. David Nigel, FCA CF** *1982;* (Tax Fac), Larking Gowen, King Street House, 15 Upper King Street, NORWICH, NR3 1RB. See also Larking Gowen Limited, Larking Gowen Corporate Finance Limited
WHITEHEAD, Mr. Frankie Ray, ACA *2011;* 4 Kelso Drive, GRAVESEND, KENT, DA12 4NR.
•**WHITEHEAD, Mr. Godfrey, FCA** *1960;* Godfrey Whitehead, The Okefield, Beaulieu Road, LYNDHURST, SO43 7DA.
WHITEHEAD, Mr. Ian Kenneth, BSc ACA *1979;* 1 Vallance Road, LONDON, N22 4UD.
•**WHITEHEAD, Mr. Ian Martin, FCA** *1973;* Whitehead & Co, Penfold, Cannington Lane, Uplyme, LYME REGIS, DT7 3SW.
WHITEHEAD, Mr. Ian Royston, BA ACA *1993;* 35 Aldridge Park, Winkfield Row, BRACKNELL, BERKSHIRE, RG42 7NU.
WHITEHEAD, Mrs. Jane, BA ACA *1993;* 17 Kendal Park, West Derby, LIVERPOOL, L12 9LS.
WHITEHEAD, Mr. Jeremy Ralph, BSc ACA *1980;* Abbey Arms Hotel, 1 The Square, New Abbey, DUMFRIES, DG2 8BX.
WHITEHEAD, Miss. Jill Tildesley, BA(Hons) ACA *2001;* 4/17 Farilight Street, MANLY, NSW 2095, AUSTRALIA.
WHITEHEAD, Mrs. Joanne Elizabeth, BSc ACA *1993;* Advertising Principles Devonshire Hall, Devonshire Avenue, LEEDS, LS8 1AW.
WHITEHEAD, Mr. John, BSc ACA *1993;* Flat C, 40 Pandora Road, LONDON, NW6 1TR.
WHITEHEAD, Mr. John Charles, BA ACA *1979;* 1 Hereford Drive, Claydon, IPSWICH, IP6 0BF.
•**WHITEHEAD, Mr. John Gresham, BA ACA CTA** *1991;* Deloitte LLP, Athene Place, 66 Shoe Lane, LONDON, EC4A 3BQ. See also Deloitte & Touche LLP
•**WHITEHEAD, Mr. John Richard, BSc ACA** *1998;* JRW, Tan-y-Llwyn, ARTHOG, GWYNEDD, LL39 1YY.
WHITEHEAD, Mr. John Robert, BA ACA *1983;* Arbutus, Grayswood Road, HASLEMERE, GU27 2BP.
WHITEHEAD, Mr. Jonathan Daniel, BA(Hons) ACA *2002;* 35 Grove Road, WINDSOR, BERKSHIRE, SL4 1JD.
•**WHITEHEAD, Mr. Laurence, BA ACA CF** *1997;* MacIntyre Hudson LLP, Moorgate House, 201 Silbury Boulevard, MILTON KEYNES, MK9 1LZ. See also MacIntyre Hudson Corporate Finance Ltd
WHITEHEAD, Miss. Louise, BSc ACA *2010;* 14/366 Military Road, CREMORNE, NSW 2090, AUSTRALIA.
WHITEHEAD, Mrs. Lynn Christine, ACA *1985;* 6 Fenhall Park, Lanchester, DURHAM, DH7 0JT.
WHITEHEAD, Mr. Malcolm, FCA *1968;* Heathcote, 93 Whittingham Lane, Broughton, PRESTON, PR3 5DB.
•**WHITEHEAD, Mr. Mark Andrew Milton, BA FCA** *1988;* (Tax Fac), Easter Green Partnership, Office A, Hoste House, Whiting Street, BURY ST. EDMUNDS, SUFFOLK IP33 1NR.
WHITEHEAD, Mr. Mark Edwin, BSc FCA *1980;* Highclere, 661 Chorley New Road, Lostock, BOLTON, BL6 4AG.
•ⓘ**WHITEHEAD, Mr. Martin John, BSc ACA** *1993;* PricewaterhouseCoopers, Rahimtulla Tower, Upper Hill Road, PO Box 43963, NAIROBI, 00100 KENYA.
WHITEHEAD, Mr. Matthew Ian, BA ACA *2003;* 1 Glebe Side, HUDDERSFIELD, HD5 0HQ.
WHITEHEAD, Mr. Matthew John, ACA *2007;* 3 Clark Spring Close, Churwell, LEEDS, LS27 9PJ.
WHITEHEAD, Mr. Michael Charles, BSc FCA *1985;* 28 Blackhill Lane, KNUTSFORD, WA16 9DD.
WHITEHEAD, Mr. Michael Ernest, BSc FCA *1963;* 41 Clay Lane, Bushey Heath, BUSHEY, WD23 1NZ.
WHITEHEAD, Mrs. Michelle, ACA *2006;* 5 Dalesman Drive, Hollymount, OLDHAM, OL1 4PU.
WHITEHEAD, Mrs. Michelle Ann, BSc ACA *2002;* 86 Westfield Lane, South Milford, LEEDS, LS25 5AL.
WHITEHEAD, Mr. Nicky, ACA *2009;* Pricewaterhousecoopers, 7 More London Riverside, LONDON, SE1 2RT.
WHITEHEAD, Mrs. Nicola, BSc ACA *1983;* 15 The Haywain, ILKLEY, LS29 8SL.
•**WHITEHEAD, Mr. Peter, BA FCA** *1990;* with RSM Tenon Audit Limited, Charterhouse, Legge Street, BIRMINGHAM, B4 7EU.
WHITEHEAD, Mr. Peter George, BSc ACA *1990;* 25 Highbury Terrace, LONDON, N5 1UP.
WHITEHEAD, Mr. Peter Timothy, LLB ACA *1981;* (Tax Fac), 61 New Adel Lane, Adel, LEEDS, LS16 6BA.
WHITEHEAD, Mr. Peter Wright, BSc FCA *1988;* 1 Firs Avenue, Parkside, East Sheen, LONDON, SW14 7NZ.
WHITEHEAD, Mr. Philip Ernest, FCA *1980;* 3 Nutfields, Ightham, SEVENOAKS, TN15 9EA.
WHITEHEAD, Mr. Raymond William, FCA *1970;* 20 The Willows, WEYBRIDGE, KT13 8EQ.
WHITEHEAD, Miss. Rebecca Helen, ACA *2008;* 15 Oaklands Avenue, LEEDS, LS13 1LH.
WHITEHEAD, Mr. Richard Andrew, BSc ACA *1979;* Department of Energy & Climate Change, 3 Whitehall Place, LONDON, SW1A 2AW.
WHITEHEAD, Mr. Robert Neil, BSc ACA *1982;* Prospect House, Lealholmside, Lealholm, WHITBY, YO21 2AF.
WHITEHEAD, Mr. Rodney John, BA ACA *1985;* Foremarke House, Thorpe Green, EGHAM, TW20 8QL.
WHITEHEAD, Mr. Roger, FCA *1964;* 7 Westminster Close, SHEFFIELD, S10 4FR.
WHITEHEAD, Mr. Russell Gregory, BA ACA *2000;* 153 Argyle Gardens, UPMINSTER, ESSEX, RM14 3EU.
WHITEHEAD, Miss. Sarah Anne, ACA *2008;* Smith & Williamson Ltd Corporate Tax, 25 Moorgate, LONDON, EC2R 6AY.
WHITEHEAD, Mr. Simon Gregory Michael, MA ACA *1989;* Nutfield House Market Street, Charlbury, CHIPPING NORTON, OXFORDSHIRE, OX7 3PH.
WHITEHEAD, Mr. Simon James, BSc ACA *2004;* with PricewaterhouseCoopers LLP, 1 Embankment Place, LONDON, WC2N 6RH.
•**WHITEHEAD, Mr. Stuart Michael, FCA** *1983;* Edwards Veeder LLP, Alex House, 260-268 Chapel Street, SALFORD, M3 5JZ. See also Edwards Veeder Payroll Ltd
WHITEHEAD, Mrs. Suzanne Jane, ACA *1999;* 4 Nightingale Close, RAYLEIGH, ESSEX, SS6 9GE.
WHITEHEAD, Mr. William Frederick, ACA *1986;* 6 Fenhall Park, Lanchester, DURHAM, DH7 0JT.
WHITEHILL, Mr. Edward David, MA FCA *1963;* 2 Shelbourne Close, PINNER, HA5 3AF.
WHITEHORN, Mr. John Leonard, FCA *1963;* Beech Croft, 10 Dinorben Beeches, FLEET, GU52 7SR. (Life Member)
WHITEHORN, Mr. Justin Michael, BA FCA *1974;* Lower Farm House, Milton-under-Wychwood, CHIPPING NORTON, OXFORDSHIRE, OX7 6EX.
WHITEHORN, Mr. Mark Jeremy, MA ACA *1982;* 3B The Grove, EPSOM, KT17 4DQ.
•**WHITEHOUSE, Mr. Alan John, FCA** *1965;* 8 Edstone Close, Dorridge, SOLIHULL, B93 8DP.
•**WHITEHOUSE, Miss. Alison, BSc ACA** *1993;* Total Accounting Solutions Limited, 68 Habgood Road, LOUGHTON, ESSEX, IG10 1HE.
WHITEHOUSE, Miss. Amanda Jayne, BSc ACA *1998;* 129 Mitre Road, Cheslyn Hay, WALSALL, WS6 7HL.
WHITEHOUSE, Mr. Andrew Peter, BSc ACA *1987;* Esure Holdings Ltd, The Observatory, Castlefield Road, REIGATE, SURREY, RH2 0SG.
WHITEHOUSE, Mr. Brian, FCA *1969;* 73 Harborne Road, OLDBURY, B68 9JF.
WHITEHOUSE, Mr. Brian Cedric, FCA *1951;* 22 Chartwell Drive, SUTTON COLDFIELD, B74 4NT. (Life Member)
•**WHITEHOUSE, Mrs. Carole Ann, FCA** *1976;* (Tax Fac), C.A. Whitehouse & Co, 5 Lowdham, Wilnecote, TAMWORTH, B77 4LX.
WHITEHOUSE, Mr. Charles Frederick, BSc ACA *1997;* 246 Lower Luton Road, Wheathampstead, ST. ALBANS, HERTFORDSHIRE, AL4 8HN.
WHITEHOUSE, Mr. Charles Raymond, FCA *1970;* 17 Mill Lane, Dorridge, SOLIHULL, B93 8PA.
WHITEHOUSE, Mr. Christopher Graham, BA ACA *2007;* Flat 4, 113 Broadhurst Gardens, LONDON, NW6 3BJ.

WHITEHOUSE, Mr. Christopher James, MSc ACA *2003;* Hardstrasse 100, 8004 ZURICH, SWITZERLAND.
WHITEHOUSE, Miss. Colette Alison, BA(Hons) ACA *2003;* 4 Riverbank Close, NANTWICH, CW5 5YF.
WHITEHOUSE, Mr. David Benton, FCA *1977;* Ropemaker Place 12th Floor, 25 Ropemaker Place, LONDON, EC2Y 9LY.
WHITEHOUSE, Mr. Derrick Frank, FCA *1969;* 6 Overbury Close, HALESOWEN, B63 3DL. (Life Member)
•WHITEHOUSE, Mr. Gavin Christopher, BSocSc FCA *1994;* Clement Keys, 39/40 Calthorpe Road, Edgbaston, BIRMINGHAM, B15 1TS. See also Professional Link Limited
WHITEHOUSE, Miss. Gemma Claire, ACA *2009;* 10 Springfield Crescent, SOLIHULL, WEST MIDLANDS, B92 9AF.
WHITEHOUSE, Mr. Gerald Michael, FCA *1971;* 2 Glebe Gardens, Cheadle, STOKE-ON-TRENT, ST10 1YW.
WHITEHOUSE, Mr. Grant Leslie, BSc ACA *1993;* Flat 12 Winter House, 38 Twickenham Road, TEDDINGTON, TW11 8AW.
•WHITEHOUSE, Mrs. Jacqueline, ACA MAAT *1996;* 2 Chelsea Drive, SUTTON COLDFIELD, WEST MIDLANDS, B74 4UG.
WHITEHOUSE, Mr. Joel Paul, BSc FCA FSI *1999;* Brook Cottage, 7 Drayton Road, Belbroughton, STOURBRIDGE, WEST MIDLANDS, DY9 0DX.
WHITEHOUSE, Mr. John Mitchell, FCA *1967;* Dales Cottage, Melford Road, Lawshall, BURY ST. EDMUNDS, IP29 4PX. (Life Member)
WHITEHOUSE, Mr. Jonathan Paul, ACA *1991;* 87 Gunnin Street, FIG TREE POCKET, QLD 4069, AUSTRALIA.
•WHITEHOUSE, Miss. Kelly, BA(Hons) ACA *2002;* Peters Elworthy & Moore, Salisbury House, Station Road, CAMBRIDGE, CB1 2LA.
•WHITEHOUSE, Mrs. Margaret Patricia, FCA *1982;* (Tax Fac), PPI Accounting Ltd, Horley Green House, Horley Green Road, Claremount, HALIFAX, WEST YORKSHIRE HX3 6AS.
WHITEHOUSE, Mr. Mark, BA ACA *1993;* 56 Pytchley Road, KETTERING, NORTHAMPTONSHIRE, NN15 6JA.
WHITEHOUSE, Mr. Mark Edward, BSc ACA *2005;* 2nd Floor Bournville Place, Cadbury Ltd PO Box 12, Bournville, BIRMINGHAM, B30 2LU.
WHITEHOUSE, Miss. Melissa Marie, BSc ACA *2007;* 47 Phoenix Way, CARDIFF, CF14 4PR.
WHITEHOUSE, Mr. Nicholas Murray, MA FCA *1978;* 40 Wardo Avenue, LONDON, SW6 6RE.
WHITEHOUSE, Mr. Nigel Douglas, BSc ACA *1989;* Riverbank House, 49 Mill Village, The Lower Mill Estate, Somerford Keynes, CIRENCESTER, GLOUCESTERSHIRE GL7 6DU.
WHITEHOUSE, Mr. Paul Edward, MSc BSc ACA *2006;* Flat 3 Turnberry Court, 5 Vicarage Road, TEDDINGTON, MIDDLESEX, TW11 8JH.
WHITEHOUSE, Mr. Paul Wilson, FCA *1959;* 44 Clifton Road, Tettenhall, WOLVERHAMPTON, WV6 9AP. (Life Member)
WHITEHOUSE, Mr. Peter George, MEng ACA *1991;* 19A Acresfield Road, Timperley, ALTRINCHAM, WA15 6HT.
WHITEHOUSE, Mr. Richard Charles, FCA *1975;* E H Bennett & Co Ltd, 33-35 High Street, Shirehampton, BRISTOL, BS11 0DX.
•WHITEHOUSE, Mrs. Rosanella, BA FCA *1994;* Phipps Henson McAllister, 22/24 Harborough Road, Kingsthorpe, NORTHAMPTON, NN2 7AZ.
WHITEHOUSE, Mr. Simon John, FCA *1986;* 4300 Brandywine St NW, WASHINGTON, DC 20016, UNITED STATES.
WHITEHOUSE, Mr. Simon Richard, BSc ACA *2000;* Woodview, Mill Road, Bethersden, ASHFORD, KENT, TN26 3DA.
WHITEHOUSE, Mr. Stuart Eric James, BA ACA *1991;* 2 Walsall Road, Four Oaks, SUTTON COLDFIELD, WEST MIDLANDS, B74 4QJ.
WHITEHOUSE, Miss. Victoria Ann, BA ACA *1998;* The Old Granary, 5 Shurnock Court Barns, Saltway, Feckenham, REDDITCH, WORCESTERSHIRE B96 6JT.
WHITEHURST, Mrs. Claire Elizabeth, BA(Hons) ACA *2001;* with Spencer Gardner Dickins Limited, 3 Coventry Innovation Village, Cheetah Road, COVENTRY, CV1 2TL.
WHITEHURST, Mr. James Peter, BA ACA *2007;* Dental Laboratories Association, 44-46 Wollaton Road Beeston, NOTTINGHAM, NG9 2NR.
WHITEHURST, Mrs. Joanne Lesley, BA ACA *1997;* 5 Quenby Drive, DUDLEY, DY1 2GX.
WHITEHURST, Mr. Mark Christopher, BA ACA *2002;* 4 Walden Close, Thelwall, WARRINGTON, WA4 2HB.
WHITEHURST, Mr. Peter Lewis, ACA *1995;* Venus, 1 Old Park Lane, Trafford Park, MANCHESTER, M41 7HA.
•WHITEHURST, Mr. Trevor Harold, FCA *1970;* Freedman Frankl & Taylor, Reedham House, 31 King Street West, MANCHESTER, M3 2PJ.
WHITELAM, Mrs. Catherine Jane, BA ACA *2004;* with PricewaterhouseCoopers LLP, Benson House, 33 Wellington Street, LEEDS, LS1 4JP.
WHITELAM, Mr. David Roy, MA ACA *1979;* 1, Park Lane, HEMEL HEMPSTEAD, HP2 4YL.
WHITELAM, Mr. Gary, BA FCA *1983;* Southfield House, Clifford Road, Boston Spa, WETHERBY, LS23 6DB.
WHITELAND-SMITH, Mrs. Ann, FCA *1968;* C/O Jabega 2, Myramar1P37c, 29640 FUENGIROLA, MALAGA, SPAIN. (Life Member)
WHITELAW, Mr. Colman Michael, FCA *1975;* 98 Old Penkridge Road, CANNOCK, WS11 1HY.
WHITELAW, Mr. David Stuart, MA FCA *1981;* Chine House, Wildhill, ESSENDON, HERTFORDSHIRE, AL9 6EB.
WHITELAW, Mr. Peter Francis, BA ACA CTA *1985;* 7 Dickens Drive, CHISLEHURST, BR7 6RU.
WHITELAW, Mrs. Rachel Helen, BSc FCA *1988;* (Tax Fac), 8 Geneva Road, KINGSTON-UPON-THAMES, KT1 2TW.
WHITELEGG, Mr. James Richard, BSc FCA *1991;* 26 Trefoil Drive, Killinghall, HARROGATE, NORTH YORKSHIRE, HG3 2WB.
WHITELEY, Miss. Angela Mary, BA(Hons) ACA CTA *2001;* 6 Upper Green Way, Tingley, WAKEFIELD, WF3 1TA.
WHITELEY, Ms. Brenda Patricia, ACA *1985;* 6 Hayfield Avenue, Oakes, HUDDERSFIELD, HD3 4FZ.
WHITELEY, Mrs. Caroline Jane, BA FCA *1985;* with ICAEW, Metropolitan House, 321 Avebury Boulevard, MILTON KEYNES, MK9 2FZ.
WHITELEY, Mr. Christopher, BSc ACA *2004;* 84 Kings Road, KINGSTON UPON THAMES, SURREY, KT2 5HS.
•WHITELEY, Mr. Christopher John, BCom BCompt(Hons) ACA CA(SA) *2011;* (Tax Fac), Creating Limited, 93 New Road, MARLOW, BUCKINGHAMSHIRE, SL7 3NN.
WHITELEY, Mr. Christopher Keith, MA FCA *1971;* Westley Cottage, Westley, Waterless, NEWMARKET, SUFFOLK, CB8 0RQ.
•WHITELEY, Mr. David Maurice, FCA *1977;* Max Montague Limited, Building D, Berkley Works, Berkley Grove, Primrose Hill, LONDON NW1 8XY.
WHITELEY, Mr. David Robert, BA FCA *1988;* Oak Apple Cottage, Westridge Green, Streatley, READING, RG8 9RG.
•WHITELEY, Mrs. Elizabeth, BSc ACA *1986;* (Tax Fac), Elizabeth Whiteley Accountancy Limited, 2 The Meade, Chorlton, MANCHESTER, M21 8FA.
WHITELEY, Mr. Fred Ainsworth, FCA *1952;* 47 Glenville Road, Rustington, LITTLEHAMPTON, WEST SUSSEX, BN16 2EA. (Life Member)
WHITELEY, Mr. James, BA ACA *2001;* Ovre Kristianstens Gate 3D, 7014 TRONDHEIM, NORWAY.
WHITELEY, Mr. James Michael, BSc ACA *1992;* 1 Eton Court, Richmond Road, STAINES, TW18 2AF.
WHITELEY, Mr. John Barry, FCA *1965;* Orontes, Shute Road, Kilmington, AXMINSTER, EX13 7ST.
WHITELEY, Mr. John Howard, BA FCA *1983;* 5 Headlands Drive, BERKHAMSTED, HERTFORDSHIRE, HP4 2PG.
•WHITELEY, Mr. John Peter, BSc FCA *1986;* 84 Pannal Ash Road, HARROGATE, NORTH YORKSHIRE, HG2 9AB.
•WHITELEY, Mr. John Stuart, FCA *1965;* Stuart Whiteley FCA CMI, 50 Alma Road, COLNE, LANCASHIRE, BB8 7JJ. See also J.S. Whiteley
WHITELEY, Mr. Jonathan Walton, LLB ACA *1982;* 9 Broadhalgh Road, ROCHDALE, OL11 5NJ.
WHITELEY, Mr. Matthew James, ACA *2009;* 84 Pannal Ash Road, HARROGATE, NORTH YORKSHIRE, HG2 9AB.
•WHITELEY, Mr. Maurice, BSc FCA FCII CTA *1974;* Maurice Whiteley, Nash House, 16 Swain Street, WATCHET, SOMERSET, TA23 0AB.
WHITELEY, Mr. Paul Martin, MSc BA ACA *1984;* Caledonia Investment Plc, 30 Buckingham Gate, LONDON, SW1E 6NN.
WHITELEY, Mr. Peter John, BA FCA *1989;* 4 Blackwall Rise, Friendly, SOWERBY BRIDGE, WEST YORKSHIRE, HX6 2UJ.
WHITELEY, Mr. Raymond Robert, MBA BA FCA *1975;* 5 Greenside Close, Merrow, GUILDFORD, GU4 7EU.
WHITELEY, Mr. Robert Allan, MEng ACA *2004;* 88 High Street, Ashwell, BALDOCK, HERTFORDSHIRE, SG7 5NS.
•WHITELEY, Mr. Simon William Alastair, BA ACA *1983;* Simon Whiteley Consulting Limited, 74 Lyndhurst Grove, LONDON, SE15 5AH.
WHITELEY, Mr. William Thomas, BSc ACA *2005;* Cabot Corporation, Suite 1300, 2 Seaport Lane, BOSTON, MA 02210, UNITED STATES.
•WHITELEY, Mrs. Winifred, BA ACA CTA *1986;* Simon Whiteley Consulting Limited, 74 Lyndhurst Grove, LONDON, SE15 5AH.
WHITELOCK, Mr. Christopher John, BA ACA *1989;* PO Box 909, VICTORIA PARK, WA 6979, AUSTRALIA.
WHITELOCK, Mr. Peter Rodney, FCA *1958;* Cranford, 2 Esholt Avenue, Park Road Guiseley, LEEDS, LS20 8AX. (Life Member)
WHITEMAN, Mr. Charles Richard, MA ACA *2003;* Flat 2, 62 Upper Richmond Road West, LONDON, SW14 8DA.
WHITEMAN, Mr. David James, ACA *1995;* 21 Avenue Matignon, 75008 PARIS, FRANCE.
WHITEMAN, Mr. Gregory Iain, BEng ACA DipCII *1997;* Les Frances, Route des Frances, St. Saviour, GUERNSEY, GY7 9RW.
•WHITEMAN, Mr. Ian Frank, BA FCA *1967;* (Tax Fac), I.F. Whiteman, 1 Ashdown, 7 Cambalt Road, LONDON, SW15 6EL.
WHITEMAN, Mr. Jeffrey Keith, BEng ACA CF *1994;* 25 View St, PADDINGTON, QLD 4064, AUSTRALIA.
WHITEMAN, Mr. Luke, ACA *2011;* 24 Glendale Avenue, EASTBOURNE, EAST SUSSEX, BN21 1UU.
WHITEMAN, Mr. Philip William, BSc FCA *1979;* SEMTA, 14 Upton Road, WATFORD, HERTFORDSHIRE, WD18 0JT.
WHITEMORE, Mr. Kevin Arthur, FCA *1973;* Yew Tree House, Watermillock, PENRITH, CUMBRIA, CA11 0JN.
WHITER, Mr. Barnaby John Wakinshaw, BA ACA *1995;* 75 Broomleaf Road, FARNHAM, GU9 8DH.
WHITER, Mrs. Claire, MA ACA *2002;* Town Dairy Cottage, Church Road, Lympstone, EXMOUTH, DEVON, EX8 5JU.
WHITER, Mrs. Janet Dulcie Sarah, FCA *1974;* Meades, Lake Street, Mark Cross, CROWBOROUGH, EAST SUSSEX, TN6 3NT.
•WHITER, Mr. John Lindsay Pearce, FCA *1973;* 62 Bishopsgate, LONDON, EC2N 4AW.
WHITER, Mr. Timothy David, BSc(Hons) ACA *2002;* Town Dairy Cottage, Church Road, Lympstone, EXMOUTH, EX8 5JU.
WHITESIDE, Mr. Christopher Mark, BSc ACA *1989;* 5 Fleming Road, Chafford Hundred, GRAYS, RM16 6YA.
•WHITESIDE, Mr. Gerard Francis, FCA *1981;* Ingalls (Kendal) Limited, Libra House, Murley Moss Business Village, Oxenholme Road, KENDAL, CUMBRIA LA9 7RL. See also Douglass Grange
WHITESIDE, Mrs. Hazel Jean, BA ACA *1983;* University of Chichester, Finance Department, College Lane, CHICHESTER, WEST SUSSEX, PO19 6PE.
WHITESIDE, Miss. Jennifer Lynn, ACA *2010;* 8 The Pastures, BLACKBURN, BB2 7QR.
•WHITESIDE, Mrs. Joanne Lesley, BA ACA *1982;* (Tax Fac), Whiteside Limited, 6 & 7 Feast Field, Horsforth, LEEDS, LS18 4TJ. See also Accounts Department Online Limited
WHITESIDE, Mr. John, FCA *1974;* 22 Swan Close, Poynton, STOCKPORT, SK12 1HX.
WHITESIDE, Mr. John Paul, ACA *1982;* 4 Moss Hall Farm Mews, Golborne Lane, High Legh, KNUTSFORD, CHESHIRE, WA16 0RD.
WHITESIDE, Mr. Neil Barry, BSc FCA *1985;* Darley Stud Management Co Ltd The Main Office, Duchess Drive, NEWMARKET, SUFFOLK, CB8 9HE.
WHITESIDE, Mr. Simon David, BA ACA *1997;* Struan House Mill of Crynoch, Maryculter, ABERDEEN, AB12 5GX.
WHITESIDE, Mr. Terence Ernest, MBE FCA *1949;* Coach House Cottage, 1 Coach House Way, STRATFORD-UPON-AVON, WARWICKSHIRE, CV31 6YJ. (Life Member)
WHITESIDE, Ms. Veronica Clare, BSc ACA *1992;* 68 Hillpark Avenue, Blackhall, EDINBURGH, EH4 7AL.
•WHITESMITH, Mr. John Dennis, FCA *1974;* 18 Fenhall Park, Lanchester, DURHAM, DH7 0JT.
WHITEWAY, Mr. David Anthony, ACA *1988;* 2 Meadow House Drive, Fulwood, SHEFFIELD, S10 3NA.
WHITEWAY, Mr. George Timothy, BA FCA *1955;* 16 Wentworth Road, SUTTON COLDFIELD, B74 2SG. (Life Member)
•WHITEWAY, Mr. Philip Anthony, BA ACA *1983;* (Tax Fac), CLB Coopers, Fleet House, New Road, LANCASTER, LA1 1EZ.
WHITEWAY, Miss. Ruth Jane, BSc ACA *1992;* The Knoll, 28 Draycot Cerne, CHIPPENHAM, WILTSHIRE, SN15 5LH.
WHITEWOOD, Mr. David Stephen, BSc ACA MCT *1983;* Lockton Companies International Ltd, The St. Botolph Buildin, 138 Houndsditch, LONDON, EC3A 7AG.
WHITEWOOD, Mr. Paul Mark, BSc ACA *1994;* 1362 Hidden Hills Drive, KELOWNA V1V 2X8, BC, CANADA.
WHITFIELD, Mr. Andrew Peter, BSc ACA *1993;* 12 Llwyn Kensington, Acton, WREXHAM, LL12 8AJ.
WHITFIELD, Mrs. Annette, BSc ACA *1992;* 39 Starbold Crescent, Knowle, SOLIHULL, B93 9LA.
WHITFIELD, Mrs. Catriona Anne, LLB FCA *1991;* Culgower House, Loth, HELMSDALE, KW8 6HP.
WHITFIELD, Ms. Christine Jane, BA(Hons) ACA FPC TEP *1991;* Bella Vista Le Mont Du Ouaisne, St. Brelade, JERSEY, JE3 8AW.
WHITFIELD, Mr. David Lister, FCA *1969;* Osterwaldstrasse 131, 80805 MUNICH, GERMANY. (Life Member)
WHITFIELD, Mr. Dylan Benjamin, ACA *2004;* 17 Dorien Road, LONDON, SW20 8EL.
WHITFIELD, Mr. Edward Henry, FCA *1968;* Weston Hall, Weston, Standon, STAFFORD, ST21 6RF.
WHITFIELD, Mrs. Elizabeth Ann, BSc ACA *1992;* 68 Silhill Hall Road, SOLIHULL, WEST MIDLANDS, B91 1JS.
WHITFIELD, Mr. Ian, BA ACA *1989;* Unit 2 City Link Industrial Park Phoenix Way Tyersal, BRADFORD, BD4 8JP.
•WHITFIELD, Mr. Ian Robert, BA FCA *1988;* with Evolution Audit LLP, 10 Evolution, Wynyard Park, BILLINGHAM, CLEVELAND, TS22 5TB.
WHITFIELD, Mrs. Joanne Claire Ranson, BA(Hons) ACA *2004;* 51 Falstone Drive, Fellside Meadows, CHESTER LE STREET, COUNTY DURHAM, DH2 3ST.
WHITFIELD, Miss. Joanne Louise, BSc ACA *1995;* 46 Mossgrove Road, Timperley, ALTRINCHAM, WA15 6LT.
WHITFIELD, Mrs. Joanne Louise, BA FCA *1989;* 3 Hildyard Close, Stokesley, MIDDLESBROUGH, TS9 5QE.
•WHITFIELD, Mr. John David, MA ACA *1981;* PricewaterhouseCoopers LLP, 1 Embankment Place, LONDON, WC2N 6RH. See also PricewaterhouseCoopers
•WHITFIELD, Mr. John Neville, BSc FCA *1992;* MCR, 43-45 Portman Square, LONDON, W1H 6LY.
WHITFIELD, Mr. Malcolm Charles Norman, FCA *1963;* 36 Northcote Road, TWICKENHAM, TW1 1PA. (Life Member)
WHITFIELD, Mr. Nicholas Stewart Berkeley, BA FCA *1999;* Abu Dhabi Commercial Bank, P.O. Box 939, ABU DHABI, UNITED ARAB EMIRATES.
WHITFIELD, Mrs. Paula Jayne, BSc FCA *1992;* with PricewaterhouseCoopers LLP, Donington Court, Pegasus Business Park, Castle Donington, DERBY, DE74 2UZ.
WHITFIELD, Mr. Peter John Haydon, MA ACA *1987;* 152 Kidmore End Road, Emmer Green, READING, RG4 8SP.
WHITFIELD, Mr. Peter Nigel, BA FCA *1991;* 39 Starbold Crescent, Knowle, SOLIHULL, WEST MIDLANDS, B93 9LA.
•WHITFIELD, Mr. Peter Storey, FCA *1966;* (Tax Fac), Peter S. Whitfield, 13 Briarwood, Westbury on Trym, BRISTOL, BS9 3SS.
WHITFIELD, Mr. Richard Ian, FCA *1971;* P.O. Box 2555, Half Moon P.O., Rose Hall, ST JAMES SJ29, JAMAICA.
•WHITFIELD, Mr. Roger David, FCA *1975;* Turner Peachey, Column House, London Road, SHREWSBURY, SY2 6NN.
WHITFIELD, Mr. Stephen Howard, BSc ACA *1997;* 1011 Estancia Lane, ALGONQUIN, IL 60102, UNITED STATES.
WHITFIELD, Mr. William George Thomas, FCA *1966;* 25 Charles Sumner House, Hobill Walk, SURBITON, SURREY, KT5 8SZ. (Life Member)
WHITHAM, Mr. Alan Frederick George, FCA *1962;* Lea Bank, Demage Lane, Lea-by-Backford, CHESTER, CH1 6NU. (Life Member)
WHITHAM, Mrs. Anita, BSc ACA *1993;* 39 Corringway, Ealing, LONDON, W5 3AB.
WHITHAM, Mr. Damian Paul, BA ACA *1994;* 39 Corringway, Ealing, LONDON, W5 3AB.
WHITHAM, Mr. Ian Edward, BA ACA *1989;* 5 Chichester Close, SALE, M33 4TR.
WHITHAM, Mr. Peter, BA ACA *1992;* 6 Park Place, Newhaven, EDINBURGH, EH6 4LB.
WHITHAM, Mr. Roy, FCA *1960;* 68 Holymoor Road, Holymoorside, CHESTERFIELD, S42 7DX. (Life Member)
WHITHAM, Mr. Stuart Richard, BA ACA *1997;* 40 Macdonalds Lane, RD3, Rangiora 7473, NORTH CANTERBURY, NEW ZEALAND.
WHITHAM, Mrs. Susan Osborne, BSc ACA *1995;* 6 Park Place, EDINBURGH, EH6 4LB.

WHITHOUSE, Mr. Michael James Norman, BSc FCA *1977;* 3 Bells Court, BISHOPS CASTLE, SHROPSHIRE, SY9 5BJ.

WHITICAR, Mr. Jonathan James, MA FCA *1981;* Maple House Consulting Ltd, Maple House, Dean Lane, WINCHESTER, HAMPSHIRE, SO22 5LS.

WHITING, Miss. Adele Kate, BA ACA *2005;* 72 Minster Moorgate, BEVERLEY, NORTH HUMBERSIDE, HU17 8HR.

WHITING, Mr. Alec, BSc ACA *1999;* 41 Muschamp Road, LONDON, SE15 4EG.

•**WHITING, Mr. Alexander, FCA** *1977;* Alexander Whiting & Co Limited, Shelthorpe Lodge, 6 Chestnuts Close, Sutton Bonington, LOUGHBOROUGH, LEICESTERSHIRE LE12 5RJ.

WHITING, Mrs. Alison Louise, BSc(Hons) ACA *2000;* Barons Keep, Pantings Lane, Highclere, NEWBURY, BERKSHIRE, RG20 9PS.

WHITING, Mr. Andrew Michael John, BSc ACA *1979;* Kia Katina, London Road, WINDLESHAM, SURREY, GU20 6PJ.

WHITING, Miss. Audrey, FCA *1953;* 10 Cecil Road, Cheam, SUTTON, SM1 2DL. (Life Member)

WHITING, Mr. David John, BSc FCA CTA *1976;* Chartered Institute of Taxation, 1st Floor, Artillery House, 11-19 Artillery Row, LONDON, SW1P 1RT.

WHITING, Mr. David Michael, BA(Hons) ACA *2003;* 3 Walnut Grove, Wooburn Green, HIGH WYCOMBE, BUCKINGHAMSHIRE, HP10 0AL.

WHITING, Mr. Dexter, MA ACA *2006;* 3 Grosvenor Mews, Grosvenor Road, EPSOM, KT18 6JL.

•**WHITING, Mrs. Elaine Margaret Crosland, BSc ACA** *1979;* Elaine Whiting, Great Gable, 225 Kitson Hill Rd, MIRFIELD, WF14 9DS.

•**WHITING, Mr. Gregory John, BA FCA** *1982;* Smith Cooper, 2 Lace Market Square, NOTTINGHAM, NG1 1PB. See also F B 40 Limited

WHITING, Mr. Ian Richard, BA ACA *1984;* 207 St. Bernards Road, SOLIHULL, B92 7DL.

•**WHITING, Mr. John William, MA FCA FCCA** *1970;* (Tax Fac), 64 Thanington Road, CANTERBURY, CT1 3XE.

WHITING, Mr. Jonathan David, BSc FCA *1989;* 29 Farmhill Lane, Douglas, ISLE OF MAN, IM2 2EF.

WHITING, Mr. Jonathan Lee, BSc ACA *1994;* 55 Elm Grove, ORPINGTON, BR6 0AA.

WHITING, Mr. Michael Keith, FCA *1966;* 16 Riddings Road, Hale, ALTRINCHAM, WA15 9DS.

WHITING, Mrs. Pauline Heather, BSc ACA *1992;* 5 Alders End Lane, HARPENDEN, HERTFORDSHIRE, AL5 2HL.

WHITING, Mr. Peter Noel Thurley, FCA *1968;* Thaw Cottage, City, COWBRIDGE, CF71 7RW.

WHITING, Mrs. Rachel Elizabeth, BSc FCA CTA *1987;* Flintwell House, Novington Lane, East Chiltington, LEWES, BN7 3AT.

WHITING, Mr. Robert Lawrence, FCA *1951;* Cernbrok House, Holford, BRIDGWATER, SOMERSET, TA5 1SD. (Life Member)

•**WHITING, Mrs. Ruth Louise, ACA FCCA DChA** *2009;* RLW Accountants, 5 Elms Paddock, Little Stretton, CHURCH STRETTON, SHROPSHIRE, SY6 6RD.

WHITING, Miss. Samantha Louise, ACA *2008;* 131 Bybrook Road, Kennington, ASHFORD, Kent, TN24 9JE.

•**WHITING, Mr. Stephen David, FCA** *1980;* (Tax Fac), S.D. Whiting & Co Limited, 76 Ouseley Road, Wraysbury, STAINES, TW19 5JH.

WHITING, Mr. Stephen Kenneth, MA FCA *1984;* Creed Catering Supplies Ltd Unit 2 Herrick Way, Staverton Technology Park Staverton, CHELTENHAM, GL51 6TQ.

WHITING, Mrs. Susan Barbara, DPh ACA *1979;* 7 Abbey View, RADLETT, WD7 8LT.

WHITING, Mrs. Susan Helen, BSc ACA *1982;* 8 Grandfield Avenue, Radcliffe-on-Trent, NOTTINGHAM, NG12 1AL.

•**WHITING, Ms. Susan Joy, BA ACA** *1988;* (Tax Fac), Dean Statham, Bank Passage, STAFFORD, ST16 2JS.

•**WHITING, Miss. Susan May, BSc FCA** *1984;* 10 Lorne Road, Southsea, PORTSMOUTH, HAMPSHIRE, PO5 1RR.

WHITLAM, Mr. Daniel, ACA *2011;* 93 Heddington Grove, Islington, LONDON, N7 9SZ.

WHITLAM, Miss. Lucy, BSc ACA *2010;* 6 Canewdon Close, WOKING, GU22 7RA.

WHITLAM, Mr. Michael George, BA(Hons) ACA *2002;* Deutsche Bank Winchester House, 1 Great Winchester Street, LONDON, EC2N 2DB.

WHITLEY, Mr. Adrian Mourant, BSc(Hons) ACA *2002;* 41 Mitchell Street, BENTLEIGH, VIC 3204, AUSTRALIA.

•**WHITLEY, Mrs. Alexia Louise, ACA** *2005;* Le Suffren, 7eme etage, 7 rue Suffren Reymond, 98000 MONACO, MONACO.

WHITLEY, Mr. Benjamin Neil, MEng ACA *2001;* 6 The Crescent, Croxley Green, RICKMANSWORTH, HERTFORDSHIRE, WD3 3DU.

WHITLEY, Mr. Brett Charles, ACA CA(SA) *2010;* 1 The Oaks, Fetcham, LEATHERHEAD, SURREY, KT22 9PP.

WHITLEY, Mr. Edward Thomas, BSc ACA *1980;* The Old Vicarage, Wilmington, POLEGATE, BN26 5SL.

WHITLEY, Mr. John Duncan, BSc FCA *1974;* Field View, Byers Lane, GODSTONE, RH9 8JL.

WHITLEY, Mr. Stuart John, BSc ACA *2004;* Le Quattrocento, 14 Quai Jean Charles REY, MC98000 MONACO, MONACO.

•**WHITLEY-JONES, Mr. Christopher David, BSc FCA** *1989;* PRB Accountants LLP, Kingfisher House, Hurstwood Grange, Hurstwood Lane, HAYWARDS HEATH, WEST SUSSEX RH17 7QX. See also PRB Martin Pollins LLP and Movie Accounting LLP

WHITLING, Mr. John Victor, FCA *1970;* Boscehan, Hannafore Lane, LOOE, CORNWALL, PL13 2DT.

WHITLOCK, Mr. Benedict Stephen James, BA ACA *2006;* 15 Hollis Wood Drive, Wrecclesham, FARNHAM, GU10 4JT.

WHITLOCK, Mr. Brian John, MA ACA *1983;* (Tax Fac), 57 Charnwood Way, LEAMINGTON SPA, CV32 7BU.

•**WHITLOCK, Mr. Ian John Philip, FCA** *1983;* Ernst & Young LLP, 1 More London Place, LONDON, SE1 2AF. See also Ernst & Young Europe LLP

•**WHITLOCK, Mrs. Jane, BA ACA** *1996;* Deloitte LLP, 4 Brindley Place, BIRMINGHAM, B1 2HZ. See also Deloitte & Touche LLP

WHITLOCK, Mr. Mark Howard, FCA *1974;* 40 Glen Rise, BRIGHTON, BN1 5LP.

WHITLOCK, Mr. Peter James, FCA *1991;* 18 Japonica Close, BICESTER, OX26 3YB.

•**WHITLOCK, Mr. Rhodri Ryland, BA ACA** *1990;* (Tax Fac), PKF (UK) LLP, Pannell House, Park Street, GUILDFORD, SURREY, GU1 4HN.

WHITLOW, Mrs. Jeanette Lindsay, BSc ACA *1984;* 48B Masters Lane, HALESOWEN, B62 9HL.

WHITMAN, Mr. Barrie Stuart, BSc ACA *1985;* 39 Kildare Terrace, LONDON, W2 5JT.

•**WHITMEE, Mrs. Deborah Joan, BA FCA** *1988;* Forest Lodge, Cages Wood Drive Egypt, Farnham Common, SLOUGH, SL2 3JZ.

•**WHITMELL, Mr. Paul Edwin, BSc(Econ) FCA** *1982;* (Tax Fac), P W Accountants Ltd, 82b High Street, Sawston, CAMBRIDGE, CB22 3HJ.

•**WHITMORE, Mr. Barry John, BSc FCA** *1985;* B.Jay & Co, 51 Porthill Drive, Copthorne, SHREWSBURY, SY3 8RS.

WHITMORE, Mr. David John Ludlow, BSc FCA *1984;* Thurnets, Lower Moushill Lane, Milford, GODALMING, GU8 5JX.

WHITMORE, Mr. David William, ACA CA(SA) *2011;* (Tax Fac), Salans, Millennium Bridge House, 2 Lambeth Hill, LONDON, EC4V 4AJ.

WHITMORE, Mr. Geoffrey Hector, FCA *1960;* 37 Victoria Road, Eton Wick, WINDSOR, SL4 6LY. (Life Member)

WHITMORE, Mr. James Robert, BSc ACA *2007;* 23 Pineway, Abbeydale, GLOUCESTER, GL4 4AE.

WHITMORE, Mrs. Lisa Marie, BSc(Hons) ACA *2003;* Ryhurst Ltd, Rydon House, Station Road, FOREST ROW, EAST SUSSEX, RH18 5DW.

WHITMORE, Mrs. Patricia Susan, BSc ACA *1979;* 22 East Sheen Avenue, LONDON, SW14 8AS.

•**WHITMORE, Mrs. Susan Jane, BA FCA** *1992;* Devonshire Advisory, 54 Huggetts Lane, EASTBOURNE, EAST SUSSEX, BN22 0LU.

•**WHITNEY, Mrs. Andrea Ruth, BSc(Hons) ACA** *2001;* Francis Gray, Ty Madog, 32 Queens Road, ABERYSTWYTH, DYFED, SY23 2HN. See also Francis, Jones & Davies Ltd

WHITNEY, Mr. Mark Roy, BSc(Hons) ACA *2002;* Goldfish Consultancy Ltd, 17 Bencroft Road, HEMEL HEMPSTEAD, HERTFORDSHIRE, HP2 5UX.

•**WHITNEY, Mr. Paul Andrew, ACA MP** *2003;* Hallidays LLP, Riverside House, Kings Reach Business Park, Yew Street, STOCKPORT, CHESHIRE SK4 2HD. See also Hallidays Accountants LLP

•**WHITNEY, Mrs. Sarah Jane, BSc ACA** *1989;* 22 The Drive, SEVENOAKS, KENT, TN13 3AE.

WHITROW, Mrs. Jane Elizabeth, PhD BSc FCA *1998;* 40 Gun Lane, KNEBWORTH, SG3 6BH.

WHITROW, Mr. Robert William Guy, BCom FCA *1990;* Kilverts Parsonage, Chippenham Road, Langley Burrell, CHIPPENHAM, SN15 4LE.

WHITSON, Mr. Rowland John, FCA *1959;* Jorvik, 35 Parkfield, Chorleywood, RICKMANSWORTH, WD3 5AZ. (Life Member)

WHITTAKER, Mrs. Allison, BA ACA *1990;* 22 Bennett Street, MAYLANDS, SA 5069, AUSTRALIA.

WHITTAKER, Mr. Andrew Graham, FCA *1983;* 101 Yarrbat Avenue, BALWYN, VIC 3103, AUSTRALIA.

WHITTAKER, Mrs. Anne Victoria, BA FCA *1990;* 32 Main Street, Mawsley, KETTERING, NORTHAMPTONSHIRE, NN14 1GA.

WHITTAKER, Mr. Charles Norris, MA FCA *1968;* 21 St Marks Road, HENLEY-ON-THAMES, RG9 1LP. (Life Member)

WHITTAKER, Miss. Claire Elizabeth, LLB FCA *1987;* 45 Salisbury Drive, Bracebridge Heath, LINCOLN, LN4 2SW.

WHITTAKER, Mr. Colin, BSc FCA *1984;* Coeur Joyeux, Rue Des Sapins, St Peter, JERSEY, JE3 7AD.

WHITTAKER, Mr. Colin David, FCA *1966;* Neathwood House, Nr. Kingswood, WOTTON-UNDER-EDGE, GL12 8JU.

WHITTAKER, Mr. Daniel James, BA ACA *2000;* 21 Waterhouse Mead, College Town, SANDHURST, GU47 0ZD.

WHITTAKER, Mr. David Kevin, LLB FCA *1965;* Field House, 26 Bownham Park, Rodborough Common, STROUD, GL5 5BZ.

WHITTAKER, Mr. Dean, BSc ACA *2000;* 104 Ticknall Road, Hartshorne, SWADLINCOTE, DERBYSHIRE, DE11 7AT.

WHITTAKER, Mrs. Deborah, BSc ACA *2007;* K P M G Edward VII Quay, Navigation Way Ashton-on-Ribble, PRESTON, PR2 2YF.

WHITTAKER, Mr. Dennis Martin, FCA *1973;* Berrow House, Berrow, MALVERN, WORCESTERSHIRE, WR13 6AE.

WHITTAKER, Mr. Edward Alexander Niles, ACA *2010;* with RSM Tenon Audit Limited, 2 Wellington Place, LEEDS, LS1 4AP.

WHITTAKER, Mr. Edward Joseph, ACA *1985;* 15 Goodhall Close, STANMORE, MIDDLESEX, HA7 4FR.

WHITTAKER, Miss. Elizabeth Anne, BA ACA *1992;* 10 Winterbrook Road, Herne Hill, LONDON, SE24 9JA.

WHITTAKER, Mr. Frederick Norman, FCA *1973;* 26 Abergeldie Street, Dulwich Hill, SYDNEY, NSW 2203, AUSTRALIA.

•**WHITTAKER, Mr. Geoffrey Brian, FCA** *1972;* Whittaker & Company Limited, 13 Doolittle Mill, Froghall Road, Ampthill, BEDFORD, MK45 2ND.

WHITTAKER, Mr. George, BSc ACA *2011;* 53a Cottenham Road, LONDON, E17 6RP.

•**WHITTAKER, Mr. George Moray, FCA** *1970;* George Whittaker FCA, 2 Twemlow Parade, Heysham, MORECAMBE, LANCASHIRE, LA3 1PD.

WHITTAKER, Mr. Graham, BA FCA *1991;* 79 Downs Park East, BRISTOL, BS6 7QG.

•**WHITTAKER, Mr. Graham Alfred, FCA** *1980;* with BDO LLP, 125 Colmore Row, BIRMINGHAM, B3 3SD.

WHITTAKER, Mr. Ian Paul, BSc FCA *1977;* Amor Group, 3 Lochside Way, EDINBURGH, EH12 9DT.

•**WHITTAKER, Mr. James Francis, MEng FCA CF** *1995;* 4 Oaklands Avenue, Adel, LEEDS, LS16 8NR.

WHITTAKER, Ms. Jill Marie, FCA *1988;* 8 Kingston Bay Road, SHOREHAM-BY-SEA, WEST SUSSEX, BN43 5HP.

WHITTAKER, Mr. John, BSc ACA *1993;* 10 Taleworth Road, ASHTEAD, KT21 2PT.

WHITTAKER, Mr. John, MA FCA *1975;* business school, Loughborough University, LOUGHBOROUGH, LEICESTERSHIRE, LE11 3TU.

WHITTAKER, Mrs. Judith Ellen, MA ACA *1987;* 3 Canterbury Road, OXFORD, OX2 6LU.

WHITTAKER, Miss. Katy, BA ACA *2004;* 6 Westbury Avenue, SALE, CHESHIRE, M33 4WQ.

WHITTAKER, Mr. Malcolm John, FCA *1962;* 11 Priory Park, Thurgarton, NOTTINGHAM, NG14 7HE.

WHITTAKER, Mr. Mark James, BA ACA *1987;* L'Oreal UK Ltd, 255 Hammersmith Road, LONDON, W6 8AZ.

WHITTAKER, Mr. Michael John, BA ACA *1987;* U B S Global Asset Management, 21 Lombard Street, LONDON, EC3V 9AH.

•**WHITTAKER, Mr. Michael Philip, FCA** *1981;* (Tax Fac), McCabe Ford Williams, 2 The Links, HERNE BAY, KENT, CT6 7GQ.

WHITTAKER, Mrs. Naomi, ACA *2008;* 55a Schubert Road, LONDON, SW15 2QT.

WHITTAKER, Mr. Neil Paul, ACA *2009;* 31 Highbank Road, NORTHWICH, CHESHIRE, CW8 4AB.

WHITTAKER, Mr. Nicholas Peter, BA ACA *1982;* 16 Ladycroft Paddock, Allestree, DERBY, DE22 2GA.

WHITTAKER, Mr. Nigel Anthony, BSc ACA *1987;* 28 Holmewood Ridge, Langton Green, TUNBRIDGE WELLS, TN3 0ED.

WHITTAKER, Mr. Oliver David, BA ACA *2007;* 5 Wilton Crescent, SOUTHAMPTON, SO15 7QN.

WHITTAKER, Mr. Peter Mark, FCA *1987;* 2 Ashford Court, Highburton, HUDDERSFIELD, HD8 0US.

•**WHITTAKER, Mr. Peter Richard, FCA** *1983;* P.R. Whittaker, 49 Woodfield Road, Cheadle Hulme, CHEADLE, CHESHIRE, SK8 7JT.

WHITTAKER, Mr. Philip David, LLB FCA *1983;* Pembroke Managing Agency Ltd, 3 Minster Court, LONDON, EC3R 7DD.

WHITTAKER, Mrs. Philippa Rosemary, MA FCA CPFA PGCertL&THE *1980;* 160 Chamber Road, OLDHAM, OL8 4BU.

WHITTAKER, Mr. Raymond Wemyss, BA FCA *1950;* Great Crouchs Farm, Rushlake Green, HEATHFIELD, EAST SUSSEX, TN21 9QD. (Life Member)

WHITTAKER, Mr. Rex Peter Albert, FCA *1953;* 8 Fairway Close, West Common, HARPENDEN, AL5 2NN.

WHITTAKER, Mr. Robert Brian, FCA *1973;* Royds Cottage, 130 Longwood Road, HUDDERSFIELD, HD3 4EJ.

•**WHITTAKER, Mr. Robert John, FCA** *1966;* (Tax Fac), R.J. Whittaker, Rivelin Cottage, Wynne Cresent, Lower Penn, WOLVERHAMPTON, WV4 4SW.

WHITTAKER, Mr. Roger Graham, FCA *1966;* 15 Spicers Field, Oxshott, LEATHERHEAD, KT22 0UT. (Life Member)

WHITTAKER, Mr. Roger Timothy, BA ACA *1981;* Holman Fenwick Willan, 65 rue d'Anjou, 75008 PARIS, FRANCE.

WHITTAKER, Mr. Simon Andrew, MEng ACA *1999;* 405 St. Davids Square, LONDON, E14 3WQ.

WHITTAKER, Mr. Simon Paul, LLB ACA *2002;* Greenfields, Francis Green Lane, Penkridge, STAFFORD, ST19 5HE.

WHITTAKER, Mr. Simon William, MA FCA *1977;* Mortgages for Business Limited, 53-55 High Street, SEVENOAKS, KENT, TN13 1JF.

WHITTAKER, Mr. Stanley Henry, FCA *1958;* Appletrees, 12 Kennylands Road, Sonning Common, READING, RG4 9JT. (Life Member)

WHITTAKER, Mr. Steven, BSc ACA *1983;* Rexcote, Bethesda Street, Upper Basildon, READING, RG8 8NU.

WHITTAKER, Mr. Thomas James, ACA MBA *1987;* The Prudential Assurance Co Ltd, 121 Kings Road, READING, RG1 3ES.

•**WHITTALL, Mr. Adrian John, BSc FCA** *1985;* Ysguborwen, Scethrog, BRECON, POWYS, LD3 7EQ.

•**WHITTALL, Mr. Graeme, ACA FCCA** *2008;* Chancery (UK) LLP, Chancery Pavilion, Boycott Avenue, Oldbrook, MILTON KEYNES, MK6 2TA.

WHITTALL, Mr. Jeffrey, BA ACA *1997;* 118 Carlingford Road, LONDON, N15 3ER.

WHITTALL, Mrs. Melanie Fiona, MSc ACA *2004;* British Telecom Delta Point, 31-35 Wellesley Road, CROYDON, CR9 2YZ.

WHITTALL, Mr. Robert Edward, ACA *1996;* PO Box 1805, MENTOR, OH 44061-1805, UNITED STATES.

WHITTAM, Miss. Amber, BSc ACA *2005;* 17 The Green, WESTERHAM, TN16 1AX.

WHITTAM, Mr. John Jerrold, BSc ACA *1990;* 4 Hanson Gardens, Bishops Cleeve, CHELTENHAM, GLOUCESTERSHIRE, GL52 7RA.

WHITTAM, Mr. Peter John, BSc FCA *1991;* with DTE Business Advisory Services Limited, DTE House, Hollins Mount, Hollins Lane, BURY, BL9 8AT.

WHITTARD, Mr. Timothy Peter Graham, BSc ACA *1993;* 11 Bridgewater Road, BERKHAMSTED, HERTFORDSHIRE, HP4 1HN.

WHITTEMORE, Mrs. Susan Jean, BSc ACA *1992;* Apartado de Correos 568, 03193 SAN MIGUEL DE SALINAS, ALICANTE, SPAIN.

WHITTEN, Mr. Colin Albert Frederick, FCA *1953;* 5 Kenneth Road, BANSTEAD, SURREY, SM7 3HQ.

WHITTEN, Mr. David John Alexander, MA ACA *1987;* 35 Wellesley Road, TWICKENHAM, TW2 5RR.

•**WHITTEN, Mr. Frank, FCA** *1974;* F. Whitten, 29 High Street, Bridge, CANTERBURY, CT4 5JZ.

WHITTEN, Mr. Michael Ian, BA ACA *1999;* 60 Wolsey Drive, KINGSTON-UPON-THAMES, KT2 5DN.

WHITTEN, Miss. Michaela Avril, ACA *2009;* 9 Howard Drive, MAIDSTONE, ME16 0QG.

WHITTEN, Mr. Robert Edward, BSc FCA *1966;* Glebe House, Ellesfield, WELWYN, HERTFORDSHIRE, AL6 9HB.

WHITTEN, Mr. Stephen Robert Boyd, BA ACA *1997;* 25 Harcourt Road, LONDON, N22 7XW.
WHITTENBURY, Mrs. Alison Mary, BSc ACA *1993;* Stocks Farm Cottage, Webbs Lane, Beenham, READING, RG7 5LH.
WHITTENBURY, Mr. John Rowsell, FCA *1962;* John Whittenbury Financial Services, 17a Gregories Road, BEACONSFIELD, BUCKINGHAMSHIRE, HP9 1HH.
WHITTENBURY, Mr. Robert James Havelock, BA ACA *1993;* Stocks Farm Cottage, Webbs Lane, Beenham, READING, RG7 5LH.
WHITTER, Mr. Gavin, ACA FCCA ACCA CTA *2007;* with Morris Crocker, Station House, 50 North Street, HAVANT, PO9 1QU.
WHITTER, Miss. Roberta Kelly, ACA *2008;* 2 Gold Street, Pent House 4, NEW YORK, NY 10038, UNITED STATES.
WHITTERN, Mr. Stephen Lee, BSc FCA *1999;* (Tax Fac), Fairway View, 121 Stafford Road, WALSALL, WS3 3PG.
WHITTICASE, Mr. Mark Daniel, ACA *2009;* with Grant Thornton UK LLP, Enterprise House, 115 Edmund Street, BIRMINGHAM, B3 2HJ.
WHITTICK, Miss. Alison Mary, BA ACA *1996;* 4 Bourne Grove Close, Lower Bourne, FARNHAM, GU10 3RA.
•WHITTICK, Mr. John Leonard, BSc FCA *1988;* HW, Bridge House, Ashley Road, Hale, ALTRINCHAM, WA14 2UT. See also Haines Watts Corporate Finance (NW) and Haines Watts
WHITTICK, Mr. Robert James, ACA *1998;* 35 Englewood Road, LONDON, SW12 9PA.
WHITTINGDALE, Mr. Thomas Jennings, FCA *1965;* 48 Raedwald Drive, BURY ST.EDMUNDS, IP32 7DD. (Life Member)
WHITTINGHAM, Miss. Aimee, BA(Hons) ACA *2011;* 1 The Beeches, Baildon, SHIPLEY, WEST YORKSHIRE, BD17 6JN.
WHITTINGHAM, Mr. Colin, BA ACA *1988;* P.O. Box 237 Tropicana Plaza, Leeward Highway, Grace Bay, PROVIDENCIALES, BWI, TURKS AND CAICOS ISLANDS.
WHITTINGHAM, Mr. Conrad Adrian, BA FCA *1999;* Equinox Wealth, PO Box 467, TUNBRIDGE WELLS, TN2 9PZ.
WHITTINGHAM, Mr. Dominic Paul, BA ACA AMCT *1997;* 76 Latchmere Road, LONDON, SW11 2JU.
WHITTINGHAM, Mr. James Ronald, BA ACA *2002;* 36 Cité am Bruch, L-8062 BERTRANGE, LUXEMBOURG.
WHITTINGHAM, Mr. John, FCA *1956;* Betley Hall House, Betley, CREWE, CW3 9AD. (Life Member)
WHITTINGHAM, Mr. John Andrew, FCA *1977;* 1 Quality Court Chancery Lane, LONDON, WC2A 1HR.
WHITTINGHAM, Mrs. Katie Sarah, BA ACA *1999;* Great Owl Barn Windmill Farm Lamberhurst Quarter Lamberhurst, TUNBRIDGE WELLS, KENT, TN3 8AL.
WHITTINGHAM, Mr. Leigh Nattrass, BA FCA *1976;* British Medical Association B M A House, Tavistock Square, LONDON, WC1H 9JP.
WHITTINGHAM, Mr. Neil Raymond, BA(Hons) ACA ATT *2006;* 262 Wigan Road, Standish, WIGAN, WN6 0AD.
WHITTINGHAM, Mr. Philip, BSc ACA *1997;* Meridian, 85 Smallbrook Queensway, BIRMINGHAM, B5 4HA.
WHITTINGHAM-JONES, Mr. William Martin, FCA *1964;* Elderberry, Frankby Green, West Kirby, WIRRAL, CH48 1PE.
•WHITTINGTON, Mrs. Catherine Susan, BSc FCA *1990;* CW Acccountants Limited, 11 Thorn Close, Barkham, WOKINGHAM, BERKSHIRE, RG41 4SQ. See also CW Accountants
•WHITTINGTON, Mrs. Cheryl Christine, FCA *1976;* (Tax Fac), Whittington & Co, 83 South Street, DORKING, RH4 2JU.
WHITTINGTON, Mr. Christopher Mark John, MA FCA *1964;* Southwood Lodge, Kingsley Place, LONDON, N6 5EA. (Life Member)
WHITTINGTON, Mr. Ernest John, BSc FCA *1975;* Le Pignolet, Folligny, 50320 LA HAYE PESNEL, FRANCE.
WHITTINGTON, Prof. Geoffrey, CBE FCA *1963;* CFAP, Judge Business School Old Addenbrookes Site, Trumpington Street, CAMBRIDGE, CB2 1AG.
WHITTINGTON, Mr. John Robert, BSc ACA *1998;* Orchard Barn The Green, Uffington, FARINGDON, OXFORDSHIRE, SN7 7SB.
WHITTINGTON, Mr. Mark David, BSc ACA *2002;* Goldman Sachs Intl, Petershill, 1 Carter Lane, LONDON, EC4V 5ER.
WHITTINGTON, Mr. Peter Alan, ACA *1978;* Willow Barn, Manor Road, Stutton, TADCASTER, LS24 9BR.
WHITTINGTON, Mr. Richard Gordon, FCA *1974;* Burchetts, Chobham, WOKING, SURREY, GU24 8SW.
WHITTLE, Miss. Anita, BSc ACA *1998;* Alizarin Broad Lane, Grappenhall, WARRINGTON, WA4 3HS.
WHITTLE, Mr. Antony John, BSc ACA *2006;* 66 Voltaire Buildings, 330 Garratt Lane, LONDON, SW18 4FQ.
WHITTLE, Mrs. Charlotte Mary, MEng ACA *1999;* Woolstrop, Bryces Lane, Brown Candover, ALRESFORD, SO24 9TL.
WHITTLE, Mr. Christopher John, MA BA(Hons) ACA *1993;* 24 Hutton Road, Shenfield, BRENTWOOD, CM15 8LB.
WHITTLE, Mr. Christopher Roy, FCA *1965;* PO Box FL 180, FLATTS FLBX, BERMUDA. (Life Member)
WHITTLE, Miss. Claire, ACA *2008;* with PricewaterhouseCoopers LLP, Donington Court, Pegasus Business Park, Castle Donington, DERBY, DE74 2UZ.
•WHITTLE, Mr. David Michael, BSc FCA *1971;* (Tax Fac), David Whittle & Co, 5 The Walk, BECCLES, SUFFOLK, NR34 9AJ.
WHITTLE, Mr. Garry Melvyn, FCA *1977;* 51 Heron Way, BLACKPOOL, FY3 8FA.
WHITTLE, Mrs. Helen Frances, BSc ACA *2001;* 74 Woodside Road, Lower Woodside, LUTON, LU1 4DQ.
WHITTLE, Mrs. Jacqueline, FCA *1986;* 6 Prince Rupert Avenue, Powick, WORCESTER, WR2 4PZ.
WHITTLE, Mr. John Lee, BA ACA *2002;* 3A, 3 Old Deer Park Gardens, RICHMOND, TW9 2TN.
WHITTLE, Mr. John Richard, FCA *1978;* Pont Du Val, Le Pont, St. Pierre Du Bois, GUERNSEY, GY7 9AJ.
WHITTLE, Mrs. Kathleen Margaret, BA FCA *1977;* Nigel Whittle Chartered Accountants, Parkside House, 167 Chorley New Road, BOLTON, BL1 4RA.
•WHITTLE, Mrs. Mary Catherine, BSc(Hons) FCA CTA *1991;* Whittles LLP, 1 Richmond Road, LYTHAM ST. ANNES, LANCASHIRE, FY8 1PE. See also Whittles
WHITTLE, Mr. Matthew Christopher, MSc(Econ) BA ACA *2002;* with Deloitte LLP, 4 Brindley Place, BIRMINGHAM, B1 2HZ.
•WHITTLE, Mr. Nigel Anthony, FCA CF *1983;* Lambert Chapman LLP, 3 Warners Mill, Silks Way, BRAINTREE, ESSEX, CM7 3GB.
WHITTLE, Mr. Nigel Edward, BA FCA *1983;* 19, Bedford Place, LONDON, WC1B 5JA.
•WHITTLE, Mr. Nigel John, FCA *1975;* (Tax Fac), Nigel Whittle, Parkside House, 167 Chorley New Road, BOLTON, BL1 4RA.
WHITTLE, Mr. Paul, FCA *1969;* 2 Courtyards, Little Shelford, CAMBRIDGE, CB22 5ER.
•WHITTLE, Mr. Paul John, BSc FCA *1975;* (Tax Fac), Whittle & Partners LLP, Century House South, North Station Road, COLCHESTER, CO1 1RE.
•WHITTLE, Mr. Paul Joseph, BA(Econ) FCA *1984;* (Tax Fac), Whittles LLP, 1 Richmond Road, LYTHAM ST. ANNES, LANCASHIRE, FY8 1PE. See also Whittles
WHITTLE, Mr. Peter, MSci ACA *2007;* Accenture, 20 Old Bailey, LONDON, EC4M 7AN.
WHITTLE, Mr. Richard Andrew, BEng ACA *1997;* 37 Mulberry Close, West Bridgford, NOTTINGHAM, NG2 7SS.
WHITTLE, Mrs. Sharon Elizabeth, BSc ACA *1986;* Nettley Dell, 26 Back Road, Linton, CAMBRIDGE, CB21 4JF.
WHITTLE, Mr. Simon Glynn, BSc ACA *1985;* Flat 43, Westminster Mansions, Great Smith Street, LONDON, SW1P 3BP.
WHITTLE, Mr. Stephen Michael, BA ACA *1999;* 74 Woodside Road, Lower Woodside, LUTON, LU1 4DQ.
WHITTLE, Mr. Stuart John, BCom ACA *1986;* Clova, 1 Glebe Lane Radcliffe-on-Trent, NOTTINGHAM, NG12 2FR.
WHITTLE, Mr. Stuart John, BA(Hons) ACA *2000;* 1 Windermere Drive, LEEDS, LS17 7UZ.
WHITTLE, Mr. Thomas Ian, BA ACA *2007;* 57 Holmdene Avenue, HARROW, HA2 6HP.
WHITTLES, Mr. Andrew James, BSocSc ACA *1993;* 12 Cross Street, RYDE, NSW 2112, AUSTRALIA.
WHITTLES, Mr. Kenneth John, FCA *1968;* Rose Dene, 415 Huddersfield Road, Shelley, HUDDERSFIELD, HD8 8NE. (Life Member)
WHITTLESEY, Mr. Kevin Stephen, ACA *2001;* 63 Barfields, Bletchingley, REDHILL, RH1 4RD.
•WHITTON, Mr. Andrew John, BSc FCA *1994;* Deloitte LLP, 2 New Street Square, LONDON, EC4A 3BZ. See also Deloitte & Touche LLP
WHITTON, Mr. Geoffrey, MSc BSc ACA *1980;* 5 Mallard Close, Burnham, SLOUGH, SL1 7DT.
WHITTON, Miss. Laura Jean, BSc ACA *1990;* 2 Lawn Cottages, Castle Lane, LINCOLN, LN1 3BH.
WHITTON, Mr. Terence Davidson, BA FCA *1969;* 8 Warren Road, Wanstead, LONDON, E11 2NA. (Life Member)
WHITTOW, Mr. Richard John, BA ACA *2000;* 180 6th Avenue, SAN FRANCISCO, CA 94118, UNITED STATES.
WHITTY, Mr. Brian Howard, FCA *1978;* Ruxley House, Rowney Green Lane, Rowney Green, Alvechurch, BIRMINGHAM, B48 7QF.
WHITVER, Miss. Heather, MSc ARCS ACA *2010;* National Audit Office, 157-197 Buckingham Palace Road, LONDON, SW1W 9SP.
WHITWAM, Mr. Jonathan Walker, BSc FCA *2001;* 81 Avenue Road, INGATESTONE, ESSEX, CM4 9HB.
WHITWAM, Miss. Lynne Barbara, FCA *1978;* 11 Llyn Tircoed Tircoed Forest Village Penllergaer, SWANSEA, SA4 9LB.
•WHITWAM, Mr. Paul Andrew, BSc FCA *1989;* BWC Business Solutions Limited, 8 Park Place, LEEDS, LS1 2RU.
WHITWAM, Mr. Robert Samuel, BA(Hons) ACA *2004;* C/O Kyagalanyi Coffee Ltd, 5th Street Bugolobi, PO Box 3181, KAMPALA, UGANDA.
WHITWELL, Mr. Michael, FCA *1967;* 17 Lindsay Road, Horfield, BRISTOL, BS7 9NP.
•WHITWELL, Miss. Olga Rachel, BA FCA *1994;* 118 Hampton Court Road, BIRMINGHAM, B17 9AG.
WHITWELL, Mr. Richard Peter, MA ACA *1992;* Wood House Curlieu Lane, Norton Lindsey, WARWICK, CV35 8JS.
WHITWOOD, Mr. David John, BSc ACA *1996;* Newsells Park Stud Ltd, Barkway, ROYSTON, HERTFORDSHIRE, SG8 8DA.
WHITWORTH, Mrs. Aliki, BA ACA *2000;* Chemin de la Croisette 12A, 1260 NYON, SWITZERLAND.
WHITWORTH, Miss. Amanda Jayne, BSc ACA *1988;* Broomleaf Cottage, Church Lane, Ewshot, FARNHAM, GU10 5BD.
WHITWORTH, Dr. Andrew Martin, FCA *1985;* 56 St. Georges Road, HARROGATE, NORTH YORKSHIRE, HG2 9DW.
WHITWORTH, Mrs. Anne, MBA BA FCA *1992;* Le Bourg House The Drove, Lower Common Road West Wellow, ROMSEY, HAMPSHIRE, SO51 6BT.
WHITWORTH, Mr. Benjamin Michael, BSc(Hons) FCA *2001;* Catesby House, 23a The Croft, Sheriff Hutton, YORK, YO60 6SQ.
WHITWORTH, Mr. David Charles Housely, BA FCA *1982;* Trefallen, Retot Lane, Castel, GUERNSEY, GY5 7EF.
WHITWORTH, Miss. Deborah Gay, BSc ACA *1986;* Data Liberation Ltd, Integra House, 138-140 Alexandra Road, LONDON, SW19 7JY.
WHITWORTH, Mr. James Christopher Bardsley, BSc FCA *1972;* Northover, Heathside Park Road, WOKING, GU22 7JE.
•WHITWORTH, Mr. Jason Paul, BA FCA *1993;* BDO LLP, 1 Bridgewater Place, Water Lane, LEEDS, LS11 5RU. See also BDO Stoy Hayward LLP
WHITWORTH, Mr. John Edward, FCA *1969;* Tara, Long Walk, CHALFONT ST. GILES, HP8 4AW.
WHITWORTH, Mr. John Michael, FCA *1971;* Catesby House, Sheriff Hutton, YORK, YO60 6SQ.
WHITWORTH, Miss. Karen Tracy, BA ACA *1994;* J Sainsbury Plc, 33 Holborn, LONDON, EC1N 2HT.
WHITWORTH, Dr. Lesley Anne, PhD BSc ACA *2004;* Tamar Valley Cottage, Gulworthy, TAVISTOCK, DEVON, PL19 8JG.
WHITWORTH, Mr. Philip John, BA ACA *1989;* 5 Spring Bank Lane, ROCHDALE, LANCASHIRE, OL11 5SE.
WHITWORTH, Mr. Richard Stanley, FCA *1970;* Upcote, Green Dene, East Horsley, LEATHERHEAD, SURREY, KT24 5RE.
WHOLEY, Mr. Kevin Paul, BSc ACA *1992;* Rose Cottage, Scotts Lane, Knowbury, LUDLOW, SY8 3JR.
WHOLLEY, Mrs. Elizabeth Anne, BA FCA *1986;* Inchape Retail, Business Support Centre, Boldon Business Park, Newcastle Road, EAST BOLDON, TYNE AND WEAR NE36 0BQ.
WHONE, Mr. John, FCA *1967;* 2 Sykes Close, Greenfield, OLDHAM, OL3 7PT.
WHONE, Mrs. Sally Elizabeth, BSc ACA *1992;* Piethorne House West, Ogden Lane, Milnrow, ROCHDALE, LANCASHIRE, OL16 3TQ.
WHONG, Ms. Shuk Ping, ACA *2008;* Flat D Floor 11 Block 2, Villa Esplanada, 8 Nga Ying Chau Street, TSING YI, NEW TERRITORIES, HONG KONG SAR.
WHOOLEY, Mr. Terry David, BA ACA *2003;* Flat 17 Lantern Court, 99 Worple Road, LONDON, SW20 8HB.
WHOOLEY, Miss. Tracey Lorraine, BA(Hons) ACA *2004;* 11 Tiepigs Lane, BROMLEY, BR2 7HJ.
•WHORLOW, Mr. Stuart Graham, BA FCA *1992;* (Tax Fac), Cassidys Limited, South Stour Offices, Roman Road, Mersham, ASHFORD, KENT TN25 7HS. See also Cassidys Payroll Limited
•WHOWELL, Mr. Jason Robert, BSc ACA *2002;* Robert Whowell & Partners, 78 Loughborough Road, Quorn, LOUGHBOROUGH, LEICESTERSHIRE, LE12 8DX.
•WHOWELL, Mr. Robert Harold, FCA *1964;* (Tax Fac), Robert Whowell & Partners, 78 Loughborough Road, Quorn, LOUGHBOROUGH, LEICESTERSHIRE, LE12 8DX.
WHY, Mrs. Christine, BSc ACA *1995;* 107 Woodward Close, Winnersh, WOKINGHAM, RG41 5UT.
WHYARD, Mr. Michael John, FCA *1968;* 13 Darley Avenue, Beeston, NOTTINGHAM, NG9 6JP.
•WHYATT, Mr. Clive Robert James, FCA *1976;* Whyatt & Co, 3 Pinford Dell, Wigmore Park, LUTON, LU2 9SD.
WHYATT, Miss. Joanne, BSc ACA *1996;* 9 Banks Road, Linthwaite, HUDDERSFIELD, HD7 5LP.
WHYATT, Mrs. Kirsten Lisa, BA ACA *1992;* 39 Crofters Fold, Galgate, LANCASTER, LA2 0RB.
WHYATT, Mr. Lyndon Buchan, FCA *1958;* 4 Swancombe, Clapton In Gordano, BRISTOL, BS20 7RR. (Life Member)
WHYATT, Mr. Paul Alan, BA ACA *1991;* 1 Aysgarth Avenue, Romiley, STOCKPORT, SK6 4PX.
WHYATT, Robert George, Esq MBE FCA *1957;* Cedar House, Broadwas-On-Teme, WORCESTER, WR6 5NE. (Life Member)
WHYATT, Miss. Sarah Anne, MEng ACA *2003;* 14 Stanbridge Road, LONDON, SW15 1DX.
WHYATT, Mr. Stephen John, BA ACA *1979;* 8 West Court, Downley, HIGH WYCOMBE, HP13 5TG.
WHYATT, Mr. Thomas John, MBE BA FCA *1974;* 26 Malford Gr, Gilwern, ABERGAVENNY, GWENT, NP7 0RN.
WHYBROW, Mr. Edward, BSc ACA *2011;* Flat D, 68 Netherwood Road, Hammersmith, LONDON, W14 0BG.
WHYBROW, Mrs. Lesley Barbara, BSc ACA *1987;* St Catherines, Cliff Road, HYTHE, CT21 5XW.
•WHYKE, Mr. Michael William Ian, FCA CF *1979;* with Anstey Bond LLP, 1 Charterhouse Mews, LONDON, EC1M 6BB.
WHYMAN, Ms. Bethan Amber, BSc ACA *2006;* 5 Lower Kings Road, KINGSTON UPON THAMES, SURREY, KT2 5JA.
WHYMAN, Mr. Philip, BA FCA *1982;* Anvil House, Front Street, Appleton Wiske, NORTHALLERTON, DL6 2AB.
WHYNACHT, Mr. Dean Richard, BA ACA *1978;* Monte Cerredo 3, Casa 11, 39700 CASTRO URDIALES, SPAIN.
WHYTE, Mr. Alan Manson, FCA *1955;* Rafters, Church Street, Great Maplestead, HALSTEAD, ESSEX, CO9 2RG. (Life Member)
WHYTE, Mr. Alan Peter, FCA *1970;* Rockfield House, Coombe Hill Road, EAST GRINSTEAD, WEST SUSSEX, RH19 4LZ.
WHYTE, Mr. Christopher Alexander, BSc ACA *2006;* Kildare, Chorleywood Road, RICKMANSWORTH, WD3 4EX.
WHYTE, Mr. Iain William, BSc ACA *1991;* Cedar Croft, Horsell Park, WOKING, SURREY, GU21 4LY.
WHYTE, Mr. James Paterson, MSc ACA *1992;* 1 Birchlands Avenue, LONDON, SW12 8ND.
WHYTE, Mr. Lawrence Robert, FCA *1975;* 6615 Buffalo Speedway, HOUSTON, TX 77005, UNITED STATES.
WHYTE, Miss. Margaret, BSc ACA *1994;* Dunvegan Cottage, Puddingate, Bishop Burton, BEVERLEY, NORTH HUMBERSIDE, HU17 8QH.
WHYTE, Mr. Michael, BSc ACA *2011;* Flat 206, Indiana Building, Deals Gateway, LONDON, SE13 7QD.
WHYTE, Ms. Natalie Victoria, BA(Hons) ACA DChA *2002;* Royal Opera House, Covent Garden, LONDON, WC2E 9DD.
WHYTE, Mr. Roland Charles, ACA *2003;* 39 Orlando Road, LONDON, SW4 0LD.
•WHYTE, Mrs. Sona Suryakant, BA FCA *1992;* Oxley Accountants and Business Advisors Limited, 17 Manor Road, EAST MOLESEY, SURREY, KT8 9JU.
WHYTESIDE, Mrs. Caroline, ACA *2008;* New Campus Glasgow Ltd, 300 Cathedral Street, GLASGOW, G1 2TA.
•WHYTON, Mr. Adrian John, ACA CTA *1991;* Whyton Roberts, Clouds, Soldridge Road, Medstead, ALTON, GU34 5JF.
WICHELOW, Mr. Phillip Arthur, FCA *1968;* Pantiles, 14 Bedford Road, Moor Park, NORTHWOOD, HA6 2AZ. (Life Member)
WICK, Mr. Derek Anthony, FCA *1962;* 8 Lane Top, Fence, BURNLEY, LANCASHIRE, BB12 9QR.
WICK, Mr. Ian Stuart, FCA *1959;* 13 Florence Drive, ENFIELD, EN2 8DG. (Life Member)
WICKE, Mr. Edward Franklin, MA FCA *1981;* 13 Dellands, Overton, BASINGSTOKE, RG25 3LD.

WICKENDEN, Mr. Christopher John, FCA *1977;* Haven Funeral Service, 13 The Broadway Gunnersbury Lane, LONDON, W3 8HR.

WICKENDEN, Mrs. Eve Michelle, BSc ACA *2003;* 160 Seven Sisters Road, EASTBOURNE, EAST SUSSEX, BN22 0PB.

WICKENDEN, Mr. Graham Roland, MA MBA ACA *1980;* Apt 20, Chalet Plein Sud, Route du Golf14, 1936 VERBIER, SWITZERLAND.

WICKENS, Mr. Brian James, MA ACA *1995;* Providence, 27 Ladder Hill, Wheatley, OXFORD, OX33 1SX.

WICKENS, Mr. Daniel, ACA *2011;* 116 Firle Road, EASTBOURNE, EAST SUSSEX, BN22 8ES.

WICKENS, Mrs. Margaret Jane, MA ACA *1984;* 14 KALKEWEE, L-7681 WALDBILLIG, LUXEMBOURG.

•WICKENS, Mr. Martin George, FCA *1974;* Watson Associates, 30-34 North Street, HAILSHAM, EAST SUSSEX, BN27 1DW.

WICKENS, Mr. Timothy Stephen, MSc FCA *1972;* 6 Academy Street, FORTROSE, ROSS-SHIRE, IV10 8TW.

WICKENS, Mrs. Tracey Kathleen, BSc ACA *1995;* with Midgley Snelling, Ibex House, Baker Street, WEYBRIDGE, SURREY, KT13 8AH.

•WICKERS, Mr. Matthew John, LLB FCA *1987;* Croit Vane, Corlea Road, Ballasalla, ISLE OF MAN, IM9 3BA.

WICKERSHAM, Mr. Mark Julian, BA FCA *1992;* The Haven, Main Road, Cutthorpe, CHESTERFIELD, DERBYSHIRE, S42 7AJ.

WICKERSON, Mr. Karl Alexander, FCA *1993;* 25 Constable Way, BROUGH, NORTH HUMBERSIDE, HU15 1GQ.

•WICKES, Mr. Alton Stewart, BA FCA *1981;* 23 Sanderling Road, Offerton, STOCKPORT, CHESHIRE, SK2 5UL.

WICKHAM, Mr. Andrew James, MA ACA AMCT *2001;* (Tax Fac), with PricewaterhouseCoopers LLP, Benson House, 33 Wellington Street, LEEDS, LS1 4JP.

WICKHAM, Mr. George William, FCA *1964;* Pond Mere, Chenies Road, Chorleywood, RICKMANSWORTH, HERTFORDSHIRE, WD3 5LU. (Life Member)

WICKHAM, Miss. Jodie Octavia, BA(Hons) ACA *2003;* 5 Porchfield Close, GRAVESEND, KENT, DA12 5PX.

WICKHAM, Miss. Maria Ann, BA ACA *1991;* (Tax Fac), 55 Wildern Lane, NORTHAMPTON, NN4 0SN.

WICKHAM, Mr. Stanley Terence, FCA *1962;* Brookview, 9 Jericho Street, Thorverton, EXETER, EX5 5PA.

•WICKHAM, Ms. Susan Carole, BA FCA *1987;* Quartrange Limited, 30 Gwynne Close, TRING, HP23 5EN.

WICKHAM, Mr. Timucin Avni, BSc ACA *2007;* T wickham, 15 Maddox Street, LONDON, W1S 2QQ.

WICKMAN, Mr. Paul Nigel, FCA *1980;* Flat 415 Anchor House, Smugglers Way, LONDON, SW18 1EN.

WICKRAMASINGHE, Miss. Ayomi, MSc BSc ACA *2009;* Flat 103 Ionian Building, 45 Narrow Street, LONDON, E14 8DX.

WICKRAMASINGHE, Mr. Eranda, ACA *2008;* 32 Eastbrook Road, LONDON, SE3 8BT.

WICKRAMASURIYA, Mr. Priyalal Nimalsri, FCA FCMA *1963;* 4107 North Pine Brook Way, HOUSTON, TX, 77059, UNITED STATES. (Life Member)

WICKREMERATNE, Mr. Nalin, BSc ACA *1991;* 35 Vicarage Grove, LONDON, SE5 7LY.

WICKS, Mr. Christopher Richard, FCA *1986;* 44 Millias Close, BROUGH, NORTH HUMBERSIDE, HU15 1GP.

•WICKS, Mr. David Ian, BSc FCA *1982;* (Tax Fac), Apsleys, 21 Bampton St, TIVERTON, EX16 6AA. See also A + B Bookkeeping Ltd

WICKS, Ms. Deborah Elizabeth, FCA *1987;* Ord Lodge The Street, Fornham St. Martin, BURY ST. EDMUNDS, SUFFOLK, IP31 1SW.

WICKS, Mr. Gerald Richard, FCA *1974;* Quinneys, 32 Peacock Lane, BRIGHTON, BN1 6WA.

WICKS, Mrs. Karen, ACA MAAT *1998;* 22 Staleys Road, Borough Green, SEVENOAKS, KENT, TN15 8RL.

WICKS, Miss. Karen, LLB ACA *2011;* Chickfield, Ridgelands Lane, Newick, LEWES, EAST SUSSEX, BN8 4RR.

WICKS, Mr. Keith Martin, BA ACA *1989;* 36 Rowlatt Drive, ST. ALBANS, HERTFORDSHIRE, AL3 4NB.

WICKS, Mrs. Lindsey, BSc(Hons) ACA CTA *2001;* (Tax Fac), 23 Saffron Close Chineham, BASINGSTOKE, HAMPSHIRE, RG24 8XQ.

WICKS, Mr. Martin Theodore, FCA *1970;* 5 Brandon Place, St Ives, SYDNEY, NSW 2075, AUSTRALIA.

WICKS, Mr. Merlin Whitfield, FCA *1951;* 10 Cavendish Avenue, BUXTON, SK17 9AE. (Life Member)

WICKS, Mr. Michael J, ACA *2009;* 10 Penstock Mews, GODALMING, GU7 1NB.

WICKS, Miss. Sarah Louise, BA ACA *1993;* 59 New Road, Ruscombe, READING, RG10 9LN.

WICKS, Mr. Steven Benjamin, FCA *1974;* Moores Management & Finance Ltd, 10 South Parade, LEEDS, LS1 5AL.

•WICKS, Mr. Terence Peter, FCA CTA TEP *1970;* (Tax Fac), with Burton Sweet, Spencer House, Morston Court, Aisecombe Way, WESTON-SUPER-MARE, BS22 8NA.

WICKSON, Mrs. Annelie Teresia, BA(Hons) ACA *2001;* 2 Patching Close, Goring-by-Sea, WORTHING, BN12 6AU.

WICKSTEAD, Mr. Christopher Anthony, ACA *2008;* 83B Yerbury Road, LONDON, N19 4RW.

WICKSTEAD, Mr. Robert Edmund, BSc ACA *1988;* 21 Hazel Drive, Wythall, BIRMINGHAM, B47 5RJ.

WICKSTEED, Mr. Jonathan Hartley, FCA *1963;* The School House, Church Lane, BAKEWELL, DE45 1DE.

•WICKSTEED, Mr. Peter, BSc FCA *1977;* Peter Wicksteed, El Calvario 12, San Lorenzo, 35018 LAS PALMAS, GRAN CANARIA, SPAIN.

WIDBERG, Mr. Stephen Ronald Farquhar, BA ACA *1987;* 17 Firsby Avenue, Shirley, CROYDON, CR0 8TP.

WIDDALL, Mr. Matthew, BSc ACA CF *1999;* 259 Bramhall Lane South Bramhall, STOCKPORT, CHESHIRE, SK7 3DP.

WIDDAS, Mr. Christopher John, BSc ACA *1988;* Elfab Ltd, Alder Road, NORTH SHIELDS, TYNE AND WEAR, NE29 8SD.

WIDDAS, Mrs. Lynn, ACA *1991;* Thompkins & Thompkins, 1 Benton Terrace, Jesmond, NEWCASTLE UPON TYNE, NE2 1QU.

•WIDDAS, Mr. Richard Leonard, BA ACA *1995;* Deloitte LLP, Stonecutter Court, 1 Stonecutter Street, LONDON, EC4A 4TR. See also Deloitte & Touche LLP

•WIDDAS, Mr. Timothy Michael, BA ACA *1991;* KPMG LLP, St. Nicholas House, 31 Park Row, NOTTINGHAM, NG1 6FQ. See also KPMG Europe LLP

WIDDEN, Mr. David Charles, BA FCA *1974;* 7 Hainult Close, Wordsley, STOURBRIDGE, DY8 5PB.

WIDDERS, Mr. Mark Lorimer, ACA *1983;* 12 Clovelly Drive, SOUTHPORT, PR8 3AJ.

WIDDICOMBE, Mr. Charles Richard, ACA *2002;* 68A Tawa Road, One Tree Hill, AUCKLAND 1061, NEW ZEALAND.

WIDDOP, Mr. Christopher Alan, BSc ACA *2009;* 122 Wentworth Road, RUGBY, WARWICKSHIRE, CV22 6BL.

WIDDOWS, Mr. Mark, BSc FCA *1989;* Beech House Crabtree Green, Collingham, WETHERBY, LS22 5AB.

WIDDOWS, Mr. Peter, ACA *1995;* 908/150 Clarendon Street, EAST MELBOURNE, VIC 3002, AUSTRALIA.

•WIDDOWSON, Mr. Adrian, MA FCA CTA *1982;* (Tax Fac), 406 Otley Road, LEEDS, LS16 8AD.

WIDDOWSON, Mr. Allen Robert, BSc ACA *1998;* 13 Alston Close, Long Ditton, SURBITON, SURREY, KT6 5QS.

WIDDOWSON, Mr. Andrew Phillip, BSc ACA *1997;* 9 Elswick Avenue, Bramhall, STOCKPORT, CHESHIRE, SK7 2PN.

WIDDOWSON, Mr. Daniel James, MSc BA ACA *2007;* Investec Bank (UK) Ltd, 2 Gresham Street, LONDON, EC2V 7QP.

WIDDOWSON, Mrs. Emma, BA ACA *1999;* 9 Elswick Avenue, Bramhall, STOCKPORT, CHESHIRE, SK7 2PN.

WIDDOWSON, Mr. Ian Michael, BA ACA CTA *1986;* 8 Coppice Close, NEWBURY, BERKSHIRE, RG14 7JX.

WIDDOWSON, Mr. John Richard, FCA *1968;* 15199 Blossom Hill Road, LOS GATOS, CA 95032, UNITED STATES.

•WIDDOWSON, Mrs. Katharine Mary, BSc ACA *1986;* Katharine Widdowson, 406 Otley Road, LEEDS, LS16 8AD.

WIDDOWSON, Mr. Keith Edward, BA ACA *1995;* 9 Leonard Way, HORSHAM, RH13 5JA.

WIDDOWSON, Mr. Kenneth John, FCA *1964;* 21 Brinklow Way, HARROGATE, NORTH YORKSHIRE, HG2 9JW.

•①WIDDOWSON, Mr. Martin Neil, BA FCA CF FABRP *1988;* Brebners, The Quadrangle, 180 Wardour Street, LONDON, W1F 8LB.

WIDDOWSON, Mr. Nigel Anthony, BSc ACA *1995;* P O BOX 30486, BUDAIYA, BAHRAIN.

WIDDOWSON, Mr. Paul Edward, BA FCA *1999;* with RSM Tenon Audit Limited, Charterhouse, Legge Street, BIRMINGHAM, B4 7EU.

•WIDDOWSON, Mr. Robert John, BA FCA *1971;* KPMG Audyt Sp. z o.o, ul. Chlodna 51, XVI Floor, WARSAW, 00-867, POLAND.

•WIDDOWSON, Mr. Roger C, BA FCA *1992;* KPMG LLP, One Snowhill, Snow Hill Queensway, BIRMINGHAM, B4 6GN. See also KPMG Europe LLP

WIDDOWSON, Mr. William Frank, BA FCA *1984;* Im Eichli 8, 6315 OBERAEGERI, SWITZERLAND.

WIDDUP, Mr. Joseph Micah, BSc ACA MSI *1998;* Windhill Manor, Leeds Road, SHIPLEY, WEST YORKSHIRE, BD18 1BP.

WIDGER, Mr. John Caisley, FCA *1957;* 14 Regent Close, KINGS LANGLEY, WD4 8TP. (Life Member)

WIDGER, Mr. Martin John, ACA *1981;* Expense Reduction Analysts, 15 Red Fox Lane, LITTLETON, CO 80127, UNITED STATES.

WIDGER, Mr. Paul Russell, ACA *2008;* Apartment 132, 1 Kelso Place, MANCHESTER, M15 4LE.

WIDNALL, Mrs. Emma-Louise, ACA CTA *2002;* 33 Stoneleigh Crescent, EPSOM, SURREY, KT19 0RW.

WIDNALL, Mr. Mark Andrew, BSc ACA *1997;* 33 Stoneleigh Crescent, EPSOM, SURREY, KT19 0RW.

WIDTMAN, Mr. Henry Emile, FCA *1942;* Toepferweg 10, CH 8224 LOEHNINGEN, SWITZERLAND. (Life Member)

WIECHERS, Ms. Julia Helen, BA ACA *1995;* Warburtons Ltd Rear of Bank House, Hereford Street, BOLTON, BL1 8HJ.

WIEGAND, Mr. Sean James, ACA *2004;* Lambert Chapman Llp, 3 Warners Mill Silks Way, BRAINTREE, CM7 3GB.

•WIELAND, Mrs. Adelaide Mary, BSc FCA *1986;* (Tax Fac), Adelaide Wieland, 9 Gerard Road, LONDON, SW13 9RQ.

WIELAND, Mr. Michael Douglas, BA ACA *1999;* Laurel House, 11 Rayleigh Road, HARROGATE, NORTH YORKSHIRE, HG2 8QR.

WIELAND, Mr. Philip Robert, BSc ACA *1999;* Sixpenny Buckle, Clodhouse Hill, WOKING, GU22 0QS.

•WIELENGA-ESSEX, Mrs. Janet, BSc FCA *1986;* Janet Essex Limited, Saville Court, 11 Saville Place, Clifton, BRISTOL, BS8 4EJ.

WIER, Mr. Andrew Peter, BA ACA *2005;* 5 The Laurels, Kingsbury, TAMWORTH, STAFFORDSHIRE, B78 2PH.

WIFFEN, Miss. Joanna Louise, BSc ACA DChA *2004;* Shelter National Campaign for the Homeless, Head Office, 1st Floor, 88 Old Street, LONDON, EC1V 9HU.

WIFFEN, Mr. Stephen John, BSc ACA CTA *1996;* (Tax Fac), with PricewaterhouseCoopers LLP, 1 Embankment Place, LONDON, WC2N 6RH.

•WIFFIN, Mrs. Deborah, BA ACA MCT *1981;* Deborah Wiffin, 3 Manor Lane, Gotherington, CHELTENHAM, GLOUCESTERSHIRE, GL52 9QX.

WIFFIN, Mr. Gary John, BA ACA *1989;* 8 Paget Road, IPSWICH, IP1 3RP.

WIGAN, Mr. Andrew Nigel, LLB ACA *1987;* 14 Finsbury Avenue, LYTHAM ST.ANNES, FY8 1BP.

WIGAN, Mr. Anthony John, FCA *1975;* Halo Trust Carronfoot, Carronbridge, THORNHILL, DUMFRIESSHIRE, DG3 5BF.

WIGAN, Mr. Christopher, FCA *1971;* PO Box 113, RED HILL SOUTH, VIC 3937, AUSTRALIA.

•WIGAN, Mr. Paul George, ACA *1981;* (Tax Fac), Goorney & Taylor, 14 Abingdon Street, BLACKPOOL, FY1 1PY.

WIGFULL, Miss. Claire, BA ACA *1992;* Abbeyfield Beaconsfield Society Bradbury House, Windsor End, BEACONSFIELD, BUCKINGHAMSHIRE, HP9 2JW.

WIGG, Mr. Andrew Miles, BSc ACA *1999;* 21 Torrington Road, BERKHAMSTED, HERTFORDSHIRE, HP4 3DB.

WIGG, Mr. Christopher Graham, BSc FCA *1977;* 16 St. Margarets Road, OXFORD, OX2 6RU.

WIGG, Mr. David George Andrew, ACA *1986;* 117 Slieau Dhoo, Tromode Park, ISLE OF MAN, IM2 5LF.

WIGG, Mr. Michael Norman, FCA *1959;* 25 Corton Road, LOWESTOFT, NR32 4PJ. (Life Member)

WIGG, Mrs. Susannah, BSc(Hons) ACA *2001;* 21 Torrington Road, BERKHAMSTED, HERTFORDSHIRE, HP4 3DB.

WIGG, Miss. Victoria Richmond, BSc(Hons) ACA *2011;* The White House, Heath Road, Whitmore, NEWCASTLE, STAFFORDSHIRE, ST5 5HB.

•WIGGETT, Mr. Andrew John, BSc FCA *1974;* (Tax Fac), Andrew Wiggett, Gainsborough House, 15 High Street, HARPENDEN, HERTFORDSHIRE, AL5 2RT.

•WIGGIN, Mr. Anthony Charles David, BSc FCA *1974;* (Tax Fac), Wiggin's, Soane Point, 6-8 Market Place, READING, RG1 2EG.

WIGGIN, Mrs. Collette, ACA *2011;* 96 Underdale Road, SHREWSBURY, SY2 5EE.

•WIGGINS, Mr. Andrew, BCom ACA *1999;* PricewaterhouseCoopers LLP, Cornwall Court, 19 Cornwall Street, BIRMINGHAM, B3 2DT. See also PricewaterhouseCoopers

WIGGINS, Miss. Catherine Sarah, ACA *2008;* 166 Eswyn Road, LONDON, SW17 8TN.

WIGGINS, Mr. James, BA ACA *2005;* 6 Croft Street, COWBRIDGE, SOUTH GLAMORGAN, CF71 7DH.

•WIGGINS, Mrs. Linda Margaret, BA FCA *1975;* Wiggins & Co., The Old Stables, East Lenham Farm, Ashford Road, Lenham, MAIDSTONE KENT ME17 2DP.

WIGGINS, Mr. Ross Alan, ACA CF *2004;* 39 Brantwood Gardens, WEST BYFLEET, SURREY, KT14 6BZ.

WIGGINTON, Mr. Robert James, ACA *2009;* 31 Forrest Road, CARDIFF, CF5 1HP.

•WIGGLESWORTH, Mr. Arthur, FCA *1962;* A Wigglesworth & Company Ltd, Wigglesworth & Co, 1 Albion Place, DONCASTER, SOUTH YORKSHIRE, DN1 2EG.

WIGHAM, Mr. Richard Paul Martin, BSc ACA *1985;* Enterprise House, Enterprise Way, EDENBRIDGE, TN8 6HF.

WIGHT, Mr. Alastair John Graham, BA ACA *2006;* 15 Beamish View, Derwent View, Birtley, DURHAM, DH3 1RS.

WIGHT, Mr. Glenn Robert Leslie, BA ACA *1997;* with Ernst & Young LLP, 1 More London Place, LONDON, SE1 2AF.

•WIGHT, Mr. Ian Auberon Nigel, FCA *1975;* Deloitte & Touche, P.O.Box 1787 GT, One Capital Place, GEORGE TOWN, GRAND CAYMAN, KY1 1109 CAYMAN ISLANDS.

WIGHT, Mr. James William Fairbairn, BSc ACA *1992;* Abbotshay Cottage, Tanyard Lane, Ayot St. Lawrence, WELWYN, HERTFORDSHIRE, AL6 9BS.

WIGHT, Mr. Peter Liddell, FCA *1953;* 37 Kelmscott Road, BIRMINGHAM, B17 8QW. (Life Member)

WIGHT, Mr. Robin Alexander Fairbairn, MA FCA *1965;* Arville Holdings Ltd, 22 Regent Terrace, EDINBURGH, EH7 5BS.

WIGHTMAN, Mr. Alan Edward, FCA *1965;* Towanroath, 11 Tickow Lane, Shepshed, LOUGHBOROUGH, LEICESTERSHIRE, LE12 9LY.

WIGHTMAN, Mr. Andrew David Mark, MSc BSc ACA *2007;* 72 Jackson Crescent, MANCHESTER, M15 5AA.

WIGHTMAN, Mr. Andrew Robin John, MA ACA *2004;* FINANCE DEPARTMENT, St. Johns College, CAMBRIDGE, CB2 1TP.

WIGHTMAN, Mr. Arthur Douglas Niall, BA(Hons) ACA *2002;* Surrey Hill, 21 St Marks Road, SMITHS FL06, BERMUDA.

WIGHTMAN, Mr. Gerald, FCA *1963;* Woodland View, 56 Knowl Road, MIRFIELD, WF14 8DL. (Life Member)

WIGHTMAN, Mr. James Henry Forbes, BSc ACA *2006;* Duddenhoe Grange, Langley Upper Green, SAFFRON WALDEN, CB11 4RY.

WIGHTMAN, Mrs. Judith Barbara, MSc FCA *1973;* (Tax Fac), Pricewaterhousecoopers, PO Box 90, EDINBURGH, EH2 4NH.

•WIGHTMAN, Mrs. Karen Margaret, LLB ACA *1994;* KPMG LLP, 15 Canada Square, LONDON, E14 5GL. See also KPMG Europe LLP

WIGHTMAN, Mr. Robert Getliff, FCA *1967;* Rychenbergstr 203, 8404 WINTERTHUR, SWITZERLAND.

WIGHTMAN, Mrs. Sally Marion, ACA *2000;* 4a Crowlees Road, MIRFIELD, WEST YORKSHIRE, WF14 9PR.

WIGHTON, Mr. Alastair Graeme, BA ACA *1995;* Flat 15 Ocean Breeze, 8-10 Studland Road, BOURNEMOUTH, BH4 8JJ.

WIGHTON, Mr. Andrew Gordon, BSc ACA *1999;* Wolseley UK Ltd The Wolseley Center, Harrison Way, LEAMINGTON SPA, WARWICKSHIRE, CV31 3HH.

•WIGHTWICK, Mr. Geoffrey Edward, BA FCA *1987;* Baker Tilly Tax & Advisory Services LLP, 3 Hardman Street, MANCHESTER, M3 3HF. See also Baker Tilly Corporate Finance LLP

WIGLEY, Mr. Alan, ACA MAAT *2010;* Coveney Nicholls The Old Wheel House, 31-37 Church Street, REIGATE, RH2 0AD.

WIGLEY, Mr. Christopher James, BA ACA *2010;* 2 Church Lane, Abington, CAMBRIDGE, CB21 6BQ.

•WIGLEY, Mr. John Clive, FCA *1965;* J.C. Wigley FCA, 68 Hilley Field Lane, Fetcham, LEATHERHEAD, KT22 9UU.

•WIGLEY, Mr. Malcolm Norman, FCA *1971;* MNW, 55 Bradley Court, Crossley Road, WORCESTER, WR5 3GH. See also Malcolm N. Wigley & Co

•WIGLEY, Mr. Martin William, MSc ACA ATII *1992;* (Tax Fac), Jones Harris Limited, 17 St. Peters Place, FLEETWOOD, LANCASHIRE, FY7 6EB.

•WIGLEY, Mr. Michael James, FCA *1971;* (Tax Fac), Norman J. Wigley & Partners, Edgar House, 12 Birmingham Road, WALSALL, WS1 2NA.

WIGLEY, Mr. Michael Jonathan O'Halloran, FCA MCT *1975;* Lower Barn, Eastcott, Morwenstow, BUDE, CORNWALL, EX23 9PL.
WIGLEY, Mr. Peter William, FCA *1967;* 87 Wolsey Drive, WALTON-ON-THAMES, KT12 3BB.
WIGLEY, Mr. Robert Charles Michael, BSc FCA *1986;* Hermitage Farmhouse, Chidden, Hambledon, WATERLOOVILLE, HAMPSHIRE, PO7 4TD.
•**WIGLEY, Mr. Robert Stanley, FCA** *1969;* with Chalmers & Co (SW) Limited, 6 Linen Yard, South Street, CREWKERNE, SOMERSET, TA18 8AB.
WIGLEY, Mr. Ronald William, FCA *1958;* 27 Ashford Drive, SUTTON COLDFIELD, B76 1EN. (Life Member)
WIGLEY, Mrs. Sharon, ACA *2004;* 8 Yarmouth Close, CRAWLEY, WEST SUSSEX, RH10 6TH.
WIGMORE, Mr. Andrew, BSc ACA *2011;* 30 Milman Road, READING, RG2 0AY.
WIGMORE, Mr. Andrew George Alexander, MA FCA *1980;* 24 Chalfont Road, OXFORD, OX2 6TH.
WIGMORE, Mr. Bryan James, BA ACA *1993;* 34 Cavendish Street, CHICHESTER, WEST SUSSEX, PO19 3BS.
WIGMORE, Mr. James Alan Edward, BSc ACA *1985;* 58 Upper Way, FARNHAM, SURREY, GU9 8RF.
WIGMORE, Mr. Michael John, BSc FCA *1975;* 32 Nore Park Drive, Portishead, BRISTOL, BS20 8EB.
WIGNALL, Mr. Andrew Ian, BA FCA *1990;* Le Forgeron Cottage Le Mont Les Vaux, St. Brelade, JERSEY, JE3 8AF.
WIGNALL, Mr. Christopher, BSc ACA *2004;* 96 Stafford Road, SOUTHAMPTON, SO15 5ED.
WIGNALL, Mr. Neville Owen, FCA *1962;* St Cleres, Hubbards Lane, Hessett, BURY ST.EDMUNDS, IP30 9BG.
•**WIGNALL, Ms. Patricia, BA FCA** *1982;* P3 Learning Limited, 30 Brudenell Drive, Stoke Mandeville, AYLESBURY, BUCKINGHAMSHIRE, HP22 5UR.
WIGNALL, Mr. Simon James, BA ACA *1999;* 1 Raffles Place, SINGAPORE, SINGAPORE.
WIGNALL, Mr. Trevor, BSc ACA *1994;* with Ernst & Young LLP, 1 More London Place, LONDON, SE1 2AF.
WIGNEY, Mr. Michael John, MA ACA *1984;* 117 Valetta Road, LONDON, W3 7TB.
WIGODER, Mr. Charles, BA ACA *1984;* Telecom Plus Plc, Dryden House, Edge Business Centre, Humber Road, LONDON, NW2 6EW.
WIGRAM, Mr. Gerrard Charles, FCA *1959;* 12 Michel Walk, MARINA DA GAMA, 7945, SOUTH AFRICA. (Life Member)
•**WIGRAM, Miss. Julia Margaret Fyers, FCA** *1992;* Woolford & Co LLP, Hillbrow House, Hillbrow Road, ESHER, SURREY, KT10 9NW. See also Dixcart International Limited
WIJAYASURIYA, Mr. Patabendi Muhandramge Wimalasena, FCA JDipMA *1958;* 19 Bagatalle Road, 3 COLOMBO, SRI LANKA. (Life Member)
WIJAYATILLEKE, Mr. Sanath Prasanna, BSc FCA *1999;* 22 Poles Hill, CHESHAM, BUCKINGHAMSHIRE, HP5 2QP.
WIJEKOON, Mr. Kumara Kashyapa, BSc ACA *2000;* Philips de Pury, 7 Howick Place, LONDON, SW1P 1BB.
WIJERATNE, Mr. Rohan James, ACA *2008;* 39 Peabody Close, LONDON, SW1V 4BA.
WIJERATNE, Mr. Vinodha Soysa, BSc ACA *1994;* Ger-Y-Llyn, 128 Lake Road East, CARDIFF, CF23 5NQ.
WIJESEKERA, Mr. Dharni Chandragupta, FCA *1957;* 21 Hedges Court, 10 COLOMBO, SRI LANKA. (Life Member)
WIJESINHA, Mr. Gayan Nishantha, BSc(Hons) ACA *2004;* 27 Collingtree Road, LONDON, SE26 4QG.
WIKE, Mr. Brian, FCA *1959;* 17 Dolphin Yard, Maidenhead Street, HERTFORD, SG14 1DR. (Life Member)
WIKRAMANAYAKE, Mr. Prenitha Srimath, BSc FCA *1976;* Wikramanayake & Co, 50 Hardy Street, DOVER HEIGHTS, NSW 2030, AUSTRALIA.
WILATHGAMUWA, Mr. Don Francis Wimaladharma, FCA *1965;* 379 Light Street, Dianella 6062, PERTH, WA 6062, AUSTRALIA. (Life Member)
•**WILBER, Ms. Rebecca, BA(Hons) CA ACA** *1994;* Rebecca Wilber, 63 Marleigh Road, Bidford-on-Avon, ALCESTER, WARWICKSHIRE, B50 4EE.
•**WILBOURN, Mr. Andrew, BA(Hons) ACA** *1986;* Andrew Wilbourn Ltd, 96 Pendle Gardens, Culcheth, WARRINGTON, WA3 4LU.
WILBRAHAM, Mr. Ian Hugh, ACA *1983;* Royalty Resorts Corporation, 7125 Fruitville Road, SARASOTA, FL 34240, UNITED STATES.
•**WILBURN, Ms. Jacqueline, FCA CTA** *1995;* J Wilburn, 10 Arnian Way, Rainford, ST. HELENS, MERSEYSIDE, WA11 8BX.
WILBY, Mr. Christopher Richard, BA ACA *1998;* 2 Carmont Street, REMUERA 1050, NEW ZEALAND.
WILBY, Mr. Dennis Frank, LLB FCA *1971;* 152 Southstand Apartments, Highbury Stadium Square, LONDON, N5 1FB. (Life Member)
WILBY, Miss. Nicola Joy, BSc ACA CTA *2001;* 108 Russell Road, NEWBURY, RG14 5LA.
•**WILBY, Mr. Paul Russell, BSc FCA** *1989;* P R Wilby, 13 Alan Drive, BARNET, EN5 2PP.
WILCE, Mr. David Alan, BSc FCA *1980;* 8 Hermes Close, Saltford, BRISTOL, BS31 3LD.
•**WILCH, Mr. Steven David, BA FCA** *1992;* Clifford Roberts, Pacioli House, 9 Brookfield, Duncan Close, Moulton Park, NORTHAMPTON NORTHAMPTONSHIRE NN3 6WL.
WILCHER, Mr. Christopher David, FCA *1961;* The Downs, Ancaster View, LEEDS, LS16 5HR.
WILCOCK, Mrs. Alison Barbara, ACA *1993;* 8 Carleton Way, POULTON-LE-FYLDE, LANCASHIRE, FY6 7LS.
WILCOCK, Mrs. Catherine Fiona, BSc ACA *1995;* Westbourne, 43 Manchester Road, BUXTON, SK17 6SR.
WILCOCK, Mr. David, BA FCA *1984;* with Ernst & Young LLP, 1 Bridgewater Place, Water Lane, LEEDS, LS11 5QR.
WILCOCK, Mr. David, BA FCA *1974;* 57 Newbury Lane, Silsoe, BEDFORD, MK45 4EX.
•**WILCOCK, Mr. David Ian, BCom FCA** *1994;* David Wilcock, Pine View, Glen Vine Road, Glen Vine, ISLE OF MAN, IM4 4HG.
WILCOCK, Mr. Gareth John, BSc ACA *2005;* Gloucester Research Ltd, Whittington House, 19-30 Alfred Place, LONDON, WC1E 7EA.
WILCOCK, Mr. Geoffrey Austin, FCA *1963;* 1564 Farrindon Circle, HEATHROW, FL 32746, UNITED STATES.
WILCOCK, Miss. Helen, BSc(Hons) ACA *2011;* 30 Morello Gardens, Stevenage Road, HITCHIN, HERTFORDSHIRE, SG4 9DW.
WILCOCK, Miss. Margaret Mary, BA ACA *1987;* Lectra UK Ltd, First Floor, Jade Building, Albion Mills, Albion Road, Greengates BRADFORD WEST YORKSHIRE BD10 9TQ.
•**WILCOCK, Mr. Mark Christopher, FCA** *1995;* Watson Buckle LLP, York House, Cottingley Business Park, BRADFORD, BD16 1PE.
WILCOCK, Mr. Nicholas John, BSc ACA *1992;* Bank Credit Suisse Moscow, 4 Romanov Pereluk, Building 2, 125009 MOSCOW, RUSSIAN FEDERATION.
WILCOCK, Mr. Richard Henry, BSc(Hons) ACA *2001;* JTI, Koppstrasse 116, 1160 VIENNA, AUSTRIA.
WILCOCK, Mr. Richard Thomas, MA ACA *1991;* Egerton House, Towers Business Park, Wilmslow Road, MANCHESTER, M20 2DX.
WILCOCK, Mr. Timothy John, MA BSc ACA *1979;* 48 Badshot Park, Badshot Lea, FARNHAM, GU9 9JZ.
WILCOCKSON, Mrs. Christina, BSc ACA *1995;* 6 Barker Close, Arborfield, READING, RG2 9NQ.
WILCOCKSON, Miss. Lorna, ACA *2011;* Look Ahead Housing & Care, 1 Derry Street, LONDON, W8 5HY.
•**WILCOX, Mr. Adrian John, BSc FCA** *1990;* KPMG LLP, 15 Canada Square, LONDON, E14 5GL. See also KPMG Europe LLP
WILCOX, Mr. Alan Frank, FCA *1957;* Redmays, 14 Grinstead Hill, Needham Market, IPSWICH, IP6 8EY. (Life Member)
WILCOX, Mr. Ashley Neil, BSc(Hons) ACA *2004;* 9-9b Milton Road, CROYDON, CR0 2BG.
WILCOX, Mr. Brian Henry, FCA *1968;* Woodside, 6 Queens Copse Lane, Holt, WIMBORNE, DORSET, BH21 7EF.
WILCOX, Miss. Christine, ACA *2008;* with KPMG, 10 Shelley Street, SYDNEY, NSW 2000, AUSTRALIA.
WILCOX, Mr. Christopher John, BA(Hons) ACA *2003;* G & J Seddon Ltd, Ploder Lane, Farnworth, BOLTON, BL4 0NN.
WILCOX, Mr. Clive John, ACA CPA *1983;* Dibru Strathallan Road, Onchan, ISLE OF MAN, IM3 1NN.
WILCOX, Mr. Daniel John, MEng ACA *2005;* The Paragon, Counterslip, BRISTOL, BS1 6BX.
WILCOX, Mrs. Donna Louise, BA ACA *1999;* with Baker Tilly UK Audit LLP, 25 Farringdon Street, LONDON, EC4A 4AB.
WILCOX, Mr. Edward Godwin, BA ACA *1991;* Mabey Holdings Ltd, Mabey House, Floral Mile, Twyford, READING, RG10 9SQ.
•**WILCOX, Mr. Graham Bernard, BA FCA** *1971;* Wilcox & Co, Smithy Farm, Twyford, Barrow on Trent, DERBY, DE73 7HJ.
WILCOX, Mr. Jason Andrew, BA(Hons) ACA *2004;* with Rogers Paulley Limited, Arclight House, 3 Unity Street, BRISTOL, BS1 5HH.
WILCOX, Miss. Jennifer, ACA *2011;* The Wren, 34 Pawson Street, Morley, LEEDS, LS27 0QA.
WILCOX, Mr. John, FCA *1967;* 11 Stafford Close, Bloxwich, WALSALL, WS3 3NW. (Life Member)
WILCOX, Mr. Leigh Antony, ACA *2008;* 18 Lindale Avenue, Whickham, NEWCASTLE UPON TYNE, NE16 5QT.
WILCOX, Mr. Martin Swootman, FCA *1969;* Cypressvagen 6B, 13552 TYRESO, SWEDEN.
①**WILCOX, Mrs. Mary Elaine, FCA** *1982;* Armstrong Watson, Fairview House Victoria Place, CARLISLE, CUMBRIA, CA10 2DF.
WILCOX, Mr. Matthew David, BSc ACA *2002;* 18 Rupert Road, SHEFFIELD, S7 1RP.
WILCOX, Mr. Michael James, BA ACA *2006;* 6 Montagu Mews North, LONDON, W1H 2JR.
WILCOX, Mr. Michael Norman, BSc FCA *1978;* Broad Oaks Langley Road, Claverdon, WARWICK, CV35 8QA.
WILCOX, Mr. Peter John, FCA *1963;* 32 Willow Drive, Cheswick Green, SOLIHULL, WEST MIDLANDS, B90 4HW.
WILCOX, Mrs. Rachel, FCA *1996;* Waltoft, 2 Old Thorne Road, Hatfield, DONCASTER, DN7 6ER.
WILCOX, Mrs. Rachel Vernie, MA ACA DChA *2000;* 5th Floor East, University College London Hospitals, 250 Euston Road, LONDON, NW1 2PG.
WILCOX, Mr. Roland Peter, BA FCA *1969;* Simonsfield, 36 Barton Hey Drive, WIRRAL, CH48 1PZ. (Life Member)
WILCOX, Mr. Sam Thomas, BA ACA *2010;* Chestal Farm, Chestal, DURSLEY, GLOUCESTERSHIRE, GL11 5HB.
WILCOX, Mr. Simon Gordon, FCA *1964;* Johnsons Veterinary Products, Ltd, 5 Reddicap Trading Estate, Coleshill Road, SUTTON COLDFIELD, B75 7DF.
WILCOX, Mr. Steven John, BSc FCA *1993;* ING Direct, Hoeksteen74-84, P.O. BOX 810, 1000AV HOOFDDORP, NETHERLANDS.
WILCOX, Mrs. Teresa Joan, BSc ACA *1984;* Romney Cottage, Cotherstone, BARNARD CASTLE, COUNTY DURHAM, DL12 9PG.
WILCOX-PATES, Mrs. Kara, ACA *2008;* One Snowhill, Snowhill Queensway, BIRMINGHAM, B4 6GH.
WILD, Mr. Adrian Frederick, BSc ACA *1990;* Smith & Williamson Ltd, 1 Bishops Wharf Walnut Tree Close, GUILDFORD, GU1 4RA.
WILD, Mrs. Alison Jane, ACA FCCA *1980;* 9 Clifton Drive, Bare, MORECAMBE, LA4 6SR.
•**WILD, Miss. Amanda, BA FCA** *1996;* 12 Crovens Close, Douglas, ISLE OF MAN, IM2 7AQ.
WILD, Mr. Andrew, BA ACA *1997;* 75 Oakhill Road, SEVENOAKS, TN13 1NU.
•**WILD, Mr. Andrew Vernon, BA ACA** *1996;* TLP, 3 Greengate, Cardale Park, HARROGATE, NORTH YORKSHIRE, HG3 1GY. See also TLP Audit Limited, TLP Consulting LLP
WILD, Mr. Anthony David, BEng ACA *2001;* 80a Temple Road, BOLTON, BL1 3LT.
WILD, Mr. Barry Edward, FCA *1959;* Mill Race Barn, Mill Lane, Aldridge, WALSALL, WS9 0LZ. (Life Member)
•**WILD, Mr. Charles Barrie, FCA** *1959;* Wild & Co., 34 Dringthorpe Road, Dringhouses, YORK, NORTH YORKSHIRE, YO24 1LG.
WILD, Mr. Christopher, BA ACA *1998;* 628 Bury Road, ROCHDALE, OL11 4AY.
WILD, Miss. Clare, ACA *2008;* 76 Stone Court, CRAWLEY, WEST SUSSEX, RH10 7RX.
WILD, Mr. David Brian, BA ACA *1997;* Royal Bank of Canada (Channel Islands) Ltd, PO Box 194, 19-21 Broad Street, St. Helier, JERSEY, JE4 8RR.
•**WILD, Mrs. Elizabeth Caroline, BSc ACA** *1996;* Wild Accountancy Limited, 16 Green Way, HARROGATE, NORTH YORKSHIRE, HG2 9LR.
•**WILD, Mrs. Gillian, BA ACA** *1983;* Ernst & Young LLP, 1 More London Place, LONDON, SE1 2AF. See also Ernst & Young Europe LLP
WILD, Mr. Gordon, FCA *1962;* 560 Bury Road, ROCHDALE, OL11 4DN. (Life Member)
•**WILD, Mr. Graham Michael, BSc FCA** *1997;* with Zolfo Cooper Ltd, 10 Fleet Place, LONDON, EC4M 7RB.
WILD, Mr. Graham Peter, FCA *1965;* 32 Daneway, Ainsdale, SOUTHPORT, MERSEYSIDE, PR8 2QW.
WILD, Ms. Hilary Frances, FCA *1971;* 493/D Giudecca, VE 30133 VENICE, ITALY.
WILD, Mr. James Alexander Lawson, BSc ACA *2006;* 16 Ashley Drive, Bramhall, STOCKPORT, CHESHIRE, SK7 1EW.
•**WILD, Mr. James Anthony, FCA** *1964;* Wilds Limited, Lancaster House, 70-76 Blackburn Street, Radcliffe, MANCHESTER, M26 2JW.
WILD, Mr. James David, FCA *1962;* 24 Hay Brow Crescent, Scalby, SCARBOROUGH, YO13 0SG.
WILD, Mr. James Watson Eyre, MA ACA *1987;* (Tax Fac), Manor House Farm, Top Street, East Drayton, RETFORD, NOTTINGHAMSHIRE, DN22 0LG.
WILD, Mr. John, FCA *1961;* 37 Oakfield Crescent, Blaby, LEICESTER, LE8 4HS. (Life Member)
WILD, Mr. John Frank, MA FCA MBA *1992;* 5 Packsaddle Park, Prestbury, MACCLESFIELD, CHESHIRE, SK10 4PU.
WILD, Mr. John Laurence Ralph, FCA *1967;* 12 Faircroft, KENILWORTH, CV8 1JT.
WILD, Mr. John Paul, BEng ACA *1997;* West Warren Warren Road, Woodley, READING, RG5 3AR.
•**WILD, Mr. John Lawson, JP BA(Hons) FCA FCCA AIIT MAAT DChA** *1969;* (Tax Fac), PKW LLP, Cloth Hall, 150 Drake Street, ROCHDALE, LANCASHIRE, OL16 1PX.
WILD, Mr. Jonathan Andrew, BSc ACA *2006;* Lush, 18-20 Market Street, POOLE, DORSET, BH15 1NF.
•**WILD, Mr. Kenneth, OBE BA FCA** *1978;* (Member of Council 1991 - 1997), Wildwood, 19 Linksway, NORTHWOOD, HA6 2XA.
WILD, Mrs. Lindsey, ACA *1988;* 16 Whitley Grange, LISKEARD, PL14 6DQ.
WILD, Mrs. Madeleine, BSc ACA *1996;* Cedar Lodge, Scotland Lane, HASLEMERE, SURREY, GU27 3AB.
WILD, Mr. Mark Steven, MA FCA *1985;* Apartment 10 Maple Gardens, Birkby Road, HUDDERSFIELD, WEST YORKSHIRE, HD2 2DR.
•①**WILD, Mr. Matthew Richard Meadley, BSc ACA** *1995;* Baker Tilly Tax & Advisory Services LLP, The Clock House, 140 London Road, GUILDFORD, SURREY, GU1 1UW. See also Baker Tilly Restructuring and Recovery LLP
WILD, Mrs. Natalie Ann, LLB ACA *2000;* WOODLAWN, 628 Bury Road, ROCHDALE, OL11 4AY.
WILD, Mrs. Nicola, ACA *2010;* 93 Grovehill Road, REDHILL, RH1 6DB.
WILD, Mr. Paul, BSc ACA *1992;* 33 Kelthorpe Close, Ketton, STAMFORD, LINCOLNSHIRE, PE9 3RS.
WILD, Mr. Peter, BA ACA *1991;* 18 Blackfield Lane, SALFORD, M7 3PD.
WILD, Mr. Peter Dayer, FCA *1969;* 37 Cottontail Road, NORWALK, CT 06854, UNITED STATES.
WILD, Mr. Philip Anthony, MA ACA *1983;* 18 Old Kiln Lane, Grotton, OLDHAM, OL4 5RZ.
WILD, Mr. Richard Anthony, ACA CTA *1998;* Palmers Cottage, The Green, Woolpit, BURY ST. EDMUNDS, SUFFOLK, IP30 9RQ.
WILD, Mr. Roderick William, BA ACA *1992;* Frosbury Farm House, Gravetts Lane, GUILDFORD, GU3 3JW.
WILD, Mr. Roger Duncan, BSc ACA *1989;* 40 Fairfax Road, TEDDINGTON, TW11 9BZ.
WILD, Mr. Ross, ACA *2011;* 269 Phoenix Way, Portishead, BRISTOL, BS20 7PB.
WILD, Ms. Stephanie Claire, BA ACA *2001;* 77 Green Lane, LONDON, W7 2PA.
WILD, Mr. Steven, FCA *1968;* 59a Schools Hill Road, CHEADLE, SK8 1JE.
WILD, Mr. Stuart Richard, BCom ACA *1996;* Rockview Cottage, La Route de L'Etacq, St. Ouen, JERSEY, JE3 2FD.
WILD, Mrs. Suzanna Jane, BSc(Hons) ACA *2000;* H M Revenue & Customs Manchester Castlefield, Albert Bridge House 1 Bridge Street, MANCHESTER, M60 9AF.
•**WILDBLOOD, Mr. Edward Stephen, BA FCA** *1992;* Talbot Hughes McKillop LLP, 6 Snow Hill, LONDON, EC1A 2AY.
WILDBLOOD, Mr. Fred Roger John, MA FCA *1957;* 4 Birchwood Grove, Higher Heath, WHITCHURCH, SHROPSHIRE, SY13 2EX. (Life Member)
WILDBORE, Mr. James, BA ACA *2002;* Flat B-e, 68 Netherwood Road, LONDON, W14 0BG.
WILDE, Mrs. Alison Frances Blake, BA FCA *1979;* 1109 Kornhill Apartments, 2 Kornhill Road, QUARRY BAY, HONG KONG SAR.
•**WILDE, Mr. Andrew Peter, BSc FCA ATII** *1990;* Deloitte LLP, PO Box 500, 2 Hardman Street, MANCHESTER, M60 2AT. See also Deloitte & Touche LLP
WILDE, Mr. Christopher David, ACA *1984;* 184 Rochdale Road, Triangle, SOWERBY BRIDGE, WEST YORKSHIRE, HX6 3PB.
WILDE, Mr. Christopher John, BA ACA *1990;* Dewhirst Group Ltd, Dewhirst House, Westgate, East Yorkshire, DRIFFIELD, NORTH HUMBERSIDE YO25 6TH.
WILDE, Dr. Christopher Louis, ACA *1988;* 7 Crondall Lane, FARNHAM, GU9 7BG.
WILDE, Miss. Debra Jane, BSc ACA *1990;* 18 Richardson Court, Hambleton, SELBY, NORTH YORKSHIRE, YO8 9GY.

WILDE, Mr. Geoffrey Spencer, FCA *1964;* 15 Grosvenor Avenue, Great Crosby, LIVERPOOL, L23 0SB. (Life Member)
WILDE, Mrs. Gillian Elizabeth, BA ACA *1990;* 2 Fixby Park Drive, Fixby, HUDDERSFIELD, HD2 2NN.
WILDE, Mr. Gordon Roger, FCA *1965;* Bahamas Realty Limited, P.O. Box N-1132, NASSAU, BAHAMAS.
WILDE, Mrs. Jane Helen, BSc ACA *1996;* 18 New Street, Donisthorpe, SWADLINCOTE, DERBYSHIRE, DE12 7PG.
WILDE, Mr. Jonathan Rodger James, ACA *2010;* Furniture Village, 238 Bath Road, SLOUGH, SL1 4DX.
WILDE, Mrs. Kelly Louise, BA ACA *2005;* Matalan Retail Ltd, Gillibrands Road, SKELMERSDALE, LANCASHIRE, WN8 9TB.
WILDE, Miss. Lucinda Alise, BA ACA *1992;* Unit 4, 17 Allison Road, CRONULLA, NSW 2230, AUSTRALIA.
•WILDE, Mr. Matthew John, BSc FCA *1991;* 5/18 Alice Street, Turramurra, SYDNEY, NSW 2074, AUSTRALIA.
WILDE, Mr. Paul Michael, ACA *2011;* Flat 8 Barnstaple House, Devonshire Drive, LONDON, SE10 8LD.
WILDE, Mr. Peter, MA ACA *1993;* 8 Ashburn Place, ILKLEY, WEST YORKSHIRE, LS29 9NW.
WILDE, Mr. Peter Frank, FCA *1969;* Wilde Timmons Michaud Inc, 32 Glendale Avenue, LOWER SACKVILLE B4C 3M1, NS, CANADA.
WILDE, Mr. Peter Geoffrey, FCA *1949;* The Garden House, 55 Trumlands Road, TORQUAY, TQ1 4RA. (Life Member)
WILDE, Mr. Robert, BSc ACA *1990;* Litchfield House, Mill Road, Kislingbury, NORTHAMPTON, NORTHAMPTONSHIRE, NN7 4BB.
WILDE, Mrs. Shelagh Joan, BSc ACA *1992;* Molescroft House, 63 Molescroft Road, BEVERLEY, NORTH HUMBERSIDE, HU17 7EG.
WILDE, Dr. Thomas Stephen, PhD MA ACA *1995;* 2 Amner Road, LONDON, SW11 6AA.
WILDEN, Miss. Nichola Jane, ACA *1983;* 12c Elsworthy Terrace, LONDON, NW3 3DR.
WILDEN, Miss. Rachel Henrietta, BA ACA *1987;* 12 Malmesbury Park, 263 Harborne RoadEdgbaston, BIRMINGHAM, B15 3JA.
•WILDEN, Mrs. Rachel Louise, BSc ACA *1997;* with Ernst & Young LLP, Compass House, 80 Newmarket Road, CAMBRIDGE, CB5 8DZ.
WILDEN, Mr. Stephen Kenneth, FCA *1975;* Lawn Cottage Rectory Road, Streatley, READING, RG8 9LE.
WILDER, Mr. Alan Peter, BSc ACA *1990;* with Menzies LLP, Heathrow Business Centre, 65 High Street, EGHAM, SURREY, TW20 9EY.
WILDER, Mr. Gary Spencer, BSc ACA *1986;* (Tax Fac), York House, 45 Seymour St, LONDON, W14 7JT.
WILDER, Mr. Stephen Andrew, BSc FCA *1973;* 3 Redcourt, WOKING, GU22 8RA.
•WILDERMUTH, Mr. Paul Edmund, FCA CTA *1972;* (Tax Fac), Paul E. Wildermuth, Pentre Farm, Pentre, Cilcain, MOLD, FLINTSHIRE CH7 5PF.
WILDERMUTH, Miss. Sheenagh Kate, LLB ACA *2006;* with Duesburys Mareeba, 67 Greenhill Road, WAYVILLE, SA 5034, AUSTRALIA.
WILDERS, Mr. Anthony James, BA ACA *2005;* 92 Mill Rise, Westdene, BRIGHTON, BN1 5GH.
WILDERSPIN, Mr. Mark Paul, BSc ACA *1990;* 2 Grantley Close, Shalford, GUILDFORD, GU4 8DL.
WILDERSPIN, Mr. Steven, BA FCA *1994;* Belluno 13 Parcq Du Rivage, La Route de la Haule St. Lawrence, JERSEY, JE3 1NA.
WILDEY, Mr. David William, BA ACA *2006;* 55a Crimsworth Road, Vauxhall, LONDON, SW8 4RJ.
WILDEY, Mr. Donald, BSc FCA *1973;* 32 Magnolia Dene, Hazlemere, HIGH WYCOMBE, HP15 7QE.
WILDEY, Miss. Frances Jane, BA ACA *1989;* Petalioti 2, 74100 RETHYMNO, CRETE, GREECE.
•WILDEY, Mr. Gary David, ACA *1985;* 80 Bedfordshire Way, WOKINGHAM, BERKSHIRE, RG41 3BA.
•WILDEY, Mrs. Sarah Ellen, BA(Hons) FCA *1988;* (Tax Fac), Rice Associates Ltd, Market Chambers, 3-4 Market Place, WOKINGHAM, BERKSHIRE, RG40 1AL.
WILDGOOSE, Mr. Guy Geoffrey, FCA *1953;* 19 Hazells Lane, Shrivenham, SWINDON, SN6 8DS. (Life Member)
WILDGOOSE, Mr. Nicholas Ian James, BA *1983;* 30 Colcokes Road, BANSTEAD, SM7 2EW.
WILDGOOSE, Mr. Oliver Leonard, MEng ACA *2004;* 37 Algarve Road, LONDON, SW18 3EQ.
WILDI, Mr. Mark Robert, BA ACA *1989;* (Tax Fac), Orchard Brook, Five Oak Green Road, TONBRIDGE, TN12 6TJ.
WILDIG, Mrs. Janet Elizabeth, BA ACA *1983;* 17 Ellesmere Place, WALTON-ON-THAMES, SURREY, KT12 5AE.
WILDIG, Mr. Mark, ACA *2010;* 17 The Orchards, Newton, RUGBY, CV23 0DS.
WILDIG, Mr. Michael Jeffrey, BSc FCA *1974;* Skreens Lodge, Shellow Road, Willingale, ONGAR, CM5 0SU.
•WILDIG, Mr. Michael John, BSc FCA *1979;* (Tax Fac), Ernst & Young LLP, 100 Barbirolli Square, MANCHESTER, M2 3EY. See also Ernst & Young Europe LLP
WILDIG, Mrs. Rachel Elen, BA ACA *2002;* 4 Dudley Street, Bondi, SYDNEY, NSW 2026, AUSTRALIA.
WILDIG, Mr. Robert, BSc ACA *2001;* MLC, 105-153 Miller St, NORTH SYDNEY, NSW 2060, AUSTRALIA.
WILDIG, Mr. Thomas, BA ACA *2011;* 97 Manchester Road, WILMSLOW, CHESHIRE, SK9 2JH.
•WILDIN, Mr. Graham Michael, FCA *1975;* (Tax Fac), Wildin & Co, Kings Buildings, Hill Street, LYDNEY, GLOUCESTERSHIRE, GL15 5HE.
•WILDIN, Miss. Jacqueline Anne, BA ACA *2006;* (Tax Fac), Wildin & Co, King's Buildings, Hill St, LYDNEY, GL15 5HE.
WILDING, Mr. Adrian, BSc ACA *1991;* Just Retirement Ltd Vale House, Roebuck Close Bancroft Road, REIGATE, RH2 7RU.
WILDING, Mr. Antoni James, LLB ACA *2001;* 126/809 PACIFIC HWY, CHATSWOOD, NSW 2067, AUSTRALIA.
•WILDING, Mrs. Christine Diana, FCA *1973;* (Tax Fac), C.Diana Wilding, Heathfield, Ffawyddog, CRICKHOWELL, NP8 1PY.
•WILDING, Miss. Diane Jane, ACA *1984;* Diane Wilding & Associates Ltd, 64 Harrow Lane, MAIDENHEAD, BERKSHIRE, SL6 7PA.
WILDING, Mr. James Nicholas, MA FCA *1986;* 5 College Street, ST. ALBANS, HERTFORDSHIRE, AL3 4PW.
•WILDING, Mr. John Richard, FCA *1966;* Wilding Hudson & Co, Saxon House, 17 Lewis Road, SUTTON, SM1 4BR.
•WILDING, Mrs. Katharine, BA(Hons) ACA *1995;* Katharine Wilding BA(Hons) ACA, Oldfield, Forestry Road, Llanferres, MOLD, CLWYD CH7 5SH.
WILDING, Dr. Linda, ACA *1987;* Tangley Way, Blackheath, GUILDFORD, GU4 8QS.
WILDING, Mrs. Margaret Jean, BSc ACA *1984;* Old Impton Farm, Norton, PRESTEIGNE, POWYS, LD8 2EN.
WILDING, Mrs. Sally Ann, FCA *1977;* Westerly Little Falmouth, Flushing, FALMOUTH, CORNWALL, TR11 5TJ.
WILDMAN, Mr. Andrew Charles, ACA *1994;* with Ernst & Young LLP, 1 More London Place, LONDON, SE1 2AF.
WILDMAN, Miss. Claire Louise, ACA MBA *1997;* 24 Crabtree Lane, HARPENDEN, HERTFORDSHIRE, AL5 5TE.
•WILDMAN, Mr. John Derek, FCA *1980;* John Wildman, 15 Grove Place, BEDFORD, MK40 3JJ.
•WILDMAN, Mr. Michael Robert, FCA *1973;* (Tax Fac), Wildman & Co, Goss Court, 36a High Street, Thrapston, KETTERING, NN14 4JH.
•WILDMAN, Mr. Stephen Ian, FCA *1973;* Goodman Jones LLP, 29-30 Fitzroy Square, LONDON, W1T 6LQ.
WILDMAN, Mr. Vincent John, BSc ACA *1996;* 28 Ainsdale Drive, PETERBOROUGH, PE4 6RL.
WILDRIDGE, Mr. Frederick Ian, BSc FCA *1971;* 31 Woodland Avenue, EASTBOURNE, BN22 0HQ.
WILDSMITH, Mr. Benjamin John, BSc ACA *2005;* 10 Mornington Avenue, CHEADLE, CHESHIRE, SK8 1NL.
WILDSMITH, Mr. Christopher James, BA(Hons) ACA *2004;* with Deloitte LLP, 1 City Square, LEEDS, WEST YORKSHIRE, LS1 2AL.
WILEMAN, Mr. Ian Edward, BSc ACA *2002;* Schroder Investment Management Ltd Garrard House, 31-45 Gresham Street, LONDON, EC2V 7QA.
WILES, Mr. Andrew Francis, BA ACA *1993;* 18 Clanalpine Street, MOSMAN, NSW 2088, AUSTRALIA.
•WILES, Mr. Benjamin John, ACA CA(AUS) *2010;* MCR, 43-45 Portman Square, LONDON, W1H 6LY.
WILES, Mr. Christopher John, FCA *1969;* 66 Woodrow Crescent, Knowle, SOLIHULL, B93 9EQ.
WILES, Mr. Darran John, BSc ACA *1995;* XL Capital, XL House, 70 Gracechurch Street, LONDON, EC3V 0XL.
•WILES, Mr. David Philip, FCA *1973;* David Wiles Associates, The Coach House, 7 Carlton Drive, Heaton, BRADFORD, BD9 4DL.
WILES, Mr. Eric Allen, BA FCA CTA FRSA *1982;* (Member of Council 1994 - 2011), The Chapel, Chapel Lane, Upton Snodsbury, WORCESTER, WR7 4NH.
•WILES, Mr. Garry Michael, FCA *1992;* Stephenson Smart & Co, Stephenson House, 15 Church Walk, PETERBOROUGH, PE1 2TP.
WILES, Miss. Juliet, ACA *2011;* 19 Lanhill Road, Maida Vale, LONDON, W9 2BS.
WILES, Mr. Matthew James, ACA *2009;* 187 Arbour Stone Crescent, CALGARY T3G 4Z9, AB, CANADA.
WILES, Mr. Peter Martin, FCA *1970;* 4 Sycamore Close, Garston, WATFORD, WD25 0DF.
WILES, Mr. Philip John, BA(Hons) ACA *1991;* Blandy Group, PO Box 408, 9001-956 FUNCHAL, MADEIRA, PORTUGAL.
•WILES, Mr. Robert Lewis, FCA *1975;* Robert L. Wiles, 33 Bush Hill, Winchmore Hill, LONDON, N21 2BT.
WILES, Mr. Ronald Sidney, FCA *1960;* 34 Butlers Court Road, BEACONSFIELD, HP9 1SG. (Life Member)
WILES, Mr. Rupert Antony, FCA *1970;* 20a Lonsdale Road, LONDON, W4 1ND.
WILES, Miss. Sarah Louise, ACA *2003;* with KPMG LLP, 1 The Embankment, Neville Street, LEEDS, LS1 4DW.
WILES, Miss. Stephanie Josephine, BA ACA *1994;* 30 Greenways, Hinchley Wood, ESHER, KT10 0QD.
WILES, Mr. Trevor Martin, BSc ACA *1992;* 18 Somerset Road, HARROW, HA1 4NG.
WILEY, Dr. Adrian Peter, ACA *2008;* 10 Durley Crescent, Totton, SOUTHAMPTON, SO40 7QA.
WILEY, Mr. Andrew James, MEng ACA *2006;* 16 Montenotte Road, LONDON, N8 8RL.
WILEY, Mr. Graham Francis Vincent, BA ACA *1993;* 3 Homewood Crescent, Hartford, NORTHWICH, CHESHIRE, CW8 1NH.
WILFORD, Mr. Albert Edward, FCA *1941;* 8 St Raphael Road, WORTHING, BN11 5HL. (Life Member)
WILFORD, Mrs. Alison Louise, BSc ACA *1989;* Red House Farm Low Road Alburgh, HARLESTON, IP20 0BZ.
WILFORD, Mr. David Michael, FCA *1966;* Jades, 50 Dyall Close, BURGESS HILL, RH15 8UD. (Life Member)
WILFORD, Mrs. Gillian Mary Elizabeth Brownrigg, BA ACA *1983;* South East Health Ltd, Kingston House, The Long Barrow, Orbital Park, ASHFORD, KENT TN24 0GP.
WILFORD, Mr. Mark William, BSc ACA *1988;* Red House Farm Low Road Alburgh, HARLESTON, IP20 0BZ.
WILFORD, Mr. Martyn Sydney, FCA *1973;* Joseph Clark & Sons (Soho) Ltd, Buscat Farm, Sigwells, SHERBORNE, DORSET, DT9 4LN.
WILFORD, Mr. Peter Leslie, FCA *1972;* 7 Chive Road, Earley, READING, RG6 5XP.
WILFRED, Mr. William Thurailingam, FCA *1979;* 806 Ashley Lane, ALLEN, TX 75002, UNITED STATES.
WILK, Mr. Michael Roy, BSc FCA *1983;* 3 The Firs, Kennford, EXETER, EX6 7TZ.
WILKENFELD, Mr. Manfred, FCA *1953;* 1 Maryrose Way, LONDON, N20 9RP. (Life Member)
WILKES, Mr. Adam Thomas, MSc BSc ACA *2009;* 32 Spencer Walk, Catshill, BROMSGROVE, WORCESTERSHIRE, B61 0NF.
•WILKES, Mr. Andrew Terence Ronald, BSc FCA CTA MSI *1992;* Smith & Williamson Ltd, 25 Moorgate, LONDON, EC2R 6AY.
WILKES, Mr. Anthony Ronald, FCA *1969;* DW Consultants, The Charterhouse, Runnymede Chase, BENFLEET, ESSEX, SS7 3DB.
•WILKES, Mr. Bernard Laurence, FCA *1971;* A.J. Eacersall & Co, Cutthorn, Parsonage Lane, Lamberhurst, TUNBRIDGE WELLS, TN3 8DR.
WILKES, Mr. Christopher John, MA ACA *1978;* 40 Bourton Road, BUCKINGHAM, MK18 1BE.
WILKES, Mr. David James, BA ACA *2004;* 3 Oswin Street, LONDON, SE11 4TF.
•WILKES, Mr. David Lawson, BA ACA *1989;* 28 Hearne Road, LONDON, W4 3NJ.
•WILKES, Mrs. Deborah Jean, BA FCA CTA *1979;* (Tax Fac), Simpson Wreford & Partners, Suffolk House, George Street, CROYDON, CR0 0YN.
WILKES, Mr. Derek, BCom ACA *1989;* 19 Priory Road, HALESOWEN, B62 0BZ.
WILKES, Mrs. Elizabeth Beatrice, BA ACA *2006;* Finsbury (Orthopaedics) Ltd Unit 12-13, Mole Business Park Randalls Road, LEATHERHEAD, SURREY, KT22 7BA.
WILKES, Mr. Gary David, BSc ACA *1998;* Eskdale Lovel Road, Winkfield, WINDSOR, SL4 2ES.
WILKES, Mr. Guy Stephen Charles, BSc ACA *2011;* 48 Biddiblack Way, BIDEFORD, DEVON, EX39 4AY.
WILKES, Mr. John, BSc ACA *1982;* 11 Buckingham Street, Grandpont, OXFORD, OX1 4LH.
WILKES, Mr. John David Hamilton, FCA *1969;* Oakland House, Brackley Avenue, Hartley Wintney, HOOK, RG27 8QX.
WILKES, Mr. John Hyde, FCA *1969;* 14 Richmond Gardens, Wombourne, WOLVERHAMPTON, WV5 0LQ.
WILKES, Mr. John Russell, MA ACA *1985;* Flat 311, Queens Quay, 58 Upper Thames Street, LONDON, EC4V 3EJ.
•WILKES, Mr. Jonathan Mark, BSc ACA *1994;* Wellington Media Ltd, 49 Rannoch Road, LONDON, W6 9SS.
WILKES, Mrs. Julia Claire, BSc ACA *1991;* Buttes House, Les Buttes, St. Pierre Du Bois, GUERNSEY, GY7 9SD.
WILKES, Mrs. Katherine Anne, BSc ACA *2003;* 10 Goldwell Drive, NEWBURY, BERKSHIRE, RG14 1HZ.
•WILKES, Mr. Marcus John, ACA FCCA *2010;* Gareth Hughes & Company Limited, The Round House, Glan-y-Mor Road, LLANDUDNO JUNCTION, GWYNEDD, LL31 9SN.
WILKES, Mrs. Maureen, BSc ACA *1985;* Ruff Farm House, Vicarage Lane, ORMSKIRK, L40 6HG.
•WILKES, Ms. Michelle Ann, MS FCA *1994;* Wilkins Kennedy FKC Limited, Stourside Place, 35-41 Station Road, ASHFORD, KENT, TN23 1PP. See also W K Finn-Kelcey & Chapman Limited
WILKES, Mr. Paul, BSc ACA *2005;* 1 Keythorpe Cottage, Hallaton Road, Tugby, LEICESTER, LE7 9WB.
WILKES, Mr. Richard Geoffrey, CBE TD DL FCA *1952;* (President 1980 - 1981) (Member of Council 1969 - 1990), Little Orchard, 26 Blackmile Lane, Grendon, NORTHAMPTON, NN7 1JR. (Life Member)
WILKES, Mrs. Sarah Louise, BA ACA *2004;* 1 Keythorpe Cottage, Hallaton Road Tugby, LEICESTER, LE7 9WB.
WILKES, Mr. Simon John, FCA *1982;* 100 E Huron St, Apartment 4301, Illinois, CHICAGO, IL 60611, UNITED STATES.
WILKES, Mr. Stephen James, BSc ACA *2001;* Finance Office, University of Warwick University House, Kirby Corner Road, COVENTRY, CV4 8UW.
WILKES, Mr. Timothy John, BA ACA *1985;* Kirklees Metropolitan Council Director of Finance, Civic Centre, HUDDERSFIELD, HD1 2NF.
•WILKIE, Mr. Alan Douglas, FCA *1965;* Alan Wilkie, 19 Edlingham Close, South Gosforth, NEWCASTLE UPON TYNE, NE3 1RH.
WILKIE, Mr. Alastair James, BA FCA *1973;* 2 Winton Road, Bowdon, ALTRINCHAM, WA14 2PG.
WILKIE, Ms. Anne Irene, BA ACA *1991;* 3 The Mount, Trumpsgreen Road, VIRGINIA WATER, SURREY, GU25 4EJ.
WILKIE, Mr. David Alexander Randall, BSc ACA *2002;* 23 Manbey Grove, LONDON, E15 1EX.
WILKIE, Mr. George, BSc ACA *1982;* 3 Denwick Close, CHESTER LE STREET, DH2 3TL.
•WILKIE, Mr. Iain Rob, BA FCA *1985;* Ernst & Young LLP, 1 More London Place, LONDON, SE1 2AF. See also Ernst & Young Europe LLP
WILKIE, Mr. Ian James George, BA ACA *1997;* 6009 Quinpool Road, 9th Floor, HALIFAX B3K 5J7, NS, CANADA.
WILKIE, Miss. Joanne Margaret, MA ACA *2003;* 14 Griffin Gate, 135 Lower Richmond Road, LONDON, SW15 1EZ.
WILKIE, Mrs. Julie, ACA MAAT *2003;* 18 Kings Acre Coggeshall, COLCHESTER, CO6 1NY.
WILKIE, Mr. Lindsay Alexander, BSc ACA *1992;* 25 Cross Lane, Clifton, BRIGHOUSE, HD6 4HG.
WILKIE, Mrs. Louise, BA ACA *1993;* 4 Beech Grove, HALTWHISTLE, NORTHUMBERLAND, NE49 9DB.
WILKIE, Mrs. Louise Elizabeth, BSc ACA *2000;* 23 Sullivans Road, PAIHIA 0200, BAY OF ISLANDS, NEW ZEALAND.
WILKIE, Mr. Mark John, BA(Hons) ACA *2010;* (Tax Fac), 9 Searles Road, LONDON, SE1 4YU.
WILKIE, Mr. Michael Howe, FCA *1965;* 5 Mere Close, Bomere Heath, SHREWSBURY, SY4 3NN. (Life Member)
WILKIE, Mr. Neil David, BSc FCA MCIM MBA *1980;* 16 Jarvis Fields, Bursledon, SOUTHAMPTON, SO31 8AF.
WILKIE, Ms. Penny Jane Gwyneth, ACA *2008;* 424 Waterside, CHESHAM, BUCKINGHAMSHIRE, HP5 1QD.
WILKIE, Mr. Peter, FCA *1973;* 11 Walrand Close, Hastings Meadow, Wigginton, TAMWORTH, B79 9EA. (Life Member)
WILKIE, Mr. Stuart Ian, FCA *1982;* 21 Heron Close, Great Glen, LEICESTER, LEICESTERSHIRE, LE8 9DZ.

WILKIE, Miss. Susan Barbara, BA ACA *1991;* Provident Personal Credit Ltd Colonnade, Sunbridge Road, BRADFORD, BD1 2LQ.
•**WILKIE, Miss. Tania, BA ACA** *1984;* Tania Wilkie & Co Ltd, 52 Portsmouth Road, LEE-ON-THE-SOLENT, HAMPSHIRE, PO13 9AG.
WILKIN, Mr. Neal Geoffrey, BA ACA *2000;* 21 Pinewood, HEBBURN, NE31 1YP.
•**WILKIN, Mr. Peter, BA ACA** *1979;* PricewaterhouseCoopers, 34 Al - Farabi Ave, Building A, 4th Floor, ALMATY 050059, KAZAKHSTAN.
WILKINS, Mr. Alfred Percy, FCA *1953;* 30 Chester Close South, Regents Park, LONDON, NW1 4JG. (Life Member)
WILKINS, Mr. Andrew Michael, BA ACA *1990;* Oulton House 22 Lancaster Lane, LEYLAND, PR25 5SN.
WILKINS, Mr. Ben Robert, LLB ACA *2001;* Flat 6 Colliton Court, 31 Cumberland Road, BROMLEY, BR2 0PP.
WILKINS, Miss. Brigid Catherine, ACA *1987;* 13 Kirkstall Road, LONDON, SW2 4HD.
WILKINS, Mr. Christopher James, FCA *1969;* Highfields House, Gills Hill Lane, RADLETT, WD7 8DB.
WILKINS, Miss. Claire, BSc ACA *2005;* Balfour Beatty Ltd, Room B203, Midland House, 1 Nelson Street, DERBY, DE1 2SA.
•**WILKINS, Mr. David Ernest, FCA** *1962;* David Wilkins, 25a Market Square, BICESTER, OX26 6AD.
WILKINS, Mr. David Hardwicke, FCA *1982;* Jem Limited, Hyde Estate Road, LONDON, NW9 6JX.
WILKINS, Mr. David Locke, FCA *1960;* 4 Pinewood Avenue, Broughton, PRESTON, PR3 5DJ. (Life Member)
WILKINS, Mrs. Eileen Mary, BSc FCA *1978;* 5 Endlebury Road, Chingford, LONDON, E4 6QB.
WILKINS, Mrs. Eleanor Grace, BA ACA *1993;* The Old Dairy, Broad Street, BAMPTON, OXFORDSHIRE, OX18 2LY.
WILKINS, Miss. Emma Louise, LLB ACA *2005;* 13 Maes Yr Hafod, Creigiau, CARDIFF, CF15 9JU.
WILKINS, Mr. Gareth Martyn, BSc ACA *1993;* 70 Rose Road, Harborne, BIRMINGHAM, B17 9LJ.
WILKINS, Mr. Gavin Lawrence, BAcc ACA *2004;* Minerva Financial Services Ltd, PO Box 218, 43/45 La Motte Street, St Helier, JERSEY, JE4 8SD.
WILKINS, Mrs. Gillian Anne, BSc FCA *1980;* James Cowper North Lea House, 66 Northfield End, HENLEY-ON-THAMES, OXFORDSHIRE, RG9 2BE.
•**WILKINS, Mr. Graham David, BSc FCA** *1981;* Third Millennium Consultants Limited, Kelly Park, St. Dominick, SALTASH, CORNWALL, PL12 6SQ.
WILKINS, Mr. Gregory, FCA MAAT *1998;* 3 Coltsfoot Close, Hedge End, SOUTHAMPTON, SO30 4UN.
WILKINS, Mrs. Heather Knight, BA ACA *2004;* Riva Bella, 81 Roseville Street St. Helier, JERSEY, JE2 4PL.
WILKINS, Mrs. Joanna Claire, BSc ACA *1994;* Myrtle Villa, 17 Updown Hill, WINDLESHAM, SURREY, GU20 6DL.
WILKINS, Mr. John George, BCom FCA *1948;* 78 Armorial Road, Styvechale, COVENTRY, CV3 6GJ. (Life Member)
WILKINS, Mrs. Katherine, LLB ACA *2007;* 2 Blott Rise, WITHAM, CM8 1DG.
WILKINS, Mr. Keith Graham, BA FCA *1972;* Elm Barn Curry Rivel, LANGPORT, SOMERSET, TA10 0HG. (Life Member)
WILKINS, Mrs. Marie Suzanne, BSc ACA *1999;* 72 Whirlow Court Road, Whirlow, SHEFFIELD, S11 9NT.
WILKINS, Mr. Mark James George, BA ACA AKC *2008;* Gartenstrasse 35, 40479 DUSSELDORF, GERMANY.
•**WILKINS, Mr. Mark Timothy, FCA** *1986;* Blue Edge Solutions Limited, 1 Dillington, Great Staughton, ST. NEOTS, CAMBRIDGESHIRE, PE19 5DH.
WILKINS, Miss. Nicola Jane, ACA *2010;* 27 Ullswater, LOWESTOFT, SUFFOLK, NR33 8WG.
•**WILKINS, Mr. Peter John David, FCA** *1974;* Peter Wilkins & Co, 16 Cathedral Road, CARDIFF, CF11 9LJ.
•**WILKINS, Mr. Richard John, FCA** *1963;* Richard J. Wilkins, 1 Wentworth Close, Barnham, BOGNOR REGIS, WEST SUSSEX, PO22 0HS.
WILKINS, Mr. Richard Michael, FCA *1960;* 5 Colemere Gardens, Highcliffe, CHRISTCHURCH, BH23 5AS. (Life Member)
WILKINS, Mr. Richard Philip, MA ACA FFin *1981;* 29 Reed Street, Cremorne, SYDNEY, NSW 2090, AUSTRALIA.
WILKINS, Mr. Richard Vaughan Lindsay, MA FCA *1983;* The Cottage, Old Rectory Lane, Denham, UXBRIDGE, UB9 5AH.
WILKINS, Mr. Robert Henry, FCA *1966;* 80 Gilbert Scott Court, Whielden Street, AMERSHAM, BUCKINGHAMSHIRE, HP7 0AR.
WILKINS, Mrs. Samantha Clare, ACA *1998;* 3 Coltsfoot Close, Hedge End, SOUTHAMPTON, SO30 4UN.
WILKINS, Mrs. Sarah Amanda, ACA *1993;* 82 Loughborough Road, Whitwick, COALVILLE, LE67 5AQ.
WILKINS, Miss. Sarah Jane Angharad, BSc ACA *1999;* Plum Tree Barn, Houghton, STOCKBRIDGE, HAMPSHIRE, SO20 6LL.
WILKINS, Mr. Simon Christopher, BA ACA *1995;* 6 bramwell place, AUCKLAND 1023, NEW ZEALAND.
WILKINS, Mr. Thomas William, BA(Hons) ACA *2010;* 31 Halstead Road, LONDON, E11 2AY.
WILKINSON, Mr. Adam Thomas, MA FCA CTA *1995;* with Deloitte LLP, 4 Brindley Place, BIRMINGHAM, B1 2HZ.
WILKINSON, Mrs. Alison Claire, MSci ACA *2010;* 14 Hesketh Way, Bromborough, WIRRAL, MERSEYSIDE, CH62 2EL.
•**WILKINSON, Mr. Alistair Keith, LLB FCA** *1975;* Fisher Wilkinson, 44 Cheltenham Mount, HARROGATE, HG1 1DL.
WILKINSON, Mr. Andrew, ACA *2011;* 315 Denison House, 20 Lanterns Way, LONDON, E14 9JG.
•ⓘ**WILKINSON, Mr. Andrew Hartley, FCA** *1975;* Wilkinson & Co, 68 Thorpe Lane, Almondbury, HUDDERSFIELD, HD5 8UF.
•**WILKINSON, Mr. Andrew James Durham, FCA** *1974;* Andrew Wilkinson & Company, The Coach House, Rectory Lane, Charlton Musgrove, WINCANTON, SOMERSET BA9 8ES.
WILKINSON, Mr. Andrew Neil, BA FCA *1995;* with RSM Tenon Audit Limited, 2 Wellington Place, LEEDS, LS1 4AP.
WILKINSON, Mr. Arthur Joseph, FCA *1966;* 391 Southborough Lane, BROMLEY, BR2 8BQ.
WILKINSON, Mr. Barry Ernest, BA FCA *1962;* Creek House, Chertsey Road, SHEPPERTON, MIDDLESEX, TW17 9LA. (Life Member)
WILKINSON, Mr. Ben, BA(Hons) ACA *2011;* Sagars Llp, Gresham House, 5-7 St. Pauls Street, LEEDS, LS1 2JG.
WILKINSON, Mr. Benjamin David, BSc ACA *2006;* Levine Capital Management Advisors Ltd, 11 Hill Street, LONDON, W1J 5LF.
•**WILKINSON, Mr. Benjamin Paul, BSc ACA** *2003;* Chavereys, Mall House, The Mall, FAVERSHAM, KENT, ME13 8JL.
WILKINSON, Miss. Beverley Anne, LLB ACA *2004;* Coal Pension Trustees Services Ltd, Ventana House, 2 Concourse Way, Sheaf Street, SHEFFIELD, S1 2BJ.
•**WILKINSON, Mr. Brent, BSc FCA** *1976;* BDO LLP, 6th Floor, 3 Hardman Street, Spinningfields, MANCHESTER, M3 3AT. See also BDO Stoy Hayward LLP
WILKINSON, Mr. Bruce Peirs, ACA *1991;* 24 Eleanor Avenue, EPSOM, SURREY, KT19 9HD.
•**WILKINSON, Mr. Bryan Ross, BA FCA** *1990;* BDO LLP, 55 Baker Street, LONDON, W1U 7EU. See also BDO Stoy Hayward LLP
WILKINSON, Mrs. Camilla Amy, BSc ACA *2002;* 30 Parish Hill, Bournheath, BROMSGROVE, WORCESTERSHIRE, B61 9JQ.
WILKINSON, Mrs. Carolyn Sian, BSc ACA *1995;* Warwick Business School, University of Warwick, Gibbet Hill Road, COVENTRY, CV4 7AL.
WILKINSON, Mr. Christopher John, BA ACA *1983;* Whitehouse Farm, Easthorpe, COLCHESTER, CO5 9HG.
•**WILKINSON, Mr. Clive Stuart, FCA** *1976;* C.S. Wilkinson, 49B Market Square, WITNEY, OX28 6AG.
•**WILKINSON, Mr. Colin Anthony, BSc(Hons) FCA** *2000;* Cadishead Accountancy Services Limited, Britannic House, 657 Liverpool Road, Irlam, MANCHESTER, M44 5XD. See also Colin Wilkinson
WILKINSON, Mr. Craig, LLB ACA *1998;* 2 William Foster Way, Burley in Wharfedale, ILKLEY, WEST YORKSHIRE, LS29 7SS.
WILKINSON, Mr. Damien Michael, BCom ACA *1993;* 1 Haw Grove Court, Hellifield, SKIPTON, NORTH YORKSHIRE, BD23 4JB.
•**WILKINSON, Mr. Daniel, ACA** *2003;* (Tax Fac), Wilkinson & Partners, Victoria Mews, 19 Mill Field Road, Cottingley Business Park, Cottingley, BINGLEY WEST YORKSHIRE BD16 1PY. See also Wilkinson & Partners Business Services Limited
WILKINSON, Miss. Danielle Elizabeth, BSc ACA *2002;* 132 Valley Road, LONDON, SW16 2XR.
WILKINSON, Mr. David Hobart, BEng ACA *1995;* 39 Lorian Close, Woodside Park, LONDON, N12 7DW.
WILKINSON, David Kenworthy, Esq OBE FCA *1975;* Barn Cottage, Hebers Ghyll Drive, ILKLEY, LS29 9QH.
WILKINSON, Mr. David Lawrence, MA FCA *1988;* Old Cross Street Farm, Westburton, PULBOROUGH, WEST SUSSEX, RH20 1HD.
•**WILKINSON, Mr. David Lindow, BA ACA** *1982;* Ernst & Young LLP, 1 More London Place, LONDON, SE1 2AF. See also Ernst & Young Europe LLP
WILKINSON, Mr. David Matthew, MEng ACA *2001;* 43 Dunmow Road, BISHOP'S STORTFORD, HERTFORDSHIRE, CM23 5HE.
WILKINSON, Mr. David Michael, MEng ACA *1996;* Brabners Chaffe Street Llp, Horton House, Exchange Flags, LIVERPOOL, L2 3YL.
WILKINSON, Mr. David Paul, MA ACA *1986;* Top Floor Flat, 3 Ifield Road, LONDON, SW10 9AZ.
WILKINSON, Mr. David Paul, ACA *2004;* with BDO LLP, Arcadia House, Maritime Walk, Ocean Village, SOUTHAMPTON, SO14 3TL.
•**WILKINSON, Mr. David Philip, FCA CF** *1979;* Deloitte LLP, One Trinity Gardens, Broad Chare, NEWCASTLE UPON TYNE, NE1 2HF. See also Deloitte & Touche LLP
WILKINSON, Mr. David Robert, BCom ACA *1999;* 55 Butt Lane, Blackfordby, SWADLINCOTE, DE11 8BG.
WILKINSON, Miss. Deborah Janet, BEng ACA *2001;* Airborne Systems, Llangeinor, BRIDGEND, MID GLAMORGAN, CF32 8PL.
WILKINSON, Ms. Deborah Josette, BA(Hons) FCA *1994;* 13 Gellatly Road, LONDON, SE14 5TU.
WILKINSON, Miss. Denise, BA ACA *1991;* 67 Manchester Road, KNUTSFORD, CHESHIRE, WA16 0LX.
WILKINSON, Mr. Derek Lewis, FCA *1953;* 25 Baldocks Road, Theydon Bois, EPPING, CM16 7EB. (Life Member)
WILKINSON, Mr. Donald, JP FCA *1953;* Dam Head, Ellel R.P, LANCASTER, LA2 0QG. (Life Member)
WILKINSON, Miss. Dorothy, MA FCA *1972;* 16 Stanford Rd, FARINGDON, SN7 7AQ. (Life Member)
WILKINSON, Mr. Edwin John, BA ACA *1990;* Sheldon Lodge, 5 Stone Lodge Walk, IPSWICH, IP2 9AP.
WILKINSON, Mrs. Eleanor, BA(Hons) ACA *2003;* Livingstone Partners LLP, 15 Adam Street, LONDON, WC2N 6RJ.
WILKINSON, Miss. Elizabeth Gillian, BA FCA *1976;* Anglican Church of Papua New Guinea, PO Box 673, LAE, MOROBE PROVINCE, MP411, PAPUA NEW GUINEA.
WILKINSON, Mrs. Elizabeth Mary, BA ACA *1991;* 7 Rushmoor Lane, Backwell, BRISTOL, BS48 3BN.
•**WILKINSON, Mrs. Fiona Helen, BA FCA** *1980;* MEMBER OF COUNCIL, Fiona Wilkinson, Little Churchill, Whimple, EXETER, EX5 2PE. See also Wilkinsons
WILKINSON, Mr. Francis, BSc ACA *2003;* 81 Woodside Avenue, Meanwood, LEEDS, LS7 2UL.
WILKINSON, Mr. Gary, BA ACA *1989;* (Tax Fac), Flat 9 Stoneygate Court, 298 London Road, LEICESTER, LE2 2AH.
WILKINSON, Mr. Gavin Leslie, ACA *2008;* Flat 2, 72 Ifield Road, LONDON, SW10 9AD.
•**WILKINSON, Mr. Geoffrey, FCA** *1975;* Tax Right, 35 Montgomery Close, Whiston Knowsley, PRESCOT, L35 3RD.
•**WILKINSON, Mr. Geoffrey Robert, ACA** *1981;* Geoff Wilkinson, Pickwick House, Bunces Lane, Burghfield Common, READING, RG7 3DL.
WILKINSON, Mr. George Stuart, BA FCA *1977;* Rushfield Barn, Dairy Lane, Darley, HARROGATE, NORTH YORKSHIRE, HG3 2QP.
WILKINSON, Mr. Gerard James, BSc ACA *1996;* (Tax Fac), 43 Belgrave Road, Great Boughton, CHESTER, CH3 5SA.
WILKINSON, Mrs. Gillian Anne, BA ACA *1997;* 32 Longacres, ST. ALBANS, HERTFORDSHIRE, AL4 0DR.
•**WILKINSON, Mr. Glenn Robert, FCA** *1976;* Wrigley Partington, Sterling House, 501 Middleton Road, Chadderton, OLDHAM, OL9 9LY.
WILKINSON, Mr. Gordon Mark, BSc ACA *1994;* Bunzl Healthcare George House, Unit 6 Delta Park Industrial Estate Millmarsh Lane, ENFIELD, MIDDLESEX, EN3 7QJ.
WILKINSON, Mr. Graham John, FCA *1968;* Apdo. 333, 07814 SANTA GERTRUDIS DE FRUITERA, IBIZA, SPAIN.
WILKINSON, Mr. Guy James Craig, BA ACA *2000;* KPMG Corporate Finance LLC, Suite 2500, 111 Congress Avenue, AUSTIN, TX 78701, UNITED STATES.
WILKINSON, Miss. Helen Joanne, BA ACA *1999;* 14 Ewenfield Avenue, AYR, KA7 2QJ.
WILKINSON, Mrs. Helen Louise, BSc ACA *1997;* with Ernst & Young LLP, 1 Bridgewater Place, Water Lane, LEEDS, LS11 5QR.
•**WILKINSON, Mrs. Helena, BSc FCA DChA** *1993;* Chantrey Vellacott DFK LLP, Russell Square House, 10-12 Russell Square, LONDON, WC1B 5LF.
WILKINSON, Henry Russell, Esq OBE MA FCA *1962;* 4 Avenue Road, EPSOM, KT18 7QT.
•**WILKINSON, Mr. Howard James, FCA** *1972;* Mercer & Hole, Gloucester House, 72 London Road, ST. ALBANS, HERTFORDSHIRE, AL1 1NS. See also Mercer & Hole Trustees Limited
WILKINSON, Mr. Howard Stephen Jeremy, MA ACA *1998;* Sakala 18 -18, TALLINN 10141, ESTONIA.
WILKINSON, Mrs. Jacqueline Margaret, BEng ACA *1992;* Bellevuestrasse 44, Spiegel bei, 3095 BERNE, SWITZERLAND.
WILKINSON, Miss. Jacqueline Phyllis, BA ACA *2004;* 1 Saxon Court, BISHOP AUCKLAND, COUNTY DURHAM, DL14 7UA.
WILKINSON, Mr. James, ACA *2008;* Flat 7 Lane End, 196 West Hill, LONDON, SW15 3SH.
WILKINSON, Mr. James, BSc ACA *1992;* 2 The Nursery, Sutton Courtenay, ABINGDON, OX14 4UA.
WILKINSON, Mr. James Andrew, ACA *2009;* Deloitte & Touche, 1 City Square, LEEDS, LS1 2AL.
WILKINSON, Mr. James Crawford, BSc FCA *1998;* 123 South Middleton, Uphall, BROXBURN, WEST LOTHIAN, EH52 5GA.
WILKINSON, Mr. James Richard, BA ACA *2002;* 10 How Field, HARPENDEN, AL5 3AU.
WILKINSON, Ms. Jane Fiona, BA FCA *1995;* 9 Allee Scheffer, L2520 LUXEMBOURG, LUXEMBOURG.
WILKINSON, Mrs. Janet, BA ACA *1993;* 32 St. Pauls Drive, Mount Pleasant, HOUGHTON LE SPRING, TYNE AND WEAR, DH4 7SH.
WILKINSON, Miss. Janet, BSc ACA *1986;* Flat 2, 9 The Avenue, ASHFIELD, NSW 2131, AUSTRALIA.
WILKINSON, Mrs. Janet Marie, MSc ACA *1986;* Earleydene Cottage, Earleydene, ASCOT, BERKSHIRE, SL5 9JY.
•**WILKINSON, Mrs. Janette Carole, BA ACA** *1991;* (Tax Fac), KPMG LLP, 15 Canada Square, LONDON, E14 5GL. See also KPMG Europe LLP
WILKINSON, Mrs. Jennifer Jane, BA FCA *1998;* with KPMG LLP, 1 The Embankment, Neville Street, LEEDS, LS1 4DW.
WILKINSON, Mrs. Joanne Susan, BSc(Hons) ACA *2001;* with Grant Thornton UK LLP, 1 Whitehall Riverside, Whitehall Road, LEEDS, WEST YORKSHIRE, LS1 4BN.
WILKINSON, Mr. John Bernard, FCA *1956;* D1413 Villa Lotto, 18 Broadwood Road, HAPPY VALLEY, HONG KONG ISLAND, HONG KONG SAR. (Life Member)
•**WILKINSON, Mr. John Charles, FCA** *1973;* 31 Southfield, HESSLE, HU13 0EL.
WILKINSON, Mr. John David, BA FCA *1992;* Haus Salita, Monbielerstrasse 57, 7250 KLOSTERS, SWITZERLAND.
WILKINSON, Mr. John Frederick, MA FCA *1977;* Flat 10 St Johns Court, St Johns Hill, SEVENOAKS, KENT, TN13 3NU.
WILKINSON, Mr. John Hartley, FCA *1970;* Hillside, Broad Campden, CHIPPING CAMPDEN, GLOUCESTERSHIRE, GL55 6UR.
WILKINSON, Mr. John Philip, BA(Hons) ACA *2010;* 48 Trevelyan Crescent, STRATFORD-UPON-AVON, WARWICKSHIRE, CV37 9LL.
WILKINSON, Mr. John Richard, FCA *1962;* 5 Willow Bank, BARNSLEY, S75 1BN. (Life Member)
WILKINSON, Mr. John Richard, MA ACA *1987;* 28 Winfrith Road, LONDON, SW18 3BD.
WILKINSON, Mr. John Richard, FCA *1960;* Abbey Cottage, 1 Elm Lane, Well End, BOURNE END, SL8 5PF. (Life Member)
WILKINSON, Mr. John Stuart, BA FCA *1959;* 65 West Hill Avenue, EPSOM, KT19 8JX. (Life Member)
•**WILKINSON, Mr. Julian Ayscough, FCA** *1978;* Moore Stephens LLP, 150 Aldersgate Street, LONDON, EC1A 4AB. See also Moore Stephens & Co
WILKINSON, Miss. Julie Anne, BSc ACA *1995;* 37 Henshaw Drive, Ingleby Barwick, STOCKTON-ON-TEES, TS17 0PN.
WILKINSON, Mrs. Karen, BSc ACA *1991;* 87 Margaret Road, BARNET, HERTFORDSHIRE, EN4 9NX.
WILKINSON, Mrs. Kathryn Hazel, BA ACA *1996;* 3 St. Peters Avenue, Caversham, READING, RG4 7DD.
WILKINSON, Miss. Katy Jane, ACA *2009;* (Tax Fac), 2 Kenilworth Road, Cumnor, OXFORD, OX2 9QP.

WILKINSON, Miss. Kay, BA ACA ATII *1994;* with DPC Accountants Limited, Vernon Road, STOKE-ON-TRENT, ST4 2QY.
WILKINSON, Mr. Keith William, MA ACA *1982;* 160 Russells Ride, Cheshunt, WALTHAM CROSS, HERTFORDSHIRE, EN8 8UP.
WILKINSON, Mr. Kenneth Edward, BSc FCA *1977;* Burnt House Farm, Cross Stone Road, TODMORDEN, LANCASHIRE, OL14 8RA.
•WILKINSON, Mr. Kevan Stuart, ACA *1984;* 32 Woodthorpe Drive, BEWDLEY, WORCESTERSHIRE, DY12 2RH.
WILKINSON, Mrs. Lananh, BSc ACA *2003;* 32 Butterfield Road, Boreham, CHELMSFORD, CM3 3BS.
WILKINSON, Miss. Laura Elizabeth, FCA *1977;* 14 Woodcrest Road, DARLINGTON, DL3 8EF.
•WILKINSON, Mr. Lawrence, BA ACA *2002;* PricewaterhouseCoopers LLP, 7 More London Riverside, LONDON, SE1 2RT. See also PricewaterhouseCoopers
WILKINSON, Mr. Lawrence Rowland, FCA *1948;* 61 Moss Lane, SALE, M33 5AP. (Life Member)
WILKINSON, Mr. Lee, ACA *2008;* 14 Ashfield Close, SHEFFIELD, S36 6EY.
WILKINSON, Mr. Liam Adrian, BA ACA *1993;* 72 Pine Tree Circle, Cedarfield, NORTH KINGSTOWN, RI 02852, UNITED STATES.
WILKINSON, Mrs. Lucy Victoria, BSc ACA *1998;* 2 William Foster Way, Burley in Wharfedale, ILKLEY, WEST YORKSHIRE, LS29 7SS.
WILKINSON, Mr. Malcolm Derek, BA FCA *1979;* 12 Croome Road, Hanbury Park, WORCESTER, WR2 4PL.
•WILKINSON, Mr. Malcolm Hadath, BA ACA *1994;* Deloitte LLP, Stonecutter Court, 1 Stonecutter Street, LONDON, EC4A 4TR. See also Deloitte & Touche LLP
WILKINSON, Mr. Mark Raymond, BA(Econ) ACA *1999;* 21 Palmerston Road, IPSWICH, IP4 2NU.
WILKINSON, Mr. Mark Robert George, BA ACA *1987;* 24 Chemin des Gascards, Charente, 16130 GENSAC LA PALLUE, FRANCE.
•WILKINSON, Mr. Matthew Maxwell, BSc FCA *1995;* Moore Green, 22 Friars Street, SUDBURY, SUFFOLK, CO10 2AA. See also Moore Green Ltd
WILKINSON, Mr. Michael, FCA *1960;* 6 Wilfred Gardens, ASHBY-DE-LA-ZOUCH, LE65 2GX. (Life Member)
WILKINSON, Mr. Michael Geoffrey, FCA *1974;* Baines Simmons Ltd, Aviation Safety Centre, The Baker Suite, Fairoaks Airport, Chobham, WOKING SURREY GU24 8HX.
WILKINSON, Mr. Michael Robin, BA ACA *1979;* Indicus Advisors Aldermary House, 15 Queen Street, LONDON, EC4N 1TX.
WILKINSON, Mr. Michael Stanley, FCA *1958;* Heatherfield, South Milton, KINGSBRIDGE, DEVON, TQ7 3JG. (Life Member)
WILKINSON, Mrs. Michelle Andrea, BA ACA *1992;* Pitney Bowes Ltd, The Pinnacles, Elizabeth Way, HARLOW, ESSEX, CM19 5BD.
WILKINSON, Mrs. Neha, BA ACA *1997;* 21 Mulgrave Road, Ealing, LONDON, W5 1LF.
WILKINSON, Mr. Neil Freeman, FCA *1960;* Larkswood, Jordans Way, Jordans, BEACONSFIELD, HP9 2SP. (Life Member)
•WILKINSON, Mr. Neil Paul, BA FCA *1990;* (Tax Fac), Knox Cropper, 153-155 London Road, HEMEL HEMPSTEAD, HP3 9SQ.
WILKINSON, Mr. Nicolas Paul, BA ACA MCT *1991;* Tomkins Plc East Putney House, 84 Upper Richmond Road, LONDON, SW15 2ST.
WILKINSON, Mr. Nigel, BSc ACA *1991;* 11 Park Street, YORK, YO24 1BQ.
WILKINSON, Mr. Nigel Geoffrey, FCA *1974;* 24 Kelcey Road, Quorn, LOUGHBOROUGH, LEICESTERSHIRE, LE12 8UU.
•WILKINSON, Mr. Nigel Richard, BA(Hons) FCA CTA FPC *1987;* 1 Damsteads, Dodworth, BARNSLEY, SOUTH YORKSHIRE, S75 3TL.
WILKINSON, Mr. Norman George, ACA *1985;* Les Rebouquets, Les Rebouquets Lane, St. Martin, GUERNSEY, GY4 6UH.
•WILKINSON, Mr. Paul, FCA *1989;* (Tax Fac), Scott & Wilkinson, Dalton House, 9 Dalton Square, LANCASTER, LA1 1WD. See also Scott & Wilkinson LLP
WILKINSON, Mr. Paul David, BA ACA *1993;* 1 Le Coin Court, La Route De St Jean, St Lawrence, JERSEY, JE3 1ND.
WILKINSON, Mr. Paul Douglas, BA FCA *1974;* 4 Cattock Hurst Drive, SUTTON COLDFIELD, B72 1XG.
•WILKINSON, Mr. Paul Stuart, ACA *1980;* (Tax Fac), Lees Accounting Limited, 53 Chapelfield Crescent, Thorpe Hesley, ROTHERHAM, SOUTH YORKSHIRE, S61 2TP.
WILKINSON, Mr. Peter, LLB FCA *1964;* 66 Bishop Street, SHREWSBURY, SHROPSHIRE, SY2 5HD.
WILKINSON, Mr. Peter, FCA *1972;* 35 Back Lane, Baxenden, ACCRINGTON, BB5 2RE.
WILKINSON, Mr. Peter, BSc ACA *1988;* (Tax Fac), Langtons The Plaza, 100 Old Hall Street, LIVERPOOL, L3 9QJ.
WILKINSON, Mr. Peter, BA ACA *1996;* (Tax Fac), Tomkins Plc East Putney House, 84 Upper Richmond Road, LONDON, SW15 2ST.
WILKINSON, Mr. Peter Robert, FCA *1965;* 5 Bedford Street, Woburn, MILTON KEYNES, MK17 9QB. (Life Member)
WILKINSON, Mr. Peter William, MC FCA *1952;* Tharfield, East Haddon, NORTHAMPTON, NN6 8DE. (Life Member)
WILKINSON, Mr. Philip John, BA ACA *1998;* 78 Aire Road, WETHERBY, LS22 7FJ.
•WILKINSON, Miss. Philippa Clare, FCA *1997;* 11 Duck Lane, Woburn, MILTON KEYNES, MK17 9PT.
WILKINSON, Miss. Rachael Maria, LLB ACA *2002;* White House Farm, Sutton cum Granby, NOTTINGHAM, NG13 9QA.
WILKINSON, Mrs. Rachel, MSocSc BA ACA *2001;* Sun Life of Canada Matrix House, Basing View, BASINGSTOKE, HAMPSHIRE, RG21 4DZ.
WILKINSON, Mr. Ralph, BCom FCA *1962;* 36 Kirkhead Road, Kents Bank, GRANGE-OVER-SANDS, CUMBRIA, LA11 7DB. (Life Member)
WILKINSON, Mrs. Rebecca Tanya, BA ACA *2000;* Madingley, Endwood Drive, SUTTON COLDFIELD, STAFFORDSHIRE, B74 3AJ.
WILKINSON, Mr. Richard, BSc ACA *1992;* 22 Packsaddle Park, Prestbury, MACCLESFIELD, CHESHIRE, SK10 4PU.
WILKINSON, Mr. Richard Brooke, BA ACA *1994;* 52a Well House Drive, Penymynydd, CHESTER, CH4 0LB.
WILKINSON, Mr. Richard Freeman, BA ACA *1994;* Airlie, Surrey Gardens, Effingham Junction, LEATHERHEAD, SURREY, KT24 5HH.
WILKINSON, Mr. Richard John, BSc ACA CTA *1998;* 36 Harvey Road, GUILDFORD, SURREY, GU1 3SE.
WILKINSON, Mr. Richard John, BA ACA *1994;* Old Lodge Farm Moons Lane, Dormansland, LINGFIELD, RH7 6PD.
WILKINSON, Mr. Richard Malcolm, BSc ACA *2009;* 12 Croome Road, WORCESTER, WR2 4PL.
WILKINSON, Mr. Richard Mark, BA FCA *1988;* Department for Business Innovation and Skills, 1 Victoria Street, LONDON, SW1H 0ET.
WILKINSON, Mr. Richard Peter, MA(Hons) ACA *2000;* Manor Farm, Scoreby, Gate Helmsley, YORK, YO41 1NR.
WILKINSON, Mr. Richard Poynton, BA FCA *1952;* 14 Elm Road, Didsbury, MANCHESTER, M20 6XD. (Life Member)
WILKINSON, Mr. Richard Vere, ACA *1983;* 10 Bourmac Avenue, NORTHBRIDGE, NSW 2063, AUSTRALIA.
WILKINSON, Mr. Robert Anthony, FCA *1966;* 89 Cascade Terrace, Niskayuna, NEW YORK, NY 12309, UNITED STATES.
WILKINSON, Mr. Robert Bawden, FCA *1956;* 25 Capricorn Place, Hotwell Road, Hotwells, BRISTOL, BS8 4UA. (Life Member)
•WILKINSON, Mr. Robert John, BA FCA *1989;* PricewaterhouseCoopers, P O Box 1531, Old Parham Road, ST JOHNS, ANTIGUA AND BARBUDA.
WILKINSON, Mr. Robert Stephen, BA ACA MCT *1985;* T H B Group Plc Bankside House, 107-112 Leadenhall Street, LONDON, EC3A 4AF.
WILKINSON, Mr. Robert William Ian, BA ACA *1997;* 25 Routh Road, LONDON, SW18 3SP.
WILKINSON, Mr. Rodney Peter, BA ACA *1987;* with KPMG LLP, Quayside House, 110 Quayside, NEWCASTLE UPON TYNE, NE1 3DX.
WILKINSON, Mr. Roger Graham, BSc ACA *1997;* 110 Bennerley Road, Battersea, LONDON, SW11 6DU.
•WILKINSON, Mr. Ryan, LLB FCA MSI *2000;* with HW Progress Accountants Ltd, 6 Charter Point Way, ASHBY-DE-LA-ZOUCH, LEICESTERSHIRE, LE65 1NF.
WILKINSON, Miss. Sally, BSc(Hons) ACA *2003;* 13 Richmond Road, STOCKPORT, CHESHIRE, SK4 3BZ.
WILKINSON, Ms. Sarah, BA ACA *1989;* Field Fisher Waterhouse LLP, 35 Vine Street, LONDON, EC3N 2AA.
WILKINSON, Miss. Sarah, BA ACA *2007;* Pricewaterhousecoopers, 101 Barbirolli Square, MANCHESTER, M2 3PW.
WILKINSON, Miss. Sarah Elizabeth, BSc ACA *1995;* Kimberley, 288 Kepa Road, MISSION BAY 1071, AUCKLAND, NEW ZEALAND.
WILKINSON, Mrs. Sarah Elizabeth, BSc FCA *1991;* White Gables, Golden Acres, East Cowton, NORTHALLERTON, NORTH YORKSHIRE, DL7 0BD.
WILKINSON, Mrs. Sarah Helen, BEng ACA *2002;* 102 Hundred Acres Lane, AMERSHAM, BUCKINGHAMSHIRE, HP7 9BN.
WILKINSON, Mrs. Sharman Patricia Morris, BSc ACA *1980;* The Old Vicarage, Cleasby, DARLINGTON, DL2 2QY.
•WILKINSON, Mrs. Shelagh Marie, ACA *1989;* Shelagh Wilkinson ACA, Runtlings Grange, Runtlings, OSSETT, WEST YORKSHIRE, WF5 8JJ.
WILKINSON, Mr. Simon Brent, ACA *2008;* Astrazeneca Plc, G441, Alderley House, Alderley Park, MACCLESFIELD, CHESHIRE SK10 4TF.
•WILKINSON, Mr. Simon David, BSc FCA *1992;* Reeves Wilkinson Ltd, 41b Beach Road, LITTLEHAMPTON, WEST SUSSEX, BN17 5JA.
WILKINSON, Mrs. Sophi, BSc ACA *1997;* Rexam Plc, 4 Millbank, LONDON, SW1P 3XR.
•WILKINSON, Mr. Stanley, FCA *1951;* (Tax Fac), Stanley Wilkinson & Co, 139 Red Bank Road, Bispham, BLACKPOOL, LANCASHIRE, FY2 9HZ.
WILKINSON, Mr. Stephen Alan, BA FCA *1977;* 16 Hartley Road, SOUTHPORT, PR8 4SA.
WILKINSON, Mr. Stephen Peter, BA ACA *1986;* 9 Lower Cribden Avenue, Rawtenstall, ROSSENDALE, BB4 6SW.
WILKINSON, Mr. Steven David, ACA *2009;* Flat B, 18 Aristotle Road, LONDON, SW4 7UZ.
WILKINSON, Mr. Steven David, BA(Hons) ACA *2003;* 4 King Edwards Court, King Edwards Square, SUTTON COLDFIELD, B73 6AP.
WILKINSON, Dr. Susan, BSc ACA *1999;* La Mellette 13, 1081 MONTPREVEYRES, SWITZERLAND.
WILKINSON, Mrs. Susan Wendy, ACA *1986;* 9 rue des Provenceaux, 77300 FONTAINEBLEAU, FRANCE.
WILKINSON, Mr. Thomas Adam, MA(Hons) ACA *2000;* Flat 2, 43-44 Nevern Square, Earls Court, LONDON, SW5 9PF.
WILKINSON, Dr. Timothy Charles, PhD BSc CMath FCA MIMA *1995;* 32 St Pauls Drive, Mount Pleasant, HOUGHTON LE SPRING, DH4 7SH.
WILKINSON, Mrs. Tracy, BA ACA *1992;* 72 Pine Tree Circle, NORTH KINGSTOWN, RI 02852, UNITED STATES.
WILKINSON, Mr. Walter, FCA *1958;* Horsley Fell, Horsley, NEWCASTLE UPON TYNE, NE15 0NT. (Life Member)
WILKINSON-KEAN, Mr. Robert John Andrew, BEng ACA *1993;* 26 Grove Farm Close, Cookridge, LEEDS, LS16 6DB.
WILKS, Mrs. Camilla Jane, MA ACA *1999;* Berry Grove House, Church Street, LISS, GU33 6JY.
WILKS, Mr. Christopher John, BSc ACA *1990;* Old Pines House, Ball Hill, NEWBURY, RG20 0NN.
WILKS, Mrs. Gemma Louisette Jaqueline, ACA *2008;* Boleyn Cottage, Forest Road, Nomansland, SALISBURY, SP5 2BW.
WILKS, Mr. Geoffrey Victor Edward, MA FCA *1971;* 28 Berkeley Road, LONDON, N8 8RU. (Life Member)
•ⒹWILKS, Mr. Harold Charles, BSc FCA *1982;* Wilks & Associates, 19 Church Lane, West Tytherley, SALISBURY, SP5 1JY.
WILKS, Mr. Jeffrey Alan, FCA *1970;* 45 Norsey View Drive, BILLERICAY, CM12 0QS.
•WILKS, Mr. Nicholas Anthony, BSc ACA *2001;* PricewaterhouseCoopers LLP, 7 More London Riverside, LONDON, SE1 2RT. See also PricewaterhouseCoopers
WILKS, Mr. Paul Duncan Hardy, BA FCA *1977;* Trinity Mirror plc, 1 Canada Square, Canary Wharf, LONDON, E14 5AP.
WILKS, Mr. Peter Geoffrey, FCA *1971;* 1278 Chavano Drive, IVINS, UT 84738-6336, UNITED STATES.
WILKS, Mr. Rodney Steven Lailey, BSc ACA *1979;* Maryland, Wilverley Road, BROCKENHURST, SO42 7SP.
WILKS, Mrs. Sara, LLB ACA *2000;* Blacks Leisure Group Plc, Cob Drive, Swan Valley, NORTHAMPTON, NN4 9BB.
•WILKS, Mr. Simon Christopher, BA ACA *1990;* haysmacintyre, Fairfax House, 15 Fulwood Place, LONDON, WC1V 6AY.
WILKS, Mr. Steven Andrew, BSc ACA *1992;* 21 Belfry Way, Edwalton, NOTTINGHAM, NG12 4FA.
WILL, Mr. Richard Edward, BSc FCA *1976;* Frick Farm House Station Road, North Chailey, LEWES, EAST SUSSEX, BN8 4HG.
WILLAMSON-CARY, Mrs. Clare Diane, BA ACA *1993;* Headson Farm, Bratton Clovelly, OKEHAMPTON, DEVON, EX20 4JP.
•WILLAN, Mr. John Anthony, FCA *1966;* John Willan FCA, 54 Hertford Street, CAMBRIDGE, CB4 3AQ.
•WILLAN, Mr. Michael John, FCA *1975;* Willan & Willan, The Old Post Office, High Street, Hartley Wintney, HOOK, HAMPSHIRE RG27 8NZ.
WILLAN, Mr. Richard Charles, BA ACA *1997;* Kent House Hudnall Lane, Little Gaddesden, BERKHAMSTED, HERTFORDSHIRE, HP4 1QQ.
WILLAN, Mrs. Sarah Lucy, BA ACA *1997;* Kent House, Hudnall Lane, Little Gaddesden, BERKHAMSTED, HERTFORDSHIRE, HP4 1QQ.
•WILLANS, Mr. Peter Robert, BSc FCA *1980;* (Tax Fac), P.R. Willans & Co, 21 The Fairway, BROMLEY, BR1 2JZ.
WILLANS, Mr. Robert John, ACA *2009;* 1048 Middleton Road, Chadderton, OLDHAM, OL9 9RZ.
WILLATS, Mr. Antony, FCA *1962;* Wyck Oast, Wyck Lane, Woods Green, WADHURST, TN5 6QS.
WILLATT, Mr. Ian Glynn, FCA *1982;* 7 St. Johns Road, ORPINGTON, BR5 1HS.
WILLBOURNE, Ms. Sian Elizabeth, MA BA ACA *2003;* 32 St. Annes Road, London Colney, ST. ALBANS, HERTFORDSHIRE, AL2 1LJ.
WILLCOCK, Mr. Carl Martin, BA ACA *2006;* 121 Montreal Avenue, BRISTOL, BS7 0NJ.
WILLCOCK, Mr. John, FCA *1952;* 10 Torkington Road, WILMSLOW, CHESHIRE, SK9 2AE. (Life Member)
WILLCOCK, Mr. Robert, BA ACA *1993;* 2 Ashpole Furlong, Loughton, MILTON KEYNES, MK5 8EA.
WILLCOCKS, Mr. Paul Kneale, BSc ACA *1990;* Partnerships in Care Unit 2, Imperial Place Maxwell Road, BOREHAMWOOD, HERTFORDSHIRE, WD6 1JN.
WILLCOCKS, Mr. Vernon Eric, FCA *1971;* 22 West Garth Road, EXETER, EX4 5AH. (Life Member)
•WILLCOX, Mr. Alan Kenneth, ACA *1978;* Willcox & Co, 10 Chilcott Court, SOUTHAMPTON, SO52 9PS.
WILLCOX, Mr. Benjamin Philip Richard, MMath ACA *2007;* 7 Kenilworth Road, WHITLEY BAY, TYNE AND WEAR, NE25 8BE.
WILLCOX, Mrs. Karen Jane, MA ACA CTA *1993;* (Tax Fac), with PricewaterhouseCoopers LLP, The Atrium, 1 Harefield Road, UXBRIDGE, UB8 1EX.
WILLCOX, Mrs. Kirsty Jane, ACA *2008;* 4 Walter Road, WOKINGHAM, RG41 3JA.
WILLCOX, Mr. Neil Richard, ACA *1993;* c/o ResMan Limited, 22 Rose Lane, LIVERPOOL, L18 5ED.
WILLCOX, Mr. Nicholas David, BEng ACA *1997;* 11a West Park Road, RICHMOND, SURREY, TW9 4DB.
WILLCOX, Mr. Richard John, BA ACA *1997;* 745 Carter Street, NEW CANAAN, CT 06840, UNITED STATES.
•WILLCOX, Mr. Ross William, FCA *1985;* Haines Watts (East Midlands) Limited, 10 Stadium Business Court, Millennium Way, Pride Park, DERBY, DE24 8HP.
•WILLCOX, Mr. Stephen Anthony, BSc FCA *1974;* (Tax Fac), The TACS Partnership, Graylaw House, Mersey Square, STOCKPORT, CHESHIRE, SK1 1AL.
•WILLCOX, Mr. Stephen Reginald, FCA *1974;* Stephen Willcox, Frogwell House, Cotesbach, LUTTERWORTH, LE17 4HZ.
WILLDRIDGE, Miss. Louise, ACA *2008;* Level 17, 383 Kent Street, SYDNEY, NSW 2000, AUSTRALIA.
WILLEMITE, Miss. Katherine Elizabeth, BSc(Hons) ACA *2002;* Unipart Group of Companies Unipart House, Garsington Road Cowley, OXFORD, OX4 2PG.
WILLENBROCK, Miss. Margaret Susan Clare, BSc ACA *1989;* Baring Asset Management, 155 Bishopsgate, LONDON, EC2M 3XY.
WILLERS, Mr. Geoffrey Alan, FCA *1962;* 10A Tinwell Road, STAMFORD, PE9 2QQ. (Life Member)
WILLETS, Miss. Jodie, ACA *2001;* Dornford Waresley Road, Hartlebury, KIDDERMINSTER, WORCESTERSHIRE, DY11 7XT.
WILLETT, Dr. Barbara, ACA *2010;* 43 St. Pauls Mews, YORK, YO24 4BR.
WILLETT, Mrs. Caroline Louise, BA ACA *1983;* Rythe House, Marine Walk, HAYLING ISLAND, PO11 9PQ.
WILLETT, Prof. Roger John, PhD BA FCA *1975;* School of Accounting & Corporate Governance, Private Bag 86, University of Tasmania, Sandy Bay, HOBART, TAS 7001 AUSTRALIA.
WILLETT, Miss. Victoria Jane, MBA BA ACA *2006;* Unit 4, 73 Shirley Road, WOLLSTONECRAFT, NSW 2065, AUSTRALIA.

WILLETTS, Mr. Adrian, BSc ACA *1987;* Lawnswood, 10 Bromwich Lane, Pedmore, STOURBRIDGE, WEST MIDLANDS, DY9 0QZ.
WILLETTS, Mr. Andrew John, BA ACA *1990;* Lloyds Pharmacy, Sapphire Court, Walsgrave Triangle, COVENTRY, CV2 2TX.
WILLETTS, Mrs. Claire Nicola, BCom ACA *1990;* Upper Wick Cottage Upper Wick Lane, Rushwick, WORCESTER, WR2 5SU.
•WILLETTS, Mr. Clark, BSc ACA *1986;* Clark Willetts & Company, 5a Newerne Street, LYDNEY, GLOUCESTERSHIRE, GL15 5RA.
WILLETTS, Mr. David Robert, BA FCA *1969;* St. Gennys, Love Lane, Shaw, NEWBURY, BERKSHIRE, RG14 2DY.
WILLETTS, Mr. Martin Gordon, BCom ACA *1985;* #26-01 Tribeca by the Waterfront, 60 Kin Seng Road, SINGAPORE 239497, SINGAPORE.
WILLETTS, Mr. Nigel John, BSc ACA *1997;* 257 Rugby Road, LEAMINGTON SPA, WARWICKSHIRE, CV32 6EB.
WILLETTS, Mr. Peter William, BA ACA *1995;* Man Financial Services plc, Frankland Road, Blagrove, SWINDON, SN5 8YZ.
WILLEY, Mr. Alistair James, MSc ACA *2002;* Cadbury Plc, Cadbury House, Sanderson Road, UXBRIDGE, MIDDLESEX, UB8 1DH.
WILLEY, Mr. Anthony Edward, FCA *1965;* 58 Kendal Green, KENDAL, CUMBRIA, LA9 5PT.
WILLEY, Mr. Gerald Jeffrey, FCA *1951;* 3 Forge End, AMERSHAM, BUCKINGHAMSHIRE, HP7 0JP. (Life Member)
WILLEY, Mrs. Jayne Elizabeth, BA ACA *2004;* 52 Coolshinney Road, MAGHERAFELT, COUNTY LONDONDERRY, BT45 5JF.
WILLEY, Mr. Michael, BA FCA *1964;* 24 Kennedy Road, SHEFFIELD, S8 0HD.
WILLEY, Mr. Michael Jeffrey, BSc FCA *1980;* 1 Bevan Court, Winslow, BUCKINGHAM, MK18 3FA.
•WILLEY, Mr. Peter Gilhespy, BSc ARCS CMath FCA CTax *1980;* Hallgarth, Lincoln Hill, Humshaugh, HEXHAM, NORTHUMBERLAND, NE46 4BE.
•WILLEY, Mr. Peter Joseph, FCA *1967;* (Tax Fac), Willey & Co, Bainbridge House, 379 Stamfordham Road, Westerhope, NEWCASTLE UPON TYNE, NE5 2LH.
•WILLEY, Mr. Philip Robert, FCA *1980;* The Swillett Portfolio Limited, Berry Cottage, Bullsland Lane, Chorleywood, RICKMANSWORTH, WD3 5BD.
•WILLEY, Mr. Stephen Charles, BCom FCA CTA *1973;* (Tax Fac), Montpelier Professional (Leeds) Limited, Sanderson House, Station Road, Horsforth, LEEDS, LS18 5NT.
WILLFORD, Mr. Anthony Charles, BSc ACA *1981;* 17 Beaconsfield Road, Knowle, BRISTOL, BS4 2JE.
•WILLGOOSE, Mr. Richard Michael, ACA *1985;* R.M. Willgoose, Chestnut End, Leddington, LEDBURY, HR8 2LG.
•WILLIAM, Mr. Charles, FCA ACCA ACMA ATII *1995;* 115 Hampstead Road, LONDON, NW1 3EE.
WILLIAMNS, Mrs. Nicola Anne, BA ACA *1993;* Field House Rock Cross, Rock, KIDDERMINSTER, WORCESTERSHIRE, DY14 9RQ.
•WILLIAMS, Mr. Abdul Razak Olatokunboh, BA FCA *1988;* Cavernham LLP, 85-87 Bayham Street, LONDON, NW1 0AG.
WILLIAMS, Mr. Adam Alan, BSc FCA MCT FSI *1997;* Park View, Copsewood, Redlands Road, Lolworth, CAMBRIDGE, CB23 8HQ.
WILLIAMS, Mr. Adam Caleb, ACA *2008;* 14 Tollhouse Point, London Road, ST. ALBANS, AL1 1NU.
WILLIAMS, Mr. Adam James, BSc(Hons) ACA *2002;* 8a St Georges Road, TOORAK, VIC 3142, AUSTRALIA.
WILLIAMS, Mr. Adam Miles, ACA *2009;* 343 Walkden Road, Worsley, MANCHESTER, M28 2RY.
WILLIAMS, Mr. Adrian, MA ACA *2005;* 56 Riverside Road, SHOREHAM-BY-SEA, WEST SUSSEX, BN43 5RB.
WILLIAMS, Mr. Adrian Mark, MA ACA *1992;* 7 Woodland Place, BLACKWOOD, NP12 3QX.
WILLIAMS, Mr. Adrian Ryley, BSc ACA *2003;* 40 Horseshoe Drive, CANNOCK, STAFFORDSHIRE, WS12 0FR.
WILLIAMS, Mr. Akintola, CBE BCom FCA *1950;* 17 Ilabere Avenue, Ikoyi South East, PO Box 1923, LAGOS, NIGERIA. (Life Member)
•WILLIAMS, Mr. Alan, FCA *1980;* (Tax Fac), Hopper Williams & Bell Limited, Highland House, Mayflower Close, Chandler's Ford, SOUTHAMPTON, HAMPSHIRE SO53 4AR. See also HWB Holdings Limited
WILLIAMS, Mr. Alan Ernest John, BA FCA FCT *1967;* Woodhatch, Cotchford Lane, HARTFIELD, TN7 4DN. (Life Member)
WILLIAMS, Mr. Alan Hugh, FCA JDipMA *1957;* 18 Rhydes Court, 199-201 Fidlas Road, Llanishen, CARDIFF, CF14 5NA. (Life Member)
WILLIAMS, Mr. Alan John, FCA *1973;* 87 Penrhos Road, BANGOR, GWYNEDD, LL57 2BQ. (Life Member)
•WILLIAMS, Mr. Alastair John, FCA *1981;* (Tax Fac), A J Williams, 39 Trafalgar Road, SOUTHPORT, PR8 2HF.
WILLIAMS, Mr. Aled Wyn, BSc FCA *1989;* 6 Nicholas Street, CHESTER, CH1 2NX.
WILLIAMS, Mr. Alex, ACA *2009;* 23 Talfourd Way, REDHILL, RH1 6GD.
WILLIAMS, Mr. Alexander Edward, BSc ACA *2002;* 11 Langdale Avenue, HARPENDEN, HERTFORDSHIRE, AL5 5QU.
WILLIAMS, Mr. Alexander Paul, BSc(Hons) ACA *2001;* Ernst & Young, 100 Barbirolli Square, MANCHESTER, M2 3EY.
WILLIAMS, Miss. Alexandra Jane, ACA *2009;* Mazars LLP The Pinnacle, 160 Midsummer Boulevard, MILTON KEYNES, MK9 1FF.
WILLIAMS, Mrs. Alison, BA ACA *2009;* Apt 303, 425 West Side Drive, GAITHERSBURG, MD 20878, UNITED STATES.
WILLIAMS, Mrs. Alison Jane, BA ACA *1991;* 98 Elwill Way, BECKENHAM, BR3 6RX.
WILLIAMS, Ms. Alison Margaret Wyn, FCA *1981;* 'St Germain', 6 The Ridge, 89 Green Lane, NORTHWOOD, MIDDLESEX, HA6 1AE.
WILLIAMS, Mr. Alistair Charles Walter, BSc FCA *1987;* 6 College Drive, THAMES DITTON, KT7 0LB.
WILLIAMS, Mrs. Allan, FCA *1951;* Pendle House, 16 Ashmount Gardens, GRANGE-OVER-SANDS, LA11 6DN. (Life Member)
WILLIAMS, Mr. Allan George, FCA DChA *1977;* Swansea Young Single Homeless Project 6a Walter Road, SWANSEA, SA1 5NF.
WILLIAMS, Mr. Alun Gwyn, MA FCA *1980;* 771 Amsterdam Road, BRIDGWATER, NJ 08807, UNITED STATES.
WILLIAMS, Mr. Alun Gwynne, MSc BA FCA *1974;* 26 Bellmans Grove, Whittlesey, PETERBOROUGH, CAMBRIDGESHIRE, PE7 1TX.
WILLIAMS, Mr. Alun Rees, BSc ACA *1993;* 24 Gipsy Lane, Irchester, WELLINGBOROUGH, NORTHAMPTONSHIRE, NN29 7DL.
•WILLIAMS, Mr. Alwyne Graham, BA FCA *1961;* A Graham Williams, 18 Shrewsbury Wood, Cabinteely, DUBLIN 18, COUNTY DUBLIN, IRELAND.
WILLIAMS, Ms. Alyson Dawn, BSc ACA *1993;* 9 Brodrick Close, Kenton, NEWCASTLE UPON TYNE, NE3 3SG.
WILLIAMS, Mrs. Amanda Caroline, MA ACA CTA *1992;* Mead House, Church Hill, Tasburgh, NORWICH, NR15 1NB.
WILLIAMS, Miss. Amanda Elizabeth Watkin, BSc ACA *1987;* Personal Finance Education Group, 14 Bonhill Street, LONDON, EC2A 4BX.
WILLIAMS, Miss. Amy, ACA *2011;* PricewaterhouseCoopers LLP, Marlborough Court, 10 Bricket Road, ST. ALBANS, HERTFORDSHIRE, AL1 3JX.
WILLIAMS, Mrs. Andrea Elizabeth, BSc ACA *1999;* A A Finance, 1 Swallowfield, Wolverhampton Road, OLDBURY, WEST MIDLANDS, B69 2BG.
WILLIAMS, Mr. Andrew, MSc ACA *2009;* S G B Group Ltd Harsco House, 299 Regent Park Kingston Road, LEATHERHEAD, KT22 7SG.
•WILLIAMS, Mr. Andrew, BSc ACA *1992;* Porter Garland Limited, Portland House, Park Street, BAGSHOT, SURREY, GU19 5PG.
WILLIAMS, Mr. Andrew, BA ACA *2005;* Flat 3 Birch House, 48 Holmesdale Road, TEDDINGTON, MIDDLESEX, TW11 9NA.
WILLIAMS, Mr. Andrew, ACA *2011;* 17 Stanfield Road, Great Barr, BIRMINGHAM, B43 7LR.
WILLIAMS, Mr. Andrew, BA ACA *2006;* Lower Hill Farm, 6 Pound Lane, Frankley Green, BIRMINGHAM, B32 4BD.
WILLIAMS, Mr. Andrew Christopher, BA ACA *2004;* Horwath Clark Whitehill Arkwright House, Parsonage Gardens, MANCHESTER, M3 2HP.
WILLIAMS, Mr. Andrew John, BSc ACA *1990;* 104 Birmingham Road, SUTTON COLDFIELD, B72 1LY.
WILLIAMS, Mr. Andrew John, BA ACA *1995;* 25 Palesides Avenue, OSSETT, WF5 9NL.
•WILLIAMS, Mr. Andrew Jonathan, BEng ACA *1992;* Haraled Consultancy Limited, 54 Bettws-y-Coed Road, Cyncoed, CARDIFF, CF23 6PN.
WILLIAMS, Mr. Andrew Paul, BA ACA *1984;* 25 Sims Lane, Quedgeley, GLOUCESTER, GL2 3NJ.
•WILLIAMS, Mr. Andrew Paul, BA ACA *1990;* Moore Stephens (South) LLP, 33 The Clarendon Centre, Salisbury Business Park, Dairy Meadow Lane, SALISBURY, SP1 2TJ. See also Moore Secretaries Limited
WILLIAMS, Mr. Andrew Paul Carlyle, BSc ACA *1999;* 6a Grayburn Close, CHALFONT ST. GILES, BUCKINGHAMSHIRE, HP8 4NZ.
WILLIAMS, Mr. Andrew Ralph, BA FCA *1992;* 12a Parsonage Street, CAMBRIDGE, CB5 8DN.
WILLIAMS, Mr. Andrew Simon, BSc ACA *2006;* 1 Westwood Close, DROITWICH, WORCESTERSHIRE, WR9 0BD.
•WILLIAMS, Mrs. Angela, BSc FCA CTA *1987;* (Tax Fac), Angela Williams & Associates Limited, 1 Meadowside, WALTON-ON-THAMES, KT12 3LS.
•WILLIAMS, Ms. Angela Elizabeth, FCA *1993;* (Tax Fac), Haysom Silverton & Partners Ltd, Norfolk House Centre, 82 Saxon Gate West, MILTON KEYNES, MK9 2DL.
WILLIAMS, Miss. Angela Jane, BA ACA *1996;* 6 Bedale Close, DURHAM, DH1 2BB.
WILLIAMS, Mrs. Ann, ACA *1982;* 67 Cote Green Road, Marple Bridge, STOCKPORT, SK6 5EN.
WILLIAMS, Mrs. Anna Elizabeth, BSc ACA *2006;* 6 Ardington Road, Abington, NORTHAMPTON, NN1 5LJ.
WILLIAMS, Mrs. Anna Elizabeth, BA FCA DChA *1992;* Birmingham Royal Ballet, 39 Thorp Street, BIRMINGHAM, B5 4AU.
WILLIAMS, Mrs. Anna Nuvit, BSc ACA *2001;* 60 Kim Seng Road, #15-02, SINGAPORE 239497, SINGAPORE.
•WILLIAMS, Mrs. Anne, BA ACA *1979;* Price Pearson Ltd, Finch House, 28-30 Wolverhampton Street, DUDLEY, DY1 1DB. See also Finch House Properties Limited
•WILLIAMS, Mrs. Anne Vivien, MA FCA *1983;* Bruton Knowles, Chartered Surveyors, Bisley House, Green Farm Business Park, Bristol Road, GLOUCESTER GL2 4LY.
WILLIAMS, Mr. Anthony David, ACA *1987;* Derwent House University Way, Cranfield Technology Park Cranfield, BEDFORD, MK43 0AZ.
•WILLIAMS, Mr. Anthony John, FCA *1969;* (Tax Fac), Anthony J Williams, 27 Forest Centre, Pinehill Road, BORDON, HAMPSHIRE, GU35 0TN.
•WILLIAMS, Mr. Anthony Philip, FCA *1974;* Robinson Rice Associates Ltd, 93 Banks Road, West Kirby, WIRRAL, MERSEYSIDE, CH48 0RB.
WILLIAMS, Mr. Anthony Robert, BSc FCA *1973;* 7 Glamis Gardens, PETERBOROUGH, PE3 9PQ.
WILLIAMS, Mr. Anthony Trewitt, FCA *1971;* 16833 Flying Jib Road, CORNELIUS, NC 28031, UNITED STATES.
WILLIAMS, Mr. Antony Brian, BA ACA *1989;* 39 All Saints Close, WOKINGHAM, BERKSHIRE, RG40 1WE.
WILLIAMS, Mr. Arthur Barrie, FCA *1961;* Cartref, 65 Hitchen Hatch Lane, SEVENOAKS, TN13 3AY.
WILLIAMS, Mr. Arthur Norman, FCA *1950;* Walnut Cottage, 36 Kilsby Road, Barby, RUGBY, CV23 8TU. (Life Member)
WILLIAMS, Mrs. Barbara Eileen, MA ACA *1985;* 21 Melrose Crescent, Poynton, STOCKPORT, CHESHIRE, SK12 1UT.
•WILLIAMS, Ms. Barbara Gigi, BA ACA *1989;* Vetiver Ltd, East Ballarobin, Kerrowkeil Road, Grenaby, ISLE OF MAN, IM9 3BB.
WILLIAMS, Mr. Ben, ACA *2011;* Ireland 2010); Uplands, Alresford Road, Wivenhoe, COLCHESTER, CO7 9JX.
WILLIAMS, Mr. Benjamin, ACA *2010;* 11 Wensleydale, Carlton Colville, LOWESTOFT, SUFFOLK, NR33 8TL.
WILLIAMS, Mr. Bernard Cooper, PhD BSc FCA *1976;* 80 High Street, Graveley, ST. NEOTS, CAMBRIDGESHIRE, PE19 6PL. (Life Member)
WILLIAMS, Mr. Bevan Edward, ACA *2009;* Flagship Private Asset Management, 1st Floor ICR House, Alphen Park, Constantia Main Road, CAPE TOWN, 7800 SOUTH AFRICA.
WILLIAMS, Mrs. Brenda Michaela, BA ACA *1991;* BDO, MERCURY COURT, CHOC ESTATE, P.O. BOX 364, CASTRIES, SAINT LUCIA.
WILLIAMS, Mr. Brian, FCA *1959;* 14 Shirley Avenue, Cheam, SUTTON, SURREY, SM2 7QR. (Life Member)
WILLIAMS, Mr. Brian, ACA *2000;* The Willows, Saltpans Road, St. Sampson, GUERNSEY, GY2 4LY.
WILLIAMS, Mr. Brian James, FCA *1967;* Les Bastets, Marsanne, 26740 DROME, FRANCE.
•WILLIAMS, Mr. Brian Thornley, FCA *1958;* Brian T. Williams, 11 Westminster Drive, Cyncoed, CARDIFF, CF23 6RD.
WILLIAMS, Mr. Bryan Rhys, MA ACA *1997;* 12 Hopefield Avenue, LONDON, NW6 6LH.
WILLIAMS, Mr. Bryn, MA FCA MCIM *1989;* 10 Maslen Road, ST. ALBANS, AL4 0GT.
WILLIAMS, Mr. Bryn Charles, BA ACA *2010;* 45 Manor Road, LONDON, W13 0JA.
WILLIAMS, Miss. Calley, BSc ACA *2011;* Ground Floor Flat, 85 Belmont Road, LONDON, N17 6AT.
WILLIAMS, Mr. Carl Ivor, BA FCA *1981;* 134a Kew Road, RICHMOND, SURREY, TW9 2AU.
WILLIAMS, Mrs. Carla, BSc ACA *1999;* (Tax Fac), 3 Buchanan Close, WIDNES, CHESHIRE, WA8 9QD.
WILLIAMS, Ms. Carol Ann, FCA *1966;* 5 Windsor Avenue, Radyr, CARDIFF, CF15 8BW.
WILLIAMS, Miss. Caroline Alice, ACA *2009;* 16 Lavender Sweep, LONDON, SW11 1HA.
WILLIAMS, Miss. Caroline Anne, BA(Hons) ACA *2010;* 21 Buryfield Road, SOLIHULL, WEST MIDLANDS, B91 2DF.
WILLIAMS, Mrs. Caroline Victoria, BSc(Hons) ACA *2000;* 53 Racecourse Road, WILMSLOW, CHESHIRE, SK9 5LJ.
WILLIAMS, Mrs. Carolyn Ann Peverel-Cooper, BSc ACA *1989;* P C B Solicitors LLP, Cypress Centre, Sitka Drive, Shrewsbury Business Park, SHREWSBURY, SY2 6LG.
WILLIAMS, Mrs. Carolyn Jane, FCA *1973;* (Tax Fac), 3 Kingston Cottages, Kingswear, DARTMOUTH, TQ6 0EG.
•WILLIAMS, Mrs. Catherine Ann, BSc ACA *1999;* (Tax Fac), Catherine A Williams Ltd, 1 High Street, CRICKHOWELL, POWYS, NP8 1BW.
WILLIAMS, Mrs. Catherine Mary, BA ACA *1991;* 93 Davis Road, Acton, LONDON, W3 7SF.
WILLIAMS, Mr. Ceri Rhys, ACA *2008;* Flat 35 Leigham Hall, Streatham High Road, LONDON, SW16 1DN.
WILLIAMS, Mr. Charles Robin Gilbert, FCA *1959;* Tan y Bryn, School Lane, Govilon, ABERGAVENNY, GWENT, NP7 9RH. (Life Member)
WILLIAMS, Mr. Charles Stephen, BA ACA *1982;* 7th floor, Natwest, 1 Princes Street, LONDON, EC2R 8BP.
WILLIAMS, Mrs. Cherry Rosalyn, BSc ACA *1984;* Animal House Justin Business Park, Sandford Lane, WAREHAM, DORSET, BH20 4DY.
WILLIAMS, Miss. Chloe Jane, ACA *2008;* 146 Beverley Road, Kirk Ella, HULL, HU10 7HA.
WILLIAMS, Miss. Christina, BA(Hons) ACA *2010;* 34 Eggbridge Lane, Waverton, CHESTER, CH3 7PE.
WILLIAMS, Mrs. Christine Susan, BSc FCA *1974;* 199 Finchampstead Road, WOKINGHAM, RG40 3HE.
WILLIAMS, Mr. Christopher, BA ACA *1993;* Foster & Partners 3 Riverside Albert Wharf, 22 Hester Road, LONDON, SW11 4AN.
•WILLIAMS, Mr. Christopher, BSc(Hons) ACA *2004;* Dow Schofield Watts Transaction Services LLP, 7700 Daresbury Park, Daresbury, WARRINGTON, WA4 4BS.
WILLIAMS, Mr. Christopher, MSci(Hons) ACA *2011;* 62 Orchard Road, Hockley Heath, SOLIHULL, WEST MIDLANDS, B94 6QR.
WILLIAMS, Mr. Christopher Alan, BSc FCA *1995;* 31 Chartwell Drive, Lisvane, CARDIFF, CF14 0EZ.
WILLIAMS, Mr. Christopher Andrew, BA ACA *1991;* Firth Rixson Ltd, Firth House, P.O. Box 644, Meadowhall Road, SHEFFIELD, S9 1JD.
•WILLIAMS, Mr. Christopher David, FCA *1972;* (Tax Fac), Thomas R. Knowles & Williams, Stanley House, Market Square, HOLYHEAD, GWYNEDD, LL65 1UF.
WILLIAMS, Mr. Christopher David, BA ACA *1991;* 11 Briarmeadow Drive, Thornhill, CARDIFF, CF14 9FB.
WILLIAMS, Mr. Christopher Henry, MA ACA *1999;* Wheat Glade House Woods Lane, Cliddesden, BASINGSTOKE, RG25 2JG.
WILLIAMS, Mr. Christopher Ian, MA ACA *1985;* Argo Management Services Ltd Exchequer Court, 33 St. Mary Axe, LONDON, EC3A 8AA.
•WILLIAMS, Mr. Christopher James, MA ACA ATII *1999;* (Tax Fac), PricewaterhouseCoopers LLP, One Kingsway, CARDIFF, CF10 3PW. See also PricewaterhouseCoopers
•WILLIAMS, Mr. Christopher James, BSc ACA *1996;* KPMG LLP, 15 Canada Square, LONDON, E14 5GL. See also KPMG Europe LLP
WILLIAMS, Mr. Christopher John, BA ACA *1989;* 1 Kings Road, BARNET, EN5 4EF.
WILLIAMS, Mr. Christopher John, BA ACA CF *1983;* Cobalt Corporate Finance LLP, 28 Brook Street, LONDON, W1K 5DH.
•WILLIAMS, Mr. Christopher John, BSc ACA *1997;* Jack Ross, Barnfield House, The Approach, MANCHESTER, M3 7BX.
WILLIAMS, Mr. Christopher John, BSc ACA *1990;* 20 Amberheart Drive, Thornhill, CARDIFF, CF14 9HA.

WILLIAMS, Mr. Christopher John, MA ACA *1993;* 3i Investments plc, 16 Palace Street, LONDON, SW1E 5JD.
•ⒹWILLIAMS, Mr. Christopher Kenneth, FCA *1975;* McTear Williams & Wood, 90 St Faiths Lane, NORWICH, NR1 1NE.
WILLIAMS, Mr. Christopher Mark, BA ACA *1991;* The White House, Main Street, East Langton, MARKET HARBOROUGH, LE16 7TW.
•**WILLIAMS, Mr. Christopher Martin, LLB ACA** *1987;* Christopher Williams, Carnoch House, Glencoe, BALLACHULISH, PH49 4HS.
•**WILLIAMS, Mr. Christopher Robert Hugh, FCA** *1979;* (Tax Fac), reidwilliams, Prince Regent House, 108 London Street, READING, RG1 4SJ.
•**WILLIAMS, Mr. Christopher Stanley, BSc FCA CTA** *1979;* (Tax Fac), Lowe McTernan Limited, Highcroft House, 81-85 New Road, Rubery, Rednal, BIRMINGHAM B45 9JR.
WILLIAMS, Mrs. Clair Marie, BSc ACA *2005;* 26 Ashover Road, NEWCASTLE UPON TYNE, NE3 3GH.
WILLIAMS, Mrs. Claire Alexander, MA ACA *2001;* Fenway, Westbury, SHREWSBURY, SY5 9QP.
WILLIAMS, Miss. Claire Michelle, BA ACA *2006;* 35 Farleigh Road, Backwell, BRISTOL, BS48 3PB.
WILLIAMS, Miss. Clare, MChem ACA *2010;* 4 Keble Road, MAIDENHEAD, BERKSHIRE, SL6 6BA.
WILLIAMS, Mrs. Clare Elizabeth, BSc FCA *1986;* (Tax Fac), 5 Blinkbonny Grove West, EDINBURGH, EH4 3HJ.
WILLIAMS, Mr. Clive, FCA *1965;* 55 Sandygate Park, SHEFFIELD, S10 5TZ.
WILLIAMS, Mr. Clive Richard, FCA *1958;* Old Scantlings, 26 Church Street, SHOREHAM-BY-SEA, BN43 5DQ. (Life Member)
WILLIAMS, Mr. Clive Robert, FCA *1968;* 13 Belvedere Avenue, Wimbledon Village, LONDON, SW19 7PP.
WILLIAMS, Mr. Colin, FCA *1958;* The Croft, 12 School Lane, Shareshill, WOLVERHAMPTON, WV10 7LE. (Life Member)
WILLIAMS, Mr. Colin, MA MBA BSc FCA *1986;* Glyn Y Bont, 7 High Street, Cwmgwrach, NEATH, SA11 5SY.
•**WILLIAMS, Mr. Colin Cecil, FCA** *1963;* C.C. Williams & Co, 38 High Street, Yatton, BRISTOL, BS49 4JA.
WILLIAMS, Dr. Colin Graeme, ACA *1985;* with Sagars LLP, Gresham House, 5-7 St. Pauls Street, LEEDS, LS1 2JG.
•**WILLIAMS, Mr. Colin Herbert, BA FCA CTA** *1983;* (Tax Fac), 1 Crowtrees Grove, Roughlee, NELSON, BB9 6NE.
WILLIAMS, Mr. Colin James Nelson, BA FCA *1968;* 141 West Town Lane, Knowle, BRISTOL, BS14 9EA. (Life Member)
WILLIAMS, Mr. Colin Jeffrey, BA ACA *1982;* 64 Berkeley Road, Westbury Park, BRISTOL, BS6 7PL.
WILLIAMS, Mr. Colin Neil, ACA *2002;* 11 Ffordd Trem y Foel, MOLD, CLWYD, CH7 1NG.
WILLIAMS, Mr. Colin Raymond, FCA *1974;* Williams Shipping, Manor House Avenue, Millbrook, SOUTHAMPTON, SO15 0LF.
WILLIAMS, Mr. Colin Victor Kenneth, LLB FCA *1964;* 7801 SW 35th Terrace, MIAMI, FL 33155, UNITED STATES. (Life Member)
•**WILLIAMS, Mr. Conrad Mark Kennedy, BEng ACA** *1996;* PricewaterhouseCoopers LLP, 7 More London Riverside, LONDON, SE1 2RT. See also PricewaterhouseCoopers
WILLIAMS, Mr. Conrad Russell, FCA *1955;* The Boat House, Portloe, TRURO, CORNWALL, TR2 5RG. (Life Member)
•**WILLIAMS, Mr. Craig Gerrard, BA FCA FRSA** *1993;* MWM, 11 Great George Street, BRISTOL, BS1 5RR. See also Mooney Williams May Limited
WILLIAMS, Mrs. Cressida Catherine, BA(Econ) ACA *2002;* Elm Cottage, Brightwalton, NEWBURY, BERKSHIRE, RG20 7BN.
WILLIAMS, Mr. Cyril Dwyer, FCA *1955;* 1 Garden Close, Devon Road, SALCOMBE, TQ8 8HF. (Life Member)
WILLIAMS, Mr. Damian Robert Lloyd, BEng ACA *1994;* R O C Systems Consulting Ltd, Abbey House, Wellington Way, WEYBRIDGE, SURREY, KT13 0TT.
WILLIAMS, Mr. Daniel, BSocSc ACA *1997;* 44 Heatherleigh, ST.HELENS, MERSEYSIDE, WA9 5SU.
WILLIAMS, Mr. Daniel Luke, ACA MAAT *2011;* 26 Foxland Close, Chelmsley Wood, BIRMINGHAM, B37 6TH.
WILLIAMS, Ms. Danielle, ACA *2010;* 13 Halkyn Avenue, LIVERPOOL, L17 2AH.
•**WILLIAMS, Mr. Darren Richard, BSc ACA** *1994;* Darren Williams & Co Ltd, Longacre House, Wilcott, SHREWSBURY, SHROPSHIRE, SY4 1BJ.
•**WILLIAMS, Mr. David, FCA** *1993;* Hazlewoods LLP, Windsor House, Barnett Way, Barnwood, GLOUCESTER, GL4 3RT.
WILLIAMS, Mr. David, BA ACA *1993;* B U P A Health Assurance, Second Floor, The Core, 40 St. Thomas Street, BRISTOL, BS1 6JX.
•**WILLIAMS, Mr. David, FCA** *1984;* Dendy Neville Limited, 3-4 Bower Terrace, 1 Tonbridge Road, MAIDSTONE, KENT, ME16 8RY.
•**WILLIAMS, Mr. David, FCA** *1978;* (Tax Fac), Abrams Ashton Williams Limited, 77Corporation Street, ST. HELENS, MERSEYSIDE, WA10 1SX. See also Abrams Financial Services LLP and Abrams Ashton Williams(Clergy Taxation Specialists)
WILLIAMS, The Revd. David, BD FCA *1965;* 153 Crompton Way, BOLTON, BL2 2SQ.
WILLIAMS, Mr. David, BA FCA *1974;* 105 Bathurst Gardens, LONDON, NW10 5JJ.
WILLIAMS, Mr. David, BSc ACA *2007;* 39 Shrubbery Avenue, WORCESTER, WR1 1QP.
•**WILLIAMS, Mr. David Anthony, FCA CTA** *1961;* 6 Cashio Lane, LETCHWORTH GARDEN CITY, SG6 1AX.
WILLIAMS, Mr. David Anthony Ellis, BA FCA *1979;* The Bursary, Charterhouse, Hurtmore Road, GODALMING, SURREY, GU7 2DF.
WILLIAMS, Mr. David Anthony James, BSc ACA *1991;* (Tax Fac), 71a Long Ashton Road, Long Ashton, BRISTOL, BS41 9HW.
WILLIAMS, Mr. David Benjamin Rhys, LLB ACA *1980;* Willow Cottage, Watery Lane, Clifton Hampdon, ABINGDON, OX14 3EL.
WILLIAMS, Mr. David Brian, FCA *1967;* 20a Forrest Road, PENARTH, SOUTH GLAMORGAN, CF64 5BT.
•**WILLIAMS, Mr. David Charles, FCA** *1972;* 533 Hurst Road, BEXLEY, KENT, DA5 3JS.
WILLIAMS, Mr. David Charles, BSc FCA *1976;* 2F 119 Che Keng Tuk Road, SAI KUNG, HONG KONG SAR.
•**WILLIAMS, Mr. David Christopher, BSc FCA DChA** *1978;* Watts Gregory LLP, Elfed House, Oak Tree Court, Mulberry Drive, Cardiff Gate Business Park Pontprennau, CARDIFF CF23 8RS. See also W G Financial Outsourcing Solutions Ltd
WILLIAMS, Mr. David Francis, MA FCA *1977;* Moore Stephens, 150 Aldersgate Street, LONDON, EC1A 4AB.
WILLIAMS, Mr. David Gareth Clive, BEng ACA *1993;* Summerhill, Luke Street, ST. ASAPH, LL17 0SE.
•**WILLIAMS, Mr. David Gavin, FCA** *1980;* I.G. Jones & Co, 12 Salem Street, Ynys Mon, AMLWCH, LL68 9BP.
WILLIAMS, Mr. David Geraint, ACA *2010;* Flat 2, 57 Kelly Avenue, LONDON, SE15 5LZ.
•**WILLIAMS, Mr. David Gwyn Jones, BA FCA** *1987;* Clay Shaw Thomas Ltd, 2 Old Field Road, Bocam Park, BRIDGEND, MID GLAMORGAN, CF35 5LJ.
WILLIAMS, Mr. David Hallett, FCA *1958;* Gulls Way, West Cliff Road, West Bay, BRIDPORT, DT6 4HR. (Life Member)
•**WILLIAMS, Mr. David Hugh Alfred, BA FCA** *1985;* David Williams & Co, 66 Belper Road, DERBY, DE1 3EN.
WILLIAMS, Mr. David Huw, BSc ACA *1989;* Tullett Prebon, Level 37, Tower 42, 25 Old Broad Street, LONDON, EC2N 1HQ.
WILLIAMS, Mr. David Ian Thomas, BA ACA MCT *1994;* Bank for Int Settlements, Centralbahnplatz 2, CH-4002 BASEL, SWITZERLAND.
WILLIAMS, Mr. David James, BSc ACA *2001;* 6 Clos Cartref, Llangybi, USK, GWENT, NP15 1QU.
WILLIAMS, Mr. David John, BEng FCA *1993;* 7 Green Place, Radyr, CARDIFF, CF15 8GF.
WILLIAMS, Mr. David John, BSc FCA *1986;* Reserve Bank of New Zealand, 2 The Terrace, PO Box 2498, WELLINGTON, NEW ZEALAND.
WILLIAMS, Mr. David John, FCA FCMA *1961;* Pippins, 22 Carroll Avenue, FERNDOWN, DORSET, BH22 8BP.
•**WILLIAMS, Mr. David John, BA ACA** *1999;* Ernst & Young LLP, 1 More London Place, LONDON, SE1 2AF. See also Ernst & Young Europe LLP
•**WILLIAMS, Mr. David John, FCA** *1975;* John Williams & Co, Westerview, Grimshaw Green Lane, Parbold, WIGAN, LANCASHIRE WN8 7BB.
WILLIAMS, Mr. David John, ACA FCCA *2009;* with Locke Williams Associates LLP, Blackthorn House, St Paul's Square, BIRMINGHAM, B3 1RL.
WILLIAMS, Mr. David John, BA ACA *1990;* Rhenus Ltd Unit 1-2 Westpoint Enterprise Park, Clarence Avenue Trafford Park, MANCHESTER, M17 1QS.
WILLIAMS, Mr. David John, BSc ACA *1998;* 2 Woodlands, Clapham Park Clapham, BEDFORD, MK41 6FS.
WILLIAMS, Mr. David Leslie, BSc FCA *1979;* 23 Yew Tree Park, Congresbury, BRISTOL, BS49 5ER.
•**WILLIAMS, Mr. David Llewelyn, FCA** *1990;* (Tax Fac), Griffith Williams & Co, 36 Stryd Fawr, PWLLHELI, LL53 5RT.
•**WILLIAMS, Mr. David Mark, ACA** *1991;* 174 Banstead Road, CARSHALTON, SURREY, SM5 4DW.
WILLIAMS, Mr. David Michael, BA FCA *1971;* Down End, 29 Fort Road, GUILDFORD, GU1 3TE.
WILLIAMS, Mr. David Michael, MA ACA *1985;* 2 Bakery Close, LONDON, SW9 0EB.
WILLIAMS, Mr. David Michael, BA ACA *2002;* Midtown, 32 High Holborn, LONDON, WC1V 7PB.
WILLIAMS, Mr. David Nash, MA FCA *1958;* 19 Chelmick Drive, CHURCH STRETTON, SHROPSHIRE, SY6 7BP. (Life Member)
•**WILLIAMS, Mr. David Nigel, FCA** *1966;* (Tax Fac), David N Williams, Chapel Lodge, Langthwaite, RICHMOND, NORTH YORKSHIRE, DL11 6RE.
WILLIAMS, Mr. David Paul Lumley, MA FCA *1972;* Westridge Shadybrook Lane, Weaverham, NORTHWICH, CHESHIRE, CW8 3PN.
WILLIAMS, Mr. David Phillip, BSc ACA CTA *1996;* 39 Partridge Road, Roath, CARDIFF, CF24 3QW.
WILLIAMS, Mr. David Rhys, FCA *1966;* Flat 8, Pembroke Court, South Edwardes Square, LONDON, W8 6HN.
WILLIAMS, Mr. David Richard, BA ACA *1991;* 3 Back Lane, Market Bosworth, NUNEATON, WARWICKSHIRE, CV13 0LD.
WILLIAMS, Mr. David Robert, BA FCA *1991;* 15 St. Stephens Road, Prenton, BIRKENHEAD, MERSEYSIDE, CH42 8PP.
•**WILLIAMS, Mr. David Scott, MA FCA** *1961;* D.S. Williams, Beaux Aires Cottage, Yelsted Road, Stockbury, SITTINGBOURNE, KENT ME9 7QY.
WILLIAMS, Mr. David Simon, BA ACA *1988;* 54 Bridle Road, Eastham, WIRRAL, CH62 8BR.
WILLIAMS, Mr. David Thomas, BA(Hons) ACA *2003;* 3 Edna Road, LONDON, SW20 8BS.
WILLIAMS, Mrs. Dawn Elizabeth, BSc ACA *1995;* 1 Bellcast Close, Appleton, WARRINGTON, WA4 5SA.
WILLIAMS, Mr. Dean, FCA *1974;* 27 Ryecroft Rise, Long Ashton, BRISTOL, BS41 9NQ.
WILLIAMS, Miss. Debbie, BA ACA *2006;* 13B Dorothy Road, LONDON, SW11 2JJ.
WILLIAMS, Miss. Deirdre Susan, BSc FCA *1992;* The Ipswich Hospital, Finance Department, Heath Road, IPSWICH, IP4 5PD.
WILLIAMS, Mr. Derek, FCA *1959;* Fair Acre, Fountains Park, Netley Abbey, SOUTHAMPTON, SO31 5HB. (Life Member)
WILLIAMS, Mr. Derek Drummond, BA FCA *1982;* Calle San Sebastian 6, 11330 JIMENA DE LA FRONTERA, SPAIN.
WILLIAMS, The Revd. Derek Ivor, JP FCA *1961;* Buteland House, Bellingham, HEXHAM, NE48 2EX. (Life Member)
WILLIAMS, Mr. Derek Stuart, FCA *1953;* 15 Gresham Court, Pampisford Road, PURLEY, SURREY, CR8 2UU. (Life Member)
WILLIAMS, Mrs. Derryl, BA ACA *1993;* 17 Waterton Close, Waterton, BRIDGEND, MID GLAMORGAN, CF31 3YE.
WILLIAMS, Mr. Donald Bruce, BA FCA *1982;* 190 Broom Road, TEDDINGTON, TW11 9PQ.
WILLIAMS, Mr. Donald James, BSc FCA *1972;* 18 Hillway, Guiseley, LEEDS, LS20 8HB.
•**WILLIAMS, Mr. Donald Scott, BA(Hons) FCA** *1993;* BDO LLP, 55 Baker Street, LONDON, W1U 7EU. See also BDO Stoy Hayward LLP
WILLIAMS, Mrs. Donna Elizabeth, BSc ACA *2002;* The Wagon Hovel, Hill Top Farm, Croxton Kerrial, GRANTHAM, LINCOLNSHIRE, NG32 1QJ.
WILLIAMS, Miss. Dorothy Alice, FCA *1964;* Apartment 11, Les Arches, La Grande Route de la Cote, St. Martin, JERSEY, JE3 6LA. (Life Member)
WILLIAMS, Mr. Duane, BSc ACA *2011;* 16 Talworth Street, CARDIFF, CF24 3EJ.
WILLIAMS, Mr. Duncan John Mathieson, FCA *1973;* Alameda Ubatuba 279, Alphaville Residencial III, Santana do Parnaiba, 06542-115 SAO PAULO, BRAZIL.
•**WILLIAMS, Mr. Edgar Norman, FCA** *1954;* (Tax Fac), Champness & Sargant, 8 The Green, HOVE, EAST SUSSEX, BN3 6TH.
•ⒹWILLIAMS, Mr. Edward, BA FCA *1999;* with PricewaterhouseCoopers, Donington Court, Pegasus Business Park, Castle Donington, DERBY, DE74 2UZ.
WILLIAMS, Mr. Edward Kesteven, FCA *1964;* Greenways, Vyse Road, Boughton, NORTHAMPTON, NN2 8RR. (Life Member)
•**WILLIAMS, Mr. Edward Mark, BSc ACA** *2009;* Williams & Co, Quietways, Old Walls, Llanrhidian, SWANSEA, SA3 1HA.
WILLIAMS, Miss. Elaine Angela, BSc ACA *1988;* 88 Princes St, RYDE, NSW 2112, AUSTRALIA.
•**WILLIAMS, Mrs. Elaine Margaret, MSc BSc(Hons) ACA** *2002;* Elaine Williams Accounting, 3 Albion Close, Moira, SWADLINCOTE, DERBYSHIRE, DE12 6EA.
WILLIAMS, Mrs. Elisabeth, BSc FCA *1991;* (Tax Fac), 50 Hawkhurst Road, Penwortham, PRESTON, PR1 9QS.
WILLIAMS, Ms. Elizabeth, BSc ACA *1992;* 9 Whitehill Cottages, Whitehill, WELWYN, AL6 9AE.
WILLIAMS, Miss. Emma, BSc ACA *2006;* Flat 2, 268 Oriental Parade, Oriental Bay, WELLINGTON 6011, NEW ZEALAND.
WILLIAMS, Miss. Emma Claire, BA ACA CFE *2006;* 4/F, 50 BLUE POOL ROAD, HAPPY VALLEY, HONG KONG SAR.
WILLIAMS, Mrs. Emma Jane, ACA *2001;* 1 Fallowfield Close, Wesham, PRESTON, PR4 3EE.
WILLIAMS, Mrs. Emma Jane, BSc ACA *2007;* 15 Stafford Road, EXETER, EX4 1EX.
WILLIAMS, Miss. Emma Louise, BA(Hons) ACA *2003;* 22 Nant y Glyn, Llanrug, CAERNARFON, GWYNEDD, LL55 4AH.
WILLIAMS, Mr. Emyr Heddwyn, BEd ACA *1984;* PO Box 73780, NAIROBI, 00200, KENYA.
WILLIAMS, Mr. Emyr Owen Francis, BA FCA *1966;* Whitegate, Grange Road, LLANGOLLEN, CLWYD, LL20 8AP.
•**WILLIAMS, Mr. Eric David, FCA** *1975;* Edmund Carr LLP, 146 New London Road, CHELMSFORD, CM2 0AW. See also EC (Management Services) Ltd
WILLIAMS, Mr. Eryl, FCA *1952;* Leahurst, Bryn Coch Lane, MOLD, CH7 1PP. (Life Member)
•**WILLIAMS, Mr. Euan John, BSc FCA** *1979;* (Tax Fac), Euan Williams, 55 Glenesk Road, Eltham, LONDON, SE9 1AH.
WILLIAMS, Mr. Eurig Dylan Jones, BSc ACA *1991;* (Tax Fac), Coedfryn, Felingwm, CARMARTHEN, DYFED, SA32 7PT.
•**WILLIAMS, Mr. Evan Richard, BA FCA** *1992;* J.Emyr Thomas & Co, Tegfan, 7 Deiniol Road, BANGOR, GWYNEDD, LL57 2UR.
WILLIAMS, Mrs. Evelyn Veronica, BA ACA *1982;* 43 Milman Road, READING, RG2 0AZ.
WILLIAMS, Miss. Fiona, ACA *2009;* 76 Anglesey Avenue, MAIDSTONE, KENT, ME15 9TD.
WILLIAMS, Mrs. Fiona Jane, BSc ACA *1998;* 1 Astwood Grange Cottage, Astwood, NEWPORT PAGNELL, BUCKINGHAMSHIRE, MK16 9JT.
WILLIAMS, Miss. Frances, BSc ACA *2011;* St. Benedicts School, 54 Eaton Rise, LONDON, W5 2ES.
•**WILLIAMS, Ms. Frances Anne Marie Everlyn Claire, FCA** *1974;* (Tax Fac), 21st Century Accounting Services Limited, 12 Silver Way, WICKFORD, SS11 7AP.
WILLIAMS, Mr. Frank Michael Basil, FCA CTA *1990;* (Tax Fac), Lindum Group Ltd, Lindum House, Station Road, North Hykeham, LINCOLN, LN6 3QX.
WILLIAMS, Mr. Gareth, BA ACA *1999;* 13 Stonells Road, Battersea, LONDON, SW11 6HQ.
WILLIAMS, Mr. Gareth, ACA *2008;* 68 Herbert Gardens, LONDON, NW10 3BU.
WILLIAMS, Mr. Gareth, BEng ACA *1998;* 35 Henleaze Avenue, Henleaze, BRISTOL, BS9 4EU.
WILLIAMS, Mr. Gareth, MEng ACA *2003;* TGPP, 42 Brook Street, LONDON, W1K 5DB.
WILLIAMS, Mr. Gareth Clwyd, BSc ACA *1998;* 14 Elkington Croft, Shirley, SOLIHULL, B90 4PB.
WILLIAMS, Mr. Gareth David, BA FCA *1984;* CDMS, Fallows Way, Whiston, LIVERPOOL, L35 1RZ.
WILLIAMS, Mr. Gareth Huw, BA ACA *2005;* Orient Business Park, Billington Road, BURNLEY, LANCASHIRE, BB11 5UB.
WILLIAMS, Mr. Gareth Michael, BSc ACA *2002;* McGrathNicol, Level 31, 60 Margaret Street, SYDNEY, NSW 2000, AUSTRALIA.
•**WILLIAMS, Mr. Gareth Richard, BSc(Econ) FCA** *1983;* Hayvenhursts, Fairway House, Links Business Park, St. Mellons, CARDIFF, CF3 0LT. See also Hayvenhursts Limited
WILLIAMS, Mr. Gareth Wyn, BA FCA *1972;* Beech Heights, 75 Owler Park Road, ILKLEY, LS29 0BG. (Life Member)
WILLIAMS, Mr. Gary, MSc BEng FCA *1994;* Trident Trust, Trident Trust Co Ltd, Po Box 398, St Helier, JERSEY, JE4 8UT.
WILLIAMS, Mr. Gary Scott, BCom ACA *1983;* St Georges House, 24 Queens Road, WEYBRIDGE, SURREY, KT13 9UX.
•**WILLIAMS, Mr. Gavin Roland, BSc(Hons) ACA DChA** *2003;* Gavin Williams, 25 Somerford Way, LONDON, SE16 6QN.
WILLIAMS, Mr. Geoffrey Gray, BSc FCA *1966;* 10 Malden Road, WATFORD, WD17 4EW.

WILLIAMS, Mr. Geoffrey James, FCA *1971;* 79 Alexandra Crescent, BAYVIEW, NSW 2104, AUSTRALIA.
WILLIAMS, Mr. George Adam, BA(Hons) ACA *2003;* Sovereign Capital Partners Llp, 25 Victoria Street, LONDON, SW1H 0EX.
WILLIAMS, Mr. George Raymond, BSc ACA *1994;* 27 Venn Grove, PLYMOUTH, PL3 5PQ.
WILLIAMS, Mr. Geraint Fraser, BSc ACA *1993;* 11 Heatherside Gardens, Farnham Common, SLOUGH, SL2 3RR.
WILLIAMS, Mr. Geraint Parry, BSc ARCS ACA *1999;* K P M G, 1 Canada Square, LONDON, E14 5AG.
WILLIAMS, Mr. Geraint Robert, BSc ACA *1992;* 47 Elm Drive, Llanellen, ABERGAVENNY, NP7 9HW.
WILLIAMS, Mr. Gerald Cecil Garside, FCA *1976;* Beechwood, Ridgley Road, Chiddingfold, GODALMING, SURREY, GU8 4QW.
WILLIAMS, Mr. Gerald William, FCA *1970;* Warren Croft, Manor Farm Lane, Tidmarsh, READING, RG8 8EX.
WILLIAMS, Mrs. Geraldine Mary, BSc FCA *1978;* Hatchways, Run Common, Shamley Green, GUILDFORD, GU5 0SY.
•WILLIAMS, Mr. Gerallt Rhys, BSc FCA *1982;* Guilfoyle Sage & Co, 21 Gold Tops, NEWPORT, NP20 4PG. See also Guilfoyle Sage LLP
•WILLIAMS, Mr. Giles Nicholas Dalgety, MA ACA *1989;* KPMG LLP, 15 Canada Square, LONDON, E14 5GL. See also KPMG Europe LLP
WILLIAMS, Mrs. Gillian, BA ACA *1984;* Fairway, Penbanc, FISHGUARD, SA65 9BJ.
WILLIAMS, Mrs. Gillian Patricia, BSc ACA *1995;* 54 Bridle Road, Eastham, WIRRAL, CH62 8BR.
WILLIAMS, Mr. Glenn Bernard Douglas, BSc FCA *1979;* 12 Lowry Close, College Town, SANDHURST, GU47 0FJ.
•WILLIAMS, Mr. Glyn David, FCA *1977;* Grant Thornton UK LLP, 4 Hardman Square, Spinningfields, MANCHESTER, M3 3EB. See also Grant Thornton LLP
•WILLIAMS, Mr. Glyn Mark, BSc FCA *1985;* Mazars LLP, Tower Bridge House, St. Katharines Way, LONDON, E1W 1DD. See also Mazars Corporate Finance Limited
WILLIAMS, Mr. Glyn Winant, BA FCA *1968;* 9 Grassington Drive, SHEFFIELD, S12 4NE. (Life Member)
WILLIAMS, Mr. Graham David, FCA *1970;* 48 Crescent Road, Rowley Park, STAFFORD, ST17 9AN.
•WILLIAMS, Mr. Graham Eric Hanson, FCA *1976;* (Tax Fac), Moore Stephens LLP, 150 Aldersgate Street, LONDON, EC1A 4AB. See also Moore Stephens & Co
WILLIAMS, Mr. Graham Thomas, FCA *1959;* 9 Abbey Rise, BARROW-UPON-HUMBER, DN19 7TF. (Life Member)
•WILLIAMS, Mr. Graham Timothy, BA FCA *1983;* PricewaterhouseCoopers LLP, 80 Strand, LONDON, WC2R 0AF. See also PricewaterhouseCoopers
WILLIAMS, Mr. Greg, ACA CA(NZ) *2010;* 41 Longdon Wood, Keston Park, KESTON, KENT, BR2 6EN.
WILLIAMS, Mr. Gregory Alun, BA ACA *2007;* with HCA International Ltd, 242 Marylebone Road, LONDON, NW1 6JL.
WILLIAMS, Mr. Griffith Owen Charles, BA FCA MBA *1974;* (Tax Fac), Chantry, Batcombe, SHEPTON MALLET, SOMERSET, BA4 6HD.
WILLIAMS, Mr. Guy David, BSc ACA *1996;* 31 Eastbourne Road, Remuera, AUCKLAND, NEW ZEALAND.
WILLIAMS, Mr. Guy James, BSc ACA *1996;* Soho House, 72-74 Dean Street, Soho, LONDON, W1D 3SG.
WILLIAMS, Miss. Gwendolyn Ann, BA(Hons) FCA *2001;* 33 Fathersfield, BROCKENHURST, HAMPSHIRE, SO42 7TH.
WILLIAMS, Miss. Gwenno Mair, BSc ACA *2000;* 23 Maes yr Annedd, Canton, CARDIFF, CF5 1GR.
WILLIAMS, Miss. Hanim, MSc ACA *2004;* 7 Fishery Road, HEMEL HEMPSTEAD, HERTFORDSHIRE, HP1 1NA.
WILLIAMS, Mrs. Hannah Lisa, BSc ACA *1996;* 5/67-69 Abbott Street, SANDRINGHAM, VIC 3191, AUSTRALIA.
WILLIAMS, Mr. Hayden Charles, BSc ACA *1994;* 16 Woodmill Close, Stalbridge, STURMINSTER NEWTON, DORSET, DT10 2ST.
WILLIAMS, Miss. Heather Cawley, ACA *2009;* 46 Elizabeth Street, Artarmon, SYDNEY, NSW 2046, AUSTRALIA.
WILLIAMS, Mrs. Heather Elizabeth, BSc ACA *1994;* H E F C E, Northavon House, Coldharbour Lane, BRISTOL, BS16 1QD.
WILLIAMS, Mrs. Heather June, BSc FCA ATII *1991;* Splinters, 27 St. Osmunds Road, POOLE, DORSET, BH14 9JT.
WILLIAMS, Mrs. Heather Ruth, BA ACA *2001;* (Tax Fac), with PricewaterhouseCoopers LLP, Cornwall Court, 19 Cornwall Street, BIRMINGHAM, B3 2DT.
WILLIAMS, Mrs. Helen Caroline, BSc ACA *1989;* E On Sherwood Park, Little Oak Drive Annesley, NOTTINGHAM, NG15 0DR.
WILLIAMS, Ms. Helen Elizabeth, MA ACA *2004;* 112 Englefield Road, LONDON, N1 3LQ.
WILLIAMS, Mrs. Helen Elizabeth, BA ACA *1992;* 73 Alexandra Road, READING, RG1 5PS.
WILLIAMS, Miss. Helen Mary, BA ACA *1998;* 3 Fullerton Road, CROYDON, CR0 6JD.
WILLIAMS, Miss. Helen Patricia, BSc ACA *1990;* 6/19 Western Harbour Terrace, EDINBURGH, EH6 6JN.
WILLIAMS, Miss. Hilary Kathryn, BSc ACA *1988;* Flat 7 Willowfield Court, Cyncoed Place, CARDIFF, CF23 6SN.
WILLIAMS, Miss. Holly, BSc ACA *2010;* 13 King Edwards Grove, TEDDINGTON, MIDDLESEX, TW11 9LY.
WILLIAMS, Mr. Howard, BSc FCA *1975;* 22 Crowhill, HAVERFORDWEST, SA61 2HL.
WILLIAMS, Mr. Howard Edward, FCA *1961;* 2 Springwood Hall, Springwood Park, TONBRIDGE, TN11 9LZ.
WILLIAMS, Mr. Hugh, FCA *1954;* 20 Meiriadog Road, Old Colwyn, COLWYN BAY, Clwyd, LL29 9NR. (Life Member)
WILLIAMS, Mr. Hugh Colclough, BA FCA *1969;* 1099 Oxford Road, READING, RG31 6YE.
•WILLIAMS, Mr. Hugh Martyn, FCA *1970;* (Tax Fac), H.M. Williams, Valley House, 53 Valley Road, Plympton, PLYMOUTH, PL7 1RF. See also Nevill Hovey & Co Limited
WILLIAMS, Mr. Huw Glyn Tudor, BA FCA *1985;* 92 Deodar Road, LONDON, SW15 2NJ.
•WILLIAMS, Mr. Huw John, BA ACA *2007;* Oury Clark, PO Box 150, Herschel House, 58 Herschel Street, SLOUGH, SL1 1HD.
WILLIAMS, Mr. Huw Llewelyn Francis, BEng ACA *1985;* Kylmar (K M C) Ltd Lambda House Unit 1, Fairview Road Weyhill, ANDOVER, SP11 0ST.
WILLIAMS, Mr. Huw Rees, LLB ACA *1989;* 11 Heath Park Avenue, CARDIFF, CF14 3RF.
•WILLIAMS, Mr. Huw Russell, BA FCA ATII *1982;* (Tax Fac), Huw Williams Limited, 217 Musters Road, West Bridgford, NOTTINGHAM, NG2 7DT.
WILLIAMS, Mr. Huw Scott, BSc ACA *2003;* 42 Reedley Road, Westbury-on-Trym, BRISTOL, BS9 3SU.
WILLIAMS, Mr. Hywel, BA ACA *2007;* Nythfa, Cardiff Road, Creigiau, CARDIFF, CF15 9NL.
WILLIAMS, Mr. Hywel Dyfrig, BA ACA *1983;* 19 Carisbrooke Way, CARDIFF, CF23 9HS.
•WILLIAMS, Mr. Iain Douglas, BSc ACA *1992;* Deloitte LLP, Athene Place, 66 Shoe Lane, LONDON, EC4A 3BQ. See also Deloitte & Touche LLP
WILLIAMS, Mr. Ian, BSc(Hons) ACA *2001;* 5 Bath Road, TETBURY, GLOUCESTERSHIRE, GL8 8EG.
WILLIAMS, Mr. Ian David, FCA *1972;* Mountain View, 65 Route Des Pecheurs, 74410 ST. JORIOZ, FRANCE. (Life Member)
•WILLIAMS, Mr. Ian Donald, BSc FCA *1973;* Benedict Mackenzie LLP, 62 Wilson Street, LONDON, EC2A 2BU. See also Crouch Chapman
•WILLIAMS, Mr. Ian Edward, FCA TEP *1980;* (Tax Fac), Campbell Dallas, Sherwood House, 7 Glasgow Road, PAISLEY, RENFREWSHIRE, PA1 3QS.
WILLIAMS, Mr. Ian Kingsley, BA FCA *1984;* 4 Brokes Road, REIGATE, RH2 9LP.
WILLIAMS, Mr. Ian Peter, BSc ACA *1990;* 3 Ivy House Close, Seagrave, LOUGHBOROUGH, LE12 7LE.
WILLIAMS, Mr. Ian Robert, BSc ACA *1998;* 8 Derwin Avenue, Stocksmoor, HUDDERSFIELD, HD4 6YA.
•WILLIAMS, Mr. Ian Robert, BSc FCA *1982;* (Tax Fac), Pritchard A'I Gwmni Cyf, 74 High Street, FISHGUARD, DYFED, SA65 9AU. See also Pritchard & Co
WILLIAMS, Mr. Ian Roderick, FCA *1957;* Westwick, Point Hill, RYE, TN31 7NP. (Life Member)
WILLIAMS, Mr. Ian Vaughan, BSc ACA *2001;* 29 Hastings Crescent, CARDIFF, CF3 5DF.
WILLIAMS, Mr. Ifor Llywelyn, MA FCA *1972;* The Haven, Mayals Green, SWANSEA, SA3 5JR.
•WILLIAMS, Mr. Iorwerth Llywelyn, BSc ACA *2007;* Dunn & Ellis, St Davids Building, Lombard Street, PORTHMADOG, GWYNEDD, LL49 9AP.
WILLIAMS, Mrs. Jacqueline, BSc ACA *1989;* Rectory Lodge 2a, Kirkwick Avenue, HARPENDEN, AL5 2QL.
WILLIAMS, Mrs. Jacqueline Ruth, BSc ACA *1992;* 2 Ladderstile Ride, KINGSTON-UPON-THAMES, KT2 7LP.
WILLIAMS, Miss. Jacqui Nadine, BA(Hons) ACA *2004;* 14 Station Road, CHINNOR, OXFORDSHIRE, OX39 4QD.
WILLIAMS, Mr. James, BSc ACA *2007;* 2 Pool Meadow, SUTTON COLDFIELD, B76 1PW.
•WILLIAMS, Mr. James Andrew Peter, BSc ACA *1997;* Deloitte LLP, Athene Place, 66 Shoe Lane, LONDON, EC4A 3BQ. See also Deloitte & Touche LLP
WILLIAMS, Mr. James Benedict, ACA *2010;* 4 Arlesey Close, LONDON, SW15 2EX.
WILLIAMS, Mr. James Jasper, BA ACA *1998;* 126 Windmill Drive, Somerton Road, Cricklewood, LONDON, NW2 1US.
WILLIAMS, Mr. James Peter, ACA *2009;* Little Place, 38 Beaucroft Lane, WIMBORNE, BH21 2PA.
WILLIAMS, Mr. Jamie, BSc FCA CISA *1997;* with PricewaterhouseCoopers, Financial Services Centre, Bishop's Court Hill, BRIDGETOWN, BARBADOS.
WILLIAMS, Mrs. Jane Elizabeth, BSc ACA *1979;* Watts Gregory Elfed House Oak Tree Court, Mulberry Drive Cardiff Gate Business Park Pontprennau, CARDIFF, CF23 8RS.
WILLIAMS, Miss. Janet Dorothy, BSc ACA *1980;* 6 Elm Street, FERNDALE, CF43 4PY.
WILLIAMS, Mr. Jason Aran, ACA *2008;* 148 Severn Street, HULL, HU8 8TH.
WILLIAMS, Mr. Jason Cyril Douglas, CA ACA CTA *2002;* 19 The Chase, WELWYN, HERTFORDSHIRE, AL6 0QT.
WILLIAMS, Mr. Jason Mark, ACA *2009;* 35 The Furrow, Littleport, ELY, CAMBRIDGESHIRE, CB6 1GL.
WILLIAMS, Mrs. Jenny, ACA *2010;* 59 Coppice Drive, High Ercall, TELFORD, SHROPSHIRE, TF6 6BX.
WILLIAMS, Mr. Jeremy Angus, BSc(Hons) ACA *2000;* Mercia Group Limited, Best Hse Grange Business Pk, Enderby Road, Whetstone, LEICESTER, LE8 6JL.
WILLIAMS, Mr. Jeremy David, MA ACA *1997;* Welcombe Thatch, Witchampton, WIMBORNE, DORSET, BH21 5AR.
WILLIAMS, Mr. Jeremy David Charles, BA ACA *1996;* 4336 Mount Paran Parkway, ATLANTA, GA 30327, UNITED STATES.
WILLIAMS, Mr. Jeremy Hugh Lyndoch, BA ACA *2009;* with KPMG LLP, 15 Canada Square, LONDON, E14 5GL.
WILLIAMS, Mr. Jeremy Mark, BA FCA *1996;* Clowance House, Bull Lane, Gerrards Cross, GERRARDS CROSS, BUCKINGHAMSHIRE, SL9 8RZ.
WILLIAMS, Mr. Jeremy Robert Ellis, FCA *1968;* 45 Newerne Street, LYDNEY, GLOUCESTERSHIRE, GL15 5RA.
WILLIAMS, Mrs. Jill, BSc ACA *1986;* The Old Dairy, The Hyde, Handcross, HAYWARDS HEATH, WEST SUSSEX, RH17 6EZ.
WILLIAMS, Mrs. Jill, LLB ACA *1984;* Blenheim, Glastonbury Road, Meare, GLASTONBURY, BA6 9SN.
WILLIAMS, Miss. Jill Caroline, MA(Oxon) ACA *2005;* with RJD Partners, 8-9 Well Court, Bow Lane, LONDON, EC4M 9DN.
WILLIAMS, Miss. Jo-Anne, ACA *2003;* Flat 18, 130 Barlby Road, LONDON, W10 6DR.
•WILLIAMS, Mrs. Joanna, FCA *1983;* (Tax Fac), Williams Accountancy Services Limited, Manor Farm, Church Road, Glatton, HUNTINGDON, CAMBRIDGESHIRE PE28 5RR.
•WILLIAMS, Miss. Joanna Louise, BA FCA *1988;* (Tax Fac), J.L. Williams, Apple Tree Cottage, 38 Rushett Close, THAMES DITTON, KT7 0UT.
WILLIAMS, Ms. Joanna Mary Katherine, MA ACA *2001;* Octavia Housing & Care, Emily House, 202-208 Kensal Road, LONDON, W10 5BN.
WILLIAMS, Mrs. Joanne, BSc ACA *1996;* 6 The Rise, Reading Road Finchampstead, WOKINGHAM, RG40 4RH.
WILLIAMS, Mrs. Joanne Marie, MEng ACA ACGI *2001;* 169 Daglish Street, WEMBLEY, WA 6014, AUSTRALIA.
WILLIAMS, Miss. Joanne Susan, ACA *1992;* 60 Park Avenue, EGHAM, SURREY, TW20 8HN.
WILLIAMS, Mr. John, FCA *1967;* 11 Penryn Close, WALSALL, WS5 3ET. (Life Member)
WILLIAMS, Mr. John, BSc ACA *1992;* Fawley Villa, Newent Lane, Huntley, GLOUCESTER, GL19 3HH.
WILLIAMS, Mr. John Brian, FCA *1960;* 9 Danescourt Road, West Derby, LIVERPOOL, L12 8RB. (Life Member)
•WILLIAMS, Mr. John Bruce, FCA *1977;* John Williams & Co, 1 The Royal, Hoylake, WIRRAL, MERSEYSIDE, CH47 1HS.
WILLIAMS, Mr. John Bryan, FCA *1955;* 206 Westmoreland Ct, SARASOTA, FL 34243, UNITED STATES. (Life Member)
WILLIAMS, Mr. John David, BA FCA *1981;* Rowan House, Pilton, OAKHAM, LEICESTERSHIRE, LE15 9PA.
WILLIAMS, Mr. John David, MSc ACA *2001;* with Deloitte LLP, PO Box 500, 2 Hardman Street, MANCHESTER, M60 2AT.
WILLIAMS, Mr. John David Rhys, BSc ACA *2002;* (Tax Fac), 33 Meadow Way, Dorney Reach, MAIDENHEAD, BERKSHIRE, SL6 0DR.
•WILLIAMS, Mr. John Frederick, FCA *1971;* John F. Williams & Co Ltd, Elizabethan House, 8 George Lane, MARLBOROUGH, SN8 4BT.
WILLIAMS, Mr. John Gordon, FCA *1965;* Wayfield, 8 Van Diemens Lane, Lansdown, BATH, BA1 5TW.
•WILLIAMS, Mr. John Graham, BCom ACA *1997;* PricewaterhouseCoopers LLP, 7 More London Riverside, LONDON, SE1 2RT. See also PricewaterhouseCoopers
WILLIAMS, Mr. John Gwynne, FCA *1966;* Perthi Bach, Berthlwyd, Pentyrch, CARDIFF, CF15 9PP.
WILLIAMS, Mr. John Hugh, BCom FCA *1957;* Brook House, Church Street, Fenny Compton, SOUTHAM, WARWICKSHIRE, CV47 2YE. (Life Member)
WILLIAMS, Mr. John Kenrick, FCA *1969;* 19 Hood Road, Wimbledon, LONDON, SW20 0SR.
WILLIAMS, Mr. John Marshall, BA FCA *1968;* 17 Birchdale Road, Appleton, WARRINGTON, WA4 5AR.
WILLIAMS, Mr. John Maurice Harrison, FCA *1952;* 9 Freshfield Road, Formby, LIVERPOOL, L37 3JA. (Life Member)
•WILLIAMS, Mr. John Michael, FCA *1965;* (Tax Fac), John M. Williams, 9 Wieland Rd, NORTHWOOD, HA6 3RD.
WILLIAMS, Mr. John Michael, BSc ACA *1986;* Deptford Chambers, 60-66 North Hill, PLYMOUTH, PL4 8EP.
•WILLIAMS, Mr. John Michael Beaumont, BSc FCA *1984;* Gully Top, ST THOMAS, BB22022, BARBADOS.
WILLIAMS, Mr. John Oliver Molyneux, MBE TD FCA *1953;* 17 Kingsway, Fenham, NEWCASTLE UPON TYNE, NE4 9UH. (Life Member)
•WILLIAMS, Mr. John Oliver Roger, FCA *1966;* Williams & Co, Longmead, 3 Heol Gwermont, Llansaint, KIDWELLY, DYFED SA17 5JA.
WILLIAMS, Mr. John Peter, BA FCA *1979;* Daily Mail & General Trust plc, Northcliffe House, 2 Derry Street, LONDON, W8 5TT.
WILLIAMS, Mr. John Philip, FCA *1959;* 12 Glendale, Bryncoch, NEATH, SA10 7PF. (Life Member)
•WILLIAMS, Mr. John Richard, FCA *1982;* JW & Co LLP, Chart House, 2 Effingham Road, REIGATE, SURREY, RH2 7JN. See also Alderstead Financial Services Ltd
•WILLIAMS, Mr. John Robert, FCA *1967;* (Tax Fac), J.R. Williams & Co, 1 Beeches Road, Heybridge, MALDON, CM9 4SL.
WILLIAMS, Mr. John Sinclair, BA ACA *1993;* 62 Greenacres Woolton Hill, NEWBURY, BERKSHIRE, RG20 9TA.
•WILLIAMS, Mr. John Stedwill, FCA *1973;* Peach Wilkinson Limited, 78 Cross Hill, Ecclesfield, SHEFFIELD, S35 9TU.
WILLIAMS, Mr. John Stuart, BA ACA *1996;* Radio House, Whittle Avenue, FAREHAM, HAMPSHIRE, PO15 5SX.
WILLIAMS, Mr. John Wynne, MBA FCA *1967;* Hartwell, Winkers Close, Chalfont St. Peter, GERRARDS CROSS, BUCKINGHAMSHIRE, SL9 0AH.
WILLIAMS, Mr. Jonathan, ACA *2004;* 6/43 Mulgrave Street, Thorndon, WELLINGTON 6011, NEW ZEALAND.
WILLIAMS, Mr. Jonathan, BSc ACA *1990;* 65 Hillingdon Road, Stretford, MANCHESTER, M32 8PH.
WILLIAMS, Mr. Jonathan, MA MSc ACA *2006;* The White House Majors Road, Longcot, FARINGDON, OXFORDSHIRE, SN7 7TR.
WILLIAMS, Mr. Jonathan Daniel, MEng ACA *2010;* Cross Cottage, Netherton, NEWTON ABBOT, DEVON, TQ12 4RW.
WILLIAMS, Mr. Jonathan Edward, LLB ACA MBA *1984;* Cicerone Press Ltd, 2 Police Square, MILNTHORPE, CUMBRIA, LA7 7PY.
•WILLIAMS, Mr. Jonathan Mark, BA FCA CF *1989;* Bishop Fleming, 16 Queen Square, BRISTOL, BS1 4NT.
WILLIAMS, Mr. Jonathan Paul, BSc ACA CTA *2004;* with Simpkins Edwards LLP, Michael House, Castle Street, EXETER, EX4 3LQ.
WILLIAMS, Mr. Jonathan Paul, BA FCA *1997;* Mariner Apartments, 1 La Route de L'Etacq, St. Ouen, JERSEY, JE3 2FB.
WILLIAMS, Mr. Joseph William, ACA *2009;* 26 Clevedon Drive, Earley, READING, RG6 5XE.
WILLIAMS, Ms. Judith Karen, BSc ACA *1993;* 52 Sutherland Avenue, LEEDS, LS8 1BZ.
WILLIAMS, Ms. Julia, BSc ACA *1999;* Flat 2, 58 Leicester Road, LOUGHBOROUGH, LE11 2AG.
WILLIAMS, Mrs. Julia, BSc ACA *1997;* 17 Reedley Road, BRISTOL, BS9 3SR.
WILLIAMS, Miss. Julia Linda, ACA *2008;* 143 Sheen Court, RICHMOND, TW10 5DQ.

WILLIAMS, Miss. Julie, BA ACA *1990;* 19 Albert Road, LONDON, N22 7AA.
WILLIAMS, Mrs. Julie Ann, BA ACA CTA *1980;* 3 Tong Close, Bishopswood, STAFFORD, ST19 9AJ.
WILLIAMS, Mrs. Julie Annette, MA ACA *1993;* 21 Brooke Gardens, BISHOP'S STORTFORD, HERTFORDSHIRE, CM23 5JF.
WILLIAMS, Ms. Julie Catherine, BSc ACA *1993;* 25 Ashdell Road, Broomhill, SHEFFIELD, S10 3DA.
WILLIAMS, Miss. Julie Helen, BA FCA CTA *1992;* HBOS Plc, Walton Street, AYLESBURY, HP21 7QW.
•WILLIAMS, Mr. Justin, BSc FCA *1985;* Williams & Co Ltd., Ebor House, 1 Knott Lane, Easingwold, YORK, YO61 3LX.
•WILLIAMS, Mrs. Kara Marie, BSc ACA *2003;* Ellis Lloyd Jones LLP, Alan House, 2 Risca Road, NEWPORT, GWENT, NP20 4JW.
WILLIAMS, Miss. Karen, BEng ACA *2011;* 1 Southfield Close, Dorney, WINDSOR, BERKSHIRE, SL4 6QN.
WILLIAMS, Ms. Karen Elizabeth, BA ACA DChA *1995;* 3 Warren Lane, Dartington Hall, TOTNES, DEVON, TQ9 6EG.
WILLIAMS, Mrs. Karen Louise, BSc(Hons) ACA *2000;* Bldg B, British Petroleum Co Plc, Chertsey Road, SUNBURY-ON-THAMES, MIDDLESEX, TW16 7LN.
WILLIAMS, Miss. Karen Louise, BSc(Hons) ACA *2001;* with Deloitte LLP, Hill House, 1 Little New Street, LONDON, EC4A 3TR.
WILLIAMS, Mrs. Karen Marie, BA ACA *1988;* University Campus Suffolk Ltd Waterfront Building, 19 Neptune Quay, IPSWICH, IP4 1QJ.
WILLIAMS, Mr. Karl Daniel, MEng ACA *2004;* 51 Old Dickens Heath Road, Shirley, SOLIHULL, B90 1SR.
WILLIAMS, Mrs. Katherine Ann, BA FCA CTA *1998;* (Tax Fac), 10 St Ann Street, SALISBURY, SP1 2DN.
WILLIAMS, Ms. Katherine Rachel, BSc ACA *1988;* 19 Conduit Mews, LONDON, W2 3RE.
•WILLIAMS, Mrs. Katrina Louise, ACA CTA TEP *2003;* Locke Williams Associates LLP, Blackthorn House, St Paul's Square, BIRMINGHAM, B3 1RL.
•WILLIAMS, Mr. Keith, MA ACA *1978;* with Acklands Limited, Waterloo House, Waterloo Street, Clifton, BRISTOL, BS8 4BT.
WILLIAMS, Mr. Keith, BA ACA *1983;* 12 Fairlawn Park, WINDSOR, SL4 4HL.
WILLIAMS, Mr. Keith James, BSc ACA *1980;* 65 Brantwood Road, LONDON, SE24 0DH.
WILLIAMS, Mr. Keith John, BA FCA *1998;* 20 Cundell Way, Kings Worthy, WINCHESTER, SO23 7NP.
WILLIAMS, Mr. Keith John, FCA *1968;* 12 The Haybarn, Walmley, SUTTON COLDFIELD, B76 1DE.
WILLIAMS, Mr. Keith Richard, BA(Econ) ACA *2002;* Altium Capital Ltd, 6th Floor Belvedere, 12 Booth Street, MANCHESTER, M2 4AW.
WILLIAMS, Mr. Keith Stanley, BA ACA *1990;* UK Steel Enterprise Ltd, The Innovation Centre, 217 Portobello, SHEFFIELD, S1 4DP.
WILLIAMS, Mr. Keith Steven, BA ACA MSFA *1989;* 33 Danefield Road, WIRRAL, CH49 3PB.
WILLIAMS, Mr. Keith Stewart, BA FCA *1989;* The London Clinic, 20 Devonshire Place, LONDON, W1G 6BW.
WILLIAMS, Mrs. Kelli, BSc ACA *1999;* 2 Knoll Avenue, Uplands, SWANSEA, SA2 0JN.
WILLIAMS, Mr. Kenneth Rigby, FCA *1958;* 15 Lime Tree Walk, VIRGINIA WATER, GU25 4SW. (Life Member)
WILLIAMS, Ms. Keren Elizabeth, BSc ACA *1987;* Randalls, 30 Greenhill Road, Otford, SEVENOAKS, TN14 5RS.
•WILLIAMS, Mr. Kevin Alan, LLB ACA *1990;* with PricewaterhouseCoopers LLP, One Kingsway, CARDIFF, CF10 3PW.
WILLIAMS, Mr. Kevin Anthony, ACA *2008;* with Barnes Roffe LLP, 16-19 Copperfields, Spital Street, DARTFORD, DA1 2DE.
WILLIAMS, Mr. Kevin David, BSc ACA *2011;* Apartment 34, Somerville Point, 305 Rotherhithe Street, LONDON, SE16 5EQ.
WILLIAMS, Mr. Kevin Glyn, BA ACA *1986;* FH Interim & Consulting, Folly Hall, Folly Hall Lane, Upper Broughton, MELTON MOWBRAY, LE14 3QB.
WILLIAMS, Mrs. Kim Marie, BSc ACA *1997;* Woodlands Farm, Narcot Lane, Chalfont St. Peter, GERRARDS CROSS, BUCKINGHAMSHIRE, SL9 8TR.
WILLIAMS, Miss. Kirsten Lee, BSc ACA *2000;* 123 Wellington Hill West, BRISTOL, BS9 4QX.
WILLIAMS, Mrs. Laura, ACA *2009;* 17 Burnside Avenue, Stockton Heath, WARRINGTON, WA4 2AW.
WILLIAMS, Miss. Laura Elizabeth, BA(Hons) ACA *2004;* Flat 8, 12 Kew Gardens Road, RICHMOND, SURREY, TW9 3HG.
WILLIAMS, Mr. Lawrence Meredith, BA FCA *1974;* Crofsway, Bombers Lane, WESTERHAM, TN16 2JA.
WILLIAMS, Mr. Leonard, FCA *1950;* 585 Ridgewood Avenue, GLEN RIDGE, NJ 07028-1932, UNITED STATES. (Life Member)
WILLIAMS, Miss. Lesley-Ann, BA ACA *2002;* 58 Taunton Road, LONDON, SE12 8PB.
WILLIAMS, Mr. Lewis James Glyn, MEng ACA *2007;* Eastcroft, 11 Le Bel Mourant, Maufant Village St Helier, JERSEY, JE2 7JJ.
•WILLIAMS, Mrs. Linda Carol, BSc ACA MBA *1990;* Bright Blue Skies Limited, 41 Cambridge Road, LONDON, E11 2PL.
WILLIAMS, Mrs. Linda Joanne, BSc ACA *1999;* 39 Tawny Way, Littleover, DERBY, DE23 7XG.
WILLIAMS, Mrs. Lisa Dawn, FCA *1993;* 28 The Spinney, Bradley Stoke, BRISTOL, BS32 8ES.
WILLIAMS, Mrs. Lisa Joanne, BA ACA *2007;* with Simpkins Edwards LLP, Michael House, Castle Street, EXETER, EX4 3LQ.
WILLIAMS, Miss. Llinos, BSc(Econ) ACA *2010;* 68 Brynteg, CARDIFF, CF14 6TT.
WILLIAMS, Mr. Lloyd, BSc ACA CF *1994;* Kuwait Finance House (Bahrain), 21st Floor, West Tower, Bahrain World Trade Center, PO Box 2066, MANAMA BAHRAIN.
WILLIAMS, Miss. Louise Michele, BA ACA *1991;* Acal Plc, 2 Chancellor Court, Occam Road, Surrey Research Park, GUILDFORD, SURREY GU2 7AH.
WILLIAMS, Miss. Lyndsay Anne, BSc ACA CTA *2002;* Ludlow Street Healthcare Group Limited, 5th Floor, Harlech Court, Bute Terrace, CARDIFF, CF10 2FE.
•WILLIAMS, Mrs. Lynn Christine, BA FCA *1981;* Landau Morley LLP, Lanmor House, 370-386 High Road, WEMBLEY, MIDDLESEX, HA9 6AX.
WILLIAMS, Mrs. Lynsey Jane, LLB ACA *2001;* Co-operative Bank Plc, PO Box 101, MANCHESTER, M60 4EP.
WILLIAMS, Mr. Marc, ACA *2008;* Highcroft, 17 Haldon Road, TORQUAY, TQ1 2LX.
WILLIAMS, Mr. Marc Lawrence, BA ACA *1999;* Flat 8 8 St. Olaves Court St. Petersburgh Place, LONDON, W2 4JY.
WILLIAMS, Mrs. Marian Therese, ACA *2000;* 13 Henleaze Avenue, BRISTOL, BS9 4EU.
WILLIAMS, Miss. Marie, BSc ACA *2005;* with KPMG LLP, 100 Temple Street, BRISTOL, BS1 6AG.
WILLIAMS, Mr. Mark, BSc ACA *1990;* 45 Avenue Carnot, 78100 ST GERMAIN-EN-LAYE, FRANCE.
•WILLIAMS, Mr. Mark, FCA *1981;* (Tax Fac), Williams & Co, 8-10 South Street, EPSOM, KT18 7PF.
WILLIAMS, Mr. Mark, BA ACA DChA *2003;* with Robinson Reed Layton, Peat House, Newham Road, TRURO, CORNWALL, TR1 2DP.
WILLIAMS, Mr. Mark, ACA MAAT *2011;* 14 Hunters Gate, OKEHAMPTON, DEVON, EX20 1SU.
WILLIAMS, Mr. Mark, BA ACA *1985;* The Hedgerows, Common Lane, Church Fenton, TADCASTER, LS24 9QR.
WILLIAMS, Mr. Mark Alexander, BA ACA *1992;* Flat G, 105 Alderney Street, LONDON, SW1V 4HE.
WILLIAMS, Mr. Mark David, BSc ACA *2006;* 20b Cambridge Park, TWICKENHAM, TW1 2JE.
WILLIAMS, Mr. Mark Hilton, MEng ACA *2006;* 22 Chancery Lane, LONDON, WC2A 1LS.
WILLIAMS, Mr. Mark Justin, BSc ACA *2002;* 15 Shepley Close, Hazel Grove, STOCKPORT, CHESHIRE, SK7 6JJ.
WILLIAMS, Mr. Mark Leslie, BSc FCA *1996;* 42 Norbury Avenue, The Reeds, WATFORD, WD24 4PJ.
WILLIAMS, Mr. Mark Pritchard, BSc FCA *1989;* Cofunds, 1 Minster Court, LONDON, EC3R 7AA.
•WILLIAMS, Mr. Mark Ronald, BSc ACA *1980;* Mark R Williams LLP, 362 Shooters Hill Road, LONDON, SE18 4LS.
•WILLIAMS, Mr. Mark Stephen, BD FCA *1984;* Williams Naylor, 1st Floor, 454 Gower Road, Killay, SWANSEA, SA2 7AL.
WILLIAMS, Mr. Marlon Fabion, BSc ACA *2005;* 30A Russell Hill, PURLEY, CR8 2JA.
•WILLIAMS, Mr. Martin, FCA *1973;* Williams Giles, 12 Conqueror Court, SITTINGBOURNE, KENT, ME10 5BH. See also Williams Giles Limited
WILLIAMS, Mr. Martin Christopher, FCA *1972;* The Old Vicarage, Moreton Morrell, WARWICK, CV35 9AT.
WILLIAMS, Mr. Martin David, BA ACA *1982;* Britannia Row Productions Ltd, 9 Osiers Road, Wandsworth, LONDON, SW18 1NL.
WILLIAMS, Mr. Martin Glyn, FCA *1976;* Q'Nim, Main Street, Howsham, MARKET RASEN, LN7 6JZ.
WILLIAMS, Mr. Martin Glyndwr Hurst, BA ACA *2007;* Mailpoint 7A Npower Cogen, Trigonos Windmill Hill Business Park, SWINDON, SN5 6PB.
WILLIAMS, Mr. Martin Gwynne, MA FCA *1972;* Flat 5 Oxford House, 52 Parkside, LONDON, SW19 5NE.
•WILLIAMS, Mr. Martin James, BSc FCA *1985;* Martin Williams & Co, Riverside House, Brymau 3, River Lane, Saltney, CHESTER CH4 8RQ.
WILLIAMS, Mr. Martin John, BA ACA *1983;* Rainbridge Timber Ltd Pye Bridge Industrial Estate, Pye Bridge, ALFRETON, DERBYSHIRE, DE55 4NX.
WILLIAMS, Mr. Martin John, MA FCA *1984;* Chaucer Syndicates Ltd, Plantation Place, 30 Fenchurch Street, LONDON, EC3M 3AD.
WILLIAMS, Mr. Martin Nicholas, BSc ACA *1993;* 43 Amorys Holt Road, Maltby, ROTHERHAM, S66 8EH.
WILLIAMS, Mr. Martin Robert, BA FCA *1978;* (Tax Fac), 28 Radcliffe Square, LONDON, SW15 6BL.
WILLIAMS, Mr. Martyn Douglas, MA(Cantab) FCA *1976;* The Round House, Riding Lane, Hildenborough, TONBRIDGE, TN11 9QL.
WILLIAMS, Mr. Matthew Alexander, BA(Econ) FCA *2001;* 8 Grafton Gardens, ACCRINGTON, LANCASHIRE, BB5 2TY.
WILLIAMS, Mr. Matthew David, BA ACA *2010;* 27 Charlestown Grove, STOKE-ON-TRENT, ST3 7WL.
•WILLIAMS, Mr. Matthew Francis, BSocSc ACA *1996;* with Ernst & Young LLP, 1 More London Place, LONDON, SE1 2AF.
•WILLIAMS, Mr. Matthew James, BSc ACA CTA *2004;* L.H. Phillips & Co, 29/30 Quay St., CARMARTHEN, SA31 3JT.
WILLIAMS, Mr. Matthew Stephen, BA(Hons) ACA *2001;* Bush Meadow, Greenways, Flordon, NORWICH, NR15 1QN.
WILLIAMS, Mr. Max Vincent, BSc ACA *1990;* 41 Ewell Downs Road, EPSOM, SURREY, KT17 3BT.
WILLIAMS, Mrs. Melissa, BA ACA *2000;* Mattash, East Williamston, TENBY, DYFED, SA70 8RT.
WILLIAMS, Miss. Melissa Catherine, BA ACA *1996;* Flat 43 China Court Asher Way, LONDON, E1W 2JF.
WILLIAMS, Dr. Melvyn John, BSc ACA *1998;* Deutsche Bank A G, Prince George House, 20 Finsbury Circus, LONDON, EC2M 1NB.
WILLIAMS, Mr. Michael, ACA *2010;* Flat 37 Meridian Court, 9 Chambers Street, LONDON, SE16 4UE.
WILLIAMS, Mr. Michael, ACA *2008;* 5 Thistle House, 2 Celsus Grove, SWINDON, SN1 4GT.
•WILLIAMS, Mr. Michael Alfred, BSc ACA *1980;* 30 Retford Drive, SUTTON COLDFIELD, B76 1DG.
WILLIAMS, Mr. Michael Andrew, BA(Hons) ACA *2001;* 7 Maes y Crofft, Morganstown, CARDIFF, CF15 8FE.
WILLIAMS, Mr. Michael David, FCA *1977;* The Old Rectory, Ipsley Lane, REDDITCH, WORCESTERSHIRE, B98 0AP.
•WILLIAMS, Mr. Michael David, ACA *1980;* (Tax Fac), Flint & Thompson Limited, 1325A Stratford Road, Hall Green, BIRMINGHAM, WEST MIDLANDS, B28 9HL.
WILLIAMS, Mr. Michael Jeffery, BSc FCA *1995;* 6 Baskerville Road, Sonning Common, READING, RG4 9LS.
WILLIAMS, Mr. Michael John, BA FCA *1972;* 27 Elizabeth Way, Uppingham, OAKHAM, LE15 9PQ.
•WILLIAMS, Mr. Michael John, FCA *1972;* Sumup Limited, 28 Pangfield Park, Allesley Park, COVENTRY, CV5 9NL.
WILLIAMS, Mr. Michael Robert Campion, ACA *2009;* 10 Floyds Lane, WOKING, GU22 8TF.
•WILLIAMS, Mr. Michael Wade, BA ACA *1988;* Deloitte LLP, Hill House, 1 Little New Street, LONDON, EC4A 3TR. See also Deloitte & Touche LLP
WILLIAMS, Mrs. Michele Mary, BSc ACA *1984;* 27 Bolton Gardens, TEDDINGTON, TW11 9AX.
WILLIAMS, Mrs. Michelle Louise, BSc ACA *1993;* 24a Helen Street, Golborne, WARRINGTON, WA3 3QR.
WILLIAMS, Mrs. Michelle Louise, BSc ACA *2007;* 2a Park View, Sutton Veny, WARMINSTER, WILTSHIRE, BA12 7AN.
WILLIAMS, Miss. Natalie Jane, ACA *2008;* 105 Beecham Road, READING, RG30 2RB.
WILLIAMS, Mrs. Natasa Miklavcic, BA ACA *1998;* 10 Oakleigh Park Avenue, CHISLEHURST, KENT, BR7 5PB.
•WILLIAMS, Mr. Neil Andrew, BA FCA *1994;* Forrester Boyd, 66-68 Oswald Road, SCUNTHORPE, SOUTH HUMBERSIDE, DN15 7PG.
WILLIAMS, Mr. Neil Andrew, ACA *2003;* with Lubbock Fine, Russell Bedford House, City Forum, 250 City Road, LONDON, EC1V 2QQ.
WILLIAMS, Mr. Neil Fraser, BSc ACA *2000;* Sunseeker International Ltd, 27-31 West Quay Road, POOLE, DORSET, BH15 1HX.
WILLIAMS, Mr. Neil James, BA ACA *1998;* 3 Cardinal Avenue, MORDEN, SM4 4TA.
WILLIAMS, Mr. Neil Pryce, BSc ACA *1989;* Beech Hurst, Tyrrells Wood, LEATHERHEAD, KT22 8QJ.
WILLIAMS, Mr. Neil Rodney, FCA *1968;* 207 Providence Square, Mill Street, LONDON, SE1 2EW.
WILLIAMS, Mr. Neil Russell, BSc ACA *1986;* 11 High Street, Abbotsley, ST. NEOTS, CAMBRIDGESHIRE, PE19 6UJ.
WILLIAMS, Mr. Neil Stuart, BSc ACA *1989;* 98 Elwill Way, BECKENHAM, BR3 6RX.
WILLIAMS, Mr. Nicholas, BA FCA *1995;* Pear Tree Lodge, Heath Ride, WOKINGHAM, RG40 3QJ.
WILLIAMS, Mr. Nicholas Anthony, BSc FCA *1993;* Hope Mill, 113 Pollard Street, MANCHESTER, M4 7JB.
•WILLIAMS, Mr. Nicholas Charles, BA(Hons) FCA CTA TEP *1981;* (Tax Fac), Carter A.J. & Co, 22B High Street, WITNEY, OX28 6RB.
WILLIAMS, Mr. Nicholas Charles, BSc ACA *1988;* Barn Owl, Holmacott, Instow, BIDEFORD, EX39 4LR.
WILLIAMS, Mr. Nicholas Clyde, FCA *1986;* Power House, The Street, Sissinghurst, CRANBROOK, KENT, TN17 2JL.
WILLIAMS, Mr. Nicholas John, BA ACA *1987;* 7 South Parade, YORK, YO23 1BF.
WILLIAMS, Mr. Nicholas Mark, ACA *1986;* Bluebay Asset Management, 77 Grosvenor Street, LONDON, W1K 3JR.
•WILLIAMS, Mr. Nicholas Owen, BA ACA *1991;* with RSM Tenon Audit Limited, Highfield Court, Tollgate, Chandlers Ford, EASTLEIGH, SO53 3TY.
WILLIAMS, Mr. Nicholas Paul, FCA *1982;* HEFCW, Linden Court, The Orchards, Ilex Close, Llanishen, CARDIFF CF14 5DZ.
WILLIAMS, Miss. Nicola, ACA MAAT *2010;* 136 Knockhall Road, GREENHITHE, DA9 9EY.
WILLIAMS, Mrs. Nicola Joanne, BSc(Hons) ACA *2004;* Worldwide House, Western Road, BRACKNELL, RG12 1RW.
•WILLIAMS, Mr. Nicolas Simon Loretz, FCA *1985;* Sully & Co, 75 South Street, SOUTH MOLTON, DEVON, EX36 4AG.
WILLIAMS, Mr. Nigel Barry, FCA *1996;* 94 Tantallon Road, LONDON, SW12 8DH.
WILLIAMS, Mr. Nigel Edward, BSc ACA *1991;* 14 Blatchington Road, TUNBRIDGE WELLS, KENT, TN2 5EG.
•WILLIAMS, Mr. Nigel Frederick, BA ACA ACCA *1982;* WH Parker, 174 High Street, Harborne, BIRMINGHAM, B17 9PP.
WILLIAMS, Dr. Nigel James, PhD BSc ACA *1978;* 5 Roebuck Villas, St Smithwick Way, Port Pendennis Village, FALMOUTH, CORNWALL, TR11 3XY.
WILLIAMS, Mr. Nigel John, BA ACA *1990;* 184D Ramsden Road, LONDON, SW12 8RE.
WILLIAMS, Mr. Nigel Leslie Morgan, BA ACA *1986;* 5 Culgaith Road, Langwathby, PENRITH, CUMBRIA, CA10 1NA.
WILLIAMS, Mr. Nigel Stephen David, BSc FCA *1977;* Rustruffin Ltd, 2100 College Drive, Suite 72, BATON ROUGE, LA 70808, UNITED STATES.
•WILLIAMS, Mr. Nigel Stuart, BCom FCA *1989;* Agincourt Limited, 9 Deryn Court, Pentwyn Business Centre, Wharfedale Road, Pentwyn, CARDIFF CF23 7HB.
•WILLIAMS, Mr. Noel Geoffrey, BSc ACA *1979;* Kilsby & Williams LLP, Cedar House, Hazell Drive, NEWPORT, GWENT, NP10 8FY. See also Noel Williams Business Services Ltd
WILLIAMS, Mr. Norman Lyn Thomas, MA ACA *1979;* Woodcote, Nairdwood Lane, Prestwood, GREAT MISSENDEN, HP16 0QH.
WILLIAMS, Mr. Oscar, BSc FCA *1974;* Pontywal Farmhouse, Bronllys, BRECON, POWYS, LD3 0LU. (Life Member)
WILLIAMS, Mr. Owen Jonathan, BSc ACA *2009;* Pacific Investments Plc, 124 Sloane Street, LONDON, SW1X 9BW.
WILLIAMS, Mrs. Pamela Mary, FCA *1963;* 1 Dyke Close, HOVE, BN3 6DB. (Life Member)
WILLIAMS, Mr. Paul, ACA *1983;* 65 Springleaze, Knowle, BRISTOL, BS4 2TY.
•WILLIAMS, Mr. Paul, FCA *1983;* Ensors, 285 Milton Road, CAMBRIDGE, CB4 1XQ.
WILLIAMS, Mr. Paul, BSc ACA *2003;* Flat 4, 13 Woodlands Road, CAMBERLEY, SURREY, GU15 3LZ.
WILLIAMS, Mr. Paul, MA FCA *1974;* 4 Woodlands, RADLETT, WD7 7NT.
WILLIAMS, Mr. Paul, BSc ACA *1990;* Unit 1.15 Alba Innovation Centre, Alba Campus, LIVINGSTON, EH54 7GA.
WILLIAMS, Mr. Paul, BSc ACA *1992;* 11 Carrs Crescent West, Formby, LIVERPOOL, L37 2EX.

•**WILLIAMS, Mr. Paul, BA ACA** *2008;* with Barnett Spooner, The Old Steppe House, Brighton Road, GODALMING, SURREY, GU7 1NS.
WILLIAMS, Mr. Paul Adam, BSc ACA *2001;* with BDO Limited, 25/F Wing On Centre, 111 Connaught Road, CENTRAL, HONG KONG ISLAND, HONG KONG SAR.
WILLIAMS, Mr. Paul Andrew, BA(Hons) ACA *2009;* 43 Redsands Drive, Fulwood, PRESTON, PR2 6GG.
WILLIAMS, Mr. Paul Anthony, BSc ACA *1990;* 191 Moss Lane, PINNER, HA5 3BE.
•**WILLIAMS, Mr. Paul Charles, BSc FCA** *1982;* (Tax Fac), Davies Williams, 21 St. Andrews Crescent, CARDIFF, CF10 3DB. See also DW Consultancy Services Ltd
WILLIAMS, Mr. Paul David, BSc(Hons) ACA *1991;* 194 Woodside Street, DOUBLEVIEW, WA 6018, AUSTRALIA.
WILLIAMS, Mr. Paul Francis, BSc FCA *1974;* 26 Monterey Road, BILGOLA PLATEAU, NSW 2107, AUSTRALIA.
WILLIAMS, Mr. Paul Geoffrey, BSc ACA *1991;* Alvarez & Marsal, 6th Floor, 600 Lexington Avenue, NEW YORK, NY 10022, UNITED STATES.
WILLIAMS, Dr. Paul Godfrey Lee, PhD MA FCA *1974;* Flat 9 Chesterford House, Southacre Drive, CAMBRIDGE, CB2 7TZ.
WILLIAMS, Mr. Paul Graham, LLB ACA *1979;* 32 Burnham Avenue, BOGNOR REGIS, WEST SUSSEX, PO21 2JU.
WILLIAMS, Mr. Paul Henry, BA FCA *1974;* The Bridge Centre, 1 St Thomas Street, LONDON, SE1 9RY.
WILLIAMS, Mr. Paul John, ACA *1982;* Hope House, Hedgerley Hill, Hedgerley, SLOUGH, SL2 3RJ.
WILLIAMS, Mr. Paul Joseph, FCA *1974;* Walnut Tree House, 20 Lower Teddington Road, Hampton Wick, KINGSTON UPON THAMES, KT1 4EU. (Life Member)
WILLIAMS, Mr. Paul Leonard, BSc ACA *1979;* Avalon, Heathside Park Road, WOKING, SURREY, GU22 7JF.
WILLIAMS, Mr. Paul Mark, BA(Hons) ACA *2003;* 52 St. Marys Road, OXFORD, OX4 1PY.
WILLIAMS, Mr. Paul Mason, BSc ACA *2009;* 3 Parkfield Way, Topsham, EXETER, EX3 0DP.
WILLIAMS, Mr. Paul Michael, BSc ACA *1995;* 79 Quicks Road, Wimbledon, LONDON, SW19 1EX.
WILLIAMS, Mr. Paul Nicholas, BSc ACA *2000;* 136 Knutsford Road, WILMSLOW, CHESHIRE, SK9 6JP.
WILLIAMS, Mr. Paul Prichard, BA FCA *1992;* Flat 2, Cassis Court, Chigwell Lane, LOUGHTON, ESSEX, IG10 3UA.
WILLIAMS, Mrs. Paula Marie, ACA ATII *1988;* (Tax Fac), Mountpumps Oast London Road, Hurst Green, ETCHINGHAM, EAST SUSSEX, TN19 7QY.
WILLIAMS, Mrs. Penelope Jane, BSc ACA *1992;* Monks Way, Haggnook Wood, Ravenshead, NOTTINGHAM, NG15 9HE.
WILLIAMS, Mrs. Penelope Susan Jane, MSc ACA *1984;* 3 Maple Grove, Worsley, MANCHESTER, M28 7ED.
WILLIAMS, Peter, Esq CBE FCA *1939;* Una, Barlaston, STOKE-ON-TRENT, ST12 9AA. (Life Member)
WILLIAMS, Mr. Peter, FCA *1957;* 5 Mason Close, EAST GRINSTEAD, WEST SUSSEX, RH19 3RR. (Life Member)
WILLIAMS, Mr. Peter, BSc FCA *1979;* Flat 18, Lansdowne, Groves Avenue, Langland, SWANSEA, SA3 4QX.
WILLIAMS, Mr. Peter, BSc ACA *2004;* Upton House, Upton Grey, BASINGSTOKE, RG25 2RE.
WILLIAMS, Mr. Peter, FCA *1974;* 34 Southdown Road, Sticker, ST. AUSTELL, CORNWALL, PL26 7EW.
WILLIAMS, Mr. Peter Anthony, FCA *1960;* Longledge, Winspit Road, Worth Matravers, SWANAGE, BH19 3LW. (Life Member)
WILLIAMS, Mr. Peter Bryan Gurmin, FCA *1969;* (Member of Council 1987 - 1994), 2 Buckingham Place, LONDON, SW1E 6HR.
WILLIAMS, Mr. Peter Dominic, BSc FCA *1989;* William Sinclair Holdings Plc, Firth Road, LINCOLN, LN6 7AH.
WILLIAMS, Mr. Peter Gruffydh, BSc FCA *1983;* 33 Barcheston Road, Knowle, SOLIHULL, B93 9JS.
WILLIAMS, Mr. Peter Hugh, FCA *1966;* 25 Hambledon Vale, Woodcote, EPSOM, KT18 7DA. (Life Member)
WILLIAMS, Mr. Peter Iwan, BSc ACA *1979;* Barbers Cottage Witts Lane, Purton, SWINDON, SN5 4ES.
WILLIAMS, Mr. Peter J, MA(Hons) ACA *2006;* 60 Kingslea Road, MANCHESTER, M20 4UA.
•**WILLIAMS, Mr. Peter John, BA FCA** *1980;* (Tax Fac), Peter Williams & Co, 68 Herbert Gardens, LONDON, NW10 3BU.
•**WILLIAMS, Mr. Peter John, FCA** *1959;* P.J.Williams, 45 Baginton Road, Styvechale, COVENTRY, CV3 6JX.
WILLIAMS, Mr. Peter John, BA ACA *1992;* 6th Floor, 34 Lime Street, LONDON, EC3M 7AT.
WILLIAMS, Mr. Peter John, BA FCA *1996;* 26 Grosvenor Road, Harborne, BIRMINGHAM, B17 9AN.
WILLIAMS, Mr. Peter John, BA ACA *2009;* Saville House, Apartment 606, 37 Potato Wharf, MANCHESTER, M3 4BD.
WILLIAMS, Mr. Peter John, BSc ACA *2007;* 11 Medlar House, Hemlock Close, LONDON, SW16 5PS.
WILLIAMS, Mr. Peter Michael, FCA *1961;* Down Hollow, Down Lane, Compton, GUILDFORD, GU3 1DQ.
WILLIAMS, Mr. Peter Rhys, BA ACA *1992;* 17 Occupation Road, Albert Village, SWADLINCOTE, DERBYSHIRE, DE11 8HA.
WILLIAMS, Mr. Peter Thomas, BA ACA *1986;* Bizmedia Ltd, 80-82 Chiswick High Road, LONDON, W4 1SY.
WILLIAMS, Mr. Peter Wodehouse, BSc ACA *1979;* 3 Rayners Road, LONDON, SW15 2AY.
WILLIAMS, Miss. Phaedra Ann, ACA *2010;* 12 St. Stephens Court, Undy, CALDICOT, GWENT, NP26 3PR.
WILLIAMS, Mr. Philip, FCA *1963;* 74 Strawberry Mead, Fair Oak, EASTLEIGH, SO50 8RG. (Life Member)
WILLIAMS, Mr. Philip, BA FCA *1976;* (Tax Fac), Mercia Group Ltd Best House Grange Business Park, Enderby Road Whetstone, LEICESTER, LE8 6EP.
WILLIAMS, Mr. Philip David, FCA *1972;* 3 Channel View, Langland, SWANSEA, SA3 4PL.
WILLIAMS, Mr. Philip Edward, BA ACA *1993;* Team Simoco, Field House, Uttoxeter Old Road, DERBY, DE1 1NH.
WILLIAMS, Mr. Philip John, BA ACA *1985;* 59 Marine Drive, BARRY, SOUTH GLAMORGAN, CF62 6QP.
•**WILLIAMS, Mr. Philip John, FCA** *1970;* (Tax Fac), Brices, Well Street, Burghclere, NEWBURY, BERKSHIRE, RG20 9HR.
WILLIAMS, Mr. Philip Stanhope Ray, MA ACA *1983;* Crofton, Park Road, HASLEMERE, GU27 2NL.
WILLIAMS, Mrs. Polly Ann, BA ACA *1989;* The Old Rectory, 81 Stoke Road, Stoke D'Abernon, COBHAM, KT11 3PU.
WILLIAMS, Mrs. Rachael Anne, LLB ACA *1986;* 29 Calabria Road, LONDON, N5 1HZ.
WILLIAMS, Miss. Rachel, ACA *2011;* Flat 2, Eaton Court, Mulroy Road, SUTTON COLDFIELD, WEST MIDLANDS, B74 2PZ.
WILLIAMS, Miss. Rachel Louise, BA ACA *2003;* Flat 81 Kings Lodge, Pembroke Road, RUISLIP, MIDDLESEX, HA4 8NJ.
WILLIAMS, Mr. Ralph Henry, FCA *1956;* 5 The Paddocks, Bourton-on-the-Water, CHELTENHAM, GLOUCESTERSHIRE, GL54 2LS. (Life Member)
WILLIAMS, Mrs. Rebecca, ACA *2009;* 19 Bluebell Mead, CORSHAM, WILTSHIRE, SN13 9FS.
WILLIAMS, Mrs. Rebecca Jane, BA ACA *2005;* with Howsons, Winton House, Stoke Road, STOKE-ON-TRENT, ST4 2RW.
•**WILLIAMS, Mrs. Rebecca Jane, BSc ACA** *2001;* Rebecca Williams BSc ACA, 62 Derbyshire Road, SALE, CHESHIRE, M33 3EL.
WILLIAMS, Miss. Rebecca Jayne, ACA *2005;* 14 Lindisfarne, Glascote, TAMWORTH, STAFFORDSHIRE, B77 2QN.
WILLIAMS, Mrs. Rebecca Louise, BA(Hons) ACA *2004;* 10 Bracken Hill View, Horbury, WAKEFIELD, WF64 6FD.
WILLIAMS, Miss. Rebecca Sian, ACA *2008;* 8 Egerton Street, CARDIFF, CF5 1RG.
WILLIAMS, Mrs. Rhiannon Nest, MA ACA *1992;* (Tax Fac), with PricewaterhouseCoopers LLP, One Kingsway, CARDIFF, CF10 3PW.
WILLIAMS, Mr. Richard, BCom ACA *1999;* 9 Batsford Close, REDDITCH, WORCESTERSHIRE, B98 7TF.
WILLIAMS, Mr. Richard, BSc ACA *2009;* 32 Gnoll Avenue, NEATH, WEST GLAMORGAN, SA11 3AB.
WILLIAMS, Mr. Richard Anthony, BCom ACA *1985;* Manor Farm, South Barrow, YEOVIL, BA22 7LN.
•**WILLIAMS, Mr. Richard Antony, BSc FCA** *1996;* with Beever and Struthers, St George's House, 215-219 Chester Road, MANCHESTER, M15 4JE.
WILLIAMS, Mr. Richard Barnaby, BA ACA *2006;* Lloyds TSB Bank Plc, Phase 2 First Floor Southeast, Canons House, Canons Way, BRISTOL, BS1 5LL.
WILLIAMS, Mr. Richard Bramley, FCA *1977;* Culvers, Pilcot Hill, Dogmersfield, HOOK, RG27 8SX.
WILLIAMS, Mr. Richard Bryn, BA ACA *1984;* 39 West Drive, PORTHCAWL, MID GLAMORGAN, CF36 3HS.
WILLIAMS, Mr. Richard Douglas, BSc ACA *1991;* Lancastle International Ltd, 73-75 High Road, Halton-on-Lune, LANCASTER, LA2 6PS.
WILLIAMS, Mr. Richard Edward Lewis, FCA *1975;* 78 Cromwell Avenue, Highgate, LONDON, N6 5HQ.
WILLIAMS, Mr. Richard Francis Howat, BA FCA *1981;* 29 Woodstock Road, LONDON, W4 1DS.
WILLIAMS, Mr. Richard George, FCA *1989;* Godfrey's Hall, Wells Road, Hindringham, FAKENHAM, NORFOLK, NR21 0PQ.
WILLIAMS, Mr. Richard Glynne, BSc ACA *1983;* 63 Wolsey Road, Moor Park, NORTHWOOD, HA6 2ER.
WILLIAMS, Mr. Richard James, BSc ACA *2006;* 24 Park Road, WILMSLOW, CHESHIRE, SK9 5BT.
•**WILLIAMS, Mr. Richard James Henry, BA FCA** *1994;* Jamalu Limited, 14 Netheravon Road, SALISBURY, SP1 3BJ.
•**WILLIAMS, Mr. Richard Jason, BA FCA** *1989;* Gordon Wood Scott & Partners, Dean House, 94 Whiteladies Road, Clifton, BRISTOL, BS8 2QX.
WILLIAMS, Mr. Richard John, BSc ACA *2000;* Flat 5 1 Twig Folly Close, LONDON, E2 0SU.
•**WILLIAMS, Mr. Richard John, BSc ACA CTA** *1996;* Deloitte LLP, 1 City Square, LEEDS, WEST YORKSHIRE, LS1 2AL. See also Deloitte & Touche LLP
WILLIAMS, Mr. Richard John Hoskyn, ACA CA(SA) *2010;* 34 Cawcott Drive, WINDSOR, BERKSHIRE, SL4 5PU.
WILLIAMS, Mr. Richard Juxon, BCom FCA *1962;* Garden Flat, 15 South Hill Park Gardens, Hampstead, LONDON, NW3 2TD. (Life Member)
•**WILLIAMS, Mr. Richard Keith, BA ACA** *1981;* 5B Watea Road, Torbay, AUCKLAND 1311, NEW ZEALAND.
WILLIAMS, The Revd. Richard Lawrence, BSc ACA *1987;* The Vicarage, Waterloo Road, CRANBROOK, TN17 3JQ.
WILLIAMS, Mr. Richard Leslie, BA ACA *1999;* C P A Management Systems Ltd, 1 Oliver's Yard, LONDON, EC1Y 1DT.
•**WILLIAMS, Mr. Richard Mark, BA FCA** *1991;* 53 Mount Harry Road, SEVENOAKS, KENT, TN13 3JN.
WILLIAMS, Mr. Richard Radway, BSc ACA *1981;* Sherborne House, 119 Cannon Street, LONDON, EC4N 5AT.
WILLIAMS, Dr. Richard Spencer, ACA *2009;* Flat 5 Barloch House, Henley Street, LONDON, SW11 5BZ.
WILLIAMS, Mr. Richard Tobias, BSc ACA *2009;* Glanrhyd, Penrhyd, AMLWCH, GWYNEDD, LL68 9TL.
WILLIAMS, Mrs. Rita, BA FCA *1971;* Down End, 29 Fort Road, GUILDFORD, GU1 3TE. (Life Member)
WILLIAMS, Mr. Robert, BSc ACA *1987;* 2 Quebec Close, Smallfield, HORLEY, RH6 9QY.
WILLIAMS, Mr. Robert, ACA *2011;* 89 Cyncoed Road, CARDIFF, CF23 5SD.
WILLIAMS, Mr. Robert Boyd, FCA *1976;* 24 St Johns Close, SAFFRON WALDEN, CB11 4AR.
WILLIAMS, Mr. Robert Charles, FCA FRSA *1961;* 2 Victoria Cottages, South Stoke, BATH, BA2 7DT. (Life Member)
•**WILLIAMS, Mr. Robert David, BSc ACA** *1999;* Greys Accountants Limited, 5 Whiteoaks, Bwlchgwyn, WREXHAM, CLWYD, LL11 5UJ.
WILLIAMS, Mr. Robert David, BSc ACA *2002;* 9 Stewards Inn Lane, LEWES, EAST SUSSEX, BN7 1XP.
WILLIAMS, Mr. Robert Edward, FCA *1980;* Fairways, 20 Abingdon Road, Tubney, ABINGDON, OXFORDSHIRE, OX13 5QQ.
WILLIAMS, Mr. Robert George, BA ACA *1993;* 11 Black Bull Road, FOLKESTONE, KENT, CT19 5QL.
•**WILLIAMS, Mr. Robert Ian, MBA BA ACA CF** *1990;* Williams & Co, New Maxdov House, 130 Bury New Road, Prestwich, MANCHESTER, M25 0AA.
WILLIAMS, Mr. Robert James, BA FCA *1969;* R.J.W. Management Consultants Ltd, Laurans, 5 Park Seymour, Penlow, NEWPORT, NP26 3AB.
WILLIAMS, Mr. Robert Johnathan Hugh, BSc ACA *2010;* Pound Farm House, Church Road, TADLEY, HAMPSHIRE, RG26 3AU.
WILLIAMS, Mr. Robert Norman, FCA *1970;* 22 Ingrebourne Gardens, UPMINSTER, RM14 1BQ.
WILLIAMS, Mr. Robert Parry, BA FCA *1976;* 8 Llys-Y-Brenin Coed Brydwen, Kingsbridge, Gorseinon, SWANSEA, SA4 6SX.
WILLIAMS, Mr. Robert Paul, BA FCA *1998;* 5 Saxon Gate, Burghfield, READING, BERKSHIRE, RG30 3BR.
•**WILLIAMS, Mr. Robert Paul, FCA** *1976;* (Tax Fac), Ensors, Warwick House, Ermine Business Park, Spitfire Close, HUNTINGDON, CAMBRIDGESHIRE PE29 6XY.
WILLIAMS, Mr. Robert Penry, LLB ACA *2001;* Flat 15 The Azure, 36 Bath Buildings, BRISTOL, BS6 5QL.
WILLIAMS, Mr. Robert Raymond, FCA *1955;* Threeways, 46 Earlsway, CHESTER, CH4 8AZ. (Life Member)
WILLIAMS, Mr. Robert Thomas, BA ACA *2005;* Sapphire Energy Recovery Ltd, Yelsway Lane, Waterhouses, STOKE-ON-TRENT, ST10 3AZ.
WILLIAMS, Mr. Robert Timothy, BSc ACA *1983;* 26 Lancet Lane, Loose, MAIDSTONE, ME15 9RY.
WILLIAMS, Mr. Robert Trevor, BSc ACA *1986;* 17 Orchard Rise, Coombe Hill, KINGSTON-UPON-THAMES, KT2 7EY.
WILLIAMS, Mr. Robin Edward, FCA *1984;* Thatched Cottage, Nottingham Road, SOUTHWELL, NOTTINGHAMSHIRE, NG25 0QW.
WILLIAMS, Mr. Robin George Waltoh, MA ACA *1982;* Flat 5, 26 Gledhow Gardens, LONDON, SW5 0AZ.
WILLIAMS, Miss. Robyn Sylvia Lianne, BSc(Hons) ACA *2010;* 26 Farmhill Meadows, Douglas, ISLE OF MAN, IM2 2LJ.
WILLIAMS, Mr. Roderick John, BSc ACA *2010;* 15 Effra Road, LONDON, SW19 8PW.
WILLIAMS, Mr. Roger Alyn, BA ACA CA(SA) *1991;* PO Box 3033, RIVONIA, 2128, SOUTH AFRICA.
•**WILLIAMS, Mr. Roger Anthony, FCA** *1972;* B.A. Khan & Co, 4 Cambridge Gardens, HASTINGS, EAST SUSSEX, TN34 1EH. See also Williams & Co
WILLIAMS, Mr. Roger Anthony, BSc FCA *1974;* 95 Kennerleigh Road, Rumney, CARDIFF, CF3 4BH.
•**WILLIAMS, Mr. Roger Charles, FCA** *1964;* Stirling International, 11th Floor, St James Centre, 111 Elizabeth Street, GPO Box 7019, SYDNEY NSW 2001 AUSTRALIA.
WILLIAMS, Mr. Roger Graham, BSc ACA *1989;* 18 Bracebridge Road, Four Oaks Park, SUTTON COLDFIELD, WEST MIDLANDS, B74 2SL.
WILLIAMS, Mr. Roger John Morris, BSc ACA *1986;* 8 Mountbatten Close, Shottery, STRATFORD-UPON-AVON, CV37 9ET.
WILLIAMS, Mr. Roger Philip, BA FCA *1978;* Chapel Farmhouse, Trelleck Grange, Nr Llanishen, CHEPSTOW, GWENT, NP16 6QR.
•**WILLIAMS, Mr. Roger W, BSc FCA CTA** *1977;* (Tax Fac), Wilkins Kennedy, Gladstone House, 77-79 High Street, EGHAM, TW20 9HY.
WILLIAMS, Miss. Rosemary Elizabeth, BSc ACA *1995;* with Smith & Williamson (Bristol) LLP, Portwall Place, Portwall Lane, BRISTOL, BS1 6NA.
WILLIAMS, Mr. Ross Antony John, ACA *2007;* 275 Barclay Road, SMETHWICK, WEST MIDLANDS, B67 5LA.
•**WILLIAMS, Mrs. Rowan Patricia, FCA** *1985;* 25 Farringdon Street, LONDON, EC4A 4AB. See also Baker Tilly Tax and Advisory Services LLP and Baker Tilly UK Audit LLP
WILLIAMS, Mr. Roy, FCA *1959;* 22 High Green, NORWICH, NR1 4AP. (Life Member)
WILLIAMS, Mrs. Ruth Mererid, BA FCA *1991;* The Hollies, Hall Close, Dronfield Woodhouse, DRONFIELD, S18 8ZA.
WILLIAMS, Mrs. Sally Angela Helen, BSc ACA *1991;* Red Roofs, Fearn Close, East Horsley, LEATHERHEAD, KT24 6AD.
WILLIAMS, Mrs. Sally-Anne, MSc BSc ACA *2004;* Corus FSS, Port Talbot Works, PORT TALBOT, WEST GLAMORGAN, SA13 2NG.
WILLIAMS, Miss. Samantha June, BSc ACA *1995;* 4a Hadley Parade, High Street, BARNET, EN5 5SX.
WILLIAMS, Mr. Samuel Anthony, BSc ACA *1990;* Sellar Property Group, 110 Park Street, LONDON, W1K 6NX.
WILLIAMS, Miss. Sarah Ann, BSc ACA *2007;* 7 De Bawdrip Road, CARDIFF, CF24 2TN.
WILLIAMS, Miss. Sarah Jane, BA ACA *1990;* 6 Cumberland Street, WORCESTER, WR1 1QE.
•**WILLIAMS, Miss. Sarah Jane, MEng ACA** *1994;* Ernst & Young LLP, 1 More London Place, LONDON, SE1 2AF. See also Ernst & Young Europe LLP
WILLIAMS, Miss. Sarah Jane, BA ACA *2001;* Flat 6, 269 East End Road, LONDON, N2 8AY.
•**WILLIAMS, Mrs. Sarah Jane, FCA** *1983;* (Tax Fac), Thwaites Blackwell Bailey & Co Limited, Delaport Coach House, Wheathampstead, ST. ALBANS, HERTFORDSHIRE, AL4 8RQ.

WILLIAMS, Miss. Sarah Louise, BSc(Hons) ACA ATII *2002;* GlaxoSmithKline plc, GSK House, 980 Great West Road, BRENTFORD, TW8 9GS.
WILLIAMS, Mr. Scott Stewart, BA(Hons) ACA *2010;* PricewaterhouseCoopers, 2 Eglin Road, Sunninghill 2157, Private Bag X36, JOHANNESBURG, SOUTH AFRICA.
•WILLIAMS, Mr. Sean, BSc ACA *1990;* PricewaterhouseCoopers LLP, 7 More London Riverside, LONDON, SE1 2RT. See also PricewaterhouseCoopers
WILLIAMS, Mrs. Sera, BSc ACA *1992;* Barn Owl, Holmacott, Instow, BIDEFORD, DEVON, EX39 4LR.
WILLIAMS, Mr. Shaun George, ACA MAAT *2009;* 28 Chartwell Gardens, SUTTON, SM3 9TQ.
WILLIAMS, Miss. Sheenagh Marie, ACA *2005;* Flat B, 69 Albany Street, LONDON, NW1 4BT.
WILLIAMS, Mrs. Shirley Anne, MA ACA *1979;* (Tax Fac), Yeoland Down, Golf Links Road, YELVERTON, PL20 6BN.
WILLIAMS, Mrs. Shirley Cecilia, FCA *1971;* 4 Davids Court, PONTYCLUN, MID GLAMORGAN, CF72 9AY. (Life Member)
WILLIAMS, Ms. Sian Elizabeth, BSc ACA *1988;* Victoria And Albert Museum, South Kensington, LONDON, SW7 2RL.
•WILLIAMS, Mrs. Sian Margaret, MBA FCA *1987;* Griffith Williams & Co, 36 Stryd Fawr, PWLLHELI, LL53 5RT.
WILLIAMS, Mr. Simon, BSc ACA *2006;* Technology Services Group, 1 Gosforth Parkway, Gosforth Business Park, NEWCASTLE UPON TYNE, NE12 8ET.
WILLIAMS, Mr. Simon, ACA *2008;* The Citco Group (Nyon Branch) Limited, 9 Route de St Cergue, 1260 NYON, SWITZERLAND.
WILLIAMS, Mr. Simon, ACA *2009;* Flat 9 Fettes House, Wellington Road, LONDON, NW8 9SU.
WILLIAMS, Mr. Simon, MA ACA *2011;* Flat 1, 4 Stoke Road, GUILDFORD, SURREY, GU1 4HW.
WILLIAMS, Mr. Simon Clyde Haydn, FCA *1996;* 31 Arlington Crescent, WILMSLOW, CHESHIRE, SK9 6BH.
WILLIAMS, Mr. Simon Daniel, BA ACA *1996;* John Lewis, Corporate Sales 8th Floor, 171 Victoria Street, LONDON, SW1E 5NN.
WILLIAMS, Mr. Simon David, BSc ACA *1989;* 3 Shires Close, RINGWOOD, BH24 3DJ.
WILLIAMS, Mr. Simon David, BSc ACA *1991;* 6 Devonshire Terrace, CARLISLE, CA3 9NB.
WILLIAMS, Mr. Simon James, BSc ACA *1984;* 1 Sparrow Lane, GREENWICH, CT 06830, UNITED STATES.
WILLIAMS, Mr. Simon Nicholas, BA FCA *1980;* 94 Coningsby Drive, KIDDERMINSTER, WORCESTERSHIRE, DY11 5LY.
WILLIAMS, Mr. Simon Owen Gibson, FCA *1975;* Lamb House, Church Street, Chiswick, LONDON, W4 2PD.
WILLIAMS, Mr. Simon Philip, BA FCA *1999;* 21 Velindre Road, CARDIFF, CF14 2TE.
WILLIAMS, Mr. Simon Robert John, BSc(Hons) ACA *2002;* 50 Baring Road, BEACONSFIELD, BUCKINGHAMSHIRE, HP9 2NE.
WILLIAMS, Mr. Spencer, BA ACA *2007;* Overbridge, Bransford Road, Rushwick, WORCESTER, WR2 5TA.
WILLIAMS, Mr. Stanley Ross Wade, FCA *1958;* Leahurst Residential Home, 20 Upperthorpe, SHEFFIELD, S6 3NA. (Life Member)
WILLIAMS, Mr. Stefan James, MSc ACA *1999;* 28 The Spinney Bradley Stoke, BRISTOL, BS32 8ES.
WILLIAMS, Mr. Stephen, FCA *1986;* 27 Parkfield Avenue, East Sheen, LONDON, SW14 8DY.
WILLIAMS, Mr. Stephen, BSc ACA *1981;* 20 Hillmont, Hinchley Wood, ESHER, KT10 9BA.
WILLIAMS, Mr. Stephen, MPhil BA ACA *1983;* (Tax Fac), Step Cottage, The Street, Finglesham, DEAL, KENT, CT14 0NE.
WILLIAMS, Mr. Stephen Andrew, FCA *1977;* D S T L, North Court, Portsdown West, Portsdown Hill Road, FAREHAM, HAMPSHIRE PO17 6AD.
•WILLIAMS, Mr. Stephen Charles, BSc ACA *1993;* Deloitte LLP, 1 City Square, LEEDS, WEST YORKSHIRE, LS1 2AL. See also Deloitte & Touche LLP
WILLIAMS, Mr. Stephen Charles, ACA *1978;* Suite 629, 48 Par-La-Ville Road, HAMILTON HM11, BERMUDA.
WILLIAMS, Mr. Stephen Derek, BSc ACA *1984;* Gulf International Bank, P.O.Box 1017, MANAMA, BAHRAIN.
WILLIAMS, Mr. Stephen Lee, BSc ACA *1997;* Poole Farm Horse & Animal Feed Poole Farm, Poole Street Great Yeldham, HALSTEAD, CO9 4HP.
WILLIAMS, Mr. Stephen Lloyd, FCA *1966;* Le Bourg, 16450 BEAULIEU-SUR-SONNETTE, FRANCE. (Life Member)
•WILLIAMS, Mr. Stephen Lynn, BSc FCA *1977;* (Tax Fac), Sheppard Rockey & Williams Ltd, Sannerville Chase, Exminster, EXETER, EX6 8AT. See also Edwina Rockey
WILLIAMS, Mr. Stephen Norman, BSc FCA *1977;* Luxfer Holdings Plc, The Victoria 150-182 Harbour City The Quays, SALFORD, M50 3SP.
WILLIAMS, Mr. Stephen Paul, BEng FCA ACT *1993;* 130 Murray Avenue, BROMLEY, BR1 3DT.
WILLIAMS, Mr. Stephen Peter, BA ACA *1985;* PO Box 309, Ugland House, GEORGE TOWN, GRAND CAYMAN, KY1-1104, CAYMAN ISLANDS.
•WILLIAMS, Mr. Stephen Thomas, FCA *1985;* Langtons, The Plaza, 100 Old Hall Street, LIVERPOOL, L3 9QJ.
WILLIAMS, Mr. Stephen Thomas Quentin, MA FCA *1975;* 4 Christchurch Crescent, RADLETT, WD7 8AH.
WILLIAMS, Mr. Stephen Willis, BA FCA *1977;* Erlenweg 28, Postfach 610, 6390 ENGELBERG, SWITZERLAND.
•WILLIAMS, Mr. Steven Alan, BSc ACA *2003;* Murray Smith LLP, Darland House, 44 Winnington Hill, NORTHWICH, CHESHIRE, CW8 1AU.
WILLIAMS, Mr. Steven Alastair, MMath ACA *2005;* with Deloitte LLP, Athene Place, 66 Shoe Lane, LONDON, EC4A 3BQ.
WILLIAMS, Mr. Steven Anthony John, ACA *2008;* 82 Jacey Road, Shirley, SOLIHULL, WEST MIDLANDS, B90 3LN.
•WILLIAMS, Mr. Steven David, BSc FCA *1989;* S D Williams FCA BSc, 20 Manor Road, RICHMOND, SURREY, TW9 1YB.
WILLIAMS, Mr. Steven John, BSc ACA *2000;* 15 Hilton Grange Bramhope, LEEDS, LS16 9LE.
WILLIAMS, Mr. Steven John, BA(Hons) ACA *2001;* Bank Machine Ltd Unit 1, The Beacons, HATFIELD, HERTFORDSHIRE, AL10 8RS.
WILLIAMS, Mr. Steven John, BA ACA *1993;* 5 The Spindles, Mossley, ASHTON-UNDER-LYNE, LANCASHIRE, OL5 9SA.
•WILLIAMS, Mr. Steven Mark, ACA *2007;* Butterfield Morgan Limited, Druslyn House, De La Beche Street, SWANSEA, SA1 3HJ.
WILLIAMS, Mr. Steven Richard, ACA *2009;* 150 Princes Mews, ROYSTON, HERTFORDSHIRE, SG8 9BN.
WILLIAMS, Mr. Steven Wyn, BSc FCA *1976;* 199 Finchampstead Road, WOKINGHAM, RG40 3HE.
WILLIAMS, Mr. Stewart, BSc ACA *1981;* 7 Eaton Place, Hartford, NORTHWICH, CHESHIRE, CW8 2PW.
WILLIAMS, Mr. Stuart John, BSocSc FCA *1975;* 38 Greenfields Rd, KINGSWINFORD, DY6 8EW.
WILLIAMS, Mr. Stuart Joseph, BSc ACA *2002;* Flat 4, 1 Grosvenor Gardens, LONDON, N10 3TB.
WILLIAMS, Mr. Stuart Kenneth Mathieson, FCA *1966;* Topps Tiles Unit 1 Meridian Trading Estate, 22 Lombard Wall, LONDON, SE7 7SW.
WILLIAMS, Mr. Subesh Ronald, ACA *1987;* 254a Randolph Avenue, LONDON, W9 1PF.
WILLIAMS, Mrs. Susan, BA ACA *1990;* 48 Tewit Well Road, HARROGATE, HG2 8JJ.
WILLIAMS, Mrs. Susan Elizabeth, BSc ACA *1992;* 9 Orchard Way, Shapwick, BRIDGWATER, TA7 9NU.
WILLIAMS, Mrs. Susan Jane, BSc ACA *1988;* Faram, 132 Commercial Street, LONDON, E1 6AZ.
•WILLIAMS, Mrs. Suzanne, BSc FCA *1987;* (Tax Fac), 30 Westernlea, CREDITON, EX17 3JQ.
WILLIAMS, Miss. Tamsyn Victoria, BSc ACA *2005;* 42 Greenwood Drive, Angmering, LITTLEHAMPTON, WEST SUSSEX, BN16 4ND.
•WILLIAMS, Mr. Terence John, FCA *1980;* T J Medano Ltd, 12 Stonehill Close, Ranskill, RETFORD, DN22 8NG. See also Terry J. Williams & Co
WILLIAMS, Mr. Thomas, BA ACA *2010;* 94 Schooner Way, CARDIFF, CF10 4EQ.
WILLIAMS, Mr. Thomas Edward, BA ACA *2010;* 12c Dartmouth Road, LONDON, NW2 4EU.
WILLIAMS, Mr. Thomas Edward, ACA *2008;* The Home Delivery Co, Dabell Avenue Blenheim Industrial Estate Bulwell, NOTTINGHAM, NG6 8WA.
WILLIAMS, Mr. Thomas Mark, LLB ACA *2009;* Havering Cottage, 9 Michel Dene Road, East Dean, EASTBOURNE, EAST SUSSEX, BN20 0HP.
•WILLIAMS, Mr. Thomas Richard James, FCA *1959;* Williams & Co, Bramley Cottage, Town Row Green, Rotherfield, CROWBOROUGH, TN6 3QU.
WILLIAMS, Mr. Timothy Huw, BCom ACA *2002;* To be advised, PARIS, FRANCE.
WILLIAMS, Mr. Timothy James, MSc ACA *1982;* 31 Woodfields, Chipstead, SEVENOAKS, KENT, TN13 2RB.
WILLIAMS, Mr. Timothy Mark John, BA FCA *1996;* Manchester Football Club Ltd, Old Trafford, Sir Matt Busby Way, MANCHESTER, M16 0RA.
WILLIAMS, Mr. Tom David, BA ACA *2005;* 1 Astwood Grange Cottage, Astwood, NEWPORT PAGNELL, BUCKINGHAMSHIRE, MK16 9JT.
•WILLIAMS, Mrs. Tracey Marie, MEng ACA *1997;* 13 Overland Road, Langland, SWANSEA, SA3 4LS.
•WILLIAMS, Miss. Tracey Marie, BA FCA CF MBA MRICS MCMI MIC *1995;* Exigo Corporate Finance Limited, Suite 1, 42 Triangle West, Park St, BRISTOL, BS8 1ES. See also Burton Sweet Corporate Finance Limited
WILLIAMS, Mr. Trevor David, FCA *1962;* 1 Old Cross Wharf, HERTFORD, SG14 1RU.
WILLIAMS, Mr. Trevor John, BSc FCA *1979;* 38 Lakes Lane, NEWPORT PAGNELL, MK16 8HR.
WILLIAMS, Mr. Trevor John, FCA *1966;* Consolidated Services Ltd, P.O. Box HM 2257, HAMILTON HMJX, BERMUDA.
WILLIAMS, Miss. Trudi Louise Owen, BA ACA *1997;* 38 Allanson Road, Rhos on Sea, COLWYN BAY, CLWYD, LL28 4HL.
•WILLIAMS, Mr. Tudor Morgan, FCA *1975;* H & W Jones & Co., 81 Bridge Street, LAMPETER, SA48 7AB.
WILLIAMS, Mrs. Valerie Joyce, BA ACA *1993;* Hill Farm, Church Road, Grafham, HUNTINGDON, CAMBRIDGESHIRE, PE28 0BE.
•WILLIAMS, Mrs. Vanda Elaine, BSc ACA *1985;* (Tax Fac), Thorne Widgery Accountancy Ltd, 33 Bridge Street, HEREFORD, HR4 9DQ. See also TW Business Solutions LLP and Thorne Widgery & Jones LLP
WILLIAMS, Mr. Vernon Keith, FCA *1959;* 12 St. Marys Close, MERTHYR TYDFIL, CF47 8YS. (Life Member)
WILLIAMS, Miss. Vicki Anna, ACA *1997;* 16 St. Julians Close, SHOREHAM-BY-SEA, WEST SUSSEX, BN43 6LF.
WILLIAMS, Mrs. Wendy Sue, BA ACA ATII *1995;* Little Pengwern, Nant-y-Faenol Road, Rhuddlan, RHYL, CLWYD, LL18 5UL.
•WILLIAMS, Mr. William Alun, BSc FCA *1997;* W J James & Co Limited, Bishop House, 10 Wheat Street, BRECON, LD3 7DG.
WILLIAMS, Mr. William David, FCA *1955;* Shearwater, Perranuthnoe, PENZANCE, TR20 9NR. (Life Member)
•WILLIAMS, Mr. William David, FCA *1975;* (Tax Fac), R. Sutton & Co, 25 Park Street, MACCLESFIELD, SK11 6SS.
WILLIAMS, Mr. William David Laurie, BSc FCA *1977;* The Green, 60 Green Lane, Burnham, SLOUGH, SL1 8EB.
WILLIAMS, Mr. William Fredrick, FCA *1952;* 1 Westwood Drive, Brooklands, SALE, M33 3QZ. (Life Member)
WILLIAMS, Mr. Winston Guinness Andrew, ACA *2001;* 12 Park Road, HUNSTANTON, PE36 5BP.
WILLIAMS-ALLDEN, Mr. David, FCA *1969;* Dalegarth, Tanwood Lane, Bluntington, Chaddesley Corbett, KIDDERMINSTER, DY10 4NR.
WILLIAMS-BAFFOE, Mrs. Phyllis, BA ACA *1993;* 38 Cranleigh Gardens, KINGSTON UPON THAMES, KT2 5TX.
WILLIAMS-FREEMAN, Mr. Derek Robeert Peere, FCA *1965;* 903 Howard House, Dolphin Square, LONDON, SW1V 3PQ. (Life Member)
WILLIAMSON, Mr. Alexander Patrick, BA(Hons) ACA *2000;* The Goodwood Estate Co Ltd, Goodwood, CHICHESTER, WEST SUSSEX, PO18 0PX.
WILLIAMSON, Miss. Amy Louise, BA(Hons) ACA *2010;* The Old Coach House Hatton Green, Hatton, WARWICK, CV35 7LA.
WILLIAMSON, Mr. Andrew Gordon, BSc ACA *1984;* Flat 20-02, Ardmore II, 1 Ardmore Park, SINGAPORE 259962, SINGAPORE.
•WILLIAMSON, Mr. Andrew Lawrence, BA ACA *1993;* Williamson Morton Thornton LLP, 47 Holywell Hill, ST. ALBANS, HERTFORDSHIRE, AL1 1HD.
WILLIAMSON, Mr. Andrew Miles, BA ACA *1989;* Mercedes Benz UK Ltd, Delaware Drive, Tongwell, MILTON KEYNES, MK15 8BA.
WILLIAMSON, Mr. Andrew Peter, BMus ACA *2004;* with Nyman Libson Paul, Regina House, 124 Finchley Road, LONDON, NW3 5JS.
WILLIAMSON, Mr. Andrew Stuart, BA FCA *1974;* (Tax Fac), 12 Greenhill Road, BURY, BL8 2LJ.
WILLIAMSON, Mr. Ben, ACA *2011;* 72 Saltwell Road South, GATESHEAD, TYNE AND WEAR, NE9 6HA.
WILLIAMSON, Mr. Benjamin George Frederick, BEng ACA *2005;* 31 Juniper Avenue, Woodlesford, LEEDS, LS26 8WP.
WILLIAMSON, Ms. Catherine Anne, BA ACA *1984;* I N G Bank NV, 60 London Wall, LONDON, EC2M 5TQ.
WILLIAMSON, Mr. Christian Andreas, BA(Hons) ACA *2003;* 5c Kidbrooke Park Road, LONDON, SE3 0LR.
WILLIAMSON, Mr. Christopher John, BA FCA *1980;* Kingswood Consultancy, Kingsview, Beachley Road, Tutshill, CHEPSTOW, GWENT NP16 7BH.
WILLIAMSON, Mr. Christopher John, FCA *1984;* (Tax Fac), Satis House, Mill Hill, Ellerker, BROUGH, HU15 2DG.
WILLIAMSON, Mr. Christopher John, BA ACA *2006;* 22 Silverdale Avenue, LEEDS, LS17 8SZ.
WILLIAMSON, Mr. Clive, FCA *1958;* 5 Broadwater Road, WALTON-ON-THAMES, KT12 5DB. (Life Member)
WILLIAMSON, Mr. Darryl Andrew, FCA *1977;* 14 Gorsey Way, ASHTON-UNDER-LYNE, OL6 9HT.
WILLIAMSON, Mr. David Alexander, BSc ACA *2005;* Benefield, Woodhall Lane, ASCOT, SL5 9QW.
WILLIAMSON, Mr. David Andrew, BSc FCA *1991;* William Grant & Sons Limited, Phoenix Crescent, Strathclyde Business Park, BELLSHILL, LANARKSHIRE, ML4 3AN.
WILLIAMSON, Mr. Donald Gordon, FCA *1963;* 25 Christchurch Road, East Sheen, LONDON, SW14 7AB. (Life Member)
WILLIAMSON, Mr. Duncan Alexander, ACA *2008;* Flat 4, 182 Sutherland Avenue, LONDON, W9 1HR.
WILLIAMSON, Mr. Edward David, BSc FCA *1969;* Kiplings, Upper Lane, Brighstone, NEWPORT, PO30 4BA.
WILLIAMSON, Dr. Gavin, BEng ACA *2003;* with Deloitte LLP, Athene Place, 66 Shoe Lane, LONDON, EC4A 3BQ.
WILLIAMSON, Mr. Gilbert John, BSc FCA *1976;* 18 Pine Copse Close, Duston, NORTHAMPTON, NN5 6NF.
WILLIAMSON, Miss. Hannah, BSc ACA *1999;* Lant Close Farm, 40 Bolehill Road, Bolehill, MATLOCK, DERBYSHIRE, DE4 4GQ.
WILLIAMSON, Mr. Iain, BA FCA *2000;* Wood Hall Farm Office, Woodhall Lane, SHENLEY, HERTFORDSHIRE, WD7 9AA.
WILLIAMSON, Mr. Ian Gordon Mcpherson, FCA *1966;* 4 Heathfield, COBHAM, SURREY, KT11 2QY. (Life Member)
WILLIAMSON, Mr. James, FCA *1957;* Ebenezer Cottage, Crawhall, BRAMPTON, CA8 1TR. (Life Member)
WILLIAMSON, Mr. James Lindsay Neil, FCA *1954;* 30 Tatachilla Road, MCLAREN VALE, SA 5171, AUSTRALIA. (Life Member)
WILLIAMSON, Mr. James Stephen, FCA *1972;* Reilth Top, Bishops Moat, BISHOPS CASTLE, SHROPSHIRE, SY9 5LL.
•WILLIAMSON, Mr. Jeffrey, BA FCA *1994;* Townends Accountants Limited, Fulford Lodge, 1 Heslington Lane, YORK, YO10 4HW. See also Townends
WILLIAMSON, Mrs. Jennifer Catherine, ACA *2008;* 8 High Street Eastry, SANDWICH, KENT, CT13 0HF.
WILLIAMSON, Mr. Jeremy Paul, BA FCA *1983;* Nunthorpe, Jesmond Park East, NEWCASTLE UPON TYNE, NE7 7BT.
WILLIAMSON, Miss. Joanne Louise, BA ACA *1999;* 14 Birkhill Crescent, Birkenshaw, BRADFORD, WEST YORKSHIRE, BD11 2LJ.
WILLIAMSON, Mr. John David, FCA *1963;* Flat 11 St Edmunds Apartments, Lower Baxter Street, BURY ST.EDMUNDS, IP33 1EF.
•WILLIAMSON, Mr. John Michael Joseph, BSc FCA *1974;* 11 Woodmere, LUTON, LU3 4DL.
•WILLIAMSON, Mr. John Stuart, FCA *1974;* (Tax Fac), J.S. Williamson & Co, Suite F20, Twyford House, Garner Street, STOKE-ON-TRENT, ST4 7AY. See also JSW Accounting Services Limited
•WILLIAMSON, Mr. Jon Adam, ACA *1994;* (Tax Fac), Levicks, West Hill, 61 London Road, MAIDSTONE, ME16 8TX. See also Somerfield Consultants Limited
WILLIAMSON, Mrs. Jonquil, BA ACA *1992;* 11 Percival Road, East Sheen, LONDON, SW14 7QE.
WILLIAMSON, Mrs. Joyce Elizabeth, BA ACA *1987;* with RSM Tenon Limited, Arkwright House, Parsonage Gardens, MANCHESTER, M3 2LF.
WILLIAMSON, Mrs. Julie Elizabeth, ACA *1987;* 17 Southam Drive, SUTTON COLDFIELD, WEST MIDLANDS, B73 5PD.
WILLIAMSON, Miss. Karen, MA ACA *2007;* 37 Calthorpe Street, LIVERPOOL, L19 1RE.
WILLIAMSON, Mr. Keith Andrew, LLB ACA *1999;* 20 North Audley Street, LONDON, W1K 6WE.

•**WILLIAMSON, Mr. Keith John, FCA** *1973;* Bell Tindle Williamson LLP, The Old Post Office, 63 Saville Street, NORTH SHIELDS, TYNE AND WEAR, NE30 1AY. See also BTW LLP and Bell Tindle Williamson Services Limited
•**WILLIAMSON, Mr. Kenneth Andrew, BA ACA** *1991;* Ernst & Young LLP, 100 Barbirolli Square, MANCHESTER, M2 3EY. See also Ernst & Young Europe LLP
•**WILLIAMSON, Mr. Kenneth Grant, BA FCA** *1992;* Ernst & Young LLP, 1 More London Place, LONDON, SE1 2AF. See also Ernst & Young Europe LLP
WILLIAMSON, Mr. Kevin, MMath ACA *2007;* 30 Trent Road, DIDCOT, OXFORDSHIRE, OX11 7RD.
WILLIAMSON, Mr. Mark, BA ACA *1999;* 30 Lartonwood, WIRRAL, MERSEYSIDE, CH48 9YG.
WILLIAMSON, Mr. Mark Andrew, MA ACA *1990;* 26 Lady Menzies Place, EDINBURGH, EH7 4BA.
WILLIAMSON, Mr. Mark James, PhD BSc ACA *2001;* 29 Wheatfield Lane, Haxby, YORK, YO32 2YX.
WILLIAMSON, Mr. Martin Grant, BA ACA *1983;* Flat 9 Branksome Chase 82 Penn Hill Avenue, POOLE, BH14 9NA.
WILLIAMSON, Mr. Martin John, FCA *1973;* (Tax Fac), Atrium Underwriting Plc, Room 790, Lloyds Building, 1 Lime Street, LONDON, EC3M 7DQ.
WILLIAMSON, Mr. Mervyn John, BSc ACA *1991;* 71 Park Road, Chiswick, LONDON, W4 3EY.
WILLIAMSON, Mr. Michael Frank, BSc ACA *1982;* 38 Roehampton Gate, LONDON, SW15 5JS.
WILLIAMSON, Mr. Michael John, ACA *1990;* Encore Envelopes Ltd, Wessyngton House, Industrial Road, Hertburn, WASHINGTON, TYNE AND WEAR NE37 2SA.
•**WILLIAMSON, Mr. Michael Newton, FCA** *1966;* (Tax Fac), Williamsons, Rosewood, Raemoir Road, BANCHORY, KINCARDINESHIRE, AB31 4ET.
WILLIAMSON, Mr. Michael Paul, FCA *1975;* Meadow House, Old End, Padbury, BUCKINGHAM, MK18 2BB.
WILLIAMSON, Mr. Michael Robert, MSc ACA *2010;* 81 Chamberlayne Road, EASTLEIGH, SO50 5JJ.
WILLIAMSON, Miss. Nathalie Charlotte, BA FCA *1997;* Garden Flat, 71 Lime Grove, LONDON, W12 8EE.
WILLIAMSON, Mr. Neil Roger, BEng ACA *2001;* Aberdeen Asset Management Plc, 1 Bow Churchyard, LONDON, EC4M 9HH.
WILLIAMSON, Mr. Nicholas David, BA FCA *1989;* 20 Devonshire Crescent, Douglas, ISLE OF MAN, IM2 3RD.
WILLIAMSON, Mr. Paul John, BSc FCA CTA *1986;* 4 Potter Close, New Oscott, BIRMINGHAM, B23 5YU.
WILLIAMSON, Mr. Paul Merrick, MA ACA *1996;* 35 Green Lane, PURLEY, SURREY, CR8 3PQ.
WILLIAMSON, Mr. Paul Ronald, BA ACA *1996;* 25, Camberton Road, LEIGHTON BUZZARD, LU7 2UN.
•**WILLIAMSON, Mr. Paul Tordoff, BSc FCA** *1982;* Deloitte LLP, One Trinity Gardens, Broad Chare, NEWCASTLE UPON TYNE, NE1 2HF. See also Deloitte & Touche LLP
•**WILLIAMSON, Mrs. Pauline Clare, BSc ACA** *1990;* (Tax Fac), Kirkpatrick & Hopes Ltd, Overdene House, 49 Church Street, Theale, READING, RG7 5BX.
•①**WILLIAMSON, Mr. Richard Ian, BA ACA FABRP** *1986;* Campbell Crossley & Davis, 348/350 Lytham Road, BLACKPOOL, FY4 1DW. See also Crossley & Davis
WILLIAMSON, Mr. Richard John, MA FCA *1977;* 9 High Street, Witcham, ELY, CB6 2LQ.
WILLIAMSON, Mr. Richard John, MA ACA *2004;* Brit Insurance, 55 Bishopsgate, LONDON, EC2N 3AS.
WILLIAMSON, Mr. Robert Douglas, BSc FCA *1975;* 35 Treves Road, DORCHESTER, DORSET, DT1 2HE.
WILLIAMSON, Mr. Robert Ian, BSc ACA *1994;* 1157 S. 7th Street, PHILADELPHIA, PA 19147, UNITED STATES.
WILLIAMSON, Mr. Robert Ian, BA(Hons) ACA *2002;* Cougar Leisure Chorley Business & Technology Centre, East Terrace Euxton Lane Euxton, CHORLEY, PR7 6TE.
WILLIAMSON, Miss. Sarah Penelope, ACA *2004;* Apartment 4, 173 Palatine Road, MANCHESTER, M20 2GH.
WILLIAMSON, Mr. Stephen, BA ACA *1992;* 93 Adams Street, LEXINGTON, MA 02420, UNITED STATES.
WILLIAMSON, Mr. Stephen, BSc ACA *2011;* 7 Mayfield Road, Grappenhall, WARRINGTON, WA4 2NP.
•**WILLIAMSON, Mr. Stuart, FCA** *1972;* (Tax Fac), Williamson West, 10 Langdale Gate, WITNEY, OX28 6EX.
•**WILLIAMSON, Mr. Stuart Alexander, FCA** *1973;* AIMS - Stuart A Williamson FCA, 8 Sydney Grove, LONDON, NW4 2EH.
WILLIAMSON, Mr. Stuart Alexander, BSc ACA AMCT *1991;* Number 102, Mail Boxes Etc, 80 High Street, WINCHESTER, SO23 9AT.
WILLIAMSON, Mr. Thomas, FCA *1967;* Cultram Holme, Main Street, Abbey Town, WIGTON, CA7 4SR.
•**WILLIAMSON, Mr. Timothy John Graham, FCA** *1968;* Tim Williamson, WG Hospitality (SA) cc, PO Box 53, ST LUCIA, KWAZULU NATAL, 3936 SOUTH AFRICA.
WILLIAMSON-CARY, Mr. Martin Howard, BA ACA *1992;* Headson Farm, Bratton Clovelly, OKEHAMPTON, DEVON, EX20 4JP.
WILLIAMSON-JONES, Mrs. Isobel Mary, BCom ACA *1996;* Wades House, Barton Stacey, WINCHESTER, SO21 3RJ.
•**WILLIES, Mr. Geoffrey David, BSc FCA** *1969;* (Tax Fac), Charles Marcus Limited, 42 Brook Street, LONDON, W1K 5DB. See also Marcus Charles
WILLIFER, Mr. Brian Lester John, FCA *1963;* Woodleigh, Horley Lodge Lane, REDHILL, RH1 5EA.
•**WILLIMER, Mr. Nigel David, FCA** *1973;* (Tax Fac), WKH, PO Box 501, The Nexus Building, Broadway, LETCHWORTH GARDEN CITY, HERTFORDSHIRE SG6 9BL. See also Virtual Business Source Limited
WILLIMOTT, Mr. Richard Andrew, BEng ACA *2010;* 32 Norton Road, STOKE-SUB-HAMDON, SOMERSET, TA14 6QW.
WILLING, Mr. Jeremy George, FCA *1958;* Neilson Lodge, Mill Wynd, HADDINGTON, EH41 4DB. (Life Member)
WILLING, Mr. Justin Dryden, BA(Hons) ACA *2004;* Firth Rixson Limited, Firth House, P.O. Box 644, Meadowhall Road, SHEFFIELD, S9 1JD.
WILLING, Mr. Paul James, BSc ACA *1992;* Monte Bello, Le Vieux Beaumont, St. Peter, JERSEY, JE3 7EA.
WILLINGHAM, Mr. David, FCA *1962;* 22 York Road, Gee Cross, HYDE, SK14 5JH.
WILLINGHAM, Mr. David Fraser, BA ACA *1998;* 11 Lichfield Road, LONDON, E3 5AT.
WILLINGS, Mr. Malcolm Robert Thomson, FCA *1960;* Rudloe, Church Lane, Ewshot, FARNHAM, GU10 5BD. (Life Member)
WILLINGTON, Mr. James Stephen Peter, MA ACA *2002;* Gagosian Gallery, 6 - 24 Britannia Street, LONDON, WC1X 9JD.
WILLINGTON, Mrs. Victoria Mary, BA(Hons) ACA *2002;* Judges Court Police Row Therfield, ROYSTON, HERTFORDSHIRE, SG8 9QE.
WILLINS, Mr. Gordon Steven, BCom ACA *1989;* Manapia, Strathkinness Low Road, ST ANDREWS, FIFE, KY16 9NG.
WILLIS, Mr. Alan Douglas, FCA *1965;* Alan Willis & Associates, 1889 Truscott Drive, MISSISSAUGA L5J 2A1, ON, CANADA.
WILLIS, Mr. Alan Raymond, FCA *1955;* River Cottage, 171 Ewen, CIRENCESTER, GL7 6BT. (Life Member)
WILLIS, Miss. Amelia, MPhys ACA *2010;* 278 Heathfield Drive, MITCHAM, SURREY, CR4 3RJ.
WILLIS, Mr. Andrew Richard, MMath ACA *2010;* 40 Axial Drive, COLCHESTER, CO4 5RY.
WILLIS, Mr. Andrew Robert, MEng ACA *1999;* Protiviti Inc., 711 Louisiana Suite 1200, HOUSTON, TX 77006, UNITED STATES.
WILLIS, Mrs. Angela Jane, BSc ACA *1982;* Linthwaite, Bailiffs Cross Road, St. Andrew, GUERNSEY, GY6 8SA.
WILLIS, Mr. Bernard John Christian, BSc ACA *1983;* North House, 27 Great Peter Street, LONDON, SW1P 3LN.
WILLIS, Mrs. Caroline, BSc ACA *2004;* 59 Woolgreaves Drive, Sandal, WAKEFIELD, WEST YORKSHIRE, WF2 6DS.
WILLIS, Mrs. Caroline Elizabeth, FCA *1974;* 29 Sunnybank, Woodcote, EPSOM, SURREY, KT18 7DY.
WILLIS, Mr. Christopher James Percival, FCA *1956;* Stickle Ghyll, One Berry Close, Langdon Hills, BASILDON, ESSEX, SS16 6BZ. (Life Member)
WILLIS, Mr. Darren Vaughan, BA ACA *1992;* 21 Betchworth Avenue, Earley, READING, RG6 7RH.
WILLIS, Mr. David Michael, ACA *1981;* Naivasha, Brook Lane, Botley, SOUTHAMPTON, SO30 2ER.
WILLIS, Mr. Denis George, BSS ACA *1991;* Total Fabrications Ltd, Units 1-6, Kingston Industrial Estate, 81-86 Glover Street, BIRMINGHAM, B9 4EN.
WILLIS, Mrs. Gemma Claire, BSc(Hons) ACA *2009;* 46 Wagtail Road, WATERLOOVILLE, HAMPSHIRE, PO8 9YD.
WILLIS, Mr. Geoffrey, FCA *1975;* 29 Sunny Bank, Woodcote, EPSOM, KT18 7DY. (Life Member)
WILLIS, Mr. Grant Alistair, BA ACA *1994;* 12 Wellhead Lane, WESTBURY, WILTSHIRE, BA13 3PW.
WILLIS, Miss. Helen Margaret, BSc ACA *1992;* 2 Merrow Road, SUTTON, SURREY, SM2 7LU.
WILLIS, Mr. John Anthony, ACA MAAT *1996;* Femcare Nikomed Ltd, Stuart Court, Spursholt Place, Salisbury Road, ROMSEY, HAMPSHIRE SO51 6DJ.
•**WILLIS, Mr. John Darrell, BA FCA** *1982;* Murrells, Cedar House, 41 Thorpe Road, NORWICH, NR1 1ES. See also Calum Ward & Co Limited
•**WILLIS, Mr. John Howard, LLB FCA** *1972;* 69 St. Johns Hill, Shenstone, LICHFIELD, STAFFORDSHIRE, WS14 0JE.
WILLIS, Mr. Jonathan Paul, BSc ACA *1997;* 35-37 South Corporate Avenue, ROWVILLE, VIC 3178, AUSTRALIA.
WILLIS, Mrs. Karen Laurel, MA FCA GradICSA *1987;* Northampton High School, Newport Pagnell Road, Hardingstone, NORTHAMPTON, NN4 6UU.
•**WILLIS, Mr. Keith Andrew, BA FCA** *1990;* Keith Willis Associates Limited, Gothic House, Barker Gate, NOTTINGHAM, NG1 1JU.
WILLIS, Mr. Keith Charles, BA FCA *1986;* Prestbury, Quarry Road, OXTED, RH8 9HF.
WILLIS, Mrs. Lara, BSc ACA *2003;* 12 Walnut Ridge Lane, STAMFORD, CT 06905, UNITED STATES.
WILLIS, Miss. Lynne Marie, LLB DipLP ACA *1999;* 10 Mount Road, LONDON, SW19 8ET.
WILLIS, Mr. Mark Andrew, MA FCA MCT *1983;* Mawsley Wood House, Mawsley WoodFaxton Turn, Old, NORTHAMPTON, NN6 9RN.
WILLIS, Mr. Mark William, BA(Hons) ACA *2001;* Vanguard Investments, Level 34, Freshwater Place, 2 Southbank Boulevard, MELBOURNE, VIC 3006 AUSTRALIA.
WILLIS, Mr. Martin Alexander, BSc(Hons) ACA *2001;* 2 Plover Close, STRATFORD-UPON-AVON, CV37 9EN.
WILLIS, Mr. Martin John, FCA *1980;* Laserline Dies Ltd, 6 Northumberland Court, Dukes Park Ind Est, CHELMSFORD, CM2 6UW.
WILLIS, Mr. Michael William, FCA *1975;* 2 Cymbeline Court, The Lawns, Mount Pleasant, ST. ALBANS, HERTFORDSHIRE, AL3 4TZ.
WILLIS, Mr. Neil, BSc ACA *1986;* 13 Village Close, Belsize Lane, LONDON, NW3 5AH.
•**WILLIS, Mr. Nicholas John, FCA** *1984;* George Hay, Brigham House, 93 High Street, BIGGLESWADE, BEDFORDSHIRE, SG18 0LD. See also GH Online Accounting Ltd
•**WILLIS, Mr. Nigel Jaques, BA ACA** *1997;* Deloitte LLP, Hill House, 1 Little New Street, LONDON, EC4A 3TR. See also Deloitte & Touche LLP
WILLIS, Mr. Oliver John, Beng ACA *2010;* Anacap Financial Partners, 25 Bedford Street, LONDON, WC2E 9ES.
WILLIS, Mrs. Pamela Barbara, LLB ACA *1991;* 13 Village Close, Belsize Lane, LONDON, NW3 5AH.
•**WILLIS, Mrs. Patricia, FCA** *1962;* (Tax Fac), P. Furmston & Co, Longburgh Farmhouse, Burgh by Sands, CARLISLE, CA5 6AF.
•**WILLIS, Mr. Paul Nigel, BA ACA** *1986;* with Burton Sweet, Pembroke House, 15 Pembroke Road, Clifton, BRISTOL, BS8 3BA.
WILLIS, Mr. Peter Garrett, BSc ACA *1993;* 4 Hither Green, Southbourne, EMSWORTH, PO10 8JA.
WILLIS, Mrs. Rachael Anne, ACA *1996;* Premier Holidays Ltd, Westbrook, Milton Road, CAMBRIDGE, CB4 1YG.
WILLIS, Miss. Rachel, BA ACA *2007;* Cherry Tree Cottage Angel Yard, High Street, MARLBOROUGH, SN8 1AG.
WILLIS, Mrs. Rachel Sarah, BA ACA CTA *2002;* with MJ Brooks Consultancy Limited, 9 Waterside, Station Road, HARPENDEN, HERTFORDSHIRE, AL5 4US.
WILLIS, Mrs. Rebecca, BA(Hons) ACA ACCA *2002;* 23 Helmton Road, Woodseats, SHEFFIELD, S8 8QJ.
•**WILLIS, Mr. Richard John, BSc ACA** *1991;* ECA Accounting Services, 78 Shirley Way, Shirley, CROYDON, CR0 8PB. See also Chantrey Vellacott DFK LLP
WILLIS, Mr. Robert Ian, BA FCA *1973;* 402 Buxton Road, MACCLESFIELD, SK11 7EP.
WILLIS, Mr. Roger Edward, FCA *1961;* 94 Downscourt Road, PURLEY, CR8 1BD. (Life Member)
WILLIS, Mrs. Roxana, ACA *2008;* 8 Ivy Road, SUTTON COLDFIELD, B73 5ED.
WILLIS, Miss. Sarah, BSc ACA *2011;* Flat 39, Sandhurst Court, Acre Lane, LONDON, SW2 5TX.
WILLIS, Miss. Sarah Louise, ACA *2009;* 4 The Hermitage, LONDON, SW13 9RF.
WILLIS, Mr. Simon James Millington, BSc ACA *1983;* 101 Pipers Lane, Heswall, WIRRAL, CH60 9HR.
WILLIS, Mr. Simon John, BA FCA *1994;* 3 The Hollows, Elburton, PLYMOUTH, PL9 8TX.
WILLIS, Mr. Stephen David, BSc ACA *2005;* 1 Police Houses, Kerries Road, SOUTH BRENT, DEVON, TQ10 9BZ.
WILLIS, Mr. Thomas Michael, BA ACA *1991;* Elmhurst, Wick Lane, DEVIZES, SN10 5DW.
•**WILLIS, Mrs. Victoria Angela, ACA** *1992;* (Tax Fac), Joy Mining Machinery Ltd, Meco Works, Bromyard Rd, WORCESTER, WR2 5EG.
•**WILLIS, Mr. William Alan, FCA** *1971;* W A Willis Ltd, Wyre Hill Cottage, Buildwas, TELFORD, SHROPSHIRE, TF8 7BX. See also WILLIS
WILLIS, Miss. Zoe Catherine, MA ACA *1988;* Overdale, Glasshouses, HARROGATE, NORTH YORKSHIRE, HG3 5QY.
WILLITS, Mr. Giles Kirkley, BA ACA *1992;* 10 Moreton End Lane, HARPENDEN, AL5 2EX.
WILLITTS, Mr. Peter James, ACA *1979;* Liberty Mutual Management Bermuda, Maxwell Robert Building, 4th Floor, P.O. Box HM 2455, HAMILTON HM JX, BERMUDA.
WILLMAN, Mr. David, MChem ACA *2004;* 13 Sydney Grove, LONDON, NW4 2EJ.
•①**WILLMONT, Mr. Jeremy Mark, BA FCA** *1994;* Moore Stephens LLP, 150 Aldersgate Street, LONDON, EC1A 4AB. See also Moore Stephens & Co
WILLMOT, Mrs. Helen Elizabeth Marian, BSc ACA *2007;* Tarawara Church Road, Alpington, NORWICH, NR14 7NU.
WILLMOT, Mr. John Nicholas, LLB ACA *2003;* with PricewaterhouseCoopers LLP, The Atrium, St. Georges Street, NORWICH, NR3 1AG.
•**WILLMOTT, Mr. Allan, FCA** *1974;* Allan Willmott, Bramley, Farthings Hill, HORSHAM, WEST SUSSEX, RH12 1TS.
WILLMOTT, Mr. Colin Morris, FCA *1949;* 12 Furness Road, EASTBOURNE, BN21 4EY. (Life Member)
WILLMOTT, Mrs. Elisabeth Sarah, BSc ACA *1992;* 92 West Street, HENLEY-ON-THAMES, OXFORDSHIRE, RG9 2EA.
WILLMOTT, Mr. George Horace, FCA *1973;* 51 Elms Crescent, Clapham Park, LONDON, SW4 8QE. (Life Member)
•**WILLMOTT, Mr. John Martin, LLB FCA** *1974;* (Tax Fac), BDO LLP, 55 Baker Street, LONDON, W1U 7EU. See also BDO Stoy Hayward LLP
•**WILLMOTT, Mr. Kevin Nash Knight, BSc FCA** *1978;* 6 Parc y Fro, Creigiau, CARDIFF, CF15 9SA.
WILLMOTT, Miss. Lorna Margaret, BA ACA *1986;* Bodrane Farmhouse, Herodsfoot, LISKEARD, PL14 4QU.
WILLMOTT, Mr. Matthew David, MSc ACA *2011;* 5 South Wing, Mansion House, Devington Park, Exminster, EXETER, EX6 8UJ.
WILLMOTT, Mr. Peter John, FCA *1956;* 5 Yeomanry Court, MARKET HARBOROUGH, LEICESTERSHIRE, LE16 9BL. (Life Member)
WILLMOTT, Mr. Richard George Greville, BA FCA *1971;* Fontaine House, Fontaine David, Alderney, GUERNSEY, GY9 3XL.
WILLMOTT, Mr. Robert William, LLB ACA *2004;* 37 High Street, Higham Ferrers, RUSHDEN, NORTHAMPTONSHIRE, NN10 8DD.
WILLOCK, Mrs. Paula Jayne, ACA *1996;* B D O Stoy Hayward Emerald House, East Street, EPSOM, KT17 1HS.
WILLOCK, Mr. Thomas Michael, BA ACA *1995;* 41 Poplar Avenue, WINDLESHAM, SURREY, GU20 6PW.
WILLOTT, Mr. David John, BA(Hons) ACA *2011;* 8 Morlais, Emmer Green, READING, RG4 8PQ.
WILLOTT, Mr. Justin Matthew, BA ACA *1996;* Gartmore Investment Management Ltd, Gartmore House, 8 Fenchurch Place, LONDON, EC3M 4PB.
WILLOTT, Mr. Nicholas Christian, MA FCA *1995;* 32 Burnside, ST. ALBANS, HERTFORDSHIRE, AL1 5RS.
WILLOTT, Mr. Robert Graham, FCA *1965;* The Old Royal Oak, High Street, Blockley, MORETON-IN-MARSH, GLOUCESTERSHIRE, GL56 9EX.
WILLOTT, Mr. Roger de Quetteville, MA ACA *1986;* (Tax Fac), 29 Beechwood Avenue, Kew, RICHMOND, TW9 4DD.
WILLOUGHBY, Mr. Andrew James, BA ACA ACII *1991;* FRD, 14 Castle Street, LIVERPOOL, Pl11 3AA.
WILLOUGHBY, Ms. Catherine Anne, MA ACA *2001;* 101 Greenside Road, LONDON, W12 9JQ.
WILLOUGHBY, Mrs. Gillian Sara, ACA *1980;* The Old Lodge, Haresfield, STONEHOUSE, GL10 3DX.
•**WILLOUGHBY, Mr. Ian, BA FCA** *1987;* P.P.S., 29 Devizes Road, SWINDON, SN1 4BG.

WILLOUGHBY, Mr. Martin John, FCA *1960;* 5901 Mount Eagle Drive, #306, ALEXANDRIA, VA 22303, UNITED STATES. (Life Member)
WILLOUGHBY, Mr. Paul Michael, BA ACA *1992;* 5 Solent Drive, Warsash, SOUTHAMPTON, SO31 9HB.
WILLOUGHBY, Mr. Peter George, BSc FCA *1976;* The Old Lodge, Haresfield, STONEHOUSE, GL10 3DX.
WILLOUGHBY, Mr. Philip John, OBE FCA *1964;* 28 Valley Road, RICKMANSWORTH, HERTFORDSHIRE, WD3 4DS.
•**WILLOUGHBY, Mr. Richard George Wilmshurst, MSc FCA DChA** *1988;* Richard Willoughby, 3 Ashlands Grove, Harpfields, STOKE-ON-TRENT, ST4 6QU.
WILLOUGHBY, Mr. Steven John, BSc ACA CTA *1985;* Zborovska 60/84, 150 00 PRAGUE, CZECH REPUBLIC.
WILLOUGHBY, Mrs. Susan, BA ACA *1980;* Little Deeracres, Bisterne Close, Burley, RINGWOOD, HAMPSHIRE, BH24 4BA.
WILLOWS, Mr. Christopher John Wallace, BA FCA *1972;* 2 Eastbourne Terrace, LONDON, W2 6LG.
•**WILLOWS, Mr. Derek Frank, FCA** *1968;* (Tax Fac), Derek Willows Ltd, 7 Priory Gate, SHEFFORD, BEDFORDSHIRE, SG17 5TX.
WILLOWS, Mr. George Foster, FCA *1963;* 348 Mauldeth Road West, Chorlton, MANCHESTER, M21 7RB.
WILLOX, Mrs. Heidi Brigitte, BA ACA *1998;* 195 Russell Road, Moseley, BIRMINGHAM, B13 8RR.
WILLOX, Mr. Henry Steven, FCA *1973;* Mott MacDonald Group Ltd, 8 Sydenham Road, CROYDON, CR0 2EE.
WILLS, Mr. Andrew Clive, BA ACA *1990;* 9 Hammersmith Close, Radcliffe-on-Trent, NOTTINGHAM, NG12 2NQ.
WILLS, Mr. Anthony Ivor Mckay, ACA *1978;* 34 Bridgewater Drive, Great Glen, LEICESTER, LE8 9DX.
WILLS, Mr. Brian, FCA *1955;* Dunnerdale, Allerston, PICKERING, YO18 7PG. (Life Member)
WILLS, Mr. Christopher Neil, BSc ACA *2005;* Moore Management Limited, Ground Floor Liberation House Castle Street, ST HELIER, JE2 3AT.
WILLS, Mrs. Claire Deborah, ACA *2003;* 1 Old Sopwell Gardens, ST. ALBANS, HERTFORDSHIRE, AL1 2BY.
WILLS, Mrs. Claire Emma, BSc(Hons) ACA *2004;* 28 Grange Road, EAST COWES, ISLE OF WIGHT, PO32 6DZ.
WILLS, Mr. David John, BSc ACA *1993;* Hindenburgstrasse 35, 64295 DARMSTADT, GERMANY.
WILLS, Miss. Deborah, BSc ACA *2003;* Flat G/3, 53 Mansionhouse Gardens, GLASGOW, G41 3DP.
•**WILLS, Mrs. Jane, MA FCA** *1991;* Haines Watts, Sterling House, 177-181 Farnham Road, SLOUGH, BERKSHIRE, SL1 4XP. See also Haines Watts Slough LLP
WILLS, Mr. Jeffrey Gilbert, BCom FCA *1968;* Accounts Department, Salvation Army International Headquarters, 101 Queen Victoria Street, LONDON, EC4V 4EH.
WILLS, Mrs. Jessica Ruth, BA ACA *2006;* with Littlejohn, 1 Westferry Circus, Canary Wharf, LONDON, E14 4HD.
WILLS, Miss. Joanna Jane McKay, ACA *2005;* 3 The Crescent, Stretton Road Great Glen, LEICESTER, LE8 9HD.
WILLS, John Robert, Esq OBE FCA *1959;* White Scaur, Bassenthwaite, KESWICK, CA12 4RL. (Life Member)
WILLS, Mr. John Roy, BA ACA *1986;* The Dower House, Forty Hill, ENFIELD, EN2 9EJ.
WILLS, Mr. Jonathan, BSc ACA *1993;* Sumitomo Mitsui Banking Corporation Ltd, 99 Queen Victoria Street, LONDON, EC4V 4EH.
•**WILLS, Mr. Julian Charles, BA ACA MCT** *1998;* Julian Wills, 25 Carlyle Street, BRIGHTON, BN2 9XU. See also Wills
WILLS, Miss. Katharine Jane, BSc ACA *2002;* Vodafone Group Plc, Vodafone House, The Connection, NEWBURY, BERKSHIRE, RG14 2FN.
WILLS, Mr. Kevin Robert, BSc ACA *1996;* 1 Hartley Avenue, WHITLEY BAY, TYNE AND WEAR, NE26 3NS.
•**WILLS, Mrs. Lesley Jane, FCA ATII MAE QDR TEP** *1983;* (Tax Fac), Brookwood, Weare Street, Paynes Green, Ockley, DORKING, RH5 5NH. See also Fact-Services LLP
WILLS, Mr. Mathew Jonathon Clifford, MBA BA ACA *1994;* Linndale, Wells Road, ILKLEY, WEST YORKSHIRE, LS29 9JH.
WILLS, Mr. Michael John, BSc FCA *1978;* 64 High Street, Greenfield, BEDFORD, MK45 5DB.
WILLS, Mr. Michael John, BSc FCA *1985;* 20a Kensal Rise, YORK, YO10 5AL.
WILLS, Mr. Nicholas Kenneth Spencer, MA FCA *1967;* The Great House, Church Road, Great Milton, OXFORD, OX44 7PD.
WILLS, Mr. Paul Andrew, BA ACA *1990;* Millgate Developments Ltd, Millgate House, Ruscombe Lane, Ruscombe, READING, RG10 9JT.
WILLS, Miss. Rachel Ann, BA(Hons) ACA *2001;* 39 Stourton View, FROME, SOMERSET, BA11 4DZ.
WILLS, Mr. Richard Thomas, LLB ACA *2005;* Microsoft Ltd, Microsoft Campus, Thames Valley Park, READING, BERKSHIRE, RG6 1WG.
•**WILLS, Mr. Robert, FCA** *1973;* R Wills Accountants Limited, Chaparral, Windsor Lane, Little Kingshill, GREAT MISSENDEN, HP16 0DP. See also Millennium Business Services Limited
WILLS, Mrs. Sarah, MEng ACA *2009;* Zurich Insurance Co The Zurich Centre 3000b, Parkway Whiteley, FAREHAM, PO15 7JZ.
•**WILLS, Mr. Shane, BSc FCA** *1994;* ESW Limited, 162-164 High Street, RAYLEIGH, ESSEX, SS6 7BS.
•**WILLS, Mr. Steven Peter, BA ACA** *1985;* Ernst & Young LLP, 1 More London Place, LONDON, SE1 2AF. See also Ernst & Young Europe LLP
•**WILLS, Mrs. Susan Patricia, BSc FCA** *1985;* (Tax Fac), Wills Accountants Limited, 10 The Crescent, PLYMOUTH, PL1 3AB.
WILLS, Mr. Timothy Ashton, MBA BA FCA *1983;* Ratcliffe Grange Farm, Mansfield Road, WORKSOP, NOTTINGHAMSHIRE, S80 3DW.
WILLS, Mr. Tom Julian Lynall, BA FCA *1992;* 16 Cherry Orchard Road, WEST MOLESEY, KT8 1QZ.
WILLS, Mr. Trevor, FCA *1956;* 8 Leam Road, LEAMINGTON SPA, CV31 3PA. (Life Member)
•**WILLS, Mr. William Eric, FCA** *1963;* (Tax Fac), Wills Bingley Limited, St. Denys House, 22 East Hill, ST. AUSTELL, CORNWALL, PL25 4TR. See also Eric Wills & Co Ltd
•**WILLS, Mr. William John, BA ACA** *1986;* Wills Accountants, 10 The Crescent, PLYMOUTH, PL1 3AB. See also Wills Accountants Limited
WILLSHER, Mr. Anthony Gordon, FCA *1976;* World Courier Group Inc., 4 High Ridge Park, STAMFORD, CT 06905, UNITED STATES.
WILLSHER, Mrs. Katharine Claire, BSc ACA *2004;* with Williams & Co, 8-10 South Street, EPSOM, KT18 7PF.
WILLSHIRE, Mrs. Catherine Louise, FCA DChA *1998;* with Price Bailey LLP, Causeway House, 1 Dane Street, BISHOP'S STORTFORD, HERTFORDSHIRE, CM23 3BT.
WILLSHIRE, Mr. Jeffrey Martin, BSc FCA *1976;* 317 Chapel Lane, New Longton, PRESTON, PR4 4AB.
WILLSMER, Mr. Craig Jonathan, BA ACA *1999;* 15 Young Street, WAHROONGA, NSW 2076, AUSTRALIA.
WILLSON, Mr. Andrew David, BSc ACA *1992;* Honeysuckle Cottage, Westbury Road, West Meon, PETERSFIELD, GU32 1LX.
WILLSON, Mr. Anthony David, FCA *1969;* Domaine du Makila, 18 Allee du Drive, 64200 BASSUSSARRY, FRANCE.
WILLSON, Mr. Brian Anthony, FCA *1974;* 56 Davies Close, MARKET HARBOROUGH, LEICESTERSHIRE, LE16 7ND.
WILLSON, Mr. Edward James, BA ACA *1994;* 61 The Drive, MORDEN, SM4 6DH.
WILLSON, Mrs. Emma Katherine, LLB ACA *2007;* 56 Beaconsfield Road, SURBITON, SURREY, KT5 9AP.
WILLSON, Mr. Gary Lee, BSc ACA *1996;* 88 Worrin Road, Shenfield, BRENTWOOD, CM15 8JL.
WILLSON, Mr. James Henry, BSc ACA *2007;* 34b Marischal Road, LONDON, SE13 5LG.
WILLSON, Mrs. Jennifer Susan, BSc ACA CTA *1994;* Kaplan Financial, Citypoint, Temple Gate, BRISTOL, BS1 6PL.
WILLSON, Miss. Lindsay Clare, ACA *2008;* 186 Ross Close, SAFFRON WALDEN, CB11 4DU.
WILLSON, Mr. Paul James, BA(Hons) ACA *2009;* 308 Upper Wickham Lane, WELLING, KENT, DA16 3ER.
•**WILLSON, Mr. Peter Edward, FCA** *1969;* Peter Willson, Bowood, The Ropewalk, Penpol Point, TRURO, TR3 6NS.
WILLSON, Mrs. Sally, BSc ACA *1996;* 61 Wray Park Road, REIGATE, RH2 0EQ.
WILLSON, Mr. Stephen John, MBA BSc FCA *1994;* T L T Solicitors, One Redcliff Street, BRISTOL, BS1 6TP.
WILLSON, Mr. Thomas James, BSc ACA *2002;* Total Lindsey Oil Refinery Ltd, Eastfield Road, North Killingholme, IMMINGHAM, SOUTH HUMBERSIDE, DN40 3LW.
WILMAN, Mr. David John, FCA *1979;* Survitec Group Ltd, Kingsway, Dunmurry, BELFAST, BT17 9AF.
WILMAN, Mrs. Jacqueline Anne, FCA *1976;* Appleshaw, Prey Heath Road, Worplesdon, WOKING, GU22 0RN.
WILMAN, Mr. Jonathan David, BSc ACA *2008;* Flat 8 Park Lofts, 63 Lyham Road, LONDON, SW2 5EB.
WILMAN, Mrs. Kirsty, BA ACA *2006;* Hermes Pensions Management Ltd Lloyds Chambers, 1 Portsoken Street, LONDON, E1 8HZ.
WILMAN, Mr. Paul Anthony, BA FCA *1976;* 10 Dunlin Close, Thorpe Hesley, ROTHERHAM, S61 2UL.
•**WILMAN, Mr. Peter, FCA** *1978;* Woolford & Co LLP, Hillbrow House, Hillbrow Road, ESHER, SURREY, KT10 9NW. See also Dixcart International Limited
WILMER, Mrs. Julie, BA FCA *1992;* Cherry Tree House, 12a West Side Rise, OLNEY, BUCKINGHAMSHIRE, MK46 5HP.
WILMER, Mr. Peter James, MMath ACA *2007;* Barclays Corporate, 2nd Floor, 1 St. Pauls Place, 121 Norfolk Street, SHEFFIELD, S1 2JW.
WILMINGTON, Mr. Andrew, ACA *2010;* WBI, Editorial Department, 3rd Floor, 6-14 Underwood Street, LONDON, N1 7JQ.
WILMINGTON, Mr. Richard Robin, BSc FCA *1972;* Wilmingtons, West Door, 18 Brock Street, BATH, BA1 2LW. (Life Member)
WILMOT, Mr. Brian Hugh, FCA *1952;* The Hollies, Beechwood Road, Combe Down, BATH, BA2 5JS. (Life Member)
WILMOT, Mrs. Catherine Rosemary, BSc ACA *2005;* 10 Warenton Way Greenside, NEWCASTLE UPON TYNE, TYNE AND WEAR, NE13 9AR.
WILMOT, Miss. Christine Ann, BA ACA *1990;* Brackenhill, 1a Crescent Close, Olivers Battery, WINCHESTER, HAMPSHIRE, SO22 4EX.
WILMOT, Mr. Christopher John, BA ACA *1998;* 34 St. Albans Road, KINGSTON UPON THAMES, SURREY, KT2 5HQ.
WILMOT, Mr. David Keith, FCA *1966;* 8 Mountview, NORTHWOOD, HA6 3NZ.
WILMOT, Mrs. Fiona, BA ACA *1998;* 60 Archel Road, LONDON, W14 9QP.
WILMOT, Mr. Ian Michael, BA FCA *1990;* 4 Benington Road, Aston, STEVENAGE, SG2 7DX.
WILMOT, Mr. Jason, BSc ACA *1998;* A L D Automotive Ltd, Oakwood Park, Lodge Causeway, BRISTOL, BS16 3JA.
WILMOT, Mr. Joseph Michael, FCA *1959;* 8 Cuba Street, SUNDERLAND, SR2 8RU. (Life Member)
WILMOT, Mr. Kenneth Frederick, FCA *1959;* Flat 110 Frinton Lodge, The Esplanade, FRINTON-ON-SEA, CO13 9HE. (Life Member)
WILMOT, Mr. Michael Anthony, ACA *1991;* 120 Goddard Avenue, HULL, HU5 2BA.
WILMOT, Mr. Michael John, BSc(Hons) FCA *2001;* Parkdean Holidays, 1 Gosforth Park Way Salters Lane, NEWCASTLE UPON TYNE, NE12 8ET.
WILMOT, Mr. Richard James, BSc ACA *1998;* 60 Archel Road, LONDON, W14 9QP.
WILMOT, Mrs. Susan Jennifer, BA ACA *1999;* 11 Park Road, ABINGDON, OXFORDSHIRE, OX14 1DA.
WILMOT-WILKINSON, Mr. Michael David, FCA *1972;* Liberty Leasing Plc, Liberty House, 37 Mitchell Point, Ensign Way, Hamble, SOUTHAMPTON SO31 4RF.
•**WILMOTT, Mr. Martin Andrew, BA FCA** *1986;* (Tax Fac), Hawsons, 5 Sidings Court, White Rose Way, DONCASTER, SOUTH YORKSHIRE, DN4 5NU.
•**WILSDON, Mr. Peter Henry Frank, FCA** *1975;* Peters Elworthy & Moore, Salisbury House, Station Road, CAMBRIDGE, CB1 2LA. See also PEM VAT Services LLP, PEM Corporate Finance LLP
WILSDON, Mr. Richard Albert, FCA *1951;* Holmcroft, 14 Clarendon Street, LEAMINGTON SPA, CV32 5ST. (Life Member)
•**WILSHAW, Mr. Andrew George, FCA CTA** *1994;* Barringtons Limited, 18 Queen Street, MARKET DRAYTON, SHROPSHIRE, TF9 1PX.
WILSHAW, Mrs. Dawn Philippa, BA ACA *1998;* with KPMG LLP, Box 10426 Pacific Centre, 777 Dunsmuir Street, VANCOUVER V7Y 1K3, BC, CANADA.
WILSHAW, Mr. Ian Derek, BA ACA *1997;* with KPMG LLP, Box 10426 Pacific Centre, 777 Dunsmuir Street, VANCOUVER V7Y 1K3, BC, CANADA.
WILSHAW, Mr. Peter, BSc FCA *1979;* 20 Douglas Drive, Quispamsis, QUISPAMSIS E2G 1Y3, NB, CANADA.
WILSHAW, Mr. Raymond, BSc FCA *1975;* 173 Kempshott Lane, BASINGSTOKE, RG22 5LF.
WILSHAW, Mr. Simon Nicholas, FCA *1967;* Westcote, Sherborne, CHELTENHAM, GLOUCESTERSHIRE, GL54 3DU.
WILSHER, Mr. Bryan Guy, FCA *1975;* 20 Abbotswood Road, LONDON, SW16 1AP.
WILSHER, Mr. Mark Andrew, BSc ACA *1986;* 28 York Way, Fort George, St. Peter Port, GUERNSEY, GY1 2SY.
WILSHER, Mr. Robert Peter, ACA *1989;* 5 Belgrave Road, Branksome Park, POOLE, DORSET, BH13 6DB.
•**WILSON, Mr. Adam Richard Nicholas, BSc FCA** *1989;* CW Fellowes Limited, Templars House, Lulworth Close, Chandlers Ford, EASTLEIGH, SO53 3TL.
WILSON, Mr. Alan, FCA *1983;* 20 Westfield Park, Elloughton, BROUGH, HU15 1AN.
WILSON, Mr. Alan Andrew, ACA *1980;* The Croft House, Slaley, HEXHAM, NORTHUMBERLAND, NE47 0AA.
WILSON, Mr. Alan James, FCA *1958;* 30 Broxbourne Road, ORPINGTON, KENT, BR6 0AY. (Life Member)
WILSON, Mr. Alan Peter, FCA *1960;* 42 Park Avenue, RUISLIP, HA4 7UH.
WILSON, Mr. Alan William, FCA *1959;* 179 / 33-93 Spinifex Avenue, TEA GARDENS, NSW 2324, AUSTRALIA. (Life Member)
WILSON, Mr. Alastair John, BSc ACA *2007;* with Deloitte Limited, PO Box 758, Merchant House, 22/24 John Mackintosh Square, GIBRALTAR, GIBRALTAR.
WILSON, Mr. Alexander Dey, BA ACA *1998;* 29 Haugh Lane, SHEFFIELD, S11 9SB.
WILSON, Mr. Alexander Duncan, FCA *1970;* Plas-Yn-Cornel, Waen, ST. ASAPH, LL17 0DY.
WILSON, Mr. Alexander Henry MacLeod, BSc ACA *1990;* Old Hall, Penley, WREXHAM, LL13 0LU.
WILSON, Mr. Alexander John, BSc ACA *2010;* 133 Waterloo Road, ROMFORD, RM7 0AA.
WILSON, Mr. Alexander Matthew, ACA *2009;* 301/45 Shelley Street, SYDNEY, NSW 2000, AUSTRALIA.
WILSON, Mr. Alexander Peter, BSc(Hons) ACA *2010;* 5 Goldfinch Close, CONGLETON, CHESHIRE, CW12 3FB.
•**WILSON, Miss. Alison Elizabeth Jane Seymour, MA FCA** *1990;* Rapid Relief Consultancy Limited, Cedar Cottage, Burrough Green, NEWMARKET, SUFFOLK, CB8 9NE.
WILSON, Ms. Andrea Jane, MA FCA CTA *1990;* B U P A, 4 Pine Trees Chertsey Lane, STAINES, TW18 3DZ.
WILSON, Mr. Andrew, BSc ACA *1993;* 18 Parkfield Avenue, AMERSHAM, BUCKINGHAMSHIRE, HP6 6BE.
•**WILSON, Mr. Andrew, FCA** *1976;* (Tax Fac), Langtons, The Plaza, 100 Old Hall Street, LIVERPOOL, L3 9QJ.
WILSON, Mr. Andrew Alan, FCA *1968;* The Dove Cote Home Farm, Water Lane Hawkhurst, CRANBROOK, KENT, TN18 5DL.
WILSON, Mr. Andrew Bryan, BSc ACA CTA *2000;* with Target Consulting Limited, Bloxam Court, Corporation Street, RUGBY, WARWICKSHIRE, CV21 2DU.
WILSON, Mr. Andrew James, BSc ACA *1991;* 20 Hallhead Road, EDINBURGH, EH16 5QJ.
WILSON, Mr. Andrew James, BA ACA *1998;* 33 Marquis Lane, HARPENDEN, HERTFORDSHIRE, AL5 5AE.
•**WILSON, Mr. Andrew James, FCA** *1982;* (Tax Fac), Assets Limited, Chiltern Chambers, St. Peters Avenue, Caversham, READING, RG4 7DH. See also Assets Outsourcing Limited, Assets Media Limited and Assets Licensed Trade Limited
WILSON, Mr. Andrew James, BSc ACA *2006;* 63 Birkdale Avenue, PINNER, MIDDLESEX, HA5 5SG.
•**WILSON, Mr. Andrew James Granville, BA FCA** *1985;* UNW LLP, Citygate, St. James Boulevard, NEWCASTLE UPON TYNE, NE1 4JE.
WILSON, Mr. Andrew John, BA ACA *1992;* 54 Chiswick Lane, LONDON, W4 2JQ.
WILSON, Mr. Andrew Malcolm, BSc ACA *2001;* 21 E 67th Street, KANSAS CITY, MO 64113, UNITED STATES.
WILSON, Mr. Andrew Philip, BSc FCA *1976;* Metaira Pty Ltd, 53 Metaira Road, BURNIE, TAS 7320, AUSTRALIA.
•**WILSON, Mr. Andrew Richard, BA(Hons) ACA** *2003;* Wesley Wilson & Associates Ltd, Parker House, 44 Stafford Road, WALLINGTON, SURREY, SM6 9AA. See also Wesley Wilson LLP
WILSON, Mrs. Angela Fay, BSc ACA *2000;* 97 Coates Way, WATFORD, HERTFORDSHIRE, WD25 9NX.
•**WILSON, Miss. Ann Chrisette, BSc ACA** *1982;* A.C. Wilson, The Kingswood, Ridgemount Road, ASCOT, BERKSHIRE, SL5 9RW.
WILSON, Mrs. Ann-Marie, LLB ACA *2004;* 61 Harte Street, CHELMER, QLD 4068, AUSTRALIA.
WILSON, Miss. Anna Elizabeth, BA ACA *2005;* 44 Holden Street, LONDON, SW11 5UP.

•WILSON, Mrs. Anne Claire Louise, BSc ACA *2006;* 55 High Street, NORTH FERRIBY, NORTH HUMBERSIDE, HU14 3EP.
WILSON, Miss. Anne Frances, MA ACA *1986;* (Tax Fac), St Bride's House, 10 Salisbury Square, LONDON, EC4Y 8EH.
WILSON, Mrs. Annette Elizabeth, ACA *1995;* 88 Wyatt Drive, LONDON, SW13 8AB.
WILSON, Sir Anthony, Kt FCA *1952;* (Member of Council 1985 - 1988), The Barn House, 89 Newland, SHERBORNE, DT9 3AG. (Life Member)
WILSON, Mr. Anthony Charles, FCA *1973;* The Manor House, Cherhill, CALNE, SN11 8xp.
•WILSON, Mr. Anthony John, FCA *1971;* (Tax Fac), Whitmill Wilson & Co., 40 Union St, RYDE, PO33 2LF.
WILSON, Mr. Anthony John, MA ACA *1986;* Deloitte & Touche, Sun Plaza, Bilim Sokak No 5, Maslak Mah Sisli, ISTANBUL 34398, TURKEY.
WILSON, Mr. Anthony William, MBA BTech ACA *1984;* Kimal Plc Unit 401, Pointon Way Hampton Lovett, DROITWICH, WORCESTERSHIRE, WR9 0LW.
WILSON, Mr. Antony Havelock, BA FCA *1980;* Lane House, Aislaby, PICKERING, YO18 8PE.
WILSON, Mr. Antony Peter, BA ACA *2003;* Fresh Approach Ltd Fin House, 1 Oakwater Avenue Cheadle Royal Business Park, CHEADLE, CHESHIRE, SK8 3SR.
WILSON, Mr. Antony Richard, FCA *1966;* Buttons Farmhouse, Monewden Road, Charsfield, WOODBRIDGE, SUFFOLK, IP13 7QE.
WILSON, Mr. Antony Roger, FCA *1974;* 32 Exchange Street, DRIFFIELD, NORTH HUMBERSIDE, YO25 6LL.
•WILSON, Mr. Archie Douglas Allan, BSc ACA *2002;* 29 Nashdom, Nashdom Lane, Burnham, SLOUGH, SL1 8NJ.
WILSON, Mr. Arthur Thomas Ralph, BSc ACA *1994;* A K Q A, 1 St. John's Lane, LONDON, EC1M 4BL.
•WILSON, Mr. Baron Wayne, FCA *1976;* (Tax Fac), B W Wilson, 4 Saturn Close, LEIGHTON BUZZARD, BEDFORDSHIRE, LU7 3UU.
WILSON, Mr. Barry, FCA *1971;* Apartment 5 Les Carrieres, La Grande Route de St. Martin, St. Martin, JERSEY, JE3 6JB. (Life Member)
WILSON, Mr. Barry Ian, ACA CA(SA) *2011;* with PricewaterhouseCoopers LLP, 1 Embankment Place, LONDON, WC2N 6RH.
WILSON, Mrs. Belinda Anne, BSc ACA *1992;* (Tax Fac), 10 Lilleshall Way, LOUGHBOROUGH, LEICESTERSHIRE, LE11 4DD.
WILSON, Mr. Ben, ACA *2008;* Kaplan Financial, 1st Floor City Exchange, 11 Albion Street, LEEDS, LS1 5ES.
WILSON, Mr. Ben, BA(Hons) ACA *2008;* 21 Dudley Street, PADDINGTON, NSW 2021, AUSTRALIA.
WILSON, Mr. Benjamin James, MA(Oxon) ACA *2005;* Flat E, 283 Trinity Road, LONDON, SW18 3SN.
WILSON, Mr. Benjamin John Ord, MA FCA *1993;* Sergels Torg 2, SE-10640 STOCKHOLM, SWEDEN.
WILSON, Mr. Bernard Cecil, FCA *1954;* 28 Bridge Road, CHESSINGTON, KT9 2EP. (Life Member)
WILSON, Mr. Brian Frederick, FCA *1975;* 30 St. Georges Road, Palmers Green, LONDON, N13 4AS.
WILSON, Mr. Brian John, FCA *1966;* Eden Lodge, Links Drive, CHELMSFORD, CM2 9AW. (Life Member)
WILSON, Mr. Brian Richard, BA ACA *1980;* Tamar, Bedwells Heath, Boars Hill, OXFORD, OX1 5JE.
WILSON, Mrs. Caroline Michelle, BA ACA *1991;* 18 Eythrope Road, Stone, AYLESBURY, HP17 8PG.
WILSON, Ms. Caroline Victoria Alexa, ACA *2009;* 10 Park Brow Close, MANCHESTER, M21 8UL.
WILSON, Miss. Carolyn Alisa, ACA *2008;* P.O. Box 905, GEORGE TOWN, KY1-1103, CAYMAN ISLANDS.
WILSON, Mrs. Catharine Simonne Anne, MA ACA *1989;* 4 Fountain Place, WORCESTER, WR1 3HW.
WILSON, Mrs. Catherine Linda, BSc FCA *1986;* Warren Cottage, Upper Warren Avenue, Caversham, READING, RG4 7EB.
WILSON, Miss. Catherine Mary, BA ACA *2004;* 1 Bafford Lane, Charlton Kings, CHELTENHAM, GL53 8DN.
WILSON, Mr. Charles Anthony Crawford, BEng ACA *1993;* 29 Sibree Close, Bussage, STROUD, GL6 8DB.
WILSON, Mr. Charles Edward, FCA *1965;* 135 Sunset Way, #03-11, SINGAPORE 597158, SINGAPORE. (Life Member)
WILSON, Mr. Charles Ian, MA ACA *1999;* Flat 8 Edmonscote, Argyle Road, LONDON, W13 0HQ.
WILSON, Mr. Chris, MA(Hons) ACA *2009;* 70 St. Georges Terrace, Jesmond, NEWCASTLE UPON TYNE, NE2 2DL.
WILSON, Mrs. Christina, BSc ACA *2007;* 63 Birkdale Avenue, PINNER, MIDDLESEX, HA5 5SG.
•WILSON, Ms. Christine Anne, BA FCA DChA *1993;* Moore and Smalley LLP, Richard House, 9 Winckley Square, PRESTON, PR1 3HP.
WILSON, Miss. Christine Louise, BSc(Hons) ACA *2001;* 88 Fennel Grove, SOUTH SHIELDS, TYNE AND WEAR, NE34 8TN.
WILSON, Mr. Christopher, FCA *1976;* 2 Leycester Close, WINDLESHAM, SURREY, GU20 6JR.
WILSON, Mr. Christopher, BSc ACA *2007;* 3 Newstead Way, LONDON, SW19 5HR.
WILSON, Mr. Christopher, BSc ACA *2010;* 18 Endean Court, Wivenhoe, COLCHESTER, CO7 9SG.
WILSON, Mr. Christopher, MSc BA(Hons) ACA *2011;* 23 Cloister Crofts, LEAMINGTON SPA, WARWICKSHIRE, CV32 6QG.
WILSON, Mr. Christopher David, CBE MC FCA *1947;* 1 Hamble Manor, The Green Hamble, SOUTHAMPTON, SO31 4GB. (Life Member)
•WILSON, Mr. Christopher Harry, FCA *1981;* Maynard Heady LLP, 40-42 High Street, MALDON, ESSEX, CM9 5PN. See also Maynard Heady
WILSON, Mr. Christopher John, BA FCA *1977;* New Inn Farm, Beckley, OXFORD, OX3 9TY.
•WILSON, Mr. Christopher John, BA ACA *1988;* KPMG LLP, Arlington Business Park, Theale, READING, RG7 4SD. See also KPMG Europe LLP
WILSON, Mr. Christopher Peter, BA ACA *1992;* 64 Walkhampton Avenue, Bradwell Common, MILTON KEYNES, MK13 8NJ.
WILSON, Miss. Claire, BSc ACA *1993;* 1 Radnor Gardens, TWICKENHAM, TW1 4NA.
WILSON, Miss. Claire Victoria, ACA *2009;* J E Draper, 23 Lumley Road, SKEGNESS, LINCOLNSHIRE, PE25 3LN.
WILSON, Miss. Clare, BA ACA *1996;* 7 Geoffrey Street, Ramsbottom, BURY, BL0 9PQ.
•WILSON, Mr. Clive Alan, FCA *1981;* Melbourne, Hubbards Lane, Hessett, BURY ST.EDMUNDS, IP30 9BG.
•WILSON, Mr. Clive Stanley, FCA *1955;* Clive Wilson & Co, 385 Boothferry Road, HESSLE, HU13 0JJ.
WILSON, Mr. Colin, BA ACA *1993;* Stadium Group Plc, Stephen House, Brenda Road, HARTLEPOOL, CLEVELAND, TS25 2BQ.
•WILSON, Mr. Colin Malcolm, BA FCA *1972;* F H P Engineering Services Solutions, 34-42 Woburn Place, LONDON, WC1H 0JR. See also Wilson CM
WILSON, Mr. Colin Michael, MA ACA *1981;* 10 Heaton Close, Baildon, SHIPLEY, BD17 5PL.
WILSON, Mr. Craig Anthony, BSc ACA *1993;* 9 Henleaze Gardens, Henleaze, BRISTOL, BS9 4HH.
•WILSON, Mr. Daniel Patrick, BSc FCA *1980;* (Tax Fac), Greenwood Wilson, The Old School, The Stennack, ST. IVES, CORNWALL, TR26 1QU.
WILSON, Mr. Daniel Scott, BA(Hons) ACA *2001;* Green Valley Villa 2301, Lane 1500, Ha Mi Road, SHANGHAI 200336, CHINA.
WILSON, Mr. Daniel Thomas, ACA *2010;* 5 Hazel Croft, SHIPLEY, BD18 2DY.
WILSON, Miss. Daniella Clare, ACA *2006;* 36 Long Row, Horsforth, LEEDS, LS18 5AA.
WILSON, Mr. Darren Anthony, BA(Hons) ACA *2002;* 10 Kennet Close, Woodland Chase, WILMSLOW, CHESHIRE, SK9 3UE.
WILSON, Mr. David, ACA *2008;* Flat 6, 1 Manchester Road Chorlton cum Hardy, MANCHESTER, M21 9JG.
WILSON, Mr. David, ACA *2010;* MM Flowers Limited, Ronald House, Fenton Way, CHATTERIS, CAMBRIDGESHIRE, PE16 6UP.
WILSON, Mr. David, FCA *1963;* Flat C2, 49 Stanley Village Road, STANLEY, HONG KONG ISLAND, HONG KONG SAR. (Life Member)
WILSON, Mr. David, BCom FCA *1975;* Im Ror 22, 8340 HINWIL, SWITZERLAND.
WILSON, Mr. David, ACA *2011;* 2 Norfolk Farm Road, Pyrford, WOKING, SURREY, GU22 8LF.
•WILSON, Mr. David, FCA *1967;* (Tax Fac), Barnett & Turner LLP, Cromwell House, 68 West Gate, MANSFIELD, NOTTINGHAMSHIRE, NG18 1RR. See also Barnett & Turner
•WILSON, Mr. David Alan, FCA *1975;* David A. Wilson, 5 Passage Road, Westbury On Trym, BRISTOL, BS9 3HN.
WILSON, Mr. David Antony, BSc ACA *1987;* 37 Middle Mead, HOOK, RG27 9TE.
WILSON, Mr. David Ardron, BA ACA *1986;* 16 Stockarth Place, Oughtibridge, SHEFFIELD, S35 0JZ.
WILSON, Mr. David Charles, FCA *1962;* 14 Edgecote, Great Holm, MILTON KEYNES, MK8 9ER. (Life Member)
WILSON, Mr. David Christopher, BSc FCA CF *1993;* 27 Wellington Road, Bollington, MACCLESFIELD, CHESHIRE, SK10 5JR.
•WILSON, Mr. David Craig Edman, CA ACA CPA *2008;* Ernst & Young LLP, 1 More London Place, LONDON, SE1 2AF. See also Ernst & Young Europe LLP
WILSON, Mr. David Ernest, FCA *1972;* 49 Wolfreton Garth, Kirk Ella, HULL, HU10 7AB.
•WILSON, Dr. David Gerald, DPhil MSc BSc FCA ATII *1985;* David Wilson Consultants Limited, 52 Fairfield Road, UXBRIDGE, MIDDLESEX, UB8 1AL.
WILSON, Mr. David Ian, BA FCA *1990;* The Cottage, Mashbury, CHELMSFORD, CM1 4TF.
•WILSON, Mr. David James, ACA *1981;* Silver Tree Financial Support (STFS) Ltd, 79 St. Leonards Road, AMERSHAM, BUCKINGHAMSHIRE, HP6 6DR.
WILSON, Mr. David James, MA ACA FCT *1987;* 4 Harefield, Hinchley Wood, ESHER, KT10 9TQ.
WILSON, Mr. David John, FCA *1968;* Brick Kiln Farm, Ticehurst, WADHURST, EAST SUSSEX, TN5 7HX.
WILSON, Mr. David John, BA ACA *1995;* (Tax Fac), 7 Rush Hill Road, Uppermill, OLDHAM, OL3 6JD.
WILSON, Mr. David Michael, BA ACA *2001;* Northern Foods Plc, Trinity Park House, Trinity Business Park, Fox Way, WAKEFIELD, WEST YORKSHIRE WF2 8EE.
WILSON, Mr. David Michael, MA FCA *1974;* West Longdens, Forty Green Road, Knotty Green, BEACONSFIELD, HP9 1XL.
WILSON, Mr. David Noel, BSc FCA *1986;* 20a Khartoum Road, Tooting, LONDON, SW17 0HZ.
WILSON, Mr. David Oliver Ross, BA ACA *1988;* 19 Grosvenor Road, Jesmond, NEWCASTLE UPON TYNE, NE2 2RL.
•WILSON, Mr. David Paul, ACA *1983;* (Tax Fac), Wilson & Co, Joseph's Well, Hanover Walk, Park Lane, LEEDS, LS3 1AB.
WILSON, Mr. David Robert Murray, MBA FCA *1977;* 4425 E Maderos Del Cuenta Dr, PARADISE VALLEY, AZ 85253-4028, UNITED STATES.
WILSON, Mr. David Sidney, FCA *1953;* 46 Heath Road, POTTERS BAR, EN6 1LW. (Life Member)
WILSON, Mr. David Steel, BSc ACA ASIP *1991;* Trafalgar House Trustees Limited, 30 Coleman Street, LONDON, EC2R 5AL.
WILSON, Mr. David Thomas, BSc FCA *1973;* 5 Vat House, Regents Bridge, Gardens, Rita Road, LONDON, SW8 1HD.
WILSON, Mr. David Trevor, BSc ACA *1978;* 16 Lyndhurst Drive, SEVENOAKS, TN13 2HQ.
•WILSON, Mr. David Wood, BA FCA *1992;* Hindle Jepson & Jennings Ltd, 10 Borough Road, DARWEN, LANCASHIRE, BB3 1PL.
WILSON, Mrs. Deborah Ann, ACA *1992;* 18 Royal Gardens, Davenham, NORTHWICH, CW9 8HB.
WILSON, Miss. Deborah Mary, BA ACA *1990;* Anglo American Plc, Anglo American House, 20 Carlton House Terrace, LONDON, SW1Y 5AN.
WILSON, Mr. Dereck, FCA *1978;* 27 Broad Lawn, New Eltham, LONDON, SE9 3XE.
WILSON, Mr. Derek Andrew, BSc ACA *1993;* 37 Steps, Orchard Road Matlock Bath, MATLOCK, DERBYSHIRE, DE4 3PF.
WILSON, Mr. Derek Malam, FCA *1971;* Riverside House, 3 Avoncliffe, Main Street, Tiddington, STRATFORD-UPON-AVON, WARWICKSHIRE CV37 7AS.
WILSON, Mrs. Dianne Catherine, BA ACA *1992;* 4 Collingwood Terrace, Jesmond, NEWCASTLE UPON TYNE, NE2 2JP.
WILSON, Mrs. Diya, BSc ACA *2003;* 10 Espirit House, Keswick Road, LONDON, SW15 2JL.
WILSON, Mr. Duncan Henry, OBE MA MPhil FCA *1986;* The Greenwich Foundation, Old Royal Naval College, 2 Cutty Sark Gardens, Greenwich, LONDON, SE10 9LW.
WILSON, Mr. Dylan Mathew, ACA *2009;* Ty Twr, Shirenewton, CHEPSTOW, GWENT, NP16 6RG.
WILSON, Mr. Edward, ACA *2010;* 2 The Courtyard, High Street Islip, KETTERING, NORTHAMPTONSHIRE, NN14 3JS.
WILSON, Mr. Edward Robert Alexander, BSc ACA *2009;* Rudge Manor Farm, Rudge, Froxfield, MARLBOROUGH, WILTSHIRE, SN8 2HN.
WILSON, Dr. Elaine Marcia Kate, PhD BSc ACA *2002;* 1st Floor Flat, 179 Redland Road, Redland, BRISTOL, BS6 6YQ.
WILSON, Mrs. Elizabeth, BSc FCA ATII *1986;* (Tax Fac), Anderson Barrowcliff, Waterloo House, Thornaby Place, Thornaby, STOCKTON-ON-TEES, CLEVELAND TS17 6SA.
WILSON, Mrs. Elizabeth Mary, BA ACA *1992;* The Orchard House, Church Lane, Croughton, BRACKLEY, NN13 5LS.
WILSON, Miss. Elizabeth Rachel, BA ACA *2005;* 58 Vaudrey Close, Shirley, SOUTHAMPTON, SO15 5PY.
WILSON, Mrs. Emma Kate, BSc ACA *2003;* 9 Scarlet Gum Street, ULLADULLA, NSW 2539, AUSTRALIA.
•WILSON, Mrs. Emma Kate, ACA *2002;* Bailey-Wilson, 12 Arnhem Close, BINGLEY, WEST YORKSHIRE, BD16 3JX.
WILSON, Mrs. Fiona Christine, BSc ACA *1982;* Gregories, Gregories Farm Lane, BEACONSFIELD, HP9 1HJ.
WILSON, Mrs. Fiona Jane, BAcc ACA CTA *1998;* 9 Monro Park, DUMFRIES, DG1 4YJ.
WILSON, Mrs. Fiona Mary, BA ACA *1989;* 219 Ashford Circle, LA GRANGE, GA 30240, UNITED STATES.
WILSON, Mrs. Franciska Christina Maria, BA ACA *2003;* Danone, International House, 7 High Street, LONDON, W5 5DB.
WILSON, Mr. Frank Brian, FCA *1956;* 21 Church Lane, Lillington, LEAMINGTON SPA, CV32 7RG. (Life Member)
WILSON, Mr. Frederick Findlay, FCA *1973;* Reviva Ltd, 35 Cambridge Road, Crosby, LIVERPOOL, L23 7TU.
WILSON, Mr. Gareth Laurence Philip, FCA *1968;* 2 Station Road, Haddenham, ELY, CAMBRIDGESHIRE, CB6 3XD. (Life Member)
WILSON, Mr. Garry, MA ACA *1993;* Endless LLP, 3 Whitehall Quay, LEEDS, LS1 4BF.
WILSON, Miss. Gemma, BSc ACA *2006;* 11 Brockwell Park Gardens, LONDON, SE24 9BL.
WILSON, The Hon. Geoffrey Hazlitt, CVO BA FCA FCMA *1955;* Bowden House, Bay Tree Yard, ALRESFORD, HAMPSHIRE, SO24 9UJ. (Life Member)
WILSON, Mr. Geoffrey Michael, FCA *1959;* Scaran, 7 Seaburn Gardens, Seaburn, SUNDERLAND, SR6 8BT. (Life Member)
WILSON, Mr. George Christopher, FCA *1970;* Po Box 9, Kekerengu, BLENHEIM 7260, NEW ZEALAND.
WILSON, Mrs. Georgina, BA ACA *2003;* Grossmatt 40, 6314 UNTERAEGERI, SWITZERLAND.
WILSON, Mr. Gerald, FCA *1963;* Ballasloe Beg, Ballafayle Road, Cornaa, Ramsey, ISLE OF MAN, IM7 1EQ. (Life Member)
WILSON, Mr. Giles Robert Bryant, BEng ACA *1999;* 14 Oakley Gardens, Brockham Park, BETCHWORTH, SURREY, RH3 7DN.
WILSON, Mr. Gillan Ranald Graham, MSc ACA *2010;* 23 Strathblaine Road, LONDON, SW11 1RG.
WILSON, Mr. Gordon, FCA *1966;* 9 Lazenby Fold, WETHERBY, LS22 6WN.
WILSON, Mr. Gordon Bruce, BSc ACA *1991;* 4 Naseby Court, BUCKINGHAM, MK18 1TS.
WILSON, Mr. Gordon Redvers, BA ACA *1999;* with KPMG LLP, 15 Canada Square, LONDON, E14 5GL.
WILSON, Mr. Graham, MA ACA *2006;* PricewaterhouseCoopers LLP, PO Box 82, Royal Trust Tower, TD Centre, 77 King Street West, TORONTO M5K 1G8 ON CANADA.
•WILSON, Mr. Graham John, BSc FCA *1976;* (Tax Fac), Liverpool Victoria Friendly Society, Frizzell House, County Gates, BOURNEMOUTH, BH1 2NF.
WILSON, Mr. Graham Matthew, BSc ACA MBA *1992;* Limetree House, Broughton Cross, COCKERMOUTH, CUMBRIA, CA13 0TY.
•WILSON, Mr. Graham Michael, BA FCA *1980;* Beever and Struthers, Central Buildings, Richmond Terrace, BLACKBURN, BB1 7AP.
WILSON, Mr. Grant, ACA *1980;* 2 Adamson Way, LAURENCEKIRK, KINCARDINESHIRE, AB30 1FS.
WILSON, Mr. Gregory James, ACA CA(NZ) *2009;* 18 Green Lane, Datchet, SLOUGH, SL3 9EX.
•WILSON, Mr. Gregory John, BA(Hons) FCA *1997;* with PricewaterhouseCoopers, Cornwall Court, 19 Cornwall Street, BIRMINGHAM, B3 2DT.
WILSON, Mr. Guy Edward Nairne Sandilands, FCA *1972;* 110 Burnthwaite Road, LONDON, SW6 5BG.
WILSON, Mr. Guy Howard, BA FCA *1988;* Aggregates Industries UK Ltd, Bardon Hill, COALVILLE, LEICESTERSHIRE, LE67 1TL.
WILSON, Mr. Guy Spedding, BSc ACA *1989;* Blakeney, 24 Church Street, Haslingfield, CAMBRIDGE, CB23 1JE.
WILSON, Mrs. Hannah, BA ACA *1998;* 3 Laburnham Road, MAIDENHEAD, BERKSHIRE, SL6 4DB.

•**WILSON, Mr. Harold Charles, ACA ATII** *1978;* Grant Thornton UK LLP, Grant Thornton House, 22 Melton Street, Euston Square, LONDON, NW1 2EP. See also Grant Thornton LLP
WILSON, Miss. Hayley Dawn, BSc ACA *2005;* 2 Hale Fen, Littleport, ELY, CB6 1EN.
WILSON, Mrs. Helen Christine, BSc ACA *1999;* Treetops, Davis Way, Hurst, READING, RG10 0TR.
WILSON, Mrs. Helen Louise, BA ACA *2003;* 147 Featherstone Grove, NEWCASTLE UPON TYNE, NE3 5RF.
WILSON, Mr. Henry Alfred Vallette, BCom FCA *1951;* 66 The Spinney, BEACONSFIELD, HP9 1SA. (Life Member)
WILSON, Dr. Henry Robertson, FCA MCT *1989;* BP Treasury 4th Floor, British Petroleum Co Plc, 20 Canada Square, LONDON, E14 5NJ.
WILSON, Mr. Henry William Humphrey, BA(Hons) ACA *2009;* 2/F 62 Hollywood Road, VICTORIA, HONG KONG SAR.
WILSON, Mrs. Hilary Claire, BSc ACA *1992;* 37 Balmoral Gardens, WINDSOR, SL4 3SG.
WILSON, Mrs. Hilary Judith, ACA *1980;* 77 Lindon Drive Alvaston, DERBY, DE24 0LP.
WILSON, Mrs. Hilary Sarah Jane, BSc ACA *1996;* (Tax Fac), Provelio Ltd, The Meeting House, Lewins Mead, BRISTOL, BS1 2NN.
WILSON, Mr. Hugh David, MA ACA CTA *1996;* Rockwood Additives Ltd, Moorfield Road, WIDNES, CHESHIRE, WA8 3AA.
WILSON, Mrs. Hylda Irene, BSc ACA *1987;* 8 Kent House, Courtlands, Sheen Road, RICHMOND, TW10 5AU.
WILSON, Mr. Iain Mackenzie, FCA *1973;* Furze Park, Polruan, FOWEY, PL23 1PS. (Life Member)
WILSON, Mr. Ian, FCA *1971;* Ivy Cottage, Holyport Street, Holyport, MAIDENHEAD, BERKSHIRE, SL6 2JR.
WILSON, Mr. Ian, BA ACA *2007;* IP Group plc West 1 Level 7, Forth Banks, NEWCASTLE UPON TYNE, NE1 3PA.
WILSON, Mr. Ian, BSc ACA *1987;* Mulgrave Castle, Estate Office Mulgrave Castle, Lythe, WHITBY, NORTH YORKSHIRE, YO21 3RJ.
WILSON, Mr. Ian Andrew Donald, FCA *1970;* Glebe Farm, Shipton-under-Wychwood, CHIPPING NORTON, OX7 6BJ.
WILSON, Mr. Ian Christopher, BSc ACA *1987;* Apartment 39C South Tower, Pacific Plaza Towers, 4th Avenue, Bonifacio Global City Taguig, MANILA 1634, METRO MANILA PHILIPPINES.
WILSON, Mr. Ian Christopher, BA ACA *1990;* 1 Weycroft, 78, Portmore Park Road, WEYBRIDGE, KT13 8HH.
WILSON, Mr. Ian David, MSc ACA *2004;* 245 Sunshine Road, TOTTENHAM, VIC 3012, AUSTRALIA.
WILSON, Mr. Ian Everard, MA FCA *1992;* 141 Walton End, MILTON KEYNES, BUCKINGHAMSHIRE, MK7 7AX.
•**WILSON, Mr. Ian Patrick Joseph, BA ACA** *1988;* Grant Thornton UK LLP, Enterprise House, 115 Edmund Street, BIRMINGHAM, B3 2HJ. See also Grant Thornton LLP
WILSON, Mr. Ian Scott, BA ACA *1991;* (Tax Fac), 28 Willow Park, HAYWARDS HEATH, WEST SUSSEX, RH16 3UA.
WILSON, Mr. James Alexander, BEng ACA *1994;* Rosales 333 Y Girasoles, Primavera 2, Cumbaya, QUITO, ECUADOR.
WILSON, Mr. James Andrew, BA FCA *1992;* 11 Marriotts Way, Haddenham, AYLESBURY, BUCKINGHAMSHIRE, HP17 8BW.
WILSON, Mr. James Arthur, BSc(Econ) ACA *1996;* Flat 2, 53 Roderick Road, LONDON, NW3 2NP.
WILSON, Mr. James Murray, FCA *1959;* Sonnestraal, Harrow Road, DIEPRIVIER, 7800, SOUTH AFRICA. (Life Member)
WILSON, Mrs. Janice Morgan, FCA *1973;* PO BOX 188, PICTON, SOUTH ISLAND, NEW ZEALAND.
•**WILSON, Mr. Jeremy James Francis, FCA** *1980;* JJW, 235 Cassiobury Drive, WATFORD, WD17 3AN.
WILSON, Mr. Jeremy Michael Charles, BSc ACA *1992;* The Orchard House, Church Lane, Croughton, BRACKLEY, NN13 5LS.
WILSON, Mr. Jeremy Simon, BSc ACA *1997;* 53 Common End Lane, Lepton, HUDDERSFIELD, HD8 0AL.
WILSON, Mrs. Joanne, BA ACA *1997;* 36 Balmoral Road, COALVILLE, LE67 4PE.
WILSON, Miss. Joanne Lee, BA ACA AMCT *1996;* Shell Chemicals Limited, 18th floor, Shell Centre, York Road, LONDON, SE1 7NA.
WILSON, Mrs. Joanne Lisa, ACA *2001;* 71 Sundew Gardens, High Green, SHEFFIELD, S35 4DQ.
WILSON, Mrs. Joanne Louise, BSc ACA *1997;* 66 Highgate Avenue, Lepton, HUDDERSFIELD, HD8 0EE.
WILSON, Miss. Joanne Rosemary, BA(Hons) ACA *2002;* Tesco Stores Ltd Cirrus Building 1a, Shires Park Kestrel Way, WELWYN GARDEN CITY, HERTFORDSHIRE, AL7 1GA.
WILSON, Ms. Joanne Susan, BA ACA *1998;* The Garden Flat, 211, Archway Road, LONDON, N6 5BN.
WILSON, Mr. John, FCA *1972;* 31 Gladstone Street, YORK, YO31 8WD.
WILSON, Mr. John Alastair, FCA *1969;* 33 White Lion Road, Coltishall, NORWICH, NR12 7AR.
WILSON, Mr. John Alexander, FCA *1975;* Mulliner House, Flanders Road, LONDON, W4 1NN.
WILSON, Mr. John Alexander Torrens, BSc FCA *1992;* 12 Ploughmans Way, MACCLESFIELD, SK10 2UN.
WILSON, Mr. John Barrington, FCA *1952;* 36A Calder Avenue, Brookmans Park, HATFIELD, AL9 7AG. (Life Member)
•**WILSON, Mr. John Bentley, BA FCA ATII** *1982;* (Tax Fac), Hallidays LLP, Riverside House, Kings Reach Business Park, Yew Street, STOCKPORT, CHESHIRE SK4 2HD. See also Hallidays Accountants LLP
•**WILSON, Mr. John Campbell, BAcc ACA ATII** *1999;* (Tax Fac), Howard Wilson, 36 Crown Rise, WATFORD, WD25 0NE.
WILSON, Mr. John Christopher, BA FCA *1965;* 1 Cobbe Place, Beddingham, LEWES, BN8 6JY.
•**WILSON, Mr. John David, MA FCA** *1985;* Revell Ward LLP, 7th Floor, 30 Market Street, HUDDERSFIELD, HD1 2HG.
WILSON, Mr. John David, BSc ACA *1993;* 19 Daylesford Avenue, LONDON, SW15 5QR.
WILSON, Mr. John Gary, BEng ACA *1989;* Drawn Metal Ltd, Swinnow Lane, Bramley, LEEDS, LS13 4NE.
WILSON, Mr. John Gilbert, FCA *1953;* Caerfai, Church Lane, South Harting, PETERSFIELD, GU31 5QF. (Life Member)
•**WILSON, Mr. John Henry, FCA** *1974;* Blythe Squires Wilson, 1-2 Vernon Street, DERBY, DE1 1FR.
WILSON, Mr. John Howitt, FCA *1957;* Herons Creek, Yealm View Road, Newton Ferrers, PLYMOUTH, PL8 1AN. (Life Member)
WILSON, Mr. John Kenneth, FCA *1958;* 33 The Warren, GRAVESEND, DA12 4DA. (Life Member)
WILSON, Mr. John Laurence Anthony Ashley, MA ACA *1989;* 46 Princes Court, LONDON, SE16 7TD.
•**WILSON, Mr. John Nevison, FCA** *1971;* (Tax Fac), J.N. Wilson, Grosvenor House, 25 St.Peter Street, TIVERTON, EX16 6NW.
WILSON, Mr. John Noel, FCA *1974;* 18 Millview Gardens, Wrawby, BRIGG, SOUTH HUMBERSIDE, DN20 8SY.
WILSON, Mr. John Owen Parker, BA FCA *1969;* 190 Church Lane, Marple, STOCKPORT, SK6 7LA.
WILSON, Mr. John Peter, BSc ACA *1978;* 38 Tilsworth Road, BEACONSFIELD, HP9 1TP.
WILSON, Mr. John Richard, BA ACA *1978;* 2 Whitemeadows, DARLINGTON, DL3 8SR.
WILSON, Mr. John Robert, FCA *1972;* True Blue Inc, 1015 A Street, TACOMA, WA 98401, UNITED STATES.
WILSON, Mr. John Vertue, FCA *1953;* Broadside, Limpsfield Chart, OXTED, RH8 0SZ. (Life Member)
WILSON, Mr. John Warwick, FCA *1964;* 27 Longlands Lane, Heysham, MORECAMBE, LANCASHIRE, LA3 2NR.
WILSON, Mr. John Werden, BA FCA *1971;* 54 King Henrys Walk, LONDON, N1 4NN. (Life Member)
WILSON, Mr. Jonathan David, BA(Econ) ACA *2003;* 78 Derby Road, South Woodford, LONDON, E18 2PS.
•**WILSON, Mr. Jonathan David, BA ACA** *2007;* (Tax Fac), Barnett & Turner LLP, Cromwell House, 68 West Gate, MANSFIELD, NOTTINGHAMSHIRE, NG18 1RR.
WILSON, Mr. Jonathan Dudley, BA ACA *1992;* Timbers, 84 Braiswick, COLCHESTER, CO4 5AY.
WILSON, Mr. Jonathan Richard, ACA *1997;* (Tax Fac), 45 Greengate Lane, KNARESBOROUGH, NORTH YORKSHIRE, HG5 9EL.
WILSON, Mr. Joseph Oliver, ACA *2009;* Pricewaterhousecoopers Llp, 1 Hays Lane, LONDON, SE1 2RD.
WILSON, Mr. Joseph Robert, FCA *1969;* The Azaleas, 8 Lilian Close, SWINDON, SN25 1XG. (Life Member)
WILSON, Mrs. Judith Anne, BA FCA *1992;* Quality Improvement Agency Friars House, Manor House Drive, COVENTRY, CV1 2TE.
WILSON, Mrs. Julia Clare, BA ACA *1997;* Freudenberg Household Products L.P., 2 Chichester Street, ROCHDALE, OL16 2AX.
WILSON, Mrs. Julia Ruth, BA ACA *1994;* Beech House, North Leys, ASHBOURNE, DERBYSHIRE, DE6 1DQ.
WILSON, Mrs. Julia Susan, BSc ACA *1994;* 3i Group plc, 16 Palace Street, LONDON, SW1E 5JD.
WILSON, Mr. Julian Robin Guy, BSc ACA *1989;* 30 Derwent Drive, PURLEY, CR8 1EQ.
WILSON, Miss. Julie, ACA *2011;* 10 Broad ING Crescent, KENDAL, CUMBRIA, LA9 6HA.
WILSON, Miss. Julie Margaret, BA ACA *1995;* 47 Normanton Rise, Anlaby Common, HULL, HU4 7SX.
WILSON, Mrs. Karen Angela, BA ACA *1992;* Lakes College, Hallwood Road, Lillyhall Business Park, WORKINGTON, CUMBRIA, CA14 4JN.
WILSON, Mrs. Karen Julia, BSc ACA *1990;* 29 Geralds Way, Chalford, STROUD, GL6 8FJ.
WILSON, Mrs. Karen June, BA ACA *1987;* 33 Holly Walk, Silsoe, BEDFORD, MK45 4EB.
WILSON, Mrs. Karen Louise, BSc ACA *1999;* 26 Tudor Drive, Otford, SEVENOAKS, KENT, TN14 5QP.
WILSON, Mr. Karl, BSc ACA *2002;* #3 Paget Court, 10 Paget Drive, PAGET PG04, BERMUDA.
WILSON, Mrs. Katherine, LLB ACA *1990;* Les Marais La Rue de la Marais A la Cocque, Grouville, JERSEY, JE3 9AT.
WILSON, Miss. Katherine Margaret, BSc ACA *2011;* Devon House, 50 Elthorne Road, UXBRIDGE, MIDDLESEX, UB8 2PS.
•**WILSON, Mrs. Kathleen Elizabeth, BSc FCA ATII** *1983;* (Tax Fac), K.E. Wilson & Co, 40 The Highway, Great Staughton, ST. NEOTS, PE19 5DA.
WILSON, Mrs. Kathryn, BA ACA *2010;* 84 Montmano Drive, MANCHESTER, M20 2EB.
WILSON, Mrs. Katie Jane, BSc ACA *1999;* 14 Oakley Gardens, Brockham Park, BETCHWORTH, SURREY, RH3 7AZ.
WILSON, Mrs. Katie Victoria, BA ACA *2002;* 23 Manor Wood Road, PURLEY, SURREY, CR8 4LG.
WILSON, Mrs. Kay Linda, BA FCA *1972;* High Cross Grange, Claybrooke Magna, LUTTERWORTH, LE17 5AU.
WILSON, Mr. Keith, FCA *1963;* 1 Hillside Road, Pannal, HARROGATE, NORTH YORKSHIRE, HG3 1JP. (Life Member)
WILSON, Mr. Keith Andrew, FCA *1966;* 21 Mandeville Close, BROXBOURNE, HERTFORDSHIRE, EN10 7PN.
WILSON, Mr. Keith Beresford, BSc ACA *1990;* 3 Burton Street, Balgowlah, SYDNEY, NSW 2093, AUSTRALIA.
WILSON, Mr. Kenneth, MA FCA *1950;* Prospect House, Castle Street, SAFFRON WALDEN, CB10 1BD. (Life Member)
WILSON, Mr. Kenneth Adrian Raymond, ACA *1981;* K Wilson, 179 Kings Road, KINGSTON UPON THAMES, KT2 5JH.
WILSON, Mr. Kenneth Ian, LLB FCA *1975;* 6A Yeomans Meadows, SEVENOAKS, TN13 2LS.
•**WILSON, Mr. Kerry Alan, BA ACA** *1998;* KW Finance Director Services, 35 Dover Road, BRIGHTON, BN1 6LP.
WILSON, Miss. Kim Anne, BSc ACA *2002;* 12 Queensdale Walk, LONDON, W11 4QQ.
WILSON, Mrs. Kimberley Anne, BA ACA *2005;* Acal Plc, 2 Chancellor Court, Occam Road, Surrey Research Park, GUILDFORD, SURREY GU2 7AH.
WILSON, Mrs. Kirsty Louise, BA ACA *2005;* 11 Harley Way, ST. LEONARDS-ON-SEA, EAST SUSSEX, TN38 8BT.
WILSON, Miss. Laura, BA(Hons) ACA *2002;* with PricewaterhouseCoopers, Riverside Centre, 123 Eagle Street, GPO Box 150, BRISBANE, QLD 4001 AUSTRALIA.
WILSON, Mr. Lee Kenneth, ACA *1995;* (Tax Fac), Flat 5 Manor Gate, 9 Bishops Down Road, TUNBRIDGE WELLS, TN4 8UY.
WILSON, Mr. Lewis Edward Arthur, BA(Hons) ACA *2002;* with BDO LLP, 55 Baker Street, LONDON, W1U 7EU.
WILSON, Miss. Linda Michelle, BSc ACA *2007;* 12 Nelson Street, OLDHAM, LANCASHIRE, OL4 5AW.
WILSON, Miss. Lindsey Deanna, ACA *2008;* with Mazars LLP, The Lexicon, Mount Street, MANCHESTER, M2 5NT.
WILSON, Mrs. Louisa Jane, LLB ACA *1994;* 209 Westcombe Hill, Blackheath, LONDON, SE3 7DR.
WILSON, Mrs. Lynette, ACA *1982;* 1 Park Cottages, Great Braxted, WITHAM, CM8 3EF.
WILSON, Mrs. Lynn Julie, ACA *1980;* 16 Lyndhurst Drive, SEVENOAKS, TN13 2HQ.
•**WILSON, Mr. Malcolm Alexander Trevor, BSc ACA** *1991;* Nicholas & Walters Limited, 54-56 Victoria Street, Shirebrook, MANSFIELD, NOTTINGHAMSHIRE, NG20 8AQ.
WILSON, Mr. Malcolm John, MA ACA *1979;* The Granary, Walnut Farm, Main Street, Great Ouseburn, YORK, YO26 9RQ.
WILSON, Mr. Malcolm Mcarthur, MA FCA *1976;* 11 Atkinson Street, Bentleigh, MELBOURNE, VIC 3204, AUSTRALIA.
•**WILSON, Mrs. Mandy Susan Elizabeth, FCA** *1984;* (Tax Fac), P R Hornsby & Company Limited, 5 Yeomans Court, Ware Road, HERTFORD, SG13 7HJ.
WILSON, Ms. Margaret, ACA *2000;* 215 Richmond Road, TWICKENHAM, TW1 2NJ.
WILSON, Mrs. Marianne Therese, BSc ARCS ACA *1995;* 9 Holroyd Road, LONDON, SW15 6LN.
WILSON, Mrs. Marilyn Linda, MA ACA *1979;* The Granary, Main Street Great Ouseburn, YORK, YO26 9RQ.
WILSON, Mr. Mark, ACA *2002;* 106 Cowper Street, HOVE, EAST SUSSEX, BN3 5BL.
•**WILSON, Mr. Mark, BSc FCA** *1995;* M Wilson Accountants Limited, 6 Twigg Crescent, Armthorpe, DONCASTER, SOUTH YORKSHIRE, DN3 2FP.
WILSON, Mr. Mark Erik, BSc ACA *1999;* DEUTSCHE BANK AG 1ST FLOOR MAILPOINT 105, 1 APPOLD STREET, LONDON, EC2A 2HE.
WILSON, Mr. Mark Geoffrey, MSc ACA *2002;* 7A Lydden Grove, LONDON, SW18 4LJ.
WILSON, Mr. Mark Henry Richard Iain, MBA BA ACA *1992;* Paddock House, Lower Dunsforth, YORK, YO26 9RZ.
WILSON, Mr. Mark Lee, ACA *1986;* The Cottage, The Green, Cross Lanes, Oscroft, Tarvin, CHESTER CH3 8NQ.
WILSON, Mr. Mark Raymond, MA ACA *1993;* 100 Kinderkamack Road, Apt 6, ORADELL, NJ 07649, UNITED STATES.
WILSON, Mr. Mark Richard, BA ACA *1983;* Sea Containers Group of Companies, PO Box 305, LONDON, SE1 9PF.
WILSON, Mr. Mark Simon, BSc ACA *1991;* 14b Cliff Road, Sherston, MALMESBURY, SN16 0LN.
WILSON, Mr. Mark St John, MA ACA *1999;* 8A Corporate Square, 35 Financial Street, Xicheng, BEIJING 100033, CHINA.
WILSON, Mr. Mark Stephen, BSc(Hons) ACA *2003;* with PricewaterhouseCoopers LLP, Benson House, 33 Wellington Street, LEEDS, LS1 4JP.
WILSON, Mr. Mark Stephen, MEng ACA *1992;* Southern Cross Health Care Plc, Southgate House, Archer Street, DARLINGTON, COUNTY DURHAM, DL3 6AH.
WILSON, Mr. Mark Terence, BA ACA *1986;* (Tax Fac), 4th Floor Peel, Home Office, 2 Marsham Street, LONDON, SW1P 4DF.
WILSON, Mr. Mark William, BSc ACA *1989;* Millstone House, 239 Millhouses Lane, Ecclesall, SHEFFIELD, S11 9HX.
WILSON, Mr. Martin, MA FCA *1989;* 63 Woodnewton Drive, LEICESTER, LE5 6NN.
WILSON, Mr. Martin Gerald, BSc ACA *1980;* 81 Strafford Gate, POTTERS BAR, EN6 1PR.
WILSON, Mr. Martin Harry, MA FCA *1984;* MTBN Direct House, Lancaster Way Wingates Industrial Park, BOLTON, BL5 3XD.
WILSON, Mr. Martin John, BA FCA *1984;* (Tax Fac), 23 Turpins Rise, WINDLESHAM, SURREY, GU20 6NG.
WILSON, Mr. Martin Paul, BA ACA *1997;* 11 Macgregor Drive, Birkdale, BRISBANE, QLD 4159, AUSTRALIA.
WILSON, Mr. Martyn Alexander, FCA *1970;* 15 Kingsway, Worsley, MANCHESTER, M28 7DE.
WILSON, Mrs. Mary Elizabeth, BA FCA *1981;* 1 Keltus Avenue, Off Park Rd. Crosshills, KEIGHLEY, BD20 8AN.
WILSON, Mrs. Mary Tracey, BA ACA CTA *2002;* BPP Professional Education, Gunner House, Neville Street, NEWCASTLE UPON TYNE, NE1 5DF.
•**WILSON, Mr. Matthew Alasdair Forster, BA FCA** *1986;* HedgeStart Partners LLP, St Albans House, 57/59 Haymarket, LONDON, SW1Y 4QX.
WILSON, Mr. Matthew Francis, BSc(Hons) CA ACA *2002;* 9 Pasture Avenue, Sherburn in Elmet, LEEDS, LS25 6LG.
•**WILSON, Miss. Melanie Jane, FCA CTA MAAT** *1999;* (Tax Fac), Systematic Tax & Accountancy, Hudson House, 8 Albany Street, EDINBURGH, EH1 3QB.
WILSON, Mrs. Melanie Jane, BA ACA *1996;* 88 Worrin Road, Shenfield, BRENTWOOD, CM15 8JL.
WILSON, Mrs. Melissa Skye, ACA *2008;* Entertaining Play, Floor 2 Suite 2, Waterport Place, GIBRALTAR, GIBRALTAR.
WILSON, Mr. Michael, BSc FCA *2000;* 2 Bluebell Way, WILMSLOW, CHESHIRE, SK9 2LF.
WILSON, Mr. Michael Joseph, BA FCA *1987;* 98 Lathom Road, East Ham, LONDON, E6 2DY.
WILSON, Mr. Michael Stuart, FCA *1963;* 22 Crescent Grove, LONDON, SW4 7AH. (Life Member)
WILSON, Mr. Michael Vincent, FCA *1976;* 54 The Riddings, Beechwood Gardens, COVENTRY, CV5 6AU.
WILSON, Miss. Michelle, ACA *2011;* Flat B, 9 Elsynge Road, LONDON, SW18 2HW.

WILSON, Miss. Michelle Joanne, BA(Hons) ACA AMCT *2000;* 7 Stanley Avenue, Shirley, SOLIHULL, WEST MIDLANDS, B90 3NJ.

WILSON, Mr. Mostyn Daniel, BSc(Hons) ACA *2004;* with KPMG LLP, 15 Canada Square, LONDON, E14 5GL.

WILSON, Mr. Neil, ACA *2008;* Kingsley Bungalow, Runcorn Road, Little Leigh, NORTHWICH, CHESHIRE, CW8 4RU.

WILSON, Mr. Neil, FCA *1983;* The Cart House, Mork Road, St. Briavels, LYDNEY, GLOUCESTERSHIRE, GL15 6QE.

•**WILSON, Mr. Neil, FCA** *1975;* McEwan Wallace, 68 Argyle Street, Birkenhead, WIRRAL, CH41 6AF. See also Premier Payroll Centre Limited

WILSON, Mr. Neil Andrew, FCA *1983;* PricewaterhouseCoopers, Darling Park Tower 2, 201 Sussex Street, GPO Box 2650, SYDNEY, NSW 1171 AUSTRALIA.

•**WILSON, Mr. Neil David Ferrers, ACA** *1989;* Neil Wilson Accountancy and Bookkeeping Limited, 42A Walnut Road, Chelston, TORQUAY, TQ2 6HS.

•**WILSON, Mr. Neil Guest, MA FCA CF** *1986;* Guest Wilson Limited, 8 Wolverton Road, Snitterfield, STRATFORD-UPON-AVON, CV37 0HB.

WILSON, Mr. Neil Philip, BSc ACA *1988;* 33 Holly Walk, Silsoe, BEDFORD, MK45 4EB.

WILSON, Mr. Neil Stuart, BSc(Hons) ACA *2003;* International Markets, R Twining & Co Ltd, South Way, ANDOVER, SP10 5AQ.

WILSON, Mr. Nicholas Hugh Murray, BA FCA *1990;* 10 Wheatens Close, Brixworth, NORTHAMPTON, NN6 9UP.

WILSON, Mr. Nicholas James, BSc ACA *2009;* 49 Winter Gardens Way, BANBURY, OXFORDSHIRE, OX16 1UX.

WILSON, Mr. Nicholas Peter, BA ACA *1999;* 520 Route des Cotes, 74290 MENTHON SAINT BERNARD, FRANCE.

WILSON, Miss. Nicola, ACA *2008;* 3 Darenth Road, LONDON, N16 6EP.

WILSON, Miss. Nicola Jane, BSc(Hons) ACA *2011;* 20 Marsden Road, BATH, BA2 2LW.

WILSON, Miss. Nicola Suzanne, BA ACA *2002;* 1st Floor Derbyshire House, St Chad's Street, LONDON, WC1H 8AG.

WILSON, Mr. Nigel, MA ACA *2001;* 24 Phipps Hatch Lane, ENFIELD, MIDDLESEX, EN2 0HN.

WILSON, Mr. Nigel Anthony, FCA *1967;* Clump Corner, Lee Common, GREAT MISSENDEN, HP16 9JW. (Life Member)

WILSON, Mr. Nigel Bruce, ACA *1983;* 58b Wood Vale, LONDON, SE23 3ED.

•**WILSON, Mr. Nigel Keith, FCA** *1983;* Wilson Stevens LLP, Third Floor, 111 Charterhouse Street, LONDON, EC1M 6AW. See also Nigel Wilson & Co

WILSON, Mr. Nigel Kenneth, BCom ACA *1983;* Alltaria AS, Postboks 353, Skoyen, 0213 OSLO, NORWAY.

WILSON, Mr. Nigel Nicholas Crawford, BA FCA *1978;* Minerva, Thales UK, Manor Royal, CRAWLEY, WEST SUSSEX, RH10 9HA.

WILSON, Mr. Nigel Peter, BSc ACA *1995;* Hoe Moor House Dodwell Lane, Bursledon, SOUTHAMPTON, SO31 1AB.

WILSON, Mr. Oliver Edward James, BA ACA *1999;* 3 Laburnham Road, MAIDENHEAD, BERKSHIRE, SL6 4DB.

WILSON, Mrs. Patricia May, MSc BA FCA *1982;* Lane House, Aislaby, PICKERING, YO18 8PE.

WILSON, Mr. Patrick, BA ACA *1987;* 9 Leafy Lane, Whiteley, FAREHAM, PO15 7HL.

WILSON, Mr. Paul, BCom FCA *1993;* 6 Larch Lane, Kingsley Park, WITNEY, OXFORDSHIRE, OX28 1AG.

WILSON, Mr. Paul Antony, BSc ACA *1997;* 410 Parrs Wood Road, MANCHESTER, M20 5GP.

WILSON, Mr. Paul Craig, BSc ACA *2003;* Knockholt Lodge Sundridge Hill, Knockholt, SEVENOAKS, TN14 7PP.

WILSON, Mr. Paul Jonathan, BA FCA *1999;* 142 Kant Straße, 10623 BERLIN, GERMANY.

•**WILSON, Mr. Paul Richard, BSc(Hons) FCA** *1984;* (Tax Fac), Beever and Struthers, St George's House, 215-219 Chester Road, MANCHESTER, M15 4JE.

WILSON, Mr. Paul Steven, BSc ACA *1996;* 16A Seabeach Avenue, MONA VALE, NSW 2103, AUSTRALIA.

WILSON, Mr. Peter, MSc BA ACA *1986;* (Tax Fac), 2 Stoneycroft, Horsforth, LEEDS, LS18 4RB.

•**WILSON, Mr. Peter, FCA** *1983;* (Tax Fac), Peter Wilson, Suite 6, Rockfield House, 512 Darwen Road, Bromley Cross, BOLTON BL7 9DX.

•**WILSON, Mr. Peter, ACA CA(AUS)** *2008;* Gateway Partners Auditing UK Limited, 2nd Floor, 43 Whitfield Street, LONDON, W1T 4HD.

WILSON, Mr. Peter, BA ACA *2009;* 21 Godmanston Close, POOLE, DORSET, BH17 8BT.

WILSON, Mr. Peter Brian, BSc ACA *1985;* Studio Cottage, 39 Farm Street, Harbury, LEAMINGTON SPA, CV33 9LS.

WILSON, Mr. Peter George Kirke, FCA *1966;* Dormers, Kiln Way, Grayshott, HINDHEAD, GU26 6JF.

WILSON, Mr. Peter Ian, MA ACA *1993;* Flat 21, De Montfort Court, Stoneygate Road, LEICESTER, LE2 2AB.

WILSON, Mr. Peter James, BSc ACA *2006;* (Tax Fac), 16 West Rise, SUTTON COLDFIELD, WEST MIDLANDS, B75 7TG.

WILSON, Mr. Peter James Bruce, ACA CA(AUS) *2009;* 95 Godstone Road, TWICKENHAM, TW1 1JY.

WILSON, The Revd. Peter John, MA FCA *1965;* 156 Monks Walk, BUNTINGFORD, HERTFORDSHIRE, SG9 9DX.

WILSON, Mr. Peter Kenneth Alston, BA ACA *1979;* 6 Yuruga Place, ALLAMBIE HEIGHTS, NSW 2100, AUSTRALIA.

WILSON, Mr. Peter Leslie, FCA *1979;* 21 Manor Court, Wolviston, BILLINGHAM, CLEVELAND, TS22 5LS.

WILSON, Mr. Peter Morris, BCom ACA DChA *1991;* Open Doors International Inc, 6 Des Roches Square, Witan Way, WITNEY, OXFORDSHIRE, OX28 4BE.

•**WILSON, Mr. Peter Perry, ACA ACCA** *2007;* Brown McLeod Limited, 51 Clarkegrove Road, SHEFFIELD, SOUTH YORKSHIRE, S10 2NH.

WILSON, Mr. Peter Raymond, FCA *1967;* Vale Court, Colerne, CHIPPENHAM, SN14 8EL.

WILSON, Mr. Peter Rowland, FCA *1982;* Brackenbury Lodge, 67 Cliff Road, OLD, FELIXSTOWE, IP11 9SQ.

WILSON, Mr. Philip, BA FCA *1958;* 11 Larkswood Rise, PINNER, HA5 2HH. (Life Member)

WILSON, Mr. Philip, BA(Hons) ACA *2011;* Puddingcake House, Puddingcake Lane, Rolvenden, CRANBROOK, KENT, TN17 4JS.

•**WILSON, Dr. Philip Alexander Daniel, BSc ACA** *1992;* AIMS - Philip Wilson, 90 Pinner Park Avenue, HARROW, MIDDLESEX, HA2 6JU.

WILSON, Mr. Philip Andrew, MA ACA *2005;* National Audit Office, 157 Buckingham Palace Road, Victoria, LONDON, SW1W 9SP.

WILSON, Mr. Philip Charles, MA ACA *1980;* Gregories, Gregories Farm Lane, BEACONSFIELD, BUCKINGHAMSHIRE, HP9 1HJ.

WILSON, Mr. Philip Dennis Nagenda, FCA MBA *1980;* UNICEF Kenya Country Office, PO Box 44145, NAIROBI, 00100, KENYA.

WILSON, Mr. Philip Derek, BA ACA *1982;* The Pensions Regulator, Napier House, Trafalgar Place, BRIGHTON, BN1 4DW.

WILSON, Mr. Philip James, ACA MAAT *2009;* 44 Dean Brook Road, Netherthong, HOLMFIRTH, HD9 3UF.

•**WILSON, Mr. Philip Riches, FCA** *1979;* Day Smith & Hunter, Globe House, Eclipse Park, Sittingbourne Road, MAIDSTONE, KENT ME14 3EN.

WILSON, Mr. Piers Leigh Stuart, BA ACA *1992;* 28 Lytton Grove, LONDON, SW15 2HB.

WILSON, Miss. Rachael Yvonne, ACA *2002;* Cork Gully LLP, 52 Brook Street, LONDON, W1K 5DS.

WILSON, Mr. Rajah Kumaran, BSc FCA *1966;* Unit 1, 36 Angus Drive, GLEN WAVERLEY, VIC 3150, AUSTRALIA.

WILSON, Mr. Raymond George, FCA JDipMA *1952;* (Member of Council 1970 - 1987), 60 John F Kennedy Estate, WASHINGTON, NE38 7AJ. (Life Member)

WILSON, Miss. Rebecca, BA ACA *1992;* 6 Ettrick Loan, EDINBURGH, EH10 5EP.

WILSON, Mrs. Rebecca Josephine, BSc ACA *2009;* 5 Empire Villas, REDHILL, SURREY, RH1 5EZ.

WILSON, Mrs. Rebecca Lucy, BSc ACA *1997;* 5 The Maltings, Tingewick, BUCKINGHAM, MK18 4LQ.

WILSON, Mr. Rex Robert, FCA *1940;* 4 Calvert Road, DORKING, RH4 1LS. (Life Member)

WILSON, Mr. Richard, BSc ACA *2010;* 6 Ryde Avenue, Heaton Moor, STOCKPORT, CHESHIRE, SK4 4ES.

WILSON, Mr. Richard, ACA *2010;* 17 Goswick Avenue, NEWCASTLE UPON TYNE, NE7 7ER.

WILSON, Mr. Richard Adrian, BSc ACA *1998;* 12 Village Mews, Wilsden, BRADFORD, BD15 0DG.

WILSON, Mr. Richard Anthony Charles, BSc FCA *1969;* 7 Avenue des Papalins, MC98000 MONACO, MONACO.

•**WILSON, Mr. Richard David, ACA** *1983;* PKF (UK) LLP, Regent House, Clinton Avenue, NOTTINGHAM, NG5 1AZ.

WILSON, Mr. Richard Mark, BA ACA *1997;* 14 The Drive, Henleaze, BRISTOL, BS9 4LD.

WILSON, Mr. Richard Miles, BSc FCA *1991;* Harron Homes Yorkshire Ltd Colton House, Temple Point Bullerthorpe Lane, LEEDS, LS15 9JL.

WILSON, Mr. Richard Timothy, ACA *2009;* Flat 373 Anchor House, Smugglers Way, LONDON, SW18 1EL.

•**WILSON, Mr. Richard William, FCA** *1976;* Ernst & Young LLP, 1 More London Place, LONDON, SE1 2AF. See also Ernst & Young Europe LLP

WILSON, Mr. Robert, BA FCA *1980;* 8 Bywater Road, South Woodham Ferrers, CHELMSFORD, CM3 7AJ.

WILSON, Mr. Robert, ACA *2011;* Apartment 127, 1 William Jessop Way, LIVERPOOL, L3 1DZ.

WILSON, Mr. Robert, ACA *2011;* 100 Nether Hall Avenue, BIRMINGHAM, B43 7ET.

WILSON, Mr. Robert, BA ACA *2000;* Buhlstrasse 19, 8125 ZOLLIKERBERG, SWITZERLAND.

WILSON, Mr. Robert Anthony, BSc FCA *1979;* Ty Twr, Ditch Hill Lane, Shirenewton, CHEPSTOW, NP16 6RG.

•**WILSON, Mr. Robert Campbell, MSc ACA** *2002;* Godfrey Wilson Ltd, Unit 5.11 Paintworks, Bath Road, BRISTOL, BS4 3EH.

WILSON, Mr. Robert Edward, BSc FCA *1997;* with PricewaterhouseCoopers LLP, Pricewaterhousecoopers, 12 Plumtree Court, LONDON, EC4A 4HT.

WILSON, Mr. Robert Graham, BSc FCA *1978;* 8 Oaklands, Darras Hall, NEWCASTLE UPON TYNE, NE20 9PH.

WILSON, Mr. Robert Ian, BA FCA *1972;* 35 Horn Park Lane, Lee, LONDON, SE12 8UX.

WILSON, Mr. Robert James, BA ACA *1990;* Sheffield Teaching Hospitals NHS Foundation Trust, Herries Road, SHEFFIELD, S5 7AU.

WILSON, Mr. Robert John, FCA *1969;* P O Box 64621-00620, NAIROBI, KENYA.

WILSON, Mr. Robert John, FCA *1966;* Moor House Farm, Frensham Lane, Wishanger, FARNHAM, GU10 2QH.

•**WILSON, Mr. Robin Francis Sidney, FCA DChA** *1976;* (Tax Fac), Wilson Sandford Ltd, 85 Church Road, HOVE, EAST SUSSEX, BN3 2BB. See also Wilson Sandford (Brighton) Limited

•**WILSON, Mr. Rodney Birkett, FCA** *1966;* 27 Makepeace Avenue, Highgate, LONDON, N6 6EL.

WILSON, Mr. Roger Edward, BA ACA *1982;* Parks Farm, Sudeley Road, Winchcombe, CHELTENHAM, GL54 5JB.

WILSON, Mr. Roger John, LLB FCA *1972;* Corner Barns, Michelmersh, ROMSEY, SO51 0NR.

WILSON, Mr. Roger Martin Raymond, BA FCA *1988;* 36 Ridout Road, SINGAPORE 248432, SINGAPORE.

WILSON, Mr. Roger Sydney William, BMet ACA *1981;* The New House, Station Road, Upper Broughton, MELTON MOWBRAY, LE14 3BQ.

WILSON, Mrs. Rosamund Christine, FCA *1970;* Buttons Farmhouse, Monewden Road, Charsfield, WOODBRIDGE, SUFFOLK, IP13 7QE.

WILSON, Mr. Roy, FCA *1966;* J'Airenee, 15 Thurstaston Road, Irby, WIRRAL, CH61 0HA.

•**WILSON, Mr. Ruskin Howard Brice, BSc FCA** *1989;* Thompson Jenner LLP, 28 Alexandra Terrace, EXMOUTH, DEVON, EX8 1BD.

WILSON, Mrs. Sally Elizabeth, LLB ACA *1988;* 19 Daylesford Avenue, LONDON, SW15 5QR.

WILSON, Miss. Sally Jean, BCom ACA *2009;* 37 De Paul Way, BRENTWOOD, CM14 4FT.

WILSON, Mrs. Samantha Clare, ACA MAAT *1998;* 16a Seabeach Avenue, MONA VALE, NSW 2103, AUSTRALIA.

WILSON, Miss. Sandra Margaret, MA ACA *1990;* 25 Rue Des Ecouffes, 75004, PARIS, FRANCE.

WILSON, Mrs. Sarah Allison, BSc ACA *2001;* 22504 NE 93rd Place, REDMOND, WA 98053-2053, UNITED STATES.

WILSON, Mrs. Sarah Caroline, BA ACA *1986;* Plymouth Hospitals NHS Trust Finance Directorate, 3 Derriford Park Derriford Business Park, PLYMOUTH, PL6 5QZ.

WILSON, Miss. Sarah Jane, MSci ACA *2004;* with Hatch Partnership LLP, 29 Wood Street, STRATFORD-UPON-AVON, CV37 6JG.

WILSON, Miss. Sarah Louise, ACA *2010;* 11 Corfe Close, Urmston, MANCHESTER, M41 6WZ.

•**WILSON, Mrs. Sarah-Jane, BA(Hons) ACA** *2000;* Wilsons Accounting Services, Cherry Lodge, West Haddon Road, Watford, NORTHAMPTON, NN6 7UN.

WILSON, Mr. Scott McCallum, BAcc ACA *1993;* with Grant Thornton UK LLP, 30 Finsbury Square, LONDON, EC2P 2YU.

WILSON, Miss. Serena Margaret Burton, BSc FCA *1999;* Top Floor Flat, 23 Raynham Road, LONDON, W6 0HY.

•**WILSON, Mr. Simon, BSc FCA** *1992;* with Zolfo Cooper Ltd, The Zenith Building, 26 Spring Gardens, MANCHESTER, M2 1AB.

WILSON, Mr. Simon Baxter, BCom ACA *1986;* 624 Lassen Park Court, SCOTTS VALLEY, CA 95060, UNITED STATES.

WILSON, Mr. Simon David, BSc ACA *1999;* (Tax Fac), Ciceley Commercials Ltd, Cicely Lane, BLACKBURN, BB1 1HQ.

WILSON, Mr. Simon James, ACA *2003;* Halma Plc, Misbourne Court, Rectory Way, AMERSHAM, BUCKINGHAMSHIRE, HP7 0DE.

WILSON, Mr. Simon Levick Garth, BA ACA *1999;* Pacific Investments Plc, 124 Sloane Street, LONDON, SW1X 9BW.

WILSON, Mr. Simon Mark, BA ACA *1996;* Renolit Cramlington Limited, Station Road, CRAMLINGTON, NORTHUMBERLAND, NE23 8AQ.

WILSON, Mrs. Stephanie A, BA ACA *2005;* 2 Tayberry Close, Red Lodge, BURY ST. EDMUNDS, SUFFOLK, IP28 8FW.

WILSON, Mr. Stephen Gerard, BSc ACA *1995;* London Bay Homes, 9130 Galleria Court, NAPLES, FL 34109, UNITED STATES.

WILSON, Mr. Stephen Graham, BSc FCA *1982;* Clover House, Old Warwick Road, Lapworth, SOLIHULL, WEST MIDLANDS, B94 6LD.

WILSON, Mr. Stephen Michael, BA ACA MCT *1991;* 10 Rivelin Road, SCUNTHORPE, SOUTH HUMBERSIDE, DN16 2BH.

•**WILSON, Mr. Stephen Patrick, BA ACA** *1985;* Waller Wilson & Co, The Forge Cottage, 2 High Street, Mildenhall, BURY ST. EDMUNDS, IP28 7EJ.

•**WILSON, Mr. Steven Leslie, BSc ACA** *1993;* Thieme & Co, 18 Thorne Road, DONCASTER, SOUTH YORKSHIRE, DN1 2HS.

•**WILSON, Mr. Stewart, FCA** *1972;* (Tax Fac), Wilson Sharpe & Co, 27 Osborne Street, GRIMSBY, NORTH LINCOLNSHIRE, DN31 1NU.

WILSON, Mr. Strahan Leonard Arthur, MA ACA *2001;* 28 Lindore Road, LONDON, SW11 1HJ.

WILSON, Mr. Stuart, BSc ACA *2003;* Deloitte & Touche, Deloitte Place Building 6, The Woodlands, 20 Woodlands Drive, Woodmead, JOHANNESBURG GAUTENG 2191 SOUTH AFRICA.

•**WILSON, Mr. Stuart, BSc ACA** *1996;* Ernst & Young LLP, 1 More London Place, LONDON, SE1 2AF. See also Ernst & Young Europe LLP

WILSON, Mr. Stuart Andrew, BA ACA *2005;* 68 Maury Road, LONDON, N16 7BT.

WILSON, Mr. Stuart Andrew McLeod, BAcc ACA *1997;* 36 Balmoral Road, COALVILLE, LE67 4PE.

WILSON, Mr. Stuart Norton, FCA *1966;* 16 Bluegun Avenue, GONUBIE, 5257, SOUTH AFRICA. (Life Member)

WILSON, Mr. Stuart Victor, FCA *1969;* with Reeves & Co LLP, 37 St. Margarets Street, CANTERBURY, KENT, CT1 2TU.

WILSON, Ms. Susan Anne, FCA *1974;* 23 Mornington, Digswell, WELWYN, HERTFORDSHIRE, AL6 0AJ.

WILSON, Mrs. Susan Mary, FCA CTA *1986;* with PricewaterhouseCoopers LLP, 1 Embankment Place, LONDON, WC2N 6RH.

WILSON, Mr. Thomas Alexander, BA ACA *2009;* 131 Cobden View Road, SHEFFIELD, S10 1HR.

WILSON, Mr. Thomas Arthur, BA ACA *1996;* TAG Aviation (UK) Limited, Tag Farnborough Airport Ltd, Farnborough Airport, FARNBOROUGH, HAMPSHIRE, GU14 6XA.

WILSON, Mr. Thomas Charles, FCA *1969;* The Old Rectory, Upper Clatford, ANDOVER, SP11 7QP.

WILSON, Mr. Thomas Martin, FCA *1970;* Broadacres, Roade Hill, Ashton, NORTHAMPTON, NN7 2JH.

WILSON, Mr. Thomas Matthew, ACA *2007;* 69 Ferguson Close, LONDON, E14 3SJ.

WILSON, Mr. Thomas Patrick Charles, BA ACA *1990;* 113 Bobbin Head Road, TURRAMURRA, NSW 2074, AUSTRALIA.

WILSON, Mr. Timothy James Martin, BSc ACA *1989;* The Old Chapel, Mapperley Village, ILKESTON, DE7 6BT.

WILSON, Mr. Timothy Peter, FCA *1955;* Flat 8, 37 Keswick Road, LONDON, SW15 2JB. (Life Member)

WILSON, Mr. Timothy Richard Fairfax, MA FCA *1985;* Boundary House, Heath Road, Southend Bradfield, READING, RG7 6HD.

WINTER, Mr. Horace Stephen, FCA *1956;* 105 Corringway, Ealing, LONDON, W5 3HD. (Life Member)
WINTER, Mr. Ian, BA ACA *1989;* Ashgate House, 6 Inkerman Cottages, Ashgate Road, CHESTERFIELD, DERBYSHIRE, S40 4BP.
WINTER, Mr. Ian Robert, BSc FCA *1988;* Orica Philippines, P.O. Box 330, Greenhills, MANILA, PHILIPPINES.
•**WINTER, Mrs. Jane Ruth, BSc ACA CTA** *1999;* Armitage - Winter Limited, Croft House, 51 Ashbourne Road, DERBY, DE22 3FS.
WINTER, Miss. Jennifer Rose, BSc ACA *1993;* Rose Cottage, Bakers Lane, Shipley, HORSHAM, WEST SUSSEX, RH13 8GF.
WINTER, Mr. John Hubert, FCA *1970;* The Hop House, Kennel Lane, Frensham, FARNHAM, SURREY, GU10 3AS.
WINTER, Mr. Jonathan Charles, BA ACA *2002;* 22 St. Ediths Road, Kemsing, SEVENOAKS, KENT, TN15 6PT.
WINTER, Mr. Jonathan Craig, BSc(Hons) ACA *2002;* 15 Crofters Lea, Yeadon, LEEDS, LS19 7WE.
WINTER, Ms. Kate, ACA *1982;* 2 Packhorse Close, ST. ALBANS, HERTS, AL4 9TQ.
•**WINTER, Mr. Keith James, FCA** *1969;* (Tax Fac), Dyke Yaxley Limited, 1 Brassey Road, Old Potts Way, SHREWSBURY, SY3 7FA.
WINTER, Mr. Keith Michael, BEng ACA *1990;* Spencer Stuart & Associates Ltd, Bain House, 16 Connaught Place, LONDON, W2 2ED.
WINTER, Miss. Leanne, BA ACA *2004;* Nyasa Le Mont Arthur, St. Brelade, JERSEY, JE3 8AH.
WINTER, Mr. Leo, FCA *1969;* 53 Green Lane, EDGWARE, HA8 7PZ.
WINTER, Miss. Louise, BA ACA *2007;* with Ellacotts LLP, Countrywide House, 23 West Bar Street, BANBURY, OXFORDSHIRE, OX16 9SA.
WINTER, Miss. Lucy Elizabeth, MSc BA ACA *2009;* 1 Fellows Lane, BIRMINGHAM, B17 9TS.
WINTER, Mr. Mark, MA MPhil ACA *1992;* 5 Collum End Rise, CHELTENHAM, GL53 0PA.
WINTER, Mr. Mark John, BA FCA *1975;* 20 Via San Pio V, 10125 TURIN, ITALY.
WINTER, Mr. Matthew Thomas, BSc ACA *2007;* New Church Farm, Grange Lane, Springthorpe, GAINSBOROUGH, LINCOLNSHIRE, DN21 5TP.
WINTER, Mr. Michael, FCA *1955;* 2 Springfield Yard, Hall Lane, Branston, LINCOLN, LN4 1LY. (Life Member)
•**WINTER, Mr. Paul Joseph, BA FCA** *1985;* (Tax Fac), SPW (UK) LLP, Gable House, 239 Regents Park Road, LONDON, N3 3LF.
•**WINTER, Mr. Peter Stephen, BA FCA** *1985;* Carter Backer Winter LLP, Enterprise House, 21 Buckle Street, LONDON, E1 8NN.
•**WINTER, Mr. Peter William, FCA** *1961;* Sully & Co (WSM) Ltd, 55b Oxford Street, WESTON-SUPER-MARE, AVON, BS23 1TW.
•**WINTER, Mr. Philip James Cooper, BSc FCA** *1973;* Winters Consulting, 59A North Street, Nailsea, BRISTOL, BS48 4BS.
WINTER, Mr. Richard Anthony, FCA *1965;* 29 Port Hall Place, BRIGHTON, BN1 5PN.
WINTER, Mr. Richard David, BCom FCA *1980;* Quam Ltd, 32/F Gloucester Tower, The Landmark, 11 Pedder Street, CENTRAL, HONG KONG ISLAND HONG KONG SAR.
WINTER, Mr. Richard Harry Blair, FCA *1968;* Ducketts Farm, Henham Road, Debden Green, SAFFRON WALDEN, ESSEX, CB11 3LZ. (Life Member)
•**WINTER, Mr. Richard Thomas George, BA FCA** *1989;* PricewaterhouseCoopers LLP, 1 Embankment Place, LONDON, WC2N 6RH. See also PricewaterhouseCoopers
WINTER, Mr. Robert Louis, BSc FCA *1966;* 67 Tankerton Road, WHITSTABLE, KENT, CT5 2AH.
WINTER, Mr. Roger James, BCom FCA *1971;* Bedfordia Group Plc Milton Parc, Milton Ernest, BEDFORD, MK44 1YU.
WINTER, Miss. Ruth Elizabeth, MSci ACA *2009;* 14 Pentire Avenue, SOUTHAMPTON, SO15 7RS.
WINTER, Mrs. Ruth Megan, BA(Hons) ACA *2002;* 22 St. Ediths Road, Kemsing, SEVENOAKS, KENT, TN15 6PT.
WINTER, Miss. Sarah Lita, LLM LLB ACA *2009;* 120 Bridge Avenue, UPMINSTER, RM14 2LR.
WINTER, Ms. Shirley Anne, BSc ACA *1993;* 7a Chester Road, NORTHWOOD, HA6 1BE.
WINTER, Mr. Simon Andrew Emile, BSc ACA *2000;* 55 Pulborough Road, LONDON, SW18 5UL.
WINTER, Mr. Terence John, FCA *1973;* Old Warden Cottage, 2 Warden Road, Ickwell, BIGGLESWADE, SG18 9EL.
WINTERBOTHAM, Mr. Derek, FCA *1969;* Kingsbridge, Hilton Road, Seamer, MIDDLESBROUGH, TS9 5LX.
WINTERBOTHAM, Mrs. Sarah, BA ACA *2001;* 63 Applegarth Avenue, GUILDFORD, SURREY, GU2 8LX.
WINTERBOTHAM, Miss. Sophie, BSc ACA *2011;* 5 Belmont Road, EXETER, EX1 2HF.
WINTERBOTTOM, Mrs. Anne Christine, BA(Hons) ACA CTA *2003;* 14 Andalus Road, Brixton, LONDON, SW9 9PF.
WINTERBOTTOM, Mr. Fraser John, MSc FCA *1981;* Old Bakery House, Main Street, Gawcott, BUCKINGHAM, MK18 4HZ.
WINTERBOTTOM, Mr. Mark Alan, BA ACA *2006;* 129 Cairnwell Road, Chadderton, OLDHAM, OL9 0NF.
WINTERBOTTOM, Mr. Mark James, MA ACA *1998;* British Sky Broadcasting, Grant Way, ISLEWORTH, MIDDLESEX, TW7 5QD.
•**WINTERBURN, Mr. Andrew Stephen, FCA** *1975;* Andrew Winterburn Ltd, Broadstreet Chambers, 18 Broad Street, BROMYARD, HEREFORDSHIRE, HR7 4BT.
•**WINTERBURN, Mr. Kevin Lewis, ACA** *1996;* Sheards Accountancy Limited, Vernon House, 40 New North Road, HUDDERSFIELD, HD1 5LS. See also Sheards
WINTERBURN, Mr. Michael, FCA *1974;* 95 Hereford Close, Barwell, LEICESTER, LE9 8HU.
WINTERBURN, Mr. Roger Nicholas, FCA *1969;* 62 Brunswick Street, DEWSBURY, WF13 4NF.
WINTERMANTEL, Ms. Andrea, ACA *2002;* 27 Ranelagh Gardens, Stamford Brook Avenue, LONDON, W6 0YE.
WINTERS, Mr. Christopher, BA ACA *1992;* Im Bünd 4, 77694 KEHL, GERMANY.
WINTERS, Mrs. Diana Margaret, BA ACA *1992;* Chequers, Heavegate Road, CROWBOROUGH, TN6 1UA.
WINTERS, Mrs. Julie Sarah, BA ACA *1991;* Nunn Hayward Sterling House, 20 Station Road, GERRARDS CROSS, BUCKINGHAMSHIRE, SL9 8EL.
WINTERS, Mr. Marc Jason, BA ACA *1996;* 6 Uphill Road, LONDON, NW7 4RB.
•**WINTERS, Mr. Nicholas Simon, BSc FCA** *1987;* with RSM Tenon Audit Limited, 66 Chiltern Street, LONDON, W1U 4JT.
WINTERS, Mr. Paul Richard, BA ACA *1998;* 12 Blandford Close, Hampstead Garden Suburb, LONDON, N2 0DH.
WINTERS, Mr. Simon Mark, ACA *1994;* with Prager and Fenton LLP, 8th Floor, Imperial House, 15-19 Kingsway, LONDON, WC2B 6UN.
WINTERS, Mr. Stephen Richard, BA ACA *1995;* Chequers, Heavegate Road, CROWBOROUGH, TN6 1UA.
WINTERSCHLADEN, Mr. Richard Emile Henry, FCA *1975;* Birch House, 18 High Green, Great Ayton, MIDDLESBROUGH, CLEVELAND, TS9 6BJ.
•**WINTERSGILL, Mr. Alan, FCA** *1974;* (Member of Council 2007 - 2011), Naylor Wintersgill Ltd, Carlton House, Grammar School Street, BRADFORD, WEST YORKSHIRE, BD1 4NS.
•**WINTERSGILL, Mr. Paul, BA(Hons) ACA** *2003;* Wintersgill Associates Limited, Suite 1, 10/12 The Grove, ILKLEY, WEST YORKSHIRE, LS29 9EG.
WINTHER, Mr. Timothy Johan, BA ACA *1996;* Oakwood House, Buchlyvie, STIRLING, FK8 3PD.
WINTHORPE, Mrs. Sarah Louise, BA ACA *2006;* 92 Wood Street, BURY, LANCASHIRE, BL8 2QU.
•**WINTLE, Mr. Graham David, ACA** *1995;* Williamson Morton Thornton LLP, 47 Holywell Hill, ST. ALBANS, HERTFORDSHIRE, AL1 1HD.
WINTLE, Mr. Jonathan Christopher, BSc ACA *2000;* 56 Brand Hill, Woodhouse Eaves, LOUGHBOROUGH, LEICESTERSHIRE, LE12 8SS.
WINTLE, Mrs. Kathryn Ann, BSc ACA *2007;* (Tax Fac), 13 St. Lukes Crescent, Green Road St. Clement, JERSEY, JE2 6QH.
WINTLE, Mrs. Katrina Margaret, ACA *1982;* The Rectory, 211 Mowbray Road, WILLOUGHBY, NSW 2068, AUSTRALIA.
WINTON, Mr. Crawford Eric, BSc ACA *1993;* Northumbrian Water Boldon House, Wheatlands Way, DURHAM, DH1 5FA.
WINTON, Miss. Diana Mary, BA FCA *1973;* Temple House, Quarry Road, OXTED, RH8 9HF.
WINTON, Mr. Graeme Walter, BSc FCA *1979;* 3 Birch View, Lutterworth Road Kimcote, LUTTERWORTH, LE17 5SD.
WINTON, Mr. Harold Maurice, FCA *1960;* 1 The Pavilions, 24/26 Avenue Road, St Johns Wood, LONDON, NW8 6BU. (Life Member)
WINTON, Mr. James, FCA *1962;* 30 Eastwood Road, LEIGH-ON-SEA, SS9 3AB. (Life Member)
WINTON, Mr. Mark Adam, ACA *1985;* The Gables, 9 Aylwards Rise, STANMORE, MIDDLESEX, HA7 3EH.
•**WINTON, Mrs. Mary, BA ACA** *1989;* with Wintons Limited, First Floor, 6 Ferranti Court, Staffordshire Technology Park, STAFFORD, ST18 0LQ.
•**WINTON, Mr. Richard Joseph, BSc ACA** *1989;* Wintons Limited, First Floor, 6 Ferranti Court, Staffordshire Technology Park, STAFFORD, ST18 0LQ.
•**WINTON, Mr. Stephen Ronald, FCA** *1983;* Stephen R Winton FCA, 17 Canterbury Close, SWINDON, SN3 1HU.
WINTOUR, Mr. Iain Arthur, ACA *2008;* Pricewaterhousecoopers Erskine House, 68-73 Queen Street, EDINBURGH, EH2 4NH.
WINWARD, Mr. Alexander, BSc ACA CFA *2002;* Wilanda House, Preston Candover, BASINGSTOKE, HAMPSHIRE, RG25 2DN.
WINWARD, Miss. Amy Jane, ACA *2008;* 154 Turton Road, BOLTON, BL2 3DY.
WINWARD, Mr. Christopher, BA(Hons) ACA *2002;* Fisher Offshore, North Meadows, Oldmeldrum, INVERURIE, ABERDEENSHIRE, AB51 0GQ.
WINWARD, Miss. Hannah Elizabeth, BA(Hons) ACA *2010;* 3 Mayfield Grove, WILMSLOW, CHESHIRE, SK9 6BU.
WINWARD, Mrs. Isabel Claire, BSc ACA *2007;* Wilanda House, Preston Candover, BASINGSTOKE, HAMPSHIRE, RG25 2DN.
WINWARD, Mr. Kenneth Greenlees, FCA *1947;* 4 Pinewoods, BEXHILL-ON-SEA, TN39 3UD. (Life Member)
•**WINWARD, Mr. William, BSc FCA** *1977;* W. Winward F.C.A, The Old Vicarage, North End Road, Yapton, ARUNDEL, WEST SUSSEX BN18 0DT.
WINWOOD, Mr. Paul Michael, BA(Hons) ACA *2010;* 110d Occupation Lane, SHEFFIELD, S12 4PQ.
WINWOOD, Mr. Steven James, BA ACA *1993;* 14 Coombe Lane, BRISTOL, BS9 2AA.
WINWOOD, Mr. Stuart James, FCA *1977;* P O Box 31502, BUDAIYA, BAHRAIN.
WINYARD, Mr. Colin Frederick, FCA *1970;* (Tax Fac), 27 High Road, Orsett, GRAYS, ESSEX, RM16 3ER.
WIRGMAN, Mr. George Edward, FCA *1973;* 12 Noel Close, BROCKENHURST, SO42 7RP.
WISCHHUSEN, Mr. Paul Stephen, ACA *1980;* Mott MacDonald South Africa Pty Ltd, Mott MacDonald House, 359 Rivonia Boulevard, Rivonia, JOHANNESBURG, 2128 SOUTH AFRICA.
WISDISH, Mr. Robert John, BA ACA *1987;* 8 York Way, HEMEL HEMPSTEAD, HERTFORDSHIRE, HP2 4JT.
•**WISDOM, Mr. Craig Anthony, ACA** *2008;* with Deloitte LLP, 3 Victoria Square, Victoria Street, ST. ALBANS, HERTFORDSHIRE, AL1 3TF.
WISDOM, Mr. Michael Alan, FCA *1966;* Furze Common, 15a Northview Road, BUDLEIGH SALTERTON, DEVON, EX9 6BZ.
WISDOM, Mr. Stephen, FCA *1995;* 55 Priory View Road, Moordown, BOURNEMOUTH, BH9 3JH.
WISE, Mr. Andrew Timothy, BSc(Econ) ACA *1999;* 12 Woodside Avenue, ESHER, SURREY, KT10 8JQ.
WISE, Mr. Christopher, BSc(Hons) ACA *2011;* 28 The Pines, LEIGH, LANCASHIRE, WN7 3JS.
•**WISE, Mr. Christopher John, ACA** *1984;* (Tax Fac), Wise & Co, The Old Star, Church Street, PRINCES RISBOROUGH, HP27 9AA. See also Money Matters (High Wycombe) Limited
WISE, Mr. Colin Arthur, FCA *1958;* 4 Springmead, LYMINGTON, HAMPSHIRE, SO41 3AA. (Life Member)
WISE, Mr. David Michael, MSc ACA *1995;* (Tax Fac), 9 Maskell Way, FARNBOROUGH, HAMPSHIRE, GU14 0PU.
WISE, Mr. David William, FCA *1973;* By The Green, Thornborough, BUCKINGHAM, MK18 2DH. (Life Member)
WISE, Mr. Jack, FCA *1956;* 7 The Clock House, 192 High Road Byfleet, WEST BYFLEET, KT14 7BT. (Life Member)
WISE, Mr. James Alexander, BSc ACA *1988;* 28 Furlong Road, LONDON, N7 8LS.
•**WISE, Miss. Janet Hazel, BSc ACA** *1987;* J H Wise & Co, 27 Wheeler Avenue, OXTED, SURREY, RH8 9LF.
WISE, Miss. Jenna Karen, BSc ACA *2007;* 777 Dunsmuir Street, PO Box 10426, Pacific Centre, VANCOUVER V7Y 1K3, BC, CANADA.
WISE, Mr. John Richard, BSc FCA *1990;* PO Box N366, Grosvenor Place, SYDNEY, NSW 2000, AUSTRALIA.
WISE, Mr. Kenneth Brian, BA ACA *1991;* 10 Knoll Court, GAVEN, QLD 4211, AUSTRALIA.
WISE, Mr. Kevin, ACA *1999;* 11 Midsummer Meadow, Caversham, READING, RG4 7XD.
WISE, Mr. Leslie Michael, JP FCA *1959;* Pitt House, North End Avenue, LONDON, NW3 7HP.
WISE, Mrs. Margaret Elizabeth, MA ACA *1983;* 31 Glebe Avenue, ENFIELD, EN2 8NZ.
WISE, Mr. Michael, FCA *1966;* Sandford Lodge 2 Seven Acres Park, BRAUNTON, DEVON, EX33 2PD.
WISE, Mr. Michael Charles, BSc ACA *1989;* 28 Trenwith Place, ST.IVES, CORNWALL, TR26 1QD.
WISE, Mr. Michael Henry, ACA *2009;* 19a Aulton Place, LONDON, SE11 4AG.
WISE, Mr. Paul William, FCA *1975;* 14 Fernwood, Marple, STOCKPORT, SK6 5BE.
•**WISE, Mr. Peter George, BA FCA** *1981;* (Tax Fac), Wise & Co., 24 Woodside Road, WOODFORD GREEN, ESSEX, IG8 0TR.
WISE, Mr. Peter George, BA ACA *1997;* 35 Napier Avenue, TAKAPUNA 0622, AUCKLAND, NEW ZEALAND.
WISE, Mr. Richard James, MA ACA FRSA *1983;* Verfides, 86 Jermyn Street, LONDON, SW1Y 6AW.
•**WISE, Mr. Roger Frank, FCA** *1971;* (Tax Fac), Wise & Co, Wey Court West, Union Road, FARNHAM, SURREY, GU9 7PT. See also Firmvalue Payrolls Ltd
WISE, Mr. Stephen John, MBA BSc ACA *1983;* Rowley Farm, Rowley Lane, BOREHAMWOOD, WD6 5PE.
WISE, Mr. Trevor Melvyn, FCA *1958;* 13 Portland Street, Dover Heights, SYDNEY, NSW 2030, AUSTRALIA.
WISELY, Mr. Ian William, FCA *1960;* Windsong, 16 Golf Place, ABOYNE, AB34 5GA.
WISELY, Mr. John Carroll, FCA *1962;* 23 Franklin Road, Maidenbower, CRAWLEY, WEST SUSSEX, RH10 7FG. (Life Member)
WISELY, Mr. Stuart William, BSc ACA *1990;* Arsenal Football Club, Highbury House, 75 Drayton Park, LONDON, N5 1BU.
WISEMAN, Mrs. Amanda Jane, BSc ACA *1995;* National Air Traffic, Corporate and Technical Centre, 4000 Parkway, Whiteley, FAREHAM, HAMPSHIRE PO15 7FL.
WISEMAN, Mr. Andrew, ACA *2009;* 59 Eden Close, YORK, YO24 2RD.
WISEMAN, Mr. Andrew Terence Peter, ACA *2009;* 55 Maraetai School Road, Maraetai, MANUKAU 2018, NEW ZEALAND.
WISEMAN, Mrs. Angela Jane, BSc ACA *1996;* c/o Hill International, PO Box 31450, DUBAI, UNITED ARAB EMIRATES.
WISEMAN, Mr. Brian Leonard, MSc FCA *1960;* 3 Heathy Close, Barton On Sea, NEW MILTON, BH25 7JP. (Life Member)
WISEMAN, Mr. Clive Andrew, FCA *1972;* 3 Pond Field End, Great Woodcote Park, LOUGHTON, IG10 4QR.
•**WISEMAN, Mr. Colin George, FCA MIPA MABRP** *1973;* Wilkins Kennedy, Bridge House, London Bridge, LONDON, SE1 9QR.
•**WISEMAN, Mr. David, BA FCA** *1984;* RL Wiseman Ltd, Fernwood House, Fernwood Road, Jesmond, NEWCASTLE UPON TYNE, NE2 1TJ. See also Robson Laidler LLP and RL David Ltd
WISEMAN, Mr. David Charles, BA ACA *1985;* 53 Dorset Drive, EDGWARE, HA8 7NT.
WISEMAN, Mr. David William, BSc ACA *1981;* 31 Beconsfield Close, Dorridge, SOLIHULL, B93 8QZ.
WISEMAN, Miss. Esther Julie, BSc ACA *1999;* 4 Abbots Close, FLEET, HAMPSHIRE, GU51 3RF.
WISEMAN, Mr. Gerald Arthur, FCA *1959;* 1 Collinswood Drive, ST. LEONARDS-ON-SEA, EAST SUSSEX, TN38 0NU. (Life Member)
•**WISEMAN, Mr. Graham Mark, FCA** *1981;* (Tax Fac), Boler Wiseman, 8 Toll Gate, Stanbridge Earls, ROMSEY, HAMPSHIRE, SO51 0HE. See also Boler Wiseman Limited and Boler Wiseman Financial Services Limited
WISEMAN, Mrs. Iryna, BA ACA *2007;* Flat 2 Spinney House, 18 Uplands Way, SOUTHAMPTON, SO17 1QW.
WISEMAN, Mr. James Neville, FCA *1961;* 605 Lytham Road, BLACKPOOL, FY4 1RG.
WISEMAN, Mr. Jonathan James, ACA *2009;* 57 Kirby Drive, Bramley, TADLEY, HAMPSHIRE, RG26 5EQ.
WISEMAN, Miss. Katherine Margaret, BA ACA *1996;* 2 The Firs, Wilburton, ELY, CAMBRIDGESHIRE, CB6 3FL.
WISEMAN, Miss. Lois Jeanette, ACA *2007;* (Tax Fac), 16 Ankerdine Crescent, LONDON, SE18 3LQ.
WISEMAN, Mrs. Marian Sheila, BSc ACA *1988;* 2 Noland Park, SOUTH BRENT, DEVON, TQ10 9DE.
WISEMAN, Mr. Michael Charles, FCA *1966;* Spinney Close, Chessetts Wood Road, Lapworth, SOLIHULL, B94 6EW. (Life Member)
WISEMAN, Mr. Michael John, BA ACA *1982;* Haunch Lane Developments Ltd, 7 Stratford Road, Shirley, SOLIHULL, B90 3LU.

WISEMAN, Mr. Paul, FCA *1956;* 10 Stanhope House, 38-40 Shepherds Hill, LONDON, N6 5RR. (Life Member)
WISEMAN, Mr. Phillip, BSc ACA *1998;* Deutsche Asset Management, 1 Appold Street, LONDON, EC2A 2UU.
WISEMAN, Mr. Phillip Andrew, BSc FCA *1978;* 26 Perwick Road, Port St. Mary, ISLE OF MAN, IM9 5PA.
WISEMAN, Mr. Richard Norman, BSc FCA *1975;* 35 Sheen Park, RICHMOND, TW9 1UN.
WISEMAN, Mr. Robert John, FCA *1967;* 11 Dunlin Close, Thorpe Hesley, ROTHERHAM, SOUTH YORKSHIRE, S61 2UL.
WISEMAN, Mr. Sol David, FCA *1968;* 2 Woodville Gardens, Ealing, LONDON, W5 2LG.
•**WISEMAN, Mr. Trevor, FCA** *1986;* Thompsons Accountants and Advisors Limited, 1 Grove Place, BEDFORD, MK40 3JJ.
WISHART, Miss. Alice Jane, BSc ACA *1992;* Watermelon Ltd, Innovate House, Lake View Drive, Annesley, NOTTINGHAM, NG15 0DT.
•**WISHART, Mr. Ian Macintosh, BSc FCA** *1989;* PricewaterhouseCoopers LLP, Savannah House, 3 Ocean Way, Ocean Village, SOUTHAMPTON, SO14 3TJ. See also PricewaterhouseCoopers
WISHART, Mr. John David, BSc ACA *2000;* Sulzer Ltd, CH-8401, WINTERTHUR, SWITZERLAND.
WISKER, Mr. Jeremy William, BSc FCA *1983;* Millstone Cottage, 79a High Street, Hampton in Arden, SOLIHULL, B92 OAE.
WISKER, Mrs. Mary Angela, BA FCA *1986;* 91 Penn Hill Road, BATH, BA1 3RT.
WISNIEWSKI, Mr. Damian Mark Alan, BSc ACA *1987;* Spring House, Southdown Road, Woldingham, CATERHAM, SURREY, CR3 7DP.
WISNIEWSKI, Mr. Edward Anthony, BSc ACA *1988;* 19 Poplar Drive, Barnt Green, BIRMINGHAM, B45 8NQ.
•**WISNIOWSKI, Mr. Robert Richard, MA FCA MBA DChA** *1996;* Anglopol Limited, Oxford House, 24 Oxford Road North, LONDON, W4 4DH.
WISSON, Mr. Michael Anthony, MEng ACA *2007;* with PricewaterhouseCoopers LLP, 1 Embankment Place, LONDON, WC2N 6RH.
WISZNIEWSKI, Mr. Adam Tomasz, BSc ACA *1996;* Ty-Carreg, Hindhayes Lane, STREET, SOMERSET, BA16 0DP.
WITCHELL, Mr. David, BA ACA *1988;* 81 Lambton Road, West Wimbledon, LONDON, SW20 0LW.
WITCHELL, Mr. John, BA ACA *1995;* 44 Church Hams, Finchampstead, WOKINGHAM, BERKSHIRE, RG40 4XF.
•**WITCHELL, Mr. Keith Roger, ACA FCCA CTA** *2006;* (Tax Fac), KRW Accountants Ltd, Home Ground Barn, Pury Hill Business Park, Alderton Road, Paulerspury, TOWCESTER NORTHAMPTONSHIRE NN12 7LS.
WITCHELL, Mrs. Teresa Joy, BA ACA *1995;* Avis Rent A Car (UK) Ltd, Avis Management Services Avis House, Park Road, BRACKNELL, RG12 2EW.
WITCHER, Mr. Christopher Raymond, BSc FCA *1972;* Westcote, Seymour Plain, MARLOW, SL7 3DA.
WITCHER, Mr. Geoffrey Alan, FCA *1971;* Trago Mills, Two Waters Foot, LISKEARD, CORNWALL, PL14 6HY.
WITCHER, Mr. Peter Winston Robert, FCA *1967;* Cambria House, 107 High Street, Worton, DEVIZES, WILTSHIRE, SN10 5RU. (Life Member)
•**WITCOMB, Mr. Simon James, FCA** *1972;* (Tax Fac), Witcombs, Turnfields Gate, THATCHAM, BERKSHIRE, RG19 4PT.
WITCOMBE, Mr. Keith Eric, FCA *1965;* 13 Homesdale Road, Petts Wood, ORPINGTON, KENT, BR5 1JS.
•**WITHALL, Mr. Keith Brian, BA ACA** *1981;* (Tax Fac), Keith Withall & Co, 303 High Street, ORPINGTON, BR6 0NN.
WITHALL, Mrs. Nicola Dawn, FCA *1992;* 58 Mornington Crescent, Nuthall, NOTTINGHAM, NG16 1QE.
•**WITHALL, Mrs. Shirley Elizabeth, BSc ACA** *1986;* Withall & Co Ltd, Squires House, 205A High Street, WEST WICKHAM, BR4 0PH. See also Withall & Co
WITHAM, Mr. Christopher John, FCA *1966;* 10 Bridleshire Road, Bridleshire Farms, NEWARK, DE 19711, UNITED STATES. (Life Member)
•**WITHAM, Mr. David James, BA FCA** *1987;* Price Deacon Witham Ltd, 9 Millar Court, Station Road, KENILWORTH, WARWICKSHIRE, CV8 1JD. See also Price Pearson Witham Ltd
•**WITHAM, Mr. Dominic, BA ACA** *1993;* Hakim Fry, 69-71 East Street, EPSOM, KT17 1BP. See also Barbican Services Limited
WITHAM, Mr. Harry, FCA *1963;* Stoke Lodge, Steels Lane, Oxshott, LEATHERHEAD, KT22 0QH.
WITHAM, Mrs. Janice Ann, BA ACA *1986;* 6 Mulberry Drive, WARWICK, CV34 5JP.
WITHAM, Mrs. Leslie Karen, BA FCA *1982;* Avalon, Ventnor Terrace, ST. IVES, CORNWALL, TR26 1DY.
WITHECOMBE, Mr. Mark, BA ACA *2007;* Anglo American Plc Anglo American House, 20 Carlton House Terrace, LONDON, SW1Y 5AN.
WITHECOMBE, Mr. Robert Darren, FCA CTA *1991;* Swanmoor, Harracott, BARNSTAPLE, DEVON, EX31 3LG.
WITHERICK, Miss. Claire Diane, BSc ACA *1998;* with PricewaterhouseCoopers, 2 Southbank Boulevard, Southbank, MELBOURNE, VIC 3006, AUSTRALIA.
WITHERICK, Mrs. Deborah Karen, BA ACA *1999;* Anchor House, 5 Station Road, ORPINGTON, KENT, BR6 0RZ.
WITHERINGTON, Mr. John Stewart, FCA *1975;* Les Pinardes, 16190 SALLES LAVALETTE, FRANCE.
WITHERINGTON, Mr. Philip James, BSc ACA *2001;* 18/F Tower 1, HSBC Centre, 1 Sham Mong Road, TAI KOK TSUI, KOWLOON, HONG KONG SAR.
WITHERS, Miss. Alison Clare, ACA *2010;* 9 Helena Road, YEOVIL, SOMERSET, BA20 2HQ.
WITHERS, Mrs. Alison Margaret, BA ACA *1991;* 291 Carter Knowle Road, SHEFFIELD, S11 9FY.
WITHERS, Mr. Andrew Philip, BA ACA *1983;* Liggard House, Ballam Road, LYTHAM ST. ANNES, LANCASHIRE, FY8 4NL.
WITHERS, Mr. Craig Stewart, BSc ACA *1998;* Morgan Stanley International, 25 Cabot Square, LONDON, E14 4QA.
•**WITHERS, Mr. David, BSc FCA CTA** *1985;* Impact Business Management Ltd, 57 The Moorlands, Weir, BACUP, LANCASHIRE, OL13 8BT.
WITHERS, Mr. David Lawrence, BSc ACA *1991;* Wildgoose Construction Ltd Fallgate, Milltown Ashover, CHESTERFIELD, DERBYSHIRE, S45 0EY.
WITHERS, Mrs. Helen Margaret, BSc ACA *1987;* The Gatehouse, Lodge Park, Lodge Lane, COLCHESTER, CO4 5NE.
WITHERS, Mr. Howard Marshall, FCA *1954;* (Tax Fac), South Wharf Investments (Portscade) Ltd, Suite 61, Innovation Centre, Highfield Drive, ST. LEONARDS-ON-SEA, EAST SUSSEX TN38 9UH.
WITHERS, Mr. James, BSc(Hons) ACA *1995;* 22 Gaydon Road, Aldridge, WALSALL, WS9 0SX.
WITHERS, Mr. John Granville, BA ACA *1985;* 36 Fern Avenue, Jesmond, NEWCASTLE UPON TYNE, NE2 2QX.
WITHERS, Mr. John Norman, FCA *1972;* H M C Brauer Ltd, Dawson Road, Bletchley, MILTON KEYNES, MK1 1JP.
WITHERS, Mr. John Robert, FCA *1975;* 19 Ranulf Croft, Cheylesmore, COVENTRY, CV3 5FB.
WITHERS, Mrs. Lesley Janet, MA ACA *1990;* Little Heath, Crays Pond, READING, RG8 7QG.
WITHERS, Miss. Maria Ann, ACA *1996;* H S B C, 8-16 Canada Square, LONDON, E14 5HQ.
WITHERS, Mrs. Melanie Jane, BA ACA *1995;* 22 Gaydon Road, WALSALL, WS9 0SX.
WITHERS, Mrs. Pamela Melesina Marion, ACA *2008;* National Trust, Kemble Drive, SWINDON, SN2 2NA.
WITHERS, Mr. Philip Ian, BSc FCA AMCT *1989;* 9 Angletarn Close, West Bridgford, NOTTINGHAM, NG2 6TB.
WITHERS, Miss. Rebecca, ACA *2009;* 19 Canton Street, SOUTHAMPTON, SO15 2DJ.
WITHERS, Mr. Robin William, FCA *1964;* 19 Woodmancourt, GODALMING, GU7 2BT.
WITHERS, Miss. Sarah Louise, BSc(Hons) FCA *2001;* BNP Paribas Securities Services, 55 Moorgate, LONDON, EC2R 6PA.
•**WITHERS, Mr. William Jonathan, BSc FCA** *1996;* (Tax Fac), William Withers & Co Limited, Town Farm, Templeton, TIVERTON, EX16 8BL.
WITHERS, Mr. William St John, BSc(Hons) ACA *2003;* 51 Queen Street, Cubbington, LEAMINGTON SPA, WARWICKSHIRE, CV32 7NB.
WITHERS, Ms. Zoe Anne, MBA BSc FCA *1991;* 79 Manchuria Road, LONDON, SW11 6AF.
WITHERS GREEN, Mr. Stephen, MA ACA *1990;* St. Edwards School, Woodstock Road, OXFORD, OX2 7NN.
•**WITHEY, Mr. Guy Damian, BA ACA** *1991;* 17 Stanhope Road, Bowdon, ALTRINCHAM, CHESHIRE, WA14 3LA.
WITHEY, Mrs. Philippa Clare, BSc ACA *1991;* 17 Stanhope Road, Bowdon, ALTRINCHAM, CHESHIRE, WA14 3LA.
WITHEY, Mr. Richard John, BA FCA *1985;* PricewaterhouseCoopers LLP, 350 South Grand Avenue, LOS ANGELES, CA 90071, UNITED STATES. See also PricewaterhouseCoopers
WITHEY, Mr. Robert, FCA *1951;* Woodside House, Farm Hill Lane, STROUD, GL5 4BX. (Life Member)
WITHINGTON, Mr. Andrew Peter David, ACA *2008;* Pricewaterhousecoopers, 101 Barbirolli Square, MANCHESTER, M2 3PW.
WITHINGTON, Mrs. Jill, ACA *1987;* 48 Woodfield Road, SHREWSBURY, SY3 8HY.
WITHINGTON, Mr. John Paul, BA(Hons) ACA *2009;* 532 Heathway, DAGENHAM, ESSEX, RM10 7RU.
WITHINGTON, Mr. Mark, ACA *1983;* Gilbody & Co, 65 Sackville Road, HOVE, EAST SUSSEX, BN3 3WE.
WITHINGTON, Mr. Peter James, MBA BA ACA *1991;* 91 Ochitree, DUNBLANE, FK15 0DQ.
WITHINSHAW, Mr. Benjamin Michael, ACA *2008;* 12 Delavor Road, WIRRAL, MERSEYSIDE, CH60 4RN.
•①**WITHINSHAW, Mr. Roderick Michael, FCA** *1979;* with Royce Peeling Green Limited, The Copper Room, Deva Centre, Trinity Way, MANCHESTER, M3 7BG.
WITHNELL, Mr. Aloysius Luke Hamilton Lowndes, BSc ACA *1981;* 35 Elms Rd, LONDON, SW4 9ER.
WITHNELL, Mr. James, MChem ACA *2011;* 60 Eelbrook Avenue, Bradwell Common, MILTON KEYNES, MK13 8RA.
WITHRINGTON, Mr. Julian Xavier, BA(Hons) ACA *2001;* Morgan Stanley, 20 Bank Street, Canary Whaf, LONDON, E14 4AD.
WITHYCOMBE, Mrs. Susan Michele Tracey, ACA *1989;* 92 Long Street, Williton, TAUNTON, SOMERSET, TA4 4RD.
WITKISS, Mr. Simon Richard George, BSc(Hons) ACA *2004;* (Tax Fac), with IRIS Software Ltd, Riding Court House, Riding Court Road, Datchet, SLOUGH, SL3 9JT.
WITKOVER, Mr. Paul Daniel, LLB ACA *1999;* 37 Lorian Close, Woodside Park, LONDON, N12 7DW.
WITT, Mr. Leon Murray, FCA *1971;* 12 Galton Road, WESTCLIFF-ON-SEA, ESSEX, SS0 8LE.
WITT, Miss. Lynsey Louise, ACA *2008;* 1 Guernsey Way, Winnersh, WOKINGHAM, RG41 5FT.
WITT, Mr. Melvin John, BA ACA *2003;* The Marlowe Academy, Stirling Way, RAMSGATE, ct1 2sx.
WITT, Mr. Robin, BSc ACA *1999;* Inspire Professional Services, 37 Commercial Road, POOLE, BH14 0HU.
WITT, Mr. William Robert Tansley, BA ACA *1998;* Zurich Financial Services UK Life Centre, Station Road, SWINDON, SN1 1EL.
WITTENBERG, Mrs. Paula Jane, BA FCA *1986;* 50 Grosmont Avenue, WORCESTER, WR4 0RD.
WITTER, Mr. Clive Philip, BA ACA *1986;* Willis Group, 51 Lime Street, LONDON, EC3M 7DQ.
WITTET, Mr. Mark, BA FCA *1986;* Symm & Co Ltd, Osney Mead, OXFORD, OX2 0EQ.
WITTET, Mr. Pascal, BSc ACA *2006;* with PricewaterhouseCoopers LLP, 1 Embankment Place, LONDON, WC2N 6RH.
WITTEVEEN, Mr. Martin Hans, BEng BCom FCA *2001;* 52 Second Avenue, Selly Park, BIRMINGHAM, B29 7HD.
•**WITTICH, Mr. Peter Charles, FCA** *1973;* (Tax Fac), Wittich & Co Limited, Holly Grove, Hatching Green, HARPENDEN, HERTFORDSHIRE, AL5 2JS.
WITTING, Miss. Julia Elizabeth, BA FCA *1990;* 4 Marsh Lane, Stanstead Abbotts, WARE, HERTFORDSHIRE, SG12 8HH.
WITTNER, Mr. Guy, ACA *2011;* 55 Northiam, LONDON, N12 7JH.
WITTRED, Mr. Nicholas John, ACA *2009;* 4 Ash Grove, South Wootton, KING'S LYNN, NORFOLK, PE30 3TS.
WITTRED, Mr. Robin John, FCA *1974;* (Tax Fac), Mopus-Smith & Lemmon LLP, 48 Kings Street, KING'S LYNN, NORFOLK, PE30 1HE.
WITTS, Mr. Allan Gavin, BCom FCA *1961;* 104 Mountbatten Avenue, Sandal, WAKEFIELD, WF2 6HH.
WITTS, Mr. Andrew, BA(Hons) ACA *2011;* 95 Chatham Road, Battersea, LONDON, SW11 6HJ.
WITTS, Mr. Ernest John, FCA *1951;* 16 Dale Close, Littleton, WINCHESTER, SO22 6RA. (Life Member)
WITTS, Mr. Graeme Alan, BSc FCA *1979;* L'Hermitage, Les Varines, St Saviour, JERSEY, JE2 7SB.
WITTS, Mr. Howard Raymond, BA FCA *1982;* 80 Clarence Road, ST. ALBANS, AL1 4NG.
WITTS, Mrs. Karen, MA FCA *1989;* 14 Kersley Street, LONDON, SW11 4PT.
WITTS, Mr. Kevin Michael, BSc FCA *1996;* c/o Group Strategy & Planning, L39 HSBC Main Building, 1 Queens Road Central, CENTRAL, HONG KONG SAR.
WITTS, Mr. Richard Arthur, FCA *1968;* Flat 5 A Tower 2, Golf Parkview, 83 Castle Peak Road, Kwu Tung, SHEUNG SHUI, NEW TERRITORIES HONG KONG SAR.
WITTS, Mr. Roger Charles, FCA *1970;* 35 College Road, LONDON, SE21 7BA.
WITTY, Mr. David Ronald, BA ACA *1979;* 182 Simmondley Lane, GLOSSOP, SK13 6LY.
WITTY, Mr. Stanley Smith, FCA *1949;* 4 Clifton Square, PETERLEE, SR8 5HQ. (Life Member)
WITZENFELD, Mr. Jeffrey Phillip, FCA *1975;* Trade & Financial Services Ltd, 72 Charlotte Street, LONDON, W1T 4QQ.
WIVELL, Mr. Robert Frederick Banks, BA FCA *1963;* 2 The Terrace, Boston Spa, WETHERBY, WEST YORKSHIRE, LS23 6AH.
WIXEY, Mr. Christopher John, FCA *1979;* C.J. Wixey, Fossil Cottage, Havyatt, GLASTONBURY, BA6 8LF.
WLAZNIK, Mr. Chris, ACA *2007;* 106 Gloucester Road, NEWBURY, BERKSHIRE, RG14 5JJ.
•**WLODYKA, Mr. George Christopher, BSc ACA** *1981;* Allan George Consultants, 107 The Grove, WEST WICKHAM, BR4 9LA. See also George Allan
WLOSZEK, Miss. Mary Kay, BSc ACA *1994;* 155 Wentworth Road, Golders Green, LONDON, NW11 0RJ.
WO, Mr. David Yuk-Sum, BSc(Hons) ACA *2009;* Flat B, 28 Fontenoy Road, LONDON, SW12 9LU.
WO, Mr. Sai Yin, ACA *2007;* Flat B 32/F Block 3, Belvedere Garden, Phase 2, TSUEN WAN, NEW TERRITORIES, HONG KONG SAR.
WOFFENDEN, Mr. Cedric John, FCA *1955;* 4 Southfield Drive, KENILWORTH, CV8 2FR. (Life Member)
WOFFENDEN, Mr. Mark David, BA ACA *1993;* 31 Cookridge Lane, LEEDS, LS16 7LQ.
WOFFENDEN, Mr. Richard Michael, BSc FCA *1975;* 12 Middle Drive, ROTHERHAM, SOUTH YORKSHIRE, S60 3DJ.
WOJACZEK, Mr. Wojciech, ACA *2011;* Top Floor Flat, 32 Albert Road, MITCHAM, SURREY, CR4 4AH.
WOJCIECHOWSKA, Miss. Magdalena, BA ACA *1986;* 56 Alburgh Close, BEDFORD, MK42 0HE.
WOJCIECHOWSKI, Mr. Paul Michal, BSc FCA *1979;* Vilvorde, Le Mont Felard, ST. LAWRENCE, JERSEY, JE3 1JA.
WOJEWODZKI, Miss. Laura Rose, ACA *2009;* with Deloitte LLP, Athene Place, 66 Shoe Lane, LONDON, EC4A 3BQ.
WOJTULEWICZ, Mr. Stefan Jan, ACA *2010;* 10 Sandalwood Drive, STAFFORD, ST16 3FX.
WOKES, Mr. Christopher Richard, FCA *1969;* Box 361, ROSEVILLE, NSW 2069, AUSTRALIA. (Life Member)
WOLAHAN, Mr. Laurence Gerard, BCom ACA *1985;* 4529 Middledale Road South, West Bloomfield, DETROIT, MI 48323, UNITED STATES.
WOLAHAN, Mrs. Susan, BA ACA *1986;* 4529 Middledale Road South, WEST BLOOMFIELD, MI 48323, UNITED STATES.
•**WOLDEGABRIEL, Mr. Taddesse, FCA** *1972;* Taddesse Woldegabriel & Co, P.O. Box 22848 - Code 1000, ADDIS ABABA, ETHIOPIA.
WOLF, Mr. Alan Charlton, FCA *1958;* 42 St Lucia Close, WHITLEY BAY, NE26 3HT. (Life Member)
WOLF, Mr. Geoffrey Michael, FCA *1958;* 2 Gleneagles, STANMORE, MIDDLESEX, HA7 3QG. (Life Member)
•**WOLF, Mr. Jacob, FCA** *1980;* Crowe Clark Whitehill LLP, Arkwright House, Parsonage Gardens, MANCHESTER, M3 2HP. See also Horwath Clark Whitehill LLP and Crowe Clark Whitehill
WOLF, Mr. Julian David, BSc FCA *1974;* 22 Portman Close, ST. ALBANS, AL4 9TW.
WOLF, Mr. Michael Lewis, BCom FCA *1960;* St. Anns Residential Care Home, The Crescent, KETTERING, NORTHAMPTONSHIRE, NN15 7HW. (Life Member)
WOLF, Mr. Peter Giles Dudley, FCA *1973;* 126 Lower Ham Road, KINGSTON UPON THAMES, KT2 5BD.
WOLF, Miss. Stephanie Maria, BA ACA *2005;* Flat 3 Banbury Court, Woodstock Avenue, LONDON, W13 9UF.
WOLFE, Mr. Andrew Stuart, ACA *2009;* 8 Chancellors Road, LONDON, W6 9RS.
WOLFE, Mr. Anthony James Garnham, BSc FCA *1978;* North Square Consulting Limited, 6 Northcote Park, Oxshott, LEATHERHEAD, SURREY, KT22 0HN.
WOLFE, Ms. Blanche, BSc ACA *1996;* 5a Martaban Road, Stoke Newington, LONDON, N16 5SJ.

WOLFE, Mr. Bryce Daniel, BSc FCA FSI *1996;* Village Roadshow Limited, 500 Chapel Street, SOUTH YARRA, VIC 3141, AUSTRALIA.
WOLFE, Mr. Colin Eric, MA FCA CTA *1973;* 220 Radcliffe Road, West Bridgford, NOTTINGHAM, NG2 5HD.
WOLFE, Mr. Harvey Alan, FCA *1968;* 143 Route De Salernes, 83510 LORGUES, FRANCE.
•WOLFE, Mr. Mark, ACA *2008;* Mark Wolfe & Co, 30 Carnoustie, Beaumont Rise, BOLTON, BL3 4TF.
WOLFE, Mr. Richard Bron, FCA *1969;* 5 Boundary Road, West Bridgford, NOTTINGHAM, NG2 7BW.
WOLFE-MURRAY, Mr. Martin Andrew, ACA *2008;* 12 Peri Court, St. Mildreds Place, CANTERBURY, KENT, CT1 3TH.
WOLFENDALE, Mr. David Arthur, FCA *1969;* Flat 4 Rostherne, Whitehall Road Rhos on Sea, COLWYN BAY, CLWYD, LL28 4ET.
WOLFENDALE, Mr. Richard, BA ACA *2010;* 33 Midfield Road, SHEFFIELD, S10 1SU.
•WOLFENDEN, Mr. Thomas Geoffrey, BA(Hons) ACA *2001;* Hillside, Forty Green, BEACONSFIELD, BUCKINGHAMSHIRE, HP9 1XS.
WOLFF, Mr. Alan, FCA *1975;* (Tax Fac), 7 Kenerne Drive, BARNET, HERTFORDSHIRE, EN5 2NW.
WOLFF, Miss. Anne Helen, BA ACA *1986;* Stone House, Stonehouse Lane, Cookham, MAIDENHEAD, BERKSHIRE, SL6 9TP.
•WOLFF, Mr. David Alexander, FCA *1975;* (Tax Fac), Banner & Associates Ltd, 29 Byron Road, HARROW, HA1 1JR.
WOLFF, Mr. Jonathan Charles, BA ACA *2006;* 20 Russell Place, LONDON, SE16 7PL.
WOLFGANG, Mr. Michael John, BSc FCA *1969;* Archways, 87 Weald Road, SEVENOAKS, TN13 1QJ.
WOLFIN, Mr. Nigel Ellis, BSc FCA *1996;* 21 The Ridgeway, WATFORD, WD17 4TH.
WOLFRAM, Mr. Thomas Mark, BSc ACA *1991;* Gut Kerschlach 1, 82396 PAEHL, GERMANY.
WOLFSON, Mr. Alan, ACA *1990;* 43 Lyndhurst Gardens, LONDON, N3 1TA.
•WOLFSON, Mr. Daniel, FCA *1986;* Guner Wolfson Ltd, 9 Beaumont Gate, Shenley Hill, RADLETT, HERTFORDSHIRE, WD7 7AR. See also Daniel Wolfson & Co Ltd
•WOLFSON, Mr. Ian, FCA *1982;* (Tax Fac), Wolfson Associates Limited, 1st Floor, 314 Regents Park Road, Finchley, LONDON, N3 2LT.
•WOLFSON, Mr. Kenneth, FCA *1981;* (Tax Fac), Wolfson Associates Limited, 1st Floor, 314 Regents Park Road, Finchley, LONDON, N3 2LT. See also Wolfson Associates Services Ltd
WOLFSON, Mr. Michael Barry, BSc ACA *1994;* 4 Abbey View, RADLETT, HERTFORDSHIRE, WD7 8LT.
WOLFSON, Mr. Raymond, BA ACA *1991;* 9 Sandmoor Lane, LEEDS, LS17 7EA.
•WOLINSKY, Mr. Daniel, BSc ACA *1984;* 34 Fursby Avenue, LONDON, N3 1PL.
•WOLKIND, Mr. Brian Jeffrey, FCA *1973;* Brian J Wolkind Limited, 35 Ballards Lane, LONDON, N3 1XW.
WOLLAN, Miss. Lynne, BA ACA *1997;* 25 Red Lion Lane, Overton, BASINGSTOKE, HAMPSHIRE, RG25 3HH.
WOLLASTON, Mr. Matthew James, BSc ACA *1994;* Corus, Shotton Works, Weighbridge Road, Deeside Industrial Park, DEESIDE, CLWYD CH5 2NH.
WOLLASTON, Mr. Thomas, ACA *2009;* Studio 47 West, Gainsborough Studios West, 1 Poole Street, LONDON, N1 5EA.
•WOLLEN, Mr. Peter Frederick, FCA *1953;* Peter F. Wollen, 7 Cleeve Lake Court, Bishops Cleeve, CHELTENHAM, GLOUCESTERSHIRE, GL52 8SN.
WOLLEY, Mr. Hugh Seymour, ACA *1982;* Lysanda Ltd Tintagel House, London Road Kelvedon, COLCHESTER, CO5 9BP.
WOLLIN, Ms. Babett, ACA *2009;* Flat 1, 15 Gladstone Terrace, BRIGHTON, BN2 3LB.
WOLLNER, Mr. Mark Edward, BSc FCA *1978;* Barnes Mill, Mill Vue Road, CHELMSFORD, CM2 6NP.
WOLMAN, Mr. Lawrence Philip, MBA BA DIC ACA *1992;* Knoll House, 1 High View, CHALFONT ST. GILES, BUCKINGHAMSHIRE, HP8 4HH.
WOLOSIUK, Miss. Philomena Jean, BSc FCA *1976;* HFI L.P., Schroders House, 3rd floor 131 Front Street, P O Box HM 2083, HAMILTON HM HX, BERMUDA.
WOLSEY, Mrs. Deborah Jane, BA ACA *2005;* 18 Brudenell Close, Cawston, RUGBY, WARWICKSHIRE, CV22 7GN.
WOLSEY, Mr. Denham Hadley, BA ACA *2002;* 18 Brudenell Close, Cawston, RUGBY, WARWICKSHIRE, CV22 7GN.
WOLSTENCROFT, Ms. Jane Allyson, BSc ACA *1984;* Hurlingham, 109 Botley Road, ROMSEY, HAMPSHIRE, SO51 5RQ.
WOLSTENCROFT, Mrs. Nicola Joanne, BSc ACA *1995;* Allan Stobart Lubricants & Fuels, Low Currigg, Raughton Head, CARLISLE, CA5 7DX.
•WOLSTENCROFT, Mr. Paul Wilfred, MA ACA *1981;* with Deloitte LLP, PO Box 500, 2 Hardman Street, MANCHESTER, M60 2AT.
WOLSTENCROFT, Mr. Roger, ACA *1981;* Croftanne, 20 Anvil Close, Portslade, BRIGHTON, BN41 2HT.
•ⓘWOLSTENHOLME, Mr. Adrian John, ACA *1991;* Amber Advisory Limited, 48 Moorfield Avenue, Knowle, SOLIHULL, WEST MIDLANDS, B93 9RA.
WOLSTENHOLME, Mrs. Amanda, BSc ACA *1997;* 25 Devonshire Park Road, Davenport, STOCKPORT, CHESHIRE, SK2 6JZ.
•WOLSTENHOLME, Mr. Colin, FCA *1973;* Colin Wolstenholme, 1 Brockholme Road, LIVERPOOL, L18 4QG.
WOLSTENHOLME, Mr. David, FCA *1965;* The Old Rectory, Quidenham, NORWICH, NR16 2PH. (Life Member)
WOLSTENHOLME, Mr. David John, BSc FCA *1978;* Sheepwash Farm Middle Bridge Road Gringley-on-the-Hill, DONCASTER, SOUTH YORKSHIRE, DN10 4SD.
WOLSTENHOLME, Mr. Iain John, BA ACA CF *1997;* 25 Devonshire Park Road, Davenport, STOCKPORT, CHESHIRE, SK2 6JZ.
WOLSTENHOLME, Mrs. Irene Joy, BA ACA *1992;* (Tax Fac), 139 Harbut Road, LONDON, SW11 2RD.
•WOLSTENHOLME, Ms. Kate Andrea, BA ACA *1995;* PricewaterhouseCoopers, 1 Embankment Place, LONDON, WC2N 6RH. See also PricewaterhouseCoopers LLP
•WOLSTENHOLME, Mrs. Katharine Julie, BA(Hons) ACA *2001;* Moore Stephens LLP, 150 Aldersgate Street, LONDON, EC1A 4AB.
WOLSTENHOLME, Miss. Lynsey, ACA *2011;* Flat 2, 16b Stamford Road, LONDON, N1 4JS.
WOLSTENHOLME, Mrs. Manjit, BSc ACA *1989;* Birtles Hall Farm, Birtles Lane, Over Alderley, MACCLESFIELD, CHESHIRE, SK10 4RU.
WOLSTENHOLME, Mrs. Marjorie Elizabeth, BSc FCA *1977;* 21 Garsdale Road, Brierdene, WHITLEY BAY, NE26 4NT.
WOLSTENHOLME, Miss. Mary, BA ACA *2003;* 25 Westbury Avenue, SALE, CHESHIRE, M33 4WQ.
WOLSTENHOLME, Mr. Neil, BSc FCA *1989;* Private Banking Training, Birtles Lane Over Alderley, MACCLESFIELD, CHESHIRE, SK10 4RU.
WOLSTENHOLME, Mr. Neil Edward, BSc ACA *1992;* 42 Lansdowne Road, LONDON, N10 2AU.
WOLSTENHOLME, Mrs. Patricia Mary, BA FCA *1977;* with Creaseys LLP, 12 Lonsdale Gardens, TUNBRIDGE WELLS, KENT, TN1 1PA.
WOLSTENHOLME, Mr. Peter Hartley, MA ACA *1990;* London Diocesan Fund, 36 Causton Street, LONDON, SW1P 4AU.
•WOLSTENHOLME, Mr. Tom Vincent, BA FCA *1967;* Wolstenholme McIlwee Limited, Marlet House, E1 Yeoman Gate, Yeoman Way, WORTHING, WEST SUSSEX BN13 1QZ.
WOLTER, Mr. Kirk, BCom ACA MBA *1999;* 14 The Lawns, Lee Terrace, Blackheath, LONDON, SE3 9TB.
WOLTON, Mr. James Ian, BSc FCA *1974;* HM Revenue & Customs Specialist Investigations 11th Floor Castle House, 31 Lisbon Street, LEEDS, WEST YORKSHIRE, LS1 4SD.
WOLTON, Miss. Suzanne Marie, LLB ACA *1996;* 39a Ronaki Road, Mission Bay, AUCKLAND, NEW ZEALAND.
WOLVAARDT, Mr. Graeme Michael, ACA CA(SA) *2010;* 105 Willow Park, Otford, SEVENOAKS, KENT, TN14 5NF.
WOLVERSON, Mrs. Lucy Jane, ACA *2006;* 9 Winchester Road, Kings Somborne, STOCKBRIDGE, SO20 6PF.
WOLVERSON, Mr. Mark, BA(Hons) ACA *2001;* 9 Winchester Road, Kings Somborne, STOCKBRIDGE, SO20 6PF.
WOLVERSON, Mr. Rodney John, FCA *1975;* 39 Cambridge Road, Abington, CAMBRIDGE, CB21 6BL. (Life Member)
WOMBELL, Mr. Anders, BA(Hons) ACA *2001;* Financial Services Authority, 25 North Colonnade, LONDON, E14 5HS.
WOMBWELL, Mr. Malcolm Thomas, FCA *1954;* 5 Mayflower Close, GAINSBOROUGH, DN21 1AU. (Life Member)
WOMERSLEY, Mrs. Emma Jane, BSc ACA CF *2000;* 5 Davies Avenue, LEEDS, LS8 1JZ.
WOMERSLEY, Mr. John Crossley, FCA *1939;* 31a Boundary Close, WOODSTOCK, OX20 1LR. (Life Member)
WOMERSLEY, Mr. Mark Elliott James, ACA *2009;* Daniels Chilled Foods Unit 4, Killingbeck Drive, LEEDS, LS14 6UF.
WOMERSLEY, Mr. Peter Christopher, FCA *1970;* Petit Mesnil, Mont Morin, St. Sampson, GUERNSEY, GY2 4JB.
WOMERSLEY, Mr. Roger Ingham, FCA *1967;* 75 Lamb Hall Road, Longwood, HUDDERSFIELD, HD3 3TJ. (Life Member)
•WOMWELL, Mr. Richard William, FCA *1975;* R.W. Womwell, Suite 11, Woodside House, 18 Walsworth Road, HITCHIN, HERTFORDSHIRE SG4 9SP.
WON, Ms. Michaela, ACA CA(NZ) *2010;* 36a Burnbury Road, LONDON, SW12 0EJ.
•WONACOTT, Mr. William George, FCA *1970;* (Tax Fac), Ford Bull Watkins, Clerks Well House, 20 Britton Street, LONDON, EC1M 5TU.
WONFOR, Mr. Martin Robert Francis, BA FCA *1971;* The Old Palace, The Green, RICHMOND, SURREY, TW9 1PB. (Life Member)
WONG, Mr. Adrian Kin-Ho, ACA *2009;* with Deloitte LLP, Abbots House, Abbey Street, READING, RG1 3BD.
WONG, Miss. Adriana Yu Ming, BA(Hons) ACA *2003;* 75 Underwood Place, Oldbrook, MILTON KEYNES, MK6 2SJ.
WONG, Mr. Alexis Tsz Tuk, BSc FCA *1992;* BOC International, 26/F BOC Tower, 1 Garden Road, CENTRAL, HONG KONG ISLAND, HONG KONG SAR.
WONG, Mrs. Amy Wan Chi, MEng ACA *2004;* 36B Tower 12 Carmel Cove, Caribbean Coast, 1 Kin Tung Road, TUNG CHUNG, NEW TERRITORIES, HONG KONG SAR.
WONG, Mr. Andrew, ACA *2008;* Flat 2, 1 Broadlands Road, Highgate, LONDON, N6 4AE.
WONG, Mr. Andrew, MBA FCA *1992;* 245 Jalan 5/48, 46000 PETALING JAYA, Selangor, MALAYSIA.
WONG, Mr. Andrew Wei Ping, ACA CA(AUS) *2008;* 184 Heytesbury Road, SUBIACO, WA 6008, AUSTRALIA.
WONG, Miss. Angela Ching Yee, BSc FCA *1994;* Morgan Stanley, Level 46, International Commerce Centre, 1 Austin Road West, TSIM SHA TSUI, KOWLOON HONG KONG SAR.
WONG, Mrs. Anne Elizabeth, BSc(Hons) ACA *2001;* with Ernst & Young, 100 Barbirolli Square, MANCHESTER, M2 3EY.
WONG, Mr. Anthony, ACA *2005;* Anthony Wong, 14C 6/F Nassau Road, MEI FOO SUN CHUEN, KOWLOON, HONG KONG SAR.
WONG, Mr. Anthony Tet Look, BSc FCA *1977;* Oriental Holdings Berhad, c/o 195 Macalister Road, 10450 GEORGE TOWN, PULAU PINANG, MALAYSIA.
WONG, Mr. Arthur Nyap Nee, ACA *2005;* Flat E 5/F Block 17, Serenity Park Two, TAI PO, NEW TERRITORIES, HONG KONG SAR.
WONG, Mr. Augustine Kum Wah, FCA *1974;* 56 Draycott Park, SINGAPORE 259399, SINGAPORE.
WONG, Mr. Baldwin, MPhys ACA CTA *2001;* 88 Lodge Crescent, ORPINGTON, BR6 0QG.
WONG, Mrs. Barbara, FCA *1976;* 68 Taman Zaaba, Taman Tun Dr. Ismail, 60000 KUALA LUMPUR, FEDERAL TERRITORY, MALAYSIA.
WONG, Mr. Bo Tong, ACA *2007;* BT Wong & Co, Unit A 6/F Rammon House, 101 Sai Yeung Choi Street, MONG KOK, KOWLOON, HONG KONG SAR.
WONG, Ms. Bonnie Kar-Man, ACA CA(AUS) *2009;* 31 Riverbank, Laleham Road, STAINES, MIDDLESEX, TW18 2QE.
WONG, Miss. Bonnie Phik Shan, BSc(Econ) ACA *2002;* with BDO LLP, Kings Wharf, 20-30 Kings Road, READING, RG1 3EX.
WONG, Miss. C Lin, FCA *1977;* 4 Margate Road, #12-01, SINGAPORE 438044, SINGAPORE.
WONG, Miss. Carolyn, ACA *2009;* 165 Windy Arbor Road, Whiston, PRESCOT, MERSEYSIDE, L35 3SE.
WONG, Ms. Catherine Yuen Man, ACA *2006;* A1 15/F Block A, The Fortune Gardens, 11 Seymour Road, CENTRAL, HONG KONG ISLAND, HONG KONG SAR.
WONG, Mr. Chak Yu John, ACA *2011;* (Tax Fac), Flat A 26/F Estoril Heights, Belair Gardens, SHA TIN, NT, HONG KONG SAR.
WONG, Mr. Chan Wai, ACA *1994;* 5th Floor, 33 Grosvenor Place, LONDON, SW1X 7HY.
WONG, Mr. Chang Khai, BSc ACA *2004;* 11A Jalan 1, Taman Tun Abdul Razak, 68000 AMPANG, SELANGOR, MALAYSIA.
WONG, Miss. Charmaine Chin Sim, LLB ACA *2002;* Flat 9 Sandy Lodge, Avenue Road, Highgate, LONDON, N6 5DQ.
WONG, Mr. Che Ming, BA ACA *1994;* IMS Health Asia Pte Ltd, 10 Hoe Chiang Road, #23-01/02 Keppel Towers, SINGAPORE 089315, SINGAPORE.
WONG, Mr. Chen Vui, BA ACA *2003;* 139 Norfolk Avenue, LONDON, N13 6AL.
WONG, Mr. Chen Yau, BSc ACA *1980;* Grand Paradise Group(HK) Ltd, Room 1001-2, China Merchants Tower, 168-200 Connaught Road, CENTRAL, HONG KONG ISLAND HONG KONG SAR.
•WONG, Mr. Cheng Keen, FCA *1977;* C K Wong & Co, Citibase, 40 Princess Street, MANCHESTER, M1 6DE.
WONG, Mr. Cheuk Him, ACA *2008;* 2503 Admiralty Centre, Tower 1, 18 Harcourt Road, ADMIRALTY, HONG KONG ISLAND, HONG KONG SAR.
WONG, Mr. Cheuk Ming, ACA *2006;* 144 Thorpe Hall Avenue, SOUTHEND-ON-SEA, ESSEX, SS1 3AR.
WONG, Mr. Cheung Lai, BA FCA *1974;* P O Box 3051, M.I.P., MARKHAM L3R 6G4, ON, CANADA. (Life Member)
•WONG, Mr. Cheung Shui, FCA *1983;* C.S. Wong, 118 High Street, Sawston, CAMBRIDGE, CB22 3HJ.
WONG, Mr. Chi Chien, BA ACA *1981;* 13 Lorong SS1/1C, 47300 PETALING JAYA, Selangor, MALAYSIA.
WONG, Mr. Chi Yuen, ACA *2007;* Flat G, 30/F, Nam Fung Court, Harbour Heights, 1 Fook Yum Road, NORTH POINT HONG KONG SAR.
WONG, Mr. Chi Lik Henry, ACA *2005;* 17/F MTR Headquateres Building, Telford Plaza, KOWLOON BAY, KOWLOON, HONG KONG SAR.
WONG, Ms. Chi Ling, ACA *2008;* Flat A 1/F. Block 2, Grandeur Villa, No. 21 Tat Chee Avenue, KOWLOON TONG, KOWLOON, HONG KONG SAR.
WONG, Mr. Chi Ming, ACA *2008;* C M Wong & Company, Flat C, 6/F, Guangdong Tours Centre, 18 Pennington Street, CAUSEWAY BAY HONG KONG SAR.
WONG, Mr. Chi Sang Derek, ACA FCCA MBA CPA *2004;* United Asia Finance Ltd, 21/F Allied Kajima Building, 138 Gloucester Road, WAN CHAI, HONG KONG ISLAND, HONG KONG SAR.
WONG, Mr. Chi Wai, ACA *2004;* Level 36, Three Pacific Place, 1 Queens Road East, ADMIRALTY, HONG KONG ISLAND, HONG KONG SAR.
WONG, Mr. Chi Wai Albert, ACA *2005;* Albert Wong & Co., Room 701A, Nan Dao Commercial Building, 359-361 Queen's Road Central, CENTRAL, HONG KONG ISLAND HONG KONG SAR.
WONG, Mr. Chi Yan, ACA *2008;* Flat 1112, Block B, Kornhill, QUARRY BAY, HONG KONG ISLAND, HONG KONG SAR.
WONG, Ms. Ching Ngor, ACA *2008;* 28B Block 5, Ocean View, 1 Po Tai Street, Ma On Shan, SHA TIN, NEW TERRITORIES HONG KONG SAR.
WONG, Mr. Chiu Yin Frederick, ACA *2007;* 126A Broadway, 10/F Mei Foo Sun Chuen, MEI FOO SUN CHUEN, KOWLOON, HONG KONG SAR.
WONG, Mr. Chiu Ming Alan, ACA *2008;* Flat A 1 Fl, Village Gardens, 21 Fa Po Street, KOWLOON TONG, HONG KONG SAR.
WONG, Ms. Chiu Yu, ACA *2008;* Flat A 2nd Floor Golden Block, 12 Cassia Road, Yau Yat Chuen, KOWLOON TONG, KOWLOON, HONG KONG SAR.
WONG, Mr. Choong Leong, FCA *1974;* 499 Jalan 17/17, 46400 PETALING JAYA, Selangor, MALAYSIA.
WONG, Mr. Choong Meng, FCA *1982;* 814 Jalan 17\24, 46400 PETALING JAYA, SELANGOR, MALAYSIA.
WONG, Mr. Christopher, BA FCA *1981;* Westcon UK Ltd, 210 Bath Road, SLOUGH, SL1 3XE.
WONG, Mr. Christopher Wing Kee, BSc ACA *1988;* 12 Wilson Road, 1/F, JARDINE'S LOOKOUT, HONG KONG ISLAND, HONG KONG SAR.
WONG, Mr. Chun, BA ACA *2011;* 34 Aldercombe Road, BRISTOL, BS9 2QL.
WONG, Mr. Chun Ming, ACA *2007;* Wong & Kwan, Room A, 7/F Queen Centre, 58-64 Queens Road East, WAN CHAI, HONG KONG ISLAND HONG KONG SAR.
WONG, Mr. Chun Bong, ACA *2007;* C.B. Wong & Co, Room 1601 Carnarvon Plaza, 20 Carnarvon Road, TSIM SHA TSUI, KOWLOON, HONG KONG SAR.
WONG, Mr. Chun Wah, ACA *2007;* Flat G 10/F, Nan Shan Mansion, Kao Shan Terrace, TAIKOO SHING, HONG KONG ISLAND, HONG KONG SAR.
WONG, Mr. Chung Kin Kenny, ACA *2009;* Flat 1, 86 Blackheath Road, LONDON, SE10 8DA.
WONG, Mr. Chung Fai Felix, ACA *2005;* Unit 12E CDW Building, 388 Castle Peak Road, TSUEN WAN, NEW TERRITORIES, HONG KONG SAR.
WONG, Mr. Chung Kin Quentin, ACA *2008;* Quentin Wong & Co Certified Public Accountants, Room 907, 9/F, Wayson Commerical Building, 28 Connaught Road West, SHEUNG WAN HONG KONG ISLAND HONG KONG SAR.

Members - Alphabetical WONG - WONG

WONG, Ms. Cindy, BSc ACA *1987;* 6 Pilgrims Lane, LONDON, NW3 1SL.
WONG, Mr. David Anthony, FCA *1969;* S F G Ltd, 134 Old Hope Road, KINGSTON 6, JAMAICA.
WONG, Mr. David Cecil Vivian, BA ACA *1978;* 14 Joan Road, SINGAPORE 298892, SINGAPORE.
WONG, Mr. David Peter, BA ACA *1983;* 30 Vista Tiburon Drive, TIBURON, CA 94920, UNITED STATES.
WONG, Ms. Denise S H, ACA *2007;* Flat 3, 10/F, Block D, 3 Long Yuet Street, TO KWA WAN, KOWLOON HONG KONG SAR.
WONG, Mr. Desmond Chun Wah, ACA *2006;* Room 314, Ming Fai House, Kwun Fai Court, HO MAN TIN, KOWLOON, HONG KONG SAR.
WONG, Mr. Desmond Siu Wai, ACA *2007;* Flat 3402, Block Q, Allway Gardens, TSUEN WAN, NEW TERRITORIES, HONG KONG SAR.
WONG, Mrs. Diana, BA MCMI FCA *1983;* 529 Boston Road, Chandler, BRISBANE, QLD 4155, AUSTRALIA.
•①**WONG, Mr. Dominic Lee Zoong, MA FCA FABRP** *1994;* Deloitte LLP, 4 Brindley Place, BIRMINGHAM, B1 2HZ. See also Deloitte & Touche LLP
WONG, Mr. Edmund Ngai Man, BSc FCA *1990;* 6 Silverflower Avenue, MARKHAM L3S4B7, ON, CANADA.
WONG, Mr. Ee Choon, FCA *1974;* 297, Bedok South Avenue 3, #09-04, Bedok Court, SINGAPORE 469297, SINGAPORE.
WONG, Mr. Ee Keen, ACA *1982;* Block 3, Marine Terrace, Apt 16-288, SINGAPORE 440003, SINGAPORE.
WONG, Ms. Elise Yuen Shan, ACA *2006;* KPMG, 8th Floor, Tower E2, Oriental Plaza, 1 East Chang An Avenue, BEIJING 100738 CHINA.
WONG, Miss. Elizabeth Maria, MA BA(Hons) ACA *2010;* 57 Oakdale Road, WATFORD, WD19 6JX.
WONG, Mr. Eric Brian, BCom ACA *1996;* 30 Warrender Way, RUISLIP, HA4 8ED.
WONG, Mr. Eric Chun Yu, MA ACA *1995;* 16B Block 20, Wonderland Villas, KWAI CHUNG, NEW TERRITORIES, HONG KONG SAR.
WONG, Miss. Fay Yin, BA ACA *2002;* Flat C 3/F. Whitfield Mansion, 15-19 Whitfield Road, NORTH POINT, HONG KONG SAR.
•**WONG, Mrs. Fiona Sheung Chun, BA ACA** *1987;* Wong & Company, 70 Airthrie Road, Goodmayes, ILFORD, IG3 9QU. See also Wong & Co
WONG, Miss. Fiona Wan Ching, BSc ACA *1993;* Flat 30A, South Tower 5, Residence Bel-Air, 38 Bel-Air Avenue, POK FU LAM, HONG KONG ISLAND HONG KONG SAR.
WONG, Miss. Florence Fook Wing, BA FCA *1962;* Flat A, 35th Floor Starcrest Tower 1, 9 Star Street WAN CHAI, Hong Kong Island, HONG KONG SAR. (Life Member)
WONG, Mr. Foo, BA ACA *1992;* 1-015 Rits Garden, Liyuan Road Tianzhu Zone, Shunyi, BEIJING 101312, CHINA.
WONG, Mr. Fook Leong, FCA *1980;* 6 Low Street, HURSTVILLE, NSW 2220, AUSTRALIA.
WONG, Mr. Francis Man Hon, ACA *2006;* Room 107, Block 23, Heng Fa Chuen, CHAI WAN, HONG KONG ISLAND, HONG KONG SAR.
WONG, Mr. Frederick Wai Keung, FCA *1983;* 16D Choi Tien Mansion, 11 Taikoo Wan Road, Taikoo Shing, QUARRY BAY, HONG KONG ISLAND, HONG KONG SAR.
WONG, Mr. Frederick Wing Tong, BCom FCA *1968;* D1 9/F, Evergreen Villa, 43 Stubbs Road, MID LEVELS, HONG KONG ISLAND, HONG KONG SAR. (Life Member)
WONG, Mr. Fuk Shing Philip, ACA *2006;* Room 902, General Commercial Building, 156-164 Des Voeux Road, CENTRAL, HONG KONG ISLAND, HONG KONG SAR.
WONG, Mr. Fung Fong, BSc FCA *1986;* 15 Purcells Avenue, EDGWARE, HA8 8DR.
WONG, Ms. Fung Yu, ACA *2007;* Flat D, 15th Floor, Woodgreen Court, DISCOVERY BAY, HONG KONG SAR.
WONG, Mr. Gah Jih, FCA *1980;* Flat G, 20th Floor, Block 15, South Horizons, AP LEI CHAU, HONG KONG ISLAND HONG KONG SAR.
WONG, Mr. Gar Man, BEng ACA *1993;* Lloyds Banking Group, Canons House Canons Way, BRISTOL, BS99 7LB.
WONG, Miss. Gar Mun, BSc(Hons) ACA *2009;* 12 Sydenham Close, ROMFORD, RM1 4HN.
WONG, Mr. Gary Yat Fung, ACA *2008;* Flat 5 Empire Place, Linden Avenue, WATFORD, WD18 7AX.
WONG, Mr. George, BSc ACA *2011;* Flat 255 North Block, 1c Belvedere Road, LONDON, SE1 7GF.
WONG, Mr. George Har-Kar, FCA *1981;* G P O Box 1315, General Post Office, CENTRAL, HONG KONG ISLAND, HONG KONG SAR.
WONG, Mr. Guang Seng, MBA FCA *1975;* Deloitte Kassimchan (AF0080), 87 Jalan Sultan Abdul Jalil, 30450 IPOH, MALAYSIA.
WONG, Ms. Hau Ling Ava, ACA *2007;* Flat F 6/F Block 4, La Cite Noble, 1 ngan 0 Road, TSEUNG KWAN O, NEW TERRITORIES, HONG KONG SAR.
WONG, Mr. Hei Chiu, ACA *2008;* H C Wong & Co, Room 1007, 10th Floor, Won Centre, 111 Connaight Road, CENTRAL HONG KONG ISLAND HONG KONG SAR.
WONG, Ms. Hei Man, ACA *2011;* Flat 6H, Block 3, South Wave Court, 3 Shum Wan Road, WONG CHUK HANG, HONG KONG ISLAND HONG KONG SAR.
WONG, Mr. Heng-Boon, ACA *1986;* 41JALAN DESA MESRA, TAMAN DESA, 58100 KUALA LUMPUR, FEDERAL TERRITORY, MALAYSIA.
WONG, Mr. Henry Kwok-Hei, ACA *1981;* A6 Coral Court 14/Fl, Tin Hau Temple Road, NORTH POINT, HONG KONG ISLAND, HONG KONG SAR.
WONG, Mr. Henry Shiu Kwan, FCA *1973;* Henry Wong & Company, 4A Ngan House, 210 Des Voeux Road, CENTRAL, HONG KONG ISLAND, HONG KONG SAR.
WONG, Mr. Hil Foon, ACA *2003;* Elisabethlaan 38, Berchem, 2600 ANTWERP, BELGIUM.
WONG, Mr. Hin Wing, ACA *2004;* Suite 1101, Shun Kwong Commercial Building, 8 Des Voeux Road West, SHEUNG WAN, HONG KONG ISLAND, HONG KONG SAR.
WONG, Mr. Hing Tat, ACA *2004;* H. T. Wong & Co., 1123A Landmark North, 39 Lung Sum Avenue, SHEUNG SHUI, NEW TERRITORIES, HONG KONG SAR.
WONG, Mr. Hing Wah, ACA *2005;* Flat C, 47/F, Tower 8, The Belcher's, 89 Pokfulam Road, POK FU LAM HONG KONG ISLAND HONG KONG SAR.
WONG, Mr. Hiu Fai Keith, ACA *2007;* Keith Wong CPA & Co, Room 903, 9/F, Parkes Commercial Centre, 2 - 8 Parkes Street, TSIM SHA TSUI KOWLOON HONG KONG SAR.
WONG, Ms. Ho Chun Karen, ACA *2007;* Allied Banking Corp. (HK) Ltd, 1402, Worldwide House, 19 Des Voeux Road, CENTRAL, HONG KONG SAR.
WONG, Mr. Ho Yuen Gary, ACA *2008;* 11/F Hong Kong Trade Centre, 161 - 167 Des Voeux Road Central, CENTRAL, HONG KONG SAR.
WONG, Ms. Hoi Ka Shirley, ACA *2007;* Flat C 28/F Block 1, Waterfront South, No. 1 Yue Wok Street, Tin Wan, ABERDEEN, HONG KONG SAR.
WONG, Mr. Hoi Kuen Edmund, ACA *2005;* Edmund Wong & Company, Unit 2301B, 23/F, BEA Harbour View Centre, 56 Gloucester Road, WAN CHAI HONG KONG SAR.
WONG, Mr. Hok Sun Joseph, ACA *2007;* 4/F Flat C, 36 Nassau Road, MEI FOO SUN CHUEN, KOWLOON, HONG KONG SAR.
WONG, Mr. Hong Sun, MA FCA *1986;* 27 Jalan Tupai, SINGAPORE 249155, SINGAPORE.
•**WONG, Mr. Hong Yuen, MA FCA** *1968;* (Member of Council 2005 - 2010), Deloitte & Touche, 35/F One Pacific Place, 88 Queensway, CENTRAL, HONG KONG ISLAND, HONG KONG SAR. See also Kwan Wong Tan & Hong
WONG, Mr. Hsing Fa, FCA *1974;* 33 Jalan SL 4/6, Bandar Sungeilong, 43000 KAJANG, SELANGOR, MALAYSIA.
WONG, Mr. Hung Tak, BSc ACA *1993;* Floor13 FlatA Kingford Height, 17-19 Babington Path, MID LEVELS, Hong Kong Island, HONG KONG SAR.
WONG, Mr. Hung Nam, ACA *2008;* with PricewaterhouseCoopers, Prince's Building, 22/F, 10 Chater Road, CENTRAL, HONG KONG ISLAND HONG KONG SAR.
WONG, Mr. Ian Yee Yan, ACA *2007;* 12 Science Park East Avenue 6/F, HONG KONG SAR Science Park, SHA TIN, NEW TERRITORIES, HONG KONG SAR.
WONG, Mr. James, BSc ACA *2008;* 41 Brazier Crescent, NORTHOLT, MIDDLESEX, UB5 6FB.
WONG, Miss. Joan Mei Yee, BSc ACA *1987;* Flat B 27/FTung Shan Mansion, 11 Taikoo Shing Road, TAIKOO SHINGHong Kong Island, HONG KONG SAR.
WONG, Mrs. Joanna Marie, BSc ACA *2005;* with Lawrence Wong & Co, 2 Parkfield Gardens, North Harrow, HARROW, HA2 6JR.
WONG, Mr. John Hon Cheung, MSc ACA *1991;* Ground Floor, Block A Fontana Garden, 25 Ka Ning Path, CAUSEWAY BAY, HONG KONG ISLAND, HONG KONG SAR.
WONG, Mr. John Wing Kit, FCA *1974;* J.W.K. Wong, Unit B 21 Floor, Two Chinachem Plaza, 68 Connaught Road, CENTRAL, HONG KONG ISLAND HONG KONG SAR.
WONG, Mr. Johnny Ka Keung, ACA *1989;* with PricewaterhouseCoopers, 33/F Cheung Kong Center, 2 Queen's Road, CENTRAL, HONG KONG ISLAND, HONG KONG SAR.
WONG, Mr. Jonathan Ying Kit, BSc(Econ) ACA *2001;* 19 Keats House Cottage Close, HARROW, MIDDLESEX, HA2 0HA.
•**WONG, Mr. Joon Hian, FCA** *1973;* J.H. Wong & Co, 68 Taman Zaaba, Taman Tun Dr Ismail, KUALA LUMPUR, FEDERAL TERRITORY, MALAYSIA.
WONG, Mr. Joseph Man Chung, BA ACA *2006;* Flat 7 Cuthbert Bell Tower, 4 Pancras Way, LONDON, E3 2SL.
WONG, Mr. Joseph Phui-Lun, BCom FCA *1959;* 36 geylang #08-01, SINGAPORE 398162, SINGAPORE.
WONG, Mr. Joshua Yee Tak, BA(Hons) ACA *2000;* 22 Avenue Crescent, LONDON, W3 8EP.
WONG, Miss. Judy Mei Wan, BSc ACA *1992;* Flat 8 Peak Gardens 16-20 Mt Austin Road, THE PEAK, HONG KONG SAR.
WONG, Miss. Ka Pui, BA ACA *2007;* Flat 4, 28 Floor Tin Hor House, Tin Ping Estate, SHEUNG SHUI, NEW TERRITORIES, HONG KONG SAR.
WONG, Mr. Ka Ho, ACA *2008;* 27/F Apt. No. 15 Celestial Heights 80 Sheung Shing Street, HO MAN TIN, HONG KONG SAR.
WONG, Mr. Ka Kit, ACA *2009;* Room 1502 Kan Wai House, Kam Fung Court, SHA TIN, NEW TERRITORIES, HONG KONG SAR.
WONG, Mr. Ka Lok, ACA *2005;* 2801 Island Place, 510 King's Road, NORTH POINT, HONG KONG ISLAND, HONG KONG SAR.
WONG, Mr. Ka Lok, ACA *2008;* Tesa Tape Greater China, Suite 712 7/F, Tower 2, The Gateway, 25 Canton Road, TSIM SHA TSUI KOWLOON HONG KONG SAR.
WONG, Ms. Ka Yi, ACA *2008;* Flat 5B Block 14, Tak Chee Yuen, 88 Tat Chee Avenue, KOWLOON TONG, KOWLOON, HONG KONG SAR.
WONG, Mr. Kah Keung Peter, ACA *1979;* 7 Lisbon Court, PARKWOOD, WA 6147, AUSTRALIA.
WONG, Mr. Kai Cheong, ACA *2005;* Champion Capital Limited, 5B CKK Commercial Centre, 289 Hennessy Road, WAN CHAI, HONG KONG SAR.
WONG, Mr. Kai Tat, ACA CF *2006;* Dickson Wong CPA Co Ltd, Room 302, 3/F, The Chinese General Chamber of Commerce Building, 24-25 Connaught Road, CENTRAL HONG KONG SAR.
WONG, Mr. Kam Chung Raymond, ACA *2008;* China Everbright International Co Ltd, Room 2703, Far East Finance Centre, 16 Harcourt Road, ADMIRALTY, HONG KONG ISLAND HONG KONG SAR.
WONG, Mr. Kam Kee Andy, ACA *2008;* Flat C 19/F. Phase 1 Blessings Garden, 95 Robinson Road, MID LEVELS, HONG KONG ISLAND, HONG KONG SAR.
WONG, Mr. Kam Piu, ACA *2005;* Wong & Associates, 5403 - 48 Street, YELLOWKNIFE X1A 1N7, NT, CANADA.
WONG, Mr. Kan-Wai, BA ACA *1992;* 1st Floor, No 156 Wing Ning New Village, Kam Tin, YUEN LONG, NEW TERRITORIES, HONG KONG SAR.
WONG, Mr. Kang Hwee, ACA *1978;* Apt 23-5 Desa Angkasa, 12 Jalan Taman U Thant, 55000 KUALA LUMPUR, FEDERAL TERRITORY, MALAYSIA.
WONG, Mr. Kang Juat, FCA *1978;* C-2-2 Vista Tasik Condo, 12 Jalan Sri Permaisuri, Bandar Sri Permaisuri, 56000 KUALA LUMPUR, FEDERAL TERRITORY, MALAYSIA.
WONG, Ms. Kar Bik, ACA *2008;* 1503 Block 49, Heng Fa Chuen, CHAI WAN, HONG KONG SAR.
WONG, Ms. Kar Men Michele, ACA *2010;* (Tax Fac), Flat B, 25/f Tower 2, 33 Conduit Road, MID LEVELS, HONG KONG SAR.
WONG, Mr. Karl Dominic, MA ACA *2002;* c/o MWA (IC) Ltd, 705A Tung Ning Building, 249-253 Des Voeux Road, CENTRAL, HONG KONG ISLAND, HONG KONG SAR.
WONG, Mr. Ke Chin, ACA *2006;* 12/F Flat C, Tower 12, Parc Royale, 8 Hin Tai Street, SHA TIN, NEW TERRITORIES HONG KONG SAR.
WONG, Mr. Keat Soon, FCA *1988;* Talisman Energy (UK) Ltd, Talisman House, 163 Holburn Street, ABERDEEN, AB10 6BZ.
•**WONG, Mr. Kee Yen, FCA** *1986;* 1176 Westdale Road, OAKVILLE L6L 6P3, ON, CANADA.
WONG, Mr. Kei Wo Janson, ACA *2008;* 1503 Block 49, Heng Fa Chuen, CHAI WAN, HONG KONG SAR.
WONG, Mr. Keng Chong, BSc ACA *2008;* Rotherhithe Street, 21 Helena Square, LONDON, SE16 5XP.
WONG, Mr. Keng Ho, MSc ACA *1991;* Flat 405 Hong Lee Court, 24 Hong Lee Road, KWUN TONG, KOWLOON, HONG KONG SAR.
WONG, Mr. Kenneth Siu Tai, ACA *2006;* Kenneth Wong & Co, Unit B & C, 20/F Full Win Commercial Centre, 573 Nathan Road, MONG KOK, KOWLOON HONG KONG SAR.
•**WONG, Mr. Kent Kam Sing, BA FCA** *1990;* Wong & Co, 2nd Floor Astoria House, 62 Shaftesbury Avenue, LONDON, W1D 6LT.
WONG, Mrs. Khrystyna, BA ACA *2007;* Pricewaterhousecoopers, 9 Greyfriars Road, READING, RG1 1JG.
WONG, Miss. Kia Yin, BSc ACA *1990;* Flat G 36/F Tower 10, Park Central, 9 Tong Tak Street, TSEUNG KWAN O, NEW TERRITORIES, HONG KONG SAR.
WONG, Mr. Kim Ming, ACA *2005;* Flat 1 16/F. Block 37 Heng Fa Chuen, CHAI WAN, HONG KONG ISLAND, HONG KONG SAR.
WONG, Mr. Kin Ming, ACA *2007;* 29 Beechmount Avenue, LONDON, W7 3AE.
WONG, Mr. Kin Chung, ACA *2011;* Room 2408, 24/Floor, Block B, Yu Yan House, Yu Chui Court, 6 Ngau Pei Sha Street SHA TIN NT HONG KONG SAR HK SHA TIN HONG KONG SAR.
WONG, Mr. Kin Leung, ACA *2008;* Ushio Hong Kong Ltd, Suites 3113-3114, 31/F Tower 6, The Gateway, 9 Canton Road, TSIM SHA TSUI KOWLOON HONG KONG SAR.
WONG, Mr. Kin Lun, ACA *2008;* K L Wong & Co, 14/F, San Toi Building, 137-139 Connaught Road, CENTRAL, HONG KONG SAR.
WONG, Mr. Kin Wai, ACA *2008;* Flat H, 16/F, Scholastic Garden, 48 Lyttleton Road, MID LEVELS, HONG KONG SAR.
WONG, Mr. King Cheung, BCom FCA *1991;* Flat E 29/F Tower 3, Summit Terrace, 1 On Yuk Road, TSUEN WAN, NEW TERRITORIES, HONG KONG SAR.
WONG, Mr. King Fung William, BEng ACA *1994;* Goldman Sachs (Asia) L.L.C, 68/F Cheung Kong Center, 2 Queens Road, CENTRAL, HONG KONG ISLAND, HONG KONG SAR.
WONG, Ms. Kit Ching Agnes, ACA *2007;* Flat B 13/F. Supernova Stand, 28 Mercury Street, TIN HAU, HONG KONG SAR.
WONG, Ms. Kitty Kam Che, ACA *2005;* Flat 6 9/F, 42 Wood Road, Wah Tao Building, WAN CHAI, HONG KONG ISLAND, HONG KONG SAR.
WONG, Mr. Kok Leong Victor, BSc ACA ACMA MBA *1991;* 15 Brockwell Avenue, BECKENHAM, KENT, BR3 3GE.
WONG, Miss. Kok Yee, CA FCA CMC *1970;* Wong Kok Yee Tax Services Pte Ltd, 78 Shenton Way, Apartment 30 - 01, Lippo Centre, SINGAPORE 079120, SINGAPORE.
WONG, Mr. Koon Fong, ACA *2005;* K.F. Wong & Co, Unit 8 13/F, Rise Commercial Building, 5-11 Granville Circuit, Granville Road, TSIM SHA TSIU KOWLOON HONG KONG SAR.
WONG, Ms. Koon Fung, ACA *2008;* Flat 28D Panorama Gardens, 103 Robinson Road, MID LEVELS, HONG KONG SAR.
WONG, Mr. Kuen Fai, ACA *2008;* Flat B, 36/F, Tower 7, South Horizons, AP LEI CHAU, HONG KONG SAR.
WONG, Mr. Kum Chew, FCA *1975;* 10 Venice Court, Dress Circle Estate, Dianella Heights, PERTH, WA 6059, AUSTRALIA.
WONG, Mr. Kwok Kit, FCA *1977;* Flat 28DBlock 4, City Garden NORTH POINT, Hong Kong Island, HONG KONG SAR.
WONG, Mr. Kwok Hong Patrick, ACA *2007;* 4A Majestic Court, 8 Tsui Man Street, HAPPY VALLEY, HONG KONG SAR.
WONG, Mr. Kwok Wai Albert, ACA *2008;* Chu and Chu, Suite 1801-5 18/F, Tower 2, China HONG KONG SAR City, 33 Canton Road, TSIM SHA TSUI KOWLOON HONG KONG SAR.
WONG, Mr. Kwok Wai Robin, ACA *2007;* Flat E 47/F Tower 2, Maritime Bay, TSEUNG KWAN O, HONG KONG SAR.
WONG, Mr. Kwok Ying, ACA *2007;* Flat 307 Block B, Peninsula Heights, 63 Broadcast Drive, KOWLOON CITY, KOWLOON, HONG KONG SAR.
WONG, Mr. Kwong Ling Terence, ACA *2004;* Castelo Investments Limited, 1592 Po Tung Road, SAI KUNG, HONG KONG SAR.
WONG, Mr. Lai Pong, ACA *2007;* 26D, BLK6, Laguna City, Cha Kwo Ling, LAM TIN, KOWLOON HONG KONG SAR.
•**WONG, Mr. Lawrence Chin Tung, ACA** *1983;* Lawrence Wong & Co, 2 Parkfield Gardens, North Harrow, HARROW, HA2 6JR.

WONG, Mr. Lawrence Yow Khan, BEng ACA *1994;* 3 Changkat Minden Lorong 8, Gelugor, 11700 PENANG, MALAYSIA.
WONG, Mr. Lee Siong, BA FCA *1982;* MSI RAGG WEIR, Level 2, 108 Power Street, HAWTHORN, VIC 3122, AUSTRALIA.
WONG, Mrs. Lee-Pa, ACA *1985;* Block 7, Dairy Farm Estate, Apt. 02-04 Dairy Farm Road, SINGAPORE 679037, SINGAPORE.
WONG, Mr. Leung Tim, ACA *2008;* Flat 4C Block 2Phase 7, Cotton Tree Mansion, 11 Tak On Street, Whampoa Gardens, HUNG HOM, KOWLOON HONG KONG SAR.
WONG, Miss. Lisa Chui Shan, BA ACA DChA *2005;* 8a Penwith Road, LONDON, SW18 4QF.
WONG, Mr. Louis Chi Kong, BA ACA *1987;* 20/B Block 7, Cavendish Heights, 33 Perkins Road, JARDINE'S LOOKOUT, HONG KONG ISLAND, HONG KONG SAR.
WONG, Miss. Lu Wern, BSc ACA *2009;* Flat 7 Yew House, 2 Woodland Crescent, LONDON, SE16 6YH.
WONG, Mr. Luen Hing, ACA *2008;* Securities and Futures Commission, 8/F, Chater House, 8 Connaught Road, CENTRAL, HONG KONG SAR.
WONG, Mr. Lukwong, FCA *1976;* 106 Mill Way, BUSHEY, WD23 2AQ.
•**WONG, Dr. Lung Tak Patrick, ACA** *2004;* Wong Lam Leung & Kwok C.P.A. Ltd, Room 1101, 11/F China Insurance Group Building, 141 Des Voeux Road Central, CENTRAL, HONG KONG ISLAND HONG KONG SAR.
WONG, Miss. Lynn Kui Lian, BA ACA *1994;* 27 Hazel Park Terrace, Unit 04-05, Hazel Park Condominium, SINGAPORE 678949, SINGAPORE.
WONG, Mr. Man On, MA ACA *1995;* 278 Ocean Drive #06-11, SINGAPORE 098450, SINGAPORE.
WONG, Mr. Man Chung Francis, ACA *2005;* Union Alpha CPA Limited, 19/F No. 3 Lockhart Road, WAN CHAI, HONG KONG ISLAND, HONG KONG SAR. See also Francis Wong CPA Co Limited
WONG, Mr. Man Kai Ricky, ACA *2008;* KPMG Huazhen, 38th Floor, Teem Tower, 208 Tianhe Road, GUANGZHOU 510620, CHINA. See also KPMG
WONG, Miss. Margaret Lu Yan, MA(Cantab) ACA *2000;* c/o Schweppes International Limited, Bankrashof 3, 1183 NP AMSTELVEEN, NETHERLANDS.
WONG, Mr. Mark, ACA *2011;* 35 Spalding Way, CAMBRIDGE, CB1 8NP.
WONG, Mr. Matthew, BSc ACA *2007;* (Tax Fac), 4 Rokeby Place, LONDON, SW20 0HU.
WONG, Miss. Mee Chun, BSc ACA *1978;* 54 B Tregunter Tower 3, 14 Tregunter Path, MID LEVELS, HONG KONG SAR.
WONG, Miss. Mei Kiu, ACA *2010;* Room 1904 19/F. Block 19, Heng Fa Chuen, 100 Shing Tai Road, CHAI WAN, HONG KONG SAR.
WONG, Ms. Mei Lai, ACA *2007;* Rm 1906 Empress Plaza, 17-19 Chatham Road South, TSIM SHA TSUI, KOWLOON, HONG KONG SAR.
WONG, Ms. Mei Sing, BSc ACA *1990;* 14128 84th Drive Apt 3H, BRIARWOOD, NY 11435, UNITED STATES.
•**WONG, Mr. Michael Seang Hock, FCA** *1979;* Michael Wong & Co, 23 Hillside Grove, LONDON, NW7 2LS.
WONG, Mrs. Michelle Wai Man, BSc ACA *1987;* 10 Clandon Road, GUILDFORD, SURREY, GU1 2DR.
WONG, Miss. Michelle Wing Kay, MSci ACA *2003;* Centennium House, 100 Lower Thames Street, LONDON, EC3R 6DL.
WONG, Miss. Michelle Yiing, ACA *2011;* No.47 Jalan Minang, Taman Sri Minang, KAJANG, MALAYSIA.
WONG, Ms. Millie Pui-Yan, BSc ACA *1994;* P.O. Box 361007, DUBAI, UNITED ARAB EMIRATES.
WONG, Ms. Ming Yun Katherine, ACA *2007;* Suite 703-8, One Pacific Place, 88 Queensway, CENTRAL, HONG KONG ISLAND, HONG KONG SAR.
WONG, Ms. Miu Ling, ACA *2007;* Flat H 17/ Floor, Block 6, Laguna City, Cha kwo Ling, LAM TIN, KOWLOON HONG KONG SAR.
WONG, Ms. Miu Ting Ivy, ACA *2008;* Wong Miu Ting Ivy, Rm. 1311 13/F. Leighton Centre, 77 Leighton Road, CAUSEWAY BAY, HONG KONG SAR.
WONG, Ms. Miu Yan Cecilia, ACA *2008;* B-2 20/F, Sunway Gardens, 989 Kings Road, QUARRY BAY, HONG KONG SAR.
WONG, Mr. Mok Siw, ACA *1979;* 61-A Jalan Perang, Taman Pelangi, 80400 JOHOR BAHRU, JOHOR, MALAYSIA.
WONG, Mr. Muk Chuen, BSc ACA *1990;* Flat 17BMacDonnell House, 6-8 MacDonnell Road, MID LEVELSHong Kong Island, HONG KONG SAR.
WONG, Mr. Mun Chee, ACA *2007;* Flat 6, 9th Floor, Wah Tao Building, 42 Wood Road, WAN CHAI, HONG KONG ISLAND HONG KONG SAR.
WONG, Miss. Nancy, BSc(Hons) ACA *2010;* 29 Summercroft Close, Golborne, WARRINGTON, WA3 3WL.
WONG, Mr. Nathan Wing Hung, BSc ACA *2004;* 76 Discovery Dock East, Marsh Wall, LONDON, E14 9RU.
WONG, Mr. Nicholas, ACA *2011;* 62 Swakeleys Road, UXBRIDGE, MIDDLESEX, UB10 8BD.
WONG, Mr. Nicholas Chi Wai, BSc ACA MInstP MBCS *2001;* 12 Cranley Road, Hersham, WALTON-ON-THAMES, SURREY, KT12 5BP.
WONG, Miss. Nicole Yuet Wan, BA ACA *2000;* 18 Lingkungan, U-Thant, Off JLN U-Thant, 55000 KUALA LUMPUR, FEDERAL TERRITORY, MALAYSIA.
WONG, Mr. Nigel Peter, BCom ACA *2000;* 21 Warrender Way, RUISLIP, HA4 8EB.
WONG, Miss. Norma Sze Man, MA ACA *2006;* Flat 9, 11 Tarves Way, LONDON, SE10 9JP.
WONG, Ms. Oi Ming, ACA *2008;* Flat G 17/F. Block 2 City Garden 233 Electric Road, NORTH POINT, HONG KONG SAR.
WONG, Mr. Pak Ling Philip, ACA *2005;* Flat 21B Tower 3, Hillsborough Court, 18 Old Peak Road, MID LEVELS, HONG KONG ISLAND, HONG KONG SAR.
WONG, Mr. Park Yun, ACA *2005;* Rooms 1001-1003 10/F. Manulife Provident Funds Place, 345 Nathan Road, TSIM SHA TSUI, KOWLOON, HONG KONG SAR.
WONG, Mr. Parkson King Fung, BA ACA *1997;* 1 Northcote Close, 3/F Sasson Road, POK FU LAM, HONG KONG ISLAND, HONG KONG SAR.
WONG, Mr. Patrick Tak-Pong, BA ACA *1989;* 40 Dunstan Road, Golders Green, LONDON, NW11 8AD.
WONG, Miss. Pek Peng, BCom ACA *2004;* 2 Lanark Place, LONDON, W9 1BS.
WONG, Miss. Pek Yee, BSc ACA *1983;* 158 Lorong Ma'arof, Bandaraya, 59000 KUALA LUMPUR, FEDERAL TERRITORY, MALAYSIA.
WONG, Mr. Peng Kian, ACA *1982;* 6 Manor Park Gardens, EDGWARE, HA8 7NA.
WONG, Mr. Peter Ernest, MA ACA *1987;* 17/F Sun and Moon Building, 45 Sing Woo Road, HAPPY VALLEY, HONG KONG ISLAND, HONG KONG SAR.
WONG, Mr. Peter Yap Ting, MBA BSc FCA *1987;* 27 Bredon Avenue, West Pennant Hills, SYDNEY, NSW 2125, AUSTRALIA.
WONG, Mr. Philip, ACA *1980;* Philip Wong & Co, 142 Jalan Datuk Sulaiman 6, Taman Tun Dr Ismail, 60000 KUALA LUMPUR, FEDERAL TERRITORY, MALAYSIA.
WONG, Mr. Philip Chi Ho, BA(Hons) ACA *2003;* with Business Link Northwest, City Office, Brian Johnson Way, PRESTON, PR2 5PE.
WONG, Mr. Philip Chiho, MBA BSc FCA *1982;* 12 Chiltern Close, NEWBURY, RG14 6SZ.
WONG, Mr. Po Chung, ACA *2005;* Flat D 2/F, Tower 11, Discovery Park, 398 Castle Peak Road, TSUEN WAN, NEW TERRITORIES 852 HONG KONG SAR.
WONG, Ms. Po Ling Pauline, ACA *2007;* Flat G 5/F, Block 5, Harmony Garden, 9 Siu Sai Wan Road, CHAI WAN, HONG KONG SAR.
WONG, Miss. Poh Har, FCA *1976;* 21 Kym Street, ATHELSTONE, SA 5076, AUSTRALIA.
WONG, Mr. Poh Weng, BSc FCA *1977;* RSM Nelson Wheeler, 29th Floor Caroline Centre, Lee Gardens Two, 28 Yun Ping Road, CAUSEWAY BAY, HONG KONG ISLAND HONG KONG SAR.
WONG, Mrs. Polly Pui Yi, ACA *2007;* 7A Block 4, Fullview Garden, CENTRAL, HONG KONG ISLAND, HONG KONG SAR.
WONG, Mr. Pong Kwok Ivan, ACA *2005;* P.K. Wong & Co, Unit 909 Tower 1, Silvercod, 30 Canton Road, TSIM SHA TSUI, KOWLOON HONG KONG SAR.
WONG, Ms. Pui Man, ACA *2008;* Room 1010, Block E, Sui Wo Court, SHA TIN, NEW TERRITORIES, HONG KONG SAR.
WONG, Ms. Pui Shan, ACA *2008;* Flat A 11/F, 23 Nassau Street, Mei Foo Sun Chuen, LAI CHI KOK, HONG KONG SAR.
WONG, Miss. Pui Yan, ACA *2009;* Flat 6 Princess Gate, 57 Market Street, BRIGHTON, BN1 1HH.
WONG, Ms. Pui Yeng, BSc ACA *2004;* 24 Jalan Desa Wangsa 2, Taman Desa Wangsa, Off Bandar Tun Hussein Onn, 43200 CHERAS, SELANGOR, MALAYSIA.
WONG, Mr. Raymond, ACA *2005;* FLAT A3, 12/F Wai Lai Mansion, 24 Yuet Wah Street, KWUN TONG, KOWLOON, HONG KONG SAR.
•**WONG, Mr. Raymond Fook Lam, FCA** *1980;* Raymond F.L. Wong, Room 130513F, Universal Trade Centre, 3-5A Arbuthnot Road, CENTRAL, HONG KONG ISLAND HONG KONG SAR.
•**WONG, Mr. Richard Chin Ho, BSc ACA** *2003;* RSW, Unit 6-17, 17 Thorp Street, BIRMINGHAM, B5 4AT.
WONG, Mr. Richard Fook Ming, FCA *1978;* 23rd Floor, 248 Queen's Road East, WAN CHAI, HONG KONG SAR.
WONG, Miss. Rose Lynn, BSc ACA *2007;* Flat 7 Welles Court, 4 Premiere Place, LONDON, E14 8SE.
WONG, Mr. Samuel See Lik, BCom ACA *1985;* 25 Cranley Gardens, LONDON, N10 3AA.
WONG, Miss. Sau Ling, BSc ACA *1998;* 263 River Valley Road, 01 24 Aspen Heights, SINGAPORE 238309, SINGAPORE.
WONG, Ms. Sau Pik, ACA *2007;* Ernst & Young Tax Services Ltd, 18/F, Two IFC, 8 Finance Street, CENTRAL, HONG KONG ISLAND HONG KONG SAR.
WONG, Ms. Sau Ying, ACA *2008;* Flat B 8th Floor, Block 7 Sereno Verde, 99 Tai Tong Road, YUEN LONG, NEW TERRITORIES, HONG KONG SAR.
WONG, Miss. Seow Wah, BSc ACA *1991;* Flat 11 25th Floor Block D, Villa Lotto, 18 Broadwood Road, HAPPY VALLEY, HONG KONG ISLAND, HONG KONG SAR.
WONG, Miss. Sheyee, BComm ACA *2009;* Flat 1 St Michaels Court, 29 Cheniston Gardens, LONDON, W8 6TG.
WONG, Ms. Shin Ming, ACA *2005;* Unit 4 No 48 Edith Street, Leichhardt, SYDNEY, NSW 2040, AUSTRALIA.
WONG, Mr. Shing Kay Oliver, ACA *2005;* Oliver Wong & Co., 12/F Goodfit Commercial Building, 7 Fleming Road, WAN CHAI, HONG KONG SAR.
WONG, Mr. Shing Nok Noah, ACA *2008;* Room 1 6/F Lok Wing Building, Whampoa Estate, HUNG HOM, KOWLOON, HONG KONG SAR.
WONG, Mr. Shu Ho Raymond, ACA *2008;* Flat G 27/F Tower 2, Island Place, 55 Tanner Road, NORTH POINT, HONG KONG SAR.
WONG, Ms. Shuk Yu, ACA *2009;* Ground Floor, 366B Queens Road West, SAI YING POON, HONG KONG ISLAND, HONG KONG SAR.
WONG, Mr. Shun Loy, ACA *2007;* S L Wong & Co, 2nd Floor, Teng Fuh Commercial Building, 333 Queen's Road Central, SHEUNG WAN, HONG KONG SAR.
WONG, Mr. Siew Kiat, BSc ACA *2006;* Flat 7 Yew House, 2 Woodland Crescent, LONDON, SE16 6YH.
WONG, Miss. Siew Lee Molly, BA ACA *1999;* with PricewaterhouseCoopers, P.O.Box 10192, Level 10 1 Sentral, Jalan Travers, 50470 KUALA LUMPUR, FEDERAL TERRITORY MALAYSIA.
WONG, Mr. Simon Hon-Chung, BA(Hons) ACA *2003;* 8 Alexandra View, #36-08 Metropolitan, SINGAPORE 158747, SINGAPORE.
WONG, Mr. Siu Fai Albert, ACA *2008;* Flat D 2/F, 180 Nam Cheong Street, SHAM SHUI PO, KOWLOON, HONG KONG SAR.
WONG, Mr. Siu Keung Kendy, ACA *2005;* 12/F Novel Industrial Building 850-870 Lai Chi Kok Road, CHEUNG SHA WAN, KOWLOON, HONG KONG SAR.
WONG, Mr. Siu Loi, ACA *2008;* Room 508 Lim Kit House, Lei Cheng Uk Estate, SHAM SHUI PO, KOWLOON, HONG KONG SAR.
WONG, Ms. Siu Yee Suzanne, MBA ACA ACCA CPA *2005;* Suzanne Wong & Co, Unit 704 Gee Tuck Building, Gee Tuck Building, 18 Bonham Strand, CENTRAL, HONG KONG SAR. See also Noble Pondus (CPA) Limited
WONG, Ms. Siu Yung, ACA *2007;* Flat B 3/F Tower 19 No. 47 Tat Chee Avenue, Parc Oasis Kowloon Tong, KOWLOON TONG, HONG KONG SAR.
WONG, Mr. Steven, ACA *2009;* Apartment 906, 8 Walworth Road, LONDON, SE1 6EE.
WONG, Ms. Sue Ling, BSc ACA *1995;* White Lodge, 170 Burntwood Lane, CATERHAM, SURREY, CR3 6TB.
WONG, Ms. Suet Fan Josephine, ACA *2008;* Flat E, 12th Floor, Block 5, Juniper Mansions, Whampoa Garden, HUNG HOM KOWLOON HONG KONG SAR.
WONG, Miss. Sui Ee, BA ACA *1995;* 37 Jalan Wangsa Budi 5, Wangsa Melawati, 53300 KUALA LUMPUR, FEDERAL TERRITORY, MALAYSIA.
WONG, Mr. Sui Chi, ACA *2008;* Flat 18E, Tower 5, Ocean Shores, TSEUNG KWAN O, NEW TERRITORIES, HONG KONG SAR.
WONG, Miss. Sui-Ting, ACA *2008;* 133 Totterdown Street, LONDON, SW17 8TE.
WONG, Ms. Suk Fan, ACA *2009;* F-3 5/Floor, 99 Mei King Street, Wyler Garden, Kowloon, TO KWA WAN, KOWLOON HONG KONG SAR.
WONG, Mr. Sun Keung, ACA *2007;* 20/F. Far East Consortium Building, 121 Des Voeux Road C, CENTRAL, HONG KONG SAR.
WONG, Miss. Susan Lai Wah, BA ACA *1995;* Flat 15E Tower 4 Les Saisons, 28 Tai On Street, SAI WAN HO, HONG KONG ISLAND, HONG KONG SAR.
WONG, Miss. Sweet Lynn, BSc ACA *2009;* Flat 36 Raleigh Court, Clarence Mews, LONDON, SE16 5GB.
WONG, Miss. Sylvia Ka Yee, BSc ACA *1990;* Flat 7A, 39 Clond View Road, NORTH POINT, Hong Kong Island, HONG KONG SAR.
WONG, Mr. Sze Lok, ACA *2007;* 1312 Tun Man House, 01 Man Estate, CENTRAL, HONG KONG ISLAND, HONG KONG SAR.
WONG, Ms. Sze Wai Basilia, ACA *2007;* PO Box No 1405, Shatin Central Post Office, SHA TIN, NEW TERRITORIES, HONG KONG SAR.
WONG, Mr. Tai Wai David, ACA *2008;* PO Box 1608, ShaTin Central Post Office, SHA TIN, NEW TERRITORIES, HONG KONG SAR.
WONG, Mr. Tak Chuen, ACA *2008;* Flat F 8/F. Block 5, One Beacon Hill, No. 1 Beacon Hill Road, KOWLOON TONG, HONG KONG SAR.
WONG, Mr. Tak Man Stephen, ACA *2005;* RSM Nelson Wheeler, 29th Floor Caroline Centre, Lee Gardens Two, 28 Yun Ping Road, CAUSEWAY BAY, HONG KONG ISLAND HONG KONG SAR.
WONG, Mr. Tak Ming Gary, ACA *2007;* WTMG, 17/F Wing Sing Commercial Building, 12-16 Wing Lok Street, SHEUNG WAN, HONG KONG ISLAND, HONG KONG SAR.
WONG, Mr. Tiew Theng, BA ACA *2010;* 81 Dickerage Road, KINGSTON UPON THAMES, KT1 3SR.
WONG, Miss. Tiffany Louise, BSc(Hons) ACA *2010;* 66 Queensdown Gardens, Brislington, BRISTOL, BS4 3JF.
WONG, Mr. Timothy Tseun Wai, ACA *2011;* 35 George Crescent, LONDON, N10 1AL.
WONG, Mr. Timothy Roong En, BA(Hons) ACA *2011;* 26, Jalan SS 25/30, Taman Mayang, 47301 PETALING JAYA, SELANGOR, MALAYSIA.
WONG, Mr. Tin Chak Samuel, ACA *2008;* Deloitte Touche Tohmatsu, 8-F Tower W2, The Towers, Oriental Plaza, 1 East Chang An Avenue, BEIJING 100738 CHINA.
WONG, Mr. Tin King Richard, ACA *2005;* Gayety Holdings Limited, 11F Ho Shun Tai Building, 10 Sai Ching Street, YUEN LONG, HONG KONG SAR.
WONG, Mr. Tin Lai, ACA *2008;* Flat A 22nd Floor, 62b Robinson Road, MID LEVELS, HONG KONG ISLAND, HONG KONG SAR.
WONG, Mr. Ting Hei Jennings, ACA *2008;* Jennings T. H. Wong & Company, Unit 406, Hua Qin International Building, 340 Queens Road, CENTRAL, HONG KONG SAR.
WONG, Mr. Toby Chung Yin, ACA *2007;* Unit B 32/F, Tower One, Lippo Centre, 89 Queensway, ADMIRALTY, HONG KONG ISLAND HONG KONG SAR.
WONG, Mr. Tong Loy, BA(Hons) ACA *2002;* 33 Swan Drive, LONDON, NW9 5DE.
WONG, Mr. Tsz Kin Patrick, FCA *1991;* B3 Villa Piubello, 3 Cape Drive, CHUNG HOM KOK, HONG KONG ISLAND, HONG KONG SAR.
WONG, Ms. Tsz Wai, ACA *2008;* Flat 28 8/F, Block A, 23 Homantin Hill Road, HO MAN TIN, KOWLOON, HONG KONG SAR.
WONG, Miss. Vivian Wai Wan, BSc ACA *1991;* 9 Briarglen Road, MARKHAM L6C 2K5, ON, CANADA.
WONG, Miss. Vivien, BA ACA *2005;* Flat 2, 82 Maida Vale, LONDON, W9 1PR.
WONG, Ms. Wah Jeanne, ACA *2005;* Flat B 26/F Tower 1, Dragon Centre, 21 Wun Sha St, TAI HANG, HONG KONG ISLAND, HONG KONG SAR.
WONG, Mrs. Wai Him Priscilla, BSc FCA *1974;* Hanford Management Ltd, 17a South China Building, Wyndham Street, CENTRAL, HONG KONG ISLAND, HONG KONG SAR.
WONG, Mr. Wai Man, ACA *2007;* Flat E 18/F. Tower 1, The Sparkle, 500 Tung Chau Street, SHAM SHUI PO, KOWLOON, HONG KONG SAR.
WONG, Mr. Wai Ming, BSc ACA *1985;* Lenovo Group Limited, 23/F Lincoln House, Taikoo Place, 979 King's Road, QUARRY BAY, HONG KONG ISLAND HONG KONG SAR.
WONG, Miss. Wai Ping, ACA *2006;* Flat D 28/F. Block 4, 398 Castle Peak Road, Discovery Park, TSUEN WAN, NEW TERRITORIES, HONG KONG SAR.

WONG, Ms. Wai Chun, ACA *2008;* G 26/F Block 1 Nan Fung Sun Chuen 32 Greig Road, QUARRY BAY, HONG KONG SAR.
WONG, Mr. Wai Kan Raymond, ACA *2007;* Flat B, No. 1 Homantin Hill Road, HO MAN TIN, KOWLOON, HONG KONG SAR.
WONG, Ms. Wai Kwan Anita, ACA *2007;* Flat 4 39/F., Block J Chui Fu House, Tin Fu Court, 15 Tin Sau Road, TIN SHUI WAI, NEW TERRITORIES HONG KONG SAR.
WONG, Mr. Wai Man, ACA *2008;* W M Wong & Co, Room 1517, 15/F, Nan Fung Centre, 264-298 Castle Peak Road, TSUEN WAN NEW TERRITORIES HONG KONG SAR.
WONG, Ms. Wai Mei Maria, ACA *2008;* Flat D, 13/F, Block 11, Sceneway Garden, LAM TIN, KOWLOON HONG KONG SAR.
WONG, Mr. Wai Ming Raymond, ACA *2008;* Flat F 23/F, Block 10, Rhythm Garden, SAN PO KONG, KOWLOON, HONG KONG SAR.
WONG, Miss. Wai Yin, ACA *2009;* Flat 7 31 Floor Block B, Cheung Wo Court, KWUN TONG, KOWLOON, HONG KONG SAR.
WONG, Miss. Wai-Kuen, BSc ACA *1991;* 40 Court Drive, SUTTON, SM1 3RG.
WONG, Mr. Wen Tak, BA ACA *2006;* 39 Jalan Suria, Taman Suria, 81100 JOHOR BAHRU, JOHOR, MALAYSIA.
WONG, Mr. Wing On, BA FCA *1992;* Flat F 7/F Block 20, 9 Laguna Street, Laguna City, KWUN TONG, KOWLOON, HONG KONG SAR.
WONG, Mr. Wing Cheong Dennis, ACA *2005;* Rooms 1610-11, C.C. Wu Building, 302-308 Hennessy Road, WAN CHAI, HONG KONG SAR.
WONG, Mr. Wing Hon Clint, ACA *2006;* W.H. Wong & Co, Room 6, 16/Floor, Enterprise Square 3, 39 Wang Chiu Road, KOWLOON BAY KOWLOON HONG KONG SAR.
WONG, Mr. Wing Kin, ACA *2008;* 19E Foong Shan Mansion, TAIKOO SHING, HONG KONG SAR.
WONG, Ms. Wing Man, ACA *2007;* Room 3909, 39/F, Fu Yuet Hse, Fu Cheong Est, SHAM SHUI PO, KOWLOON HONG KONG SAR.
WONG, Mr. Wing Seong, ACA CPA *2010;* BDO International, 12th Floor Menara Uni. Asia, Jalan sultan Ismail, 1008 KUALA LUMPUR, FEDERAL TERRITORY, MALAYSIA.
WONG, Mr. Wing Yin, ACA *2006;* Room 3104, Tung Hiu House, Tung Yuk Court, SHAU KEI WAN, HONG KONG ISLAND, HONG KONG SAR.
WONG, Mr. Wing-Hong Angus, BCom ACA *1989;* Flat 20G, Block 2 Academic Terrace, 101 Pokfulam Road, POK FU LAM, HONG KONG ISLAND, HONG KONG SAR.
WONG, Mr. Wo Cheung, ACA *2006;* RSM Nelson Wheeler, 29th Floor Caroline Centre, Lee Gardens Two, 28 Yun Ping Road, CAUSEWAY BAY, HONG KONG ISLAND HONG KONG SAR.
WONG, Mr. Yan Fai, ACA *2007;* Units 1005-6 10/F, Cigna Tower, 482 Jaffe Road, CAUSEWAY BAY, HONG KONG ISLAND, HONG KONG SAR.
WONG, Mrs. Yee Ling, BA(Hons) ACA *2002;* 20 Heath Drive, Raynes Park, LONDON, SW20 9BG.
WONG, Mr. Yeng Kiat, BSc ACA *2002;* 6 Herbert Place, ISLEWORTH, MIDDLESEX, TW7 4BU.
WONG, Mr. Yew Meng, BSc FCA *1977;* 2F Bishopsgate, Singapore 249994, SINGAPORE, SINGAPORE.
WONG, Mr. Yien Kim, ACA *1982;* No.8 Jalan 11/3, 46200 Petaling Jaya, 46200 PETALING JAYA, SELANGOR, MALAYSIA.
WONG, Mr. Yim Pan, ACA *2005;* Room 1403 Po Chui House, Po Pui Court, Tsui Ping Road, KWUN TONG, KOWLOON, HONG KONG SAR.
WONG, Mr. Yin Chung, BSc ACA *1994;* 31 Lorong Datuk Sulaiman 3, Taman Tun Dr Ismail, 60000 KUALA LUMPUR, FEDERAL TERRITORY, MALAYSIA.
WONG, Mr. Ying Kit Alex, ACA *2011;* Flat 16A, HONG KONG SAR Garden, 8 Seymour Road, CENTRAL, HONG KONG ISLAND, HONG KONG SAR.
WONG, Mr. Yiu Kwan, MBA MSc BSc FCA AMCT *1993;* Flat D 18/F Block 3, Scenic View, 63 Fung Shing Street, NGAU CHI WAN, KOWLOON, HONG KONG SAR.
WONG, Mr. Yiu Kit, ACA *2008;* Unit 1903 19/F, Bank of East Asia Harbour View Centre, 56 Gloucester Road, WAN CHAI, HONG KONG ISLAND, HONG KONG SAR.
WONG, Mr. Yiu Tat Stephen, MBA BA(Hons) ACA FCCA MSI *2005;* Flat A 13/F, Trillion Court, 1 Dragon Terrace, TIN HAU, HONG KONG SAR.
WONG, Mr. Yoke Ming, ACA *1979;* 4B-3-3A Southwinds Ara Hill, PJU1A/31 Ara Damansara, 47301 PETALING JAYA, MALAYSIA.
WONG, Mr. Yu Kwong, ACA *2006;* Room 1603 Block 1 Lane 477 Xin Chang Road, SHANGHAI 200003, CHINA.
WONG, Mr. Yu Shan Eugene, ACA *2007;* ON Capital, Suite 2102 Tower 2, Prosper Center, No. 5 Guanghua Road, Chaoyang District, BEIJING 100020 CHINA.
WONG, Mr. Yue Ting Thomas, ACA *2005;* Nexia Charles Mar Fan & Co, 11/F Fortis Tower, 77-79 Gloucester Road, WAN CHAI, HONG KONG ISLAND, HONG KONG SAR.
WONG, Ms. Yuen Ching, ACA *2007;* 1/F 43 C, Luso Apartment, 5 Warwick Road, Beacon Hill, KOWLOON TONG, KOWLOON HONG KONG SAR.
WONG, Miss. Yuen Ching Mary, ACA *2007;* 171 Aberdeen Main Road, 29F Flat H, Kam Fung Building, ABERDEEN, HONG KONG ISLAND, HONG KONG SAR.
WONG, Miss. Yuen Mei Jade, BSc ACA *2005;* FLAT D 11/F CANNON GARDEN, 68 KINGS ROAD, NORTH POINT, HONG KONG SAR.
WONG, Mr. Yuet, ACA *2006;* Pantheon Ventures Ltd, Norfolk House, 31 St. James's Square, LONDON, SW1Y 4JR.
WONG, Miss. Yuk Ling, BA ACA *1991;* 3388 SUN HUNG KAI CENTRE, 30 HARBOUR ROAD, WAN CHAI, HONG KONG SAR.
WONG, Ms. Yuk King Olivia, ACA *2005;* Flat 2A Block 19, Baguio Villa, POK FU LAM, HONG KONG ISLAND, HONG KONG SAR.
WONG, Mr. Yuk Ming Aaron, ACA *2005;* Aaron Wong & Co, Room 1002, 10/F Summit Insurance Building, 789 Nathan Road, MONG KOK, KOWLOON HONG KONG SAR.
WONG, Ms. Yuk-ying, ACA *2005;* Flat E 42/F Tower 1, The Metropolis, 8 Mau Yip Road, Tseung Kwan O, SAI KUNG, NEW TERRITORIES HONG KONG SAR.
WONG, Ms. Yuki, ACA *2007;* 25C BANYAN MANSION, TAIKOO SHING, QUARRY BAY, HONG KONG SAR.
WONG, Miss. Yvonne, ACA *1978;* 43 Jalan Bawang, Taman Cheras, 56100 KUALA LUMPUR, FEDERAL TERRITORY, MALAYSIA.
WONG CHEUNG, Mrs. Carmen Wai Lan, ACA *2004;* c/o Canada Lands Company CLC Limited, 1 University Avenue, Suite 1200, TORONTO M5J 2P1, ON, CANADA.
WONG-CHUNG-LUNG, Mr. Mang Chong, ACA *1980;* 7 Kain Avenue, MATRAVILLE, NSW 2036, AUSTRALIA.
WONG LEE, Mrs. Sok Chi, ACA *2009;* PO Box 11432, Central Post Office, CENTRAL, HONG KONG ISLAND, HONG KONG SAR.
WONG MIN, Miss. Marie Charlene, BSc ACA *2006;* with PricewaterhouseCoopers LLP, Pricewaterhousecoopers, 12 Plumtree Court, LONDON, EC4A 4HT.
WONG PING LUN, Mrs. Margaret, BA FCA *1983;* University of Mauritius, REDUIT, MAURITIUS.
WONG SHIU LEUNG, Mr. Terence, BSc(Hons) ACA *2001;* Langley Waterside, 7 Whitstone Lane, BECKENHAM, BR3 3GY.
WONG SICK WAH, Mr. Laval, FCA *1988;* 4A Saraca Hill, SINGAPORE 807491, SINGAPORE.
WONG SUN THIONG, Mr. Cyril Tchang Fa, BSc ACA *1988;* 12 Pope Hennessy Street, Curepipe Road, CUREPIPE, MAURITIUS.
WONG SUN-WAI, Mr. Wan Tay Tat, BSc ACA *1993;* 3039 Simpson Street, EVANSTON, IL 60201, UNITED STATES.
WONG TO WING, Mr. Ah Tse, ACA *1988;* 54 Dauphine Street, PORT LOUIS, MAURITIUS.
WONG TOO YEN, Mr. Sew Sin, FCA *1980;* Level 25 580 George Street, SYDNEY, NSW 2000, AUSTRALIA.
WONG TOO YUEN, Mr. Ah Chay Khinchow, MBA FCA *1977;* A.C.K. Wong Too Yuen, P.O.Box 5184, CHATSWOOD, NSW 1515, AUSTRALIA.
WONG TSZE SHOW, Mr. Georges Laval, ACA ACCA *2002;* with Ernst & Young LLP, 1 More London Place, LONDON, SE1 2AF.
WONG YUEN TIEN, Mr. Jimmy Michael, FCA *1992;* 10th Floor, Raffles Tower, 19 Cybercity, EBENE, MAURITIUS.
WONG YUN SHING, Mr. Joseph Tommy, BSc FCA *1993;* 81 Rue Du Gouverneur, Le Bout Du Monde, EBENE, MAURITIUS.
WONGSAM, Miss. Stephanie, BSc ACA *2011;* 8 Estella Apartments, 20 Grove Crescent Road, LONDON, E15 1AQ.
WONGSOO, Mr. Frank Von Hin, ACA *1986;* 99 - 3880, Westminster Highway, RICHMOND V7C 5S1, BC, CANADA.
WONNACOTT, Mr. Andrew Robert, BSc FCA *1987;* Craigievar, Palm Hall Close, St Giles Hill, WINCHESTER, SO23 0JL.
WONS, Mrs. Yvonne Tina, BSc ACA *1987;* Barn Ridge, South Cheriton, TEMPLECOMBE, BA8 0BG.
WONTNER-SMITH, Mr. Christopher Michael, BA FCA *1974;* 16 Farfield Road, SHIPLEY, WEST YORKSHIRE, BD18 4QP.
WONTNER-SMITH, Mr. Robert Michael, BA ACA *2004;* Ulitsa Popovicha 100 4 Floor, YUZHNO SAKHALINSK, RUSSIAN FEDERATION.
WOO, Mr. Alex, BSc ACA *2003;* Flat 23/B South Tower 7, Residence Bel-Air, POK FU LAM, HONG KONG ISLAND, HONG KONG SAR.
WOO, Mr. Chi Mun, MA ACA *1997;* 3 Quince Street Lofts, Private Bag X23, AUCKLAND PARK, 2006, SOUTH AFRICA.
WOO, Dr. Dawson Ka Chung, BSc MBBS ACA *1994;* 2nd Floor, Kailey Tower, 14 Stanley Street, CENTRAL, HONG KONG ISLAND, HONG KONG SAR.
WOO, Mr. Hing Kwen, ACA MBA *2005;* 502/38 Alfred Street, Milsons Point, SYDNEY, NSW 2061, AUSTRALIA.
WOO, Mr. Hock Chong, ACA *1981;* 88 Hillview Avenue, Apt 09-03 Hillbrooks, SINGAPORE 669590, SINGAPORE.
WOO, Mr. King Hang, ACA *2005;* Hip Hing Construction Co Ltd, 27/F New World Tower, 18 Queen's Road, CENTRAL, HONG KONG ISLAND, HONG KONG SAR.
WOO, Ms. Kit Ping Fanny, ACA *2008;* Flat B 12th Floor, Block 15, Charming Garden, 8 Hoi Ting Road, MONG KOK, KOWLOON HONG KONG SAR.
WOO, Mr. Richard Bing Han, MBA BSc ACA CTA AMCT *1999;* 41 Hole Farm Road, Northfield, BIRMINGHAM, B31 2BP.
WOO, Miss. Teick Koon, BA ACA *1988;* Blk 558 No 12-459 Street 42, Jurone West, SINGAPORE 2264, SINGAPORE.
WOO-MING, Mr. Peter Anthony, MA ACA *1985;* 46 Ridgeview Road, LONDON, N20 0HJ.
•**WOOD, Mr. Adrian David, BSc FCA** *1984;* Wadock Limited, 2nd Floor, 33a High Street, Stony Stratford, MILTON KEYNES, MK11 1AA.
•**WOOD, Mr. Adrian William, FCA** *1986;* O'Hara Wood Limited, 29 Gay Street, BATH, BA1 2NT.
WOOD, Mr. Alan, ACA *1983;* The Hollies, 87 Maylam Gardens, Borden, SITTINGBOURNE, ME10 1GA.
WOOD, Mr. Alan Smith, BSc ACA *1980;* Trevor Mottram Ltd, 33-41 The Pantiles, TUNBRIDGE WELLS, TN2 5TE.
WOOD, Mr. Alexander Basil John, MSci ACA *2004;* with KPMG LLP, St. Nicholas House, 31 Park Row, NOTTINGHAM, NG1 6FQ.
WOOD, Mrs. Alexis Claire, BSc(Hons) BA(Hons) ACA *1997;* ECCU (Legal) - Faraday building, B G Group Plc, 100 Thames Valley Park Drive, READING, RG6 1PT.
WOOD, Miss. Alison, BA ACA *1996;* 34A Amaroo Avenue, MOUNT COLAH, NSW 2079, AUSTRALIA.
WOOD, Mrs. Alison Jane, MSc BEng ACA *1998;* 33 Eddington Road, BRACKNELL, RG12 8GF.
WOOD, Mrs. Alison Mary, BCom ACA *1999;* Saxon House Moreton Paddox, Moreton Morrell, WARWICK, CV35 9BT.
•①**WOOD, Mr. Alistair Steven, BA FCA MABRP** *1985;* Mazars LLP, 45 Church Street, BIRMINGHAM, B3 2RT.
WOOD, Mr. Allen Thornton, FCA *1959;* 119 Woodhouse Lane, SALE, M33 4LW. (Life Member)
WOOD, Miss. Allison Jennifer, BA ACA *2004;* Abnormal Load Engineering Ltd, New Road, Hixon, STAFFORD, ST18 0PE.
WOOD, Miss. Ami Jane, ACA *2008;* Flat B, 23 Deronda Road, LONDON, SE24 9BQ.
•**WOOD, Mr. Andrew, BA ACA** *1996;* Grant Thornton UK LLP, 1 Whitehall Riverside, Whitehall Road, LEEDS, WEST YORKSHIRE, LS1 4BN. See also Grant Thornton LLP
WOOD, Mr. Andrew Brian, BA ACA *1985;* 51A Worminghall Road, Ickford, AYLESBURY, HP18 9JB.
•**WOOD, Mr. Andrew David, BA FCA** *1981;* (Tax Fac), Salway & Wright, 32 The Crescent, SPALDING, LINCOLNSHIRE, PE11 1AF. See also Salway and Wright (Spalding) Limited
WOOD, Mr. Andrew David, MA BSc ACA *1998;* Rock International Holdings Ltd, 500 Chiswick High Road, LONDON, W4 5RG.
WOOD, Mr. Andrew David, BEng ACA *2002;* The Farm, St. Hilary, COWBRIDGE, SOUTH GLAMORGAN, CF71 7DP.
WOOD, Mr. Andrew Dennis, BSc ACA *1989;* 18 Stillman Lane, GREENWICH, CT 06831, UNITED STATES.
WOOD, Mr. Andrew Edward John, BSc ACA *1997;* Hilden King Street, Odiham, HOOK, RG29 1NJ.
WOOD, Mr. Andrew Jeremy, BEng ACA MABRP *2004;* Edogawa-ku, Naka Kasai, 5-32-5. 6th Floor, TOKYO, 134-0083 JAPAN.
•**WOOD, Mr. Andrew John, BA ACA** *1994;* 25 Winkins Lane, Great Somerford, CHIPPENHAM, WILTSHIRE, SN15 5HY.
WOOD, Mr. Andrew John, BSc FCA *1991;* 10 Catisfield Road, FAREHAM, HAMPSHIRE, PO15 5QE.
WOOD, Mr. Andrew John, BA FCA *1988;* T H Q Dukes Court, Duke Street, WOKING, SURREY, GU21 5BH.
WOOD, Mr. Andrew Jonathan, MA MEng ACA *1998;* with Deloitte LLP, Stonecutter Court, 1 Stonecutter Street, LONDON, EC4A 4TR.
WOOD, Mr. Andrew McFarlane, BCom ACA *2002;* 21 Newlay Grove, Horsforth, LEEDS, LS18 4LQ.
WOOD, Mr. Andrew Mitchell, BSc ACA *2000;* 5 Archway Street, LONDON, SW13 0AS.
WOOD, Mr. Andrew Nicholas Scott, BA ACA *1991;* 44 Corymbia Circuit, OXFORD FALLS, NSW 2100, AUSTRALIA.
WOOD, Mr. Andrew Simon, BSc ACA *1989;* 5 Shaplands Stoke Bishoo, BRISTOL, BS9 1AY.
WOOD, Mr. Andrew Stuart, MA FCA MIIA(Aust) *1995;* 8 Blossom Drive, ORPINGTON, BR6 0AS.
WOOD, Mrs. Angela Anna, BSc ACA *2003;* ARUP, 13 Fitzroy Street, LONDON, W1T 4BQ.
WOOD, Mrs. Anne Macdonald, MA ACA *1995;* 2/2 33 Falkland Street, GLASGOW, G12 9QZ.
WOOD, Mr. Anthony James, FCA *1956;* Greystones, Hill Lane, Hathersage, HOPE VALLEY, S32 1AY. (Life Member)
WOOD, Mr. Ashley Stafford, BSc ACA *2003;* with PricewaterhouseCoopers, Darling Park Tower 2, 201 Sussex Street, GPO Box 2650, SYDNEY, NSW 1171 AUSTRALIA.
WOOD, Mr. Benjamin Joseph Berry, LLB ACA *1992;* 94 Ramsden Road, LONDON, SW12 8QZ.
WOOD, Mr. Benjamin Richard, ACA *2010;* 6 Walpole Mews, LONDON, NW8 6EZ.
•**WOOD, Mr. Bertie Dennis, FCA** *1952;* B Dennis Wood, 42 Fort Road, GOSPORT, PO12 2BU.
•**WOOD, Mrs. Beverley, ACA MAAT** *2004;* (Tax Fac), Allen Sykes Limited, 5 Henson Close, South Church Enterprise Park, BISHOP AUCKLAND, COUNTY DURHAM, DL14 6WA.
WOOD, Mr. Brian Bowran, MA FCA *1962;* The Byre, Pound Court, Earls Lane Deddington, BANBURY, OX15 0LA. (Life Member)
WOOD, Mr. Brian Dixon, FCA *1953;* 5 Bickerton Road, ALTRINCHAM, CHESHIRE, WA14 4LA. (Life Member)
WOOD, Mr. Brian John, FCA *1965;* 6 Gresham Road, BOURNEMOUTH, BH9 1QR.
•**WOOD, Mr. Brian Michael, FCA** *1970;* B.M. Wood, 44b High Street, STEVENAGE, SG1 3EF.
WOOD, Mr. Brian Norman, FCA *1952;* 6 Padstow Place, FORDINGBRIDGE, SP6 1BT. (Life Member)
•**WOOD, Mrs. Caroline Dulcie, BA ACA** *1987;* Caroline Wood A.C.A., Low Field House, Bleach Mill Lane, Menston, ILKLEY, WEST YORKSHIRE LS29 6AW.
WOOD, Ms. Caroline Mary, ACA *2002;* 25 Chillagoe Street, FISHER, ACT 2611, AUSTRALIA.
WOOD, Mrs. Catriona Anne, ACA *1989;* Cerris House, 5 New Road, Mistley, MANNINGTREE, ESSEX, CO11 2AE.
WOOD, Mrs. Celine Donna, MSci ACA *2005;* 45 Ryder Crescent, Aughton, ORMSKIRK, L39 5EY.
WOOD, Mr. Charles Raymond, FCA *1958;* Skyways, Icknield Road, Goring, READING, RG8 0DG.
WOOD, Mr. Charles Richard, BSc ACA *1999;* Floor 24, Barclays Bank Plc, 1 Churchill Place, LONDON, E14 5HP.
WOOD, Mr. Charles William Overend, BA ACA *1990;* Unit 9, Holford Way, Holford, BIRMINGHAM, B6 7AX.
WOOD, Mrs. Charlotte Lauren, MMath ACA *2006;* The School House, 2 Chapel Rise, Wilford Road, Ruddington, NOTTINGHAM, NG11 6EN.
WOOD, Mr. Christopher, FCA *1982;* Pemberley, North Green, West Hanney, WANTAGE, OX12 0LQ.
WOOD, Mr. Christopher, BA ACA *2010;* U N W Llp Citygate, St. James Boulevard, NEWCASTLE UPON TYNE, NE1 4JE.
WOOD, Mr. Christopher Gilbert, BSc FCA *1990;* 41 The Chancery, Bramcote, NOTTINGHAM, NG9 3AJ.
WOOD, Mr. Christopher Mark, BA(Hons) ACA *2000;* 13 The Jays, Highwoods, COLCHESTER, CO4 9TW.
WOOD, Mr. Christopher Nigel, BSc ACA *1992;* 7 Kings Road, ASCOT, SL5 9AD.

WOOD, Mr. Christopher Peter, ACA *1988;* The Nuance Group A.G, Unterrietstrasse ZA, 8152 GLATTBRUGG, SWITZERLAND.
•**WOOD, Mr. Christopher Richard, FCA** *1991;* 48 Bright Meadow, Halfway, SHEFFIELD, S20 4SY.
WOOD, Miss. Claire Louise, BSc ACA *2003;* 76 Elleray Road, SALFORD, M6 7GZ.
WOOD, Mrs. Claire Sylvia, BSc ACA *1989;* 7 Tremorvah Barton, TRURO, CORNWALL, TR1 1NN.
WOOD, Mr. Clifford Robert Dennis, BA ACA *1988;* 25 Rowanwood Avenue, SIDCUP, DA15 8WL.
•**WOOD, Mr. Colin, FCA** *1958;* (Tax Fac), Colin Wood, 15 Ronneby Close, Oatlands Chase, WEYBRIDGE, KT13 9SB.
WOOD, Mr. Colin George, FCA *1954;* 43 Eaton Street, NORWICH, NR4 7LD. (Life Member)
WOOD, Mr. Cyril Christopher, FCA *1970;* 13 Merino Green, MILTON KEYNES, MK14 6FL.
WOOD, Mr. Daniel Philip, ACA *2008;* Seefeldstrasse 26, 8008 ZURICH, SWITZERLAND.
WOOD, Mr. Danny, ACA *2009;* 531 Helmshore Road, Helmshore, ROSSENDALE, BB4 4JJ.
•**WOOD, Mr. David Alastair Thomas, FCA** *1977;* Champion Business Advisors Limited, 4 Nile Close, Nelson Court Business Centre, Riversway, PRESTON, PR2 2XU. See also Champion Business Solutions Limited
WOOD, Mr. David Anthony, MA FCA *1986;* The Institute of Chartered Accountants of Scotland C A Hous, 21 Haymarket Yards, EDINBURGH, EH12 5BH.
WOOD, Mr. David Bernard, BA FCA *1968;* 26 Garstons, Bathford, BATH, BA1 7TE.
WOOD, Mr. David Edwin, BA ACA *1981;* Taylor Wimpey IT, 2 Trinity Park Bickenhill Lane, BIRMINGHAM, B37 7ES.
WOOD, Mr. David Geoffrey, FCA *1976;* with Menzies LLP, Heathrow Business Centre, 65 High Street, EGHAM, SURREY, TW20 9EY.
WOOD, Mr. David Gerald, FCA *1971;* Am Kleff 4, 40699 ERKRATH, GERMANY. (Life Member)
WOOD, Mr. David Jack, BSc FCA *1982;* 310 Langer Lane, Wingerworth, CHESTERFIELD, S42 6UB.
WOOD, Mr. David James Cecil, FCA *1952;* 5 Phillimore Terrace, Allen Street, LONDON, W8 6BJ. (Life Member)
WOOD, Mr. David John, FCA *1967;* 15 Bellfield Avenue, Harrow Weald, HARROW, HA3 6ST.
WOOD, Mr. David John, BA ACA *2009;* 5 Banbury Close, LEIGH, WN7 3NZ.
WOOD, Mr. David John, BA ACA *1985;* Carlac Ltd, 16-17 Ashfield Way, Whitehall Estate, LEEDS, LS12 5JB.
•**WOOD, Mr. David Jonathan, BA ACA** *1993;* 17 Lee View, The Oaks, Whitley, GOOLE, NORTH HUMBERSIDE, DN14 0FH.
WOOD, Mr. David Keith Charles, BSc(Hons) ACA *2003;* 6 New Street, KENILWORTH, WARWICKSHIRE, CV8 2EZ.
WOOD, Mr. David Lewis, BSc ACA *1998;* Rowan Rough, The Drive, GODALMING, GU7 1PD.
WOOD, Mr. David Raymond, FCA *1971;* 15 Westbrook Gardens, BRACKNELL, BERKSHIRE, RG12 2JD.
WOOD, Mr. David Roy, BA ACA *1985;* North House, 27 Great Peter Street, LONDON, SW1P 3LN.
WOOD, Mr. David Thomas, FCA *1973;* Crofters Court, 145 Rosemary Hill Road, Little Aston, SUTTON COLDFIELD, B74 4HP.
•**WOOD, Mrs. Deborah Stuart, BSc FCA** *1988;* Moore and Smalley LLP, Fylde House, Skyways Commercial Campus, Amy Johnson Way, BLACKPOOL, FY4 3RS.
WOOD, Ms. Debra Anne, BCom ACA *1988;* Apartment 201, Berkeley Tower, 48 Westferry Circus, LONDON, E14 8RP.
WOOD, Mr. Derek William, BSc FCA CFA *1974;* 451 Caesar Avenue, OAKVILLE L6J 3Z1, ON, CANADA.
WOOD, Mr. Donald, FCA *1952;* 6 Wootton Court, Lillington Avenue, LEAMINGTON SPA, CV32 5UU. (Life Member)
WOOD, Mrs. Donna Sharon, MA ACA *1987;* Pemberley, North Green, West Hanney, WANTAGE, OX12 0LQ.
WOOD, Mr. Douglas Reay Waring, FCA *1967;* 48 Oakland Drive, DAWLISH, DEVON, EX7 9RX.
WOOD, Mr. Duncan, LLB ACA *1989;* 39 Ruswarp Drive, Barrons Hill Lea Estate, Tunstall Village, SUNDERLAND, SR3 2PH.
WOOD, Mr. Duncan Francis, MA FCA *1974;* 185 Balsam Avenue, TORONTO M4E 3C2, ON, CANADA.
•**WOOD, Mr. Edmund Michael, FCA** *1968;* Mercer & Hole Trustees Limited, Gloucester House, 72 London Road, ST. ALBANS, AL1 1NS.
WOOD, Mr. Edward Charles, BSc ACA *1993;* The Bar House, Arthington Lane, Pool in Wharfedale, OTLEY, WEST YORKSHIRE, LS21 1LG.
WOOD, The Hon. Edward Orlando Charles, JP ACA *1981;* Dorn Priory, Dorn, MORETON-IN-MARSH, GLOUCESTERSHIRE, GL56 9NS.
WOOD, Mrs. Elizabeth, BSc ACA *2003;* 58 Ron Lawton Crescent, Burley in Wharfedale, ILKLEY, LS29 7ST.
WOOD, Miss. Elizabeth Anna, BSc ACA *2008;* 44 Wilberforce Road, LONDON, N4 2SR.
WOOD, Dr. Emily Jane, ACA *2003;* Close Premium Finance, 21st Floor, Tolworth Tower, Ewell Road, SURBITON, SURREY KT6 7EL.
WOOD, Mr. Eric Michael, FCA *1975;* Oxford Analytica, 5 Alfred Street, OXFORD, OX1 4EH.
WOOD, Mr. Ewart Walter, FCA *1963;* Ashlands, Brockbridge, Droxford, SOUTHAMPTON, SO32 3QT. (Life Member)
WOOD, Mrs. Fiona Anne Murray, BSc ACA *1987;* 27 Roehampton Lane, LONDON, SW15 5LS.
WOOD, Mrs. Fiona Geal, MSc BA(Hons) ACA *2002;* GlaxoSmithKline, HW8113 New Frontiers Science Park Third Avenue, HARLOW, ESSEX, CM19 5AW.
•**WOOD, Miss. Fiona Margaret Warburton, ACA** *1987;* Page Kirk, Sherwood House, 7 Gregory Boulevard, NOTTINGHAM, NG7 5JD.
WOOD, Mr. Frank, FCA *1952;* 21 Rombalds Crescent, Silsden, KEIGHLEY, WEST YORKSHIRE, BD20 0LE. (Life Member)
WOOD, Mr. Frederick William, FCA *1969;* Pleasant House, Pleasant Place, LOUTH, LN11 0NA.
WOOD, Mr. Gavin Hilary James, BA ACA *1997;* 13 Hurst Close, WALLINGFORD, OXFORDSHIRE, OX10 9BQ.
WOOD, Mr. Gavin Peter, BEng ACA *1998;* 48 Colwith Road, LONDON, W6 9EY.
WOOD, Mr. Geoff Peter, MA ACA *1983;* (Tax Fac), 32 Victoria Road, LONDON, N22 7XB.
WOOD, Mr. Geoffrey Claud, FCA *1948;* Apartment 2, 646 Sandy Bay Road, Sandy Bay, HOBART, TAS 7005, AUSTRALIA. (Life Member)
WOOD, Mr. Geoffrey Michael, BSc FCA *1983;* 1a Monmouth Street, LONDON, WC2H 9DA.
WOOD, Mr. George David, FCA *1969;* 1 Hays Walk, CHEAM, SURREY, SM2 7NQ. (Life Member)
WOOD, Mr. George Edmund Richard, BSc ACA *1993;* Man Group Plc, Sugar Quay, Lower Thames Street, LONDON, EC3R 6DU.
WOOD, Mr. Gerald Anthony, FCA *1971;* 7 Rodgers Avenue, CONSTANTIA, C.P., 7806, SOUTH AFRICA.
WOOD, Mr. Gerald Norman, FCA *1968;* 1 Fallingbrook Woods, TORONTO M1N 1B7, ON, CANADA. (Life Member)
WOOD, Mr. Gervase Roger, FCA *1961;* 70 Hartley Crescent, Birkdale, SOUTHPORT, MERSEYSIDE, PR8 4SQ.
WOOD, Mrs. Gillian, BA ACA *1984;* 2 Honeysuckle Close, Prestbury, CHELTENHAM, GL52 5LN.
WOOD, Mr. Gordon James, FCA *1966;* Abernantyffin, Brechfa, CARMARTHEN, SA32 7RE.
WOOD, Mr. Graeme Alan, BA FCA *1981;* (Tax Fac), 7725 Indian Hill Road, CINCINNATI, OH 45243, UNITED STATES.
WOOD, Mr. Graham, BSc ACA *1985;* 14 Avoncroft Rd, Stoke Heath, BROMSGROVE, B60 4NG.
WOOD, Mr. Gregory Mark, DBA BA(Hons) FCA *1980;* Cameron House, Shire Lane, Chorleywood, RICKMANSWORTH, HERTFORDSHIRE, WD3 5NT.
WOOD, Mrs. Hannah, ACA *2011;* 65 Bushmead Avenue, BEDFORD, MK40 3QW.
•**WOOD, Mr. Haydn Calvin, BA ACA** *1999;* Steele Robertson Goddard, 28 Ely Place, LONDON, EC1N 6AA.
WOOD, Mrs. Heather Carol, BSc(Hons) ACA *2001;* 45 Enmore Gardens, East Sheen, LONDON, SW14 8RF.
WOOD, Miss. Helen Victoria, ACA *2011;* 3 Darfield Close, Owlthorpe, SHEFFIELD, S20 6SW.
WOOD, Mr. Henry James Prescott, BSc FCA CTA *1980;* (Tax Fac), with Ensors, Saxon House, Moseleys Farm, Business Centre, Fornham All Saints, BURY ST. EDMUNDS SUFFOLK IP28 6JY.
WOOD, Mr. Howard Graham, FCA *1962;* 12 Park Wood Rise, LIFTON, DEVON, PL16 0LA. (Life Member)
•**WOOD, Mr. Iain Donald, BSc FCA** *1995;* Celtic Associates Limited, The Red House, One The Parade, Castletown, ISLE OF MAN, IM9 1LG.
WOOD, Mr. Ian David Hadfield, BSc ACA *2005;* 1 Horsell Dene, Ridgeway Horsell, WOKING, GU21 4QR.
WOOD, Mr. James Marcus Fisher, ACA *2002;* 16 Crondace Road, LONDON, SW6 4BB.
WOOD, Mr. James Robert, MA ACA *2004;* (Tax Fac), with Wingrave Yeats Limited, 101 Wigmore Street, LONDON, W1U 1QU.
WOOD, Mr. James William, BSc(Hons) ACA *2009;* 25 Mead Row, LONDON, SE1 7JG.
WOOD, Mr. Jamie Peter, MA BA ACA *1995;* Odey Asset Management Ltd, 12 Upper Grosvenor Street, LONDON, W1K 2ND.
WOOD, Miss. Jane Tracey, BCom ACA *1994;* Jane Wood & Associates Ltd, 70 Sterndale Road, LONDON, W14 0HU.
WOOD, Mrs. Janet Elizabeth, BA ACA *1986;* 39 The Uplands, HARPENDEN, AL5 2PA.
•**WOOD, Mr. Jeremy Anthony Cassillis, FCA** *1965;* (Tax Fac), NJJT Limited, 95a Connaught Avenue, FRINTON-ON-SEA, ESSEX, CO13 9PS.
WOOD, Mr. John, BSc ACA *1979;* 3 Birch Mews, Adel, LEEDS, LS16 8NX.
•**WOOD, Mr. John, ACA** *2007;* Glencross Wood & Co, 247 Seymour Grove, Old Trafford, MANCHESTER, M16 0DS.
•**WOOD, Mr. John Alan, FCA** *1959;* Saunders Wood & Co., The White House, 140A Tachbrook Street, LONDON, SW1V 2NE.
WOOD, Mr. John Anthony, FCA *1956;* Spout Close, Millbeck, Underskiddaw, KESWICK, CA12 4PS. (Life Member)
WOOD, Mr. John Edward, FCA *1963;* 16 Windmill Drive, Marchington, UTTOXETER, ST14 8JP. (Life Member)
•**WOOD, Mr. John Gregory, BA FCA** *1981;* Wood & Co, 53b Calle Romo, Jimena de la Frontera, 11330 CADIZ, SPAIN.
WOOD, Mr. John Hadfield, BCom FCA *1974;* Brooklands, The Pitchens, Wroughton, SWINDON, SN4 0RU.
WOOD, Mr. John Paul, BA ACA *1990;* 1 Howcroft Gardens, Sandal, WAKEFIELD, WEST YORKSHIRE, WF2 6TW.
WOOD, Mr. John William, FCA *1966;* 12 Seagate View, Sewerby, BRIDLINGTON, YO15 1ET. (Life Member)
WOOD, Mr. Jonathan, BA(Econ) ACA *1987;* Via G. Frua 7, 20146 MILAN, ITALY.
WOOD, Mr. Jonathan Barrington, BEng ACA *2007;* 503/9-15 Central Avenue, MANLY, NSW 2095, AUSTRALIA.
WOOD, Mr. Jonathan Brian Vincent, BSc ACA *1990;* Waverley, Sheath Lane, Oxshott, LEATHERHEAD, SURREY, KT22 0RA.
WOOD, Mr. Jonathan Mark, BSc ACA *1993;* 34 Taman Nakhoda, Villa Delle Rose, SINGAPORE 257760, SINGAPORE.
WOOD, Mr. Joseph William, FCA *1960;* 39 Dunsmoor Road, LONDON N6K 1T6, ON, CANADA. (Life Member)
WOOD, Mrs. Julia Doris, MSc ACA APMI *1979;* 6 Lincoln Green, ALTON, HAMPSHIRE, GU34 1SX.
WOOD, Mr. Julian, BSc ACA *1990;* 75 Moor Road North, Gosforth, NEWCASTLE UPON TYNE, NE3 1RJ.
WOOD, Miss. Julie Patricia, BSc ACA *1985;* Dean + Chapter of Canterbury Cathedral, Cathedral House The Precincts, CANTERBURY, CT1 2EH.
WOOD, Miss. Karen, BA ACA *1992;* Liberty Hall, Chatham Green, Little Waltham, CHELMSFORD, CM3 3LQ.
WOOD, Mrs. Karen Emma, BSc(Hons) ACA *2003;* 111 Edison Way, Arnold, NOTTINGHAM, NG5 7NE.
WOOD, Mrs. Kathryn Jane, BA ACA *1992;* Railston Design Ltd, Whitehill Lane, Wootton Bassett, SWINDON, SN4 7DB.
WOOD, Mr. Keith, FCA *1970;* 9 Willow Lane, Goostrey, CREWE, CW4 8PP.
WOOD, Mr. Keith, BA ACA *2003;* 45 Ryder Crescent, Aughton, ORMSKIRK, L39 5EY.
WOOD, Mr. Keith David, FCA *1971;* Bankdam, St. Georges Road, BROMLEY, BR1 2AU.
WOOD, Mr. Keith Derek, FCA *1962;* 6 Moorside Rise, CLECKHEATON, BD19 6AA.
WOOD, Mr. Keith Robert, BA FCA *1992;* 29 Braganza Way, Beaulieu Park, CHELMSFORD, CM2 5AP.
WOOD, Mr. Kenneth Ian, BSc ACA *1989;* Three Gables, The Leaze, Ashton Keynes, SWINDON, SN6 6PE.
•**WOOD, Mr. Kenneth Vincent, ACA** *1986;* Planet Business Services Limited, 6B Planet Business Centre, Planet Place, Killingworth, NEWCASTLE UPON TYNE, NE12 6DY.
WOOD, Mr. Kevin David, MEng ACA *1992;* Old Grange Farm, Old Lane, Bramhope, LEEDS, WEST YORKSHIRE, LS16 9HT.
•**WOOD, Mr. Kevin Stuart, BA ACA** *1987;* PricewaterhouseCoopers, Building No 4, Arundel Office Park, Norfolk Road Mount Pleasant, HARARE, ZIMBABWE.
WOOD, Miss. Lara Joanne, BA ACA *1994;* with Ernst & Young LLP, 1 More London Place, LONDON, SE1 2AF.
WOOD, Mrs. Laura Claire, BA ACA *1986;* 45 Cassiobury Park Avenue, WATFORD, HERTFORDSHIRE, WD18 7LD.
WOOD, Mr. Leslie, BA FCA *1985;* 35 York Fields, BARNOLDSWICK, LANCASHIRE, BB18 5DA.
WOOD, Mr. Leslie Thomas, BSc ACA *1993;* Level 13, 100 St Georges Terrace, PERTH, WA 6000, AUSTRALIA.
WOOD, Mrs. Linda, BA ACA *1991;* 1 Howcroft Gardens, Sandal, WAKEFIELD, WEST YORKSHIRE, WF2 6TW.
WOOD, Mrs. Lindsay, ACA *2003;* La Mare Ballam, La Rue de la Mare Ballam, St. John, JERSEY, JE3 4EJ.
WOOD, Mrs. Lindsay Fiona, BA ACA *1983;* 7725 Indian Hill Road, CINCINNATI, OH 45243, UNITED STATES.
WOOD, Miss. Lisa Diane, BSc(Hons) ACA CTA *2000;* 16 Hathaway Close, Balsall Common, COVENTRY, CV7 7EP.
WOOD, Miss. Lois Sara, ACA *2011;* 5 West Hill, EPSOM, SURREY, KT19 8JN.
•**WOOD, Mrs. Lynne Marie, BA ACA CTA** *1994;* LM Wood, 22 John Aubrey Close, Yatton Keynell, CHIPPENHAM, WILTSHIRE, SN14 7EG.
WOOD, Mr. Malcolm Antony, FCA *1962;* (Tax Fac), Hague Bank, 7 Hague Road, Broadbottom, HYDE, SK14 6DU.
WOOD, Mr. Malcolm Hugh, FCA *1968;* Walton House, Wendling Road, Longham, DEREHAM, NORFOLK, NR19 2RD. (Life Member)
WOOD, Mr. Malcolm John, FCA *1965;* Woodpecker Cottage, 12a Ashley Place, WARMINSTER, WILTSHIRE, BA12 9QJ.
•**WOOD, Mr. Malcolm Stanley, FCA** *1975;* W Accountancy Limited, 74 Victoria Road, Knaphill, WOKING, SURREY, GU21 2AA.
WOOD, Mr. Marcus Charles, BSc ACA *1994;* 175 Berglen Court, 7 Branch Road, LONDON, E14 7JY.
WOOD, Mr. Marcus James, BSc ACA *1992;* 9 Southside Common, LONDON, SW19 4TL.
WOOD, Miss. Margaret Juliana, BA FCA *1966;* 139 Crossley Lane, MIRFIELD, WF14 0NX. (Life Member)
WOOD, Ms. Marie, BSc ACA *1995;* 15 Riversleigh Avenue, LYTHAM ST. ANNES, LANCASHIRE, FY8 5QZ.
WOOD, Mr. Mark Andrew Kenneth, MA ACA *1994;* The Oaks, 52 Leeds Road, SELBY, YO8 4JQ.
WOOD, Mr. Mark Duncan, BA ACA *1987;* Low Field House, Bleach Mill Lane, Menston, ILKLEY, WEST YORKSHIRE, LS29 6AW.
WOOD, Mr. Mark Jonathan, BA ACA *2004;* with Deloitte LLP, 3 Victoria Square, Victoria Street, ST. ALBANS, HERTFORDSHIRE, AL1 3TF.
WOOD, Mr. Martin John, BSc ACA *1996;* Flat 5 Highland Lodge, Fox Hill, LONDON, SE19 2UJ.
•**WOOD, Mr. Martin Joseph, BA(Hons) MCMI ACA FCCA MAAT MEWI** *2007;* (Tax Fac), Gross Klein, 6 Breams Buildings, LONDON, EC4A 1QL.
WOOD, Mr. Martin Richard, BA ACA *1989;* 14 Manor Wood Gate, Lower Shiplake, HENLEY-ON-THAMES, OXFORDSHIRE, RG9 3BY.
WOOD, Mr. Martyn Leslie, BSc FCA *1975;* 1 Bartongate, LOUTH, LN11 8EU.
WOOD, Mr. Matthew, BA(Hons) ACA *2000;* Combined Management Services Ltd, 11 Grosvenor Crescent, LONDON, SW1X 7EE.
WOOD, Mr. Matthew Lawrence, BSocSc ACA *2011;* 43 Westbury Terrace, UPMINSTER, ESSEX, RM14 3LU.
WOOD, Mr. Matthew Peter, BSc(Hons) ACA *2003;* First floor, Dorey Court, Admirals Park, St Peter Port, GUERNSEY, GY1 6HJ.
•**WOOD, Mr. Michael, MMath ACA** *2004;* MCBW Limited, 6 Wellington Drive, WELWYN GARDEN CITY, HERTFORDSHIRE, AL7 2NJ. See also MCBW Consulting Ltd
•**WOOD, Mr. Michael Alan, FCA** *1982;* (Tax Fac), Michael Wood, 22a Bank Street, ASHFORD, KENT, TN23 1BE.
•**WOOD, Mr. Michael Alan, FCA** *1980;* Robinson & Co, 72 Lowther Street, WHITEHAVEN, CA28 7AH. See also Robinson J.F.W. & Co
WOOD, Mr. Michael Colin, MA FCA ACII *1983;* 11 Horseshoe Close, BILLERICAY, ESSEX, CM12 0YA.
WOOD, Mr. Michael Frederick, ACA *2010;* 20 Perch Street, LONDON, E8 2EG.
WOOD, Mr. Michael Harlow, BSc ACA *2005;* 51a Atheldene Road, LONDON, SW18 3BN.
WOOD, Mr. Michael James, FCA *1962;* 1 Garden Cottages, Church Walk, Bredon, TEWKESBURY, GLOUCESTERSHIRE, GL20 7FG.
•**WOOD, Mr. Michael John, FCA** *1970;* M W Medical, 2 Westbury Mews, Westbury Hill, Westbury on Trym, BRISTOL, BS9 3QA.

WOOD, Mr. Michael Paul, BA ACA CTA *2001;* 88 Mill Rise, Swanland, NORTH FERRIBY, NORTH HUMBERSIDE, HU14 3PW.
WOOD, Mr. Michael Robert, BA ACA *1988;* Tesco Personal Finance, 22 Haymarket Yards, EDINBURGH, EH12 5BH.
WOOD, Mr. Michael Thomas, FCA *1969;* 8 Clydesdale Close, DROITWICH, WR9 7SB.
•WOOD, Mr. Michael Warburton, MA FCA *1958;* with Page Kirk LLP, Sherwood House, 7 Gregory Boulevard, NOTTINGHAM, NG7 6LB.
WOOD, Miss. Natalie, ACA *2010;* 107 Park Road, Hagley, STOURBRIDGE, WEST MIDLANDS, DY9 0QH.
•WOOD, Mr. Neil Timothy, MBE BSc FCA *1990;* Deloitte LLP, Hill House, 1 Little New Street, LONDON, EC4A 3TR. See also Deloitte & Touche LLP
WOOD, Mr. Nicholas, BAcc ACA *1999;* 10 Blenheim Road, BROMLEY, BR1 2HA.
WOOD, Mr. Nicholas John, ACA *1988;* Fieldfare, Hampton-on-the-Hill, WARWICK, CV35 8QR.
WOOD, Mr. Nicholas Robert Harvey, ACA *1986;* 17 Wallace Fields, EPSOM, SURREY, KT17 3AX.
WOOD, Mrs. Nicola Claire, BA ACA *1993;* Grange Farm Old Lane, Bramhope, LEEDS, LS16 9HT.
WOOD, Mrs. Nicola Jane, BSc ACA *1997;* Meadow Cottage Ferbies, Speldhurst, TUNBRIDGE WELLS, KENT, TN3 0NS.
WOOD, Mr. Nigel Charles, BSc FCA *1980;* 41 Norton Road, INGATESTONE, CM4 0AB.
WOOD, Mr. Nigel Harley, ACA TEP *1983;* Isle of Man Assurance Ltd, Ioma House, Hope Street, Douglas, ISLE OF MAN, IM1 1AP.
•WOOD, Mr. Nigel John, FCA *1981;* (Tax Fac), Saunders Wood & Co., The White House, 140A Tachbrook Street, LONDON, SW1V 2NE.
WOOD, Mr. Nigel Richard Watson, BSc ACA *1985;* 101 Film & TV Accountants, 101 Wardour Street, LONDON, W1F 0UG.
WOOD, Mr. Norman Davies, FCA *1955;* The Old Rectory, Little Horsted, UCKFIELD, TN22 5TS. (Life Member)
WOOD, Mr. Norman Frederick, FCA *1954;* 69 Meadow Drive, Prestbury, MACCLESFIELD, SK10 4EY. (Life Member)
WOOD, Mr. Paul Christopher, FCA *1967;* Promenade de Gournet, 11190 COUIZA, FRANCE. (Life Member)
•WOOD, Mr. Paul David, BSc ACA *1990;* Ernst & Young Advisory, Faubourg de l'arche, La Defense cedex, 92037 PARIS, FRANCE. See also Ernst & Young Europe LLP
•WOOD, Mr. Paul Graham, BCom ACA *1982;* Holmwood, 6 Bracebridge Road, Four Oaks, SUTTON COLDFIELD, WEST MIDLANDS, B74 2SB.
WOOD, Mr. Paul Gregory, LLB ACA *2002;* 16 New Street, Horsforth, LEEDS, LS18 4BH.
•WOOD, Mr. Paul Nicholas, FCA *1974;* (Tax Fac), Reeves & Co LLP, 37 St. Margarets Street, CANTERBURY, KENT, CT1 2TU.
WOOD, Mr. Paul Richard, FCA ATII *1986;* (Tax Fac), with PricewaterhouseCoopers LLP, Pricewaterhousecoopers, 12 Plumtree Court, LONDON, EC4A 4HT.
WOOD, Mr. Peter, FCA *1967;* 4 SILVER STREET, SILVER HILLS SUBDIVISION, TALAMBAN, CEBU CITY 6000, CEBU, PHILIPPINES.
WOOD, Mr. Peter Anthony, FCA *1967;* Tarnwater, Tunstall, CARNFORTH, LA6 2QP. (Life Member)
•WOOD, Mr. Peter Brendan, BSc FCA *1976;* Kauai Limited, Broombarn Lane, GREAT MISSENDEN, BUCKINGHAMSHIRE, HP16 9JD. See also Middlegate Services Ltd
WOOD, Mr. Peter Bruce, FCA *1951;* The Castle, Thornham, HUNSTANTON, PE36 6LZ. (Life Member)
WOOD, Mr. Peter Charles, BSc ACA *1992;* 18 Queens Road, STONEHAVEN, AB39 2HQ.
•WOOD, Mr. Peter Charles, BSc FCA *1991;* Jackson & Graham, Lake Road, WINDERMERE, LA23 2JJ.
WOOD, Mr. Peter David, ACA *2009;* Malkin Bower, Chop Gate, MIDDLESBROUGH, CLEVELAND, TS9 7LG.
WOOD, Mr. Peter Edwin, FCA *1964;* 9 North Drive, Ancaster, GRANTHAM, NG32 3RB.
WOOD, Lieut.-Colonel Peter James, FCA *1962;* 407 Wickham Road, Shirley, CROYDON, CR0 8DP.
WOOD, Mr. Peter Jason, BSc ACA AMCT *1993;* 145 Copers Cope Road, BECKENHAM, BR3 1NZ.
WOOD, Mr. Peter John, FCA *1962;* 3 Knapps Close, WINSCOMBE, BS25 1BN. (Life Member)
WOOD, Mr. Peter John Friederich, BA FCA *1976;* Copperhurst, Knoll Hill, Aldington, ASHFORD, KENT, TN25 7BZ.
•WOOD, Mr. Peter Lawrence, FCA *1977;* Benson Wood Limited, 10 Yarm Road, STOCKTON-ON-TEES, CLEVELAND, TS18 3NA. See also Benson Wood & Co Limited and Benson Wood Bureau Services Limited
•WOOD, Mr. Peter Lawton, FCA *1957;* (Tax Fac), P.L. Wood, 20 Lonsdale Meadows, Boston Spa, WETHERBY, LS23 6DQ.
WOOD, Mr. Peter Michael, BEd BCom FCA FCMA *1968;* 7 The Grange Road, West Park, LEEDS, LS16 6HA.
WOOD, Mr. Peter Richard, FCA *1972;* 13 The Jays, Highwoods, COLCHESTER, ESSEX, CO4 9TW.
WOOD, Mr. Peter Scott, FCA *1968;* 31 Newall Hall Park, OTLEY, LS21 2RD.
•WOOD, Mr. Philip Anthony, BA ACA *2006;* Meadfoot, Westgate Drive, BRIDGNORTH, WV16 4QF.
•①WOOD, Mr. Philip Barrington, FCA CTA FABRP *1979;* (Tax Fac), Barringtons Limited, 570-572 Etruria Road, NEWCASTLE, ST5 0SU. See also Barringtons Corporate Recovery Limited
WOOD, Mr. Philip Basil, LLB ACA *1997;* 8 Redwood Lodge, Grange Road, CAMBRIDGE, CB3 9AR.
WOOD, Mr. Philip Declan, BA ACA *1991;* 18 Tavistock Close, ST. ALBANS, HERTFORDSHIRE, AL1 2NS.
WOOD, Mr. Philip Edward, BA FCA *1982;* Philip Wood & Co Ltd, 12 Main North Road, Woodend 7610, NORTH CANTERBURY, NEW ZEALAND.
WOOD, Mr. Philip John, FCA *1972;* 41 Y Ffridd, Morfa Bychan, PORTHMADOG, GWYNEDD, LL49 9YR.
WOOD, Mr. Philip John, BA(Hons) ACA *2004;* 27 Robbery Bottom Lane, WELWYN, HERTFORDSHIRE, AL6 0UL.
WOOD, Mr. Philip Kenneth, MA(Oxon) FCA MCT *1980;* 4 Middlings Wood, Kippington Road, SEVENOAKS, TN13 2LF.
WOOD, Mr. Philip Miles, BSc FCA MCT *1991;* 29 Langham Place, Highwoods, COLCHESTER, CO4 9GB.
WOOD, Mr. Philip Timothy Charles, BSc(Hons) ACA *2000;* 38 Springfield Avenue, ABERDEEN, AB15 8JD.
WOOD, Mr. Phillip David, BA(Hons) ACA *2004;* 195 College Street, Long Eaton, NOTTINGHAM, NG10 4GF.
•WOOD, Miss. Rachel Emma, ACA *2006;* Jan McDermott & Co Limited, Third Floor, 51 Hamilton Square, BIRKENHEAD, MERSEYSIDE, CH41 5BN. See also Jan McDermott & Associates Limited
WOOD, Mr. Raymond Kenneth, FCA *1961;* Grange Court, New Road, TEIGNMOUTH, DEVON, TQ14 8UD. (Life Member)
WOOD, Mrs. Rebecca Elise, ACA *2010;* 29 Broom Road, ROTHERHAM, SOUTH YORKSHIRE, S60 2SW.
WOOD, Miss. Rebecca Louise, BSc(Hons) ACA *2003;* 3 Talma Gardens, TWICKENHAM, TW2 7RB.
WOOD, Miss. Rebecca Tania Sophie, BSc ACA *1996;* 66 Wandsworth Common West Side, LONDON, SW18 2ED.
WOOD, Mr. Richard Anthony, FCA *1979;* with Smailes Goldie, Regents Court, Princess Street, HULL, HU2 8BA.
•WOOD, Mr. Richard Frost, FCA *1973;* (Tax Fac), Richard F Wood Ltd, Oakwood House, 51a Lucknow Avenue, Mapperley Park, NOTTINGHAM, NG3 5AZ.
WOOD, Mr. Richard James, BSc ACA *1993;* West Reidford, Drumoak, BANCHORY, KINCARDINESHIRE, AB31 5AU.
WOOD, Mr. Richard John, BSc FCA *1997;* 11 Ashley Close, KINGSWINFORD, DY6 9SX.
WOOD, Mr. Richard John Leonard, MA ACA *1992;* PricewaterhouseCoopers, Communications House, 1 Colville Street, PO Box 882, KAMPALA, UGANDA.
WOOD, Mr. Richard Neil, BA(Hons) ACA *2009;* 9 Botham Grove, DARLINGTON, COUNTY DURHAM, DL3 0YA.
WOOD, Mr. Richard Piers Karslake, BSc ACA *1978;* Apartment 2 Searle House, 98 Battersea Park Road, LONDON, SW11 4LQ.
WOOD, Mr. Robert, BSc ACA *1989;* 19 Furber Court, BRISTOL, BS5 8PU.
WOOD, Mr. Robert, BSc ACA *1992;* Home Farm, Raithby-cum-Maltby, LOUTH, LINCOLNSHIRE, LN11 9RR.
WOOD, Mr. Robert Jameson, FCA *1952;* 37 Innisfree Way, CONSTANTIA, C.P., 7806, SOUTH AFRICA. (Life Member)
•WOOD, Mr. Robert MacGregor Warburton, BA ACA *1990;* (Tax Fac), Robert M W Wood, 27 Silver Birch Drive, Hollywood, BIRMINGHAM, B47 5RB.
WOOD, Mr. Robert Matthew, ACA *2006;* Flat 61, New Caledonian Wharf, 6 Odessa Street, LONDON, SE16 7TW.
WOOD, Mr. Robert Nicholas, BA FCA *1978;* Wychwood, White Horse Road, East Bergholt, COLCHESTER, CO7 6TR.
WOOD, Mr. Robert William, MA FCA *1976;* 9 Northumberland Street, EDINBURGH, EH3 6LL.
WOOD, Mr. Roderick Edward, FCA *1970;* Red Rose, Maxwelltown Station, DUMFRIES, DG2 9RH.
•WOOD, Mr. Roger Anthony John, FCA *1970;* R.W. & CO Ltd, Bishops Farm, Coldharbour, WEYMOUTH, DORSET, DT3 4BG.
WOOD, Mr. Roger John, BSc ACA *1991;* 120 Holme Road, West Bridgford, NOTTINGHAM, NG2 5AE.
WOOD, Mr. Roger Norman Alexander, BSc FCA *1972;* Leybourne Securities Limited, High Leybourne, Hascombe Road, GODALMING, GU8 4AD.
WOOD, Mr. Roger Paul Gregory, FCA *1972;* Durford Cottage, 12b Sladesbrook, BRADFORD-ON-AVON, BA15 1SH.
WOOD, Mr. Roger Vernon, BA ACA *1998;* Midven Ltd, Cavendish House, 39-41 Waterloo Street, BIRMINGHAM, B2 5PP.
WOOD, Mr. Roland Frederick, FCA *1949;* 21 Charnwood Road, LOUGHBOROUGH, LE11 2BN. (Life Member)
•WOOD, Mrs. Sandra Elaine, BSc FCA *1987;* (Tax Fac), S.E.Wood, Fieldings, 6 Wheelers Way, Felbridge, EAST GRINSTEAD, RH19 2QJ.
WOOD, Ms. Sandra Melanie, BCom ACA *1987;* (Tax Fac), 61 Knowle Wood Road, Dorridge, SOLIHULL, B93 8JP.
WOOD, Mrs. Sara, MMath ACA *2003;* 10 Wren Close, WINCHESTER, SO22 4HX.
WOOD, Mrs. Sarah Jane, BCom ACA *2000;* 21 Newlay Grove, Horsforth, LEEDS, LS18 4LQ.
WOOD, Miss. Sarah Louise, FCA *1989;* 94 Town Lane, Mobberley, KNUTSFORD, CHESHIRE, WA16 7HW.
WOOD, Mr. Sebastian Courtney, BA FCA *1996;* 79 Petworth Road, LONDON, N12 9HE.
WOOD, Mr. Simon Andrew, ACA *2009;* Flat 12 Grosvenor Court, 135-139 The Grove, LONDON, W5 3SL.
WOOD, Mr. Simon Christopher, BSc ACA *1987;* (Tax Fac), Hillcrest, 176 Hall Road, NORWICH, NR1 2PP.
WOOD, Mr. Simon James, MBA BSc ACA CPA *1992;* G Tech Corporation, 8th Floor, G Tech Center, 10 Memorial Boulevard, PROVIDENCE, RI 02903 UNITED STATES.
WOOD, Mr. Simon Joseph, BEng ACA *1991;* Emmetts Hill, Whichford, SHIPSTON-ON-STOUR, CV36 5PG.
WOOD, Mr. Simon Vincent, BSc ACA *1992;* 11 Woodside Avenue, ESHER, SURREY, KT10 8JQ.
WOOD, Mr. Stephen Charles, ACA *2008;* 31 May Street, ILKESTON, DERBYSHIRE, DE7 8NJ.
WOOD, Mr. Stephen David, BA ACA *1992;* 27 Lindow Fold Drive, WILMSLOW, CHESHIRE, SK9 6DT.
WOOD, Mr. Stephen John, BSc FCA *1976;* Tower House, Dittons Road, Stone Cross, PEVENSEY, BN24 5ER.
•WOOD, Mr. Stephen John, BA FCA *1985;* (Tax Fac), Newton Magnus Ltd, Arrowsmith Court, Station Approach, BROADSTONE, BH18 8AT. See also Newton Magnus & Co
WOOD, Mr. Stephen Robert, BA ACA *1992;* C B Imports Plc Ardsley Mills, Common Lane East Ardsley, WAKEFIELD, WEST YORKSHIRE, WF3 2DW.
WOOD, Mr. Steve, BA ACA *2004;* 13 Raine Road, PADSTOW, NSW 2211, AUSTRALIA.
•WOOD, Mr. Steven John, FCA *1982;* Hargreaves Brown & Benson, 1 Bond Street, COLNE, LANCASHIRE, BB8 9DG.
WOOD, Mr. Stuart, FCA *1956;* 16 Tudor Close, Chope Road, Northam, BIDEFORD, EX39 3QD. (Life Member)
•WOOD, Mr. Stuart Charles, FCA *1989;* with KPMG LLP, One Snowhill, Snow Hill Queensway, BIRMINGHAM, B4 6GN.
WOOD, Mr. Stuart Francis, FCA *1961;* Edificio Javea Esc 1 No 11, Avda de Lepanto 1, PUERTO DE JAVEA, 03730 ALICANTE, SPAIN. (Life Member)
WOOD, Mr. Stuart Paul, BSc ACA *2004;* 43 Ashworth Park, KNUTSFORD, CHESHIRE, WA16 9DG.
•WOOD, Mrs. Suzanne, FCA *1992;* (Tax Fac), Price & Company, 30/32 Gildredge Road, EASTBOURNE, BN21 4SH.
•WOOD, Mr. Terence, FCA *1966;* T Wood & Co (Birmingham) Limited, 129 Hazelhurst Road, Kings Heath, BIRMINGHAM, B14 6AG.
WOOD, Mr. Thomas Francis, LLB ACA *1998;* Tower House, 26A Kent Road, HARROGATE, HG1 2LE.
WOOD, Mr. Thomas Nicholas, FCA *1981;* Bahrain Airport Company (S.P.C.), P.O. Box 24924, MUHARRAQ, BAHRAIN.
WOOD, Mr. Timothy Frank, FCA *1969;* The Gables Church Lane, Utterby, LOUTH, LINCOLNSHIRE, LN11 0TH.
WOOD, Mr. Timothy Garbett, FCA *1967;* 17 Grassfield Way, KNUTSFORD, CHESHIRE, WA16 9AF. (Life Member)
•WOOD, Mr. Timothy Nicolas, FCA *1974;* Tim Wood FCA, Moresdale Lodge, Lambrigg, KENDAL, CUMBRIA, LA8 0DH.
WOOD, Mr. Tod Ryan, MSc ACA *2001;* 51 Apsley Road, OLDBURY, B68 0QY.
WOOD, Mr. Tom Patrick, BA ACA *2004;* 309 Hatherley Road, CHELTENHAM, GLOUCESTERSHIRE, GL51 6HT.
•WOOD, Ms. Tracy Michelle, ACA *2000;* Ernst & Young LLP, Apex Plaza, Forbury Road, READING, RG1 1YE. See also Ernst & Young Europe LLP
•WOOD, Mrs. Valerie Ann, BA FCA *1992;* DPC Accountants Limited, Vernon Road, STOKE-ON-TRENT, ST4 2QY. See also The DPC Group Limited
WOOD, Ms. Victoria Jane, ACA *2008;* Flat 6, 1 Manchester Road Chorlton cum Hardy, MANCHESTER, M21 9JG.
•WOOD, Mr. Vincent Philip, BSc FCA *1991;* (Tax Fac), Baker Tilly Tax and Advisory Services LLP, 25 Farringdon Street, LONDON, EC4A 4AB.
•WOOD, Mr. William Henry Alan, BA ACA *2005;* Accsys Accountants Limited, Rm 1 North Wing, Turkey Court, Turkey Mill, MAIDSTONE, KENT ME14 5PP.
WOOD, Mr. William Henry Luke, MA FCA *1962;* Deerswood, Sheephouse Lane, Abinger Common, DORKING, SURREY, RH5 6LP. (Life Member)
WOOD, Mr. William John, BSc ACA ARe ARM *1992;* 7 Belmont Hills Drive, WARWICK WK06, BERMUDA.
WOOD, Mr. William Michael, MA MBA FCA *1965;* Greycote, Little Barrington, Burford, BURFORD, OX18 4TE. (Life Member)
•WOOD, Mrs. Yvonne Alison, FCA *1979;* Bennett Brooks & Co Ltd., St. Georges Court, Winnington Avenue, NORTHWICH, CHESHIRE, CW8 4EE.
•WOOD-MITCHELL, Mr. James Harold, FCA *1970;* J.H. Wood-Mitchell, 3rd Floor, 22 Devonshire Place, HARROGATE, HG1 4AA.
WOOD-ROE, Mr. Nicholas William Clifton, BA ACA *1999;* 4 Mathon Lodge, Cross Lanes, GUILDFORD, GU1 1SY.
WOOD-ROE, Mr. William Robert, FCA *1968;* The Spinney, Bagshot Road, Worplesdon Hill, WOKING, GU22 0QY.
WOODAGE, Mr. David Arthur, FCA *1965;* (Tax Fac), 34 Swan Way, Church Crookham, FLEET, HAMPSHIRE, GU51 5TT.
WOODALL, Mr. Christopher Francis, BA ACA *1991;* 36 Kennylands Road, Sonning Common, READING, RG4 9JT.
WOODALL, Mrs. Elaine Nicola Rose, BA ACA *1995;* MRIB Ltd, Eagle House, 25 Amersham Hill, HIGH WYCOMBE, BUCKINGHAMSHIRE, HP13 6NU.
WOODALL, Mr. Gary, FCA *1985;* 58 City Way, ROCHESTER, ME1 2AB.
WOODALL, Mr. John Barry, BSc(Econ) FCA FRSA *1972;* 1, Summercourt Square, KINGSWINFORD, DY6 9QJ.
WOODALL, Mr. Mark Andrew, BA ACA *1989;* A Vontade, Les Quatres Vents, St. Martin, GUERNSEY, GY4 6SS.
WOODALL, Mr. Mark James, BA ACA *1996;* 19 Wallis Road, BASINGSTOKE, RG21 3DN.
WOODALL, Mr. Peter Llewellyn, BEng ACA ATII *1994;* 60 Redgrove Park, CHELTENHAM, GLOUCESTERSHIRE, GL51 6QY.
WOODARD, Mr. Stuart James, MA ACA *1991;* Burnley House, 37 High Street, Needham Market, IPSWICH, IP6 8AL.
WOODARDS, Mr. Luke Simon, ACA *2008;* 15 Glenfield Road, Brockham, BETCHWORTH, SURREY, RH3 7HR.
WOODBERRY, Miss. Claire Joanne, BSc ACA *2004;* with Deloitte LLP, 3 Rivergate, Temple Quay, BRISTOL, BS1 6GD.
WOODBINE, Mr. David, BA ACA *1994;* 18 Holly Grove, LONDON, SE15 5DF.
WOODBRIDGE, Mr. Carl James, BSc(Hons) ACA *2011;* 68 Scotlands Drive, COALVILLE, LEICESTERSHIRE, LE67 3SU.
WOODBRIDGE, Mrs. Caroline Lesley, BSc ACA *2001;* Npower, 2 Princes Way, SOLIHULL, B91 3ES.
WOODBRIDGE, Mr. John Charles Harold, FCA *1965;* Mirembe, Cliff Road, Gorran Haven, ST AUSTELL, CORNWALL, PL26 6JW.
•WOODBRIDGE, Mr. Jonathan Charles, LLB FCA *1983;* J.C. Woodbridge, Oak House, Partridge Lane, Rusper, HORSHAM, WEST SUSSEX RH12 4RW.
•WOODBRIDGE, Mr. Matthew James, ACA *2000;* Matthew J Woodbridge ACA, PO Box 6400, Pitstone, LEIGHTON BUZZARD, BEDFORDSHIRE, LU7 6DS.
WOODBRIDGE, Mrs. Natalie, MSc ACA *2011;* 68 Scotlands Drive, COALVILLE, LEICESTERSHIRE, LE67 3SU.
WOODBRIDGE, Mr. Robert James, BA FCA *1971;* 6A Langford Place, St Johns Wood, LONDON, NW8 0LL.

WOODBRIDGE, Mr. Robert Thomas, BA ACA *2005;* 36 Queen Victoria Road, BRISTOL, BS6 7PE.
WOODBURN, Mr. Christopher Hugh, FCA *1972;* Oak House, Heathfield Road, Burwash, ETCHINGHAM, EAST SUSSEX, TN19 7HN.
WOODBURN, Mr. David Matthew, BA ACA *1988;* 38 Cromwell Avenue, Highgate, LONDON, N6 5HL.
•WOODBURN, Miss. Janine Clare, BSc FCA *1991;* J C Woodburn Limited, 37 Brookland Road, Phippsville, NORTHAMPTON, NN1 4SN.
•WOODBURN, Mrs. Nicola Jane, BA ACA *1990;* (Tax Fac), Nicola Woodburn, 100 Station Road, Bannockburn, STIRLING, FK7 8JP.
•WOODBURN, Mr. Paul, BCom FCA *1989;* (Tax Fac), Wallwork Nelson & Johnson, Chandler House, 7 Ferry Road Office Park, Riversway, PRESTON, PR2 2YH.
WOODBURN, Mr. Philip John, BA ACA *1987;* No 188 Mingyue Road, Shimao Lakeside Garden, Block 67 Appt 301, Pudong District, SHANGHAI 200135, CHINA.
•WOODBURN, Miss. Rebecca Jane, BA FCA *1996;* Iota Accountancy Services Limited, 1 Factory Cottages, Pound Green, Cowlinge, NEWMARKET, SUFFOLK CB8 9QQ.
WOODBURN, Mrs. Ruth Caroline, MA ACA *1990;* 38 Cromwell Avenue, Highgate, LONDON, N6 5HL.
WOODBURN, Mr. Stephen Sealy, LLB ACA *2001;* Crown Cottage West End, Wootton, WOODSTOCK, OXFORDSHIRE, OX20 1DL.
WOODBURY, Mr. Kenneth Ian, BA FCA *1975;* Beech Cottage, Front Street, Churchill, WINSCOMBE, AVON, BS25 5NG.
WOODCOCK, Mrs. Cathy Ann, BA(Hons) ACA *2000;* Shelley House, 2-4 York Road, MAIDENHEAD, BERKSHIRE, SL6 1SR.
WOODCOCK, Mr. Christopher Charles, BA ACA *1984;* Harpendon, 21 Keats Avenue, Littleover, DERBY, DE23 7EE.
WOODCOCK, Mrs. Davina Abigail, BSc ACA *1998;* 59 Richmond Road, SOLIHULL, WEST MIDLANDS, B92 7RR.
WOODCOCK, Mr. Derek Charles, ACA *1978;* Apulgarth, Meadows Road, East Wittering, CHICHESTER, PO20 8NW.
WOODCOCK, Mr. Derek Nicholas Philip, BSc FCA *1974;* 25 Howard Drive, Tarleton, PRESTON, PR4 6DA.
WOODCOCK, Mr. Duncan, BSc ACA *2011;* 43 Currells Lane, Felton, BRISTOL, BS40 9XF.
•WOODCOCK, Mr. Jason Charles, FCA *1999;* Berry & Warren Ltd, 54 Thorpe Road, NORWICH, NR1 1RY.
WOODCOCK, Mr. John, FCA *1975;* 1 Horksley Gardens, Hutton, BRENTWOOD, ESSEX, CM13 1YP.
WOODCOCK, Mr. Jonathan, BSc ACA *1978;* Lower Cladswell Farm, Cookhill, ALCESTER, B49 5LA.
WOODCOCK, Miss. Linda Deborah Mitchell, BSc ACA *1995;* 5 Wrigleys Close, Freshfield Formby, LIVERPOOL, L37 7DT.
WOODCOCK, Mr. Michael John, BSc ACA *1998;* 45 Bawdale Road, LONDON, SE22 9DL.
WOODCOCK, Mr. Nigel Kevin Mitchell, BA FCA *1989;* 5 Wrigleys Close, Freshfield Formby, LIVERPOOL, L37 7DT.
WOODCOCK, Mr. Norman Marshall, FCA *1963;* 61 Eastcliff, PORTISHEAD, BS20 7AB. (Life Member)
•WOODCOCK, Mr. Paul John, BA ACA *1993;* PJW Accounting Limited, Suite 15, Hawkesyard Hall, Armitage Park, Armitage, RUGELEY STAFFORDSHIRE WS15 1PU.
WOODCOCK, Mr. Peter Glyn, BSc ACA *1980;* 30 Egremont Drive, Lower Earley, READING, RG6 3BS.
WOODCOCK, Mr. Peter Richard, BA ACA *1985;* 42 rue Victor Hugo, 11000 CARCASSONNE, FRANCE.
WOODCOCK, Mr. Peter Stephen, FCA *1975;* 59 Priory Way, MIRFIELD, WF14 9EB.
WOODCOCK, Mr. Roger Alistair, BA(Hons) FCA *2001;* 1 Widbury, Langton Green, TUNBRIDGE WELLS, KENT, TN3 0HW.
WOODCOCK, Mrs. Serena Louise, BA(Hons) ACA CTA *2000;* 1 Widbury, Langton Green, TUNBRIDGE WELLS, TN3 0HW.
WOODCOCK, Ms. Sheila Mary, BSc ACA *1990;* 23 Guardhouse Road, Radford, COVENTRY, CV6 3DU.
•WOODCOCK, Mr. Stephen Ronald, BSc FCA *1977;* Stephen Woodcock, 69 Maudlin Drive, TEIGNMOUTH, DEVON, TQ14 8SB.
WOODCOCK, Mr. Stuart Peter, BA(Hons) ACA *2002;* with PricewaterhouseCoopers SA, Birchstrasse 160, 8050 ZURICH, SWITZERLAND.
WOODCOCK, Mr. Timothy David, BCom ACA *1995;* 71 Popes Avenue, TWICKENHAM, MIDDLESEX, TW2 5TD.
WOODCRAFT, Mr. Steven, ACA *2006;* Flat 6, Mount Arlington, 37 Park Hill Road, BROMLEY, BR2 0LB.
•WOODDISSE, Mr. Paul Arthur, FCA *1967;* Paul Wooddisse, 2 Chantry Road, STOURBRIDGE, DY7 6SA.
WOODESON, Mr. Donald Richard Albert, FCA *1957;* 7 Rodenhurst Road, Clapham Park, LONDON, SW4 8AE. (Life Member)
WOODFIELD, Ms. Sarah Caroline, BSc ACA *1984;* Dragonfly, 130 High Street, BECKENHAM, BR3 1EB.
WOODFINE, Mr. Neville George, FCA *1958;* The Wynd, Low Town Road, Longframlington, MORPETH, NE65 8BA.
WOODFORD, Mrs. Deborah Ann, BA ACA *1996;* 9 Residence Noaille, 142 Avenue du Generale de Gaulle, 78600 MAISONS LAFFITTE, FRANCE.
WOODFORD, Mr. Gerald Anthony, FCA *1956;* 2 Bennion Road, Newstead, Bushby, LEICESTER, LE7 9QF.
•WOODFORD, Mr. Graham Richard, FCA *1975;* GRW Consultancy Limited, The Old Rectory, Brisley, DEREHAM, NORFOLK, NR20 5LJ.
WOODFORD, Mr. John Kenneth William, BA ACA *1992;* 25 Jennings Road, ST. ALBANS, HERTFORDSHIRE, AL1 4NU.
WOODFORD, Mr. Julian Ray, BSc FCA *1989;* 36 Huntingdon Road, LONDON, N2 9DU.
WOODFORD, Mrs. Juliet, BSc ACA *1992;* 25 Jennings Road, ST. ALBANS, HERTFORDSHIRE, AL1 4NU.
WOODFORD, Mr. Kenneth Robert, FCA *1961;* The Stables, Reynoldston, Gower, SWANSEA, SA3 1AE.
WOODFORD, Mr. Malcolm James, FCA *1968;* 31 Grangewood, Little Heath, POTTERS BAR, HERTFORDSHIRE, EN6 1SJ.
•WOODFORD, Mr. Nicholas Andrew, BA ACA *1991;* (Tax Fac), PricewaterhouseCoopers LLP, 1 Embankment Place, LONDON, WC2N 6RH. See also PricewaterhouseCoopers
WOODGATE, Mr. Charles William Lyndon, MBA BSc FCA *1977;* Pendennis Clevedon Road, West Hill Wraxall, BRISTOL, BS48 1PN.
WOODGATE, Mrs. Ksenia, BSc ACA *1999;* 21 Onslow Gardens, WIMBORNE, DORSET, BH21 2QG.
•WOODGATE, Mr. Mark Lee, FCA *1995;* John Crook & Partners, 255 Green Lanes, Palmers Green, LONDON, N13 4XE.
WOODGATE, Miss. Natalie Sarah, ACA *2003;* 25 Tringham Close, Knaphill, WOKING, SURREY, GU21 2FB.
•WOODGATE, Mr. Philip Harcourt, BSc FCA *1994;* Goodman Jones LLP, 29-30 Fitzroy Square, LONDON, W1T 6LQ.
WOODGATE, Mr. Richard Miles, RD MA FCA FSI *1966;* 6 Westfield Close, Dorridge, SOLIHULL, B93 8DY.
WOODGATE, Mrs. Susan Alison, BSc ACA *1994;* 70 Whyteleafe Hill, WHYTELEAFE, SURREY, CR3 0AB.
•WOODGATE, Mrs. Susan Mary, BSc ACA *1990;* (Tax Fac), Sue Woodgate, 42 St. Nicholas Drive, SHEPPERTON, MIDDLESEX, TW17 9LD.
WOODGATES, Mr. Paul Jonathan, BA ACA *1992;* 7 Westfield Road, SURBITON, KT6 4EL.
WOODGER, Mr. Alastair John, BSc ACA *1986;* with PricewaterhouseCoopers Pvt. Ltd, 5th Floor Tower D The Millenia, 1 & 2 Murphy Road, Ulsoor, BANGALORE 560008, KARNATAKA INDIA.
WOODGETT, Mr. Sidney Raven, FCA *1934;* 41 High Street, Milton, ABINGDON, OXFORDSHIRE, OX14 4ER. (Life Member)
•WOODHALL, Mr. Gary, ACA *2009;* Kilby Fox, 4 Pavilion Court, 600 Pavilion Drive, NORTHAMPTON, NN4 7SL.
WOODHALL, Mr. Geoffrey Kelvin, FCA *1965;* 22 Bowgreave Drive, Bowgreave, PRESTON, PR3 1TD. (Life Member)
WOODHALL, Miss. Jane Frances, BSc(Hons) ACA *2003;* 13 Thorn Bank Lodge, 150 Heaton Moor Road, STOCKPORT, CHESHIRE, SK4 4LA.
WOODHALL, Mr. Michael John, FCA *1966;* 2 Elder Court, 83 Heaton Moor Road, STOCKPORT, CHESHIRE, SK4 4FX.
•WOODHALL, Mr. Michael John, BA FCA *1970;* Orchard Lodge, Backsideans, Wargrave, READING, RG10 8JP.
•WOODHALL, Mr. Peter Michael, BSc FCA *1992;* WKH, PO Box 501, The Nexus Building, Broadway, LETCHWORTH GARDEN CITY, HERTFORDSHIRE SG6 9BL. See also Virtual Business Source Limited
WOODHALL, Mr. Richard Edward, FCA *1970;* Penrhos Garage, ABERDOVEY, GWYNEDD, LL35 0NR. (Life Member)
WOODHAM, Mr. Stephen James, BSc FCA *1996;* 28 Springfield Road, SWINDON, SN1 4EP.
WOODHAMS, Mr. Ernest James, FCA *1954;* 5 Rectory Close, EASTBOURNE, BN20 8AQ. (Life Member)
WOODHAMS, Mrs. Jennifer Margaret, BA ACA *2006;* 13 Springfield, Clifford, WETHERBY, LS23 6HQ.
WOODHAMS, Mr. Peter John, FCA *1978;* 7 Sunset View, BARNET, HERTFORDSHIRE, EN5 4LB.
WOODHAMS, Mr. Steven James, BA ACA *2005;* Tara Topcliffe Lane, Morley, LEEDS, LS27 9BB.
WOODHEAD, Mr. Andrew Clifford, BSc(Hons) ACA *2002;* 13 Clos Llewellyn, Creigiau, CARDIFF, CF15 9JR.
WOODHEAD, Mrs. Anne Denise, BA FCA *1977;* 26 Castlefields, Bournmoor, HOUGHTON-LE-SPRING, DH4 6HH.
WOODHEAD, Anthony John Keith, Esq CBE FCA *1958;* Old Orchard, 32 Albion Hill, LOUGHTON, IG10 4RD. (Life Member)
WOODHEAD, Mr. Ben, ACA *2008;* with KPMG LLP, 15 Canada Square, LONDON, E14 5GL.
•WOODHEAD, Mr. Christopher John, BA FCA *1985;* C J Woodhead & Co Limited, 158 Hemper Lane, Greenhill, SHEFFIELD, S8 7FE.
WOODHEAD, Mr. David, FCA *1973;* Frisky Place, Eastbury, HUNGERFORD, RG17 7JL.
WOODHEAD, Mr. David John, BSc ACA *1986;* 7 Essex Park, EDINBURGH, EH4 6LH.
WOODHEAD, Mr. Keith James, BA(Hons) ACA *2002;* 72 Cronk Coar, Douglas, ISLE OF MAN, IM2 5LY.
WOODHEAD, Mrs. Louise Michelle, BA ACA *2005;* with KPMG LLP, Quayside House, 110 Quayside, NEWCASTLE UPON TYNE, NE1 3DX.
WOODHEAD, Miss. Lyn, BSc ACA *1980;* 28 Pymmes Green Road, New Southgate, LONDON, N11 1BY.
WOODHEAD, Mr. Martin Richard, BA ACA *1982;* 52 Roberta Avenue, Glendowie, AUCKLAND, NEW ZEALAND.
WOODHEAD, Mr. Matthew David, BSc ACA *2009;* 46 Delamere Drive, MANSFIELD, NOTTINGHAMSHIRE, NG18 4DF.
WOODHEAD, Mr. Michael John, FCA *1968;* Manor Holme, Linden Road, HALIFAX, HX3 0BS. (Life Member)
WOODHEAD, Mr. Niall James, BSc ACA *1994;* 63 Fernside Road, Balham, LONDON, SW12 8LH.
WOODHEAD, Norman Arthur, Esq MBE MC FCA *1947;* 4 Victoria Road, Formby, LIVERPOOL, L37 7AG. (Life Member)
WOODHEAD, Mr. Raymond, FCA *1951;* Keld, Plough Road, Tibberton, DROITWICH, WR9 7NQ. (Life Member)
WOODHEAD, Mr. Robert Charles, FCA *1973;* 38 Clare Road, HALIFAX, WEST YORKSHIRE, HX1 2HX.
WOODHEAD, Mrs. Ruth Helen, BA ACA *1992;* 28 Alvaston Avenue, STOCKPORT, CHESHIRE, SK4 4EW.
WOODHEAD, Mrs. Sarah Elizabeth, BA(Hons) ACA *2009;* Tudor John Nightingale House, 46-48 East Street, EPSOM, KT17 1HQ.
WOODHEAD, Mr. Thomas Michael Parkin, BA ACA *1983;* 438 El Cielito Road, SANTA BARBARA, CA 93105, UNITED STATES.
WOODHOUSE, Mr. Andrew David, BSc ACA *1993;* S A B Miller Plc, S A B Miller House, Church Street West, WOKING, SURREY, GU21 6HS.
WOODHOUSE, Mr. Anthony William, FCA *1953;* 6 Linkswood, Compton Place Rd, EASTBOURNE, BN21 1EE. (Life Member)
•WOODHOUSE, Mr. Charles Rudiger, ACA *2004;* Charles Wong & Co., Room A, 6th Floor, Kiu Fu Commercial Building, 300 - 306 Lockhart Road, WAN CHAI HONG KONG ISLAND HONG KONG SAR.
WOODHOUSE, Mr. Christopher Kevin, BSc FCA AMCT *1986;* 28 Chester Square, LONDON, SW1W 9HT.
WOODHOUSE, Dr. David Robert Sterry, MA ACA *1999;* with Fauchier Partners Ltd, 72 Welbeck Street, LONDON, W1G 0AY.
WOODHOUSE, Mrs. Deborah Mary, FCA *1978;* 14 Carmalt Gardens, LONDON, SW15 6NE.
WOODHOUSE, Miss. Diana Alison, FCA *1976;* At Last, East Street, Addington, WEST MALLING, KENT, ME19 5DE.
•WOODHOUSE, Mr. Geoffrey William, BA FCA *1988;* Moore Stephens LLP, 150 Aldersgate Street, LONDON, EC1A 4AB. See also Moore Stephens & Co
WOODHOUSE, Mr. Graham, BSc ACA *1988;* 29 St. Peter's Street, LONDON, N1 8JP.
WOODHOUSE, Mr. Graham Harvey, FCA *1971;* Queen Alexandra College, 49 Court Oak Road, Harborne, BIRMINGHAM, B17 9TG.
WOODHOUSE, Mr. James Alexander, BA ACA *1992;* Culmannstrasse 21, 8006 ZURICH, SWITZERLAND.
WOODHOUSE, Mr. John Edward, BSc ACA *1982;* Ul Jorskiego 48, WARSAW, 03-593, POLAND.
•WOODHOUSE, Mr. Justin Jonathan Thomas, BA FCA *1981;* PricewaterhouseCoopers LLP, Hays Galleria, 1 Hays Lane, LONDON, SE1 2RD. See also PricewaterhouseCoopers
WOODHOUSE, Mr. Laurence Daniel, BA ACA *2007;* Flat 16, 41 Carlton Drive, LONDON, SW15 2DG.
WOODHOUSE, Miss. Lee Shelley, BA ACA *1991;* St Aubin, Albert Road, Alexandra Park, NOTTINGHAM, NG3 4JD.
WOODHOUSE, Mr. Matthew Wilfrid, BA FCA *1996;* 4229 Swarthmore, HOUSTON, TX 77005, UNITED STATES.
WOODHOUSE, Mr. Paul Duncan, BA ACA *1989;* 10 Hodder Close Crich, MATLOCK, DERBYSHIRE, DE4 5NH.
WOODHOUSE, Mr. Philip Laurence, BA ACA *1984;* 66 Surbiton Hill Park, SURBITON, KT5 8ER.
WOODHOUSE, Mrs. Rachel Lucy, BA(Hons) ACA *2001;* The White House, High Street, Iron Acton, BRISTOL, BS37 9UG.
WOODHOUSE, Mr. Robert Boam, BA FCA *1981;* The Grange, The Grove, Houghton Conquest, BEDFORD, MK45 3JU.
WOODHOUSE, Mrs. Sarah Caroline, BSc ACA *1985;* Deloitte Touche Tohmatsu, PO Box N250, 225 George Street, GROSVENOR PLACE, NSW 1217, AUSTRALIA.
WOODHOUSE, Mr. Stephen, BSc(Hons) ACA *2001;* 4 Adelaide Grove, STOCKTON-ON-TEES, CLEVELAND, TS18 5BU.
WOODHOUSE, Mr. Stephen Charles, BA FCA *1983;* 12 Blackford Hill View, EDINBURGH, EH9 3HD.
WOODHOUSE, Mr. Timothy John, MBA BA ACA *1988;* 39 Great Ellshams, BANSTEAD, SURREY, SM7 2BA.
WOODHOUSE, Mr. Vincent Spencer, FCA *1957;* 80 Upgang Lane, WHITBY, YO21 3JW. (Life Member)
WOODHOUSE, Mrs. Virginia Anne Mary, BA ACA *2002;* Holly Tree House Sarson Lane, Amport, ANDOVER, SP11 8AA.
WOODING, Mr. Andrew Paul, ACA *2010;* Target Chartered Accountants, 14 Floor 76 Shoe Lane, LONDON, EC4A 3JB.
WOODING, Mr. Eric Harrison, BSc FCA *1978;* Deloitte & Touche Hill House, 1 Little New Street, LONDON, EC4A 3TR.
WOODING, Mr. Ian Christopher, FCA *1954;* Uplands, Stourbridge Road, Wombourne, WOLVERHAMPTON, WV5 9BN. (Life Member)
WOODING, Miss. Mona Virginia, BSc ACA *2006;* Flat 3, 10 St. Andrews Road, SURBITON, SURREY, KT6 4DT.
WOODING, Mr. Simon James, BSc ACA *2006;* 25 Maunsel Street, LONDON, SW1P 2QN.
•WOODINGS, Mr. Anthony John, BA FCA *1991;* Hurst & Company Accountants LLP, Lancashire Gate, 21 Tiviot Dale, STOCKPORT, CHESHIRE, SK1 1TD.
WOODINGS, Miss. Teresa Lillian, BSc ACA *1987;* Elm House, Spridlington, MARKET RASEN, LN8 2DE.
WOODISSE, Mr. Michael Helm, FCA *1965;* 3 The Brambles, Girton, CAMBRIDGE, CB3 0NY.
•WOODLAND, Mrs. Allison Mary, BSc ACA *1991;* Woodland & Woodland Limited, Dragon House, Princes Way, Bridgend Industrial Estate, BRIDGEND, MID GLAMORGAN CF31 3AQ.
WOODLAND, Mr. Andrew Charles, ACA *1987;* 25 Turnoak Avenue, WOKING, GU22 0AJ.
•WOODLAND, Mr. David Barrie, BA ACA *1991;* Woodland & Woodland Limited, Dragon House, Princes Way, Bridgend Industrial Estate, BRIDGEND, MID GLAMORGAN CF31 3AQ.
•WOODLAND, Mr. Guy Geoffrey Edward, FCA *1982;* Guy Woodland Ltd, Renwood, Vale Road, High Kelling, HOLT, NORFOLK NR25 6RA.
WOODLAND, Miss. Helen Frances, BSc ACA *1993;* Skandia Investment Group, PO Box 37, Skandia House, Portland Terrace, SOUTHAMPTON, SO14 7AY.
WOODLAND, Mr. Simon Roger, BBS ACA *1993;* 24 Victoria Avenue, Melrose, JOHANNESBURG, GAUTENG, 2196, SOUTH AFRICA.
WOODLEY, Mr. Brian Peter, FCA *1972;* 13 Welland Road, Barrow On Soar, LOUGHBOROUGH, LE12 8NA.
WOODLEY, Mr. Ian Christopher George, BA ACA *1996;* Finance Department, University of Derby, Kedleston Road, DERBY, DE22 1GB.
WOODLEY, Mrs. Jill, LLB ACA *1986;* 57 Claremont Road, Highgate, LONDON, N6 5DA.
WOODLEY, Miss. Justine Kate, BA ACA *1991;* 39 Grace Gardens, CHELTENHAM, GLOUCESTERSHIRE, GL51 6QE.

WOODLEY, Mrs. Keely-Anne, BSc ACA *2004;* with Grant Thornton UK LLP, Grant Thornton House, 22 Melton Street, Euston Square, LONDON, NW1 2EP.
WOODLEY, Mr. Keith Spencer, FCA *1963;* (President 1995 - 1996) (Member of Council 1989 - 1998), Rectory Cottage, Combe Hay, BATH, BA2 7EG.
WOODLEY, Mr. Paul Jonathan, BSc ACA *1980;* Broadoak, West Park Road, Copthorne, CRAWLEY, RH10 3EX.
WOODLEY, Mr. Quentin Nash, BSc FCA *1986;* McKinsey & Co Inc, 1 Jermyn Street, LONDON, SW1Y 4UH.
WOODLEY, Mr. Richard William, BA FCA *1963;* Flower Wood, Pillaton, SALTASH, PL12 6QS.
WOODLIFFE, Mr. David Leonard, FCA *1959;* 10 Clearview, Shirenewton, CHEPSTOW, NP16 6AX.
•WOODLOCK, Mr. Peter James, FCA *1970;* 20 Leopold Road, St Andrews, BRISTOL, BS6 5BS.
WOODMAN, Mr. Anthony Robin, FCA *1968;* Samhchair, The Oa, ISLE OF ISLAY, PA42 7AX. (Life Member)
WOODMAN, Mr. David John, BA FCA *1985;* 12 Tabor Grove, Wimbledon, LONDON, SW19 4EB.
WOODMAN, Mrs. Fiona Mary, ACA *1984;* P E P Ltd, 58 Coinagehall Street, HELSTON, CORNWALL, TR13 8EL.
WOODMAN, Mr. James Alexander, BA ACA *2010;* Flat 7, Webster House, 26 Gloucester Street, LONDON, SW1V 2DN.
•WOODMAN, Mr. John, BSc FCA *1973;* John Woodman, 3 Cadman House, Off Peartree Road, COLCHESTER, CO3 0NW.
•WOODMAN, Mr. John Charlton, FCA *1988;* (Tax Fac), Dalewood Limited, 42-44 Brunswick Road, SHOREHAM-BY-SEA, WEST SUSSEX, BN43 5WB.
WOODMAN, Mr. John Crawford, CA *2001; (CA Scotland 1979);* Elford Farmhouse, Elford, SEAHOUSES, NORTHUMBERLAND, NE68 7UT.
WOODMAN, Mrs. Laura Jane, ACA *2003;* with KPMG, 10 Shelley Street, SYDNEY, NSW 2000, AUSTRALIA.
WOODMAN, Mr. Michael Geoffrey, BSc FCA CTA *1985;* (Tax Fac), NewSmith Financial Products LLP, Lansdowne House, 57 Berkeley Square, LONDON, W1J 6ER.
WOODMAN, Mr. Michael John, FCA *1966;* PO Box 1048, Woodmanery, Elbow Rise, BRAGG CREEK T0L 0K0, AB, CANADA. (Life Member)
WOODMAN, Miss. Nicola Jane, BSc ACA *1990;* 5 Robinia Close, Charlton Kings, CHELTENHAM, GL53 8PR.
WOODMAN, Dr. Paul Richard, PhD ACA *2002;* with Deloitte LLP, PO Box 403, Lord Coutanche House, 66-68 Esplanade, St Helier, JERSEY JE4 8WA.
•WOODMAN, Mr. Robert James, FCA *1978;* (Tax Fac), 9 Church Close, Cranham, GLOUCESTER, GL4 8HT.
WOODMAN, Miss. Susan Jane, FCA *1981;* Engbakkevej 18, 8800 VIBORG, DENMARK.
WOODMAN, Mrs. Susan Jane, BSc ACA *1993;* 41 Cheswick Way Shirley, SOLIHULL, WEST MIDLANDS, B90 4HF.
WOODMANSEY, Mr. Nicholas John, ACA *2008;* 17A Rawhitiroa Road, Kohimarama, AUCKLAND 1071, NEW ZEALAND.
WOODROFFE, Miss. Alison, BSocSc ACA *1997;* 9 Shelvers Way, TADWORTH, SURREY, KT20 5QJ.
WOODROFFE, Miss. Carolyn Rose, BSc ACA *2007;* 50 Elm Grove, Hildenborough, TONBRIDGE, KENT, TN11 9HF.
WOODROFFE, Mr. Christopher Martin, BSc(Hons) ACA *2010;* 14 The Meadows, Riccall, YORK, YO19 6RR.
WOODROFFE, Mrs. Janet Sarah, FCA *1969;* Petan, Wistanstow, CRAVEN ARMS, SY7 8DG.
WOODROFFE, Mr. Nigel Anthony, FCA *1971;* (Tax Fac), Jersey Financial Services Commission, PO Box 267, JERSEY, JE4 8TP.
WOODROOF, Mr. Paul Andrew, LLB ACA *1995;* First Floor Flat, 320 Goring Road, WORTHING, WEST SUSSEX, BN12 4PE.
•WOODROW, Mr. James Radclyffe, FCA *1972;* (Tax Fac), Radclyffe & Woodrow Limited, 52 St John Street, ASHBOURNE, DERBYSHIRE, DE6 1GH.
WOODROW, Mr. John Graham, MVO FCA *1963;* Crookswood Stud Farm, Wycombe Road, Studley Green, HIGH WYCOMBE, HP14 3XB. (Life Member)
WOODROW, Mr. John Rodger, FCA *1968;* Coach House, Hadlow Wood, Willaston, NESTON, CH64 2UN.
•WOODROW, Mr. Jonathan Woolf, BSc FCA *1979;* J.W. Woodrow & Co, 141 Station Road, Hendon, LONDON, NW4 4NJ.
WOODROW, Miss. Kerrie, ACA *2010;* 33 White Oak Way, Nailsea, BRISTOL, BS48 4YS.
WOODROW, Dr. Kevin Peter, ACA *1992;* Planning Inspectorate, Temple Quay House, 2 The Square, Temple Quay, BRISTOL, BS1 6PN.
WOODROW, Mr. Neil Keith, BCom FCA *1988;* 3 Falstaff Gardens, ST. ALBANS, HERTFORDSHIRE, AL1 2AL.
WOODROW, Mr. Phillip Andrew, FCA *1971;* (Tax Fac), Low House, Smithy Greaves, Addingham, ILKLEY, LS29 0SB.
WOODROW, Mr. Rowland Kevin Lindley, BSc ACA *1984;* 15 Sylvester Avenue, CHISLEHURST, KENT, BR7 5ED.
WOODRUFF, Mr. Andrew, BSc ACA *2011;* Ernst & Young Llp, 1 More London Place, LONDON, SE1 2AF.
WOODRUFF, Mr. Ian, BSc ACA CTA *1998;* (Tax Fac), with Grant Thornton UK LLP, 30 Finsbury Square, LONDON, EC2P 2YU.
•WOODRUFF, Mr. Nigel Roy, BSc ACA *1990;* Read Woodruff Limited, 24 Cornwall Road, DORCHESTER, DORSET, DT1 1RX.
WOODS, Mr. Alan, BA ACA *1996;* 41 Allington Street, Aigburth, LIVERPOOL, L17 7AE.
WOODS, Mr. Alan Arthur, FCA *1968;* Harehill Farm, Twisses Bank, Boylestone, DERBY, DE6 5AA.
WOODS, Miss. Amanda, BSc ACA *2005;* 26 Second Avenue, Horbury, WAKEFIELD, WEST YORKSHIRE, WF4 6HB.
•WOODS, Mr. Andrew James, BA ACA CTA *1999;* (Tax Fac), Ratiocinator Limited, Cholmondeley House, Dee Hills Park, CHESTER, CH3 5AR.
WOODS, Mr. Andrew James, BA ACA *2002;* Broadwood La Rue A la Dame, St. Saviour, JERSEY, JE2 7NH.
WOODS, Mr. Andrew Kindebee, MA FCA *1969;* P O Box 3565, 224 Tansy Hill Road, STOWE, VT 05672, UNITED STATES. (Life Member)
WOODS, Mr. Andrew Nicholas, BSc FCA *1988;* 18 Hollybush Lane, HARPENDEN, HERTFORDSHIRE, AL5 4AT.
WOODS, Mr. Ben, ACA *2011;* 25 Humberston Avenue, Humberston, GRIMSBY, SOUTH HUMBERSIDE, DN36 4SL.
WOODS, Mr. Brian Edwin, FCA *1965;* 13 Windrush Avenue, BEDFORD, MK41 7BS.
WOODS, Mrs. Catherine Anna, BSc ACA *1996;* Caramore, 44 Lynch Road, FARNHAM, SURREY, GU9 8BY.
WOODS, Mr. Charles Henry, BA FCA *1989;* Thimble Cottage, School Lane, Warmington, BANBURY, OX17 1DE.
WOODS, Miss. Christine Mary, BSc ACA ATII *1988;* Tay Commercial Services Ltd, PO Box 36, BURY, BL8 2NH.
WOODS, Mr. Christopher Gerard, BSc ACA *1991;* 134d Route de Veyrier, 1234 Vessy, GENEVA, SWITZERLAND.
•WOODS, Mr. Darren James, ACA *1991;* Woods & Co, 1 Fordyce Close, HORNCHURCH, ESSEX, RM11 3LE. See also Synergy Business Solutions UK Limited
•WOODS, Mr. David, FCA *1966;* Trefreock, Hatfield Heath, BISHOP'S STORTFORD, CM22 7DL.
WOODS, Mr. David Ian, ACA *2003;* 79 Wheatlands, FAREHAM, PO14 4SU.
WOODS, Mrs. Deborah Jane, BSc ACA *1990;* 128 Fidlas Road, CARDIFF, CF14 0NE.
WOODS, Miss. Denise Olga, BSc ACA *1992;* 43 Tunley Road, Balham, LONDON, SW17 7QH.
•WOODS, Mr. Edward James, BSc ACA *1994;* with PricewaterhouseCoopers, Prince's Building, 22/F, 10 Chater Road, CENTRAL, HONG KONG ISLAND HONG KONG SAR.
WOODS, Miss. Eileen Louise, BSc ACA *1996;* 4 Sandend Place, Ardgowan View, Inverkip, GREENOCK, PA16 0HU.
WOODS, Ms. Elisa, BA ACA *2006;* 37 Prospect Road, Longwood, HUDDERSFIELD, HD3 4UY.
WOODS, Miss. Elizabeth Ann, ACA *2008;* 10 Acorn Close, HAMPTON, MIDDLESEX, TW12 3DX.
WOODS, Mrs. Emma Alice, BA ACA *2006;* 12 Rhosleigh Avenue, BOLTON, BL1 6PP.
WOODS, Miss. Georgina Roselle, ACA *2008;* The Maisonette, 7 Sutherland Road, TUNBRIDGE WELLS, TN1 1SE.
WOODS, Miss. Helen Josephine, BA(Hons) ACA *2010;* 32 Stone Hill, ST. NEOTS, CAMBRIDGESHIRE, PE19 6AA.
WOODS, Mr. Ian Paul, FCA *1982;* 17 Wold Road, Burton Latimer, KETTERING, NN15 5PN.
WOODS, Mrs. Iris Lily, FCA *1948;* 38 Lincoln Drive, Pyrford, WOKING, GU22 8RR. (Life Member)
WOODS, Mr. James Noel, FCA *1967;* PO Box 298, Klapmuts, PAARL, 7625, SOUTH AFRICA. (Life Member)
WOODS, Mrs. Janelle, BSc ACA *1999;* 45 The Fairway, GRAVESEND, DA11 7LN.
WOODS, Miss. Jennifer, ACA *2009;* 39 Holmefield Road, LIVERPOOL, L19 3PE.
WOODS, Mr. Jeremy Alexander, BA ACA *1994;* 95 White Hart Lane, Barnes, LONDON, SW13 0PW.
WOODS, Mr. John Christopher, BA ACA *1998;* 48 Knightlow Road, Harborne, BIRMINGHAM, B17 8QB.
WOODS, Mr. John David, BMus ACA *2004;* 174 St. Albans Avenue, LONDON, W4 5JU.
WOODS, Mr. John Frederick, FCA *1955;* 53 Bodley Road, NEW MALDEN, KT3 5QD. (Life Member)
WOODS, Mr. Jonathan, BSc ACA *1992;* Auburn, 1 New England Close, St Ippolyts, HITCHIN, SG4 7NQ.
WOODS, Ms. Kathryn Louise, BA ACA *1995;* 17 Royles Head Lane, Longwood, HUDDERSFIELD, HD3 4TU.
WOODS, Mr. Kenneth John, FCA *1963;* 389 Mountnessing Road, BILLERICAY, CM12 0EU. (Life Member)
WOODS, Mrs. Lalena, BA ACA *1999;* (Tax Fac), 48 Knightlow Road, Harborne, BIRMINGHAM, B17 8QB.
WOODS, Mr. Mark, BA ACA *2007;* Plexus Cotton Ltd, Cotton Place, 2 Ivy Street, BIRKENHEAD, MERSEYSIDE, CH41 5EF.
•WOODS, Mr. Mark Anthony, BSc FCA *1989;* (Tax Fac), Berry Accountants, Bowden House, 36 Northampton Road, MARKET HARBOROUGH, LEICESTERSHIRE, LE16 9HE.
WOODS, Mr. Mark Kevin, ACA *1984;* XBG Fleet Remarketing Ltd, 206 Popham Court Lane, Micheldever, WINCHESTER, HAMPSHIRE, SO21 3BJ.
WOODS, Mr. Martin John, FCA *1982;* 7 Garth Way Close, DRONFIELD, DERBYSHIRE, S18 1SZ.
WOODS, Mr. Martin Walter, FCA *1961;* Mead House, Weston Patrick, BASINGSTOKE, HAMPSHIRE, RG25 2NX.
WOODS, Mrs. Melissa Clare, BSc ACA *2002;* 9 West Clyst, EXETER, EX1 3TP.
WOODS, Mr. Michael Martin, FCA *1970;* Catomance Technologies Ltd, 4 Caxton Place Caxton Way, STEVENAGE, HERTFORDSHIRE, SG1 2UG.
WOODS, Miss. Michelle Katherine, BSc ACA *2007;* Flat 1, 3 Wilbury Grove, HOVE, EAST SUSSEX, BN3 3JQ.
WOODS, Mr. Nicholas, BSc ACA *1997;* 146 Pepys Road, LONDON, SW20 8NR.
WOODS, Mr. Nicholas John Dillon, BSc ACA *1997;* Earlswood House, 30 Main Road, Hanwell, BANBURY, OXFORDSHIRE, OX17 1HR.
WOODS, Mrs. Nicola Jayne, BSc ACA *2000;* Manhattan, Pensarn, CARMARTHEN, DYFED, SA31 2JY.
WOODS, Mrs. Penny Jane, ACA *2005;* Deloitte Touche Tohmatsu, Level 17 11 Waymouth Street, ADELAIDE, SA 5000, AUSTRALIA.
WOODS, Mr. Peter, ACA *2008;* 9 Deanway, WILMSLOW, CHESHIRE, SK9 2JT.
WOODS, Mrs. Rachel Mary, MA ACA *1997;* with KPMG LLP, 15 Canada Square, LONDON, E14 5GL.
•WOODS, Mr. Richard Lester, BSc FCA *1978;* (Tax Fac), Richard Woods & Co, Southwold House, Boston Road, Swineshead, BOSTON, PE20 3HB.
WOODS, Mr. Robin Charles, BA ACA *2008;* Old Rectory Frilsham, Hermitage, THATCHAM, RG18 9XH.
WOODS, Mr. Rodney Alan, BA ACA *1990;* 3A Mulberry Avenue, Chatterpur, NEW DELHI 110030, INDIA.
WOODS, Mr. Roger Lewis, BEng ACA *1993;* Go Outdoors Ltd, Hill Street, Bramall Lane, SHEFFIELD, S2 4SZ.
WOODS, Mr. Simon Alasdair, BSc ACA *1996;* 3 Dairy Meadow, Garford, ABINGDON, OX13 5PH.
WOODS, Mr. Simon Richard Jonathan, MA ACA *2000;* 11 Erpingham Road, LONDON, SW15 1BE.
WOODS, Mr. Spencer John, BA(Hons) ACA *2010;* Top of Th Knotts Farm, Tottington Road, BOLTON, BL2 4LL.
WOODS, Mrs. Stephanie, ACA *2007;* 19 Heron Close, GUILDFORD, GU2 9PH.
WOODS, Mr. Stephen, LLB ACA *2010;* Apartment 265, Block 5 Spectrum, Blackfriars Road, SALFORD, M3 7BT.
WOODS, Mr. Stephen Matthew, BA FCA *1997;* Howmet Ltd Kestrel Way, Sowton Industrial Estate, EXETER, EX2 7LG.
WOODS, Mr. Thomas James, ACA *2009;* 12 Heathfield Mews, Martlesham Heath, IPSWICH, IP5 3UF.
WOODS, Mr. Timothy Stuart, BA ACA *2003;* A E S Engineering Ltd, Mill Close, ROTHERHAM, SOUTH YORKSHIRE, S60 1BZ.
WOODS, Mrs. Valerie Sheila, MA FCA *1988;* 75 Five Mile Drive, OXFORD, OX2 8HW.
WOODS, Miss. Victoria Jane Mulliner, BA ACA *1996;* Rowland Farmhouse Rowland Farm Hensil Lane Hawkhurst, CRANBROOK, KENT, TN18 4QH.
WOODS, Mr. Warren, BA ACA *2002;* 2 Copthall Gardens, TWICKENHAM, TW1 4HJ.
WOODS BALLARD, Mr. Hugh William, MA ACA *1996;* Kyuquot House, Lower Haugh Lane, WOODBRIDGE, SUFFOLK, IP12 4NJ.
WOODS BALLARD, Mrs. Judith Jane, MA ACA *2002;* with Pricewaterhousecoopers, 12 Plumtree Court, LONDON, EC4A 4HT.
WOODS-SCAWEN, Dr. Brian Dennis, CBE DL LLD MA FCA FRSA *1974;* The Stables, Hunt Paddocks, Rouncil Lane, KENILWORTH, WARWICKSHIRE, CV8 1NL.
WOODS-SCAWEN, Mrs. Jane, BCom FCA *1974;* The Stables, Hunt Paddocks, Rouncil Lane, KENILWORTH, CV8 1NL.
WOODSFORD, Mr. Noel Clive, BSc FCA *1978;* 30 Wellington Street West, P.O. Box 400, Stn Commerce Court, TORONTO M5L 1B1, ON, CANADA.
WOODSIDE, Mr. Brian, BSc ACA *1988;* PO Box 66546, 1st Floor Crescent Tower, Al Buheirah Corniche, SHARJAH, UNITED ARAB EMIRATES.
WOODSIDE, Miss. Janine Claire Alexandra, BSc ACA *2001;* 74 Richardson Street, Edge Hill, CAIRNS, QLD 4870, AUSTRALIA.
•ⒹWOODSIDE, Mr. Jeremy, LLB ACA *2000;* with RSM Tenon Limited, Arkwright House, Parsonage Gardens, MANCHESTER, M3 2LF.
WOODSTOCK, Ms. Varsha, BA ACA *2000;* Flat 18 Hanger Court, Hanger Green, Ealing, LONDON, W5 3ER.
WOODTHORPE, Mr. Anthony Edmund, FCA *1964;* Rossmere House, Lower Laines, The Furlongs, Alfriston, POLEGATE, BN26 5XS. (Life Member)
WOODTHORPE, Miss. Catherine Joan, BSc FCA *1996;* (Tax Fac), 15 Rooks View, Bobbing, SITTINGBOURNE, KENT, ME9 8GB.
WOODTHORPE, Mr. Christopher Philip, BSc ACA *2011;* 22 Millard Way, HITCHIN, SG4 0QE.
WOODTHORPE, Mr. Ian Craig, ACA CA(SA) *2008;* Gap Placements Unit 5, 1p Brewhouse Street, LONDON, SW15 2JX.
WOODTHORPE, Mrs. Jayne Stephanie, BA ACA *1987;* 8 Moorlands Road, Mount Outlane, HUDDERSFIELD, HD3 3UH.
WOODTHORPE, Mr. John Desmond, BA FCA *1951;* Atherfield, Park View Road, Woldingham, CATERHAM, CR3 7DJ. (Life Member)
•WOODTHORPE, Mr. Kevin Norton, FCA CTA *1970;* Rawlinsons, Ruthlyn House, 90 Lincoln Road, PETERBOROUGH, PE1 2SP.
WOODTHORPE, Mr. Peter Crispin, FCA *1975;* 52c Maresfield Gardens, Hampstead, LONDON, NW3 5RX.
WOODTHORPE, Miss. Sarah Katherine, MA ACA *2004;* 41a St. James Road, SURBITON, KT6 4QN.
WOODWARD, Mr. Alexander James, BA ACA *1990;* General Josep Moragues 27 Baixos D, Gava, 08850 BARCELONA, SPAIN.
WOODWARD, Miss. Amy, ACA *2011;* 72 Wymersley Road, HULL, HU5 5LL.
WOODWARD, Mrs. Angela Margaret, BA(Hons) ACA *2004;* Green Tree Farm, Green lane, Rudyard, LEEK, STAFFORDSHIRE, ST13 8PN.
WOODWARD, Mr. Arthur, BA(Hons) ACA *2011;* 19 Hazel Grove, WINCHESTER, HAMPSHIRE, SO22 4PQ.
WOODWARD, Mr. Benjamin Peter, BSc ACA *1997;* The Croft, Station Road, Bledington, CHIPPING NORTON, OXFORDSHIRE, OX7 6UR.
WOODWARD, Mrs. Caroline Melanie, ACA *1979;* Minnesota, Ashford Hill Road, Headley, THATCHAM, RG19 8AB.
WOODWARD, Mr. Christopher James, BA ACA *2003;* with Ernst & Young LLP, 100 Barbirolli Square, MANCHESTER, M2 3EY.
WOODWARD, Mr. Christopher Peter, BSc FCA *1978;* WGD LLP, 900 Elveden House, 717-7 Seventh Avenue SW, CALGARY T2P 0Z3, AB, CANADA.
WOODWARD, Mrs. Claire Marianne, BSc ACA *2000;* 1 Grasscroft, HUDDERSFIELD, HD5 8XG.
WOODWARD, Miss. Clare, ACA *2010;* 19 Lockhart Street, LONDON, E3 4BL.
WOODWARD, Mr. David Alan, BSc ACA *1990;* Fairline Boats Head Office, Nene Valley Business Park, Oundle, PETERBOROUGH, PE8 4HN.
WOODWARD, Mr. David John, FCA *1965;* Tunley Farm, Tunley, Sapperton, CIRENCESTER, GL7 6LW. (Life Member)
WOODWARD, Mr. David Roger, FCA *1983;* Landors, Venn Lane, Wichenford, WORCESTER, WR6 6XY.
•WOODWARD, Mr. Edmund Harold, BSc ACA *1989;* E.H. Woodward, Hall Farm, Risley, DERBY, DE72 3TT.
WOODWARD, Miss. Felicity, BA ACA *2004;* Flat 16 Newlyn, 69 Oatlands Avenue, WEYBRIDGE, KT13 9TL.

•**WOODWARD, Mr. Gareth John, BSc FCA** *1979;* Begbies Traynor, 340 Deansgate, MANCHESTER, M3 4LY. See also Begbies Traynor Limited
WOODWARD, Mr. George Leo, LLB ACA *2003;* Pumpkin Patch, 439 East Tamaki Road, East Tamaki, AUCKLAND, NEW ZEALAND.
WOODWARD, Mrs. Gina, BSc ACA *2002;* 77 Peel Road, LONDON, E18 2LJ.
WOODWARD, Mr. Grahame Keith Paul, BCom ACA *1989;* Henderson House, 133 Sandford Road, BIRMINGHAM, B13 9DA.
WOODWARD, Mr. Gwynne James, BA(Econ) FCA *1969;* 10255 Cape Roman Road, BONITA SPRINGS, FL 34135, UNITED STATES. (Life Member)
WOODWARD, Miss. Jessica, ACA *2009;* Prime Plc 5 The Triangle, Wildwood Drive, WORCESTER, WR5 2QX.
WOODWARD, Mrs. Joanne Mary, BA ACA *1999;* 29 Eager Way, Exminster, EXETER, EX6 8TJ.
WOODWARD, Mr. John Frederick, FCA *1971;* Harbour View, Windsor Hill, Glounthaune, CORK, COUNTY CORK, IRELAND.
WOODWARD, Mr. John Scott, BSc ACA *1990;* George Batemans & Son Ltd Salem Bridge Brewery, Mill Lane Wainfleet, SKEGNESS, LINCOLNSHIRE, PE24 4JE.
WOODWARD, Mr. John Vincent, FCA *1970;* (Tax Fac), Fairfield, Old Hall Avenue, Littleover, DERBY, DE23 6EN.
WOODWARD, Miss. Julie Louise, BA ACA *1998;* Talbot Validus Group, 60 Threadneedle Street, LONDON, EC2R 8HP.
WOODWARD, Mrs. Laura, ACA *2001;* 17 Elswick Gardens, Mellor, BLACKBURN, BB2 7JD.
WOODWARD, Miss. Laura Hamilton, ACA *2008;* 28 St. Peters Wharf, NEWCASTLE UPON TYNE, NE6 1TW.
WOODWARD, Miss. Lee, ACA *2010;* 1 Ashcombe Drive, EDENBRIDGE, TN8 6JY.
WOODWARD, Mr. Lee Gareth, BSc ACA *1997;* 22 Chapel View, Loveclough, ROSSENDALE, LANCASHIRE, BB4 8FN.
WOODWARD, Mrs. Lynn, BSc ACA *1995;* 3 Townshend Road, RICHMOND, TW9 1XH.
WOODWARD, Mr. Mark, MA ACA *2002;* Ashleigh, Eaton Road, ST. ALBANS, HERTFORDSHIRE, AL1 4UE.
WOODWARD, Mr. Mark Simon, BSc(Hons) ACA *2002;* 77 Peel Road, LONDON, E18 2LJ.
WOODWARD, Mrs. Mary Teresa, BSc ACA *1994;* Hagg Foot Farm, Burneside, KENDAL, CUMBRIA, LA8 9AB.
•**WOODWARD, Mr. Michael Raymond, BA FCA** *1990;* KPMG LLP, 15 Canada Square, LONDON, E14 5GL. See also KPMG Europe LLP
WOODWARD, Mrs. Michelle, ACA *1997;* Holly Lodge, Burnside, Witton Gilbert, DURHAM, DH7 6SE.
•**WOODWARD, Mr. Paul Leslie, BSc FCA** *1993;* H.L. Barnes & Sons, Barclays Bank Chambers, Bridge Street, STRATFORD-UPON-AVON, WARWICKSHIRE, CV37 6AH.
WOODWARD, Mr. Paul Michael, BSc ACA *1999;* 5 Connemara Crescent Whiteley, FAREHAM, HAMPSHIRE, PO15 7BN.
WOODWARD, Mr. Paul Scott, FCA *1973;* Fairfield, Limes Lane, Buxted, UCKFIELD, EAST SUSSEX, TN22 4PB.
WOODWARD, Mr. Peter Graham, FCA *1966;* Burlam, Brenchley Road, Matfield, TONBRIDGE, KENT, TN12 7PP.
WOODWARD, Mr. Peter Tristram Ridgeway, MEng ACA *1990;* (Tax Fac), Fishmongers Co Fishmongers Hall, London Bridge, LONDON, EC4R 9EL.
WOODWARD, Mrs. Rebecca Jane, BSc(Hons) ARCS ACA AMCT *2002;* 3rd Floor Collinsons Building, Halifax Plc, Trinity Road, HALIFAX, WEST YORKSHIRE, HX1 2RG.
WOODWARD, Mr. Richard Brian, BA ACA *2003;* 40 Pennythorne Drive Yeadon, LEEDS, LS19 7DS.
WOODWARD, Mr. Richard Guthrie, FCA *1969;* 24 Piccadilly Way, Prestbury, CHELTENHAM, GLOUCESTERSHIRE, GL52 5DQ.
WOODWARD, Mr. Robert Stephen, FCA *1972;* 229 Varsity Estates, Mews N.W., CALGARY T3B 3C9, AB, CANADA.
WOODWARD, Mrs. Rosemary Anne, BA ACA *1991;* 8 Persian Drive, Whitley, FAREHAM, PO15 7BJ.
WOODWARD, Ms. Sarah Louise, BSc ACA *1992;* 16 The Crescent, MAIDENHEAD, BERKSHIRE, SL6 6AB.
WOODWARD, Mr. Stephen Andrew, BA ACA *1991;* (Tax Fac), Quality Assurance Agency for Higher Education, Southgate House Southgate Street, GLOUCESTER, GL1 1UB.
WOODWARD, Mr. Stephen David, MEng FCA *1992;* with KPMG, Crown House, 4 Par-la-Ville Road, HAMILTON HM 08, BERMUDA.
•**WOODWARD, Mr. Stuart Neil, MA FCA** *1982;* Deloitte LLP, 3 Rivergate, Temple Quay, BRISTOL, BS1 6GD. See also Deloitte & Touche LLP
WOODWARD, Mrs. Susan Anne, BSc FCA *1977;* WGD LLP, 900 Elveden House, 717-7 Seventh Avenue SW, CALGARY T2P 0Z3, AB, CANADA.
WOODWARD, Mrs. Susan Claire, BA ACA *1984;* Bindon House, 118 St Cross Road, WINCHESTER, SO23 9RE.
WOODWARD, Mr. Tim James, BA ACA *1990;* Flat 2a Block13, Wonderland Villas, 9 Wah King Hill Road, KWAI CHUNG, NEW TERRITORIES, HONG KONG SAR.
•**WOODWARD, Mr. Tim James, BA FCA** *2002;* Moore Stephens LLP, 150 Aldersgate Street, LONDON, EC1A 4AB.
WOODWARD, Miss. Vanessa Jayne, BSc ACA *1999;* (Tax Fac), 24 Dunton Close, SUTTON COLDFIELD, WEST MIDLANDS, B75 5QD.
WOODWARD, Mr. William Alan, BSc ACA *1990;* Classic Lodges Ltd, Conway House, Ackhurst Business Park, Foxhole Road, CHORLEY, LANCASHIRE PR7 1NY.
WOODWARD, Mr. Xavier James, BA ACA *1998;* 52-54 Main Street, Menston, ILKLEY, WEST YORKSHIRE, LS29 6LF.
WOODWARD, Mrs. Yvonne Yee Fun, BSc ACA *1979;* 18 Ringmer Avenue, Fulham, LONDON, SW6 5LW. (Life Member)
WOODWARD-SMITH, Miss. Philippa, ACA *2008;* 58 Pettinger Gardens, SOUTHAMPTON, SO17 2WL.
WOODWARDS, Mr. Daniel Richard, BSc ACA *2002;* 40 Hall Lane, Horsforth, LEEDS, LS18 5JF.
WOODWARDS, Mr. Robert, BA ACA *2009;* Flat 6 Coachmans Terrace, 80-86 Clapham Road, LONDON, SW9 0JR.
WOODWARDS, Ms. Tracey Jane, BEd ACA *1993;* Tresgyrch Farm, Rhyd-Y-Fro, Pontardawe, SWANSEA, SA8 4RU.
WOODWARK, Mr. William James, BSc ACA *1980;* Level 12, 280 Bishopsgate, LONDON, EC2M 4RB.
WOODWORTH, Mr. John Kevin, BA ACA *1983;* 1 Gorse Corner, Townsend Drive, ST. ALBANS, AL3 5SH.
WOODWORTH, Mr. Michael Robert, BSc ACA *1997;* 30 Clayton Way Clayton le Moors, ACCRINGTON, LANCASHIRE, BB5 5WT.
WOODYATT, Miss. Amber, ACA *2010;* 26 Halyard Drive, BRIDGWATER, SOMERSET, TA6 3SG.
WOODYER, Mr. Neil, FCA *1969;* Monte Carlo Palace, Bureau 76, 7 Boulevard des Moulins, 98000 MONACO, MONACO.
•①**WOODYET, Mr. Graham Edward, FCA** *1971;* 47 Miller Drive, FAREHAM, HAMPSHIRE, PO16 7LY.
•**WOOF, Mr. Michael, FCA** *1972;* MWForensics, Beech Cottage, Slad, STROUD, GLOUCESTERSHIRE, GL6 7QA.
WOOFF, Ms. Deborah, BSc ACA *1999;* 27 Bradley Gardens, Ealing, LONDON, W13 8HE.
WOOFFINDEN, Mr. Mark Andrew, BA ACA *2005;* Apartment 39, 1 Jordan Street, MANCHESTER, M15 4QU.
WOOFFINDIN, Mrs. Andrea, BSc(Hons) ACA *2000;* 19 Newton Drive, WAKEFIELD, WF1 3HZ.
WOOKEY, Mr. Charles Michael Harry, BA ACA *1983;* Catholic Bishops Conference of England & Wales, 39 Eccleston Square, LONDON, SW1V 1BX.
WOOKEY, Mr. David Henry, BA FCA *1986;* 26 Rokeby Avenue, Redland, BRISTOL, BS6 6EL.
WOOKEY, Mr. James Joseph, ACA *2009;* 1 Hillcrest, SOUTHWELL, NOTTINGHAMSHIRE, NG25 0AQ.
WOOKEY, Mr. Nicolas Mark, BA(Hons) ACA *2002;* PP01 Phase 1, Department for Work & Pensions Peel Park Control Centre, Brunel Way Blackpool & Fylde Industrial Estate, BLACKPOOL, FY4 5ES.
WOOLARD, Mr. Andrew Charles, BSc ACA *1986;* 24 Hayward Close, Walkington, BEVERLEY, HU17 8YB.
WOOLAWAY, Mr. Reginald Thomas, FCA *1953;* 5 Chamberlain Road, Hanbury Park, WORCESTER, WR2 4PP. (Life Member)
WOOLCOCK, Miss. Joanna Elizabeth, ACA *2008;* First Floor Flat, 30 Greenside Road, LONDON, W12 9JG.
WOOLCOCK, Mr. Matthew Paul, ACA *2009;* 5 Old Park Road, PLYMOUTH, PL3 4PY.
WOOLCOCK, Mr. Richard Alan, ACA MAAT *2005;* P.O. Box 1085, 5th Floor Queensgate House, 113 South Church Street, GEORGETOWN, KY1-1102, CAYMAN ISLANDS.
•**WOOLCOTT, Miss. Catherine Jane, BSc ACA** *1999;* PricewaterhouseCoopers LLP, Hays Galleria, 1 Hays Lane, LONDON, SE1 2RD. See also PricewaterhouseCoopers
WOOLCOTT, Mr. Justin Ralph, BSc ACA *1986;* 135 Stoothoff Road, East Northport, NEW YORK, NY 11731, UNITED STATES.
WOOLDRIDGE, Mr. James Christopher Marchant, MSci ACA *2006;* F W Smith Riches & Co, 18 Pall Mall, LONDON, SW1Y 5LU.
WOOLDRIDGE, Ms. Rebecca Louise, BA ACA *2010;* Barley Barn, Chesterton Farm Barns, Chesterton, BRIDGNORTH, SHROPSHIRE, WV15 5NX.
WOOLDRIDGE, Mrs. Rhian Lynn, BSc ACA *1990;* 38 Parkside, LONDON, SW19 5NB.
WOOLDRIDGE, Mr. Robert Ian, BA ACA *1990;* 38 Parkside, LONDON, SW19 5NB.
WOOLDRIDGE, Mr. Robin, BA ACA *1993;* 27 Upper Grotto Road, TWICKENHAM, TW1 4NG.
•**WOOLDRIDGE, Mr. Stuart John, BSc ACA** *1993;* PricewaterhouseCoopers LLP, Hays Galleria, 1 Hays Lane, LONDON, SE1 2RD. See also PricewaterhouseCoopers
WOOLDRIDGE, Mr. Thomas Michael Scott, BA(Hons) ACA *2001;* 12 Ivy Road, Gosforth, NEWCASTLE UPON TYNE, NE3 1DB.
WOOLER, Mr. Andrew Robert, ACA *2008;* Flat 309, The Magdalen, 278 Magdalen Road, Earlsfield, LONDON, SW18 3NY.
WOOLES, Mr. Jonathan Christian, BSc ACA *1989;* 1 The Close, DUNMOW, CM6 1EW.
WOOLF, Mr. Andrew, ACA *2008;* 3 Chapel Lane, Hale Barns, ALTRINCHAM, CHESHIRE, WA15 0HJ.
WOOLF, Mr. Antony Barrie, MA FCA *1973;* with Tony Woolf Associates, 3 Chapel Lane, Hale Barns, ALTRINCHAM, CHESHIRE, WA15 0HJ.
WOOLF, Mr. Arnold Robert, FCA *1954;* 3 Taverners Lodge, 20 Cockfosters Road, BARNET, HERTFORDSHIRE, EN4 0DU. (Life Member)
WOOLF, Miss. Caroline, BSc ACA *2011;* Flat 5, Colinsdale, Camden Walk, Islington, LONDON, N1 8DZ.
•**WOOLF, Mr. David, FCA** *1969;* Hyde Hill House, Hyde Hill Lane, Beaulieu, BROCKENHURST, HAMPSHIRE, SO42 7YN.
•**WOOLF, Mr. Derrick Stephen, FCA FCCA FSPI** *1971;* with RSM Tenon, 66 Chiltern Street, LONDON, W1U 4JT.
WOOLF, Mr. Emile Harold, FCA *1962;* Greenacres, 19 Greenacre Walk, Southgate, LONDON, N14 7DB.
WOOLF, Mr. Gordon, FCA *1954;* 5 Hartfield Close, Elstree, BOREHAMWOOD, WD6 3JD. (Life Member)
•**WOOLF, Mr. Howard Michael, BSc FCA** *1996;* with DTE Business Advisory Services Limited, Park House, 26 North End Road, LONDON, NW11 7PT.
WOOLF, Mr. Ian Bernard, FCA *1973;* 15 Chadwick Road, WESTCLIFF-ON-SEA, SS0 8LS.
WOOLF, Mr. James Lewis, BSc ACA *1990;* Flow East, Vaclavske Namesti 11, 110 00 PRAGUE, CZECH REPUBLIC.
•**WOOLF, Mr. James Peter Lewis, BA FCA** *1992;* KPMG LLP, 15 Canada Square, LONDON, E14 5GL. See also KPMG Europe LLP
•**WOOLF, Mr. Keith Harris, BA FCA CTA** *1982;* (Tax Fac), Adler Shine LLP, Aston House, Cornwall Avenue, LONDON, N3 1LF.
WOOLF, Miss. Kerry, BA ACA *2004;* 11 Oakmead Road, LONDON, SW12 9SN.
WOOLF, Mr. Leonard, FCA *1951;* 1036 South Holt Avenue, Apt 4, LOS ANGELES, CA 90035, UNITED STATES. (Life Member)
WOOLF, Mrs. Linda Mary, BA MBA ACA *1986;* P G L Group Ltd, Alton Court, Penyard Lane, ROSS-ON-WYE, HEREFORDSHIRE, HR9 5GL.
•**WOOLF, Mr. Nicholas, BSc FCA CTA** *1971;* Wyngates, Portsmouth Road, ESHER, SURREY, KT10 9JA.
WOOLF, Mr. Peter John, FCA *1958;* PO Box 7283, Hutt Street, ADELAIDE, SA 5000, AUSTRALIA. (Life Member)
WOOLF, Mr. Rafe, BSc ACA *1987;* Le Petit Chene, Le Mont de la Rosiere, St. Saviour, JERSEY, JE2 7HF.
WOOLF, Mr. Robert Anthony, BA FCA *1976;* 2 Berkeley Road, Barnes, LONDON, SW13 9LZ.
•**WOOLF, Mr. Roger Brian, FCA** *1970;* Felton Associates, 112 Wembley Park Drive, WEMBLEY, MIDDLESEX, HA9 8HS. See also Felton Associates Limited
WOOLFE, Mr. Geoffrey, FCA *1947;* Cambashaw Cottage, 130C Simister Lane, Middleton, MANCHESTER, M24 4SJ. (Life Member)
WOOLFE, Mr. Nicholas Edward, ACA *2009;* Flat 4, 24a Uplands Park Road, ENFIELD, MIDDLESEX, EN2 7PT.
WOOLFE, Mr. Stephen Johnathon, BSc ACA *1980;* Conductix Wampfler Ltd, 1 Michigan Avenue, SALFORD, M50 2GY.
WOOLFENDEN, Mr. Edward, FCA *1952;* 7 Selham Close, CHICHESTER, PO19 5BZ. (Life Member)
WOOLFENDEN, Mr. John Granville, BA FCA *1972;* The Anchorage, Coombelands Lane, PULBOROUGH, WEST SUSSEX, RH20 1AG.
WOOLFMAN, Mr. Graham Jeffrey, BSc FCA CF *1983;* Sawford Benedict Plc, 33 Wigmore Street, LONDON, W1U 2HA.
•**WOOLFORD, Mr. Michael John, FCA** *1983;* The Lawford Company, Lawford House, Leacroft, STAINES, TW18 4NN.
•**WOOLFORD, Mr. Robert Percy, FCA** *1967;* Dixcart House, PO Box 161, Sir William Place, St Peter Port, GUERNSEY, GY1 4EZ.
•**WOOLFSON, Mr. Leslie Ian, FCA** *1968;* (Tax Fac), 25 School Lane Limited, Profex House, 25 School Lane, BUSHEY, HERTFORDSHIRE, WD23 1SS.
•**WOOLFSON, Mr. Philip Alan, BA FCA** *1980;* (Tax Fac), Tuchbands, 925 Finchley Road, LONDON, NW11 7PE. See also Tuchbands Accounting Services Ltd
•**WOOLFSON, Mr. Robert Melvyn, FCA** *1972;* The Lawrence Woolfson Partnership, 1 Bentinck Street, LONDON, W1U 2ED.
•**WOOLFSON, Miss. Suzanne Lindsay, BSc FCA** *1990;* PricewaterhouseCoopers, West London Office, The Atrium, 1 Harefield Road, UXBRIDGE, UB8 1EX. See also PricewaterhouseCoopers LLP
WOOLFSON, Mr. Tony Ivor, FCA *1960;* 4 Westford Villas, 11 Milton Crescent, CHEADLE, SK8 1NT. (Life Member)
WOOLGAR, Mr. Adam Mark, ACA *2008;* 55 Morley Street, SHEFFIELD, S6 2PL.
WOOLGAR, Mr. Howard Thomas, BA ACA *1988;* Bonshaw Mains, Kirtlebridge, LOCKERBIE, DUMFRIESSHIRE, DG11 3NB.
WOOLGAR, Mr. Owen Thomas, ACA *2008;* 102 La Providence, La Vallee de St. Pierre St. Lawrence, JERSEY, JE3 1PR.
WOOLGAR, Mr. Robert James, FCA *1974;* 6 Neath Street, SURREY HILLS, VIC 3127, AUSTRALIA.
•**WOOLHEAD, Mr. Alan Edward, FCA** *1977;* Ryecroft Glenton, 32 Portland Terrace, Jesmond, NEWCASTLE UPON TYNE, NE2 1QP.
WOOLHOUSE, Mrs. Anne, BSc ACA *1988;* 47 Scotgate Road, Honley, HOLMFIRTH, HD9 6RE.
WOOLHOUSE, Mr. James Robert, BA ACA *1991;* 41 Dalebury Road, LONDON, SW17 7HQ.
WOOLHOUSE, Ms. Sally, BA ACA *2000;* 242 Ryebank Road, Chorlton cum Hardy, MANCHESTER, M21 9LU.
WOOLHOUSE, Mr. Stephen, BA(Hons) ACA *2004;* 21 Honeypots Road, WOKING, GU22 9QW.
WOOLHOUSE, Mr. Terence Harry Lawrence, FCA *1961;* 52 Mymms Drive, Brookmans Park, HATFIELD, AL9 7AF. (Life Member)
WOOLLACOTT, Mr. John Mark, BSc ACA *2000;* C/O DP World, PO Box 17000, DUBAI, UNITED ARAB EMIRATES.
WOOLLACOTT, Mrs. Lucy Joanna, BSc ACA *2003;* C/o John Woollacott, DP World, 5th Floor JAFZA 17, Jebel Ali Freezone, DUBAI, 17000 UNITED ARAB EMIRATES.
WOOLLACOTT, Mr. Michael Richard, BSc(Hons) ACA *2002;* with Deloitte LLP, Stonecutter Court, 1 Stonecutter Street, LONDON, EC4A 4TR.
WOOLLAND, Mr. John Layton, BA ACA *1980;* UBS Limited, 1 Finsbury Avenue, LONDON, EC2M 2PA.
WOOLLARD, Mr. David Alan, FCA *1978;* 15 Uplands Way, LONDON, N21 1DH.
WOOLLARD, Mr. David Beresford, ACA *1987;* Arcall Plc, 1 Westminster Road, WAREHAM, DORSET, BH20 4SR.
•**WOOLLARD, Mr. Ian Martyn, ACA** *2006;* Pearson Buchholz Limited, North House, Farmoor Court, Cumnor Road, Farmoor, OXFORD OX2 9LU.
WOOLLARD, Mr. Matthew, ACA *2010;* Flat 4, 86 Holland Road, LONDON, W14 8BN.
WOOLLARD, Mrs. Patricia Clare, MA ACA *1994;* 9 Fordham Avenue, STRATFORD-UPON-AVON, WARWICKSHIRE, CV37 6XD.
WOOLLARD, Mr. Paul James, MBA BCom CA ACA AOQ *1981;* University of Queensland, Bel Faculty, BRISBANE, QLD 4072, AUSTRALIA.
WOOLLARD, Mrs. Rachel, BCom ACA *2002;* 9 Chaffinch Drive, CLEETHORPES, SOUTH HUMBERSIDE, DN35 0ST.
•**WOOLLARD, Mrs. Rosalind Ann, BTech FCA** *1980;* (Tax Fac), R.A. Woollard, 19 Annetyard Drive, SKELMORLIE, PA17 5BN.
WOOLLARD, Mr. Scott Martin, BA ACA *2006;* 37 Tudor Manor Gardens, WATFORD, WD25 9TQ.

•**WOOLLATT, Mrs. Clare, ACA** *2000;* Clare Woollatt, 8 Almeys Lane, Earl Shilton, LEICESTER, LE9 7AJ.
WOOLLATT, Mr. Matthew James, BSc ACA *1998;* 9 Miles Close, Ham Green, BRISTOL, BS20 0LH.
WOOLLER, Mr. Joseph Arnold, BA ACA *1986;* Shell International Petroleum Co Ltd, Shell Centre, York Road, LONDON, SE1 7NA.
WOOLLETT, Mr. Peter Leonard, BA ACA *1985;* 10 Chestnut Drive, Shenstone, LICHFIELD, WS14 0JH.
WOOLLEY, Mr. Alastair John Lomond, BA FCA *1990;* 21 Alexander Chase, ELY, CAMBRIDGESHIRE, CB6 3SN.
WOOLLEY, Mr. Andrew Moger, BA ACA *1989;* Travelex Ltd, 65 Kingsway, LONDON, WC2B 6TD.
WOOLLEY, Mr. Anthony, BSc ACA *2006;* 35 Burnell Gate, CHELMSFORD, CM1 6ED.
•**WOOLLEY, Miss. Caroline Louise, BA ACA CFE** *2000;* 82 Grove End Gardens, Grove End Road, St Johns Wood, LONDON, NW8 9LP.
WOOLLEY, Mr. Christopher James Russell, BSc(Econ) ACA *2004;* 8 Inholmes Cottages, Whitemans Green Cuckfield, HAYWARDS HEATH, WEST SUSSEX, RH17 5DB.
•**WOOLLEY, Mr. Christopher John, FCA** *1983;* 12 Marriott Lodge Close, ADDLESTONE, SURREY, KT15 2XD.
WOOLLEY, Mr. Eric Rhys, BA FCA *1983;* 29 Palace Street, LONDON, SW1E 5HW.
WOOLLEY, Mr. Geoffrey LLoyd, BSc ACA *1995;* 26 Skomer Island Way, CAERPHILLY, MID GLAMORGAN, CF83 2AR.
WOOLLEY, Mr. Giles William, FCA *1980;* Domus, 20 Upper Carlisle Road, EASTBOURNE, BN20 7TN.
WOOLLEY, Miss. Jacqueline, ACA *1994;* STANDARD CHARTERED BANK, DUBAI, PO BOX 999, UNITED ARAB EMIRATES.
WOOLLEY, Mr. James Christopher Michael, BA ACA *2004;* with Endless LLP, 3 Whitehall Quay, LEEDS, LS1 4BF.
WOOLLEY, Mr. James Geoffrey, FCA *1965;* 12 Redesmere Drive, ALDERLEY EDGE, SK9 7UR.
WOOLLEY, Mr. Jonathan Frank, BA FCA *1977;* 12 Castle Road, WEYBRIDGE, KT13 9QN.
WOOLLEY, Miss. Kim, BA ACA *2011;* Flat A, 7 Melbourne Avenue, LONDON, N13 4SY.
WOOLLEY, Mr. Mark Christopher, BA ACA *2010;* 47 Lindfield Gardens, GUILDFORD, GU1 1TS.
WOOLLEY, Mr. Mark Stefan, MA ACA *1995;* Ecosse Films Ltd, Brigade House, 8 Parsons Green, LONDON, SW6 4TN.
WOOLLEY, Mr. Matthew, BA ACA *2005;* Deloitte Forensic, Grosvenor Place, 225 George Street, SYDNEY, NSW 2000, AUSTRALIA.
WOOLLEY, Mr. Matthew John, BA ACA *1999;* Level 34, Bankwest Tower, 106 St Georges Terrace, PERTH, WA 6000, AUSTRALIA.
WOOLLEY, Mr. Michael John Desmond, BA FCA *1967;* 34 Thame Road, Warborough, WALLINGFORD, OXFORDSHIRE, OX10 7DA.
WOOLLEY, Mr. Nigel Mark, BA ACA *1989;* 44 Anne William Drive, West Pennant Hills, SYDNEY, NSW 2125, AUSTRALIA.
WOOLLEY, Mr. Peter Frederick, FCA *1970;* 78 Cranborne Avenue, WARRINGTON, WA4 6DE.
WOOLLEY, Mr. Peter George, BA FCA *1997;* 4 St. Peters Way, STRATFORD-UPON-AVON, WARWICKSHIRE, CV37 0RU.
WOOLLEY, Mr. Peter John, BSc FCA *1975;* The Library, Thorndon Hall, Ingrave, BRENTWOOD, ESSEX, CM13 3RJ. (Life Member)
WOOLLEY, Mr. Peter Thomas Griffith, BCom ACA *1987;* Derivale, 38 Pen-Y-Pound Road, ABERGAVENNY, NP7 7RN.
WOOLLEY, Mr. Philip John, ACA *1985;* 76 Perrinsfield, LECHLADE, GLOUCESTERSHIRE, GL7 3SD.
WOOLLEY, Mr. Raymond Arthur, BSc FCA *1978;* 19 Bayport Circuit, MINDARIE, WA 6030, AUSTRALIA.
•**WOOLLEY, Mrs. Rebecca, BA ACA** *2004;* Pareto Tax and Wealth LLP, 8 St. John Street, MANCHESTER, M3 4DU.
WOOLLEY, Mr. Richard Downing, FCA *1970;* Windylands Tormarton Road, Old Sodbury, BRISTOL, BS37 6RP.
•**WOOLLEY, Mr. Richard George, MA ACA CTA** *1987;* (Tax Fac), Callow Matthewman & Co., Atholl House, 29-31 Hope Street, Douglas, ISLE OF MAN, IM1 1AR.
WOOLLEY, Mr. Richard Neil, FCA *1970;* 144 Spies Lane, HALESOWEN, B62 9SR.
•**WOOLLEY, Mr. Robert William, BA MCMI FCA MAAT DChA** *1983;* HPH, 54 Bootham, YORK, YO30 7XZ.
WOOLLEY, Mr. Roderic Harry, FCA *1970;* Hill Place House, 55A High Street, Wimbledon, LONDON, SW19 5BA.
•**WOOLLEY, Mr. Roger Laurie, FCA** *1980;* 31 Camelot Way, Narborough, LEICESTER, LE19 3BT.
WOOLLEY, Mr. Russell Roy, BSc FCA *1975;* Gloucester House, 399 Silbury Boulevard, MILTON KEYNES, MK9 2AH.
WOOLLEY, Mr. Stuart James, BA ACA *2003;* 95 Mablins Lane, Coppenhall, CREWE, CW1 3RG.
WOOLLEY, Mr. Timm, BA FCA *1976;* 1708 Black Lake Drive, LADY LAKE, FL 32162, UNITED STATES.
WOOLLEY, Miss. Zowie, BA ACA *2011;* 67 Park Lane, Pinxton, NOTTINGHAM, NG16 6PR.
WOOLLGAR, Mr. Keith Raymond, MA FCA *1976;* Ben Lawers, 33 Lord Street, HODDESDON, EN11 8NA.
WOOLLHEAD, Mrs. Aileen, LLB ACA *1988;* 23 Ruxley Ridge, Claygate, ESHER, KT10 0HZ.
WOOLLISCROFT, Mr. Dermot Francis, BA ACA *1986;* (Tax Fac), Waters Edge, Tithe Barn Drive, Bray, MAIDENHEAD, SL6 2DF.
WOOLLON, Mr. Timothy Terence, BSc ACA *1995;* 42a Ainger Road, LONDON, NW3 3AT.
WOOLMAN, Miss. Gillian Frances, MA FCA *1990;* Audit Scotland, Osborne House, 1-5 Osborne Terrace, EDINBURGH, EH12 5HG.
WOOLMAN, Mr. Roger Ivan, ACA *1994;* Ballygarran Cottage, ANNESTOWN, COUNTY WATERFORD, IRELAND.
•**WOOLMER, Mr. Philip Trevor, FCA** *1981;* Woolmer & Kennedy, 30 Star Hill, ROCHESTER, ME1 1XB.
WOOLMER, Miss. Ruth Elizabeth, BSc ACA CTA *2003;* with Deloitte LLP, PO Box 500, 2 Hardman Street, MANCHESTER, M60 2AT.
WOOLMER, Mr. Stephen, BA ACA *2003;* with BDO LLP, 55 Baker Street, LONDON, W1U 7EU.
•**WOOLMER, Mr. Trevor John, FCA** *1973;* (Tax Fac), Layton Train Limited, 1 Town Quay Wharf, Abbey Road, BARKING, ESSEX, IG11 7BZ.
WOOLMORE, Miss. Georgina May, ACA *2007;* 49 Allnutts Road, EPPING, CM16 7BE.
WOOLNER, Mrs. Katherine Jeannette, BA ACA *1990;* with Sheppard Rockey & Williams Ltd, Sannerville Chase, Exminster, EXETER, EX6 8AT.
WOOLNER, Ms. Tzigane Abigail, BSc(Econ) FCA *1999;* Pasta Foods Ltd, Pasteur Road, GREAT YARMOUTH, NORFOLK, NR31 0DW.
WOOLNOUGH, Mr. John Paul, BA ACA *2004;* 22 Grenville Street, St. Helier, JERSEY, JE2 4UF.
•**WOOLNOUGH, Miss. Susan Jane, BA ACA** *1998;* 72 Brinklow Road, Binley, COVENTRY, CV3 2HY.
WOOLRICH, Mr. Kevin, BA ACA *1987;* 2 Harmer Crescent, Cringleford, NORWICH, NR4 7RX.
WOOLRIDGE, Mr. Robert James, BSc ACA *2003;* 3 Bradley Street, TONBRIDGE, TN9 1HW.
WOOLRYCH, Mr. Toby Richard, BA ACA *1992;* The Old Vicarage Dye House Road, Thursley, GODALMING, GU8 6QD.
WOOLSEY, Mr. Richard John, BEng FCA *1998;* Flat 171 Princess Park Manor, Royal Drive, LONDON, N11 3FR.
WOOLSTON, Mr. David Andrew, BSc(Hons) ACA *2009;* 102 Shepherds Walk, Bradley Stoke, BRISTOL, BS32 9AY.
•**WOOLSTON, Mr. Jonathan David, FCA** *1986;* (Tax Fac), Larking Gowen, King Street House, 15 Upper King Street, NORWICH, NR3 1RB. See also Larking Gowen Limited, Larking Gowen Corporate Finance Limited
WOOLSTON, Miss. Sarah Elizabeth, BA(Hons) ACA *2005;* 7 Bunbury Avenue, Great Barton, BURY ST. EDMUNDS, SUFFOLK, IP31 2SZ.
WOOLSTON, Mrs. Teresa Sybil, BA(Hons) ACA *2002;* 61 Gayville Road, LONDON, SW11 6JW.
WOOLSTON, Mr. William Hall, MA FCA *1963;* PO Box 722, Rua DAs Acacias 859c, Vale Do Lobo, 8135-034 ALMANCIL, ALGARVE, PORTUGAL. (Life Member)
WOOLVEN, Mr. Stephen John, BSc ACA *1987;* 3 The Birches, TONBRIDGE, TN9 2UR.
WOOLVERIDGE, Miss. Catherine Susan, BA ACA *1991;* The Warren, Bois Lane, Chesham Bois, AMERSHAM, HP6 6DF.
WOON, Ms. Siew Choo, ACA *1980;* 16 Jalan BU 11/9, Bandar Utama, 47800 PETALING JAYA, SELANGOR, MALAYSIA.
WOON, Mr. Wai Phang, ACA *1980;* 7 Nassim Road #03-01, SINGAPORE 258374, SINGAPORE. (Life Member)
•**WOOSEY, Mr. Andrew David, MA ACA** *1992;* Ernst & Young LLP, 1 More London Place, LONDON, SE1 2AF. See also Ernst & Young Europe LLP
WOOSNAM, Mr. Nick, BSc ACA *2010;* 11 Childs Hall Road, Bookham, LEATHERHEAD, SURREY, KT23 3QD.
WOOSNAM, Mr. Stephen, BSc ACA *1996;* with Deloitte Touche Tohmatsu, Grosvenor Place, 225 George Street, P.O. Box N 250, SYDNEY, NSW 2000 AUSTRALIA.
WOOTON, Mrs. Natasha Elizabeth, BSc ACA *2005;* 5 Benbow Gardens Calmore, SOUTHAMPTON, SO40 2SX.
•**WOOTTEN, Mr. Dean Robert, FCA CTA** *1988;* (Tax Fac), Highlands, 13 The Ridgeway, Friston, EASTBOURNE, BN20 0EU.
WOOTTEN, Mr. John James, FCA *1976;* 55 Grasmere Road, BEXLEYHEATH, KENT, DA7 6PL.
WOOTTEN, Mrs. Nicola Jane, ACA MAAT *1997;* Unit 2, A P I Europe Ltd Unit 2a-2b Cornbrash Park, Bumpers Way Bumpers Farm, CHIPPENHAM, SN14 6RA.
•**WOOTTEN, Mr. Stephen Richard, MBA BSc FCA** *1981;* PricewaterhouseCoopers LLP, First Point, Buckingham Gate, London Gatwick Airport, GATWICK, WEST SUSSEX RH6 0NT. See also PricewaterhouseCoopers
WOOTTON, Mr. Eric Graham, FCA *1972;* Leybourne Mill, 13 Castle Way, Leybourne, WEST MALLING, ME19 5HF.
WOOTTON, Mr. Geoffrey, FCA *1975;* 22 Walpole Road, TWICKENHAM, TW2 5SN.
WOOTTON, Mr. Geoffrey Phillip, MC FCA *1948;* 2 The Mews Hall Lane, Colston Bassett, NOTTINGHAM, NG12 3FB. (Life Member)
WOOTTON, Mr. Jack, BSc ACA *2011;* 33 Stanley Close, LONDON, SE9 2BA.
WOOTTON, Mr. Jeremy Charles, BA ACA *1991;* 85b Bradford Street, Bocking, BRAINTREE, ESSEX, CM7 9AU.
WOOTTON, Mr. Michael John, FCA *1965;* Pool Cottage, Radmore Lane, Gnosall, STAFFORD, ST20 0EG.
WOOTTON, Mr. Ralph, BA ACA *2010;* 92 Westcombe Hill, LONDON, SE3 7DT.
WOOTTON WOOLLEY, Mr. Robin Michael, MBA FCA *1971;* Denehurst, Pyrford Road, West Byfleet, WEST BYFLEET, KT14 6QY.
WORBEY, Mr. Richard Charles, FCA *1961;* 33 Bell Acre, LETCHWORTH GARDEN CITY, SG6 2BS.
WORBOYS, Mr. Andrew Greville, BA ACA *1990;* 26 Heymede, LEATHERHEAD, KT22 8PG.
WORBOYS, Mr. David Ruff, FCA *1965;* 28 Dunwood Court, Boyn Valley Road, MAIDENHEAD, SL6 4JE.
WORBOYS, Mr. Liam Michael, ACA *2008;* Flat 1098, 19 St George Wharf, LONDON, SW8 2FG.
•**WORBOYS, Mr. Richard David, FCA** *1989;* (Tax Fac), Spencer Fellows & Co, 169 New London Road, CHELMSFORD, CM2 0AE.
WORBOYS, Mr. Simon Anthony, BA ACA *1990;* Oakfield House, The Rickyard, Newton Blossomville, BEDFORD, MK43 8AF.
WORBY, Mrs. Eleanor, MA ACA *2004;* 8 Station Road, DUNMOW, ESSEX, CM6 1EJ.
WORBY, Mr. Graham Frederick, FCA *1964;* PO Box 60640, Paphos Central Post Office, 8106 PAPHOS, CYPRUS.
WORBY, Mr. John Graham, BSc FCA *1975;* Southway, Stoke Park Ave, Farnham Royal, SLOUGH, SL2 3BJ.
WORBY, Mr. Peter John, BSc ACA *1981;* 11 Cherrywood Close, KINGSTON UPON THAMES, KT2 6SF.
WORBY, Mrs. Shelagh Anne, FCA *1977;* Southway, Stoke Park Avenue, Farnham Royal, SLOUGH, SL2 3BJ.
WORDEN, Mrs. Jayne Mary, BSc ACA *1996;* 69 St Leonards Road, LONDON, SW14 7NW.
WORDEN, Miss. Sarita Dolores, BSc ACA *1999;* 16 Treseders Gardens, Moresk, TRURO, CORNWALL, TR1 1TR.
WORDEN, Mrs. Susan Erica Ann, MA FCA *1997;* Riverside Housing Association, 2 Estuary Boulevard, Estuary Commerce Park, Speke, LIVERPOOL, L24 8RF.
WORDIE, Mr. Andrew George Lyon, RD BSc ACA *1988;* The Anchorage, 12 Easthorpe Drive, Nether Poppleton, YORK, YO26 6NS.
•**WORDINGHAM, Mr. Nigel John, BA FCA** *1978;* (Tax Fac), Nigel Wordingham Ltd, 5 Recorder Road, NORWICH, NR1 1NR.
WORDSWORTH, Mr. Andrew Thomas, ACA *2009;* with Ryecroft Glenton, 32 Portland Terrace, Jesmond, NEWCASTLE UPON TYNE, NE2 1QP.
WORDSWORTH, Mrs. Sally Frances, ACA *1985;* NOMS South West Office, H M Prison Channings Wood, Denbury, NEWTON ABBOT, DEVON, TQ12 6DW.
WORGAN, Mr. Ian James, BA ACA *1986;* 6 New Row, Kirby Wiske, THIRSK, NORTH YORKSHIRE, YO7 4EX.
WORGAN, Mr. Martin John, BA ACA *1994;* Waters Edge Cottage, Lower Common, Aylburton, LYDNEY, GLOUCESTERSHIRE, GL15 6DU.
WORGAN, Mrs. Ruth Elizabeth, MSc ACA *2003;* with BDO LLP, Arcadia House, Maritime Walk, Ocean Village, SOUTHAMPTON, SO14 3TL.
WORGER, Mr. Peter David, FCA *1962;* 15 Uplands Crescent, Clayton Heights, BRADFORD, BD13 1EP.
•**WORICKER, Mr. Adam Kenneth, ACA MAAT** *2002;* Fisher Phillips, Summit House, 170 Finchley Road, LONDON, NW3 6BP. See also Fisher Phillips 2010 Ltd
WORIFAH, Mr. Gene Mbanwei, BSc ACA *1991;* Citibank NA South Africa, 145 West Stree, Sandton, JOHANNESBURG, 2196, SOUTH AFRICA.
WORK, Mr. Magnus David, BSc ACA *1994;* 6 Chandos Road, STAINES, TW18 3AT.
WORKER, Mr. Keith Mark, ACA *1983;* 35 Old Post Lane, LITITZ, PA 17543, UNITED STATES.
WORKMAN, Miss. Helen Marie, BSc ACA *2007;* 76 Petteril Street, CARLISLE, CA1 2AJ.
WORKMAN, Mrs. Joanne Lesley, BSc ACA *1998;* 150 Ringwood Road, VERWOOD, DORSET, BH31 7AP.
WORKMAN, Mr. Jonathan Mark, BSc ACA *1996;* Haskins Garden Centre Ltd, Head Office Building, Longham, FERNDOWN, DORSET, BH22 9DJ.
WORKMAN, Mr. Richard John, BSc ACA *1990;* 30a Lambton Road, LONDON, SW20 0LT.
WORKMAN, Mr. William Arthur Fergus, BA FCA *1977;* 39 Independence Drive, Pinchbeck, SPALDING, PE11 3TR.
WORLAND, Mr. Richard Stanley, MA FCA *1973;* 14 Eghams Wood Road, BEACONSFIELD, HP9 1JU.
WORLEY, Mr. Christopher John, BA FCA *1969;* 1606 South Le Homme Dieu Dr., ALEXANDRIA, MN 56308, UNITED STATES. (Life Member)
WORLEY, Mr. Craig, BA ACA *1994;* Dempsey Dyer Ltd, Langthwaite Grange Ind Estate, South Kirkby, PONTEFRACT, WEST YORKSHIRE, WF9 3AP.
WORLEY, Mr. Geoffrey Walter Ernest, FCA *1954;* 39 Tudor Stacks, 1 Dorchester Drive, Herne Hill, LONDON, SE24 0DL. (Life Member)
WORLEY, Mr. Ian Clifford Francis, FCA *1967;* Birch House, 16 Broad Walk, CRANLEIGH, SURREY, GU6 7LS.
WORLEY, Mr. Julian Ralph, BSc FCA *1971;* Apt 5B Scenic Villas, 4 Scenic Villa Drive, Pokfulam, POK FU LAM, HONG KONG ISLAND, HONG KONG SAR. (Life Member)
WORLIDGE, Mr. David John, MA ACA *1982;* Merchant Securities Limited, 51-55 Gresham Street, LONDON, EC2V 7HQ.
WORLLEDGE, Mr. Peter John Franklin, BSc ACA *1994;* Fettes College, 2 Carrington Road, EDINBURGH, EH4 1QX.
WORLLEDGE, Mr. Timothy John, BSc FCA *1980;* 82 Home Park Road, Wimbledon Park, LONDON, SW19 7HR.
WORMALD, Mr. Carl Edmund, BA ACA *1993;* Beech House, 52 Eagle Brow, LYMM, CHESHIRE, WA13 0LZ.
WORMALD, Miss. Claire Louise, BA(Hons) ACA *2001;* Flat 59 Anchor Brewhouse, 50 Shad Thames, LONDON, SE1 2LY.
WORMALD, Mr. David Michael, BA ACA *1993;* Babbage House, The Connection, NEWBURY, RG14 2FN.
WORMALD, Mr. Eric John Charles, FCA *1960;* with Wormald & Partners, Redland House, 157 Redland Road, BRISTOL, BS6 6YE. (Life Member)
WORMALD, Mr. Jonathan Michael, MA ACA *2004;* 3 The Cedars, BOLTON, BL1 7HT.
WORMALD, Mr. Simon James, BA(Hons) ACA *2004;* with Deloitte LLP, 1 City Square, LEEDS, WEST YORKSHIRE, LS1 2AL.
WORMALD, Mr. Stephen, BA ACA *1985;* (Tax Fac), 6 Duncombe Close, MALTON, YO17 7YY.
WORMALD, Miss. Zoe, ACA *2008;* Astra Zeneca Ltd, 2 Kingdom Street, LONDON, W2 6BD.
WORMLEIGHTON, Mr. Ian Colin, BSc ACA *2005;* Bramblings, Horsell Way, WOKING, GU21 4UJ.
•**WORMLEIGHTON, Mr. Michael Bryan, FCA** *1975;* 3 Clifton Drive, Lytham, LYTHAM ST. ANNES, FY8 5QY.
WORMWELL, Mr. Alan, FCA *1972;* Nanny Brow, Old Lane, Hawksworth, Guiseley, LEEDS, LS20 8PD.
WORNE, Mr. Michael John, FCA *1974;* 2 Clifton Road, Clifton, CAPE TOWN, 8005, SOUTH AFRICA.
WORNER, Mr. Richard, MSci ACA *2003;* 10 Virginia Court, Station Parade, VIRGINIA WATER, GU25 4AF.
WORRAKER, Mr. Adam Timothy, MEng ACA *2004;* 51 Priory Road, LONDON, W4 5JA.

WORRALL, Ms. Anastasia T, ACA *2010;* 29 Garrick Avenue, WIRRAL, MERSEYSIDE, CH46 6DY.

•**WORRALL, Mr. Andrew James, ACA FCCA** *2007;* (Tax Fac), Brooks Mayfield, 12 Bridgford Road, West Bridgford, NOTTINGHAM, NG2 6AB. See also Brooks Mayfield Audit Limited

WORRALL, Mr. Brian Andrew, ACA *1986;* The White House, York Road, Skipwith, SELBY, NORTH YORKSHIRE, YO8 5SF.

WORRALL, Mr. Darren, BA ACA *1997;* 23 Old Hall Knowe Terrace, BATHGATE, WEST LOTHIAN, EH48 2TT.

WORRALL, Mr. Donald, FCA *1961;* 1 Kings Close, Grove Park, ILKLEY, LS29 9NT. (Life Member)

WORRALL, Mrs. Elisabeth Ann, BA ACA *1991;* 37 Springwell Avenue, Beighton, SHEFFIELD, S20 1XD.

WORRALL, Mr. Iain Martin, BSc FCA *1994;* 14 Wilcannia Elbow, CURRAMBINE, WA 6028, AUSTRALIA.

WORRALL, Mrs. Jennifer Elizabeth, BSc ACA DChA *2003;* 25 Lowland Road, Denmead, WATERLOOVILLE, HAMPSHIRE, PO7 6YR.

WORRALL, Mr. John, BSc FCA *1978;* PO Box 364, SOUTH FREMANTLE, WA 6162, AUSTRALIA. (Life Member)

WORRALL, Ms. Katharine, BSc(Hons) ACA PGCE *2002;* 5 Jubilee Close, Middletown Hailey, WITNEY, OXFORDSHIRE, OX29 9UL.

WORRALL, Mrs. Katie Frances, BSc ACA *2007;* Saucemeres Farm Mallows Green, Manuden, BISHOP'S STORTFORD, HERTFORDSHIRE, CM23 1BS.

WORRALL, Mrs. Lauren Elizabeth, BSc ACA *2006;* 39 Springbank Gardens, LYMM, CHESHIRE, WA13 9GR.

WORRALL, Mr. Malcolm, FCA *1956;* 15 Whitegate Drive, Astley Bridge, BOLTON, BL1 8SF. (Life Member)

WORRALL, Mrs. Marion Jean, BA ACA *1985;* 4620 Cumbrian Lakes Drive, KISSIMMEE, FL 34746, UNITED STATES.

•**WORRALL, Mr. Michael John, BSc ACA** *1992;* (Tax Fac), The Counting House Partnership LLP, 6 Hanover Road, TUNBRIDGE WELLS, KENT, TN1 1EY.

WORRALL, Mr. Oliver Stanley, BA ACA *2004;* 39 Springbank Gardens, LYMM, CHESHIRE, WA13 9GR.

WORRALL, Mr. Peter Brian, MA ACA *1980;* Owlswood, Tennysons Lane, HASLEMERE, GU27 3AF.

WORRALL, Mr. Richard, ACA *2011;* 3 Tenlands, Middleton Cheney, BANBURY, OXFORDSHIRE, OX17 2NL.

•**WORRALL, Mr. Russell Peter, BA ACA** *1996;* PricewaterhouseCoopers LLP, Cornwall Court, 19 Cornwall Street, BIRMINGHAM, B3 2DT. See also PricewaterhouseCoopers

WORRALL, Mr. Simon Robert Slater, BA ACA *1987;* 40 Cross Keys Drive Whittle-le-Woods, CHORLEY, LANCASHIRE, PR6 7TF.

WORRALL, Mr. Stephen David, MM ACA *2002;* 27 Wellington House, 398-400 Wilmslow Road, MANCHESTER, M20 3LU.

•**WORROW, Mr. David John, BSc FCA** *1977;* Baker Tilly Tax & Advisory Services LLP, The Clock House, 140 London Road, GUILDFORD, SURREY, GU1 1UW. See also Baker Tilly Corporate Finance LLP

•**WORSDALE, Mr. Alan, FCA** *1980;* Rickard Keen LLP, 7 Nelson Street, SOUTHEND-ON-SEA, SS1 1EH. See also MGI Rickard Keen LLP

WORSDELL, Mr. Matthew Woolford, BA ACA *1998;* 28 Godwin Drive Nailsea, BRISTOL, BS48 2XF.

WORSEY, Mrs. Jayne, BSc ACA *1982;* 10 Pritchard Close, Danescourt, Llandaff, CARDIFF, CF5 2QS.

•**WORSEY, Mr. Mark Charles, BA FCA** *1986;* Buzzacott LLP, 130 Wood Street, LONDON, EC2V 6DL.

WORSEY, Mrs. Veronica Myfanwy, BSc ACA *1995;* The White House, Valley Lane, Markyate, ST. ALBANS, AL3 8AS.

•**WORSFOLD, Mr. Graham Robert Gerard, BSc FCA** *1980;* Graham Worsfold, 102 Hawthorn Road, WOKING, GU22 0BD.

WORSFOLD, Miss. Katherine, BA ACA *2003;* 168 Charlton Lane, LONDON, SE7 8AA.

WORSFOLD, Mr. Lee, BA(Hons) ACA *2002;* Derwent Holdings, Celtic House, Victoria Street, Douglas, ISLE OF MAN, IM99 1PL.

WORSFOLD, Mrs. Trudi Mia, BSc ACA *2000;* (Tax Fac), 112 Coriander Drive, Bradley Stoke, BRISTOL, BS32 0DL.

WORSFOLD-MORRIS, Mrs. Claire Elizabeth Louise, BSc FCA ATII *1992;* 22 Grounds Road, SUTTON COLDFIELD, B74 4SE.

WORSH, Mr. Christopher Stephen, MBA BSc FCA *1992;* 62 Stowe Drive, SOUTHAM, CV47 1NP.

WORSLEY, Mr. Adam Robert, BSc ACA *2006;* 201 Heywood Road, Prestwich, MANCHESTER, M25 1LB.

WORSLEY, Mr. Alexander Francois, ACA *2008;* 180 Leamore Court, Meath Crescent, Bethnal Green, LONDON, E2 0QQ.

WORSLEY, Mrs. Bridgetta, BA ACA *1994;* Moore House, 13 Black Lion Street, BRIGHTON, WEST SUSSEX, BN1 1ED.

WORSLEY, Ms. Catharine Jane, BA ACA *1999;* Apartment 3 Westwood Hall, Peregrine Way, BRADFORD, WEST YORKSHIRE, BD6 3YT.

WORSLEY, Francis Edward, Esq OBE FCA *1964;* (President 1988 - 1989) (Member of Council 1977 - 1996), 10 Whitehills Green, Goring-on-Thames, READING, RG8 0EB.

WORSLEY, Miss. Lucy, BA ACA *2003;* with KPMG LLP, 15 Canada Square, LONDON, E14 5GL.

•**WORSLEY, Mr. Mark Duncan, BA FCA** *1992;* CLB Coopers, Laurel House, 173 Chorley New Road, BOLTON, BL1 4QZ.

•**WORSLEY, Mr. Neil William, ACA** *2002;* Ford Campbell Corporate Finance LLP, Bass Warehouse, 4 Castle Street, Castlefield, MANCHESTER, M3 4LZ.

WORSLEY, Mr. Paul James, BSc(Hons) ACA *2001;* 11/42 Grove Street, LILYFIELD, NSW 2040, AUSTRALIA.

WORSLEY, Mr. Simon David, ACA *2009;* 34 Thurston Close, BURY, LANCASHIRE, BL9 8NW.

WORSLEY, Mr. Simon David, BSc ACA *2002;* 105 Broad Oak Way, Hatherley, CHELTENHAM, GLOUCESTERSHIRE, GL51 3LL.

WORSLEY, Mrs. Tanya Lorraine, BA ACA *2003;* Financial Training Co Ltd, St. James Buildings, 6th Floor, 79 Oxford Street, MANCHESTER, M1 6FQ.

WORSLEY, Mrs. Vanessa, BA(Hons) ACA *2003;* T D G European Chemicals Euroterminal, Westinghouse Road Trafford Park, MANCHESTER, M17 1PY.

WORSNIP, Mr. James Charles, BA FCA *1999;* with PricewaterhouseCoopers LLP, 1 Embankment Place, LONDON, WC2N 6RH.

WORSNUP, Mr. Ian Stuart, BA(Hons) ACA *2002;* 134 Hightown Road, LIVERSEDGE, WEST YORKSHIRE, WF15 8BZ.

WORSNUP, Mr. Peter Jonathan, ACA *1980;* H & L Garages Ltd, Humber Road, SOUTH KILLINGHOLME, LINCOLNSHIRE, DN40 3DL.

WORSTER, Mr. Matthew David, BA ACA *2001;* 136 Davies Road, West Bridgford, NOTTINGHAM, NG2 5HY.

WORSTER, Mrs. Nazneen, MSc(Econ) ACA *1997;* 9 Wallace Way, ROMFORD, RM1 4TG.

WORSTER, Mrs. Victoria Louise, BA ACA *1998;* 5 Spriggs Oak, Palmers Hill, EPPING, CM16 6SE.

WORSWICK, Mr. Richard, FCA *1987;* Secure Options Group, Mitchell Hey Place, College Road, ROCHDALE, LANCASHIRE, OL12 6AE.

WORSWICK, Miss. Sara Helen, BSc ACA *1994;* Caer Bwlch, Mynydd Nefyn, PWLLHELI, GWYNEDD, LL53 6TN.

•**WORSWICK, Mr. Simon John, BA FCA** *1991;* R P Smith & Co Ltd, 71 Chorley Old Road, BOLTON, LANCASHIRE, BL1 3AJ. See also Smith R.P. & Co

WORT, Miss. Frances Stella, BA ACA *1990;* (Tax Fac), 2 Hamilton Close, PURLEY, SURREY, CR8 1AW.

WORTERS, Mr. David Keith, BSc(Hons) ACA *2004;* 38 Louis Road, Lake, NEWPORT, ISLE OF WIGHT, PO36 9HT.

•**WORTH, Mr. Anthony Sandever Richard, BA FCA** *1999;* Summerland, 60 Balsall Street, Balsall Common, COVENTRY, CV7 7AP.

WORTH, Mr. Brian Leslie, FCA FCIArb *1960;* (Member of Council 1985 - 1993), The Cottage, Tiltups End, Horsley, STROUD, GLOUCESTERSHIRE, GL6 0QE. (Life Member)

WORTH, Miss. Brigitte Susan, BA ACA *2001;* 4 Rugby Mews, BELFAST, BT7 1SS.

WORTH, Miss. Eleanor Jasmine, BSc ACA *2010;* 64 Gladesmore Road, LONDON, N15 6TB.

WORTH, Mr. Ian Lee, FCA *1976;* 2 Wilkinson View, Backbarrow, ULVERSTON, CUMBRIA, LA12 8RE.

WORTH, Mr. John Alexander, BA FCA *1988;* Barclays Bank Plc, 1 Churchill Place, LONDON, E14 5HP.

WORTH, Mr. John Tudor, FCA *1965;* 5 Sanderstead Avenue, Cricklewood, LONDON, NW2 1SE. (Life Member)

WORTH, Mr. Paul Nicholas, ACA *1982;* 38 rue de bourlinster, L-6112 JUNGLINSTER, LUXEMBOURG.

WORTH, Mr. Peter St John, FCA *1976;* The Leaze, Crocker End, Nettlebed, HENLEY-ON-THAMES, RG9 5BJ.

WORTH, Mr. Richard James Sandever, FCA *1973;* 4 Kingshurst, Radford Semele, LEAMINGTON SPA, CV31 1TG. (Life Member)

WORTH, Mr. Richard Peter, BA ACA CTA *2000;* 18 Eglamour Way, Heathcote, WARWICK, CV34 6GE.

WORTH, Mr. William John, FCA *1959;* Stradbroke House, Melford Road, Cavendish, SUDBURY, CO10 8AD. (Life Member)

•**WORTHAM, Mr. David Gerald, BA FCA** *1985;* Wortham Jaques, 130a High Street, CREDITON, DEVON, EX17 3LQ.

WORTHINGTON, Mr. Alan, FCA *1950;* 22 Charlton Gardens, COULSDON, CR5 1AS. (Life Member)

•**WORTHINGTON, Mr. Andrew Easton, FCA** *1974;* Gardner Brown, Calderwood House, 7 Montpellier Parade, CHELTENHAM, GL50 1UA.

WORTHINGTON, Miss. Anna Charlotte, BA ACA *2001;* 258 Dacre Park, LONDON, SE13 5DD.

WORTHINGTON, Mrs. Cherry Ann, BA ACA *1989;* 152 Midhurst Road, LONDON, W13 9TP.

WORTHINGTON, Mr. David Anthony, BA(Hons) ACA *2010;* 17 Northfield Lane, Kirkburton, HUDDERSFIELD, HD8 0QT.

WORTHINGTON, Mr. David Frank, FCA *1955;* 3 Curtis House, 57 Blackwater Road, EASTBOURNE, BN20 7DL. (Life Member)

WORTHINGTON, Mr. David Mark, BA FCA *1984;* 35/149 Soi 7/13, Ladawan Housing Estate, Srinakarin Road, SAMUT PRAKAN 10540, THAILAND.

WORTHINGTON, Mrs. Elisabeth Anne, BSc ACA *1980;* 115 Chessetts Wood Road, Lapworth, SOLIHULL, B94 6EL.

WORTHINGTON, Miss. Heather, BA(Hons) ACA *2011;* 49 Windmill Lane, Inkberrow, WORCESTER, WR7 4HG.

WORTHINGTON, Miss. Helen Louisa, MChem ACA *2009;* 5 Heyes Mount, Rainhill, PRESCOT, MERSEYSIDE, L35 0LU.

WORTHINGTON, Mr. John, ACA *2007;* 3 Elm Tree Rise, Hampton-In-Arden, SOLIHULL, B92 0AG.

WORTHINGTON, Mr. Keith Alan, FCA *1977;* 97 Church Road, Sandford-On-Thames, OXFORD, OX4 4YA.

WORTHINGTON, Mr. Lee James, BSc ACA *2001;* with PricewaterhouseCoopers, Darling Park Tower 2, 201 Sussex Street, GPO Box 2650, SYDNEY, NSW 1171 AUSTRALIA.

WORTHINGTON, Mr. Martin, BSc(Hons) ACA *2010;* Floor 10, King Sturge Llp, 45 Church Street, BIRMINGHAM, B3 2RT.

WORTHINGTON, Mr. Martin Richard, BSc ACA *2003;* Flat 6, 19 Percy Circus, LONDON, WC1X 9EE.

WORTHINGTON, Mr. Michael Henry, FCA *1963;* 10 The Crescent, STONE, ST15 8JN.

WORTHINGTON, Mr. Michael James, FCA *1953;* The Roost, Worcester Road, Chadbury, EVESHAM, WORCESTERSHIRE, WR11 4TD. (Life Member)

WORTHINGTON, Mr. Paul John, BSc ACA *1996;* The Limes, Orchards Court, Upper Wardington, BANBURY, OXFORDSHIRE, OX17 1SP.

WORTHINGTON, Mrs. Rebecca Jane, BA ACA *1998;* 97 High Street, Wargrave, READING, RG10 8DD.

•**WORTHINGTON, Mr. Roger Guy, FCA** *1980;* Robson & Co Limited, Kingfisher Court, Plaxton Bridge Road, Woodmansey, BEVERLEY, NORTH HUMBERSIDE HU17 0RT.

WORTHINGTON, Mr. Ronald, FCA *1966;* Box 819, ARTHUR N0G 1A0, ON, CANADA.

WORTHINGTON, Mr. Stuart, BSc ACA *1993;* Nestec Ltd, Avenue Nestle 55, CH 1800 VEVEY, SWITZERLAND.

•**WORTHINGTON-EYRE, Mr. Roland, MA FCA** *1970;* (Tax Fac), Roland Worthington-Eyre, Quartz Lodge, Kildalton, Port Ellen, ISLE OF ISLAY, ARGYLL PA42 7EF.

•**WORTHY, Mr. Christopher Robin, FCA** *1965;* (Tax Fac), Weston Whalley & Jackson, 12 Skipton House, Thanets Yard, SKIPTON, NORTH YORKSHIRE, BD23 1EE.

WORTHY, Ms. Judith Margaret Ann, ACA *1992;* Flat 16, Newton Mansions, Queens Club Gardens, LONDON, W14 9RR.

WORTHY, Mr. Stephen Douglas, MA(Cantab) ACA *2001;* Balfour Beatty Capital Ltd, 350 Euston Road, LONDON, NW1 3AX.

WORTLEY, Mr. Jonathan Charles, BA(Hons) ACA *2001;* 4982 River Reach, DELTA V4K 4A4, BC, CANADA.

•**WORTLEY, Mr. Michael George, BSc FCA** *1979;* M.G. Wortley & Co, Bramble Lodge, Colstrope Lane, Hambleden, HENLEY-ON-THAMES, RG9 6SL.

WORTLEY, Mrs. Viju, BSc ACA *1991;* Mala, Sandy Lane, Pamber Heath, TADLEY, RG26 3PA.

•**WORTON, Mr. Derrick John, FCA** *1979;* Wortons, 23 Bull Plain, HERTFORD, SG14 1DX.

WORTON, Mr. Graham Andrew, BA ACA *1996;* 9D Stourbridge Road, BRIDGNORTH, WV15 5AY.

WORTON, Mr. John, FCA *1957;* 4 The Glen, Farnborough Park, ORPINGTON, BR6 8LR. (Life Member)

WORTON, Mr. Nigel Howard, BSc(Econ) ACA *1998;* Greenways Carlton Road, South Godstone, GODSTONE, SURREY, RH9 8LE.

WORTS, Mr. Robert Kevin, FCA *1970;* F15, 59 Forest Approach, WOODFORD GREEN, IG8 9BP. (Life Member)

•**WORWOOD, Mr. Hedley Scott, FCA** *1976;* Hedley S. Worwood, 8 Showell Lane, Penn, WOLVERHAMPTON, WV4 4UA.

WOSKI, Ms. Sonia, BSc ACA *1988;* Fusion Corportae Finance, The Crescent, King Street, LEICESTER, LE1 6RX.

WOSNER, Mr. John Leslie, BA FCA *1972;* 3 Haslemere Avenue, LONDON, NW4 2PU.

WOSNER, Mr. Michael Dennis, BSc FCA *1976;* 10 Haslemere Avenue, LONDON, NW4 2PX. (Life Member)

WOTHERSPOON, Mrs. Lesley, BSc ACA *1988;* 20 Upper Hall Park, BERKHAMSTED, HP4 2NW.

WOTHERSPOON, Mrs. Melanie Melrose, BSc ACA *1995;* Jupiter Asset Management, 1 Grosvenor Place, LONDON, SW1X 7JJ.

WOTHERSPOON, Mr. Robert John William, BEng ACA *1992;* Flat 20, Lawrence House, Cureton Street, LONDON, SW1P 4ED.

WOTTON, Mr. Andrew Stace, BSc ACA *1990;* PricewaterhouseCoopers, 113-119 The Terrace, PO Box 243, WELLINGTON 6011, NEW ZEALAND.

WOTTON, Mr. Kenneth Michael, BA ACA *2000;* 20 Broomsleigh Street, LONDON, NW6 1QH.

WOTTON, Mr. Stephen James, BA(Hons) ACA *2001;* HSBC 21/F Citibank Tower, 3 Garden Road, CENTRAL, HONG KONG SAR.

WOTTON, Mr. Thomas, BA(Hons) ACA *2010;* 40 Oakwood Grove, Alderbury, SALISBURY, SP5 3BN.

•**WOUDSTRA, Mr. Bret Shane, FCA** *1988;* Bret Woudstra & Co, 69 Chesilton Road, LONDON, SW6 5AA. See also Woudstra B.S.

WOULD, Miss. Nicola, BA(Hons) ACA *2006;* 7/47-53 Dudley Street, COOGEE, NSW 2034, AUSTRALIA.

WOULDHAM, Mr. David Graham, BSc ACA *1993;* Volac International, 50 Fishers Lane Orwell, ROYSTON, HERTFORDSHIRE, SG8 5QX.

WOULDHAM, Mrs. Emma Frances, BSc ACA *1992;* 11 Glinton Road, Helpston, PETERBOROUGH, PE6 7DG.

WOULDHAVE, Mr. Mark, BA(Hons) ACA *2001;* 2 Greenwell Drive, Prudhoe, NEWCASTLE UPON TYNE, NE4 5QR.

WOULDS, Mr. William Ivan, FCA *1958;* 9 Wadham Close, Wellington, TELFORD, TF1 3PU. (Life Member)

WOYDA, Mr. Jeffrey David, BA FCA *1987;* Partingdale Manor, Partingdale Lane, Mill Hill, LONDON, NW7 1NS.

WOZENCROFT, Mr. Andrew John, FCA *1976;* Temple Cottage, Pleasant Stile, Littledean, CINDERFORD, GL14 3NX.

WOZENCROFT, Mrs. Nutan, BSc ACA *1990;* 947 Petite Route Des Jardins, 13210 ST REMY DE PROVENCE, FRANCE.

WOZNIAK, Mr. Stanley Paul, FCA *1976;* Stonefall Grange, 213 Wetherby Road, HARROGATE, HG2 7AE.

WRAFTER, Mr. Mark Patrick, BA ACA *2000;* 5 Victoria Close, East Dulwich, LONDON, SE22 0BF.

WRAGG, Mr. Alistair Charles, BA ACA *1992;* Hollybank, Station Road, Upper Broughton, MELTON MOWBRAY, LE14 3BQ.

•**WRAGG, Mr. David Clive, BA FCA** *1986;* (Tax Fac), Saffery Champness, Beaufort House, 2 Beaufort Road, Clifton, BRISTOL, BS8 2AE.

WRAGG, Mr. George Dennis, FCA *1953;* 15 Meadowside, Whaley Bridge, HIGH PEAK, DERBYSHIRE, SK23 7AZ. (Life Member)

WRAGG, Mr. James David, BEng ACA *1998;* 12 Couldrey Street Bardon, BRISBANE, QLD 4065, AUSTRALIA.

WRAGG, Mr. John Leslie, BCom FCA *1974;* The Old Coach House, Church Hill, Kinver, STOURBRIDGE, WEST MIDLANDS, DY7 6HY.

WRAGG, Mr. Jonathan Peter, BSc ACA *1993;* Rensburg Sheppards Plc, Beech House, 61 Napier Street, SHEFFIELD, S11 8HA.

WRAGG, Mr. Keith, BSc FCA *1984;* 9 Stone Close, Coal Aston, DRONFIELD, DERBYSHIRE, S18 3AS.

WRAGG, Mrs. Linda Kay, FCA *1970;* 64F Brighowgate, GRIMSBY, DN32 0QW.

WRAGG, Mr. Martin George, FCA *1968;* Poulton House, 89A Main Street, Bushby, LEICESTER, LE7 9PL. (Life Member)

•**WRAGG, Mr. Michael, FCA** *1983;* Lings, Provident House, 51 Wardwick, DERBY, DE1 1HN.

•**WRAGG, Mr. Paul Simon, BA FCA** *1995;* (Tax Fac), Focus Accounting Limited, Unit 9, Basepoint Waterlooville, waterberry drive, WATERLOOVILLE, HAMPSHIRE PO7 7Th. See also Direct Payroll
WRAGG, Miss. Sarah Jessica, BA(Hons) ACA *2002;* 7 Slingsby Close, Apperley Bridge, BRADFORD, BD10 0UJ.
WRAIGHT, Mr. Alan Spencer, BA ACA DChA *1991;* Alan Wraight 52 Lucas Avenue, HARROW, MIDDLESEX, HA2 9UJ.
WRAIGHT, Mr. Keith Vincent Andrew, BSc ACA *1991;* The Old Bakery, High Road, High Cross, WARE, SG11 1AB.
WRAIGHT, Miss. Nicola, BSc ACA *2007;* with KPMG LLP, 55 Second Street, Suite 1400, SAN FRANCISCO, CA 94105, UNITED STATES.
WRAITH, Miss. Sarah, ACA *2011;* 5 Christopher Road, Walkergate, NEWCASTLE UPON TYNE, NE6 4AQ.
WRANEK, Mr. Paul Victor, BSc ACA *1993;* 10 New Street, WOODBRIDGE, SUFFOLK, IP12 1DU.
WRATHALL, Ms. Janet Claire, FCA MBA *1977;* 4 Langsett Croft, HUDDERSFIELD, HD2 1PP.
WRATTEN, Mr. Donald Alfred, FCA *1958;* 9 Christie Close, BROXBOURNE, EN10 7RB. (Life Member)
•**WRATTEN, Mr. Geoffrey, FCA** *1966;* G. Wratten & Co, 8 Higham Lane, TONBRIDGE, TN10 4JA.
WRAY, Mr. Andrew Michael, BSc FCA *1972;* Knockmullane, Innishannon, CORK, COUNTY CORK, IRELAND.
WRAY, Mr. Anthony Edward, FCA *1969;* Woodlands 9 Rushclose, SHANKLIN, ISLE OF WIGHT, PO37 7NW.
WRAY, Mrs. Catherine Ann, BA ACA *1992;* 19 Connaught Road, HARPENDEN, HERTFORDSHIRE, AL5 4TW.
WRAY, Mr. Christopher John, BA ACA *1987;* Howber Hill, Langbar, ILKLEY, WEST YORKSHIRE, LS29 0EX.
WRAY, Mr. Colin Malcolm, FCA *1983;* 26 North Common, Redbourn, ST. ALBANS, AL3 7BU.
WRAY, Mr. Ian David, BA(Hons) ACA *2004;* 10 Mallards Reach, WEYBRIDGE, KT13 9HQ.
WRAY, Mr. Ian Webster, FCA *1960;* 85 Falconwood Road, Addington, CROYDON, CR0 9BF. (Life Member)
WRAY, Mr. Jonathan Adam, BSc ACA *1998;* 6 Starling Walk, Walton Cardiff, TEWKESBURY, GL20 7TB.
WRAY, Mrs. Karen Jane, BSc ACA *1998;* 6 Starling Walk, Walton Cardiff, TEWKESBURY, GL20 7TB.
WRAY, Mr. Mark Christopher, ACA *1979;* The Granary, Church Lane, Nether Poppleton, YORK, YO26 6LF.
WRAY, Mr. Martin Jonathan, ACA *1985;* 26 Kerria Way, West End, WOKING, GU24 9XA.
WRAY, Mr. Michael John, FCA *1958;* 7 Stevens Close, Eastcote, PINNER, HA5 2SN. (Life Member)
WRAY, Mrs. Miriam, MA ACA *1993;* 56 Oakwood Avenue, PURLEY, CR8 1AQ.
WRAY, Mr. Neil Douglas, BSc ACA AMCT *1989;* BP Plc, 20 Canada Square, LONDON, E14 5NJ.
WRAY, Mr. Neil Timothy, BA ACA *1997;* 48 Sundridge Road, CROYDON, CR0 6RH.
WRAY, Mr. Nicholas James, BSc(Hons) ACA *2004;* c/o Capital G Bank, Finance 5th Floor, Phillips House Building, 21 - 25 Reid Street, P.O. Box HM 1194, HAMILTON HM 12 BERMUDA.
•**WRAY, Mr. Paul Frank, FCA** *1980;* Wray Accountants Ltd, PO Box 413, KEIGHLEY, BD22 9WX.
WRAY, Mr. Philip Michael, BA ACA *2005;* 5 Foxglove Close, Winkfield Row, BRACKNELL, BERKSHIRE, RG42 7NW.
WRAY, Miss. Rachael, BSc ACA *2003;* Haweswater House, United Utilities Lingley Green Avenue, Lingley Mere Business Park Great Sankey, WARRINGTON, WA5 3LP.
WRAY, Miss. Sara Jane, BA ACA *2000;* 29 Route de Guignonville, 78550 BAZAINVILLE, FRANCE.
•**WRAY, Mr. Simon Charles Blagbrough, BA FCA** *1989;* PricewaterhouseCoopers, Thomas R. Malthusstraat 5, P O Box 90351, 1006 BJ AMSTERDAM, NETHERLANDS.
WRAY, Mr. Stuart James, ACA *1994;* C/O 50 Martello Gardens, Cochrane Park, NEWCASTLE UPON TYNE, NE7 7LE.
•**WREFORD, Mr. Dominic John Yardley, MA FCA FSI** *1997;* FTI Forensic Accounting Limited, 322 High Holborn, LONDON, WC1V 7PB.
WREFORD, Mr. John Alan David, FCA *1965;* Vine Cottage, Bainton Green Road, Ashton, STAMFORD, PE9 3BA.
WREFORD, Mr. Matthew Thomas Yardley, ACA *2001;* Garban-Intercapital Plc, 2 Broadgate, LONDON, EC2M 7UR.
•**WREFORD, Mr. Nigel Graham Felton, FCA** *1981;* Percy Gore & Co, 39 Hawley Square, MARGATE, KENT, CT9 1NZ.
WREFORD, Mr. Peter Jonathan, BA ACA *1988;* Ellerslie, 35 Balsall Street East, Balsall Common, COVENTRY, CV7 7FQ.
WREFORD, Mr. Roger John, FCA *1960;* Appletree House, Marshside, Brancaster, KING'S LYNN, PE31 8AD. (Life Member)
WREFORD, Mr. Spencer James, BSc ACA *1998;* 57 Beaconsfield Road, TWICKENHAM, TW1 3HX.
WREFORD, Mr. Steven Mark, BSc ACA *1998;* 8 Benfleet Close, COBHAM, KT11 2NR.
WREN, Mr. Anthony Edward, FCA *1959;* 12 Church Mount, Guilsborough, NORTHAMPTON, NN6 8QA. (Life Member)
WREN, Mr. David Joseph, ACA *2008;* Flat 8, School House, 2 Pelling Street, LONDON, E14 7DT.
•**WREN, Miss. Gillian, BA(Hons) ACA** *2004;* Wren Accountancy, 26 Saxton Lane, Saxton, TADCASTER, NORTH YORKSHIRE, LS24 9QD.
WREN, Miss. Laura Ann, BA ACA *2009;* Flat 2, 150 Chapel Street, SALFORD, M3 6AF.
WREN, Mr. Maurice Arthur, FCA *1954;* 12 Mountdale Gardens, LEIGH-ON-SEA, ESSEX, SS9 4AU.
WREN, Mr. Michael Hainsworth, ACA *1985;* 10 Solent Drive, Warsash, SOUTHAMPTON, SO31 9HB.
WREN, Mr. Simon, BSc ACA *1992;* 29 Barleycroft Road, WELWYN GARDEN CITY, AL8 6JX.
WRENCH, Mr. David James, MA ACA *2009;* 2 Dover Close, BASINGSTOKE, HAMPSHIRE, RG23 8EG.
WRENCH, Mr. Paul, FCA *1978;* 3 Camblez House, Queens Road, St. Peter Port, GUERNSEY, GY1 1PS.
WRENCH, Mr. Richard William, BA ACA *1995;* Town House 14, 30A The Crescent, DEE WHY, NSW 2099, AUSTRALIA.
WRENN, Ms. Susan Christine, MA ACA *2000;* 22 Eachard Road, CAMBRIDGE, CB3 0HY.
WRENN, Mr. Thomas Laurence, BA ACA *2003;* with E C I Partners, Brettenham House, Lancaster Place, LONDON, WC2E 7EN.
WRENNALL, Mr. David Lupton, FCA *1960;* 82 Eastgrove Avenue, Sharples, BOLTON, BL1 7HA. (Life Member)
WRESCHNER, Mr. Benjamin Mark, BSc(Econ) ACA *2001;* 40 Brent Street, LONDON, NW4 2ET.
WRESCHNER, Mr. Michael Montague, FCA *1967;* 35/2 Rechov Ben Maimon, JERUSALEM, 92262, ISRAEL.
WRIDE, Mr. David William, FCA *1971;* 1 Court Meadow, StoneNr., BERKELEY, GL13 9LR.
WRIDE, Mr. Kevan Mark, BEng ACA *1993;* 15 Weavers Croft, Westwoodside, DONCASTER, SOUTH YORKSHIRE, DN9 2HE.
WRIGGLESWORTH, Mr. Geoffrey Robert, FCA *1972;* 8 Ashfield Avenue, Skelmanthorpe, HUDDERSFIELD, HD8 9BW.
WRIGGLESWORTH, Mr. Mark Alan, MA ACA *2010;* A24 78 Park Terrace, CHRISTCHURCH 8013, NEW ZEALAND.
•**WRIGGLESWORTH, Mr. Mark Richard, BA FCA** *1991;* (Tax Fac), Brunswick Trustees Limited, Suite 26 Century Buildings, Brunswick Business Park, Tower Street, LIVERPOOL, L3 4BJ. See also ERC Accountants & Business Advisers Limited and The Tax Place Solutions LLP
WRIGGLESWORTH, Mr. Simon John, BSc ACA *2009;* 21 Wike Ridge Mount, LEEDS, LS17 9NP.
WRIGHT, Mr. Adrian Cary, FCA *1956;* Birbecks, 9 Redgates Lane, Sewards End, SAFFRON WALDEN, CB10 2LW. (Life Member)
WRIGHT, Mr. Adrian John, FCA *1971;* 38 Eastern Way, Darras Hall, Ponteland, NEWCASTLE UPON TYNE, NE20 9PF.
WRIGHT, Mr. Adrian Paul, BA ACA *1994;* 10 Sandale Close, Gamston, NOTTINGHAM, NG2 6QG.
WRIGHT, Mr. Alan Arthur, BSc FCA *1967;* 9-861 Shelborne Street, LONDON N5Z 5C5, ON, CANADA. (Life Member)
•**WRIGHT, Mr. Alan Peter, BCom FCA** *1964;* Wright & Co, 2 Longrood Road, Bilton, RUGBY, CV22 7RG.
WRIGHT, Miss. Alison Elizabeth, BSc ACA *1999;* 52 Millpond Estate, West Lane, LONDON, SE16 4LZ.
WRIGHT, Mrs. Alison Jane, BSc ACA *1983;* 31 Bankart Avenue, LEICESTER, LEICESTERSHIRE, LE2 2DD.
WRIGHT, Mr. Alistair, MEng ACA *2011;* Apartment 3, 20 Newhall Hill, BIRMINGHAM, B1 3JA.
WRIGHT, Mr. Allan William, BA ACA *1999;* 52 Verona Drive, SURBITON, SURREY, KT6 5AL.
WRIGHT, Miss. Amanda, BA ACA *2004;* A & J Fabtech Ltd, Unit 700, Bretton Park Way, DEWSBURY, WEST YORKSHIRE, WF12 9BS.
WRIGHT, Mrs. Andrea Elizabeth, LLB ACA *1993;* Stoke Abbot, 24A Abbotswood, GUILDFORD, GU1 1UY.
WRIGHT, Mr. Andrew David, BA(Hons) ACA *2001;* 188 Woodseer Street, LONDON, E1 5HQ.
WRIGHT, Mr. Andrew Graham, BSc ACA *1991;* Tomkins Plc, East Putney House, 84 Upper Richmond Road, LONDON, SW15 2ST.
•**WRIGHT, Mr. Andrew Mark, BA(Hons) ACA** *2000;* Rowan House, 94 Bristol Road, Frampton Cotterell, BRISTOL, BS36 2AY.
WRIGHT, Mr. Andrew Merlay, BA ACA *1986;* 60 Elmbourne Road, LONDON, SW17 8JJ.
WRIGHT, Mr. Andrew Phillip Dettmar, MSci ACA *2006;* Flat 1 Dickens Court, 3 Makepeace Road, LONDON, E11 1UR.
•**WRIGHT, Mr. Andrew Stephen, ACA** *1991;* Wold House, 3 Vicarage Lane, North Newbald, YORK, YO43 4RR.
WRIGHT, Mr. Andrew Walter Yorkstone, MA FCA *1968;* Croft Butts, 9 Smiddy Burn, Kingsbarns, ST. ANDREWS, FIFE, KY16 8SN.
WRIGHT, Miss. Angela Barbara, BSc ACA *2001;* 2 Greenan Place, AYR, KA7 4ER.
WRIGHT, Mrs. Annabel Portia, BA ACA *1999;* Brandt Holding Ltd, 20 Barclay Road, CROYDON, CR0 1JN.
•①**WRIGHT, Mr. Anthony John, BA ACA** *1999;* Baker Tilly Restructuring And Recovery LLP, 25 Farringdon Street, LONDON, EC4A 4AB. See also Baker Tilly Tax and Advisory Services LLP
WRIGHT, The Revd. Anthony John, FCA *1970;* The Vicarage, 6 The Green, TETBURY, GLOUCESTERSHIRE, GL8 8DN.
•**WRIGHT, Mr. Anthony John Phillip, ACA** *2002;* Edwards, 15 Station Road, ST. IVES, CAMBRIDGESHIRE, PE27 5BH.
WRIGHT, Mr. Arthur John, FCA JDipMA *1968;* 8 Rookery Rise, Wombourne, WOLVERHAMPTON, WV5 0NP.
•**WRIGHT, Mr. Barrie William, ACA** *1989;* (Tax Fac), McCabe Ford Williams, Invicta Business Centre, Monument Way, Orbital Park, ASHFORD, KENT TN24 0HB.
WRIGHT, Mr. Barry Lendon, FCA *1953;* 19 Broadway Furlong, Anstey, LEICESTER, LE7 7TL. (Life Member)
WRIGHT, Mr. Ben, BSc ACA *2002;* Flat 3, 5 Tower Street, MANLY, SYDNEY, NSW 2095, AUSTRALIA.
WRIGHT, Mr. Benjamin, MA BA ACA *2006;* 32 Almond Tree Road, Cheadle Hulme, CHEADLE, CHESHIRE, SK8 6HW.
WRIGHT, Mr. Benjamin James, ACA *2008;* Apartment 5 4 Breezyway Lane, SMITHS FL06, BERMUDA.
WRIGHT, Mr. Branton, FCA *1965;* 46 West Meadows Rd, Cleadon, SUNDERLAND, SR6 7TU.
WRIGHT, Mr. Brian, ACA *2007;* 77 Springfields, Mickle Trafford, CHESTER, CH2 4EG.
•**WRIGHT, Mr. Brian, FCA** *1975;* (Tax Fac), B. Wright & Co, 28 Bycullah Avenue, ENFIELD, EN2 8DN.
WRIGHT, Mr. Brian Charles Gordon, FCA *1956;* 69 Ramsay Drive, EASTBOURNE, BN23 6DF. (Life Member)
WRIGHT, Mr. Brian Michael, FCA *1963;* Sunnyside Cottage, Plough Road, Tibberton, DROITWICH, WR9 7NL.
WRIGHT, Mr. Bruce Sean, BA ACA *1991;* Pennington, Ashwells Way, CHALFONT ST.GILES, HP8 4HR.
WRIGHT, Mrs. Caroline Fiona, BA ACA *1999;* 12 College Way, East Garston, HUNGERFORD, RG17 7EP.
WRIGHT, Miss. Catherine Mary Gardiner, ACA *2008;* 35 The Oval, Wood Street Village, GUILDFORD, GU3 3DL.
WRIGHT, Mr. Charles, BA ACA *2005;* Little Beck, 15 Sands Lane, Ellerker, BROUGH, NORTH HUMBERSIDE, HU15 2DR.
WRIGHT, Mr. Charles Naunton, BA ACA *1982;* Flat 7 Loxham House, Loxham Street, LONDON, WC1H 8HS.
WRIGHT, Mr. Charles Stuart, FCA *1957;* Apt 7218, 50080 ZARAGOZA, SPAIN. (Life Member)
•**WRIGHT, Mr. Charles Stuart, BA FCA CF** *1986;* Needle's Eye Limited, 14 Catherine Drive, SUTTON COLDFIELD, B73 6AX.
WRIGHT, Mrs. Christina Margaret, BA ACA *2003;* Ernst & Young, 100 Barbirolli Square, MANCHESTER, M2 3EY.
•**WRIGHT, Miss. Christine, BA ACA** *1987;* C. Wright, 39 Court Farm Road, NEWHAVEN, BN9 9DH.
•**WRIGHT, Mrs. Christine Dorothy, BSc ACA** *1987;* (Tax Fac), C.D. Wright, Mains of Balfour, Birse, ABOYNE, ABERDEENSHIRE, AB34 5DB.
WRIGHT, Mr. Christopher John, BA ACA *1992;* 236 Ashby Road, HINCKLEY, LEICESTERSHIRE, LE10 1SW.
WRIGHT, Mr. Christopher John, ACA *2008;* 1st Floor, The Co-operative Group (C W S) Ltd Old Bank Building, Hanover Street, MANCHESTER, M60 0AB.
•**WRIGHT, Mr. Christopher John, FCA** *1975;* Brough Kirkman, 8 High Skellgate, RIPON, NORTH YORKSHIRE, HG4 1BA.
WRIGHT, Mr. Christopher John, BSc ACA CTA *1983;* 4 Ash Lea, Castleton, WHITBY, NORTH YORKSHIRE, YO21 2EW.
WRIGHT, Mr. Christopher Neil, BSc ACA *1995;* McManus Pub Co Ltd, Kingsthorpe Road, NORTHAMPTON, NN2 6HT.
•**WRIGHT, Mr. Christopher Stephen, FCA** *1973;* (Tax Fac), Chris Wright & Co Limited, 217 Hallgate, COTTINGHAM, NORTH HUMBERSIDE, HU16 4BG. See also Accountancy & Secretarial Services Ltd
WRIGHT, Mr. Christopher Thomas, BA(Econ) ACA *2004;* 21 Meadow Bank, MANCHESTER, M21 8EF.
•**WRIGHT, Mr. Christopher Thomas, FCA** *1976;* Keelings Limited, Broad House, 1 The Broadway, Old Hatfield, HATFIELD, HERTFORDSHIRE AL9 5BG.
•**WRIGHT, Mr. Christopher William, FCA CTA** *1991;* Moore Thompson, Monica House, St. Augustines Road, WISBECH, CAMBRIDGESHIRE, PE13 3AD.
•**WRIGHT, Mrs. Claire Elizabeth, BA ACA** *1990;* with Smailes Goldie, Regents Court, Princess Street, HULL, HU2 8BA.
WRIGHT, Mrs. Claire Frances, BSc ACA ATII *1998;* 9 Wycombe Road, PRINCES RISBOROUGH, BUCKINGHAMSHIRE, HP27 0EE.
WRIGHT, Miss. Claire Lesley, BA ACA *1992;* Milton Gate, 60 Chiswell Street, LONDON, EC1Y 4SA.
WRIGHT, Mrs. Claire Lily, BSc ACA *1988;* The Limes, South Lane, Southbourne, EMSWORTH, HAMPSHIRE, PO10 8PP.
WRIGHT, Mrs. Claire Louise, BCom ACA *2002;* 2 Aldeburgh Gardens, IPSWICH, SUFFOLK, IP4 5HJ.
WRIGHT, Mrs. Claire Mary, BSc ACA CTA *1995;* (Tax Fac), Old Mill Rowden Lane, Hampsthwaite, HARROGATE, NORTH YORKSHIRE, HG3 2ER.
WRIGHT, Mr. Colin Dennis, BSc FCA *1972;* 21 High View, Cheam, SUTTON, SM2 7DZ.
WRIGHT, Mr. Colin John, ACA *1986;* 28 Bramble Tye, Laindon, BASILDON, SS15 5GS.
WRIGHT, Mr. Colin Redvers, FCA *1968;* 2 Tippett Avenue, STOWMARKET, IP14 1TE.
WRIGHT, Mr. Craig Richard, BA *1996;* Charlecote House, Weaverlake Drive, Yoxall, BURTON-ON-TRENT, DE13 8AD.
WRIGHT, Mr. Curtis Lee, BSc ACA *1981;* Mr C L Wright, The Garth, Lands Lane, KNARESBOROUGH, NORTH YORKSHIRE, HG5 9DE.
WRIGHT, Mr. Damian James Edward, BSc(Econ) ACA *2002;* 320 West 38th Street, Apt 2405, NEW YORK, NY 10017, UNITED STATES.
WRIGHT, Mr. Daniel James, BSc ACA *2006;* 48 South Oak Lane, WILMSLOW, CHESHIRE, SK9 6AT.
WRIGHT, Mr. Daniel Michael, ACA *2011;* Apartment 1, 48a Nelson Street, LIVERPOOL, L1 5DN.
WRIGHT, Miss. Danielle Alexandra, BA ACA *2006;* 29 Bishops Gate, LYTHAM ST. ANNES, FY8 4FR.
WRIGHT, Mr. Darren, ACA MAAT *2003;* Targetfollow Estates Ltd, Riverside House, 11-12 Riverside Road, NORWICH, NR1 1SQ.
•**WRIGHT, Mr. David, FCA** *1979;* Thompson Wright Limited, Ebeneezer House, Ryecroft, NEWCASTLE, STAFFORDSHIRE, ST5 2BE.
WRIGHT, Mr. David, BSc ACA *1986;* 59 Beckenham Road, WEST WICKHAM, BR4 0QS.
WRIGHT, Mr. David, MA ACA *1998;* 111 Stephen Lane, Grenoside, SHEFFIELD, S35 8QZ.
WRIGHT, Mr. David, BA FCA *1967;* 2 The Beeches, Beechfield Gardens, SPALDING, LINCOLNSHIRE, PE11 1UE.
WRIGHT, Mr. David Adrian Llewellyn, BSc ACA *1990;* Waskerley, Stowhill, Childrey, WANTAGE, OXFORDSHIRE, OX12 9XQ.
•**WRIGHT, Mr. David Anthony, BSc FCA** *1993;* David Anthony & Co, 5 The Gateway, Rathmore Road, LONDON, SE7 7QW.
WRIGHT, Mr. David Antony, BSc ACA *2000;* Flat 4, 110 Drayton Gardens, LONDON, SW10 9RL.
WRIGHT, Mr. David Charles, BSc ACA *1978;* 21 Rothley Avenue, Ainsdale, SOUTHPORT, PR8 2SS.
WRIGHT, Mr. David Edward, BSc FCA *1967;* Marine Aviation & General Ltd, 10 Eastcheap, LONDON, EC3M 1AJ.

WRIGHT, Mr. David Franklin, BMus ACA *2002;* 162 Tenniswood Road, ENFIELD, MIDDLESEX, EN1 3LX.
WRIGHT, Mr. David James, BSc ACA *2005;* 56 Reedley Road, BRISTOL, BS9 3SU.
WRIGHT, Mr. David James, BA ACA *1983;* Lloyds TSB Bank Plc Faryners House, 25 Monument Street, LONDON, EC3R 8BQ.
•**WRIGHT, Mr. David John, FCA** *1978;* (Tax Fac), The Walker Brown Partnership LLP, 32 Trafalgar Road, Portslade, BRIGHTON, BN41 1LD.
WRIGHT, Mr. David John, BA FCA *1983;* 14 Lordsbury Field, WALLINGTON, SM6 9PE.
WRIGHT, Mr. David John, BA(Hons) ACA *2003;* Sita UK Ltd Unit 301-304, Park Way Worle, WESTON-SUPER-MARE, AVON, BS22 6WA.
WRIGHT, Mr. David John, BA ACA *1992;* 69 Hambalt Road, LONDON, SW4 9EQ.
•**WRIGHT, Mr. David John, BSc FCA** *1976;* (Tax Fac), David Wright Accountants Limited, 1st Floor, Nathaniel House, David Street, BRIDGEND, CF31 3SA.
WRIGHT, Mr. David John, FCA *1964;* 241 Darras Road, Ponteland, NEWCASTLE UPON TYNE, NE20 9AJ. (Life Member)
WRIGHT, Mr. David Leonard, BSc FCA *1978;* Mistletoe Cottage, Westhope, HEREFORD, HR4 8BU.
WRIGHT, Mr. David Leslie Inns, ACA *2010;* Flat 37 Thanet Lodge, 10 Mapesbury Road, LONDON, NW2 4JA.
•**WRIGHT, Mr. David Maxwell, FCA** *1981;* (Tax Fac), David M. Wright, Woodlands Works, Woodlands Road, Thundridge, WARE, SG12 0SP.
WRIGHT, Mr. David Michael, ACA *1981;* Guardian Accountancy Services, 41 High Street, SANDBACH, CHESHIRE, CW11 1AL.
•**WRIGHT, Mr. David Paul, ACA FCCA** *2010;* Lowe McTernan Limited, Highcroft House, 81-85 New Road, Rubery, Rednal, BIRMINGHAM B45 9JR.
WRIGHT, Mr. David Peter, BSc(Hons) ACA *2003;* 83 Cromwell Road, NORWICH, NR7 8XJ.
WRIGHT, Mr. David Robert, BSc(Hons) ACA *2006;* 8 Hazel Road, BERKHAMSTED, HERTFORDSHIRE, HP4 2JN.
•**WRIGHT, Mr. David Trevor, BSc FCA** *1983;* Chantrey Vellacott DFK LLP, Russell Square House, 10-12 Russell Square, LONDON, WC1B 5LF.
•**WRIGHT, Mr. David William, FCA** *1973;* Moore & Co, Belvoir House, 1 Rous Road, NEWMARKET, SUFFOLK, CB8 8DH.
WRIGHT, Miss. Deborah Jayne, BA(Hons) ACA *2011;* 198 Baltic Quay, Mill Road, GATESHEAD, TYNE AND WEAR, NE8 3QZ.
WRIGHT, Mr. Declan Joseph, BEng ACA *1992;* Larsen Building Ltd, 4 West Bank Road, BELFAST, BT3 9JL.
WRIGHT, Mrs. Denise Jane, BA(Hons) FCA CTA *1989;* Carrara 2 - Financial Accounting, Surrey Street, NORWICH, NORFOLK, NR1 3NS.
WRIGHT, Mr. Derek Michael, FCA *1967;* PO BOX 305, Simonstown, CAPE TOWN, 7995, SOUTH AFRICA. (Life Member)
WRIGHT, Mr. Deryck Edward, BA FCA *1974;* 25 The Fieldings, Southwater, HORSHAM, WEST SUSSEX, RH13 9LY.
WRIGHT, Miss. Donna, ACA *2006;* 35 Holmewood, Holme, PETERBOROUGH, PE7 3PG.
WRIGHT, Mr. Dylan Matthew, BA FCA *1998;* 8 Chesnut Cottages, Wallingford Road, Streatley, READING, RG8 9JQ.
WRIGHT, Mr. Edward James, BA ACA *2007;* 30a Hartopp Road, SUTTON COLDFIELD, WEST MIDLANDS, B74 2QX.
•**WRIGHT, Mr. Edward Kenneth Hockley, ACA** *2008;* Hockley Wright & Co Limited, Berkeley House, 18 Station Road, EAST GRINSTEAD, WEST SUSSEX, RH19 1DJ. See also Pinard Wright & Co Ltd
WRIGHT, Mr. Edward Malcolm, BA(Hons) ACA CTA *2003;* with Deloitte LLP, 2 New Street Square, LONDON, EC4A 3BZ.
WRIGHT, Mrs. Felicia, BSc ACA *2006;* 196c Kings Hall Road, BECKENHAM, KENT, BR3 1LJ.
WRIGHT, Mr. Freddie Richard, BA ACA *1993;* 34 Spencer Street, Cathays, CARDIFF, CF24 4PG.
WRIGHT, Mr. Gareth Richard, BSc ACA *1998;* Informa Group Plc, Informa House, 30-32 Mortimer Street, LONDON, W1W 7RE.
WRIGHT, Mr. Gary Robert, BCom ACA *2005;* with KPMG LLP, Quayside House, 110 Quayside, NEWCASTLE UPON TYNE, NE1 3DX.
WRIGHT, Mr. Gavin Richard, BA ACA *1991;* 70a Kent Road, HARROGATE, NORTH YORKSHIRE, HG1 2NH.
WRIGHT, Mr. George Frederick Dennis, FCA *1963;* 28 Roundwood View, BANSTEAD, SM7 1EQ.
WRIGHT, Mr. George Frederick Henry, FCA *1949;* 13 West Common Road, UXBRIDGE, UB8 1NZ. (Life Member)
WRIGHT, Miss. Geraldine Helen, BA ACA *1987;* 71 Barnfield Wood Road, BECKENHAM, BR3 6ST.
WRIGHT, Miss. Gillian, BSc FCA CTA *1988;* 25 Strathearn Drive, Westbury-on-Trym, BRISTOL, BS10 6TJ.
WRIGHT, Mrs. Gillian Claire, BA(Hons) ACA *2002;* 152 Highbury Grove, Clapham, BEDFORD, MK41 6DU.
WRIGHT, Mr. Gordon Ronald Charles, FCA *1969;* 40 Crescent Way, Norbury, LONDON, SW16 3AJ.
WRIGHT, Mr. Gordon William Patrick, BSc FCA *1973;* c/o KPMG, PO Box 82 Post International, Suite 2 Global House, Payle Road, Colnbrook, SLOUGH BERKSHIRE SL3 0AY.
WRIGHT, Mr. Graham, BA FCA DChA *1988;* School House Farm, The Gravel, Mere Brow, PRESTON, LANCASHIRE, PR4 6JX.
WRIGHT, Mr. Graham Alexander Neale, MA ACA *1985;* B-52 Kapoorthala Crossing, Mahanagar, LUCKNOW 226006, UTTAR PRADESH, INDIA.
WRIGHT, Mr. Graham Christopher, BSc ACA *1978;* 57 Chester Drive, HARROW, HA2 7PX.
WRIGHT, Mr. Graham Mark, BSc ACA CTA *1999;* with Ernst & Young LLP, 100 Barbirolli Square, MANCHESTER, M2 3EY.
WRIGHT, Mr. Graham Marvel, FCA *1971;* 1 Pilgrims Court, Cuckoo Hill, BURES, SUFFOLK, CO8 5LF.
WRIGHT, Mr. Graham Rodney, FCA *1969;* 173 Green Lane, LEIGH-ON-SEA, SS9 5QL. (Life Member)
WRIGHT, Mr. Gregory Arthur, FCA *1970;* Paddock House, 31 Cedar Drive, Market Bosworth, NUNEATON, CV13 0LW.
WRIGHT, Miss. Hannah, BSc ACA *2010;* Apartment 90, Avoca Court, 25 Moseley Road, BIRMINGHAM, B12 0HJ.
WRIGHT, Mrs. Helen Jane, BA(Hons) ACA *2003;* 29 Beverley Road, Kirk Ella, HULL, HU10 7AA.
WRIGHT, Miss. Helen Sarah, BSc ACA *1993;* 7a Rozel Road, Clapham, LONDON, SW4 0EY.
WRIGHT, Mr. Hubert, FCA *1959;* 34 Oakwood Green, North Lane, LEEDS, LS8 2QU. (Life Member)
WRIGHT, Mr. Iain Andrew, BA ACA FSI *1990;* Sun Life of Canada Matrix House, Basing View, BASINGSTOKE, RG21 4DZ.
WRIGHT, Mr. Iain David, LLB FCA CTA *2000;* (Tax Fac), RSM Tenon Plc, Bentley Jennison Charter House, Legge Street, BIRMINGHAM, B4 7EU.
WRIGHT, Mr. Iain David, BA ACA MP *2003;* 9 Cornflower Close, HARTLEPOOL, CLEVELAND, TS26 0WJ.
WRIGHT, Mr. Iain Stuart, ACA *2008;* Pricewaterhousecoopers, 8 Princes Parade, LIVERPOOL, L3 1QJ.
•**WRIGHT, Mr. Ian, BA FCA** *1983;* Ian Wright & Co, 15 Stretton Drive, SOUTHPORT, PR9 7DR.
WRIGHT, Mr. Ian Christopher, BSc ACA *1998;* 53 Blacketts Wood Drive, Chorleywood, RICKMANSWORTH, HERTFORDSHIRE, WD3 5PY.
WRIGHT, Mr. Ian Donald, BSc FCA *1990;* Mendip House, Beacon, Doulting, SHEPTON MALLET, SOMERSET, BA4 4LA.
WRIGHT, Mr. Ian Duncan, BSc ACA *1982;* 4 St. Brelade Close, Le Mont Gras D'Eau, St. Brelade, JERSEY, JE3 8ED.
WRIGHT, Mr. Ian Nicholas Molyneux, MA ACA *2002;* 13 Churchill Road, ST. ALBANS, HERTFORDSHIRE, AL1 4HH.
WRIGHT, Mr. Ian Robert, FCA *1981;* 44 Mitchell Road, ST.HELENS, MERSEYSIDE, WA10 3EX.
WRIGHT, Mr. Jake Stephen Hockley, BSc ACA *1997;* Tribal Education Ltd, 1-4 Portland Square, BRISTOL, BS2 8RR.
WRIGHT, Mr. James, ACA *2009;* 10 Laurel Avenue Onchan, ISLE OF MAN, IM3 3JD.
WRIGHT, Mr. James, ACA *2009;* 35 Tyneham Road, LONDON, SW11 5XH.
WRIGHT, Mr. James De Garis, MLitt BA ACA *1999;* British Steel Pension Fund, 17th Floor, 125 Old Broad Street, LONDON, EC2N 1AR.
WRIGHT, Mr. James Douglas Weatherley, FCA *1972;* The White House, 41 High Street, Codicote, HITCHIN, HERTFORDSHIRE, SG4 8XB.
WRIGHT, Mr. James Leonard, FCA *1958;* 32 Devonshire Avenue, GRIMSBY, DN32 0BW. (Life Member)
WRIGHT, Mr. James Macdonald, BA FCA *1962;* 5 Broomans Court, Broomans Lane, LEWES, BN7 2LT. (Life Member)
WRIGHT, Mr. James Martin Charles, BSc ACA *2003;* 55 Bolton Road, Maidenbower, CRAWLEY, WEST SUSSEX, RH10 7LR.
WRIGHT, Mr. James Matthew, BSc ACA *1993;* 84 High Street, Gilling West, RICHMOND, DL10 5JW.
•**WRIGHT, Mr. James Nicholas, BA FCA** *1996;* Deloitte LLP, 2 New Street Square, LONDON, EC4A 3BZ. See also Deloitte & Touche LLP
WRIGHT, Mr. James Peter Charles, MSci ACA *2004;* J P Morgan Chase, 125 London Wall, LONDON, EC2Y 5AJ.
WRIGHT, Mr. James William, FCA *1961;* Flat D. 10, Sloane Avenue Mansions, Sloane Avenue, LONDON, SW3 3JH. (Life Member)
WRIGHT, Mr. Jamie, BA(Hons) ACA *2011;* 1 Bowden Close, NEWCASTLE UPON TYNE, NE13 9GB.
WRIGHT, Mr. Jamie Alexander, BSc ACA *2010;* Baker Tilly, St. Philips Point, Temple Row, BIRMINGHAM, B2 5AF.
WRIGHT, Mrs. Jane Elizabeth, BSc ACA *1985;* The Old School House, Stratford Road, Wootton Wawen, SOLIHULL, B95 6BB.
WRIGHT, Mrs. Janet Elizabeth Mark, BSc FCA *1991;* First Floor, Guild House, Guild Street, I.F.S.C., DUBLIN 1, COUNTY DUBLIN IRELAND.
WRIGHT, Mr. Jason Mark, BA ACA *1994;* 98 The Street, Poringland, NORWICH, NR14 7JX.
WRIGHT, Miss. Jennifer Louise, BCom ACA *2004;* Springfield House, 17 Shrewsbury Fields, SHIFNAL, SHROPSHIRE, TF11 8AL.
WRIGHT, Mr. Jeremy Nicholas, BA FCA *1989;* 14 Roedhelm Road, East Morton, KEIGHLEY, WEST YORKSHIRE, BD20 5RF.
•**WRIGHT, Mrs. Jill Lorraine, BA FCA** *1990;* Kirk Newsholme Ltd, 4315 Park Approach, Thorpe Park, LEEDS, LS15 8GB.
WRIGHT, Miss. Joanna Clare, BCom ACA *1997;* Nick UK Rathbone House, 15-16 Rathbone Place, LONDON, W1T 1HU.
WRIGHT, Mrs. Joanna Louise, BA ACA *1995;* Flat 1 Middlewood Hall, Doncaster Road, Darfield, BARNSLEY, S73 9HQ.
WRIGHT, Mrs. Joanne, BSc ACA *2004;* Bewers Turner & Co, Portland House, 12 Station Road, KETTERING, NORTHAMPTONSHIRE, NN15 7HH.
WRIGHT, Mr. Jody Duncan Alexander, BA(Hons) ACA *2002;* 5 College Road, Colliers Wood, LONDON, SW19 2BP.
WRIGHT, Mr. John, BA ACA *1989;* (Tax Fac), 22 St Johns Road, ALTRINCHAM, WA14 2NA.
WRIGHT, Mr. John, FCA *1969;* 21 The Paddocks, Kirk Ella, HULL, HU10 7PF.
WRIGHT, Mr. John Alexander, FCA *1975;* Bramleys, Manor Lane, WEDMORE, SOMERSET, BS28 4EL.
WRIGHT, Mr. John Charles, FCA *1959;* 24 Park Drive, ROMFORD, RM1 4LH. (Life Member)
WRIGHT, Mr. John Clark, FCA *1958;* 2 Shirley Gardens, SUNDERLAND, SR3 1YD. (Life Member)
•**WRIGHT, Mr. John Michael, BSc FCA** *1986;* Stoten Gillam Limited, Alban House, Stoten Gillam, 99 High Street South, DUNSTABLE, BEDFORDSHIRE LU6 3SF.
WRIGHT, Mr. John Michael, FCA *1960;* 1488 Woodward Avenue, OTTAWA K1Z 7W6, ON, CANADA. (Life Member)
WRIGHT, Mr. John Stuart, FCA *1980;* Welham Hall, Welham, MALTON, YO17 9QF.
WRIGHT, Mr. John Stuart, MA FCA *1976;* 16 Barratts Hill, BROSELEY, SHROPSHIRE, TF12 5NJ.
WRIGHT, Mr. John Thomas, FCA *1951;* The Martins, 18 The Green, Marsh Baldon, OXFORD, OX44 9LJ. (Life Member)
•**WRIGHT, Mr. John William James, FCA** *1983;* John W J Wright FCA, 13 Market Place, UTTOXETER, STAFFORDSHIRE, ST14 8HY.
WRIGHT, Mr. Jonathan David, BSc ACA *1997;* 28 Redland Court Road, BRISTOL, BS6 7EQ.
WRIGHT, Mr. Jonathan Hugh Timothy, BA FCA *1978;* Oak Tree House, Delarue Close, TONBRIDGE, KENT, TN11 9NN.
•**WRIGHT, Mr. Jonathan Maitland, FCA** *1979;* Maitland Wright Limited, 55 East Budleigh Road, BUDLEIGH SALTERTON, DEVON, EX9 6EW.
WRIGHT, Mr. Joseph Francis, MA ACA *1978;* 8 Wedgewood Way, Upper Norwood, LONDON, SE19 3AS.
•**WRIGHT, Mr. Joseph Hockley, MBA FCA** *1972;* Hockley Wright & Co Limited, Berkeley House, 18 Station Road, EAST GRINSTEAD, WEST SUSSEX, RH19 1DJ.
•**WRIGHT, Mrs. Judith, BTech FCA** *1978;* 31 Norfolk Road, SUTTON COLDFIELD, WEST MIDLANDS, B75 6SQ.
WRIGHT, Mrs. Judith, BSc ACA *1999;* 1 Abbey Close, Bowdon, ALTRINCHAM, CHESHIRE, WA14 3NA.
WRIGHT, Miss. Julie, BSc ACA *1991;* Doroken Court, Locko Road, Lower Pilsley, CHESTERFIELD, S45 8DN.
WRIGHT, Mrs. Julie Ann, BA ACA *2004;* St. Catherines Farm, Catlins Lane, PINNER, MIDDLESEX, HA5 2HE.
WRIGHT, Mrs. Julie Elizabeth, BSc ACA *1983;* Saverley House, Saverley Green, STOKE-ON-TRENT, ST11 9QX.
WRIGHT, Mrs. Justine Caroline, BA ACA *1993;* 4 Hartwell Gardens, HARPENDEN, HERTFORDSHIRE, AL5 2RW.
WRIGHT, Mrs. Karen Louise, BSc ACA *1999;* 5 Downsview, Edington, WESTBURY, WILTSHIRE, BA13 4QL.
WRIGHT, Mrs. Katharine Hannah, BA ACA *2005;* Concateno PLC, 92 Milton Park, ABINGDON, OXFORDSHIRE, OX14 4RY.
WRIGHT, Mrs. Kathryn Jane, MSc BA ACA *2003;* Axa Life, PO Box 1810, BRISTOL, BS99 5SN.
WRIGHT, Mrs. Katie, BSocSc ACA *1997;* Reconnaissance International Ltd Unit 4, Windmill Business Village Brooklands Close, SUNBURY-ON-THAMES, TW16 7DY.
WRIGHT, Mrs. Katie, BSc ACA *2007;* 45 The Circuit, WILMSLOW, CHESHIRE, SK9 6DA.
WRIGHT, Mrs. Kelly Frances, ACA *2001;* 53 Churchfields, Hethersett, NORWICH, NR9 3PH.
•①**WRIGHT, Mr. Kenneth John, FCA CTA MAE QDR FABRP** *1968;* Wright Associates, First Floor, 56-57 High Street, STOURBRIDGE, WEST MIDLANDS, DY8 1DE.
•**WRIGHT, Mr. Kevin John, BA ACA** *1990;* Leftley Rowe & Company, The Heights, 59-65 Lowlands Road, HARROW, MIDDLESEX, HA1 3AW. See also Mountsides Limited
WRIGHT, Mr. Kevin Trevor, FCA *1984;* 65 Sandown Drive, CHIPPENHAM, SN14 0YA.
WRIGHT, Mr. Kim Alexander, BSc FCA *1981;* Chandlers, Farnham Royal, SLOUGH, BUCKINGHAMSHIRE, SL2 3EF.
WRIGHT, Mrs. Kirsten Mhairi, BA(Hons) ACA *2003;* 19 Coates Close, Brighton Hill, BASINGSTOKE, RG22 4EE.
•**WRIGHT, Mr. Leo William Paul, ACA** *1981;* Wright & Co, 51 Oxhey Avenue, WATFORD, WD19 4HB.
•**WRIGHT, Mr. Malcolm John, FCA** *1976;* (Tax Fac), Elpizo Limited, 13 Village Road, Bebington, WIRRAL, MERSEYSIDE, CH63 8PP.
WRIGHT, Mrs. Margaret Patricia, BA ACA *1988;* Edward Cheshire & Co Ltd, 18 Chesford Grange, WARRINGTON, WA1 4RQ.
WRIGHT, Miss. Maria-Pia, ACA *2009;* 23 Russet Close, BEDFORD, BEDFORDSHIRE, MK41 7GB.
WRIGHT, Mr. Mark Anthony, BSc ACA *2002;* Lombard Asset Finance Group, 3 Princess Way, REDHILL, RH1 1NP.
WRIGHT, Mr. Mark Anthony, BSc FCA *1985;* 17 Milverton Road, Knowle, SOLIHULL, B93 0HX.
WRIGHT, Mr. Mark Bleakley, BSc(Hons) ACA *2003;* Garden Cottage The Street, Shackleford, GODALMING, GU8 6AH.
WRIGHT, Mr. Martin, BSc FCA *1978;* The Lodge, Purton Stoke, SWINDON, SN5 4JF.
WRIGHT, Mr. Martin Anthony, MA FCA *1985;* 27 Oatlands Drive, HARROGATE, HG2 8JT.
WRIGHT, Mr. Martin Charles, FCA *1970;* Sea Glympse, 6 Western Avenue, FELIXSTOWE, IP11 9SB.
WRIGHT, Mr. Martin David, FCA *1964;* 24 Fairlands Road, SALE, CHESHIRE, M33 4AY.
WRIGHT, Mr. Martin Ian, BSc ACA *1987;* 8 Shetland, Braemar Heights 7 Wai Tsui Crescent, Braemar Hill, NORTH POINT, HONG KONG ISLAND, HONG KONG SAR.
•**WRIGHT, Mr. Martin James, FCA** *1972;* MW Martin J Wright, Grove House, Pond Hall Road, Hadleigh, IPSWICH, SUFFOLK IP7 5PQ.
•**WRIGHT, Mr. Martin James, BA ACA** *1993;* Critchleys LLP, Greyfriars Court, Paradise Square, OXFORD, OX1 1BE.
•**WRIGHT, Mr. Martin John, FCA MAE** *1982;* ECL Howard Watson Smith LLP, E C L House, Lake Street, LEIGHTON BUZZARD, BEDFORDSHIRE, LU7 1RT.
WRIGHT, Mr. Martin John, BSc ACA *1991;* Melville Cottage, 10 Melville Road, BIRMINGHAM, B16 9LN.
WRIGHT, Mr. Martin Paul, BSc ACA *1997;* Northall Lodge, Northall Green, DEREHAM, NORFOLK, NR20 4BA.
•**WRIGHT, Mr. Matthew George, BA ACA** *1990;* Matthew Wright, 701-137 West 17th Street, NORTH VANCOUVER V7M 1 V5, BC, CANADA.
WRIGHT, Mr. Matthew Lee, BA ACA *1999;* 45 Norton Road, Knowle, BRISTOL, BS4 2EZ.
•**WRIGHT, Mr. Matthew William, FCA** *1993;* Sayers Butterworth LLP, 3rd Floor, 12 Gough Square, LONDON, EC4A 3DW.
WRIGHT, Miss. Melanie Frances, ACA *2004;* with Lovewell Blake LLP, 89 Bridge Road, Oulton Broad, LOWESTOFT, SUFFOLK, NR32 3LN.

WRIGHT, Mr. Michael Arthur, FCA *1954;* Stillwater, 69 Orchard Road, Melbourn, ROYSTON, SG8 6BB. (Life Member)
WRIGHT, Mr. Michael Charles, ACA *1984;* Church Farm House, Ellesborough Road, Little Kimble, AYLESBURY, HP17 0XR.
WRIGHT, Mr. Michael David, ACA *1990;* 29 Hawkhurst Way, Cooden, BEXHILL-ON-SEA, TN39 3SG.
•**WRIGHT, Mr. Michael Gordon, FCA FInstD** *1966;* MG Wright FCA FInstD, 22 Charlton Close, Charlton Kings, CHELTENHAM, GLOUCESTERSHIRE, GL53 8DJ.
•**WRIGHT, Mr. Michael James, FCA** *1992;* Littlestone Martin Glenton, 73 Wimpole Street, LONDON, W1G 8AZ.
WRIGHT, Mr. Michael Jiro Dales, MSci ACA *2009;* 34 St. David's Drive, Englefield Green, EGHAM, SURREY, TW20 0BA.
WRIGHT, Mr. Michael John, BA ACA *1993;* Ernst And Young, Ernst & Young Centre, 680 George Street, SYDNEY, NSW 2000, AUSTRALIA.
WRIGHT, Mr. Michael John, FCA *1962;* 4 Longwood Drive, Roehampton, LONDON, SW15 5DL.
•**WRIGHT, Mr. Michael Leslie, FCA** *1969;* Kavanagh Knight & Co. Ltd, Chaldean House, 7 Chandos Close, CHESTER, CH4 7BJ.
WRIGHT, Mr. Neil Andrew, BA ACA *1986;* (Tax Fac), 6 Stourton Close, Fivewell Lodge, Wilby Way, WELLINGBOROUGH, NN8 2LG.
•**WRIGHT, Mr. Neil Joseph, FCA** *1975;* Neil Wright & Co, 166 Linacre Road, Litherland, LIVERPOOL, L21 8JU.
WRIGHT, Mr. Nicholas Anthony, BSc FCA *1980;* 3 Cartland Road, Kings Heath, BIRMINGHAM, B14 7NS.
WRIGHT, Mr. Nicholas David, BA FCA *1982;* 8 West Riding, Tewin Wood, WELWYN, HERTFORDSHIRE, AL6 0PD.
WRIGHT, Mr. Nicholas Edward Weatherley, FCA *1964;* 7 Parthenia Road, LONDON, SW6 4BD.
WRIGHT, Mr. Nicholas James, BA(Hons) ACA *2001;* Hideaway House, Croquet Gardens, Wivenhoe, COLCHESTER, CO7 9PQ.
WRIGHT, Mr. Nicholas John, BSc FCA *1991;* Conifers, Bristol Road, West Harptree, BRISTOL, BS40 6HG.
WRIGHT, Mr. Nicholas Kenneth, BA FCA *1983;* Andrews & partners Limited, The Clockhouse, Bath Hill, Keynsham, BRISTOL, BS31 1HL.
WRIGHT, Mr. Nicholas Mark, BSc ACA *1998;* 13 Eric Avenue, Emmer Green, READING, RG4 8QU.
WRIGHT, Mr. Nick, BSc ACA *1995;* 6 Rievaulx Avenue, KNARESBOROUGH, NORTH YORKSHIRE, HG5 8LD.
•**WRIGHT, Mrs. Nicola, BA(Hons) ACA** *2001;* with PricewaterhouseCoopers LLP, 89 Sandyford Road, NEWCASTLE UPON TYNE, NE1 8HW.
WRIGHT, Miss. Nicola, BSc ACA *2007;* with Ernst & Young LLP, 100 Barbirolli Square, MANCHESTER, M2 3EY.
WRIGHT, Mrs. Nicola Ann, BSc ACA *1999;* Unit 16, 78A Old Pittwater Road, BROOKVALE, NSW 2100, AUSTRALIA.
WRIGHT, Mr. Nigel Anthony, BSc ACA *1987;* with Nigel Wright Consultancy Ltd, Lloyds Court, 78 Grey Street, NEWCASTLE UPON TYNE, NE1 6AF.
•**WRIGHT, Mr. Nigel Charles Comstive, FCA** *1973;* Nigel Wright Corporate Finance, 11 Danemere Street, LONDON, SW15 1LT.
WRIGHT, Mr. Nigel David, BA ACA *1988;* 7 Walsingham Place, LONDON, SW4 9RR.
WRIGHT, Mr. Nigel John, BSc ACA *1989;* 24 Kopiko Road, TITIRANGI 0604, NEW ZEALAND.
WRIGHT, Mr. Nigel John, FCA *1976;* 19 The Manor, Badgers Holt Blackhurst Lane, TUNBRIDGE WELLS, TN2 3ET.
•**WRIGHT, Mr. Nigel John, BSc FCA** *1992;* with RSM Tenon Audit Limited, Cedar House, Sandbrook Business Park Sandbrook Way, ROCHDALE, LANCASHIRE, OL11 1LQ.
WRIGHT, Mr. Nigel Kevin, BEng ACA *1996;* 31 Hitherwood Drive, LONDON, SE19 1XA.
WRIGHT, Mr. Norman Gainsford, FCA *1951;* 6 Walkers Road, Longwick, PRINCES RISBOROUGH, BUCKINGHAMSHIRE, HP27 9SS. (Life Member)
WRIGHT, Mr. Oliver Gerard, BA ACA *1996;* Five Corporate Finance LLP, The Innovation Centre, Cranfield Technology Park, Cranfield, BEDFORD, BEDFORDSHIRE MK43 0BT.
WRIGHT, Mr. Oliver Stuart, BA ACA *2007;* with PricewaterhouseCoopers LLP, 101 Barbirolli Square, Lower Mosley Street, MANCHESTER, M2 3PW.
WRIGHT, Mrs. Patricia, LLB FCA *1960;* 26 Westfield Road, Wheatley, OXFORD, OX33 1NG. (Life Member)
•**WRIGHT, Mr. Patrick Charles, BSc FCA** *1980;* RSM Tenon Audit Limited, Vantage, Victoria Street, BASINGSTOKE, HAMPSHIRE, RG21 3BT. See also Tenon Audit Limited
WRIGHT, Mr. Paul, ACA *2011;* 44 Sherwood Road, Crosby, LIVERPOOL, L23 7UF.
WRIGHT, Mr. Paul David, BSc ACA *1981;* 15 Tanner Avenue, CARLTON, NSW 2218, AUSTRALIA.
•**WRIGHT, Mr. Paul Edward Henry, ACA DChA** *1989;* Sheen Stickland LLP, 7 East Pallant, CHICHESTER, WEST SUSSEX, PO19 1TR.
•**WRIGHT, Mr. Paul James, LLB ACA** *2002;* Allens Accountants Limited, 123 Wellington Road South, STOCKPORT, SK1 3TH.
•**WRIGHT, Mr. Paul Jonathan, BA ACA** *2008;* Swallow Associates (Stokesley) Limited, Commercial House, 10 Bridge Road, Stokesley, MIDDLESBROUGH, CLEVELAND TS9 5AA.
WRIGHT, Mr. Paul Keith, BA FCA *1981;* 73 York Avenue, East Sheen, LONDON, SW14 7LQ.
WRIGHT, Mr. Paul Michael, BSc ACA *1994;* Andrew Weir Shipping Ltd Dexter House, 2 Royal Mint Court, LONDON, EC3N 4XX.
WRIGHT, Mr. Paul Stephen, ACA *1984;* 1 Lingfield Grange, Streetly, SUTTON COLDFIELD, WEST MIDLANDS, B74 3GB.
WRIGHT, Mr. Paul Timothy, FCA *1982;* Stonescot, 83 Janes Lane, BURGESS HILL, RH15 0QP.
WRIGHT, Mr. Paul Vernon, MA FCA *1978;* Towry Ltd Towry House, Western Road, BRACKNELL, RG12 1TL.
WRIGHT, Mr. Peter, BA ACA *1982;* 25 Meadow Park Crescent, Stanningley, PUDSEY, WEST YORKSHIRE, LS28 7TN.
•**WRIGHT, Mr. Peter, BSc ACA** *1990;* Na Hrebenech II, 1163/3B, 147 00 PRAGUE, CZECH REPUBLIC.
WRIGHT, Mr. Peter Giles, MA ACA *1990;* 73 Victoria Road, Mortimer, READING, RG7 3SL.
•**WRIGHT, Mr. Peter Ian, BSc FCA** *1982;* HW, 7-11 Station Road, READING, BERKSHIRE, RG1 1LG. See also Haines Watts
WRIGHT, Mr. Peter James, FCA *1980;* 10 Hemingford Road, COVENTRY, CV2 2RE.
WRIGHT, Mr. Peter Kenneth, FCA *1976;* 322 Main Western Road, NORTH TAMBORINE, QLD 4272, AUSTRALIA.
WRIGHT, Mr. Peter Malcolm Vanner, BSc ACA *1979;* Ley Farm, Bere Ferrers, YELVERTON, DEVON, PL20 7JF.
WRIGHT, Mr. Philip, BA ACA *1986;* 5 Towers Avenue, Jesmond, NEWCASTLE UPON TYNE, NE2 3QE.
WRIGHT, Mr. Philip, BSc(Hons) ACA *2010;* Apartment, 12 Ribble Gardens, FAREHAM, HAMPSHIRE, PO16 8FJ.
WRIGHT, Mr. Philip David, BSc ACA *1994;* 51 Easedale Avenue, Melton Park Gosforth, NEWCASTLE UPON TYNE, NE3 5TA.
•**WRIGHT, Mr. Philip Duncan, MA ACA** *1979;* PricewaterhouseCoopers LLP, 1 Embankment Place, LONDON, WC2N 6RH. See also PricewaterhouseCoopers
WRIGHT, Mr. Philip James, ACA *2005;* 88 Trusley Brook, Hilton, DERBY, DE65 5LA.
WRIGHT, Mr. Philip James Kenneth, BSc ACA *1987;* 3 Pond Road, Horsford, NORWICH, NR10 3SW.
WRIGHT, Mr. Philip John, BSc ACA *1993;* 29 Garrett Close, Kingsclere, NEWBURY, RG20 5SD.
•**WRIGHT, Mr. Philip John, BSc ACA** *1992;* Russell & Bromley Ltd, 24-34 Farwig Lane, BROMLEY, BR1 3RB.
WRIGHT, Mr. Philip Michael, MSc DIC ACA *1989;* 8 Sorbie Close, WEYBRIDGE, KT13 0TP.
WRIGHT, Mrs. Philippa Jane, BSc ACA *1990;* Hundred House, Cornard Tye, SUDBURY, CO10 0QA.
WRIGHT, Miss. Philippa Jane, BA ACA *2006;* Top Floor Flat 4 Worcester Gardens, LONDON, SW11 6LR.
WRIGHT, Mr. Phillip Charles, FCA *1973;* Brooklands, 49 Chester Road, CHIGWELL, IG7 6AN.
WRIGHT, Mr. Piers Waite, MEng ACA *2005;* 1 Richmond Court, Richmond Dale, BRISTOL, BS8 2UX.
WRIGHT, Miss. Rachel, BA(Hons) ACA *2010;* 7 Dalmorton Road, WALLASEY, MERSEYSIDE, CH45 1LE.
WRIGHT, Miss. Rachel Louise, ACA *2009;* Saul Fairholm & Co, 12 Tentercroft Street, LINCOLN, LN5 7DB.
WRIGHT, Mr. Richard Arthur Frederick, BA FCA *1977;* Church House Farm, Dog Lane, Nether Whitacre, Coleshill, BIRMINGHAM, B46 2DT. (Life Member)
WRIGHT, Mr. Richard David, MA ACA *1992;* 39c The Common, Langley Burrell, CHIPPENHAM, WILTSHIRE, SN15 4LQ.
WRIGHT, Mr. Richard Hilton, BA ACA *1987;* 14 The Hawthorns, Cam, DURSLEY, GLOUCESTERSHIRE, GL11 5LJ.
WRIGHT, Mr. Richard Lewis, FCA *1958;* 20 Hillstead Court, Cliddesden Road, BASINGSTOKE, HAMPSHIRE, RG21 3PT. (Life Member)
WRIGHT, Mr. Rikki Zeus Paul, BSc ACA *2001;* 249 River Side Drive, OAKVILLE L6K 3N1, ON, CANADA.
WRIGHT, Mr. Robert David, BSc ACA *1981;* Midhurst, 22 Beechwood Avenue, WEYBRIDGE, SURREY, KT13 9TB.
WRIGHT, Mr. Robert George, FCA *1952;* 10 Early Bank, STALYBRIDGE, SK15 2RU. (Life Member)
WRIGHT, Mr. Robert Stephen, BSc FCA *1975;* 11 Galtres Road, NORTHALLERTON, NORTH YORKSHIRE, DL6 1QN.
WRIGHT, Mr. Robin Edward, FCA *1969;* Cottage Farm, Sandford Orcas, SHERBORNE, DORSET, DT9 4RU. (Life Member)
WRIGHT, Mr. Robin Henry, FCA *1958;* Flat 14, Lipton Court, 196 Chase Side, Southgate, LONDON, N14 5HG. (Life Member)
WRIGHT, Mr. Robin James Morrison, BA ACA *1991;* 7 Buckland Gate, Wexham, SLOUGH, SL3 6LS.
•**WRIGHT, Mr. Roderick Edmund, BSc FCA DChA** *1975;* (Tax Fac), Edmund Wright & Co, 1 Allum Way, Totteridge, LONDON, N20 9QL.
WRIGHT, Mr. Rollo Andrew Johnstone, BA ACA *2003;* GCP, 53/54 Grosvenor Street, LONDON, W1K 3HU.
WRIGHT, Mrs. Rowena, BSc ACA *1989;* 17 Westminster Croft, BRACKLEY, NN13 7ED.
WRIGHT, Mr. Russell James Edwards, BSc ACA *1991;* 4/17 Pittwater Road, MANLY, NSW 2095, AUSTRALIA.
WRIGHT, Miss. Samantha, ACA *2008;* 10 Hereward Avenue, BIRCHINGTON, KENT, CT7 9LY.
WRIGHT, Mrs. Samantha Joy, BSc ACA *1996;* Southwood, 14 Newbridge Hill, BATH, BA1 3PU.
WRIGHT, Miss. Sarah Abigail, BSc ACA *2005;* 34 Jubilee Road, Knowle, BRISTOL, BS4 2LP.
WRIGHT, Mrs. Sarah Anne, BA ACA *1995;* 10 Sandale Close, Gamston, NOTTINGHAM, NG2 6QG.
WRIGHT, Mrs. Sarah Louise, BSc ACA *1992;* Beiersdorf UK Ltd Unit 2010, Solihull Parkway Birmingham Business Park, BIRMINGHAM, B37 7YS.
WRIGHT, Mrs. Sarah Lucy, BA ACA *1989;* Bennetts, Donhead St. Mary, SHAFTESBURY, DORSET, SP7 9DJ.
WRIGHT, Miss. Sarah Nicola Janet, MA ACA *1990;* 7 Ringwood Avenue, LONDON, N2 9NT.
WRIGHT, Mr. Simon, BSc ACA *2011;* 11 / 77 West Esplanade, MANLY, NSW 2095, AUSTRALIA.
WRIGHT, Mr. Simon Jonathan, BSc FCA *1991;* 3 Ghyll Farm, Mill Lane, Bradley, KEIGHLEY, WEST YORKSHIRE, BD20 9EE.
•**WRIGHT, Mr. Spencer Geoffrey, BSc ACA CF** *1996;* Dains LLP, Unit 306, Third Floor, Fort Dunlop, Fort Parkway, BIRMINGHAM B24 9FD.
WRIGHT, Miss. Stefanie, ACA *2006;* 28 Fellows Road, Beeston, NOTTINGHAM, NG9 1AQ.
WRIGHT, Mrs. Stephanie Jane, BSc FCA DChA *1978;* with Menzies LLP, Victoria House, 50-58 Victoria Road, FARNBOROUGH, HAMPSHIRE, GU14 7PG.
WRIGHT, Mr. Stephen, MA MPhil BA(Hons) ACA *2005;* with National Audit Office, 157-197 Buckingham Palace Road, Victoria, LONDON, SW1W 9SP.
WRIGHT, Mr. Stephen, ACA *2001;* 18 Roseberry Gardens, ORPINGTON, KENT, BR6 9QE.
WRIGHT, Mr. Stephen Ayrton, FCA *1971;* Fourways, 589 Bradford Road, Bradley Bar, HUDDERSFIELD, HD2 2LA.
WRIGHT, Mr. Stephen David, BSc ACA *1989;* 10 The Pines, SUNBURY-ON-THAMES, TW16 6HT.
WRIGHT, Mr. Stephen Dennis, BA ACA *1982;* Gastons, 1 Beaconsfield Road, Claygate, ESHER, KT10 0PN.
WRIGHT, Mr. Stephen Noble, BPhil FCA *1965;* 207 Ballestier Road, 17-02 Ballestier Towers, SINGAPORE S329683, SINGAPORE.
WRIGHT, Mr. Stephen Paul, FCA *1982;* 12 East Chapel, Tattenhoe, MILTON KEYNES, MK4 3AR.
WRIGHT, Mr. Stephen William, FCA *1965;* 22 Kelsey Way, BECKENHAM, KENT, BR3 3LL.
WRIGHT, Mr. Steven Antony, BA ACA *2005;* 48 Paradise Road, Writtle, CHELMSFORD, CM1 3HP.
WRIGHT, Mr. Stewart Henry, BSc ACA *1980;* 26 Lincoln Avenue, Southgate, LONDON, N14 7LG.
WRIGHT, Mr. Stewart William, BA FCA *1973;* 7 Charterhouse Close, Nailsea, BRISTOL, BS48 4PU.
WRIGHT, Mr. Stuart Andrew, BSc ACA *1997;* GMO WMR Level 40, H S B C, 8-16 Canada Square, LONDON, E14 5HQ.
WRIGHT, Mr. Stuart Anthony, BEng ACA *2006;* Flat 3, 8 St. Marys Walk, HARROGATE, NORTH YORKSHIRE, HG2 0LW.
•**WRIGHT, Mr. Stuart John, BAcc FCA** *2000;* Barnbrook Sinclair Limited, 1 High Street, Knaphill, WOKING, SURREY, GU21 2PG. See also The Barnbrook Sinclair Partnership LLP
WRIGHT, Mr. Stuart Laurence, BA FCA *1992;* 3 Moore Close, Appleby Magna, SWADLINCOTE, DE12 7AT.
•**WRIGHT, Mr. Stuart Neil Harold, BSc ACA** *1991;* Stuart Wright, 79 Churchill Road, THETFORD, IP24 2JZ.
WRIGHT, Mrs. Tara Marie, BA ACA *1998;* 10 Engadine Street, LONDON, SW18 5BH.
WRIGHT, Mr. Thomas Charles Alexanderson, ACA *2009;* Flat A, 44 Devonshire Street, LONDON, W1G 7AL.
WRIGHT, Mr. Thomas Desmond, BA FCA *1975;* 140 Kings Hall Road, BECKENHAM, BR3 1LN.
WRIGHT, Mr. Timothy, BSc FCA *1974;* West Headley Mount, Headley, BORDON, GU35 8AG.
WRIGHT, Mr. Timothy Charles Vipan, BSc ACA *1980;* 10 Marlborough Place, ST.IVES 2075, NSW 2075, AUSTRALIA.
WRIGHT, Mr. Timothy Michael, BSc FCA *1986;* 4 Baldwin Crescent, Merrow Park, GUILDFORD, GU4 7XW.
•**WRIGHT, Mr. Timothy Michael, FCA** *1974;* AIMS - Tim Wright, 3 Holly Orchard, STRATFORD-UPON-AVON, WARWICKSHIRE, CV37 6RJ.
•**WRIGHT, Mr. Timothy Peter, FCA** *1987;* (Tax Fac), 396 Elphin, LAIRG, SUTHERLAND, IV27 4HH.
WRIGHT, Mr. Timothy Russell, MA ACA *2003;* 58 Front Street, Lockington, DRIFFIELD, NORTH HUMBERSIDE, YO25 9SH.
•**WRIGHT, Mr. Tobias Christopher Francis, BA FCA** *1996;* Deloitte LLP, Mountbatten House, 1 Grosvenor Square, SOUTHAMPTON, SO15 2BZ. See also Deloitte & Touche LLP
WRIGHT, Mrs. Tracey Deanne, BSc ACA *1993;* 43 Colton Road, Shrivenham, SWINDON, SN6 8AZ.
•**WRIGHT, Mr. Trevor, FCA** *1967;* Trevor Wright, 2 Wayside Drive, Oadby, LEICESTER, LE2 4NU.
WRIGHT, Miss. Vanessa Louise, ACA *2000;* 3 Carlton Drive, Guiseley, LEEDS, LS20 9NQ.
WRIGHT, Miss. Victoria, BBA ACA *2006;* 16 Town Lane, Much Hoole, PRESTON, PR4 4GJ.
WRIGHT, Mrs. Victoria Irene, BA(Hons) ACA *2001;* Total Produce Enterprise Way, Pinchbeck, SPALDING, LINCOLNSHIRE, PE11 3YR.
WRIGHT, Mrs. Vivienne Louise Halsey, BSc ACA CTA *2005;* (Tax Fac), The Manor House, Main Street, Harborough Magna, RUGBY, WARWICKSHIRE, CV23 0HS.
WRIGHT, Mr. Walter Innes, BSc FCA *1992;* Bennetts, Donhead St. Mary, SHAFTESBURY, SP7 9DJ.
WRIGHT, Miss. Wendy Joy, BA ACA *1990;* 79 High Street, Burgh Le Marsh, SKEGNESS, PE24 5JZ.
•①**WRIGHT, Mr. William, BSocSc ACA** *2003;* with KPMG LLP, One Snowhill, Snow Hill Queensway, BIRMINGHAM, B4 6GN.
WRIGHT, Mr. William Brian, BA FCA *1955;* 5 Earlscliffe Court, Bowdon, ALTRINCHAM, WA14 2BX. (Life Member)
WRIGHT, Mr. William Charlton, ACA *2009;* Apartment 9, 1 High Street, Shirley, SOLIHULL, WEST MIDLANDS, B90 1HA.
WRIGHT, Mr. William James, BA FCA *1985;* 27 Carmen Crescent, Holton Le Clay, GRIMSBY, DN36 5DD.
WRIGHT, Mr. William Mansell, FCA *1975;* Chemin du Tournesol 10, 1131 TOLOCHENAZ, SWITZERLAND.
WRIGHT-WASTELL, Mr. James, BA ACA *2005;* 6 Brookside, WOKINGHAM, BERKSHIRE, RG41 2SU.
WRIGHTMAN, Mr. Jacob, BA(Hons) ACA *2011;* 57 Preston Road, BRIGHTON, BN1 4QE.
•**WRIGHTON, Mr. Christopher Arthur, FCA** *1983;* (Tax Fac), Harold Sharp, Holland House, 1-5 Oakfield, SALE, M33 6TT.
WRIGHTON, Mr. Nicholas Richard, BA ACA *1999;* 2 Fairford Close, HAYWARDS HEATH, RH16 3EF.
WRIGHTSON, Mr. Brian Alfred, FCA *1963;* 5 Purley Rise, PURLEY, SURREY, CR8 3AU. (Life Member)
WRIGHTSON, Mr. David George, ACA *1988;* Amari Metals Ltd, 25 High Street, COBHAM, KT11 3DH.

WRIGHTSON, Mr. David Wilmot, BSc FCA *1965;* 194 Queen Alexandra Road, SUNDERLAND, SR3 1XQ.
WRIGHTSON, Mrs. Fiona Isabel, MA ACA *1988;* 12 Old Lane, Bramhope, LEEDS, LS16 9AZ.
•**WRIGHTSON, Mr. Ian Geoffrey, BA FCA** *1996;* Mazars LLP, Mazars House, Gelderd Road, Gildersome, LEEDS, LS27 7JN.
WRIGHTSON, Mr. James Anthony, BA ACA *1994;* 30 Broomfield Road, Heaton Moor, STOCKPORT, SK4 4ND.
WRIGLEY, Miss. Amy Christine Lawson, BA FCA *1955;* 206 Upper Road, Kennington, OXFORD, OX1 5LR. (Life Member)
WRIGLEY, Mrs. Diana Meriel, BA ACA *1992;* 17 West Common Way, HARPENDEN, HERTFORDSHIRE, AL5 2LH.
WRIGLEY, Mr. Edmund James Borgen, MA ACA *1992;* 17 West Common Way, HARPENDEN, HERTFORDSHIRE, AL5 2LH.
•**WRIGLEY, Mrs. Gillian Audrey, BSc ACA** *1994;* with RSM Tenon Limited, York House, 20 York Street, MANCHESTER, M2 3BB.
WRIGLEY, Mr. Henry, BA ACA *2006;* with BDO LLP, 55 Baker Street, LONDON, W1U 7EU.
WRIGLEY, Mr. Jeremy Charles, BSc ACA *1990;* European Credit Management Ltd, 34 Grosvenor Street, LONDON, W1K 4QU.
WRIGLEY, Miss. Jill Maxine, BA FCA *1993;* 6 Harry Rowley Close, MANCHESTER, M22 1HY.
WRIGLEY, Mr. John Gordon, FCA *1958;* Belmont, Church Road, Earsham, BUNGAY, NR35 2TL. (Life Member)
WRIGLEY, Mr. Jonathan, FCA *1974;* National Trust, Eastleigh Court, Bishopstrow, WARMINSTER, WILTSHIRE, BA12 9HW.
WRIGLEY, Mr. Jonathan George, BA ACA CTA *1995;* L'Ancienne Maison La Route de Trodez, St. Ouen, JERSEY, JE3 2GA.
WRIGLEY, Miss. Lynsey Rosemary, ACA *2009;* Flat 8 Lymington Mansions, Lymington Road, LONDON, NW6 1SF.
WRIGLEY, Mr. Martin Paul, FCA *1977;* 10 Frogmore Avenue, HYDE, CHESHIRE, SK14 5JE.
WRIGLEY, Mr. Miles St John, FCA *1970;* Tythe Cottage, 8-9 Teindhillgreen, DUNS, BERWICKSHIRE, TD11 3DX.
WRIGLEY, Mr. Nicholas Donald, BA(Hons) ACA *2004;* 12 The Pound, Almondsbury, BRISTOL, BS32 4EG.
WRIGLEY, Mr. Nicholas Hugh Tremayne, ACA *1979;* N.M. Rothschild & Sons Ltd., New Court, St.Swithins Lane, LONDON, EC4P 4DU.
WRIGLEY, Mr. Philip Anderson, FCA CTA *1969;* Apartment 9, City Point, Standard Hill, NOTTINGHAM, NG1 6FX. (Life Member)
WRIGLEY, Miss. Sarah Zoe, LLB ACA *2003;* with Ernst & Young LLP, 1 More London Place, LONDON, SE1 2AF.
WRIGLEY, Mr. Thomas James Borgen, FCA *1960;* The Old Malt House, St. Peter Street, MARLOW, SL7 1NQ. (Life Member)
WRINCH, Mr. Ronald Peter, BA FCA *1954;* Brook Farm, Hough Lane, ALDERLEY EDGE, SK9 7JD. (Life Member)
•**WRITER, Mrs. Anna Pauline, BSc ACA** *1995;* Gyro Limited, Tarn House, 58 Kelsey Lane, BECKENHAM, KENT, BR3 3NE.
WRIXON, Mr. Bernard, FCA *1971;* 4a Lakeway Street, Claremont, PERTH, WA 6010, AUSTRALIA.
WRIXON, Mr. Peter, FCA *1970;* 6 Holcombe Drive, Paraparaumu Beach, WELLINGTON 5032, NEW ZEALAND. (Life Member)
WROE, Mrs. Helen Margaret, BA ACA *1984;* Foxwell, 18 Hounds Close, Chipping Sodbury, BRISTOL, BS37 6EG.
•**WROE, Mr. Ian Malcolm, BSc ACA** *1979;* (Tax Fac), Crossley & Davis, 348-350 Lytham Road, BLACKPOOL, FY4 1DW. See also Campbell Crossley & Davis
WROE, Mr. John Vincent, BSc FCA *1983;* BT Group plc, BT Centre, 81 Newgate Street, LONDON, EC1A 7AJ.
WROE, Mrs. Marie Geraldine Monica, BSc ACA *1988;* 1 Robins Orchard, Chalfont St. Peter, GERRARDS CROSS, SL9 0HQ.
WROE, Mr. Michael John, BSc FCA *1992;* Just Eat.Co.UK Ltd Grosvenor House, 1 High Street, EDGWARE, MIDDLESEX, HA8 7TA.
WU, Ms. Alice Sel-Yen, BSc ACA *1991;* 14 Fowey Close, LONDON, E1W 2JP.
WU, Mr. Anthony Ting-Yuk, FCA *1979;* with Ernst & Young, 18/F, Two International Finance Centre, 8 Finance Street, CENTRAL, HONG KONG ISLAND HONG KONG SAR.
WU, Mr. Charles Kok Seng, ACA *1980;* Suite 5 365 High Road, PARKWOOD, WA 6147, AUSTRALIA.
WU, Mr. Chung Ming, ACA *2006;* Deloitte Touche Tohmatsu, 35/F One Pacific Place, 88 Queensway, CENTRAL, HONG KONG ISLAND, HONG KONG SAR.
WU, Miss. Dan, MPhil ACA *2007;* 2 Observatory Mews, LONDON, E14 3AZ.
WU, Mr. Geoffrey Ho Yin, ACA *2010;* Flat 2312 23/F Block P, Kornhill, QUARRY BAY, HONG KONG SAR.
WU, Mr. Ho Wai, ACA *2008;* Flat G 17/F Tower 8, Banyan Garden, 863 Lai Chi Kok Road, CHEUNG SHA WAN, HONG KONG SAR.
WU, Mr. Hsu Lung, BA ACA *1992;* 111 Sai Yee Street, 2nd Floor, MONG KOK, KOWLOON, HONG KONG SAR.
WU, Ms. Hui Hsuan, MA BSc ACA *2011;* Flat 29 Elektron Tower, 12 Blackwall Way, LONDON, E14 9GB.
WU, Mrs. Jane Louise, LLB ACA *1999;* 9 Church Hams, Finchampstead, WOKINGHAM, BERKSHIRE, RG40 4XF.
WU, Mr. Julian Vardy, BA(Hons) ACA ACMA *1994;* PTS Consulting Group, #37-00 Singapore Land Tower, 50 Raffles Place, SINGAPORE 048623, SINGAPORE.
WU, Ms. Ka Lai Cary, ACA *2008;* with Ernst & Young, 18/F, Two International Finance Centre, 8 Finance Street, CENTRAL, HONG KONG ISLAND HONG KONG SAR.
WU, Ms. Kit Man Athena, ACA *2005;* 15A Block 10, Tsuen King Garden, TSUEN WAN, NEW TERRITORIES, HONG KONG SAR.
WU, Mrs. Li Qun, ACA *2008;* Petrochina Company Ltd, Finance Department D2009, 9 Dongzhimen North Street, Dongcheng District, BEIJING 100007, CHINA.
WU, Mr. Lucian Ho Lap, BSc ACA *1991;* A8, 4th Floor, Block A, Carolina Gardens, 20-26 Coombe Road, The Peak ADMIRALTY HONG KONG ISLAND HONG KONG SAR.
WU, Ms. Mei, ACA *2011;* 39 Shipwright Road, LONDON, SE16 6QA.
•**WU, Miss. Melissa Mao Chin, BCom FCA** *1992;* KPMG, 8/F Prince's Building, 10 Chater Road, CENTRAL, HONG KONG ISLAND, HONG KONG SAR.
WU, Mr. Mingfeng, ACA *2011;* Room 506 No.24, 1400 Daduhe Road, Puto Area, SHANGHAI 200333, CHINA.
WU, Mr. Suk Chuen, ACA *2008;* Room 1206 Choi Mui House, Choi Ming Court, TSEUNG KWAN O, NEW TERRITORIES, HONG KONG SAR.
WU, Mr. Sze Yin, ACA *2006;* S.Y. Yu, Unit 1007 10/F, Focal Industrial Building, 21 Man Lok Street, HUNG HOM, KOWLOON HONG KONG SAR.
WU, Mr. Wai On, ACA *2007;* c/o CMT 12/F China Taiping Tower Phase 2 8 Sunning Road, CAUSEWAY BAY, HONG KONG SAR.
WU, Ms. Wing Kam Kennis, ACA *2008;* Flat B 16/F Block 2, Phoenix Court, 39 Kennedy Road, WAN CHAI, HONG KONG ISLAND, HONG KONG SAR.
WU, Mr. Yanson, BSc ACA *2002;* Houlihan Lokey Howard & Zukin (UK) Ltd, 83 Pall Mall, LONDON, SW1Y 5ES.
WU, Mr. Yi, BSc ACA *2009;* Apartment 17, Somerville Point, 305 Rotherhithe Street, LONDON, SE16 5EQ.
WU, Ms. Yin Fong, ACA *2008;* with Ernst & Young, 18/F, Two International Finance Centre, 8 Finance Street, CENTRAL, HONG KONG ISLAND HONG KONG SAR.
WU, Mr. Zhedong, ACA *2011;* Zhedong Wu c/o Barclays Capital, 60B Orchard Road #10-00, The Atrium@Orchard, SINGAPORE 238891, SINGAPORE.
•**WULFF, Mrs. Andrea Sarah, BSc FCA** *1990;* Moore Stephens (South) LLP, City Gates, 2-4 Southgate, CHICHESTER, WEST SUSSEX, PO19 8DJ. See also Moore Secretaries Limited
WULFSOHN, Mr. Harry Joshua, BSc ACA *1998;* 180 Great Portland Street, LONDON, W1W 5QZ.
WUN, Mr. Kwok Leung, ACA *2007;* Flat F 27 Floor, Nam Fung Sun Chueng, 38 Greig Road, QUARRY BAY, HONG KONG SAR.
WUNDRAM, Miss. Julia Magdalena, BA(Hons) ACA *2003;* 50 St. Leonards Drive, Timperley, ALTRINCHAM, CHESHIRE, WA15 7RS.
WUT, Ms. Ivy Oi Fan, ACA *2006;* Room 2904 29/F, Park Axis Aoyama Ichome Tower, 1-3-1 Minami Aoyama, Minato-Ku, TOKYO, 107-0062 JAPAN.
WYARD, Mr. Michael, BA FCA *1988;* The Nurse's House, Park Lane, Reepham, NORWICH, NR10 4JZ.
WYATT, Mr. Alan Robert, FCA *1975;* Shaw Consultants Limited, Witan Gate House, 500-600 Witan Gate West, MILTON KEYNES, MK9 1BA.
WYATT, Mrs. Alison Anne, BCom ACA *1992;* 9 Cliveden Road, Wimbledon, LONDON, SW19 3RD.
WYATT, Miss. Ann Louise, MEng ACA *2004;* The Old Barn, Ironmonger Lane High Street, MARLBOROUGH, SN8 1HN.
WYATT, Mr. Anthony, FCA *1960;* 9 Tyrrell Road, TIVERTON, EX16 5BB. (Life Member)
WYATT, Mr. Christopher, FCA *1976;* 24 Stevens Lane, Claygate, ESHER, SURREY, KT10 0TE.
WYATT, Mr. Christopher Mark, BSc ACA *2000;* Blaides Knaresborough Road, Bishop Monkton, HARROGATE, NORTH YORKSHIRE, HG3 3QG.
WYATT, Mr. Ernest William, FCA *1951;* 29 Mount Pleasant, Keyworth, NOTTINGHAM, NG12 5EP. (Life Member)
•**WYATT, Mr. Gary Charles, FCA** *1984;* (Tax Fac), Wyatts, York House, 1 Seagrave Road, LONDON, SW6 1RP.
WYATT, Mr. Gary Paul, BSc ACA *1992;* 9 Cliveden Road, Wimbledon, LONDON, SW19 3RD.
•**WYATT, Mr. Ian Edward Andrew, FCA** *1974;* Wyatt Husler Cook(Accountants) Limited, 50-51 Albemarle Crescent, SCARBOROUGH, NORTH YORKSHIRE, YO11 1XX. See also Wyatt & Co
WYATT, Mr. Ian Martin, BSc FCA *1985;* 12 Parma Crescent, Battersea, LONDON, SW11 1LT.
WYATT, Mr. James Richard, BA(Hons) ACA *2000;* British Gas Plc, 30 The Causeway, STAINES, MIDDLESEX, TW18 3BY.
WYATT, Mr. Jamie Richard, ACA *1998;* 37 Manor Road, TEDDINGTON, MIDDLESEX, TW11 8AA.
•**WYATT, Mr. John Leslie, FCA** *1965;* (Tax Fac), Betmathel Limited, 6 College Road, BROMSGROVE, B60 2NE.
WYATT, Mr. Jonathan Paul, BA ACA *1998;* Protiviti Grand Buildings, 1-3 Strand, LONDON, WC2N 5AB.
•**WYATT, Mrs. Karen Mary, FCA** *1984;* Wyatts, York House, 1 Seagrave Road, LONDON, SW6 1RP.
WYATT, Miss. Marina May, MA FCA *1989;* 44 Duncan Terrace, LONDON, N1 8AL.
•**WYATT, Mr. Mark George, BSc ACA** *1996;* Icarus Wyatt Consulting Limited, 8 Sovereign Court, 8 Graham Street, BIRMINGHAM, B1 3JR.
WYATT, Mr. Mark Sunder, BSc ACA *1992;* 7 Rue Georges Ville, 75116 PARIS, FRANCE.
•**WYATT, Mr. Martin, FCA** *1986;* (Tax Fac), Whitley Stimpson LLP, Penrose House, 67 Hightown Road, BANBURY, OXFORDSHIRE, OX16 9BE.
•**WYATT, Mr. Matthew Paul, ACA** *2005;* Wellers, Stuart House, 55 Catherine Place, LONDON, SW1E 6DY.
WYATT, Mr. Michael, PhD BSc FCA *1977;* 33 New Road, Twyford, READING, RG10 9PS. (Life Member)
WYATT, Miss. Natalie Elizabeth, ACA *2009;* 8/104 Darley Road, MANLY, NSW 2095, AUSTRALIA.
WYATT, Mr. Nicholas Clive, BA ACA *1992;* Lex Pty Ltd, PO Box 1451, OSBORNE PARK, WA 6916, AUSTRALIA.
WYATT, Mr. Nicholas James, BSc ACA *2011;* 26 Ashfield Crescent, Billinge, WIGAN, LANCASHIRE, WN5 7TE.
•**WYATT, Mr. Nigel Peter Lynn, BSc FCA** *1986;* Nigel Wyatt & Company Limited, 125 Main Street, Garforth, LEEDS, LS25 1AF.
WYATT, Mr. Oliver James, ACA *2008;* Flat 1, 105 Fentiman Road, LONDON, SW8 1JZ.
WYATT, Miss. Olivia Therese, BSc ACA *2009;* 13 Watermarque, 100 Browning Street, BIRMINGHAM, B16 8GY.
•**WYATT, Mr. Peter Edward, LLB FCA** *1975;* FD Management Services Limited, New Inn Cottage, Dereham Road, Litcham, KING'S LYNN, PE32 2NT.
WYATT, Mr. Peter Edward James, BSc ACA *1985;* 48 The Avenue, Cheam, SUTTON, SURREY, SM2 7QE.
WYATT, Mr. Peter John, BA FCA *1988;* 29 Longleaf Drive, BRAINTREE, CM7 1XS.
WYATT, Mr. Peter Walter Ernest, FCA *1962;* 86 Charnwood Avenue, NORTHAMPTON, NN3 3DY.
•**WYATT, Mr. Philip Thomas Stanbury, FCA** *1975;* (Tax Fac), R.E. Stratford & Co, 100 Queen Street, NEWTON ABBOT, DEVON, TQ12 2EU.
WYATT, Miss. Rebecca Louise, BSc ACA *1997;* 52 Marston Gate, WINCHESTER, HAMPSHIRE, SO23 7DS.
•**WYATT, Mr. Richard David, FCA** *1972;* (Tax Fac), Richard Wyatt & Co., 109c High Street, CHESHAM, HP5 1DE.
WYATT, Mr. Richard Edward, BSc ACA *1988;* 12 St. Peters Road, HUNTINGDON, CAMBRIDGESHIRE, PE29 7AA.
WYATT, Mr. Roland Ian, MA FCA *1982;* (Tax Fac), Royal Bank of Canada Trust Corporation Ltd, 71 Queen Victoria Street, LONDON, EC4V 4DE.
•**WYATT, Mr. Simon David, BA FCA** *1985;* (Tax Fac), SDW Associates, 57 Brockhurst Road, GOSPORT, HAMPSHIRE, PO12 3AP.
WYATT, Mr. Stephen Emlyn, FCA *1968;* 59 The Highway, Hawarden, DEESIDE, CH5 3DG.
WYATT, Mr. Thomas Arthur, FCA *1950;* 4 Knebworth Court, 44 Petitor Road, TORQUAY, TQ1 4QF. (Life Member)
WYATT, Miss. Tracey Jane, BA ACA *1997;* The Chantry High Street, Girton, NEWARK, NG23 7JA.
WYATT, Mr. Victor John, FCA *1958;* 52 Crown Lane, Southgate, LONDON, N14 5ER. (Life Member)
WYATT-INGRAM, Mr. Stuart George, BA FCA *1992;* 14032 Lissadell Circle, CHARLOTTE, NC 28277, UNITED STATES.
WYBER, Mr. Harold, ACA *2011;* 7 Mornington Close, WOODFORD GREEN, ESSEX, IG8 0TT.
WYBER, Mrs. Jean Margaret, FCA *1975;* U R C Thames North Synod, Ipalo House, 32-34 Great Peter Street, LONDON, SW1P 2DB.
WYBER, The Revd. Richard John, MA FCA *1973;* 7 Mornington Close, WOODFORD GREEN, IG8 0TT. (Life Member)
WYBORN, Mr. Alan Irvine, FCA *1943;* Flat 5, 1 Hyde Park Square, LONDON, W2 2JZ. (Life Member)
WYBORN, Mr. Matthew James, BSc ACA *1992;* PricewaterhouseCoopers, Sumitomo Fudosan Shiodome Hamarikyu Bldg, 8-21-1 Ginza, Chuo-ku, TOKYO, 104-0061 JAPAN.
WYBORN, Mr. Stephen John, BA ACA *2002;* 45 Fitzgerald Place, CAMBRIDGE, CB4 1WA.
WYBROW, Mr. Robert James, ACA *2011;* 11 Sedgemoor, Shoeburyness, SOUTHEND-ON-SEA, SS3 8AX.
WYBURD, Mr. Harry, ACA *2011;* 9 Ravensdon Street, LONDON, SE11 4AQ.
•**WYBURN, Mr. Charles Louis, FCA** *1973;* (Tax Fac), Charles L. Wyburn & Co, 23 Bellfield Avenue, HARROW, HA3 6ST.
WYCHE, Mr. David Mark, BSc FCA *1979;* Aus Bore Aus Bore House, 19-25 Manchester Road, WILMSLOW, CHESHIRE, SK9 1BQ.
WYCHERLEY, Mr. Graham S, FCA *1952;* The Hattons, 181 Penn Road, WOLVERHAMPTON, WV3 0EQ. (Life Member)
WYCHERLEY, Mr. William Francis, BSc ACA *1997;* (Tax Fac), 23 Fleming Drive, Winwick Park, WARRINGTON, WA2 8XY.
•**WYE, Mr. Andrew Frederick, BA FCA** *1988;* (Tax Fac), Andrew F. Wye Limited, 24 Marlyns Drive, Burpham, GUILDFORD, GU4 7LT.
•**WYE, Mr. David, FCA** *1981;* (Tax Fac), 56 Stanstead Road, HODDESDON, HERTFORDSHIRE, EN11 0RJ.
WYER, Mrs. Catherine Louise, BA ACA *2006;* 11 Ripley Close, Kingsmead, MILTON KEYNES, MK4 4HJ.
WYER, Miss. Elizabeth Jane, ACA *2009;* K P M G Llp, 15 Canada Square, LONDON, E14 5GL.
WYER, Mr. John Daryl, LLB FCA *1977;* Tudor House, Romsley, BRIDGNORTH, SHROPSHIRE, WV15 6HP.
WYER, Mr. Mark Andrew, BSc ACA *2002;* Hatch Associates 9th Floor Portland House, Bressenden Place, LONDON, SW1E 5BH.
•**WYETH, Mr. Richard John, BA ACA CPA** *1989;* R.J.W. Associates, 44 Kirby Drive, Bramley Green, TADLEY, HAMPSHIRE, RG26 5FN.
WYKE, Miss. Victoria, ACA *2007;* Woodford, Eel Pie Island, TWICKENHAM, TW1 3DY.
WYKEMAN, Mr. Nicolas Alexander Ulrich, BSc ACA *1991;* 100 Inglethorpe Street, LONDON, SW6 6NX.
WYKES, Miss. Christina Ann, BSc ACA *1990;* Tudor House, Alma Road, Headley Down, BORDON, GU35 8JR.
WYKES, Mr. Graham Thomas, BSc FCA *1979;* Kouterstraat 51, 3090 OVERIJSE, BELGIUM.
WYLD, Mr. William Thomas Whitcliffe, ACA *2010;* 10 Tintern Close, LONDON, SW15 2HF.
•**WYLDE, Mr. Nicholas William, ACA** *1992;* Stuart Dick & Co Limited, Suite 8 & 9, Courtyard House, Mill Lane, GODALMING, SURREY GU7 1EY.
WYLDES, Mrs. Gail Linda, BSc ACA *1985;* Holly Grange, 89 Marsh Lane, SOLIHULL, B91 2PE.
WYLDES, Mr. Richard Thomas, ACA *1984;* Greenways, 124 Northampton Road, Earls Barton, NORTHAMPTON, NN6 0HF.
WYLE, Mr. Ivan Gordon, FCA *1969;* 11 Europa Avenue, Sandwell Valley, WEST BROMWICH, B70 6TL.
WYLES, Mr. Damian, BSc ACA *2005;* 18 Sandleford Lane, Greenham, THATCHAM, RG19 8XW.
WYLES, Mrs. Lindsay Susan Jane, BSc FCA *1989;* (Tax Fac), 29 Brantwood Road, LONDON, SE24 0DH.
WYLES, Mr. Steven Graeme, BSc ACA *2007;* Flat 3, Gemini Court, 852 Brighton Road, PURLEY, SURREY, CR8 2FD.
WYLIE, Mr. Adrian Nigel, FCA *1974;* Highland, 29 Old Glebe, Fernhurst, HASLEMERE, GU27 3HT.
•**WYLIE, Mr. Alan Robert, BSc FCA** *1981;* AR Wylie & Co, Armagh Business Centre, 2 Loughgall Road, ARMAGH, BT61 7NH.

WYLIE, Mr. Andrew John, BA ACA *2003;* 50 Vicarage Avenue, Cheadle Hulme, CHEADLE, CHESHIRE, SK8 7JP.
WYLIE, Mrs. Annette Lena, BSc ACA *1997;* 47 Wimborne St. Giles, WIMBORNE, DORSET, BH21 5NF.
WYLIE, The Revd. David Victor, BA BSc ACA *1989;* Little Elms, Ilchester, YEOVIL, BA22 8NQ.
WYLIE, Miss. Jacqueline, BA ACA *1995;* Crofton, 10 Ewhurst Avenue, Sanderstead, SOUTH CROYDON, SURREY, CR2 0DG.
WYLIE, Mr. Jeffrey Jackson, MA FCA CF *1991;* 394 Belmont Road, BELFAST, BT4 2NH.
WYLIE, Mr. John Patrick, MBA BSc FCA *1993;* 20 Howells Crescent, Llandaff, CARDIFF, CF5 2AJ.
WYLIE, Mrs. Leigh, BSc ACA *1999;* 12 Rochester Drive, Timperley, ALTRINCHAM, CHESHIRE, WA14 5BQ.
WYLIE, Mrs. Lilla Ajgaonkar, BA FCA *1978;* 17A Redgrave Road, NORMANHURST, NSW 2076, AUSTRALIA.
WYLIE, Mr. Malcolm Stewart, FCA *1969;* 1 The Croft, Bishopstone, SALISBURY, SP5 4DF.
WYLIE, Mr. Michael Charles, BA ACA *1985;* 11 Ravenwood Drive, Halebarns, ALTRINCHAM, WA15 0JA.
WYLIE, Mr. Owen Philip, LLB FCA *1976;* 42 Spencer Drive, Llandough, PENARTH, CF64 2LR. (Life Member)
WYLIE, Mr. Philip Nicholas, MSc FCA *1990;* Fifth Floor, Building # 101, Street 494, Near Russian Market, PHNOM PENN, CAMBODIA.
WYLIE, Mr. Robert James, ACA *2008;* 3 The Priors, ASHTEAD, SURREY, KT21 2QF.
WYLLIE, Mrs. Susan Valerie, FCA *1964;* 4 Mawby Close, Whetstone, LEICESTER, LE8 6XA.
WYMAN, Mr. Neal Alastair, BSc ACA *1979;* 54 Emmanuel Road, LONDON, SW12 0HP.
•WYMAN, Mr. Peter Lewis, CBE FCA *1973;* (President 2002 - 2003) (Member of Council 1991 - 2009), Plainsfield Court, Plainsfield, Over Stowey, BRIDGWATER, TA5 1HH.
WYMER, Miss. Joanna Elizabeth, ACA MAAT *2004;* Larking Gowen Kingstreet House, 15 Upper King Street, NORWICH, NR3 1RB.
•WYN, Mrs. Gwenno Mair, BA(Hons) ACA *2003;* Gwenno Mair Wyn ACA, Cilgerran, 8 Llys Gwyn, CAERNARFON, GWYNEDD, LL55 1EN.
•WYNCOLL, Mr. Julian George, ACA *1982;* Tile & Co, Warden House, 37 Manor Road, COLCHESTER, CO3 3LX.
WYND, Mr. Alexander, BSc ACA *1988;* 452 Fifth avenue, NEW YORK, NY 10018, UNITED STATES.
WYND, Miss. Elspeth Mary, ACA *2009;* 70 A East Hill, Wandsworth, LONDON, SW18 2HQ.
WYNDE, Mr. Stephen Norman, FCA *1977;* 31 Lynn Close, Leigh Sinton, MALVERN, WR13 5DU.
WYNN, Mr. James Edward Meynell, MA ACA *2001;* Field House, Bridge Road, GODALMING, GU7 3DT.
WYNN, Mr. Mark David, BSc ACA *1989;* Little Wain Wells, Cuckoo Lane, Wraxall, BRISTOL, BS48 1PJ.
WYNN, Mr. Martin Stuart, BSc FCA *1987;* Fernbank, East Street, Rusper, HORSHAM, RH12 4RE.
•WYNN, Mr. Mathew, BSc ACA *2007;* Welland Medical Ltd, Unit 7-8, The Brunel Centre, Newton Road, CRAWLEY, WEST SUSSEX RH10 9TU.
WYNN, Mr. Peter Barrington, FCA *1968;* Home Farm, Fowlmere Road, Heydon, ROYSTON, SG8 8PZ.
WYNN, Mr. Robert, BSc ACA *2003;* Rosemere, Publow Lane, Woollard, Pensford, BRISTOL, BS39 4HY.
WYNN JONES, Miss. Helena Sophia, BSc ACA *1992;* Domestic & General Insurance, 11 Worple Road, Wimbledon, LONDON, SW19 4JS.
WYNNE, Mr. Christopher John, BA ACA *1992;* Avda de la Circunvalacion 321, Miramadrid, Paracuellod De Jarama, 28860 MADRID, SPAIN.
WYNNE, Mr. Derek Longworth, FCA *1959;* 62 Alinora Avenue, WORTHING, BN12 4LX. (Life Member)
WYNNE, Mr. Derrick Paul Mckenzie, BA ACA *1986;* 6 Garth Terrace, Penybont Road, KNIGHTON, POWYS, LD7 1HB.
•WYNNE, Mr. Edward Craig, FCA *1977;* AIMS - Craig Wynne FCA, 29 Meadowcroft, Higher Kinnerton, CHESTER, CH4 9AY.
WYNNE, Mr. Geoffrey, BCom FCA *1983;* 16 Peach Field, Caldy Village, CHESTER, CH3 5RF.
WYNNE, Mr. James Robert Owen, BSc ACA *1990;* Carreg Wen54 West Farm Road, Ogmore By Sea BRIDGEND, Mid Glamorgan, CF32 0PU.
WYNNE, Mr. Jonathan, FCA *1955;* 900 East Madrid Avenue, Unit APT.55, LAS CRUCES, NM 88001, UNITED STATES. (Life Member)
WYNNE, Mr. Jonathan George, BSocSc ACA *2002;* Surrenda Link Ltd, 8-11 Grosvenor Court Foregate Street, CHESTER, CH1 1HG.
WYNNE, Miss. Michelle Hazel, BSc ACA *2011;* 70 Morrison Street, LONDON, SW11 5LS.
WYNNE, Mrs. Rosalind Mary, BA ACA *1997;* Appin Lodge Vicarage Lane, Ropley, ALRESFORD, HAMPSHIRE, SO24 0DU.
WYNNE, Mrs. Sarah Jenna, ACA *2006;* 30 St. Nons Avenue, CARMARTHEN, DYFED, SA31 3DL.
WYNNE, Mr. Steven John, MA MSc BA ACA FHEA *2006;* MMUBS, Room 421 Aytoun Building, Aytoun Street, MANCHESTER, M1 3GH.
WYNNE-EYTON, Ms. Elizabeth Kate, ACA *2000;* 19 Dean Path Buildings, EDINBURGH, EH4 3AZ.
WYNNE-GRIFFITH, Mr. Richard Christopher, ACA *1985;* The Old Vicarage, Church Street, Effingham, LEATHERHEAD, SURREY, KT24 5LX.
WYNNE-JONES, Mrs. Jane Linda Ann, BA ACA *1987;* 31 Ribblesdale Road, Sherwood, NOTTINGHAM, NG5 3GY.
WYNNE-JONES, Mrs. Juliette Helena, BA ACA *2004;* with PricewaterhouseCoopers LLP, 1 Embankment Place, LONDON, WC2N 6RH.
WYNNE-JONES, Mr. Martin, BSc ACA *1985;* 31 Ribblesdale Road, Sherwood, NOTTINGHAM, NG5 3GY.
•WYNNIATT-HUSEY, Mr. Reginald James, FCA *1959;* (Tax Fac), Wynniatt-Husey Ltd, The Old Coach House, Horse Fair, RUGELEY, STAFFORDSHIRE, WS15 2EL. See also WPA Audit Limited and Tax Assured Limited
WYNTER, Mr. Lindsay Anton, BA ACA *1993;* 7150 Pincone Court, LONGMONT, CO 80503, UNITED STATES.
•WYNTER, Mr. Mark Talbot, MA FCA *1971;* M T Wynter MA FCA, Thornton Cottage, Puckpool Hill, RYDE, PO33 1PJ.
WYON, Mr. Adam, BSc ACA *2005;* Building 11, Glaxo Smithkline UK Ltd, 1-3 Iron Bridge Road Stockley Park, UXBRIDGE, UB11 1BT.
WYRE, Mr. Adam James, BCom ACA *2008;* Flat 233 Scafell Court, Nod Rise, COVENTRY, CV5 7JN.
•WYRLEY-BIRCH, Mr. Nigel Ralph, FCA *1982;* Ryecroft Glenton, 32 Portland Terrace, Jesmond, NEWCASTLE UPON TYNE, NE2 1QP.
WYRLEY-BIRCH, Mr. Paul, BA ACA *1987;* (Tax Fac), 55 Valnay Street, LONDON, SW17 8PS.
•WYSE, Mr. John Howard, FCA *1963;* with Roger Lugg & Co, 12/14 High Street, CATERHAM, CR3 5UA.
WYTHE, Mr. Paul Stephen, BA ACA *1985;* Breidden View, Grimpo, West Felton, OSWESTRY, SHROPSHIRE, SY11 4HL.
WYTON, Mr. Robert Frederick, BA FCA *1965;* 14 Warboys Crescent, Highams Park, LONDON, E4 9HR. (Life Member)
XAVIER, Mr. Eustace Egbert James, ACA *2008;* Flat 34, Crayford House, Tabard Garden Estate, LONDON, SE1 4BU.
XAVIER, Miss. Sabina Dilhara, BSc FCA *1991;* Coface UK, Eagle 1, 80 St Albans Road, WATFORD, WD17 1RP.
XAVIER, Miss. Sonali Rochelle, BA FCA CTA *1991;* 75 Laureate Way, HEMEL HEMPSTEAD, HP1 3RW.
XENIDES, Mr. Andreas Georgiou, FCA *1974;* 32 Kotzia Street, P.Penteli, 15236 ATHENS, GREECE.
XENOPHONTOS, Mr. Alexis, BEng ACA MBA ACGI *1997;* Soboh House 2nd Floor, 377 28th October Street, 3107 LIMASSOL, CYPRUS.
XENOPHONTOS, Mr. Andreas, ACA *2003;* 7A Foinikoudon Street, Apartment 2, Geri, 2201 NICOSIA, CYPRUS.
XENOPHONTOS, Mr. Antonis, BSc ACA *2006;* 28A Andrea Panagide, Dasoupolis, 2024 NICOSIA, CYPRUS.
XENOPHONTOS, Mr. Evdokimos, FCA CF *1963;* 3 Kalamatas Street, Acropolis, 2002 STROVOLOS, CYPRUS.
XENOPHONTOS, Mr. Kyriacos, BA ACA *2006;* NEOCLEOUS HOUSE, 195 Archbishop Makarios III Avenue, 3030 LIMASSOL, CYPRUS.
•XENOPHONTOS, Mr. Polydoros Kyriacou, BA FCA *1984;* Polydoros Xenophontos Ltd, Athienitis Building, 8 Kennedy Avenue Suite 305, 1087 NICOSIA, CYPRUS.
XENOPOULOU, Mrs. Christina, MBA BSc MCMI ACA *1996;* 42 Omerou Street, Monarch 4 Flat 202, 2121 NICOSIA, CYPRUS.
XHINDOLI, Miss. Ortiola, BSc ACA *2010;* 7a, Woodlands Avenue, LONDON, N3 2NS.
XHOLLO, Mrs. Elena Achilleas, ACA *2011;* Kissavou 28 - 30, Flat 102, Strovolos, NICOSIA, CYPRUS.
XHOLLO, Ms. Evi, ACA *2011;* Stylianou Lena 11, Apt 202, 2019 NICOSIA, CYPRUS.
XI, Mr. Victor Zhenjie, ACA *2010;* 42 Soo Chow Rise, SINGAPORE 575483, SINGAPORE.
XIAO, Mr. Shaoping, MA ACA CICPA *2011;* General Manager Office, Zhuzhou CSR Times Electric Co. Ltd, Shidai Road, Shifeng District, ZHUZHOU 412001, HUNAN PROVENCE CHINA.
XIAO, Mr. Zuhe, ACA *2008;* Room 1404, Block B, Kam Tai Court, Ma On Sha, SHA TIN, NEW TERRITORIES HONG KONG SAR.
XIE, Mrs. Fang, BA ACA *2007;* with KPMG LLP, One Snowhill, Snow Hill Queensway, BIRMINGHAM, B4 6GN.
XIE, Miss. Fei, BSc ACA *2011;* 3 Sunlight Square, LONDON, E2 6LD.
XIE, Mr. Si, ACA *2011;* with KPMG, 7th Floor, China Resources Building, 5001 Shennan East Road, SHENZHEN 518001, CHINA.
XIFARAS, Mr. Paul George, BSc ACA *1994;* Lion Nathan Limited, Level 7, 68 York Street, SYDNEY, NSW 2000, AUSTRALIA.
XIN, Miss. Ran, ACA *2011;* PricewaterhouseCoopers, 7 More London Riverside, LONDON, SE1 2RT.
XING, Mr. Zhe, ACA *2007;* 172 St. Davids Square, LONDON, E14 3WD.
XIPSITIS, Mr. Andreas, ACA *2010;* 2 Ellados Street, Palechori, 2740 NICOSIA, CYPRUS.
XIRADAKIS, Miss. Pamela Electra, ACA *2011;* 15 Dundas Gardens, WEST MOLESEY, SURREY, KT8 1RX.
XU, Mrs. Jingjin Jane, BA ACA *1997;* 131 Terregles Avenue, GLASGOW, G41 4DG.
XU, Mr. Sheng, ACA CA(NZ) *2010;* Flat 11 Wealden House, Capulet Square, LONDON, E3 3NG.
XU, Mr. Zhining, MSc ACA *2007;* 22 Ashdown Gardens, SOUTH CROYDON, SURREY, CR2 9DR.
XUE, Mr. Jiao, ACA *2009;* Apartment 2, 28 Martin Lane, LONDON, EC4R 0DR.
XUE, Miss. Wan Ru, ACA *2009;* Room 2303, Central International Plaza, No.105-6 North Zhongshan Road, NANJING 210009, CHINA.
XUEREB, Mr. Karl Robert, BA FCA *1986;* Kllopstockstrasse 14, 14163 BERLIN, GERMANY.
YAAKUB, Mr. Azlan, BSc(Hons) ACA *2003;* 8 Jalan SS 4B/3, Kelana Jaya, 47301 PETALING JAYA, SELANGOR, MALAYSIA.
YABSLEY, Mr. Alexander Roy, FCA *1973;* R D Industries Ltd, Drake Hill Bus Park, Estover Road, Estover, PLYMOUTH, PL6 7PS.
YACOB, Mr. Khalid, ACA *1974;* 304 Upper Mall Road, LAHORE, PAKISTAN.
•YADAV, Mrs. Varsha Ramnik, FCA *1984;* Yadav & Co, 87 Lansdowne Road, Seven Kings, ILFORD, IG3 8NG.
YADOO, Mr. Gerald, FCA *1967;* 2 Eastmont Road, Hinchley Wood, ESHER, KT10 9AZ.
YAFFE, Mr. Bernard Max, BA FCA *1981;* 6 Holden Road, SALFORD, MANCHESTER, M7 4WD.
YAFFE, Mr. Ian Carlton, FCA *1976;* 1 Rochford Close, Whitefield, MANCHESTER, M45 7QR.
YAGCIOGLU, Mr. Mehmet, ACA *2009;* Yeni Yol Sokak, Murat Apartmani, No:4/10, Bostanci, Kadiko, ISTANBUL TURKEY.
YAGER, Mr. Raymond Simon, ACA *1987;* 15 Old Forge Close, STANMORE, HA7 3EB.
YAHIAOUI, Mr. Samir, ACA *2009;* with Deloitte LLP, 2 New Street Square, LONDON, EC4A 3BZ.
YAHYA, Mr. Didi Syafruddin, MA ACA *1992;* Menara Dion Level 27, Jalan Sultan Ismail, 50250 KUALA LUMPUR, FEDERAL TERRITORY, MALAYSIA.
YAHYA, Mr. Mirza, FCA *1969;* 1 Saint Thomas Street, Apt 16B, TORONTO M5S3M5, ON, CANADA.
YAHYA, Mr. Mohamed Azman, BSc ACA *1989;* 1 Jalan Setiabakti 2, Damansara Heights, 50490 KUALA LUMPUR, FEDERAL TERRITORY, MALAYSIA.
•YAKOOB, Mr. Jawaid, MA FCA *1997;* Alhambra Accounting Limited, Crown House, 28 George Street, BIRMINGHAM, B12 9RG.
YAKUB, Mrs. Alison Jane, BA ACA *1991;* 23 St Johns Road, Petts Wood, ORPINGTON, BR5 1HS.
YALDREN, Miss. Margaret Ann, BSc FCA *1978;* 11 Ashcombe Drive, EDENBRIDGE, TN8 6JY.
YALDRON, Mr. David John, LLB FCA *2001;* 52 Chestnut Road, LONDON, SE27 9LE.
YALE, Miss. Mary Anora, FCA *1961;* (Member of Council 1979 - 1995), (Tax Fac), 4 Wallgrave Road, LONDON, SW5 0RL.
YALIZ, Miss. Nia Emel, BSc(Hons) ACA *2010;* Flat 18 Edison Court, Exchange Mews Culverden Park Road, TUNBRIDGE WELLS, KENT, TN4 9TR.
YALLOP, Mrs. Fiona Alison, BA FCA *1992;* 36 Grand Avenue, WORTHING, BN11 5AJ.
YALLOP, Mr. John Christopher, BSc FCA *1978;* 8 Richmond Heights, BATH, BA1 5QJ.
YALLOP, Mrs. Louisa Jane, ACA CTA *2003;* Grey Gables, Claxton Church Road, Ashby St. Mary, NORWICH, NR14 7BZ.
YALLOP, Mr. Paul Graeme, BEng ACA *2001;* 4 Cook Close, Walton Park, MILTON KEYNES, MK7 7JA.
YAM, Mr. Colin Chin Kwan, FCA *1973;* 900 Dunearn Road, #03-18 The Blossomvale, SINGAPORE 589473, SINGAPORE.
YAM, Miss. Gladys Oi Yan, ACA *2008;* 20b Broadlands Road, Highgate, LONDON, N6 4AN.
YAM, Ms. Hoi Yin Cecilia, ACA *2007;* Flat D, 9th Floor, Tower 10, Park Avenue, 18 Hoi Ting Road, TAI KOK TSUI KOWLOON HONG KONG SAR.
YAM, Miss. Jacqueline, MEng ACA *2011;* 20b Broadlands Road, Highgate, LONDON, N6 4AN.
•YAM, Mr. Kenneth King Tai, MEng BA ACA *2004;* with PricewaterhouseCoopers LLP, 1 Embankment Place, LONDON, WC2N 6RH.
YAM, Mr. Kenneth Tse Kin, BEng ACA *1991;* 19th Floor Nokia Tower, Pacific Century Place, No 2A Gong Ti Bei Lu, Chaoyang District, BEIJING 100027, CHINA.
YAM, Mr. Robert Mow Lam, FCA *1971;* Robert Yam & Co, Fortune Centre, Apt. 16-03, 190 Middle Road, SINGAPORE 188979, SINGAPORE.
YAM, Mr. Ronald Tak Fai, ACA *2006;* RSM Nelson Wheeler, 29th Floor Caroline Centre, Lee Gardens Two, 28 Yun Ping Road, CAUSEWAY BAY, HONG KONG ISLAND HONG KONG SAR.
YAM, Miss. Tracy Wing San, MA ACA *2002;* Royal London Mutual Insurance, 55 Gracechurch Street, LONDON, EC3V 0RL.
YAM, Mr. Tsz Yu Revson, ACA *2008;* F S Li & Co, 1001 Admiralty Centre Tower 1, 18 Harcourt Road, ADMIRALTY, HONG KONG SAR.
YAMADA, Miss. Mariko, ACA *2009;* 7-130 Shiba cho, Kanazawa Ku, YOKOHAMA, 236-0012 JAPAN.
•YAMAKIS, Mr. Ninos Antoni, FCA *1962;* Yamakis & Co, Regaena House, 4a Regaena Street, PO Box 21082, 1501 NICOSIA, CYPRUS.
YAMANAKA, Miss. Rowan Kimiko, MSc ACA *2004;* 100a Elgin Avenue, LONDON, W9 2HD.
YAMASHITA, Miss. Satoko, ACA MBA *1998;* Star Royal Nakano, JP 1003 58-7, Chuo 4-Chome, TOKYO, 164-0011 JAPAN.
YAMASHITA, Miss. Takako, MPhil FCA *1996;* Ernst & Young, Becket House, 1 Lambeth Palace Road, LONDON, SE1 7EU.
YAMATO, Ms. Junko, ACA *1995;* with PricewaterhouseCoopers, Kasumigaseki Building 15F, Kasumigaseki 3-2-5, Chiyoda-Ku, TOKYO, 100-6015 JAPAN.
YAMAWAKI, Miss. Sachika, BSc ACA *2007;* 49 Crescent Road, BARNET, HERTFORDSHIRE, EN4 9RD.
•YAMAWAKI, Miss. Tomoko, FCA *1993;* Kaiser Yamawaki LLP, Unit 4, 17 Plumbers Row, LONDON, E1 1EQ.
YAN, Mr. Isaac Lap Kei, BA FCA *1987;* KPMG, 8th Floor, Tower E2, Oriental Plaza, 1 East Chang An Avenue, BEIJING 100738 CHINA.
YAN, Mr. Kwok Sun, ACA *2008;* Li Tang Chen & Co., 10/F Sun Hung Kai Centre, 30 Harbour Road, WAN CHAI, HONG KONG ISLAND, HONG KONG SAR.
YAN, Mr. Shui Lau Francis, ACA *2008;* Francis S L Yan & Co, Room 101 1st Floor, Tak Fung Building, 79-81 Connaught Road West, SAI YING PUN, HONG KONG ISLAND HONG KONG SAR.
YAN, Mr. Tat Wah, ACA *2007;* LKY China, 5/F, Dah Sing Life Building, 99-105 Des Voeux Road, CENTRAL, HONG KONG SAR.
YAN, Mr. Yiu Kwong Eddy, ACA *2004;* 34/F The Lee Gardens, 33 Hysan Avenue, CAUSEWAY BAY, HONG KONG SAR.
YAN-KAI HEW KHEE, Ms. Marie Kathleen Sandra, BA ACA *1996;* Church Road, POINTE AUX PIMENTS, MAURITIUS.
YAN MAN SHING, Miss. Mary Jane, BSc ACA *2005;* 43 Cambridge Road, MITCHAM, CR4 1DW.
YANDELL, Mr. Andrew, ACA *2009;* Flat 7 Wallace Court, 288 Balham High Road, LONDON, SW17 7AT.
YANDELL, Mr. David Bawden, FCA *1971;* RenaissanceRe Syndicate Management Limited 18th Floor, 125 Old Broad Street, LONDON, EC2N 1AR.
YANDLE, Miss. Catherine Mary, BA ACA *1991;* Mid Devon District Council, Phoenix House, Phoenix Lane, TIVERTON, DEVON, EX16 6PP.
YANG, Mr. Adrian Chi-Ming, BSc ACA *1982;* 18 Mount Carmel Chambers, Dukes Lane, LONDON, W8 4JW.
YANG, Miss. Anita Chuen Sing, BSc ACA *1995;* 3 Brightlingsea Place, LONDON, E14 8DB.

YANG, Miss. Anna Hon Pik, BSc ACA *1988;* 122 Holland Grove View, SINGAPORE 276278, SINGAPORE.
YANG, Mr. Charles Chuen Liang, MBA ACA *1986;* S Y-Yang & Company, Room 1 02, Seaview Building Block A, 2-8 Watson Road, NORTH POINT, HONG KONG ISLAND HONG KONG SAR.
YANG, Mr. Chiu Ming, FCA *1971;* 133 HEMMANT ROAD #04-09 SINGAPORE 438686, SINGAPORE, SINGAPORE.
YANG, Mr. Fei, ACA *2008;* Flat 307, Latitude Court, 3 Albert Basin Way, LONDON, E16 2QP.
YANG, Mr. Guang, ACA *2009;* No 29 - Room 802, Lane 395 ShuangYang North Road, SHANGHAI 200433, CHINA.
YANG, Miss. Guang, ACA *2010;* 12 Frederick Square, LONDON, SE16 5XR.
YANG, Mr. Hong Lye, FCA *1976;* 903/21 Elizabeth Bay Road, ELIZABETH BAY, NSW 2011, AUSTRALIA.
YANG, Mrs. Qun, MSc BSc ACA CFA *2005;* 30 St. Bartholomews Court, Riverside, CAMBRIDGE, CB5 8HG.
•**YANG, Mr. Silas Siu Shun, BSc FCA** *1982;* PricewaterhouseCoopers, Prince's Building, 22/F, 10 Chater Road, CENTRAL, HONG KONG ISLAND HONG KONG SAR.
YANG, Mr. Tianxiu, BA ACA *2011;* 20 Lisle Close, Tooting Bec, LONDON, SW17 6LB.
YANG, Mrs. Weilin, ACA CA(SA) *2009;* 17 St. Clairs Road, CROYDON, CR0 5NE.
YANG, Mr. Wilbur, BEng ACA *2004;* Flat 29, Woolcombes Court, Princes Riverside Road, LONDON, SE16 5RQ.
YANG, Miss. Ying, ACA *2008;* Flat H 16th Floor, Three Island Place, 61 Tanner Road, NORTH POINT, HONG KONG SAR.
YANG, Mr. Yufu, BSc ACA *2009;* 26 Pioneer Close, LONDON, E14 6BF.
YANG, Mr. Zhiwen, ACA *2011;* Deloitte & Touche Llp City House, 126-130 Hills Road, CAMBRIDGE, CB2 1RY.
YANNAKOUDAKIS, Miss. Stephanie Anastasia, BA ACA *2010;* Flat 9 Orchard Mead House, Finchley Road, LONDON, NW11 8DJ.
YAO, Mr. Gang, ACA *2010;* Room11-1-301, Zhong Hai Feng Lian Villa, Xi Bei Wang Town, Haidian District, BEIJING 100094, CHINA.
YAO, Miss. Karen Ka Yen, BA ACA *1994;* 8A, Y Z, No 10 Tai Hang Road, TAI HANG, HONG KONG ISLAND, HONG KONG SAR.
YAO, Mr. Lee Jian, ACA CA(AUS) *2009;* 1406 Audubon Trace, JEFFERSON, LA 70121, UNITED STATES.
YAO, Miss. Qian Vivien, MEng ACA *2011;* 27 Roman Way, LONDON, N7 8XE.
YAO, Ms. Xing, ACA *2009;* Flat 30 Topaz Court, 580 High Road Leytonstone, LONDON, E11 3GA.
YAO, Mrs. Yan, ACA *2009;* Room 302 Buiding 16, Shang Di Moma, No 1 An Ning Zhuang Road, Hai Dian District, BEIJING 100085, CHINA.
YAO, Mr. Yan Ping Francis, ACA *2008;* Yao & Co, 14B Wing Cheong Comm. Bldg, 19 Jervois Street, SHEUNG WAN, HONG KONG SAR.
YAP, Miss. Ai Yong, BSc ACA *1992;* 57 Jalan BU11/6, Bandar Utama Dasmansara, 478000 PETALING JAYA, Selangor, MALAYSIA.
YAP, Mr. Aik Hwee, ACA *1983;* 51 Kingussie Avenue, CASTLE HILL, NSW 2154, AUSTRALIA.
YAP, Miss. Amanda Ruoh Kim, BA LLB ACA *1998;* 8A Orange Grove Road, #15-01, SINGAPORE 258343, SINGAPORE.
YAP, Mr. Beng Kui, FCA *1974;* 4457 Fortune Avenue, RICHMOND V7E 5J7, BC, CANADA.
YAP, Mr. Boh Pin, FCA *1966;* B.P.Y. Pte Ltd, 190 Middle Road, #13-01 Fortune Centre, SINGAPORE 188979, SINGAPORE.
YAP, Mr. Chee Fatt, BA ACA *1981;* Unit E-02-03 Block E, Villa Hijauan, Jalan Silat Harimua 34, Bandar Selesa Jaya, 81300 JOHOR BAHRU, JOHOR MALAYSIA.
YAP, Mr. Chee Meng, FCA *1981;* 327 River Valley Road # 15-02, SINGAPORE 238359, SINGAPORE.
YAP, Mr. Derrick Tian Heng, BA ACA ATII *1993;* (Tax Fac), 20 Rosebery Road, SUTTON, SM1 2BW.
YAP, Mr. E Hock, BSc ACA *1982;* 26H Shouson Hill Road, SHOUSON HILL, HONG KONG ISLAND, HONG KONG SAR.
YAP, Miss. Ee-Lin, ACA CA(AUS) *2010;* (Tax Fac), with Ernst & Young LLP, 1 More London Place, LONDON, SE1 2AF.
YAP, Miss. Elisa Seok Eng, BSc ACA *1995;* 17 JALAN KENYALANG 11/7A, PJU5 KOTA DAMANSARA, 47810 PETALING JAYA, MALAYSIA.
YAP, Miss. Eng Li, BSc ACA *2007;* Flat 3/A Welles Court, 4 Premiere Place, LONDON, E14 8SE.
YAP, Mr. Henry Fat Suan, FCA MBA *1972;* 15 Braga Circuit, MONG KOK, KOWLOON, HONG KONG SAR.
YAP, Miss. Huey Ling, BA ACA *1991;* 8 Westbourne Park Villas, LONDON, W2 5EA.
YAP, Mr. Kah On, BSc FCA *1988;* Unit 0897 Tower 18, HK Parkview, 88 Tai Tam Reservoir Road, TAI TAM, HONG KONG ISLAND, HONG KONG SAR.
YAP, Mr. Ken Vui Edwin, ACA *2007;* 23G Tung Hoi Mansion, 8 Taikoo Shing Road, TAIKOO SHING, HONG KONG ISLAND, HONG KONG SAR.
YAP, Dr. Kim Fay, DBA BCom ACA ATII ACIS MBA CPA CA(NZ) *2011;* (Tax Fac), K F Yap & Company, 53 Tingkat 1, Bandar Raub Perdana, 27600 RAUB, PAHANG, MALAYSIA.
YAP, Mr. Kim Foo, BSc ACA *1990;* 153C, Jalan Besar, Kepong, 52100 KUALA LUMPUR, FEDERAL TERRITORY, MALAYSIA.
•**YAP, Mr. Koi Ming, ACA** *1979;* Suite 05-03 Wisma Tan Kim San 518A Jalan Ipoh, 51200 KUALA LUMPUR, FEDERAL TERRITORY, MALAYSIA. See also K M Yap & Company
YAP, Mr. Kok Keong, BSc ACA *1981;* 24 Cantex Court, RICHMOND HILL L4S 1B1, ON, CANADA.
YAP, Miss. Koon Chai, BA ACA *1983;* E2-05-1 BUKIT UTAMA 1, NO.3 CHANGKAT BUKIT UTAMA, PJU6 BANDAR UTAMA, 47800 PETALING JAYA, SELANGOR, MALAYSIA.
YAP, Mr. Ngen Siak, BSc(Hons) ACA *2002;* J Walter Thompson, 1 knightsbridge Green, LONDON, SW1X 7NW.
YAP, Mr. Raymond Quan Meng, BA ACA *1989;* 70 Jalan Terasik 3, Bangsar Baru, 59100 KUALA LUMPUR, FEDERAL TERRITORY, MALAYSIA.
•**YAP, Mr. Shen Siak, BSc ACA** *2002;* Barnes Roffe LLP, Leytonstone House, Leytonstone, LONDON, E11 1GA.
YAP, Mr. Shoong Wah, ACA *1986;* Botania, 29A West Coast Park, #01-16, SINGAPORE 127723, SINGAPORE.
YAP, Miss. Siew-Keng, BSc ACA *2004;* 107 Jalan USJ 4/1A, 47600 SUBANG, SELANGOR, MALAYSIA.
YAP, Mr. Steve Peng Leong, BA ACA *1983;* Unit 38-02 Mont Kiara Damai, No 3 Jalan Kiara 2, Mont Kiara, 50480 KUALA LUMPUR, FEDERAL TERRITORY, MALAYSIA.
YAP, Mr. Tse-Juie, ACA *2011;* A-22-3 The Maple at Sentul West, No.1A Persiaran Parkview, off Jalan Ipoh, 51100 KUALA LUMPUR, MALAYSIA.
YAP, Dr. Violetta Patricia, MSc BSc ACA *2006;* Flat 10, 10 Alexandra Road, LONDON, SW19 7JZ.
•**YAPP, Mr. David Sandiford, ACA** *1979;* (Tax Fac), Sexty & Co., 124 Thorpe Road, NORWICH, NR1 1RS.
YAPP, Mr. John Peter, FCA *1973;* 8 Manor Farm, Farm Lane, South Littleton, EVESHAM, WR11 8UA.
YAQOOB, Mr. Mohammed, BSc FCA *1982;* 29 Armadale Road, Ladybridge, BOLTON, BL3 4QE.
•**YAQUB, Mr. Manzar, BA FCA** *1991;* Yaqub & Co Limited, 274 Stapleton Road, Easton, BRISTOL, BS5 0NW.
YAQUB, Mr. Mohammed, BEng ACA *1993;* 23 Greswolde Road, BIRMINGHAM, B11 4DJ.
YAQUB, Mr. Mohammed Arif, BSc ACA *1982;* Crisp, House Number 40 A & B, Street 27, ISLAMABAD, ISLAMABAD CAPITAL TERRITORY, PAKISTAN.
YAQUB, Mr. Shoaib, ACA *2010;* 3 Sovereign Court, Unwin Road, STANMORE, HA7 1FH.
•**YARAS, Mr. Andrew John, BA FCA** *1977;* (Tax Fac), Andrew Yaras & Co, 2 Fishpool Street, ST. ALBANS, HERTFORDSHIRE, AL3 4RT.
YARD, Mr. Barry Alan, BSc ACA *1979;* 7 Nurseries Close, Exton, EXETER, EX3 0PG.
YARD, Mr. John Gilbert, FCA *1955;* 74 Fruitfields Close, DEVIZES, WILTSHIRE, SN10 5JY. (Life Member)
YARD, Mr. Matthew James, BA ACA *2006;* 22 Pennant Place, Portishead, BRISTOL, BS20 7AA.
YARDLEY, Mr. Adrian Mark Miller, MBA MSc BSc FCA *1982;* 25-27 Mill Street, NEWPORT PAGNELL, BUCKINGHAMSHIRE, MK16 8ER.
YARDLEY, Mr. Daniel John, BSc(Hons) ACA *2003;* 21a Dingwall Road, LONDON, SW18 3AZ.
•**YARDLEY, Mr. Martin, BA FCA** *1991;* Martin Yardley FCA, 10 Horizon Close, TUNBRIDGE WELLS, KENT, TN4 0AW.
•**YARDLEY, Ms. Miranda Jane, BA FCA** *1994;* Yardley & Co, 27 Hoxton Street, LONDON, N1 6NH.
•**YARDLEY, Mr. Noel Peter, BSc ACA** *1984;* Outsourced Accountancy Services Ltd, Flat 11, Randolph Court, 11 The Avenue, Hatch End, PINNER MIDDLESEX HA5 4HQ.
YARDLEY, Mr. Oliver Henry Thomas, ACA *2010;* Flat 7, 7 St. Gregorys Road, STRATFORD-UPON-AVON, WARWICKSHIRE, CV37 6UH.
YARDLEY, Mr. Robert John, BSc ACA *1978;* 168 Penns Lane, Wylde Green, SUTTON COLDFIELD, B76 8JT.
YARDLEY, Mr. Rupert Michael, MA ACA *1988;* Flat 1 The Briars, 50 Alma Road, REIGATE, SURREY, RH2 0DN.
YARDY, Mr. Philip, BA FCA *1975;* Palos Verdes Footwear, 1010 Sandhill Ave, CARSON, CA 90027, UNITED STATES.
YARNALL, Mr. Michael David, ACA *2008;* Apartment 157 N V Building, 98 The Quays, SALFORD, M50 3BD.
YARR, Mr. Jonathan, BA ACA *2007;* 28 Ferndale Road, LONDON, SW4 7SF.
•**YARR, Mrs. Margaret, ACA** *1979;* (Tax Fac), M. Yarr, 105 Cedar Drive, Parklands, CHICHESTER, PO19 3EL.
YARROW, Mr. Guy Frederick James, BEng ACA *2010;* 14 Ewald Road, LONDON, SW6 3ND.
YARROW, Mr. John Paul, BSc ACA *2001;* Allen Sykes Ltd, 5 Henson Close South Church Enterprise Park, BISHOP AUCKLAND, COUNTY DURHAM, DL14 6WA.
YARROW, Mr. Nicholas John, BSc ACA *1992;* 27 Cobbetts Ride, TRING, HERTFORDSHIRE, HP23 4BZ.
YARROW, Mr. Philip James, BA ACA *1993;* Ormiston Lodge, Bunch Lane, HASLEMERE, SURREY, GU27 1AJ.
•**YARSLEY, Mr. David, FCA** *1972;* D. Yarsley, 10 Quail Green, WOLVERHAMPTON, WEST MIDLANDS, WV6 8DF. See also D Yarsley(Tax and Accountancy) Ltd and Yarsley D.
YARWOOD, Ms. Frances, BSc ACA *1987;* 22 Fitzjames Avenue, CROYDON, CR0 5DH.
•**YARWOOD, Mr. Ian Roy, FCA** *1970;* Ian Yarwood & Co, 2 Station Road, SOLIHULL, B91 3SB.
YARWOOD, Mr. Paul Anthony, ACA *2009;* 22 Heathfield Road, BURY, LANCASHIRE, BL9 8HB.
YARWOOD, Ms. Sarah Sally Anne, BSc ACA *1984;* 20 Haydon Park Road, Wimbledon, LONDON, SW19 8JY.
YARWOOD, Mr. Simon Paul, BA(Hons) ACA *2002;* 25 Priory View Road, Moordown, BOURNEMOUTH, BH9 3JQ.
YARWOOD, Mr. Stephen John, BA ACA *1986;* Brock House, Brock Road, Great Eccleston, PRESTON, LANCASHIRE, PR3 0XD.
YASHIN, Mr. Stepan, ACA *2011;* Udarnaya 22 - 26, 440028 PENZA, RUSSIAN FEDERATION.
YASHKOV, Mr. Alexey, ACA *2008;* ZAO PricewaterhouseCoopers Audit 10 Butyrsky Val, 125047 MOSCOW, RUSSIAN FEDERATION.
YASIN, Mr. Muzammal, BSc ACA *1995;* 21 Pavenham Drive, BIRMINGHAM, B5 7TN.
•**YASIN, Mr. Waseem, BSc FCA** *1995;* Riley Moss Limited, Riley House, 183-185 North Road, PRESTON, PR1 1YQ. See also Riley Moss Audit LLP
YASIN, Miss. Zarka, BSc ACA *2007;* 336-338 Fulham Palace Road, LONDON, SW6 6HS.
•**YASUE, Ms. Rachel Miako, BSc FCA** *1992;* KPMG LLP, 15 Canada Square, LONDON, E14 5GL. See also KPMG Europe LLP
YASUE, Miss. Rebecca Michiko, BA ACA *1988;* 2a The Nook, Hallowes Park Road, Cullingworth, BRADFORD, BD13 5AS.
YASUI, Mrs. Yuki, MSc BSc(Econ) ACA *2000;* UNEP Finance Initiative, International Environment House D-513, 15 Chemin des Anemones, CH-1219 GENEVA, SWITZERLAND.
YATEMAN-SMITH, Miss. Amy Louise, BA ACA *2009;* 8 Isaac Way, LONDON, SE1 1EE.
YATES, Mr. Adam, BSc ACA *2011;* 317 Hotwell Road, BRISTOL, BS8 4NQ.
YATES, Mr. Andrew Barclay, BA(Hons) FCA *2000;* 8 Pearman's Hill, WARWICK WK03, BERMUDA.
YATES, Mr. Andrew David, BSc FCA *1987;* 21 Wilton Crescent, LONDON, SW19 3QY.
YATES, Mr. Andrew Desmond, BA FCA *1973;* Flat A, 70 Castlebar Road, LONDON, W5 2DD.
YATES, Mr. Andrew Glyn, BSc ACA *2000;* PO Box 248, Collins Street West, MELBOURNE, VIC 8007, AUSTRALIA.
YATES, Mr. Andrew James Vincent, BSc ACA *1987;* 10 Cobbittee Street, MOSMAN, NSW 2088, AUSTRALIA.
YATES, Mr. Andrew John, LLB ACA *2004;* with Deloitte LLP, Athene Place, 66 Shoe Lane, LONDON, EC4A 3BQ.
YATES, Mr. Andrew Joseph, ACA *1984;* 9 Edenhurst Avenue, LONDON, SW6 3PD.
YATES, Mr. Andrew Temple, FCA *1975;* 83 Pembroke Road, Clifton, BRISTOL, BS8 3EA.
•**YATES, Mr. Brian John, FCA** *1969;* 14 Worcester Road, Lodge Moor, SHEFFIELD, S10 4JJ.
YATES, Mr. Christopher Henry Francis, MA FCA *1999;* Nexus Vehicle Management, 141 Richardshaw Lane, Stanningley, PUDSEY, WEST YORKSHIRE, LS28 6AA.
YATES, Mr. Christopher John, MA ACA *1979;* 60 Minster Road, LONDON, NW2 3RE.
YATES, Mr. Christopher Paul, BA ACA *1995;* 9 Pontoise Close, SEVENOAKS, TN13 3ES.
YATES, Mrs. Claire Marie, ACA *1994;* 63 Stowe Avenue, West Bridgford, NOTTINGHAM, NG2 7HQ.
YATES, Mrs. Clare Therese, ACA *1987;* 9 Milner Road, LYTHAM ST. ANNES, FY8 4EY.
YATES, Mr. Clifford, FCA *1972;* 11 Southcliffe, Great Harwood, BLACKBURN, BB6 7PP.
•**YATES, Mr. Colin Michael, ACA** *1989;* (Tax Fac), Yates & Co, 27 Rosewood Gardens, Marchwood, SOUTHAMPTON, SO40 4YX.
YATES, Mr. David, BA ACA *2007;* 19 Lawrence Close, GUILDFORD, SURREY, GU4 7RD.
YATES, Mr. David Andrew, BA ACA *2007;* with PricewaterhouseCoopers LLP, 1 Embankment Place, LONDON, WC2N 6RH.
YATES, Mr. Dominique Robert De Lisle, BSc ACA *1991;* Acorn Lodge, St. Huberts Lane, GERRARDS CROSS, BUCKINGHAMSHIRE, SL9 7BP.
YATES, Mr. Douglas Martin, BSc FCA *1967;* 29 Grange Gardens, PINNER, HA5 5QD.
YATES, Mrs. Eleanor, LLB ACA *2003;* 2 Broom Way, KETTERING, NORTHAMPTONSHIRE, NN15 7RB.
YATES, Miss. Elizabeth, BSc ACA *2001;* with Allotts, The Old Grammar School, 13 Moorgate Road, ROTHERHAM, SOUTH YORKSHIRE, S60 2EN.
YATES, Mrs. Elizabeth Mary, BSc FCA *1989;* 1 Olton Court, 89 St Bernard's Road, Olton, SOLIHULL, B92 7EN.
YATES, Miss. Emily, ACA *2009;* MBIA, Hiscox Underwriting Ltd, 1 Great St. Helen's, LONDON, EC3A 6HX.
YATES, Mr. Eric Nicolas, BA ACA *1990;* Im Erlich 48, 64291 DARMSTADT, GERMANY.
YATES, Mrs. Fiona Elizabeth, BSc ACA *1987;* 10 Cobbittee Street, MOSMAN, NSW 2088, AUSTRALIA.
YATES, Mrs. Fiona Jane, BA ACA *1991;* South Wing, Yewden Manor, Hambleden, HENLEY-ON-THAMES, RG9 6RJ.
YATES, Mr. Geoffrey John, FCA *1951;* Speldhurst, 15 Dr Browns Road, Minchinhampton, STROUD, GL6 9DD. (Life Member)
YATES, Mr. Geoffrey Michael, FCA *1954;* 2 Daisy Bank Crescent, Audlem, CREWE, CW3 0HD. (Life Member)
YATES, Mrs. Helen, BA ACA AMCT *2000;* 108 Hollin Lane, Styal, WILMSLOW, CHESHIRE, SK9 4LD.
YATES, Mr. Howard Mark, MA ACA *1998;* 8 Orchard Road, BRENTFORD, MIDDLESEX, TW8 0QX.
YATES, Mr. James William, BA ACA *1997;* 20 Onslow Avenue, RICHMOND, SURREY, TW10 6QB.
•**YATES, Mr. John Alexander, DBA FCA MBA** *1975;* No 2 Old Farmhouse Drive, Oxshott, LEATHERHEAD, KT22 0EY.
YATES, Mr. John Anthony, FCA *1970;* 20 Leo Court, Augustus Close, BRENTFORD, Middlesex, TW8 8QX.
YATES, Mr. John Frederick, BSc FCA *1974;* Willow Way, Free Green Lane, Over Peover, KNUTSFORD, WA16 9QY. (Life Member)
YATES, Mr. John Gipson, FCA *1957;* 76 Forest Rd, Narborough, LEICESTER, LE19 3EQ. (Life Member)
YATES, Mr. John Oliver, FCA *1970;* 9 Hamilton Road, OXFORD, OX2 7PY. (Life Member)
YATES, Mr. John Richard, BSc FCA *1982;* JRY Associates, 86 Victoria Road, Hale, ALTRINCHAM, CHESHIRE, WA15 9AB.
YATES, Mr. John Richard Stevenson, FCA *1956;* Little Paddock, Middletown Lane, STUDLEY, B80 7PW. (Life Member)
YATES, Mr. John Thomas, FCA *1968;* 11 Friary Avenue, LICHFIELD, STAFFORDSHIRE, WS13 6QQ.
YATES, Mrs. Julia Lindsay, BA ACA *2005;* with PricewaterhouseCoopers, Strathvale House, PO Box 258, GEORGE TOWN, GRAND CAYMAN, KY1-1104 CAYMAN ISLANDS.
•**YATES, Mr. Julian Anthony, MA ACA** *1993;* with Ernst & Young LLP, 100 Barbirolli Square, MANCHESTER, M2 3EY.
YATES, Miss. Katherine Ann, BSc ACA *1995;* A T & T Highfield House, Headless Cross Drive, REDDITCH, WORCESTERSHIRE, B97 5EQ.

•**YATES, Mrs. Lorraine, LLB ACA** *2001;* 64 Somerset Road, New Barnet, BARNET, EN5 1JD.
YATES, Mr. Mark, BA ACA *2007;* with Clash-Media Advertising Limited, Totara Park House, 34-36 Gray's Inn Road, LONDON, WC1X 8HR.
YATES, Mr. Martin Harold, FCA *1977;* 69 Laburnum Park, BOLTON, BL2 3BX.
YATES, Mr. Paul Anthony, FCA *1970;* Summerfield, Higher Park Road, BRAUNTON, EX33 2LG. (Life Member)
YATES, Mr. Paul Brian, ACA *2002;* Manheim Auctions Central House, Pontefract Road Rothwell, LEEDS, LS26 0JE.
•**YATES, Mr. Peter Charles, FCA** *1960;* Peter C. Yates, 100 Baker Street, POTTERS BAR, HERTFORDSHIRE, EN6 2EP.
YATES, Mr. Peter Francis Seymour, BSc ACA *1992;* 80 Eastmoor Park, HARPENDEN, AL5 1BP.
YATES, Mr. Peter Malcolm, BSc FCA *1980;* Font Hill, Le Mont De La Trinite, St. Helier, JERSEY, JE2 4NX.
•**YATES, Mr. Peter Richard, FCA** *1973;* P.O.Box 1111, GEORGETOWN, GRAND CAYMAN, KY1 - 1102, CAYMAN ISLANDS.
YATES, Miss. Philippa Jayne, ACA *2009;* 32 Wilson Road, READING, RG30 2RN.
•**YATES, Mr. Raymond Derek, FCA** *1969;* UL Wesola 29, 05-510 KONSTANCIN-JEZIORNA, POLAND.
•**YATES, Mr. Richard Charles, LLB(Hons) FCA CTA AIIT** *1985;* (Tax Fac), Richard C. Yates, 16 Arnold Grove, Shirley, SOLIHULL, WEST MIDLANDS, B90 3JR. See also Rytax Consultants Ltd
YATES, Mr. Richard James, ACA *2008;* 3 Glenowen House, Lansdown Road, CHELTENHAM, GLOUCESTERSHIRE, GL50 2JA.
YATES, Mr. Richard James, BCom ACA *1997;* Credit Suisse, Controllers (Product Control), 1 Raffles Link, #03/#04-01 South Lobby, SINGAPORE 039393, SINGAPORE.
YATES, Mr. Robert, BA ACA *2010;* 83 Pembroke Road, Clifton, BRISTOL, BS8 3EA.
YATES, Mr. Robert William Frederick, FCA *1970;* Crows Nest, Helford Passage, FALMOUTH, CORNWALL, TR11 5LB.
YATES, Mr. Rodney Brooks, FCA *1962;* 4 Greatford Road, Uffington, STAMFORD, LINCOLNSHIRE, PE9 4SW. (Life Member)
YATES, Mr. Roger Andrew, BSc ACA *1983;* East London Bus Group Ltd, Stephenson Street, LONDON, E16 4SA.
YATES, Mrs. Ruth Elizabeth, MSc BA ACA *1996;* 10 Wood End Hill, HARPENDEN, HERTFORDSHIRE, AL5 3EZ.
YATES, Mrs. Samantha Louise, BCom ACA *1998;* Brackenwood, 164 Thornhill Road, SUTTON COLDFIELD, WEST MIDLANDS, B74 2EH.
YATES, Miss. Sarah Elizabeth, BSc ACA *2000;* Flat 6 Chimneys Court 119, Ridgway, Wimbledon, LONDON, SW19 4RE.
YATES, Miss. Sarah Jane, ACA *2008;* Flat 2/B, Sir John Lyon House, 8 High Timber Street, LONDON, EC4V 3PA.
YATES, Mrs. Stella Maria, BSc ACA *2003;* George Commercial Department, George House, Hunter Boulevard, Magna Park, LUTTERWORTH, LEICESTERSHIRE LE17 4XN.
YATES, Mr. Stephen Bradshaw, BSc FCA ATII TEP *1989;* (Tax Fac), Rawlinson & Hunter, 6 New Street Square, LONDON, EC4A 3AQ.
YATES, Mr. Stephen Luke, MA MLitt ACA *2002;* 42 Perivale Way, STOURBRIDGE, DY8 4ND.
YATES, Mr. Stuart William, BA ACA *1993;* Robin Hill Water End, Stokenchurch, HIGH WYCOMBE, BUCKINGHAMSHIRE, HP14 3XQ.
YATES, Mr. Thomas Henry, MA ACA *2009;* Flat 2 133 Bennerley Road, LONDON, SW11 6DX.
YATES, Mr. Tim, BSc ACA *2007;* Eidos Technologies Ltd Wimbledon Bridge House, 1 Hartfield Road, LONDON, SW19 3RU.
•**YATES, Mr. Timothy Benjamin, BSc ACA** *2002;* Holeys, Stuart House, 15/17 North Park Road, HARROGATE, HG1 5PD. See also Holeys Limited
YATES-MERCER, Mr. David Robert George, BA ACA *1993;* 15 Foster Close, STEVENAGE, HERTFORDSHIRE, SG1 4SA.
YATES-MERCER, Mr. George Lewis, FCA *1957;* 209 Lavender Hill, ENFIELD, EN2 8RW. (Life Member)
YATSUN, Miss. Oksana, BA ACA *2010;* Flat 10, 60 Sinclair Road, LONDON, W14 0NH.
YAU, Ms. Amelia Yu Xin, ACA *2005;* with PricewaterhouseCoopers, Prince's Building, 22/F, 10 Chater Road, CENTRAL, HONG KONG ISLAND HONG KONG SAR.
YAU, Mr. Chi Fai Kenny, ACA *2007;* King Field Shipyard Limited, 76 Tam Kon Shan Road, TSING YI, NEW TERRITORIES, HONG KONG SAR.
YAU, Mr. Christopher, ACA *2010;* Flat 7 31/F Ka Oi House, Ka Keng Court, SHA TIN, HONG KONG SAR.
YAU, Mr. David Chung Man, BA FCA *1983;* with Deloitte Touche Tohmatsu, 30th Floor, Bund Centre, 222 Yan An Road East, SHANGHAI 20002, CHINA.
YAU, Ms. Emily, BA ACA *2009;* 3 The Mount, Alwoodley, LEEDS, LS17 7RH.
YAU, Mr. Fook Chuen Stephen, ACA *2005;* Room 2101A, Nan Fung Centre, 264-298 Castle Peak Road, TSUEN WAN, NEW TERRITORIES, HONG KONG SAR.
YAU, Mr. Henry Clement Hok-Wai, MSc BSc ACA *1992;* Flat E 13/F Ilford Court Perth Garden, 5 Perth Street, HO MAN TIN, KOWLOON, HONG KONG SAR.
YAU, Miss. Kok-Yee, BSc ACA *2007;* Ingenious Media Plc, 15 Golden Square, LONDON, W1F 9JG.
•**YAU, Ms. Lai Man, ACA** *2006;* Room 2818, China Merchants Tower, Shun Tak Centre, 168-200 Connaught Road, CENTRAL, HONG KONG ISLAND HONG KONG SAR.
YAU, Ms. Lai Ngo, ACA *2005;* Flat B 18/F, Hilary Court, 63G Bonham Road, MID LEVELS, HONG KONG ISLAND, HONG KONG SAR.
YAU, Miss. Linda Wong Kiu, BSc ACA *1994;* Flat C 12th Floor, The Leighton Hill, 2B Broadwood Road, HAPPY VALLEY, HONG KONG ISLAND, HONG KONG SAR.
YAU, Mr. Robin, BSc ACA *2007;* Pricewaterhousecoopers Llys Tawe, Kings Road, SWANSEA, SA1 8PG.
YAU, Mr. Rudi, BA ACA *2005;* 69 Basin Approach, LONDON, E14 7JB.
YAU, Mr. Sai Ming, ACA *2008;* 2602 26/F Technology Plaza, 29-35 Sha Tsui Road, TSUEN WAN, NEW TERRITORIES, HONG KONG SAR.
YAU, Mr. Stephen Wai-Hing, BSc ACA *1987;* 19 Floor Seaview Commercial Building, 21-24 Connaught Road West, SHEUNG WAN, HONG KONG ISLAND, HONG KONG SAR.
YAU, Ms. Wan Wah Lindy, ACA *2005;* C K Yau & Partners CPA Limited, 11-13/F Pico Tower, 66 Gloucester Road, WAN CHAI, HONG KONG SAR.
YAU, Mr. Yan-Man, BSc ACA *1980;* Far East Consortium Building, Room 1501, 121 Des Voeux Road, CENTRAL, HONG KONG ISLAND, HONG KONG SAR.
YAU, Mr. Ying Fai Eddie, ACA *2005;* Rm J1 9/F, Kaiser Estate II, 47-53 Man Yue Street, HUNG HOM, KOWLOON, HONG KONG SAR.
YAVARI, Mr. Justin Bahram, BSc ACA *2005;* 75 Cheddington Road, Edmonton, LONDON, N18 1LU.
YAWAR BAKHSHI, Mr. Muneeb, ACA *2008;* 59/1 Khayaban e Ghazi, Phase 5, Defence Housing Authority, KARACHI 75500, PAKISTAN.
•**YAXLEY, Mrs. Carolyne, BSc ACA** *1999;* (Tax Fac), Carolyne Yaxley ACA, 5 St. Wilfrids Drive, Grappenhall, WARRINGTON, WA4 2SH.
•**YAXLEY, Mr. Christopher William, LLB FCA CTA** *1971;* 55 Porthill Road, SHREWSBURY, SY3 8RN.
YAZDABADI, Mr. Alan, BA ACA *2006;* 32 Oval Road, CROYDON, CR0 6BJ.
YAZDANI, Mr. Neil, BA ACA *2005;* with Deloitte LLP, 2 New Street Square, LONDON, EC4A 3BZ.
YAZGI, Mr. Robert Joseph, BSc FCA *1961;* Avenue Perdtemps 19, 1260 Nyon, VAUD, SWITZERLAND. (Life Member)
YDLIBI, Mr. John Abdo Rowland, BA ACA *1990;* 46 Mansfield Road, Brinsley, NOTTINGHAM, NG16 5AE.
YDLIBI, Mr. Nicholas Abdo Rodney, BA ACA *1991;* 14 Wallace Avenue, Carlton, NOTTINGHAM, NG4 3AS.
YE, Mr. Jun, ACA *2010;* Room 728, Zhongda International Mansion, 30 Nan Da Street, XI'AN 710002, CHINA.
YE, Mr. Kan, ACA *2011;* 70 Netherwood Green, NORWICH, NORFOLK, NR1 2JG.
YEADON, Mrs. Jane Margaret, BA ACA *1993;* with Princecroft Willis LLP, Towngate House, 2-8 Parkstone Road, POOLE, DORSET, BH15 2PW.
YEADON, Mr. Kenneth Edward, FCA *1952;* October Cottage, Claphill Lane, Rushwick, WORCESTER, WR2 5TP. (Life Member)
YEADON, Mr. Tom Henry, ACA *2009;* Flat 2, 114 St. Dunstans Road, LONDON, W6 8RA.
YEALLAND, Mr. Richard Ian, FCA *1963;* JL Teratai VII Blok O, No 10, Tanjung Barat Indah, 12530 JAKARTA, MALAYSIA.
YEANDLE, Mr. Colin John, FCA *1969;* Le Bois Renault, 61320 LA LACELLE, FRANCE.
YEANDLE, Miss. Emily Louise, BSc ACA *2009;* 17 Foster Drive, Penylan, CARDIFF, CF23 9BD.
•**YEANDLE, Mr. George Robb, BSc FCA** *1983;* Pricewaterhousecoopers, 1 Embankment Place, LONDON, WC2N 6RH. See also PricewaterhouseCoopers LLP
YEANDLE, Mr. Henry Squire, FCA *1951;* West Darwood, Darwood Place, ST.IVES, CAMBRIDGESHIRE, PE27 5PG. (Life Member)
YEANDLE, Mr. Simon Peter, BSc ACA *1992;* 26 Heather Street, WHEELER HEIGHTS, NSW 2097, AUSTRALIA.
YEAP, Mr. Cavin Khoo Hong, BA(Econ) ACA *1999;* 72 Jalan SS22/34, 47400 PETALING JAYA, MALAYSIA.
YEAP, Mr. Dah Shen, BCom ACA *2001;* 42 Jalan BU12/6, Bandar Utama, 47800 PETALING JAYA, MALAYSIA.
YEAP, Mr. Edwin Khoo Soon, BSc ACA *1995;* Lot 8 Lingkaran Sultan Mohamed 1, Bandar Sultan Suleiman, PO Box 93, 42008 PORT KLANG, SELANGOR, MALAYSIA.
YEARDSLEY, Mr. Robert William, FCA *1977;* 5 Tyers Avenue, Lydiate, LIVERPOOL, L31 4LD.
YEARLEY, Mrs. Patricia Ann, BSc FCA DChA *1993;* 9 Sheridan Crescent, CHISLEHURST, KENT, BR7 5RZ.
YEARSLEY, Mr. Andrew Mark, BA(Hons) ACA *2010;* 38 Park Road, Congresbury, BRISTOL, BS49 5HN.
YEARSLEY, Miss. Francesca Clare, BSc ACA *2005;* with Deloitte LLP, 2 New Street Square, LONDON, EC4A 3BZ.
YEARSLEY, Mr. Geoffrey Bradburn, FCA *1958;* 7 Ruskin Court, KNUTSFORD, WA16 6HN. (Life Member)
YEARSLEY, Mr. Joseph, BA ACA *2002;* Apartment 20, 4 Wolf Grange, ALTRINCHAM, CHESHIRE, WA15 9TS.
YEATES, Mr. Andrew, BSc(Hons) ACA *2011;* 66 Foss Road, DERBY, DERBYSHIRE, DE65 5BH.
YEATES, Mr. Christopher John William, ACA *2008;* 53 Bracondale, NORWICH, NR1 2AT.
YEATES, Mrs. Claire Helen, ACA *2008;* 55 Lambourne Way, Tongham, FARNHAM, SURREY, GU10 1AB.
YEATES, Mr. David James, BSc ACA *2003;* 4 Jumb Beck Close, Burley in Wharfedale, ILKLEY, WEST YORKSHIRE, LS29 7RE.
YEATES, Mr. Jeremy, MMath ACA *2011;* 59 Thurlestone Avenue, ILFORD, ESSEX, IG3 9DX.
•**YEATES, Mrs. Joanne Carol, FCA** *1993;* Joanne Yeates, 4 Basted Mill, Basted Lane, Crouch, SEVENOAKS, KENT TN15 8LP.
YEATES, Mr. Paul Graham, BSc ACA *1995;* 33 Somerton Road, Cricklewood, LONDON, NW2 1RJ.
•**YEATES, Mr. Roger, FCA** *1967;* (Tax Fac), Roger Yeates, 4 Petrel Croft, Kempshott, BASINGSTOKE, RG22 5JY.
YEATES, Mrs. Stephanie Lisa, BSc ACA *2006;* 5 Ridgewood Gardens, NEWCASTLE UPON TYNE, NE3 1SB.
•**YEATES, Mr. Stephen Peter, ACA** *1983;* Midgley Snelling, Ibex House, Baker Street, WEYBRIDGE, SURREY, KT13 8AH.
YEATES, Mr. Thomas Richard, BSc ACA *2003;* with PricewaterhouseCoopers LLP, 89 Sandyford Road, NEWCASTLE UPON TYNE, NE1 8HW.
YEATMAN, Miss. Gillian Margaret, BSc FCA *1967;* Orchard House, Cot Lane, Chidham, CHICHESTER, WEST SUSSEX, PO18 8ST. (Life Member)
YEATMAN, Mr. Graham Edward, BSc FCA *1991;* 7 Holm Oak Close, Littleton, WINCHESTER, SO22 6PJ.
YEATMAN, Dr. Stuart Gregory, PhD BSc ACA *2005;* 64 Fair Close, BECCLES, SUFFOLK, NR34 9QR.
YEE, Mr. Chee Kong William, FCA *1972;* 4578 Mayfair Ave., MONTREAL H4B 2E5, QC, CANADA. (Life Member)
YEE, Mr. Chi Hang Andrew, ACA *2008;* Flat H, 24/F Block 9, Fullview Garden, 18 Siu Sai Wan Road, CHAI WAN, HONG KONG ISLAND HONG KONG SAR.
YEE, Mr. Fook Loong, ACA *1980;* 18-1 Bangsar Peak, 17 Jalan Medang Serai, 59100 KUALA LUMPUR, FEDERAL TERRITORY, MALAYSIA.
YEE, Mr. George, FCA *1969;* Flat 4, 7th Floor, 2M Cornwall Street, KOWLOON TONG, KOWLOON, HONG KONG SAR. (Life Member)
YEE, Mr. Kit Hong, BA ACA *1986;* 371 Beach Road, Apt 19-06, Keypoint, SINGAPORE 199597, SINGAPORE.
•**YEE, Mr. Pak Young, BSc FCA** *1976;* (Tax Fac), Pak Yee & Co, 6 The Cleave, HARPENDEN, AL5 5SJ.
YEE, Miss. Suzanne Catherine, BSc ACA *1992;* c/o Goldman Sachs Intl, Peterborough Court, 133 Fleet Street, LONDON, EC4A 2BB.
YEE, Ms. Wai Bo, ACA *2008;* Flat 3902 Tung King House, Tung Yuk Court, SHAU KEI WAN, HONG KONG SAR.
YEE, Ms. Wendy Wai Fong, ACA *2006;* 7/F Tin Fung Industrial Mansions, 63 Wong Chuk Hang Road, WONG CHUK HANG, HONG KONG ISLAND, HONG KONG SAR. See also Wendy W F Yee
YEE, Mr. Yoon Chong, BSc FCA *1982;* 2 Jalan Rahim Kajai, Taman Tun Dr Ismail, 60000 KUALA LUMPUR, FEDERAL TERRITORY, MALAYSIA.
•**YEE, Mr. Yue Thye, FCA** *1974;* Y.T. Yee & Co, 8-12-11a Menara Bangsar, Jalan Liku, P.O. Box 12536, 50782 KUALA LUMPUR, FEDERAL TERRITORY MALAYSIA.
YEE CHEN HING, Miss. Lan Foon Stephanie, BSc ACA *2001;* 123 Avondale Road, BROMLEY, BR1 4HR.
•**YEELES, Mr. Adrian Trannack, LLB ACA** *1990;* PricewaterhouseCoopers LLP, The Atrium, 1 Harefield Road, UXBRIDGE, UB8 1EX. See also PricewaterhouseCoopers
YEELES, Mr. Jonathan Neil, BA ACA *1996;* 2 Colton Square, LEICESTER, LE1 1QH.
YEELES, Mr. Michael Trannack, FCA *1961;* Saturday Cottage, 68 Lincoln Drive, Pyrford, WOKING, GU22 8RR. (Life Member)
YEH, Mr. King Yeung Albrecht Carl, ACA *2007;* 23/F Wing Hang Finance Centre, 60 Gloucester Road, WAN CHAI, HONG KONG SAR.
YELDHAM, Mr. David John, BSc FCA *1976;* Flat 6, 24 Rathbone Street, LONDON, W1T 1NY.
YELDHAM, Mr. John Geoffrey, MA MSc ACA *2002;* with BDO LLP, 55 Baker Street, LONDON, W1U 7EU.
YELDON, Mrs. Elizabeth Anne, BSc ACA *1988;* 146 The Mount, YORK, YO24 1BW.
YELLAND, Mr. Allen Percy, FCA *1961;* 40 Avenue D'Aire, 1203 GENEVA, SWITZERLAND. (Life Member)
YELLAND, Mr. Christopher, BSc ACA *1993;* 39 Tilford Road, FARNHAM, GU9 8DN.
•**YELLAND, Mr. John Anthony, OBE FCA** *1962;* (Tax Fac), John Yelland & Company, 22 Sansome Walk, WORCESTER, WR1 1LS.
•**YELLAND, Mr. Simon James, BSc ACA** *2002;* Bostock White Limited, Unit 1, Cabourn House, Station Street, Bingham, NOTTINGHAM NG13 8AQ.
YELLAND, Mr. Stephen Clive, BSc ACA *1989;* with Swiss Re, 30 St. Mary Axe, LONDON, EC3A 8EP.
YELLEN, Mr. Philip, BA ACA *2006;* Flat 108 Boston Building, Deals Gateway, LONDON, SE13 7RW.
•**YELLOWLEES, Mr. Nicholas John, ACA** *1981;* 43 High Street, MARLOW, BUCKINGHAMSHIRE, SL7 1BA.
YEN, Miss. Catherine Kai Shun, BA ACA *1989;* Ernst & Young, 18/F, Two International Finance Centre, 8 Finance Street, CENTRAL, HONG KONG ISLAND HONG KONG SAR.
YEN, Mr. Heng Fook, ACA *1982;* Ernst & Young, One Raffles Quay, North Tower, Level 18, SINGAPORE 048583, SINGAPORE. See also Evan Wong & Co and Ee Peng Liang & Co
YEN, Ms. Sau Yin Emily, ACA *2007;* Deloitte Touche Tohmatsu, 35/F One Pacific Place, 88 Queensway, CENTRAL, HONG KONG ISLAND, HONG KONG SAR.
YEN, Miss. Siw Kuin, BSc ACA *1983;* 64 Jalan SS2/91, 47300 PETALING JAYA, SELANGOR, MALAYSIA.
YENAGRITES, Mr. Marios, BSc ACA *2004;* 14 Esperidon Street, 1087 NICOSIA, CYPRUS.
YENDLE, Mr. Anthony, FCA *1959;* Bryn Parkia, Bangor Road, CAERNARFON, GWYNEDD, LL55 1TP. (Life Member)
YENDLE, Miss. Nicola Jo, BA(Hons) ACA *2000;* 5 Wemberham Crescent, Yatton, BRISTOL, BS49 4BD.
YENNEMADI, Mr. Vinod Gurudatta, FCA *1970;* 303 B Wing Hasmukh Mansion, Junction of 14th Road and CD Road, Khar (W), MUMBAI 400052, INDIA.
YENTOB, Mr. Robert, FCA *1970;* 18 Cumberland Terrace, LONDON, NW1 4HS.
YEO, Mrs. Alison Clare, BSc ACA ACCA *1997;* 23 St. Leonards Road, AMERSHAM, BUCKINGHAMSHIRE, HP6 6DT.
YEO, Mrs. Amy Margaret, BSc ACA *1997;* Barclaycard House, Barclaycard, 1234 Pavilion Drive, NORTHAMPTON, NN4 7SG.
YEO, Mr. Andrew Frederick, BCom ACA *1985;* 34 Cheverton Road, LONDON, N19 3AZ.
YEO, Mr. Andrew Richard, MEng ACA *1995;* 4 Longmoor Close, Finchampstead, WOKINGHAM, RG40 4DZ.
YEO, Mr. Chee Chiow, FCA *1973;* 802 Dunearn Road, SINGAPORE 289670, SINGAPORE.
YEO, Mr. Clive Richard, BSc ACA *1994;* DPIA, The Coal Exchange, Mount Stuart Square, CARDIFF, CF10 5EB.
YEO, Mr. David Alexander, MA ACA *2003;* Flat 1, 102 Bulwer Road, BARNET, HERTFORDSHIRE, EN5 5EY.

YEO, Mr. David Seng Lee, BSc ACA *1984;* 14 SS 2/94, 47300, PETALING JAYA, SELANGOR, MALAYSIA.
YEO, Miss. Elizabeth Mary, FCA *1957;* Greensleeves, Clarence Road East, WESTON-SUPER-MARE, BS23 4BT. (Life Member)
YEO, Mr. Eng Swee, FCA *1969;* 10B Braddell Hill, Apt.07-07, SINGAPORE 579721, SINGAPORE.
YEO, Mr. Hian Chong, BAcc ACA *2006;* Block 248 Choa Chu Kang Avenue 2 #13-496 Singapore 680248, SINGAPORE, SINGAPORE.
YEO, Mr. John Jih-Jong, BA ACA *1990;* 44 Milton Park, Highgate, LONDON, N6 5QA.
YEO, Mr. Kar Teck, ACA *2008;* Blk 20 Telok Blangah Crescent #05-88, SINGAPORE 090020, SINGAPORE.
YEO, Mrs. Marie-Claire, BSc ACA *2005;* 20 Combedale Road, LONDON, SE10 0LG.
YEO, Mr. Martin John, FCA *1974;* 63 Chadwick Road, GIBSONS V0N 1V6, BC, CANADA.
YEO, Ms. Monique Cheng Yee, BSc ACA *1995;* 4 Hollytrees, Church Crookham, FLEET, GU51 5NL.
•**YEO, Mr. Ooi Leng, FCA** *1972;* O.L. Yeo & Co, 110 A & B, Jalan Melaka Raya 25, Taman Melaka Raya, 75000 MALACCA CITY, MALACCA STATE MALAYSIA.
YEO, Miss. Patricia Wei Ping, BSc ACA *1989;* 57 University Road, SINGAPORE 297883, SINGAPORE.
YEO, Mr. Robert Philip, BSc FCA *1999;* 340 W72nd Street, Apartment 4BC, NEW YORK, NY 10023, UNITED STATES.
YEO, Miss. Su-Lynn, ACA *1996;* 1001 Bukit Timah Road #10-15, The Sterling, SINGAPORE 596288, SINGAPORE.
YEO, Mr. Tee Kiat, ACA *2007;* Blk 699C Hougang Street 52, #12-37, SINGAPORE 533699, SINGAPORE.
YEOH, Miss. Chit Ghee, BSc FCA *1996;* 132 Graham Road, Wimbledon, LONDON, SW19 3SJ.
YEOH, Mr. Chong Keat, FCA *1982;* 53 Lengkok Aminuddin Baki, Taman Tun Dr. Ismail, 60000 KUALA LUMPUR, FEDERAL TERRITORY, MALAYSIA.
YEOH, Miss. Christina Su Mei, LLB ACA *1995;* Credit Suisse, One Raffles Quay, SINGAPORE 048583, SINGAPORE.
YEOH, Miss. Guat Ee, ACA *1980;* 2 Pekeliling Sempadan, Padang Tembak, 11400 PENANG, MALAYSIA. (Life Member)
YEOH, Mr. Johnny Sin Poh, BA FCA *1984;* 27 Mainroyal Court, RABY BAY, QLD 4163, AUSTRALIA.
YEOH, Mr. Lip Keong, ACA *1992;* 136A Malacca Street, 10400 PENANG, MALAYSIA.
YEOH, Mr. Oon Jin, BCom ACA *1986;* PricewaterhouseCoopers LLP, 17-00 PWC Building, 8 Cross Street, SINGAPORE 048424, SINGAPORE.
YEOH, Mr. Raymond Cheng Seong, BA ACA *1989;* 5 Taman U-Thant Tiga, 55000 KUALA LUMPUR, FEDERAL TERRITORY, MALAYSIA.
YEOH, Mr. Seng Hock, FCA *1976;* 1st & 2nd Floor Maisonette, 68 Gloucester Terrace, LONDON, W2 3HH.
YEOH, Miss. Swee Yen, BA ACA *2005;* 43 Mott Street, Apartment 10, NEW YORK, NY 10013, UNITED STATES.
YEOH, Mr. Tee Aun, BA FCA *1983;* 29 Alexandra Avenue, Canterbury, MELBOURNE, VIC 3126, AUSTRALIA.
YEOH, Mr. Tiang Eng, BA ACA *1988;* 21 West Avenue, Finchley, LONDON, N3 1AU.
YEOH ENG HOCK, Mr. William, ACA ACCA *2001;* 4 Jalan SS 24/12, Taman Megah, 47301 PETALING JAYA, SELANGOR, MALAYSIA.
YEOMAN, Mr. Ian Robert Malcolm, FCA *1949;* 3 Beverley Court, Aldrington Close, New Church Road, HOVE, BN3 5UB. (Life Member)
YEOMAN, Mr. John David, BA FCA *1991;* PricewaterhouseCoopers, Freshwater Place, 2 Southbank Boulevard, MELBOURNE, VIC 3006, AUSTRALIA.
YEOMANS, Mr. Alan Richard, BA FCA *1978;* Latimer Associates Ltd, Winnowing Barn, High Street, Sherington, NEWPORT PAGNELL, MK16 9QP.
YEOMANS, Mr. Andrew, ACA *2009;* 707/99 Jones Street, ULTIMO, NSW 2007, AUSTRALIA.
YEOMANS, Mr. Andrew Hamilton, FCA *1974;* 25 Exeter Close, TONBRIDGE, TN10 4NT.
YEOMANS, Mr. Brian, MA FCA *1979;* The Latch, White Lane, GUILDFORD, GU4 8PS.
YEOMANS, Mr. Brian, FCA *1970;* 17 Havelock Street, Desborough, KETTERING, NORTHAMPTONSHIRE, NN14 2LU.
YEOMANS, Mr. David Anthony, BSc ACA *1988;* 87 Watermarque, 100 Browning Street, BIRMINGHAM, B16 8GZ.
•**YEOMANS, Mr. Derek Mark, ACA** *1981;* Advantis Services Limited, 144 Birchfield Road, REDDITCH, WORCESTERSHIRE, B97 4LT.
YEOMANS, Mr. Frazer John, MA BSc ACA *2000;* 45 Sandmoor Place, LYMM, CHESHIRE, WA13 9GR.
•**YEOMANS, Mr. Geoffrey, FCA** *1964;* G. Yeomans & Co, 4 Poplar Way, High Lane, STOCKPORT, SK6 8ES.
YEOMANS, Mrs. Kathryn Barbara, BA ACA *1999;* Spire Cheshire Hospital, Fir Tree Close Stretton, WARRINGTON, WA4 4LU.
•**YEOMANS, Mr. Neil, BA ACA** *1987;* Deloitte LLP, 3 Victoria Square, Victoria Street, ST. ALBANS, HERTFORDSHIRE, AL1 3TF. See also Deloitte & Touche LLP
YEOMANS, Mrs. Olivia Charlotte, BSc ACA *2006;* 10 Bevington Road, BECKENHAM, BR3 5LD.
YEOMANS, Miss. Rebecca, ACA *2011;* 499 Streetsbrook Road, SOLIHULL, WEST MIDLANDS, B91 1LA.
YEOMANS, Mr. Rodger Walter Pattinson, FCA *1970;* PO Box 1584, GEORGETOWN, GRAND CAYMAN, KY1-1110, CAYMAN ISLANDS.
YEOMANS, Mr. Russell James, BSc ACA *1985;* c/o Reed Personnel Services FZ-LLC, Kowledge Village, Block 4 F15, PO Box 501734, DUBAI, UNITED ARAB EMIRATES.
YEOMANS, Mrs. Shelagh Margaret, BA ACA *1982;* The Latch, White Lane, GUILDFORD, GU4 8PS.
YEOMANS, Mr. Tod, BSc ACA *2011;* 18 Mirabel Road, LONDON, SW6 7EH.
YEOW, Mr. Keck Yam, FCA *1966;* No. 99, Lorong 1, Jalan Sentosa 14, Taman Sentosa, 75150 MALACCA CITY, MALACCA STATE MALAYSIA. (Life Member)
YEOWARD, Mr. David James, MA ACA ATII *1994;* 119B Brook Drive, LONDON, SE11 4TQ.
YERASSIMOU, Mr. Nicholas Andreas, BSc ACA *1995;* 9 Pondfield Road, ORPINGTON, BR6 8HJ.
YERBURY, Mrs. Gillian Mary, BA ACA *1992;* The Rectory New Road, Penkridge, STAFFORD, ST19 5DN.
YEROLEMOU, Mr. Loizos, BSc(Hons) ACA *2001;* 58 Cavalry Square, LONDON, SW3 4RB.
YETMAN, Mr. John Albert, FCA *1965;* Welton House, La Grande Route De Faldouet, St Martin, JERSEY, JE3 6UD.
YETMAN, Mrs. Maria Susan, BSc ACA *1992;* 10 Grange Road, GRAVESEND, DA11 0EU.
YEU, Miss. Hyun Joo, BSc(Hons) ACA *2010;* Flat 121 Ocean Wharf, 60 Westferry Road, LONDON, E14 8JF.
YEUNG, Miss. Ada Kwok Wai, ACA *2010;* Shop 2C, G/F Fung Shing Building, 168 Connaught Road West, SHEUNG WAN, HONG KONG ISLAND, HONG KONG SAR.
YEUNG, Mr. Allen, FCA *1975;* 1125 Schubert, BROSSARD J4X 1X6, QUE, CANADA.
YEUNG, Mr. Chak Chi, MSc LLB BA(Hons) ACA CPA *2008;* with PricewaterhouseCoopers, 21/F Edinburgh Tower, 15 Queen's Road Central, CENTRAL, HONG KONG ISLAND, HONG KONG SAR.
YEUNG, Mr. Cheuk Kwong, ACA *2006;* Flat C, 30th Floor, Block 3, Kai Tak Garden, 121 Choi Hung Road, WONG TAI SIN KOWLOON HONG KONG SAR.
YEUNG, Mr. Chi Hang, ACA *2008;* Flat 9E Block 3, Cheerful Garden, Siu Sai Wan, CHAI WAN, HONG KONG SAR.
YEUNG, Mr. Chi Hung, ACA *2005;* Yeung Chan & Associates CPA Limited, 1703-1705 Easey Commercial Building, 253-261 Hennessy Road, WAN CHAI, HONG KONG SAR.
YEUNG, Mr. Chi Kwong Matthias, ACA *2004;* 22/F Bank of China Tower, 1 Garden Road, CENTRAL, HONG KONG ISLAND, HONG KONG SAR.
YEUNG, Mr. Chi Tat, ACA *2007;* 60/E Floor, Tower 3, Vision City, 1 Yeung Uk Road, TSUEN WAN, NEW TERRITORIES HONG KONG SAR.
YEUNG, Mr. Chi Wai Edwin, ACA *2005;* Edwin Yeung & Co(CPA) Ltd, 12/F, Lucky Building, 39 Wellington Street, CENTRAL, HONG KONG ISLAND HONG KONG SAR.
YEUNG, Ms. Ching Mei Anna, ACA *2008;* Flat A60th FloorTower 6, Albany Cove, Caribbean Coast, 1 Kin Tung Road, TUNG CHUNG, NEW TERRITORIES HONG KONG SAR.
YEUNG, Mr. Choi Sang, ACA *2008;* C S Yeung & Co, Room 204, 2/F Lyndhurst Building, 29 Lyndhurst Terrace, CENTRAL, HONG KONG SAR.
YEUNG, Mr. David Mui Kwan, ACA *2005;* David M.K. Yeung & Co, 14/F San Toi Building, 137-139 Connaught Road Central, CENTRAL, HONG KONG ISLAND, HONG KONG SAR.
YEUNG, Mr. Ho Kong Christopher, ACA *2005;* Flat 9D Hung Fook Court, 169 Tin Hau Temple Road, NORTH POINT, HONG KONG ISLAND, HONG KONG SAR.
YEUNG, Mr. Jar Wing Louis, ACA *2005;* Louis Yeung & Co., Room 706 Grand City Plaza, 1 Sai Lau Kok Road, TSUEN WAN, 9999, HONG KONG SAR.
•**YEUNG, Mr. Jonathan Mark, BA ACA** *1999;* with PricewaterhouseCoopers LLP, 1 Embankment Place, LONDON, WC2N 6RH.
YEUNG, Miss. Josje, BSc(Econ) ACA *2004;* Flat 17C The Broadville, 4 Broadwood Road, HAPPY VALLEY, HONG KONG ISLAND, HONG KONG SAR.
YEUNG, Mr. Ka Keung, BCom ACA *1987;* PO Box 84465, Hunghom Bay Post Office, HUNG HOM, KOWLOON, HONG KONG SAR.
YEUNG, Mr. Ka Bo, ACA *2008;* K.B. Yeung & Co., Unit 6206/F Tower A, New Mandarin Plaza, No. 14 Science Museum Road, TSIM SHA TSUI, KOWLOON HONG KONG SAR.
YEUNG, Mr. Ka Chun, ACA *2008;* KPMG Advisory (China), 4th Floor, Inter Royal Building, 15 Donghai West Road, QINGDAO 266071, CHINA. See also KPMG
YEUNG, Mr. Ka Sing, ACA *2008;* 10H, Block 2, Banyan Mansions, Whampoa Garden, HUNG HOM, KOWLOON HONG KONG SAR.
YEUNG, Mr. Kai Cheung, ACA *2007;* Suite 1006, Bank of America Tower, 12 Harcourt Road, CENTRAL, HONG KONG ISLAND, HONG KONG SAR.
YEUNG, Mr. Kam Ming, ACA *2008;* Flat 1504 Block 43, Heng Fa Chuen, CHAI WAN, HONG KONG SAR.
YEUNG, Mr. Kelvin Tik Ka, MSc ACA *2002;* Barclays Capital Asia Limited, 41/F. Cheung Kong Center, 2 Queen's Road Central, CENTRAL, HONG KONG SAR.
•**YEUNG, Mr. Kenneth King Wah, BCom FCA ATII MCT** *1987;* (Tax Fac), Yeung & Co, 14 Grange Drive, CHISLEHURST, BR7 5ES.
YEUNG, Mr. Kevin Kai Yin, BSc ACA *1999;* Allendorferstr. 7, 60433 FRANKFURT AM MAIN, GERMANY.
YEUNG, Mr. Kin Wai, ACA *2007;* Room 802-804, Bank Centre, 636 Nathan Road, MONG KOK, KOWLOON, HONG KONG SAR.
YEUNG, Mr. King Yuk, ACA *2006;* CC Consortium CPA Limited, Unit 1703, Vicwood Plaza, 199 Des Voeux Road, CENTRAL, HONG KONG SAR. See also Azure Limited
YEUNG, Ms. Kit Man, ACA *2006;* KM Yeung & Co, Room 405, Dominion Centre, 43-59 Queens Road E, WAN CHAI, HONG KONG ISLAND HONG KONG SAR.
YEUNG, Mr. Kwok-Kwong Philip, BA ACA *1990;* Flat F 6/F Block 11, Sceneway Garden, LAM TIN, KOWLOON, HONG KONG SAR.
YEUNG, Mr. Lai, ACA *2007;* 289 Tai Yuan Road, Room 603 Block 2, SHANGHAI 201203, CHINA.
YEUNG, Ms. Lai Man Sandy, ACA *2007;* Flat C 18/F Block 4, Maywood Court, Kingswood Villas, TIN SHUI WAI, NEW TERRITORIES, HONG KONG SAR.
YEUNG, Mr. Lai Woo Noohu, ACA *2007;* Chung & Yeung, Suite 1001, Centre point, 181-185 Gloucester Road, WAN CHAI, HONG KONG SAR.
YEUNG, Mr. Lawrence Lok Lun, BA ACA *1995;* 162 Grand Avenue, SURBITON, KT5 9JA.
YEUNG, Ms. Lesley Kit Kam, ACA *2008;* BDO McCabe Lo Ltd, 25/F Wing On Centre, 111 Connaught Road, CENTRAL, HONG KONG SAR.
YEUNG, Ms. Mona Yuen Chun, ACA *2007;* C/O ITE (Holdings) Limited, Units 1005-07 Level 10, Manulife Provident Funds Place, 345 Nathan Road, MONG KOK, KOWLOON HONG KONG SAR.
YEUNG, Mr. Pui Yuen, BA FCA *1991;* 907 Block 46, Heng Fa Chuen, 100 Shing Tai Road, CHAI WAN, HONG KONG ISLAND, HONG KONG SAR.
YEUNG, Mr. Sai Ho Nelson, ACA *2009;* Room 1810, Heung Tung House, Yu Tung Court, TUNG CHUNG, NEW TERRITORIES, HONG KONG SAR.
YEUNG, Miss. Salina Clare, ACA *2010;* Flat 7, 94 Camberwell Grove, LONDON, SE5 8RF.
YEUNG, Mr. Sau Yin, ACA *2007;* Room 2304 23/F., Far East Consortium Building, 121 Des Voeux Road, CENTRAL, HONG KONG ISLAND, HONG KONG SAR.
YEUNG, Ms. See Man, ACA *2008;* 43D Tower 7, Park Central, TSEUNG KWAN O, HONG KONG SAR.
YEUNG, Mr. Shang, BA FCA *1973;* 17 Chisenhale, Orton Waterville, PETERBOROUGH, PE2 5FP.
YEUNG, Ms. Shuk Ching, ACA *2008;* B1 12/F Wilshire Towers, 200 Tin Hau Temple Road, NORTH POINT, HONG KONG SAR.
YEUNG, Mr. Shun Hing, ACA *2008;* Flat B 34/F Block 9 Beverly Garden, TSEUNG KWAN O, HONG KONG SAR.
YEUNG, Ms. Sim Kuen, ACA *2008;* Chu and Chu, Suite 1801-5 18/F, Tower 2, China HONG KONG SAR City, 33 Canton Road, TSIM SHA TSUI KOWLOON HONG KONG SAR.
YEUNG, Ms. Siu Ching, BSc ACA *1990;* Asia Satellite Telecommunications Ltd, 19/F, Sunning Plaza, 10 Hysan Avenue, CAUSEWAY BAY, HONG KONG ISLAND HONG KONG SAR.
YEUNG, Ms. Siu Hung, ACA *2005;* Cheng Yeung & Co. CPA, Room 1001-2, 10th Floor, Chow Tai Fook Centre, No 580 A-F Nathan Road, MONG KOK KOWLOON HONG KONG SAR.
YEUNG, Mr. Sui Por Paul, ACA *2007;* 6 Dolan Street, RYDE, NSW 2112, AUSTRALIA.
YEUNG, Miss. Susan, BA ACA *1983;* 7 Lytham Close, LIVERPOOL, L10 1NF.
YEUNG, Mr. Sze Leung Roy, ACA *2011;* Flat 704, Landmark West Tower, 22 Marsh Wall, LONDON, E14 9AF.
YEUNG, Mr. Tat Man, ACA *2007;* 45D Tower 6, Ocean Shores, 88 O King Road, TSEUNG KWAN O, NT, HONG KONG SAR.
YEUNG, Miss. Tsui Shu, MSc LLB(Hons) ACA *2003;* Flat 612, Hanover House, 7 St George Wharf, LONDON, SW8 2JA.
YEUNG, Mr. Wai Kee, BEng ACA *1993;* 39/F Flat B, La Place De Victoria, 632 King's Road, NORTH POINT, HONG KONG ISLAND, HONG KONG SAR.
YEUNG, Mr. Wai Lon, BEng ACA *1995;* 8 Wensleydale Drive, CAMBERLEY, SURREY, GU15 1SP.
YEUNG, Ms. Wai Yan, ACA *2008;* Flat F 13/F Block 4 Metro City Phase 1 1 Wan Hang Road, TSEUNG KWAN O, HONG KONG SAR.
YEUNG, Mr. William Kin Sing, BSc ACA *1990;* 4A Alpine Court, 12 Kotewall Road, MID LEVELS, HONG KONG ISLAND, HONG KONG SAR.
YEUNG, Mr. Wing Kwong, BSc ACA *1987;* PO Box 210369, SAN FRANCISCO, CA 94121, UNITED STATES.
YEUNG, Ms. Yee Wah, ACA *2008;* Flat D18/F, Block 3 Scenic View, 63 Fung Shing Street, NGAU CHI WAN, KOWLOON, HONG KONG SAR.
YEUNG, Mr. Yu Man, ACA *2007;* Deloitte Touche Tohmatsu, Shenzhen Branch, 13/F China Resources Building, 5001 Shennan Road East, SHENZHEN 518010, CHINA.
YEUNG SIK YUEN, Mrs. Laura, BSc ACA *1989;* Kemp Chatteris Deloitte, 7th. Floor, Raffles Tower, 19 Cybercity, EBENE, MAURITIUS.
YEUNG SIK YUEN, Miss. Stephanie, BSc ACA *2005;* 8/382 Miller Street, CAMMERAY, NSW 2062, AUSTRALIA.
YEUNG WING YEN, Mr. Hin Vee, ACA *1994;* Avenue Des Roses, Morcellement Swan, Tombeau Bay, TOMBEAU BAY, MAURITIUS.
YEUNG YAM WAH, Mr. Sit Kow, BSc ACA *1983;* Penny Hitch, Sandy Lane, Rushmore, FARNHAM, GU10 2ET.
YEW, Mr. Alexander, ACA *1981;* Summers Place, Upper Bordean, PETERSFIELD, HAMPSHIRE, GU32 1ET.
YEW HIN CLAIR, Ms. Corrinne, BSc(Hons) ACA *2001;* 2/24 Maroo Street, HUGHESDALE, VIC 3166, AUSTRALIA.
•**YEWDALL, Mr. John Christopher, FCA** *1980;* Spenser Wilson & Co, Equitable House, 55 Pellon Lane, HALIFAX, WEST YORKSHIRE, HX1 5SP.
YEWDALL, Mr. Neil Stuart, FCA *1981;* 31 St. Helens Lane, Adel, LEEDS, LS16 8BR.
YEWEN, Mrs. Sharon Ann, BA ACA *1996;* 21 Elm Close, NEWQUAY, TR7 2LN.
YHEARM, Mr. Allen John, ACA *1988;* Saddleback The Cross, Buckland Dinham, FROME, SOMERSET, BA11 2QS.
YI, Miss. Man-Sau, BA ACA MCT AMCT *1992;* 333 East 79th Street, No 19Z, NEW YORK, NY 10075, UNITED STATES.
•**YIACOUMI, Mr. Petros Nicou, MBA BA FCA CF** *1993;* Yiakoumi & Partners Ltd, 1 Ayias Lavras Street, Office 304 Engomi, 2414 NICOSIA, CYPRUS.
•**YIAKOUMI, Mr. Iacovos Nicou, BA FCA** *1993;* Yiakoumi & Partners Ltd, 1 Ayias Lavras Street, Office 304 Engomi, 2414 NICOSIA, CYPRUS.
•**YIALLOURIDES, Mr. George, BA FCA** *1996;* 16 Spyrou Kyprianou Street, Divine Clock Tower, 1st floor, 3070 LIMASSOL, CYPRUS.
•**YIALLOURIS, Mr. Frank, ACA FCCA** *2008;* JF Francis, Francis House, 2 Park Road, BARNET, HERTFORDSHIRE, EN5 5RN.
YIALLOUROS, Mr. Alexander, BA ACA *2005;* 2 Clydesdale, ENFIELD, EN3 4RJ.

YIALLOUROS, Mr. Andreas, BA ACA *2003;* with PricewaterhouseCoopers LLP, Hays Galleria, 1 Hays Lane, LONDON, SE1 2RD.
YIAMAKIS, Mr. Ninos Albert, FCA *1977;* 25 Herodou Atticou, 106 74 ATHENS, GREECE.
•YIAMBIDES, Mr. Kyriakos Nicola, FCA *1968;* Kyriakos Yiambides, 1 Sophoulis Street, Acropolis, 2008 NICOSIA, CYPRUS.
YIAMBIDES, Mr. Nicos, BSc(Hons) ACA *2002;* European Investment Bank, 100 Boulevard Conrad Adenauer, L2950 LUXEMBOURG, LUXEMBOURG.
YIANGOULLIS, Ms. Froso, BSc ACA *2006;* Trizinas 1, Strovolos, TT2040 NICOSIA, CYPRUS.
YIANNAKI, Mr. Andrew, BA ACA *1992;* 42 Durlston Road, KINGSTON UPON THAMES, KT2 5RT.
YIANNAKIS, Mr. Dimitrios, ACA CA(AUS) *2010;* Flat 26, The Ambassador, London Road, Sunningdale, ASCOT, BERKSHIRE SL5 0LJ.
YIANNAKOU, Miss. Maria, ACA *2009;* Flat 18 Hill Quays, 1 Jordan street, MANCHESTER, LANCASHIRE, M15 4QU.
YIANNAS, Mr. Panayiotis, BA ACA *2009;* Flat 101, 18 Kafkasou Street, Palouriotissa, 1041, NICOSIA, CYPRUS.
YIANNIKOURIS, Mr. Michalis, BSc ACA *2002;* Flat 301, 4 Ellados Street, 2003 STROVOLOS, CYPRUS.
•YIANNOPOULOS, Mr. Aimilios, FCA *1980;* PricewaterhouseCoopers, 268-270 Kifissias Avenue, Halandri, 15232 ATHENS, GREECE.
YIANNOUKAS, Mr. Joseph, BA ACA *2010;* Antigonou 10, 6036 LARNACA, CYPRUS.
YIASEMIDES, Mr. Anastassis, BSc ACA *2005;* 8 Kekropa Street, Anavargos, 8026 PAPHOS, CYPRUS.
YIASEMIDES, Mr. Andreas, BA ACA *2003;* Flat 204, 4 Gorgiou Street, 1076 NICOSIA, CYPRUS.
YIASOUMI, Mr. Thomas Andreas, BSc ACA *1995;* 106 Alcester Road South, BIRMINGHAM, B14 7PR.
YIASSEMIDES, Mr. Spyros C, MSc BA ACA *2009;* 14 Kosti Palama Street, 2121 NICOSIA, CYPRUS.
YIK, Ms. Mei Ling, ACA *2008;* Intertrust Hong Kong, 38/F Central Plaza, 18 Harbour Road, WAN CHAI, HONG KONG SAR.
YIK, Miss. Yvonne Po Yee, BA FCA *1997;* Block 14, Flat 21B, Braemar Hill Mansion, 41 Braemar Hill Road, NORTH POINT, HONG KONG ISLAND HONG KONG SAR.
YILDIRIM, Ms. Samiye, BA ACA CPA *2000;* 205 West 54st Apt 2E, NEW YORK, NY 10019, UNITED STATES.
YIM, Mr. Chun Leung, ACA *2005;* New Heritage Holdings Ltd, Room 2301 23/F Fortis Tower, 77-79 Gloucester Road, WAN CHAI, HONG KONG SAR.
YIM, Mr. Chun Yu, ACA *2010;* Flat 1706 Yiu on House, Yiu Tung Estate, SHAU KEI WAN, HONG KONG SAR.
YIM, Miss. Joyce Ka Yee, LLM MBA MPhil BSc ACA CFA *1992;* Dynasty Court, 5B Tower 4, 23 Old Peak Road, MID LEVELS, HONG KONG ISLAND, HONG KONG SAR.
YIM, Mr. Lui Fai Gerry, BA ACA *1985;* B902 Villa Verde, 12 Guildford Road, THE PEAK, HONG KONG ISLAND, HONG KONG SAR.
YIM, Miss. Mun Foon, BSc ACA *1986;* 2/128 Paritai Drive, Orakei, AUCKLAND, NEW ZEALAND.
YIM, Mr. See Hau, BA ACA MCT *2002;* 10 Jalan Wangsa Perkasa 1, Wangsa Melawati, 53300 KUALA LUMPUR, MALAYSIA.
YIM, Mr. Ting Cheong Anthony, ACA *2007;* 3791 Jalan Burit Nerah, Apt 07-05, E-Centre Redhill, SINGAPORE 159471, SINGAPORE.
YIM, Mr. Wai Chung Michael, ACA *2007;* 8A Jasmine Court, 111 Song Lin Road, PUDONG 200120, CHINA.
YIM, Mr. Weng Tat, BSc FCA *1990;* Northern Trust Management Services, 50 Bank Street, LONDON, E14 5NT.
YIM, Miss. Yuen Wa Claudia, BA ACA *1987;* Flat 26HBlock 3, Tanner Gardens NORTH POINT, Hong Kong Island, HONG KONG SAR.
YIN, Mr. Gregory Kam-Chong, BA ACA *1979;* 24 Knoll Drive, Southgate, LONDON, N14 5LT.
YIN, Mr. Richard Yingneng, FCA *1974;* Wanthorpe House, 39 Hing Lung Street, CENTRAL, HONG KONG ISLAND, HONG KONG SAR.
YIN SHING YUEN, Mr. Kian Chung, ACA *1984;* c/o Le Mauricien Limited, 8 Saint Georges Street, PORT LOUIS, MAURITIUS.
YIP, Miss. Appy Fei Yin, ACA *1983;* (Tax Fac), C/O APPY YIP, 01 KIM SENG WALK, TIARA #35-06, SINGAPORE 239403, SINGAPORE.
YIP, Mr. Brian John Sze Hain Wing, BSc ACA *2001;* 8 Manor Park Close, Moseley, BIRMINGHAM, B13 9SL.
YIP, Miss. Carol Bik Kay, MA ACA *2009;* 69a Howberry Road, EDGWARE, MIDDLESEX, HA8 6TD.
YIP, Mr. Chan Sing, ACA *1982;* B15-2 The Istara Condominium1 Lorong Utara B, 46200 PETALING JAYA, MALAYSIA.
YIP, Mr. Che Man William, ACA *2005;* Flat A1, 2/F Arts Mansion, 31 Conduit Road, MID LEVELS, HONG KONG ISLAND, HONG KONG SAR. (Life Member)
YIP, Mr. Cheung, ACA *2007;* 12/F, Cheung Kong Centre, 2 Queen's Road Central, CENTRAL, HONG KONG ISLAND, HONG KONG SAR.
YIP, Mr. Chi-Tou, ACA *2008;* 59 Longheath Gardens, CROYDON, CR0 7TD.
YIP, Mr. Chun Ho Martin, ACA *2008;* Room 2105, Block E, Mount Parker Lodge, QUARRY BAY, HONG KONG ISLAND, HONG KONG SAR.
YIP, Miss. Donna Do Ling, BSc ACA *2006;* 11 Lindley Wood Grove, YORK, YO30 4SR.
YIP, Ms. Fung Ling, ACA *2008;* Flat 1311, 13/F Block K, Telford Gardens, 33 Wai Yip Street, Kowloon Bay, KOWLOON BAY KOWLOON HONG KONG SAR.
YIP, Mr. Heung Yin, ACA *2006;* Nan Pao Group Holdings Ltd, Room 13, 10/F Block B, Tonic Industrial Centre, 19 Lam Hing Street, KOWLOON BAY KOWLOON HONG KONG SAR.
YIP, Miss. Joyce Sui Hing, BA ACA *1992;* Unit 1601 16/F Malaysia Building 50 Gloucester Road, WAN CHAI, HONG KONG ISLAND, HONG KONG SAR.
YIP, Mr. Kai Yung, ACA *2008;* Deloitte Touche Tohmatsu, Shenzhen Branch, 13/F China Resources Building, 5001 Shennan Road East, SHENZHEN 518010, CHINA.
YIP, Mr. Kam Keung, ACA *2007;* Flat E12/F, Tower 2, Jubilant Place, 99 Pau Chung Street, TO KWA WAN, KOWLOON HONG KONG SAR.
YIP, Mr. King Tung Clive, ACA *2007;* Flat A 20/F, Block 1, Granville Garden, Tai Wai, SHA TIN, NT HONG KONG SAR.
YIP, Mr. Kok Lok, ACA *1985;* 3 Mint Street, WANTIRNA, VIC 3152, AUSTRALIA.
YIP, Mr. Kok Tho, FCA *1972;* 84 Neram Road, SINGAPORE 807779, SINGAPORE.
YIP, Mrs. Kwai Fong Florence, BSc ACA *1986;* PricewaterhouseCoopers, 21/F Edinburgh Tower, 15 Queen's Road Central, CENTRAL, HONG KONG ISLAND, HONG KONG SAR.
YIP, Mr. Man Tin, ACA *2005;* Inter-Link CPA Limited, 15/F OTB Building, 259-265 Des Voeux Road Central, CENTRAL, HONG KONG ISLAND, HONG KONG SAR.
YIP, Mrs. Margaret Chi Man, BSc FCA *1998;* 10, Ridgeway, Highwoods, COLCHESTER, CO4 9UW.
•YIP, Mrs. Nathalie, ACA *1990;* Elliotts Shah, 2nd Floor, York House, 23 Kingsway, LONDON, WC2B 6UJ.
YIP, Mr. Peter Hing Lam, BSc ACA *1979;* Yip Leung & Co, Unit D, 12/F Tak Lee Commercial Building, 113-117 Wan Chai Road, WAN CHAI, HONG KONG ISLAND HONG KONG SAR.
YIP, Ms. Pui Ling Rebecca, ACA *2008;* Flat A 18/F, Lotus Mansion, 6 Taikoo Wan Road, TAIKOO SHING, HONG KONG ISLAND, HONG KONG SAR.
YIP, Ms. Sau Kuen, ACA *2007;* Flat E5, 9/F Wei Chien Court, 6 Wai King Street, TO KWA WAN, KOWLOON, HONG KONG SAR.
YIP, Mr. See Kem, BSc(Econ) ACA *2001;* 65 Colebrook Road, LITTLEHAMPTON, WEST SUSSEX, BN17 7NU.
YIP, Mr. Shiu Kwong James, ACA *2007;* KHI Management Limited, 19/F, Fairmont House, 8 Cotton Tree Drive, CENTRAL, HONG KONG SAR.
YIP, Mr. Simon Ka-Yui, BSc(Eng) ACA *1987;* Simon K Y Yip & Co, 6/F Greenwich Centre, 260 Kings Road, NORTH POINT, HONG KONG SAR.
YIP, Miss. Stella Chui Wan, BSc ACA *1993;* Flat 1308 Block P, Kornhill, QUARRY BAY, Hong Kong Island, HONG KONG SAR.
YIP, Miss. Syn Yee, BA ACA *1995;* Ms S Freedman - GROUP AUDIT (mailstop 403), Deutsche Bank Winchester House, 1 Great Winchester Street, LONDON, EC2N 2DB.
YIP, Mr. Tai Him, ACA *2006;* Yip Tai Him, 7/F New York House, 60 Connaught Road, CENTRAL, HONG KONG ISLAND, HONG KONG SAR.
YIP, Mr. Tak On George, ACA *2005;* 5/F Effectual Bldg, 16 Hennessy Road, WAN CHAI, HONG KONG ISLAND, HONG KONG SAR.
YIP, Mr. Ting Yu, ACA *2008;* Room 909 Lung Yiu House, Kam Lung Court, Ma on Shan, SHA TIN, HONG KONG SAR.
YIP, Miss. Wai Fong, BSc ACA *2001;* 22 Midship Close, LONDON, SE16 6BT.
YIP, Mr. Wai Ming, ACA *2008;* Flat H, 38/F Tower 6, Sorrento, 1 Austin Road West, TSIM SHA TSUI, KOWLOON HONG KONG SAR.
YIP, Mr. Wai Sang, ACA *2008;* Room 2307 Siu Ping House, Siu Hong Court, TUEN MUN, NEW TERRITORIES, HONG KONG SAR.
YIP, Mr. Yau, ACA *2008;* 13G Block 7, Discovery Park, TSUEN WAN, NEW TERRITORIES, HONG KONG SAR.
YIP, Mr. Ying Chee John, ACA *2005;* 4/F Full View Commercial Building, 140-142 Des Voeux Road Central, CENTRAL, HONG KONG ISLAND, HONG KONG SAR.
YIP, Miss. Yuk Lin Susan, ACA *1985;* Morrison CPA Limited, 2308 Dominion Centre, 43-59 Queens Road East, WAN CHAI, HONG KONG ISLAND, HONG KONG SAR.
YIU, Ms. Cheuk Tsai, ACA *2009;* Flat B 16/F, Royal Court, 9M Kennedy Road, WAN CHAI, HONG KONG SAR.
YIU, Mr. Chi Shing, ACA *2008;* 5D Garve Court, Perth Garden, 9 Perth Street, HO MAN TIN, KOWLOON, HONG KONG SAR.
YIU, Mr. Chung Patrick, ACA *2008;* Flat B3, 20/F Block B, Kingsfield Tower, 64-68 Pokfulam Road, POK FU LAM, HONG KONG ISLAND HONG KONG SAR.
YIU, Mr. David Yuk Lun, ACA *1981;* Cavendish Heights, Flat B Block 2 28th Floor, 33 Perkins Road, JARDINE'S LOOKOUT, HONG KONG ISLAND, HONG KONG SAR.
YIU, Mr. Fai Ming Thomas, ACA *2008;* Flat 7B, Block 18, Wonderland Villas, KWAI CHUNG, HONG KONG SAR.
YIU, Ms. Helen, BA ACA *1989;* c/o Credit Suisse, 1 Raffles Link, #03-01 South Lobby, SINGAPORE 039393, SINGAPORE.
YIU, Mr. Hi Cheong, ACA *2006;* A1 15F Block A, The Fortune Gardens, 11 Seymour Road, MID LEVELS, HONG KONG ISLAND, HONG KONG SAR.
YIU, Ms. Hoi Lun Hellen, ACA *2008;* with Ernst & Young, 18/F, Two International Finance Centre, 8 Finance Street, CENTRAL, HONG KONG ISLAND HONG KONG SAR.
YIU, Mr. Joe Cho Yan, BSc ACA *1992;* Flat G, 27/F Chi Sing Mansion, TaiKoo Shing, QUARRY BAY, HONG KONG ISLAND, HONG KONG SAR.
YIU, Mr. Kam Man, ACA *2007;* Room 2105 21/F, Good Hope Building, 5 Sai Yeung Choi Street South, MONG KOK, KOWLOON, HONG KONG SAR.
YIU, Mr. Kin Wah Stephen, ACA *2006;* KPMG, 8/F Prince's Building, 10 Chater Road, CENTRAL, HONG KONG ISLAND, HONG KONG SAR.
YIU, Ms. O'San, ACA *2006;* Flat A, 25/F Golden Pavillion, 66 Caine Road, CENTRAL, HONG KONG ISLAND, HONG KONG SAR.
YIU, Mr. Tsz Yin, ACA *2008;* Room A, 25/F, Block 5, Greenfield Garden, TSING YI, NEW TERRITORIES HONG KONG SAR.
YIU, Miss. Valerie Yoi-Ling, BSc(Hons) ACA *2008;* 16 Bayr Cam, Douglas, ISLE OF MAN, IM2 2HT.
YIU, Mr. Wing Him, ACA *2009;* 24B Block 12, Wonderland Villas, KWAI CHUNG, NEW TERRITORIES, HONG KONG SAR.
YIU, Mr. Yau Kee Patrick, ACA *2008;* Flat 02 24/F, Choi To House, Choi Ming Court, TSEUNG KWAN O, NEW TERRITORIES, HONG KONG SAR.
YOE, Mrs. Jennifer Elizabeth, ACA *2002;* 16 Russell Gardens Mews, LONDON, W14 8EU.
YOE, Mr. Tony Tsen Wei, BA ACA *1990;* Cineworld Cinemas, Power Road Studios, Chiswick, LONDON, W4 5PY.
YOGA-WILLETTS, Mrs. Nalini, BA ACA *1992;* 25 Leonie Hill, Apt 22-04, Leonie Gardens, SINGAPORE 239225, SINGAPORE.
YOGANATHAN, Mr. Sathasivam, FCA *1972;* 17 Southfield Way, ST. ALBANS, HERTFORDSHIRE, AL4 9JJ.
YOKOI, Ms. Kumiko Judith, ACA *1998;* Arizona Golf Resort, Villa 162, PO Box 8080, RIYADH, 11482, SAUDI ARABIA.
YOKOYAMA, Mr. Ryotaro, BA ACA *2005;* Flat 111, 41 Millharbour, LONDON, E14 9ND.
YONG, Mr. Alan Yit Fong, FCA *1975;* 171 Jalan Athinahapan Dua, Taman Tun Dr. Ismail, 60000 KUALA LUMPUR, FEDERAL TERRITORY, MALAYSIA. (Life Member)
YONG, Mr. Choon Kong, BSc ACA *1987;* Pico House, No 4 Dai Fu Street, Tai Po Industrial Estate, TAI PO, NEW TERRITORIES, HONG KONG SAR.
YONG, Mr. Edmund Kin Kwong, ACA *1990;* 7 Holt Road. #9-01., SINGAPORE 249445, SINGAPORE.
YONG, Mr. Kam Fei, ACA *2008;* RSM Robert Teo Kuan & Co, Penthouse Wisma RKT Block A No2, Jalan Raja Abdullah, Off Jalan Sultan Ismail, 50300 KUALA LUMPUR, FEDERAL TERRITORY MALAYSIA.
YONG, Mr. Ket Inn, BSc ACA *1987;* No.7 Taman Rafflesia, Jalan Bundusan, 88300 KOTA KINABALU, SABAH, MALAYSIA.
YONG, Mr. Kok Choong, BSc ACA *2000;* 13 Lorong Mengkudu Satu, Jalan Ampang, 55000 KUALA LUMPUR, FEDERAL TERRITORY, MALAYSIA.
YONG, Mr. Kok Fong, ACA FCCA *2010;* 1 JALAN SETIA TROPIKA 6/8, TAMAN SETIA TROPIKA, 81200 JOHOR BAHRU, JOHOR, MALAYSIA.
YONG, Ms. Mei Ling Sarina, ACA *2005;* 20/F. Nexxus Building, 41 Connaught Road Central, CENTRAL, HONG KONG SAR.
•YONG, Mr. Richard Chu Keon, FCA *1974;* Richard Yong & Co, 100 Hale Lane, LONDON, NW7 3SE.
YONG, Mr. Robert Kuen Loke, FCA *1978;* 71 Jalan PJU1A/36, Ara Damansara, 47301, PETALING JAYA, MALAYSIA.
YONG, Mr. Shing Cheong, BA(Hons) ACA ACCA *2002;* 29 & 29a Jalan Dedap 19, Taman Johor Jaya, 81100 JOHOR BAHRU, JOHOR, MALAYSIA.
YONG, Ms. Soke, ACA *2008;* 8 Grace Mews, BECKENHAM, KENT, BR3 1BF.
YONG KIANG YOUNG, Mr. Christian Pierre, BSc ACA *2006;* Flat 172 Berglen Court, 7 Branch Road, LONDON, E14 7JY.
YONGE, Mr. Alan Geoffrey, BSc ACA *2000;* 42 Beech Avenue, CHICHESTER, WEST SUSSEX, PO19 3DS.
YONGE, Mrs. Elizabeth Shara, BSocSc ACA *2000;* 42 Beech Avenue, CHICHESTER, WEST SUSSEX, PO19 3DS.
YONGE, Mr. William James Beaumont, BA ACA *1982;* 298 Upper Elmers End Road, BECKENHAM, BR3 3HF.
YOO, Mr. Jin-Woo, BEng ACA *2008;* Apartment 8, 7 Bewley Street, LONDON, SW19 1XF.
•YOON, Mr. Kwok Ching, ACA *1980;* Casey Yoon & Co, Level 5, 231 Adelaide Terrace, PERTH, WA 6000, AUSTRALIA.
YOONG, Miss. Joyce Nyuk Fong, BSc ACA *2003;* #86 Jalan SS23/9, Taman Sea, 47400 PETALING JAYA, SELANGOR, MALAYSIA.
YOONG, Miss. Mei Lan, BSc ACA *2006;* 1st Floor, 1 Appold, Deutsche Bank, PO Box 135, LONDON, EC2A 2HE.
YOONG, Miss. Yui Ven, ACA *2011;* Apartment 613 Islington Gates, 110 Newhall Street, BIRMINGHAM, B3 1JN.
YORK, Mr. Andrew Dexter, FCA *1977;* H S B C, 8-16 Canada Square, LONDON, E14 5HQ.
YORK, Mr. Andrew Roland, FCA *1970;* 6 Magnolia Close, Aylestone, LEICESTER, LE2 8PS.
YORK, Miss. Camilla Melanie, BA ACA *1998;* 4 Chatsworth Avenue, LONDON, SW20 8JZ.
YORK, Mr. David Alan, BA FCA FCCA *1977;* 71 Freegrove Road, LONDON, N7 9RG.
•YORK, Mr. Edward Leslie, BEng ACA *1994;* Kampstrasse 82, 42781 HAAN, GERMANY.
YORK, Mrs. Elizabeth Ann, ACA MAAT *1996;* Kampstrasse 82, 42781 HAAN, GERMANY.
YORK, Mrs. Jay Paula, BSc ACA *1990;* with James Cowper LLP, Mill House, Overbridge Square, Hambridge Lane, NEWBURY, BERKSHIRE RG14 5UX.
YORK, Mr. John Timothy Langham, MA FCA *1962;* 11 Clos de la Fontaine, 1380 OHAIN, BELGIUM.
YORK, Mr. Peter Michael, FCA *1976;* Tbayco Limited, 9 Seven Ash Green, CHELMSFORD, CM1 7SE.
YORK, Mr. Richard Kenneth Patrick, BSc ACA PGCE *2002;* Aimia Foods Ltd Penny Lane, Haydock, ST. HELENS, MERSEYSIDE, WA11 0QZ.
YORK, Mr. Robert, BSc ACA *2007;* 9 Red Lion Court, Great North Road, HATFIELD, HERTFORDSHIRE, AL9 6LB.
YORK, Dr. Thomas John, MSci ACA *2008;* Barnes Roffe Llp Leytonstone House, Hanbury Drive, LONDON, E11 1GA.
YORK, Mr. Toby Sebastian, ACA *1991;* 114 The Avenue, LONDON, NW6 7NN.
YORK-SMITH, Mr. Paul Mahoney, BSc ACA *1996;* 8, Pimpernel Mead, Bradley Stoke, BRISTOL, BS32 8ET.
YORKE, Mr. Ben, BSc ACA *2002;* Cranswick Plc, 74 Helsinki Road, Sutton Fields, HULL, HU7 0YW.
•YORKE, Mr. Ian Stuart, FCA *1978;* Clement Keys, 39/40 Calthorpe Road, Edgbaston, BIRMINGHAM, B15 1TS.
YORKE, Mr. John David, FCA *1959;* Beckfoot, Cragg Vale, HEBDEN BRIDGE, HX7 5RX. (Life Member)
YORKE, Mr. John Sarne, BA FCA *1965;* Forthampton Court, GLOUCESTER, GL19 4RD.
YORKE, Mr. Jonathan Paul, BA ACA *1997;* Image Polymers Company, 100 Burtt Road, Suite 115, ANDOVER, MA 01810, UNITED STATES.
YORKE, Mr. Neil Robert, BA ACA *1984;* The Coach House, Frederick Road, Edgbaston, BIRMINGHAM, B15 1JN.

YORKE, Mr. Raymond Horace, FCA *1958;* 9 The Priory, Sedgley, DUDLEY, WEST MIDLANDS, DY3 3UB. (Life Member)
YORKE, Mr. William, FCA *1956;* Lowfields Cottage, London Road, Hartley Wintney, HOOK, RG27 8HY. (Life Member)
YORKE-ROBINSON, Mrs. Christine Helen Anne, BA ACA *1994;* 3 Green Bank, Simmondley, GLOSSOP, DERBYSHIRE, SK13 6XT.
YORSTON, Mr. Gordon Malcolm, FCA *1970;* Hernando de Magallanes 1651, Dpto 702 Las Condes, SANTIAGO, CHILE.
YOSHIDA, Miss. Chie, MSc ACA *1999;* 5A Russell Parade, Golders Green, LONDON, NW11 9NN.
•**YOU, Miss. Jacqueline, BSc FCA** *1989;* Norman You, 72 Rodney Street, LIVERPOOL, L1 9AF.
YOU, Miss. Lan, MA ACA *2002;* Flat 12B, 2 Old Peak Road, MID LEVELS, HONG KONG ISLAND, HONG KONG SAR.
YOUD, Mr. Brian Michael Frank, FCA *1958;* 32 Princes Avenue, WOODFORD GREEN, IG8 0LN. (Life Member)
YOUD, Mr. Michael John, BA ACA *1995;* 30 Christopher Way, LIVERPOOL, L16 1JQ.
YOUD, Mr. Simon Anthony, BSc ACA *1997;* 3 Green View Cottages, The Green, Theydon Bois, EPPING, ESSEX, CM16 7JD.
YOUDAN, Mrs. Laura, ACA *2008;* 37 Ferryhill Road, Epsom, AUCKLAND 1023, NEW ZEALAND.
•**YOUDEN, Mr. James Cowper, ACA** *1991;* Youden & Co, Old Stocks, Crowbrook Road, Monks Risborough, PRINCES RISBOROUGH, HP27 9LW.
YOUDS, Miss. Jane Louise, BA ACA *2010;* 4 Wilmslow Avenue, Great Sutton, ELLESMERE PORT, CH66 3JB.
YOUDS, Mrs. Siobhan, BSc ACA *2006;* 8/59 Garfield Street, FIVE DOCK, NSW 2046, AUSTRALIA.
YOUEL, Mr. Gary Malcolm, BSc ACA *1991;* 39 Nether Royd View Silkstone Common, BARNSLEY, S75 4QQ.
YOUELL, Mr. Christopher Alan, BSc FCA *1983;* 4 The Briars, Sarratt, RICKMANSWORTH, WD3 6AU.
YOUELL, Mrs. Jacqueline Mary, BSc ACA *1987;* 4 The Briars, Sarratt, RICKMANSWORTH, WD3 6AU.
YOUELL, Mr. Simon Edward, ACA *1981;* Finance Department, University of the West of England Frenchay Campus, Coldharbour Lane, BRISTOL, BS16 1QY.
YOUENS, Mr. Robert Noel, ACA *1986;* 65 St Andrews Road, COLWYN BAY, CLWYD, LL29 6DL.
YOUL, Mr. Christopher Simon, BA ACA *2006;* 37 Winchester Road, TWICKENHAM, TW1 1LE.
•**YOUL, Mr. Simon Robert, BSc FCA** *1976;* Bicknell Sanders, Alresford House, 60 West Street, FARNHAM, GU9 7EH.
•**YOULE, Mr. Edward Robin Godfrey, FCA** *1961;* Robin Youle, 6 Malpas Drive, PINNER, MIDDLESEX, HA5 1DF.
•**YOULE, Mrs. Kim Helen, BSc(Hons) ACA** *2004;* Citroen Wells, Devonshire House, 1 Devonshire Street, LONDON, W1W 5DR.
•**YOULES, Mr. Andrew James, FCA** *1993;* Andrew Youles, 20 Kingswood Road, MARCH, CAMBRIDGESHIRE, PE15 9RT.
YOUNAS, Mr. Mohammed Irfan, BSc ACA *2004;* 36 Parkland Grove, ASHFORD, TW15 2JR.
YOUNG, Mrs. Abigail, BA ACA *2008;* 57 Ashfurlong Road, SHEFFIELD, S17 3NL.
•**YOUNG, Mr. Adam John, ACA** *1994;* MacIntyre Hudson LLP, Peterbridge House, The Lakes, NORTHAMPTON, NN4 7HB.
YOUNG, Mr. Adrian Donald, FCA *1970;* 21 Wollombi Road, NORTHBRIDGE, NSW 2063, AUSTRALIA.
YOUNG, Mr. Alan Charles, ACA *1987;* Roundway Sheerwater Avenue, Woodham, ADDLESTONE, KT15 3DR.
YOUNG, Mr. Alan Godfrey, FCA *1959;* Thryft House Farm, Ringinglow Road, SHEFFIELD, S11 7TA. (Life Member)
YOUNG, Mr. Alasdair Robin Lockstone, FCA *1969;* 3 Wellington Square, YARMOUTH, ISLE OF WIGHT, PO41 0LB.
YOUNG, Mr. Alex Charles, BA ACA *2007;* with The Mudd Partnership, Lakeview House, 4 Woodbrook Crescent, BILLERICAY, ESSEX, CM12 0EQ.
YOUNG, Mr. Alexander, PhD BCom FCA JDipMA *1958;* 4 Wynnstay Gardens, Marlow Bottom, MARLOW, SL7 3NR. (Life Member)
YOUNG, Mr. Alexander John, BA ACA *2001;* 27 Links View Road, Hampton Hill, HAMPTON, MIDDLESEX, TW12 1LA.
YOUNG, Mr. Alistair John Cunningham, ACA *1989;* 8 Cherrington Close, Hurstpierpoint, HASSOCKS, WEST SUSSEX, BN6 9AY. (Life Member)
YOUNG, Mr. Allister Wilson, BSc ACA *2001;* 44 British Road, BRISTOL, BS3 3BJ.
YOUNG, Mr. Andrew, ACA *2008;* 12a Middleton Hall Road, BIRMINGHAM, B30 1BY.
YOUNG, Mr. Andrew, FCA *1970;* Spiral (UK) Limited, 7 Fieldings Suite, Whitwell Hatch, Scotland Lane, HASLEMERE, SURREY GU27 3AW.
YOUNG, Mr. Andrew Charles, BA ACA *1981;* Stefano Toselli SAS, ZI Espace Zuckerman B.P. 56, 14270 MEZIDON CANON, FRANCE.
YOUNG, Mr. Andrew David, BA FCA *1977;* Woodlands Cottage, 74 Eastwick Drive, Bookham, LEATHERHEAD, KT23 3NX.
•**YOUNG, Mr. Andrew David, FCA** *1985;* Cummins Young Ltd, 39 Westgate, THIRSK, NORTH YORKSHIRE, YO7 1QR.
YOUNG, Mr. Andrew Haley, BSc CA ACA *1996;* with Deloitte Touche Tohmatsu, Grosvenor Place, 225 George Street, P.O. Box N 250, SYDNEY, NSW 2000 AUSTRALIA.
•**YOUNG, Mr. Andrew James, FCA** *1988;* (Tax Fac), Dyke Yaxley Limited, 1 Brassey Road, Old Potts Way, SHREWSBURY, SY3 7FA.
YOUNG, Mr. Andrew James, BA FCA *1995;* 7 Cherry Hill Grove, Upton, POOLE, BH16 5LP.
YOUNG, Mr. Andrew James Bruce, BSc ACA *1991;* Boldrewood Cottage, Jordans Lane, Burghfield Common, READING, RG7 3LP.
YOUNG, Mr. Andrew Neil, FCA *1969;* Raveloe, Beech Avenue, Anderton, CHORLEY, PR6 9PQ.
YOUNG, Mr. Andrew Paul, BSc ACA *1985;* 58 Park Road, Stevington, BEDFORD, MK43 7QG.
YOUNG, Mr. Andrew Peter, FCA *1979;* 4 Walney Lane, Aylestone Hill, HEREFORD, HR1 1JD. (Life Member)
YOUNG, Mr. Andrew Thomas, BA(Hons) ACA *2004;* 9 Avenue Gardens, LONDON, SW14 8BP.
YOUNG, Mr. Andrew Timothy, BA ACA *1996;* PO Box 2454, Abu Dhabi, ABU DHABI, UNITED ARAB EMIRATES.
YOUNG, Mrs. Anna Louise, BA ACA *2001;* Xchanging, 13 Hanover Square, LONDON, W1S 1HN.
•**YOUNG, Mrs. Annabel, BSc ACA** *1998;* Annabel Young, 26 Spencer Road, LONDON, W3 6DW.
YOUNG, Mrs. Anne Margaret, BSc ACA *1989;* 6 Village Hall Yard, The Green, Long Itchington, SOUTHAM, WARWICKSHIRE, CV47 9QH.
YOUNG, Mr. Anthony Keith Mcleod, BA FCA *1976;* 26 Denmark Avenue, LONDON, SW19 4HQ.
YOUNG, Mr. Arthur, FCA *1959;* Pear Tree House, Peter Lane, Burton Leonard, HARROGATE, NORTH YORKSHIRE, HG3 3RZ. (Life Member)
YOUNG, Miss. Ashley Victoria, BA ACA *2011;* 25 Holmewood Road, LONDON, SW2 3RP.
•**YOUNG, Mr. Benjamin Thomas, BA ACA** *1999;* Mazars LLP, The Pinnacle, 160 Midsummer Boulevard, MILTON KEYNES, MK9 1FF.
YOUNG, Mr. Brian William, FCA *1962;* Apart 6A, Manor Court, Manor Park, KINGSTON 8, JAMAICA.
YOUNG, Mr. Bryn Mansell Lewis, BSc ACA *2003;* 161 Trentham Street, LONDON, SW18 5DH.
YOUNG, Mr. Carleton Adrian, BSc ACA *1979;* Santis, Bathwick Hill, BATH, BA2 6EX.
YOUNG, Mrs. Catherine Anne, BA ACA *1993;* 3 Lady Hay, WORCESTER PARK, KT4 7LT.
•**YOUNG, Mrs. Catherine Elizabeth, BA FCA** *1988;* 23 Lyndhurst Road, NEWCASTLE UPON TYNE, NE12 9NT.
YOUNG, Mrs. Chan Seong Ching, FCA *1970;* 3072 West 28th Avenue, VANCOUVER V6L 1X5, BC, CANADA. (Life Member)
YOUNG, Mrs. Charlotte Felicity, BA ACA *2001;* with Peters Elworthy & Moore, Salisbury House, Station Road, CAMBRIDGE, CB1 2LA.
YOUNG, Mr. Christopher, FCA *1997;* 24 Claremont Field, OTTERY ST. MARY, DEVON, EX11 1NP.
YOUNG, Mr. Christopher Arthur, BSc ACA *2007;* Flat 58 Becket House, Tabard Street, LONDON, SE1 4XZ.
YOUNG, Mr. Christopher George, MA FCA *1977;* Red Lodge, Cokes Lane, CHALFONT ST. GILES, HP8 4UD. (Life Member)
YOUNG, Mr. Christopher Huxley, MA ACA *1983;* Philippine Long Distance Telephone, 12th Flr Ramon Cojuanglo Bldg, Makati Avenue, MAKATI CITY, PHILIPPINES.
YOUNG, Mr. Christopher James, BEng ACA *2007;* 29 Stepney Causeway, LONDON, E1 0JW.
YOUNG, Mr. Christopher John, BA ACA *1979;* 76 Riversmeet, HERTFORD, SG14 1LE.
YOUNG, Mr. Christopher John, ACA *2008;* R412/183 West Coast Highway, SCARBOROUGH, WA 6019, AUSTRALIA.
YOUNG, Mr. Christopher John, BSc FCA *1975;* Beedon Lodge, Beedon Common, NEWBURY, BERKSHIRE, RG20 8TU.
YOUNG, Mr. Christopher Paul, BA ACA *1998;* 88 Baracchi Crescent, GIRALANG, ACT 2617, AUSTRALIA.
YOUNG, Mr. Christopher Thomas, BSc(Econ) ACA *2009;* BDO LLP, 55 Baker Street, LONDON, W1U 7EU.
•**YOUNG, Mr. Colin Clifford, BSc ACA** *1993;* (Tax Fac), C C Young & Co Ltd, 1st Floor, 48 Poland Street, LONDON, W1F 7ND. See also Young C C & Co Ltd
YOUNG, Mr. Colin Leslie, BSc FCA *1993;* 2 Roundhay, Leybourne, WEST MALLING, ME19 5QF.
•**YOUNG, Mr. Colin Stewart, BA FCA** *1990;* Hilton Sharp & Clarke, 30 New Road, BRIGHTON, BN1 1BN.
YOUNG, Mr. Cristian, BA ACA *2007;* Smedvig Capital Ltd, 20 St. James's Street, LONDON, SW1A 1ES.
YOUNG, Mr. Danny Chi, BA ACA *1997;* 4 Brownspring Drive, LONDON, SE9 3JX.
YOUNG, Mr. Darryl Anthony Rolf, BA ACA *1992;* 5 Highfields, ASHTEAD, KT21 2NL.
YOUNG, Mr. David, ACA *1985;* 6 Glenburn Close, Ayton, WASHINGTON, NE38 8PE.
YOUNG, Mr. David, FCA *1964;* Fieldside, Back Lane, Hathersage, HOPE VALLEY, S32 1AR. (Life Member)
YOUNG, Mr. David Eric, FCA *1969;* (Tax Fac), Wolverson X-Ray Ltd, 51 Walsall Street, WILLENHALL, WV13 2DY.
YOUNG, Mr. David Frank, MBE FCA *1956;* 132 Eastmoor Park, HARPENDEN, AL5 1BP. (Life Member)
YOUNG, Mr. David George Macgregor, FCA *1969;* 26 Aspley Court, 1 Warwick Avenue, BEDFORD, MK40 2UH.
YOUNG, Mr. David James, FCA *1964;* 5 Hill Terrace, MOSMAN PARK, WA 6012, AUSTRALIA. (Life Member)
YOUNG, Mr. David Kenneth, LLB FCA *1982;* Lambshield, HEXHAM, NORTHUMBERLAND, NE46 1SF.
YOUNG, Mr. David Maitland, FCA *1968;* 26 Chertsey Road, Chobham, WOKING, GU24 8NB.
•**YOUNG, Mr. David Michael, FCA** *1972;* David Young & Co, 89 Gillards Close, Rockwell Green, WELLINGTON, SOMERSET, TA21 9DX.
YOUNG, Mr. David Michael, BSc ACA *1992;* 5 Fortune Hill, KNARESBOROUGH, HG5 9DG.
YOUNG, Mr. David Thomas McAree, BA FCA CTA *1987;* Maisemore Consultants Ltd, The Old Coach House, Church Lane, Shotteswell, BANBURY, WARWICKSHIRE OX17 1JD.
YOUNG, Mr. David Tyrrell, FCA *1961;* (Member of Council 1980 - 1981), Yewtree Cottage Church End, Ashdon, SAFFRON WALDEN, CB10 2HG.
YOUNG, Mr. David William James, FCA *1955;* Little Glen, 19 Leigh Hill Road, COBHAM, KT11 2HS. (Life Member)
YOUNG, Mr. Dennis Walter, BSc FCA *1976;* Mayflower House, 3 Quaker Row, Coates, CIRENCESTER, GLOUCESTERSHIRE, GL7 6JX.
YOUNG, Mr. Derek Roy, FCA *1961;* Waterside, Main Road, Inkberrow, WORCESTER, WR7 4HH.
YOUNG, Miss. Diana Harding, FCA *1948;* Fairholm, Higher Brimley, Bovey Tracey, NEWTON ABBOT, TQ13 9JT. (Life Member)
YOUNG, Mr. Douglas Charles, BA ACA *1995;* 71 Kirby Road, PORTSMOUTH, PO2 0PF.
YOUNG, Mr. Douglas James, BEng ACA *1994;* Ettrick, Maitland Street, LEVEN, FIFE, KY8 4RE.
YOUNG, Mr. Edward James Gilzean, FCA *1968;* 17 Juer Street, LONDON, SW11 4RE. (Life Member)
YOUNG, Miss. Emma, MA BA(Hons) ACA *2010;* Grant Thornton - BRS, 30 Finsbury Square, LONDON, EC2P 2YU.
YOUNG, Miss. Emma Caroline, BSc(Hons) ACA *2002;* 76 Gassiot Road, LONDON, SW17 8LA.
YOUNG, Mr. Eric Cecil, FCA *1959;* 52 Sutton Court, Sutton Court Road, Chiswick, LONDON, W4 3JE. (Life Member)
YOUNG, Miss. Fiona Denise, FCA DChA *1992;* 56 Churchill Road, SOUTH CROYDON, SURREY, CR2 6HA.
YOUNG, Miss. Flora Caroline, LLB ACA *2005;* 133 Athenlay Road, LONDON, SE15 3EJ.
•**YOUNG, Mr. Gary, ACA** *1981;* G. Young & Co, 49 Deaconsfield Road, HEMEL HEMPSTEAD, HP3 9HZ.
YOUNG, Mr. Gary Richard, BSc FCA *1986;* Wisteria Cottage, Sudbury Lane, Longworth, ABINGDON, OXFORDSHIRE, OX13 5EL.
YOUNG, Mr. George Brian, FCA *1946;* 12 Ashcombe Gardens, EDGWARE, MIDDLESEX, HA8 8HS. (Life Member)
YOUNG, Mr. George Horatio, BA ACA *1993;* with PricewaterhouseCoopers LLP, 1 Embankment Place, LONDON, WC2N 6RH.
YOUNG, Mr. George Malcolm, FCA *1973;* 17 rue Gabriel Peri, 92300 LEVALLOIS-PERRET, FRANCE.
YOUNG, Miss. Gillian, BSc ACA *2004;* UEC Limited, 18 Oxford Road, MARLOW, BUCKINGHAMSHIRE, SL7 2NL.
YOUNG, Mr. Gordon Douglas, BA ACA *2010;* Flat 16 Nofax House, 11 Voltaire Road, LONDON, SW4 6DQ.
YOUNG, Mr. Gordon John, FCA *1957;* Parkfield, Valley Road, Fawkham, LONGFIELD, KENT, DA3 8NA. (Life Member)
•**YOUNG, Mr. Graeme Lindsay, FCA** *1980;* MacIntyre Hudson Llp, 30-34 New Bridge Street, LONDON, EC4V 6BJ.
•**YOUNG, Mr. Graham, FCA** *1980;* (Tax Fac), Hazlemere Tax Consultancy Ltd, 35 Jackson Court, Hazlemere, HIGH WYCOMBE, BUCKINGHAMSHIRE, HP15 7TZ.
YOUNG, Mr. Harold, FCA *1968;* 38 Woodland Rise, Studham, DUNSTABLE, BEDFORDSHIRE, LU6 2PF.
•**YOUNG, Miss. Hazel Diana Reeve, BSc FCA** *1982;* Reeve-Young & Co, Silverbirch Cottage, Watford Road, Elstree, BOREHAMWOOD, WD6 3BE.
YOUNG, Ms. Helen, ACA *2007;* Flat 1 6/F, Man Ying Building, 1 Man Yuen Street, TSIM SHA TSUI, KOWLOON, HONG KONG SAR.
YOUNG, Miss. Helen Carole, BSc ACA *2004;* 38 Nantes Close, LONDON, SW18 1JL.
YOUNG, Miss. Helen Margaret, LLB ACA *1990;* 9 Glenwood Drive, Rouken Glen, GLASGOW, G46 7EN.
YOUNG, Mr. Hugh Christopher, BSc ACA *1986;* 97 Newberries Avenue, RADLETT, HERTFORDSHIRE, WD7 7EN.
YOUNG, Mr. Ian Kirkpatrick, BA FCA *1975;* (Tax Fac), with ICAEW, Chartered Accountants' Hall, Moorgate Place, LONDON, EC2P 2BJ.
YOUNG, Mr. Ian Terence Bernard, FCA *1972;* 59 Ilex Drive, NEWBURY PARK, CA 91320, UNITED STATES.
YOUNG, Mr. Jack, FCA *1959;* 42 Devonshire Avenue, Allestree, DERBY, DE22 2AT. (Life Member)
YOUNG, Mr. James Alastair, MA ACA *1994;* 7 Craiglockhart Road, EDINBURGH, EH14 1HJ.
YOUNG, Mr. James Andrew, MSci ACA *2004;* 115 Abbey Road, BRISTOL, BS9 3QJ.
•**YOUNG, Mr. James Cameron Cunningham, BA FCA** *1993;* Feist Hedgethorne Limited, Preston Park House, South Road, BRIGHTON, BN1 6SB.
YOUNG, Mr. James Frederick Cameron, BA(Hons) ACA *2001;* 25 Woodlea Lane, Meanwood, LEEDS, LS6 4SX.
YOUNG, Mr. James Robert Gillmore, MEng ACA *2006;* 135a Maplewell Road, Woodhouse Eaves, LOUGHBOROUGH, LEICESTERSHIRE, LE12 8QY.
YOUNG, Mrs. Janet Ann, BSc ACA *1995;* 72 Watten Estate Road, SINGAPORE 287552, SINGAPORE.
YOUNG, Ms. Jenifer Ann, BA ACA *1991;* 22 New River Head, 173 Rosebery Avenue, LONDON, EC1R 4UL.
YOUNG, Mrs. Jennifer, BA ACA *2002;* 52 St. Marks Avenue, HARROGATE, NORTH YORKSHIRE, HG2 8AE.
YOUNG, Mrs. Jenny Louise, BA ACA *2006;* Tarmac Ltd Millfields Road, Ettingshall, WOLVERHAMPTON, WV4 6JP.
•**YOUNG, Mr. Jeremy George Thomas, BA ACA** *1998;* with Ernst & Young LLP, 1 More London Place, LONDON, SE1 2AF.
YOUNG, Mr. Jeremy James, BA ACA *1983;* 161 Wakehurst Road, LONDON, SW11 6BW.
YOUNG, Mrs. Joan Elizabeth Mary, MSc BSc ACA *1995;* 105 Castlewellan Road, Rathfriland, NEWRY, BT34 5EP.
YOUNG, Miss. Johanne, BSc ACA *1999;* Apartment 3603, 301 Deansgate, MANCHESTER, M3 4LU.
YOUNG, Mr. John Anthony, FCA *1972;* Mullion Plaistow Road, Loxwood, BILLINGSHURST, WEST SUSSEX, RH14 0TU.
YOUNG, Mr. John Anthony Marshall, FCA *1967;* Im Zaeundli, CH-3804 HABKERN, SWITZERLAND. (Life Member)
YOUNG, Mr. John Baldwin, BSc FCA *1953;* 9 Glen Eyre Road, Bassett, SOUTHAMPTON, SO16 3GA. (Life Member)
YOUNG, Mr. John Cedric Keith, FCA *1965;* 22 Holme Chase, St Georges Ave, WEYBRIDGE, KT13 0BZ.
•**YOUNG, Mr. John Douglas, FCA** *1971;* MurraYoung Limited, 15 Home Farm, Luton Hoo Estate, LUTON, LU1 3TD.

YOUNG, Mr. John Malcolm, FCA *1959;* 30 Birtley Rise, Bramley, GUILDFORD, SURREY, GU5 0HZ. (Life Member)
YOUNG, Mr. John Michael, FCA *1958;* 7 Hayfield Close, BUSHEY, WD23 3SX.
YOUNG, Mr. John Michael Douglas, FCA *1976;* Amec Plc, 76-78 Old Street, LONDON, EC1V 9RU.
YOUNG, Mr. John Smithson, BSc FCA *1976;* 28 Northumberland Avenue, Gosforth, NEWCASTLE UPON TYNE, NE3 4XE.
•①**YOUNG, Mr. John William, BSc ACA MABRP** *1998;* with BDO, Lindsay House, 10 Callender Street, BELFAST, BT1 5BN.
•**YOUNG, Mr. Jon Conrad Shepherd, BA ACA ATII** *1987;* Deloitte LLP, Hill House, 1 Little New Street, LONDON, EC4A 3TR. See also Deloitte & Touche LLP
YOUNG, Mr. Jonathan David Robert, BSc ACA *2003;* 98 Leathwaite Road, LONDON, SW11 6RR.
YOUNG, Mr. Jonathan George, BA ACA *2005;* 19 Eastlands, Lacey Green, PRINCES RISBOROUGH, BUCKINGHAMSHIRE, HP27 0QB.
YOUNG, Mr. Jonathan James, BEng ACA *2003;* Interserve Project Services Ltd, 395 George Road Erdington, BIRMINGHAM, B23 7RZ.
•**YOUNG, Mr. Julian Arthur, BSc ARCS ACA** *1997;* Ernst & Young LLP, 1 More London Place, LONDON, SE1 2AF. See also Ernst & Young Europe LLP
YOUNG, Miss. Karen, BA ACA *1994;* GM (China) Investment Co. Ltd., No 56 Jinwan Road, Pudong, SHANGHAI 201206, CHINA.
YOUNG, Mrs. Karen Bridget, BSc ACA *1992;* 3120, Milk Link Great Western Court, Hunts Ground Road Stoke Gifford, BRISTOL, BS34 8HP.
YOUNG, Mr. Karsten William, ACA *2010;* 33 High Street, Burcott, LEIGHTON BUZZARD, BEDFORDSHIRE, LU7 0JS.
YOUNG, Miss. Katherine Maire, MA ACA *2009;* Flat 20 168 Clapham High Street, LONDON, SW4 7UG.
YOUNG, Mrs. Kathryn Jane, BA ACA *1991;* 15 Scizdons Climb, GODALMING, GU7 1NL.
•**YOUNG, Mrs. Kathryn Mary, BSc FCA** *1976;* Kathryn M. Young, Lake Cottage, Southbury Lane, Ruscombe, READING, RG10 9XN.
YOUNG, Miss. Katy Isabella, BA ACA *2006;* 2 Purcell Avenue, NUNEATON, CV11 4SN.
YOUNG, Miss. Katy Sarah, ACA *2008;* 5 Franklin Place, LONDON, SE13 7ES.
•**YOUNG, Mr. Keith Alan, FCA** *1971;* (Tax Fac), K.A. Young, 2A Fenwick Close, Goldsworth Park, WOKING, GU21 3BY.
YOUNG, Mr. Keith Martin, LLB ACA *2002;* 33 Rodwell Road, LONDON, SE22 9LF.
YOUNG, Mr. Kenneth, BA FCA *1991;* 30/F. Flat B Grand Deco Tower, 26 Tai Hang Road, CAUSEWAY BAY, HONG KONG SAR.
YOUNG, Mr. Kenneth Albert, FCA *1958;* 25 Trotsworth Avenue, VIRGINIA WATER, SURREY, GU25 4AN. (Life Member)
•**YOUNG, Mr. Kenneth Robert, BA FCA** *1983;* (Tax Fac), Wilkins Kennedy, Mount Manor House, 16 The Mount, GUILDFORD, SURREY, GU2 4HN.
YOUNG, Mr. Kevin Andrew, BSc ACA *1987;* 35 Dean Close, Pyrford, WOKING, GU22 8NX.
YOUNG, Mrs. Laura Gail, BSc ACA *1991;* with KPMG LLP, Management Services Centre, 58 Clarendon Road, WATFORD, WD17 1DE.
YOUNG, Mr. Lindsay Ian Green, BEng ACA *1994;* Flat E, 98 Repulse Bay Road, REPULSE BAY, HONG KONG SAR.
YOUNG, Mrs. Ling Kit, BA ACA *1997;* 10 Cabin Moss, Forest Park, BRACKNELL, BERKSHIRE, RG12 0WB.
•**YOUNG, Mr. Lionel Henry, BSc FCA** *1981;* Hayes House, 25 Hayes Lane, KENLEY, CR8 5LE.
YOUNG, Mrs. Lorraine Angela, ACA *2010;* 19 Kepple Place, BAGSHOT, SURREY, GU19 5NB.
YOUNG, Mr. Malcolm Craig, FCA *1962;* 70 Birchover Way, Allestree, DERBY, DE22 2QL.
YOUNG, Mr. Marc, LLB ACA *2005;* Flat 1, 24 Stanhope Gardens, LONDON, SW7 5QX.
YOUNG, Mr. Mark, BSc ACA *2005;* 1 St. Johns Avenue, KENILWORTH, WARWICKSHIRE, CV8 1FW.
YOUNG, Mr. Mark Halifax Graham, FCA *1974;* 22 Arundel Rd, TUNBRIDGE WELLS, TN1 1TB.
YOUNG, Mr. Mark Terence, BA ACA *1992;* 4 Wayside Avenue, Scarcroft, LEEDS, LS14 3BE.
YOUNG, Mr. Mark William, ACA *2006;* H M Revenue & Customs, South West Wing, Bush House, Strand, LONDON, WC2B 4RD.
YOUNG, Mr. Martin Charles, MA ACA *1994;* 10 Caldervale Road, Clapham, LONDON, SW4 9LZ.
YOUNG, Mr. Martin Henry, FCA *1970;* 21 Broomhouse Road, LONDON, SW6 3QU.
YOUNG, Mr. Martin Paul, BSc ACA *1989;* Perseus House, 3 Chapel Court Holly Walk, LEAMINGTON SPA, CV32 4YS.
•**YOUNG, Mr. Michael Charles, FCA** *1971;* (Tax Fac), Tilbury Young Limited, Almac House, Church Lane, Bisley, WOKING, GU24 9DR.
YOUNG, Mr. Michael Christopher, BA ACA *2007;* 19 Kepple Place, BAGSHOT, SURREY, GU19 5NB.
•**YOUNG, Mr. Michael Denoon, BSc FCA** *1991;* Peplows, Sterling House, Wavell Drive, Rosehill, CARLISLE, CA1 2SA.
YOUNG, Mr. Michael Raymond, FCA *1969;* Aldridge's Farm, Maple Lane, Wimbish, SAFFRON WALDEN, CB10 2XG. (Life Member)
YOUNG, Mr. Michael Robert, PhD BSc FCA *1975;* 17 Prior Park Buildings, BATH, BA2 4NP.
YOUNG, Miss. Natalie Jane Hedley, ACA *2009;* 21 Oakwood Drive, ST. ALBANS, HERTFORDSHIRE, AL4 0UL.
YOUNG, Mr. Neil Edward, LLB ACA *2004;* Deutsche Bank AG - Asia Pacific Head Office, One Raffles Quay, #20-00 South Tower, SINGAPORE 048583, SINGAPORE.
YOUNG, Mr. Nicholas, FCA *1970;* 1 Balmoral Close, Fernhill Heath, WORCESTER, WR3 7XQ.
YOUNG, Mr. Nicholas Daniel, BA ACA *1988;* 79 Crabtree Lane, HARPENDEN, HERTFORDSHIRE, AL5 5PX.
YOUNG, Mrs. Nicola Annabel, BSc ACA *1999;* Twll y Grafel, Ysceifiog, HOLYWELL, CLWYD, CH8 8NJ.
YOUNG, Mrs. Nicola Frances, ACA *1981;* 119 Cambridge Road, LONDON, SW20 0PU.
YOUNG, Mr. Nigel John, FCA *1980;* 32 Sandhurst Road, Four Oaks, SUTTON COLDFIELD, B74 4UE.
YOUNG, Mr. Nigel Jonathan, BCom ACA *1986;* PO Box 22500, DOHA, QATAR.
YOUNG, Mr. Nigel Robert, BSc FCA *1979;* Rosemullion, Bulstrode Way, GERRARDS CROSS, SL9 7QU.
YOUNG, Miss. Nina Sasha, BSc ACA *2005;* 2 Skelf Street, Church Fenton, TADCASTER, NORTH YORKSHIRE, LS24 9RX.
YOUNG, Miss. Olivia, ACA *2009;* Engøysnaget 24, 4085 Hundvåg, STAVANGER, NORWAY.
YOUNG, Mr. Osie Lindsay, BA ACA *2006;* Swarovski UK Ltd, Unit 10, Perrywood Business Park, Honeycrock Lane, REDHILL, RH1 5JQ.
•**YOUNG, Mrs. Pamela Ann, FCA** *1994;* Celtic Associates Limited, The Red House, One The Parade, Castletown, ISLE OF MAN, IM9 1LG.
YOUNG, Mr. Paul, BCom ACA *1995;* Flat E36/F Tower 16, South Horizon AP LEI CHAU, Hong Kong Island, HONG KONG SAR.
YOUNG, Mr. Paul Alfred, FCA *1981;* 110 Longfields, Marden Ash, ONGAR, CM5 9DF.
•**YOUNG, Mr. Paul Anthony, FCA** *1971;* Young & Phillips, 77 Bute Street, TREORCHY, MID GLAMORGAN, CF42 6AH. See also Young & Phillips Limited
YOUNG, Mr. Paul Antony, MA ACA CF *1981;* 5 Longview Street, BALMAIN, NSW 2041, AUSTRALIA.
YOUNG, Mr. Paul George, BA(Hons) ACA *2001;* 14 Essex Rise, Warfield, BRACKNELL, BERKSHIRE, RG42 3XG.
YOUNG, Mr. Paul Henry, BA FCA *1970;* 6 Millbrook Walk, Inchbrook, Nailsworth, STROUD, GLOUCESTERSHIRE, GL5 5HE. (Life Member)
YOUNG, Mr. Paul Michael, BA ACA *1998;* SSL International, 101 Thomson Road, #26-05 United Square, SINGAPORE 307591, SINGAPORE.
YOUNG, Mr. Paul Sinclair, BA ACA *1992;* 3 Lady Hay, WORCESTER PARK, KT4 7LT.
YOUNG, Mr. Peter Alan, BSc ACA *1994;* Milton Cottage Rectory Lane, Milton Malsor, NORTHAMPTON, NN7 3AQ.
YOUNG, Mr. Peter Arthur, FCA *1970;* The Mill House, 166 Birmingham Road, BROMSGROVE, B61 0HB.
•**YOUNG, Mr. Peter Colin Robert, ACA** *1979;* (Tax Fac), Peter Young, Orchard Cottage, Stanford Lane, Hadlow, TONBRIDGE, TN11 0JP.
•**YOUNG, Mr. Peter Douglas, FCA** *1985;* Lovewell Blake LLP, 102 Prince of Wales Road, NORWICH, NORFOLK, NR1 1NY.
YOUNG, Mr. Peter George, FCA *1958;* 3 Partridge Drive, ORPINGTON, BR6 8PE. (Life Member)
YOUNG, Mr. Peter William, FCA *1958;* 1 Tasmania Way, Sovereign Harbour North, EASTBOURNE, BN23 5PA. (Life Member)
YOUNG, Mr. Philip, ACA *1984;* Paymaster (1836) Ltd, Sutherland House, Russell Way, CRAWLEY, WEST SUSSEX, RH10 1UH.
YOUNG, Mr. Philip Bruce Andrew, BSc FCA *1973;* 5 Scholar Mews, Marston Ferry Road, OXFORD, OX2 7GY.
YOUNG, Mr. Philip David, BSc ACA *1995;* 7 Howard Drive, YORK, YO30 5UX.
YOUNG, Mr. Philip James, BSc ACA *1980;* 29 Kings Road, Ealing, LONDON, W5 2SD.
YOUNG, Mr. Philip James, ACA *1985;* 5 The Bramblings, Rustington, LITTLEHAMPTON, BN16 2DA.
•**YOUNG, Mr. Philip James, BSc FCA** *1989;* Ernst & Young LLP, 1 More London Place, LONDON, SE1 2AF. See also Ernst & Young Europe LLP
YOUNG, Mr. Philip John, BSc ACA *1990;* The Green Transport Co Ltd The White House, 111 New Street, BIRMINGHAM, B2 4EU.
YOUNG, Mrs. Rachel Clare, BA ACA *2003;* 29 Tudor Road, HAMPTON, MIDDLESEX, TW12 2NG.
YOUNG, Ms. Rebecca Ann, BSc ACA *1991;* (Tax Fac), Building 37, University of Southampton, University Road, SOUTHAMPTON, SO17 1BJ.
YOUNG, Mr. Richard, BSc FCA *1991;* 29 Badger Way, Hazlemere, HIGH WYCOMBE, BUCKINGHAMSHIRE, HP15 7LJ.
YOUNG, Dr. Richard, PhD MSci ACA *2011;* 8 Riverdale Road, Stanley, WAKEFIELD, WEST YORKSHIRE, WF3 4LA.
•**YOUNG, Mr. Richard John, ACA** *1991;* Deeks Evans, 3 Boyne Park, TUNBRIDGE WELLS, TN4 8EN. See also Deeks Evans Audit Services Limited, R J Young Limited
•**YOUNG, Mr. Richard Stanford Kilburn, FCA** *1970;* Little Foxes, 3 Gong Hill Drive Lower Bourne, FARNHAM, GU10 3HG.
YOUNG, Mr. Richard William Shirley, BA FCA *1974;* Whyr Farm, Winterbourne Bassett, SWINDON, SN4 9QE. (Life Member)
•**YOUNG, Mr. Robert Alan, BSc FCA** *1977;* (Tax Fac), The Young Company, Ground Floor, 2B Vantage Park, Washingley Road, HUNTINGDON, CAMBRIDGESHIRE PE29 6SR.
YOUNG, Mr. Robert David Gordon, BA(Hons) ACA *2010;* 5 The Mount, Wrenthorpe, WAKEFIELD, WEST YORKSHIRE, WF2 0NZ.
YOUNG, Mr. Robert Graeme Meeres, BA FCA *1965;* St. Martins House, Church Lane, Preston, HITCHIN, SG4 7TP.
•**YOUNG, Mr. Robert James Russell, BCom ACA** *2002;* (Tax Fac), SB&P LLP, Oriel House, 2-8 Oriel Road, BOOTLE, MERSEYSIDE, L20 7EP. See also Satterthwaite Brooks & Pomfret LLP and SB&P Corporate Finance Ltd
YOUNG, Mr. Robert Thomas Joseph, MSc BA(Hons) ACA *2001;* Flat 2, 50 Warwick Gardens, LONDON, W14 8PP.
YOUNG, Mr. Robin Timothy, BA(Hons) ACA *2006;* 29 Kavanaghs Road, BRENTWOOD, CM14 4NB.
YOUNG, Mr. Roderick Neil, MA FCA *1959;* Down Farm House, Lamberhurst Down, Lamberhurst, TUNBRIDGE WELLS, KENT, TN3 8HA. (Life Member)
YOUNG, Mr. Ronald James, FCA *1956;* 27 Manor Road, Cheam, SUTTON, SM2 7AG. (Life Member)
YOUNG, Mr. Ruairi Peter, BA ACA *1999;* 15/F Citibank Tower;, 3 Garden Road;, CENTRAL, HONG KONG SAR.
YOUNG, Mr. Russell John, BA FCA *1992;* 35 Franklin Road, BIRMINGHAM, B30 2HJ.
•**YOUNG, Mrs. Sarah Ann, ACA** *1987;* 2 Kings Avenue, FALMOUTH, TR11 2QH.
YOUNG, Mrs. Sarah Jane, BA(Hons) ACA *1999;* Edwards Angell Palmer & Dodge, Dashwood House, 69 Old Broad Street, LONDON, EC2M 1QS.
YOUNG, Mrs. Sarah Jayne, MSc BSc(Econ) ACA *2002;* 25 Woodchester Avenue, Richmond, CHRISTCHURCH, NEW ZEALAND.
YOUNG, Mrs. Sarah Katharine, BSc FCA *1987;* Wisteria Cottage, Sudbury Lane, Longworth, ABINGDON, OX13 5EL.
YOUNG, Mr. Scott Charles, FCA *1987;* 1301 Ocean Manor Lane, LEAGUE CITY, TX 77573, UNITED STATES.
YOUNG, Mr. Sebastian Joseph, ACA *2009;* 38 Hatherleigh Gardens, POTTERS BAR, HERTFORDSHIRE, EN6 5HZ.
YOUNG, Mr. Shaun Martin, ACA *1990;* Apartment 1141, King Edwards Wharf, 25 Sheepcote Street, BIRMINGHAM, B16 8AH.
YOUNG, Mrs. Sheenagh, MA ACA *1990;* 2 Birch Grove, Rusholme, MANCHESTER, M14 5JY.
YOUNG, Mr. Simon Alexander, BSc ACA *1985;* Nationwide Bldg Soc, Kings Park Road, Moulton Park Industrial Estate, NORTHAMPTON, NN3 6NW.
•**YOUNG, Mr. Simon Christopher, BA FCA** *1988;* 13 Castle Street, ST HELIER, JE4 5UT.
•**YOUNG, Mr. Simon Christopher Craig, BA FCA** *1992;* Clive Owen & Co LLP, 140 Coniscliffe Road, DARLINGTON, COUNTY DURHAM, DL3 7RT.
•**YOUNG, Mr. Simon Jonathan, FCA** *1981;* (Tax Fac), Milton Avis, Wellington Building, 28-32 Wellington Road, St John's Wood, LONDON, NW8 9SP. See also Crowley Young Associates Ltd
YOUNG, Ms. So Hung, ACA *2008;* Flat A, 15/F, Block 2, Villa Athena, Ma On Shan, SHA TIN NEW TERRITORIES HONG KONG SAR.
YOUNG, Mrs. Sophie Elizabeth Denny, BSc ACA *2008;* Yew Tree Cottage, Church Hill, Beighton, NORWICH, NR13 3JZ.
•**YOUNG, Mr. Stephen Burchell Martin, BA ACA** *1982;* KPMG, Vesetas iela 7, RIGA LV 1013, LATVIA.
YOUNG, Mr. Stephen James, BSc ACA *1990;* SES S.A, Chateau de Betzdorf, L- 6815 LUXEMBOURG, LUXEMBOURG.
•**YOUNG, Mr. Stephen Mark, BSc FCA** *1993;* Derek Young & Co, Estate House, Evesham Street, REDDITCH, B97 4HP.
YOUNG, Mr. Stephen Paul, BSc ACA *2002;* Flat 3 Christopher Court, Ashburton Road, CROYDON, CR0 6AN.
YOUNG, Mr. Stephen Robert, BA ACA *1980;* La Tuque Neuve, 47800 PUYSSERAMPION, FRANCE.
YOUNG, Mr. Stewart Grant, BSc FCA *1970;* Park Rock Management Ltd, 1 Conduit Street, LONDON, W1R 9TG.
YOUNG, Mr. Stuart, FCA *1964;* Hotel Bristol, Narrowcliff, NEWQUAY, TR7 2PQ.
YOUNG, Mr. Stuart Anthony, MA FCA *1982;* Flat 12, Darling House, 35 Clevedon Road, TWICKENHAM, TW1 2TU.
YOUNG, Mr. Stuart Livingston, ACA *2005;* Flat 104 Kestrel House, Pickard Street, LONDON, EC1V 8EL.
YOUNG, Miss. Susan, BA(Hons) ACA CTA *2003;* with Ernst & Young LLP, 100 Barbirolli Square, MANCHESTER, M2 3EY.
•**YOUNG, Mrs. Susan Carole, BA ACA** *1982;* Merrywinds, 8-10 Northfield, Timsbury, BATH, BA2 0JT.
YOUNG, Mrs. Susan Patricia, BA FCA RRP MBCI SIRM *1987;* Flat B, 7 Cumberland Park, Acton, LONDON, W3 6SY.
YOUNG, Mrs. Susanna Renee, BSc ACA *2006;* 50 Valley Crescent, WOKINGHAM, RG41 1NP.
YOUNG, Mrs. Suzanna Penny, BA ACA *1998;* (Tax Fac), 11 Capitol Close, Smithills, BOLTON, BL1 6LU.
YOUNG, Mr. Terence John, FCA *1965;* 3 Knowle Road, Weeping Cross, STAFFORD, ST17 0DN. (Life Member)
•**YOUNG, Mr. Thomas Knibb, MA FCA CTA** *1986;* S Y Accountancy Services Ltd, Unit 6D Planet Business Centre, Planet Place, West Moor, NEWCASTLE UPON TYNE, NE12 6DY.
YOUNG, Mr. Thomas Robertson, MA(Oxon) ACA *1979;* Scotch Bonnet Limited, Old Post House, Radford Road, Flyford Flavell, WORCESTER, WR7 4DL.
•**YOUNG, Mr. Timothy Christopher, BA ACA** *2000;* with BDO LLP, 55 Baker Street, LONDON, W1U 7EU.
YOUNG, Mr. Timothy James, BSc FCA *1979;* KPMG Auditores Independentes, Av Almirante Barroso 52 4th, RIO DE JANEIRO, 20031-000, BRAZIL.
•**YOUNG, Mrs. Tracey Louise, BSc(Hons) ACA DChA** *2001;* haysmacintyre, Fairfax House, 15 Fulwood Place, LONDON, WC1V 6AY.
YOUNG, Mr. Tung Shing Samuel, ACA *2005;* Flat B 16/F Block 3, Bayview Garden, 633 Castle Peak Road, TSEUNG KWAN O, NEW TERRITORIES, HONG KONG SAR.
YOUNG, Mrs. Valerie, BSc FCA *1980;* 58 St. James Road, CARLISLE, CA2 5PD.
•**YOUNG, Mr. Victor John, BSc FCA** *1979;* (Tax Fac), Thomas & Young LLP, 240-244 Stratford Road, Shirley, SOLIHULL, WEST MIDLANDS, B90 3AE. See also Thomas & Young
YOUNG, Mr. Wayne Paul, BSc(Hons) ACA *2001;* 5 Shearling Drive, Lower Cambourne, CAMBRIDGE, CB23 6BZ.
YOUNG, Mr. William Read, FCA *1950;* 10 White Hill Close, Lower Hardres, CANTERBURY, CT4 7AQ. (Life Member)
YOUNG SHIN KWONG, Mr. Jean-Pierre, BSc ACA *1995;* 51 Sir Virgil Naz Street, PORT LOUIS, MAURITIUS.
YOUNGER, Mr. Alexander, BSc ACA *2002;* 8 Karen Close, Hethersett, NORWICH, NR9 3DG.
YOUNGER, Miss. Heather, ACA *2010;* 170 The Chandlers, LEEDS, LS2 7EZ.
YOUNGER, Mr. Michael James, BSc ACA *1987;* Ian Macleod Distillers Ltd Russell House, Dunnet Way East Mains Industrial Estate, BROXBURN, WEST LOTHIAN, EH52 5BU.
YOUNGER, Mr. Nick, BA(Hons) ACA *2003;* EMI, Vogelsanger Str. 321, 50827 COLOGNE, GERMANY.

YOUNGER, Mr. Paul, ACA *2008;* Flat 41 Cedar House, 35 Melliss Avenue, RICHMOND, TW9 4BG.
YOUNGER, Mr. Paul Martin, ACA *2007;* 22 Firlands, Stanwix, CARLISLE, CA3 9FB.
YOUNGHUSBAND, Mrs. Susan Margaret, BSc FCA *1987;* Four Seasons, 18 Priory Way, HITCHIN, SG4 9BL.
YOUNGMAN, Mr. Brian Christopher, FCA *1963;* 4 Glasspool, Denmead, WATERLOOVILLE, PO7 6EA. (Life Member)
•YOUNGMAN, Mr. Brian John, FCA *1959;* (Tax Fac), Youngman & Co, 11 Lynn Road, ELY, CB7 4EG.
YOUNGMAN, Mrs. Gillian Mary, FCA *1976;* The Pines, Thakeham Copse, Storrington, PULBOROUGH, WEST SUSSEX, RH20 3JW.
YOUNGMAN, Mr. Mark Owen, BSc FCA *1984;* 10 Wynmore Dv, Bramhope, LEEDS, LS16 9DQ.
•YOUNGMAN, Mr. Nigel Cleaver, FCA CTA MCT *1977;* (Tax Fac), N.C. Youngman, The Pines, Thakeham Copse, Storrington, PULBOROUGH, WEST SUSSEX RH20 3JW.
YOUNGMAN, Mr. Stephen Roy, ACA *1983;* Neptunusstraat 41-63, 2132JA HOOFDDORP, NETHERLANDS.
YOUNGS, Miss. Emily Kate, BSc ACA *2007;* Lily Cottage, 10 Beach Road, Sea Palling, NORWICH, NR12 0UJ.
YOUNIE, Mr. Alasdair Relph, BSc ACA *2002;* P.O. Box HM 2532, HAMILTON, BERMUDA.
YOUNIE, Mr. Cameron Peter, MA ACA *1980;* Cameron Peters Fine Lighting Ltd, Home Farm Ardington, WANTAGE, OX12 8PD.
YOUNIS, Mr. Adam, BA ACA *1997;* Copedale Limited, Headland, North Drive, Sandfield Park, LIVERPOOL, L12 1LD.
YOUNIS, Mr. Nahidh Mohammed Tahir, BSc FCA *1974;* 10 Royton Close, The Ithens, WREXHAM, LL13 7EP.
YOUNIS, Ms. Salma, BSc ACA *2004;* 39 Brantwood Oval, BRADFORD, WEST YORKSHIRE, BD9 6QN.
YOUNIS, Miss. Yasmin, MA BA ACA *2009;* Flat 5, 39 Tierney Road, LONDON, SW2 4QL.
YOUNUS, Mr. Imran Azam, BSc ACA *2010;* General Stores & Newsagent, 2 Grays Road, Headington, OXFORD, OX3 7QA.
•YOUNUS, Mr. Irfan, BA ACA *2001;* (Tax Fac), Paragon, 155 Normanton Road, DERBY, DE23 6UR. See also IWC
YOUSAF, Mr. Habib-Ur-Rehman, BA ACA *1989;* 16 Westminster Avenue, ASHTON-UNDER-LYNE, OL6 8DD.
YOUSAFALI, Mr. Qutub, FCA *1979;* Arab Banking Corporation, PO Box 5698, MANAMA, BAHRAIN.
YOUSFANI, Mr. Khawar Azam, BA ACA *2007;* 45 St. Helens Grove, Monkston, MILTON KEYNES, MK10 9FG.
•YOUSHANI, Mr. Abol Hassan, BSc(Hons) ACA FCCA *2008;* (Tax Fac), Sterling Partners LLP, Grove House, 774-780 Wilmslow Road, Didsbury, MANCHESTER, M20 2DR. See also Sterling Pay Limited and Sterling Informia Limited
•YOUSSEFI, Mr. Hossein, BSc ACA *1986;* Overdraft Limited, 124 Valley Road, RICKMANSWORTH, HERTFORDSHIRE, WD3 4BP. See also H.Y Stevens & Co
YOUSUF, Mr. Haroon, BA ACA *2011;* 35 Parkdale Close, BIRMINGHAM, B24 8JU.
YOUSUF, Mrs. Khurshid, ACA MAAT *2004;* (Tax Fac), with Howard Worth, Drake House, Gadbrook Park, NORTHWICH, CHESHIRE, CW9 7RA.
YOUSUF, Mr. Zahed, MSc BSc ACA *2003;* Flat 5, 400-402 Brixton Road, LONDON, SW9 7AW.
YOXON, Mr. Michael Neville, BSc FCA *1979;* Vilmorin et Cie, BP1, 63720 CHAPPES, FRANCE.
YU, Mr. Albert Kwok Man, ACA *2007;* A13 Block 12, Nan Fung Sun Chuen, 15 Greig Crescent, QUARRY BAY, HONG KONG ISLAND, HONG KONG SAR.
YU, Mr. Andrew Ka-Leung, BSc ACA *1988;* 20A Tower II, Elegant Terrace, 36 Conduit Road, MID LEVELS, HONG KONG ISLAND, HONG KONG SAR.
YU, Miss. Anita, BSc ACA *1994;* 19B Block 1, Victoria Gardens, 301 Victoria Road, POK FU LAM, HONG KONG ISLAND, HONG KONG SAR.
YU, Miss. Bing, ACA *2003;* 70 Thistley Court, Glaisher Street, LONDON, SE8 3JW.
YU, Mr. Calvin Seng Yap, BA ACA *2005;* KPMG Level 16 Riparian Plaza, 71 Eagle Street, BRISBANE, QLD 4000, AUSTRALIA.
YU, Mr. Carl Yin Wah, BSc ACA *1999;* 39 Merrydale Drive, LIVERPOOL, L11 4UD.
YU, Mrs. Carrie, ACA *1986;* PricewaterhouseCoopers, Prince's Building, 22/F, 10 Chater Road, CENTRAL, HONG KONG ISLAND HONG KONG SAR.
YU, Mr. Che-Chia, ACA CA(SA) *2008;* 238A Thomson Road, #25-04/05 Novena Square, SINGAPORE 307684, SINGAPORE.
YU, Mr. Chi Fat, ACA *2007;* HLB Hodgson Impey Cheng, 31/F Gloucester Tower, The Landmark, 11 Pedder Street, CENTRAL, HONG KONG ISLAND HONG KONG SAR.
YU, Mr. Chi Kit, ACA *2008;* Flat 7 14/Fl, Block E, Kornhill, 13 - 15 Hong Shing Street, QUARRY BAY, HONG KONG ISLAND HONG KONG SAR.
YU, Mr. Chun Kau, ACA *2005;* Flat E 43/F, L'Hiver (Tower 4), Les Saisons, 28 Tai On Street, SAI WAN HO, HONG KONG ISLAND HONG KONG SAR.
YU, Mr. Chung Sang, ACA *2007;* UTi (HK) Ltd, 23/F, Tower 2, Ever Gain Plaza, 88 Container Port Road, KWAI CHUNG NEW TERRITORIES HONG KONG SAR.
YU, Ms. Chung Yang, ACA *2011;* 29 Coombe Gardens, LONDON, SW20 0QU.
YU, Mr. David Hon-To, FCA *1976;* 7 th Floor, 9 Queen's Road, CENTRAL, HONG KONG ISLAND, HONG KONG SAR.
YU, Mr. Eric Ho Yui, BA ACA *1986;* 15 Peartree Lane, LONDON, E1W 3SR.
YU, Mr. George Hung-Hing, ACA *2007;* 10/F 17 Waterloo Road, HO MAN TIN, KOWLOON, HONG KONG SAR.
YU, Mr. Hailiang, ACA *2009;* Flat 38 Aura House, 39 Melliss Avenue, RICHMOND, TW9 4BX.
YU, Mr. How Yuen, ACA *2005;* Yu How Yuen & Co., Room 1104-1105 New Victory House, 93-103 Wing Lok Street, CENTRAL, HONG KONG ISLAND, HONG KONG SAR.
YU, Miss. Jiameng, LLB ACA *2010;* 5 Clay Walk, Hermitage, THATCHAM, BERKSHIRE, RG18 9WW.
YU, Mr. Johnny Ching Yan, MBA BSc ACA CFA *1998;* Flat 21C, Bon-Point, 11 Bonham Road, MID LEVELS, HONG KONG ISLAND, HONG KONG SAR.
YU, Miss. Judith, BSc ACA *1993;* Hong Kong Intl Grp of COS, 9/F HKI Building, 56 Hung To Road, KWUN TONG, KOWLOON, HONG KONG SAR.
YU, Mr. Kam Tim, ACA *2007;* Flat E 36/F Tower 12, Ocean Shores, TSEUNG KWAN O, NEW TERRITORIES, HONG KONG SAR.
YU, Mr. King Yip, ACA *2009;* Flat 6 11/F Block D, Treasure Garden, TAI PO, NEW TERRITORIES, HONG KONG SAR.
YU, Mr. Kwok Kuen Harry, ACA *2004;* c/o Golden Meditech Holdings Limited, 48/F Bank of China Tower, 1 Garden Road, CENTRAL, HONG KONG ISLAND, HONG KONG SAR.
YU, Mr. Kwong Man, ACA *2005;* 21/F. Tai Yau Building, 181 Johnston Road, WAN CHAI, HONG KONG SAR.
YU, Ms. Lai Chu, ACA *2007;* Flat F, 53rd Floor, Block 3, The Pacifica, 9 Sham Shing Road, Cheung Sha Wan SHAM SHUI PO KOWLOON HONG KONG SAR.
YU, Ms. Lai Lin, ACA *2008;* 16/F Flat C, Block 4, Lily Mansion, Whampoa Garden, HUNG HOM, HONG KONG SAR.
YU, Mr. Leo Yiu Sing, ACA *2009;* 26 Hickory Gardens, West End, SOUTHAMPTON, SO30 3RN.
YU, Ms. Lily Fiona, ACA *2007;* Flat A 43rd Floor, Tower 3 The Belcher's, 89 Pokfulam Road, POK FU LAM, HONG KONG ISLAND, HONG KONG SAR.
YU, Miss. Lora Lee See, BSc(Hons) ACA *2010;* 8 Altham Close, BURY, LANCASHIRE, BL9 9NN.
YU, Ms. Mei, ACA *2010;* Unit 1501 Tower 1 Henderson Center, No.18 Jian Guo Men Nei Ave Dong Cheng district, BEIJING 100005, CHINA.
YU, Miss. Mei Yen, ACA *2009;* 34 Haywood Oaks Lane, Blidworth, MANSFIELD, NOTTINGHAMSHIRE, NG21 0TP.
YU, Mr. Michael, MEng ACA *2010;* 6 Primley Park Close, LEEDS, LS17 7LT.
YU, Mr. Ming Tak Eric, ACA *2009;* Room 1509 C C Wu Building, 302 - 308 Hennessy Road, WAN CHAI, HONG KONG SAR.
YU, Ms. Miu Yee Iris, ACA *2008;* Flat G 23/F, Block 6, Discovery Park, TSUEN WAN, NEW TERRITORIES, HONG KONG SAR.
YU, Mr. Shi Kuen, ACA *2004;* PWPlus CPA Limited, Room 2003, CC Wu Building, 302-308 Hennersey Road, WAN CHAI, HONG KONG ISLAND HONG KONG SAR. See also Kam Ching Yu CPA Limited
YU, Miss. Sze Min, BA(Hons) ACA *2003;* 7 Julan Layang Layang, SINGAPORE 598474, SINGAPORE.
YU, Mrs. Sze Wing, MSc ACA *2004;* 11 Collette Court, Eleanor Close, LONDON, SE16 6PW.
YU, Mr. Tak Yuen, ACA *2007;* Room 919, Wah Sin House, Wah Kwai Estate, ABERDEEN, HONG KONG SAR.
YU, Ms. Tak Yee Beryl, ACA *2005;* T.K. Choi & Co, 15th Floor, Empire Land Commercial Centre, 81-85 Lockhart, WAN CHAI, HONG KONG ISLAND HONG KONG SAR. See also YWC & Partners
YU, Mr. Wai Man, ACA *2008;* W M Yu & Co, Flat B1, 11/F, Loyong Court Commercial Building, 212-220 Lockhart Road, WAN CHAI HONG KONG SAR.
YU, Ms. Wai Ling Loretta, ACA *2005;* Flat B 11/F. South Tower 3 Residence Bel-Air Island South 38 Bel-Air Avenue, POK FU LAM, HONG KONG SAR.
YU, Mr. Wei, ACA MBA *2005;* Room 802 No 38 Lane 155, Bao Cheng Road, SHANGHAI 201100, CHINA.
YU, Miss. Wendy, BSc ACA CTA *1997;* Flat B 18/F Panorama Gardens, 103 Robinson Road, MID LEVELS, HONG KONG ISLAND, HONG KONG SAR.
YU, Mr. Wing Fu Philip, ACA *2008;* Suite 6, 3 Curban Street, UNDERWOOD, QLD 4119, AUSTRALIA.
YU, Miss. Yan, BA BSc ACA *2009;* JinHe Road Lane 99 Number 18 1201 Pudong, SHANGHAI 200127, CHINA.
•YU SAK KAN, Mr. Kin Lew, FCA *1974;* 4 Asterix Road, BEAU BASSIN, MAURITIUS.
YU SAK KAN, Miss. Lynn Lee Fah, BSc ACA *2003;* Flat 44, Anderson Heights, 1260 London Road, Norbury, LONDON, SW16 4EH.
YUAN, Ms. Rebecca, MSc ACA *2009;* 104 Ferguson Close, LONDON, E14 3SJ.
•YUDT, Mr. David Hilary, FCA *1973;* (Tax Fac), 3 Goldcrest Way, BUSHEY, WD23 1AL.
YUE, Mr. Bonaventure Ming Wai, ACA FCPA *2005;* Flat A, 11/F, Block 1, Royal Knoll, FANLING, NEW TERRITORIES HONG KONG SAR.
YUE, Mr. King-Man, BA ACA *1990;* Flat 505 Block A, Ming Yuen Mansion, 1-7 Peacock Road, NORTH POINT, HONG KONG ISLAND, HONG KONG SAR.
YUE, Mr. Shik Yin, ACA *2007;* Flat A1/F, Tower 23, Parcoasis, KOWLOON TONG, KOWLOON, HONG KONG SAR.
YUE TING SHING, Mr. Lindsay KianFat, ACA *1993;* Bishops Farmhouse, 24 High Street, Drayton, ABINGDON, OXFORDSHIRE, OX14 4JL.
YUEN, Ms. Chi Kwan, MA BSc FCA *1991;* 61 Lor Sarhad, #04-11, SINGAPORE S119174, SINGAPORE.
YUEN, Mr. Chi Hung Francis, ACA *2005;* 28/F Two International Finance Centre, 8 Finance Street, CENTRAL, HONG KONG SAR.
YUEN, Mr. Chi Shing, ACA *2007;* Flat E 16/F Tower 3, Vista Paradiso, 2 Hang Ming Street, Ma On Shan, SHA TIN, HONG KONG SAR.
YUEN, Mr. Daniel Shu Mun, FCA *1961;* Flat A 7th Floor Tower 2, Redhill Peninsula Phase 4, 18 Pak Pat Shan Road, TAI TAM, HONG KONG ISLAND, HONG KONG SAR. (Life Member)
YUEN, Mr. Eldon Ka Lung, ACA *2006;* Lang & Yuen, 270-5655 Cambie Street, VANCOUVER V5Z 3A4, BC, CANADA.
YUEN, Mrs. Hee-Kwee Dominique, FCA *1978;* 3988 W 27th Avenue, VANCOUVER V6S 1R5, BC, CANADA.
YUEN, Mr. James Wai Yin, MBA MSc BA FCA *1995;* Flat H 57/F Tower 5, Manhattan Hill, 1 Po Lun Street, MEI FOO SUN CHUEN, KOWLOON, HONG KONG SAR.
YUEN, Mr. Ka Cheong Samuel, ACA *2005;* Ernst & Young, 18/F Two International Finance Centre, No. 8 Finance Street, CENTRAL, HONG KONG ISLAND, HONG KONG SAR.
YUEN, Mr. Kingsley King Mun, FCA *1968;* Yuen Tang & Co, 301 Bangunan Lee Yan Lian, Jalan Tun Perak, 50050 KUALA LUMPUR, FEDERAL TERRITORY, MALAYSIA.
YUEN, Mr. Kwok Wan, ACA *2007;* Flat D 27/F. Block 3, Lok Hin Terrace, 350 Chai Wan Road, CHAI WAN, HONG KONG SAR.
YUEN, Mr. Man Kin, ACA *2006;* Prudential Corporation Asia, 13/F, One International Centre, 1 Harbour View Street, CENTRAL, HONG KONG ISLAND HONG KONG SAR.
YUEN, Mr. Ming Fai, BSc FCA *1990;* Flat 19B, La Place de Victoria, 632 King's Road, NORTH POINT, HONG KONG ISLAND, HONG KONG SAR.
YUEN, Mr. Nai Lun Ulysses, ACA *2005;* Ulysses Yuen & Co., 13/F Foo Hoo Centre, 3 Austin Avenue, TSIM SHA TSIU, KOWLOON, HONG KONG SAR.
YUEN, Mr. Pak Lau, ACA *2008;* 28 th Floor, Manhattan Place, 23 Wan Tai Road, KOWLOON BAY, KOWLOON, HONG KONG SAR.
YUEN, Mr. Philip Ewe Jin, BSc ACA *1990;* with Deloitte & Touche, 6 Shenton Way, 32-00, DBS Building Tower Two, SINGAPORE 068809, SINGAPORE.
YUEN, Mr. Shu Tong, ACA *2007;* 3/F. Malaysia Building, 50 Gloucester Road, WAN CHAI, HONG KONG SAR.
YUEN, Mr. Tai Leung, ACA *2007;* Ernst & Young Tax Services Ltd, 18/F, Two IFC, 8 Finance Street, CENTRAL, HONG KONG ISLAND HONG KONG SAR.
YUEN, Mr. Tak Ching, ACA *2008;* Flat 7 11/F Yan Pak House, Hong Pak Court, LAM TIN, HONG KONG SAR.
YUEN, Mr. Tin On, ACA *2005;* 16th Floor, Flat F Block 8, Site 3 Whampoa Garden, 120 Baker Street, HUNG HOM, KOWLOON HONG KONG SAR.
YUEN, Mr. Tsz Chun, ACA *2008;* KLC Kennic Lui & Co, 5/F, Ho Lee Commercial Building, 38 - 44 D' Aguilar Street, CENTRAL, HONG KONG SAR. See also Kennic L H Lui & Co Ltd
YUEN, Mr. Vui Hau, BA ACA *2003;* 10 Islip Gardens, EDGWARE, HA8 9EX.
YUEN, Mr. Wai Ho, ACA *2007;* Flat B 12/Floor, Block 3, Hong Fai Court, 190 Tsat Tsz Mui Road, NORTH POINT, HONG KONG ISLAND HONG KONG SAR.
YUEN, Mr. Wai Leung, BSc FCA *1977;* 72D Tower 2, The Harbourside, 1 Austin Road West, TSIM SHA TSUI, KOWLOON, HONG KONG SAR.
YUEN, Ms. Wai Yee, ACA *2008;* Flat 15D, 86 Broadway, MEI FOO SUN CHUEN, KOWLOON, HONG KONG SAR.
YUEN, Ms. Wing Han Shirley, ACA *2005;* Flat G 14/F, Block 23, South Horizons, AP LEI CHAU, HONG KONG ISLAND, HONG KONG SAR.
YUEN, Ms. Wing Man Yvonne, ACA *2005;* 9C Knight Court, 38 Shing Tai Road, VTC Staff Quarters, CHAI WAN, HONG KONG ISLAND, HONG KONG SAR.
YUEN, Mr. Yiu Leung, ACA *2006;* Fin Div CCB HK, 15/F Tai Yau Building, 181 Johnston Rd, WAN CHAI, HONG KONG SAR.
YUEN, Ms. Yuk Yin, ACA *2008;* Flat D, 8/F, Yan Oi Building, Yan Oi Street, SAN PO KONG, HONG KONG SAR.
YUILE, Mr. Anthony, FCA *1986;* 241 Buckley Road, Island Bay, WELLINGTON 6023, NEW ZEALAND.
YUILL, Mr. Andrew James, BSc FCA *1995;* Wayside The Street, Shotesham All Saints, NORWICH, NR15 1YL.
YUILL, Miss. Gemma, BA ACA *2007;* 5 Fisher Street, CAMBRIDGE, CB4 3DJ.
YUILL, Miss. Heather Louise, BA(Hons) ACA *2005;* 33 Byards Green, Potton, SANDY, BEDFORDSHIRE, SG19 2SB.
YUILL, Mr. Stewart John, ACA *1997;* Fox Murphy Ltd t/a Balloon Dog, Norfolk Tower, Surrey Street, NORWICH, NR1 3PA.
•YULE, Mr. Andrew Herlyn, FCA *1961;* (Tax Fac), Andrew Yule & Co, 1564 Pershore Rd, Stirchley, BIRMINGHAM, B30 2NL. See also Yule A.H.
YULE, Mrs. Angela, MSc ACA *1993;* 246 Pahiatua Track, Aokautere, PALMERSTON NORTH RD1, NEW ZEALAND.
YULE, Miss. Michelle Louise, BSc ACA *2004;* 77 Crown Woods Way, LONDON, SE9 2NL.
YUMASHEVA, Ms. Olga, ACA *2011;* Apt 9, 8ya Sovietskaya Street, 42, 191144 ST PETERSBURG, RUSSIAN FEDERATION.
YUN, Mr. Hon Man, ACA *2005;* Room 1345, Yue Shun House, Yue Wan Estate, CHAI WAN, HONG KONG ISLAND, HONG KONG SAR.
YUN, Mr. Lok Ming, ACA *2007;* Aquamarine 8, Sham Shing Road, Block 5 19F Room A, CHEUNG SHA WAN, KOWLOON, HONG KONG SAR.
YUNG, Ms. Choi Wing Cecilia, ACA *2008;* Flat H 33/F, Block 1, Bel Air Heights, 1 Lung Poon Street, DIAMOND HILL, KOWLOON HONG KONG SAR.
YUNG, Miss. Christine, MA ACA *2011;* 9 Sailacre House, Woolwich Road, GREENWICH, SE10 0JD.
YUNG, Mr. Chun Lu Sam, ACA *2007;* Flat E Block5, Harbour Green, 8 Sham Mong Road, TAI KOK TSUI, KOWLOON, HONG KONG SAR.
YUNG, Ms. Hui Ling, BSc ACA *1994;* 22C The Grand Sethiwan, 82 Soi 24 Sukhumvit Road, Klongtoey, BANGKOK 10110, THAILAND.
YUNG, Mr. Hung Man, ACA *2008;* Room 3504 35/F, Block B Yuk Mei House, Yau Chui Court, YAU TONG, KOWLOON, HONG KONG SAR.
YUNG, Ms. Jessie Mei Chun, ACA *2005;* Jessie Yung CPA, 17/F Yue On Commercial Building, 385-387 Lockhart Road, WAN CHAI, HONG KONG ISLAND, HONG KONG SAR.
YUNG, Mr. Ka Chun, ACA *2005;* Flat B 9th Floor Tower 7 Pacific Palisades, No. 1 Braemar Hill Road, NORTH POINT, HONG KONG ISLAND, HONG KONG SAR.
YUNG, Mr. Kin Chan Sae, BCom FCA *1964;* 31 Watkins Road, DALKEITH, WA 6009, AUSTRALIA. (Life Member)

YUNG, Ms. Miu Pik, ACA *2008;* Flat G 8/F Block 2, Illumination Terrace, No.7 Tai Hang Road, CAUSEWAY BAY, HONG KONG SAR.
YUNG, Ms. Tsui Yee Linda, ACA *2008;* AIP Partners CPA Ltd, Room 1304, C C Wu Building, 302-308 Hennessy Road, WAN CHAI, HONG KONG SAR.
YURAVLIVKER, Mrs. Anita Shirke, BSc ACA *2006;* 10301 Grosvenor Place, Apt 1506, NORTH BETHESDA, MD 20852, UNITED STATES.
YURKWICH, Mr. Adrian Michael, BSc ACA *1995;* 38 Topstreet Way, HARPENDEN, AL5 5TT.
YUSOF, Mr. Hilmi, MA ACA *2003;* Shell Malaysia, Damansara Heights, 50490 KUALA LUMPUR, FEDERAL TERRITORY, MALAYSIA.
YUSOF, Mr. Mohammed Rashdan, MA ACA ACT *1996;* 5 Jalan SS4B/1, Kelana Jaya, 47301 PETALING JAYA, SELANGOR, MALAYSIA.
YUSOF, Mr. Mohd Sharif, FCA *1966;* No 5 Jalan 22/38, Taman Lian Seng, 46300 PETALING JAYA, Selangor, MALAYSIA.
•YUSSOF, Mr. Mohd Yussof, FCA *1972;* 54 Jalan Kolek 19/29, 40300, SHAH ALAM, SELANGOR, MALAYSIA.
•YUSSOUF, Mr. Falak, BA ACA FCCA *2008;* Accountancy Services London Ltd, Suite 401/402, Cumberland House, 80 Scrubs Lane, LONDON, NW10 6RF. See also Matrix
YUSUF, Mr. Atif, ACA *2003;* 28 Downsview Avenue, WOKING, GU22 9BT.
YUSUF, Mr. Mahmood, FCA *1976;* 1004 AL_WASL TOWER, SHEIKH ZAYED ROAD, PO BOX 29332, DUBAI, UNITED ARAB EMIRATES.
YUSUF, Mr. Mohammad Abdullah, FCA *1972;* House No 744, Street No 83, Sector I-8/4, ISLAMABAD, PAKISTAN.
YUSUF, Mr. Mosiudi Alani Olaya, FCA *1970;* 58 Rawlinson Road, Maiden Bower, CRAWLEY, WEST SUSSEX, RH10 7DP.
YUSUF, Miss. Ololade Bilikis, LLM BA(Hons) ACA *2011;* 121 Great Meadow Road, Bradley Stoke, BRISTOL, BS32 8DF.
YUSUF, Mr. Shiraz Mohomed Faruk, ACA *1991;* Ernst & Young, Apex House Kidney Crescent, PO Box 530, BLANTYRE, 3, MALAWI.
YUSUFI, Mr. Aurangzaib Khan, ACA *2009;* Flat 8 Johns Court, Gillian Street, LONDON, SE13 7AL.
ZABELL, Mr. Barry Norman, FCA *1962;* 23 Little Forest Road, BOURNEMOUTH, BH4 9NN. (Life Member)
ZABEO, Mr. Gino, ACA *2001;* 18 Oak Close, Bishop's Cannings, DEVIZES, SN10 2RZ.
ZACHARIADES, Mr. Andreas, BSc ACA *1994;* 8 Evdaimonias, Archangelos, 2331 NICOSIA, CYPRUS.
ZACHARIAH, Mr. Kelvin Joseph, BA ACA *1993;* 4 Foley Road, Claygate, ESHER, SURREY, KT10 0ND.
ZACHARIAS, Ms. Eleni Alexia, BA(Hons) ACA *2003;* 3 Willow Way, RADLETT, HERTFORDSHIRE, WD7 8DU.
ZACHARIOU, Mr. Zacharias, BSc ACA *2006;* Liberty House, Flat 1605, PO Box 506829, DIFC, DUBAI, UNITED ARAB EMIRATES.
ZACK, Mr. Malcolm Robert, MBA BCom FCA *1990;* Brakes, Tower House, 10 Southampton Street, LONDON, WC2E 7HA.
ZACKHEIM, Mr. Irving Robin Jules, FCA *1972;* 27 Oak Tree Drive, Totteridge, LONDON, N20 8QJ.
ZADANFARROKH, Mr. Farshid, BSc ARCS ACA *1996;* 754 E 6th Street, Apt 3B, NEW YORK, NY 10009, UNITED STATES.
ZADUCK, Mrs. Kelly Anne Leman, ACA CA(SA) *2009;* 57 Bellairs, Sutton, ELY, CAMBRIDGESHIRE, CB6 2RW.
ZAFAR, Dr. Amir, BSc ACA *1992;* 14 Goodby Road, BIRMINGHAM, B13 8NJ.
ZAFAR, Mr. Asim, ACA ACMA *1993;* Arcapita Bank, PO BOX, 1406, MANAMA, BAHRAIN.
ZAFAR, Mr. Azhar, ACA CF *1984;* with Ernst & Young, Level 28, AL Attar Bus Tower, Sheikh Zayed Road, P.O. Box 9267, DUBAI UNITED ARAB EMIRATES.
ZAFAR, Mr. Islam, MEng ACA *2007;* Ernst & Young, P.O.Box 164, Al Abdulghani Tower, Airport Road, DOHA, QATAR.
ZAFAR, Mr. Khalid, ACA *2008;* 1723 Albunist, #1086, VANCOUVER V66 369, BC, CANADA.
ZAFAR, Mr. Masood, FCA *1977;* Gulf International Bank, P.O.Box 1017, MANAMA, BAHRAIN.
ZAFAR, Mr. Naveed, BSc ACA *1993;* 15 Springkell Gate, GLASGOW, G41 4BY.
ZAFAR, Mr. Rizvan Ali, BA ACA *1994;* New Butts Cottage, Congleton Road, Nether Alderley, MACCLESFIELD, SK10 4TP.
•ZAFFAR, Mr. Muhammad Azhar, ACA FCCA *2009;* Maz & Co, 63 Beehive Lane, ILFORD, ESSEX, IG1 3RL.
ZAFRULLAH, Mr. Mohammad, ACA *1986;* Glaxosmithkline, Gulf & Near East Regional Office, 28 Floor API Tower, Sheikh Zayed Road, PO Box 50199, DUBAI UNITED ARAB EMIRATES.
ZAHARI, Ms. Juniza, BA(Hons) ACA *2002;* No 11 Jalan Puncak Kiara 4, Kiara View, Desa Sri Hartamas, 50480 KUALA LUMPUR, FEDERAL TERRITORY, MALAYSIA.
ZAHARIA, Ms. Vasoulla, ACA *1998;* ANDROKLEOUS 16, AGLANTZIA, 2103 NICOSIA, CYPRUS.
•ZAHEDI, Mrs. Carol Yuen Hie, FCA *1975;* Shoaie Zahedi & Co, 1 Mayfields, WEMBLEY, HA9 9PW.
•ZAHEDI, Mr. Seyed Mohammad Amir, FCA *1974;* Shoaie Zahedi & Co, 1 Mayfields, WEMBLEY, HA9 9PW.
ZAHEDIEH, Mr. Ahmad, BSc FCA *1977;* 310 Liverpool Road, LONDON, N7 8PU.
ZAHID, Mr. Ahmad Zubir, BSc ACA *2004;* A-8-1 The Park Residence 1, No. 2A Jalan 1/112H, Off Jalan Kerinchi, Bangsar South, 59200 KUALA LUMPUR, FEDERAL TERRITORY MALAYSIA.
ZAHID, Mr. Farhan Mohammad, BSc ACA CISA *2010;* 338 Wilbraham Road, MANCHESTER, M21 0UX.
ZAHID, Mr. Mohammad Taha, ACA *2010;* Scotland 95/11 24th Street, off Khayaban - e Rahat, Phase 6, KARACHI, SINDH, PAKISTAN.
ZAHID HASSAN, Mr. Hamid, BSc ACA *2010;* 37 Du Cros Drive, STANMORE, MIDDLESEX, HA7 4TL.
ZAHIDI, Mr. Aamir, FCA CF *1977;* Fullerton Financial Holdings Ltd, 60b Orchard Road, unit 06-18, Tower 2, The Atrium e, Orchard SINGAPORE 238891 SINGAPORE.
ZAHIDI, Mr. Syed Omar, BSc(Hons) ACA *2011;* 38 Alma Court, BRISTOL, BS8 2HH.
ZAHIR, Mr. Amirul Feisal Wan, BSc ACA *1997;* Permodalan Nasional Berhad, 3rd Floor Balai PNB, 201-A Jalan Tun Razak, 50400 KUALA LUMPUR, FEDERAL TERRITORY, MALAYSIA.
ZAHIR, Mr. Mohammed, BSc ACA *1988;* BNP Paribas Global Securities Operations, Menon Eternity, 3rd Floor, 165 St Mary's Road, Alwarp, CHENNAI 600 018 TAMIL NADU INDIA.
ZAHIRI, Mr. Hooshang, ACA *1980;* 2441 Yorktown Circle, MISSISSAUGA L5M 5Y1, ON, CANADA.
ZAHN, Miss. Johanna, ACA *2011;* Vanity Park Cottage, North Street, Norton St. Philip, BATH, BA2 7LE.
ZAHN, Mr. Oskar, ACA CA(SA) *2010;* 36 Allen House Park, WOKING, SURREY, GU22 0DB.
ZAHOOR, Miss. Shafia, BSc FCA *1996;* 89 Cassiobury Park Avenue, WATFORD, WD18 7LH.
•ZAHUR, Mr. Muhammad, FCA *1979;* (Tax Fac), Altman Smith & Co, Leverton House, 461-463 London Road, Heeley, SHEFFIELD, S2 4HL.
ZAHUR, Mr. Shahid, FCA *1977;* 690 Auger Terrace, MILTON L9T 5M2, ON, CANADA.
ZAIDI, Mr. Adnan, ACA *2011;* Villa 84, Garden View Villa's, Jebel Ali, DUBAI, 212445, UNITED ARAB EMIRATES.
ZAIDI, Mr. Ali, ACA FCCA *2011;* Flat 83 Dominion House, The Avenue, Ealing, LONDON, W13 8AE.
ZAIDI, Mr. Ali Abbas, ACA *1993;* PO Box 215161, DUBAI, UNITED ARAB EMIRATES.
ZAIDI, Mr. Amir Hassan, ACA *2008;* 48 Windermere Avenue, WEMBLEY, MIDDLESEX, HA9 8SF.
ZAIDI, Mrs. Amna, BSc ACA *2004;* 9 Twyford Road, HARROW, MIDDLESEX, HA2 0SH.
ZAIDI, Mrs. Asfiya, ACA *2004;* 42 Malden Green Avenue, WORCESTER PARK, KT4 7SQ.
•ZAIDI, Mr. Mannan Husain, BSc(Hons) ACA *2004;* Zaidi & Co, Amen Corner, 241 Mitcham Road, LONDON, SW17 9JQ.
•ZAIDI, Mr. Misdaq Husain, FCA *1975;* (Tax Fac), Zaidi & Co, Amen Corner, 241 Mitcham Road, LONDON, SW17 9JQ.
ZAIDI, Mr. Mohammed Akhtar, FCA *1973;* Flat 4, 22-26 Ovington Square, LONDON, SW3 1LR.
ZAIDI, Miss. Nadia, ACA *2009;* 140a Wallwood Road, LONDON, E11 1AN.
ZAIDI, Mr. Saiyed Hidayat Husain, FCA *1971;* 33 Oakwood Park Road, LONDON, N14 6QD.
ZAIDI, Mrs. Sajida Batool, BSc(Hons) ACA *2002;* Lacrosse Global Fund Services UK Ltd Munro House, Portsmouth Road, COBHAM, KT11 1TF.
•ZAIDI, Mr. Syed Raza Haider, FCA *1970;* 68b Sistova Road, LONDON, SW12 9QS.
•ZAIM, Mr. Atif, ACA *1996;* with KPMG LLP, 345 Park Avenue, NEW YORK, NY 10154, UNITED STATES.
ZAIN, Mr. Asad, ACA *1997;* c/o Olayan Financing Company, PO Box 8772, Riyadh 11492, RIYADH, 11492, SAUDI ARABIA.
ZAIN, Mr. Azmir, BA(Hons) ACA *2003;* 2A Jalan 203B 20trees, Taman Melawati Indah, 53100 GOMBAK, MALAYSIA.
ZAIN, Mr. Masud, FCA *1962;* House no 5A-2, 19th Street, Phase-V, Defence Housing Society, KARACHI, PAKISTAN.
ZAIN, Mr. Sarmad, ACA FCCA *2009;* 23 Dartnell Park Road, WEST BYFLEET, KT14 6PN.
ZAINAL-ABIDIN, Miss. Mona Sirin Zam, BA ACA *1995;* 90 Archel Road, West Kensington, LONDON, W14 9QP.
ZAINOL, Mr. Azlan Bin, FCA *1975;* c/o Employees Provident Fund, 25th Floor EPF Building, Jalan Raja Laut, 50350 KUALA LUMPUR, FEDERAL TERRITORY, MALAYSIA.
ZAINOL ABIDIN, Miss. Noor Aza, BA ACA *2005;* Plot 5Yemen Street, Area 5, Diplomatic Enclave, Daiya, P.O Box: 4105, SAFAT 13042 KUWAIT.
ZAINUDIN, Mr. Irman Shah, BSc ACA *2001;* 65 Jalan Villa 11, Anggerik Villa Off Jalan Semenyih, 43000 KAJANG, SELANGOR, MALAYSIA.
ZAINUL ABIDIN, Mr. Sufian, BSc ACA *2009;* Apartment 9, 11 Sheldon Square, LONDON, W2 6DQ.
ZAJAC, Mr. Piotr Antoni, BA ACA AMCT *1999;* Standard Chartered, 1 Basinghall Avenue, LONDON, EC2V 5DD.
ZAJAC, Mrs. Susan Gayner, BSc ACA *1999;* 27 Wellington Road, Wanstead, LONDON, E11 2AS.
•ZAKARIYA, Mr. Adnan, BSc(Hons) FCA *2000;* Zakariya & Company, Al Shaheed Tower, 4th Floor, Khaled Ben Al Waleed Street, PO Box 1773, SAFAT 13018 KUWAIT.
ZAKARIYA, Miss. Bushra, ACA *2008;* 31 Hitherwell Drive, HARROW, MIDDLESEX, HA3 6JD.
•ZAKI, Mr. Shahid, BSc ACA *1989;* Orbis Partners LLP, Third Floor, 35 Newhall Street, BIRMINGHAM, B3 3PU.
ZAKIEWICZ, Mr. Michael Bronislaw Wood, BCom FCA *1974;* (Tax Fac), Radcliffes Le Brasseur, 5 Great College Street, LONDON, SW1P 3SJ.
•ZAKIR, Mr. Zulfikarhusein Fazleabbas, ACA *1979;* HMS International Fabrics Corp., 51 Hartz Way, SECAUCUS, NJ 07094, UNITED STATES.
ZAKOVA, Miss. Victoria, BSc ACA *2010;* 15 Landons Close, LONDON, E14 9QQ.
ZAKRZEWSKA, Mrs. Aleksandra Zofia, PhD ACA *1990;* 16 Avondale Avenue, WORCESTER PARK, KT4 7PD.
ZALAGENAS, Mr. Tomas, ACA *2009;* Flat 4 Moore House, Cassilis Road, LONDON, E14 9LN.
ZALKIN, Mr. Paul Andrew, BA(Hons) ACA *2004;* with Baker Tilly Restructuring And Recovery LLP, 25 Farringdon Street, LONDON, EC4A 4AB.
ZAMAN, Mr. Amjid Hussain, BA ACA *1998;* 21 London Road, Loughton, MILTON KEYNES, MK5 8AB.
ZAMAN, Miss. Farah, MSci ACA *2006;* MTV NE, UK House, 180 Oxford Street, LONDON, W1D 1DS.
ZAMAN, Mr. Mohamed Nasir-Uz, FCA *1971;* PO Box 358605, DUBAI, UNITED ARAB EMIRATES. (Life Member)
ZAMAN, Miss. Rohi, BA ACA *2010;* Flat 17, Clarion House, Moreton Place, LONDON, SW1V 2NN.
•ZAMAN, Mr. Tariq, BA ACA *1980;* Zaman & Co., 27 Dollis Hill Lane, LONDON, NW2 6JH.
ZAMARIA, Mr. John Victor, FCA *1975;* Lane End Cottage, Cargreen, SALTASH, CORNWALL, PL12 6PA.
ZAMBAS, Mr. Pavlos, BA(Hons) ACA *2002;* PO Box 29007, CY 1620 NICOSIA, CYPRUS.
ZAMBONI, Mr. Edward Charles, MA MSc ACA *1987;* H M Revenue & Customs, 100 Parliament Street, Westminster, LONDON, SW1A 2BQ.
ZAMBONI, Mr. Richard Frederick Charles, FCA *1954;* The Old Vicarage, 80 Church Street, LEATHERHEAD, KT22 8ER. (Life Member)
ZAMHOT, Ms. Aida, BA ACA *2005;* Flat 17, Charnwood House, Rembrandt Way, READING, RG1 6QR.
ZAMIR, Mr. Asim, BSc ACA *2007;* 33 Budgen Drive, REDHILL, RH1 2QB.
ZAMMIT TABONA, Mr. Joseph, FCA *1971;* 16 Kensington Square, LONDON, W8 5HH.
ZAMMIT VASILIEVA, Mrs. Tatiana, ACA *2004;* 46 The Strand, SLIEMA SLM1022, MALTA.
ZAMOJSKI, Mr. Jan William, BA ACA *1981;* 290 Windmill Road, Ealing, LONDON, W5 4DL.
ZAMPELAS, Mr. Michalakis Herodotou, FCA *1966;* 18 Napoleontos St., Kaimkali, CY-1020 NICOSIA, CYPRUS.
ZAMURD, Mrs. Shabnam, BSc(Econ) ACA *2002;* Opportunity International, 81 St. Clements Street, OXFORD, OX4 1AW.
ZANE, Mr. David Alan, BCom FCA *1965;* 14 Friern Mount Drive, LONDON, N20 9DN.
•ZANETTOS, Mr. Adonis, FCA *1981;* (Tax Fac), A S Zanettos & Co Limited, 4 Croxted Mews, Croxted Road, LONDON, SE24 9DA.
•ZANGOULOS, Mr. Kyriakos Andreas, BSc ACA *1990;* BDO Limited, Antonis Zenios Tower, 1 Erehthiou Street Engomi, PO Box 25277, 2413 NICOSIA, CYPRUS. See also BDO Philippides Limited
ZANI, Mrs. Rachel Sarah, BSc ACA *1999;* 26 Goldney Road, CAMBERLEY, GU15 1DH.
ZANKER, Mr. Martin Mortimore, BCom FCA *1965;* (Tax Fac), 1 Moorland Street, AXBRIDGE, BS26 2BA. (Life Member)
ZAPHIRIOU-ZARIFI, Mr. Ari Charles, BSc FCA *1970;* The Mews, 1A Birkenhead Street, LONDON, WC1H 8BA.
ZAPITIS, Mr. Antonis, BA ACA *1997;* Antonis Zapitis, 13 Michalaki Karaoli, Omorphita, 1025 NICOSIA, CYPRUS.
ZAPITIS, Mr. Christakis, BSc ACA *2010;* 6 Nemeseos, 2045 Strovolos, NICOSIA, CYPRUS.
ZAPPAROV, Mr. Marat, ACA *2008;* HSBC, Floor 15, HSBC Main Building, 1 Queen's Road, CENTRAL, HONG KONG ISLAND HONG KONG SAR.
ZARA, Ms. Joanna Mary, BSc ACA *1987;* 1 Burton Walk, HOVE, BN3 6EZ.
ZARAC, Mr. Neil, MSc BBA ACA *2010;* 13 Longbridge Road, LICHFIELD, STAFFORDSHIRE, WS14 9EL.
•ZARACH, Mr. Barrington Philip, FCA *1966;* (Tax Fac), Barrington Zarach & Company, 23 Kings Road, ASCOT, SL5 9AD.
ZARB, Mr. Michael, ACA *2011;* 1 San Lawrenz, Triq A.Ferris, ZEBBUG ZBG 1430, MALTA.
ZARBALIAN, Mr. Ali-Akbar, ACA *1981;* 15 Sheen Common Drive, RICHMOND, SURREY, TW10 5BW.
ZAREMBA, Mr. Bogdan Mark, BA ACA *1983;* 28 Oxford Gardens, Chiswick, LONDON, W4 3BW.
•ZAREMBA, Mr. Martin Antoni, ACA *1985;* (Tax Fac), James Worley & Sons, 9 Bridle Close, Surbiton Road, KINGSTON UPON THAMES, SURREY, KT1 2JW.
ZARNO, Mr. Michael, ACA *2009;* Wilderness Edge, The Green, Hilton, HUNTINGDON, CAMBRIDGESHIRE, PE28 9NB.
ZAROOVABELI, Mr. Daniel, BSc ACA *2006;* 35 Stoneyfields Lane, EDGWARE, MIDDLESEX, HA8 9SH.
•ZAROOVABELI, Mr. Moosa, FCA *1981;* 6 Weymouth Avenue, LONDON, NW7 3JE.
ZARZOUR, Mr. Antoine Ezzat Fouad, BCom FCA *1954;* 121 14th Street, Roxboro, MONTREAL H8Y 1N3, QUE, CANADA. (Life Member)
ZATMAN, Mr. Merton Sydney, FCA *1958;* 5 Balmoral Close, Park Street, ST. ALBANS, HERTFORDSHIRE, AL2 2AF. (Life Member)
•ZATOUROFF, Mr. Justin Alan, BA FCA CF *1993;* KPMG LLP, 15 Canada Square, LONDON, E14 5GL. See also KPMG Europe LLP
ZAUM, Mr. Benjamin Bruno, FCA *1961;* 1 Rabina Street, TEL AVIV, 69395, ISRAEL.
ZAUSMER, Mr. Anthony David, BSc ACA *1981;* Pandy, Llan Ffestiniog, BLAENAU FFESTINIOG, GWYNEDD, LL41 4PH.
ZAVERI, Mr. Manesh, ACA *1995;* 3 Siglap Road, 02-28 Mandarin Gardens, SINGAPORE 448907, SINGAPORE.
ZAVOU CHRISTOFOROU, Mrs. Anna, ACA FCCA *2009;* Democratias 5, Egomi, 2406 NICOSIA, CYPRUS.
ZAWISTOWSKI, Ms. Marcella Lucia, ACA *2008;* PO Box 32127 SMB, SEVEN MILE BEACH, GRAND CAYMAN, KY1-1208, CAYMAN ISLANDS.
•ZBIROHOWSKA-KOSCIA, Mrs. Linda Joy, BSc FCA *1982;* Linda Koscia Ltd, Wedgewood, Mapledrakes Road, Ewhurst, CRANLEIGH, GU6 7QW.
ZDRZALKA, Mr. Nick, BA(Hons) ACA *2011;* 37 Temple Sheen Road, LONDON, SW14 7QF.
ZEALE, Mr. Timothy John Christopher, BSc ACA *2007;* Moonrakers La Vieille Charriere, Trinity, JERSEY, JE3 5AT.
ZEDGITT, Mr. Martyn John, BSc ACA *1990;* Tetra Laval International Switzerland, Av. General-Guisan 70, CH-1009 PULLY, SWITZERLAND.
ZEE, Ms. Ching Man Tiffany, ACA *2007;* 16 D Block 8 Site 3, Whampoa Garden, HUNG HOM, KOWLOON, HONG KONG SAR.
ZEFF, Prof. Stephen A, FCA(Honorary) Herbert S. Autrey Professor of Accounting, Jesse H. Jones Graduate School of Management, Rice University - MS 531, 6100 Main Street, HOUSTON, TX 77005 UNITED STATES.
ZEFFERTT, Mr. Robert James, BSc ACA *1998;* with Kaplan Financial, Broadcasting House, 10 Havelock Road, SOUTHAMPTON, SO14 7FY.

•**ZEIDERMAN, Mr. Gavin Warren, BA(Hons) ACA** *2004;* FMCB, Hathaway House, Popes Drive, Finchley, LONDON, N3 1QF.

•**ZEIDERMAN, Mr. Leonard, BSc FCA** *1981;* (Tax Fac), Leonard Mann & Co., 28 Marlborough Road, ST. ALBANS, AL1 3XQ.

•**ZEIN, Mrs. Michaela Catherine, ACA CA(NZ)** *2009;* Zein Contractors Limited, Unit 71, 61 Praed Street, LONDON, W2 1NS.

ZEIN-IDDIN, Mrs. Rula, BSc ACA *1995;* Evolve, P O Box 850252, AMMAN, 11185, JORDAN.

ZEITAL, Mr. Simon Maurice, BA ACA *2000;* 47 Hale Drive, LONDON, NW7 3EL.

ZEITOUNE, Mr. Barry, BA ACA *2005;* Flat 5, Tudor Court, Crewys Road, Cricklewood, LONDON, NW2 2AA.

•**ZEKIA, Mr. Engin, BSc FCA** *1990;* with Gerald Edelman, Edelman House, 1238 High Road, Whetstone, LONDON, N20 0LH.

•**ZELKHA, Mr. Morris Sion, FCA** *1970;* 6 Melina Place, LONDON, NW8 9SA.

ZELTSER, Mr. Lionel Harvey, BA(Econ) FCA *1987;* (Tax Fac), Heron House, 4 Bentinck Street, LONDON, W1U 2EF.

ZEMLYANOV, Mr. Andrey, ACA *2010;* Apt 8, Bolotni Kovskay Street 712, MOSCOW, RUSSIAN FEDERATION.

ZENG, Mr. Stephen Xianlong, MSc ACA *2010;* 36 Germander Way, LONDON, E15 3AB.

ZENIERI, Mr. Antonis, BSc ACA *2008;* 51A Iasonos Str, 6052 LARNACA, CYPRUS.

ZENIOS, Mr. Jonathan David, MA FCA ATII *1994;* (Tax Fac), Barclays Capital, 5 North Colonnade, LONDON, E14 4BB.

ZENKER, Mr. Robert Michael, FCA *1977;* Rütistrasse 10b, 9325 ROGGWIL, SWITZERLAND.

ZENKEROVA, Mrs. Claire Louisa, BA ACA *1991;* Frani Sramka 36/1918, Smichov, 15000 PRAGUE, CZECH REPUBLIC.

ZEPLER, Mr. Paul Eric, MSc FCA *1993;* (Tax Fac), 53 Mayfair Gardens, SOUTHAMPTON, SO15 2TW.

ZERTALIS, Mr. Constantinos, ACA *2010;* 35D Brecknock Road, LONDON, N7 0BT.

ZETLIN, Mr. Paul, BA ACA *1989;* Maher Bird Associates, 82 Charing Cross Road, LONDON, WC2H 0BA.

•**ZEVEDEOU, Miss. Marina, BSc FCA ACA** *1992;* Athinodorou & Zevedeou Ltd, Elia House, 77 Limassol Avenue, 2121 NICOSIA, CYPRUS.

ZEVLARIS, Mr. Ioannis Miki, BSc ACA *1989;* P O Box 23278, 1680 NICOSIA, CYPRUS.

ZHANG, Mr. An, ACA *2010;* Flat 93 Abbott's Wharf, 93 Stainsby Road, LONDON, E14 6JN.

ZHANG, Mr. Gang Gang, ACA *2010;* 6 Oak Grove, Emmer Green, READING, RG4 8AW.

ZHANG, Mr. Guangle, ACA CPA *2010;* Room 1401 No.3, Lane 176 Zhenping Road, Putuo District, SHANGHAI 200061, CHINA.

ZHANG, Miss. Han, ACA *2011;* No 511, 5 unit Building 7, Shuangyushu Xili, Community Haidian District, BEIJING 100086, CHINA.

ZHANG, Ms. Huifang, ACA *2009;* 27-3-501 Biguiyuan Changyang Road, Fangshan District, BEIJING 100240, CHINA.

ZHANG, Mr. James Jian, BSc ACA *1999;* Flat 2702 No 9 Lane 168, Shun Chang Road Lakeville Regency, SHANGHAI 200010, CHINA.

ZHANG, Mr. Jing, BEng ACA *2006;* 117 Leopold Avenue, BIRMINGHAM, B20 1EX.

ZHANG, Ms. Jing, MA ACA *2010;* Room 1101, South Building Tower C, Raycom InfoTech Park Haidian District, BEIJING 100190, CHINA.

ZHANG, Miss. Lei, ACA *2011;* Flat 3F Tower 10, Island Harbour View, 11 Hoi Fan Road, TAI KOK TSUI, KOWLOON, HONG KONG SAR.

ZHANG, Mr. Liang, ACA *2009;* 5 Fielden Terrace, Northfleet, GRAVESEND, DA11 8FN.

ZHANG, Mr. Lilai, MSc ACA *2010;* Flat 2 Kilby Court, Child Lane, LONDON, SE10 0PZ.

ZHANG, Miss. Lu, ACA *2009;* with Deloitte LLP, 2 New Street Square, LONDON, EC4A 3BZ.

ZHANG, Mr. Peng, ACA *2011;* Room 701Building 13, Shanshui Garden, Jinxiuxiangjiang Garden, Yingbin Road Panyu District, GUANGZHOU 511442, GUANGDONG PROVINCE CHINA.

ZHANG, Ms. Qian, ACA *2011;* Flat 9, Wellwood Court, 390 Upper Richmond Road, LONDON, SW15 6JH.

ZHANG, Ms. Su, ACA *2008;* 9 Alma Grove, YORK, YO10 4DH.

ZHANG, Mr. Wei, BSC ACA *2011;* Flat 3 Sussex House, 86 Raymond Road, LONDON, SW19 4AH.

ZHANG, Miss. Wendy Hanqing, ACA *2009;* Coller Capital Limited, 33 Cavendish Square, LONDON, W1G 0TT.

ZHANG, Miss. Xiaoti, BSc ACA *2011;* Deloitte & Touche Ltd Global House, High Street, CRAWLEY, WEST SUSSEX, RH10 1DL.

ZHANG, Mr. Yi, MSc ACA *2009;* 39 Holders Gardens, BIRMINGHAM, B13 8NW.

ZHANG, Miss. Yi-Ye, ACA *2009;* 30 Highgate Edge, Great North Road, LONDON, N2 0NT.

ZHANG, Mr. Yifan, MA ACA *2009;* Universal Pictures International Entertainment Ltd, Prospect House 80-110 New Oxford Street, LONDON, WC1A 1HB.

ZHANG, Miss. Yu, ACA *2011;* 5AC Huang Jia Cui Yuan, Fuzhong Road, Futian District, SHENZHEN 518026, GUANGDONG PROVINCE, CHINA.

ZHANG, Miss. Yuanchao, ACA *2010;* Flat 44, 18 Great Suffolk Street, LONDON, SE1 0UG.

ZHANG, Miss. Yufan, ACA *2010;* #05-10 Blk 553 Woodlands Drive 44, SINGAPORE 730553, SINGAPORE.

ZHANG, Miss. Zengyan, ACA *2008;* 93 Cherry Tree Lane, RAINHAM, ESSEX, RM13 8TR.

ZHAO, Miss. Amanda, ACA *2009;* 79 Shirland Road, LONDON, W9 2EL.

ZHAO, Miss. Bingnan, ACA *2008;* Flat 5 Buckland House, 18 The Moors, REDHILL, RH1 2PE.

ZHAO, Mr. Bo, BSc ACA *2011;* 18 Munster Road, LONDON, SW6 4EN.

ZHAO, Mr. Hairong, MBA ACA *2009;* 6th floor, xinghu business building, xixi road 128, HANGZHOU 310007, CHINA.

ZHAO, Miss. Ivy Xin, ACA *2009;* Flat 35 Bombay House, 59 Whitworth Street, MANCHESTER, M1 3AB.

ZHAO, Ms. Jin, BSc ACA *2011;* Flat 97, New Atlas Wharf, 3 Arnhem Place, LONDON, E14 3ST.

ZHAO, Miss. Meng, ACA *2011;* Zurich London Ltd, 3 Minster Court, LONDON, EC3R 7DD.

ZHAO, Miss. Qing, BA(Hons) ACA *2010;* Flat D171 Parliament View Apartments, 1 Albert Embankment, LONDON, SE1 7XQ.

ZHAO, Miss. Yanlin, ACA *2008;* Nomura International (HK) Limited, 22/F Two IFC, 8 Finance Street, CENTRAL, HONG KONG ISLAND, HONG KONG SAR.

ZHAO, Mr. Yuming, ACA *2009;* Barclays Capital, 10 South Colonnade, LONDON, E14 4PU.

ZHENG, Mr. Jeremy Binman, MBiochem ACA *2010;* Wilkins & Kennedy, Gladstone House, 77-79 High Street, EGHAM, SURREY, TW20 9HY.

ZHIKA, Miss. Elona, BA ACA *2005;* Acision, 1430 Arlington Business Park Theale, READING, RG7 4SA.

ZHOU, Ms. Biyu, ACA *2011;* Flat 104, Baquba Building, Conington Road, LONDON, SE13 7FF.

ZHOU, Miss. Fangfang, ACA *2009;* Flat 7, Cotterell Court, Hop Street, LONDON, SE10 0QR.

ZHOU, Ms. Jie, ACA *2010;* ChengDeXin accountants company, ZhongYuan Road 58#, PU Yang, HENAN 457001, CHINA.

ZHOU, Ms. Lin, ACA *2011;* Room 601, No 25, Lane 1225, Xian Xia Road, SHANGHAI 200336, CHINA.

ZHOU, Mr. Lupeng, MBA ACA *2006;* 99 Telegraph Place, LONDON, E14 9XA.

ZHOU, Mr. Teli, MSc ACA *2009;* Beijing ChaoYangQu, NanMoFang Road Dong Si Huan Yao Wa Hu Gong Yuan Hua Han Guo Ji D-3 Danyuan -1101, BEIJING 100023, BEIJING, CHINA.

ZHOU, Miss. Wei, BCom ACA *2011;* Flat 9 Westfield House, Rotherhithe New Road, LONDON, SE16 2AB.

ZHU, Mr. Enlei, ACA *2011;* Room 1709 Building 8 (#8-1709), Niu Jie Dong Li Xiao Qu, BEIJING 100053, CHINA.

ZHU, Miss. Nan, MA ACA *2010;* Flat 1, 227 Winchester Road, SOUTHAMPTON, SO16 6TP.

ZHU, Ms. Shu, BSc ACA *2009;* Flat 16 Sail Court, 15 Newport Avenue, LONDON, E14 2DQ.

ZHU, Ms. Shu, ACA *2010;* Room 1501 Unit 2 Building 4 Da He Zhuang Yuan No. 3 Suzhou Street Haidian District, BEIJING 100086, CHINA.

ZHU, Miss. Xiaowei, MSc ACA *2006;* Travelex UK Ltd, 65 Kingsway, LONDON, WC2B 6TD.

ZHU, Miss. Yibing, MSc ACA *2004;* NO. 32, Lane 333, Qingtong Road, Pudong District, SHANGHAI 201203, CHINA.

ZHU, Mr. Youyi, BBA ACA *2010;* 19F Shuiping Building, No.2088 Nanyou Road Nanshan District, SHENZHEN, CHINA.

ZIA, Mr. Mohsen, BSc ACA *1986;* IBM United Kingdom Ltd, 1175 Century Way Thorpe Park, LEEDS, LS15 8ZB.

ZIA, Mr. Omar, ACA FCCA *2007;* House 153, Street 47, Sector F-11/3, ISLAMABAD 44000, PAKISTAN.

ZIA KHAN, Mr. Murad, BSc ACA *2007;* 19 Meanley Road, LONDON, E12 6AP.

ZICKEL, Mr. Clive Benjamin Atkins, FCA *1978;* 20 Highwoods Court, SAINT JAMES, NY 11780, UNITED STATES.

ZIEGLER, Mr. Graham Anthony, FCA *1968;* 47 Arthur Road, Wimbledon, LONDON, SW19 7DN. (Life Member)

ZIEGLER, Mr. Michael Robert, BSc ACA *1989;* Care of Kazakhmys Services Ltd, 69-A Samal 2, ALMATY 050059, KAZAKHSTAN.

ZIELINSKI, Mr. Andrew John, BA ACA *1993;* 48 Wycliffe Road, Abington, NORTHAMPTON, NN1 5JF.

ZIELINSKI, Mr. Andrew Michael, BA ACA *1982;* Wyndgates, 47 Foley Road, Claygate, ESHER, KT10 0LU.

•**ZIELINSKI, Mr. George Christopher, FCA** *1971;* Little Oaks, Castlebar Hill, LONDON, W5 1TA.

ZIEVE, Mr. Alon Joel, BA ACA *2006;* 121 Moshav Azriel, 45825 AZRIEL, ISRAEL.

•**ZIFF, Mr. Brian Norman, FCA** *1977;* Brian Ziff Limited, 3 Lakeland Crescent, LEEDS, LS17 7PS.

ZIFF, Mr. Simon Maxwell, BA ACA *1982;* Flat 5, St. Albans Mansions, Kensington Court Place, LONDON, W8 5QH.

ZILLWOOD, Mr. Jason Leonard, BSc ACA *1995;* 46 Asquith Road, GILLINGHAM, KENT, ME8 0JD.

ZIMBA, Mrs. Rosalyn, ACA *2009;* Flat 17 Weymouth House, Hill House Mews, BROMLEY, BR2 0DD.

ZIMBE, Miss. Juliette, BA ACA *2010;* Flat 3, Vectis Court, Borrodaile Road, LONDON, SW18 2LE.

ZIMBLER, Mr. Andrew Mark, FCA *1970;* Whispers, 1 Lock Close, Woodham, ADDLESTONE, KT15 3QP.

ZIMMER, Miss. Natalie, MMath ACA *2001;* Ernst & Young, Suite 1600, 560 Mission Street, SAN FRANCISCO, CA 94105, UNITED STATES.

•**ZIMMERMAN, Mr. Paul Eliot, BSc ACA CF** *1987;* Deloitte LLP, Athene Place, 66 Shoe Lane, LONDON, EC4A 3BQ. See also Deloitte & Touche LLP

ZIMMERMAN, Mr. Peter Michael, MEng FCA *2000;* 3 Ilkley Road, Caversham, READING, RG4 7BD.

ZIMMERMANN, Mr. Jacek Alfred, BSc FCA *1957;* Flat 2 Elm House, 97 Ducks Hill Road, NORTHWOOD, HA6 2WG. (Life Member)

ZIMMERMANN, Mr. Jan, BSc ACA *2007;* 4 Station Road, Hagley, STOURBRIDGE, WEST MIDLANDS, DY9 0NU.

ZIMMERMANN, Ms. Janina Malgorzata, MA ACA *1984;* 14 Sweetcroft Lane, UXBRIDGE, UB10 9LD.

ZIMMERN, Mr. Michael Gregory, BA ACA *2005;* with Ernst & Young LLP, 1 Colmore Square, BIRMINGHAM, B4 6HQ.

ZIMNIAK, Mrs. Lina-Rose, ACA *1993;* Am Wasserbaum 2, 65817 EPPSTEIN, GERMANY.

ZIMNY, Mrs. Lorna, BA ACA *2003;* Northern Trust Guernsey, PO Box 255, Trafalgar Court, Les Banques, St Peter Port, GUERNSEY GY1 3DA.

ZINAR, Mr. Roger Mark, BSc(Econ) ACA *1999;* Zenith Optimedia (UK) Ltd, 24 Percy Street, LONDON, W1T 2BS.

ZINGAS, Mr. Kyriacos, FCA *1977;* P.O.Box 25303, 1308 NICOSIA, CYPRUS.

•**ZINKIN, Mr. Jeffrey David, FCA** *1971;* FMCB, Hathaway House, Popes Drive, Finchley, LONDON, N3 1QF.

ZINOBER, Miss. Madeleine, BSc ACA *2002;* 5 Applesham Avenue, HOVE, EAST SUSSEX, BN3 8JF.

ZIOBER, Miss. Monica, ACA *2011;* Flat 28, Halstead Court, 4 Murray Grove, LONDON, N1 7QF.

ZIRAKNEJAD, Miss. Morvarid, MA BA ACA *2009;* Apex Fund Services Ltd., 3 Burnaby Street, 1st Floor T.J. Pearman Building, P.O. Box 2460 HMJX, HAMILTON HM12, BERMUDA.

ZIRKER, Mr. David Michael, FCA *1971;* Brookfields, Venn Ottery Road, Newton Poppleford, SIDMOUTH, DEVON, EX10 0BU.

ZISARUK, Mr. Jonathan, LLB ACA *2005;* Enstar (EU) Ltd 6th Floor, America House 2 America Square, LONDON, EC3N 2LU.

ZISSELL, Mr. Andrew Malcolm, BA ACA *1993;* 6 Aldermary Road, BROMLEY, BR1 3PH.

ZISSELL, Miss. Catherine Julie, BA ACA *1994;* H S B C, 8 Canada Square, Canary Wharf, LONDON, E14 5HQ.

ZISSELSBERGER, Miss. Isabel Andrea, BCom ACA *2005;* with KPMG, 8/F Prince's Building, 10 Chater Road, CENTRAL, HONG KONG ISLAND, HONG KONG SAR.

ZISSMAN, Mr. Derek, FCA *1971;* 35 Viceroy Court, Prince Albert Road, LONDON, NW8 7PR.

ZOGRAPHOS, Miss. Katherine, MSci ACA *2004;* Flat 75 Eton Hall, Eton College Road, LONDON, NW3 2DH.

ZOIS, Mr. George, ACA *2004;* 28 C.Palaiologou Avenue, Kifissia, 14563 ATHENS, GREECE.

ZOLDAN, Mr. Ronald Anthony, FCA *1968;* 14 Pipers Green Lane, EDGWARE, HA8 8DG.

ZOLFAGHARNIA, Mr. Pouyan, ACA *2009;* 117 Coresbrook Way, Knaphill, WOKING, SURREY, GU21 2TR.

ZOPIATIS, Miss. Polina, MSc BSc ACA *2010;* 22 Themistocleous Street, Strovolos, 2060 NICOSIA, CYPRUS.

ZORKO, Mr. Michael Alexander, ACA *2010;* 55 Tasman Road, LONDON, SW9 9LZ.

ZORKOCZY, Mr. Paul, BEng ACA *1995;* Astra Zeneca UK Ltd, 600 Capability Green, LUTON, LU1 3LU.

ZOSO, Mr. Andrea, ACA *2005;* C/O DAP-Italy S.r.L., via Flaminia 999, 00189 ROME, ITALY.

ZOTTI, Mr. Attilio Valentino, BSc ACA *1998;* 82 Yeldham Road, Hammersmith, LONDON, W6 8JG.

ZOU, Mrs. Ming, ACA *2008;* Flat B29/F., Tower 1, The Dynasty, 18 Yeung Uk Road, TSUEN WAN, NEW TERRITORIES HONG KONG SAR.

ZOUEIHED, Mr. Rashid, ACA *2009;* Flat 2, 1 Queensberry Place, LONDON, SW7 2DL.

ZOUMARAS, Mr. Andreas, ACA *2009;* 28 Cleveland Road, St. Helier, JERSEY, JE2 4PB.

ZSIGO, Mr. John Michael, BA ACA *1989;* Tynholme, Salters Lane, TAMWORTH, STAFFORDSHIRE, B79 8BH.

ZUBAIDA, Miss. Dahlia, ACA *1982;* 440 Elm Avenue, Westmount, MONTREAL H3Y 3J1, QUE, CANADA.

ZUBAIR, Mr. Syed Saad, ACA *1981;* 460 Champ De Mars, Apt 404, MONTREAL H2Y 1B4, QUE, CANADA.

ZUBAIRI, Mr. Hamid Jamil, FCA *1978;* 23 Halland Way, NORTHWOOD, HA6 2BY.

•**ZUBERI, Mr. Rafat Ullah Khan, FCA** *1974;* 321 Malden Road, NEW MALDEN, SURREY, KT3 6AH.

ZUCCONI, Mr. Anthony, ACA *1995;* (Tax Fac), 203 Kings Avenue, LONDON, SW12 0AT.

ZUCKER, Mr. Daniel Efraim, ACA *2008;* Nachal Shimshon 12/2, 99622 RAMAT BEIT SHEMESH, ISRAEL.

ZUK, Mr. Robert, ACA *2009;* 25 Whitbourne Close, BARNSLEY, SOUTH YORKSHIRE, S71 1NJ.

ZULBERG, Mr. Martin Ian, ACA CA(SA) *2010;* Hampstead Safe Depository, 573-575 Finchley Road, LONDON, NW3 7BN.

ZUNIGA, Mrs. Emily, BSc ACA *2011;* Cleasby Hall Old Hall Farm, Boathouse Lane Cleasby, DARLINGTON, COUNTY DURHAM, DL2 2RA.

ZUO, Miss. Liya, ACA *2011;* Flat 532 New Providence Wharf, 1 Fairmont Avenue, LONDON, E14 9PL.

ZUURBIER, Mr. Jacques Stendert Adrianus Marinus, BA FCA *1979;* 179 Queens Road, WEYBRIDGE, KT13 0AH.

ZUYDAM, Mr. David Mel, BSc FCA *1991;* Utrechtseweg 87, 1213 TM, HILVERSUM, NETHERLANDS.

•**ZUZGA, Mr. Michael Francis, BA FCA** *1982;* Apaz Ltd, Gretton House, Waterside Court, Third Avenue, Centrum 100, BURTON-ON-TRENT STAFFORDSHIRE DE14 2WQ.

ZWETSLOOT, Mr. Karl Dominic, BA ACA *1992;* Flamingo, Great North Road, SANDY, BEDFORDSHIRE, SG19 2AJ.

ZWICKY, Mr. Jean-Jaques Charles, FCA *1949;* 29 Friars Walk, Southgate, LONDON, N14 5LR. (Life Member)

ZWIERZYNSKI, Mr. Lech, MA FCA *1975;* 13 Acland Crescent, LONDON, SE5 8EQ.

ZWIGGELAAR, Mr. John Lucas, BSc ACA *1990;* 7 Arnside Close, Gatley, CHEADLE, CHESHIRE, SK8 4QU.

ZYLSTRA, Mr. Brian Anton, FCA *1959;* PO Box 21723, Kloofstreet, CAPE TOWN, 8008, SOUTH AFRICA. (Life Member)

THE OFFICIAL ICAEW LIST OF MEMBERS 2012

TAX FACULTY MEMBERS

Tax Faculty Members - Alphabetical

ABASY, Mr. Waris
ABBOTT, Mrs. Diane Patricia
ABBOTT, Mr. John Gavin Campbell
ABBOTT, Mr. Philip George
ABEL, Mr. Lawrence James
ABERY, Miss. Christine
ABJI, Mr. Kurban Ahmed Murji
ABRAHAM, Mr. Edward Charles
ABREHART, Mr. David Charles
ABREHART, Mr. David John
ABREY, Mr. Ian Nicholas
ACHARYA, Mr. Vijay
ACHILLEA, Mr. George
ACOTT, Mr. David Alan
ACRES, Mrs. Sharon Lesley
ACTON, Mr. Adrian Harold Alan
ADAIR, Mr. Robert Fredrik Martin
ADAM, Mr. David Nicholas Goddard
ADAM, Mr. Iftikar Hassen Mohamed
ADAM, Mr. Richard John
ADAMJEE, Mr. Habel Akberali
ADAMS, Mrs. Cheryl Diane
ADAMS, Mr. David Norman
ADAMS, Mrs. Gillian May
ADAMS, Mr. Glen Samuel
ADAMS, Mrs. Helen Anna Tansy
ADAMS, Ms. Hilary Janet
ADAMS, Mrs. Jacqueline Mary
ADAMS, Mr. John Trevor
ADAMS, Mr. Laura Jane
ADAMS, Mr. Michael Edward
ADAMS, Mr. Roland John
ADAMS, Mr. Roy William
ADAMS, Mrs. Sharon Aideen Mei Mei
ADAMSON, Mr. Roland John
ADDISON, Mr. David John
ADKINS, Mr. Simon Paul
AELLIG, Mr. Martin
AGER, Mrs. Helen Rosemary
AGER, Mr. Jonathan Peter
AGG, Mrs. Jacqueline Sarah
AGGARWAL, Mr. Ashwani Kumar
AGGARWAL, Mr. Eesh Kumar
AGGARWAL, Mrs. Gita Harilal
AGGARWAL, Mr. Vinesh
AGGARWALL, Mr. Kamal
AGUTTER, Miss. Helen Elizabeth
AHAMMAD, Mrs. Ursula Castillo
AHERNE, Mrs. Joanne Elizabeth
AHMAD, Mr. Mahmood
AHMED, Mr. Abmr
AHMED, Mr. Forhad
AHMED, Mr. Naim
AHMED, Mr. Nauman
AHMED, Mr. Samar
AHMEDABADI, Mrs. Seema
AHMEDANI, Mr. Mohammad Tahir
AHSON, Dr. Mahmood Umar
AITKEN, Mrs. Beverley Ann
AITKEN, Mrs. Roopa
AKANDE, Mrs. Ayoyinka Mobolaji
AKDAG, Mr. Metin
AKHTAR, Mr. Mirza Hasnain
AKHTARUZZAMAN, Mr. Mohammed
AKIN, Mr. Barrie Simon
AKRAM, Mr. Aftab Muhammad
AKRAM, Mr. Muhammad
ALBORNO, Mr. Nabil Emran Mousa
ALDER, Mr. Nicholas John
ALDERSON, Mr. Stephen
ALDERSON, Mr. Stephen John
ALDERWICK, Mr. George Alexander Matthew
ALDOUS, Mr. Bryan James
ALDRIDGE, Mr. Mark Lionel
ALDWORTH, Mrs. Sandra
ALESBURY, Mr. David Norman Edwin
ALEXANDER, Mr. David John
ALEXANDER, Mr. Martin
ALEXANDER, Mr. Paul David
ALEXANDER, Mr. Simon Leonard
ALEXANDROU, Mr. Photos
ALFORD, Dr. Elizabeth Anne
ALIBHAI, Mr. Hussein
ALLAN, Miss. Charlotte
ALLEN, Mrs. Alison Janet
ALLEN, Miss. Carolyn Sarah
ALLEN, Mr. David John
ALLEN, Mr. David John
ALLEN, Mr. David Keith
ALLEN, Mr. David Stewart
ALLEN, Mr. Geoffrey William
ALLEN, Mr. Michael John
ALLEN, Mr. Peter John
ALLEN, Mrs. Priscilla Jane
ALLEN, Mr. Richard John
ALLEN, Mr. Richard Nigel De Garrs
ALLEN, Mr. Robert William Edward
ALLEN, Mrs. Sian Elise
ALLEN, Mr. Stephen Raymond
ALLEN, Mr. Steven David
ALLEN, Mrs. Tanya Louise
ALLEN-CHITWA, Mrs. Audrey Marie
ALLI, Mr. Ronald Muntaz
ALLIBAN, Mr. Richard Douglas
ALLISON, Mr. Nigel Douglass
ALLMAN, Mr. David Malcolm
ALLSOP, Mr. Paul David
ALLWOOD, Mrs. Catherine Margaret
ALTMAN, Mr. Jeffrey Allen
ALVIS, Mr. Raymond Blair
AMERICANOS, Mr. Antonio
AMIN, Mr. Pratapbhanu Ambalal
AMIN, Mr. Rajesh
AMIN, Mrs. Shima
AMINIAN, Mr. Massoud
AMLANI, Mr. Kushil
ANDERSON, Mr. Colin Clive
ANDERSON, Mr. Dennis John George
ANDERSON, Mr. Duncan Ross
ANDERSON, Mr. Frederick John Haiste
ANDERSON, Mr. Ian Henry
ANDERSON, Mr. Ian Stephen
ANDERSON, Mr. Kenneth Andrew
ANDERSON, Mr. Mark Raymond
ANDERSON, Miss. Muriel Elizabeth
ANDERSON, Mr. Robert
ANDERSON, Mr. Robert David
ANDERSON, Mrs. Rosemary Annie
ANDERSON, Mrs. Sarah
ANDERSON, Mr. Stuart
ANDIC, Mr. Stephen George
ANDO, Mr. Roderic David Clarence
ANDREW, Mr. Christopher John
ANDREW, Mr. John
ANDREW, Mr. Jonathan Garnett
ANDREW, Mr. Nicholas Anthony Samuel
ANDREW, Mrs. Victoria Elizabeth
ANDREWARTHA, Mrs. Elaine Bridget
ANDREWS, Mr. Christopher John
ANDREWS, Mr. David Hugh
ANDREWS, Mr. David Ross
ANDREWS, Mr. Glenn Martin
ANDREWS, Mrs. Jane Margaret
ANDREWS, Mr. Jeremy Marc
ANDREWS, Miss. Kirsty Rachel
ANDREWS, Mr. Mark Richard
ANGELIS, Mr. Anthony George
ANNELLS, Miss. Deborah
ANNESLEY, Mr. Mark
ANSON, Mr. Alexander Lothian
ANTHISTLE, Mr. Michael Peter
ANTHONY, Mr. John Stuart Frazer
ANTHONY, Mr. Michael Andrew
ANTHONY, Mr. Steven Ronald
ANTIPPA, Mr. Angelo George
ANTONIA, Mr. David John
ANTONIS, Mr. Simon Maughan
ANTROBUS, Mrs. Barbara Ann
ANTROBUS, Mr. Colin Paul
ANWAR, Mr. Javed
APLIN, Mr. David Charles
APLIN, Mr. Paul Stephen
APPLEBY, Mrs. Deborah Margaret
APPLEBY, Mr. Robert Paul
APPLETON, Mr. Paul Robert
AQUINO, Mr. David James
ARANIYASUNDARAN, Ms. Sundareswary
ARCHER, Mr. Clive Philip
ARCHER, Mr. Lawrence Charles
ARCHER, Mr. Paul Michael
ARCHER, Mr. Robin Thomas Edward
ARIAN, Mr. Imtiaz Ali
ARIARATNAM, Mr. Namasivayam
ARIS, Mr. Menelaos Aristodemou
ARIS, Ms. Natalie
ARK, Mr. Balvinder Singh
ARK, Mr. Gurnek
ARKLE, Miss. Jane
ARKLEY, Mr. David Robert
ARMER, Mrs. Annette Patricia
ARMES, Mr. Nicholas
ARMSTRONG, Mr. Anthony Daniel
ARMSTRONG, Mr. David Maurice
ARMSTRONG, Mr. Mark Franklin
ARMSTRONG, Mr. Nigel James
ARNOLD, Mr. Geoffrey
ARNOLD, Mrs. Jill Anita
ARNOLD, Mr. John
ARNOLD, Mr. John Harold Eveleigh
ARNOLD, Mr. Julian Cary
ARNOLD, Miss. Marie Claire
ARNOLD, Mr. Nigel Kenneth
ARNOLD, Mrs. Patricia Jillian Ruth
ARNOLD, Mrs. Sarah Ann
ARNOTT, Mr. Andrew George David
ARROWSMITH, Mr. Peter
ARTHUR, Mrs. Amanda
ARTHUR, Mr. David Robson
ASCROFT, Mrs. Jane
ASGHAR, Mr. Sajjad
ASHALL, Miss. Rosemary Denise
ASHBRIDGE, Mr. Anthony Frederick
ASHBROOK, Mr. Michael Keith
ASHBY, Mr. Geoffrey Frank
ASHCROFT, Mr. Martin Spencer
ASHCROFT, Mr. Paul Michael
ASHFIELD, Mr. Robert Mark
ASHFORD, Mr. Derek Francis
ASHFORD, Mr. Jon Gardiner
ASHFORTH, Mrs. June Guat Imm
ASHING, Mr. Darryl Douglas
ASHLEY, Mr. John Andrew
ASHMAN, Mr. David James
ASHMAN, Mr. Gerald Henry William
ASHMORE, Mr. Howard Charles Selby
ASHRAF, Ms. Masheed
ASHTON, Mr. Frank Martin Scott
ASHTON, Mr. Mark
ASHTON, Mr. Nicholas Lewis
ASHTON, Dr. Raymond Keighley
ASKEW, Mr. Stephen James Thomas
ASLAM KHAN, Mr. Mohammad
ASPROU, Mr. George Demetriou
ASTON, Mr. David William
ATHANASIOU, Mr. Athanasios Manoli
ATHANASIOU, Mr. Miltiades
ATHERDEN, Mr. John Edward
ATKIN, Miss. Catherine Elizabeth
ATKINS, Ms. Deborah
ATKINS, Mr. Ian Clark
ATKINS, Mr. Richard Farquhar
ATKINS, Mrs. Stephanie Louise
ATKINS, Mrs. Susan Jane
ATKINSON, Miss. Gillian Heather
ATKINSON, Mr. John Spencer
ATKINSON, Mr. John William
ATKINSON, Mr. Nigel Peter
ATKINSON, Mr. Paul Alan
ATKINSON, Mr. Peter Graham
ATKINSON, Mr. Richard Duncan
ATKINSON, Mr. Robert Bruce
ATKINSON, Mr. Thomas Andrew
ATTRIDGE, Miss. Lisa Karen
ATTWOOD, Mr. Martin Percival
AUBER, Mr. John Richard Gerratt
AUERO-FOX, Mrs. Heidi Marina
AUGHTERSON, Mr. James Richard
AUGUSTE, Mr. Peter
AUREN, Mr. Johan
AUSTIN, Mr. Anthony Julian
AUSTIN, Mr. John Jeremy Robison
AUSTIN, Miss. Kathryn Mary
AUSTIN, Mr. Michael John Charles
AUSTIN, Mr. Robert John
AUSTIN, Mr. Simon John
AUSTIN-BAILEY, Mr. Peter George
AUSTRENG, Mr. Trevor
AUSTWICK, Mr. Steven John
AUTON, Mr. Michael Colin
AVIS, Mr. Nicholas John
AVRAAM, Mr. Costas Loizos
AVRAAM, Mr. Paraskevas
AXCELL, Mr. Paul Steven
AYLOTT, Mr. Colin Paul
AYLWARD, Mr. Brian Stewart Millett
AYLWARD, Mr. John Hopkin Thomas
AYRE, Mr. Andrew Nicholas
AYRE, Mr. Peter Barrowford
AYRES, Mr. Christopher Robert
AYRTON, Mr. Jawahar Bomi
AYTON, Mr. David Nigel
AYTON, Mr. Rupert Harry Derrick
AZIZ, Mr. Ibrahim Ismail
BACH, Mr. Alan Rene
BACON, Mr. Michael Albert
BACON, Mr. Richard Francis
BADCOCK, Mr. Ian Leslie
BADCOCK, Miss. Sophia Belinda
BADGER, Mr. Ross Wyndham
BADHWAR, Mr. Sharad
BAER, Miss. Lucy Alix St Clair
BAGINSKY, Mr. Sidney
BAGSHAWE, Mr. Rohan Eric
BAHL, Mr. Ajay Kumar
BAILEFF, Mrs. Nicola
BAILEY, Mr. Alan
BAILEY, Miss. Ann Jeannette
BAILEY, Mrs. Anne
BAILEY, Mr. Forbes Anthony Barnes
BAILEY, Mr. Gerald
BAILEY, Mr. Richard Charles
BAILEY, Mr. Robert Christian
BAILEY, Mr. Robert Ian
BAILEY, Mr. Simon Alexander Farquhar
BAILEY, Mr. Timothy
BAILLIE, Mr. Scott Anthony
BAILY, Mr. Stephen
BAINES, Mrs. Hilary Pauline
BAINES, Dr. Malcolm Ian
BAINES, Mr. Thomas Charles
BAIROLIYA, Mr. Rajib
BAJARIA, Mr. Chandrasinh Hansraj
BAJER, Mr. David Alan
BAKER, Mr. Clifford John
BAKER, Ms. Dawn Julia
BAKER, Mr. Donald Matthew Burton
BAKER, Mr. Edward James
BAKER, Mr. Hilary David
BAKER, Mr. Howard Lindon
BAKER, Miss. Katherine Rose
BAKER, Mrs. Nina Ann
BAKER, Mr. Paul Anthony
BAKER, Mr. Richard Charles
BAKER, Mr. Richard James Malcolm Louis
BAKER, Mr. Rowan Clare
BAKSHI, Mr. Pankaj Shantilal
BAL, Mr. Jastinder Singh
BALCH, Mrs. Denise Margaret
BALDING, Mr. Charles Leonard
BALDWIN, Ms. Anne Louise
BALDWIN, Mrs. Marla
BALDWIN, Mr. Paul
BALDWIN, Mr. Robert Paul
BALDWIN, Mr. Steven Robert
BALE, Mr. Nicholas Malyn
BALFOUR, Mr. Mark David
BALL, Mr. Adrian
BALL, Mr. Russell Mark
BALL, Mr. Stephen Thomas Lintern
BALLANCE, Mr. Anthony Nevill Peter
BALLANCE, Miss. Morag McIntyre
BALLANTINE, Mr. Alan Thomas
BALLARD, Mr. Geoffrey William
BALLARD, Mr. Keith Bryan
BALSHAW, Mr. John Frederick
BALSOM, Mr. Peter James
BAMBER, Mr. Norman
BAMBRIDGE, Mr. Alistair John
BAMFORD, Mr. Miles Oliver
BANBURY, Miss. Rosalind Janet Manuela
BANDAY, Mr. Arif Saleem
BANGA, Mr. Rajinder Singh
BANKS, Mr. Geoffrey Laurence
BANKS, Mrs. Gillian Morag
BANKS, Mrs. Lynette Susan
BANKS, Mr. Stephen Craig
BANKS, Mr. Stuart Paul
BANNISTER, Mr. Andrew Charles
BANNISTER, Ms. Kate Emma
BANSAL, Mr. Tejinder Singh
BANWELL, Mr. Gary Paul
BANWELL, Mr. Geoffrey Wilfrid
BARBER, Mr. Ian
BARBER, Mr. Jonathan Stephen
BARBER, Mr. Peter John
BARD, Mr. Laurence David
BARDSLEY, Mr. Martin John
BAREHAM, Mr. Colin Anthony
BARFOOT, Miss. Carol Elizabeth
BARGERY, Mr. Stuart James
BARKER, Alan Douglas
BARKER, Ms. Angela Mary
BARKER, Mr. Anthony John
BARKER, Mrs. Helen Dorothy
BARKER, Mr. John Arthur
BARKER, Mr. Kenneth
BARKER, Miss. Louise Claire
BARKER, Mr. Robert John Swinburn
BARKER, Mr. Stephen
BARKER, Mr. Timothy James
BARKER-BENFIELD, Mr. Charles Vere
BARLTROP, Mr. Christopher Charles
BARNARD, Mr. William Thomas
BARNBROOK, Mr. Gareth Neil
BARNES, Mrs. Andrea Karen
BARNES, Mrs. Barbara Joyce
BARNES, Mr. David John Delacourt
BARNES, Mr. Geoffrey Kenneth
BARNES, Mr. Geoffrey Norman
BARNES, Mr. Graham Paul
BARNES, Mr. John Charles Radcliffe
BARNES, Mr. Michael John
BARNES, Mr. Philip Michael
BARNES, Mr. Stephen Charles
BARNETT, Mrs. Carole Julie
BARNETT, Mr. David Jeffrey
BARNETT, Mr. Wayne
BARNFIELD, Mr. Stephen Gerald
BARNISH, Mr. David John
BARNWELL, Miss. Susan Mary
BARR, Mr. Alan Murray
BARR, Mrs. Penelope Ann
BARR, Mr. Roger
BARRATT, Mr. Colin Edward
BARRATT, Mr. Peter Douglas
BARRELL, Mr. Simon Lee
BARRETT, Mr. Andrew John
BARRETT, Mr. Austin Francis
BARRETT, Mrs. Gillian Ann
BARRETT, Mr. Ian Peter
BARRETT, Mr. Michael
BARRETT, Mr. Philip John
BARRETT, Mrs. Renee Teresa
BARRETT, Mr. Stephen Andrew
BARRETT, Mrs. Susan Marie
BARRETT ROGERS, Mrs. Marianne Patricia
BARRIGAN, Mr. Robert
BARRINGTON, Mr. Christian Mark
BARRON, Mrs. Joan
BARRON, Mr. Martin David
BARROW, Mrs. Amanda Helen
BARROWMAN, Mr. David Alexander
BARRY, Mrs. Lorraine Kate
BARRY, Mr. Michael Edward
BARTARYA, Mr. Ajeet
BARTER, Mr. James Terence
BARTHOLOMEW, Mrs. Alison Elizabeth
BARTHOLOMEW, Mr. Lee Barry Andrew
BARTLETT, Anthony Henry Peter
BARTLETT, Mr. Guy Paul
BARTLETT, Mr. James Michael Gilbert
BARTLETT, Miss. Karen Teresa
BARTLETT, Mr. Kenneth David
BARTLETT, Mr. Peter Michael Arnold
BARTLETT, Mrs. Voon Pow Cathy
BARTON, Mr. Alan
BARTON, Mr. Clive Neil Stewart

B3

BARTON, Mr. John Victor
BARTON, Mrs. Judith Helen
BARTON, Mr. Kenneth
BARTON, Mr. Michael William
BARTON, Mr. Peter Francis
BARTON, Mr. Peter John
BARTON, Mr. Roy
BARTRAM, Mrs. Wendy Patricia
BARTROP, Mr. Peter John
BARWELL, Mr. Nicholas Mark
BASS, Mr. Derek Michael
BASS, Mrs. Keren Joy Irene
BASS, Mr. Robert James
BASSETT, Mr. Andrew Graham
BASSFORD, Mr. Ian
BASSIL, Mr. John Edward
BATCHELOR, Mr. Peter Andrew
BATE, Mr. Andrew Joseph
BATER, Mr. Campbell Paul
BATES, Mr. Giles Langley
BATES, Mrs. Jane Challoner
BATES, Mr. Stuart John
BATH, Mr. Charles Roger
BATH, Mrs. Julie Ann
BATT, Mr. Ian Gregory
BATTARBEE, Mr. Edward
BATTYE, Mr. Anthony Charles Norton
BAUJI, Mr. Hassan Abdul Latif
BAULF, Mr. Adrian John
BAVEJA, Mr. Jagdish
BAXENDALE, Mr. David James
BAXTER, Mr. Christopher John
BAXTER, Mr. Clive Martin
BAXTER, Mr. David Tennant Harry
BAXTER, Mr. Harold
BAXTER, Mrs. Sylvie Gabrielle
BAYCROFT, Mr. Mark Anthony
BAYER, Mr. Michael Moshe
BAYLEY, Mr. Carl
BAYLEY, Mr. Graeme Charles Roger
BAYLEY, Ms. Rowan
BEACHELL, Miss. Clare Louise
BEADLE, Mr. Michael
BEAHAN, Mr. Michael Peter
BEAK, Mr. Geoffrey Alan
BEAK, Mr. Terence John
BEALE, Mr. Robert Andrew
BEALE, Mr. Stephen George John
BEAN, Mr. Lawrence Philip
BEANEY, Mrs. Margaret Valerie
BEARD, Miss. Jacqueline
BEARD, Mr. Sebastian James
BEARDALL, Mr. Ian Malcolm
BEARDON, Mr. Douglas
BEARE, Mr. Kevin Leslie
BEARPARK, Miss. Jennifer Kathryn
BEATTIE, Mrs. Imogen Mary
BEATTIE, Mrs. Joanne Lindsey
BEATTIE, Mr. John
BEATTIE, Mr. Michael George
BEATTIE, Miss. Roslyn
BEATTY, Mr. Stephan Christoph
BEATY-POWNALL, Mr. Michael Christopher
BEAUMONT, Mr. David
BEAUMONT, Mr. John Harvey
BEAUMONT, Mrs. Katherine Jane Victoria
BEAVEN, Mr. Peter Francis
BEBBINGTON, Mrs. Pauline Margaret
BECK, Mr. Neil Spencer
BECK, Mr. Nigel Robin
BECKMAN, Mrs. Lindsay
BECKMAN, Mr. Peter David Joseph
BECKWITH, Mr. David Martin
BEDDOES, Miss. Christina
BEDFORD, Mr. Howard Martin
BEDINGFIELD, Mr. Geoffrey James
BEEBY, Mr. Jonathan Derek
BEECH, Mr. Sydney John
BEECROFT, Mr. Thomas Michael
BEEDHAM, Mr. Peter John Geoffrey
BEEFORTH, Mr. Michael Allan
BEELEY, Mr. Philip Michael
BEENY, Mr. David John
BEESLEY, Mr. Stuart Nicholas
BEEVERS, Mr. John
BEEVERS, Mr. Timothy
BEGLEY, Mr. Kevin George
BEHNAM, Mr. Shahrokh
BELBIN, Mr. David Mark
BELFIELD, Mr. Richard Craig
BELINGER, Mr. John Joseph Robert
BELK, Mr. Brian Henry
BELL, Mr. Alan Douglas
BELL, Mr. Alexander William John
BELL, Mr. Christopher
BELL, Mr. David Thomas
BELL, Mr. Garry James
BELL, Mr. James Douglas
BELL, Mr. John
BELL, Mr. John Graham Kearton
BELL, Mr. Michael Ernest
BELL, Mr. Michael John
BELL, Mr. Nicholas William
BELL, Mr. Patrick John
BELL, Miss. Rachel Angharad
BELL, Mr. Roger Wallace
BELL, Mr. Rowell

BELL, Mr. Simon Jeremy
BELL, Mr. Stephen John
BELL, Mr. Stephen Richard
BELLAMY, Mr. Edward Gordon
BELLAMY, Mr. Jeffrey
BELLAMY, Mrs. Nicola Karen
BELLINI, Mr. Peter Joseph
BELSMAN, Mr. Paul Simon
BEMAN, Mr. David Garrick
BEMBRIDGE, Mr. William Harry
BEMMENT, Mr. Anthony Peter
BEN-NATHAN, Mr. Colin Victor
BENAIM, Mr. Shalom
BENDALL, Mr. Peter Stanley
BENDING, Mrs. Delyth Clare
BENFORD, Mr. Jonathan Richard
BENNETT, Mr. Andrew Neil
BENNETT, Mr. Andrew William
BENNETT, Mr. Calum John
BENNETT, Mr. David Alastair
BENNETT, Mr. David Anthony
BENNETT, Mr. David John
BENNETT, Mr. David Paul
BENNETT, Mr. Harry
BENNETT, Mr. John Stuart
BENNETT, Mr. Marc Stephen
BENNETT, Miss. Sarah Elizabeth
BENNETTS, Mr. Peter Lawrence
BENNEWITH, Mr. Anthony John
BENNEY, Mr. Paul
BENNEYWORTH, Mrs. Rebecca Anne
BENOSIGLIO, Mr. Adrian Howard
BENOY, Mr. William Oscar Robin
BENSON, Mrs. Anita Julie Sheelagh
BENSON, Mrs. Cynthia Sin Yi
BENTALL, Mrs. Jane Elizabeth
BENTLEY, Mr. Laurence John
BENTLEY, Mr. Michael Scott
BENTLEY, Mr. Stephen Johnson
BENTON, Mr. Alan
BENTON, Mr. Martin Jeremy
BENVENISTE, Mr. Barry Phillip
BERENS, Mr. Andrew Wayne
BERGER, Mr. Stephen Howard
BERRIDGE, Mrs. Amanda Mary
BERRIMAN, Mr. Stuart Graham
BERRY, Mr. Douglas Mark
BERRY, Mr. Frank Thurstan
BERRY, Mrs. Helen Jane
BERRY, Miss. Kathryn Charlotte
BERRY, Mr. Keith Julian
BERRY, Mr. Martin Curtis
BERRY, Mr. Michael Richard
BERTRAM, Mr. Anthony David Weguelin
BESHAHWRED, Mr. Getachew
BEST, Mrs. Jaine
BESTLEY, Miss. Sarah Elizabeth
BETHEL, Mr. Peter David
BETTANEY, Mrs. Sheila Helen
BETTINSON, Mr. Michael Charles Edgar
BETTS, Mr. Nigel Rolf
BETTS, Mr. Richard John
BEVAN, Mr. Christopher John
BEVAN, Mr. David Charles
BEVAN, Mr. Richard Charles
BEVIS, Mr. Geoffrey David
BEXLEY, Mr. Kevin Howard
BEYNON, Dr. Emma Margaret
BEYNON, Mr. Robert Charles
BHAGI, Mr. Anil Kumar
BHAMM, Mr. Anup Kumar
BHAMRA, Mr. Ravinder Singh
BHANOT, Mr. Anil Kumar
BHATTI, Mr. Paramjit
BHAVNANI, Mr. Manjeet
BHIMJEE, Mr. Anwar Ali
BHOGADIA, Mr. Mahmood Reza
BHOVAN, Mr. Prashant
BICK, Mr. James David
BICKENSON, Mrs. Teresa Ellen
BICKLEY, Mr. Peter Charles
BIDDELL, Mr. Vaughan Alan
BIDMEAD, Mr. Ian Trevor
BIFULCO, Mr. Vincent
BIGAIGNON, Mr. Noel Maurice Robert
BIGGIN, Mr. Alan Keith
BIGGS, Mr. John Simon
BIGGS, Mr. Kenneth Alan
BIGLAND, Mr. David Harry
BIGWOOD, Mrs. Penelope Ann
BILLINGHAM, Mr. Barry John
BILLINGS, Mr. John Graham
BILLINGTON, Mr. Mark Anthony
BINGHAM, Mr. David Paul
BINGHAM, Mr. Ian Anthony
BIRCH, Mr. Christopher Charles
BIRCH, Mr. David Clifford
BIRCH, Mr. David William
BIRCH, Mr. Nigel Milne
BIRD, Miss. Fiona Mary
BIRD, Mr. Nicholas Charlton Penrhys
BIRD, Mr. Simon Christopher
BIRDSALL, Mr. Eric Graham
BIRKETT, Mr. Simon James
BIRKIN, Mr. David William Thomas
BIRLEY, Mr. Thomas Spencer
BIRNS, Mr. Raymond

BIRTLES, Mr. Eric Roydon
BISHOP, Mr. John Andrew
BISHOP, Mrs. Kathy Lee Carol
BISHOP, Mr. Simon Andrew
BISSEKER, Mr. Tilden John
BISSELL, Mrs. Ceri Sian
BISSET, Mr. Andrew Patrick
BISWAS, Mr. Debashish
BLACK, Mr. David Peter
BLACK, Mr. Michael Anthony
BLACKBURN, Mr. Barrie
BLACKBURN, Mr. Colin Andrew
BLACKBURN, Mr. Paul Adrian
BLACKBURN, Mr. Vernon Frederick Neil
BLACKFORD, Ms. Caroline Jane
BLACKMORE, Mr. Gary Fenton
BLACKMORE, Mr. Mark Rupert
BLACKMORE, Mr. Steven Mark
BLACKSTONE, Mr. Andrew Simon
BLACKSTONE, Mr. Lance Roy
BLACKWELL, Mr. Christopher Michael
BLACKWELL, Mr. John William George
BLACKWOOD, Mr. Andrew Robert
BLACKWOOD, Mr. Iain Stuart
BLAIKIE, Lord Paul John
BLAIR, Mr. Graeme James
BLAIR, Mrs. Helen Margaret
BLAKE, Mr. Douglas
BLAKE, Mrs. Emma Maria
BLAKE, Mr. James Samuel
BLAKE, Mr. Kevin Neil
BLAKE, Mr. Matthew Jon
BLAKE, Mr. Michael David
BLAKE, Mrs. Susan Ruth
BLAKE, Mr. Timothy John
BLAND, Mr. David Victor
BLAND, Mr. Maurice Nathan
BLAXLAND, Mrs. Rowan Fiona
BLEAZARD, Mr. Keith
BLISS, Mr. Christopher Jan Andrew
BLOCKSIDGE, Mr. Peter Anthony
BLOOMBERG, Mr. Joseph Morris
BLOOMER, Mrs. Lynda Jane
BLOOMER, Mr. Roger Charles
BLOOMFIELD, Mr. Jonathan Charles
BLOY, Mrs. Susan Anne
BLUEITT, Mrs. Catherine
BLUNDELL, Mrs. Catherine
BLUNDELL, Mrs. Rosemary
BLYTH, Mr. Crispin Richard
BLYTHE, Mr. Jonathan David
BOAGE, Mr. Ian Neal
BOAR, Mr. Graham
BOATENG, Miss. Leona Asaah
BOBER, Miss. Lynnette Joy Christina Margaret Therese
BOBY, Mr. Alan Richard
BODIMEADE, Mr. Colin Henry
BOGGON, Mr. Roland John
BOGHANI, Mr. Nashir Nurmohamed
BOLD, Mr. Simon Mercer
BOLDEN, Mr. John Charles
BOLSOM, Mr. Alan Norman
BOLTON, Mr. Alan Keith
BOLTON, Miss. Carol Elizabeth
BOLTON, Mr. Henry Alan
BOLTON, Dr. Lina Wai Yue
BOLTON, Mr. Michael John
BOLTON, Mr. Nicholas John Canning
BOLTON, Mr. Philip Charles
BOLTON, Mr. Timothy David
BOLTSA, Mr. Michael
BOMBER, Miss. Jennifer Ann
BOND, Mr. David William
BOND, Mr. Phillip Raymond
BOND, Miss. Rosemary Anne Louise
BONDS, Mr. Graham Baynard
BONNERT, Mr. David Victor
BONNETT, Mr. Robert James
BONNEY, Mr. Stephen Andrew
BONNEY, Miss. Susan Philippa
BOOKER, Mr. David Francis
BOOKER, Mr. Malcolm Marc
BOOKER, Mr. Roger Denys
BOORMAN, Mr. Ian Hugh
BOOTH, Mr. Alan
BOOTH, Mr. Geoffrey Charles
BOOTH, Mr. Richard Mark Sinclair
BOOTH, Mr. Russell
BOOTH, Mr. Steven John
BOOTH, Mr. William Thomas
BOOTHBY, Mr. Geoffrey Guy
BOOTHROYD, Mr. Peter Alexander John
BOR, Mr. Jeffrey Anthony
BORALESSA, Mr. Harsha
BORDOLEY, Mr. Michael
BORLAND, Mr. Andrew Herbert
BORN, Mr. Simon Henry Graham
BORTHWICK, Mr. Patrick James Joseph
BOSE, Mr. Samar
BOSLEY, Mrs. Eleanor Catherine Rose
BOSMAN, Mrs. Birka Thordis Reinhild
BOTHAMLEY, Mr. Paul Justin Robert
BOTROS, Mrs. Victoria
BOTTING, Mr. Anthony Ernest William
BOTTOMLEY, Mr. David Robert
BOUCHER, Mr. Andrew Paul

BOULTER, Mrs. Jennifer
BOURNE, Mr. Christopher John
BOURNE, Mr. Jonathan Hartle
BOUSTEAD, Mr. Ian Bryan
BOWDEN, Mrs. Jacqueline
BOWEN, Mr. Delme Roger
BOWEN, Mr. Howel Isaac
BOWEN, Mr. Ian David
BOWEN, Mr. William Charles Rodney
BOWEN-DAVIES, Mr. David Ian
BOWLER, Mr. Peter Bruce
BOWMAN, Mrs. Angela Michele
BOWMAN, Mr. Graham Reavley
BOWMAN, Mrs. Kathryn Jane
BOWMAN, Mr. Neil Robert
BOWMAN, Mr. Nicholas John
BOWMAN, Mr. Stephen Lindsay
BOWYER, Mr. David Clive
BOWYER, The Revd. Geoffrey
BOXALL, Mr. Malcolm James
BOYD, Mr. Christopher Nigel
BOYD, Mrs. Judith Helen
BOYD, Mr. Michael Iain Macbryde
BOYD, Mr. William Michael
BOYES, Mr. Graham Gardner
BOYLE, Mrs. Alexandra Helen
BOYLE, Mr. Gerald Patrick
BOYLE, Mr. Mark Robert
BOYTON, Mr. John Leonard
BRADFORD, Mr. James Peter Blunden
BRADFORD, Mr. Justin Nicholas
BRADFORD, Ms. Sarah Diane
BRADING, Mr. Ian
BRADISH, Mr. Martyn Henry Stewart
BRADLEY, Mrs. Jennifer Ruth
BRADLEY, Mrs. Karen Anne
BRADLEY, Mr. Mark Mason
BRADLEY, Mr. Matthew Gurney
BRADLEY, Mr. Paul Edward
BRADSHAW, Mr. Ian
BRADSHAW, Mr. Jeffrey Roy
BRADSHAW, Mr. Keith
BRADSHAW, Mr. Kenneth Morton
BRADSHAW, Miss. Lynsey Karen
BRADSHAW, Mr. Mark Philip
BRADSHAW, Mr. Peter David
BRADSHAW, Mr. Raymond James
BRADSHAW, Miss. Rebecca Ann
BRADSHAW, Mr. Roger Harold
BRAGANZA, Mr. Maurice Arnold
BRAGG, Mr. Andrew Stewart
BRAGG, Mrs. Sophie Clare
BRAIDWOOD, Mrs. Christine Elizabeth
BRAILEY, Mr. Colin William
BRAIN, Mr. John
BRAIN, Mr. Raymond Howard
BRAJKOVICH, Mr. Nikola
BRAMALL, Mr. George Michael
BRAMALL, Mr. Paul John
BRAMLEY, Mr. Kevin
BRAMWELL, Mrs. Ann Helen
BRAMWELL, Mr. Kenneth
BRANAGAN MATTHEWS, Mrs. Gillian Amy Louise
BRAND, Mr. Derek Jack
BRANDL, Mr. Peter Leonard Joseph
BRANDRETH, Mr. Stuart
BRANNIGAN, Mr. Eric
BRANSBURY, Mr. David
BRANSBY-ZACHARY, Mr. Stefan Victor Henri
BRANSON, Mr. Andrew David
BRASSINGTON, Miss. Victoria
BRAWN, Mr. Richard William
BRAY, Mrs. Dawn Susan
BRAY, Mrs. Deborah Faith
BRAY, Mr. Iain Myles
BRAZELL, Mr. Raymond
BRAZIER, Mr. Anthony Benjamin
BREARLEY, Mr. Thomas
BREEN, Mr. Jeremy Mark
BREEZE, Mr. Alan Leonard
BREEZE, Mr. Thomas George
BRENNAN, Mr. Nicholas John
BRENNAN, Mrs. Pamela Anne
BRENNAN, Mr. Roger Fergus
BRETT, Mrs. Margaret Jean
BRETT, Mr. Raymond Michael Ashby
BREW, Mr. Joseph Edward
BREWER, Mr. David Douglas
BREWER, Mr. Stephen Paul
BREWERTON, Mr. John Charles
BREWSTER, Mr. David
BRIANTI, Mr. Roberto Vittorio Francis
BRIDDON, Mr. John David
BRIDGE, Mr. Thomas Edward
BRIDGE, Mr. Peter Anthony
BRIDGER, Mr. Robert George Cameron
BRIDGES, Mr. Peter Anthony
BRIDGFORD, Ms. Julie Margaret
BRIERLEY, Mrs. Jeanette Alexia
BRIGGS, Mr. Christopher James
BRIGGS, Mr. Graham
BRIGGS, Mr. Kevin Edward
BRIGGS, Mr. Martin Stephen
BRIGGS, Mr. Paul William
BRIGHAM, Mr. Peter John
BRIGHT, Mr. Stephen John

BRIGHTLING, Mrs. Nicola Lynn
BRIGHTMORE, Mr. Andrew Robert Paul
BRIGHTON, Mr. Richard Thomas
BRILEY, Mr. Stephen Andrew
BRIMMELL, Mr. Peter James
BRINAN, Mr. David George
BRISENDEN, Mr. Robert John
BRISLEY, Mr. Roger Alan
BRISTOW, Mrs. Claire Margaret
BRISTOW, Mr. Roy Philip
BRITTAIN, Mr. John Jeremy Mitchell
BRITTON, Mrs. Angela Winifred
BRITTON, Mrs. Heather Dawn
BROAD, Mr. Gary Peter
BROADBENT, Mr. Darren Wayne
BROADHEAD, Mr. James Edward
BROADHEAD, Mr. Mark
BROADWAY, Mr. Alistair Brice
BROCK, Ms. Sarah Jane
BROCKHURST, Mr. Anthony John
BROCKHURST, Mrs. Nicola Hayley
BROCKLEHURST, Mrs. Jacqueline
BROCKLESBY, Mr. Donald Ian
BROCKWELL, Mr. Colin James
BRODER, Mr. Kevin
BRODIE, Mr. David Sidney
BRODIE, Mr. Jonathan David
BROERS, Mr. Jerome Adrian Paul
BROKE, Mr. Adam Vere Balfour
BROLLY, Mr. Martin
BROMELL, Mr. Walter Mark
BROMLEY, Mr. Stuart Richard Squire
BROOK, Mr. Philip Dudley Anthony
BROOK, Mr. Robert Paul
BROOKE, Mr. Michael Richard William
BROOKER, Miss. Annette
BROOKES, Mr. Alan
BROOKES, Mr. David
BROOKES, Mr. David Russell
BROOKS, Mr. Gerald Richard
BROOKS, Mr. Peter David
BROOM, Mr. John Anthony
BROSNAN, Mr. Bernard Joseph
BROWN, Mr. Alan David
BROWN, Mrs. Alison Dawn
BROWN, Mr. Allan Keith
BROWN, Mr. Andrew
BROWN, Miss. Caroline Louise
BROWN, Mr. Christopher Mark
BROWN, Mr. Christopher Raymond
BROWN, Mr. Christopher Stuart
BROWN, Mr. David Trevor
BROWN, Miss. Diane Elizabeth
BROWN, Mr. Douglas John
BROWN, Mrs. Elizabeth Kate
BROWN, Mr. Graham Douglas
BROWN, Mr. Ian William
BROWN, Mr. James Graham
BROWN, Mr. John
BROWN, Mr. John Craig
BROWN, Mr. Martin Timothy
BROWN, Mr. Philip Norman
BROWN, Mr. Richard Graham
BROWN, Mr. Richard Seymour
BROWN, Mr. Robert Thomas
BROWN, Mr. Robert Warburton
BROWN, Mr. Roger Garrett
BROWN, Mr. Roy Spencer
BROWN, Mrs. Sandra Kay
BROWN, Mr. Stephen Paul
BROWN, Mr. Steven Allen John
BROWN, Miss. Susan Elizabeth
BROWN, Mr. Timothy David
BROWN, Mr. Trevor Alan
BROWN, Ms. Valerie
BROWNE, Mr. Clive Acteson
BROWNE, Mr. Kevin Paul
BROWNE, Mr. Nicholas Valentine
BROWNE, Mr. Patrick Alexander Howe
BROWNE, Mr. Peter Graham
BROWNHILL, Miss. Alison Mary
BROWNING, Mr. Robin Nicholas
BROWNLEE, Mr. Charles
BROWNSON, Mr. Henry Mark
BROWNSON, Mr. Jonathan Selwyn
BRUCE, Mrs. Helen Patricia
BRUCE, Mrs. Sabrina Marion Christine
BRUCE-MORGAN, Mr. Claes Owen Llewellyn
BRUCH, Mr. David Ernst
BRUNDELL, Mrs. Faye
BRUNTON, Mr. Peter Howard James
BRYAN, Mr. Neil Peter
BRYAN-BROWN, Miss. Jennifer Anne
BRYANT, Mr. Peter George
BRYDEN, Mr. Kenneth Antony
BRYDONE, Mr. Christopher Malcolm
BRYSON, Mr. Graeme William Bruce
BRYSON, Mrs. Mary Margaret
BUCHHOLZ, Mrs. Lynne Fiona
BUCHSBAUM, Mr. Abraham Jacob
BUCKELL, Mr. Graham John
BUCKLE, Mr. Alan Edric
BUCKLER, Mr. John Mark
BUCKLEY, Mrs. Marie-Therese
BUCKMAN, Ms. Bianca
BUCKWORTH, Mr. Edward William

BUDDHDEV, Mr. Krutsnadeek Devjibhai
BUDHDEO, Mr. Jayprakash Lalitrai
BUFFERY, Mr. Mark Charles
BUGDEN, Mr. Christopher Anthony
BUIST, Mrs. Penny Anne
BULL, Mr. Gordon Richard
BULLARD, Mr. Andrew Stuart
BULLEN, Mrs. Karen Margaret Mary
BULLETT, Mr. Michael Leonard Searchfield
BULLING, Mr. Stephen Francis Langlands
BULMAN, Mr. Thomas Emmet
BULMER, Mrs. Yuen Man Anna
BUNN, Mr. Alan Leslie
BUNT, Mr. Christopher John
BUNTING, Mr. David Arthur
BUNTING, Mr. William Keith
BURDASS, Mr. James Edward Bradshaw
BURDEN, Mrs. Elizabeth Jane
BURDEN, Ms. Susan Patricia
BURDER, Mr. Stephen Basil
BURDIN, Mr. Paul Boscoe Leo
BURFORD, Mr. Ryan Robert
BURGE, Mr. Nigel David Ritchie
BURGE, Mr. Nigel Martin
BURGESS, Mr. Peter John
BURGESS, Mrs. Rima
BURGIN, Miss. Michele Claudia
BURGOINE, Mr. John Keith
BURKE, Mr. Brian Michael
BURKE, Mr. Gerald Michael
BURKINSHAW, Mrs. Lynda Jane
BURLEY, Mr. Philip Nigel
BURLISON, Mr. Michael
BURMAN, Mr. Andrew Marc
BURNHAM, Mr. Graeme Michael
BURNHAM, Mrs. Patricia Ann
BURNIE, Mr. Joseph Robert
BURNS, Mr. Gordon MacGregor
BURRILL, Mr. Fraser Stuart
BURROUGHS, Mr. Nigel John
BURROWES, Mr. David William
BURROWS, Mr. Christopher Nigel
BURROWS, Mr. David Howard
BURROWS, Mr. David John
BURROWS, Mr. Nicholas John
BURROWS, Mr. Peter George
BURROWS, Mr. Peter Henry
BURROWS, Mr. Richard John Freeman
BURSACK, Mr. Graeme Philip
BURT, Mr. Michael John
BURT, Mrs. Rosemary Ethel
BURTON, Mrs. Ann Elizabeth
BURTON, Mr. Christopher John Charles
BURTON, Ms. Helen Anne
BURTON, Ms. Julie Marion
BURTON, Mr. Mark Andrew
BURTON, Mr. Stanley Philip James
BURTON, Mr. Tony Lawrence
BURY, Mr. Leslie
BUSBY, Mr. Alan George
BUSH, Mr. Christopher John
BUSH, Miss. Sally Ann
BUSHNELL, Mrs. Marsha Ann
BUSSETIL, Mr. Emmanuel Leonard
BUTCHER, Miss. Susan Emma
BUTLER, Mr. Alan Francis
BUTLER, Mr. David George
BUTLER, Mrs. Delia Marie
BUTLER, Miss. Elizabeth Jane
BUTLER, Miss. Frances Helen
BUTLER, Mr. Geoffrey Robert
BUTLER, Mr. John William
BUTLER, Ms. Julie Elizabeth
BUTLER, Mrs. Julie Marion
BUTLER, Mr. Keith David
BUTLER, Mr. Roger John
BUTLER, Mr. Shaun
BUTLER, Mr. Stephen Leslie
BUTLER-ADAMS, Mr. Richard
BUTT, Mr. Brian Mervyn
BUTT, Mr. Jeffrey Neil
BUTT, Mr. Nigel Bevan
BUTTERLEY, Miss. Diane Elizabeth
BUTTERS, Mr. Jonathan Richard
BUTTERWORTH, Mr. David Martin
BUTTERWORTH, Mr. Mark Bernard
BUTTERWORTH, Mr. Philip John
BUXTON, Mr. David William
BUXTON, Mrs. Priscilla Caroline
BUYS, Mr. Marais
BYERS, Mr. Jeremy Richard
BYFIELD, Mr. Nicholas Donald
BYGOTT, Mr. John James
BYGRAVE, Mr. Clifford
BYRNE, Mr. Peter Edward
BYWATER, Mr. David
CABLE, Mr. Charles Hylton
CADBURY, Mrs. Pamela Kathleen
CAIN, Mrs. Sheryl Margaret
CAINE, Mr. Philip Peter
CAIRA, Mrs. Donna Louise
CAISLEY, Mr. Quentin
CALCUTT, Mr. Martin Leonard
CALDARA, Ms. Angela Jane
CALDERBANK, Ms. Allison Margaret
CALEY, Mr. Andrew Maitland
CALLOW, Mr. Roy Stanley

CALVERT, Mr. Paul Anthony
CAMBRAY, Mr. Philip Anthony
CAMDEN, Mr. Edward James
CAMERON, Mr. Roger Alan
CAMERON-CLARKE, Mr. Robert
CAMISSAR, Mr. Brian Bentzien
CAMPBELL, Mr. Barrie
CAMPBELL, Mr. John Oliver
CAMPBELL, Mr. Jonathan Francis
CAMPBELL, Mr. Patrick James
CAMPBELL, Mrs. Rosemary Ann
CAMPBELL, Miss. Sarah Ann
CAMPBELL, Mr. William John
CANE, Mr. David Alexander
CANE, Miss. Marion Hazel
CANFIELD, Mr. Gerald Thomas
CANN, Mr. David Francis
CANN, Miss. Susan Elizabeth
CANNAN, Mr. Jonathan Michael
CAPLAN, Mr. Philip Michael
CARDEN, Mr. Philippe O'Neill
CARDER, Mr. Roger William
CAREW, Mr. David Alun
CAREY, Ms. Alison Aithna
CAREY, Mr. Robin Frederick
CAREY, Mr. Steven Howard
CAREY, Mr. Timothy William
CARLESS, Mrs. Jean Margaret
CARLETON, Mrs. Rosemary
CARLIN, Mr. Peter David
CARMEL, Mr. Barrie Alan
CARMICHAEL, Mr. Keith Stanley
CARNE, Mr. Charles Nicholas
CARPENTER, Mr. Kevin Michael
CARPENTER, Mr. Stuart David
CARR, Mrs. Janet Mary
CARR, Mrs. Teresa
CARRIGAN, Miss. Anne Kathleen
CARROLL, Mr. Brian Charles
CARROLL, Mr. Brian John
CARROLL, Mr. Julian Markham
CARROLL, Mrs. Sally Ann
CARROLL, Mrs. Tanya Katrina
CARRUTH, Mr. John Christian Claasen
CARSLAKE, Mr. John Alfred Lawrence
CARSON, Mr. Paul John
CARTER, Mr. Alan John
CARTER, Mr. Brian
CARTER, Mr. David Reeves
CARTER, Mr. Dominic Alan
CARTER, Mrs. Gillian Mary
CARTER, Mr. Jason Lee
CARTER, Mr. John Anthony
CARTER, Mr. John Richard
CARTER, Mr. Martin Arthur Charles
CARTER, Mr. Richard Matthew
CARTMAN, Mr. Ashley
CARTWRIGHT, Mr. Anthony Robert John
CARTWRIGHT, Mr. Graham Alan
CARTWRIGHT, Mr. Hugh Walter Matheson
CARTWRIGHT, Mr. Ian Crossley
CARTWRIGHT, Mr. Nicholas John
CARTY, Mr. David
CARUANA, Mr. Joseph Lewis
CARVELL, Mr. Paul
CARVER, Mrs. Corinne Suzanne
CARY, Mr. David William
CASCIOLI, Mr. Michele
CASHMAN, Mr. Michael Allan
CASILLAS, Mrs. Terase Nora Anne
CASIMO, Mrs. Julia
CASSERLY, Mr. Ian Vincent James
CASSIDY, Mr. John Bernard
CASTLE, Mr. Paul Richard
CASTLEDINE, Mr. Alan Douglas
CASTLEMAN, Mr. Christopher John
CASTON, Mr. Leslie Ernest
CATER, Miss. Stephanie Jane
CATER, Mrs. Suzanne Louise
CATES, Mr. Dean Richard
CATON, Mrs. Christine Ann
CATT, Mr. Timothy Charles
CATTELL, Mr. Ian James
CATTERALL, Mr. Stephen John Cliffe
CATTERMOLE, Miss. Marguerite Clare
CATTERMOLE, Mr. Peter Alexander
CAVE, Mr. Andrew Jonathan
CAVE, Mr. Nicholas Edward
CAVEY, Mr. Martin Cameron
CAVILL, Mr. Alan Robert
CELIA, Mr. Roger
CHADDA, Mr. Parveen
CHADWICK, Mr. Michael
CHADWICK, Mr. Wallace George
CHAKRABORTY, Mr. Dilip Kumar
CHALK, Mr. Rupert Alexander
CHALK, Mr. Stephen Edward
CHALLINOR, Mr. David John
CHAMBERLAIN, Mr. Clive Douglas
CHAMBERLAIN, Mr. John Robert
CHAMBERLAIN, Mr. Neil Howard
CHAMBERLAIN, Mr. Paul Jonathan
CHAMBERLAIN, Mr. Simon John
CHAMBERS, Mr. Graham Leonard
CHAMBERS, Miss. Helen
CHAMBERS, Mr. Jennifer Mary
CHAMBERS, Mr. Steven Michael

CHAMPKEN, Mr. Graham Roy
CHAN, Mr. Chi Kong
CHAN, Mr. Chun Kit Ivan
CHAN, Miss. Josephine Yin-On
CHAN, Mr. Kit Wang
CHAN, Ms. Mandy Man-Fong
CHAN, Mr. Peter Wing Kai
CHAN, Miss. Rosemary Chung Yan
CHAN, Mr. Wai Chung
CHAN, Mr. William Kam Wing
CHANDLER, Mr. Clifford Roy
CHANDLER, Mr. John Geoffrey
CHANDLEY, Miss. Anna Maria
CHANDLEY, Mr. Charles William Duncan
CHANG, Ms. Win Yin Anita
CHANNA, Mr. Pritpal Singh
CHANNER, Mr. Colin Patrick
CHANT, Mr. Peter John
CHANT, Mr. Richard
CHANTER, Mr. David John
CHAPLIN, Mrs. Deborah
CHAPLIN, Mr. Mark Douglas Lekay
CHAPLIN, Mr. Mark Peter
CHAPLIN, Mr. Russell Ian
CHAPLIN, Mr. Stanley Frederick
CHAPLING, Miss. Veronica Ruth
CHAPMAN, Mr. Andrew
CHAPMAN, Miss. Annette Louise
CHAPMAN, Miss. Cara
CHAPMAN, Mr. Christopher Stanley
CHAPMAN, Mr. David Lindsay
CHAPMAN, Mr. Keith John
CHAPMAN, Mr. Matthew
CHAPMAN, Mr. Paul Graham
CHAPMAN, Mrs. Penny Dawn
CHAPPELL, Mr. Andrew David
CHAPPELL, Mrs. Rachel Mary
CHAPPELL, Mrs. Yvonne Marie
CHAPPLE, Mr. Andrew Graham
CHAPPLE, Mr. Jonathan Richard
CHARALAMBOS, Mrs. Claire Louise
CHARALAMBOUS, Miss. Effie
CHARGE, Mr. Philip
CHARING, Mr. Simon Lawrence
CHARLTON, Miss. Cecilia Claire
CHARLTON, Mr. David William
CHARLTON, Mr. Kenneth Reginald
CHARLTON, Mr. Mark
CHARLTON, Mr. Stephen Gordon
CHARTERS, Mr. John Alan
CHARTRES, Michael Duncan
CHASTON, Mr. David Carl Anthony
CHATOO, Mr. Shabbir Abdulhusein
CHATWANI, Mrs. Hansa Satish
CHAUDHRI, Mr. Muhammad Aslam
CHAUHAN, Mr. Ashok Uttamlal
CHAUHAN, Mr. Sarbjit Singh
CHAVE, Mr. Philip Thomas
CHEADLE, Mr. Anthony Peter
CHEADLE, Mr. Martin Richard
CHEEMA, Mr. Darbara Singh
CHEESMAN, Miss. Carol Ann
CHEETHAM, Mr. John Buchanan
CHEETHAM, Mrs. Sonia Michelle
CHENEY, Mr. Francis Peter
CHERNOFF, Mr. Barry Grant
CHESTERTON, Miss. Lynne Mary
CHESWORTH, Mr. Andrew
CHESWORTH, Mr. Philip Leonard
CHETWOOD, Mrs. Caroline Margaret Denise
CHEUNG, Mr. Simon Kam Loi
CHEUNG, Mr. Ting Pong
CHEUNG, Mr. Tung Kwong
CHEVERN, Mr. Stephen
CHEW, Mr. Fook Aun
CHIANG, Mr. Alexander Jong-Luan
CHIANG, Mr. Sham Lam Anthony
CHICK, Mr. Derek Michael
CHICKEN, Mrs. Rosemary Jane
CHICKSAND, Mr. Stanley Barry
CHILD, Mrs. Anne Elizabeth Mary
CHILD, Mr. John
CHILD, Mr. Roger
CHILDS, Mr. Nicholas John
CHILVERS, Mr. Julian David John
CHILVERS, Mr. Martyn Leslie
CHING, Mr. Gavin Chin-Ngai
CHISHOLM, Mrs. Norma Margaret
CHISNALL, Mr. Clive Antony
CHITTENDEN, Dr. Stella Jane Rebecca
CHIU, Mr. Kwok Kit
CHIU, Mr. Pak Hei William
CHIVERS, Mr. Jeremy Charles Alistair
CHIVERS, Mr. Nicholas James
CHO, Mr. Kui Keung Gilbert
CHOPRA, Mr. Sunil
CHOTHANI, Mr. Devshi
CHOUHAN, Mrs. Sushmadevi
CHOWDHARY, Mr. Bhupindar Singh
CHOWEN, Mr. Matthew Jonathan
CHOWN, Mr. Ian Jack
CHOWN, Mr. John Beresford
CHRISFIELD, Mr. Lawrence John
CHRISTIE, Mr. John Campbell
CHRISTIE, Mrs. Lorna Bisset
CHRISTOPHER, Mrs. Melissa Jane

CHRISTOPHER, Mr. Nicholas
CHRISTOPHER, Mr. Simon John
CHRISTOU, Mr. Achilleas
CHRISTY, Mrs. Morisha Kim
CHRISTY, Mr. Norman David
CHUHAN, Mr. Abdul Majeed
CHUNG NIEN CHIN, Mr. William
CHURCH, Mr. William Edward
CHURCHILL, Mr. Adrian Francis
CHURCHILL, Mr. Martin John
CHURCHILL, Miss. Rhiannon
CICCONE, Mr. Peter Vincent
CINI, Mr. Jonathan Anthony
CINNAMON, Mr. Allan
CITRON, Mr. Richard Jonathan
CLADD, Mr. Roger John
CLAGUE, Miss. Joanne
CLAISSE, Mrs. Paula Irena
CLAMP, Mr. Thomas Michael
CLAPSHAW, Mr. Russell Ernest Aquila
CLAPTON, Mr. Eric
CLARANCE, Mr. Leon Alexander
CLARK, Mr. Allan Leonard
CLARK, Mr. Alun
CLARK, Mr. Andrew Aidan
CLARK, Mr. Cameron Mccallum
CLARK, Miss. Catherine Louise
CLARK, Mr. David Anthony
CLARK, Mr. Derek
CLARK, Mr. Frances Helen
CLARK, Mrs. Helen
CLARK, Mr. Ian
CLARK, Mr. Jeremy Francis
CLARK, Mrs. Karen Frances
CLARK, Mr. Malcolm Ian
CLARK, Mr. Michael Stuart
CLARK, Mr. Peter Morten
CLARK, Mr. Richard James
CLARK, Mrs. Susan Jane
CLARKE, Mr. Andrew Charles Simon
CLARKE, Mrs. Carole Leslie
CLARKE, Mrs. Caroline June
CLARKE, Mr. David
CLARKE, Miss. Faye Nicola
CLARKE, Mr. Gerard Joseph John
CLARKE, Mr. Iain Christopher
CLARKE, Mr. Iain Kenneth John
CLARKE, Mr. Ian Michael
CLARKE, Mr. John Leonard
CLARKE, Mr. Kenneth Edwin
CLARKE, Mr. Paul Mervyn
CLARKE, Mrs. Rachel Louise
CLARKE, Mr. Richard Brian
CLARKE, Mr. Richard David
CLARKE, Mr. Stephen Timothy
CLARKSON, Mr. Ashley Mark Edward
CLARKSON, Mrs. Chrysoulla Louise
CLARKSON, Mrs. Fiona Jane
CLARKSON, Mr. Robert Hollings
CLARKSON, Mrs. Sarah Virginia
CLAVANE, Mr. Martin
CLAVELL, Mr. Anthony Roger
CLAXTON, Mrs. Elizabeth Jane
CLAY, Mr. Peter
CLAYDEN, Mr. Anthony Louis
CLAYTON, Mr. Andrew John
CLAYTON, Mr. Nicholas Edward
CLEATON-ROBERTS, Mrs. Hannah Lucia
CLEAVER, Mr. Barry Keith
CLEAVER, Mrs. Clare Janine
CLEAVER, Mr. David Charles
CLEDEN, Mr. John Lloyd
CLEGG, Mr. Brian
CLEGG, Miss. Helen
CLEGG, Mrs. Mary Clare
CLEGG, Mr. Paul
CLEGG, Mr. Peter Dixon
CLEMAS, Mr. Vincent Edward
CLEMENT, Mr. Jeremy James
CLEMENTS, Mrs. Alexandra Susan
CLEMENTS, Mr. John William
CLEMENTS, Mrs. Sandra
CLEVERDON, Mr. Jonathan James
CLEWES, Mrs. Emma Jane
CLEWETT, Mr. Charles James
CLIFF, Mr. Peter Brian Maurice
CLIFFORD, Mrs. Audrey Elizabeth
CLIFFORD, Mr. Daniel Sean Patrick
CLIFFORD, Mrs. Lynn Diane
CLIFT, Mr. David Scott
CLIMPSON, Mr. Trevor Sidney
CLINTON, Mr. Ian Louis
CLITHEROE, Mr. Alan James
CLOAKE, Mr. Roger Sidney
CLOKE, Mr. Ian Frank
CLORLEY, Mrs. Helen Louise
CLOUGHTON, Miss. Karen Teresa
CLOW, Mr. Robert Christopher
CLOW, Mr. Roger Heber
CLUBB, Mr. Thomas James
CLUER, Miss. Bronya Joy
CLYNE, Mr. Gordon Roger
COAKLEY, Mrs. Anne Barbara
COATES, Mr. Anthony
COATES, Mr. Roger John
COATES, Mr. Steven Richard
COATES, Mrs. Susan

COATH, Mr. Michael
COBB, Mr. Christopher Paul
COBDEN, Mr. Ian Howard
COBDEN, Mr. Philip Malcolm
COCHRANE, Ms. Elizabeth Jane
COCKMAN, Mr. Ian Francis
COCKWELL, Mr. Mark Julian
COESHALL, Miss. Elizabeth Jane
COFFEY, Mr. Charles Edward
COGAN, Miss. Heather Dawn
COHEN, Mr. Adam George Joseph
COHEN, Mr. Alan Ivan
COHEN, Miss. Amanda Ruth
COHEN, Mr. Andrew Simon Reisler
COHEN, Mr. Andrew Trevor
COHEN, Mr. Anthony Jeremy
COHEN, Mr. Anthony Joseph Henry
COHEN, Mr. David Elliot
COHEN, Mr. David Michael
COHEN, Mr. Errol Frederick
COHEN, Mr. Ian Michael
COHEN, Mr. Jonathan Brett
COHEN, Mr. Samuel David
COISH, Mrs. Janet Ann
COKE, Mr. Stephen John
COLACO, Mr. Nelson Rosario
COLBECK, Mr. Andrew
COLE, Mr. Andrew Albert
COLE, Mr. Andrew Stephen
COLE, Mr. David Anthony
COLE, Miss. Elizabeth-Anne
COLE, Mr. Geoffrey Stanley John
COLE, Mr. Leslie Ronald
COLE, Mr. Mark Christopher Nicholas
COLE, Mr. Michael Eric
COLE, Mr. Sheldon Andrew
COLE, Mrs. Tracey Michelle
COLEMAN, Miss. Ann Georgina
COLEMAN, Mr. Martin Anthony
COLEMAN, Mrs. Michelle
COLEMAN, Mr. Paul David
COLEMAN, Mrs. Rachel
COLINSWOOD, Mrs. Carol Rosemary Ethel
COLLERTON, Mr. Timothy Edwin Albert
COLLETT, Mr. Alan
COLLETT, Mr. Aubrey James
COLLEY, Mr. Michael Anthony
COLLIER, Miss. Jane Ann
COLLIER, Mr. Jeffrey Steven
COLLIER, Mr. Michael Andrew
COLLIER, Mr. Stephen Francis
COLLIER, Mr. Stewart Cyril
COLLINGS, Mr. Patrick Nigel
COLLINGS, Mr. Peter Richard
COLLINGWOOD, Mr. Roland Frank
COLLINS, Mrs. Amy
COLLINS, Mr. Gary Milo
COLLINS, Mr. Geoffrey
COLLINS, Mr. Iain Alistair
COLLINS, Miss. Jacqueline Brenda
COLLINS, Mr. Michael Nathan
COLLINS, Mr. Patrick Hugh
COLLINS, Mr. Peter Richard
COLLINS, Miss. Samantha Louise
COLLINSON, Mr. Anthony John Urquhart
COLLINSON, Mrs. Judith Irene
COLLINSON, Mr. Stephen
COLLIS, Mr. Ronald Stephen Paul
COLLISON, Mr. David William
COLLISTER, Mr. Adrian James
COLLISTER, Mr. Carlton Keith Kinrade
COLLYER, Mr. Simon Aron
COLMER, Mr. Douglas John
COLSON, Mr. Darren John
COLVILLE, Mr. David Hulton
COLVILLE, Dr. John Robert
COMBE, Mr. Brian Francis
COMENS, Mr. Martin John
CONCANON, Mr. Brian Anthony Ross
CONDER, Miss. Elizabeth Joan
CONDON, Mr. Richard Simon
CONLAN, Mr. John James William
CONLON, Miss. Anne Marie
CONNELL, Mrs. Caroline Anne
CONNELL, Mrs. Claire Elizabeth
CONNER, Mr. David
CONNOLLY, Mrs. Juliet Gay
CONNOLLY, Mrs. Margaret Mary
CONNOLLY, Mr. Peter
CONNOR, Mr. Howard Arthur
CONNOR, Mr. Ian Richard Marcel
CONRAD, Mr. Stephen
CONRADI, Mr. Paul Hammond
CONSTABLE, Mr. Andrew Stephen
CONSTANT, Mr. Simon
CONSTANTINIDES, Mr. George Ioannis
CONSTANTINIDES, Mr. Michael Ioannis
CONWAY, Mr. Arthur Noel
CONWAY, Mr. David Jeffrey
CONWAY, Mr. George
COOK, Mr. Andrew Richard
COOK, Mr. Christopher John
COOK, Mr. Graham Irvin
COOK, Dr. Jeanette Claire
COOK, Mrs. Jennie Margaret
COOK, Mr. John Charles
COOK, Mr. Kenneth John Charles

COOK, Mr. Kevin Richard
COOK, Mr. Philip Thomas
COOK, Mr. Stuart Donald
COOK, Mr. Stuart James
COOK, Mr. Trevor
COOKE, Mr. Anthony Richard
COOKE, Mr. Christopher George
COOKE, Mr. Jonathan Barry
COOKE, Mr. Keith Felix
COOKE, Mrs. Louise Susanne
COOKE, Miss. Sharon Julie
COOKE, Mr. Stephen John
COOKE, Mrs. Susanna Hope
COOKLIN, Mr. Jonathan Laurence
COOKSON, Mrs. Gillian Louise
COOKSON, Mr. Michael John Edwin
COOKSON, Mr. Peter John
COOLEY, Mr. Christopher Martin
COOMBS, Mr. John Leslie
COOMBS, Mr. Richard Christopher Philemon
COOMBS, Mr. Roger Alan
COOMER, Mr. Edward Alan
COOPER, Mr. Adam
COOPER, Mr. Alan Albert
COOPER, Mrs. Alison Ann
COOPER, Mr. Andrew
COOPER, Mr. Barry James
COOPER, Mr. Christopher
COOPER, Mr. Edward James Ashley
COOPER, Mr. Jeffrey Stanton
COOPER, Mr. John Anthony
COOPER, Mrs. Lesley Ann
COOPER, Mr. Mark Andrew
COOPER, Mr. Mark Anthony
COOPER, Mr. Martin Howard
COOPER, Mr. Michael
COOPER, Mr. Michael Francis Robert
COOPER, Miss. Nicola Ann
COOPER, Mr. Robert
COPE, Miss. Emma Jane
COPE, Mr. Michael Hugh
COPPARD, Mr. David John
COPPARD, Mr. Kevin Andrew
COPSEY, Mr. David Russell
CORBIN, Mr. Phillip Andrew
CORBITT, Miss. Margaret Anne
CORCORAN, Mrs. Melva Jane
CORCORAN, Mr. Stephen Albert Martin
CORDEN, Mr. Nicholas John
CORFIELD, Mr. Philip David
CORK, Mr. David Jenner
CORKING, Mr. Brian Martin
CORLETT, Mr. George James Brian
CORLETT, Mr. John Kenneth
CORNE, Mr. Stephen
CORNELIUS, Mr. Paul Anthony
CORNER, Mr. Stephen Ashley
COSMA, Mr. Marios
COSSLETT, Mrs. Kim
COSTA, Mr. Amilios Christodoulos
COSTA, Mr. David
COSTAS, Mr. Eraklis
COSTER, Mr. Stephen William
COTILLARD, Mr. Christopher Billot
COTTAM, Miss. Sarah Jayne
COTTERILL, Dr. Linda Ann
COTTINGHAM, Mr. Stephen Richard
COTTON, Mr. Wilson Peter
COTTRELL, Mr. David
COUCH, Mr. Mark Andrew
COUCH, Mr. Stephen John
COUGHLAN, Mrs. Sally Ann
COUGHTREY, Mr. Michael Thomas
COULTRUP, Mr. Timothy Jon
COUNSELL, Mrs. Alison Judy
COUNSELL, Mr. David John
COUNSELL, Mr. David William
COUPEE, Mr. David Harry
COUPLAND, Mr. William David
COURT, Mrs. Jane Elizabeth
COURTNEY, Mr. Philip George
COURTS, Mrs. Jill Marion
COUSINS, Mr. Andrew Neil
COUSSENS, Mr. Michael Charles
COUTINHO, Mr. Jason
COUTINHO, Mr. John Baptist
COUZENS, Mr. William Hugh
COVELL, Mr. Beverley Michael
COWAN, Mr. John Andrew
COWAN, Mr. Nigel Ian
COWAN, Mrs. Sally Ann
COWAN, Mr. Stanley
COWDY, Mr. Peter Edward Mason
COWEN, Mrs. Claire
COWEN, Mrs. Julie Dawn
COWGILL, Mr. Andrew Anthony
COWLAND, Mr. Mark James
COWLEY, Mrs. Annette Maria
COWLEY, Mr. Barry David
COWLEY, Mr. John
COWLING, Mr. John Hugh
COX, Mr. Andrew David
COX, Mr. Brian John
COX, Mr. David
COX, Mr. David Charles
COX, Mr. David John

COX, Mr. David Nigel
COX, Mrs. Eleana
COX, Mr. Frank Arthur
COX, Mr. John
COX, Mr. Leslie James
COX, Mr. Martin Christopher
COX, Mr. Michael John
COX, Miss. Rebecca Marie
COX, Mrs. Susan Anne
COXE, Mr. Clifford Arthur Michael
COXON, Ms. Lisa Marie
COYLE, Mr. Timothy Joseph
COZENS, Mrs. Dorothy Jean
CRACKETT, Mr. David
CRAGG, Mr. Mark Stephen
CRAGGS, Mr. Ian Arthur
CRAIG, Mr. Peter Ross
CRAMB, Mr. Andrew Paul Duncan
CRAMP, Mr. David William
CRANE, Miss. Jemma
CRANE, Mr. Peter Alan
CRANLEIGH-SWASH, Mr. Philip Anthony
CRANNESS, Mr. David John
CRAUGHWELL, Mr. John
CRAVEN, Mr. Brian
CRAWFORD, Mr. Alan Michael
CRAWFORD, Mr. Daniel Dundas Euing
CRAWFORD, Mr. James Duncan
CRAWFORD, Mrs. Sarah Kate Mary
CRAWLEY, Mr. Andrew Stephen
CRAWLEY, Miss. Jill
CRAWLEY, Mr. John David
CRAWLEY, Mr. Martyn Andrew
CRAWTE, Mr. Antony Mitchell
CREAL, Mr. David Alexander
CREASEY, Mr. Anthony Philip
CREASY, Mr. Paul
CREDALI, Mr. Giuseppe Antonio
CREEVY, Mr. Matthew John Bamborough
CREMIN, Mr. Denis James Paul
CRESSEY, Dr. Jonathan Tony
CRESSWELL, Mrs. Barbara
CRESSWELL, Mrs. Fiona Jean
CRESSWELL, Mr. John Robert
CRESSWELL, Mr. Michael Ian
CRESSWELL, Mr. Stephen Amos
CREW, Mr. Robert Paul
CRICHTON, Mr. Andrew David Denzil
CRIDLAND, Mr. Marcus James
CRILLY, Mr. Aidan Joseph
CRIPPS, Mr. Brian Edward
CRISP, Mr. Tony Graham
CROCKER, Mr. Neil Jesse
CROCKER, Mr. Richard Anthony
CROFTS, Mr. Simon John
CROMBIE, Mr. David John
CROMPTON, Mr. John Stewart
CROMWELL, Mrs. Clare Elizabeth
CRONIN, Mr. Peter John Edmund
CRONK, Mrs. Janet Sheila
CROOK, Mr. David Ford
CROOK, Mr. John
CROOK, Mr. Stuart Peter
CROOKS, Mr. Toby Lloyd
CROOMBS, Mr. Paul David
CROSBY, Mr. Richard William Villiers
CROSBY, Mr. Roy
CROSS, Mr. Denis
CROSS, Mrs. Helen Marie
CROSS, Mr. Ian Alexander Robertson
CROSS, Mr. James Mark
CROSS, Mr. Jonathan Nicholas
CROSS, Mr. Simon Gerrard
CROSSLEY, Mr. Steven David
CROTTY, Miss. Jane
CROUCH, Mr. Roland Paul
CROWE, Mr. John
CROWE, Miss. Margaret Anne
CROWLEY, Mr. Colin John
CROWLEY, Mr. Paul James
CROWN, Mr. Irvin Russell
CROWTHER, Mrs. Amanda Geraldine
CROWTHER, Mr. Daniel Bryan Elon
CROWTHER, Mr. John Nicholas
CROWTHER, Mr. Jonathan Douglas
CROWTHER, Mr. Jonathan James
CROZIER, Mr. Gavin Hugh
CROZIER, Mr. Michael Shaun
CRUICKSHANK, Mr. James William Alexander
CRUMP, Mr. Ralph
CRUSE, Mr. Ian Francis
CRUTCHFIELD, Mr. Donovan Ashley
CRUTTENDEN, Mr. Eric James
CUE, Mr. Bernard Godfrey
CULLEY, Miss. Katharine Julia
CULLINANE, Mr. Peter Michael
CULLINGWORTH, Mr. Robert
CULLUM, Mr. Philip James
CULSHAW, Mr. Martin John
CULVER, Mr. Peter James
CULVER, Mr. Robert
CULVERHOUSE, Mr. John Robert
CULWICK, Mrs. Elaine
CUMMINGS, Mrs. Alice Sarah Louise
CUMMINS, Mrs. Jane
CUNNINGHAM, Mr. Declan Thomas

Tax Faculty Members - Alphabetical

CUNNINGHAM, Mr. John Leslie
CUNNINGHAM, Mr. Michael Robert
CUNNINGHAM, Mr. Richard Leslie
CUNYNGHAME, Sir Andrew (David Francis)
CURD, Mr. Jeremy Kenneth Edward
CURRIE, Miss. Fiona Alexandra
CURRIE, Mrs. Isobel Jane
CURRIE, Mr. Oliver Humphrey Raphael
CURRY, Miss. Fiona Alexandra
CURRY, Mr. Mark Andrew
CURRY, Mr. Peter Jonathan
CURTHOYS, Mr. Lee Richard
CURTIS, Mr. Derek Reginald
CURTIS, Mr. Henry Farquharson
CURTIS, Mr. Lee
CURTIS, Mr. Paul James
CURTIS, Mr. Peter John
CURTIS, Mr. Roger William Holbrook
CURTIS, Mr. Ronald Frank
CURZON, Mr. Terence Stuart
CUTHBERTSON, Mr. Simon Alexander
CUTLER, Mr. Gordon
CUTLER, Mr. John Ernest
CUTLER, Mrs. Shona Mary
CUTTER, Mr. Paul James
CUTTING, Miss. Hannah Claire
CUTTING, Mrs. Kerry June
CUTTING, Mrs. Samantha Jane
CYMERMAN, Mr. Selwyn
CYPHER, Mrs. Yvonne
D'INVERNO, Mrs. Isobel Jane
DA ROZA, Mr. Mark Anthony
DABEK, Mr. Julian Richard
DACK, Mr. Michael John
DACOMBE, Mr. David William
DADA, Mr. Feeroze Ahmad
DAEMI, Mr. Vahid
DAFINONE, Mr. Igho Omueya
DAGG, Mrs. Charlotte Amy
DAGLESS, Mr. Andrew Edward
DAKIN, Mrs. Jennifer Mary
DALBY, Mr. Anthony Hedley Burkitt
DALBY, Mr. Brian
DALE, Mr. Christopher James
DALE, Mr. Douglas Brian
DALE, Mrs. Lorraine Stephanie
DALGLEISH, Mr. Robert Henry
DALLAS, Mrs. Joanna Victoria
DALMAN, Mr. Robert Alistair
DALTON, Mr. Jesse
DALTON, Mr. John Leslie
DALTON, Dr. Michael
DALZELL, Mr. Ian Robert
DALZIEL, Mr. Andrew James
DAMER, Mr. Anthony Joseph Charles
DAMERY, Mr. Aynsley Norman
DANAHER, Mr. Stephen Paul
DANCE, Mr. Andrew Kevin
DANES, Mr. Desmond Hector John
DANIEL, Mr. Harry Jonathan
DANIEL, Mr. Peter Roger
DANIELS, Mr. Daniel
DANIELS, Mr. Keith Barry
DANIELS, Mr. Stephen
DANIELS, Mr. William Roger
DANN, Mr. Phillip Andrew
DANN, Mr. William Edward
DANTON, Mr. Mark Paul
DANVERS, Mrs. Gillian Mary
DARBY, Mr. Andrew Thomas
DARBY, Mrs. Barbara Joan
DARBY, Mr. Raymond
DARBYSHIRE, Mr. Robin Vivian
DARGUE, Mr. Roger Thomas
DARNBROUGH, Mr. John Alister
DARUKHANAWALA, Mrs. Selina Percy
DARUWALLA, Mr. Paurus Cawas
DARVELL, Mr. Malcolm Lawton
DARVELL, Mr. Michael John
DATOO, Mr. Mustafa Aunali Lalji
DATTA, Mr. Gour Sadhan
DATTANI, Mr. Nitin
DATTANI, Mr. Vijaykumar
DAUNCEY, Mr. John Anthony
DAUPPE, Mr. Victor Andre Francois
DAVE, Mr. Anil
DAVE, Mr. Dineshchandra Jatashanker Bhavani Shanker
DAVENPORT, Mr. Anthony Henry
DAVENPORT, Mr. Leigh
DAVENPORT, Mr. Paul
DAVERN, Mr. Fergal Gerard John
DAVEY, Mr. John Lester
DAVEY, Mr. Michael Graham
DAVEY, Mr. Richard John Chatterton
DAVIDSEN, Ms. Elizabeth Bulow
DAVIDSON, Ms. Ann Lloyd
DAVIDSON, Mrs. Fiona Christine
DAVIES, Mr. Andrew Norman
DAVIES, Mr. Anthony Desmond
DAVIES, Mr. Anthony Paul
DAVIES, Ms. Caroline Margaret
DAVIES, Miss. Catherine Elaine
DAVIES, Mr. Daniel Ivor
DAVIES, Mr. David Craig
DAVIES, Mr. David Hatfield
DAVIES, Mr. David Michael Barry

DAVIES, Mr. Gareth Huw
DAVIES, Mr. Gareth John
DAVIES, Mr. Geoffrey
DAVIES, Mr. Geoffrey Brian
DAVIES, Mr. Geraint Vaughan
DAVIES, Mr. Hefin Lewis
DAVIES, Mr. Jack
DAVIES, Mr. John Alan
DAVIES, Mr. John Peter
DAVIES, Mr. Jonathan Edward
DAVIES, Mr. Jonathan William Edward
DAVIES, Mr. Leslie Edward
DAVIES, Mr. Martin John
DAVIES, Mr. Mervyn Neil
DAVIES, Mr. Neil
DAVIES, Mr. Nicholas John
DAVIES, Mr. Paul Walton
DAVIES, Mr. Peter Walters
DAVIES, Mr. Robert Goyne
DAVIES, Mr. Robert William
DAVIES, Ms. Sheena Elizabeth
DAVIES, Mr. Solomon
DAVIES, Mr. Steven Michael
DAVIES, Mr. Stuart James
DAVIES, Mr. Timothy Grenville
DAVIES, Mr. Trevor Charles
DAVIES, Mrs. Wendy Susan
DAVIS, Mr. Christopher Philip
DAVIS, Mr. David Paul
DAVIS, Miss. Mariette Catherine
DAVIS, Mr. Paul Anthony
DAVIS, Mr. Ray Alan
DAVIS, Mr. Richard James
DAVISON, Mr. Colin Andrew
DAVY, Mr. Martyn George
DAWES, Mr. Michael Harvey
DAWKINS, Mr. Jeremy Stephen
DAWSON, Mr. David Andrew
DAWSON, Mr. Jeremy Alan Courtenay
DAWSON, Mr. Michael Forbes
DAWSON, Mr. Peter Joseph
DAWSON, Mr. Richard Godfrey
DAWSON, Mr. Stephen
DAY, Mr. Andrew
DAY, Mr. Clifford
DAY, Mr. Geoffrey Allan
DAY, Mrs. Heather Kathryn
DAY, Mrs. Sarah Louise
DAYA, Mr. Ahmed Abdulhusein
DAYE, Mrs. Susan Ann
DE, Mr. Debaprasad
DE BACKER, Mr. Damian Paul
DE BACQ ROSE, Mr. Malcolm
DE BARR, Mr. Richard Jeremy
DE BRUYN, Mr. Christiaan Leonard
DE DOMBAL, Dr. Richard Francis
DE JAGER, Mr. Gary Vigne
DE-LACY ADAMS, Mr. Simon Downing
DE LANGE, Mrs. Madele
DE MELLO, Mr. Rodney Hugh
DE PALMA, Miss. Maria Rosa
DE RENZO, Mrs. Novella
DE-RHUNE, Mr. Michael Anthony
DE WILTON, Mr. Jonathan
DEACON, Ms. Sandra Karen
DEAKIN, Mrs. Anne Catherine
DEAKIN, Mrs. Anne Marie
DEAN, Mr. Charles Robert
DEANE, Mr. Peter Michael
DEANS, Mr. Robin William Lauder
DEAR, Mr. David Michael
DEARDEN, Mrs. Helen Clare
DEARDEN, Mr. Phillip Edward
DEARING, Mrs. Kathryn Margaret
DEBSON, Mr. Jon Godfrey
DEE, Mr. Nicholas Charles
DELAHUNTY, Mr. John Joseph
DELAMERE, Miss. Louise Anne
DELF, Mr. Peter James
DELLER, Mrs. Diane Frances
DEMETRIOU, Mr. Constantinos
DEMETRIOU, Mr. Dimitrakis George
DEMETRIOU, Ms. Margarita
DEMUTH, Ms. Helen Veronica
DENBY, Mr. Paul Justin
DENCHER, Mr. John Stanley
DENISON, Mr. Michael John
DENLEY, Mr. Andrew John
DENNARD, Mr. Roger Frederick
DENNIS, Mr. Gordon Frank
DENNIS, Mrs. Jane
DENNIS, Mrs. Michelle Alexandra
DENNIS, Mr. Paul James
DENNIS, Mr. Philip Gavril
DENNIS, Mr. Timothy
DENNISS, Mr. Neil Michael
DENT, Miss. Elizabeth Ann
DENT, Mr. Nicholas Michael
DENT, Mr. Simon Jeffrey Michael
DENTON, Ms. Laurie Lesley
DENTON, Mr. Roger
DENTON, Mr. Simon Mark
DENYE, Mr. Simon Antony
DENZA, Mr. John
DERBY, Mr. Alan James
DERBY, Mrs. Polly Elizabeth
DESAI, Mr. Dineshchandra Kalidas

DESAI, Mr. Jayanti
DESAI, Mr. Kaushik Jayantilal Sunderlal
DESAI, Mr. Narendra Kumar Dhirajlal
DESAI, Mr. Vinodrai Kikubhai
DESOUZA, Mr. Querobino Leo
DESSAIN, Mr. Paul Mark
DETHERIDGE, Mr. John
DEUTSCH, Mr. Stephen Soloman
DEVANI, Mr. Shashikant Chandulal
DEVEREUX, Mrs. Pallavi
DEVEREUX, Mr. Ronald
DEVERILL, Mr. Ian Stuart
DEVERSON, Mrs. Nicola
DEVJI, Mrs. Nasim Mohamed
DEWANI, Mr. Ragesh Kantilal
DEWHIRST, Mrs. Susan Elizabeth
DEY, Mr. Joseph William
DHALIWAL, Mr. Harvinder Singh
DHALIWAL, Mr. Randeep Singh
DHANANI, Mr. Bharat-Kumar Premchand
DHARSI, Mr. Taha Mohammed
DHILLON, Mr. Navjyot Singh
DI FRANCO, Mr. Marco
DI GIUSEPPE, Mr. Peter Ettore
DI LETO, Mr. Michael
DIAS, Mr. Denver Aloysius
DICK, Mr. William Robert Andrew
DICKENS, Mr. Kevin
DICKENS, Mr. Mark Christopher
DICKENSON, Mr. Maurice
DICKER, Mr. Samuel Sidney
DICKINSON, Mr. Alan Geoffrey
DICKINSON, Mr. David Anthony
DICKINSON, Mr. Gary
DILENA, Mr. Salvatore
DILLAMORE, Mr. Robin Mark
DILLOW, Mr. Nicholas John
DIMMICK, Mr. Christopher
DINER, Mr. Jeffrey Martin
DINES, Miss. Helen Elizabeth
DINGLEY, Mr. Leslie George
DINGWALL, Mr. Roger David
DINNAGE, Mrs. Jennifer Clare
DIOLA, Ms. Christiana
DISHMAN, Mr. James David
DISLEY, Mr. Andrew Guy
DISNEY, Mr. Peter
DISTON, Mr. Robert
DITCHFIELD, Mrs. Helen Margaret
DIXON, Mr. Andrew Paul
DIXON, Mr. Gary Frank
DIXON, Mr. James Wolryche
DIXON, Mrs. Jane Louise
DIXON, Mr. Lee Howard
DIXON, Mr. Philip John
DIXON, Mrs. Stephanie Susan
DIXON, Mr. Stuart Roy
DIXON, Mr. Thomas Mark
DIZADJI, Mr. Farhad
DOBBIN, Mr. Anthony Michael Chetwynd
DOBSON, Mrs. Geraldene Lea
DOBSON, Mr. Robert Kirton
DOCHERTY, Miss. Kathleen
DOCKERILL, Mrs. Caroline Mary
DOCTOR, Ms. Parizad
DODD, Mr. Michael Thomas Fulton
DODD, Mr. Michael William
DODD, Mr. Nigel George
DODD, Mr. Simon John
DODDS, Mr. Alastair James
DODDS, Mr. David Anthony
DODDS, Mr. Richard John
DODGSON, Mr. David Henry
DODHIA, Mr. Rasmikant Premchand
DOE, Mr. Philip Malcolm
DOGGETT, Mr. Ashley
DOHERTY, Mr. Cecil Norman
DOHERTY, Mrs. Joanne Susan
DOHERTY, Mr. Michael Anthony Peter
DOLPHIN, Mr. Nicholas Albert
DONALD, Mrs. Lynne Alison
DONEY, Mr. Robert George William
DONNAN, Mr. Michael
DONNELLY, Mrs. Tracey Anne
DONOGHUE, Mr. Mark Richard
DOOLEY, Miss. Nicola Gillian
DOOTSON, Mr. John Kevin
DORE, Mr. Andrew Michael
DOUCE, Mr. Andrew James
DOUGLAS, Ms. Katrina
DOUGLAS, Mrs. Ruth Ingela Astrid
DOUGLASS, Mr. Ian
DOUST, Mr. Clive Howard
DOVE, Mrs. Diana Mary
DOVER, Mr. Daniel Isaac
DOVEY, Mr. Charles Frederick
DOWLER, Mr. Jeremy
DOWLING, Mr. Anthony John
DOWLING, Mr. Robert Wheatley
DOWN, Mr. Terence John
DOWNES, Mr. Gareth
DOWNING, Mr. Michael Thomas
DOWSON, Mr. David William
DOYLE, Mr. Peter Edward
DOYLE, Mr. Richard Howard
DRAFFAN, Mr. Michael
DRAGE, Mr. Colin John Fleming

DRAKE, Mr. Keith Robert
DRAKE, Mr. Raymond John
DRANSFIELD, Mr. Anthony James
DRAPER, Mr. Derek George
DRAPER, Mr. Jeremy Paul
DREESE, Miss. Sarah
DRENNAN, Mr. Richard Gordon
DREW, Miss. Anna Marian
DREW, Mr. Barry John
DREW, Mrs. Julie Amanda
DREW, Mr. Patrick Keith
DREWERY, Mr. Gary
DRIFFIELD, Mr. Alan Edward
DRISCOLL, Mr. Christopher John
DRUMMOND, Mr. Hugh Redvers
DRURY, Mr. Edward Martin
DRURY, Mrs. Emma
DRURY, Mr. John Joseph
DRURY, Mr. Sean Michael
DU PREEZ, Mr. Vivian Rabey
DUA, Mr. Rakesh Kumar
DUBENS, Mr. Timothy Samuel Daiches
DUBOIS, Mrs. Johanna Elizabeth
DUCKWORTH, Mr. David John
DUCKWORTH, Mr. Philip Roy
DUDFIELD, Mr. Simon Thomas
DUDGEON, Mr. Jonathan Robert
DUDHIA, Mrs. Radha
DUDLEY, Mr. Johnathan Geoffrey
DUDLEY, Mr. Martin Paul
DUDLEY, Mr. Robert Howard
DUFFILL, Mr. Robert Frank
DUFFIN, Mr. Christopher John
DUFFY, Mrs. Amanda Jane
DUFFY, Mr. Thomas William
DUGGAN, Mr. Christopher Peter
DUGGAN, Ms. Diana Margaret
DUGGAN, Mr. John
DUKER, Mr. Steven Gregory
DUNBAR, Mr. David Randolph Michell
DUNCAN, Mr. John Paul
DUNCAN, Miss. Lucy Jane
DUNCOMBE, Mr. Jeremy Robert
DUNCUMB, Mrs. Nicola Jenny
DUNGARWALLA, Mr. Hatimalli
DUNKLEY, Mr. Adrian Paul
DUNN, Mrs. Anne-Maree
DUNN, Mrs. Hayley Marie
DUNN, Miss. Joanna
DUNN, Mr. Robert John
DUNNE, Mr. Joseph Charles
DUNNE, Mr. Martin Conrad
DUNNING, Mr. Barrie John
DUNNING, Mr. Nicholas Anthony Robert
DUNSTAN, Mrs. Lisa
DURANCE, Mr. Peter Anthony
DURBIN, Mr. Peter Charles Robertson
DURDIN, Mrs. Margaret Anne
DURRANI, Mr. Farouk Salim Khan
DURRANT, Mrs. Alexandra Beryl
DURRANT, Miss. Elaine Margaret
DURRANT, Mrs. Patricia Chorlton Prichard
DURST, Mr. Michael Bernard
DURTNALL, Mr. Alan Robert
DURY, Mr. Michael Raymond
DUSGATE, Mr. Christopher Ian
DUTTON, Mr. Ian
DYER, Mr. Mark Edward
DYER, Mr. Michael Karl Remane
DYER, Mr. William Edward
DYER-SMITH, Mr. Christopher Simon Paul
DYKE, Mr. Christopher John
DYMEK, Mr. Christopher John
DYSON, Mr. Alan Campbell
DYSON, Mr. Patrick John
EAGER, Miss. Anne
EAGLE, Mr. Philip James
EALES, Mrs. Helen
EAPEN, Mr. Mammen
EARL, Mrs. Fiona Diane
EASTAWAY, Mr. Nigel Antony
EASTMOND, Mr. Stephen Reginald
EASTWOOD, Mr. Anthony George
EASTWOOD, Miss. Elizabeth Jane
EASTWOOD, Mr. Paul
EASUN, Miss. Lorraine Jennifer
EATON, Mr. David Andrew
EATON, Mr. Mark Charles
EATOUGH, Mrs. Diane Louise
EAVES, Mr. Mark
EAVES, Mr. Paul Nigel Thomas
EBELING, Mr. Michael George
EBERT, Mr. Ahron
EBRAHIM, Mr. Sherali
ECCLES, Mr. Jonathan Philip
ECOB, Mrs. Josephine Simone
EDDINS, Mr. Paul Francis Rowe
EDDISON, Mrs. Catherine Sophie
EDENBOROUGH, Mr. Kevin
EDGE, Mr. Francis Andrew
EDGE, Mr. Malcolm Clive Greenhalgh
EDGSON, Mr. Daniel Paul
EDIE, Mrs. Greta Maud
EDMOND, Mr. James Michael
EDMONDSON, Mr. Paul Robert
EDWARDS, Mr. Anthony Brian
EDWARDS, Mr. Arthur

EDWARDS, Mr. David Cottelle
EDWARDS, Mr. Esmond Barry
EDWARDS, Mr. Geoffrey Ivor
EDWARDS, Mr. Ian Nigel
EDWARDS, Mr. Keith Geoffrey
EDWARDS, Mr. Peter James
EDWARDS, Mr. Peter John
EDWARDS, Mr. Peter John
EDWARDS, Mr. Philip James
EDWARDS, Mr. Richard Andrew
EDWARDS, Mr. Robert Mark
EDWARDS, Mr. Simon Jeremy
EDWARDS, Mr. Stephen George
EDWARDS, Mr. Stephen Richard
EDWARDS, Mr. Stuart
EDWARDS, Mr. Stuart Ian
EDWARDS, Mr. Terence
EDWORTHY, Mr. David William
EGAN, Mr. Michael
EGAN, Mr. Michael
EGGERS, Miss. Sara
EGGLESTONE, Mr. Edward
EGINTON, Mr. Anthony Charles Thomas
EGLINTON, Mr. Timothy Read
EISEN, Mr. Russell David
EKERMANS, Mrs. Issebel
ELCOCK, Mr. Derek Frank
ELDER, Mr. David John
ELDER, Mr. Robert Bruce
ELFORD, Mr. Julian Francis
ELGAR, Mr. Simon John
ELIAS, Mr. Antoun
ELLIOTT, Mrs. Beverley Anne
ELLIOTT, Mr. Colin Robert
ELLIOTT, Miss. Dawn
ELLIOTT, Miss. Diane Clare
ELLIOTT, Miss. Isabel Rose
ELLIOTT, Mrs. Joyce Elspeth Bain
ELLIOTT, Mr. Keith Malcolm
ELLIOTT, Mr. Peter Albert
ELLIOTT, Mr. Philip John
ELLIOTT, Mr. Robert Tregellas
ELLIOTT, Mr. Simon Timothy
ELLIS, Mr. Andrew Timothy
ELLIS, Mr. Charles Robert
ELLIS, Miss. Chloe Jade
ELLIS, Mr. Clive Edward
ELLIS, Mr. Geoffrey
ELLIS, Mr. Guy Butterworth
ELLIS, Mr. John Andrew Jackson
ELLIS, Mrs. June
ELLIS, Mr. Mark Richard
ELLIS, Mr. Mervyn Brian
ELLIS, Mr. Paul James
ELLIS, Mr. Paul Stuart
ELLIS, Mr. Philip Harold
ELLIS, Mrs. Rachel Caroline
ELLIS, Mr. Richard David
ELLIS, Mr. Simon Kevin
ELLISON, Mrs. Susan Theresa
ELSDEN, Mr. Neil Richard
ELSEY, Mr. Christopher
ELSWORTH, Mrs. Elizabeth Joanna
ELWICK, Mr. Brian
EMERY, Mr. Kenneth John
EMERY, Mr. Paul Stephen
EMSDEN, Mr. Reginald Christopher
EMSLIE, Mrs. Caroline Patricia
ENDACOTT, Mr. Jonathan Leonard
ENDEACOTT, Mr. Jonathan Craig
ENDICOTT, Mr. David John
ENGLAND, Mr. Andrew Mark
ENGLAND, Mr. Graham Martyn
ENGLISH, Mrs. Ellen Margaret Mary
ENRIGHT, Mr. Peter Maurice
ENSOR, Miss. Alison Lindsay
ENSOR, Miss. Debbie Jayne
ENSOR, Mr. Jonathan Arthur
ENTWISTLE, Mr. Leonard
EPSTEIN, Mr. Gary John
EPTON, Mr. Anthony John Walter
ERASMUS, Ms. Magdalena Maria
ESMAIL, Mr. Salim
ESSAM, Mr. Jonathan Charles Seymour
ESTCOURT, Mr. Paul
ETHERIDGE, Mr. Mark Charles
EVAGORA, Mr. Evagoras
EVANS, Mr. Alan George
EVANS, Mr. Alan Martin
EVANS, Mr. Alan Morgan
EVANS, Mr. Alun
EVANS, Mrs. Carol Ann
EVANS, Mrs. Claire Jane
EVANS, Mr. David Edward
EVANS, Mr. David Humphrey
EVANS, Mr. David Lloyd
EVANS, Mr. David Robert
EVANS, Mr. Dylan Vaughan
EVANS, Mrs. Georgina Ellen
EVANS, Mr. Ian Malcolm
EVANS, Miss. Jane Thompson
EVANS, Mr. John Arnold
EVANS, Mr. John Michael
EVANS, Miss. Katharine Julia
EVANS, Mr. Keith
EVANS, Mr. Malcolm David
EVANS, Mr. Mark Christopher

EVANS, Mr. Michael John
EVANS, Mr. Nicholas Stewart
EVANS, Mr. Paul Herbert
EVANS, Mr. Philip John
EVANS, Mrs. Sara Catrin
EVANS, Mrs. Sarah Jane
EVANS, Mrs. Susan Elizabeth
EVANS, Mrs. Suzanne Joan
EVANS, Mrs. Tahira
EVANS, Mrs. Yvonne Ann
EVE, Mr. Dennis Paul
EVE, Mr. Maurice Anthony
EVENDEN, Miss. Jill Marie
EVENS, Mrs. Alison Ruth
EVERALL, Mr. Richard James
EVERATT, Mr. David James
EVEREST, Mrs. Jane Mary
EVEREST, Mr. Philip James
EVERETT, Mr. Chai Hung
EVERITT, Mrs. Amanda Jane
EWEN, Mr. Norman Edward
EXWOOD, Mr. Roger John William
FAGELMAN, Mr. Michael Joseph
FAHY, Mr. Brendan Patrick
FAIL, Mrs. Pauline Lesley
FAINT, Miss. Carol Elizabeth
FAIRBAIRN, Mr. Noel Kenneth
FAIZ-MAHDAVI, Mr. Behzad
FALK, Mr. Leslie
FALVEY, Mr. Paul Timothy
FANTHOME, Mrs. Heather Christine
FAQUIR, Mr. Nazir Naveed
FARAM, Mr. David Paul
FARANDA BELLOFIGLIO, Dr. Nunzio
FARAZMAND, Mr. Habib Sayed
FARDELL, Mrs. Penelope Joyce
FARGHER, Mr. Anthony Eric
FARLEY, Mr. Ian Thomas
FARMER, Mr. David
FARMER, Mr. Nicholas Michael
FARNDON, Mr. Michael Alan
FARNWORTH, Mr. Oliver George
FAROOQ, Mr. Umar
FAROOQI, Mr. Shajar Ahmad
FARQUHAR, Mrs. Ann
FARQUHAR, Mr. Robert Mackenzie
FARR, Miss. Kathryn Olwen
FARR, Mr. Nicholas Edward
FARRAND, Mr. Colin Eric
FARRAND-LAINE, Mrs. Colette Marilynne
FARRANT, Mr. Matthew Granby
FARRAR, Mr. Christopher
FARRELL, Mr. Colin Andrew
FARROW, Mr. Nicholas Charles
FARROW, Mr. Paul Edward
FASSAM, Mr. Christopher John
FATONA, Mr. Emmanuel Aibinu
FATTORINI, Mr. Michael James
FAULKNER, Mr. Hugh Edmund Brooke
FAULKNER, Mr. Richard Ian
FAULKNER, Mr. Russell John
FAULKNER, Mrs. Sharon
FAUNCE, Mr. Charles Edmund
FAUTLEY, Mr. Robin Graham
FAWTHROP, Mr. Russell Howard
FAY, Mr. Paul
FAYERS, Mrs. Susan Lesley
FEARN, Mr. Peter Stuart
FEARNSIDE, Mr. David John Richard
FEASEY, Mrs. Michelle Anne Elizabeth
FEATHER, Mr. Roy
FEGAN READ, Mrs. Alexandra Claire
FEINGOLD, Mr. Eliot Hugh
FEIST, Mr. Paul Richard
FELLOWS, Mr. Nigel John
FELTON, Mr. David John
FENN, Mr. David Robert
FENNER, Mr. Vere Anthony
FENNER, Mrs. Yvonne Bridget
FENTON, Mr. Ian Jonathan
FENTON, Mr. Richard John
FEORE, Mrs. Angela Barbara
FERGUSON, Mr. Keith
FERGUSON, Mr. Michael William
FERGUSON, Mrs. Sally Ruth
FERNANDES, Mr. Gavin Anthony
FERNANDES, Mr. Jonathan Anthony Ivan
FERNANDO, Mr. Sunil Anthony
FERNYHOUGH, Mr. Nicholas Francis
FERRARI, Mr. Robert Christopher
FERREDAY, Mr. Michael John
FERRIS, Mr. Roger
FERRY, Mr. John Douglas
FFITCH, Mr. Paul Eldon
FIELD, Mr. Anthony David
FIELD, Mrs. Caroline Patricia
FIELD, Mr. Derek Bernard Melvin
FIELD, Mr. Martin Victor
FIELD, Mr. Paul Michael Antony
FIELD, Ms. Susan
FIELDING, Mrs. Christine Carol
FIELDS, Mr. Stephen Andrew
FILBEE, Mr. Andrew Philip
FILBY, Mr. Christopher Brian Terrence
FILOSE, Mr. Nicholas John
FINCH, Mr. Michael Clifford
FINERTY, Mr. Bernard Francis

FINESILVER, Mr. Jack Malcolm
FINGLETON, Mr. Paul John
FINK, Mr. Mark Richard
FINNEMORE, Mr. Jeffrey Michael
FIRTH, Mr. John Barry
FIRTH, Miss. Nicola
FIRTH, Mrs. Sally Ann
FISH, Mr. Colin Andrew Everitt
FISHBURN, Mr. Michael James Engledew
FISHER, Mr. Don
FISHER, Mr. John Michael
FISHER, Mr. Jonathan David
FISHER, Miss. Karen
FISHER, Mrs. Nicola Jane
FISHER, Mr. Philip
FISHER, Mr. Richard Welby
FISHLEIGH, Mr. Martin John
FITCH, Mr. Ian Robert
FITZPATRICK, Mr. Kevin Paul
FITZPATRICK, Mr. Maurice Charles
FLACK, Ms. Debby Marie
FLANIGAN, Mr. Martin Barrie
FLANNAGAN, Mr. Terence Michael
FLATTERS, Mrs. Jacqueline Anne
FLAVELL, Mr. John Stanley
FLEET, Mrs. Caroline Ruth
FLEET, Mrs. Emma
FLEETWOOD, Mr. Martin Christopher
FLEMING, Mr. John Christopher
FLEMONS, Mr. Graham Barry
FLETCHER, Mrs. Amanda Jill
FLETCHER, Mr. Charles Malcolm
FLETCHER, Mr. David Clifford
FLETCHER, Mr. Ian Jack
FLETCHER, Dr. James
FLETCHER, Mr. Marek Christopher
FLETCHER, Mr. Mark Timothy
FLETCHER, Mr. Sean Andrew
FLETCHER, Ms. Sharron
FLOOD, Miss. Judith
FLOOD, Mr. Paul Andrew
FLOOK, Mrs. Lisa Diane
FLORINGER, Mr. Brian James
FLORSHEIM, Mr. Daniel Robert
FLORY, Mr. Simon John
FLOWERDEW, Mrs. Lesley Ann
FLOWERS, Mr. Richard Dominic
FLOYDD, Mr. Maxwell John
FLYNN, Mr. Anthony Joseph
FLYNN, Mr. William Brendan
FOLEY, Mr. Anthony John
FOLEY, Mr. Martin John
FOOT, Mr. Richard William David
FOOTE, Mr. Malcolm George
FORBES, Mr. Ian Robert
FORBES, Mr. John David
FORBES, Mr. Jonathan Paul
FORBES, Mr. Richard Nicol
FORBES-CABLE, Mr. John Michael
FORD, Mr. Christopher Barry
FORD, Mr. Christopher John
FORMBY, Mr. Richard Francis
FORREST, Mr. Andrew Derek
FORSTER, Mr. Stewart John
FORSYTH, Mr. David Thomas
FORSYTH, Mr. Nicholas
FORTUNE, Mrs. Lisa Joanne
FORWOOD, Mr. Antony Alexander
FOSKETT, Mr. James Ronald
FOSSA, Mr. Riccardo Clifford
FOSTER, Mrs. Kathryn Louise
FOSTER, Mr. Leslie Raymond
FOSTER, Mr. Stephen Mark
FOSTER, Mrs. Susan Martha
FOULKES, Mr. Stephen John
FOWKES, Mr. Timothy
FOWLER, Mr. Malcolm
FOWLER, Mr. Raymond Charles
FOWLER-COLWELL, Mrs. Anne
FOWLES, Miss. Christine Margaret
FOX, Mr. Andrew Michael
FOX, Mr. Edward Michael
FOX, Mr. John William Alfred
FOX, Ms. Krista Margaret
FOX, Mr. Sean Joseph
FOX, Mrs. Victoria Ann
FOX, Mr. William James Staley
FOY, Miss. Jane Barbara
FRAIN, Mrs. Pamela Anne
FRAIS, Mr. Adam Richard
FRANCIS, Mrs. Anzo Gloreen
FRANCIS, Mr. Christopher Joseph Sutherland-Campbell
FRANCIS, Mr. Jeremy Inglesby
FRANCIS, Mr. Julian Paul
FRANCIS, Mr. Nicholas Hugh
FRANGOU, Mr. Iacovos Kyriacos
FRANKLIN, Mrs. Penelope Jane
FRANKLIN, Mr. Stephen
FRANKS, Miss. Jessica
FRANKS, Mr. Marc Ian
FRANKTON, Mr. Terence John
FRASER, Mr. Geoffrey
FRASER, Mr. Ian James
FRASER, Mr. Ian Stuart
FRAYNE-JOHNSON, Mr. Paul

FRECKNALL HUGHES, Dr. Jane
FREED, Mr. Mark Robin
FREEDMAN, Mr. Barry Stephen
FREEDMAN, Mr. David Charles Nathaniel
FREEDMAN, Mr. Michael Jacob
FREEDMAN, Mr. Richard Allen
FREEMAN, Mr. Charles Truscott
FREEMAN, Mr. Crispin Patrick
FREEMAN, Mr. David Derek
FREEMAN, Mrs. Elaine Joy
FREEMAN, Mr. Paul Michael
FREEMAN, Mr. Paul Stephen
FREEMAN, Mr. Peter Edward
FREEMAN, Miss. Stephanie Elizabeth
FREEMAN, Mr. Stephen Andrew
FREEMANTLE, Mr. Gavin Harry
FREER, Mr. Andrew Malcolm Bruce
FRENCH, Mr. Colin Edward Marfleet
FRENCH, Mr. John
FRENCH, Mr. Michael Frank
FRENCH, Mr. Robert Arnold
FRESSON, Mr. Mark Gerald
FRICKER, Mr. Harry William
FRIDLINGTON, Mr. Stephen Andrew
FRIEDE, Mr. Philip Mark
FRIEL, Mr. Edward James
FRIEL, Mr. John
FRITH, Mr. Robert Michael
FRIXOU, Mr. John
FROOD, Mr. David Graham
FROOM, Mr. Robert Howard
FROST, Ms. Caroline Mary Frances
FROUD, Mr. Nicholas Edward
FRUMIN, Mr. David Hilbre
FRY, Mr. Christopher Ramon
FRY, Mr. Peter Graham
FRYER, Mr. Kenneth Wade
FRYER, Mr. Stephen Mark
FUDGE, Mrs. Diana Marion
FUGE, Mr. Jeffrey Peter
FULENA, Mr. Rewtiraman
FULFORD, Mr. Graham Ronald
FULLARD, Mr. Stephen William
FULTON, Mr. Keith Stewart
FUNG, Mr. Chiu Kit
FURRER, Mr. Paul Steven
FURSDON, Mr. Jonathan Malcolm
FURST, Mrs. Susan
FUSSELL, Mr. Stewart Raymond
FYLES, Mr. Stephen
GAINEY, Mr. Stephen Leslie
GALAIYA, Mr. Hiten Ratilal
GALE, Mr. John Robert
GALE, Mr. Kevin Alexander
GALE, Mr. Nicholas David
GALE, Mr. Peter Bradley
GALE, Mr. Philip Antony
GALE, Mr. Robert
GALLAGHER, Mrs. Donna Louise
GALLAGHER, Mr. James Joseph
GALLANT, Mr. John Claude James
GALLER, Mr. Alfred Michael
GALLIERS, Mr. Colin Steven
GAMAGE, Mr. Nigel John
GAMBLE, Mr. Simon Richard
GAMBLEN, Mr. Nigel John
GAMBOLD, Mr. Matthew William
GAMMON, Miss. Sara Jane
GANDHI, Mr. Jayant Bhikhabhai
GANDZ, Mr. Melvyn
GANT, Mr. Ian Tetley
GANT, Mrs. Jane Farley
GARABEDIAN, Mr. Garo
GARCIA, Mr. Daniel Alexis
GARDINER, Mr. Michael Henry
GARDNER, Miss. Ann Georgina
GARDNER, Mr. Graham Alan James
GARDNER, Mr. John Derrick
GARDNER, Mr. John Richard
GARDNER, Mr. Stephen Watson
GARDNER, Mr. Stuart John Lawson
GAREZE, Mr. Thomas Andrew George
GARFEN, Mr. David Leon
GARFEN, Mr. Gerald
GARFIELD, Mr. Alfred Marcel
GARLICK, Mrs. Kathryn Ann
GARNER, Mr. Stephen Charles John
GARNER, Mr. Thomas Ian
GARRATT, Mr. Mark Jonathan
GARRETT, Miss. Fiona Marie
GARRETT, Mrs. Helen Joan
GARRETT, Mr. Mark John Adam
GARRETT-BOWES, Mrs. Rosalind Josephine
GARRINGTON, Miss. Sandra
GARROD, Mr. Paul John
GARSIDE, Mr. Stephen Brian
GARTON, Mr. Philip Miles
GARWOOD, Mr. Paul Frederick
GASCOYNE, Mr. Barry
GASCOYNE-RICHARDS, Mrs. Rebecca Jane
GASKELL, Miss. Fiona Elizabeth
GASSON, Mr. Thomas William
GATES, Mr. Stephen John
GATLAND, Mr. Paul
GATTER, Mr. Stephen Martin
GAUSDEN, Mrs. Sally Anne

GAUTREY, Mr. Christopher
GAYLER, Mr. Andrew Martin
GAYMER, Mr. Nigel Anthony Plumptre
GE, Mr. Jia
GEARY, Mr. Andrew John
GEARY, Mr. Christopher Mark
GEARY, Mr. Peter Moray Grattan
GEDDES, Mr. Philip John
GEDGE, Mr. David Russell
GEDLING, Mr. Nicholas James
GEE, Mrs. Maureen Grace
GEE, Mr. Nicholas
GEE, Mr. Philip James
GEE, Mr. Stephen Malcolm
GEELAN, Miss. Lorraine Ann
GENDERS, Mr. David Boulton
GEORGE, Mr. Adrian Craven
GEORGE, Mr. Andrew Christopher
GEORGE, Mrs. Anna Helena Olesiuk
GEORGE, Mrs. Jeanette Anne
GEORGE, Mr. Michael David
GEORGE, Mr. Michael Richard
GEORGE, Mr. Richard Frank
GEORGE, Mrs. Victoria Anne
GEORGE, Mr. William John
GEORGIADES, Mr. Harris
GEORGIOU, Mr. Georgios
GEORGIOU, Mr. John
GERAGHTY, Mr. Thomas Patrick
GHATAURAY, Mr. Sundeep Singh
GHOSAL, Mr. Arnab Kumar
GHOSH, Mr. Pronab Kumar
GHUMRA, Mr. Yusuf Omar
GIBBONS, Mrs. Jennifer Ann Cathleen
GIBBONS, Mr. Michael Frederick
GIBBS, Mr. David Christopher
GIBBS, Mr. Mark Peter
GIBSON, Mr. David Anthony
GIBSON, Mr. David Arthur
GIBSON, Mrs. Joanna Clare
GIBSON, Mrs. Joelle
GIBSON, Mr. John Christopher
GIBSON, Mr. Martin
GIBSON, Mr. Matthew David
GIBSON, Mr. Robert Baird
GIBSON, Mr. Simon John
GIDDENS, Mr. Mark
GIESSLER, Mr. Paul Christopher
GIGG, Mrs. Kathryn Healy
GILBERT, Mr. Benjamin Charles
GILBERT, Mr. Brian John
GILBERT, Mr. Geoffrey Roy Freeman
GILBERT, Mr. Graham Geoffrey
GILBERT, Mr. Iain
GILBERT, Mr. Kevin Mark
GILBERT, Mr. Michael Harvey
GILBERTSON, Mr. John Gordon
GILBURN, Mr. David Alan
GILCHREASTE, Mr. Thomas Anthony
GILDERSLEEVES, Mr. Paul Simon
GILES, Mr. Alan Keith
GILES, Mrs. Linda
GILES, Mrs. Lorraine Ann
GILL, Mr. Charles
GILL, Mr. David Kevin
GILL, Mr. Gordon Melvyn
GILL, Mr. Jeffrey Edward
GILL, Mr. Robert James
GILL, Mr. Timothy Stuart
GILLAM, Mr. Neil Malcolm
GILLANI, Mr. Shamsher Esmail
GILLARD, Mr. David John
GILLARD, Mr. Roger
GILLBANKS, Mr. Neale William
GILLBE, Mrs. Jane Helen
GILLESPIE, Mr. Alexander
GILLETT, Mr. Timothy John
GILLIS, Mrs. Rosalyn
GILLIS, Mrs. Ruth Jane Prescott
GILLMORE, Mr. Frederick Charles
GILLOTT, Prof. Elizabeth
GILLOTT, Mrs. Elizabeth Sharon
GILMARTIN, Dr. Mark
GILMARTIN, Mr. Matthew Francis
GILMORE, Mr. Michael Joseph
GILMOUR, Mr. Walter Allison
GILROY, Mrs. Julie
GILROY, Mr. Nigel Howard
GIRDLESTONE, Mr. John
GIRLING, Mr. Roger Malcolm
GITTINS, Mr. Edward Watkin
GLADDERS, Mr. Kevin Michael
GLADWIN, Miss. Pamela
GLASMAN, Mr. Leslie
GLASMAN, Mr. Mark
GLASNER, Mr. Jonathan David
GLASS, Miss. Jenny Louise
GLASSMAN, Mr. David
GLASSON, Mr. Christopher James
GLATTER, Mrs. Helen
GLAZIER, Mr. Alan
GLEAVE, Mr. David Geraint
GLENCAIRN-CAMPBELL, Mr. Diarmid Cecil Brinton
GLOVER, Mrs. Emma Catharine
GLOVER, Mr. John Martin
GLOVER, Mr. Lindsey Richard

GLOVER, Mr. Neil Jonathan
GLYN-SMITH, Mr. Philip Anthony
GLYNN, Mr. Michael Boyde
GOAD, Mr. Ian Richard
GOATCHER, Mr. James
GODDARD, Mr. Anthony Michael
GODDARD, Mr. Iain Jackson
GODDEN, Mrs. Diana Mary
GODDEN, Mrs. Ruth Mary
GODFREY, Mr. Hugo John
GODFREY, Mr. Stephen
GODSELL, Mr. James Martin
GODSMARK, Mr. Martin Richard
GOFF, Mr. Brian Leslie
GOFFE, Mr. James Robert
GOH, Mr. John Oon Par
GOKOOL, Miss. Joanna Santos
GOLAN, Mr. Simon
GOLBEY, Mr. Geoffrey Philip
GOLD, Mr. Jeffrey David
GOLDBERG, Mr. David
GOLDICH, Mr. Lance Spencer
GOLDING, Mr. Anthony Peter
GOLDING, Mr. Nicholas Francis
GOLDING, Mr. Sean Thomas
GOLDSHMID, Mrs. Galit
GOLDSMITH, Mr. Peter
GOLDSMITH, Mr. William Richard Morgan
GOLDSTEIN, Mr. Michael
GOLDSTEIN, Mr. Michael David
GOLDSTEIN, Mr. Philip
GOLLOP, Geoffrey Richard
GOMPELS, Mrs. Susan Irene
GONZALEZ, Mrs. Margaret
GOOCH, Mr. Alan John
GOOD, Mr. Jonathan William
GOOD, Mr. Timothy James
GOODALL, Mr. Timothy Michael Charles
GOODCHILD, Mr. Martin Roy
GOODEY, Mr. Mark James Nicholas
GOODKIND, Mr. Clive Warren
GOODMAN, Mr. David
GOODMAN, Mr. Jonathan Harrison Moss
GOODMAN, Mr. Paul Joseph
GOODMAN, Mr. Peter Albert
GOODSON, Mrs. Suzanne Marie
GOODWIN, Mr. Christopher
GOODWIN, Mr. Glynn Leslie
GOODWIN, Mr. Robert Edward Osbon
GOODWIN, Mr. Stephen Paul
GOODYEAR, Mr. Geoffrey George
GOOLD, Mrs. Jane Louise
GOPSILL, Mr. Michael Clement
GORDON, Mr. Barry Allan
GORDON, Mr. Keith William
GORDON, Mr. Martyn John
GORDON, Mr. Stuart Thomas
GORDON-SMITH, Mr. David Robyn
GORDON STEWART, Mr. Julian Alistair
GORE, Mrs. Sharon Amanda
GOREHAM, Mr. Alan Charles
GORING, Mr. Anthony Robert
GORING, Mr. Keith Solomon
GORNALL, Mr. Michael James
GORROD, Mr. David Charles
GORROD, Mr. Philip Jeffrey
GORSE, Mr. John
GORTON, Mr. Jim
GORWALA, Miss. Khushnaz Feroze
GOSLING, Mr. Graham Martin
GOTHAM, Mr. Peter John
GOULD, Mr. David Mark Thomas
GOULD, Mr. Mark Philip
GOULD, Miss. Victoria Anne
GOUW, Mr. Peter Jan
GOVAN, Mr. Philip Morrison
GOVENDER, Mr. Bhashkaran
GOWDY, Mr. Barry Anthony
GOWER, Mr. Stuart Walton
GOWER-SMITH, Mr. Nicholas Mark
GRAFF, Mr. Howard Lester
GRAFF, Mrs. Sara Jane
GRAHAM, Mr. Carl Antony
GRAHAM, Mr. Colin Frank
GRAHAM, Mr. Darragh Michael Peter
GRAHAM, Mr. David Maurice
GRAHAM, Mr. David Michael
GRAHAM, Mr. Francis Leslie
GRAHAM, Mr. Glyn David
GRAHAM, Miss. Jane Wendy
GRAHAM, Mr. Jeffrey Malcolm
GRAHAM, Mr. John
GRAHAM, Mr. John Howard
GRAHAM, Miss. Lesley Anne
GRAHAM, Mrs. Marion
GRAHAM, Mr. Murray Maclellan
GRAHAM, Mr. Neil Robert
GRANAT, Mr. Joy Elizabeth
GRANGE, Mrs. Anthea Janice
GRANGER, Mr. Christopher Francis Kendall
GRANGER, Mr. Simon John
GRANT, Mr. Daniel Chaim
GRANT, Mr. Ian Jonathan
GRANT, Mrs. Janine
GRANT, Mr. Leon John
GRANT, Newton Keene
GRANT, Mr. Robert Raymond

GRANT, Mr. Stephen Paul
GRANT, Ms. Wendy Jane
GRASSAN, Mr. John Frederick
GRASSBY, Mr. Stephen Duncan
GRAVES, Mr. John Anthony
GRAVES, Mr. John Michael
GRAVES, Mr. Simon Peter
GRAVES, Mrs. Susan Menzies
GRAVETT, Mr. Michael Louis
GRAY, Mrs. Alexandra Judith
GRAY, Mr. Bruce Malcolm Lee
GRAY, Mrs. Claire Laura
GRAY, Mr. Colin Richard
GRAY, Mr. Derek Richard
GRAY, Mr. Gary Alan
GRAY, Miss. Hazel Margaret
GRAY, Mrs. Helen Judith
GRAY, Mr. Ian Stephen
GRAY, Mr. Matthew Grant
GRAY, Mrs. Sarah Lynn
GRAY, Mr. Stephen
GREATOREX, Mr. Raymond Edward
GREAVES, Mr. Cameron Geoffrey
GREELEY, Mr. Paul William
GREEN, Mr. Alexander Sonny
GREEN, Mr. Andrew Jonathan
GREEN, Mr. Charles Richard
GREEN, Mr. Clifford Charles
GREEN, Mr. David Michael
GREEN, Dr. Judith Margaret
GREEN, Mr. Keith Anthony
GREEN, Mr. Keith Charles
GREEN, Mr. Michael
GREEN, Miss. Natalie Ursula
GREEN, Mr. Norman Frank
GREEN, Mr. Paul Steven
GREEN, Mr. Raymond Michael
GREEN, Mr. Stephen Michael
GREEN, Miss. Susan Margaret
GREENBERG, Mr. Brian Stephen
GREENE, Mr. Christopher Randall
GREENE, Mr. David Antony
GREENE, Mr. Michael Edwin
GREENER, Mrs. Pamela Anne
GREENHALF, Mr. Niven Coats
GREENHALGH, Mr. Geoffrey Frank
GREENHALGH, Mr. Melvyn
GREENHALGH, Mr. Melvyn Ellis
GREENHALGH, Mr. Nigel Kent
GREENSILL, Mr. David Thomas
GREENSILL, Mr. Steven Mark
GREENSMITH, Mr. Peter
GREENWAY, Mr. Anthony William
GREENWOOD, Mr. Andrew
GREENWOOD, Mr. David Michael
GREENWOOD, Mr. David Scott
GREENWOOD, Mr. James Hall
GREENWOOD, Miss. Joanne Alison
GREENWOOD, Mr. John
GREENWOOD, Mr. Jonathan
GREENWOOD, Mr. Robert
GREEVES, Mr. Christopher John
GREEVES, Mr. Edward William
GREGORIADES, Mr. Angelos Michael
GREGORY, Mr. Adrian
GREGORY, Mrs. Alison Clare
GREGORY, Mrs. Catherine Ann
GREGORY, Mr. Clive
GREGORY, Mr. David Michael
GREGORY, Mrs. Helen Diana
GREGORY, Mr. Keith Anthony
GREGORY, Mrs. Linda Carol
GREGORY, Mrs. Margaret Elizabeth
GREGORY, Mr. Peter Michael
GREGORY, Mr. Robin Guy
GREGORY, Mr. Timothy Mark Thomas
GREGORY-JONES, Mrs. Anne Marie
GREIG, Mr. Michael William
GRENVILLE-BARKER, Mrs. Carol Ann
GRETTON, Mr. Richard John
GRICKS, Mr. Daniel David Thomas
GRIEVSON, Mr. Allen
GRIFFIN, Mr. Ben Charles
GRIFFIN, Mr. Terence James
GRIFFITH, Mr. Campbell Lloyd
GRIFFITH, Mr. George Henry Wilson
GRIFFITH, Mr. Paul Jeremy
GRIFFITH, Mrs. Samantha Georgina
GRIFFITHS, Mr. Andrew Bartholomew
GRIFFITHS, Mrs. Anne Thompson
GRIFFITHS, Mr. Anthony Charles
GRIFFITHS, Mr. David
GRIFFITHS, Mr. David Morley Arthur
GRIFFITHS, Mrs. Deborah
GRIFFITHS, Mr. Dorian Lyn
GRIFFITHS, Mr. Jolyon David Hewer
GRIFFITHS, Mrs. Julia Clare
GRIFFITHS, Mr. Peter Williams
GRIFFITHS, Mr. Stephen
GRIFFITHS, Mr. Stephen Clive
GRIGG, Miss. Jean Margaret
GRIGG, Mr. Robert Neil
GRIGGS, Mr. Geoffrey John
GRIGGS, Mrs. Julie Anita
GRIGGS, Mr. Stuart Arthur
GRIMES, Mr. Malcolm Patrick
GRIMLEY, Mr. Peter Anton Ninian

GRIMMER, Mrs. Julie Gail
GRIMSDELL, Mrs. Helen Margaret
GRIMSON, Mr. Neil Bernard Stuart
GRINSTED, Mr. Sean Andrew
GRIST, Miss. Helen Elizabeth
GROCOTT, Mr. Paul Martin
GROCOTT, Miss. Sarah Lindsay
GROENEWALD, Mr. Christo
GROMAN, Mr. Anthony Israel
GROSELEY, Mr. Reginald Keith
GROSS, Mr. Bernard
GROSS, Mr. Howard Anthony
GROSSMAN, Mr. Edward
GROUT, Mr. Andrew Philip
GROVE, Ms. Annette Veronica
GROVE, Mr. Graham Slater
GROVER, Mr. Rajesh
GROVES, Mr. Peter James
GRUBE, Miss. Sarah Jane
GRUNDY, Mr. John Richard
GUDKA, Mrs. Palvi
GUEST, Mr. David Anthony
GUEST, Mr. David Thomas
GUIDUZZI, Mr. Pierluigi
GUILFOYLE, Mr. Paul St John
GUILLIATT, Mr. Glenn William
GUINN, Mr. Peter Charles
GUIRY, Mr. Vincent Edward
GULABIVALA, Mr. Rajesh
GULLIVER, Mr. Peter
GUMBLEY, Mr. Christopher David
GUMMOW, Mr. Clive Frances
GUNARATNASINGAM, Ms. Athena Meera
GUNGAH, Mr. Dharmanand Neil
GUNN, Miss. Alice
GUNNEY, Mr. Colin Hugh
GUNNINGHAM, Mr. James Douglas
GUNSON, Mr. Martin Edward
GUNTER, Mrs. Amanda Jane
GUPTA, Mr. Brijinder Kumar
GUPTA, Mr. Simon
GUPTA, Mr. Sudheer
GURAV, Mr. Subhash Nivrutti
GURNEY, Mr. Martin Stuart
GUTHRIE, Mr. George Richard
GUY, Mr. Joseph Henry George
GUY, Mr. Kevin Andrew
GUY, Mr. Richard Benjamin
GWATKIN, Mr. Philip
GWILT, Mr. Jonathan Simon
GWYTHER, Miss. Julie Anne
GYDE, Mr. Mark David Andrew
HACKNEY, Mr. Howard Stanley
HACKNEY, Mr. John Christopher
HADDOW, Miss. Rachel Helen Pirie
HADFIELD, Mr. Nicholas James
HADFIELD, Mr. Philip James
HADJIHANNAS, Mr. Marios Felix
HADJINICOLAOU, Mr. Nicholas
HADJINICOLAOU, Mr. Yiangos
HADJIPAVLOU, Mr. George
HADLEY, Mr. David Iain
HADLEY, Mr. John Henry
HAFFENDEN, Mr. Richard Ian
HAGG, Mr. John Bevil
HAGGER, Mr. Barry Thomas
HAGON, Mr. Richard John
HAGUE, Mr. John Michael Richard
HAIGH, Miss. Alison Sarah
HAIGH, Mr. Peter Joseph
HAINING, Mr. Peter
HAINSWORTH, Mr. Robert James
HAKIM, Mr. Azra Ramsay
HALDER, Mr. Christopher William
HALE, Mr. John Stuart
HALE, Mr. Richard Kenneth
HALEY, Mr. Timothy John
HALFORD, Mr. Mark
HALL, Mrs. Caroline Heather
HALL, Miss. Catherine Ann
HALL, Mr. David Cameron
HALL, Mr. George Henry
HALL, Mrs. Jacqueline Lesley
HALL, Mr. Jan Yanick Stephen
HALL, Mr. Jason William
HALL, Mr. Julian
HALL, Mr. Keith
HALL, Mr. Kevin Robert
HALL, Mr. Mark James
HALL, Mr. Nathan Jamie
HALL, Mr. Nicholas Malcolm
HALL, Mr. Philip Jonathan
HALL, Mr. Richard Martin
HALL, Mr. Steven John
HALL, Mrs. Susan Linda
HALL-TOMKIN, Mr. Clive Neil
HALLETT, Mr. David
HALLETT, Mr. Stephen Charles
HALLIDAY, Mr. Paul
HALLIDAY, Mr. Philip Michael
HALLIDAY, Mrs. Susan Jane
HALLMARK, Mr. John Frederick
HALLS, Mrs. Nicola Ann
HALLSWORTH, Mr. Christopher
HALLYBONE, Mr. Michael John
HALSTEAD, Mr. John Stephen
HAM, Mr. John

JUDSON SMITH - LEFEVRE — Tax Faculty Members - Alphabetical

JUDSON SMITH, Mrs. Julia Margaret
JUKES, Mr. Brian Charles
JULIAN, Mr. John Terence
JULIAN, Miss. Suzanne Margaret
JULLEEKEEA, Mr. Rajesh Kumar
JUMP, Mr. Roger
JUNEMAN, Mr. Richard John
JUPP, Dr. Andrew Peter
JUPP, Mrs. Jane Elizabeth
JUPP, Dr. Sonia
JUSTICE, Mr. Robert George
JUTHANI, Mr. Kanak Kumar Rugnath
KABAN, Mr. Tugrul
KABINI, Mr. Alfred Freddy
KACHHELA, Miss. Trusha
KACHWALLA, Mrs. Nafisa
KADIRI, Mrs. Tasneem
KAGDADIA, Mr. Ashwin Govindji
KAHAN, Mr. Shlomo Alex
KAINTH, Mr. Sanjev
KAISER, Mrs. Julie Caroline
KAKKAD, Mr. Dilip Tulsidas
KALE, Mr. Yashodhan Madhusudan
KALRA, Mr. Anil
KAMAL, Mr. Javed
KAMBO, Mr. Harjinder Singh
KANAGARAJAH, Mr. Sutharman
KANAS, Mr. Philip Ellis
KANCZULA, Miss. Helena
KANE, Mr. Christopher
KANERIA, Mr. Amit
KANJI, Mr. Nizar Tajuddin
KAPADIA, Mr. Vijay Vissonji
KAPASI, Mr. Enayathusein Akbarali
KAPOOR, Miss. Meenakshi
KAPUR, Mr. Bankim Krishan
KARAGEORGHIS, Mr. Panayiotis
KARN, Mr. Lawrence William
KAROLIA, Mr. Ebrahim Bashir
KARSAN, Mr. Hassan Popat
KASSAMALI, Mr. Rizwan
KATARIA, Mr. Ashok
KATTE, Mr. Ian Paul
KATZ, Mr. Peter David
KAUFMAN, Miss. Rachelle Esther
KAVANAGH, Mr. Peter John
KAVANAGH, Mr. Steven Paul
KAY, Mr. Adam Michael
KAY, Mr. Adrian Charles Donald
KAY, Mr. Brian Richard
KAY, Mr. Melvin Clifford
KAY, Mr. Michael
KAY, Mr. Peter
KAY, Mr. Robert Gerald Charles
KAY, Mr. Stewart Jeffrey
KAY, Mr. Stuart James
KAYE, Mr. Jonathan Mark
KAYE, Mr. Martin Wallace
KAZI, Mr. Mohammed Aamir
KAZMI, Mr. Syed Humayun
KEARNEY, Mr. Kevin Gerard
KEAST, Mr. Wayne Bruce
KEATES, Mr. Brian Edward
KEATING, Mr. John Arthur
KEEBLE, Mr. Graham Charles
KEEBLE, Mr. Richard Francis
KEEHAN, Mrs. Jill
KEEL, Mr. Douglas Vincent
KEELEY, Mr. John
KEEN, Mr. Malcolm Fraser
KEENAN, Mr. Anthony William
KEENE, Mr. Adrian Charles
KEFFORD, Miss. Jennifer May
KEITH, Mrs. Lizanne Jayne
KEITH, Mr. Richard Anthony
KELLAND, Mr. Ian Michael
KELLEDY, Mrs. Deborah Ann
KELLEWAY, Mr. Noel Christopher
KELLEY, Mr. Anthony Leonard
KELLIE-SMITH, Mr. David Anthony
KELLY, Mrs. Jane Rosemary
KELLY, Mr. Jeffrey Neil
KELLY, Miss. Julie Dawn
KELLY, Mr. Lee Martin
KELLY, Ms. Mary Ellen
KELLY, Mr. Paul Anthony
KELLY, Mr. Peter
KELLY, Mr. Stephen
KELLY, Mr. Stephen John
KELSALL, Mrs. Sarah Louise
KEMAL, Mr. Altan
KEMBER, Mr. Matthew William
KEMP, Mr. Harry Charles
KEMP, Mrs. Susan Margaret
KEMPSTER, Mr. Peter
KENCH, Mr. Eric Arthur
KENDAL, Mr. Jonathan David
KENDALL, Mrs. Lynda
KENDALL, Mr. Richard John
KENDALL, Mr. Robert Norman
KENDELL, Mr. Philip John
KENNAN, Mr. Peter John
KENNARD, Mr. Andrew Marc Julian
KENNEDY, Mr. Stephen Michael James
KENNEDY, Mr. Daniel James
KENNEDY, Mr. Michael Andrew
KENNEDY, Mr. Paul Michael

KENNETT, Mrs. Melanie Anne
KENNY, Mr. Stephen Phillip
KENT, Ms. Judith Amanda
KENT, Mr. Martyn Robert
KENT, Mr. Michael Alan
KENT, Mr. Peter
KENT, Mr. Ronald Victor
KENT, Mr. Simon Andrew David
KENT, Mr. Stephen Michael
KENTAS, Mr. Michael
KENTON, Mr. Howard Neil
KENWELL, Mr. Robert
KENYON, Mr. Michael James
KENYON, Mr. Ronald James
KEOGAN, Mr. Anthony Gerard
KERBY, Mr. Stephen Michael
KERIN, Mrs. Fiona Ann
KERNON, Mr. Barry Patrick Waring
KERR, Mr. Andrew Thomas
KERR, Mr. John Francis Edward
KERRIDGE, Mr. Michael John
KERRY, Mrs. Adrienne Mary
KERRY, Mr. Stephen John
KERSHEN-FISHER, Mrs. Deborah Leah
KERSWILL, Miss. Leonie Christiane
KESBY, Mr. Stephen William
KESHANI, Mr. Mahmood
KESHANI, Mr. Mehboob
KETLEY, Mr. John Christopher
KETTLEWELL, Mr. John Simon
KEYTE, Mr. Malcolm William
KEYWORTH, Mr. Timothy David George
KHAKHRIA, Mr. Hilesh
KHALIL, Mr. Mohammad Kamran
KHALIQ, Mr. Hafiz Junaid
KHAN, Mr. Ferdous Ahmed
KHAN, Mr. Noor-Ul-Moobeen Sohail
KHAN, Mr. Parvez Aslam
KHAN, Mr. Rehan Shah
KHAN, Mr. Sarmad Ahmad
KHAN, Mr. Yasar Usman
KHAN-AHMED, Mrs. Saba Mahjabeen
KHANDERIA, Mr. Vinodray Savchand Narbheram
KHANNA, Mr. Atul
KHATIBI, Dr. Iraj
KHATRI, Mr. Mukesh Vallabh
KHATTAB, Mr. Basim
KHOKHAR, Mr. Khurshid Alam
KHOKHAR, Mr. Mohammad Irshad
KHONG, Ms. Yee Voon
KIBEL, Mr. Simon David
KIDSON, Mr. Charles Graham Douglas
KIEDISH, Mr. Mark James
KIEL, Mr. Eric Stanley
KIERNAN, Miss. Anne Maria
KIERNANDER, Mr. John Anthony
KILBURN, Mr. Martin Graham
KILBY, Mr. John David
KILCZEWSKI, Ms. Natasha Marion
KILMARTIN, Mr. Steven John
KILNER, Mr. David Leonard
KILROY, Mrs. Tina Arleene
KILSBY, Mr. Andrew James
KILSHAW, Mr. Andrew Donald
KILSHAW, Mr. Samuel James
KIMBERLEY, Mr. David Oliver
KINDRED, Mr. Alan Stuart
KING, Mr. Adrian Paul
KING, Mr. Colin Andrew
KING, Mr. David
KING, Mr. David William
KING, Mr. Duncan
KING, Mrs. Elizabeth Ann
KING, Mrs. Eshani Malika
KING, Mr. Jason
KING, Mr. John Rupert Charles
KING, Mr. Lionel
KING, Mrs. Mary Clare Augusta
KING, Mr. Michael Sidney
KING, Mr. Nicholas James
KING, Mr. Robert Forbes
KING, Mr. Robert Harvey Leeder
KING, Mr. Wayne Thomas
KING, Mr. William Roger
KINGDOM, Mr. Paul Anthony
KINGETT, Mr. Ian Nicholas
KINGON, Mrs. Wendy Margaret
KINGSLEY, Miss. Martine Clare
KINGSLEY, Mr. Michael John
KINGSLEY, Mr. Nigel
KINGSTON, Mr. Anthony John
KINGSTON, Mrs. Gaynor Elizabeth Verna
KINSEY, Mr. Martin Lowther
KIPLING, Mr. Geoffrey Paul
KIRALFY, Mr. Roger
KIRBY, Miss. Cecilia Ann
KIRBY, Mr. Michael Francis
KIRBY, Mr. Neil Gordon
KIRK, Mr. Bruce Anthony
KIRK, Mr. David Kirk
KIRK, Mr. Graham
KIRK, Mr. Martin Frederick
KIRK, Mr. Ronald Derek
KIRK, Mr. Timothy David
KIRKBRIDE, Mr. Mark Major Bowes
KIRKHAM, Mrs. Carolyn Jill

KIRKHAM, Mr. Frank David
KIRKHAM, Mr. Jeffery Allen
KIRKHAM, Mr. Stephen Paul John
KIRKHAM PARRY, Mr. Jeremy Patrick
KIRKLAND, Miss. Shelagh
KIRKLAND, Mr. David John
KIRKWOOD, Mr. David Ian
KIRKWOOD, Mr. John
KIRTON, Mr. Shane Edward
KISBY, Mr. Edward John
KITCHEN, Miss. Sarah
KITCHEN, Mr. William Vernon
KITE, Mrs. Barbara Patricia
KITE, Mr. Timothy James
KLEIN, Mr. Anthony Philip
KLEIN, Mr. Nicholas Jeffrey
KLEINMAN, Mr. Paul Raymond
KLEPZIG, Mr. Roland Peter
KNAGGS, Mr. Colin
KNAPTON, Mr. Anthony John
KNEE, Mr. Simon David
KNIGHT, Mr. Ashley Thomas
KNIGHT, Mrs. Christina Frances
KNIGHT, Mr. Colin Clifford
KNIGHT, Mr. David John
KNIGHT, Mr. David John
KNIGHT, Mrs. Elizabeth
KNIGHT, Mr. Geoffrey William
KNIGHT, Mrs. Krystyna Maria
KNIGHT, Mr. Philip Ivan
KNIGHT, Mr. Steven Andrew
KNIGHT-EVANS, Mr. Nigel David
KNIGHTS, Mr. Michael Timothy
KNIGHTS, Mr. Paul Andrew
KNOWLES, Mr. Anthony
KNOWLES, Mr. Nigel Mark
KNOWLES, Mr. Steven Dudley
KOCHANSKI, Mrs. Laura
KOCKELBERGH, Mr. Mark Charles
KOON KAM KING, Mr. David
KORMAN, Mr. Victor
KOTECHA, Mrs. Bindu
KOTECHA, Mr. Bipin
KOTECHA, Mr. Mukundrai Kanjibhai
KOTECHA, Mr. Pritesh Dharshi
KOTECHA, Miss. Shenai
KOTSOMITIS, Mr. Aristedes
KOZUBA-KOZUBSKA, Miss. Danuta Ann
KRAITT, Mr. Michael Stanley
KRANTZ, Mr. Martyn Ralph
KRIPALANI, Mr. Mohan
KROL, Mr. Christopher Jan
KRONBERGS, Mr. Zigurds Guntis
KUMAR, Mr. Ranjan
KUMAR, Ms. Susan
KURCHENKO, Mrs. Anna
KURESHI, Mr. Kamal Ahmed
KURZ, Mr. Stuart Leon
KUTTEN, Mrs. Lindsey Lee
KWAN, Mr. Sai Leung
KYLE, Miss. Renee Sheffield
KYPRIANOU, Mr. Chrysostomos
KYRIAKIDES, Mr. Christakis Nicolaou
KYRIAKIDES, Mr. Michael
LABATON, Mr. Adrian
LACEY, Mr. Ian John
LACEY, Mr. Neville Denis
LACEY, Mr. Richard Donald
LACOME, Mr. Gerald Anthony
LADANOWSKI, Miss. Kathryn
LADIMEJI, Mr. Oladapo Alani
LAGERBERG, Mrs. Francesca Clare
LAI-PAT-FONG, Miss. Suzanne
LAITNER, Mr. Stewart Anthony
LAITY, Mr. Jason Scott
LAKE, Mrs. Gillian Patricia
LAKE, Ms. Jane Anne
LAKE, Mr. Simon Neville
LAKHA, Mr. Azim Mohamedali Sunderji
LAKHANI, Mr. Jayendra Sunderji
LAKHANI, Mr. Kaushik Jagjivan
LAKHANI, Mr. Satish
LAKHANI, Miss. Sonal
LAKIN, Mr. Keith
LALLEMAND, Mr. Christopher John
LAM, Mrs. Linda Chay Leng
LAM, Ms. Pik Kwan
LAMB, Mr. Anthony Noel
LAMB, Mr. Charles Sebastian
LAMB, Mr. Ian Robert
LAMB, Mr. Stephen
LAMB, Mr. Stephen James
LAMBDEN, Mr. James Percival
LAMBERT, Mr. Christopher James
LAMBERT, Mrs. Kathryn Ruth
LAMBERT, Mr. Michael Anthony
LAMBERT, Mr. Richard John
LAMBERTH, Mrs. Joanne Elizabeth
LAMBOURNE, Mr. John Horace
LAMBSON, Mrs. Margaret Elizabeth
LAMONT, Mr. Graham William
LAMPARD, Mr. Anthony
LAMSTAES, Mr. Pierre Gaetan
LANCASTER, Mr. Arthur John
LANCASTER, Mrs. Carolyn Jane
LANCASTER, Mr. David Michael
LANCASTER, Mr. Ian Callander

LAND, Mr. Christopher John
LAND, Mr. Maurice Jack
LAND, Mr. Paul Douglas
LANDERGAN, Mr. Philip Martin
LANDES, Mr. Steven Harry
LANDON, Mr. James Frederic
LANDON, Mr. Peter Lawrence
LANDON, Mr. Robin Edward
LANE, Mr. Andrew Charles
LANE, Mr. Christopher John
LANE, Mr. Geoffrey Charles
LANE, Mr. Julian Dai
LANE, Mr. Norman Arnold
LANG, Mr. Andrew Charles D'arcy
LANGDON, Mr. Patrick John
LANGDON, Mr. Paul Frederick
LANGER, Mr. Eric Graham
LANGFIELD, Mr. John Michael
LANGFORD, Mr. Reginald
LANGLANDS, Mr. Robert
LANGRIDGE, Mr. David Henry
LANGTON-DAVIES, Mrs. Melanie Jane
LANKESTER, Mr. Clive Arthur
LANSDELL, Mr. Michael Roy
LANSDOWN, Mr. Ian Gregory
LANT, Mr. Stephen
LAPTHORN, Mr. David Edwin Richard
LARGE, Mr. David John
LARSEN, Mr. David Brinsley
LARSEN, Mr. Michael Joseph
LASK, Mr. Hugh Michael
LAST, Mrs. Kay Barbara
LATHAM, Mr. Graham William
LATHAM, Mr. Neil Andrew
LATIF, Mr. Quazi Abdul
LATIMER, Mrs. Gillian Valerie
LATIMER, Mr. Nicholas John
LAU, Mr. Cheong Seng
LAU, Mr. Peter Wing Wing
LAVENTURE, Mr. Brian George
LAVERTY, Mr. Patrick John
LAW, Ms. Lorraine Nicola
LAW, Mrs. Louise Marie
LAW, Miss. Yee Man
LAWES, Mr. Christopher William
LAWES, Mrs. Susan Jacqueline
LAWLAN, Mr. John Ross Binks
LAWLOR, Mr. Paul Joseph
LAWRENCE, Mr. John Robert
LAWRENCE, Mr. Martin
LAWRENCE, Mrs. Sally
LAWSON, Mr. Charles Bruce Farquharson
LAWSON, Miss. Lucy Anne
LAWSON, Mr. Marc
LAWSON, Mr. Tony Harold
LAY, Mr. Richard John
LAYLAND, Miss. Tracy-Lee
LAYZELL, Mr. Thomas Richard
LAZAROU, Mr. Yiannakis Phidia
LAZDA, Mrs. Angela Christine
LE BRAS, Mr. Stephen Jean Armand James
LE CLAIRE, Mr. Bernard Michael
LE FLEMING, Mrs. Barbara Maria
LE GRYS, Mrs. Carol Annn
LE MAITRE, Mrs. Jane Anne
LE POIDEVIN, Miss. Fiona Louise Amy
LE RAY, Mr. Stephen
LEA, Mrs. Desirie Dolores
LEA, Mr. Michael David
LEA, Mrs. Sally Elizabeth
LEACH, Mr. Huw Mostyn
LEACH, Mr. Robert
LEACH, Mr. Simon
LEADBEATER, Mr. David
LEAF, Mr. Michael John
LEAKE, Mr. John David
LEAR, Mr. Andrew Nicholas
LEAR, Mr. Christopher Martin
LEAR, Mr. David Alan
LEARMONTH, Mr. Christopher James
LEATHEM, Mrs. Susan Elizabeth
LEATHER, Mr. Michael Robert
LEAVER, Mr. Kevin John
LEDINGHAM, Mr. Nicholas Orme
LEE, Mr. Andrew Chiu Man
LEE, Mr. Antoine Yim Ok
LEE, Mr. Brian Martin
LEE, Mr. Charles Robert
LEE, Mr. David Leslie
LEE, Mr. Derek John
LEE, Mr. Howard Patrick
LEE, Mr. John David
LEE, Mr. Mark Nigel
LEE, Mr. Michael John
LEE, Mr. Patrick William
LEE, Mr. Paul Anthony
LEE, Mr. Peter John
LEE, Mr. Phillip
LEE, Mr. Robin
LEE, Mr. Roger David
LEE, Mr. Yoke Hing
LEECH, Mr. Christopher John
LEEMAN, Mr. Timothy Guy
LEES, Mr. David Arthur
LEES-BUCKLEY, Mr. Lewis Gary
LEESE, Mr. David Brian
LEFEVRE, Mrs. Ellen Margaret

LEGGETT, Mr. Robert David
LEGGETT, Mr. Russell Alan
LEIBOVITCH, Mr. Barry
LEIGH, Mr. Barry
LEIGH, Mr. Barry Malcolm
LEIGH, Mr. Gareth John
LEIGH, Mr. Graham Charles
LEIGH, Mr. Ian
LEIGH, Mr. John Raymond
LEIGH, Mr. Michael Arnold
LEIGH, Mr. Michael Richard
LEIGHTON, Mr. Richard Martin
LELLIOTT, Mr. Timothy John
LEMON, Mr. David
LENNEY, Mrs. Susanna Loretta
LEONARD, Mr. John Douglas
LEONARD, Mr. Richard John
LEONG, Mr. Michael Chee Loke
LEONIDOU, Mr. Leonidas Anastasis
LERMAN, Mr. Michael
LERMER, Mr. Jeffrey Ian
LERMON, Mr. David Nicholas
LERNER, Mr. Michael Anthony
LERNER, Mr. Stephen Ian
LESLIE, Mrs. Nadine Lucy
LESLIE, Mr. Richard Andrew
LESSER, Mr. Stephen Morris
LESTER, Mr. Mark Adrian
LESTER, Mr. Michael Patrick
LEVER, Mr. Simon Alan
LEVER, Mrs. Susan
LEVI, Mr. Philip John
LEVINE, Mr. Anthony Ronald
LEVINE, Mr. Steven Richard
LEVINE, Mrs. Tanya Sima
LEVINSON, Mr. Pesah David
LEVITT, Mr. Mark Joseph
LEVY, Mr. Anthony
LEVY, Mr. Brian Francis
LEVY, Mr. Jason Paul
LEVY, Mr. Julian Isaac
LEVY, Mr. Neville
LEW, Mr. David Norman
LEWIN, Mr. Raymond John
LEWINDON, Mr. Kenneth
LEWIS, Mr. Alan John
LEWIS, Mr. Barnaby James
LEWIS, Mr. Barry David
LEWIS, Mr. Christopher
LEWIS, Mr. David Michael
LEWIS, Miss. Elizabeth Jayne
LEWIS, Mr. Gethin William
LEWIS, Mr. Graham
LEWIS, Miss. Helen Louise
LEWIS, Mr. Ian Macintyre
LEWIS, Mr. James Barrow
LEWIS, Mr. John Ernest
LEWIS, Mr. Kenneth Raymond
LEWIS, Mr. Martin Allen
LEWIS, Mr. Matthew John
LEWIS, Mr. Michael Victor
LEWIS, Mr. Nicholas Charles
LEWIS, Miss. Patricia
LEWIS, Mr. Paul William
LEWIS, Mr. Philip Andrew John
LEWIS, Mr. Richard Wayne
LEWIS, Mr. Robert Price
LEWIS, Mr. Simon Mark Henry
LEWIS - JAMES, Mrs. Rhian
LEYHANE, Mr. Dennis Frederick
LI, Mr. George Wing Chung
LI, Mr. Kwan Hung
LIDDELL, Mr. Nigel John
LIDDLE, Miss. Joyce Rosanne
LIEW, Miss. Suet Fei
LIGGATT, Mr. Andrew Alexander
LILADHAR, Mr. Anup
LILLINGSTON, Mr. Andrew Harry
LILLYCROP, Mr. Robert
LIM, Mr. Kheng Hock
LINARD, Mr. Keith William
LINCROFT, Dr. Christopher David
LINDFORD, Mr. Terence John
LINDLEY, Mr. Michael Denis
LINDLEY, Mr. Steven
LINDSAY, Mr. David Robert Hamish
LINDSAY, Mr. Grahame Duncan Gordon
LINDSAY, Mr. John McGlashan
LINDSAY, Mr. Keith
LINDSAY, Mrs. Patricia May
LINDSAY, Mr. Peter John
LINDSELL, Miss. Denise Rebecca
LINDSEY, Mr. Alan Michael
LINDSEY, Mr. Brian
LINDSEY, Mr. Simon Nicholas Merry
LINGHAM, Mr. Nagalingam Thiyaga
LINGHAM, Mr. Peter
LINK, Mr. Charles Richard Stephen
LINLEY, Mr. Simon Timothy
LINNELL, Miss. Kay Catherine Sheila Hilary
LINTOTT, Mr. Andrew Douglas
LINTOTT, Mr. Martin Stephen David
LIPKIN, Mr. Edward Barry
LIPOWICZ, Mr. Leslie Michael
LISHAK, Mr. Jeffrey
LISLE, Mr. Stuart Roger
LISTER, Mr. Andrew

LISTER, Mr. Anthony Francis
LISTER, Miss. Deborah
LISTER, Mr. John Prentice
LITCHFIELD, Mrs. Julia Anne
LITHERLAND, Mr. Guy
LITTEN, Mr. Mathew Francis
LITTLE, Mr. Anthony
LITTLE, Mr. Charles William
LITTLE, Mr. Geoffrey Michael
LITTLE, Mr. James
LITTLE, Mr. Richard Anthony
LITTLECHILD, Mr. Robert John
LITTLEFAIR, Ms. Linda Frances
LITTLEJOHNS, Mr. Simon
LITTLER, Mr. Philip John
LIU, Mr. Nicholas Ying Shan
LIVESEY, Miss. Gwendoline Ann
LIVINGSTON, Mr. Steven Charles
LIVINGSTONE, Mr. Andrew
LLOYD, Mr. Andrew John
LLOYD, Mr. Anthony Joseph
LLOYD, Mr. Bedford Steven Miles
LLOYD, Mrs. Clare
LLOYD, Mr. David Martin
LLOYD, Mr. Martin Richard
LLOYD, Mr. Timothy John
LLOYD, Mr. Trevor Graham
LLOYD, Mr. William David
LLOYDBOTTOM, Mr. Mark Gabriel
LO SEEN CHONG, Mr. Deans Tommy
LOAKE, Mr. Richard Ashwell
LOBBENBERG, Mrs. Kathryn Eluned John
LOCK, Mr. Cyril John
LOCK, Mr. Michael Derrick
LOCK, Mr. Richard Alan
LOCKE, Mrs. Mary Elizabeth
LOCKEY, Mr. Eric
LOCKS, Mr. John George Melbourne
LODGE, Mr. Graham John
LODGE, Mr. Toby Daniel
LODGE, Mr. Trevor Drabes
LOE, Mrs. Penelope Sara
LOEBL, Mr. John Charles
LOESCHER, Mr. Jonathan Andrew
LOFTHOUSE, Mr. John Stephen
LOFTHOUSE, Mr. Philip John
LOFTS, Mr. Malcolm Charles
LOGAN, Mr. Dean Russell
LOGAN, Mr. Mark Derek
LOGAN, Mr. Ross
LOIZIDES, Miss. Sylvia A
LOIZOU, Mr. Panayiotis George
LOMAS, Mr. Paul James
LOMAS, Mr. Philip Guy
LOMAX, Mr. Clifford Kenneth
LONERGAN, Mr. Roy John
LONG, Mr. Alan Edward
LONG, Mr. Christopher John
LONG, Mr. Gordon Andrew
LONG, Mr. Paul
LONG, Mr. Philip
LONG, Mr. Raymond John Ian
LONG, Mr. Robert Edward
LONGHILL, Mrs. Sarah Ann
LONGLEY, Mr. Michael Richard
LONGMAN, Mr. Michael John
LONGTON, Mr. David Russell
LONSDALE, Mrs. Pauline Ann
LOOCHIN, Mr. Ivor Bernard
LOPIAN, Mr. David Zvi
LOPIAN, Mr. Simon Abner
LORAM, Mr. Jonathan Jeffrey
LORD, Miss. Rachel
LORD, Mr. Stephen John
LORIMER, Mr. Andrew Charles
LOUGHNANE, Mrs. Terence John
LOUGHREY, Mr. Mark John
LOUTIT, Mr. Paul Morris
LOVELADY, Mr. Andrew Robert
LOVELL, Mrs. Julia Susan
LOVERING, Mr. Roger Vincent
LOVETT, Mr. Andrew Barrington
LOVITT, Mr. Robert John Clarke
LOWE, Mr. David
LOWE, Mr. Gareth Lloyd
LOWE, Mr. Merryck Brandon
LOWER, Mr. Paul Richard
LOWTHORPE, Mr. Michael
LUCAS, Mr. Giles David
LUCAS, Mr. Michael Robert
LUCAS, Mr. Peter Reginald
LUCAS, Miss. Rosemary Carol
LUCK, Mr. George Anton
LUCKETT, Mr. Philip Jeffery
LUCKING, Mr. William Raymond
LUGG, Mr. Roger Bruce
LUHRS, Mrs. Nicola Katharine
LUK, Mr. Yui Chow
LUKE, Mrs. Ann
LUKE, Mr. Colin Douglas
LUKE, Mr. Jason Howard
LUKES, Mr. David Ronald Mark
LUKES, Mr. Jonathan Charles
LUNDERVOLD, Mr. Chris Alexander
LUNG, Mr. Raymond Ka-Hon
LUNN, Mr. Melvyn
LUNT, Miss. Diane Margaret

LUNT, Mr. Martin Henry Charles
LUNT, Mr. Martin Keith
LUSCOMBE, Mr. Gerald Arthur
LUTHRA, Mr. Vishwa Nath
LUXFORD, Mr. Keith
LWIN, Mr. Kevin Timothy David
LYDDON, Mr. John William
LYFORD, Mr. Timothy John
LYMN, Mr. Anthony John
LYMN, Miss. Carolyn Jane
LYNAM, Mrs. Gemma
LYNCH, Mr. Barry Michael
LYNCH, Mrs. Clare Elizabeth
LYNCH, Mr. David John
LYNCH, Mr. John Anthony
LYNCH, Mr. John David
LYNCH, Mr. Roger John Christopher
LYND, Mrs. Anoushka
LYNN, Miss. Catherine Ann
LYON, Mr. Donald Malcolm
LYON, Mrs. Nicolena Ella
LYON, Mr. Stephen John
LYONS, Mrs. Cheryl Anne
LYONS, Mr. Christopher John
LYONS, Mr. David Albert
LYONS, Mr. John Robert
LYONS, Mr. Richard Anthony
LYONS, Mr. Timothy Rayner
LYTHGOE, Mr. John Stephen
MAAS, Mr. Robert William
MABEY, Mr. John Colin
MACAREE, Mrs. Kathryn Eluned John
MACARTHUR, Miss. Jane Linda
MACASKILL, Mrs. Caroline Elaine
MACAULAY, Mr. David John
MACCALLUM, Mr. Neil Herbertson
MACCORKINDALE, Mr. Peter Duncan
MACDONALD, Mr. Alistair John
MACDONALD, Mr. David Charles
MACDONALD, Mr. Lawson Ranald
MACDONALD, Mr. Mervyn John
MACDONALD, Mr. Philip John
MACDOUGALL, Mr. Diarmuid Joseph Declan
MACDOUGALL, Mr. Forbes Duncan Rogers
MACEY, Mr. Christopher Eric
MACEY, Miss. Hazel
MACFARLANE, Mr. Norman Barclay
MACGILLIVRAY, Mr. Alasdair Duncan
MACGILLIVRAY, Mr. Ian Alistair
MACGREGOR, Mr. Ian David
MACGREGOR, Mr. Neil Holden
MACHARG, Mr. Walter Maitland
MACHELL, Mr. Ronald
MACHIN, Mr. Howard Neil
MACHIN, Mr. Ronald Thomas
MACINTOSH, Mrs. Tracey Anne
MACK, Mrs. Jacqueline Holt
MACKAY, Mrs. Antonia Jane
MACKENZIE, Mr. Anthony Thomas Dorman Buist
MACKENZIE, Mr. Iain Stuart
MACKENZIE, Mrs. Rachel Louise
MACKENZIE, Mr. Ruairidh Iain
MACKIE, Mr. Alan Graham
MACKIE, Mrs. Andrea
MACKIE, Mr. John Taylor
MACKINLAY, Mr. Craig
MACKINNON, Mr. Iain Francis
MACKLIN, Mr. Joseph David
MACLEOD, Mr. Donald Iain
MACLUCAS, Mr. Ian David
MACNAY, Mr. Bruce William
MACORISON, Mrs. Valerie Susan
MACRAE, Mr. Gregor Charles William
MACRAE, Mrs. Susan Joanna
MADAMS, Mr. James Richard
MADANI, Mr. Jignesh Shashikant Amilal
MADDEN, Mr. Edward Timothy
MADDERS, Miss. Rosemary Margaret
MADDISON, Mr. Edward John
MADDOX, Mr. Geoffrey
MADDRELL, Mr. Joe Hankin
MADEWELL, Mr. William Guy
MADGE, Mr. Christopher Bartholomew
MADGIN, Mrs. Catharine Jane
MADON, Mr. Khurshed Russy
MAEER, Mrs. Jane Elizabeth
MAEER, Miss. Tracey Jane
MAGAGNIN, Miss. Amanda Louise
MAGGS, Mr. Roger Philip
MAGINNIS, Mr. Robert
MAGRATH, Mr. Mark Robert George
MAGUIRE, Mr. Martin Patrick
MAHABIR-SINGH, Mr. Mohan
MAHADEO, Mr. Hemraj
MAHALLATI-KAZEMEINI, Mr. Abdol-Majid
MAHMUD, Mr. Nasir
MAHOMED, Mrs. Shamim
MAHON, Mr. Andrew Philip
MAHON, Mr. John Macmahon
MAHONEY, Mr. Anthony Gerard
MAIDMENT, Mr. Bruce William
MAIDSTONE, Mr. Andrew John
MAITLAND, Mr. Andrew Reginald Campbell
MAJAINAH, Mr. Nowzer
MAJOR, Mr. Guy Alexander

MAJOR, Mrs. Sarah Dawn
MAKAN, Mr. Dhirajlal
MALCOLM, Mr. Andrew James
MALCOLM, Mr. Gary Neil
MALDE, Miss. Anita
MALDE, Mr. Kirankumar Vaghji
MALDE, Mr. Nishith
MALDE, Mr. Rajiv Pravinlal
MALEWICZ, Mr. David John
MALEWSKI, Mr. Peter Stanislaw
MALIK, Mr. Jamshed
MALKIN, Mr. Roland Spencer Norman
MALL, Mr. Lekh Raj
MALLAGHAN, Mr. Gerard John
MALLETT, Mr. Kevin Anthony
MALLEY, Mr. Paul Mathew
MALLON, Mr. Timothy John
MALONEY, Mr. Christopher George
MALTHOUSE, Mr. John Christopher
MAMDANI, Mr. Shabir Roshanali
MAMUJEE, Mr. Azam Najmudin
MAN, Mr. Chiu Ming
MAN, Mr. Shing Chun
MAN, Mr. Victor Tsinkeung
MANAKTALA, Mr. Pradeep
MANCHANDA, Mr. Rajiv
MANDAIR, Miss. Baldish Kaur
MANDALE, Miss. Nicola
MANFREDI, Mrs. Tracy
MANGAN, Mrs. Lucy Victoria
MANGAT, Mr. Harminder Singh
MANJRA, Mr. Mohamed Yacoob
MANKELOW, Mr. Peter Kenneth
MANLEY, Mrs. Julia Anne
MANN, Mr. David Jonathan
MANN, Mr. Richard John
MANN, Mr. Richard William
MANNAN, Mr. Salman Ahmad
MANNANI, Miss. Zohra
MANNING, Mrs. Pauline Rose
MANNION, Mr. Richard Francis
MANNOOCH, Mr. David James
MANOLESCUE, Mr. George Victor
MANSBRIDGE, Mr. Adrian Charles
MANSER, Mr. Peter Andrew Ronald
MANSON, Mr. Jeremy
MANTON, Mr. Simon Paul
MANTZ, Mr. William Stewart
MARAIA, Mr. Antonio
MARCHANT, Mr. Geoffrey Keith
MARCHANT, Mr. Roger
MARCOU, Mr. Aristides
MARCUS, Mr. Michael David
MARDLE, Mr. Alain Richard
MARGETTS, Mr. Peter
MARJORAM, Mr. John Charles
MARJORAM, Mrs. Sarah
MARK, Mrs. Lesley Carolyn
MARKHAM, Mr. Howard Saul
MARKHAM, Mr. John Michael Gervase
MARKHAM, Mr. Matthew Anthony
MARKLEY, Mr. Stuart James
MARKOU, Mr. Demetrios
MARKOU, Mr. Pieris
MARKS, Mr. David
MARKS, Mr. David Norman
MARKS, Mrs. Jennifer Helen
MARKS, Mr. Michael
MARKS, Mr. Michael John
MARKS, Mr. Philip Conrad
MARLOW, Mrs. Doreen Vivienne
MARR, Mr. Robert Andrew
MARRIOTT, Mr. David Paul
MARRIOTT, Mr. Martin John
MARRIS, Mr. Robert Frederick
MARRISON, Mr. Andrew James
MARSDEN, Miss. Caroline
MARSDEN, Mr. Michael Frank
MARSDEN, Mr. Peter Charles
MARSDEN, Mr. Robert Greig
MARSH, Mr. Brian Colin
MARSH, Mr. Christopher John
MARSH, Mrs. Gaynor
MARSH, Mr. Howard
MARSH, Mr. Michael John
MARSH, Mrs. Rowena Mary
MARSH, Mr. Terence George
MARSHALL, Mr. Anthony John
MARSHALL, Mr. David Clifford
MARSHALL, Mrs. Deirdre Patricia
MARSHALL, Mr. Duncan Richard
MARSHALL, Mr. Edward
MARSHALL, Mrs. Jennifer Ann
MARSHALL, Mr. John
MARSHALL, Mr. Jonathan Marcus
MARSHALL, Mr. Paul
MARSHALL, Mr. Paul Ernest Francis
MARSHALL, Mr. Paul Francis
MARSHALL, Mr. Philip Norman
MARSHALL, Mr. Richard Leslie Barnett
MARSON, Mr. Francis John
MARTELL, Mr. John Peter
MARTIN, Mrs. Alison Marie
MARTIN, Mr. Andrew Thomas
MARTIN, Mr. Anthony Graham
MARTIN, Mr. Anthony Patrick
MARTIN, Mrs. Barbara Elizabeth

MARTIN, Mrs. Clare Louise
MARTIN, Mr. Craig
MARTIN, Mr. David William
MARTIN, Mr. Frank
MARTIN, Mr. Ian Frederick
MARTIN, Mr. John William Rolfe
MARTIN, Mr. Malcolm
MARTIN, Mrs. Marilyn
MARTIN, Mr. Mark John
MARTIN, Mr. Michael Leigh
MARTIN, Mr. Nicholas Ford
MARTIN, Mr. Philip Jeremy
MARTIN, Mr. Roy Christopher
MARTIN, Mrs. Sheila Isabel
MARTIN, Mrs. Shirley Anne
MARTIN, Mr. Timothy Ian
MARTIN, Mr. Trevor Caleb
MARTIN-LONG, Mrs. Valerie Anne
MARTIN-SKLAN, Mr. Alexander
MARTINS, Mr. Steven Mark
MARWOOD, Mr. Philip David La Borde
MASLEN, Mr. Christopher John
MASLEN, Mrs. Susan Elaine
MASON, Mr. Colin Andrew
MASON, Mr. Colin John Stewart
MASON, Frank Charles
MASON, Mrs. Patricia Mary
MASON, Mr. Peter Robert
MASON, Mr. Peter William
MASON, Mr. Richard David
MASON, Mr. Richard John Spencer
MASON, Mr. Richard Michael
MASSEY, Mrs. Alison Eve
MASSEY, Mr. Anthony Stephen
MASSEY, Mr. Paul Andrew
MASSEY, Mr. Simon James
MASSINGALE, Mrs. Moira
MASSINGBERD-MUNDY, Mrs. Janet
MASSON, Mr. Kenneth Ely Brooke
MASTERMAN-SMITH, Mrs. Fiona
MASTERS, Mr. Robert
MASTERS, Mr. Roger Gerald
MATE, Mr. Andrew Paul
MATEJTSCHUK, Mrs. Susan Carol
MATHARU, Mrs. Rominda
MATHERS, Mr. Alastair McLeod
MATHEWS, Mr. Roger Gordon
MATHIESON, Mrs. Elizabeth Anne
MATHIESON, Mrs. Kristina Annette
MATLEY, Mr. David Nuttall
MATTHAMS, Mr. William James
MATTHEWS, Mr. Anthony John
MATTHEWS, Mr. Barry John
MATTHEWS, Miss. Elizabeth Anne
MATTHEWS, Mr. Janek Paul
MATTHEWS, Miss. Lucia Mary Caitriona
MATTHEWS, Mr. Nicholas George
MATTHEWS, Miss. Philippa Anne
MATTHEWS, Mr. Richard John
MATTHEWS, Mr. Robert Edmund
MATTHEWS, Mr. Rupert Nicholas Charles
MATTHIAE, Ms. Judith
MAUGHAM, Mr. Alan Bryan
MAULTBY, Mr. David Herbert
MAULTBY, Mrs. Ella Joy
MAUNDRELL, Mr. Colin Neil
MAUNSULTY, Mr. Robin Guy Debonnaire
MAURICE, Mr. Paul Gary
MAVANI, Mr. Rajesh Anantray
MAVRON, Mr. Panycos Chris
MAW, Mr. David John
MAW, Mr. Peter Loseby Trentham
MAWBY, Mr. Timothy Joseph
MAWHOOD, Mr. Richard
MAXFIELD, Mr. Andrew Michael
MAXWELL, Mrs. Helen Mary
MAY, Mr. Kenton Charles
MAY, Mr. Martin Irvin
MAY, Mr. Michael Robert
MAYERS, Mr. Patrick Guy
MAYES, Mr. Raymond John
MAYFIELD, Mr. David Thomas
MAYFIELD, Mr. Kim
MAYLED, Mr. Stephen John
MAYNARD, Mrs. Jane Carter
MAYNES, Mr. Jeremy John
MAYOR, Mr. Sandeep
MAYSTON, Mr. Albert Peter
MAZZOTTI, Mr. Gary Wheatley
MCADAM, Mrs. Helen Mott
MCALEAVY, Mr. Francis
MCALPINE, Mrs. Pauline Blair
MCANOY, Mr. Gordon Ashley
MCARDLE, Mr. Eamonn Michael
MCAREAVEY, Mr. Paul George
MCAUGHEY, Mr. Peter John
MCBRIDE, Mr. Peter
MCBRIDE, Mr. Richard Thomas John
MCBURNEY, Mr. James
MCCANDLESS, Mr. Christopher Paul
MCCANN, Mr. Ian
MCCARTHY, Mr. Timothy Joseph Mary
MCCARTHY, Mr. Denis Fighin Knox
MCCARTNEY, Mr. Alan Leonard
MCCAY, Mr. James Brendan
MCCLURE, Mrs. Teresa Ann
MCCLUSKY, Mr. Andrew

MCCOMBE, Mr. Gary Stephen
MCCORMICK, Mrs. Andrea Elizabeth
MCCORMICK, Ms. Nora
MCCOUBREY, Miss. Anne Elizabeth
MCCOWIE, Mr. George
MCCOY, Mr. Colin Edward
MCCULLOCH, Mr. Robert
MCCULLOUGH, Mr. John Patrick
MCDERMOTT, Mr. Brian Patrick
MCDERMOTT, Miss. Jannine Sandra
MCDONAGH, Mr. Raymond Thomas
MCEVILLY, Mr. Robin Angelo
MCEWAN, Mrs. Emma Margaret Jeanne
MCFADYEN, Mr. Christopher Alec
MCFARLANE, Mr. Iain Alexander
MCFARLANE, Miss. Roslyn Grace
MCFIE, Mr. Peter Andrew Charles
MCGARRY, Mr. Mark Dominic
MCGHEE, Mr. Alexander Freeburn
MCGHIE, Mr. Graham Thomas
MCGINLEY, Mr. James Benedict
MCGINTY, Mr. Robert Gerard Anton
MCGLADE, Mrs. Marie-Claire
MCGOVERN, Mr. Anthony Gerard
MCGOWAN, Dr. Victoria Anne
MCGREGOR, Mrs. Anne Maxwell
MCGUINNESS, Mr. Stephen John
MCGURGAN, Mr. Dennis Anthony
MCHALE, Mr. James Joseph
MCHATTIE, Mr. Frederick
MCHUGH, Mrs. Lynne Diane
MCILRATH, Ms. Lisa Jayne
MCINERNEY, Mr. Robert Andrew
MCINNES, Mr. Timothy Ian
MCINTOSH, Mr. Philip Ian
MCKAY, Miss. Fiona Jean
MCKAY, Ms. Gillian Jamieson
MCKELVIE, Mr. Allan William
MCKENNA, Mr. Mark
MCKENNA, Mr. Michael David
MCKENZIE, Lord William David
MCKENZIE, Mr. William Ernest
MCKERAN, Mr. Alexander Charles
MCKIE, Mr. Simon Peter
MCKINNELL, Mr. Malcolm William
MCLAREN, Miss. Alison
MCLAUGHLIN, Mr. Ian Stuart
MCLAUGHLIN, Mr. James Henry Philip
MCLEAN, Mr. Alan Daniel
MCLEAN, Mr. Alan James
MCLEAN, Mrs. Sandra Vivienne
MCLEAN, Mr. Simon Andrew
MCLELLAN, Mr. Andrew
MCLELLAN, Miss. Jeannette
MCLELLAN, Mr. Richard Martin Stuart
MCLEOD, Mr. Robert Alexander
MCLINTOCK, Mr. John Alexander
MCMANNERS, Mr. Thomas William
MCMANUS, Mr. Andrew John
MCMILLAN, Mr. Alistair James
MCMULLEN, Mr. Mark Kerry
MCNAIR, Mr. Iain Peter
MCNALLY, Mr. Emond John
MCNEIL, Mrs. Catherine Jane
MCNEILL, Mr. Hugh
MCNEILL, Mr. Philip
MCNULTY, Mr. Francis Joseph
MCPHAIL, Mr. Philip Anthony
MCPHERSON, Mr. Keith Robert
MCQUATER, Mr. Alastair
MCVEIGH, Mr. Peter William
MEAD, Mrs. Carol Anne
MEAD, Mr. David Henry
MEAD, Mrs. Pearl Lesley
MEADOWS, Mr. Thomas Rory St John
MEE, Mr. Darren
MEE, Mr. Michael John Robert
MEECHAN, Miss. Margaret Mary
MEEK, Mr. Robert Charles
MEERE, Mrs. Julia Claire
MEETEN, Mr. Jonathan Philip
MEGHJEE-CAINE, Mrs. Shama
MEHIGAN, Mr. John Anthony
MEHTA, Mr. Bipinchandra Babulal
MEHTA, Mr. Jagdish Amritlal
MEHTA, Mr. Jayantkumar Dasubhai
MEHTA, Mr. Jehangir Jamshed
MEHTA, Mr. Paresh Lalchand
MEHTA, Mr. Vinaychandra Kantilal
MEIN, Mr. Alastair William
MELIA, Mr. Philip James
MELLAR, Mrs. Susan
MELLER, Mr. Richard James
MELLETT, Mr. John Hilton
MELLING, Miss. Sarah Louise
MELLOR, Mr. Anthony David Gordon
MELLOR, Mr. David Craig
MELLOR, Mr. David Charles
MELLOR, Mr. David John
MELLOR, Mr. Peter Stuart
MENDELSON, Mr. Philip Mark
MENDELSSOHN, Mr. Ronald Guy
MENDES, Mr. Antonio Francisco Remedio
MENZIES-CONACHER, Mr. Ian Duncan
MERALI, Mr. Mahmud Pyarali Kassamali
MERCHANT, Mr. Mahboob Ali
MERCHANT, Mr. Sadruddin Ashraf

MEREDITH, Mr. Christopher Thomas Arthur
MEREDITH, Mr. Darren Craig William
MEREDITH, Mr. Duncan Gabriel
MEREDITH, Mr. Nigel Headley
MERRELL, Mr. Paul David
MERRITT, Mr. Michael William
MERRY, Mr. Leigh
MERRY, Mr. Stewart Scott
MESSORE, Mr. John Salvadore
METHARAM, Mr. Paul
METHERELL, Mr. John
METSON, Mr. Adrian William
METT, Mr. Ian
MEYERS, Mr. Martin Leigh
MIAH, Mr. Ali Ahmed Thoskir
MICHAEL, Mr. Adrian John
MICHAEL, Mr. John
MICHAEL, Mr. Michael Cosmas
MICHAEL, Mr. Michalakis
MICHELL, Miss. Joan Millicent
MICHELMORE, Miss. Jennifer Mary
MIDDLETON, Mrs. Julie Louise
MIDDLETON, Mr. Richard Stephenson
MIDGLEY, Mr. Richard James
MIDGLEY-CARVER, Mr. Philip David
MILES, Mr. Andrew Ronald
MILES, Mrs. Ceri Louise
MILES, Mr. Christopher John
MILES, Mr. David John
MILES, Mr. Dennis Brian
MILES, Mr. Geoffrey William
MILES, Mr. Ian David
MILES, Mr. Nicholas Christopher Francis
MILES, Mrs. Raina Margaret
MILES, Mr. Steven William
MILES, Mr. Victor Alfred
MILLAR, Mrs. Ceri
MILLARD, Mr. Anthony John
MILLARD, Mrs. Catherine Rachel
MILLENER, Mr. Paul Anthony
MILLER, Mr. Andrew Blake
MILLER, Mr. Andrew Gordon
MILLER, Mr. Andrew Horne
MILLER, Mr. David Paul
MILLER, Mr. Ian Robert
MILLER, Mrs. Karen Anne
MILLER, Mr. Keith John
MILLER, Mr. Kevin George
MILLER, Mrs. Nicola Ruth
MILLER, Mr. Paul Anthony
MILLER, Mr. Robert Leslie
MILLER, Mr. Robin
MILLER, Mr. Stephen Charles
MILLETT, Mr. Timothy Peter
MILLIKEN, Mr. Terence John
MILLINGTON, Mr. John Peter
MILLINGTON, Mr. John Robert
MILLION, Mr. David Paul
MILLMAN, Mr. Eric
MILLS, Mr. Anthony
MILLS, Mr. Anthony James
MILLS, Mr. Clifford John
MILLS, Mr. Dominic
MILLS, Mr. Edward Richard
MILLS, Mr. John Charles Harvey
MILLS, Mr. John William
MILLWARD, Mrs. Judith
MILNE, Mr. Alan Martin
MILNE, Mr. Alan Meldrum
MILNE, Mr. David Geoffrey
MILNER, Mrs. Haydee Ann
MILNER, Mr. Ian
MILROY, Mr. Alasdair
MILSOM, Miss. Donna Louise
MINA, Mr. Paolo
MINDHAM, Mr. Anthony John
MINERS, Miss. Dawn Kathleen
MINES, Mr. Thomas John
MINETT, Mr. Keith
MINFORD, Mr. Allen John
MINNS, Mr. Gavin Brent
MINSHALL, Mr. Alan Anthony
MINSHULL, Mrs. Andrea
MINSON, Ms. Ann Louise
MINTON, Mr. Brian Arthur
MIROW, Mr. John Charles Henry
MISSEN, Mr. David Christopher
MISTRY, Mr. Gulabrai
MISTRY, Mr. Harish Bhagwanji
MISTRY, Miss. Jyoti
MISTRY, Mr. Narendrakumar Narendrakumar
MITCHAM, Mr. Arthur David
MITCHELL, Ms. Eithne Catherine
MITCHELL, Mr. Anthony Eamonn
MITCHELL, Mr. Christopher David
MITCHELL, Mr. Colin Stuart
MITCHELL, Mr. David Nigel
MITCHELL, Mr. Derek James
MITCHELL, Mr. Ian Bruce
MITCHELL, Mr. Ian Randall
MITCHELL, Mr. James Russell Ian
MITCHELL, Mr. Nicholas James
MITCHELL, Mrs. Patricia M.D
MITCHELL, Mr. Peter John David
MITCHELL, Mr. Sean Damian
MITCHELL, Mr. Stuart Ernest

MITCHELL, Mrs. Susan Lynne
MITHANI, Miss. Priti Chimanlal
MODI, Mr. Umesh Jamnadas
MODIRI HAMEDAN, Mr. Mehrdad
MOFFAT, Mrs. Sheilagh
MOFFAT, Mr. William
MOGILNER, Mr. Leonard
MOHAMED, Mr. Iqbal Shamsudin
MOHAMED, Mr. Sultanali Kassamali
MOHAMMAD, Mr. Shah
MOHINDRA, Mr. Manoj
MOK, Mr. David Hung Heng
MOLD, Mr. John Kenneth
MOLE, Mr. Adrian Nicholas
MONCRIEFF, Mr. Ronald Mcculloch
MONDY, Mr. Steven Derek
MONFRIES, Mrs. Mary Cicely Florence
MONK, Miss. Elizabeth Ann
MONSON, Mr. Kevin
MONTAGUE-FULLER, Mr. Peter Malcolm
MONTEITH, Mrs. Anita
MONTGOMERY, Mr. Ian
MOODY, Mr. Christopher John
MOON, Mr. Gerald
MOON, Mr. Nigel William George
MOONEY, Mr. Giles Edward
MOONEY, Miss. Marie Therese
MOORBY, Mr. Andrew John
MOORCROFT, Mr. James Langford
MOORE, Mrs. Bethan Alison
MOORE, Mrs. Eira Monica Elisabeth
MOORE, Mr. George Frank
MOORE, Mr. Harry Charles
MOORE, Mr. Herbert John
MOORE, Mr. James Robert
MOORE, Miss. Jane Maureen
MOORE, Mr. John Edward
MOORE, Mr. John Francis
MOORE, Mr. Justin Michael
MOORE, Mr. Laurence Philip
MOORE, Mr. Michael John
MOORE, Mr. Paul Leslie
MOORE, Mr. Robert Keith
MOORE, Mr. Roger Kevin
MOORE, Mrs. Rosaleen Anne
MOORE, Mr. Stephen Jeremy
MOORE, Mrs. Susan Elizabeth
MOORE, Ms. Susan Jennifer
MOORES, Mr. Ian David
MOOREY, Mr. Philip Ian
MOORHOUSE, Mr. Peter
MOORS, Mr. Gareth Shone
MORAN, Mrs. Amanda Jane
MORAN, Mr. Carl Patrick
MORAN, Mr. William
MORARBHAI, Mr. Naresh Harilal
MORDAN, Mrs. Keren Elizabeth
MORELAND, Mrs. Pamela Ann
MOREY, Mr. Colin
MORGAN, Mr. Alan Martin
MORGAN, Mr. Andrew Raymond John
MORGAN, Mr. Andrew Robert Quayle
MORGAN, Miss. Charlotte Elisabeth Diana
MORGAN, Dr. David Andrew
MORGAN, Mr. Gerald Charles
MORGAN, Mr. Graham Anthony
MORGAN, Mr. Ian David
MORGAN, Mr. John Jeffrey
MORGAN, Mrs. June Elizabeth
MORGAN, Mrs. Margaret Elizabeth
MORGAN, Mrs. Margaret Mary
MORGAN, Mr. Nigel
MORGAN, Mr. Peter Hellings
MORGAN, Mr. Richard John Craig
MORGAN, Mr. Roger
MORGAN-OWEN, Miss. Sally Jane
MORJARIA, Mr. Bijesh
MORLAND, Mrs. Claire Celia
MORLAND, Mr. Derek
MORLEY, Mr. Jonathan
MORLEY, Mr. Mark Christopher James
MORLEY, Mr. Stephen Robert
MORPHAKIS, Mr. Stelios
MORPHEW, Mr. John Bernard
MORREALE, Mr. Tony
MORRELL, Mrs. Sheila Jayne
MORRIS, Mr. Adrian William
MORRIS, Mr. Andrew
MORRIS, Mr. Andrew David
MORRIS, Mr. Andrew Robert
MORRIS, Mr. Christopher Glyn
MORRIS, Mrs. Glynis Dawn
MORRIS, Mr. Gregory David
MORRIS, Mr. James Edward
MORRIS, Mr. James William
MORRIS, Mr. Jeremy Rich
MORRIS, Mr. John Richard
MORRIS, Mr. John Stanley
MORRIS, Mrs. Kaye
MORRIS, Mrs. Lynda Jane
MORRIS, Mrs. Lynn
MORRIS, Mr. Matthew Edward
MORRIS, Mr. Patrick James
MORRIS, Mr. Paul Andrew
MORRIS, Mr. Paul David
MORRIS, Mr. Peter Christopher
MORRIS, Mr. Roger

MORRIS, Mr. Roger Paul
MORRIS, Mr. Stephen Anthony
MORRIS, Mr. Timothy Richard Thomas
MORRISH, Mr. Phillip Anthony
MORRISON, Mr. Kenneth Stephen
MORRISON, Mrs. Rachel Jane
MORROW, Mr. Andrew Martin
MORROW, Mrs. Pamela
MORTELL, Mr. David James
MORTER, Mr. Gerald Raymond
MORTON, Mr. Tom Martyn
MORWOOD-LEYLAND, Mr. Antony Michael
MOSCROP, Mr. Gerald Ian
MOSES, Mr. Hugh Frederick
MOSS, Mr. Andrew Gary
MOSS, Mr. Gary Jonathan
MOSS, Mr. Howard Simon
MOSS, Mr. John Webster
MOSS, Mr. Phillip John
MOSS, Mrs. Jane Dummott
MOSS, Mrs. Patricia Jill
MOSS, Mr. Robert Harold
MOSSMAN, Mr. Peter Lawrence
MOTASHAW, Mehernosh Murzban
MOTT, Mr. Dennis Phillip
MOTTERSHEAD-NEEDS, Mr. Jonathan Cary
MOUAT, Miss. Carolyn Emma
MOUKTARIS, Mr. George Anastasiou
MOULDING, Mr. David James
MOULSDALE, Mr. Robert Alan
MOULTON, Miss. Angela
MOUNSEY, Miss. Sarah Anne
MOUNTER, Mr. Robert Neil
MOUSSA, Ms. Sarah Anne
MOY, Mr. Philip James
MOYLE, Mr. Christopher Anthony
MOYNIHAN, Mr. Edward James
MOYSEY, Mr. Nigel Peter
MUIR, Mrs. Judith Anne Elizabeth
MUIRHEAD, Mr. Martin Andrew
MULDERRIG, Mr. Brian David
MULLAN, Mr. George Timothy
MULLEN, Mr. Neil
MULLEY, Mrs. Sharon Virginia
MULLIGAN, Mr. Luke Thomas
MULLIN, Mr. Martin Thomas
MUMBY, Mr. Jeremy Andrew D'arcy
MUNDAY, Mr. Jonathan Martin
MUNDY, Mr. Andrew Stephen
MUNDY, Mr. Christopher Michael
MUNDY, Mrs. Margaret Mary
MUNDY, Mr. Nigel Rodney
MUNIR, Mr. Cemal Teki
MUNRO, Mr. Robert Kenneth Campbell
MUNSON, Mrs. Alma Russell
MURAT, Mr. Mehmet Yilmaz Hilmi
MURCOTT, Mr. Peter William
MURPHY, Mr. Andrew Peter
MURPHY, Mr. George Anthony
MURPHY, Mr. John
MURPHY, Miss. Rachel
MURPHY, Mr. Richard James
MURPHY, Mrs. Sally Ann
MURPHY, Mr. Seamus
MURPHY, Mr. Sean Patrick
MURPHY, Mr. Vincent Michael
MURRALL, Mr. Gary Christopher William
MURRAY, Mr. Graham John
MURRAY, Mr. Martin Daniel
MURRAY, Mr. Simon Nicolas
MURRAY-WILLIAMS, Mr. Simon
MURRIN, Mr. Richard John
MURTAGH, Mrs. Lesley Ann Katie
MURTY, Mr. Anthony Leslie
MUSCHAMP, Mr. Michael
MUSGROVE, Miss. Marie Elizabeth
MUSKETT, Mr. Michael James
MUTKIN, Mr. Malcolm
MUTLOW, Mr. Roy Wilton
MUTTER, Mr. Christopher George
MUXWORTHY, Mr. Peter Rice
MYATT, Miss. Nicola Dora
MYERS, Mr. Daniel Barry
MYERS, Mr. Graham Lloyd
MYERS, Mr. Kevin
MYERS, Mr. Martin Andrew
MYERS, Mr. Rodney Saul
MYERSCOUGH, Mrs. Helen Jane
NABARRO, Mr. Anthony Keith
NAGELE, Mrs. Melanie Joy Emma
NAIK, Mr. Hitendra Ramanlal
NAIRN, Mr. David Albert
NAJEFY, Mr. Shiraz
NALLY, Mr. Eamon Philip Peter
NAPIER, Mr. Stephen
NARAGHI-SHAH, Miss. Lida
NARAIN, Mrs. Lakshmi
NARULA, Mr. Sam
NASH, Mr. Alistair Dennis
NASH, Mr. Andrew Meyrick
NASH, Mr. Charles John
NASH, Mr. David Harwood
NASH, Mr. Jeffery Frederick
NASH, Mr. Philip Jonathan
NASH, Mrs. Sarah Jane
NASON, The Revd Canon Thomas David

NATHAN, Mr. Christopher David John
NATHWANI, Mr. Kaushik Chunilal
NATHWANI, Mr. Meeten
NATHWANI, Mr. Vijay Mukundlal
NAUDI, Mr. Christopher Joseph
NAVESEY, Mr. Michael Anthony
NAYLER, Mr. Jonathan Mark
NAYLOR, Mrs. Anne-Marie
NAYLOR, Mrs. Katharine
NEAL, Mr. Adrian Charles
NEAL, Mr. Ian Keith
NEEDHAM, Mr. David Kevin
NEEDHAM, Miss. Helen Anne
NEEDS, Dr. Richard Leslie
NEEDS, Mrs. Jacqueline Elizabeth
NEEDS, Mr. Robert Edward
NEEVE, Mr. Robert
NEICHO, Mrs. Fiona Gordon
NEIL, Mr. Simon Duncan
NELKON, Mr. Nigel Clifford Alastair
NELSON, Mr. David Howard
NELSON, Mr. David William
NELSON, Mr. Robert Anthony
NEOGY, Mr. Abhijit
NESBIT, Mr. Simon
NEUHOFF, Mrs. Marianne Elisabeth
NEVILL, Mr. Richard Anthony Charles
NEVILLE, Mr. Roger Drummond
NEVIN, Mr. Mark
NEWBERRY, Mr. Alan Edward
NEWBIGIN, Mr. Michael Paul
NEWBOLD, Mr. Paul Robert
NEWCOMBE, Mr. Stephen Thomas
NEWELL, Mr. Trevor Lewis
NEWING, Mr. Kenneth John
NEWMAN, Mr. Christopher James
NEWMAN, Mr. Jeremy William Gare
NEWMAN, Mr. Joel
NEWMAN, Mr. Leslie Robert
NEWMAN, Mr. Peter Herbert Heinz
NEWMAN, Mrs. Rani
NEWMAN, Ms. Tracy Lorraine
NEWNES-SMITH, Mr. Roger
NEWNHAM, Mr. Eric Robert
NEWNHAM, Mr. John Roger
NEWSAM, Mrs. Julie Anne
NEWSAM, Mr. Peter Frederick
NEWSHAM, Mrs. Heather
NEWSHAM, Miss. Kay
NEWSUM, Mr. Richard Nevin
NEWSUM-SMITH, Mr. Andrew Maltby
NEWTON, Mr. Richard
NEWTON, Mr. Richard John Ernest
NEWTON, Mr. Timothy
NEWTON, Miss. Tracy Ann
NG, Mr. Chee Khoon
NG, Mr. Kin-Chung
NG, Mr. Ko Seng
NG, Mr. Paul Hon Sun
NGAI, Ms. Pui Ming Juni
NICHOL, Mr. Derek
NICHOLLS, Mrs. Wendy Elisabeth
NICHOLSON, Mrs. Helen Jane
NICHOLSON, Mr. Kevin James
NICHOLSON, Mr. Mark Alan
NICKS, Mrs. Diane Margaret
NICKSON, Mr. David Anthony
NICOL, Mr. Andrew John Diarmid
NICOL, Mr. John
NICOLL, Mr. Bruce Kenneth
NICOLLE, Mr. Jean-Pierre William Sarre
NICOLSON, Ms. Jennifer Ann
NIELSEN, Mr. Gorm Ward
NILSEN, Mr. John Peter
NIMAN, Mr. Edmund Brian
NIREN, Mr. Charles Jeffrey
NISNER, Mr. Maxwell John
NIVEN, Mr. Euan Niall Macnaughton
NIXON, Mr. Ian Lindsay
NIXON, Mr. John Michael
NIXON, Mr. Philip John
NOAD, Mr. Stuart Ian
NOAKES, Mr. Stuart Robert
NOBLE, Mrs. Doreen
NOBLE, Mrs. Elisabeth Jane
NOBLE, Ms. Elizabeth
NOBLE, Mr. Lee
NOBLE, Mr. Stuart Jason
NOCKELS, Mr. Aubrey George
NOEL, Mr. Clive
NOLAN, Mrs. Vanessa Maria
NOON, Mrs. Teresa Anne
NOONE, Mrs. Caroline Anne
NORGATE, Ms. Lucy
NORMAN, Miss. Charlotte Mary
NORMAN, Mr. David John
NORMAN, Mr. Michael Barney
NORMAN, Mr. Stewart Stanley
NORRIS, Mr. David John
NORRIS, Miss. Deborah Joy
NORRIS, Mr. Ian William
NORRIS, Mr. Robert
NORTH, Mr. Barry Edward
NORTH, Mrs. Judith Anne
NORTHOVER, Mr. Michael Alan
NORTON, Mr. Anthony James
NORTON, Mr. Geoffrey Norman
NORTON, Mr. Richard Jonathan

NORTON, Miss. Sarah
NORTON, Mr. Stephen John
NOTT, Mr. Clive Gilbert
NOTT, Mr. Peter Charles
NOTTAGE, Mr. George Henry
NOTTINGHAM, Miss. Donna Lorelle
NOVITT, Mr. Brian
NOVITT, Mr. Mark Simon
NOWN, Mrs. Patricia Ann
NOYES, Mr. Adrian Dennis
NUFRIO, Mr. Harry
NUNN, Mr. Christopher John
NUNN, Mr. Derrick James
NUNN, Mrs. Jacqueline Elizabeth
NUNN, Mr. Simon Maxwell
NUNN, Mrs. Susan Claire
NUNN, Miss. Trina Jane
NURSE, Mr. Christopher Hart
NUTTING, Mrs. Lynda
NYE, Mr. David William
NYE, Mr. John Elliott
O'BRIEN, Ms. Cathryn Janet
O'BRIEN, Mrs. Cora Mary
O'BRIEN, Mr. Dermot Timothy James
O'BRIEN, Mr. James Charles
O'BRIEN, Mr. Jonathan Spencer Andrew
O'BRIEN, Mrs. Kay
O'BRIEN, Mr. Paul Gerard
O'BRIEN, Mr. Peter Michael
O'CALLAGHAN, Mr. Michael Henry Desmond
O'CONNELL, Mr. Timothy Stuart
O'CONNOR, Mr. Edward Brendan
O'CONOR, Mr. Patrick Francis
O'DONNELL, Mr. Brendan Daniel
O'DONNELL, Mr. Michael Richard
O'GORMAN, Mr. Simon John
O'HARA, Miss. Rachael Elizabeth
O'HARE, Mr. John Daniel
O'HARE, Mr. Sean Gerald Eugene
O'KEEFFE, Mr. Timothy Michael
O'MAHONY, Mrs. Lucy Caroline Eleanor
O'MALLEY, Mr. Graham Robert
O'MALLEY, Mr. Liam James Paul
O'NEILL, Mr. Garry
O'REILLY, Mrs. Kay Francis
O'ROURKE, Mr. Paul Aloysius
O'SHEA, Mr. Ian David
O'SULLIVAN, Mr. Joseph Michael
OAKES, Mr. Anthony Clarke
OATES, Mrs. Christine Ann
ODAM, Mr. Simon
ODDIE, Ms. Elaine Anne
ODDY, Mr. Philip Douglas
OFFER, Mr. Kevin James
OGILVIE, Mr. David Charles Nasmith
OGILVIE, Mr. Michael James Davidson
OGLE, Mrs. Elaine Charlotte
OGLE, Mr. Robert Charles
OGLE, Mr. Simon David
OGLEY, Mr. Adrian Edward
OHARE, Mrs. Kathryn Vivien
OHLSEN, Mr. Mark
OLDFIELD, Mr. Stephen Robin
OLIVER, Ms. Alison
OLIVER, Mr. Nicholas Simon Anthony
OLIVER, Mr. Peter
OLIVER, Mr. Stephen John
OLLEY, Mr. Charles William
OLLIER, Mr. Jonathan Matthew
OLLIFFE, Mr. Graham Hedley
OLSBERG, Mr. Bernard
ONONA, Mr. Eric James
OPPENHEIM, Mr. Martin John Marcus
OPPENHEIM, Mr. Nicholas Stephen
ORME, Mrs. Delia Joan
ORNSTEIN, Mr. Gerald Richard
ORR, Mr. Derrek James
ORR, Mr. Thorsten John
ORRIN, Mr. Mark Andrew
ORRISS, Mrs. Melanie Zoe
ORWIG, Mrs. Eirwen
OSBORN, Mr. Charles Eric
OSBORN, Mr. Charles Robert
OSBORN, Mrs. Christine
OSBORN, Mr. Michael Vincent Isted
OSBORNE, Mr. Martin Paul
OSBORNE, Mr. Peter James
OSBORNE, Mr. Raymond John
OSBORNE, Mr. Tobias Charles
OSLER, Mr. Nicholas Charles
OSMENT, Mr. Robert John
OSSMAN, Mr. Mohamed Hassan Lutfy
OSTER, Mr. Benjamin Mark
OSTROWSKI, Mr. Adrian Ilbert Tadeusz
OSWELL, Mr. Jeremy Nicholas
OVEREND, Mr. David Melvin
OWEN, Mr. Adam
OWEN, Mr. Eric Thomas
OWEN, Mr. Gary David
OWEN, Mr. Giles James
OWEN, Mr. John Herbert
OWEN, Mr. Martyn
OWEN, Mr. Stuart Guy
OWENS, Mr. Christopher John
OWENS, Mr. Gareth Thomas
OWENS, Mr. Julian Spencer

OWERS, Mr. David John
OXENHAM, Mr. Andrew Charles John
OXLEY, Mr. Gary William
OXLEY, Mr. Leslie Thomas
OZIN, Mr. Stephen Daryl
PACHE, Mr. John Bower
PACK, Miss. Anna Elizabeth
PACKER, Mr. Andrew
PACKER, Mr. William Rees
PACKMAN, Mr. Jeremy David
PADAMSEY, Mr. Abdulaziz Pyarali
PADOL, Miss. Irena Elzbieta
PADUA, Miss. Elizabeth Ann
PAGELLA, Mr. Maurice Vondy
PAGET, Mrs. Susan Pamela
PAIGE, Mr. Michael
PAIN, Mr. Robert William
PAINTER, Mr. Iain Anderson
PALER, Mrs. Lesley Anne
PALETHORP, Mr. Ian
PALETHORPE, Mrs. Elizabeth Anne
PALFREYMAN, Mr. Donald Edward
PALLACE, Mrs. Janet Elizabeth
PALLESCHI, Mrs. Emma
PALLISTER, Mr. Richard Lorne
PALMER, Mr. Christopher Michael John
PALMER, Miss. Jennifer Sara
PALMER, Mr. Jeremy
PALMER, Mrs. Jill Susan
PALMER, Mr. John Frederick
PALMER, Mr. Lee Jonathan
PALMER, Mr. Richard Neil
PALMER, Mr. Robert Stephen
PALMER, Mr. Robin George
PALMER, Mr. Simon Robin
PAMPLIN, Mr. Neil Charles
PANDEY, Mr. Daleep
PANDYA, Mr. Dhananjay Ramanlal
PANDYA, Mr. Manoj Vinayak
PANDYA, Mr. Milan
PANG, Mr. Michael Lik Thien
PANG, Mr. Tze Fung
PANGBOURNE, Mr. Rodney Bryan
PANGBURN, Miss. Lesley Elaine
PANNETT, Mr. John Christopher
PANTELI, Ms. Angelie
PANTLING, Mr. Kevin Andrew
PAPADAMOU, Mr. Adam Kosta
PAPADEMETRIS, Mrs. Nicoletta
PARAMESWARAN, Mr. Kandaswami
PARCELL, Mr. Nicholas Roch
PARDOE, Mr. Colin
PARE, Mr. Gordon Daniel
PAREKH, Mr. Girish Ishvarlal
PAREKH, Mr. Sanjay Girdharlal
PARISH, Mr. Rick
PARK, Mr. Andrew Martin
PARK, Mr. Ian Bruce
PARKER, Mr. Ashley
PARKER, Mr. Clive William
PARKER, Mr. David William
PARKER, Mr. John Dobson
PARKER, Mr. Michael John
PARKER, Mr. Nicholas Duncan
PARKER, Sir Peter
PARKER, Mrs. Sharon Nerys
PARKER, Mr. Sydney Seymour
PARKES, Mr. David John William
PARKHOUSE, Mr. Derek Francis
PARKHOUSE, Mr. Keith Ian
PARKIN, Mr. Robert David
PARKINSON, Mrs. Jacqueline Lindsay
PARKINSON, Mr. Richard Horrox
PARKINSON, Mr. Robert
PARKINSON, Miss. Victoria Susan
PARKS, Miss. Elizabeth Anne
PARLONS, Miss. Alison
PARMAR, Mr. Haresh
PARMAR, Mr. Mahendra Amratlal
PARMAR, Mr. Rashpal Singh
PARMAR, Mr. Ravindra Babulal
PARMAR, Mr. Udaibir Singh
PARNELL, Miss. Victoria Heather
PARNESS, Mr. Paul
PARR, Mr. Jeffrey John
PARR, Mr. Philip Henry Arthur
PARRISH, Mr. Gabriel John
PARROTT, Mr. Graham William
PARRY, Mrs. Jane
PARRY, Mr. Laurence Edward
PARRY, Mr. Philip John
PARRY, Mr. Roland George
PARRY, Mr. William
PARRY-WINGFIELD, Mr. Maurice Andrew
PARSEY, Mrs. Katherine Mary
PARSONS, Mr. Dale Nicholas
PARSONS, Mr. Ian William
PARSONS, Mr. Philip Roger
PARSONS, Mrs. Sarah Josephine
PARTINGTON, Miss. Jane Cressida
PARTNER, Mr. Graham Robert
PARTRIDGE, Mr. Mark
PARYLO, Mrs. Violetta Elizabeth
PASCALL, Mr. Ian Derek
PASCOE, Mr. Charles Lionel
PASCOE, Mr. Trevor William
PASS, Miss. Heather Elizabeth

PASSINGHAM, Mr. Matthew
PATARA, Mr. Talwinder Singh
PATCHETT, Mr. Edgar William
PATEL, Mrs. Aarti
PATEL, Mr. Ajay
PATEL, Mr. Ashok Ranchhodbhai
PATEL, Mr. Balwant Natubhai
PATEL, Miss. Bina Jashvantlal
PATEL, Mrs. Dawn Michelle
PATEL, Mr. Dilipkumar Ramanbhai
PATEL, Mr. Dipak
PATEL, Mr. Dipak Purusottam
PATEL, Mr. Farook Ahmed
PATEL, Mr. Gulam Mohamed Ismail
PATEL, Mr. Hasmuk
PATEL, Mr. Himatlal Vashrambhai
PATEL, Mr. Jashwantkumar Nathubhai
PATEL, Mr. Jayesh
PATEL, Mr. Kirankumar Dullabhbhai
PATEL, Mr. Latish
PATEL, Mr. Mahendra Babubhai
PATEL, Mr. Mukund Rambhai Shivabhai
PATEL, Mr. Narendra Natwarlal
PATEL, Mr. Narendrakumar Jashbhai
PATEL, Mr. Neal Mahen
PATEL, Mr. Nilesh Chimanbhai
PATEL, Mr. Pankaj Rameshchandra
PATEL, Miss. Paru
PATEL, Mr. Pradipkumar Durlabhbhai
PATEL, Mr. Praful
PATEL, Mr. Pravin Gordhanbhai
PATEL, Mr. Raj
PATEL, Mr. Rajendrakumar Chhotabhai
PATEL, Mr. Rajendrakumar Govind
PATEL, Mr. Rajnikant Chhotabhai
PATEL, Mr. Raman
PATEL, Mr. Ramesh Kashibhai
PATEL, Mr. Ravindra Gordhanbhai
PATEL, Mr. Rinku
PATEL, Mr. Rohit Shanabhai
PATEL, Miss. Saraswati
PATEL, Mr. Shailen Chandulal
PATEL, Mr. Shashi
PATEL, Mrs. Sonal
PATEL, Mr. Suresh Jashbhai
PATEL, Mr. Ullas Ambalal
PATEL, Mr. Umeshchandra Dahyabhai
PATEL, Mr. Vikram Shirishchandra
PATEL, Mr. Vipul Surendra
PATEL, Mr. Viral
PATEL, Mr. Yogan Apabhai
PATER, Miss. Caroline Mary
PATERSON, Miss. Janet Treacy
PATERSON, Mr. Rowland William Ormiston
PATRY, Mr. Maurice Robert Louis
PATSTON-LILLEY, Mr. Gerald
PATTEN, Mr. Bernard Philip
PATTERSON, Mr. Alan James
PATTERSON, Mr. Donald Robert
PATTERSON, Mr. Frederick
PATTERSON, Mr. Ian Antony
PATTERSON, Mr. Michael
PATTINSON, Mr. David
PATWARI, Miss. Jagriti
PATWARI, Mr. Mohammed Abdul Wadud
PAU, Mr. Anilkumar Haridas
PAUL, Mr. David Graham
PAUL, Mr. Narinder
PAUL, Mr. Viresh Kumar
PAWLOWSKI, Mr. Robert John
PAWSON, Mr. Nicholas Charles Thoresby
PAYDON, Mr. Barry Harvey
PAYNE, Mr. Brian Peter
PAYNE, Mrs. Dana Claire
PAYNE, Mr. David John Charles
PAYNE, Mrs. Deborah Anne
PAYNE, Mr. Douglas
PAYNE, Mr. Guy Stephen John
PAYNE, Mrs. Jennifer Margaret
PAYNE, Mr. John
PAYNE, Mr. John Christopher
PAYNE, Mr. Julian Antony
PAYNE, Mr. Leonard
PAYNE, Mr. Martin David
PAYNE, Mr. Stephen Emmerson
PAYNE, Mr. Stephen Kevin
PAYNE, Mr. Stephen Vear
PEACHMAN, Mr. Phillip Andrew
PEACOCK, Mr. Ian Gordon
PEACOCK, Mr. Michael John
PEACOCKE, Mrs. Heather Anne Hope
PEARCE, Mr. Albert Henry
PEARCE, Mr. Andrew James
PEARCE, Mr. Charles Francis
PEARCE, Mr. Geoffrey William
PEARCE, Mr. George Alan
PEARCE, Mr. Graham
PEARCE, Mr. Olusola Aderohunmu
PEARCE, Mr. Robert Gordon
PEARCE, Mr. Stephen Douglas
PEARCY, Miss. Sara Elizabeth
PEARLMAN, Mr. Gerald Alan
PEARMAN, Mr. Michael Tom Smith
PEARN, Mr. Stephen Charles
PEARS, Miss. Carolyn
PEARSE, Mr. Christopher Andrew Sainthill
PEARSON, Miss. Amanda Jane

PEARSON, Mr. Anthony John
PEARSON, Mr. Laurence John
PEARSON, Mr. Roger David
PEAT, Mr. Nicholas James
PECK, Mr. Geoffrey Michael
PECK, Mr. Robert Stephen
PECK, Mr. Stephen Charles
PEDLER, Mr. Garth
PEERS, Mr. Mark Robert Ernest
PEET, Mr. Richard Martin
PEGG, Miss. Sharon Elizabeth
PEGLER, Mr. Stephen Raymond
PEIRCE, Mr. Arthur Randall Malcolm
PEIRSON, Mr. David Martin
PENASA, Mr. Giovanni Vigilio
PENGELLY, Mr. Clive Eric
PENGELLY, Mr. Malcolm John
PENN, Mr. Jonathan Howard
PENN, Mrs. Zuzanka Daniella
PENNEY, Mrs. Katharine Anne Louise
PENNEY, Mr. Mark Stephen
PENNEYCARD, Mr. Peter Kenneth
PENNIFOLD, Mr. Matthew John
PENNINGTON, Mr. Andrew John
PENNINGTON, Mr. Richard Brian
PENNOCK, Mr. James Nicholas
PENNY, Miss. Miranda Jane Comyns
PENTELOW, Mr. Lindsay Roy
PEPLOW, Mr. Nicholas Robert
PEPPER, Mr. David Ian
PERCIVAL, Mr. James William
PEREIRA, Mrs. Janice Belinda
PERERA, Mr. Brandon Jayalath
PERERA, Mr. Francis Gerard
PERINPANAYAGAM, Miss. Roshini
PERKIN, Mr. Leon Melvin
PERKINS, Mr. John Michael
PERKINS, Mr. Kevin Mark
PERKINS, Mr. Richard Clive
PERKS, Mr. Alan Trevor
PERLIN, Mr. Paul Leslie
PERRIAM, Mr. Andrew John
PERRINS, Mr. John Neville
PERRY, Mr. Colin Charles
PERRY, Mr. Jonathan Henry
PERRY, Ms. Kate Louise
PERRY, Mrs. Louise Emma
PERRY, Mr. Michael Joseph
PERRY, Mr. Richard
PERRY, Mr. Richard Michael Langman
PERRY, Mr. Robert Edward
PERRY, Ms. Theresa
PESCHARDT, Mr. John William Hagbarth
PESCUD, Mr. George Brian
PESTELL, Mr. Paul David
PETER, Mr. Andre Colin
PETERMAN, Mr. David Michael
PETERS, Mr. Christopher
PETERS, Miss. Elizabeth Helen
PETERS, Mr. John Fabian
PETERS, Mr. Keith Leslie
PETERS, Mr. Philip Michael
PETHA, Mrs. Anne Cornelia
PETHERICK, Mr. Mark Julian
PETKOV, Mr. Vesselin Plamenov
PETRICCIONE, Mr. Mario Stefano
PETRIDES, Mr. Ian
PETROU, Mr. Kyriacos
PETROU, Mr. Stavros
PETTMAN, Miss. Katherine Zoe Vivian
PETTS, Mrs. Lynn
PETTY, Mr. Christopher John
PETTY, Mr. Ian Stewart
PEXTON, Mr. Peter Leslie
PHELAN, Mrs. Lesley Anne
PHELPS, Mr. David Simon
PHILIPPS, Mrs. Caroline Anne
PHILLIPS, Mr. Andrew
PHILLIPS, Mr. Andrew Goodwyn
PHILLIPS, Mr. Anthony
PHILLIPS, Mrs. Fiona Elizabeth
PHILLIPS, Mrs. Jane Elizabeth Margaret
PHILLIPS, Mrs. Janette May
PHILLIPS, Ms. Juliet
PHILLIPS, Mr. Keith Arthur
PHILLIPS, Miss. Maxine Lindsay
PHILLIPS, Mr. Neil Christopher
PHILLIPS, Mr. Richard William
PHILLIPS, Mr. Stephen Rupert
PHILLIPS-BAKER, Mr. Hugh
PHILLIPSON, Mrs. Elaine
PHILPOTT, Ms. Gill
PHILPOTT, Mr. Raymond John
PICK, Mr. Douglas
PICKERING, Mrs. Denise
PICKERING, Mr. John Christopher Gordon
PICKERING, Mr. John Philip
PICKLES, Mr. John Timothy Basil
PICKLES, Mr. Roger Albert
PICKUP, Mr. Roland
PIDGEON, Mr. Christopher Milner Fosbrooke
PIERCE, Mr. David Richard
PIERI, Mr. Chris
PIGGOTT, Mr. Andrew
PILCHER, Mr. Grant Stanley
PILGRIM, Mr. Colin John

PILLOW, Mrs. Jessica
PIMBLOTT, Mr. Christopher
PINDER, Mr. Stephen John
PINDORIA, Mr. Ravji Kanji
PINK, Mr. Alan David
PINKHAM, Mr. David John
PINSENT, Mr. Oliver Clive
PINTON, Mr. Timothy John
PIPER, Mr. Jack Leon
PIRILIDOU, Mrs. Katia
PIRMOHAMED, Mr. Amir Gulamhussein
PISSARRO, Mrs. Carolynn Pryse
PITAYANUKUL, Mr. Sangyai
PITCHFORD, Mr. Kevin Michael
PITRAKKOU, Mr. George Nicholas
PITT, Mr. Andrew Michael
PITTALIS, Mr. John Kyriacos
PITTOCK, Mr. Frederick
PLANT, Miss. Joanne Helen
PLANT, Mrs. Judy Catherine
PLATT, Ms. Victoria Catherine
PLAW, Mr. Anthony Charles
PLINSTON, Mr. John Anthony
PLOWS, Mr. John George
PLUMB, Miss. Louise
PLUMMER, Mr. Clive Howard
PLUMMER, Mr. Oliver John
PLUMMER, Mr. Ronald Anthony
PLUMTREE, Mrs. Jenny Rebecca
POCKNELL, Mr. Colin Michael
POCOCK, Mrs. Michelle Odette
PODMORE, Mr. Edward
POLE, Mr. Christopher Joseph
POLEY, Mr. Simon John
POLLARD, Mrs. Claire Sylvia
POLLARD, Mrs. Judith Ann
PONS, Mr. Francis Joseph Ramon
POOLE, Mr. Mark
POOLE, Mr. Martyn Richard
POOLE, Mr. Michael
POOLE, Mr. Trevor Barry
POOLEY, Mr. David Henry
POON, Mr. Simon Yuen Choi
POORUN, Mr. Rajesh
POPAT, Mr. Kiritkumar Dhirajlal
POPAT, Mr. Rajendra Nanalal
POPE, Mr. John Benjamin
POPE, Mr. Keith
POPE, Mr. Matthew Russell
POPE, Ms. Sarah Joanne Elizabeth
POPKIN, Mr. Alexander Guy
POPPLEWELL, Mr. Noel
PORTER, Mr. Anthony Giles
PORTER, Mrs. Clare Noelle
PORTER, Mr. Geoffrey William
PORTER, Mr. Graham David
PORTER, Mr. Jonathan Howard
PORTER, Mr. Kelvin Robert
PORTER, Mrs. Lucie
PORTER, Mr. Noil
PORTMAN, Mr. Richard Harry
POSNER, Mr. Jack Louis
POST, Mr. David Kenneth
POSTLETHWAITE, Mr. David
POTJEWIJD, Mr. Yme Alexander
POTT, Mrs. Julie Maxine
POTTER, Mr. Graham Henry
POTTER, Mr. James Anthony
POTTER, Mr. John Michael
POTTER, Mr. Michael Frederick
POTTER, Mr. Philip
POTTER, Mr. Robert John
POTTER, Mr. Terence Sefton
POTTINGER, Mr. Thomas Charles Alston
POTTS, Mr. Raymond David
POULTER, Mr. Barrie
POULTER, Mr. John Alfred
POULTER, Mr. Jonathan
POULTER, Mr. Steven Matthew
POVEY, Mr. Alan Michael
POWELL, Mr. David
POWELL, Mr. Ian Edward
POWELL, Mr. Kevin Stephen
POWELL, Mr. Robert William
POWELL, Mrs. Sarah Alexandra Walwyn
POWELL, Mr. Timothy March
POWER, Mr. Simon Christopher
POYIADJIS, Mr. Ioannis Pavlou
PRASHAD, Mr. Shashi Amal
PRATT, Mr. John Peter
PRECIOUS, Mr. Martin David
PREECE, Mr. Kevin John
PREECE, Mrs. Linda Anne
PRENTIS, Mr. Nigel Anthony
PRESCOTT, Mr. Jeffrey
PRESKY, Mr. Howard Mark
PRESTON, Mr. Iain William
PRESTON, Mr. John David
PRESTON, Mr. Kevin Henry Duncan
PRESTON, Mr. Malcolm Hunter
PRESTON, Mr. Paul John
PRETTEJOHN, Mr. Philip Muir
PREVETT, Mr. Anthony James
PREVOST, Mr. John Peter Raymond
PRICE, Mr. Andrew David
PRICE, Mr. David Edward
PRICE, Mr. David Nigel

PRICE, Mr. John Lucas
PRICE, Ms. Linda
PRICE, Mr. Matthew Geoffrey
PRICE, Mr. Michael John Edward
PRICE, Mrs. Nia Wynne
PRICE, Mr. Richard William
PRICE, Mr. Ronald Dennis
PRICE, Mr. Steven Glenn
PRICE, Mr. Steven James
PRICHARD, Mr. Andrew John
PRIDHAM, Mrs. Rebecca Louise
PRIDMORE, Mr. Wilfred John
PRIEST, Mr. Kenneth Peter
PRIEST, Mr. Martin Roy
PRIMICERIO, Mr. Andrea
PRINCE, Miss. Iris Ann
PRING, Mr. Brian John
PRING, Mr. Peter Thomas
PRIOR, Mrs. Emily Margaret
PRIOR, Mr. Malcolm Beverley Charles
PRIOR, Mr. Paul Stephen
PRIOR, Mr. Roger Jonathan
PRIOR, Mrs. Sarah Wilkes
PRIORE, Mr. Angelo
PRITCHARD, Mr. Eric Richard
PRITCHARD, Mr. John Morris
PRITCHARD, Mrs. Kathleen Mary
PRITCHARD, Mr. Nigel
PRITCHARD, Mr. Oliver Frank John
PRITCHARD, Mr. Paul James
PRITCHARD, Mr. Robert Michael
PRITCHARD, Miss. Sally Victoria
PRITCHETT, Mr. David Henry
PROBERT, Miss. Helen Margaret
PROBERT, Mrs. Kathryn Mary
PROBERT, Mr. Trevor John
PROCTER, Mr. Andrew John
PROCTER, Mr. Michael Sheriden Tuxworth
PROCTER, Mr. Simon
PROCTOR, Mrs. Li Jean
PROCTOR, Mrs. Patricia Anne
PROCTOR, Mr. Richard Norman
PROSSER, Mr. Robert John
PROTO, Mr. Peter Richard
PROUDFOOT, Mr. Keith Michael
PUCA, Dr. Claudio
PUDNEY, Mr. Jeffrey John
PUGH, Mr. David John
PUGH, Mr. Neil
PUGH, Mr. Peter Brandon
PULFORD, Mr. John David
PULLAN, Mrs. Nicola Elizabeth
PULLAR, Mr. Simon Denis Hedley
PULLEN, Mr. David
PULLEN, Mrs. Jane Elizabeth
PULLEN, Mr. John Arthur
PULLEY, Mr. Brian John
PULMAN, Mr. Ernest Wayne
PUN LAI YUEN, Mr. Antoine Gilles Foong Lin
PUNCHARD, Miss. Elizabeth Jane
PURCELL, Mr. Michael Joseph Martin
PURDHAM, Mr. Paul
PURDY, Mr. Clive Robert
PURDY, Mr. Keith Neil
PURKIS, Mr. John William
PURSER, Mr. David Keith
PUSEY, Mr. Simon Keith
PUTTICK, Mr. Raymond Eric
PYE, Mr. Allan
PYE, Mrs. Kerry Jane
PYE, Mr. Rupert James
PYLIOTIS, Mr. Rolandos Socratous
PYPLACZ, Mr. Brian
QAYYUM, Mr. Abdul
QIDWAI, Mr. Mohammad
QUAIL, Mrs. Shiromani Sharda Devi
QUEK, Mr. Jin Peng
QUEST, Mrs. Michelle Ann
QUICK, Mr. Christopher David
QUICKE, Mr. Andrew Charles
QUINE, Mr. David John
QUINLAN, Mr. John Joseph
QUINLAN, Mr. Michael John
QUINN, Mr. Peter William
QURESHI, Mr. Nisar Ahmed
QURESHI, Mr. Shaikh Muhammed Hafeez
RABET, Mr. Adrian Denis
RADFORD, Mr. Alan Clive
RADFORD, Mr. David Michael
RADFORD, Mrs. Eve Taylor
RADIA, Mr. Yogesh Dhirajlal
RADLETT, Mr. Stephen John
RAE, Mr. Ian Kenyon
RAFFAN, Mr. Richard Keith
RAFFLE, Mrs. Georgina
RAGHU, Mr. Bharat Deo Persaud
RAHMAN, Mr. Sheikh Anisur
RAHMAT-SAMII, Mr. Gholam-Reza
RAHMATULLAH, Mr. Mohammed
RAICHURA, Mr. Rashmikant Narbheram
RAICHURA, Mr. Sanjay Chunilal Chhaganlal
RAINSFORD, Mrs. Valerie Maud
RAISTRICK, Mrs. Anne Louise
RAJA, Mr. Mahendra Khimjibhai
RAJA, Mr. Muhammad Afzal
RAJA, Mr. Rajnikant Kakubhai

RAJAN, Mr. Benoy Thomas
RALPH, Mr. Ian Peter
RAMALINGUM, Mr. Richard
RAMSBOTTOM, Mr. George Loynd
RAMSEY, Mr. Michael Stephen
RAMSHAW, Mr. David Shaun
RANA, Mr. Major Singh
RANCHHOD, Mr. Dilip Mohan
RAND, Mr. Andrew Stanes
RAND, Mr. Jonathan David
RANDALL, Mrs. Alsion Edna
RANDALL, Mr. John Alexander
RANDALL, Mr. Kevin Andrew
RANDALL, Mrs. Pamela Marion
RANDALL, Mr. Peter George
RANDALL, Mr. Robert Andrew
RANDALL, Mr. Ross Woolfrey
RANDLE, Mr. Adrian Edward
RANDLES, Mr. David Frank
RANDOLPH, Mr. Ian Anthony
RANGELEY, Mr. Robert David Alexander
RANIWALA, Mr. Zaffer Fazleabbas Hassanali
RANKIN, Mr. Ian Thomas
RANSOM, Mr. Jonathan Peter
RANSOME, Mr. Michael William
RANSTED, Mr. David Andrew
RASHID, Mr. Khalil
RASHID, Miss. Salma Shireen
RASTALL, Mr. Walter Guy
RATCLIFFE, Mr. Alan George
RATCLIFFE, Mr. Nigel Terence
RATFORD, Mr. Alan George
RATIGAN, Mr. Paul Andrew
RAVEN, Mr. Colin John
RAVEN, Mr. Gary John
RAVEN, Mr. Peter Micheal
RAWI, Mr. Radwan Al
RAWLE, Mr. John Edward
RAWLINGS, Mr. Mark Anthony
RAWLINGS, Mr. Stephen Bruce
RAWLINGS, Mr. Stuart Andrew
RAWSON, Mr. Nicholas
RAY, Mr. Alan Charles
RAY, Mr. Christopher
RAY, Mrs. Joanne Mary
RAY-JONES, Mr. Philip Raymond
RAYMOND, Mr. William George
RAYNER, Mr. Benjamin Thomas William
RAYNER, Mr. Mark
RAYNER, Mr. Paul Edward
RAYNEY, Mr. Peter Cyril
RAYNOR, Mr. Hubert George
REA, Mr. Norman Thomas
READ, Mr. David Arthur
READ, Mr. Michael John
READ, Mr. Stephen Robert
READE, Miss. Barbara Mary Hamilton
READER, Mr. Michael
REASON, Mrs. Heather Louise
REAST, Mr. Peter Barradell
REBELLO, Mr. Trevor Peter
REDDEN, Mr. Alan Raymond
REDDIHOUGH, Mr. Malcolm Paul
REDFERN, Mr. Simon Anthony
REDFORD, Mr. Marcus James
REDMAN, Mr. Graham
REDSTON, Ms. Anne
REDWOOD, Mr. Derek Gordon
REECE, Mr. Adam David
REED, Mr. Christopher Mark
REED, Mr. Martin Haynes
REES, Mrs. Ceri Haf
REES, Mr. David Bilbie
REES, Mr. Richard Jonathan Owen
REES, Mr. Simon Philip
REES, Mrs. Sonya Faye
REESE, Mr. Trevor Ellison
REEVE-TUCKER, Mr. Charles Stanley
REEVES, Mr. Roy Arnold
REGAL, Mr. Richard Neill
REGAN, Mr. John
REHNCY, Mr. Jasdev Singh
REID, Mr. Allan McLean
REID, Mr. Christopher
REID, Mr. David Michael
REID, Mr. Ewan David
REID, Mrs. Frances Mary
REID, Mr. Graham Alexander
REID, Mr. Ian Clive
REID, Miss. Joanna Mary
REIFER, Mr. Abraham
REILLY, Mr. Peter Alexander
REILLY, Dr. William Mark
REITH, Mrs. Deborah Jayne
RELF, Mr. Clive Neil
RENGERT, Mr. Christopher
RENNISON, Ms. Yvonne
RENTON, Mr. Adam John
RETOUT, Mr. Paul George
REUBEN, Mr. Howard Robert
REVEL-CHION, Mr. Gary
REVILL, Mr. Stewart
REYERSBACH, Mr. John Quentin
REYES, Mr. Stephen Joseph
REYLAND, Mrs. Deborah Louise
REYNAERT, Mr. Paul Anthony

REYNOLDS, Mr. David Alan
REYNOLDS, Mr. Hugh Michael Peter
REYNOLDS, Mr. James Alan
REYNOLDS, Mr. Mark
REYNOLDS, Mr. Michael Stanley
REYNOLDS, Mr. Neil Anthony William
REYNOLDS, Mr. Nigel Philip
REYNOLDS, Mr. Peter Kinsey
REYNOLDS, Mr. Timothy Edward
RHIND, Mr. Kevin John
RHODES, Mr. John Howard
RHODES, Mr. Jonathan
RHODES, Mr. Richard Spencer
RHODES, Mr. Steven Lewis
RIBCHESTER, Mr. Robert William
RICE, Mr. David Arthur
RICE, Ms. Gill
RICE, Mr. Kirk Andrew Stephen
RICE, Miss. Lynn
RICE, Mr. Stephen Euston
RICHARDS, Mr. Alan David
RICHARDS, Mr. Alun
RICHARDS, Mr. Andrew Henry
RICHARDS, Mr. Andrew Paul
RICHARDS, Mr. Brian
RICHARDS, Mrs. Caroline Ann
RICHARDS, Mrs. Cathrin Mary
RICHARDS, Mr. Colin Edward George
RICHARDS, Mr. David John
RICHARDS, Mr. David William Ryman
RICHARDS, Mr. Keith Spenser
RICHARDS, Mrs. Pamela Vanessa Roberta
RICHARDS, Mr. Ralph Henry Arthur
RICHARDS, Mr. Stephen John
RICHARDS, Mr. Steven Mark
RICHARDS, Mr. Timothy Roy
RICHARDS, Mrs. Yvonne
RICHARDSON, Mr. Dale
RICHARDSON, Mr. Edward Andrew
RICHARDSON, Mrs. Jennifer Mary
RICHARDSON, Mr. Jonathan
RICHARDSON, Mrs. Judith Anne
RICHARDSON, Mr. Kenneth Larry
RICHARDSON, Mrs. Linda Louise
RICHARDSON, Mr. Martin James
RICHARDSON, Mr. Timothy John
RICHES, Mrs. Tina Elizabeth
RICHINGS, Mrs. Julie
RICHMAN, Mr. Marcus
RICKARD, Mr. Christopher Colin
RICKERS, Mr. Simon
RICKETTS, Mr. Christopher Mark Walker
RIDD-JONES, Mr. Gary Royston
RIDDLE, Mr. Rodney Keith
RIDING, Mr. Ian David
RIDING, Mrs. Karen Ann
RIDING, Mr. Philip Alan
RIGDEN, Mr. Stephen Peter
RILEY, Mrs. Alison Patricia
RILEY, Mrs. Angela Kathryn
RILEY, Mr. David Neil
RILEY, Mrs. Elizabeth Jane
RILEY, Ms. Helen Doone
RILEY, Mr. Michael John
RILEY, Mr. Peter William
RILEY, Mr. Philip Ian
RIMINGTON, Mr. Christopher Laurence
RIMMER, Mrs. Clare Frances
RIMMER, Mr. Jonathan
RIMMER, Mr. Malcolm Robert
RIORDAN, Mr. Timothy Michael
RIPPINGALE, Mr. Simon John
RISSBROOK, Mrs. Susan Mary
RISSEN, Mr. Howard Theo
RITCHIE, Mr. Stuart David
RITZEMA, Mr. Gary
RIVETT, Mr. Nicholas William
RIZAN, Mrs. Patricia Mary
ROACH, Mr. John Roger Murray
ROBB, Mrs. Gillian Fiona
ROBBINS, Mr. Anthony Thomas
ROBBINS, Miss. Laura Catherine
ROBBINS, Mr. Paul John Gilbert
ROBBINS, Mr. Stephen Frederick
ROBERTS, Mr. Alan
ROBERTS, Mr. Alistair Dominic
ROBERTS, Mr. Arthur George
ROBERTS, Miss. Barbara Elizabeth
ROBERTS, Mr. Brian John
ROBERTS, Mr. Charles Anthony
ROBERTS, Mr. Christopher
ROBERTS, Mr. David Brian
ROBERTS, Mr. David Gareth
ROBERTS, Mr. David Graham
ROBERTS, Mr. Eifion
ROBERTS, Miss. Jane
ROBERTS, Mrs. Joan Lucille
ROBERTS, Mr. John Arthur
ROBERTS, Mr. Keith
ROBERTS, Mrs. Louisa
ROBERTS, Mr. Meurig Wyn
ROBERTS, Mr. Michael William
ROBERTS, Mr. Philip Michael
ROBERTS, Mrs. Rachel Jane Scott
ROBERTS, Mr. Richard Andrew
ROBERTS, Mrs. Zoe Michelle
ROBERTSON, Mrs. Elizabeth Mary

ROBERTSON, Mr. Peter Anthony
ROBERTSON, Mr. Shaun Archibald
ROBINSON, Mrs. Alison Ruth
ROBINSON, Mr. Andrew Paul
ROBINSON, Mrs. Ann Katrina
ROBINSON, Mr. Ben
ROBINSON, Mr. David Howard
ROBINSON, Mr. David James Ian
ROBINSON, Mr. David John
ROBINSON, Mr. Douglas
ROBINSON, Mrs. Eleni
ROBINSON, Mr. Francis
ROBINSON, Mrs. Helen Ann Elizabeth
ROBINSON, Mrs. Hilary Anne
ROBINSON, Mr. Ian
ROBINSON, Mrs. Janet
ROBINSON, Mr. John Edwin
ROBINSON, Mr. John Stewart
ROBINSON, Mr. Jonathan Howard
ROBINSON, Mr. Martin Edward
ROBINSON, Ms. Nicola Jane
ROBINSON, Mr. Peter Edward
ROBINSON, Mr. Peter Graham
ROBINSON, Mr. Phillip David
ROBINSON, Mr. Robert William
ROBINSON, Mrs. Ruth Anne
ROBINSON, Ms. Sandra
ROBINSON, Mrs. Sarah Doris
ROBINSON, Mr. Stephen Beresford
ROBINSON, Ms. Susan Ann
ROBINSON, Mrs. Susan Mary
ROBLIN, Mr. Lynn Anthony
ROBSON, Mrs. Ann Sylvia
ROBSON, Ms. Fiona
ROBSON, Mr. John Sutherland
ROBSON, Mrs. Karen Margaret
ROBSON, Mr. Philip Martyn
ROCHE, Mr. Dale
ROCHE, Mr. Richard Anthony
ROCHESTER, Mr. Stephen Gordon
ROCHMAN, Mr. Paul Henry
ROCKETT, Mr. Nicholas Anthony
ROCKEY, Mrs. Edwina Tamsin
RODNEY, Mr. David Howard
RODNEY, Mr. Peter Allan
RODWAY, Mr. Alan James
ROE, Mr. Peter Howard
ROGAN, Mr. Haydn
ROGERS, Mrs. Christina
ROGERS, Mr. Francis John
ROGERS, Mrs. Helen
ROGERS, Mr. Iain Michael
ROGERS, Mr. Kenneth Albert
ROGERS, Mr. Neil Derek
ROGERS, Mr. Peter Mervyn
ROGERS, Mrs. Susan
ROGOFF, Mr. Samuel
ROLES, Mr. Kenneth Brian
ROLFE, Mrs. Susan Jane
ROLLIN, Mr. Charles Austin Noble
ROLLISTON, Mr. Guy Charles
ROLPH, Mr. John Richard
ROMANS, Miss. Shelley Ann
ROME, Mr. John Jack
RONALD, Mrs. Sharon Ann
RONKOWSKI, Mr. Philip Konrad
ROOHI LARIJANI, Mrs. Michele Elizabeth
ROOK, Mrs. Jane Alison
ROOK, Mr. Peter Philip
ROONEY, Mr. Martin James
ROPER, Mr. David Anthony
ROPER, Mr. Ian
ROPER, Mr. Jonathan Paul
ROSBROOK, Mrs. Janet Mary
ROSE, Mr. Anthony David
ROSE, Mr. Douglas Charles
ROSE, Mr. Ian Simon
ROSE, Mr. Jeffrey Sydney
ROSE, Mr. Marcus John
ROSE, Mr. Matthew Saul
ROSE, Mr. Paul William
ROSE, Mr. Robert Geoffrey
ROSE, Mr. Trevor
ROSEN, Mr. Stephen
ROSENTHAL, Miss. Catherine Charlotte
ROSENTHAL, Mr. Meir
ROSENTHAL, Mr. Robert Charles
ROSMARIN, Mr. Ian Mark
ROSS, Mr. Alistair David
ROSS, Mr. Harry Jonathan
ROSS, Mr. Ian Harvey
ROSS, Mr. Lewis Ian
ROSS, Mr. Nicholas Sydney
ROSS, Mr. Simon Nicholas
ROSS MARTIN, Miss. Nichola
ROSSI MERLI, Mr. Pier Marco
ROSSIDES, Mr. Kyriacos
ROSSITER, Mrs. Carolyn Ann
ROSSITER, Mr. Paul
ROSSOR, Mr. Michael Keith
ROSTANCE, Mr. David Anthony
ROSTEN, Mr. Alan David
ROTHENBERG, Mr. Robert Michael
ROTHENBERG, Mr. Walter David
ROTHERA, Mr. Derek John
ROTHERAM, Mr. Keith
ROTHMAN, Miss. Rebecca Louise Elizabeth

ROUNSEFELL, Mr. Terence Martin
ROUSE, Mr. Gary Paul
ROUSE, Mr. Geoffrey Frederick Roland
ROUSE, Mr. Steven John
ROUTLEDGE, Mrs. Trudi Ann
ROUZEL, Mr. Alan Keith
ROWAN, Mr. Kevin Christopher
ROWBOTTOM, Mrs. Rachelle
ROWDEN, Mrs. Penelope Ann
ROWE, Mr. John Neil
ROWE, Mr. Kevan
ROWE, Mrs. Rosalind
ROWELL, Mr. Peter William
ROWLAND, Mr. Anthony Bernard
ROWLAND, Mr. Mark Andrew
ROWLAND, Mr. Matthew
ROWLAND, Mr. Neil
ROWLAND, Mrs. Rosemary Helen
ROWLAND, Mr. Stephen
ROWLANDS, Mr. Anthony Joseph
ROWNTREE, Mr. Alan Thomas
ROWSELL, Mrs. Cheryl Anne
ROXBURGH, Mr. Douglas Selwyn
ROY, Mrs. Susan Jennifer Ruth
ROYLE, Mr. John Cartwright
ROYLE, Mr. Jonathan
ROZARIO, Mr. Clive Joseph Lawrence
RUBACK, Mr. Sidney Martin
RUBAKUMAR, Mr. Sivasubramaniam
RUBENSTEIN, Mr. Raymond Alan
RUBIDGE, Miss. Tina Michelle
RUBIN, Mr. David Antony
RUCKLIDGE, Mr. James Francis
RUDD, Mr. Steven Graham
RUDDEN, Mr. Stephen James
RUDDICK, Mr. Brian
RUDDOCK, Mr. Paul Geoffrey
RUDDOCK, Mrs. Sarah Margaret
RUDDY, Mr. John Michael
RUDGE, Mr. Malcolm Arthur
RUDGE, Mr. Paul Anthony
RUDICH, Mr. Daniel Yehudi
RUFFONI, Mr. Peter Conrad
RUGHANI, Miss. Seema
RULE, Mrs. Lindsay Dawn
RULTEN, Miss. Claire Ann
RUMPH, Mr. Alan
RUNDELL, Mr. Ian
RUNDLE, Mr. John David
RUNNEGAR, Mr. Antony James
RUOCCO, Mr. Salvatore
RUPAL, Mr. Raj Gopal
RUPP, Mr. Christopher David
RUSHD, Mr. Asad Ali
RUSHEN, Mr. Keith Douglas
RUSHTON, Mr. Christopher Charles St John
RUSHTON, Mr. Peter Shaun
RUSHTON-TURNER, Mr. John Martin
RUSHWORTH, Mr. Stephen John
RUSKELL, Miss. Diane Jane
RUSMAN, Mr. David Jacob
RUSSELL, Mr. Allan
RUSSELL, Mr. Christopher James
RUSSELL, Mr. Christopher Mark
RUSSELL, Mr. James Robert
RUSSELL, Mr. John Oliver
RUSSELL, Mr. Kevin John
RUSSELL, Mr. Robert Haran
RUSSELL, Mr. Timothy
RUSSELL-SMITH, Mrs. Susanna Gibson
RUSSETT, Mrs. Barbara Joan
RUST, Miss. Sara Katrine
RUTT, Mr. Michael Logan
RUZZON, Mr. Alberto
RYAN, Mr. Clifford Anthony
RYAN, Mr. Matthew Alexander
RYAN, Mrs. Sharon Rosemary
RYDER, Mr. Geoffrey Winston
SAADY, Mr. Stephen Jon
SACHDEV, Mr. Ripan
SACHER, Mr. Brad Jonathan
SACKS, Mr. Alan Leon Barry
SADIQ, Mr. Muhammad
SADLER, Mr. Graham Edward Joseph
SADLER, Mr. Robert Alistair
SADOFSKY, Mr. Melvyn Warren
SADRA, Mr. Kamiljit Singh
SAFFER, Mr. Michael Jonathan
SAGE, Mr. Roderick Noel Anthony
SAGOO, Mrs. Fiona Gwendoline
SAHADEVAN, Mr. Sajit
SAHAMI, Mr. Firooz
SAKER, Mr. Hitendra
SALE, Mr. Christopher John Norman
SALE, Mr. Michael Derek
SALEEMI, Mr. Mohammad Ashfaq
SALLOWS, Mr. Daniel Edward
SALMON, Mr. Brian Edward
SALMON, Mr. Derek Harry
SALMON, Mr. Rupert Edward Fitzjohn
SALTER, Mr. Kevin Nigel
SAMAR, Mr. Raza Ullah
SAMJI, Mr. Abdulmohamed Mohamedali Premji
SAMJI, Mr. Sadrudin Noordin
SAMOTHRAKIS, Mrs. Deborah Mary
SAMPSON, Mr. Michael Anthony

SAMPSON, Mr. Michael Oliver
SAMRAH, Mr. Paul Edward Marshall
SAMUEL, Mr. David Lawrence
SANDELLS, Mr. David
SANDERS, Mr. David Andrew
SANDERS, Mr. John Michael
SANDERS, Mr. Mark Charles
SANDERS, Mr. Simon Barry
SANDERS, Mrs. Vanessa
SANDERSON, Mr. Iain Richard
SANDERSON, Mrs. Philippa Amy Clare
SANDFORD, Mr. Anthony Charles
SANDGROUND, Mr. David Kenton
SANDS, Mr. Jonathan Richard
SANDS, Mr. Paul
SANGANI, Mr. Manish Rasiklal
SANGANI, Mr. Rakesh Natwarlal
SANGANI, Mr. Sunil Kumar
SANGER, Mr. Christopher
SANGHA, Mr. Kalvir Singh
SANGHRAJKA, Mr. Jayant
SANSOM, Mr. Anthony John
SANSOM, Mr. Brian Thomas
SANSOM, Mr. Bryan Kingsley
SANT, Dr. Helen Kathryn
SAPAT, Mr. Dipak Ratansinh
SAPKOTA, Mr. Saroj
SARA, Mr. Derek Richard Tomlin
SARESSALO, Mr. Mikko Juhana
SARGEANT, Mr. Gary Andrew
SARGENT, Mr. Alfred Charles
SARJANT, Mr. David
SARRAU, Mrs. Carolyn Patricia
SARTIN, Mr. Scott John
SAUNDERS, Mr. Alan John
SAUNDERS, Mrs. Christine Judith
SAUNDERS, Mr. Michael David
SAUNDERS, Mr. Paul Barry
SAVADIA, Mr. Nitin Devchand
SAVAGE, Ms. Jacqueline Elizabeth Franziska
SAVAGE, Mr. Leo
SAVAGE, Mr. Mark John
SAVAGE, Mr. Paul Reginald
SAVILL, Mr. David Charles
SAVVA, Mr. Savvas Antoniou
SAVVIDES, Mr. George
SAVVIDES, Mr. Savvas Epiphaniou
SAW, Miss. Mary Biq Shyuan
SAWBRIDGE, Mr. Neil John
SAWDON, Mrs. Audrey Jean
SAWYER, Mr. Mark Stephen
SAXBY, Mr. Nicholas Syred
SAXON, Mr. Anthony Alfred
SAXON, Mr. Timothy John
SAYAGH, Miss. Abigail
SAYED, Mr. Rizwan Hassan
SAYERS, Mrs. Karen Patricia
SAZAN, Mr. Abdul Mohamed Akbarali Ismail
SCALLY, Mrs. Julie Elaine
SCANLAN, Mr. William Andrew
SCANLON, Mr. Christopher Peter
SCARBOROUGH, Mr. Paul
SCARGILL, Mr. Stewart
SCARLETT, Mr. Michael
SCHEERMANN, Mr. Steven Anthony
SCHICK, Mr. Stephen Edward
SCHILLER, Mr. Michael Frank
SCHINDLER, Mr. Richard Franz
SCHOFIELD, Miss. Katie
SCHOFIELD, Mr. Mark
SCHOFIELD, Mr. Michael Gregory
SCHOLL, Mr. Jeremy Simon
SCHOTTLER, Mr. Klaus
SCHUMAN, Mr. Martin Paul
SCHUMAN, Mr. Norman
SCLAVERANO, Mr. Peter Victor
SCODIE, Mr. Michael
SCOTT, Mr. Alexander
SCOTT, Mr. Brian Godfrey
SCOTT, Mr. Clive Anthony
SCOTT, Mr. David John
SCOTT, Mr. David Michael
SCOTT, Mr. Ian Paul
SCOTT, Mr. Justin Joseph
SCOTT, Mr. Kenneth
SCOTT, Mr. Mathew Robert
SCOTT, Miss. Melanie
SCOTT, Mr. Michael Howard
SCOTT, Mr. Nigel Glazier
SCOTT, Mrs. Rachel Elizabeth
SCOTT, Mr. Stephen Lindsay
SCOTT, Mr. William Robert
SCOTT-KERR, Miss. Fiona Margaret
SCRIVENS, Mr. Gary Stuart
SCRUTTON, Mrs. Carolyn Mary
SCULL, Mr. Nicholas John
SCURRY, Mr. George Martin
SEABRIDGE, Mr. Stephen James
SEAGRAVE, Mr. Steven Peter
SEAL, Mr. Paul John
SEALS, Mr. Russell
SEARLE, Mr. David John
SEARLE, Mr. James Francis
SEARLE, Miss. Rona Sian Teague
SEARLE, Mrs. Shona Claire
SEATON, Mr. Michael David

SEDDON, Mrs. Claire Louise
SEDDON, Mr. David Clive
SEDDON, Mr. Richard James
SEDDON, Mr. Ronald Kelsall
SEDGWICK, Mrs. Caroline Suzanne
SEDGWICK, Mrs. Susan Margaret
SEELEY, Mr. David William
SEEYAVE, Mr. Gilbert Louis Kim Fa Cheh
SEFTON, Mrs. Lucinda Jane
SEFTON, Mr. Simon Jerome
SEGAL, Mrs. Alexandra Charlotte
SEGAL, Mrs. Amanda Heather
SEGAL, Mr. David Ashley
SEIDLER, Mr. Andrew Francis
SEJPAL, Mr. Mukesh Ranchhoddas
SELF, Ms. Heather
SELIG, Mr. Jason Henry
SELIGMAN, Mr. Philip Michael
SELLENS, Mr. Keith
SELLERS, Mr. Stephen
SELLEY, Mr. Peter Frederick
SELVARAJAH, Mr. Ravindran
SELVARAJAH, Miss. Sarasavi
SEN, Mr. Aditya Kumar
SEN, Mr. Subrata
SENIOR, Mr. Andrew James
SENNETT, Mr. Barry Rodney
SENNITT, Mrs. Karen Andrea
SERFATY, Mr. Mesod William
SERGENT, Mr. Aidan William
SERGI, Mr. Michael Demetrios
SETCHELL, Mr. James Henry
SEWARD, Miss. Claire
SEWELL, Mr. Robin George
SEWELL, Mr. Sidney John
SEWELL, Mr. Timothy Michael
SHABBIR, Mr. Ghulam
SHABBIR, Mr. Muhammed
SHACKLETON, Mrs. Marilyn Freda
SHAFFER, Mr. Geoffrey Saul
SHAH, Mr. Alkesh Suryakant
SHAH, Mr. Arvind Kumar Velji
SHAH, Mr. Ashok Kawas
SHAH, Mr. Ashvinkumar Meghji Karman
SHAH, Mr. Ashvinrai Govindji Shamat
SHAH, Mrs. Bibi Shamim
SHAH, Mr. Bimal
SHAH, Mr. Dhirajlal Fulchand
SHAH, Mr. Dhiresh Jayantilal
SHAH, Mr. Dinesh Ambalal
SHAH, Mr. Dipan Mahendra
SHAH, Mr. Dipun Velji
SHAH, Mr. Harish Hirji
SHAH, Mr. Hemel Arvindal
SHAH, Mr. Jayendra
SHAH, Mr. Jitendra Meghji
SHAH, Mr. Kanaiyalal Kashalchand Jagjivan
SHAH, Mr. Kanubhai Nagindas
SHAH, Mr. Kaushik Kanji
SHAH, Mr. Ketan Pravin
SHAH, Mr. Kishorilal
SHAH, Mrs. Kokila
SHAH, Mr. Mahesh Shantilal
SHAH, Mr. Navinchandra Dharamshi
SHAH, Mr. Neel Kamal
SHAH, Mr. Nilesh
SHAH, Mr. Nilesh
SHAH, Mr. Nileshkumar Harakchand
SHAH, Mr. Nitesh Bhagwanji
SHAH, Mr. Nitin Premchand
SHAH, Mr. Pankaj
SHAH, Mr. Pankaj Nathalal
SHAH, Mr. Paresh L
SHAH, Mr. Pradip Kumar
SHAH, Mr. Praphulchandra Raichand
SHAH, Mr. Rajan Shantilal
SHAH, Mr. Rajesh Hiralal
SHAH, Mr. Rajesh Keshavlal
SHAH, Mr. Rajesh Natwerlal
SHAH, Mr. Rameshchandra Manilal Dharamshi
SHAH, Mr. Rasiklal Ladhabhai
SHAH, Mr. Rizwan Ul-Hassan
SHAH, Mr. Sanjay Gosar
SHAH, Mr. Sanjay Rameshchandra
SHAH, Mr. Sanjiv Mohanlal
SHAH, Mr. Satishchandra Baburaj
SHAH, Mr. Satishchandra Z
SHAH, Mr. Shakunt Vinodrai
SHAH, Mr. Siddharth Kantilal
SHAH, Mr. Subhash Chimanlal
SHAH, Mr. Vijal Premchand
SHAH, Mr. Vipin Ambalal
SHAH, Mr. Vipin Shantilal
SHAH, Mr. Vipool Khetshi Nathoobhai
SHAHMOON, Mr. Ran Charles
SHAIK, Mr. Abdul Aziz
SHAIKH, Mr. Mohommad
SHAKESPEARE, Miss. Anne Muriel Carter
SHAMSI, Mrs. Rasheeda Ambereen
SHAND, Mr. John Philip
SHANKS, Mr. James Douglas Douglas
SHANNON, Mr. John Richard
SHAPIRO, Mrs. Barbara
SHAPIRO, Mr. David
SHAPIRO, Mr. Jeffrey Israel Joseph
SHAREEF, Mr. Naeem Mohammed

SHARIF, Mr. Ashfaq
SHARKEY, Mrs. Melanie Ann Menzies
SHARMA, Mr. Adarsh Kumar Dev Prakash Gurbux Rai
SHARMA, Mrs. Anugrah
SHARMA, Mr. Vivek
SHARMAN, Mr. Neil
SHARMAN, Mr. Patrick Michael
SHARMAN, Mr. Paul David
SHARNOCK, Mr. Philip John
SHARP, Mrs. Hilary Frances
SHARP, Mr. Paul John
SHARP, Mr. Peter John
SHARPE, Mrs. Hilary Frances
SHARPE, Mr. Matthew David
SHARRATT, Mrs. Julie Patricia
SHAUL, Mr. Richard John Leslie
SHAUL, Mr. William
SHAVE, Mr. Martin David Reid
SHAW, Mr. Andrew Nigel
SHAW, Mr. Andrew Rhead
SHAW, Mr. Anthony Vause
SHAW, Mr. Ashley Mark
SHAW, Mr. David Adam
SHAW, Mr. David Hamilton
SHAW, Mr. Graham
SHAW, Mr. Graham Philip
SHAW, Mr. Ian Gordon
SHAW, Mr. James Leslie
SHAW, Mr. John Joseph
SHAW, Mr. Martyn Alan
SHAW, Mr. Michael John
SHAW, Mr. Peter
SHAW, Mr. Peter Robert
SHAW, Mr. Richard Gardner
SHAW, Mrs. Susan Elizabeth
SHAW, Mr. Timothy Martin
SHAW, Mrs. Tracy Jane
SHAWCROSS, Mr. Robert Edward Newlove
SHAWYER, Mr. David Martin
SHEA, Mr. John Brian
SHEA, Mrs. Margaret Louise
SHEAR, Mr. Alexander Michael
SHEARAN, Mr. Michael John
SHEARD, Mr. Andrew Philip Snell
SHEARD, Mr. Graham
SHEARER, Mr. Andrew Charles
SHEARN, Mr. David Anthony
SHEATHER, Mr. John Donald
SHEEHAN, Mr. John Paul
SHEEN, Mr. Mark Richard Churchill
SHEIKH, Mr. Kamran Iftikhar
SHELDON, Mr. Jonathan Paul
SHELLEY, Mrs. Geraldine Anne
SHELLEY, Mr. Stephen Michael
SHENKER, Mr. Michael Martin
SHEPHARD, Ms. Pamela Ann
SHEPHERD, Mr. Peter William
SHEPHERD, Mr. Andrew Paul
SHEPHERD, Mrs. Anne Elizabeth
SHEPHERD, Mrs. Claire
SHEPHERD, Miss. Jane Nicola
SHEPHERD, Mr. John Kenneth
SHEPHERD, Mr. Richard James
SHEPHERD, Mr. William Ralph
SHEPHERD-THEMISTOCLEOUS, Miss. Helen Louise
SHEPHERDSON, Mr. John
SHEPPARD, Mrs. Barbara Lyn
SHEPPARD, Mr. Derrick Richard Adam
SHEPPARD, Mr. Ian Francis
SHEPPARD, Mr. John Kenneth
SHEPPARD, Mr. Peter Michael
SHEPPARD, Mr. Reginald Thomas
SHERET, Mr. William Allen
SHERIDAN, Mr. Alan Peter
SHERIDAN, Ms. Hayley
SHERLOCK, Mrs. Estelle Gaye
SHERRINGTON, Mr. David
SHERRY, Mr. Michael Gabriel
SHERWOOD, Mrs. Anny Kirkegaard
SHERWOOD, Mr. John Seton
SHETH, Mr. Vipul Pravinchandra
SHETLY, Mr. David Lewis
SHEW, Mr. Edmund Jeffrey
SHIELDS, Mr. Barry Joseph Mark
SHIERS, Mr. Paul Thomas
SHILLINGLAW, Mr. Peter
SHILSTON, Miss. Nichola Jayne
SHINN, Mr. David John Brooklyn
SHIPLEY, Mr. Thomas John
SHIRLEY, Mr. David John
SHIRLEY, Mr. Philip Evelyn
SHIRTCLIFFE, Mr. Stephen James
SHOESMITH, Mr. David Edward
SHONCHHATRA, Mr. Ashvinkumar M
SHONE, Miss. Amanda Jane
SHONE, Mrs. Marcella Jane
SHOOTER, Mr. Richard Graham
SHORE, Mr. Charles Nicholas
SHORE, Mr. Laurence Charles
SHORT, Mr. Ian George
SHORT, Mr. Paul Richard
SHORT, Mr. Paul Trevor
SHORTRIDGE, Mr. Andrew Lancaster
SHORTRIDGE, Mr. Anthony John
SHRINGARPURE, Mr. Atul Jagannath

SHRUBB, Mr. Christopher John
SIBA, Mr. Miroslav
SIBCY, Mrs. Eileen Patricia
SIBLEY, Mr. James William
SIDAWAY, Mr. Jeremy Frederick John
SIDDIQI, Mr. Amir
SIDDIQUI, Mr. Mohammed Imran
SIDDIQUI, Mr. Mohammed Javed
SIDDLE, Mr. Richard James
SILINS, Miss. Zinaida Biruta
SILK, Mr. Antony Peter
SILVER, Mr. Alan John
SILVER, Mr. Gordon Robert
SILVER, Mr. Peter John
SILVERMAN, Mr. Irving
SIM, Mr. Michael Cher Khuan
SIM, Mr. Peter William John
SIMCOX, Mr. David
SIMCOX, Mr. Joseph Richard Maurice
SIMLER, Mr. Gerald Joseph
SIMM, Mrs. Jenifer Harley
SIMMONDS, Mr. John Anthony Edward
SIMMONS, Mr. Mark Andrew
SIMMONS, Mr. Paul Jonathan
SIMMS, Mr. Greig Thomas
SIMONS, Mr. Anthony Victor
SIMONS, Mr. Gavin Ronald Maurice
SIMONS, Mr. Richard Alan
SIMPKINS, Mr. John
SIMPSON, Mr. Charles Haddon McBratney
SIMPSON, Mr. Dale Howard
SIMPSON, Mr. Graham Cooper
SIMPSON, Mr. Ian Stanley
SIMPSON, Mr. Neil Ferguson
SIMPSON, Mr. Richard Neil
SIMPSON, Mr. Robert Mark
SIMPSON-PRICE, Mrs. Dianne Elizabeth
SIMS, Mr. Julian Leslie
SINCLAIR, Mr. Deryck Allan Peter
SINCLAIR, Mr. Michael Nathan
SINCLAIR, Mr. Walter Isaac
SINDEN, Mr. Alan Jeremy
SINDEN, Mrs. Janis Sylvia
SINDLE, Mr. Graham James
SINFIELD, Mr. Michael John
SINGH, Mr. Balbir
SINGH, Mr. Harpal
SINGH, Mr. Harsharan Francis William Jeeves
SISSONS, Mr. Damien Stephen John
SITCH, Mr. David Charles
SIVA-PRAKASAM, Mr. Christopher Nesakumar
SKARPARIS, Mr. Christakis
SKEATES, Mr. Alan John
SKEELES, Mr. John William
SKELLS, Mrs. Rachel Marion
SKELTON, Mr. Malcolm James
SKINGLE, Mr. David Nevile
SKIPPER, Mr. Paul Arthur Rees
SKOLNICK, Mr. Ian Nathan
SLACK, Mr. Kevin
SLATER, Mr. Colin David
SLATER, Mr. Frederick Charles
SLATER, Mr. Geoffrey David
SLATER, Mr. Gerald Robert
SLATER, Miss. Jacqueline Suzanne
SLATER, Mr. Paul
SLATER, Mr. Stephen Peter
SLATER, Mr. Timothy William
SLAVIN, Mr. Laurence Mark
SLEIGHT, Mr. Mark James
SLOAN, Mr. Sean William
SLONEEM, Mr. Jeffrey
SLUCKIS, Mr. Ian
SMALL, Mr. Matthew George
SMALLEY, Mr. Michael
SMART, Mr. Christopher Stephen Kaye
SMART, Mrs. Laura Jane
SMART, Mr. Robert Kevin
SMEDLEY, Mr. Richard John
SMEDLEY, Mr. Richard William
SMEDLEY, Mr. Robert Charles Boleyne
SMETHURST, Mr. Ian Thomas
SMITH, Mr. Adrian Dagley
SMITH, Mr. Alan Gregson
SMITH, Mr. Albert Malcolm
SMITH, Mrs. Alison Heather
SMITH, Mr. Allan Esler
SMITH, Mrs. Amanda Anne
SMITH, Ms. Amanda Elizabeth
SMITH, Mr. Andrew David
SMITH, Mr. Andrew Nathan
SMITH, Mr. Andrew Peter
SMITH, Mrs. Anita Janine Mary
SMITH, Mrs. Beverley Louise
SMITH, Miss. Catherine Anne
SMITH, Mr. Colin Harold Pottier
SMITH, Mr. David Austin
SMITH, Mr. David Charles
SMITH, Mr. David George
SMITH, Mr. David John
SMITH, Mr. David John
SMITH, Mr. David Mark
SMITH, Mr. David Owen
SMITH, Miss. Diane Joy
SMITH, Mrs. Elizabeth Anne

Tax Faculty Members - Alphabetical

SMITH, Mr. Geoffrey
SMITH, Mr. Geoffrey Dennis
SMITH, Mrs. Gillian Erica
SMITH, Miss. Gillian Wendy
SMITH, Mr. Glen Warren
SMITH, Miss. Hazel Marie
SMITH, Mr. Hazel Sharon
SMITH, Mr. Ian
SMITH, Mr. Ian William
SMITH, Mr. Jeremy Charles Allan
SMITH, Mr. John Nigel
SMITH, Mr. John Simon Bertie
SMITH, Mr. Jonathan Francis
SMITH, Mr. Jonathan Frederick
SMITH, Mrs. Kathryn Anne
SMITH, Mr. Kerry Ann
SMITH, Mr. Kimball Robyn Gordon
SMITH, Mr. Leslie Frederick
SMITH, Mrs. Lorna Claire
SMITH, Mr. Mark Robert
SMITH, Mr. Martin Anthony
SMITH, Mr. Martin Phillip
SMITH, Mr. Martyn Douglas
SMITH, Mr. Martyn Stuart
SMITH, Mr. Michael Frank Torble
SMITH, Mr. Michael John
SMITH, Mr. Michael John
SMITH, Mr. Neil David
SMITH, Mr. Nigel David
SMITH, Mr. Oliver Samuel
SMITH, Mr. Paul Bernard
SMITH, Mr. Paul Martin
SMITH, Mrs. Penelope Jayne
SMITH, Mr. Peter
SMITH, Mr. Peter
SMITH, Mr. Philip Mckelvie
SMITH, Mr. Richard George
SMITH, Mr. Richard Marfell
SMITH, Mr. Roderick James Anthony
SMITH, Mr. Roger John
SMITH, Mr. Ronald Charles Peter
SMITH, Mr. Sean Russell
SMITH, Mr. Stephen Andrew
SMITH, Mr. Stephen Paul
SMITH, Mr. Stephen Roger
SMITH, Mr. Terence Albert
SMITH, Mr. Thomas Edward James
SMITH, Mr. Thomas James
SMITH, Mr. Timothy Guy Knowles
SMITH, Mr. Timothy John
SMITH, Mr. Trevor John
SMITH, Mr. Wayne Philip
SMITHAM, Mrs. Shirin Sarah
SMITHSON, Mr. Anthony John Michael
SMY, Mr. Michael David
SMYK, Mrs. Catherine
SMYLLIE, Mr. Alastair James
SNAITH, Mr. Christopher James
SNAPE, Mr. George
SNELGAR, Mrs. Alison Margaret
SNELLING, Mr. Jean-Philippe Albion
SNOOK, Mr. Alan
SNOWDEN, Mr. John Frederick Hugh
SNOWLING, Mr. Martin James
SNYDER, Sir Michael (John)
SOBER, Mr. Anthony Lionel
SODEN, Mr. Matthew James
SODHA, Mr. Kamal
SOHOR, Mr. Michael Eugene
SOKHAL, Mr. Jagdish Paul Roy
SOLANKI, Mr. Ashwin Damji
SOLANKI, Mr. Vijay
SOLAZZO, Mr. Salvatore
SOLOMON, Miss. Alison Elizabeth Ann
SOLOMON, Mr. Sefton Alexander
SOLOMONS, Mr. Kenneth Sidney
SOMERFIELD, Mrs. Adrienne B
SOMERSTON, Mr. Malcolm Steven
SOMERVILLE, Mr. Ian Christopher
SOMERVILLE-WOODWARD, Mrs. Lynn Patricia
SOMJI, Mr. Akberali Fazel
SOMMERS, Miss. Catherine Louise
SONN, Mr. Michael Anthony
SONNEBORN, Mr. Peter Michael
SOOD, Mr. Sanjeev
SOPHER, Mr. Victor
SOTERI, Mr. Philippos Kalli
SOTERIOU, Mr. Panicos
SOTERIOU, Mr. Robert
SOTIRIOU, Mr. Achilleas
SOUTAR, Mr. James
SOUTER, Ms. Gwen Henderson
SOUTHERINGTON, Mr. Nigel James
SOUTHGATE, Mr. Robert James
SOUTHWARD, Mr. Eric James
SOUTHWORTH, Mr. Ian Gerard
SOWTER, Mr. Timothy James
SPANO, Mr. Marco
SPARKE, Mr. Michael
SPARKES, Mr. Richard William
SPARROW, Mrs. Heather
SPASH, Mrs. Susan
SPAULS, Mrs. Helen Jayne
SPECTERMAN, Mr. Darren
SPECTERMAN, Mr. David Barry
SPEDDING, Mr. David Newman

SPELLER, Mr. Christopher Kenneth
SPELLER, Mr. John Stanley
SPENCE, Mr. Maxwell Stanley
SPENCE CLARKE, Mr. Alistair Marino Archibald
SPENCER, Mr. Anthony Edward Tully
SPENCER, Mrs. Carolyn Mary
SPENCER, Miss. Christa Andrea Elizabeth
SPENCER, Mr. Keith Terence
SPENCER, Mr. Martin Russell William
SPENCER, Mr. Philip
SPICER, Mr. Barry Leslie
SPICER, Mrs. Michelle
SPICER, Mr. Paul Frederick
SPICER, Mr. Russell
SPINKS, Mr. Gordon
SPITTLE, Mr. Martin Henry Peter
SPOFFORTH, Mr. David Mark
SPOKES, Mr. Christopher Daniel
SPOONER, Mr. Andrew Charles
SPOTTISWOODE, Mr. David Martin
SPRAGUE, Miss. Carole Evette
SPRIGGS, Mr. Harvey John William
SPRING, Mr. Ian David
SPRINGBETT, Ms. Jill Louise
SPRINGER, Mr. Nigel Frank
SPURR, Mr. Geoffrey Stuart
STABBINS, Mr. Derek Henry
STABLES, Miss. June Christine
STABLES, Mr. Peter
STACEY, Mr. Ian
STACKHOUSE, Mr. Andrew
STADIUS, Mrs. Judith Margaret
STAFFORD, Mr. Julian Robert
STAFFORD, Mr. Kenneth James
STAFFORD, Mr. Michael
STAFFORD, Mr. Roger Thomas
STAFFORD, Mr. Scott John
STAINTON, Mrs. Helen
STAIT, Mr. Philip Gordon
STALLARD, Mr. Philip Adrian
STANBRA, Mr. Graham Michael
STANFORD, Mr. Paul
STANIFORTH, Mr. Adrian Charles Dominic
STANIFORTH, Mr. Philip Guy
STANLEY, Mr. Roger Clayton Holbrook
STANLEY, Mr. Terence John
STANNARD, Mr. Wayne
STANT, Mr. Andrew Warren
STANTON, Mr. John
STANTON, Mrs. Marion Janet
STANTON, Mr. Robert John
STANWORTH, Miss. Tanya Maria
STAPLEHURST, Mr. Trevor
STAPLETON, Mr. Graham Martin
STAPLETON, Mr. Paul David
STARK, Mr. Paul Graeme
STARKEY, Mrs. Sophie Anne
STARKIE, Mr. Thomas Oliver Matthew
STARLEY, Mr. John Keith
STARR, Mr. Christopher
STARR, Mr. Lionel
STARTIN, Mr. Frank David
STAVRINIDES, Mr. Nicolaos
STEAD, Mr. Alan George
STEAN, Mr. Michael Frank
STEBBINGS, Mr. Alan John
STEBBINGS, Mr. Dudley James
STECHLER, Mr. Alain Leon
STEDMAN, Miss. Philippa Ann
STEED, Mr. Anthony Jos
STEELE, Mr. Nigel Peter
STEEN, Mr. Colin
STEINBERG, Mr. Ian Beverley
STEINBERG, Mr. Nathan Anthony
STEINSON, Mrs. Rosemary Jane
STEINTHAL, Mr. Anthony Paul Richard
STEMP, Miss. Kelly
STENT, Mr. John Henry
STEPHENS, Mr. David Geoffrey
STEPHENS, Mr. David William
STEPHENS, Mr. Ian Richard
STEPHENSON, Mr. David John
STEPHENSON, Mr. John Wilson
STEPHENSON, Mr. Roger Anthony
STEPNEY, Mr. Robert Adam
STERN, Mr. Iain James
STERN, Mr. Michael Charles
STERN, Mr. Simon Dan
STERNLICHT, Mr. Asher
STEVART, Mr. John Edward Douglas
STEVENS, Mrs. Alison Mary
STEVENS, Mr. Clive Robert
STEVENS, Mr. Colin Roland
STEVENS, Mr. David John
STEVENS, Ms. Grace Elanor
STEVENS, Mr. Ivan Hardy
STEVENS, Mr. John Frederick
STEVENS, Mr. Nigel Brent
STEVENS, Mr. Patrick Tom
STEVENSON, Mr. Alan Leonard
STEVENSON, Mrs. Janet Mary
STEVENSON, Mr. Nicholas Raymond
STEWARD, Mr. Clive James
STEWARD, Mr. John Andrew
STEWART, Mr. Alastair James
STEWART, Mr. Christopher John

STEWART, Mr. Christopher Norman
STEWART, Mr. Iain Elliott
STEWART, Mr. Ian Peter
STEWART, Mr. Jeremy David
STEWART, Mr. John Sanderson
STEWART, Miss. Lauren Louise
STEWART, Mr. Michael George
STEWART, Mr. Richard Charles
STIMPSON, Mr. John Robert
STIRLING, Mrs. Judith Ann
STITT, Mr. Anthony Vincent Portman
STITT, Mr. Paul Benedict Anderson
STOCK, Mr. Lynton Robert
STOCKER, Mr. Russell Victor
STOCKFORD, Mrs. Rosemary Heather
STOCKLEY, Mr. Timothy Robert
STODDART, Mr. Peter
STOKER, Mr. Peter Jeffrey
STOKES, Miss. Deborah Anne
STOKES, Mr. Donald Clifford
STOKOE, Ms. Anna Marie
STOLTZ, Mr. David Albert
STONE, David
STONE, Mr. Geoffrey George
STONE, Miss. Jennifer Anne
STONE, Ms. Lisa
STONE, Mr. Michael Ralph
STONE, Mr. Richard Andrew
STONE, Mr. Robert Edwin
STONE, Mr. Stephen Courtney
STONEFIELD, Mr. David Anthony
STONIER, Mr. Christopher
STOPFORD, Mrs. Anne Louise
STOPFORD, Mr. Brian John
STOPFORD, Mrs. Prudence Jane Louise
STOPPARD, Mr. Richard Frederick
STOPPS, Mr. Kevin Peter
STOPYRA, Mrs. Jacqueline Elizabeth
STOREY, Mrs. Julia
STOREY, Mr. Michael Charles
STOTT, Mr. Michael Moreton
STRANGE, Mr. Ian Michael
STRATTON-BROWN, Mrs. Helen Celia
STRAUGHAN, Mr. Brian Jonathan
STRAUSS, Mr. Steven Michael
STRAW, Mr. Anthony Robert James
STRAWSON, Mrs. Kay Vanessa
STREET, Miss. Theresa Anne
STRIKE, Mr. Duncan John
STRINGER, Mr. Anthony Charles
STRONACH, Mr. Adam James
STRONG, Mr. Neil William
STROUD, Miss. Ruth Julia
STUBBS, Mr. Gary
STUDHAM, Mr. Michael David
STURMEY, Mr. Neil John
STURROCK, Ms. Laura-Ann
STYLES, Mr. Leslie
SUCHAK, Mr. Anant
SUCHAK, Mr. Shailesh Manilal
SUCKLING, Mr. David John
SUDWORTH, Mr. John
SUFRAZ, Mr. Hassam
SUFRIN, Mr. Michael Maurice
SUGARMAN, Mr. Clive Jonathan
SUGARMAN, Mr. Jack
SUGARWHITE, Mr. Jeffrey
SUGDEN, Mr. Anthony Brendan
SUHAIL, Mr. Nazmil
SULEMAN, Mr. Abdul Kayoom
SULEMAN, Mr. Ebrahim
SULLIVAN, Mr. Christopher Robin
SULLIVAN, Mr. David John
SULLIVAN, Mr. David Mark
SULLIVAN, Miss. Susan Ann
SUMARIA-SHAH, Mr. Surendra Kumar Devshi
SUMMERFIELD, Mrs. Judith Ann
SUMMERS, Mr. Alistair Gerald
SUMMERS, Mr. David
SUMMERS, Mr. Robin
SUNDERLAND, Mr. David Grahame
SURFLEET, Mr. Robert John
SURRALL, Mr. Peter Howard
SURRIDGE, Miss. Alison Mary
SURRY, Mr. Keith Raymond Stewart
SUSGAARD-VIGON, Mr. Marc James
SUSSMAN, Mr. Ian Anthony
SUSSMAN, Mr. Keith Andrew
SUSSMAN, Mr. Steven Anthony
SUTHERLAND, Bruce Wilson
SUTTON, Mr. Barry Read
SUTTON, Mr. John Edward
SUTTON, Miss. Lesley Jane
SUTTON, Mr. Peter James
SUTTON, Mr. Robert David
SUTTON, Mr. Rodney Maginess
SUTTON, Mr. Roger William
SUTTON, Mr. Steven Maxwell
SWAFFIELD, Mr. Roger
SWAIN, Mr. Frank Colin
SWAINE, Mrs. Heather
SWALES, Mr. John William
SWANNELL, Mrs. Barbara
SWANSON, Mrs. Carol Elspeth
SWARBRICK, Mr. Peter
SWASH, Mr. Peter Charles

SWATMAN, Mr. Derek James
SWEENEY, Mrs. Kaye
SWIFT, Mr. Joseph John
SWIFT, Dr. Michael Joseph Robert
SWIFT, Mr. Susan Winifred
SWINGLEHURST, Mr. Alan John
SYKES, Mr. Christopher John
SYKES, Mr. Eric
SYKES, Mr. Geoffrey Howarth
SYKES, Mr. John Buchanan
SYKES, Mr. Leslie Joseph
SYKES, Ms. Suzanne Louise
SYMES, Mr. Peter Sigourney
SYMONS, Mr. Paul
SYNGHAL, Mr. Manoj Kumar
SYREE, Mr. Jeremy Anton
SYRON, Mr. Derek Vincent
SYSON, Mr. Russell Nigel
SZCZEPANSKI, Mr. Jan
SZE, Mr. Hua Ming
SZMIGIN, Mr. Christopher Richard
TABERNER, Mr. Robert John
TABOR, Mr. Robert Mark
TACCONI, Mr. Henry
TADMAN, Mr. Moray Roger
TAGGART, Mr. John Michael
TAILOR, Mr. Bhasker
TAILOR, Mr. Paresh
TAILOR, Mrs. Vanita Bhupendra
TAIT, Mrs. Hazel Margaret
TAIT, Mr. Michael John Hewson
TAIT, Mr. Nicholas Sebastian Charles
TAKAHASHI, Mrs. Fiona Helen
TAKHAR, Mrs. Kamaljit Kaur
TALBERT, Mrs. Alison Clare
TALBOT, Mrs. Fiona Margaret
TALBOT, Mr. John Guy
TALBOT, Mr. Stephen
TALBOTT, Mr. Richard John
TALL, Mr. Andrew Brian Orme
TALLON, Mr. David Seymour
TALLON, Mr. John Mark
TALLON, Mrs. Paula Christina
TALUKDAR, Mr. Muhammad Noorul Huda
TAMURI, Mr. Shamim Uddin
TAN, Miss. E Hun
TAN, Mr. Ghee Kiat
TAN, Mr. Keng Nam
TANG, Mr. Chin Wun
TANG, Mr. Long-Sing Raymond
TANG, Mr. Renold Lee On
TANNA, Mr. Piyush Jayantilal
TANNA, Mr. Sunil
TANNER, Mr. Henry John
TANNER, Mr. Stephen Paul
TAPPIN, Mr. Andrew Brice
TARAZ, Mr. Afshin
TARBARD, Mr. Christopher John
TARREN, Mr. Peter
TASKER, Mrs. Gillian Maxine
TATE, Mr. Adrian John Anthony
TATE, Mr. Harold Bryan Keith
TATTON, Mr. Malcolm
TATTUM, Mrs. Susan Ruth
TATTUM, Mr. Paul Nigel
TAYLER, Mr. Hugh Edgar
TAYLOR, Mr. Alastair James
TAYLOR, Miss. Anthea Jane
TAYLOR, Mr. Brian Charles
TAYLOR, Mr. Brian David
TAYLOR, Mr. Colin Jeffrey
TAYLOR, Mr. Damian Peter
TAYLOR, Dr. David Alan
TAYLOR, Mr. David Albert
TAYLOR, Mr. David Lee
TAYLOR, Mr. Donald Thomas
TAYLOR, Mrs. Dorothy Ruth
TAYLOR, Mr. Duncan Andrew
TAYLOR, Mr. Ian David
TAYLOR, Mr. Ian Richard
TAYLOR, Ms. Joanne Elizabeth
TAYLOR, Mr. John David
TAYLOR, Mrs. Laura
TAYLOR, Mr. Mark Owen
TAYLOR, Mr. Martin Anthony
TAYLOR, Mr. Michael Colin
TAYLOR, Mr. Michael Denis
TAYLOR, Mr. Neville Kenneth John
TAYLOR, Mr. Nicholas Albert
TAYLOR, Mr. Nicholas Roy
TAYLOR, Mr. Paul Anthony
TAYLOR, Mr. Paul Edwin
TAYLOR, Mr. Paul Norman
TAYLOR, Mr. Peter Alan
TAYLOR, Mr. Peter Geoffrey
TAYLOR, Mr. Philip Charles
TAYLOR, Mr. Philip Harry
TAYLOR, Mr. Richard Cecil Charlton
TAYLOR, Mr. Richard John
TAYLOR, Mr. Robert Anthony Steven
TAYLOR, Miss. Suzanne Elizabeth
TAYLOR, Mr. Timothy John
TAYLOR, Mrs. Vanessa Wellings
TAYLOR REA, Mr. David Gordon
TAYUB, Mr. Abdul Aziz
TEASDALE, Mr. Paul Raymond
TEATHER, Mr. Richard Paul

TECKOE, Mr. David Alfred
TEGG, Mr. Malcolm Frederick
TELFORD, Mr. Gary Alan
TEMLETT, Mr. John Christopher
TEMPEST, Ms. Kylie May
TEMPLEMAN, Ms. Clare Elisabeth
TENZER, Mr. Russell Paul
TERRY, Mr. Christopher
TERRY, Mr. James Richard
TERRY, Mr. Michael Charles William
TESHOME, Ms. Sarah
TETLEY, Mrs. Christine Mary
TETLEY, Mr. James Robert
TEVERSON, Miss. Lisa Helen
TEW, Miss. Serena Elizabeth
THACKABERRY, Mrs. Clare Anne
THACKERAY, Miss. Vivien Amanda
THAKKAR, Mr. Mayur Chinubhai
THAKRAR, Mr. Ajit Kalidas
THAKRAR, Mr. Harish Mathuradas
THAKRAR, Mr. Jaysukh Amritlal
THAKRAR, Mr. Jentilal Prabhudas
THAKRAR, Mr. Pradeep Girdharlal
THAKRAR, Mr. Rajni Gordhandas
THAKRAR, Mr. Subhash Vithaldas
THAMMANNA, Mr. Subbash Chandra
THANAWALA, Mr. Atul Maneklal
THANTREY, Mr. Shabir-Ud-Deen
THARMARATNAM, Ms. Nandhini
THEAKER, Mr. Stephen Michael
THEBRIDGE, Mr. David Lawrence
THEMISTOCLI, Mr. Themis
THEXTON, Mr. Michael John
THICKPENNY, Mr. Roger John
THIMONT, Ms. Ann Mary
THIND, Mr. Jitender Singh
THIRKETTLE, Mr. Roger
THIRLWALL, Mrs. Nicola Jane
THIRUVASAGAM, Mr. Maniccavasagan
THOBURN, Mrs. Fiona Jane
THOMAS, Mr. Adrian Anthony Michael
THOMAS, Mr. Anthony Haydn
THOMAS, Mrs. Catherine Helen
THOMAS, Mr. David Arthur
THOMAS, Mr. David Philip Glyn
THOMAS, Mrs. Deirdre Anne
THOMAS, Miss. Emma Jayne
THOMAS, Mr. Fitzroy Leroy Conroy
THOMAS, Miss. Hazel Claire
THOMAS, Mr. Huw
THOMAS, Mr. Huw
THOMAS, Mr. Hywel Meredith Winston
THOMAS, Mrs. Janet Linda
THOMAS, Mr. Jeffrey Raymond
THOMAS, Mr. Keith
THOMAS, Mr. Keith Michael
THOMAS, Mr. Kevin Patrick
THOMAS, Ms. Lesley Anne
THOMAS, Miss. Maureen Ann
THOMAS, Mr. Nicholas Simon
THOMAS, Mr. Nigel John
THOMAS, Mr. Richard Alun
THOMAS, Mr. Richard Brian
THOMAS, Mr. Robin Grenville
THOMAS, Mr. Russell Leslie
THOMAS, Mrs. Sally-Ann
THOMAS, Mr. Simon Reginald
THOMAS, Mrs. Susan Teresa
THOMAS, Mr. Wayne Douglas
THOMAS, Mr. William Edward Lloyd
THOMPSON, Mr. Andrew
THOMPSON, Mrs. Ann Margaret
THOMPSON, Mr. David Andrew
THOMPSON, Mr. David D'arcy
THOMPSON, Mr. David Elliott
THOMPSON, Mr. Graham Philip
THOMPSON, Mr. Graham William
THOMPSON, Mr. Ian
THOMPSON, Mr. Ian Barry
THOMPSON, Mr. Michael John
THOMPSON, Mr. Philip Geoffrey
THOMPSON, Mr. Richard
THOMPSON, Mr. Richard William
THOMPSON, Mr. Richard William Graham
THOMSON, Mr. Alan Alexander
THOMSON, Mr. Alexander John
THOMSON, Miss. Margaret Jane
THOMSON, Mr. Robert Brian
THORN, Mr. Peter
THORNTON, Mr. Graham
THORNTON, Mr. James Paul
THORNTON, Mr. John Richard
THORNTON, Mrs. Margaret Rosemary
THORPE, Mrs. Carole Elizabeth
THORPE, Mr. Nicholas Andrew
THORPE, Mr. Phillip Arthur
THORPE, Mr. Stuart Kenneth
THOULASS, Mrs. Emma
THROSSELL, Mr. Andrew
THRUSH, Mr. Giles Anthony
THURSFIELD, Mr. David John
TICE, Mr. Colin
TICKEL, Mrs. Amanda Judith
TIDBURY, Mr. Nigel Oliver
TIDMARSH, Mr. Richard John Studley
TIERNAY, Mrs. Nicola Ferris
TIERNEY, Mrs. Mary Ann

TILEY, Mr. Mark Stephen
TILMAN, Miss. Joan Ann
TILSON, Ms. Hannah Lindsay
TIMBRELL, Mrs. Sarah Elizabeth
TIMMINS, Mrs. Gail
TIMMS, Mr. Peter John
TINDLE, Mr. Robert Ralph
TING, Mrs. Christina Kiik Ing
TING, Miss. Ei Leen
TINKLER, Mrs. Yvonne Karen
TINNER, Mr. Richard
TIPPETT, Mr. Jonathan Charles Morley
TIPPING, Mr. Andrew
TIPPING, Mr. John Alfred
TIPPING, Mr. Paul Richard
TISH, Mr. Harvey Lester
TITMUSS, Miss. Rachel
TIZARD, Mr. Michael Robert
TOBIN, Mrs. Maria Angela
TODD, Mr. Andrew William
TODD, Mr. Colin Michael William
TODD, Mr. Martyn Walter
TOGHILL, Mr. Malcolm Stewart
TOINTON, Mr. Stephen Leslie
TOLAN, Mr. John Peter
TOLAT, Mr. Suresh
TOLLEY, Mrs. Claire Helen
TOMASZEWSKI, Mr. Christopher Ryszard Gregory
TOMKINS, Mr. Nicholas Graeme
TOMKINSON, Mr. Derek William
TOMLIN, Mrs. Rebecca Catherine
TOMLINSON, Mr. Ian Edward
TOMLINSON, Miss. Joanne Marguerite
TOMLINSON, Ms. Rosemary Olive
TOMPSETT, Mr. Michael Frederick
TOMSETT, Alan Jeffrey
TOMSETT, Mr. Eric George
TONG, Mr. James Edward
TONKS, Mr. George Howard
TOOLEY, Mrs. Lesley Ann
TOOVEY, Mr. Richard
TOPPER, Mr. Alan
TOPPERMAN, Mr. Simon
TOPPING, Mrs. Janet
TORBITT, Mr. Geoffrey Colin
TOSH, Mr. Peter McLaren
TOSTEVIN, Mr. Philip James
TOULSON, Mr. Stephen Reginald
TOWERS, Mrs. Julie Ann
TOWERS, Mr. Neil William
TOWLSON, Mr. Malcolm Richard
TOZER, Mr. Richard
TRAMONTINI, Mr. Clive
TRAN, Mr. William
TRANTER, Mrs. Angela Elizabeth
TRANTER, Mr. Jim
TRANTER, Mr. Paul Alistair
TRANTER, Mr. Stephen Ernest William
TRAVERS, Mr. Anthony Howard
TRAYLEN, Mr. Geoffrey Francis
TRAYNOR, Mr. John Thomas
TREADGOLD, Mr. Peter William
TREHARNE, Mr. Myles Gregory Dale
TREMBLING, Mr. Mark Philip
TRENFIELD, Mr. Dennis Walter Stuart
TRENT, Mr. Jeremy Steven
TREVELYAN, Mr. Nigel David
TREVOR, Mr. Christopher John
TRIGG, Mr. Michael Jonathan
TRILL, Mr. David John
TRIMBY, Mr. James Edward
TRIMM, Mr. Michael James
TRINHAM, Mr. John Dennis
TROBIA, Mr. Alessandro
TROISE, Mr. Christopher Joseph James
TROMANS, Mr. David Brian
TROUGHTON, Mr. Roger
TROUT, Mr. David Harold
TRUELOVE, Mr. Charles Richard
TRUEMAN, Mr. Richard John
TRUMAN, Miss. Elizabeth
TRUMAN, Mr. Leslie Samuel Alfred
TRUMFIELD, Miss. Diane Marie
TRUNCHION, Mr. Robert William
TRUSCOTT, Mr. Andrew Thomas
TRY, Mr. Christopher Colin
TSAI, Mr. Philip Wing Chung
TSANG, Ms. Wai Lui
TSE, Mrs. Sylvia Sau-Bing
TSE YOUNG SUN, Mr. Joseph
TSUI, Mr. Edward
TUBBY, Mr. Kevin Eric
TUCK, Dr. Penelope Ann Louise
TUCKER, Mr. Alan William
TUCKER, Mr. Peter David
TUCKER, Mr. Robert John
TUCKEY, Mr. Michael Anthony
TUDOR PRICE, Mr. Simon Hywel
TUFF, Mrs. Lyn Caroline
TUFFIN, Mr. Peter Jonathan
TUFFIN, Mr. Roger Quentin Allon
TUFNELL, Mr. Mark Henry
TULLETT, Mr. Peter John
TULLOCH, Mr. Clive William
TULLY, Mr. Edward Christopher
TUNG SING, Mr. Cheong Mou Yuen

TUPPER, Mr. Robin Charles
TURFORD, Mr. Andrew John
TURK, Mr. Darrell John
TURLAND, Mr. Alan John
TURLAND, Mr. Kevin John
TURLEY, Mrs. Janet Valerie
TURLEY, Mr. William Jonathan
TURNBULL, Mrs. Alison Jane
TURNBULL, Mr. Michael Roy
TURNBULL-HALL, Mrs. Caroline Sarah
TURNER, Mrs. Christine Janet
TURNER, Mrs. Christine Marie
TURNER, Mr. Christopher Michael
TURNER, Mr. David Daniel
TURNER, Mr. Grahame Howard Jonathan
TURNER, Mr. Hugh David
TURNER, Mr. Ian Andrew
TURNER, Mr. James
TURNER, Mrs. Karen Anita
TURNER, Mr. Kevin William
TURNER, Mr. Mark Richard Charles
TURNER, Mr. Michael Richard
TURNER, Mr. Nicholas Fyers
TURNER, Mr. Raymond Charles
TURNER, Mr. Richard David
TURNER, Mr. Stephen Paul
TURNER, Mrs. Susan Natalie
TURNER, Dr. Thomas Stephen
TURTON, Mrs. Angela Clare
TUTIN, Mr. Richard Philip
TUTT, Mr. Antony Timothy David
TWADDLE, Mr. Andrew Bryan
TWEEDIE, Mr. Matthew Stuart
TWISSELL, Mr. Michael John
TWYDLE, Mr. Robert Michael
TYACKE, Ms. Sara Louise
TYAS, Mr. Stephen Richard
TYDEMAN, Mr. Robert Kenneth
TYLER, Mr. Philip Geoffrey
TYSON, Mr. Matthew Ronald
TYZZER, Mr. Andrew Thomas
TZOULIOU, Mr. Tzoulios Andreas
UDALL, Mrs. Stephanie Pamela
UDANI, Mr. Paresh
ULLMANN, Mr. Herman
ULLYOTT, Mrs. Samantha Jane
ULRICH, Mr. Michael Philip
UMBLEJA, Mr. Evan Peter
UNDERHILL, Mr. Alan
UNDERHILL, Mr. John Lewis Laird
UNDERWOOD, Mr. Gary
UNSWORTH, Mr. Peter Maurice
UNTHANK, Mrs. Rosemary Anne
UPCOTT, Mr. Simon Christopher
UPPAL, Mr. Balbir Singh
UPSTONE, Mr. David Robert
UPTON, Mr. Dean Vearncombe
URBAN, Ms. Helena Claire
URMSTON, Mr. Philip
USHER, Miss. Joan Beatrice
USHER-SOMERS, Mr. Robert John
UTTING, Miss. Helen Louise
VAHORA, Mr. Zakir Hussain Moosa
VAINES, Mr. Peter Stephen
VAINKER, Mr. Nicholas Marcel
VALE, Mr. Christopher John
VALJI, Mr. Nazir Mohamed Hussein
VAN VEEN, Mr. Christopher Willem
VAN VLIET, Mr. Richard Christopher
VANAGS, Mrs. Samantha Joanne
VANDERPUIJE, Mrs. Antoinette
VANN SMITH, Mrs. Joanna
VANNOZZI, Mr. Paul
VARNEY, Mr. Adrian Simon
VARNEY, Mr. Keith Bernard
VARTY, Mr. Paul Andrew
VASEY, Mr. Charles Harold
VASWANI, Mr. Mahesh
VAUGHAN, Mr. Alan John
VAUGHAN, Mr. David Robin
VAUGHAN, Mrs. Mary
VAUGHAN, Mr. Richard Leslie
VAUGHAN, Mr. Roger Albert
VEALL, Mr. Malcolm Peter
VEARES, Mr. Howard Richard
VED, Mr. Jayendra Janardan
VENITT, Mr. Malcolm Alan
VERKADE-CAVE, Mrs. Rebecca Ann
VERNEY, Mr. Frederick Charles
VERRALL, Mr. Bernard Peter
VESEY, Mr. Thomas Francis
VICCAJEE, Mr. Rutton Behram
VICE, Mr. David Patrick
VICKERS, Mr. Jeremy Philip Hilton
VICKERS, Mr. Stephen
VICTORY, Mrs. Stella Barbara
VIDLER, Edwin Norman
VIGAR, Miss. Amanda Adele
VIGAR, Mr. Richard Leonard James
VIGORS, Mr. Patrick Mervyn Doyne
VIJH, Mr. Deepak
VILLIS, Mrs. Deborah Anne
VINCENT, Mr. John Stephen
VINCENT, Mr. Paul Malcolm John
VINE, Miss. Clare Marie
VINE, Mr. Paul Simon
VINER, Mr. Simon Keith

VINES, Mr. Jonathan Edwin
VINSON, Mr. Simon Geoffrey
VISRAM, Mr. Aniz
VITEZ, Mr. Charles Oscar
VOGAN, Mr. Ian
VOICE, Mr. Hugh Alistair
VOIGTS, Mr. Allen Keith
VOISEY, Mr. Howard Gwyn
VOLLER, Mr. Kevin Nicholas
VON BERGEN, Mr. Hugh Robert
VON BERTELE, Mr. Maurice
VON FURER-HAIMENDORF, Mr. Nicholas Cristoph
VORA, Mr. Rajendra Shivalal
VOWLES, Mrs. Hilary Frances
VOWLES, Mr. Richard Anthony
WACKS, Mr. Anthony Charles
WACZKOW, Mrs. Zabetz Enge
WADDELL, Mrs. Gayle Christine
WADDINGTON, Mr. David
WADE, Mr. Michael Musgrave
WADE, Mr. Philip William
WADE-JONES, Mrs. Amanda Jayne
WADEY, Ms. Claire Frances
WADHAM, Miss. Jennifer Susan
WADKIN, Mr. Douglas John
WADSWORTH, Mr. Howard Peter
WAGER, Mr. Edwin John
WAGSTAFF, Mr. David Christopher
WAHID, Miss. Nasreen
WAHNON, Mr. Joshua
WAIGHT, Mr. Peter Charles Staward
WAINE, Mr. Benjamin James
WAINE, Mr. Nigel Jeremy
WAINWRIGHT, Mr. Philip
WAITE, Mr. Paul David
WAITES, Mr. Nicholas Stuart
WAKEFIELD, Mr. John David Christopher
WAKEFIELD, Mrs. Susan Louise
WAKEFORD, Mrs. Julie Carol
WAKEFORD, Mr. Michael Ian
WAKELING, Miss. Margaret Anne
WALA, Mrs. Gwyneth
WALBERTON, Mr. Michael Andrew
WALDEN, Mr. David Simon
WALDRON, Mr. Bernard William
WALDUCK, Mr. Alexander Harold Edward Peter
WALES, Mr. Christopher John
WALES, Mr. Jonathan Robert Hamilton
WALKER, Mr. Adrian
WALKER, Mr. Andrew
WALKER, Mr. Arthur Edward
WALKER, Mr. David Allan
WALKER, Mr. David Ernest John
WALKER, Mr. David Gordon
WALKER, Mr. David William
WALKER, Mrs. Elaine
WALKER, Mr. Graeme Neill
WALKER, Mr. Henry Iain Stancliffe
WALKER, Mr. Philip
WALKER, Mr. Robert Fenwick
WALKER, Mrs. Sally Anne
WALKER, Mrs. Susan Lilian
WALKER, Mr. Terence John
WALKER-SHARP, Mr. Timothy Charles
WALKLETT, Mr. Christopher
WALL, Mrs. Gillian Lesley
WALLACE, Mr. Graham Moncrieff
WALLACE, Mr. Ian Wingrave
WALLACE, Mr. Mark Arthur
WALLACE, Mr. Paul Alexander
WALLER, Mr. John Joseph De-Warrenne
WALLER, Mr. Patrick
WALLER, Mr. Philip
WALLER, Mrs. Rebecca Elizabeth
WALLIS, Mr. John Stanley
WALLIS, Mr. Michael John
WALPOLE, Mrs. Tracy Jane
WALSH, Miss. Deborah Karen
WALSH, Mr. Francis
WALSH, Mr. Gary Michael
WALSH, Mr. Ian James
WALSH, Mr. Ian Roland
WALSH, Mr. Kevin Michael
WALSH, Miss. Sheila Mary
WALTERS, Mr. Alun John
WALTERS, Mr. Clive Anthony
WALTERS, Mr. David Ian
WALTERS, Miss. Julia
WALTERS, Mr. Michael
WALTERS, Mr. Michael Godfrey
WALTHO, Mr. Paul Kenneth Stanley
WALTON, Mrs. Ann Carol
WALTON, Miss. Anna-Marie
WALTON, Mrs. Dawn Catherine
WALTON, Mr. Jeffrey Andrew
WALTON, Neil
WALZER, Miss. Bernice Frances
WANDERER, Mr. Denis Harold
WANSEL, Mr. Florian Fred
WANSTALL, Mrs. Rebecca Rhee
WARBURTON, Mrs. Anita Susan
WARBURTON, Mr. Philip George
WARD, Mr. Anthony Maurice
WARD, Mrs. Catherine Alison
WARD, Mr. David Matthew

WARD, Mr. James
WARD, Mr. John David
WARD, Mr. Michael
WARD, Mr. Michael John
WARD, Mr. Nigel Graham
WARD, Mr. Nigel Richard
WARD, Mr. Peter Murray
WARDLE, Mr. Eric Adrian
WARDROPE, Mrs. Natalie
WARING, Mr. Christopher Thomas
WARNE, Mr. Simon
WARNEFORD, Mr. Brian Richard
WARNER, Mrs. Anita
WARNER, Mr. John
WARNER, Mrs. Linda Ann
WARR, Mr. Timothy Vaughan
WARREN, Mr. Anthony Brian
WARREN, Mr. Benjamin Jack
WARREN, Mr. David Edgar
WARREN, Mr. Derek
WARREN, Mrs. Gillian Evelyn Florence
WARREN, Mr. Martyn Jeffrey Gomer
WARSOP, Mr. Jonathan Philip
WARWICK, Mr. Alan Harold
WASDEN, Mrs. Jane Anita
WASHBOURNE, Mr. Ian Garth
WASU, Mr. Jatinder Singh
WATERHOUSE, Mrs. Amanda Elizabeth
WATERMAN, Mr. Mark Vernon
WATERS, Mr. David Anthony
WATERWORTH, Mr. Martin
WATKIN, Mr. Andrew Bedford
WATKINS, Mr. Alan James
WATKINS, Mr. James Angus Wellwood
WATKINS, Mr. John
WATKINS, Mr. Keith John
WATKINS, Mr. Mark David
WATKINS, Mr. Timothy John
WATKINSON, Mr. Barry Ian
WATKINSON, Mr. David John
WATKINSON, Mrs. Janet Ann
WATSON, Mr. Alexander William
WATSON, Mr. Andrew Muirhead
WATSON, Mr. Anothony Robert
WATSON, Mr. Barry
WATSON, Mr. Brian David
WATSON, Mr. Christopher Michael
WATSON, Miss. Hazel Anne Marie
WATSON, Mr. John David
WATSON, Mrs. Lorna
WATSON, Mr. Michael Raymond
WATSON, Mr. Michael Steven
WATSON, Mr. Peter George
WATSON, Mr. Richard
WATSON, Mr. Robert Michael
WATSON, Mrs. Sian Elizabeth
WATSON, Mr. Stephen Andrew
WATSON, Mr. Stuart Maxwell
WATSON, Mrs. Susan Carol
WATSON, Mr. Timothy
WATSON, Ms. Valerie Diane
WATT, Mrs. Cheryl Ann
WATT, Mr. David Alexander
WATT, Mr. Ian Stewart
WATTS, Miss. Angela Jean
WATTS, Mr. Charles Michael
WATTS, Mr. David James
WATTS, Mr. Graham James
WATTS, Mr. Jeremy James
WATTS, Mr. John Garratt
WATTS, Miss. Kathryn Anne
WATTS, Mr. Michael David
WATTS, Mr. Paul John
WATTS, Mr. Sean Alexander
WAUGH, Mr. David Gary
WAXMAN, Mr. Frank Stephen
WAXMAN, Mr. Stephen Anthony
WAY, Mrs. Elaine Frances
WAYMONT, Mrs. Jacqueline Yvonne
WEARDEN, Mr. Peter Francis
WEATHERILL, Mr. Andrew James
WEAVER, Miss. Christine Anne
WEAVER, Mr. Wayne Geoffrey
WEBB, Mr. Arthur Richard
WEBB, Mrs. Caroline Ann
WEBB, Mr. Colin Thomas
WEBB, Mr. David Charles Patrick
WEBB, Mr. David Rodney
WEBB, Mr. Frank William
WEBB, Mr. Martin
WEBB, Mr. Michael Frederick
WEBB, Mr. Nicholas
WEBB, Mr. Richard Neil
WEBB, Miss. Sharron Elizabeth
WEBB, Mr. Simon John
WEBER, Miss. Angela Louise
WEBSTER, Mr. Ian Stuart
WEBSTER, Mr. Jonathan Paul
WEBSTER, Mrs. Kathleen Winifred
WEBSTER, Mr. Lawrence Andrew
WEBSTER, Mr. Martyn
WEBSTER, Mr. Nigel Buckley
WEBSTER, Mr. Paul
WEBSTER, Mr. Paul Alan
WEBSTER, Mr. Paul Oliver
WEBSTER, Mr. Peter
WEBSTER, Mr. Robert James

WEBSTER, Mr. Simon Paul
WEBSTER, Mr. Timothy Martin
WEBSTER, Mrs. Tina
WEDGE, Mr. Andrew Neil
WEDGWOOD, Mr. Stuart Thomas
WEEDEN, Mr. David William
WEEDEN, Mrs. Dawn
WEIMANN, Mr. Brett Alan
WEINBERG, Mr. Graham
WEINTROB, Mr. Howard Frank
WEISS, Mr. Peter Alfred Mervyn
WEIST, Mr. Derek Jonathan
WELCH, Mr. James David
WELCH, Mr. Martin Brian
WELLAND, Mr. Ross Adrian
WELLS, Miss. Hazel Anne
WELLS, Mr. Timothy Adrian
WELSH, Mr. Brian Frank
WELSH, Mr. Simon Frederick
WEM, Mr. Alistair Ian
WERTH, Mr. Gavin Lawrence
WEST, Mr. Angus
WEST, Mr. Brian William
WEST, Mrs. Gloria Heather
WEST, Mr. Graham John
WEST, Mrs. Rosemary Ada Christina
WESTBURY, Mrs. Sharon
WESTCOTT, Miss. Helen Margaret
WESTCOUGH, Mrs. Anne Elizabeth
WESTMAN, Mr. Nigel Christopher
WESTON, Mr. Joseph Harry Lawrence
WESTON, Mr. Keith Andrew
WESTON, Mr. Michael Arthur
WESTON, Mr. Richard Harry
WESTWOOD, Mr. Graham Phillip
WESTWOOD, Mr. Neil Adrian
WETHERALL, Mr. Stephen John
WEVILL, Mr. Michael John
WHALE, Mrs. Barbara Jean
WHALLEY, Mr. David Johnson
WHALLEY, Mr. Peter James
WHARTON, Mr. Neil Charles
WHATELEY, Mr. Christopher Robert Kelvin
WHATELEY, Mr. David John
WHEATON, Mrs. Jacqueline Anne
WHEELER, Mrs. Caroline Jane
WHEELER, Mr. John Edward
WHEELER, Mr. John Kenneth
WHEELER, Mr. Peter John
WHEELER, Mr. Richard
WHELAN, Mr. John Patrick
WHELAN, Mrs. Julia Alison
WHILEY, Mrs. Vivienne Elizabeth
WHITAKER, Mr. John Barry
WHITBURN, Mrs. Louise
WHITCOMBE, Mr. Paul Jeffrey
WHITE, Mr. Alfred Andrew
WHITE, Mr. Benjamin Peter
WHITE, Mrs. Esther Mary
WHITE, Mr. Graham Mcgillivray
WHITE, Mrs. Hazel
WHITE, Mr. James
WHITE, Mrs. Janet Margaret
WHITE, Mr. John Leslie
WHITE, Mr. John Nigel
WHITE, Mr. John Richard
WHITE, Mr. Nicholas
WHITE, Mr. Peter Richard
WHITE, Mr. Simon Robert Franklin
WHITE, Mr. Timothy Leigh
WHITE-ADAMS, Mr. Colin John
WHITEAR, Mr. Mark Anthony
WHITEFIELD, Mr. David
WHITEHEAD, Mr. Allan David
WHITEHEAD, Mr. Anwyl Richard
WHITEHEAD, Mr. David Nigel
WHITEHEAD, Mr. Mark Andrew Milton
WHITEHEAD, Mr. Peter Timothy
WHITEHOUSE, Mrs. Carole Ann
WHITEHOUSE, Mrs. Margaret Patricia
WHITELAW, Mrs. Rachel Helen
WHITELEY, Mr. Christopher John
WHITELEY, Mrs. Elizabeth
WHITEMAN, Mr. Ian Frank
WHITESIDE, Mrs. Joanne Lesley
WHITEWAY, Mr. Philip Anthony
WHITFIELD, Mr. Peter Storey
WHITING, Mr. John William
WHITING, Mr. Stephen David
WHITING, Ms. Susan Joy
WHITLOCK, Mr. Brian John
WHITLOCK, Mr. Rhodri Ryland
WHITMELL, Mr. Paul Edwin
WHITMORE, Mr. David William
WHITTAKER, Mr. Michael Philip
WHITTAKER, Mr. Robert John
WHITTERN, Mr. Stephen Lee
WHITTINGTON, Mrs. Cheryl Christine
WHITTLE, Mr. David Michael
WHITTLE, Mr. Nigel John
WHITTLE, Mr. Paul John
WHITTLE, Mr. Paul Joseph
WHORLOW, Mr. Stuart Graham
WHOWELL, Mr. Robert Harold
WICKHAM, Mr. Andrew James
WICKHAM, Miss. Maria Ann

WICKS, Mr. David Ian
WICKS, Mrs. Lindsey
WICKS, Mr. Terence Peter
WIDDOWSON, Mr. Adrian
WIELAND, Mrs. Adelaide Mary
WIFFEN, Mr. Stephen John
WIGAN, Mr. Paul George
WIGGETT, Mr. Andrew John
WIGGIN, Mr. Anthony Charles David
WIGHTMAN, Mrs. Judith Barbara
WIGLEY, Mr. Martin William
WIGLEY, Mr. Michael James
WILD, Mr. James Watson Eyre
WILD, Mr. John Lawson
WILDER, Mr. Gary Spencer
WILDERMUTH, Mr. Paul Edmund
WILDEY, Mrs. Sarah Ellen
WILDI, Mr. Mark Robert
WILDIG, Mr. Michael John
WILDIN, Mr. Graham Michael
WILDIN, Miss. Jacqueline Anne
WILDING, Mrs. Christine Diana
WILDMAN, Mr. Michael Robert
WILKES, Mrs. Deborah Jean
WILKIE, Mr. Mark John
WILKINSON, Mr. Daniel
WILKINSON, Mr. Gary
WILKINSON, Mr. Gerard James
WILKINSON, Mrs. Janette Carole
WILKINSON, Miss. Katy Jane
WILKINSON, Mr. Neil Paul
WILKINSON, Mr. Paul
WILKINSON, Mr. Paul Stuart
WILKINSON, Mr. Peter
WILKINSON, Mr. Peter
WILKINSON, Mr. Stanley
WILLANS, Mr. Peter Robert
WILLCOX, Mrs. Karen Jane
WILLCOX, Mr. Stephen Anthony
WILLEY, Mr. Peter Joseph
WILLEY, Mr. Stephen Charles
WILLIAMS, Mr. Alan
WILLIAMS, Mr. Alastair John
WILLIAMS, Mrs. Angela
WILLIAMS, Ms. Angela Elizabeth
WILLIAMS, Mr. Anthony John
WILLIAMS, Mrs. Carla
WILLIAMS, Mrs. Carolyn Jane
WILLIAMS, Mrs. Catherine Ann
WILLIAMS, Mr. Christopher David
WILLIAMS, Mr. Christopher James
WILLIAMS, Mr. Christopher Robert Hugh
WILLIAMS, Mr. Christopher Stanley
WILLIAMS, Mrs. Clare Elizabeth
WILLIAMS, Mr. Colin Herbert
WILLIAMS, Mr. David
WILLIAMS, Mr. David Anthony James
WILLIAMS, Mr. David Llewelyn
WILLIAMS, Mr. David Nigel
WILLIAMS, Mr. Edgar Norman
WILLIAMS, Mrs. Elisabeth
WILLIAMS, Mr. Euan John
WILLIAMS, Mr. Eurig Dylan Jones
WILLIAMS, Ms. Frances Anne Marie Everlyn Claire
WILLIAMS, Mr. Frank Michael Basil
WILLIAMS, Mr. Graham Eric Hanson
WILLIAMS, Mr. Griffith Owen Charles
WILLIAMS, Mrs. Heather Ruth
WILLIAMS, Mr. Hugh Martyn
WILLIAMS, Mr. Huw Russell
WILLIAMS, Mr. Ian Edward
WILLIAMS, Mr. Ian Robert
WILLIAMS, Mrs. Joanna
WILLIAMS, Miss. Joanna Louise
WILLIAMS, Mr. John David Rhys
WILLIAMS, Mr. John Michael
WILLIAMS, Mr. John Robert
WILLIAMS, Mr. Katherine Ann
WILLIAMS, Mr. Mark
WILLIAMS, Mr. Martin Robert
WILLIAMS, Mr. Michael David
WILLIAMS, Mr. Nicholas Charles
WILLIAMS, Mr. Paul Charles
WILLIAMS, Mrs. Paula Marie
WILLIAMS, Mr. Peter John
WILLIAMS, Mr. Philip
WILLIAMS, Mr. Philip John
WILLIAMS, Mrs. Rhiannon Nest
WILLIAMS, Mr. Robert Paul
WILLIAMS, Mr. Roger W
WILLIAMS, Mrs. Sarah Jane
WILLIAMS, Mrs. Shirley Anne
WILLIAMS, Mr. Stephen
WILLIAMS, Mr. Stephen Lynn
WILLIAMS, Mrs. Suzanne
WILLIAMS, Mrs. Vanda Elaine
WILLIAMS, Mr. William David
WILLIAMSON, Mr. Andrew Stuart
WILLIAMSON, Mr. Christopher John
WILLIAMSON, Mr. John Stuart
WILLIAMSON, Mr. Jon Adam
WILLIAMSON, Mr. Martin John
WILLIAMSON, Mr. Michael Newton
WILLIAMSON, Mrs. Pauline Clare
WILLIAMSON, Mr. Stuart
WILLIES, Mr. Geoffrey David

WILLIMER, Mr. Nigel David
WILLIS, Mrs. Patricia
WILLIS, Miss. Victoria Angela
WILLMOTT, Mr. John Martin
WILLOTT, Mr. Roger de Quetteville
WILLOWS, Mr. Derek Frank
WILLS, Mrs. Lesley Jane
WILLS, Mrs. Susan Patricia
WILLS, Mr. William Eric
WILMOTT, Mr. Martin Andrew
WILSON, Mr. Andrew
WILSON, Mr. Andrew James
WILSON, Miss. Anne Frances
WILSON, Mr. Anthony John
WILSON, Mr. Baron Wayne
WILSON, Mrs. Belinda Anne
WILSON, Mr. Daniel Patrick
WILSON, Mr. David
WILSON, Mr. David John
WILSON, Mr. David Paul
WILSON, Mrs. Elizabeth
WILSON, Mr. Graham John
WILSON, Mrs. Hilary Sarah Jane
WILSON, Mr. Ian Scott
WILSON, Mr. John Bentley
WILSON, Mr. John Campbell
WILSON, Mr. John Nevison
WILSON, Mr. Jonathan David
WILSON, Mr. Jonathan Richard
WILSON, Mrs. Kathleen Elizabeth
WILSON, Mr. Lee Kenneth
WILSON, Mrs. Mandy Susan Elizabeth
WILSON, Mr. Mark Terence
WILSON, Mr. Martin John
WILSON, Miss. Melanie Jane
WILSON, Mr. Paul Richard
WILSON, Mr. Peter
WILSON, Mr. Peter
WILSON, Mr. Peter James
WILSON, Mr. Robin Francis Sidney
WILSON, Mr. Simon David
WILSON, Mr. Stewart
WILSON, Miss. Victoria Jayne
WILSON, Mr. William John
WILTSHIRE, Mr. Iain Stuart Edward
WIMALENDRA, Mr. Muttyah Manickam
WIMPENNY, Mrs. Kathryn Louise
WINCH, Mr. David Robert
WINCKLESS, Mr. Neil Anthony Roger
WINDELINCKX, Mr. Dion
WINDMILL, Mr. Andrew Lewis
WINEARLS, Mr. Andrew Paul
WINFIELD, Mr. Kenneth John
WINGHAM, Mr. Michael
WINN, Mr. Paul Bernard
WINNARD, Mr. Leslie Clarke David
WINROW, Mr. Andrew Stuart
WINSTANLEY, Mr. John Douglas
WINSTON, Mr. Anton Jacoby
WINSTON, Mr. Paul
WINSTONE, Mr. Martin
WINTER, Mr. Christopher Philip Akers
WINTER, Mr. Keith James
WINTER, Mr. Paul Joseph
WINTLE, Mrs. Kathryn Ann
WINYARD, Mr. Colin Frederick
WISE, Mr. Christopher John
WISE, Mr. David Michael
WISE, Mr. Peter George
WISE, Mr. Roger Frank
WISEMAN, Mr. Graham Mark
WISEMAN, Miss. Lois Jeanette
WITCHELL, Mr. Keith Roger
WITCOMB, Mr. Simon James
WITHALL, Mr. Keith Brian
WITHERS, Mr. Howard Marshall
WITHERS, Mr. William Jonathan
WITKISS, Mr. Simon Richard George
WITTICH, Mr. Peter Charles
WITTRED, Mr. Robin John
WOLFF, Mr. Alan
WOLFF, Mr. David Alexander
WOLFSON, Mr. Ian
WOLFSON, Mr. Kenneth
WOLSTENHOLME, Mrs. Irene Joy
WONACOTT, Mr. William George
WONG, Mr. Chak Yu John
WONG, Ms. Kar Men Michele
WONG, Mr. Matthew
WOOD, Mr. Andrew David
WOOD, Mrs. Beverley
WOOD, Mr. Colin
WOOD, Mr. Geoff Peter
WOOD, Mr. Graeme Alan
WOOD, Mr. Henry James Prescott
WOOD, Mr. James Robert
WOOD, Mr. Jeremy Anthony Cassillis
WOOD, Mr. Malcolm Antony
WOOD, Mr. Martin Joseph
WOOD, Mr. Michael Alan
WOOD, Mr. Nigel John
WOOD, Mr. Paul Nicholas
WOOD, Mr. Paul Richard
WOOD, Mr. Peter Lawton
WOOD, Mr. Philip Barrington
WOOD, Mr. Richard Frost
WOOD, Mr. Robert MacGregor Warburton

WOOD, Mrs. Sandra Elaine
WOOD, Ms. Sandra Melanie
WOOD, Mr. Simon Christopher
WOOD, Mr. Stephen John
WOOD, Mrs. Suzanne
WOOD, Mr. Vincent Philip
WOODAGE, Mr. David Arthur
WOODBURN, Mrs. Nicola Jane
WOODBURN, Mr. Paul
WOODFORD, Mr. Nicholas Andrew
WOODGATE, Mrs. Susan Mary
WOODMAN, Mr. John Charlton
WOODMAN, Mr. Michael Geoffrey
WOODMAN, Mr. Robert James
WOODROFFE, Mr. Nigel Anthony
WOODROW, Mr. James Radclyffe
WOODROW, Mr. Phillip Andrew
WOODRUFF, Mr. Ian
WOODS, Mr. Andrew James
WOODS, Mrs. Lalena
WOODS, Mr. Mark Anthony
WOODS, Mr. Richard Lester
WOODTHORPE, Miss. Catherine Joan
WOODWARD, Mr. John Vincent
WOODWARD, Mr. Peter Tristram Ridgeway
WOODWARD, Mr. Stephen Andrew
WOODWARD, Miss. Vanessa Jayne
WOOLF, Mr. Keith Harris
WOOLFSON, Mr. Leslie Ian
WOOLFSON, Mr. Philip Alan
WOOLLARD, Mrs. Rosalind Ann
WOOLLEY, Mr. Richard George
WOOLLISCROFT, Mr. Dermot Francis

WOOLMER, Mr. Trevor John
WOOLSTON, Mr. Jonathan David
WOOTTEN, Mr. Dean Robert
WORBOYS, Mr. Richard David
WORDINGHAM, Mr. Nigel John
WORMALD, Mr. Stephen
WORRALL, Mr. Andrew James
WORRALL, Mr. Michael John
WORSFOLD, Mrs. Trudi Mia
WORT, Miss. Frances Stella
WORTHINGTON-EYRE, Mr. Roland
WORTHY, Mr. Christopher Robin
WRAGG, Mr. David Clive
WRAGG, Mr. Paul Simon
WRIGGLESWORTH, Mr. Mark Richard
WRIGHT, Mr. Barrie William
WRIGHT, Mr. Brian
WRIGHT, Mrs. Christine Dorothy
WRIGHT, Mr. Christopher Stephen
WRIGHT, Mrs. Claire Mary
WRIGHT, Mr. David John
WRIGHT, Mr. David John
WRIGHT, Mr. David Maxwell
WRIGHT, Mr. Iain David
WRIGHT, Mr. John
WRIGHT, Mr. Malcolm John
WRIGHT, Mr. Neil Andrew
WRIGHT, Mr. Roderick Edmund
WRIGHT, Mr. Timothy Peter
WRIGHT, Mrs. Vivienne Louise Halsey
WRIGHTON, Mr. Christopher Arthur
WROE, Mr. Ian Malcolm
WYATT, Mr. Gary Charles

WYATT, Mr. John Leslie
WYATT, Mr. Martin
WYATT, Mr. Philip Thomas Stanbury
WYATT, Mr. Richard David
WYATT, Mr. Roland Ian
WYATT, Mr. Simon David
WYBURN, Mr. Charles Louis
WYCHERLEY, Mr. William Francis
WYE, Mr. Andrew Frederick
WYE, Mr. David
WYLES, Mrs. Lindsay Susan Jane
WYNNIATT-HUSEY, Mr. Reginald James
WYRLEY-BIRCH, Mr. Paul
YALE, Miss. Mary Anora
YAP, Mr. Derrick Tian Heng
YAP, Miss. Ee-Lin
YAP, Dr. Kim Fay
YAPP, Mr. David Sandiford
YARAS, Mr. Andrew John
YARR, Mrs. Margaret
YATES, Mr. Colin Michael
YATES, Mr. Richard Charles
YATES, Mr. Stephen Bradshaw
YAXLEY, Mrs. Carolyne
YEATES, Mr. Roger
YEE, Mr. Pak Young
YELLAND, Mr. John Anthony
YEUNG, Mr. Kenneth King Wah
YIP, Miss. Appy Fei Yin
YOUNG, Mr. Andrew James
YOUNG, Mr. Colin Clifford
YOUNG, Mr. David Eric
YOUNG, Mr. Graham

YOUNG, Mr. Ian Kirkpatrick
YOUNG, Mr. Keith Alan
YOUNG, Mr. Kenneth Robert
YOUNG, Mr. Michael Charles
YOUNG, Mr. Peter Colin Robert
YOUNG, Ms. Rebecca Ann
YOUNG, Mr. Robert Alan
YOUNG, Mr. Robert James Russell
YOUNG, Mr. Simon Jonathan
YOUNG, Mrs. Suzanna Penny
YOUNG, Mr. Victor John
YOUNGMAN, Mr. Brian John
YOUNGMAN, Mr. Nigel Cleaver
YOUNUS, Mr. Irfan
YOUSHANI, Mr. Abol Hassan
YOUSUF, Mrs. Khurshid
YUDT, Mr. David Hilary
YULE, Mr. Andrew Herlyn
ZAHUR, Mr. Muhammad
ZAIDI, Mr. Misdaq Husain
ZAKIEWICZ, Mr. Michael Bronislaw Wood
ZANETTOS, Mr. Adonis
ZANKER, Mr. Martin Mortimore
ZARACH, Mr. Barrington Philip
ZAREMBA, Mr. Martin Antoni
ZEIDERMAN, Mr. Leonard
ZELTSER, Mr. Lionel Harvey
ZENIOS, Mr. Jonathan David
ZEPLER, Mr. Paul Eric
ZUCCONI, Mr. Anthony

THE OFFICIAL ICAEW LIST OF MEMBERS 2012

MEMBERS IN PRACTICE AND FIRMS:

ALPHABETICAL

Members in Practice and Firms - Alphabetical 02Vie Ltd - A.G. Eastwood & Co

Ⓟ**02Vie Ltd** *(K P Rashleigh)* 43 Oxshott Way, COBHAM, SURREY, KT11 2RU.

1.2.1 Accountancy Services *(P A Megson)* 4 Railway Cottages, Low Row, BRAMPTON, CA8 2LG.

Ⓟ**108 Taxes, trading name of 108 Taxes Limited** *(M J E Fishburn)* Northend, Malbrook Road, Putney, LONDON, SW15 6UH.

Ⓟ**1234 Accountancy, trading name of 1234 Accountancy Limited** *(S M Higgins)* 54 Clarendon Road, WATFORD, WD17 1DU.

Ⓟ**1st Consult Ltd** *(P F Mills)* Rowley Stables, Combe Hay, BATH, BA2 7EF.

Ⓟ**1st Contact Accountants Limited** *(A M Deakin)* Castlewood House, 77-91 New Oxford Street, LONDON, WC1A 1DG.

Ⓟ**1st Finance Solutions Limited** *(S Basra)* Acorn House, Broomfield Park, Sunningdale, ASCOT, BERKSHIRE, SL5 0JT.

★Ⓟ**1st Option Accounting Services Limited** *(S H Tudor Price)* Bank House, 23 Warwick Road, COVENTRY, CV1 2EZ.

★Ⓟ**1st Option Consulting, trading name of 1st Option Consulting Services Limited** *(S H Tudor Price)* Bank House, 23 Warwick Road, COVENTRY, CV1 2EZ. and at LONDON

Ⓟ**2020 CA Ltd** *(S Hay, S J Kelly)* 1 St. Andrew's Hill, LONDON, EC4V 5BY.

Ⓟ**21st Century Accounting Services Limited** *(F A M E C Williams)* 12 Silver Way, WICKFORD, SS11 7AP.

Ⓟ**2AG Solutions Limited** *(A M Flemons, G B Flemons)* 76 Birches Lane, KENILWORTH, WARWICKSHIRE, CV8 2AG.

ⒻⓅⒶ**360, trading name of 360 Accountants Limited** *(A M Steele)* Melton Court, Gibson Lane, Melton, HULL, HU14 3HH.

39A Financial Direction *(S Bentley)* 38 Strother Close, Pocklington, YORK, YO42 2GR.

39a Financial Direction, trading name of 39a Business Solutions LLP *(S Bentley)* 38 Strother Close, Pocklington, YORK, YO42 2GR.

Ⓟ**3CA, trading name of 3CA Limited** *(S J Jones)* Kent Cottage, Bridge Lane, KENDAL, CUMBRIA, LA9 7DD.

Ⓟ**3S Accountancy Services, trading name of Third Sector Accountancy Services Limited** *(C F Milbanke)* 12 The Greenhouse, Greencroft Industrial Park, Annfield Plain, STANLEY, COUNTY DURHAM, DH9 7XN.

4J Services Ltd *(J M White)* 43 Sparch Hollow, May Bank, NEWCASTLE, STAFFORDSHIRE, ST5 9PE.

Ⓟ**5 Four Payroll Bureau Limited** *(A M Steele)* Melton Court, Gibson Lane, Melton, NORTH FERRIBY, NORTH HUMBERSIDE, HU14 3HH.

Ⓟ**757 Ltd** *(D P Hoskins)* 123 Priests Lane, Shenfield, BRENTWOOD, ESSEX, CM15 8HJ.

ⓅⒶ**80K Limited** *(A T Knight)* 45 Days Lane, Biddenham, BEDFORD, MK40 4AE.

Ⓟ**8M3, trading name of 8M3 Limited** *(K P Bonney)* K.P. Bonney & Co LLP, 50 Cleasby Road, Menston, ILKLEY, WEST YORKSHIRE, LS29 6JA.

★ⓉⓅ**9ine, trading name of 9ine Accounting Limited** *(R Mason)* 76 Bridgford Road, West Bridgford, NOTTINGHAM, NG2 6AX.

ⓉⓅ**A & A Accounting Services Ltd** *(A Shababi)* 2 Acorn Grove, Kingswood, TADWORTH, SURREY, KT20 6QT.

Ⓟ**A & C Christofi Ltd** *(C Christofi)* 37 Nicou and Despinas Pattichi Avenue, Evi Court, 3rd Floor, Offices 302-303, CY-3071 LIMASSOL, CYPRUS.

ⓅⒶ**A & L Audit Services Ltd** *(A Panayiotou)* Checknet House, 153 East Barnet Road, BARNET, HERTFORDSHIRE, EN4 8QZ.

Ⓟ**A & N Accountancy Solutions Limited** *(A A James)* Willowbend, Dunwood Hill, East Wellow, ROMSEY, HAMPSHIRE, SO51 6FD.

ⓉⒻⓅⒶ**A & N, trading name of A & N (Haslemere) Limited** *(A Sharma)* Aruna House, 2 Kings Road, HASLEMERE, SURREY, GU27 2QA.

A & S Accountants *(M A A Maudarbocus)* 135 Belgrave Road, Walthamstow, LONDON, E17 8QF.

Ⓟ**A & S Associates, trading name of A & S Associates Limited** *(A Jones, S C Jones)* P O Box 3310, 126 Fairlie Road, SLOUGH, BERKSHIRE, SL1 0AG.

Ⓟ**A + B Bookkeeping Ltd** *(P A Morrish, D I Wicks)* 21 Bampton Street, TIVERTON, DEVON, EX16 6AA.

Ⓟ**A A Jamal Tax Consultants Limited** *(A A Jamal)* 28 Fairlop Road, LONDON, E11 1BN.

A Allcock Corporate Finance *(A C Allcock)* 59 Granary Way, SALE, CHESHIRE, M33 4GF.

ⓅⒶ**A Allen & Son, trading name of A Allen & Son Limited** *(D C Cooper)* Union Road, 45 Union Road, New Mills, HIGH PEAK, DERBYSHIRE, SK22 3EL.

Ⓟ**A B Accounting and Consulting Limited** *(Huang)* 34 Langbourne Place, LONDON, E14 3WN.

ⓅⒶ**A Brightmore & Co, trading name of ARP Brightmore Limited** *(A R P Brightmore)* Fairholme Bungalow, Hathersage Road, Bamford, HOPE VALLEY, DERBYSHIRE, S33 0EB.

Ⓕ**A C Drennan** *(A C Drennan)* 73 Ashgate Avenue, CHESTERFIELD, DERBYSHIRE, S40 1JD.

A C M Crombie *(A C M Crombie)* 20 Sandfield Road, Headington, OXFORD, OX3 7RQ.

ⓅⒶ**A C Ralph Ltd** *(A C Ralph)* c/o The Old Police Station, Whitburn Street, BRIDGNORTH, SHROPSHIRE, WV16 4QP.

Ⓟ**A C Tucker & Co, trading name of A C Tucker & Co Limited** *(Alan Tucker)* Manor Cottage, 18a Waxwell Lane, PINNER, MIDDLESEX, HA5 3EN.

A Chow & Partners *(W Chow, S Li)* 17/F, Amtel Building, 144-148 Des Voeux Road Central, CENTRAL, HONG KONG SAR.

Ⓟ**A D Financial Services Ltd** *(J M L Hankinson, D R Tossell)* Avaland House, 110 London Road, Apsley, HEMEL HEMPSTEAD, HERTFORDSHIRE, HP3 9SD.

ⓉⒶ**A D Parks & Co** *(A D Parks)* 30 High Street, Wendover, AYLESBURY, HP22 6EA.

Ⓕ**A F Kabini & Co** *(A F Kabini)* 14 Conlan Street, LONDON, W10 5AR.

A Fielding & Co, trading name of Alan Fielding *(A Fielding)* 18 The Walk, ROCHDALE, LANCASHIRE, OL16 1EP.

A G Plumb *(A G Plumb)* 10 South Road, SAFFRON WALDEN, CB11 3DH.

Ⓟ**A Graham Accountancy Services Ltd** *(A Graham)* The Vicarage, Church Street, Eccleshall, STAFFORD, ST21 6BY.

A Graham Williams *(A G Williams)* 18 Shrewsbury Wood, Cabinteely, DUBLIN 18, COUNTY DUBLIN, IRELAND.

A H Delahunt *(A H Delahunt)* Wembury, 4A Green Lane, PURLEY, CR8 3PG.

ⒻⓅ**A H Montpelier, trading name of Montpelier Professional (West End) Ltd** *(I Fishman, J S Marco, I A Randolph, H R Reuben)* 58-60 Berners Street, LONDON, W1T 3JS.

A H Olley BSc ACA *(A Olley)* Thyme Cottage, The Green, Whiteparish, SALISBURY, SP5 2RP.

Ⓟ**A H Tudor Limited** *(A H Tudor)* 20 St. Johns Hill, SHREWSBURY, SY1 1JJ.

ⓉⓅⒶ**A I Cherry, trading name of A I Cherry Limited** *(A I Cherry)* 26 Winckley Square, PRESTON, PR1 3JJ.

ⓅⒶ**A I Cohen & Associates Ltd** *(A I Cohen)* 61 Crowstone Road, WESTCLIFF-ON-SEA, ESSEX, SS0 8BG.

Ⓟ**A I M S Edinburgh, trading name of Robert Maclaren Ltd** *(R P M Maclaren)* 16 Ainslie Place, EDINBURGH, EH3 6AU.

ⒻⓅ**A J Accountancy Limited** *(A C Jones)* The Old Surgery, Spa Road, LLANDRINDOD WELLS, POWYS, LD1 5EY.

Ⓟ**A J Brown Limited** *(A J Brown)* 91 Front Street, Acomb, YORK, YO24 3BU.

Ⓟ**A J Burton Ltd** *(A J Burton)* 16 Lapwings, LONGFIELD, KENT, DA3 7NH.

Ⓐ**A J Measures** *(A J Measures)* 157-197 Buckingham Palace Road, LONDON, SW1W 9SP.

Ⓟ**A J Peach & Co Limited** *(A J Peach)* 104 Grasshopper Avenue, WORCESTER, WR5 3TB.

A J Robinson & Co *(A J Robinson)* Saddleworth Business Centre, Huddersfield Road, Delph, OLDHAM, OL3 5DF.

A J Shah & Company *(A J Shah)* 8 Pinner View, HARROW, HA1 4QA.

ⒻⓅⒶ**A J Shortridge, trading name of A J Shortridge Limited** *(A J Shortridge)* Wessex House, Teign Road, NEWTON ABBOT, DEVON, TQ12 4AA.

Ⓟ**A J Solway Limited** *(A J Solway)* 37 Bosvean Road, Shortlanesend, TRURO, CORNWALL, TR4 9DX.

★**A J Topping LLP** *(A J Topping)* 6 High Lea, Marsden, HUDDERSFIELD, HD7 6DZ.

A J Williams *(A J Williams)* 39 Trafalgar Road, SOUTHPORT, PR8 2HF.

Ⓟ**A K & K Limited** *(K M Gladders)* 40 Gildale, Werrington, PETERBOROUGH, PE4 6QY.

★Ⓟ**A K Associates, trading name of A.K. Limited** *(J A Kokkinos)* 8 Percy Road, North Finchley, LONDON, N12 8BU.

Ⓐ**A M J Ball** *(A M J Ball)* 75 Banner Cross Road, Ecclesall, SHEFFIELD, S11 9HQ.

A M Porbunderwalla *(A M Porbunderwalla)* PO Box 40248, NAIROBI, 00100, KENYA.

Ⓐ**A M Robinson** *(A M Robinson)* 3 Hospital Cottages, Crescent Road, BRENTWOOD, ESSEX, CM14 5JA.

A M Rogers *(A M Rogers)* Yorkshire House, 7 South Lane, HOLMFIRTH, HD9 1HN.

Ⓟ**A M Sherman & Co, trading name of A M Sherman & Co Limited** *(A R Effendi, M J Johnson, A M Sherman)* 199 Roundhay Road, LEEDS, LS8 5AN.

Ⓟ**A Mendes & Co Limited** *(A F R Mendes)* 55A London Road, LEICESTER, LE2 0PE.

A Miller & Co *(A Miller)* Evans House, 107 Marsh Road, PINNER, MIDDLESEX, HA5 5PA.

Ⓐ**A Mitra & Co** *(A K Mitra, J G Mitra)* 137 Cassiobury Drive, WATFORD, WD17 3AH.

Ⓐ**A Nichol & Co** *(A J Nichol)* 191 New Ridley Road, STOCKSFIELD, NORTHUMBERLAND, NE43 7QD.

Ⓟ**A P Bemment & Co Limited** *(A P Bemment, M Cator)* 101 Bridge Road, Oulton Broad, LOWESTOFT, SUFFOLK, NR32 3LN.

Ⓟ**A P Carter & Co, trading name of ABT Services (UK) Limited** *(A P Carter)* 50 Haygate Road, Wellington, TELFORD, SHROPSHIRE, TF1 1QN.

ⓉⒶ**A P Robinson LLP** *(A P Robinson)* 107 Cleethorpe Road, GRIMSBY, SOUTH HUMBERSIDE, DN31 3ER.

Ⓟ**A Plus Accountants Limited** *(Y K Tinkler)* 10 Canberra House, Corby Gate Business Park, CORBY, NORTHAMPTONSHIRE, NN17 5JG.

A Q Accounting *(P J Waters)* Tall Trees, 26 Tranby Lane, Anlaby, HULL, HU10 7DS.

▽**A Qasem & Co** *(K I Choudhury, A S Kasem)* Gulshan Pink City, Suites 01-03 Level 7, Plot No. 15 Road No. 103, Gulshan Avenue, DHAKA 1212, BANGLADESH.

Ⓟ**A R Avann and Co Ltd** *(A R Avann)* 33 Wood Lane, Sonning Common, READING, RG4 9SJ.

ⓅⒶ**A S Howes & Co Limited** *(A S Howes)* Unit 3a, Minton Place, Victoria Road, BICESTER, OXFORDSHIRE, OX26 6QB.

★Ⓟ**A S Kalsi & Co Limited** *(U K Ghosh)* 124 Rookery Road, Handsworth, BIRMINGHAM, B21 9NN.

A S Mundy *(A S Mundy)* 73 High Street, Shoreham, SEVENOAKS, TN14 7TB.

ⓉⒻⓅⒶ**A S Zanettos & Co, trading name of A S Zanettos & Co Limited** *(A Zanettos)* 4 Croxted Mews, Croxted Road, LONDON, SE24 9DA.

A Shamsi & Co *(R A Shamsi)* 11 Stone Close, TAUNTON, SOMERSET, TA1 4YG.

Ⓟ**A Shaw & Co, trading name of A Shaw & Co Ltd** *(D A Shaw)* 21 Bushy Park Road, TEDDINGTON, MIDDLESEX, TW11 9DQ.

Ⓟ**A T Accounting Services, trading name of A & T Accounting Services Limited** *(J Caplen)* The Office, Oaklands, La Rue Du Coin Varin, St. Peter, JERSEY, JE3 7ZG.

Ⓟ**A T P, trading name of Accountancy Training Partnership Limited** *(M E Bishop)* Merryhills, Dulcote, WELLS, SOMERSET, BA5 3NU.

Ⓟ**A Team Finance Limited** *(S M Begbey)* 34 Beaufort Crescent, Stoke Gifford, BRISTOL, BS34 8QY.

★Ⓟ**A U Chauhan Limited** *(A U Chauhan, J J Ved)* 5 Theobald Court, Theobald Street, ELSTREE, WD6 4RN.

ⒻⒶ**A W. Beckinsale & Co** *(A W Beckinsale)* 1 St. Peters Road, BRAINTREE, CM7 9AN.

A Wade Tax Consultancy *(A J Wade-Jones)* 2 Plough Cottages, Great Munden, WARE, HERTFORDSHIRE, SG11 1HS.

Ⓐ**A West & Co** *(A West)* 550 Valley Road, Basford, NOTTINGHAM, NG5 1JJ.

ⓅⒶ**A Wigglesworth and Company Ltd** *(A Wigglesworth)* Wigglesworth & Co, 1 Albion Place, DONCASTER, SOUTH YORKSHIRE, DN1 2EG.

ⓉⓅ**A&C, trading name of Armitt & Company Limited** *(P Hoszowskyj)* Marsland Chambers, 1a Marsland Road, Sale Moor, SALE, M33 3HP.

A&L *(A Panayiotou)* Checknet House, 153 East Barnet Road, BARNET, HERTFORDSHIRE, EN4 8QZ.

A. Butnick & Co *(A E Butnick)* 18 Barn Crescent, STANMORE, HA7 2RY.

A. Caldara *(A J Caldara)* 10 Crossway, West Wimbledon, LONDON, SW20 9JA.

A. David Conner *(D Conner)* 19 Lower Elms, St. Minver, WADEBRIDGE, CORNWALL, PL27 6QB.

Ⓕ**A. E. Ioannou & Co** *(A E Ioannou)* 407 Green Lanes, LONDON, N4 1EY.

A. Elias *(A Elias)* Coldharbour House, Coldharbour Lane, Bletchingley, SURREY, RH1 4NA.

A. F. McGhee & Co *(A F McGhee)* First Floor Offices, 54 Main Road, WINDERMERE, CUMBRIA, LA23 1DX.

Ⓟ**A. G. Accounting Services Limited** *(A D Gill)* 24 Mount Durand, St. Peter Port, GUERNSEY, GY1 1ED.

A. Green *(A Green)* Dal Ghorm House, Ardtoe, ACHARACLE, ARGYLL, PH36 4LD.

Ⓟ**A. Hadley Ltd** *(J H Hadley)* 28 Littlegreen Road, Woodthorpe, NOTTINGHAM, NG5 4LN.

A. Hodson *(A R Hodson)* 40 The Glades, Aldridge, WALSALL, WS9 8RN.

ⓉⒻⒶ**A. Hughes-Jones, Dyson & Co** *(B Hughes, I R Parry, E Pursglove)* Bryn Afon, Segontium Terrace, CAERNARFON, LL55 2PN.

A. Hurley *(A Hurley)* 4 Friars Crescent, NEWPORT, NP20 4EY.

A. Jackson-Jakubowski *(A Jackson-Jakubowski)* 5 Lowfield Road, Acton, LONDON, W3 0AY.

ⒻⒶ**A. Macdonald & Co** *(S Scargill)* 21 Parliament Street, HULL, HU1 2BL.

A. Mannan & Co *(A Mannan)* 14 Norman Road, Leytonstone, LONDON, E11 4PX.

A. Omar & Co *(A A I Omar)* 23 Jalan Merah Saga, Apt 04-05, Mera Saga, SINGAPORE 278102, SINGAPORE.

A. Phillips & Co. *(A P Mahon)* Wilsons Park, Monsall Road, Newton Heath, MANCHESTER, M40 8WN.

A. Pringle *(A Pringle)* P O Box 49561, NAIROBI, KENYA.

Ⓕ**A. R. Goring** *(A R Goring)* 91a Hassock Lane North, Shipley, HEANOR, DERBYSHIRE, DE75 7JB.

A. R. Hunt & Co *(A R Hunt)* 50 Ridge Crest, ENFIELD, EN2 8JX.

A. Razzaq & Company *(A Razzaq)* Suite #40 3rd floor, landmark Plaza, Jail Road, LAHORE, PAKISTAN.

A. von Gebsattel *(A von Gebsattel)* S. Polo 2733, 30125 VENICE, ITALY.

A.A. Ball *(A A Ball)* 4 Lidgate Walk, Westbury Park, Clayton, NEWCASTLE, STAFFORDSHIRE, ST5 4LT.

Ⓐ**A.A. Bromhead & Co** *(A A Bromhead)* P.O. Box 709, ADDIS ABABA, ETHIOPIA.

A.A. Liggatt *(A A Liggatt)* Dark Haven, Witham Friary, FROME, SOMERSET, BA11 5HF.

Ⓟ**A.B. Griffiths & Co Ltd** *(A B Griffiths)* 93 Ersham Road, HAILSHAM, EAST SUSSEX, BN27 3LH.

A.B. Mercer *(A B Mercer)* Broad Dale, Pennington Lane, ULVERSTON, LA12 7SE.

A.C. Camplejohn *(A C Camplejohn)* The Old Rectory, Main Street, Frolesworth, LUTTERWORTH, LE17 5EE.

A.C. Fletcher *(A C Fletcher)* 4 Copperfield Way, CHISLEHURST, BR7 6RY.

A.C. Luckman & Co *(A C Luckman)* 5 Hollybank Road, BIRMINGHAM, B13 0RF.

ⓉⒻⒶ**A.C. Mole & Sons** *(P S Aplin, C P Glover, S Golby, A J Gunter, P A Kingdom, C P Loveluck, M Perry, I Pinder)* Stafford House, Blackbrook Park Avenue, TAUNTON, SOMERSET, TA1 2PX. and at BRIDGWATER

A.C. Wain & Company *(A C Wain)* 3 Highlands Close, Chalfont St Peter, GERRARDS CROSS, SL9 0DR.

Ⓐ**A.C. Wilson** *(A C Wilson)* The Kingswood, Ridgemount Road, ASCOT, BERKSHIRE, SL5 9RW.

A.C.Cripps *(A C Cripps)* 5 Kingcup Drive, Bisley, WOKING, SURREY, GU24 9HH.

A.C.K. Wong Too Yuen *(A C K Wong Too Yuen)* P.O.Box 5184, CHATSWOOD, NSW 1515, AUSTRALIA.

Ⓟ**A.C.O.L Business Matters, trading name of A.C.O.L. Business Matters Limited** *(K D A Jones)* 27 Heol-y-Bryn, Rhiwbina, CARDIFF, CF14 6HX.

A.C.Reichwald *(A C Reichwald)* 239 Richmond Road, TWICKENHAM, TW1 2NN.

A.D. Kiddle *(A D Kiddle)* Newlands Farm, Wickham Bishops, WITHAM, ESSEX, CM8 3JH.

A.D. Michelson *(A D Michelson)* 33 North Avenue, Gosforth, NEWCASTLE UPON TYNE, NE3 4DQ.

A.D. Noyes *(A D Noyes)* 22 Truro Road, Ashton, BRISTOL, BS3 2AE.

A.D.G. Jones & Co *(A D G Jones)* Osmunda, Wells Road, Hallatrow, BRISTOL, BS39 6EJ.

A.D.Harverd *(A D Harverd)* c/o Carter Backer Winter, Enterprise House, 21 Buckle Street, LONDON, E1 8NN.

Ⓐ**A.E. Dowd** *(A E Dowd)* Roentgen Court, Roentgen Road, Daneshill, BASINGSTOKE, HAMPSHIRE, RG24 8NT.

A.E. Jones *(A E Jones)* 51 Kelston Road, Whitchurch, CARDIFF, CF14 2AH.

Ⓐ**A.E. Mitchell & Co** *(A E Mitchell)* The Coach House, Fields Road, Chedworth, CHELTENHAM, GL54 4NQ.

A.E.C Scruton *(A E C Scruton)* 271 State Street, BROOKLYN, NY 11201, UNITED STATES.

A.E.M. Jones *(A E M Jones)* Tai Cochion, Brynsiencyn, LLANFAIRPWLLGWYNGYLL, LL61 6TQ.

★Ⓣ**A.F. Ferguson & Co** *(Z I Bhatti, S Hasan, S Hussain, Z A Qureshi, K Rafi, M S Sadiq)* State Life Building 1C, Off I.I. Chundrigar Road, P.O. Box 4716, KARACHI 74000, PAKISTAN. and at ISLAMABAD, LAHORE

▽**A.F. Ferguson & Co** *(B P Shroff)* Hansalaya, Barakhamba Road, NEW DELHI 110 001, INDIA. and at BANGALORE, CALCUTTA, CHENNAI, DUBAI, HYDERABAD, JAMSHEDPUR, MUMBAI, MUSCAT, PUNE, VADODARA

A.G. Barnes & Co *(A G B Barnes)* 147 Forest Road, TUNBRIDGE WELLS, TN2 5EX.

A.G. Eastwood & Co *(A G Eastwood)* 2 Brook Place Cottages, Ide Hill, SEVENOAKS, TN14 6BL.

Afford Bond LLP - AIMS **Members in Practice and Firms - Alphabetical**

★ⓉⒻⒶ**Afford Bond LLP** *(J E Atkinson, D Bailey, J G Curwen, G Greer, J E Phibbs)* 31 Wellington Road, NANTWICH, CHESHIRE, CW5 7ED. and at WILMSLOW

★Ⓟ**AFH Price Pearson Wheatley Limited** *(J S Wheatley)* Clarendon House, 14 St. Andrews Street, DROITWICH, WORCESTERSHIRE, WR9 8DY.

Afimar, trading name of Afimar Accountants, SLU *(M Franco Carr)* c/- Alfonso XIII s/n, Edf Terminal 1 3-8, 29640 FUENGIROLA, Malaga, SPAIN.

AFM *(M J Pactat)* Unit 4 Kernel Court, Walnut Tree Close, GUILDFORD, GU1 4UD.

ⒻⓅ**Afortis Limited** *(G Dallimore)* 2 Pennyblack Court, Barton Road, Worsley, MANCHESTER, M28 2PD.

AFT, trading name of Alan F. Trinder *(A F Trinder)* 22 Laburnham Gardens, UPMINSTER, ESSEX, RM14 1HU.

Aftab Nabi & Co *(A Ahmad)* Alshajar, Nila Gubad, Anarkali, LAHORE, PAKISTAN.

Afzal & Co, trading name of J. Afzal & Co *(J Afzal)* 23 Grove Hall Court, Hall Road, LONDON, NW8 9NR.

AG Associates *(H I Mirza)* Cantium House, Railway Approach, WALLINGTON, SURREY, SM6 0DZ.

★**Agahan & Co** *(H Namvari)* PO Box 11365-4731, 32/1 Shadab Street, Gharani Avenue, TEHRAN, 15989, IRAN.

Ⓟ**AGB Services Ltd** *(A G B Barnes)* 147 Forest Road, TUNBRIDGE WELLS, TN2 5EX.

★ⓉⓅⒶ**Aggarwal & Co, Edwards & Co, Foreman & Co, trading names of Aggarwal & Co Ltd** *(R C Abel, A Aggarwal)* 3-5 London Road, Rainham, GILLINGHAM, KENT, ME8 7RG. and at ASHFORD, SHEERNESS

Ⓟ**AGH Audit Ltd** *(G Hadjipieris)* 58 Agiou Athanasiou Avenue, El Greco Building, 2nd Floor, Office 201, 4102 LIMASSOL, CYPRUS.

ⓅⒶ**AGHS, trading name of AGHS Accounting & Taxation Services Limited** *(R K Parsons)* 14 Progress Business Centre, Whittle Parkway, SLOUGH, SL1 6DQ.

ⒻⓅⒶ**Agincourt, trading name of Agincourt Limited** *(W E Evans, N S Williams)* 9 Deryn Court, Pentwyn Business Centre, Wharfedale Road, Pentwyn, CARDIFF, CF23 7HB.

ⒻⓅⒶ**Agincourt, trading name of Agincourt Practice Limited** *(M Anderson, R N Mounter)* 6 Agincourt Street, MONMOUTH, GWENT, NP25 3DZ.

★**Agisilaos E. Demetriou FCA** *(A E Demetriou)* 9 Marathovounou Str, P.O. Box 53159, 3071 LIMASSOL, CYPRUS.

ⓉⒻⒶ**AGL** *(S D Donovan, S C Morgan)* Prudence House, Ashleigh Way, Langage Business Park, PLYMOUTH, PL7 5JX.

ⒻⓅ**AGL Accountants Limited** *(S D Donovan, S C Morgan)* 89 Fore Street, KINGSBRIDGE, TQ7 1AB.

Ⓐ**AGM** *(A G Moss)* Rockware Business Centre, Rockware Avenue, GREENFORD, MIDDLESEX, UB6 0AA.

★**AGM Partners LLP** *(J R Ayton, C Gregory, J R Jackson)* Suite 9, Innovation Centre, 23 Cambridge Science Park, CAMBRIDGE, CB4 0EY.

★ⓉⒻⒶ**AGP** *(I A Black, R K Lloyd, S A McLean)* Sycamore House, Sutton Quays Business Park, Sutton Weaver, RUNCORN, CHESHIRE, WA7 3EH. and at CHESTER, WARRINGTON

Ⓟ**AGS Accountants and Business Advisors Ltd** *(P Squire)* Castle Court 2, Castlegate Way, DUDLEY, WEST MIDLANDS, DY1 4RH.

Agutter, Helen ACA *(H E Agutter)* 48 Albany Villas, HOVE, EAST SUSSEX, BN3 2RW.

ⒻⒶ**Agutter-Khanderia** *(K D Khanderia)* First Floor, 85a Great Portland Street, LONDON, W1W 7LT.

Ⓟ**AH Accounting Limited** *(A Heath)* 41 Kingfisher Road, BUCKINGHAM, MK18 7EX.

ⓅⒶ**AH Partnership, trading name of AH Partnership Limited** *(J A Gibbs)* Stanley House, 49 Dartford Road, SEVENOAKS, KENT, TN13 3TE.

Ⓟ**Ahead for Business Pty Ltd** *(W R Hancox, B N Jones)* Level 10, 420 St Kilda Road, MELBOURNE, VIC 3004, AUSTRALIA.

AHLN Associates *(S Abbas)* First Floor, 182-184 Wolverhampton Street, DUDLEY, WEST MIDLANDS, DY1 3AD.

Ⓟ**Ahmad & Co, trading name of Ahmad Accountancy Services Limited** *(M Ahmad)* 232 Whitchurch Road, CARDIFF, CF14 3ND.

Ahmad Mustapha & Co *(A M Ghazali)* 37-2 Block C Jaya One, 72A Jalan Universiti, 46200 PETALING JAYA, SELANGOR, MALAYSIA.

Ⓐ**Ahmed & Co** *(T Ahmed)* Ferrari House, 2nd Floor, 102 College Road, HARROW, HA1 1ES.

Ⓐ**Ahmedani & Co** *(Mohammad Ahmedani)* 46 Wycliffe Road, LONDON, SW11 5QR.

Ⓟ**Ahmed-Cliffords, trading name of Ahmed-Cliffords Limited** *(H Ahmed)* 153 Beehive Lane, ILFORD, ESSEX, IG4 5DX.

Ⓟ**Ahmedi & Co Limited** *(M A Ahmedi)* 1 Marlow Copse, Walderslade, CHATHAM, KENT, ME5 9DP.

Ahmet Ozdal *(A Ozdal)* 135 Sht Huseyin Amca, Caddesi, Gonyeli, PO Box 478, LEFKOSA MERSIN 10, TURKEY.

Ⓟ**AHS & Co Limited** *(A H Sharpe)* 5 Spinney Close, Douglas, ISLE OF MAN, IM2 1NF.

★**Aib, Fatona & Co** *(E A Fatona)* 13 Jibowu Street, P.O. Box 461, YABA, NIGERIA. and at IBADAN

AIC Accountancy *(C E Johnson)* 97 Normandy Avenue, BEVERLEY, HU17 8PR.

Ⓟ**Ailsa Sadler Ltd** *(A C Sadler)* 4 Shaftesbury Avenue, Chandler's Ford, EASTLEIGH, HAMPSHIRE, SO53 3BS.

AIMS - Accountants for Business *(S S Kalirai)* 2 Pinfold Lane, Penn, WOLVERHAMPTON, WV4 4EE.

AIMS - Accountants For Business, trading name of AIM - Russell Thomas FCA *(R L Thomas)* 9 Bullfinch Lane, SEVENOAKS, KENT, TN13 2DY.

Ⓟ**AIMS - Accountants for Business, trading name of Cowbridge Finance Ltd** *(S P Kavanagh)* Aeolian House, Piccadilly, Llanblethian, COWBRIDGE, SOUTH GLAMORGAN, CF71 7JL.

Ⓟ**Aims - Accountants for Business, trading name of Jeremy Clark Accountants Ltd** *(J F Clark)* The Moat House, Sallow Lane, Wacton, NORWICH, NR15 2UL.

AIMS - Alan Reay *(A Reay)* 3 Hartley Avenue, WHITLEY BAY, NE26 3NS.

AIMS - Alastair Cameron *(A L C Cameron)* 48 Lowther Road, Barnes, LONDON, SW13 9NU.

AIMS - Andrew Fay *(A P A Fay)* 30 West Street, Dunster, MINEHEAD, SOMERSET, TA24 6SN.

AIMS - Andrew Tyzzer *(A T Tyzzer)* 3 Foden Close, Shenstone, LICHFIELD, STAFFORDSHIRE, WS14 0LE.

AIMS - Anthony Mackenzie FCA *(A T D B Mackenzie)* 77 St. Helens Park Road, HASTINGS, EAST SUSSEX, TN34 2JW.

Ⓟ**AIMS - Anthony Millner BSc(Hons) ACA, trading name of TM Accountancy Ltd** *(A E Millner)* 54 Milverton Road, Knowle, SOLIHULL, B93 0HY.

AIMS - Bryan Crystol *(B M Crystol)* 13 Walham Court, 111 Haverstock Hill, LONDON, NW3 4SD.

AIMS - Chris Poullis *(C Poullis)* 30 Tolworth Rise South, SURBITON, SURREY, KT5 9NN.

AIMS - Chris Tarbard *(C J Tarbard)* 5 Huxley Close, MACCLESFIELD, SK10 3DG.

AIMS - Colin Elliott *(C G G Elliott)* The Paddock, Bishopsbourne, CANTERBURY, CT4 5HT.

AIMS - Craig Wynne FCA *(E C Wynne)* 29 Meadowcroft, Higher Kinnerton, CHESTER, CH4 9AY.

AIMS - David Dyson *(D M Dyson)* 115 Crosland Road, Oakes, HUDDERSFIELD, HD3 3PW.

AIMS - David F Hodgson *(D F Hodgson)* 7 School Lane, Laneshawbridge, COLNE, BB8 7JB.

AIMS - David M. Cottam, trading name of David M. Cottam *(D M Cottam)* 40 Gilderdale Close, Gorse Covert, Birchwood, WARRINGTON, WA3 6TH.

Ⓟ**Aims - David Smith, Aims - Guy Berkeley, trading names of Cranfield Associates Ltd** *(R G Berkeley, D P A Smith)* Church Street House, Church Street, Rudgwick, HORSHAM, WEST SUSSEX, RH12 3EH. and at CRANLEIGH, HAYWARDS HEATH

AIMS - David Turner *(D C Turner)* 38 Caxton House, Northampton Science Park, Kings Park Road, Moulton Park, NORTHAMPTON, NN3 6LG.

AIMS - Elizabeth Bingham *(E E Bingham)* The Thatched House, The Downs, LEATHERHEAD, SURREY, KT22 8LH.

AIMS - Eric Anderson *(E H Anderson)* Rhos Fach Farm, Cross Hands, LLANELLI, DYFED, SA14 6DG.

AIMS - Graham Biggs *(G Briggs)* Peak View, Stevens Cross, Sidford, SIDMOUTH, EX10 9QL.

AIMS - Graham Eardley *(J G Eardley)* 17 Wilsthorpe Road, Breaston, DERBY, DERBYSHIRE, DE72 3EA.

Aims - Gregory Walker, trading name of Aims - Gregory Walker FCA *(G L Walker)* Yew Tree Farmhouse, Linton Road, Hadstock, CAMBRIDGE, CB21 4NU.

AIMS - Guy Smith ACA *(T G K Smith)* 5 Oakwood Park, LEEDS, LS8 2PJ.

AIMS - Harry Jeffs *(H Jeffs)* 1 Beacon Buildings, Yard 23 Stramongate, KENDAL, LA9 4BH.

AIMS - Hilary Dinsdale *(H J Dinsdale)* Pathways, Highland Street, IVYBRIDGE, DEVON, PL21 9AG.

Ⓟ**Aims - Jackie Bonella Ltd** *(J A Bonella)* Avonlea, Bush Lane, Send, WOKING, SURREY, GU23 7HP.

AIMS - Jeremy Eastwood ACA *(J C Eastwood)* 10 Broad Close, Barford St. Michael, BANBURY, OXFORDSHIRE, OX15 0RW.

Ⓐ**AIMS - John E Appleby FCA** *(J E Appleby)* 82 Upper Hanover Street, SHEFFIELD, S3 7RQ.

AIMS - John Mace *(J A Mace)* 54 King Edwards Road, MALVERN, WORCESTERSHIRE, WR14 4AJ.

AIMS - John Starley FCA *(J K Starley)* Moonrakers, Back Lane, Birdingbury, RUGBY, WARWICKSHIRE, CV23 8EN.

AIMS - Jon Smith *(J F Smith)* Mid Thatch, Boon Street, Eckington, PERSHORE, WORCESTERSHIRE, WR10 3BL.

AIMS - Jonathan Lynn *(J D Lynn)* Coach House, Warren House, Eridge Green, TUNBRIDGE WELLS, KENT, TN3 9JR.

AIMS - Jonathan Porter *(J H Porter)* 8 Bassett Dale, SOUTHAMPTON, SO16 7GT.

AIMS - M J Gordon *(M J Gordon)* 57 Taunton Road, BRIDGWATER, TA6 3LP.

Ⓟ**AIMS - Mike Barnes ACA, trading name of Mike Barnes Ltd** *(M J Barnes)* Unit 3 Waterford Industrial Estate, Mill Lane, Great Massingham, KING'S LYNN, NORFOLK, PE32 2HT.

AIMS - Neil Crossland Hinchliffe *(N. Crossland-Hinchliffe)* 16 Devonshire Road, Eastcote, PINNER, HA5 1TX.

AIMS - Nick Frost *(N W Frost)* 1 The Maples, Great Alne, ALCESTER, WARWICKSHIRE, B49 6HL.

AIMS - Nigel Newman ACA *(N P C Newman)* 4 Monmouth Close, CHARD, SOMERSET, TA20 1HQ.

AIMS - Nigel Taylor *(N F G Taylor)* Lower Farm, Green Lane, Ellisfield, BASINGSTOKE, RG25 2QL.

AIMS - Paul Whelan FCA *(P C Whelan)* Ashby House, Bernard Lane, Green Hammerton, YORK, YO26 8BP.

Ⓟ**AIMS - Richard Noble, trading name of RN Consultancy Ltd** *(R M Noble)* 4 Butterbur Place, CARDIFF, CF5 4QZ.

Aims - Robert Bull, trading name of R. Bull *(R A Bull)* 4 Park Lodge, 80 Auckland Road, LONDON, SE19 2DF.

AIMS - Robert W Field BSc ACA *(R W Field)* 9 Hinton Wood Avenue, CHRISTCHURCH, DORSET, BH23 5AB.

AIMS - Roger Thomas Owen *(R T Owen)* 69 Laurel Drive, Eccleston, ST. HELENS, WA10 5JB.

AIMS - Ronald Pollock *(Ronnie Pollock)* 7 Ellison Road, Barnes, LONDON, SW13 0AD.

AIMS - Sara E Pearcy *(S E Pearcy)* PO Box 108, The Ferry, FELIXSTOWE, SUFFOLK, IP11 9WF.

Ⓟ**AIMS - Simon Cox, trading name of Simon Cox (Norfolk) Ltd** *(S Cox)* 134 Norwich Road, Stoke Holy Cross, NORWICH, NR14 8QJ.

AIMS - Simon Fishburn FCA *(S E Fishburn)* 10 The Old Convent, EAST GRINSTEAD, WEST SUSSEX, RH19 3RS.

Ⓟ**AIMS - Steve Hallett, trading name of Gapfillers Limited** *(S C Hallett)* 5 Chargot Road, Llandaff, CARDIFF, SOUTH GLAMORGAN, CF5 1EW.

AIMS - Stuart A Williamson FCA *(S A Williamson)* 8 Sydney Grove, LONDON, NW4 2EH.

AIMS - Tim Carney *(T J Carney)* Tudor House, The Green, Great Bentley, COLCHESTER, CO7 8PG.

Ⓟ**AIMS - Tim Taylor FCA, trading name of Tim Taylor & Co Ltd** *(T M Taylor)* 24 Brynfield Road, Langland, SWANSEA, SA3 4SX.

AIMS - Tim Wright *(T M Wright)* 3 Holly Orchard, STRATFORD-UPON-AVON, WARWICKSHIRE, CV37 6RJ.

AIMS - Trevor Mills *(T J Mills)* High Dyke, Church Lane, Bury, PULBOROUGH, WEST SUSSEX, RH20 1PB.

AIMS - Virginia Pearson FCA *(V A Pearson)* 69 Tyne Park, TAUNTON, SOMERSET, TA1 2RP.

AIMS - William Hall *(W G Hall)* Sarratt House, Bridle Lane, Loudwater, RICKMANSWORTH, HERTFORDSHIRE, WD3 4JA.

Ⓟ**AIMS Accountant for Business - Chris Halder, trading name of Chris Halder Limited** *(C W Halder)* 23 Ingham Road, LONDON, NW6 1DG.

AIMS Accountant for Business, trading name of Michael Ball *(M E Ball)* James House, Newport Road, Albrighton, WOLVERHAMPTON, WV7 3FA.

AIMS Accountants *(P A D Wilson)* 90 Pinner Park Avenue, HARROW, MIDDLESEX, HA2 6JU.

Aims Accountants for Business *(A P Lloyd)* 107 Humber Doucy Lane, IPSWICH, IP4 3NU.

AIMS Accountants for Business *(R A Johnson)* 3 Grindleford Close, Desborough, KETTERING, NORTHAMPTONSHIRE, NN14 2FG.

Aims Accountants for Business *(K A Davies)* PO Box 6419, Earl Shilton, LEICESTER, LE9 7ZJ.

AIMS Accountants for Business - Ian Burton *(I M Burton)* 7 Dover Road, Birkdale, SOUTHPORT, MERSEYSIDE, PR8 4TF.

AIMS Accountants for Business, trading name of AIMS - Andrew Garran *(A A Garran)* 61 Beckwith Road, LONDON, SE24 9LQ.

AIMS Accountants for Business, trading name of AIMS - Andrew Tilbrook *(A C Tilbrook)* 47 Scraptoft Lane, LEICESTER, LE5 2FD.

Aims Accountants for Business, trading name of AIMS - Christopher van Veen *(C W van Veen)* 420 Outwood Common Road, BILLERICAY, CM11 1ET.

AIMS Accountants for Business, trading name of AIMS - David Mather *(D Mather)* 19 St Christophers Close, Upton, CHESTER, CH2 1EJ.

Aims Accountants for Business, trading name of AIMS - Geraldine Shelley FCA *(G A Shelley)* 45 Kimberley Road, Nuthall, NOTTINGHAM, NG16 1DA.

Ⓟ**Aims Accountants for Business, trading name of Bennington Finance Limited** *(N Totham)* 30 Church Street, Long Bennington, NEWARK, NOTTINGHAMSHIRE, NG23 5EN.

Aims Accountants For Business, trading name of Chris Bird *(C D Bird)* Porth Y Castell, Ravenspoint Road, Trearddur Bay, HOLYHEAD, GWYNEDD, LL65 2AQ.

AIMS Accountants for Business, trading name of Chris Burton *(C C Burton)* 13 Warren Way, Digswell, WELWYN, HERTFORDSHIRE, AL6 0DQ.

Ⓟ**Aims Accountants for Business, trading name of Duttellis Productions Ltd** *(M R Ellis)* 1 Ramsay Court, Kingfisher Way, Hinchingbrooke Business Park, HUNTINGDON, CAMBRIDGESHIRE, PE29 6FY.

Aims Accountants for Business, trading name of Gordon Maughan *(G Maughan)* 15 Bellister Park, PETERLEE, COUNTY DURHAM, SR8 1PH.

Ⓟ**AIMS Accountants for Business, trading name of Guidewise Ltd** *(A D Betley)* 27 Redwood Glade, LEIGHTON BUZZARD, BEDFORDSHIRE, LU7 3JT.

Ⓟ**Aims Accountants for Business, trading name of Laura Sturrock Ltd** *(L Sturrock)* 39 Church Street, Nether Heyford, NORTHAMPTON, NN7 3LH.

Ⓟ**AIMS Accountants for Business, trading name of M.H. Smith Ltd** *(M H Smith)* 3 Ambassador Drive, Halewood Village, LIVERPOOL, L26 6LT.

Ⓟ**Aims Accountants For Business, trading name of MGF Associates Limited** *(M G Fairbotham)* 11 Simpkins Close, Weston Under Wetherley, LEAMINGTON SPA, CV33 9GE.

Aims Accountants For Business, trading name of Michael E Mason FCA *(M E Mason)* PO Box 268, UCKFIELD, TN22 9DE.

Ⓟ**Aims Accountants for Business, trading name of Spider Associates Limited** *(M J Drinkwater)* 1 Hamlet Way, STRATFORD-UPON-AVON, WARWICKSHIRE, CV37 0AL. and at HORSHAM

AIMS Accountants For Business, trading name of Tania Oxley *(T K V Oxley)* 26 York Street, Harborne, BIRMINGHAM, B17 0HG.

Ⓟ**AIMS Accountants for Business, trading name of Westdale Associates Limited** *(J D Lawson)* 44 Dale Lee, Captain Lees Road, Westhoughton, BOLTON, BL5 3YE.

AIMS Accountants, trading name of Ian Anderson *(I M Anderson)* 24 Leigh View, Tingley, WAKEFIELD, WEST YORKSHIRE, WF3 1NJ.

AIMS Accountants, trading name of JN Oldfield LLP *(J N Oldfield)* Broomedge Post Office, 286 Higher Lane, LYMM, CHESHIRE, WA13 0RW.

Ⓟ**AIMS Accountants, trading name of RLM Accountants Ltd** *(R L Murphy)* 84 Crantock Road, LONDON, SE6 2QP.

Ⓟ**Aims Accountants, trading name of Roy Farrant & Co Ltd** *(R D Farrant)* 14 Le Corte Close, KINGS LANGLEY, HERTFORDSHIRE, WD4 9PS.

AIMS Helen Palmer *(H E Palmer)* 22 Croftdown Road, BIRMINGHAM, B17 8RB.

Ⓐ**AIMS, trading name of A.J. Charik & Co** *(A J Charik)* 24 Churchill Crescent, Headley, BORDON, GU35 8ND.

Ⓟ**AIMS, trading name of AIMS - CD 68 Enterprises Limited** *(C T Darby)* 18 Kinnoul Road, LONDON, W6 8NQ.

AIMS, trading name of AIMS - Seamus Clarke ACA *(S P Clarke)* Unit X1, European House, Rudford Industrial Estate, Ford Arundel, ARUNDEL, WEST SUSSEX BN18 0BF.

Members in Practice and Firms - Alphabetical **AIMS - Alex Picot**

Ⓟ**AIMS, trading name of AIMS - Tim Kemp Accountancy Services Limited** *(T J Kemp)* Top Barn, Rectory Road, Steppingley, BEDFORD, MK45 5AT.

AIMS, trading name of Anthony D'Arcy FCA *(A R H D'Arcy)* Bourne House, 10 Sandrock Hill Road, Wrecclesham, FARNHAM, SURREY, GU10 4NS.

Ⓟ**AIMS, trading name of Kevin Llewelyn-Evans Limited** *(M K L Evans)* 21 Northampton Square, LONDON, EC1V 0AJ.

Aims, trading name of Peter Mason *(P D Mason)* 35 New Road, Great Kingshill, HIGH WYCOMBE, BUCKINGHAMSHIRE, HP15 6DR.

Ⓟ**AIMS, trading name of Simon Hennell Limited** *(S J A Hennell)* Newhaven, Penn Street, AMERSHAM, BUCKINGHAMSHIRE, HP7 0PY.

AIMS, trading name of Stephen Plowman FCA *(S J Plowman)* 2 Sunflowers Close, Egerton Road, Pluckley, ASHFORD, KENT, TN27 0PD.

AIMS-Martin Foley, trading name of Zandan Limited *(M J Foley)* 4 Grotes Place, Blackheath, LONDON, SE3 0QH.

Ainley Cookson & Co *(P F Ainley, J J Cookson)* 102 Market Street, Hoylake, WIRRAL, MERSEYSIDE, CH47 3BE.

Ⓣ**Ainsleys** *(M F Schiller)* Suite 2, 40 Compton Rise, PINNER, MIDDLESEX, HA5 5HR.

Ⓟ**Ainsleys Limited** *(M F Schiller)* Suite 2, 40 Compton Rise, PINNER, MIDDLESEX, HA5 5HR.

Ⓟ**Ainsworth & Co, Ox Systems, trading names of Ainsworth Accountants Limited** *(P R Ainsworth)* 19 Sandringham Park Drive, New Longton, PRESTON, PR4 4ZS.

★ⓉⒻⓅⒶ**Ainsworths, trading name of Ainsworths Limited** *(P F Carney, I M W Dugmore, J Storey)* Charter House, Stansfield Street, NELSON, LANCASHIRE, BB9 9XY. and at ACCRINGTON

Ⓟ**AIP Partners CPA Ltd** *(K K Kwan, T Y Yung Linda)* Room 1304, C C Wu Building, 302-308 Hennessy Road, WAN CHAI, HONG KONG SAR.

Ⓐ**Airde Accountancy** *(R D Enticott)* Brant House, 83 Church Road, ADDLESTONE, KT15 1SF.

Ⓟ**Aitken Corporate Finance, trading name of Aitken Corporate Finance Limited** *(G M Aitken)* 18 High Street, NORTH FERRIBY, NORTH HUMBERSIDE, HU14 3JP.

AJ *(A D Jarvis)* 6a Deacon Road, LONDON, NW2 5QH.

Ⓟ**AJ & S Associates, trading name of AJ & S Associates Ltd** *(K Jordanou, S A Savva)* 289a High Street, WEST BROMWICH, WEST MIDLANDS, B70 8ND. and at NOTTINGHAM

AJ Clark *(A J Clark)* 14 Cricket Lawns, OAKHAM, LEICESTERSHIRE, LE15 6HT.

Ⓕ**AJ Rowlands & Co** *(A J Rowlands)* Suite 17, 4th Floor, 1 Crown Square, Church Street East, WOKING, SURREY GU21 6HR.

AJ Shone & Co *(A J Shone)* Ashley House, Unit 3, Brickfields Business Park, GILLINGHAM, DORSET, SP8 4PX.

Ⓟ**AJ, trading name of AJV Consultancy Limited** *(A J Vernon)* 4 The Ridings, WILMSLOW, CHESHIRE, SK9 6ES.

Ajay Kaushik *(A Kaushik)* Chrysalia Court, 206 Makarios Avenue, P O Box 50465, 3605 LIMASSOL, CYPRUS.

Ⓟ**AJB Accounting Services Ltd** *(A J Bishop)* 2 Ruskin Lodge, 20 Victor Drive, LEIGH-ON-SEA, SS9 1PP.

AJB Consultancy *(A J Brockhurst)* Ashby Pastures Farm, Great Dalby Road, Ashby Folville, MELTON MOWBRAY, LEICESTERSHIRE, LE14 2TU.

AJC Accountancy Services *(A J Cook)* Basepoint Business Centre, 110 Butterfield, LUTON, LU2 8DL.

Ⓟ**AJCK Limited** *(A J Clifford-King)* 29 Eghams Wood Road, BEACONSFIELD, BUCKINGHAMSHIRE, HP9 1JU.

AJD Accounting *(A J Davison)* 17 Apperley Avenue, High Shincliffe, DURHAM, DH1 2TY.

AJE *(A J Evans)* Little Garth, St. Johns Road, Bishop Monkton, HARROGATE, NORTH YORKSHIRE, HG3 3QU.

AJH Accountancy *(A J Hardy)* 10 Westgate Park, Hough, CREWE, CW2 5GY.

Ⓟ**AJH Limited** *(M A Assman)* Trinity House, Bath Street, St. Helier, JERSEY, JE2 4ST.

Ⓟ**AJH Resourcing, trading name of AJH Resourcing Limited** *(A J Thomas)* Trinity House, Bath Street, St. Helier, JERSEY, JE2 4ST.

★**Ajibade Durojaiye & Co** *(S A Durojaiye)* 27 Ajay Aina Street, Ifako Gbagada, PO Box 70305 Victoria Island, LAGOS, NIGERIA.

AJM Accountancy & Taxation *(A J Martin)* 20 Kensington Drive, WOODFORD GREEN, ESSEX, IG8 8LR.

AJM Business Services *(A J McEvoy)* Holmleigh, Eastham Street, CLITHEROE, LANCASHIRE, BB7 2HY.

Ⓟ**AJM Grant Services, trading name of AJM Grant Services Limited** *(J G Sweet)* Q E D Centre, Main Avenue, Treforest Industrial Estate, PONTYPRIDD, MID GLAMORGAN, CF37 5YR.

ⓅⒶ**AJP Corporate Accountants Ltd** *(A J Pearce)* Unit 9, Brenton Business Complex, Bond Street, BURY, LANCASHIRE, BL9 7BE.

ⓉⓅ**AJR & Co Ltd** *(A J G Richardson)* 1 Sandhill Farm, Middle Claydon, BUCKINGHAM, MK18 2LD.

★**AJS & Associates** *(E L Barty)* 43 Battery Hill, Fairlight, HASTINGS, EAST SUSSEX, TN35 4AP.

Ⓟ**AK Accountancy Ltd** *(A K Green)* 64 Coronation Road, Downend, BRISTOL, BS16 5SL. and at BATH

ⓉⒶ**AKA** *(L A Khan)* 803 Stratford Road, Springfield, BIRMINGHAM, B11 4DA.

Ⓟ**AKA Consulting Limited** *(J A Anderson, J Kidger)* 6 Esplanade Crescent, SCARBOROUGH, NORTH YORKSHIRE, YO11 2XB.

Ⓟ**AKA, trading name of AK Associates Limited** *(L A Khan)* 803 Stratford Road, Springfield, BIRMINGHAM, B11 4DA.

Ⓐ**Akber & Co** *(A F Somji)* 451 Moseley Road, BIRMINGHAM, B12 9BX.

ⒻⓅⒶ**AKC, trading name of KKMJ Limited** *(M Aslam Khan, K A Khokhar)* 42 Charles Street, MANCHESTER, M1 7DB. and at GLASGOW

Ⓟ**Akdag & Co, trading name of Akdag & Co Limited** *(M Akdag)* 1st Floor South, 332-336 Holloway Road, LONDON, N7 6NJ.

ⒻⒶ**Akhtar & Co** *(N Akhtar)* 454-458 Chiswick High Road, LONDON, W4 5TT.

Ⓟ**Akhtar & Co, trading name of Akhtar & Co Limited** *(M H Akhtar)* 11 Regent Place, RUGBY, WARWICKSHIRE, CV21 2PJ.

★**Akintola Williams Adetona Isichei & Co** *(I T Isichei)* P.O.Box 965, Town Planning Way/ Ade, Akinsanya Street Ilupeju, LAGOS, NIGERIA. and at ABIDJAN, BENIN CITY, DOUALA, ENUGU, JOS, KADUNA, KANO, MAIDUGURI, MBABANE, OWERRI, PORT HARCOURT

Ⓟ**AKK Consultants Limited** *(A Khosla)* 45 Mymms Drive, Brookmans Park, HATFIELD, AL9 7AE.

Ⓐ**AKM** *(A Manota)* 10 Deyncourt Road, Wednesfield, WOLVERHAMPTON, WV10 0SQ.

AKM Consulting *(A K Meadows)* PO Box 84, LEWES, EAST SUSSEX, BN8 4XB.

Akram Siddiqi & Co *(M A Siddiqi)* 58 Almond Way, MITCHAM, SURREY, CR4 1LN.

ⓅⒶ**Alacrity Accountancy, trading name of Alacrity Accountancy Ltd** *(V Kotecha)* 21 High View Close, Hamilton, LEICESTER, LE4 9LJ.

Alan A.M. Robinson *(A A M Robinson)* New Glenmore, Sliders Lane, Furners Green, UCKFIELD, EAST SUSSEX, TN22 3RU.

Alan B Higgs *(A B Higgs)* 9 Redwood Mount, REIGATE, SURREY, RH2 9NB.

Alan Baines *(A L Baines)* Church House, Thorpe, ASHBOURNE, DERBYSHIRE, DE6 2AW.

ⒻⒶ**Alan Barker & Co** *(A D Barker)* Barnhill, Wetherby Road, Collingham, WETHERBY, LS22 5AY.

Alan Barr & Co *(A M Barr)* 146/148 Bury Old Road, Whitefield, MANCHESTER, M45 6AT.

Ⓣ**Alan Boddy & Co** *(A D Boddy)* Damer House, Meadoway, WICKFORD, SS12 9HA.

Alan Bonham *(A J Bonham)* 2 Crabtree Lane, HARPENDEN, AL5 5TB.

ⓅⒶ**Alan C Prendergast, trading name of Alan C Prendergast Ltd** *(A C Prendergast)* Leicester House, Castle Street, Hay-on-Wye, HEREFORD, HR3 5DF.

Alan C Radford *(A C Radford)* Needham Cottage, Needham Green, Hatfield Broad Oak, BISHOP'S STORTFORD, HERTFORDSHIRE, CM22 7JT.

Alan C. Prendergast *(A C Prendergast)* Leicester House, Castle Street, Hay On Wye, HEREFORD, HR3 5DF.

Alan Charles Associates *(A C Goreham)* Abacus House, 19 Manor Close, TUNBRIDGE WELLS, TN4 8YB.

Alan Clarke FCA *(A Clarke)* Heawood House, Congleton Road, Nether, Alderley, MACCLESFIELD, SK10 4TN.

★ⓉⒻⒶ**Alan Cooper Saunders Angel** *(A A Cooper, M Schuz, R V Stocker)* Kenton House, 666 Kenton Road, HARROW, HA3 9QN.

Ⓐ**Alan Corbett** *(A Corbett)* 45 Rooker Avenue, Parkfields, WOLVERHAMPTON, WV2 2DT.

Alan David Arthur BSc (Econ) *(A D Arthur)* 76 Hallowes Park Road, Cullingworth, BRADFORD, WEST YORKSHIRE, BD13 5AR.

Alan Day BA (Hons) ACA *(A A Day)* 55 Bournside Road, CHELTENHAM, GLOUCESTERSHIRE, GL51 3AL.

Alan D'Silva & Co *(A.J.S.D'silva)* Paseo De La Castellana, 43, 28046 MADRID, SPAIN.

Alan E. Buckle *(A E Buckle)* 39 The Croft, Haddenham, AYLESBURY, HP17 8AS.

Ⓕ**Alan Glazier & Co** *(A Glazier)* 36 Upton Road, Claughton, BIRKENHEAD, MERSEYSIDE, CH41 0DF.

Alan Goold *(A C W Goold)* 16 Bayliss Road, Wargrave, READING, RG10 8DR.

Ⓟ**Alan Green & Co, trading name of Alan Green Accountancy Limited** *(A D Green)* Verna House, 9 Bicester Road, AYLESBURY, BUCKINGHAMSHIRE, HP19 9AG.

Alan H.K.Shing & Co *(H Shing)* Unit B 15/F, Kiu Yin Commercial Building, WAN CHAI, HONG KONG ISLAND, HONG KONG SAR.

Alan Hartley *(A Hartley)* 5 West Lane, Pirton, HITCHIN, SG5 3RA.

ⒻⒶ**Alan Heywood & Co** *(A Heywood, S G Parekh)* 78 Mill Lane, West Hampstead, LONDON, NW6 1JZ.

Ⓕ**Alan Holloway** *(A Holloway)* 18 Lumley Drive, Tickhill, DONCASTER, SOUTH YORKSHIRE, DN11 9QE.

Alan Howell *(A W Howell)* 4 South View Road, ASHTEAD, KT21 2NB.

Ⓕ**Alan Hussey Accountants** *(A Hussey)* Unit 4, Parsonage Business Centre, Church Street, Ticehurst, WADHURST, EAST SUSSEX TN5 7DL.

Alan J Harland *(A J Harland)* 380 Wokingham Road, Earley, READING, RG6 7HX.

Alan J. Carter *(A J Carter)* Goddards, 46 Maltese Road, CHELMSFORD, CM1 2PA.

ⒻⒶ**Alan James & Co** *(K G Edwards, A G James)* Quantum House, 59-61 Guildford Street, CHERTSEY, SURREY, KT16 9AX.

Alan Jon Cohen *(A J Cohen)* 2 Ganton Avenue, Whitefield, MANCHESTER, M45 7LT.

Alan Jones & Co *(A V Jones)* 59 Meadow Road, Kingswood, WATFORD, WD25 0JB.

Ⓐ**Alan Jones & Co.** *(A Jones)* 15 Killegland Street, ASHBOURNE, COUNTY MEATH, IRELAND.

Alan K. Jackson *(A K Jackson)* 63 Church Hill Road, East Barnet, BARNET, EN4 8SY.

ⓅⒶ**Alan Kitson & Company, trading name of Alan Kitson & Company Limited** *(A P Kitson)* 65 Kingswood Chase, LEIGH-ON-SEA, SS9 3BB.

Ⓐ**Alan Lindsey & Co** *(A M Lindsey)* 23 Gresham Gardens, LONDON, NW11 8NX.

ⒻⓅ**Alan M Crawford & Co Limited** *(A M Crawford)* 10 Frankscroft, PEEBLES, EH45 9DX.

Alan Miller & Co *(A Miller)* 5 Ranelagh Drive, EDGWARE, MIDDLESEX, HA8 8HJ.

Ⓟ**Alan Minshall Accountants Ltd** *(A A Minshall)* 222 Woodlands Road, Woodlands, SOUTHAMPTON, SO40 7GL.

Ⓟ**Alan Moulsdale Limited** *(R A Moulsdale)* Dale House, Tewitfield, CARNFORTH, LANCASHIRE, LA6 1JH.

Alan Pardoe *(A P Pardoe)* 52 Owen Gardens, WOODFORD GREEN, ESSEX, IG8 8DJ.

Ⓐ**Alan Patient & Co** *(A S Patient)* 9 The Shrubberies, George Lane, South Woodford, LONDON, E18 1BD.

Alan Pink Tax, trading name of Pink Consultants LLP *(A D Pink)* 44 The Pantiles, TUNBRIDGE WELLS, KENT, TN2 5TN.

Ⓐ**Alan Poole & Co** *(J A Poole)* 51 Colwyn Drive, Knypersley, STOKE-ON-TRENT, ST8 7BJ.

ⓉⒻ**Alan R. Grey & Co** *(L J Abel)* The Old Forge, Beck Place, Gosforth, SEASCALE, CA20 1AT.

Alan R. Moyse *(A R Moyse)* 12 Shepherds Croft, Withdean, BRIGHTON, BN1 5JF.

Alan Ratford & Co *(A G Ratford)* 20 School Lane, Herne, HERNE BAY, CT6 7AL. and at CANTERBURY

ⒻⓅ**Alan Reed, trading name of Alan Reed (ACT) Limited** *(A R Reed)* 4 Kent View, KENDAL, CUMBRIA, LA9 4DZ.

ⓅⒶ**Alan Reynolds & Co Ltd** *(J A Reynolds)* Walnut House, 34 Rose Street, WOKINGHAM, BERKSHIRE, RG40 1XU.

Alan Rumph & Co *(A Rumph)* Jubilee House, Altcar Road, Formby, LIVERPOOL, L37 8DL.

ⓉⒻⒶ**Alan Rush & Co.** *(R N Raichura)* 1349/1353 London Road, LEIGH-ON-SEA, SS9 2AB.

Alan S Johnson *(A S Johnson)* 173 College Road, LIVERPOOL, L23 3AT.

Ⓐ**Alan S. Kindred** *(A S Kindred)* Normans Corner, 41 Church Lane, Fulbourn, CAMBRIDGE, CB21 5EP.

ⒻⒶ**Alan Sacks & Co** *(A L B Sacks)* Little Red Court, 7 St. Ronans Close, Hadley Wood, BARNET, HERTFORDSHIRE, EN4 0JH.

Alan Salt *(A C Salt)* Rose Croft, Fauls Green, Fauls, WHITCHURCH, SHROPSHIRE, SY13 2AS.

Alan Sears *(A Sears)* 2 Hartsbourne Park, 180 High Road, Bushey Heath, BUSHEY, WD23 1SD.

ⓉⒻⒶ**Alan Secker & Co.** *(A Secker)* 209 Albury Drive, PINNER, MIDDLESEX, HA5 3RH.

Ⓟ**Alan Shanson & Co, trading name of Bryal Commercial & Financial Facilities Ltd** *(A Shanson)* Flat 6, 71 Park Road, New Barnet, BARNET, EN4 9QD.

Alan Solomons & Co. *(A J Solomons)* 2 Gayton Road, HARROW, MIDDLESEX, HA1 2XU.

Alan Taylor *(A T Taylor)* 28 Aldrich Drive, Willen, MILTON KEYNES, MK15 9LU.

Alan Vause *(A C Vause)* Wood End, High Cotts Lane, West Clandon, GUILDFORD, GU4 7XA.

Ⓐ**Alan W Hooper FCA CTA** *(A W Hooper)* 21 Hartshill Close, Hillingdon, UXBRIDGE, UB10 9LH.

ⓅⒶ**Alan W Simons & Co, trading name of Alan W Simons Limited** *(A W Simons)* Hillview Business Centre, 2 Leybourne Avenue, BOURNEMOUTH, BH10 6HF.

Alan W. Denham *(A W Denham)* Glen Lea, 25 Manor Close, Edwalton, NOTTINGHAM, NG12 4BH.

Alan W. Docker *(A W Docker)* 8 Milton Close, Headless Cross, REDDITCH, WORCESTERSHIRE, B97 5BQ.

Alan Waterhouse *(A Waterhouse)* 106 Mount Albany, Newtownpark Avenue, BLACKROCK, COUNTY DUBLIN, IRELAND.

Alan Wilkie *(A D Wilkie)* 19 Edlingham Close, South Gosforth, NEWCASTLE UPON TYNE, NE3 1RH.

ⓅⒶ**Alanbrookes Ltd** *(A S Fisher)* PO Box 258, STROUD, GLOUCESTERSHIRE, GL6 8WZ. and at BRISTOL

Alanthwaite & Co *(T R Alanthwaite)* The Linden Building, Regent Park, Booth Drive, WELLINGBOROUGH, NORTHAMPTONSHIRE, NN8 6GR.

Ⓟ**Alastair Walmsley Consulting Limited** *(A S Walmsley)* Rosehill, Chapel Fold, Wiswell, CLITHEROE, LANCASHIRE, BB7 9DE.

Ⓟ**Alathea Audit Limited** *(A Liasides)* PO Box 53590, CY 3303 LIMASSOL, CYPRUS.

Ⓟ**Albeck Limited** *(J D A Cowan)* 112 Green Lane, EDGWARE, MIDDLESEX, HA8 8EJ.

ⓉⒻⓅⒶ**Albert Goodman CBH, trading name of Albert Goodman CBH Limited** *(R G Bugler, A J Goracy, D H Griffin, J A Hall, M J Howard, A E Newberry, I W Walton)* The Lupins Business Centre, 1-3 Greenhill, WEYMOUTH, DORSET, DT4 7SP. and at DORCHESTER

★ⓉⒻⒶ**Albert Goodman LLP** *(R G Bugler, S A Cole, D H Griffin, N J Hancock, J Hopkins, A J Kerr, K J Miller, P Sargent)* Mary Street House, Mary Street, TAUNTON, SOMERSET, TA1 3NW. and at BRIDGWATER, CHARD, YEOVIL

Albert J. Pope *(P M Roberts)* Unit 4 Westfield Court, Third Avenue, Westfield Inds Est, Midsomer Norton, RADSTOCK, BA3 4XD.

★**Albert Wong & Co.** *(C W A Wong)* Room 701A, Nan Dao Commercial Building, 359-361 Queen's Road Central, CENTRAL, HONG KONG ISLAND, HONG KONG SAR.

★Ⓟ**Alchemy Business Solutions, trading name of Alchemy Business Solutions Limited** *(M J McCafferty)* The Axis Building, Maingate, Team Valley, GATESHEAD, TYNE AND WEAR, NE11 0NQ.

Alcock Watson Associates *(M R Watson)* 15 High Street, LYDNEY, GLOUCESTERSHIRE, GL15 5DP.

Ⓟ**Alcon Limited** *(A Twamley)* Enterprise House, 7 Coventry Road, Coleshill, BIRMINGHAM, B46 3BB.

Alder Dodsworth & Co *(S G Alder)* 22 Athol Street, Douglas, ISLE OF MAN, IM1 1JA.

ⒻⒶ**Aldersons** *(S J Alderson)* 4 The Moorings, Mossley, ASHTON-UNDER-LYNE, LANCASHIRE, OL5 9BZ.

Ⓟ**Alderstead Financial Services Ltd** *(J R Williams)* Chart House, 2 Effingham Road, REIGATE, SURREY, RH2 7JN.

ⓉⒻⓅ**Alderwick James & Co, trading name of Alderwick James & Co Limited** *(G A M Alderwick)* 4 The Sanctuary, 23 Oak Hill Grove, SURBITON, SURREY, KT6 6DU.

Ⓟ**Aldington Navesey & Co Ltd** *(M A Navesey)* 19 Billericay Road, Herongate, BRENTWOOD, Essex, CM13 3PS.

Ⓟ**Aldridge Taxation & Accountancy Services Ltd** *(M L Aldridge)* Woodlands Lodge, 2 Penfold Drive, Great Billing, NORTHAMPTON, NN3 9EQ.

Aleathia Mann *(A M Mann)* Springwood Church Lane, Sparham, NORWICH, NR9 5PP.

Ⓟ**Aleathia Mann Ltd** *(A M Mann)* Springwood, Church Lane, Sparham, NORWICH, NR9 5PP.

Ⓟ**Alef Tuf Limited** *(M F Schiller)* Suite 2, 40 Compton Rise, PINNER, MIDDLESEX, HA5 5HR.

Alex Ewin *(A D Ewin)* Flat 7 Strathaird Court, 39 Grove Road, SUTTON, SURREY, SM1 2AH.

★ⓉⒶ**Alex Picot** *(A D Le Cheminant, S J Phillips, J D Rhodes)* 95-97 Halkett Place, St. Helier, JERSEY, JE1 1BX.

Ⓟ**Alex Picot Ltd** *(A D Le Cheminant, S J Phillips, C Purcell, J D Rhodes)* 95-97 Halkett Place, St. Helier, JERSEY, JE1 1BX.

ⓉⒻⒶ**Alexander & Co** *(F Atkinson, A H Berg, S Jolley, G S Kramrisch, S Topperman, S Verber)* 17 St Ann's Square, MANCHESTER, M2 7PW.

Ⓟ**Alexander & Co (Accountancy) Ltd** *(S L Alexander)* 7 Murray Crescent, PINNER, MIDDLESEX, HA5 3QF.

Ⓐ**Alexander & Company** *(B Dzialowski)* 220 The Vale, LONDON, NW11 8SR.

ⓅⒶ**Alexander Ash & Co Ltd** *(P Dell)* 1st Floor, Bristol & West House, 100 Crossbrook Street, Cheshunt, WALTHAM CROSS, HERTFORDSHIRE EN8 8JJ.

★**Alexander Bursk** *(B Fine, B M Shafar)* Parkgates, Bury New Road, Prestwich, MANCHESTER, M25 0JW.

Ⓐ**Alexander Dave** *(A Dave)* 76 Belmont Avenue, BARNET, HERTFORDSHIRE, EN4 9LA.

Ⓟ**Alexander Lawson Jacobs, trading name of Alexander Lawson Jacobs Ltd** *(N I Koumettou, Y Koumettou)* 1 Kings Avenue, LONDON, N21 3NA.

Ⓟ**Alexander Maitland Limited** *(T A Steiner)* 50 Cowick Street, St Thomas, EXETER, EX4 1AP.

ⓉⒻⒶ**Alexander Myerson & Co** *(P R Burns, J K McCormick, R G Myerson, P Rothwell, I Swerdlow)* Alexander House, 61 Rodney Street, LIVERPOOL, L1 9ER. and at ORMSKIRK

Ⓐ**Alexander Partnership** *(M S Dashfield, P W Griffiths)* Barclays Bank Chambers, 18 High Street, TENBY, PEMBROKESHIRE, SA70 7HD. and at LLANELLI

ⒻⓅ**Alexander Rosse, trading name of Alexander Rosse Limited** *(A Dhanda, R Joshi)* 10 Linford Forum, Rockingham Drive, Linford Wood, MILTON KEYNES, MK14 6LY.

Alexander Whiting & Co Limited *(A Whiting)* Shelthorpe Lodge, 6 Chestnuts Close, Sutton Bonington, LOUGHBOROUGH, LEICESTERSHIRE, LE12 5RJ.

Alexander, Moore & Co. *(J R Moore)* 2nd Floor, Monument House, 215 Marsh Road, PINNER, MIDDLESEX, HA5 5NE.

Ⓟ**Alexander-Passe & Co, trading name of Alexander-Passe Ltd** *(G Alexander-Passe)* 44 North Crescent, LONDON, N3 3LL.

Ⓟ**Alexanders Strategic Planning Ltd** *(C R G Tomaszewski)* Redhill Chambers, 2d High Street, REDHILL, RH1 1RJ.

ⒻⓅⒶ**Alexanders, trading name of Alexanders Professional Services Ltd** *(C R G Tomaszewski)* Redhill Chambers, High Street, REDHILL, RH1 1RJ.

ⓉⒻⒶ**Alexandra Durrant** *(A B Durrant)* 10A/12A High Street, EAST GRINSTEAD, RH19 3AW.

Alexandros Charalambous *(A Charalambous)* 3 Prokopiou street, 2000 STROVOLOS, CYPRUS.

Ⓟ**Alextra Accountants Ltd** *(M G Price)* Units 12-14 Macon Court, Herald Drive, CREWE, CW1 6EA.

Alfred E Redden FCA *(A E Redden)* 42 Drylla, DINAS POWYS, SOUTH GLAMORGAN, CF64 4UL.

Alfred HK Huen & Company *(A H K Huen)* 14/F Wing On Cheong Building, 5 Wink Lok Street, CENTRAL, KOWLOON, HONG KONG SAR.

Alfred Neill & Co *(R E Glencross)* 34 Hollington Crescent, NEW MALDEN, KT3 6RR.

★**ALG** *(M R Hilton)* Brook Point, 1412-1420 High Road, LONDON, N20 9BH.

Algonquin Trust S.A. *(B K Stamps)* Cour du Moulin, 5-9 Route de L'Etat, 1380 LASNE, BELGIUM.

Alicia Howell BSc (Hons) ACA *(A C Howell)* 13 Ipswich Grove, NORWICH, NR2 2LU.

Alison Brooker *(A M Brooker)* 19 Calmore Crescent, Calmore, SOUTHAMPTON, SO40 2RJ.

Alison Gurkin Consultants *(A Gurkin)* 41 Culmington Road, Ealing, LONDON, W13 9NJ.

Ⓕ**Alison J Counsell** *(A J Counsell)* Meadow House, 2 Chapel Close, Empingham, OAKHAM, RUTLAND, LE15 8BX.

Alison J Dodd *(A J Dodd)* 39 Rosebery Road, Aston Clinton, AYLESBURY, BUCKINGHAMSHIRE, HP22 5JY.

Alison Maquire *(A Maguire)* 10 Clovelly Avenue, WARLINGHAM, SURREY, CR6 9HZ.

Ⓟ**Alison Rogers Limited** *(A V Rogers)* 4 Longborough Close, REDDITCH, WORCESTERSHIRE, B97 5QN.

Alison Rought & Co *(A M Rought)* 16 Appleton Avenue, Pedmore, STOURBRIDGE, WEST MIDLANDS, DY8 2JZ.

Alison Stevens & Co *(A M Stevens)* 1 Churchfield, Appledore, BIDEFORD, DEVON, EX39 1RL.

Ⓐ**Alison Vickers** *(A Vickers)* Bevan & Buckland, Langdon House, Langdon Road, SA1 Swansea Waterfront, SWANSEA, SA1 8QY.

Alison White FCA *(A B White)* Combe Cottage, Stortford Road, Leaden Roding, DUNMOW, ESSEX, CM6 1RB.

Alistair Barclay *(A Barclay)* 28 Cartha Place, DUMFRIES, DG1 4LW.

Alistair D. Ross *(A D Ross)* 21 Hylton Road, West Park, HARTLEPOOL, TS26 0AG.

ⓉⒻⓅ**AlixPartners Ltd** *(S S Dubey, D C Lovett, S J Taylor)* 20 North Audley Street, LONDON, W1K 6WE.

Ⓕ**AlixPartners UK LLP** *(S G Bailur, A T D L Grantham, D A Hewish, D C Lovett, H C H Munro, S J Taylor)* 20 North Audley Street, LONDON, W1K 6WE.

Al-janabi Al-rubaie *(B A Al-Janabi)* No 66, St 14 Ave 902, Al -Wathiq Sq, BAGHDAD, IRAQ.

All Accountancy *(C Shing)* 377 Edgware Road, LONDON, W2 1BT.

Allan Brown & Co *(A K Brown)* 18/22 Church Street, Great Malvern, MALVERN, WR14 2AY.

Ⓟ**Allan Brown Accountancy & Taxation Services Limited** *(A K Brown)* 18/22 Church Street, MALVERN, WR14 2AY.

Allan Browne *(A Browne)* 34 Frankland Crescent, Parkstone, POOLE, BH14 9PX.

★Ⓐ**Allan G. Whittle & Co** *(G T Ferguson)* Alum House, 5 Alum Chine Road, Westbourne, BOURNEMOUTH, BH4 8DT.

Allan George Consultants *(G C Wlodyka)* 107 The Grove, WEST WICKHAM, BR4 9LA.

Allan Pye *(A Pye)* 12th Floor, Bank House, Charlotte Street, MANCHESTER, M1 4ET.

Ⓟ**Allan Smith Accounting & Tax Ltd** *(A E Smith)* 5 The Green, Codicote, HITCHIN, HERTFORDSHIRE, SG4 8UR.

Ⓐ**Allan Steinberg & Co** *(A M Steinberg)* 25A York Road, ILFORD, IG1 3AD.

Allan Willmott *(A Willmott)* Bramley, Farthings Hill, HORSHAM, WEST SUSSEX, RH12 1TS.

Ⓟ**Allans The Accountants, trading name of Allans The Accountants Ltd** *(D M Patel)* 1st Floor, 21 Victoria Road, SURBITON, SURREY, KT6 4JZ.

Ⓟ**Allchild Accounting Limited** *(M B Allchild)* 4 Howland Court, 20 The Avenue, Hatch End, PINNER, MIDDLESEX, HA5 4ET.

ⓉⒻⓅⒶ**Allchurch Bailey Limited** *(R I Bailey, D A Brown)* 93 High Street, EVESHAM, WORCESTERSHIRE, WR11 4DU. and at PERSHORE

Ⓟ**Allen & Co, trading name of First Call Accounting Ltd** *(K T Spencer)* 2nd Floor, Chantrey House, 8-10 High Street, BILLERICAY, ESSEX, CM12 9BQ.

Allen Accountancy Services *(T L Allen)* Unit 13 Gwenfro Units, Wrexham Technology Park, WREXHAM, CLWYD, LL13 7YP.

Allen Accounting *(S J Allen)* 57 Dartmouth Road, RUISLIP, MIDDLESEX, HA4 0DE.

★**Allen Ainsworth Associates, trading name of K.C. Allen** *(K C Allen)* 49B Post Street, Godmanchester, HUNTINGDON, PE29 2AQ.

Allen Consulting *(V M Allen)* 96a Hillside Road, Portishead, BRISTOL, BS20 8LJ.

Ⓟ**Allen Consulting Limited** *(M S Allen)* 9 St. Helier Close, WOKINGHAM, BERKSHIRE, RG41 2HA.

Ⓟ**Allen Martin & Company Limited** *(T A Martin)* 9 Ravenhill Park Gardens, BELFAST, BT6 0DH.

★**Allen Mills Howard & Co** *(J C H Mills)* 23 Stockport Road, ASHTON-UNDER-LYNE, OL7 0LA. and at HYDE

ⒻⓅ**Allen Mills Howard Ltd** *(D K Allen, K G Allen)* 56 Manchester Road, ALTRINCHAM, WA14 4PJ.

ⓉⓅⒶ**Allen Sykes Limited** *(G R Herbert, J F Hindmarsh, P Lamb, D Stanwix, B Wood)* 5 Henson Close, South Church Enterprise Park, BISHOP AUCKLAND, COUNTY DURHAM, DL14 6WA. and at BARNARD CASTLE

Allen Thornton Springer *(R M J Allen)* 67 Westow Street, Upper Norwood, LONDON, SE19 3RW.

ⓉⒻⓅⒶ**Allens, trading name of Allens Accountants Limited** *(P E Collier, R G Dawson, B Furness, P N Horrocks, P G Leah, S J Leigh, P J Wright)* 123 Wellington Road South, STOCKPORT, SK1 3TH.

Alliance Associates *(D T Lo Seen Chong)* Suite 401, St James Court, St Denis Street, PORT LOUIS, MAURITIUS.

ⓉⓅ**Alliott Partellas Kiliaris Ltd** *(A A Partellas)* 77 Strovolou Strovolos Center, Office 201, 2018 NICOSIA, CYPRUS.

Ⓟ**Alliott Tsoi CPA Limited** *(T W D Tsoi)* 22nd Floor, Hing Yip Commercial Centre, 280 Des Voeux Road, CENTRAL, HONG KONG ISLAND, HONG KONG SAR.

ⓉⒶ**Alliotts** *(N J Armstrong, C S Cairns, R S Curtis, I Davies, P J Edwards, C C Farmer, I Gibbon, P C Guinn, S Gupta, R D E Hopes, Y C Luk, S J Meredith)* Friary Court, 13-21 High Street, GUILDFORD, SURREY, GU1 3DL. and at HARROW, LONDON

Allison & Associates *(D M Allison)* 31 Mentone Road, PO Box 30, PORT ALFRED, 6170, SOUTH AFRICA.

Ⓟ**Allon Schick-Maier, trading name of ASM Accounting Services Limited** *(A Schick-Maier)* 21 Culverlands Close, STANMORE, HA7 3AG.

ⓉⒶ**Allotts** *(A E Grice, N S Highfield, S Pepper, J N Saunders, M S Watson)* The Old Grammar School, 13 Moorgate Road, ROTHERHAM, SOUTH YORKSHIRE, S60 2EN. and at DONCASTER

Ⓟ**Allways Accounting, Bevis Accountants, trading names of Bevis Accountants Ltd** *(G D Bevis)* First Floor, 32-34 High Street, RINGWOOD, HAMPSHIRE, BH24 1AG.

Allwell Brown & Co *(S Allwell-Brown)* 73 Ikwerre Road, P.O. Box 242, PORT HARCOURT, NIGERIA.

Ⓟ**Almas Consulting Ltd** *(B Amin)* 195 Stoke Pages Lane, SLOUGH, BERKSHIRE, SL1 3LU.

Aloke Bosu *(A Bosu)* 17880 Skypark Circle, Suite 120, IRVINE, CA 91614-4498, UNITED STATES.

Ⓟ**Alpha Accountancy Evesham Limited** *(G B Robinson)* 35 Badsey Road, Willersey, BROADWAY, WORCESTERSHIRE, WR12 7PR.

Alpha Advice *(S F Westmacott)* Greenacre, Meopham Green, GRAVESEND, DA13 0PY.

Ⓟ**Alpha Business Services, trading name of Alpha Business Services Limited** *(C S Hall)* Inverebrie, ELLON, ABERDEENSHIRE, AB41 8PX.

Ⓟ**Alsford Limited** *(A S Ford)* 306 The Greenway, EPSOM, SURREY, KT18 7JF.

Ⓟ**Altash Consultants, trading name of Altash Consultants & Partners Ltd** *(E San-Juan Martin)* Shaw House, Pegler Way, CRAWLEY, WEST SUSSEX, RH11 7AF. and at MADRID

ⓉⒶ**Altman, Blane & Co** *(A Blane, G H Owen)* Middlesex House, 29/45 High Street, EDGWARE, HA8 7LH.

ⒻⒶ**Altman, Smith & Co** *(M Zahur)* Leverton House, 461-463 London Road, Heeley, SHEFFIELD, S2 4HL.

ⓉⒶ**Alton & Co** *(A Kemal)* 237 Kennington Lane, LONDON, SE11 5QU.

Ⓟ**Altorfer Financial Management Ltd** *(M P Chaplin)* 5 Regent Gate, WALTHAM CROSS, HERTFORDSHIRE, EN8 7AF.

Altus Accounting Service, trading name of Altus Business Consulting *(R J Ashmore)* 76 High Street, STOURBRIDGE, WEST MIDLANDS, DY8 1DX.

Alun Dunning *(A Dunning)* 25 Front Street, Hetton-le-Hole, HOUGHTON LE SPRING, DH5 9PF.

Ⓐ**Alun Evans** *(A Evans)* 45 High Street, HAVERFORDWEST, DYFED, SA61 2BP.

Alun G Hicks *(A G Hicks)* Westways, Tintagel Road, Finchampstead, WOKINGHAM, RG40 3JJ.

Alun Walters & Co *(A J Walters)* Llanddewi Castle, Llanddewi, Reynoldston, SWANSEA, SA3 1AU.

Alvarez & Marsal Transaction Advisory Group Europe LLP *(A K Balcombe, C J A McLelland, P Mitchell)* 1 Finsbury Circus, LONDON, EC2M 7EB.

Ⓟ**Alvery Ltd** *(J E F Savage)* Capital Business Centre, Suite 126, 22 Carlton Road, SOUTH CROYDON, SURREY, CR2 0BS.

Ⓐ**Alwyn Thomas** *(A Thomas)* Glenaub House, Old School Road, PORTHCAWL, MID GLAMORGAN, CF36 3AW.

ⓉⒻⒶ**Alwyns, trading name of Alwyns LLP** *(T Applin, D I Kirkwood, R D Neville, J A Rickler, D N C Stanley)* Crown House, 151 High Road, LOUGHTON, ESSEX, IG10 4LG.

AM & Associates *(A Manzoor)* 201 Manor Road, Grange Hill, CHIGWELL, ESSEX, IG7 4JY.

ⓅⒶ**AM & Co, trading name of A Maqbool & Co Limited** *(M Maqbool)* 192 Haydons Road, Wimbledon, LONDON, SW19 8TR. and at HOUNSLOW

Ⓟ**AM Accountancy Services, trading name of AM Accountancy Services Limited** *(A Millar)* 6 Brunel Court, TRURO, TR1 3AE.

AM Griffin BSc FCA *(A M Griffin)* Ladyacre, Stag Lane, Chorleywood, RICKMANSWORTH, HERTFORDSHIRE, WD3 5HD.

AM Pitt MA FCA *(A M Pitt)* 14 Queen Square, BATH, BA1 2HN.

Ⓟ**AM Tax Services Ltd** *(A J McMillan)* 24a Priory Lane, WEST MOLESEY, SURREY, KT8 2PS.

Amanda J Moran *(A J Moran)* 7 Goosebrook Close, Comberbach, NORTHWICH, CHESHIRE, CW9 6BX.

Amanda Loizou *(A L Loizou)* 44 Penwortham Road, SOUTH CROYDON, SURREY, CR2 0QS.

Ⓟ**Amanda Stead, trading name of Amanda Stead Limited** *(A J Stead)* Weavers Cottage, Holt Lane, Brindle, CHORLEY, LANCASHIRE, PR6 8NE.

Amanda Thornton *(A L Thornton)* Saltwood, Onslow Crescent, WOKING, SURREY, GU22 7AU.

ⒻⒶ**AMAS, trading name of Keith Graham** *(A J Pusey, S K Pusey)* Suite 2, Wesley Chambers, Queens Road, ALDERSHOT, HAMPSHIRE, GU11 3JD.

Ⓟ**Amati UK, trading name of Amati UK Ltd** *(J L Macarthur)* 25A Plover Way, LONDON, SE16 7TS.

Ⓟ**AMBC, trading name of A & M Bryant Consulting Ltd** *(A J Bryant)* 6 Pheasants Way, RICKMANSWORTH, HERTFORDSHIRE, WD3 7ES.

Ⓟ**Amber Corporate Advisory, trading name of Amber Advisory Limited** *(A J Wolstenholme)* 48 Moorfield Avenue, Knowle, SOLIHULL, WEST MIDLANDS, B93 9RA.

Ⓟ**Ambitious Minds Limited** *(A P C Berkley, I Cornelius)* 4 Shaw Green Lane, Prestbury, CHELTENHAM, GLOUCESTERSHIRE, GL52 3BP.

Ⓟ**Ambler & Co Limited** *(J M Konczyk)* 107 Northern Lights, Salts Mill Road, SHIPLEY, WEST YORKSHIRE, BD17 7DG.

★**Amcan** *(A J Macdonald)* 31 Heol Cefn Onn, Lisvane, CARDIFF, CF14 0TP.

Ⓟ**Amchins, trading name of Amchin Management Services Limited** *(B S Champsi)* 23 Northiam, LONDON, N12 7ET.

Amey & Associates *(S L Amey)* 32a St. Benedicts Street, NORWICH, NR2 4AQ.

Ⓐ**Amey Kamp LLP** *(M B Patel)* 310 Harrow Road, WEMBLEY, MIDDLESEX, HA9 6LL.

ⒻⓅⒶ**Amherst & Shapland Limited** *(K H D Preston)* 4 Irnham Road, MINEHEAD, SOMERSET, TA24 5DG.

Ⓐ**Amherst & Shapland, trading name of Amherst & Shapland (Taunton & Wiveliscombe)** *(A G Porter)* Unit 2, Old Brewery Road, Wiveliscombe, TAUNTON, SOMERSET, TA4 2PW.

Ⓟ**Amicustax Limited** *(S Friend, E A Moss)* 16 Dover Street, Mayfair, LONDON, W1S 4LR.

Ⓟ**Amies & Co.** *(J S Amies)* 205 High Street, Brownhills, WALSALL, WS8 6HE.

Amin & Co *(P A Amin)* 781-783 Harrow Road, Sudbury Town, WEMBLEY, MIDDLESEX, HA0 2LP.

Ⓣ**Amin Mudassar & Co** *(M Amin)* 4th Floor 97-B/D-I, Main Building, Gulberg III, LAHORE, PAKISTAN.

★**Amin Patel & Shah** *(N S Amin)* 1st Floor, 334-336 Goswell Road, LONDON, EC1V 7RP.

Aminian & Co *(M Aminian)* Unit 2 Edison Business Centre, 52 Edison Road, AYLESBURY, HP19 8TE.

Amir Kassam *(A A A Kassam)* Suite 207, 1911 Kennedy Road, SCARBOROUGH M1P 2L9, ON, CANADA.

Amir Khan & Co *(M A Khan)* 9 Michni Road, Peshawar Cantt, PESHAWAR, PAKISTAN.

Amir M. Jazayeri *(A M Jazayeri)* 15 Fleming Street, Vari, 16672 ATHENS, GREECE.

Ⓕ**Amiri Associates** *(S A Amiri)* 57 Princess Street, MANCHESTER, M2 4EQ.

Amjad Hussain BSc ACA *(A Hussain)* 74 Hazelwood Road, Walthamstow, LONDON, E17 7AL.

★Ⓟ**AMK Russell Marks Limited** *(A Marcou)* 21 Aylmer Parade, Aylmer Road, LONDON, N2 0AT.

Ⓟ**AML, trading name of Amlbenson Limited** *(A J Axelsen, C J Mills)* AML Maybrook House, 97 Godstone Road, CATERHAM, CR3 6RE.

Ⓟ**AMP & Partners Limited** *(A Sharma)* Suite 8 Ellesmere House, 29 City Mill Lane, PO Box 1467, GIBRALTAR, GIBRALTAR.

Ⓟ**AM-PM Accounting Solutions Limited** *(R K Jurd)* Building 6000, Langstone Technology Park, Langstone Road, HAVANT, HAMPSHIRE, PO9 1SA.

Ⓟ**AMR Accounting Services Limited** *(C D Root)* Rutland House, 114-116 Manningham Lane, BRADFORD, WEST YORKSHIRE, BD8 7JF.

Ⓟ**AMS Accountancy Ltd** *(P J Bromiley)* Delta 606, Welton Road, Delta Office Park, SWINDON, SN5 7XF.

Ⓟ**AMT Consulting Limited** *(A M Tuck)* 26 Kings Hill Avenue, Kings Hill, WEST MALLING, KENT, ME19 4AE.

Amy Taylor Accountancy *(M A Taylor)* 10 Blackbird Street, Potton, SANDY, BEDFORDSHIRE, SG19 2LT.

Anas Ng *(A Ng)* Room 1506-1508, 15/F Asia Orient Tower, 33 Lockhart Road, WAN CHAI, HONG KONG ISLAND, HONG KONG SAR.

Ⓟ**Anavrin Limited** *(R J Griffiths)* 51 Penyston Road, MAIDENHEAD, BERKSHIRE, SL6 6EJ.

Ⓟ**Anchor Accounting Services Ltd** *(R G Pester)* 67 Old Woking Road, WEST BYFLEET, SURREY, KT14 6LF.

Anchorage *(V Barnacle)* 17 Red Lion Court, Victoria Street, HEREFORD, HR4 0BZ.

ⒻⒶ**Anderson & Co** *(F J H Anderson, A R Doggett)* Sumpter House, 8 Station Road, Histon, CAMBRIDGE, CB24 9LQ.

Ⓐ**Anderson & Shepherd** *(M E Anderson, P A Shepherd)* Shepson House, Stockwell Street, LEEK, STAFFORDSHIRE, ST13 6DH.

ⓉⒻⒶ**Anderson Barrowcliff, trading name of Anderson Barrowcliff LLP** *(B S Blakey, J Q J P Bury, D J Robertson, R G Robinson, D R Shawcross, N P Upton)* Waterloo House, Thornaby Place, Thornaby on Tees, STOCKTON-ON-TEES, CLEVELAND, TS17 6SA.

Ⓟ**Anderson Griffin Limited** *(A W Davies)* Rotunda Buildings, Montpellier Exchange, CHELTENHAM, GLOUCESTERSHIRE, GL50 1SX.

Ⓐ**Anderson Musaamil & Co** *(A M Musaamil)* 101 Epsom Road, SUTTON, SURREY, SM3 9EY.

ⓅⒶ**Anderson Neal, trading name of Anderson Neal Limited** *(M A Corbitt)* 1 The Mews, 6 Putney Common, LONDON, SW15 1HL.

★ⓉⒻⒶ**Anderson Ross, trading name of Anderson Ross LLP** *(N Savomy, P F L Ten)* Waltham Forest Business Centre, 5 Blackhorse Lane, LONDON, E17 6DS.

Ⓟ**Andersons Accountants and Business Advisors, trading name of Andersons Accountants Limited** *(R H Anderson)* Bank Chambers, Market Place, Melbourne, DERBY, DE73 8DS.

★Ⓟ**Andersons, trading name of Anderson Brownlie Ltd** *(T A Anderson)* 53 Wellhall Road, HAMILTON, LANARKSHIRE, ML3 9BY.

Andertons *(J A Manjoo)* Hytec House, 27 Burgess Wood Road South, BEACONSFIELD, BUCKINGHAMSHIRE, HP9 1EX.

ⓉⒻⓅⒶ**Andertons Liversidge & Co, trading name of Alco Audit Limited** *(J Cousins Woodrow, J Healy, R M Johnson)* 12-14 Percy Street, ROTHERHAM, SOUTH YORKSHIRE, S65 1ED. and at WORKSOP

Andon Freres *(A Jones)* Cavendish House, St Andrew's Court, Burley Street, LEEDS, LS3 1JY.

ⓉⒻⓅⒶ**Andorran Limited** *(R F Downes, S E Garside)* 6 Manor Park Business Centre, Mackenzie Way, CHELTENHAM, GL51 9TX.

Andre Peter *(A C Peter)* First Floor, The Old Auction Rooms, Marine Walk Street, HYTHE, KENT, CT21 5NW.

Andrea Ellis *(A Ellis)* 6 Shaftesbury Avenue, Radcliffe-on-Trent, NOTTINGHAM, NG12 2NH.

Andrea Law *(A L Law)* Sandrock Farmhouse, Limes Lane, Buxted, UCKFIELD, EAST SUSSEX, TN22 4PE.

Andrea Szalanczi *(A M Szalanczi)* 3 Brooksville Avenue, LONDON, NW6 6TH.

Andrea Terroni *(A J Terroni)* 28 Beechdale, Winchmore Hill, LONDON, N21 3QG.

Ⓣ**Andreas Prodromou & Co** *(A Prodromou)* Prodromou Court, 54 Sittica Hanoum Street, P.O. Box 40163, 6301 LARNACA, CYPRUS.

Ⓟ**Andrew B Sharkey Ltd** *(A B Sharkey)* Jasmine Cottage, Rowland, BAKEWELL, DERBYSHIRE, DE45 1NR.

Andrew B Tappin *(A B Tappin)* 18 East Sheen Avenue, LONDON, SW14 8AS.

Andrew Bagnall *(C A S J Bagnall)* Wyndham House, The Street, Market Weston, DISS, IP22 2NZ.

ⒻⓅ**Andrew Bates Accountancy, trading name of Ceilic Ltd** *(A W A Bates)* 5 Miles Garth, Bardsey, LEEDS, LS17 9BW.

Andrew Blencowe *(A Blencowe)* 18 Pleasant Avenue, PO Box 108, ERSKINEVILLE, NSW 2043, AUSTRALIA.

Ⓕ**Andrew Borland** *(A H Borland)* 75 Newnham Street, ELY, CB7 4PQ.

Andrew C.M. Sime *(A C M Sime)* 6 The Courtyard(The Farmhouse), The Outwoods, Burbage, HINCKLEY, LEICESTERSHIRE, LE10 2UD.

Andrew Clarke MA FCA FITI *(A P Clarke)* 15 Palmerston Road, Rathmines, DUBLIN 6, COUNTY DUBLIN, IRELAND.

Andrew Clements *(A V Clements)* 19 Page Furlong, Dorchester-on-Thames, WALLINGFORD, OX10 7PU.

Andrew Colbeck *(A Colbeck)* 313a Ipswich Road, COLCHESTER, CO4 0HN.

ⓅⒶ**Andrew Cooper & Company, trading name of Andrew Cooper & Company Limited** *(A Cooper)* 650 Anlaby Road, HULL, HU3 6UU.

★Ⓕ**Andrew Cross & Co** *(A C Cross)* The Plaza Building, Lee High Road, Lewisham, LONDON, SE13 5PT.

ⓉⒶ**Andrew D. Kilshaw** *(A D Kilshaw)* 99 Stanley Road, BOOTLE, MERSEYSIDE, L20 7DA.

Andrew Donaldson *(A F W Donaldson)* Oak Tree House, 17 Lake Walk, Adderbury, BANBURY, OXFORDSHIRE, OX17 3PF.

Andrew E. Bain *(A E Bain)* 8 Scotland Bridge Road, New Haw, ADDLESTONE, KT15 3HD.

Ⓐ**Andrew E.S. Sherrey** *(A E S Sherrey)* Laburnum House, Adams Hill, Clent, STOURBRIDGE, DY9 9PS.

Ⓟ**Andrew F. Wye Limited** *(A F Wye)* 24 Marlyns Drive, Burpham, GUILDFORD, GU4 7LT.

Andrew G Binns *(A G Binns)* 5 Kings Croft, Ealand, SCUNTHORPE, DN17 4GA.

Andrew G. Bishop *(A G Bishop)* 24 Ebley Road, Ryeford, STONEHOUSE, GL10 2LQ.

Andrew Grass *(A R Grass)* Vallehermoso 82, Baso, Izqda, Espana, 28015 MADRID, SPAIN.

▽Ⓐ**Andrew Hamilton & Co** *(A N Hamilton)* 38 Dean Park Mews, EDINBURGH, EH4 1ED.

Andrew Hitchcock *(A P Hitchcock)* 5 Ashburnham Close, CHICHESTER, WEST SUSSEX, PO19 3NB.

Ⓟ**Andrew Hobbs, trading name of Andrew Hobbs Limited** *(A R Hobbs)* 17 Suckling Green Lane, Codsall, WOLVERHAMPTON, WV8 2BL.

Andrew Hulme *(A J Hulme)* 12 Tunbridge Lane, Bottisham, CAMBRIDGE, CB25 9DU.

ⓉⒻⒶ**Andrew Jones & Co** *(A C Jones)* The Old Surgery, Spa Road, LLANDRINDOD WELLS, POWYS, LD1 5EY.

Andrew K.C. Lai & Company *(K C A Lai)* Room 1901-1902 Hong Kong Trade Centre, 161-167 Des Voeux Road, CENTRAL, HONG KONG ISLAND, HONG KONG SAR.

Andrew Lillingston *(A H Lillingston)* Hurlingham Studios, Ranelagh Gardens, LONDON, SW6 3RT.

Ⓐ**Andrew Lim** *(A M T Lim)* 111 Parsonage Lane, ENFIELD, EN2 0AB.

Andrew M Sherling FCA *(A M Sherling)* 100 Green Lane, EDGWARE, HA8 8EJ.

Andrew Martin & Co *(A P Martin)* Unit 28, The Mansley Business Centre, Timothys Bridge Road, STRATFORD-UPON-AVON, WARWICKSHIRE, CV37 9NQ.

Ⓐ**Andrew Miller & Co** *(A G Miller)* The Mews, Stratton Cleeve, Cheltenham Road, CIRENCESTER, GL7 2JD.

Ⓟ**Andrew Morgan, trading name of Andrew R Q Morgan Ltd** *(A R Q Morgan)* Oaklea, LLANSANTFFRAID, SY22 6TE.

Andrew Mullett FCA *(A K Mullett)* 10 Highbury Place, Camden, BATH, BA1 2JW.

ⓉⒻⒶ**Andrew Murphy** *(A P Murphy)* Sovereign House, 82 West Street, ROCHFORD, SS4 1AS.

★Ⓐ**Andrew Murray & Co** *(N K D Desai, A K G Modi)* 144-146 Kings Cross Road, LONDON, WC1X 9DU.

Andrew Naylor & Co *(A C Naylor)* 51 Glastonbury Drive, MIDDLEWICH, CW10 9HR.

Ⓐ**Andrew Ogg FCA** *(A A Ogg)* Holme Farm, Chapel Lane, Spalford, NEWARK, NOTTINGHAMSHIRE, NG23 7HD.

Andrew Olesiuk & Co *(A Olesiuk)* 9 Norley Drive, Sale Moor, SALE, M33 2JE.

Andrew Oxenham *(A C J Oxenham)* Pylewell House, Field Way, Compton Down, WINCHESTER, SO21 2AF.

Andrew PD Cramb BSc *(A P D Cramb)* 26/7 Eildon Terrace, EDINBURGH, EH3 5LU.

Andrew Piggott *(A Piggott)* 10 Station Close, Leckhampton, CHELTENHAM, GLOUCESTERSHIRE, GL53 0AB.

Andrew Pollock *(R A Pollock)* 3rd Floor, The Triangle, Exchange Square, MANCHESTER, M4 3TR.

ⒻⓅ**Andrew Price & Co, trading name of Andrew Price & Co Limited** *(A D Price)* Haldon House, 4 Castle Road, TORQUAY, TQ1 3BG.

Andrew R Hall & Co *(A R Hall)* 71 Dominies Close, ROWLANDS GILL, TYNE AND WEAR, NE39 1PB.

Andrew R Lovelady *(A R Lovelady)* 50 Tollemache Road, PRENTON, MERSEYSIDE, CH43 8SZ.

Ⓐ**Andrew R Shaw** *(A R Shaw)* Windsmoor, School Lane, Chittering, CAMBRIDGE, CB25 9PW.

Ⓐ**Andrew Ratcliffe** *(A N Ratcliffe)* 1 Hays Lane, LONDON, SE1 2RD.

Andrew Rolls *(A E Rolls)* 3 Pound Lane, LEAMINGTON SPA, WARWICKSHIRE, CV32 7RT.

Ⓐ**Andrew S. Parker** *(A S Parker)* 2 Meadow Court, Allerton, BRADFORD, BD15 9JZ.

Andrew Saunders *(A D Saunders)* Scotchcoultard, HALTWHISTLE, NORTHUMBERLAND, NE49 9NH.

ⒻⒶ**Andrew Sharma & Co** *(A K D P G Sharma)* Wembley Point, 2nd Floor, 1 Harrow Road, WEMBLEY, MIDDLESEX, HA9 6DE.

Andrew Shearer *(A C Shearer)* Town House, 16-18 Town Street, Horsforth, LEEDS, LS18 4RJ.

Andrew St J Ellis *(A St J Ellis)* 1 High Street, Bramham, WETHERBY, WEST YORKSHIRE, LS23 6QQ.

Andrew Taffs *(A B Taffs)* 6 Barrons Close, ONGAR, ESSEX, CM5 9BJ.

Andrew Taylor & Co *(A J Taylor)* Thames Court, 1 Victoria Street, WINDSOR, BERKSHIRE, SL4 1YB.

ⒻⒶ**Andrew Thurburn & Co** *(A J Thurburn)* 38 Tamworth Road, CROYDON, CR0 1XU.

Andrew Todd *(A W Todd)* Highcroft, Deadmans Ash Lane, Sarratt, RICKMANSWORTH, WD3 6AL.

Andrew Tse & Company *(S A Tse)* Suite 610, 6th Floor Tower1, Silvercord, 30 Canton Road, TSIM SHA TSUI, KOWLOON HONG KONG SAR.

Ⓟ**Andrew Turford & Co Limited** *(A J Turford)* 33 Stow Park Avenue, NEWPORT, NP20 4FN.

Ⓟ**Andrew Turvey Solutions Limited** *(A R Turvey)* 23 Cartwright Way, Beeston, NOTTINGHAM, NG9 1RL.

Andrew W Berens FCA *(A W Berens)* 48 Ringley Drive, Whitefield, MANCHESTER, M45 7LR.

Andrew W. Hunt & Co *(A W Hunt)* 13 Lowthian Terrace, WASHINGTON, TYNE AND WEAR, NE38 7BA.

Ⓟ**Andrew Waters & Associates Ltd** *(A F Waters)* 16 Westfield Road, Westbury-On-Trym, BRISTOL, BS9 3HG.

Ⓟ**Andrew Watson Consulting Ltd** *(A Watson)* Lane Cottage, Pound Green, Arley, BEWDLEY, WORCESTERSHIRE, DY12 3LF.

Andrew Webster Associates *(A G Webster)* 48 St. Martins Hill, CANTERBURY, KENT, CT1 1PP.

ⒻⒶ**Andrew Wiggett** *(A J Wiggett)* Gainsborough House, 15 High Street, HARPENDEN, HERTFORDSHIRE, AL5 2RT.

Ⓟ**Andrew Wilbourn Ltd** *(A Wilbourn)* 96 Pendle Gardens, Culcheth, WARRINGTON, WA3 4LU.

Andrew Wilkinson & Company *(A J D Wilkinson)* The Coach House, Rectory Lane, Charlton Musgrove, WINCANTON, SOMERSET, BA9 8ES.

Ⓟ**Andrew Winterburn Ltd** *(A S Winterburn)* Broadstreet Chambers, 18 Broad Street, BROMYARD, HEREFORDSHIRE, HR7 4BT.

Ⓐ**Andrew Yaras & Co** *(A J Yaras)* 2 Fishpool Street, ST. ALBANS, HERTFORDSHIRE, AL3 4RT.

Andrew Youles *(A J Youles)* 20 Kingswood Road, MARCH, CAMBRIDGESHIRE, PE15 9RT.

Andrew Yule & Co *(A H Yule)* 1564 Pershore Rd, Stirchley, BIRMINGHAM, B30 2NL.

Andrews & Co, trading name of Andrews & Associe CA SENC *(R W Kennish, R S Lodge)* 151 Boulevard Hymus, POINTE CLAIRE H9R 1E9, QC, CANADA. and at OTTAWA

ⒻⓅⒶ**Andrews & Palmer, trading name of Andrews & Palmer Limited** *(R D Andrews, P L Bevis, C H Jarratt)* 32 The Square, GILLINGHAM, DORSET, SP8 4AR.

★ⓉⓅ**Andrews Orme & Hinton Limited** *(E A Crook, N J Hinton)* 4 Darwin Court, Oxon Business Park, SHREWSBURY, SY3 5AL.

Andy Blackstone *(A S Blackstone)* 106 Chatsworth Road, LONDON, NW2 5QU.

Ⓟ**Andy Clarke Motor, trading name of Andy Clarke Motor Limited** *(A D Clarke)* 23 Brownlow Road, CAMBRIDGE, CB4 3NG.

Andy Gill, trading name of Andy Gill Accounting Services *(A D Gill)* 24 Mount Durand, St. Peter Port, GUERNSEY, GY1 1ED.

Angel Accountancy Services *(P Angel)* 3 Stobart Avenue, Prestwich, MANCHESTER, M25 0AJ.

Angela Bowness *(A E Bowness)* 44 Stoughton Drive, LEICESTER, LE5 6AN.

Angela Britton Consulting *(A W Britton)* 22 Sennen Place, Port Solent, PORTSMOUTH, HAMPSHIRE, PO6 4SZ.

Angela Hayward *(A J Hayward)* 17 High Street, Needham Market, IPSWICH, IP6 8AL.

Ⓟ**Angela Monti Accountancy Services Limited** *(A H Monti)* 84 Elmhurst Road, READING, RG1 5HY.

Ⓟ**Angela Paull & Co Ltd** *(A M Webb)* 1 New Barn, Manor Farm Courtyard, Southam, CHELTENHAM, GLOUCESTERSHIRE, GL52 3PB.

Ⓟ**Angela Williams & Associates, trading name of Angela Williams & Associates Limited** *(A Williams)* 1 Meadowside, WALTON-ON-THAMES, KT12 3LS.

ⒻⓅⒶ**Angell Pinder Limited** *(M Angell, S J Pinder)* 1 Victoria Street, DUNSTABLE, BEDFORDSHIRE, LU6 3AZ. and at AYLESBURY

Angus Handasyde Dick *(A H Dick)* Lower Shearlangstone, Modbury, IVYBRIDGE, PL21 0TQ.

Anil & Co *(A C Jobanputra)* 220 Maplin Way North, Thrope Bay, SOUTHEND-ON-SEA, SS1 3NT.

Anil Aneja & Co *(A Aneja)* F213C Lado Sari, 1st Floor, NEW DELHI 110030, INDIA.

Ⓐ**Anil K. Bhagi** *(A K Bhagi)* 91 Soho Hill, Hockley, BIRMINGHAM, B19 1AY.

Ⓐ**Aniz Visram & Co** *(A Visram)* Pinfold Lodge, 32a Hampton Lane, SOLIHULL, B91 2PY.

Ⓟ**Aniz Visram Accountancy Services Limited** *(A Visram)* Pinfold lodge, 32a Hampton Lane, SOLIHULL, WEST MIDLANDS, B91 2PY.

Anja Fairbairn *(A Fairbairn)* 26 Kimberley Road, SOUTHSEA, HAMPSHIRE, PO4 9NS.

Anjous, Uku, Eweka & Co *(Sir (Chief) Babatunde Anjous)* 4 Ladipo Labinjo Crescent, Off Bode Thomas Street, Suru Lere, LAGOS, PMB 12020, NIGERIA. and at BENIN CITY, JOS, SAPELE, WARRI

Ann Burnett ACA *(A K Burnett)* 23 Tanfield Drive, Burley in Wharfedale, ILKLEY, WEST YORKSHIRE, LS29 7RT.

Ⓟ**Ann Coleman Accountancy Ltd** *(A G Coleman)* Ground Floor, 5c Parkway, Valley Road, Porters Wood, ST. ALBANS, HERTFORDSHIRE AL3 6PA.

Ann Everin *(A Everin)* 24 Victoria Ave, Saltaire, SHIPLEY, BD18 4SQ.

Ann Greenwood *(A M Greenwood)* Wood Farm Cottage, Barton Lane, Thrumpton, NOTTINGHAM, NG11 0AU.

Ann K Robinson *(A K Robinson)* 13b Market Place, Caistor, MARKET RASEN, LINCOLNSHIRE, LN7 6TW.

Ann Luke *(A Luke)* 15 Richard Hind Walk, STOCKTON-ON-TEES, TS18 3LU.

Ann Massey FCA *(A Massey)* 229 Ombersley Road, WORCESTER, WR3 7BY.

Anna Long *(V A Long)* 58 Crescent Lane, LONDON, SW4 9PU.

Anna Preedy *(A L Nolan)* 45 Anne Boleyns Walk, Cheam, SUTTON, SURREY, SM3 8DE.

Annabel Young *(A Young)* 26 Spencer Road, LONDON, W3 6DW.

Anne Alderman *(A Alderman)* 13 Mill Vale Meadows, Milland, LIPHOOK, HAMPSHIRE, GU30 7LZ.

Anne Colvin *(A L Colvin)* Hollendene, Goodrich, ROSS-ON-WYE, HR9 6JA.

Ⓟ**Anne Colwell Accountancy, trading name of Lightlink Ltd** *(A Fowler-Colwell)* 15 Kingston Street, DERBY, DE1 3EZ.

Anne Conneely & Co *(A M Conneely)* 199 Friern Barnet Lane, Whetstone, LONDON, N20 0NN.

Anne Corfield *(A H Corfield)* 15 Curzon Way, Chelmer Village, CHELMSFORD, CM2 6PF.

Ⓟ**Anne Dobson Limited** *(A E Dobson)* 133 Comiston Road, EDINBURGH, EH10 6AQ.

Anne Good *(A Good)* 51 St. James Avenue, FARNHAM, SURREY, GU9 9QF.

Anne Griffiths *(A T Griffiths)* Lant Lodge Farm, Tansley, MATLOCK, DE4 5FW.

Anne Kiernan *(A M Kiernan)* Apt 1, 9 Otley Road, HARROGATE, NORTH YORKSHIRE, HG2 0DJ.

Anne Tutt *(A C Tutt)* Jasmine Cottage, The Green, Hook Norton, BANBURY, OXFORDSHIRE, OX15 5LE.

Anneliese Garrett *(A E Garrett)* 110 Speldhurst Road, TUNBRIDGE WELLS, KENT, TN4 0JD.

Anne-Marie Waddingham *(A Waddingham)* 4 Spruce Close, Fulwood, PRESTON, PR2 9WB.

Annesley Tory & Co *(R M A Tory)* Clock House, Tandridge Lane, OXTED, RH8 9NJ.

Ⓟ**Anning and Co** *(P A Anning)* 5 High Street, Westbury-On-Trym, BRISTOL, BS9 3BY.

Anova *(R Y C Leung, L M S Mi)* Unit 505 5/F Tower II, Cheung Sha Wan Plaza, 833 Cheung Sha Wan Road, KOWLOON TONG, KOWLOON, HONG KONG SAR.

Ansari & Associates *(A Ansari)* 126 Sepehr Street, Farahzadi Boulevard, Shahrak Goods, TEHRAN, 1468673951, IRAN.

Ansax Business Solutions *(A L Baldwin)* Brickfield Cottage, Hurn, CHRISTCHURCH, DORSET, BH23 6AR.

ⓉⓅⒶ**Ansers!, trading name of Anser Solutions Limited** *(A Packer)* Suite 3, Warren House, Main Road, HOCKLEY, ESSEX, SS5 4QS.

Ansons *(G C D G Anderson)* Parker House, 104a Hutton Road, Shenfield, BRENTWOOD, ESSEX, CM15 8NB.

ⒻⒶ**Anstey Bond LLP** *(M W I Whyke)* 1 Charterhouse Mews, LONDON, EC1M 6BB.

★ⒻⓅⒶ**Anthistle Craven, trading name of Anthistle Craven Ltd** *(M P Anthistle)* 31 High Street, BUCKINGHAM, MK18 1NU.

ⓉⒻⒶ**Anthonisz Neville LLP** *(I H Anthonisz)* 1st Floor, 105-111 Euston Street, LONDON, NW1 2EW.

Ⓟ**Anthony Abbott & Co, trading name of Anthony Abbott Limited** *(A R Abbott)* 48 St. Marys Street, BUNGAY, SUFFOLK, NR35 1AX.

ⒻⒶ**Anthony Alford** *(A P R Alford)* Shepherd's Crook, Netherbury, BRIDPORT, DT6 5LY.

Anthony Battye *(A C N Battye)* 8 Ashlyns Road, FRINTON-ON-SEA, ESSEX, CO13 9ED.

Ⓟ**Anthony Blackstock Limited** *(A B Blackstock)* 37 High Street, Eydon, DAVENTRY, NN11 3PP.

Anthony C J Humphreys *(A C J Humphreys)* 25 Crestwood Drive, SCARBOROUGH M1E 1E6, ON, CANADA.

Anthony G. Fine *(A G Fine)* 9 The Regents, Norfolk Road, BIRMINGHAM, B15 3PP.

Ⓟ**Anthony Golding, trading name of Anthony Golding Limited** *(A P Golding)* Blue Haze, Down Road, TAVISTOCK, DEVON, PL19 9AG.

Anthony Gray & Co *(A Gray)* 28 Church Lane, Culcheth, WARRINGTON, WA3 5DJ.

Anthony H Lusman & Co *(A H Lusman)* 20 John Keats Lodge, Chase Side Crescent, ENFIELD, EN2 0JZ.

Anthony Iliff *(A Iliff)* Westgate, 55 Milestone Drive, Hagley, STOURBRIDGE, DY9 0LH.

Anthony J Williams *(A J Williams)* 27 Forest Centre, Pinehill Road, BORDON, HAMPSHIRE, GU35 0TN.

Anthony J. Knapton *(A J Knapton)* 6 St. Johns Close, Bovey Tracey, NEWTON ABBOT, DEVON, TQ13 9BU.

Ⓟ**Anthony Kam & Associates Ltd** *(A Kam)* 2/05 Wing On Centre, 111 Connaught Road, CENTRAL, HONG KONG ISLAND, HONG KONG SAR.

Anthony M. Myers & Co *(A M Myers)* 28 West End Avenue, PINNER, MIDDLESEX, HA5 1BJ.

Ⓟ**Anthony Markham & Company, trading name of A.M. Accountants Limited** *(M A Markham)* 63 Highgate High Street, LONDON, N6 5JX.

ⓉⒻⓅⒶ**Anthony Marshall Ltd** *(A Marshall)* 70 Market Street, Tottington, BURY, BL8 3LJ.

Anthony Mills *(A J Mills)* 5 Fox & Hounds Close, Thurston, BURY ST. EDMUNDS, SUFFOLK, IP31 3NS.

Ⓟ**Anthony Mundy & Co, trading name of Anthony Mundy & Co Ltd** *(R W Thompson)* 14 High Street, EAST GRINSTEAD, WEST SUSSEX, RH19 3AW.

Anthony N. Bristow *(A N Bristow)* 84 Wisbech Road, Outwell, WISBECH, CAMBRIDGESHIRE, PE14 8PF.

★**Anthony Ononye & Co** *(A Ononye)* 2 Iya-Agan Lane, Ebute-Metta (West), P O Box 74774 Victoria Island, LAGOS, NIGERIA.

Anthony P Dobrin FCA *(A P Dobrin)* 31 Church Mount, LONDON, N2 0RW.

Anthony P. Linton *(A P Linton)* 8 Croome Drive, West Kirby, WIRRAL, CH48 8AH.

Anthony Peter Deegan *(A P Deegan)* Via Verdi 64, 27058 VOGHERA, ITALY.

Anthony R Vincent BSc FCA FCIE *(A R Vincent)* 79 Foxgrove Road, BECKENHAM, KENT, BR3 5BB.

Anthony R.J. Cartwright *(A R J Cartwright)* 16 Taleworth Park, ASHTEAD, SURREY, KT21 2NH.

Anthony Rosenshine & Co *(A P Rosenshine)* 17 Castle Street, DALKEY, COUNTY DUBLIN, IRELAND.

ⓉⒻⓅⒶ**Anthony Russel Ltd** *(W R Hockley, A C Metcalf)* Winghams House, 9 Freeport Office Village, Century Drive, BRAINTREE, ESSEX, CM77 8YG.

Anthony Slann *(A Slann)* 52A Walsall Road, Aldridge, WALSALL, WS9 0JL.

Ⓟ**Anthony Smithson Limited** *(A J M Smithson)* 20 Larch Close, TAUNTON, SOMERSET, TA1 2SF.

Anthony Taylor & Co. *(A C Taylor)* 25 Lordswood Road, Harborne, BIRMINGHAM, B17 9RP.

ⒻⒶ**Anthony Tiscoe & Co** *(A M Tiscoe)* Brentmead House, Britannia Road, LONDON, N12 9RU.

ⓅⒶ**Anthony Wacks Ltd** *(A C Wacks)* Stanton House, 41 Blackfriars Road, SALFORD, M3 7DB.

ⓉⒻⓅⒶ**Anthony Williams & Company, trading name of Anthony Williams & Co Ltd** *(D G Stephens)* 14 North Parade, PENZANCE, TR18 4SL.

Anthony Wong *(A Wong)* 14C 6/F Nassau Road, MEI FOO SUN CHUEN, KOWLOON, HONG KONG SAR.

Anthony Y.T.Tse & Co *(Y A Tse)* Room 711, Argyle Centre, 7th Floor, 688 Nathan Road, MONG KOK, KOWLOON HONG KONG SAR.

Anthony, Wells & Co *(A A Wells)* 19 Norrice Lea, LONDON, N2 0RD.

Ⓟ**Antippa & Company Ltd** *(A G Antippa)* 17 Copthall Gardens, TWICKENHAM, TW1 4HH.

Antoine S Calfa *(A Calfa)* 18 Crown Steel Drive, Suite 201, MARKHAM L3R 9X8, ON, CANADA.

Antonios Vrahimis *(A Vrahimis)* P O Box 21936, 1515 NICOSIA, CYPRUS.

Antony Batty & Company LLP *(W A Batty)* 3 Field Court, Gray's Inn, LONDON, WC1R 5EF. and at BRENTWOOD

Ⓟ**Antony Norris ACA Ltd** *(A A Norris)* 31 Vicarage Crescent, Grenoside, SHEFFIELD, S35 8RE.

★ⒻⒶ**Antrams** *(D E Brown, A L Henton)* 44-46 Old Steine, BRIGHTON, BN1 1NH.

★**Antrams Taxation** *(T A Colverd)* 44-46 Old Steine, BRIGHTON, BN1 1NH.

ⒻⓅⒶ**Antrobus, trading name of Antrobus Accountants Limited** *(M F Kirby)* Antrobus House, 18 College Street, PETERSFIELD, HAMPSHIRE, GU31 4AD.

ⒻⒶ**Anwar Chaudhary & Co** *(A U H Chaudhary)* 9 Littleton Road, HARROW, MIDDLESEX, HA1 3SY.

Anwar Islam & Co *(A L M A Islam)* 12 Cheyne Walk, LONDON, NW4 3QJ.

Ⓟ**AP Associates, trading name of AP & Associates Limited** *(A P Padamsey)* 7 Merrows Close, NORTHWOOD, MIDDLESEX, HA6 2RT.

AP Smith Atkins and Co *(A Hickson)* 18 Tewkesbury Close, MIDDLEWICH, CHESHIRE, CW10 9HT.

Ⓟ**APBS Limited** *(R Neal)* Westgate House, Royland Road, LOUGHBOROUGH, LEICESTERSHIRE, LE11 2EH.

Ⓟ**APC Interim Solutions Ltd** *(A P Chandler)* 30 Parkhurst Road, BEXLEY, DA5 1AR.

ⓅⒶ**APC, trading name of APC Accountants Limited** *(A P Cripps)* 7 St. John Street, MANSFIELD, NOTTINGHAMSHIRE, NG18 1QH.

Ⓟ**Apex CPA Limited** *(C Chai, M C Leigh)* Units 2205-07, 22/F China Merchants Building, 303-307 Des Voeux Road Central, SHEUNG WAN, HONG KONG SAR.

Ⓟ**APH Accounting Limited** *(A P P Handford)* 1 The Hamlet, Hough Green, CHESTER, CH4 8JW.

Ⓟ**APL Accountants Limited** *(P Hodges, S L Jeffries)* 9 St Georges Street, CHORLEY, PR7 2AA.

Ⓣ**APL Accountants LLP** *(P Hodges, S L Jeffries)* 9 St. Georges Street, CHORLEY, LANCASHIRE, PR7 2AA.

Apley Accounting *(L C Foster)* 4 Apley Road, Wollaston, STOURBRIDGE, WEST MIDLANDS, DY8 4PA.

ⒻⒶ**APP & Co** *(A P Padamsey)* 7 Merrows Close, NORTHWOOD, MIDDLESEX, HA6 2RT.

★Ⓐ**Apperley Rowley & Co** *(R G Rowley)* Bell House, Bell Street, Great Baddow, CHELMSFORD, CM2 7JS.

Ⓟ**Applause Accountancy Services Limited** *(J D Relf)* 60 Beamish View, BIRTLEY, COUNTY DURHAM, DH3 1RS.

Ⓟ**Apple Leonard Limited** *(L D Courts)* PO Box 928, ST. ALBANS, HERTFORDSHIRE, AL1 9GB.

Ⓟ**Apple Tree Accountancy & Taxation Services Ltd** *(V A Gould)* The Barn, The Old Manor House, Poffley End, Hailey, WITNEY, OXFORDSHIRE OX29 9UW.

Ⓐ**Appleby & Wood** *(S F Knowles)* Bolton Enterprise Centre, Washington Street, BOLTON, BL3 5EY.

★ⓉⒶ**Appleby & Wood** *(R R Oswald)* 40 The Lock Building, 72 High Street, LONDON, E15 2QB.

Ⓟ**Appleby & Wood Consulting Ltd** *(R R Oswald)* 40 The Lock Building, 72 High Street, LONDON, E15 2QB.

Ⓟ**Appleby & Wood Ltd** *(S F Knowles)* Bolton Enterprise Centre, Washington Street, BOLTON, BL3 5EY.

Ⓐ**Appleby Mall** *(L R Mall)* 86 Tettenhall Road, WOLVERHAMPTON, WV1 4TF.

ⓅⒶ**Appleby Mall, trading name of Appleby Mall Limited** *(L R Mall)* 86 Tettenhall Road, WOLVERHAMPTON, WV1 4TF.

Ⓐ**Appleby Windsor** *(E K Aggarwal)* 100 Hibernia Road, HOUNSLOW, TW3 3RN.

ⒻⓅ**Appleday Associates, trading name of Appleday Associates Limited** *(A V Malde)* Premier House, 112-114 Station Road, EDGWARE, MIDDLESEX, HA8 7BJ.

Ⓟ**Appleton Dale Limited** *(A Cliffe, P J Cliffe)* Orchard House, 347c Wakefield Road, Denby Dale, HUDDERSFIELD, HD8 8RT.

Appletons *(E G Appleton, R J Ellerton)* Suite 1, Armcon Business Park, London Road South, Poynton, STOCKPORT, CHESHIRE SK12 1LQ.

Applewood LLP *(L J Heraty, S E Stevens)* Sycamore House, Church Street, Bentworth, ALTON, HAMPSHIRE, GU34 5RB. and at SUDBURY

Ⓟ**Apps Bookkeeping Services, trading name of Apps Accountancy Services Ltd** *(D E Apps)* 130 - 140 Old Shoreham Road, BRIGHTON, EAST SUSSEX, BN3 7BD. and at HAILSHAM

ⓉⒻⒶ**Apsleys** *(P A Morrish, D I Wicks)* 21 Bampton St, TIVERTON, EX16 6AA.

Ⓟ**Aquarius Tax Consultancy Ltd** *(M C Dawson, E Mohmed)* Atria Building, Spa Road, BOLTON, BL1 4AG.

Ⓟ**AR & JE Hull Partnership, Buckley & Co, Buckley & Co Strategies, trading names of ABC 123 Limited** *(P L Buckley, P T Pring)* 41 Park Road, Freemantle, SOUTHAMPTON, SO15 3AW. and at SALISBURY

ⒻⓅ**ar accountants, trading name of Alan Roberts & Company Limited** *(A Roberts)* Chartered Chambers, 294 Balby Road, Balby, DONCASTER, SOUTH YORKSHIRE, DN4 0QF.

AR Consulting *(R Selvarajah)* 57 Abbots Lane, KENLEY, SURREY, CR8 5JG.

AR Wylie & Co *(A R Wylie)* Armagh Business Centre, 2 Loughgall Road, ARMAGH, BT61 7NH.

Arawn Johnson *(A A Johnson)* PO Box 14574, RAS AL-KHAIMAH, UNITED ARAB EMIRATES.

Ⓟ**ARCD Associates Ltd** *(A J Bailey)* 42 Wright Lane, Kesgrave, IPSWICH, IP5 2FA.

Ⓟ**Archangel Accounting, trading name of Archangel Accounting Limited** *(J F Brown)* Burnham House, Splash Lane, Wyton, HUNTINGDON, CAMBRIDGESHIRE, PE28 2AF.

Ⓐ**Archer Associates** *(H S Archer)* 1 Olympic Way, WEMBLEY, MIDDLESEX, HA9 0NP.

Ⓟ**Archer Associates (Finchley) Ltd** *(H S Archer)* 1 Olympic Way, WEMBLEY, MIDDLESEX, HA9 0NP.

Archer Hayes *(L R Nandlal)* Castle House, 39 Nork Way, BANSTEAD, SURREY, SM7 1PB.

★**Archie Jenner Consultants** *(S K Jenner)* The Old Post Office, 109 Northampton Road, Brixworth, NORTHAMPTON, NN6 9BU.

Ⓟ**Arden Tax & Accountancy Limited** *(J M Hawker)* 2nd Floor, Cavendish House, 39-41 Waterloo Street, BIRMINGHAM, B2 5PP.

Ⓟ**Ardhurst Accountants Limited** *(G A Morrison)* 200 Brook Drive, Green Park, READING, RG2 6UB.

Ⓟ**Ardiesse Consultants Limited** *(R D Spurling)* 18 Marlborough Drive, WEYBRIDGE, SURREY, KT13 8PA.

ⒻⒶ**Ardners** *(S K D Sumaria-Shah)* 18 Hand Court, LONDON, WC1V 6JF.

Arena Business Solutions LLP *(N C Tunnard)* 42 Chapel Street, KING'S LYNN, NORFOLK, PE30 1EF.

Argent & Company *(S Argent)* 20 Burgess Hill, LONDON, NW2 2DA.

Ⓟ**Argenta Associates, trading name of Argenta Associates Ltd** *(R J H Hayward)* 15 Ernle Road, Wimbledon Common, LONDON, SW20 0HH.

Ⓟ**Argenta Tax & Corporate Services Limited** *(D L Powell)* Fountain House, 130 Fenchurch Street, LONDON, EC3M 5DJ.

Ⓟ**Argentica Limited** *(N J McDonald)* 356 Broadway, Horsforth, LEEDS, LS18 4RE. and at STANFORD-LE-HOPE

ⓉⒻⒶ**Argents** *(M A Johnstone, G Miller, J B Spoor)* 15 Palace Street, NORWICH, NR3 1RT.

Argot Accounting and Business Services *(J Owens)* 16 Queen Street, REDCAR, CLEVELAND, TS10 1AF.

Ⓟ**Argyll Street Management Services Ltd** *(L Angel, S R N Fenton, S H Jaffe, M M Krieger, R P Tenzer)* Palladium House, 1-4 Argyll Street, LONDON, W1F 7LD.

Ⓟ**Aria Personal Tax Consultancy Ltd** *(R Meizoso)* 4 Penyston Road, MAIDENHEAD, BERKSHIRE, SL6 6EH.

Ⓟ**Arian Accountants Limited** *(A L Davies)* 19 Sundew Close, Radyr Cheyne, CARDIFF, CF5 2SE.

★**Arian Asghar & Co** *(S Asghar)* 295 Whitechapel Road, LONDON, E1 1BY.

Ⓟ**Aries & Co, trading name of Aries Accountants Limited** *(R McCulloch)* 10 Boundary Business Park, Garsington, OXFORD, OX44 9DY.

Aries Consultants LLP *(N C Keeble, S J Keeble)* Ivanhoe, Maitland Close, WEST BYFLEET, SURREY, KT14 6RF.

ⓉⒻⒶ**Arif Malida** *(A Malida)* 66 Moyser Road, LONDON, SW16 6SQ.

★ⓉⒶ**Arithma, trading name of Arithma LLP** *(N N Mistry)* 9 Mansfield Street, LONDON, W1G 9NY.

Ⓟ**ARJ Accountancy, trading name of ARJ Accountancy Limited** *(A R Johnson)* 9 Loreille Gardens, Rownhams, SOUTHAMPTON, SO16 8LP.

ⓉⒻⓅⒶ**Ark Aurora, trading name of Ark Aurora Ltd** *(B S Ark)* Capital House, 172-176 Cape Hill, BIRMINGHAM, WEST MIDLANDS, B66 4SJ.

Ⓟ**Arkadia, trading name of Arkadia Limited** *(R Kiralfy)* 159 Rochester Road, Burham, ROCHESTER, KENT, ME1 3SF.

★**Arkan & Ergin Grant Thornton, trading name of Eren Bagimsiz Dentetim Ve YMM AS** *(A Halit)* Abidei Hurriyet Cad, No 285 Bolkan Center, C Blok, Sisli, ISTANBUL, TURKEY.

Ⓟ**Arlene Castle Limited** *(A Castle)* 31 Redcrest Gardens, CAMBERLEY, SURREY, GU15 2DU.

Ⓟ**Armada Computer Accounting Ltd** *(G Atkin, R T McDonagh)* Leonard House, 5-7 Newman Road, BROMLEY, BR1 1RJ.

Armida Business Recovery LLP *(T Maton, F E Monson, B R Stevens)* Bell Walk House, High Street, UCKFIELD, EAST SUSSEX, TN22 5DQ.

ⓉⒻⓅⒶ**Armida Limited** *(T Maton, B R Stevens)* Bell Walk House, High Street, UCKFIELD, TN22 5DQ.

Ⓟ**Armitage - Winter, trading name of Armitage - Winter Limited** *(J R Winter)* Croft House, 51 Ashbourne Road, DERBY, DE22 3FS.

Ⓟ**Armitage & Co, trading name of Armitage & Co Limited** *(P D Armitage)* 1 New Street, Slaithwaite, HUDDERSFIELD, HD7 5AB.

Ⓐ**Armitage Davis & Co.** *(D A Barker)* 81b High Street, WARE, SG12 9AD.

ⓅⒶ**Armitages Limited** *(N R Howard)* 9 Archbell Avenue, BRIGHOUSE, WEST YORKSHIRE, HD6 3SU.

Ⓐ**Armstrong & Co** *(A D Armstrong)* Unit 4A, Printing House Yard, Hackney Road, LONDON, E2 7PR.

Armstrong & Co *(A T How)* Pegaxis House, Suite 8, 61 Victoria Road, SURBITON, SURREY, KT6 4JX.

Armstrong Bell, trading name of Amanda Bell MA (Cantab) FCA *(A F Bell)* Suite 122, 5 High Street, MAIDENHEAD, BERKSHIRE, SL6 1JN.

Ⓐ**Armstrong Chase** *(P W Mason)* Suite 1, Winwood Court, Norton Road, STOURBRIDGE, WEST MIDLANDS, DY8 2AE.

Armstrong Rogers & Co *(P K Shenton)* 18 Etnam Street, LEOMINSTER, HR6 8AQ.

Ⓟ**Armstrong Rose, trading name of Armstrong Rose Limited** *(S W Armstrong)* 21 Langholm Road, EAST BOLDON, TYNE AND WEAR, NE36 0ED.

★ⓉⒶ**Armstrong Watson** *(C P Barrett, W J Booth, J E Carroll, M E Hill, A J Johnston, S R Palmer, L Parker, S Pinguey, R A Rankin, A C Robinson, D Samson, G W Sewell, G P Smith, A M Taylor, D J Threlkeld, H L Utting, D Warwick, R M Watson, A J Watts)* 15 Victoria Place, CARLISLE, CA1 1EW. and at DUMFRIES, HEXHAM, KENDAL, LANCASTER, LEEDS, NORTHALLERTON, PENRITH, SKIPTON, WORKINGTON

★ⒻⓅⒶ**Armstrongs, trading name of Armstrongs Accountancy Ltd** *(P Georgiades, M Shabbir)* 1 & 2 Mercia Village, Torwood Close, Westwood Business Park, COVENTRY, CV4 8HX. and at HINCKLEY

Ⓣ**Arnold Hill & Co** *(M J Bostelmann, L J Duncan, J M Moore, T J Straw, R J Usher-Somers)* Craven House, 16 Northumberland Ave, LONDON, WC2N 5AP.

ⒻⒶ**Arnold Hill & Co LLP** *(L J Duncan, J M Moore, T J Straw, R J Usher-Somers)* Craven House, 16 Northumberland Avenue, LONDON, WC2N 5AP.

★**Arnold Hill Sp zoo** *(M J Bostelmann)* UL Nowogrodzka 13 M3, WARSAW, POLAND.

Arnold Hillier F.C.A, trading name of Arnold Hillier *(A Hillier)* Dalkeith, 82 Bridge Lane, Bramhall, STOCKPORT, SK7 3AW.

Arnold Winter *(A Winter)* 13 Glendale Avenue, EDGWARE, HA8 8HF.

ⓅⒶ**Arora & Co, trading name of The Corporate Practice Limited** *(D Arora)* 65 Delamere Road, HAYES, MIDDLESEX, UB4 0NN.

★ⓉⒶ**Arram Berlyn Gardner** *(P P Berlyn, V A F Dauppe, J Donohoe, G Jackson, P G S Morris, J A Piper)* 30 City Road, LONDON, EC1Y 2AB.

Ⓟ**Artaius Ltd** *(R S Berry, R M Coe, S S Landy)* Oxford House, Campus 6, Caxton Way, STEVENAGE, HERTFORDSHIRE, SG1 2XD. and at LONDON

Arthur C Custance *(A C Custance)* Tigh na Bruaich, Garbhein Road, KINLOCHLEVEN, ARGYLL, PH50 4SE.

★Ⓐ**Arthur Daniels & Company** *(R E Madden, B K Plumb)* 227a West Street, FAREHAM, PO16 0HZ.

ⓉⓅⒶ**Arthur G Mead Limited** *(G F J McKey)* Adam House, 1 Fitzroy Square, LONDON, W1T 5HE.

ⓉⒶ**Arthur Gait & Company** *(D E Hayes, C J Pritchard)* 18 Gold Tops, NEWPORT, NP20 5WJ.

Ⓟ**Arthur Gow Ltd** *(M J A Gow)* 21 Queens Road, Hale, ALTRINCHAM, CHESHIRE, WA15 9HE.

★**Arthur Morris & Co** *(D R Cottingham)* P.O. Box HM 1806, Century House, 16 Par La Ville Road, HAMILTON HM HX, BERMUDA.

Ⓟ**Arthur Sampson Aims Accountants for Business, trading name of Bramley Place Limited** *(A R Sampson)* Bramley Place, Orchard Road, 45 The Scarr, NEWENT, GLOUCESTERSHIRE, GL18 1DQ.

Ⓟ**Arthur Wappat** *(A Wappat)* The Old Granary, Dilston Steadings, CORBRIDGE, NE45 5RF.

Members in Practice and Firms - Alphabetical | Artume - Auckland & Associates Limited

Ⓟ**Artume, trading name of Artume Limited** *(P V Watts)* 97 Burge Crescent, Cotford St. Luke, TAUNTON, SOMERSET, TA4 1NU.

Arul & Associates *(A B Arulnayagam)* 10 Lynngrove Crescent, RICHMOND HILL L4B 2B7, ON, CANADA.

ⓉⒻⒶ**Arundales** *(P A Beddard, B Pulley)* Stowe House, 1688 High Street, Knowle, SOLIHULL, B93 0LY.

ASA & Co *(A Sahay)* Regent House Business Centre, 24/25 Nutford Place, Marble Arch, LONDON, W1H 5YN.

ⒻⒶ**Asad A. Rushd & Co** *(A A Rushd)* 74 Walton Road, HARROW, HA1 4UU.

Asante-Wiredu & Associates *(K Asante-Wiredu)* 4 Feo Eyeo Link, off Dadeban Road, North Industrial Area, PO Box AN 19196, ACCRA, GHANA.

Ⓟ**ASAP Accounting Services Ltd** *(M K Burwood)* The Old Cartlodge, Warrens Farm, Great Tey, COLCHESTER, CO6 1JG.

Ⓟ**ASCA Limited** *(A L B Sacks)* Little Red Court, 7 St. Ronans Close, Hadley Wood, BARNET, HERTFORDSHIRE, EN4 0JH.

Ⓟ**Ascendant Accounting Limited** *(P Webster)* 44 Stamford Street, STALYBRIDGE, CHESHIRE, SK15 1LQ.

ⓅⒶ**Ascendis Audit Limited** *(D L Clegg)* 42-44 Chorley New Road, BOLTON, BL1 4AP.

Ⓟ**Ascent Accountancy, trading name of Ascent Accountancy Limited** *(A J Manson)* 13 Park Road, GODALMING, SURREY, GU7 1SQ.

Ⓟ**Ascent Accounting Ltd** *(C Surgett)* 33 Dover Road, BRIGHTON, BN1 6LP.

ⓉⒻⒶ**ASE Audit LLP** *(P C Daly, M D Fazal, M A Jones, R A Jones, M J Sanchez Montes)* Rowan Court, Concord Business Park, MANCHESTER, M22 0RR.

ⓅⒶ**ASE Group Ltd** *(M A Jones)* Rowan Court, Concord Business Park Threapwood Road, MANCHESTER, M22 0RR.

ⒻⒶ**Ash & Associates** *(A K Aggarwal)* 2 London Wall Buildings, London Wall, LONDON, EC2M 5PP.

Ⓟ**Ash & Co Accountants Ltd** *(A K Shah)* Acorn House, 74-94 Cherry Orchard Road, CROYDON, SURREY, CR9 6DA.

Ash Pullan *(H Pullan, A P Shukla)* Epworth House, 25 City Road, LONDON, EC1Y 1AR.

Ⓐ**Ash Shaw LLP** *(G J Burton, T Jarvis)* 180 Piccadilly, LONDON, W1J 9HF.

Ⓟ**Ash Tree Accounting Limited** *(H L Barham)* 1 Ash Tree Close, HEATHFIELD, EAST SUSSEX, TN21 8BF.

Ⓐ**Ashall & Co** *(R D Ashall)* 4 Locksley Close, Heaton Norris, STOCKPORT, SK4 2LW.

ⓅⒶ**Ashburns, trading name of Ashburns Accountants Ltd** *(S S A Haji)* 79 Victoria Road, Ruislip Manor, RUISLIP, MIDDLESEX, HA4 9BH.

Ashby & Company *(J W N Ashby)* North Bank, 14 Bishearne Gardens, LISS, HAMPSHIRE, GU33 7SB.

ⓉⒶ**Ashby, Berry & Co** *(G Hay, T A Jones)* 48/49 Albemarle Crescent, SCARBOROUGH, YO11 1XU. and at MALTON, YORK

ⓉⓅⒶ**Ashbys, trading name of Ashbys Business Consultants Limited** *(J Andrews, R D Goodridge)* Morton House, 9 Beacon Court, Pitstone Green Business Park, Pitstone, LEIGHTON BUZZARD, BEDFORDSHIRE LU7 9GY.

★**Ashcroft Anthony** *(D Anthony)* Heydon Lodge, Flint Cross, Newmarket Road, Heydon, ROYSTON, HERTFORDSHIRE SG8 7PN.

ⓉⒻⓅⒶ**Ashcroft Anthony, trading name of Ashcroft Anthony Ltd** *(D Anthony, A L Weber)* Heydon Lodge, Flint Cross, Newmarket Road, Heydon, ROYSTON, HERTFORDSHIRE SG8 7PN.

Ashcrofts *(A D Patel)* 34 Hartsbourne Drive, HALESOWEN, B62 8ST.

Ⓟ**Ashdene Accountancy Limited** *(A Shah)* 17 Thorndene Avenue, LONDON, N11 1ET.

Ashdens *(M S Sandercombe)* Pennyroyal, Stour Lane, Stour Row, SHAFTESBURY, DORSET, SP7 0QJ.

ⓉⒻⒶ**Ashdown Hurrey, trading name of Ashdown Hurrey LLP** *(P A Bradbury, P W Lee, J R Moore)* 20 Havelock Road, HASTINGS, EAST SUSSEX, TN34 1BP. and at BEXHILL-ON-SEA

ⓅⒶ**Ashdown Price, trading name of Accountsource Ltd** *(F A Edge)* 4 Beaufort, Parklands, Railton Road, GUILDFORD, SURREY, GU2 9JX.

Ⓐ**Ashford & Co** *(J G Ashford)* 186 Reservoir Road, GLOUCESTER, GL4 6SB.

Ashford & Co *(D F Ashford)* 95A High Street, Lees, OLDHAM, OL4 4LY.

Ashford & Partners *(C H K Shah, N K Shah)* 2nd Floor, Kings House, 202 Lower High Street, WATFORD, WD17 2EH.

ⒻⒶ**Ashford Read** *(A C Read)* Unit 4, Basepoint Enterprise Centre, Andersons Road, SOUTHAMPTON, SO14 5FE.

Ⓟ**Ashfords Accountants Ltd** *(S A Shah)* 1378 Leeds Road, BRADFORD, WEST YORKSHIRE, BD3 8NE.

Ashforth LLP *(J G I Ashforth)* 93 Bramley Road, Ealing, LONDON, W5 4ST.

★**Ashgates** *(A T Halls, A J Lymn, D M Newborough)* 5 Prospect Place, Millennium Way, Pride Park, DERBY, DE24 8HG. and at LEICESTER

Ⓟ**Ashgates Corporate Finance Limited** *(A T Halls, A J Lymn, D M Newborough, M I Selby)* 5 Prospect Place, Millennium Way, Pride Park, DERBY, DE24 8HG.

Ⓟ**Ashgates Corporate Services Limited** *(A T Halls, A J Lymn, D M Newborough, M I Selby)* 5 Prospect Place, Millennium Way, Pride Park, DERBY, DE24 8HG.

Ashgroves *(J R Grundy, G A Lockwood)* 14 Albert Street, Douglas, ISLE OF MAN, IM1 2QA.

ⒻⓅⒶ**Ashings Limited** *(D D Ashing, N Kachwalla)* Northside House, Mount Pleasent, BARNET, HERTFORDSHIRE, EN4 9EB.

Ⓐ**Ashlei Associates** *(I N Patel)* 7 Heath Drive, SUTTON, SM2 5RP.

Ⓟ**Ashleigh Accountancy Ltd** *(P P Hampton)* 1 Ashleigh Rise, BOURNEMOUTH, BH10 4FB.

Ashleigh, Norrington & Co *(J A Campkin)* PO Box 816, HORSHAM, WEST SUSSEX, RH12 9EJ.

Ashley Dawes FCA *(A G Dawes)* 8 Cleland Court, Manor Road, Bishopsteignton, TEIGNMOUTH, DEVON, TQ14 9SX.

Ⓐ**Ashley Doggett & Co** *(A Doggett)* 5 Crossborough Gardens, Crossborough Hill, BASINGSTOKE, HAMPSHIRE, RG21 4LB.

Ashley J. B. Meredith *(A J B Meredith)* 22 Riverside Road, West Moors, FERNDOWN, BH22 0LQ.

ⒻⓅⒶ**Ashley King Limited** *(R G Patel)* 68 St. Margarets Road, EDGWARE, MIDDLESEX, HA8 9UU.

Ⓟ**Ashley Nathoo & Co, trading name of Ashley Nathoo & Co Ltd** *(A D Bharakda)* 250 High Road, HARROW, MIDDLESEX, HA3 7BB.

ⓉⒻ**Ashleys** *(M J Bradly Russell, B Burke)* Invision House, Wilbury Way, HITCHIN, HERTFORDSHIRE, SG4 0TY.

★ⒻⓅⒶ**Ashleys (Hitchin) Limited** *(M J Bradly Russell, B Burke, L McCole)* Invision House, Wilbury Way, HITCHIN, HERTFORDSHIRE, SG4 0TY.

Ⓐ**Ashmans** *(A M Sodha)* Zone G, Salamander Quay West, Park Lane, Harefield, UXBRIDGE, MIDDLESEX UB9 6NZ.

Ⓟ**Ashmar & Co, trading name of Ashmar & Co (London) Ltd** *(N H Shah)* Marlborough House, 159 High Street, Wealdstone, HARROW, MIDDLESEX, HA3 5DX.

★**Ashmole & Co** *(D M T Gould, A G Hawthorn, C H Rees, D R Vaughan)* Williamston House, 7 Goat Street, HAVERFORDWEST, DYFED, SA61 1PX. and at AMMANFORD, CARDIGAN, CARMARTHEN, LLANDOVERY, NEWCASTLE EMLYN, SWANSEA

Ashoke Roy *(A Roy)* 3rd Floor, Baroda Bank Building, Sir William Newton St, PORT LOUIS, MAURITIUS.

ⓅⒶ**Ashon, trading name of Ashon Limited** *(A M Shonchhatra)* Sental House, 66 Waldeck Road, Strand on the Green, LONDON, W4 3NU.

Ashraf & Co. *(M Ashraf)* 30 Crescent Road, SHEFFIELD, S7 1HL.

Ashraf Ahmed & Co *(A U Ahmed)* 112 Dickenson Road, Rusholme, MANCHESTER, M14 5HS.

★**Ashton Hart David Lee** *(H P Koslover)* Sterling House, Langston Road, LOUGHTON, ESSEX, IG10 3FA.

Ashtons *(V M Nathwani)* 79 Ashness Gardens, GREENFORD, MIDDLESEX, UB6 0RW.

Ⓟ**Ashville Henderson, trading name of Ashville Accountancy Limited** *(A C Finnegan)* 33-35 Old Chester Road, Bebington, WIRRAL, MERSEYSIDE, CH63 7LE.

Ⓟ**Ashway Accountants Limited** *(M A Saul)* Willow Garth, Field House Close, WETHERBY, WEST YORKSHIRE, LS22 6UD.

Ashworth Accountancy & Bookkeeping Services *(J R Ashworth)* 7 Stanford Hall Crescent, Ramsbottom, BURY, LANCASHIRE, BL0 9FD.

★ⓅⒶ**Ashworth Bailey Limited** *(G Bailey)* 20a Racecommon Road, BARNSLEY, SOUTH YORKSHIRE, S70 1BH.

ⓉⒻⒶ**Ashworth Moulds** *(C Harrison, M Holmes, D A Pickles, J Roberts)* 11 Nicholas Street, BURNLEY, BB11 2AL. and at ROSSENDALE

ⒻⓅⒶ**Ashworth Treasure (BOC) Limited** *(B C O'Cleirigh)* 17-19 Park Street, LYTHAM ST. ANNES, LANCASHIRE, FY8 5LU.

★ⓉⒻⓅⒶ**Ashworth Treasure, trading name of Ashworth Treasure Limited** *(A J Cooney, R G Ingle)* 17-19 Park Street, LYTHAM ST. ANNES, LANCASHIRE, FY8 5LU.

Askey & Co *(J S Askey)* 25 Whitebridge Parkway, Gosforth, NEWCASTLE UPON TYNE, NE3 5LU.

ⓅⒶ**ASL Partners Ltd** *(I Hussain)* 14 Honister Gardens, STANMORE, MIDDLESEX, HA7 2EH.

Ⓟ**ASM Company Secretaries Limited** *(A Schick-Maier)* 21 Culverlands Close, STANMORE, MIDDLESEX, HA7 3AG.

ⒻⓅⒶ**Aspen Waite Limited** *(P D Waite)* Rubis House, 15 Friarn Street, BRIDGWATER, SOMERSET, TA6 3LH. and at FAREHAM

ⓅⒶ**Aspens, trading name of Aspens Ltd** *(A N Fox)* Suite G/4, Waterside Centre, North Street, LEWES, EAST SUSSEX, BN7 2PE.

★**Aspen-Waite** *(P D Waite)* Rubis House, 15 Friarn Street, BRIDGWATER, SOMERSET, TA6 3LH. and at TAUNTON, WELLINGTON

Ⓟ**Aspinall Accountancy Limited** *(M Aspinall)* 5 Hockery View, Hindley, WIGAN, LANCASHIRE, WN2 3JX.

ⓅⒶ**A-spire Business Partners, trading name of A-spire Business Partners Limited** *(B Shapiro, A J Silver)* 32 Byron Hill Road, HARROW, MIDDLESEX, HA2 0HY.

Ⓟ**Assets Licensed Trade Limited** *(A J Wilson)* Chiltern Chambers, 37 St. Peters Avenue, Caversham, READING, RG4 7DH.

ⓉⓅⒶ**Assets Limited** *(D D Patel, A J Wilson)* Chiltern Chambers, St. Peters Avenue, Caversham, READING, RG4 7DH. and at THATCHAM

Ⓟ**Assets Media Limited** *(A J Wilson)* Chiltern Chambers, 37 St. Peters Avenue, Caversham, READING, RG4 7DH.

Ⓟ**Assets Outsourcing Limited** *(D D Patel, A J Wilson)* Chiltern Chambers, 37 St. Peters Avenue, Caversham, READING, RG4 7DH.

Ⓣ**Assured Accountancy** *(A S Bullard)* 14 Market Place, Pocklington, YORK, YO42 2AR.

Ⓟ**Astbury Accountants Limited** *(C Astbury)* Regent House, Bath Avenue, WOLVERHAMPTON, WV1 4EG.

Aster Accountants *(K Ladanowski)* 7 Aster Crescent, Beechwood, RUNCORN, CHESHIRE, WA7 3HS.

Ⓟ**Astley Private Clients Ltd** *(P R Newbold)* 53 Old Mill Road, Broughton Astley, LEICESTER, LE9 6PQ.

Ⓐ**Aston & Co** *(D W Aston)* 132 Walham Green Court, Moore Park Road, Fulham, LONDON, SW6 2PX.

Aston Business Consultancy *(J B Aston)* 69 Bolton Avenue, RICHMOND, DL10 4BA.

ⓉⒻ**Aston Draycott** *(C Atalianis)* Caprini House, 163/173 Praed Street, LONDON, W2 1RH.

▽ⓉⒻⒶ**Aston Hughes & Co** *(A D Erasmus, G G Hickerton, G L Lowe, J C Lukes)* Selby Towers, 29 Princes Drive, COLWYN BAY, LL29 8PE. and at LLANDUDNO

ⓉⓅⒶ**Astute Services, trading name of Astute Services Ltd** *(R B Henderson)* 4 Daventry Road, Dunchurch, RUGBY, WARWICKSHIRE, CV22 6NS.

Ⓟ**ATA Accountants Limited** *(R W Jones)* Fetcham Park House, Lower Road, Fetcham, LEATHERHEAD, SURREY, KT22 9HD.

Ata Khan & Co *(A A U Khan)* 67 Motijheel Commercial Area, DHAKA 1000, BANGLADESH.

ATC Accountants *(S H L Chang)* 5 Castle Court, 1 Brewhouse Lane, LONDON, SW15 2JJ.

Athar Khan & Co *(F Farouk)* Pixfield, Greencourt Road, Crockenhill, SWANLEY, BR8 8JG.

ⓅⒶ**Athawes & Company Limited** *(A K Athawes)* Stirling House, Sunderland Quay, Culpeper Close, Medway City Estate, ROCHESTER, KENT ME2 4HN.

Ⓟ**Athena & Co, trading name of Athena & Company Accountancy Limited** *(A C K Wan)* Unit 1 Marble House, 20 Grosvenor Terrace, LONDON, SE5 0DD. and at EDINBURGH

Ⓐ**Atherden & Co** *(J E Atherden)* PO Box 660, ALTRINCHAM, CHESHIRE, WA14 3UZ.

Atherton Bailey, Maxwell Davis, trading names of Atherton Bailey LLP *(M P Fillmore, N T Paul, C R Purdy, M P Riley)* Arundel House, 1 Amberley Court, Whitworth Road, CRAWLEY, WEST SUSSEX, RH11 7XL. and at EASTLEIGH, GUILDFORD, LEIGH-ON-SEA, MAIDSTONE, WORTHING

Ⓟ**Atherton Bailey, trading name of East Park Services Ltd** *(M P Fillmore)* Arundel House, 1 Amberley Court, Whitworth Road, County Oak, CRAWLEY, WEST SUSSEX RH11 7XL. and at WORTHING

Ⓣ**Athinodorou & Zevedeou Ltd** *(A Athinodorou, M Zevedeou)* Elia House, 77 Limassol Avenue, 2121 NICOSIA, CYPRUS.

Ⓟ**Aticus Recovery Limited** *(D P Hennessy)* 5th Floor, Horton House, Exchange Flags, LIVERPOOL, L2 3PF. and at CHESTER

Atkin & Co *(C E Atkin)* 75 The Chase, Clapham, LONDON, SW4 0NR.

ⓉⓅⒶ**Atkin Macredie and Co, trading name of Atkin Macredie & Co Ltd** *(P S Boden, S L Brock, S J Hartley, N C Oates)* Westbourne Place, 23 Westbourne Road, SHEFFIELD, S10 2QQ.

Ⓟ**Atkins & Co, trading name of Atkins Accountancy Services Limited** *(D Atkins)* 15 Yarbury Way, WESTON-SUPER-MARE, AVON, BS24 7EP.

ⒻⒶ**Atkins & Partners** *(A M Thanawala)* 3rd Floor Brent House, 214 Kenton Road, HARROW, HA3 8BT.

★ⒻⒶ**Atkins Ferrie** *(A P Ferrie)* 1 Water-Ma-Trout, HELSTON, CORNWALL, TR13 0LW.

Ⓟ**Atkinson & Co, trading name of Atkinson & Co Ltd** *(J Mellor-Jones)* Victoria House, 87 High Street, TILLICOULTRY, CLACKMANNANSHIRE, FK13 6AA.

Ⓟ**Atkinson Accountancy, trading name of Atkinson Accountancy Limited** *(G Atkinson)* 137 Manor Road North, SOUTHAMPTON, SO19 2DX.

Ⓣ**Atkinson Accounts** *(P Atkinson)* The Grange, 1 Hoole Road, CHESTER, CH2 3NQ.

ⓅⒶ**Atkinson Finch & Co** *(G R Bolton, S G Bolton)* Central Chambers, 45-47 Albert St, RUGBY, CV21 2SG.

ⒻⒶ**Atkinson Hunter & Co.** *(S F Hunter)* Weir Bank, Monkey Island Lane, Bray, MAIDENHEAD, BERKSHIRE, SL6 2EA.

Ⓟ**Atkinson Saul Fairholm Limited** *(R M Atkinson, S L Tointon, R M Welsh, R M White)* 21a Newland, LINCOLN, LN1 1XP.

ⒻⒶ**Atkinsons** *(D N Atkinson)* The Red House, 10 Market Square, AMERSHAM, HP7 0DQ.

Atkinsons *(M D F Atkinson, P R Atkinson)* 32 Hiltingbury Road, EASTLEIGH, SO53 5SS.

ⓉⒶ**Atkinsons** *(R B Atkinson)* Palmeira Avenue Mansions, 19 Church Road, HOVE, BN3 2FA. and at NEW MALDEN

ⒻⓅ**Atkinsons (Bishopstone) Ltd** *(J Atkinson)* The Old Chapel, Chapel Lane, Bishopstone, SALISBURY, SP5 4BT.

ⒻⓅⒶ**Atkinsons (Hull), trading name of Atkinsons (Hull) Ltd** *(S A Atkinson)* 60 Commercial Road, HULL, HU1 2SG.

ⓉⒻⓅⒶ**Atkinsons, R. M Locking & Co, trading names of J W Smith & Co Ltd** *(J Morley)* 17a Yorkersgate, MALTON, NORTH YORKSHIRE, YO17 7AA. and at BRIDLINGTON, SCARBOROUGH

ⒻⓅ**Atkinsons, trading name of Atkinsons Consulting Limited** *(P G Atkinson)* Innovation Centre, University Road, Heslington, YORK, YO10 5DG.

Ⓟ**ATL Accountants Ltd** *(T G Lloyd)* 3 Tynan Close, KETTERING, NORTHAMPTONSHIRE, NN15 5YA.

Atlantic Advisors *(S L George)* 3 Thornton Road, LONDON, SW19 4NB.

Ⓟ**Atlas Euro Limited** *(A M Thanawala)* 3rd Floor, Brent House, 214 Kenton Road, HARROW, MIDDLESEX, HA3 8BT.

ⒻⓅⒶ**Atom Consulting Limited** *(C J Fassam)* Premier House, 50-52 Cross Lances Road, HOUNSLOW, TW3 2AA.

Ⓟ**ATP Associates, trading name of ATP Associates Limited** *(A T Perks)* 7 Upper Aston, Claverley, WOLVERHAMPTON, WV5 7EE.

Ⓟ**Atraxa Consulting Limited** *(J D Bamforth, M Walker)* Brooke's Mill, Armitage Bridge, HUDDERSFIELD, HD4 7NR.

ATS Accounting & Tax Solutions *(M Shotter)* 6 Corfield Close, Finchampstead, WOKINGHAM, BERKSHIRE, RG40 4PA.

ATS Associates, trading name of ATS Associates - Roger Harris *(R Harris)* Denebank, 117 Bolton Road, Hawkshaw, BURY, BL8 4JF.

ATSA CPA & Co *(M F Fung)* Room B 19/F, 88 Commercial Building, 28-34 Wing Lok Street, SHEUNG WAN, HONG KONG ISLAND, HONG KONG SAR.

Ⓟ**ATTS Ltd** *(J E Lewis)* 42-48 Charlbert Street, St Johns Wood, LONDON, NW8 7BU.

Ⓐ**Attwood & Co** *(D Attwood)* Harrison House, Marston Road, WOLVERHAMPTON, WV2 4NJ.

Attwoods *(M P Attwood)* 12 Palfrey Close, ST. ALBANS, HERTFORDSHIRE, AL3 5RE.

Ⓟ**Au Yeung & Au Yeung CPA Limited** *(L S L Au Yeung)* Room C 18/F, Nathan Commericial Bldg, 430-436 Nathan Road, YAU MA TEI, KOWLOON, HONG KONG SAR.

Au Yeung Huen Ying & Co *(H Y Au-Yeung)* 8th Floor, Shum Tower, 268 Des Voeux Road, CENTRAL, HONG KONG ISLAND, HONG KONG SAR.

★**Au Young, Tse & Wu** *(R M Au Young)* 3500 Yorkshire Road, PASADENA, CA 91107, UNITED STATES.

Ⓟ**Auckland & Associates Limited** *(K H Auckland)* Guppys Lodge, Fishpond Bottom, BRIDPORT, DORSET, DT6 6NN.

Ⓟ**Audit & Compliance Solutions, trading name of Audit & Compliance Solutions Limited** *(C E Johnson)* Charwell House, The Alton Business Centre, Wilsom Road, ALTON, HAMPSHIRE, GU34 2PP.

ⓅⒶ**Audit England, trading name of Audit England Limited** *(A R Gibson)* Blackburn House, 32 Crouch Street, COLCHESTER, ESSEX, CO3 3HH. and at CHELMSFORD

ⓅⒶ**Audit Network Limited** *(K Dadfarma, B Faiz-Mahdavi)* 23 Mountside, STANMORE, MIDDLESEX, HA7 2DS.

Ⓟ**Auditex, trading name of Auditex Limited** *(S Esmail)* 20 Broadwick Street, LONDON, W1F 8HT.

Audition Accounting & Tax Services *(M S Johnson)* 11 Sutherland House, Royal Herbert Pavilions, Gilbert Close, LONDON, SE18 4PS.

Ⓟ**Auditpro Services Ltd** *(M Larkos)* 28th October Avenue No. 1, Engomi Business Centre Block B, Office 104, Engomi Nicosia, CYPRUS, 2413 NICOSIA CYPRUS.

Aughtersons *(J R Aughterson)* 1 Wheatsheaf Close, WOKING, SURREY, GU21 4BL.

Ⓟ**Augmenture Ltd** *(M Di Franco)* 20 Links Side, ENFIELD, MIDDLESEX, EN2 7QZ.

Ⓐ**Auker Hutton** *(D A Kirk)* The Stables, Little Coldharbour Farm, Tong Lane, Lamberhurst, TUNBRIDGE WELLS, KENT TN3 8AD.

Ⓟ**Auker Hutton Limited** *(D A Kirk)* The Stables, Little Coldharbour Farm, Tong Lane, Lamberhurst, TUNBRIDGE WELLS, KENT TN3 8AD.

ⓅⒶ**Auker Rhodes Accounting, trading name of Auker Rhodes Accounting Ltd** *(D H Akester, J A Pedley)* Devonshire House, 32 North Parade, BRADFORD, WEST YORKSHIRE, BD1 3HZ.

ⒾⒶ**Auker Rhodes Professional Services LLP** *(R H Doyle, R J Kenyon, G A Rudloff)* Sapphire House, Albion Road, Greengates, BRADFORD, WEST YORKSHIRE, BD10 9TQ.

Ⓟ**Auker Rhodes Tax & Financial Planning Ltd** *(D H Akester, R H Doyle, R J Kenyon, J A Pedley, G A Rudloff)* Sapphire House, Albion Mills, Albion Road, Greengates, BRADFORD, WEST YORKSHIRE BD10 9TQ.

Aukett & Co *(D R Aukett)* Gildredge House, 5 Gildredge Road, EASTBOURNE, EAST SUSSEX, BN21 4RB.

Aundhia & Parikh *(B K G Aundhia, G B P Parikh)* 81 Cachet Parkway, MARKHAM L6C 1C7, ON, CANADA.

Aundhia & Parikh *(B K G Aundhia, G B P Parikh)* 265 Rimrock Road, Suite 1, NORTH YORK M3J 3C6, ON, CANADA.

ⓅⒶ**Auren & Co Limited** *(J Auren)* Sweden House, 5 Upper Montagu Street, LONDON, W1H 2AG.

★**Auria** *(S J Hall, B D Sochall)* 9 Wimpole Street, LONDON, W1G 9SR.

Aurora *(D L Houghton)* 26 Netherwood Grove, Winstanley Wigan, WIGAN, LANCASHIRE, WN3 6NF.

Ⓐ**Austen & Co** *(M Cascioli)* 57 Upper Fant Road, MAIDSTONE, ME16 8BU.

Ⓟ**Austen Prince Limited** *(D A Prince)* 59 St. Johns Hill, Shenstone, LICHFIELD, STAFFORDSHIRE, WS14 0JD.

Austin & Co *(H L Austin)* 18 Angram Drive, SUNDERLAND, SR2 7RD.

Ⓐ**Austins** *(J E Austin, S J Austin)* Pine House, Chandlers Way, SOUTHEND-ON-SEA, SS2 5SE.

Austral Crosby *(R Crosby)* 20 Norgetts Lane, Melbourn, ROYSTON, SG8 6HS.

★ⒻⓅⒶ**Austral Ryley, trading name of Austral Ryley Limited** *(G J Ashmore, R P Bradley, M J Rose)* 416-418 Bearwood Road, SMETHWICK, WEST MIDLANDS, B66 4EZ.

Ⓟ**AV Accountants Limited** *(A M Gunaratnasingam)* 19 Harewood Road, ISLEWORTH, MIDDLESEX, TW7 5HB.

★Ⓘ**Avais Hyder Liaquat Nauman** *(W Avais)* Nizam Chambers, Level 4, 7 Fatima Jinah Road, LAHORE, PAKISTAN. and at ISLAMABAD, KARACHI

Ⓐ**Avalon Accounting** *(D O Horgan)* 11 Penny Close, Longlevens, GLOUCESTER, GL2 0NP.

Ⓐ**Avalon Accounting** *(J M North)* Equity House, 4-6 School Road, Tilehurst, READING, RG31 5AL.

Ⓟ**Avantica Ltd** *(S Proctor)* 3 The Grange, Flaxby, KNARESBOROUGH, NORTH YORKSHIRE, HG5 0RJ.

ⒾⒻⓅ**Avar & Company Limited** *(A Varma)* Avar Suite 2.8, Central House, 1 Ballards Lane, LONDON, N3 1LQ.

Ⓟ**Avar Consulting Ltd** *(A Varma)* Central House, 1 Ballards Lane, LONDON, N3 1LQ.

Ⓟ**Avassets Limited** *(A N Vincent)* Uplands, Mythe Road, TEWKESBURY, GLOUCESTERSHIRE, GL20 6EA.

ⓅⒶ**Avenue Business Services** *(C D Bielckus)* 1 Silvertrees, Lady Bettys Drive, Titchfield, FAREHAM, HAMPSHIRE, PO15 6RJ.

Ⓟ**Aver, trading name of Aver Corporate Advisory Services Ltd** *(E S L Porter)* 21 York Place, EDINBURGH, EH1 3EN.

Ⓐ**Averillo & Associates** *(D L Averillo, P M Nellemose)* 16 South End, CROYDON, CR0 1DN.

Ⓟ**Averillo Taxation Services Limited** *(D L Averillo, P M Nellemose)* 16 South End, CROYDON, CR0 1DN.

Ⓟ**Avery West, trading name of Avery West Ltd** *(T Brearley)* 334 Blossomfield Road, SOLIHULL, WEST MIDLANDS, B91 1TF.

Ⓟ**Aviaccs Limited** *(Y A Evans)* 29 Moor Close Lane, Queensbury, BRADFORD, WEST YORKSHIRE, BD13 2NS.

Ⓟ**Avicenna Tax, trading name of Avicenna Consulting Ltd** *(F Mohammed)* 124 Yardley Road, Acocks Green, BIRMINGHAM, B27 6LG.

ⒾⓅⒶ**AVN Arena Limited** *(N C Tunnard)* 42 Chapel Street, KING'S LYNN, NORFOLK, PE30 1EF. and at SWAFFHAM

ⒾⒻⓅⒶ**AVN Beyond Profit, trading name of Profit Plus (UK) Limited** *(C R Martin)* Queens Chambers, Eleanors Cross, DUNSTABLE, BEDFORDSHIRE, LU6 1SU.

ⒾⒻⓅⒶ**AVN Picktree, trading name of AVN Picktree Limited** *(R M Peet)* Picktree House, The Barn, Tilford Road, FARNHAM, SURREY, GU9 8HU.

ⒾⓅ**AVN Wickershams, trading name of Wickersham Ltd** *(S E Key)* Unit 114, Westthorpe Business Innovation Centre, Westthorpe Fields Road, Killamarsh, SHEFFIELD, DERBYSHIRE S21 1TZ.

ⒻⓅ**Avonglen Limited** *(W S Harris, T J Hilton, T W Ricketts)* 2 Venture Road, Southampton Science Park, Chilworth, SOUTHAMPTON, SO16 7NP.

★Ⓟ**Avonhurst, trading name of Avonhurst Accountancy Services Limited** *(V M E Lawson)* Severn View Villa, Gloucester Road, Tutshill, CHEPSTOW, GWENT, NP16 7DH. and at BRISTOL

ⒾⒶ**Avraam Associates** *(C L Avraam)* 495 Green Lanes, Palmers Green, LONDON, N13 4BS.

AW *(M A Waters)* 117 Beech Road, ST. ALBANS, HERTFORDSHIRE, AL3 5AW.

ⓅⒶ**AWM Accountancy & Taxation Limited** *(A Warner)* Old Chambers, 93-94 West Street, FARNHAM, SURREY, GU9 7EB.

Axel *(A T Ellis)* 3 Minshull Street, KNUTSFORD, WA16 6HG.

Axel Consulting *(K Axelrod)* 6 Upper Heath Road, ST. ALBANS, HERTFORDSHIRE, AL1 4DN.

Ⓟ**Axiom Capital Limited** *(D G Sinclair)* Roman House, 296 Golders Green Road, LONDON, NW11 9PT.

Ⓟ**Axis Accounts Limited** *(J P Ransom)* Office 7, Unit 16, Dinan Way Trading Estate, Concorde Road, EXMOUTH, DEVON EX8 4RS.

Ⓐ**Axtons** *(C J Axton)* The Mews, St Nicholas Lane, LEWES, BN7 2JZ.

Ayew Agyeman Turkson & Co *(J K Ayew)* Mobil House, P.O. Box 3599, ACCRA, GHANA.

Ⓟ**Aylmore Limited** *(S A Clark)* 6 Long Mark Road, LONDON, E16 3TH.

ⒾⓅ**Aynesley Walters Cohen Ltd** *(G Cohen)* 16 South End, CROYDON, CR0 1DN. and at LONDON

Ⓟ**AYP Advisory Limited** *(M A Nicholson)* Windrush House, 15 Marshall Avenue, WORTHING, BN14 0ES.

ⒾⒶ**Ayres Bright Vickers** *(P A Stone, A N Vickers)* Bishopstone, 36 Crescent Road, WORTHING, BN11 1RL.

Aytons *(J Mehta)* 32 Bathurst Road, ILFORD, IG1 4LA.

Ⓟ**Azadi & Co, trading name of Azadi & Company Limited** *(M Rahman)* 765 Pershore Road, Selly Park, BIRMINGHAM, B29 7NY.

Azlan & Co *(F Ashraf)* 55 Sherwood Avenue, GREENFORD, MIDDLESEX, UB6 0PQ.

ⒻⓅⒶ**AZR Limited** *(A Raniwala, Z F H Raniwala)* 79 College Road, HARROW, MIDDLESEX, HA1 1BD.

Azumba *(S Leppard)* 43 De Paul Way, Weald Park, BRENTWOOD, ESSEX, CM14 4FT.

Azur Consultancy *(M L Nettleton)* Gouvia Lodge, Chollacott Lane, Whitchurch, TAVISTOCK, DEVON, PL19 9DD.

★Ⓐ**B & A Associates** *(S Case, M G Jones, R S Preece, L J Reed, I R Thomas)* Ty Derw, Lime Tree Court, Cardiff Gate Business Park, CARDIFF, CF23 8AB.

Ⓟ**B & M Accountancy Limited** *(P Metharam)* 52 Dale View Avenue, Chingford, LONDON, E4 6PL.

ⒾⓅ**B & P Accounting, trading name of B&P Accounting Limited** *(B E Pritchett)* Kingsley House, Church Lane, Shurdington, CHELTENHAM, GL51 5TQ.

B A Howlett *(B A Howlett)* Aleys Barn, Swan Chase, Swan Street, Sible Hedingham, HALSTEAD, ESSEX CO9 3RB.

B Dennis Wood *(B D Wood)* 42 Fort Road, GOSPORT, PO12 2BU.

B G Laventure FCA *(B G Laventure)* Monard, High Lane, HASLEMERE, SURREY, GU27 1BD.

Ⓟ**B G Swain & Co, trading name of Kppbusiness Limited** *(K P Priest)* 115 Huddersfield Road, OLDHAM, OL1 3NY. and at ROCHDALE

B H White & Co *(B H White)* 51 Fordington Road, Highgate, LONDON, N6 4TH.

Ⓕ**B H.J. French** *(B H J French)* Ancholme house, Hall Lane, Elsham, BRIGG, DN20 0SX.

Ⓟ**B J Jarvis & Co, trading name of B J Jarvis & Co Limited** *(B J Jarvis)* 109 Churchill Road, Earls Barton, NORTHAMPTON, NN6 0RE.

B J Mistry & Co *(B J Mistry)* Flat 7, Hanover Court, 112-116 Bessborough Road, HARROW, MIDDLESEX, HA1 3DU.

ⒾⒶ**B J Straughan & Partners** *(B J Straughan, J N Straughan)* Epworth House, 7 Lucy Street, CHESTER LE STREET, DH3 3UP. and at STANLEY

B L Chancellor *(B L Chancellor)* 29 rue des Petits Champs, 75001 PARIS, FRANCE.

B L Picton *(B L Picton)* 4 Laburnum Road, SANDY, BEDFORDSHIRE, SG19 1HQ.

B M Dunk *(B M Dunk)* 70 Windermere Road, WEST WICKHAM, BR4 9AW.

ⒾⓅⒶ**B M Howarth Limited** *(C Bell, C R Moorby)* West House, Kings Cross Road, HALIFAX, WEST YORKSHIRE, HX1 1EB.

B Olsberg *(B Olsberg)* 2nd Floor Newbury House, 401 Bury New Road, SALFORD, M7 2BT.

ⒻⒶ**B P & Co** *(B Pyplacz)* 6 Bexley Square, SALFORD, M3 6BZ.

ⓅⒶ**B R & S Sutton Limited** *(B R Sutton)* 1a Fernville Avenue, Sunniside, Whickham, NEWCASTLE UPON TYNE, NE16 5PE.

Ⓐ**B S Ingleby** *(B S Ingleby)* 157-197 Buckingham Palace Road, Victoria, LONDON, SW1W 9SP.

B S Rose & Co *(B S Rose)* Milford Lodge, 38a Talbot Avenue, Talbot Woods, BOURNEMOUTH, BH3 7HZ.

★**B W Chatten LLP** *(B W Chatten)* Room 44 Millfield Busines Centre, Ashwells Road, Pilgrims Hatch, BRENTWOOD, ESSEX, CM15 9ST.

B W Wilson *(B W Wilson)* 4 Saturn Close, LEIGHTON BUZZARD, BEDFORDSHIRE, LU7 3UU.

B. Blewett *(B F Blewett)* 13 Cedar Avenue, Blackwater, CAMBERLEY, GU17 0JE.

B. Dunton & Co *(B Dunton)* Millstone, Off Barleyfields, Wooburn Moor, HIGH WYCOMBE, HP10 0NH.

B. Ehreich & Co *(B Ehreich)* 113 Manor Road, LONDON, N16 5PB.

B. Fleetwood *(B Fleetwood)* 62 Chapel Street, BILLERICAY, CM12 9LS.

★**B. Koten & Co (Accountants)** *(B Koten)* 16 Whitethorn Gardens, HORNCHURCH, ESSEX, RM11 2AL.

B. R. Sheth & Co *(Bharat Sheth)* 15 Rosecroft Walk, PINNER, HA5 1LJ.

Ⓕ**B. Wainwright & Co.** *(B F Wainwright)* 1st Floor, Harveys Depot, Daveys Lane, LEWES, EAST SUSSEX, BN7 2BQ.

B. Wright & Co *(B Wright)* 28 Bycullah Avenue, ENFIELD, EN2 8DN.

B.A. Abraham *(B A Abraham)* 40A Primrose Gardens, LONDON, NW3 4TP.

B.A. Khan & Co *(R M Jones, R A Williams)* 4 Cambridge Gardens, HASTINGS, EAST SUSSEX, TN34 1EH.

Ⓐ**B.A. Kirk & Co** *(B A Kirk)* 21A Ulundi Road, Blackheath, LONDON, SE3 7UQ.

B.B. Mehta & Co *(B B Mehta)* 28 Lindsay Drive, Kenton, HARROW, HA3 0TD.

B.C Taylor *(B C Taylor)* The Bungalow, The Avenue, Rowington, WARWICK, CV35 7BX.

B.C. Green *(B C Green)* Neumattstrasse 13, 6313 MENZINGEN, SWITZERLAND.

Ⓟ**B.C.S.B.C Ltd** *(V S Green)* 7 Inchlaggan Road, Fallings Park, WOLVERHAMPTON, WV10 9QX.

B.E.M.Carter *(B E M Carter)* Russetts, Coach and Horses Lane, Dane Hill, HAYWARDS HEATH, RH17 7JF.

ⓅⒶ**B.H. Accountancy Limited** *(B Howarth)* Design Works, William Street, Felling, GATESHEAD, TYNE AND WEAR, NE10 0JP. and at NEWCASTLE UPON TYNE

B.H. Belk & Co *(B H Belk)* 35 Hainton Avenue, GRIMSBY, DN32 9AY.

B.H. Kwan *(B H Kwan)* 16 Pontinscale Close, Leigh Lane Walshaw, BURY, BL8 1RL.

B.J. Bone *(B J Bone)* 14 Hurst Farm Road, Weald, SEVENOAKS, TN14 6PE.

B.J. Patel *(B J Patel)* 76 Buckingham Road, Bletchley, MILTON KEYNES, MK3 5HL.

B.J. Robinson *(B J Robinson)* 10 Bishops Avenue, Llandaff, CARDIFF, CF5 2HJ.

B.J. Roth *(B J Roth)* 10 Whitby Close, BURY, BL8 2TX.

B.J. Scott *(B J Scott)* High Barn, Hunters Meadow, Great Shefford, HUNGERFORD, RG17 7EQ.

B.J. Tutin & Co *(B J Tutin)* 141 Ashwood Road, POTTERS BAR, EN6 2QD.

B.L. Spicer FCA *(B L Spicer)* 3 Inwood Kilns, The Street, Binsted, ALTON, GU34 4PB.

B.M. May & Co *(B M May)* 41 Salisbury Road, CARSHALTON, SM5 3HA.

B.M. Wood *(B M Wood)* 44b High Street, STEVENAGE, SG1 3EF.

Ⓕ**B.N. Redpath & Co** *(B N Redpath)* 42 Berkeley Square, LONDON, W1J 5AW.

Ⓐ**B.R. Bamford** *(B R Bamford)* Old School Cottage, 6-7 Moulton Road, Pitsford, NORTHAMPTON, NN6 9AU.

B.R. Dunn *(B R Dunn)* Manton Cottage, Westhorpe, SOUTHWELL, NOTTINGHAMSHIRE, NG25 0NE.

B.R. Johnstone & Co *(B R Johnstone)* Errwood House, 212 Moss Lane, Bramhall, STOCKPORT, CHESHIRE, SK7 1BD.

Ⓐ**B.S. Greenberg & Co.** *(B S Greenberg)* 2 The Reddings, Mill Hill, LONDON, NW7 4JR.

B.S. Mangat & Company *(B S Mangat)* 20 Cecil Street, 15-08 Equity Plaza, SINGAPORE 049705, SINGAPORE.

B.S. Uppal & Co *(B S Uppal)* 31 Oak Avenue, Ickenham, UXBRIDGE, UB10 8LR.

ⒾⒶ**B.T. Hagger** *(B T Hagger)* Shirebrook House, Fen Street, Buxhall, STOWMARKET, IP14 3DQ.

Ⓐ**B.W. Holman & Co** *(B W Holman)* First Floor Suite, Enterprise House, 10 Church Hill, LOUGHTON, IG10 1LA.

B.W. West & Co *(B W West)* 150 Haydn Road, Sherwood, NOTTINGHAM, NG5 2LB.

B.W.J. Crane *(B W J Crane)* 24 Korimako Street, St. Leonards, DUNEDIN 9022, NEW ZEALAND.

B.Z. Alexander *(S V H Bransby-Zachary)* The Old Post Cottage, Denston, NEWMARKET, Suffolk, CB8 8PW.

ⒻⒶ**B2B** *(H J Dell)* 82/84 High Street, Stony Stratford, MILTON KEYNES, MK11 1AH.

Ⓟ**BA Taxation Services Ltd** *(B A Antrobus)* Lyndhurst, Main Street, Peasmarsh, RYE, EAST SUSSEX, TN31 6YA.

Ⓕ**Baccma Consulting (MG Bacchus)** *(M G Bacchus)* 92 Jerningham Road, Telegraph Hill, LONDON, SE14 5NW.

Baccus *(A Baccus)* 391 Cranbrook Road, ILFORD, ESSEX, IG1 4UH.

Bacha & Co *(P Bacha)* 62 S.S.R. Avenue, QUATRE-BORNES, MAURITIUS.

ⒾⒶ**Bacha and Bacha** *(Y Bacha, Y Bacha)* Steamhouse, 555 White Hart Lane, LONDON, N17 7RP. and at PORT LOUIS

Ⓟ**Bache Brown & Co, trading name of Bache Brown & Co Ltd** *(I R Baker, P G Simpson)* Swinford House, Albion Street, BRIERLEY HILL, WEST MIDLANDS, DY5 3EE.

Ⓐ**Backhouse Yong Partnership** *(S R Gaynor)* Broomwood, Cambridge Road, Quendon, SAFFRON WALDEN, CB11 3YN.

ⓅⒶ**Badcock Business Solutions Limited** *(I L Badcock)* 4 Prince William Close, WORTHING, WEST SUSSEX, BN14 0AZ.

Badhwar & Co *(V Badhwar)* C-28 East of Kailash, NEW DELHI 110065, INDIA.

ⒾⒻⒶ**Baginsky Cohen** *(D Cohen, J Michael)* 930 High Road, North Finchley, LONDON, N12 9RT.

Bahram Alimoradian & Co *(B Alimoradian)* 76 Braithwaite Tower, Hall Place, LONDON, W2 1LR.

Ⓟ**Bahrams Ltd** *(B Mavahebi)* 46 Bushey Way, Park Langley, BECKENHAM, KENT, BR3 6TB.

Bailey Oster *(B M Oster)* Grosvenor House, St. Thomas's Place, STOCKPORT, CHESHIRE, SK1 3TZ.

Ⓐ**Bailey Phillips** *(K M Bailey)* 17 Hanbury Close, Cheshunt, WALTHAM CROSS, HERTFORDSHIRE, EN8 9BZ.

ⓅⒶ**Bailey Philpott Limited** *(D J Bailey, T J Philpott)* 30 Medlicott Way, Swanmore, SOUTHAMPTON, SO32 2NE.

ⒻⒶ**Bailey Watts** *(F U Rehman)* Meridian House, 62 Station Road, LONDON, E4 7BA.

Bailey-Wilson *(E K Wilson)* 12 Arnhem Close, BINGLEY, WEST YORKSHIRE, BD16 3JX.

Ⓟ**Bainbridge Lewis Limited** *(G A Bainbridge, C Lewis)* 13 Kingsway House, 134-140 Church Road, HOVE, EAST SUSSEX, BN3 2DL.

ⒾⒻⒶ**Baines Jewitt** *(D Adams, M R Bigley, T Cook, A L Cowley, J Lester)* Barrington House, 41-45 Yarm Lane, STOCKTON-ON-TEES, CLEVELAND, TS18 3EA.

ⒾⒻⒶ**Bairstow & Atkinson** *(A Bamforth, P Dyson)* Carlton House, Bull Close Lane, HALIFAX, HX1 2EG.

Bajaj & Company. *(P K Bajaj)* 111 Imperial Drive, North Harrow, HARROW, HA2 7HW.

ⒾⒻ**Bajaria, Gibbs & Co** *(C S Lau)* 72 Plumstead High Street, LONDON, SE18 1SL.

Members in Practice and Firms - Alphabetical | Baker & Co - Barnard Sampson

Baker & Co *(J M Baker)* Golden Meadow, 21 Dennyview Road, Abbots Leigh, BRISTOL, BS8 3RD.

★**Baker & Co** *(C Carter)* Arran House, 42 Gravel Hill, LUDLOW, SHROPSHIRE, SY8 1QR.

Baker Accounting *(R Baker)* Knutcroft, Knutscroft Lane, Thurloxton, TAUNTON, TA2 8RL.

ⓅⒶ**Baker Britt Helm, trading name of Baker Britt Helm Ltd** *(P E Britt)* Westcliff House, 106 Southlands Road, BROMLEY, BR2 9QY.

ⒻⒶ**Baker Chapman & Bussey** *(J Frost, V Jones, A C Taylor)* Magnet House, 3 North Hill, COLCHESTER, CO1 1DZ. and at BRAINTREE

Ⓟ**Baker Consultancy Ltd** *(A G Lakhani)* 25 Station Road, Desford, LEICESTER, LE9 9FN.

ⒻⓅⒶ**Baker Fox, trading name of Baker Fox Limited** *(A Hitch)* Owl Cotes Barn, Mire Close Lane, Cowling, KEIGHLEY, WEST YORKSHIRE, BD22 0LE.

Baker Homyard *(S Ballands, S A Homyard)* Ingouville House, Ingouville Lane, St Helier, JERSEY, JE2 4SG.

ⓅⒶ**Baker Noel, trading name of Baker Noel Limited** *(C Noel)* Cheribourne House, 45A Station Road, Willington, BEDFORD, MK44 3QL.

Ⓟ**Baker Tilly & Co Limited** *(J C Chapman, D J Punt, N J Tristem)* 25 Farringdon Street, LONDON, EC4A 4AB.

Ⓟ**Baker Tilly (BVI) Limited** *(J J Greenwood, N B Macphail)* P.O. Box 650, Tropic Isle Building, Nibbs Street, Road Town, TORTOLA, VIRGIN ISLANDS (BRITISH). and at ROAD TOWN

★ⓉⓅ**Baker Tilly (Gibraltar) Limited** *(I P Collinson, A Linares, J Olivera, C D Serruya)* Regal House, Queensway, PO Box 191, GIBRALTAR, GIBRALTAR.

ⓉⓅ**Baker Tilly Channel Islands Limited** *(D J Hopkins, B M Le Claire, E J Spraggon)* PO Box 437, 13 Castle Street, St Helier, JERSEY, JE4 0ZE.

★Ⓕ**Baker Tilly Corporate Finance LLP** *(A Aneizi, J P Banks, A J Clifford, K Denham, R H Donaldson, P T Elliot, J Y Farmbrough, C R Fray, N E Harber, G Houghton, M A Huggins, A S R Hynd, P R Johnson, J A H Killick, D B Knapp, I Latham, M J List, S J Mason, D G McCulloch, H M Morrison, S J Orriss, A D Pierre, M V Pownall, C R V Taylor, D A Thorpe, N J Tristem, P R Watts, N H Weston, I S Wherry, R White, G E Wightwick, D J Worrow)* 25 Farringdon Street, LONDON, EC4A 4AB. and at BIRMINGHAM, BRISTOL, BURY ST. EDMUNDS, CRAWLEY, EDINBURGH, GLASGOW, GUILDFORD, HOVE, LEEDS, LIVERPOOL, MANCHESTER, MILTON KEYNES, NEWCASTLE UPON TYNE, STOKE-ON-TRENT, WATFORD

Ⓟ**Baker Tilly Hong Kong Limited** *(K Choi, P A Phenix)* 2nd Floor, 625 Kings Road, NORTH POINT, HONG KONG SAR.

ⓉⒶ**Baker Tilly Isle of Man LLC** *(W L Bennett, A J Collister, F J Kirkham, R J Kirkham, Ian Radford, A S Roy)* PO Box 95, 2a Lord Street, Douglas, ISLE OF MAN, IM99 1HP.

ⓉⓅ**Baker Tilly Klitou and Partners, trading name of Baker Tilly Klitou and Partners Ltd** *(A Philippou)* 11 Bouboulinas Street, 1060 NICOSIA, CYPRUS. and at LARNACA

Ⓣ**Baker Tilly Mauritius** *(B Lim, D T Lo Seen Chong)* Level 3, Alexander House, 35 Cybercity, EBENE, MAURITIUS.

Baker Tilly MKM *(A M J Al-Rubaie)* P.O. Box 46283, ABU DHABI, UNITED ARAB EMIRATES.

Baker Tilly Monteiro Heng *(Michael Joseph Monteiro)* Monteiro & Heng Chambers, No. 22-1 Jalan Tun Sambanthan 3, 50470 KUALA LUMPUR, FEDERAL TERRITORY, MALAYSIA. and at BATU PAHAT

★**Baker Tilly Poland** *(J Smoczynski)* Hrubieszowska 2, 01 209 WARSAW, POLAND.

Ⓕ**Baker Tilly Restructuring and Recovery LLP** *(A D Allen, P H Allen, J D Ariel, S L Batchelor, M A Blakemore, G P Bushby, R S Cash, A Chapman, A J Clifford, L J Cooper, P G Cooper, J Y Farmbrough, A Lovett, R G Maclaverty, G E B Mander, N Millar, P E Pierce, A D Pillmoor, M N Ranson, M B Rodgers, N J Tristem, M R M Wild, A J Wright)* 25 Farringdon Street, LONDON, EC4A 4AB. and at BIRMINGHAM, BRISTOL, BURY ST. EDMUNDS, CRAWLEY, EDINBURGH, GUILDFORD, HULL, LEEDS, MANCHESTER, MILTON KEYNES, PETERBOROUGH, WATFORD

Ⓟ**Baker Tilly Revas Limited** *(D C Buxton, M J A Holland)* The Clock House, 140 London Road, GUILDFORD, SURREY, GU1 1UW. and at HOVE, IPSWICH, MANCHESTER

Ⓣ**Baker Tilly TFWLCL** *(D C Foong)* 15 Beach Road, Apt. 03-10 Beach Centre, SINGAPORE 189677, SINGAPORE.

ⒻⓅ**Baker Tilly, trading name of Baker Tilly Tax and Accounting Limited** *(N J Tristem)* 12 Gleneagles Court, Brighton Road, CRAWLEY, WEST SUSSEX, RH10 6AD. and at BASINGSTOKE, BATH, BIRMINGHAM, BRISTOL, BROMLEY, BURY ST. EDMUNDS, CHELMSFORD, CHESTER, EDINBURGH, GLASGOW, GUILDFORD, HEREFORD, HOVE, HULL, LEEDS, LIVERPOOL, LONDON, MANCHESTER, MILTON KEYNES, NEWCASTLE UPON TYNE, SHETLAND, SHIPLEY, STOKE-ON-TRENT, TUNBRIDGE WELLS, WARRINGTON, WATFORD

★Ⓕ**Baker Tilly, trading name of Baker Tilly Tax and Advisory Services LLP** *(C P Abrahams, E R Aitken, A P Allchin, A D Allen, A Aneizi, J D Ariel, H L Arthurs, A H Baker, L J Ballard, E C Banks, J P Banks, D Bardell, J T Barnes, D R Barton, K A Barwick, S L Batchelor, P G Beckett, G J Bedingfield, I A Bell, S H Berger, M L I Blain, M A Blakemore, J C Bleach, G P Bond, S M Brown, J R Burnie, G P Bushby, D C Buxton, P Byrne, G D Carrington, S Carter, R S Cash, A Chapman, D S Clark, K F Clark, R G Clark, A J Clifford, R J Coates, J W Conlan, L J Cooper, P G Cooper, G M Craig Waller, I F Cruse, N Davenport, R M Davies, K Denham, R H Donaldson, A Duley, R J Eastell, P T Elliot, G Elliott, J M Ericson, M C Fairhurst, P T Falvey, J Y Farmbrough, D J Fenton, R W Fisher, R A Foreman, G J Francies, C R Fray, H Freedman, T G Fussell, P W Geldeard, P R Ginman, D J Glossop, R J Goodwin, N J Gowans, M J Gregg, P J Groves, J L Hall, R M Hamlin, N E Harber, N J Hardy, R Harvey, M E Harwood, M B Hearne, D A Heaton, K R Hillam, S J Hinds, M J A Holland, A Hollands, K C Holliday, G Houghton, P A B Howard, M A Huggins, C J Humphrey, J J Humphries, C I Hurren, A S R Hynd, M A Jackson, E W Jarvis, P R Johnson, J M Jones, J C Kaiser, J A H Killick, R H King, D B Knapp, A Lakin, I Latham, A D Lawes, B G Lawrance, C Leece, T L Lerwill, D Lewis, K A Lickorish, M J List, A J Lloyd, L P Longe, A Lovett, R G Maclaverty, G E B Mander, J H Mann, S E Mason, S J Mason, D G McCulloch, N Millar, A C Monteith, G K Moreton, T R Morgan, H M Morrison, A Mould, S Mullins, P S Newman, K P O'Connor, M Z Orriss, S J Orriss, M L Owen, W B Owen, T F X Parr, D A Payne, K J Phillips, P E Pierce, A D Pierre, A D Pillmoor, H A Platt, G Potts, M V Pownall, G G Purdy, M N Ranson, J D A Read, K Reid, A Richardson, S J Robb, C D Roberts, M B Rodgers, J S Rushton, T J Saunders, D J Searle, E B Simon, S Singh, N P Sladden, R H Spooner, M J Standish, M F Stean, D C Stewart, A R Summers, C Sutherland, C R V Taylor, N J Thomas, P J Thorburn, D A Thorpe, A A Tranter, N J Tristem, D C W Unwin, N D Ware, A E Waterhouse, P R Watts, N H Weston, H J Wheelhouse, I S Wherry, J E White, R White, G E Wightwick, M R M Wild, R P Williams, V P Wood, D J Worrow, A J Wright)* 25 Farringdon Street, LONDON, EC4A 4AB. and at BASINGSTOKE, BATH, BIRMINGHAM, BRISTOL, BROMLEY, BURY ST. EDMUNDS, CHELMSFORD, CHESTER, CRAWLEY, EDINBURGH, GLASGOW, GUILDFORD, HEREFORD, HOVE, HULL, LEEDS, LIVERPOOL, MANCHESTER, MILTON KEYNES, NEWCASTLE UPON TYNE, SHETLAND, SHIPLEY, STOKE-ON-TRENT, TUNBRIDGE WELLS, WARRINGTON, WATFORD

★ⓉⒻ**Baker Tilly, trading name of Baker Tilly UK Audit LLP** *(E R Aitken, A P Allchin, H L Arthurs, A H Baker, E C Banks, D Bardell, J T Barnes, K A Barwick, G J Bedingfield, I A Bell, J C Bleach, G P Bond, P Byrne, D S Clark, R G Clark, R J Coates, G M Craig Waller, R M Davies, G Elliott, J M Ericson, M C Fairhurst, J Y Farmbrough, D J Fenton, R W Fisher, R A Foreman, G J Francies, C R Fray, H Freedman, R J Goodwin, N J Gowans, M J Gregg, R M Hamlin, N J Hardy, M E Harwood, K R Hillam, S J Hinds, A Hollands, P A B Howard, J M W Hudson, M A Huggins, C I Hurren, M A Jackson, E W Jarvis, J M Jones, R H King, A Lakin, A D Lawes, B G Lawrance, C Leece, T L Lerwill, K A Lickorish, J H Mann, S E Mason, A C Monteith, G K Moreton, T R Morgan, S Mullins, P S Newman, W B Owen, A D Pierre, G G Purdy, J D A Read, K Reid, A Richardson, C D Roberts, J S Rushton, T J Saunders, E B Simon, D E Simpson-Price, S Singh, N P Sladden, M J Standish, D C Stewart, A R Summers, C Sutherland, D C Taylor, N J Thomas, D A Thorpe, A A Tranter, N J Tristem, N D Ware, P R Watts, H J Wheelhouse, R White, G E Wightwick, R P Williams, D J Worrow)* 25 Farringdon Street, LONDON, EC4A 4AB. and at BASINGSTOKE, BATH, BIRMINGHAM, BRISTOL, BROMLEY, BURY ST. EDMUNDS, CHELMSFORD, CHESTER, CRAWLEY, EDINBURGH, GLASGOW, GUILDFORD, HEREFORD, HOVE, HULL, LEEDS, LIVERPOOL, MANCHESTER, MILTON KEYNES, NEWCASTLE UPON TYNE, SHETLAND, SHIPLEY, STOKE-ON-TRENT, TUNBRIDGE WELLS, WARRINGTON, WATFORD

ⓉⒻⒶ**Baker Watkin** *(J Abbott, R B Baker, C P Craggs, A B Watkin)* Middlesex House, Rutherford Close, STEVENAGE, SG1 2EF.

Baker-Gordon *(E A Gordon)* 23 Lindhurst Drive, Hockley Heath, SOLIHULL, WEST MIDLANDS, B94 6QD.

★ⒻⓅⒶ**Bakers, trading name of Baker (Midlands) Limited** *(M V Ballinger, J Davis, M J Dickson, M B Harris, P H Taylor)* Arbor House, Broadway North, WALSALL, WS1 2AN.

Bakewell Accountancy Services *(S L Bakewell)* 4 Coed Terfyn, Penymynydd, CHESTER, CH4 0XB.

Balance Response, trading name of Paul Bedford *(P N Bedford)* 36 Princes Road, TEDDINGTON, MIDDLESEX, TW11 0RW.

ⓉⒻⓅⒶ**Balance, trading name of Balance Accountants Limited** *(R A Barrowclough)* Victoria Court, 91 Huddersfield Road, HOLMFIRTH, HD9 3JA.

Ⓐ**Balanced Accounting, trading name of Balanced Accounting LLP** *(C R Bendall, H A Wells)* Unit Q, The Brewery, Bells Yew Green, TUNBRIDGE WELLS, KENT, TN3 9BD.

Ⓣ**Baldhu Consulting** *(A K Denton)* 20 Pantbach Road, Birchgrove, CARDIFF, CF14 1UA.

ⒻⒶ**Baldwin Cox & Co.** *(M J Cox)* 15-17 Foster Avenue, Beeston, NOTTINGHAM, NG9 1AE.

★Ⓟ**Baldwin Cox Limited** *(A P Crossley)* 15 Foster Avenue, Beeston, NOTTINGHAM, NG9 1AE.

★Ⓐ**Baldwin Scofield & Co** *(N M Baldwin)* 3 New House Farm Business Centre, Old Crawley Road, HORSHAM, WEST SUSSEX, RH12 4RU.

★**Baldwyn Ward** *(L J Ward)* Pinewood, Crockford Lane, Chineham Business Park, Chineham, BASINGSTOKE, HAMPSHIRE RG24 8AL.

Bales *(C R Bales)* 15 Cheddar Close, Nailsea, BRISTOL, BS48 4YA.

ⒻⓅⒶ**Balfour Sanson, trading name of Sanson Limited** *(N L Balfour)* 17 Bourne Court, Southend Road, WOODFORD GREEN, ESSEX, IG8 8HD.

★ⒻⒶ**Ballams** *(S L Fayers, M K Howes, S C Marriage)* Crane Court, 302 London Road, IPSWICH, IP2 0AJ.

Ⓣ**Ballamy Woodhouse** *(M E Ballamy, N J J Lindsay)* Albert Buildings, 49 Queen Victoria Street, LONDON, EC4N 4SA.

Ballard Campbell, trading name of Fraser Campbell LLP *(J R H Hoyle, E M McCrink)* Direct House, Lancaster House, Wingates Inds Est, Westhoughton, BOLTON, BL5 3XD.

ⓉⒻⒶ**Ballard Dale Syree Watson LLP** *(G W Ballard, D B Dale, E H Peters, J A Syree, J E Syree, M A Watson)* Oakmoore Court, Kingswood Road, Hampton Lovett, DROITWICH, WORCESTERSHIRE, WR9 0QH.

ⓉⓅ**Ballard Evans Corporate Finance, trading name of Ballard Evans Corporate Finance Limited** *(J Ballard, C Evans)* Lowry House, 17 Marble Street, MANCHESTER, M2 3AW.

ⒻⓅⒶ**Ballards Newman, trading name of Ballards Newman (Finchley) Limited** *(L D Cohen, R Muller, L M Perkin)* Apex House, Grand Arcade, Tally Ho Corner, LONDON, N12 0EH.

Ⓟ**Balme Kitchen and Pearce Ltd** *(A Gessey)* 25 Lemon Street, TRURO, TR1 2LS.

Balvaird Consulting Services *(E J Panczak)* Meadowview, Westbrook, Boxford, NEWBURY, BERKSHIRE, RG20 8DJ.

Ⓟ**Bambridge Accountants, trading name of Bambridge Accountants Ltd** *(A J Bambridge)* 34 South Molton Street, LONDON, W1K 5RG.

Bambury & Co *(S P Cracroft-Brennan)* Flat 4, Goodwood House, Park Court, Lawrie Park Road, LONDON, SE26 6EQ.

ⓉⒻⒶ**Bamforth & Co** *(A L Bamforth, D Pettinger)* Douglas House, 24 Bridge Street, Slaithwaite, HUDDERSFIELD, HD7 5JN.

Ⓟ**Bance, trading name of Bance Consultants Limited** *(S Bance)* 46a Station Road, North Harrow, HARROW, MIDDLESEX, HA2 7SE.

Ⓟ**Banday Limited** *(A S Banday)* 47 Park Chase, WEMBLEY, MIDDLESEX, HA9 8EQ.

ⓉⒻⒶ**Banham Graham** *(J A Banham, M M Graham, R H Jarrold, S C Mary, S J Rolfe)* Windsor Terrace, 76-80 Thorpe Road, NORWICH, NR1 1BA. and at GREAT YARMOUTH

Ⓟ**Banham Graham Corporate Limited** *(J A Banham, M M Graham, R H Jarrold, S C Mary, S J Rolfe)* Windsor Terrace, 76-80 Thorpe Road, NORWICH, NR1 1BA.

Ⓟ**Bankim Patel & Co Ltd** *(B C Patel)* 42 Anglesmede Crescent, PINNER, HA5 5SP.

ⓉⓅⒶ**Banks Sheridan, trading name of Banks Sheridan Limited** *(S P Banks)* Datum House, Electra Way, CREWE, CW1 6ZF.

ⓉⓅⒶ**Banks, trading name of Banks Limited** *(R Bluh, N R Elsden)* 14 Devizes Road, Old Town, SWINDON, SN1 4BH.

Ⓟ**Banner & Associates Ltd** *(R Banerjee, D A Wolff)* 29 Byron Road, HARROW, HA1 1JR.

Ⓟ**Bannerdale Accountancy Services Limited** *(S Douglas)* Cornwell House, Amotherby, MALTON, NORTH YORKSHIRE, YO17 6UN.

Barbara A. Simmonds *(B A Simmonds)* 3 Cotton Row, Plantation Wharf Battersea, LONDON, SW11 3UG.

Barbara Cresswell *(B Cresswell)* 7 Baillieswells Grove, Bieldside, ABERDEEN, AB15 9BH.

Ⓟ**Barbara Ewin Ltd** *(B A Ewin)* Pear Tree Cottage, Old Durham, DURHAM, DH1 2RY.

Barbara Forrest *(B A Forrest)* 17 Orchard Way, Hurst Green, OXTED, RH8 9DJ.

Barbara Gabriel *(B Gabriel)* 156 Clarence Avenue, NEW MALDEN, KT3 3DY.

Barbara J. Russett *(B J Russett)* Lamara, 29 Duporth Bay, ST AUSTELL, CORNWALL, PL26 6AF.

Barbara L. Sheppard *(B L Sheppard)* 23 Brookdene Drive, NORTHWOOD, HA6 3NS.

Barbara le Fleming *(B M Le Fleming)* 14 Cliveden Mead, MAIDENHEAD, BERKSHIRE, SL6 8HE.

Barbara M H Reade & Co *(B M H Reade)* May Tree Hollow, 10 Crownfields, SEVENOAKS, KENT, TN13 1EF.

★**Barbara M Thompson FCCA** *(A J Meikle)* Summerdale, Head Dyke Lane, Pilling, PRESTON, PR3 6SJ.

Ⓟ**Barbara Martin and Co, trading name of Cooks Accountancy Services Limited** *(B E Martin)* 28 Clappers Meadow, Alfold, CRANLEIGH, SURREY, GU6 8HH.

Ⓟ**Barbara Rowland Limited** *(B M Rowland)* Summer House, Knowle Hill, EVESHAM, WR11 7EL.

Ⓟ**Barbel Consulting Limited** *(R Stevens)* Bridge House, Restmor Way, WALLINGTON, SURREY, SM6 7AH.

★ⓉⒶ**Barber & Co** *(P J Barber, C Horsley)* 2 Jardine House, The Harrovian Bus' Village, Bessborough Road, HARROW, HA1 3EX.

★Ⓐ**Barber & Co, trading name of Barber & Co LLP** *(P M Jones, J P Surrey)* Level 5, City Tower, 40 Basinghall Street, LONDON, EC2V 5DE. and at WELWYN

Ⓟ**Barbican Computer Services Ltd** *(N C Patel, D Witham)* 69-71 East Street, EPSOM, SURREY, KT17 1BP.

Ⓟ**Barbican Services Limited** *(N C Patel, D Witham)* 69-71 East Street, EPSOM, SURREY, KT17 1BP.

ⓉⒶ**Barcant Beardon LLP** *(D Beardon, M V Khatri)* 8 Blackstock Mews, Islington, LONDON, N4 2BT.

Barcrofts *(S J Barcroft)* 157 Bolton Road, BURY, LANCASHIRE, BL8 2NW.

Ⓟ**Bardsley Accountants, trading name of Bardsley Accountants Limited** *(J B Guy)* 7 Newton Road, Great Barr, BIRMINGHAM, B43 6AA.

Baree Pear & Khan *(P Ali)* 154KA Mohammadpur, Pisciculture, Housing Society Ltd, 2nd Floor, Syamolly, DHAKA 1207 BANGLADESH.

★**Barker & Bunster** *(J Bunster)* 24 Hillway, Guiseley, LEEDS, LS20 8HB.

ⒻⓅⒶ**Barker & Co, trading name of Barkers Accountants Limited** *(K Barker, C A Dexter)* Street Ashton Farm House, Stretton Under Fosse, RUGBY, WARWICKSHIRE, CV23 0PH.

ⓉⓅ**Barker Maule & Co, trading name of Barker Maule Limited** *(T P Geraghty, H A Rashid)* 27/33 Castle Gate, NEWARK, NOTTINGHAMSHIRE, NG24 1BA.

ⒻⒶ**Barkers** *(S B Barker)* Council Offices, College Road, CAMELFORD, PL32 9TL.

ⓉⒻⒶ**Barlow Andrews, trading name of Barlow Andrews LLP** *(J D Barden, D A Kay, G W Leigh, M J Pearson, P A Riding, M R C Sheen, A G Smith)* Carlyle House, 78 Chorley New Road, BOLTON, BL1 4BY. and at DARWEN

★ⓉⒶ**Barlow, Mendham & Co** *(L H Jones)* Glandover House, 67 Bute Street, ABERDARE, SOUTH GLAMORGAN, CF44 7LD.

Ⓐ**Barnard Sampson, trading name of Barnard Sampson LLP** *(N L Marsham, R Sullivan)* 3a Quay View Business Park, Barnards Way, LOWESTOFT, SUFFOLK, NR32 2HD.

ⓅBarnbrook Sinclair, trading name of Barnbrook Sinclair Limited (G N Barnbrook, A S Holmes, M E Sinclair, S J Wright) 1 High Street, Knaphill, WOKING, SURREY, GU21 2PG.

ⒶBarnbrook Sinclair, trading name of The Barnbrook Sinclair Partnership LLP (G N Barnbrook, M E Sinclair, S J Wright) 1 High Street, Knaphill, WOKING, SURREY, GU21 2PG.

ⒻⓅⒶBarnes Business Services Ltd (J C R Barnes) 30 Blake Hall Road, MIRFIELD, WEST YORKSHIRE, WF14 9NS.

★ⓉⒻⒶBarnes Roffe LLP (P Bonnell, A Cheason, M P Cientanni, S A Corner, S M Davis, P W Hughes, M Ibbotson, S D Liggins, K J Mason, M A Parkinson, M B Smith, D Stannett, G M Wallace, S S Yap) Leytonstone House, Leytonstone, LONDON, E11 1GA. and at DARTFORD, UXBRIDGE

ⒻBarnett & Co (M A Barnett) 19-21 New Road, WILLENHALL, WV13 2BG.

ⓉBarnett & Turner (Y Lovett, D Wilson) Cromwell House, 68 West Gate, MANSFIELD, NG18 1RR.

ⒻⒶBarnett & Turner LLP (Y Lovett, D Wilson, J D Wilson) Cromwell House, 68 West Gate, MANSFIELD, NOTTINGHAMSHIRE, NG18 1RR.

ⓅBarnett DM Limited (C E Clift, T G Davies, N J Mayers, M A Minchella, N S Smith) Pillar House, 113-115 Bath Road, CHELTENHAM, GLOUCESTERSHIRE, GL53 7LS.

ⒻⒶBarnett Ravenscroft LLP (P A Barnett, R H D Gold) 13 Portland Road, Edgbaston, BIRMINGHAM, B16 9HN.

ⓉⒻⒶBarnett Spooner (A J Barnett, M G Farrant) The Old Steppe House, Brighton Road, GODALMING, SURREY, GU7 1NS.

Barnett, Hill & Co (G J Taylor) 1 Hazelbury Crescent, LUTON, LU1 1DS.

ⒻⒶBarr & Associates (P A Barr) 22 Westcott, WELWYN GARDEN CITY, HERTFORDSHIRE, AL7 2PP.

Barra Accountancy Services (T Halton) Kisimul, 9 Argyll Close, Horsforth, LEEDS, LS18 5SP.

Barrett & Co (S M Barrett) Cheriton, Basingstoke Road, Riseley, READING, RG7 1QL.

ⓅBarrett & Co, trading name of R C Barrett & Co (Wokingham) Ltd (S A Barrett) Tithe House, 15 Dukes Ride, CROWTHORNE, BERKSHIRE, RG45 6LZ.

ⓅBarrett Accounting and Tax Services, trading name of Barrett ATS Limited (J B Raymond) 1 Ellis Barn, The Old Dairy, Badbury, SWINDON, SN4 0EU.

ⓅBarrette, trading name of Barrette Limited (K F B Lau, K W Y Lau) 144 Thatto Heath Road, Thatto Heath, ST. HELENS, MERSEYSIDE, WA9 5PE. and at MANCHESTER

Barretts (P J Barrett) 1 St.Marys House, St.Marys Road, SHOREHAM-BY-SEA, BN43 5ZA.

ⒻⓅⒶBarretts, trading name of Check Book Ltd (I P Barrett, M P Barrett Rogers) 22 Union Street, NEWTON ABBOT, DEVON, TQ12 2JS.

Barrie Harding & Co (B D Harding) Hollyoak House, Mead Pastures, Woodham Walter, MALDON, CM9 6PY.

Barrie M. Smith (B M Smith) 10a Winchester Street, BASINGSTOKE, RG21 7DY.

ⓅBarrington House Solutions, trading name of Barrington House Solutions Limited (D Adams, M R Bigley, T Cook, A L Cowley, J Lester) Barrington House, 41-45 Yarm Lane, STOCKTON-ON-TEES, CLEVELAND, TS18 3EA.

Barrington Zarach & Company (B P Zarach) 23 Kings Road, ASCOT, SL5 9AD.

ⓅⒶBarringtons Limited (A M Bridge, N B Cooper, A G Wilshaw, P B Wood) 570-572 Etruria Road, NEWCASTLE, ST5 0SU. and at MARKET DRAYTON, NANTWICH, NEWPORT

ⓉⒻⒶBarron & Barron (R C Bailey, G S Ward) Bathurst House, 86 Micklegate, YORK, YO1 6LQ.

ⓉBarron & Co (M Antoniou, G Preece) 175 Cole Valley Road, Hall Green, BIRMINGHAM, B28 0DG.

★ⓉⒻⒶBarrons (G J Raven) Monometer House, Rectory Grove, LEIGH-ON-SEA, ESSEX, SS9 2HN.

ⓅBarrons Limited (G J Raven) Monometer House, Rectory Grove, LEIGH-ON-SEA, ESSEX, SS9 2HN.

ⒻⒶBarrow LLP (R M Barrow) Jackson House, Station Road, Chingford, LONDON, E4 7BU. and at BISHOP'S STORTFORD

ⓅBarrowby Accountants Limited (M J Pennifold) Kobia, Low Road, Barrowby, GRANTHAM, LINCOLNSHIRE, NG32 1DJ.

Barry Caldwell & Co (B M Caldwell) 135 Hillside, GREYSTONES, COUNTY WICKLOW, IRELAND.

Barry Compton & Co (B C C Compton) 14 Hallsland Way, OXTED, SURREY, RH8 9AL.

Barry Dwyer & Co (B Dwyer) 25 Pishiobury Drive, SAWBRIDGEWORTH, HERTFORDSHIRE, CM21 0WT.

Barry Hampson (B E Hampson) 63 Passmore, Tinkers Bridge, MILTON KEYNES, MK6 3DY.

Barry Hill & Co (B P Hill) The Brighton Forum, 95 Ditchling Road, BRIGHTON, BN1 4ST.

Barry J Nudds (B J Nudds) PO Box 667, 56 Hepworth Avenue, BURY ST. EDMUNDS, SUFFOLK, IP33 9EU.

Barry J. Northcott (B J Northcott) Langstone Manor Cottage, Brentor, TAVISTOCK, DEVON, PL19 0NE.

Barry Lee & Co (C K Lee) Unit C, 8th Floor, Charmhill Centre, 50 Hillwood Road, TSIM SHA TSUI, KOWLOON HONG KONG SAR.

Barry McCann (B J McCann) Westfield, 10 Westfield Gardens, Westcott Road, DORKING, SURREY, RH4 3DX.

Barry Mitchell & Company (B G Mitchell) Pentre Farm House, Mamhilad, PONTYPOOL, NP4 0JH.

ⒶBarry P. Bennis & Co (B P Benveniste) 9 Chilton Road, EDGWARE, MIDDLESEX, HA8 7NJ.

Barry Page & Co (B D Page) 72 Pentyla Baglan Road, PORT TALBOT, SA12 8AD.

ⒻBarry Paydon & Co. (B H Paydon) 28 Church Road, STANMORE, MIDDLESEX, HA7 4AW. and at LONDON

ⓅBarry Paydon Ltd (B H Paydon) 28 Church Road, STANMORE, MIDDLESEX, HA7 4AW.

Barry Peek & Co (B J J Peek) Clock House, Stonham Parva, STOWMARKET, IP14 5JP.

Barry Roback & Co (B P Roback) 17 Parkside Drive, EDGWARE, MIDDLESEX, HA8 8JU.

ⓅBarry Watkinson & Co, trading name of Barry Watkinson & Co Limited (B I Watkinson) 683 Galleywood Road, CHELMSFORD, CM2 8BT.

Barry.R. Coleman (B R Coleman) 28 Dufferin Street, CAMPBELLTON E3N 2N2, NB, CANADA.

ⓉⒶBarter Durgan (K A Green, J B Pache, K J Watkins) 10 Victoria Road South, SOUTHSEA, PO5 2DA.

ⒻⓅⒶBarter Durgan & Muir, trading name of Barter Durgan & Muir Limited (C Elsey) 35 Lavant Street, PETERSFIELD, GU32 3EL.

★ⓉⒻⓅⒶBartfields, trading name of Bartfields (UK) Limited (G M A Bell, R S Davidson, M Gibson, P F Goddard, D P Miller) Burley House, 12 Clarendon Road, LEEDS, LS2 9NF.

ⒻBartfields, trading name of Bartfields Business Services LLP (G M A Bell, M Cawley, R S Davidson, P F Goddard, D P Miller) Burley House, 12 Clarendon Road, LEEDS, LS2 9NF.

ⒻⒶBartlett Kershaw Trott (J M G Bartlett) 4 Pullman Court, Great Western Road, GLOUCESTER, GL1 3ND.

★Bartlett Platt & Company (C J Bartlett) 1 Oak Farm, Long Lane, Haughton, TARPORLEY, CHESHIRE, CW6 9RN.

Barton Little & Co (P F Barton) 1 Fernhurst Road, LONDON, SW6 7JN.

★ⓉⒻⒶBartrum Lerner (S I Lerner) 39A Welbeck Street, LONDON, W1G 8DH.

Base Stone (R Powell) 159 College Road, College Town, SANDHURST, BERKSHIRE, GU47 0RG.

ⓅⒶBasra & Basra Ltd (H Basra, R Mandair) 9 London Road, SOUTHAMPTON, SO15 2AE.

ⒻBass & Co (A J Bass) 123 Riddlesdown Road, PURLEY, CR8 1DL.

★ⒶBassett Herron, Chipchase Nelson, Willis Scott, trading names of Willis Scott Group (S K Hutton, K Scott) 27/28 Frederick Street, SUNDERLAND, SR1 1LZ. and at BISHOP AUCKLAND, HEXHAM, NEWCASTLE UPON TYNE, SOUTH SHIELDS

ⓅBASSL, trading name of Crana Trading Limited (N McLaughlin) 133 Bath Road, STROUD, GLOUCESTERSHIRE, GL5 3LL.

ⒶBatchelor & Co (M K Batchelor) 14 Wellington Square, HASTINGS, EAST SUSSEX, TN34 1PB.

ⓅⒶBatchelor Coop, trading name of Batchelor Coop Ltd (M A Batchelor, R C Coop) The New Barn, Mill Lane, Eastry, SANDWICH, CT13 0JW.

ⓉⒻⓅⒶBates & Co, trading name of Bates & Company Shrewsbury Limited (B M Bates) 10 Park Plaza, Battlefield Enterprise Park, SHREWSBURY, SY1 3AF.

★Bates Accountants (B G J Bates) Wulfrun Chambers, 17 Lawton Road, Alsager, STOKE-ON-TRENT, ST7 2AA.

★ⓉBates Weston LLP (G J Buckell, R J Carman, G Evans, I K Neal, R J Smith, W D Thomas) The Mills, Canal Street, DERBY, DE1 2RJ.

ⓉⓅⒶBates Weston, trading name of Bates Weston Audit Limited (R J Carman, G Evans, I K Neal, R J Smith, W D Thomas) The Mill, Canal Street, DERBY, DE1 2RJ.

Batesons (J R Bradshaw) 2 Statham Court, Statham Street, MACCLESFIELD, SK11 6XN.

Batt & Co (I G Batt) 11 Woolaston Drive, Alsager, STOKE-ON-TRENT, ST7 2PL.

ⓅBatten Hughes & Co Ltd (A F Hughes, N A Hughes) 173 College Road, Crosby, LIVERPOOL, L23 3AT.

ⒻⓅBatterbee Thompson, trading name of Batterbee Thompson & Co Limited (M Thompson) Units 7&8, Cargo Workspace, 41 - 43 George Place, PLYMOUTH, PL1 3DX.

ⓉⒶBaty Casson Long (J A Baty) 23 Moorhead Terrace, SHIPLEY, WEST YORKSHIRE, BD18 4LB.

ⓉⒻⓅⒶBaverstocks, trading name of Baverstocks Limited (P Lawrence) Dickens House, 3-7 Guithavon Street, WITHAM, ESSEX, CM8 1BJ. and at BRAINTREE, COLCHESTER

Baws and Co (A R Baws) 70 Elm Road, LEIGH-ON-SEA, SS9 1SJ.

ⓅBaxter & Co, trading name of Christopher Baxter Limited (C J Baxter) 7 Ashby Road, SPILSBY, LINCOLNSHIRE, PE23 5DS.

ⓉⓅBaxter, Payne & Haigh Limited (P J Parmar, S V Payne) Claremont House, Deans Court, BICESTER, OX26 6BW.

ⒶBaxters (D N Baxter) Mill Road Farmhouse, Low Road, North Tuddenham, DEREHAM, NR20 3AB.

ⒻⒶBaxters (A G Baxter) 3 Nightingale Place, Pendeford Business Park, Wobaston Road, WOLVERHAMPTON, WV9 5HF.

Bay Tree Bookkeeping (S J Leitch) 2 Minnis Green, Stelling Minnis, CANTERBURY, KENT, CT4 6AA.

ⓅBAY, trading name of Bay Accountants Ltd (B Mahmood, A Samad) 215 Bacchus Road, BIRMINGHAM, B18 4RE.

★ⓅBayley Miller Ltd (C Bayley) 16b Queen Street, EDINBURGH, EH2 1JE.

ⒶBayliss & Co (P D Bayliss) 25 Lordswood Road, Harborne, BIRMINGHAM, B17 9RP.

ⓅⒶBayliss Ware Ltd (P Bayliss) 9 Stratfield Park, Elettra Avenue, WATERLOOVILLE, HAMPSHIRE, PO7 7XN.

ⓅBaze, trading name of Enpeyz Consulting Limited (N N Pattni) Team House, St. Marys Road, WATFORD, WD18 0EE.

BBG Professionals (H Jahangir) 13 Nevill Lodge, Ferndale Close, TUNBRIDGE WELLS, KENT, TN2 3RP.

★ⓉⒻⒶBBK Partnership (D M Beckwith, A D Kaye, S S Sahota) 1 Beauchamp Court, Victors Way, BARNET, HERTFORDSHIRE, EN5 5TZ. and at CHATTERIS, CROYDON, LONDON

ⓅBBML, trading name of Bosworth Business Management Limited (H Skeat) 37 Northumberland Avenue, Market Bosworth, NUNEATON, WARWICKSHIRE, CV13 0RJ.

ⓈBBS Computing Ltd (K N Salter) 30 Bear Street, BARNSTAPLE, EX32 7DD.

ⓉⓅBC & A, trading name of Business Consulting & Accounting Limited (T Ahmed) 161 Elm Grove, SOUTHSEA, HAMPSHIRE, PO5 1LU.

ⓅBC & C Ltd (N T Chaudhary) 50 Mansfield Road, ILFORD, ESSEX, IG1 3BD.

ⓅBCG Accountancy Company Ltd (K A Guy) 111 South Road, Waterloo, LIVERPOOL, L22 0LT.

ⓅⒶBCG, trading name of BCG Accountants Limited (K A Guy) 111 South Road, Waterloo, LIVERPOOL, L22 0LT.

ⓉⓅⒶBCL Accountants Ltd (C J Nunn) 30-38 Dock Street, LEEDS, LS10 1JF.

ⓅBCR, trading name of Barringtons Corporate Recovery Limited (N B Cooper, K Lucas, P B Wood) 570-572 Etruria Road, NEWCASTLE, STAFFORDSHIRE, ST5 0SU.

ⓉⓅBDHC, trading name of SWC4Limited (R J Chicken) 11 Moor Street, CHEPSTOW, GWENT, NP16 5DD. and at CARDIFF

BDO (K Se) Suite 18-04 Level 18, Menara Maa, No 15 Julan Dato, Abdullah Tahir, 80300 JOHOR BAHRU, MALAYSIA.

★BDO (G C Culmer) P.O. Box N10144, East Street, NASSAU, BAHAMAS.

ⓉⓅⒶBDO Alto Limited (M J Corbin, C L Treharne) Windward House, La Route de la Liberation, St Helier, JERSEY, JE1 1BG.

▽ⓉBDO Auditores y Consultores S.R.L., BDO Binder B.V., BDO Espana, BDO Khaled & Co, BDO Minas Ioannou, BDO Nelson Parkhill, BDO Scanrevision Aktieselskab, BDO Spencer Steward, BDO Visura Treuhand Gesellschaft, Collins Barrow Ottawa LLP, Hernandez Lozano Marron Lebraja, S.C., Lodha & Co, Murphy & Associates, Pazos, Lopez De Romana Rodriguez S.C., Saleh, Barsoum & Abdel Aziz, trading names of BDO International (M Ashraf, I I Bahemia, R Balasburamaniam, R B Benge, C J Bray, W A Chan, P D Cook, J P Crowley, T M Khaled, H Lim, B Mayo-Smith, T Ooi, S Patel, W Wong) Boulevard de la Woluwe 60, B-1200 BRUSSELS, BELGIUM. and at AALBORG, AARAU, AARHUS, ABU DHABI, ADELAIDE, AFFOLTERN AM ALBIS, ALEXANDRIA, ALPHEN AAN DEN RIJN, ALTDORF, ANKARA, ANTWERP, APELDOORN, ARNHEM, AUCKLAND, AVIGNON, BADEN-DAETTWIL, BANDUNG, BANGKOK, BARCELONA, BEAUVAIS, BEIJING, BEIRUT, BERLIN, BOGOTA, BONN, BORKOP, BOSTON, BREDA, BREMEN, BRISBANE, BROCKVILLE, BRONDERSLEV, BUCARAMANGA, BUENOS AIRES, BURGDORF, CAIRO, CALCUTTA, CALEXICO, CALI, CAPE TOWN, CELAYA, CHARLESTOWN, CHARLOTTE, CHATHAM, CHICAGO, CHRISTCHURCH, COBOURG, COLOGNE, COPENHAGEN, CORNWALL, CRANBROOK, CUREPIPE, DORDRECHT, DRYDEN, DUBAI, DURBAN, DUSSELDORF, EINDHOVEN, EJSTRUPHOLM, EKERO, EL PASO, EMBRUN, EMPANGENI, ERFURT, ESSEN, FAABORG, FLENSBURG, FREDERIKSHAVN, FREIBURG, FRIBOURG, GABORONE, GARDNER, GLARUS, GOSFORD, GRAND RAPIDS, GRENCHEN, GRONINGEN, GUATEMALA CITY, GUAYAQUIL, GUELPH, HAIFA, HAMBURG, HAMILTON, HANOVER, HAPARANDA, HELSINKI, HERNING, HIGH POINT, HIRTSHALS, HOBRO, HOFORS, HOUSTON, HUNTSVILLE, IBAGUE, IKAST, IQUIQUE, ISTANBUL, JAIPUR, JAKARTA, JERUSALEM, JOHANNESBURG, JORN, KALMAR, KAMLOOPS, KARACHI, KARLSHAMN, KARLSKRONA, KENORA, KIEL, KINGSTON, KOBLENZ, KRISTINEHAMN, KUALA LUMPUR, LA PAZ, LAGOS, LANGLEY, LAUFEN, LEIDEN, LIEGE, LIESTAL, LILLE, LIMA, LINDSAY, LINKOPING, LISBON, LONG ISLAND, LUBECK, LUDVIKA, LUZERN, MACAU, MADRAS, MADRID, MANIZALES, MANOTICK, MARKHAM, MEMPHIS, MEXICO CITY, MILWAUKEE, MIRANDA, MISSISSAUGA, MONTEVIDEO, MONTREAL, MOSCOW, MOUNT FOREST, MUMBAI, MUSCAT, MUSKEGON, NAALDWIJK, NAIROBI, NELSPRUIT, NEW DELHI, NEW YORK, NICOSIA, NIJMEGEN, OAKVILLE, OLTEN, OPORTO, ORANGEVILLE, ORILLIA, ORLANDO, OSHAWA, OTTAWA, OWEN SOUND, PADBORG, PENANG, PERTH, PETERBOROUGH, PIETERMARITZBURG, PORT ELGIN, PORT LOUIS, PRETORIA, QUITO, RANDERS, RECIFE, RED LAKE, REVELSTOKE, RICHMOND, RIDGETOWN, RIO DE JANEIRO, ROAD TOWN, ROOSENDAAL, ROTORUA, ROTTERDAM, S'HERTOGENBOSCH, SAEBY, SAN FRANCISCO, SANTIAGO, SAO PAULO, SARNEN, SARNIA, SAULT STE. MARIE, SEATTLE, SEOUL, SEREMBAN, SHENZHEN, SILKEBORG, SINGAPORE, SKAGEN, SKELLEFTEA, SOLLEFTEA, SOLLENTUNA, SOLOTHURN, SOUTH AUCKLAND, SQUAMISH, ST CATHARINES, ST GALLEN, STANS, STUTTGART, SURREY, SURSEE, SYDNEY, TAIPEI, TEL AVIV, THE HAGUE, THUNDER BAY, TIJUANA, TILBURG, TIMRA, TOKYO, TOLUCA, TORONTO, TOULOUSE, TROY, TUPELO, UTRECHT, VALLETTA, VANCOUVER, VASTERAS, VERACRUZ, VIBORG, VICTORIA, WALKERTON, WARSAW, WELLAND, WEST PALM BEACH, WETZIKON, WIARTON, WIESBADEN, WILLEMSTAD, WINCHESTER, WINDHOEK, WINDSOR, WINNIPEG, WOODBRIDGE, ZURICH

BDO Corporate Finance (Middle East) LLP (I R Plunkett) DIFC, Gate Village 10, Level 03, Office 33, PO Box 125115, DUBAI UNITED ARAB EMIRATES.

★ⓉBDO De Chazal du Mee (A A A Ebrahim, K Hawabhay, J Pougnet, A B Ramdin, M Y A Ramtoola, G L K F C Seeyave, Y K Teng Hin Voon) P.O. Box 799, 10 Frere Felix, De Valois Street, PORT LOUIS, MAURITIUS.

ⓉBDO Ebrahim & Co (Q E Causer) 2nd Floor, Block C, Lakson Square Building No1, Sarwar Shahead Road, KARACHI 74200, PAKISTAN. and at ISLAMABAD, LAHORE

ⓅBDO Limited (A Lee, S Lo, S H Ng) 25/F Wing On Centre, 111 Connaught Road, CENTRAL, HONG KONG ISLAND, HONG KONG SAR.

ⓉⓅⒶBDO Limited (Y Kapetanios, R Potamitis, K A Zangoulos) Antonis Zenios Tower, 1 Erehthiou Street Engomi, PO Box 25277, 2413 NICOSIA, CYPRUS. and at LIMASSOL

★ⓉⒶBDO LLP (R D Adams, M A Anslow, P N Anthony, D M Ashman, J Aston, J P Austin, R S Aziz, J L Barker, P J Bates, D E Bawtree, I Beaumont, A H Beckingham, S B Benaim, S Bevan, M Bomer, S W Brooker, D Brookes, G M Brooks, J L H Brown, N F

Burbidge, D K Campbell, N H Carter-Pegg, P C J Chidgey, R J Citron, C D Clark, T P Clarke, G C Clayworth, M Cohen, K R Cook, I P Cooper, M J Copley, A V Cottle, K D Crossthwaite, D N W Dartnaill, P R Davies, M F Dawson, J M Dennison, D I Dover, A H Draper, A M Dumbleton, P M Eagland, D M Eagle, N A Eastaway, G S Elsworth, R E Farr, J P Fearon, F E Fernie, A L Foyle, A R Frais, J C H Frost, N A R Fung-On, S Gerber, D H Gilbert, J L Gilbey, S E J Girling, M H Goldstein, N S Goldstone, C J Grove, G E Hanson, A W Harris, K H Hayward, C Heatlie, P J Hemington, I A R Henderson, S J Herring, M E Hunt, D Isherwood, L S Jefferson, G H Jones, M Joy, R N Kelly, S W Knight, E K Kulczycki, G D Lane, P A Lannagan, P R Lavercombe, T W Lawton, J Le Poidevin, R J Levy, S R Lisle, M B Lowe, D I C Lowson, G Macgregor, T A Macintosh, A D Marsden, S R G McNaughton, R L Miller, J S Newman, A D Nygate, J I Parkinson, A J Perkins, A R Perrett, S S Plaha, C Pooles, A Porter, D A Porter, D J Power, P N A M Prince, G D Quigley, C K Rayment, P D Rego, M Reinecke, J A Rice, J A Roberts, R Rose, P B Russell, J T Rye, C J Searle, H L Sharma, M J Shaw, M A Sherfield, P E H Smith, E P Solomons, P Spencer, J A Stephan, A J Stickland, K M Storan, P C Storer, A C D Tapp, D M Taylor, N J Taylor, M B Thixton, N A Udal, A S Viner, S B Ward, A J A Ware, S D Watson, N G Wharton, A C White, M R White, J P Whitworth, B Wilkinson, B R Wilkinson, D S Williams, J M Willmott) 55 Baker Street, LONDON, W1U 7EU. and at BIRMINGHAM, BRISTOL, CAMBRIDGE, CHELMSFORD, EPSOM, GATWICK, GLASGOW, HATFIELD, LEEDS, MANCHESTER, READING, SOUTHAMPTON

Ⓣ**BDO LLP** *(S H Chia, S M Lim)* 21 Merchant Road, 05-01 Royal Merukh, S.E.A Building, SINGAPORE 058267, SINGAPORE.

Ⓟ**BDO Services Limited** *(M A Sherfield)* 55 Baker Street, LONDON, W1U 7EU.

★**BDO, trading name of BDO Limited** *(C P Summerfield)* PO Box 1200, Montagu Pavilion, 8-10 Queensway, GIBRALTAR, GIBRALTAR.

ⓉⓅⒶ**BDO, trading name of BDO Limited** *(P M Burnard, I R Damarell, J M Hallett, R P Jackson, R M Searle)* PO Box 180, Place du Pre, Rue du Pre, St Peter Port, GUERNSEY, GY1 3LL.

Ⓟ**BDP Oribita Limited** *(B J Proffitt)* Ioma House, Hope Street, Douglas, ISLE OF MAN, IM1 1AP.

ⓅⒶ**BDWM Limited** *(S E M Bishop, A J Millard)* Ground Floor, Hallow Park, Hallow, WORCESTER, WR2 6PG.

BE Roberts & Co *(B E Roberts)* 3 Kirkleas Road, SURBITON, SURREY, KT6 6QJ.

Beadman & Co *(P M F Beadman)* Maple Lodge, Paines Hill, Steeple Aston, BICESTER, OXFORDSHIRE, OX25 4SQ.

ⓉⒻⒶ**Beak Kemmenoe** *(C Mackinlay, R D Price)* 1-3 Manor Road, CHATHAM, ME4 6AE.

Ⓐ**Beales & Co** *(D Beales)* Oaken Coppice, Bears Den, Kingswood, TADWORTH, KT20 6PL.

Bear Space LLP *(L A Wall)* 59 Lambeth Walk, LONDON, SE11 6DX.

Ⓟ**Bear Space Projects Limited** *(L A Wall)* 59 Lambeth Walk, LONDON, SE11 6DX.

Ⓟ**Beasley & Co, trading name of Trevor Beasley & Co Ltd** *(I J Parry)* 25 Market Place, NUNEATON, WARWICKSHIRE, CV11 4EG.

ⓉⒻⒶ**Beatdebt, trading name of Muras Baker Jones** *(D J Baker, M J Botwood, T P Brueton, J H Marks, C A Morris, M H Parker, O Ross, S Ross)* Regent House, Bath Avenue, WOLVERHAMPTON, WV1 4EG.

ⓉⒻⓅ**Beatons Limited** *(R A Beaton, S Hammond, J Oakley)* York House, 2-4 York Road, FELIXSTOWE, IP11 7QG.

Ⓟ**Beattie & Co, trading name of JMBt Limited** *(J M Beattie, S A Knapp)* The Old Studio, High Street, West Wycombe, HIGH WYCOMBE, HP14 3AB.

ⓅⒶ**Beattie Moulds, McIntosh, trading names of McIntosh (Ilkeston) Limited** *(I A McIntosh)* 20 Burns Street, ILKESTON, DERBYSHIRE, DE7 8AA. and at STOKE-ON-TRENT

Ⓟ**Beaty-Pownall Associates Limited** *(M.C. Beaty-Pownall)* 5 Fir Close, WALTON-ON-THAMES, SURREY, KT12 2SX.

ⒻⒶ**Beauchamp Charles** *(C C Barltrop)* 145a Ashley Road, Hale, ALTRINCHAM, WA14 2UW.

Beaufort Chancery *(R E Moore)* 27a High Street, ESHER, SURREY, KT10 9RL.

Beaumont Tew & Co *(C C Tew)* Forsythia Cottage, 4 Sefton Paddock, Stoke Poges, SLOUGH, SL2 4PT.

Ⓐ**Beaumonts** *(S N Mountford)* 29-31 Moorland Road, Burslem, STOKE-ON-TRENT, ST6 1DS.

ⒻⒶ**Beaumonts** *(J H Beaumont, P M Samuel)* 8 Navigation Court, Calder Park, WAKEFIELD, WEST YORKSHIRE, WF2 7BJ.

Ⓐ**Beavers** *(M J Beaver)* 3 The Shrubberies, George Lane, LONDON, E18 1BD.

ⓉⓅⒶ**Beavis Morgan Audit Limited** *(M J Burge, B J Dunning, R S Thacker)* 82 St. John Street, LONDON, EC1M 4JN.

Ⓕ**Beavis Morgan LLP** *(P K Ashton, M J Burge, P L Drown, B J Dunning, P F Jackson, C C Roberts, R S Thacker)* 82 St. John Street, LONDON, EC1M 4JN.

Bebbington & Co *(A J P Bebbington)* 13 Rushside Road, Cheadle Hulme, CHEADLE, SK8 6NW.

Beck Financial, trading name of Paul Becksmith FCA *(D P Becksmith)* 14 Oldfield Wood, WOKING, GU22 8AN.

Ⓟ**Beckenham Business Services Ltd** *(J E Scally)* 3 Mackenzie Road, BECKENHAM, KENT, BR3 4RT.

Becketts *(D E Beckett)* Suite 8, 12 Devon Place, NEWPORT, GWENT, NP20 4NN.

Ⓐ**Becketts** *(A R H Beckett)* Unit 1 Waterside, Old Boston Road, WETHERBY, WEST YORKSHIRE, LS22 5NB.

ⓉⒶ**Becketts, trading name of The Beckett Partnership LLP** *(L T McLoughney)* Beckett House, Sovereign Court, Wyrefields, Poulton Industrial Estate, POULTON-LE-FYLDE, LANCASHIRE FY6 8JX.

Ⓟ**Bedford Place Tax Shop Limited** *(R C B Smallman)* 30a Bedford Place, SOUTHAMPTON, SO15 2DG.

Ⓟ**Beech Business Services Limited** *(J D Barden, D A Kay, G W Leigh, P A Riding, M R C Sheen, A G Smith)* Carlyle House, 78 Chorley New Road, BOLTON, BL1 4BY.

Ⓟ**Beech Sanderson Ltd** *(L R Sanderson)* 70 St. Andrews Road, HENLEY-ON-THAMES, OXFORDSHIRE, RG9 1JE.

ⓉⒻⒶ**Beechams LLP** *(R B Parmar, S M Ufland)* 3rd Floor, 167 Fleet Street, LONDON, EC4A 2EA.

ⒻⓅ**Beechcroft Associates Limited** *(T J Gerhard, F A Lilley, S Mollett, J R Terry)* Greencoat House, Francis Street, LONDON, SW1P 1DH. and at EAST GRINSTEAD

Beecroft & Associates *(R D Beecroft)* The Laurels, Wickham Heath, NEWBURY, BERKSHIRE, RG20 8PG.

Ⓟ**Beelams, trading name of Beelams Accountancy Limited** *(S M Beelam)* 93 Burlescoombe Road, Thorpe Bay, SOUTHEND-ON-SEA, SS1 3PT.

ⓉⒻⓅⒶ**Beeley Hawley & Co, trading name of Beeley Hawley & Co Ltd** *(G M Beeley, P M Beeley, R M Callingham)* 44 Nottingham Road, MANSFIELD, NOTTINGHAMSHIRE, NG18 1BL. and at SOUTHWELL

ⓉⒻⒶ**Beever and Struthers** *(J M Adams, S Boyes, L Bury, W J Campbell, M M Hallows, D N Hunter, J R Jones, C M Kennedy, S L Lomax, C C S Macmillan, A J McLaren, C R Monk, C Porritt, S Rahman, P J Roberts, I E Round, A T Rowntree, P Shaw, A J Speakman, N W Stevens, A S B Thom, G Wilson, P R Wilson)* St George's House, 215-219 Chester Road, MANCHESTER, M15 4JE. and at BLACKBURN, WEMBLEY

★**Beevers & Co, trading name of Beevers & Moreno LLP** *(T Beevers)* 44 Chatsworth Gardens, LONDON, W3 9LW.

Ⓟ**Beevers Accounting Services Ltd** *(T Beevers)* 44 Chatsworth Gardens, LONDON, W3 9LW.

ⓉⒶ**Begbies Playfoot, trading name of Begbies Chettle Agar** *(R G Maples, J Payne, D M Valentine, C P Wain)* Epworth House, 25 City Road, LONDON, EC1Y 1AR. and at CRANBROOK

Ⓣ**Begbies Traynor (Central) LLP** *(N G Atkinson, P D Bekisz, P R Dewey, A R Fanshawe, D Hill, N R Hood, W J Kelly, E Klempka, G M Krasner, S J Lundy, N J Mather, R A H Maxwell, C Morris, R E Penn-Newman, J N R Pitts, R N I Pughe, G W Rhodes, A J Roberts, M E G Saville, P Stanley, A H Tomlinson, R W Traynor, I E Walker)* 340 Deansgate, MANCHESTER, M3 4LY. and at ABERDEEN, BATH, BIRMINGHAM, BLACKPOOL, BOURNEMOUTH, BRIGHTON, BRISTOL, CAMBRIDGE, CARDIFF, CHESTERFIELD, DERBY, DONCASTER EAST, DUNDEE, DUNGANNON, EDINBURGH, EXETER, GEORGE TOWN, GLASGOW, HALIFAX, HULL, LEEDS, LEICESTER, LINCOLNSHIRE, LIVERPOOL, LONDON, MIDDLESBROUGH, NEWCASTLE UPON TYNE, NOTTINGHAM, PLYMOUTH MEETING, PORTSMOUTH, PRESTONPANS, SALISBURY, SHEFFIELD, SOUTHAMPTON, STOCKTON-ON-TEES, STOKE-ON-TRENT, YORK

Ⓟ**Begbies Traynor (Channel Islands) Limited** *(J E Pirouet, A J Roberts)* Charles House, Charles Street, St. Helier, JERSEY, JE2 4SF. and at GUERNSEY

ⓉⓅ**Begbies Traynor, trading name of Begbies Traynor Limited** *(N G Atkinson, S L Conn, P R Dewey, D Hill, N R Hood, W J Kelly, G N Lee, N J Mather, R A H Maxwell, C Morris, J N R Pitts, G W Rhodes, M E G Saville, P Stanley, R W Traynor, I E Walker, G J Woodward)* 340 Deansgate, MANCHESTER, M3 4LY. and at BIRMINGHAM, BRIGHTON, BRISTOL, CARDIFF, CHESTER, EDINBURGH, EXETER, GLASGOW, HALIFAX, HULL, LEEDS, LIVERPOOL, LONDON, NEWPORT, NOTTINGHAM, PLYMOUTH, PRESTON, SALISBURY, SOUTHEND-ON-SEA, STOKE-ON-TRENT

Ⓟ**Beginning 2 End Limited** *(A Patel)* 11 Amberside House, Wood Lane, Paradise Industrial Estate, HEMEL HEMPSTEAD, HERTFORDSHIRE, HP2 4TP.

★Ⓣ**Beh L.H. & Co** *(Dato' Beh)* Suite B-2-1A, North Point Office, Mid Valley City, 1 Medan Syed Putra Utara, 59200 KUALA LUMPUR, FEDERAL TERRITORY MALAYSIA.

Behrman Swindell & Co. *(J Behrman)* 4b Shenley Road, BOREHAMWOOD, HERTFORDSHIRE, WD6 1DL.

Ⓟ**Beldon Brook Limited** *(P Walker)* Sanderson House, Jubilee Way, Grange Moor, WAKEFIELD, WEST YORKSHIRE, WF4 4TD.

Ⓟ**Belfield & Co Ltd** *(R C Belfield)* 15 Medlock Road, Woodhouses, Failsworth, MANCHESTER, M35 9UA.

Belgrave Accountants *(D S Press)* 5 Belgrave Gardens, St Johns Wood, LONDON, NW8 0QY.

Ⓟ**Belhus Limited** *(D J Orr)* 14 Dublin Crescent, Henleaze, BRISTOL, BS9 4NA.

Belinda Bettam ACA *(B C Bettam)* 16 Sandy Lane, Little Neston, NESTON, CH64 4DR.

Bell & Co *(N A Bell)* 37 The Vale, Southgate, LONDON, N14 6HR.

Ⓟ**Bell & Co, trading name of Bell & Co (Accountancy Services) Ltd** *(J D Bell)* 4 Jermyns Lane, Ampfield, ROMSEY, SO51 0QA.

★Ⓐ**Bell & Company** *(S J Clear, G B Moore)* 64 Harpur Street, BEDFORD, MK40 2ST.

ⓉⒻⓅⒶ**Bell Anderson, trading name of Bell Anderson Limited** *(M B Anderson, G Little)* 264-266 Durham Road, GATESHEAD, NE8 4JR.

Ⓐ**Bell Dinwiddie & Co** *(P J Bell)* Glenavon House, 39 Common Road, Claygate, ESHER, KT10 0HG.

Bell Howley LLP *(O M Howley)* 1 Laurel Road, Chalfont St. Peter, GERRARDS CROSS, BUCKINGHAMSHIRE, SL9 9SL.

Ⓟ**Bellanco Limited** *(T L Bell)* 32 The Yonne, CHESTER, CH1 2NH.

Ⓟ**BellGranger, trading name of BellGranger Limited** *(M J Stant)* Copperfield, Grey Road, ALTRINCHAM, CHESHIRE, WA14 4BT.

Ⓟ**Bellstar Associates Ltd** *(A R Hakim)* 727-729 High Road, LONDON, N12 0BP.

Ⓟ**Beman & Co** *(D G Beman)* The Bungalow, Llantrithyd House, Llantrithyd, COWBRIDGE, CF71 7UB.

Ⓟ**Beman & Co Tax Consultants, trading name of Astonworth Limited** *(D G Beman)* The Bungalow, Llantrithyd House, Llantrithyd, COWBRIDGE, SOUTH GLAMORGAN, CF71 7UB.

Ben Adler Associates *(J B Adler)* 4c Unity House, 3-5 Accommodation Road, LONDON, NW11 8ED.

Ben Y S Ho & Co *(Y Ho)* Unit B, 20/F, Nathan Comm Building, 430 - 436 Nathan Road, YAU MA TEI, KOWLOON HONG KONG SAR.

Ⓣ**Benady Cohen & Co** *(M M Benady, S V M Cohen)* 21 Engineer Lane, GIBRALTAR, GX11 1AA, GIBRALTAR.

Bendel & Company *(A P Bendel)* 5 Whitegate Gardens, Harrow Weald, HARROW, HA3 6BW.

Ⓐ**Benedict Leff & Co, trading name of Reed Taylor Benedict** *(P H Benedict)* First Floor, Trinominis House, 125-129 High Street, EDGWARE, HA8 7DB.

ⓉⒻⒶ**Benedict Mackenzie, Benedict McQueen, trading names of Crouch Chapman** *(A P M Benedict, K J Chapman, K L Foster, N M Heath, R P Howard, L Pagden, I D Williams)* 62 Wilson Street, LONDON, EC2A 2BU.

Benedict Mackenzie, trading name of Benedict Mackenzie LLP *(A P M Benedict, V L Neave, L Pagden, I D Williams)* 62 Wilson Street, LONDON, EC2A 2BU. and at BANSTEAD, BRISTOL, CRAWLEY, EASTLEIGH, PORTSMOUTH, TEWKESBURY

Ⓣ**Benjamin Morris & Co** *(B H Morris)* Brook House, 18a Brook Street, NESTON, CHESHIRE, CH64 9XL.

ⓉⒻⒶ**Benjamin, Kay & Brummer** *(S C P Kapoor, M Mohammadi, J J Rome)* York House, Empire Way, WEMBLEY, HA9 0QL.

ⓉⒻⒶ**Benjamin, Taylor & Co** *(J Diner, P Goldstein)* 201 Great Portland Street, LONDON, W1W 5AB.

★Ⓟ**Bennett & Co** *(M D Hurren)* 16 Upland Road, Dulwich, LONDON, SE22 9GG.

ⓉⒻⓅⒶ**Bennett Brooks, The Payroll Centre, trading names of Bennett Brooks & Co Ltd** *(M Day, S D Littler, A Moulton, G M Swift, N J A White, Y A Wood)* St. Georges Court, Winnington Avenue, NORTHWICH, CHESHIRE, CW8 4EE. and at LONDON, MACCLESFIELD, MOLD, WIRRAL

Ⓐ**Bennett Jolly** *(T A Jolly)* 4 Hollies Way, Thurnby, LEICESTER, LE7 9RJ.

Ⓟ**Bennett Jolly Ltd** *(T A Jolly)* 4 Hollies Way, Thurnby, LEICESTER, LE7 9RJ.

ⓉⒶ**Bennett Jones & Co** *(T A M Allen, R J Healey, M S Spence)* 94 Fore Street, BODMIN, PL31 2HR. and at ST. AUSTELL

Ⓣ**Bennett Verby LLP** *(S L Rhodes, J R M Sutcliffe)* 7 St Petersgate, STOCKPORT, CHESHIRE, SK1 1EB.

Ⓟ**Bennett Verby, trading name of De La Wyche Baker Limited** *(C N Jackson, K P McCay, S L Rhodes, J R M Sutcliffe)* 7 St. Petersgate, STOCKPORT, CHESHIRE, SK1 1EB.

Ⓟ**Benson Flynn, trading name of Benson Flynn Ltd** *(A J Flynn)* 4 Abbey Square, CHESTER, CH1 2HU.

★**Benson Walker & Co** *(A J Walker)* 1 Bachelor Lane, Horsforth, LEEDS, LS18 5NA.

Ⓟ**Benson Wood (Darlington) Ltd** *(G W Thompson, P L Wood)* 21 Coniscliffe Road, DARLINGTON, COUNTY DURHAM, DL3 7EE.

Ⓟ**Benson Wood Bureau Services Limited** *(G W Thompson, P L Wood)* 10 Yarm Road, STOCKTON-ON-TEES, CLEVELAND, TS18 3NA.

ⒻⓅⒶ**Benson Wood Limited** *(G W Thompson, P L Wood)* 10 Yarm Road, STOCKTON-ON-TEES, CLEVELAND, TS18 3NA.

★**Benten & Co.** *(G L Goodwin)* Abbey House, 51 High Street, SAFFRON WALDEN, ESSEX, CB10 1AF.

ⓉⒻⒶ**Bentleys** *(J C Hargraves, J J Shaw, M A Turner)* Hazlemere, 70 Chorley New Road, BOLTON, BL1 4BY.

★ⓉⒻⒶ**Beresfords** *(R W Adams)* Castle House, Castle Hill Avenue, FOLKESTONE, CT20 2TQ.

ⓉⒻⒶ**Berg Kaprow Lewis LLP** *(D M B Landau)* 35 Ballards Lane, LONDON, N3 1XW.

ⒻⓅⒶ**Berke Fine Fussell Limited** *(S R Fussell)* Beren Court, Newney Green, CHELMSFORD, CM1 3SQ.

ⓉⒻⓅ**Berkeley Bate Limited** *(J S Bate, C J Bush)* Cheviot House, 71 Castle Street, SALISBURY, WILTSHIRE, SP1 3SP. and at BATH

ⓉⒻⓅⒶ**Berkeley Hall Limited** *(S A Ronald)* Vallis House, 57 Vallis Road, FROME, SOMERSET, BA11 3EG.

ⓉⒻⓅⒶ**Berkeley Hall Marshall Limited** *(B A Marshall, M G Small)* 6 Charlotte Street, BATH, BA1 2NE.

ⒻⒶ**Berkeley Hamilton LLP** *(T C Baines, A Edwards, K W Felton, R Lewis)* 5 Pullman Court, Great Western Road, GLOUCESTER, GL1 3ND.

★**Berkeley Lifford Hall** *(S P Brewer)* Greengate House, Pickwick Road, CORSHAM, SN13 9BY. and at LONDON, WARMINSTER

Ⓟ**Berkeley Tax Consultants (UK) Limited** *(J A B Talfourd-Cook)* Berkeley Square House, Berkeley Square, LONDON, W1J 6BD.

★ⓉⒶ**Berkeley Townsend** *(D J Aquino)* Hunter House, 150 Hutton Road, Shenfield, BRENTWOOD, CM15 8NL.

Ⓟ**Berkeley-Tax Limited** *(R Patel)* Berkeley House, 5 Roman Way, BRACKNELL, RG42 7UT.

ⒻⒶ**Berley** *(J H Berman, M Levy)* 76 New Cavendish Street, LONDON, W1G 9TB.

Bernard Atkins *(B Atkins)* 205 Wells Road, Knowle, BRISTOL, BS4 2DF.

Ⓟ**Bernard Atkins Limited** *(B Atkins)* Eight Bells House, 14 Church Street, TETBURY, GLOUCESTERSHIRE, GL8 8JG.

ⒻⒶ**Bernard Edge & Co** *(B M Edge)* The Old Courts, 147 All Saints Road, NEWMARKET, SUFFOLK, CB8 8HH.

Bernard Hawes *(B H Hawes)* 52 Maids Causeway, CAMBRIDGE, CB5 8DD.

Bernard Joseph *(B M Joseph)* PO Box 199, EDGWARE, MIDDLESEX, HA8 7FG.

ⒻⓅ**Bernard Rogers & Co, trading name of Kenilworth Accountancy Limited** *(B A Rogers)* Bank Gallery, 13 High Street, KENILWORTH, WARWICKSHIRE, CV8 1LY.

ⓅⒶ**Bernie Anson Limited** *(B L Anson)* 2a Alton House Office Park, Gatehouse Way, Gatehouse Industrial Area, AYLESBURY, BUCKINGHAMSHIRE, HP19 8YF.

★Ⓕ**Berry & Co** *(A D Cornish)* 7 Clarendon Place, King Street, MAIDSTONE, ME14 1BQ. and at TENTERDEN

Berry & Hotson, trading name of Berry & Hotson LLP *(I Berry)* Cherrytree Suite 2, Union Road, Nether Edge, SHEFFIELD, S11 9EF.

ⒻⒶ**Berry & Partners** *(S W Miles)* West Walk House, 99 Princess Road East, LEICESTER, LE1 7LF.

ⓅⒶ**Berry & Warren, trading name of Berry & Warren Ltd** *(T Chapman, D J Mann, J C Woodcock)* 54 Thorpe Road, NORWICH, NR1 3DY. and at WYMONDHAM

★ⒻⒶ**Berry Accountants** *(A C Neal, M A Woods)* Bowden House, 36 Northampton Road, MARKET HARBOROUGH, LEICESTERSHIRE, LE16 9HE.

Ⓟ**Berry Kearsley Stockwell Limited** *(M J Stockwell)* Sterling House, 31/32 High Street, WELLINGBOROUGH, NN8 4HL. and at MARKET HARBOROUGH

ⒻⓅ**Berrys, trading name of Berrys Business Services Limited** *(J K Berry, K J Berry)* Caddywell Yard, Caddywell Lane, TORRINGTON, DEVON, EX38 7EL.

ⒻⒶ**Bertram Burrows** *(C N Burrows)* 10 Grange Road, West Kirby, WIRRAL, CH48 4HA.

Ⓐ**Bertram Todd** *(N A Nicolaou-Todd)* 5 Oxford House, Oxford Road, WOKINGHAM, RG41 2YE.

Berwell Consultancy *(C Bamber)* Bowbridge House, 23 Kings Drive, Bishopston, BRISTOL, BS7 8JW.

Ⓕ**Bespoke Tax Accountants LLP** *(N M Denniss)* Westmoreland House, 80-86 Bath Road, CHELTENHAM, GLOUCESTERSHIRE, GL53 7JT.

ⓉⒻⒶ**Bessler Hendrie** *(P A Bessler, N I Bolt, J M Hendrie, P R Nicholls, R G E Watkins)* Albury Mill, Mill Lane, Chilworth, GUILDFORD, SURREY, GU4 8RU.

ⓉⒻⒶ**Best For Business, Dean Statham, trading names of Dean Statham LLP** *(D W Beardmore, R W Bladen, P A Dann)* 29 King Street, NEWCASTLE, STAFFORDSHIRE, ST5 1ER.

★Ⓟ**Bestwick Bone & Allbut, trading name of BBA Limited** *(R S Behan, N C Bone, M J Godel, C R Le Marquand, S A Rentsch)* Beachside Business Centre, La Rue du Hocq, St Clement, JERSEY, JE2 6LF.

Ⓟ**Beta Ways Limited** *(B M H Reade)* May Tree Hollow, 10 Crownfields, SEVENOAKS, KENT, TN13 1EF.

BeTRUSTTed, Monks, trading names of PricewaterhouseCoopers *(V Abrams, D W Adair, C M Adshead, A M Ahmad, P D Aitken, S Ali, D Allen, S C Amiss, M Amitrano, H Anderson, S Anderson, B R Andrews, J D Arden-Davis, G I A Armfield, N A Atkinson, R S Auluk, R F Bacon, G A Bagley, C J Baker, J K Baker, G A Barker, J Barker, P A Barkus, M Barling, S Barnes, P V Barrow, C A Bates, M C Batten, M E Batten, L J Beal, D A Beer, S W Beet, A N Bell, S Bellars, T N Bentham, A M Berridge, J R L Berriman, J Bertolotti, C Billington, M Binney, D C Bishop, N G Blackwood, P Bloomfield, S H Boadle, N W E Boden, M C Bolton, M N Bolton, J C Booker, P Boorman, A P Boucher, J S Bourdeaux, C E B Bowman, R C Boys-Stones, S A Bradley, J A Bradshaw, R J Bridson, G D Briggs, J R Bromfield, F M Brooker, R Bunter, J Burkitt, D J Burn, C J Burns, K J Burrowes, C Butter, P J L Calnan, J R Calvert-Davies, N A V Campbell-Lambert, A J L Casley, R L Casson, S J Cater, J W P Chalmers, I R Chambers, D L Charles, A P Clark, B L Clark, R J Clark, C S Clarke, J Clarke, P E C Clarke, R S Collier, R D Collier-Keywood, D J H Cooke, N C Coomber, J E Cooper, P D Copley, N C Corp, S Cosgrove, A D Cottis, S J Couch, M R Cowan, P J Coward, J S Cowling, D J Cox, E H L Cox, P R Cragg, G Crawford, M M Cross, P C Cussons, Y Cypher, S H Dale, H J Daubeney, G M Davies, S T Davies, I F Davis, M J Dawson, R F De Peyrecave, S L De Young, A M Debell, S J Denison, S Devenney, A E Devoy, C M Dewar, J Dickson, I E Dilks, D M Docker, J M S Dowty, S M Drury, K L Dukes, I W Durrans, I F Dykes, N R Edwards, A M Eldridge, I H Elliott, J M Ellis, K J D Ellis, M C Ellis, S A Ellis, K Evans, P A Evans, C M L Everest, G W C Eversfield, S C Fairchild, N N Faquir, P A F Figgis, J S J Fillingham, A W G Finn, K E Finn, S J Fish, J J N W Fisher, M C Fleetwood, N J Fletcher, J D Forbes, J M R Foster, S M Fraser, N Freeman, R A J French, S D A Friend, B J Furness, P R Galpin, M C J Gardiner, I L Gardner, C G Gentle, P D George, S R Gilder, M A Gill, C S Gillespie, R P Girdlestone, C J Glazier, R J Gledhill, D K Godbee, R N A Gordon, N J P Gower, D W Grace, C F Graham, A J Gray, I D Green, R J Green, I J L Griffiths, A E Grimbly, N C Grimes, A P W Groves, N T Groves, T J Groves, D P Guly, C S M Hallett, N C Hammans, A R Hammond, G P Hannam, M A Hannam, J A Hare, K D Harrington, J G Harrison, P R Harrold, S J S Hawes, L H Hayward, M A Heath, C F Hemmings, A J Hemus, A J M Henderson, S A Herbert, D J L Hewer, C D Hibbs, J Higgins, S Higgins, M A Higginson, A G Hill, I A Hill, C P Hinds, L M Hine, M N Hine, J P A Hines, L Frazer, J C F Hitchins, A E Hodgson, M A Hodgson, M R Hodgson, R P Hodson, P Hogarth, P A Holgate, J J Holloway, J A Hook, L J Hooker, T V Hopcroft, N D Hopes, N Hopkin, M E W Hoskyns-Abrahall, J P Howe, D A Howell, N J Howlett, H R A Hudson, M C Hughes, R W Hughes, R J Hunt, M A F Hunter, R A Hunter, Z Hussain, S T Hyde, S T Isted, C J Jackson, P Jackson, W Jackson-Moore, P C Jeffrey, J S Jenkins, S M Jennings, J R Jensen, M J A Jervis, D M J Jessup, S Jiang, D C John, C P Jones, M N Jones, M Jordan, C L Joseland, D Jukes, R K Julleekeea, T Kachhela, A Kail, M B Karp, R J Keers, F E Kelsey, A C Kemp, D F Kenmir, S Kentish, W Kenyon, V A Kerrigan, L C Kerswill, D G Ketteringham, J S King, M King, M A King, S B Kundu, G J Lagerberg, K S Laing-Williams, G J Lambert, J W Lambert, A P Latham, D J A Law, A Lees, J L Leeson, M J Legg, P J Lennon, A Levack, A J Lever, R N Lewis, T E Lewis, B G Lochead, A V Lomas, I M Looker, G S Lord, A J Lyon, D J D Macdougall, J C Mackintosh, O Mackney, S D Maddison, M J Magee, C J Maidment, J B G Maitland, P Mankin, K J Mansfield, L J Manson-Smith, Q Marikar, I C Marsden, R Marsh, B J Marshall, J F Martin, C Maw, P C Maybrey, E C McCann, A H McCrae, A J McCrosson, A D McGill, D J McNab, R E Meakin, D L Meek, A G R Meeke, F Meijs, R J Milburn, R Mills, J E B Minards, M W Moffat, M C F Monfries, J G Mongan, A Moore, A R Morgan, J D Morgan, W J Morgan, A C M Morris, K D Morris, I J Morrison, S G Mount, M R Mullins, F P F Murphy, P H Nash, P J Newberry, M P Newman, S B Newman, D M Newton, U Newton, M S Nichols, P Nixon, H M Nixseaman, P J Norbury, S A O'Brien, C O'Hare, S G E O'Hare, G S Oakland, R Oldfield, S J Ormiston, T S Owusu-Adjei, A Packman, N R Page, S R Page, A R Palmer, R G Palmer, A Parker, J G Parr, G J Parsons, S J Partridge, Z U Patel, A F C Paynter, S A Pearson, D A Pedropillai, C A Penwarden, S M Perry, D S Phelps, D M H Phillips, G M Phillips, G P N Phillips, J M Picton, G K Pike, R J Pollard, A J Popham, R J Porter, C W Potter, G J Powell, I C Powell, J D Preston, M H Preston, I R A Prideaux, D T Prosser, R M L Pugh, P S Purewal, R S Radia, M G Rajani, Z P Randeria, N J Ransome, A N Ratcliffe, J Ratcliffe, P S Rawlinson, J P Rayner, N L S Rea, N H Reynolds, C D Richardson, J Richardson, N J Richens, J C Rickett, S M Rissbrook, P G Rivett, T M Robb, G E Roberts, G T Robinson, M W Robinson, R M Rollinshaw, C D Romans, D A Roper, A J B Rose, R Rowe, S Rowe, C C Rowland, D A Russell, S J Russell, G A Rutter, M A Ryan, P S Samaratunga, G A Sanderson, J A Sansum, J S Sarai, M A Saunders, I Schneider, J M D Schofield, D Y Schwarzmann, J L Scott, I M Selfridge, R V Y Setchim, R G Sexton, S R Shah, R J Shapland, J R Sheer, P A Shepherd, N J E Shield, G S L Shiels, E M Shires, C J F Silcock, A E Simpson, G M Singer, J Singh, D J A Skailes, A S M Skrzypecki, P Slater, A N Smith, B K Smith, C D Smith, H K Smith, I R Smith, J L Smith, M L Smith, N A Smith, P B Smith, R A C Smith, S A Smith, D A Snell, J S Southgate, R J Spilsbury, P N Spratt, R Sriskandan, L E Stapleton, T M Stephen, A M Stephenson, J K Steveni, R D Stevens, N P Stevenson, P J A Stokes, G R Stoner, W N Sutton, H Swanston, R J Sykes, D I Tapnack, P Taurae, C H Taylor, D J Taylor, D Tecwyn, G A Telford, C J Temple, J P Terry, N J D Terry, P G Tew, H Thomas, M C M Thomas, R Thomas, C E Thompson, R C W Thompson, S J Thompson, K Tilson, C P Tompsett, T R Troubridge, G L Tucker, K L Turner, S P Udall, C E F van den Arend, N J Vooght, J C Wakelam, P Wallace, K N Walsh, D R W Walters, S M Walton, N M Ward, G L Ward-Thompson, S N Warriner, J M Waters, L J Watts, J T Wayman, R C G Weaver, N M Webster, J D Whitfield, A Wiggins, L Wilkinson, N A Wilks, C J Williams, C M K Williams, G T Williams, J G Williams, S Williams, R T G Winter, I M Wishart, K A Wolstenholme, N A Woodford, J J T Woodhouse, C J Woolcott, S J Wooldridge, S L Woolfson, S R Wootten, R P Worrall, P D Wright, G R Yeandle, A T Yeeles)* 1 Embankment Place, LONDON, WC2N 6RH. and at ABERDEEN, ARMAGH, BELFAST, BIRMINGHAM, BOURNEMOUTH, BRISTOL, CAMBRIDGE, CARDIFF, CRAIGAVON, DERBY, DUNGANNON, EDINBURGH, FELTHAM, GATWICK, GLASGOW, GLOUCESTER, HULL, LEEDS, LIVERPOOL, LONDONDERRY, MANCHESTER, MILTON KEYNES, NEWCASTLE UPON TYNE, NORWICH, OMAGH, PLYMOUTH, READING, SHEFFIELD, SOUTHAMPTON, ST. ALBANS, SWANSEA, UXBRIDGE

Bettridge & Co *(M G Bettridge)* 28 Broad Street, WOKINGHAM, BERKSHIRE, RG40 1AB.

Ⓟ**Beverley Simpson & Co Ltd** *(K N Lloyd-Simpson)* 10 Russett Hill, GERRARDS CROSS, SL9 8JY.

Beverton & Co. *(N D Beverton)* 3 The Old Print House, Russell Street, DOVER, CT16 1PX.

ⒻⒶ**Bevis & Co** *(C J Bevis)* Apex House, 6 West Street, EPSOM, SURREY, KT18 7RG.

Ⓟ**Bew & Co Limited** *(B K Froud, A P King)* 130 High Street, MARLBOROUGH, WILTSHIRE, SN8 1LZ.

ⓅⒶ**Bewers Turner & Co, trading name of Bewers Turner & Co Ltd** *(P A Bewers)* Portland House, Station Road, KETTERING, NORTHAMPTONSHIRE, NN15 7HH.

ⓅⒶ**Bexons, trading name of Bexons Accountants Limited** *(J P Bexon)* 24 Rectory Road, West Bridgford, NOTTINGHAM, NG2 6BG.

★ⓅⒶ**BFCA Limited** *(B H R Alidina)* Barbican House, 26-34 Old Street, LONDON, EC1V 9QQ.

ⓉⒻⓅⒶ**BFE Brays, trading name of BFE Brays Ltd** *(L J Bentley, D W Eadon, J M Farndale)* 6 Cambridge Crescent, HARROGATE, NORTH YORKSHIRE, HG1 1PE. and at OTLEY

Ⓐ**BG Audit LLP** *(R A Beaton, J Oakley)* 2/4 York Road, FELIXSTOWE, IP11 7QG.

Ⓟ**BG Outsourcing Ltd** *(R A Beaton, S Hammond, J Oakley)* York House, 2-4 York Road, FELIXSTOWE, SUFFOLK, IP11 7QG.

BGS Accountancy & Taxation Services *(B G Swain)* 127 Dale Street, Milnrow, ROCHDALE, LANCASHIRE, OL16 3NW.

Ⓟ**BH White & Co, trading name of Business Assistance Services Ltd** *(B H White)* 51 Fordington Road, LONDON, N6 4TH.

Bhana & Co *(I O Bhana)* 410 Raheja Chambers, Plot No 213 Nariman Point, MUMBAI 400 021, MAHARASHTRA, INDIA.

Bhanot Partnership, trading name of Bhanot & Co *(A K Bhanot)* First Floor, 126-128 Uxbridge Road, Ealing, LONDON, W13 8QS.

Bharat Malhotra & Co *(B Malhotra)* 20-6 Bangur Avenue, Block C, KOLKATA 700 055, INDIA.

Ⓐ**Bharat Shah & Co** *(B P M Shah)* 786 London Road, THORNTON HEATH, SURREY, CR7 6JB.

Bharati Patel *(B Patel)* 27b Priory Road, NEWBURY, RG14 7QS.

ⓅⒶ**Bhaskar Bhavsar Limited** *(B D A Bhavsar)* 36 Tottenhall Road, LONDON, N13 6HX.

★**Bhatia, Sonnadara & Co** *(V Bhatia)* Tower House, 17 Tower Road, Strawberry Hill, TWICKENHAM, TW1 4PD. and at LONDON

Bhatt & Co *(S L Bhatt)* 20 College Close, Harrow Weald, HARROW, HA3 7BZ.

Bhatti & Co *(P Bhatti)* 60 Waterloo Road, WOLVERHAMPTON, WV1 4QP.

ⒻⒶ**BHG, trading name of BHG LLP** *(P B Harrington)* 77 Shrivenham Hundred Business Park, Majors Road, Watchfield, SWINDON, SN6 8TY.

ⓉⒻⒶ**BHP Mitchells, trading name of Barber Harrison & Platt** *(P C Allsop, D W Charlton, P Cross, D Forrest, D H Gray, C Haw, S Ingram, L A Leighton, J E Marshall, D C Mitchell, C H Ringrose, A C D Staniforth, J Warner)* 2 Rutland Park, SHEFFIELD, S10 2PD. and at CHESTERFIELD, HARROGATE, LEEDS

ⓅⒶ**Bibby & Legge Limited** *(R N Bibby)* Unit 3D, Dreadnought Trading Estate, Magdalen Lane, BRIDPORT, DT6 5BU.

ⓉⒻⓅⒶ**Bibbys, trading name of Michael Trigg Accounting Limited** *(M J Trigg)* 19 Old Exeter Street, Chudleigh, NEWTON ABBOT, DEVON, TQ13 0LD.

ⓉⒻⓅⒶ**Bick Accountants Ltd** *(J D Bick)* 52 Longbrook Street, EXETER, EX4 6AH. and at EXMOUTH

ⓉⒶ**Bicknell Sanders** *(B S M Lloyd, S R Youl)* Alresford House, 60 West Street, FARNHAM, GU9 7EH.

★**Bicknell Sanders** *(B S M Lloyd, S R Youl)* Alresford House, 60 West Street, FARNHAM, GU9 7EH.

Biddle Matthews *(R J Biddle)* Mulberry House, 18a Ashfield Lane, CHISLEHURST, KENT, BR7 6LQ.

Biggs Doran *(Biggs)* 55 Irene Avenue, LANCING, WEST SUSSEX, BN15 9NY.

Bignold & Co *(R C Bignold)* Lester House, 7 Bridge Street, STURMINSTER NEWTON, DT10 1AP.

Bijan Sheibani *(B Sheibani)* 18C Radisson Plaza, Al Makthoum Street, PO Box 51130, DUBAI, UNITED ARAB EMIRATES.

Ⓟ**Bilimoria & Co Limited** *(J D Bilimoria)* 171 Raeburn Avenue, SURBITON, KT5 9DE.

Bill Couzens *(W H Couzens)* 40 Digswell Road, WELWYN GARDEN CITY, AL8 7PA.

Bill Fone *(W J Fone)* Bear Place Farm, Blakes Lane, Hare Hatch, READING, RG10 9TA.

Bill Ritchie FCA *(W J Ritchie)* 18 Westbury Road, CROYDON, CR0 2ES.

Bill Thomas & Co *(W E L Thomas)* 58 France Street, Westhoughton, BOLTON, BL5 2HP.

Ⓟ**Billard & Co, trading name of Trevor Billard and Company Limited** *(T Billard)* 1 Webster Crescent, Kimberworth, ROTHERHAM, SOUTH YORKSHIRE, S61 2BS.

Ⓟ**Billingham & Co, trading name of Billingham & Co Limited** *(B J Billingham)* 4 Masons Yard, Mill Street, KIDDERMINSTER, WORCESTERSHIRE, DY11 6UY.

Ⓟ**Binary Accounting Limited** *(D J F Jones)* 10 Aire View Avenue, BINGLEY, WEST YORKSHIRE, BD16 1NS.

Ⓟ**Binks, trading name of TTP Business Services Limited** *(P A Binks)* 84 Manor Road, LANCING, WEST SUSSEX, BN15 0HD.

Bipin Kotecha *(B Kotecha)* 123 Queen Alexandra Mansions, Tonbridge Street, LONDON, WC1H 9DW.

ⒻⒶ**Bipin Vyas & Co** *(B C Vyas)* 34 Butler Road, HARROW, HA1 4DR.

ⒻⓅ**Birch Riddle & Co Limited** *(G N Birch, B J Riddle)* Pond House, Weston Green, THAMES DITTON, SURREY, KT7 0JX.

Ⓐ**Birchall & Co** *(S R Birchall)* 42 Church Street, LEIGH, LANCASHIRE, WN7 1AZ.

Ⓐ**Birchall & Co** *(F J Birchall)* 5 Penrhos Road, Hoylake, WIRRAL, MERSEYSIDE, CH47 1HU.

Ⓟ**Birchway Tax Ltd** *(P S Cornish)* Birchway Farm, Mundham, NORWICH, NR14 6HE.

ⓉⒻⓅⒶ**Bird Luckin, trading name of Bird Luckin Limited** *(A Barnwell, J Gallant, J Osborne, C Pardoe, I J Plunkett, G A Smith, K P Thomas)* Aquila House, Waterloo Lane, CHELMSFORD, CM1 1BN. and at DUNMOW

Ⓐ**Birdsall & Bennett LLP** *(E G Birdsall, N J Birdsall)* 1 Tranquility, Crossgates, LEEDS, LS15 8QU.

Birkett, Tomlinson & Co. *(R D Dingwall)* Regency House, 67 Albert Road, COLNE, BB8 0BP.

Ⓟ**Birkinshaw Raven Limited** *(C S Birkinshaw)* 54a Lightfoot Lane, Fulwood, PRESTON, PR2 3LR.

ⓅⒶ**Birtley Business Services, trading name of Torbitt & Co Ltd** *(G C Torbitt)* 27 Durham Road, Birtley, CHESTER LE STREET, COUNTY DURHAM, DH3 2QG.

Ⓟ**Bishop CLS Limited** *(C A Bishop)* 93 Beaumont Road, Petts Wood, ORPINGTON, KENT, BR5 1JH.

★ⓉⒶ**Bishop Fleming** *(R E T Borton, R G Davey, J J Finnegan, I J Fraser, W J Hanbury, M D Lee, J A O'Sullivan, A Oliver, D C Savill, J H Scaife, C P Thomson, P W A Tuckett, N K Warren, J M Williams)* Stratus House, Emperor Way, Exeter Business Park, EXETER, EX1 3QS. and at BRISTOL, PLYMOUTH, TORQUAY, TRURO

Ⓐ**Bishop Jones** *(M E Bishop)* 13a Broad Street, WELLS, SOMERSET, BA5 2DJ.

★ⓅⒶ**Bishop Simmons, trading name of Bishop Simmons Limited** *(J Simmons)* Mitre House, School Road, Bulkington, BEDWORTH, WARWICKSHIRE, CV12 9JB.

★ⓉⒻⓅⒶ**Bishops, trading name of Bishop & Partners Ltd** *(A J Tabernacle)* Phoenix Park, Blakewater Road, BLACKBURN, BB1 5BG. and at BLACKPOOL

ⒻⓅⒶ**Bishops, trading name of Bishops Accountancy Practice Limited** *(K M Bishop)* 2 Water End Barns, Water End, Eversholt, MILTON KEYNES, MK17 9EA.

Ⓟ**Bissell & Brown Birmingham, trading name of Bissell & Brown Birmingham Ltd** *(B J Matthews, D L Thebridge)* 12 Portman Road, Kings Heath, BIRMINGHAM, B13 0SL.

★ⓉⒻⓅ**Bissell & Brown Ltd** *(J M Malkin, B J Matthews, D L Thebridge, P M Tremayne)* Charter House, 56 High Street, SUTTON COLDFIELD, WEST MIDLANDS, B72 1UJ.

ⓉⒻⓅⒶ**BJ Dixon Walsh, trading name of BJ Dixon Walsh Limited** *(J B Lewis, R A O'Donnell, H S Papworth, T A Routledge)* St. Marys House, Magdalene Street, TAUNTON, SOMERSET, TA1 1SB. and at WELLINGTON

Ⓟ**BJ Hammond & Co, trading name of BJ Hammond & Co Ltd** *(B J Hammond)* 10c West Station Yard, MALDON, ESSEX, CM9 6TR.

BJB Tax *(B J Bedford)* The Hayloft, Grange Farm, Gartree Road, STOUGHTON, LEICESTERSHIRE, LE2 2FB.

Ⓟ**BJCA Limited** *(H S Papworth, T A Routledge)* Rumwell Hall, Rumwell, TAUNTON, SOMERSET, TA4 1EL.

BKAS *(M D Viney)* 45 Deerstone Ridge, WETHERBY, WEST YORKSHIRE, LS22 7XN.

Ⓟ**BKB Services Limited** *(J J Rome)* York House, Empire Way, WEMBLEY, MIDDLESEX, HA9 0QL.

BKK Accounting, trading name of Lorraine Kerr ACA *(L Kerr)* 2 Tompkins Close, Aston Clinton, AYLESBURY, BUCKINGHAMSHIRE, HP22 5WH.

BLA Consulting, trading name of BLA Consulting LLP *(M B Anderson, D Bradshaw, G Little)* 264-266 Durham Road, GATESHEAD, TYNE AND WEAR, NE8 4JR.

Black & Co *(D G Black)* Gorse Cottage, Harborough Hill, West Chiltington, PULBOROUGH, RH20 2PW.

ⒻⓅⒶ**Blackborn Limited** *(S L Bowman)* 131 High Street, Chalfont St. Peter, GERRARDS CROSS, BUCKINGHAMSHIRE, SL9 9QJ.

Blackborn Services *(S L Bowman)* 131 High Street, Chalfont St. Peter, GERRARDS CROSS, BUCKINGHAMSHIRE, SL9 9QJ.

Ⓟ**Blackburn & Blackburn, trading name of Blackburn & Blackburn Ltd** *(C A Blackburn)* Glenroyd, Keighley Road, COLNE, LANCASHIRE, BB8 7HF.

Blackfriars Tax Solutions, trading name of Backfriars Tax Solutions LLP *(J A Bryant)* 30-34 New Bridge Street, LONDON, EC4V 6BJ.

★**Blackler & Co** *(A L Blackler)* The Barn Office, Tredivett Mill, Little Comfort, LAUNCESTON, PL15 9NA.

Ⓐ**Blackman Terry, trading name of Blackman Terry LLP** *(J M Terry)* Bolney Place, Cowfold Road, Bolney, HAYWARDS HEATH, WEST SUSSEX, RH17 5QT.

Blackmore & Company *(M R Blackmore)* Pier Cottage, Pier Road, Portishead, BRISTOL, BS20 7HG.

ⓉⒶ**Blackstone Franks Corporate Finance, trading name of Blackstone Franks LLP** *(L R Blackstone, R W Maas, S V Thakrar)* Barbican House, 26-34 Old Street, LONDON, EC1V 9QR.

Blackwell P.B. *(P B Blackwell)* 8 Bramley Close, LYMINGTON, HAMPSHIRE, SO41 3TE.

Ⓐ**Blackwood Futcher & Co** *(I S Blackwood, I R Futcher)* 9 St. Georges Yard, Castle Streeet, FARNHAM, SURREY, GU9 7LW.

Blake & Co *(D Blake)* Rasdens, The Street, Halvergate, NORWICH, NR13 3AJ.

Ⓐ**Blake Weltman & Co** *(B L Weltman)* Sovereign House, 1 Albert Place, LONDON, N3 1QB.

Ⓐ**Blanche & Co.** *(J E Gill, J W Jewson)* The Lanterns, 16 Melbourn Street, ROYSTON, HERTFORDSHIRE, SG8 7BX.

ⒻⓅⒶ**Bland & Wood, trading name of Planet Business Services Limited** *(K V Wood)* 6B Planet Business Centre, Planet Place, Killingworth, NEWCASTLE UPON TYNE, NE12 6DY.

ⒻⒶ**Bland Baker** *(D M B Baker, K B Roles)* 21 Lodge Lane, GRAYS, RM17 5RY.

Blease Lloyd Associates *(G P Angus, D L H Cole)* Banholzsirasse 16, Box 381, FL 9490 VADUZ, LIECHTENSTEIN.

Bleazard K *(K Bleazard)* 5 Chapel Street, POULTON-LE-FYLDE, FY6 7BQ.

★ⓅⒶ**Blencowes, trading name of Blencowe & Partners Limited** *(R F Blencowe, T L Burton)* 15 High Street, BRACKLEY, NORTHAMPTONSHIRE, NN13 7DH.

Ⓟ**Blenheim Consulting Limited** *(C D Godden)* PO Box 464, BRISTOL, BS34 8SE.

Blenkinsop & Co *(J Blenkinsop)* 1 Shardlow Gardens, Bessacarr, DONCASTER, DN4 6UB.

Bles & Co *(R M Garforth-Bles)* Lower Moor Farm, Charlton, MALMESBURY, SN16 9DY.

Ⓟ**Bles & Partners CPA Limited** *(Y F Ip)* Unit 802, 8/F Bright Way Tower, 33 Mongkok Road, MONG KOK, KOWLOON, HONG KONG SAR.

BLG Accounts *(B A Godfrey)* 18 Hall Park, Barlby, SELBY, NORTH YORKSHIRE, YO8 5XR.

ⓉⒶ**Blick Rothenberg** *(J A Brown, S M Bruck, R M Fabian, M E Hart, D G Jordan, C I Lehmann, S J Mayston, J A Newman, M Pandya, R M Rothenberg, A J Sanford, M G D Scoltock, N Shah, T M Shaw, C J Shepherd, S Wagman)* 12 York Gate, Regent's Park, LONDON, NW1 4QS.

★ⓉⒻⒶ**Blinkhorns** *(D M Cramer, M A L Datoo, G S Stern, S J Wharton)* 27 Mortimer Street, LONDON, W1T 3BL.

Blocks *(P R Block)* Roseworth, Roseworth Crescent, Gosforth, NEWCASTLE UPON TYNE, NE3 1NR.

ⓅⒶ**Blomfields, Stephen Foster, trading names of S Foster (BOA) Ltd** *(I M Burford, S Foster)* The Courtyard, 33 Duke Street, TROWBRIDGE, WILTSHIRE, BA14 8EA.

ⓅⒶ**Bloomer Heaven Payroll, trading name of Bloomer Heaven Limited** *(C Barlow, S E Law, C M Stephen-Haynes)* Rutland House, 148 Edmund Street, BIRMINGHAM, B3 2FD.

ⓅⒶ**Bloomfield & Co, trading name of Bloomfield Business Services Limited** *(J C Bloomfield)* 9 Queen Street, GREAT YARMOUTH, NORFOLK, NR30 2QP.

ⓉⓅⒶ**Blow Abbott Ltd** *(D S Blow, G N Dawson)* 36 High Street, CLEETHORPES, SOUTH HUMBERSIDE, DN35 8JN.

ⒻⓅⒶ**Blue Cube Business, trading name of Blue Cube Business Ltd** *(J D Foster)* 10 Cheyne Walk, NORTHAMPTON, NN1 5PT.

Ⓟ**Blue Dot Consulting Limited** *(M J C Austin)* Riverbank House, Business Centre, 1 Putney Bridge Approach, LONDON, SW6 3JD.

Ⓟ**Blue Edge Solutions Limited** *(M T Wilkins)* 1 Dillington, Great Staughton, ST. NEOTS, CAMBRIDGESHIRE, PE19 5DH.

Blue Note Solutions *(F J K Plumley)* 4 St. Annes Road, Headington, OXFORD, OX3 8NL.

Ⓟ**Blue Skies Accountancy Limited** *(M Graves)* 17 Millbrook Drive, Broughton Astley, LEICESTER, LE9 6UX.

Ⓟ**Blue Sky Corporate Finance (Midlands) Ltd** *(P M Heaven)* 2nd Floor, 3 Brindley Place, BIRMINGHAM, B1 2JB. and at BROMSGROVE

★ⓉⒻⒶ**Blue Spire South LLP** *(G R Beer, G C Fairclough, G A Frost, M J N Goodey, Z Hogg, C A Hunt, M P Middleton, J O'Rourke, J C Ragg, S J Scurr)* Cawley Priory, South Pallant, CHICHESTER, WEST SUSSEX, PO19 1SY. and at HOVE, SOUTHSEA

Ⓟ**Blue Surf Consulting, trading name of Blue Surf Consulting Ltd** *(R N West)* Darvells Farm, Dunt Avenue, Hurst, READING, RG10 0SY.

Ⓟ**Blueface Consulting, trading name of Blueface Consulting Limited** *(A Cutts)* Mill Farm, Allendale, HEXHAM, NORTHUMBERLAND, NE47 9EQ.

Ⓟ**BlueSky Consulting, trading name of BlueSky Consulting (Scotland) Limited** *(I Pritchard)* 9 McLauchlan Rise, Aberdour, BURNTISLAND, FIFE, KY3 0SS.

Ⓟ**BlueSky Corporate Finance Ltd** *(C J Varley)* Milestone Farm, 56-58 Westgate, North Cave, BROUGH, NORTH HUMBERSIDE, HU15 2NJ.

Blueworm *(A L R Roberts)* Winnington Hall, Winnington, NORTHWICH, CHESHIRE, CW8 4DU.

★Ⓟ**Blusky, trading name of Blu Sky Tax Ltd** *(J R Dudgeon)* 17 Northumberland Square, NORTH SHIELDS, TYNE AND WEAR, NE30 1PX.

Ⓐ**Blyth & Co** *(C J J Blyth)* Sental House, 66 Waldeck Road, Strand-on-the-Green, LONDON, W4 3NU.

Ⓟ**Blyth & Co, trading name of Blyth & Co Corporate Services Ltd** *(C R Blyth)* Church View Cottage, Fordon Road, Burton Fleming, DRIFFIELD, YO25 3PS.

Ⓕ**Blythe & Co** *(J D Blythe)* 206 Upper Richmond Road West, East Sheen, LONDON, SW14 8AH.

Ⓟ**Blythe & Co, trading name of DWB Limited** *(D W Blythe)* 41 Oldfields Road, SUTTON, SURREY, SM1 2NB. and at MITCHAM

Ⓟ**Blythe Financial Ltd** *(J D Blythe)* 206 Upper Richmond Road West, East Sheen, LONDON, SW14 8AH.

ⓉⒻⒶ**Blythe Squires Wilson** *(A D Castledine, D S Jackson, R G Squires, J H Wilson)* 1-2 Vernon Street, DERBY, DE1 1FR.

Ⓟ**BMS (Silchester) Limited** *(E M McArdle)* Whistlers Barn, Whistlers Lane, Silchester, READING, RG7 2NE.

Ⓟ**BND Audits Limited** *(B T Denholm, A B Noble)* York House, Empire Way, WEMBLEY, MIDDLESEX, HA9 0PA.

Ⓐ**Boardman & Co** *(Susan Boardman)* Lakeside, 36 Reynards Road, WELWYN, AL6 9TP.

ⒻⒶ**Boardman Conway** *(S J Conway)* 23A High Street, Weaverham, NORTHWICH, CHESHIRE, CW8 3HA.

Boardwell & Company *(D N Boardwell)* Oakdene, Barrowford Road, BURNLEY, BB12 9AT.

Bodsworth & Co *(P Bodsworth)* 55 Mowbray Street, SHEFFIELD, S3 8EZ.

ⓅⒶ**Body Dubois, trading name of Body Dubois Limited** *(R Amin, J Dubois)* The Bellbourne, 103 High Street, ESHER, SURREY, KT10 9QE.

Body Dudois, trading name of Body Dubois Associates LLP *(R Amin)* The Belbourne, 103 High Street, ESHER, KT10 9QE.

★Ⓐ**Bolden & Long** *(J C Bolden)* 36a Goring Road, Goring-by-Sea, WORTHING, BN12 4AD.

Boldero & Co *(I G M Boldero)* Ivy House, The Market Place, Reepham, NORWICH, NR10 4LZ.

ⓉⒶ**Boler Wiseman** *(G M Wiseman)* 8 Toll Gate, Stanbridge Earls, ROMSEY, HAMPSHIRE, SO51 0HE.

Ⓟ**Boler Wiseman Financial Services Limited** *(G M Wiseman)* 8 Tollgate, Stanbridge Earls, ROMSEY, HAMPSHIRE, SO51 0HE.

Ⓟ**Boler Wiseman Limited** *(G M Wiseman)* 8 Tollgate, Stanbridge Earls, ROMSEY, HAMPSHIRE, SO51 0HE.

Bollands *(D E Delve)* Minerva Mill, Station Road, ALCESTER, WARWICKSHIRE, B49 5ET.

ⒻⓅⒶ**Bolton & Co Accountants Ltd** *(T D Bolton)* Squirrels Wood, Reigate Road, LEATHERHEAD, SURREY, KT22 8QY.

ⒻⓅⒶ**Bolton & Co, trading name of A Bolton & Co. Business Advisers Ltd** *(A K Bolton)* 14 Warrington Street, Ashton-Under-Lyne, MANCHESTER, OL6 6AS. and at ASHTON-UNDER-LYNE

Ⓟ**Bolton Consulting Ltd** *(H Bolton)* 16 Lee Fold, Tyldesley, MANCHESTER, M29 7FQ.

Ⓟ**Bolton Smith & Co Limited** *(D Smith)* 158 High Street, Wealdstone, HARROW, HA3 7AX.

Bond & Co *(P R Bond)* 110 Kenilworth Road, COVENTRY, CV4 7AH.

Ⓟ**Bond & Co, trading name of Bondeastleigh Limited** *(B Venney)* 59B Leigh Road, EASTLEIGH, HAMPSHIRE, SO50 9DF.

Ⓣ**Bond Group LLP** *(M D Marcus, C Morfakis, T Papanicola)* The Grange, 100 High Street, LONDON, N14 6TB.

Bond Partners LLP *(C T Brewster, B G Cue, C Morfakis, T Papanicola)* The Grange, 100 High Street, LONDON, N14 6TB. and at ALCESTER, BATH, BOSTON, BUNTINGFORD, DONCASTER, EAST BOLDON, HARWICH, HASSOCKS, HESSLE, NORWICH, STOKE-ON-TRENT

ⓉⓅⒶ**Bonelle & Co Limited** *(A D Bonelle)* 1 Wyecliffe Terrace, Bath Street, HEREFORD, HR1 2HG.

Bonham Bagshaw *(R D Bagshaw)* 25 Greenfield Avenue, NORTHAMPTON, NN3 2AA.

Ⓟ**Book Manager Limited** *(A K Robinson)* 13b Market Place, Caistor, MARKET RASEN, LINCOLNSHIRE, LN7 6TW.

Bookey & Co *(B S Bookey)* 319 Trafalgar House, Grenville Place, LONDON, NW7 3SA.

Ⓟ**Book-Keeping & Accountancy Taxation Services Limited** *(A Doggett)* 5 Crossborough Gardens, BASINGSTOKE, HAMPSHIRE, RG21 4LB.

Ⓟ**Bookkeeping & Beyond Limited** *(S L Cook)* Kinta Cottage, Edwin Road, West Horsley, LEATHERHEAD, SURREY, KT24 6LN.

ⓉⒶ**Booth Ainsworth LLP** *(M Booth, P J Bradbury, G Cook, C I Goldman, P Howard, A A Malik, D Powell, S J Pullen, J N Ward)* Alpha House, 4 Greek Street, STOCKPORT, CHESHIRE, SK3 8AB.

Ⓟ**Booth Finance Consulting Limited** *(S G Booth)* 2 Bradley Drive, WOKINGHAM, BERKSHIRE, RG40 3HZ.

ⓅⒶ**Booth Parkes & Associates Limited** *(D N Booth)* Southolme, Trinity Street, GAINSBOROUGH, DN21 2EQ.

Ⓐ**Boothby Baker & Co** *(G G Boothby)* 12 Mountway Close, WELWYN GARDEN CITY, HERTFORDSHIRE, AL7 4JZ.

Boothmans *(D A Boothman)* Millennium House, Summerhill Business Park, Victoria Road, Douglas, ISLE OF MAN, IM2 4RW.

ⓅⒶ**Borderbay Limited** *(A J P Bebbington)* 13 Rushside Road, Cheadle Hulme, CHEADLE, CHESHIRE, SK8 6NW.

ⓉⒻⓅⒶ**Born & Co, trading name of Born Associates Limited** *(G I Born, S H G Born)* 4 Bloomsbury Place, LONDON, WC1A 2QA.

★**Boroughs** *(P M Prettejohn)* 6 New Street Square, New Fetter Lane, LONDON, EC4A 3AQ. and at SYDNEY

★**Boroumand & Associates** *(H Noorizadeh)* 6th Floor, 94-96 Wigmore Street, LONDON, W1U 3RF.

ⓉⒶ**BOSeCo** *(R Bose, S Bose)* 309 Regents Park Road, LONDON, N3 1DP.

ⓉⓅⒶ**Bostockwhite, trading name of Bostockwhite Limited** *(A C Bostock, S L White, S J Yelland)* Unit 1, Cabourn House, Station Street, Bingham, NOTTINGHAM, NG13 8AQ.

ⒻⓅⒶ**Botham Accounting, trading name of Botham Accounting Limited** *(A J Botham)* 14 Clarendon Street, NOTTINGHAM, NG1 5HQ.

Ⓐ**Botros & Co** *(S E Botros)* 4 Northwest Business Park, Servia Hill, LEEDS, LS6 2QH.

Ⓟ**Botting & Co** *(A E W Botting)* 8 Clifton Moor Business Village, James Nicolson Link, YORK, YO30 4XG.

ⓉⓅⒶ**Botting & Co Ltd** *(A E W Botting)* 8 Clifton Moor Bus.Village, James Nicolson Link, YORK, YO30 4XG.

Ⓟ**Botting and Co, trading name of Reeves Wilkinson Ltd** *(S D Wilkinson)* 41b Beach Road, LITTLEHAMPTON, WEST SUSSEX, BN17 5JA.

Bottomley and Co *(D H Bottomley)* Glenwood House, 5 Arundel Way, Cawston, RUGBY, WARWICKSHIRE, CV22 7TU.

Ⓟ**Boundary Accounting Limited** *(G K Corbett)* Bank Farm, Leigh, WORCESTER, WR6 5LA.

▽**Bourke Quinn O'Mara & Co** *(R A J Quinn)* Arran House, James Street, BALLINA, COUNTY MAYO, IRELAND.

ⓉⒶ**Bourne & Co** *(J J Delaney, M J Edwards, N D Gale, I Hill, D Meadows, M R Nutt)* 6 Lichfield Street, BURTON-ON-TRENT, DE14 3RD. and at DERBY

Bourne & Company *(A C A Bourne)* 19 High Street, LEATHERHEAD, SURREY, KT23 4AA.

ⓉⒻⒶ**Bourner Bullock** *(M S Brooks, D B Matkins, P J M Watts)* Sovereign House, 212-224 Shaftesbury Avenue, LONDON, WC2H 8HQ.

Bowden Smith *(R W Bowden-Smith)* 6 Roedeer Copse, HASLEMERE, SURREY, GU27 1RF.

Ⓟ**Bowen Accountants Ltd** *(W C R Bowen)* Griffon House, Seagry Heath, Great Somerford, CHIPPENHAM, WILTSHIRE, SN15 5EN.

Bowen-Jones, Watkins & Partners *(A J Watkins)* 17 Dan-Y-Graig Avenue, Newton, PORTHCAWL, MID GLAMORGAN, CF36 5AA.

Bowers & Co *(E N Bowers)* 13 Peel Road, Douglas, ISLE OF MAN, IM1 4LR.

ⒻⒶ**Bowker Orford** *(R S Parmar)* 15/19 Cavendish Place, LONDON, W1G 0DD.

Ⓕ**Bowker, Stevens & Co** *(P D Jackson)* Suite No. 2, Centre Court, Vine Lane, HALESOWEN, B63 3EB.

Bowles & Co. *(M B Bowles)* 14 Westerham Road, SEVENOAKS, TN13 2PU.

Ⓟ**Bowman & Co, trading name of N J Bowman Ltd** *(N J Bowman)* Bowman & Hillier Building, The Old Brewery, Priory Lane, BURFORD, OX18 4SG.

Ⓟ**Bowmans Accountants Limited** *(K J Bowman)* 1 Woodridge Close, Edgmond, NEWPORT PAGNELL, SHROPSHIRE, TF10 8JF.

Boyd Roberts & Co *(D G Roberts)* The Tallett, Ewen, CIRENCESTER, GLOUCESTERSHIRE, GL7 6BU.

Ⓐ**Boydell & Co** *(M B Boydell)* 89 Chiswick High Road, LONDON, W4 2EF.

ⒻⓅⒶ**Boyds, trading name of TWY Limited** *(C N Boyd)* 20 Sansome Walk, WORCESTER, WR1 1LR.

ⒻⓅ**BPB, trading name of BPB (Accountants) Limited** *(B P Baxter)* The Gatehouse, Gloucester Lane, Mickleton, CHIPPING CAMPDEN, GLOUCESTERSHIRE, GL55 6SD.

ⓅⒶ**BPC Chandarana & Co, trading name of BPC Chandarana & Co Ltd** *(B P Chandarana, R Chandarana)* Prebend House, 72 London Road, LEICESTER, LE2 0QR.

ⓉⓅⒶ**BPC Partners, trading name of BPC Partners Limited** *(M A G Bull, P K Cadbury)* 1 Rockfield Business Park, Old Station Drive, Leckhampton, CHELTENHAM, GLOUCESTERSHIRE, GL53 0AN.

Ⓟ**bpo accounting, turnround practice, trading names of arca group Ltd** *(R M Frost)* The Old Chapel, Union Way, WITNEY, OXFORDSHIRE, OX28 6HD.

ⓉⒻⓅⒶ**BPU, trading name of BPU Limited** *(M D Bishop, J H Palin, C Russell, N M Toye, E P Umbleja)* Radnor House, Greenwood Close, Cardiff Gate Business Park, CARDIFF, CF23 8AA. and at LLANTWIT MAJOR

BRAAMS LLP *(M Y Jooma, S R Voralia)* First Floor, Allied Sainif House, 412 Greenford Road, GREENFORD, UB6 9AH.

Brabners Stuart LLP *(S Stuart)* Horton House, Exchange Flags, LIVERPOOL, L2 3YL.

Ⓕ**Brackman & Co LLP** *(S Brackman)* 2nd Floor, 421a Finchley Road, LONDON, NW3 6HJ.

ⓉⒻⒶ**Brackman Chopra LLP** *(A J Azarang, S Chopra)* 8 Fairfax Mansions, Finchley Road Swiss Cottage, LONDON, NW3 6JY.

Ⓟ**Bradavon Consultants Limited** *(P H Crook)* Bradavon, 45 The Dales, COTTINGHAM, NORTH HUMBERSIDE, HU16 5JS.

★**Bradford Accountancy Services** *(M A Choudhury)* Valley Point, Valley Road, BRADFORD, WEST YORKSHIRE, BD1 4AA.

Brading & Co *(I Brading)* 5 Kilncroft, HEMEL HEMPSTEAD, HP3 8HH.

Bradley & Co *(J P Bradley)* 110 High Street, ALFRETON, DERBYSHIRE, DE55 7HH.

Bradley & Co *(P Bradley)* 4b Christchurch House, Beaufort Court, ROCHESTER, KENT, ME2 4FX.

Bradley & Co *(M J Brizzolara)* 18 Kingfisher Reach, Boroughbridge, YORK, YO51 9JS.

Ⓟ**Bradley Cave, trading name of Bradley Cave Ltd** *(M W Todd)* 18 Jordan Close, KENILWORTH, WARWICKSHIRE, CV8 2AE.

Bradley Soni & Co *(P L Soni)* 365 South Coast Road, Telscombe Cliffs, PEACEHAVEN, EAST SUSSEX, BN10 7HA.

Bradley-Hoare & Co *(J Bradley-Hoare)* 31 Harley Street, LONDON, W1G 9QS.

Bradshaw Johnson - Brooks Green **Members in Practice and Firms - Alphabetical**

Bradshaw Johnson *(N Harding, S Pike)* 13 Bancroft, HITCHIN, HERTFORDSHIRE, SG5 1JQ. and at ST. NEOTS

ⓉⓅⒶ**Bradshaws, trading name of Bradshaws Ltd** *(A J Bradshaw)* Charter Court, 2 Well House Barns, Chester Road, Bretton, CHESTER, CH4 0DH.

Bradwell & Partners *(A Khan)* 158 Bradwell Common Boulevard, Bradwell Common, MILTON KEYNES, MK13 8BE.

★**Bradwood (South Yorkshire) Unlimited** *(P Hebblethwaite, A P Jackson, J A Midgley)* 24-26 Mansfield Road, ROTHERHAM, SOUTH YORKSHIRE, S60 2DT.

Brady & Co *(W M Brady)* 19 Wentworth Crescent, Alwoodley, LEEDS, LS17 7TW.

Ⓟ**Brady Scrace Limited** *(E B Scrace)* Willowdale, 57 Rooksbury Road, ANDOVER, HAMPSHIRE, SP10 2LP.

★Ⓣ**Braham Noble Denholm & Co.** *(B T Denholm, A B Noble)* York House, Empire Way, WEMBLEY, HA9 0PA.

Brahams & Co *(B P Brahams)* 43 Wren Crescent, BUSHEY, WD23 1AN.

★**Brahmayya & Co** *(P S Kumar)* 48 Masilamani Road, Balaji Nagar, Royapettah, CHENNAI 600 014, INDIA. and at BANGALORE, VIJAYAWADA

Ⓐ**Braidwood & Company** *(C E Braidwood)* Willow Grange, The Street, BETCHWORTH, SURREY, RH3 7DJ.

Ⓟ**Braken, trading name of Braken Limited** *(S J Rakestraw)* 28 Edward Gardens, Martinscroft, WARRINGTON, WA1 4QT.

Ⓟ**BRAL, trading name of BRAL Limited** *(A L Boronte, J A Brown, R M Rothenberg)* 12 York Gate, Regents Park, LONDON, NW1 4QS.

★**Bramil Associates** *(S B Brougham, M Miltiadous)* Rex House, 354 Ballards Lane, North Finchley, LONDON, N12 0DD.

Bramleys *(W N Bramley)* 380 Ecclesall Rd South, SHEFFIELD, S11 9PY.

ⓉⒻⒶ**Bramwell Morris** *(A D Morris)* 133 Albert Road, WIDNES, CHESHIRE, WA8 6LB.

Ⓕ**Brannans** *(A J Prevett, P G Warburton)* 61 Warren Road, LEIGH-ON-SEA, ESSEX, SS9 3TT. and at COLCHESTER

Bransby & Co *(R J Bransby)* 5 Bedales, Lewes Road, HAYWARDS HEATH, RH17 7TE.

Ⓐ**Brassington & Co** *(I R Brassington)* 600 High Rd, WOODFORD GREEN, IG8 0PS.

Bratton A.J. *(A J Bratton)* 2 Priory Court, Priory Farm, STUDLEY, B80 7BB.

Ⓐ**Bray Giffin, trading name of Bray Giffin LLP** *(I M Bray, L A Giffin)* Langford Hall Barn, Witham Road, Langford, MALDON, ESSEX, CM9 4ST.

Ⓟ**Bray Management Services Limited** *(P D Longstaff, R Parish)* 1 Paper Mews, 330 High Street, DORKING, SURREY, RH4 2TU.

ⓉⒻⓅⒶ**Brays, trading name of Brays Ltd** *(I D Parkinson, S Taylor)* 23 Market Place, WETHERBY, WEST YORKSHIRE, LS22 6LQ.

ⓉⒻⓅⒶ**BRC Accountants, Swift Accounting, trading names of Beck Randall & Carpenter Limited** *(D P Carpenter)* Aldwych House, Winchester Street, ANDOVER, HAMPSHIRE, SP10 2EA.

Ⓟ**Breakthrough Finance Limited** *(B Brake)* Suite 303 Princess House, 50-60 East Castle Street, LONDON, W1W 8EA.

Ⓕ**Brealey Foster & Co** *(P I Brealey)* Edwards Centre, The Horsefair, HINCKLEY, LE10 0AN.

Breavis Consultants *(B J Rea-Palmer)* Boissiere, St Andre Nord, 47360 MONTPEZAT D'AGENAIS, FRANCE.

Ⓡ**Brebner, Allen & Trapp Assoc Serv. Ltd** *(J Craig)* The Quadrangle, 180 Wardour Street, LONDON, W1V 4LB.

★ⓉⒶ**Brebners** *(M R J Burton, J B Chamberlain, J Craig, M C Davis, K V Doshi, R S Gregory, P J Heath, C N Pomeroy, T E J Smith, A J S Sturgeon, M N Widdowson)* The Quadrangle, 180 Wardour Street, LONDON, W1F 8LB. and at SEVENOAKS, TUNBRIDGE WELLS

Ⓟ**Brebners Limited** *(J R Chamberlain, J Craig, C N Pomeroy)* The Quadrangle, 2nd Floor, 180 Wardour Street, LONDON, W1F 8LB. and at SEVENOAKS, TUNBRIDGE WELLS

ⒻⒶ**Breen & Co** *(J M Breen)* 12 Church Square, LEIGHTON BUZZARD, BEDFORDSHIRE, LU7 1AE.

ⒻⓅⒶ**Breeze & Associates Ltd** *(A L Breeze, A C George, C K Marsh)* 5 Cornfield Terrace, EASTBOURNE, EAST SUSSEX, BN21 4NN. and at BRIGHTON

Ⓟ**Breeze & Co, trading name of Breeze & Co (Llandudno) Ltd** *(M D Evans)* 9 Lloyd Street, LLANDUDNO, CONWY, LL30 2UU.

ⓉⓅ**Brehon Limited** *(S A G Hancock)* Mayfield House, Grand Rue, St Martin, GUERNSEY, GY4 6AA.

ⓅⒶ**Bremakumars, trading name of Ossmans Limited** *(M H L Ossman)* 591 London Road, North Cheam, SUTTON, SURREY, SM3 9BX.

Brenda Cannon *(B C Cannon)* West House, West Street, HASLEMERE, SURREY, GU27 2AB.

Brenda Forrest *(B Forrest)* 33 St. Georges Terrace, EAST BOLDON, TYNE AND WEAR, NE36 0LU.

Brenda Mooney *(B T Mooney)* The Oast House, The Street, Brook, ASHFORD, KENT, TN25 5PG.

Brendan O'Connor *(B O'Connor)* Rock Cottage, Kilnaclasha, SKIBBEREEN, COUNTY CORK, IRELAND.

ⓉⒶ**Brennan Neil & Leonard** *(M E Brennan, J Hall, J D Leonard)* 32 Brenkley Way, Blezard Business Park, Seaton Burn, NEWCASTLE UPON TYNE, NE13 6DS.

ⒻⒶ**Brennan Pearson & Co** *(N A Hewitt)* 110-112 Lancaster Road, BARNET, EN4 8AL.

Brenner & Co *(A M Brenner)* 7 Pavilion Court, Mount Vernon, Frognal Rise, LONDON, NW3 6PZ.

Ⓟ**Brent King, trading name of Brent King Limited** *(E M King)* 18 Gosport Business Centre, Frater Gate, GOSPORT, HAMPSHIRE, PO13 0FQ. and at WINCHESTER

ⓅⒶ**Breslins, trading name of Breslins Birmingham Ltd** *(P J Breslin)* Albion Court, 18-20 Frederick Street, BIRMINGHAM, B1 3HE. and at COVENTRY, SOLIHULL

Bret Woudstra & Co *(B S Woudstra)* 69 Chesilton Road, LONDON, SW6 5AA.

ⓉⒻⒶ**Brett Adams** *(J B Cohen, S Davidson)* 25 Manchester Square, LONDON, W1U 3PY.

★Ⓟ**Brett Pittwood, trading name of Brett Pittwood Limited** *(M J Brett)* Suite 8, Bourne Gate, 25 Bourne Valley Road, POOLE, DORSET, BH12 1DY.

Ⓟ**Brewer & Company, trading name of Brewer & Company Limited** *(C W Brewer)* 1 Abbotsleigh House, 3 Dalton Road, EASTBOURNE, EAST SUSSEX, BN20 7NP.

ⒻⒶ**Brewers** *(A M Skilton)* Bourne House, Queen Street, Gomshall, GUILDFORD, SURREY, GU5 9LY.

★**Brewster & Brown** *(I Robertson)* 129 New Bridge Street, NEWCASTLE UPON TYNE, NE1 2SW.

ⓅⒶ**Brewster & Co, trading name of Brewster & Co (NE) Ltd** *(C T Brewster)* 5a Station Terrace, EAST BOLDON, TYNE AND WEAR, NE36 0LJ.

Brian a Braiden ACA *(B A Braiden)* 59 Lansdowne Place, HOVE, EAST SUSSEX, BN3 1FL.

ⒻⓅⒶ**Brian Bell Meyer & Co, trading name of Brian Bell Meyer & Co Limited** *(A G Howell, P J H Meyer)* Plymouth Chambers, 23 Bartlett Street, CAERPHILLY, MID GLAMORGAN, CF83 1JS.

Brian Ben Camissar & Co *(B B Camissar)* 38 Hendon Lane, LONDON, N3 1TT.

ⓅⒶ**Brian Berg Limited** *(B Berg)* Berg Kaprow Lewis LLP, 35 Ballards Lane, LONDON, N3 1XW.

Brian Bewick, trading name of B.N. Bewick *(B N Bewick)* 5 Radway Close, Whiteholme, THORNTON-CLEVELEYS, FY5 3EZ. and at BLACKPOOL

Brian Carter & Co *(B Carter)* River House, 6 Firs Path, LEIGHTON BUZZARD, BEDFORDSHIRE, LU7 3JG.

Brian Clarke *(B Clarke)* 5 Downsway, ORPINGTON, BR6 9NU.

Brian Cohen *(B J Cohen)* 88 Camden Road, LONDON, NW1 9EA.

★**Brian Cook Associates** *(B T Cook)* Marine House, 151 Western Road, HAYWARDS HEATH, WEST SUSSEX, RH16 3LH.

Brian Cox & Co *(B J Cox)* Crown Buildings, 18 Market Hill, CHATTERIS, PE16 6BA.

Brian D Jones *(B D Jones)* 59 Little Sutton Lane, SUTTON COLDFIELD, WEST MIDLANDS, B75 6SJ.

Brian D. Hogg *(B D Hogg)* Brookside, Walgrave Road, Hannington, NORTHAMPTON, NN6 9SX.

Brian D. Watson *(B D Watson)* 1A Windsor Sq, EXMOUTH, EX8 1JU.

Brian Drake & Co *(B Drake)* The Counting House, Forest Road, New Ollerton, NEWARK, NG22 9QS.

Brian E Hawthorn *(B E Hawthorn)* 12 Cotham Road, BRISTOL, BS6 6DR.

Brian E Ray *(B E Ray)* 30 Old Sneed Avenue, Stoke Bishop, BRISTOL, BS9 1SE.

Ⓟ**Brian Elwick and Co Limited** *(B Elwick)* 35 Mill Road, Swanland, NORTH FERRIBY, NORTH HUMBERSIDE, HU14 3PJ.

Brian G. Neale *(B G Neale)* Was-Thatched, Hambleton, OAKHAM, LE15 8TH.

Brian Harris & Co *(B E Harris)* Grosvenor Gardens House, 35-37 Grosvenor Gardens, LONDON, SW1W 0BS.

ⓅⒶ**Brian J Wolkind Limited** *(B J Wolkind)* Berg Kaprow Lewis LLP, 35 Ballards Lane, LONDON, N3 1XW.

Brian James *(B R James)* 45 Wide Bargate, BOSTON, PE21 6SH.

ⓉⓅⒶ**Brian Kelsey & Co Limited** *(B Kelsey)* 7A Court Street, FAVERSHAM, KENT, ME13 7AN.

Ⓕ**Brian Lewis FCA** *(B J Lewis)* 146 Queens Road, WATFORD, WD17 2NX.

Brian Lloyd *(B Lloyd)* Holly Cottage, Millington Lane, Millington, ALTRINCHAM, WA14 3RR.

Ⓟ**Brian M Parrott** *(B M Parrott)* Stonecroft, Beadon Road, SALCOMBE, TQ8 8LU.

Brian Meakin *(B Meakin)* Ward Cottage, 83 Main Street, Papplewick, NOTTINGHAM, NG15 8FE.

ⓉⒻⓅⒶ**Brian Paul Limited** *(B.M. O'Leary, P J Phillips)* Chase Green House, 42 Chase Side, ENFIELD, MIDDLESEX, EN2 6NF.

Brian Payne & Company *(B P Payne)* The Old Coach House, R/O 89-91 Mildmay Road, CHELMSFORD, CM1 0DS.

Brian Perkins FCA *(B K Perkins)* 11 Ilmington Close, Hatton Park, WARWICK, CV35 7TL.

Brian Roberts & Co *(B J Roberts)* 7/8 Raleigh Walk, Brigantine Place, CARDIFF, CF10 4LN.

Brian T. Williams *(B T Williams)* 11 Westminster Drive, Cyncoed, CARDIFF, CF23 6RD.

Brian Taylor FCA *(B Taylor)* 4 Lee Lane, Lumbutts, TODMORDEN, OL14 6HS.

Brian Thurlbeck *(E B Thurlbeck)* Beechmount, 33 Beechwood Terrace, SUNDERLAND, SR2 7LY.

Brian W. Howard *(B W Howard)* Argel Vean, Parknoweth, Churchtown Cury, HELSTON, CORNWALL, TR12 7BW.

Ⓟ**Brian Ziff Limited** *(B N Ziff)* 3 Lakeland Crescent, LEEDS, LS17 7PS.

Briant, Elmore & Co. *(D J Elmore)* 155 Station Road, Histon, Impington, CAMBRIDGE, CB24 9NP.

ⓉⒻⒶ**Briants** *(T A C Briant)* Maritime House, Discovery Quay, FALMOUTH, CORNWALL, TR11 3XA.

Ⓟ**Bridge Accountancy Ltd** *(A D Chappell)* Westfield House, Bratton Road, WESTBURY, WILTSHIRE, BA13 3EP.

Ⓟ**Bridge Accounting Limited** *(S Miller)* 1 The Old Brushworks, 56 Pickwick Road, CORSHAM, WILTSHIRE, SN13 9BX.

Bridge Business Recovery, trading name of Bridge Business Recovery LLP *(J P Bradney)* 3rd Floor, 39-45 Shaftesbury Avenue, LONDON, W1D 6LA. and at BEDFORD, TUNBRIDGE WELLS

Ⓟ**Bridge Renewables Ltd** *(N J R Mullan)* 19 St Gabriels Manor, 25 Cormont Road, LONDON, SE5 9RH.

Ⓕ**Bridgeman** *(P Bridgeman)* Dell House, Lower Buckland Road, LYMINGTON, HAMPSHIRE, SO41 9DS.

Bridger, Smart & Co. *(R C Smart)* Unitek House, Churchfield Road, Chalfont St. Peter, GERRARDS CROSS, BUCKINGHAMSHIRE, SL9 9EW.

Ⓟ**Brieley Grimsdell Ltd** *(H M Grimsdell)* 12 James Street, Kimberley, NOTTINGHAM, NG16 2LP.

Bright Accounts & Tax, Longleys, trading names of Longley & Co *(M R Longley)* 81 Melton Road, West Bridgford, NOTTINGHAM, NG2 6EN.

Ⓟ**Bright Blue Skies Limited** *(L C Williams)* 41 Cambridge Road, LONDON, E11 2PL.

★ⓉⓅⒶ**Bright Brown, trading name of Bright Brown Limited** *(R Barton, R B Fokias, M G Russell, F T Seabourne)* Exchange House, St. Cross Lane, NEWPORT, ISLE OF WIGHT, PO30 5BZ.

ⓉⒻⒶ**Bright Grahame Murray** *(M Colclough, M C N Cole, L A Delamere, R L Feld, K L Levine, A Miraj, R K Moore, P A Rodney, A P Rotman, J D C Wakefield)* 131 Edgware Road, LONDON, W2 2AP.

ⓉⒶ**Bright Partnership** *(M P Gillibrand, M G Senior)* Yarmouth House, Trident Business Park, Daten Avenue, Birchwood, WARRINGTON, WA3 6BX.

Ⓟ**Bright Star Accounting Limited** *(D J Strike)* 3 Branksome Park House, Branksome Business Park, Bourne Valley Road, POOLE, DORSET, BH12 1ED.

Brightling & Co *(N L Brightling)* Vine Hall Farm, Bethersden, ASHFORD, KENT, TN26 3JY.

Brij K Sharma *(B K Sharma)* 175 Old Surrey Lane, RICHMOND HILL L4K 2P5, ON, CANADA.

ⓅⒶ**Brindley Goldstein Ltd** *(C H Goldstein)* 103 High Street, WALTHAM CROSS, EN8 7AN.

ⓅⒶ**Brindley Millen, trading name of Brindley Millen Limited** *(M W Brindley, G K Jacob)* 167 Turners Hill, Cheshunt, WALTHAM CROSS, HERTFORDSHIRE, EN8 9BH.

★ⓉⓅⒶ**Brindleys, trading name of Brindleys Limited** *(S C Chumber, S Sumar)* 2 Wheeleys Road, Edgbaston, BIRMINGHAM, B15 2LD.

Brine & Co *(J Brine)* PO Box 6210, LEIGHTON BUZZARD, BEDFORDSHIRE, LU7 0ZN.

Brinsmead Maden *(C Maden)* The Loft House, Meadow Lane, Hamble, SOUTHAMPTON, SO31 4RB.

ⒻⓅ**Bristol Tax Shop, Lloydbottoms, trading names of Lloydbottoms Limited** *(A M Watson)* 118 High Street, Staple Hill, BRISTOL, BS16 5HH.

Briston Johnson & Co *(E C Johnson)* 8 Carrington Avenue, COTTINGHAM, HU16 4DU.

ⓉⒻⒶ**Bristow Burrell** *(G W Hetherington, W B D Sleap, R Spicer)* 4 Riverview, Walnut Tree Close, GUILDFORD, GU1 4UX.

Ⓐ**Bristow Still** *(I Cleaver, D R Still)* 39 Sackville Road, HOVE, BN3 3WD.

Ⓟ**Brite Accounting Limited** *(K E Tribe)* 26 St. Nicholas Road, Copmanthorpe, YORK, YO23 3UX.

Ⓐ**Britt & Keehan** *(M Britt, J Keehan)* 33 Grimwade Avenue, CROYDON, CR0 5DJ.

Britton & Co *(D O Britton)* 1 Chatsworth Manor, Ladybrook Road, Bramhall, STOCKPORT, CHESHIRE, SK7 3NB.

Ⓟ**Broad Reach Partnership Limited** *(C J Burr)* 49 High Street, West Mersea, COLCHESTER, CO5 8JE.

★ⒻⓅⒶ**Broadhead Peel Rhodes, trading name of Broadhead Peel Rhodes Ltd** *(M R Andrews, R P Brook)* 27a Lidget Hill, PUDSEY, WEST YORKSHIRE, LS28 7LG. and at LEEDS

Ⓟ**Broadside Business Services Limited** *(R S Condon, D A Dickinson)* Hawkstone House, Portland Mews, Portland Street, LEAMINGTON SPA, WARWICKSHIRE, CV32 5HD.

Ⓟ**Broadsides, Francis Webbs, trading names of Broadsides Limited** *(R S Condon, D A Dickinson)* Hawkstone House, Portland Mews, Portland Street, LEAMINGTON SPA, WARWICKSHIRE, CV32 5HD. and at COVENTRY

Ⓟ**Broadthunder Accounting Limited** *(C E Lucas)* 164 Walkden Road, Worsley, MANCHESTER CENTER, M28 7DP.

Broadway & Co *(A B Broadway)* Nadder House, Lower Road, Bemerton, SALISBURY, SP2 9NB.

Ⓟ**Brockhurst Davies Limited** *(A J Bentley, N H Brockhurst, J E Davies)* 11 The Office Village, North Road, LOUGHBOROUGH, LEICESTERSHIRE, LE11 1QJ.

Ⓕ**Brodericks** *(J M Broderick)* 1 Heslington Court, Heslington, YORK, YO10 5EX.

Ⓟ**Brodericks GBC, trading name of Axholme Associates Limited** *(S Garbutt)* Melbourne House, 27 Thorne Road, DONCASTER, SOUTH YORKSHIRE, DN1 2EZ.

Ⓕ**Brody Lee Kershaw & Co** *(L S Goldich, L S Kershaw, G D Lee)* 2nd Floor, Hanover House, 30-32 Charlotte Street, MANCHESTER, M1 4EX.

ⒻⓅ**Brody Lee Kershaw Ltd** *(L S Goldich, L S Kershaw, G D Lee)* 2nd Floor, Hanover House, 30-32 Charlotte Street, MANCHESTER, M1 4EX.

ⓉⒻⓅⒶ**Bromhead, trading name of Bromhead Limited** *(L Curtis, J A Groves, P J B Hamon)* Harscombe House, 1 Darklake View, Estover, PLYMOUTH, PL6 7TL.

ⒻⓅⒶ**Bromley Clackett, trading name of Bromley Clackett Limited** *(S R S Bromley, L D Clackett)* 76 Aldwick Road, BOGNOR REGIS, WEST SUSSEX, PO21 2PE.

★ⓉⒻⒶ**Bronsens** *(P J Burton, B R Sennett)* 6 Langdale Court, WITNEY, OXFORDSHIRE, OX28 6FG. and at CHIPPING NORTON

Ⓟ**Brookes & Company, trading name of Brookes & Company(UK) Limited** *(C A Barker)* Trafalgar House, Fullbridge, MALDON, ESSEX, CM9 4LE.

ⓅⒶ**Brookes O'Hara Limited** *(A Brookes)* Old Hall Farmhouse, Barthomley, CREWE, CHESHIRE, CW2 5PE.

Ⓟ**Brookes Sivyer Limited** *(M A Sivyer)* The Old Chapel, High Street, East Hoathly, LEWES, EAST SUSSEX, BN8 6DR.

Ⓟ**Brookes Stephens, trading name of LTS Consulting Limited** *(L T Stephens)* New Media House, Davidson Road, LICHFIELD, STAFFORDSHIRE, WS14 9DU.

Ⓐ**Brookfield & Co** *(J A Brookfield)* 52 Church Road, Crystal Palace, LONDON, SE19 2EZ.

ⓉⒻⓅⒶ**Brooking Ruse & Co, trading name of Brooking Ruse & Co Limited** *(L D Cox, E Knight, R D Orr, M Paphitis)* 3 Beaconsfield Road, WESTON-SUPER-MARE, SOMERSET, BS23 1YE. and at BRISTOL

★ⓉⒻⒶ**Brooks & Co** *(S Araniyasundaran, K J Dixon, M J Harding)* Hampton House, High Street, EAST GRINSTEAD, WEST SUSSEX, RH19 3AW. and at SUTTON

Ⓐ**Brooks & Co** *(G R Brooks)* 9A Leicester Road, Blaby, LEICESTER, LE8 4GR.

Brooks & Co *(M R Goldman)* 27 Stanley Road, SALFORD, M7 4FR.

★**Brooks & Jeal** *(N M Brooks)* Eddystone Road, WADEBRIDGE, CORNWALL, PL27 7AL.

Ⓐ**Brooks Green** *(R Aarons, D J Harris)* Abbey House, 342 Regents Park Rd, LONDON, N3 2LJ.

Ⓟ**Brooks Johnson, trading name of Brooks Johnson Consultancy Services Limited** *(M B Brooks)* Northumberland House, Drake Avenue, STAINES, MIDDLESEX, TW18 2AP.

★Ⓕ**Brooks Mayfield** *(W Oates, N W Turner, A J Worrall)* 12 Bridgford Road, West Bridgford, NOTTINGHAM, NG2 6AB.

ⓅⒶ**Brooks Mayfield Audit Limited** *(W Oates, N W Turner, A J Worrall)* 12 Bridgford Road, West Bridgford, NOTTINGHAM, NG2 6AB.

Ⓟ**Brookson Projects Ltd** *(M J Hesketh)* Brunel House, 340 Firecrest Court, Centre Park, WARRINGTON, WA1 1RG.

Ⓟ**Brookson, trading name of Brookson Limited** *(M J Hesketh)* Brunel House, 340 Firecrest Court, Centre Park, WARRINGTON, WA1 1RG.

ⓉⒻⓅⒶ**Broomfield & Alexander, trading name of Broomfield & Alexander Limited** *(S Case, D L George, M G Jones, R S Preece, L J Reed, J F Spencer, I R Thomas)* Ty Derw, Lime Tree Court, Cardiff Gate Business Park, CARDIFF, CF23 8AB. and at NEWPORT, SWANSEA

Ⓟ**Brooms, trading name of Brooms Professional Services Limited** *(S I Shah)* Broom House, 39-43 London Road, Hadleigh, BENFLEET, ESSEX, SS7 2QL.

ⓉⓅ**Brosnans, trading name of Brosnans Limited** *(A J Brosnan, B J Brosnan)* Birkby House, Bailiff Bridge, BRIGHOUSE, WEST YORKSHIRE, HD6 4JJ. and at TODMORDEN

★**Brough Kirkman** *(C J Wright)* 8 High Skellgate, RIPON, NORTH YORKSHIRE, HG4 1BA.

ⓉⒻⒶ**Brown & Batts LLP** *(F Khan, Z U Khan)* 25-29 Harper Road, LONDON, SE1 6AW.

Brown & Co *(S J Blamire-Brown)* Maple House, Bayshill Road, CHELTENHAM, GLOUCESTERSHIRE, GL50 3AW.

ⓅⒶ**Brown & Co Audit Ltd** *(P A Brown, C I Cook)* Brown & Co House, 4 High Street, Brasted, WESTERHAM, KENT, TN16 1JA. and at BASILDON

★Ⓣ**Brown & Co, trading name of Brown & Co LLP** *(P A Brown, C I Cook)* 2 Lords Court, Cricketers Way, BASILDON, ESSEX, SS13 1SS. and at WESTERHAM

ⓉⓅ**Brown & Lonsdale, Denisons, Martindale Kingham, trading names of Kingham Accountancy Ltd** *(P Kingham, N Y S Liu)* Kingham Chambers, 3-5 Nelson Street, LIVERPOOL, L1 5DW. and at BIRKENHEAD, LEYLAND, ST. HELENS

Ⓟ**Brown Accountants Ltd** *(R S S Brown)* 1 High Street, Roydon, HARLOW, ESSEX, CM19 5HJ.

★ⓉⒻⒶ**Brown Butler** *(J W Brear, D Cross, S J Hornshaw, R M Solyom, J R White)* Leigh House, 28-32 St Paul's Street, LEEDS, LS1 2JT.

Brown McLeod & Berrie *(J D Berrie)* 12 Spring Lane, Bottisham, CAMBRIDGE, CB25 9BL.

ⓉⓅ**Brown McLeod Limited** *(J Roddison, P P Wilson)* 51 Clarkegrove Road, SHEFFIELD, SOUTH YORKSHIRE, S10 2NH. and at LONDON

ⓉⒻⒶ**Brown Peet & Tilly, trading name of Barker Hibbert & Co** *(C J Brockwell, R S Clarke)* 133 Cherry Orchard Road, CROYDON, CR0 6BE.

★ⒻⓅ**Brown Russell, trading name of Brown Russell Ltd** *(M J Russell)* 71a and 71c High Street, HEATHFIELD, EAST SUSSEX, TN21 8HU. and at ST. LEONARDS-ON-SEA

★ⓉⓅⒶ**Browne Craine & Co, trading name of Browne Craine Associates Limited** *(B D Bielich, D P Craine, C Mitchell, M Singer)* Burleigh Manor, Peel Road, Douglas, ISLE OF MAN, IM1 5EP.

Ⓐ**Browning Hotchkiss & Partners** *(C R Browning, A J Hotchkiss)* Buckhurst Chambers, Coppid Beech Hill, London Road, WOKINGHAM, RG40 1PD.

Ⓟ**Brownlows Accountants, trading name of Brownlow Consulting Limited** *(S Brownlow)* 428 Preston Old Road, Cherry Tree, BLACKBURN, BB2 5LP.

Ⓐ**Browns** *(J Brown)* 42 Greenhaugh, West Moor, NEWCASTLE UPON TYNE, NE12 7WA.

Ⓟ**Browns Accountancy & Taxation Ltd** *(L E Brown)* Rowan Cottage, 74 Hailey Road, WITNEY, OXFORDSHIRE, OX28 1HF.

Bruce Burford *(B W Burford)* 8 Beechfield Road, BROMLEY, BR1 3BU.

Ⓕ**Bruce M.L. Gray** *(B M L Gray)* Suite 122, Airport House, Purley Way, CROYDON, CR0 0XZ.

ⓅⒶ**Bruce Morley Limited** *(B K Morley)* TWP Accounting LLP, The Old Rectory, Church Street, WEYBRIDGE, SURREY, KT13 8DE.

Ⓟ**Bruce Roberts & Co Limited** *(B S S Roberts)* 18 Ruabon Road, WREXHAM, LL13 7PB.

Bruce Sutherland & Co *(J A Nelder, B W Sutherland)* Moreton House, MORETON-IN-MARSH, GL56 0LH.

★Ⓕ**Bruce Sutherland & Co** *(J A Nelder, B W Sutherland)* Moreton House, MORETON-IN-MARSH, GL56 0LH.

ⓉⒻⓅⒶ**Bruch & Co Limited** *(D E Bruch)* 1 School Lane, WISBECH, CAMBRIDGESHIRE, PE13 1AW.

Ⓟ**Brunswick Trustees Limited** *(R W J Brown, M R Wrigglesworth)* Suite 26 Century Buildings, Brunswick Business Park, Tower Street, LIVERPOOL, L3 4BJ.

▽ⓉⒻⒶ**Bruton Charles** *(J C R Lawrence-Archer, K A Roberts)* The Coach House, Greys Green Business Centre, Rotherfield Greys, HENLEY-ON-THAMES, OXFORDSHIRE, RG9 4QG.

★ⓉⒶ**Bryan and Ridge** *(R G Norfolk, E M Ridge, N B Ridge)* The Gatehouse, 2 Devonhurst Place, Heathfield Terrace, LONDON, W4 4JD.

ⒻⓅⒶ**Bryan Grey & Co, trading name of Bryan Grey & Co Limited** *(B W Grey)* Broadfield House, 18 Broadfield Road, SHEFFIELD, S8 0XJ.

Bryan Jones *(B Jones)* 5 Longmans Lane, COTTINGHAM, NORTH HUMBERSIDE, HU16 4EA.

Bryan K H Rogers *(B K H Rogers)* 1 Cranleigh Gardens, Sanderstead, SOUTH CROYDON, Surrey, CR2 9LD.

★Ⓣ**Bryan Redhead & Co** *(B B Redhead)* Market Street, BROUGHTON-IN-FURNESS, LA20 6HP.

Bryant & Co *(L M Bryant)* 3 Burcott Gardens, New Haw, ADDLESTONE, KT15 2DE.

Ⓐ**Bryant & Co** *(P G Bryant)* 35 Ashurst Road, Ash Vale, ALDERSHOT, HAMPSHIRE, GU12 5AF.

Ⓟ**Bryant & Co, trading name of Bryant & Co Limited** *(D J Bryant)* North Houghton Mill, North Houghton, STOCKBRIDGE, HAMPSHIRE, SO20 6LF.

Bryant, Mayl & Co *(G R Bryant)* 24 South Street, VALLETTA VLT 1102, MALTA.

Ⓐ**Bryars & Co.** *(M J Bryars)* Cloverfield, Houghton Down, STOCKBRIDGE, SO20 6JR.

Bryden & Co *(K A Bryden)* 17 Mornington Road, SALE, M33 2DA.

ⓉⒶ**BRYDEN JOHNSON** *(G R Bull, N F K Johnson)* Kings Parade, Lower Coombe Street, CROYDON, CR0 1AA.

Ⓟ**Bryden Johnson Payroll Services Limited** *(G R Bull, N F K Johnson)* Kings Parade, Lower Coombe Street, CROYDON, CR0 1AA.

Brydone & Co *(C M Brydone)* 65 Meersbrook Road, SHEFFIELD, S8 9HU.

Bryn Griffith *(B J Griffith)* 24 Carleton Road, Poynton, STOCKPORT, CHESHIRE, SK12 1TL.

Bryony Gaskell Accountancy Services *(B Gaskell)* Monteverde, Stocks Road, Alfrick, WORCESTER, WR6 5HD.

★ⓉⒶ**BSG Valentine** *(A M Athanasiou, M Benson, D S Burke, N R Colaco, M Gandz, R Gulrajani, D L Lee, M Nicolaou, N Patel, S C Poluck, N Strong)* Lynton House, 7/12 Tavistock Square, LONDON, WC1H 9BQ.

ⓅⒶ**BSN Associates Holdings Limited** *(H E Justice, S M Richards)* 3b Swallowfield Courtyard, Wolverhampton Road, OLDBURY, WEST MIDLANDS, B69 2JG.

ⓉⒻⓅⒶ**BSN, trading name of BSN Associates Limited** *(H E Justice, S M Richards)* 3b Swallowfield Courtyard, Wolverhampton Road, OLDBURY, WEST MIDLANDS, B69 2JG.

ⓉⒻⒶ**BSR Bespoke** *(K J R Buckland, N F Looseley, A Roberts)* Linden House, Linden Close, TUNBRIDGE WELLS, KENT, TN4 8HH.

ⓉⒻⓅⒶ**BSR Bespoke Limited** *(P R Chewter, N Deverson, N F Looseley, P K Matthews)* Hilden Park House, 79 Tonbridge Road, Hildenborough, TONBRIDGE, KENT, TN11 9BH.

★Ⓟ**BSS & Co, trading name of BSS & Co (Bridgnorth) Limited** *(C Astbury)* 12 Northgate, BRIDGNORTH, SHROPSHIRE, WV16 4ER.

ⓅⒶ**BSS Associates Limited** *(A R J Cartwright, F H Khundkar)* Gresham House, 116 Sussex Gardens, LONDON, W2 1UA.

BT Wong & Co *(B T Wong)* Unit A 6/F Rammon House, 101 Sai Yeung Choi Street, MONG KOK, KOWLOON, HONG KONG SAR.

Ⓕ**BTG Corporate Finance, trading name of BTG Financial Consulting LLP** *(C J Appleby, J M Barber, S Bone, D Irwin, I J Lownes, R E Penn-Newman, D R Wilton)* 340 Deansgate, MANCHESTER, M3 4LY. and at BIRMINGHAM, LEEDS, LONDON, NEWCASTLE UPON TYNE, SOUTHAMPTON

Ⓣ**BTG Tax LLP** *(L D Bard)* 11 Haymarket, LONDON, SW1Y 4BP.

ⓉⒻⓅ**BTP Associates, trading name of BTP Associates Limited** *(H L Baker, R D Taylor)* 84-86 High Street, MERTHYR TYDFIL, MID GLAMORGAN, CF47 8UG.

Ⓟ**BTP Business Ltd** *(H L Baker, R D Taylor)* 84-86 High Street, MERTHYR TYDFIL, MID GLAMORGAN, CF47 8UG.

BTR Accountancy *(B T Rajan)* 2 Hornsby Square, Southfields Business Park, BASILDON, ESSEX, SS15 6SD.

ⓉⒻⒶ**BTW, trading name of Bell Tindle Williamson LLP** *(J Bell, E J Hartshorne-Ferguson, M Tindle, K J Williamson)* The Old Post Office, 63 Saville Street, NORTH SHIELDS, TYNE AND WEAR, NE30 1AY.

Ⓟ**BTW, trading name of Bell Tindle Williamson Services Limited** *(J Bell, E J Hartshorne-Ferguson, M Tindle, K J Williamson)* The Old Post Office, 63 Saville Street, NORTH SHIELDS, TYNE AND WEAR, NE30 1AY.

Ⓟ**Buchanan Bonds Limited** *(G B Bonds)* 39 Braehead Crescent, STONEHAVEN, KINCARDINESHIRE, AB39 2PP.

Buchhaltungsburo Rabea Leake *(R I Leake)* Kleinburgwedeler Str. 6B, 30938 BURGWEDEL, GERMANY.

Buchlers LLP *(D J Buchler)* 6 Grosvenor Street, LONDON, W1K 4PZ. and at TUNBRIDGE WELLS

ⒻⓅ**Buckingham Corporate Finance Limited** *(S S Bennett, I D Leaman)* 57A Catherine Place, LONDON, SW1E 6DY.

Ⓟ**Buckinghams, trading name of Buckinghams (Accountants) Ltd** *(R G C Kay)* 7 The Cottages, Biddlesden, BRACKLEY, NORTHAMPTONSHIRE, NN13 5TR.

ⓅⒶ**Buckler Spencer, trading name of Buckler Spencer Limited** *(J M Buckler, R J Spencer, T J Spencer)* Old Police Station, Church Street, SWADLINCOTE, DERBYSHIRE, DE11 8LN. and at BURTON-ON-TRENT

ⒻⒶ**Buckley Watson** *(S F Watson)* 57a The Broadway, LEIGH-ON-SEA, SS9 1PE.

Buckleys *(M Moore)* Marshall House, 124 Middleton Road, MORDEN, SURREY, SM4 6RW.

Bucksbookkeeper, Porters Chartered Accountants, trading names of Porters *(J Porter)* 127 Fairacres, Prestwood, GREAT MISSENDEN, BUCKINGHAMSHIRE, HP16 0LF.

ⒻⓅⒶ**Buffery & Co, trading name of Buffery & Co Ltd** *(M C Buffery)* 25 Hart Street, HENLEY-ON-THAMES, OXFORDSHIRE, RG9 2AR.

Bukhari & Co *(S F H Bukhari)* 389 Wilbraham Road, Chorlton Cum Hardy, MANCHESTER, M21 0UT.

ⓉⒻⒶ**Bulcock & Co** *(M J Bulcock)* 10 The Bull Ring, NORTHWICH, CW9 5BS.

★ⒻⒶ**Bulley Davey** *(A R Atkins, M A Burden, D R Webb)* 4 Cyrus Way, Cygnet Park, Hampton, PETERBOROUGH, PE7 8HP. and at HUNTINGDON, MELTON MOWBRAY, SPALDING, WISBECH

Ⓣ**Bulley Davey & Co** *(A R Atkins, M A Burden, D R Webb)* 6 North Street, Oundle, PETERBOROUGH, PE8 4AL. and at HUNTINGDON, SPALDING, WISBECH

ⓉⒻⒶ**Bullimores** *(G A Luscombe)* 50 South Street, SOUTH MOLTON, DEVON, EX36 4AG.

ⓉⒻⒶ**Bullimores, trading name of Bullimores LLP** *(N Boot, M J Brett, T Edwards)* Old Printers Yard, 156 South Street, DORKING, SURREY, RH4 2HF.

ⒻⓅ**Bunting & Co, trading name of Bunting Accountants Limited** *(D A Bunting, V J Checkley)* 5 Orchard Close, Wheatley, OXFORD, OX33 1US. and at FARINGDON

Ⓐ**Burchill & Co** *(G R Birditt)* Reed House, 16 High Street, West Wratting, CAMBRIDGE, CB21 5LU.

Ⓐ**Burford and Partners LLP** *(M D V Beauclerk, D J Colson)* Suite 75, London Fruit Exchange, Brushfield Street, LONDON, E1 6EP.

ⓅⒶ**Burge Accountancy, trading name of Burge Accountancy Limited** *(N M Burge)* Whitecroft House, Hatton Hill, WINDLESHAM, SURREY, GU20 6AB.

★ⓉⒻⒶ**Burgess Hodgson** *(P Gatland, K Jones, K C May, A R Miles, C S Reid, C D Slater, R C Stewart, M P Sutton, S M Sutton)* Camburgh House, 27 New Dover Road, CANTERBURY, CT1 3DN.

Ⓟ**Burgin & Co, trading name of D Burgin Limited** *(A D Burgin)* The Little Grey House, 8 Melton Road, Langham, OAKHAM, RUTLAND, LE15 7JN. and at GRANTHAM

★ⓉⒻⒶ**Burgis & Bullock** *(A K Chadaway, S J Chapman, T J Day, J S W Farnell, G M Howard, S Littlejohns)* 2 Chapel Court, Holly Walk, LEAMINGTON SPA, CV32 4YS. and at NUNEATON, RUGBY

ⒻⓅ**Burgis & Bullock Corporate Finance Ltd** *(S J Chapman, J S W Farnell, G M Howard)* 2 Chapel Court, Holly Walk, LEAMINGTON SPA, CV32 4YS.

★ⒻⒶ**Burke Wallace** *(P A Wallace)* 146 High Street, HOLYWOOD, COUNTY DOWN, BT18 9HS.

★Ⓐ**Burleys (Midlands) LLP** *(S A Tanna)* Unit 9 St Matthew's Business Centre, Gower Street, LEICESTER, LEICESTERSHIRE, LE1 3LJ.

ⓅⒶ**Burlinson Shaw & Co, trading name of Accountancy Services (Batley) Limited** *(J H Shaw)* 21 Henrietta Street, Batley, BATLEY, WEST YORKSHIRE, WF17 5DN.

ⓉⒻⒶ**Burman & Co** *(D R Burman, N Farmer)* Brunswick Hse, Birmingham Rd, REDDITCH, B97 6DY.

ⓅⒶ**Burnley & Evans, trading name of Burnley & Evans Limited** *(R M Pritchard)* 7 Centre Court, Vine Lane, HALESOWEN, WEST MIDLANDS, B63 3EB.

ⓉⒻⒶ**Burns Waring** *(S J T Askew, R J Calderwood)* Roper Yard, Roper Road, CANTERBURY, CT2 7EX.

ⒻⓅ**Burns Waring, trading name of Burns Waring Ltd** *(S J T Askew, R J Calderwood)* Denning House, 1 London Road, MAIDSTONE, KENT, ME16 8HS. and at CANTERBURY

ⒻⓅ**Burnside, trading name of Burnside (Bristol) Limited** *(S A Burnside)* 8 Pipe Lane, St. Augustines, BRISTOL, BS1 5AJ.

Burr Pilger & Mayer LLP *(K J Dansie)* 110 Stony Point Road, Suite 210, SANTA ROSA, CA 95401, UNITED STATES.

Ⓟ**Burrells Accountancy Limited** *(S J Burrell)* Jubilee House, Jubilee Court, Dersingham, KING'S LYNN, PE31 6HH.

ⒻⓅⒶ**Burrow & Crowe Limited** *(M A Crowe)* 8-9 Feast Field, Horsforth, LEEDS, LS18 4TJ.

Ⓟ**Burrowmoor Consulting Limited** *(J Bradshaw)* 200 Broadway, PETERBOROUGH, PE1 4DT.

ⒻⓅⒶ**Burrows Scarborough, trading name of Burrows Scarborough Silk Limited** *(N J Burrows, M W Dockerty)* Sovereign House, 12 Warwick Street, Earlsdon, COVENTRY, CV5 6ET.

ⒻⒶ**Burton & Co** *(R Feather, I T Phillips, A Pope)* Sovereign House, Bradford Road, Riddlesden, KEIGHLEY, BD20 5EW.

Ⓟ**Burton Accountancy Services Limited** *(D J Wagstaff)* 26 Little Burton West, BURTON-ON-TRENT, STAFFORDSHIRE, DE14 1PP.

Ⓟ**Burton Davy, trading name of Lund Consulting Ltd** *(D J Lund)* Silverdale Suite, Clawthorpe Hall Business Centre, Burton in Kendal, CARNFORTH, LANCASHIRE, LA6 1NU.

ⓉⒻⒶ**Burton Sweet** *(G H Cole, N M Kingston)* Pembroke House, 15 Pembroke Road, Clifton, BRISTOL, BS8 3BA. and at SHEPTON MALLET, WESTON-SUPER-MARE

ⒻⓅⒶ**Burton Sweet, trading name of Burton Sweet Limited** *(G H Cole, N M Kingston)* Prospect House, 5 May Lane, DURSLEY, GLOUCESTERSHIRE, GL11 4JH. and at GLOUCESTER

Ⓟ**Burwood (Pinner) Ltd** *(A J Peters)* 17 Little Moss Lane, PINNER, MIDDLESEX, HA5 3BA. and at NORTHWOOD

★Ⓣ**Busbys** *(D J R Meredith)* Unit 7, Pickhill Business Centre, Smallhythe Road, TENTERDEN, KENT, TN30 7LZ.

ⓉⒻⒶ**Bush & Co** *(N Bamber, R P Carne, I E Powell, S Truran)* 2 Barnfield Crescent, EXETER, EX1 1QT.

ⓉⓅⒶ**Bushells, trading name of Robert Alice Limited** *(P W Bushell)* 6 Victoria Avenue, HARROGATE, NORTH YORKSHIRE, HG1 1ED.

ⓅⒶ**Business & Risk Solutions, trading name of Business & Risk Solutions Limited** *(M G Brindley)* Forge House, Stodmarsh Road, CANTERBURY, KENT, CT3 4AG.

Ⓟ**Business & Tax Solutions Limited** *(G Roberts)* Watergate House, 85 Watergate Street, CHESTER, CH1 2LF.

Ⓟ**Business Advantage Limited** *(A L Bamforth, D Pettinger)* Douglas House, 24 Bridge Street, Slaithwaite, HUDDERSFIELD, HD7 5JN.

Ⓟ**Business and Tax Cures Limited** *(K R Lewis)* 22 Gelliwastad Road, PONTYPRIDD, MID GLAMORGAN, CF37 2BW.

Ⓟ**Business Builders, trading name of Business Builders (UK) Limited** *(J Y S Hall)* Omnia One, 125 Queen Street, SHEFFIELD, S1 2DU.

Business Consultancy Services *(S Waller)* 1st Floor, 2c St Mary's Green, Front Street, Whickham, NEWCASTLE UPON TYNE, NE16 4DN.

ⒻⓅ**Business Equilibrium Solutions Limited** *(R S Brown, S A Ferguson)* Business Equilibrium Ltd, 5 Straiton View, Straiton, LOANHEAD, MIDLOTHIAN, EH20 9QZ.

Business Experts *(T M Trainer)* 40 Womersley Road, LONDON, N8 9AN.

ⓉⒻⓅⒶ**Business Focus & Systems Limited** *(N Firth, A M Massarella)* 4 Chevin Mill, Leeds Road, OTLEY, WEST YORKSHIRE, LS21 1BT.

Ⓟ**Business Information Systems, trading name of Bizis Limited** *(P W Bates)* 11 Upper Church Park, Mumbles, SWANSEA, SA3 4DD.

Ⓠ**Business Interface Ltd** *(P K Crumpton)* 7 Garden Court, Wheathampstead, ST.ALBANS, AL4 8RE.

Ⓟ**Business Issue Solutions Ltd** *(M R Aldridge)* 2A Crown Street, Redbourn, ST. ALBANS, HERTFORDSHIRE, AL3 7JX.

Ⓟ**Business Matters (UK) Ltd** *(M A Clark, R F John, P T Minchell)* Chancery House, St. Nicholas Way, SUTTON, SURREY, SM1 1JB.

Ⓟ**Business Nurture, trading name of Business Nurture Limited** *(K L Engel)* 54 Farmleigh Gardens, Great Sankey, WARRINGTON, WA5 3FA.

ⓉⒻⓅⒶ**Business Orchard, trading name of The Business Orchard Consultancy Limited** *(H T Rissen)* 3a Chestnut House, Farm Close, Shenley, RADLETT, HERTFORDSHIRE, WD7 9AD.

Ⓟ**Business Support Matters, trading name of Business Support Matters Limited** *(D I Lockett)* 1 Pottery Yard, Liverton, NEWTON ABBOT, DEVON, TQ12 6LR. and at EXETER

Ⓟ**Business Tax Services Ltd** *(J D Moss)* 58 Vineyard Hill Road, Wimbledon, LONDON, SW19 7JH.

Ⓟ**Business Wizards Limited** *(T S O'Connell)* 12 Darley Mead Court, Hampton Lane, SOLIHULL, WEST MIDLANDS, B91 2QA.

ⒻⓅ**Businessvision, trading name of Marc Lawson & Co Limited** *(M Lawson)* Unit 7, Brooklands, Budshead Road, PLYMOUTH, PL6 5XR.

Ⓟ**But Do Yeung C.P.A. Limited** *(Y But, W Chan)* 3/F Kam Sang Building, 257 Des Voeux Road Central, CENTRAL, HONG KONG ISLAND, HONG KONG SAR.

Butcher and Company *(E J Butcher)* 3-7 Wyndham Street, ALDERSHOT, HAMPSHIRE, GU12 4NY.

ⓉⒻⒶ**Butler & Co** *(J M Butler, S J Slater)* Bennett House, The Dean, ALRESFORD, HAMPSHIRE, SO24 9BH.

Butler & Co *(K D Butler)* 1 Manor Park, Arkendale, KNARESBOROUGH, HG5 0QH.

Butler & Co *(M S Desai, R V Patel, S Y Phadke)* Third Floor, 126-134 Baker Street, LONDON, W1U 6UE.

ⓉⒻⓅⒶ**Butler & Co (Bishops Waltham) Ltd** *(J M Butler, S J Slater)* Avalon House, Waltham Business Park, Brickyard Road, Swanmore, SOUTHAMPTON, SO32 2SA.

Ⓐ**Butler & Co LLP** *(M S Desai, R V Patel, S Y Phadke)* 3rd Floor, 126-134 Baker Street, LONDON, W1U 6UE.

★Ⓐ**Butler & Speller** *(J S Speller)* 1436 London Road, LEIGH-ON-SEA, ESSEX, SS9 2UL.

Ⓟ**Butler Accountancy Services Ltd** *(D A Butler)* Suite 1 Telford House, Riverside, Warwick Road, CARLISLE, CA1 2BT.

Ⓟ**Butler Cook, trading name of Butler Cook Accountants Ltd** *(A F Butler)* 30/32 High Street, Codnor, RIPLEY, DE5 9QB.

Butler Fancourt *(C E Butler, M P Fancourt)* Boon Court, Papyrus Road, Werrington, PETERBOROUGH, PE4 5HQ.

Butlers *(J W Butler, L Butler)* Little Garth, Tirley Lane, Utkinton, TARPORLEY, CHESHIRE, CW6 0JZ.

Butlers *(J D Butler)* 4 Oakwood Gardens, Knaphill, WOKING, SURREY, GU21 2RX.

Ⓟ**Butlers, trading name of Butlers Financial Limited** *(H A Meagher)* 10 Dobsons Close, RAYLEIGH, ESSEX, SS6 7NZ.

ⓉⒻⒶ**Butt Cozens, Hard Dowdy, Heathcote & Coleman, trading names of Chantrey Vellacott DFK LLP** *(S S Aulak, I C Blackman, S J Bonner, M J Cannon, G A Cartwright, P A Clark, M F R Cooper, F J Cross, D V Devalia, W S Devitt, T C Evans, P Fenner, E S Harris, M R Hewitt-Boorman, C W Hindle, D Ince, C D James, I B Johnson, G M Jones, J A Keating, M E Lamb, D T Lay-Flurrie, S R Levine, C N Malacrida, K A McCaffrey, K A Murphy, R P R O'Beirne, D J Oprey, J H Owen, C J Povey, N J Simkins, M J Simpson, I B Staunton, A P R Steinthal, M F Stevens, A K Syrocki, R H Toone, M J Tovey, H Wilkinson, R J Willis, D T Wright)* Russell Square House, 10-12 Russell Square, LONDON, WC1B 5LF. and at BIRMINGHAM, COLCHESTER, CROYDON, HOVE, LEICESTER, NORTHAMPTON, READING, SOUTHAMPTON, STEVENAGE

ⓅⒶ**Butt Miller, trading name of Butt Miller Limited** *(N B Butt)* 92 Park Street, CAMBERLEY, SURREY, GU15 3NY.

ⓉⒻⓅⒶ**Butterfield Morgan Limited** *(C Harry, S M Williams)* Druslyn House, De La Beche Street, SWANSEA, SA1 3HJ.

ⒻⒶ**Butters & Company** *(P S Butters)* 129 High St, TEDDINGTON, TW11 8HJ.

ⒻⒶ**Butters Gates & Company** *(J R Butters)* 107 Bell Street, LONDON, NW1 6TL.

Butterworth Barlow *(B C Barlow, G Butterworth)* Prescot House, 3 High Street, PRESCOT, MERSEYSIDE, L34 3LD.

Ⓟ**Butterworth Barlow, trading name of Butterworth Barlow Limited** *(G Butterworth)* Prescot House, 3 High Street, PRESCOT, MERSEYSIDE, L34 3LD.

★ⓉⒻⒶ**Butterworth Jones** *(P J Butterworth, D R John, J D Parker, D H Stabbins)* 7 Castle St, BRIDGWATER, SOMERSET, TA6 3DT. and at BURNHAM-ON-SEA, LANGPORT, WESTON-SUPER-MARE

Ⓟ**Butterworths Accountants Limited** *(M B Butterworth)* Windsor House, 26 Mostyn Avenue, Craig-y-Don, LLANDUDNO, GWYNEDD, LL30 1YY.

ⓉⓅ**Butterworths, trading name of Mark Butterworth Limited** *(M B Butterworth)* Windsor House, 26 Mostyn Avenue, LLANDUDNO, GWYNEDD, LL30 1YY.

Buxton & Co *(P Buxton)* Le Pallion, La Route Des Landes, St Ouen, JERSEY, JE3 2AA.

Buxton Accounting LLP *(D W Buxton)* 98 Middlewich Road, NORTHWICH, CHESHIRE, CW9 7DA.

Ⓟ**Buzzacott Livingstone Ltd** *(M P Farmar)* 130 Wood Street, LONDON, EC2V 6DL.

ⒻⒶ**Buzzacott, Buzzacott Expatriate Tax Services, trading names of Buzzacott LLP** *(J P Ager, C R Cooper, A.De Lacey, M P Farmar, E A Finch, A S Francis, D N Jarman, A McQuater, K Patel, A K Savjani, G F M Wheatley, M C Worsey)* 130 Wood Street, LONDON, EC2V 6DL.

Ⓟ**BW Bradley & Associates, trading name of Radclyffe and Woodrow Limited** *(J R Woodrow)* 52 St John Street, ASHBOURNE, DERBYSHIRE, DE6 1GH.

BW Gale *(B W Gale)* Yew Tree House, Penn Lane, Kings Stanley, STONEHOUSE, GLOUCESTERSHIRE, GL10 3PT.

Ⓟ**BWC, trading name of BWC Business Solutions Limited** *(G E Blackburn, P A Whitwam)* 8 Park Place, LEEDS, LS1 2RU. and at STOCKTON-ON-TEES

Ⓐ**BWH and Company** *(B W Harley)* Iveco House, Station Road, WATFORD, WD17 1DL.

ⒻⒶ**BWMacfarlane LLP** *(K J L Green, A T R Macfarlane, L M Malkin, A P Morris, P H Taaffe)* 3 Temple Square, LIVERPOOL, L2 5BA.

Ⓐ**BWW, trading name of Bridgen Watkins & Wainwright** *(R C Bridgen, D R Watkins)* 10 Dashwood Avenue, HIGH WYCOMBE, HP12 3DN.

ⒻⒶ**Bygott & Co** *(S W Bygott)* 1-3 Dudley Street, GRIMSBY, LINCOLNSHIRE, DN31 2AW.

Byrne and Co *(T B Byrne)* Trenhaile Bungalow, St Newlyn East, NEWQUAY, TR8 5JL.

★ⒻⒶ**Byrne, Palmer & Co** *(P J Cobb)* 14 Queens Road, Hersham, WALTON-ON-THAMES, KT12 5LS.

byte size accounting *(M Vaughan)* 70 Pilley Crescent, CHELTENHAM, GLOUCESTERSHIRE, GL53 9ET.

C & C Accountants *(M I Coulter)* 1st Floor, 4 Sherrard Street, MELTON MOWBRAY, LEICESTERSHIRE, LE13 1XJ.

Ⓟ**C & M Scott Ltd** *(J Vann Smith)* Unit 1, Leylands Farm Business Park, Colden Common, WINCHESTER, HAMPSHIRE, SO21 1TH.

Ⓟ**C & S Associates Ltd** *(C Simpkins)* 3 Wessex Way, Highworth, SWINDON, SN6 7NT.

Ⓟ**C & S Christie Ltd** *(C J Christie)* 1 Nalton Close, Copmanthorpe, YORK, NORTH YORKSHIRE, YO23 3YY.

C A Cameron ACA *(C A Cameron)* Opera Close, 22b Court Street, HADDINGTON, EAST LOTHIAN, EH41 3JA.

Ⓣ**C A Pitts & Co** *(M A Khan, S M Khan-Ahmed)* Omnibus Business Centre, 39-41 North Road, LONDON, N7 9DP.

C B Hunt *(C B Hunt)* 52 Roundway, CAMBERLEY, SURREY, GU15 1NU.

ⓉⒻⓅⒶ**C B Reid Limited** *(P A Cattermole, D R Gordon-Smith, D C W Reid)* 48 High West Street, DORCHESTER, DORSET, DT1 1UT.

C Biggs *(C Biggs)* 1 Malcolm Drive, SURBITON, SURREY, KT6 6QS.

Ⓟ**C Bragg & Co Ltd** *(C J Bragg)* Rose Villa, Cherry Chase, Tiptree, COLCHESTER, CO5 0AE.

ⓅⒶ**C C Young & Co Ltd** *(C C Young)* 1st Floor, 48 Poland Street, LONDON, W1F 7ND.

Ⓟ**C D Nash Limited** *(C D Nash)* 1st Floor, 15a Hill Avenue, AMERSHAM, BUCKINGHAMSHIRE, HP6 5BD.

ⒻⓅ**C E Hill & Co (UK) Limited** *(C E Hill)* Fairacre, Chiltern Road, Ballinger, GREAT MISSENDEN, BUCKINGHAMSHIRE, HP16 9LJ.

ⓅⒶ**C H Ivens & Co, trading name of Ivensco Limited** *(D B Thomson, L R Thomson)* 50 Regent Street, RUGBY, WARWICKSHIRE, CV21 2PU.

★ⓅⒶ**C H London Limited** *(D A I Cooper)* The Ground Floor, Suite G1, Buckingham Court, 78 Buckingham Gate, LONDON, SW1E 6PE.

ⒻⒶ**C J Dyke & Company** *(C J Dyke)* The Old Police Station, Priory Road, ST. IVES, CAMBRIDGESHIRE, PE27 5BB.

Ⓐ**C J Bailey & Co** *(C J Bailey)* 145 High Street, NEWTON-LE-WILLOWS, WA12 9SQ.

Ⓟ**C J Lawman FCA, trading name of Deblaw Limited** *(C J Lawman)* 44 Hall Orchard Lane, Frisby-On-The-Wreake, MELTON MOWBRAY, LE14 2NH.

Ⓟ**C J Petty Limited** *(C J Petty)* 175 High Street, Brownhills, WALSALL, WS8 6HG.

Ⓟ**C J Smith Accountancy Limited** *(C J Smith)* 92 Hamilton Road, TAUNTON, SOMERSET, TA1 2ES.

ⒻⓅⒶ**C J Woodhead & Co Limited** *(C J Woodhead)* 158 Hemper Lane, Greenhill, SHEFFIELD, S8 7FE.

C Jefferson FCA *(C P Jefferson)* 20 The Paddocks, WEYBRIDGE, SURREY, KT13 9RJ.

★**C K Lam & Co** *(C M Lam, M Wai)* Unit 704, Fourseas Building, 208-212 Nathan Road, KOWLOON CITY, KOWLOON, HONG KONG SAR.

C K Speller *(C K Speller)* 2 Claremont Court, Rose Hill, DORKING, SURREY, RH4 2EE.

Ⓐ**C K Wong & Co** *(C K Wong)* Citibase, 40 Princess Street, MANCHESTER, M1 6DE.

Ⓟ**C K Yau & Partners CPA Limited** *(W L Yau)* 11-13/F Pico Tower, 66 Gloucester Road, WAN CHAI, HONG KONG SAR.

Ⓟ**C Kounnis Ltd** *(C Kounnis)* 100 Yiannis Kranidiotis Avenue, Office 102, Latsia, 2235 NICOSIA, CYPRUS.

Ⓟ**C M Tax Consultants Limited** *(C S Mitchell)* 95 Wellington Road North, STOCKPORT, CHESHIRE, SK4 2LP.

C M Wong & Company *(C Wong)* Flat C, 6/F, Guangdong Tours Centre, 18 Pennington Street, CAUSEWAY BAY, HONG KONG SAR. and at TSUEN WAN

C Micklewright & Co *(C M Micklewright)* High Sheriff's House, Trenowth, Grampound Road, TRURO, TR2 4EH.

Ⓟ**C P Lovells Ltd** *(P J Lovell)* 44 Elthorne Park Road, Hanwell, LONDON, W7 2JA.

ⒻⒶ**C P Waites** *(N S Waites)* 24 St Cuthberts Way, DARLINGTON, DL1 1GB.

Ⓕ**C Pimblott & Co** *(C Pimblott)* 341/343 Park Lane, MACCLESFIELD, SK11 8JR.

C Priestley & Co *(C Priestley)* 37 Minchenden Crescent, LONDON, N14 7EP.

Ⓟ**C S James & Co Limited** *(C S James)* 88 New Road, Skewen, NEATH, WEST GLAMORGAN, SA10 6HG.

Ⓐ**C S Pomroy & Co** *(C S Pomroy)* Unit A1, Weltech Centre, Ridgeway, WELWYN GARDEN CITY, HERTFORDSHIRE, AL7 2AA.

C S Yeung & Co *(C Yeung)* Room 204, 2/F Lyndhurst Building, 29 Lyndhurst Terrace, CENTRAL, HONG KONG SAR.

C T Jones & Co *(C T Jones)* Suite 108A, Glenfield Park, Philips Road, BLACKBURN, BB1 5PF.

C W Leung & Co *(T Ho, L T Hui, C Tam, C N Tse)* Room 403, Wing on House, 71 Des Voeux Road, CENTRAL, HONG KONG ISLAND, HONG KONG SAR.

C W Turner *(C W Turner)* 28 Wilman Road, TUNBRIDGE WELLS, TN4 9AP.

ⓅⒶ**C Wiltshire & Co, trading name of C Wiltshire & Co Stratford Limited** *(P A Jones, C Wiltshire)* 17 Greenhill Street, STRATFORD-UPON-AVON, WARWICKSHIRE, CV37 6LF.

C Y Chan & Co *(C Chan)* Room B, 5/F, Kiu Yin Com Building, 361-363 Lockhart Road, WAN CHAI, HONG KONG SAR.

Ⓟ**C&M Services (Bristol) Ltd** *(K Docherty)* 19 The Park, Bradley Stoke, BRISTOL, BS32 0AP.

C. Bajaria & Co *(C H Bajaria)* 42 Bromley Common, BROMLEY, BR2 9PD.

C. Chaplow & Co, trading name of C. Chaplow *(C Chaplow)* 32 Granville Road, ACCRINGTON, BB5 2LA.

C. Cooper *(C Cooper)* 24 Haughgate Close, WOODBRIDGE, IP12 1LQ.

C. Dusgate & Co *(C I Dusgate)* Fir Tree Cottage, Llanmadoc, Gower, SWANSEA, SA3 1DB.

C. K. Liu & Company *(C Liu, C L Liu)* 13th Floor, Wah Kit Commercial Centre, 302 Des Voeux Road, CENTRAL, HONG KONG ISLAND, HONG KONG SAR.

Ⓟ**C. Leventis Ltd** *(H Leventis)* 33 Apostolou Pavlou Avenue, Andreas - Niki Court, Office 204, 8046 PAPHOS, CYPRUS.

C. McDonald & Co *(I M McDonald)* Ditton Lodge, 16 Southborough Road, SURBITON, SURREY, KT6 6JN.

Ⓐ**C. Mitchell & Co** *(C D Mitchell)* Deremar, 33 Faesten Way, BEXLEY, DA5 2JB.

C. Neate *(C M Neate)* 15 Mill Road, STEYNING, WEST SUSSEX, BN44 3LN.

C. Roughton *(C Roughton)* 10 The Orchard, LONDON, W4 1JX.

C. Terry & Co. *(C Terry)* The Birches, Todds Green, STEVENAGE, SG1 2JE.

C. Umpleby & Co *(C Umpleby)* Westbourne House, 60 Bagley Lane, Farsley, PUDSEY, WEST YORKSHIRE, LS28 5LY.

★**C. V. Book Keeping** *(S W Valentine)* Unit 2, Ferry Road Office Park, Ferry Road, Riversway, PRESTON, PR2 2YH.

C.A. Brown *(C A Brown)* 24 Woodlands Road, HAYWARDS HEATH, RH16 3JU.

C.A. Cox *(C A Cox)* 18 Chambers Close, MARKFIELD, LE67 9NB.

Ⓐ**C.A. Evans & Company** *(C A Evans)* Spring Royd, Clapham Road, Austwick, LANCASTER, LA2 8BE.

C.A. Whitehouse & Co *(C A Whitehouse)* 5 Lowdham, Wilnecote, TAMWORTH, B77 4LX.

C.A.M.Ashton *(C A M Ashton)* Marwood, 8 Townsend, Curry Rivel, LANGPORT, SOMERSET, TA10 0HN.

C.B. Hayman *(C B Hayman)* 9 Sutton Road, SEAFORD, BN25 1RU.

ⓉⒶ**C.B. Heslop & Co** *(T Allen, S J Coke, C B Heslop, J P R Prevost)* 1 High Street, THATCHAM, RG19 3JG. and at LYMINGTON

Ⓐ**C.B. Hoare** *(C B Hoare)* 10b The Green, Cheddington, LEIGHTON BUZZARD, BEDFORDSHIRE, LU7 0RJ.

C.B. Wong & Co *(C Wong)* Room 1601 Carnarvon Plaza, 20 Carnarvon Road, TSIM SHA TSUI, KOWLOON, HONG KONG SAR.

C.Babs-Jonah & Co *(C B Jonah)* Central House, 1 Ballards Lane, Finchley, LONDON, N3 1LQ.

C.C. Kwong & Co *(C C Kwong)* Room 601 6/F, Tai Tung Building, No 8 Fleming Road, WAN CHAI, HONG KONG ISLAND, HONG KONG SAR.

C.C. Williams & Co *(C C Williams)* 38 High Street, Yatton, BRISTOL, BS49 4JA.

C.D. Hindley & Co *(C D Hindley)* 29 Captain Lees Garden, Westhoughton, BOLTON, BL5 3YF.

C.D. Hunt & Co *(C D Hunt)* Unit 3.07, Q West, Great West Road, BRENTFORD, MIDDLESEX, TW8 0GP.

C.D. Wright *(C D Wright)* Mains of Balfour, Birse, ABOYNE, ABERDEENSHIRE, AB34 5DB.

C.Diana Wilding *(C D Wilding)* Heathfield, Ffawyddog, CRICKHOWELL, NP8 1PY.

C.E. Akeroyd *(D E G Akeroyd)* Sherwood House, 7 Gregory Boulevard, NOTTINGHAM, NG7 6LB.

C.E. Johnson *(C E Johnson)* 2 Friary Gardens, LICHFIELD, WS13 6QU.

C.E. Murphy *(C E Murphy)* Hale Bank, 40 Bridgeman Terrace, WIGAN, LANCASHIRE, WN1 1TT.

C.E. Okobi & Co *(C E Okobi)* Fed. Govt. Girls College Road, P O Box 555, IBUSA, NIGERIA.

C.E. Petty & Co *(C E Petty)* 1 Effingham Court, Constitution Hill, WOKING, SURREY, GU22 7RX.

C.F. Chan & Company *(C F Chan)* 28th Floor, Times Tower, 393 Jaffe Road, WAN CHAI, HONG KONG SAR.

C.G. Walton *(C G Walton)* The Tynings, Ham Lane, Kingston Seymour, CLEVEDON, AVON, BS21 6XE.

C.G.Harwood *(C G Harwood)* 2 Rochester Gardens, CROYDON, CR0 5NN.

★**C.H. Jefferson & Co** *(A L Clark)* 108 Oswald Road, SCUNTHORPE, SOUTH HUMBERSIDE, DN15 7PA.

C.H. Pearson *(C H Pearson)* 7 Moore Close, Aller Park, NEWTON ABBOT, TQ12 4TH.

C.H. Siskin & Co *(C H Siskin)* Mulberry Cottage, Church Lane, PINNER, HA5 3AA.

C.H.Ong & Co *(C H Ong)* 110 Jalan Jurong Kechil, Apt 02-01 Sweebi House, SINGAPORE 2159, SINGAPORE.

C.J. Beeston *(C J Beeston)* The Laurels, Reeth, RICHMOND, DL11 6TX.

Ⓕ**C.J. Cook & Co** *(C J Cook)* 24A Suffolk Road, Barnes, LONDON, SW13 9NB.

ⒻⒶ**C.J. Driscoll** *(C N Clarke, C J Driscoll)* The Old Surgery, 19 Mengham Lane, HAYLING ISLAND, PO11 9JT.

C.J. Fisher & Co. *(C J Fisher, S A Fisher)* 11 Oakwood Road, Henleaze, BRISTOL, BS9 4NP.

Ⓟ**C.J. Lansdown & Co Limited** *(C J Lansdown)* 7 Terrey Road, SHEFFIELD, S17 4DD.

Ⓕ**C.J. Leech & Company** *(C J Leech)* 88 Sheep Street, BICESTER, OX26 6LP.

C.J. Leggate & Associates *(C J Leggate)* 15 New Road, HIGH WYCOMBE, HP12 4LH.

ⓉⒶ**C.J. Lucking & Co** *(M J Lucking)* 34 Cross Street, Long Eaton, NOTTINGHAM, NG10 1HD.

C.J. O'Brien & Co *(C J O'Brien)* Batemill Farmhouse, Batemill Lane, Over Peover, MACCLESFIELD, CHESHIRE, SK11 9BW.

Ⓕ**C.J. Patel & Co** *(C J Patel)* 112 Hamilton Avenue, ILFORD, IG6 1AB.

C.J. Wells & Co *(C J Wells)* 84 Western Road, LEWES, EAST SUSSEX, BN7 1RP.

Members in Practice and Firms - Alphabetical
C.J. Wixey - Carson & Company

C.J. Wixey *(C J Wixey)* Fossil Cottage, Havyatt, GLASTONBURY, BA6 8LF.

C.J.Jones *(C J Jones)* 45 Cwm Cwddy Drive, Rhiwderin Heights, NEWPORT, NP10 8JN.

C.K. Chui & Co. *(C K Chui)* 1st Floor, 2 Waterloo Street, MANCHESTER, M1 6HX.

C.K. Shum & Co *(C K Shum)* 20/F, 88 Lockhart Road, WAN CHAI, HONG KONG ISLAND, HONG KONG SAR.

C.L. Batsford *(Colin Batsford)* 69 Grange Park Avenue, Winchmore Hill, LONDON, N21 2LN.

C.M. Dalby *(C M Dalby)* 18 Merstow Green, EVESHAM, WR11 4BD.

C.M. Mitchell *(C M Mitchell)* 111 Wolsey Drive, KINGSTON UPON THAMES, KT2 5DR.

C.M. Wilson *(C M Wilson)* 7 Saunders Copse, Saunders Lane, Mayford, WOKING, GU22 0NS.

C.M.A. Simon *(C M A Simon)* 13 Malt House Close, Old Windsor, WINDSOR, BERKSHIRE, SL4 2SD.

C.M.F. Pidgeon *(C M F Pidgeon)* Sandaway, Daleside Park, Darley, HARROGATE, HG3 2PX.

★**C.M.G. Associates** *(P R Clements, S Foster, H A Goldstein)* 5th Floor, Chalfont Square, Old Foundry Road, IPSWICH, IP4 2AJ.

Ⓐ**C.P. O'Donnell & Co.** *(C P O'Donnell)* Homeland, Hempstead Road, Bovingdon, HEMEL HEMPSTEAD, HP3 0HF.

Ⓟ**C.R. Jones, trading name of C.R. Jones & Co Limited** *(C R Jones)* 45 Staplegrove Road, TAUNTON, TA1 1DG.

C.R. Needham *(C R Needham)* Watersmeet, Westfield Drive, Ramsey, ISLE OF MAN, IM8 3ER.

C.R. Stevens *(C R Stevens)* 57 Station Road, TRING, HP23 5NW.

C.R. Walker *(C R Walker)* 8 Longford Park, Longford, NEWPORT, SHROPSHIRE, TF10 8LW.

C.R.S. Link *(C R S Link)* 4 Brunswick Gardens, LONDON, W8 4AJ. and at CROYDON

Ⓐ**C.R.V. Gudka & Co** *(C R V Gudka)* 306 Neasden Lane, LONDON, NW10 0AD.

Ⓟ**C.Rengert & Company, trading name of C. Rengert & Company Limited** *(C Rengert)* 24 High Street, SAFFRON WALDEN, ESSEX, CB10 1AX.

C.S. Cocks *(C S Cocks)* 45 Rannoch Drive, Lakeside, CARDIFF, CF23 6LP.

★**C.S. Fenton & Co** *(C S Fenton)* The Old Rectory, Kirby Underdale, YORK, YO41 1QY.

ⒻⒶ**C.S. Wilkinson** *(C S Wilkinson)* 49B Market Square, WITNEY, OX28 6AG.

C.S. Wong *(C S Wong)* 118 High Street, Sawston, CAMBRIDGE, CB22 3HJ.

ⓉⒻⓅⒶ**CAAS, trading name of Complete Audit and Accounting Solutions Ltd** *(L Berko, G M Burnham)* Unit 203, China House, 401 Edgware Road, LONDON, NW2 6GY.

Cabinet Galley Manterfield *(L M Manterfield)* Anatoth, 19 Allee de la Gare, Le Vesinet, 78110 PARIS, FRANCE.

Ⓟ**Cable Financial Directions Limited** *(J E Cable)* 5 Downs Road, West Stoke, CHICHESTER, PO18 9BQ.

Ⓟ**Cadham & Carter, trading name of Cadham & Carter Limited** *(C Delicata)* 7 Lethbridge Road, SWINDON, SN1 4BY.

Ⓟ**Cadishead Accountancy Services Limited** *(C A Wilkinson)* Britannic House, 657 Liverpool Road, Irlam, MANCHESTER, M44 5XD.

Ⓕ**Cadwallader & Co LLP** *(M J Cadwallader)* Eagle House, 25 Severn Street, WELSHPOOL, POWYS, SY21 7AD.

Ⓟ**Caerus Financial Management Limited** *(S Guy)* 23 Larch Rise, Easingwold, YORK, NORTH YORKSHIRE, YO61 3RZ.

ⓉⒻⒶ**Caerwyn Jones** *(A J Barker, D C Blofield, I A Painter)* Emstrey House, Shrewsbury Business Park, SHREWSBURY, SY2 6LG.

Ⓟ**Cairn Business Solutions Limited** *(I W Jones)* Ground Floor, 24 Hill Street, St. Helier, JERSEY, JE2 4UA.

★ⓉⒶ**Cairns Bailey & Co** *(J C Cairns, M A Cairns)* 3 Beacon Court, Birmingham Road, Great Barr, BIRMINGHAM, B43 6NN.

Ⓟ**Calculus International Limited** *(P Calcutteea)* 4 Manita House, Broad Avenue, Belle Rose, Quatre Bornes, ROSE HILL, MAURITIUS.

ⓉⓅⒶ**Calcutt Matthews, trading name of Calcutt Matthews Ltd** *(N M Hume)* 2nd Floor, Cardine House, 30 North Street, ASHFORD, KENT, TN24 8JR.

ⓉⒻⒶ**Calder & Co** *(T Badiani, P K S Ewen, D J Gallagher, D J Lyon, I M Rosmarin)* 1 Regent Street, LONDON, SW1Y 4NW.

Ⓐ**Caldwell Crompton** *(J S Crompton)* Alderley, 33 Whitehall Road, SALE, CHESHIRE, M33 3NL. and at WIRRAL

★ⓉⒻ**Caldwell Penn** *(M J Martin)* 1 Bramley Business Centre, Station Road, Bramley, GUILDFORD, SURREY, GU5 0AZ.

Ⓟ**Callen Company Secretarial Services Ltd, Nick Callen, trading names of Callen Consultants Ltd** *(N E Callen)* 146 Bath Road, Longwell Green, BRISTOL, BS30 9DB.

Callicott & Co *(M Callicott)* 46 Fairacres, Prestwood, GREAT MISSENDEN, HP16 0LE.

Callin & Co *(G C Boyde)* 6-7 Fort William, Head Road, Douglas, ISLE OF MAN, IM1 5BG.

★Ⓐ**Callow & Holmes** *(C Breeze)* Tattershall House, 19 St Catherine's Road, GRANTHAM, NG31 6TT.

Ⓣ**Callow Matthewman & Co.** *(D M Callin, C Matthewman, R G Woolley)* Atholl House, 29-31 Hope Street, Douglas, ISLE OF MAN, IM1 1AR.

Calthorn & Co *(M S R Thornton)* Headwell House, Headwell, Curry Mallet, TAUNTON, TA3 6SX.

Ⓟ**Calum Ward & Co Limited** *(J D Willis)* Cedar House, 41 Thorpe Road, NORWICH, NR1 1ES.

ⓉⒻⓅⒶ**Calvert Dawson Limited** *(P A Calvert, B Dawson)* 288 Oxford Road, Gomersal, CLECKHEATON, WEST YORKSHIRE, BD19 4PY.

Caly Accountants, trading name of A.J. Carte *(A J Carte)* 215 Nanpantan Road, LOUGHBOROUGH, LE11 3YD.

CAM Holdings LLP *(K L White)* The Pavilions, Eden Park, Ham Green, BRISTOL, BS20 0DD.

Ⓟ**Camamile Associates Ltd** *(C J Shelbourne, R L J Vigar)* 15 Newland, LINCOLN, LN1 1XG.

Ⓟ**Camamile Limited** *(P D Harrison, J E O'Hern, N M Roberts, C J Shelbourne, R L J Vigar)* 15 Newland, LINCOLN, LN1 1XG.

Ⓐ**Cambrian Partnership, trading name of J Gareth Morgan & Co** *(D Jones, D L Rees)* Clun House, 11 Morgan Street, TREDEGAR, GWENT, NP22 3NA.

Cambridge Financial Partners LLP *(K L Clark)* St. Johns Innovation Park, Cowley Road, CAMBRIDGE, CB4 0WS.

Ⓟ**Cambridge Recovery Services Limited** *(R H Barker)* St Johns Innovation Centre, Cowley Road, CAMBRIDGE, CB4 0WS. and at BEWDLEY

Cambridge Recovery Services, trading name of RH Barker & Co *(R H Barker)* T/A Cambridge Recovery Services, St John's Innovation Centre, Cowley Road, CAMBRIDGE, CB4 0WS. and at BEWDLEY

Ⓟ**Cambus Consulting Ltd** *(Y P Marsden)* 24 Lodge Close, COBHAM, SURREY, KT11 2SQ.

ⓅⒶ**Cameron & Associates Ltd** *(R S Basra, M A Shah, D Wadhwani)* 35-37 Lowlands Road, HARROW, MIDDLESEX, HA1 3AW.

ⓉⒻⒶ**Cameron Baum** *(D I Baum, G Hollander)* 88 Crawford Street, LONDON, W1H 2EJ.

Ⓐ**Cameron Baum Davis, trading name of Cameron Baum Davis LLP** *(D P Davis)* 88 Crawford Street, LONDON, W1H 2EJ.

ⒻⓅⒶ**Cameron Baum Limited** *(D I Baum, G Hollander)* 88 Crawford Street, LONDON, W1H 2EJ.

★**Cameron Browne** *(R L Dick)* 3a Headley Road, Woodley, READING, RG5 4JB.

ⓉⒻⓅ**Cameron Cavey Consulting Limited** *(M C Cavey)* 3 Branksome Park House, Branksome Business Park, Bourne Valley Road, POOLE, DORSET, BH12 1ED.

Cameron Cavey LLP *(D J Strike)* Suite 3, Branksome Park House, Branksome Business Park, Bourne Valley Road, POOLE, DORSET BH12 1ED.

Cameron Clark *(C M Clark)* Prinlaws House, 12 Walkerton Drive, Leslie, GLENROTHES, FIFE, KY6 3BT.

Cameron Cunningham LLP *(D T Cunningham)* 145 High Street, SEVENOAKS, KENT, TN13 1XJ.

ⓅⒶ**Cameron Hughes, trading name of Cameron Hughes Ltd** *(G S Gilbert, M Hayton)* 16 Jubilee Parkway, Jubilee Business Park, DERBY, DE21 4BJ.

ⒻⓅⒶ**Cameron Valentine Ltd** *(S W Valentine)* Unit 2, Ferry Road Office Park, Ferry Road, Riversway, PRESTON, PR2 2YH.

ⒻⒶ**Cameron, Ferriby & Co** *(R A Cameron)* Bridge House, 41 Wincolmlee, HULL, HU2 8AG.

ⓉⒻⓅⒶ**Camerons Accountancy Consultants Limited** *(E O'Donnell)* 9 Worton Park, Worton, WITNEY, OXFORDSHIRE, OX29 4SX.

ⒻⓅⒶ**Camfield Chapman Lowe, trading name of Camfield Chapman Lowe Limited** *(A J Camfield, C D Lowe)* 9 High Street, Woburn Sands, MILTON KEYNES, MK17 8RF.

Campagna-Smith *(G Campagna, M J Smith)* Fernleigh House, 10 Uttoxeter Road, Mickleover, DERBY, DE3 0DA.

Campbell Crossley & Davis *(S D Mondy, P G C Riley, P Swarbrick, R I Williamson, I M Wroe)* 348/350 Lytham Road, BLACKPOOL, FY4 1DW. and at NORTHWICH

Campbell Park *(E C Park)* 54 Woods Avenue, HATFIELD, HERTFORDSHIRE, AL10 8LY.

★**Campbell, Saunders & Co** *(R N M Farrier)* Suite 500-1055, West Broadway, VANCOUVER V6H 1E2, BC, CANADA.

Campion Accountancy *(D L Morgan)* St. Marys House, Clifton Road, WINCHESTER, HAMPSHIRE, SO22 5BP.

ⓅⒶ**Camplejohn Rowan, trading name of R L & Associates Limited** *(K Fretwell, S Sequerra)* Unit 9 Acorn Business Park, Woodseats Close, SHEFFIELD, S8 0TB.

ⓅⒶ**Campling & Co, trading name of Campling & Co Ltd** *(N J Campling)* 4 Burges Close, SOUTHEND-ON-SEA, SS1 3JW.

Ⓟ**Camrose Consulting Limited** *(D M Lewis)* 61 St. Margarets Road, EDGWARE, MIDDLESEX, HA8 9UT.

★**Camwells, trading name of Camwell Consulting** *(C R Challis)* Arena 119, 5 High Street, MAIDENHEAD, BERKSHIRE, SL6 1JN.

Canfield & Co., *(G T Canfield)* Bankfield, 38 The Orchards, SAWBRIDGEWORTH, HERTFORDSHIRE, CM21 9BB.

Ⓟ**Cann Polus, trading name of DBS Accounting Services Limited** *(D B Specterman)* Parade House, 135 The Parade, WATFORD, WD17 1NA.

ⓉⒻⓅⒶ**Cannon Moorcroft Limited** *(P H Cannon, J L Moorcroft)* 3 Manor Courtyard, Hughenden Avenue, HIGH WYCOMBE, HP13 5RE.

ⓉⒻⒶ**Cansdales** *(F M Bowers, N S Evans, J R Foskett)* Bourbon Court, Nightingales Corner, Little Chalfont, AMERSHAM, HP7 9QS.

Ⓟ**Cansdales Ltd** *(F M Bowers, N S Evans, J R Foskett)* Bourbon Court, Nightingales Corner, Little Chalfont, AMERSHAM, HP7 9QS.

ⓅⒶ**Cantium Consulting Limited** *(A R Bradley)* 162 High Street, TONBRIDGE, KENT, TN9 1BB.

CAP *(J Y Chan)* 6 Holly Road, High Lane, STOCKPORT, CHESHIRE, SK6 8HW.

Ⓟ**CAP Accountancy Limited** *(J Y Chan)* 6 Holly Road, High Lane, STOCKPORT, CHESHIRE, SK6 8HW.

Cape and Dalgleish *(G C A Morphitis)* 22 Melton Street, Euston Square, LONDON, NW1 2BT.

★**Capel Cavendish & Co** *(P Webster)* 27 Cavendish Road, SUTTON, SURREY, SM2 5EY.

Ⓟ**Capes Gittins, trading name of Capes Gittins Limited** *(T Capes)* 28 Mount Grace Road, POTTERS BAR, EN6 1RD.

Ⓟ**Capitax Financial Limited** *(S V Shah)* Devonshire House, 582 Honeypot Lane, STANMORE, MIDDLESEX, HA7 1JS.

Caplan Associates *(P M Caplan)* Cardinal Point, Park Road, RICKMANSWORTH, HERTFORDSHIRE, WD3 1RE.

Ⓟ**Capshire, trading name of Capshire Consulting Limited** *(N U Choudhary)* 15 Heath Mead, Wimbledon, LONDON, SW19 5JP.

Captus *(P M Langdon)* Flat G104, Gilbert Scott Building, Scott Avenue, LONDON, SW15 3SG.

Cara Chapman *(C Chapman)* 6 Wingfield Close, Ewelme, WALLINGFORD, OXFORDSHIRE, OX10 6JY.

Cardiff Bay Accountancy *(R J M Gardener)* Braeside, 7 Heol Y Pentre, Pentyrch, CARDIFF, CF15 9QD.

Ⓟ**Care Home Accounting Limited** *(P E Nurick)* 66 Longfield Avenue, LONDON, NW7 2EG.

Ⓟ**Carew & Co, trading name of Alun Carew Limited** *(D A Carew)* Cyder House, 11 Pilgrims Way, GUILDFORD, SURREY, GU4 8AD.

★**Carl Associates** *(N A Smeed)* 186 Wanstead Park Road, ILFORD, ESSEX, IG1 3TR.

Carla Holmes *(C Holmes)* 15 Guernsey Way, Winnersh, WOKINGHAM, BERKSHIRE, RG41 5FT.

Ⓐ**Carless Stebbings & Co** *(P J Stevens)* 31 Westminster Palace Gardens, Artillery Row, LONDON, SW1P 1RR.

Ⓟ**Carleys Integrated Solutions Ltd** *(A J Gooch, B J Hensman, B Owen)* St. James House, 8 Overcliffe, GRAVESEND, KENT, DA11 0HJ.

Carlo Salford *(C P Salford)* Via Passo Di Fargorida 6, 20148 MILAN, ITALY.

Ⓟ**Carmichael & Co, trading name of Carmichaels Insolvency Ltd** *(M J Landsman)* 2nd Floor, Portland Tower, Portland Street, MANCHESTER, M1 3LF.

ⒻⓅ**Carnelian, trading name of Carnelian Business Services Limited** *(S Aggarwal)* 7a Wyndham Place, LONDON, W1H 1PN.

Carol Colinswood & Co *(C R E Colinswood)* Ground Floor, Dorchester House, 15 Dorchester Place, THAME, OXFORDSHIRE, OX9 2DL.

Carol Dunlop *(C E Dunlop)* Pinnolds, Upton Lane, Brookthorpe, GLOUCESTER, GL4 0UT.

Carol Gardner *(Gardner)* 13 High Green, Thorpe Hamlet, NORWICH, NR1 4AP.

Carol Jones FCA *(C Jones)* 35 Dean Close, Rhosnesni, WREXHAM, LL13 9EP.

Carol Le Grys *(C.A. Le Grys)* 19 Amberley Road, Bush Hill Park, ENFIELD, EN1 2QX.

Carol Waters *(C A Waters)* Trefoil, Boucher Close, Shottery, STRATFORD-UPON-AVON, CV37 9YX.

Carole A Barton FCA *(C A Barton)* 5 Grange Park Road, CHEADLE, CHESHIRE, SK8 1HQ.

Carole J. Barnett *(C J Barnett)* 102 Kimberley Park Road, FALMOUTH, TR11 2DQ.

Carole Judd *(C E Judd)* 82a Winchester Road, ANDOVER, SP10 2ER.

Carole Walker *(C A Walker)* 47 Brookdale, New Longton, PRESTON, PR4 4XL.

Ⓐ**Caroline A. Vickery FCA** *(C A Vickery)* Wealden Farm, Parrock Lane, Upper Hartfield, HARTFIELD, EAST SUSSEX, TN7 4AT.

Caroline Barnes *(C J Barnes)* College Farm, Creeting Hills, Creeting St. Mary, IPSWICH, IP6 8PX.

Caroline Chetwood *(C M D Chetwood)* Banacle Field, Church Lane, Brook, GODALMING, SURREY, GU8 5UQ.

Caroline Dockerill *(C M Dockerill)* 487 Chemin de la Contettaz, 74110 MORZINE, FRANCE.

Caroline Fox *(C S Fox)* Limeburners, Old Horsham Road, Beare Green, DORKING, RH5 4PW.

Caroline Hartley FCA *(C E Hartley)* 21 Anglesey Drive, Poynton, STOCKPORT, SK12 1BT.

Caroline J Beresford Pratt ACA *(C J Pratt)* The Manor House, High Street, BILLINGSHURST, WEST SUSSEX, RH14 9PH.

Caroline Meredith *(C L Meredith)* 9 Bowling Green Lane, Purley on Thames, READING, RG8 8EJ.

Caroline Pritchard *(C M Pritchard)* 16 Huron Drive, LIPHOOK, GU30 7TZ.

Caroline Sedgwick *(C S Sedgwick)* 163 Powder Mill Lane, TWICKENHAM, TW2 6EQ.

ⓉⒶ**Caroline Wilson** *(C E Kirkwood-Wilson)* 45 Kensington Road, SOUTHPORT, MERSEYSIDE, PR9 0RT.

Caroline Wood A.C.A. *(C D Wood)* Low Field House, Bleach Mill Lane, Menston, ILKLEY, WEST YORKSHIRE, LS29 6AW.

Carolyn Austin *(C S Austin)* 5 Barnfield Close, Cookham, MAIDENHEAD, BERKSHIRE, SL6 9DY.

Ⓟ**Carolyn Churchill, trading name of Solent Accountancy Services Limited** *(C J Churchill)* 7 Captains Parade, EAST COWES, ISLE OF WIGHT, PO32 6GU. and at RYDE

Carolyne Yaxley ACA *(C Yaxley)* 5 St. Wilfrids Drive, Grappenhall, WARRINGTON, WA4 2SH.

Caron M Kehoe *(C M Kehoe)* 53 Brabourne Rise, Park Langley, BECKENHAM, KENT, BR3 6SD.

★ⓉⒻⒶ**Carpenter Box, trading name of Carpenter Box LLP** *(P M Archer, J G Billings, K N Blake, R W Dowling, C H Eve, M R Godsmark, E M Goff, H J Julian, S R Noakes)* Amelia House, WORTHING, WEST SUSSEX, BN11 1QR.

ⒻⒶ**Carpenter Keen LLP** *(S D Carpenter, M F Keen)* Grand Prix House, 102-104 Sheen Road, RICHMOND, SURREY, TW9 1UF.

Ⓟ**Carr Jemmett (Cleethorpes) Ltd** *(R J Jemmett)* 66 St Peters Avenue, CLEETHORPES, DN35 8HP.

Ⓟ**Carr Jemmett Limited** *(R J Jemmett)* 66 St. Peters Avenue, CLEETHORPES, SOUTH HUMBERSIDE, DN35 8HP.

ⒻⓅⒶ**Carr, Jenkins & Hood, trading name of Redwood Wales Limited** *(P E Carr, J C Hood)* Redwood Court, Tawe Business Village, Swansea Enterprise Park, SWANSEA, SA7 9LA.

Ⓕ**Carrick** *(B B Carrick)* 10 Oxford Street, MALMESBURY, SN16 9AZ.

Ⓟ**Carrie Stokes Limited** *(C L Stokes)* 2 Mountbatten Close, SHIFNAL, SHROPSHIRE, TF11 8TU.

Ⓟ**Carrington Dean, Easy Debt Solutions, The Debt Experts, trading names of Carrington Dean Group Limited** *(P C Dean)* 135 Buchanan Street, GLASGOW, G1 2JA.

★ⒻⒶ**Carringtons** *(R N Morjaria)* Carrington House, 170 Greenford Road, HARROW, HA1 3QX.

ⒻⓅⒶ**Carringtons Ltd** *(A K Bhamm)* 6 Maple Grove Business Centre, Lawrence Road, HOUNSLOW, TW4 6DR.

Carroll & Co *(J M Carroll)* 6 Willow Drive, Twyford, READING, RG10 9DD.

ⒻⓅ**Carroll & Co, trading name of Carroll Business Consulting Ltd** *(A J Carroll, J F Socci)* 335 Jockey Road, SUTTON COLDFIELD, WEST MIDLANDS, B73 5XE.

Ⓐ**Carson & Company** *(A R Carson)* Unit 3, Dukes Court, Wellington Street, LUTON, LU1 5AF. and at LONDON

Ⓟ**Carston Holdings Ltd** *(K M Munn, R J O Rees)* Tudor House, 16 Cathedral Road, CARDIFF, CF11 9LJ.

ⓉⒻⓅⒶ**Carston, Gordon Sealey & Associates, Hoyles, Peter Wilkins & Co, Sullivans, Waldron Auditing, trading names of Carston & Co Limited** *(K M Munn, R J O Rees)* First Floor, Tudor House, 16 Cathederal Road, CARDIFF, CF11 9LJ. and at BATH, PONTYPRIDD

Carter & Co *(G M Carter)* 7 Downs Road, Westbury-on-Trym, BRISTOL, BS9 3TX.

ⒻⒶ**Carter & Coley** *(A A Clark, A Cooke)* 3 Durrant Road, BOURNEMOUTH, BH2 6NE.

ⒻⒶ**Carter A.J. & Co** *(A J Carter, M D A Gyde, N C Williams)* 22B High Street, WITNEY, OX28 6RB.

★ⒻⒶ**Carter Backer Winter LLP** *(J A G Alexander, M J Carter, R H Davis, D P Kramer, P D Smethurst, M S Somerston, E Tsui, A A White, P Winter)* Enterprise House, 21 Buckle Street, LONDON, E1 8NN. and at HIGH WYCOMBE, LEICESTER, SOUTHEND-ON-SEA, WEYBRIDGE

★**Carter Clark** *(A J Clark)* Meridian House, 62 Station Road, North Chingford, LONDON, E4 7BA.

ⓉⒻⓅⒶ**Carter Dutton, trading name of Carter Dutton Limited** *(J M Duffill, R W Dutton, R L Mander)* 65-66 St. Mary Street, CHIPPENHAM, WILTSHIRE, SN15 3JF.

Ⓟ**Carter Gold Ltd** *(A Chapman, S B Howarth)* 27 Landport Terrace, PORTSMOUTH, PO1 2RG.

ⓅⒶ**Carter Nicholls Consultants Ltd** *(M D Chilvers)* 415 Limpsfield Road, WARLINGHAM, SURREY, CR6 9HA.

ⒻⓅⒶ**Carter Nicholls, trading name of Carter Nicholls Limited** *(S D Potter)* Victoria House, Stanbridge Industrial Park, Staplefield Lane, Staplefield, HAYWARDS HEATH, WEST SUSSEX RH17 6AS.

Ⓟ**Cartlidge & Co Ltd** *(J W Cartlidge)* 137 Laughton Road, Dinnington, SHEFFIELD, S25 2PP.

Cartner & Co. *(A E Cartner)* 47 Sandy Lodge Way, NORTHWOOD, HA6 2AR.

ⓅⒶ**Cartwrights Accountants Holdings Limited** *(A D C Hill)* Regency House, 33 Wood Street, BARNET, HERTFORDSHIRE, EN5 4BE.

Ⓟ**Cartwrights Advisory Services Limited** *(A D C Hill)* Regency House, 33 Wood Street, BARNET, HERTFORDSHIRE, EN5 4BE.

★ⒻⓅⒶ**Cartwrights Audit, trading name of Cartwrights Audit Limited** *(A D C Hill)* Regency House, 33 Wood Street, BARNET, HERTFORDSHIRE, EN5 4BE.

Ⓟ**Caryl Chambers Limited** *(C A Chambers)* Kamara, 6a Church Street, Burton Latimer, KETTERING, NN15 5LU.

ⓅⒶ**CAS, trading name of CAS House Limited** *(I T Ibrahim)* 69-71 High Street, CHATHAM, KENT, ME4 4EE.

Case & Co *(T R Case)* 20 Goodwood Way, Cepen Park South, CHIPPENHAM, WILTSHIRE, SN14 0SY.

★Ⓐ**Casey Lester** *(H L Tish)* Equity House, 57 Hill Avenue, AMERSHAM, BUCKINGHAMSHIRE, HP6 5UN.

Casey Yoon & Co *(K C Yoon)* Level 5, 231 Adelaide Terrace, PERTH, WA 6000, AUSTRALIA.

Caseys *(S N Casey)* Wild Acre, Old Green Lane, CAMBERLEY, SURREY, GU15 4LG.

Ⓟ**Cashability, trading name of Cashability Limited** *(I Cornelius)* The Office, 4 Shaw Green Lane, Prestbury, CHELTENHAM, GLOUCESTERSHIRE, GL52 3BP.

Ⓐ**Cashmore & Co** *(M J Cashmore)* Third Floor, The Robbins Building, Albert Street, RUGBY, CV21 2SD.

Ⓟ**Casserley Accounting Limited** *(I V J Casserly)* 16 Tilsworth Road, BEACONSFIELD, BUCKINGHAMSHIRE, HP9 1TR.

Cassidy & Co. *(P G Cassidy)* 1 Grasmere Avenue, Locksbottom, ORPINGTON, KENT, BR6 8HD.

Ⓟ**Cassidys Payroll Limited** *(S G Whorlow)* South Stour Offices, Roman Road, Mersham, ASHFORD, KENT, TN25 7HS.

ⓉⒻⓅⒶ**Cassidys, trading name of Cassidys Limited** *(S G Whorlow)* South Stour Offices, Roman Road, Mersham, ASHFORD, KENT, TN25 7HS.

ⓉⒻⓅⒶ**Casson Beckman, trading name of Casson Beckman Business and Tax Advisers Limited** *(S R Walter)* Murrills House, 48 East Street, Portchester, FAREHAM, HAMPSHIRE, PO16 9XS.

Ⓟ**Casson Beckman, trading name of Cassonbeckman.co.uk Limited** *(R A Vaughan)* Rose Villa, Reading Road, Mattingley, HOOK, HAMPSHIRE, RG27 8JZ.

ⓉⒶ**Cassons** *(C G Cooper, S Greenwood, A Hayman, L Nutter, N C Stockton, C Tice)* St Crispin House, St. Crispin Way, Haslingden, ROSSENDALE, LANCASHIRE, BB4 4PW. and at MANCHESTER

★**Cassons & Associates** *(S Greenwood, A Hayman, L Nutter, N C Stockton, C Tice)* St. Crispin House, 4 St. Crispin Way, Haslingden, ROSSENDALE, LANCASHIRE, BB4 4PW.

Ⓟ**Castaing & Co, trading name of Castaing & Co Limited** *(H C Fairpo)* The Chapel, Silver Street, Witcham, ELY, CAMBRIDGESHIRE, CB6 2LF.

Castle Accountancy *(G S Dolby)* 51 Bower Street, BEDFORD, BEDFORDSHIRE, MK40 3RD.

Ⓟ**Castle Accountancy Limited** *(D H Burrows)* Parkfield House, Park Street, STAFFORD, ST17 4AL.

ⒻⓅ**Castle Corporate Finance Limited** *(M A Norrie)* 158 High Street, TONBRIDGE, KENT, TN9 1BB.

Castle Johns *(P J Castle)* 1 Warwick Row, LONDON, SW1E 5ER.

★ⒻⓅ**Castle Park Services Limited** *(G L Banks)* 39 Castle Street, LEICESTER, LE1 5WN.

★Ⓐ**Castle Ryce** *(P Davda, S C Shah, S M Suchak)* The Clockhouse, 87 Paines Lane, PINNER, MIDDLESEX, HA5 3BY.

Ⓟ**Castle Training Ltd** *(A R Clavell)* 2 Whitbred Road, SALISBURY, SP2 9PE.

CAT Accounting Services *(C A Tonkin)* 50 Great Woodford Drive, Plympton, PLYMOUTH, PL7 4RL.

★ⒻⓅⒶ**Catalyst Business Support, LDP Luckmans, trading names of Luckmans Duckett Parker Limited** *(T J Frankton, G P Parker, A K Rishiraj, S A Twigger)* Victoria House, 44-45 Queens Road, COVENTRY, CV1 3EH.

Catalyst Corporate Finance LLP *(M Birri, J P R Crowther, J A Currie, S P Currie, A B Davis, J Harrison, R A D Holden, J R Hope, M S Humphries, T E Hurley, E J Keating, B D McGowan, K A Pickering, J A Sanders, R J Sanders, P D Vanstone)* 9th Floor, Bank House, 8 Cherry Street, BIRMINGHAM, B2 5AL. and at LONDON, NOTTINGHAM

Cate Allwood *(C M Allwood)* 12 Church Close, Pulham St. Mary, DISS, NORFOLK, IP21 4RR.

Catharine Madgin *(C J Madgin)* 33 Murray Road, Wimbledon, LONDON, SW19 4PD.

ⓅⒶ**Catherine A Williams Ltd** *(C A Williams)* 1 High Street, CRICKHOWELL, POWYS, NP8 1BW.

Catherine Bennett *(C Bennett)* 6 Green Lane, Redruth, CORNWALL, TR15 1JT.

Catherine Goudge *(C A Goudge)* 33 Well Close, Long Ashton, BRISTOL, BS41 9NB.

Catherine Hussey *(A C Hussey)* 3 O'Rahilly Row, Fermoy, CORK, COUNTY CORK, IRELAND.

Catherine Metcalfe *(C H Metcalfe)* October House, Jonas Lane, WADHURST, TN5 6UJ.

Ⓐ**Catherine Monaghan** *(C Monaghan)* South View, Clairemorris Road, BALLA, COUNTY MAYO, IRELAND.

Catherine Smith & Co *(C E Smith)* 3 Campsie View Drive, Blanefield, GLASGOW, G63 9JE.

Cathy Hood *(C Hood)* 137 Barlows Lane, LIVERPOOL, L9 9HZ.

ⓅⒶ**Caton Fry & Co Limited** *(J E Caton)* Essex House, 7-8 The Shrubberies, George Lane, LONDON, E18 1BD.

Cattaneo LLP *(C E Cattaneo)* One Victoria Square, BIRMINGHAM, B1 1BD.

Ⓟ**Caulkhead Investments Ltd** *(N A Dixon)* Manor Farm House, Winterslow Road, Porton, SALISBURY, SP4 0JZ.

★**Cavendish** *(S Henry, D I Lawrence)* 4th Floor, Centre Heights, 137 Finchley Road, LONDON, NW3 6JG.

ⒻⒶ**Cavernham LLP** *(P I Macorison, A R O Williams)* 85-87 Bayham Street, LONDON, NW1 0AG.

★**Caversham** *(R P Surcouf, S Whale)* Elizabeth House, 9 Castle Street, St Helier, JERSEY, JE4 2QP.

★**CB Partnership** *(M O Prosser)* 119 Bury Old Road, Whitefield, MANCHESTER, M45 7AY.

Ⓟ**cba (Accountants) Ltd** *(C S Brown, S P Jenkinson)* 72 Lairgate, BEVERLEY, NORTH HUMBERSIDE, HU17 8EU.

Ⓟ**CBA Financial Services Limited** *(C S Brown, S P Jenkinson)* 72 Lairgate, BEVERLEY, HU17 8EU.

Ⓟ**CBAC Limited** *(A J Weatherill)* Hamelin, Bell Hill, Finedon, WELLINGBOROUGH, NORTHAMPTONSHIRE, NN9 5ND.

Ⓟ**C-BAS Accountancy and Taxation Services Ltd** *(R W Adams)* Castle House, Castle Hill Avenue, FOLKESTONE, KENT, CT20 2TQ.

★ⓉⒶ**CBHC LLP** *(D M Belbin, J A Boyden, D Bransbury, R E Bransbury, I Harris, R F Jarrard, M R W Spencer)* Riverside House, 1-5 Como Street, ROMFORD, RM7 7DN. and at CHELMSFORD

Ⓟ**CBS (Nottingham) Ltd** *(J Henderson)* 5 The Old Stables, Bestwood Country Park, NOTTINGHAM, NG5 8ND.

Ⓟ**CBS Accountants, trading name of CBS Accountants Ltd** *(N Majeed)* 27 Stratford Way, WATFORD, WD17 3DL.

Ⓟ**CBS Global, trading name of ML CA Complete Business Solutions Ltd** *(M Louka)* 16 Olympou Street, PO Box 12193, Lakatamia, 2322 NICOSIA, CYPRUS.

★ⓅⒶ**CBSL Accountants Limited** *(A J Barker)* Rowan House North, 1 The Professional Quarter, Shrewsbury Business Park, SHREWSBURY, SY2 6LG.

ⓅⒶ**CBSL Group Limited** *(A J Barker)* Rowan House, 1 The Professional Quarter, Shrewsbury Business Park, SHREWSBURY, SY2 6LG.

Ⓟ**CC Accountants Limited** *(I Bradshaw)* Business Suite 5, 3rd Floor, Castle Circus House, 136 Union Street, TORQUAY, TQ2 5QG.

CC Ching & Co *(C Ching)* Rooms 801-2, The Centre Mark, 287-299 Queen's Road Central, CENTRAL, HONG KONG SAR.

Ⓟ**CC Consortium CPA Limited** *(K Y Yeung)* Unit 1703, Vicwood Plaza, 199 Des Voeux Road, CENTRAL, HONG KONG SAR.

CC Panayi & Co LLP *(E Charalambous)* 2nd Floor, 44-46 Whitfield Street, LONDON, W1T 2RJ.

Ⓟ**CC Secretaries Limited** *(D T Cunningham)* 145 High Street, SEVENOAKS, KENT, TN13 1XJ.

CCH & Co *(C C Hull, J E Hull)* PO Box 827, London Colney, ST. ALBANS, HERTFORDSHIRE, AL1 9AB.

Ⓟ**CCIF CPA Limited** *(P Y Fung)* 1/F Sunning Place, 10 Hysan Avenue, CAUSEWAY BAY, HONG KONG ISLAND, HONG KONG SAR.

Ⓟ**CCIF CPA Limited** *(P Y Fung)* 34/f The Lee Gardens, 33 Hysan Avenue, CAUSEWAY BAY, HONG KONG ISLAND, HONG KONG SAR.

ⓅⒶ**CCM Accountancy Limited** *(V Cresswell)* Mede House, St. Judes Road, Englefield Green, EGHAM, SURREY, TW20 0DH.

Ⓟ**CCW Trust, trading name of CCW Trust Limited** *(R G Barrs, P S Bird, J A Cowan)* 6th Floor, Victory House, Prospect Hill, Douglas, ISLE OF MAN, IM1 1EQ.

ⓅⒶ**CCW, trading name of CCW Limited** *(S M Barr, Lord Blaikie)* 295-297 Church Street, BLACKPOOL, FY1 3PJ.

CDTL *(C F Dumbrell)* GPO Box 5360, SYDNEY, NSW 2001, AUSTRALIA.

Ⓟ**CE&GE Professional Services Ltd** *(C Eliades, G Evangelou)* 7 Dositheou Street, Parabuilding Block C, 1st Floor, Office C102, 1071 NICOSIA, CYPRUS.

Cecil Sanderson *(C R Sanderson)* 4 Lansdown Parade, CHELTENHAM, GL50 2LH.

★ⓅⒶ**CED Accountancy Services Limited** *(C E Davidson)* Unit 1, Lucas Bridge Business Park, 1 Old Greens Norton Road, TOWCESTER, NORTHAMPTONSHIRE, NN12 8AX.

Ⓟ**Cedar Solutions, trading name of Cedar Solutions (Management) Ltd** *(C K Varley)* Prospect House, 2 Sinderland Road, Broadheath, ALTRINCHAM, CHESHIRE, WA14 5ET.

Ⓐ**Cedric Douse & Co, trading name of Gardiner, Hunter & Catt** *(T C Catt)* 13 Station Approach, ASHFORD, MIDDLESEX, TW15 2GH.

ⒻⓅ**Celarben Ventures Limited** *(C D Carr)* 4 Whiteley Close, Dane End, WARE, HERTFORDSHIRE, SG12 0NB.

Ⓟ**Celia Adams Associates Ltd** *(C M Adams)* Eastham Court, TENBURY WELLS, WR15 8NW.

Ⓟ**Celtic Associates Limited** *(I D Wood, P A Young)* The Red House, One The Parade, Castletown, ISLE OF MAN, IM9 1LG.

ⒻⒶ**Censis** *(S M Close, K T E Harrison, R A Sullivan)* Exchange Building, 66 Church Street, HARTLEPOOL, TS24 7DN. and at MIDDLESBROUGH

Ⓟ**Centre For Education & Finance Management Limited** *(C R Dickson, R Martin)* Red Lion House, 9-10 High Street, HIGH WYCOMBE, BUCKINGHAMSHIRE, HP11 2AZ.

Ⓟ**Centre Stage, Michael Brookes & Co, National Private Hire Accountancy Services, Pub Plan, trading names of Michael Brookes & Co Ltd** *(M Brookes)* Hampton House, Oldham Road, Middleton, MANCHESTER, M24 1GT.

Ⓟ**Centrecourt Limited** *(Colin Batsford)* 23 Beechdale, LONDON, N21 3QE.

Ⓟ**Century Accounting Ltd** *(R D Featherstone)* PO Box 56 Century House, Victoria Street, Alderney, GUERNSEY, GY9 3UF.

ⒻⓅ**Ceri Millar & Co, trading name of Ceri Millar Ltd** *(C Millar)* 39 John Street, PORTHCAWL, MID GLAMORGAN, CF36 3AP.

Ceri Schinella *(C D Schinella)* 74 The Maultway, CAMBERLEY, SURREY, GU15 1QF.

Certax Accounting *(M J Lee)* Charwell House Business Centre, Wilsom Road, ALTON, HAMPSHIRE, GU34 2PP.

Ⓟ**Certax Accounting (Doncaster), trading name of Certax Accounting (Doncaster) Limited** *(J Newton)* 117 Wivelsfield Road, DONCASTER, SOUTH YORKSHIRE, DN4 0UY.

Ⓟ**Certax Accounting (Reigate), trading name of GMR Accounting Limited** *(M Robinson)* Castle Court, 41 London Road, REIGATE, RH2 9RJ.

★ⓉⓅ**Certax Accounting Ltd** *(K Bradshaw, J Newton)* Maynard House, 40 Clarence Road, CHESTERFIELD, DERBYSHIRE, S40 1LQ. and at COLCHESTER, MARGATE, SAXMUNDHAM

Ⓟ**Certax Accounting, trading name of Certax Accounting (Chelmsford) Ltd** *(A J Chivers)* 44 Oak Lodge Tye, Springfield, CHELMSFORD, CM1 6GZ.

Ⓟ**Certax Accounting, trading name of Certax Northampton Ltd** *(D M Haden)* 180 Bants Lane, NORTHAMPTON, NN5 6AH.

CF Cheung *(C Cheung)* 19th Floor, Cameron Commercial Centre, 468 Hennessy Road, CAUSEWAY BAY, HONG KONG SAR.

CFA *(C Christodoulou)* 10 Parton Street, 6051 LARNACA, CYPRUS.

Ⓟ**CFC Accountancy Services Ltd** *(K Fretwell, S Sequerra)* Unit 9, Acorn Business Park, Woodseats Close, SHEFFIELD, S8 0TB.

Ⓟ**CFO Consulting Ltd** *(P H Rossiter)* Flat 2, 27 Disraeli Road, Putney, LONDON, SW15 2DR.

Ⓟ**CFO Partners Ltd** *(M H Billington)* PO Box 28560, Remuera, AUCKLAND 1541, NEW ZEALAND.

Ⓟ**CFO Services Asia, trading name of CFO Services Asia Pte Limited** *(J D E Alliston)* 114 Taman Permata, Yew Lian Park, SINGAPORE 575237, SINGAPORE.

Ⓟ**CFO Solutions Limited** *(N R Lee, N Y Souster)* 47 Maplehurst Road, CHICHESTER, WEST SUSSEX, PO19 6QL.

★**CFW** *(J A C Gibbons, D G Sharrock, A C Stevens)* 1 Sterling Court, Loddington, KETTERING, NN14 1RZ.

Ⓟ**CG Accounting Limited** *(C R Guy)* 70 Eddington Crescent, WELWYN GARDEN CITY, HERTFORDSHIRE, AL7 4SQ.

ⓉⒻⒶ**CGC Associates** *(A Feighery)* 272 Harolds Cross Road, Harolds Cross, DUBLIN 6W, COUNTY DUBLIN, IRELAND.

Ⓟ**CGR Sussex Ltd** *(C G Ranson)* 1 Naseby Cottages, Fletching, UCKFIELD, EAST SUSSEX, TN22 3TB.

CGSM Accountants *(C Gricks)* 1 Engayne Gardens, UPMINSTER, ESSEX, RM14 1UY.

★ⓉⒻⒶ**CH Internal Audit, CHR Outsourcing, Cowgill Holloway, trading names of Cowgill Holloway LLP** *(A J Ball, P A Cowgill, J Marshall, M J Murphy, M M Parmar, P Stansfield, S P Stead, P W Stringer)* Regency House, 45-51 Chorley New Road, BOLTON, BL1 4QR. and at MANCHESTER

Ⓟ**CH4 Accounts Limited** *(R J Flook)* 13 Seymore Mews, New Cross Road, LONDON, SE14 6AG.

Ⓟ**CHA Business Advisors Limited** *(J R L Coy, S Hall)* Great Clough House, Goodshaw Fold Close, Loveclough, ROSSENDALE, LANCASHIRE, BB4 8PZ.

★**Chaddesley Sanford LLP** *(M W Gambold)* Longcroft House, 2-8 Victoria Avenue, LONDON, EC2M 4NS.

ⒻⓅⒶ**Chadwick & Company, trading name of Chadwick & Company (Manchester) Ltd** *(M Chadwick)* Capital House, 272 Manchester Road, Droylsden, MANCHESTER, M43 6PW.

ⓅⒶ**Chadwicks, trading name of Chadwicks Accountants Limited** *(B Chadwick)* 16a Menston Old Lane, Burley in Wharfedale, ILKLEY, WEST YORKSHIRE, LS29 7QQ.

Chagani *(A Chagani)* 37 Kingfishers, Orton Wistow, PETERBOROUGH, PE2 6YH.

Ⓟ**Chaimel Limited** *(M T Warwick)* 55 Longford Road, Bradway, SHEFFIELD, S17 4LP.

Chakraborty & Co *(D K Chakraborty)* 19 Elmfield Road, East Finchley, LONDON, N2 8EB.

ⓉⒻⓅⒶ**Chalmers & Co, trading name of Chalmers & Co (SW) Limited** *(S M Bachrach, D N Parsons, H E Tayler)* 6 Linen Yard, South Street, CREWKERNE, SOMERSET, TA18 8AB. and at YEOVIL

★ⓉⒻⓅⒶ**Chalmers HB, trading name of Chalmers HB Limited** *(P A Ballan-Whitfield, A P Paine, D C Winter)* 20 Chamberlain Street, WELLS, BA5 2PF.

Ⓟ**Chamberlain & Co, trading name of Michael Chamberlain & Co Limited** *(M Chamberlain)* Aireside House, 24-26 Aire Street, LEEDS, LS1 4HT.

Members in Practice and Firms - Alphabetical **Chamberlains - Chhaya Hare Wilson Limited**

Ⓐ**Chamberlains** *(P J Chamberlain)* 3 Burford Lea, Elstead, GODALMING, SURREY, GU8 6HT.

ⓉⒻⒶ**Chamberlains, trading name of Chamberlains UK LLP** *(M R Shah, R M D Shah, S B Shah)* 173-175 Cleveland Street, LONDON, W1T 6QR.

★Ⓟ**Chambers Cope & Partners Limited** *(S M Chambers)* 121 Smedley Street, MATLOCK, DE4 3JG.

★ⓉⒻⒶ**Champion Accountants LLP** *(G Cosgrove, A J Flanagan, A M Hopwood, M P Jackson, D L Thorn, M Turner)* 1 Worsley Court, High Street, Worsley, MANCHESTER, M28 3NJ. and at BLACKPOOL, CHESTER, PRESTON, SOUTHPORT

Ⓟ**Champion Business Advisors Limited** *(G Cosgrove, D A T Wood)* 4 Nile Close, Nelson Court Business Centre, Riversway, PRESTON, PR2 2XU.

Ⓟ**Champion, trading name of Champion Allwoods Limited** *(G Cosgrove, A M Hopwood, M P Jackson)* Refuge House, 33-37 Watergate Row South, CHESTER, CH1 2LE.

Ⓟ**Champion, trading name of Champion Business Solutions Limited** *(G Cosgrove, D A T Wood)* 71/73 Hoghton Street, SOUTHPORT, MERSEYSIDE, PR9 0PR. and at MANCHESTER

Ⓟ**Champion, trading name of Champion Consulting Ltd** *(G Cosgrove)* 1 Worsley Court, High Street, Worsley, MANCHESTER, M28 3NJ.

Ⓟ**Champion, trading name of Champion Haworth Moore Limited** *(G Cosgrove, D L Thorn)* 54 Caunce Street, BLACKPOOL, LANCASHIRE, FY1 3LJ. and at MANCHESTER

Champness & Sargant *(E N Williams)* 8 The Green, HOVE, EAST SUSSEX, BN3 6TH.

★**Chan & Man** *(S Y L Chan, K L Man)* 1603 16/F Island Place Tower, 510 King's Road North Point, WAN CHAI, HONG KONG SAR.

Chan & Wat *(C W Wat)* Suite A, 19th Floor, Ritz Plaza, 122 Austin Road, TSIM SHA TSUI, KOWLOON HONG KONG SAR.

★**Chan Chee Cheng & Co** *(K T A Cheng)* 19/F Beverly House, 93-107 Lockhart Road, WAN CHAI, HONG KONG ISLAND, HONG KONG SAR.

★**Chan Chee Hong & Co** *(W Chan)* No. 6 & 8 Jalan Gereja, 2nd Floor, Bangunan Keng, 50100 KUALA LUMPUR, FEDERAL TERRITORY, MALAYSIA.

Chan Chor Hung & Co *(C Chan)* Room 1801A, Sunbeam Commercial Building, 469-474 Nathan Road, YAU MA TEI, KOWLOON, HONG KONG SAR.

Chan Chun Kwong & Co *(C Chan, H Ho)* 904 Wellborne Commercial Centre, 8 Java Road, NORTH POINT, HONG KONG SAR.

Chan Lai Pang & Co *(S T Lai)* 28/F Times Tower, 393 Jaffe Road, WAN CHAI, HONG KONG ISLAND, HONG KONG SAR.

Chan Li Law & Co *(C B Chan, F C Li)* Unit 402, 4/F Malaysia Building, 50 Gloucester Road, WAN CHAI, HONG KONG ISLAND, HONG KONG SAR. and at YUEN LONG

Chan Yip Keung & Co *(Y K Chan)* Unit 1702-03, 17/F Skyline Commercial Centre, 71-77 Wing Lok Street, SHEUNG WAN, HONG KONG ISLAND, HONG KONG SAR.

★ⓉⒶ**Chancellers** *(R A Owen, N K Sarna)* 38/39 Bucklersbury, HITCHIN, SG5 1BG. and at LONDON

ⓉⒶ**Chancery (UK) LLP** *(R Dearing, R N Eddowes, J D Shanks, G Whittall)* Chancery Pavilion, Boycott Avenue, Oldbrook, MILTON KEYNES, MK6 2TA.

ⒻⒶ**Chancery Hartwell LLP** *(R N Eddowes)* 30 Ashby Road, TOWCESTER, NORTHAMPTONSHIRE, NN12 6PG.

Chancery Hopkins LLP *(R Dearing)* Chancery Pavilion, Boycott Avenue, Oldbrook, MILTON KEYNES, MK6 2TA.

Chanda Associates *(R Chanda)* 23 King Edward Walk, LONDON, SE1 7PR.

ⒻⓅⒶ**Chandler & Georges, trading name of API Partnership Limited** *(C T Jobanputra, P Karageorghis, A Sotiriou)* 75 Westow Hill, Crystal Palace, LONDON, SE19 1TX.

Chandler Backer & Co. *(M Mahe)* PO Box 63, Unit 3, Houmet House, Rue Des Houmets, Castel, GUERNSEY GY1 4BH.

Chandlers *(R J L Shaul)* 85-87 Bayham Street, LONDON, NW1 0AG.

ⒻⓅⒶ**Chandley Robinson, trading name of Chandley Robinson Ltd** *(N J Chandley, P G Robinson)* 33 Church Road, Gatley, CHEADLE, CHESHIRE, SK8 4NG.

Chandra Shah & Co *(C L Shah)* 64 Belmont Lane, STANMORE, MIDDLESEX, HA7 2PZ.

Ⓟ**Chang Leung Hiu & Li CPA Limited** *(C Leung, S Y Luk)* 12th Floor, No 3, Lockhart Road, WAN CHAI, HONG KONG ISLAND, HONG KONG SAR.

Chanter, Browne & Curry *(D J Chanter)* PO Box 6, DELABOLE, CORNWALL, PL33 9ET.

ⒻⒶ**Chanter, Browne & Curry** *(P G Browne)* 1 Plato Place, 72-74 St Dionis Road, LONDON, SW6 4TU.

Ⓟ**Chapel Grange Associates Ltd** *(B R Warneford)* College House, 17 King Edwards Road, RUISLIP, MIDDLESEX, HA4 7AE.

Chapman & Chapman *(C R J Chapman, P N Chapman)* Satley House, Satley, BISHOP AUCKLAND, COUNTY DURHAM, DL13 4HU.

Ⓕ**Chapman & Co** *(M S Chapman)* 39 Ferndene Road, Whitefield, MANCHESTER, M45 6RB.

Ⓟ**Chapman Associates, trading name of Chapman Associates (CA) Limited** *(K V Malde)* 31 Northwick Circle, HARROW, MIDDLESEX, HA3 0EE.

ⒻⒶ**Chapman Davis LLP** *(J C Davis, R J Palmer)* 2 Chapel Court, LONDON, SE1 1HH.

Chapman Higgs *(P A Higgs)* 58 Birchwood Road, LICHFIELD, STAFFORDSHIRE, WS14 9UW.

Chapman Nash, trading name of Chapman Nash LLP *(J S Chapman, E Nash)* Unit 4, Barford Exchange, Wellesbourne Road, Barford, WARWICK, CV35 8AQ.

ⒻⒶ**Chapman Pugh** *(D J Chapman, P B Pugh)* 4 Tregarne Terrace, ST. AUSTELL, CORNWALL, PL25 4BE.

ⓉⒻⓅⒶ**Chapman Robinson & Moore Limited** *(J R Moore)* 30 Bankside Court, Stationfields, KIDLINGTON, OX5 1JE.

ⓅⒶ**Chapman Worth, trading name of Chapman Worth Limited** *(A M Chapman, M Chapman)* 6 Newbury Street, WANTAGE, OXFORDSHIRE, OX12 8BS.

ⓅⒶ**Chapmans, trading name of Chapmans Associates Limited** *(P Patel)* 3 Coombe Road, LONDON, NW10 0EB.

Chappell & Co *(G G Chappell)* Baysfield House, Silfield Road, WYMONDHAM, NR18 9AZ.

ⓅⒶ**Chappell Associates, trading name of Chappell Associates Limited** *(A D Chappell)* Westfield House, Bratton Road, WESTBURY, WILTSHIRE, BA13 3EP.

Ⓐ**Charcroft Baker** *(M G Baker, G M Thorneycroft)* 5 West Court, Enterprise Road, MAIDSTONE, KENT, ME15 6JD. and at TUNBRIDGE WELLS

Charing & Company *(S L Charing)* 6 Sewardstone Road, WALTHAM ABBEY, EN9 1NA.

ⓉⓅ**Chariot House Ltd** *(M Partridge)* Gunpowder House, 66/68 Great Suffolk Street, LONDON, SE1 0BL. and at BRIGHTON

Charity Management Services *(M Wallbank)* 18 Park Road, Chandler's Ford, EASTLEIGH, HAMPSHIRE, SO53 2EU.

Ⓟ**Charles & Company(Services) Ltd** *(D C Craft, J A Pullen)* 1st Floor, 16 Massetts Road, HORLEY, SURREY, RH6 7DE.

Ⓟ**Charles & Company, trading name of Charles & Co Accountancy Services Ltd** *(G Georgiou)* 66 Cross Street, SALE, CHESHIRE, M33 7AN.

ⒻⓅ**Charles A Wood & Co, trading name of Charles A Wood & Co Ltd** *(A W Ingham, P Ingham, P D Webster)* 14 Wellington Road, BRIDLINGTON, NORTH HUMBERSIDE, YO15 2BH.

Charles A. Sherrey F.C.A. *(C A Sherrey)* Falcons Rest, Fairfield Lane, Wolverley, KIDDERMINSTER, DY11 5QJ.

Charles Associates *(A P Charles)* 32 Coleraine Road, LONDON, N8 0QL.

Charles Brownlee *(C Brownlee)* 11 Graffham Close, CHICHESTER, WEST SUSSEX, PO19 5AW.

Ⓟ**Charles Crehan Ltd** *(S C Crehan)* 51 Victor Road, TEDDINGTON, MIDDLESEX, TW11 8SP.

Charles D.B. Pugh *(C D B Pugh)* 2 Priory Walk, LONDON, SW10 9SP.

Charles E Lucas *(C E Lucas)* 9 Holly Dene Drive, Lostock, BOLTON, BL6 4NP.

Ⓐ**Charles E. Coffey & Co** *(C E Coffey)* Unicredit House, Irwell Street Entrance, 16 Paley Road, BRADFORD, BD4 7EJ.

Ⓐ**Charles Ellinas & Co** *(C G Ellinas)* 15 York Gate, Southgate, LONDON, N14 6HS.

Charles Fargher *(J C Fargher)* Ballafreer House, Union Mills, Douglas, ISLE OF MAN, IM4 4AT.

Charles Frieze MA(Oxon) FCA *(C A Frieze)* 5 The Miltons, 13 Milton Crescent, CHEADLE, CHESHIRE, SK8 1NT.

Charles Harvey ACA *(C W Harvey)* 74 Wragby Road, Bardney, LINCOLN, LN3 5XW.

ⒻⒶ**Charles L. Wyburn & Co** *(C L Wyburn)* 23 Bellfield Avenue, HARROW, HA3 6ST.

Charles Lamb ACA *(R C Lamb)* 3 Queen Street, Dorchester-on-Thames, WALLINGFORD, OXFORDSHIRE, OX10 7HR.

ⓅⒶ**Charles Lamb, trading name of Charles Lamb Professional Services Ltd** *(C S Lamb)* 3 Blacklands Crescent, FOREST ROW, EAST SUSSEX, RH18 5NN.

Ⓟ**Charles Marcus, trading name of Charles Marcus Limited** *(G D Willies)* 42 Brook Street, LONDON, W1K 5DB. and at FAREHAM

ⒻⒶ**Charles R. Dean BSc ACA** *(C R Dean)* Limbers Mead, Old Barn Lane, South Chailey, LEWES, BN8 4AS.

ⓉⒻ**Charles Rippin & Turner** *(V Acharya)* Middlesex House, 130 College Road, HARROW, MIDDLESEX, HA1 1BQ.

Charles Smith & Co *(C A Smith)* Hillside, Gills Hill Lane, RADLETT, HERTFORDSHIRE, WD7 8DB.

Charles Stringer *(C G G Stringer)* 17 Frith Way, HINCKLEY, LE10 0JE.

Charles Tait Accounting *(N S C Tait)* 124 Sharps Lane, RUISLIP, MIDDLESEX, HA4 7JB.

Charles Tweedale *(C E W Tweedale)* Dangerous Corner, PO Box 605, Brookledge Lane, Adlington, MACCLESFIELD, CHESHIRE SK10 4JX.

Charles Vasey & Co *(C H Vasey)* 75 Richmond Park Road, East Sheen, LONDON, SW14 8JY.

Charles Vitez & Co *(C O Vitez)* 37 Preston Road, WEMBLEY, HA9 8JZ.

Ⓕ**Charles Wakeling & Co** *(H R Johnson)* 72-73 Wilton Road, Victoria, LONDON, SW1V 1DE.

Charles Wong & Co. *(C R Woodhouse)* Room A, 6th Floor, Kiu Fu Commercial Building, 300 - 306 Lockhart Road, WAN CHAI, HONG KONG ISLAND HONG KONG SAR.

Charlie Carne & Co *(C N Carne)* 49 Windmill Road, LONDON, W4 1RN.

Ⓟ**Charlotte Dagg Financial Services Ltd** *(C A Dagg)* 14 Haverhill Road, LONDON, SW12 0HA.

Ⓟ**Charlotte Ready, trading name of C Ready Limited** *(C Ready)* The Oast, Stone Green Farm, Mersham, ASHFORD, KENT, TN25 7HE.

Charlotte Tucker *(C R L Tucker)* 92 Craiglea Drive, EDINBURGH, EH10 5PH.

ⓉⒻⒶ**Charlton & Co** *(M Charlton, G A Gray)* Saville Chambers, 4 Saville Street, SOUTH SHIELDS, NE33 2PR.

★ⓉⓅ**Charlton Baker Limited** *(S J Sartin)* 1 Fordbrook House, Fordbrook Business Centre, Marlborough Road, PEWSEY, SN9 5NU. and at DEVIZES

ⒻⒶ**Charlton Williamson, trading name of The Charlton Williamson Partnership LLP** *(D Charlton)* 77 Osborne Road, Jesmond, NEWCASTLE UPON TYNE, NE2 2AN.

★Ⓟ**Charter Tax Consulting Limited** *(J T Paterson)* 11 St. James's Place, LONDON, SW1A 1NP. and at TONBRIDGE

ⒻⒶ**Charterhouse, Charterhouse Whittenbury, trading names of Charterhouse (Accountants) LLP** *(M Ackenson, J M Edmond, H A Harris, M J Siddiqui)* 88-98 College Road, HARROW, MIDDLESEX, HA1 1RA. and at BEACONSFIELD

Ⓟ**Charterwells, trading name of JP Money Ltd** *(M P Pandya)* Premier House, 112 Station Road, EDGWARE, MIDDLESEX, HA8 7BJ.

Chartwell, trading name of Chartwell Accountants LLP *(R Evans)* 79 High Street, SAFFRON WALDEN, ESSEX, CB10 1DZ.

Ⓐ**Chartwells** *(N E Lyon)* Knightlands, North Benfleet, WICKFORD, SS12 9JR.

ⓉⓅ**Chase Reeves & Co Limited** *(D Bubb)* Chase House, 90 Springbank Road, LONDON, SE13 6SX.

★Ⓣ**Chater Allan LLP** *(S G Berriman, G M D Day)* Beech House, 4a Newmarket Road, CAMBRIDGE, CB5 8DT.

Chater Financial Consultants, trading name of M J Kerridge & Co *(M J Kerridge)* Unit 8, Midshires House, Midshires Business Park, Smeaton Close, AYLESBURY, BUCKINGHAMSHIRE HP19 8HL.

Chatoo & Co *(S A Chatoo)* 22 Sherington Ave, Hatch End, PINNER, HA5 4DT.

Chatur L. Ali *(L R Chatur)* 601 1088 - 6 Avenue SW, CALGARY T2P 5N3, AB, CANADA.

Chaucer *(S Dhillon)* 64a Shelley Crescent, HOUNSLOW, TW5 9BJ.

Ⓐ**Chaudhri & Chaudhri** *(M A Chaudhri)* 47 Hodder Drive, Perivale, GREENFORD, UB6 8LL.

ⓉⒻⒶ**Chavereys** *(M A Crawley, R J Davis, N Holmes, I D Morris, H A Mullens, B Wilkinson)* Mall House, The Mall, FAVERSHAM, KENT, ME13 8JL. and at CAMBRIDGE

ⒻⒶ**Chaytor, Steele & Co** *(P A Atherton, G M Dobson)* 9a Derby Street, ORMSKIRK, L39 2BJ.

Ⓐ**CHD Associates LLP** *(D J Evans-Dudley)* Ground Floor, Eden Point, Three Acres Lane, Cheadle Hulme, CHEADLE, CHESHIRE SK8 6RL.

Ⓟ**Cheadle Business Services Ltd** *(M R Cheadle)* Telegraph House, 59 Wolverhampton Road, STAFFORD, ST17 4AW.

★**Cheadles** *(M R Cheadle)* Telegraph House, 59 Wolverhampton Road, STAFFORD, ST17 4AW.

Ⓟ**CheapAccounting, trading name of KLS Business Consultants Limited** *(N Herring)* 21 Coniscliffe Road, DARLINGTON, COUNTY DURHAM, DL3 7EE.

Ⓟ**CheapAccounting.co.uk, trading name of All on the Web Limited** *(E C Clark)* 51 Hambledon Drive, WIRRAL, MERSEYSIDE, CH49 2QH.

Ⓟ**CheapAccounting.co.uk/Andrea Dobson, trading name of Andrea Dobson Limited** *(A Dobson)* 10 Freshfields, KNUTSFORD, CHESHIRE, WA16 0NR.

Cheatley and Co *(K M Cheatley)* 90 West Street, Oundle, PETERBOROUGH, PE8 4EF.

ⒻⓅ**Chedzoy Butterworth, trading name of Chedzoy Butterworth Limited** *(D R John, J D Parker, D H Stabbins)* 2 Chartfield House, Castle Street, TAUNTON, SOMERSET, TA1 4AS.

ⓉⒶ**Cheema Goffe & Co** *(D S Cheema)* 26 Plashet Grove, East Ham, LONDON, E6 1AE.

ⓉⒻⒶ**Cheesmans** *(C A Cheesman)* 4 Aztec Row, Berners Road, LONDON, N1 0PW.

Cheetah Management Services *(R J Benn)* Rua 31 de Janiero 81A - 3E, 9050-011 FUNCHAL, MADEIRA, PORTUGAL.

Cheetham & Co *(D J C Cheetham)* Holmlea House, Quarrier's Village, BRIDGE OF WEIR, RENFREWSHIRE, PA11 3SX.

★Ⓐ**Cheetham Allen** *(J B Cheetham)* 17 Wright St., HULL, HU2 8HU.

ⓉⒻⒶ**Chegwidden & Co** *(B T Buckley, M A Harris, P G Harris, C Otter)* Priestley House, Priestley Gardens, Chadwell Heath, ROMFORD, RM6 4SN.

Ⓐ**Chelepis & Co** *(G Georgiou)* 67 Westow Street, Upper Norwood, LONDON, SE19 3RW.

★ⒻⓅⒶ**Chelepis Watson, trading name of Chelepis Watson Limited** *(P S Dunn, G Georgiou, N F Springer, M G Tsielepis, P L Wallyn)* 67 Westow Street, Upper Norwood, LONDON, SE19 3RW.

Chenery & Company *(T J Chenery)* 36 Palliser Road, CHALFONT ST. GILES, HP8 4DL.

ⒻⒶ**Cheney & Co** *(R I Higginson, P A Sparks)* 310 Wellingborough Road, NORTHAMPTON, NN1 4EP.

Ⓟ**Cheng Yuen Ching Jennifer & Associates CPA Limited** *(Y J Cheng)* 10/F, Dawning House, 145-6 Connaught Road Central, CENTRAL, HONG KONG SAR.

★**Cheng, Kwok & Chang** *(P Chang)* 5/F, Wah Kit Commercial Centre, 302 Des Voeux Road, CENTRAL, HONG KONG ISLAND, HONG KONG SAR.

Cheng, Yeung & Co. CPA *(S Cheng, S H Yeung)* Room 1001-2, 10th Floor, Chow Tai Fook Centre, No 580 A-F Nathan Road, MONG KOK, KOWLOON HONG KONG SAR.

Cheong Youne E.K. *(E K Cheong Youne)* 7 Remy Ollier Street, BEAU BASSIN, MAURITIUS.

Ⓟ**Chequers Tax Bureau Limited** *(C Rengert)* 24 High Street, SAFFRON WALDEN, ESSEX, CB10 1AX.

Cheryl Major BA(Hons) ACA *(C J Major)* 7 Phipps Close, Whetstone, LEICESTER, LE8 6YN.

Cheryl Reeve *(C A Reeve)* 4 Ennion Close, Soham, ELY, CB7 5GU.

Ⓟ**Chesapeake Associates Limited** *(J J Parr)* Unit 5, Evans Business Centre, Jessop Close, Brunel Business Park, NEWARK, NOTTINGHAMSHIRE NG24 2AG.

Ⓟ**Chessman Limited** *(E M A Bishop)* Wrenfield, The Chase, Oxshott, LEATHERHEAD, SURREY, KT22 0HR.

★**Chester Accounting Services** *(S M Greensill, J A Hunt, F Patterson, C N H Pursglove)* Military House, 24 Castle Street, CHESTER, CH1 2DS.

Cheung & Co *(D C Cheung)* 342 Windmill Road, LONDON, W5 4UR.

Cheung Lee Ng & Co *(K A Cheung)* Room 1208, Two Grand Tower, 625 Nathan Road, MONG KOK, KOWLOON, HONG KONG SAR.

Cheung Pui Chung & Co *(P Cheung)* Office A, 21/F, Crawford Tower, 99 Jervois Street, SHEUNG WAN, HONG KONG SAR.

Ⓟ**Chew, trading name of T Chew & Co Limited** *(N Chew)* Second Floor, Cathay Building, 86 Holloway Head, BIRMINGHAM, B1 1NB.

Ⓟ**Cheyette & Co, trading name of Cheyettes Ltd** *(K L Cheyette)* 167 London Road, LEICESTER, LE2 1EG.

Ⓟ**CHF Accountancy Limited** *(P C F Howes)* Omnia One, 125 Queen Street, SHEFFIELD, S1 2DU.

Ⓟ**Chhaya Hare Wilson Limited** *(R E Day)* Redmead House, Uxbridge Road, Hillingdon Heath, UXBRIDGE, MIDDLESEX, UB10 0LT.

ⓅⒶ**Chicksand Gordon Avis, trading name of Chicksand Gordon Avis Limited** *(S B Chicksand, A J Taylor)* 12 Northfields Prospect, Putney Bridge Road, LONDON, SW18 1PE.

ⓉⓅ**Child & Child, Theo Jones & Co, trading names of Child & Child Accountants Limited** *(J Child, R J Child)* 49 Somerset Street, ABERTILLERY, GWENT, NP13 1DL. and at LONDON

ⓉⒻⒶ**Child & Co** *(A E Child, M J Child, R Child, J S Dawson, J P Monaghan)* 20 Kirkgate, Sherburn In Elmet, LEEDS, LS25 6BL.

Ⓟ**Chiltern Accountancy Services Limited** *(R H Cambrook)* 29 Highmoor, AMERSHAM, BUCKINGHAMSHIRE, HP7 9BU.

Ching Shun Fu & Company *(S F Ching)* Block B 14/F, Hillier Commercial Building, 89-91 Wing Lok Street, SHEUNG WAN, HONG KONG ISLAND, HONG KONG SAR.

ⓉⒶ**Chipchase Manners** *(G R Boagey, M Firth, C S Gorman)* 384 Linthorpe Road, MIDDLESBROUGH, TS5 6HA.

Chipchase, Robson & Co *(R E Robson)* 3 Springfield Park, DURHAM, DH1 4LS.

Ⓐ**Chisnall & Co** *(C H Chisnall)* 17 Stowell Close, ASHFORD, KENT, TN23 5HS.

★ⒻⒶ**Chisnall Comer Ismail & Co** *(R Gibb, T G Humphries)* Maria House, 35 Millers Road, BRIGHTON, BN1 5NP.

ⓅⒶ**Chittenden Horley Limited** *(G Horley, P Smith)* 456 Chester Road, Old Trafford, MANCHESTER, M16 9HD.

ⒻⓅⒶ**Chittenden Horley, trading name of CHCA Limited** *(G Horley, A C Roxburgh)* 456 Chester Road, MANCHESTER, M16 9HD.

Ⓟ**Chittenden Horley, trading name of Chittenden Horley Consulting Limited** *(G Horley)* 456 Chester Road, Old Trafford, MANCHESTER, M16 9HD.

Ⓟ**Chiu Choy & Chung CPA Ltd** *(K Y Chung)* Unit A 5/F Yu Fung Commercial Centre, 289-295 Hennesey Road, WAN CHAI, HONG KONG ISLAND, HONG KONG SAR.

Chivers & Co *(J C A Chivers)* 15 St. James Road, LONDON, E15 1RL.

ⒻⓅⒶ**CHL, trading name of Christopher Harden Ltd** *(C P Harden)* 122a Nelson Road, TWICKENHAM, TW2 7AY.

Chloe Fletcher *(C E Fletcher)* 4 West View Orchard, Freshford, BATH, BA2 7TT.

▽**Choksey Bhargava & Co.** *(K H Vachha)* P22, Bondel Road, CALCUTTA 700 019, INDIA. and at MADRAS, MUMBAI, NEW DELHI

Choksy Associates *(H A Choksy)* PO Box 11529, DUBAI, 75500, UNITED ARAB EMIRATES.

Chong & Co *(C H Low)* Flat 4, 55 Lancaster Gate, LONDON, W2 3NA.

ⒻⒶ**Chotai & Co** *(M M Chotai)* 3 Ambassador House, Wolseley Road, HARROW, HA3 5RT.

ⓅⒶ**Chowdhary & Co, trading name of Chowdhary & Co (Morden) Ltd** *(B S Chowdhary)* 23 London Road, MORDEN, SURREY, SM4 5HT.

ⓉⒶ**Chowdhary & Co.** *(B S Chowdhary)* 46 Syon Lane, Osterley, ISLEWORTH, TW7 5NQ.

Chowdhury Ahammad & Co *(U C Ahammad)* 4th Floor, 36 East Castle Street, LONDON, W1W 8DP.

Chown Dewhurst LLP *(K J S Desai, K J Offer)* 51 Lafone Street, LONDON, SE1 2LX.

Ⓟ**Chris Barkess FCA, trading name of Barkess & Co Limited** *(C Barkess)* Stockton Business Centre 70-74, Brunswick Street, STOCKTON-ON-TEES, CLEVELAND, TS18 1DW.

Chris Bawtree FCA *(C O Bawtree)* 8 Kingsmill Road, BASINGSTOKE, RG21 3JJ.

Ⓟ**Chris Charlton, trading name of Chris Charlton Ltd** *(C Charlton)* 38 Middlehill Road, Colehill, WIMBORNE, DORSET, BH21 2SE.

Chris Cunningham *(C J Cunningham)* The Wheelwrights, Silver Street, Abthorpe, TOWCESTER, NORTHAMPTONSHIRE, NN12 8QR.

Ⓐ**Chris Duckett** *(C D N Duckett)* Thorn Office Centre, Straight Mile Road, Rotherwas, HEREFORD, HR2 6JT.

Ⓟ**Chris Duckett Limited** *(C D N Duckett)* Thorn Office Centre, Straight Mile Road, Rotherwas, HEREFORD, HR2 6JT.

ⒻⒶ**Chris Edwards** *(C Edwards)* Clamarpen, 17 Napier Court, Gander Lane, Barlborough, CHESTERFIELD, DERBYSHIRE S43 4PZ.

Chris Edworthy *(C J Edworthy)* St John House, Trusham, NEWTON ABBOT, TQ13 0NR.

Chris Gumbley and Co *(C D Gumbley)* 5 Mercury Quays, Ashley Lane, SHIPLEY, WEST YORKSHIRE, BD17 7DB.

Chris Haworth & Co *(C G T Haworth)* The Gables, Goostrey Lane, Twemlow Green, Holmes Chapel, CREWE, CW4 8BH.

Chris Hope *(C I Hope)* Roselea, 82 Cleveland Avenue, DARLINGTON, DL3 7BE.

Chris Langham Consulting *(C R D Langham)* 17 Springs Road, KESWICK, CUMBRIA, CA12 4AQ.

Chris Lavis & Co. *(C A Lavis)* Pineapple Business Park, Salway Ash, BRIDPORT, DORSET, DT6 5DB.

Chris Lo *(L K T Lo Neng Fong)* 23 Rowsley Avenue, LONDON, NW4 1AP.

Ⓟ**Chris Makin Mediator Limited** *(C Makin)* Well Cottage, 39 Water Royd Lane, MIRFIELD, WEST YORKSHIRE, WF14 9SF.

Chris Marsh *(C J Marsh)* 3 Sherringham Court, 13 The Ridgeway, ENFIELD, MIDDLESEX, EN2 8NS.

Ⓟ**Chris Reid Ltd** *(G A Baker, C Reid)* Brick House, 150A Station Road, Woburn Sands, MILTON KEYNES, MK17 8SG. and at LONDON, STOCKPORT

Ⓟ**Chris Sinclair Accountants Limited** *(C G Sinclair)* 17 Upper Batley Low Lane, BATLEY, WEST YORKSHIRE, WF17 0AP.

ⓉⓅⒶ**Chris Skarparis & Co Ltd** *(C Skarparis)* 2nd Floor, 10(b) Aldermans Hill, Palmers Green, LONDON, N13 4PJ.

Chris Skinner *(C P Skinner)* 27 Albatross Way, DARLINGTON, COUNTY DURHAM, DL1 1DN.

Chris Swinson *(C Swinson)* Roseheath Wood, Bullbeggars Lane, BERKHAMSTED, HERTFORDSHIRE, HP4 2RS.

Chris Sykes *(C J Sykes)* 22 Hollin Lane, Weetwood, LEEDS, LS16 5LZ.

ⓉⓅ**Chris Wright & Co Limited** *(C S Wright)* 217 Hallgate, COTTINGHAM, NORTH HUMBERSIDE, HU16 4BG.

Chris Wright, trading name of C. Wright *(C Wright)* 39 Court Farm Road, NEWHAVEN, BN9 9DH.

Christchurch Accountants, trading name of Christchurch Accountants LLP *(C M Rusden, S R Rusden)* 3 The Paddock, 73a Mudeford, CHRISTCHURCH, DORSET, BH23 3NJ.

ⓉⓅ**Christian & Co Ltd** *(N E Christian, N H G Christian)* 26 High Street, HOLYWELL, FLINTSHIRE, CH8 7LH.

★**Christian Dodd, trading name of Christian Dodd LLP** *(W D Dodd)* PO Box 208, PENRITH, CUMBRIA, CA11 1DB.

ⓉⒻⒶ**Christian Douglass, trading name of Christian Douglass LLP** *(D J Burton, R J Massey, G H C Storey)* 2 Jordan Street, Knott Mill, MANCHESTER, M15 4PY. and at ALTRINCHAM, CARLISLE, TWICKENHAM

Christie Buchanan *(H A Adamjee)* Bridge House, 11 Creek Road, EAST MOLESEY, SURREY, KT8 9BE.

★**Christie Proud Thompson** *(L B Christie)* 64 Duke Street, DARLINGTON, DL3 7AN.

Christina Lyle BSc Hons ACA *(C M Lyle)* 26 St. James Avenue, West Ealing, LONDON, W13 9DJ.

Christine Clark ACA, trading name of Christine Clark *(C Roberts)* 6 Rowan Grove, Huyton With Roby, LIVERPOOL, L36 5XX.

Ⓟ**Christine Clark Accountants, trading name of Christine Clark Accountants Ltd** *(C M Clark)* 43 Poplar Avenue, WETHERBY, WEST YORKSHIRE, LS22 7RA.

Ⓐ**Christine Dickson** *(C R Dickson)* Red Lion House, 9-10 High Street, HIGH WYCOMBE, BUCKINGHAMSHIRE, HP11 2AZ.

Ⓐ**Christine Tetley** *(C M Tetley)* 195 Bramhall Lane, STOCKPORT, SK2 6JA.

Christmas & Co *(P A Christmas)* El Molino de la Nina, Casarabonela, 29566 MALAGA, SPAIN.

★**Christodoulides Shakallis & Co** *(G Savvides)* Christodoulides Building, 8 Alasias Street, P.O.Box 4428, LIMASSOL, CYPRUS.

ⒻⒶ**Christopher & Co** *(N Christopher)* 51A Anson Road, LONDON, N7 0AR.

Christopher B. Fry & Co *(C B Fry)* Claire House, Bridge Street, LEATHERHEAD, SURREY, KT22 8BZ.

Christopher Bailey *(C N Bailey)* Yoden House, 30 Yoden Way, PETERLEE, COUNTY DURHAM, SR8 1AL.

Christopher Bennett *(C R E Bennett)* Summer Pool Meadow, High Street, Bramley, GUILDFORD, SURREY, GU5 0HB.

Christopher C Jenkins & Co *(C C Jenkins)* Birchden Corner, Station Road, Groombridge, TUNBRIDGE WELLS, KENT, TN3 9NG.

Christopher C. Stone *(C C Stone)* 3 Tormead, 27 Dene Road, NORTHWOOD, MIDDLESEX, HA6 2BX.

Christopher D Jones *(C D Jones)* Strawberry Cottage, Strawberry Lane, Mollington, CHESTER, CH1 6LL.

Christopher Dean & Co *(C N Dean)* Ivy Cottage, Bakers Lane, Tadmarton, BANBURY, OX15 5TB.

Christopher Dix *(C J Dix)* Eskdale, The Street, Claxton, NORWICH, NR14 7AS.

Christopher E.J. Burman FCA *(C E J Burman)* Ardmhor House, 3 The Paddocks, Ampfield, ROMSEY, HAMPSHIRE, SO51 9BG.

Christopher G Glover *(C G Glover)* 2 New Road, Cookham, MAIDENHEAD, BERKSHIRE, SL6 9HD.

Ⓟ**Christopher Goldie & Co, trading name of Christopher Goldie & Co Limited** *(C B Goldie)* 11 Kings Road, BARNET, EN5 4EF.

Christopher Harvey *(C Harvey)* Rue de la Neuville 58, 1348 LOUVAIN LA NEUVE, BELGIUM.

Christopher Hyde-Cooper *(C Hyde-Cooper)* 74 Claverton Street, LONDON, SW1V 3AX.

Christopher J Holmes *(C J Holmes)* 27 Cootes Avenue, HORSHAM, WEST SUSSEX, RH12 2AD.

Christopher J. Snaith *(C J Snaith)* Tarn House, 55 The Meadows, Leven, BEVERLEY, HU17 5LX.

Ⓟ**Christopher Jenner & Co Ltd** *(C J Jenner)* 4 Walcote Place, High Street, WINCHESTER, HAMPSHIRE, SO23 9AP.

Christopher Jewell *(C A Jewell)* Torvista, Heathfield Road, Sands, HIGH WYCOMBE, BUCKINGHAMSHIRE, HP12 4DG.

Christopher Kent *(C T Kent)* 23 Rivergreen Crescent, Bramcote, NOTTINGHAM, NG9 3ET.

Christopher M. Stephen-Haynes *(C M Stephen-Haynes)* Malvern View Barn, Shrawley, WORCESTER, WR6 6TS.

Christopher Maslen *(C J Maslen)* Old Tan House, Cottingley Bridge, BINGLEY, BD16 1NB.

Ⓟ**Christopher R. Brown Limited** *(C R Brown)* 24 Albert Road, CLEVEDON, BS21 7RR.

Christopher R. Clarke *(C R Clarke)* 26 Elm Court, Highburton, HUDDERSFIELD, HD8 0TB.

Christopher Thubron *(C R S Thubron)* Avenue Louise 251, Bte 14, B 1050 BRUSSELS, BELGIUM.

Christopher Williams *(C M Williams)* Carnoch House, Glencoe, BALLACHULISH, PH49 4HS.

Ⓐ**Christou & Co** *(A Christou)* 132 Salmon Street, LONDON, NW9 8NT.

Christou & Co *(A Christou)* P.O. Box 25297, NICOSIA, CYPRUS.

Ⓟ**Chrysostomou & Co, trading name of Chrysostomou & Co Ltd** *(K Chrysostomou)* 407 Green Lanes, Palmers Green, LONDON, N13 4JD.

Chu & Lo Co. *(N C Lo)* Room 1701-2, 17/F ING Tower, 308 Des Voeux Road, CENTRAL, HONG KONG ISLAND, HONG KONG SAR.

★**Chu and Chu** *(K P Chan, K T Chan, K A Wong, S Yeung)* Suite 1801-5 18/F, Tower 2, China HONG KONG SAR City, 33 Canton Road, TSIM SHA TSUI, KOWLOON HONG KONG SAR.

Ⓟ**Chua Lowe & Co, trading name of Chua Lowe (JB) Limited** *(L L Lowe)* 5 Crookhill Road, Conisbrough, DONCASTER, SOUTH YORKSHIRE, DN12 2AD.

ⓉⓅⒶ**Chuhan & Singh, trading name of Chuhan & Singh Partnership Limited** *(A M Chuhan, G H Singh)* 81 Borough Road, MIDDLESBROUGH, CLEVELAND, TS1 3AA.

★**Chui & Kwok** *(C Chui, S K J Kwok)* Room 705 & 706, 7th Floor, China Insurance Group Building, No 141 Des Voeux Road Central, CENTRAL, HONG KONG ISLAND HONG KONG SAR.

★**Chung & Partners Limited** *(Y S Chung)* Room 2408, 24/F Hopewell Centre, 183 Queens Road East, WAN CHAI, HONG KONG SAR.

Church & Co *(S A Church)* 1st Floor, Burleigh House, 357 Strand, LONDON, WC2R 0HS.

Church & Co, trading name of Church & Partners SL *(P A Church)* El Rosario 143, 29600 MARBELLA, MALAGA, SPAIN.

Ⓕ**Church & Young** *(W E Church)* 11 Station Road, Headcorn, ASHFORD, Kent, TN27 9SB.

Ⓟ**Churchgate Accountants, trading name of Churchgate Accountants Limited** *(R B Jackson)* 18 Langton Place, BURY ST. EDMUNDS, SUFFOLK, IP33 1NE.

Ⓐ**Churchills** *(I S Brown, M Tomlinson)* 1st Floor, Shenstone Station, Station Road, Shenstone, LICHFIELD, STAFFORDSHIRE WS14 0NW.

Ⓐ**Churchills** *(B M Stevens)* Lindens House, 16 Copse Wood Way, NORTHWOOD, MIDDLESEX, HA6 2UE.

ⒻⓅⒶ**Churchmill House Ltd** *(D C Speller)* Churchmill House, Ockford Road, GODALMING, SURREY, GU7 1QY.

Ⓟ**CIG CPA Limited** *(W Chung)* Unit 702 7th Floor, Tung Hip Commercial Building, 244 Des Voeux Road, CENTRAL, HONG KONG SAR.

Cilla Watts FCA *(P C Buxton)* Vectis House, Banbury Street, Kineton, WARWICK, WARWICKSHIRE, CV35 0JS.

ⒻⓅ**Cinderhall Limited** *(C G G Smith)* Moor End, Silkstone Common, BARNSLEY, S75 7RA.

Ⓟ**Cindy & Co Limited** *(C J Adegbile)* The Weston Centre M6, Weston Road, CREWE, CHESHIRE, CW1 6FL.

Circs Insolvency & Recovery *(C F Smethurst)* Dallam Court, Dallam Lane, WARRINGTON, CHESHIRE, WA2 7LT.

Ⓟ**Cirrus Accounting, trading name of Cirrus Accounting & Bookkeeping Ltd** *(J C Thomson)* 39 Linden Road, Westbury Park, BRISTOL, BS6 7RN.

Citadel Tax Consultants LLP *(M R Leigh)* 3 The Glen, BOLTON, BL1 5DB.

★ⓉⒻⒶ**Citroen Wells** *(M S Bailey, N J Brennan, H M Charles, M Higgins, D J B Kidd, M J Levy, D Marks, J W Prevezer, D H Rodney, S Simou, K H Youle)* Devonshire House, 1 Devonshire Street, LONDON, W1W 5DR.

ⓅⒶ**City Wise Accountants Limited** *(V Jayaweerasingham)* 19 Tintern Avenue, LONDON, NW9 0RH.

ⓉⒻⓅⒶ**City, trading name of Citycas Limited** *(P M Cullen, S Pahwa)* Fifth Floor, Linen Hall, 162-168 Regents Street, LONDON, W1B 5TF.

ⓉⒻ**Civvals** *(L N Fagan, M A Kazi, S Pollack, A N Siganporia)* 50 Seymour Street, LONDON, W1H 7JG.

ⒻⓅⒶ**Civvals Ltd** *(L N Fagan, M A Kazi, S Pollack, A N Siganporia, M D Tullett)* 50 Seymour Street, LONDON, W1H 7JG.

CJ Accountancy and Bookkeeping Services *(C J Martin)* 31 Crescent Drive North, BRIGHTON, BN2 6SP.

CJM Consultancy Limited *(C J Moody)* Oriel House, Thames Road, Goring, READING, RG8 9AH.

ⓉⒻⒶ**CK Accounting Services, CK Audit, CK Corporate Finance, CK Systems, trading names of CK** *(L C Barnes, P J Davies, W J Davies, I J M Johnstone, B J Morgan)* No 4 Castle Court 2, Castlegate Way, DUDLEY, WEST MIDLANDS, DY1 4RH.

★**CK Law & Co.** *(C K Law)* 1101 Bank Centre, 630-636 Nathan Road, MONG KOK, KOWLOON, HONG KONG SAR.

ⒻⓅⒶ**CK Partnership Limited** *(G Christou, R Koppa)* 1 Old Court Mews, 311a Chase Road, LONDON, N14 6JS.

Ⓟ**CKA Consultancy Limited** *(B R Clark)* Pen Afon, Maunsel Road, North Newton, BRIDGWATER, SOMERSET, TA7 0BS.

★ⒻⓅⒶ**CKLG Accountants, trading name of CKLG Ltd** *(J S Cronk, L J Golding)* 9 Quy Court, Colliers Lane, Stow-cum-Quy, CAMBRIDGE, CB25 9AU.

CKP *(C S Choo Kim Pin)* 141 Queen Anne Avenue, BROMLEY, BR2 0SH.

CKP Services *(K E Prestwich)* Weavers Cottage, Porters Lane, Fordham Heath, COLCHESTER, CO3 9TX.

ⓅⒶ**CKS, trading name of CKS Accountancy Limited** *(A J Clarke)* 1 Church Hill, LEIGH-ON-SEA, ESSEX, SS9 2DE.

★**CL Finance Associates** *(C L Kennedy)* 3 Dodford Lane, Christian Malford, CHIPPENHAM, WILTSHIRE, SN15 4DE.

Ⓟ**Clacton Business Services Ltd** *(M K Burwood)* 61 Station Road, CLACTON-ON-SEA, ESSEX, CO15 1SB. and at COLCHESTER

Cladd Beck *(S M Beck)* 56a London Road, Apsley, HEMEL HEMPSTEAD, HP3 9SB.

ⓅⒶ**Cladd Beck Limited** *(S M Beck)* 56a London Road, Apsley, HEMEL HEMPSTEAD, HERTFORDSHIRE, HP3 9SB.

Claire Bisset *(C Bisset)* Beech Tree Cottage, The Street, Bacton, STOWMARKET, SUFFOLK, IP14 4LF.

Claire Charalambos *(C L Charalambos)* 59 Northaw Road East, Cuffley, POTTERS BAR, HERTFORDSHIRE, EN6 4LY.

Claire Connell *(C E Connell)* 195 Silverdale Road, Earley, READING, RG6 7NY.

Claire Hurrell ACA *(C L Hurrell)* Oaktree Cottage, The Street, Swanton Abbott, NORWICH, NR10 5DU.

Claire Ibbitson BSc(Hons) FCA *(C Ibbitson)* 24 Bryn Dreinog, Capel Hendre, AMMANFORD, DYFED, SA18 3RJ.

Claire Mosey ACA *(C A Mosey)* Woodstock, Bigby Road, BRIGG, SOUTH HUMBERSIDE, DN20 8HN.

Claire Savage Accountancy Services, trading name of Claire Savage *(H C Savage)* 37 Olney Road, Emberton, OLNEY, BUCKINGHAMSHIRE, MK46 5BX.

Claire Smith ACA Accountancy Services *(C Smith)* 77 Rosebery Road, Langley Vale, EPSOM, SURREY, KT18 6AB.

ⓅⒶ**Clamp Gogarty Ltd** *(R J Gogarty)* Bank House, Southwick Square, Southwick, BRIGHTON, BN42 4FN. and at HOVE

Clare & Co *(J Clare)* Bannisters, Chorley Road, Withnell, CHORLEY, LANCASHIRE, PR6 8BG.

Clare E Johns *(C E Johns)* 13 Banks Way, GUILDFORD, SURREY, GU4 7NL.

Clare F. Rimmer FCA *(C F Rimmer)* Fir Tree House, Truemans Way, Hawarden, DEESIDE, CH5 3LS.

Clare Woollatt *(C Woollatt)* 8 Almeys Lane, Earl Shilton, LEICESTER, LE9 7AJ.

★Ⓐ**Clarity** *(C J Bush)* 2 Lancaster Close, Weston Heights, STEVENAGE, HERTFORDSHIRE, SG1 4RX.

Clark & Co *(D Clark)* 22 Leaman Close, Chipping Sodbury, BRISTOL, BS37 6HA.

Ⓔ**Clark & Co** *(A Clark)* 4 Broad Street, BUILTH WELLS, LD2 3DT.

Ⓟ**Clark & Co Accountants Ltd** *(G Sisman)* Red Sky House, Fairclough Hall, Halls Green, Weston, HITCHIN, HERTFORDSHIRE SG4 7DP.

Ⓐ**Clark & Deen LLP** *(P G Salisbury-Jones)* Benson House, Suite D, 98-104 Lombard Street, BIRMINGHAM, B12 0QR.

Clark & Horner LLP *(R J Horner)* Dundee Place, 1 Adelaide Street East, Suite 2340, PO Box 181, TORONTO M5C 2V9, ON CANADA.

Clark Accounting Services *(A Clark)* 18 Homevale Cottages, Main Road, Knockholt, SEVENOAKS, KENT, TN14 7JE.

ⒺⓅⒶ**Clark Brownscombe, trading name of Clark Brownscombe Limited** *(V M R Anderson, N W H Ericsson, D R Scrivins, P J Thacker)* 8 The Drive, HOVE, EAST SUSSEX, BN3 3JT. and at LEWES

★ⓉⓅⒶ**Clark Howes Auditing Solutions Limited** *(F E O Porter)* 2 Minton Place, Victoria Road, BICESTER, OXFORDSHIRE, OX26 6QB.

Clark R. Durbin & Co *(C R Durbin)* 92 Western Avenue, NEWPORT, NP20 3QZ.

★**Clark Willetts & Company** *(C Willetts)* 5a Newerne Street, LYDNEY, GLOUCESTERSHIRE, GL15 5RA.

ⓉⒶ**Clarke & Co** *(P A Cambray, N Law Pak Chong, K K Pandya, M T Stower)* Acorn House, 33 Churchfield Road, Acton, LONDON, W3 6AY.

Ⓔ**Clarke & Co** *(J L Clarke)* 59 Curzon Road, Muswell Hill, LONDON, N10 2RB.

Ⓟ**Clarke Bell Limited** *(J P Bell)* Parsonage Chambers, 3 The Parsonage, MANCHESTER, M3 2HW.

Ⓐ**Clarke Dowzall & Balding** *(C L Balding)* 6 Old Main Street, BINGLEY, WEST YORKSHIRE, BD16 2RH.

★**Clarke Henning LLP** *(V M Raja)* 10 Bay Street, Suite 801, TORONTO M5J 2R8, ON, CANADA.

★**Clarke Jefferies** *(J Jefferies)* 105 Duke Street, BARROW-IN-FURNESS, CUMBRIA, LA14 1RH.

ⓉⒺⒶ**Clarke Nicklin, trading name of Clarke Nicklin LLP** *(A Baggott, G Clarke, P Draper, S Humphries, A S Jakara, P B Mellor, G C F Travis)* Clarke Nicklin House, Brooks Drive, Cheadle Royal Business Park, CHEADLE, CHESHIRE, SK8 3TD.

Ⓐ**Clarkes** *(P J Clarke)* Shaw House, 54 Bramhall Lane South, Bramhall, STOCKPORT, CHESHIRE, SK7 1AH.

ⓉⒺⒶ**Clarke's** *(P M Clarke, P J E Cronin)* First Floor, 5 Walker Terrace, GATESHEAD, NE8 1EB.

ⓉⒺⒶ**Clarkson & Co** *(R H Clarkson)* Centre of Excellence, Hope Park, Trevor Foster Way, BRADFORD, WEST YORKSHIRE, BD5 8HH.

ⓉⓅ**Clarkson Cleaver & Bowes Ltd** *(S J Clarkson)* 8A Wingbury Courtyard Business Village, Wingrave, AYLESBURY, BUCKINGHAMSHIRE, HP22 4LW.

ⒺⒶ**Clarkson Hyde, trading name of Clarkson Hyde LLP** *(M A Clark, M E Coomber, C R Green, R F John, P T Minchell, G Speck)* 3rd Floor, Chancery House, St. Nicholas Way, SUTTON, SURREY, SM1 1JB. and at LONDON

Ⓟ**Clarkson Mayer, trading name of Clarkson Mayer Limited** *(T J Bates)* Queensgate House, 48 Queen Street, EXETER, EX4 3SR.

Ⓟ**Classique Consultants LTD** *(M N Rae)* 4 Frere Street, LONDON, SW11 2JA.

Clavane & Company *(M Clavane)* 6 Trans Walk, Church Fenton, TADCASTER, LS24 9RR.

Ⓔ**Clavering & Co** *(R J Clavering)* Crew-yard House, Water Lane, Stainby, GRANTHAM, LINCOLNSHIRE, NG33 5QZ.

Claverley Accountancy Services *(J Bailey)* 22 The Wold, Claverley, WOLVERHAMPTON, WV5 7BD.

Ⓟ**Clay Ratnage Daffin & Co Ltd** *(Y Dedat, I S Laird)* Suite D, The Business Centre, Faringdon Avenue, ROMFORD, RM3 8EN. and at WICKFORD

★Ⓣ**Clay Ratnage Strevens & Hills** *(Y Dedat, I S Laird)* Construction House, Runwell Road, WICKFORD, ESSEX, SS11 7HQ. and at ROMFORD

ⓉⓅⒶ**Clay Shaw Butler, trading name of Clay Shaw Butler Ltd** *(D G Butler)* 24 Lammas Street, CARMARTHEN, DYFED, SA31 3AL. and at PORTHCAWL

ⓉⓅⒶ**Clay Shaw Thomas Ltd** *(D G J Williams)* 2 Old Field Road, Bocam Park, BRIDGEND, MID GLAMORGAN, CF35 5LJ.

ⓉⒺⒶ**Clayman & Co** *(M Kabel, D S Mildener, I Mildener)* 189 Bickenhall Mansions, Bickenhall Street Baker Street, LONDON, W1U 6BX.

ⓉⒺⒶ**Clayton & Brewill** *(Y J Jackson, N F South, J R Wilson-Mawer)* Cawley House, 149-155 Canal Street, NOTTINGHAM, NG1 7HR. and at MELTON MOWBRAY

Clayton & Co *(A S Brown)* 9 Lynton Close, KNUTSFORD, CHESHIRE, WA16 8BH.

ⒺⒶ**Clayton, Stark & Co** *(J L Budhdeo, N J Kariya, A Mitchell)* 5th Floor Charles House, 108-110 Finchley Road, LONDON, NW3 5JJ.

Claytons *(R J Bonnett)* 39 Harewood Avenue, NORTHOLT, MIDDLESEX, UB5 5DB.

Ⓟ**Claytons, trading name of Nick Clayton Ltd** *(N E Clayton)* 44 Drewitt House, 865 Ringwood Road, BOURNEMOUTH, DORSET, BH11 8LW.

★ⓉⒺⒶ**CLB Coopers** *(D R Clift, M G Garrett, G K Rigby, I T Smethurst, D J Travis, R Wardle, P A Whiteway, M D Worsley)* Ship Canal House, 98 King Street, MANCHESTER, M2 4WU. and at BOLTON, LANCASTER

ⓉⒺⒶ**Clear & Lane** *(D A Hope, I Hunt, A M Lane)* 340 Melton Road, LEICESTER, LE4 7SL.

Ⓟ**Clear Vision Consultancy(UK) Ltd** *(R D Walsh)* 1 Abacus House, Newlands Road, CORSHAM, WILTSHIRE, SN13 0BH.

ⓉⓅⒶ**Clear Vision, trading name of Clear Vision Accountancy Ltd** *(R D Walsh)* 1 Abacus House, Newlands Road, CORSHAM, WILTSHIRE, SN13 0BH.

Clearline Business Consultants *(L F Smith)* 552-554 Bristol Road, Selly Oak, BIRMINGHAM, B29 6BD.

Ⓟ**Clearly Read Limited** *(D P S Bedi)* 18 Neofytou Nicolaidi Avenue, 8011 PAPHOS, CYPRUS.

Clearscope *(J Thirukailayanathan)* 63 Lanercost Road, CRAWLEY, WEST SUSSEX, RH11 8YA.

Clearview Book Keeping & Accountancy Services *(A D Read)* Little Brockley, Broadway, Shipham, WINSCOMBE, SOMERSET, BS25 1UF.

Clearwater Corporate Finance LLP *(P J Burns, P Jones, A D Moore, P A Newell, P Nuttall, M H Reeves)* 7th Floor, Chancery Place, 50 Brown Street, MANCHESTER, M2 2JT. and at BIRMINGHAM, LONDON, NOTTINGHAM

Ⓟ**Cleden Howard and Company Limited** *(J L Cleden)* 121 Albert Street, FLEET, HAMPSHIRE, GU51 3SR.

Ⓟ**Cleethorpes Accountancy Limited** *(P J Curtis)* 3 Wardall Street, CLEETHORPES, DN35 8HA.

Ⓟ**Cleeve Accounting and Taxation Services Limited** *(G A McAnoy)* Hunters End, Southam Lane, Southam, CHELTENHAM, GLOUCESTERSHIRE, GL52 3NY.

ⓉⓅⒶ**Cleland & Co Limited** *(A H G Dick-Cleland, C M Harvey)* 1st Floor, Harbour Court, Les Amballes, St. Peter Port, GUERNSEY, GY1 1WU.

Clement C. W. Chan & Co. *(C W Chan)* 3/F & 5/F, Heng Shan Centre, 145 Queen's Road East, WAN CHAI, HONG KONG ISLAND, HONG KONG SAR.

★ⓉⒺⒶ**Clement Keys** *(S Atkins, J R Bates, R A Cocker, P T Cook, S M Cutler, F T Holden, D A McNab, M T Meakin, A T Robertson, G C Whitehouse, I S Yorke)* 39/40 Calthorpe Road, Edgbaston, BIRMINGHAM, B15 1TS.

ⒺⓅⒶ**Clement Rabjohns Limited** *(P S Emsley, P R Parsons)* 111-113 High Street, EVESHAM, WORCESTERSHIRE, WR11 4XP.

Ⓔ**Clements & Co** *(I R Clements)* 2 Eslington Terrace, Jesmond, NEWCASTLE UPON TYNE, NE2 4RJ.

ⓉⒺⓅⒶ**Clements Jones, trading name of Clements Jones Limited** *(J S Clements, T J Clements)* 1 Picton Lane, SWANSEA, SA1 4AF.

ⒺⒶ**Clemmence & Co.** *(J W Clemmence)* Linton, Rawdon Hall Drive, Rawdon, LEEDS, LS19 6HD.

Ⓐ**Clemrab LLP** *(P S Emsley, P R Parsons)* 111-113 High Street, EVESHAM, WORCESTERSHIRE, WR11 4XP.

ⓅⒶ**Clenshaw Minns, trading name of Clenshaw Minns Ltd** *(G B Minns)* 30 Market Place, SWAFFHAM, PE37 7QH. and at KING'S LYNN

Ⓟ**Cleverdon & Co, trading name of Thomas Moffatt & Co Ltd** *(R S Harding, T Moffatt)* 3rd Floor, The Sion, Crown Glass Place, BRISTOL, BS48 1RB. and at NAILSEA

ⓉⒺⓅ**Cleverdons, trading name of J Cleverdons Limited** *(J J Cleverdon)* 7 The Broadway, BROADSTAIRS, KENT, CT10 2AD.

Cliff White *(N C White)* Notre Coin, 31 Jardin De L'Epine, Collings Road, ST PETER PORT, GY11TX.

ⒺⓅ**Cliffe Catterall Limited** *(S J C Catterall)* 21 Dick Place, EDINBURGH, EH9 2JU.

Clifford & Co *(L D Clifford)* 11 Manor Farm Drive, Hinstock, MARKET DRAYTON, SHROPSHIRE, TF9 2SN.

Clifford Bygrave *(C Bygrave)* The Rustlings, Valley Close, Studham, DUNSTABLE, LU6 2QN.

Ⓔ**Clifford C. Palmer & Co** *(C J Pilgrim)* 61-67 Rectory Road, Wivenhoe, COLCHESTER, CO7 9ES.

Clifford Coxe *(C A M Coxe)* Greensted Hall, ONGAR, CM5 9LD.

Clifford Day *(C Day)* 21 Pinfold, South Cave, BROUGH, HU15 2HE.

Ⓟ**Clifford Fry & Co (Payroll) Limited** *(S M Allenby)* St Marys House, Netherhampton, SALISBURY, SP2 8PU.

★ⒺⒶ**Clifford Fry & Co, trading name of Clifford Fry & Co LLP** *(S M Allenby, L M Hallsworth)* St. Marys House, Netherhampton, SALISBURY, SP2 8PU.

ⓉⒺⒶ**Clifford Roberts** *(M V Field, L.J.P. O'Malley, J A Payne, S D Wilch)* Pacioli House, 9 Brookfield, Duncan Close, Moulton Park, NORTHAMPTON, NORTHAMPTONSHIRE NN3 6WL. and at WELLINGBOROUGH

Ⓐ**Clifford Sharp & Co** *(C J K Sharp)* 42 Park Road, BURGESS HILL, WEST SUSSEX, RH15 8ET.

ⓅⒶ**Clifford Sharp & Co, trading name of Clifford Sharp & Co Ltd** *(C J K Sharp)* 42 Park Road, BURGESS HILL, WEST SUSSEX, RH15 8ET.

ⒺⓅⒶ**Clifford Towers, trading name of Clifford Towers (Accountants) Limited** *(M R Lynds, S G C Towers)* 1st Floor Suites, Units 8-9, Webb Ellis Business Park, RUGBY, CV21 2NP. and at MILTON KEYNES

Ⓟ**Clifton Financial Solutions Limited** *(R H Louw)* 110 Coombe Lane, LONDON, SW20 0TH.

ⓉⒺⒶ**Clifton House Partnership** *(A K Aggarwal, S J Arthur, P C Bolton, D G Redwood)* Clifton House, Four Elms Road, CARDIFF, CF24 1LE.

Ⓐ**Clifton Page Wood** *(I P J Clifton)* 36a West Hill Road, BRIGHTON, EAST SUSSEX, BN1 3RT.

ⒺⒶ**Clifton-Crick Sharp & Co** *(P C Dann)* 40 High Street, PERSHORE, WORCESTERSHIRE, WR10 1DP.

Ⓟ**Clipper Accounting Limited** *(N S Wallis)* PO Box 5503, 11 Derwent Street, Draycott, DERBY, DE72 3ZH.

★Ⓟ**Clive Atkins & Co Ltd** *(V L Neave)* 60 Mansel Street, SWANSEA, SA1 5TF.

Ⓟ**Clive Bowyer Limited** *(D C Bowyer)* 18 Old Well Gardens, PENRYN, CORNWALL, TR10 9LF.

Clive Gummow *(C F Gummow)* Cottage Farm, Pinley Green, Claverdon, WARWICK, CV35 8LX.

Clive Howard Doust *(C H Doust)* 63 Pampisford Road, PURLEY, CR8 2NJ.

Clive Kettley *(C Kettley)* 80 Nettleham Road, LINCOLN, LN2 1RR.

ⓉⒺⒶ**Clive Owen & Co LLP** *(A I Allan, N Baldry, C P Beaumont, N J Bellerby, T A Doyle, G J Ellis, P A Hogan, A W Luckett, C F Owen, S C C Young)* 140 Coniscliffe Road, DARLINGTON, COUNTY DURHAM, DL3 7RT. and at DURHAM, YORK

Ⓐ**Clive Parker & Co** *(C W Parker)* 70 Graeme Road, ENFIELD, EN1 3UT.

Clive Parritt *(C A Parritt)* 34 Eton Avenue, LONDON, NW3 3HL.

Ⓐ**Clive Shedd & Co** *(C L Shedd)* 232 Sladepool Farm Road, Highters Heath, BIRMINGHAM, B14 5EE.

Ⓟ**Clive Steward, trading name of Clive Steward Limited** *(C J Steward)* 7 Spoonbill Road, BRIDGWATER, SOMERSET, TA6 5QZ.

Clive Thomas *(C R Thomas)* 16 Quat Goose Lane, Swindon Village, CHELTENHAM, GLOUCESTERSHIRE, GL51 9RX.

Ⓐ**Clive Tomes & Co** *(A C Le Brun, C P L B Tomes)* PO Box 771, Ground Floor, Colomberie Close, St. Helier, JERSEY, JE4 0RX.

ⓅⒶ**Clive Tramontini & Co, trading name of C & M Tramontini Limited** *(C Tramontini)* Bruce House, 15 The Street, Hatfield Peverel, CHELMSFORD, CM3 2DP.

Clive Wilson & Co *(C S Wilson)* 385 Boothferry Road, HESSLE, HU13 0JJ.

Ⓟ**CLK Payrolls Limited** *(M Kenyon)* Ashview, 88A Knutsford Road, WILMSLOW, CHESHIRE, SK9 6JD.

Ⓟ**CLL CPA Limited** *(M P Lee)* Suite A, 8/F Ritz Plaza, 122 Austin Road, TSIM SHA TSUI, KOWLOON, HONG KONG SAR.

Clockwork Tax & Accountancy *(C A Thackaberry)* 15 Ormonds Close, LICHFIELD, STAFFORDSHIRE, WS13 8EG.

Ⓟ**Clouders, trading name of Clouders (Audit & Accounts) Limited** *(C E Binnie)* Charter House, 103-105 Leigh Road, LEIGH-ON-SEA, ESSEX, SS9 1JL.

★ⓉⒺⒶ**Clough & Company, Clough Business Development, trading names of Clough & Company LLP** *(N C Bullas, N Gash, S Gash, L A Kendrew, R H Thompson, N C Westman)* New Chartford House, Centurion Way, CLECKHEATON, WEST YORKSHIRE, BD19 3QB. and at KEIGHLEY

★**Clough Management Services, trading name of Clough Management Services LLP** *(N C Bullas, S Gash, L A Kendrew, R H Thompson, N C Westman)* New Chartford House, Centurion Way, CLECKHEATON, BD19 3QB.

Clough Taxation Solutions LLP *(N C Bullas, N Gash, S Gash, L A Kendrew, R H Thompson, N C Westman)* New Chartford House, Centurion Way, CLECKHEATON, WEST YORKSHIRE, BD19 3QB. and at KEIGHLEY

Ⓔ**Clough, Tomblin & Co** *(D A Crowther, D N Riley, J Spenceley)* Nat.Westminster Bank Chmbrs, The Grove, ILKLEY, LS29 9LS.

Ⓟ**Cloverleaf Accountancy Services Ltd** *(N M Reese)* 48 Dalkeith Grove, STANMORE, MIDDLESEX, HA7 4SF.

Ⓟ**CLPC, trading name of CLPC Limited** *(C S Blaxall)* 41 Shaws Park, HEXHAM, NORTHUMBERLAND, NE46 3BJ.

ⒺⓅⒶ**Clyne & Co, trading name of Clyne & Co Ltd** *(G R Clyne)* 3 Mountain Road, CAERPHILLY, MID GLAMORGAN, CF83 1HG.

★**CM Adamides & Co** *(C M Adamides)* P.O. BOX 57167, 3313 LIMASSOL, CYPRUS.

Ⓟ**CM Payrolls Limited** *(G R Boagey, M Firth, C S Gorman)* 384 Linthorpe Road, MIDDLESBROUGH, CLEVELAND, TS5 6HA.

CMB Partners LLP *(H I Mirza)* 34 Ely Place, LONDON, EC1N 6TD.

ⒺⒶ**CMB Partnership** *(R M Brown, C P Campbell, P Martin)* Chapel House, 1 Chapel Street, GUILDFORD, SURREY, GU1 3UH.

ⒺⓅ**CMEASY Limited** *(V Korman)* Anglo Dal House, 5 Spring Villa Park, EDGWARE, MIDDLESEX, HA8 7EB.

Ⓔ**Coakley & Co** *(A B Coakley, D B Coakley)* West House, Milford Road, Elstead, GODALMING, SURREY, GU8 6HF.

★**Coalraven** *(M L Welbourne)* 127 Station Road, Hugglescote, COALVILLE, LEICESTERSHIRE, LE67 2GD.

Ⓟ**Coastal Accountants Ltd** *(D J Rudd)* Unit C, Oxford Court, Cambridge Road, Granby Industrial Estate, WEYMOUTH, DORSET DT4 9GH.

Ⓟ**Coates & Co, trading name of Tony Coates & Co Limited** *(A Coates)* 2 Fairhope Avenue, Bare, MORECAMBE, LA4 6JZ.

ⓉⓅ**Coates and Partners Limited** *(M I Blake, H H Bourchier, H Dowson, M Hathaway)* 51 St. John Street, ASHBOURNE, DERBYSHIRE, DE6 1GP.

Ⓟ**Coates Franklin Ltd** *(S R Coates)* Accountancy House, Station Road, Upper Broughton, MELTON MOWBRAY, LEICESTERSHIRE, LE14 3BQ.

Ⓟ**Cobalt Accountancy Limited** *(S F Brocklehurst)* Forest Lodge, Forest Road, Pyrford, WOKING, SURREY, GU22 8NA.

ⒺⒶ**Cobb Burgin & Co** *(N A Burgin, C P Cobb)* 129a Middleton Boulevard, Wollaton Park, NOTTINGHAM, NG8 1FW.

Ⓟ**Cobham House Management Services Ltd** *(R A Pick)* 9 Warwick Court, LONDON, WC1R 5DJ.

ⒺⓅⒶ**Cobham Murphy Limited** *(P D Harrison, E Roberts)* 116 Duke Street, LIVERPOOL, L1 5JW.

Ⓟ**Cobhams Limited** *(J E Harper)* 73 Liverpool Road, Crosby, LIVERPOOL, MERSEYSIDE, L23 5SE.

Ⓟ**Cobley & Co, trading name of Oakwood Accountancy Limited** *(B A Cobley)* 26 Beechwood Avenue, MELTON MOWBRAY, LEICESTERSHIRE, LE13 1RT.

ⓅⒶ**Cochrane & Co, trading name of Cochrane & Co Accountants Limited** *(J L Cochrane)* 38 Kings Road, LEE-ON-THE-SOLENT, HAMPSHIRE, PO13 9NU.

Ⓐ**Cocke, Vellacott & Hill** *(C W Brailey, J A Russell)* Unit 3, Dock Offices, Surrey Quays Road, Surrey Quays, LONDON, SE16 2XU.

ⓅⒶ**Cockett & Co Limited** *(L D Cockett)* 2e Rainbow Street, LEOMINSTER, HEREFORDSHIRE, HR6 8DQ.

Ⓟ**COG Accountancy Limited** *(N Steed)* 4 Heol Tre Forys, PENARTH, SOUTH GLAMORGAN, CF64 3RE.

ⓅⒶ**Cognitor Audit Services Limited** *(M R Eden)* Cognitor Ltd, 3 Birch House, Harris Business Park, Hanbury Road, Stoke Prior, BROMSGROVE WORCESTERSHIRE B60 4DJ.

★ⓉⒺⒶ**Cohen Arnold** *(D M Birns, M Broner-Cohen, A J Cohen, D Goldberg, D Z Harris, B Leigh, D B Myers, J A Neumann, J N Schwarz, A Sternlicht)* New Burlington House, 1075 Finchley Road, Temple Fortune, LONDON, NW11 0PU.

ⒺⓅⒶ**Cohen Corkery, trading name of Cohen Corkery Limited** *(E F Corkery)* 30 Chertsey Road, WOKING, SURREY, GU21 5AJ.

Colclough, Harrall & Co *(J C Harrall)* 50 King Street, NEWCASTLE, ST5 1HX.

Cole & Co *(A A Cole)* 15 Emperor Close, BERKHAMSTED, HP4 1TD.

ⒺⒶ**Cole & Co** *(M C E Bettinson, L R Cole)* 400 Harrow Rd, LONDON, W9 2HU. and at ASHFORD

Ⓔ**Cole Associates Corporate Finance** *(J B Cole, D R Middleton)* 19 Spring Gardens, MANCHESTER, M2 1FB.

★Ⓟ**Cole Bishop & Co, trading name of Cole Bishop & Co Limited** *(M Bishop)* Market Square Chambers, BROMYARD, HEREFORDSHIRE, HR7 4BP.

★ⒺⓅⒶ**Cole Marie, trading name of Cole Marie Partners Ltd** *(A C Marie)* Priory House, 45-51 High Street, REIGATE, SURREY, RH2 9AE.

Coleman & Co. *(N J Coleman)* 57 West End Lane, PINNER, HA5 1AH.

Ⓐ**Coleman & Company** *(P D Coleman)* 8A Alfred Square, DEAL, CT14 6LU.

Ⓟ**Coleopterus Limited** *(G Cardew)* 10 Main Street, Bilton, RUGBY, WARWICKSHIRE, CV22 7NB.

Ⓟ**Colesgrove Trustees Ltd** *(Richard Lane, T G Somers)* Springfield House, 99-101 Crossbrook Street, Cheshunt, WALTHAM CROSS, HERTFORDSHIRE, EN8 8JR.

Ⓔ**Colin Barker** *(C S Barker)* 11 Felton Close, Hollins, BURY, BL9 8BJ.

Ⓟ**Colin C Andrews Limited** *(C C Andrews)* 44 Armingford Crescent, Melbourn, ROYSTON PARK, HERTFORDSHIRE, SG8 6NG.

Colin C Evans, trading name of C.C.Evans *(C C Evans)* 25 Clarefield Drive, Pinkneys Green, MAIDENHEAD, SL6 5DW.

Colin D Clark *(C D Clark)* Riverside House, Off Glen Road, Laxey, ISLE OF MAN, IM4 7AT.

Ⓐ**Colin D Luke & Co** *(C D Luke)* 79 Northumberland Road, New Barnet, BARNET, HERTFORDSHIRE, EN5 1EB.

Colin Dalton *(C B W Dalton)* Hillside, 3 Tinacre Hill, West Midlands, WOLVERHAMPTON, WV6 8DB.

★**Colin Dowson** *(Colin Dowson)* 1748 West 2nd Avenue, VANCOUVER V6J 1H6, BC, CANADA.

Colin E Jones *(C E Jones)* Fernwood, Christchurch Rd, VIRGINIA WATER, GU25 4QB.

Ⓟ**Colin F Whitfield & Co, trading name of Colin F Whitfield & Co Limited** *(S G Haynes)* Redbrook View, Redbrook, WHITCHURCH, SHROPSHIRE, SY13 3AD.

Colin Faiers *(C C Faiers)* 4 Elm Way, Willingham, CAMBRIDGE, CB24 5JS.

Colin Fowler *(C P Fowler)* The Woodlands, Mold Road, Cefn-y-Bedd, WREXHAM, CLWYD, LL12 9YG.

Colin G. Horwood *(C G Horwood)* The Bungalow, Glebelands, Mildenhall, MARLBOROUGH, SN8 2LR.

Colin Glover & Co *(C S Glover)* 23 Carlyle Court, Chelsea Harbour, LONDON, SW10 0UQ.

Colin Gray & Co *(C Gray)* 26 Lower Kings Road, BERKHAMSTED, HP4 2AE.

ⒺⓅⒶ**Colin Gray & Co, trading name of Colin Gray & Co Limited** *(C Gray)* 26 Lower Kings Road, BERKHAMSTED, HERTFORDSHIRE, HP4 2AE.

Colin H P Smith *(C H P Smith)* Little Twitten, Mount Street, BATTLE, EAST SUSSEX, TN33 0EG.

ⓅⒶ**Colin J B Spinks & Co, trading name of Colin J B Spinks & Co Ltd** *(S A Portman)* St James House, 65 Mere Green Road, SUTTON COLDFIELD, WEST MIDLANDS, B75 5BY.

ⓅⒶ**Colin J Howe Limited** *(C J Howe)* Charter Court, Midland Road, HEMEL HEMPSTEAD, HERTFORDSHIRE, HP2 5GE.

ⒺⓅ**Colin Meager & Co Limited** *(C G Meager)* 32-35 Hall Street, BIRMINGHAM, B18 6BS.

Colin Morey *(C Morey)* 22 Charlock Way, Burpham, GUILDFORD, SURREY, GU1 1YB.

Colin Pearson FCA *(C M Pearson)* 10 The Rowans, St. Mary's Park, Portishead, BRISTOL, BS20 6SR.

Colin Rees Professional Corporation *(C J Rees)* 101 14020-128th Avenue, EDMONTON T5L 4M8, AB, CANADA.

Colin Rofe & Company *(C Rofe)* 12 Hatherley Road, SIDCUP, DA14 4BG.

Colin Stacey Associates *(C J Stacey)* 39 Silk Mill Road, Redbourn, ST. ALBANS, HERTFORDSHIRE, AL3 7GE.

Colin Steen *(C Steen)* 19 Polwarth Drive, Brunton Park, NEWCASTLE UPON TYNE, NE3 5NH.

Colin Tiffin FCA *(C M Tiffin)* Oak Lodge, Livermere Road, Great Barton, BURY ST. EDMUNDS, SUFFOLK, IP31 2RZ.

Colin W. Hoy *(C W Hoy)* 12 Millfield, Wadesmill, WARE, SG12 0TU.

Ⓟ**Colin Warren Accountants Limited** *(C Warren)* The Warren, 30 Tewkesbury Close, Poynton, STOCKPORT, CHESHIRE, SK12 1QJ.

Ⓐ**Colin Wilkinson** *(C A Wilkinson)* Britannic House, 657 Liverpool Road, Irlam, MANCHESTER, M44 5XD.

Colin Wolstenholme *(C Wolstenholme)* 1 Brockholme Road, LIVERPOOL, L18 4QG.

Colin Wood *(C Wood)* 15 Ronneby Close, Oatlands Chase, WEYBRIDGE, KT13 9SB.

Ⓟ**Collard Associates Limited** *(J G Collard)* 26 Orleans Road, TWICKENHAM, TW1 3BL.

★ⒹⒺⒶ**Collards** *(J C Addison, C J Brigstocke)* 2 High Street, KINGSTON UPON THAMES, KT1 1EY. and at HORSHAM

Ⓟ**Colledge & Co, Kontracta.com, Sole Trader Accountants.com, trading names of MPC Financial Consulting Ltd** *(M P Colledge)* 16 Conaglen Road, Aylestone, LEICESTER, LE2 8LD.

Ⓟ**Colleen Hammond ACA, trading name of CEH Consulting and Accounting Limited** *(C E Hammond)* 41 Weeping Cross, STAFFORD, ST17 0DG.

Ⓟ**Collenette Jones, trading name of Collenette Jones Limited** *(J P Collenette, M J Collenette, C S Falla)* Crossways Centre, Braye Road, Vale, GUERNSEY, GY3 5PH.

Collett Hulance, trading name of Collett Hulance LLP *(A J Collett)* 40 Kimbolton Road, BEDFORD, MK40 2NR.

Collett Smith, Elliott & Co *(P A Elliott, R T Elliott)* The Old Coach House, 179 Moss Lane, PINNER, HA5 3AL.

Collier & Co *(J S Collier)* PO Box 3450, BARNET, HERTFORDSHIRE, EN5 9GD.

Collingbourne Consultants *(J L L Underhill)* Glebe View House, Collingbourne Kingston, MARLBOROUGH, WILTSHIRE, SN8 3SE.

Collings & Co *(P N Collings)* Treen, Perranwell, Goonhavern, TRURO, TR4 9PD.

Ⓐ**Collins & Co** *(P J Collins)* 73a New Court Way, Ormskirk Business Park, ORMSKIRK, L39 2YT.

Ⓐ**Collins & Company** *(M N Collins)* 2nd Floor, 116 College Road, HARROW, HA1 1BQ.

Ⓟ**Collins Chapple & Co. Limited** *(A G Chapple)* Van Gaver House, 48 Bridgford Rd, West Bridgford, NOTTINGHAM, NG2 6AP.

Ⓟ**Collins Davies, trading name of Collins Davies Ltd** *(R H Collins, D H Davies)* 371 Exeter Road, EXMOUTH, DEVON, EX8 3NS. and at EXETER

Ⓐ**Collins Hart** *(N J Collins)* Victoria House, 437 Birmingham Road, SUTTON COLDFIELD, B72 1AX.

ⓅⒶ**Collinsons, trading name of Collinsonsplus Limited** *(S J Bosley)* 55 Newhall Street, BIRMINGHAM, B3 3RB.

Collyer & Co *(R C Collyer)* 17A Fairacres, RUISLIP, HA4 8AN.

ⒹⒺⒶ**Colman, Whittaker & Roscow** *(J Bellamy, A P Bracewell)* The Close, Queen Square, LANCASTER, LA1 1RS. and at MORECAMBE

ⒹⒺⒶ**Colston Bush** *(I S Petty, D Postlethwaite, M H P Spittle)* Lacemaker House, 5-7 Chapel Street, MARLOW, BUCKINGHAMSHIRE, SL7 3HN.

Colton & Co *(J E Colton)* Honeysuckle House, 17 Field Lane, LETCHWORTH GARDEN CITY, HERTFORDSHIRE, SG6 3LF.

Colville & Co *(D S W Colville)* Rhoscwm, BUILTH WELLS, POWYS, LD2 3PT.

Ⓟ**Comac Accounting Services, trading name of Richard A Crocker Ltd** *(R A Crocker)* 181 Chester Road, Hazel Grove, STOCKPORT, CHESHIRE, SK7 6EN.

ⒹⓅ**Combined Business Solutions Limited** *(A J Barker)* Rowan House North, 1 The Professional Quarter, Shrewsbury Business Park, SHREWSBURY, SY2 6LG.

Ⓟ**Command Accountancy Limited** *(C M Davis)* 7 Tennyson Avenue, Gedling, NOTTINGHAM, NG4 3HJ.

Ⓟ**Community Accountancy Service Ltd** *(E L Anderson)* The Grange, Pilgrim Drive, Beswick, MANCHESTER, M11 3TQ.

Ⓟ**Company Secretarial Services UK Ltd** *(P Bradley)* Unit 4/B, Christchurch House, Beaufort Court, Sir Thomas Longley Road, Medway City Est, ROCHESTER KENT ME2 4FX.

Ⓟ**Company Solutions Limited** *(R Beattie)* 2 Festival Square, Little Germany, BRADFORD, WEST YORKSHIRE, BD1 5BD.

ⒺⓅⒶ**Compass Accountants Limited** *(J A Walton)* Venture House, The Tanneries, East Street, Titchfield, FAREHAM, HAMPSHIRE PO14 4AR.

Compelling Solutions Consulting *(R A Toner)* 29 Lamb Close, WATFORD, WD25 0TB.

Ⓟ**Complete Payroll Services Ltd** *(A M Povey)* 12 Hatherley Road, SIDCUP, KENT, DA14 4DT.

Ⓟ**Complete Payroll Solutions Ltd** *(G M Burnham)* Second Floor, Cardiff House, Tilling Road, LONDON, NW2 1LJ.

Ⓟ**Complete Solutions 4U Limited** *(G G Gibbons)* 44a High Street, Pelsall, WALSALL, WS3 4LT.

★**Complete Tax Solutions** *(G M Burnham)* Second Floor, Cardiff House, Tilling Road, LONDON, NW2 1LJ.

Ⓟ**Completion Accounts Ltd** *(N J Thornton)* 19 St. Margarets Road, LONDON, SE4 1YL.

Compliance Financial *(C M W Todd)* 36 Tor Bryan, INGATESTONE, CM4 9JZ.

Ⓟ**Compliant Accounting Limited** *(E G Appleton, R J Ellerton)* Carpenter Court, Maple Road, Bramhall, STOCKPORT, CHESHIRE, SK7 2DH.

Composure Accounting & Taxation *(C J Burchell)* 9 Tennyson Close, HORSHAM, WEST SUSSEX, RH12 5PN.

Ⓟ**Compubook Services Ltd** *(S Cowan, J Diner, P Goldstein)* 201 Great Portland Street, LONDON, W1W 5AB.

★ⒹⒺⒶ**Condy Mathias** *(R Baker, S W Emery, J C Fry, J M Hillier)* 6 Houndiscombe Road, PLYMOUTH, PL4 6HH. and at TAVISTOCK

Ⓟ**Confin Interim Management Ltd** *(R B Kotlarzewski)* 95 Crofters Way, DROITWICH, WORCESTERSHIRE, WR9 9HU.

Confluence Tax LLP *(C Hailey)* Fosters Wing, Anstey Hall, Maris Lane, Trumpington, CAMBRIDGE, CB2 9LG. and at PETERBOROUGH

★**Conley Ward** *(T D Fowler)* 1168/1170 Melton Road, Syston, LEICESTER, LE7 2HB.

Ⓟ**Connect Financial Management Ltd** *(S G Bailey)* 29 Beverley Rise, ILKLEY, WEST YORKSHIRE, LS29 9DB.

ⒹⒺⓅⒶ**Connelly & Co, trading name of Connelly & Co Limited** *(D S Greenwood, A J McCarthy, G S Roebuck)* Permanent House, 1 Dundas Street, HUDDERSFIELD, HD1 2EX. and at TODMORDEN

★**Connellys** *(D G Burton)* Trident House, 222 Katherine Street, ASHTON-UNDER-LYNE, OL6 7AS.

Connor Richardson *(I R M Connor)* Victoria Buildings, 9 Silver Street, BURY, BL9 0EU.

Connor Spencer & Co *(J L Spencer)* Unit 5, Waterside, Station Road, HARPENDEN, HERTFORDSHIRE, AL5 4US.

ⒹⒺⒶ**Connor Warin Limited** *(G H Connor)* Trinity House, Sewardstone Road, WALTHAM ABBEY, ESSEX, EN9 1PH. and at BISHOP'S STORTFORD

Ⓐ**Conrad Ruffoni** *(P C Ruffoni)* Suite 14, Kent House, Old Bexley Business Park, 19 Bourne Road, BEXLEY, KENT DA5 1LR.

Ⓟ**Conradi Morrison & Co** *(J Bowen, P H Conradi)* 4 Summerhill Road, DARTFORD, DA1 2LP.

★ⒹⒺⒶ**Conradi Morrison, trading name of Thornton Springer LLP** *(P S Dunn, G Georgiou, S A Kaye, N F Springer, M G Tsielepis, P L Wallyn)* 67 Westow Street, Upper Norwood, LONDON, SE19 3RW.

★**Conrich & Associates** *(L M Conrich)* 65 Castellan Avenue, Gidea Park, ROMFORD, RM2 6EB.

Conrich & Co *(L M Conrich)* 65 Castellan Avenue, Gidea Park, ROMFORD, RM2 6EB.

Ⓟ**Conroy & Lermer, trading name of New Thinking Leaders Limited** *(J I Lermer)* 42 Lytton Road, New Barnet, BARNET, HERTFORDSHIRE, EN5 5BY.

Ⓟ**Consacc Accounting & Tax Services, R.H. Henkhuzens & Co, trading names of R.H. Henkhuzens Limited** *(R H Henkhuzens)* PO Box 643, Ground Floor Office Suite, Colomberie Close, JERSEY, JE4 0YS.

Ⓟ**Consergo Limited** *(M J Feeney)* Regency House, 3 Albion Place, NORTHAMPTON, NN1 1UD.

Ⓟ**Constant & Co, trading name of Constant & Co Accountancy Services Ltd** *(C Constantinou)* 344 Croydon Road, BECKENHAM, KENT, BR3 4EX.

★ⒹⒶ**Constantin** *(R J A Legon, P A Smith)* 25 Hosier Lane, LONDON, EC1A 9LQ.

Constantinos Tsiolakkis *(C Tsiolakkis)* Agion Ioxkim 10, Archangelos, STROVOLOS, CYPRUS.

Ⓟ**consult.Autus Limited** *(R Bell)* 5 Eskdale Avenue, Bramhall, STOCKPORT, CHESHIRE, SK7 1DS.

Ⓟ**Conte Davies & Co Ltd** *(L B Conte)* 60 Walter Road, SWANSEA, SA1 5PZ.

Ⓟ**Continuum Limited** *(C J Keene)* Gild House, 66 Norwich Avenue West, BOURNEMOUTH, BH2 6AW.

Ⓟ**Contractor Taxation Services Limited** *(I P Stewart)* Emstrey House, Sitka Drive, Shrewsbury Business Park, SHREWSBURY, SY2 6LG.

Control Accountancy Services *(D P Faram)* 1 Hawkwood Close, St Margaret's Banks, ROCHESTER, KENT, ME1 1HW.

Ⓓ**Conway & Co, trading name of Ian F Conway & Co** *(I F Conway)* 6 Blue Water Drive, Elborough Village, WESTON-SUPER-MARE, AVON, BS24 8PF.

ⒺⓅ**Conway Davis Ltd** *(G Conway)* Greenfield, The Causeway, Undy, CALDICOT, GWENT, NP26 3DP.

★ⒹⒺⓅⒶ**Conway Fielden Gough, trading name of Conway Fielden Gough Limited** *(P Conway, D J Verney)* Colne House, Guithavon Street, WITHAM, CM8 1BL.

★**Cook & Partners** *(K D Barker, M G Cook, M Jones)* Manufactory House, Bell Lane, HERTFORD, SG14 1BP. and at BISHOP'S STORTFORD, STEVENAGE

★ⒹⒺⓅⒶ**Cook & Partners Limited** *(K D Barker, M G Cook, M Jones)* Manufactory House, Bell Lane, HERTFORD, SG14 1BP. and at BISHOP'S STORTFORD, STEVENAGE

Ⓔ**Cook Sutton** *(D J Rusman)* Tay Court, Blounts Court Road, Sonning Common, READING, RG4 9RS.

ⒺⓅⒶ**Cook Trotter Ltd** *(G P Trotter)* 3 Sceptre House, Hornbeam Square North, Hornbeam Park, HARROGATE, NORTH YORKSHIRE, HG2 8PB.

Ⓟ**Cooke, Cooke & Co, trading name of 2Cookes Limited** *(C M Cooke, J M Cooke)* 1 Cranesfield, Sherborne St. John, BASINGSTOKE, RG24 9LN.

Cookes *(E Cooke)* 4 Powys Avenue, Oadby, LEICESTER, LE2 2DP.

Ⓔ**Cooks** *(J K H Cook)* 61 Thurstaston Road, Heswall, WIRRAL, CH60 6SA. and at PRENTON

ⓅⒶ**Cooks, trading name of Amyas Limited** *(P A R Cook)* 32 Argyll Road, EXETER, EX4 4RY.

Cooksey Perry & Co *(C J Cooksey)* Wayside, Old Horsham Road, Beare Green, DORKING, RH5 4RB.

ⒺⒶ**Cooley & Co** *(C M Cooley)* Sampuran House, 3a Chislehurst Road, ORPINGTON, BR6 0DF.

Ⓔ**Coombes, trading name of Coombes Corporate Finance LLP** *(D J Coombes)* Adamson House, Towers Business Park, Wilmslow Road, MANCHESTER, M20 2YY.

ⓅⒶ**Coombs, trading name of Coombs (Bedford) Limited** *(R S Bhamra)* 164 Bedford Road, Kempston, BEDFORD, MK42 8BH.

ⒺⒶ**Coope, Badman & Co.** *(J Badman)* 209 Church Street, BLACKPOOL, FY1 3TE.

Ⓐ**Cooper & Co** *(C A Cooper)* 18 Magdalen Grove, ORPINGTON, KENT, BR6 9WE.

Cooper & Co *(G S Cooper)* Level 15, Lumley House, 309 Kent Street, SYDNEY, NSW 2000, AUSTRALIA.

ⓅⒶ**Cooper Adams, trading name of Cooper Adams Limited** *(R A Adams, D C Cooper)* 12 Payton Street, STRATFORD-UPON-AVON, WARWICKSHIRE, CV37 6UA.

ⒹⒺⓅ**Cooper Dawn Jerrom Limited** *(M Amos, R J Cooper, S Meghjee-Caine)* Units SCF 1 & 2, Western International Market, Hayes Road, SOUTHALL, MIDDLESEX, UB2 5XJ. and at EPSOM

ⒺⒶ**Cooper Murray** *(J M Cooper, K E Grafton, N Murray, P J Watts)* Fifth Floor, Tennyson House, 159-165 Great Portland Street, LONDON, W1W 5PA.

Ⓟ**Cooper Parry Wealth Strategies Limited** *(J J Bowler)* 14 Park Row, NOTTINGHAM, NG1 6GR.

ⒹⒺⒶ**Cooper Parry, trading name of Cooper Parry LLP** *(J J Bowler, D A Browne, S R Bryan, A P Cheatham, T S Courtman, N J Edwards, K J Harris, A Honarmand, G M Jones, R Jones, D Parker, M A Pashley, E C Rands, P D Rowley, C R Shaw, P R Sterling, A H Timms)* 3 Centro Place, Pride Park, DERBY, DE24 8RF. and at LEICESTER, LONDON, NOTTINGHAM

ⒹⒺⒶ**Cooper Paul** *(B M Conway, C N Corrigan, B P Jones, G H Olliffe)* Abacus House, 14-18 Forest Road, LOUGHTON, IG10 1DX.

Cooper Rylatt, trading name of Cooper Rylatt LLP *(C Rylatt, J J C Rylatt)* 6 Teasel Drive, ELY, CAMBRIDGESHIRE, CB6 3WJ.

ⒹⒺⒶ**Cooper Young** *(Z Iqbal, M R Sangani)* Hunter House, 109 Snakes Lane West, WOODFORD GREEN, ESSEX, IG8 0DY.

Coopers *(R Cooper)* Apex House, Grand Arcade, Tally Ho Corner, LONDON, N12 0EH.

Cope Consulting *(E J Cope)* 15 One End Lane, Benson, WALLINGFORD, OXFORDSHIRE, OX10 6PA.

★ⒹⒺⒶ**Coplestons, Haydn Hughes & Co, trading names of The HHC Partnership** *(A J Copleston, H P Hughes)* 52 High Street, PINNER, MIDDLESEX, HA5 5PW. and at SEVENOAKS

Coppers & Co *(D A Copperwheat)* Green End Farmhouse, 22 Green End, Granborough, BUCKINGHAM, MK18 3NT.

Ⓟ**Coppersun Accountants, trading name of Coppersun Accountants Limited** *(D Kotecha)* 7 Wynlie Gardens, PINNER, MIDDLESEX, HA5 3TN.

Ⓟ**Coppin-Hughes Limited** *(C H J Hughes)* The Croft, Pit Lane, Treflach, OSWESTRY, SHROPSHIRE, SY10 9HB.

Ⓐ**Coppins-Hughes** *(C H J Hughes)* The Croft, Pit Lane, Treflach, OSWESTRY, SY10 9HB.

ⒻⒶ**Copplestone Unsworth & Co** *(P M Unsworth, J E Wain)* 9 Abbey Square, CHESTER, CH1 2HU.

ⓉⓅⒶ**Copson Grandfield Ltd** *(S R Copson)* 30-31 St James Place, Mangotsfield, BRISTOL, BS16 9JB.

Copthorne *(J Payne)* Copthorne House, The Broadway, ABERGELE, LL22 7DD.

Ⓟ**Cor Limited** *(A Taramides)* 1 Lampousas Street, 1095 NICOSIA, CYPRUS.

Core Resolutions LLP *(M D Marcus)* 63 Grosvenor Street, LONDON, W1K 3JG.

Corinne S. Carver *(C S Carver)* Pippin Lodge, Church Road, Snitterfield, STRATFORD-UPON-AVON, CV37 0LF.

Cork Gully Restructuring LLP *(J P Considine)* 52 Brook Street, LONDON, W1K 5DS.

Ⓟ**Corlett & Co Ltd** *(J K Corlett)* Ellan Vannin, Baldrine, ISLE OF MAN, IM4 6HA.

Cornaby & Stanley *(T J Stanley)* 18 Bath Rd, Old Town, SWINDON, SN1 4BA.

ⓅⒶ**Cornel Partners, trading name of Cornel Partners Limited** *(P N Jenkinson, R P Jones)* 115 Alexandra Park Road, LONDON, N10 2DP.

Ⓐ**Cornelius, Barton & Co** *(H P Sethi)* Mitre House, 44-46 Fleet Street, LONDON, EC4Y 1BN.

Ⓟ**Cornerstone Accountancy & Taxation Solutions Limited** *(C P Thomas)* B8 The Liverpool Centre, 23 Goodlass Road, LIVERPOOL, L24 9HJ.

Ⓕ**Cornish Accounting Solutions** *(P A Miller)* 20 Crockwell Street, BODMIN, PL31 2DS.

ⒻⓅⒶ**Cornish Accounting Solutions, trading name of Cornish Accounting Solutions Ltd** *(P A Miller)* 20 Crockwell Street, BODMIN, CORNWALL, PL31 2DS.

Ⓟ**Corporate Accountancy Solutions Ltd** *(J M Roylance)* Georges Court, Chestergate, MACCLESFIELD, CHESHIRE, SK11 6DP.

Ⓐ**Corporate Audit Solutions** *(J M Roylance)* Georges Court, Chestergate, MACCLESFIELD, SK11 6DP.

Corporate Finance and Strategy LLP *(A J Vickery)* Cherwell, St. Aldhelms Road, POOLE, DORSET, BH13 6BS.

Corporate Finance Services, trading name of Corporate Finance Services LLP *(N C Bullas, N Gash, S Gash, R H Thompson, N C Westman)* New Chartford House, Centurion Way, CLECKHEATON, WEST YORKSHIRE, BD19 3QB.

ⓉⒶ**Corrigan Associates, trading name of Corrigan Associates Bristol LLP** *(E J Corrigan)* Venturers House, King Street, BRISTOL, BS1 4PB.

Ⓟ**CosmoCo Services Ltd** *(S Ioannou)* Kyriacou Matsi 10, Liliana Court, Office 104, 1082 NICOSIA, CYPRUS.

Ⓟ**Cosmos Certified Public Accountants Limited** *(C Ng)* 808 8th Floor, Sun Hung Kai Centre, 30 Harbour Road, WAN CHAI, HONG KONG SAR.

ⓉⓅ**Costas Tsielepis & Co Limited** *(G C Tsielepis)* 205, 28th October Avenue, Louloupis Court, 1st Floor, PO Box 51631, 3507 LIMASSOL CYPRUS.

★**Costouris, Michaelides & Co(Overseas)** *(G Hadjispyrides, A A Savva)* 1 Deligeorgi Street, Cosmo Building, P O Box 23907, 1687 NICOSIA, CYPRUS. and at DUBAI

Ⓟ**Cotham Practice Management, trading name of Cotham Practice Management Limited** *(P E O Cox)* 17a Cotham Park, BRISTOL, BS6 6BZ.

ⓅⒶ**Cotterell & Co, trading name of Cotterell Partnership Limited** *(B Roberts, A R W Storey)* The Curve, 83 Tempest Street, WOLVERHAMPTON, WV2 1AA.

★ⒻⒶ**Cottons, trading name of Cottons Accountants LLP** *(G N Pain, M W Palmer, D O Smith, N C Warne)* The Stables, Church Walk, DAVENTRY, NORTHAMPTONSHIRE, NN11 4BL. and at BANBURY, NORTHAMPTON, RUGBY, SOLIHULL, SOUTHAM

ⓉⒻⒶ**Couch Bright King & Co** *(D R Cates, A C Oakes, A P Shepherd)* 91 Gower Street, LONDON, WC1E 6AB.

ⓉⒻⒶ**Coulsons** *(D J Bryden, P B Hodgson)* 2 Belgrave Crescent, SCARBOROUGH, NORTH YORKSHIRE, YO11 1UB.

★Ⓣ**Coulter & Co** *(M I Coulter)* 1st Floor, 4 Sherrard Street, MELTON MOWBRAY, LE13 1XJ.

ⓉⒻⒶ**Coulthards Mackenzie** *(M J Church, P L Gittins, C J Pexton)* 9 Risborough Street, LONDON, SE1 0HF. and at CAMBERLEY, HAYWARDS HEATH

★**Cound & Co LLP** *(K W Bunney, D R Gradon, J R King)* 27 Granby Street, LOUGHBOROUGH, LE11 3DU. and at ASHBY-DE-LA-ZOUCH

ⒻⒶ**Counsells** *(D J Counsell)* Smithbrook Kilns, CRANLEIGH, GU6 8JJ.

Ⓟ**Counterpoint, trading name of Counterpoint Limited** *(G J Loveday)* Harberts Cottage, 1 Back Street, Ashton Keynes, SWINDON, WILTSHIRE, SN6 6PD.

Ⓟ**Counting Tree Limited** *(R Ruparel)* 118 Massingberd Way, LONDON, SW17 6AH.

Ⓟ**Court Park Financial Services Limited** *(G A Todesco)* 11 Court Drive, HILLINGDON, MIDDLESEX, UB10 0BL.

Ⓕ**Courtland Financial Services, trading name of Ian Robinson** *(I Robinson)* Electroline House, 15 Lion Road, TWICKENHAM, TW1 4JH.

Ⓟ**Courtlands, trading name of Courtland Ltd** *(J Berger)* Courtlands Cottage, 62 Copsem Lane, Oxshott, LEATHERHEAD, KT22 0NT.

ⓉⓅ**Cousins & Co Limited** *(A R Cousins)* The Vanguard Suite, Broadcasting House, Newport Road, MIDDLESBROUGH, TS1 5JA.

Cousins Brett *(J E Cousins)* 20 Bulstrode Street, LONDON, W1U 2JW.

Ⓕ**Coussens** *(M C Coussens)* Chimneys, Boughton Hall Avenue, Send, WOKING, GU23 7DD.

Cova & Co *(A J Cova)* Pedlars March, 4 Meadway, Oxshott, LEATHERHEAD, SURREY, KT22 0LZ.

ⓉⒻⒶ**Coveney Nicholls** *(J N Kelly, J Mabey)* The Old Wheel House, 31/37 Church Street, REIGATE, RH2 0AD.

Ⓟ**Coveney Nicholls Limited** *(S Beaton, M Bennett, J N Kelly, J Mabey)* The Old Wheel House, 31/37 Church Street, REIGATE, RH2 0AD.

Ⓟ**Cowbridge Investments Limited** *(N J Hickling)* Aeolian House, Piccadilly, Llanblethian, COWBRIDGE, SOUTH GLAMORGAN, CF71 7JL.

Cowbridge Tax Services, trading name of R. H Bradshaw *(R H Bradshaw)* Mill Brow, Brookfield Park Road, COWBRIDGE, CF71 7HJ.

Ⓟ**Cowden Consulting Ltd** *(A R Gourlay)* Ruthin House, Southgate, Eckington, SHEFFIELD, S21 4FT.

Cowgill Holloway & Co *(P A Cowgill, M J Murphy, P Stansfield)* 10 Bolton Street, Ramsbottom, BURY, BL0 9HX.

Ⓟ**Cowgill Holloway Care 1 Limited** *(A J Ball, P A Cowgill, J Marshall, P Stansfield, S P Stead, P W Stringer)* Regency House, 45-51 Chorley New Road, BOLTON, BL1 4QR.

ⒻⒶ**Cowgill Holloway, trading name of Cowgill Holloway Liverpool LLP** *(A J Ball, J Marshall, P Stansfield)* The Plaza, 100 Old Hall Street, LIVERPOOL, L3 9QJ.

Cowley & Co *(A M Cowley)* 73 Arthur Road, LONDON, SW19 7DP.

Cowley Holmes Accountants LLP *(B D Cowley)* 9 Goldington Road, BEDFORD, MK40 3JY.

Cox *(E Cox)* PO Box 1241, BLACKPOOL, FY1 9FD.

Ⓟ**Cox & Browning, trading name of Cox & Browning Limited** *(C E Browning)* 35 Manor Road, Bladon, WOODSTOCK, OX20 1RU.

Ⓟ**Cox & Co(Management Consultancy) Ltd** *(D A Cox)* The Granary, High Street, BEDFORD, MK43 8DB.

Ⓟ**Cox & Co, trading name of Cox & Co (Accountancy) Limited** *(D A Cox)* The Granary, High Street, Turvey, BEDFORD, MK43 8DB.

ⓉⒻⓅⒶ**Cox Costello & Horne Limited** *(M F Cox)* Langwood House, 63-81 High Street, RICKMANSWORTH, HERTFORDSHIRE, WD3 1EQ.

Ⓐ**Cox Costello & Horne, trading name of Cox Costello & Horne Partners LLP** *(M F Cox)* Langwood House, 63-81 High Street, RICKMANSWORTH, HERTFORDSHIRE, WD3 1EQ.

★**Cox Hinkins & Co** *(M H Hinkins)* Charterford House, 75 London Road, Headington, OXFORD, OX3 9BB.

★ⒻⒶ**Cox Jerome** *(G F Wain)* Churchill House, 59 Lichfield Street, WALSALL, WS4 2BX.

★ⓉⒻⓅⒶ**Coxeys, McAleavy & Co, trading names of M D Coxey & Co Limited** *(G H Atkinson, M D Coxey, F McAleavy, P W McVeigh)* 25 Grosvenor Road, WREXHAM, CLWYD, LL11 1BT. and at CHESTER

CP Antrobus FCA *(C P Antrobus)* 20 North Meade, Green Park, Maghull, LIVERPOOL, L31 8DP.

Ⓐ**CPP** *(P V Ciccone)* 81 Essex Road, Islington, LONDON, N1 2SF.

ⓉⒶ**CPS & Co** *(C Pantazis)* 10a Aldermans Hill, Palmers Green, LONDON, N13 4PJ.

Ⓟ**CQ Accountancy Services Limited** *(M C Quenault)* First Floor Centre Office, Charles House, Charles Street, St. Helier, JERSEY, JE2 4SF.

Ⓟ**CQ Secretaries Limited** *(M C Quenault)* First Floor Centre Office, Charles House, Charles Street, St. Helier, JERSEY, JE2 4SF.

Ⓟ**Craggs & Co, trading name of Craggs & Co Ltd** *(S V Clarkson)* Hollydene, 58 Otley Road, LEEDS, LS6 4DL.

Ⓟ**Craig Callum Associates Ltd** *(S W Jones)* 51 Sandhills Lane, LIVERPOOL, L5 9XJ.

▽**Craig, McIntyre & Peacock** *(K A Cox)* 33 Lewis Street, STRANRAER, DG9 7LB.

Ⓟ**Craigton Limited** *(E N M Niven)* 13 Greville Park Road, ASHTEAD, SURREY, KT21 2QU.

Ⓟ**Craigwest Consulting Ltd** *(K S Chalk)* Hilltop Meadow, Cuck Hill, Shipham, WINSCOMBE, AVON, BS25 1RB.

Craker Business Solutions *(D L Craker)* 7A Ventnor Villas, HOVE, EAST SUSSEX, BN3 3DD.

Ⓟ**Cramp & Harding Ltd** *(D W Cramp)* 192D Huddersfield Road, MIRFIELD, WEST YORKSHIRE, WF14 8AU.

Ⓐ**Cramptons** *(J R Crampton)* Delgrae House, 25A St Matthews Road, Chelston, TORQUAY, TQ2 6JA.

ⒻⓅ**Crane & Johnston Limited** *(P A Crane)* 11 Alverton Terrace, PENZANCE, TR18 4JH.

ⓉⒶ**Crane & Partners** *(G Atkin, G A Collett, R T McDonagh)* Leonard House, 5-7 Newman Road, BROMLEY, BR1 1RJ.

ⒻⒶ**Crane, Cox & Co** *(M R Crane)* Hele Farmhouse, Hele Road, Marhamchurch, BUDE, EX23 0JB.

ⓅⒶ**Cranenburgh Limited** *(P J Cranenburgh)* 88 College Road, HARROW, MIDDLESEX, HA1 1BQ.

Craner & Co *(J E Craner)* PO Box 5196, STRATFORD-UPON-AVON, WARWICKSHIRE, CV37 1JJ.

Ⓐ**Cranfields** *(R F Cocoracchio, B S Duffell)* Suite 2, 3rd Floor, Leon House, 233 High Street, CROYDON, CR0 9XT.

Ⓟ**Cranford Computer Services Ltd** *(P J Hadfield, P R Hadfield)* 17 King Street, KNUTSFORD, CHESHIRE, WA16 6DW.

ⓉⒻⓅ**Cranleys Consulting Limited** *(C A Davison)* Winton House, Winton Square, BASINGSTOKE, HAMPSHIRE, RG21 8EN.

ⓅⒶ**Craufurd Hale, trading name of Craufurd Hale Audit Services Ltd** *(J A Daniell, C J Krol)* Ground Floor, Belmont Place, Belmont Road, MAIDENHEAD, BERKSHIRE, SL6 6TB.

Ⓟ**Crawford + Co, trading name of Clearwater Accountancy Ltd** *(D R Crawford)* 10 Worsley Place, Theale, READING, RG7 5QP.

ⒻⒶ**Crawfords, trading name of Crawfords Accountants LLP** *(R A Becker, A Kachani, D N Kaye, A C Wacks)* Stanton House, 41 Blackfriars Road, SALFORD, M3 7DB.

Ⓕ**Crawley** *(J D Crawley)* 23 Keswick Avenue, Gatley, CHEADLE, SK8 4LE.

Crawley & Co *(J Crawley)* 47 Newton Street, MANCHESTER, M1 1FT.

Ⓟ**Creaction limited** *(J K McDonald)* 27 Meads Road, GUILDFORD, SURREY, GU1 2NB.

ⓉⒻⒶ**Creasey Alexander & Co** *(A P Creasey)* Parkgate House, 33A Pratt St, LONDON, NW1 0BG.

ⓉⒻⒶ**Creasey Son & Wickenden** *(A N Davies, M K Lunt)* Hearts of Oak House, 4 Pembroke Road, SEVENOAKS, TN13 1XR.

★ⓉⒻⒶ**Creaseys, Creaseys IT Consulting, Creaseys Tax Consulting, trading names of Creaseys LLP** *(R A Blundell, R H B Holme, M A Howard, J Pearce, E M Robertson, G J Turpin, R P Ward)* 12 Lonsdale Gardens, TUNBRIDGE WELLS, KENT, TN1 1PA.

Ⓟ**Creative FD Limited** *(C M Day)* 6 Pigott Drive, Shenley Church End, MILTON KEYNES, MK5 6BY.

Ⓟ**Credor Point Ltd** *(J Record)* Arford Lodge, Bowcott Hill, Headley, BORDON, HAMPSHIRE, GU35 8DF.

ⒻⒶ**Cresswells Accountants LLP** *(J Dakin, G Roper, P S Vine)* Barclays Bank Chambers, 12 Market Street, HEBDEN BRIDGE, WEST YORKSHIRE, HX7 6AA.

Cresten Preddy, trading name of Cresten Preddy - AIMS Accountants for Business *(A C Preddy)* Firle Cottage, Chapel Lane, Iden Green, CRANBROOK, KENT, TN17 4HQ.

★ⒻⒶ**Crew & Hammond** *(R P Crew)* 13 Park Hill Road, TORQUAY, DEVON, TQ1 2AL. and at BRISTOL

Crick & Co *(D W Crick)* 15a Silver Street, BARNSTAPLE, EX32 8HR. and at HOLSWORTHY

Crilly & Co *(A J Crilly)* Wyvern House, 1 Church Road, Bookham, LEATHERHEAD, SURREY, KT23 3PD.

Cripps & Co *(P R S Cripps)* 8-10 Heronsgate Road, Chorleywood, RICKMANSWORTH, HERTFORDSHIRE, WD3 5BW.

Ⓐ**Cripps Dransfield** *(B E Cripps, A J Dransfield)* 206 Upper Richmond Road West, LONDON, SW14 8AH.

★**Critchley, Cole & Co.** *(M M Critchley)* 20 Lansdown, STROUD, GL5 1BG.

Ⓐ**Critchleys, trading name of Critchleys LLP** *(K C Byrne, A P Stein, M J Wright)* Greyfriars Court, Paradise Square, OXFORD, OX1 1BE. and at ABINGDON

Critical Path Solutions *(R J Clouter)* The Mews, Canaan Lane, EDINBURGH, EH10 4SG.

CRM *(C R Munday)* 33 New Road, BROXBOURNE, HERTFORDSHIRE, EN10 7LN.

Ⓟ**Crofts & Co, trading name of Porticum Limited** *(D J Crofts)* 7 Orestes Court, 39 Woodford Road, South Woodford, LONDON, E18 2EF.

★**Cromack & Co** *(P C Jones)* 29 High Street, Morley, LEEDS, LS27 9AL.

★Ⓟ**Crombies Corfield Accountants Limited** *(I J Cattell, M Fletcher)* 34 Waterloo Road, WOLVERHAMPTON, WV1 4DG. and at WALSALL

★ⓉⒻⓅⒶ**Crombies, trading name of Crombies Accountants Limited** *(I J Cattell, M Fletcher, P G Taylor)* 34 Waterloo Road, WOLVERHAMPTON, WV1 4DG. and at WALSALL

ⒻⓅⒶ**Crompton & Co, trading name of Crompton & Co Financial Solutions Ltd** *(A J Atkins)* 42 Queens Road, COVENTRY, CV1 3DX.

Ⓟ**Cromwell Accountants, trading name of Cromwell Accountants Ltd** *(C Haria)* 29 Lansdowne Road, STANMORE, MIDDLESEX, HA7 2RX.

Ⓟ**Crook & Co, trading name of Crook & Co (Accounts) Ltd** *(J Crook)* Pencoed, Sheets Heath Lane, Brookwood, WOKING, GU24 0EL.

Ⓟ**Croombs, trading name of Croombs C.A. Limited** *(P D Croombs)* Ilex House, The Green, Upper Clatford, ANDOVER, HAMPSHIRE, SP11 7PS.

Croshaw & Co *(N J Croshaw)* 19 Windmill Road, ATHERSTONE, WARWICKSHIRE, CV9 1HP.

ⒻⒶ**Cross & Bowen** *(T P Hopkins, R G Margetts)* 11 Calvert Terrace, SWANSEA, SA1 6AT.

Cross & Company Business Development and Support *(J M Cross)* Grove End, Upper Brailes, BANBURY, OXFORDSHIRE, OX15 5BA.

ⓅⒶ**Cross & Fairhead, trading name of Cross & Fairhead Business Consultants Limited** *(N S Toon)* 5 Queen Street, GREAT YARMOUTH, NORFOLK, NR30 2QP.

Ⓟ**Crossbrook Property Services Limited** *(T G Somers)* 24 New Road, Bongon, HERTFORD, SG14 3JL.

★ⒻⓅⒶ**Crossfields, trading name of Crossfields Limited** *(M G Bullock)* 85/87 High Street West, GLOSSOP, DERBYSHIRE, SK13 8AZ.

Ⓐ**Crossley & Co** *(N R C Standeven)* Royal Mews, St. Georges Place, CHELTENHAM, GLOUCESTERSHIRE, GL50 3PQ.

ⓉⒶ**Crossley & Co** *(R A Brown, T Rose)* Star House, Star Hill, ROCHESTER, KENT, ME1 1UX.

ⓉⒻⒶ**Crossley & Davis** *(S D Mondy, P G C Riley, P Swarbrick, R I Williamson, I M Wroe)* 348-350 Lytham Road, BLACKPOOL, FY4 1DW.

ⓉⒻⒶ**Crossley & Davis** *(R J Monks, P Shaw)* 52 Chorley New Road, BOLTON, BL1 4AP.

ⓉⒻⒶ**Crossley Lomas, trading name of Crossley Lomas LLP** *(J M Davenport, G N Lomas)* 25 Ryecroft, Manor Park Road, GLOSSOP, DERBYSHIRE, SK13 7SQ.

Ⓟ**Crossleys LLC** *(A J Pennington)* Portland House, Station Road, Ballasalla, ISLE OF MAN, IM9 2AE.

Crossmount *(P S Welsford)* Highland House, 165 The Broadway, Wimbledon, LONDON, SW19 1NE.

★**Crowe Clark Whitehill** *(M J Anderson, R Austin, T J Baines, R F Baker, R J M L Baker, N D Bostock, D W K Chitty, J S Cooper, L M Cooper, G R Cranston, W I C Dale, R D Darlaston, J E C Davidson, D J Devon, H C Drew, J G Dudley, P Fay, P R Framjee, D A Furst, S J Gale, M A Hall, J F Hancox, S A Harvie, N Hashemi, J A Hetherington, M E Hicks, M A Hunt, M A B Israel, M J H Jayson, S J Kirby, A C Lazda, S C Livingston, A R Lyon, C L Malcolm, D C Mellor, J L Mitchell, P Moore, G J Morgan, K A Newman, P E F O'Neill, A Penketh, A J Pianca, M Regan, J L Stalker, G J P E Struyven, D V Szulist, P Varley, S Warne, I Weekes, R I J Wherton, J Wolf)* St. Brides House, 10 Salisbury Square, LONDON, EC4Y 8EH. and at CHELTENHAM, KIDDERMINSTER, MAIDSTONE, MANCHESTER, READING, TUNBRIDGE WELLS, WALSALL

Ⓐ**Crowe Clark Whitehill Audit LLC** *(R G Barrs, P S Bird, J A Cowan)* 6th Floor, Victory House, Prospect Hill, Douglas, ISLE OF MAN, IM1 1EQ.

ⓉⓅ**Crowe Clark Whitehill LLC** *(R G Barrs, P S Bird, J A Cowan)* 6th Floor, Victory House, Prospect Hill, Douglas, ISLE OF MAN, IM1 1EQ.

★ⓉⒶ**Crowe Clark Whitehill LLP** *(D M Anderson, M J Anderson, R Austin, T J Baines, R F Baker, R J M L Baker, N D Bostock, S M Bullock, A S Campbell, D W K Chitty, H C Clarke, J S Cooper, L M*

Cooper, G R Cranston, W I C Dale, R D Darlaston, J E C Davidson, S A Daye, J W Dent, D J Devon, H C Drew, J G Dudley, S A Eden, P Fay, P R Framjee, D A Furst, S J Gale, M A Hall, J F Hancox, S A Harvie, N Hashemi, J A Hetherington, M E Hicks, F C Hotston Moore, M A Hunt, M A B Israel, M J H Jayson, S J Kirby, A C Lazda, S C Livingston, A R Lyon, C L Malcolm, R L Malkin, D C Mellor, J L Mitchell, P Moore, G J Morgan, K A Newman, P E F O'Neill, A Penketh, A J Pianca, M Regan, J L Stalker, M C Stallabrass, R Stevens, G J P E Struyven, D V Szulist, P Varley, S Warne, I Weekes, S R Weekes, R I J Wherton, J Wolf) St Bride's House, 10 Salisbury Square, LONDON, EC4Y 8EH. and at CHELTENHAM, MAIDSTONE, MANCHESTER, OLDBURY, READING, TUNBRIDGE WELLS, WALSALL

★ⓉⒶ**Crowe Morgan** *(M F G Crowe, D J Morgan, A L Slee)* 8 St. George's Street, Douglas, ISLE OF MAN, IM1 1AH.

ⓉⒻⓅⒶ**Crowfoot and Company, trading name of Crowfoot and Company Limited** *(A Crowfoot, A E Humphreys, R A Platt)* Lonsdale House, High Street, LUTTERWORTH, LEICESTERSHIRE, LE17 4AD.

ⓅⒶ**Crowley Young, trading name of Crowley Young Associates Ltd** *(S J Young)* 10 Berkeley Street, LONDON, W1J 8DP.

Ⓟ**Crown & Co Accountants Limited** *(I R Crown)* Apex House, Wonaston Road, MONMOUTH, MONMOUTHSHIRE, NP25 5JB.

ⓅⒶ**Crown Chambers Limited** *(R J Horner)* Crown Chambers, Princes Street, HARROGATE, NORTH YORKSHIRE, HG1 1NJ.

ⓉⒻⒶ**Crowther Beard LLP** *(S E Costello-Byrne, J H Painter)* Suite 1A, Shire Business Park, Wainwright Road, WORCESTER, WORCESTERSHIRE, WR4 9FA. and at TEWKESBURY

ⒻⓅⒶ**Crowther Jordan Ltd** *(S Gray)* 39 High Street, Wednesfield, WOLVERHAMPTON, WV11 1ST.

ⓉⒻⓅⒶ**Crowthers, trading name of Crowthers Accountants Limited** *(R F Beard, I P Cooke, J J Crowther, N L Walding)* The Courtyard, 19 High Street, PERSHORE, WORCESTERSHIRE, WR10 1AA. and at LEDBURY

Ⓟ**Croydon Business Centre Limited** *(G Cohen)* 16 South End, CROYDON, SURREY, CR0 1DN.

★**Crozier Jones & Co** *(M S Crozier)* 9/13 Thorne Road, DONCASTER, SOUTH YORKSHIRE, DN1 2HJ.

Ⓟ**Crozier Kemp Ltd** *(J E Crozier)* 7 Ball Grove Drive, COLNE, LANCASHIRE, BB8 7HY.

ⒻⓅⒶ**Crumpton & Co Limited** *(N D Crumpton)* 682 Anlaby Road, HULL, HU3 6UZ.

ⒻⒶ**Crunchers Scotland, trading name of The Long Partnership** *(A E Long)* 1 Castle Street, KIRKWALL, ORKNEY, KW15 1HD. and at THURSO

ⓅⒶ**Cryer Sandham Limited** *(J D Cryer, B P Sandham)* Epping House, 55 Russell Street, READING, RG1 7XG.

ⓅⒶ**Crystal Business Services Limited** *(A Dedat)* 264 Stoney Stanton Road, COVENTRY, CV1 4FP.

Ⓟ**Crystal Business Services, trading name of P & C E Services Limited** *(P Estcourt)* 1 Cheyney Avenue, Salhouse, NORWICH, NR13 6RJ.

Ⓟ**Crystal Clear Accountancy Limited** *(J P Sharratt)* 11 Whitehall Drive, Hartford, NORTHWICH, CHESHIRE, CW8 1SJ.

Ⓟ**CS Lawrence & Co Limited** *(C A L Hall)* 10 Swan Bank, CONGLETON, CHESHIRE, CW12 1AH.

Ⓟ**CS Taxation and Accountancy Limited** *(C Sage)* 41 High Cross Drive, Rogerstone, NEWPORT, GWENT, NP10 9AB.

★ⓉⒻⒶ**CTC** *(P Cole, A B Twaddle)* 13 Portland Terrace, Jesmond, NEWCASTLE UPON TYNE, NE2 1SN.

ⓅⒶ**CTM Partnership Limited** *(C T Munir)* 838 Wickham Road, CROYDON, CR0 8ED.

Ⓐ**Cuan O'Shea** *(R.K.C. O'Shea)* Bevan & Buckland, Langdon House, Langdon Road, SA1 Swansea Waterfront, SWANSEA, SA1 8QY.

ⓉⓅⒶ**Cube Partners Limited** *(G C Cochran, K F O'Reilly)* 5 Giffard Court, Millbrook Close, NORTHAMPTON, NN5 5JF.

Cuckoo *(L Thomas)* 2 Station Road, Portskewett, CALDICOT, MONMOUTHSHIRE, NP26 5SF.

Ⓟ**Cue & Co Ltd** *(B G Cue)* 201 Newbridge Road, BATH, BA1 3HH.

Ⓐ**Cullingworth & Co** *(R Cullingworth)* 96 High Street, HENLEY-IN-ARDEN, WARWICKSHIRE, B95 5BY.

Cullum and Co *(P J Cullum)* 24 Home Field Close, Emersons Green, BRISTOL, BS16 7BH.

Cultra C T S *(G J C Wharton)* 102b Bangor Road, HOLYWOOD, COUNTY DOWN, BT18 0LR.

★ⓅⒶ**Culverhouse & Co, trading name of Culverhouse & Co Ltd** *(J R Culverhouse)* 7 High Street, Farnborough, ORPINGTON, KENT, BR6 7BQ.

Ⓟ**Culwick Consultancy Services Limited** *(J S Culwick)* 9 Uplands Road, HOCKLEY, ESSEX, SS5 4DL.

Ⓟ**Cundy Solutions Limited** *(D Cundy)* Birch Hollow, Netherhope Lane, Tidenham, CHEPSTOW, NP16 7JE.

Ⓟ**Cunningham Wishart, trading name of Back Office People Ltd** *(M J Corcoran)* 66 Pwllmelin Road, CARDIFF, CF5 2NH.

★ⒻⒶ**Cunninghams** *(B J Lynes, M A Smith)* 61 Alexandra Road, LOWESTOFT, SUFFOLK, NR32 1PL.

ⓉⓅⒶ**Curo, trading name of Curo Professional Services Limited** *(A Madden, J A Whelan)* Curo House, Greenbox, Westonhall Road, Stoke Prior, BROMSGROVE, WORCESTERSHIRE B60 4AL.

Ⓟ**Curran & Co, trading name of Curran Tax Consultants Limited** *(M E Curran)* The Cottage, Donkey Lane, Bradmore, NOTTINGHAM, NG11 6PG.

ⓅⒶ**Currie Accountancy Limited** *(I J Currie)* 13a High Street, EDENBRIDGE, KENT, TN8 5AB.

Curtis & Co *(P J Curtis)* 14 Crossfell Road, HEMEL HEMPSTEAD, HERTFORDSHIRE, HP3 8RF.

Curtis & Co *(H Curtis)* Bank Chambers, 1-3 Woodford Avenue, Gants Hill, ILFORD, IG2 6UF.

Curtis & Co *(R F Curtis)* 16 Middlefield, Bardsley, OLDHAM, OL8 2TP.

Ⓟ**Curtis Bowden & Thomas, trading name of Curtis Bowden & Thomas Limited** *(J L Thomas)* First Floor, 101 Dunraven Street, TONYPANDY, MID GLAMORGAN, CF40 1AR.

Ⓟ**Curwen & Co, trading name of Curwen & Co Limited** *(C Curwen)* 44 Queens Drive, Heaton Mersey, STOCKPORT, CHESHIRE, SK4 3JW.

Ⓟ**Cuthbertson Hewitt Limited** *(C Cuthbertson)* 5 Hill Gardens, MARKET HARBOROUGH, LE16 9EB.

Cutler & Co PC *(D J C Cutler)* 2460 West 26th Avenue, Suite 380C, DENVER, CO 80211, UNITED STATES.

CV Capital, trading name of CV Capital LLP *(I C Blackman)* 10-12 Russell Square, LONDON, WC1B 5LF.

ⒻⒶ**CW & G Partnership LLP** *(A T Coomber, A L Weiner)* 68 Great Portland Street, LONDON, W1W 7NG.

Ⓟ**CW Acccountants Limited** *(C S Whittington)* 11 Thorn Close, Barkham, WOKINGHAM, BERKSHIRE, RG41 4SQ.

CW Burton & Co *(C W Burton)* 3 Meadowcroft, Draughton, SKIPTON, BD23 6EG.

CW Energy LLP *(P R Greatrex, S S Norman, M P Rogerson)* 4th Floor, 40 Queen Street, LONDON, EC4R 1DD.

Ⓟ**CW Energy Tax Consultants Ltd** *(P R Greatrex, S S Norman, M P Rogerson)* 4th Floor, 40 Queen Street, LONDON, EC4R 1HN.

ⓉⒻⓅⒶ**CW Fellowes Limited** *(K M G Beazley, P G Blades, B A Elkins, R L Green-Wilkinson, C A E Spencer, A R N Wilson)* Templars House, Lulworth Close, Chandlers Ford, EASTLEIGH, SO53 3TL. and at PORTSMOUTH

CW Ip & Co *(C W Ip)* 9/F Times Media Centre, 133 Wanchai Road, WAN CHAI, HONG KONG ISLAND, HONG KONG SAR.

CW Noel & Co *(C W Noel)* 97 Harbord Street, LONDON, SW6 6PN.

Ⓐ**CWM** *(M A Cooper)* 1a High Street, EPSOM, KT19 8DA.

Ⓟ**CWS Accounting Limited** *(C W Smit)* 50 Skylark Way, Shinfield, READING, RG2 9AJ.

Ⓟ**CWW Limited** *(D Warren)* 149-151 Mortimer Street, HERNE BAY, KENT, CT6 5HA.

Cyfrifon Cadog Accounts *(E A Price)* Trehelyg, Heol yr Orsaf, LLANGADOG, DYFED, SA19 9LS.

Ⓐ**D & A Hill** *(A Hill)* 18 T8/9 Brookes Mill, Armitage Bridge, HUDDERSFIELD, HD4 7NR.

ⓉⒻⓅⒶ**D & J Randles Limited** *(D F Randles)* 203 Askern Road, Bentley, DONCASTER, SOUTH YORKSHIRE, DN5 0JR. and at LEEDS

Ⓐ**D & L Accountancy Services** *(D P Radford)* 1 Mearns Place, CHELMSFORD, CM2 6TT.

Ⓟ**D & S Plumb Accountants Limited** *(D J Plumb)* 19A/B Blackwell Business Park, Blackwell, SHIPSTON-ON-STOUR, WARWICKSHIRE, CV36 4PE.

ⓅⒶ**D A & C M Rowe Limited** *(D A Rowe)* Woodfield House, Castle Walk, NEATH, WEST GLAMORGAN, SA11 3LN.

ⓉⓅ**D A Clark & Co Limited** *(D A Clark, S P McManus)* 4 Peel House, Barttelot Road, HORSHAM, WEST SUSSEX, RH12 1DE.

D A Seccombe FCA *(D A Seccombe)* Boyden House, 6a Avenue Road, STRATFORD-UPON-AVON, WARWICKSHIRE, CV37 6UW.

ⓅⒶ**D B Foot Limited** *(D Foot)* 10 Prestwick Road, KINGSWINFORD, WEST MIDLANDS, DY6 9DZ.

Ⓟ**D B Jones & Co Limited** *(D B Jones)* 14 Providence Street, Earlsdon, COVENTRY, WEST MIDLANDS, CV5 6ED.

D Bowen-Davies & Co *(D I Bowen-Davies)* 67 Elmcroft Close, FELTHAM, TW14 9HJ.

Ⓟ**D C Howard, trading name of Stoneygate Consulting Ltd** *(D C Howard)* 16 Morland Avenue, Stoneygate, LEICESTER, LE2 2PE.

D C Hughesdon *(D C Hughesdon)* 165 Newbridge Hill, BATH, BA1 3PX.

ⒻⓅⒶ**D E Ball & Co Ltd** *(R M Ball, A Jefferies)* 15 Bridge Road, Wellington, TELFORD, SHROPSHIRE, TF1 1EB.

Ⓟ**D Gupta & Company, trading name of Financial Accounts Limited** *(D Das Gupta)* 88 Howberry Road, EDGWARE, MIDDLESEX, HA8 6SY.

Ⓕ**D H Salmon** *(D H Salmon)* 25 Mayfield Drive, KENILWORTH, CV8 2SW.

Ⓟ**D H Salmon (Consultants) Ltd** *(D H Salmon)* 25 Mayfield Drive, KENILWORTH, WARWICKSHIRE, CV8 2SW.

D I Davies FCA *(D I Davies)* 3 Gwynfan, Nantycaws, CARMARTHEN, DYFED, SA32 8HF.

D J Dean *(D J Dean)* 62 Reservoir Road, Elburton, PLYMOUTH, PL9 8NJ.

Ⓟ**D J Macaulay, trading name of D J Macaulay Accountancy Ltd** *(D J Macaulay)* Morcroft, Ellington Road, Taplow, MAIDENHEAD, SL6 0BA.

D J R Associates *(D J Robshaw)* 1 Bowden Way, Failand, BRISTOL, BS8 3XA.

D J. Robinson *(D J Robinson)* 58 Peartree Walk, Cheshunt, WALTHAM CROSS, EN7 6RE.

D K Mak & Co *(K D Mak)* Rooms 2101-3, China Insurance Group Building, 141 Des Voeux Road Central, CENTRAL, HONG KONG SAR.

D M Flather *(D M Flather)* 15 Goodwood, Owler Park Road, ILKLEY, LS29 0BY.

D M Jones *(D M Jones)* 2 Burnside Road, Gatley, CHEADLE, CHESHIRE, SK8 4NA.

Ⓟ**D Morjaria & Co, trading name of D Morjaria & Co Ltd** *(D M Morjaria)* 69 Lynwood Road, Ealing, LONDON, W5 1JG.

D N Accounting Solutions *(D Needham)* Brynawel, Velindre, LLANDYSUL, DYFED, SA44 5UU.

D N Ayton *(D N Ayton)* 5 Jenkins Drive, BISHOP AUCKLAND, COUNTY DURHAM, DL14 6XJ.

D P Howell *(D P Howell)* 33 Grove Road, Coombe Dingle, BRISTOL, BS9 2RJ.

Ⓟ**D Rogers & Co, trading name of D Rogers & Co Limited** *(D M Rogers)* St. Edith's View, High Street, Kemsing, SEVENOAKS, KENT, TN15 6NA.

D T S Bolton *(D T S Bolton)* Laurels Back Lane, Goudhurst, CRANBROOK, TN17 1AN.

ⒻⓅⒶ**D V Marlow & Co Limited** *(D V Marlow)* 72 West Street, Portchester, FAREHAM, HAMPSHIRE, PO16 9UN.

Ⓟ**D Yarsley(Tax and Accountancy) Ltd** *(D Yarsley)* 10 Quail Green, WOLVERHAMPTON, WV6 8DF.

D. Basu & Co *(A Chatterjee)* 10 Old Post Office Street, CALCUTTA 700001, INDIA.

D. Berry *(D Berry)* 41 Elmstead Lane, CHISLEHURST, BR7 5EG.

D. Clamp & Co *(D Clamp)* Park Farm, Church Road, Ashton Hayes, CHESTER, CH3 8AB.

D. Dave & Co. *(D J B S Dave)* 60 Kenwyn Drive, LONDON, NW2 7NT.

D. Freeman & Co *(D D Freeman)* Gateways Lodge, 76A Oakleigh Park North, LONDON, N20 9AS.

D. Hall & Co *(D Halberstadt)* 46 Broom Lane, SALFORD, M7 4FJ.

D. Little *(D Little)* 1 Orchard Road, Burnham Green Tewin, WELWYN, AL6 0HE.

Ⓐ**D. M. Linell & Co** *(D M Linell)* Design House, 27 Chesterfield Road, DRONFIELD, DERBYSHIRE, S18 2WZ.

Ⓐ**D. Matley & Co** *(D N Matley)* 500 Hartshill Road, Hartshill, STOKE-ON-TRENT, ST4 6AD.

★**D. Montgomery & Co** *(D G Montgomery)* P O Box 119, 118 Abercromby Street, PORT OF SPAIN, TRINIDAD AND TOBAGO.

Ⓐ**D. Seeley & Company** *(D W Seeley)* 40 Bear Hill, Alvechurch, BIRMINGHAM, B48 7JX.

Ⓐ**D. Shah & Co** *(D K Shah)* 40 Anmersh Grove, STANMORE, HA7 1PA.

★ⒻⒶ**D. Stoker & Co** *(G M Chappell, D B Stoker)* Abacus House, 367 Blandford Road, BECKENHAM, BR3 4NW.

D. Swindlehurst *(D Swindlehurst)* Flat 2, 67 Stockport Road, Timperley, ALTRINCHAM, WA15 7LH.

D. Tanna & Co *(D C Tanna)* 32 Berry Hill, STANMORE, MIDDLESEX, HA7 4XS.

Ⓐ**D. Velida & Co** *(D R W Velida)* Centurion House, Central Way, Walworth Business Park, ANDOVER, SP10 5AN.

D. Yarsley *(D Yarsley)* 10 Quail Green, WOLVERHAMPTON, WEST MIDLANDS, WV6 8DF.

Ⓐ**D.& I. Walton** *(I Walton)* 17 Lancaster Drive, Vicars Cross, CHESTER, CH3 5JW.

Ⓕ**D.A. Creal** *(D A Creal)* Peterkin House, 76 Botley Road, Swanwick, SOUTHAMPTON, SO31 7BA.

Ⓐ**D.A. Hopkins** *(D A Hopkins)* 7 King Street, WREXHAM, LL11 1HF.

D.A. Scott *(D A Scott)* 1 Merryhill Park, Belmont, HEREFORD, HR2 9SS.

Ⓐ**D.B. Jones & Co** *(D B Jones)* 14 Providence Street, Earlsdon, COVENTRY, WEST MIDLANDS, CV5 6ED.

D.B. Lye & Co *(I F Cloke, J F Moate)* 34 Cheriton Gardens, FOLKESTONE, CT20 2AX.

D.B. Simpson Consultancy, trading name of D.B. Simpson *(D B Simpson)* Prospect House, Prospect Street, HUDDERSFIELD, HD1 2NU.

D.C. Brown *(D C Brown)* 48 Airedale Avenue, Tickhill, DONCASTER, DN11 9UD.

D.C. Evans *(D C Evans)* Cae Nant, Llandyrnog, DENBIGH, CLWYD, LL16 4HB.

D.C. Marshall & Co *(D C Marshall)* Giles Croft, 1a Ferriby High Road, NORTH FERRIBY, NORTH HUMBERSIDE, HU14 3LD.

D.E. Boulter *(D E Boulter)* New Mills Cottage, Ermington, IVYBRIDGE, PL21 0LH.

D.E. Jones *(D E Jones)* 22 The Drive, Chorleywood, RICKMANSWORTH, WD3 4EB.

D.E. Palfreyman *(D E Palfreyman)* 176 Leach Green Lane, Rednal, BIRMINGHAM, B45 8EH.

D.G. Burton *(D G Burton)* 3 The Green, WOODFORD GREEN, IG8 0NF.

D.G. Pangbourne *(D G Pangbourne)* High Trees, Gustard Wood, Wheathampstead, ST. ALBANS, AL4 8RP.

D.H.Shaw & Co, trading name of D.H.Shaw *(D H Shaw)* 7 Chapel Row, Wilsden, BRADFORD, BD15 0EQ.

D.I. Brocklesby & Co *(D I Brocklesby)* Kiln How, Rosthwaite, KESWICK, CUMBRIA, CA12 5XB.

D.I. Garland *(D I Garland)* 7 Highlands Road, Long Ashton, BRISTOL, BS41 9EN.

Ⓟ**D.J Duckworth & Co, trading name of D.J. Duckworth Limited** *(D J Duckworth)* 20 Bank Street, ACCRINGTON, BB5 1HH.

D.J. Coleman *(D J Coleman)* 2 Redcar Street, ROCHDALE, OL12 0PU.

D.J. Colson *(D J Colson)* 35 Pebworth Road, HARROW, HA1 3UD.

D.J. Jones *(D J Jones)* 10 Beacon Court, Southcote Road, READING, RG30 2ER.

Ⓕ**D.J. Lewis** *(D J Lewis)* 23 Heol Eglwys, Ystradgynlais, SWANSEA, SA9 1EY.

D.J. Oates & Co *(D J Oates)* Suite 59, 42 St Johns Road, SCARBOROUGH, NORTH YORKSHIRE, YO12 5ET.

D.J. Quine *(D J Quine)* 27 Claremont Drive, Aughton, ORMSKIRK, LANCASHIRE, L39 4SP.

D.J. Ranson *(D J Ranson)* 17 Willets Rise, Shenley Church End, MILTON KEYNES, MK5 6JW.

ⒻⒶ**D.J. Reynolds & Co** *(D J Reynolds)* 15 Alverton Street, PENZANCE, CORNWALL, TR18 2QP.

Ⓕ**D.J. Smith** *(D J Smith)* 23 Welford Road, Kingsthorpe, NORTHAMPTON, NN2 8AQ.

D.J. Swatman *(D J Swatman)* 24 Wilkinson Way, NORTH WALSHAM, NR28 9BB.

D.J. Weaver & Co, trading name of D.J. Weaver *(D J Weaver)* 4 Amis Avenue, New Haw, ADDLESTONE, KT15 3ET.

D.J.Rockall *(D J Rockall)* 14 MacLean Close, Abington, NORTHAMPTON, NN3 3DJ.

D.K. Deniz & Co *(D K Deniz)* 2 Memduh Asaf Sokak, LEFKOSA, CYPRUS.

ⒻⒶ**D.K. Gardiner & Co.** *(D K Gardiner)* 15F Postgate, GLENROTHES, KY7 5LH.

D.L. Thompson *(D L Thompson)* c/- P O Box 294, CIVIC SQUARE, ACT 2608, AUSTRALIA.

D.M. Clinton *(D M Clinton)* 116 Rosia Plaza, P O Box 677, GIBRALTAR, GIBRALTAR.

Ⓐ**D.M. Kirke-Smith** *(D M Kirke-Smith)* Springhill House, Pilgrims Way, WESTERHAM, TN16 2DU.

D.M. Richards *(D M Richards)* 17 Whittington Road, Norton, STOURBRIDGE, DY8 3DB.

D.M. Shah *(D M Shah)* 3 Alicia Avenue, Kenton, HARROW, HA3 8HW.

★**D.P. Marshall** *(D P Marshall)* 25 Highfield Road, Bickley, BROMLEY, BR1 2JN.

D.P. Rooze *(D P Rooze)* 122 Glenfield Frith Drive, Glenfield, LEICESTER, LE3 8PS.

D.R. Andrews *(D R Andrews)* Northacre, Deerleap Road, Westcott, DORKING, RH4 3LE.
D.R. Carter *(D R Carter)* Park Farm, Mileham, KING'S LYNN, PE32 2RD.
D.R. Hicks *(D R Hicks)* 107 Penn Hill Road, Weston, BATH, BA1 3RU.
Ⓕ**D.R. Pandya** *(D R Pandya)* Porch House, Little Raveley, HUNTINGDON, PE28 2NQ.
★ⓅⒶ**D.R.E. & Co (Audit) Limited** *(L M Fitton, C H Hall, M R Kent, A J Matthews)* 7 Lower Brook Street, OSWESTRY, SHROPSHIRE, SY11 2HG. and at SHREWSBURY
D.S A-Walia & Co *(D S Ahluwalia)* 5 Amery Road, HARROW, HA1 3UH.
D.S Booth & Co *(D S Booth)* 19 Tower Estate, Point Clear, St Osyth, CLACTON-ON-SEA, ESSEX, CO16 8NG.
ⒻⒶ**D.S. & Co** *(D F Shah)* DS House, 306 High Street, CROYDON, CR0 1NG.
D.S. Williams *(D S Williams)* Beaux Aires Cottage, Yelsted Road, Stockbury, SITTINGBOURNE, KENT, ME9 7QY.
Ⓕ**D.T. Rodgers** *(D T Rodgers)* 3 Ruscote, Cross Oak Road, BERKHAMSTED, HP4 3NA.
Ⓕ**D.V. Marlow & Co** *(D V Marlow)* 72 West Street, Portchester, FAREHAM, PO16 9UN.
D.V. Udall & Co *(D V Udall)* Dukes Edge, Lunghurst Road, Woldingham, CATERHAM, CR3 7HE.
D.W. Charlton *(D W Charlton)* 20 Canterbury Avenue, SHEFFIELD, S10 3RT.
D.W. Edworthy BSc FCA *(D W Edworthy)* The Old Rectory, Rectory Way, Lympsham, WESTON-SUPER-MARE, AVON, BS24 0EW.
DA Locke & Co *(D A Locke)* 3 Flaxen Field, Weston Turville, AYLESBURY, BUCKINGHAMSHIRE, HP22 5GJ.
Ⓟ**DA Roberts Accountancy Services Limited** *(D A Roberts)* 41 Newbury Drive, DAVENTRY, NORTHAMPTONSHIRE, NN11 0WQ.
DAC Accountancy Services *(D A Clarke)* 8 Vernon Crescent, Galgate, LANCASTER, LA2 0LX.
Dadabhoy & Co. *(K R Dadabhoy)* 7 Darbhanga Mansions, 12 Carmichael Road, MUMBAI 400026, MAHARASHTRA, INDIA.
Daeche Dubois & Plinston *(J A Plinston)* Mansfield House, 139 Shirley Road, CROYDON, CR0 7LR.
ⒾⒻⒶ**Dafferns LLP** *(R J Miller)* 1 Eastwood, Harry Weston Road, Binley Business Park, COVENTRY, CV3 2UB.
Dafferns Resource LLP *(G R Cox, B C Jukes, B A King)* 1 Eastwood Business Village, Harry Weston Road, Binley Business Park, COVENTRY, CV3 2UB.
Daggatt & Co *(J Daggatt)* 21 Conchar Road, SUTTON COLDFIELD, B72 1LW.
Ⓟ**Daggerlux Limited** *(P D Armitage)* 1 New Street, Slaithwaite, HUDDERSFIELD, HD7 5AB.
ⒻⒶ**Daggett and Company** *(T M Daggett)* 516 Wilmslow Road, Withington, MANCHESTER, M20 4BS.
ⓅⒶ**Dai David Ltd** *(D W P David)* Critchleys LLP, Greyfriars Court, Paradise Square, OXFORD, OX1 1BE.
ⒾⒻⒶ**Dains LLP** *(P D Bradshaw, M Castree, R E Farmer, M C Hargate, A P Morris, M F P Smith, S G Wright)* St. Johns Court, Wiltell Road, LICHFIELD, STAFFORDSHIRE, WS14 9DS. and at BIRMINGHAM, BURTON-ON-TRENT, DERBY, RUGELEY
Ⓟ**Daishow Limited** *(S A Brison)* Hirado 4-5-23, Totsuka-ku, YOKOHAMA, 244-0802 JAPAN.
ⒾⒻⒶ**Dale Pickard & Co** *(D Pickard)* Bank House, 4 Wharf Rd, SALE, M33 2AF.
ⒻⓅ**Dales Evans & Co Limited** *(P D Makin)* 88/90 Baker Street, LONDON, W1U 6TQ.
ⓅⒾ**Dalewood, trading name of Dalewood Limited** *(J C Woodman)* 42-44 Brunswick Road, SHOREHAM-BY-SEA, WEST SUSSEX, BN43 5WB.
Ⓕ**Daly & Co** *(P M Daly)* The Portergate, Ecclesall Road, SHEFFIELD, S11 8NX.
ⒻⒶ**Daly Mandel** *(P W B Mandel)* 105 Southlands Road, BROMLEY, BR2 9QT. and at ST. ALBANS
ⒾⒶ**Daly, Hoggett & Co** *(D J Bartlett, R V F Brianti)* 5-11 Mortimer Street, LONDON, W1T 3HS. and at RICKMANSWORTH
Dan Hartley Business Consulting *(D Hartley)* Manor Farm House East, Knaresborough Road, Follifoot, HARROGATE, NORTH YORKSHIRE, HG3 1DT.
Dana Payne Accountant ACA *(D C Payne)* 4 Cryfield Heights, COVENTRY, WEST MIDLANDS, CV4 7LA.
Dangoor & Company *(R P Dangoor)* 36 Chester Close North, Regents Park, LONDON, NW1 4JE.
Daniel Djanogly *(D Djanogly)* 25 Southampton Buildings, LONDON, WC2A 1AL.
Ⓟ**Daniel Freeman & Co, trading name of Financialmodelling.com Ltd** *(D M Freeman)* 19 South View, East Preston, LITTLEHAMPTON, WEST SUSSEX, BN16 1PX.
Ⓐ**Daniel Jeyes** *(D J Jeyes)* 23 Abington Park Crescent, NORTHAMPTON, NN3 3AD.
Daniel Lally *(D B Lally)* Flat 3, 76 Shooters Hill Road, Blackheath, LONDON, SE3 7BG.
ⓅⒶ**Daniel Prais Ltd** *(D Prais)* Stanton House, 41 Blackfriars Road, SALFORD, M3 7DB.
Ⓟ**Daniel Whitefield Ltd** *(D Whitefield)* New Arch House, 57b Catherine Place, LONDON, SW1E 6DY.
Ⓟ**Daniel Wolfson & Co, DW, trading names of Daniel Wolfson & Co Ltd** *(D Wolfson)* 9 Beaumont Gate, Shenley Hill, RADLETT, HERTFORDSHIRE, WD7 7AR.
Daniels & Co *(K B Daniels)* 111a Station Road, WEST WICKHAM, BR4 0PX.
ⒾⓅⒶ**Daniels & Co (Accountants) Limited** *(J R Byers)* 111a Station Road, WEST WICKHAM, KENT, BR4 0PX.
Ⓐ**Daniels Accounts, trading name of Daniels Accounts LLP** *(W R Daniels)* Unit B1 Laser Quay, Culpeper Close, Medway City Estate, ROCHESTER, ME2 4HU.
★**Danmirr Consultants** *(M Rahmatullah)* 170 Church Road, MITCHAM, SURREY, CR4 3BW. and at LONDON
★ⒻⒶ**Danzig & Co** *(J J Danzig)* 8-12 Torphichen Street, EDINBURGH, EH3 8JQ.
Ⓟ**DAP Limited** *(S A Lever)* 6 Regent Gate, 83 High Street, WALTHAM CROSS, HERTFORDSHIRE, EN8 7AF.
Ⓟ**D'Arcy Howard & Co, trading name of D'Arcy Howard Castleford Limited** *(B F Martyn)* 7A Pontefract Road, CASTLEFORD, WF10 4JE.
Ⓟ**Darlaston Taxshop, trading name of Darlaston Taxshop Ltd** *(T Afzal)* 210a-212a Darlaston Road, Darlaston, WEDNESBURY, WEST MIDLANDS, WS10 7TQ.
ⒻⓅ**Darnbrough & Co, trading name of Darnbrough & Co Ltd** *(J A Darnbrough)* 8 York Place, KNARESBOROUGH, NORTH YORKSHIRE, HG5 0AA.
★ⒾⒻⒶ**Darnells** *(L Dickinson, N J Holmes, S P Murphy, D G Smith)* Quay House, Quay Road, NEWTON ABBOT, TQ12 2BU. and at TOTNES
Darrell H. Webb *(D H Webb)* 1st Floor, 88 Charles Street, KEW, VIC 3101, AUSTRALIA.
Ⓟ**Darren Williams & Co Ltd** *(D R Williams)* Longacre House, Wilcott, SHREWSBURY, SHROPSHIRE, SY4 1BJ. and at ROCHFORD
Darvin & Co *(A G Patel)* 62 Redbridge Lane East, Redbridge, ILFORD, IG4 5EZ.
Ⓐ**Darwins** *(A S Sahota)* 54 Batchworth Lane, NORTHWOOD, HA6 3HG.
ⓅⒶ**DAS, trading name of DAS UK Limited** *(P M Shah)* 1st Floor, Windsor House, 1270 London Road, LONDON, SW16 4DH.
Ⓟ**Datacomp Consultants Ltd** *(V F Mather)* 4 Houldsworth Square, STOCKPORT, CHESHIRE, SK5 7AF.
Ⓟ**Datacount Limited** *(P A Cambray, K K Pandya, M T Stower)* Chalfont House, 35 Churchfield Road, LONDON, W3 6AY.
Ⓟ**Dataplan Payroll Limited** *(N Ellis, P S Fearn)* 26 South St. Marys Gate, GRIMSBY, SOUTH HUMBERSIDE, DN31 1LW.
Datta & Co *(G S Datta)* 58 Whittington Road, LONDON, N22 8YF.
Ⓐ**Dattani** *(N Dattani)* Scottish Provident House, 76-80 College Road, HARROW, MIDDLESEX, HA1 1BQ.
Ⓐ**Dattani & Co.** *(V Dattani)* 47 Hill Road, PINNER, HA5 1LB.
★**Dattani, & Co** *(K M Dattani)* 2218 Lombard Street, SAN FRANCISCO, CA 94123, UNITED STATES.
ⓅⒶ**Dauman & Co Limited** *(E A Kapasi, C W Roberts, G F Styburski)* 9 Station Parade, Uxbridge Road Ealing Common, LONDON, W5 3LD.
★**D'Auria, Quick & Tanna** *(K B Tanna)* Antonia House, 262 Holloway Road, LONDON, N7 6NG.
Dave & Co *(A Dave)* 18 Fitzhardinge Street, Manchester Square, LONDON, W1H 6EQ. and at HARROW
Dave Kwok & Co *(S N D Kwok)* Room 902, General Commercial Building, 156-164 Des Voeux Road, CENTRAL, HONG KONG ISLAND, HONG KONG SAR.
★Ⓐ**Davenport Hodgkiss** *(D J Walford)* 1a Wilton Street, Manchester Road, Hollinwood, OLDHAM, OL9 7NZ.
ⓅⒶ**Daverns Audit Services Limited** *(F G J Davern, M J McKay)* 149-151 Sparrows Herne, BUSHEY, WD23 1AQ.
Ⓐ**Davert Banks & Co** *(R T Hecquet)* 11 St. Saviours Wharf, Mill Street, LONDON, SE1 2BE.
Ⓟ**Davey Grover Limited** *(J J Windsor)* 4 Fenice Court, Phoenix Business Park, Eaton Socon, ST. NEOTS, CAMBRIDGESHIRE, PE19 8EP.
David A Acott *(D A Acott)* 12 The Farthings, CROWBOROUGH, TN6 2TW.
David A Lees *(D A Lees)* 8 Fosters Grove, WINDLESHAM, GU20 6JZ.
David A Taylor *(D A Taylor)* The Old Rectory, Boltongate, WIGTON, CUMBRIA, CA7 1DA.
David A. Clarke *(D A Clarke)* 20 Longhill Drive, SALISBURY, SP2 8TD.
David A. Dodds & Co *(D A Dodds)* Boundary Farm, South Scarle Lane, Swinderby, LINCOLN, LN6 9JA.
Ⓕ**David A. Rose & Co** *(D A Rose)* Unit 404 Centennial Avenue, Centennial Park, Elstree, BOREHAMWOOD, HERTFORDSHIRE, WD6 3TN.
David A. Thomas & Co *(D A Thomas)* Garden Reach, 5 Hurn Close, Ashley, RINGWOOD, BH24 2AD.
David A. Wilson *(D A Wilson)* 5 Passage Road, Westbury On Trym, BRISTOL, BS9 3HN.
ⒾⒻⒶ**David Allen** *(S D Allen)* Dalmar House, Barras Lane Estate, Dalston, CARLISLE, CA5 7NY. and at PENRITH, WORKINGTON
David Allen Associates *(D S Allen)* 122 Hill Top Road, Thornton, BRADFORD, BD13 3QX.
Ⓐ**David Anthony & Co** *(D A Wright)* 5 The Gateway, Rathmore Road, LONDON, SE7 7QW.
David Ashley & Co *(D A Segal)* PO Box 716, BOREHAMWOOD, HERTFORDSHIRE, WD6 9GD.
David Atkinson LLP *(D B Atkinson)* 25 Harley Street, LONDON, W1G 9BR.
★ⒾⒻⒶ**David Bailey** *(W E Hodgson)* 28 Landport Terrace, PORTSMOUTH, PO1 2RG.
★**David Banks Associates** *(D E Banks)* Douelis House, 49 Ben Rhydding Road, ILKLEY, WEST YORKSHIRE, LS29 8RN.
David Barton *(D J Barton)* 8 Bevan Street, Islington, LONDON, N1 7DY.
Ⓕ**David Beagent & Co** *(P C Ballard, D J Beagent)* The Old Rectory, Mill Lane, Tempsford, SANDY, SG19 2AT.
Ⓟ**David Beaumont Ltd** *(D Beaumont)* 58 Valley Prospect, NEWARK, NG24 4QW.
David Beckman & Co *(D J Beckman)* 62 The Street, ASHTEAD, SURREY, KT21 1AT.
Ⓟ**David Beckman & Co, trading name of David Beckman & Co Ltd** *(D J Beckman)* 62 The Street, ASHTEAD, SURREY, KT21 1AT.
David Bennett BA FCA *(D A Bennett)* 46 Old Wool Lane, Cheadle Hulme, CHEADLE, CHESHIRE, SK8 5JA.
David Blaxter *(D Blaxter)* Wood Cottage, Barton Hartshorne, BUCKINGHAM, MK18 4JT.
David Boldy *(A D Boldy)* 6 Spring Farm Mews, Wilsden, BRADFORD, BD15 0EF.
David Bottomley *(D R Bottomley)* The Old Rectory, Owmby Cliff Road, Owmby-by-Spital, MARKET RASEN, LINCOLNSHIRE, LN8 2HL.
Ⓐ**David Bowden & Co** *(D M A Brownrigg)* 19 Den Avenue, BOGNOR REGIS, PO21 1HE.
David Bunker *(D A L Bunker)* Kings House, 14 Orchard Street, BRISTOL, BS1 5EH.
David C Cleaver *(D C Cleaver)* Blackden Heath Farm, Blackden Lane, Holmes Chapel, CREWE, CW4 8DG.
ⒻⓅ**David C Gorrod, trading name of Gorrod Nominees Ltd** *(D C Gorrod)* 68 Ship Street, BRIGHTON, BN1 1AE.
David C. Minshaw *(D C Minshaw)* 3501 Parkside, 88 Queensway, ADMIRALTY, HONG KONG ISLAND, HONG KONG SAR.
David Cairns *(D H Cairns)* Bramblewood, Turville Heath, HENLEY-ON-THAMES, OXFORDSHIRE, RG9 6JY.
David Campbell & Co. *(D Campbell)* 8 New Heys Way, Bradshaw, BOLTON, BL2 4AR.
ⒻⓅⒶ**David Cane, trading name of Business Assurance & Taxation Services Limited** *(D A Cane)* 10 Sundial Court, Barnsbury Lane, SURBITON, SURREY, KT5 9RN.
David Cann *(D F Cann)* 22 Chartwell Place, EPSOM, SURREY, KT18 5JH.
Ⓕ**David Carty & Co** *(D Carty)* 234 Manchester Road, WARRINGTON, WA1 3BD.
Ⓟ**David Chapman Accountancy Limited** *(D L Chapman)* 18 Stoneleigh Avenue, SALE, M33 5FF.
David Clark *(D J Clark)* 1st Floor, Church House, 61 College Road, BROMLEY, BR1 3QG.
David Cleaver & Co *(D K Cleaver)* 25 Heycroft, COVENTRY, CV4 7HE.
David Clewin Hughes *(D C Hughes)* Silverleigh House, 3 Silver Lane, PURLEY, SURREY, CR8 3HJ.
David Cooke & Co *(D C S Cooke)* 6 Seacourt Road, Botley, OXFORD, OX2 9LD.
David Cornish *(D A Cornish)* Marlins, Back Lane, CHALFONT ST. GILES, HP8 4PF.
ⒻⒶ**David Cottrell & Company** *(D Cottrell)* The Old Bakery, 11a Canford Lane, Westbury-on-Trym, BRISTOL, BS9 3DE.
Ⓕ**David Coupee** *(D H Coupee)* Holmes House, The Green, Sedlescombe, BATTLE, TN33 0QA.
Ⓐ**David Crackett** *(D Crackett)* Viale Coni Zugna 17, 20144 MILAN, ITALY.
David Crammer & Co *(D J Crammer)* 20 Courtland Drive, CHIGWELL, IG7 6PW.
David Crook & Co. *(D F Crook)* 6 Martineau Close, BOGNOR REGIS, WEST SUSSEX, PO21 4BT.
David Cutter & Co *(P J Cutter, K Jones)* 2 Lyttleton Court, Birmingham Street, HALESOWEN, WEST MIDLANDS, B63 3HN.
Ⓟ**David Cutter & Co, trading name of Cutter & Co Limited** *(P J Cutter, K Jones)* 2 Lyttleton Court, Birmingham Street, HALESOWEN, WEST MIDLANDS, B63 3HN.
Ⓟ**David Earley (2005) Limited** *(D W Earley)* Ketts House, Winchester Road, Chandler's Ford, EASTLEIGH, HAMPSHIRE, SO53 2FZ.
David Edge *(A D Edge)* 2 Sandlebridge Lane, KNUTSFORD, WA16 7SD.
Ⓟ**David Edmonds FCA CTA, trading name of David Edmonds Ltd** *(D K Edmonds)* Land Court Lane House, Tytherley Road, Winterslow, SALISBURY, SP5 1PZ.
Ⓟ**David Elliott & Co, trading name of David S M Elliott & Company Limited** *(D S M Elliott)* Southdown, 59 Grove Road, Coombe Dingle, BRISTOL, BS9 2RT.
Ⓟ**David Elliott Associates, trading name of Elliott Business Advisory Services Limited** *(D C Elliott)* Manchester Business Park, 3000 Aviator Way, MANCHESTER, M22 5TG.
Ⓕ**David Endicott** *(D J Endicott)* 47 Ashwood Drive, BROADSTONE, DORSET, BH18 8LN.
David Evans & Co *(D E Evans)* PO Box 113, FRODSHAM, WA6 7WS.
Ⓐ**David Evans & Co** *(J D Evans)* Stowegate House, 37 Lombard Street, LICHFIELD, STAFFORDSHIRE, WS13 6DP.
David Exell Associates *(D J Exell)* PO Box 1601, Broad Street, Wrington, BRISTOL, BS40 5WA. and at CHICHESTER, CHRISTCHURCH, CWMBRAN, EXETER, GLOUCESTER, LONDON, SOUTHAMPTON, ST COLUMB, STRATFORD-UPON-AVON, SWANSEA
Ⓐ**David F. Edwards** *(D F Edwards)* Victoria House, Victoria Street, CWMBRAN, NP44 3JS.
David Fine & Co *(S D Fine)* Dolphin House, 12 Beaumont Gate, RADLETT, HERTFORDSHIRE, WD7 7AR.
ⒻⓅ**David Fishel Accountancy Services Limited** *(D H Fishel)* 59A Brent Street, LONDON, NW4 2EA.
ⒻⓅ**David Frumin & Associates, trading name of DFA (Accountancy) Ltd** *(D H Frumin)* 48 Queen Street, EXETER, EX4 3SR.
David G.Rouse *(D G Rouse)* 18 Four Pools Road, EVESHAM, WR11 1EF.
ⒻⒶ**David Gamblin** *(D M Gamblin)* David Gamblin, 71 The Hundred, ROMSEY, HAMPSHIRE, SO51 8BZ.
David Gedge & Co *(D R Gedge)* 38 Sirdar Road, LONDON, N22 6RG.
David Golby *(D C Golby)* High Street Cottage, Compton, NEWBURY, RG20 6NL.
David Grant *(D N Grant)* 22 Alba Gardens, Golders Green, LONDON, NW11 9NR.
★Ⓟ**David Grey & Co Ltd** *(D W Grey)* 175/177 Temple Chambers, Temple Avenue, LONDON, EC4Y 0DB.
David Griffiths *(D Griffiths)* Westville, Ober Road, BROCKENHURST, SO42 7ST.
David Grimwade *(D R Grimwade)* Watermead, St Mary's Road, Mortimer, READING, RG7 3UE.
ⒾⓅⒶ**David H Evans Limited** *(D H Evans)* Unit 2, The Old Sawmill, Shaw Bridge Street, CLITHEROE, LANCASHIRE, BB7 1LY.
Ⓐ**David Hancock & Co** *(D J C Hancock)* Webb House, 20 Bridge Road, Park Gate, SOUTHAMPTON, SO31 7GE.
ⒻⒶ**David Harris** *(D F Harris)* Lyn House, 39 The Parade, Oadby, LEICESTER, LE2 5BB.
ⒻⓅ**David Herbert Limited** *(D J Herbert)* Regus Centre, Windmill Hill Business Park, Whitehill Way, SWINDON, SN5 6QR.
David Herskine & Co *(D Herskine)* 45 Hurstwood Road, Temple Fortune, LONDON, NW11 0AX.
David Hillel *(D Hillel)* Flat 2, Stanview Court, 5 Queens Road, LONDON, NW4 2TH.
David Hilliam *(D P Hilliam)* The Lodge, Oak Lawn, Woodside, Wootton, RYDE, ISLE OF WIGHT PO33 4JR.
Ⓟ**David Holl, trading name of Holl Cameron & Co Ltd** *(D J Holl)* Ground Floor, Beresford House, Bellozanne Road, St. Helier, JERSEY, JE2 3JW.
ⒻⓅ**David Holm Ltd** *(D T Holm)* Plum Cottage, Mersea Road, COLCHESTER, CO2 7SG.
★ⒻⒶ**David Howard** *(S A Bishop, N King)* 1 Park Road, Hampton Wick, KINGSTON UPON THAMES, KT1 4AS. and at WEYBRIDGE
David Ingall *(D A Ingall)* 40 Garth Lane, Hambleton, SELBY, NORTH YORKSHIRE, YO8 9QA.

David Isaacs & Company - Davis & Co
Members in Practice and Firms - Alphabetical

David Isaacs & Company *(D Isaacs)* 2nd Floor, Walsingham House, 1331-1337 High Road, Whetstone, LONDON, N20 9HR.

Ⓐ**David J Barnett** *(D J Barnett)* The Point, Granite Way, Mountsorrel, LOUGHBOROUGH, LEICESTERSHIRE, LE12 7TZ.

Ⓟ**David J Conway & Co, trading name of Trafalgar Associates Limited** *(D J Conway)* Unit 24, Bury Business Centre, Kay Street, BURY, LANCASHIRE, BL9 6BU.

David J Hackett *(D J Hackett)* 100 Newland, LINCOLN, LN1 1YA.

Ⓟ**David J House Limited** *(D J House)* 21 Barton Court Avenue, Barton on Sea, NEW MILTON, HAMPSHIRE, BH25 7EP.

David J Miller & Co *(D Miller, D J Miller)* 8 Savoy Grove, Blackwater, CAMBERLEY, SURREY, GU17 9JW.

David J Musker *(D J Musker)* Tullich, Forest Lane, Hightown Hill, RINGWOOD, HAMPSHIRE, BH24 3HF.

ⒻⓅⒶ**David J Payne Ltd** *(D J C Payne)* Room 42, 19b Moor Road, BROADSTONE, DORSET, BH18 8AZ.

David J Peacock BSc(Hons) FCA CTA *(D J Peacock)* 58 Ballybeen Road, Comber, NEWTOWNARDS, COUNTY DOWN, BT23 5PZ.

Ⓟ**David J. Cox, trading name of David J Cox (Midlands) Limited** *(D J Cox)* 45 The Ridgeway, STOURPORT-ON-SEVERN, DY13 8XT.

David J. East *(D J East)* Ashcroft House, 1 St Pauls Road, NEWTON ABBOT, DEVON, TQ12 2HP.

David J. Gingell *(D J Gingell)* 15 Raddenstile Lane, EXMOUTH, EX8 2JL.

David J. Hill & Co *(D J Hill)* Museum Buildings, Church Road, Port Erin, ISLE OF MAN, IM9 6AH.

David J. Townend *(D J Townend)* 17 Stoneleigh Road, SOLIHULL, WEST MIDLANDS, B91 1DG.

David J. Trill *(D J Trill)* Thorley Houses Farm, Thorley Lane West, BISHOP'S STORTFORD, HERTFORDSHIRE, CM23 4BN.

David J. Watts *(D J Watts)* White Wheels, Aston Abbotts, AYLESBURY, HP22 4LU.

David J. Wenham & Co *(D J Wenham)* 7 Victoria Road, LONDON, E4 6BY.

Ⓟ**David Jeffreys, trading name of David Jeffreys Ltd** *(D C Jeffreys)* First Floor, 4 Princes Street, HUNTINGDON, PE29 3PA.

David Jones & Co *(D J F Jones)* Spring Mill, 2 Main Street, Wilsden, BRADFORD, WEST YORKSHIRE, BD15 0DX.

Ⓟ**David Joseph & Co Ltd** *(J M Bloomberg)* Suite 109, Atlas Business Centre, Oxgate Lane, LONDON, NW2 7HJ.

David Josephs *(D L M Josephs)* 2 Queens Avenue, Whetstone, LONDON, N20 0JE.

David K Meggitt *(D K Meggitt)* 5 Parkside, 172 Kew Road, RICHMOND, TW9 2AS.

David K. Hardiman *(D K Hardiman)* 36-38 Meadow Street, WESTON-SUPER-MARE, AVON, BS23 1QQ.

David Keffler & Co *(D P Keffler)* 30 Greenway Lane, Charlton Kings, CHELTENHAM, GLOUCESTERSHIRE, GL52 6LB.

David Kellie-Smith *(D A Kellie-Smith)* 50 Peterborough Road, LONDON, SW6 3EB.

David King *(D C King)* The Old King William, Nettleton, CHIPPENHAM, SN14 7NW.

David Kirk *(D G Kirk)* 91 Bawtry Road, Bessacarr, DONCASTER, SOUTH YORKSHIRE, DN4 7AG.

David Kirk & Co *(D K Kirk)* 183 Fraser Road, SHEFFIELD, S8 0JP.

David L. Hohnen, trading name of Hohnen David Leslie *(D L Hohnen)* Cedars Lodge, Church Road, WINDLESHAM, GU20 6BL.

David L. Kilner *(D L Kilner)* 7 Eldon Square, NEWCASTLE UPON TYNE, NE1 7JG.

David Langley *(D J Langley)* 82 Marine Crescent, Goring-by-Sea, WORTHING, WEST SUSSEX, BN12 4JH.

Ⓕ**David Langridge** *(D H Langridge)* 77A High Street, Lindfield, HAYWARDS HEATH, RH16 2HN.

David Lederer *(D A Lederer)* Riverdale, 32 Kings Road, Pownall Park, WILMSLOW, SK9 5PZ.

Ⓐ**David Lee** *(D E Lee)* 26 Old London Road, HYTHE, KENT, CT21 4DQ.

David Leverett *(D M Leverett)* Crugybar, 66 St. Marys Road, KETTERING, NORTHAMPTONSHIRE, NN15 7BW.

David Lewis & Co *(D M Lewis)* Flat 1, 16 Lindfield Gardens, Hampstead, LONDON, NW3 6PU.

★Ⓐ**David Lindon & Co** *(J M L Hankinson, D R Tossell)* Avaland House, 110 London Road, Apsley, HEMEL HEMPSTEAD, HP3 9SD.

Ⓐ**David Lloyd** *(D E Lloyd)* 148 Lugtrout Lane, SOLIHULL, B91 2RX.

Ⓐ**David Lloyd & Co** *(D M Lloyd)* Century House, 100 Church Street, STAINES, MIDDLESEX, TW18 4DQ.

Ⓟ**David Lloyd Medical Accountant Limited** *(D E Lloyd)* 148 Lugtrout Lane, SOLIHULL, B91 2RX.

ⓅⒶ**David M Rees & Associates Limited** *(D M Rees, S C Rees)* Hawkswick House, Hawkswick, Harpendon Road, ST. ALBANS, HERTFORDSHIRE, AL3 6JG.

David M. Othick *(D M Othick)* 12 Parr Fold Avenue, Worsley, MANCHESTER, M28 7HD.

David M. Pullan *(D M Pullan)* Highfield House, Highfield Road, Idle, BRADFORD, BD10 8QY.

David M. Wallis & Co *(D M Wallis)* 10 Badminton Place, BROXBOURNE, HERTFORDSHIRE, EN10 7PA.

David M. Wright *(D M Wright)* Woodlands Works, Woodlands Road, Thundridge, WARE, SG12 0SP.

David M.K. Yeung & Co *(D M K Yeung)* 14/F San Toi Building, 137-139 Connaught Road Central, CENTRAL, HONG KONG ISLAND, HONG KONG SAR.

ⒻⒶ**David Marston & Co.** *(D L Marston)* Suite A8 Kebbell House, Delta Gain, Carpenders Park, WATFORD, WD19 5BE.

David Moed *(D D Moed)* 8 Hart Grove, LONDON, W5 3NB.

David Moffatt *(M D Moffatt)* Windy Ridge, Station Hill, WIGTON, CA7 9BJ.

David Mok *(D H H Mok)* 10 Queensberry Mews West, South Kensington, LONDON, SW7 2DU.

ⒻⒶ**David Morgan & Co** *(D L T Morgan)* 52 High Street, Harrow-on-the-Hill, HARROW, HA1 3LL.

David Moulding *(D J Moulding)* The Atrium, Park Street West, LUTON, LU1 3BE.

David N Skingle *(D N Skingle)* 8 Glengarry Way, Friars Cliff, CHRISTCHURCH, BH23 4EQ.

Ⓟ**David N W Shore, trading name of DS Management Consultants Ltd** *(D N W Shores)* Hill Rise, Hare Lane, Hordle, LYMINGTON, HAMPSHIRE, SO41 0GE.

David N Williams *(D N Williams)* Chapel Lodge, Langthwaite, RICHMOND, NORTH YORKSHIRE, DL11 6RE.

David Nason *(T D Nason)* 1 St Richards Walk, Canon Lane, CHICHESTER, PO19 1QA.

David Norris - AIMS Pangbourne, trading name of AIMS - David Norris *(D W W Norris)* Tidmarsh House, Tidmarsh Lane, Pangbourne, READING, RG8 8HA.

David Northfield *(D N Northfield)* 412 Daws Heath Road, BENFLEET, ESSEX, SS7 2UD.

Ⓟ**David Osman, trading name of David Osman Ltd** *(D R Osman)* 20 Rougemont Avenue, TORQUAY, TQ2 7JP.

★ⓉⒻⒶ**David Owen & Co** *(P Bennett, M E Buckland, D Wiltshire)* 17 Market Place, DEVIZES, SN10 1BA. and at MARLBOROUGH

Ⓣ**David Pattinson** *(D Pattinson)* 233 London Road, Balderton, NEWARK, NG24 3HA.

Ⓐ**David Paul** *(D J Paul)* 5 Aldermary Road, BROMLEY, BR1 3PH.

David Payne *(D Payne)* 60 The Green, EPSOM, SURREY, KT17 3JJ.

★**David Payne** *(D J Payne)* Sportsman Farm, St Michaels, TENTERDEN, TN30 6SY.

Ⓟ**David Peake Ltd** *(D R Peake)* Butley Cottage, Chestnut Way, Longwick, PRINCES RISBOROUGH, BUCKINGHAMSHIRE, HP27 9SD. and at BUCKINGHAM

David Pennington *(D M Pennington)* Suite Four, The Old Station Business Park, Station Road, PERRANPORTH, CORNWALL, TR6 0LH.

Ⓟ**David Phipps Consultancy Limited** *(D G Phipps)* Thurlestone, 11 Hillcrest, Thornbury, BRISTOL, BS35 2JA.

David Pinder & Co *(D Pinder)* Woodford Lodge, 70 Larkham Lane, Woodford, PLYMOUTH, PL7 4PL.

ⓅⒶ**David Pinder & Co Limited** *(D Pinder)* 23 Lockyer Street, PLYMOUTH, PL1 2QZ.

Ⓟ**David Poole, trading name of David Poole Accountants Ltd** *(D A Poole, A G Sealey)* Hemdean House, 39 Chapel Road, SOUTHAMPTON, SO30 3FG.

ⒻⒶ**David Pullan & Co** *(D J S Pullan)* 24a Brook Street, ILKLEY, LS29 8DE.

David Pullen *(D Pullen)* 24 Katherine Drive, Toton, Beeston, NOTTINGHAM, NG9 6JB.

David R Hazzard FCA *(D R Hazzard)* Dobsons Farm, Sandygate Lane, Broughton, PRESTON, PR3 5LA.

David R S Welch *(D R S Welch)* 3 Alvington Grove, Hazel Grove, STOCKPORT, SK7 5LS.

David R. Robson *(D R Robson)* 143 Sidecliff Road, Roker, SUNDERLAND, SR6 9NE.

David Ray *(D W Ray)* 4 Walk Mill, Dalston, CARLISLE, CA5 7QW.

David Reeve *(D M Reeve)* Harvern, Colber Lane, Bishop Thornton, HARROGATE, HG3 3JR.

ⒻⓅ**David Reid Accountancy Ltd** *(D M Reid)* Unit 4, The Bardfield Centre, Braintree Road, Great Bardfield, BRAINTREE, ESSEX CM7 4SL.

David Richardson & Co *(D Richardson)* 4a London Road, STROUD, GL5 2AG.

★Ⓟ**David Ridley Associates, trading name of David Ridley Associates Limited** *(R Hilling)* Manor House, 1 Macaulay Road, BROADSTONE, DORSET, BH18 8AS.

★**David Roberton & Co** *(S J Cook)* 84 Whiting Street, BURY ST. EDMUNDS, IP33 1NZ.

David Rogers FCA *(D G Rogers)* The Old Malt House, Church Street, BROSELEY, SHROPSHIRE, TF12 5DA.

David Rubin & Partners LLP *(P R Appleton, S M Katz, H K Lan, A D Miller, D A Rubin)* Pearl Assurance House, 319 Ballards Lane, North Finchley, LONDON, N12 8LY.

David S Riding FCA *(D S Riding)* Sherwood House, Division Lane, BLACKPOOL, FY4 5DZ.

David S. Sutcliffe & Co *(D S Sutcliffe)* 14 First Avenue, Church, ACCRINGTON, BB5 5EH.

David Sarjant & Co *(D Sarjant)* Suite 21, Oliver House, Hall Street, CHELMSFORD, CM2 0HG.

David Scott *(D V Scott)* 440 Carnation Lane, Bowerhill, MELKSHAM, WILTSHIRE, SN12 6RD.

David Scott & Co *(D T Scott)* 15 Colburn Avenue, NEWTON AYCLIFFE, COUNTY DURHAM, DL5 7HX.

Ⓟ**David Seabright, trading name of David E Seabright & Co (Nailsea) Limited** *(D E Seabright)* 126a High Street, Nailsea, BRISTOL, BS48 1AH.

David Shaw *(D Shaw)* 9 Gorsty Hill Close, Balterley, CREWE, CW2 5QS.

★ⓉⓅ**David Shawyer & Co Ltd** *(D M Shawyer)* 6 Lodge Place, Thunder Lane, NORWICH, NR7 0LA.

ⒻⒶ**David Smith & Co** *(D C Smith)* 41 Welbeck Street, LONDON, W1G 8HH.

David Sorrell & Company, trading name of Redmayne & Co *(J J Czerwonka)* The Old Bank House, Harris Court, Wellgate, CLITHEROE, BB7 2DP. and at PRESTON

ⓅⒶ**David Starbuck, trading name of David Starbuck Limited** *(D C Starbuck)* 609 Delta Office Park, Welton Road, SWINDON, SN5 7XF.

David Stone *(D Stone)* 16 Goldhurst Terrace, LONDON, NW6 3HU.

Ⓟ**David Stonefield & Co, trading name of David Stonefield & Company Limited** *(D A Stonefield)* 70 Grasmere Road, Gatley, CHEADLE, CHESHIRE, SK8 4RS.

ⓅⒶ**David Summers & Co, trading name of H and S Accountants Ltd** *(C Haria, D Summers)* Argo House, Kilburn Park Road, LONDON, NW6 5LF.

David T Forsyth *(D T Forsyth)* 13 Barn Crescent, MARGATE, KENT, CT9 5HF.

David T W Fong & Co *(T D Fong)* Unit B 23/F, North Cape Commercial Building, 388 Kings Road, NORTH POINT, HONG KONG SAR.

David T. Guest *(D T Guest)* Woodmeadow, Bishopswood Lnane, Crossway Green, STOURPORT-ON-SEVERN, DY13 9SE.

David Taylor *(D A Taylor)* 15 Hill Rise, WOODSTOCK, OXFORDSHIRE, OX20 1AA.

David Tooley *(D A Tooley)* 68 Westbury Road, NORTHWOOD, HA6 3BY.

Ⓐ**David Turner & Co** *(D R B Turner)* Studio 701, 17 Princess Street, HULL, HU2 8BJ.

Ⓐ**David Upstone** *(D R Upstone)* 9 Market Place, BRACKLEY, NORTHAMPTONSHIRE, NN13 7AB.

ⓉⓅⒶ**David V Elston & Co, trading name of David V Elston & Co Ltd** *(D V Elston)* 51 Molesworth Street, WADEBRIDGE, CORNWALL, PL27 7DR.

Ⓟ**David Verney Limited** *(D J Verney)* 83 Curtis Way, Kesgrave, IPSWICH, IP5 2FF.

Ⓟ**David W Graves, trading name of Profitright Ltd** *(D W Graves)* 29 Wyatt Drive, LONDON, SW13 8AL.

Ⓐ**David W T Birkin & Co, trading name of D W T Birkin & Co** *(D W T Birkin)* Ivy House, Nantwich Road, Audley, STOKE-ON-TRENT, ST7 8DW.

Ⓟ**David W T Birkin Ltd** *(D W T Birkin)* Ivy House, Nantwich Road, Audley, STOKE-ON-TRENT, ST7 8DW.

David W. Adams *(D W Adams)* 12 Epping Close, Rainhill, PRESCOT, L35 0QE.

Ⓕ**David W. Morgan** *(D W Morgan)* 32 Llanforda Rise, OSWESTRY, SY11 1SY.

David Wadsworth & Co *(D J Wadsworth)* 47 Merthyr Terrace, Barnes, LONDON, SW13 8DL.

David Walker *(D I Walker)* Trebarwith, 91 Ashbourne Road, Cowers Lane, BELPER, DERBYSHIRE, DE56 2LF.

David Ward *(D S Ward)* 2 Ingleton Close, Holmes Chapel, CREWE, CW4 7LF.

Ⓟ**David Warren & Co, trading name of David Warren & Co Limited** *(D E Warren)* 32 Phipps Hatch Lane, ENFIELD, MIDDLESEX, EN2 0HN.

David Watson *(D I Watson)* Knoll Farm, Aston Lane, Hope, HOPE VALLEY, S33 6RA.

Ⓐ**David Wells** *(D R Wells)* 33 Purnells Way, Knowle, SOLIHULL, WEST MIDLANDS, B93 9JN.

David Wells FCA *(D J R Wells)* 14 Dukes Court, 77 Mortlake High Street, LONDON, SW14 8HS.

David West *(D J West)* 24 The Woodlands, LONDON, N14 5RN.

David Wharrie & Co. *(D R Wharrie)* Woodside House, Ashton, CHESTER, CH3 8AE.

David White & Co *(D B White)* Karen 76 Dagoretti Road, P.O. Box 24911 NAIROBI, 00502, KENYA.

David Whittle & Co *(D M Whittle)* 5 The Walk, BECCLES, SUFFOLK, NR34 9AJ.

David Wilcock *(D I Wilcock)* Pine View, Glen Vine Road, Glen Vine, ISLE OF MAN, IM4 4HG.

David Wiles Associates *(D P Wiles)* The Coach House, 7 Carlton Drive, Heaton, BRADFORD, BD9 4DL.

David Wilkins *(D E Wilkins)* 25a Market Square, BICESTER, OX26 6AD.

ⓅⒶ**David William Walker, trading name of Manor Close Limited** *(D W Walker)* 114-116 High Street, Gosforth, NEWCASTLE UPON TYNE, NE3 1HB.

Ⓐ**David Williams & Co** *(D H A Williams)* 66 Belper Road, DERBY, DE1 3EN.

Ⓟ**David Wilson Consultants Limited** *(D G Wilson)* 52 Fairfield Road, UXBRIDGE, MIDDLESEX, UB8 1AL.

David Young & Co *(D M Young)* 89 Gillards Close, Rockwell Green, WELLINGTON, SOMERSET, TA21 9DX.

Ⓐ**Davidson & Company** *(B J Davidson)* Anchor's Rest, Barnlake Point, Burton, MILFORD HAVEN, DYFED, SA73 1PF.

★**Davidsons** *(S Davidson)* 23 Comfrey Close, FARNBOROUGH, HAMPSHIRE, GU14 9XX.

Davies & Co *(L E Davies)* 136 Bridge Street, LEDBURY, HR8 2AS.

Ⓟ**Davies & Co, trading name of Davies and Co(Accountants) Limited** *(R W Davies)* 15 Rhyd-Y-Defaid Drive, Sketty, SWANSEA, SA2 8AH.

Davies & Crane *(J E Stopyra)* 80 Lytham Road, Fulwood, PRESTON, PR2 3AQ.

Ⓟ**Davies & Crane Accounting Services Ltd** *(J E Stopyra)* Unit 10, 80 Lytham Road, Fulwood, PRESTON, PR2 3AQ.

Davies Associates *(J Davies)* 77 Rue Charlemagne, L-1328 LUXEMBOURG, LUXEMBOURG.

★**Davies Edwards & Co** *(R W Davies)* West Lodge, Rainbow Street, LEOMINSTER, HR6 8DQ. and at KINGTON

Ⓟ**Davies Financial Management Ltd** *(S M Davies)* 29 Solva Avenue, Llanishen, CARDIFF, CF14 0NP.

Ⓕ**Davies Gimber Brown LLP** *(R L Brown, M J Davies)* Ryebrook Studios, Woodcote Side, EPSOM, SURREY, KT18 7HD.

Ⓐ**Davies Grindrod & Co** *(A M Grindrod)* 11 Queen Street, Wellington, TELFORD, TF1 1EH.

ⓉⒻⒶ**Davies Mayers Barnett LLP** *(C E Clift, T G Davies, N J Mayers, M A Minchella, N S Smith)* Pillar House, 113-115 Bath Road, CHELTENHAM, GLOUCESTERSHIRE, GL53 7LS.

★Ⓐ**Davies McLennon** *(G A Davies)* 93 Wellington Road North, STOCKPORT, SK4 2LR.

Davies Rowbotham & Co *(C G Rowbotham)* 1 St Lawrence Court, 81 High Street, Chobham, WOKING, GU24 8LX.

Ⓐ**Davies Sigley** *(M P Sigley)* Dresden House, The Strand, Longton, STOKE-ON-TRENT, ST3 2PD.

ⒻⓅⒶ**Davies Tracey & Co, trading name of Davies Tracey Ltd** *(C Davies)* 3rd Floor, Newport House, Thornaby Place Thornaby, STOCKTON-ON-TEES, CLEVELAND, TS17 6SE.

ⓉⒻⒶ**Davies Williams** *(S Johns, B A Minton, P Williams)* 21 St. Andrews Crescent, CARDIFF, CF10 3DB.

Davies, Downs & Co. *(J P Davies)* Kemmel House, 6 Red Lane, Appleton, WARRINGTON, WA4 5AD.

ⒻⓅⒶ**Davies, trading name of Davies & Associates Limited** *(G V Davies)* Sherwood House, 2 Albert Road, TAMWORTH, B79 7JN.

Davis & Co *(M E Davis)* 66 Garner Drive, East Malling, WEST MALLING, ME19 6NF.

ⒻⓅ**Davis & Co, trading name of Davis & Co (Management Consultants) Ltd** *(P G Davis)* The Lodge, 101 Clarkehouse Road, SHEFFIELD, S10 2LN.

Ⓟ**Davis & Co, trading name of The Four Pages Limited** *(C P Davis)* Canada House, 272 Field End Road, RUISLIP, HA4 9NA.

Davis & Company *(S M Chilton)* Room 11, 1-5 Warstone Lane, Hockley, BIRMINGHAM, B18 6JE.

★**Davis Bonley** *(D Daniels, A S Davis)* Northside House, Mount Pleasant, BARNET, EN4 9EE.

Davis Grant LLP *(B G Chernoff, N M Driver)* Treviot House, 186-192 High Road, ILFORD, ESSEX, IG1 1LR.

Ⓟ**Davis Lombard, trading name of Davis Lombard (UK) Ltd** *(R A Davis)* Whittington House, 64 High Street, FAREHAM, HAMPSHIRE, PO16 7BG.

ⓉⒻⒶ**Davison & Shingleton** *(R Davison, A K Shingleton)* Boundary House, 91-93 Charterhouse Street, LONDON, EC1M 6HR.

★ⓉⒻⓅⒶ**Davisons Ltd** *(M F Joslin, E A Plume, E Smith, J C Ward)* Lime Court, Pathfields Business Park, SOUTH MOLTON, DEVON, EX36 3LH. and at BARNSTAPLE, BIDEFORD

ⓉⒻⒶ**Daw White Murrall** *(P Daw, I E Gregory, C S Jones, G C W Murrall)* 1 George Street, WOLVERHAMPTON, WV2 4DG.

Ⓐ**Dawes & Sutton** *(L G Sutton)* Springfield House, 4 Millicent Road, West Bridgford, NOTTINGHAM, NG2 7LD.

Dawkins Lewis & Soar *(P Clay, J S Dawkins, A J Sawdon)* 4 Cowdown Business Park, Micheldever, WINCHESTER, SO21 3DN.

Dawn Cann Accounting Service *(D E Cann)* 26 Dawley Road, Wall Heath, KINGSWINFORD, DY6 9BH.

Dawn Miners *(D K Miners)* 34 Fairfield Avenue, BATH, BA1 6NH.

Ⓟ**Day & Co (High Peak) Ltd** *(O J Day)* 1 Hunters Green Close, Chinley, HIGH PEAK, DERBYSHIRE, SK23 6DF.

Ⓐ**Day & Company** *(G A Day)* 23 Park Road, GLOUCESTER, GL1 1LH.

ⓉⒻⒶ**Day, Smith & Hunter** *(B A Aitken, A Bell, M Cassidy, R Coates, D G Cochrane-Dyet, S Ellmers, S J Farrant, D Jones, R Lim, J G Moore, M Startup, G D Thomas, P Wilson)* Globe House, Eclipse Park, Sittingbourne Road, MAIDSTONE, KENT, ME14 3EN. and at RICKMANSWORTH

Ⓐ**Daykins** *(P J Daykin)* 6 Abergavenny Road, USK, MONMOUTHSHIRE, NP15 1SB.

Ⓟ**Daymar Ltd** *(D J Pugh)* 15 Partridge Way, Merrow Park, GUILDFORD, GU4 7DW.

ⓅⒶ**DB Associates Limited** *(D T Brown)* 4th Floor, Imperial House, 15 Kingsway, LONDON, WC2B 6UN.

Ⓟ**DB Payroll Services Limited** *(W E Hodgson)* 28 Landport Terrace, PORTSMOUTH, PO1 2RG.

ⒻⓅ**DBA Group limited** *(D M Blair)* 6 Varrier Jones Drive, Papworth Everard, CAMBRIDGE, CB23 3GJ.

ⓉⒻⓅ**DBA, trading name of Duncan Barr Associates Limited** *(D C A Barr)* Canalside Buildings, Graingers Way, Roundhouse Business Park, LEEDS, LS12 1AH.

ⓉⒶ**DBF Associates** *(D Chothani)* South Cheetham Business Centre, 10 Park Place, MANCHESTER, M4 4EY.

★**DBH** *(A D Trowbridge)* 16 Dorcan Business Village, Murdock Road Dorcan, SWINDON, SN3 5HY.

Ⓟ**DC Accounting Solutions Ltd** *(D W Counsell)* Heron House, 39 - 41 Higher Bents Lane, Bredbury, STOCKPORT, SK6 1EE.

Ⓟ**DC Payroll Solutions Limited** *(D W Counsell)* Heron House, 39-41 Higher Bents Lane, Bredbury, STOCKPORT, CHESHIRE, SK6 1EE.

Ⓟ**DCA Associates Limited** *(D C Abrehart)* 3 Great Pitchers, Earls Colne, COLCHESTER, CO6 2SP.

Ⓟ**DCN & Co. Limited** *(G D Boulton, S L Gainey, T P Reed)* Peat House, Newham Road, TRURO, CORNWALL, TR1 2DP.

D'Cruz & Co. *(V.C. D'cruz)* 21 Hanworth Road, REDHILL, RH1 5HS.

Ⓟ**DDR Securities Limited** *(D C Rose)* 22 New Upperton Road, EASTBOURNE, EAST SUSSEX, BN21 1NU.

Ⓐ**de Freitas & Co** *(A E de Freitas)* 39 Berwyn Road, RICHMOND, SURREY, TW10 5BU.

Ⓟ**de Freitas & Co, trading name of de Freitas & Co. Accountants Limited** *(A E de Freitas)* 39 Berwyn Road, RICHMOND, SURREY, TW10 5BU.

Ⓐ**De La Wyche Travis & Co** *(D R M Lukes)* Crown House, Trafford Park Road, Trafford Park, MANCHESTER, M17 1HG.

Ⓣ**de Longa & Company** *(P C De Longa, R H De Longa)* Ffordd Celyn, Lon Parcwr Business Park, RUTHIN, CLWYD, LL15 1NJ.

Ⓕ**De Susman & Co** *(D De)* 9th Floor, Hyde House, Edgware Road Hendon, LONDON, NW9 6LH.

ⓉⒻⓅⒶ**De Vines, trading name of DeVines Accountants Limited** *(R M D Collini, C R Purdy)* DeVine House, 1299-1301 London Road, LEIGH-ON-SEA, ESSEX, SS9 2AD.

ⓅⒶ**De Warrenne Waller and Co Limited** *(J J D Waller)* White Hart House, High Street, Limpsfield, OXTED, RH8 0DT. and at LONDON

Ⓐ**de Wit & Co** *(T P De Wit)* Audit House, Oakwellgate West, GATESHEAD, NE8 2AU.

ⓅⒶ**Deacon Jewell Limited** *(G A Deacon, M J Jewell)* 7 West Street, LISKEARD, CORNWALL, PL14 6BW.

ⓉⒻⒶ**Deacon's** *(S K Deacon)* The Stables, Shipton Bridge Farm, Widdington, SAFFRON WALDEN, ESSEX, CB11 3SU.

Dean & Co *(M A Mohiuddin)* 48 Norbury Hill, LONDON, SW16 3LB.

ⓉⒻⒶ**Dean Statham** *(M R Heenan, J G Hodgkiss, R N Stonier, S J Whiting)* Bank Passage, STAFFORD, ST16 2JS.

Ⓟ**Deanbrook Accounting Services Ltd** *(S D Cohen)* Lear House, 259 Cranbrook Road, ILFORD, ESSEX, IG1 4TG.

Ⓟ**Deane Consulting Limited** *(J A Varley)* 42 Deane Croft Road, PINNER, MIDDLESEX, HA5 1SR.

Deavin & Co *(H Deavin)* 3 Russell-Cotes Road, BOURNEMOUTH, BH1 3AB.

Ⓣ**DEB** *(J Edwards-Brown, J Edwards-Brown)* DEB House, 19 Middleswood Way, Wharncliffe Business Park, Carlton, BARNSLEY, SOUTH YORKSHIRE S71 3HR.

Ⓟ**Deben Accounting Services, trading name of Deben Financial Services Ltd** *(R A Simons)* 270 Colchester Road, IPSWICH, IP4 4QX.

Deborah Dean *(D M Dean)* 30 Postern Road, Tatenhill, BURTON-ON-TRENT, STAFFORDSHIRE, DE13 9SJ.

Deborah O'Keefe (ACA) *(D O' Keeffe)* 23 Fairfield Avenue, Victoria Park, CARDIFF, CF5 1BR.

Deborah Wiffin *(D Wiffin)* 3 Manor Lane, Gotherington, CHELTENHAM, GLOUCESTERSHIRE, GL52 9QX.

Debra Clark & Co *(D Clark)* 128 Rawreth Lane, RAYLEIGH, SS6 9RR.

Debra Morris ACA *(D L Morris)* 9 Grosvenor Road, LONDON, N3 1EY.

ⒻⒶ**Debson & Co.** *(J G Debson)* Galley House, Second Floor, Moon Lane, BARNET, HERTFORDSHIRE, EN5 5YL.

Ⓟ**Debt Free Direct Limited** *(D J Oakley)* Fairclough House, Church Street, Adlington, CHORLEY, LANCASHIRE, PR7 4EX.

Ⓟ**Debt Lifeboat Limited** *(P H Allen, G E B Mander, A D Pillmoor)* Centre City Tower, 7 Hill Street, BIRMINGHAM, B5 4UU.

ⓉⒶ**Debt Lifeline, trading name of Bevan & Buckland** *(H J Lloyd Davies, C J Wheeler)* Langdon House, Langdon Road, SA1 Swansea Waterfront, SWANSEA, SA1 8QY. and at HAVERFORDWEST, PEMBROKE

Ⓟ**Debtmatters Limited** *(G N Ratcliffe)* Mansell House, Aspinall Way, Middlebrook Business Park, BOLTON, BL6 6QQ.

★ⓉⒻ**Deeks Evans** *(P J Delaney, J M Fisher, P E Garside, S R Toulson, R J Young)* 3 Boyne Park, TUNBRIDGE WELLS, TN4 8EN. and at HASTINGS

ⓅⒶ**Deeks Evans Audit Services Limited** *(P E Garside, S R Toulson, R J Young)* 3 Boyne Park, TUNBRIDGE WELLS, KENT, TN4 8EN. and at HASTINGS

Deepak Idnani Accountancy Services *(D Idnani)* 83 Selwood Road, CROYDON, CR0 7JW.

ⒻⓅⒶ**Defries Weiss, trading name of Defries Weiss (Accountants) Ltd** *(G M Defries, W R Weiss)* 311 Ballards Lane, North Finchley, LONDON, N12 8LY.

Ⓟ**DEH Accounting Ltd** *(D E Hickin)* Charnwood, Berry Hall Road, Barton Turf, NORWICH, NR12 8BE.

ⓉⒶ**Deighan Perkins LLP** *(A W Deighan, K M Perkins)* 6th Floor, Newbury House, 890-900 Eastern Avenue, ILFORD, ESSEX, IG2 7HH.

ⒻⒶ**Deirdre A Thomas** *(D A Thomas)* 45a Cottenham Park Road, LONDON, SW20 0SB.

Deirdre L Booth *(D L Booth)* Fairview, Marley Lane, Hoath, CANTERBURY, CT3 4JY.

★**Deitch Cooper** *(K K Shah)* 54-58 High Street, EDGWARE, HA8 7EJ.

ⓉⒻⓅⒶ**DEKM, trading name of DEKM Limited** *(P E Bradley, J H Downes, P J Fletcher)* 5 Trinity Terrace, London Road, DERBY, DE1 2QS. and at ASHBY-DE-LA-ZOUCH

Delahunty & Co *(J J Delahunty)* 4 Eagle Terrace, DUNDRUM 14, COUNTY DUBLIN, IRELAND.

ⓉⒻ**Delia Orme** *(D J Orme)* Branksome House, Filmer Grove, GODALMING, SURREY, GU7 3AB.

Ⓟ**Delightful Managment Services Ltd** *(D A L Bunker)* Kings House, 14 Orchard Street, BRISTOL, BS1 5EH.

Dellal & Co. *(D Dellal)* 5 Park Drive, LONDON, SW14 8RB.

★**Deloitte** *(J S Melrose)* P.O.Box 931, Indebank House, BLANTYRE, MALAWI.

★**Deloitte & Touche** *(A J Wilson)* Attar Sokak No. 9/1-3, Gaziosmanpasa, ANKARA, 06700, TURKEY. and at ISTANBUL

Deloitte & Touche *(A G B Teare)* Dozsa Gyorgy ut 84/C, 1068 BUDAPEST, HUNGARY.

▽**Deloitte & Touche** *(K E McKelvie, P W C Tsai, H Y Wong)* 35/F One Pacific Place, 88 Queensway, CENTRAL, HONG KONG ISLAND, HONG KONG SAR.

★**Deloitte & Touche** *(D M Ndonye)* Patel Building 4th Floor, Maktaba Street, (P O Box 1559), DAR ES SALAAM, TANZANIA.

▽**Deloitte & Touche** *(M J Hartwell)* Deloitte & Touche House, Earlscourt Terrace, DUBLIN 2, COUNTY DUBLIN, IRELAND. and at CORK, LIMERICK

★**Deloitte & Touche** *(R E Douglas, M W Pilling, I A N Wight)* P.O.Box 1787 GT, One Capital Place, GEORGE TOWN, GRAND CAYMAN, KY1 1109, CAYMAN ISLANDS.

Deloitte & Touche *(G J Branch, R A Garrard)* The Old Courthouse, PO Box 250, Athol Street, Douglas, ISLE OF MAN, IM99 1XJ. and at LONDON

★**Deloitte & Touche** *(G Sokota)* Kafue House, 1 Nairobi Place, P O Box 30030, LUSAKA, ZAMBIA. and at CHINGOLA, KITWE, LUANSHYA, MUFULIRA, NDOLA

★Ⓣ**Deloitte & Touche** *(M M Booker, N J Captur, C R Curmi)* Deloitte Place, Mriehel Place, Mriehel Bypass, MRIEHEL BKR3000, MALTA.

★**Deloitte & Touche** *(D M Ndonye, S O Onyango)* Deloitte Place, Waiyaki Way, Muthangari, P O Box 40092, GPO 00100, NAIROBI KENYA. and at KAMPALA

★**Deloitte & Touche** *(M J Jennings)* Tyn 641/4, 110 00, 1 PRAGUE, CZECH REPUBLIC.

★**Deloitte & Touche** *(M I S Chapman)* James Frett Building, Wickhams Cay 1, P O Box 3083, ROAD TOWN, TORTOLA ISLAND, VIRGIN ISLANDS (BRITISH).

★Ⓣ**Deloitte & Touche** *(P J Baldock, T C Chong, E Y Kan)* 6 Shenton Way, # 32-00, DBS Building Tower Two, SINGAPORE 068809, SINGAPORE. and at BANDAR SERI BEGAWAN

★Ⓣ**Deloitte & Touche** *(M J Barrington)* Al Jana Pawla 19, 00854 WARSAW, POLAND.

Deloitte & Touche (M.E) *(C P Corby)* 1001 City Tower 2, Sheikh Zayed Rod, PO Box 4254, DUBAI, UNITED ARAB EMIRATES.

Deloitte & Touche (M.E.) *(S Y Sindaha)* P.O.Box 990, Bin Ghanem Tower, Hamdan Street, ABU DHABI, UNITED ARAB EMIRATES.

★Ⓣ**Deloitte & Touche Bakr Abulkhair & Co** *(N Ahmed, H J Mondon-Ballantyne)* P O Box 442, JEDDAH, 21411, SAUDI ARABIA. and at DAMMAM

★Ⓣ**Deloitte & Touche GmbH** *(A D Crampton)* Schwannstrasse 6, 40476 DUSSELDORF, GERMANY.

Deloitte & Touche LLP *(R Basu, J H Cottrell, C J Pimlott)* Two World Financial Center, NEW YORK, NY 10281-1414, UNITED STATES. and at ALBUQUERQUE, ANN ARBOR, ATLANTA, BATON ROUGE, BIRMINGHAM, BOISE, BOSTON, BRADENTON, BUFFALO, CHARLOTTE, CHEYENNE, CHICAGO, CINCINNATI, CLEVELAND, COLUMBUS, COSTA MESA, DALLAS, DAVENPORT, DAYTON, DENVER, DES MOINES, DETROIT, DURHAM, ELIZABETHTOWN, FORT LAUDERDALE, FORT WORTH, FRESNO, GRAND RAPIDS, GREENSBORO, HARTFORD, HERMITAGE, HONOLULU, HOUMA, INDIANAPOLIS, JACKSONVILLE, JERICHO, LAS VEGAS, LINCOLN, LOS ANGELES, LOUISVILLE, MCLEAN, MELVILLE, MOBILE, MORRISVILLE, NASHVILLE, NEW ORLEANS, OMAHA, ORLANDO, PALM SPRINGS, PARSIPPANY, PHILADELPHIA, PHOENIX, PITTSBURGH, PORTLAND, RALEIGH, RENO, RICHMOND, ROCHESTER, SAIPAN, SALEM, SALT LAKE CITY, SAN DIEGO, SAN FRANCISCO, SANTA ROSA, STEUBENVILLE, TAMPA, TOPEKA, WASHINGTON, WILTON, WINSTON-SALEM, WOODLAND HILLS

Deloitte & Touche LLP *(J B Cawthorne, J A F Cook, R Krishnamoorthy, Y N Pavri)* Suite 1400, 181 Bay Street, TORONTO M5J 2V1, ON, CANADA. and at AMOS, BAIE COMEAU, CALGARY, CHIBOUGAMAU, CORNWALL, DARTMOUTH, EDMONTON, FARNHAM, GRANBY, GRAND-MERE, HAWKESBURY, LA BAIE, LAC-ETCHEMIN, LANGLEY, LONGUEUIL, MATANE, MISSISSAUGA, MONTREAL, NORTH YORK, PRINCE ALBERT, PRINCE GEORGE, RIMOUSKI, SAINT JOHN, SAINT-HYACINTHE, SARNIA, SASKATOON, SHAWINIGAN, ST FELICIEN, ST JOHN'S, TROIS-PISTOLES, VANCOUVER, VILLE SAINT-GEORGES, WINNIPEG

★Ⓣ**Deloitte Hadjipavlou Sofianos & Cambanis S.A** *(A Agathocleous, P Efthymiades, M Hadjipavlou, C Karsas, N Sofianos)* 3a Fragoklissias & Granikou Str, Maroussi, 15125 ATHENS, GREECE.

▽**Deloitte Haskin & Sells** *(B P Shroff)* 12 Dr A Besant Road, Wonli, MUMBAI 400018, INDIA. and at BARODA, NEW DELHI

★**Deloitte Haskins & Sells** *(B P Shroff)* 12 Dr Annie Besant Road, Opp Shiv Sagar Estate, MUMBAI 400 018, INDIA. and at BANGALORE, CALCUTTA, HYDERABAD, JAMSHEDPUR, MADRAS, NEW DELHI

ⓉⓅ**Deloitte Limited** *(J L Caruana, D Delgado, S J Reyes, J M Tricker)* PO Box 758, Merchant House, 22/24 John Mackintosh Square, GIBRALTAR, GIBRALTAR.

ⓉⓅ**Deloitte Ltd** *(A Andreou, C M Christoforou, N S Kyriakides, M C Lambrou, P Markou, P Papadopoulos, N D Papakyriacou, P Papamichael, E N Philippou)* 24 Spyrou Kyprianou Avenue, P.O.Box 21675 CY-1512, 1075 NICOSIA, CYPRUS. and at LARNACA, LIMASSOL

Deloitte Ross Tohmatsu *(S R Konfortion)* 7th Floor, Raffles Tower, 19 Cybercity, EBENE, MAURITIUS.

Ⓣ**Deloitte Touche Tohmatsu** *(S K Chiu, W K C Chou, T D Keung, E W Phipps, T S Wong, Y M Yeung)* 8-F Tower W2, The Towers, Oriental Plaza, 1 East Chang An Avenue, BEIJING 100738, CHINA. and at GUANGZHOU, NANJING, SHANGHAI, SHENZHEN

★**Deloitte Touche Tohmatsu** *(W J Chan, H Fong, A Glen, C K H Hung, C Ip, L T G Khaw, W C Lam, M Li, K E McKelvie, C D Pak, S Taylor, E Tong, Y Tse, G R White, C M Wu, S E Yen, K Yip)* 35/F One Pacific Place, 88 Queensway, CENTRAL, HONG KONG ISLAND, HONG KONG SAR. and at BEIJING, MACAU, SHANGHAI

★**Deloitte Touche Tohmatsu** *(J R T Oram)* Cxa Postal 2922 CEP 01051, SP Avenida Ipiranga, 324-6 andar, SAO PAULO, BRAZIL. and at RECIFE, RIO DE JANEIRO, SALVADOR

★**Deloitte Touche Tohmatsu** *(S M Holdstock)* Grosvenor Place, 225 George Street, P.O. Box N 250, SYDNEY, NSW 2000, AUSTRALIA. and at ADELAIDE, AIRLIE BEACH, ALICE SPRINGS, BRISBANE, CANBERRA, DARWIN, HOBART, LAUNCESTON, MACKAY, MELBOURNE, MIDLAND, MOORABBIN, NELSON BAY, NEWCASTLE, PARRAMATTA, PERTH, PORT MORESBY, QUEANBEYAN, SHEPPARTON, SURFERS PARADISE, WOLLONGONG

★**Deloitte Touche Tohmatsu Jaiyos** *(S Krishnamra)* 25th Fl Rajanakarn Bldg, 183 South Sathorn Road Yanawa, BANGKOK 10120, THAILAND.

Ⓟ**Deloitte Touche Tohmatsu Jaiyos Co Ltd** *(S Krishnamra)* Rajanakarn Building, 25 Floor 183 South Sathorn Rd, Yannawa, BANGKOK 10120, THAILAND.

Deloitte West & Central Africa *(E A Chatburn)* 235 Ikorodu Road, Llupeeju, PO Box 965, Marina, LAGOS, NIGERIA.

Delta Accountancy Services *(D B Evans)* 57 Stotfold Road, Maypole, BIRMINGHAM, B14 5JD.

Ⓟ**Delta Tax Services Limited** *(G D Tongue)* 6 Fair Field, Waltham on the Wolds, MELTON MOWBRAY, LEICESTERSHIRE, LE14 4AX.

Delwin Groves *(J D Groves)* 7 Mill Close, Broom, ALCESTER, WARWICKSHIRE, B50 4HT.

Ⓟ**Delyth Bending Accountancy Limited** *(D C Bending)* 4 The Paddock, Lower Boddington, DAVENTRY, NORTHAMPTONSHIRE, NN11 6YF.

Denby & Associates *(P A Denby)* Ravensbourne Business Centre, Westerham Road, KESTON, KENT, BR2 6HE.

★ⓉⒻⓅⒶ**Dendy Neville, Payroll.biz, trading names of Dendy Neville Limited** *(D M Hill, D Williams)* 3-4 Bower Terrace, 1 Tonbridge Road, MAIDSTONE, KENT, ME16 8RY.

Denis Farman *(D J Farman)* 28 Park Gate, Mount Avenue, Ealing, LONDON, W5 1PX.

★**Deniz-Gumus & Co** *(D K Deniz)* 111/5 Mehmet Aki f Caddesi, LEFKOSA MERSIN 10, TURKEY.

ⓅⒶ**Denmark Forrester Limited** *(R P Easby)* First Floor, 1A High Street, SOUTHMINSTER, ESSEX, CM0 7AA.

Ⓟ**Dennis & Turnbull Holdings, trading name of Dennis & Turnbull Holdings Limited** *(B P Herbert, C S Reader)* Swatton Barn, Badbury, SWINDON, SN4 0EU.

★ⒻⓅⒶ**Dennis & Turnbull, trading name of Dennis & Turnbull Limited** *(N L Dennis, B P Herbert, C S Reader)* Swatton Barn, Badbury, SWINDON, SN4 0EU.

Dennis Chi In Chow *(D C I Chow)* 35th Floor, One Pacific Place, 88 Queensway, CENTRAL, HONG KONG ISLAND, HONG KONG SAR.

Dennis Cross - Dinesh Desai
Members in Practice and Firms - Alphabetical

Dennis Cross *(J D Cross)* Sycamore House, 5 Vine Close, Stapleford, CAMBRIDGE, CB22 5BZ.

Dennis Leyhane *(D F Leyhane)* Greenleaf, 46 The Gables, ONGAR, ESSEX, CM5 0GA.

Ⓐ**Dennis Mott & Co** *(D P Mott)* 6a The Pavement, ST. IVES, PE27 5AD.

Dennis Payne FCA *(D Payne)* 9 Kingfisher Close, West Moors, FERNDOWN, DORSET, BH22 0DX.

ⒻⒶ**Denny Sullivan & Associates LLP** *(A W Denny)* Blackwell House, Guildhall Yard, LONDON, EC2V 5AE.

Dent & Co *(E A Dent)* Beacon House, 1 Willow Walk, Woodley Park, SKELMERSDALE, WN8 6UR.

★**Dental Business Solutions** *(G V Manolescue, N D Stewart)* Network House, Station Yard, THAME, OXFORDSHIRE, OX9 3UH.

Derby & Co *(A J Derby)* 52 Hickmans Close, GODSTONE, RH9 8EB.

Ⓟ**Derby Payroll Services Limited** *(D J Mellor, R E Minns)* 81 Burton Road, DERBY, DE1 1TJ.

Dereck C. Sale *(D C Sale)* 4015 Cormack Crescent, PRINCE GEORGE V2N 5K8, BC, CANADA.

Derek A Naylor FCA *(D A Naylor)* Woodthorpe House, Packington Lane, Hopwas, TAMWORTH, B78 3AY.

Derek A Parry *(D A Parry)* 82 Tyne Crescent, Brickhill, BEDFORD, MK41 7UL.

Derek Brian Murton *(D B Murton)* Baden-croft, Falmouth Avenue, NEWMARKET, SUFFOLK, CB8 0NB.

Ⓟ**Derek Cousens Limited** *(D A Cousens)* 58 Kestell Parc, BODMIN, CORNWALL, PL31 1HP.

Derek Draper *(D G Draper)* The Glen, Adsett, WESTBURY-ON-SEVERN, GL14 1PH.

Derek F. Parkhouse *(D F Parkhouse)* 10 Plas Derwen Close, ABERGAVENNY, NP7 9SQ.

★ⒻⒶ**Derek Field & Co** *(D B M Field)* 2nd Floor, Crown House, 37 High Street, EAST GRINSTEAD, RH19 3AF.

Derek Fieldhouse *(D Fieldhouse)* 39 Newton Court, Oakwoood Grange Lane, LEEDS, LS8 2PH.

Derek Greene & Co *(D L Greene)* 33 Minoan Drive, Apsley, HEMEL HEMPSTEAD, HERTFORDSHIRE, HP3 9WA.

Derek Hill *(D Hill)* 38 Knowsley Road, Hazel Grove, STOCKPORT, SK7 6BW.

ⓉⓅ**Derek J. Stenner Ltd** *(D J Stenner)* The Mews, Hounds Road, Chipping Sodbury, BRISTOL, BS37 6EE.

Derek Longden *(D Longden)* 47 West Parade, WORTHING, BN11 5EF.

Derek Ng & Company *(K K D Ng)* Room 702, Hollywood Plaza, 610 Nathan Road, MONG KOK, KOWLOON, HONG KONG SAR.

ⒻⒶ**Derek Owram** *(D Owram)* Meadow Bank, 2 Hall Rise, Bramhope, LEEDS, LS16 9JG.

Derek Payne *(D Payne)* Alwynne, 48 The Ridgeway, Astwood Bank, REDDITCH, WORCESTERSHIRE, B96 6LT.

Derek R James & Co *(D R James)* 10 Hercies Road, Hillingdon, UXBRIDGE, MIDDLESEX, UB10 9NA.

ⒻⒶ**Derek Rothera & Company** *(D J Rothera)* Units 15 & 16, 7 Wenlock Road, LONDON, N1 7SL.

Derek W Miles *(D W Miles)* 6 Wybourne Rise, TUNBRIDGE WELLS, TN2 5JG.

Ⓟ**Derek Willows, trading name of Derek Willows Ltd** *(D F Willows)* 7 Priory Gate, SHEFFORD, BEDFORDSHIRE, SG17 5TX.

★Ⓐ**Derek Young & Co** *(G M Adams, S M Young)* Estate House, Evesham Street, REDDITCH, B97 4HP.

Ⓐ**Derrick J. Nunn** *(D J Nunn)* 54 Shirley Street, HOVE, BN3 3WG.

ⓅⒶ**Derrick Newman & Co., trading name of Derrick Newman Limited** *(P J Crowley, D J Horne)* 29 Bath Road, Old Town, SWINDON, SN1 4AS.

Ⓕ**Derrick Sheppard & Co** *(D R A Sheppard)* Orchard House, Back Lane, Garboldisham, DISS, IP22 2SD.

Ⓟ**Desai & Co Accountants Ltd** *(N K D Desai)* Desai House, 9-13 Holbrook Lane, COVENTRY, CV6 4AD.

Desai & Co. *(N N Desai)* 1 Tanjong Rhu Road, 05-01, SINGAPORE 436879, SINGAPORE.

Ⓟ**Deseret Accountants Ltd** *(R G Hough)* 4 Thorpe Court, Thorpe Waterville, KETTERING, NORTHAMPTONSHIRE, NN14 3DE.

Ⓟ**Devcomp, trading name of Devcomp Limited** *(I S Deverill)* 18 Elgin Road, POOLE, DORSET, BH14 8ER.

ⓅⒶ**Devereux Accountants Ltd** *(R Devereux)* Empire House, Edgar Street, ACCRINGTON, LANCASHIRE, BB5 1PT.

Devon Finance Director LLP *(D J Large, M A Large, R M Tickell)* 13 Silver Street, BARNSTAPLE, DEVON, EX32 8HR.

Ⓟ**Devon Square Partners Limited** *(M J W White)* 14 Torquay Road, NEWTON ABBOT, DEVON, TQ12 1AJ.

Ⓟ**Devonhurst Accounting Ltd** *(E M Ridge, N B Ridge)* The Gatehouse, 2 Devonhurst Place, LONDON, W4 4JD.

Devonshire Advisory *(S J Whitmore)* 54 Huggetts Lane, EASTBOURNE, EAST SUSSEX, BN22 0LU.

Ⓟ**Devonshire Corporate Finance Limited** *(M A Burchmore, D Fecher, M J Meadows, S Neal, M J Snyder)* Devonshire House, 60 Goswell Road, LONDON, EC1M 7AD.

Devonshire Corporate Services LLP *(D A Benton, N M Birch, N S J Brooks, M A Burchmore, E M Carder, P Chadda, S T Clark, A P Craddock, J T L Cross, J M Dawson, S J De Lord, D Fecher, N M Finlayson, A G D Follows, D J Goodridge, I J Graham, K E Halstead, R M Heap, M K Hindson, P R Holgate, A J Houstoun, C C Hughes, C W Ireton, C J Lane, D T Martine, M J Meadows, A Merron, D J Montgomery, T J Moore, G A Morgan, M A Muirhead, S Neal, T Park, M B Penfold, B R Pope, H M Powell, J R Riches, P E M Samrah, J P Seymour, A N Shaw, M N Sinclair, M J Snyder, J Staniforth, T F J Stovold, R N Surman, J Sutcliffe, P J Timms, M Twum-Ampofo, G A Tyler, J I Walsh)* Devonshire House, 60 Goswell Road, LONDON, EC1M 7AD.

ⓅⒶ**Dewanis, trading name of Dewanis Limited** *(R K Dewani)* Westbury House, 23-25 Bridge Street, PINNER, MIDDLESEX, HA5 3HR.

Ⓐ**Dewey & Co** *(P R Dewey)* 17 St Andrews Crescent, CARDIFF, CF10 3DB.

★**Dexter & Sharpe** *(S A Fridlington)* The Old Vicarage, Church Close, BOSTON, LINCOLNSHIRE, PE21 6NE. and at BOURNE, HORNCASTLE, LOUTH, SLEAFORD, SPILSBY

Ⓟ**Dey & Co Ltd** *(J W Dey)* Brookdale, 41 Clarence Road, CHESTERFIELD, S40 1LH.

Ⓟ**DF Taxation Services Ltd** *(D Fisher)* 309 Winston House, 2 Dollis Park, LONDON, N3 1HF.

ⓉⒻⒶ**DFC** *(P G Dennis, S M H Lewis)* First Floor Unit 4C, Village Way, GreenMeadow Springs Business Park, CARDIFF, CF15 7NE.

ⓉⓅ**DFK Demetriou Trapezaris Ltd** *(C Constantinou)* 59-61 Acropolis Avenue, 3rd Floor, 2012 NICOSIA, CYPRUS.

Ⓟ**DG Accountancy Services Limited** *(D A Gingles)* 1 Canterbury Close, WORCESTER PARK, SURREY, KT4 8GR.

Ⓟ**DG Accounting & Business Administration Ltd** *(D A Lear)* Orchard House, Three Elm Lane, Golden Green, TONBRIDGE, KENT, TN11 0BE.

Ⓟ**DH Tuck & Co Ltd** *(D H Tuck)* 167 Park Street, CLEETHORPES, SOUTH HUMBERSIDE, DN35 7LX.

Dharsi & Co *(T M Dharsi)* Woodview, 92a Broadwood Avenue, RUISLIP, MIDDLESEX, HA4 7XT.

Ⓟ**Dharun & Co Accountants & Auditors Limited** *(V Jayaweerasingham)* 19 Tintern Avenue, LONDON, NW9 0RH.

ⓉⓅⒶ**DHB Accountants, trading name of DHB Accountants Limited** *(D S Bray, S P Horrigan)* 110 Whitchurch Road, CARDIFF, CF14 3LY.

Ⓟ**DHF Accounting Limited** *(F G Drainey, H C Drainey)* 20 Market Street, ALTRINCHAM, CHESHIRE, WA14 1PF.

★Ⓐ**DHH** *(N Webb)* Wychbury Chambers, 78 Worcester Road, Hagley, STOURBRIDGE, DY9 0NJ.

Dhillons *(A A Dhillon)* 139 Blendon Road, BEXLEY, DA5 1BT.

ⒻⒶ**dhjh, trading name of dhjh LLP** *(N C Danks, P T Johnston, J L Swann)* Springhill House, 94-98 Kidderminster Road, BEWDLEY, WORCESTERSHIRE, DY12 1DQ.

DHL Accountancy Services *(D H Lane)* 30 Willowbank Gardens, TADWORTH, SURREY, KT20 5DS.

ⓅⒶ**Dialmode (328) Limited** *(M L Burgess, R M Simpson)* Ground Floor, Maclaren House, Talbot Road, Old Trafford, MANCHESTER, M32 0FP.

Ⓟ**Diamond Accounting Group, trading name of Diamond RBA Ltd** *(R C Bettany)* G9 Enterprise House, Navigation Park, Abercynon, Rhondda Cynon Taf, MOUNTAIN ASH, MID GLAMORGAN CF45 4SN. and at SWANSEA

Diamond Accounting Services *(H L Court)* 23 Melford Drive, MAIDSTONE, KENT, ME16 0UN.

ⓉⒶ**Diamond Advisory Services, Monks, Saratoga, trading names of PricewaterhouseCoopers LLP** *(V Abrams, D W Adair, C M Adshead, A M Ahmad, P D Aitken, S Ali, D Allen, S C Amiss, M Amitrano, H Anderson, S Anderson, B R Andrews, J D Arden-Davis, G I A Armfield, N A Atkinson, R S Auluk, R F Bacon, G A Bagley, C J Baker, J K Baker, G A Barker, J Barker, P A Barkus, M Barling, S Barnes, P V Barrow, C A Bates, M C Batten, M E Batten, L J Beal, D A Beer, S W Beet, A N Bell, S Bellars, T N Bentham, A M Berridge, J R L Berriman, S Berryman, J Bertolotti, J W E Bichard, C Billington, M Binney, D C Bishop, N G Blackwood, P Bloomfield, S H Boadle, N W E Boden, M C Bolton, M N Bolton, J C Booker, P Boorman, A P Boucher, J S Bourdeaux, C E B Bowman, R C Boys-Stones, S A Bradley, J A Bradshaw, R J Bridson, J R Bromfield, F M Brooker, D J Brown, R Bunter, J Burkitt, D J Burn, C J Burns, K J Burrowes, R W Burton, C Butter, P J L Calnan, J R Calvert-Davies, N A V Campbell-Lambert, A J L Casley, R L Casson, S J Cater, J W P Chalmers, I R Chambers, D L Charles, A P Clark, B L Clark, R J Clark, C S Clarke, J Clarke, P E C Clarke, R S Collier, R D Collier-Keywood, D J H Cooke, N C Coomber, J E Cooper, P D Copley, N C Corp, S Cosgrove, A D Cottis, S J Couch, M R Cowan, P J Coward, J S Cowling, D J Cox, E H L Cox, P R Cragg, G Crawford, M M Cross, P C Cussons, Y Cypher, A J Dale, S H Dale, H J Daubeney, G M Davies, S T Davies, I F Davis, M J Dawson, R F De Peyrecave, S L De Young, A M Debell, S J Denison, S Devenney, A E Devoy, C M Dewar, J Dickson, I E Dilks, D M Docker, J M S Dowty, S M Drury, K L Dukes, I W Durrans, I F Dykes, N R Edwards, A M Eldridge, I H Elliott, J M Ellis, K J D Ellis, M C Ellis, S A Ellis, K Evans, P A Evans, C M L Everest, G W C Eversfield, S C Fairchild, M G Falconer, N N Faquir, P A F Figgis, J S J Fillingham, A W G Finn, K E Finn, S J Fish, J J N W Fisher, M C Fleetwood, N J Fletcher, J D Forbes, J M R Foster, S M Fraser, N Freeman, R A J French, S D A Friend, B J Furness, P R Galpin, M C J Gardiner, I L Gardner, C G Gentle, P D George, D C Gibbs, S R Gilder, M A Gill, C S Gillespie, R P Girdlestone, C J Glazier, R J Gledhill, D K Godbee, R N A Gordon, N J P Gower, D W Grace, C F Graham, A J Gray, I D Green, K D P Green, R J Green, I J L Griffiths, A E Grimbly, N C Grimes, A P W Groves, N T Groves, T J Groves, D P Guly, C S M Hallett, N C Hammans, A R Hammond, G P Hannam, M A Hannam, J A Hare, K D Harrington, J G Harrison, P R Harrold, S J S Hawes, L H Hayward, M A Heath, C F Hemmings, A J Hemus, A J M Henderson, S A Herbert, D J L Hewer, C D Hibbs, J Higgins, S Higgins, M A Higginson, A G Hill, I A Hill, C P Hinds, L M Hine, M N Hine, J P A Hines, L Frazer, J C F Hitchins, A E Hodgson, M A Hodgson, M R Hodgson, R P Hodson, P Hogarth, P A Holgate, J J Holloway, J A Hook, L J Hooker, T V Hopcroft, N D Hopes, N Hopkin, M E W Hoskyns-Abrahall, J P Howe, D A Howell, N J Howlett, H R A Hudson, M C Hughes, R W Hughes, R J Hunt, S D Hunt, M A F Hunter, R A Hunter, Z Hussain, S T Hyde, S T Isted, C J Jackson, P Jackson, W Jackson-Moore, P C Jeffrey, J S Jenkins, S M Jennings, J R Jensen, M J A Jervis, D M J Jessup, S Jiang, D C John, C P Jones, M N Jones, C L Joseland, D Jukes, R K Julleekeea, T Kachhela, A Kail, M B Karp, R J Keers, F E Kelsey, A C Kemp, D F Kenmir, S Kentish, W Kenyon, V A Kerrigan, L C Kerswill, D G Ketteringham, J S King, M King, M A King, S B Kundu, G J Lagerberg, K S Laing-Williams, G J Lambert, J W Lambert, A P Latham, D J A Law, A Lees, J L Leeson, M J Legg, P J Lennon, A Levack, A J Lever, R N Lewis, T E Lewis, B G Lochead, A V Lomas, I M Looker, G S Lord, A J Lyon, D J D Macdougall, J C Mackintosh, O Mackney, S D Maddison, M J Magee, C J Maidment, J B G Maitland, P Mankin, K J Mansfield, L J Manson-Smith, Q Marikar, I C Marsden, R Marsh, B J Marshall, J F Martin, M T Martin, C Maw, P C Maybrey, E C McCann, A H McCrae, A J McCrosson, A D McGill, D J McNab, R E Meakin, D L Meek, A G R Meeke, F Meijs, R J Milburn, R Mills, J E B Minards, M W Moffat, M C F Monfries, J G Mongan, A Moore, A R Morgan, J D Morgan, W J Morgan, A C M Morris, K D Morris, I J Morrison, S G Mount, M R Mullins, F P F Murphy, E L Myall-Schofield, P H Nash, P J Newberry, M P Newman, S B Newman, D M Newton, U Newton, M S Nichols, P Nixon, H M Nixseaman, P J Norbury, S A O'Brien, C O'Hare, S G E O'Hare, G S Oakland, R Oldfield, D I Oliver, S J Ormiston, T S Owusu-Adjei, A Packman, N R Page, S R Page, A R Palmer, R G Palmer, A Parker, J G Parr, G J Parsons, S J Partridge, Z U Patel, A F C Paynter, S A Pearson, D A Pedropillai, C A Penwarden, S M Perry, D S Phelps, D M H Phillips, G M Phillips, G P N Phillips, J M Picton, G K Pike, R J Pollard, A J Popham, R J Porter, C W Potter, G J Powell, I C Powell, J D Preston, M H Preston, I R A Prideaux, D T Prosser, R M L Pugh, P S Purewal, R S Radia, M G Rajani, Z P Randeria, N J Ransome, A N Ratcliffe, J Ratcliffe, P S Rawlinson, J P Rayner, N L S Rea, N H Reynolds, C D Richardson, J Richardson, N J Richens, J C Rickett, S M Rissbrook, P G Rivett, T M Robb, G E Roberts, G T Robinson, M W Robinson, R M Rollinshaw, C D Romans, D A Roper, A J B Rose, R Rowe, S Rowe, C C Rowland, D A Russell, S J Russell, G A Rutter, M A Ryan, P S Samaratunga, G A Sanderson, J A Sansum, J S Sarai, M A Saunders, I Schneider, J M D Schofield, D Y Schwarzmann, J L Scott, I M Selfridge, R V Y Setchim, R G Sexton, S R Shah, R J Shapland, J R Sheer, P A Shepherd, P Sheward, N J E Shield, G S L Shiels, E M Shires, C J F Silcock, A E Simpson, G M Singer, J Singh, D J A Skailes, A S M Skrzypecki, P Slater, A N Smith, B K Smith, C D Smith, H K Smith, I R Smith, J L Smith, M L Smith, N A Smith, P B Smith, R A C Smith, S A Smith, J M Smithies, D A Snell, S R Snook, J S Southgate, R J Spilsbury, P N Spratt, R Sriskandan, L E Stapleton, T M Stephen, A M Stephenson, J K Steveni, R D Stevens, N P Stevenson, P J A Stokes, G R Stoner, G E Stylianides, W N Sutton, H Swanston, R J Sykes, D I Tapnack, P Taurae, C H Taylor, D J Taylor, D Tecwyn, G A Telford, C J Temple, J P Terry, N J D Terry, P G Tew, H Thomas, M C M Thomas, R Thomas, C E Thompson, R C W Thompson, S J Thompson, K Tilson, C P Tompsett, T R Troubridge, G L Tucker, K L Turner, S P Udall, C E F van den Arend, R J Veysey, N J Vooght, J C Wakelam, P Wallace, K N Walsh, D R W Walters, S M Walton, N M Ward, G L Ward-Thompson, S N Warriner, J M Waters, L J Watts, J T Wayman, R C G Weaver, N M Webster, J D Whitfield, A Wiggins, L Wilkinson, N A Wilks, C J Williams, C M K Williams, G T Williams, J G Williams, S Williams, R T G Winter, I M Wishart, K A Wolstenholme, N A Woodford, J J T Woodhouse, C J Woolcott, S J Wooldridge, S L Woolfson, S R Wootten, R P Worrall, P D Wright, G R Yeandle, A T Yeeles)* 1 Embankment Place, LONDON, WC2N 6RH. and at ABERDEEN, BELFAST, BIRMINGHAM, BOURNEMOUTH, BRISTOL, CAMBRIDGE, CARDIFF, CHESHAM, DERBY, DUNGANNON, EDINBURGH, GATWICK, GLASGOW, GLOUCESTER, HULL, LEEDS, LIVERPOOL, MANCHESTER, MILTON KEYNES, MUSCAT, NEWCASTLE UPON TYNE, NORWICH, OMAGH, PLYMOUTH, READING, SHEFFIELD, SOUTHAMPTON, ST. ALBANS, SWANSEA, UXBRIDGE

Diana Dove *(D M Dove)* 115 High Street, Prestwood, GREAT MISSENDEN, HP16 9EU.

Ⓐ**Diana Duggan & Co** *(D M Duggan)* 27 East Street, HEREFORD, HR1 2LU.

Diana Godden *(D M Godden)* 65 Alzey Gardens, HARPENDEN, AL5 5SY.

Diana L Ma & Co *(L D Ma)* Room 1708 17/F Hart Avenue Plaza, 5-9 Hart Avenue, TSIM SHA TSUI, KOWLOON, HONG KONG SAR.

Diane J Nichols BSc FCA *(D J Nichols)* Little Moss Farm, Red Cat Lane, Crank, ST. HELENS, MERSEYSIDE, WA11 8QZ.

Diane J. Bryant *(D J Bryant)* Eversley, Gorse Way, Hartley, LONGFIELD, DA3 8AF.

Ⓟ**Diane Wilding & Associates Ltd** *(D J Wilding)* 64 Harrow Lane, MAIDENHEAD, BERKSHIRE, SL6 7PA.

Dianne Walker & Co *(D G D Walker)* The White House, Alvanley Road, Helsby, FRODSHAM, WA6 9PS.

Dick Germain *(R M C Germain)* 37 Springfield Close, ANDOVER, HAMPSHIRE, SP10 2QR.

Ⓐ**Dick Maule** *(R J R Maule)* Little Bosullow Cottage, Little Bosullow, PENZANCE, CORNWALL, TR20 8NS.

ⓉⒻⒶ**Dickinsons** *(P G Abbott, J Birch, N S Spalton, P D Tucker, P F Wagstaff)* Enterprise House, Beesons Yard, Bury Lane, RICKMANSWORTH, WD3 1DS. and at BRACKNELL

Ⓟ**Dickson Wong CPA Co Ltd** *(K Wong)* Room 302, 3/F, The Chinese General Chamber of Commerce Building, 24-25 Connaught Road, CENTRAL, HONG KONG SAR.

ⓅⒶ**Dilena Limited** *(S Dilena)* Nicholson House, 41 Thames Street, WEYBRIDGE, SURREY, KT13 8JG.

Ⓐ**Dillamore & Co** *(R M Dillamore)* The Stables Offices, Stansty Park, Summerhill Road, WREXHAM, LL11 4YW.

ⓉⓅ**Dillamore & Co Limited** *(R M Dillamore)* The Stables Offices, Stansty Park, Summerhill Road, WREXHAM, LL11 4YW.

Ⓟ**Dilloways Ltd** *(L D Dilloway)* Weavers, 6 Hamlet Road, HAVERHILL, SUFFOLK, CB9 8EE.

★**Dimbleby & Dale** *(L J Morley)* Junction House, 58 High Street, Beighton, SHEFFIELD, S20 1ED.

Dinesh Desai *(D K Desai)* 31 Ennerdale Avenue, STANMORE, MIDDLESEX, HA7 2LB.

Dion Mailich & Co *(D P Mailich)* 2 Tynedale, London Colney, ST. ALBANS, HERTFORDSHIRE, AL2 1TF.
Direct Payroll *(P S Wragg)* Unit 9, Basepoint Waterdrive, Waterbury Drive, WATERLOOVILLE, HAMPSHIRE, PO7 7TH.
Ⓟ**Disclosure Solutions Ltd** *(S G Hastie)* The Old Smithy, Radwinter Road, Ashdon, SAFFRON WALDEN, ESSEX, CB10 2ET.
Ⓟ**Distinctive Accountancy Limited** *(S R Voralia)* First Floor, Allied Sainif House, 412 Greenford Road, GREENFORD, UB6 9AH.
ⓅⒶ**Diverset, trading name of Diverset Ltd** *(H M H Britter, M C H Britter)* Canada House, 272 Field End Road, RUISLIP, MIDDLESEX, HA4 9NA.
ⓅⒶ**Dix Vogan Limited** *(C W Dix, I Vogan)* 2 Chancery Lane, WAKEFIELD, WEST YORKSHIRE, WF1 2SS.
Ⓟ**Dixcart, trading name of Dixcart International Limited** *(L Binge, J C Dunne, J M F Wigram, P Wilman)* Hillbrow House, Hillbrow Road, ESHER, SURREY, KT10 9NW.
Ⓟ**Dixie Associates Ltd** *(D R Dixie)* AIMS Accountants for Business, 34 Swarthmore Road, Selly Oak, BIRMINGHAM, B29 4JS.
Dixon & Company, trading name of Dixon & Co *(R Dixon)* Bird in Eye Farm, Bird in Eye Hill, Framfield, UCKFIELD, EAST SUSSEX, TN22 5HA.
Ⓟ**Dixon & Stone, trading name of Dixon & Stone Limited** *(A Dixon)* Fielding House, 43 Thornbury Close, Rhiwbina, CARDIFF, CF14 1UT.
ⒾⒻⒶ**Dixon Wilson** *(J R Benford, J L Boatfield, G L Chambers, H Clark, B C Grist, J K Kidgell, D C Mellor, D H Nelson, S F Rees, S M Rose, G Spinks, J L Sutton, S J Wakefield, M V Waterman)* 22 Chancery Lane, LONDON, WC2A 1LS. and at PARIS
Ⓟ**DJ Colom & Co, trading name of DJ Colom & Co Ltd** *(D J Colom)* Hillside House, 2-6 Friern Park, North Finchley, LONDON, N12 9BT.
ⒻⓅ**DJB Accontancy Limited** *(D J Brown)* Sandy Farm Business Centre, The Sands, FARNHAM, SURREY, GU10 1PX.
Ⓟ**DJB Tax Ltd** *(D J Brown)* Gravel Hill, Chalfont St. Peter, GERRARDS CROSS, BUCKINGHAMSHIRE, SL9 9QP.
Ⓟ**DJH Accountants Ltd** *(F E Green)* Porthill Lodge, High Street, Wolstanton, NEWCASTLE, STAFFORDSHIRE, ST5 0EZ.
Ⓐ**DJM Accountants LLP** *(D Jacobs, J H Mendlesohn)* Fourth Floor, Brook Point, 1412 High Road, LONDON, N20 9BH.
Ⓟ**DKF Accountants Ltd** *(D L Kershen-Fisher)* Kingsgate House, 12-50 Kingsgate Road, KINGSTON UPON THAMES, SURREY, KT2 5AA.
Ⓟ**DKP Consultants Limited** *(D Papachristodoulou)* PO Box 24856, 1304 NICOSIA, CYPRUS.
DKS *(D K Sandground)* 30a Station Road, Cuffley, POTTERS BAR, HERTFORDSHIRE, EN6 4HE.
Ⓟ**DL Accountancy, trading name of DL Accountancy Limited** *(D M Leonard)* 2 Brunel Way, Church Gresley, SWADLINCOTE, DERBYSHIRE, DE11 9LE.
DLM Accountancy Services *(D L Meneses)* 19 Warren Road, BANSTEAD, SURREY, SM7 1LG.
DLP, trading name of DL Partnership LLP *(A Denham)* Suite 5, 90 New North Road, HUDDERSFIELD, HD1 5NE.
Ⓟ**DLS Accounting Services Ltd** *(P Clay, J S Dawkins, A J Sawdon)* 4 Cowdown Business Park, Micheldever, WINCHESTER, HAMPSHIRE, SO21 3DN.
ⒾⓅ**DM Globus Audit Services Ltd** *(M Papademetris)* Afentrikas 3, PC 6018 LARNACA, CYPRUS.
Ⓟ**DM, trading name of Dexter Matthews Ltd** *(M J Matthews, E W Pulman)* 99 Walter Road, SWANSEA, SA1 5QE.
DMA Business Improvement Services *(A D Thakrar)* Business Box, Oswin Road, LEICESTER, LE3 1HR.
Ⓟ**DMB Davies Ltd** *(D M B Davies)* Broyan House, Priory Street, CARDIGAN, DYFED, SA43 1BU.
Ⓐ**DMC Accounting** *(D S Roberts)* Olympic House, 63 Wallingford Road, UXBRIDGE, UB8 2RW.
Ⓟ**DMC Corporate Services, trading name of DMC Recovery Ltd** *(A M Bland)* 41 Greek Street, STOCKPORT, CHESHIRE, SK3 8AX.
★ⒻⒶ**DMC Partnership** *(P N B Cunningham, E G Sherlock)* Yew Tree House, Lewes Road, FOREST ROW, RH18 5AA.
DMP Accounting *(D M Potts)* 5a Parkway, Porters Wood, ST. ALBANS, HERTFORDSHIRE, AL3 6PA.
DMS Partners *(A E Morrison)* 31 Rutland Square, EDINBURGH, EH1 2BW.
Ⓟ**DMS, trading name of Darwen Management Services Ltd** *(G T Melia)* 27 Bolton Road, DARWEN, LANCASHIRE, BB3 1DF.
Ⓟ**DN Consultancy Limited** *(D M Patel)* Nakatcha, Over Wallop, STOCKBRIDGE, HAMPSHIRE, SO20 8HN.
Ⓟ**DNA Accountants, trading name of DNA Accountants Limited** *(G E A French, I French)* Regency House, 61a Walton Street, Walton on the Hill, TADWORTH, SURREY, KT20 7RZ.
Ⓟ**DNA Accountants, trading name of DNA Logistics Limited** *(A L Fitch)* 2 Toft Villas, Kites Hardwick, RUGBY, WARWICKSHIRE, CV23 8AD.
Ⓟ**DNB, DNB Accounting, trading names of DNB Accounting Limited** *(E C Currie)* 33 Luccombe Road, SOUTHAMPTON, SO15 7RJ.
★ⒾⒻⒶ**DNG Dove Naish** *(V W Griffiths, J R Henderson, A M McGregor, I C Robson, P J Smith)* Eagle House, 28 Billing Road, NORTHAMPTON, NN1 5AJ. and at DAVENTRY
ⒾⓅⒶ**Dodd & Co.** *(F Armstrong, I W Brown, J Brown, A M Johnston, D Johnston, A McViety, M S Ward, R M Wharton)* Fifteen Rosehill, Montgomery Way, Rosehill Estate, CARLISLE, CA1 2RW. and at PENRITH
ⒻⒶ**Dodd Harris** *(J D Epstein, D A Jaye)* 35/37 Brent Street, Hendon, LONDON, NW4 2EF.
Ⓟ**Dodgson & Co, trading name of Dodgson & Co Limited** *(D H Dodgson)* The Meredith Building, 23-33 Reform Street, HULL, HU2 8EF.
Dodhia & Co *(J V Dodhia)* 3 Tewkesbury Terrace, LONDON, N11 2LT.
Doggett & Co *(R J Doggett)* 26 Laurence Street, DROGHEDA, COUNTY LOUTH, IRELAND.
Doherty & Co *(J S Doherty)* Riddingdyke, Cummertrees, ANNAN, DUMFRIESSHIRE, DG12 5PU.
Ⓟ**Dolfinblue Business Advisory Services Limited** *(A S Coulson)* 6 Marlborough Place, LUTTERWORTH, LEICESTERSHIRE, LE17 4DE.
Dolman Accountancy Services *(P Dolman)* Ashleaze, Sodbury Road, Horton, BRISTOL, BS37 6PN.
Ⓟ**Dolphin Business Strategies Ltd** *(J Stevens)* Unit 1a, Little Braxted Hall, Little Braxted, ESSEX, CM8 3EU.
Ⓟ**Dolphin Business Strategies, trading name of DB Strategies LLP** *(J Stevens)* Unit 1a, Little Braxted Hall, Little Braxted, ESSEX, CM8 3EU.
Dolphin Tax LLP *(R A Adams, J H Boyd)* 195 Loughborough Road, LEICESTER, LE4 5PL.
Dominic Cheung and Company *(W D Cheung)* Room 1502, 15/F, Harcourt House, No.39, Gloucester Road, WAN CHAI HONG KONG SAR.
ⒻⓅⒶ**Dominic Hill, trading name of Dominic Hill Associates Ltd** *(P D Hill)* Archer House, Britland Estate, Northbourne Road, EASTBOURNE, BN22 8PW.
Dominic K. N. Tai & Company *(D K N Tai)* 16E Neich Tower, 128 Gloucester Road, WAN CHAI, HONG KONG ISLAND, HONG KONG SAR.
Dominic K.F. Li & Co *(D K F Li)* Room 2107-8 21/F, Kai Tak Commercial Building, 317-319 Des Voeux Road, CENTRAL, HONG KONG ISLAND, HONG KONG SAR.
Dominic Mills *(D Mills)* 66b High Street, Black Swan Yard, ANDOVER, SP10 1NG.
ⒻⒶ**Don Fisher & Co** *(D Fisher)* 309 Winston House, 2 Dollis Park, Finchley, LONDON, N3 1HF.
Donal Lucey Lawlor *(P J Lawlor)* 43 Highfield Road, DARTFORD, DA1 2JS.
ⒻⒶ**Donald Jacobs & Partners** *(A Cohen, C J Taylor)* Suite 2 1st Floor, Fountain House, 1a Elm Park, STANMORE, HA7 4AU.
Donald M. Smith *(D M Smith)* Hadleigh House, 5 Rivercourt Road, LONDON, W6 9LD.
ⓅⒶ**Donald Owen & Co, trading name of Donald Owen Ltd** *(G P G Jones)* 34 Quay Street, CARMARTHEN, CARMARTHENSHIRE, SA31 3JT.
ⒾⒻⓅⒶ**Donald Reid & Co, trading name of Donald Reid Limited** *(D R Gordon-Smith, D C W Reid)* Prince Albert House, 20 King Street, MAIDENHEAD, BERKSHIRE, SL6 1DT.
Donald Stokes *(D C Stokes)* 33 Mossy Bank Close, Queensbury, BRADFORD, BD13 1PX.
Ⓟ**Dongworth Limited** *(F P Dongworth)* First Floor, 30 London Road, SAWBRIDGEWORTH, HERTFORDSHIRE, CM21 9JS.
Ⓟ**Donnan Calderbank (Warrington) Ltd** *(A M Calderbank)* 25 Sandmoor Place, LYMM, CHESHIRE, WA13 0LQ.
ⒻⓅⒶ**Donnellys, trading name of Donnellys C.A. Limited** *(N L Baxendale, A J Donohoe)* Peel House, 2 Chorley Old Road, BOLTON, BL1 3AA.
Doreen Noble *(D Noble)* 81 Woodcot Avenue, Baildon, SHIPLEY, BD17 6QR.
ⒻⓅⒶ**Dorrell Oliver Ltd** *(P E Lea, E A Moore)* 26 Monk Street, ABERGAVENNY, GWENT, NP7 5NF.
Ⓟ**Dorset Business Services Ltd** *(N G Depper, M R G Magrath)* Unit 4 Brackley Close, South East Sector, Bournemouth International Airport, Hurn, CHRISTCHURCH, DORSET BH23 6SE.
Ⓟ**Dorset FD Limited** *(B T Hooley)* 25 Olga Road, DORCHESTER, DORSET, DT1 2LY.
Ⓟ**Double Espresso & Friends Ltd** *(D C Fletcher)* 3 The Paddock, Timperley, ALTRINCHAM, CHESHIRE, WA15 7NR.
Ⓟ**Doubleday & Co** *(T J Doubleday)* The Swallows, Marsh Green Farm, Vicarage Lane Elworth, SANDBACH, CW11 3BU.
Ⓟ**Douglas & Co Limited** *(F D Newton)* Broadway House, 8-10 Broadway, Douglas, ISLE OF MAN, IM2 4EL.
Ⓟ**Douglas & Co, trading name of James Douglas Accounting Limited** *(J A Douglas)* 21 Trent View Gardens, Radcliffe-on-Trent, NOTTINGHAM, NG12 1AY.
★**Douglas & Reaves** *(K D Reaves)* Dundock, 15 Ancrum Bank, Eskbank, DALKEITH, MIDLOTHIAN, EH22 3AY.
Douglas Colmer & Co *(D J Colmer)* Orwell Lodge, 13 Lesney Park Road, ERITH, DA8 3DQ.
Douglas Forsyth *(D C S Forsyth)* Roydon Cottage, Sandy Down, Boldre, LYMINGTON, HAMPSHIRE, SO41 8PL.
ⓅⒶ**Douglas Home & Co, trading name of Douglas Home & Co Limited** *(L C Mark)* 47-49 The Square, KELSO, ROXBURGHSHIRE, TD5 7HW. and at HAWICK
ⓅⒶ**Douglas Shaw, trading name of Douglas Shaw Limited** *(G T Douglas)* 7 Brenkley Way, Blezard Business Park, Seaton Burn, NEWCASTLE UPON TYNE, NE13 6DS.
Ⓟ**Douglas Wadkin, trading name of Douglas Wadkin Limited** *(D J Wadkin)* 11 Amwell Street, LONDON, EC1R 1UL.
ⒾⒻⒶ**Douglass Grange** *(A J Grange, G F Whiteside)* Stanley House, Phoenix Park, Blakewater Road, BLACKBURN, BB1 5RW.
Ⓟ**Dover Accountancy Ltd** *(T W Pascoe)* 4 River Meadow, River, DOVER, KENT, CT17 0XA.
ⒾⓅ**Dow Schofield Watts Corporate Finance Limited** *(A G Dodd, J A T Dow, P C Price, C S Richardson, J H Schofield, M S Watts)* 7700 Daresbury Park, Daresbury, WARRINGTON, CHESHIRE, WA4 5BS. and at PRESTON
Dow Schofield Watts Transaction Services LLP *(E J Brentnall, C M Lang, C S Richardson, C Williams)* 7700 Daresbury Park, Daresbury, WARRINGTON, WA4 4BS.
Ⓟ**Downer & Co Associates Limited** *(M J Downer)* 125 Broadclyst Gardens, Thorpe Bay, SOUTHEND-ON-SEA, ESSEX, SS1 3QY.
ⒾⒻⓅⒶ**Downham Mayer Clarke & Co, trading name of Downham Mayer Clarke Limited** *(A M Bland, A Clarke, I C Clarke)* 41 Greek Street, STOCKPORT, CHESHIRE, SK3 8AX.
Ⓟ**Downspark Consulting Limited** *(M W Griffiths)* 8 Norland Road, Clifton, BRISTOL, BS8 3LP.
Ⓟ**Dowsett & Moore, trading name of Dowsett & Moore Ltd** *(A J Dowsett, B A Moore)* 24A Coton Road, NUNEATON, CV11 5TW.
Dowsett Moore *(A J Dowsett, B A Moore)* 17 Station Road, HINCKLEY, LE10 1AW.
Dowsons *(P Goswell)* 195 Main Road, HARWICH, CO12 3PH.
Doyle & Co *(P J Doyle)* 7 The Courtyard, Gaulby Lane, Stoughton, LEICESTER, LE2 2FL.
★ⒾⒻⓅⒶ**DPC, trading name of DPC Accountants Limited** *(D Griffiths, C Kane, M M Reynolds, S J Webster, V A Wood)* Vernon Road, STOKE-ON-TRENT, ST4 2QY.
Ⓟ**DPM Accounting Services Ltd** *(D P Marriott)* Suite 2B Ribble Court, 1 Mead Way, Padiham, BURNLEY, LANCASHIRE, BB12 7NG.
ⒻⓅ**DPMC Business Advisory Ltd** *(N M Hamilton)* Flat Third Floor North, 6 Raymond Buildings, Gray's Inn, LONDON, WC1R 5BN.
Ⓟ**DPN Consulting Services Ltd** *(D P Nichol)* 5 Gravel Hill, UXBRIDGE, UB8 1PB.
Ⓟ**DPS, trading name of DP Solutionz Limited** *(D Price)* 1 The Old Drive, WELWYN GARDEN CITY, HERTFORDSHIRE, AL8 6TB.
Dr P A Vickers *(P A Vickers)* Loydons, 17 Hitchin Road, LETCHWORTH GARDEN CITY, HERTFORDSHIRE, SG6 3LX.
Dr R K Ashton *(R K Ashton)* Upton Cottage, Nairdwood Lane, Prestwood, GREAT MISSENDEN, BUCKINGHAMSHIRE, HP16 0QH.
Ⓐ**Drabble & Co** *(P Drabble)* 1 Wellington Road, Bollington, MACCLESFIELD, SK10 5JR.
Drage & Co. *(C J F Drage)* 62 The Rise, SEVENOAKS, TN13 1RN.
ⒻⒶ**Drake & Co** *(R J Drake)* Drake House, 80 Guildford Street, CHERTSEY, KT16 9AD.
Drake Fletcher & Co *(K R Drake)* Sheaf House, 1-3 Sheaf Street, DAVENTRY, NN11 4AA.
ⒻⓅ**Drake.Com Limited** *(R J Drake)* Drake House, 80 Guildford Street, CHERTSEY, SURREY, KT16 9AD.
ⒻⒶ**Draycott & Kirk** *(R M Draycott, R D Kirk)* Cleveland House, 92 Westgate, GUISBOROUGH, CLEVELAND, TS14 6AP.
Ⓟ**DRC Accountancy, trading name of DRC Accountancy Services Ltd** *(D R Chew)* Hafotty Bach, Cyffylliog, RUTHIN, CLWYD, LL15 2DY.
Ⓟ**DRC Forensics Limited** *(D R Cook, C J Gahagan)* Kestrel Court, Harbour Road, PORTISHEAD, BS20 7AN.
★ⒾⒻ**DRE & Co** *(L M Fitton, C H Hall, M R Kent, A J Matthews)* 7 Lower Brook Street, OSWESTRY, SY11 2HG. and at LUDLOW, NEWTOWN, SHREWSBURY
★Ⓟ**DRE & Co, trading name of DRE & Co Limited** *(L M Fitton, C H Hall, M R Kent, A J Matthews)* Number 5, The Business Quarter, Eco Park Road, LUDLOW, SHROPSHIRE, SY8 1FD. and at NEWTOWN
Ⓐ**Drennan & Co** *(R G Drennan)* 64 Belsize Park, LONDON, NW3 4EH.
Ⓟ**Drennan Management Services Limited** *(R G Drennan)* 64 Belsize Park, LONDON, NW3 4EH.
Driffield & Co *(A E Driffield)* 11 Grenfell Close, Parkgate, NESTON, CH64 6TU.
ⒾⒶ**Driver Jonas Deloitte, trading name of Deloitte LLP** *(A H Abhyankar, J A Adam, M J D Adams, M K Adams, S M P Adcock, S Almond, D S Anthony, J L Antoniazzi, T W Archer, A J Arterton, C A Atha, G P Atkins, S G Austin, T M Awan, J W F Baird, E L S Bairstow, M R Barber, D J Barnes, I J Barnes, S W Barnett, S J Barratt, J A Bates, M N Batham, D C Beanland, A W Beardsworth, S J Beech, C R Bell, M R Bell, J C Bentley, D S Bettesworth, P Biddle, P M Birch, J W Bird, J E Birkett, R J Blackwell, J A Boardman, S Z H Bokhari, A J Bond, A L Bond, D N Boocock, P L Booth, M J Boyle, R A Bradbury, N S Bramwell, G J Branch, C L Britton, C W Brough, D E Brown, I Brown, S Brown, C A Buck, R A Buck, G J Bullock, G Bunting, S D Burnhope, D F Butters, A R Butterworth, H A Bygrave, C D Cahill, N D Carrington, J Casson, R B Cattell, M S Chahal, J W Charlton, A Chaudhuri, R K Chopra, J G Clacy, A P Clark, I E Clark, M J Clatworthy, D N Claxton, J Clennett, S L Cleveland, D F Cobb, J P Colborne-Baber, N O Coles, R P Collins, D S Cook, S J Cottee, M J Cowlishaw, E J Cox, J F Cox, W R T Crane, D J O Cruickshank, N S Cruickshanks, S D Cuerden, J P Cullinane, G Culshaw, H D Da Silva, H J Davies, J Davies, R S Davis, T R Davis, W K Dawson, H E Athey, W J I Dodwell, J M Dodworth, M F Doleman, M E Donaldson, G P Dootson, A J Downes, T G M Downing, M J Drysdale, M R H Duckworth, E J Dungworth, T Edge, N G Edwards, R W H Esler, D J Evans, M Ewing, A J Farnworth, C Faulkner, P E Feechan, A D Fendall, J R Ferguson, K Folwell-Davies, P Franek, S J Fraser, P C Gallimore, R A Garrard, K J Garrison, E J Gill, M Goodey, A P Goulden, D E Graham, P W R Gratton, M Gregory, B M Griffin, D Griffiths, G J Griffiths, S Griggs, A J Grimstone, D Grosvenor, O W Grundy, S E Gutteridge, A G Gwyther, K A Hackshall, T M Haden, K A Hale, D Hall, D E M Halstead, A M Hamilton, J R Hammond, E J Hanson, S C Hardy, D Haria, A S Harris, N R Harris, W H Harvey, R M Hawes, D Heaton, D Hedditch, S J B Henderson, M P Hill, C W Hindle, J W Hinton, J A Holden, O P Holder, G T Hollis, S E Holmes, I M Hook, K J Houldsworth, R I Howard, M J Howell, C G Hudson, N A Hudson, C D Hughes, D S Hughes, M W Hughes, D J Hume, C J Hyams, F L Ilett, W R H Inglis, D R James, N J Jeal, M A Jenkins, D M Johnson, N R Johnson, D Johnston, A P M Jones, C P Jones, D C R Jones, M E Jones, M W Jones, N G Jones, N B Kahn, P K Kakoullis, P R Kaye, D K Keeble, A J Kelly, N J Kerr, S H Kerton-Johnson, D J King, R J Knight, S R Knight, R C Knights, Y Konii, I S Krieger, J I Leake, M R Lee-Amies, J A Leigh, S D Letts, T O Lewthwaite, S G Ley, M J Lloyd, R A Lloyd-Owen, A Lloyd-Taylor, P M Lobb, G C Loftus, P J Loftus, D S Longley, N Lovejoy, S A Lucas, P N C Lupton, T J Macdonald, C D Mackinnon, I A Macmillan, T M Mahapatra, P F Maher, P J Maher, L A Manning, S P Manning, M Y Manuel, A L Marks, N H A Marsden, D J Marsh, A M Martin, R A Matthews, J F Maxey, N R McCrea, K I McFarlane, M McIlquham, D K McNeil, K McNicholls, M P McQueen, N J Mercer, P D Mills, K J Mitchell, N M Mitchell, P K Moller, J D Moore, A D Morris, A J Morris, B Moseley, P R Muir, M*

Driver Jonas Deloitte - Eddison & Co Ltd   Members in Practice and Firms - Alphabetical

A M Mullins, J G Murphy, R R J Muschamp, F Nagari, V Naidoo, K L Newman, A J Newsome, J V Niblett, H M H Nicholson, P G Nicklin, D A Noon, D C Norton, S J Nuttall, P S J O'Donoghue, D O'Leary, C G Oswald, N R Owen, A G Paisley, Z Patel, D J Paterson, V A Pereira, M D Perkins, C C H Phillips, P N Pickard, G C Pickett, A J Pollock, V Poole, C D Powell, N J Prior, R K Punt, D Quantrill, P B Quigley, D J Quinlin, W A Ramsay, M Rana, C C Rawlings, M R Rea, J C Reid, M M Reilly, M G Rhys, J D Richards, P D E Richards, G O Richardson, G A Robb, C D Robertson, A P Rothery, S M Routledge, D J Rush, L G Russell, M P Rust, I F Sadler, J S Sahota, M A Saluveer, N J Sandall, D R Sanders, S Sanders, I G Sargeant, M F K Saunders, P J A Saunders, P J Schofield, D D Scott, R D Seldon, A Shah, M R Shah, H J Shekle, S L Shillingford, A K J Simmonds, N Slater, J P Small, A Smith, I J Smith, I S Smith, M D Smith, M J Smith, W R Smith, I R Sparshott, A J Spooner, D Sproul, T D Steel, S J Stephens, M Stephenson, P R Stephenson, I M Stone, L J Stott, S L Sturt, M D Sullivan, A T Swarbrick, R W Syratt, V C Thakrar, C T Thomas, G M Thomas, J S Thomas, N J Thomas, P M Thompson, C M Thomson, P J Thomson, M Thorne, A G Todd, R J Topley, W G Touche, N F Tratalos, P R Trickett, V Vedi, H Vega-Lozano, P Waldron, F J Walker, I P Waller, M D Ward, S A Ward, N G Warner, C N Warren, D B Watkinson, W G Weaver, R H Webber, A J Westbrook, S G Weston, B H White, B J White, B Whitehead, J G Whitehead, J Whitlock, A J Whitton, R L Widdas, A P Wilde, D P Wilkinson, M H Wilkinson, I D Williams, J A P Williams, M W Williams, R J Williams, S C Williams, P T Williamson, N J Willis, D L Z Wong, N T Wood, S N Woodward, J N Wright, T C F Wright, N Yeomans, J C S Young, P E Zimmerman) 2 New Street Square, LONDON, EC4A 3BZ. and at ABERDEEN, BASEL, BATH, BELFAST, BIRMINGHAM, BRISTOL, CAMBRIDGE, CARDIFF, CRAWLEY, EDINBURGH, EPSOM, GENEVA, GLASGOW, GUERNSEY, ISLE OF MAN, JERSEY, LAUSANNE, LEEDS, LIVERPOOL, MANCHESTER, MILTON KEYNES, NEWCASTLE UPON TYNE, NOTTINGHAM, READING, SLOUGH, SOUTHAMPTON, ST. ALBANS, ZURICH

ⒻⒶ**DRP & Co** *(E Davies, N W Price)* 6 St. Johns Court, Upper forest Way, SWANSEA, SA6 8QQ.

★**DRT Denet** *(S Sevket)* Buyukdere Cad.121 Ercan Han, Kat 4-6 Gayrettepe ISTANBUL, 80300, TURKEY. and at ANKARA

Ⓐ**Drummonds** *(H R Drummond)* Heritage House, 235 Main Street, GIBRALTAR, GIBRALTAR.

Ⓕ**DS Management Consultants, trading name of D.N.W. Shores** *(D N W Shores)* Hillrise, Hare Lane, Hordle, LYMINGTON, SO41 0GE.

Ⓟ**DSA Taxation, trading name of Donald Scott Associates Limited** *(N D Byfield, D S Macleod)* PO Box 7785, HUNGERFORD, RG17 1DB.

DSC Wealth Management LLP *(J O Campbell)* Tattersall House, East Parade, HARROGATE, NORTH YORKSHIRE, HG1 5LT.

ⓅⒶ**DSC, trading name of DSC Accountants Limited** *(J O Campbell, G S French, J P Garbutt)* Tattersall House, East Parade, HARROGATE, NORTH YORKSHIRE, HG1 5LT.

Ⓟ**DSCO Limited** *(David Suckling)* The Old Boardroom, Collett Road, WARE, HERTFORDSHIRE, SG12 7LR.

Ⓟ**DSG Accountancy and Taxation Services Limited** *(I Douglas, J M Ellis, P Hyland, A D Moss, L Staniforth, C Wheatley)* Stratford House, 149 Stanley Road, BOOTLE, MERSEYSIDE, L20 3DL.

Ⓐ**DSJ Partners LLP** *(B P Dhanani, V M Jamal, R L Shah)* 2nd Floor, 1 Bell Street, LONDON, NW1 5BY.

Ⓟ**DSL Accountancy, trading name of DSL Accountancy Ltd** *(D S M Lonnen)* 3 Ridgeview, Long Ashton, BRISTOL, BS41 9EQ.

Ⓟ**DTA Services Ltd** *(H L Engelsman)* The Estate House, 201 High Road, CHIGWELL, ESSEX, IG7 5BJ.

ⒻⒶ**DTB Associates LLP** *(D T Brown)* Imperial House, 4th Floor, 15 Kingsway, LONDON, WC2B 6UN.

ⓉⒻⓅⒶ**DTE, trading name of DTE Business Advisory Services Limited** *(N J Fail, S Rosen, R I Taylor)* DTE House, Hollins Mount, Hollins Lane, BURY, BL9 8AT. and at LONDON, MANCHESTER

Ⓟ**Du Gua, trading name of Du Gua Limited** *(L E Alexander)* 36 Ferrymans Quay, William Morris Way, LONDON, SW6 2UT.

ⒻⓅⒶ**Dua & Co, trading name of Dua & Co Limited** *(R K Dua, B A Gordon)* 3 Century Court, Tolpits Lane, WATFORD, WD18 9PU.

Dua LLP *(R K Dua, B A Gordon)* 3 Century Court, Tolpits Lane, WATFORD, WD18 9RS.

★**Dub & Co** *(J A Thakrar)* 7 Torriano Mews, LONDON, NW5 2RZ.

Dubell & Co *(M Dubell)* 16 Hartfield Avenue, Elstree, BOREHAMWOOD, WD6 3JE.

Duboff & Co *(P E Duboff)* Trafalgar House, Grenville Place, LONDON, NW7 3SA.

Ⓟ**Dudhia Lewin Myers Associates Limited** *(Z Dudhia)* 98 Chingford Mount Road, South Chingford, LONDON, E4 9AA.

★Ⓕ**Dudley & Co.** *(J C Thompson)* 33 New Street, CARNFORTH, LA5 9BX.

ⒻⓅⒶ**Dufton Kellner, trading name of Dufton Kellner Limited** *(A J Biddle, S D Kellner)* Barnston House, Beacon Lane, Heswall, WIRRAL, CH60 0EE.

▽**Duggan Wood, trading name of M W Medical** *(M P Caulfield, M J Wood)* 2 Westbury Mews, Westbury Hill, Westbury on Trym, BRISTOL, BS9 3QA.

ⓅⒶ**Dunbar & Co (Corporate Services) Limited** *(R E Long)* 70 South Lambeth Road, LONDON, SW8 1RL.

★ⓉⒻⒶ**Duncan & Toplis** *(J S Alexander, J D Andrew, M J Argyle, D A Brain, J B Chappelle, M H Chatterton, M H Cope, N P Cudmore, T G Godson, D A J Gratton, J E Green, R J Hardy, M T Hindmarch, J R Hodson, I Phillips, K Phillips, A N Reynolds, S N Syddall, P S Townsend)* Duncan & Toplis, 3 Castlegate, GRANTHAM, LINCOLNSHIRE, NG31 6SF. and at BOSTON, LINCOLN, LOUTH, MELTON MOWBRAY, NEWARK, OAKHAM, SKEGNESS, SLEAFORD, SPALDING, STAMFORD

ⒻⒶ**Duncan Anderson & Company** *(D R Anderson)* Temple Chambers, 4 Abbey Road, GRIMSBY, DN32 0HF.

Duncan Gaskell *(D W Gaskell)* Pace Sports Management, 6 The Causeway, TEDDINGTON, MIDDLESEX, TW11 0HE.

Duncan Godden ACA *(D J Godden)* 38 Sandringham Close, Haxby, YORK, YO32 3GL.

Ⓐ**Duncan Joyce & Associates** *(D N Joyce)* 36-38 Cross Hayes, MALMESBURY, WILTSHIRE, SN16 9BG.

Ⓐ**Duncan King** *(D King)* 2 Macneice Drive, Barton Park, MARLBOROUGH, SN8 1TR.

Ⓟ**Duncan Noice, trading name of Duncan Noice Limited** *(B S Duncan, K E Noice)* 5 Cherrytree, Union Road, Nether Edge, SHEFFIELD, S11 9EF.

ⓉⒻⒶ**Duncan Sheard Glass** *(I Douglas, J M Ellis, P Hyland, A D Moss, L Staniforth, C Wheatley)* Castle Chambers, 43 Castle St, LIVERPOOL, L2 9TL. and at DEESIDE, SOUTHPORT

Duncombe & Co *(J R Duncombe)* Beech Hill, Glassenbury Road, CRANBROOK, TN17 2QJ.

Dunelm *(C E Sprague)* The Chase, Flempton Road, Risby, BURY ST. EDMUNDS, SUFFOLK, IP28 6QJ.

ⓉⒻⓅⒶ**Dunkley & Co, Dunkleys, Matrix Accounting and Taxation Solutions, trading names of Dunkley & Co Limited** *(M R P Dunkley)* Woodlands Grange, Woodlands Lane, Bradley Stoke, BRISTOL, BS32 4JY.

ⓉⒻⒶ**Dunn & Ellis** *(C T Brown, P Roberts, I L Williams)* St Davids Building, Lombard Street, PORTHMADOG, GWYNEDD, LL49 9AP.

Durrant & Company *(R N Durrant)* Tankard Hall, Morton, OSWESTRY, SHROPSHIRE, SY10 8BQ.

Ⓐ**Durrants** *(A K Batra, I V Bessant)* 24 Wellington Business Park, Dukes Ride, CROWTHORNE, RG45 6LS.

ⓉⒶ**Dutchmans** *(M A Poile)* 3 Station Parade, Cherry Tree Rise, BUCKHURST HILL, ESSEX, IG9 6EU.

Ⓟ**Dutchmans Payroll Services, trading name of Dutchmans Consultants Limited** *(M A Poile)* 3 Station Parade, Cherry Tree Rise, BUCKHURST HILL, ESSEX, IG9 6EU.

★ⓉⒻⒶ**Dutton Moore** *(A R Bullock, J Gilleard, D McGarry, C J D Moore, J M Waters)* 6 Silver Street, HULL, HU1 1JA. and at BEVERLEY

DVernon Accounting Services *(D Vernon)* 30 High Mount, Station Road, LONDON, NW4 3SS.

Ⓟ**DVS, trading name of DVS Tax Limited** *(D V Shah)* 13 Hillbury Avenue, Kenton, HARROW, MIDDLESEX, HA3 8EP.

Ⓟ**DW Consultancy Services Ltd** *(S Johns, B A Minton, P Williams)* 21 St. Andrews Crescent, CARDIFF, CF10 3DB.

Ⓟ**DWA, trading name of David Wright Accountants Limited** *(D J Wright)* 1st Floor, Nathaniel House, David Street, BRIDGEND, CF31 3SA.

DWS, trading name of De Winter Smith LLP *(M A De Winter)* 22 The Green, Flore, NORTHAMPTON, NN7 4LG.

ⓅⒶ**Dyer & Co, trading name of Dyer & Co Audit Services Ltd** *(N J Thirlwall)* Onega House, 112 Main Road, SIDCUP, KENT, DA14 6NE.

★ⓉⓅ**Dyer & Co, trading name of Dyer & Co Services Limited** *(N A Dyer, N J Thirlwall)* Onega House, 112 Main Road, SIDCUP, KENT, DA14 6NE.

Ⓟ**Dyer-Smith & Company** *(C S P Dyer-Smith)* 7A High Street, EMSWORTH, PO10 7AQ.

Ⓟ**Dyke Ruscoe & Hayes Limited** *(P K Reynolds)* 110 Corve Street, LUDLOW, SHROPSHIRE, SY8 1DJ. and at CRAVEN ARMS, TENBURY WELLS

ⓉⒻⓅⒶ**Dyke Yaxley Limited** *(M Bramwell, H P Bruce, A P Davies, M F Griffiths, W L Riley, C H Thomas, K J Winter, A J Young)* 1 Brassey Road, Old Potts Way, SHREWSBURY, SY3 7FA.

Ⓟ**E A Mathieson Associates Ltd** *(E A Mathieson)* 97 Broomleaf Road, FARNHAM, SURREY, GU9 8DH.

Ⓕ**E Barry Lipkin** *(E B Lipkin)* Manor Lawn, 15 Normans Place, ALTRINCHAM, CHESHIRE, WA14 2AB.

Ⓟ**E C C Limited** *(E G Cobb)* 73 Chapel Lane, Hale Barns, ALTRINCHAM, CHESHIRE, WA15 0BN.

E F Cohen & Co *(E F Cohen)* 21A Russell Gardens, LONDON, NW11 9NJ.

Ⓐ**E Georgas & Co.** *(E Georgas)* 40 Kilmarnock Drive, Bushmead, LUTON, LU2 7YP.

E H Goater *(E H Goater)* 71 Burtons Road, Hampton Hill, HAMPTON, MIDDLESEX, TW12 1DE.

E Heys & Co. *(E Heys)* 229 Coppull Moor Lane, Coppull, CHORLEY, PR7 5JA.

E Hodgkinson & Co *(E Hodgkinson)* Brooklyn House, Brook Street, Shepshed, LOUGHBOROUGH, LEICESTERSHIRE, LE12 9RG.

Ⓟ**E Hopson, trading name of E Hopson Ltd** *(E Hopson)* Red Roof Cottage, 27 Sands Lane, Barmston, DRIFFIELD, NORTH HUMBERSIDE, YO25 8PQ.

E J Butler *(E J Butler)* Manor Road House, 42 Manor Road, BECKENHAM, BR3 5LE.

E J Camden *(E J Camden)* 3 Trews Weir Court, Trews Weir Reach, EXETER, EX2 4JS.

E J Owen *(E J Owen)* 1 Beech Cliffe, WARWICK, CV34 5HY.

Ⓐ**E Johnston & Co** *(Mrs Elaine Johnston)* 17 Crowhill, Godmanchester, HUNTINGDON, PE29 2LP.

E Mary Grove *(E M Grove)* Beechwood, Stoke Prior, LEOMINSTER, HEREFORDSHIRE, HR6 0LN.

★ⓉⒻⓅⒶ**E R Grove & Co Limited** *(N S Thomas)* Grove House, Coombs Wood Court, Steel Park Road, HALESOWEN, WEST MIDLANDS, B62 8BF.

ⒻⓅ**E R Lloyd & Company Limited** *(E R Lloyd)* Regent House, Bath Avenue, WOLVERHAMPTON, WV1 4EG.

ⓉⒻⒶ**E T Peirson & Sons** *(A A Bentley, S E Faire)* 21 The Point, Rockingham Road, MARKET HARBOROUGH, LEICESTERSHIRE, LE16 7NU.

Ⓟ**E W Owen & Co, trading name of E W Owen Limited** *(D M B Davies, E W Owen)* Broyan House, Priory Street, CARDIGAN, DYFED, SA43 1BZ.

E W Thomas *(E W Thomas)* Cwmffwrd Villa, Tirycoed Road, Glanamman, AMMANFORD, DYFED, SA18 2YG.

ⓅⒶ**E Wayne Pulman & Co Ltd** *(E W Pulman)* 19 Church Street, MERTHYR TYDFIL, MID GLAMORGAN, CF47 0AY. and at MOUNTAIN ASH

Ⓟ**E&R Consulting Limited** *(R A Gillett)* 5 Highfield Park, MARLOW, BUCKINGHAMSHIRE, SL7 2DE.

Ⓟ**E. B. Taylor, trading name of E. B. Taylor Limited** *(E B Taylor)* Haven Lea, Canterbury Road, Chilham, CANTERBURY, KENT, CT4 8AE.

E. Dawood & Co *(E E Dawoodbhai)* 27 Wilbury Avenue, Cheam, SUTTON, SM2 7DU.

E.A.LITTLE *(E A Little)* Larkmount, Walmersley, BURY, BL9 6TD.

E.G. Hughes & Co *(E G Hughes)* Glynderi, Batchworth Lane, NORTHWOOD, HA6 3HE.

E.G. Jones & Co *(E G Jones)* 2 Colwyn Avenue, Rhos-on-Sea, COLWYN BAY, LL28 4RB.

E.H. Cohen & Co *(E H Cohen)* 58 Anthony Road, BOREHAMWOOD, HERTFORDSHIRE, WD6 4NG.

E.H. Woodward *(E H Woodward)* Hall Farm, Risley, DERBY, DE72 3TT.

E.J. Cochrane, trading name of Jane Cochrane *(E J Cochrane)* 35 Thornton Hill, EXETER, EX4 4NN.

E.M. McManus *(E M McManus)* 2 Heatherlands Thakeham Road, Storrington, PULBOROUGH, RH20 3NE.

E.S.Solomon FCA *(E S E Solomon)* Le Chalet, Long Lane, Bovingdon, HEMEL HEMPSTEAD, HP3 0NE.

★Ⓣ**EA Associates** *(E Evagora, T Vassiliades)* 869 High Road, North Finchley, LONDON, N12 8QA.

ⒻⒶ**EA Associates, trading name of EA (UK) LLP** *(E Evagora, M Michaelides, S Sapkota, T Vassiliades)* 869 High Road, LONDON, N12 8QA.

ⓉⓅ**E-Accountants Limited** *(P K Teh)* 36 Bardolph Road, RICHMOND, SURREY, TW9 2LH.

★ⓉⒻ**Eacotts** *(N M Curtis, M Gatehouse, M A Newbold, J B Smith)* Grenville Court, Britwell Road, Burnham, SLOUGH, SL1 8DF.

★ⒻⓅⒶ**Eacotts Limited** *(N M Curtis, M Gatehouse, M A Newbold, J B Smith)* Grenville Court, Britwell Road, Burnham, SLOUGH, SL1 8DF.

Ⓟ**Eadie Young Ltd** *(D Y Eadie, T S Eadie)* Chart House, Milton Road, Bloxham, BANBURY, OXFORDSHIRE, OX15 4HD.

Eafton & Co *(E A Fatona)* 143 Varley Road, LONDON, E16 3NR.

Ⓟ**East Ayton Accountancy Limited** *(D F Mansell)* 4 Castlegate, East Ayton, SCARBOROUGH, NORTH YORKSHIRE, YO13 9EJ.

★**East London Accountancy Services** *(E A Oloyede)* 7 Norbury Road, LONDON, E4 8JX.

East London Accountancy Services, trading name of Emmanuel Stephens & Co *(E A Oloyede)* 62 Beechwood Road, LONDON, E8 3DY.

Ⓟ**East Partnership Limited** *(D J Elder)* Mill House, 103 Holmes Avenue, HOVE, BN3 7LE.

East Riding Accounts *(P Benn)* 48 New Village Road, COTTINGHAM, HU16 4NA.

Ⓟ**Eastbury Accounting Solutions Limited** *(C C Green)* Beechwood, Balnain, Drumnadrochit, INVERNESS, IV63 6TJ.

Easter Green Partnership *(M A M Whitehead)* Office A, Hoste House, Whiting Street, BURY ST. EDMUNDS, SUFFOLK, IP33 1NR.

ⓉⒻⓅⒶ**Easterbrook Eaton Limited** *(S Childs, C J Hodge, M Jones, R Puttick, C M Timms)* Cosmopolitan House, Old Fore Street, SIDMOUTH, DEVON, EX10 8LS. and at OTTERY ST. MARY

Ⓟ**Eastgate Accounts Office Limited** *(S E Leathem, A Markham)* Eastgate House, 11 Cheyne Walk, NORTHAMPTON, NN1 5PT.

ⓉⓅⒶ**Eastmonds, trading name of Eastmond & Co Limited** *(S R Eastmond)* 4 Cordwallis Street, MAIDENHEAD, BERKSHIRE, SL6 7BE.

Ⓟ**Easy Accounts Ltd** *(R J Cooper)* Unit 6, Heritage Business Centre, Derby Road, BELPER, DERBYSHIRE, DE56 1SW.

Ⓟ**Easypay Limited** *(D S George)* 246 High Road, HARROW, MIDDLESEX, HA3 7BB.

★Ⓕ**Eaves and Co** *(P N T Eaves)* 11 Part Street, SOUTHPORT, MERSEYSIDE, PR8 1HX. and at LEEDS

Ebert & Co *(A Ebert)* 9 Windsor Court, Golders Green Road, LONDON, NW11 9PP.

Ebrahim *(A Ebrahim)* 252 Uxbridge Road, RICKMANSWORTH, WD3 8EA.

Ebrahim Mulla & Co *(E T Mulla)* P.O. Box 81518, MOMBASA, KENYA.

ⒻⓅⒶ**EBS, trading name of EBS Accountants Ltd** *(J M Evenden)* Gothic House, Barker Gate, NOTTINGHAM, NG1 1JU.

Ⓟ**EC (Management Services) Ltd** *(R Crace, D C Drain, S Martin, D J Wakefield, F V Whitbread, E D Williams)* 146 New London Road, CHELMSFORD, CM2 0AW.

Ⓟ**EC Accountancy, trading name of E.Chapman Limited** *(E A Chapman)* Clearways, Colley Way, REIGATE, SURREY, RH2 9JH.

ECA Accounting Services *(R J Willis)* 78 Shirley Way, Shirley, CROYDON, CR0 8PB.

e-ccountant, trading name of G Salomon & Co *(G Salomon)* 89 Hullah Lane, WREXHAM, CLWYD, LL13 9AT.

★ⓉⒻⒶ**ECL Howard Watson Smith, trading name of ECL Howard Watson Smith LLP** *(M L Clark, B J Smith, M J Wright)* E C L House, Lake Street, LEIGHTON BUZZARD, BEDFORDSHIRE, LU7 1RT.

ⓅⒶ**Eclipse Consultancy Limited** *(J P C Harding-Edgar, D Patel)* 9 Limes Road, BECKENHAM, KENT, BR3 6NS.

Ⓟ**Economical Accountant & Bookkeeper Limited** *(S Luthra)* 2 Ross Close, HAYES, MIDDLESEX, UB3 1TS.

Ⓟ**Economize Accounting & Tax Solutions Limited** *(S R Akbar)* 1st Floor Rear, Hamilton House, 84-86 High Street, Rainham, GILLINGHAM, ME8 7JH.

Ⓐ**Ed Connolly & Co** *(E F Connolly)* 126 Bassett Avenue, SOUTHAMPTON, SO16 7EZ.

Ⓟ**Eddison & Co Ltd** *(T R W Eddison)* 16-18 Devonshire Street, KEIGHLEY, WEST YORKSHIRE, BD21 2DG.

Members in Practice and Firms - Alphabetical **Eddisons - Engineer & Mehta**

ⒾⒶ**Eddisons** *(T R W Eddison)* 16-18 Devonshire Street, KEIGHLEY, WEST YORKSHIRE, BD21 2DG.

Ⓟ**Eden Consultants Limited** *(C F Musgrave)* 24 Cloth Fair, LONDON, EC1A 7JQ.

ⒾⒻⓅⒶ**Eden Currie, trading name of Eden Currie Limited** *(P J Mannion, C A Webb)* Pegasus House, Solihull Business Park, SOLIHULL, WEST MIDLANDS, B90 4GT.

Ⓟ**Eden Outsourcing Limited** *(P J Giltrap)* Tuscam House, Trafalgar Way, CAMBERLEY, SURREY, GU15 3BN.

Ⓟ**Eden, trading name of Eden Wood Accountants Limited** *(K Edenborough)* 2 Beaconsfield Road, Knowle, BRISTOL, BS4 2JF.

EDF Accountancy *(E D Fisher)* 78 Brocket Road, WELWYN GARDEN CITY, HERTFORDSHIRE, AL8 7TU.

ⒾⒻ**EDF Tax, trading name of EDF Tax LLP** *(K E Macdonald, K A Mountain)* 7 Regan Way, Chetwynd Business Park, Chilwell, NOTTINGHAM, NG9 6RZ.

ⒻⒶ**Edgar Elias & Co** *(E Elias)* Trinominis House, First Floor, 125-129 High Street, EDGWARE, HA8 7DB.

Edith Jessup *(E E Jessup)* Nobles Green, Mill Lane, Dormansland, LINGFIELD, SURREY, RH7 6NL.

Edmonds & Co *(A G Edmonds)* 9 Clun Terrace, Cathays, CARDIFF, CF24 4RB.

Ⓐ**Edmondson & Co** *(P R Edmondson)* 170A London Road, Hazel Grove, STOCKPORT, SK7 4DJ.

Ⓟ**Edmondsons, trading name of Edmondson's Associates Ltd** *(P T Edmondson)* 1 Tye Green Paddock, Glemsford, SUDBURY, SUFFOLK, CO10 7TS.

ⒾⒻⒶ**Edmund Carr, trading name of Edmund Carr LLP** *(R Crace, D C Drain, S Martin, D J Wakefield, F V Whitbread, E D Williams)* 146 New London Road, CHELMSFORD, CM2 0AW.

Edmund Lau & Co *(W M Lau)* Unit 1403, President Commercial Centre, 608 Nathan Road, MONG KOK, KOWLOON, HONG KONG SAR.

★**Edmund Wong & Company** *(H K E Wong)* Unit 2301B, 23/F, BEA Harbour View Centre, 56 Gloucester Road, WAN CHAI, HONG KONG SAR.

ⒻⒶ**Edmund Wright & Co** *(R E Wright)* 1 Allum Way, Totteridge, LONDON, N20 9QL.

Ⓟ**Edmunds Richmond Limited** *(H R Edmunds)* Suite 404, Albany House, 324-326 Regent Street, LONDON, W1B 3HH.

EDW, trading name of Ellis Dennis Warwick LLP *(P J Dennis, J Warwick)* 59 Berks Hill, Chorleywood, RICKMANSWORTH, HERTFORDSHIRE, WD3 5AJ.

Edward Battarbee *(E Battarbee)* 195 Longlands Road, SIDCUP, KENT, DA15 7LB.

Edward Bridge *(T E Bridge)* Oak Cottage, London Road, Walgherton, NANTWICH, CHESHIRE, CW5 7LA.

ⒾⒻ**Edward Egglestone & Company** *(E Egglestone)* 3-5 Scarborough Street, HARTLEPOOL, TS24 7DA.

ⓅⒶ**Edward Friel & Co Limited** *(E J Friel)* James House, 40 Lagland Street, POOLE, DORSET, BH15 1QG.

Edward Hamon *(E C Hamon)* Mirador, 1 Rue de L'Est, St. Helier, JERSEY, JE2 4UD.

Ⓟ**Edward Howells Associates Limited** *(E J Howells)* 20a High Street, GLASTONBURY, SOMERSET, BA6 9DU.

ⒻⓅⒶ**Edward J. Baker Ltd** *(E J Baker)* Badgers Bank, Hastings Hill, Churchill, CHIPPING NORTON, OX7 6NA.

Edward Lau & Co. *(H M E Lau)* 16A Eib Centre, 40 Bonham Strand, SHEUNG WAN, HONG KONG ISLAND, HONG KONG SAR.

★**Edward Moore & Partners** *(G E Moore)* Le Pont De Vaux, 86150 MILLAC, FRANCE.

Edward O Kirwan *(E O Kirwan)* 3 Pine Tree Garden, Oadby, LEICESTER, LE2 5UT.

Ⓟ**Edward Ramsden Ltd** *(D W Eadon, J M Farndale)* 6 Cambridge Crescent, HARROGATE, NORTH YORKSHIRE, HG1 1PE.

Edward Ratnam FCA *(E I Ratnam)* 23 Chetwynd Park, Rawnsley, CANNOCK, STAFFORDSHIRE, WS12 0NZ.

ⒻⒶ**Edward Trews & Co, Eric Nabarro & Co, Leslie A Ward & Partners, trading names of Nabarro** *(R F Atkins, M F Gibbons, C P Mason)* 3/4 Great Marlborough Street, LONDON, W1F 7HH.

Edward Watkins & Co *(E W Watkins)* Glenmoir, New Street, LEDBURY, HR8 2DX.

ⒾⒶ**Edwards** *(J Duggan)* 409-411 Croydon Road, BECKENHAM, KENT, BR3 3PP.

★ⒾⒶ**Edwards** *(E C Tully, A J P Wright)* 15 Station Road, ST. IVES, CAMBRIDGESHIRE, PE27 5BH.

★ⒾⒻⒶ**Edwards** *(N J Taylor, D C P Webb)* Harmony House, 34 High Street, Aldridge, WALSALL, WS9 8LZ.

Edwards & Co *(R E M Edwards)* 2 Stud Farm, Burrough Green, NEWMARKET, Suffolk, CB8 9NH.

★**Edwards & Hartley** *(C T M Hartley)* PO Box 237, Peregrine House, Peel Road, Douglas, ISLE OF MAN, IM99 1SU.

Ⓟ**Edwards & Hartley Limited** *(D J Edwards, C T M Hartley)* PO Box 237, Peregrine House, Peel Road, Douglas, ISLE OF MAN, IM99 1SU.

★ⒾⒻⒶ**Edwards & Keeping** *(I M Carrington, R J A Edwards, K Hobbs)* Unity Chambers, 34 High East Street, DORCHESTER, DT1 1HA.

★ⒾⒶ**Edwards Veeder LLP** *(J H Law, P A O'Brien, D Shapiro, T Veeder, S M Whitehead)* Alex House, 260-268 Chapel Street, SALFORD, M3 5JZ.

Ⓟ**Edwards Veeder Payroll Ltd** *(S M Whitehead)* Alex House, 260-268 Chapel Street, SALFORD, M3 5JZ.

★ⒾⒻⒶ**Edwards Veeder, trading name of Edwards Veeder (Oldham) LLP** *(A G Basger, E B Edwards, G Leinhardt)* Block E, Brunswick Square, Union Street, OLDHAM, OL1 1DE.

ⒻⒶ**Edwards, Rowley & Co** *(P A Reilly)* 168A Hoylake Road, Moreton, WIRRAL, CH46 8TQ.

Edwin C. Brown *(E C Brown)* 15 St Joseph, Carouge-GE, CH-1227 GENEVA, SWITZERLAND.

Edwin Cheung & Siu *(K E Cheung, Y L Siu)* Room A, 7/F, China Overseas Building, 139 Hennessy Road, WAN CHAI, HONG KONG ISLAND HONG KONG SAR.

Edwin Fussell & Co. *(A Fussell)* 109 Footshill Road, Hanham, BRISTOL, BS15 8HB.

Edwin G. Monger *(E G Monger)* 49 West End, Sherborne St. John, BASINGSTOKE, RG24 9LE.

Edwin Oyinze & Associates *(E I Oyinze)* 29 Ogui Road, P.O. Box 2555, ENUGU, NIGERIA.

ⒾⒻⒶ**Edwin Smith** *(D L Barnes, P J Nixon)* 32 Queens Road, READING, RG1 4AU.

Ⓟ**Edwin Yeung & Co(CPA) Ltd** *(C W E Yeung)* 12/F, Lucky Building, 39 Wellington Street, CENTRAL, HONG KONG ISLAND, HONG KONG SAR.

Ⓟ**Edzell Lindsay Limited** *(P M Lindsay)* 8 Ashgrove Road, Redland, BRISTOL, BS6 6LY.

★**Ee Peng Liang & Co** *(K K Kwok, S H Lee, Y H Ong, H F Yen)* 10 Collyer Quay, 21-01, Ocean Building, SINGAPORE 0104, SINGAPORE.

ⒾⒻⓅⒶ**Egan Roberts, trading name of Egan Roberts Limited** *(K Roberts)* Glenfield House, Philips Road, BLACKBURN, BB1 5PF.

Eggleston Wiley LLP *(A K Eggleston)* 20 Anchor Terrace, 3-13 Southwark Bridge Road, LONDON, SE1 9HQ. and at CHAMONIX

Ⓟ**EH Consulting Limited** *(E Horton)* 30 Castle Lane, Chandlers Ford, EASTLEIGH, HAMPSHIRE, SO53 4AG.

★**Ehiemua & Co** *(E O Ehiemua)* 24 Commercial Road, Capl House, 1st Floor Apapa, P O Box 8096, Marina, LAGOS NIGERIA.

Eileen Crockett ACA *(E L Crockett)* The Cottage, Preston Lane, Lydeard St. Lawrence, TAUNTON, SOMERSET, TA4 3QQ.

Eileen M. Quinn *(E M Quinn)* Chelford, Glendyke Road, LIVERPOOL, L18 6JR.

Ⓐ**Eira Moore** *(E M E Moore)* 1 Church Meadow, SHIFNAL, SHROPSHIRE, TF11 9AD.

Ⓟ**EIS Advisors Limited** *(M Peters)* Millennium House, Victoria Road, Douglas, ISLE OF MAN, IM2 4RW.

Ⓟ**ejbc, trading name of EJ Business Consultants Ltd** *(E J Thomas)* 2b Northbrook Court, Park Street, NEWBURY, BERKSHIRE, RG14 1EA. and at HENLEY-ON-THAMES

Ⓟ**EJK Associates Limited** *(E J Kirkwood)* Unit SF09, City Mills Business Centre, City Mills, Peel Street, Morley, LEEDS LS27 8QL.

EKAS *(S C H Jennings)* Link Asia House, Penthouse Suite, 127- 129 Commercial Road, LONDON, E1 1PX.

Ⓟ**Ekkeshis Ierodiakonou, trading name of Ekkeshis Ierodiakonou Ltd** *(C Ekkeshis, C Ierodiakonou)* 39 Themistocles Dervis Street, Office 102, CY-1066 NICOSIA, CYPRUS.

Elaine Chatterton *(E Chatterton)* 5 Heathbank Avenue, WALLASEY, CH44 3AS.

Ⓕ**Elaine Hawkins** *(E Hawkins)* Merok, 34 Camp Road, GERRARDS CROSS, BUCKINGHAMSHIRE, SL9 7PD.

Elaine Horsley & Co *(E Horsley)* Ivy House, 687 Ormskirk Road, Pemberton, WIGAN, WN5 8AQ.

Elaine Jones Book-Keeping *(E Jones)* 8 Fusilier Way, Weedon, NORTHAMPTON, NN7 4TH.

Elaine M Hulse *(E M Hulse)* 6 Manor Park Drive, Great Sutton, ELLESMERE PORT, CH66 2ET.

ⒻⓅ**Elaine Philipson, trading name of Elaine Philipson Ltd** *(E Phillipson)* Forest Way, Waste Lane, Kelsall, TARPORLEY, CHESHIRE, CW6 0PE.

Elaine Whiting *(E M C Whiting)* Great Gable, 225 Kitson Hill Rd, MIRFIELD, WF14 9DS.

Elaine Williams Accounting *(E M Williams)* 3 Albion Close, Moira, SWADLINCOTE, DERBYSHIRE, DE12 6EA.

Elbourne & Company *(C W Elbourne)* 5 St. Marys Place, Meppershall, SHEFFORD, BEDFORDSHIRE, SG17 5NL.

Ⓟ**Eleanor Rice Ltd** *(E A Rice)* 13 Buckingham Road, NEWBURY, RG14 6DH.

Ⓟ**Electronic Tax Limited** *(R B Thomson)* 2 Oakfield Lane, KESTON, KENT, BR2 6BY.

ⒻⓅ**Element Consulting, Element Corporate Finance, trading names of Element Leadership Consulting Ltd** *(G C Element)* Woodlands, Home Farm, Cefn Mably, CARDIFF, CF3 6LP.

Ⓟ**Elisabeth Larner Limited** *(E Larner)* Meadow Croft, Pouk Lane, Hilton, LICHFIELD, STAFFORDSHIRE, WS14 0ET.

Elizabeth A Pile *(E A Pile)* Flat 2, 10 Frognal Gardens, LONDON, NW3 6UX.

Elizabeth A. Johnson *(E A Johnson)* 5 Lee Road, Hollywood, BIRMINGHAM, B47 5NY.

ⒻⒶ**Elizabeth A. Matthews & Co** *(E A Matthews)* Parklands, Barton Road, WISBECH, PE13 1LE.

Elizabeth Blake ACA *(E J Blake)* 27 Tudor Road, Ainsdale, SOUTHPORT, MERSEYSIDE, PR8 2RY.

Ⓐ**Elizabeth Burden** *(E J Burden)* 254 Coggeshall Road, Little Tey, COLCHESTER, CO6 1HT. and at SAWBRIDGEWORTH

Ⓟ**Elizabeth Eyre Limited** *(E L Eyre)* 112-114 West Malvern Road, MALVERN, WORCESTERSHIRE, WR14 4NB.

Elizabeth M Anfield *(E M Anfield)* 6 Tudor Road, NEWBURY, RG14 7PU.

Elizabeth Padua & Co *(E A Padua)* 21 Bangalore Street, Putney, LONDON, SW15 1QD.

Elizabeth Palethorpe *(E A Palethorpe)* 4 Chanters Hill, BARNSTAPLE, DEVON, EX32 8DQ.

Ⓟ**Elizabeth Pittman Accountancy Limited** *(E K Pittman)* 8 Rectory Close, Swinford, LUTTERWORTH, LEICESTERSHIRE, LE17 6BR.

Elizabeth Pooley *(E A Pooley)* Norfolk House, Station Road, CHESHAM, HP5 1DH.

ⓅⒶ**Elizabeth R Dean, trading name of ERD Services Limited** *(E R Dean)* West Lodge, Hall Court, Bishops Frome, WORCESTER, HEREFORDSHIRE, WR6 5BY.

Elizabeth Rose, trading name of Elizabeth Rose FCA ATT *(E Rose)* 12 Forest Dean, FLEET, HAMPSHIRE, GU51 2UQ.

Elizabeth Stevenson *(E A Stevenson)* Mullion, Westfield Road, Oakley, BEDFORD, MK43 7SU.

Ⓟ**Elizabeth Whiteley Accountancy Limited** *(E Whiteley)* 2 The Meade, Chorlton, MANCHESTER, M21 8FA.

Ella Cooper *(E F Cooper)* Owl Cottage, 6 Knox Lane, HARROGATE, NORTH YORKSHIRE, HG1 3AP.

ⒾⒻⒶ**Ellacotts LLP** *(A R Boby, D M Boughton, P H Clayton, M W Dickin, D B Saunders, J R S Thame)* Countrywide House, 23 West Bar Street, BANBURY, OXFORDSHIRE, OX16 9SA.

★**Ellam Oxtoby & Peck, trading name of Ellam Oxtoby & Peck LLP** *(H I S Walker)* Malthouse Farm, Brooke Road, Shotesham All Saints, NORWICH, NR15 1XL. and at OXFORD, TIVERTON

Ellaway-Smith *(B L Smith)* Frights Bridge Farm, Woodchurch, ASHFORD, KENT, TN26 3PR.

Ellay *(L A Rawlings)* Maple Court, Quarry Lane, Cricket Hill, YATELEY, HAMPSHIRE, GU46 6XW.

Ellen English *(E M M English)* 99 St. James's Drive, LONDON, SW17 7RP.

ⒾⒶ**Elliot & Co LLP** *(J A Elliot)* 84 Portland Road, Wyke Regis, WEYMOUTH, DORSET, DT4 9AB.

★ⒻⒶ**Elliot, Woolfe & Rose** *(M P Horsnell, M L Rose, S N Seifert, F S Waxman)* Equity House, 128-136 High Street, EDGWARE, MIDDLESEX, HA8 7TT.

Elliott & Co *(P G L Elliott)* 15 Dragon Close, BURNHAM-ON-CROUCH, CM0 8PW.

Ⓐ**Elliott & Company** *(A R Elliott)* 1a Station Buildings, Station Road, Gobowen, OSWESTRY, SY11 3LX.

Ⓐ**Elliott & Partners** *(L J Elliott, R Spedding)* 1 Sudley Terrace, High Street, BOGNOR REGIS, WEST SUSSEX, PO21 1EY.

ⒻⓅⒶ**Elliott Bunker Ltd** *(P Cridland, N Michael)* 3-8 Redcliffe Parade West, BRISTOL, BS1 6SP.

Ⓟ**Elliott Clark & Hayes, trading name of Elliott Clark Limited** *(C R Elliott)* 1 Lamorna Court, 43 Wollaton Road, Beeston, NOTTINGHAM, NG9 2NG.

Ⓐ**Elliott Stewart & Co** *(I E Stewart)* 35 Cambridge Road, BROMLEY, KENT, BR1 4EB. and at LONDON

Ⓟ**Elliott Upton Limited** *(N Upton)* 30 St. Annes Crescent, LEWES, EAST SUSSEX, BN7 1SB.

★ⒻⒶ**Elliott, Mortlock Busby & Co** *(A G Busby)* Abacus House, 7 Argent Court, Sylvan Way, Southfields Business Park, BASILDON, ESSEX SS15 6TH.

ⒾⒻⒶ**Elliotts Shah** *(M Haria, A R Shah, N Shah, P R Shah, W Wan, N Yip)* 2nd Floor, York House, 23 Kingsway, LONDON, WC2B 6UJ.

ⒻⒶ**Ellis & Co** *(J R Ellis)* 1 Peach Street, WOKINGHAM, BERKSHIRE, RG40 1XJ.

ⒾⒻⒶ**Ellis & Co.** *(C R Ellis)* 114/120 Northgate Street, CHESTER, CH1 2HT. and at WREXHAM

ⒾⒻⒶ**Ellis Atkins** *(P D Longstaff, R Parish)* 1 Paper Mews, 330 High Street, DORKING, SURREY, RH4 2TU.

Ellis Banks *(C E Ellis-Banks)* 49 Sandbeck Court, Kingswood, Bawtry, DONCASTER, SOUTH YORKSHIRE, DN10 6XP.

ⒾⒶ**Ellis Lloyd Jones LLP** *(N T Ellis, R D Ellis, K C Jones, K M Williams)* Alan House, 2 Risca Road, NEWPORT, GWENT, NP20 4JW.

Ⓟ**Ellis Management Services Limited** *(R P Ellis)* 29 Hartington Close, Dorridge, Knowle, SOLIHULL, WEST MIDLANDS, B93 8SU.

Ellisfoster LLP *(J R Ellis)* 1 High Street, Lindfield, HAYWARDS HEATH, WEST SUSSEX, RH16 2HG.

ⒾⒻⓅⒶ**Elman Wall, Elman Wall Solutions, Elman Wall Travel Accountants, trading names of Elman Wall Limited** *(R D Eisen, I R Palmer, J Wall)* 5-7 John Princes Street, LONDON, W1G 0JN.

Ⓟ**Elpizo, trading name of Elpizo Limited** *(M J Wright)* 13 Village Road, Bebington, WIRRAL, MERSEYSIDE, CH63 8PP.

Ⓟ**Els Accounting & Business Consultants, trading name of ElsAcc Limited** *(J E A Els)* 18 The Hemsleys, Pease Pottage, CRAWLEY, WEST SUSSEX, RH11 9BX.

ⓅⒶ**Elsby & Co, trading name of Elsby & Co (Sywell) Ltd** *(C A Elsby)* Thistledown Barn, Holcot Lane, Sywell, NORTHAMPTON, NN6 0BG.

★**Elsby & Co, trading name of Elsby & Co(Northampton) LLP** *(C A Elsby)* Thistledown Barn, Holcot Lane, Sywell, NORTHAMPTON, NN6 0BG.

Elspeth Consulting *(J E Jones)* 50 Denton Avenue, LEEDS, LS8 1LE.

Elver Consultancy *(S M Blackmore)* 1 Smallshaw Close, Ashton-in-Makerfield, WIGAN, WN4 9LW.

Elwell Watchorn & Saxton LLP *(P A Saxton, D J Watchorn)* 109 Swan Street, Sileby, LOUGHBOROUGH, LE12 7NN. and at LONDON, NORTHAMPTON, NOTTINGHAM, PETERBOROUGH

ⒻⓅ**EM Costas & Co, trading name of Easebay Limited** *(E Costas)* Unit 3, Gateway Mews, Ringway, LONDON, N11 2UT.

Ⓟ**Emerson & Co, trading name of GN Emerson Ltd** *(C Emerson)* Common House, Gelt Road, BRAMPTON, CUMBRIA, CA8 1QQ.

Emma J Sonia BSc(Hons) ACA *(E J Sonia)* 13 Tarn Hows Walk, Ackworth, PONTEFRACT, WEST YORKSHIRE, WF7 7QS.

Emma Sutcliffe *(E C Sutcliffe)* 9 Low Mill, Caton, LANCASTER, LA2 9HY.

Emma Veelenturf BSc ACA *(E L Veelenturf)* 51 Victoria Road, OXFORD, OX2 7QF.

Emmanuel Okechukwu & Co *(Chief Ojike)* 55 Western Avenue, P.O. Box 7923, LAGOS, NIGERIA.

EMMAS, trading name of East Midlands Managed Account Service *(E J Goodwin)* 9 Trent View Gardens, Radcliffe-on-Trent, NOTTINGHAM, NG12 1AY.

Ⓟ**Emmaus, trading name of Emmaus Accountants Ltd** *(S E Shearer)* Westmead House, Westmead, FARNBOROUGH, HAMPSHIRE, GU14 7LP.

Ⓟ**Emmett & Co (Nelson) Ltd** *(C Emmett)* 11 Market Square, NELSON, BB9 7LP.

ⒻⓅ**Employer Covenant Solutions, R P Rendle & Co, Rendle & Co, trading names of R P Rendle & Co Limited** *(R P Rendle)* No 9 Hockley Court, Hockley Heath, SOLIHULL, WEST MIDLANDS, B94 6NW.

Ⓟ**enCONCERT, trading name of Enconcert Ltd** *(S Hancock)* 47 Upper High Street, WORTHING, WEST SUSSEX, BN11 1DR.

Endless LLP *(D W Forshaw, G Wilson)* 3 Whitehall Quay, LEEDS, LS1 4BF. and at BIRMINGHAM, LONDON, MANCHESTER

★**Engelsman & Co** *(H L Engelsman)* The Estate House, 201 High Road, CHIGWELL, ESSEX, IG7 5BJ.

★**Engineer & Mehta** *(F J Engineer)* 45/47 Bombay Samachar Marg, Bank of Maharashtra Building, 5th Floor, MUMBAI 400 023, MAHARASHTRA, INDIA.

Ⓐ**England & Co** *(T M T England)* 18 Trevecca Terrace, LISKEARD, CORNWALL, PL14 6RH.

★ⓉⓅⒶ**Ensors** *(I C Brookman, J A Card, D S P Clifford, I D Gorman, R W Hatch, S M Law, R D Leggett, J O Matthews, M R McGready, G D Page, H S Rumsey, S M Runnacles, D P Scrivener, P Williams, R P Williams)* Cardinal House, 46 St Nicholas Street, IPSWICH, IP1 1TT. and at BURY ST. EDMUNDS, CAMBRIDGE, HUNTINGDON, SAXMUNDHAM

Ⓟ**Enterprise Solutions (England) Ltd** *(A J Robinson)* March House, 44 The Avenue, TADWORTH, KT20 5AT. and at BROMLEY

Ⓟ**Entigy Ltd** *(D N Mitchell)* Imperial Chambers, Prince Albert Street, CREWE, CW1 2DX.

Ⓟ**Epiphany Business Solutions Limited** *(J B Chown, K W Jones, G Moses)* 4 Ynys Bridge Court, Gwaelod-y-Garth, CARDIFF, CF15 9SS.

e-practice *(A Miller)* The Studio, Drift Road, BORDON, HAMPSHIRE, GU35 9DZ.

Ⓟ**Epsom Accounting Limited** *(D C Shepherd)* 93 High Street, EPSOM, KT19 8DR.

Epstein Consultancy *(E R Epstein)* 1 Oakwell Drive, SALFORD, M7 4PY.

★**EQ, trading name of EQ Accountants LLP** *(K Hopkins, A W Tucker)* Westby, 64 West High Street, FORFAR, ANGUS, DD8 1BJ. and at DUNDEE

Ⓟ**Eqeria Limited** *(J H Smith)* 83 Lightfoot Lane, Fulwood, PRESTON, PR2 3LS.

Equal Accounting *(S M Antrobus)* 22 Cranmere Road, PLYMOUTH, PL3 5JY.

Ⓟ**Equal IP, trading name of Equal IP Ltd** *(R Sengupta)* 60 Park Road, BECKENHAM, KENT, BR3 1QH.

Er & Co *(B C Er)* 336 Smith Street, 04-302 New Bridge Centre, SINGAPORE 050336, SINGAPORE.

ⓉⓅⒶ**ERC Accountants & Business Advisers Limited** *(R W J Brown, M R Wrigglesworth)* Suite 26, Century Building, Tower Street, Brunswick Business Park, LIVERPOOL, L3 4BJ.

Erdal & Co *(E Erdal, H Erdal, F H Fehmi)* 100 Bedrettin Demirel CAD, PO Box 410, LEFKOSA MERSIN 10, TURKEY.

Eric Bone *(E Bone)* Offshore House, Euroseas Centre, Albert Street, BLYTH, NORTHUMBERLAND, NE24 1LZ.

Eric G. Bolam *(E G Bolam)* 14 Fox Covert, River View Park, Colwick, NOTTINGHAM, NG4 2DD.

Eric Kiel & Co *(E S Kiel)* 49 Ravenscroft Avenue, WEMBLEY, MIDDLESEX, HA9 9TE.

Eric M. Cobley *(E M Cobley)* Great Dalby House, Great Dalby, MELTON MOWBRAY, LEICESTERSHIRE, LE14 2EY.

Eric R. Jenkins *(E R Jenkins)* 104 Southover, LONDON, N12 7HD.

Eric Southwick & Co *(E Southwick)* 51 The Avenue, SEAHAM, COUNTY DURHAM, SR7 8NS.

Eric Sykes *(E Sykes)* 62 Higher Lane, LYMM, WA13 0BG.

Eric T. Owen F.C.A *(E T Owen)* 25 Lynton Green, Woolton, LIVERPOOL, L25 6JB.

Ernest Clark & Co *(A E Clark)* 26 St.Catherines Close, LONDON, SW17 7UA.

Ernest Eng *(E Eng)* Lynwood, Mayfield Road, WEYBRIDGE, KT13 8XD.

Ernie Thorn *(E J Thorn)* 47 Buttermere Drive, Onchan, ISLE OF MAN, IM3 2EB.

★**Ernst & Young** *(M Chourdakis, A Hadjidamianou, C Panayidou, C C Seferis, Y Theoklitou)* Ilission 3-5, 115 28 ATHENS, GREECE. and at METAMORFOSIS

★Ⓣ**Ernst & Young** *(C S Glavanis)* 11Klm National Road, Athens-Lamia, Metamorphosi, 14451 ATHENS, GREECE. and at BUCHAREST, PIRAEUS, THESSALONIKI

★**Ernst & Young** *(A B Dent)* PO Box 261, BRIDGETOWN, BARBADOS. and at PORT OF SPAIN

★**Ernst & Young** *(J P Hartley, M J Keson-Lee, A B Stewart)* P.O. Box 656, CAPE TOWN, C.P., 8000, SOUTH AFRICA. and at BLOEMFONTEIN, DURBAN, GABORONE, GEORGE, ILLOVO, JOHANNESBURG, KRUGERSDORP, MAFIKENG, MASERU, MBABANE, NEWCASTLE, ORANGE COUNTY, PAARL, PIETERMARITZBURG, PORT ELIZABETH, PRETORIA, SWAKOPMUND, VEREENIGING, WALVIS BAY, WINDHOEK

★**Ernst & Young** *(M J Buxton, Y Chan, K Lau, M H Lee, E H P Lee To, C Leung, K K A Leung, C R E Saunderson, T M Tsang, C K S Yen)* 15/F Hutchison House, 10 Harcourt Road, CENTRAL, HONG KONG ISLAND, HONG KONG SAR. and at BANGKOK, JAKARTA, QUARRY BAY, SEOUL, SHANGHAI, TSIM SHA TSUI

★**Ernst & Young** *(M P Bentley, M M Coll, A Cotton, I M Eddleston, A K Gupta, R D Moncrieff)* 2000 National City Center, 1900 East Ninth Street, CLEVELAND, OH 44114, UNITED STATES. and at ABILENE, ALBANY, ATLANTIC CITY, AUSTIN, BIRMINGHAM, BOSTON, BRIDGEPORT, BUFFALO, CENTURY CITY, CHARLESTON, CHARLOTTE, CHATTANOOGA, CHICAGO, CINCINNATI, CLOVIS, COLUMBUS, DALLAS, DENVER, DES MOINES, DETROIT, FAYETTEVILLE, FORT WAYNE, FRESNO, GREENVILLE, HARTFORD, HOUSTON, INDIANAPOLIS, JACKSON, JACKSONVILLE, KANSAS CITY, LAWRENCEVILLE, LONG BEACH, LONG ISLAND, LOS ANGELES, LOUISVILLE, MANCHESTER, METROPARK, MIAMI, MINNEAPOLIS, NASSAU, NEW ORLEANS, NEW YORK, NEWPORT BEACH, OMAHA, ORLANDO, PALO ALTO, PANAMA CITY, PHILADELPHIA, PHOENIX, RICHMOND, RIVERSIDE, ROANOKE, SACRAMENTO, SAN ANTONIO, SAN FRANCISCO, SAN JOSE, SCOTTSDALE, SEATTLE, SOUTH BEND, ST PETERSBURG, ST THOMAS, SYRACUSE, TAMPA, TOLEDO, TULSA, WALNUT CREEK, WOODLAND HILLS

▽**Ernst & Young** *(M R Green, A H Issa, A E Kasparian)* Level 28, AL Attar Bus Tower, Sheikh Zayed Road, P.O. Box 9267, DUBAI, UNITED ARAB EMIRATES. and at ABU DHABI, BEIRUT, CAIRO, DHAHRAN, DOHA, MANAMA, MUSCAT, SAFAT, SANAA, SHARJAH, TEHRAN

Ernst & Young *(N L Hodgson)* Ernst & Young Building, Harcourt Centre, Harcourt Street, DUBLIN 2, COUNTY DUBLIN, IRELAND.

Ⓣ**Ernst & Young** *(A Y Lai Wan Loong, C Y M Leung Hing Wah, P G Lincoln, P Ng Tseung, L Pookimlifu)* 9th Floor, Tower 1, NextTeracom, Cybercity, EBENE, MAURITIUS.

★**Ernst & Young** *(T G M Hooley)* Angwa City, cnr Julius Nyerere & Union Ave, Box 62, HARARE, ZIMBABWE. and at BULAWAYO, GWERU, KWE KWE, MUTARE

★Ⓣ**Ernst & Young** *(H Abdul, A R Rashid, M S Sardon)* 4th Floor, Kompleks Antarabangsa, P O Box 10068, 50704 KUALA LUMPUR, FEDERAL TERRITORY, MALAYSIA. and at IPOH, JOHOR BAHRU, KOTA KINABALU, KUANTAN, KUCHING, MALACCA CITY, PENANG, SANDAKAN, SIBU, TAWAU

★**Ernst & Young** *(P L Pang, M S Sardon)* Level 23A, Menara Milenium, Jalan Damanlela, Pusat Bandar Damansara, Damansara Heights, 50490 KUALA LUMPUR FEDERAL TERRITORY MALAYSIA. and at IPOH, JOHOR BAHRU, KUCHING, LABUAN, MALACCA CITY, MIRI, PENANG, SANDAKAN, SIBU, TAWAU

▽Ⓣ**Ernst & Young** *(N R Abid, A Adil, P J Griffiths, A A H Rudman, M T Sadiq Akbar)* P.O. Box 140, MANAMA, BAHRAIN. and at BAGHDAD, BEIRUT, RAMALLAH

★**Ernst & Young** *(A D Robertson)* Via Wittgens 6, 20123 MILAN, ITALY.

★Ⓣ**Ernst & Young** *(N R Abid, K A Mian)* Al Faisaliah Office Tower, Level 14, PO Box 2732, RIYADH, 11461, SAUDI ARABIA. and at AL KHOBAR, AMMAN, DAMASCUS, DHAHRAN, JEDDAH

★**Ernst & Young** *(N Shafi)* P.O. Box 74, SAFAT, 13001, KUWAIT.

★Ⓣ**Ernst & Young** *(S Y Ho, K K Kwok, Y H Ong, N Sivaram, H F Yen)* One Raffles Quay, North Tower Level 18, SINGAPORE 048583, SINGAPORE.

★**Ernst & Young** *(M B Bryant, A Islam, S R Lomas, J M Prentice, I J Rodin)* The Ernst & Young Building, 680 George Street, SYDNEY, NSW 2000, AUSTRALIA. and at ADELAIDE, BRISBANE, CANBERRA, DARWIN, MELBOURNE, PERTH

★**Ernst & Young** *(G H C De Meris)* (P.O. Box 90636), Wassenaarseweg 80, 2509 LP THE HAGUE, Zuid Holland, NETHERLANDS. and at ALKMAAR, ALMELO, AMERSFOORT, AMSTERDAM, APELDOORN, ARNHEM, ASSEN, BREDA, DIEGEM, EDE, EINDHOVEN, EMMEN, ENSCHEDE, GOES, GOUDA, GRONINGEN, HEERENVEEN, HEERLEN, HILVERSUM, HONSERERSDIJK, LEEUWARDEN, LIEGE, LUXEMBOURG, MAASTRICHT, MILAN, NAALDWIJK, NIJMEGEN, PARAMARIBO, ROTTERDAM, SINGAPORE, TERNEUZEN, TIEL, UTRECHT, VENLO, WILLEMSTAD, WINSCHOTEN, ZWOLLE

Ernst & Young *(G R Slater)* P.O. Box 91873, TRIPOLI, LIBYAN ARAB JAMAHIRIYA.

Ernst & Young Advisory *(P D Wood)* Faubourg de l'arche, La Defense cedex, 92037 PARIS, FRANCE.

Ernst & Young Audit & Associados SROC S.A *(M A Bean, J V Mackey)* Avenida da Republica 90-6, 1600-206 LISBON, PORTUGAL.

★**Ernst & Young Audit SP zoo** *(D A Aluwihare)* U1 Sienna 39, WARSAW, 00 121, POLAND.

Ernst & Young Beograd d.o.o *(M G Evry)* 115d Bulevar, Miharjla Pupina, 11070 BELGRADE, SERBIA.

ⓉⓅ**Ernst & Young Cyprus Limited** *(A Avraamides, A Demetriou, G Kourris, N Neophytou, G Onisiforou, S Pantzaris, C Stylianou, Y Theoklitou)* Nicosia Tower Centre, 36 Byron Avenue, P.O Box 21656, 1511 NICOSIA, CYPRUS. and at LIMASSOL

Ⓟ**Ernst & Young Cyprus Limited** *(A Avraamides, A Demetriou, G Kourris, P L Liassides, N Neophytou, G Onisiforou, S Pantzaris, C Stylianou)* Nicosia Tower Centre, 36 Byron Avenue, P O Box 21656, 1511 NICOSIA, CYPRUS. and at LIMASSOL

Ⓐ**Ernst & Young Europe LLP** *(L J Sass, C P Alexander, K A Alexander, S Allport, D A Aluwihare, G Anderson, J E L Anderson, A Anthony, D P J Arnold, N Bacon, I J J Baggs, V Balakrishnan, H W Ball, M R Bane, K L Barrow, J A Bates, R M Battersby, A A Beecher, I S Beer, S D Bell, A J Belton, M D Benson, I Best, M Bevington, R Bhuchar, R D M Birch, J G Blackie, A R Bloom, J Bourne, J Bowden-Williams, C S Bowles, D Brewin, A R Brogan, R Brown, R S Brown, M P Burke, D P Burnham, M J Buxton, B T Cairns, S L Callaghan, D G Canning-Jones, J M Carlyle, E H Carruthers, M J Carter, C G Cartmell, B A Castell, J R Charlton, M Choурdakis, J S Clayton, H L Cleaton-Roberts, A S Clewer, A R E Clifford, S E Clifford, J D E Close, D P Coats, J G Cole, D P Cooper, M J D Corson, A D Coups, C H H Cowling, T M Cradock-Watson, R Cubbage, P J D'Arcy, A J Dann, S M Date, O Davidson, A D Davies, G C B Davies, T N Davison, N J Dawes, G H C De Meris, J W Dean, A Demetriou, A J Denton, G J Deuchar, T D G Dewar, R M Dobson, S M Dobson, L M Downham, A Duncan, L J Ed, R J Engineer, M Evans, M G Evry, D A Eyre, N Eyton, C Fairhurst, D G Fairhurst, J Faiz, D E Feather, P A Ferrigno, S J Fish, M Fishman, J C Flaherty, M P Flanagan, B Flynn, S A Fowler, R N A Franchini, E W Gardner, D A Gaunt, H T Gill, K D Gill, D J Gittleson, A J Glover, A Godfrey, N K Gomer, T J Goodman, T R Gordon, A H F Grant, J J Gray, N J Gray, R J Gray, P J Green, S R Gregory, A J Griffiths, P Haberman, A Hadjidamianou, D M Hales, N L Halkes, R A Hall, N D Handler, G Harding, R A Harding, N J Harrison, M N Harvey, M A B Hatton, K J Havers, M J Hawkins, J A Headley, R D J Heath, R S D Heron, K R Hills, I R Hobson, Z I Holgate, S J Holt, N A Holyoake, K M Honey, C G Honnywill, C Hooper, M D J Hornsby, J A Houlden, C W O Hughes, G H Hughes, J Hughes, N A Hughes, M Hurst, N J Hutt, R K Indge, S G Ivermee, T A Jack, J N W Jennings, M F Jones, N G O Jones, R P Jones, R D Jowitt, N Kaul, S J Keen, J D Kelly, M J Keson-Lee, G Kourris, S C Lamb, D W Lambert, S C Lang, D J Larnder, R Laverick, D W Leather, T J Leggett, J A Lenton, J R Lester, R P Lewis, T J Link, J R Liver, A J Love, R J Lowe, S P Lucey, T Lukic, M D Lynch-Bell, K P Macauley, P J Mapleston, C Marsden, L Marston-Weston, H D Martin, P H Martin, C J Matthews, A M Mawji, C E McAree, T B McCartney, M D A McCormick, R R McCracken, E J McGrath, K McGregor, A J McIntyre, J E Meader, M C Mealey, T M Medak, N J Meredith, S P Michaelson, J W Middup, A J Millar, A S Millings, M E Mills, R J Moody, D R J Moore, J E W Morris, T J Morris, M Moses, D A Murray, E Mustafa, S A Nash, G L Nattrass, C J Naudi, N C A Nelkon, N Neophytou, A C Nicholls, A C P Noble, A J R Nuttall, D O'Connor, E O'Donnell, D A O'Hanlon, P.M. O'Neill, S D O'Neill, C A Oates, A Ogram, D Oldknow, M D Otty, R Overend, C Panayiodou, S Pantzaris, A D Papadopoulos, S J Parkinson, G W Parrott, A B Patel, K Paterson, S M Pearson, S T Perry, R A J Phillip, S J Phizackerley, M J Portnoy, N C Powell, M R Price, M Purrington, D G Ramm, L S Rattigan, D L Read, G M Reid, A L Roberts, L K Roberts, A D Robertson, J A Robertson-Kellie, S C Robinson, R A C Roman, T J Rooke, D L Royce, C Sanger, J L Santinon, P E R Sater, I A Scott, C C Seferis, M A Semple, K W Senior, R A Shah, H S Sidhu, A Singh, J J Skingley, F D Small, B K Smith, P G Smith, A D Smyth, J Soar, A Spence, P H Spence, E Stanton, T J Steel, C S Steppler, P T Stevens, M A Stilwell, A T Stokes, N J Strathdee, A Swarbrick, C D Tattersall, M H Taylor, S C Taylor, Y Theoklitou, J D Thurbin, A D Tivey, D P Trotman, R E Upton, J Uranic, D L Vaughan, J Vaughan, C J Voogd, R C Walker, P I Wallace, P D Wallek, A Walton, A Ward, R J Ward, P E Warn, S J Wasley, L W Watson, S W Watson, P J Wells, T J A West, D J Whitecross, I J P Whitlock, G Wild, M J Wildig, I R Wilkie, D L Wilkinson, D J Williams, S J Williams, K A Williamson, K G Williamson, S P Wills, D C E Wilson, R W Wilson, S Wilson, R F Winchester, P D Wood, T M Wood, A D Woosey, J A Young, P J Young)* Becket House, 1 Lambeth Palace Road, LONDON, SE1 7EU.

Ⓣ**Ernst & Young Ford Rhodes Sidat Hyder** *(S Chinoy, M Junaid, M Khandwala, M A Khandwala)* 601 Progressive Plaza, Beaumont Road, KARACHI 75530, SINDH, PAKISTAN. and at LAHORE, RAWALPINDI, SHARJAH

★Ⓣ**Ernst & Young GmbH** *(M D Benson, P A Bradley, S Didam, M Hurst)* Merghentalerallee 10-12, 65760 ESCHBORN, GERMANY. and at DUSSELDORF, FRANKFURT AM MAIN, HAMBURG, HANNOVER, LEIPZIG, MUNICH, NURNBERG, STUTTGART

Ⓟ**Ernst & Young Limited** *(R D J Heath, P T Stevens)* 1 More London Place, LONDON, SE1 2AF.

ⓉⒶ**Ernst & Young LLP** *(L J Sass, C P Alexander, K A Alexander, S Allport, G Anderson, J E L Anderson, A Anthony, D P J Arnold, N Bacon, I J J Baggs, V Balakrishnan, H W Ball, M R Bane, K L Barrow, J A Bates, R M Battersby, A A Beecher, I S Beer, S D Bell, A J Belton, I Best, M Bevington, R Bhuchar, R D M Birch, J G Blackie, A R Bloom, J Bourne, J Bowden-Williams, C S Bowles, D Brewin, A R Brogan, R Brown, R S Brown, M P Burke, M J Buxton, B T Cairns, S L Callaghan, D G Canning-Jones, J M Carlyle, E H Carruthers, M J Carter, C G Cartmell, B A Castell, J R Charlton, J S Clayton, H L Cleaton-Roberts, A S Clewer, A R E Clifford, S E Clifford, J D E Close, J G Cole, D P Cooper, M J D Corson, A D Coups, C H H Cowling, R Cubbage, P J D'Arcy, A J Dann, S M Date, O Davidson, A D Davies, G C B Davies, T N Davison, N J Dawes, J W Dean, A J Denton, G J Deuchar, T D G Dewar, S M Dobson, L M Downham, A Duncan, L J Ed, R J Engineer, M Evans, D A Eyre, N Eyton, C Fairhurst, D G Fairhurst, J Faiz, D E Feather, M Fishman, J C Flaherty, M P Flanagan, B Flynn, S A Fowler, E W Gardner, D A Gaunt, H T Gill, K D Gill, D J Gittleson, A J Glover, A Godfrey, N K Gomer, T J Goodman, T R Gordon, A H F Grant, J J Gray, N J Gray, R J Gray, P J Green, S R Gregory, P Haberman, D M Hales, N L Halkes, R A Hall, N D Handler, G Harding, R A Harding, N J Harrison, M N Harvey, M A B Hatton, K J Havers, J A Headley, R D J Heath, R S D Heron, K R Hills, I R Hobson, Z I Holgate, S J Holt, N A Holyoake, K M Honey, C G Honnywill, C Hooper, J A Houlden, C W O Hughes, G H Hughes, J Hughes, N J Hutt, R K Indge, S G Ivermee, T A Jack, M F Jones, N G O Jones, R P Jones, R D Jowitt, N Kaul, S J Keen, S C Lamb, D W Lambert, S C Lang, D J Larnder, R Laverick, D W Leather, T J Leggett, J A Lenton, J R Lester, J R Liver, A J Love, R J Lowe, S P Lucey, T Lukic, M D Lynch-Bell, K P Macauley, P J Mapleston, C Marsden, L Marston-Weston, H D Martin, P H Martin, C J Matthews, A M Mawji, C E McAree, T B McCartney, M D A McCormick, R R McCracken, E J McGrath, K McGregor, A J McIntyre, J E Meader, M C Mealey, T M Medak, N J Meredith, S P Michaelson, J W Middup, A J Millar, A S Millings, M E Mills, R J Moody, D R J Moore, J E W Morris, T J Morris, M Moses, D A Murray, E Mustafa, S A Nash, G L Nattrass, N C A Nelkon, A C Nicholls, A C P Noble, A J R Nuttall, E O'Donnell, D A O'Hanlon, P.M. O'Neill, S D O'Neill, C A Oates, A Ogram, D Oldknow, M D Otty, R Overend, S J Parkinson, G W Parrott, A B Patel, K Paterson, S M Pearson, S T Perry, R A J Phillip, S J Phizackerley, M J Portnoy, N C Powell, M R Price, M Purrington, L S Rattigan, D L Read, G M Reid, A L Roberts, L K Roberts, J A Robertson-Kellie, S C Robinson, R A C Roman, T J Rooke, D L Royce, C Sanger, J L Santinon, P E R Sater, I A Scott, M A Semple, K W Senior, R A Shah, H S Sidhu, A Singh, J J Skingley, F D Small, B K Smith, A D Smyth, J Soar, A Spence, P H Spence, E Stanton, T J Steel, C S Steppler, P T Stevens, M A Stilwell, A T Stokes, N J Strathdee, A Swarbrick, M H Taylor, S C Taylor, A D Tivey, D P Trotman, R E Upton, D L Vaughan, J Vaughan, C J Voogd, R C Walker, P I Wallace, P D Wallek, A Walton, A Ward, R J Ward, P E Warn, S J Wasley, L W Watson, S W Watson, T J A West, D J Whitecross, I J P Whitlock, G Wild, M J Wildig, I R Wilkie, D L Wilkinson, D J Williams, S J Williams, K A Williamson, K G Williamson, S P Wills, D C E Wilson, R W Wilson, S Wilson, R F Winchester, T M Wood, A D Woosey, J A Young, P J Young)* 1 More London Place, LONDON, SE1 2AF. and at ABERDEEN, BELFAST, BIRMINGHAM, BRISTOL, CAMBRIDGE, EDINBURGH, EXETER,

Members in Practice and Firms - Alphabetical · Ernst & Young LLP - FD-UK

GLASGOW, GUERNSEY, HULL, INVERNESS, JERSEY, LEEDS, LIVERPOOL, LUTON, MANCHESTER, NEWCASTLE UPON TYNE, NOTTINGHAM, READING, SOUTHAMPTON

★**Ernst & Young Orenda Corporate Finance Inc, trading name of Ernst & Young** *(G P Kaye)* P.O Box 251, Ernst & Young Tower, TORONTO M5K 1J7, ON, CANADA. and at ABILENE, ALBANY, ALBUQUERQUE, AMARILLO, ANCHORAGE, ATLANTA, ATLANTIC CITY, AUSTIN, BAKERSFIELD, BALTIMORE, BATON ROUGE, BELO HORIZONTE, BEVERLY HILLS, BIRMINGHAM, BOSTON, BRIDGEPORT, BUFFALO, CALGARY, CEDAR RAPIDS, CHARLESTON, CHARLOTTE, CHICAGO, CINCINNATI, CLEVELAND, COLUMBIA, COLUMBUS, COSTA MESA, CURITIBA, DALLAS, DAYTONA BEACH, DENVER, DES MOINES, DETROIT, EDMONTON, FAYETTEVILLE, FORT LAUDERDALE, FORT SMITH, FORT WORTH, FORTALEZA, FRESNO, GREENSBORO, GREENVILLE, HALIFAX, HARTFORD, HATO REY, HONOLULU, HOUSTON, INDIANAPOLIS, JACKSONVILLE, JONESBORO, KANSAS CITY, KITCHENER, LAVAL, LITTLE ROCK, LONDON, LOS ANGELES, LOUISVILLE, MADISON, MANCHESTER, MIAMI, MILWAUKEE, MINNEAPOLIS, MONTREAL, NAPERVILLE, NASHVILLE, NEW ORLEANS, NEW YORK, NEWARK, NORFOLK, OAKLAND, OKLAHOMA CITY, OMAHA, ORANGE COUNTY, ORLANDO, OTTAWA, PALO ALTO, PHILADELPHIA, PHOENIX, PINE BLUFF, PITTSBURGH, PORTLAND, PORTO ALEGRE, PRINCETON, PROVIDENCE, QUEBEC CITY, RALEIGH, RECIFE, RENO, RESTON, RICHMOND, RIO DE JANEIRO, SACRAMENTO, SADDLE BROOK, SAINT JOHN, SALT LAKE CITY, SALVADOR, SAN ANTONIO, SAN DIEGO, SAN FRANCISCO, SAN JOSE, SAN JUAN, SANTA FE, SAO PAULO, SCHAUMBURG, SEATTLE, SPRINGDALE, SPRINGFIELD, ST LOUIS, ST PETERSBURG, STAMFORD, STUTTGART, TALLAHASSEE, TAMPA, THORNHILL, THUNDER BAY, TOLEDO, TRENTON, TULSA, VANCOUVER, WALNUT CREEK, WASHINGTON, WEST PALM BEACH, WICHITA, WINNIPEG, WOODLAND HILLS, WORCESTER

Ⓟ**Ernst & Young Tax Services Ltd** *(K N Chan, S Wong, T Yuen)* 18/F, Two IFC, 8 Finance Street, CENTRAL, HONG KONG ISLAND, HONG KONG SAR.

ⓉⒶ**Ernst & Young, trading name of Ernst & Young LLC** *(P F Duffy, J D Kelly)* Rose House, 51-59 Circular Road, Douglas, ISLE OF MAN, IM1 1AZ.

ⒺⒶ**Errington Langer Pinner** *(R N Errington, M S Pinner)* Pyramid House, 956 High Road, Finchley, LONDON, N12 9RX.

Errol Martin *(J E T Martin)* 2nd Floor, 272 London Road, WALLINGTON, SURREY, SM6 7DJ.

ESampson *(E J Sampson)* 59 Heyes Lane, ALDERLEY EDGE, CHESHIRE, SK9 7LA.

Eskays & Co *(S K Mohamed)* 34 Bellfield Avenue, HARROW, MIDDLESEX, HA3 6SX.

Ⓟ**Espira Limited** *(Y M A Chu)* 74 Castleton Road, Lightwood, STOKE-ON-TRENT, ST3 7TD.

Ⓟ**Esther White, trading name of Pickled Parsnip Limited** *(E M White)* 236 Henleaze Road, Henleaze, BRISTOL, BS9 4NG.

ⒺⓅⒶ**ESW Limited** *(S J Cracknell, S Wills)* 162-164 High Street, RAYLEIGH, ESSEX, SS6 7BS.

Ⓟ**Ethos Corporate Finance Ltd** *(A J Walls)* 1 City Square, LEEDS, LS1 2ES.

Ⓟ**ETM Consulting Limited** *(K N Mathieson, P G Power)* The Old Stables, Hendal Farm, Groombridge, TUNBRIDGE WELLS, KENT, TN3 9NU.

Etyek Consulting *(M N Dudgeon)* Dorottya utca 11, 1051 BUDAPEST, HUNGARY.

Euan Williams *(E J Williams)* 55 Glenesk Road, Eltham, LONDON, SE9 1AH.

Ⓣ**Eura Audit UK, trading name of Lishman Sidwell Campbell & Price LLP** *(E J Maclean, D M Naylor, B Price, P Tarren)* Eva Lett House, 1 South Crescent, RIPON, HG4 1SN. and at DARLINGTON, HARROGATE, MORECAMBE, NORTHALLERTON, SHEFFIELD, SHIPLEY, TADCASTER, WETHERBY

Ⓟ**Eura Audit UK, trading name of Lishman Sidwell Campbell & Price Ltd** *(B Price)* Eva Lett House, 1 South Crescent, RIPON, HG4 1SN.

Ⓟ**Euro Capital Ventures Ltd** *(D T Singh)* 26 Cypress Avenue, WELWYN GARDEN CITY, HERTFORDSHIRE, AL7 1HN.

Eurocontrol Asesores Contables *(A R Hall)* Oficina 48, Edificio Burgosol, Comunidad de Madrid 35 bis, Las Rozas de Madrid, 28230 MADRID, SPAIN.

Eurocontrol Auditores S.L.P *(A R Hall)* Oficina 48 Edificio Burgosol, c/Comunidad de Madrid 35 bis, Las Rozas de Madrid, 28230 MADRID, SPAIN.

Ⓟ**Eurofin Taxation Services Limited** *(T A Wells)* Telford House, Hamilton Close, BASINGSTOKE, HAMPSHIRE, RG21 6YT.

★**Eurorevision** *(R J Panday)* Pez Volador 32, 28007 MADRID, SPAIN.

★**Evan Wong & Co** *(K K Kwok, S H Lee, Y H Ong, H F Yen)* P.O. Box 384, 10 Collyer Quay, 21-01 Ocean Building, SINGAPORE 0104, SINGAPORE. and at IPOH, JOHOR BAHRU, KOTA KINABALU, KUALA LUMPUR, KUCHING, MALACCA CITY, MIRI, PENANG, SANDAKAN, SIBU, TAWAU

Evans & Co *(C J Poulton)* 51 Brunswick Road, GLOUCESTER, GL1 1JS.

ⓉⒺⒶ**Evans & Partners** *(O J Evans, D Morland)* 9 Bank Road, Kingswood, BRISTOL, BS15 8LS.

Ⓟ**Evans Mockler, trading name of Evans Mockler Limited** *(M Evans)* Highstone House, 165 High Street, BARNET, HERTFORDSHIRE, EN5 5SU.

ⓉⒺⓅ**Evans Weir, trading name of Evans Weir Limited** *(R Swaffield)* The Victoria, 25 St. Pancras, CHICHESTER, WEST SUSSEX, PO19 7LT. and at PORTSMOUTH

ⓉⓅⒶ**Evens & Co. Ltd** *(A R Evens, B K Evens)* Hamilton House, Hamilton Terrace, MILFORD HAVEN, PEMBROKESHIRE, SA73 3JP.

ⓉⒺⒶ**Everett & Son** *(J K Barclay, J N Cross, J Griffin, M S Lamb)* 35 Paul Street, LONDON, EC2A 4UQ.

Ⓟ**Everett Horder Limited** *(J N Cross, C Horder)* 35 Paul Street, LONDON, EC2A 4UQ.

ⓉⓅ**Everett Wong Limited** *(C H Everett)* 51 The Mall, Southgate, LONDON, N14 6LR.

Ⓔ**Everetts** *(S J Kay)* 86 Bury Old Road, Cheetham Village, MANCHESTER, M8 5BW.

ⓉⒶ**Evergreen** *(J S Bal)* 2 London Wall Buildings, London Wall, LONDON, EC2M 5UU.

Everitt, James & Co. *(D T Everitt)* 7 Ison Close, Biddenham, BEDFORD, MK40 4BH.

Ⓟ**Evolution Accounting, trading name of Evolution Accounting Limited** *(G L Kennaugh, C M Quayle)* West Suite, Ragnall House, 18 Peel Road, Douglas, ISLE OF MAN, IM1 4LZ.

ⓉⒺⒶ**Evolution Audit LLP** *(G Fitzgerald, J R Lindsay, J Regan)* 10 Evolution, Wynyard Park, BILLINGHAM, CLEVELAND, TS22 5TB.

Ⓔ**Evolution Business and Tax Advisors LLP** *(D S Burns, G A Fotheringham, R Priestman)* 10 Evolution, Wynyard Park, Wynyard, BILLINGHAM, CLEVELAND, TS22 5TB. and at HARTLEPOOL

Ⓟ**Evolve FD Ltd** *(D Ewing)* 11 North Road, LIVERPOOL, L19 0LP.

Ⓟ**Evolve, trading name of Evolve Legal Business Solutions Limited** *(J R P Miller)* 20 Bonville Chase, ALTRINCHAM, CHESHIRE, WA14 4QA.

Evolvement *(E J Riley, S Riley)* 12 The Vinery, New Longton, PRESTON, PR4 4YB.

Ewart Roots *(E H Roots)* Trethullan Cottage, Trethullan, Sticker, ST. AUSTELL, CORNWALL, PL26 7EH.

EWE, LOKE & PARTNERS *(P K Ewe)* 8 Robinson Road #08-800, ASO Building, SINGAPORE 048544, SINGAPORE.

Ⓟ**Ewing Commercial Brokers Ltd** *(J D Crawley)* 23 Keswick Avenue, Gatley, CHEADLE, CHESHIRE, SK8 4LE.

Ⓟ**Exalter, trading name of Exalter Limited** *(H Ijaz)* Second Floor, Berkeley Square House, Berkeley Square, LONDON, W1J 6BD.

ⒺⓅⒶ**Excalibur, trading name of DPR Accountancy Limited** *(S J Lawes, S M Lawes)* 3 Station Road, HAVERHILL, SUFFOLK, CB9 0EU.

ⒺⓅ**Exceed, trading name of Exceed UK Limited** *(A Phillips, G Visagie)* Bank House, 81 St Judes Road, Englefield Green, EGHAM, SURREY, TW20 0DF.

Excelsior CPA & Company *(W A Ip)* Unit 1, 15th Floor, Workingbond Commercial Centre, 162 Prince Edward Road West, CENTRAL, HONG KONG ISLAND HONG KONG SAR.

ⒺⓅ**Exigo Corporate Finance, trading name of Exigo Corporate Finance Limited** *(T M Williams)* Suite 1, 42 Triangle West, Park St, BRISTOL, BS8 1ES.

ⓅⒶ**Expecto Patronum Limited** *(M Fisher)* 1st Floor, Monument House, 215 Marsh Road, PINNER, MIDDLESEX, HA5 5NE.

Ⓟ**Expert Accountancy Limited** *(C G Foster)* 341 Lytham Road, BLACKPOOL, FY4 1DS.

EYOP LLP *(R D J Heath, T V Howard)* 1 More London Place, LONDON, SE1 2AF.

Ⓟ**F & A Consulting Limited** *(J Fellows)* 2 Dublin Crescent, Henleaze, BRISTOL, BS9 4NA.

Ⓟ**F & A Solutions, trading name of Creating Limited** *(C J Whiteley)* 93 New Road, MARLOW, BUCKINGHAMSHIRE, SL7 3NN.

Ⓔ**F A Kerin** *(F A Kerin)* 92 Woodgrange Avenue, North Finchley, LONDON, N12 0PS.

ⓅⒶ**F C Gillmore & Co Limited** *(F C Gillmore)* 198 Leesons Hill, CHISLEHURST, KENT, BR7 6QH.

F C Rees *(F C Rees)* Michaelmas, 13 Oatlands Chase, WEYBRIDGE, KT13 9RQ.

★**F E Metcalfe & Co** *(J L Crabtree, G L Evans)* 40A Market Place, RIPON, NORTH YORKSHIRE, HG4 1BZ.

F F Leach & Co *(W Sandford)* Oak Lodge, Beedon Hill, Beedon, NEWBURY, BERKSHIRE, RG20 8SJ.

F Kelly & Co *(F A Kelly)* 43 Carpenters Wood Drive, Chorleywood, RICKMANSWORTH, HERTFORDSHIRE, WD3 5RN.

F S Law & Co *(C Law)* Room 1315, Leighton Centre, 77 Leighton Road, CAUSEWAY BAY, HONG KONG SAR.

Ⓟ**F&L Expatriate Tax Consulting Limited** *(A H Law, G J Parrish)* 8 Lincoln's Inn Fields, LONDON, WC2A 3BP.

Ⓟ**F&L International Limited** *(A H Law, G J Parrish)* 8 Lincoln's Inn Fields, LONDON, WC2A 3BP.

F. Heaney *(F Heaney)* 22 Hillcrest Road, LOUGHTON, ESSEX, IG10 4QQ.

ⓉⒶ**F. Mazloomian & Co** *(F Mazloomian)* 73/75 Princess Street, MANCHESTER, M2 4EG.

F. Pittock & Co *(F Pittock)* Tremlett Villa, London Road, Pitsea, BASILDON, SS13 2DB.

F. Whitten *(F Whitten)* 29 High Street, Bridge, CANTERBURY, CT4 5JZ.

ⒺⒶ**F. Winter & Co LLP** *(H Khakhria, R Patel)* Ramillies House, 1-2 Ramillies Street, LONDON, W1F 7LN.

F.A. Dawoodkhan & Co *(F A Dawoodkhan)* 3 Wildacres, NORTHWOOD, HA6 3JD.

Ⓐ**F.A. Magee & Co.** *(A Davies, W S Davies)* Wimborne House, 4-6 Pump Lane, HAYES, MIDDLESEX, UB3 3NB.

F.Ahmed *(F Ahmed)* 232 Perth Road, ILFORD, ESSEX, IG2 6DY.

F.C.R. Moule & Co *(J K Sheppard)* Westminster Buildings, Theatre Square, NOTTINGHAM, NG1 6LG.

F.D. Earl *(F D Earl)* 3 Harvey Drive, SITTINGBOURNE, ME10 4UR.

ⒺⒶ**F.E. Sidaway, Son & Co** *(R F Homer, G F Sidaway, K J Sims)* 5-6 Long Lane, ROWLEY REGIS, B65 0JA.

Ⓐ**F.F. Leach & Co** *(D D Golton)* Kestrel House, 111 Heath Road, TWICKENHAM, TW1 4AH.

F.G. Kluyver *(F G Kluyver)* Moor End, Bridge Street, Lower Moor, PERSHORE, WORCESTERSHIRE, WR10 2PL.

ⒺⒶ**F.P. Delaunay** *(F P Delaunay)* 49 Beggarmans Lane, KNUTSFORD, WA16 9BA.

F.P. Johnson *(F P Johnson)* Suite 75, 24 St Leonards Road, WINDSOR, BERKSHIRE, SL4 3BB.

Ⓐ**F.P.Leach & Co** *(W M Scott)* Northumbria House, 62/64 Northumbria Drive, Henleaze, BRISTOL, BS9 4HW.

ⓉⓅⒶ**F.S. Dalal & Co, trading name of Blandfords & Co Limited** *(S Chaudhry)* 284 Station Road, HARROW, MIDDLESEX, HA1 2EA.

F.T. Giebel & Co *(F T Giebel)* 26 Menelik Road, LONDON, NW2 3RP.

ⒺⒶ**F.W. Berringer & Co** *(P Allan, J Cardnell, A G Foxwell, C J Raven, P Tymms)* Lygon House, 50 London Road, BROMLEY, BR1 3RA.

ⓉⒺⒶ**F.W. Smith, Riches & Co** *(D Crawford, A Jackson, M J Rooney)* 15 Whitehall, LONDON, SW1A 2DD.

F.W. Tyler *(F W Tyler)* 9 Colby Drive, Thurmaston, LEICESTER, LE4 8LD.

Ⓔ**Fact-S, trading name of Fact-Services LLP** *(L J Wills)* Brookwood, Paynes Green, Weare Street, Ockley, DORKING, SURREY RH5 5NH.

Ⓟ**Fadavi & Co Limited** *(M Fadavi-Ardekani)* 8b Accommodation Road, LONDON, NW11 8ED.

ⓅⒶ**FAI Audit Ltd** *(P J Chamberlain)* 142 Buckingham Palace Road, LONDON, SW1W 9TR.

Fairfax *(G Patston-Lilley)* 12 Malvern Close, SURBITON, KT6 7UG.

★ⓉⒺⒶ**Fairhurst** *(Peter J Cheetham, J Dennis, G Edgerton, J B S Fairhurst, P J Morris, R M Smith)* Douglas Bank House, Wigan Lane, WIGAN, WN1 2TB.

Fairlead Forensic Accounting *(P F Daniel)* Roseleigh, New Street, BANBURY, OX15 0SS.

ⓉⒶ**Fairman Davis** *(A R Virji)* Crown House, 72 Hammersmith Road, LONDON, W14 8TH.

ⓉⒶ**Fairman Law** *(I E Mawji, F Meghani, F G Ramji)* Fairman Law House, 1-3 Park Terrace, WORCESTER PARK, SURREY, KT4 7JZ.

ⓅⒶ**Faiz & Co, trading name of Faiz & Co Limited** *(B Faiz-Mahdavi)* 8b Accommodation Road, Golders Green, LONDON, NW11 8ED.

Ⓟ**Fala Accounting Limited** *(A T Ballantine)* Haughhead House, Fala Dam, PATHHEAD, MIDLOTHIAN, EH37 5SW.

ⓉⒺⓅⒶ**Fallows & Company, trading name of Guy Fallows Enterprises Limited** *(G R Fallows)* Archway House, 81-82 Portsmouth Road, SURBITON, SURREY, KT6 5PT.

Ⓟ**Farley Kaye Limited** *(F D Kaye)* Caradene, Gills Hill Lane, RADLETT, HERTFORDSHIRE, WD7 8DB.

ⓉⒺⒶ**Farmiloes LLP** *(C R Osborn, S Y C Poon, D K Purser, D R T Sara)* Winston Churchill House, 8 Ethel Street, BIRMINGHAM, B2 4BG.

ⓅⒶ**Farooq & Co, trading name of Farooq & Co (London) Limited** *(U Farooq)* Wembley Point, 1 Harrow Road, WEMBLEY, MIDDLESEX, HA9 6DE.

Farouk Ibrahim *(F Ibrahim)* 12 North Crescent, Finchley, LONDON, N3 3LL.

★**Farquhar Partnership LLP** *(A Farquhar)* Saville Court, Saville Place, Clifton, BRISTOL, BS8 4EJ.

Farrand & Co *(C E Farrand)* Canada Del Tejar 3, Alhaurin el Grande, 29120 MALAGA, SPAIN.

Ⓟ**Farrand-Laine Limited** *(C M Farrand-Laine)* 81 High Street, Little Paxton, ST. NEOTS, CAMBRIDGESHIRE, PE19 6QH.

ⓅⒶ**Farrar Smith, trading name of Farrar Smith Limited** *(J M Konczyk, C P Lydon, M W F Ringrose, P R Smith)* 2 Woodside Mews, Clayton Wood Close, LEEDS, LS16 6QE.

Ⓐ**Farrars** *(C Farrar, T E Farrar)* 8 Hillcrest Drive, LOUGHBOROUGH, LEICESTERSHIRE, LE11 2GX. and at LINCOLN

Ⓟ**Farrars, trading name of Farrars Limited** *(T E Farrar)* 8 Hillcrest Drive, LOUGHBOROUGH, LEICESTERSHIRE, LE11 2GX.

Ⓟ**Farrell & Co Accountants Limited** *(A Patel)* 11 Amberside House, Wood Lane, Paradise Industrial Estate, HEMEL HEMPSTEAD, HERTFORDSHIRE, HP2 4TP.

Farrell Accountants *(M D Farrell)* 175 Mead Way, BROMLEY, BR2 9ES.

Ⓟ**Farrow Accounting, trading name of Farrow Accounting & Tax Ltd** *(N C Farrow)* Worple Court, 94-95 South Worple Way, LONDON, SW14 8ND.

Ⓟ**Fast Accounting Services Limited** *(A E McCormick)* PO Box 803, Ampthill, BEDFORD, MK45 9AJ.

Faulkner Assoicates *(B S Faulkner)* The Maltings, 36 Beanacre, Hook Norton, BANBURY, OX15 5UA.

Ⓣ**Faust Loveday Bell LLP** *(G M Bell, G W Ryder)* 5 Curfew Yard, Thames Street, WINDSOR, BERKSHIRE, SL4 1SN.

★ⓉⒺⒶ**Fawcetts** *(R M V Allen, T Austreng, S J L Ellingham)* Windover House, St Ann Street, SALISBURY, SP1 2DR.

★**Fawley Judge & Easton** *(M W Marsden)* 1 Parliament Street, HULL, HU1 2AS.

Ⓟ**Fawthrop Williams** *(R H Fawthrop)* Old Buttermere Works, 15 Buttermere Road, SHEFFIELD, S7 2AX.

★Ⓣ**Fazal Mahmood & Company** *(F Mahmood)* 147 Shadman Colony 1, LAHORE 54000, PAKISTAN.

ⓉⒺⒶ**FBR McGarry Harvey** *(M E S Finlayson, R G Harvey)* 38-39 New Forest Enterprise Ctr, Rushington Business Park, Totton, SOUTHAMPTON, SO40 9LA.

Ⓟ**FC Partners CPA Limited** *(S Fok)* Room 1902-4, 19/F Rightful Centre, 11-12 Tak Hing High Street, TSIM SHA TSUI, KOWLOON, HONG KONG SAR.

Ⓟ**FCA Solutions, trading name of FCA Solutions Ltd** *(R C P Freeman)* 44 Kelling Way, Broughton, MILTON KEYNES, MK10 9NW.

Ⓟ**FCF Limited** *(J B S Fairhurst)* 11 Stoney Lane, Wrightington, WIGAN, LANCASHIRE, WN6 9QE.

FD Accounting Solutions *(J M G Richards)* New Nutwalls, Aylesbeare, EXETER, EX5 2JL.

Ⓟ**FD Management Services Limited** *(P E Wyatt)* New Inn Cottage, Dereham Road, Litcham, KING'S LYNN, PE32 2NT.

FD OnBoard *(J C Collett)* 36 Amherst Road, SEVENOAKS, KENT, TN13 3LS.

Ⓟ**FD Solutions, HR Director Solutions, trading names of DFM Limited** *(M G Durham, S H Walters)* 100 Fenchurch Street, LONDON, EC3M 5JD. and at BIRMINGHAM, BRISTOL, MANCHESTER

Ⓟ**FD-UK, trading name of Wellington Media Ltd** *(J M Wilkes)* 49 Rannoch Road, LONDON, W6 9SS.

ⒻⓅⒶ**Fearns Marriott Ltd** *(P Grindey, P Marriott)* Ford House, Market Street, LEEK, STAFFORDSHIRE, ST13 6JA.

★Ⓐ**Fearnside & Co** *(D J R Fearnside)* 6 Foundry Yard, Boroughbridge, YORK, YO51 9AX.

Feeley & Co *(M J E Cookson)* 11 Glenpark Drive, Hesketh Bank, PRESTON, PR4 6TA.

Feilding & Co *(P R Feilding)* Highfields, 11 Marlow Road, HIGH WYCOMBE, HP11 1TA.

Feingold & Co *(B D Adler)* 349 Bury Old Road, Prestwich, MANCHESTER, M25 1PY.

ⓉⒻⓅⒶ**Feist Hedgethorne, trading name of Feist Hedgethorne Limited** *(P R Feist, K R Hall, P J Hedgethorne, J C C Young)* Preston Park House, South Road, BRIGHTON, BN1 6SB.

ⓉⓅⒶ**FEL Accounts, trading name of FE Laughlin Ltd** *(F E Laughlin)* 23 The Crescent, WHITLEY BAY, TYNE AND WEAR, NE26 2JG.

Felix Chun Ning Leung *(F C N Leung)* 16027 Ventura Boulevard, Suite 400, ENCINO, CA 91436, UNITED STATES.

Felix Ng *(T W F Ng)* Dascom Technology Limited, Room 1811-12, Nan Fung Center, 298 Castle Peak Road, TSEUNG KWAN O, NEW TERRITORIES HONG KONG SAR.

Felix W.S. Lo & Co *(F W S Lo)* Room 810, HSH Mongkok Plaza, 794-802 Nathan Road, MONG KOK, KOWLOON, HONG KONG SAR.

Ⓟ**Felstra, trading name of Felstra Limited** *(S K Purohit)* Saunders House, 52-53 The Mall, LONDON, W5 3TA.

ⒻⒶ**Felton Associates** *(C L Stupack, R B Woolf)* 112 Wembley Park Drive, WEMBLEY, MIDDLESEX, HA9 8HS.

Ⓟ**Felton Associates Limited** *(C L Stupack, R B Woolf)* 112 Wembley Park Drive, WEMBLEY, MIDDLESEX, HA9 8HS.

ⓉⒶ**Felton Pumphrey, trading name of Feltons** *(R S Rhodes, J J Watts)* 12 Sheet Street, WINDSOR, SL4 1BG.

★ⓉⓅ**Felton Pumphrey, trading name of Feltons Limited** *(R S Rhodes, J J Watts)* 12 Sheet Street, WINDSOR, BERKSHIRE, SL4 1BG.

Ⓟ**Felton Pumphrey, trading name of LW Feltons Limited** *(R S Rhodes, J J Watts)* 12 Sheet Street, WINDSOR, BERKSHIRE, SL4 1BG.

ⓉⒻⓅⒶ**Felton Pumphrey, trading name of Pumphrey Dasalo Limited** *(D N E Alesbury, R J Carter, J A Hamblin, R S Rhodes, J J Watts)* 1 The Green, RICHMOND, SURREY, TW9 1PL.

ⓉⒻⓅⒶ**Feltons, trading name of Feltons (Bham) Limited** *(D W Farnsworth, J Powell)* 8 Sovereign Court, 8 Graham Street, BIRMINGHAM, B1 3JR.

Fenczuk & Co *(A J Fenczuk)* 6 Sefton Drive, WILMSLOW, SK9 4EL.

ⒻⒶ**Fenleys** *(S Fyles)* 1st Floor, 168 High Street, WATFORD, WD17 2EG.

Fenton & Co *(A Feigenbaum)* 7 Bancroft Avenue, LONDON, N2 0AR.

Ⓟ**Fenwick Advisory, trading name of Fenwick Advisory Limited** *(M A Fenwick)* 19 Tredelerch Road, Rumney, CARDIFF, CF3 3AJ.

Feore & Co. *(A B Feore)* 7 Ingram Avenue, AYLESBURY, BUCKINGHAMSHIRE, HP21 9DW.

ⓉⒻⒶ**Ferguson Maidment & Co** *(J Kamal, V Kapoor, A H E Smith)* Sardinia House, Sardinia Street, Lincolns Inn Fields, LONDON, WC2A 3LZ.

Ⓟ**Fergusson & Co Ltd** *(M E Fergusson)* 5-7 Northgate, CLECKHEATON, WEST YORKSHIRE, BD19 4LE. and at STOCKTON-ON-TEES

Fernandez *(S F Fernandez)* 35 Tudor Close, LONDON, NW3 4AG.

Fernley Nankivell *(F Nankivell)* 1 St. Pauls Road, NEWTON ABBOT, DEVON, TQ12 2HP.

★**Feroze Sharif & Co** *(F Qaiser)* 7-G, Block 6, P. E. C. H. S., KARACHI 75400, SINDH, PAKISTAN.

Ⓟ**Fetherstones, trading name of Fetherstones Ltd** *(S Bance)* 46a Station Road, North Harrow, HARROW, MIDDLESEX, HA2 7SE.

Ⓟ**FFM, trading name of Fellows Financial Management Limited** *(C Fellows, R T Fellows)* 10 Hall Lane, KETTERING, NORTHAMPTONSHIRE, NN15 7LJ.

FGS Accountancy & Taxation *(F G Sagoo)* 39 Woodland Way, Theydon Bois, EPPING, ESSEX, CM16 7DY.

ⓉⒻⒶ**Fiander Tovell LLP** *(D Harper, P F Meacher, J C Mills, A C Quicke, C Revis)* Stag Gates House, 63/64 The Avenue, SOUTHAMPTON, SO17 1XS.

Ⓟ**Fidelico Limited** *(C Economides)* G Pavlides Court, 5th Floor, 2 Arch Kyprianou & Ayiou Andreou Street, 3036 LIMASSOL, CYPRUS.

Fidentia, trading name of Fidentia Services LLP *(M J Argyle, M T Hindmarch)* Duncan & Toplis, 3 Castlegate, GRANTHAM, LINCOLNSHIRE, NG31 6SF.

★**Fidirevisa Italia S.P.A** *(M E Golding)* Via Senato 12, 20121 MILAN, ITALY.

Ⓟ**Fieldwick Kemsley & Partners Limited** *(D M Fieldwick)* 12 Heathfield South, TWICKENHAM, TW2 7SS.

Ⓟ**Fifty Business Services Ltd** *(M A C Evans)* 5th Floor, 63 St Mary Axe, LONDON, EC3A 8AA.

★**Fikri & Co** *(A T Fikri)* Ali Tanner Fikri Building, Kyrenia Avenue No.78, LEFKOSA MERSIN 10, TURKEY.

★ⓉⒻⒶ**Filer Knapper LLP** *(S Ellson, L J Filer)* 10 Bridge Street, CHRISTCHURCH, DORSET, BH23 1EF.

Finacc *(O A Rawat)* 3rd Floor PCL Building, 43 Sir William Newton Street, PORT LOUIS, MAURITIUS.

Finance and Management Consulting *(P J W Smith)* 32 Belle Vue Avenue, Gosforth, NEWCASTLE UPON TYNE, NE3 1AH.

ⒻⓅⒶ**Finance Associates Limited** *(E S Steiner)* 65 London Wall, LONDON, EC2M 5TU.

Ⓟ**Finance Directors Ltd** *(A N Lamb)* 14 The Droveway, Lucastes Lane, HAYWARDS HEATH, RH16 1LL.

Finance Mix LLP *(P G Atkinson)* The Innovation Centre, Innovation Way, Heslington, YORK, YO10 5DG.

Ⓟ**Financial Advisory Services and Training Limited** *(L S Hodgson)* PO Box 4182, Boulevard de l'Umuganda, KIGALI, RWANDA.

ⓅⒶ**Financial Angels Ltd** *(S K R Tulsidas)* 7 Plaza Parade, Maida Vale, LONDON, NW6 5RP.

Ⓟ**Financial Consulting & Accounting Ltd** *(J S Nicholson)* Grosvenors Square, Unit 3-213, 23 Lime Tree Bay Avenue, PO Box 1976, GEORGE TOWN, GRAND CAYMAN CAYMAN ISLANDS.

Financial Consulting Services *(M S Konfortion)* 3rd Floor Cerne House, La Chaussee, PORT LOUIS, MAURITIUS.

Financial Direction *(J R H Perkins)* Unit 1C, Membury Logistics Centre, Ramsbury Road, Lambourn Woodlands, HUNGERFORD, BERKSHIRE RG17 7TJ.

Financial Direction, trading name of Malcolm Wilton & Co. *(M C Wilton)* Ty Gwyn, Catbrook, CHEPSTOW, NP16 6ND.

Financial Forensics LLP *(D A Small, R M Stow)* 6 Snow Hill, LONDON, EC1A 2AY. and at BRIGHTON

Ⓟ**Financial Management Solutions, trading name of Financial Management Solutions UK Limited** *(S J Bentley)* 42a High Street, SUTTON COLDFIELD, B72 1UJ.

Ⓟ**Financial Planners Co UK Limited** *(B E Keates FIFP CFP)* Studio 3, Waterside Court, Third Avenue Centrum 100, BURTON-ON-TRENT, DE14 2WQ.

Ⓐ**Financial Professional Support Services, trading name of Financial Professional Support Services LLP** *(S J Cramer, K R Malcouronne, E J Noble)* The Old Church, Quicks Road, Wimbledon, LONDON, SW19 1EX.

Ⓟ**Financial Progression Limited** *(A L T Jenkins)* 16 Marlin Court, MARLOW, BUCKINGHAMSHIRE, SL7 2AJ.

Financial Project Consulting *(A W Jones)* Egerton House, Chilton Business Park, Chilton, AYLESBURY, BUCKINGHAMSHIRE, HP18 9LS.

Financial Reporting Services *(H L Hughes)* 1a Main Street, Thornton, COALVILLE, LEICESTERSHIRE, LE67 1AF.

Financial Support for Schools *(T Peplinski)* High Trees, Ty'r Winch Road, Old St. Mellons, CARDIFF, CF3 5UW.

Ⓟ**Finansure Limited** *(R M Dillamore)* The Stables Offices, Stansty Park, Summerhill Road, WREXHAM, CLWYD, LL11 4YW.

ⓅⒶ**Finch House Properties Limited** *(V Brassington, C Cooper, N C Davis, S Garrington, F J McKay, D E Price, P C Rayney, K A Turner, A Williams)* Finch House, 28-30 Wolverhampton Street, DUDLEY, WEST MIDLANDS, DY1 1DB.

Ⓟ**Finch Lynton, trading name of Finch Lynton Limited** *(R J Stebbings)* 2/4 Ash Lane, Rustington, LITTLEHAMPTON, WEST SUSSEX, BN16 3BZ.

Findlay James *(A J F Findlay)* Saxon House, Saxon Way, CHELTENHAM, GLOUCESTERSHIRE, GL52 6QX. and at BOURNEMOUTH, CANTERBURY, DARLINGTON, EASTBOURNE, ELY, EXETER, LEICESTER, MAIDSTONE, MANSFIELD, NEWCASTLE, NORTHWICH, PLYMOUTH, READING, SHIPLEY, SOUTHEND-ON-SEA, ST. HELENS, YORK

ⓉⒻⒶ**Findlay, Wetherfield, Scott & Co** *(K Hopson)* 135/137 Station Road, Chingford, LONDON, E4 6AG.

Ⓐ**Finer Heymann LLP** *(I M Finer, R Heymann)* Premier House, 112 Station Road, EDGWARE, HA8 7BJ.

ⒻⒶ**Finerty Brice** *(N A Brice, B F Finerty)* Endeavour House, 78 Stafford Road, WALLINGTON, SM6 9AY.

Finite *(S Jalaf)* 88 Burnley Road, Dollis Hill, LONDON, NW10 1EH.

ⒻⓅⒶ**Finlay Robertson, trading name of Finrob Limited** *(N C P Bird, R S Owen)* Suite 5b, Brook House, 77 Fountain Street, MANCHESTER, M2 2EE.

Ⓟ**Finn Associates, trading name of Finn Associates (Businesscare) Limited** *(P H Finn)* Central Administration, Tong Hall, Tong Lane, BRADFORD, WEST YORKSHIRE, BD4 0RR. and at LONDON

ⒻⒶ**Finnemores** *(J M Finnemore)* 10 St Edwards Walk, Charlton Kings, CHELTENHAM, GL53 7RS.

Ⓟ**Finnemores Ltd** *(J M Finnemore)* 10 St. Edwards Walk, Charlton Kings, CHELTENHAM, GLOUCESTERSHIRE, GL53 7RS.

ⒻⓅⒶ**Finnieston Berry Partnership Limited** *(E L Berry, C M Finnieston)* Europa House, 72-74 Northwood Street, BIRMINGHAM, B3 1TT.

Ⓟ**Fino Accounting, trading name of Fino Limited** *(D Z Webb)* 29 Cleveleys Avenue, ROCHDALE, LANCASHIRE, OL16 4PD.

Fintax *(S Fayyaz)* 2 Hebe Court, Montpelier Road, SUTTON, SURREY, SM1 4PE.

Ⓟ**Fintech, trading name of Fintech Associates Limited** *(C P Scanlon)* Ballards, Jobs Lane, MAIDENHEAD, BERKSHIRE, SL6 9TX.

Finton Doyle *(M T Forshaw)* Preston Technology Centre, Marsh Lane, PRESTON, PR1 8UQ.

Fiona *(F F Fraser)* 33 Talisker Place, PERTH, PH1 3GW.

Fiona Curry & Co *(F A Curry)* 9 Crookfur Road, Newton Mearns, GLASGOW, G77 6DY.

Fiona E Davies *(F E Ellwood)* 3 Barton Common Lane, NEW MILTON, HAMPSHIRE, BH25 5PS.

Fiona Evans *(F L Evans)* 11 Perches Close, Membland, Newton Ferrers, PLYMOUTH, PL8 1HZ.

Fiona Wilkinson *(F H Wilkinson)* Little Churchill, Whimple, EXETER, EX5 2PE.

Ⓟ**Firmvalue Payrolls Ltd** *(M J Dickinson, R A Lock, S M South, R F Wise)* Wey Court, Union Road, FARNHAM, SURREY, GU9 7PT.

Ⓟ**First Class Accounting.com, trading name of First Class Accounting Limited** *(M I Lewis)* Suite 15, 20 Churchill Square, Kings Hill, WEST MALLING, KENT, ME19 4YU.

★**First Payroll & Accounting** *(R A Brown, T Rose)* Star House, 8 Star Hill, ROCHESTER, KENT, ME1 1UX.

FirstFD *(J P Frost)* Greengables, Peterston-super-Ely, CARDIFF, CF5 6LH.

ⓉⒻⒶ**Firth Parish** *(G Beaumont, L R Brain, S Hudson)* 1 Airport West, Lancaster Way, Yeadon, LEEDS, LS19 7ZA.

Ⓟ**Fiscal Solutions Ltd** *(A.De Lacey, M P Farmar, A K Savjani)* 130 Wood Street, LONDON, EC2V 6DL.

Ⓟ**Fiscalis, trading name of Fiscalis Management Ltd** *(P Edwards)* Dunraven House, 6 Meadow Court, 41-43 High Street, WITNEY, OX28 6ER.

★ⓉⒶ**Fish Partnership LLP** *(M J Sheehy)* The Mill House, Boundary Road, Loudwater, HIGH WYCOMBE, BUCKINGHAMSHIRE, HP10 9QN.

★ⒻⓅⒶ**Fisher & Company Limited** *(P Fisher)* Kingfisher House, 65 Market Place, Market Weighton, YORK, YO43 3AN.

Ⓟ**Fisher Corporate plc** *(P A C Beber, P A Beer, C J Hazard, G A Miller)* Acre House, 11/15 William Road, LONDON, NW1 3ER.

★ⓉⒻⒶ**Fisher Forensic, Fisher Partners, trading names of H W Fisher & Company** *(P A C Beber, P A Beer, A J Bernstein, D L Birne, D W Breger, S Burns, J S Challis, M B Davis, C J Hazard, A K Lester, B Lindsey, S P Mehta, G A Miller, S M Mott-Cowan, R Nathan, A R W Parfitt, A G Rich, N S Samani, R A Saville, D S Selwyn, N N Siganporia, A Subramaniam, M A Taylor, N J Thaker, J S Trent)* Acre House, 11-15 William Road, LONDON, NW1 3ER. and at WATFORD

Ⓐ**Fisher Michael** *(N Carpenter, A S Kaley, N Shaw)* Boundary House, 4 County Place, New London Road, CHELMSFORD, CM2 0RE.

Ⓟ**Fisher Ng, trading name of Fisher Ng Limited** *(L M Ng)* 2 Kings Road, London Colney, ST. ALBANS, HERTFORDSHIRE, AL2 1EN.

ⓉⒻⒶ**Fisher Phillips** *(S P Frost, G R Ornstein, P P Sykes, R Ward, A K Woricker)* Summit House, 170 Finchley Road, LONDON, NW3 6BP.

Ⓟ**Fisher Phillips 2010 Ltd** *(S P Frost, G R Ornstein, P P Sykes, R Ward, A K Woricker)* Summit House, 170 Finchley Road, LONDON, NW3 6BP.

Ⓕ**Fisher Wilkinson** *(D J Fisher, A K Wilkinson)* 44 Cheltenham Mount, HARROGATE, HG1 1DL.

ⓉⒻⒶ**Fisher, Sassoon & Marks** *(J Marks, A Rose, N P Rose)* 43-45 Dorset Street, LONDON, W1U 7NA.

Ⓟ**FisherEase Limited** *(D W Breger, M B Davis, M K Shah, A Subramaniam, N J Thaker)* Acre House, 3-5 Hyde Road, WATFORD, WD17 4WP.

Ⓟ**Fisk & Co, trading name of Dallas (East Anglia) Ltd** *(A J Bailey)* 42 Wright Lane, Kesgrave, IPSWICH, IP5 2FA.

ⓉⒻⒶ**Fitzgerald and Law LLP** *(A H Law, G J Parrish)* 8 Lincoln's Inn Fields, LONDON, WC2A 3BP. and at SAN FRANCISCO

★**Fitzgerald Mithia** *(A J Fitzgerald)* Newgate House, 431 London Road, CROYDON, CR0 3PF.

▽**Fitzgerald Power** *(M Hill)* Greyfriars, WATERFORD, COUNTY WATERFORD, IRELAND. and at DUBLIN

Fitzgeralds *(T J Fitzgerald)* 40 Ringford Road, LONDON, SW18 1RR.

Fitzpatrick *(W J Fitzpatrick)* 88 Church Road, HOLYWOOD, COUNTY DOWN, BT18 9BX.

Ⓟ**Fitzpatrick & Kearney Ltd** *(M Reynolds)* 10 Marcus Square, NEWRY, COUNTY DOWN, BT34 1AE.

Fitzpatrickroyle *(J C Fitzpatrick, J Royle)* 105 Moorside North, Fenham, NEWCASTLE UPON TYNE, NE4 9DY. and at NORTH SHIELDS

Fiveoaks Accountancy Services *(A D Rennie)* Fiveoaks, Gatelawbridge, THORNHILL, DUMFRIESSHIRE, DG3 5EA.

Ⓟ**Fixedfeetaxreturn.co.uk, uk-tax-return.co.uk, uklandlordtax.co.uk, trading names of Thandi Nicholls Ltd** *(K W Nicholls)* Wolverhampton Science Park, Creative Industries Centre, Glaisher Drive, WOLVERHAMPTON, WV10 9TG.

Ⓟ**Fizz Accounting Limited** *(G J Lovett, J E Park)* Meteor House, Eastern Bypass, THAME, OXFORDSHIRE, OX9 3RL.

Ⓕ**FJA** *(F Anayi)* 1 Shalford Road, GUILDFORD, SURREY, GU1 3XL.

FL Tang & Company *(K Cheung)* 12/F, Yat Chau Building, 262 Des Voeux Road Central, CENTRAL, HONG KONG SAR.

Flanders & Company *(J B Flanders)* Bunkers, 8 Ladycroft Paddock, Allestree, DERBY, DE22 2GA.

Ⓟ**Flannagans, trading name of MD Accountants Ltd** *(T M Flannagan)* Frederick House, Dean Group Business Park, Brenda Road, HARTLEPOOL, CLEVELAND, TS25 2BW.

Flanton & Co *(F Liu)* Second Floor, Berkeley Square House, Berkeley Square, LONDON, W1J 6BD.

Flavelle & Co *(C Flavelle)* Penventinnie Barn, TRURO, CORNWALL, TR4 9EG.

Flaxton Ventures LLP *(R W Smedley)* Oakford House, 291 Low Lane, Horsforth, LEEDS, LS18 5NU.

Ⓟ**FLC, trading name of F L Consultancy Ltd** *(C F Lim)* 63 Greenway, Totteridge, LONDON, N20 8EL. and at BARNET

ⓉⒶ**Flemmings** *(H C Shah, S Shah, S P Shah)* 76 Canterbury Road, CROYDON, SURREY, CR0 3HA.

Ⓟ**Flemons & Co Limited** *(J D Groves)* 70 Priory Road, KENILWORTH, WARWICKSHIRE, CV8 1LQ.

Fletcher & Co *(S Fletcher)* 25 York Close, Freshfield, LIVERPOOL, L37 7HZ.

ⓉⒻⒶ**Fletcher & Partners** *(J Fletcher, N A Halls, P A Proctor, M F Tompsett)* Crown Chambers, Bridge Street, SALISBURY, SP1 2LZ.

ⒻⒶ**Fletcher Greenwood & Co** *(I J Fletcher)* 11-13 Broad Street, BRADFORD, WEST YORKSHIRE, BD1 4QT.

Fletcher Naessens *(A C Fletcher)* 4 Copperfield Way, CHISLEHURST, BR7 6RY.

Ⓕ**Fletcher Thompson** *(K J Fletcher)* Mill House, 21 High Street, Wicken, ELY, CAMBRIDGESHIRE, CB7 5XR.

ⓉⒶ**Fletchers** *(C M Fletcher)* Albion House, 163-167 King Street, DUKINFIELD, CHESHIRE, SK16 4LF.

ⒻⓅⒶ**Flint & Thompson, trading name of Flint & Thompson Limited** *(D H Neville, M D Williams)* 1325A Stratford Road, Hall Green, BIRMINGHAM, WEST MIDLANDS, B28 9HL.

ⓉⒻⒶ**Flinthams** *(A L McCartney)* 277-279 Chiswick High Road, Chiswick, LONDON, W4 4PU.

Ⓟ**Fluency Solutions Limited** *(A L Boronte, J A Brown, R M Rothenberg)* Regents Park, 12 York Gate, LONDON, NW1 4QS.

▽**FM Associates** *(B E Thorp)* 49 Newall Terrace, DUMFRIES, DG1 1LN.

★ⓉⒻⒶ**FMCB** *(S N Freeda, G W Zeiderman, J D Zinkin)* Hathaway House, Popes Drive, Finchley, LONDON, N3 1QF.

Ⓟ**Focus Accounting, trading name of Focus Accounting Limited** *(P S Wragg)* Unit 9, Basepoint Waterlooville, waterberry drive, WATERLOOVILLE, HAMPSHIRE, PO7 7Th.

Ⓟ**Focus Systems Development Ltd** *(R I Payne)* 4 Ravens House, Charter Quay, KINGSTON UPON THAMES, SURREY, KT1 1HR.

Ⓟ**Fok Chan Leung Wan CPA Ltd** *(S W Leung)* Rooms 904-8 & 403-4, Kai Tak Commercial Building, 317-319 Des Voeux Road, CENTRAL, HONG KONG ISLAND, HONG KONG SAR.

Foley & Co *(M J M Foley)* 44A Oriental Road, WOKING, GU22 7AR.

Ⓐ**Folkes Worton & Wood** *(A A Walker)* 56-58A Warwick Road, KENILWORTH, WARWICKSHIRE, CV8 1HH.

Ⓟ**Folkes Worton & Wood ltd** *(S K Jones, A A Walker)* 56-58 Warwick Road, KENILWORTH, WARWICKSHIRE, CV8 1HH.

ⓉⒻⒶ**Folkes Worton LLP** *(N H Meredith, N C Smith)* 15-17 Church Street, STOURBRIDGE, WEST MIDLANDS, DY8 1LU.

★Ⓣ**Folks DFK & Co** *(P L Khoo)* 12th Floor, Wisma Tun Sambanthan, No. 2 Jalan Sultan Sulaiman, 50000 KUALA LUMPUR, FEDERAL TERRITORY, MALAYSIA.

Folorunso Olaleye & Co *(F A Kasumu-Olaleye)* 17th Floor(Right Wing), Western House, 8-10 Broad Street, LAGOS, NIGERIA.

Foo Kon & Tan *(S Leong)* 1st Floor Unit No 15, Lot 7191Bgn Haji Hassa, Hj Abd. Ghani Dan Anak-anak, Jalan Jaya Negara, Kg Pandan, KUALA BELAIT KA 1931 BRUNEI DARUSSALAM. and at BANDAR SERI BEGAWAN

★Ⓣ**Foo Kon Tan Grant Thornton LLP** *(S B Chin)* 47 Hill Street, 5th Fl. Unit 01, Chinese Chamber of Comm & Industry Bldg, SINGAPORE 179365, SINGAPORE.

Foot & Ellis-Smith *(I E Foot, S P Mitchell)* Abacus House, 68A North Street, ROMFORD, RM1 1DA.

ⓅⒶ**Foot & Ellis-Smith, trading name of Foot & Ellis-Smith Ltd** *(I E Foot, S P Mitchell)* Abacus House, 68A North Street, ROMFORD, RM1 1DA.

ⓉⒶ**Foot Davson** *(T T Clay, R W D Foot)* 17 Church Road, TUNBRIDGE WELLS, TN1 1LG.

ⓉⓅ**Forbes, trading name of Forbes Ltd** *(J D Forbes)* Suite 5, Melville House, High Street, DUNMOW, ESSEX, CM6 1AF.

Ⓟ**Forbes-Cable Ltd** *(J M Forbes-Cable)* 8 Albert Place, ABERDEEN, AB25 1RG.

ⓅⒶ**Ford & Co, Guy Rastall Financial Services, KPS, Raymarsh Ford, trading names of Raymarsh Ford Limited** *(C B Ford)* Ground Floor, 41 High Street, Kingswood, BRISTOL, BS15 4AA.

Ⓟ**Ford Campbell Corporate Finance LLP** *(N H Blake, D A Cheetham, A J Ford, C J Froggatt, A J Richardson, N W Worsley)* Bass Warehouse, 4 Castle Street, Castlefield, MANCHESTER, M3 4LZ.

Ⓟ**Ford Campbell Corporate Finance Ltd** *(N H Blake, D A Cheetham, C J Froggatt)* Ford Campbell Corporate Finance LLP, Bass Warehouse, 4 Castle Street, Castlefield, MANCHESTER, M3 4LZ.

ⓉⒻⒶ**Ford Campbell Freedman LLP** *(J Barnard, J R Butcher, A J Ford, K M Frisby)* 34 Park Cross Street, LEEDS, LS1 2QH.

Ford, Bull, Watkins *(L Barry, W G Wonacott)* Clerks Well House, 20 Britton Street, LONDON, EC1M 5TU.

★ⒻⒶ**Fordhams & Co** *(M Akhtaruzzaman, I F Nurbhai)* Second Floor, 61 Old Street, LONDON, EC1V 9HX.

Forecast Flow *(L E Munday)* 107 New Road, CHATTERIS, CAMBRIDGESHIRE, PE16 6BT.

Ⓟ**Foremans Company Services Ltd** *(A L Ensor)* Clayton House, Sandpiper Court, Chester Business Park, CHESTER, CH4 9QU.

Foremans LLP *(A L Ensor)* Clayton House, Sandpiper Court, Chester Business Park, CHESTER, CH4 9QU.

Forensic Accounting Services *(B W Draper)* 1st Floor Aztec Centre, Aztec West, Almondsbury, BRISTOL, BS32 4TD.

★**Forensic Accounting Solutions** *(S L Segal)* 315 Regents Park Road, Finchley, LONDON, N3 1DP. and at MANCHESTER

Foreshore Accountancy *(N L Cordle, L E Golding)* Balmoral, Shotley Road, Chelmondiston, IPSWICH, IP9 1EE.

★**Forrest & Co** *(P A Forrest)* 30 Heron Close, BLACKBURN, BB1 8NU.

ⓉⒶ**Forrest Burlinson** *(C S B Sheard, E Suleman)* 20 Owl Lane, DEWSBURY, WEST YORKSHIRE, WF12 7RQ.

Ⓟ**Forrest Consultancy Ltd** *(P A Forrest)* 30 Heron Close, BLACKBURN, BB1 8NU.

Ⓕ**Forrester & Co.** *(N Forrester)* 33 Graham Road, MALVERN, WR14 2HU.

Ⓟ**Forrester & Company (Malvern) Limited** *(N Forrester)* 33 Graham Road, MALVERN, WORCESTERSHIRE, WR14 2HU.

★ⓉⒶ**Forrester Boyd** *(M A Beckett, S A Czornyj, N Ellis, D J Everatt, P S Fearn, S A Fields, K S Hopper, C P Hunt, A G Nesbitt, T I Robinson, M R G Smith, N A Williams)* 26 South Saint Mary's Gate, GRIMSBY, NORTH LINCOLNSHIRE, DN31 1LW. and at LOUTH, SCUNTHORPE

Forresters *(W J Sheppard)* 8 Gayton Road, Lower Heswall, WIRRAL, CH60 8PE.

ⒻⒶ**Forshaws** *(A K Goddard, M B Solomon, H K C Thakkar)* Railex Business Centre, Crossens Way, Marine Drive, SOUTHPORT, MERSEYSIDE, PR9 9LY.

ⒻⒶ**Forster, Stott & Co** *(L P Bean, S J Kilmartin, I W Wallace)* Langton House, 124 Acomb Road, Holgate, YORK, NORTH YORKSHIRE, YO24 4EY. and at THIRSK

ⓉⓅ**Forths Forensic Accountants, trading name of Forth Associates Ltd** *(R I E Forth)* The Station, 77 Canal Road, LEEDS, LS12 2LX. and at MANCHESTER

Ⓟ**Fortisratio Limited** *(R A Brown, T Rose)* Star House, 8 Star Hill, ROCHESTER, KENT, ME1 1UX.

Fortune Hart *(L J Fortune)* Green Hay Barn, Pershall, Eccleshall, STAFFORD, ST21 6NE.

Ⓕ**Forty-Two Consulting LLP** *(N G Jones)* Percivals Barn, Fairfield Farm, Upper Weald, MILTON KEYNES, MK19 6EL.

Ⓟ**Forward Financial Accounting, trading name of Forward Financial Accounting Ltd** *(S W Ainley)* Catalyst House, 720 Centennial Court, Centennial Park, Elstree, BOREHAMWOOD, HERTFORDSHIRE WD6 3SY.

Ⓟ**Forward Financials, trading name of Forward Financials Ltd** *(R Singh)* Kemp House, 152-160 City Road, LONDON, EC1V 2NX.

Forwil Services, trading name of J R Palmer *(J R Palmer)* 16 The Crescent, Colwall, MALVERN, WR13 6QN.

Foskett & Co. *(C J C Foskett)* Beechcroft, Northleigh Lane, Colehill, WIMBORNE, BH21 2PN.

Foster & Co *(L R Foster)* 144 Malvern Avenue, NUNEATON, CV10 8NB.

Foster & Co *(B A Foster)* Foxbourne Business Centre, Heath Mill Close, Wombourne, WOLVERHAMPTON, WV5 8EX.

ⓅⒶ**Foster & Co, trading name of Foster & Co Ltd** *(N W Atkin, J K Foster)* 80 Lytham Road, Fulwood, PRESTON, PR2 3AQ.

Ⓕ**Foster & Company** *(A T Foster)* 5 South Terrace, Moorgate, ROTHERHAM, S60 2EU.

★**Foster Lewis Stone** *(M L Lewis)* 302-308 Preston Road, HARROW, HA3 0QP.

Ⓣ**Fosters** *(H D Foster)* Unit 3, Friends School, Low Green Rawdon, LEEDS, LS19 6HB.

ⓉⓅⒶ**FOTAS, trading name of Four Oaks Taxation & Accounting Services Limited** *(M J Rudd)* Suite D, Astor House, 282 Lichfield Road, SUTTON COLDFIELD, WEST MIDLANDS, B74 2UG.

Ⓟ**Fouette Accountancy Solutions Limited** *(K Grice)* White Rose House, 5 Walnut Grove, Cotgrave, NOTTINGHAM, NG12 3AU.

Ⓟ**Fountain Accountancy Limited** *(R D P Jones, D G Roberts)* Great Western House, The Sidings, Chester Street, Saltney, CHESTERFIELD, CH4 8RD.

ⓅⒶ**four fifty (holdings) Limited** *(J R Boswell, N J B Gravell, P K Ison)* 34 Boulevard, WESTON-SUPER-MARE, AVON, BS23 1NF.

ⓉⒻⓅⒶ**Four Fifty Partnership Limited** *(J R Boswell, N J B Gravell, P K Ison)* 34 Boulevard, WESTON-SUPER-MARE, AVON, BS23 1NF. and at CHEDDAR

Four J's *(R D James)* 46 Chester Road, Stockton Heath, WARRINGTON, CHESHIRE, WA4 QRX.

ⓉⓅ**Fourways, trading name of Fourways 4 Business Ltd** *(R N C Matthews)* 1a Melbourn Street, ROYSTON, HERTFORDSHIRE, SG8 7BP.

Ⓟ**Fourwood Services Limited** *(G Reid-Marr)* 18 Cedar Drive, Barming, MAIDSTONE, KENT, ME16 9HD.

Fowler & Co *(V Steer-Fowler)* 1st Floor Norton House, 41 Arbory Street, Castletown, ISLE OF MAN, IM9 1LL.

Ⓟ**Fowler & Co, trading name of Competex Ltd** *(C R S Fowler)* Orchard House, Park Lane, REIGATE, SURREY, RH2 8JX.

ⓉⒻ**Fowler & Hare** *(P E H Fowler)* Pennant House, Glyndwr, LLANGEFNI, LL77 7EF.

Fowler & Trembling *(R C Fowler, M P Trembling)* 2 Forge Close, Chipperfield, KINGS LANGLEY, WD4 9DL. and at ST. ALBANS

ⒻⓅⒶ**Fox & Co (Accountants) Ltd** *(I Gilbert)* Atticus House, 2 The Windmills, Turk Street, ALTON, HAMPSHIRE, GU34 1EF.

ⒻⓅ**Fox & Co (Anglia) Limited** *(A M Fox)* The Priory, Church Street, DEREHAM, NORFOLK, NR19 1DW.

Fox & Company *(B G Fox)* 15 Merton Avenue, Hartley, LONGFIELD, DA3 7EB.

ⒻⒶ**Fox Associate, trading name of Fox Associate LLP** *(H Fox)* Britannic House, 17 Highfield Road, LONDON, NW11 9LS. and at DERBY

ⓉⒻⓅⒶ**Fox Evans, trading name of Fox Evans Limited** *(R Anderson, J A Banbrook, J M Higgitt, M R McLean)* Abbey House, 7 Manor Road, COVENTRY, CV1 2FW.

ⓅⒶ**Fox Jennings, trading name of A & R Accountancy Limited** *(A D Ormondroyd)* Tarn House, 77 High Street, Yeadon, LEEDS, LS19 7SP.

Ⓟ**Fox Reynard Ltd** *(S J Fox)* PO Box 963, AYLESBURY, HP22 9JL.

ⒻⒶ**Fox Sharer LLP** *(A E Sharer)* Britannic House, 17 Highfield Road, LONDON, NW11 9LS.

★**Foxborough Consulting** *(S R Edwards, A J Parsons)* 30 Camp Road, FARNBOROUGH, HAMPSHIRE, GU14 6EW.

★Ⓟ**Foxleigh Knight & Co, trading name of Foxleigh Knight & Co Limited** *(J L G Smith)* PO BOX 162, Ground Floor, Anley House, 5 Anley Street, St. Helier, JERSEY JE4 5NZ.

Foxley Kingham Medical, trading name of Foxley Kingham Medical LLP *(P M Bithrey, C L Howe, S R Mason)* Prospero House, 46-48 Rothesay Road, LUTON, LU1 1QZ.

★ⓉⒻⓅⒶ**Foxley Kingham, trading name of FKCA Limited** *(P M Bithrey, C L Howe, S R Mason)* Prospero House, 46-48 Rothesay Road, LUTON, LU1 1QZ.

Ⓟ**Foxmain Associates Limited** *(J P Fuge)* 60 Stoke Lane, Westbury-on-Trym, BRISTOL, BS9 3SW.

Ⓟ**FPSS Ltd** *(S J Cramer, K R Malcouronne)* The Old Church, Quicks Road, Wimbledon, LONDON, SW19 1EX.

★**Frampton Pitt** *(J M Pitt)* 19 York Road, NORTHAMPTON, NN1 5QG.

Frances A Haynes *(F A Haynes)* 1 Church Hill Road, Hooe, PLYMOUTH, PL9 9SE.

Ⓟ**Franchise Logistics Ltd** *(A Needham)* Waterside House, Station Road, Mexborough, ROTHERHAM, S64 9AQ.

Ⓟ**Francis & Co, trading name of Francis & Co Limited** *(W B Francis)* Festival House, Jessop Avenue, CHELTENHAM, GLOUCESTERSHIRE, GL50 3SH.

ⓅⒶ**Francis & Co, trading name of W Francis & Co Ltd** *(W B Francis)* Festival House, Jessop Avenue, CHELTENHAM, GLOUCESTERSHIRE, GL50 3SH.

Francis & Co. *(G E Francis)* 100 Clarence Road, LONDON, E5 8HB.

Ⓟ**Francis Clark Tax Consultancy Ltd** *(L M Burnett, M S Clark, P A Collings, S M Probyn, A H Richards)* Sigma House, Oak View Close, Edginswell Park, TORQUAY, TQ2 7FF.

★ⒻⒶ**Francis Clark, Francis Clark with Winter Rule, trading names of Francis Clark LLP** *(A G Allen, L J Banfield, R M T Beard, L M Bennett, M S Bentley, I L Burnard, L M Burnett, C J Bush, M S Clark, P B M Cliff, P A Collings, C G Cooke, N S Cowen, R R Cowie, J L Endacott, C D Evans, P C Giessler, N H W Gooch, M A Greaves, S A Grinsted, S J Henshaw, C L Hicks, S J Hobson, R J Hussey, R I Kennedy, D E Lannon, M P Lock, J M Michelmore, J P Mitchell, S M Probyn, A H Richards, T W Roach, J N Rowe, P Serjeant, J G Talbot, J A Towers)* Sigma House, Oak View Close, Edginswell Park, TORQUAY, TQ2 7FF. and at EXETER, PLYMOUTH, SALISBURY, TAUNTON, TAVISTOCK, TRURO

ⒻⓅⒶ**Francis Gray, trading name of Francis Gray Limited** *(R J Gray, A R Whitney)* Ty Madog, 32 Queens Road, ABERYSTWYTH, DYFED, SY23 2HN.

Francis HL Sham & Co *(H F Sham)* Room 1416, 14/F, Hollywood Plaza, 610 Nathan Road, MONG KOK, KOWLOON HONG KONG SAR.

Ⓟ**Francis J Woods & Company Limited** *(A C Milsom)* Balbriggan Business Campus, BALBRIGGAN, COUNTY DUBLIN, IRELAND.

ⒻⒶ**Francis James & Partners LLP** *(P J Elman, J P Francis, D Petrassi, C D Salmon)* 1386 London Road, LEIGH-ON-SEA, ESSEX, SS9 2UJ.

Francis S L Yan & Co *(S F Yan)* Room 101 1st Floor, Tak Fung Building, 79-81 Connaught Road West, SAI YING PUN, HONG KONG ISLAND, HONG KONG SAR.

Ⓟ**Francis Wong CPA Co Limited** *(M C F Wong)* 19/F 3 Lockhart Road, WAN CHAI, HONG KONG ISLAND, HONG KONG SAR. and at YUEN LONG

Ⓟ**Frank Bebbington Accountants Ltd** *(F D Bebbington)* Bridge House, 9 Fowley Common Lane, Glazebury, WARRINGTON, WA3 5JJ.

Frank Benson *(F Benson)* 199 Carr Lane, Tarleton, PRESTON, PR4 6BY.

ⓉⒻⒶ**Frank Brown & Walford** *(A Walker)* 314 Linthorpe Road, MIDDLESBROUGH, TS1 3QX.

Ⓟ**Frank Hirth plc** *(C N Shore)* 236 Gray's Inn Road, LONDON, WC1X 8HB.

Frank Kirkham *(F D Kirkham)* Greetwell Place, 2 Limekiln Way, LINCOLN, LN2 4US.

Ⓕ**Frank Newman & Co** *(F R Newman)* Flat 3, Elderberry Court, 39b Bycullah Road, ENFIELD, MIDDLESEX, EN2 8FF.

Ⓐ**Frank P Dongworth & Co** *(F P Dongworth)* First Floor, 30 London Road, SAWBRIDGEWORTH, CM21 9JS.

Ⓐ**Frank S Lachman** *(F S Lachman)* Nachal Sorek 33-16, Remat Beit, SHEMESH-ALEPH, ISRAEL. and at LONDON

Ⓟ**Franklin and Co Limited** *(D A Franklin)* Manor Cottage, Delmonden Lane, Hawkhurst, CRANBROOK, KENT, TN18 4XJ.

ⓉⒻⒶ**Franklin Chartered Accountants** *(A J Franklin, S R Franklin)* 320 Garratt Lane, Earlsfield, LONDON, SW18 4EJ. and at LOUTH

★**Franklin Underwood** *(G Underwood)* 1 Pinnacle Way, Pride Park, DERBY, DE24 8ZS.

Ⓐ**Franklins** *(D J Franklin)* Bury Road, Hitcham, IPSWICH, IP7 7PP.

ⒻⓅⒶ**Franklins Accountants Limited** *(R C Franklin)* Astor House, 2 Alexandra Road, Mutley Plain, PLYMOUTH, PL4 7JR.

ⓉⒻ**Franklins Accountants LLP** *(R C Franklin)* Astor House, 2 Alexandra Road, Mutley, PLYMOUTH, PL4 7JR.

Franklyn & Co *(R F Davies)* 9 Elm Close, Wheatley, OXFORD, OXFORDSHIRE, OX33 1UW.

Fraser & Associates *(M E Fraser)* 1 Imperial Square, CHELTENHAM, GLOUCESTERSHIRE, GL50 1QB.

Fraser Hayes Pickard *(E J H Pickard)* 7 Nimbus Way, Watnall, NOTTINGHAM, NG16 1FP.

Ⓟ**Fraser Price Consulting Limited** *(N G Fraser)* Suite 1, Enness Building, East Street, Bingham, NOTTINGHAM, NG13 8DS.

Ⓟ**Frategists, trading name of Financial Strategists Limited** *(C J Akwaeze)* 20 Sandwick Close, LONDON, NW7 2AX.

Frearson & Co *(J S S Frearson)* 187 Ringwood Road, EASTBOURNE, EAST SUSSEX, BN22 8UW.

ⒻⓅⒶ**Fredericks Limited** *(S G Duker)* 5th Floor, Newbury House, 890-900 Eastern Avenue, Newbury Park, ILFORD, ESSEX IG2 7HH.

Ⓟ**Fredericks, trading name of Fredericks 2001 Limited** *(J F Grassan, J E Hollington)* Highgate Business Centre, 33 Greenwood Place, LONDON, NW5 1LB.

Fredk A.J. Couldery *(F A J Couldery)* 81 Hove Park Road, HOVE, BN3 6LN.

ⓉⒻⒶ**Freedman, Frankl & Taylor** *(A S R Cohen, R I Frankl, I Sluckis, P J Stoker, K Taylor, T H Whitehurst)* Reedham House, 31 King Street West, MANCHESTER, M3 2PJ.

ⒻⒶ**Freedmans** *(H S Freedman)* Northway House, 5th Floor Suite 504-505, 1379 High Road, Whetstone, LONDON, N20 9LP.

★**Freedom Business Services** *(D J Burrows, P J Trinham)* 36 Vicar Street, DUDLEY, WEST MIDLANDS, DY2 8RG.

ⒻⓅⒶ**Freeman and Partners Limited** *(G R Cranston, F A Dada, W I C Dale, M E Hicks, A J Pianca)* St. Brides House, 10 Salisbury Square, LONDON, EC4Y 8EH.

★ⓉⒻⒶ**Freeman Baker Associates** *(S C Bird, S L Hay)* The Old Church, 48 Verulam Road, ST. ALBANS, AL3 4DH.

ⒻⓅ**Freeman Lawrence & Partners, trading name of Freeman Lawrence & Partners Ltd** *(S A Freeman)* Spectrum Studios, 2 Manor Gardens, LONDON, N7 6ER.

Ⓟ**Freeman Rich Limited** *(J R Duckworth, W J Turley)* 284 Clifton Drive South, LYTHAM ST. ANNES, LANCASHIRE, FY8 1LH. and at NEWCASTLE UPON TYNE

Freemans, trading name of Freemans Partnership LLP *(G Makris, C Petrides)* Solar House, 282 Chase Road, LONDON, N14 6NZ.

Ⓟ**Freeport Management Ltd** *(M.C. Beaty-Pownall)* 5 Fir Close, WALTON-ON-THAMES, SURREY, KT12 2SX.

★Ⓕ**Freestone & Co** *(R C Freestone)* 1 The Centre, The High Street, GILLINGHAM, Dorset, SP8 4AB. and at WINCANTON

Ⓐ**French Associates** *(E Cole, R H French)* The Swan Centre, Fishers Lane, Chiswick, LONDON, W4 1RX.

Ⓟ**French Ludlam & Co Ltd** *(J J French)* 661 High Street, KINGSWINFORD, DY6 8AL.

ⒻⓅ**Frenkels Forensics, Frenkels Westbury Forensics, trading names of Frenkels Limited** *(J R Frenkel)* Churchill House, 137 Brent Street, LONDON, NW4 4DJ.

Ⓐ**Friedmans** *(J R Friedman)* Summit House, 13 High Street, Wanstead, LONDON, E11 2AA.

ⓉⓅⒶ**Friend & Grant Ltd** *(M A Friend, A I Grant)* Bryant House, Bryant Road, Strood, ROCHESTER, KENT, ME2 3EW.

ⒻⒶ**Friend LLP** *(D Friend, M D Friend, F Upton)* Eleven Brindley Place, 2 Brunswick Square, BIRMINGHAM, B1 2LP.

★ⓅⒶ**Friend-James, trading name of Friend-James Ltd** *(R H Clow, S J Forster, J D Warner)* 169 Preston Road, BRIGHTON, BN1 6AG.

Friends Accounting Services *(P H Friend)* 51 Elm Park, STANMORE, MIDDLESEX, HA7 4AU.

ⓅⒶ**Frisby Wishart, trading name of Frisby Wishart Ltd** *(C Frisby)* 2 Lavender Lane, Rowledge, FARNHAM, SURREY, GU10 4AY.

ⒻⒶ**Frith & Co** *(R M Frith)* Moorgate House, 7b Station Road West, OXTED, SURREY, RH8 9EE.

Ⓟ**Frith Accountants Limited** *(R M Frith)* Moorgate House, 7b Station Road West, OXTED, SURREY, RH8 9EE.

Ⓐ**Frixou & Co** *(J Frixou)* 71 Goldhawk Road, Shepherds Bush, LONDON, W12 8EG.

ⒻⓅ**Frost & Company, trading name of Frost & Company (CA) Limited** *(S J Frost)* Redcotts House, 1 Redcotts Lane, WIMBORNE, DORSET, BH21 1JX.

ⓅⒶ**Frosts, trading name of Frosts C. A. Limited** *(S Frost)* 51 Bernard Street, EDINBURGH, EH6 6SL.

Ⓣ**FRP Advisory LLP** *(P L Armstrong, J D Baker, J S French, G R Morris, G C Smith, C I Vickers)* 10 Furnival Street, LONDON, EC4A 1YH. and at BEXLEYHEATH, BIRMINGHAM, BRISTOL, HORNCHURCH, LEICESTER, MANCHESTER, ST. ALBANS, WORTHING

Fryers Bell & Co *(G A Bell, K W Fryers)* 27 Athol Street, Douglas, ISLE OF MAN, IM1 1LB.

Ⓟ**FSP (UK) Ltd** *(A C Ray)* 87 Firs Park Avenue, Winchmore Hill, LONDON, N21 2PU.

FT Accounts, trading name of F H Takahashi *(F H Takahashi)* 2/2 287 Wilton Street, GLASGOW, G20 6DD.

Ⓟ**FTW & Partners CPA Limited** *(H Fung)* Suite 1001-3, 10th Floor, Manulife Provident Funds Place, 345 Nathan Road, KOWLOON CITY, HONG KONG SAR.

Fulcrum *(R J Murphy)* The Old Orchard, Bexwell Road, DOWNHAM MARKET, NORFOLK, PE38 9LJ.

ⒻⓅⒶ**Full Circle Accountancy, trading name of Full Circle Accountancy Limited** *(J M B Miller)* 29-30 Cornmarket, PENRITH, CUMBRIA, CA11 7HS.

Fullard Duffill *(E L Duffill, C D Fullard)* 106 Birmingham Road, BROMSGROVE, B61 0DF.

ⓅⒶ**Fuller Spurling, trading name of Fuller Harvey Ltd** *(M T C Harvey, S M Keane)* Mill House, 58 Guildford Street, CHERTSEY, SURREY, KT16 9BE. and at SANDHURST

ⓅⒶ**Fuller, trading name of Fuller Accountants Limited** *(J S Fuller, S Roper)* The Counting House, Church Farm Business Park, Corston, BATH, BA2 9AP.

Fullers *(J Fuller, K Fuller)* The Glebe, Shipley Hills Road, Meopham, GRAVESEND, DA13 0AD.

Ⓐ**Fullertons** *(J R Fullerton)* Westbourne House, 60 Bagley Lane, Farsley, PUDSEY, WEST YORKSHIRE, LS28 5LY.

Ⓟ**Fundi Professional Services Limited** *(C R Hawkins)* Hambrook, Bethesda Street, Upper Basildon, Pangbourne, READING, RG8 8NT.

Ⓟ**Fung & Pang CPA Limited** *(W Y Fung)* 1/F & 2/F Xiu Ping Commercial Building, 104 Jervois Street, SHEUNG WAN, HONG KONG ISLAND, HONG KONG SAR.

Fung Hoi Fung & Co *(H F Fung)* Flat B, 8/F, THY (Yuen Long) Commercial Building, 2 - 8 Tai Cheung Street, YUEN LONG, NEW TERRITORIES HONG KONG SAR.

★**Fung Lau & Co.** *(Y L Lau)* Room 2604 26/F, C. C. Wu Building, 302-308 Hennessy Road, WAN CHAI, HONG KONG ISLAND, HONG KONG SAR.

Fung Leung & Co *(C Leung)* Room 1606, Nan Fung Centre, 264-298 Castle Peak Road, TSEUNG KWAN O, NEW TERRITORIES, HONG KONG SAR.

★**Fung, Yu & Co** *(S L Fung)* Hong Kong Trade Centre 7/F, 161-7 Des Voeux Road Central, CENTRAL, HONG KONG ISLAND, HONG KONG SAR.

Furness Consultancy *(A J Furness)* 30 Sonning Meadows, Sonning - on -Thames, READING, RG4 6XB.

Ⓟ**Fursdon Tax Consulting, trading name of Fursdon Consulting Ltd** *(J M Fursdon)* The Old Stables, Grange Manor, Shipley Bridge Lane, Shipley Bridge, HORLEY, SURREY RH6 9TL.

Futers Accountancy & Finance *(A Futers)* 1 Westwood Avenue, NEWCASTLE UPON TYNE, NE6 5QT.

Ⓟ**Future Solutions, trading name of FSCA Limited** *(F Micheli)* Regency House, 2 Wood Street, Queen Square, BATH, BA1 2JQ.

Ⓟ**FWPL Accounting Limited** *(F W P Lea)* 58 Manor Road, WOODSTOCK, OXFORDSHIRE, OX20 1XJ.

Ⓟ**Fylde Tax Accountants, trading name of Fylde Tax Accountants Limited** *(S M Fay)* Offices 11 & 12, Bisphan Village Chambers, 335 Red Bank Road, BLACKPOOL, FY2 0HJ.

Ⓟ**G & Co, trading name of G & Co Molesey Ltd** *(D Koshal)* Gautam House, 1-3 Shenley Avenue, Ruislip Manor, RUISLIP, MIDDLESEX, HA4 6BP. and at WEST MOLESEY

ⓅⒶ**G & E (Holdings) Ltd** *(R J Green, A M Sidebottom)* Garbutt & Elliott, Arabesque House, Monks Cross Drive, Huntington, YORK, YO32 9GW.

ⓅⒶ**G & E Professional Services Limited** *(R J Green, A M Sidebottom)* Arabesque House, Monks Cross Drive, Huntington, YORK, YO32 9GW.

G A Briggs FCA *(G A Briggs)* Manor Farm, Farnham, KNARESBOROUGH, NORTH YORKSHIRE, HG5 9JE.

G A Hellings Ltd *(G A Hellings)* 53 Queens Road, Wimbleon, LONDON, SW19 8NP.

G Capstick & Co *(G Capstick)* Ashwood Lodge, Berry Hill Road, Adderbury, BANBURY, OXFORDSHIRE, OX17 3HF.

ⒻⒶ**G D Hakin & Co** *(R B Gibson, T J Herbert)* 9 Stanley Street, BLYTH, NORTHUMBERLAND, NE24 2BS.

ⓅⒶ**G D O'Hehir & Co Ltd** *(G D O'Hehir)* 22/23 Clyde Terrace, SPENNYMOOR, DL16 7SE.

Ⓟ**G D Parkes Ltd** *(G D Parkes)* 10 Simon House, 39 St. Marys Road, IPSWICH, SUFFOLK, IP4 4SP.

Ⓟ**G Feldman & Co Limited** *(G I Feldman)* 5 Stone Hall Road, LONDON, N21 1LR.

G Foxwell & Co *(R A Foxwell, R L Johnson)* Foxwell House, Libanus Road, EBBW VALE, GWENT, NP23 6YY.

Ⓟ**G H Wala & Co, trading name of Mainard Limited** *(V K Gulamhuseinwala)* 7 Kingfield Road, LONDON, W5 1LD.

ⒻⓅⒶ**G J Jackson Accountants Limited** *(G J Jackson)* 5 Victoria Avenue, BISHOP AUCKLAND, COUNTY DURHAM, DL14 7JH.

G J Kirk LIP *(G J Kirk)* 6 The Crescent, PLYMOUTH, PL1 3AB.

G J Myers FCA *(G J Myers)* 22 Bracknell Gardens, LONDON, NW3 7ED.

Ⓟ**G J Taggart Ltd** *(G J Taggart)* Fach Uchaf, Cwmllinau, MACHYNLLETH, POWYS, SY20 9PF.

Ⓟ**G K Hewkin, trading name of G K Hewkin & Co Ltd** *(M A Hewkin)* The Croft, Water End Lane, Beeston, KING'S LYNN, NORFOLK, PE32 2NL.

G K Prince ACA *(G K Prince)* 151 Grove Road, HARPENDEN, HERTFORDSHIRE, AL5 1SY.

Ⓟ**G L Ramsbottom & Co Ltd** *(G L Ramsbottom)* Kenmore, Bolton Road, Bradshaw, BOLTON, BL2 3EU.

Ⓟ**G L Taylor & Co(Accountants) Limited** *(G L Taylor)* 10 Tudor Close, Cheam, SUTTON, SURREY, SM3 8QS.

G Lunt *(G Lunt)* 9 Gordon Road, CHELMSFORD, CM2 9LL.

★**G M Agencies** *(R F Millett)* Orchard Cottage, Old Apley, MARKET RASEN, LINCOLNSHIRE, LN8 5JQ.

Ⓕ**G M Aitken** *(G M Aitken)* 18 High Street, NORTH FERRIBY, NORTH HUMBERSIDE, HU14 3JP.

ⓅⒶ**G Murphy Limited** *(G Murphy)* Whittingham Riddell LLP, Hafren House, 5 St Giles Business Park, NEWTOWN, POWYS, SY16 3AJ. and at SHREWSBURY

ⒶⓅ**G P Boyle & Co** *(G P Boyle)* Old Fire Station, Cecil Street, NEWRY, COUNTY DOWN, BT35 6AU.

Ⓟ**G P Ivory & Co, trading name of G P Ivory & Co Ltd** *(G Ivory)* 344 Croydon Road, BECKENHAM, KENT, BR3 4EX.

G Pritchard FCA *(G Pritchard)* 6 County View, Clifton, BANBURY, OXFORDSHIRE, OX15 0PZ.

G R Forbes *(G R Forbes)* 20 Harrowby Lane, GRANTHAM, LINCOLNSHIRE, NG31 9HX.

G R Gadsby *(G R Gadsby)* The Orchard, Manor Park, CHISLEHURST, KENT, BR7 5QE.

ⓅⒶ**G R Stone, trading name of G R Stone Limited** *(G R Stone)* 1 Union Street, FAREHAM, HAMPSHIRE, PO16 7XX.

G S Grove *(G S Grove)* 7 Hillwood Common Road, Four Oaks, SUTTON COLDFIELD, B75 5QJ.

ⒻⒶ**G W Dick & Co LLP** *(G W Dick, W R A Dick)* Earl Grey House, 11 Beach Road, SOUTH SHIELDS, TYNE AND WEAR, NE33 2QA.

G W Langfield *(G W Langfield)* 55 Seaburn Road, Toton, Beeston, NOTTINGHAM, NG9 6HN.

Ⓟ**G&T Accountancy Services Ltd** *(C L Turner)* Denby Dale Business Park, Wakefield Road, Denby Dale, HUDDERSFIELD, HD8 8QH.

G. Dufton and Co, trading name of Gareth Dufton ACA *(G N Dufton)* 61 Page Hill, WARE, HERTFORDSHIRE, SG12 0RZ.

Ⓕ**G. Hilder** *(G Hilder)* The Alde Suite, 8 Wherry Lane, IPSWICH, SUFFOLK, IP4 1LG.

G. Maddox *(G Maddox)* 21 Honeysuckle Gardens, Everton, LYMINGTON, HAMPSHIRE, SO41 0EH.

G. Moon & Co *(G Moon)* 74 Duke Street, BARROW-IN-FURNESS, CUMBRIA, LA14 1RX.

G. O'Brien *(G O'Brien)* Ullenwood, Manor Close, East Horsley, LEATHERHEAD, KT24 6SA.

G. Quinn ACA Accountant *(G J Quinn)* 134 Lincoln Avenue, NEWCASTLE, STAFFORDSHIRE, ST5 3AR.

G. Reeves *(G Reeves)* 11 Percy Terrace, Beltring Road, TUNBRIDGE WELLS, TN4 9RH.

Ⓟ**G. Spratt Accountancy Limited** *(P A Ronan)* 3 Abbeylands, High Street, DUNBAR, EH42 1EH. and at EYEMOUTH

G. Tan & Co *(G H Tan)* 88 Ventnor Drive, LONDON, N20 8BS.

G. Wratten & Co *(G Wratten)* 8 Higham Lane, TONBRIDGE, TN10 4JA.

G. Yeomans & Co *(G Yeomans)* 4 Poplar Way, High Lane, STOCKPORT, SK6 8ES.

G. Young & Co *(G Young)* 49 Deaconsfield Road, HEMEL HEMPSTEAD, HP3 9HZ.

G.A. Maile *(G A Maile)* 7333 L & A Road, VERNON V1B 3S6, BC, CANADA.

G.A. Pearlman *(G A Pearlman)* 159 Wynchgate, LONDON, N21 1QT.

Ⓟ**G.A.Harris & Co Limited** *(G A Harris)* Brulimar House, Jubilee Road, Middleton, MANCHESTER, M24 2LX.

Ⓟ**G.A.P. Leigh-Pollitt, trading name of G.A.P. Leigh-Pollitt Ltd** *(G A P Leigh-Pollitt)* The Old Post Office, Polstead Street, STOKE BY NAYLAND, SUFFOLK, CO6 4SA.

G.C. Das & Co. *(G C Das)* 57 Icknield Drive, Gants Hill, ILFORD, IG2 6SE.

G.C. Reid & Co *(G C Reid)* 57 Hull Road, COTTINGHAM, NORTH HUMBERSIDE, HU16 4PT.

G.D. Deverell *(G D Deverell)* Asthill House, Aldbrough St. John, RICHMOND, NORTH YORKSHIRE, DL11 7ST.

★**G.D. Price & Co.** *(S F Hardy)* 25 Mill Lane, Newbold Verdon, LEICESTER, LE9 9PT.

★ⒻⓅⒶ**G.H. Attenborough & Co., trading name of G.H. Attenborough & Co. Limited** *(Howard Connor)* 1 Tower House, Tower Centre, HODDESDON, HERTFORDSHIRE, EN11 8UR.

G.H. Murray & Co *(I C Thomas)* St John's House, Barrington Road, ALTRINCHAM, WA14 1TJ.

G.H.Herbert & Co *(G H Herbert)* 227 Marlpool Lane, KIDDERMINSTER, DY11 5DL.

Ⓐ**G.H.W.Ashman** *(G H W Ashman)* 109a North Street, Burwell, CAMBRIDGE, CB25 0BB.

G.Iliffe *(G C Iliffe)* 6 Greystoke Court, 29 Albemarle Road, BECKENHAM, BR3 5HL.

G.J. Bishop *(G J Bishop)* 16 Stewarts Close, ABBOTS LANGLEY, WD5 0LU.

G.J. Fennell *(G J Fennell)* 41 River Way, LOUGHTON, ESSEX, IG10 3LJ.

G.J.Burgess & Co. *(G J Burgess)* 175 Jersey Road, Osterley, ISLEWORTH, TW7 4QJ.

G.K.Swarup & Co *(G K Swarup)* Shyam Kutir, 12/11 Station Road, Teen Batti, JAMNAGAR 361001, INDIA.

G.L. Aston *(G L Aston)* 23 Church Lane, Old Arley, COVENTRY, CV7 8FW.

★**G.L. Barker & Co LLP** *(G P Greenfield, P A Holleran)* 45-49 Austhorpe Road, Crossgates, LEEDS, LS15 8BA.

G.L. Taylor & Co *(G L Taylor)* 10 Tudor Close, Cheam, SUTTON, SM3 8QS.

Ⓐ**G.P. Brookes** *(G P Brookes)* 24 Abbotsford Drive, DUDLEY, WEST MIDLANDS, DY1 2HD.

Ⓕ**G.P. Cole & Co** *(G P Cole)* Suite 2 Ground Floor, 5 Hercules Way, Leavesden, WATFORD, WD25 7GS.

G.P. Holland *(G P Holland)* 44 Rowney Croft, Hall Green, BIRMINGHAM, B28 0PL.

ⒻⒶ**G.R. Potton & Co** *(G R Potton)* 2 Harestone Valley Road, CATERHAM, SURREY, CR3 6HB.

G.R. Webb *(G R Webb)* 107 Canterbury Road, MARGATE, KENT, CT9 5AX. and at DOVER

G.S. Cook *(G S Cook)* 2 Hall Orchards Avenue, WETHERBY, WEST YORKSHIRE, LS22 6SN.

G.S. Shergill *(G S Shergill)* 30 Bell Road, WALSALL, WS5 3JW.

G.S. West & Company *(G S West)* 2 Inglewood, Kemnal Road, CHISLEHURST, KENT, BR7 6NF.

★**G.S.Tan & Co** *(G S Tan)* 116 Middle Road, #06-01 ICB Enterprise House, SINGAPORE 188972, SINGAPORE.

G.T. Associates *(R K Green)* The Limes, 1339 High Road, Whetstone, LONDON, N20 9HR.

ⓉⒶ**G.T. Grant & Co** *(J R B Lawlan)* 79 High Street, Gosforth, NEWCASTLE UPON TYNE, NE3 4AA.

G.V. Fisher FCA *(G V Fisher)* Flint House, 58 Worple Road, EPSOM, SURREY, KT18 5EL.

Gabriel Tse *(G C W Tse)* Unit 1601, 16/F Malaysia Building, 50 Gloucester Road, WAN CHAI, HONG KONG ISLAND, HONG KONG SAR.

Gadsden Grillo & Co *(B L Gadsden)* P.O.Box 35931, LUSAKA, ZAMBIA.

Gaffneys *(C N Gaffney)* 2 Longsight Road, Holcombe Brook, BURY, LANCASHIRE, BL0 9TD.

Gainsford, Bell & Co. *(B Bell)* 111 Arlosoroff St, TEL AVIV, 62098, ISRAEL.

Gairdners *(J A C Gairdner)* 17 Larpent Avenue, Putney, LONDON, SW15 6UP.

GALA CPA *(K Lin)* Unit 1005 10/F Tower B, Hunghom Comm Ctr, 37 Ma Tau Wai Road, HUNG HOM, KOWLOON, HONG KONG SAR.

Ⓟ**Gale Gardner & Co Limited** *(T J F Gardner)* Kencot House, Kencot, LECHLADE, OXFORDSHIRE, GL7 3QX.

Gallagher & Brocklehurst *(S E Brocklehurst, J E M Gallagher)* 4 Plantagenet Road, BARNET, EN5 5JQ.

Gallagher & Co *(P R Gallagher)* Ivydene House, Uckinghall, TEWKESBURY, GL20 6ES.

Ⓐ**Gallaghers** *(J J Gallagher)* 33a High Street, Stony Stratford, MILTON KEYNES, MK11 1AA.

★ⓉⒻⓅ**Gallaghers, trading name of The Gallagher Partnership LLP** *(I A Arian, S D Clarke, M J Palmer, R S Palmer)* PO Box 698, 2nd Floor, Titchfield House, 69/85 Tabernacle Street, LONDON, EC2A 4RR.

Gallant Accountancy Services *(L A J Gallant)* 4 Johnsons Drive, HAMPTON, MIDDLESEX, TW12 2EQ.

Galliers & Co. *(C S Galliers)* Wizzard's Knoll, 33 Cockshot Road, MALVERN, WR14 2TT.

Galloway Smith & Company *(J M G Smith)* 9 Hope Street, Douglas, ISLE OF MAN, IM1 1AQ.

Gambit Corporate Finance LLP *(S S Heer, J F Holmes, A L Jones, G A Rowe)* 3 Assembly Square, Britannia Quay, Cardiff Bay, CARDIFF, CF10 4PL. and at BIRMINGHAM

Gandhi & Co *(J B Gandhi)* 113 Kingsley Road, HOUNSLOW, TW3 4AJ.

Gane Jackson Scott LLP *(G.R. O'Malley)* 144 High Street, EPPING, ESSEX, CM16 4AS.

Ganley Burt, trading name of Kay *(L S Burt)* 59/63 Station Road, NORTHWICH, CHESHIRE, CW9 5LT.

Gant Massingale *(J F Gant, M Massingale)* Fairlight, Meadway, BERKHAMSTED, HP4 2PN.

Ⓟ**Ganymede Business Services Limited** *(C E Tall)* Long Field House, Station Road, Bratton Fleming, BARNSTAPLE, DEVON, EX31 4TZ.

ⓉⒻⒶ**Garbutt & Elliott, trading name of Garbutt & Elliott LLP** *(D J Dickson, R J Green, C Manson, A M Sidebottom)* Arabesque House, Monks Cross Drive, Huntington, YORK, YO32 9GW. and at LEEDS

ⒻⒶ**Gardezi Jay & Co** *(P C N Jayawardene)* Hamilton House, 4a The Avenue, LONDON, E4 9LD.

ⒻⓅⒶ**Gardiner Fosh, trading name of Gardiner Fosh Limited** *(S A Fosh, G P Gardiner)* 31 St. Johns, WORCESTER, WR2 5AG.

Gardiner Karbani Audy & Partners *(Z K Tejpar)* 4107-99 Street, EDMONTON T6E 3N4, AB, CANADA.

ⓉⓅⒶ**Gardiners, trading name of Gardiners Limited** *(B Cleaver, S J R Roy)* Hutton House, Dale Road, Sheriff Hutton, YORK, YO60 6RZ.

Gardner Brown *(J D Gardner, A E Worthington)* Calderwood House, 7 Montpellier Parade, CHELTENHAM, GL50 1UA.

Ⓟ**Gardner Steward Limited** *(C E Johnson)* Charwell House, Wilsom Road, ALTON, HAMPSHIRE, GU34 2PP.

ⓉⒻⓅⒶ**Gardners, trading name of Gardners Accountants Ltd** *(A P Filbee, J R Gardner, M J Langton-Davies)* Brynford House, Brynford Street, HOLYWELL, CLWYD, CH8 7RD.

Ⓟ**Gareth Davies, trading name of Gareth A Davies Limited** *(G A Davies)* Spec House, 83 Elm Road, LEIGH-ON-SEA, ESSEX, SS9 1SP.

ⒻⓅⒶ**Gareth Hughes & Co, trading name of Gareth Hughes & Company Limited** *(G W Hughes, M J Wilkes)* The Round House, Glan-y-Mor Road, LLANDUDNO JUNCTION, GWYNEDD, LL31 9SN.

Gareth Jones *(G Jones)* Ger-y-garth, Tyddyngwyn, Manod, BLAENAU FFESTINIOG, LL41 4AL.

Ⓟ**Garlands, trading name of Garlands CA Ltd** *(R Gadhvi)* 6 Oakroyd Avenue, POTTERS BAR, HERTFORDSHIRE, EN6 2EH.

Garner & Co *(M R Garner)* Rest Harrow, Welland, MALVERN, WORCESTERSHIRE, WR13 6NQ.

ⒻⒶ**Garner Pugh & Sinclair** *(D P Evison, M P Evison, J F Hughes)* 3 Belgrave Place, 19 Salop Road, OSWESTRY, SHROPSHIRE, SY11 2NR.

ⓉⒻⓅⒶ**Garners, trading name of Garners Limited** *(S W Francis, J C Temlett)* Bermuda House, 45 High Street, Hampton Wick, KINGSTON UPON THAMES, SURREY, KT1 4EH.

ⒻⒶ**Garner-Stevens & Co, trading name of Segrave & Partners** *(I Hay, A D Pateman, J N Smith)* Turnpike House, 1208/1210 London Road, LEIGH-ON-SEA, SS9 2UA.

Ⓕ**Garo & Co.** *(G Garabedian)* 27 Daventry Street, LONDON, NW1 6TD.

ⓉⒻⓅⒶ**Garratts, trading name of Garratts Wolverhampton Limited** *(A D Brabazon, R Chaggar, J T Hitchen, J Reed, J Roden)* 29 Waterloo Road, WOLVERHAMPTON, WV1 4DJ.

ⒻⓅⒶ**Garrod, Beckett & Co Ltd** *(P J Garrod)* 10 Town Quay Wharf, Abbey Road, BARKING, ESSEX, IG11 7BZ.

ⓉⒶ**Garside & Co LLP** *(S B Garside, D Russell)* 6 Vigo Street, LONDON, W1S 3HF.

Garth Pedler & Co *(G Pedler)* Hay Hill, TOTNES, TQ9 5LH.

ⒻⒶ**Garton Graham & Co** *(P M Garton, D W Graham)* 56 Grammar School Yard, HULL, HU1 2NB.

Gary Bush *(G R Bush)* Badgers Hollow, 40 Badgers Hall Avenue, BENFLEET, ESSEX, SS7 1TN.

Gary C.C. Lam & Co *(C C Lam)* Room 1501 15th Floor, Shanghai Industrial Investment Building 48-62 Hennessy Road, WAN CHAI, HONG KONG ISLAND, HONG KONG SAR.

Gary Drewery *(G Drewery)* 27 Canewdon Road, WESTCLIFF-ON-SEA, ESSEX, SS0 7NE.

Ⓐ**Gary J. Cansick & Co** *(G J Cansick)* Janelle House, 6 Hartham Lane, HERTFORD, SG14 1QN.

Gary Jobsey & Co *(G N J Jobsey)* 3 Barnsway, Love Lane, KINGS LANGLEY, WD4 9PW.

Ⓟ**Gary Malcolm & Co Ltd** *(G N Malcolm)* 9 Chandlers Court, Eaton, NORWICH, NR4 6EY.

Gary Revel-Chion *(G Revel-Chion)* 35 Benett Drive, HOVE, EAST SUSSEX, BN3 6US.

★ⓉⒻⒶ**Gary Sargeant + Company** *(E L Beal, A D Hughes, G A Sargeant)* 5 White Oak Square, London Road, SWANLEY, BR8 7AG.

Gary Sisman *(G Sisman)* Woodlands, Todds Green, STEVENAGE, HERTFORDSHIRE, SG1 2JE.

ⒻⓅⒶ**Gascoynes, trading name of Gascoynes Limited** *(B Gascoyne, C Reeve)* 15 Whiting Street, BURY ST. EDMUNDS, SUFFOLK, IP33 1NX.

Ⓐ**Gates Freedman & Company** *(D C N Freedman)* 9th Floor, Hyde House, The Hyde, LONDON, NW9 6LQ.

ⒻⓅⒶ**Gateway Partners, trading name of Gateway Partners Auditing UK Limited** *(A Epstein, A Greengarten, R I Hasseck, P Wilson)* 2nd Floor, 43 Whitfield Street, LONDON, W1T 4HD.

Ⓟ**Gateway, trading name of Gateway Advisors Limited** *(S Sexton)* 4 York Place, LEEDS, LS1 2DR.

★ⓉⒻⒶ**Gatley, Read** *(D A Read, C White)* Prince of Wales House, 18/19 Salmon Fields Business Village, Royton, OLDHAM, OL2 6HT.

ⒻⓅ**Gauzebrook, trading name of Gauzebrook Limited** *(D J Smith)* The Old Barton, Rodbourne Rail Business Centre, Grange Lane, Rodbourne, MALMESBURY, WILTSHIRE SN16 0ES.

Ⓐ**Gavin G. Curtis** *(G G Curtis)* 24 Ashley Gardens, Green Street Green, ORPINGTON, BR6 9NH.

Gavin Williams *(G R Williams)* 25 Somerford Way, LONDON, SE16 6QN.

Gaythorn Administrative Services *(J R Hiley, N J Nixon)* Athena House, 35 Greek Street, STOCKPORT, CHESHIRE, SK3 8BA.

Ⓐ**GB & Co** *(G Beshahwred)* Brent House, 214 Kenton Road, HARROW, MIDDLESEX, HA3 8BT.

Ⓟ**GBAC, trading name of GBAC Limited** *(A J Boyle)* Old Linen Court, 83-85 Shambles Street, BARNSLEY, SOUTH YORKSHIRE, S70 2SB.

ⓉⒶ**GBJ, trading name of GBJ LLP** *(N I Green)* Sterling House, 27 Hatchlands Road, REDHILL, RH1 6RW.

GBM Accounting Services *(G Murugesan)* 8 Bulstrode Avenue, HOUNSLOW, MIDDLESEX, TW3 3AB.

Ⓟ**GCA, trading name of GCA (Surrey) Ltd** *(P M O'Halloran)* Beacon House, South Road, WEYBRIDGE, SURREY, KT13 9DZ.

ⒻⒶ**Geary Partnership** *(A J Geary, C M Geary)* 2nd Floor, 159a Chase Side, ENFIELD, MIDDLESEX, EN2 0PW. and at CANTERBURY

Ⓟ**Gee Aggar & Co, trading name of Gee Aggar & Co Limited** *(G H Aggarwal)* 10A Osram Road, East Lane Business Park, WEMBLEY, MIDDLESEX, HA9 7NG.

Gee Kar & Co *(S Kar)* 22 Kohinoor, 105 Park Street, CALCUTTA 700 016, INDIA.

ⓉⒻⒶ**Geens** *(S J Archer, K V Lowe)* 68 Liverpool Road, STOKE-ON-TRENT, ST4 1BG.

Geetika Jain Accountancy Services *(G Jain)* 123 Thornbury Road, 15 Leworth, ISLEWORTH, MIDDLESEX, TW7 4ND.

Ⓟ**Genial Systems Ltd** *(D Beardon, M V Khatri)* 8 Blackstock Mews, Islington, LONDON, N4 2BT.

Geoff Butler & Co, The Accounting Surgery, trading names of G.W Butler *(G W Butler)* 5 Rothsbury Drive, Valley Park, Chandlers Ford, EASTLEIGH, SO53 4QQ.

Geoff Croft *(G Croft)* 28 Hollins Road, Hindley, WIGAN, WN2 4JZ.

Ⓟ**Geoff Davies Associates Ltd** *(G M Davies)* 27 Main Street, PEMBROKE, DYFED, SA71 4JS.

ⓅⒶ**Geoff Gollop & Co Limited** *(G R Gollop)* St Brandon's House, 29 Great George Street, BRISTOL, BS1 5QT.

Geoff Mitchell *(G Mitchell)* 40 Eastgate Street, BURY ST. EDMUNDS, SUFFOLK, IP33 1YW.

Ⓟ**Geoff Spurr & Co Limited** *(G S Spurr)* 41 Fore Hill, ELY, CB7 4AA.

Geoff Wilkinson *(G R Wilkinson)* Pickwick House, Bunces Lane, Burghfield Common, READING, RG7 3DL.

Geoffrey Alan Whaley *(G A Whaley)* 23 Hillfield Road, Chalfont St Peter, GERRARDS CROSS, SL9 0DU.

Geoffrey Carson *(G Carson)* Twin Pines, Devenish Road, ASCOT, BERKSHIRE, SL5 9PH.

ⒻⓅⒶ**Geoffrey Cole & Co, trading name of Geoffrey Cole & Co Ltd** *(G S J Cole)* 4 Reading Road, Pangbourne, READING, RG8 7LY.

Ⓟ**Geoffrey Collins & Co, trading name of Geoffrey Collins Ltd** *(G Collins)* Parallel House, 32 London Road, GUILDFORD, SURREY, GU1 2AB.

ⓅⒶ**Geoffrey Cox Limited** *(G R Cox)* Dafferns LLP, 1 Eastwood, Harry Weston Road, Binley Business Park, COVENTRY, CV3 2UB.

Geoffrey Ellis & Co. *(S J Bolton, G Ellis)* Kirby Grange, Cold Kirby, THIRSK, NORTH YORKSHIRE, YO7 2HL. and at HALIFAX

Ⓟ**Geoffrey F. Stephens, trading name of Markamber Ltd** *(G F Stephens)* 2 Haydock Close, Cheadle, STOKE-ON-TRENT, ST10 1UE.

Geoffrey Fowler-Tutt *(G Fowler-Tutt)* 22 St. Heliers Avenue, HOVE, EAST SUSSEX, BN3 5RE.

Geoffrey G Wall, trading name of G.G. Wall *(G G Wall)* Brynglas, St Andrews Road, DINAS POWYS, CF64 4AT.

ⓉⒻⓅⒶ**Geoffrey Hannam Limited** *(G Hannam)* 103 Castle Street, Edgeley, STOCKPORT, CHESHIRE, SK3 9AR.

Geoffrey Hodge *(G D Hodge)* 30 Market Place, HITCHIN, SG5 1DY.

Ⓕ**Geoffrey J. Griggs** *(G J Griggs)* 66 Lynwood Grove, ORPINGTON, BR6 0BH.

Geoffrey Little & Co. *(G M Little)* 22 Orford Road, LONDON, E18 1PY.

Geoffrey M. Spencer *(G M Spencer)* The Wincombe Centre, Wincombe Business Park, SHAFTESBURY, DORSET, SP7 9QJ.

ⒻⒶ**Geoffrey Marchant & Co** *(G K Marchant)* Rathbond House, High Street, Staplehurst, TONBRIDGE, TN12 0AD.

★**Geoffrey Martin & Co** *(J H Twizell)* 4th Floor, St Andrew House, 119-121 The Head Row, LEEDS, LS1 5JW. and at LONDON

★ⒻⒶ**Geoffrey N. Barnes** *(G N Barnes)* 12 Fratton Road, PORTSMOUTH, PO1 5BX.

Ⓟ**Geoffrey Nathan International Limited** *(G Nathan)* Le Roccabella, 24 Avenue Princess Grace, 98000 MONTE CARLO, MONACO.

Geoffrey Peck Consultants LLP *(G M Peck)* PO Box 3, EDENBRIDGE, TN8 5ZF.

Geoffrey R Butler *(G R Butler)* The Mullions, New Road, Beer, SEATON, EX12 3EB.

Geoffrey Rogers *(G Rogers)* Metropolitan House, 37 The Millfields, Stonehouse, PLYMOUTH, PL1 3JB.

Geoffrey Scotton FCA *(G Scotton)* 29 Stoneleigh Park, WEYBRIDGE, SURREY, KT13 0DZ.

Geoffrey W Pillar & Co *(L D Johns)* Erme House, Station Road, PLYMOUTH, PL7 2AU.

George & Co *(D S George)* 246 High Road, Harrow Weald, HARROW, HA3 7BB.

George & Co *(G Kapaya)* 16 Berberis Close, Walnut Tree, MILTON KEYNES, MK7 7DZ.

Ⓕ**George & Co (audit) Limited** *(G H Charilaou)* Thornhill House, 26 Fisher Street, MAIDSTONE, ME14 2SU.

George A. Kitcher & Company *(G A Kitcher)* 1 Cyncoed Crescent, Cyncoed, CARDIFF, CF23 6SW.

George A. Strovolides *(G A Strovolides)* Hermes Building Office 501, 31 Chr Sozos Street, PO Box 22104, 1517 NICOSIA, CYPRUS.

Ⓟ**George Achillea Limited** *(George Achillea)* 49 Ash Grove, Bush Hill Park, ENFIELD, EN1 2LB.

George Allen & Co *(W G A Coward)* 6 Lakeside View, Rawdon, LEEDS, LS19 6RN.

ⒻⓅⒶ**George Arthur, trading name of George Arthur Limited** *(J A Rook, P P Rook)* York House, 4 Wigmores South, WELWYN GARDEN CITY, HERTFORDSHIRE, AL8 6PL.

George Bates Consultancy *(D G Bates)* 79 Tempest Avenue, POTTERS BAR, HERTFORDSHIRE, EN6 5LD.

George Cassell *(G Cassell)* Old Abbey Farm House, Quarr Lane, RYDE, ISLE OF WIGHT, PO33 4ER.

George Charlton *(G Charlton)* 11 Stoneleigh Court, Woodham Village, NEWTON AYCLIFFE, DL5 4TL.

George Dougherty *(G J Dougherty)* Chestnuts, Lower Farm Road, Effingham, LEATHERHEAD, SURREY, KT24 5JJ.

George Edwards *(G Edwards)* 10 Starts Close, Locksbottom, ORPINGTON, BR6 8NU.

George Egaddu *(G W Egaddu)* 6 Clement Hill Road, PO Box 3736, KAMPALA, UGANDA.

★ⓉⒻⒶ**George Hay** *(R C Dilley, B D Jefferd, A P Newman, N J Willis)* Brigham House, 93 High Street, BIGGLESWADE, BEDFORDSHIRE, SG18 0LD. and at HUNTINGDON, LETCHWORTH GARDEN CITY

ⓉⒻⒶ**George Hay & Company** *(N D Christy, J P P Craik, M G Davis, A P C Fox, P A Ventham)* 83 Cambridge Street, Pimlico, LONDON, SW1V 4PS.

George K W Ho & Co *(K G Ho)* Suite 1016 10/F, Chinachem Golden Plaza, 77 Mody Road, TSIM SHA TSUI, KOWLOON, HONG KONG SAR.

George M.C. Mak & Company *(G M Mak)* Office 907, 9/F, Kai Wong Commercial Building, 222-226 Queen's Road Central, SHEUNG WAN, HONG KONG ISLAND HONG KONG SAR.

George Palmer *(G I Palmer)* 53 Marlin Drive, WONGA BEACH, QLD 4873, AUSTRALIA.

George Panayiotou FCA *(G Panayiotou)* Corner 25th March Avenue, & Mystra Street, Papapetrou Building, Office 101 1st Floor, Egomi, 2408 NICOSIA CYPRUS.

George Pearce & Co *(G A Pearce)* The Forge, Langham, COLCHESTER, CO4 5PX.

Ⓟ**George Pearce & Co Ltd** *(G A Pearce)* The Forge, Langham, COLCHESTER, CO4 5PX.

George Rogers & Co. *(G W Rogers)* 12 Landor Road, Knowle, SOLIHULL, B93 9HZ.

George Ronson FCA *(G R Ronson)* 11 Healy Drive, ORPINGTON, KENT, BR6 9LB.

George Scurry & Co *(G M Scurry)* Suite B, Western House, St James Place, CRANLEIGH, SURREY, GU6 8RL.

★Ⓐ**George Snape** *(G Snape)* 214 High Street, WINSFORD, CW7 2AU.

George T. Ehlers *(G T Ehlers)* Trendlewood, Ditchling Common, BURGESS HILL, RH15 0SE.

George Tavares *(G F J Tavares)* 55 Purtell Street, EAST BENTLEIGH, VIC 3165, AUSTRALIA.

George Tso & Co *(K P G Tso)* 807 Fortress Tower, 250 King's Road, NORTH POINT, HONG KONG ISLAND, HONG KONG SAR.

George Whittaker FCA *(G M Whittaker)* 2 Twemlow Parade, Heysham, MORECAMBE, LANCASHIRE, LA3 1PD.

Ⓣ**Georgiades Charalambou & Co LLP** *(H Charalambou)* 283 Green Lanes, LONDON, N13 4XS.

Georgina Raffle *(G Raffle)* Warringtons, Gelsmoor Road, Coleorton, COALVILLE, LEICESTERSHIRE, LE67 8JF.

Georgiou & Prasanna LLP *(S Georgiou, A Prasanna)* 100 Pall Mall, St James, LONDON, SW1Y 5NQ.

★**GEP Associates** *(W T Gong, E C H Tan)* 25 Jalan 1/42A, Dataran Prima, 47301 PETALING JAYA, Selangor, MALAYSIA. and at JOHOR BAHRU, PENANG

Geraint Humphreys & Co *(G Humphreys)* 5-7 Beatrice Street, OSWESTRY, SY11 1QE.

Gerald Bailey *(G Bailey)* 6 St Martins Close, Firbeck, WORKSOP, S81 8JU.

Gerald Berlyn FCA *(G Berlyn)* Flat 10 Elderberry Court, 39b Bycullah Road, ENFIELD, MIDDLESEX, EN2 8FF.

Gerald Duthie & Co *(P Anderson)* 525 Windsor Avenue, WINDSOR N9A 1J4, ON, CANADA.

ⒻⓅ**Gerald Edelman Transaction Services Ltd** *(D B Atkinson, R H Kleiner)* 25 Harley Street, LONDON, W1G 9BR.

ⒻⓅⒶ**Gerald Holmes & Co, Nigel Webster & Co, trading names of Nigel Webster & Co Ltd** *(A J McSweeny, N B Webster)* 129 North Hill, PLYMOUTH, PL4 8JY.

ⓉⒻⒶ**Gerald Kreditor & Co** *(M Rosen, I S Sivlal, J Smulovitch, P P Smulovitch)* Hallswelle House, 1 Hallswelle Road, LONDON, NW11 0DH.

ⓉⒶ**Gerald Thomas & Co** *(J M Evans, B G Garland, M E Jones)* Furze Bank, 34 Hanover Street, SWANSEA, SA1 6BA.

Ⓐ**Gerroll & Co** *(A F Gerroll)* 10 Brockley Close, STANMORE, MIDDLESEX, HA7 4QL.

Gethin Lewis FCA CTA *(G W Lewis)* 24 Chiltern Drive, Royton, OLDHAM, OL2 5TD.

ⒻⒶ**GGDD llp** *(D J A Driver, G S Good)* 2nd Floor, Compton House, 29-33 Church Road, STANMORE, MIDDLESEX, HA7 4AR.

ⓅⒶ**GGS Consulting Limited** *(M V Lewis, W R L Oastler)* 12a Marlborough Place, BRIGHTON, BN1 1WN.

Ⓟ**GH Business & Accountancy Services, trading name of 360 Solutions (Cambridge) Ltd** *(G Hochmuth)* Ridgeways, 47a Lambs Lane, Cottenham, CAMBRIDGE, CB24 8TB.

Ⓟ**GH Online Accounting Ltd** *(R C Dilley, B D Jefferd, A P Newman, N J Willis)* Brigham House, 93 High Street, BIGGLESWADE, BEDFORDSHIRE, SG18 0LD.

Ghatan & Co. *(N Ghatan)* 4 Park Lodge Close, CHEADLE, CHESHIRE, SK8 1HU.

ⓉⓅ**Ghiaci Goodhand Smith, trading name of Ghiaci Goodhand Smith Limited** *(M V Lewis)* 12a Marlborough Place, BRIGHTON, EAST SUSSEX, BN1 1WN.

ⓉⓅ**Ghumra & Co Limited** *(Y O Ghumra)* 24 Vulcan House, Vulcan Road, LEICESTER, LE5 3EF.

Ⓟ**Ghumra Accounting Limited** *(Y O Ghumra)* 24 Vulcan House, Vulcan Road, LEICESTER, LE5 3EF.

Ⓟ**Gibbens Waterfield Ltd** *(D L Gibbens, H C Gibbens)* Priory House, 2 Priory Road, DUDLEY, WEST MIDLANDS, DY1 1HH.

ⓉⒶ**Gibbons** *(G Carty, L H Dixon, T Hindmoor, B C Sheard, M J Stanger, E Taylor, P F Tew, R J Thwaites)* Carleton House, 136 Gray Street, WORKINGTON, CUMBRIA, CA14 2LU. and at COCKERMOUTH, MARYPORT, WHITEHAVEN

ⓉⒻⒶ**Gibbons Mannington, Phipps & Co, trading names of Gibbons Mannington & Phipps** *(C E Barfoot, N S Cunliffe, D S S Hawkins, K M Luck, R Robinson, C A Rowsell, D E Sallows)* 82 High Street, TENTERDEN, KENT, TN30 6JG. and at BEXHILL-ON-SEA, RYE

Ⓟ**Gibbors** *(B J Gibbor)* 19 Ardross Avenue, NORTHWOOD, HA6 3DS.

ⓅⒶ**Gibbors Limited** *(B J Gibbor)* 19 Ardross Avenue, NORTHWOOD, MIDDLESEX, HA6 3DS.

ⓉⒶ**Gibson Appleby** *(S C Johnson, P J Watts)* 1-3 Ship Street, SHOREHAM-BY-SEA, WEST SUSSEX, BN43 5DH.

★ⓉⒶ**Gibson Booth** *(G Dickinson, S Lindley, S P Mell, A R J Russell, R Umbers, R I Watson, E C Wetton)* 12 Victoria Road, BARNSLEY, SOUTH YORKSHIRE, S70 2BB. and at HUDDERSFIELD

ⓉⓅ**Gibson Hewitt, trading name of Gibson Hewitt & Co** *(L Gibson, R D Hewitt)* 5 Park Court, Pyrford Road, WEST BYFLEET, SURREY, KT14 6SD.

Gibson McKerrell Brown LLP *(J Cordery)* 14 Rutland Square, EDINBURGH, EH1 2BD.

Gibsons *(M D Gibson)* Belmont, Church Road, St Mary's, ISLES OF SCILLY, TR21 0NA.

ⒻⓅⒶ**Gibsons Accountants Ltd** *(D A Gibson)* 226 Oldham Road, ROCHDALE, LANCASHIRE, OL11 2ER.

★Ⓟ**Gibsons Financial Limited** *(G C Gibbs, S.C. O'Neill, C O Ogunsola)* Foresters Hall, 25-27 Westow Street, LONDON, SE19 3RY.

Gidley Accounting *(Z L Gidley)* 1 Thornton Close, CRICK, NORTHAMPTONSHIRE, NN6 7GE.

ⓉⒶ**Giess Wallis Crisp LLP** *(G Armitage, T Crisp, A B Taffs, M J Wallis)* 10-12 Mulberry Green, HARLOW, ESSEX, CM17 0ET.

Ⓟ**Gil Black Ltd** *(G B Black)* 28 Chaise Meadow, LYMM, CHESHIRE, WA13 9UP.

Ⓐ**Gilbert & Co** *(B J Gilbert)* Suite 2, Hilton Hall, Hilton Lane, WOLVERHAMPTON, WV11 2BQ.

ⒻⒶ**Gilbert Allen & Co** *(J Duncan)* Churchdown Chambers, Bordyke, TONBRIDGE, TN9 1NR.

Ⓟ**Gilbert Allen Ltd** *(J Duncan)* Churchdown Chambers, Bordyke, TONBRIDGE, KENT, TN9 1NR.

Gilbert Finance & Accounting LLP *(N J Gilbert)* Amarna, Hillam Common Lane, Hillam, LEEDS, LS25 5HU.

ⒻⒶ**Gilbert, Allan & Co** *(W S Gilbert)* 8 Rodborough Road, LONDON, NW11 8RY.

ⓉⒻⒶ**Gilberts** *(R Hatrell, R Keeble, A Lovett, A J Ruggles)* Pendragon House, 65 London Road, ST. ALBANS, AL1 1LJ.

ⓉⒻⒶ**Gilchrist Tash** *(C T McBride, F M Parkin, L D Steel)* Cleveland Bldgs., Queen's Square, MIDDLESBROUGH, TS2 1PA.

Ⓐ**Gilderson & Co** *(J E Gilderson)* Hawthorn House, High Levels, Sandtoft, DONCASTER, DN8 5SJ. and at RETFORD

Ⓕ**Giles** *(A K Giles)* 32 High Street, Winterbourne, BRISTOL, BS36 1JN.

Giles & Co *(D B Giles)* Humphrystown House, BLESSINGTON, COUNTY WICKLOW, IRELAND.

Ⓟ**Giles & Co, trading name of Giles Accounting Services Ltd** *(M B Patel)* 7d Hill Avenue, AMERSHAM, BUCKINGHAMSHIRE, HP6 5BD.

▽**Gill & Johnson** *(S O Onyango)* Kirungii, Ring Road, Westlands (P.O. Box 40092), NAIROBI, KENYA. and at KAMPALA, MOMBASA

Gill Orchard ACA *(G M Orchard)* Warreston House, Slade Cross, Cosheston, PEMBROKE DOCK, SA72 4SX.

Ⓟ**Gill Peer & Co, trading name of Gill Peer & Company Limited** *(V D Shah)* 13 Alwyn Close, Elstree, BOREHAMWOOD, HERTFORDSHIRE, WD6 3LF.

Gill Sinkinson *(G M Sinkinson)* Fairview, 16 Wickwar Road, Kingswood, WOTTON-UNDER-EDGE, GLOUCESTERSHIRE, GL12 8RF.

ⓉⒻⒶ**Gillani & Co** *(R W Boulton)* Conduit House, Conduit Lane, HODDESDON, EN11 8EP.

Gillard Watson *(T Watson)* 7 The Pagets, Newick, LEWES, EAST SUSSEX, BN8 4PW.

Ⓟ**Gillards, trading name of Gillards Limited** *(D J Gillard)* 4 Heath Square, Boltro Road, HAYWARDS HEATH, RH16 1BL.

★ⒻⒶ**Gillespie Inverarity & Co** *(A Gillespie)* 33 Leslie Street, Blairgowie, PERTH, PH10 6AW. and at EDGWARE, EDINBURGH

Ⓟ**Gillespie's, trading name of Gillespie BS Limited** *(M Gillespie)* Henleaze House, Harbury Road, BRISTOL, BS9 4PN.

Gillian Barrett *(G R Barrett)* 34 Greenfield Avenue, SURBITON, SURREY, KT5 9HR.

Gillian Charles *(G S Charles)* 29 Aldbourne Avenue, Earley, READING, RG6 7DB.

Gillian Edwardes-Ker *(G C Edwardes-Ker)* 29 Shalstone Road, Mortlake, LONDON, SW14 7HP.

Gillian Evans *(G Evans)* 71 allee du Largado, 13190 ALLAUCH, FRANCE.

Gillian Jones & Company *(G Jones)* Ballykeane, GEASHILL, COUNTY OFFALY, IRELAND.

Gillian McKay Accountancy Services *(G J McKay)* 13 Pasquier Road, Walthamstow, LONDON, E17 6HB.

Gillian Nowell FCA *(G Nowell)* Clifton House, Hill Head, Bradwell, HOPE VALLEY, DERBYSHIRE, S33 9HY.

Gillian Taylor *(G Taylor)* 49 Creighton Avenue, Muswell Hill, LONDON, N10 1NR.

Gillian Tyerman & Co *(G C Tyerman)* 2-3 Robinson Terrace, WASHINGTON, TYNE AND WEAR, NE38 7BD.

ⒻⒶ**Gilpin and Harding** *(M J Gilpin, I Harding)* 15 St. Johns Place, Birtley, CHESTER LE STREET, COUNTY DURHAM, DH3 2PW.

ⒻⒶ**Gilroy & Brookes** *(L J Powell)* Ground Floor, Interpower House, Windsor Way, ALDERSHOT, HAMPSHIRE, GU11 1JG. and at ALTON

Gittins & Co *(C D Gittins)* 3 Tebbit Mews, Winchcombe Street, CHELTENHAM, GLOUCESTERSHIRE, GL52 2NF.

Ⓐ**Gittins Mulderrig** *(B D Mulderrig)* 6 High Street, NORTHWOOD, MIDDLESEX, HA6 1BN.

★**Giwa-Osagie DFK & Co** *(A R O O Giwa-Osagie)* 6 Ugbague Street, P.O. Box 16, BENIN CITY, NIGERIA. and at LAGOS, ONITSHA, YOLA

GJ Almond *(G J Almond)* 3 Topfield, Popes Lane, COLCHESTER, CO3 3JR.

Ⓟ**GJ Consultancy Services Ltd** *(G Jones)* 55 Siskin Road, Offerton, STOCKPORT, CHESHIRE, SK2 5JX.

GJ Duda *(G J Duda)* Tree Tops, Outwood Common, Outwood, REDHILL, RH1 5PW.

Ⓟ**GJH Accountancy & Taxation Services, trading name of GJH Accountants Ltd** *(G J Harding)* Five Ways, 57-59 Hatfield Road, POTTERS BAR, HERTFORDSHIRE, EN6 1HS.

GJH Accountancy and Taxation Services, trading name of Gary J. Harding *(G J Harding)* 24 Brickfield Avenue, Leverstock Green, HEMEL HEMPSTEAD, HP3 8NP. and at POTTERS BAR

Ⓟ**GK Abbott & Co, trading name of GK Abbott & Co Limited** *(G K Abbott)* 25 Wollaton Road, Beeston, NOTTINGHAM, NG9 2NG.

Ⓟ**GKM Associates Limited** *(N K Montague)* 8 Caspian Close, PURFLEET, ESSEX, RM19 1LH.

ⓅⒶ**GKP Partnership Ltd** *(C E Carter, A Sharma)* 109-110 Viglen House, Alperton Lane, WEMBLEY, MIDDLESEX, HA0 1HD.

ⓉⓅ**GKP Partnership, trading name of CPL Audit Limited** *(C E Carter, A Sharma)* 110 Viglen House, Alperton Lane, WEMBLEY, MIDDLESEX, HA0 1HD.

ⒻⒶ**GKP, trading name of Graham Keeble Partnership LLP** *(G C Keeble)* First Floor, 5 Doolittle Yard, Froghall Road, Ampthill, BEDFORD, MK45 2NW.

Glaister Jones & Co *(R J Jones)* 1a The Wool Market, Dyer Street, CIRENCESTER, GLOUCESTERSHIRE, GL7 2PR.

Ⓕ**Glassman & Company** *(D Glassman)* 8 Holywell Hill, ST. ALBANS, HERTFORDSHIRE, AL1 1BZ.

Ⓟ**Glassman & Company Limited** *(D Glassman)* 8 Holywell Hill, ST. ALBANS, HERTFORDSHIRE, AL1 1BZ.

★ⒻⒶ**Glazers** *(R Black, P G Herszaft, S B Okin, D Specterman)* 843 Finchley Road, LONDON, NW11 8NA.

★Ⓟ**Glazers, trading name of Glazers Ltd** *(R Black, P G Herszaft, S B Okin, D Specterman)* 843 Finchley Road, LONDON, NW11 8NA.

Ⓟ**Gleek Cadman Ross Limited** *(C Cadman, D J Gleek, M L Ross)* Credcoll House, 96 Marsh Lane, LEEDS, LS9 8SR.

ⓉⒻⒶ**Gleek Cadman Ross LLP** *(C Cadman, D J Gleek, M L Ross)* Credcoll House, 96 Marsh Lane, LEEDS, LS9 8SR.

Glen C Davis BA ACA *(G C Davis)* 22 High Road, Essendon, HATFIELD, HERTFORDSHIRE, AL9 6HW.

ⓉⓅⒶ**Glen C Rodger Limited** *(R A Purvis, E Watson)* Cragside House, Heaton Road, NEWCASTLE UPON TYNE, NE6 1SE.

Ⓟ**Glenburgh, trading name of Glenburgh Limited** *(R A Harris)* 136 Boden Street, GLASGOW, G40 3PX.

★**Glencoe Accounting** *(A W Webb)* Maxwell Road, LANGHOLM, DUMFRIESSHIRE, DG13 0DX.

Glencross Wood & Co *(J Wood)* 247 Seymour Grove, Old Trafford, MANCHESTER, M16 0DS.

Ⓟ**Glenoaks Accounting Services Ltd** *(P R W Smith)* 120 Bull Head Street, WIGSTON, LEICESTERSHIRE, LE18 1PB.

ⓉⒻⒶ**Glew, Dunn & Co** *(J C Fleming)* 83 Spring Bank, HULL, HU3 1AG.

ⓉⒶ**GLF Richards & Co** *(D M Parry-Richards)* Unit 8, Connect Business Village, 24 Derby Road, LIVERPOOL, L5 9PR.

★**GLK Financial Services S.L.** *(P A Lawrence)* Cl. Imaculada Conception 7, Edif Europa of 1, Arroyo De La Hiel, 29631 MALAGA, SPAIN.

ⓅⒶ**glm Ghest Lloyd Limited** *(A C Marsh)* 103-105 Brighton Road, COULSDON, SURREY, CR5 2NG.

Ⓟ**Global Payroll Services Ltd** *(G I Topol)* 102 Selby Road, West Bridgford, NOTTINGHAM, NG2 7BA.

Globe Accounting *(A T Watts)* 19 Isaacson Road, Burwell, CAMBRIDGE, CB25 0AF.

ⓉⒶ**Glover & Co** *(J S Mellor, P S Mellor)* 13/15 Netherhall Road, DONCASTER, DN1 2PH.

ⓉⒻ**Glover & Co** *(B Campbell)* 50A Oswald Road, SCUNTHORPE, DN15 7PQ. and at DONCASTER

ⓉⓅ**Glover & Co, trading name of Accountancy and Tax Solutions Ltd** *(L R Glover)* Unit 2, Hockliffe Business Park, Hockliffe, LEIGHTON BUZZARD, BEDFORDSHIRE, LU7 9NB.

ⓉⒶ**Glover Stanbury & Co** *(N A Bennett, M J Chance, S D Pearce, B C Ross, K N Salter, M R Shute)* 30 Bear Street, BARNSTAPLE, DEVON, EX32 7DD. and at BIDEFORD

★ⓉⒶ**GLS, GLS Wealth Management, trading names of Geo Little Sebire & Co** *(G A Cleaver, R J Crawley)* Oliver House, 19-23 Windmill Hill, ENFIELD, MIDDLESEX, EN2 7AB.

Glyn Hewitt *(R G Hewitt)* Network House, St Ives Way, Sandycroft, DEESIDE, CLWYD, CH5 2QS.

Glyn Pike *(G M Pike)* 10 Mark Road, Hightown, LIVERPOOL, L38 0BH.

Glynis D. Morris *(G D Morris)* Cae Ceffylau, Drefach, LLANYBYDDER, DYFED, SA40 9SX.

Glynis I. Hayton FCA *(G I Hayton)* 92 Valley Park, WHITEHAVEN, CUMBRIA, CA28 8BA.

Ⓟ**GM Accountancy Services Ltd** *(K B March)* 308 London Road, Hazel Grove, STOCKPORT, CHESHIRE, SK7 4RF.

GM Associates *(G I Moscrop)* 7 Viga Road, Grange Park, LONDON, N21 1HH.

★Ⓐ**GMAK** *(Guy Mayers)* 5-7 Vernon Yard, Portobello Road, LONDON, W11 2DX.

★ⓅⒶ**GMAK Services Limited** *(Guy Mayers)* Flat 1, 26 Lansdowne Road, LONDON, W11 3LL.

ⒻⓅ**GMC Accountancy Limited** *(G M Chipp)* 18 North End, BEDALE, NORTH YORKSHIRE, DL8 1AB.

ⒻⒶ**GMG Roberts** *(H A Mehdyoun, A J Sansom)* 47 Queen Anne Street, LONDON, W1G 9JG.

Ⓟ**GNG Accountants Limited** *(G Georgiades)* 176 Makarios III Avenue, Pashalis Court 201, PO Box 57161, 3027 LIMASSOL, CYPRUS.

Ⓟ**Go Matilda, trading name of Go Matilda (Accounting and Tax) Pty Limited** *(A Collett)* L27 Rialto South Tower, 525 Collins Street, MELBOURNE, VIC 3000, AUSTRALIA.

ⓅⒶ**Goatcher Chandler, trading name of Goatcher Chandler Limited** *(C R Chandler, J Goatcher)* 10 Overcliffe, GRAVESEND, KENT, DA11 0EF.

Ⓟ**Goddard & Co, trading name of Peter Goddard & Co Ltd** *(P B Goddard)* 125 High Street, Odiham, HOOK, RG29 1LA.

Goddards *(K J Goddard)* 54 New Road, ESHER, SURREY, KT10 9NU.

Godfrey *(D J Godfrey)* 75 Queens Park Avenue, BOURNEMOUTH, BH8 9LJ.

Godfrey Accounting *(H J Godfrey)* 1 Farnham Road, GUILDFORD, SURREY, GU2 4RG.

Ⓕ**Godfrey Anderson & Co.** *(S Godfrey)* 6 Latchmoor Way, GERRARDS CROSS, SL9 8LP.

★Ⓣ**Godfrey Edwards** *(R A Godfrey)* Park Lodge, Rhosddu Road, WREXHAM, LL11 1NF.

Ⓟ**Godfrey Holland, trading name of Godfrey Holland Limited** *(A N Vause)* Venture House, 341 Palatine Road, Northenden, MANCHESTER, M22 4FY.

ⓉⒻⓅⒶ**Godfrey Laws & Co Limited** *(H C S Ashmore)* 69 Knowl Piece, Wilbury Way, HITCHIN, HERTFORDSHIRE, SG4 0TY. and at BEDFORD

Ⓟ**Godfrey Mansell & Co Ltd** *(G I Cook, G Mansell)* Hales Court, Stourbridge Road, HALESOWEN, WEST MIDLANDS, B63 3TT.

Ⓐ**Godfrey Mansell & Co, trading name of Godfrey Mansell & Co LLP** *(G I Cook, G Mansell)* Hales Court, Stourbridge Road, HALESOWEN, WEST MIDLANDS, B63 3TT.

Godfrey Whitehead *(G Whitehead)* The Okefield, Beaulieu Road, LYNDHURST, SO43 7DA.

ⓅⒶ**Godfrey Wilson Ltd** *(A Godfrey, R C Wilson)* Unit 5.11 Paintworks, Bath Road, BRISTOL, BS4 3EH.

ⒻⒶ**Godley & Co.** *(D Malde, V K N Shah)* Congress House, 14 Lyon Road, HARROW, MIDDLESEX, HA1 2EN.

Ⓕ**Godson & Co** *(R G Godson)* 6/7 Pollen Street, LONDON, W1S 1NJ.

Godwin & Company *(D P Godwin)* 16 Railway Place, High Street, CORK, COUNTY CORK, IRELAND.

Godwin Harby *(N E Harby)* Grays Court, 5 Nursery Road, BIRMINGHAM, B15 3JX.

★**Goff and Company** *(B L Goff)* 89 Havant Road, EMSWORTH, HAMPSHIRE, PO10 7LF.

★ⓉⒻⓅⒶ**Goldblatts, trading name of Goldblatts Limited** *(S Ferguson)* 171-173 Gray's Inn Road, LONDON, WC1X 8UE. and at CHATHAM

ⒻⒶ**Goldin & Co** *(I A Goldin)* 105 Hoe Street, Walthamstow, LONDON, E17 4SA. and at GRAYS

ⓅⒶ**Golding West & Co Limited** *(M J Golding)* 16 Station Road, CHESHAM, BUCKINGHAMSHIRE, HP5 1DH.

Goldsmith & Co *(P Goldsmith)* 61 Highgate High Street, LONDON, N6 5JX.

Ⓟ**Goldsmiths Bayley Ltd** *(W R M Goldsmith)* 7 Glentworth Road, Clifton, BRISTOL, BS8 4TB.

ⓉⓅⒶ**Goldstar, trading name of Goldstar Accountants Ltd** *(M Z Iqbal)* Ibex House, 85 Southampton Street, READING, RG1 2QU.

★**Goldwells** *(J E Sutton)* Heaton House, 4 Gordon Street, NAIRN, IV12 4DQ.

ⓅⒶ**Goldwins, trading name of Goldwins Limited** *(A I Benosiglio, A J W Epton, S P Goodwin)* 75 Maygrove Road, West Hampstead, LONDON, NW6 2EG.

★ⓉⒻⒶ**Goldwyns** *(M T Motyer, M A Myers)* 13 David Mews, Porter Street, LONDON, W1U 6EQ.

ⓉⒻⓅⒶ**Goldwyns, trading name of Goldwyns (Bristol) Ltd** *(C M Brown)* 9 Portland Square, BRISTOL, BS2 8ST.

★Ⓟ**Goldwyns, trading name of Goldwyns (London) Limited** *(M T Motyer, M A Myers)* 13 David Mews, Porter Street, LONDON, W1U 6EQ.

ⓉⒻⓅⒶ**Goldwyns, trading name of Goldwyns Limited** *(B Maini, A R Millman, D J Reynolds, I S Simpson)* Rutland House, 90-92 Baxter Avenue, SOUTHEND-ON-SEA, SS2 6HZ.

Gomez & Co *(J G Gomez)* 16-A 1st Fl, Jalan Tun Sambanthan 3, Brickfields, 50470 KUALA LUMPUR, FEDERAL TERRITORY, MALAYSIA.

ⓉⓅ**Gompertz Kendall, trading name of Gompertz Kendall & Co Limited** *(M W Pearsall)* 1st Floor, Trigate, 210-222 Hagley Road West, OLDBURY, WEST MIDLANDS, B68 0NP.

Good & Co *(J W Good)* The White House, 6 Nottingham Road, Cropwell Bishop, NOTTINGHAM, NG12 3BQ.

Good Financial Management *(G J Good)* 18 Aylesbury Close, New Catton, NORWICH, NR3 3LB.

Ⓟ**Good Payroll Services Ltd** *(P Stewart)* Lyndhurst, 1 Cranmer Street, Long Eaton, NOTTINGHAM, NG10 1NJ.

ⒻⓅ**Goodale Mardle Limited** *(A R Mardle)* Greens Court, West Street, MIDHURST, WEST SUSSEX, GU29 9NQ.

ⒻⒶ**Goodall & Co** *(T M C Goodall)* Abacus House, Manor Road, LONDON, W13 0AS.

ⓉⒻⒶ**Goodband Viner Taylor** *(E M C Goodband, M D Viner)* Ellin House, 42 Kingfield Road, SHEFFIELD, S11 9AS.

Ⓟ**Goodbridge Ltd** *(R K Lung)* 17 Hemingford Close, LONDON, N12 9HF.

Goodheads *(C Goodhead)* Oceans End, Rose Hill, MARAZION, CORNWALL, TR17 0HB.

ⓉⓅⒶ**Goodier, Smith and Watts Limited** *(D J Mead, A B Turner)* Devonshire House, Manor Way, BOREHAMWOOD, HERTFORDSHIRE, WD6 1QQ.

Goodin Reid & Co *(M C Reid)* 7 Woodside Road, NEW MALDEN, KT3 3AH.

Ⓐ**Goodman & Co** *(P C Goodman)* 14 Basing Hill, Golders Green, LONDON, NW11 8TH.

ⓉⒻⒶ**Goodman Jones, trading name of Goodman Jones LLP** *(M P G Austin, J C Bates, G J Blair, G P Bursack, J M Finesilver, J R Flitter, M D Goldstein, W E Grossman, L M Phillips, P J Rogol, A Sharma, S I Wildman, P H Woodgate)* 29-30 Fitzroy Square, LONDON, W1T 6LQ.

Goodmans *(R A Goodman)* 138 Bury Old Road, Whitefield, MANCHESTER, M45 6AT.

Ⓟ**Goodmans, trading name of Goodmans Accounting and Advisory Ltd** *(P M Goodman)* The Waterfront (ADI Office), Salts Mill Road, Saltaire, SHIPLEY, WEST YORKSHIRE, BD17 7EZ.

Goodrich Morrison & Co *(S R Goodrich)* 10 Durfold Road, HORSHAM, RH12 5HZ.

ⓉⒻⒶ**Goodwin Shaw** *(N S Chandler, R E O Goodwin)* 39 Market Place, CHIPPENHAM, SN15 3HT.

ⓅⒶ**Goodwins, trading name of L J Goodwin & Co Limited** *(L J Goodwin)* 6 Parkside Court, Greenhough Road, LICHFIELD, STAFFORDSHIRE, WS13 7AU.

Ⓐ**Goorney & Taylor** *(R G Taylor, P G Wigan)* 14 Abingdon Street, BLACKPOOL, FY1 1PY.

Gopal & Co *(G S Iyengar)* 349 Hagley Rd, Edgbaston, BIRMINGHAM, B17 8DL.

Gordon A. Smith *(G A Smith)* The Gables, 14 Beech Road, Saltford, BRISTOL, BS31 3BE.

Ⓟ**Gordon Consultancy Limited** *(R W Gordon)* Hamilton, 13 The Nurseries, Linstock, CARLISLE, CA6 4RR.

Ⓟ**Gordon Cutler & Co Limited** *(G Cutler)* The Maybird Suite, The Maybird Centre, Birmingham Road, STRATFORD-UPON-AVON, WARWICKSHIRE, CV37 0HZ.

Ⓟ**Gordon Down & Company Ltd** *(L S Cohen)* 144 Walter Road, SWANSEA, SA1 5RW.

★Ⓐ**Gordon Down & Partners** *(L S Cohen)* 144 Walter Road, SWANSEA, SA1 5RW. and at CARDIFF

Ⓟ**Gordon Leighton Limited** *(M S Somerston)* Enterprise House, 21 Buckle Street, LONDON, E1 8NN.

Ⓟ**Gordon Levy Limited** *(G H Levy)* Arthur House, Chorlton Street, MANCHESTER, M1 3FH.

Gordon Moss *(G L Moss)* 159 Pencisely Road, Llandaff, CARDIFF, CF5 1DN.

Gordon Pennington & Co *(G Pennington)* 1 Hall View Close, Gorstage, NORTHWICH, CW8 2GB.

Gordon Spencer *(G T Spencer)* 70A Victoria Road, WORTHING, BN11 1UN.

Ⓐ**Gordon Wood, Scott & Partners** *(J D Moorcraft, R J Williams, E G Winstone)* Dean House, 94 Whiteladies Road, Clifton, BRISTOL, BS8 2QX.

Ⓟ**Gordons Knight & Co Ltd** *(G P D'silva)* Pendragon House, 170 Merton High Street, LONDON, SW19 1AY.

Gore & Company *(K S Girn)* QWest, International House, Great West Road, BRENTFORD, MIDDLESEX, TW8 0GP. and at BIRMINGHAM, CARDIFF, READING

ⒻⒶ**Gorings** *(M R Allen, D H Bigland, D A Grace)* The Laurels, St. Mary Street, ILKESTON, DE7 8BQ. and at NOTTINGHAM

Ⓟ**Gorman Darby & Co Limited** *(A T Darby)* 74 Chancery Lane, LONDON, WC2A 1AD.

ⓉⒻⒶ**Gormley & Co** *(J B A Gormley)* Plurenden Manor Farm, Plurenden Road, High Halden, ASHFORD, KENT, TN26 3JW.
ⒻⓅⒶ**Gorrie Whitson, trading name of Gorrie Whitson Limited** *(G W Bowler, J R Russell, K E Upsdell)* 18 Hand Court, LONDON, WC1V 6JF. and at SANDERSTEAD
Ⓐ**Gort & March** *(K B March)* 308 London Road, Hazel Grove, STOCKPORT, CHESHIRE, SK7 4RF.
ⓉⒻⒶ**Gortons** *(D J Gorton, J Gorton)* Stanmore House, 64-68 Blackburn Street, Radcliffe, MANCHESTER, M26 2JS.
Ⓕ**Gosling Consulting** *(G H Gosling)* Unit 15, Hockley Court, 2401 Stratford Road, Hockley Heath, SOLIHULL, WEST MIDLANDS B94 6NW.
ⒻⓅⒶ**Gostling Ltd** *(P J Gostling)* Unit 6, Acorn Business Park, Keighley Road, SKIPTON, NORTH YORKSHIRE, BD23 2UE. and at KENDAL, MORECAMBE
ⓉⒶ**Gotham Erskine, trading name of Gotham Erskine LLP** *(J M Ball, S D Erskine, J Gare, P J Gotham)* Friendly House, 52-58 Tabernacle Street, LONDON, EC2A 4NJ.
Gould & Mansford *(M Gillibrand)* P O Box 151, Anvil Cottage, Anvil Lane, Letcombe Regis, WANTAGE, OXFORDSHIRE OX12 9LA.
Gowards *(S P Davies)* 102 Burnmill Road, MARKET HARBOROUGH, LEICESTERSHIRE, LE16 7JG.
ⓉⒻⓅⒶ**Gowers Limited** *(M L S Bach, I A Carter, D M Green)* The Old School House, Bridge Road, Hunton Bridge, KINGS LANGLEY, HERTFORDSHIRE, WD4 8SZ.
Gower-Smith and Co *(N M Gower-Smith)* Grosvenor Lodge, 72 Grosvenor Road, TUNBRIDGE WELLS, TN1 2AZ.
GP & Co *(G Patel)* 105 Streatfield Road, Kenton, HARROW, MIDDLESEX, HA3 9BL.
Ⓟ**GP Tax Limited** *(G M Peck)* Kempston, Mill Hill, EDENBRIDGE, KENT, TN8 5DQ.
ⒻⓅⒶ**GPFM, trading name of G P Financial Management Limited** *(T D Tribe, T Warren)* 8-9 The Old Yard, Lodge Farm Business Centre, Wolverton Road, Castlethorpe, MILTON KEYNES, MK19 7ES.
ⒻⓅ**GPMA, trading name of GPMA Limited** *(G T Psara)* Devon House, Church Hill, LONDON, N21 1LE.
GPS Accounting Services *(G P Snape)* 172 Croston Road, Farington Moss Leyland, PRESTON, PR26 6PQ.
Ⓟ**GRA Enterprises Ltd** *(K I Trocki)* 15 Perry Road, Sherwood, NOTTINGHAM, NG5 3AD.
ⒻⒶ**Graeme Bruce & Partners** *(G A Davis)* 911 Green Lanes, LONDON, N21 2QP.
Ⓟ**Graeme M. Pike Ltd** *(G M Pike)* 48 Prince Charles Avenue, CHATHAM, ME5 8EY.
Graham Anderson *(G Anderson)* Holwell, Stainfield Road, Kirkby Underwood, BOURNE, LINCOLNSHIRE, PE10 0SG.
★**Graham Associates AG** *(A J Ashurst)* Breitackerstr 1, 8702 ZOLLIKON, SWITZERLAND.
Ⓟ**Graham B Walker Ltd** *(G B Walker)* 1 Westfield Cottages, Newton on Derwent, YORK, YO41 4DG.
ⒻⓅ**Graham Barber Accountancy Limited** *(G C Barber)* Westcross House, 73 Midford Road, BATH, BA2 5RT.
Ⓐ**Graham Barnes** *(G P Barnes)* 19A The Nook, Anstey, LEICESTER, LE7 7AZ.
Ⓐ**Graham Best & Co** *(G R Best)* 189 Lynchford Road, FARNBOROUGH, HAMPSHIRE, GU14 6HD.
Graham Bravo & Co *(G P Bravo)* 27 Tudor Manor Gardens, WATFORD, WD25 9TQ.
Graham Brooker FCA *(G Brooker)* River Hill Cottage, River Hill, Flamstead, ST. ALBANS, HERTFORDSHIRE, AL3 8BY.
Graham Brown & Co. *(J G Brown)* 2 Bathwick Terrace, Bathwick Hill, BATH, BA2 4EL.
Graham Carter FCA *(G W V Carter)* 20 Hardys Field, Kingsclere, NEWBURY, BERKSHIRE, RG20 5EU.
Ⓟ**Graham Cohen & Company, trading name of Graham Cohen & Co Limited** *(G Cohen)* 16 South End, CROYDON, SURREY, CR0 1DN.
Graham Cruickshank BA FCA *(G D Cruickshank)* 35 Whittingstall Road, LONDON, SW6 4EA.
Graham Dawes *(G K Dawes)* 117 Nottingham Road, Kimberley, NOTTINGHAM, NG16 2ND.
★Ⓕ**Graham Dent & Co** *(C J Dent)* Compton House, 104 Scotland Road, PENRITH, CUMBRIA, CA11 7NR.
Graham Gosling & Co *(G M Gosling)* 1 Fawns Keep, Mottram Rise, STALYBRIDGE, SK15 2UL.
Graham H Y Chan & Co *(S Chan)* Unit 1, 15/F, The Center, 99 Queen's Road Central, CENTRAL, HONG KONG SAR.
Graham H Y Chan & Co *(G H Y Chan, S K R Chan)* Unit 1, 15/F The Center, 99 Queens Road, CENTRAL, HONG KONG ISLAND, HONG KONG SAR.
ⓉⒻⒶ**Graham H. Wood & Co** *(S J Booth)* 225 Market Street, HYDE, CHESHIRE, SK14 1HF.
Graham Hunn & Company *(G M G Hunn)* Field Walls, The Avenue, SHERBORNE, DORSET, DT9 3AH. and at SUTTON
Ⓐ**Graham Hunt & Co** *(G A Hunt)* Unit 15, Hockliffe Business Park, Watling Street Hockliffe, LEIGHTON BUZZARD, LU7 9NB.
Graham I. Ryder *(G I Ryder)* 120 Ashton Road, Denton, MANCHESTER, M34 3JE.
Graham J Taylor *(G J Taylor)* 25 Index Drive, DUNSTABLE, BEDFORDSHIRE, LU6 3TU.
Graham J. Cryer *(G J Cryer)* 3 Humpty Dumpty Meadow, St. Thomas Hill, CANTERBURY, CT2 8HN.
Graham J. Lodge & Co *(G J Lodge)* 12 Main Road, Brookville, THETFORD, IP26 4RB.
Ⓟ**Graham Jones, trading name of GJCA Limited** *(A C Mulley, G Jones)* 15 The South Street Centre, 16-20 South Street, Hythe, SOUTHAMPTON, SO45 6EB.
ⒻⓅ**Graham Latham Limited** *(G W Latham)* Hedge House, Hangersley Hill, Hangersley, RINGWOOD, HAMPSHIRE, BH24 3JW.
Graham Laycock & Associates *(G J Laycock)* 152 Eastern Road, BRIGHTON, BN2 0AE.
Ⓐ**Graham Long** *(G Long)* 107 The Broadway, LEIGH-ON-SEA, SS9 1PG.
Graham M. Cooper & Co *(G M Cooper)* Peek Building, George St., P.O. Box N8160, NASSAU, BAHAMAS.
★ⒻⓅⒶ**Graham Martin & Co, trading name of Eastleigh Accountants Limited** *(G P Martin)* 89 Leigh Road, EASTLEIGH, HAMPSHIRE, SO50 9DQ.
Ⓐ**Graham Meager** *(G S Meager)* 12 Wendover Close, ST. ALBANS, HERTFORDSHIRE, AL4 9JW.
Graham P Thompson *(G P Thompson)* Beaufoys, Firle Road, SEAFORD, BN25 2HU.
ⓉⒻⓅⒶ**Graham Paul, trading name of Graham Paul Limited** *(A S Lee, D G Paul, B G Scott, J D Squire, I G Washbourne)* 10-12 Dunraven Place, BRIDGEND, MID GLAMORGAN, CF31 1JD. and at CARDIFF
Graham Price *(J G V Price)* 18 Trotsworth Avenue, VIRGINIA WATER, GU25 4AL.
Graham Shaw *(G Shaw)* 2 St Paul's Close, CLITHEROE, BB7 2NA.
Ⓟ**Graham Sherling and Co, trading name of Graham Sherling and Co Limited** *(G C Sherling)* 36 The Avenue, Hatch End, PINNER, MIDDLESEX, HA5 4EY.
ⒻⒶ**Graham Smith** *(M T Staddon)* 11 Green Lane, REDRUTH, TR15 1JY.
Ⓟ**Graham Sunley & Co, trading name of Graham Sunley & Co Limited** *(M E Brooke-Taylor)* 52 Front Street, Acomb, YORK, YO24 3BX.
Ⓕ**Graham Winstanley** *(G Winstanley)* North Barn, Torgate Farm, Torgate Lane, Bassingham, LINCOLN, LN5 9JG.
Ⓟ**Graham Winstanley Ltd** *(G Winstanley)* Manor Farm, Moor Lane, Aubourn, LINCOLN, LN5 9DX.
★**Graham Wood Partnership** *(S J Booth)* 225 Market Street, HYDE, CHESHIRE, SK14 1HF.
Graham Worsfold *(G R G Worsfold)* 102 Hawthorn Road, WOKING, GU22 0BG.
Graham, Smith & Partners *(J H Graham)* Hemonystraat 11, 1074 BK AMSTERDAM, NETHERLANDS.
Grahame Isard *(G R H Isard)* 129 Southgate Street, BURY ST. EDMUNDS, SUFFOLK, IP33 2AF.
ⓅⒶ**Grahame J Harbour Limited** *(G J Harbour)* 1 Windrush Road, Keynsham, BRISTOL, BS31 1QL.
Ⓟ**Granary Accounting Ltd** *(F P A Reid)* The Granary, Wheatlands Manor, Park Lane, Finchampstead, WOKINGHAM, BERKSHIRE RG40 4QL.
★**Granite Morgan Smith** *(C J Smith)* 122 Feering Hill, Feering, COLCHESTER, CO5 9PY.
ⓉⓅ**Grant & Co (Accountants) Limited** *(M G Gray)* 7 Manor Park Business Centre, Mackenzie Way, CHELTENHAM, GLOUCESTERSHIRE, GL51 9TX.
ⓅⒶ**Grant Franklin Limited** *(G D Franklin)* 64 Clarendon Road, WATFORD, WD17 1DA.
ⒻⓅⒶ**Grant Sellers, trading name of Grant Sellers Limited** *(S Sellers)* Bank Court, Manor Road, VERWOOD, DORSET, BH31 6DY.
★**Grant Thornton** *(Y Hsiang, N Lo, H Y H Ng)* 6th Floor, Nexus Building, 41 Conaught Road, CENTRAL, HONG KONG SAR. and at CAUSEWAY BAY
ⓉⒶ**Grant Thornton** *(D A McGurgan, R C Ratcliffe)* PO Box 307, 3rd Floor, Exchange House, 54-58 Athor Street, Douglas, ISLE OF MAN IM99 2BE.
★**Grant Thornton** *(P A Billingham)* Level 2, 215 Spring Street, MELBOURNE, VIC 3000, AUSTRALIA. and at SYDNEY
★**Grant Thornton** *(V Chandiok, P Grover)* L41 Connaught Circus, NEW DELHI 110001, INDIA.
Ⓣ**Grant Thornton** *(A S Hajee Abdoula, Y Thacoor)* 2nd Floor, Fairfax House, 21 Mgr Gonin Street, PORT LOUIS, MAURITIUS.
ⓉⓅ**Grant Thornton (Gibraltar) Limited** *(M A Hayday)* 6A Queensway, PO Box 64, GIBRALTAR, GIBRALTAR.
★ⓅⒶ**Grant Thornton Limited** *(M A Colver, A Langley)* Kensington Chambers, 46/50 Kensington Place, JERSEY, JE1 1ET. and at GUERNSEY
Grant Thornton LLP *(J T Holdstock)* Grant Thornton Place, Suite 1600 - 333 Seymour Street, VANCOUVER V6B 0A4, BC, CANADA. and at TORONTO, VICTORIA
Grant Thornton Spain *(D M Radley-Searle)* Jose Abascal 56, 28003 MADRID, SPAIN.
★ⓉⒶ**Grant Thornton UK LLP** *(R Aitken, S J Akers, M L Aldridge, N M Armstrong, D P Ascott, T A J Back, S R Baker, D L Barnes, S Barnes, P J Barrett, J A Bartlett, E J Best, D G N Bolton, J Bowler, J R Brown, M J Burt, P S Burton, M R Byers, M J Cardiff, I S Carr, A J Chande, R J Chaplin, C M S J Clements, P A Cooper, J Corbishley, C E Corner, S J Cornmell, P J Crooks, S K Croston, J G Davies, W H W Davies, P M Dawson, D J Dunckley, M Dunham, J Earp, M G Ellis, K M Engel, P M D Etherington, I M Evans, N E Farr, P Flatley, C J N Frostwick, K A Gale, P J Gamson, M N Gardner, M P Gerrard, M A Goddard, K M Godfree, J C Golding, M A Gomersall, J M Grant, D K Grundy, P J Hall, H Hamedani, W E Hart, C S Hartnell, K V Hiddleston, K Hinds, M J Hore, P R Houghton, O C Hutton-Potts, D A Ingram, T D James, I R Johnson, S J Jones, C Kemsley, F C Lagerberg, D A Lamb, A Lees, T J W Lincoln, J C Loebl, S L Longworth, S J Lowe, I R Marwood, S Maslin, D M Mason, D A S Maxwell, M A M Merali, G L Mesher, J D Mew, D F Miller, S J Mills, S C Morris, N Morrison, J R Morter, C M Mundy, D P Munton, S Muskett, R F Napper, P P Naylor, D A Newstead, J Newton, W E Nicholls, J O'Mahony, G Odlin, N S Page, P S Prior, R N Proctor, A C Rasmussen, M Redfern, A N Richards, S J Robinson, J N Rogers, S V Romanovitch, L Ross, C A Rudge, N M Rutledge, N R Savory, P J Secrett, A D Seekings, A A Sharifi, M D Sheppard, J M Shinnick, I V Smart, C Smith, D R W Smith, A L Stopford, P D Storey, N J Sturmey, M J Swales, D S Taylor, M A Taylor, M J Thornton, J M Toone, S J Vanags, M R Ward, A G Wardell, N J Watson, R Welsby, P R Westerman, D P White, G D Williams, H C Wilson, I P J Wilson, T J L Wilson, A Wood)* Grant Thornton House, 22 Melton Street, Euston Square, LONDON, NW1 2EP. and at BELFAST, BIRMINGHAM, BRISTOL, CAMBRIDGE, CARDIFF, CRAWLEY, EDINBURGH, GLASGOW, HIGH WYCOMBE, IPSWICH, KETTERING, LEEDS, LEICESTER, LIVERPOOL, MANCHESTER, MILTON KEYNES, NEWCASTLE UPON TYNE, NORTHAMPTON, NORWICH, OXFORD, READING, SHEFFIELD, SLOUGH, SOUTHAMPTON
★ⒻⒶ**grantharrodparkinson, trading name of Grant Harrod Parkinson LLP** *(A H Grant, J B Grant, J L Parkinson)* 49a High Street, RUISLIP, MIDDLESEX, HA4 7BD.
ⒻⒶ**Grants** *(I J Grant)* 11 Park Place, LEEDS, LS1 2RX.
Ⓕ**Grashoff & Co** *(T Grashoff)* 35 Whellock Road, LONDON, W4 1DY.
Ⓟ**Grashoff & Co, trading name of Grashoff & Co Ltd** *(T Grashoff)* 35 Whellock Road, LONDON, W4 1DY.
Ⓕ**Grassbys** *(S D Grassby)* Lindsay House, 15 Springfield Way, Anlaby, HULL, HU10 6RJ.
ⒻⓅⒶ**Gravestock & Owen Ltd** *(K Evans, M Owen)* 75 New Road, WILLENHALL, WV13 2DA.
Ⓐ**Gray & Co** *(I S Gray)* Springvale, Police Station Square, Mildenhall, BURY ST. EDMUNDS, IP28 7ER.
Ⓟ**Gray Carpendale Ltd** *(A F R Mendes)* 55A London Road, LEICESTER, LE2 0PE.
ⓉⒻⓅⒶ**Graybrowne Limited** *(N V Browne, A L Gray)* The Counting House, Nelson Street, HULL, HU1 1XE.
★ⒻⒶ**Grays** *(M W Marsden)* 1 Parliament Street, HULL, HU1 2AS.
Ⓟ**Grays Accountants Limited** *(F M Cox, R S Gray)* Kings Works, Kings Road, TEDDINGTON, MIDDLESEX, TW11 0QB.
Ⓟ**Great Life Limited** *(R M Howell)* Shoreston Cottage, Shoreston, SEAHOUSES, NORTHUMBERLAND, NE68 7SX.
Ⓟ**Great Scotts Limited** *(B J Scott)* High Barn, 3 Hunters Meadow, Great Shefford, HUNGERFORD, BERKSHIRE, RG17 7EQ.
Greaves & Co *(J Buckland)* 41 North Seaton Rd, ASHINGTON, NE63 0AG.
Greaves & Co *(C M Greaves)* White Lodge, 33 Woodside Road, WOODFORD GREEN, IG8 0TW.
ⓉⒻⒶ**Greaves Grindle** *(A Clark, J Harvey)* Victoria House, Bondgate Within, ALNWICK, NE66 1TA.
▽ⓉⒶ**Greaves West & Ayre** *(A N Ayre, P B Ayre, R M Bennett, R H Dalgleish, A J Patterson, H M Smith)* 1-3 Sandgate, BERWICK-UPON-TWEED, TD15 1EW.
ⓅⒶ**Green & Co, trading name of GPMG Limited** *(E L Gooderham)* 7 New Street, Pontnewydd, CWMBRAN, GWENT, NP44 1EE.
ⓉⒻⒶ**Green & Peter** *(R K Green, D R Peter)* The Limes, 1339 High Road, Whetstone, LONDON, N20 9HR.
ⒻⓅⒶ**Green & Seager, trading name of Orrin Accountancy Limited** *(M A Orrin)* 12 Tavern Street, STOWMARKET, SUFFOLK, IP14 1PH.
Ⓟ**Green Accounting Solutions Limited** *(L G Green)* 82 Vaughan Williams Way, Warley, BRENTWOOD, ESSEX, CM14 5WT.
Ⓟ**Green Corporates Limited** *(C P Bodimeade)* Brandon House, King Street, KNUTSFORD, CHESHIRE, WA16 6DX.
Green Square, trading name of Green Square Partners LLP *(K E Twyning)* 33 Cavendish Square, LONDON, W1G 0PW.
ⓉⒻⒶ**Greenaway** *(R J C Lovitt, G J Matthews)* 150 High Street, SEVENOAKS, TN13 1XE.
★ⓉⒻⒶ**Greenback Alan LLP** *(M K Christy, S A Dabby, A S Green)* 11 Raven Wharf, Lafone Street, LONDON, SE1 2LR.
Ⓟ**Greenbank, trading name of Greenbank Accountancy Services Ltd** *(J Dobson)* 23 Littlejohn Avenue, EDINBURGH, EH10 5TG.
Greene Miller & Co *(L Greene)* 14 Woburn Close, Bushey, WATFORD, WD23 4XA. and at BUSHEY
Greenhalf & Associates *(N C Greenhalf)* Elm Tree House, Britwell Salome, WATLINGTON, OXFORDSHIRE, OX49 5LG.
★ⓉⓅⒶ**Greenhalgh, trading name of Greenhalgh Business Services Ltd** *(G Brockway, P A Handley, M Henshaw, C Peacock)* 2a Peveril Drive, NOTTINGHAM, NG7 1DE. and at BURTON-ON-TRENT, UTTOXETER
Greenhead *(D R Beaumont)* Ridgewood, 7 Park Drive South, Greenhead, HUDDERSFIELD, HD1 4HT.
Greenhow & Co *(C A N Rollin)* Montague House, 258 Kings Road, READING, RG1 4HP.
Ⓐ**Greenwood & Co** *(J Greenwood)* 5 Cherry Grove, ROCHDALE, LANCASHIRE, OL11 5YT.
★**Greenwood Wilson** *(D P Wilson)* The Old School, The Stennack, ST. IVES, CORNWALL, TR26 1QU.
★**Greenwood, Barton & Co** *(E Ineson)* Barclays Bank Chambers, 2 Northgate, CLECKHEATON, WEST YORKSHIRE, BD19 5AA.
Gregory & Co *(A J Gregory)* 80 Bowling Hall Road, BRADFORD, WEST YORKSHIRE, BD4 7TH.
Gregory & Co *(M G Gregory)* 12 Kikas & Frosos Sountia Street, 6016 LARNACA, CYPRUS.
ⒻⒶ**Gregory Michaels & Co** *(M C Ioannou)* 6 Southwick Mews, Paddington, LONDON, W2 1JG.
Gregory Morris *(G D Morris)* 160 Tamworth Road, SUTTON COLDFIELD, WEST MIDLANDS, B75 6DJ.
★ⓉⒻⒶ**Gregory Priestley & Stewart** *(P Stewart)* Lyndhurst, 1 Cranmer Street, Long Eaton, NOTTINGHAM, NG10 1NJ.
★Ⓐ**Gregory Priestley & Stewart** *(P Stewart)* Alexandra House, 123 Priestsic Road, SUTTON-IN-ASHFIELD, NG17 4EA.
★ⒻⒶ**Gregory Wildman** *(L C Gregory, H A Jones, D M Lewsley)* The Granary, Crowhill Farm, Ravensden Road, Wilden, BEDFORD, MK44 2QS.
Ⓟ**Grencodrive Limited** *(S A Waxman)* Canada House, 29 Hampton Road, TWICKENHAM, TW2 5QE.
ⒻⒶ**Grenfell James** *(E G D James)* 2 Shottery Brook Office Park, Timothys Bridge Road, Stratford Enterprise Park, STRATFORD-UPON-AVON, WARWICKSHIRE, CV37 9NR.
ⓅⒶ**Grenfell James Investments.com Limited** *(E G D James)* 2 Shottery Brook Office Park, Timothy's Bridge Road, STRATFORD-UPON-AVON, WARWICKSHIRE, CV37 9NR.
Ⓟ**Grenfell James Limited** *(E G D James)* 2 Shottery Brook Office Park, Timothys Bridge Road, Stratford Enterprise Park, STRATFORD-UPON-AVON, WARWICKSHIRE, CV37 9NR.

Ⓟ**Grenville Barker & Co Limited** *(C A Grenville-Barker)* 15 Lingfield Avenue, KINGSTON UPON THAMES, SURREY, KT1 2TL.

Grenville Wheelhouse *(G Wheelhouse)* 14 Rochdale Road, Milnrow, ROCHDALE, OL16 3LN.

Ⓟ**Greys Accountants Limited** *(R D Williams)* 5 Whiteoaks, Bwlchgwyn, WREXHAM, CLWYD, LL11 5UJ.

ⓉⒶ**Greystone, trading name of Greystone LLC** *(I A Cook, G A Wiltcher)* 18 Athol Street, Douglas, ISLE OF MAN, IM1 1JA.

Ⓟ**Greywalls, trading name of Greywalls Accountants Limited** *(N Fox)* Greywalls, Silver Street, Minety, MALMESBURY, WILTSHIRE, SN16 9QU.

ⓅⒶ**Griffin & Associates, trading name of Griffin & Associates Limited** *(G L F Griffin)* 312 Uxbridge Road, RICKMANSWORTH, HERTFORDSHIRE, WD3 8YL.

Ⓟ**Griffin & King, trading name of Griffin & King Limited** *(T F Corfield)* 26/28 Goodall Street, WALSALL, WS1 1QL.

★ⓉⒺⒶ**Griffin Chapman** *(C Pissarro, N W Raven, G Tarr)* Blackburn House, 32a Crouch Street, COLCHESTER, CO3 3HH.

ⓉⒺⒶ**Griffin Stone Moscrop & Co.** *(C I T Brecht, G S Hill, R J Hill, J L Tolmie, D Wells)* 41 Welbeck Street, LONDON, W1G 8EA.

Ⓔ**Griffin Sutton & Partners** *(A P Sutton)* 207/215 High Street, ORPINGTON, BR6 0PF.

★**Griffins** *(T J Bramston, K A Goldfarb)* Tavistock House South, Tavistock Square, LONDON, WC1H 9LG. and at DUBAI

ⒺⒶ**Griffins, trading name of Griffins Business Advisers LLP** *(T G Boothby, C P Duggan, B A Elliott, J Piercy, N S Pomroy, K H Weeks)* Griffins, 24-32 London Road, NEWBURY, BERKSHIRE, RG14 1JX. and at READING

GriffinTax *(T A G Gareze)* Gravelye Farm House, Hanlye Lane, Cuckfield, HAYWARDS HEATH, WEST SUSSEX, RH17 5HR.

ⓅⒶ**Griffith & Griffith, trading name of George H W Griffith Limited** *(G H W Griffith)* Century House, 31 Gate Lane, SUTTON COLDFIELD, WEST MIDLANDS, B73 5TR.

ⓉⒺⒶ**Griffith Clarke** *(P J Griffith, J S Owens)* 701 Stonehouse Business Park, Sperry Way, STONEHOUSE, GLOUCESTERSHIRE, GL10 3UT.

ⓉⒺⒶ**Griffith, Williams & Co** *(E A Daly, E Griffiths, P O Horwood, D L Williams, S M Williams)* 36 Stryd Fawr, PWLLHELI, LL53 5RT. and at DOLGELLAU

Ⓟ**Griffiths & James Limited** *(D P Griffiths)* Suite 5, Brecon House, Llantarnam Park, CWMBRAN, NP44 3AB.

ⒺⒶ**Griffiths & Pegg** *(B F Arch, A A B Grainger)* 42-43 Reddal Hill Road, CRADLEY HEATH, B64 5JS.

ⓅⒶ**Griffiths Limited** *(D M A Griffiths)* Number One, 272 Kensington High Street, LONDON, W8 6ND.

Griffiths Preston *(A C J Preston)* Aldbury House, Dower Mews, 108 High Street, BERKHAMSTED, HERTFORDSHIRE, HP4 2BL. and at BUCKINGHAM

★ⓉⒶ**Griffiths, Green, Arnold** *(R Arnold, K Davies)* 11 New Street, Pontnewydd, CWMBRAN, NP44 1EE.

Grimsdell & Co *(M H Grimsdell)* P.O. Box 8080, Sitteen Street, RIYADH, 11482, SAUDI ARABIA.

Ⓟ**Grindrod & Company Limited** *(A M Grindrod)* 11 Queen Street, Wellington, TELFORD, SHROPSHIRE, TF1 1EH.

ⓉⓅ**Grineaux Accountants Ltd** *(D Hammersley)* 20 Market Hill, SOUTHAM, WARWICKSHIRE, CV47 0HF.

★Ⓐ**Grineaux Hammersley** *(D Hammersley)* 20 Market Hill, SOUTHAM, CV47 0HF.

ⒺⒶ**Groman & Company** *(A I Groman)* 5 Violet Hill, St. Johns Wood, LONDON, NW8 9EB.

ⓉⒶ**Gross Klein** *(H A Gross, A P Klein, M J Wood)* 6 Breams Buildings, LONDON, EC4A 1QL. and at PETERBOROUGH

★**Gross, Klein & Partners** *(H A Gross, A P Klein)* 6 Breams Buildings, LONDON, EC4A 1QL.

Ⓔ**Grosvenor Business Services (Tunbridge Wells) Limited** *(N M Gower-Smith)* Grosvenor Lodge, 72 Grosvenor Road, TUNBRIDGE WELLS, KENT, TN1 2AZ.

ⓉⒶ**Grosvenor Partners LLP** *(J A Horne, K Petrou)* 6-7 Ludgate Square, LONDON, EC4M 7AS.

ⓉⓅⒶ**Groucott Moor Limited** *(A J Groucott)* Lombard House, Cross Keys, LICHFIELD, STAFFORDSHIRE, WS13 6DN.

★**Groupe Agora** *(M W D Harrisson)* 2 rue Joseph Sansboeuf, 75008 PARIS, FRANCE. and at ARGENTEUIL, BASTIA, CHELLES, CRE-PY-EN-VALOIS, RESNY-SUR-SEINE

Ⓐ**Grover & Co** *(R Grover)* Anmol House, 173 Uxbridge Road, Hanwell, LONDON, W7 3TH.

Groves & Co *(D D Groves)* 141 Cyncoed Road, CARDIFF, CF23 6AF.

ⓉⓅ**Groves Davey, trading name of Groves Davey Limited** *(J L Davey)* 34 Wellfield Road, CARDIFF, CF24 3PB.

Ⓟ**GRS Accounting Limited** *(G A Barrett)* 17 Birley Brook Drive, Newbold, CHESTERFIELD, S41 8XN.

ⓉⒺⓅⒶ**Grugeon Reynolds Limited** *(K Cheeseman, A Roberts)* Rutland House, 44 Masons Hill, BROMLEY, BR2 9JG.

★ⒺⓅⒶ**Grunberg & Co, trading name of Grunberg & Co Limited** *(R D Bean, D Grunberg, A L Stechler)* 10-14 Accommodation Road, Golders Green, LONDON, NW11 8ED.

ⒺⓅⒶ**Grundy Anderson & Kershaw, trading name of Grundy Anderson & Kershaw Limited** *(M Chadwick, M S J Royle)* 123-125 Union Street, OLDHAM, OL1 1TG.

Ⓟ**GRW Consultancy Limited** *(G R Woodford)* The Old Rectory, Brisley, DEREHAM, NORFOLK, NR20 5LJ.

GS *(G Singh)* 2 Woodfarm Road, Rouken Glen, GLASGOW, G46 7JJ.

Ⓟ**GS Ltd** *(A G Griffiths)* Shiraz Loft Suite, Belvedere Hill, St. Saviour, JERSEY, JE2 7RP.

Ⓟ**GS, trading name of Grave Solutions Limited** *(J C Grave)* River Bend, Culgaith, PENRITH, CUMBRIA, CA10 1QE.

Ⓟ**GSR Consultancy (UK) Limited** *(G S Ridewood)* Leigh Cottage, Mount Road, DINAS POWYS, SOUTH GLAMORGAN, CF64 4DG.

★**GSW Bureau** *(D J Mead)* 33 Cairns Avenue, WOODFORD GREEN, ESSEX, IG8 8DH.

Ⓟ**GT Management Consultancy Limited** *(G M Tapping)* 19 Cheriton Avenue, BOURNEMOUTH, BH7 6SD.

Guard D'Oyly *(D A Ash, J N White)* 4 Mansell Street, STRATFORD-UPON-AVON, WARWICKSHIRE, CV37 6NR.

Ⓟ**Guardian Business Recovery (VA) Ltd** *(M P Bassford)* First Floor, 3 Queens Road, BRIGHTON, BN1 3WA.

Guardian Business Recovery LLP *(M P Bassford)* 6-7 Ludgate Square, LONDON, EC4M 7AS.

Guardians *(A H Gadhia)* 24 Spencer Walk, RICKMANSWORTH, HERTFORDSHIRE, WD3 4EE.

ⓉⒶ**Guest & Company** *(J A Guest)* 91 Princess Street, MANCHESTER, M1 4HT.

ⓅⒶ**Guest & Company, trading name of J A Guest Ltd** *(J A Guest)* 91 Princess Street, MANCHESTER, M1 4HT.

ⓅⒶ**Guest Wilson Limited** *(N G Wilson)* 8 Wolverton Road, Snitterfield, STRATFORD-UPON-AVON, CV37 0HB.

ⒺⒶ**Guilfoyle Sage Gloucester** *(M G Spashett)* 58 Eastgate Street, GLOUCESTER, GL1 1QN.

Guilfoyle Sage LLP *(D L Evans, G R Williams)* 21 Gold Tops, NEWPORT, GWENT, NP20 4PG.

ⒺⒶ**Guilfoyle, Sage & Co** *(D L Evans, G R Williams)* 21 Gold Tops, NEWPORT, NP20 4PG.

ⒺⓅⒶ**Guner Associates, trading name of Guner Associates Ltd** *(G Mustafa)* 9 Beaumont Gate, Shenley Hill, RADLETT, HERTFORDSHIRE, WD7 7AR.

ⓉⓅ**Guner Wolfson Ltd** *(G Mustafa, D Wolfson)* 9 Beaumont Gate, Shenley Hill, RADLETT, HERTFORDSHIRE, WD7 7AR.

Guram & Co *(N K Guram)* 173 Homesdale Road, BROMLEY, KENT, BR1 2QL.

Ⓐ**Guryel & Co** *(S Guryel)* 214 Lower Addiscombe Road, CROYDON, SURREY, CR0 7AB.

Ⓟ**Guthrie Accountancy Services Limited** *(G R Guthrie)* Unit 1, 11 Eagle Parade, BUXTON, DERBYSHIRE, SK17 6EQ.

Ⓐ**Gutteridge Scanlan** *(W A Scanlan)* 5 High View Close, Hamilton Office Park, Hamilton, LEICESTER, LE4 9LJ.

Guy & Co *(J E Guy)* Beechwood, 5 Hale End, Hook Heath, WOKING, GU22 0LH.

Ⓟ**Guy Payne & Co (Accounting Services) Limited** *(G S J Payne)* Hale Buildings, 5 Parkgate Road, NESTON, CH64 9XF.

Ⓟ**Guy Payne & Co Ltd** *(G S J Payne)* Hale Buildings, 5 Parkgate Road, NESTON, CH64 9XF.

★ⓉⒶ**Guy Walmsley & Co** *(J D Bevan, N Fryer, S Griffiths, M D Lindley)* 3 Grove Road, WREXHAM, LL11 1DY.

Ⓟ**Guy Woodland Ltd** *(G G E Woodland)* Renwood, Vale Road, High Kelling, HOLT, NORFOLK, NR25 6RA.

Gwatkin & Co *(P Gwatkin)* 98 Meols Parade, Meols, WIRRAL, CH47 5AY.

ⓅⒶ**Gwatkin & Co Limited** *(P Gwatkin)* 98 Meols Parade, WIRRAL, MERSEYSIDE, CH47 5AY.

Gwenno Mair Wyn ACA *(G M Wyn)* Cilgerran, 8 Llys Gwyn, CAERNARFON, GWYNEDD, LL55 1EN.

Gwilym R Morgan *(G R Morgan)* 25 Seafield Close, East Wittering, CHICHESTER, WEST SUSSEX, PO20 8DP.

Ⓐ**Gwyn Thomas & Co** *(G T Thomas)* 1 Thomas Buildings, New Street, PWLLHELI, LL53 5HH.

Gwynne-Evans & Co *(D Gwynne-Evans)* 49 Sandy Lodge Way, NORTHWOOD, MIDDLESEX, HA6 2AR.

Gwyther B Perseus & Co *(H Gwyther)* 4 Heath Halt Court, Heath Halt Road, CARDIFF, CF23 5QB.

Ⓟ**Gyro Limited** *(A P Writer)* Tarn House, 58 Kelsey Lane, BECKENHAM, KENT, BR3 3NE.

Ⓟ**H & D Consultants Ltd** *(S M Hawes)* Braefield, Castle Walk, WADHURST, EAST SUSSEX, TN5 6DB.

Ⓐ**H & E Johnson** *(S A N Milburn)* Sandall House, 230 High Street, HERNE BAY, KENT, CT6 5AX.

ⓅⒶ**H & M Ltd** *(H Z Burrows)* 1-5 Alma Terrace, Otley Street, SKIPTON, NORTH YORKSHIRE, BD23 1EJ.

Ⓣ**H & W Jones & Co.** *(D R Bowen, T G H Bowen, T M Williams)* 81 Bridge Street, LAMPETER, SA48 7AB. and at CARMARTHEN

Ⓟ**H A Hyatt & Co, trading name of H A Hyatt & Co Limited** *(H A Hyatt)* 4-5 King Street, RICHMOND, SURREY, TW9 1ND.

Ⓟ**H B Counters Ltd** *(S Kettridge)* 182 Manor Road, BENFLEET, ESSEX, SS7 4HY.

ⓅⒶ**H B Mistry & Co, trading name of H B Mistry & Co Limited** *(H B Mistry)* Tudor House, Mill Lane, Calcot, READING, RG31 7RS.

H C Wong & Co *(H Wong)* Room 1007, 10th Floor, Won Centre, 111 Connaight Road, CENTRAL, HONG KONG ISLAND HONG KONG SAR.

ⓉⒺⓅⒶ**H Davies & Co, trading name of Howell Davies Limited** *(R Jebb, R G Jeff, C J Pole)* 37a Birmingham New Road, WOLVERHAMPTON, WV4 6BL.

ⓅⒶ**H Decruz Ltd** *(H De Cruz)* 26 Oakleigh Avenue, EDGWARE, MIDDLESEX, HA8 5DT.

Ⓟ**H F D Professional Services Ltd** *(R A Hickie)* Unit 4, Dovedale Studios, 465 Battersea Park Road, LONDON, SW11 4LR.

Ⓟ**H G Accounting Solutions Limited** *(H J Garrett)* 17 St. James's Avenue, BECKENHAM, KENT, BR3 4HF.

Ⓟ**H K Ng, trading name of K Consulting(Surrey) Limited** *(H K Ng)* Suite 1, Central House, Woodside Park Commerical Centre, Catteshall Lane, GODALMING, SURREY GU7 1LG.

Ⓟ**H Martin Smith & Co Limited** *(H M Smith)* 40 Springfield Gardens, Hirwaun, ABERDARE, MID GLAMORGAN, CF44 9LY.

H Nair FCA *(H Nair)* Flat 3 Cuckoos Nest, 60 Crawley Green Road, LUTON, LU2 0QW.

Ⓟ**H R Accountancy Limited** *(B C Hogg)* 2 Market Lane, SELBY, NORTH YORKSHIRE, YO8 4QA.

H R C Lewis & Co *(H R C Lewis)* 54 Amersham Hill Drive, HIGH WYCOMBE, HP13 6QY.

★ⒺⓅⒶ**H R Harris & Partners, trading name of H R Harris & Partners (2010) Limited** *(S J Burkinshaw, J M Evans)* 44 St. Helens Road, SWANSEA, SA1 4BB. and at TADLEY

H S Accounting *(H C Shears)* 47 All Hallows Road, Preston, PAIGNTON, DEVON, TQ3 1DX.

Ⓟ**H Summers Ltd** *(H Summers)* 26 Lake View, EDGWARE, MIDDLESEX, HA8 7RU.

ⓉⒺⒶ**H W** *(C M Fletcher, A E Golding, G A Heywood, M G Watkins)* Sterling House, 5 Buckingham Place, Bellfield Rd West, HIGH WYCOMBE, HP13 5HQ.

★Ⓔ**H W** *(G C Fairclough, M Porter)* Enterprise House, Timbrell Street, TROWBRIDGE, WILTSHIRE, BA14 8PL.

★ⒺⓅⒶ**H W Fisher & Company Limited** *(P A C Beber, P A Beer, A J Bernstein, D L Birne, D W Breger, S Burns, J S Challis, M B Davis, C J Hazard, A K Lester, B Lindsey, S P Mehta, G A Miller, S M Mott-Cowan, R Nathan, A R W Parfitt, A G Rich, N S Samani, R A Saville, D S Selwyn, N N Siganporia, A Subramaniam, M A Taylor, N J Thaker, J S Trent)* Acre House, 11/15 William Road, LONDON, NW1 3ER.

ⒺⓅⒶ**H W Vaughan & Co, Watkins Bradfield & Co, trading names of WBV Limited** *(R J Halliday, S Harries, P L Hunkin, S R Lopez, D A Rowe)* Woodfield House, Castle Walk, NEATH, WEST GLAMORGAN, SA11 3LN. and at SWANSEA

H. Amara Makalanda *(H A Makalanda)* 11 Drapers Road, ENFIELD, EN2 8LT.

Ⓔ**H. Bennett** *(H Bennett)* East Park, Woodland Road, ST AUSTELL, CORNWALL, PL25 4QZ.

H. Bingham & Co *(H Bingham)* 39 Andrew Avenue, Rawtenstall, ROSSENDALE, BB4 6EU.

H. Garrison *(H Garrison)* 10 Bickley Court, Aran Drive, STANMORE, MIDDLESEX, HA7 4NA.

H. Gosrani *(H Gosrani)* 12 Blakesley Road, Yardley, BIRMINGHAM, B25 8XU.

ⒺⒶ**H. Graham King & Co** *(K Holden)* Southernhay Suite 7, 207 Hook Road, CHESSINGTON, KT9 1HJ.

H. Guderley & Co *(H Guderley)* 67 Lancaster Avenue, BARNET, EN4 0ER.

★**H. H. Liu & Co.** *(H H Liu)* 3/F Yue on Commercial Centre, 387 Lockhart Road, WAN CHAI, HONG KONG SAR.

H. I. Bowen *(H I Bowen)* Llwynbedw, Bethlehem Road, St. Clears, CARMARTHEN, DYFED, SA33 4AN.

Ⓟ**H. K. Popat & Co, trading name of HKP Kabason Limited** *(H K Popat)* Kabason House, 30 Greenbank Drive, Oadby, LEICESTER, LE2 5RP.

H. Kings *(H Kings)* 18 Birchfield Gdns, Harlow Green, GATESHEAD, NE9 7TJ.

H. Morris & Co *(H L Morris)* 6 Shirehall Park, Hendon, LONDON, NW4 2QL.

★**H. P. Wan & Company** *(H P Wan)* 711A Ocean Centre, Canton Road, TSIM SHA TSIU, KOWLOON, HONG KONG SAR.

ⒺⒶ**H. Rainsbury & Co.** *(A N Bolsom, R L Hodge)* 15 Duncan Terrace, LONDON, N1 8BZ.

H. Royce *(H Royce)* 6 Filleigh, 2 Barry Rise, Bowdon, ALTRINCHAM, CHESHIRE, WA14 3JS.

★**H. T. Wong & Co.** *(H T Wong)* 1123A Landmark North, 39 Lung Sum Avenue, SHEUNG SHUI, NEW TERRITORIES, HONG KONG SAR. and at TSIM SHA TSUI

H.A. Burton *(H A Burton)* 17 Hertford Avenue, East Sheen, LONDON, SW14 8EF.

H.A. Christie & Co *(H A Christie)* 36 Robinson Road, 14-03, City House, SINGAPORE 068877, SINGAPORE.

H.B. Dhondy & Co *(H B Dhondy)* Taj Building, 2nd Floor, 210 Dr. Dadabhai Naoroji Road, MUMBAI 400 001, INDIA.

H.C. Monk *(H C Monk)* 49 Barrow Road, Burton-on-the-Wolds, LOUGHBOROUGH, LEICESTERSHIRE, LE12 5TB.

H.C.Koh & Co *(H C Koh)* 190 Middle Road, 14-02 Fortune Centre, SINGAPORE 188979, SINGAPORE.

H.C.Samuel & Co. *(J D Hattersley)* Glen View, Epsom Road, West Horsley, LEATHERHEAD, KT24 6AL.

H.D. Lloyd *(H D Lloyd)* Pen Y Graig, Cilcain Road, Pantymwyn, MOLD, CH7 5NJ.

ⒺⒶ**H.D. Shah & Co** *(H D V Shah)* 2 The Avenue, WEMBLEY, MIDDLESEX, HA9 9QJ.

H.E. Dunning *(H E Dunning)* Highleigh Nant-Y-Gamar Road, Craig-Y-Don LLANDUDNO, Clwyd, LL30 3BD.

H.E. Midwinter FCA *(H E Midwinter)* 13 St. Peters Road, ABINGDON, OX14 3SJ.

★Ⓐ**H.G.Field & Co** *(J A Ensor, A Rodrigues)* 2 Guildford Street, CHERTSEY, KT16 9BQ.

H.H.Lam & Co *(H H Lam)* Yu To Sang Bldg 9/F, 37 Queens Road, CENTRAL, Hong Kong Island, HONG KONG SAR.

Ⓟ**H.I. Associates Limited** *(A Bailey)* 17 The Orchards, Cheswick Green, Shirley, SOLIHULL, WEST MIDLANDS, B90 4HP.

H.K. Day & Co *(H K Day)* 18 Leith View, North Holmwood, DORKING, SURREY, RH5 4TG.

H.Kershner *(H Kershner)* 18 New Hall Road, SALFORD, M7 4EL.

ⓉⒺⒶ**H.L. Barnes & Sons** *(R W P Bowen, D M Buxton, P L Woodward)* Barclays Bank Chambers, Bridge Street, STRATFORD-UPON-AVON, WARWICKSHIRE, CV37 6AH.

Ⓣ**H.L. Hong & Co** *(H L Hong)* 1B-3 Plaza Mayang, Jalan SS26/9, 47301 PETALING JAYA, SELANGOR, MALAYSIA.

ⓉⒶ**H.M. Williams** *(T J Smith, H M Williams)* Valley House, 53 Valley Road, Plympton, PLYMOUTH, PL7 1RF.

H.M.K. Rehmani *(H M K Rehmani)* Farmaniyeh Rouhani St., Koy Ferdos No 32, TEHRAN, 19547, IRAN.

H.Martin Smith & Co *(H M Smith)* 40 Springfield Gardens, Hirwaun, ABERDARE, MID GLAMORGAN, CF44 9LY.

H.S. Kong & Co *(H S Kong)* Sovereign Manor, Gover View, Gover Hill, TONBRIDGE, TN11 9SQ.

H.V.Bamford & Co *(M O Bamford)* 99 Main Street, Wilsden, BRADFORD, BD15 0DZ.

Ⓟ**H.W.M. Cartwright LTD** *(H W M Cartwright)* 22 Shrewsbury Mews, Chepstow Road, LONDON, W2 5PN.

H.Y. Stevens & Co, trading name of Overdraft Limited *(H Youssefi)* 124 Valley Road, RICKMANSWORTH, HERTFORDSHIRE, WD3 4BP.

ⓉⓅ**H2O Accounting Ltd** *(H J Oliver)* Ground Floor, 1000 Lakeside North Harbour, Western Road, PORTSMOUTH, PO6 3EZ.

Habib Alam & Co. *(H Alam)* 249 Jinnah Colony Rehman Hospital Road, Opposite Pakistan Academy, FAISALABAD, PAKISTAN.

Members in Practice and Firms - Alphabetical **Hadfield & Co - Harpersheldon**

Hadfield & Co *(P J Hadfield, P R Hadfield)* 17 King Street, KNUTSFORD, CHESHIRE, WA16 6DW.

Ⓣ**Hadfields** *(M A Hadfield)* Commerce House, 658B Chatsworth Road, CHESTERFIELD, S40 3JZ.

Ⓐ**Hadleighs** *(P A Hadani)* Sai Krupa, 27 Beechcroft Road, BUSHEY, WD23 2JU.

Hadley & Co *(J M Graham)* 1-7 Harley Street, LONDON, W1G 9QD.

Ⓐ**Hadley & Co** *(P J Barlow, J R D Gummerson, J G Hyland)* Adelphi Chambers, 30 Hoghton Street, SOUTHPORT, PR9 0NZ. and at LIVERPOOL

ⒻⒶ**Hadleys & Co** *(K Mehmood)* 5 Malvern House, 199 Marsh Wall, Meridan Gate, LONDON, E14 9YT.

Ⓟ**Hadlow & Harborow Ltd** *(P J Hudson)* 454-458 Chiswick High Road, LONDON, W4 5TT.

Hafeez & Co *(M Hafeez)* 2 Minto Street, EDINBURGH, EH9 1RG.

Ⓣ**Hafeez & Co.** *(S M H Qureshi)* 41 Willesden Lane, LONDON, NW6 7RF.

ⒻⒶ**Haffner Hoff LLP** *(A L Haffner)* 86 Princess Street, MANCHESTER, M1 6NP.

★**Hager Stenhouse & Co** *(S Y Steinhaus)* 206 High Road, LONDON, N15 4NP.

★Ⓣ**Haggards Crowther** *(A D D Haggard, T M D Haggard)* Heathmans House, 19 Heathmans Road, LONDON, SW6 4TJ.

Haider Naqvi & Co *(S Z H H Naqvi)* Concept House, 225 Hale Lane, EDGWARE, MIDDLESEX, HA8 9QF.

ⓉⓅⒶ**Hailwood & Co, trading name of Hailwood Accountants Ltd** *(Danny French)* 392-394 Hoylake Road, WIRRAL, MERSEYSIDE, CH46 6DF.

ⒻⓅⒶ**Haines & Co, trading name of Carlton Haines Ltd** *(N P Griggs, S N James)* Carlton House, 28/29 Carlton Terrace, Portslade, BRIGHTON, BN41 1XF.

ⓉⒻⒶ**Haines Watts (Lancashire) LLP** *(F J Cresswell, G C Fairclough, D M Fort, J E Pomfret)* Northern Assurance Buildings, 9-21 Princess Street, MANCHESTER, M2 4DN. and at LEYLAND

Ⓕ**Haines Watts Consulting** *(S R Edwards, A J Parsons, B J Potter)* 30 Camp Road, FARNBOROUGH, HAMPSHIRE, GU14 6EW.

★ⓉⒻⒶ**Haines Watts Gatwick LLP** *(A M Bodkin, F S K Durrani, M R Neve, J C Pannett, J A Peach, P Simmons)* 3rd Floor, Consort House, Consort Way, HORLEY, SURREY, RH6 7AF.

ⓉⒻⒶ**Haines Watts Wales LLP** *(A S Cunningham, C S Edwards, D T Green)* 7 Neptune Court, Vanguard Way, CARDIFF, CF24 5PJ. and at NEWPORT

ⓉⒻⒶ**Haines Watts, HW, Lee Associates, trading names of HW Lee Associates LLP** *(R Husband, M Perry, S Rawal, P Simmons)* New Derwent House, 69-73 Theobalds Road, LONDON, WC1X 8TA.

ⒻⓅⒶ**Haines Watts, HW, trading names of Haines Watts Glasgow Limited** *(A S Minifie)* 231-233 St. Vincent Street, GLASGOW, G2 5QY.

ⓉⒻⒶ**Haines Watts, HW, trading names of Haines Watts Kent LLP** *(A D Brand, G C Fairclough, F C James, P J Sutton)* 4-5 Kings Row, Armstrong Road, MAIDSTONE, KENT, ME15 6AQ.

ⒻⒶ**Haines Watts, HW, trading names of Haines Watts London LLP** *(J R P Moughton, M Perry, P Simmons, R A Welland)* New Derwent House, 69-73 Theobalds Road, LONDON, WC1X 8TA. and at SLOUGH

ⒻⒶ**Haines Watts, HW, trading names of Haines Watts Slough LLP** *(J R P Moughton, M Perry, K Sanghera, P Simmons, R A Welland, J Wills)* 177/181 Farnham Road, SLOUGH, BERKSHIRE, SL1 4XP. and at LONDON

Ⓕ**Haines Watts, HW, trading names of Haines Watts Wimbledon LLP** *(A M Bodkin, D G Demetriou, S Hussein, P Simmons)* 158-160 Arthur Road, LONDON, SW19 8AQ.

ⒻⓅⒶ**Haines Watts, HW, trading names of HWEA Ltd** *(E K Klingaman, A S Minifie, M Neale, N S Ross, P D Sumpter)* 8 Hopper Way, DISS, NORFOLK, IP22 4GT. and at THETFORD

★ⒻⒶ**Hakim Fry** *(N C Patel, D Witham)* 69-71 East Street, EPSOM, KT17 1BP.

Ⓟ**Hakim Fry International Limited** *(N C Patel, D Witham)* 69-71 East Street, EPSOM, SURREY, KT17 1BP.

Ⓟ**Halcyon, trading name of Halcyon Accountants & Business Adviser Ltd** *(A Passingham)* PO Box 9953, LEICESTER, LE7 3UX.

Ⓣ**Hale & Company, trading name of Hale & Company LLP** *(D Cole, S M Egan, C J Krol)* Ground Floor, Belmont Place, Belmont Road, MAIDENHEAD, BERKSHIRE, SL6 6TB.

ⓉⒻⒶ**Hale Jackson Knight** *(L Hale, S L Jackson, P E Knight)* Montague House, 4 St. Marys Street, ROSS-ON-WYE, HEREFORDSHIRE, HR9 5HT.

Ⓟ**Halex, trading name of Halex Business Risk Services Limited** *(C J Burt)* 20 Fletcher Gate, NOTTINGHAM, NG1 2FZ.

ⓉⓅⒶ**Haleys, trading name of Electspace Limited** *(T J Haley)* Thomas House, Meadowcroft Business Park, Pope Lane, Whitestake, PRESTON, PR4 4AZ.

Halford & Co *(K A Halford)* Unit 14, Home Farm Business Centre, East Tytherley Road, Lockerley, ROMSEY, HAMPSHIRE SO51 0JT.

Ⓟ**Halford Accountancy Services Ltd** *(K A Halford)* Unit 14, Home Farm Rural Industries, East Tytherley Road, Lockerley, ROMSEY, HAMPSHIRE SO51 0JT.

ⒻⒶ**Hall & Co** *(G Hall, I Richardson)* 59 The Avenue, SOUTHAMPTON, SO17 1XS.

Ⓟ**Hall Accountancy Services Limited** *(G P Hall)* Sunnycroft, Glasshouses, Pateley Bridge, HARROGATE, NORTH YORKSHIRE, HG3 5QY.

Hall Farm Accountancy Services *(N D Smith)* 2 Hall Farm Cottage, Main Street, Netherseal, SWADLINCOTE, DERBYSHIRE, DE12 8BZ.

Hall Hayes & Co *(J A Flatters)* Prospect House, 24 Prospect Road, OSSETT, WEST YORKSHIRE, WF5 8AE.

ⒻⓅ**Hall Liddy Ltd** *(D J Hall, D P Liddy, A J Pow)* 12 St. John Street, MANCHESTER, M3 4DY.

★ⓉⒻⒶ**Hall Livesey Brown** *(N Carr, B Dunbavand, R Evans, S J Jeffrey, C P Parsons, S Welsh)* 68 High Street, TARPORLEY, CW6 0AT. and at CHESTER, SHREWSBURY, WREXHAM

Ⓟ**Hall Robinson, trading name of Hall Robinson Limited** *(G W Midgley)* 25 Teak Drive, Kearsley, BOLTON, BL4 8RR.

Hall Warren *(S E Warren)* 23 Braehead Road, EDINBURGH, EH4 6BN.

Ⓟ**Hallett & Co, trading name of NPH Accountants Ltd** *(N P Hallett)* The Old Rectory, Church Road, Gisleham, LOWESTOFT, SUFFOLK, NR33 8DS.

Halliday & Co *(J F Halliday)* Victoria House, 45 Rutland Park, Botanical Gardens, SHEFFIELD, S10 2PB.

ⓉⒻⒶ**Hallidays, trading name of Hallidays LLP** *(A E Bennett, N D Bennett, P J Eagle, P A Whitney, J B Wilson)* Riverside House, Kings Reach Business Park, Yew Street, STOCKPORT, CHESHIRE, SK4 2HD.

Halliwell & Horton *(R.B. Rodrigues-Pereira)* 29 Burnley Road East, Waterfoot, ROSSENDALE, BB4 9AG.

Ⓕ**Halpern and Co** *(D Halpern)* 20 Berkeley Street, LONDON, W1J 8EE.

Halstead & Co *(J S Halstead, M E Halstead)* 434 Hale Road, Hale Barns, ALTRINCHAM, WA15 8TH.

Ⓐ**Hamid & Co** *(H Pervez)* 35 Tintern Way, HARROW, MIDDLESEX, HA2 0RZ.

Hamilton & Co *(D N P Hamilton)* The White Cottage, Stock Lane, Landford Wood, SALISBURY, SP5 2ER.

Hamilton & Co. *(R C Hamilton)* 7 Greave Close, The Grange Wenvoe, CARDIFF, CF5 6BU.

Hamilton Associates *(D N P Hamilton)* The White Cottage, Stock Lane, Landford, SALISBURY, SP5 2ER.

ⓉⒶ**Hamilton Brading** *(A J Brading, D H Hamilton)* 1 Sopwith Crescent, WICKFORD, SS11 8YU.

Hamilton Thomas *(D H Thomas)* 29 Camus Close, Church Crookham, FLEET, HAMPSHIRE, GU52 0UT.

ⓉⒻⒶ**Hamilton-Eddy & Co.** *(D W Weeden)* 39 Tamworth Road, CROYDON, CR0 1XU.

★**Hamlyn Mike and Co** *(H R Mike)* 13 Mayfield Road, VALSAYN, TRINIDAD AND TOBAGO.

ⓉⒻⒶ**Hamlyns, trading name of Hamlyns LLP** *(D G Cooper, C J Shrubb)* Sundial House, 98 High Street, Horsell, WOKING, SURREY, GU21 4SU.

ⓅⒶ**Hammer & Co, trading name of Hammer & Co Accountants Ltd** *(A Hammer)* 13 Alba Court, Alba Gardens, LONDON, NW11 9NP.

Ⓟ**Hammett Associates, trading name of Hammett Associates Ltd** *(A Horton)* 8-10 Queen Street, SEATON, DEVON, EX12 2NY.

Hammond Knight *(A A A Balouch)* 2nd Floor, 145-157 St. John Street, LONDON, EC1V 4PY.

★**Hammond McNulty** *(A G Martin, P McNulty)* Bank House, Market Square, CONGLETON, CW12 1ET. and at CREWE

Ⓐ**Hammonds** *(G W Miles)* Burnhill Business Centre, Provident House, Burrell Row, BECKENHAM, BR3 1AT.

ⓅⒶ**Hammonds, trading name of Hammonds Consultants Ltd** *(R T Shah)* 21The Broadwalk, Pinner Road, HARROW, MIDDLESEX, HA2 6ED.

ⒻⓅ**Hampden Tax Consultants, Just Tax, Seymour Taylor, trading names of ST Hampden Limited** *(C J Baker, J F R Hayes, F W Johnston, R P Maggs, S J Turner)* 57 London Road, HIGH WYCOMBE, BUCKINGHAMSHIRE, HP11 1BS. and at GREAT MISSENDEN, LONDON

Ⓟ**Hampstead Accountants Ltd** *(B S Sahni)* 55 Maresfield Gardens, LONDON, NW3 5TE.

ⓅⒶ**Hamptans Limited** *(P G Thakrar)* Compton House, 20(a) Selsdon Road, SOUTH CROYDON, SURREY, CR2 6PA.

Ⓟ**Hampton & Co, trading name of Woodbury Accounting Ltd** *(P J Cumming)* Warwick House, Church Lane, Little Witley, WORCESTER, WR6 6LP.

Ⓟ**Hampton Management Resources Ltd** *(R Campbell)* 37 Linden Road, HAMPTON, TW12 2JG.

Hampton Wells *(A Gulati)* 2 Woolhampton Way, CHIGWELL, IG7 4QH.

ⒻⒶ**Hamshaw & Co** *(D J Hamshaw)* 100 Wide Bargate, BOSTON, PE21 6SE.

ⒻⒶ**Hamsun & Hogate** *(A M S Lakha)* 2 Bramber Court, 2 Bramber Road, LONDON, W14 9PA.

Hanafin Klein *(M J Hanafin)* The House, High Street, Brenchley, TONBRIDGE, TN12 7NQ.

ⒻⒶ**Hanby & Co** *(P M Brierley, I C Cartwright)* 209 High Street, NORTHALLERTON, DL7 8LW.

Ⓕ**Hancock & Company** *(R J Hancock)* 47 Winchester Road, ANDOVER, HAMPSHIRE, SP10 2EF.

Hancock M.E. *(M E Hancock)* 2 Burls Yard, Crown Street, Needham Market, IPSWICH, IP6 8AJ.

★ⓉⒶ**Hancock, Gilbert, Morris & Partners, Mayor Cuttle & Co, trading names of William Evans & Partners** *(G A Clarke, S W Evans, S G Shah)* 20 Harcourt Street, LONDON, W1H 4HG. and at CHELMSFORD

Ⓟ**Hancox & Co Limited** *(J J Hancox)* 62 Market Street, Milnsbridge, HUDDERSFIELD, HD3 4HT.

ⓅⒶ**Hand in Hand Business Solutions Ltd** *(J R Stimpson)* 1 & 2 Hillbrow House, Linden Drive, LISS, HAMPSHIRE, GU33 7RJ.

Handley & Co *(J Handley)* Fern Dene, Savile Rd, HALIFAX, HX1 2BA.

★Ⓕ**Handley Roberts** *(W J Handley)* 1 The Courtyard, Chalvington, HAILSHAM, EAST SUSSEX, BN27 3TD. and at GUILDFORD

Handyside & Company *(R G Handyside)* Bank Chambers, 92 Newport Road, CARDIFF, CF24 1DG.

Ⓐ**Hanley & Co** *(M A Booth, J G Gilbertson)* 25 Main Street, Staveley, KENDAL, LA8 9LU.

ⓅⒶ**Hanley & Co, trading name of Hanley & Co Ltd** *(D R Logan)* 18 Church Street, ASHTON-UNDER-LYNE, LANCASHIRE, OL6 6XE.

ⓅⒶ**Hanleys, trading name of Hale Financial Limited** *(J G Harris, A Knowles, F Minaeian)* Spring Court, Spring Road, Hale, ALTRINCHAM, CHESHIRE, WA14 2UQ.

ⒻⓅⒶ**Hannaways, trading name of Hannaways Business Support Limited** *(C J Northwood)* Trios House, Reform Road, MAIDENHEAD, BERKSHIRE, SL6 8BY.

Ⓟ**Hannay & Co Limited** *(N Gaul)* Norwood House, 73 Elvetham Road, FLEET, HAMPSHIRE, GU51 4HL.

ⓉⒻⓅⒶ**Hansons, trading name of PGU Accounting Ltd** *(G Guilliatt, R M Smith, M A Upex)* St. Oswald House, St. Oswald Street, CASTLEFORD, WEST YORKSHIRE, WF10 1DH.

HAQ AND CO *(S H Haq)* Via Lombardia 30, 00187 ROME, ITALY.

Ⓟ**Haraled Consultancy Limited** *(A J Williams)* 54 Bettws-y-Coed Road, Cyncoed, CARDIFF, CF23 6PN.

★ⒻⓅⒶ**Harben Barker Limited** *(D C Minett, P Scott, P Stanford)* Drayton Court, Drayton Road, SOLIHULL, WEST MIDLANDS, B90 4NG. and at BIRMINGHAM

▽**Harbinson Mulholland** *(B T P Dwyer)* IBM House, 4 Bruce Street, BELFAST, BT2 7JD.

Ⓟ**Harbor Limited** *(J Hamilton)* 2 Mundy Street, HEANOR, DERBYSHIRE, DE75 7SB. and at ASHBOURNE

ⒻⒶ**Hardcastle Burton** *(M J Anthony, C J Hayfield)* 166 Northwood Way, NORTHWOOD, MIDDLESEX, HA6 1RB.

ⒻⓅⒶ**Hardcastle Burton (Redbourn) Limited** *(K Myers)* Old School, The Common, Redbourn, ST. ALBANS, HERTFORDSHIRE, AL3 7NG.

ⓉⒶ**Hardcastle Burton LLP** *(K C Bouttell, B P Homent, M J Law, D R Lindsell, J C Tulloch)* Lake House, Market Hill, ROYSTON, HERTFORDSHIRE, SG8 9JN.

★ⓉⓅⒶ**Hardcastle Burton, trading name of Hardcastle Burton (Newmarket) Limited** *(P J Tostevin)* 90 High Street, NEWMARKET, SUFFOLK, CB8 8FE.

ⓉⒻⒶ**Hardcastle France** *(C G Payne)* 30 Yorkersgate, MALTON, YO17 7AW.

Hardie Brown & Co *(G M Hardie-Brown)* Hilltown, BALLYMITTY, COUNTY WEXFORD, IRELAND.

Harding & Co *(L M Harding)* Tiptree Cottage, 1 King Street, Markyate, ST. ALBANS, HERTFORDSHIRE, AL3 8JY.

ⓅⒶ**Harding Accountants Limited** *(B R Harding)* 23 Frogmore Park Drive, Blackwater, CAMBERLEY, GU17 0PG.

Harding Higgins *(P G Taylor)* 36 Church Street, UTTOXETER, STAFFORDSHIRE, ST14 8AD.

ⒻⓅⒶ**HardingRedmans, trading name of HardingRedmans Limited** *(S J Harding)* Bridge House, Court Road, SWANAGE, DORSET, BH19 1DX.

Ⓐ**Hardings** *(B S Baggaley, E M Fox, T R McNeal)* 6 Marsh Parade, NEWCASTLE, ST5 1DU.

Ⓟ**Hards Tax Services, trading name of Hards Tax Services Limited** *(A J Hards)* Stanford House, Stanford Close, Frampton Cotterell, BRISTOL, BS36 2DG.

Ⓐ**Hardwick & Morris, trading name of The 41GP Partnership LLP** *(S J Hardwick, J A Hollett, L N Morris)* 41 Great Portland Street, LONDON, W1W 7LA.

ⒻⒶ**Hardwickes** *(D Hall, D R Harper, P L Robinson, D R Shaw)* Etruria Old Road, STOKE-ON-TRENT, ST1 5PE.

ⓅⒶ**Hardwicks, trading name of Hardwicks Accountants Ltd** *(N A Hardwick)* Sarsfield House, Gillott Lane, Wickersley, ROTHERHAM, S66 1EH.

ⓉⒻⒶ**Hardy & Company** *(R S Khan)* 166 Streatham Hill, LONDON, SW2 4RU.

Ⓟ**Hardy & Company Limited** *(R S Khan)* 166 Streatham Hill, LONDON, SW2 4RU.

Hardy Pearman LLP *(K J Hardy, T E Hardy)* Hurst House, High Street, Ripley, WOKING, GU23 6AY.

Ⓟ**Harford Michaels Kaye Limited** *(A J Kaye)* 250 Hendon Way, LONDON, NW4 3NL.

ⓉⒻⓅⒶ**Hargreaves & Woods, trading name of Ratiocinator Limited** *(J A Hargreaves, A J Woods)* Cholmondeley House, Dee Hills Park, CHESTER, CH3 5AR.

ⓉⒶ**Hargreaves, Brown & Benson** *(M J Evans, S J Wood)* 1 Bond Street, COLNE, LANCASHIRE, BB8 9DG.

ⓉⒻⓅⒶ**Harish Thakrar Limited** *(H M Thakrar)* 29 - 31 Finedon Road, WELLINGBOROUGH, NORTHAMPTONSHIRE, NN8 4AS.

ⓅⒶ**Harland Accountants (Newquay) Limited** *(D J Edwards)* 42 East Street, NEWQUAY, CORNWALL, TR8 5NG.

ⒻⓅⒶ**Harmer Slater, trading name of Harmer Slater Limited** *(R Agyei-Boamah, C Harmer, T W Slater)* Salatin House, 19 Cedar Road, SUTTON, SURREY, SM2 5DA.

Ⓐ**Harnettaccountants** *(H D Harnett)* Weir Cottage, Teddington Studios, Broom Road, Teddington, TWICKENHAM, TW11 9NT.

Harold D. Nass *(H D Nass)* 20 Heath View, LONDON, N2 0QA.

ⓉⒶ**Harold D. Pritchard & Co** *(B C Carroll, T J Evans, R D Thomas)* Old Oak House, 49-51 Lammas Street, CARMARTHEN, DYFED, SA31 3AL.

ⒻⒶ**Harold Duckworth & Co** *(G A Beak)* 41 Houndiscombe Road, Mutley, PLYMOUTH, PL4 6EX.

ⓉⒻⒶ**Harold Everett Wreford LLP** *(M Bayer, S Cymerman, G P Golbey, M D Isaacs, D J Scott, J Sloneem)* 1st Floor, 44-46 Whitfield Street, LONDON, W1T 2RJ.

Harold K Porter & Co *(H K Porter)* Honor House, Honor End Lane, Prestwood, GREAT MISSENDEN, BUCKINGHAMSHIRE, HP16 9QZ.

ⓉⒶ**Harold Sharp** *(A C Copping, H R Cunningham, R M Evans, A J Lane, C A Wrighton)* Holland House, 1-5 Oakfield, SALE, M33 6TT.

ⓉⒶ**Harold Smith** *(L C Archer, N L Ashton, N J Hulson, C I Jones, S Murray-Williams, B J M Shields)* Unit 32, Llys Edmund Prys, St. Asaph Business Park, ST. ASAPH, LL17 0JA. and at CRICCIETH, PRESTATYN

ⓉⒻⒶ**Harper Broom** *(J A Broom, F Masterman-Smith)* Aston House, York Road, Maidenhead, MAIDENHEAD, BERKSHIRE, SL6 1SF.

ⒻⓅⒶ**Harper Cavendish, trading name of Harper Cavendish (International) Ltd** *(J S Thind)* 16 Holywell Row, LONDON, EC2A 4XA. and at HAMPTON

ⓉⒻⓅⒶ**Harpersheldon, trading name of THS Accountants Limited** *(J Harper, S Sheldon)* The Old School House, Leckhampton Road, CHELTENHAM, GLOUCESTERSHIRE, GL53 0AX.

Ⓟ**Harries Watkins & Jones Ltd** *(N Harries, C D Jones)* First Floor, 85 Taff Street, PONTYPRIDD, MID GLAMORGAN, CF37 4SL. and at BRIDGEND

★Ⓐ**Harrington & Co** *(J R Harrington)* 7 Hawthorn Wood, KENMARE, COUNTY KERRY, IRELAND.

Ⓣ**Harris** *(L Harris)* 10th Floor, Alberton House, St. Marys Parsonage, MANCHESTER, M3 2WJ.

Ⓣ**Harris & Clarke, trading name of Harris & Clarke LLP** *(R F Clarke, J T G Harris)* 7 Billing Road, NORTHAMPTON, NN1 5AN.

ⓉⒻⒶ**Harris & Co** *(P J Harris)* 2 Pavilion Court, 600 Pavillion Drive, NORTHAMPTON, NN4 7SL.

★ⓉⒻⒶ**Harris & Co, trading name of Harrisaccounts LLP** *(M A Barratt, T I Garner, P Hinchliffe)* Marland House, 13 Huddersfield Road, BARNSLEY, SOUTH YORKSHIRE, S70 2LW.

Ⓟ**Harris & Company, trading name of Harris & Company (C.A.) Limited** *(N B Harris)* 4-6 Canfield Place, LONDON, NW6 3BT.

★Ⓟ**Harris & Harris Accountancy, trading name of Harris & Harris Accountancy Services CIC** *(H L Harris)* Fort Dunlop, Fort Parkway, BIRMINGHAM, B24 9FE.

Ⓟ**Harris & Screaton Ltd** *(B E Harris, B Screaton)* 49 Station Street, ATHERSTONE, WARWICKSHIRE, CV9 1DB.

★ⓉⒻⒶ**Harris & Trotter LLP** *(S M Garbutta, S E Haffner, C E Harris, R M Harris, H M Lask, N J Newman, R M Selwyn, D R Walters, M Webber)* 65 New Cavendish Street, LONDON, W1G 7LS.

ⒻⓅⒶ**Harris Bassett, trading name of Harris Bassett Limited** *(N W Bassett)* 5 New Mill Court, Phoenix Way, Enterprise Park, SWANSEA, SA7 9FG.

ⓅⒶ**Harris Carr Ltd** *(O R Smyth)* Cheriton, Farnham Lane, HASLEMERE, SURREY, GU27 1HD.

★ⓉⒶ**Harris Coombs & Company** *(R C P Coombs)* 5 Jaggard Way, LONDON, SW12 8SG.

★ⓉⒶ**Harris Kafton** *(D N Thakrar)* Ground Floor, Elizabeth House, 54-58 High Street, EDGWARE, HA8 7EJ.

Harris Kafton *(M Halford, M B Harris)* 11a Norwich Street, FAKENHAM, NORFOLK, NR21 9AF.

★ⓉⒻⒶ**Harris Lipman, trading name of Harris Lipman LLP** *(M J Atkins, M D T Bernstein, N D Chajet, F Khalastchi, P D Kurup, B D Lewis)* 2 Mountview Court, 310 Friern Barnet Lane, LONDON, N20 0YZ. and at CARDIFF, ST. ALBANS

ⒻⒶ**Harris, Lacey and Swain** *(R Adamson, R D Lacey, F C Swain)* 8 Waterside Business Park, Livingstone Road, HESSLE, NORTH HUMBERSIDE, HU13 0EN.

Ⓐ**Harrison & Co** *(C A Harrison)* St. Johns Kirk, Symington, BIGGAR, LANARKSHIRE, ML12 6JU.

ⓅⒶ**Harrison & Co, trading name of Harrison & Co Accountants Limited** *(R J Harrison)* 531 Denby Dale Road West, Calder Grove, WAKEFIELD, WEST YORKSHIRE, WF4 3ND.

★**Harrison Beale & Owen Management Services** *(M Ashfield, P G Ewing, R N Kendall)* 15 Queens Road, COVENTRY, CV1 3DE.

ⓉⒻⓅⒶ**Harrison Beale & Owen, Harrison Beale & Owen Management Services, trading names of Harrison Beale & Owen Limited** *(M Ashfield, P G Ewing, R N Kendall)* Harrison Beale, 15 Queens Road, COVENTRY, CV1 3DE. and at LEAMINGTON SPA

ⓅⒶ**Harrison Bernstein Ltd** *(R M Patel)* 10 Harmer Street, GRAVESEND, DA12 2AX.

ⓉⒻⓅⒶ**Harrison Black, trading name of Harrison Black Limited** *(E Dack, A Garner, G K Ricketts)* Pyle House, 137 Pyle Street, NEWPORT, ISLE OF WIGHT, PO30 1JW.

ⒻⒶ**Harrison Farrow** *(B K Farrow, A J Harrison)* Newnham House, 3 Kings Road, NEWARK, NG24 1EW.

ⒻⒶ**Harrison Hill Castle & Co.** *(P R Castle, M D French)* Melbury House, 34 Southborough Road, Bickley, BROMLEY, BR1 2EB.

Ⓐ**Harrison Holt** *(P J H Holt)* High Park Farm, Kirkbymoorside, YORK, YO62 7HS.

★ⓅⒶ**Harrison Hutchinson Ltd** *(P Hutchinson)* 246 Park View, WHITLEY BAY, TYNE AND WEAR, NE26 3QX.

Harrison Ingham & Co *(P Harrison, A W Ingham)* Riggs House, Riggs Head, SCARBOROUGH, YO12 5TG.

Ⓟ**Harrison Jasper Limited** *(C W Pickin)* 3 The Close, Corseley Road, Groombridge, TUNBRIDGE WELLS, KENT, TN3 9SE.

ⒻⒶ**Harrison Jones & Co** *(P Harrison)* Excelsior House, Mucklow Hill, HALESOWEN, B62 8EP.

ⒻⒶ**Harrison Latham & Company** *(M Harrison, N A Latham)* 97 Tulketh Street, SOUTHPORT, PR8 1AW.

Ⓐ**Harrison Reeds** *(K R Sodha)* 59 Kynance Gardens, STANMORE, HA7 2QJ.

Ⓟ**Harrison Smith Ltd** *(K A Smith)* The Spinney, Bracken Park, Scarcroft, LEEDS, LS14 3HZ.

Harrison Walker *(W N Harrison)* Enterprise House, 2 Pass Street, OLDHAM, OL9 6HZ.

ⓉⒻⒶ**Harrison, Priddey & Co** *(C J Hammond, S Priddey)* 22 St John Street, BROMSGROVE, B61 8QY.

ⒻⒶ**Harrisons** *(N G Depper, M R G Magrath)* 4 Brackley Close, South East Sector, Bournemouth International Airport, CHRISTCHURCH, DORSET, BH23 6SE.

Ⓟ**Harrisons Accountancy, trading name of Harrisons Accountancy Limited** *(D J Harrison)* 14 Saffron Road, BIGGLESWADE, BEDFORDSHIRE, SG18 8DJ.

Ⓐ**Harrod Neilson & Company** *(D Harrod)* 14 Woodstock Road, Bushey Heath, BUSHEY, HERTFORDSHIRE, WD23 1PH.

Ⓐ**Harrop Marshall** *(T G Bowler, C J Westbury)* Ashfield House, Ashfield Road, CHEADLE, CHESHIRE, SK8 1BB.

Ⓟ**Harrovian Business Services Limited** *(K G Patel, R M Robinson, M C Thakkar)* 1 Warner House, Harrovian Business Village, Bessborough Road, HARROW, MIDDLESEX, HA1 3EX.

Harry Alvarez FCA *(H L Alvarez)* 51 Ranelagh Road, Ealing, LONDON, W5 5RP.

Harry C.L. Poon *(C L H Poon)* PO Box 9047, General Post Office, 2 Connaught Place, CENTRAL, HONG KONG ISLAND, HONG KONG SAR.

ⒻⓅ**Harry Jeffery & Co Ltd** *(H E Jeffery)* St Lawrence, 28 Station Road, Bardney, LINCOLN, LINCOLNSHIRE, LN3 5UD.

Harry Moore *(H C Moore)* 2 Limekiln Close, Claydon, IPSWICH, IP6 0AW.

Ⓟ**Harry Nicolaou & Co Ltd** *(H Nicolaou)* 38b Stroud Green Road, LONDON, N4 3ES.

Harry Nicolaou & Co. *(H Nicolaou)* 38b Stroud Green Road, LONDON, N4 3ES.

Ⓟ**Hart Moss Doyle Ltd** *(A S Doyle)* 69 High Street, Dodworth, BARNSLEY, SOUTH YORKSHIRE, S75 3RQ.

ⒻⒶ**Hart Nurse** *(C H Nurse)* The Old Coach House, Southern Road, THAME, OXFORDSHIRE, OX9 2ED.

Ⓟ**Hart Nurse Limited** *(C H Nurse)* The Old Coach House, Southern Road, THAME, OXFORDSHIRE, OX9 2ED.

ⓉⒻⒶ**Hart Shaw, trading name of Hart Shaw LLP** *(P Dawson, A J Maybery, M McDonagh, J H Robinson, S Vickers, M Wharin)* Europa Link, Sheffield Business Park, SHEFFIELD, S9 1XU.

Ⓟ**Hartington Accountancy Services Ltd** *(D J Cousin)* Upper Holme, Holme Court, Matlock Street, BAKEWELL, DERBYSHIRE, DE45 1GQ.

ⓉⒻⒶ**Hartley Fowler LLP** *(J Askew, P R Collins, D M Fennell-Crouch, I R Gilchrist, G C Rolliston, J K Upson)* 4th Floor, Tuition House, 27-37 St. Georges Road, Wimbledon, LONDON, SW19 4EU. and at BRIGHTON, HORSHAM

Ⓐ**Hartmans** *(M T Hamid)* Trenleigh House, 3 Woodbridge Road, Moseley, BIRMINGHAM, B13 8EH.

ⓉⒻⒶ**Harts** *(J M Hart)* 3 Churchgates, Church Lane, BERKHAMSTED, HERTFORDSHIRE, HP4 2UB.

ⒻⓅⒶ**Harts Limited** *(A Naylor, D A J Taylor)* Westminster House, 10 Westminster Road, MACCLESFIELD, CHESHIRE, SK10 1BX.

★ⓉⒻ**Harts LLP** *(A Naylor, D A J Taylor)* Westminster House, 10 Westminster Road, MACCLESFIELD, CHESHIRE, SK10 1BX.

Ⓟ**Harvester Consultants Limited** *(S A Kahan, D Z Lopian)* 6th Floor, Cardinal House, 20 St. Marys Parsonage, MANCHESTER, M3 2LG.

Harvey & Co *(H S Dhaliwal)* 76a Uxbridge Road, Ealing, LONDON, W13 8RA.

ⒻⒶ**Harvey & Co** *(M Harvey)* 7 Dryden Close, Ashley Heath, RINGWOOD, BH24 2JB.

Harvey Marcus & Conway *(D I Conway)* 30 Dene Gardens, STANMORE, MIDDLESEX, HA7 4TD.

Harvey Spriggs *(H J W Spriggs)* Dovecote House, 11 Malvern Close, KETTERING, NORTHAMPTONSHIRE, NN16 9JP.

Harvey Tish *(H L Tish)* Whispers, Dog Kennel Lane, Chorleywood, RICKMANSWORTH, HERTFORDSHIRE, WD3 5EE.

Harwood & Ball *(R S N Malkin)* 23 Rectory Road, West Bridgford, NOTTINGHAM, NG2 6BE.

★ⓅⒶ**Harwood Hutton Limited** *(J C Cable, G C Corney, R J Hutton, D E Jones, A J Stronach)* 22 Wycombe End, BEACONSFIELD, BUCKINGHAMSHIRE, HP9 1NB.

★**Harwood Hutton, trading name of Harwood Hutton Tax Advisory LLP** *(J C Cable, G C Corney, R J Hutton, D E Jones, A J Stronach)* 22 Wycombe End, BEACONSFIELD, BUCKINGHAMSHIRE, HP9 1NB.

ⓉⒻⒶ**Harwood Lane & Co** *(R C Cook, D C Cox)* Units 1-4 Crossley Farm Business Centre, Swan Lane, Winterbourne, BRISTOL, BS36 1RH.

ⓉⒻⒶ**Harwoods** *(R F W Harwood)* 1Trinity Place, Midland Drive, SUTTON COLDFIELD, WEST MIDLANDS, B72 1TX.

ⓅⒶ**HAS Ltd** *(H Schwalbe)* Prince Albert House, 2b Mather Avenue, Prestwich, MANCHESTER, M25 0LA.

★ⓅⒶ**Haslehursts, trading name of Haslehursts Limited** *(T W Haslehurst, W K G Haslehurst)* 88 Hill Village Road, SUTTON COLDFIELD, WEST MIDLANDS, B75 5BE.

★ⓉⒻⒶ**Haslers Insolvency Services LLP, trading name of Haslers** *(L A Ambrose, M J Anderson, C Georgiou, R A J Hooper, L A Jacobs, C Munro, L E Shafier)* Old Station Road, LOUGHTON, ESSEX, IG10 4PL.

Ⓟ**Haslocks Limited** *(C G Haslock)* 46-48 East Smithfield, LONDON, E1W 1AW.

Hasmuk Patel & Co *(H Patel)* Lalita Buildings, 378 Walsall Road, Perry Barr, BIRMINGHAM, B42 2LX.

Ⓟ**Hassapis & Co, trading name of Hassapis & Co (Accountants Auditors) Ltd** *(P Hassapis)* Doma Building, 227 Arch Makarios III Avenue, PO Box 53104, 3300 LIMASSOL, CYPRUS.

Ⓟ**Hassard-Jones Limited** *(H Hassard-Jones)* 9 Northmead Road, Allerton, LIVERPOOL, L19 5NN.

Ⓟ**Hassell & Co, trading name of Hassell Forensic Accounting Limited** *(S R Hassell)* Erry Lodge, 3 Wilkins Green Lane, HATFIELD, HERTFORDSHIRE, AL10 9RT.

Ⓟ**Hasties, trading name of Dawpool Accountancy Services Limited** *(C P Hastie)* 48 Brimstage Road, Heswall, WIRRAL, MERSEYSIDE, CH60 1XG.

Ⓟ**HAT Group of Accountants, trading name of Holborn Accountancy Tuition Limited** *(I Atkins, O A H W Dodd, N M C Light, R Morris, M J Shaw)* 12 Cock Lane, LONDON, EC1A 9BU.

ⓉⒻⒶ**Hatch, trading name of Hatch Partnership LLP** *(S B Walsh, N J Warden)* 29 Wood Street, STRATFORD-UPON-AVON, WARWICKSHIRE, CV37 6JG. and at BRISTOL

Hatche & Co *(T J Hatche)* 8 Streamside, TONBRIDGE, KENT, TN10 3PU.

Ⓟ**Hatfield & Co, trading name of Hatfield & Co Accounting Services Ltd** *(I Hatfield)* South Normanton Business Centre, 40 High Street, NORMANTON, DERBYSHIRE, DE55 2BP. and at ALFRETON

ⒻⓅ**Hatfield & John Ltd** *(D A Hatfield, M John)* 2 Market Street, ABERAERON, DYFED, SA46 0AS.

Ⓟ**HATS Gloucester Ltd** *(A G Evans)* 162 Hucclecote Road, GLOUCESTER, GL3 3SH.

Ⓕ**Hattersley Clark** *(J C H Clark)* Copthall Bridge House, Station Bridge, HARROGATE, NORTH YORKSHIRE, HG1 1SP.

Ⓐ**Haviland & Co** *(A Haviland-Nye, J C Stables)* 11 Biddulph Road, LONDON, W9 1JA.

Hawdon Bell & Co *(J Bell, M Tindle, K J Williamson)* The Old Post Office, 63 Saville Street, NORTH SHIELDS, TYNE AND WEAR, NE30 1AY.

Ⓕ**Hawes Richards & Co** *(A N Lear)* 17 The Terrace, TORQUAY, TQ1 1BN.

Hawes Strickland *(T J Hawes, T B Strickland)* Federation House, 36/38 Rockingham Road, KETTERING, NORTHAMPTONSHIRE, NN16 8JS.

Hawkes Law *(C J Ling)* Hawkes Law House, PO Box 146, PORT VILA, VANUATU.

Hawkins *(K R Hawkins)* Dunelm, Longden Common Lane, Longden Common, SHREWSBURY, SY5 8AQ.

ⓉⒶ**Hawkins Scott** *(K P Brown, N J Clarke, W R Scott)* Wyvern House, 55-61 Frimley High Street, Frimley, CAMBERLEY, SURREY, GU16 7HJ.

Ⓟ**Hawkins Tilly Limited** *(G C Hawkins)* 5 Canterbury Street, GILLINGHAM, KENT, ME7 5TP.

ⒻⒶ**Hawley and Company** *(G S Hawley)* First Floor Suite, 23 Trinity Square, LLANDUDNO, LL30 2RH.

ⓉⓅ**Haworth & Co, trading name of Haworth & Co Limited** *(P J Haworth)* 21 Market Place, DEREHAM, NORFOLK, NR19 2AX. and at NORWICH

ⓅⒶ**Haworths Holdings Ltd** *(M Schofield)* The Old Tannery, Eastgate, ACCRINGTON, LANCASHIRE, BB5 6PW.

ⒻⓅⒶ**Haworths, trading name of Haworths Limited** *(M Schofield)* The Old Tannery, Eastgate, ACCRINGTON, LANCASHIRE, BB5 6PW. and at LANCASTER, SETTLE

ⓉⒻⒶ**Hawsons Corporate Finance, Hawsons IT Services, trading names of Hawsons** *(R M Burkimsher, D T Cairns, R A Frost, K Gregory, C I Hill, P J Kennan, P G Lomas, R W Marsh, M J Weatherall, M Wilmott)* Pegasus House, 463a Glossop Road, SHEFFIELD, S10 2QD. and at DONCASTER, NORTHAMPTON

Hawthorns *(J A Pullen)* Ist Floor, 16 Massetts Road, HORLEY, SURREY, RH6 7DE.

ⒻⓅ**Hawthorns, trading name of Charles & Company Accountancy Ltd** *(D C Craft, J A Pullen)* 1st Floor, 16 Massetts Road, HORLEY, SURREY, RH6 7DE.

ⓅⒶ**Hay Audit Ltd** *(L D F Hill)* Berkeley House, Dix's Field, EXETER, EX1 1PZ.

★ⒻⒶ**Hayes & Co** *(G T Hughes, A N Totham, A J Wardle)* St Andrews House, 11 Dalton Court, Commercial Road, Blackburn Interchange, DARWEN, LANCASHIRE BB3 0DG. and at MANCHESTER, PRESTON

Hayes & Company *(A G Hayes)* 76 Old Woking Road, WEST BYFLEET, KT14 6HU.

★ⒻⒶ**Hayhow & Co** *(R S Peck)* 19 King St, KING'S LYNN, PE30 1HB.

ⓅⒶ**Hayhursts, trading name of SPD Accountants Limited** *(S Delmege, S W Pollard)* First Floor, Hampshire House, 169 High Street, SOUTHAMPTON, SO14 2BY.

ⒻⓅⒶ**Hayles & Partners Limited** *(G L Banks, S P Davies, P J Morris)* 39 Castle Street, LEICESTER, LE1 5WN.

ⓉⒻⒶ**haysmacintyre** *(A Ball, J R Beard, A M Broome, K E Burton, I J R Cliffe, D Cox, G A Crowther, I A Daniels, A Frangos, N M Gillam, A M Gregory-Jones, A M Halsey, M F Jessa, A P Jupp, B A E King, D R Riley, D J E Sewell, R N Simpson, B A Watson, R J Weaver, S C Wilks, T L Young)* Fairfax House, 15 Fulwood Place, LONDON, WC1V 6AY.

ⒻⓅⒶ**Haysom Silverton & Partners, trading name of Haysom Silverton & Partners Ltd** *(R F Haysom, D A Silverton, A E Williams)* Norfolk House Centre, 82 Saxon Gate West, MILTON KEYNES, MK9 2DL.

Ⓟ**Hayton Accountancy, trading name of Hayton Accountancy Limited** *(J P Hayton)* 22 The Boyle, Barwick in Elmet, LEEDS, LS15 4JN.

Hayton Accounts *(I R Delany)* 20 Hayton Close, Bramingham, LUTON, LU3 4HD.

Ⓟ**Haytons, trading name of Haytons Ltd** *(S Hayton)* 20 Melbourne Avenue, FLEETWOOD, LANCASHIRE, FY7 8AY.

Hayvenhursts *(N J V Morris)* Lermon Court Fairway House, Links Business Park, St. Mellons, CARDIFF, CF3 0LT.

Hayvenhursts *(S F Cox, M D Felman, P T Felman, H Smith, G R Williams)* Fairway House, Links Business Park, St. Mellons, CARDIFF, CF3 0LT.

ⓅⒶ**Hayvenhursts (Holdings) Limited** *(S F Cox)* Fairway House Links Business Park, Fortran Road, St. Mellons, CARDIFF, CF3 0LT.

ⓉⓅ**Hayvenhursts Limited** *(S F Cox, M D Felman, P T Felman, H Smith, G R Williams)* Fairway House, Links Business Park, St Mellons, CARDIFF, CF3 0LT.

Hayward & Co *(D W Hayward)* 49 Dundalk Lane, Cheslyn Hay, WALSALL, WS6 7AZ.

Ⓐ**Hayward Cooper & Co** *(M E Hayward)* 30 Bolton Road, Aspull, WIGAN, WN2 1YY.

Ⓟ**Hayward Williams Limited** *(M B Hayward)* 85a High Street, BARRY, SOUTH GLAMORGAN, CF62 7DW.

ⓅⒶ**Hayward Wright Ltd** *(A G Hayward-Wright)* Prospect House, Church Green West, REDDITCH, WORCESTERSHIRE, B97 4BD.

Haywards *(P Bannister)* 4 Bridgeman Terrace, WIGAN, LANCASHIRE, WN1 1SX.

ⓉⒶ**Haywood & Co LLP** *(C W Haywood, M H Haywood)* Kevan Pilling House, 1 Myrtle Street, BOLTON, BL1 3AH.

Ⓟ**Haywood & Co Ltd** *(C W Haywood, M H Haywood)* Kevan Pilling House, 1 Myrtle Street, BOLTON, BL1 3AH.

ⓉⒻⒶ**Haywood & Co.** *(P Hebblethwaite, A P Jackson, J A Midgley, D Robinson)* 18 Stalker Walk, SHEFFIELD, S11 8NF. and at HARROGATE, ROTHERHAM

Hazel White *(H White)* 25 Ridge Hall Close, Caversham, READING, RG4 7EP.

Ⓐ**Hazell Minshall, trading name of Hazell Minshall LLP** *(D N Joyce)* 2 Clarendon Court, Over Wallop, STOCKBRIDGE, HAMPSHIRE, SO20 8HU.

Ⓟ**Hazlemere Tax Consultancy Ltd** *(G Young)* 35 Jackson Court, Hazlemere, HIGH WYCOMBE, BUCKINGHAMSHIRE, HP15 7TZ.

ⓉⒻⒶ**Hazlems Fenton LLP** *(L Angel, J M Barron, S R N Fenton, S H Jaffe, M M Krieger, M J Levitt, L J Siskind, R P Tenzer)* Palladium House, 1-4 Argyll Street, LONDON, W1F 7LD.

★ⓉⒶ**Hazlewoods LLP** *(A W Brookes, D S Clift, N F Dee, R Dooley, P R J Frost, P Fussell, N M Haines, M J Howard, P A Kinahan, S M Lawrence, D G Main, D R*

Pierce, G T Rew, P A Swan, D Williams) Windsor House, Barnett Way, Barnwood, GLOUCESTER, GL4 3RT. and at CHELTENHAM

ⒹⒻⓅⒶ**HB Accountants, trading name of HBAS Limited** *(J S Clarke, B D Claxton, K A Grover, J F T Neighbour)* Amwell House, 19 Amwell Street, HODDESDON, HERTFORDSHIRE, EN11 8TS.

HBA Accountancy *(V E Andrew)* 47 Oxenden Wood Road, Chelsfield Park, ORPINGTON, KENT, BR6 6HP.

ⓅⒶ**HBB Audit Limited** *(P A R Skipper)* Bridge House, 25 Fiddle Bridge Lane, HATFIELD, HERTFORDSHIRE, AL10 0SP.

ⒹⒻⒶ**HBD Accountancy Services LLP** *(A Beasley, S Buckley, H Macey, B J Russell)* Gladstone House, 2 Church Road, Wavertree, LIVERPOOL, L15 9EG.

★Ⓐ**HBH, trading name of Holmes Beaumont & Holroyd** *(K Bramwell, M K Brooke)* 15 Ropergate End, PONTEFRACT, WF8 1JT.

HCB Solutions *(H C Brunt)* Keys Cottage, Woodgate Road, Lower Bentley, BROMSGROVE, WORCESTERSHIRE, B60 4HA.

ⒻⒶ**HDC, trading name of Hollows Davies Crane** *(J S Bond, M Lowe)* Hoghton Chambers, Hoghton Street, SOUTHPORT, PR9 0TB.

Ⓟ**Headland Accounting Solutions Ltd** *(D J Edwards)* 42 East Street, NEWQUAY, CORNWALL, TR7 1BE.

ⒹⓅ**Heady & Co Limited** *(J N Heady)* 27 City Business Centre, Hyde Street, WINCHESTER, SO23 7TA.

Ⓟ**Heady & Company(Business Services) Limited** *(J N Heady)* 27 City Business Centre, Hyde Street, MANCHESTER, SO23 7TA.

Ⓟ**Healthcare Accounting Solutions Ltd** *(J B Cooke)* 11 Calton Road, New Barnet, BARNET, HERTFORDSHIRE, EN5 1BY.

HearnKelly Consulting *(M E Kelly)* 67 Ebery Grove, PORTSMOUTH, HAMPSHIRE, PO3 6HG.

Heath House Business Services *(A J Goodman)* 14 Willow Close, Mylor Bridge, FALMOUTH, CORNWALL, TR11 5SG.

Ⓟ**Heathcoates, trading name of Heathcoates Limited** *(S Ahmad)* Carr Chambers, 24-26 Carr Road, NELSON, LANCASHIRE, BB9 7JS.

Ⓟ**Heather & Co Ltd** *(S J Heather)* Longlac, White House Lane, Jacobs Well, GUILDFORD, GU4 7PT.

Heather Barnes *(H J Barnes)* 1 Nottingham Road, Ravenshead, NOTTINGHAM, NG15 9HG.

Heather Lea Business Services *(D K P Mangles)* 49 Heather Lea Avenue, SHEFFIELD, S17 3DL.

Heather Newton *(H C Newton)* Court Cottage, Little Heath Lane, Potten End, BERKHAMSTED, HP4 2RT.

Ⓟ**Heathfield Tax Consultancy Ltd** *(R J Halliday, S R Lopez)* 33 Heathfield, SWANSEA, SA1 6HD.

★ⒹⒻⒶ**Heaton Lumb Lisle** *(A M Carr, D P Lewis)* Thorpe House, 61 Richardshaw Lane, PUDSEY, LS28 7EL. and at BRADFORD

ⒹⒻⒶ**Hebblethwaites** *(R Brennan, R W Murdoch, A Throssell)* Westbrook Court, Sharrow Vale Road, SHEFFIELD, S11 8YZ.

Hedges & Co *(D A R Hedges)* The Leighs, Weston, SIDMOUTH, EX10 0PH.

Ⓟ**Hedges Bull Commercial Finance Ltd** *(T S G Hedges)* Hamlet House, 366-368 London Road, WESTCLIFF-ON-SEA, ESSEX, SS0 7HZ.

Hedges Chandler *(I J Chandler)* 36 The Westerings, HOCKLEY, ESSEX, SS5 4NY.

Ⓟ**Hedges Chandler, trading name of Hedges Chandler (Sudbury) Ltd** *(I J Chandler, T S G Hedges)* Hamlet House, 366-368 London Road, WESTCLIFF-ON-SEA, ESSEX, SS0 7HZ.

ⒹⒻⓅⒶ**Hedges Chandler, trading name of Hedges Chandler (Westcliff) Limited** *(I J Chandler, T S G Hedges)* Hamlet House, 366/368 London Road, WESTCLIFF-ON-SEA, SS0 7HZ.

HedgeStart, trading name of HedgeStart Partners LLP *(R B Edwards, M A F Wilson)* St Albans House, 57/59 Haymarket, LONDON, SW1Y 4QX.

ⒹⒻⓅⒶ**Hedley Dunk, trading name of Hedley Dunk Limited** *(S M Fryer, J Outram)* Trinity House, 3 Bullace Lane, DARTFORD, DA1 1BB.

Ⓐ**Hedley S. Worwood** *(H S Worwood)* 8 Showell Lane, Penn, WOLVERHAMPTON, WV4 4UA.

Hedworth Moore *(C H Moore)* Hollybank Cottage, Mill Lane, Audlem, CREWE, CW3 0AY.

Heena Patel BA ACA *(H Patel)* 25 Burghley House, Somerset Road, LONDON, SW19 5JB.

Heenans *(S J Heenan)* KBC Kingston Exchange, 12-50 Kingsgate Road, KINGSTON UPON THAMES, SURREY, KT2 5AA.

Helen Bardle *(H L Bardle)* 7 Cliff Street, CHEDDAR, SOMERSET, BS27 3PT.

Helen Calder *(H M Calder)* Black Cat Cottage, Broadwell Road, Oddington, MORETON-IN-MARSH, GL56 0UX.

Helen Curran *(H C Curran)* 35 Hawthorn Avenue, WILMSLOW, CHESHIRE, SK9 5BR.

Helen Gray Accounting Services *(H L Gray)* Hideaway House, Wilderness Rise, Dormans Park, EAST GRINSTEAD, WEST SUSSEX, RH19 2LN.

Helen J Senior *(H J Senior)* The Azaleas, Norchard Lane, Crossway Green, STOURPORT-ON-SEVERN, WORCESTERSHIRE, DY13 9SN.

Helen Lee *(H M Lee)* 55 Wodeland Avenue, GUILDFORD, SURREY, GU2 4LA.

Helen Miller Accountancy Services *(H L Miller)* 5 Bincleaves Road, WEYMOUTH, DORSET, DT4 8RL.

Ⓟ**Helen Phenix & Co, trading name of Hyperons Limited** *(H L Phenix)* 61 Greensleeves Avenue, BROADSTONE, DORSET, BH18 8BJ.

Helen Rumsey *(H R Rumsey)* 18 Plough Close, DAVENTRY, NORTHAMPTONSHIRE, NN11 0NX.

Ⓟ**Helen Sida, trading name of Helen Sida Ltd** *(H V Sida-Page)* Bramble Cottage, Middle Road, Denton, HARLESTON, NORFOLK, IP20 0AJ.

Helen Tombs *(H M Tombs)* 50 Wellfield Road, Culcheth, WARRINGTON, WA3 4JT.

Helena Kay *(H C D Kay)* North Lodge, Ironsbottom, Sidlow, REIGATE, SURREY, RH2 8PU.

Helliwell Handscomb *(G D Handscomb, L Handscomb)* 15 Littlethorpe Hill, Hartshead, LIVERSEDGE, WF15 8AZ.

★ⒹⒻⒶ**Helmores, trading name of Helmores UK LLP** *(M J V Guillem, W H Hertzberg, N C Hough, J B McGinley)* Grosvenor Gardens House, 35-37 Grosvenor Gardens, LONDON, SW1W 0BY.

ⒹⓅⒶ**Hem Mahadeo Limited** *(H Mahadeo)* 47 Hazelgrove Road, HAYWARDS HEATH, WEST SUSSEX, RH16 3PH.

Hemant Patel *(H J Patel)* The Manor House, 1028 Melton Road, Syston, LEICESTER, LE7 2NN.

Ⓟ**Hemisphere Accounting Limited** *(G L Dobson)* Mornington, Maybourne Rise, WOKING, SURREY, GU22 0SH.

Ⓐ**Hemming Vincent, trading name of Hemming Vincent LLP** *(A N Parker, P M J Vincent)* 31 Abbey Road, GRIMSBY, SOUTH HUMBERSIDE, DN32 0HQ.

ⒻⒶ**Hemsley Miller & Co** *(N G Dodd)* Old Telephone Exchange, Kingsway, Farnham Common, SLOUGH, SL2 3ST.

★**Henderson Loggie** *(J M Stevenson)* 34 Melville Street, EDINBURGH, EH3 7HA.

Ⓐ**Hendersons** *(S Faid)* Sterling House, Brunswick Industrial Estate, NEWCASTLE UPON TYNE, NE13 7BA.

Ⓟ**Hendersons, trading name of Ward Goodman (Wareham) Limited** *(G G Ball, D E R Lapthorn, T D Riley)* 4 Cedar Park, Cobham Road, Ferndown Industrial Estate, WIMBORNE, DORSET, BH21 7SF. and at WAREHAM

Hendry Lau & Co. *(H Y Lau)* Room 704, 7/F Landwide Commercial Building, 118-120 Austin Road, TSIM SHA TSUI, KOWLOON, HONG KONG SAR.

Henley Accounting Services *(D I Quigley)* Chiltern House, 45 Station Road, HENLEY-ON-THAMES, OXFORDSHIRE, RG9 1AT.

Ⓐ**Henn & Westwood** *(R W Aldridge, E Lockey)* Rumbow House, Rumbow, HALESOWEN, B63 3HU. and at WOLVERHAMPTON

Ⓟ**Henry and Banwell, trading name of Henry and Banwell Limited** *(M P Winkelmann)* 26 Berkeley Square, Clifton, BRISTOL, BS8 1HP.

ⒹⒶ**Henry Bach & Co** *(A R Bach)* Suite 2, 15 Broad Court, Covent Garden, LONDON, WC2B 5QN.

Henry Guy *(J H G Guy)* 20 Belmont Close, UXBRIDGE, UB8 1RF.

Ⓟ**Henry Jarvis Fleming, trading name of HJF (Personal Tax) Limited** *(R H Thistle)* First Floor, 74 Chancery Lane, LONDON, WC2A 1AD.

★**Henry Law & Company** *(H H H Law)* Room 301-2, Hang Seng Wanchai Building 3rd Floor, No. 200 Hennessy Road, WAN CHAI, HONG KONG ISLAND, HONG KONG SAR.

Henry Lunt *(M H C Lunt)* Ashburn, Woodhart Lane, Eccleston, CHORLEY, PR7 5TB.

ⒻⒶ**Henry R. Davis & Co** *(A H Travers)* 33 Chester Road West, Queensferry, DEESIDE, CH5 1SA.

Henry Wong & Company *(H S K Wong)* 4A Ngan House, 210 Des Voeux Road, CENTRAL, HONG KONG ISLAND, HONG KONG SAR.

★ⒹⒻⒶ**Henton & Co, trading name of Henton & Co LLP** *(A Ahmad, N Ahmed, S Gray, I P Hart, C Howitt)* St. Andrews House, St. Andrews Street, LEEDS, LS3 1LF. and at SHEFFIELD

Hepplewhite & Co *(M F Hepplewhite)* 20 Selborne Road, Southgate, LONDON, N14 7DH.

Hepworth Griffiths *(P D Griffiths, J A Hepworth)* 47/49 Grove Street, RETFORD, NOTTINGHAMSHIRE, DN22 6LA.

Herbert J. Moore *(H J Moore)* 35 Edgcumbe Park Drive, CROWTHORNE, RG45 6HU.

Ⓐ**Herbert Parnell** *(A W Hodgetts, A M Peckham)* Station House, Connaught Road, Brookwood, WOKING, SURREY, GU24 0ER.

ⒹⒻⓅⒶ**Herbert Parnell, trading name of HPCA Limited** *(A W Hodgetts, A M Peckham, L G Redman)* Station House, Connaught Road, Brookwood, WOKING, SURREY, GU24 0ER.

Herbert W Tuckey FCA *(H W Tuckey)* 17 Avonside, Mill Lane, STRATFORD-UPON-AVON, CV37 6BJ.

ⒻⓅⒶ**Heriot Hughes, trading name of Heriot Hughes Limited** *(J M Hughes)* 42 Crosby Road North, Crosby, LIVERPOOL, L22 4QQ.

Herman & Co *(I Herman)* Clapper Cottage, Bondleigh, NORTH TAWTON, DEVON, EX20 2AU.

Herown Ltd, trading name of Carol Jefferis *(C R Jefferis)* 3 Upper Station Road, RADLETT, WD7 8BY.

Ⓟ**Heslops, trading name of Taxpal Ltd** *(J P R Prevost)* 111 Milford Road, LYMINGTON, HAMPSHIRE, SO41 8DN.

★ⒻⒶ**Hetherington & Co,** *(K B Ballard)* Second Floor, 289 Green Lane, Palmers Green, LONDON, N13 4XS.

ⒻⓅⒶ**Hewitt Warin Ltd** *(J Warin)* Harlow Enterprise Hub, Edinburgh Way, HARLOW, ESSEX, CM20 2NQ.

★ⒻⒶ**Hewitts** *(B Clegg)* 11 Venture One Business Park, Long Acre Close, SHEFFIELD, S20 3FR.

Hewitts *(N A Hewitt)* 6 The Spindles, Great Wyrley, WALSALL, WS6 6GD.

ⒹⒻⒶ**Hewson and Howson** *(I J Hewson, A Howson)* 8 Shepcote Office Village, Shepcote Lane, SHEFFIELD, S9 1TG.

ⓅⒶ**Hewsons, trading name of Hewsons (UK) Limited** *(N D Hewson)* 80 Woodhurst Avenue, Petts Wood, ORPINGTON, KENT, BR5 1AT.

ⒹⒻⓅⒶ**Hextall Meakin, trading name of Hextall Meakin Limited** *(G R Meakin)* Argon House, Argon Mews, LONDON, SW6 1BJ. and at SALISBURY

Heydon & Co. *(D W Heydon)* 6 Templar Mews, Black Jack Street, CIRENCESTER, GLOUCESTERSHIRE, GL7 2AA.

ⒻⒶ**Heywards** *(S Patel, P N Samuels, H B Strudwick)* 6th Floor, Remo House, 310-312 Regent Street, LONDON, W1B 3BS.

★ⒹⒶ**Heywood Shepherd** *(N W Hutchings, N A Kennington, D Southall)* 1 Park Street, MACCLESFIELD, CHESHIRE, SK11 6SR.

ⒻⒶ**Heywoods** *(A R Payne)* Countrywide House, Knights Way, Battlefield Enterprise Park, SHREWSBURY, SY1 3AB.

ⓅⒶ**HG Professional, trading name of HG Professional Limited** *(H E Gandy)* Office F5, Building 67, Europa Business Park, Bird Hall Lane, Cheadle Heath, STOCKPORT CHESHIRE SK3 0XA.

Ⓟ**HGR Secretaries Limited** *(G G Stern)* Stern & Co, 12-15 Hanger Green, LONDON, W5 3AY.

Ⓕ**HGT Management LLP** *(D A Hallgarten)* 20 Manchester Square, LONDON, W1U 3PZ.

HH Lam & Co *(O V Lam)* Room 905-909 Yu To Sang Building, 37 Queens Road, CENTRAL, HONG KONG SAR.

Ⓟ**HHG Business Services Ltd** *(M H Rhodes, S Rhodes)* Hill House, Shelton Road, Upper Dean, HUNTINGDON, CAMBRIDGESHIRE, PE28 0NQ.

Hibbert & Co. *(T N Hibbert)* 480a Roundhay Road, LEEDS, LS8 2HU.

Hibbit & Partners *(M O D Hibbit)* The Tithe Barn, Lillington, SHERBORNE, DORSET, DT9 6QX.

★ⒻⓅ**Hicks & Co** *(P M Cobden)* 53 Lampton Road, HOUNSLOW, TW3 1LY.

Ⓐ**Hicks and Company** *(M F Corrie, P Dean)* Vaughan Chambers, Vaughan Road, HARPENDEN, AL5 4EE. and at HEMEL HEMPSTEAD

ⒹⒻⒶ**Higgins Day** *(S N Higgins)* 19 York Rd, MAIDENHEAD, SL6 1SQ.

Ⓐ**Higgins Fairbairn & Co** *(F W Higgins, B C Patel)* 1st Floor, 24/25 New Bond Street, LONDON, W1S 2RR.

Ⓟ**Higgins Harvey Ltd** *(P A Higgins)* 93 Long Row, Horsforth, LEEDS, LS18 5AT.

ⒻⓅⒶ**Higginson & Co (UK) Ltd** *(D M Brown)* 3 Kensworth Gate, 200-204 High Street South, DUNSTABLE, BEDFORDSHIRE, LU6 3HS.

ⒹⒻⒶ**Higgisons** *(D J Frampton, J J McHale, I Shillinglaw)* Higgison House, 381/383 City Road, LONDON, EC1V 1NW.

High Path VAT Consultancy *(H R Mitchell)* 14 High Path, WELLINGTON, SOMERSET, TA21 8NH.

Highgrove Accountants *(A T Kent)* 1st Floor, Unit 13, Victoria Way, Pride Park, DERBY, DE24 8AN.

Ⓟ**Highview Management Services Limited** *(M E Brown)* 35 Broad Meadows, NEWCASTLE UPON TYNE, NE3 4PZ.

ⒹⒻⒶ**Higson & Co** *(D V Bonnert, W E Messom, S C R Skill, G J Strickland, D R Wallwork)* White House, Wollaton St, NOTTINGHAM, NG1 5GF.

★ⒻⒶ**Higsons** *(K Higson)* 93 Market Street, Farnworth, BOLTON, BL4 7NS.

★**Hii & Lee** *(S Lim)* 2nd Floor Lot 2765, Block 10, Jalan Tun Ahmad Zaidi Adruce, 93150 KUCHING, SARAWAK, MALAYSIA.

ⒹⓅⒶ**Hilary Adams Ltd** *(H J Adams, F N Clarke)* 158 High Street, HERNE BAY, KENT, CT6 5NP. and at ROCHESTER

Ⓟ**Hilary Bell, trading name of Hilary Bell Limited** *(H Bell)* North Mosses, Asby, WORKINGTON, CA14 4RP.

Hilary D Baker *(H D Baker)* 28 Lansdowne Road, STANMORE, MIDDLESEX, HA7 2SA.

Ⓟ**Hilary Harper Accountancy Services Ltd** *(H R Harper)* The Pines, Cranhill Farm, Harborough Road, Billesdon, LEICESTER, LE7 9EL.

Hilary Parmenter ACA *(H J Parmenter)* 1 The Willows, North Warnborough, HOOK, HAMPSHIRE, RG29 1DR.

Ⓟ**Hilary Seaward Limited** *(H J Seaward)* 9 Sherlock Road, CAMBRIDGE, CB3 0HR.

ⒹⒻ**Hill & Roberts** *(H P Baines, D V Evans, R A Roberts)* 1 Tan-Y-Castell, Dog Lane, RUTHIN, LL15 1DQ. and at BALA, MOLD

Hill Barn Management *(S P Lovett)* Hill Barn, Gore Lane, Uplyme, LYME REGIS, DORSET, DT7 3RJ.

Hill Day *(C R Hill)* Wayside House, Bedford Road, Ravensden, BEDFORD, MK44 2RA.

ⓅⒶ**Hill Eckersley & Co, trading name of Hill Eckersley & Co Limited** *(I Hampson, A M Nicholls)* 62 Chorley New Road, BOLTON, BL1 4BY.

★ⒹⒻⓅⒶ**Hill Osborne, trading name of Hill Osborne Ltd** *(A R Hill)* Tower House, Parkstone Road, POOLE, DORSET, BH15 2JH.

ⒹⒻⓅⒶ**Hill Wooldridge & Co Limited** *(I B Park, L Perdoni, J E Soughton)* 107 Hindes Road, HARROW, MIDDLESEX, HA1 1RU.

ⒹⒶ**Hillier Hopkins LLP** *(R W Badger, J A Barker, A M Bottom, P A Burnham, P Collins, J L Franks, C Leach)* Charter Court, Midland Road, HEMEL HEMPSTEAD, HERTFORDSHIRE, HP2 5GE. and at AYLESBURY, LONDON, WATFORD

★**Hills** *(S M Hill)* Eddystone House, Aberderfyn, Johnstown, WREXHAM, LL14 1PB.

ⒻⒶ**Hills & Burgess** *(P R Dodson, J Roberts)* 20 Bridge Street, LEIGHTON BUZZARD, LU7 1AL.

Ⓐ**Hillyates** *(P W Hill, V Hill)* Hill House, 27 Meadowford, Newport, SAFFRON WALDEN, CB11 3QL.

ⒻⓅⒶ**Hilton Consulting, trading name of Hilton Consulting Limited** *(B J Warren)* 119 The Hub, 300 Kensal Road, LONDON, W10 5BE.

ⓅⒶ**Hilton Holdings, trading name of Hilton Holdings (UK) Limited** *(B J Warren)* 119 The Hub, 300 Kensal Road, LONDON, W10 5BE.

ⒹⒻⒶ**Hilton Sharp & Clarke** *(D G Bishop, R K Moore, F C Roberts, C S Young)* 30 New Road, BRIGHTON, BN1 1BN. and at BILLINGSHURST, HOVE

★ⓅⒶ**Hindle Jepson & Jennings Ltd** *(D W Wilson)* 10 Borough Road, DARWEN, LANCASHIRE, BB3 1PL.

Hindley & Co *(J S Hindley)* 733 Manchester Road, Over Hulton, BOLTON, BL5 1BA.

ⒹⒶ**Hindocha & Co** *(L V Hindocha)* V16 Howitt Building, Lenton Business Park, Lenton Boulevard, NOTTINGHAM, NG7 2BY.

ⓅⒶ**Hindocha & Co, trading name of Hindocha & Co Limited** *(Y P Hindocha)* 34 Queensbury Station Parade, EDGWARE, MIDDLESEX, HA8 5NN.

ⒻⒶ**Hindocha & Co.** *(A D Hindocha)* 19 Harewood Road, Deepdale, PRESTON, PR1 6XH.

Hindsight Tax Partners, trading name of Hindsight Tax Partners LLP *(P J Fava, M Swansbury)* 12 The Riverside Studios, Amethyst Road, NEWCASTLE UPON TYNE, NE4 7YL.

Ⓟ**Hines Harvey Woods Limited** *(J T Hines)* Queens Head House, The Street, Acle, NORWICH, NR13 3DY.

Hirons & Co *(D R Jones)* 2 Corfton Drive, WOLVERHAMPTON, WV6 8NR.

ⓉⒶ**Hitchcock Frank & Co** *(B A Hitchcock)* Highfield House, White Horse Road, Holly Hill, Meopham, GRAVESEND, DA13 0UF.

Hitchenors *(R J Hitchenor, T L Hitchenor)* School Farm, Barton Lane, Bradley, STAFFORD, ST18 9EF.

Ⓟ**Hitchin Practice Limited** *(A J W Brown)* Hemmings, Kings Walden, HITCHIN, HERTFORDSHIRE, SG4 8NW.

Hitesh Patel *(H R Patel)* 14 Denehurst Gardens, WOODFORD GREEN, IG8 0PA.

Ⓟ**Hixsons Limited** *(N V Hixson)* 24 Cecil Avenue, BOURNEMOUTH, BH8 9EJ.

ⒻⓅⒶ**HJP, trading name of All About Business Limited** *(C M Harris, A Peden)* Audley House, Northbridge Rd, BERKHAMSTED, HERTFORDSHIRE, HP4 1EH.

ⓉⒻⓅⒶ**HJS Recovery, trading name of Hunt Johnston Stokes Ltd** *(S A Hunt, G J Johnston, A R Ponting, J L Sims, G A Stokes)* 12-14 Carlton Place, SOUTHAMPTON, SO15 2EA.

HKP, trading name of Hainsworth Kerry Practice *(K J Hainsworth)* Old Links Rectory, Links Green, Hinstock, MARKET DRAYTON, TF9 2NH.

HLA Accounting *(H L Anderson)* The Gleanings, Church Road, Glatton, HUNTINGDON, CAMBRIDGESHIRE, PE28 5RR.

ⓉⓅ**HLB Afxentiou Limited** *(C Afxentiou, M F Hadjihannas, P Polyviou, S Prodromitis)* Palaceview House, Corner of Prodromos St & Zinonos Kitieos, POBox 16006, CY-2085 NICOSIA, CYPRUS. and at LIMASSOL

★**HLB Hodgson Impey Cheng** *(R C C Cheng, J T S Lai, C F Yu)* 31/F Gloucester Tower, The Landmark, 11 Pedder Street, CENTRAL, HONG KONG ISLAND, HONG KONG SAR.

ⓉⓅ**HLB Jackson Fox, trading name of HLB Jackson Fox Limited** *(G P Angus, L M M Bracken-Smith, A J Rothwell, N F Walker)* PO Box 264, Union House, Union Street, JERSEY, JE4 8TQ. and at JERSEYVILLE

HLB Jivanjee & Company *(M K Jivanjee)* P.O. Box 3401, ABU DHABI, UNITED ARAB EMIRATES.

Ⓟ**HLM Resources Ltd** *(B M Buss)* School House, Healaugh, TADCASTER, NORTH YORKSHIRE, LS24 8DB.

Ⓟ**HLM Secretaries Limited** *(C K Varley)* Prospect House, 2 Sinderland Road, Broadheath, ALTRINCHAM, CHESHIRE, WA14 5ET.

Ⓟ**HLM, trading name of HLM Accountancy Limited** *(H B H Luc)* 108 Parsonage Manorway, BELVEDERE, KENT, DA17 6LY.

HMA Accountancy Services *(H M Ainsworth)* Ranmore, Waterhouse Lane, Kingswood, TADWORTH, KT20 6DT.

Ⓟ**HMC Associates, trading name of H.M.C. Associates Limited** *(S W McGuire)* 9 Guipavas Road, CALLINGTON, CORNWALL, PL17 7PL.

Ⓐ**HMJT** *(T J Hawes)* Federation House, 36/38 Rockingham Road, KETTERING, NORTHAMPTONSHIRE, NN16 8JS.

Ⓟ**HMN Accountants Ltd** *(I D Howes)* Woodlands, Bourne Lane, Hamstreet, ASHFORD, KENT, TN26 2HH.

ⓉⒶ**HMT Assurance, trading name of HMT Assurance LLP** *(D I Hurst, G B Hurst, J M Mitchell)* 5 Fairmile, HENLEY-ON-THAMES, OXFORDSHIRE, RG9 2JR.

Ⓕ**HMT Corporate Finance, Hurst Morrison Thomson, trading names of Hurst Morrison Thomson Corporate Finance LLP** *(P J Barrand, C B Morrison, A D Thomson)* The Hub, 14 Station Road, HENLEY-ON-THAMES, OXFORDSHIRE, RG9 1AY.

HMW *(H E Webster)* 1 Stuarts Green, Pedmore, STOURBRIDGE, WEST MIDLANDS, DY9 0XR.

Ⓟ**Ho Sneddon Chow CPA Ltd** *(S K Ho, S Y Y Sneddon Chow)* Unit 1202 Mirror Tower, 61 Mody Road, TSIM SHA TSUI, HONG KONG SAR.

Ho Wai Ki & Co *(W Ho)* Unit C 11th Floor, Gaylord Commercial Building, 114-118 Lockhart Road, WAN CHAI, HONG KONG SAR.

Hobbs & Co *(A A Hobbs)* 27 Albany Road, ST. LEONARDS-ON-SEA, EAST SUSSEX, TN38 0LP.

Ⓐ**Hobday & Company** *(H E Hobday, P C Hobday)* 20a Plantagenet Road, BARNET, HERTFORDSHIRE, EN5 5JG.

Ⓟ**Hobson & Co Accountants Limited** *(S Hobson)* 37 Wollaton Road, Beeston, NOTTINGHAM, NG9 2NG.

Ⓟ**Hobson, trading name of Hobson Tax Consulting Limited** *(D C Hobson)* 106 Old Coppice Side, HEANOR, DERBYSHIRE, DE75 7DJ.

ⓉⒻⒶ**Hobsons** *(M C Berry, S G Foster, J Scully, M J Szolin-Jones, P Tagg)* Alexandra House, 43 Alexandra Street, NOTTINGHAM, NG5 1AY. and at NEWARK

ⓉⓅ**Hockley Wright & Co Limited** *(E K H Wright, J H Wright)* Berkeley House, 18 Station Road, EAST GRINSTEAD, WEST SUSSEX, RH19 1DJ.

Hockmans *(B D Kester)* Cardinal Point, Park Road, RICKMANSWORTH, HERTFORDSHIRE, WD3 1RE.

ⒻⓅⒶ**Hodge Bakshi, trading name of Hodge Bakshi Limited** *(P S Bakshi, K J Bamji)* Churchgate House, 3 Church Road, Whitchurch, CARDIFF, CF14 2DX.

Hodges & Co *(J E Hodges)* 62 Norwich Street, DEREHAM, NR19 1AD.

ⒻⒶ**Hodgson & Co** *(J B Hodgson)* Lydgate Farm, Ashopton Road, Bamford, HOPE VALLEY, DERBYSHIRE, S33 0AZ.

★ⒻⒶ**Hodgson & Oldfield** *(D J Gostelow)* 20 Paradise Square, SHEFFIELD, S1 1UA.

Ⓐ**Hodgson Hickie** *(R A Hickie)* Unit 4, Dovedale Studios, 465 Battersea Park Road, LONDON, SW11 4LR.

Ⓣ**Hodgsons** *(D E M Mond)* Nelson House, Park Road, Timperley, ALTRINCHAM, CHESHIRE, WA14 5BZ.

★ⓉⒻⒶ**Hodgsons** *(J P D Hodgson, P J D Hodgson, P J M Stevenson)* 12 Southgate Street, LAUNCESTON, PL15 9DP. and at FALMOUTH

ⒻⒶ**Hodson & Co** *(B F Hodson, M J Hodson)* Wiston House, 1 Wiston Avenue, WORTHING, BN14 7QL.

★**Hodsons Accountants** *(M J Hodson)* Wiston House, 1 Wiston Avenue, WORTHING, WEST SUSSEX, BN14 7QL.

★**Hogg Shain & Scheck** *(V D Bright)* Suite 404, 2255 Sheppard Avenue East, WILLOWDALE M2J 4Y1, ON, CANADA.

ⓉⓅⒶ**Holbrook Curtis Ltd** *(R W H Curtis)* 1 Imperial Square, CHELTENHAM, GLOUCESTERSHIRE, GL50 1QB.

Ⓐ**Holden & Co** *(E G Holden)* PO Box 229, LONDON, SW6 4UX.

Holden & Co *(R Holden)* Ashleigh House, 81 Birmingham Road, WEST BROMWICH, WEST MIDLANDS, B70 0PX.

Ⓐ**Holden Granat, trading name of Holden Granat LLP** *(J E Granat, R Granat)* 13 Walton Park, WALTON-ON-THAMES, SURREY, KT12 3ET.

Ⓟ**Holden Tax Consulting, trading name of Holden Tax Consulting Limited** *(E J Holden)* 12 Spring Close, SOUTHPORT, MERSEYSIDE, PR8 2BA.

Ⓟ**Holden Thomas Limited** *(J E Granat, R Granat)* 12 Lion & Lamb Yard, FARNHAM, SURREY, GU9 7LL.

Ⓐ**Holding & Company** *(G R Holding)* Birchwood House, Shaws Lane, Southwater, HORSHAM, WEST SUSSEX, RH13 9BX.

★ⒻⒶ**Holdstock Nicholls Train & Co** *(C S Wright)* 593 Anlaby Road, HULL, HU3 6ST.

ⓉⒻⓅⒶ**Holeys, trading name of Holeys Limited** *(P C P Durrant, B G Robinson, P Stephenson, T B Yates)* Stuart House, 15-17 North Park Road, HARROGATE, NORTH YORKSHIRE, HG1 5PD.

Holford Training and Accountancy *(S E Holford)* 5 Shutford Road, North Newington, BANBURY, OXFORDSHIRE, OX15 6AL.

Ⓟ**Holiday Gordon Limited** *(P M Holiday)* 44 Western Road, Urmston, MANCHESTER, M41 6LF.

Ⓣ**Holland & Co** *(N Holland)* 102/104 Widnes Road, WIDNES, WA8 6AX.

ⓉⒻⒶ**Holland Harper LLP** *(N S G Harper, R M Holland)* 26 High Street, BATTLE, EAST SUSSEX, TN33 0EA.

Ⓐ**Holland MacLennan & Co.** *(R P Holland, R E MacLennan)* 115 Crockhamwell Road, Woodley, READING, RG5 3JP.

ⓅⒶ**Hollingdale Pooley, trading name of Hollingdale Pooley Limited** *(P A Barry, M Pooley)* Bramford House, 23 Westfield Park, Clifton, BRISTOL, BS6 6LT.

★ⓉⒻ**Hollings Crowe Storr & Co** *(P J Fardell)* 14 Beech Hill, OTLEY, LS21 3AX. and at LEEDS

Ⓕ**Hollingsworth & Co** *(J A Hollingsworth)* Coppice House, Halesfield 7, TELFORD, SHROPSHIRE, TF7 4NA.

Hollis & Co *(A V H Farmer)* The Rookery, Freasley, TAMWORTH, B78 2EZ.

ⒻⓅⒶ**Hollis and Co, trading name of Hollis and Co Ltd** *(P J Hollis)* 35 Wilkinson Street, SHEFFIELD, S10 2GB.

ⓉⒶ**Hollows & Hesketh** *(M W Dunning, J Keeley)* 9 Sandy Lane, SKELMERSDALE, WN8 8LA.

Ⓕ**Holmes & Co** *(J R Holmes)* 10 Torrington Road, Claygate, ESHER, KT10 0SA.

Ⓐ**Holmes & Co** *(A Holmes)* 3a Bell Street, ROMSEY, SO51 8GY.

ⒻⓅⒶ**Holmes Peat Thorpe, trading name of HPT (Luton) Limited** *(Peter Cooper)* Unit F21, Basepoint Business & Innovation Centre, 110 Butterfield, Great Marlings, LUTON, LU2 8DL.

ⓉⒻⓅⒶ**Holmes Widlake Limited** *(T W Holmes, A J Powell)* 3 Sharrow Lane, SHEFFIELD, S11 8AE.

Ⓟ**Holton Partners Limited** *(K J Holton)* Treelands, Landscape Road, WARLINGHAM, SURREY, CR6 9JB.

★**Homer & Co** *(E J Nunes)* 27A Saddle Road, MARAVAL, TRINIDAD AND TOBAGO.

Homer Knott & Co *(C J Knott)* Hawthorne House, Charlotte Street, DUDLEY, DY1 1TD.

★ⓉⒻⓅⒶ**Honey Barrett, trading name of Honey Barrett Limited** *(G W Coleman, E H Densley, P A J Knight)* 53 Gildredge Road, EASTBOURNE, EAST SUSSEX, BN21 4SF. and at BEXHILL-ON-SEA, WADHURST

Ⓟ**Honeywell & Company, trading name of Honeywell (Monmouth) Limited** *(P R Honeywell)* 9 Whitecross Street, MONMOUTH, NP25 3BY.

Ⓟ**Hood & Co, trading name of Hood Financial Ltd** *(R M Hood)* 168 Shay Lane, Walton, WAKEFIELD, WEST YORKSHIRE, WF2 6NP.

Hoogewerf & Co *(F N Hoogewerf)* PO Box 878, 19 Rue Aldringen, L-2018 LUXEMBOURG, LUXEMBOURG.

Ⓟ**Hooley Counsulting Limited** *(J G Hooley)* La Maison D'Aval, Rue Des Messuriers, St. Pierre Du Bois, GUERNSEY, GY7 9SL.

Hooper & Co *(M R P Hooper)* Little Shipton, London Road, Charlton Kings, CHELTENHAM, GLOUCESTERSHIRE, GL52 6UY.

Ⓟ**Hooper & Co, trading name of Hooper & Co (Financial Management) Ltd** *(D W Hooper)* 5 Marlowe Way, COLCHESTER, CO3 4JP.

ⓅⒶ**Hope Agar, Jacksons, trading names of Hope Agar Limited** *(K T Rhodes)* 24a Marsh Street, Rothwell, LEEDS, LS26 0BB. and at OSSETT

Ⓐ**Hope Jones** *(P G Edwards, A B Maugham, P D Root)* Lymington House, 73 High St, LYMINGTON, SO41 9ZA. and at NEW MILTON

Ⓟ**Hope Shaw Ltd** *(D J L Robinson)* 21 The Old Yarn Mills, Westbury, SHERBORNE, DT9 3RQ.

ⒻⓅ**Hopefield** *(G Fielding)* The Summer House, Soldiers Field Lane, Findon, WORTHING, WEST SUSSEX, BN14 0SH.

ⒻⓅ**Hopkins & Hopkins, trading name of Hopkins & Hopkins Limited** *(M P Hopkins)* 8 The Square, Aspley Guise, MILTON KEYNES, MK17 8DG.

★ⓅⒶ**Hopkins Allen Procter, trading name of Hopkins Allen Procter Limited** *(J F B Hopkins, S Procter)* 4th Floor, St James House, Vicar Lane, SHEFFIELD, S1 2EX.

★**Horace Ho & Company** *(Horace M K Ho)* Unit 1608 Tower 1 Silvercord, 30 Canton Road, TSIM SHA TSUI, HONG KONG SAR. and at CENTRAL, WAN CHAI

ⓉⒻⒶ**Horder Adey** *(L B Adey, N I Horder)* 13 Princeton Court, 53-55 Felsham Road, Putney, LONDON, SW15 1AZ.

★**Horgan, Barrett & Co** *(R F Barrett)* Evergreen House, Congress Road, CORK, COUNTY CORK, IRELAND.

Ⓟ**Horley Enterprises Limited** *(G Horley)* 456 Chester Road, Old Trafford, MANCHESTER, M16 9HD.

ⓉⓅ**Horley Green, trading name of PPI Accounting Ltd** *(S D Crossley, R Redhead, M P Whitehouse)* Horley Green House, Horley Green Road, Claremount, HALIFAX, WEST YORKSHIRE, HX3 6AS.

ⓉⒻⓅⒶ**Hornbeam Accountancy Services Ltd** *(A R Bloy, P Needham)* Hornbeam House, Bidwell Road, Rackheath, NORWICH, NR13 6PT.

★ⓉⒶ**Horne Brooke Shenton** *(T Coulson, D Garlick, D Walsh)* 21 Caunce Street, BLACKPOOL, FY1 3LA.

Ⓐ**Horner Christopher** *(G D Christopher, A J D Horner)* First House, Altrincham Road, Styal, WILMSLOW, SK9 4JE.

★ⓅⒶ**Horner Downey & Company, trading name of Horner Downey & Company Limited** *(C P Thomas)* 30 Bromborough Village Road, Bromborough, WIRRAL, MERSEYSIDE, CH62 7ES.

Horscroft Turner Byrne & Co *(J R Byrne)* 78 The Green, TWICKENHAM, TW2 5AG.

ⓉⒻⓅⒶ**Horsfield & Smith, trading name of Horsfield-Smith Limited** *(S F Collier, P G Nicol, C A Nuttall, J Staples)* Tower House, 269 Walmersley Road, BURY, LANCASHIRE, BL9 6NX.

★**Horsfields** *(J H C Lee)* Belgrave Place, 8 Manchester Rd, BURY, BL9 0ED.

ⒻⒶ**Horsley & Co** *(J M P Horsley)* 4 Palmerston House, 60 Kensington Place, LONDON, W8 7PU.

ⒻⒶ**Horsley Spry** *(J L Horsley)* 3 Heath Road, Gamlingay, SANDY, BEDFORDSHIRE, SG19 2JD.

Ⓟ**Horsmans, trading name of Horsmans Limited** *(J E Horsman)* Stoney Down Farm, Rushall Lane, Corfe Mullen, WIMBORNE, DORSET, BH21 3RS.

Horvath Accountants *(A P Horvath)* 26 Knighton Road, Bournville, BIRMINGHAM, B31 2EH.

★**Horwath & Associados SROC Lda** *(A M Kennard)* Avenida Miquel Bombarda, 21 3 Esq, 1050 161 LISBON, PORTUGAL.

★**Horwath Belize** *(S J P Ermeav)* 35a Regent Street, P O Box 756, BELIZE CITY, BELIZE.

▽**Horwath Dafinone** *(P K Bhasin, D O Dafinone, D O Dafinone, D O Dafinone, E O Dafinone, I O Dafinone)* Ceddi Towers 16 Wharf Road, Apapa PO Box 2151, Marina, LAGOS, NIGERIA.

★Ⓣ**Horwath Mak** *(Z Maniar)* P.O. Box 6747, DUBAI, UNITED ARAB EMIRATES.

Houghton & Co, trading name of Lynn M Houghton *(L M Houghton)* 86 Holme Park Avenue, Upper Newbold, CHESTERFIELD, DERBYSHIRE, S41 8XB.

★Ⓣ**Houghton Stone** *(F V Bell-Scott, I Keeley)* The Conifers, Filton Road, Hambrook, BRISTOL, BS16 1QG. and at NOTTINGHAM

Ⓟ**Houghton Stone De Cymru Limited** *(F J Davies)* The Executive Centre, Temple Court, Cathedral Road, CARDIFF, CF11 9HA.

Ⓟ**Hourihan Limited** *(A Hourihan)* 21 Millbrook Road, DINAS POWYS, SOUTH GLAMORGAN, CF64 4BZ.

Ⓟ**Hovnan & Co Limited** *(H Hampartsoumian)* 106 Ashurst Road, Cockfosters, BARNET, HERTFORDSHIRE, EN4 9LG.

How Wall Morris *(A L Wall Morris)* Willow Corner, School Lane, Chearsley, AYLESBURY, BUCKINGHAMSHIRE, HP18 0BT.

★ⓉⒶ**Howard & Co** *(N J Howard)* 10-12 Wellington Street, (St Johns), BLACKBURN, BB1 8AG.

Howard & Co *(D H Robinson)* Bridge House, High Street, Horam, HEATHFIELD, TN21 0EY.

ⓉⓅⒶ**Howard & Company, trading name of G M Howard & Company Ltd** *(G M Howard)* Unit 17, Park Farm Business Centre, Fornham St. Genevieve, BURY ST. EDMUNDS, SUFFOLK, IP28 6TS.

ⒻⒶ**Howard & Stapleton** *(G M Stapleton)* 1st Floor Offices, Natwest Bank, Market Square, ROCHFORD, SS4 1AJ.

Ⓟ**Howard & Stapleton Ltd** *(G M Stapleton)* 1st Floor Offices, Natwest Bank, Market Square, ROCHFORD, ESSEX, SS4 1AJ.

Howard + Co Accountants LLP *(M R Howard)* 6 Market Street, Birstall, BATLEY, WEST YORKSHIRE, WF17 9EN.

Ⓟ**Howard Atkins Limited** *(H T Atkins)* 49 The Drive, RICKMANSWORTH, WD3 4EA.

★**Howard Atkins Partnership** *(H T Atkins)* 49 The Drive, RICKMANSWORTH, HERTFORDSHIRE, WD3 4EA.

Howard Attree Smith & Co *(A H Attree)* 12 Park Court, Park Road, BURGESS HILL, RH15 8EY.

Ⓟ**Howard Baker Limited** *(H L Baker)* 30 Christchurch Road, BOURNEMOUTH, BH1 3PD.

Howard Cohen *(H J Cohen)* Tall Trees, 15a Dean Park Road, BOURNEMOUTH, BH1 1HU.

ⒻⓅⒶ**Howard Frank, trading name of Howard Frank Limited** *(J S Bennett, P R Kleinman)* Turnberry House, 1404-1410 High Road, Whetstone, LONDON, N20 9BH.

Ⓟ**Howard Hackney LLP** *(H S Hackney)* Firscroft, Firs Lane, Appleton, WARRINGTON, CHESHIRE, WA4 5LD.

Howard I. Day *(H I Day)* 75 Barton Road, Headington, OXFORD, OX3 9JE.

Ⓟ**Howard J Weare & Co, trading name of Howard J Weare & Co Limited** *(H J Weare)* 34 Llwyn y Pia Road, Lisvane, CARDIFF, CF14 0SY.

ⓉⒶ**Howard Lee, Fellows & Co** *(R K Fellows, H P Lee)* 11-13 First Floor, The Meads Business Centre, 19 Kingsmead, FARNBOROUGH, HAMPSHIRE, GU14 7SR.

Howard Long *(H J Long)* 41 St Peters Road, CROYDON, CR0 1HN.

Ⓕ**Howard Lyon FCA** *(H F Lyon)* 18 Laneside Drive, Bramhall, STOCKPORT, CHESHIRE, SK7 3AR.

ⒻⒶ**Howard M Bedford & Co** *(H M Bedford)* 1st Floor, 27 Norton Road, STOCKTON-ON-TEES, CLEVELAND, TS18 2BW.

Howard M. Radley *(Howard M Radley)* P.O.Box 1644, Independence Square 11, NETANYA, 42115, ISRAEL.

Howard Marks & Co *(H J Marks)* 21 Bodley Road, NEW MALDEN, KT3 5QD.

ⓉⒻⒶ**Howard Matthews Partnership** *(A G Crowther, H J Matthews)* Queensgate House, 23 North Park Road, HARROGATE, HG1 5PD. and at LEEDS

Howard N. Kenton *(H N Kenton)* 79 College Road, HARROW, MIDDLESEX, HA1 1BD.

ⒻⓅⒶ**Howard Painter & Company Ltd** *(H N Painter)* 26 Sansome Walk, WORCESTER, WR1 1LX.

Ⓕ**Howard Perlin** *(H S Perlin)* 66 Hawtrey Road, LONDON, NW3 3SS.

ⓅⒶ**Howard Presky Limited** *(H M Presky)* 21 Bedford Square, LONDON, WC1B 3HH.

Ⓟ**Howard Royse Limited** *(H W S Royse)* 11 Warren's Way, Tacolneston, NORWICH, NR16 1DH.

ⒻⓅⒶ**Howard Smith & Co Limited** *(J R Stimpson)* 1 & 2 Hillbrow House, Linden Drive, LISS, HAMPSHIRE, GU33 7RJ.

Howard Walker Business Services, trading name of Howard Walker *(P Walker)* Ivy House, Goodmanham Road, Middleton on the Wolds, DRIFFIELD, NORTH HUMBERSIDE, YO25 9DE.

Ⓐ**Howard Wallis LLP** *(H J Wallis)* 25 Harley Street, LONDON, W1G 9BR.

Ⓐ**Howard Wilson** *(Gary Howard, John Wilson)* 36 Crown Rise, WATFORD, WD25 0NE.

★ⓉⒶ**Howard Worth** *(M A P Doherty, M Donnan, A J Hague, R H Rowland, C J Swallow, J H Whalley)* Drake House, Gadbrook Park, NORTHWICH, CHESHIRE, CW9 7RA. and at NANTWICH

Ⓟ**Howards, trading name of Howards Limited** *(C P Archer)* Newport House, Newport Road, STAFFORD, ST16 1DA.

Howarth & Co *(M Howarth)* 49 Fields Road, Haslingden, ROSSENDALE, BB4 6QA.

Howarth Armsby *(A J Armsby)* New Broad Street House, 35 New Broad Street, LONDON, EC2M 1NH. and at WALTHAM CROSS

Ⓟ**Howarth Corporate Finance Limited** *(M Hughes, C J Roulston, J M Stubbs)* 64 Wellington Street, LEEDS, LS1 2EE.

ⓉⒻⒶ**Howell Wade** *(A B Warren)* 55 Church Road, Wimbledon Village, LONDON, SW19 5DQ.

Ⓟ**Howells & Co, trading name of Howells & Co Limited** *(G W Howells)* 39 Glenferrie Road, ST. ALBANS, HERTFORDSHIRE, AL1 4JT.

ⓉⓅ**Howlader & Company, trading name of Howlader & Associates Ltd** *(H R Howlader)* 56 Leman Street, LONDON, E1 8EU.

Ⓟ**Howlader & Company, trading name of Howlader & Company Ltd** *(H R Howlader)* 56 Leman Street, LONDON, E1 8EU.

Ⓟ**Howletts, trading name of Howlett Accounts Limited** *(S O Howlett)* Mistletoe Corner, 4 Oatlands, Elmstead, COLCHESTER, CO7 7EN.

ⓉⒻⒶ**Howsons** *(N J Armstrong, S Eardley, J P Eyre-Walker, A C Kennedy, C J Parry, S E Preston, A C Riley)* Winton House, Stoke Road, STOKE-ON-TRENT, ST4 2RW. and at LEEK, NEWPORT, UTTOXETER

ⓉⒻⓅ**Howsons, trading name of Howsons Accountants Limited** *(N J Armstrong, S Eardley, J P Eyre-Walker, A C Kennedy, C J Parry, S E Preston, A C Riley)* 18-20 Moorland Road, STOKE-ON-TRENT, ST6 1DW.

Hoyle & Co *(J A Hoyle)* Wootton Farm, Pencombe, BROMYARD, HR7 4RR.

Ⓟ**HPBS Ltd** *(S C Holder)* 17 Wren Garth, Sandal, WAKEFIELD, WEST YORKSHIRE, WF2 6SL.

ⓉⒻⒶ**HPH** *(A C Rodaway, P A Thake, C M S Walker, R W Woolley)* 54 Bootham, YORK, YO30 7XZ. and at HARROGATE

HPW, trading name of H P Wadsworth *(H P Wadsworth)* 9 Hey Cliff Road, HOLMFIRTH, HD9 1XD. and at HUDDERSFIELD

HR Accountancy *(H C Rhodes)* 25 High Meadows, Greetland, HALIFAX, WEST YORKSHIRE, HX4 8QF.

★ⓅⒶ**HSA & Co, trading name of R M Chancellor & Company Ltd** *(P A Baker)* Lewis House, Great Chesterford Court, Great Chesterford, SAFFRON WALDEN, ESSEX, CB10 1PF.

★Ⓐ**HSA Associates** *(A G Harrison)* 89 Chorley Road, Swinton, MANCHESTER, M27 4AA.

Ⓟ**HSA Bookkeeping Limited** *(P A Baker)* Lewis House, Great Chesterford Court, Great Chesterford, SAFFRON WALDEN, ESSEX, CB10 1PF.

Ⓟ**HSJ Accountants, trading name of HSJ Accountants Limited** *(R J Hughes, B J Masters)* Severn House, Hazell Drive, NEWPORT, GWENT, NP10 8FY. and at PONTYCLUN

ⓅⒶ**HSJ Audit and Assurance, trading name of HSJ Audit Limited** *(R J Hughes)* Severn House, Hazell Drive, NEWPORT, GWENT, NP10 8FY.

Ⓟ**HSK Accountancy Services Ltd** *(S Khalil)* Advantage Business Centre, 132-134 Great Ancoats Street, MANCHESTER, M4 6DE.

ⓉⓅⒶ**HSKS, trading name of HSKS Limited** *(P W Hanson, A Mehan, K Singh)* 18 St. Christophers Way, Pride Park, DERBY, DE24 8JY.

Ⓕ**HSP Nicklin** *(C R Cook, H J Owen)* Church Court, Stourbridge Road, HALESOWEN, WEST MIDLANDS, B63 3TT.

Ⓟ**HSP, trading name of HSP Tax Ltd** *(P A Glyn-Smith)* Whiteacres, Cambridge Road, Whetstone, LEICESTER, LE8 6ZG.

HT Group S.A. *(K Horsburgh, F G Thomas)* 15-17 av Gaston Diderich, L-1420 LUXEMBOURG, LUXEMBOURG.

Ⓟ**HTT Audit Limited** *(C Hadjiioannou)* Elrini Tower, 27 Evagorou Street, 6th Floor, Office 61, 1066 NICOSIA, CYPRUS.

★ⓉⒻⒶ**Hubbard Lloyd** *(D S Hubbard)* 8 The Courtyard, Wyncolls Road, Severalls Industrial Park, COLCHESTER, ESSEX, CO4 9PE.

Ⓕ**Hudson & Co** *(D E Hudson)* Sterling House, 20 Station Road, GERRARDS CROSS, SL9 8EL.

Hudson Accountants *(D L Hudson)* 14 West Town Road, Backwell, BRISTOL, BS48 3HH.

Hugh Cochrane and Co *(H J Cochrane)* 26B High Street, SAXMUNDHAM, SUFFOLK, IP17 1AJ.

Hugh D Turner *(H D Turner)* Kirk Syke, High Street, Gargrave, SKIPTON, BD23 3RA.

ⓅⒶ**Hugh Davies & Co Limited** *(H W Davies, I C Sheekey)* 35 Chequers Court, Brown Street, SALISBURY, SP1 2AS.

Hugh Gregory *(H R H Gregory)* 112 South Street, TAUNTON, TA1 3AG.

ⒻⓅ**Hughes Collett Limited** *(F H Hughes)* Bridge House, 11 Creek Road, EAST MOLESEY, SURREY, KT8 9BE.

ⒻⒶ**Hughes Parry & Co** *(J G Pritchard)* 121 High Street, BANGOR, GWYNEDD, LL57 1NT.

★ⒻⓅⒶ**Hughes Waddell, trading name of Hughes Waddell Limited** *(A J Daniels, N G Dodd, N R Miller)* Hughes Waddell, 2 Meadrow, GODALMING, SURREY, GU7 3HN.

Ⓟ**Hugill Gordon, trading name of Round Numbers Limited** *(G Round)* The Maples, Fydell Court, ST. NEOTS, CAMBRIDGESHIRE, PE19 1UJ.

Hugo & Co *(H F Moses)* 198 Cookham Road, MAIDENHEAD, BERKSHIRE, SL6 7HN.

Hui Ka Hung Raymond *(K Hui)* 1902 Westley Square, 48 Hoi Yuen Road, KWUN TONG, KOWLOON, HONG KONG SAR.

Ⓟ**Hull Matthewson, trading name of Hull Matthewson Ltd** *(J A Matthewson)* 33 Boston Road, Holbeach, SPALDING, LINCOLNSHIRE, PE12 7LR.

★ⓉⒻⒶ**Humphrey & Co** *(N D Ellison, E W Hylton, M J Macefield, R J F McTear, C P Potter, A M Robinson, I B Simpson, P G Skilbeck, A G Smith)* 7-9 The Avenue, EASTBOURNE, EAST SUSSEX, BN21 3YA. and at HOVE

Humphrey Johnson FCA *(H Johnson)* 53 Edisford Road, CLITHEROE, LANCASHIRE, BB7 3LA.

Humphreys & Gates *(J F Gates)* Piazza IV Novembre 4, 20124 MILAN, ITALY.

Ⓟ**Hunot & Co Limited** *(G A Hunot)* The Gate House, Underhill, Maresfield, UCKFIELD, TN22 3AX.

ⓉⓅ**Hunt Blake, trading name of Hunt Blake Ltd** *(S R Blake, M Hunt)* Jubilee House, The Oaks, RUISLIP, MIDDLESEX, HA4 7LF.

ⒻⒶ**Hunter & Co.** *(I M S Hunter)* 415 Blackburn Road, BOLTON, BL1 8NJ.

ⓉⒻⓅ**Hunter Gee Holroyd, trading name of Hunter Gee Holroyd Limited** *(N P Atkinson, N C Everard, M R Grewer)* Club Chambers, Museum Street, YORK, YO1 7DN. and at FILEY

ⓅⒶ**Hunter Healey, trading name of Hunter Healey Limited** *(N R Healey)* Abacus House, 450 Warrington Road, Culcheth, WARRINGTON, WA3 5QX.

Ⓣ**Hunter Jones Alton** *(A G R Alton, F E C Alton)* 36 Bridge Street, BELPER, DERBYSHIRE, DE56 1AX.

Hunter Smith *(S A Smith)* Allens Wall, Black Hill, Lindfield, HAYWARDS HEATH, WEST SUSSEX, RH16 2HE.

ⓉⒻⓅⒶ**Hunter Stevens Limited** *(Michel Stevens)* 5-6 Maiden Lane, STAMFORD, LINCOLNSHIRE, PE9 2AZ.

Ⓟ**Hunter, Marshall & Co, trading name of Hunter, Marshall & Co Ltd** *(D J Hunter)* Suite C, 1st Floor, Hinksey Court, West Way, Botley, OXFORD OX2 9JU.

Ⓐ**Hunters** *(M D Hunter)* 10 Catlin Gardens, GODSTONE, SURREY, RH9 8NT.

ⒻⓅⒶ**Hunters Accountants, trading name of Hunter Accountants Limited** *(D M Hunter)* 3 Kings Court, Little King Street, BRISTOL, BS1 4HW.

ⒻⒶ**Hunters, trading name of C.A. Hunter & Partners** *(K Rotheram, D Ruane)* Britannia Chambers, George Street, ST. HELENS, MERSEYSIDE, WA10 1BZ.

Ⓟ**Hunton & Co, trading name of Hunton Bros Ltd** *(D Hunton)* 23 Rossway, DARLINGTON, DL1 3RD.

Hunziker Associates SA *(R F Hunziker)* 100 rue du Rhone, PO Box 1624, 1204 GENEVA, SWITZERLAND.

ⓉⓅⒶ**Hurkan Sayman & Co, trading name of HSCA Limited** *(E Hurer)* 291 Green Lanes, Palmers Green, LONDON, N13 4XS. and at CHATHAM

ⓉⓅⒶ**Hurshens, trading name of Hurshens Limited** *(S M Moustafa)* 14 Theobald Street, BOREHAMWOOD, HERTFORDSHIRE, WD6 4SE.

Hurst & Co *(G Hurst)* 74/76 High St, WINSFORD, CW7 2AP.

Hurst Morrison Thomson *(C B Morrison, A D Thomson)* The Hub, Station Road, HENLEY-ON-THAMES, OXFORDSHIRE, RG9 1AY.

ⓉⒻⒶ**Hurst, Hurst Corporate Finance, trading names of Hurst & Company Accountants LLP** *(P N Barratt, H A Besant-Roberts, A Milnes, R Murphy, M P Patt, T J Potter, S E Salton, A J Woodings)* Lancashire Gate, 21 Tiviot Dale, STOCKPORT, CHESHIRE, SK1 1TD.

ⒻⒶ**Husain Bulman & Co** *(S T J Lutfullah)* 258 Merton Road, LONDON, SW18 5JL.

Husbands & Co *(C M W Husbands)* Forge House, Forge Road, Osbaston, MONMOUTH, GWENT, NP25 3AZ.

Hussain A. Hashambhoy *(H A Hashambhoy)* 244 Lawrence Hargrave Drive, THIRROUL, NSW 2515, AUSTRALIA.

Hussain Mirza *(H Mirza)* 78 Crawford Terrace, New Rochelle, NEW YORK, NY 10804, UNITED STATES.

Ⓟ**Hutchins and Co, trading name of Hutchins and Co Limited** *(T Hutchins)* 371 Wood Lane, Stannington, SHEFFIELD, S6 5LR.

Hutchinson & Co *(W J Hutchinson)* 3 Scot Grove, PINNER, HA5 4RT.

Ⓐ**Hutokshi Madon** *(H R Madon)* 1 Bellamy Close, KNEBWORTH, SG3 6EH.

ⓉⒻⓅⒶ**Huw J Edmund, trading name of Huw J Edmund Limited** *(H J Edmund)* Garth House, Unit 7, Ty-Nant Court, Morganstown, CARDIFF, CF15 8LW.

ⒻⓅ**Huw John & Co Ltd** *(H S John)* Upper Floor, 5-7 Mill Street, PONTYPRIDD, MID GLAMORGAN, CF37 2SN.

Ⓐ**Huw Jones & Co** *(H W L Jones)* Larchfield, Pregge Lane, CRICKHOWELL, POWYS, NP8 1SE.

Huw Thomas *(H Thomas)* 14 Severn Road, PORTHCAWL, MID GLAMORGAN, CF36 3LW.

ⓉⒻⓅ**Huw Williams, trading name of Huw Williams Limited** *(H R Williams)* 217 Musters Road, West Bridgford, NOTTINGHAM, NG2 7DT.

Ⓕ**HW** *(S R Edwards, A S Minifie, A J Parsons, B J Potter)* Berkeley House, Amery Street, ALTON, HAMPSHIRE, GU34 1HN.

ⓉⒻⒶ**HW** *(G C Fairclough, C A Graham, J L Whittick)* Bridge House, Ashley Road, Hale, ALTRINCHAM, WA14 2UT.

★ⓉⒻⒶ**HW** *(R Hammond, A S Minifie)* 136-140 Bedford Road, Kempston, BEDFORD, BEDFORDSHIRE, MK42 8BH.

ⓉⒻⒶ**HW** *(D M Bulmer, P Collingwood, R P Duncan, D H Maultby, S Richardson, J C Scott)* Sterling House, 22 St. Cuthberts Way, DARLINGTON, COUNTY DURHAM, DL1 1GB. and at NEWCASTLE UPON TYNE

ⓉⒻⒶ**HW** *(S R Edwards, R G McFarlane, A J Parsons, B J Potter)* 30 Camp Road, FARNBOROUGH, HAMPSHIRE, GU14 6EW. and at BASINGSTOKE

ⓉⒻⒶ**HW** *(C G Dedman, A S Minifie, M L Stothard, J A Toulson)* 117-119 Cleethorpe Road, GRIMSBY, LINCOLNSHIRE, DN31 3ET. and at SCUNTHORPE

ⓉⒻⒶ**HW** *(S H Garrett, R H Style, D A Teckoe)* Sterling House, 19-23 High Street, KIDLINGTON, OXFORDSHIRE, OX5 2DH.

ⓉⒻⒶ**HW** *(G C Fairclough, M J Forshaw, F J Murphy, L R Silverman)* Pacific Chambers, 11-13 Victoria Street, LIVERPOOL, MERSEYSIDE, L2 5QQ.

★ⓉⒻⒶ**HW** *(J E Bailey, G C Fairclough, P I Wright)* 7-11 Station Road, READING, BERKSHIRE, RG1 1LG.

★Ⓕ**HW** *(C G Dedman, A S Minifie)* 23 Algitha Road, SKEGNESS, LINCOLNSHIRE, PE25 2AG.

ⓉⒻⒶ**HW** *(G C Fairclough, M S Gurney, S E Plumb)* Old Station House, Station Approach, Newport Street, SWINDON, WILTSHIRE, SN1 3DU.

ⒻⒶ**HW** *(S P Butler, A S Minifie)* Sterling House, 97 Lichfield Street, TAMWORTH, STAFFORDSHIRE, B79 7QF.

ⓉⒻⒶ**HW** *(M P Brown, A K Gardner, G T Hopwood, A S Minifie)* Keepers Lane, The Wergs, WOLVERHAMPTON, WEST MIDLANDS, WV6 8UA.

ⓉⒻⒶ**HW Associates** *(M Hjertzen, F Reid)* Portmill House, Portmill Lane, HITCHIN, HERTFORDSHIRE, SG5 1DJ.

★ⓉⒻⒶ**HW Berry & Co, trading name of HW Edinburgh** *(S J Hodgson, A S Minifie)* Q Court, 3 Quality Street, Davidsons Mains, EDINBURGH, EH4 5BP. and at KIRKCALDY

★**HW Controls & Assurance LLP** *(A J Parsons, B J Potter)* 30 Camp Road, FARNBOROUGH, HAMPSHIRE, GU14 6EW. and at TAMWORTH

Ⓕ**HW Corporate Finance** *(G C Fairclough, A M W Godfrey)* First Floor, 19 Neptune Court, Vanguard Way, CARDIFF, SOUTH GLAMORGAN, CF24 5PJ.

HW Corporate Finance LLP *(J E Bailey, G C Fairclough, C M Fletcher, R J W Hall, D P Lock, B J Potter, R H Style)* 13-21 High Street, GUILDFORD, SURREY, GU1 3DG. and at READING

★Ⓕ**HW Corporate Finance, trading name of Haines Watts Corporate Finance (NW)** *(G C Fairclough, D M Fort, S T Moriarty, G A Pendlington, J L Whittick)* 1st Floor, Northern Assurance Buildings, Albert Square, 9-21 Princess Street, MANCHESTER, M2 4DN.

HW Corporate Finance, trading name of HW Transaction Services LLP *(D J Holdway, G T Hopwood, C Key, A S Minifie)* Sterling House, 71 Francis Road, Edgbaston, BIRMINGHAM, B16 8SP.

★**HW Forensic** *(A S Minifie, D M Oliver)* Keepers Lane, The Wergs, WOLVERHAMPTON, WV6 8UA.

★ⓉⒻⒶ**HW, trading name of Haines Watts** *(A M Bodkin, D M Dear, P Self, P Simmons)* Airport House, Purley Way, CROYDON, CR0 0XZ.

Ⓕ**HW, trading name of Haines Watts** *(M Neale, P D Sumpter)* 170 High Street, Gorleston, GREAT YARMOUTH, NORFOLK, NR31 6RG.

ⒻⒶ**HW, trading name of Haines Watts** *(I M Gorsuch, P Simmons)* Interwood House, Stafford Avenue, HORNCHURCH, RM11 2ER.

★Ⓕ**HW, trading name of Haines Watts** *(M Neale, P D Sumpter)* 9-10 Byford Court, Crockatt Road, Hadleigh, IPSWICH, IP7 6RD.

★ⓉⒻⒶ**HW, trading name of Haines Watts** *(A M Bodkin, D G Demetriou, D W Morgan, P Simmons)* 2nd Floor, Argyll House, 23 Brook Street, KINGSTON UPON THAMES, SURREY, KT1 2BN.

ⒻⒶ**HW, trading name of Haines Watts** *(J R P Moughton, M Perry, P Simmons, R A Welland)* New Derwent House, 69-73 Theobalds Road, LONDON, WC1X 8TA. and at SLOUGH

★Ⓕ**HW, trading name of Haines Watts** *(M Neale, P D Sumpter)* Vision House, 5-6 Beech Avenue, Taverham, NORWICH, NR8 6HW.

ⓉⒻⒶ**HW, trading name of Haines Watts** *(L W Davies, P J Eardley)* Sterling House, 11 Omega Court, 350 Cemetery Road, SHEFFIELD, SOUTH YORKSHIRE, S11 8FT.

★ⓉⒻⒶ**HW, trading name of Haines Watts** *(J R P Moughton, M Perry, K Sanghera, P Simmons, R A Welland, J Wills)* Sterling House, 177-181 Farnham Road, SLOUGH, BERKSHIRE, SL1 4XP. and at LONDON

ⓉⒻⓅⒶ**HW, trading name of Haines Watts (East Midlands) Limited** *(M J Bowles, T Clewes, A S Minifie, R W Willcox)* 10 Stadium Business Court, Millennium Way, Pride Park, DERBY, DE24 8HP.

ⒻⓅⒶ**HW, trading name of Haines Watts (Preston) Limited** *(P C Newsham)* 120-124 Towngate, LEYLAND, PR25 2LQ.

★ⒻⓅ**HW, trading name of Haines Watts Colchester Ltd** *(M Neale, P D Sumpter)* Graphic House, 11 Magdalen Street, COLCHESTER, CO1 2JT.

ⓉⒻⒶ**HW, trading name of Haines Watts Exeter LLP** *(B De Cruz, G C Fairclough, P J Tigwell)* 3 Southernhay West, EXETER, EX1 1JG.

ⒻⓅⒶ**HW, trading name of Haines Watts Liverpool Limited** *(G C Fairclough, M J Forshaw, F J Murphy, L R Silverman)* Pacific Chambers, 11-13 Victoria Street, LIVERPOOL, L2 5QQ.

ⓉⒻⒶ**HW, trading name of HW (Leeds) LLP** *(P L Bancroft, A S Minifie, J F Sutton)* Sterling House, 1 Sheepscar Court, Meanwood Road, LEEDS, WEST YORKSHIRE, LS7 2BB.

★ⒻⒶ**HW, trading name of HW Birmingham LLP** *(H F Briggs, D J Holdway)* Sterling House, 71 Francis Road, BIRMINGHAM, B16 8SP.

ⓉⒻⓅⒶ**HW, trading name of HW Bristol Limited** *(M J Bracher, G C Fairclough)* Hyland, 21 High Street, Clifton, BRISTOL, BS8 2YF.

ⒻⓅ**HW, trading name of HW Finance Function Limited** *(C M Fletcher, G A Heywood)* Sterling House, 5 Buckingham Place, Bellfield Road West, HIGH WYCOMBE, BUCKINGHAMSHIRE, HP13 5HQ.

★ⒻⓅ**HW, trading name of HW Flitwick Limited** *(A S Minifie)* 42 High Street, Flitwick, BEDFORD, BEDFORDSHIRE, MK45 1DU.

ⒻⓅ**HW, trading name of HW Hereford Ltd** *(D J Holdway, K C McLellan, A S Minifie)* Charlton House, St. Nicholas Street, HEREFORD, HR4 0BG.

★ⒻⓅ**HW, trading name of HW Huntingdon Ltd** *(A S Minifie)* 4 St. Clements Passage, High Street, HUNTINGDON, CAMBRIDGESHIRE, PE29 3TP.

ⒹⒻⒶ**HW, trading name of HW Leicester LLP** *(S K Khullar, A S Minifie)* Hamilton Office Park, 31 High View Close, LEICESTER, LE4 9LJ.

★ⒻⒶ**HW, trading name of HW Northamptonshire LLP** *(G J Goss, A S Minifie)* 78 Tenter Road, Moulton Park Industrial Estate, NORTHAMPTON, NN3 6AX. and at KETTERING

ⒻⓅ**HW, trading name of HW Progress Accountants Ltd** *(S P Butler, A S Minifie)* 6 Charter Point Way, ASHBY-DE-LA-ZOUCH, LEICESTERSHIRE, LE65 1NF.

HW, trading name of HW Tax Compliance LLP *(A M Bodkin, D J Holdway, P J Malin, A S Minifie)* Sterling House, 71 Francis Road, Edgbaston, BIRMINGHAM, B16 8SP.

★ⒹⒻⒶ**HW, trading name of R.F. Miller & Co** *(T A Crossley, P C Newsham)* 102 Duke Street, BARROW-IN-FURNESS, LA14 1RD. and at ULVERSTON

ⒹⓅⒶ**HW, Westernshare, trading names of HW Westernshare Limited** *(F M S Ashton, C M Fletcher, G A Heywood)* 48 Totteridge Drive, HIGH WYCOMBE, BUCKINGHAMSHIRE, HP13 6JJ.

ⓅⒶ**HWB Holdings Limited** *(A R Bell, R A Hurst, A Williams)* Highland House, Mayflower Close, Chandler's Ford, EASTLEIGH, HAMPSHIRE, SO53 4AR.

ⒹⒻⓅⒶ**HWB, trading name of Hopper Williams & Bell Limited** *(A R Bell, R A Hurst, A Williams)* Highland House, Mayflower Close, Chandler's Ford, SOUTHAMPTON, HAMPSHIRE, SO53 4AR. and at EASTLEIGH

Ⓟ**HWFCA Ltd** *(H W Fricker)* Flat 1, 32 Clifftown Parade, SOUTHEND-ON-SEA, SS1 1DL.

ⒻⒶ**HWS** *(A G Freeman, M P Maguire)* 1st Floor, St Giles Hse, 15/21 Victoria Rd, Bletchley, MILTON KEYNES, MK2 2NG.

★**Hyland Johnson Keane** *(L P Johnson)* Library House, 18 Dyke Parade, Mardyke, CORK, COUNTY CORK, IRELAND.

Hyman Associates *(H J Hyman)* 1 Cato Street, LONDON, W1H 5HG.

Ⓟ**Hyman Capital, trading name of Hyman Capital Services Limited** *(C M Hyman)* 33 West Common Way, HARPENDEN, HERTFORDSHIRE, AL5 2LH. and at LONDON

ⒻⓅ**Hynes & Company (Newbury) Limited** *(G T Hynes)* Anstell House, Donnington Square, NEWBURY, BERKSHIRE, RG14 1PP.

ⒹⒻⒶ**Hysons** *(M E K Hyson)* 14 London Street, ANDOVER, SP10 2PA.

Ⓟ**I 4 Business Limited** *(S H Tudor Price)* 4 The Close, Leckhampstead Road, Akeley, BUCKINGHAM, MK18 5HD. and at COVENTRY

Ⓟ**I A Osman & Company Ltd** *(I A Osman)* 16 Leicester Road, Blaby, LEICESTER, LE8 4GQ.

I Alam *(I Alam)* 7 Tash Place, New Southgate, LONDON, N11 1PA.

I C Hobbs *(I C Hobbs)* 51 Cambridge Road, SOUTHEND-ON-SEA, SS1 1ET.

Ⓟ**I Count Limited** *(R P Bernstein)* 26 Boundary Road, PINNER, MIDDLESEX, HA5 1PN.

I D Child ACA *(I D Child)* 68 Cherry Garden Road, MALDON, ESSEX, CM9 6ET.

Ⓟ**I D MacLucas & Co** *(I D MacLucas)* 104b Malthouse Yard, West Street, FARNHAM, SURREY, GU9 7EN.

I F Davies *(I F Davies)* 1 Ellesmere Drive, SHREWSBURY, SY1 2QU.

I G. Hussein & Company *(I Gulam Hussein)* 3 Magdalen Place, DUNDEE, DD1 4NN.

I Sassoon & Co *(I D Sassoon)* 79 Windmill Lane, BUSHEY, WD23 1NE.

I Watson & Co *(I M Watson)* Cuckolds Green, Wrentham, BECCLES, SUFFOLK, NR34 7NB.

I. Hussain & Company *(I Hussain)* 11 George Street West, LUTON, LU1 2BJ.

I. Stokes & Co *(I Stokes)* Oxenleaze Farm, 88 Keevil, TROWBRIDGE, WILTSHIRE, BA14 6NH.

I. Thompson & Co *(I Thompson)* The Arcade, Belsay, NEWCASTLE UPON TYNE, NE20 0DY.

I.A. Anderson & Co *(I A Anderson)* 1 Three Pears Road, Merrow, GUILDFORD, GU1 2XU.

Ⓐ**I.A. Kay & Co** *(I A Khan)* 420 Cranbrook Road, ILFORD, ESSEX, IG2 6HW.

I.A. Machin *(I A Machin)* 19 Seer Mead, Seer Green, BEACONSFIELD, HP9 2QL.

I.C. Matthews *(I C Matthews)* Ivor House, 200 London Road North, Merstham, REDHILL, RH1 3BG.

ⒻⒶ**I.D. Bowen & Co** *(I D Bowen)* 19 Alexandra Road, Gorseinon, SWANSEA, SA4 4NW.

I.F. Whiteman *(I F Whiteman)* 1 Ashdown, 7 Cambalt Road, LONDON, SW15 6EL.

I.G. Chambers *(I G Chambers)* Compass House, 15 West Meade, Milland, LIPHOOK, GU30 7NB.

Ⓐ**I.G. Jones & Co** *(D L Jones, D G Williams)* 12 Salem Street, Ynys Mon, AMLWCH, LL68 9BP. and at LLANGEFNI

I.H. Butler & Co *(I H Butler)* 25 Gainsborough Drive, Adel, LEEDS, LS16 7PF.

I.H. Rampersad & Co *(I H Rampersad)* 4 Aruac Road, VALSAYN, TRINIDAD AND TOBAGO.

I.H. Stevens & Co *(I H Stevens)* 14 Westover Farm, Goodworth Clatford, ANDOVER, HAMPSHIRE, SP11 7LF.

I.J. Brownstein & Co *(I J Brownstein)* 59 Deacons Hill Road, Elstree, BOREHAMWOOD, WD6 3HZ.

I.K. Sethia *(I K Sethia)* 6 Arundel Road, Cheam, SUTTON, SM2 7AD.

I.M. Parlane *(I M Parlane)* 2 Magazine Mews, The Garrison, Shoeburyness, SOUTHEND-ON-SEA, SS3 9QB.

I.N. Mokhtar & Co *(I N Mokhtar)* 7 Chartfield, HOVE, EAST SUSSEX, BN3 7RD.

I.P. Scott *(I P Scott)* 81 Hawes Lane, WEST WICKHAM, BR4 0DF.

I.S.Bahrani *(I S El-Bahrani)* Faris Building, South Gate, BAGHDAD, IRAQ.

I.T. Copeland *(I T Copeland)* 4 Heather Close, Werrington, STOKE-ON-TRENT, ST9 0LB.

Iain D. Muspratt *(I D Muspratt)* Backwater House, 50 Common Lane, Hemingford Abbots, HUNTINGDON, PE28 9AW.

Iain McGrory *(I R C McGrory)* Le Bourg, 24610 ST MEARD DE GURCON, FRANCE.

Iain Murray *(I J S Murray)* Broomhill, Uckfield Road, CROWBOROUGH, EAST SUSSEX, TN6 3SU.

Iain S.E. Wiltshire *(I S E Wiltshire)* 111 High Street, Hanham, BRISTOL, BS15 3QG.

Ⓟ**Iain S.E. Wiltshire Limited** *(I S E Wiltshire)* 111 High Street, Hanham, BRISTOL, BS15 3QG.

Ian Afflick *(I Afflick)* 336A Wellington Road North, Heaton Chapel, STOCKPORT, CHESHIRE, SK4 5DA.

ⒹⓅ**Ian B Thompson & Co, trading name of Ian B Thompson Limited** *(I B Thompson)* Blades Enterprise Centre, John Street, SHEFFIELD, S2 4SU.

ⒻⒶ**Ian B. Steinberg** *(I B Steinberg)* 40 Woodford Avenue, Gants Hill, ILFORD, IG2 6XQ.

Ian Boage & Co *(I N Boage)* Rookery Barn, Yew Tree Farm, Low Ham, LANGPORT, SOMERSET, TA10 9DW.

Ian C Cummings *(I C Cummings)* 9 Parkland Drive, ST. ALBANS, HERTFORDSHIRE, AL3 4AH.

Ⓐ**Ian Cobden & Co** *(I H Cobden)* Rowlandson House, 289-293 Ballards Lane, LONDON, N12 8NP.

★Ⓟ**Ian Couzens, trading name of Ian Couzens Limited** *(I Couzens)* 4 Denbigh Road, NORWICH, NR2 3AA.

ⓅⒶ**Ian Dalzell Ltd** *(I R Dalzell)* Broughton Lodge Mews, Field Broughton, GRANGE-OVER-SANDS, CUMBRIA, LA11 6HL.

Ian Deverill *(I S Deverill)* 18 Elgin Road, POOLE, DORSET, BH14 8ER.

Ian E. Tomlinson *(I E Tomlinson)* 11 Hitherwood, CRANLEIGH, GU6 8BW.

Ian Faulkner & Co *(R I Faulkner)* Esker Cottage, Quab Lane, WEDMORE, SOMERSET, BS28 4AR.

ⓅⒶ**Ian Fenton Limited** *(I J Fenton)* 21 Bedford Square, LONDON, WC1B 3HH.

★**Ian Franses Associates** *(I S R Franses)* 24 Conduit Place, LONDON, W2 1EP.

Ian Hall FCA *(I T Hall)* Brackendale House, Roundwell, Bearsted, MAIDSTONE, KENT, ME14 4HJ.

Ian Harrower *(I Harrower)* 45 Ashlone Road, Putney, LONDON, SW15 1LS.

Ian Hinckley *(I M Hinckley)* 3 Balfour Place, MARLOW, SL7 3TB.

Ⓟ**Ian Holland + Co, trading name of Ian Holland Co Limited** *(I D Holland)* The Clock House, 87 Paines Lane, PINNER, MIDDLESEX, HA5 3BZ.

Ian J. Senior *(I J Senior)* 18 Market Place, Chapel-en-le-Frith, HIGH PEAK, SK23 0EN.

Ian J. Shanks FCA *(I J Shanks)* 25 Lancaster Avenue, South Woodford, LONDON, E18 1QF.

Ian Jones MA (Cantab) FCA *(I Jones)* 17 Long Street, DEVIZES, WILTSHIRE, SN10 1NN.

Ⓐ**Ian Katte & Co** *(I P Katte)* Lyndale House, 24 High Street, ADDLESTONE, SURREY, KT15 1TN.

Ian L. Cameron *(I L Cameron)* 100 Northwood Lane, Darley Dale, MATLOCK, DERBYSHIRE, DE4 2HR.

Ⓟ**Ian Lancaster, trading name of Ian Lancaster Limited** *(I Lancaster)* 108 Needingworth Road, ST. IVES, CAMBRIDGESHIRE, PE27 5JY.

Ⓟ**Ian Leigh Limited** *(I Leigh)* 16 Cyprus Avenue, LONDON, N3 1ST.

Ian Marfell FCA *(R I W Marfell)* 2 Knightley Road, EXETER, EX2 4SR.

Ian Mason *(I Mason)* 17 Glebe Park, Balderton, NEWARK, NG24 3GN.

Ian McCann & Co *(I McCann)* 4 Rowan Close, The Paddocks, PENARTH, CF64 5BU.

Ⓟ**Ian McKechnie & Company, trading name of Ian McKechnie and Company Ltd** *(I McKechnie)* 21 Birchwood Drive, Rushmere St. Andrew, IPSWICH, IP5 1EB.

Ian Milner *(I Milner)* 2 Langthorne Court, Morley, LEEDS, LS27 9DR.

Ⓕ**Ian Murray & Co** *(Anthony Damer, I C Murray)* 18 Poplar Road, New Denham, UXBRIDGE, MIDDLESEX, UB9 4AW. and at LONDON

Ian N. Edwards *(I N Edwards)* 141 Grasmere Way, LEIGHTON BUZZARD, LU7 2QH.

Ian Peacock *(I G Peacock)* 11 Manor Lane, MAIDENHEAD, SL6 2QN.

Ⓐ**Ian Pickup & Co** *(I C Pickup)* 123 New Road Side, Horsforth, LEEDS, LS18 4QD.

ⒻⓅ**Ian Pratt Limited** *(P A R Skipper)* Bridge House, 25 Fiddle Bridge Lane, HATFIELD, HERTFORDSHIRE, AL10 0SP.

ⒻⓅⒶ**Ian Pratt, trading name of Wincroft Pratt Limited** *(I G Pratt)* 7 Forum Place, Fiddlebridge Lane, HATFIELD, HERTFORDSHIRE, AL10 0RN.

★ⒻⒶ**Ian R. Collins & Co.** *(W P Bartram)* The Bridge House, Mill Lane, DRONFIELD, S18 2XL.

Ⓐ**Ian R. North** *(I R North)* 12 Manvers House, Pioneer Close, Wath-upon-Dearne, ROTHERHAM, SOUTH YORKSHIRE, S63 7JZ.

Ian Rankin & Co *(I T Rankin)* 4 Blades Close, LEATHERHEAD, KT22 7JY.

Ian Recordon *(I C Recordon)* 25A Bromfelde Road, LONDON, SW4 6PP.

ⓅⒶ**Ian Richmond Limited** *(I V Richmond)* Chapel Ash House, 6 Compton Road, WOLVERHAMPTON, WV3 9PH.

Ian Roper & Company *(I Roper)* 37 Fore Street, SIDMOUTH, DEVON, EX10 8AQ.

ⒻⒶ**Ian S Anderson** *(I S Anderson)* Chartam House, 16 College Avenue, MAIDENHEAD, BERKSHIRE, SL6 6AX.

Ⓟ**Ian S Duncan Limited** *(I S Duncan)* 68 Brecon Way, BEDFORD, MK41 8DE.

Ian Sainsbury *(I L Sainsbury)* 62 Branksome Hill Road, BOURNEMOUTH, BH4 9LG.

Ian See & Co *(I H Y See)* Suite1602 Bangkok Bank Building, 18 Bonham Strand West, SHEUNG WAN, HONG KONG ISLAND, HONG KONG SAR.

Ian Shaw *(D I Shaw)* Mandalay, Chelmsford Road, Felsted, DUNMOW, CM6 3EP.

Ian Skolnick & Co *(I N Skolnick)* Langley House, Park Road, LONDON, N2 8EX.

Ian Smith *(I Smith)* 54 Cockshutts Lane, Oughtibridge, SHEFFIELD, S35 0FX.

Ian Smith & Co *(I D S Smith)* Lockram Villas, 7 Collingwood Road, WITHAM, CM8 2DY.

Ⓐ**Ian Todd & Co** *(I D E Todd)* Holdford Road, Witton, BIRMINGHAM, B6 7EP.

Ian W. Smith *(I W Smith)* 6 The Hawthorns, Nettleham, LINCOLN, LN2 2GD.

Ⓕ**Ian Walker & Co** *(I D Walker)* The Ron Cooke Hub, Suite 122, University of York, Heslington, YORK, YO10 5GE.

Ian Walter *(I A Walter)* 9 Holly Tree Close, Ley Hill, CHESHAM, HP5 3QT.

Ian Wright & Co *(I Wright)* 15 Stretton Drive, SOUTHPORT, PR9 7DR.

Ⓐ**Ian Yarwood & Co** *(I R Yarwood)* 2 Station Road, SOLIHULL, B91 3SB.

Ⓟ**Ibbotson and Company, trading name of Ibboco Contracting Limited** *(N J Ibbotson)* 66 Jordan Road, Four Oaks, SUTTON COLDFIELD, WEST MIDLANDS, B75 5AD.

Ⓟ**IBIS Consult, trading name of IBIS Consult Ltd** *(G D Hill)* 1 Hall Drive, Bramhope, LEEDS, LS16 9JF.

Ibrahim, Shaikh & Co *(Z A Shaikh)* 259-260 Panorama Centre, Fatima Jinnah Road, KARACHI 74400, PAKISTAN.

IBT Consulting LLP *(N Savomy, P F L Ten)* Waltham Forest Business Centre, 5 Blackhorse Lane, LONDON, E17 6DS.

Ⓟ**Icarus Wyatt Consulting Limited** *(M G Wyatt)* 8 Sovereign Court, 8 Graham Street, BIRMINGHAM, B1 3JR.

Ⓟ**Icke & Co, trading name of Icke & Co Limited** *(K J Icke)* The Old Barn, Avoncroft Farm, Gibbs Lane, Offenham, EVESHAM, WORCESTERSHIRE WR11 8RR.

Ⓟ**Icknield, trading name of Icknield Limited** *(S B Gulamali)* 3rd Floor, 63-66 Hatton Garden, LONDON, EC1N 8LE.

Ⓟ**ICON Corporate Finance, trading name of ICON Corporate Finance Limited** *(A C Bristow)* 53 Davies Street, LONDON, W1K 5JH.

Ⓜ**Iden Business Services Limited** *(T M J Kendrick)* 2 Garden Close, Staplehurst, TONBRIDGE, TN12 0EW.

IDG Accountancy *(I D George)* 59 St. Marys Avenue, Purley on Thames, READING, RG8 8BJ.

Ⓟ**IFA Accountancy Services, trading name of IFA Accountancy Services Limited** *(A Pervez)* 18 Clitheroe Road, MANCHESTER, M13 0GE.

Ⓟ**IFD Consulting Ltd** *(T Arthur)* 10 Perry Court, CAMBRIDGE, CB3 0RS.

Ifield Keene Associates *(S J Ifield)* 11 Whitchurch Parade, Whitchurch Lane, EDGWARE, MIDDLESEX, HA8 6LR.

Ⓟ**IFRS 2009 Ltd** *(S Muncaster)* Heron House, 45 Riversdale Grove, EDINBURGH, EH12 5QS.

Ⓟ**ifrs consulting.com, trading name of Accounting Policy Advisory Limited** *(R S Johal)* 15b Addington Close, WINDSOR, BERKSHIRE, SL4 4BP.

Igweojike & Co *(Chief Ojike)* 55 Western Avenue, GPO Box 7923, Marina, LAGOS, NIGERIA.

Ⓟ**IKF Business Services Limited** *(I K Frangou)* 84 Crescent Road, BARNET, HERTFORDSHIRE, EN4 9RJ.

ⒻⒶ**Iliffe Poulter & Co.** *(T J Iliffe, A M Poulter)* 1A Bonnington Road, Mapperley, NOTTINGHAM, NG3 5JR.

IMG *(I R Goad)* The Studio, 1 Wilkins Way, BEXHILL-ON-SEA, EAST SUSSEX, TN40 2RD.

Ⓟ**Immovation Ltd** *(M I Imms)* 2 Greywethers Avenue, SWINDON, SN3 1QF.

IMN & Co *(M Nuckchady)* 53 Queen Annes Grove, Bush Hill Park, ENFIELD, MIDDLESEX, EN1 2JS.

Imogen Beattie & Co *(I M Beattie)* 5 Douglas Drive, Cambuslang, GLASGOW, G72 8NG.

Imogen Taylor *(I C Taylor)* Hilldene, Paddock Lane, Audlem, CREWE, CW3 0DP.

Ⓟ**IMP Taxation, trading name of IMP Business Consulting Limited** *(R A N Foster)* The Homestead, 60 Church Street, Willingham, CAMBRIDGE, CB24 5HT.

Impact Accounting (SW), trading name of Impact Accounting (South West) LLP *(K J Freeman, M G Freeman)* 2 Coombe Lane, Cargreen, SALTASH, CORNWALL, PL12 6PB.

Ⓟ**Impact Accounting Services Ltd** *(J J Dix)* The Gatehouse, Llanvithyn, Llancarfan, BARRY, SOUTH GLAMORGAN, CF62 3AT.

Ⓟ**Impact Business Management Ltd** *(D Withers)* 57 The Moorlands, Weir, BACUP, LANCASHIRE, OL13 8BT.

ⒻⓅ**Impact Totnes Limited** *(B K Nicoll)* 2 Warland, TOTNES, DEVON, TQ9 5EL.

Ⓟ**Imperial Company Formations and Business Services, Robert Ollman & Co, trading names of Company Contracts and Services Limited** *(R I Ollman, S Simmons)* 11 The Shrubberies, George Lane, LONDON, E18 1BD.

IMS, trading name of Income Made Smart LLP *(G W Smith)* 9-13 Fulham High Street, LONDON, SW6 3JH.

Inbizz.com, Inn Business, Inn Business 2, Tax Management Group, trading names of A N Horner & Co *(A N F J Horner)* Croft House, East Road, Oundle, PETERBOROUGH, PE8 4BZ.

Ⓟ**InC Blue Ltd** *(W R Harman)* 100 Pall Mall, LONDON, SW1Y 5NQ.

Ⓟ**Incisive Accounting, trading name of Abacus 36 Limited** *(Y U Khan)* Cantium House, Railway Approach, WALLINGTON, SURREY, SM6 0DZ.

★Ⓐ**Independent Auditors LLP** *(J P Dale, I P Stewart)* Emstrey House, Sitka Drive, Shrewsbury Business Park, SHREWSBURY, SY2 6LG.

Ⓟ**Independent Drivers Ltd** *(A S Bullard)* 15 Lawford Road, RUGBY, WARWICKSHIRE, CV21 2DZ.

Ⓟ**Independent Forensic Accounting Ltd** *(D B Prior)* PO Box 158, LEEDS, LS8 5FF.

Indigo Management, trading name of P.L Downs *(P L Downs)* Michaelmas Cottage, Roundle Square Road, Felpham, BOGNOR REGIS, PO22 8JX.

Ⓟ**Indigo Tax & Accountancy Ltd** *(T A Noon)* The Barn, Brighton Road, Lower Beeding, HORSHAM, WEST SUSSEX, RH13 6PT. and at ALTON, LIPHOOK, LITTLEHAMPTON, PULBOROUGH, SANDHURST

Ⓟ**Indigo, trading name of Indigo Accountants (UK) Limited** *(G S Sandhu)* 17 Cecil Road, LONDON, W3 0DA.

Ⓟ**Indus Gold Limited** *(K C Attawar)* 17 Belmont Close, MAIDSTONE, KENT, ME16 9DY.

Ⓟ**Infinitude, trading name of Infinitude Services Limited** *(M J Brady)* 24 Fernham Road, FARINGDON, OXFORDSHIRE, SN7 7LB.

Infinity Asset Management LLP *(S A Butler, D J Finestein)* 26th Floor, City Tower, Piccadilly Plaza, MANCHESTER, M1 4BD.

Members in Practice and Firms - Alphabetical Ingalls - J J Finney

ⒻⓅⒶ**Ingalls, trading name of Ingalls (Kendal) Limited** *(A J Grange, G F Whiteside)* Libra House, Murley Moss Business Village, Oxenholme Road, KENDAL, CUMBRIA, LA9 7RL.

Inger & Company *(R C Patel)* 7 Redbridge Lane East, Redbridge, ILFORD, IG4 5ET.

ⓉⒻⒶ**Ingham & Co** *(A W Ingham, P Ingham, P D Webster)* George Stanley House, 2 West Parade Road, SCARBOROUGH, NORTH YORKSHIRE, YO12 5ED.

ⒻⒶ**Ingle Bhatti & Co** *(R A Bhatti)* RAB House, 102-104 Park Lane, CROYDON, CR0 1JB.

Inglis Accountancy Services *(L Inglis)* Craike View, 3 The Terrace, Kirby Hill, Boroughbridge, YORK, YO51 9DQ.

Ⓟ**Ingram & Terry Limited** *(K A Phillips)* Sullivan House, 72-80 Widemarsh Street, HEREFORD, HR4 9HG.

Ⓟ**Ingram Accountancy Services Ltd** *(R A Ingram)* 29 Wellesley Road, COLCHESTER, CO3 3HE.

Ⓟ**Ingram Consulting Limited** *(S Toumadj)* 9 Milton Close, LONDON, N2 0QH.

Ingram Forrest Corporate Finance LLP *(D Forrest, S Ingram)* 2 Rutland Park, SHEFFIELD, S10 2PD.

Inimex Associates Limited *(H J Osper)* 33 Anthony Road, BOREHAMWOOD, WD6 4NF.

Ⓐ**Inman & Co** *(I Inman)* 17 Abinger Court, Ealing, LONDON, W5 2AF.

Ⓟ**Inman & Co Accountants Limited** *(R A N Inman)* 24 Green Lane, Clifton, YORK, YO30 5QX.

ⓅⒶ**Inman & Co, trading name of Inman Business Advisors Limited** *(I Inman)* 235 St. John Street, LONDON, EC1V 4NG.

Ⓟ**Inman Waverley Ltd** *(J J Inman)* 36 New Road, Milford, GODALMING, GU8 5BE.

ⓅⒶ**Innovata Business Solutions Limited** *(S Dhanani, S D Dhanani)* 26 Rofant Road, NORTHWOOD, MIDDLESEX, HA6 3BE.

Innovation Professional Services LLP *(J S Messore, P J Moroz, R J Powis)* Merlin House, Priory Drive, Langstone, NEWPORT, GWENT, NP18 2HJ. and at BIRMINGHAM, LONDON, UXBRIDGE

Ⓟ**Inside Out, trading name of Gibson Hewitt Outsourcing Ltd** *(L Gibson, R D Hewitt)* 5 Park Court, Pyrford Road, WEST BYFLEET, KT14 6SD.

★**Insight NE** *(J Griffiths)* The Exchange, Manor Court, Jesmond, NEWCASTLE UPON TYNE, NE2 2JA.

Insight Practice Services *(E P Herbert)* 1 Castleton Road, Hazel Grove, STOCKPORT, CHESHIRE, SK7 6LB.

Ⓟ**Insight to Impact, trading name of Insight to Impact Consulting Ltd** *(S H R Walsh)* 7 King Edward's Court, NOTTINGHAM, NOTTINGHAMSHIRE, NG1 1EW.

Ⓟ**Insignia Finance Solutions Ltd** *(H Lumb)* Barnside House, 9 Rookery Close, Alwyn Road Yoxall, BURTON-ON-TRENT, STAFFORDSHIRE, DE13 8QH.

Ⓟ**Insite Corporate Management Limited** *(L Godber, S R Turner)* DeVirgo House, Valepits Road, Garretts Green, BIRMINGHAM, B33 0TD.

ⓉⓅ**Inspire Audit Ltd** *(L P Bulstrode)* 37 Commercial Road, POOLE, DORSET, BH14 0HU.

ⓅⒶ**Inspire Compliance Limited** *(M D McKenna)* 20 Kingsway House, Team Valley, GATESHEAD, TYNE AND WEAR, NE11 0HW.

Inspire Finance Partners LLP *(S J Potter)* 36 Lucerne Avenue, BICESTER, OXFORDSHIRE, OX26 3EL.

Ⓟ**Inspire, trading name of Inspire Your Business Limited** *(M D McKenna)* 20 Kingsway House, Team Valley, GATESHEAD, TYNE AND WEAR, NE11 0HW. and at DARLINGTON

ⓅⒶ**Inspired, trading name of Inspired Accountants (UK) Limited** *(M J Kinson)* 4 Parkside Court, Greenhough Road, LICHFIELD, STAFFORDSHIRE, WS13 7AU.

Ⓟ**Inspired Accounting Ltd** *(K Sharma)* 24 Gardenia Drive, Allesley, COVENTRY, CV5 9BN.

Inspired Tax Solutions *(G Lovell)* Bobs Old House, Hatton Lane, Hatton, WARRINGTON, WA4 4DB.

Ⓟ**Instant Accounting Solutions Ltd** *(A J Walsh)* Suite 404, 324 Regents Street, LONDON, W11 3HH.

Intandem Business Services *(C Burton)* c/o Fiduciaire Chavaz SA, Rue Jacques-Grosselin 8, Case Postale 1835, CH-1227 CAROUGE, SWITZERLAND.

Ⓟ**Intangible Business, trading name of Intangible Business Ltd** *(T A Forbes)* 9 Maltings Place, 169 Tower Bridge Road, LONDON, SE1 3JB.

Ⓟ**InTax Libya Ltd** *(E P P Nally)* Cutlers Farm House, Marlow Road, Lane End, HIGH WYCOMBE, BUCKINGHAMSHIRE, HP14 3JW.

ⓅⒶ**Intega, trading name of Intega Ltd** *(M J Palmer)* 106 Mill Studio, WARE, HERTFORDSHIRE, SG12 9PY.

ⒻⒶ**Integer** *(C L Gray)* Unit 3, Uphall Farm, Salmons Lane, Coggeshall, COLCHESTER, CO6 1RY.

Integer *(M P Connors)* Highview, Latimer Road, GODALMING, SURREY, GU7 1BW.

Ⓟ**Integer Finance Limited** *(H Patel)* 32 Tilley Close, Thorpe Astley, Braunstone, LEICESTER, LE3 3TD.

Ⓟ**Integer, trading name of Integer Accountants Ltd** *(C L Gray)* Unit 3, Uphall Farm, Salmons Lane, Coggeshall, COLCHESTER, ESSEX CO6 1RY.

Integra Advisers, trading name of Integra Advisers Limited Liability Partnership *(D J Brownhill)* The Cedars, Barnsley Road, Hemsworth, PONTEFRACT, WEST YORKSHIRE, WF9 4PU.

ⓅⒶ**Integra Corporate Finance, trading name of Integra Corporate Finance Limited** *(N J Duxbury)* 1 Whitehall Quay, Whitehall Road, LEEDS, LS1 4HR.

★Ⓟ**Integra, trading name of Integra Accounting Solutions Limited** *(F A G Karbani)* The Station Masters House, 168 Thornbury Road, Osterley Village, ISLEWORTH, MIDDLESEX, TW7 4QE.

Ⓟ**Integrated Mailing Limited** *(A M Morwood-Leyland)* Suite 48, 88-90 Hatton Garden, LONDON, EC1N 8PN.

Ⓟ**Integri-FD Limited** *(G M Stockill)* The Old Toll House, Hill Top, Barlby, SELBY, NORTH YORKSHIRE, YO8 5JQ.

Integrity Tax and Accounting Solutions *(R J Southgate)* May Cottage, Ashfield Road, Norton, BURY ST. EDMUNDS, SUFFOLK, IP31 3NF.

Ⓟ**Intelligent Facilities Limited** *(J M Sanders)* Badgers Croft, Hive Road, Bushey Heath, BUSHEY, WD23 1JG.

Intelligent Tax Solutions, trading name of Intelligent Tax Solutions LLP *(A D Rose)* New Broad Street House, 35 New Broad Street, LONDON, EC2M 1NH.

Ⓟ**Inter Forensics Ltd** *(P A Teasdale)* 3 Meadowfield, TARPORLEY, CHESHIRE, CW6 9XD.

Ⓟ**Interbusiness Services Ltd** *(N Savomy, P F L Ten)* Waltham Forest Business Centre, 5 Blackhorse Lane, LONDON, E17 6DS.

Ⓟ**Interim Business Management Ltd** *(C R Thomas)* 16 Quat Goose Lane, Swindon Village, CHELTENHAM, GLOUCESTERSHIRE, GL51 9RX.

Ⓟ**Inter-Link CPA Limited** *(M T Yip)* 15/F OTB Building, 259-265 Des Voeux Road Central, CENTRAL, HONG KONG ISLAND, HONG KONG SAR.

Ⓟ**International Financial Services Limited** *(C Basanta Lala, K Joory, R A Toorawa)* IFS Court, TwentyEight, Cybercity, Ebene, REDUIT, MAURITIUS.

ⓉⓅ**Interquality Ltd** *(N Agathocleous)* 4 Isavellas Katholikis, Office 2, Anavargos, 8025 PAFOS, CYPRUS.

Ⓟ**InterTaxAudit, trading name of Ledra Audit Services Limited** *(E Kassapis, A Tamani-Phella)* Kyrenia House, 5 Skra Street, Agios Andreas, 1100 NICOSIA, CYPRUS.

Ⓟ**InTouch Accounting, trading name of InTouch Accounting Limited** *(P W Gough)* Bristol & West House, Post Office Road, BOURNEMOUTH, BH1 1BL.

Ⓟ**Investment Recovery Services Limited** *(R C Oaten)* Second Floor, 23 Westfield Park, Redland, BRISTOL, BS6 6LT.

Ⓟ**Invocas Business Recovery and Insolvency Limited** *(C A A Murdoch)* 2nd Floor, Capital House, 2 Festival Square, EDINBURGH, EH3 9SU. and at ABERDEEN, ALTRINCHAM, GLASGOW

Ⓟ**Invocas Group Plc** *(J M Hall, C A A Murdoch)* 2nd Floor, Capital House, Festival Square, EDINBURGH, EH3 9SU. and at ABERDEEN, GLASGOW

ⓉⒻⒶ**Ioannou & Co** *(C E Ioannou)* 13-15 High Street, BARNET, HERTFORDSHIRE, EN5 5UJ.

Iona Edwards *(I E Edwards)* Hen Dy, Plas Madoc, Llansannan, DENBIGH, CLWYD, LL16 5LF.

Ⓟ**Iota Accountancy Services Limited** *(R J Woodburn)* 1 Factory Cottages, Pound Green, Cowlinge, NEWMARKET, SUFFOLK, CB8 9QQ.

Ⓟ**IP-Config, trading name of IP-Config Limited** *(P G Poyner)* 12 Creek End, EMSWORTH, HAMPSHIRE, PO10 7EX.

Ⓟ**IQ Accountants Limited** *(G Brown)* 1 Seamer Road Corner, SCARBOROUGH, NORTH YORKSHIRE, YO12 5BB.

Ⓟ**IQ Business Consulting Chartered Accountants, trading name of IQ Business Consulting Ltd** *(P D G Stacey)* The Old Police House, Damerham, FORDINGBRIDGE, HAMPSHIRE, SP6 3HB.

Ⓟ**IQAS, trading name of Investment Quality Services Limited** *(A B Smit)* Hacienda, Church Hill, Lawford, MANNINGTREE, ESSEX, CO11 2JX.

ⓉⒶ**Ireland & Longhill** *(J W Ireland, S A Longhill)* 10 Station Street, Kibworth Beauchamp, LEICESTER, LE8 0LN.

Iris Prince B.Sc FCA *(I A Prince)* 23 Grove Crescent, Kingsbury, LONDON, NW9 0LS.

Irons Accountancy *(E A Irons)* 56 Appletrees Crescent, BROMSGROVE, WORCESTERSHIRE, B61 0UE.

Ⓐ**Irvine & Co** *(G P J Irvine)* 10 Dikes Lane, Great Ayton, MIDDLESBROUGH, TS9 6HJ.

Irving D. Schryber *(I D Schryber)* Flat 3, Opal Court, 120 Regents Park Road, LONDON, N3 3HY.

ⒻⓅ**Irving Ramsay Limited** *(M Irving)* The Axis Building, Maingate, Kingsway North, Team Valley, GATESHEAD, TYNE AND WEAR NE11 0NQ.

Ⓐ**Irving Silverman** *(I Silverman)* 52 Mayflower Lodge, Regents Park Road, LONDON, N3 3HX.

Ⓟ**IS Associates Ltd** *(I I Swycher)* 37 Friars Avenue, LONDON, N20 0XG.

ISCA Accountancy Services *(O C Davies)* 40 Ballymartin Road, Killinchy, NEWTOWNARDS, COUNTY DOWN, BT23 6QR.

ⒻⒶ**Isherwood & Co** *(R J Isherwood)* 15 London Road, Stockton Heath, WARRINGTON, WA4 6SG.

Ⓟ**Islam & Ahmed Ltd** *(J U Ahmed, M N Islam)* 68 Seymour Grove, Old Trafford, MANCHESTER, M16 0LN.

★Ⓐ**Isles & Storer** *(A F Storer)* 129 High Street, Needham Market, IPSWICH, IP6 8DH.

Ⓟ**Isles & Storer Ltd** *(A F Storer)* 129 High Street, Needham Market, IPSWICH, IP6 8DH.

★**Ismail Chong & Associates, trading name of Moore Stephens** *(T O Chong)* 8A Jalan Sri Semantan Satu, Damansara Heights, 50490 KUALA LUMPUR, FEDERAL TERRITORY, MALAYSIA.

Ⓟ**Isosceles, trading name of Isosceles Finance Limited** *(M J O'Connell)* PO Box 502, STAINES, MIDDLESEX, TW18 9AG.

Issifu Ali & Co. *(I Ali)* PO Box 6037, ACCRA, GHANA.

Ⓟ**ISW Accountancy Limited** *(S L Walker)* 17 Leighfields Avenue, LEIGH-ON-SEA, ESSEX, SS9 5NN.

ⒻⓅ**ITAccounting, trading name of Goodhaven Limited** *(R J Cooper)* SCF1QZ, Western International Market, Hayes Road, Southall, SOUTHALL, MIDDLESEX UB2 5XJ.

Ⓟ**ITR, trading name of ITR Service Limited** *(V B Welsh)* 40 Plater Drive, OXFORD, OX2 6QU.

Ⓟ**ITSInternational Limited** *(M Marks)* 105 Baker Street, LONDON, W1U 6NY.

Ivan F Kew & Co *(I F Kew)* 130 Ambleside Road, LIGHTWATER, SURREY, GU18 5UN.

Ivan J Parry *(I J Parry)* 2nd Floor, 25 Market Place, NUNEATON, WARWICKSHIRE, CV11 4EG.

ⒻⒶ**Ivan Rendall & Co** *(S C Rendall)* Torre Lea House, 33 The Avenue, YEOVIL, BA21 4BN.

Ⓟ**Ivan Rendall & Co, trading name of Rendalls Limited** *(S C Rendall)* Torre Lea House, 33 The Avenue, YEOVIL, SOMERSET, BA21 4BN.

Ⓟ**Iverley Management Services Limited** *(S E Rice)* Iverley Lodge, 186 Norton Road, Iverley, STOURBRIDGE, WEST MIDLANDS, DY8 2RT.

Ivor G. Quincey *(I G Quincey)* 50 Offington Avenue, WORTHING, BN14 9PJ.

Ⓐ**Izod Bassett** *(C L Bassett, A H Izod)* 105 High Street, Needham Market, IPSWICH, IP6 8DQ.

Ⓟ**J & A W Sully & Co, trading name of Sully & Co (WSM) Ltd** *(P W Winter)* 55b Oxford Street, WESTON-SUPER-MARE, AVON, BS23 1TW.

Ⓟ**J & B Carroll Limited** *(J P Carroll)* 52 Brighton Road, SURBITON, SURREY, KT6 5PL.

Ⓟ**J & D associates cpa limited** *(C Lo)* Room 2611-12, 26/F, C C Wu Building, 302-308 Hennessy Road, WAN CHAI, HONG KONG ISLAND HONG KONG SAR.

ⓅⒶ**J & D Pennington Limited** *(J Pennington)* 30 Union Street, SOUTHPORT, MERSEYSIDE, PR9 0QE.

Ⓟ**J A Charters & Co, trading name of J A Charters & Co Ltd** *(J A Charters)* 1 Chapel Street North, COLCHESTER, CO2 7AT.

Ⓐ**J A Cini** *(J A Cini)* 6 Birnam Close, Ripley, WOKING, SURREY, GU23 6JH.

Ⓟ**J A E Simmonds & Company Ltd** *(J A E Simmonds)* 24 Garth Road, SEVENOAKS, KENT, TN13 1RU.

★ⓉⒻⒶ**J A Fell & Company** *(J A Fell)* White Cross, South Road, LANCASTER, LA1 4XQ. and at SOUTHPORT

Ⓟ**J A Hollow & Co, trading name of J A Hollow & Co Ltd** *(J A H Hollow)* 1 Ventnor Terrace, ST. IVES, CORNWALL, TR26 1DY.

Ⓐ**J Allen & Co** *(J Allen)* Suite 3&4 Rood End House, 6 Stortford Road, DUNMOW, ESSEX, CM6 1DA.

ⓉⒻⓅⒶ**J Austerberry & Co, trading name of John Goulding & Co Ltd** *(S Gardiner, A Hilton, B A Rigby)* 4 Southport Road, CHORLEY, LANCASHIRE, PR7 1LD. and at WARRINGTON

J B Davern & Co *(F G J Davern)* 149-151 Sparrows Herne, Bushey Heath, WATFORD, WD23 1AQ.

Ⓟ**J B Davern & Co, trading name of J B Davern & Co Ltd** *(F G J Davern)* 149-151 Sparrows Herne, BUSHEY, WD23 1AQ.

J B Norfolk & Co *(J B Norfolk)* 12 Chatsworth Grove, Boroughbridge, YORK, YO51 9BB.

J B Stephenson *(J B Stephenson)* Third Floor, 3 Field Court, Grays Inn, LONDON, WC1R 5EF.

ⓅⒶ**J Brian Harrison, trading name of J Brian Harrison Limited** *(J B Harrison)* 4 Locks Common Road, PORTHCAWL, MID GLAMORGAN, CF36 3HU.

J C Neame *(J C Neame)* The Elders, 52 Ham Shades Lane, Tankerton, WHITSTABLE, CT5 1NX.

Ⓟ**J C Woodburn Limited** *(J C Woodburn)* 37 Brookland Road, Phippsville, NORTHAMPTON, NN1 4SN.

J Camilo & Associados SROC *(G M Fletcher)* Rua Odette de Saint-Maurice 3 L, Piso -1 Escritorio A, 1700-921 LISBON, PORTUGAL.

Ⓟ**J Casey & Co, trading name of J Casey & Co Ltd** *(J A L Casey)* Langstone Gate, Solent Road, HAVANT, HAMPSHIRE, PO9 1RL.

ⒻⓅ**J D 2000 Ltd** *(J P Draper)* Glan-yr-Afon, Clocaenog, RUTHIN, LL15 2BB.

J D Associates, trading name of J.H.P. Devereux *(J H P Devereux)* 7 Whitfield Road, Hughenden Valley, HIGH WYCOMBE, HP14 4NZ.

Ⓟ**J D Ferry & Co, trading name of JDF Services Ltd** *(J D Ferry)* 52 Parkway, WELWYN GARDEN CITY, HERTFORDSHIRE, AL8 6HH.

J D Frost Accountants *(J D Frost)* 7 Links View, CIRENCESTER, GLOUCESTERSHIRE, GL7 2NF.

Ⓟ**J Daniels & Co Ltd** *(J A Daniels)* 10 Wallers Hoppet, LOUGHTON, ESSEX, IG10 1SP.

J Davies FCA *(J Davies)* 96 Belgrave Road, Gorseinon, SWANSEA, SA4 6RE.

Ⓐ**J Digby-Rogers** *(J Digby-Rogers)* 13 Gipsy Hill, LONDON, SE19 1QG.

J E Butler & Co. *(J E Butler)* 222 The Avenue, Highams Park, LONDON, E4 9SE.

J E Draper *(J E Draper)* 15 Main Street, Addingham, ILKLEY, WEST YORKSHIRE, LS29 0PD.

Ⓟ**J E R Accounting Services Limited** *(M H Harding)* 32 Ramblers Way, WATERLOOVILLE, HAMPSHIRE, PO7 8RE.

J Evans *(J Evans)* 10 Walmer Crescent, WORCESTER, WR4 0ES.

Ⓟ**J F Guyers, trading name of J F Guyers Limited** *(J F Guyers)* 1 Hornby Chase, Old Hall Gardens, LIVERPOOL, L31 5PP.

★ⓉⒻ**J F Hornby & Co** *(J.F. Hornby, P Hornby)* The Tower, Daltongate Business Centre, Daltongate, ULVERSTON, LA12 7AJ.

Ⓟ**J F O'Brien FCA, trading name of J F O'Brien Taxation Services Ltd** *(J F O'Brien)* 7 Abbey Court, WALTHAM ABBEY, EN9 1RF.

Ⓟ**J F White Ltd** *(J F White)* 36 Cotland Acres, Redhill Surrey, REDHILL, RH1 6JZ.

J Forsyth *(J C Forsyth)* 19 Cutenhoe Road, LUTON, LU1 3NB.

Ⓟ**J Gareth Morgan/Cambrian Partnership, trading name of J Gareth Morgan & Co Ltd** *(D Jones, D L Rees)* Clun House, 11 Morgan Street, TREDEGAR, GWENT, NP22 3NA. and at NEATH

Ⓟ**J Gibson & Co Limited** *(J Gibson)* 12 Foxhills Close, Appleton, WARRINGTON, CHESHIRE, WA4 5DH.

Ⓟ**J Glynn & Associates Ltd** *(J A Glynn)* 24 Valley Road, Bramhall, STOCKPORT, SK7 2NN.

Ⓟ**J Goodman Accounting Services Limited** *(J H M Goodman)* 24 Lyndhurst Gardens, LONDON, N3 1TB.

J H Wise & Co *(J H Wise)* 27 Wheeler Avenue, OXTED, SURREY, RH8 9LF.

Ⓐ**J Hagg & Co** *(J B Hagg)* 75 Camborne Avenue, LONDON, W13 9QZ.

Ⓟ**J Ham & Co, trading name of J Ham & Co Ltd** *(J Ham)* 114 Heol Llanishen Fach, Rhiwbina, CARDIFF, CF14 6LG.

J J Cook & Co *(J J Cook)* 50-51 Albemarle Crescent, SCARBOROUGH, NORTH YORKSHIRE, YO11 1XX.

J J Drury *(J J Drury)* 65 Wattleton Road, BEACONSFIELD, HP9 1RY.

J J Finney *(J J Finney)* 4 Chiltern Drive, Winstanley, WIGAN, WN3 6DY.

J Johnson BA(Hons) ACA *(J A Johnson)* 6 Church Farm Close, Bierton, AYLESBURY, BUCKINGHAMSHIRE, HP22 5EL.

J Jones & Co, trading name of John Jones *(J R Jones)* 30 Woodvale Avenue, Cyncoed, CARDIFF, CF23 6SQ.

Ⓟ**J L Glass Ltd** *(J L Glass)* Trafalgar House, Trafalgar Wharf, 223 Southampton Road, PORTSMOUTH, PO6 4PY.

J L Irving *(J L Irving)* Woodside, Kirkandrews-on-Eden, CARLISLE, CA5 6DL.

Ⓟ**J L Wyatt & Co, trading name of Betmathel Limited** *(J L Wyatt)* 6 College Road, BROMSGROVE, B60 2NE.

ⓉⒻⒶ**J Llywelyn Hughes & Co** *(D E Thomas, R A Thomas)* Ty'r Bont, LLANRWST, LL26 0EY.

Ⓟ**J Locks Limited** *(J G M Locks)* 18 Willowmead, HERTFORD, SG14 2AT.

Ⓟ**J M H Financials Limited** *(F G Neicho)* Cumbrae, Brittains Lane, SEVENOAKS, KENT, TN13 2NF.

J M Holland *(J M Holland)* 53 Elmhurst Drive, HORNCHURCH, ESSEX, RM11 1NZ.

J M Kaye *(J M Kaye)* 12 Embry Way, STANMORE, HA7 3AZ.

J M Pitman & Co *(P G Jethwa)* Dometo House, Molesey Road, Hersham, WALTON-ON-THAMES, KT12 3PW.

J M Shah and Company LLP *(J M Shah)* Causeway House, 1 Dane Street, BISHOP'S STORTFORD, HERTFORDSHIRE, CM23 3BT. and at LONDON

ⓅⒶ**J Mark Evans Limited** *(J M Evans)* 44 St. Helens Road, SWANSEA, SA1 4BB.

Ⓟ**J Matthiae & Co Limited** *(J Matthiae)* The Tythings, The Plantation, West Winterslow, SALISBURY, SP5 1RE.

J Mays *(J P Mays)* 10 Kirkdale Crescent, LEEDS, LS12 6AS.

Ⓟ**J McLoughlin Ltd** *(J C McLoughlin)* Signpost Cottage, The Camp, STROUD, GLOUCESTERSHIRE, GL6 7HN.

ⓉⓅ**J Michael & Co Ltd** *(J Michael, L Michael)* 274 Northdown Road, Cliftonville, MARGATE, CT9 2PT.

J Morgan & Co *(J Morgan)* 3 Woodford Way, Wombourne, WOLVERHAMPTON, WV5 8HD.

J N Roff & Co *(J N Roff)* Swinholme Farm, Bowes, BARNARD CASTLE, COUNTY DURHAM, DL12 9NB.

J Newsam & Co *(J A Newsam)* 22 Broadlands Crescent, Bramley, ROTHERHAM, SOUTH YORKSHIRE, S66 1WE.

★**J P Consulting** *(P A Bessler)* Albury Mill, Mill Lane, Chilworth, GUILDFORD, SURREY, GU4 8RU.

J P Crook & Co *(J P Crook)* 11a Austin Street, STAMFORD, LINCOLNSHIRE, PE9 2QR.

Ⓟ**J P Martell & Co Limited** *(J P Martell)* 22 Bushby Avenue, Rustington, LITTLEHAMPTON, BN16 2BY.

Ⓐ**J P Mills & Co** *(J P K Mills)* 6 Suffolk Street, DUBLIN 2, COUNTY DUBLIN, IRELAND.

ⓉⒶ**J P Walters & Co** *(J P Walters)* 67 Duke Street, DARLINGTON, COUNTY DURHAM, DL3 7SD.

ⓅⒶ**J P Walters & Co, trading name of J P Walters & Co Ltd** *(J P Walters)* 67 Duke Street, DARLINGTON, COUNTY DURHAM, DL3 7SD.

Ⓟ**J R Brown (Accountants) Ltd** *(J R Brown)* Rose Cottage, 3 Pasture Land, Gaddesby, LEICESTER, LE7 4XB.

J R Carroll *(J R Carroll)* 8 Arthur Kennedy Close, Boughton, FAVERSHAM, ME13 9BQ.

Ⓕ**J R Gillingwater** *(J R Gillingwater)* 15 Pelham Avenue, GRIMSBY, DN33 3NA.

J R I Mitchell FCA *(J R I Mitchell)* 44 Lucastes Road, HAYWARDS HEATH, WEST SUSSEX, RH16 1JP.

Ⓟ**J R Jones & Company Limited** *(J R Jones)* 30 Woodvale Avenue, CARDIFF, CF23 6SQ.

J Raggett Accounting *(J D Raggett)* 1 Belmont Crescent, SWINDON, SN1 4EY.

J Roebuck & Co *(J Roebuck)* 148 Droylsden Road, Audenshaw, MANCHESTER, M34 5SJ.

ⓉⒻⒶ**J S Bethell & Co** *(T J Day, W P Smith, J A Thompson)* 70 Clarkehouse Road, SHEFFIELD, S10 2LJ.

J S Carling Accountancy *(J S Carling)* 41 Knaith Close, YARM, CLEVELAND, TS15 9TL.

ⓅⒶ**J S Gulati & Co, trading name of J S Gulati & Co Ltd** *(J Singh)* 4 Peter James Business Centre, Pump Lane, HAYES, MIDDLESEX, UB3 3NT.

ⒻⓅ**J Tanna & Co, trading name of Orbital Insurance Services Ltd** *(V M Shah)* 180 London Road, KINGSTON UPON THAMES, SURREY, KT2 6QW.

J V Wilson & Co *(S Chong, M J Christie)* 41a Chambers Street, HERTFORD, SG14 1PL.

J W H Martin *(J W H Martin)* 1 Cherry Tree Walk, BECKENHAM, BR3 3PF.

ⓉⒻⒶ**J W Hinks** *(R R Barnes, J A Bomber, P O H Jones, D J Thursfield)* 19 Highfield Road, Edgbaston, BIRMINGHAM, B15 3BH.

ⓉⒻⓅⒶ**J W Scrivens, trading name of J W Scrivens & Co Limited** *(G Litherland)* Grays Court, 5 Nursery Road, Edgbaston, BIRMINGHAM, B15 3JX.

ⓉⒻⓅⒶ**J W Walsh Accountants Ltd** *(J W Walsh)* Albion House, 163-167 King Street, DUKINFIELD, CHESHIRE, SK16 4LF.

J White *(J S White)* 3 Wentworth Crescent, Mayals, SWANSEA, SA3 5HT.

J Wilburn *(J Wilburn)* 10 Arnian Way, Rainford, ST. HELENS, MERSEYSIDE, WA11 8BX.

Ⓟ**J&S Accountants Limited** *(E M Jones, B A P Stevenson)* 6 Northlands Road, SOUTHAMPTON, HAMPSHIRE, SO15 2FL.

Ⓟ**J. Aubin Ltd** *(D J H Aubin)* 4 Old Barn Close, CHRISTCHURCH, BH23 2QZ.

J. Barnard *(J C Barnard)* Brelston Court, Marstow, ROSS-ON-WYE, HEREFORDSHIRE, HR9 6HF.

J. Beattie & Co *(J Beattie)* 23 Bowling Green Road, KETTERING, NN15 7QW.

Ⓕ**J. Brain** *(J Brain)* 8 Whitegates, Shopping Centre, Flaxpits Lane Winterbourne, BRISTOL, BS36 1JX.

ⒻⒶ**J. D. Bregman & Co** *(J D Bregman)* 25a York Road, ILFORD, ESSEX, IG1 3AD. and at LONDON

J. Darbyshire *(J Darbyshire)* 31 York Road, Grappenhall, WARRINGTON, WA4 2EH.

J. Davies *(J Davies)* 9 Dunes House, 1 Fairhaven Road, LYTHAM ST. ANNES, LANCASHIRE, FY8 1NN.

J. Davison & Co *(J J Davison)* The Firs, Cold Newton, LEICESTER, LE7 9DA.

J. F. Balshaw & Co *(J F Balshaw, K L Hodgkiss)* 20 Old Kiln Lane, Heaton, BOLTON, BL1 5PD.

★ⓉⓅ**J. H. Greenwood & Company, trading name of James H. Greenwood & Co Ltd** *(J H Greenwood)* Ava Lodge, Castle Terrace, BERWICK-UPON-TWEED, TD15 1NP.

Ⓟ**J. Hall & Co Limited** *(J Hall)* 255 Breightmet Fold Lane, BOLTON, BL2 5NB.

J. Hinkins *(J Hinkins)* Acorn Cottage, Abingdon Road, Tubney, ABINGDON, OXFORDSHIRE, OX13 5QQ.

Ⓐ**J. Humphrey Jones & Co** *(P Jackson, J M Pantling)* Suite 3C, St Christopher House, Wellington Road South, STOCKPORT, SK2 6NG.

J. L. Fisher *(J L Fisher)* 15 Portsmouth Court, Harbour Views, GIBRALTAR, 111111, GIBRALTAR.

J. Martin *(J Martin)* P O Box 695, KENMORE, QLD 4069, AUSTRALIA.

J. Pearson & Co *(J F R Pearson)* Patch Elm House, Patch Elm Lane, Rangeworthy, BRISTOL, BS37 7LT.

J. Raine *(J Raine)* 25 Barlows Road, Edgbaston, BIRMINGHAM, B15 2PN.

J.& A.W. Sully & Co *(S R Allan)* The Old Wagon House, Bullocks Lane, Kingston Seymour, North Somerset, CLEVEDON, AVON BS21 6XA.

J.A. Cound & Co. *(J A Vanston)* Caple Mead, How Caple, HEREFORD, HR1 4TA.

J.A. Dawson *(J A Dawson)* Old Post Office Chambers, St. Michaels Way, MIDDLEWICH, CHESHIRE, CW10 9QN.

J.A. Drake *(J A Drake)* 51 High Street, Cheveley, NEWMARKET, Suffolk, CB8 9DQ.

J.A. Finch *(J A Finch)* 30 Sweetings Road, Godmanchester, HUNTINGDON, PE29 2JS.

J.A. Heard & Co *(J A Heard)* 36 The Green, Long Whatton, LOUGHBOROUGH, LEICESTERSHIRE, LE12 5DB.

J.A. Hemming *(J A Hemming)* Unit 9a, High Grosvenor, Worfield, BRIDGNORTH, SHROPSHIRE, WV15 5PN.

J.A. Marvin *(J A Marvin)* 378 Thurmaston Boulevard, LEICESTER, LE4 9LE.

J.A. McElholm *(J A McElholm)* 71 Beech Avenue, Newton Mearns, GLASGOW, G77 5QR.

J.A. Mitchley *(J A Mitchley)* 17 Frogs Hall, Bluntisham, HUNTINGDON, PE28 3XD.

J.A.George *(J A George)* The Old School House, 108 Low St, Collingham, NEWARK, NG23 7NL.

Ⓕ**J.A.Gordon Stewart & Co** *(J A Gordon Stewart)* 29 Greenside Road, LONDON, W12 9JQ.

Ⓕ**J.B. Cooke & Co** *(J B Cooke)* 2nd Floor, Hillside House, 2-6 Friern Park, North Finchley, LONDON, N12 9BT.

J.B. Coutinho & Co *(J B Coutinho)* 46 Eleanor Road, LONDON, N11 2QS.

J.B. Dale *(J B Dale)* The Black Cottage, Bell Common, EPPING, ESSEX, CM16 4DZ.

J.B. Sheppard & Co *(S J Rudden)* 206 Chesterfield Drive, Riverhead, SEVENOAKS, TN13 2EH.

J.C Beames & Co. *(J C Beames)* 4 The Crossway, Mottingham, LONDON, SE9 4JJ.

★**J.C. Barker & Co** *(N J Regnauld)* 6 Richmond Terrace, Shelton, STOKE-ON-TRENT, STAFFORDSHIRE, ST1 4ND.

Ⓐ**J.C. Barton & Co** *(J C Barton)* Martland Buildings, Mart Lane, Burscough, ORMSKIRK, L40 0SD.

J.C. Brewerton & Co *(J C Brewerton)* Ashcombe House, 4 Morville Close, Dorridge, SOLIHULL, B93 8SZ.

J.C. Gibson & Company *(J C Gibson)* Harbour Office, Gunsgreen Basin, EYEMOUTH, BERWICKSHIRE, TD14 5SD.

J.C. Goddard *(J C Goddard)* 30 Sansome Walk, WORCESTER, WR1 1LX. and at TENBURY WELLS

J.C. Jenner *(J C Jenner)* 4 Timberling Gardens, Sanderstead, SOUTH CROYDON, SURREY, CR2 0AW.

ⒻⒶ**J.C. Marjoram & Co** *(J C Marjoram)* 486 London Road South, LOWESTOFT, NR33 0LB.

J.C. Seabrook *(J C Seabrook)* 56 Woodland Way, WEST WICKHAM, BR4 9LR. and at SOUTH CROYDON

J.C. Wigley FCA *(J C Wigley)* 68 Hilley Field Lane, Fetcham, LEATHERHEAD, KT22 9UU.

J.C. Woodbridge *(J C Woodbridge)* Oak House, Partridge Lane, Rusper, HORSHAM, WEST SUSSEX, RH12 4RW.

J.Caplan & Co *(J Caplan)* 39 Silverston Way, STANMORE, HA7 4HS.

J.D. Gardiner & Co *(J D Gardiner)* Chisholm House, 9 Queens Square, CORBY, NORTHAMPTONSHIRE, NN17 1PD.

J.D. Gardiner Company *(J D Gardiner)* Chisholm House, 9 Queens Square, CORBY, NN17 1PD.

J.D. Hewitson FCA *(J D Hewitson)* 1 Monks Heath Hall Farm, Chelford Road, Nether Alderley, MACCLESFIELD, CHESHIRE, SK10 4SY.

ⓉⓅ**J.D. Mercer & Co Ltd** *(J D Mercer)* 9 Chapel Street, POULTON-LE-FYLDE, FY6 7BQ.

J.D. Mistri *(J D Mistri)* 701 Sharda Chambers, 15 New Marine Lines, MUMBAI 400 020, MAHARASHTRA, INDIA.

J.D. Moorcraft *(J D Moorcraft)* 8 Cloisters, 22 College Road, Clifton, BRISTOL, BS8 3HZ.

J.D. Ware *(J D Ware)* 52 The Fairway, Burnham, SLOUGH, SL1 8DS.

J.D.G. Holme *(J D G Holme)* 40 Littleheath Lane, COBHAM, KT11 2QN.

J.E. Benneyworth *(J E Benneyworth)* 7 Broome Close, YATELEY, GU46 7SY.

J.E. Elliott *(J E B Elliott)* 63 Greenhill Road, Moseley, BIRMINGHAM, B13 9SU.

J.E. Pallace *(J E Pallace)* 19 Private Road, ENFIELD, EN1 2EH.

J.E. Wheeler *(J E Wheeler)* The Barn, Duck End, Offord Road, Graveley, ST. NEOTS, CAMBRIDGESHIRE PE19 6PP.

J.E.M. Caldwell *(J E M Caldwell)* 105 Carrowreagh Road, Garvagh, COLERAINE, COUNTY LONDONDERRY, BT51 5LH.

J.E.S. Dunn *(J E S Dunn)* Yew Tree Cottage, Unthank Lane, Holmesfield, DRONFIELD, S18 7WF.

ⓉⒻⒶ**J.Emyr Thomas & Co** *(E Orwig, E R Williams)* Tegfan, 7 Deiniol Road, BANGOR, GWYNEDD, LL57 2UR.

J.F. Adams *(J F Adams)* 29 Pensford Avenue, RICHMOND, TW9 4HR.

Ⓐ**J.F. Banks & Co** *(J F Banks)* 76 Huddersfield Road, BRIGHOUSE, WEST YORKSHIRE, HD6 3RD.

J.F. Jackman *(J F Jackman)* Tilthams Farm, Tilthams Corner Road, GODALMING, GU7 3DE.

J.F. Mallabar & Co *(A M Ridge)* 24a West Street, EPSOM, KT18 7RJ.

Ⓟ**J.F. Socci & Co, trading name of J.F. Socci & Co Limited** *(J F Socci)* 83 Blackwood Road, Streetly, SUTTON COLDFIELD, WEST MIDLANDS, B74 3PW.

J.G. Allbut & Co. *(J G Allbut)* Stonefield Lodge, Newcastle Road, STONE, STAFFORDSHIRE, ST15 8LB.

Ⓐ**J.G. Rhodes** *(J G Rhodes)* Lodge Park, Hortonwood 30, TELFORD, SHROPSHIRE, TF1 7ET.

J.G. Smith *(J G Smith)* 74 Knight Street, Pinchbeck, SPALDING, LINCOLNSHIRE, PE11 3RB.

J.G. Thornton *(J G Thornton)* Elfrey, 157 Holly Lane, Erdington, BIRMINGHAM, B24 9LA.

J.G.C. Abbott *(J G C Abbott)* 6 Stoney Field, Highnam, GLOUCESTER, GL2 8LY.

J.G.K. Bell *(J G K Bell)* 1 Westwood Gardens, Barnes, LONDON, SW13 0LB.

Ⓐ**J.H. Greenwood F.C.A** *(J H Greenwood)* Ava Lodge, Castle Terrace, BERWICK-UPON-TWEED, TD15 1NP.

J.H. Reynolds *(J H Reynolds)* 2 Insole Gardens, CARDIFF, CF5 2HW.

J.H. Thompson & Co *(J H Thompson)* 5 Burns Close, Long Crendon, AYLESBURY, BUCKINGHAMSHIRE, HP18 9BX.

ⓅⒶ**J.H. Thompson & Co., trading name of JHT Business Consultants Limited** *(J H Thompson)* 5 Burns Close, Long Crendon, AYLESBURY, BUCKINGHAMSHIRE, HP18 9BX.

J.H. Wood-Mitchell *(J H Wood-Mitchell)* 3rd Floor, 22 Devonshire Place, HARROGATE, HG1 4AA.

J.I.Collinson *(J I Collinson)* 12 Windsor Place, Mangotsfield, BRISTOL, BS16 9DD.

J.J. Clement *(J J Clement)* 57 Boulevard, WESTON-SUPER-MARE, AVON, BS23 1PG.

Ⓕ**J.J. Keefe** *(J J Keefe)* 77 The Wheel House, Burrells Wharf, Westferry Road, LONDON, E14 3TB.

J.J. Staniland *(J J Staniland)* 28 Peveril Drive, Riddings, ALFRETON, DE55 4AP.

Ⓟ**J.K. Research Ltd** *(K A Hunt, J A Tipping)* 6-8 The Wash, HERTFORD, SG14 1PX.

J.Kirkwood & Co *(J Kirkwood)* School End, Rowton Bridge Road, Christleton, CHESTER, CH3 7BD.

J.L. Baines & Co *(J L Baines)* Chalklands, Hatherden, ANDOVER, SP11 0HJ.

J.L. Hastings *(J L Hastings)* 3 Bewlbridge Close, Flimwell, WADHURST, TN5 7NL.

J.L. Jepson *(J L Jepson)* 5 Valley Way, STALYBRIDGE, SK15 2QZ.

J.L. White & Co *(J L White)* 46 Engine Lane, Nailsea, BRISTOL, BS48 4RL.

J.L. Williams *(J L Williams)* Apple Tree Cottage, 38 Rushett Close, THAMES DITTON, KT7 0UT.

★ⓉⒻⒶ**J.L. Winder & Co.** *(G M Haythornthwaite, S J Roberts, G Smith, J L Winder)* 125 Ramsden Square, BARROW-IN-FURNESS, LA14 1XA.

J.M. Associates *(J M Marshall)* 21A Craven Terrace, LONDON, W2 3QH.

J.M. Chapman *(J M Chapman)* 22 St. Albans Road, Codicote, HITCHIN, SG4 8UT.

J.M. Kerr & Co *(J M R S Kerr)* 26 Spencer Avenue, LEEK, STAFFORDSHIRE, ST13 5PA.

J.M. MacKenzie *(J M Mackenzie)* 119 Coverside Road, Great Glen, LEICESTER, LE8 9EB.

J.M. Page & Co *(J M Page)* 14 Tudor Grove, SUTTON COLDFIELD, WEST MIDLANDS, B74 2LL.

J.M. Ruddy *(J M Ruddy)* Long Acre, Pattingham, WOLVERHAMPTON, WV6 7AD.

J.M. Sanders & Co *(J M Sanders)* Badgers Croft, Hive Road, Bushey Heath, BUSHEY, WD23 1JG.

ⒻⒶ**J.M. Shah & Company** *(J M Shah)* 24 Old Bond Street, LONDON, W1S 4AP.

J.M. Taggart *(J M Taggart)* 64 Eshe Road North, Blundellsands, LIVERPOOL, L23 8UF.

J.M. Tildesley *(J M Tildesley)* 5 Pednandrea, St. Just, PENZANCE, TR19 7UA.

J.M. Wellington *(J M Wellington)* 13 Lancing Road, ORPINGTON, BR6 0QS.

J.M.M. Wale *(J M M Wale)* Flat 11, Apartment Buildings 66, Kabanbai Batyr Street, ALMATY, KAZAKHSTAN.

J.Martin James *(J M James)* 101A High Street, YARM, TS15 9BB.

ⓉⒻⒶ**J.N Straughan & Co** *(P R Craig, W H Sawyer)* Fram Well House, Framwelgate, DURHAM, DH1 5SU.

J.N. Lyons *(J N Lyons)* 13 Woodbury Park Road, Ealing, LONDON, W13 8DD.

J.N. Wilson *(J N Wilson)* Grosvenor House, 25 St.Peter Street, TIVERTON, EX16 6NW. and at CREDITON

J.N.Vickery *(J N Vickery)* 39 Green Lane, Blackwater, CAMBERLEY, SURREY, GU17 9DG.

J.Neville Beckman & Co *(J N Beckman)* 7 Osidge Lane, LONDON, N14 5JD.

Ⓐ**J.O. Evans** *(J O Evans)* Green Banks, The Hill, Merrywalks, STROUD, GLOUCESTERSHIRE, GL5 4EP.

J.O. Russell *(J O Russell)* 38 Leathway, Ormesby St. Margaret, GREAT YARMOUTH, NR29 3QA.

J.P. Stewart *(J P Stewart)* Devenish Cottage, Devenish Road, Sunningdale, ASCOT, SL5 9QP.

J.P. Surrey *(J P Surrey)* Mulberry House, 8 Horseshoe Lane West, GUILDFORD, SURREY, GU1 2SX.

Ⓕ**J.P. Thornton & Co** *(J P Thornton)* The Old Dairy, Adstockfields, Adstock, BUCKINGHAM, MK18 2JE.

ⒻⒶ**J.P.B. Harris & Co** *(V A Miles, A S Robinson)* 54 St. Marys Lane, UPMINSTER, ESSEX, RM14 2QT.

Ⓟ**J.P.B. Harris & Co Ltd** *(V A Miles, A S Robinson)* Harmile House, 54 St Mary's Lane, UPMINSTER, ESSEX, RM14 2QT.

J.R. Allsop *(J R Allsop)* 32 Bryanston Avenue, Whitton, TWICKENHAM, TW2 6HP.

Ⓣ**J.R. Atkins & Co** *(A J Heard)* 3 Beech Lane, MACCLESFIELD, SK10 2DR.

J.R. Crichard & Co *(J R Crichard)* 23 Pennyford Court, Henderson Drive, LONDON, NW8 8UF.

J.R. Grace & Co *(J R Grace)* Tanglin, 3A Highfield Road, SHANKLIN, ISLE OF WIGHT, PO37 6PP.

J.R. Howland *(J R Howland)* 15 Bear Lane, North Moreton, DIDCOT, OX11 9AS.

J.R. Hunter F.C.A *(J R Hunter)* 12 Church Meadow, Sherburn in Elmet, LEEDS, LS25 6NX.

J.R. Mayor *(J R Mayor)* 39 Pear Tree Park, Holme, CARNFORTH, LANCASHIRE, LA6 1SD.
★ⓉⓅ**J.R. Watson & Co** *(S E Leathem, A Markham, P J Robinson)* Eastgate House, 11 Cheyne Walk, NORTHAMPTON, NN1 5PT. and at RUGBY
Ⓐ**J.R. Williams & Co** *(J R Williams)* 1 Beeches Road, Heybridge, MALDON, CM9 4SL.
J.R. Winfield *(J R Winfield)* 62 Glendon Drive, NOTTINGHAM, NG5 1FP.
J.R. Winslet *(J R Winslet)* Windyridge, Borers Arms Road, Copthorne, CRAWLEY, RH10 3LJ.
ⒻⒶ**J.R.Antoine & Partners** *(G J Hipgrave, R King)* 75 Rickmansworth Road, AMERSHAM, HP6 5JW.
Ⓟ**J.S. Management Ltd** *(H Jacobs)* 87 Westfield, Kidderpore Avenue, Hampstead, LONDON, NW3 7SG.
J.S. Phillips *(J S Phillips)* Mill House, Dewlish, DORCHESTER, DORSET, DT2 7LT. and at LONDON
ⒻⒶ**J.S. Rose & Co** *(J S Rose)* Fiosam House, 25 Station Road, New Barnet, BARNET, EN5 1PH.
J.S. Slater *(J S Slater)* The Old House, 28 Bradford Street, SHIFNAL, TF11 8AU.
J.S. Tiley *(J S Tiley)* Spignalls, Woodlands Road, BROMLEY, BR1 2AE.
J.S. Weber & Co. *(J S Weber)* 29 Woodvale Avenue, Cyncoed, CARDIFF, CF23 6SP.
Ⓐ**J.S. Williamson & Co** *(J S Williamson)* Suite F20, Twyford House, Garner Street, STOKE-ON-TRENT, ST4 7AY.
ⒻⒶ**J.Srinivasan Crouch & Co** *(J S Crouch)* 40A Rutland Gardens, HOVE, BN3 5PB.
J.T. Kinsley *(J T Kinsley)* 28 Harfield Road, SUNBURY-ON-THAMES, TW16 5PT.
ⓉⒶ**J.T. Thomas & Co** *(J T Thomas, M I T Thomas)* 70 High Street, CRICCIETH, LL52 0HB. and at BLAENAU FFESTINIOG, LLANDUDNO
J.T. Whalley & Co *(J T Whalley)* 41 Leywood Close, BRAINTREE, ESSEX, CM7 3NP.
Ⓣ**J.V. Banks** *(P Chau, C E Davies, P J Hughes, J H McKee)* Banks House, Paradise Street, RHYL, LL18 3LW.
J.V. Botterell *(J V Beeston)* 10 Congleton Road, SANDBACH, CHESHIRE, CW11 1HJ.
J.W. Arnold & Co. *(J Arnold)* 59A Station Road, Winchmore Hill, LONDON, N21 3NB.
J.W. Binsted & Co *(J W Binsted)* Brueton House, 34 Brueton Avenue, SOLIHULL, B91 3EN.
J.W. Minton & Co. *(J W Minton)* 103a High Street, Lees, OLDHAM, OL4 4LY.
J.W. Perry & Co *(J W Perry)* 2nd Floor Hyde House, The Hyde, Edgware Road, LONDON, NW9 6LH.
ⒻⒶ**J.W. Ridgeway & Co** *(J W Ridgeway)* 106a High Street, CHESHAM, HP5 1EB.
Ⓐ**J.W. Woodrow & Co** *(J W Woodrow)* 141 Station Road, Hendon, LONDON, NW4 4NJ.
J.W.G. Blackwell *(J W G Blackwell)* 6 Hallfields, Radford Semele, LEAMINGTON SPA, CV31 1TS.
Ⓟ**J.W.Swales & Co Ltd** *(J W Swales)* The Grange, Yatton Keynell, CHIPPENHAM, SN14 7BA.
Ⓟ**J2U Consulting Ltd** *(A A M Johnson)* 239 Moor End Lane, BIRMINGHAM, B24 9DS.
JA *(J Anwar)* 9 Hudswell Close, Whitefield, MANCHESTER, M45 7UD.
JA Granger BSc ACA *(J A Granger)* 13 Howard Road, Great Bookham, LEATHERHEAD, SURREY, KT23 4PW.
Ⓟ**JA Simpson & Co, trading name of J A Simpson & Co Ltd** *(J A Simpson)* 48 Bredbury Green, Romiley, STOCKPORT, SK6 3DN.
JAC Accountancy *(J A J Charlwood)* Flat 6, 62 Woodbury Park Road, TUNBRIDGE WELLS, KENT, TN4 9NG.
Jack & Co *(M Green)* The Old Coach House, 40 Carey Street, READING, RG1 7JS.
★**Jack A. Alli, Sons & Co** *(K G Alli, R M Alli)* 145 Crown Street, GEORGETOWN, 6, GUYANA.
Jack MacDonald & Co *(J M MacDonald)* 1 Aldersyde, TAYNUILT, ARGYLL, PA35 1AG.
ⓉⒻⒶ**Jack Ross** *(D P Black, U A Memon, C J Williams)* Barnfield House, The Approach, MANCHESTER, M3 7BX.
Ⓟ**JackalAdvisory, trading name of Jackal Advisory Ltd** *(R Cacho, A S Duncan)* Level 19, Portland House, Bressenden Place, LONDON, SW1E 5RS. and at BRIGHTON
Jackie Brewer *(J R Brewer)* 71 Elgin Road, Pwll, LLANELLI, CARMARTHENSHIRE, SA15 4AF.
Jackie Pritchet *(J A Pritchet)* 17 Ashley Close, Hightown, RINGWOOD, BH24 1QX.
ⓉⒻ**Jackson & Graham** *(J M R Hague, P C Wood)* Lynn Garth, Gillinggate, KENDAL, CUMBRIA, LA9 4JB. and at SEDBERGH, WINDERMERE
ⓅⒶ**Jackson & Jackson, trading name of Jackson & Jackson Accountants Limited** *(H R Jackson)* 33 Chingford Mount Road, LONDON, E4 8LU.
Ⓟ**Jackson Birch, trading name of Jackson Birch Limited** *(B J Couzens)* 31 Woodland Way, WOODFORD WELLS, ESSEX, IG8 0QQ. and at WOODFORD GREEN
ⓅⒶ**Jackson Calvert, trading name of M J One Limited** *(M Jackson)* Jackson Calvert, 33 Coleshill Street, SUTTON COLDFIELD, WEST MIDLANDS, B72 1SD.
★**Jackson Feldman & Co** *(J P Nettleton, A Parker)* Alexander House, 3 Shakespeare Road, Finchley, LONDON, N3 1XE.
ⓅⒶ**Jackson Green Carter Limited** *(M A C Carter)* 6 Cumberland Gate, PORTSMOUTH, PO5 1AG.
Ⓟ**Jackson Mitchell Limited** *(E Mitchell)* 5 Bell Lane, Syresham, BRACKLEY, NORTHAMPTONSHIRE, NN13 5HP.
★ⓉⓅ**Jackson Robson Licence, trading name of Jackson Robson Licence Limited** *(R M Miles, G R Mountain, P M Robson)* 33/35 Exchange Street, DRIFFIELD, NORTH HUMBERSIDE, YO25 6LL. and at BRIDLINGTON
★ⓉⒻⒶ**Jackson Stephen LLP** *(E P Atkinson, C M Barrington, H M Jackson, J S Jackson)* James House, Stonecross Business Park, 5 Yew Tree Way, Golborne, WARRINGTON, CHESHIRE WA3 3JD.
Ⓕ**Jacksons** *(H Jackson)* The Old Bakehouse, Course Road, ASCOT, SL5 7HL.
Ⓐ**Jacksons** *(M Jackson)* 1 The Pathway, Alfred Gelder Street, HULL, HU1 1XJ.
Jacksons Contables S.L *(D A Mayer)* C/ Explanada Cervantes No4 1st Floor, Denia, 03700 ALICANTE, SPAIN.
ⒻⓅⒶ**Jacksons, trading name of Jacksons Accountants (Midlands) Limited** *(D A Mayer, D McDonald)* Deansfield House, 98 Lancaster Road, NEWCASTLE, STAFFORDSHIRE, ST5 1DS.
Jacky Gregory *(J A Gregory)* Church Lodge, Church Road, Warsash, SOUTHAMPTON, SO31 9GF.
ⓉⒻⒶ**Jacob Cavenagh & Skeet** *(R I Haffenden, A R Hazael, M R Hickson)* 5 Robin Hood Lane, SUTTON, SURREY, SM1 2SW.
Ⓕ**Jacob Charles & Co** *(J C Lax)* Sentinel House, Sentinel Square, Brent Street, LONDON, NW4 2EP.
Ⓐ**Jacob, Ting & Co** *(S R Jacob, C K I Ting)* 40 Homer Street, LONDON, W1H 4NL.
Jacobs & Co *(A H Jacobs)* Credcoll House, 96 Marsh Lane, LEEDS, LS9 8SR.
Jacobs & Company *(R S Jacobs)* 152-154 Coles Green Road, LONDON, NW2 7HD.
ⓅⒶ**Jacobs Allen, trading name of is business ltd** *(K F Senior)* 59 Abbeygate Street, BURY ST. EDMUNDS, SUFFOLK, IP33 1LB.
ⒻⓅⒶ**Jacquards, trading name of Jacquards Limited** *(J Patel)* 2 Wannions Close, CHESHAM, BUCKINGHAMSHIRE, HP5 1YA.
Ⓕ**Jacqueline Brocklehurst** *(J Brocklehurst)* 21 Poulton Avenue, LYTHAM ST. ANNES, FY8 3JR.
Jacqueline Davidson *(J R Davidson)* 17 Wykeham Road, LONDON, NW4 2TB.
Jacqueline Nunn FCA *(J E Nunn)* 271 St. Albans Road, HEMEL HEMPSTEAD, HERTFORDSHIRE, HP2 4RP.
Jacqueline Sewell *(J A Sewell)* 4 School Road, Twyford, WINCHESTER, SO21 1QQ.
ⒻⓅ**JAD Associates Ltd** *(D Crombie, W J Draper)* 4 Bloors Lane, Rainham, GILLINGHAM, KENT, ME8 7EG.
ⓅⒶ**JAD Audit Ltd** *(D Crombie, W J Draper)* 4 Bloors Lane, Rainham, GILLINGHAM, KENT, ME8 7EG.
ⒻⓅ**Jade Securities Limited** *(P A C Beber, M A Shulman)* Acre House, 11/15 William Road, LONDON, NW1 3ER.
Ⓟ**Jade, trading name of Jade Financial Management Ltd** *(D M E Green)* 2 Tone Road, CLEVEDON, BS21 6LG.
Ⓟ**Jadir & Co, trading name of Jadir & Co Ltd** *(R A Al Jadir)* 23 Parkway, CROWTHORNE, BERKSHIRE, RG45 6EP.
★**Jaffer & Co** *(R Kassamali)* 7 Hazlitt Mews, Hazlitt Road, LONDON, W14 0JZ.
Ⓐ**Jafferies** *(R U Shah)* 134a Maybury Road, WOKING, SURREY, GU21 5JR.
Ⓟ**Jafferies Financial Management Ltd** *(R U Shah)* 132 Maybury Road, WOKING, SURREY, GU21 5JR.
Jaffery's *(M M K Jaffer)* 113 Devonshire Road, Mill Hill, LONDON, NW7 1EA.
Jake Davies & Company *(J H Davies)* Haleswood, 2 The Crescent, St Stephens, CANTERBURY, CT2 7AG.
Ⓟ**Jamalu Limited** *(R J H Williams)* 14 Netheravon Road, SALISBURY, SP1 3BJ.
Ⓐ**Jamen Jones** *(T S Bansal)* 77 Manor Way, HARROW, MIDDLESEX, HA2 6BZ.
Ⓐ**James** *(C L Bettridge)* 6 Beaconsfield Road, Clifton, BRISTOL, BS8 2TS.
Ⓐ**James & Co** *(A A James)* The Old Vineyard, 52 Stevenage Road, KNEBWORTH, SG3 6NN.
James & Company *(A R James)* 15 Queens Walk, Thornbury, BRISTOL, BS35 1SR.
ⓉⓅ**James & Uzzell Limited** *(A E James)* Axis 15, Axis Court, Mallard Way, Riverside Business Park, Swansea Vale, SWANSEA SA7 0AJ.
ⓅⒶ**James A Hedges, trading name of James A Hedges Limited** *(J A Hedges)* Westwood Cottage, Lower Gustard Wood, Wheathampstead, ST. ALBANS, HERTFORDSHIRE, AL4 8RU.
James A. Sadler *(J A Sadler)* 13 Fountain Place, Barbourne, WORCESTER, WR1 3HW.
Ⓟ**James Accounting Limited** *(N C James)* 6 Blenheim Mews, MINEHEAD, TA24 5QZ.
Ⓟ**James Billett Ltd** *(J G Billett)* 2 Bowbank Cottage, Eddleston, PEEBLES, PEEBLESSHIRE, EH45 8QR.
James Borthwick FCA *(P J J Borthwick)* 35 Anxey Way, Haddenham, AYLESBURY, BUCKINGHAMSHIRE, HP17 8DJ.
James Carpenter & Co *(J E Carpenter)* 73 Cricketers Lane, Herongate, BRENTWOOD, ESSEX, CM13 3QB.
James Carter Consulting Limited *(J S Carter)* 28 Lingarth Street, Remuera, AUCKLAND, NEW ZEALAND.
James Coward ACA *(J A Coward)* 4 Fairview, North Brewham, BRUTON, SOMERSET, BA10 0JT.
Ⓕ**James Cowper Corporate Finance LLP** *(S A Lambert)* 3 Wesley Gate, Queens Road, READING, RG1 4AP.
★ⒻⒶ**James Cowper, trading name of James Cowper LLP** *(S L Bedford, M N Farwell, T J Goodsell, R C Holland, I D Miles, A R Peal, A Rann, N A Rogers, S R Staunton, B Watson, A P Whalley)* 3 Wesley Gate, Queens Road, READING, RG1 4AP. and at HENLEY-ON-THAMES, NEWBURY, OXFORD, SOUTHAMPTON
ⒻⓅⒶ**James de Frias, trading name of James de Frias Limited** *(D R Bowden, P R de Frias, D A James)* Llanover House, Llanover Road, PONTYPRIDD, CF37 4DY.
James Dinsdale FCA *(A J Dinsdale)* 206A Lawn Lane, HEMEL HEMPSTEAD, HP3 9JF.
James E. Conway *(J E Conway)* 12 Marchant Road, WOLVERHAMPTON, WV3 9QG.
James Eckhardt *(J D Eckhardt)* 2 Queensborough Court, North Circular Road, LONDON, N3 3JP.
Ⓟ**James F. Searle FCA, trading name of James F. Searle Limited** *(J F Searle)* 176 Spixworth Road, NORWICH, NR6 7EQ.
James Francis & Company *(A G Francis)* 32 Wontner Road, Upper Tooting, LONDON, SW17 7QT.
James G Ruddock-Broyd *(J G Ruddock-Broyd)* 2 Mayfield Lodge, 28 Brackley Road, BECKENHAM, KENT, BR3 1RQ.
James H.P. McLaughlin *(J H P McLaughlin)* 34 Ludlow Close, Willsbridge, BRISTOL, BS30 6EB.
Ⓐ**James Harman & Co** *(H J W Harman)* The Atrium, Curtis Road, DORKING, SURREY, RH4 1XA.
ⒻⓅⒶ**James Holyoak & Parker, trading name of James Holyoak & Parker Limited** *(K W Edwards, S N Parker, J Rimmer)* 1 Knights Court, Archers Way, Battlefield Enterprise Park, SHREWSBURY, SHROPSHIRE, SY1 3GA.
James Howes & Co Selas *(J Howes)* 54-56 Avenue Hoche, 75008 PARIS, FRANCE.
James Jackson & Co. *(J G Jackson)* Barberry Cottage, Waterhouse Lane, Kingswood, TADWORTH, KT20 6DT.
James K. Lee *(J K Lee)* 22 Dorian Place, THORNHILL L4J 2M3, ON, CANADA.
James Kenney & Co *(G H G Hayward, J Kenney)* 202-204 Swan Lane, COVENTRY, CV2 4GD.
James King *(J F King)* 5 Ashmore Avenue, Eckington, SHEFFIELD, S21 4AH.
James Knighton *(A J K McDade)* 2 Copythorne Road, BRIXHAM, DEVON, TQ5 8QQ.
James Little & Co *(J Little)* Leaside, Whittingham, ALNWICK, NORTHUMBERLAND, NE66 4UP.
James Magee *(B P M Magee)* 34 Bower Mount Road, MAIDSTONE, ME16 8AU.
James Mandeville *(J G Mandeville)* 6 Ridgeway, WELLINGBOROUGH, NORTHAMPTONSHIRE, NN8 4RX.
Ⓟ**James Neve & Co Limited** *(J A Neve)* 5 Wessington Court, CALNE, WILTSHIRE, SN11 0SS.
James O Hew *(J O Hew)* 16 Cassandra Boulevard, TORONTO M3A 1S4, ON, CANADA.
James Oram & Co. *(J S Oram)* Cadoro, Roman Drive, Chilworth, SOUTHAMPTON, SO16 7HT.
James P Cunnington *(J P Cunnington)* Highcroft Cottage, 33 Berridges Lane, Husbands Bosworth, LUTTERWORTH, LEICESTERSHIRE, LE17 6LE.
James Percival *(J W Percival)* The Old Orchard, Otford Lane, Halstead, SEVENOAKS, TN14 7EE.
James Pollard *(T J C Pollard)* The Old Farm, Trolliloes, Cowbeech, HAILSHAM, BN27 4QR. and at PEACEHAVEN
James Richardson *(J E Richardson)* Sirama, Little Boundes Close, TUNBRIDGE WELLS, TN4 0RS.
James Small, trading name of J.D. Small *(J D Small)* 7 Niall Close, Edgbaston, BIRMINGHAM, B15 3LU.
Ⓟ**James Smith (Accountant) Ltd** *(J E Smith)* 43 East St. Helen Street, ABINGDON, OXFORDSHIRE, OX14 5EE.
James Soo & Co *(J W F Soo)* 65 Jalan Lanjut, SINGAPORE 577708, SINGAPORE.
James Soutar & Co *(J Soutar)* Firland, High Street, Othery, BRIDGWATER, TA7 0QA.
James Stewart & Co *(J B Stewart)* St Marys, Forches Cross, Bovey Road, NEWTON ABBOT, TQ12 6PU.
James Stewart & Co. *(J A H Stewart)* 72 Church Road, WINSCOMBE, BS25 1BJ.
★**James T. W. Kong & Co.** *(J T W Kong)* Room 1901 19/F C C Wu Building, 302-308 Hennessy Road, WAN CHAI, HONG KONG ISLAND, HONG KONG SAR.
James Terry *(J R Terry)* Flat 29, Holly Lodge, 90 Wimbledon Hill Road, LONDON, SW19 7PB.
ⓉⒶ**James Todd & Co** *(R H Brain, J E Standing, J R Stirrup)* Greenbank House, 141 Adelphi Street, PRESTON, PR1 7BH.
ⒻⓅⒶ**James Todd & Co, trading name of James Todd & Co Limited** *(K A Coppard, M J Daniels, D L Shetly)* 1-2 The Barn, West Stoke Road, West Lavant, CHICHESTER, WEST SUSSEX, PO18 9AA.
James Trimby *(J E Trimby)* Woodruffs, Wingfield, TROWBRIDGE, WILTSHIRE, BA14 9LE.
James Trippett *(J Trippett)* 12 Bluebells, WELWYN, AL6 0XD.
ⓅⒶ**James W A Cruickshank & Co, trading name of James W A Cruickshank Business Services Limited** *(J W A Cruickshank)* Inglewood, Wreay, CARLISLE, CA4 0RL.
James Westacott ACA *(A J Westacott)* 478 Hendrefoilan Road, Killay, SWANSEA, SA2 7NU.
★ⓉⒻⒶ**James Worley & Sons** *(J A Spalton, M A Zaremba)* 9 Bridle Close, Surbiton Road, KINGSTON UPON THAMES, SURREY, KT1 2JW.
ⓉⒶ**James, Stanley & Co** *(A E S James)* 1733 Coventry Road, South Yardley, BIRMINGHAM, B26 1DT.
★ⒻⓅⒶ**Jamesons Consulting, trading name of Jamesons Ltd** *(R J Allen, A K Lyon, M J Neilon)* Jamesons House, Compton Way, WITNEY, OXFORDSHIRE, OX28 3AB.
ⓉⒻⓅⒶ**Jamesons, trading name of The Jamesons Partnership Limited** *(A D Brown, S J Garner, R Kerry, J Short, W J Wilson)* 92 Station Road, CLACTON-ON-SEA, CO15 1SG.
ⒻⒶ**Jamieson Stone** *(M R Stone)* Windsor House, 40-41 Great Castle Street, LONDON, W1W 8LU.
Ⓐ**Jan G Gromadzki** *(J G Gromadzki)* 13 Wolverhampton Road, Codsall, WOLVERHAMPTON, WEST MIDLANDS, WV8 1PT.
ⓉⓅ**Jan McDermott & Co Limited** *(J S McDermott, R E Wood)* Third Floor, 51 Hamilton Square, BIRKENHEAD, MERSEYSIDE, CH41 5BN.
Ⓐ**Jan Watkinson & Co** *(J A Watkinson)* 8 Mallinson Close, HORNCHURCH, RM12 5HA.
Ⓟ**Jane Allen, trading name of Smartie & Co Limited** *(P J Allen)* Rosewood, Gt. Ponton Road, Boothby Pagnell, GRANTHAM, NG33 4DH.
ⓅⒶ**Jane Ascroft Accountancy Limited** *(J Ascroft)* Dale House, Hutton Magna, RICHMOND, NORTH YORKSHIRE, DL11 7HH.
Jane B Rose *(J B Rose)* Growle Abbey, High Road, Briston, MELTON CONSTABLE, NORFOLK, NR24 2JH.
Jane Bragg ACA *(J Bragg)* 59 Nelson Road, RAYLEIGH, ESSEX, SS6 8HQ.
Ⓟ**Jane Court, trading name of Barn Owl Enterprises Ltd** *(J E Court)* Beechwood, Perrys Lane, Cawston, NORWICH, NR10 4HJ.
Ⓟ**Jane Evans Taxation Limited** *(J T Evans)* 20 St. Leonards Road, EXETER, EX2 4LA.
Jane Fabes *(C J Fabes)* Frilford Lodge, Sheepstead Road, Marcham, ABINGDON, OXFORDSHIRE, OX13 6QG.
Jane Foy & Co *(J B Foy)* 24 Mosswood Road, WILMSLOW, CHESHIRE, SK9 2DR.
Jane Gardner *(J Gardner)* 13 Great Oaks Park, Rogerstone, NEWPORT, GWENT, NP10 9AT.
Jane H. Gillbe *(J H Gillbe)* Annfield House, 5 Maori Road, GUILDFORD, GU1 2EG.

Jane Hatton *(C J Hatton)* Neville Lodge, 53 Newbridge Crescent, WOLVERHAMPTON, WV6 0LH.

Ⓟ**Jane Jenner Taxation & Accounting Services, trading name of JJ Accounts Limited** *(F J Jenner)* Redroofs, Berrington Road, TENBURY WELLS, WORCESTERSHIRE, WR15 8EN.

Jane M. Andrews *(J M Andrews)* 9 Nimrod Close, Sandpit Lane, ST. ALBANS, AL4 9XY.

Jane Miners *(J Miners)* 2 Turlake Mews, Cowley, EXETER, EX5 5ER.

Jane Moore *(J E Moore)* 3 John Morgan Close, HOOK, HAMPSHIRE, RG27 9RP.

Jane Palmer *(J I Palmer)* 18 Exeter Drive, Haughton Grange, DARLINGTON, DL1 2SE.

Jane Smith *(J M Smith)* 8 Kingland Drive, LEAMINGTON SPA, WARWICKSHIRE, CV32 6BL.

Jane Waksman ACA *(J M Waksman)* 1 Parkhill Road, Hale, ALTRINCHAM, CHESHIRE, WA15 9JX. and at LONDON

Ⓟ**Jane Wasden, trading name of Jane Wasden Limited** *(J A Wasden)* 77a South Hill Road, Thorpe St Andrew, NORWICH, NR7 0LR.

Ⓐ**Janelle Lankester** *(C A Lankester)* The Foundry, 9 Park Lane, Puckeridge, WARE, SG11 1RL.

Janet Ainsworth Accountancy Services *(J Ainsworth)* 18 Weylands Grove, Pendleton, SALFORD, M6 7WU.

Janet Coish *(J A Coish)* 2 Paradise Square, BEVERLEY, HU17 0HG.

Ⓟ**Janet Essex, trading name of Janet Essex Limited** *(J Wielenga-Essex)* Saville Court, 11 Saville Place, Clifton, BRISTOL, BS8 4EJ.

Janet Hobbs *(J E Hobbs)* Rush Court Nurseries, WALLINGFORD, OX10 8LJ.

Janet Jesson *(J C Jesson)* 31 Withenfield Road, MANCHESTER, M23 9BT.

Janet M. White ACA *(J M White)* 43 Sparch Hollow, May Bank, NEWCASTLE, STAFFORDSHIRE, ST5 9PE.

Janet R. Banning *(J R Banning)* 11 Teresa Walk, Muswell Hill, LONDON, N10 3LL.

Janet Roberts *(J M Roberts)* 112 - 114 St. Marys Road, MARKET HARBOROUGH, LEICESTERSHIRE, LE16 7DX.

Janet Robinson & Co *(J Robinson)* Victoria Loft, Hill Furze, Bishampton, PERSHORE, WR10 2NB.

Janet Turley FCA *(J V Turley)* Manor Barn, 4 The Rickyard, Newton Blossomville, BEDFORD, MK43 8AF.

ⓅⒶ**Jani Taylor Associates Limited** *(R C Jani)* Office 6A, Popin Business Centre, South Way, WEMBLEY, HA9 0HF.

Janice Hill Accounting Services *(J L Hill)* 41 Forsythia Drive, CARDIFF, CF23 7HP.

Janice Lightley *(J E Lightley)* 36 Graham Park Road, NEWCASTLE UPON TYNE, NE3 4BJ.

Janine Wallage *(J Wallage)* 53 Ducksett Lane, Eckington, SHEFFIELD, S21 4BS.

Janis Webster *(J Kennard)* Tannery Cottage, Style Loke, Barford, NORWICH, NR9 4BE.

ⒻⒶ**Jaquest & Co** *(G N Jaquest)* 29 Little Meadow, Loughton, MILTON KEYNES, MK5 8EH.

Jar & Associates *(H Ng Hing Cheung)* Hillgate Place, 8 Nahaboo Solim Street, PORT LOUIS, MAURITIUS.

Ⓟ**Jarvis & Co Business Services Ltd** *(K L Jarvis)* 75 Main Road, ROMFORD, RM2 5EL.

Ⓕ**Jasani & Co** *(M A M Jasani)* 380 Cherry Hinton Road, CAMBRIDGE, CB1 8BA.

Jasani & Co *(A Jasani)* 23 Wetherby Close, Queniborough, LEICESTER, LE7 3FR.

ⒻⓅ**Jasper Corporate Finance, trading name of Jasper CF Limited** *(M Asplin, G R Hemington, D A Tucker)* 80 Caroline Street, BIRMINGHAM, B3 1UP.

Ⓕ**Jassal & Company** *(R K Jassal)* 829 Stratford Road, Springfield, BIRMINGHAM, B11 4DA.

ⓉⒶ**Javed & Co** *(Z Haq, R Javed, M A A Nomani)* 109 Hagley Road, Edgbaston, BIRMINGHAM, B16 8LA.

Jay & Co *(J D Patel)* 12 Cherry Tree Close, Hughenden Valley, HIGH WYCOMBE, HP14 4LP.

Jay & Co *(A J Jay)* 28 Fishpool Street, ST. ALBANS, HERTFORDSHIRE, AL3 4RT.

Jay & Co, trading name of B.Jay & Co *(B J Whitmore)* 51 Porthill Drive, Copthorne, SHREWSBURY, SY3 8RS.

Ⓟ**Jay & Company, trading name of Jay & Co London Limited** *(J M Chitroda)* 15 Alexandria Road, Ealing, LONDON, W13 0NP.

Ⓕ**Jay Patel & Co** *(J G Patel)* 278 Northfield Avenue, Ealing, LONDON, W5 4UB.

Jaya Accountancy *(N M Jayakumar)* 283a Turf Lane, Royton, OLDHAM, OL2 6ET.

ⓅⒶ**Jaydee Secretarial Ltd** *(D E Watler)* Crown Chambers, Princes Street, HARROGATE, NORTH YORKSHIRE, HG1 1NJ.

Jayes Freed *(W M Freed, H R Jayes)* C P House, Otterspool Way, WATFORD, WD25 8HP.

ⓉⒶ**Jaynes & Co** *(E J Coeshall)* 20 New Street, BRAINTREE, CM7 1ES.

ⒻⓅ**Jayson Consulting, trading name of Jayson Business Consultants Limited** *(G R Jayson)* Hillsdown House, 32 Hampstead High Street, LONDON, NW3 1QD.

★**JBS Accountants LLP** *(M A Thomas)* 2 Fairfield Road, Ainsdale, SOUTHPORT, MERSEYSIDE, PR8 3LH.

Ⓟ**JC Payroll Services Ltd** *(S L Bedford, M N Farwell, T J Goodsell, R C Holland, A R Peal, A Rann, N A Rogers, S R Staunton, A P Whalley)* Mill House, Overbridge Square, Hambridge Lane, NEWBURY, BERKSHIRE, RG14 5UX.

★**JCK Shum Leung Luk & Co.** *(J C K Leung, W W R Luk)* 2nd Floor, Jonsim Place, 228 Queen's Road East, WAN CHAI, HONG KONG ISLAND, HONG KONG SAR.

JD Accountants *(J Danan)* Katzenelbogen, St. 48/1, 93871 JERUSALEM, ISRAEL.

JD Price Consulting Ltd *(J D Price)* 6 Isis Close, Long Hanborough, WITNEY, OXFORDSHIRE, OX29 8JN.

ⒻⓅ**JDC, JDC Corporate Finance, trading names of Jon Dodge & Co Ltd** *(J R Dodge)* Dencora Court, 2 Meridian Way, NORWICH, NR7 0TA.

ⓅⒶ**JDH Business Services Ltd** *(J D Henry)* Carreg Lwyd, Cefn Bychan Road, Pantymwyn, MOLD, CLWYD, CH7 5EW.

JDK Accounting *(D N Kennard)* 16 Crown Acres, East Peckham, TONBRIDGE, KENT, TN12 5HB.

Ⓟ**Jeal & Co, trading name of Jeal & Co Limited** *(I R Jeal)* Sovereign House, 51 High Street, WETHERBY, LS22 6LR.

Ⓟ**Jean Ingram, trading name of Jean Ingram Limited** *(J P Ingram)* 106a High Street, CHESHAM, BUCKINGHAMSHIRE, HP5 1EB.

Jean M. Carless *(J M Carless)* Tudor Cottage, Leamoor Common, Wistanstow, CRAVEN ARMS, SY7 8DN.

Jeff Butt & Co *(J A Butt, J N Butt)* Broadacres, The Ridge, Woodfalls, SALISBURY, SP5 2LQ.

ⓅⒶ**Jeff Hartstone Limited** *(J L Hartstone)* Berg Kaprow Lewis LLP, 35 Ballards Lane, LONDON, N3 1XW.

Ⓟ**Jeffers & Stock, trading name of Jeffers & Stock Ltd** *(I S Jefferies)* The Orchard, Mithian, ST. AGNES, CORNWALL, TR5 0QF.

Jeffery Edelman & Co. *(J Edelman)* 22 Draycot Road, LONDON, E11 2NX.

Jefferys, Houghton & Co *(J K Houghton)* The Commercial Centre, 6 Green End, Comberton, CAMBRIDGE, CB23 7DY.

ⒻⒶ**Jeffrey A Huddart** *(J A Huddart)* 164 Walkden Road, Worsley, MANCHESTER, M28 7DP.

ⒻⒶ**Jeffrey Altman & Company** *(J A Altman, M D Altman)* Wayman House, 141 Wickham Road, Shirley, CROYDON, CR0 8TE.

Jeffrey Gold & Co *(J D Gold)* Turnberry House, 1404-1410 High Road, Whetstone, LONDON, N20 9BH.

Ⓐ**Jeffrey H. Kahan** *(J H Kahan)* 5 Aprey Gardens, LONDON, NW4 2RH.

Ⓕ**Jeffrey James** *(J Kaye)* First Floor, 421A Finchley Road, Hampstead, LONDON, NW3 6HJ.

Ⓕ**Jeffrey Nedas & Co** *(J L Nedas)* 24 Upper Brook Street, LONDON, W1K 7QB.

Ⓐ**Jeffreys Henry & Co** *(A J Harvey)* Finsgate, 5-7 Cranwood Street, LONDON, EC1V 9EE.

ⓉⒻⒶ**Jeffreys Henry LLP** *(A J Harvey, J Isaacs, N P Michaels, S R Parmar, J Randall, M S Tenzer)* Finsgate, 5-7 Cranwood Street, LONDON, EC1V 9EE.

★**Jeffreys Livemore** *(D Jeffreys)* 112 The Lindens, LOUGHTON, ESSEX, IG10 3HU. and at WOODFORD GREEN

Jellybean Accounts *(L C Jessop)* White House Farm, Church Lane, East Cottingwith, YORK, YO42 4TL.

Ⓟ**Jen Consulting Ltd** *(J Shah)* 30 Deane Croft Road, PINNER, MIDDLESEX, HA5 1SR.

Ⓟ**Jenemi Associates Ltd** *(R M F Pola)* The Dormers, Low Road, Congham, KING'S LYNN, NORFOLK, PE32 1AE.

Jenifer H Simm *(J H Simm)* Tun Mead, Gussage All Saints, WIMBORNE, BH21 5ET.

Jenkin & Co *(R Jenkin)* 28 Waterloo Street, WESTON-SUPER-MARE, AVON, BS23 1LN.

Ⓟ**Jenkins & Co, trading name of Jenkins & Co 2004 Limited** *(P K Jenkins)* 86 Mildred Avenue, WATFORD, WD18 7DX.

Ⓟ**Jenner & Co, trading name of Jenner Accountants Ltd** *(G R Jenner)* 245 Queensway, Bletchley, MILTON KEYNES, MK2 2EH.

Jennifer Cole *(J D Cole)* The Rookery, Burton Hill, MALMESBURY, WILTSHIRE, SN16 0EL.

Jennifer Hanlon *(J E I Hanlon)* Wisteria Cottage, Mendlesham Road, Cotton, STOWMARKET, SUFFOLK, IP14 4RB.

Jennifer Jones ACA *(J L Jones)* 2 Sandholes, Farnsfield, NEWARK, NOTTINGHAMSHIRE, NG22 8HQ.

Jennifer Paul *(J C Paul)* 8 Southall Drive, Hartlebury, KIDDERMINSTER, WORCESTERSHIRE, DY11 7LD.

ⓅⒶ**Jennifer Richardson, trading name of Jennifer M Richardson Limited** *(J M Richardson)* 43A High Street, Newington, SITTINGBOURNE, KENT, ME9 7JR.

Jennifer Sturt *(J M Sturt)* 16 North Street, Rothersthorpe, NORTHAMPTON, NN7 3JB.

Jennifer Todd *(J Todd)* Fairgreen Cottage, Clamhunger Lane, Mere, KNUTSFORD, WA16 6QG.

Jennings & Co *(P W Jennings)* The Sharman Law Building, 1 Harpur Street, BEDFORD, MK40 1PF.

Jennings & Co *(I P Jennings, J Jennings)* 6 New Laithe Close, SKIPTON, BD23 6AZ.

Jennings T. H. Wong & Company *(T J Wong)* Unit 406, Hua Qin International Building, 340 Queens Road, CENTRAL, HONG KONG SAR.

Ⓟ**Jenny Barnes & Co Limited** *(J C Barnes)* 1st Floor Offices, 2A Highfield Road, RINGWOOD, HAMPSHIRE, BH24 1RQ.

Jenny Kun & Co., CPA *(M J Kun)* Room 1112, 11/F, Hollywood Plaza, 610 Nathan Road, MONG KOK, KOWLOON HONG KONG SAR.

Ⓐ**Jenny Regan** *(J Regan)* Ffoslas, Penuwch, TREGARON, DYFED, SY25 6RA.

ⒻⓅ**Jenson Solutions, trading name of Jenson Solutions Limited** *(P N Jenkinson)* Communications House, 26 York Street, LONDON, W1U 6PZ.

Jeremy Barnes & Co *(J J K Barnes)* Outmoor Barn, Hale House Lane, Churt, FARNHAM, GU10 2NG.

Jeremy Benjamin *(J D Benjamin)* Ground Floor Flat, 47 Bynes Road, SOUTH CROYDON, SURREY, CR2 0PY.

Jeremy Ellison BSc FCA *(J S Ellison)* Delamore, Long Lane, Shaldon, TEIGNMOUTH, DEVON, TQ14 0HB.

★**Jeremy Francis** *(J I Francis)* 8 De Freville Avenue, CAMBRIDGE, CB4 1HR.

Jeremy G. Stone *(J G T Stone)* 197 Bristol Point, LONGWOOD, FL 32779, UNITED STATES.

Jeremy Hopkinson & Co *(J S F Hopkinson)* 12 Heath Road, Great Brickhill, MILTON KEYNES, MK17 9AL.

Ⓣ**Jeremy Knight & Co, trading name of Jeremy Knight & Co LLP** *(R E Floyd, W J J Knight)* 68 Ship Street, BRIGHTON, BN1 1AE. and at GUILDFORD

Ⓐ**Jeremy Marc Andrews** *(J M Andrews)* Milroy House, Sayers Lane, TENTERDEN, KENT, TN30 6BW.

ⓅⒶ**Jeremy Richards Limited** *(J B Richards)* Dafferns LLP, 1 Eastwood, Harry Weston Road, Binley Business Park, COVENTRY, CV3 2UB.

ⒻⒶ**Jeremy Scholl & Company** *(J S Scholl)* 20-21 Jockey's Fields, LONDON, WC1R 4BW.

Ⓐ**Jeremy Stewart** *(J D Stewart)* Basepoint Centre, 70 The Havens, IPSWICH, IP3 9BF.

ⓉⒻⒶ**Jeremy Williams & Co, trading name of Griffiths Marshall** *(R G Apted, C J Bourne, S J Humphries, I J Price)* Beaumont House, 172 Southgate Street, GLOUCESTER, GL1 2EZ. and at LYDNEY

Ⓟ**Jeremy Windows, trading name of Jeremy Windows Ltd** *(J F G Windows)* 5 Beauley Road, BRISTOL, BS3 1PX.

Ⓟ**Jerrett, trading name of Accountants You Can Talk With Limited** *(C H Jerrett)* 38 Worple Road, STAINES, TW18 1EA.

Ⓣ**Jerroms LLP** *(N Currie)* The Exchange, Haslucks Green Road, Shirley, SOLIHULL, B90 2EL.

Jerroms, trading name of Alan Thompson *(A R Thompson)* Brockhampton House, Brockhampton Park, Bringsty, WORCESTER, WR6 5TB.

ⓉⓅⒶ**Jervis & Partners, trading name of Jervis Limited** *(M J Mead, N R Picton)* 20 Harborough Road, Kingsthorpe, NORTHAMPTON, NN2 7AZ. and at RUSHDEN, WELLINGBOROUGH

Jessie Yung CPA *(J M C Yung)* 17/F Yue On Commercial Building, 385-387 Lockhart Road, WAN CHAI, HONG KONG ISLAND, HONG KONG SAR.

Ⓟ**Jessop & Barnes Business Advisers Ltd** *(M N Jessop)* 32 Coppin Hall Lane, MIRFIELD, WEST YORKSHIRE, WF14 0EJ.

Jessup & Co *(B E Jessup)* 44 Athol Street, Douglas, ISLE OF MAN, IM1 1JB.

Ⓟ**Jewkes Consulting Limited** *(D W Jewkes)* Red Lodge, The Village, Kingswinford, DUDLEY, WEST MIDLANDS, DY6 8AY.

JF Clarkson *(J F Clarkson)* 16 Ffynone Drive, SWANSEA, SA1 6DD.

ⓅⒶ**JFA, trading name of JFA Accountancy Limited** *(J P Flanaghan)* 24 Foregate Street, WORCESTER, WR1 1DN.

JFU CPA *(C J Fu)* Suite 2808, 28F Exchange Tower, 33 Wang Chiu Road, KOWLOON BAY, KOWLOON, HONG KONG SAR.

JGA *(A Grogan, J F Grogan)* St James's Court, Brown Street, MANCHESTER, M2 1DH.

Ⓟ**JGCA Limited** *(J M Glover)* Yew Tree Cottage, Northchapel, PETWORTH, WEST SUSSEX, GU28 9HL.

JGM Accounting Services *(J G Marks)* 71 Church Road, HAYLING ISLAND, PO11 0NR.

Ⓟ**JH Boston & Co, trading name of JH Boston & Co Limited** *(J H Boston)* Ebor Cottage, 80 High Street, Bempton, BRIDLINGTON, YO15 1HP.

JH Maddrell ACA *(J H Maddrell)* 1 Meadowfield, Port Erin, ISLE OF MAN, IM9 6PH.

JHH Mounsey FCA *(J H H Mounsey)* Owl Cote, 12 Park West, Heswall, WIRRAL, CH60 9JF.

JHS Associates *(J H Simpson)* 37 Cricklewood Drive, Penshaw, HOUGHTON LE SPRING, TYNE AND WEAR, DH4 7EA.

Jill Bolton Professional Services *(J H Bolton)* 69 Broomfield, LEEDS, LS16 7AD.

Jim Carpenter *(J J Carpenter)* 12 Juniper Road, Boreham, CHELMSFORD, CM3 3DB.

Jimmy C H Cheung & Co *(C H J Cheung)* 1607 Dominion Centre, 43 Queen's Road East, WAN CHAI, HONG KONG SAR.

Ⓟ**Jiva Capital, trading name of Jiva Capital Limited** *(A Paliwal)* 9 Crondal Place, Edgbaston, BIRMINGHAM, B15 2LB. and at LONDON

Ⓟ**JJ Accountancy Ltd** *(I H Restell)* 41 Alma Way, FARNHAM, SURREY, GU9 0QN.

JJ Walker LLP *(J J Walker)* 16 Old Queen Street, LONDON, SW1H 9HP.

JJW *(J J F Wilson)* 235 Cassiobury Drive, WATFORD, WD17 3AN.

Ⓐ**JK Accountancy (Manchester), Tax Support, trading names of Kevin M Pitchford & Co** *(K M Pitchford)* Building 67, Europa Business Park, Bird Hall Lane, Cheadle Heath, STOCKPORT, SK3 0XA.

JK Randle International Ltd *(J K Randle)* XKPMG House, King Ologunkuntere Street, Park View Estate, Ikoyi, LAGOS, NIGERIA.

Ⓟ**JKCA Business Support Ltd** *(J F E Kerr)* 375 Eaton Road, West Derby, LIVERPOOL, L12 2AH.

JL Advisory, trading name of JL Advisory LLP *(R L Judson, E M Little)* 48 Chester Road, Poynton, STOCKPORT, CHESHIRE, SK12 1HA.

JLA Accounting *(J L Allan)* 32 Collingsway, West Park, DARLINGTON, COUNTY DURHAM, DL2 2FD.

Ⓟ**JM Accountancy Ltd** *(K Scott)* 5 Beach Road, SOUTH SHIELDS, TYNE AND WEAR, NE33 2QA.

Ⓟ**JM Accountants Limited** *(J M Malloy)* 137 Cherry Crescent, ROSSENDALE, LANCASHIRE, BB4 6DS.

Ⓟ**JMA Solutions, trading name of JMA Solutions Ltd** *(J M Astles)* 22 Dunmow Hill, FLEET, HAMPSHIRE, GU51 3AN.

Ⓟ**JMC Accountants Limited** *(J M Cooke)* The Old Bell, Bell Lane, Nuthampstead, ROYSTON, HERTFORDSHIRE, SG8 8ND.

Ⓟ**JMG Accountancy Services Ltd** *(J M Godsell)* 7 The Brookmill, Coley Park Farm, READING, RG1 6DD.

Ⓟ**JML Accountancy, trading name of JML Business Services Ltd** *(J E Cast)* 25 Church Street, GODALMING, SURREY, GU7 1EL.

JMP Accounting *(J M Przybycin)* 36a Warsash Road, Warsash, SOUTHAMPTON, SO31 9HX.

Ⓟ**JMR Financial Consultancy Ltd** *(M M Raval)* Flat 5, Embassy Court, 76 Kenton Road, HARROW, MIDDLESEX, HA3 8BB.

JN Oswell *(J N Oswell)* Church View House, Becketts Lane, Chilmark, SALISBURY, SP3 5BD.

JND Accounting, trading name of Jon Dawson and Company *(J N Dawson)* Midland Works, Station Road, Carlton, NOTTINGHAM, NG4 3AT.

Joan L. Freiwald & Co *(J L Roberts)* 60 Pangbourne Drive, STANMORE, HA7 4RB.

Ⓟ**Joanna Williams, trading name of Williams Accountancy Services Limited** *(J Williams)* Manor Farm, Church Road, Glatton, HUNTINGDON, CAMBRIDGESHIRE, PE28 5RR.

Joanne Adolphus FCA *(J Adolphus)* Aigburth, 1 Seymour Place, Mile Path, WOKING, SURREY, GU22 0JX.

Joanne Bellew *(J L Bellew)* 1 Pier Close, Portishead, BRISTOL, BS20 7BU.

Joanne Marsh & Co *(J Marsh)* 24 Amaroo Avenue, ELANORA HEIGHTS, NSW 2101, AUSTRALIA.

Joanne Olley *(J N Olley)* 31 Denton Crescent, Black Notley, BRAINTREE, ESSEX, CM77 8ZZ.

Joanne Yeates *(J C Yeates)* 4 Basted Mill, Basted Lane, Crouch, SEVENOAKS, KENT, TN15 8LP.

ⓉⓅ**Joannides & Co Limited** *(C Loizou, E Papakyriacou)* 13 Agiou Prokopiou Street, PO Box 25411, CY-1309 NICOSIA, CYPRUS. and at LARNACA, LIMASSOL

Ⓟ**Jody Associates Limited** *(J J Joseph, A Kahan)* 923 Finchley Road, LONDON, NW11 7PE.

Joe Saldanha & Co *(J M Saldanha)* 164 Rochdale Road, Royton, OLDHAM, OL2 6QF.

John & Anne Hudson *(A E Hudson, J C M Hudson)* 15 Neville Close, BASINGSTOKE, RG21 3HG.

Ⓐ**John & Co** *(D P Grammer)* 60 Lansdowne Place, HOVE, BN3 1FG.

John A Grou *(J A Grou)* Finches, Little Hill, West Chiltington, PULBOROUGH, RH20 2PU.

John A Newman MA FCA MAAT *(J A Newman)* Thornford House, Church Road, Thornford, SHERBORNE, DORSET, DT9 6QE.

ⒻⓅⒶ**John A Roberts & Co, trading name of John A Roberts & Co Ltd** *(A K Fawbert)* 42 Sheffield Road, CHESTERFIELD, DERBYSHIRE, S41 7LL.

ⓉⒻⒶ**John A Tuffin & Co LLP** *(P J Tuffin, R Q A Tuffin)* 12-13 Ship Street, BRIGHTON, BN1 1AD.

John A. Edgar & Company *(R D Lonsdale)* 7 Merefield, Astley Village, CHORLEY, PR7 1UP.

John A.L.Carslake *(J A L Carslake)* 29 Beckett Road, WORCESTER, WR3 7NH.

John Adcock & Co *(O J W Adcock)* 7 Marlborough Road, EXETER, EX2 4TJ.

Ⓐ**John Alderdice & Son** *(M Brolly, J N Straughan)* 21 Sherburn Terrace, CONSETT, DH8 6ND.

John Andrew *(J Andrew)* Green Tree Barn, Faraday Road, KIRKBY STEPHEN, CUMBRIA, CA17 4QL.

John Armistead *(J G H L Armistead)* 9 West Park Road, Scalby, SCARBOROUGH, YO13 0PX.

Ⓕ**John Ashley** *(J A Ashley)* Oake House, The Tolleys, Mill Street, CREDITON, DEVON, EX17 1HG.

Ⓟ**John Ayre Limited** *(J L Ayre)* 29a Shaw Lane, Holbrook, BELPER, DERBYSHIRE, DE56 0TG.

John B Pheby *(J B Pheby)* 44 Flint Way, PEACEHAVEN, EAST SUSSEX, BN10 8GN.

John Beaumont & Co *(J Beaumont)* 159 Stamford Street, ASHTON-UNDER-LYNE, LANCASHIRE, OL6 6XW.

ⓉⒻⓅⒶ**John Belford & Co Ltd** *(P R Bailey, J Belford, L B Tattersall)* 14a Main Street, COCKERMOUTH, CUMBRIA, CA13 9LQ.

★ⓉⒻⓅⒶ**John Benson & Company, trading name of JBC Accountants Ltd** *(J A Benson)* First Floor, Swift House, 26 Falcon Court, Preston Farm Industrial Estate, STOCKTON-ON-TEES, CLEVELAND TS18 3TX.

John Bevan *(J G Bevan)* Underhill, SOUTH BRENT, TQ10 9DZ.

Ⓣ**John Bird** *(J W Bird)* 38 Northgate Street, LEICESTER, LE3 5BY.

Ⓟ**John Buckley Limited** *(J A Plinston)* Mansfield House, 139 Shirley Road, CROYDON, CR0 7LR.

John Bunster *(J Bunster)* 24 Hillway, Tranmere Park, Guiseley, LEEDS, LS20 8HB.

John Buse & Co *(J A Buse)* Shears Farmhouse, Umborne, Shute, AXMINSTER, EX13 7QL.

Ⓟ**John C Kirk, John C Kirk Taxation Service, trading names of Cottage Properties Ltd** *(R C Ogle)* The Elms, Doncaster Road, ROTHERHAM, SOUTH YORKSHIRE, S65 1DY.

John C Walker *(J C Walker)* 11 Allergill Park, Upperthong, HOLMFIRTH, West Yorkshire, HD9 3XH.

Ⓕ**John C. Briggs** *(J C Briggs)* 54 Church Street, Warsop, MANSFIELD, NOTTINGHAMSHIRE, NG20 0AR.

★**John C. Emery & Co** *(J C Emery)* 20 Bodiam Road, Greenmount, BURY, BL8 4DW.

John C. Glover *(J C Glover)* 2 Deepdale, Wilnecote, TAMWORTH, B77 4PD.

John Cannon & Co *(J W Cannon)* The Gables, 47 Efflinch Lane, Barton-under-Needwood, BURTON-ON-TRENT, STAFFORDSHIRE, DE13 8EU.

John Capper & Co *(J A Capper)* 12 West Drive, Cheddleton, LEEK, STAFFORDSHIRE, ST13 7DW.

John Clarke & Co *(J D Clarke)* 22 Hope Street, Douglas, ISLE OF MAN, IM1 1AP.

John Cossins & Co *(J C Cossins)* Mulberry House, 11 Oxfield Close, BERKHAMSTED, HP4 3NE.

John Cowley *(J Cowley)* Bramleys, Bath Road, STURMINSTER NEWTON, DORSET, DT10 1EB.

Ⓐ**John Cowling & Co** *(J H Cowling)* 1 Britten Close, Great Berry, Langdon Hills, BASILDON, ESSEX, SS16 6TB.

John Cracknell *(J D Cracknell)* Mark House, Aviary Road, Pyrford, WOKING, GU22 8TH.

ⓉⒻⒶ**John Crook & Partners** *(P Bridges, B D Hunt, I A Hunt, G G Prosser, M Woodgate)* 255 Green Lanes, Palmers Green, LONDON, N13 4XE.

Ⓟ**John Cumming Ross Limited** *(B B Patel)* 1st Floor, Kirkland House, 11-15 Peterborough Road, HARROW, MIDDLESEX, HA1 2AX.

John D Capewell *(J D Capewell)* 47 Hockley Lane, Netherton, DUDLEY, DY2 0JW.

★ⒻⓅⒶ**John D Kilby & Co, trading name of John D Kilby & Co Limited** *(J D Kilby)* Mutfords, Hare Street, BUNTINGFORD, HERTFORDSHIRE, SG9 0ED.

John D Lancaster & Co *(J D Lancaster)* Tenpenny House, Colchester Main Road, Alresford, COLCHESTER, CO7 8DJ.

John D Trinham *(J D Trinham)* 30a South Road, STOURBRIDGE, WEST MIDLANDS, DY8 3YB.

John D. Coleman *(J D Coleman)* Howards, Middle Street, Nazeing, WALTHAM ABBEY, EN9 2LH.

Ⓕ**John D. Owen** *(J D Owen)* Commerce House, 34-38 King Street, NEWCASTLE, STAFFORDSHIRE, ST5 1HX.

Ⓕ**John Dauncey FCA** *(J A Dauncey)* New Farm, Colesden, BEDFORD, MK44 3DB.

★ⒻⒶ**John Davies and Co** *(T J Howard Davies)* St Andrews House, Yale Business Village, Ellice Way, WREXHAM, CLWYD, LL13 7YL.

John Davis & Associates *(D J Davis)* 24 Pentwyn Isaf, Energlyn, CAERPHILLY, MID GLAMORGAN, CF83 2NR.

★Ⓐ**John Davis & Co** *(J C Arnold)* 172 Gloucester Road, BRISTOL, BS7 8NU.

Ⓟ**John E Gayer Limited** *(J E Gayer)* Glebe House, Danby Wiske, NORTHALLERTON, NORTH YORKSHIRE, DL7 0LY.

John E. Lavender *(J E Lavender)* 4 Fox Lane, BROMSGROVE, WORCESTERSHIRE, B61 7NL.

John E. Powell *(J E Powell)* 24 Colebrook Road, BRIGHTON, BN1 5JH.

Ⓣ**John Ellis & Co** *(K J Chester, J G Ellis)* The Barn, 173 Church Road, Northfield, BIRMINGHAM, B31 2LX.

John F Hallmark *(J F Hallmark)* Moonrakers, 29 Overton Shaw, EAST GRINSTEAD, RH19 2HN.

ⓉⒻⓅⒶ**John F Harvey, trading name of John F Harvey Limited** *(J Husband)* Dynevor House, 5-6 De la Beche Street, SWANSEA, SA1 3HA.

Ⓐ**John F. Kennedy** *(J Kennedy)* Fiteco - Sevres, 25 Avenue De L Europe, BP 56, 92312 SEVRES, FRANCE.

John F. McGlinchey *(J F McGlinchey)* 1st Floor, Champleys Mews, Market Place, PICKERING, YO18 7AE.

Ⓐ**John F. Mould & Co** *(M Thomas)* 19/20 Baxter Gate, LOUGHBOROUGH, LE11 1TG.

John F. Peters *(J F Peters)* 1 Peacewood Mews, Montville Drive, Les Vardes, St. Peter Port, GUERNSEY, GY1 1BY.

Ⓟ**John F. Williams & Co Ltd** *(J F Williams)* Elizabethan House, 8 George Lane, MARLBOROUGH, SN8 4BT.

John F.D. Ashby *(J F D Ashby)* Braeside, 39 Silverdale Road, EASTBOURNE, EAST SUSSEX, BN20 7AT.

John Fenton-Jones *(J F Fenton-Jones)* 50 Taleworth Road, ASHTEAD, SURREY, KT21 2PY.

John Foley *(J Foley)* 5 Sedge Mead, Netley Abbey, SOUTHAMPTON, SO31 5EY.

John Foster & Co *(J M Foster)* Office Four, 3 Edgar Buildings, BATH, BA1 2FJ.

John G. Jones *(J G Jones)* 8 Briars Close, COVENTRY, CV2 5JR.

Ⓐ**John Gale Associates** *(J R Gale)* 415 Hillcross Avenue, MORDEN, SM4 4BZ.

Ⓟ**John Galpert, S L Galpert & Co, trading names of S.L. Galpert & Co Ltd** *(J B Galpert)* 6 Montpelier Rise, LONDON, NW11 9SS.

ⒻⒶ**John Girdlestone** *(J Girdlestone)* Waterside Court, Falmouth Road, PENRYN, TR10 8AW.

John Graham & Co *(J Graham)* The Mews House, Mordiford, HEREFORD, HR1 4LN.

★ⒻⒶ**John Graham & Co** *(A S Fisher, J M Graham)* 30 Birkenhead Road, Hoylake, WIRRAL, CH47 3BW.

John Graves FCA *(J M Graves)* Heatherlea House, East End, LYMINGTON, SO41 5ST.

John H Fox & Co *(J H Fox)* 14 North Park Grove, Roundhay, LEEDS, LS8 1JJ.

John H Smith *(J H Smith)* Little Acre, Perryfields Road, BROMSGROVE, B61 8QW.

John H. Hadley *(J H Hadley)* 28 Littlegreen Road, Woodthorpe, NOTTINGHAM, NG5 4LN.

Ⓐ**John H. Miller & Co** *(J H Miller)* 21 Elm Road, ORPINGTON, KENT, BR6 6BA.

John H. Nixon & Co *(J R Hiley, N J Nixon)* Athena House, 35 Greek Street, STOCKPORT, SK3 8BA.

John Halsall *(J A S Halsall)* Cherwell, Remenham Lane, Remenham, HENLEY-ON-THAMES, RG9 3DB.

John Hardcastle *(J Hardcastle)* 3 Church Green, Stanford in the Vale, FARINGDON, OXFORDSHIRE, SN7 8LQ.

John Harrild & Co. *(J Harrild)* 501A Prescot Road, Old Swan, LIVERPOOL, L13 3BU.

Ⓟ**John Harrison & Co, trading name of John Harrison (Worksop) Limited** *(J Harrison)* 78 Carlton Road, WORKSOP, S80 1PH.

John Hayes FCA, trading name of J.A. Hayes *(J A Hayes)* Les Chalumaux, Val Au Bourg, St. Martins, GUERNSEY, GY4 6EP.

John Hayward Associates *(J A I Hayward)* 4 Marco Road, Hammersmith, LONDON, W6 0PN.

John Hine & Company *(J S Hine)* Slade House, Kirtlington, OXFORD, OXFORDSHIRE, OX5 3JA.

Ⓟ**John Hine Partnership Limited** *(J S Hine)* Slade House, Kirtlington, KIDLINGTON, OXFORDSHIRE, OX5 3JA.

John Holdaway *(J E Holdaway)* Plum Cottage, Honeysuckle Lane, Headley Down, BORDON, GU35 8JA.

John Horton FCA *(J T Horton)* PO Box 52020, 4060 LIMASSOL, CYPRUS.

Ⓟ**John Horton Ltd** *(J P Horton)* 15 Malham Drive, LINCOLN, LINCOLNSHIRE, LN6 0XD.

ⓅⒶ**John Hubbard Ltd** *(J M Hubbard)* 3 St. Marys Street, WORCESTER, WR1 1HA.

John Ingham *(J Ingham)* 5 Victoria Street, GLOSSOP, SK13 8HT.

John J McKenna *(J J McKenna)* 16 Wilder Grove, HARTLEPOOL, CLEVELAND, TS25 4PB.

John J. Sheahan & Co *(J J Sheahan)* Blackwater House, Mallow Business Park, MALLOW, COUNTY CORK, IRELAND. and at COACHFORD

John Jenkins & Co *(J M Jenkins)* Seal Lodge, Simms Lane, Mortimer, READING, RG7 2JP.

John K Hicks & Co *(J K Hicks)* 81 Penn Place, Northway, RICKMANSWORTH, HERTFORDSHIRE, WD3 1QG.

John K Shepherd FCA *(J K Shepherd)* 33 Beechwood Avenue, MELTON MOWBRAY, LEICESTERSHIRE, LE13 1RT.

ⓉⒶ**John Kerr** *(J Casimo, D S Glover)* 369-375 Eaton Road, West Derby, LIVERPOOL, L12 2AH.

John Kershaw *(Lord Kershaw)* 38 High View, Hempsted, GLOUCESTER, GL2 5LN.

John L Bird *(J L Bird)* The Old Vicarage, Loves Green, Highwood, CHELMSFORD, CM1 3QG.

ⓅⒶ**John L Dalton & Co Ltd** *(J L Dalton)* 47 St. Pauls Close, Farington Moss, LEYLAND, PR26 6RT.

John L Davies *(J L Davies)* 24 Thirlestane Close, KENILWORTH, CV8 2PW.

Ⓕ**John L. Hinkley** *(J L Hinkley)* 4 Greenacres, Ponteland, NEWCASTLE UPON TYNE, NE20 9RT. and at CORBRIDGE

John Lea & Co *(J E Lea)* Naldretts Tower House, Mill Lane, Hurstpierpoint, HASSOCKS, WEST SUSSEX, BN6 9HL.

Ⓐ**John Lloyd & Co.** *(J C Lloyd)* Coles House, 64d Central Road, WORCESTER PARK, KT4 8HY.

Ⓟ**John Lyddon Limited** *(J W Lyddon)* Uplands, Manor Estate, Horrabridge, YELVERTON, DEVON, PL20 7RS.

John Lyons & Co *(J G Lyons)* Unit 44B, Capital Court, Ffordd William Morgan, St. Asaph Business Park, ST. ASAPH, CLWYD LL17 0JG.

John M Hanks *(J M Hanks)* 50 Thames Street, OXFORD, OX1 1SU.

John M Nixon & Company *(J M Nixon)* 39 Wynford Avenue, West Park, LEEDS, LS16 6JN.

John M. Williams *(J M Williams)* 9 Wieland Rd, NORTHWOOD, HA6 3RD.

John Manners *(J M Manners)* 3 Field Hurst, Scholes Lane Scholes, CLECKHEATON, BD19 6NG.

Ⓟ**John Martyn Limited** *(J H Martyn)* Cages Farm, Tuffields Road, Whepstead, BURY ST. EDMUNDS, SUFFOLK, IP29 4TL.

Ⓟ**John McCarthy Consulting Limited** *(J G M McCarthy)* 53 Watson Drive, KILLINEY, COUNTY DUBLIN, IRELAND.

Ⓟ**John Morgan FCA, trading name of John Morgan (Accountancy) Ltd** *(J J Morgan)* Ivy Cottage, Sennybridge, BRECON, LD3 8PG.

John Murrell FCA *(J Murrell)* 8 Lawn Crescent, Thorpe End, NORWICH, NR13 5BP.

John Murrin FCA MIoD *(R J Murrin)* 6 Church Street, PADSTOW, CORNWALL, PL28 8BG.

John N. Allen *(J N Allen)* 15 Ellis Avenue, Onslow Village, GUILDFORD, GU2 7SR.

John N.G. Howitt *(J N G Howitt)* 2 The Paddock Attenborough, Beeston, NOTTINGHAM, NG9 6AR.

ⒻⒶ**John Needham & Co.** *(John Needham)* Shefford Business Centre, 71 Hitchin Road, SHEFFORD, SG17 5JB.

Ⓕ**John Nicol & Co** *(J Nicol)* 161 Park Lane, MACCLESFIELD, SK11 6UB.

Ⓟ**John Nicol Ltd** *(J Nicol)* 161 Park Lane, MACCLESFIELD, CHESHIRE, SK11 6UB.

John P Lister *(J P Lister)* Bay Tree House, 8 Oak Lawn, NEWTON ABBOT, DEVON, TQ12 1QP.

Ⓐ**John P. Murtagh & Co** *(L A K Murtagh, R D Murtagh)* 36 Arden Close, Balsall Common, COVENTRY, CV7 7NY.

John Phillips *(J I Phillips)* 387 Chartridge Lane, CHESHAM, BUCKINGHAMSHIRE, HP5 2SL.

Ⓟ**John Plinston Limited** *(J A Plinston)* Mansfield House, 139 Shirley Road, CROYDON, CR0 7LR.

John Plows *(J G Plows)* 30 Carlton Road, Caversham Heights, READING, RG4 7NT.

★ⓅⒶ**John Potter & Harrison, trading name of JPH Ltd** *(J A Hyde, I D Riding)* 112-114 Whitegate Drive, BLACKPOOL, FY3 9XH. and at LYTHAM ST. ANNES

John Pratt & Co *(J P Pratt)* Basford House, 29 Augusta Street, LLANDUDNO, Clwyd, LL30 2AE.

John Price *(J B Price)* 1b Oxford Street, CHELTENHAM, GLOUCESTERSHIRE, GL52 6DT.

Ⓟ**John Price & Co, trading name of John Price & Co Ltd** *(J L Price)* 18 Archer Road, PENARTH, SOUTH GLAMORGAN, CF64 3HW.

Ⓟ**John Pulford & Co Ltd** *(J D Pulford)* 21 Picksley Crescent, Holton le Clay, Grimsby, LINCOLNSHIRE, DN36 5DR.

ⒻⒶ**John Purvis & Co** *(J Purvis)* Riverbank House, 1 Putney Bridge Approach, Fulham, LONDON, SW6 3JD.

John R Chamberlain *(J R Chamberlain)* Westcott, 16 Western Road, HENLEY-ON-THAMES, RG9 1JL.

John R Hetherington *(J R Hetherington)* 7 Seafield Road, LONDON, N11 1AR.

John R. Agnew *(J R Agnew)* 11 Waterloo Drive, Scartho Top, GRIMSBY, NORTH LINCOLNSHIRE, DN33 3SQ.

John Reyersbach & Co *(J Q Reyersbach)* The Old Post Office, High Street, Hartley Wintney, HOOK, HAMPSHIRE, RG27 8NZ.

John Richards Accountancy Services *(J E Richards)* Westgate House, 134-136 Westgate, GUISBOROUGH, NORTH YORKSHIRE, TS14 6NB.

John Ritchie *(J A Ritchie)* Downsview, 1 Brambles, HASSOCKS, BN6 8EQ.

John Robson *(J S Robson)* PO Box 56958, Muswell Hill Broadway, LONDON, N10 9AY.

John Roger Murray Roach *(J R M Roach)* 1 St. Andrew's Drive, Holmes Chapel, CREWE, CW4 7DN.

John Roulstone *(J A Roulstone)* 12 Silver Street, Chacombe, BANBURY, OXFORDSHIRE, OX17 2JR.

John Roux *(J Roux)* 25 Old Woods Hill, TORQUAY, TQ2 7NR.

Ⓐ**John S Culwick** *(J S Culwick)* 9 Uplands Road, HOCKLEY, ESSEX, SS5 4DL.

John S Danson & Co *(J S Danson)* 35 Salisbury Road, DRONFIELD, DERBYSHIRE, S18 1UG.

John S McCuin Bsc FCA *(J S McCuin)* 21 Repton Gardens, ROMFORD, RM2 5LS.

John S Ward & Co LLP *(S J Rouse)* 1 London Road, KETTERING, NN16 0EF.

John S. Morris *(J S Morris)* Rowan House, New Lane Hill, Tilehurst, READING, RG30 4JJ.

John S.G. Carew *(J S G Carew)* 20 Brunel Drive, Upton Grange, Upton, NORTHAMPTON, NN5 4AF.

Ⓕ**John Simpkins & Co** *(J Simpkins)* 12 Stake Lane, FARNBOROUGH, HAMPSHIRE, GU14 8NP.

Ⓣ**John Smart** *(J W Smart)* Delfan, New Park Terrace, Treforest, PONTYPRIDD, CF37 1TH.

Ⓟ**John Smith & Co, trading name of J S Accountants Ltd** *(J A Smith)* 11 Upper Hollis, GREAT MISSENDEN, HP16 9HP.

Ⓟ**John Snell Ltd** *(M J Snell)* 302 Hursley Road, Chandlers Ford, EASTLEIGH, SO53 5PF.

John Sowerby *(J Sowerby)* 9 Dyson Drive, KETTERING, NN16 9HR.

Ⓐ**John Stent** *(J H Stent)* 30 Elizabeth Drive, Hartford, HUNTINGDON, CAMBRIDGESHIRE, PE29 1WA.

Ⓐ**John Stephenson** *(J W Stephenson)* 3 Bank Cottages, Teeton, NORTHAMPTON, NN6 8LL.

John Stone *(J C Stone)* Hillcrest, Main Street, Elton, MATLOCK, DE4 2BU.

Ⓕ**John Sudworth** *(J Sudworth)* 5 The Street, Molash, CANTERBURY, CT4 8HH.

John T. Hill *(J T Hill)* Sycamore House, Church Street, Birlingham, PERSHORE, WR10 3AQ.

John T. Noble *(J T Noble)* 273 High Street, EPPING, ESSEX, CM16 4DA.

John Taylor *(H J C Taylor)* 11 Jacobean Lane, Copt Heath, SOLIHULL, B93 9LP.

Ⓟ**John Tiller Consulting, trading name of John Tiller Associates Limited** *(J A Tiller)* Glenthorne, Elmstead Road, WEST BYFLEET, SURREY, KT14 6JB.

Ⓕ**John Traynor & Co** *(J T Traynor)* 35 Stockdale Drive, Whittle Hall, WARRINGTON, WA5 3RU.

John Turner FCA *(J J Turner)* Berkshire House, 252/256 Kings Road, READING, RG1 4HP.

John V Blakeborough *(J V Blakeborough)* 5 Adel Park Croft, LEEDS, LS16 8HT.

John V. Barton *(J V Barton)* 29 Garstang Road, PRESTON, PR1 1LA.

John W A Fox *(J W A Fox)* 270 Singlewell Road, GRAVESEND, KENT, DA11 7RE.

ⓅⒶ**John W Atkinson FCA, trading name of J W Atkinson Ltd** *(J W Atkinson)* First Floor, Gloucester House, Clarence Court, Rushmore Hill, ORPINGTON, KENT BR6 7LZ.

John W J Wright FCA *(J W J Wright)* 13 Market Place, UTTOXETER, STAFFORDSHIRE, ST14 8HY.

Ⓟ**John W Timmis, trading name of John W Timmis Ltd** *(J W Timmis)* Beggars Roost, Whitegates Lane, WADHURST, EAST SUSSEX, TN5 6QG.

ⒻⒶ**John W. Hirst & Co** *(J W Moss)* 62 Wellington Road South, STOCKPORT, SK1 3SU.

John W. Pack *(J W Pack)* 3 Leydens Court, Hartfield Road, EDENBRIDGE, KENT, TN8 5NH.

John Ward & Co *(J D Ward)* 10 Steelstown Road, LONDONDERRY, COUNTY LONDONDERRY, BT48 8EU.

John Warwick & Co. *(J A Warwick)* Flat 308 Peninsula Apartments, 4 Praed Street, Paddington, LONDON, W2 1JE.

John Watkins *(J Watkins)* 67 Park Road, WOKING, GU22 7DH.

John Weston *(J T Weston)* Rhodenwood, 40 Hillcrest Road, CAMBERLEY, GU15 1LG.

ⒻⓅ**John Wheeler, trading name of J. W. C. A Ltd** *(J R Wheeler)* 1 Victoria Road, EXMOUTH, DEVON, EX8 1DL.

John White *(J R White)* 1 Egliston Road, LONDON, SW15 1AL.

Ⓐ**John Wildman** *(J D Wildman)* 15 Grove Place, BEDFORD, MK40 3JJ.

John Willan FCA *(J A Willan)* 54 Hertford Street, CAMBRIDGE, CB4 3AQ.

John William Haley *(J W Haley)* Hame, Stodmarsh Road, CANTERBURY, CT3 4AP.

John Williams & Co *(D J Williams)* Westerview, Grimshaw Green Lane, Parbold, WIGAN, LANCASHIRE, WN8 7BB.

John Williams & Co *(J B Williams)* 1 The Royal, Hoylake, WIRRAL, MERSEYSIDE, CH47 1HS.

ⒻⒶ**John Williams & Co, trading name of JW & Co LLP** *(J R Williams)* Chart House, 2 Effingham Road, REIGATE, SURREY, RH2 7JN.

Ⓕ**John Winlo Hoar** *(J W Hoar)* Spinney Cottage, 68 Brattlewood, SEVENOAKS, TN13 1QU.

John Woodman *(J Woodman)* 3 Cadman House, Off Peartree Road, COLCHESTER, CO3 0NW.

ⓉⒻⒶ**John Yelland & Company** *(J A Yelland)* 22 Sansome Walk, WORCESTER, WR1 1LS.

Johnny Ho & Co *(J C K Ho)* Suite 3108 A, Tower 2 Lippo Centre, 89 Queensway, ADMIRALTY, HONG KONG SAR.

ⒻⓅⒶ**Johns Jones & Lo, trading name of Johns Jones & Lo Limited** *(D K W Lo)* 14 Lambourne Crescent, Cardiff Business Park, Llanishen, CARDIFF, CF14 5GF.

Johnson & Co *(A A M Johnson)* 239 Moor End Lane, BIRMINGHAM, B24 9DS.

Johnson & Co *(D R Johnson, G A Johnson)* Hawthorne House, 28 Cowgate, Welton, BROUGH, NORTH HUMBERSIDE, HU15 1NB.

Johnson & Co *(J W Ferguson)* 14 Parkgate Road, Neston, NESTON, CH64 9XE.

Ⓐ**Johnson & Co** *(D V Johnson)* 5 Lothian Wood, TADWORTH, SURREY, KT20 5DQ.

ⓉⒻⒶ**Johnson Holmes & Co.** *(G R H Holmes, P A Johnson)* Towlers Court, 30a Elm Hill, NORWICH, NR3 1HG.

Ⓟ**Johnson Hunt (UK) Ltd** *(C B Hunt, J N White)* Pelham Business Centre, 16 Dudley Street, GRIMSBY, SOUTH HUMBERSIDE, DN31 2AB.

ⓉⒻⒶ**Johnson Murkett & Hurst** *(P J Nash, A W Stant, A J Turland)* Rawdon House, Rawdon Terrace, ASHBY-DE-LA-ZOUCH, LE65 2GN. and at LEICESTER

ⓉⓅⒶ**Johnson Smith & Co, trading name of Johnson Smith & Co Ltd** *(M B Brooks)* Northumberland House, Drake Avenue, STAINES, MIDDLESEX, TW18 2AP.

Ⓟ**Johnson Smith Associates Ltd** *(C D Johnson)* PO Box 2499, Elizabethan Square, 80 Shedden Road, GEORGE TOWN, GRAND CAYMAN, KY1-1104 CAYMAN ISLANDS.

ⓉⒻⒶ**Johnson Tidsall** *(D Hobbs, D J Mellor, R E Minns, S P Robotham, B A Scott)* 81 Burton Road, DERBY, DE1 1TJ.

ⓉⓅⒶ**Johnson Walker, trading name of The Johnson Walker Partnership Limited** *(A Needham)* Horizon House, 2 Whiting Street, SHEFFIELD, S8 9QR.

Ⓟ**Johnson White Accounting Ltd** *(C M White)* 7 Highcliffe Close, Woodley, READING, BERKSHIRE, RG5 4RE.

Ⓟ**Johnson, Murkett & Hurst (Computer Services) Ltd** *(P J Nash, A W Stant, A J Turland)* Rawdon House, Rawdon Terrace, 1-3 Station Road, ASHBY-DE-LA-ZOUCH, LEICESTERSHIRE, LE65 2GN.

ⒻⓅⒶ**Johnsons Accountants Limited** *(K Seaton, D J Walker)* 2 Hallgarth, PICKERING, NORTH YORKSHIRE, YO18 7AW.

ⓉⒻⓅⒶ**Johnsons, trading name of Johnsons Financial Management Ltd** *(D M Turner)* 2nd Floor, 109 Uxbridge Road, LONDON, W5 5TL.

★Ⓣ**Johnston Carmichael** *(E J Atkinson, I M Lewis, B Main, J Waugh)* Bishops Court, 29 Albyn Place, ABERDEEN, AB10 1YL. and at EDINBURGH

★ⓉⒶ**Johnstone Howell & Co** *(A M Bagnall, L Glasman)* Fairfield House, 104 Whitby Road, ELLESMERE PORT, CHESHIRE, CH65 0AB.

Ⓟ**Jolliffe Cork Consulting Limited** *(J S Crossley, T Hill, A D Hydes, C L Lawton, A R N Perkin)* 33 George Street, WAKEFIELD, WEST YORKSHIRE, WF1 1LX.

ⒻⒶ**Jolliffe Cork Hardy, trading name of Jolliffe Cork Hardy LLP** *(J P Hardy, A D Hydes, C L Lawton, A R N Perkin)* Market Place, OSSETT, WEST YORKSHIRE, WF5 8BQ.

ⓉⒻⒶ**Jolliffe Cork, trading name of Jolliffe Cork LLP** *(J S Crossley, T Hill, A D Hydes, C L Lawton, A R N Perkin)* 33 George Street, WAKEFIELD, WEST YORKSHIRE, WF1 1LX.

Jolly & Co *(B S Jolly)* Aashiana, Broomfield Close, GREAT MISSENDEN, HP16 9HX.

ⒻⒶ**Jon Catty & Company** *(J Catty)* 12 Durham Road, LONDON, N2 9DN.

Ⓟ**Jon Catty Consultants Limited** *(J Catty)* 12 Durham Road, LONDON, N2 9DN.

Ⓟ**Jon Chapple & Co, trading name of Chapple Accounting Services Ltd** *(J R Chapple)* 77 Chapel Street, BILLERICAY, ESSEX, CM12 9LR.

ⓉⒻⒶ**Jon Child & Co** *(S J Child, D W Remington)* 107 Oldham Street, MANCHESTER, M4 1LW.

Ⓟ**Jon Endeacott Ltd** *(J C Endeacott)* 66 Meols Drive, Hoylake, WIRRAL, MERSEYSIDE, CH47 4AW.

ⓉⒻⓅⒶ**Jon Essam & Co Ltd** *(J C S Essam)* 23 Cottingham Way, Thrapston, KETTERING, NORTHAMPTONSHIRE, NN14 4PL.

ⓅⒶ**Jon Glasner Limited** *(J D Glasner)* 21 Bedford Square, LONDON, WC1B 3HH.

Jon Mills FCA *(J C Mills)* The Old School House, Church Lane, Easton, WINCHESTER, HAMPSHIRE, SO21 1EH.

ⒻⒶ**Jon Ransom** *(J P Ransom)* Office 7a, Unit 16, Dinan Way Trading Estate, Concorde Road, EXMOUTH, DEVON EX8 4RS.

Jonathan Andrew *(J G Andrew)* 1A The Homend, LEDBURY, HR8 1BN.

ⓅⒶ**Jonathan Carter Ltd** *(W J Carter)* 50-52 Aire Street, GOOLE, NORTH HUMBERSIDE, DN14 5QE.

Jonathan Chaytor *(J Chaytor)* The Old Vicarage, Lord Sefton Way, Great Altcar, LIVERPOOL, L37 5AA.

ⓉⒻⓅ**Jonathan Ford & Co Limited** *(J R Ford)* The Coach House, 31 View Road, Rainhill, PRESCOT, MERSEYSIDE, L35 0LF.

Jonathan G. Simons *(J G Simons)* Office No 1, Paris House, Market Square, RUGELEY, WS15 2BL.

Jonathan Kendal & Co *(J D Kendal)* 4 Holt Close, LONDON, N10 3HW.

Ⓟ**Jonathan Loescher, trading name of Jonathan Loescher & Co Ltd** *(J A Loescher)* Cherry Trees, 17 Flats Lane, Weeford, LICHFIELD, WS14 9QQ.

Ⓟ**Jonathan Orchard, trading name of Jonathan Orchard Ltd** *(J R Orchard)* 2 Ash View, Randwick, STROUD, GLOUCESTERSHIRE, GL6 6JF.

Jonathan P B Harris FCA *(J P B Harris)* The Paddock, Ulting Lane, Ulting, MALDON, CM9 6QY.

Jonathan Penn and Company *(J H Penn)* Firs Farmhouse, Fishponds Way, Haughley, STOWMARKET, IP14 3PJ.

ⓉⓅ**Jonathan Round Accountancy Services Ltd** *(J P Round)* 14-15 Regent Parade, HARROGATE, NORTH YORKSHIRE, HG1 5AW.

Ⓟ**Jonathan Sands, trading name of Jonathan Sands Associates Limited** *(J R Sands)* 12 Fratton Road, PORTSMOUTH, HAMPSHIRE, PO1 5BX.

Jonathan Shelley & Co *(J Shelley)* 15 Alconbury Close, BOREHAMWOOD, HERTFORDSHIRE, WD6 4QG.

Jonathan T Cox *(J T Cox)* 26 Anagh Coar Close, Douglas, ISLE OF MAN, IM2 2BG.

Ⓣ**Jonathan Vowles** *(J C Vowles)* 114 High Street, Cranfield, BEDFORD, MK43 0DG.

Ⓟ**Jonathan Vowles Bookkeeping Services Ltd** *(J C Vowles)* 114 High Street, Cranfield, BEDFORD, MK43 0DG.

Ⓟ**Jonathan Vowles Payroll Services Ltd** *(J C Vowles)* 114 High Street, Cranfield, BEDFORD, MK43 0DG.

Jonathan W. Roberts *(J W Roberts)* Blackford Barn, Pillerton Priors, WARWICK, CV35 0PE.

Ⓟ**Jonathan Webster, trading name of J P Webster Limited** *(J P Webster)* 5 Nethergate Street, BUNGAY, SUFFOLK, NR35 1HE.

Jones & Co *(R R Jones)* Analyst House, Penthouse Suite, Peel Road, Douglas, ISLE OF MAN, IM1 4LZ.

Jones & Co Business Performance Solutions *(A N Jones, H Jones)* 333 Station Road, Dorridge, SOLIHULL, B93 8EY.

ⓅⒶ**Jones & Co, trading name of Jones & Co of York Limited** *(N Jones)* Prospect House, 148 Lawrence Street, YORK, YO10 3EB.

Jones & Dodd, trading name of Jones & Dodd LLP *(J M Dodd)* 17-19 Crabtree House, CLITHEROE, LANCASHIRE, BB7 9BU.

ⒻⒶ**Jones & Partners** *(J R Cresswell, J Lishak)* Fifth Floor, 26-28 Great Portland Street, LONDON, W1W 8AS.

Jones & Petty LLP *(E C Jones)* 21 Kelvedon Close, RAYLEIGH, ESSEX, SS6 9SQ.

ⓉⒻⓅⒶ**Jones Avens Limited** *(N D Lacey, T P Millett, C C Norwood, M Sparke)* Piper House, 4 Dukes Court, Bognor Road, CHICHESTER, WEST SUSSEX, PO19 8FX. and at SOUTHSEA

Ⓐ**Jones Boyd** *(M J Boyd, M C Jones)* 103 Station Road, ASHINGTON, NORTHUMBERLAND, NE63 8RS. and at CONSETT, DURHAM

★Ⓐ**Jones Fisher Downes** *(K J Brockwell)* Corner House, 21 Coombe Road, Chiswick, LONDON, W4 2HR.

★**Jones Harper** *(S Jones)* 25 Roseberry Road, BILLINGHAM, CLEVELAND, TS23 2SD.

ⒻⓅⒶ**Jones Harris, trading name of Jones Harris Limited** *(C F Bryning, P Neill, A D Newbold, M W Wigley)* 17 St. Peters Place, FLEETWOOD, LANCASHIRE, FY7 6EB.

Ⓟ**Jones Kinsey, trading name of Jones Kinsey Limited** *(M A Jones)* 86 The Mount, SHREWSBURY, SY3 8PL.

Jones R.A. *(R A Jones)* Tynycoed, Penybontfawr, OSWESTRY, SY10 0PB.

ⓉⒶ**Jones, Hunt & Company** *(M Jones)* Ickleford Manor, Turnpike Lane, Ickleford, HITCHIN, SG5 3XE.

Ⓟ**JonesGiles Limited** *(R I B Jones)* 11 Coopers Yard, Curran Road, CARDIFF, CF10 5NB. and at PLYMOUTH, SUTTON COLDFIELD

Ⓟ**Jonesward Ltd** *(J Ward)* 6 St. Catherine Street, CARMARTHEN, DYFED, SA31 1RE.

ⓉⒻⒶ**Jordan & Company** *(M A Jordan)* Knighton House, 62 Hagley Road, STOURBRIDGE, DY8 1QD.

Ⓟ**Jordans International, trading name of Jordans International Limited** *(R P Crew, I A Harbottle, H G M Leighton, N D Rees)* 21 St. Thomas Street, BRISTOL, BS1 6JS.

Joseph Anderson Beadle & Co *(J F Aluko, E A Fatona)* 196 High Road, LONDON, N22 8HH.

Joseph Brown *(J Brown)* The Mount, Church Lane, Kingsbury, TAMWORTH, B78 2LR.

Joseph Goh & Co *(S C Goh)* Charlene House, 44 St Margarets Road, EDGWARE, HA8 9UU.

Ⓟ**Joseph Kahan Associates Payroll Services Ltd** *(J J Joseph, A Kahan)* 923 Finchley Road, LONDON, NW11 7PE.

Ⓟ**Joseph Kahan Associates Taxation Services ltd** *(J J Joseph, A Kahan)* 923 Finchley Road, LONDON, NW11 7PE.

Ⓐ**Joseph Kahan Associates, trading name of Joseph Kahan Associates LLP** *(J J Joseph, A Kahan)* 923 Finchley Road, LONDON, NW11 7PE.

Ⓕ**Joseph Khedoory** *(J Khedoory)* Office 110, 250 York Road, Battersea, LONDON, SW11 3SJ.

Ⓟ**Joseph Kokkinos & Co Ltd** *(J A Kokkinos)* 22 Ajax Street, Ayioi Omoloyites, 1082 NICOSIA, CYPRUS. and at LONDON

ⓉⒻⒶ**Joseph Miller & Co** *(M I Cook, U Fagandini, D R Gold, C Reah, P A Robson)* Floor A, Milburn House, Dean Street, NEWCASTLE UPON TYNE, NE1 1LE.

ⓅⒶ**Joseph Morris & Co Ltd** *(J M Bloomberg)* Suite 109, Atlas Business Centre, Imex House, Oxgate Lane, LONDON, NW2 7HJ.

ⓅⒶ**Joseph Paul & Co, Roy Paul & Co, trading names of Joseph Paul & Co Ltd** *(J R Paul)* 21 Oakleigh Road North, LONDON, N20 9HE.

Ⓕ**Joseph Tseyoungsun** *(J Tse Young Sun)* Tempo House, 15 Falcon Road, LONDON, SW11 2PH.

ⓉⒶ**Josephs** *(L A Flasher)* Suite 2, Chapel Allerton House, 114 Harrogate Road, LEEDS, LS7 4NY.

Joshi & Co *(K N V Joshi)* 3A Upgate, Poringland, NORWICH, NR14 7SH.

ⓉⒻⒶ**Josolyne & Co** *(A J Earnshaw, K W McAulay, N M Pace)* Silk House, Park Green, MACCLESFIELD, CHESHIRE, SK11 7QW.

Ⓟ**Josolyne Medical Services Ltd** *(A J Earnshaw, K W McAulay, N M Pace)* Silk House, Park Green, MACCLESFIELD, CHESHIRE, SK11 7QW.

ⒻⒶ**Josolyne Rogers** *(R D Munday)* The Acorn, 10 Little Lane, Clophill, BEDFORD, MK45 4BG.

Ⓕ**Joy, Lane & Co** *(T R Stockley)* 4 South Terrace, South Street, DORCHESTER, DT1 1DE.

Joyce E. Bonney & Co. *(J E Bonney)* 30 Basin Approach, Limehouse, LONDON, E14 7JA.

Ⓟ**JP Accountancy & Taxation Solutions Ltd** *(D M Panton)* 17 St. Leonards Avenue, Kenton, HARROW, MIDDLESEX, HA3 8EJ.

JP Accounting Services *(J Price)* 15 The Paddock, Newbold Verdon, LEICESTER, LE9 9NW.

JP Associates *(Sir Jonathan Portal)* Burley Wood, Ashe, BASINGSTOKE, RG25 3AG.

JPB Bradford & Co *(J P B Bradford)* Walnut Lodge, 31 Beaumont Avenue, ST. ALBANS, HERTFORDSHIRE, AL1 4TL.

Ⓟ**JPCA Limited** *(G A J Gardner)* 15a City Business Centre, Lower Road, LONDON, SE16 2XB.

★Ⓐ**JPL** *(J P Lishak)* 110 Chandos Avenue, LONDON, N20 9DZ.

Ⓟ**JPL, trading name of JPL Accountancy Services Limited** *(J P Lishak)* 110 Chandos Avenue, LONDON, N20 9DZ.

ⓅⒶ**JPO Accountancy Limited** *(P Owen)* 5th Floor, Hanover House, Hanover Street, LIVERPOOL, L1 3DZ.

Ⓟ**JPO Associates Limited** *(M A Barnett)* 19-21 New Road, WILLENHALL, WV13 2BG.

JR *(J D Reeves, R A Reeves)* Avondale, Ellesmere Road, Wem, SHREWSBURY, SY4 5TU.

Ⓟ**JRG Auber, trading name of JRG Auber Limited** *(J R G Auber)* 2 Castle Business Village, Station Road, HAMPTON, MIDDLESEX, TW12 2BX.

JRW *(J R Whitehead)* Tan-y-Llwyn, ARTHOG, GWYNEDD, LL39 1YY.

Ⓟ**JS Outsource Solutions Limited** *(E P Atkinson)* James House, Stonecross Business Park, 5 Yew Tree Way, Golborne, WARRINGTON, CHESHIRE WA3 3JD.

Ⓣ**JS Sherwood** *(J S Sherwood)* West Cottage, Newborough End, Newborough, BURTON-ON-TRENT, STAFFORDSHIRE, DE13 8SR.

Ⓟ**JS Weber & Co Limited** *(J S Weber)* 29 Woodvale Avenue, CARDIFF, CF23 6SP.

ⓉⓅ**JS2 Limited** *(J R Sanders, J A B Speed)* 1 Crown Square, Church Street East, WOKING, SURREY, GU21 6HR. and at LONDON

Ⓟ**JSG Accountants Limited** *(J Singh)* 4 Peter James Business Centre, Pump Lane, HAYES, MIDDLESEX, UB3 3NT.

ⓉⓅⒶ**JSP Accountants, trading name of JSP Accountants Limited** *(B Singh)* First Floor, 10 College Road, HARROW, MIDDLESEX, HA1 1BE.

Ⓟ**JSW Accounting Services Limited** *(J S Williamson)* Suite F20, Twyfords House, Garner Street, STOKE-ON-TRENT, ST4 7AY.

Ⓟ**JSW Associates, trading name of JSW Associates Limited** *(J S Wasu)* Talbot House, 204-226 Imperial Drive, HARROW, HA2 7HH.

JT Financial Services *(J M Taylor)* 163 Lily Hill Street, Whitefield, MANCHESTER, M45 7SP.

JTAnalytics *(J M Teller)* 4 Leadale Road, LONDON, N16 6DA.

Ⓟ**Jude Ballard, trading name of JB Accountancy Solutions Limited** *(J Ballard)* 28 Deane Croft Road, PINNER, MIDDLESEX, HA5 1SR.

Judith Kingston *(J C Kingston)* 7 The Manor, Potton, SANDY, SG19 2RN.

Judith McMillin BSc FCA CTA *(J D Q McMillin)* Stoneleigh, Ferncliffe Drive, KEIGHLEY, WEST YORKSHIRE, BD20 6HN.

Judith Millward *(J Millward)* 31 Augustus Road, Edgbaston, BIRMINGHAM, B15 3PQ.

Ⓟ**Judy Muir, trading name of Holmcott Ltd** *(J A E Muir)* 82 High Street, TENTERDEN, KENT, TN30 6JG.

Judy Stirling *(J A Stirling)* Holly Lodge, 28 Norwich Road, Hethersett, NORWICH, NR9 3DD.

Julia Davey *(J Davey)* 60 Fen Road, Timberland, LINCOLN, LN4 3SD.

ⓉⓅⒶ**Julia New Limited** *(J B New)* Tudor House, Loxley Road, STRATFORD-UPON-AVON, WARWICKSHIRE, CV37 7DP.

Ⓟ**Julia Podmore, trading name of GCP Accountancy Services Limited** *(J B Podmore)* 54 Nelson Road, Crouch End, LONDON, N8 9RT.

Ⓟ**Julia Walters, trading name of JA Walters Limited** *(J Walters)* The Dairy, Buckwell Lane, Clifton-Upon-Dunsmore, RUGBY, CV23 0BJ.

Members in Practice and Firms - Alphabetical

Julian A Hirst - Kathleen Corbett

Julian A Hirst *(J A Hirst)* 13 York Road, SOUTHWOLD, SUFFOLK, IP18 6AN.

ⒻⒶ**Julian Chilvers** *(J D J Chilvers)* 72 Cavendish Avenue, CAMBRIDGE, CB1 7UT.

Julian Ellis *(J Ellis)* 15A Bull Plain, HERTFORD, SG14 1DX.

Julian Hall *(J Hall)* Larkfield, Ashlawn Road, RUGBY, CV22 5QE.

Ⓟ**Julian Hobbs, trading name of JLH Financial Consultancy Ltd** *(J L Hobbs)* 2 The Quadrangle, WELWYN GARDEN CITY, HERTFORDSHIRE, AL8 6SG.

Ⓘ**Julian Paul & Co.** *(J B Paul)* The Mount House, Brasted, WESTERHAM, KENT, TN16 1JB.

Ⓟ**Julian R Gronow Limited** *(J R Gronow)* Field House, Field Lane, Kemberton, SHIFNAL, SHROPSHIRE, TF11 9LR.

Ⓟ**Julian Thomas Ltd** *(J A G Thomas)* Limes Road, Kemble, CIRENCESTER, GL7 6FS.

Julian Todd *(J Todd)* Rue De France 36, B4800 VERVIERS, BELGIUM.

Julian Wills *(J C Wills)* 25 Carlyle Street, BRIGHTON, BN2 9XU.

Julie Dingwall *(J P Dingwall)* 93 Willian Way, LETCHWORTH GARDEN CITY, HERTFORDSHIRE, SG6 2HY.

Julie Hanson *(J E Hanson)* The Heights, High Molewood, HERTFORD, SG14 2PL.

Julie K Hewer *(J K Hewer)* 17 Arran Avenue, SALE, M33 3NQ.

Ⓟ**Julie Lewis, trading name of Windrush AEC Limited** *(J Lewis)* The Cottage, Fordwells, WITNEY, OXFORDSHIRE, OX29 9PP.

Julie Lucas *(J P Lucas)* Woodhouse Farm, Anson Road, Poynton, STOCKPORT, SK12 1TD.

Julie Oates ACA *(J Oates)* 2 Camlork Place, Union Mills, ISLE OF MAN, IM4 4NY.

Julie Wakeford *(J C Wakeford)* 7 The Lawns, Yatton, BRISTOL, BS49 4BG.

Juniper Accountancy *(A Cartman)* The Yews, Sandy Lane, Lower Failand, BRISTOL, BS8 3SH.

Junius C T Lung & Co *(C J Lung)* 16th Floor, Kailey Tower, 16 Stanley Street, CENTRAL, HONG KONG SAR.

Ⓟ**Jupps, trading name of Jupps Limited** *(N G A Jupp)* County House, 3 Shelley Road, WORTHING, WEST SUSSEX, BN11 1TT.

ⒾⓅⒶ**Just Audit Limited** *(R A Davis)* Unit 14, Riverside Business Centre, Foundry Lane, Milford, BELPER, DERBYSHIRE DE56 0RN.

Justin C Smith *(J C Smith)* 5 The Crescent, LYMM, CHESHIRE, WA13 0JY.

Justin Colligan ACA *(J T Colligan)* 5 Farm House Close, Whittle-le-Woods, CHORLEY, LANCASHIRE, PR6 7QN.

Justin Page Accountancy *(J R S Page)* Red Lodge, High Street, High Littleton, BRISTOL, BS39 6HW.

Ⓟ**Justwell Agencies Limited** *(B Dzialowski)* 56 Highfield Avenue, LONDON, NW11 9UD.

Ⓟ**JVP Consultants Limited** *(V M Pell)* 19 Apley Way, Lower Cambourne, CAMBRIDGE, CB23 6DF.

★ⒾⒶ**JVSA Accountants** *(C Sales)* 20 Derby Street, ORMSKIRK, LANCASHIRE, L39 2BY.

★Ⓘ**JWPCreers** *(D E Dorman, J A Farmer, S R Headley, F A Johnson, J W Machin, R Smith)* 20-24 Park Street, SELBY, NORTH YORKSHIRE, YO8 4PW. and at YORK

ⒻⒶ**JWPCreers LLP** *(D E Dorman, J A Farmer, S R Headley, F A Johnson, J W Machin, R Smith)* 20-24 Park Street, SELBY, NORTH YORKSHIRE, YO8 4PW. and at YORK

Ⓟ**K E Tubby Limited** *(K E Tubby)* Showell, New Road, NEWBURY, BERKSHIRE, RG14 7RY.

Ⓟ**K E Tubby Limited** *(K E Tubby)* Showell, New Road, Greenham, NEWBURY, RG14 7RY.

K F Yap, trading name of K F Yap & Company *(K F Yap)* 53 Tingkat 1, Bandar Raub Perdana, 27600 RAUB, PAHANG, MALAYSIA.

K Fofaria *(K N Fofaria)* 30 Ilmington Road, HARROW, MIDDLESEX, HA3 0NH.

★**K J Eaton & Company** *(P D Eaton)* 32 Main Street, Lambley, NOTTINGHAM, NG4 4PN.

ⒾⒶ**K J Pittalis & Co, trading name of K J Pittalis LLP** *(J K Pittalis)* First Floor, Global House, 303 Ballards Lane, LONDON, N12 8NP.

K K Associates *(K A Kureshi)* 5 Perivale Lodge, Perivale Lane, GREENFORD, MIDDLESEX, UB6 8TW. and at LONDON

★**K K Leong & Partners** *(K K Leong)* 7500A Beach Road, 12-313 The Plaza, SINGAPORE 199591, SINGAPORE.

K L Richardson & Co *(K L Richardson)* 20 South Close, CANNOCK, WS11 1EH.

K L Wong & Co *(K Wong)* 14/F, San Toi Building, 137-139 Connaught Road, CENTRAL, HONG KONG SAR.

K M Yap & Company *(K M Yap)* 34 Peartree Circuit, WEST PENNANT HILLS, NSW 2125, AUSTRALIA.

K N TAN *(K N Tan)* 54 Weald Lane, HARROW, MIDDLESEX, HA3 5EX.

K P M, trading name of Kevin P Moorhouse ACA *(K P Moorhouse)* 6 Royston Avenue, MANCHESTER, M16 8AL.

Ⓟ**K P Tanner Limited** *(K P Tanner)* 3-4 Westbourne Grove, HOVE, EAST SUSSEX, BN3 5PL.

Ⓟ**K R Cahill & Co, trading name of K R Cahill & Co Ltd** *(K R Cahill)* The Old Granary, Lilbourne Road, Clifton upon Dunsmore, RUGBY, WARWICKSHIRE, CV23 0BD.

Ⓕ**K S Carmichael** *(K S Carmichael)* 117 Newberries Avenue, RADLETT, WD7 7EN.

K S Sawhney *(K S Sawhney)* 104 Britannic Park, 15 Yew Tree Road, Moseley, BIRMINGHAM, B13 8NF.

Ⓟ**K W Barron Limited** *(K W Barron)* 27 Grove Road, LEE-ON-THE-SOLENT, HAMPSHIRE, PO13 9JA.

K W Lau CPA Limited *(K W Lau)* 9th Floor, Chiyu Bank Building, 78 Des Voeux Road Central, CENTRAL, HONG KONG SAR.

K Y Luk & Co *(K Y Luk)* Room 910, 9/F, 655 Nathan Road, HUNG HOM, KOWLOON, HONG KONG SAR.

Ⓟ**K&S Quality Audit, trading name of K&S Quality Audit Ltd** *(P A Koutsoftas)* PO Box 23404, CY 1683 NICOSIA, CYPRUS. and at STROVOLOS

K. Barnard *(K Barnard)* 25 Rosemary Drive, Napsbury Park, ST. ALBANS, HERTFORDSHIRE, AL2 1UD.

K. Clifford Cook *(K C Cook)* Kingsmead, Upton Road, PRENTON, CH43 7QQ.

K. F. Wong & Co *(K F Wong)* Unit 8 13/F, Rise Commercial Building, 5-11 Granville Circuit, Granville Road, TSIM SHA TSIU, KOWLOON HONG KONG SAR.

K. L. Lam & Co. *(K L Lam)* 2/F Xiu Ping Commercial Building, 104 Jervois Street, SHEUNG WAN, HONG KONG ISLAND, HONG KONG SAR.

K. Narain & Co *(K Narain)* 6A Belsize Square, LONDON, NW3 4HT.

Ⓕ**K. Robinson** *(K Robinson)* Willowcroft, Brasted Chart, WESTERHAM, TN16 1LX.

★**K. W. Wan & Company** *(K W Wan)* Room 605, 6 Floor Kai Wong Commercial Building, 222-226 Queen's Road Central, CENTRAL, HONG KONG ISLAND, HONG KONG SAR.

ⒻⒶ**K.A, trading name of Khatibi & Associates** *(I Khatibi)* 57 Hemstal Road, West Hampstead, LONDON, NW6 2AD.

Ⓐ**K.A. Johnson** *(K A Johnson)* Norfolk House, Norfolk Rd, RICKMANSWORTH, WD3 1RD.

K.A. Stokes *(K A Stokes)* 52 Liverpool Road, STOKE-ON-TRENT, ST4 1AZ.

K.A. Young *(K A Young)* 2A Fenwick Close, Goldsworth Park, WOKING, GU21 3BY.

ⒻⒶ**K.A.Farr & Co** *(K O Farr)* 6-8 Botanic Road, Churchtown, SOUTHPORT, PR9 7NG.

ⒻⒶ**K.A.Jeffries & Company** *(S A Jeffries, D C Sitch)* 18 Melbourne Grove, LONDON, SE22 8RA.

K.B. Jones *(K B Jones)* 6 Strathmore Close, Holmes Chapel, CREWE, CW4 7PP.

K.B.Tam & Co *(K B Tam)* Rooms C-F, 5th Floor, Shing Lee Commercial Building, 6-12 Wing Kut Street, CENTRAL, HONG KONG ISLAND HONG KONG SAR.

K.C. Oh & Company *(K Oh)* 8th Floor New Henry House, 10 Ice House Street, CENTRAL, HONG KONG ISLAND, HONG KONG SAR.

K.D. Mistry & Co *(K D Mistry)* 70 Station Road, NORTH HARROW, MIDDLESEX, HA2 7SJ.

K.D. Popat & Co *(K D Popat)* Kashi Nivas, 65 Ashley Park Avenue, WALTON-ON-THAMES, KT12 1EU.

K.E. Briggs *(K E Briggs)* Dukes Hagg Farmhouse, Moor Road, PRUDHOE, NE42 5PA.

K.E. Ludford *(K E Ludford)* 17 Stibbs Way, Bransgore, CHRISTCHURCH, BH23 8HG.

Ⓐ**K.E. Mathers & Co** *(K E Mathers)* Nethercroft, Upper Batley Lane, BATLEY, WF17 0AR.

ⒻⒶ**K.E. Wilson & Co** *(K E Wilson)* 40 The Highway, Great Staughton, ST. NEOTS, PE19 5DA.

ⒾⒶ**K.G. Solanki & Co** *(K G Solanki)* Hamilton House, 315 St.Saviours Road, LEICESTER, LE5 4HG.

Ⓟ**K.I.M. Business Services Ltd** *(I J H Hooper)* 111 Tankerville Drive, LEIGH-ON-SEA, ESSEX, SS9 3DB.

K.J. Dalton *(K J Dalton)* Long Lane Farm, Ickenham, UXBRIDGE, UB10 8QT.

Ⓐ**K.J. Desai & Co** *(K J S Desai)* 51 Lafone Street, LONDON, SE1 2LX.

Ⓐ**K.J. Van-Doren** *(K J Van-Doren)* The Northdown, Cranbrook Road, Goudhurst, CRANBROOK, TN17 1DP.

Ⓐ**K.J.C. Cook** *(K J C Cook)* Cuckoo Cottage, Cuckoo Lane, TONBRIDGE, TN11 0AG.

Ⓟ**K.J.Eaton & Co (Accountants) Ltd** *(P D Eaton)* Edwinstowe House, High Street, Edwinstowe, MANSFIELD, NOTTINGHAMSHIRE, NG21 9PR.

K.L. Brealey & Co. *(K L Brealey)* 26 Market Place, Huthwaite, SUTTON-IN-ASHFIELD, NG17 2QX.

K.M. Chan & Company *(K M Chan)* Room 1702, One Peking, 1 Peking Road, TSIM SHA TSUI, KOWLOON, HONG KONG SAR.

Ⓟ**K.M. Vickers & Co Ltd** *(K M Vickers)* Avon Court, 82-84 Hotwell Road, Hotwells, BRISTOL, BS8 4UB.

K.M.Elliott *(K M Elliott)* 8 The Spinney, BEACONSFIELD, BUCKINGHAMSHIRE, HP9 1SB.

Ⓐ**K.N. Shah & Co** *(K N Shah)* 232a Northolt Road, HARROW, MIDDLESEX, HA2 8DU.

★**K.P. Bonney & Co LLP** *(K P Bonney)* 50 Cleasby Road, Menston, ILKLEY, WEST YORKSHIRE, LS29 6JA.

Ⓐ**K.P. Doherty & Co** *(K P Doherty)* 22 Harlesden Walk, ROMFORD, RM3 9HS.

★**K.P. Ho & Associates** *(M K P Ho)* 80 South Bridge Road 03-01, Golden Castle Building, SINGAPORE 058710, SINGAPORE.

K.R. Burgin *(K R Burgin)* 1 Nightjar Close, Ewshot, FARNHAM, SURREY, GU10 5TQ.

K.R. Charlton *(K R Charlton)* 17 Butt Lane, Laceby, GRIMSBY, SOUTH HUMBERSIDE, DN37 7BB.

K.R. Ford FCA *(K R Ford)* Brook House, Main Street, Beckley, RYE, EAST SUSSEX, TN31 6RL.

K.R.Ham *(K R Ham)* Brambles, Noman's Chapel, Thorverton, EXETER, EX5 5JP.

ⒻⒶ**K.S. Goring & Co** *(K S Goring)* 35 Coombe Road, KINGSTON UPON THAMES, SURREY, KT2 7BA.

Ⓟ**K.S. Liu & Company, CPA Limited** *(K S Liu)* Unit 1003 10/F, Rightful Centre, 12 Tak Hing Street, TSIM SHA TSIU, KOWLOON, HONG KONG SAR.

K.S. Solomons & Co *(K S Solomons)* 6 Raleigh Close, Hendon, LONDON, NW4 2TA.

K.S. Tan & Co *(K S Tan)* 1st Floor, 10/12 New College Parade, Finchley Road, LONDON, NW3 5EP.

K.T. Low Management Services *(K T Low)* 86 Lorong Tamarino, 41500 KLANG, SELANGOR, MALAYSIA.

K.V. Laden *(K V Laden)* 7 St. Marys Road, BENFLEET, SS7 1NR.

ⒾⒶ**K.W. Bunkell & Co** *(K W Bunkell)* The Counting House, 1A Furze Hill, PURLEY, CR8 3LB.

K.W. Gordon & Co *(K W Gordon)* 32 Hillcrest, WEYBRIDGE, KT13 8EB.

K.W. Seeds FCA, trading name of K.W. Seeds *(K W Seeds)* 3 Leche Croft, BELPER, DERBYSHIRE, DE56 0DD.

Ka Lun Lam & Co *(K Lam)* Unit F 15th Floor, Seabright Plaza, 9 -23 Shell Street, NORTH POINT, HONG KONG SAR.

ⒾⓅⒶ**Kaban & Company, trading name of Percepture Ltd** *(T Kaban)* Marquis House, 68 Great North Road, HATFIELD, HERTFORDSHIRE, AL9 5ER.

ⒾⒻⓅⒶ**Kagdadia & Co, trading name of AGK Limited** *(A G Kagdadia)* 246 Narborough Road, LEICESTER, LE3 2AP. and at LEAMINGTON SPA

Kaiser Yamawaki LLP *(Z S K Husein, T Yamawaki)* Unit 4, 17 Plumbers Row, LONDON, E1 1EQ.

Kaizen Projects LLP *(W R Hockley, A C Metcalf)* Winghams House, 9 Freepost Office Village, Century Drive, Essex, COLCHESTER, CM77 8YG.

ⒾⓅⒶ**Kajaine Limited** *(J K Shah, P Shah, A Singh)* First Floor, Alpine House, Unit 2, Honeypot Lane, LONDON, NW9 9RX.

Kaleem Malik & Co *(K Malik)* House No. 9, A-Street, Off Khayaban-e-Shaheen, Defence Hsing Auth, Phase V, KARACHI PAKISTAN.

ⒾⓅ**Kallias & Associates, trading name of M Kallias & Co Ltd** *(M Kallias)* Office 202, 10 Gregoriou Xenapoulou Street, 1061 NICOSIA, CYPRUS.

★**Kallis & Partners** *(C Pieri)* Mountview Court, 1148 High Road, Whetstone, LONDON, N20 0RA.

★**Kam & Cheung** *(P S Cheung, Y T Kam)* Room 401 4th Floor, Wah Yuen Building, 149 QueenÆs Road, CENTRAL, HONG KONG SAR.

Ⓟ**Kam Ching Yu CPA Limited** *(S K Yu)* Rooms 801-2, The Centre Mark, 287-299 Queen's Road Central, CENTRAL, HONG KONG ISLAND, HONG KONG SAR.

Ⓐ**Kamal Hossain & Co** *(M M Hossain)* Suite 24, Fitzroy House, Lynwood Drive, WORCESTER PARK, KT4 7AT.

Ⓐ**Kamal J. Chopra** *(K J Chopra)* 46 Drake Road, CHESSINGTON, SURREY, KT9 1LW.

ⒻⒶ**Kambo & Co** *(H S Kambo)* 109-111 Malling Road, SNODLAND, KENT, ME6 5AB.

Ⓟ**Kamboj Associates Ltd** *(H P Kamboj)* 29 New Broadway, UXBRIDGE, UB10 0LL.

ⒻⓅⒶ**Kamini Fletcher Limited** *(K Fletcher)* Russett House, Northampton Road, Chapel Brampton, NORTHAMPTON, NN6 8AE.

Ⓐ**Kanak Juthani** *(K K R Juthani)* 209A Headstone Lane, HARROW, MIDDLESEX, HA2 6ND.

Kane Consultancy *(P M Kane)* 5 Parkgate Crescent, Hadley Wood, BARNET, HERTFORDSHIRE, EN4 0NW.

KAO Financial Management Services *(K A Oates)* 16 Buckfast Road, SALE, M33 5QB.

Ⓐ**Kapasi & Co** *(E A Kapasi)* 20 Highland Avenue, Hanwell, LONDON, W7 3RF.

Ⓟ**KAR Accountancy & Business Solutions, trading name of KAR Accountancy Services Limited** *(K A Roberts)* 11 Benedict Green, Warfield, BRACKNELL, RG42 3DW.

Karen A Sennitt FCA CTA *(K A Sennitt)* 181a Knapp Lane, Ampfield, ROMSEY, HAMPSHIRE, SO51 9BT.

Karen Anderson *(K Anderson)* 18 Brampton Chase, Lower Shiplake, HENLEY-ON-THAMES, OXFORDSHIRE, RG9 3BX.

Karen Baber *(K S Baber)* 18 Mariners Drive, Backwell, BRISTOL, BS48 3HS.

Ⓟ**Karen Crawford Limited** *(K L Crawford)* 2 Highbank, Slaughterford, CHIPPENHAM, SN14 8RG.

Karen Golden *(K V Golden)* 18 Crossley Drive, Heswall, WIRRAL, MERSEYSIDE, CH60 9JA.

Karen Hanlan Independent Examiner *(K M Hanlan)* Hollyoakes, School Lane, Lea Marston, SUTTON COLDFIELD, WEST MIDLANDS, B76 0BW.

Karen Hobday *(K L Hobday)* 24 Lynwood Grove, SALE, CHESHIRE, M33 2AN.

Karen Meades *(K L Meades)* The Old Rectory, Chipping Warden, BANBURY, OX17 1LR.

Karen Mountain *(K J Mountain)* 4/6 Royd View, Windy Bank Lane, Amblerthorn Queensbury, BRADFORD, BD13 2NW.

Ⓟ**Karen Sayers Limited** *(K P Sayers)* 29 Silver Street, Colerne, CHIPPENHAM, WILTSHIRE, SN14 8DY.

Karen Swash *(K Swash)* Hillside, Woolstone, FARINGDON, OXFORDSHIRE, SN7 7QL.

Karen Wastling BSc ACA *(K J Wastling)* 4 Dale Rise, Burniston, SCARBOROUGH, NORTH YORKSHIRE, YO13 0EG.

Karim & Co *(A Z F Karim)* 142 Edgware Way, EDGWARE, HA8 8JY.

Karl Jermyn *(K Jermyn)* 10a Whitlingham Hall, NORWICH, NORFOLK, NR14 8QH.

Ⓟ**Karrek Accountants, trading name of Karrek Accountants Limited** *(L M Mackenzie)* 9 Hilgrove Road, NEWQUAY, CORNWALL, TR7 2QY.

Ⓟ**Karsan Consulting Limited** *(H P Karsan)* Karsan Business Centre, 15 Thrale Road, (Entrance Penwortham Road), Streatham, LONDON, SW16 1NS.

Ⓟ**KAS & Co (UK) Limited** *(K Sodha)* 95 Vivian Road, BIRMINGHAM, B17 0DR.

KAS, Kelmanson Accounting Solutions, trading names of KCAS LLP *(A C Costa)* 3rd Floor, Brook Point, 1412-1420 High Road, LONDON, N20 9BH.

Ⓟ**Kase Accountancy Services Limited** *(J Shroff)* Excel House, 1 Hornminster Glen, HORNCHURCH, ESSEX, RM11 3XL.

Kate Berryman *(K Berryman)* Micklebeck, Burtons Lane, CHALFONT ST. GILES, BUCKINGHAMSHIRE, HP8 4BN.

Ⓟ**Kate Brown Accountancy Ltd** *(K M Brown)* 81 Gurney Court Road, ST. ALBANS, AL1 4QX.

Kate Brown BA ACA *(C L Brown)* The Annexe, Rectory Farm, Cranford Road, Great Addington, KETTERING, NORTHAMPTONSHIRE NN14 4BH.

Ⓟ**Kate Haynes Limited** *(K A Haynes)* 129 Woodlands Road, Little Bookham, LEATHERHEAD, KT23 4HN.

Kate Hutchins ACA *(K E M Hutchins)* 4 Brixton Terrace, HELSTON, CORNWALL, TR13 8TW.

Kate Noakes & Co *(K S Noakes)* 3 Darell Road, Caversham, READING, RG4 7AY.

Kates Accountancy Services *(K J Bowman)* 1 Woodridge Close, Edgmond, NEWPORT, SHROPSHIRE, TF10 8JF.

Ⓟ**Katharine Moss Consulting, trading name of Katharine Moss Consulting Limited** *(K M Moss)* Greyfriars Court, Paradise Square, OXFORD, OX1 1BE.

Katharine Widdowson *(K M Widdowson)* 406 Otley Road, LEEDS, LS16 8AD.

Katharine Wilding BA(Hons) ACA *(K Wilding)* Oldfield, Forestry Road, Llanferres, MOLD, CLWYD, CH7 5SH.

Katherine Mowbray *(K V Mowbray)* 17 High Street, Wainfleet, SKEGNESS, LINCOLNSHIRE, PE24 4BP.

Ⓟ**Katherine Scott Limited** *(K Scott)* 1 Landseer Drive, Marple Bridge, STOCKPORT, CHESHIRE, SK6 5BL.

Katherine Slater ACA *(K A Slater)* 29 Lime Street, RUSHDEN, NORTHAMPTONSHIRE, NN10 6DY.

Kathleen Corbett *(K S Corbett)* 44a Barclay Road, LONDON, SW6 1EH.

Kathleen M Mannion *(K M Mannion)* 221 Chamber Road, OLDHAM, OL8 4DJ.

Kathrine Stewart *(K G Stewart)* Fieldview, La Rue de Samares, St. Clement, JERSEY, JE2 6LZ.

Kathryn Garlick *(K A Garlick)* 15 Waterslea Drive, BOLTON, BL1 5FA.

ⒻⒶ**Kathryn Gigg** *(K H Gigg)* The Office, 20 Kings Lynn Road, HUNSTANTON, PE36 5HP.

Kathryn M. Young *(K M Young)* Lake Cottage, Southbury Lane, Ruscombe, READING, RG10 9XN.

Kathryn Pickering *(K L Pickering)* 15 Top Birches, ST. NEOTS, CAMBRIDGESHIRE, PE19 6BD.

Katia Barber Associates *(K Barber)* West View, Wood Lane, Bardsey, LEEDS, LS17 9AW.

Ⓟ**Katon CPA Limited** *(K Lee)* Office B, 21st Floor, Legend Tower, 7 Shing Yip Street, KWUN TONG, KOWLOON HONG KONG SAR.

Katrina Douglas *(K Douglas)* The Chapel House, The Cross, Nympsfield, STONEHOUSE, GLOUCESTERSHIRE, GL10 3TU.

Katz & Co *(S A Katz)* 135 Notting Hill Gate, LONDON, W11 3LB.

Ⓟ**Kauai, trading name of Kauai Limited** *(P B Wood)* Broombarn Lane, GREAT MISSENDEN, BUCKINGHAMSHIRE, HP16 9JD.

Kavanagh Brown & Co *(N Q Kavanagh-Brown, P Kavanagh-Brown)* 30 Wentworth Close, WATFORD, WD17 4LW.

Ⓟ**Kavanagh Knight & Co. Ltd** *(M L Wright)* Chaldean House, 7 Chandos Close, CHESTER, CH4 7BJ.

ⓅⒶ**Kavanagh Ltd** *(P J Kavanagh)* Battlefield House, Kidderminster Road, Dodford, BROMSGROVE, B61 9AD.

ⓅⒶ**Kavanaghs, trading name of Accounting Centre Eynsham Ltd** *(J S Kavanagh, K S Kavanagh)* 7-14 Station Point, Old Station Way, Eynsham Road, WITNEY, OXFORDSHIRE, OX29 4DL.

ⓉⒻⒶ**Kay Johnson Gee** *(J E Avery-Gee, J L V Beressi, R Blaskey)* Griffin Court, 201 Chapel Street, MANCHESTER, M3 5EQ.

Kay Linnell *(K C S H Linnell)* Brick Kiln Cottage, The Avenue, Herriard, BASINGSTOKE, RG25 2PR.

Ⓟ**Kay Linnell & Company Limited** *(K C S H Linnell)* Brick Kiln Cottage, The Avenue, Herriard, BASINGSTOKE, HAMPSHIRE, RG25 2PR.

Ⓟ**Kay V. Strawson & Co Limited** *(K V Strawson)* Red Cottage, Moor Road, Walesby, MARKET RASEN, LINCOLNSHIRE, LN8 3UR.

KB Accountancy *(K Bull)* Croft House Farm, Biggin Lane, Little Fenton, LEEDS, LS24 6HQ.

Ⓟ**KB Accountancy Services Ltd** *(K Burgess)* Swan Meadow Cottage, Mere Lake Road, Talke, STOKE-ON-TRENT, ST7 1UE.

★Ⓟ**KB Ferguson, trading name of KB Ferguson Limited** *(K B Ferguson, T Jones)* 95 High Street, Gorseinon, SWANSEA, SA4 4BL.

★Ⓟ**KB Ferguson, trading name of Keith B Ferguson Limited** *(K B Ferguson)* 95 High Street, Gorseinon, SWANSEA, SA4 4BL.

★Ⓐ**KBDR** *(L Butler, S J A Drummond, B R Kay)* The Old Tannery, Hensington Road, WOODSTOCK, OXFORDSHIRE, OX20 1JL.

Ⓟ**KBH Accountants Ltd** *(T Pritchard)* 255 Poulton Road, WALLASEY, MERSEYSIDE, CH44 4BT.

★ⒻⒶ**KBSP Partners LLP** *(T F Berkley, T Curzon, J Landau, M L Marks)* Harben House, 13a Harben Parade, Finchley Road, LONDON, NW3 6JP.

Ⓕ**KBSP Tax Services LLP** *(J H Simmons)* Harben House, 13a Harben Parade, Finchley Road, LONDON, NW3 6JP.

K-C Accounts, trading name of Kay Cheal *(K E Cheal)* 4 Chilcomb, BURGESS HILL, WEST SUSSEX, RH15 0DJ.

Ⓟ**KC Commercial Finance Ltd** *(D T Scott)* 15 Colburn Avenue, NEWTON AYCLIFFE, COUNTY DURHAM, DL5 7HX.

KC Ng & Company *(K C Ng)* Suite B, 13th Floor, Tak Lee Commercial Building, 113-117 Wanchai Road, WAN CHAI, HONG KONG ISLAND HONG KONG SAR.

ⓉⒶ**KC Partners** *(K B J Clive, Y V Khong)* 1st Floor, 76 New Bond Street, LONDON, W1S 1RX.

★**KCG & Co** *(C G Huynh, K C Leung)* Rooms 1401-2, 253-261 Hennessy Road, WAN CHAI, HONG KONG ISLAND, HONG KONG SAR.

Ⓟ**KCL Management Services, trading name of KCL Management Services Ltd** *(Tim Reynolds)* Kinchyle, Church Lane, Great Holland, FRINTON-ON-SEA, CO13 0JS.

Ⓕ**Keebles** *(N C Keeble)* Ivanhoe, Maitland Close, WEST BYFLEET, SURREY, KT14 6RF.

ⓉⒻⓅⒶ**Keelings, trading name of Keelings Limited** *(J Faulkner, E Pritchard, C T Wright)* Broad House, 1 The Broadway, Old Hatfield, HATFIELD, HERTFORDSHIRE, AL9 5BG.

ⓉⒻⒶ**Keen Dicey Grover** *(G J G Davies, A G Roberts)* Bathurst House, 50 Bathurst Walk, IVER, SL0 9BH.

ⓉⒶ**Keenan** *(A W Keenan)* 89-91 Marsden Road, BLACKPOOL, FY4 3BY.

Ⓐ**Keens Shay Keens Letchworth** *(B J Nicholl)* 5 Gernon Walk, LETCHWORTH GARDEN CITY, HERTFORDSHIRE, SG6 3HW.

ⓉⒻⓅⒶ**Keens Shay Keens Limited** *(P Howkins, W R Kingston, C W Little, G P C Saunders, J J Tyrrell, J S Vincent)* Christchurch House, Upper George Street, LUTON, LU1 2RS. and at BEDFORD, BIGGLESWADE

★ⓉⒻⒶ**Keens Shay Keens MK** *(P A Davis, M Rayner)* Sovereign Court, 230 Upper Fifth Street, MILTON KEYNES, MK9 2HR.

Ⓟ**Keighwood Limited** *(F K McMorran)* 12 The Range, Langham, OAKHAM, LEICESTERSHIRE, LE15 7EB.

Keith Adams *(K M Adams)* Tarn Hows, Vinegar Hill, Milford on Sea, LYMINGTON, HAMPSHIRE, SO41 0RZ.

Keith Arundale *(K Arundale)* 8 Chestnut Drive, St Leonards Hill, WINDSOR, BERKSHIRE, SL4 4UT.

Ⓟ**Keith Blaxill, trading name of Keith Blaxill Limited** *(K D Blaxill)* 12 Stevenage Road, KNEBWORTH, SG3 6AW.

Ⓐ**Keith Bridgford & Co** *(J M Bridgford)* 17 The Grove, ILKLEY, LS29 9LW.

Keith Chambers *(K Chambers)* 24 Westgate, SLEAFORD, NG34 7PN.

Ⓟ**Keith Coulson & Co Ltd** *(K D Coulson)* Benvenut, 61 Norfield Road, DARTFORD, DA2 7NY.

Keith English & Co *(N K English)* Kings Cote, 151B Kings Road, WESTCLIFF-ON-SEA, ESSEX, SS0 8PP.

Keith G Taylor FCA *(K G Taylor)* 22 Western Way, WHITLEY BAY, TYNE AND WEAR, NE26 1JE.

Keith Gregory *(K A Gregory)* 26 Barley Close, Little Eaton, DERBY, DE21 5DJ.

Keith J. Shulman *(K J Shulman)* 11 Harley Court, High Road Whetstone, LONDON, N20 0QD.

Keith Jones *(K J Jones)* 3 Tudor Grove, Church Crescent, LONDON, N20 0JW.

Keith Keyte *(K W Keyte)* Uplands, Church Hill, West Monkton, TAUNTON, SOMERSET, TA2 8QZ.

Ⓕ**Keith Lanchbury** *(K Lanchbury)* 6 West Street, Moulton, NORTHAMPTON, NN3 7SB.

Keith Lawrence *(K B Lawrence)* Haven Court, 5 Library Ramp, PO Box 900, GIBRALTAR, GIBRALTAR.

Keith McDonald *(J K McDonald)* 27 Meads Road, GUILDFORD, GU1 2NB.

Keith Older & Company *(K W Older)* 8 Barford Close, Ainsdale, SOUTHPORT, PR8 2RS.

Keith Powers *(K B Powers)* P O Box 241, Sarisbury Green, SOUTHAMPTON, SO31 1DF.

ⓉⓅ**Keith Raffan & Co, trading name of Keith Raffan & Co Limited** *(R K Raffan)* 2nd Floor, 36 Great Russell Street, LONDON, WC1B 3QB.

Ⓐ**Keith Reynolds Associates** *(J K Reynolds)* Ground Floor, 135 Bermondsey Street, LONDON, SE1 3UW.

Ⓟ**Keith Richards Limited** *(K T J Richards)* 12 Turbary Gardens, TADLEY, HAMPSHIRE, RG26 4HS.

Ⓟ**Keith Rimmer, trading name of K Rimmer Services Ltd** *(K Rimmer)* 15 Condon Road, Barrow upon Soar, LOUGHBOROUGH, LEICESTERSHIRE, LE12 8NQ.

Keith Robson *(K Robson)* 117 Roman Road, MIDDLESBROUGH, CLEVELAND, TS5 5QB.

Keith S Chapman *(K S Chapman)* 37 Church Row, BURY ST. EDMUNDS, SUFFOLK, IP33 1NT.

Ⓟ**Keith S Johnson Consulting Ltd** *(K S Johnson)* Brookside, Smiddyhill, ALFORD, ABERDEENSHIRE, AB33 8NA.

Keith S Potter, FCA, trading name of K.S. Potter *(K S Potter)* 16 Peckarmans Wood, LONDON, SE26 6RY.

Keith Saunders *(K A Saunders)* Fairview, 22 Ottershaw Park, Ottershaw, CHERTSEY, KT16 0QG.

Keith Tebbett *(K A Tebbett)* 357 Coppice Road, Arnold, NOTTINGHAM, NG5 7HH.

Keith Usher *(K Usher)* High View, 81a Main Street, Greetham, OAKHAM, RUTLAND, LE15 7NJ.

Ⓟ**Keith Vincent, trading name of Keith Vincent Limited** *(K H D Vincent)* Y Felin, Fforest, Pontardulais, SWANSEA, SA4 0YJ.

★ⒻⓅ**Keith Willis Associates Limited** *(K A Willis)* Gothic House, Barker Gate, NOTTINGHAM, NG1 1JU.

Keith Withall & Co *(K B Withall)* 303 High Street, ORPINGTON, BR6 0NN.

Keith Wong CPA & Co *(H K Wong)* Room 903, 9/F, Parkes Commercial Centre, 2 - 8 Parkes Street, TSIM SHA TSUI, KOWLOON HONG KONG SAR.

Ⓐ**Keith, Vaudrey & Co** *(J I E Borucki, T H Vaudrey)* First Floor, 15 Young Street, LONDON, W8 5EH.

Ⓟ**Kelevra, trading name of Kelevra Ltd** *(A M J Kennard)* 1 Queens Mews, Queens Road, BUCKHURST HILL, ESSEX, IG9 5AZ. and at LONDON

Kelledy & Co *(D A Kelledy)* 4 Cecil Way, Hayes, BROMLEY, BR2 7JU.

Ⓟ**Keller & Co, trading name of Keller Accountancy Services Limited** *(R F Keller)* 367b Church Road, Frampton Cotterell, BRISTOL, BS36 2AQ.

★ⓉⒻⓅⒶ**Kelley & Lowe Limited** *(B E Kelley)* Gwynfa House, 677 Princes Road, DARTFORD, KENT, DA2 6EF.

Ⓟ**Kelly Accounting Limited** *(D J Kelly)* 42 Comrie Street, CRIEFF, PERTHSHIRE, PH7 4AX.

★Ⓐ**Kelly Associates** *(S Kelly)* 4 Club Lane, Rodley, LEEDS, LS13 1JG.

★**Kelly Molyneux & Co** *(R S Molyneux)* Security House, 1 Queen Street, Burslem, STOKE-ON-TRENT, ST6 3EL.

Ⓐ**Kelly Williams** *(P Kelly)* 135/137 Queen Street, Morley, LEEDS, LS27 8HE.

Ⓟ**Kelmscott Consulting Limited** *(R D Rison)* 43 Kelmscott Road, Harborne, BIRMINGHAM, B17 8QW.

ⓉⓅⒶ**Kelsall Steele, trading name of Kelsall Steele Limited** *(M D Hutchinson, R Martin, M G Peters, B B Pooley)* Woodlands Court, Truro Business Park, Threemilestone, TRURO, CORNWALL, TR4 9NH. and at CAMBORNE

Kelvin Archer *(K Archer)* Cob Suite Old Swan House, 29 High Street, HEMEL HEMPSTEAD, HP1 3AA.

Ⓟ**Kelvin Archer Limited** *(K Archer)* Cob Suite, Old Swan House, 29 High Street, HEMEL HEMPSTEAD, HERTFORDSHIRE, HP1 3AA.

ⒻⓅⒶ**Kelvin Burke & Co Ltd** *(W H Tomlinson)* 81a Stanley Road, WAKEFIELD, WF1 4LH.

Ⓟ**Kelvin Burke & Co, trading name of Financial Consulting Services Ltd** *(W H Tomlinson)* 81A Stanley Road, WAKEFIELD, WF1 4LH.

★ⒻⒶ**Kemp & Co** *(M A Todd)* Room 2-02, The Cotton Exchange Building, Old Hall Street, LIVERPOOL, L3 9LQ.

★**Kemp Accountants** *(S M Kemp)* Little Compton, Rannoch Road, CROWBOROUGH, EAST SUSSEX, TN6 1RB.

Ⓜ**Kemp Chatteris Associates Ltd** *(S R Konfortion)* P.O. Box 322, Cerne House, La Chaussee, PORT LOUIS, MAURITIUS.

Ⓣ**Kemp Chatteris Deloitte** *(M J Burgess, T Butonkee, W Chung Nien Chin, J.P.R.De Chasteigner Du Mee, S R Konfortion, L Yeung Sik Yuen)* 7th. Floor, Raffles Tower, 19 Cybercity, EBENE, MAURITIUS.

Ⓟ**Kemp Le Tissier Limited** *(C Le Tissier)* Suite 2 Houmet House, Rue Des Houmets, Castel, GUERNSEY, GY5 7XZ.

ⓉⒶ**Kemp Taylor LLP** *(P N Foxon, G W Newbury, A K Taylor)* The Oval, 14 West Walk, LEICESTER, LE1 7NA.

Ⓟ**Kemps, trading name of Kemps Accounting Solutions Limited** *(H C Kemp)* 84 High Street, BROADSTAIRS, KENT, CT10 1JJ. and at SOUTHAMPTON

Kempster & Dale Partnership *(C E M Dale, J P Kempster)* Prospect House, 20 High Street, WESTERHAM, KENT, TN16 1RG. and at CAMBRIDGE

Ⓕ**Kempton, Emsden & Co** *(T D Wingham)* 34 Napier Road, BROMLEY, BR2 9JA.

Ⓐ**Kemsley & Co.** *(R W Kemsley)* Upper North Court, Bullens Farm Business Centre, Bullens Lane, East Peckham, TONBRIDGE, KENT TN12 5LX.

Kemsley and Company *(M Kemsley)* 12 Heathfield South, TWICKENHAM, TW2 7SS.

Ken Brew & Co *(K T Brew)* 32 Hallville Road, Mossley Hill, LIVERPOOL, L18 0HR.

Ken Chan & Co *(S K Chan)* Office No. 1818, 18/F, Beverley Commercial Centre, 87-105 Chatham Road South, TSIM SHA TSUI, KOWLOON HONG KONG SAR.

ⒻⒶ**Ken Fryer** *(K W Fryer)* 8 Coronation Road, BATH, BA1 3BH.

ⓉⒻⓅⒶ**Kench, trading name of Kench & Co Ltd** *(E A Kench)* 10 Station Road, HENLEY-ON-THAMES, OXFORDSHIRE, RG9 1AY.

ⓉⒻⒶ**Kendall Wadley, trading name of Kendall Wadley LLP** *(M A Ashworth, C W Brickell, T C P Calder, J T Marston, E D Needham)* Granta Lodge, 71 Graham Road, MALVERN, WORCESTERSHIRE, WR14 2JS. and at HEREFORD, WORCESTER

Kennedy & Co *(E S Kennedy)* 5 Gauden Road, LONDON, SW4 6LR.

Kennedy & Co *(S J D Kennedy)* ul Godebskiego 65, RASZYN, 05 090, POLAND.

Kenneth Cordeiro *(K A Cordeiro)* 26 Baronsmere Road, LONDON, N2 9QE.

Kenneth D. Elliott *(K D Elliott)* 22 Oaklands Avenue, ISLEWORTH, TW7 5PX.

ⓉⒻⒶ**Kenneth Easby LLP** *(R W Dunning, K Graham, C Hutson, M Mayman, S J Rainbow, C D Syers)* Oak House, Market Place, 35 North End, BEDALE, NORTH YORKSHIRE, DL8 1AQ. and at DARLINGTON, NORTHALLERTON

Kenneth Emery *(K J Emery)* 7 Stencills Drive, WALSALL, WS4 2HP.

Ⓕ**Kenneth H. Blears** *(K H Blears)* Church Green, 4 Church Lane, BROMSGROVE, B61 8RB.

Kenneth J Cooper FCA *(K J Cooper)* Griffin Dene, 16 Kimberley Road, Nuthall, NOTTINGHAM, NG16 1DF.

Kenneth J Winfield *(K J Winfield)* Sunnybank, Adams Hill, Clent, STOURBRIDGE, DY9 9PS.

Ⓟ**Kenneth Jones & Co, trading name of Kenneth Jones & Co Ltd** *(K E Jones)* 8 Church Avenue, Clent, STOURBRIDGE, WEST MIDLANDS, DY9 9QT.

Ⓐ**Kenneth Law Sowman & Co** *(C S Sowman)* 3 Leicester Road, Oadby, LEICESTER, LE2 5BD.

Kenneth Lewis & Co *(K R Lewis)* 22 Gelliwastad Rd, PONTYPRIDD, CF37 2BW. and at BRIDGEND

Kenneth M. Bradshaw *(K M Bradshaw)* 44 Pashley Road, EASTBOURNE, BN20 8EA.

Kenneth P Shea & Co *(K P Shea)* 25 Durnford Close, Norden, ROCHDALE, OL12 7RX.

Kenneth Wong & Co *(K S T Wong)* Unit B & C, 20/F Full Win Commercial Centre, 573 Nathan Road, MONG KOK, KOWLOON, HONG KONG SAR.

Kenny & Co *(M F Kenny)* 39 Wallace Fields, Ewell, EPSOM, KT17 3AX.

Ⓟ**Kensington Trading Co Limited** *(T S Patara)* Financial House, 352 Bearwood Road, Bearwood, BIRMINGHAM, B66 4ET.

Ⓟ**Kent & Co Ltd** *(S A D Kent)* Evans House, 107 Marsh Road, PINNER, MIDDLESEX, HA5 5PA.

Ⓟ**Kent Accounting Limited** *(A C Goreham)* Abacus House, 19 Manor Close, TUNBRIDGE WELLS, KENT, TN4 8YB.

Kent Consultancy *(R A Brooks)* PO Box 261, ST. NEOTS, PE19 9DE.

Ⓟ**Kentwell Corporation Limited** *(M I A Howell)* 86 Musters Road, West Bridgford, NOTTINGHAM, NG2 7PS.

ⓉⒻⒶ**Kershen Fairfax** *(D G Hooper, A S Kirshen)* Beacon House, 113 Kingsway, LONDON, WC2B 6PP.

ⒻⓅ**Kershen Fairfax Limited** *(D G Hooper, A S Kirshen)* Beacon House, 113 Kingsway, LONDON, WC2B 6PP.

Ⓕ**Keshani & Co** *(M Keshani, M Keshani)* 506 Kingsbury Road, LONDON, NW9 9HE. and at EDGWARE

Ⓟ**Keshani Consultancy Ltd** *(M Keshani, M Keshani)* 42 Station Road, EDGWARE, MIDDLESEX, HA8 7ZZ.

Ⓟ**Keswick Accountants Limited** *(F H Clark)* Bracken Hue, Millbeck, KESWICK, CUMBRIA, CA12 4PS.

Ⓟ**Kesworth, trading name of Kesworth Limited** *(G J Hermiston)* 8 Highgate Drive, TELFORD, SHROPSHIRE, TF2 9FE.

Ketan Patel & Co *(K Patel)* A L'Avenier, 40a Britwell Road, Burnham, SLOUGH, SL1 8AQ.

Kevan Dunn *(K P Dunn)* 18 Clavering Walk, BEXHILL-ON-SEA, TN39 4TN.

ⒻⓅ**Kevin Alderton & Team, trading name of Kevin Alderton & Team Limited** *(K R Alderton)* 14 South Way, NEWHAVEN, EAST SUSSEX, BN9 9LL.

Kevin and Anne Edwards *(K W Edwards)* Moor End, Hyde, FORDINGBRIDGE, HAMPSHIRE, SP6 2QH.

ⓉⒻⓅ**Kevin Beare & Co, trading name of Invest in UK Limited** *(K L Beare)* Forest House, 3-5 Horndean Road, BRACKNELL, BERKSHIRE, RG12 0XQ. and at LONDON

Kevin Flain Accountancy Services *(K Flain)* 52 Woodlands Road, Baughurst, TADLEY, HAMPSHIRE, RG26 5NS.

Kevin Guinness & Co *(K M Guinness)* Sibberton Lodge, Leicester Road, Thornhaugh, PETERBOROUGH, PE8 6NH.

Ⓐ**Kevin H Rourke** *(K H Rourke)* 35 Hillington Road, SALE, M33 6GQ.

Kevin How & Co *(K K How)* PO Box 11209, KOTA KINABALU, SABAH, MALAYSIA.

ⒻⒶ**Kevin J Rhind** *(K J Rhind)* Corner Cottage, Heath Road, Hempstead, NORWICH, NR12 0SH.

Ⓟ**Kevin Kearnery Associates, trading name of Kevin Kearnery Associates Ltd** *(K G Kearney)* Suite 3, Weybridge Business Centre, 66 York Road, WEYBRIDGE, KT13 9DY.

Kevin Lane *(K E Lane)* 7 Yew Tree Close, Silsoe, BEDFORD, MK45 4EQ.

Ⓟ**Kevin Loy Limited** *(I G Short)* Victoria Buildings, High Street, TAIN, ROSS-SHIRE, IV19 1AE.

Kevin M Gladders *(K M Gladders)* 40 Gildale, Werrington, PETERBOROUGH, PE4 6QY.

Kevin Whatley & Co *(K V Whatley)* 16 Gellihaf Road, Fleur de Lis, BLACKWOOD, GWENT, NP12 3UY.

Key, Pearson & Co *(G H Pearson)* 12a The Broadway, WOKING, GU21 5AP.

Ⓟ**Keynes Marshall, trading name of Leading Performance Limited** *(D French)* 21 Driftwood Avenue, ST. ALBANS, HERTFORDSHIRE, AL2 3DE.

ⓅⒶ**Keyte & Co, trading name of Keyte & Co Accountants Ltd** *(M W Keyte)* Coombe Avenue, CROYDON, CR0 5SD.

★**KFPW Pty Ltd (Knight Frank Price Waterhouse, trading name of PricewaterhouseCoopers** *(M E Batten, C Billington, M A Bridge, M J Codling, M S Colderick, C M Cuthbert, T Goldsmith, S J D Humphries, C Johnson, M J A Laithwaite, B P Lawrence, A J Loveridge, R J Millen, J.P. O'Connor, R E Prosser, K D Reeves, K R Reid, D C Romans, N A Wilson)* Darling Park Tower 2, 201 Sussex Street, GPO Box 2650, SYDNEY, NSW 1171, AUSTRALIA. and at ADELAIDE, BRISBANE, CAIRNS, CANBERRA, FORREST, HOBART, MANLY, MELBOURNE, NEWCASTLE, PERTH, SOUTH BANK, TOWNSVILLE

★Ⓣ**Khalid Majid Rehman** *(K Majid)* 1st Floor, Modern Motors House, Beaumont Road, KARACHI 46000, PAKISTAN. and at ISLAMABAD

★**Khan Wahab Shafique Rahman & Co** *(M Rahman)* 55 Dilkusha, Commercial Area, DHAKA 1000, BANGLADESH. and at CHITTAGONG, KHULNA

ⓉⓅⒶ**Khanna & Co, trading name of Khanna & Co Limited** *(A Khanna)* 6 Vicarage Road, Edgbaston, BIRMINGHAM, B15 3ES.

Ⓣ**Khans** *(M I Khan)* Bishop House, 28 Second Cross Road, TWICKENHAM, TW2 5RF.

KHMM *(K W M Man)* Lison House, 173 Wardour Street, LONDON, W1F 8WT. and at CROYDON

ⓉⒶ**Khokhar & Co** *(M I Khokhar)* 85 Shepherds Hill, Highgate, LONDON, N6 5RG.

Khoo & Associates *(E L Khoo)* 51 Jalan Alpha SS 20/1, Damansara Utama, 47400 PETALING JAYA, Selangor, MALAYSIA.

ⒻⒶ**Khoshaba & Co.** *(R K Khoshaba)* 15 Harefield Road, MAIDENHEAD, SL6 5EA.

Kl Tob *(J Wahnon)* 125 Wolmer Garden, EDGWARE, HA8 8QF.

Kiama Consulting *(M J Thomas)* 105 Lower Camden, CHISLEHURST, KENT, BR7 5JD.

Ⓐ**Kian & Co** *(K Dadfarma)* 23 Mountside, STANMORE, MIDDLESEX, HA7 2DS.

Kiat & Associates *(T K Lim)* 1st Floor 25 Seberang, Jalan Putera, 05150 ALOR STAR, KEDAH, MALAYSIA. and at KUALA LUMPUR, PENANG

Ⓐ**Kiddy & Co** *(A Kiddy)* 61 Cowbridge Road East, CARDIFF, CF11 9AE.

Ⓕ**Kidson** *(C G D Kidson)* The Harrop, 19 Anglesey Drive, Poynton, STOCKPORT, CHESHIRE, SK12 1BT.

Kieran Pierce & Co *(R K Pierce)* 15 Butterfield Park, Rathfarnham, DUBLIN 14, COUNTY DUBLIN, IRELAND.

Kierse *(E P Kierse)* 8a Convent Hill Centre, Convent Hill, KILLALOE, COUNTY CLARE, IRELAND.

★ⓉⒻⒶ**Kilby Fox** *(C Adkins, C P Beavan, G Woodhall)* 4 Pavilion Court, 600 Pavilion Drive, NORTHAMPTON, NN4 7SL.

Ⓟ**Kilda Ltd** *(L Watson)* 80 Warwick Street, OXFORD, OX4 1SY.

ⓉⓅ**Killicks Ltd** *(M Stafford)* 35/37 Kingsway, Kirkby-in-Ashfield, NOTTINGHAM, NG17 7DR.

Ⓟ**Kiloview Ltd** *(R J Baines, J Bragg, S J Caten)* Matrix House, 12-16 Lionel Road, CANVEY ISLAND, ESSEX, SS8 9DE.

ⓉⒻⒶ**Kilsby & Williams LLP** *(A Kilsby, M A McDonagh)* Cedar House, Hazell Drive, NEWPORT, GWENT, NP10 8FY.

Ⓟ**Kim Bowler & Co Limited** *(K D Bowler)* 32 Clarence Street, YORK, YO31 7EW.

Kim D Hooper *(K D Hooper)* 58 Knebworth Avenue, LONDON, E17 5AJ.

ⓅⒶ**Kimberlee & Co, trading name of Kimberlee Limited** *(N I Kimberlee)* Hunt House Farm, Frith Common, Eardiston, TENBURY WELLS, WORCESTERSHIRE, WR15 8JY.

ⒻⒶ**Kimbers** *(M D Kimber)* 20 Scillonian Road, GUILDFORD, SURREY, GU2 7PS.

ⓅⒶ**Kime O'Brien, trading name of Kime O'Brien Limited** *(G H Kime, N.D. O'Brien)* 1 Church Mews, Churchill Way, MACCLESFIELD, CHESHIRE, SK11 6AY.

Ⓟ**Kimeon Limited** *(F A Saeed)* 7 Peregrine Way, Wimbledon, LONDON, SW19 4RN.

Ⓟ**Kinetic Partners (Cayman) Limited** *(N P Matthews)* The Harbour Centre, 42 North Church Street, PO Box 10387, GEORGE TOWN, GRAND CAYMAN, KY1 1004 CAYMAN ISLANDS.

★Ⓣ**Kinetic Partners LLP** *(J W Korek, C L Mascarenhas, N P Matthews)* One London Wall, Level 10, LONDON, EC2Y 5HB.

Ⓐ**Kinetic Partners, trading name of Kinetic Partners Audit Ireland** *(M Carroll)* 1 London Wall, LONDON, EC2Y 5HB.

Ⓐ**Kinetic Partners, trading name of Kinetic Partners Audit LLP** *(M Carroll, N G Griggs, J W Korek)* One London Wall, Level 10, LONDON, EC2Y 5HB.

King & Co *(M C A King)* The Dell, Old Farm Road, HAMPTON, TW12 3RJ.

Ⓟ**King & Company, trading name of Daffurn & Co Ltd** *(P R Daffurn)* 132 Parkwood Road, BOURNEMOUTH, BH5 2BN. and at SALISBURY

★ⒻⒶ**King & King** *(R C Patel, J L Piper, J Sugarman)* Roxburghe House, 273-287 Regent Street, LONDON, W1B 2HA.

ⓉⒻⒶ**King & Taylor** *(L Chesterton, T S Climpson, K Hayman, R G H Hiscock, P Humphries)* 10-12 Wrotham Road, GRAVESEND, DA11 0PE.

Ⓟ**King Fook Business Link Ltd** *(H Ng Hing Cheung)* 8 Nahaboo Solim Street, PORT LOUIS, MAURITIUS.

ⓉⒻⒶ**King Freeman** *(T J Freeman, G D King, J W Sibley)* 1st Floor, Kimberley House, Vaughan Way, LEICESTER, LE1 4SG.

ⒻⒶ**King Loose & Co** *(H C Fanthome)* 5 South Parade, Summertown, OXFORD, OX2 7JL.

Ⓟ**King Watkins Limited** *(J A W Watkins)* The Island House, Midsomer Norton, RADSTOCK, BA3 2DZ.

ⓉⒻⒶ**King, Hope & Co** *(S Anderson, S W Gardner)* 31 Victoria Road, DARLINGTON, DL1 5SB. and at HARTLEPOOL, NORTHALLERTON

ⓉⒶ**King, Morter, Proud & Co** *(R W Brawn, J L Bromley, K M Bromley, G R Morter)* Kings Arms Vaults, The Watton, BRECON, LD3 7EF. and at BUILTH WELLS

Kingdom Powell *(J G Powell)* The Greyhound, Back Street, Reepham, NORWICH, NR10 4SJ.

ⒻⒶ**Kingett's** *(I N Kingett)* Carolyn House, 5 Dudley Road, HALESOWEN, B63 3LS.

Kingly Brookes *(M N Jones)* 415 Linen Hall, 162-168 Regent Street, LONDON, W1B 5TF.

Ⓐ**Kingly Brookes, trading name of Kingly Brookes LLP** *(M N Jones, J E Moore, J A Parsons)* 415 Linen Hall, 162-168 Regent Street, LONDON, W1B 5TE.

Ⓕ**Kingon & Co** *(N B Kingon, W M Kingon)* Green Pastures, Bullocks Farm Lane, Wheeler End, HIGH WYCOMBE, HP14 3NQ.

Ⓟ**Kings Accountancy Services Ltd** *(G G King)* 23 Porters Wood, ST. ALBANS, HERTFORDSHIRE, AL3 6PQ.

★Ⓟ**Kings Accounting House Limited** *(R H L King)* 37 Gayfere Road, EPSOM, SURREY, KT17 2JY.

ⒻⓅⒶ**Kingscott Dix (Cheltenham) Limited** *(S W Fullard, G Wala)* Malvern View Business Park, Stella Way, Bishops Cleeve, CHELTENHAM, GLOUCESTERSHIRE, GL52 7DQ.

ⒻⓅⒶ**Kingscott Dix Limited** *(S Baily, J Gorse, P H Morgan, M J Pitt, P A Reynaert, D J Turk)* 60 Kings Walk, GLOUCESTER, GL1 1LA.

Kingsley *(E J Strickland)* 25 Kingsley Drive, Cheadle Hulme, CHEADLE, CHESHIRE, SK8 5LZ.

Kingsley Accountancy *(N L Mayhew)* 18 Kingsley Way, Whiteley, FAREHAM, HAMPSHIRE, PO15 7NL.

Kingsley Sansom *(B K Sansom)* Highfield, 8 Church Hill, Shepherdswell, DOVER, KENT, CT15 7NR.

Ⓟ**Kingsleybusiness Online Limited** *(H Curtis)* Bank Chambers, 1-3 Woodford Avenue, ILFORD, ESSEX, IG2 6UF.

Ⓟ**Kingsmead Accounting Ltd** *(P H Ellis, L Leggatt)* 3 North Street, Oadby, LEICESTER, LE2 5AH.

Ⓟ**Kingsmill Ltd** *(P Haining, D J Mitchell, P A Taylor)* 75 Park Lane, CROYDON, CR9 1XS.

Ⓕ**Kingston & Co** *(A J Kingston)* Rush Lane End, Sudthorpe Hill, Fulbeck, GRANTHAM, LINCOLNSHIRE, NG32 3LE.

★**Kingston Smith & Partners LLP** *(D A Benton, N M Birch, N S J Brooks, M A Burchmore, E M Carder, P Chadda, A P Craddock, J T L Cross, S J De Lord, I M Defty, D Fecher, N M Finlayson, A G D Follows, D J Goodridge, I J Graham, K E Halstead, M G Hayes, R M Heap, M K Hindson, P R Holgate, A J Houstoun, C C Hughes, C W Ireton, C J Lane, D T Martine, M J Meadows, A Merron, D J Montgomery, T J Moore, G A Morgan, M A Muirhead, S Neal, T Park, M B Penfold, B R Pope, H M Powell, J R Riches, I Robert, P E M Samrah, J P Seymour, A N Shaw, M N Sinclair, M J Snyder, J Staniforth, T F J Stovold, R N Surman, J Sutcliffe, P J Timms, M Twum-Ampofo, G A Tyler, J I Walsh)* Devonshire House, 60 Goswell Road, LONDON, EC1M 7AD. and at ST. ALBANS

Kingston Smith Consulting LLP *(D A Benton, N M Birch, N S J Brooks, M A Burchmore, E M Carder, P Chadda, S T Clark, A P Craddock, J T L Cross, J M Dawson, S J De Lord, D Fecher, N M Finlayson, A G D Follows, D J Goodridge, I J Graham, K E Halstead, R M Heap, M K Hindson, P R Holgate, A J Houstoun, C C Hughes, C W Ireton, C J Lane, D T Martine, M J Meadows, A Merron, D J Montgomery, T J Moore, G A Morgan, M A Muirhead, S Neal, T Park, M B Penfold, B R Pope, H M Powell, J R Riches, P E M Samrah, J P Seymour, A N Shaw, M N Sinclair, M J Snyder, J Staniforth, T F J Stovold, R N Surman, J Sutcliffe, P J Timms, M Twum-Ampofo, G A Tyler, J I Walsh)* Devonshire House, 60 Goswell Road, LONDON, EC1M 7AD.

Ⓟ**Kingston Smith Services Limited** *(N S J Brooks, S Neal, M J Snyder)* Devonshire House, 60 Goswell Road, LONDON, EC1M 7AD.

★ⓉⒻⒶ**Kingston Smith W1, trading name of Kingston Smith LLP** *(D A Benton, N M Birch, N S J Brooks, M A Burchmore, E M Carder, P Chadda, S T Clark, A P Craddock, J T L Cross, J M Dawson, S J De Lord, D Fecher, N M Finlayson, A G D Follows, D J Goodridge, I J Graham, K E Halstead, R M Heap, M K Hindson, P R Holgate, A J Houstoun, C C Hughes, C W Ireton, C J Lane, D T Martine, M J Meadows, A Merron, D J Montgomery, T J Moore, G A Morgan, M A Muirhead, S Neal, T Park, M B Penfold, B R Pope, H M Powell, J R Riches, P E M Samrah, J P Seymour, A N Shaw, M N Sinclair, M J Snyder, J Staniforth, T F J Stovold, R N Surman, J Sutcliffe, P J Timms, M Twum-Ampofo, G A Tyler, J I Walsh)* Devonshire House, 60 Goswell Road, LONDON, EC1M 7AD. and at HAYES, REDHILL, ROMFORD, ST. ALBANS

Ⓟ**Kingston Smith(Bangladesh) Limited** *(M K Hindson, J Staniforth, T F J Stovold)* Devonshire House, 60 Goswell Road, LONDON, EC1M 7AD.

ⓉⒶ**Kingswood** *(J F Massing, H S Moss)* 3 Coldbath Square, LONDON, EC1R 5HL.

Ⓟ**Kingswood Corporate Finance Limited** *(J F Massing, H S Moss)* 3 Coldbath Square, LONDON, EC1R 5HL.

ⓉⓅ**Kinloch Corporate Finance Limited** *(T R Cottier)* 1 Whitehall, 1 Whitehall Road, LEEDS, LS1 4HR.

ⓉⒻⒶ**Kinnair & Company** *(M L C Mak, G Murray)* Aston House, Redburn Road, NEWCASTLE UPON TYNE, NE5 1NB.

★ⓉⒶ**Kinnaird Hill** *(A J Hurford, T P Johnson)* Montagu House, 81 High Street, HUNTINGDON, CAMBRIDGESHIRE, PE29 3NY. and at ST. IVES

★ⒻⓅⒶ**Kinsella Clarke, trading name of 61 Stanley Road Limited** *(G J J Clarke)* 61 Stanley Road, BOOTLE, MERSEYSIDE, L20 7BZ.

Ⓟ**Kinsey Jones, trading name of Learchild Limited** *(D S Kinsey, G Luke)* 4 Lansdowne Terrace, Gosforth, NEWCASTLE UPON TYNE, NE3 1HN.

★**Kinson CPA & Co.** *(C K Chow)* Room 901, Hang Seng Castle Peak Road Building, 339 Castle Peak Road, CHEUNG SHA WAN, KOWLOON, HONG KONG SAR. and at MONG KOK

ⓉⒻⓅⒶ**Kirby and Haslam, trading name of Kirby and Haslam Limited** *(A F Haslam, N G Kirby, M J Roberts)* 11 King Street, KING'S LYNN, NORFOLK, PE30 1ET.

ⒻⓅⒶ**Kirby Rookyard & Co, trading name of Kirby Rookyard Ltd** *(G L Rookyard)* 1 Castle Court, St. Peters Street, COLCHESTER, CO1 1EW.

ⓉⒻⒶ**Kirk Hills** *(S L Chamberlain, A P Hills, D G Kirk)* 5 Barnfield Crescent, EXETER, EX1 1QT.

Ⓟ**Kirk Hills Insolvency Ltd** *(S L Chamberlain, A P Hills, D G Kirk)* 5 Barnfield Crescent, EXETER, EX1 1QT.

★**Kirk Hughes Medlock** *(P K S Waltho)* Willson House, 25-31 Derby Road, NOTTINGHAM, NG1 5AW.

★ⓉⒻⓅⒶ**Kirk Newsholme, trading name of Kirk Newsholme Ltd** *(G Kirk, N A Rayland, M D Templeton, J L Wright)* 4315 Park Approach, Thorpe Park, LEEDS, LS15 8GB.

ⓉⒶ**Kirk Rice, trading name of Kirk Rice LLP** *(K A S Rice)* The Courtyard, High Street, ASCOT, BERKSHIRE, SL5 7HP.

Ⓟ**Kirkcaldy Accountancy Ltd** *(V J Kirkcaldy)* 5 Hazel Close, Chandler's Ford, EASTLEIGH, HAMPSHIRE, SO53 5RF.

ⒻⓅ**Kirkham Parry, trading name of Kirkham Parry Limited** *(J P Kirkham Parry)* Stoneybridge House, Twardreath, PAR, CORNWALL, PL24 2TY.

Ⓐ**Kirkness & Co.** *(D J Kirkness)* 21 Silver Street, OTTERY ST. MARY, EX11 1DB.

ⒻⓅⒶ**Kirkpatrick & Hopes Ltd** *(P C Williamson)* Overdene House, 49 Church Street, Theale, READING, RG7 5BX.

ⒻⒶ**Kirtley Qureshi & Co** *(N A Qureshi)* 75 Herries Road, SHEFFIELD, S5 7AS. and at BIRMINGHAM

ⒻⒶ**Kirton & Co** *(S E Kirton)* 3 Primrose Close, HEMEL HEMPSTEAD, HP1 2DL.

ⓅⒶ**Kishens, trading name of Kishens Limited** *(U V Patel)* 3 Montpelier Avenue, BEXLEY, KENT, DA5 3AP.

★ⓉⒻⒶ**Kitchen & Brown** *(B J Drew, D Goodman)* Alpha House, 40 Coinagehall Street, HELSTON, TR13 8EQ.

Ⓟ**Kite & Co Accountants Limited** *(J F Rideal)* 9 Clive House, 80 Prospect Hill, REDDITCH, WORCESTERSHIRE, B97 4BS.

Kite & Company *(J F Rideal)* 9 Clive House, 80 Prospect Hill, REDDITCH, B97 4BS.

KJ Accounting Services *(K L Jooste)* Dragons Lye, Tollgate Lane, Whitemans Green, Cuckfield, HAYWARDS HEATH, WEST SUSSEX RH17 5DJ.

KJ Consulting *(K Thomas)* Exchange Building, 66 Church Street, HARTLEPOOL, CLEVELAND, TS24 7DN.

ⓅⒶ**KJA Huque Chaudhry Limited** *(A R Effendi, M J Johnson)* 199 Roundhay Road, LEEDS, LS8 5AN.

ⓅⒶ**KJA Kilner Johnson Limited** *(N Effendi, J R Kilner)* Network House, Stubs Beck Lane, Bradford, CLECKHEATON, WEST YORKSHIRE, BD19 4TT.

KLC Kennic Lui & Co *(P Choy, L K Lui, T Yuen)* 5/F, Ho Lee Commercial Building, 38 - 44 D' Aguilar Street, CENTRAL, HONG KONG SAR.

★**Klein Evangelou** *(N J Klein)* 368 Forest Road, LONDON, E17 5JF.

ⒻⒶ**Kleinman Graham** *(J S Bennett, P R Kleinman)* Turnberry House, 1404 -1410 High Road, Whetstone, LONDON, N20 9BH.

★ⓉⒻⒶ**KLSA LLP** *(A M K Shah, H R Shah, K D Shah, S V Shah)* Klaco House, 28-30 St. John's Square, LONDON, EC1M 4DN.

★Ⓟ**KLSA Taxation Services Limited** *(H R Shah, K D Shah, S V Shah)* Klaco House, 28-30 St. John's Square, LONDON, EC1M 4DN.

Ⓟ**KM Business Advisors Limited** *(K P Muthalagappan)* 149 Warwick Road, KENILWORTH, WARWICKSHIRE, CV8 1HY.

KM Yeung & Co *(K M Yeung)* Room 405, Dominion Centre, 43-59 Queens Road E, WAN CHAI, HONG KONG ISLAND, HONG KONG SAR.

★ⓉⒻⓅⒶ**KM, trading name of K M Business Solutions Limited** *(A J Davies, R S Rothwell)* 4-6 Grimshaw Street, BURNLEY, LANCASHIRE, BB11 2AZ.

★ⒻⓅⒶ**KM, trading name of Kenneth Morris Ltd** *(T J Griffin, R S Waller)* 9-11 New Road, BROMSGROVE, WORCESTERSHIRE, B60 2JF.

Ⓟ**KMS CPA Limited** *(K M So)* Suite 1912, 19th Floor, Tower 1 The Gateway, 25 Canton Road, TSIM SHA TSUI, KOWLOON HONG KONG SAR.

ⓅⒶ**Knav, trading name of Knav UK Limited** *(I Hussain, J K Shah, A Singh)* 1st Floor, Alpine House Unit 2, Honeypot Lane, LONDON, NW9 9RX.

Ⓐ**Kneill & Co** *(M A Kneill)* Mayfield, Back Gate, Ingleton, CARNFORTH, LANCASHIRE, LA6 3BT.

★ⒻⒶ**Knight & Company** *(G W Knight)* 11 Castle Hill, MAIDENHEAD, BERKSHIRE, SL6 4AA.

ⒻⓅ**Knight Evans, trading name of Knight Evans Limited** *(N D Knight-Evans)* 11 Church Street, GODALMING, SURREY, GU7 1EQ.

ⓉⓅⒶ**Knight Goodhead, trading name of Knight Goodhead Limited** *(C J Goodhead, P I Knight)* 7 Bournemouth Road, Chandler's Ford, EASTLEIGH, HAMPSHIRE, SO53 3DA.

ⓅⒶ**Knight Wheeler & Co, trading name of Knight Wheeler Limited** *(P M P Heywood, S N Ross)* 54 Sun Street, WALTHAM ABBEY, ESSEX, EN9 1EJ.

Ⓐ**Knight-Gregson** *(M D Knight-Gregson)* 40 Kingsmere Close, Erdington, BIRMINGHAM, B24 8QL.

Knights *(T Knight)* Baxter House, 48 Church Road, ASCOT, SL5 8RR.

Knights *(S A Knight)* Europort 932, GIBRALTAR, GIBRALTAR.

Ⓟ**Knights and Company, trading name of Knights & Company(Hampton) Limited** *(V Tanna)* 280 Cooden Drive, BEXHILL-ON-SEA, EAST SUSSEX, TN39 3AB.

ⒻⓅⒶ**Knights Lowe, trading name of Knights Lowe Limited** *(P A Knights)* Eldo House, Kempson Way, BURY ST. EDMUNDS, SUFFOLK, IP32 7AR.

ⓉⒻⒶ**Knill James** *(S L Craig, S M Foster, J C Ketley, D W Martin, K S Powell, N Rawson)* One Bell Lane, LEWES, EAST SUSSEX, BN7 1JU.

Ⓟ**Knipe Whiting Heath & Associates Limited** *(J M Humby)* 1 Blackfriars Street, HEREFORD, HR4 9HS.

Ⓟ**Knipe Whiting Heath Ltd** *(C J Heath)* Turpins, St. Weonards, HEREFORD, HR2 8QG.

Ⓟ**Knoll Accounting Limited** *(H L Lever)* 30 Swanmore Road, Littleover, DERBY, DE23 3SD.

Knott Tax and Accountancy Services, trading name of Deborah Knott BA (Hons) ACA *(D Knott)* 3 Oakfield Lane, Hemingbrough, SELBY, NORTH YORKSHIRE, YO8 6RH.

ⓅⒶ**Knowles Warwick Group Limited** *(S D Knowles)* 183-185 Fraser Road, SHEFFIELD, S8 0JP.

Ⓟ**Knox & Eames, trading name of Knox & Eames Limited** *(R M Eames)* The Business Centre, Greys Green Farm, Rotherfield Greys, HENLEY-ON-THAMES, RG9 4QG.

ⓉⒻⒶ**Knox Cropper** *(J D Jones, K P Lally, B E Marshall, G N C D Stevenson, N P Wilkinson)* 8-9 Well Court, LONDON, EC4M 9DN. and at HASLEMERE, HEMEL HEMPSTEAD

Ⓟ**KNS, trading name of KNS Limited** *(K N Shah)* 11 Trinity Close, NORTHWOOD, MIDDLESEX, HA6 2AF.

Kohkar Moughal & Jackson *(K A Khokhar)* 2 Fitzroy Place, Sauciehall Street, GLASGOW, G3 7RH.

ⓉⒻⒶ**Koshal Associates** *(D Koshal)* Gautam House, 1-3 Shenley Avenue, Ruislip Manor, RUISLIP, HA4 6BP.

Ⓐ**Koten & Co** *(B Koten)* Suite 7, Essex House, Station Road, UPMINSTER, RM14 2SJ.

★**Kothari & Co** *(J J D Kothari)* Unit 1, Acton Hill Mews Business Centre, 310/328 Uxbridge Road, LONDON, W3 9QN.

Koumettou Tackoushis & Ioannou *(M C Ioannou, N I Koumettou)* Suites 204/205, 2 Katsoni Street, 150 NICOSIA, CYPRUS. and at LARNACA

Ⓟ**Kounnis and Partners Ltd** *(A C Stylianou)* Sterling House, Fulbourne Road, Walthamstow, LONDON, E17 4EE.

Ⓟ**KP Accounting Limited** *(K Blythe-Bartram)* 25 Broad View, Thorpe End, NORWICH, NR13 5DZ.

KP Cheng & Co *(K Cheng)* Room 2707, 27/F, Shui On Centre, 6-8 Harbour Road, WAN CHAI, HONG KONG SAR. and at SHANGHAI

KPA & Co *(K Parkinson-Atherton)* 41 Oakfield Road, Poynton, STOCKPORT, SK12 1AS.

Ⓟ**KPB Limited** *(K R Barry)* 30 Broadwalk, Caerleon, NEWPORT, GWENT, NP18 1NQ.

Ⓟ**KPD Business Services Limited** *(K Davies)* The Old Shippon, Bradley, FRODSHAM, CHESHIRE, WA6 7EP.

Ⓟ**KPF, trading name of KPF Accountancy Limited** *(K P Fagan)* 13 Cambridge Street, EXETER, EX4 1BY.

ⓅⒶ**KPH Audit & Assurance Services Limited** *(T Pritchard)* 255 Poulton Road, WALLASEY, MERSEYSIDE, CH44 4BT.

▽**KPMG** *(D H Calder, S A Martin, I R Moyser, P C R Ruiz, S J Scudamore)* 115 Grenfell Street, (GPO Box 2499), ADELAIDE, SA 5000, AUSTRALIA. and at ALBURY, ALICE SPRINGS, BRISBANE, CAIRNS, CANBERRA, DARWIN, KALGOORLIE, LAUNCESTON, MELBOURNE, NEDLANDS, PARRAMATTA, PERTH, SYDNEY, WANGARATTA

★**KPMG** *(A F Brame, P D Herrod)* KPMG Centre, 18 Viaduct Harbour Avenue, P.O. Box 1584, AUCKLAND 1140, NEW ZEALAND. and at CHRISTCHURCH, HAMILTON, TAURANGA, WELLINGTON

★**KPMG** *(S Sulaiman)* Unit 402-403A, Wisma Jaya, Jalan Pemanca, BANDAR SERI BEGAWAN, BS8811, BRUNEI DARUSSALAM.

▽**KPMG** *(P J Brough, J P Chattock, D J Collins, N J Debnam, S J E Gleave, A C Grassick, P Y L Kan, C W Ko, P W Kung, S H Y Lee, E S Y Li, T B Liu, Y Liu, A A Macpherson, B Nikzad, I C O'Brien, W K Siu, M J Wardle, A W B R Weir, M M C Wu)* 8/F Prince's Building, 10 Chater Road, CENTRAL, HONG KONG ISLAND, HONG KONG SAR.

KPMG *(C L Flynn)* 1 Stokes Place, St. Stephen's Green, DUBLIN 2, COUNTY DUBLIN, IRELAND. and at BELFAST, CORK

KPMG *(G T L Bullmore, S L C Whicker)* P O Box 493 Century Yard, Cricket Square, GEORGE TOWN, GRAND CAYMAN, KY1-1106, CAYMAN ISLANDS.

KPMG *(N Shah)* KPMG Crescent, 85 Empire Road, Parktown, JOHANNESBURG, 2193, SOUTH AFRICA.

★**KPMG** *(S A Sattar)* Edificio Monumental, Av. Praia da Vitoria 71-A-11o, 1069-006 LISBON, PORTUGAL. and at FUNCHAL, PORTO

★**KPMG** *(S A Poyner, A P Quinton)* Naberezhnaya Tower Complex, Block C, 10 Presnenskaya Naberezhnaya, 123317 MOSCOW, RUSSIAN FEDERATION.

Ⓣ**KPMG** *(K M Ansari)* 4th Floor HSBC Building, Muttrah Business District, PO Box 641, 112 MUSCAT, OMAN.

Ⓣ**KPMG** *(V N Malhotra, A W Robinson)* P O Box 641, 112 MUSCAT, OMAN. and at ABU DHABI, DOHA, DUBAI, SHARJAH

★**KPMG** *(J L C Carne, D J Henderson, R Lightowler, C R Thresh)* Montague Sterling Centre, East Bay Street, PO Box N123, NASSAU, BAHAMAS. and at BRIDGETOWN, CASTRIES, FREEPORT, HAMILTON, KINGSTON, MONTEGO BAY, ORANJESTAD, PORT OF SPAIN, PROVIDENCIALES, ST JOHNS, TORTOLA, WILLEMSTAD

★**KPMG** *(S P Medora, R Singh)* 511 World Trade Centre, Babar Road, NEW DELHI 110001, INDIA. and at BANGALORE, GURGAON, MUMBAI

★**KPMG** *(M Antoniades, A K Christofides, A M Gregoriades, E Z Hadjizacharias, C A Kalias, M A Loizides, S A Loizides, P G Loizou, P A Peleties, A I Shiammoutis, N Syrimis, D S Vakis, C Vasiliou)* 14 Esperidon Street, 1087 NICOSIA, CYPRUS. and at LARNACA, LIMASSOL, PAPHOS

★Ⓣ**KPMG** *(Y K Chin, A L W Lee)* Level 10, KPMG Tower, 8 First Avenue, Bandar Utama, 47800 PETALING JAYA, MALAYSIA. and at JOHOR BAHRU, KOTA KINABALU, KUCHING, PENANG, SANDAKAN, TAWAU

★Ⓣ**KPMG** *(J Chung Chung Wai)* KPMG Centre, 30 St George Street, PORT LOUIS, MAURITIUS.

★**KPMG** *(E Doyle, R J Gascoigne, E R Stelfox, A Sutherland)* Pobrezni 1a, 186 00 PRAGUE, CZECH REPUBLIC.

★**KPMG** *(S J Austwick, S B M Young)* Vesetas iela 7, RIGA LV 1013, LATVIA.

Ⓟ**KPMG (BVI) Limited** *(K Beighton, S L C Whicker)* PO Box 4467, 3rd Floor Benco Popular Building, Road Town, TORTOLA, VG-1110, VIRGIN ISLANDS (BRITISH).

★**KPMG Accountants N.V.** *(G Ramanathan)* Laan van Langerhuize 1, 1186 DS Amstelveen, P O Box 74500, 1070 DB AMSTERDAM, NETHERLANDS. and at ALKMAAR, ALMERE, AMERSFOORT, APELDOORN, ARNHEM, BREDA, DEVENTER, DORDRECHT, DRACHTEN, EINDHOVEN, GOUDA, GRONINGEN, HEERLEN, HOORN, LEEUWARDEN, MIDDELBURG, NIJMEGEN, ROTTERDAM, S'HERTOGENBOSCH, S-GRAVENHAGE, THE HAGUE, TILBURG, UTRECHT, ZWOLLE

★**KPMG Advisory (China), trading name of KPMG** *(P J Brough, J P Chattock, D J Collins, N J Debnam, S C Donowho, C Y Fung, Y K P Fung, S J E Gleave, A C Grassick, K M Ho, P Y L Kan, C W Ko, P W Kung, F K H Lee, S H Y Lee, E S Y Li, T B Liu, Y Liu, A A Macpherson, P K McSheaffrey, C Muk, K L Ng, B Nikzad, I C O'Brien, I M Parker, W K Siu, L G Y Y Tang, M J Wardle, A W B R Weir, E Y S Wong, M M C Wu, I L K Yan, K Yeung, K S Yiu)* 8/F Prince's Building, 10 Chater Road, CENTRAL, HONG KONG ISLAND, HONG KONG SAR. and at QINGDAO, SHANGHAI

★**KPMG Advisory Kft** *(M D Bownas)* Vaci ut 99, BUDAPEST, H-1139, HUNGARY.

★**KPMG AG Wirtschaftsprufungsgesellschaft** *(J G M Evans, V Lakshman, J Schindler)* Tersteengenstrasse19-31, 40474 DUSSELDORF, GERMANY. and at AUGSBURG, BERLIN, BIELEFELD, BINGEN AM RHEIN, BOCHUM, BREMEN, BRUNSWICK, COLOGNE, DRESDEN, ERFURT, ESCHBORN, FRANKFURT AM MAIN, FREIBURG, HAMBURG, HANNOVER, HOF, KAISERSLAUTERN, LEIPZIG, LUBECK, MAINZ, MANNHEIM, MULHEIM, MUNICH, NURNBERG, REGENSBURG, SCHWERIN, STUTTGART, WIESBADEN

★**KPMG Al Fozan & Al Sadhan** *(A T P Jackson)* 13th Floor, Al Subeaei Towers, King Abdulaziz Street, PO Box 4803, AL KHOBAR, 31952 SAUDI ARABIA.

★**KPMG Al Fozan Al Sadhan** *(I A Al-Bayaa, S H Shaikh)* PO Box 55078, JEDDAH, 21534, SAUDI ARABIA.

★Ⓣ**KPMG Audit** *(R K Beegun, J E H Li How Cheong, S J B Nye)* 9 Allee Scheffer, 2520 LUXEMBOURG, LUXEMBOURG.

ⓅⒶ**KPMG Audit Holdings Limited** *(R Bennison, A G Cates, J G Griffith-Jones, P Long)* 15 Canada Square, LONDON, E14 5GL.

Ⓐ**KPMG Audit LLC** *(N A Duggan, M J Fayle, M R Kelly, D K McGarry)* Heritage Court, 39-41 Athol Street, Douglas, ISLE OF MAN, IM1 1LA.

ⓅⒶ**KPMG Audit plc** *(R J Ackland, M S J Ashley, J L T Bell, R Bennison, S G Bligh, A G Cates, A J M Cole, I M Goalen, J G Griffith-Jones, P Long, S C A Masters, B Michael, O R Tant)* 15 Canada Square, LONDON, E14 5GL. and at ABERDEEN, BIRMINGHAM, BRISTOL, CAMBRIDGE, CARDIFF, CRAWLEY, EDINBURGH, GLASGOW, IPSWICH, LEEDS, LEICESTER, LIVERPOOL, MANCHESTER, MILTON KEYNES, NEWCASTLE UPON TYNE, NOTTINGHAM, PLYMOUTH, PRESTON, READING, SOUTHAMPTON, ST. ALBANS

★**KPMG Auditores Independentes** *(T J Young)* Rua Dr Renato Paes de Barros33, Itaim Bibi, CEP 04530-904, SAO PAULO, BRAZIL. and at BELO HORIZONTE, PORTO ALEGRE, RIO DE JANEIRO, SALVADOR, SAO CARLOS

KPMG Bayat Rayan *(M Bayat, A R Jam, A Merati)* 3rd Floor, 239 Motahari Ave, TEHRAN, 15876, IRAN.

★Ⓣ**KPMG Certified Auditors AE** *(M Kokkinos, M T Kyriacou)* 3 Stratigou Tombra Street, Aghia Paraskevi, GR 153 42 ATHENS, GREECE.

ⓉⓅⒶ**KPMG Channel Islands Limited** *(E J Bertrand, S D Hunt, R A Hutchinson, N D Jehan, R J Kirkby, J S Laity, Mrs M J MacCallum, A C Paxton, A P Quinn, N L Stevens, M R Thompson)* 5 St. Andrew's Place, Charing Cross, St. Helier, JERSEY, JE4 8WQ. and at GUERNSEY

★**KPMG d.o.o Beograd** *(J Thornley)* Kraljice Natalije 11, 11000 BELGRADE, SERBIA.

★Ⓐ**KPMG Europe B.V.** *(M S J Ashley)* 15 Canada Square, LONDON, E14 5GL. and at AMSTELVEEN

★Ⓐ**KPMG Europe Cooperatie U.A** *(M S J Ashley)* 15 Canada Square, LONDON, E14 5GL. and at AMSTELVEEN

Ⓐ**KPMG Europe LLP** *(P G Abram, I A Al-Bayaa, A J Aldridge, N Amin, K R Anderson, N D Andrews, A Antonius, A I Argyle, G P Armitage, R Aronson, M S J Ashley, T Aston, T Aw, J B Ayrton, M A Bacon, M R Baillache, G L T Bainbridge, I R Bannatyne, K I R Bannister, S C Barker, M F Barradell, E A Bassett, A D Bates, R K Beegun, C V Ben-Nathan, R Bennison, D J Bills, P Bishop, T J Blake, S G Bligh, I K Bone, S P Bonney, I J Borley, D A Bowen, J M Boyers, A J Brennan, R J Brent, A Brett, K S Briggs, K J Britten, R D Broadbelt, I J Brokenshire, P D A Brook, T J Brown, A A Buckle, S Burdass, D R Burgess, D J Burlison, J D Cain, R M Campbell, B K Carter, F J P Carter, A G Cates, D S Cazeaux, A R Cecil, N Chandler, P D Charles, A P Cheadle, N J Chism, P I Claisse, A R N Clarke, R J Clarke, E A Claydon, M J Cockwell, G M Collins, S J Collins, S J Cooper, S R Cormack, J J Costello, D J Costley-Wood, A J L Cottam, P J Cotton, M T Coughtrey, S Courtney, A F Cox, W R Cox, A D Coxshall, S H Craik, D J Crawshaw, I A Cummings, J Daboo, P M Davidson, N G S Davies, D M Defroand, I A Dewar, H L Dickinson, B J Dilley, A C Dray, J D Driver, S T Dumasia, K J Durward, D G R Eastwood, K P Edge, M C G Edge, N J Edmonds, J O Edwards, L S Edwards, J L Ellacott, D Elliott, D J Elms, W A Enevoldson, R V Evans, M T Farlow, J G Farnell, R J Fenton, S R F Figgis, M G Firmin, R D Fleming, D I Fletcher, S D T Foster, T K Franks, M C Froom, N M Frost, C R Fry, F C Fry, P E Furneaux, R K Gabbertas, D P Gascoigne, N R P Gibb, I M Goalen, I P Gomes, R J A Gorsuch, A W Graham, I R Gravestock, I G Greaves, B Green, H G D Green, P R Gresham, J G Griffith-Jones, J A H Groom, J J Guppy, K K Haji, N P Hall, J A Hallsworth, A M Halsey, R J Hampshire, R E Hanger, T Harding, N E Harman, M J Harper, R G Hathaway, C R Hearld, R Heis, J A Hendley, C D Hewson, H R Heyns, S P Heywood, L G Hickey, D N Hicks, R J Hill, S E Hill, J L Hills, R S Hills, A J Hodgson, W E J Holland, S P Hollis, J M Holt, M T Hopton, H R Horgan, G Horner, J Hughes, J E Hughes, P R Hughes, J Hughff, A J Hunter, S Hunter, J P F Hurst, M E J Hutchinson, A T P Jackson, P R Johnson, S R Jones, S L Jonsson, J H Kelly, R S Kharegat, P A Kirkbright, P A Korolkiewicz, C H W Le Strange Meakin, J S Leach, J D Leech, M J Lewis, R P Lewis, J E H Li How Cheong, S A Liddell, R A Little, D J Littleford, A Lobo, P Long, M A Longworth, J A Lovell, J L Lowes, J K Luke, D Macaskill, J Machin, L J Main, M V Maloney, A G Marshall, C S Martin, S C A Masters, M V Matthewman, D V Matthews, C Mayo, D I McAllan, S J M McCallion, R G McCarthy, M J McDonagh, K M McKay, J D McKinven, S K G McNaught, P N Meehan, J P Meeten, N D Meredith, W R C Meredith, M J Metcalf, B Michael, M Michael, J M Mills, A C Milner, J D T Milsom, R I Moffatt, K P Moore, A R J Morgan, J J Morgan, J A Morris, A J Morrison, M M L Morrissey, D Morritt, C J G Moulder, S J S Muncey, H M Munro, S J N Murphy, G Neale, F V H Neate, A F J Neden, M Newsholme, A M Nicholson, D A Nickson, J O'Brien, N T O'Brien, B O'Donovan, R O'Dwyer, W P J O'Reilly, R I Ohrenstein, J N Oldcorn, K T Orr, S P Osmer, J J Outen, C J Oxborough, S R Oxley, S R Palmer, S Parker, S M Pashby, H N Patel, N Paul, B L Pearcy, A J Pearson, R J Peberdy, M A Peck, G M Penfold, R Pinckard, A Plavsic, N J Plumb, I D Pontefract, R C Powell, S A Poyner, N W J Pratt, R S Price, N B Priestley, S Purkess, A J Pyle, N Quayle, M A Quest, A P Quinton, M R Rahman, G Ramanathan, P G Read, T M E Rees, R H Reid, C L Richmond, A P Rieveley, P D Robb, M S Robinson, A M Rocker, M J Roden, D W Rogers, M J Rowley, S D Ryder, P A G Sanderson, H K Sant, P K Sawdon, D A Sayer, A J Sayers, R M Seale, S J Secker, P Selvey, D J Shah, S Shah, S H Shaikh, R J Sharman, W Shaul, F F M Short, P Smart, N S Smith, S G Smith, M Soeting, W E Southwood, C J Spall, R W Spedding, S G Spellman, P F Spicer, J S Spratt, J R Stamp, N C Standen, I M Starkey, V J Stevens, M H Stevenson, M A Steventon, A C Stirling, A J Stone, A Suchak, M Summerfield, T D N Surridge, A J Sykes, O R Tant, S Thakkar, S A Tharani, D K S Thomas, J H E Thompson, M H Thompson, M R Thompson, A J Tickel, S M Tiernan, D A T Todd, P J Tombleson, J R Tucker, D K Turner, A Vials, J E Vines, H R Von Bergen, A J Walker, S R Walker, S J Wardell, G R Warrington, G A Watts, J R M White, T M Widdas, R C Widdowson, K M Wightman, A J Wilcox, J C Wilkinson, C J Williams, G N D Williams, C J Wilson, M R Woodward, J P L Woolf, R M Yasue, J A Zatouroff)* KPMG LLP, 15 Canada Square, LONDON, E14 5GL.

★Ⓣ**KPMG Fakhro** *(O Mahmood)* 5th Floor, Chamber of Commerce Building, P O Box 710, MANAMA, BAHRAIN.

ⓅⒶ**KPMG Holdings Limited** *(R Bennison, A G Cates, J G Griffith-Jones, P Long)* 15 Canada Square, LONDON, E14 5GL.

★Ⓣ**KPMG Huazhen, trading name of KPMG** *(T Cheung, Y K P Fung, M R Wong, I L K Yan)* Level 16 China World Tower 2, China World Trade Centre, No 1 Jian Guo Men Wai Avenue, BEIJING 100004, CHINA. and at GUANGZHOU, SHENZHEN

★**KPMG Hungaria Kft** *(D W M Thompson)* Vaci ut 99, H 1139 BUDAPEST, HUNGARY.

KPMG Kenya *(P C C Appleton, A Pringle)* P.O. Box 40612, 16 Floor Lonrho HS, Standard Street, NAIROBI, 00100, KENYA.

★Ⓟ**KPMG Limited** *(N A Duggan, M R Kelly, D K McGarry)* PO Box 1197, Suite 3C, Eurolife Building, 1 Corral Road, GIBRALTAR, GIBRALTAR.

Ⓟ**KPMG Limited** *(M E Jerome)* 16th Floor Pacific Place, 83B Ly Thuong Kiet Street, Hoan Kiem District, HANOI, VIETNAM.

ⓉⓅ**KPMG Limited** *(M Antoniades, A K Christofides, I Ghalanos, A M Gregoriades, E Z Hadjizacharias, C Kalli, M Karantoni, M A Loizides, P G Loizou, P A Peleties, G P Savva, A I Shiammoutis, S Sofocleous, N Syrimis, D S Vakis, C Vasiliou)* P O Box 21121, 1502 NICOSIA, CYPRUS. and at LARNACA, LIMASSOL, PAPHOS, PARALIMNI

Ⓣ**KPMG LLC** *(N A Duggan, M J Fayle, M R Kelly, D K McGarry)* Heritage Court, 41 Athol Street, Douglas, ISLE OF MAN, IM99 1HN. and at GIBRALTAR

ⓉⒶ**KPMG LLP** *(P G Abram, R J Ackland, A J Aldridge, N Amin, K R Anderson, M S Andrews, N D Andrews, A Antonius, A I Argyle, G P Armitage, R Aronson, M S J Ashley, T Aston, T Aw, J B Ayrton, M A Bacon, M R Baillache, G L T Bainbridge, I R Bannatyne, K I R Bannister, S C Barker, M F Barradell, E A Bassett, A D Bates, J L T Bell, G M Bellamy, C V Ben-Nathan, R Bennison, D J Bills, J Bingham, P Bishop, T J Blake, S G Bligh, I K Bone, S P Bonney, I J Borley, J M Boyers, A J Brennan, R J Brent, M Brereton, K S Briggs, K J Britten, R D Broadbelt, I J Brokenshire, P D A Brook, T J Brown, A A Buckle, S Burdass, D R Burgess, D J Burlison, J D Cain, R M Campbell, B K Carter, F J P Carter, A G Cates, D S Cazeaux, A R Cecil, N Chandler, P D Charles, A P Cheadle, N J Chism, P I Claisse, R J Clarke, E A Claydon, M J Cockwell, G M Collins, S J Collins, J D Coltman, S J Cooper, S R Cormack, J J Costello, D J Costley-Wood, A J L Cottam, P J Cotton, M T Coughtrey, S Courtney, A F Cox, W R Cox, S H Craik, D J Crawshaw, I A Cummings, J Daboo, P M Davidson, N G S Davies, D M Defroand, I A Dewar, H L Dickinson, B J Dilley, J M Dowie, A C Dray, J D Driver, S T Dumasia, K J Durward, D G R Eastwood, K P Edge, M C G Edge, N J Edmonds, J O Edwards, L S Edwards, J L

Ellacott, D Elliott, D J Elliott, D J Elms, W A Enevoldson, R V Evans, M G Fallon, M T Farlow, R J Fenton, S R F Figgis, M G Firmin, R D Fleming, D I Fletcher, T K Franks, M C Froom, N M Frost, A E Fry, C R Fry, F C Fry, P E Furneaux, R K Gabbertas, D P Gascoigne, N R P Gibb, I M Goalen, I P Gomes, R J A Gorsuch, A W Graham, I R Gravestock, I G Greaves, B Green, H G D Green, P R Gresham, J G Griffith-Jones, J A H Groom, J J Guppy, K K Haji, N J Hall, N P Hall, J A Hallsworth, A M Halsey, R J Hampshire, R E Hanger, T Harding, N E Harman, M J Harper, R G Hathaway, C R Hearld, R Heis, J A Hendley, C D Hewson, H R Heyns, S P Heywood, L G Hickey, D N Hicks, R J Hill, S E Hill, J L Hills, R S Hills, A J Hodgson, W E J Holland, S P Hollis, J M Holt, M T Hopton, H R Horgan, G Horner, J Hughes, J E Hughes, P R Hughes, J Hughff, A J Hunter, S Hunter, J P F Hurst, M E J Hutchinson, P R Johnson, S R Jones, S L Jonsson, J H Kelly, R S Kharegat, P A Kirkbright, P A Korolkiewicz, C H W Le Strange Meakin, J S Leach, J D Leech, M J Lewis, R P Lewis, S A Liddell, A Lister, R A Little, D J Littleford, A Lobo, P Long, M A Longworth, J A Lovell, J L Lowes, J K Luke, D Macaskill, J Machin, L J Main, M V Maloney, A G Marshall, C S Martin, S C A Masters, M V Matthewman, D V Matthews, C Mayo, D I McAllan, S J M McCallion, R G McCarthy, M J McDonagh, K M McKay, S K G McNaught, W W Mead, P N Meehan, J P Meeten, N D Meredith, W R C Meredith, M J Metcalf, B Michael, M Michael, J M Mills, A C Milner, J D T Milsom, R I Moffatt, K P Moore, A R J Morgan, J J Morgan, J A Morris, A J Morrison, M M L Morrissey, D Morritt, C J G Moulder, S J S Muncey, H M Munro, S J N Murphy, G Neale, F V H Neate, A F J Neden, M Newsholme, A M Nicholson, D A Nickson, J O'Brien, N T O'Brien, B O'Donovan, R O'Dwyer, W P J O'Reilly, R I Ohrenstein, J N Oldcorn, K T Orr, S P Osmer, J J Outen, C J Oxborough, S R Oxley, S R Palmer, S Parker, S M Pashby, H N Patel, N Paul, B L Pearcy, A J Pearson, R J Peberdy, M A Peck, G M Penfold, R Pinckard, A Plavsic, N J Plumb, I D Pontefract, R C Powell, N W J Pratt, R S Price, N B Priestley, S Purkess, A J Pyle, N Quayle, M A Quest, M R Raddan, M R Rahman, P G Read, T M E Rees, R H Reid, C L Richmond, P H Ricketts, P D Robb, M S Robinson, A M Rocker, M J Roden, D W Rogers, M J Rowley, P A G Sanderson, H K Sant, P K Sawdon, D A Sayer, A J Sayers, R M Seale, S J Secker, P Selvey, D J Shah, S Shah, N K Sharma, R J Sharman, W Shaul, F F M Short, P Smart, N S Smith, S G Smith, W T Smith, W E Southwood, C J Spall, R W Spedding, S G Spellman, P F Spicer, J S Spratt, J R Stamp, N C Standen, I M Starkey, V J Stevens, M H Stevenson, M A Steventon, A C Stirling, A J Stone, C J Stott, A Suchak, M Summerfield, T D N Surridge, A J Sykes, O R Tant, M J Taylor, S Thakkar, S A Tharani, D K S Thomas, J H E Thompson, M H Thompson, M R Thompson, A J Tickel, S M Tiernan, D A T Todd, P J Tombleson, J R Tucker, D K Turner, A Vials, J E Vines, H R Von Bergen, A J Walker, S R Walker, S J Wardell, G R Warrington, G A Watts, J R M White, T M Widdas, R C Widdowson, K M Wightman, A J Wilcox, J C Wilkinson, C J Williams, G N D Williams, C J Wilson, M R Woodward, J P L Woolf, R M Yasue, J A Zatouroff) 15 Canada Square, LONDON, E14 5GL. and at ABERDEEN, BIRMINGHAM, BRISTOL, CAMBRIDGE, CARDIFF, CRAWLEY, EDINBURGH, GLASGOW, IPSWICH, LEEDS, LEICESTER, LIVERPOOL, MANCHESTER, MILTON KEYNES, NEWCASTLE UPON TYNE, NOTTINGHAM, PLYMOUTH, PRESTON, READING, SOUTHAMPTON, ST. ALBANS

★Ⓣ**KPMG LLP** *(D A Leaver, W Y Tan, S Tham, D J Waller)* 16 Raffles Quay, # 22-00, Hong Leong Building, SINGAPORE 048581, SINGAPORE.

KPMG LLP *(A S R Kanji)* 333 Bay Street, Suite 4600, TORONTO M5H 2S5, ON, CANADA. and at ABBOTSFORD, AMOS, BROCKVILLE, BURNABY, CALGARY, CAMBRIDGE, CHILLIWACK, EDMONTON, ELLIOT LAKE, FREDERICTON, GRIMSBY, HALIFAX, HAMILTON, KELOWNA, KINGSTON, LA SHARPE, LAVAL, LETHBRIDGE, LONDON, MISSISSAUGA, MONCTON, MONTREAL, NEW WESTMINSTER, NORTH BAY, NORTH YORK, OTTAWA, PENTICTON, PORTAGE LA PRAIRIE, QUEBEC CITY, ROUYN, SAINT JOHN, SASKATOON, SAULT STE. MARIE, SEPT-ILES, ST CATHARINES, ST JOHN'S, SUDBURY, SYDNEY, THUNDER BAY, VAL D'OR, VANCOUVER, VERNON, VICTORIA, WATERLOO, WILLOWDALE, WINDSOR, WINNIPEG, YARMOUTH

KPMG Mexico Cardenas Dosal, trading name of KPMG LLP *(C E L Clark, R M Hanley, A D Parsons, H Pratten, G J C Reader)* Two Financial Center, 60 South Street, BOSTON, MA 02111, UNITED STATES. and at ALBUQUERQUE, ALLENTOWN, ATLANTA, AUSTIN, BALTIMORE, BATON ROUGE, BEAVERTON, BELLEVUE, BENNINGTON, BILLINGS, BIRMINGHAM, BURLINGTON, CHARLESTON, CHARLOTTE, CHICAGO, CINCINNATI, CLARKSBURG, CLEARWATER BEACH, CLEVELAND, COLUMBUS, CORPUS CHRISTI, DALLAS, DENVER, DES MOINES, DETROIT, DULUTH, FORT WORTH, FRESNO, GREENEVILLE, GREENVILLE, HACKENSACK, HARRISBURG, HARTFORD, HILO, HONOLULU, HOUSTON, INDIANAPOLIS, JACKSON, JACKSONVILLE, KANSAS CITY, LEXINGTON, LINCOLN, LONG BEACH, LOS ANGELES, LOUISVILLE, LUBBOCK, MCLEAN, MELVILLE, MEMPHIS, MEXICO CITY, MIAMI, MILWAUKEE, MINNEAPOLIS, MONTVALE, MOUNTAIN VIEW, NASHVILLE, NEW JERSEY, NEW ORLEANS, NEW YORK, NEWPORT BEACH, NORFOLK, OAKLAND, OKLAHOMA CITY, OMAHA, ORLANDO, PHILADELPHIA, PITTSBURGH, PORTLAND, PRINCETON, PROVIDENCE, RICHMOND, ROANOKE, SACRAMENTO, SALEM, SALT LAKE CITY, SAN ANTONIO, SAN DIEGO, SAN FRANCISCO, SAN JUAN, SAN MATEO, SANTA FE, SEATTLE, SHORT HILLS, SHREVEPORT, SOUTH BEND, ST LOUIS, ST PETERSBURG, STAMFORD, SYRACUSE, TAMPA, TOPEKA, TRENTON, TUCSON, VERO BEACH, VESTAL, VIENNA, WACO, WALNUT CREEK, WAYNE, WOODLAND HILLS

★**KPMG Peat Marwick** *(T E Knowles)* PO Box N123, Montague Sterling Centre, East Bay Street, NASSAU, BAHAMAS.

★Ⓣ**KPMG S.A.** *(R Devlin, C N Hamilton-Jones, M C McLarty, J B Nirsimloo, P D Shah)* 1 Cours Valmy, Paris La DÚfense Cedex, 92923 PARIS LA DÉFENSE, FRANCE. and at BORDEAUX, LEVALLOIS-PERRET, LYON, NANCY, NANTES, NEUILLY-SUR-SEINE, PARIS LA DEFENCE CEDEX, RENNES

★**KPMG Slovensko** *(M Lodi-Fe)* Dvorakovo nabrezie 10, P. O. Box 7, 811 02 BRATISLAVA, SLOVAK REPUBLIC.

★**KPMG Somekh Chaikin** *(J D Fisher, W D Krisman, R I Lavender, A D Schijveschuurder)* 17 Ha'arba'a Street, TEL AVIV, 64739, ISRAEL. and at HAIFA, JERUSALEM

★Ⓣ**KPMG Taseer Hadi & Co** *(A H Basrai)* 1st Floor, Sheikh Sultan Trust Bldg Apt 2, Beaumont Road, KARACHI 75530, PAKISTAN. and at ISLAMABAD, LAHORE

ⒻⓅ**KPMG United Kingdom Plc** *(M S J Ashley, R Bennison, A G Cates, J G Griffith-Jones, P Long)* 15 Canada Square, LONDON, E14 5GL.

KPSA *(N Kastellanis, S Saphiris)* 15 Themistokli Dervi Street, 1st Floor, Margarita House, PO Box 27040, 1641 NICOSIA, CYPRUS.

KR Accountancy *(K M Rogers)* Bank Bottom Farm, Broadhead Road, Turton, BOLTON, LANCASHIRE, BL7 0JN.

ⓉⓅⒶ**Krogh & Partners Ltd** *(P Krogh Petersen)* 823 Salisbury House, 29 Finsbury Circus, LONDON, EC2M 5QQ.

Krupski & Krupski *(G M Krupski)* The Maples, Almshouse Croft, Bradley, STAFFORD, ST18 9DF.

ⓉⒻⓅⒶ**KRW Accountants, trading name of KRW Accountants Ltd** *(K R Witchell)* Home Ground Barn, Pury Hill Business Park, Alderton Road, Paulerspury, TOWCESTER, NORTHAMPTONSHIRE NN12 7LS.

★**Krycler Ervin Taubman & Walheim** *(M J Krycler)* 15303 Ventura Boulevard, Suite 1040, SHERMAN OAKS, CA 91403, UNITED STATES.

KS Accountncy *(S J Smith)* 32 Wilderness Heights, West End, SOUTHAMPTON, SO18 3PS.

KSEG *(E S Gudka, K S Shah)* Belfry House, Champions Way, Hendon, LONDON, NW4 1PX.

Ⓟ**KTC Partners CPA Limited** *(K Chan, L H Tong)* Unit 501 502 &508, 5/F, Mirror Tower, 61 Mody Road, TSIM SHA TSUI, KOWLOON HONG KONG SAR.

Ⓐ**KTNG** *(K T Ng)* 3rd Floor, 12-13 Little Newport Street, LONDON, WC2H 7JJ.

ⓉⒻⓅⒶ**KTS Owens Thomas, trading name of KTS Owens Thomas Limited** *(E R Birtles, R J Jenkins, D W Owens, C S Warburton)* The Counting House, Dunleavy Drive, CARDIFF, CF11 0SN. and at ABERDARE

ⒻⒶ**Kubinski** *(A K Kubinski, J A Kubinski)* Eldon House, 201 Penistone Road, Kirkburton, HUDDERSFIELD, HD8 0PE.

Kuhrt Leach LLP *(R A Leach)* 81-82 Akeman Street, TRING, HERTFORDSHIRE, HP23 6AF.

Ⓟ**Kumar & Co Tax & Business Accountants, trading name of Kumar & Co Accountants Ltd** *(S Kumar)* 85 Rydens Road, WALTON-ON-THAMES, SURREY, KT12 3AN.

Ⓟ**Kumar, trading name of Kumar Strategic Consultants Ltd** *(A A Mohanlal)* 255-261 Horn Lane, Acton, LONDON, W3 9EH.

Kung Lok Lam & Co *(L Kung)* Office G2, 17/F Legend Tower, No 7 Shing Yip Street, KWUN TONG, KOWLOON, HONG KONG SAR.

Kunle Ladejobi & Co *(I A Ladejobi)* G.P.O. Box 6816, LAGOS, NIGERIA.

★**Kunle Oshinaike & Co** *(J A Oshinaike)* P.O. Box 8930, Marina, LAGOS, NIGERIA.

Kurban Abji *(K A M Abji)* 46 Westbourne Road, LUTON, LU4 8JD.

Ⓟ**Kusa Limited** *(D M Cunningham)* The Wheelwrights, Silver Street, Abthorpe, TOWCESTER, NORTHAMPTONSHIRE, NN12 8QR.

Kusa, trading name of Dave Cunningham *(D M Cunningham)* The Wheelwrights, Silver Street, Abthorpe, TOWCESTER, NORTHAMPTONSHIRE, NN12 8QR.

KW Finance Director Services *(K A Wilson)* 35 Dover Road, BRIGHTON, BN1 6LP.

Ⓟ**Kwan Chan & Co, trading name of Kwan Chan Accounting Services Ltd** *(S L Kwan)* 352a Carlton Hill, Carlton, NOTTINGHAM, NG4 1JB.

Kwan Wong Tan & Hong *(H Fong, H Y Wong)* 15 Scotts Road Suite 04-01/03, Thong Teck Building, SINGAPORE 228218, SINGAPORE. and at CENTRAL

ⓅⒶ**KWG Ltd** *(A D Kasmir, R Struggles)* Millstream House, 39a East Street, WIMBORNE, DORSET, BH21 1DX.

Kwok & Partners *(K Kwok)* Room 4101, 41st Floor, Tower Two Lippo Centre, 89 Queensway, ADMIRALTY, HONG KONG SAR.

★**Kwong & Co** *(L W Kwong)* 260 Lorong Maarof, Bukit Bandaraya, 59100 KUALA LUMPUR, FEDERAL TERRITORY, MALAYSIA.

★Ⓐ**KWSR & Co** *(M Rahman, S Rahman)* 136 Merton High Street, LONDON, SW19 1BA.

ⓉⓅⒶ**Kybert Carroll, trading name of Kybert Carroll Ltd** *(J P Carroll)* 52 Brighton Road, SURBITON, SURREY, KT6 5PL.

★**Kyffin & Co.** *(I M G Hedges)* The Old Convent, Llanbadarn Road, ABERYSTWYTH, SY23 1EY.

Ⓕ**Kyles & Co** *(T H R Waite)* 11 Weston Road, SOUTHEND-ON-SEA, SS1 1AS.

ⓉⓅⒶ**Kyles, trading name of KWK Limited** *(T H R Waite)* 11 Weston Road, SOUTHEND-ON-SEA, SS1 1AS.

Ⓣ**Kyprianides, Nicolaou & Associates** *(P K Kyprianides, N Nicolaou)* 48 Thermistoclis Avenue, Office 401, 1066 NICOSIA, CYPRUS. and at LIMASSOL

Kyprianides, Nicolaou & Economides *(E Economides, G I Economides, P K Kyprianides, N Nicolaou)* 4 Evagora Papachristoforou, Themis Court, Office 301, 3030 LIMASSOL, CYPRUS.

Kyriakos Yiambides *(K N Yiambides)* 1 Sophoulis Street, Acropolis, 2008 NICOSIA, CYPRUS.

Ⓟ**KZS, trading name of KZS Limited** *(L J Hillman)* 60 Fallowfield, WELLINGBOROUGH, NORTHAMPTONSHIRE, NN9 5YY.

★**L & J Lawrie** *(J L Lawrie)* 23 Buckingham Terrace, West End, EDINBURGH, EH4 3AE.

L E Marshall & Co *(L E Marshall)* Unit C3, Fairoaks Airport, Chobham, WOKING, SURREY, GU24 8HU.

Ⓟ**L G Accountants, trading name of L G Accountants Limited** *(R J Langdon)* PO Box 447, Stone Court, Helmdon Road, Sulgrave, BANBURY, OXFORDSHIRE OX17 2EF.

L J Accountancy *(L A Jones)* 7 Newman Lane, Drayton, ABINGDON, OXFORDSHIRE, OX14 4LP.

L J O'Brien *(L J O'Brien)* Hawthorne Farmhouse, Ince Lane, Wimbolds Trafford, CHESTER, CH2 4JP.

L Morris FCA *(L Morris)* 5 Greystokes, Aughton, ORMSKIRK, L39 5HE.

ⓅⒶ**L Y Y N, trading name of L Y Y Ng Accounting Services Limited** *(L Y Y Ng)* 65 Lower Essex Street, BIRMINGHAM, B5 6SN.

Ⓟ**L&J Accounting Services Ltd** *(L J Davison)* 22 The Grove, Benton, NEWCASTLE UPON TYNE, NE12 9PE.

L. Harris *(L E Harris)* 38 Rehov Habrosh, BINYAMINA, 30500, ISRAEL.

Ⓕ**L. Kaffel** *(L Kaffel)* Helmsdale, Green Lane, STANMORE, HA7 3AH.

L.A. Gurrie *(L A Gurrie)* 203 Collingwood House, Dolphin Square, LONDON, SW1V 3ND.

L.E. Friedmann *(L E Friedmann)* 110 Achuza Street, RA'ANANA, 43450, ISRAEL.

ⒻⒶ**L.H. Newman & Co** *(L H Newman)* 148 Walton Street, LONDON, SW3 2JJ.

ⒻⒶ**L.H. Phillips & Co** *(D E Humphreys, H M W Thomas, M J Williams)* 29/30 Quay St., CARMARTHEN, SA31 3JT.

L.J. Chrisfield *(L J Chrisfield)* 29 The Meadow, CHISLEHURST, KENT, BR7 6AA.

L.June Hughes *(L J Hughes)* 34 Weirdale Av, Whetstone, LONDON, N20 0AG.

L.P.H. Bennett *(L P H Bennett)* 11 Daisy Road, HILTON, KWAZULU NATAL, 3245, SOUTH AFRICA.

L.R. Fong *(L R Fong)* 1050 Schubert Street, BROSSARD J4X 1X1, QUE, CANADA.

L.R. Hall-Strutt *(L R Hall-Strutt)* 25 Cloudesley Close, SIDCUP, KENT, DA14 6TF.

L.S. Lanning *(L S Lanning)* 2 Eton Court, STAINES, TW18 2AF.

L.T.J Smith *(L T J Smith)* 3 Manor Farm Walk, Portesham, WEYMOUTH, DORSET, DT3 4PH.

★**L.V. Gough & Co** *(P B Gough)* 7 West Drive, Cheam, SUTTON, SM2 7NB.

Ⓟ**LA Business Recovery, trading name of LA Business Recovery Limited** *(P M Levy)* 3 Beasleys Yard, 126a High Street, UXBRIDGE, MIDDLESEX, UB8 1JT.

Ⓟ**Laburnum Consultants Ltd** *(D Plummer)* 20 Laburnum Close, Chapeltown, SHEFFIELD, S35 1QU.

Ⓐ**Lachman Livingstone** *(R I Jacob, N G Lachman)* 136 Pinner Road, NORTHWOOD, MIDDLESEX, HA6 1BP.

Ⓟ**Lachman Smith Ltd** *(F S Lachman)* 16b North End Road, Golders Green, LONDON, NW11 7PH.

Lackmaker & Co *(D H Lackmaker)* 10 Bradden Lane, Gaddesden Row, HEMEL HEMPSTEAD, HP2 6HZ.

ⓅⒶ**Lacome & Co, trading name of Lacome & Co Limited** *(G A Lacome)* Sapphire House, 73 St Margarets Avenue, LONDON, N20 9LD.

★ⓉⒻⒶ**Lacy Watson** *(C F Mellalieu, S M Tattersall)* Carlyle House, 107 Wellington Road South, STOCKPORT, SK1 3TL.

ⓉⒻⒶ**Ladimeji & Co** *(O A Ladimeji)* Five Kings House, 1 Queen Street Place, LONDON, EC4R 1QS.

★**Lai & Wong** *(Y H Lai)* Unit B 8th Floor, Success Commercial Building, 245-251 Hennessy Road, WAN CHAI, HONG KONG ISLAND, HONG KONG SAR.

Ⓐ**LaiPeters & Co** *(M S Lai)* New Broad Street House, 35 New Broad Street, LONDON, EC2M 1NH.

Ⓟ**LaiPeters Limited** *(M S Lai)* New Broad Street House, 35 New Broad Street, LONDON, EC2M 1NH.

★**Lak & Associates C.P.A. Ltd** *(L Fung)* 1603-1606 Alliance Building, 130-136 Connaught Road, CENTRAL, HONG KONG SAR.

ⓉⒻⒶ**Lake & Co** *(S Lakhani)* 25a Kenton Park Parade, Kenton Road Kenton, HARROW, HA3 8DN.

Lakers *(K J Lakhani)* 3 Galley House, Moon Lane, BARNET, HERTFORDSHIRE, EN5 5YL.

★**Lakes Accountancy Limited** *(S A Bloy)* 11 Church Street, WINDERMERE, CUMBRIA, LA23 1AQ.

ⓅⒶ**Lakesel Ltd** *(C A Doyle)* PO Box 47168, LONDON, W6 6AY.

Lakhani & Co *(A G Lakhani)* 25 Station Road, Desford, LEICESTER, LE9 9FN.

Lakin & Co *(K Lakin)* The Neuk, 46 Caryl Road, LYTHAM ST. ANNES, FY8 2QB.

Lakin & Co. *(M P Lakin)* Rest Hill House, Over Worton, CHIPPING NORTON, OXFORDSHIRE, OX7 7EN.

★Ⓟ**Lakin Accounting Services Limited** *(D Lakin)* Manor Lodge, Teeton, NORTHAMPTON, NN6 8LH.

ⓉⒻ**Lakin Clark** *(A R Amlot, N J Cripps)* Delandale House, 37 Old Dover Road, CANTERBURY, CT1 3JF. and at MARGATE

ⒻⓅⒶ**Lakin Clark, trading name of Lakin Clark Limited** *(A R Amlot, N J Cripps, C L Parry)* Delandale House, 37 Old Dover Road, CANTERBURY, KENT, CT1 3JF. and at MARGATE

★ⓉⓅⒶ**Lakin Rose, trading name of Lakin Rose Limited** *(C Beaumont, C P J Dougherty, S P Rose)* Pioneer House, Vision Park, Histon, CAMBRIDGE, CB24 9NL.

★**Lalor Holohan & Company** *(E Lalor)* Church Street, WICKLOW, COUNTY WICKLOW, IRELAND.

★**LAM** *(M W Carpenter)* Oakwood, The Paddock, Melmerby, RIPON, NORTH YORKSHIRE, HG4 5HW.

Lam & Co *(L C L Lam)* 94 Orchard Gate, GREENFORD, UB6 0QP.

Lam Siu Hung & Co *(S H Lam)* Room 1602, Chit Lee Commercial Building, 30-36 Shau Kei Wan Road, SHAU KEI WAN, HONG KONG ISLAND, HONG KONG SAR.

Lam Yik Yin & Co *(Y Lam)* Room 802, 8/F, Lee Kiu Building, 51 Jordan Road, YAU MA TEI, KOWLOON HONG KONG SAR.

★**Lamb & Co.** *(B Lamb)* 18 South Close, LONDON, N6 5UQ.

Lambert & Co *(R J Lambert)* The Malt House, Mortimer Hill, Cleobury Mortimer, KIDDERMINSTER, WORCESTERSHIRE, DY14 8QQ.

★ⓉⒻⒶ**Lambert Chapman, trading name of Lambert Chapman LLP** *(N Forsyth, P R Short, J M Smith-Daye, N A Whittle)* 3 Warners Mill, Silks Way, BRAINTREE, ESSEX, CM7 3GB. and at MALDON

Lambert Lewis *(C L Lewis)* 401 Cowbridge Road East, Canton, CARDIFF, CF5 1JG.

Ⓟ**Lambert Mann Limited** *(K P F Mann)* 33 Corfe Way, BROADSTONE, BH18 9ND.

ⓉⒻⓅⒶ**Lambert Roper & Horsfield Limited** *(N I Frost, S W E Mitchell, D A Roper)* The Old Woolcombers Mill, 12-14 Union Street South, HALIFAX, WEST YORKSHIRE, HX1 2LE.

ⒻⒶ**Lambous & Co** *(E Charalambous)* 327 Bowes Road, LONDON, N11 1BA.

Lambrou & Co *(L Lambrou)* 223 Cavendish Avenue, Ealing, LONDON, W13 0JZ.

Ⓐ**Lamburn & Turner** *(M D Lamburn, B E Turner)* Riverside House, 1 Place Farm, Place Farm, Wheathampstead, ST. ALBANS, AL4 8SB.

ⓅⒶ**Lamey & Co, trading name of Lamey & Co Limited** *(D R Lamey)* Ridge Cottage, Speldhurst, TUNBRIDGE WELLS, KENT, TN3 0LE.

Ⓐ**Lamont Pridmore** *(C I Lamont, G W Lamont, W J Pridmore)* Milburn House, 3 Oxford Street, WORKINGTON, CA14 2AL. and at CARLISLE, KENDAL, KESWICK

Ⓟ**Lamont Pridmore, Neil Webster & Co, trading names of Lamont Pridmore (South Cumbria) Limited** *(C I Lamont, G W Lamont, W J Pridmore)* 136 Highgate, KENDAL, CUMBRIA, LA9 4HW.

Ⓟ**Lamont Pridmore, Philip Jones Consulting, trading names of Lamont Pridmore Limited** *(C I Lamont, G W Lamont, W J Pridmore)* Arkle House, 31 Lonsdale Street, CARLISLE, CA1 1BJ.

Ⓕ**Lamont Pridmore, trading name of E.J. Williams & Co** *(G W Lamont, W J Pridmore, M Uppard)* 31 Lonsdale Street, CARLISLE, CA1 1BJ.

ⓉⓅ**Lamont Pridmore, trading name of Lamont Pridmore (West Cumbria) Limited** *(G W Lamont, S W Nixon, W J Pridmore)* Milburn House, 3 Oxford Street, WORKINGTON, CUMBRIA, CA14 2AL. and at CARLISLE

Ⓟ**Lanacre Management Services Limited** *(A Warner)* Barn Court, Washfield, TIVERTON, DEVON, EX16 9QY.

Ⓟ**Lancashire Accountants Ltd** *(J E Lancashire)* 3 Osborne Street, Bredbury, STOCKPORT, CHESHIRE, SK6 2BT.

ⒻⒶ**Lancaster & Co, trading name of Lancaster Haskins LLP** *(M Ashton, S N Beesley, D J Evans, B D Nicholson, E G M Thompson)* Granville House, 2 Tettenhall Road, WOLVERHAMPTON, WV1 4SB.

Ⓟ**Lancaster Clements Limited** *(P L Smith)* Stanley House, 27 Wellington Road, BILSTON, WV14 6AH.

ⓅⒶ**Lancasters (Accountants) Ltd** *(R V Griggs)* Manor Courtyard, Aston Sandford, Nr Haddenham, AYLESBURY, HP17 8JB.

Lance Havell *(L S Havell)* 77 Cumberland Avenue, GUILDFORD, GU2 9RH.

Ⓟ**Lance House Services Ltd** *(R H Hartley)* 142 Broadhurst Gardens, LONDON, NW6 3BH.

★ⒻⓅⒶ**Landau Baker Limited** *(M B Durst, D N Lew)* Mountcliff House, 154 Brent Street, LONDON, NW4 2DR.

ⒻⒶ**Landau Morley LLP** *(G B Davies, S Dunn, P Faber, M G Freedman, M Haberfeld, R M Jezierski, P L Kutner, R Lampert, D R Passey, B R Thakrar, L C Williams)* Lanmor House, 370-386 High Road, WEMBLEY, MIDDLESEX, HA9 6AX.

Landergan & Co *(P M Landergan)* 42 Whetstone Road, LONDON, SE3 8PX.

ⓉⒻⓅⒶ**Landers the Accountants, trading name of Landers Accountants Ltd** *(R Brown)* Church View Chambers, 38 Market Square, Toddington, DUNSTABLE, BEDFORDSHIRE, LU5 6BS.

ⓉⒻⒶ**Landin Wilcock & Co** *(R M Grierson, J Markham, G Marshall, K J Parkes, M J S Webster)* Queen St Chmbrs, 68 Queen St, SHEFFIELD, S17 4BD.

Ⓟ**Landlords Tax Services Limited** *(M R L Patry)* Davenport House, 16 Pepper Street, LONDON, E14 9RP.

Landsman *(R R Landsman)* 43 Broadway, CHEADLE, CHESHIRE, SK8 1LB.

landtax, trading name of landtax LLP *(K C Byrne, C K K Collister, A B Edwards, R M Kirtland, C R Lovibond, M A Maycroft)* Mitre House, Lodge Road, Long Hanborough, Business Park, WITNEY, OXFORDSHIRE OX29 8SS.

Lane & Co *(R J Lane)* 4 Saville Grove, KENILWORTH, WARWICKSHIRE, CV8 2PR.

Ⓟ**Lane Accounting Limited** *(R W Lane)* Thornbury House, 16 Woodlands, GERRARDS CROSS, BUCKINGHAMSHIRE, SL9 8DD.

ⒻⓅⒶ**Lane Monnington Welton, trading name of LMW Limited** *(M A Lane, C J Monnington, K A Randall, C F Welton)* Riverside View, Basing Road, Basing, BASINGSTOKE, HAMPSHIRE, RG24 7AL.

Lang & Yuen *(E K L Yuen)* 270-5655 Cambie Street, VANCOUVER V5Z 3A4, BC, CANADA.

ⓉⒻⒶ**Lang Bennetts** *(J S Mashen, I D Moores, C R E Truscott)* The Old Carriage Works, Moresk Road, TRURO, CORNWALL, TR1 1DG.

Ⓟ**Lang Bennetts, trading name of Lang Bennetts (Falmouth) Limited** *(J S Mashen)* Greenbank Quay, FALMOUTH, CORNWALL, TR11 2SR.

Ⓜ**Langdale Restructuring LLP** *(W S Martin)* Langdale, Legh Road, KNUTSFORD, CHESHIRE, WA16 8NT.

Ⓐ**Langdon Gray LLP** *(R N Chapman, J S Hine, R J Langdon)* PO Box 447, Stone Court, Helmdon Road, Sulgrave, BANBURY, OXFORDSHIRE OX17 2EF. and at LONDON, OXFORD

ⓅⒶ**Langdon West Williams plc** *(K E Brickley, I S Watt)* Curzon House, 24 High Street, BANSTEAD, SM7 2LJ.

Langdons *(R J Langdon)* Stone Court, Helmdon Road, Sulgrave, BANBURY, OXFORDSHIRE, OX17 2SQ.

★ⓉⒻⓅⒶ**Langdowns DFK, trading name of Langdowns DFK Limited** *(D J Ings, R P Law, G E Taylor, C S Thorpe-Manley, R Warwick)* Fleming Court, Leigh Road, EASTLEIGH, HAMPSHIRE, SO50 9PD. and at ANDOVER, BASINGSTOKE

ⒻⒶ**Langer & Co** *(E G Langer)* 8-10 Gatley Road, CHEADLE, SK8 1PY.

Ⓟ**Langers, trading name of Langer & Co Limited** *(E G Langer)* 8-10 Gatley Road, CHEADLE, CHESHIRE, SK8 1PY.

Ⓕ**Langford & Co** *(C J Langford)* 93 Western Road, TRING, HP23 4BN.

ⓅⒶ**Langford Sykes Ltd** *(F M L Sykes)* Cullaford House, Lower Coombe, BUCKFASTLEIGH, TQ11 0HT.

Ⓕ**Langham & Co** *(D M Langham)* 54 Westmorland Drive, Desborough, KETTERING, NORTHAMPTONSHIRE, NN14 2XB.

Ⓣ**Langley Associates** *(G K Barnes)* Milton Heath House, Westcott Road, DORKING, SURREY, RH4 3NB.

Ⓟ**Langrick Accounting & Finance, trading name of Langrick Accounting Limited** *(C J Langrick)* Suite 9C, Caledonian House, Tatton Street, KNUTSFORD, CHESHIRE, WA16 6AG.

Ⓟ**Langrick Consulting Limited** *(C J Langrick)* Caledonian House, Tatton Street, KNUTSFORD, CHESHIRE, WA16 6AG.

ⓉⒻⒶ**Langtons** *(D T Jackson, A J McCall, S Talbot, S T Williams, A Wilson)* The Plaza, 100 Old Hall Street, LIVERPOOL, L3 9QJ.

★ⓅⒶ**Lanham and Company, trading name of Lanham and Company Limited** *(H C Lanham, S J Wakefield)* 9 Great Chesterford Court, London Road, Gt Chesterford, SAFFRON WALDEN, CB10 1PF.

Ⓟ**Lapworth Consultants Ltd** *(S K Jones)* 56-58 Warwick Road, KENILWORTH, WARWICKSHIRE, CV8 1HH.

Ⓟ**Larchcroft Limited** *(G J Beever)* 12 Market Street, HEBDEN BRIDGE, WEST YORKSHIRE, HX7 6AD.

Ⓟ**Large, trading name of LCA Services Ltd** *(D J Large, M A Large, R M Tickell)* 13 Silver Street, BARNSTAPLE, DEVON, EX32 8HR.

★ⓉⒶ**Larking Gowen** *(M D Balfour, I R Fitch, R M Girling, C J Greeves, J G Grimmer, D Jefford, D C Missen, P J Moy, G S Pilcher, B J Pring, J A Richardson, R G Rose, S G Rudd, I S Webster, D N Whitehead, J D Woolston)* King Street House, 15 Upper King Street, NORWICH, NR3 1RB. and at BUNGAY, COLCHESTER, CROMER, DEREHAM, DISS, FAKENHAM, HOLT

Ⓟ**Larking Gowen Corporate Finance Limited** *(I R Fitch, D N Whitehead, J D Woolston)* King Street House, 15 Upper King Street, NORWICH, NR3 1RB.

ⓅⒶ**Larking Gowen, trading name of Larking Gowen Limited** *(R M Girling, J G Grimmer, G S Pilcher, B J Pring, R G Rose, D N Whitehead, J D Woolston)* Unit 1, Claydon Business Park, Great Blakenham, IPSWICH, IP6 0NL.

Ⓕ**Larkings, trading name of Larkings (S.E) LLP** *(J Gransby, C G Mills, M J Moore, J E Sherwood, G D Smith)* Cornwallis House, Pudding Lane, MAIDSTONE, KENT, ME14 1NH. and at CANTERBURY

★ⒻⓅ**Larkings, trading name of Larkings Ltd** *(A J Childs, S Coates, C G Mills, M J Moore, G D Smith)* 180 Upper Pemberton, Eureka Business Park, ASHFORD, KENT, TN25 4AZ.

Ⓟ**Larsen & Co, trading name of Larsens Accountants Limited** *(R A Larsen)* 2 High Brighton Street, WITHERNSEA, NORTH HUMBERSIDE, HU19 2HL.

Lasi Associates *(B Lasi)* 7 Vernon Drive, STANMORE, MIDDLESEX, HA7 2BP.

Last & Co *(P F Last)* 269 Newmarket Road, CAMBRIDGE, CB5 8JE.

Ⓐ**Latham Lambourne** *(J H Lambourne)* First Floor, Priory Buildings, Church Hill, ORPINGTON, KENT, BR6 0HH.

▽Ⓐ**Latham Lees Costa** *(D Costa)* 12 Park St, Lytham, LYTHAM ST. ANNES, FY8 5LU.

Latif & Company *(Q A Latif)* Chestnut House, 101A High Street, Old Town, STEVENAGE, SG1 3HR.

Latimer Advisory Services LLP *(S E Malin)* 6 Shaw Street, WORCESTER, WR1 3QQ.

Latimers *(S E Malin)* 6 Shaw Street, WORCESTER, WR1 3QQ.

Ⓟ**Latrigg Limited** *(H E Grist)* Latrigg, The Glen, Saltford, BRISTOL, BS31 3JP.

Lau Cheung Fung & Chan *(Y Cheung)* 1707, Chinachem Plaza, 338 King's Road, NORTH POINT, HONG KONG SAR.

★**Lau SY & Co.** *(S Y Lau)* Room 1802 Dominion Centre, 43-59 Queen's Road East, WAN CHAI, HONG KONG ISLAND, HONG KONG SAR.

★Ⓐ**Laud Meredith & Co** *(D E Hughes)* 94 High Street, PORTHMADOG, LL49 9NW.

Ⓟ**Launceston Limited** *(T M Riordan)* 2 Barley Fields, Dark Lane, East Grafton, MARLBOROUGH, WILTSHIRE, SN8 3DR.

Laura Cusick *(L J Cusick)* 27 Midholm, LONDON, NW11 6LL.

Laura Davey Bookkeeping & Business Services *(L Davey)* 6 Lime Grove, Elton, CHESTER, CH2 4PX.

Laura Kenyon & Associates *(L M Kenyon)* 12 Southville Road, THAMES DITTON, SURREY, KT7 0UL.

Laurence A Cohen *(L A Cohen)* 25 Hartfield Avenue, Elstree, BOREHAMWOOD, WD6 3JB.

Ⓕ**Laurence B Butters** *(L B Butters)* 28 Elm Avenue, WATFORD, WD19 4BE.

Laurence Benson & Co *(L M Benson)* 19 Southerton Way, Shenley, RADLETT, HERTFORDSHIRE, WD7 9LJ.

Ⓕ**Laurence J. Pearson** *(L J Pearson)* 5 Tweed Street, BERWICK-UPON-TWEED, TD15 1NG.

Laurence Linchis *(L S Linchis)* 32 Greenway Close, Colney Hatch Lane, LONDON, N11 3NS.

Laurence Myears *(L C Myears)* 6 Beechcroft Road, Longlevens, GLOUCESTER, GL2 9HF.

Laurence S.Ross *(L S Ross)* 12 Kings Close, LONDON, NW4 2JT.

Ⓕ**Laurence Scodie** *(L Scodie)* P.O. Box 11194, 35B Flower Lane, LONDON, NW7 2JG.

Laurence Tanner *(L J Tanner)* 9 Grove Way, ESHER, KT10 8HH.

Laurence Taylor *(L Taylor)* 9 Handel Close, EDGWARE, HA8 7QZ.

Laurence W. Gardiner *(L W Gardiner)* Fermain, 124 Glaziers Lane, Normandy, GUILDFORD, GU3 2DQ.

Laurie Cowan *(L Cowan)* 4 Chase Side, ENFIELD, EN2 6NF.

★ⓉⒻⒶ**Laverick Walton & Co** *(D H Richardson, O E Sandy, K M Thomson)* 10 Grange Terrace, SUNDERLAND, SR2 7DF. and at GATESHEAD

Laverty & Co *(P J Laverty)* Rectory Cottage, Church Road, Hascombe, GODALMING, SURREY, GU8 4JD.

Ⓐ**Law & Co** *(P I Murray, K L Peters)* Pool House, Arran Close, 106 Birmingham Road, Great Barr, BIRMINGHAM, B43 7AD.

Ⓟ**Law & Partners CPA Limited** *(E Law)* 8/F Chinachem Tower, 34-37 Connaught Road, CENTRAL, HONG KONG ISLAND, HONG KONG SAR.

Law Kam Wing & Company *(K W Law)* 9th Floor, Full View Commercial Bldg, 140-142 Des Voeux Road, CENTRAL, HONG KONG ISLAND, HONG KONG SAR.

ⓉⒻⓅⒶ**Lawes, Lawes & Co, trading names of Lawes & Co UK Limited** *(K L Lawes)* Boyces Building, 42 Regent Street, Clifton, BRISTOL, BS8 4HU.

Lawford & Co *(S A Silcock)* Creek Lights, 23 Cliff Parade, LEIGH-ON-SEA, ESSEX, SS9 1AS.

Lawford & Co *(C J Dymek)* Union House, Walton Lodge, Bridge Street, WALTON-ON-THAMES, SURREY, KT12 1BT.

ⓉⓅⒶ**Lawfords Consulting, trading name of Lawfords Consulting Limited** *(C J Dymek, S L Ive, S A Silcock)* Union House, Walton Lodge, Bridge Street, WALTON-ON-THAMES, SURREY, KT12 1BT.

ⒻⒶ**Lawrence & Co** *(J P Chatwani, R N Popat)* 132/134 College Road, HARROW, HA1 1BQ.

Ⓟ**Lawrence & Co, trading name of Lawrence & Co Professional Limited** *(G A Lawrence)* 2 Albany Park, Cabot Lane, POOLE, DORSET, BH17 7BX.

Lawrence B Ladenheim *(L B Ladenheim)* 5 Yehuda Halevi Street, 43555 RA'ANANA, ISRAEL.

Lawrence Chan & Co *(T L Chan)* Suite 601A, Fourseas Building, 208 - 212 Nathan Road, TSIM SHA TSUI, KOWLOON, HONG KONG SAR.

Ⓟ**Lawrence Cheung C P A Company Limited** *(S K Cheung)* 20th Floor, Euro Trade Centre, 21-23 Des Voeux Road, CENTRAL, HONG KONG SAR.

Lawrence Davison FCA *(L G Davison)* Rushwyck House, Old Road, Herstmonceux, HAILSHAM, EAST SUSSEX, BN27 1PU.

★ⒻⒶ**Lawrence Grant** *(G Busch, P G Levy)* 2nd Floor, Hygeia House, 66 College Road, HARROW, MIDDLESEX, HA1 1BE.

Lawrence Hurst & Co *(L D Hurst)* 2nd Floor Morritt House, 10/12 Love Lane, PINNER, HA5 3EF.

ⒻⒶ**Lawrence Johns** *(T M O'Keeffe)* 202 Northolt Road, HARROW, HA2 0EX.

Lawrence P. Coppock *(L P Coppock)* The Close, Church Lane, Braishfield, ROMSEY, SO51 0QH.

Lawrence Phillips & Company *(L A Phillips)* 42 Lipizzaner Fields, Whiteley, FAREHAM, HAMPSHIRE, PO15 7BH.

Ⓟ**Lawrence Rose Limited** *(I R Lawrence)* 53 Basepoint Business Centre, Rivermead Drive, SWINDON, WILTSHIRE, SN5 7EX.

Ⓕ**Lawrence W. Karn & Co** *(L W Karn)* Rosebank House, Shripney Road, BOGNOR REGIS, PO22 9PA.

ⓉⒻⒶ**Lawrence Wong & Co** *(L C T Wong)* 2 Parkfield Gardens, North Harrow, HARROW, HA2 6JR.

Ⓐ**Lawrence, Nudds & Co** *(J D Lawrence, T R Nudds)* Alpha House, 176a High Street, BARNET, HERTFORDSHIRE, EN5 5SZ.

Lawrie Berry FCA *(L A G Berry)* Oakleigh, Paynes Lane, Nazeing, WALTHAM ABBEY, ESSEX, EN9 2EU.

Lawson & Co *(T H Lawson)* Little Hide, 18 The Lagger, CHALFONT ST. GILES, HP8 4DG.

Ⓐ**Lawson & Co** *(J I Lawson)* FPCI Group Building, Ellerbeck Way, Stokesley Ind Park, Stokesley, MIDDLESBROUGH, TS9 5JZ.

Ⓟ**Lawson Accounting Ltd** *(S Lawson)* 34 Feldspar Close, SITTINGBOURNE, KENT, ME10 5FE.

Ⓟ**Lawsons Accountants Limited** *(T H Lawson)* Little Hide, 18 The Lagger, CHALFONT ST. GILES, BUCKINGHAMSHIRE, HP8 4DG.

Ⓟ**Layfield & Co Ltd** *(P R Layfield)* The Lodge, Whitehouse Lane, NANTWICH, CHESHIRE, CW5 6HQ.

ⓉⒶ**Layton Lee, trading name of Layton Lee LLP** *(R A Layton, D A Lee)* 6 Manchester Road, BUXTON, DERBYSHIRE, SK17 6SB.

Ⓟ**Layton Train, trading name of Layton Train Limited** *(T J Woolmer)* 1 Town Quay Wharf, Abbey Road, BARKING, ESSEX, IG11 7BZ.

ⓉⓅⒶ**LB Group, LB Group Limited, trading names of LB Group Ltd** *(C D Annis, R C A Francis, M E Lake, T M Lake, M Middleton)* 82 East Hill, COLCHESTER, CO1 2QW. and at CHELMSFORD, IPSWICH, LONDON

Ⓟ**LBC Investigative Accounting (Suisse) sarl** *(G Senogles)* Route de St-Cergue 15, CH-1260 NYON, SWITZERLAND.

★ⓅⒶ**LBCA Limited** *(D A Cole, E M Hart)* 8 Waterside, Station Road, HARPENDEN, HERTFORDSHIRE, AL5 4US.

ⓅⒶ**LBW, trading name of Jimalice Limited** *(L B Webster)* Enterprise House, The Courtyard, Old Courtyard Road, Bromborough, WIRRAL, MERSEYSIDE CH62 4UE.

★**LC & JA Charge** *(J A Charge)* 6 Hawk Close, WALTHAM ABBEY, ESSEX, EN9 3NE.

Ⓟ**LC Debt Solutions Ltd** *(A Poxon, J M Titley)* Hollins Mount, Hollins Lane, BURY, LANCASHIRE, BL9 8DG.

Ⓟ**LCM Accountancy Services, trading name of Louise Marsden Ltd** *(L C Marsden)* 20 Poppyfields, Horsford, NORWICH, NR10 3SR.

Ⓟ**Le Cache Accounting Limited** *(M J Norman)* Le Courtil Cache Rue de la Cache, St. Andrew, GUERNSEY, GY6 8TH.

Ⓕ**Le Forts** *(A R Le Fort)* Britannia House, Roberts Mews, ORPINGTON, BR6 0JP.

Ⓢ**Le Rossignol, Scott Warren and Partners** *(C H Taylor)* Thomas Edge House, Tunnell Street, St Helier, JERSEY, JE2 4LU.

ⓉⒻⒶ**Leach & Co** *(M A Boundy, S P Burden, R J C Gidlow)* Ashley House, 136 Tolworth Broadway, SURBITON, SURREY, KT6 7LA.

Lean, Newton & Cary *(W J Newton)* 58 York Gardens, WALTON-ON-THAMES, SURREY, KT12 3EW.

ⓉⒶ**Leapman Weiss** *(H J Leapman, P A M Weiss)* Hillside House, 2-6 Friern Park, LONDON, N12 9BT.

Ⓟ**Learmonth & Co, trading name of Learmonth & Co Limited** *(C J Learmonth)* The Granary, 39 Bell Street, SAWBRIDGEWORTH, HERTFORDSHIRE, CM21 9AR.

Ⓐ**Leat Thorn & Partners** *(A K Jaitly)* 64 High View, PINNER, MIDDLESEX, HA5 3PB.

ⓉⒻⒶ**Leathers LLP** *(M R Leather)* 17th Floor, Cale Cross House, 156 Pilgrim Street, NEWCASTLE UPON TYNE, NE1 6SU.

Ⓟ**Lecram Consultancy Ltd** *(A M Garfield)* 120 Salmon Street, Kingsbury, LONDON, NW9 8NL.

★**Ledbury Business Services** *(L E Davies)* 136 Bridge Street, LEDBURY, HEREFORDSHIRE, HR8 2AS.

Ⓟ**Leddra Perry & Co, trading name of Leddra Perry & Co Ltd** *(J A H Hollow)* The Malakoff, ST. IVES, CORNWALL, TR26 2BH.

Ledger & Co *(M Ledger)* Brackendene, Lower Daggons, FORDINGBRIDGE, SP6 3EE.

Ⓟ**Ledgers Accountancy Services Limited** *(C A Collins)* 15 Sedgmoor Close, Flackwell Heath, HIGH WYCOMBE, BUCKINGHAMSHIRE, HP10 9BH.

ⓉⒻⓅⒶ**Lee & Co, trading name of Lee Accounting Services Limited** *(J D Lee, P Lee)* 26 High Street, RICKMANSWORTH, HERTFORDSHIRE, WD3 1ER.

ⒻⒶ**Lee & Company** *(P Lee, A M McClean)* Crown House, Armley Road, LEEDS, LS12 2EJ.

Lee Associates *(Y H Lee)* 30 Malpas Drive, PINNER, MIDDLESEX, HA5 1DQ.

Ⓟ**Lee Consulting Limited** *(J M North)* Equity House, 4-6 School Road, Tilehurst, READING, RG31 5AL.

Lee Financial Management P/L *(K H L Lee)* 18 Grevillea Cresent, HORNSBY, NSW 2077, AUSTRALIA.

Lee Ka Man & Co *(K Lee)* 10/F Hang Seng Wan chai Building, 200 Hennessy Road, WAN CHAI, HONG KONG SAR.

Lee Sik Wai & Co *(S W B Lee)* Offices 1612-17, Hollywood Plaza, 610 Nathan Road, Kowloon, MONG KOK, HONG KONG SAR.

Lee Stevens *(L S Stevens)* Tyelands, Parsonage Lane, Margaretting, INGATESTONE, ESSEX, CM4 9JL.

Ⓣ**Lee Teck Leong & Co** *(T L Lee)* 47 Jalan Batai Laut 5, Kawasan 16, Taman Intan, 41300 KLANG, SELANGOR, MALAYSIA.

Lee Yuen Kwong & Company *(Y Lee)* Unit 1301 13/F, Lemmi Centre, 50 Hoi Yuen Road, KWUN TONG, KOWLOON, HONG KONG SAR.

★**Lee, Dicketts & Co** *(R B Lugg)* York House, 37 High Street, Seal, SEVENOAKS, TN15 0AW.

Ⓟ**Lees Accounting Limited** *(P S Wilkinson)* 53 Chapelfield Crescent, Thorpe Hesley, ROTHERHAM, SOUTH YORKSHIRE, S61 2TP.

Ⓟ**Lees, trading name of CG Lee Ltd** *(C G Bidgood, I Clayton, J L Hyde)* Ingram House, Meridian Way, NORWICH, NR7 0TA.

ⓉⓅ**Lees, trading name of Lees Limited** *(K Holden, D J Lee, R D Lee)* The Granary, Brewer Street, Bletchingley, REDHILL, RH1 4QP.

ⒻⓅⒶ**Lees-Buckley & Co, trading name of LBCo Ltd** *(L G Lees-Buckley)* 16 Northfields Prospect Business Centre, Putney Bridge Road, LONDON, SW18 1PE.

Leesing Marrison Lee & Co *(D V Bland)* P O Box 341, Oldcotes, WORKSOP, NOTTINGHAMSHIRE, S80 4HW.

Ⓟ**Leesing Marrison Lee & Co, trading name of Leesing Marrison Lee Limited** *(D V Bland)* 46 Main Street, MEXBOROUGH, SOUTH YORKSHIRE, S64 9DU.

Ⓟ**Lefevres, trading name of Lefevres Limited** *(E M Lefevre)* 4 Huddington Glade, YATELEY, HAMPSHIRE, GU46 6FG.

★ⓉⒶ**Leftley Rowe & Company** *(H Alibhai, C J Andrews, J W Rowe, K J Wright)* The Heights, 59-65 Lowlands Road, HARROW, MIDDLESEX, HA1 3AW. and at LONDON

Legg & Co *(M Patterson)* 8 Greenrigg Close, Faverdale, DARLINGTON, COUNTY DURHAM, DL3 0EF.

Legg & Co. *(T Legg)* 589 Marton Road, MIDDLESBROUGH, CLEVELAND, TS4 3SD.

Ⓟ**Leggate Associates, trading name of Leggate Associates Limited** *(A Leggate)* Bencroft Dassels, Braughing, WARE, HERTFORDSHIRE, SG11 2RW.

Ⓕ**Leggatt Bell** *(P J Reeve, D V Thomason)* 14 Railway Street, CHELMSFORD, CM1 1QS.

Leggott J.E. *(J E Leggott)* Wayside Cottage, Cross Street, Great Hatfield, HULL, HU11 4UR.

Ⓐ**Leibovitch & Co** *(B Leibovitch)* 249 Cranbrook Road, ILFORD, IG1 4TG.

ⒻⒶ**Leigh Adams LLP** *(M H Linton)* Brentmead House, Britannia Road, LONDON, N12 9RU.

★ⓉⒻⒶ**Leigh Carr** *(R A De Souza, P Herelle, J S Natt, R.J. O'Gorman, I P Sugarman)* 72 New Cavendish Street, LONDON, W1G 8AU.

★Ⓐ**Leigh Graham Associates** *(G S J Beach)* 10 John Street, STRATFORD-UPON-AVON, WARWICKSHIRE, CV37 6UB.

Leigh Marx *(B M Leigh)* 11 Kensington Place, BRIGHTON, BN1 4EJ.

ⓉⒻⒶ**Leigh Philip & Partners** *(D E Butterley, L A Genis, A M Shaw)* 1/6 Clay Street, LONDON, W1U 6DA.

★ⒻⒶ**Leigh Saxton Green** *(D R Leigh, T L Saxton)* Clearwater House, 4-7 Manchester Street, LONDON, W1U 3AE.

Ⓟ**Leighton & Co** *(R M Leighton)* 40 Alexandra Road, WISBECH, PE13 1HQ.

Leighton & Leighton *(N Leighton)* 4 Rue Des Orchidees, MC98000 MONACO, MONACO.

★**Leiwy Sherman & Co** *(D H A Leiwy)* 19 Downalong, BUSHEY, WD23 1HZ.

★ⓉⒻ**Lemans** *(T Bailey, D P Groves, D Marshall)* 29 Arboretum Street, NOTTINGHAM, NG1 4JA.

★ⒻⒶ**Lemon & Co** *(B Horne)* 221 Shoreditch High Street, LONDON, E1 6PP.

Len Dainty & Co *(L Dainty)* 10 Glastonbury Close, STAFFORD, ST17 0PB.

Ⓟ**Len Entwistle, trading name of Wistle Limited** *(L Entwistle)* 290 Blackburn Road, Lynwood, DARWEN, LANCASHIRE, BB3 0AA.

ⒻⒶ**Lennard Dakin** *(M J Lennard)* 88 Great King Street, MACCLESFIELD, CHESHIRE, SK11 6PW.

★ⓉⒻⓅⒶ**Lentells, trading name of Lentells Limited** *(P H Bedford, N J Gamblen, I M Kelland, P A Stallard)* 17-18, Leach Road, Chard Business Park, CHARD, SOMERSET, TA20 1FA. and at LYME REGIS, SEATON, TAUNTON

Ⓟ**Lentongate Ltd** *(M P Horsnell, M L Rose, S N Seifert, F S Waxman)* Equity House, 128-136 High Street, EDGWARE, MIDDLESEX, HA8 7TT.

ⒻⓅⒶ**Leon Charles Ltd** *(L B Charalambides, K Schofield)* 247 Gray's Inn Road, LONDON, WC1X 8QZ.

ⒻⒶ**Leon, Schiller** *(J L Posner)* 100 High Ash Drive, LEEDS, LS17 8RE.

ⒻⒶ**Leonard Brown Ltd** *(L Brown, R W Lane)* Thornbury House, 16 Woodlands, GERRARDS CROSS, SL9 8DD.

ⓉⒻⒶ**Leonard Bye** *(D R Arkley, R A Brisley, J E Hill)* 80 Borough Road, MIDDLESBROUGH, TS1 2JN. and at NORTHALLERTON

Ⓟ**Leonard Curtis Limited** *(A Poxon, J M Titley)* 1 Great Cumberland Place, LONDON, W1H 7LW.

Ⓟ**Leonard Curtis, trading name of Leonard Curtis Recovery Limited** *(P D Masters, J F Mercer, A Poxon, J M Titley)* Hollins Lane, BURY, LANCASHIRE, BL9 8DG. and at BIRMINGHAM, BLACKBURN, BRISTOL, LONDON, MANCHESTER, NEWCASTLE UPON TYNE, WOLVERHAMPTON

ⒻⓅⒶ**Leonard Finn & Co Services Ltd** *(D M Finn, L I Finn)* Brentmead House, Britannia Road, LONDON, N12 9RU.

★ⓉⒶ**Leonard Gold** *(A Chapman, S B Howarth)* 24 Landport Terrace, PORTSMOUTH, PO1 2RG.

ⒻⒶ**Leonard Jones & Co** *(A L Carter, D A Lyons)* 1 Printing House Yard, LONDON, E2 7PR.

ⒻⒶ**Leonard Mann & Co.** *(L Zeiderman)* 28 Marlborough Road, ST. ALBANS, AL1 3XQ.

ⒻⒶ**Leonard Mogilner & Co** *(L Mogilner)* 30 Leys Gardens, Cockfosters, BARNET, EN4 9NA.

★Ⓐ**Leonard Wilson & Co** *(I C Turner)* Colinton House, Leicester Road, BEDWORTH, WARWICKSHIRE, CV12 8AB.

★ⒻⒶ**Leonherman** *(D A Swann)* 7 Christie Way, Christie Fields, MANCHESTER, M21 7QY.

Leonie Hopcraft *(L Hopcraft)* The Old Cornershop, The Green, Everdon, DAVENTRY, NORTHAMPTONSHIRE, NN11 3BL.

ⒻⓅⒶ**Lerman Jacobs Davis, trading name of Starplayer Limited** *(S D Davis, M Lerman)* 510 Centennial Park, Centennial Avenue, Elstree, BOREHAMWOOD, HERTFORDSHIRE, WD6 3FG.

★ⒻⒶ**Lerman Quaile** *(G Potts)* 56 Hamilton Square, BIRKENHEAD, MERSEYSIDE, CH41 5AS.

Les Haynes *(L C Haynes)* 30 Kemps Road, Twyford, BANBURY, OXFORDSHIRE, OX17 3JS.

ⒻⒶ**Leskin Galler** *(A M Galler)* The Linney, Oak Farm, Waddicombe, DULVERTON, SOMERSET, TA22 9RX.

Lesley Alexander *(L E Alexander)* 36 Ferrymans Quay, William Morris Way, LONDON, SW6 2UT.

Lesley Ann Cooper *(L A Cooper)* 160 Whitmore Road, HARROW, HA1 4AQ.

Lesley Clark *(L M Clark)* The Beeches, Manor Court, Carlton-le-Moorland, LINCOLN, LN5 9JJ.

★**Lesley Jane Baldwyn** *(L J Ward)* Pinewood, Crockford Lane, Chineham Business Park, Chineham, BASINGSTOKE, HAMPSHIRE RG24 8AL.

Lesley M. Lunnon *(L M Lunnon)* The Pightle, Alscot Lane, Princes Risborough, PRINCES RISBOROUGH, HP27 9RU.

Lesley Nears *(L E Nears)* 8 St Johns Road, Hazel Grove, STOCKPORT, SK7 5HG.

Lesley Pasricha *(L A Pasricha)* 8 Blanchard House, 28 Clevedon Road, TWICKENHAM, TW1 2TD.

Lesley White FCA *(L White)* Yew Tree Barn, Loads Road, Holymoorside, CHESTERFIELD, DERBYSHIRE, S42 7EU.

Leslie Burgess *(L Burgess)* 87 Shirley Avenue, CROYDON, CR0 8SP.

Ⓟ**Leslie Couldwell & Co, trading name of Mitchells (Knaresborough) Limited** *(L S Couldwell, D C Mitchell)* 37 High Street, KNARESBOROUGH, NORTH YORKSHIRE, HG5 0HB.

Leslie E. Caston *(L E Caston)* 8 Bower Close, Eaton Bray, DUNSTABLE, BEDFORDSHIRE, LU6 2DU.

Leslie Hinder *(L J Hinder)* Dairy House, 59 Cheapside Road, ASCOT, BERKSHIRE, SL5 7QR.

ⒻⒶ**Leslie Michael Lipowicz & Co** *(L M Lipowicz)* Accounts House, 16 Dalling Road, Hammersmith, LONDON, W6 0JB.

Leslie R. Ball *(L R Ball)* 28 Dunkirk Road, Birkdale, SOUTHPORT, PR8 4RQ.

Leslie Winnard *(L C D Winnard)* 32 Valley Rise, Shaw, OLDHAM, OL2 7QF.

ⒻⓅⒶ**Leslie Woolfson & Co, trading name of 25 School Lane Limited** *(L I Woolfson)* Profex House, 25 School Lane, BUSHEY, HERTFORDSHIRE, WD23 1SS.

ⓉⒶ**Leslie, Ward & Drew** *(J A Drew)* Kingston House, Pierrepont Street, BATH, BA1 1LA.

ⓉⒻⒶ**Lesser & Co** *(S M Lesser)* 147 Station Road, North Chingford, LONDON, E4 6AG.

Ⓟ**Lesser Business Services Ltd** *(S M Lesser)* 147 Station Road, North Chingford, LONDON, E4 6AG.

ⒻⒶ**Lester & Co** *(M A Lester, M P Lester)* 25 Station Road, HINCKLEY, LEICESTERSHIRE, LE10 1AP.

Lethenty Accounts *(C N B Nash)* Burnside, Lethenty, INVERURIE, ABERDEENSHIRE, AB51 0HQ.

Leung & Chan *(K S Chan)* Room 1203 Valley Centre, 80-82 Morrison Hill Road, WAN CHAI, HONG KONG SAR.

Ⓟ**Leung & Puen CPA Ltd** *(J N Leung)* 6th Floor, Kwan Chart Tower, 6 Tonnochy Road, WAN CHAI, HONG KONG ISLAND, HONG KONG SAR.

Leung Ming Chi *(M C Leung)* Unit D 5th Floor, China Insurance Building, 48 Cameron Road, TSIM SHA TSIU, KOWLOON, HONG KONG SAR.

Leung Yau Wing & Co *(Y Leung)* Unit 1006, 10/F, Cigna Tower, 482 Jaffe Road, CAUSEWAY BAY, HONG KONG ISLAND HONG KONG SAR.

★ⓉⒻⒶ**Lever Bros & Co** *(G J Marrett)* The Station Masters House, 168 Thornbury Road, ISLEWORTH, MIDDLESEX, TW7 4QE.

ⒻⒶ**Levett, Charles & Co** *(T C Clark)* Abacus House, 70-72 High Street, BEXLEY, DA5 1AJ.

★ⓉⒻⒶ**Levicks** *(M A Collier, J A Griggs, M J Hurdman, K Luxford, J A Williamson)* West Hill, 61 London Road, MAIDSTONE, ME16 8TX. and at BROADSTAIRS, CANTERBURY

Ⓟ**Levin Harris & Co Limited** *(G A Harris)* 21 Butt Hill Road, Prestwich, MANCHESTER, M25 9NJ.

ⓉⒻⒶ**Levy & Co, trading name of Roger Lugg & Co** *(H D Barrett, B W Chapman, R B Lugg)* 12/14 High Street, CATERHAM, CR3 5UA. and at LINGFIELD

ⒻⓅⒶ**Levy & Partners, trading name of Levy + Partners Limited** *(R N Bhargava, A L Joshi)* 86-88 South Ealing Road, LONDON, W5 4QB.

★Ⓐ**Levy Cohen & Co** *(R C Shahmoon)* 37 Broadhurst Gardens, LONDON, NW6 3QT.

Ⓐ**Levys** *(B F Levy)* Number One Trinity, 161 Old Christchurch Road, BOURNEMOUTH, BH1 1JU.

Ⓟ**Lewin Accounts Ltd** *(C Lewin)* Mercury House, 19-21 Chapel Street, MARLOW, BUCKINGHAMSHIRE, SL7 3HN.

Lewis & Co *(N H Lewis)* Walden, Widcombe Hill, BATH, BA2 6ED.

ⒻⒶ**Lewis & Co** *(R W Lewis)* 19 Goodge Street, LONDON, W1T 2PH.

ⒻⓅ**Lewis & Co (Financial Management) Ltd** *(P J Lewis)* 2 Doughty Buildings, Crow Arch Lane, RINGWOOD, HAMPSHIRE, BH24 1NZ.

Ⓟ**Lewis & Co, trading name of B J Lewis & Co Ltd** *(B J Lewis)* 134 London Road, Southborough, TUNBRIDGE WELLS, TN4 0PL.

Lewis & Lewis, trading name of Morris John Catlin *(M J Catlin)* 209 High Town Road, LUTON, LU2 0BZ.

Ⓟ**Lewis Accounting Ltd** *(I R Lewis)* 26 Brookfields Way, East Leake, LOUGHBOROUGH, LEICESTERSHIRE, LE12 6HD.

ⒻⒶ**Lewis Alexander & Connaughton** *(M D Alexander, V P Connaughton, D E Pennington, C J Sugarman)* Second Floor, Boulton House, 17-21 Chorlton Street, MANCHESTER, M1 3HY.

ⓉⒶ**Lewis Brownlee** *(S M Alexander, J D Green, M Merritt, W J C Neville)* Avenue House, Southgate, CHICHESTER, WEST SUSSEX, PO19 1ES.

ⓅⒶ**Lewis Curtis Limited** *(A M Chandley)* 10 Durham Avenue, Gidea Park, ROMFORD, RM2 6JS.

Lewis Dyson, trading name of Lewis Dyson LLP *(M A Lewis)* 10 Fleet Place, LONDON, EC4M 7RB.

★ⓉⒻⒶ**Lewis Golden & Co** *(N W Benson, D C Edwards, A G Moss, A R Parker, S J Webber)* 40 Queen Anne Street, LONDON, W1G 9EL.

Lewis Hassell *(L I Hassell)* 235 Bury New Road, Whitefield, MANCHESTER, M45 8QP.

Lewis Mead *(A D Lewis)* The Mead, 143 Pilgrims Way, Kemsing, SEVENOAKS, TN15 6TR.

Lewis Nestel & Co *(L A L Nestel)* 17 Woodside Avenue, LONDON, N12 8AN.

ⓉⒻⒶ**Lewis Rowell** *(M A Millard, P W Rowell)* 20 Springfield Road, CRAWLEY, WEST SUSSEX, RH11 8AD.

Ⓐ**Lewis-Simler** *(G J Simler)* 83 Baker Street, LONDON, W1U 6AG.

Leybourne & Co *(S Leybourne)* 25 Crossley Hill, HALIFAX, HX3 0PL.

ⓉⒻⒶ**LF Creative, trading name of Lubbock Fine** *(S C Banks, L C Facey, J Gitter, G G Goodyear, R Majithia, L D Newman, R M Rich, N D P Shah, P N Shah, M Turner)* Russell Bedford House, City Forum, 250 City Road, LONDON, EC1V 2QQ.

LHK *(G Q Khan)* First Floor Offices, 167 Sutton Road, Wylde Green, SUTTON COLDFIELD, B23 5TN.

★**Li, Tang, Chen & Co.** *(W H Chan, P C Law, E K Li, K F D Li, K Yan)* 10/F Sun Hung Kai Centre, 30 Harbour Road, WAN CHAI, HONG KONG ISLAND, HONG KONG SAR.

Ⓟ**Libcus Limited** *(N E Riley)* Wye House, Water Street, BAKEWELL, DERBYSHIRE, DE45 1EW.

Ⓟ**Liberty Financial Solutions, trading name of Liberty Financial Solutions Group Ltd** *(S Thomson)* Cranfield Innovation Centre, University Way, Cranfield Technology Park, Cranfield, BEDFORD, MK43 0BT.

Ⓟ**Libra** *(Philip Gross)* 30 St Vincents Way, POTTERS BAR, EN6 2RF.

Ⓟ**Libra Wealth Management Limited** *(W C Humphreys)* 18 Mitchell Road, WEST MALLING, KENT, ME19 4RF.

Ⓟ**Libris, trading name of Libris Accounting Limited** *(E J Kane)* 25 Nursery Close, Potton, SANDY, BEDFORDSHIRE, SG19 2QE.

Ⓟ**Lichfield & Co, trading name of APRP Ltd** *(P B Patel)* 91 Sunnyhill Road, Streatham, LONDON, SW16 2UG.

Liddiard & Co *(S P Liddiard)* Arcturus, The Vallance, Lynsted, SITTINGBOURNE, KENT, ME9 0RP.

Liew & Co *(S N C Liew)* G/F 7 Mulgrave Chambers, 26-28 Mulgrave Road, SUTTON, SURREY, SM2 6LE.

ⓅⒶ**Liles Morris, trading name of Liles Morris Ltd** *(T R T Morris)* Park House, 233 Roehampton Lane, LONDON, SW15 4LB.

Ⓐ**Lilley & Co.** *(B M Lilley)* 125 John Wilson Business Park, Chestfield, WHITSTABLE, KENT, CT5 3QT.

★**Lim Chong & Co** *(K K Lim)* P.O. Box 13661, 88841 KOTA KINABALU, SABAH, MALAYSIA.

Lim Han Ho & Co *(H H S N Lim)* 502-A Jalan Pintu Sepuluh, 05100 ALOR STAR, KEDAH, MALAYSIA.

Lim Hon Chew & Co *(H C Lim)* 25 Jalan Ampang Hilir, KUALA LUMPUR, FEDERAL TERRITORY, MALAYSIA.

Lim Teoh & Co *(T E Teoh)* 503-A Jalan Pintu Sepuluh, 05100 ALOR STAR, KEDAH, MALAYSIA.

Ⓟ**Lime Accountancy, trading name of Lime Accountancy Limited** *(V Bayman)* 10 Upper Bourne Lane, Wrecclesham, FARNHAM, SURREY, GU10 4RQ.

Ⓟ**Limelight Accountancy Limited** *(C L Steadman)* 60 Midhurst Road, LIPHOOK, GU30 7DY. and at HASLEMERE

ⒻⓅⒶ**Lince Salisbury Limited** *(M J Fattorini, G G Robert)* Avenue House, St Julians Avenue, St Peter Port, GUERNSEY, GY1 1WA.

ⓅⒶ**Lincroft & Company Limited** *(C D Lincroft)* Langsyght, 160 Burntwood Lane, CATERHAM, SURREY, CR3 6TB.

Ⓟ**Linda Cotterill, trading name of LCCA Limited** *(L A Cotterill)* Hopton Corner House, Alfrick, WORCESTER, WR6 5HP.

Linda Dunning *(J L Dunning)* The Dormers, 92 Bell Lane, AMERSHAM, HP6 6PG.
Linda Gibson *(L A Gibson)* 44 Hillfield Road, Selsey, CHICHESTER, WEST SUSSEX, PO20 0LF.
Ⓕ**Linda Giles** *(L Giles)* 12 The Gap, Marcham, ABINGDON, OX13 6NJ.
Linda J. Sharpin *(L J Sharpin)* Mayfield House, 2 Ganghill, GUILDFORD, GU1 1XE.
Ⓟ**Linda Koscia Ltd** *(L J Zbirohowska-Koscia)* Wedgewood, Mapledrakes Road, Ewhurst, CRANLEIGH, GU6 7QW.
Ⓟ**Linden Asset Management Limited** *(T R Alanthwaite)* The Linden Building, Regent Park, 37 Booth Drive, Park Farm Industrial Estate, WELLINGBOROUGH, NORTHAMPTONSHIRE NN8 6GR.
ⓉⒶ**Lindeyer Francis Ferguson** *(M W Ferguson, J S Francis, J P Healey, S Wells)* North House, 198 High Street, TONBRIDGE, TN9 1BE.
Ⓟ**Lindeyer Francis Ferguson Limited** *(M W Ferguson, J S Francis)* North House, 198 High Street, TONBRIDGE, KENT, TN9 1BE.
Ⓟ**Lindford & Company, trading name of HH Accounting & Tax Solutions Limited** *(P A Burnham, C J Howe, T J Lindford, R J Malone)* 64 Clarendon Road, WATFORD, WD17 1DA. and at LONDON
★**Lindley & Co** *(S K Lindley)* 17 Millbrook Drive, Shenstone, LICHFIELD, WS14 0JL. and at CANNOCK
★ⓉⒻⓅⒶ**Lindley Adams, trading name of Lindley Adams Limited** *(D C Adams, T A Kelliher)* 28 Prescott Street, HALIFAX, WEST YORKSHIRE, HX1 2LG.
Lindsay & Co *(D R H Lindsay)* 119 Boundary Road, WALLINGTON, SURREY, SM6 0TE.
Lindsay Beckman & Co *(L Beckman)* 8 Bloxham Road, BROADWAY, WR12 7EU.
Ⓟ**Lindsay Beckman & Co Limited** *(L Beckman)* 8 Bloxham Road, BROADWAY, WR12 7EU.
Ⓟ**Lindsell Business Solutions Ltd** *(P E Lindsell)* 2 Crabtree Cottages, Savernake, MARLBOROUGH, WILTSHIRE, SN8 3HP.
★**Lindsey & Co** *(B Lindsey)* 9 Chapel Mews, WOODFORD GREEN, ESSEX, IG8 8GP.
Lindsey-Renton & Co *(A P Lindsey-Renton)* 43 Waterlow Road, REIGATE, SURREY, RH2 7EY.
Ⓟ**LindseyTye, trading name of LindseyTye Limited** *(S N M Lindsey)* The Stables, Manor Farm Drive, Sutton Benger, CHIPPENHAM, WILTSHIRE, SN15 4RW.
★ⓉⒻⒶ**Ling Phipp** *(P N Horton-Turner, D J Lockwood)* Cliffe Hill House, 22-26 Nottingham Road, Stapleford, NOTTINGHAM, NG9 8AA.
Linger & Co *(A C Linger)* Barrycliffe House, 2 Park View Road, Four Oaks, SUTTON COLDFIELD, B74 4PP.
Ⓟ**Linger Associates Limited** *(A C Linger)* Barrycliffe House, 2 Park View Road, Four Oaks, SUTTON COLDFIELD, WEST MIDLANDS, B74 4PP.
Lingfield Partners LLP *(T J Gerhard, F A Lilley, S Mollett, J R Terry)* The Barn, Park Farm, Felbridge, EAST GRINSTEAD, WEST SUSSEX, RH19 2RB.
Lingham & Co *(N T Lingham)* 65 Higher Drive, PURLEY, SURREY, CR8 2HR.
ⓅⒶ**Linghams, trading name of The Lingham Consultancy Ltd** *(P Lingham)* 7 Raleigh Walk, Brigantine Place, CARDIFF, CF10 4LN.
ⓉⒻⒶ**Lings** *(C L Howard, F J Marson, A Smith, M Wragg)* Provident House, 51 Wardwick, DERBY, DE1 1HN.
★Ⓟ**Link Kaplan, trading name of Link Kaplan Limited** *(M Tarragano)* 166 Upper Richmond Road, LONDON, SW15 2SH.
ⓅⒶ**Link, trading name of Linkca Ltd** *(J Kotecha)* 1 Admiral House, Cardinal Way, HARROW, MIDDLESEX, HA3 5TE.
ⓉⒶ**Linn Maggs Goldwin** *(P R Goldwin)* 2-4 Great Eastern Street, LONDON, EC2A 3NT.
Lionel C Harber *(L C Harber)* 37 Charnhill Drive, Mangotsfield, BRISTOL, BS16 9JR.
Liong Kong *(K L Kong)* 2195 Westhill Wynd, VANCOUVER V7S 2Z3, BC, CANADA.
Ⓟ**Liric Accountants Ltd** *(L H Compton)* Wyndmere House, Ashwell Road, Steeple Morden, ROYSTON, HERTFORDSHIRE, SG8 0NZ.
Lisa Darby ACA *(L J Darby)* 18 Church Road, BUCKHURST HILL, ESSEX, IG9 5RU.
Lisa Gadsby Book Keeping Services *(L M Gadsby)* Barn Owl Cottage, 32 Agates Lane, ASHTEAD, SURREY, KT21 2ND.
Lisa James *(L A James)* 20 Gander Green, HAYWARDS HEATH, WEST SUSSEX, RH16 1RB.
Lisa M Stretton *(L M Stretton)* 9 Felstead Close, Dosthill, TAMWORTH, STAFFORDSHIRE, B77 1QD.
Lisa McIlrath ACA *(L J McIlrath)* 116 Offington Avenue, WORTHING, WEST SUSSEX, BN14 9PR.
Lisa Scott *(L H Scott)* 22 St Augustines Road, LONDON, NW1 9RN.
Lister, Gilleard & Co *(D R Moore)* Standard House, George Street, HUDDERSFIELD, HD1 2JF.
ⓉⒻⒶ**Litchfields** *(R H Shah)* 5 Luke Street, LONDON, EC2A 4PX.
ⓉⒻⒶ**Lithgow Perkins LLP** *(M E Briggs, R J Horner, J Perkins, D E Watler)* Crown Chambers, Princes Street, HARROGATE, HG1 1NJ.
ⓉⒻⒶ**Lithgow, Nelson & Co** *(R Barr, P J Gee)* Unit F/1, Moor Hall, Sandhawes Hill, EAST GRINSTEAD, WEST SUSSEX, RH19 3NR.
Ⓟ**Litting Associates Ltd** *(M B Litting)* 74 Abbotsford Road, LICHFIELD, STAFFORDSHIRE, WS14 9XL.
ⓉⒻⒶ**Little & Company** *(S T Dudfield, N G Gratton)* 45 Park Road, GLOUCESTER, GL1 1LP.
Ⓟ**Little & Neal, trading name of Fourward Developments (UK) Ltd** *(L A Wall)* 37-38 Market Street, FERRYHILL, COUNTY DURHAM, DL17 8JH.
Little Accounting Solutions *(T Little)* Tewthwaite House, Tewthwaite Green, Blackford, CARLISLE, CA6 4EZ.
Little Acorns Accounting Services, trading name of Rebecca Marie Lord ACA MAAT *(R M Lord)* 52 Sparrowmire Lane, KENDAL, CUMBRIA, LA9 5PX.
★ⓉⒻⒶ**Littlejohn, trading name of Littlejohn LLP** *(P Alexander, J E Brew, N A Coulson, I M Cowan, D R M Frame, E H Hindson, P W Hopper, A J Knapp, N M C Light, M R Ling, S Morrison, J C Needham, C A Palmer, C Papa, A M Rana, M P Reddihough, A D Roberts, D W Roberts, J P Rummins, A J Sheridan, M T Stenson, D A Thompson, D H Tout)* 1 Westferry Circus, Canary Wharf, LONDON, E14 4HD.
Ⓟ**Littlestone Golding, trading name of Littlestone Golding Limited** *(V Humphrey)* 29 Hawthorn Crescent, Hazlemere, HIGH WYCOMBE, HP15 7PL.
ⓉⒻⒶ**Littlestone Martin Glenton** *(V R Drexler, D G Humphrey, R H Weston, M J Wright)* 73 Wimpole Street, LONDON, W1G 8AZ.
Ⓟ**Live Wire Business Management, trading name of Jeanstock Limited** *(L Murphy)* Canal House, 26 Grove Island, Corbally, LIMERICK, COUNTY LIMERICK, IRELAND.
ⓅⒶ**Livesey Spottiswood Holdings Ltd** *(N Bamber, J E Derbyshire, D J Hudd, H J Jesse)* 17 George Street, ST. HELENS, MERSEYSIDE, WA10 1DB.
★ⒻⓅⒶ**Livesey Spottiswood, trading name of Livesey Spottiswood Limited** *(N Bamber, J E Derbyshire, D J Hudd, H J Jesse)* 17 George Street, ST.HELENS, WA10 1DB.
Ⓐ**Livingstone & Co** *(A Livingstone)* 123 Oatlands Drive, WEYBRIDGE, KT13 9LB.
Ⓟ**Lixin CPA Limited** *(P C A Chan)* Unit 1602, Malaysia Building, 50 Gloucester Road, WAN CHAI, HONG KONG SAR.
Liz Clark *(E Clark)* 32 Sandhurst Avenue, West Didsbury, MANCHESTER, M20 1ED.
Liz Glaser *(E J Glaser)* Rookery, Pitney, LANGPORT, SOMERSET, TA10 9AS.
Liz Noble FCA CTA *(E Noble)* Westerlands, Belle Cross Road, KINGSBRIDGE, DEVON, TQ7 1NL.
Liz Owen Accounting Services *(E J Owen)* 24 Knighton Road, Woodthorpe, NOTTINGHAM, NG5 4FL.
Liz Stonebridge *(E Stonebridge)* 38 Manners Road, Balderton, NEWARK, NOTTINGHAMSHIRE, NG24 3HW.
LJ Accountancy Services Ltd *(L J Fisher)* 45 Riversleigh Drive, STOURBRIDGE, WEST MIDLANDS, DY8 4YQ.
LJ Mills FCA *(L J Mills)* Lower Church Farm, Church Lane, Cockfield, BURY ST. EDMUNDS, SUFFOLK, IP30 0LA.
Ⓟ**LJ Smith Accountants Limited** *(L J Smith)* Orwell House, 50 High Street, HUNGERFORD, BERKSHIRE, RG17 0NE.
Ⓟ**LJT Financial Management Limited** *(L J Taylor)* 31 Lloyd Road, Handsworth Wood, BIRMINGHAM, B20 2ND.
ⒻⒶ**LK** *(P M A Bartlett)* Suite D, Pinbrook Court, Venny Bridge, Pinhoe, EXETER, EX4 8JQ.
Ⓟ**LK Davies, trading name of LK Davies Limited** *(L K Davies)* 3 The Courtyard, Shapwick, BRIDGWATER, SOMERSET, TA7 9LQ.
Ⓟ**LK Tax & Accountancy Services Ltd** *(L Kidd)* 27 St. Ternans Road, Newtonhill, STONEHAVEN, KINCARDINESHIRE, AB39 3PF.
Ⓟ**LKCA Limited** *(P M A Bartlett)* Suite D, Pinbrook Court, Venny Bridge, EXETER, EX4 8JQ.
ⒻⒶ**LKP, trading name of The LK Partnership LLP** *(L Dunstan, K M Rigby)* Rowan House, Hill End Lane, ST. ALBANS, HERTFORDSHIRE, AL4 0RA.
Ⓟ**LKT, trading name of LKT Limited** *(A S Tennant)* Ravenshill Cottage, Yewleigh Lane, Upton-upon-Severn, WORCESTER, WR8 0QW.
Llandaff Accountancy & Business Services *(A R Biss)* 5 Insole Close, CARDIFF, CF5 2HQ.
ⓉⒶ**Llewelyn Davies** *(C R John, K J Randall)* Bank House, St.James Street, NARBERTH, PEMBROKESHIRE, SA67 7BX. and at PEMBROKE DOCK, TENBY, WHITLAND
ⓉⒶ**Lloyd & Co** *(M R Lloyd, M L Martin)* 103-105 Brighton Road, COULSDON, SURREY, CR5 2NG.
Lloyd Accounting *(G A Lloyd)* Chapel Cottage, Chapel Lane, Westhumble, DORKING, RH5 6AY.
ⓉⒻⓅⒶ**Lloyd Dowson & Co, trading name of Lloyd Dowson Limited** *(D W Dowson, J E Manson, S J Nuttall)* Medina House, 2 Station Avenue, BRIDLINGTON, YO16 4LZ.
Lloyd G Raskina CA *(L G Raskina)* 5 McIntosh Drive, Suite 218, MARKHAM L3R 8C7, ON, CANADA.
ⓉⒻⓅⒶ**Lloyd Piggott, trading name of Lloyd Piggott Limited** *(G L Dodds, S J Redmond)* Wellington House, 1st Floor, 39-41 Piccadilly, MANCHESTER, M1 1LQ. and at STOCKPORT
Lloyd, Thompson & Carl *(D M Thompson)* 41 Eastwood Road, The Mount, SHREWSBURY, SY3 8YJ.
ⓉⒶ**Llyr James** *(C L James)* 25 Bridge Street, CARMARTHEN, SA31 3JS.
Ⓟ**LM Ebdon, trading name of L M Ebdon Ltd** *(L M Ebdon)* Lund Farm, The Lund, Easingwold, YORK, YO61 3PA.
LM Wood *(L M Wood)* 22 John Aubrey Close, Yatton Keynell, CHIPPENHAM, WILTSHIRE, SN14 7EG.
Ⓟ**LMAC LTD** *(E McOwat)* Lower Ground Floor, 5 Brunswick Place, HOVE, EAST SUSSEX, BN3 1EA.
Ⓟ**LMDB Accountants, trading name of LMDB Limited** *(R M S Booth, S Diomedou)* Railview Lofts, 19c Commercial Road, EASTBOURNE, EAST SUSSEX, BN21 3XE.
LMG Taxation & Accountancy *(L M Glitherow)* 5 Foreman Way, Kemp Street, Crowland, PETERBOROUGH, PE6 0DJ.
LML Accounting Solutions *(L M Loader)* Copse Cottage, Pondcopse Lane, Loxwood, BILLINGSHURST, WEST SUSSEX, RH14 0XF.
LMS, trading name of Life Management Services *(N C Saker)* 69 Littleton Street, LONDON, SW18 3SZ.
Ⓟ**Lo & Lo CPA Limited** *(K M C Lo)* Room 2111, Wing on Centre, 111 Connaught Road, CENTRAL, HONG KONG ISLAND, HONG KONG SAR.
Lock & Co *(C J Lock)* Silverwood, Withyham Rd, Groombridge, TUNBRIDGE WELLS, TN3 9QR.
ⒻⒶ**Locke Williams Associates LLP** *(C B Locke, K L Williams)* Blackthorn House, St Paul's Square, BIRMINGHAM, B3 1RL.
Ⓟ**Locum Accounting, trading name of Locum Accounting Limited** *(J Patwari)* 39 High Street, LEATHERHEAD, SURREY, KT22 8AE.
Ⓟ**Lofthouse & Co** *(J S Lofthouse)* 36 Ropergate, PONTEFRACT, WF8 1LY.
Lofts & Co. *(M C Lofts)* 6 South Terrace, South Street, DORCHESTER, DORSET, DT1 1DE.
Logicum *(A L Stuart)* Longcroft House, 2-8 Victoria Avenue, LONDON, EC2M 4NS.
Logicum, trading name of A L Stuart ACA *(A L Stuart)* Longcroft House, 2-8 Victoria Avenue, LONDON, EC2M 4NS.
Ⓟ**Logika Solutions India Pvt Limited** *(M P Smith)* 4 Floor Statesman House, Connaught Place, Barakhamba Road, NEW DELHI 110001, INDIA.
★ⓅⒶ**Logika, trading name of Logika Limited** *(M P Smith)* 12 Romney Place, MAIDSTONE, KENT, ME15 6LE. and at RYDE
Ⓟ**Logivat Ltd** *(R K Lung)* 17 Hemingford Close, LONDON, N12 9HF.
★**Loizou & Loizou** *(J S N Loizou)* P. Valdaseride 33, PO Box 42501, 6500 LARNACA, CYPRUS.
★**Lok Ki Ho & Co.** *(L K Ho)* Suite No 2325, 8888 Odlin Crescent, RICHMOND V6X 3Z8, BC, CANADA.
Lomas & Co. *(M E Percival)* 28a Hardwick Street, BUXTON, DERBYSHIRE, SK17 6DH.
ⒻⓅⒶ**Lomas & Company, trading name of Lomas and Company Accountants Limited** *(P J Lomas)* Bridge House, 12 Market Street, GLOSSOP, DERBYSHIRE, SK13 8AR.
Lombard *(C A Lombard)* 20 Pine Drive, INGATESTONE, ESSEX, CM4 9EF.
Ⓟ**Lomond Accountancy, trading name of Lomond Accountancy Ltd** *(M J Greener)* Acre Cottage, Clynder, HELENSBURGH, DUNBARTONSHIRE, G84 0QQ.
Ⓟ**London & Bath Limited** *(A M Pitt)* 14 Queen Square, BATH, BA1 2HN. and at LONDON
Ⓟ**London Financial & Management Services Limited** *(W J Palmer)* PO Box 306, STANMORE, MIDDLESEX, HA7 4ZN.
Lonergan & Co. *(D P Lonergan)* 107A London Road, LEICESTER, LE2 0PF.
Loney & Co *(D S Loney)* 13 Berrishill Grove, Red House Farm, WHITLEY BAY, NE25 9XU.
ⓉⒻⒶ**Long & Co** *(J B Whitaker)* PO Box 109, BINGLEY, BD16 1ZQ.
Ⓟ**Long & Co, trading name of Long & Co Limited** *(G R Long)* 65a High Street, STEVENAGE, HERTFORDSHIRE, SG1 3AQ.
Long & Co.(Harrogate) *(A Scholefield)* 17 Wensley Road, HARROGATE, NORTH YORKSHIRE, HG2 8AQ.
Longboat Tax Advisers LLP *(P J Brook, I Herzenshtein)* St. James House, 13 Kensington Square, LONDON, W8 5HD.
Longboat VAT Advisers LLP *(P J Brook, I Herzenshtein)* St. James House, 13 Kensington Square, LONDON, W8 5HD.
Longden & Cook Dental Accountancy Practice *(H M Brownson)* 113 Union Street, OLDHAM, OL1 1RU.
ⒻⒶ**Longden & Cook Dental Accountancy Practice, trading name of S.D. Woolf & Co** *(H M Brownson)* 113 Union Street, OLDHAM, OL1 1RY.
Ⓟ**Longdon Asset Management Ltd** *(C R Ayres)* The Old Barrel Store, Draymans Lane, MARLOW, BUCKINGHAMSHIRE, SL7 2FF. and at LONDON
Longhill Accounting *(C C Thring)* 1 Longhill Lodge, Ditcheat, SHEPTON MALLET, SOMERSET, BA4 6QR.
Ⓟ**Longley Consulting Limited** *(V G T Longley)* 16 Highfield Drive, KINGSBRIDGE, DEVON, TQ7 1JR.
Ⓟ**Longman Accountancy Services Limited** *(B Longman)* Waterloo House, 141 Albion Road, New Mills, HIGH PEAK, DERBYSHIRE, SK22 3JP.
ⓉⒻⒶ**Lonsdale & Marsh** *(O J Grills, E F McElroy, N J O'Donovan, J R M Simcox, A C Thompson)* Orleans House, Edmund Street, LIVERPOOL, L3 9NG. and at ORMSKIRK
ⓉⒻⒶ**Lopian, Gross, Barnett & Co** *(J D Brodie, S A Kahan, D Z Lopian, S A Lopian, J H Selig)* 6th Floor, Cardinal House, 20 St. Marys Parsonage, MANCHESTER, M3 2LG.
Loraine & Boleat *(R M Boleat, G S Loraine)* First Floor, 7 Bond Street, St. Helier, JERSEY, JE2 3NP.
Lord & Co *(M Silver)* 31 Waterpark Road, SALFORD, M7 4FT. and at ROCHDALE
Ⓟ**Lord Associates Limited** *(I E Philip)* Caxton House, Old Station Road, LOUGHTON, ESSEX, IG10 4PE.
Ⓟ**Lordsbury Consulting Ltd** *(M K Clifford-King)* 29 Eghams Wood Road, BEACONSFIELD, BUCKINGHAMSHIRE, HP9 1JU.
Lorelie Staines *(L M Staines)* 2 Garrick Close, WALTON-ON-THAMES, KT12 5NY.
ⓉⓅ**Lorna Glenister Limited** *(L A Glenister)* 5 The Square, BAGSHOT, SURREY, GU19 5AX.
Lou Simans & Co *(L Simans)* 35 Court Road, SOUTHPORT, MERSEYSIDE, PR9 9ET.
Ⓟ**Loughrey & Co, trading name of Loughrey & Co Ltd** *(M J Loughrey)* 38 Market Street, Hoylake, WIRRAL, MERSEYSIDE, CH47 2AF.
Ⓟ**Louis Broadbent, trading name of Louis Broadbent Limited** *(W L F Broadbent)* Cleevehead, Old Coach Road, Cross, AXBRIDGE, SOMERSET, BS26 2EG.
★**Louis Yeung & Co.** *(J W L Yeung)* Room 706 Grand City Plaza, 1 Sai Lau Kok Road, TSUEN WAN, 9999, HONG KONG SAR.
Louise Bowran Accountancy *(C L Bowran)* 14 Kendal Close, PETERBOROUGH, PE4 7GN.
Louise Girvin *(L A Girvin)* Fieldsway, 4A Pikemere Road, Alsager, STOKE-ON-TRENT, ST7 2SB.
Louise Higson ACA *(L Higson)* Dean House Farm, Dean House Lane, Stainland, HALIFAX, WEST YORKSHIRE, HX4 9LG.
Louise Hollands *(L Hollands)* 1 Chapel Loke, Hargham Road, Old Buckenham, NORFOLK, NR17 1PY.
Louise Sharif *(L J Sharif)* The White Hart, 80 Main Road, Hackleton, NORTHAMPTON, NN7 2AD.
Ⓟ**Lovelawn Limited** *(J R Newnham)* Lawn Cottage, Portsmouth Road, Milford, GODALMING, GU8 5HZ.
Lovells *(P J Lovell)* 44 Elthorne Park Road, Hanwell, LONDON, W7 2JA.
Lovelock & Lewes *(P Mitra)* 4 Lyons Range, CALCUTTA 700001, INDIA. and at MUMBAI
ⓉⒻⓅ**Lovetts, trading name of FBL Services Limited** *(A B Lovett, P A R Skipper)* Bridge House, 25 Fiddle Bridge Lane, HATFIELD, HERTFORDSHIRE, AL10 0SP.
★ⓉⒶ**Lovewell Blake LLP** *(P J Blythe-Bartram, P Briddon, D J Buller, S De-Lacy Adams, C A E Fish, B J Floringer, R J Gascoyne-Richards, R A Leggett, R Morris, N P Orford, M Proctor, M D L Smith, P D Young)* Sixty Six, North Quay, GREAT YARMOUTH, NORFOLK, NR30 1HE. and at HALESWORTH, LOWESTOFT, NORWICH, THETFORD

★**Lowe & Whitwell** *(D W Nelson)* 134 Highgate, KENDAL, LA9 4HL.
Ⓟ**Lowe Henwood, trading name of Lowe Henwood Limited** *(E J Henwood, L R Lowe)* The Lodge, 149 Mannamead Road, PLYMOUTH, PL3 5NU.
ⓉⒺⓅⒶ**Lowe McTernan, trading name of Lowe McTernan Limited** *(C S Williams, D P Wright)* Highcroft House, 81-85 New Road, Rubery, Rednal, BIRMINGHAM, B45 9JR.
Ⓐ**Lowndes & Co** *(T G Lowndes)* The Blackberry Patch, Parkstone Road, Ropley, ALRESFORD, HAMPSHIRE, SO24 0EP.
Ⓟ**Lowndes & Co Limited** *(T G Lowndes)* The Blackberry Patch, Parkstone Road, Ropley, ALRESFORD, HAMPSHIRE, SO24 0EP.
ⒺⓅⒶ**Lowson Ward, trading name of Lowson Ward Limited** *(P R Ward)* 292 Wake Green Road, BIRMINGHAM, B13 9QP.
Ⓟ**LSD Accountants Ltd** *(D K Matharu)* 21 Stockwood Business Centre, REDDITCH, WORCESTERSHIRE, B96 6SX.
Lubbock, Fine *(G G Goodyear, R Majithia, R P Surcouf, S Whale)* Elizabeth House, 9 Castle Street, JERSEY, JE4 2QP.
Lucas & Co. *(A D Lucas)* 1 Mint Street, GODALMING, GU7 1HE.
ⒺⓅ**Lucas Accountancy Ltd** *(K J Lucas)* The Dell, 4 Ingleby Paddocks, Enslow, KIDLINGTON, OXFORDSHIRE, OX5 3ET.
★ⓅⒶ**Lucas Reis Limited** *(S F Reis)* Landmark House, Station Road, Cheadle Hulme, CHEADLE, CHESHIRE, SK8 7BS.
ⓉⒺⓅⒶ**Lucentum, trading name of Lucentum Limited** *(M N P A Atkinson, B A Hill, T A Kelk)* Kensal House, 77 Springfield Road, CHELMSFORD, CM2 6JG.
ⒺⓅ**Lucking Accountancy, trading name of Lucking Accountancy Ltd** *(W R Lucking)* The Lodge, Beacon End Farmhouse, London Road, Stanway, COLCHESTER, CO3 0NQ.
ⓉⒺⒶ**Lucraft, Hodgson & Dawes** *(G M Butterworth, P J Everest, C J Ford, W Taylor)* Ground Floor, 19 New Road, BRIGHTON, BN1 1UF. and at LITTLEHAMPTON
Ⓟ**Lucy Haggar Limited** *(L I Thomas)* Home Barn, 1 The Park, Westwood Lane, Askham Bryan, YORK, YO23 3FW.
Ⓟ**Lucy Jones, trading name of Lucy Jones Ltd** *(L J Jones)* First Floor, Pier House, Pier Road, Hobbs Point, PEMBROKE DOCK, DYFED SA72 6TR.
Lucy R Hill *(L R Hill)* Woodlands, Falcon Lane, LEDBURY, HEREFORDSHIRE, HR8 2JW.
Ludlam Accountancy *(A C Ludlam)* 2 Church Walk, Little Driffield, DRIFFIELD, NORTH HUMBERSIDE, YO25 5XP.
Lui & Mak *(S Lo)* Unit 19, 20/F The Fortune Commerical Building, No 326 Sha Tsui Road, TSUEN WAN, HONG KONG SAR.
Luminary Finance LLP *(T G Breeze)* PO Box 135, LONGFIELD, KENT, DA3 8WF. and at LIVERPOOL
Luna Lam & Co *(L L Lam)* Room 801, The Centre Mark, 287-299 Queen's Road Central, CENTRAL, HONG KONG SAR.
Lurie & Associates LLP *(G Lewis)* 2nd Floor, 7 Newcombe Park, LONDON, NW7 3QN.
Lustig & Co *(R H Lustig)* PO Box 59842, LONDON, SW14 9BF.
ⓉⓅⒶ**Lustigman & Company, trading name of Lustigman & Company Limited** *(A R Lustigman)* 27 Manor Park Crescent, EDGWARE, MIDDLESEX, HA8 7NH.
Ⓟ**LV Hogan & Co, trading name of LV Hogan & Co Ltd** *(L V Hogan)* Monaleen Road, Castleroy, LIMERICK, COUNTY LIMERICK, IRELAND.
LWA, trading name of Liu Ward & Associates *(H M H Liu)* Trafalgar House, 1 Grenville Place, Mill Hill, LONDON, NW7 3SA.
Ⓟ**Lymm Tax Ltd** *(J Penny)* 6 Meadow View, LYMM, CHESHIRE, WA13 9AX.
Ⓟ**Lymore Partnership Limited** *(I C Pople, S J Pople)* The Mount, Lymore Lane, Milford on Sea, LYMINGTON, HAMPSHIRE, SO41 0TX.
★Ⓟ**Lynam Tax Limited** *(G Lynam)* Embankment House, 35 Edwalton Lodge Close, Edwalton, NOTTINGHAM, NG12 4DT.
Ⓐ**Lynch & Co** *(D J Lynch)* 194 Lonsdale Avenue, Newham, LONDON, E6 3PP.
Lynda Vijh *(L M L Vijh)* 11 Everett Close, Cheshunt, WALTHAM CROSS, HERTFORDSHIRE, EN7 6XD.
Ⓟ**Lyndoe Reeve** *(P M Reeve)* 34/36 Maddox Street, LONDON, W1S 1PD.
Lynette Barling *(L Barling)* 4 Wych Elm Rise, GUILDFORD, SURREY, GU1 3TH.
Lynham & Co *(P J Lynham)* 9 Hampton Lane, Blackfield, SOUTHAMPTON, SO45 1ZA.
Lynne Gittens ACA *(L Gittens)* 5 Crystal Wood Road, Heath, CARDIFF, CF14 4HU.
Lynton Consultancy *(A J Sansom)* Lynton, 48 Park Road, Stanwell, STAINES, TW19 7NY.
ⓉⓅⒶ**Lyon Griffiths, trading name of Lyon Griffiths Limited** *(R Morris, A Weaver)* 17 Alvaston Business Park, Middlewich Road, NANTWICH, CHESHIRE, CW5 6PF.
Lyons & Co *(C J Lyons)* 18 Barn Owl Way, Stoke Gifford, BRISTOL, BS34 8RZ.
ⒺⓅⒶ**Lyons & Co, trading name of Lyons & Co Limited** *(J R Lyons)* 23 Yarm Road, STOCKTON-ON-TEES, CLEVELAND, TS18 3NJ.
Ⓐ**Lyons Leonidou** *(L A Leonidou)* Galla House, 695 High Rd, North Finchley, LONDON, N12 0BT.
M & J Lawrence Business Services *(M Lawrence)* 39 Chester Road, Castle Bromwich, BIRMINGHAM, B36 9DL.
★Ⓟ**M + A Partners (North Norfolk), trading name of M + A Partners (North Norfolk) Limited** *(I Barber, C I H Mawson)* 12 Church Street, CROMER, NORFOLK, NR27 9ER.
M A Ahmedi *(M A Ahmedi)* 1 Marlow Copse, Walderslade, CHATHAM, KENT, ME5 9DP.
ⓅⒶ**M A Barratt Limited** *(M A Barratt)* 161 Melton High Street, Wath-upon-Dearne, ROTHERHAM, SOUTH YORKSHIRE, S63 6RQ.
ⓅⒶ**M A Edwards Accountants Limited** *(M A Edwards)* 30a The Green, Kings Norton, BIRMINGHAM, B38 8SD.
Ⓐ**M A Financial & Tax Consultants** *(M Arora)* 1 Ramsey House, Fawley Road, LONDON, NW6 1SN.
Ⓐ**M A Raja & Co** *(M A Raja)* 20 Bowring Drive, Parkgate, NESTON, CH64 6ST.
Ⓐ**M Akram & Co** *(A S Akram, M Akram)* 413 Lea Bridge Road, LONDON, E10 7EA.
M B Anderson & Co *(M B Anderson)* Lindum, 264-266 Durham Road, GATESHEAD, TYNE AND WEAR, NE8 4JR.
M B Noronha *(M B Noronha)* 15 Sandy Lane, West Kirby, WIRRAL, MERSEYSIDE, CH48 3HY.
Ⓟ**M Beadle & Co, trading name of M Beadle & Co Limited** *(M Beadle)* 53 Peacocks Close, Cavendish, SUDBURY, SUFFOLK, CO10 8DA.
ⒺⓅ**M C Clegg & Co, trading name of Merganser Limited** *(M C Clegg)* 51 Priestnall Road, STOCKPORT, CHESHIRE, SK4 3HW.
Ⓐ**M C Michael** *(M C Michael)* 32 Avondale Road, Hoylake, WIRRAL, CH47 3AS.
M Cooper & Co *(M Cooper)* 18 Habankim Street, 33265 HAIFA, ISRAEL.
Ⓐ**M Cridland & Associates** *(M Cridland)* Home Farm, Lilford, Oundle, PETERBOROUGH, PE8 5SG.
Ⓟ**M Cubed, trading name of M Cubed Limited** *(A N Mamujee, K N A Mamujee)* 186 London Road, LEICESTER, LE2 1ND.
M D Jones *(M D Jones)* 96 Skip Lane, WALSALL, WS5 3LR.
Ⓟ**M D Lobo Limited** *(M D Lobo)* 118 Radford Road, LEAMINGTON SPA, WARWICKSHIRE, CV31 1LF.
Ⓟ**M Fullwood & Co, trading name of Alphaline Consultants Ltd** *(M Fullwood)* 8 Histons Drive, Codsall, WOLVERHAMPTON, WV8 2ET.
ⒺⓅⒶ**M G Beattie & Co Limited** *(M G Beattie)* 6 Main Avenue, Moor Park, NORTHWOOD, HA6 2HJ.
Ⓟ**M G Trustees Ltd** *(D N Cox, P L Mead)* Burn View, BUDE, CORNWALL, EX23 8BX.
Ⓟ**M G Walters & Co Ltd** *(M G Walters)* 21 Drake Road, WESTCLIFF-ON-SEA, ESSEX, SS0 8LP.
M G White & Co *(M G White)* 48 Brook Lane Field, HARLOW, ESSEX, CM18 7AU.
M H D O'Callaghan *(M.H.D. O'Callaghan)* 36 Seymour Street, CAMBRIDGE, CB1 3DQ.
M Howe Accountancy Services *(M R Howe)* 6 Henders, Stony Stratford, MILTON KEYNES, MK11 1RB.
Ⓐ**M I Hasan** *(M I Hasan)* Beechwood, 25 Upper Shirley Road, Shirley, CROYDON, CR0 5EB.
M I Petty *(M I Petty)* 4-6 Upper Green Avenue, Scholes, CLECKHEATON, WEST YORKSHIRE, BD19 6PD.
Ⓟ**M J Beynon & Co, trading name of M J Beynon Limited** *(M J Beynon)* 7 Pennard Drive, Pennard, SWANSEA, SA3 2BL.
ⒺⓅⒶ**M J Bushell, trading name of M J Bushell Ltd** *(J Loryman, I S Warwick)* 8 High Street, BRENTWOOD, ESSEX, CM14 4AB.
Ⓟ**M J Calderbank Limited** *(M J Calderbank)* Rustic Ridge, Benton Green Lane, Berkswell, COVENTRY, CV7 7DB.
M J Coombs, trading name of Michael J. Coombs *(M J Coombs)* 27 Ty Nant, Rotcombe Lane, High Littleton, BRISTOL, BS39 6JP.
M J Foulkes, trading name of Manchula Ltd *(M J Foulkes)* 7 Fulwith Close, HARROGATE, NORTH YORKSHIRE, HG2 8HP.
M J Golz & Company *(M J Golz)* Odeon House, 146 College Road, HARROW, HA1 1BH.
M J Harding *(M J Harding)* 7 Broad Elms Lane, Ecclesall, SHEFFIELD, S11 9RQ.
M J Kiedish *(M J Kiedish)* 24 Rosebery Road, CHELMSFORD, ESSEX, CM2 0TU.
M J Leaf & Co *(M J Leaf)* Melville House, 8-12 Woodhouse Road, Finchley, LONDON, N12 0RG.
Ⓐ**M J Rhodes & Co** *(M J Rhodes)* First Floor, 8 Poole Hill, BOURNEMOUTH, BH2 5PS.
Ⓐ**M J Riley & Co** *(M J Riley)* 22 Church Street, KIDDERMINSTER, DY10 2AW.
Ⓟ**M J Roberts Associates Ltd** *(M J Roberts)* Regency House, Kings Place, BUCKHURST HILL, ESSEX, IG9 5EB.
ⓉⓅⒶ**M J Shapcott & Company Limited** *(K F Shapcott, M J Shapcott)* Charter House, Wyvern Court, Stanier Way, Wyvern Business Park, DERBY, DE21 6BF.
ⓅⒶ**M J Smith & Co Ltd** *(M J Smith)* Woodbury House, Green Lane, Exton, EXETER, EX3 0PW.
M L Cliffe *(M L Cliffe)* 7 Lime Tree Road, NORWICH, NR2 2NF.
M L Eastwood *(M L Eastwood)* P.O. Box 2033, REEDS SPRING, MO 65737, UNITED STATES.
M L Hursthouse BA ACA *(M L Hursthouse)* 85 Derwent Close, Alsager, STOKE-ON-TRENT, ST7 2EL.
ⓉⒶ**M Lawrence & Co** *(H L Lawrence, M Lawrence)* 213 Station Road, Stechford, BIRMINGHAM, B33 8BB.
M M Morgan & Co *(M M Morgan)* 34 Wolverton Road, NEWPORT PAGNELL, BUCKINGHAMSHIRE, MK16 8HU.
M M Patel & Co *(M M Patel)* 59 Carr Road, NORTHOLT, MIDDLESEX, UB5 4RB.
Ⓟ**M N Jenks & Co Limited** *(M N Jenks, T Lane)* 72 Commercial Road, Paddock Wood, TONBRIDGE, KENT, TN12 6DP.
Ⓟ**M P Grimes & Co Ltd** *(M P Grimes)* 154a Eltham High Street, Eltham, LONDON, SE9 1BJ.
Ⓟ**M R Dury & Co Ltd** *(M R Dury)* 51 Peaslands Road, SIDMOUTH, DEVON, EX10 9BE.
M R Richardson *(M R Richardson)* Four Ways, Rake Lane, ULVERSTON, CUMBRIA, LA12 9NG.
ⒺⓅⒶ**M R Salvage, trading name of M R Salvage Limited** *(R Davies, M E Field, A L Horton, M R Salvage, G R Sutton, J Taylor)* 7-8 Eghams Court, Boston Drive, BOURNE END, BUCKINGHAMSHIRE, SL8 5YS.
M R Thomas *(M R Thomas)* 5 Church Meadow, Milton-under-Wychwood, CHIPPING NORTON, OX7 6JG.
M Reynolds *(M J Reynolds)* 42 Temple Rhydding Drive, Baildon, SHIPLEY, WEST YORKSHIRE, BD17 5PU.
Ⓟ**M S & K Financial Services Limited** *(M Alam)* 144 Motspur Park, NEW MALDEN, SURREY, KT3 6PF.
M Short & Co LLP *(M J Short)* 7 Waterloo Road, WHITSTABLE, KENT, CT5 1BP.
M T Buckley & Co *(M Buckley)* 2 Beulah Walk, Woldingham, CATERHAM, SURREY, CR3 7LL.
★ⒺⒶ**M Tatton & Co, trading name of Walletts** *(M Tatton)* 2-6 Adventure Place, Hanley, STOKE-ON-TRENT, ST1 3AF.
M Tumbridge & Co *(M Tumbridge)* 20 Anderson Close, LONDON, N21 1TH.
Ⓐ**M Ulrich** *(M P Ulrich)* 24 Highfield Road, Tolworth, SURBITON, KT5 9LP.
M Underwood Accountancy Services *(M Underwood)* 2 Oakhurst Road, Wylde Green, SUTTON COLDFIELD, B72 1EJ.
M W Bray *(M W Bray)* Byndes Farn, Pebmarsh, HALSTEAD, ESSEX, CO9 2LZ.
ⓅⒶ**M W Dodd & Associates Limited** *(M W Dodd)* 26 High Street, ROCHESTER, KENT, ME1 1PT.
M W R Lysaght *(M W R Lysaght)* Hazlewood House, MALLOW, COUNTY CORK, IRELAND.
★**M. & B. J. Conroy** *(M Conroy)* Fishponds House, 700 Wellingborough Road, Billing Park, NORTHAMPTON, NN3 9BQ.
Ⓐ**M. Ahmed & Co** *(M Ahmed)* 83 Park Road, Chilwell, NOTTINGHAM, NG9 4DE.
M. Akhtar *(M Akhtar)* 171 Shah Jamal, Colony, LAHORE, PAKISTAN.
ⓉⒺ**M. Aris & Co** *(M A Aris, N Aris)* Northway House, 1379 High Road, Whetstone, LONDON, N20 9LP.
M. Aslam *(M Aslam)* 259 Mansfield Road, NOTTINGHAM, NG1 3FT.
Ⓣ**M. Athanasiou** *(M Athanasiou)* PO Box 54320, 3723 LIMASSOL, CYPRUS.
M. Boltsa *(M Boltsa)* Premier House, 112-114 Station Road, EDGWARE, HA8 7BJ.
M. Cooper *(M Cooper)* 18 Habankim Street, HAIFA, 33265, ISRAEL.
M. Dine *(M Dine)* Stoke Lodge, Aldersey Road, GUILDFORD, GU1 2ES.
M. Emanuel *(M S Emanuel)* 5 Lexham Gardens Mews, Kensington, LONDON, W8 5JQ.
Ⓐ**M. Epstein & Co** *(R S Myers)* 250 Middleton Road, Crumpsall, MANCHESTER, M8 4WA.
★**M. Franklins** *(M S Franklin)* 84 Albion Court, Attleborough Road, NUNEATON, WARWICKSHIRE, CV11 4JJ.
★**M. Goddard & Co** *(M P Goddard)* 69 Tupwood Lane, CATERHAM, CR3 6DD.
M. Holroyd *(M Holroyd)* 11 Headley Gardens, Great Shelford, CAMBRIDGE, CB22 5JZ.
M. Ingram *(M Ingram)* Teal Cottage, 5 Holt View, Great Easton, MARKET HARBOROUGH, LEICESTERSHIRE, LE16 8TN.
M. Lilani & Co *(M N Lilani)* 1c Church Road, CROYDON, CR0 1SG.
M. P. Beahan & Co *(M P Beahan)* 57 Laughton Road, Dinnington, SHEFFIELD, S25 2PN.
M. Papadakis & Co *(A I Ioannou, M Papadakis)* Maria House 5th Floor, 1 Avlonos Street, 1075 NICOSIA, CYPRUS.
ⓉⒶ**M. Parmar & Co** *(M A Parmar)* 1st Floor, 244 Edgware Road, LONDON, W2 1DS.
ⒺⒶ**M. Pattni & Co** *(M M Pattni)* 21 Kingshill Drive, Kenton, HARROW, HA3 8TD.
Ⓟ**M. Proudlock & Co. Limited** *(S G Carley)* Mazhar House, 48 Bradford Road, Stanningley, LEEDS, WEST YORKSHIRE, LS28 6DF.
M. Qidwai & Company *(M Qidwai)* 29 Highfield Gardens, WESTCLIFF-ON-SEA, ESSEX, SS0 0SY.
Ⓟ**M. R. Barrett F.C.A, trading name of M. R. Barrett Limited** *(M R Barrett)* 1 Commonside Cottages, Salle, NORWICH, NR10 4EP.
Ⓐ**M. Rabin & Co.** *(H S M Rabin)* 22 Hillcrest Avenue, EDGWARE, HA8 8PA.
M. Robinson *(M Robinson)* 10 Greet Park Close, SOUTHWELL, NG25 0EE.
M. Seitler & Co *(M P Seitler)* Unit 4, The Cottages, Deva Centre, Trinity Way, SALFORD, M3 7BE.
Ⓐ**M. Wasley Chapman & Co** *(P Cuthbert, A G Manser, R Reynolds, A M Stokes, N Taylor)* 3 Victoria Square, WHITBY, NORTH YORKSHIRE, YO21 1EA. and at MIDDLESBROUGH, SALTBURN-BY-THE-SEA
M. Wechsler *(M Wechsler)* 48 Brookside Road, LONDON, NW11 9NE.
M. Yarr *(M Yarr)* 105 Cedar Drive, Parklands, CHICHESTER, PO19 3EL.
Ⓟ**M.A. Brawn & Co, trading name of M.A. Brawn & Company Limited** *(M A Brawn)* 2a Acland Road, BRIDGEND, MID GLAMORGAN, CF31 1TF.
M.A. Brecknell *(M A Brecknell)* Flat 72, 8 New Crane Place, LONDON, E1W 3TX.
M.A. Sutcliffe *(M A Sutcliffe)* 213 Castle Hill Road, Totternhoe, DUNSTABLE, LU6 2DA.
Ⓐ**M.A. Tobin** *(M A Tobin)* 17 Wilbury Avenue, Cheam, SUTTON, SM2 7DU.
M.A. Wakeling *(M A Wakeling)* Picketts Mead, High Street, Cowden, EDENBRIDGE, TN8 7JH.
Ⓟ**M.C. Accounting Ltd** *(A C Goreham)* Abacus House, 19 Manor Close, TUNBRIDGE WELLS, TN4 8YB.
Ⓟ**M.C. Associates Ltd** *(P M Enright)* 80c Asquith Road, Wigmore, GILLINGHAM, KENT, ME8 0JB.
M.C. Billington & Co *(M C Billington)* 17 Barford Close, SOUTHPORT, PR8 2RS.
M.C. Bogard *(M C Bogard)* 22 Dukes Avenue, LONDON, W4 2AE.
M.C. Ng & Co *(M S Ng)* Room 1502 Double Building, 22 Stanley Street, CENTRAL, HONG KONG ISLAND, HONG KONG SAR.
★**M.C. Patel & Co** *(M C Patel)* Hillingdon House, 386/388 Kenton Road, Kenton, HARROW, HA3 9DP.
M.D. Kleinberg & Co *(M D Kleinberg)* 12 Gill's Hill Lane, RADLETT, WD7 8DF.
Ⓐ**M.D. Sale & Co** *(M D Sale)* 7 Carlisle Road, Birkdale, SOUTHPORT, PR8 4DJ.
Ⓟ**M.E. Ball & Associates Limited** *(M E Ball)* Global House, 1 Ashley Avenue, EPSOM, SURREY, KT18 5AD.
M.E. Bryan *(M E Bryan)* Croft House, Gt. Finborough, STOWMARKET, IP14 3BG.
Ⓟ**M.E. Greenhalgh FCA, trading name of MeIG Limited** *(M E Greenhalgh)* Boscarn, 2 Clijah Croft, South Downs, REDRUTH, CORNWALL, TR15 2NR.
M.F. French *(M F French)* Coleridge, 92 Leamington Road, KENILWORTH, CV8 2AA.
ⓉⒶ**M.F. Khan & Co** *(N S Khan)* 25 Parkdale Close, Erdington, BIRMINGHAM, B24 8JU.
Ⓐ**M.G Archbold** *(M G Archbold)* 63 Castlefields, Bournmoor, HOUGHTON LE SPRING, DH4 6HJ.
M.G. Fellows *(M G Fellows)* 1 Rhodfa Heilyn, Gwelfor Park, Dyserth, RHYL, CLWYD, LL18 6LW.
Ⓐ**M.G. Quelch & Co** *(M G Quelch)* 5 Brewers Way, MANSFIELD, NOTTINGHAMSHIRE, NG18 3GL.
M.G. Wortley & Co *(M G Wortley)* Bramble Lodge, Colstrope Lane, Hambleden, HENLEY-ON-THAMES, RG9 6SL.
Ⓟ**M.G.G. Hadden & Co Ltd** *(M G G Hadden)* 46A Grosvenor Road, Birkdale, SOUTHPORT, PR8 2ET.
M.G.H. Sanders *(M G H Sanders)* 15 Raisins Hill, PINNER, HA5 2BU.

Ⓕ**M.H. Jones & Co** *(M H Jones)* Stuart House, Valepits Road, Garretts Green, BIRMINGHAM, B33 0TD.

M.Huque & Co *(A K M M Hossain, M Huque)* 70/C Purana Paltan Line, 3rd Floor, DHAKA 1000, BANGLADESH.

M.I Murray F.C.A *(M I Murray)* The Hollins, Manor Close, PRESTATYN, CLWYD, LL19 9PH.

M.I. Bundhun *(M I Bundhun)* Apartment 3, 15 Wedderburn Road, LONDON, NW3 5QS.

Ⓐ**M.J. Churchill** *(M J Churchill)* 5 Bracken Dell, RAYLEIGH, ESSEX, SS6 8LP.

M.J. Comens *(M J Comens)* Maritime House, Basin Road North, HOVE, EAST SUSSEX, BN41 1WR.

M.J. Curtis & Co *(M J Curtis)* 222 Broadgate House, Broadgate, COVENTRY, CV1 1NG.

M.J. Forshaw *(M J Forshaw)* 7 Oak Drive, Burscough, ORMSKIRK, LANCASHIRE, L40 5BQ.

M.J. Harris & Co *(M J Harris)* 35 Whitehill Road, GRAVESEND, KENT, DA12 5PE.

M.J. Harvey & Co *(M J Harvey)* The Old Mill House, Willow Avenue, New Denham, UXBRIDGE, MIDDLESEX, UB9 4AF.

M.J. Hazel & Co *(M J Hazel)* 30 Brookfield, NEATH, SA10 7EH.

M.J. Keizer *(M J Keizer)* 2113 Castle View Road, MANSFIELD, TX 76063, UNITED STATES.

M.J. Pinches *(M J Pinches)* 3 Rose Hill Arch Mews, Rose Hill, DORKING, RH4 2ER.

ⒻⒶ**M.J. Read & Co** *(N J Wharton)* 1 Cobden Road, SEVENOAKS, TN13 3UB.

Ⓟ**M.J. Startup & Co Ltd** *(M J Startup)* 4 New Cottages, Furzedown Lane, Amport, ANDOVER, SP11 8BQ.

M.J. Ward & Co. *(M J Ward)* 6 Chislehurst Place, West Park, LYTHAM ST. ANNES, LANCASHIRE, FY8 4RU.

M.J. Whelan *(M J Whelan)* 85 Lime Walk, Moulsham Lodge, CHELMSFORD, CM2 9NJ.

M.J.Cook & Co *(M J Cook)* Sutton House, 4 Coles Lane, SUTTON COLDFIELD, B72 1NE.

Ⓐ**M.J.Hosmer** *(M J Hosmer)* Barfords, Standford Hill, Standford, BORDON, HAMPSHIRE, GU35 8QU.

M.J.N. Goodey *(M J N Goodey)* 109 Arundel Road, PEACEHAVEN, BN10 8HE.

Ⓐ**M.K. Ashbrook** *(M K Ashbrook)* 59-61 Sea Lane, Rustington, LITTLEHAMPTON, WEST SUSSEX, BN16 2RQ.

M.K. Blundell & Co. *(M K Blundell)* 15 Carlton Croft, Sandal, WAKEFIELD, WEST YORKSHIRE, WF2 6DA.

M.K. Chowdhury & Co *(M K H Chowdhury)* 250 Bethnal Green Road, LONDON, E2 0AA.

M.K.B. Hussain *(M K B Hussain)* Unit 1003 Level 10 Block A, Pusat Perdagangan Phileo, Damansara 2, No 15 Jalan 16/11, Off Jalan Damansara, 46350 PETALING JAYA SELANGOR MALAYSIA.

M.M. Vekaria & Co *(M M Vekaria)* 36 St. Andrews Drive, STANMORE, MIDDLESEX, HA7 2NB.

★Ⓐ**M.O. Sampson & Co** *(M O Sampson)* 42 Kew Court, Richmond Road, KINGSTON UPON THAMES, SURREY, KT2 5BF.

M.P. Curtis *(M P Curtis)* New Barn Farm, Lindsell, DUNMOW, CM6 3QH.

M.P. Day Accounting Services *(M P Day)* 19 Orchard Lane, Brampton, HUNTINGDON, PE28 4TF.

M.P. Dorling *(M P Dorling)* The Firs, Levens Green, Old Hall Green, WARE, SG11 1HD.

Ⓐ**M.P. Grimes & Co** *(M P Grimes)* 154a Eltham High Street, Eltham, LONDON, SE9 1BJ.

M.P. Saunders & Co. *(M P Saunders)* 2nd Floor, Walsingham House, 1331-1337 High Road, Whetstone, LONDON, N20 9HR.

M.R Cooper *(M R Cooper)* 1 Cheddar Close, Nailsea, BRISTOL, BS48 4YA.

M.R. Aldridge *(M R Aldridge)* 2a Crown Street, Redbourn, ST. ALBANS, HERTFORDSHIRE, AL3 7JX.

M.R. Beaumont & Co *(M R Beaumont)* The Birches, 28A High Street, Standlake, WITNEY, OX29 7RY.

M.R. Cowdrey & Co *(M R Cowdrey)* 125 Nottingham Road, Stapleford, NOTTINGHAM, NG9 8AT.

M.R. Evans & Co *(M R Evans)* Birchwood, 5 Castle Way, Ewell, EPSOM, KT17 2PG.

M.R. Henderson *(M R Henderson)* 32 Granard Avenue, LONDON, SW15 6HJ.

M.R. Pooley *(M R Pooley)* 91 Church Lane, Eaton, NORWICH, NR4 6NY.

M.R.Desai *(M R Desai)* Suite 201-5990 Fraser Street, VANCOUVER V5W 2Z7, BC, CANADA.

M.R.F.Miles *(M R F Miles)* 191a High Street, STREET, SOMERSET, BA16 0NE.

Ⓐ**M.R.S. Patel & Co** *(M R S Patel)* Compton House, 20a Selsdon Road, SOUTH CROYDON, SURREY, CR2 6PA.

Ⓟ**M.Ramsey Ltd, trading name of Topline Ltd** *(M S Ramsey)* 9 Bridge Street, NEWCASTLE EMLYN, DYFED, SA38 9DX.

Ⓟ**M.S. Caister & Co Ltd** *(M S Caister, N S Caister)* Prosperity House, 121 Green Lane, DERBY, DE1 1RZ.

M.S. Iacovou & Co *(M S Iacovou)* 6 Thyra Grove, North Finchley, LONDON, N12 8HB.

M.S. Paul *(M S Paul)* Henmead Hall, Staplefield Road, Cuckfield, HAYWARDS HEATH, WEST SUSSEX, RH17 5HY.

Ⓟ**M.S. Ramsey Ltd, Topline Ltd, trading names of Michael S Ramsey Ltd** *(M S Ramsey)* 9 Bridge Street, NEWCASTLE EMLYN, DYFED, SA38 9DX.

M.S.Alinek *(M S Alinek)* 7 Upton Lodge Close, BUSHEY, WD23 1AG.

M.S.Buhariwalla & Co *(M S Buhariwalla)* 35a Norton Road, WEMBLEY, HA0 4RG.

M.Sim & Co *(M C K Sim)* 233 Princes Gardens, LONDON, W3 0LU.

Ⓐ**M.U. Ahmed & Co** *(M U Ahmed)* 28 Christian Fields, Norbury, LONDON, SW16 3JZ.

M.W. Amor *(M W Amor)* 4 The Colliers, Heybridge Basin, MALDON, CM9 4SE.

ⓉⒻⒶ**M.W. Burrough & Co** *(S Dorrington-Ward)* 10 South St, BRIDPORT, DT6 3NJ.

M.W. Consultancy Services *(M J V Ward)* 8 James Martin Close, Denham, UXBRIDGE, MIDDLESEX, UB9 5NN.

M.W. Dale *(M W Dale)* 10 Hillfort Close, DORCHESTER, DT1 2QT.

M.W. Horner & Co *(M W Horner)* Cilgerran, Eglwysbach, COLWYN BAY, Clwyd, LL28 5UA.

M.W.B. Edwards *(M W B Edwards)* Gracegarth, Wetherby Road, KNARESBOROUGH, HG5 8LQ.

ⓉⒻⒶ**M+A Partners, trading name of MA Partners LLP** *(C J Dugdale, A J Fish, W P F Hill, C I H Mawson, M Sargeant, F M E Shippam)* 7 The Close, NORWICH, NORFOLK, NR1 4DJ. and at ATTLEBOROUGH

M1 Insolvency, trading name of M1 Insolvency LLP *(M Rose)* Cumberland House, 35 Park Row, NOTTINGHAM, NG1 6EE.

Ⓟ**M2, trading name of M2 Tax and Accountancy Limited** *(C M A Makhoul, R Masters)* The Counting House, High Street, TRING, HERTFORDSHIRE, HP23 5TE. and at HARPENDEN

MA Hawkins BA ACA *(M A Hawkins)* 212 Norcot Road, Tilehurst, READING, RG30 6AE.

MA Swinson *(M A Swinson)* 46 Glenmore Avenue, LIVERPOOL, L18 4QF.

Ⓟ**MA, trading name of Mycock Associates Limited** *(P D Mycock)* 129 Middleton Boulvard, Wollaton Park, NOTTINGHAM, NG8 1FW.

★ⒻⒶ**ma2** *(A Mills)* 5 Crescent East, THORNTON-CLEVELEYS, LANCASHIRE, FY5 3LJ.

Maass & Co *(J C Maass)* 20 Queens Road, Hoylake, WIRRAL, MERSEYSIDE, CH47 2AH.

ⓉⒶ**Mabe Allen LLP** *(D J Allen, J P Allen, C J Hopkinson, K Slack, B Sutton)* 50 Osmaston Road, DERBY, DE1 2HU. and at ILKESTON, RIPLEY

Mabel Chan & Co *(M M Chan)* Suite 2208-11, 22/F Tower One, Times Square, 1 Matheson Street, CAUSEWAY BAY, HONG KONG SAR.

Ⓟ**MAC Consulting Limited** *(C McGuinness)* 38 Rosemoor Gardens, Appleton, WARRINGTON, WA4 5RG.

Ⓟ**Mac Kotecha & Co Ltd** *(M K Kotecha)* Lichfield House, 2 Lichfield Grove, LONDON, N3 2JP.

★Ⓣ**Mac Kotecha & Co.** *(M K Kotecha, P Kotecha)* Lichfield House, 2 Lichfield Grove, LONDON, N3 2JP.

ⓉⓅⒶ**Macario Lewin, trading name of Macario Lewin Ltd** *(M W Macario)* Bellarmine House, 14 Upper Church Street, CHEPSTOW, GWENT, NP16 5EX. and at SWANSEA

Ⓕ**Maccallum & Co** *(N H Maccallum)* 127 Atherstone Avenue, PETERBOROUGH, PE3 9UJ.

Ⓕ**Maccallum Slator** *(T Slator)* Claverton House, Love Lane, CIRENCESTER, GL7 1YG. and at LONDON

★**MacCorkindale International Partners** *(P D Maccorkindale)* 2 South Barn, Chrishall Grange, Heydon, ROYSTON, HERTFORDSHIRE, SG8 7NT.

Macdonald & Co. *(L.R. Macdonald)* 209 Barnwood Road, GLOUCESTER, GL4 3HS.

Ⓕ**Mace And Partners** *(R A Huckridge)* 52 Talbot Road, Talbot Green, PONTYCLUN, MID GLAMORGAN, CF72 8AF.

MacGillivray & Co *(A.D.MacGillivray)* 1 Coniston Road, CAMBRIDGE, CB1 7BZ.

ⒻⒶ**Machin & Co** *(H N Machin)* 19 Seer Mead, Seer Green, BEACONSFIELD, BUCKINGHAMSHIRE, HP9 2QL.

★ⓉⒻⒶ**Macilvin Moore Reveres LLP** *(S V Patel, P K Rajani, R Shaw)* 7 St John's Road, HARROW, HA1 2EY.

Ⓟ**MacIntyre Hudson Corporate Finance Ltd** *(A C Cook, L Whitehead)* Moorgate House, 201 Silbury Boulevard, MILTON KEYNES, MK9 1LZ. and at HIGH WYCOMBE, LONDON

★ⓉⒻⒶ**MacIntyre Hudson, trading name of MacIntyre Hudson LLP** *(K J Arnott, C T Baker, J M Ball, M J Ball, L M Barling, I C Betteridge, M J Brown, J A Bryant, A E Burnham, J C Burwood, P J Byrne, A C Cook, D J Coppard, J Coverdale, V A F Dauppe, P M Davis, S Dodds, M T Dowding, K A Edwards, S D Erskine, J Gare, H S Gill, G C Gleghorn, P J Gotham, M S Herron, G B Ives, C K Jackson, I G Jacobs, M J Kay, H K Lewis, S J Manning, S Moore, G C Morley, R A Nelson, Y A Patel, M D Payne, R Powell, B N Richens, F C Satow, B M Sharkey, R Shaunak, B K Silva, C F Stratton, C N Sutton, R W Trunchion, C P Walker, L Whitehead, A J Young, G L Young)* Moorgate House, 201 Silbury Boulevard, MILTON KEYNES, MK9 1LZ. and at BEDFORD, CHELMSFORD, HIGH WYCOMBE, LEICESTER, LONDON, NORTHAMPTON, PETERBOROUGH, ROCHESTER

Ⓟ**Mack Business Services Ltd** *(A Grant)* Mack Business Services, 36a Gordon Road, DARTFORD, DA1 2LQ.

Mackenzie & Co *(I S Mackenzie)* 34 Hazelmoor, Hebburn Village, HEBBURN, TYNE AND WEAR, NE31 1DH.

ⒻⒶ**Mackenzie Field** *(D M Andrews, P I V Galloway)* Hyde House, The Hyde, Edgware Road, LONDON, NW9 6LA.

Ⓟ**Mackenzie Spencer Limited** *(C Sellars)* 61 Huntley Road, Ecclesall, SHEFFIELD, S11 7PB.

Mackinlay *(C Mackinlay)* 8 Manor Road, CHATHAM, ME4 6AG.

Ⓟ**Mackinlay Phipps, trading name of Mackinlay Phipps Ltd** *(C Mackinlay)* 8 Manor Road, CHATHAM, KENT, ME4 6AG.

★**Macleod & Tonkin** *(J C Coulson)* 54 Coinagehall Street, HELSTON, CORNWALL, TR13 8EL.

ⓉⓅⒶ**MacMahon Leggate, trading name of MacMahon Leggate Ltd** *(K Flanagan, R W Robinson)* Charter House, 18-20 Finsley Gate, BURNLEY, LANCASHIRE, BB11 2HA.

Ⓒ**Maco Administration Ltd** *(A P M Myers, M A Silver)* 1 Hyde Park Place, Marble Arch, LONDON, W2 2LH.

★**MacPhail & Co** *(D B MacPhail)* 12 rue Pierre-Fatio, P.O. Box 3453, 1211 GENEVA, SWITZERLAND. and at LUXEMBOURG

Ⓟ**MacWilliams Consulting Limited** *(A R Lawton)* 2 Ardival East, STRATHPEFFER, ROSS-SHIRE, IV14 9DY.

Ⓟ**Maddocks & Gamble Limited** *(R A Stemmer)* 1a Warrington Road, Ashton-in-Makerfield, WIGAN, LANCASHIRE, WN4 9PL.

ⒻⒶ**Madon & Co.** *(K R Madon)* 8th Floor, Tolworth Tower, Ewell Road, SURBITON, SURREY, KT6 7EL.

ⓉⒻⓅⒶ**Magee Gammon, trading name of Magee Gammon Corporate Limited** *(J M Gammon, R G Parry, A T D Tutt)* Henwood House, Henwood, ASHFORD, KENT, TN24 8DH.

★Ⓕ**Magee Gammon, trading name of Magee Gammon Partnership LLP** *(J M Gammon, R G Parry, A T D Tutt)* Henwood House, Henwood, ASHFORD, KENT, TN24 8DH.

Maggie Holland *(M I Holland)* 4 Church View, Moulton, NORTHAMPTON, NN3 7FZ.

Ⓐ**MAGI Associates** *(P G Chapman)* Holly Cottage, Berden, BISHOP'S STORTFORD, HERTFORDSHIRE, CM23 1AE.

Magnes Accountants *(M H Jones)* 52 Fruitlands, MALVERN, WR14 4XA.

Ⓟ**Magnet Associates Ltd** *(M T Seery)* 4 Brookes Lane, Whalley, CLITHEROE, LANCASHIRE, BB7 9RG.

Ⓟ**Maguires, trading name of Hilary Maguire Ltd** *(H G Maguire)* Sunny Bank, Sibford Ferris, BANBURY, OXFORDSHIRE, OX15 5RG.

Ⓐ**Magus** *(Y Amin, P J Tanna)* 140 Buckingham Palace Road, LONDON, SW1W 9SA.

Magus Partners LLP *(C S Sanford)* 101 Wigmore Street, LONDON, W1U 1QU.

Ⓟ**MAH Professional Services Limited** *(M A Haque)* 80-83 Long Lane, Barbican, LONDON, EC1A 9ET.

Mahajan & Aibara *(H S Aibara, M K Mahajan)* 1 Chawla House, 62 Wodehouse Road Colaba, MUMBAI 400 005, INDIA.

★**Mahajan & Aibara Associates** *(M K Mahajan)* 1 Chawla House, 62 Wodehouse Road Colaba, MUMBAI 400005, MAHARASHTRA, INDIA.

Ⓟ**Mahon & Co, trading name of Mahon & Co Ltd** *(J M Mahon)* Marston House, Priors Marston, SOUTHAM, WARWICKSHIRE, CV47 7RP.

Maiden Accountancy Services *(S Maiden)* 22A Cornfield Road, EASTBOURNE, EAST SUSSEX, BN21 4QE.

Ⓐ**Mainstream Accountancy Services** *(F B B Galia)* 9 Crondal Place, Edgbaston, BIRMINGHAM, B15 2LB.

Ⓕ**Mainwaring Dean Associates** *(R E K Mainwaring)* Millfield House, Eaton Bishop, HEREFORD, HR2 9QS.

ⒻⓅⒶ**Maitland Limited** *(A R C Maitland)* Office C, Maple Barn, Buckham Hill, UCKFIELD, EAST SUSSEX, TN22 5XZ.

Ⓟ**Maitland Wright Limited** *(J M Wright)* 55 East Budleigh Road, BUDLEIGH SALTERTON, DEVON, EX9 6EW.

ⓅⒶ**Majainah Sadra Limited** *(N Majainah, K S Sadra)* 2 Martin House, 179/181 North End Road, LONDON, W14 9NL.

ⓉⒻⓅⒶ**Majors, trading name of Majors Limited** *(M Major)* 8 King Street, Trinity Square, HULL, HU1 2JJ.

Mak Cheung & Co *(L Mak)* Unit 1105, Hua Qin International Building, 340 Queen's Road, CENTRAL, HONG KONG ISLAND, HONG KONG SAR.

Makan & Makan *(D Makan)* Dukes Court, 91 Wellington Street, LUTON, LU1 5AF.

★ⒻⒶ**Makinson & Co** *(K Watkins)* 1 Hill Street, LYDNEY, GLOUCESTERSHIRE, GL15 5HB.

Malcolm Bass & Co *(M R Bass)* 53 Bentfield Causeway, STANSTED, ESSEX, CM24 8HU.

Malcolm Bengston *(M Bengston)* 27 Partridge Close, Ayton Green, WASHINGTON, NE38 0ES.

Malcolm Bird *(M K Bird)* 1 Kendals Close, RADLETT, WD7 8NQ.

Malcolm Clark & Co *(M I Clark)* 39 Grange Road, DARLINGTON, COUNTY DURHAM, DL1 5NB.

Malcolm F. Tegg *(M F Tegg)* The Old Gun House, Sedlescombe, BATTLE, TN33 0QJ.

Malcolm Fowler *(M Fowler)* 21 St. Johns Square, Wilton, SALISBURY, SP2 0DW.

Ⓟ**Malcolm Franke & Co Ltd** *(M D Franke)* Campania, Links Road, South Milton, KINGSBRIDGE, DEVON, TQ7 3JR.

ⒻⒶ**Malcolm G. Fry** *(M G Fry)* 12 Oak Grove, HERTFORD, SG13 8AT.

Malcolm High *(M High)* Pantiles, Braughing Friars, WARE, SG11 2NS.

Ⓟ**Malcolm Horton & Co, trading name of Malcolm Horton & Co Limited** *(M C Horton)* 57 Windmill Street, GRAVESEND, KENT, DA12 1BB.

Malcolm Jones & Co LLP *(M P Jones)* West Hill House, Allerton Hill, Chapel Allerton, LEEDS, LS7 3QB.

Ⓟ**Malcolm Man Accountancy Limited** *(K W M Man)* Lison House, 173 Wardour Street, LONDON, W1F 8WT.

Ⓟ**Malcolm Marsh & Co, trading name of Malcolm Marsh & Co. Ltd** *(M R Marsh)* 13 Burnieboozle Crescent, ABERDEEN, AB15 8NN.

Malcolm Mildren *(M K Mildren)* 1 Tanfield Lane, NORTHAMPTON, NN1 5RN.

Malcolm N. Wigley & Co *(M N Wigley)* 55 Bradley Court, Crossley Road, WORCESTER, WR5 3GH.

Ⓟ**Malcolm Paget Limited** *(M G Paget)* 117 Whitchurch Gardens, EDGWARE, HA8 6PG.

Malcolm Patrick *(M L Patrick)* 170 Chesterton Road, CAMBRIDGE, CB4 1DA.

ⓅⒶ**Malcolm Piper & Company Limited** *(A P Horvath, M J Piper)* Business Services Centre, 446-450 Kingstanding Road, BIRMINGHAM, WEST MIDLANDS, B44 9SA.

Ⓟ**Malcolm Piper Accounting Services Limited** *(A P Horvath, M J Piper)* Business Services Centre, 446-450 Kingstanding Road, BIRMINGHAM, B44 9SA.

ⒻⒶ**Malcolm Prior & Co** *(M B C Prior)* 4 Timber Lane, CATERHAM, SURREY, CR3 6LZ.

Malcolm Reid & Co *(M Reid)* Caudle Street, High Street, HENFIELD, WEST SUSSEX, BN5 9DQ.

Malcolm Roussak & Co. *(M Roussak)* 52 Bury Old Road, Whitefield, MANCHESTER, M45 6TL.

Ⓟ**Malcolm Veall & Co Ltd** *(M P Veall)* 60 Howard Road, LEICESTER, LE2 1XH.

Malcolm Wood & Co. *(S I Edwards)* Shrubbery House, 47 Prospect Hill, REDDITCH, WORCESTERSHIRE, B97 4BS.

Mall & Co *(L M Cheung, L J Howe)* PO Box 433, MANCHESTER, M28 8AT.

ⓉⒻⒶ**Mallett, Jones & Co** *(D M Mason)* Lee House, 6a Highfield Road, Edgbaston, BIRMINGHAM, B15 3ED.

ⒻⓅ**Malmesbury Accountancy Limited** *(A R Cavill)* 46 High Street, MALMESBURY, WILTSHIRE, SN16 9AT.

Ⓟ**Maltby Accountancy Services Ltd, Wickersley Accountancy & Taxation Services, trading names of WATS Limited** *(J R Parkin)* 63 Bawtry Road, Bramley, ROTHERHAM, SOUTH YORKSHIRE, S66 2TN.

Ⓟ**Maltey Limited** *(M T Chirume)* 57 Waylands, SWANLEY, KENT, BR8 8TN.

ⓉⒻⓅⒶ**Malthouse & Company, trading name of Malthouse & Company Ltd** *(C M French, M J Herbert, J C Malthouse)* America House, Rumford Court, Rumford Place, LIVERPOOL, L3 9DD.

ⒻⒶ**Man & Co** *(V T Man)* 114 Hamlet Court Road, WESTCLIFF-ON-SEA, ESSEX, SS0 7LP.

Ⓟ**Man & Co (UK) Ltd** *(S Y Man)* 3 Garrick House, 63 St Martin's Lane, LONDON, WC2N 4JS.

Ⓟ**Manaktala & Co, trading name of Manaktala & Co Limited** *(P Manaktala)* 17 Leeland Mansions, Leeland Road West Ealing, LONDON, W13 9HE.

Manchanda And Co *(R Manchanda)* 22 Doneraile Street, Fulham, LONDON, SW6 6EN.

Manchar Lall & Rai, trading name of Subhash C. Handa *(S C Handa)* PO Box 25223, NAIROBI, 00603, KENYA.

Ⓟ**Manchester Accountancy Services Limited** *(M P Seitler)* Unit 4, The Cottages, Deva Centre, Trinity Way, SALFORD, M3 7BE.

Ⓟ**Manchman Limited** *(M Keshani)* 10 Park Road, RICKMANSWORTH, HERTFORDSHIRE, WD3 1HT.

Ⓟ**Mancini Limited** *(R S Bhopal)* 10 Shallowford Grove, Furzton, MILTON KEYNES, MK4 1ND.

Ⓟ**Mandair & Co, trading name of Mandair Ltd** *(T S Mandair)* Partnership House, 84 Lodge Road, Portswood, SOUTHAMPTON, SO14 6RG.

Mandy Sanders *(M Sanders)* 6 Waldeck Road, Chiswick, LONDON, W4 3NP.

ⓅⒶ**Manex, trading name of Manex Accountants Limited** *(C J Meehan)* 9 Castle Court, 2 Castlegate Way, DUDLEY, WEST MIDLANDS, DY1 4RD.

ⓅⒶ**Manleys, trading name of M T Manley & Co Ltd** *(G E Collins, C J Windsor)* 696 Yardley Wood Road, Billesley, BIRMINGHAM, B13 0HY.

Mannac *(J B Shooter)* MGS House, Circular Road, Douglas, ISLE OF MAN, IM1 1BL.

ⓉⒻⒶ**Manningtons** *(D J Ames, R F Dennard, P J Langdon, C E Slatter, A E J Staples, A J Thomson)* 7-9 Wellington Square, HASTINGS, EAST SUSSEX, TN34 1PD. and at BATTLE, HEATHFIELD

Mannooch & Co *(D J Mannooch)* 5 Briton Hill Road, Sanderstead, SOUTH CROYDON, Surrey, CR2 0JG.

Ⓐ**Manser Hunot** *(M P Crimmin)* Highland House, Albert Drive, BURGESS HILL, RH15 9TN.

ⓉⒻ**Mansfield & Co** *(D F L Mansfield)* 55 Kentish Town Road, Camden Town, LONDON, NW1 8NX.

★Ⓟ**Manson Boxa Limited** *(J Manson)* 8 Kings Road, Clifton, BRISTOL, BS8 4AB.

Ⓟ**Maple Accounting & Taxation Services Limited** *(S H Magecha)* 10 Lulworth Close, HARROW, MIDDLESEX, HA2 9NR.

★**MapleWoods Partnership** *(P B Lakhani)* 74 The Drive, North Harrow, HARROW, MIDDLESEX, HA2 7EJ.

Ⓐ**Mapperson Price** *(N J Childs, S J Price)* 286a High Street, DORKING, RH4 1QT.

ⓉⒻⒶ**Mapus-Smith & Lemmon LLP** *(S T Boote, S J Edwards, P E Farrow, J W Hall, M J Jay)* 48 King Street, KING'S LYNN, NORFOLK, PE30 1HE. and at DOWNHAM MARKET

Ⓟ**Maratea Limited** *(S D Butler, N R Wheat)* 19 Holbrook Lane, CHISLEHURST, KENT, BR7 6PE.

March:Engenus *(S Corne)* 5B The Stables, Newby Hall, Ripon, KNARESBOROUGH, NORTH YORKSHIRE, HG4 5AE.

Marchant & Co *(D G Marchant)* 2 Court Farm Road, NEWHAVEN, BN9 9DH.

Marchwoods *(N M James)* 3 Berry Lane, Blewbury, DIDCOT, OX11 9QJ.

ⒻⓅ**Marcus & Co, Taxcare, trading names of Taxcare Ltd** *(D Markou)* Bank House, 36-38 Bristol Street, BIRMINGHAM, B5 7AA.

Ⓐ**Marcusfield Dodia, trading name of Marcusfield Dodia & Co** *(J H Marcusfield)* 19 Cumberland Road, STANMORE, HA7 1EL.

Marek & Co *(M T Szczesniak)* Kensington House, 7 Roe Lane, Hesketh Park, SOUTHPORT, PR9 9DT.

Ⓟ**Maretts Limited** *(D W Marett)* Tall Trees House, Westwood Road, Tilehurst, READING, RG31 5PX.

Margaret E. Gregory *(M E Gregory)* 5 Bryn Castell, Radyr, CARDIFF, CF15 8RA.

Margaret Emery *(M R Emery)* Tretawn, St Christopher Close, Little Kingshill, GREAT MISSENDEN, HP16 0DU.

Margaret Ferris LLP *(M Ferris)* Ladyroyd, Busker Lane, Scissett, HUDDERSFIELD, HD8 9JU.

Margaret Morgan *(M E Morgan)* Barnspiece, 60A Church Lane, North Bradley, TROWBRIDGE, BA14 0TA.

Ⓟ**Margaret Mundy ACA, trading name of Margaret Mundy Limited** *(M M Mundy)* 5 Beauley Road, BRISTOL, BS3 1PX.

Margaret Pearson *(M Pearson)* 2 Mayfield, Hipperholme, HALIFAX, HX3 8JY.

Margaret Thomson *(M J Thomson)* 6 Broadpark, Brampford Speke, EXETER, EX5 5HP.

Ⓟ**Marginn, trading name of Marginn Limited** *(M Schofield)* The Old Tannery, Eastgate, ACCRINGTON, LANCASHIRE, BB5 6PW. and at SKIPTON

Marian Hemsted *(M B Hemsted)* Reed House, The Street, Plaxtol, SEVENOAKS, TN15 0QL.

Marianne Dadd ACA *(M Dadd)* PO Box 856, Yalding, MAIDSTONE, KENT, ME18 6WE.

Ⓟ**Marie-Anne Rose, trading name of Marie-Anne Rose Limited** *(M Rose)* Bay Tree Cottage, Crabbswood Lane, Sway, LYMINGTON, SO41 6EQ.

Marion King *(M P King)* 13 Pinecroft, HEMEL HEMPSTEAD, HP3 8AW.

Ⓐ**Marios Aristou Kriticos & Co** *(M A Kriticos)* The Box Works, Loft 201, 4 Worsley Street, Castlefield, MANCHESTER, M15 4NU. and at NICOSIA

Mark A. Guthrie & Co. *(M A Guthrie)* 43-45 Acre Lane, LONDON, SW2 5TN.

ⒻⓅⒶ**Mark Ainley, trading name of Mark Ainley Limited** *(M W Ainley)* Regent House, Heaton Lane, STOCKPORT, CHESHIRE, SK4 1BS.

Ⓟ**Mark Anderson, trading name of Mark Anderson Limited** *(M R Anderson)* 68 Crawley Road, WITNEY, OXFORDSHIRE, OX28 1HU.

Mark Annesley & Co *(M Annesley)* Heather Lodge, Kingston Hill, KINGSTON UPON THAMES, SURREY, KT2 7LX.

Mark Azzopardi-Holland *(M Azzopardi-Holland)* Valletta Buildings Flat 20, South Street, VALLETTA VLT 1103, MALTA.

Ⓟ**Mark Bale, trading name of Mark Bale Limited** *(M P B Bale)* 106 Staunton Road, Headington, OXFORD, OX3 7TN.

Ⓟ**Mark Best, trading name of Charles Best Limited** *(C L M Best)* 12 Henley Close, Rawdon, LEEDS, LS19 6QB.

Mark Doig Nuturing Business Growth *(M S Doig)* 13b County Grove, LONDON, SE5 9LE.

Mark Fink Chartered Tax Adviser *(M R Fink)* Grove House, Back Rowarth, GLOSSOP, DERBYSHIRE, SK13 6ED.

Ⓟ**Mark G Wells, trading name of Mark Wells Consulting Ltd** *(M G Wells)* 84 Mill Street, Steventon, ABINGDON, OX13 6SP.

Ⓟ**Mark Garrett Tax & Accountancy Ltd** *(M Garrett)* 1st Floor, 11 Laura Place, BATH, BA2 4BL.

Ⓟ**Mark Greeve Accounting Limited** *(M J Greeve)* 10 Keswick Drive, FRODSHAM, WA6 7LU.

ⒻⒶ**Mark Haslam, Sons & Co** *(C Haslam, C A Haslam)* 17 Wood Street, BOLTON, BL1 1EB.

ⓉⒻⓅⒶ**Mark Holt & Co Ltd** *(P S Hill, M S Holt, N R Huntley)* Marine Building, Victoria Wharf, PLYMOUTH, PL4 0RF.

Mark Hooton *(M F Hooton)* 2 Butlers Close, Lockerley, ROMSEY, HAMPSHIRE, SO51 0LY.

Mark J Davison *(M J Davison)* PO Box 7150, CHRISTCHURCH, BH23 9FZ.

ⓉⒶ**Mark J Rees** *(S C Collier, M R Harrison, P Hollinshead, R King, A Rhodes, A R Turner, D P Vice)* Granville Hall, Granville Road, LEICESTER, LE1 7RU.

Mark J Ruffles & Co *(M J Ruffles)* 4 Baron Court, Werrington, PETERBOROUGH, PE4 7ZE.

Ⓟ**Mark James Hall, trading name of Halls (UK) Limited** *(M J Hall)* 49 Windsor Avenue, Ashton-on-Ribble, PRESTON, LANCASHIRE, PR2 1JD.

Mark Jenner & Co *(M A Jenner)* PO Box 628, YORK, YO1 0EQ.

Mark Jones & Co *(M P Jones)* 9a Southside Common, LONDON, SW19 4TL.

★**Mark K. Lam & Co.** *(K M Lam)* Room A3 13th Floor, Wing Chzong Commercial Building, 19-25 Jervis Street, CENTRAL, HONG KONG ISLAND, HONG KONG SAR.

Ⓟ**Mark Kennett & Co Limited** *(M Kennett)* Market Gate, Salop Road, OSWESTRY, SHROPSHIRE, SY11 2NR.

★**Mark Kirkbride & Co Limited** *(M M B Kirkbride)* Greenbanks, Hoo Lane, CHIPPING CAMPDEN, GL55 6AZ.

Mark L. Aldridge & Co *(M L Aldridge)* Woodlands Lodge, 2 Penfold Drive, Great Billing, NORTHAMPTON, NN3 9EQ.

Mark Lomax *(M Lomax)* 496 Darwen Road, Bromley Cross, BOLTON, BL7 9DX.

Mark Merrill *(M Merrill)* PO Box 2164, 142 The Borough, Downton, SALISBURY, WILTSHIRE, SP2 2ES.

Ⓐ**Mark O'Brien & Co** *(M T O'Brien)* 22 New Street, CHIPPING NORTON, OX7 5LJ.

Ⓕ**Mark R Williams LLP** *(M R Williams)* 362 Shooters Hill Road, LONDON, SE18 4LS.

Mark Rawlings *(M A Rawlings)* Summerfield House, Upper Wield, ALRESFORD, SO24 9RT.

Mark Richardson *(M J E Richardson)* 25 Valerie Court, Bath Road, READING, RG1 6HP.

Ⓕ**Mark Riley & Co** *(M P Riley)* 4 Cruikshank Lea, SANDHURST, BERKSHIRE, GU47 0FX.

Mark Robinson *(M S Robinson)* 36 Queen Victoria Avenue, HOVE, EAST SUSSEX, BN3 6WN.

Mark Robinson *(M G Robinson)* Trullwell, Box, STROUD, GLOUCESTERSHIRE, GL6 9HD.

Mark Sassoon *(M R Sassoon)* 8 Sheraton Close, Elstree, BOREHAMWOOD, WD6 3PZ.

Mark Satterley *(M D Satterley)* 58 Clyde Avenue, EVESHAM, WORCESTERSHIRE, WR11 3FE.

Mark Seldon & Co *(M G K Seldon)* 10 Sherwood Close, Lily Hill, BRACKNELL, RG12 2SB.

Mark Smith & Co. *(R I Smith)* Rear of, 8 The Shubberies, George Lane South Woodford, LONDON, E18 1BD.

Ⓟ**Mark Thompson Ltd** *(M A Thompson)* 12 Beech Road, Stockton Heath, WARRINGTON, WA4 6LT.

Mark Thornley Associates *(M S Thornley)* 3 Wain Close, Little Heath, POTTERS BAR, EN6 1NF.

Mark Vickers FCA *(M S Vickers)* Hyfrydle, Station Road, Valley Anglesey, HOLYHEAD, GWYNEDD, LL65 3EB.

Mark W Watson *(M W Watson)* 4 Malus Close, MALVERN, WORCESTERSHIRE, WR14 2WD.

Mark Watson *(M A Watson)* 37 Beacon Way, SKEGNESS, LINCOLNSHIRE, PE25 1HJ.

Ⓟ**Mark Wilson, trading name of M Wilson Accountants Limited** *(M Wilson)* 6 Twigg Crescent, Armthorpe, DONCASTER, SOUTH YORKSHIRE, DN3 2FP.

Mark Wolfe & Co *(M Wolfe)* 30 Carnoustie, Beaumont Rise, BOLTON, BL3 4TF.

ⒻⓅⒶ**Markhams, trading name of Markhams Accountants Limited** *(H S Markham)* 10 Perrins Lane, LONDON, NW3 1QY.

Markley Davis *(L A Davis)* 31 Edinburgh Avenue, Sawston, CAMBRIDGE, CB22 3DW.

Ⓐ**Marks & Co** *(D C Hall, M J Marks)* 100 Church St, BRIGHTON, BN1 1UJ.

ⒻⓅⒶ**Marks Bloom, trading name of Marks Bloom Limited** *(D R Evans, P Weinberg, A J Whelan)* 60 Old London Road, KINGSTON UPON THAMES, SURREY, KT2 6QZ.

ⒻⓅ**Marks Hills & Co, trading name of Marks Hills & Co Limited** *(A J Hills)* 52 Warwick Gardens, THAMES DITTON, SURREY, KT7 0RB.

Marlowe & Co *(M C Kockelbergh)* 22 Shawe Avenue, NUNEATON, WARWICKSHIRE, CV10 0EL.

★ⒻⒶ**Marray & McIntyre** *(M J Marray)* Hawthorn House, 1 Medlicott Close, CORBY, NORTHAMPTONSHIRE, NN18 9NF.

Marriots Business Rescue and Recovery, trading name of Marriots Recovery LLP *(K T Brown)* Allan House, 10 John Princes Street, LONDON, W1G 0AH.

★**Marriott Gibbs Rees Wallis** *(L G G Allen)* 13-17 Paradise Square, SHEFFIELD, S1 2DE.

Ⓐ**Marriotts** *(D S Maraj)* 32 Westfield Road, Ealing, LONDON, W13 9JL.

Ⓟ**Marroon Accounts, trading name of Maroon Accounts Limited** *(J Patwari)* 39 High Street, LEATHERHEAD, SURREY, KT22 8AE.

ⒻⒶ**Marsden & Co** *(P M Mendelson, M B Rostron)* 41 Knowsley Street, BURY, LANCASHIRE, BL9 0ST.

Ⓟ**Marsdens, trading name of Marsdens Limited** *(S I Marsh)* Tudor House, High Road, Thornwood, EPPING, ESSEX, CM16 6LT.

ⒻⓅⒶ**Marsh & Moss, trading name of Marsh & Moss Limited** *(N C Harris)* The Gables, Bishop Meadow Road, LOUGHBOROUGH, LEICESTERSHIRE, LE11 5RE.

Marsh Accountancy *(C T Webb)* Preston House, 51 East Street, WARMINSTER, WILTSHIRE, BA12 9BY.

ⒻⓅ**Marsh Accounting & Consulting Ltd** *(M Buys)* Suite 298, Kemp House, 152-160 City Road, LONDON, EC1V 2NX.

ⓉⒶ**Marshall & Co** *(E E Marshall-Birks)* St. Mary's House, Crewe Road, Alsager, STOKE-ON-TRENT, ST7 2EW.

Marshall & Co Accountants LLP *(E E Marshall-Birks)* St. Mary's House, Crewe Road, Alsager, STOKE-ON-TRENT, ST7 2EW.

Ⓟ**Marshall & Co, trading name of Marshall & Co (Hull) Limited** *(D W Marshall)* The Jenko Building, 21 Hessle Road, Clive Sullivan Way, HULL, HU3 2AA.

Marshall Beaven *(P F Beaven)* Christchurch Business Centre, Grange Road, CHRISTCHURCH, DORSET, BH23 4JD.

Marshall Friedner & Co *(M A B Friedner)* 9 Tycehurst Hill, LOUGHTON, ESSEX, IG10 1BX.

Ⓟ**Marshall Keen, trading name of Marshall Keen Limited** *(A M Warren, C E Warren)* Pinewood, Crockford Lane, Chineham, BASINGSTOKE, HAMPSHIRE, RG24 8AL.

ⒻⓅⒶ**Marshall Roche, trading name of Marshall Roche Limited** *(A J Marshall)* 1 Portland Buildings, Stoke Road, GOSPORT, HAMPSHIRE, PO12 1JH. and at WATERLOOVILLE

Ⓟ**Marshall Smalley, trading name of Marshall Smalley Accountants Limited** *(J B Hibbert)* Unit 15, Carlton Business Centre, Station Road, NOTTINGHAM, NG4 3AA.

Marshals Accounting *(S M Sutcliffe)* 26 Chandlers Road, Marshalswick, ST. ALBANS, HERTFORDSHIRE, AL4 9RS.

★**Martell Associates** *(K J Pye)* 28 Elizabeth Avenue, BAGSHOT, SURREY, GU19 5NX.

Martin & Co *(M K Niemann)* 71 Ashcroft Road, Stopsley, LUTON, LU2 9AX.

ⒻⒶ**Martin & Company** *(M Golden, G A Long)* 158 Richmond Park Road, BOURNEMOUTH, BH8 8TW.

ⓉⒻⓅ**Martin & Company, trading name of Martin & Company (Bridport) Limited** *(N D Letheren)* 2 Victoria Grove, BRIDPORT, DORSET, DT6 3AA.

ⒻⒶ**Martin + Heller** *(A Heller, F Martin)* 5 North End Road, LONDON, NW11 7RJ.

▽**Martin Aitken & Co** *(J F Clifford)* Caledonia House, 89 Seaward Street, GLASGOW, G41 1HJ.

★ⓉⒻⓅⒶ**Martin and Company, trading name of Martin and Company Accountants Limited** *(D J C Barr, J A Burnett, S P McLaughlin, W A Nixey)* 25 St. Thomas Street, WINCHESTER, HAMPSHIRE, SO23 9HJ. and at PETERSFIELD, THAME

Martin Beck *(M W Beck)* 7 Hurnard Drive, COLCHESTER, CO3 3SH.

Ⓐ**Martin Briggs & Co** *(M S Briggs)* Banbury House, 121 Stonegrove, EDGWARE, MIDDLESEX, HA8 7TJ.

Ⓟ**Martin Bruno, trading name of KPRM Limited** *(K Parkinson)* 94 Saltergate, CHESTERFIELD, DERBYSHIRE, S40 1LG.

Ⓟ**Martin C Cook & Co, trading name of Martin C Cook & Co Limited** *(M C Cook)* 19 The Fairways, Cold Norton, CHELMSFORD, CM3 6JJ.

Martin C. Galvin *(M C Galvin)* 1 Duke Street, GLOSSOP, SK13 8JD.

Martin D. Flowers *(M D Flowers)* 1 Paradise Square, SHEFFIELD, S1 2DE.

Martin Dodsworth Associates *(M Dodsworth)* 1 Richmond Drive, GOOLE, DN14 5LF.

Ⓕ**Martin Edward Gunson** *(M E Gunson)* Bank House, 9 Dicconson Terrace, Lytham, LYTHAM ST. ANNES, FY8 5JY.

Martin Edwards & Co *(M W Edwards)* La Fantaisie, St Martin, JERSEY, JE3 6HE.

ⓅⒶ**Martin Foster & Co Limited** *(M Foster)* Offices 2 & 3, Shannon Court, High Street, SANDY, BEDFORDSHIRE, SG19 1AG.

Martin G. Lewin & Co. *(M G Lewin)* 35 Thamespoint, Fairways, TEDDINGTON, TW11 9PP.

Ⓐ**Martin Gee** *(M Gee, M J Gee)* 17 Angel Courtyard, High Street, LYMINGTON, HAMPSHIRE, SO41 9AP.

Ⓐ**Martin Greene Ravden** *(D A Greene, P Simnock, N J Walfisz)* 55 Loudoun Road, St Jonh's Wood, LONDON, NW8 0DL.

★ⓉⒻ**Martin Greene Ravden, MGR, MGR Media, trading names of Martin Greene Ravden LLP** *(D A Greene, N H Muir, T S Sharman, P Simnock, T A Sullivan, I Thomas, N J Walfisz)* 55 Loudoun Road, St John's Wood, LONDON, NW8 0DL.

Ⓐ**Martin Hayward** *(M B Hayward)* 85 (a) High Street, BARRY, SOUTH GLAMORGAN, CF62 7DW.

Martin J. Fishleigh *(M J Fishleigh)* Mount Cottage, Mount Pleasant, Westleigh, BIDEFORD, EX39 4LJ.

Martin J. Reich & Co *(M J Reich)* 41 Boyne Ave, LONDON, NW4 2JL.

Martin Jackson FCA, ACIArb, MAE *(M Jackson)* 33 Coleshill Street, SUTTON COLDFIELD, WEST MIDLANDS, B72 1SD.

Martin Jermy Accountants *(M P Jermy)* 14 Royalist Drive, Thorpe St Andrew, NORWICH, NR7 0YN.

Martin Jones *(M O Jones)* 10 Seggs Lane, ALCESTER, B49 5HJ.

Martin JW Venning *(M J W Venning)* The Alma, School Lane, Baslow, BAKEWELL, DERBYSHIRE, DE45 1RZ.

ⒻⓅⒶ**Martin May, trading name of MMAS Limited** *(M I May)* 399 Hendon Way, LONDON, NW4 3LH.

Martin Milner & Co *(M P Milner)* Riverdale, 89 Graham Road, SHEFFIELD, S10 3GP.

Martin Nance *(M Nance)* P.O. Box 223, CORNWALL, CT 06796, UNITED STATES.

★**Martin Nye & Co** *(J E Nye)* 186 High Street, Winslow, BUCKINGHAM, MK18 3DQ. and at DERBY, HEREFORD

ⒻⓅ**Martin Schuman Accountancy, trading name of Martin Schuman Accountancy Ltd** *(M P Schuman)* 13 Oakfields, WALTON-ON-THAMES, SURREY, KT12 1EG.

ⓉⒻⒶ**Martin Sklan & Co** *(A Martin-Sklan)* 133 Golders Green Road, LONDON, NW11 8HJ.

Martin Smith *(M J Smith)* 17 Garbridge Court, APPLEBY-IN-WESTMORLAND, CUMBRIA, CA16 6JE.

Martin T. Mullin FCA *(M T Mullin)* 120 Bloomsbury Lane, Timperley, ALTRINCHAM, WA15 6NT.

Martin Telfer *(M R Telfer)* 5 Brookfields, Pavenham, BEDFORD, MK43 7QA.

ⒻⒶ**Martin Tiano & Co** *(M Tiano)* 2nd Floor, Highview House, 165-167 Station Road, EDGWARE, MIDDLESEX, HA8 7JU.

ⓅⒶ**Martin Waterworth Limited** *(M Waterworth)* Bronwylfa, Llangunnor Road, CARMARTHEN, SA31 2PB.

Martin Williams & Co *(M J Williams)* Riverside House, Brymau 3, River Lane, Saltney, CHESTER, CH4 8RQ.

Martin Yardley FCA *(M Yardley)* 10 Horizon Close, TUNBRIDGE WELLS, KENT, TN4 0AW.

ⒻⓅⒶ**Martlet Audit Limited** *(D C Macdonald)* Martlet House, Unit E1, Yeoman Gate, Yeoman Way, WORTHING, WEST SUSSEX BN13 3QZ.

Martyn Bradish *(M H S Bradish)* 31 Dugdale Hill Lane, POTTERS BAR, EN6 2DP.

Martyn Chilvers & Co *(M L Chilvers)* Long Lane Studios, 142-152 Long Lane, LONDON, SE1 4BS.

Martyn Davy *(M G Davy)* North Pole, Gorsley, ROSS-ON-WYE, HR9 7BJ.

Martyn G Perkins *(M G Perkins)* 166 Portland Street, SOUTHPORT, MERSEYSIDE, PR8 6RB.

Martyn Ingles & Co *(M R Ingles)* 50 High Street, Stoke Goldington, NEWPORT PAGNELL, MK16 8NR.

Ⓕ**Martyn Lewis** *(M L Lewis)* 1 Brewery House, Brook Street, Wivenhoe, COLCHESTER, CO7 9DS.

Martyn Poole & Co *(M R Poole)* 35 St Olav's Court, Lower Road Rotherhithe, LONDON, SE16 2XB.

Mary Asfour *(T M Asfour)* 21 Fremantle Road, BRISTOL, BS6 5SY.

Mary Deeming *(M J Deeming)* 34 Queensway, Sawston, CAMBRIDGE, CB22 3DJ.

Mary E. Locke *(M E Locke)* 3 Flaxen Field, Weston Turville, AYLESBURY, BUCKINGHAMSHIRE, HP22 5GJ.

Ⓟ**Mary Eckland Accounting Services, trading name of Decameas Ltd** *(M Eckland)* 17 Berceau Walk, WATFORD, WD17 3BL. and at PINNER

Ⓕ**Mary Matthews** *(L M C Matthews)* 140 Clifton, YORK, YO30 6BH.

Mary-Louise Wedderburn *(M Wedderburn)* 57 Beryl Road, LONDON, W6 8JS.

Ⓟ**Maskat Financial Solutions, trading name of Maskat Limited** *(D J Farrimond)* 7 Cedargrove, Hagley, STOURBRIDGE, WEST MIDLANDS, DY9 0DR.

Maslins, trading name of Maslins Accountants LLP *(C J Maslin)* 140 Camden Road, TUNBRIDGE WELLS, KENT, TN1 2QZ.

Mason + Co *(G Mason)* Somerville House, 20-22 Harborne Road, Edgbaston, BIRMINGHAM, B15 3AA. and at SOLIHULL

ⒻⓅ**Mason Dharsi Limited** *(C J S Mason)* 29 Cuthbert Road, CROYDON, CR0 3RB.

ⓉⒶ**Mason Law LLP** *(R E Law, R G Lindsay)* 9 Frederick Road, Edgbaston, BIRMINGHAM, B15 1TW.

★**Masons** *(A Jeffries)* 337 Bath Road, SLOUGH, SL1 5PR.

Ⓟ**Masons Forensic Accounting Services Limited** *(A Jeffries)* 337 Bath Road, SLOUGH, SL1 5PR.

ⒻⓅⒶ**Masons, trading name of Masons Audit Limited** *(S P Barker, D J Seymour)* 4 Hadleigh Business Centre, 351 London Road, Hadleigh, BENFLEET, ESSEX, SS7 2BT.

★**Massey & Massey** *(J S Massey)* Au Castillon, 32340 PLIEUX, FRANCE. and at BOURNEMOUTH

Masters *(R G Masters)* Knoll Cottage, 15 Gills Hill, RADLETT, WD7 8DA.

ⓅⒶ**Mathie, Neal, Dancer & Co, MG Group, trading names of MG Audit Services Ltd** *(G A Fernandes)* 93-95 Gloucester Place, LONDON, W1U 6JG. and at RUISLIP

Ⓐ**Matravers** *(M D Matravers)* Bridgewater House, Caspian Road, Atlantic Street, Broadheath, ALTRINCHAM, CHESHIRE WA14 5HH.

Ⓐ**Matrix** *(N Raizada, F Yussouf)* 112/113 Cumberland House, 80 Scrubs Lane, LONDON, NW10 6RF.

Ⓟ**Matrix Accountancy and Taxation Services Ltd** *(M R P Dunkley)* Woodlands Grange, Woodlands Lane, Bradley Stoke, BRISTOL, BS32 4JY.

Ⓐ**Matthams & Co** *(G H West)* 41 Clarence Street, SOUTHEND-ON-SEA, SS1 1BH.

ⓅⒶ**Matthew Craig Associates Limited** *(J D Kelleher)* 10 Riversdale, Llandaff, CARDIFF, CF5 2QL.

Ⓐ**Matthew Edwards & Co** *(N R Morris)* Clinches House, Lord Street, Douglas, ISLE OF MAN, IM1 4LN. and at DUBLIN, LONDON

Matthew Wright *(M G Wright)* 701-137 West 17th Street, NORTH VANCOUVER V7M 1 V5, BC, CANADA.

Matthews & Co. *(D G Matthews)* 40 Ferrers Road, Yoxall, BURTON-ON-TRENT, DE13 8PS.

Matthews & Company *(N G Matthews)* 52 Killigrew Street, FALMOUTH, CORNWALL, TR11 3PP. and at PADSTOW

Matthews Accounting *(S A Matthews)* 125 Cranbrook Road, Redland, BRISTOL, BS6 7DE.

Ⓟ**Matthews Cooper, trading name of Matthews Cooper Limited** *(N G Matthews)* 52 Killigrew Street, FALMOUTH, CORNWALL, TR11 3PP.

ⓅⒶ**Matthews Sutton & Co Ltd** *(S M Matthews, P M Sutton)* 48-52 Penny Lane, LIVERPOOL, L18 1DG.

ⓉⒻⒶ**Matthews, Mist & Co** *(C J Matthews, J W J Mist)* Westbury House, 14 Bellevue Road, SOUTHAMPTON, SO15 2AY.

ⒻⒶ**Mattison & Co.** *(S A Hanrahan, J Mattison)* 10A Royal Parade, CHISLEHURST, BR7 6NR.

ⓅⒶ**Mattocks Grindley, trading name of Mattocks Grindley Limited** *(G Mattocks)* Unit 25, Enterprise Greenhouse, Salisbury Street, ST. HELENS, MERSEYSIDE, WA10 1FY.

Maughan *(S M Antonis)* 9/2 Viewforth Square, EDINBURGH, EH10 4LW.

ⓅⒶ**Maughans Limited** *(N J Maughan)* Norfolk House, 75 Bartholomew Street, NEWBURY, BERKSHIRE, RG14 5DU.

Maurice & Co *(P C Q C Chow Yick Cheung)* 71 Coldershaw Road, Ealing, LONDON, W13 9DU.

ⒻⒶ**Maurice Andrews** *(B G Elliott, M J Pettit)* Grove House, 25 Upper Mulgrave Road, Cheam, SUTTON, SM2 7BE.

ⓉⒻⒶ**Maurice Apple** *(A P M Myers, M A Silver)* 3rd Floor, Marlborough House, 179-189 Finchley Road, LONDON, NW3 6LB.

Maurice Bland & Co *(M N Bland)* Suite One First Floor, Blue Pit Business Centre, Queensway, ROCHDALE, LANCASHIRE, OL11 2PG.

ⓅⒶ**Maurice Braganza & Co, trading name of MABCO Limited** *(M A Braganza)* 1 Lancaster Place, LONDON, WC2E 7ED.

ⓅⒶ**Maurice Bruno Ltd** *(M Bruno)* Wyndham House, Sunning Avenue, ASCOT, BERKSHIRE, SL5 9PW.

Maurice Dawes *(M S G Dawes)* Glen View, Boughton Hall Avenue, Send, WOKING, SURREY, GU23 7DF.

Maurice Edward Granger *(M E Granger)* 143 Burley Lane, Quarndon, DERBY, DE22 5JS.

★**Maurice Fong & Company** *(Y M Fong)* Unit 2201-2 22/F, Chinachem Johnston Plaza, 178-186 Johnston Road, WAN CHAI, HONG KONG ISLAND, HONG KONG SAR.

ⓉⒶ**Maurice G. Wood Partnership** *(H P Karsan, N M Khan)* 69 Plumstead Common Road, Plumstead, LONDON, SE18 3AX.

Maurice Glover *(M G J Glover)* 31 Burnaby Gardens, LONDON, W4 3DR.

Ⓐ**Maurice Golend & Co** *(L M Golend)* 271 Green Lanes, LONDON, N13 4XP.

ⓉⒻⒶ**Maurice J. Bushell & Co** *(P R Clements, S Foster, H A Goldstein)* Curzon House, 64 Clifton Street, LONDON, EC2A 4HB.

Maurice W. Moussa *(M W Moussa)* Suite 51 Bourg El Zamalek, 18 Shargarret El Dorr Street, Zamalek, CAIRO, 11211, EGYPT.

Ⓕ**Maurice Whiteley** *(M Whiteley)* Nash House, 16 Swain Street, WATCHET, SOMERSET, TA23 0AB. and at TAUNTON

Mavis Lucas *(M Lucas)* Bolgoed Isaf, Bolgoed Road, Pontardulais, SWANSEA, SA4 8JP.

Maws & Associates *(M A Walker-Smith)* 18 Aquinas Street, LONDON, SE1 8AE.

★**Mawson Breskal & Co** *(G Breskal)* Bishops House, Monkville Avenue, LONDON, NW11 0AH.

Max Bayes *(M W Bayes)* 33 Main Road, Hackleton, NORTHAMPTON, NN7 2AD.

Ⓟ**Max Montague, trading name of Max Montague Limited** *(D M Whiteley)* Building D, Berkley Works, Berkley Grove, Primrose Hill, LONDON, NW1 8XY.

Ⓕ**MaxAim LLP** *(T C Cormack, T E Hayes, M C A Peters, I Robinson)* United Business Centre, 1 Mariner Court, Calder Park, WAKEFIELD, WEST YORKSHIRE, WF4 3FL.

Maxama *(M J Maxfield)* Kirkland, Longdown Road, FARNHAM, SURREY, GU10 3JS.

Maxine Higgins *(M Higgins)* Pentire, Orchard Close, East Horsley, LEATHERHEAD, KT24 5EZ.

ⓅⒶ**Maxwell & Co, trading name of Maxwell & Co Limited** *(H W G Maxwell)* 10 St. Georges Yard, FARNHAM, SURREY, GU9 7LW.

★Ⓐ**Maxwell-Gumbleton & Co, trading name of Keymer Haslam & Co** *(M N Haslam, R V Maxwell-Gumbleton)* 4/6 Church Road, BURGESS HILL, RH15 9AE. and at LEWES

ⓉⒻⒶ**Maxwells** *(S T L Ball, M R Berry, N Blannin, C N Hall-Tomkin, P J Littler, A W Turrell, D A Villis, M S J Villis)* 4 King Square, BRIDGWATER, SOMERSET, TA6 3YF.

May Associates, trading name of John J May *(J J May)* 2 Belmont Mews, CAMBERLEY, GU15 2PH.

Maya's *(V Bhandari)* 11 Bunyana Avenue, WAHROONGA, NSW 2076, AUSTRALIA.

Maycall & Co *(A L Hill)* 4 Marchwood Close, BRIDGNORTH, SHROPSHIRE, WV16 4SA.

Ⓟ**Mayes Business Partnership Ltd** *(N H Snodgrass, G J Taylor)* 22-28 Willow Street, ACCRINGTON, LANCASHIRE, BB5 1LP.

ⓅⒶ**Mayfair Wealth Management Limited** *(N S Posnansky)* 1st Floor, Monument House, 215 Marsh Road, PINNER, MIDDLESEX, HA5 5NE.

Ⓟ**Mayfield & Co (Accountants) Ltd** *(A N Downes, D T Mayfield)* 2nd Floor, 27 The Crescent, King Street, LEICESTER, LE1 6RX. and at MARKET HARBOROUGH

ⓉⒻⒶ**Mayfield & Company** *(A N Downes, D T Mayfield)* 2nd Floor, 27 The Crescent, King Street, LEICESTER, LE1 6RX. and at MARKET HARBOROUGH

Ⓟ**Mayfield Accounting Ltd** *(J L Southwell)* 36 Chiswick Green Studios, 1 Evershed Walk, LONDON, W4 5BW.

Ⓟ**Mayfield Business Services Ltd** *(K D Davis)* 3 Crimicar Lane, SHEFFIELD, S10 4FA.

ⓅⒶ**Mayfield, Portland, trading names of Portland Business Consulting Ltd** *(M Shabir)* 16th Floor, Portland House, Bressenden Place, LONDON, SW1E 5RS. and at BIRMINGHAM

ⒻⒶ**Maynard Heady LLP** *(R J Baines, N J Bragg, S J Caten, D M Curtis, D Datson, P B Dixon, R M Port, D J Smith, G Tidbury, C H Wilson)* Matrix House, 12-16 Lionel Road, CANVEY ISLAND, ESSEX, SS8 9DE. and at MALDON

ⓉⒻⓅ**Maynard Johns, trading name of Jane Maynard Limited** *(A S Maynard, J C Maynard)* 37 Mill Street, BIDEFORD, DEVON, EX39 2JJ.

Mayne & Company *(K R Mayne)* Beach House, Petit Port, St. Brelade, JERSEY, JE3 8HL.

Maytree Accountancy *(T A Turigel)* 148 Neale Avenue, KETTERING, NORTHAMPTONSHIRE, NN16 9HD.

Maz & Co *(M A Zaffar)* 63 Beehive Lane, ILFORD, ESSEX, IG1 3RL.

Ⓣ**Mazars** *(S N Bitar)* Al Nassr Plaza, Offices 218 219 220, PO Box 6212, DUBAI, UNITED ARAB EMIRATES.

Mazars *(K K Sharma)* 133 Cecil Street, 15-02 Keck Seng Tower, SINGAPORE 069535, SINGAPORE.

Ⓟ**Mazars Corporate Finance Limited** *(K B Hurst, R A Karmel, A J Millington, G M Williams)* Tower Bridge House, St. Katharines Way, LONDON, E1W 1DD. and at BEDFORD, BIRMINGHAM, BRIGHTON, BRISTOL, DUDLEY, EDINBURGH, GLASGOW, LEEDS, LUTON, MANCHESTER, MILTON KEYNES, NOTTINGHAM, OXFORD, POOLE, SOUTHAMPTON, SUTTON

Ⓟ**Mazars CPA Limited** *(Y Kwok)* 42nd Floor, Central Plaza, 18 Harbour Road, WAN CHAI, HONG KONG ISLAND, HONG KONG SAR.

★ⓉⒻⒶ**Mazars LLP** *(A J Alexander, T A Askham, T C H Ball, R M Benson, J M Berry, D C Birch, D R A Bott, S A Brice, T L A Brichieri-Colombi, L A Brook, S R Brown, R J F Burrows, W N Bussey, A Carey, L Cartwright, D G Chapman, S Davies, P L Dawes, S Eames, D J Evans, L J Fox, A J Fraser, P R Gilmour, A M W Godfrey, A J Goldsworthy, S J Govey, M J Grice, N C Grummitt, G J Hall, A Heffron, D R P Herbinet, G J Hitchmough, M G Hodges, O G Hoffman, I G M Holder, G R T Hollander, J C Holroyd, R A Hopkins, A J Hubbard, T W Hudson, K B Hurst, B P Hutchinson, C A Jackson, N A Johnson, G B Jones, R A Karmel, K F J Lam Hung, R Lang, M D Leary, S J Lewis, P M Lucas, R W Metcalfe, A J Millington, R H Neate, G Oliver, L R Pentelow, M D Pickard, M J Rogers, S M G Russell, C A Scarr, R B Scott, J D Seaman, K P Simmons, A G Smith, D Smithson, T J Stanbrook, M A Stewart, M P J Taylor, P Terry, R C Tidbury, S M Tubb, P A Verity, N J Wakefield, P Waller, R J Weston, G M Williams, A S Wood, I G Wrightson, B T Young)* Tower Bridge House, St. Katharines Way, LONDON, E1W 1DD. and at BIRMINGHAM, BRIGHTON, BRISTOL, EDINBURGH, GLASGOW, LEEDS, LIVERPOOL, LUTON, MANCHESTER, MILTON KEYNES, NOTTINGHAM, POOLE, SOUTHAMPTON, SUTTON

Mazars LLP *(T W Cheng, L K Lee)* 133 Cecil Street, Apt.15-02 Keck Seng Tower, SINGAPORE 048545, SINGAPORE.

ⓉⓅⒶ**Mazars, trading name of Mazars Channel Islands Limited** *(A T Budworth)* International House, 3rd Floor, 41 The Parade, St. Helier, JERSEY, JE2 3QQ.

Ⓟ**Mazuma, trading name of Mazuma (North London) Limited** *(S L Stern)* 344-354 Gray's Inn Road, LONDON, WC1X 8BP.

Ⓟ**MB Accountancy Limited** *(M A Bushnell)* Peacehaven, Coltstaple Lane, Newfoundout, HORSHAM, WEST SUSSEX, RH13 9BB.

MB Consulting *(M W Batty)* 21 Oakland Close, Glais, SWANSEA, SA7 9EW.

MBA & Co *(C U Mba)* B19 Admirality Towers, 8 Gerrard Road, P O Box 51847, Ikoyi, LAGOS, NIGERIA.

MBA Michael Bishop & Associates *(M I Bishop)* Elderns, 19b Kings Weston Road, Henbury, BRISTOL, BS10 7QT.

Ⓟ**MBI, trading name of MBI Coakley Ltd** *(D B Coakley)* Second Floor, Tungsgate Square, 98-110 High Street, GUILDFORD, SURREY, GU1 3HE.

ⓉⒻⓅⒶ**MCA Breslins, trading name of MCA Breslins Banbury Ltd** *(M C Cox, D Handley)* Greenway House, Sugarswell Business Park, Shenington, BANBURY, OXFORDSHIRE, OX15 6HW.

ⓅⒶ**MCA Breslins, trading name of MCA Breslins Holdings Ltd** *(M C Cox)* 5-7 Newbold Street, LEAMINGTON SPA, WARWICKSHIRE, CV32 4HN.

ⒻⓅⒶ**MCA Breslins, trading name of MCA Breslins Leamington Ltd** *(M C Cox)* 5-7 Newbold Street, LEAMINGTON SPA, WARWICKSHIRE, CV32 4HN.

ⒻⓅⒶ**MCA Breslins, trading name of MCA Breslins Solihull Ltd** *(K M Walsh)* 8 The Courtyard, 707 Warwick Road, SOLIHULL, WEST MIDLANDS, B91 3DA.

MCA Papademetres LLP *(M Papademetris)* Loukis Pierides Street, Lysion Court, Flat 1, 6021 LARNACA, CYPRUS.

McAdam And Company *(D McAdam)* 7 Chalmers Road, AYR, KA7 2RQ.

Ⓟ**McBoyle & Co, trading name of C F McBoyle Ltd** *(C F McBoyle)* Omega Court, 370 Cemetery Road, SHEFFIELD, S11 8FT.

Ⓕ**McBrides** *(P McBride)* 31 Harley Street, LONDON, W1G 9QS.

ⒻⓅ**McBrides Corporate Finance Limited** *(T Baldwin, J E Eldridge, N P Kimber, B L Moleshead, N L Paterno, A J Warren)* Nexus House, 2 Cray Road, SIDCUP, KENT, DA14 5DA.

ⓉⒻⒶ**McBrides, trading name of McBrides Accountants LLP** *(T Baldwin, J E Eldridge, N P Kimber, B L Moleshead, N L Paterno, A J Warren)* Nexus House, 2 Cray Road, SIDCUP, KENT, DA14 5DA.

McBroom & Co *(A I McBroom)* Unit 12, South West Centre, Troutbeck Road, SHEFFIELD, S7 2QA.

Ⓟ**MCBW Consulting Ltd** *(M Wood)* 6 Wellington Drive, WELWYN GARDEN CITY, HERTFORDSHIRE, AL7 2NJ.

Ⓟ**MCBW Limited** *(M Wood)* 6 Wellington Drive, WELWYN GARDEN CITY, HERTFORDSHIRE, AL7 2NJ.

Ⓕ**MC-CA** *(M P Cooke)* 19 Kendrick Close, SOLIHULL, B92 0QD.

★ⓉⒶ**McCabe Ford Williams** *(D N A Boobbyer, A C Callow, D J Cork, G A Deacon, I Ellis, P R Frowde, N R Hayward, D J Kendall, L M McHugh, I D Pascall, C L Rayner, J D Sheather, T J Shipley, M P Whittaker, B Wright)* Market House, 17 Hart Street, MAIDSTONE, KENT, ME16 8RA. and at ASHFORD, CRANBROOK, DOVER, HERNE BAY, SITTINGBOURNE

★**McCambridge Duffy LLP** *(D Rule)* Templemore Business Park, Northland Road, Derry, LONDONDERRY, BT48 0LD. and at BELFAST, CARDIFF, POOLE, SEVENOAKS

McCarthy & Co *(P P McCarthy)* 17 The Village, Knockboy, WATERFORD, COUNTY WATERFORD, IRELAND.

ⒻⒶ**McCartney & Co** *(A M McCartney)* Grove House, 27 Hawkin Street, LONDONDERRY, BT48 6RE.

McChesney Indirect Tax Consultancy, trading name of McChesney LLP *(N R McChesney)* 22 Lonsdale Road, LONDON, SW13 9EB.

Members in Practice and Firms - Alphabetical McColm Cardew Ltd - Michael Donnely & Co

Ⓟ**McColm Cardew Ltd** *(G Cardew)* 10 Main Street, Bilton, RUGBY, WARWICKSHIRE, CV22 7NB.

★**Mccormack & Associates** *(N M Patani, H H Shah, R Shah)* Euro House, 1394-1400 High Road, LONDON, N20 9BH.

★ⒻⒶ**McCowie & Co** *(G McCowie)* 52-54 Leazes Park Rd, NEWCASTLE UPON TYNE, NE1 4PG.

ⓉⓅⒶ**McCranors, trading name of McCranors Limited** *(P R Chapman, R Perry, C J Squire)* Clifford House, 38-44 Binley Road, COVENTRY, CV3 1JA.

McCullough & Co *(J Reed)* 163 Smiths Green, Sherborne St. John, BASINGSTOKE, HAMPSHIRE, RG24 9JA.

ⓉⓅⒶ**McDade Roberts, trading name of McDade Roberts Accountants Limited** *(K R Carey, S A Denye, J A Roberts, J Stokes)* 316 Blackpool Road, Fulwood, PRESTON, PR2 3AE.

McDermott & Co *(B P McDermott)* 1 Hardwick's Square, LONDON, SW18 4AW.

McDowell CPA PC *(A McDowell)* 410 Park Avenue, 15th Floor, NEW YORK, NY 10022, UNITED STATES.

★**McDwyer, Lennon & Co** *(M R McDwyer)* Esker Place, Cathedral Road, CAVAN, COUNTY CAVAN, IRELAND.

Ⓐ**McEllin Kelly** *(L M Kelly)* Abacus House, 35 Cumberland Street, MACCLESFIELD, CHESHIRE, SK10 1DD.

ⓉⒻⒶ**McEwan Wallace** *(T P Cochrane, A C Gould, A D Richards, N Wilson)* 68 Argyle Street, Birkenhead, WIRRAL, CH41 6AF.

Ⓟ**McEwen & Co Ltd** *(L M J McEwen)* Forum House, Stirling Road, CHICHESTER, WEST SUSSEX, PO19 7DN.

ⓉⒻⒶ**McGills** *(S G Nuttall, A I Palmer)* Oakley House, Tetbury Road, CIRENCESTER, GL7 1US.

Ⓐ**McGoverns** *(A G McGovern)* 24 Westpole Avenue, Cockfosters, BARNET, EN4 0AY.

ⓅⒶ**McGregors Business Network Ltd** *(P S Cudworth, C J Holder)* i2 Mansfield, Office Suite 2.1, Oakham Business Park, MANSFIELD, NOTTINGHAMSHIRE, NG18 5BR.

★ⓉⓅⒶ**McGregors Corporate, trading name of McGregors (Mansfield) Ltd** *(C B Chadwick, C J Holder)* i2 Mansfield, Office Suite 2.1, Oakham Business Park, MANSFIELD, NOTTINGHAMSHIRE, NG18 5BR.

ⓅⒶ**McGregors Corporate, trading name of Mcgregors Corporate (Lincoln) Ltd** *(C B Chadwick, C J Holder)* Unit 8, Checkpoint Court, Sadler Road, LINCOLN, LN6 3PW.

★ⓅⒶ**McGregors Corporate, trading name of McGregors Corporate (Nottingham) Ltd** *(P S Cudworth, C J Holder, S R Mugglestone)* 13-15 Regent Street, NOTTINGHAM, NG1 5BS.

McKellens Outsourcing LLP *(C R Booth, J P Roper, J P Sandford)* 11 Riverview, The Embankment Business Park, Heaton Mersey, STOCKPORT, CHESHIRE, SK4 3GN.

ⒻⓅⒶ**McKellens, trading name of McKellens Ltd** *(C R Booth, J P Roper)* 11 Riverview, The Embankment Business Park, Heaton Mersey, STOCKPORT, CHESHIRE, SK4 3GN.

ⒻⒶ**McKelvie & Company** *(A W McKelvie)* 82 Wandsworth Bridge Road, Fulham, LONDON, SW6 2TF.

McKenzie Lindsay *(G D G Lindsay)* 5 Dodds Court, Preston Street, FAVERSHAM, ME13 8PE.

ⓉⒻⒶ**McKenzies** *(P S Baker, C E McCoy)* 14-16 Station Road West, OXTED, SURREY, RH8 9EP.

McKie & Co (Advisory Services) LLP *(S P McKie)* Rudge Hill House, Rudge, FROME, SOMERSET, BA11 2QG.

Ⓟ**McKie & Co Limited** *(S P McKie)* Rudge Hill House, Rudge, FROME, SOMERSET, BA11 2QG.

Ⓐ**McLachlan & Tiffin** *(R C Tiffin)* Clifton House, Craigard Road, CRIEFF, PH7 4BN.

Ⓟ**McLarens, trading name of Mclaren Cornel Limited** *(H R M Watling)* Penhurst House, 352-356 Battersea Park Road, LONDON, SW11 3BY.

Ⓟ**McLean Business Solutions Limited** *(T D McLean)* 4 Poise Brook Drive, Offerton, STOCKPORT, CHESHIRE, SK2 5JG.

ⒻⒶ**McLean Reid** *(J Champion, A M Reid)* 1 Forstal Road, AYLESFORD, ME20 7AU.

★ⓉⒻⒶ**McLintocks Partnership** *(M W Caputo, A J Jeffcott, P F McGerty, J A McLintock, T J Mitchell)* 2 Hilliards Court, Chester Business Park, CHESTER, CH4 9PX. and at WREXHAM

★ⒻⓅⒶ**McLintocks, trading name of McLintocks Ltd** *(M W Caputo, J C Hughes, A J Jeffcott, P F McGerty, J A McLintock, T J Mitchell)* 56 Hamilton Street, BIRKENHEAD, MERSEYSIDE, CH41 5HZ.

McManus Hall *(M J McManus)* Office 8, Consett Innovation Centre, Ponds Court Business Park, Genesis Way, CONSETT, COUNTY DURHAM DH8 5XP.

Ⓟ**McMillan & Co Accounting Services Ltd** *(J F D McMillan)* 28 Eaton Avenue, Matrix Office Park, Buckshaw Village, CHORLEY, LANCASHIRE, PR7 7NA.

ⓉⒻⒶ**McMillan & Co LLP** *(A B McLaughlin, J F D McMillan, N R D McMillan)* 28 Eaton Avenue, Buckshaw Village, CHORLEY, LANCASHIRE, PR7 7NA.

McNaught & Co *(A J McNaught)* 189 Wokingham Road, Earley, READING, RG6 1LT.

ⒻⓅⒶ**mcpherson*s, trading name of McPherson Accountancy Limited** *(K R McPherson)* 60 Chertsey Street, GUILDFORD, GU1 4HL.

ⓉⒻⓅⒶ**McPhersons CFG Limited** *(M Finch, A Gill)* 23 St. Leonards Road, BEXHILL-ON-SEA, EAST SUSSEX, TN40 1HH. and at HASTINGS

★Ⓣ**MCR** *(S G Clancy, P F Duffy, A G Stoneman, J N Whitfield, B J Wiles)* 43-45 Portman Square, LONDON, W1H 6LY. and at BIRMINGHAM, MANCHESTER

Ⓟ**MCS, trading name of Management Consultancy Services Limited** *(N S G Harper)* Carters Corner Farm, Cowbeech Hill, Cowbeech, HAILSHAM, EAST SUSSEX, BN27 4JA.

ⓉⒻⒶ**MCT Partnership** *(K G Patel, R M Robinson, S P Ruparellia, M C Thakkar)* 1 Warner House, Harrovian Business Village, Bessborough Road, HARROW, HA1 3EX.

★**McTear Williams & Wood** *(C N McKay, A I McTear, C K Williams)* 90 St Faiths Lane, NORWICH, NR1 1NE. and at CAMBRIDGE, CHELMSFORD, COLCHESTER, IPSWICH, LONDON

Ⓟ**MD Accounting Ltd** *(M H Denny)* 53 Irwin Road, BEDFORD, MK40 3UN.

Ⓟ**MDJ Accountancy Limited** *(M D Jordan)* Timaru, Corseley Road, Groombridge, TUNBRIDGE WELLS, KENT, TN3 9SG.

ⒻⓅⒶ**MDP, trading name of Michael Dufty Partnership Limited** *(D J Whale)* 61 Charlotte Street, St Paul's Square, BIRMINGHAM, B3 1PX.

ⒻⓅⒶ**Meacher-Jones, trading name of Meacher-Jones & Company Limited** *(D R Meacher-Jones)* 6 St. Johns Court, Vicars Lane, CHESTER, CH1 1QE. and at OLDHAM

Meades Consulting LLP *(P J Allen)* 39 The Metro Centre, Tolpits Lane, WATFORD, WD18 9SB.

★ⓉⒻⒶ**Meadows, trading name of Meadows & Co** *(D P Childs, D H Kirkland, D O H Parker, N Rowland)* Headlands House, 1 Kings Court, Kettering Parkway, KETTERING, NORTHAMPTONSHIRE, NN15 6AA.

Meco Accountancy Services *(A M Evans)* Holmwood, Pentwyn, TREHARRIS, MID GLAMORGAN, CF46 5BS.

Med Act *(R H Russell)* 36 Lancaster Road, Wimbledon, LONDON, SW19 5DD.

ⒻⓅ**Media Finance, trading name of Media Finance Ltd** *(C N Spurgeon)* Riverside Studios, Crisp Road, LONDON, W6 9RL.

Ⓟ**Medrus UK Limited** *(C E Byrne)* 43 Parkfields, Penyfai, BRIDGEND, MID GLAMORGAN, CF31 4NQ.

ⓉⒶ**Meer & Co** *(H Rafique)* 1 Cochrane House, Admirals Way, Canary Wharf, LONDON, E14 9UD.

Mehra Dhir Bhatia & Co *(P Dhir)* 248 Hauz Rani, Opp Modi Hospital Saket, NEW DELHI 110017, INDIA.

ⒻⒶ**Mehta & Tengra** *(J J Mehta, P B Tengra)* 24 Bedford Row, LONDON, WC1R 4TQ.

ⒻⒶ**Mehta and Company** *(R H L Mehta)* 221 Cranbrook Road, ILFORD, ESSEX, IG1 4TD.

Melanie Haywood *(M K Haywood)* 5 Essendine Road, LONDON, W9 2LS.

Melanie Nagele ACA *(M J E Nagele)* Christmas Cottage, Chapel Hill, Speen, PRINCES RISBOROUGH, BUCKINGHAMSHIRE, HP27 0SP.

Melanie Shepherd *(M G Dickens)* 1 Vine Cottage, Village Green, Northchapel, PETWORTH, WEST SUSSEX, GU28 9HU.

Ⓐ**Melinekfine, trading name of Melinek Fine LLP** *(D B Fine, A Y Melinek)* Ground Floor, Forframe House, 35-37 Brent Street, LONDON, NW4 2EF.

Mellor & Co *(A D G Mellor)* 1st Floor, 31 Sandiway, KNUTSFORD, WA16 8BU.

Mellor Oxland, trading name of Mellor Oxland LLP *(D S Oxland)* 2 King Street, NOTTINGHAM, NG1 2AS.

ⒻⒶ**Melville & Co** *(J R Goffe, D R Longton)* Unit 17/18, Trinity Enterprise Centre, Furness Business Park, Ironworks Road, BARROW-IN-FURNESS, CUMBRIA LA14 2PN.

Ⓐ**Melville Morris** *(M Morris)* 3rd Floor, Trident House, 31-33 Dale Street, LIVERPOOL, L2 2HF.

Ⓐ**Melvyn Davies & Co** *(J M Davies)* 9 Limes Road, BECKENHAM, BR3 6NS.

Melvyn F. Goddard & Co *(M F Goddard)* 1 Peerswood Court, Little Neston, NESTON, CH64 0US.

Melvyn Greenhalgh *(M Greenhalgh)* 34 Cedar Grove, North Runcton, KING'S LYNN, PE33 0QZ.

Melvyn Lunn *(M Lunn)* 49 Church Street, Darton, BARNSLEY, S75 5HF.

Menezes & Co *(M P Menezes)* 16 Kings Avenue, BROMLEY, BR1 4HW.

Ⓟ**Menzies Cameron & Co, trading name of Menzies Cameron Limited** *(S G C Menzies)* Rowden House, 25 Rowden Hill, CHIPPENHAM, SN15 2AQ.

★ⓉⒻⒶ**Menzies, trading name of Menzies LLP** *(J B Adams, S I Amico, J L Biffen, C J Chowney, A J Cook, M J Dawe, A J Denley, J Detheridge, T P Dunn, P P Earle, N M Farmer, J A Flewitt, T M Gale, D J Gibbons, R A R Godmon, M D Grayer, P R Hickson, A M Hookway, J R Jagger, P King, M I Lucas, S J Massey, R M Mitchison, S Mitchison, P R Noyce, M D Peddie, M A Perrin, A Price, S G Pritchard, L L Richardson, M G Sands, G R Seddon)* Woking Office, Midas House, 62 Goldsworth Road, WOKING, SURREY, GU21 6LQ. and at EGHAM, FAREHAM, FARNBOROUGH, KINGSTON UPON THAMES, LEATHERHEAD, LONDON

ⓉⒻⒶ**Meralis** *(M P K Merali)* First Floor, Scottish Provident House, 76-80 College Road, HARROW, MIDDLESEX, HA1 1BQ.

ⓉⒶ**Mercer & Hole** *(H Cain, A J Crook, J Dobbin, G C Farnes, P J Godfrey-Evans, R I Jamieson, M G Joy, C Laughton, P A Maberly, D Mansell, M A Reed, S L Smith, P Webster, H J Wilkinson)* Gloucester House, 72 London Road, ST. ALBANS, HERTFORDSHIRE, AL1 1NS. and at LONDON, MILTON KEYNES

ⒻⓅ**Mercer & Hole Trustees Limited** *(R E Capon, H J Wilkinson, E M Wood)* Gloucester House, 72 London Road, ST. ALBANS, AL1 1NS. and at LONDON, MILTON KEYNES

ⓉⒻⒶ**Mercer Lewin, trading name of Mercer Lewin Ltd** *(A Churchill Stone, P M Mercer)* 41 Cornmarket Street, OXFORD, OX1 3HA.

ⒻⒶ**Merchant & Co.** *(D W Ford, G H Freemantle)* 84 Uxbridge Road, West Ealing, LONDON, W13 8RA.

Meredith Tax LLP *(D G Meredith)* Unit 16, Clifton Moor Business Village, Clifton Moor, YORK, YO30 4XG.

Ⓕ**Meredith Thomas** *(C T A Meredith)* Suite No 1, Royal Arcade, PERSHORE, WR10 1AG.

Ⓟ**Meridian Corporate Finance LLP** *(M G Barcia)* The Coach House, Rownhams House, Rownhams, SOUTHAMPTON, SO16 8LS.

Merkler, Sharp & Co. *(L H A Sharp)* Crown Lodge, Crown Road, MORDEN, SURREY, SM4 5BY.

Ⓟ**Merlin Accountancy Services Ltd** *(G M Corby)* 4 Charnley Avenue, Redhills, EXETER, EX4 1RE.

Ⓟ**Merryhill Accountancy Services Ltd** *(L E M Partridge)* 73 High Street, Braunston, DAVENTRY, NORTHAMPTONSHIRE, NN11 7HS.

Messrs W Edwards & Co *(M Y E Lau)* 15 Cedar Drive, PINNER, HA5 4BY.

ⒻⓅ**Meta Corporate Finance Limited** *(P M Counsell, M D Ledger-Beadell)* Hop House, Lower Green Road, Pembury, TUNBRIDGE WELLS, TN2 4HS.

★Ⓐ**Metcalfes** *(H Marsh)* 1-3 St. Marys Place, BURY, LANCASHIRE, BL9 0DZ.

Ⓐ**Metherell Gard** *(J B Kitson, K E Mordan)* Old Memorial Hall, Morval, LOOE, CORNWALL, PL13 1PN.

★ⓅⒶ**Metherell Gard Ltd** *(D N Cox, P L Mead)* Burn View, BUDE, CORNWALL, EX23 8BX.

★Ⓟ**Metric Accountants, trading name of Metric Accountants Ltd** *(J L Richardson)* 85B Bedford Road, East Finchley, LONDON, N2 9DB.

Ⓟ**Metsons, trading name of Metsons Accountants Limited** *(A W Metson)* 13a The Parade, Wrotham Road, Meopham, GRAVESEND, KENT, DA13 0JL.

★ⓉⒻⒶ**Meyer Williams** *(S A Heaney, N R Jones, J L Meyer)* Queen Alexandra House, 2 Bluecoats Avenue, HERTFORD, HERTFORDSHIRE, SG14 1PB.

ⓉⓅⒶ**MFA, trading name of MFA Accountants Limited** *(M J Fagelman)* 6a The Gardens, FAREHAM, HAMPSHIRE, PO16 8SS.

ⓅⒶ**MFG Holdings Limited** *(M F Gilmartin)* 102 Bowen Court, St. Asaph Business Park, ST. ASAPH, CLWYD, LL17 0JE.

ⓅⒶ**MG Associates, trading name of MG Associates Ltd** *(M E G Ghersie)* 7a Ilsham Road, TORQUAY, TQ1 2JG. and at DARTMOUTH

Ⓟ**MG Contractor Services, MG Group, trading names of MG Contractor Services Ltd** *(G A Fernandes)* 93-95 Gloucester Place, LONDON, W1U 6JG.

Ⓟ**MG Group, Taxation Services MG Group, trading names of Taxation Services (London) Ltd** *(G A Fernandes)* 93-95 Gloucester Place, LONDON, W1U 6JG.

MG Group, trading name of MG Accountants & Co *(G A Fernandes)* Audit House, 260 Field End Road, RUISLIP, MIDDLESEX, HA4 9LT. and at LONDON

Ⓟ**MG Group, trading name of MG Accountants & Co Limited** *(G A Fernandes)* Audit House, 260 Field End Road, RUISLIP, MIDDLESEX, HA4 9LT. and at LONDON

ⓉⓅ**MG Group, trading name of MG Group (Professional Services) Ltd** *(G A Fernandes)* 93-95 Gloucester Place, LONDON, W1U 6JG. and at RUISLIP

MG Wright FCA FInstD *(M G Wright)* 22 Charlton Close, Charlton Kings, CHELTENHAM, GLOUCESTERSHIRE, GL53 8DJ.

ⓉⓅ**MGI Gregoriou & Co Ltd** *(G N Petsas)* Greg Tower, 7 Florina Street, P.O. Box 24854, 1304 NICOSIA, CYPRUS. and at LARNACA, LIMASSOL

Ⓟ**MGM Accountancy Ltd** *(M A Henison)* 3rd Floor, 20 Bedford Street, LONDON, WC2E 9HP.

ⓅⒶ**MGR Audit Limited** *(D A Greene, P Simnock, N J Walfisz)* 55 Loudoun Road, St Johns Wood, LONDON, NW8 0DL.

Ⓟ**MGW Accounting Services ltd** *(M G Wiltshire)* 39 Cardiff Road, DINAS POWYS, SOUTH GLAMORGAN, CF64 4DH.

Ⓟ**MGW Consultants Ltd** *(M G Ware)* 2 Norbury Avenue, WATFORD, WD24 4PJ.

Ⓟ**MH Mortimer, trading name of MH Mortimer Ltd** *(M H Mortimer)* 27 Beaumont Road, Petts Wood, ORPINGTON, KENT, BR5 1JL.

MHA Fieldings *(G Fielding)* The Post House, Astley Abbotts, BRIDGNORTH, SHROPSHIRE, WV16 4SW.

Ⓟ**MHL Consulting Ltd** *(H L Loke)* 7/F Allied Kajima Building, 138 Gloucester Road, SAR, HONG KONG SAR.

Mian & Malik *(O H Malik)* 28 Sarum, Roman Wood, BRACKNELL, BERKSHIRE, RG12 8XZ.

Michael A Colley *(M A Colley)* Leicester House, 6 Hamilton Terrace, Main Street, PEMBROKE, SA71 4DE.

ⒻⒶ**Michael A. Jarvis & Co** *(J A Cawley, M A Jarvis)* Edenthorpe, Grove Road, ROTHERHAM, S60 2ER.

Michael Adamson & Co *(P M Potter)* 224 Ferry Road, Hullbridge, HOCKLEY, ESSEX, SS5 6ND.

Ⓐ**Michael Alan Northover** *(M A Northover)* 130 Bournemouth Road, Chandler's Ford, EASTLEIGH, HAMPSHIRE, SO53 3AL.

Michael B Temple *(M B Temple)* 56 Allandale Crescent, POTTERS BAR, HERTFORDSHIRE, EN6 2JZ.

ⒻⒶ**Michael Barrs and Company** *(M Barrs)* 395 Hoe Street, Walthamstow, LONDON, E17 9AP.

ⒻⒶ**Michael Bell & Co** *(M E Bell)* 4 Greenfield Road, HOLMFIRTH, WEST YORKSHIRE, HD9 2JT.

Michael Brown *(M Brown)* 36 Blackmile Lane, Grendon, NORTHAMPTON, NN7 1JR.

Michael Bune & Co *(M J Bune)* 16c South Street, WAREHAM, DORSET, BH20 4LT.

ⒻⓅⒶ**Michael Burke & Company Limited** *(M J Burke)* 12 Littleworth Road, ESHER, SURREY, KT10 9PD.

Michael C Hayes *(M C Hayes)* 1 Fielding Mews, LONDON, SW13 9EY.

Michael Charlton *(M Charlton)* 19 Lodge Road, Fleckney, LEICESTER, LE8 8BX.

Michael Cole & Co *(M M Cole)* 10 Cecil Road, LONDON, N14 5RJ.

Michael Costa Correa & Co. *(M F Costa Correa)* 7 Windermere Road, WEST WICKHAM, BR4 9AN.

Ⓟ**Michael Cox Accounting Services Limited** *(M D Cox)* 13b Westfield Road, BARTON-UPON-HUMBER, SOUTH HUMBERSIDE, DN18 5AA.

Michael Croston *(M J Croston)* 33 Black Bull Lane, Fulwood, PRESTON, PR2 3PX.

Michael D. Cox *(M D Cox)* Rostrevor, Vicarage Lane, Water Orton, BIRMINGHAM, B46 1RX.

Michael D. Jones *(M D Jones)* Chelwood, Carrhouse Road, Belton, DONCASTER, DN9 1PG.

Michael D. Nichols *(M D Nichols)* 28 Boughton Lane, Loose, MAIDSTONE, ME15 9QN.

Michael D.H. Illingworth *(M D H Illingworth)* 36 Ormiston Grove, LONDON, W12 0JT.

Ⓐ**Michael Dack & Company** *(M J Dack)* 75 Great George Street, LEEDS, LS1 3BR.

Ⓐ**Michael Donnely & Co** *(M Donnely)* Clevelands, Fordwater Road, CHICHESTER, PO19 6PS.

Michael E Bancroft *(M E Bancroft)* 19 Hurricane Court, Hurricane Drive, International Business Park, Speke, LIVERPOOL, L24 8RL.
Michael E C Taylor *(M E C Taylor)* 3 Sandalwood, GUILDFORD, SURREY, GU2 7NZ.
Michael E Greene *(M E Greene)* 48 Western Road, BRENTWOOD, ESSEX, CM14 4SS.
Ⓕ**Michael E. Blake & Co** *(M E Blake)* Evans Corner, Woodmansterne Lane, CARSHALTON, SURREY, SM5 4DQ.
Michael F Keevil *(D P Chinn-Shaw, M F Keevil)* Park House, 10 Osborne Road, POTTERS BAR, EN6 1RZ.
Michael F. Atherton *(M F Atherton)* 12 Hollies Close, Feniscowles, BLACKBURN, BB2 5AJ.
Ⓟ**Michael F. Clift-Matthews Limited** *(M F Clift-Matthews)* 21 Clarence Street, PENZANCE, TR18 2NZ.
Ⓐ**Michael F.G. Cope** *(M F G Cope)* 21 Godfrey Avenue, Whitton, TWICKENHAM, TW2 7PE.
Ⓟ**Michael Farley & Associates Limited** *(M W Farley)* 426-428 Holdenhurst Road, BOURNEMOUTH, DORSET, BH8 9AA.
Ⓟ**Michael Fenton & Co Limited** *(M D Fenton)* Maltkiln House, Main Street, West Stockwith, DONCASTER, SOUTH YORKSHIRE, DN10 4HB.
Ⓟ**Michael G Weemys, trading name of Finax Limited** *(M G Weemys)* 28 Church Lea, Whitchurch, TAVISTOCK, PL19 9PS.
Michael G Wiltshire *(M G Wiltshire)* 39 Cardiff Road, DINAS POWYS, SOUTH GLAMORGAN, CF64 4DH.
ⒻⓅⒶ**Michael Gale & Co, trading name of Michael Gale & Co Limited** *(M J Gale)* 1 Chaloner Street, GUISBOROUGH, CLEVELAND, TS14 6QD.
Michael Gallant & Co *(M D Gallant)* 95 Sutton Heights, Albion Road, SUTTON, SURREY, SM2 5TD.
Michael Gaskell *(M A Gaskell)* 1 Woods Cottage, Farringdon, EXETER, EX5 2HY.
Ⓕ**Michael George & Co** *(M D George)* 1 Southborough Close, Southborough, SURBITON, KT6 6PU.
ⒻⓅⒶ**Michael George & Co, trading name of Michael George & Co Limited** *(M R George)* Dawes Court House, High Street, ESHER, SURREY, KT10 9QD.
Michael Gledhill *(M Gledhill)* New Court Cottage, Whitsbury, FORDINGBRIDGE, SP6 3QB.
Ⓐ**Michael Golding** *(M E Golding)* Pacazzo Surgente 5th Floor, via Serafino Balestra C, 6900 LUGANO, SWITZERLAND.
Michael Goldstein & Co *(M Goldstein)* 1 Harley Street, LONDON, W1G 9QD.
ⓅⒶ**Michael Good Ltd** *(M S Good)* Critchleys LLP, Greyfriars Court, Paradise Square, OXFORD, OX1 1BE.
ⓉⓅ**Michael Greenhalgh & Co Ltd** *(M Greenhalgh)* Elland House, 22 High Street, Burgh le Marsh, SKEGNESS, LINCOLNSHIRE, PE24 5JT.
Michael Gunton Consulting *(M F Gunton)* chemin de la Colline 4, Case Postale 39, 1197 PRANGINS, SWITZERLAND.
Michael H Fielder *(M H Fielder)* Sutie One The Gomez Building, PO Box N1608, NASSAU, BAHAMAS.
Michael H. Scott & Company *(M H Scott)* 107 Kenton Road, Kenton, HARROW, HA3 0AN.
Ⓟ**Michael Hamment & Associates, trading name of MH (Oxford) Ltd** *(M G Hamment)* 16 Wentworth Road, OXFORD, OX2 7TQ.
Michael Hardman *(M R Hardman)* Oak House, Botley Road, CHESHAM, BUCKINGHAMSHIRE, HP5 1XG.
Michael Harwood *(M Harwood)* Tinkers Halt, Sandy Lane, NORTHWOOD, MIDDLESEX, HA6 3ES.
ⓉⒶ**Michael Harwood & Co** *(M D Harwood, M L Harwood)* Greville House, 10 Jury Street, WARWICK, CV34 4EW.
ⓉⒻⓅⒶ**Michael Heaven & Associates Limited** *(M V R Heaven)* Quadrant Court, 48 Calthorpe Road, Edgbaston, BIRMINGHAM, B15 1TH.
Michael Hollis *(M A Hollis)* Woodland House, 24 Meadowbrook Road, Kibworth Beauchamp, LEICESTER, LE8 0HU.
Michael Huelin *(M C Huelin)* 6 Warwick Close, CAMBERLEY, SURREY, GU15 1ES.
Michael I. Kayser *(M I Kayser)* 12A Belsize Park Gardens, LONDON, NW3 4LD.
Michael Israel FCA *(M A Israel)* 22 Tenterden Drive, LONDON, NW4 1ED.
★**Michael J Dodden & Co** *(M J Dodden, R W Gliddon)* 34 & 38 North Street, BRIDGWATER, TA6 3YD.
ⓉⓅⒶ**Michael J Emery & Co Limited** *(M J Emery)* 22 St. John Street, NEWPORT PAGNELL, BUCKINGHAMSHIRE, MK16 8HJ.
Ⓟ**Michael J Gornall Ltd** *(M J Gornall)* The Office at Woodcroft, 6 Byerworth Lane North, Garstang, PRESTON, PR3 1QA.
Ⓟ**Michael J Murphy, trading name of Marche Enterprises Limited** *(M J Murphy)* Flat 7, 49 Barnes High Street, Barnes, LONDON, SW13 9JY.
Ⓟ**Michael J Owen and Company Ltd** *(M J Owen)* 2 Haygate Drive, Wellington, TELFORD, TF1 2BY.
Michael J Saffer & Co *(M J Saffer)* Northern House, 87 Town Street, Horsforth, LEEDS, LS18 5BP.
Michael J. Antoniou *(M J Antoniou)* Flat 7, 29 Aeschylus Street, 1011 NICOSIA, CYPRUS.
Michael J. Leahy *(M J Leahy)* 47 Vicars Road, Chorlton-Cum-Hardy, MANCHESTER, M21 9JB.
Michael J. Perry & Co *(M J Perry)* Flat 7, Castleham Court, 180 High Street, EDGWARE, MIDDLESEX, HA8 7EX.
Michael J. Ridgway *(M A J Ridgway)* Avenue du Maelbeek 7 bte 11, 1000 BRUSSELS, BELGIUM.
Michael J. Scott *(M J Scott)* 68 Heath Row, BISHOP'S STORTFORD, CM23 5DF.
Michael J. Ventham *(M J Ventham)* Unit 22A, West Station Yard, Spital Road, MALDON, ESSEX, CM9 6TS.
Michael J.G. Taylor *(M J G Taylor)* Hunters End, Uvedale Road, OXTED, RH8 0EN.
Ⓕ**Michael J.R. Heatley** *(M J R Heatley)* 4 Gentian Glade, HARROGATE, HG3 2NT.
Michael James Kenyon *(M Kenyon)* Ashview, 88A Knutsford Road, WILMSLOW, SK9 6JD.
Michael January *(M January)* 7 Birklands Park, London Road, ST. ALBANS, HERTFORDSHIRE, AL1 1TS.
ⒻⒶ**Michael Jellicoe** *(M J Jellicoe)* 59 Knowle Wood Road, Dorridge, SOLIHULL, B93 8JP.
Michael John Bolton FCA *(M J Bolton)* 2 St. Andrews Drive, DROITWICH, WORCESTERSHIRE, WR9 8BS.
Michael Jones *(M Jones)* St Bernards, 28 The Ridgeway, Rothley, LEICESTER, LE7 7LE.
Ⓐ**Michael K** *(M Kyriakides)* 7 Forest Road, SUTTON, SURREY, SM3 9NT.
Michael K Rossor *(M K Rossor)* 5 Courts Mount Road, HASLEMERE, SURREY, GU27 2PR.
★ⓉⒻⒶ**Michael Kay & Company** *(M H P Daly, M Kay)* 2 Water Court, Water Street, BIRMINGHAM, B3 1HP.
ⓉⒻⓅⒶ**Michael Kentas & Co, trading name of Michael Kentas & Co Ltd** *(M Kentas)* 72 Wimpole Street, LONDON, W1G 9RP.
★Ⓐ**Michael King & Co** *(M S King)* Suite 4, Stanmore Towers, 8-14 Church Road, STANMORE, MIDDLESEX, HA7 4AW.
Michael L Foote FCA *(M L Foote)* 8 Bates Lane, Weston Turville, AYLESBURY, BUCKINGHAMSHIRE, HP22 5SL.
ⓅⒶ**Michael L Tripp & Co, trading name of Michael L. Tripp & Co Limited** *(M L Tripp)* 29 Nutter Road, THORNTON-CLEVELEYS, LANCASHIRE, FY5 1BQ.
ⓉⓅⒶ**Michael Leong and Company, trading name of Michael Leong and Company Limited** *(M C L Leong)* 43 Overstone Road, LONDON, W6 0AD.
Ⓐ**Michael Levy & Co** *(M S Levy)* Suite 3 First Floor, Stanmore House, 15-19 Church Road, STANMORE, MIDDLESEX, HA7 4AR.
ⓅⒶ**Michael Lewis Audit Limited** *(M Lewis)* William James House, Cowley Road, CAMBRIDGE, CB4 0WX.
Ⓟ**Michael Lewis Ltd** *(M Lewis)* Unit 20, William James House, Cowley Road, CAMBRIDGE, CB4 0WX.
Michael Lindner *(M M Lindner)* The Gallery Room, The Old Police Station, High Street, CHIPPING CAMPDEN, GLOUCESTERSHIRE, GL55 6HB.
Michael Lister Associates *(V C M Lister)* Buttons Barn, Magpie Street, Charsfield, WOODBRIDGE, SUFFOLK, IP13 7QE.
Michael M.C. Chan & Co *(M Chan)* Room 2401, 24/F, 280 Portland Street Commercial Building, 276-280 Portland Street, MONG KOK, KOWLOON HONG KONG SAR.
Michael Mann & Co *(J M Mann)* 71 White Horse Road, WINDSOR, BERKSHIRE, SL4 4PG.
★**Michael May** *(M A May)* 47 Algitha Road, SKEGNESS, PE25 2AJ.
Michael Michalopoulos FCA *(M Michalopoulos)* 70 Kennedy Avenue, Papavasilou Building, 3rd Floor, Office 304, PO Box 28783, CY2082 NICOSIA CYPRUS.
Michael Morrice FCA *(M J Morrice)* 14B Kennington Oval, LONDON, SE11 5SG.
Michael Morton & Co *(M T Morton)* Strathmore, The Nap, KINGS LANGLEY, WD4 8ES.
Michael N. Daniel & Co *(M N Daniel)* 4 Mill Street, CRICKHOWELL, POWYS, NP8 1BA.
Ⓟ**Michael Norman & Co, trading name of M B Norman Limited** *(M B Norman)* 46-48 Nelson Road, TUNBRIDGE WELLS, KENT, TN2 5AN.
Michael Paige *(M Paige)* Limeshaw, Wappingthorn, STEYNING, BN44 3AB.
Ⓟ**Michael Parker, trading name of MP UK Ltd** *(M Parker)* 21 Sunningdale Drive, THORNTON-CLEVELEYS, LANCASHIRE, FY5 5AD.
ⓅⒶ**Michael Pawson Ltd** *(M A Pawson)* Stanton House, 41 Blackfriars Road, SALFORD, M3 7DB.
Michael Peacock ACA *(M J Peacock)* 22 Elsted Close, Ifield, CRAWLEY, WEST SUSSEX, RH11 0BH.
Michael Plant FCA *(Michael Plant)* 11 High Street, BALDOCK, SG7 6AZ.
Michael Pritchard & Co *(M A P Pritchard)* Nascot House, Church Lane, Wroxham, NORWICH, NR12 8SH.
Michael Reeves & Co *(C M Reeves)* 12 Harmsworth Way, Totteridge, LONDON, N20 8JU.
Michael Russell *(M C Russell)* Waterloo House, Don Street, JERSEY, JE2 4TQ.
Michael S. Reynolds *(M S Reynolds)* 14 Great Thrift, ORPINGTON, BR5 1NG.
Michael Scarlett & Co *(M Scarlett)* 66 Norman Road, ST. LEONARDS-ON-SEA, EAST SUSSEX, TN38 0EJ.
Michael Sinclair *(M Schachter)* Trafalgar House, Grenville Place, Mill Hill, LONDON, NW7 3SA.
Michael Singleton *(M H T Singleton)* 7 Rudry Road, Lisvane, CARDIFF, CF14 0SN.
Michael Smy *(M D Smy)* 12 Woodditton Road, NEWMARKET, Suffolk, CB8 9BQ.
ⓉⓅⒶ**Michael Sohor & Co, trading name of Michael Sohor & Co Ltd** *(M E Sohor)* 74 St. Georges Road, BOLTON, BL1 2DD.
Michael Somers & Co *(M I Somers)* 60 Croham Valley Road, SOUTH CROYDON, SURREY, CR2 7NB.
Michael Sonn & Company *(M A Sonn)* 140 Hall Lane, UPMINSTER, RM14 1AL.
Michael Stern & Co *(M C Stern)* 61 Shalimar Gardens, Acton, LONDON, W3 9JG.
Michael T. Parker *(M T Parker)* 2 St. Aubyns Mansions, Kings Esplanade, HOVE, EAST SUSSEX, BN3 2WQ.
Ⓐ**Michael Tarrant** *(M F Tarrant)* 22 Updown Hill, HAYWARDS HEATH, WEST SUSSEX, RH16 4GD.
Michael Thompson & Co *(M A Thompson)* 10 Auckland Terrace, Parliament Street, Ramsey, ISLE OF MAN, IM8 1AF.
ⓉⓅ**Michael Thompson Accountants Ltd** *(R A Goel, M J Thompson)* 32 Surrey Street, NORWICH, NR1 3NY.
Michael Tsoi and Company *(M Tsoi)* Unit 101, 1st Floor Silicon Tower, 88 Larch Street, MONG KOK, KOWLOON, HONG KONG SAR.
Ⓐ**Michael Tuckey** *(M A Tuckey)* The Dutch House, 24 The Downsway, SUTTON, SM2 5RN.
Michael Turner & Co *(M B Turner)* 17 Hope Street, Douglas, ISLE OF MAN, IM1 1AQ.
Michael W. Beard *(M W Beard)* 62 Hermitage Road, SOLIHULL, B91 2LP.
Michael Warner & Company *(M J P Warner)* 37 Southgate Street, WINCHESTER, HAMPSHIRE, SO23 9EH.
Michael Warnes *(M R Warnes)* 2a High Haden Road, CRADLEY HEATH, WEST MIDLANDS, B64 7PE.
Michael Waterson *(M Waterson)* Fenay Cottage, Fenay Lane, Fenay Bridge, HUDDERSFIELD, HD8 0LJ.
Michael Watts *(C M Watts)* Raven Gill, Parkhead, Renwick, PENRITH, CA10 1JQ.
★**Michael Watts & Co** *(M D Watts)* 1 Upper Maltings Place, BIRCHINGTON, KENT, CT7 9PW.
Ⓟ**Michael Welfare & Company Ltd** *(R J Chandler, M D Harknett)* 100 High Road, Byfleet, WEST BYFLEET, SURREY, KT14 7QT.
Michael Wheeler *(M J Wheeler)* 8 Hall Drive, Sydenham, LONDON, SE26 6XB.
Michael Wong & Co *(M S H Wong)* 23 Hillside Grove, LONDON, NW7 2LS.
ⒻⒶ**Michael Wood** *(M A Wood)* 22a Bank Street, ASHFORD, KENT, TN23 1BE.
Ⓟ**Michaelides Warner & Co Ltd** *(P D Michaelides)* 102 Fulham Palace Road, LONDON, W6 9PL.
Michele Webb *(M Webb)* Woodpecker, Fir Tree Close, St. Leonards, RINGWOOD, HAMPSHIRE, BH24 2QW.
Michelle Baggaley *(M J Baggaley)* 17 Walsingham Road, Childwall, LIVERPOOL, L16 3NR.
Michelle Everitt *(M D Everitt)* 37 North Hill, LONDON, N6 4BS.
Ⓟ**Michelle Feasey & Co Limited** *(M A E Feasey)* Unit 1, West Street Business Park, West Street, STAMFORD, LINCOLNSHIRE, PE9 2PR.
Ⓟ**Middlegate Services Ltd** *(P B Wood)* Broombarn Lane, GREAT MISSENDEN, BUCKINGHAMSHIRE, HP16 9JD.
ⓉⒻⒶ**Midgley Snelling** *(J R Beecher, J M Farrow, A P Grout, R G Sewell, S P Yeates)* Ibex House, Baker Street, WEYBRIDGE, SURREY, KT13 8AH.
ⒻⓅ**Midicorp, trading name of Midicorp Corporate Finance Ltd** *(D R Jones, M J T Stackpoole)* New Bond House, 124 New Bond Street, LONDON, W1S 1DX.
Ⓟ**Midland Accountancy Group Limited** *(C M Stephen-Haynes)* 15 New Street, STOURPORT-ON-SEVERN, WORCESTERSHIRE, DY13 8UW.
Midlands Business Recovery *(P R Brindley)* Alpha House, Tipton Street, Sedgley, DUDLEY, WEST MIDLANDS, DY3 1HE.
Midsummer Consultants *(J H Setchell)* 28 Parsonage Street, CAMBRIDGE, CB5 8DN.
Ⓟ**Mike Barrett, trading name of Barrett & Co (Carlisle) Ltd** *(M Barrett)* 56 Warwick Road, CARLISLE, CA1 1DR.
Ⓕ**Mike Black** *(M A Black)* 9 Crockwell Close, BICESTER, OXFORDSHIRE, OX26 2HG.
ⓅⒶ**Mike Bramall & Co. Limited** *(G M Bramall)* Mayfield View, 60 School Green Lane, SHEFFIELD, S10 4GR.
ⓉⒶ**Mike Egan & Co** *(M Egan)* 166-170 Lee Lane, Horwich, BOLTON, BL6 7AF.
Ⓐ**Mike Gibson, trading name of Cooper Gibson** *(M R Gibson)* 32 Parkfield Gardens, HARROW, HA2 6JR.
Mike Haddock FCA *(M S Haddock)* 94 Oxford Road, CAMBRIDGE, CB4 3PL.
Ⓟ**Mike Harper Tax & Accountancy Services Ltd** *(M A Harper)* 58a High Street, Watton, THETFORD, NORFOLK, IP25 6AH.
Ⓟ**Mike J R Twiddle & Co Limited** *(M J R Twiddle)* 5 Iona Close, Langsett Road, Sutton, HULL, HU8 9XU.
Mike Lowe *(M M Lowe)* Lydford, Level Mare Lane, Eastergate, CHICHESTER, WEST SUSSEX, PO20 3SA.
Mike Spiers Associates *(M J Spiers)* 2 Crouch Farm Cottages, Bloxham Road, BANBURY, OXFORDSHIRE, OX16 9UN.
Ⓐ**MILES cmc** *(C J Miles)* Stanley House, 33-35 West Hill, Portishead, BRISTOL, BS20 6LG.
Milford & Co *(K Morton)* Duke Street, SETTLE, BD24 9DJ.
Ⓟ**Mill House, trading name of Mill House Accountancy Limited** *(L Dyas)* Medical Life, Priestly Court, Gillette Close, Staffordshire, STAFFORD HEIGHTS, ST18 0LQ.
Ⓟ**Mill Scott, trading name of Mill Scott Ltd** *(N S Caton)* 3a Market Hill, SAFFRON WALDEN, ESSEX, CB10 1HQ.
Millar & Co *(I D G Millar)* 17 Farm View, Tupton, CHESTERFIELD, DERBYSHIRE, S42 6BD.
Ⓟ**Millbank Financial Services Limited** *(L Petts)* 4th Floor, Swan House, 17-19 Stratford Place, LONDON, W1C 1BQ.
Ⓐ**Millener Davies** *(G E Davies, P A Millener)* Southfield House, Southfield Road, Westbury On Trym, BRISTOL, BS9 3BH.
Ⓟ**Millennium Business Services Limited** *(R Wills)* Chaparral, Windsor Lane, Little Kingshill, GREAT MISSENDEN, HP16 0DP.
Miller & Co *(K A Miller)* 2 The Pavilions End, CAMBERLEY, GU15 2LD.
Ⓟ**Miller & Co, trading name of M & CCA Limited** *(R A Cox, P Stevenson)* 2 Victoria Road, HARPENDEN, HERTFORDSHIRE, AL5 4EA.
ⓉⒻⒶ**Miller & Co.** *(R A Cox, P Stevenson)* 86 Princess Street, LUTON, LU1 5AT.
Ⓕ**Miller & Company** *(L D Miller)* 17 Grove Place, BEDFORD, MK40 3JJ.
ⓉⒻⒶ**Miller Davies** *(R J Bedford, I M Cole, M R Davies)* Unit A3, Broomsleigh Business Park, Worsley Bridge Road, LONDON, SE26 5BN.
Ⓟ**Miller Kent & Co, trading name of Miller Kent & Co Limited** *(A Miller)* Evans House, 107 Marsh Road, PINNER, MIDDLESEX, HA5 5PA.
ⓅⒶ**millhall consultants ltd** *(W B D Hall)* Carlson Suite, Vantage Point Business Village, MITCHELDEAN, GLOUCESTERSHIRE, GL17 0DD.
ⓉⒶ**Milliken & Co** *(T J Milliken)* 9 Vennel Street, Stewarton, KILMARNOCK, KA3 5HL.
Ⓟ**Millington & Russell Limited** *(A J Russell)* Sovereign House, 4 Machon Bank, SHEFFIELD, S7 1GP.
Ⓟ**Millington Hore** *(C D B Millington-Hore, R S Millington-Hore)* 9 Arlesey Road, Ickleford, HITCHIN, SG5 3UN.
★Ⓐ**Mills & Black** *(R S Hardy, I M Hayes, S Nicholson)* Derwent House, 141-143 Dale Road, MATLOCK, DE4 3LU.
ⓉⒻⓅⒶ**Mills Pyatt, trading name of Mills Pyatt Limited** *(G J Mills, H G Pyatt)* Unit 11, Kingfisher Business Park, Arthur Street, REDDITCH, WORCESTERSHIRE, B98 8LG.
Millweb *(R J Webster)* 49 Sheldon Road, Ickford, AYLESBURY, BUCKINGHAMSHIRE, HP18 9HY.
Ⓟ**Milncraig Ltd** *(Sir Andrew Cunynghame)* 12 Vicarage Gardens, LONDON, W8 4AH.
Milne & Co *(K M Milne)* 1 Highlever Road, LONDON, W10 6PP.
ⒻⒶ**Milne Eldridge & Co** *(R J Smith)* The Little House, 88A West Street, FARNHAM, SURREY, GU9 7EN.

Milne Thomas & Co *(A M Milne, S V Thomas)* 27 Seller Street, CHESTER, CH1 3NA.

ⒻⓅⒶ**Milner Boardman Limited** *(E E Jess, G R Mackridge)* MBL House, 16 Edward Court, Altrincham Business Park, George Richards Way, ALTRINCHAM, CHESHIRE WA14 5GL.

ⓅⒶ**Milnes & Co, trading name of David Milnes Limited** *(D J Milnes, S Westbury)* Premier House, Bradford Road, CLECKHEATON, WEST YORKSHIRE, BD19 3TT.

ⓉⒻⒶ**Milsted Langdon LLP** *(T A Close, S M Denton, E M Durrant, G J Freeman, N P Fry, S P Horton, R A S Isaacs, D S Jacobs, S R Jenkins, J C Langdon, N P Moysey, G Salter, J W Stocker)* Winchester House, Deane Gate Avenue, TAUNTON, SOMERSET, TA1 2UH. and at BRISTOL, YEOVIL

Milston & Co *(J Milston)* 57 Wolmer Gardens, EDGWARE, MIDDLESEX, HA8 8QB.

Milton & Co. *(D J Milton)* Cranford, Wheal Venture Road, ST. IVES, TR26 2PQ.

Milton Accounting *(M A Curry)* 10 Lawn Farm Close, Milton Lilbourne, PEWSEY, WILTSHIRE, SN9 5QA.

★**Milton Avis** *(S C Goh, S J Young)* Wellington Building, 28-32 Wellington Road, St John's Wood, LONDON, NW8 9SP.

Ⓟ**Milton Financial Management Limited** *(P D Milton)* 16 Berkshire Green, Shenley Brook End, MILTON KEYNES, MK5 7FL.

Ⓟ**Minayan & Co Limited** *(F Minaeian)* 8B Accomodation Road, LONDON, NW11 8ED.

Minerva Business Advisors *(L Webber)* 123 Ellerton Road, SURBITON, SURREY, KT6 7UA.

ⓉⒶ**Minford** *(A J Minford)* Moyola House, 31 Hawthorn Grove, YORK, YO31 7UA.

ⒻⒶ**Minney & Co** *(L Minney)* 59 Union Street, DUNSTABLE, LU6 1EX.

ⒻⓅⒶ**Minshalls, trading name of Minshalls Limited** *(M R Minshall)* 370-374 Nottingham Road, Newthorpe, NOTTINGHAM, NG16 2ED.

Mirza Arshed Baig *(M A Baig)* 190-R, LCCHS, LAHORE 54792, PAKISTAN.

Miss Denise Thomas *(D Thomas)* 10 Fleming Close, FARNBOROUGH, HAMPSHIRE, GU14 8BT.

Miss E A Parks *(E A Parks)* 68 Murray Road, Wimbledon, LONDON, SW19 4PE.

Miss J.M. Hacking *(J M Hacking)* 5 Mill Mead, Wendover, AYLESBURY, HP22 6BY.

Ⓟ**Miss MPenny, trading name of MM Bookkeeping Ltd** *(H E Agutter)* 48 Albany Villas, HOVE, EAST SUSSEX, BN3 2RW.

Ⓕ**Miss Patricia Lewis FCA** *(P Lewis)* 207 Clevedon Road, Tickenham, CLEVEDON, AVON, BS21 6RX.

ⒻⓅⒶ**Mistry & Co, trading name of Mistry Accountants Ltd** *(G Mistry)* 89 B & C Far Gosford Street, Gosford Green, COVENTRY, CV1 5EA.

Mitch Castle *(M Castle)* 30 Radway Close, Church Hill North, REDDITCH, B98 8RZ.

ⓉⒻⓅⒶ**Mitchams, trading name of Mitchams Accountants Limited** *(L E Cox, T I Maclellan, M H Parsons, J H Perry, A L Whaites)* 1 Cornhill, ILMINSTER, SOMERSET, TA19 0AD.

Mitchell & Co *(A R Mitchell)* 13 Verran Road, Watchetts Lake, CAMBERLEY, GU15 2ND.

Ⓐ**Mitchell & Co** *(S E Mitchell)* 143/147 High Street, NEWTON-LE-WILLOWS, WA12 9SQ.

Ⓐ**Mitchell Brittain** *(J J M Brittain)* 6 Lon Farchog, Upper Breeze Hill, Benllech, TYN-Y-GONGL, GWYNEDD, LL74 8UL.

ⓉⒶ**Mitchell Charlesworth** *(D J Antonia, P N Booth, A Buckley, D Darlington, R L Davies, D Frangleton, P L Griffiths, R J Hall, R W Johnson, A J Lavelle, C H Plummer, P N Wainwright)* 5 Temple Square, Temple Street, LIVERPOOL, L2 5RH. and at CHESTER, MANCHESTER, WARRINGTON, WIDNES

ⒻⒶ**Mitchell Gordon, trading name of Mitchell Gordon LLP** *(M D Gordon, N A Vassilounis)* 43 Coniscliffe Road, DARLINGTON, COUNTY DURHAM, DL3 7EH.

ⓉⒻⓅⒶ**Mitchell Meredith, trading name of Mitchell Meredith Limited** *(I Mitchell, T Richardson)* The Exchange, Fiveways, Temple Street, LLANDRINDOD WELLS, POWYS, LD1 5HG. and at BRECON, MERTHYR TYDFIL

ⓉⒻ**Mitchells** *(T G Leeman, R J Trueman)* 91-93 Saltergate, CHESTERFIELD, S40 1LA.

ⒻⒶ**Mitchells** *(D N Mitchell, S J Vigus)* St Johns House, Castle Street, TAUNTON, SOMERSET, TA1 4AY.

Ⓐ**Mitchells** *(M Turner)* The Old Stables, Fox Hole Lane, WADHURST, EAST SUSSEX, TN5 6NB.

ⓉⒻⒶ**Mitchells** *(J Cheesman, D R Gair, F Robinson)* Suite 4, Parsons House, Parsons Road, WASHINGTON, TYNE AND WEAR, NE37 1EZ.

ⒻⓅⒶ**Mitchells Grievson, trading name of Mitchells Grievson Limited** *(A Grievson, N Rea)* Kensington House, 3 Kensington, BISHOP AUCKLAND, COUNTY DURHAM, DL14 6HX. and at BARNARD CASTLE

ⒻⓅⒶ**Mitchells, trading name of MCABA Limited** *(T G Leeman, R J Trueman)* 91-97 Saltergate, CHESTERFIELD, DERBYSHIRE, S40 1LA.

ⒻⓅⒶ**Mitchells, trading name of Mitchell Glanville Limited** *(J R D Glanville, N J Mitchell)* 41 Rodney Road, CHELTENHAM, GL50 1HX.

Ⓟ**Mitrod, trading name of Mitchell Rodrigues & Co Limited** *(C T Simmons)* Suite 14, Zeal House, 8 Deer Park Road, LONDON, SW19 3GY.

ⓉⓅⒶ**Mitten Clarke Limited** *(R A P Clarke, S D Heath, M Mitten, T P J Virgo)* The Glades, Festival Way, Festival Park, STOKE-ON-TRENT, STAFFORDSHIRE, ST1 5SQ.

MJ Accountants *(M J Atkinson)* 43 Gloucester Road, WALSALL, WS5 3PL.

Ⓟ**MJ Brooks Consultancy Limited** *(M J Brooks)* 9 Waterside, Station Road, HARPENDEN, HERTFORDSHIRE, AL5 4US.

Ⓟ**MJ Business Services Ltd** *(M J Ghanti)* 9 Kenilworth Avenue, GLOUCESTER, GL2 0QJ.

MJ Finn & Co *(M J Finn)* Salters Brook Cottage, Stanton Wick, Pensford, BRISTOL, BS39 4DA.

Ⓟ**MJ Goldman, trading name of MJG Accounts Ltd** *(M J Goldman, B Nyman)* Hollinwood Business Centre, Albert Street, OLDHAM, OL8 3QL.

MJ Iqbal *(M J Iqbal)* 127 Hoe Street, LONDON, E17 4RX.

MJ Lermit *(M J Lermit)* 9 Tennyson Mansions, Queen's Club Gardens, LONDON, W14 9TJ.

Ⓟ**MJ Results Ltd** *(I K Johnson, P S Moulton)* 25a Crown Street, BRENTWOOD, ESSEX, CM14 4BA.

MJF *(M J Freedman)* 23 Oaks Way, Long Ditton, SURBITON, SURREY, KT6 5DX.

★**MJF Accountancy** *(J A Davies)* 59a Booker Avenue, Mossley Hill, LIVERPOOL, L18 4QZ.

Ⓟ**MJR Taxation Services Limited** *(M J Read)* 1 Cobden Road, SEVENOAKS, KENT, TN13 3UB.

Ⓟ**MJS Accountancy, trading name of MJS Accountancy Services (Fangfoss) Limited** *(M J Skelton)* Hillcroft, Fangfoss, YORK, YO41 5QJ.

MJT Accountancy Services *(M J Tufton)* 9 Elmleigh, YEOVIL, SOMERSET, BA21 3UJ.

Ⓟ**MJV & Co Ltd** *(M J Ventham)* Unit 22A, West Station Yard, Spital Road, MALDON, ESSEX, CM9 6TS.

ⒻⓅ**MK Sheridan & Co, trading name of Sheridan Strategic Services Limited** *(M K Sheridan)* Oakways, Tubbs Lane, Highclere, NEWBURY, BERKSHIRE, RG20 9PQ.

ML & JP Rutt, trading name of ML and JP Rutt *(M L Rutt)* 7 Shepherds Fold, Holmer Green, HIGH WYCOMBE, HP15 6XZ.

MLR Accountancy *(M L Robinson)* Hold House Farm Cottage, ponteland, NEWCASTLE UPON TYNE, NE20 9TS.

MM Accountancy Services *(M C Milsom)* Lychgate House, Tyr Winch Road, Old St Mellons, CARDIFF, CF3 5UW.

MMC Accountancy Services *(M J McCullagh)* 6 Linenhall Street, LIMAVADY, COUNTY LONDONDERRY, BT49 0HQ.

ⒻⓅⒶ**MMO Limited** *(G McIntosh, S P Murray, M J Winsor)* Wellesley House, 204 London Road, WATERLOOVILLE, PO7 7AN.

MMS *(M Mahabir-Singh)* 11 Lower Hillside Street, SAN FERNANDO, TRINIDAD AND TOBAGO.

Ⓟ**MMTI, trading name of MMTI Limited** *(T A Bhatti)* 44 Carlton Avenue West, WEMBLEY, HA0 3QU.

ⒻⓅ**MN Accountants Limited** *(H McNeill)* The Lilacs, West Hill Road North, South Wonston, WINCHESTER, HAMPSHIRE, SO21 3HJ.

Ⓟ**MN Tax Consulltants Limited** *(H McNeill)* The Lilacs, West Hill Road North, South Wonston, WINCHESTER, HAMPSHIRE, SO21 3HJ.

MND Training & Consultancy *(N R Davies)* 2 Hillgrove Gardens, KIDDERMINSTER, WORCESTERSHIRE, DY10 3AN.

Ⓟ**Modi & Co Ltd** *(B V Modi)* 27 High View Close, Hamilton Office Park, LEICESTER, LE4 9LJ.

Ⓐ**Modiri, trading name of Modiri & Co** *(M Modiri Hamedan)* Tapton Park Innovation Centre, Brimington Road, Tapton, CHESTERFIELD, DERBYSHIRE, S41 0TZ.

ⓉⒶ**Moffat Gilbert** *(G R F Gilbert, S Moffat)* 5 Clarendon Place, LEAMINGTON SPA, CV32 5QL.

ⓉⒶ**Moffatt & Co** *(P F Mundy, J C Saxon)* 396 Wilmslow Road, Withington, MANCHESTER, M20 3BN.

Mohamed Abdel Halim & Co *(M A H Mohamed)* PO Box 1595, KHARTOUM, 11111, SUDAN.

Mohammad Kamran Khalil *(M K Khalil)* Unit 12 Swan Centre, Rosemary Road, LONDON, SW17 0AR.

★**Mohammad Shah & Co** *(A Muhith)* 209 Merton Road, South Wimbledon, LONDON, SW19 1EE.

Mohammed Shiraz *(M Shiraz)* 23 Abbotsfield Court, MANCHESTER, M8 0AW.

Mohindra & Co *(M Mohindra)* Finance Place, 9 Widecombe Gardens, ILFORD, IG4 5LR.

★**Mojabi & Co** *(M M Mojabi)* 205 Crescent Road, BARNET, HERTFORDSHIRE, EN4 8SB.

Ⓟ**Mojo Financial Services Limited** *(J J Dearing, K A Dearing)* Brookland Cottage, Birchgrove Road, Glais, SWANSEA, SA7 9ER.

Ⓟ**Mok & Fong CPA Limited** *(K T Mok)* Flats 2 & 3, 21/F Chung Kiu Commercial Building, 47-51 Shantung Street, MONG KOK, KOWLOON, HONG KONG SAR.

Mokhtar Edwards & Co *(I N Mokhtar)* 7 Chartfield, HOVE, BN3 7RD.

Ⓟ**Mole Valley Accountants Limited** *(J M Stadius)* Windrush, 25 Riverside Drive, ESHER, SURREY, KT10 8PG.

★**Mollart & Co** *(M I Clark)* 39 Grange Road, DARLINGTON, DL1 5NB.

ⓉⒻⒶ**Monahans** *(D I Black, L A Boss, D B Bourquin, A J H Cohen, S M Cooper, R F Formby, S G Fraser, S A Fry, H M Hilliard, M J Longmore, P E Lugg, M Shawyer, R M Snelus)* 38-42 Newport Street, SWINDON, SN1 3DR. and at BATH, CHIPPENHAM, GLASTONBURY, TROWBRIDGE

ⒻⓅⒶ**Monahans, trading name of Monahans Limited** *(L A Boss, H M Hilliard, M J Longmore)* Lennox House, 3 Pierrepont Street, BATH, BA1 1LB. and at CHIPPENHAM

ⓉⒻⒶ**Moncrieff & Co** *(R M Moncrieff)* 13 Freda Avenue, Gedling, NOTTINGHAM, NG4 4FY.

Ⓟ**Moncur Charles & Co Ltd** *(A C M Sime)* 6 The Courtyard(The Farm House), The Outwoods, Burbage, HINCKLEY, LEICESTERSHIRE, LE10 2UD.

Monday Papakyriacou DFK *(G D Papakyriacou)* 340 Kifissias Avenue, Psyhico, 15451 ATHENS, GREECE.

Ⓕ**Money Manager At Home** *(A J Hughes)* 3 Guernsey Farm Drive, Horsell, WOKING, SURREY, GU21 4BE.

Ⓟ**Money Matters (High Wycombe) Limited** *(C J Wise)* The Old Star, Church Street, PRINCES RISBOROUGH, BUCKINGHAMSHIRE, HP27 9AA.

Money Partner *(N A Bream)* 29 Kings Road, EMSWORTH, HAMPSHIRE, PO10 7HN.

Ⓟ**Money Talks, trading name of Money Talks Training Ltd** *(D A Stead)* 52 Horsley Court, Montaigne Close, LONDON, SW1P 4BF.

Monica C.A. James *(M C A James)* 2 Scots Cottages, Kington, Thornbury, BRISTOL, BS35 1NF.

Monica Irwin *(M S Irwin)* 1 Barn Close, Cumnor Hill, OXFORD, OX2 9JP.

Monica P Doherty Accountancy Services *(M Doherty)* 3 The Cobbles, Whixley, YORK, YO26 8EY.

Monique Law *(J M Law)* 129 Randolph Avenue, LONDON, W9 1DN.

Monk & Co *(K Monk)* 114 Stock Road, BILLERICAY, ESSEX, CM12 0RT.

Ⓟ**Monkspath Financial Management Limited** *(A D Jones)* 25 Horton Grove, Shirley, SOLIHULL, WEST MIDLANDS, B90 4UZ.

Monkton Accounting Services *(C P Grindell)* Yetholmlaw House, Town Yetholm, KELSO, ROXBURGHSHIRE, TD5 8SH.

Monson Accountants *(K Monson)* 72 Commonside West, MITCHAM, SURREY, CR4 4HB.

ⒻⒶ**Montgomery & Co** *(S A Bell)* Norham House, Mountenoy Road, Moorgate, ROTHERHAM, S60 2AJ.

Ⓐ**Montgomery McNally & Co** *(A C Pope)* 4 Greenstede Avenue, EAST GRINSTEAD, WEST SUSSEX, RH19 3HZ.

Ⓟ**Montgomery Tax Services Ltd** *(C B F Lawson)* Hendomen Farmhouse, Hendomen, MONTGOMERY, SY15 6HB.

ⓅⒶ**Montpelier Accountancy Limited** *(D C Gould)* 7 Montpelier, Quarndon, DERBY, DE22 5JW.

★ⓅⒶ**Montpelier Audit Limited** *(P J Fingleton, I Fishman, J S Marco, S McDonald, P R Nuttall, I A Randolph, H R Reuben, B W F Spence)* Montpelier House, 62-66 Deansgate, MANCHESTER, M3 2EN. and at LEEDS, LONDON, PRESTON, SHEFFIELD

★Ⓟ**Montpelier Professional (Borders) Limited** *(B W F Spence)* Unit 18 petteril Side, Harraby Green, Business Park, Carlisle, CARLISLE, CA1 2SQ. and at CASTLE DOUGLAS, DUMFRIES

★ⒻⓅ**Montpelier Professional (Fylde) Limited** *(B W F Spence)* 13 Rossall Road, THORNTON-CLEVELEYS, LANCASHIRE, FY5 1AP.

★ⒻⓅ**Montpelier, trading name of Montpelier Professional (Galloway) Limited** *(G F Moore)* 1 Dashwood Square, NEWTON STEWART, WIGTOWNSHIRE, DG8 6EQ. and at STRANRAER

★ⒻⓅ**Montpelier, trading name of Montpelier Professional (Lancashire) Limited** *(P J Fingleton, S McDonald, J L Teece)* Charter House, Pittman Way, Fulwood, PRESTON, PR2 9ZD.

★ⒻⓅ**Montpelier, trading name of Montpelier Professional (Leeds) Limited** *(M J Dalton, P R Nuttall, S C Willey)* Sanderson House, Station Road, Horsforth, LEEDS, LS18 5NT.

★ⓉⒻⓅ**Montpelier, trading name of Montpelier Professional (Manchester) Limited** *(B W F Spence)* Montpelier House, 62-66 Deansgate, MANCHESTER, M3 2EN.

★ⒻⓅ**Montpelier, trading name of Montpelier Professional (Sheffield) Limited** *(B W F Spence)* Suite 8, Velocity Village, 7 Solly Street, SHEFFIELD, S1 4GE.

ⓉⒻⓅⒶ**Montrose Book-Keeping Bureau, trading name of Duncan Boxwell & Company Limited** *(D H Boxwell, C J Taylor)* Montrose House, Clayhill Industrial Park, NESTON, CH64 3RU.

Ⓕ**Moore & Co** *(D J Cranness, D W Wright)* Belvoir House, 1 Rous Road, NEWMARKET, SUFFOLK, CB8 8DH.

Ⓟ**Moore & Co, trading name of Moore & Sharples Limited** *(D A Sharples)* 37 Warner Street, ACCRINGTON, LANCASHIRE, BB5 1HN.

Moore & Co. *(P L Moore)* Unit 22, Mountbatten Business Centre, Millbrook Road East, SOUTHAMPTON, SO15 1HY.

ⓉⒶ**Moore & Smalley, trading name of Moore and Smalley LLP** *(D A Bennett, M J Briggs, K Hain, D M Ingram, T N Johnson, R A Kenmare, T Medcalf, R A Norman, M E Proudfoot, N R Stevenson, J Tombs, J S Treadwell, D J Walmsley, C A Wilson, D S Wood)* Richard House, 9 Winckley Square, PRESTON, PR1 3HP. and at BLACKPOOL, KENDAL, LANCASTER, NOTTINGHAM

Ⓟ**Moore Accountancy, trading name of Moore Accountancy Limited** *(S S Moore)* 1 Northway, ALTRINCHAM, CHESHIRE, WA14 1NN.

Moore Accounting & Tax Solutions *(P V Moore)* 28 Good Road, Parkstone, POOLE, DORSET, BH12 3PJ.

Ⓟ**Moore Emmerson Accountants Ltd** *(C M Jones)* 69 Main Road, Collyweston, STAMFORD, LINCOLNSHIRE, PE9 3PQ.

ⓉⒻⒶ**Moore Green** *(V P Chandler, N Farr, M M Wilkinson)* 22 Friars Street, SUDBURY, SUFFOLK, CO10 2AA.

Ⓟ**Moore Green Ltd** *(N Farr, M M Wilkinson)* 22 Friars Street, SUDBURY, SUFFOLK, CO10 2AA.

Ⓕ**Moore Pearman** *(M T S Pearman)* The Old Barn, The Bridge, Lower Eashing, GODALMING, SURREY, GU7 2QF.

ⓅⒶ**Moore Scarrott Audit Limited** *(S R Headon, C M S Longbottom)* Calyx House, South Road, TAUNTON, SOMERSET, TA1 3DU.

Moore Scott & Co *(I P McNair)* Aden Chambers, South Crescent, LLANDRINDOD WELLS, LD1 5DH.

ⓅⒶ**Moore Secretaries Limited** *(A Coldwell, K R Cooper, G J Francis, A D Henshaw, S Lucas, R Newman, M J Scott, A L Stevens, M I Wakeford, M F J Weil, A Williams, A S Wulff)* City Gates, 2-4 Southgate, CHICHESTER, WEST SUSSEX, PO19 8DJ.

ⓉⒻⒶ**Moore Stephens** *(R J Branch, M P Burnett, D T Slocombe, A J Vince)* 30 Gay Street, BATH, BA1 2PA.

★**Moore Stephens** *(P W Rundle)* GPO Box 1144, 5th Floor, 255 Adelaide Street, BRISBANE, QLD 4001, AUSTRALIA. and at GLEN IRIS

★**Moore Stephens** *(C N S Barton, C O L Dixon, B L Hazell, A T J Moll, J T B Pickles, L E Spurrier)* Suite 5, Watergardens 4, Waterport, P O Box 743, GIBRALTAR, GIBRALTAR.

★ⓉⒶ**Moore Stephens** *(C N S Barton, C O L Dixon, B L Hazell, A T J Moll, J T B Pickles, D J Shadwell, L E Spurrier)* P O Box 25, 26-28 Athol Street, Douglas, ISLE OF MAN, IM99 1BD.

★ⓉⒶ**Moore Stephens** *(C N S Barton, P Callow, C O L Dixon, B L Hazell, B Lambert, A T J Moll, J T B Pickles, N J Solt, L E Spurrier)* P O Box 236, First Island House, Peter Street, St. Helier, JERSEY, JE4 8SG. and at GUERNSEY

★ⓉⒻⒶ**Moore Stephens** *(N J Bairstow, M E Lumsden, G J Mallaghan, F Murphy, A Page, C A Rossiter, R P S Sandbach, P J Simons, A C Urquhart, P D Walding)* Kings House, 40 Billing Road, NORTHAMPTON, NN1 5BA. and at CORBY, PETERBOROUGH

★**Moore Stephens** *(C Constantinou, D Constantinou)* (P.O.Box No. 80 132), 93 Akti Miaouli, GR-185 38, PIRAEUS, GREECE.

ⓉⒻⒶ**Moore Stephens** *(S A Watson)* 12/13 Alma Square, SCARBOROUGH, YO11 1JU. and at PICKERING, YORK

Moore Stephens *(C B Johnson)* 10 Anson Road, Apt 29-15, International Plaza, SINGAPORE 079903, SINGAPORE.

ⓉⒻⒶ**Moore Stephens** *(M H Abdulali, J D Clough)* 6 Ridge House, Ridge House Drive, STOKE-ON-TRENT, ST1 5TL. and at SHREWSBURY

★**Moore Stephens** *(H L H Tang)* 905 Silvercord, Tower 2, 30 Canton Road, TSIM SHA TSUI, KOWLOON, HONG KONG SAR.

★**Moore Stephens & Butterfield** *(R H J D C Moore)* Suite 600, 12 Church Street, HAMILTON HM11, BERMUDA.

★Ⓐ**Moore Stephens & Co** *(C R Alliston-Greiner, L M Bay, S N Bill, M J C Butler, D M Chopping, P A Clark, S P Gallagher, A Galli, N D Hilton, J S Hurrell, C Lazarevic, G A Luck, S J Markley, R J S Mason, C R Moore, R H J D C Moore, P Osborne, P H A Parr, A Potts, D A Rolph, P T Short, M E Simms, G W Smith, P D Stewart, P R Stockton, P R Sykes, T S Ward, V D Watson, J A Wilkinson, G E H Williams, J M Willmont, G W Woodhouse)* 150 Aldersgate Street, LONDON, EC1A 4AE.

Moore Stephens & Company *(M J C Butler, A J Gallagher, N D Hilton, C R Moore, R H J D C Moore, P Osborne, P H A Parr, D A Rolph, P D Stewart, P R Stockton)* L' Estoril Bloc C, 31 Avenue Princesse Grace, MONTE CARLO, MC 98000, MONACO. and at HAMILTON

ⒻⓅⒶ**Moore Stephens Enfield Limited** *(D P Anderson)* 57 London Road, ENFIELD, MIDDLESEX, EN2 6SW.

Moore Stephens FS *(C R S Thubron)* Blue Tower, Avenue Louise 326, Box 30, B 1050 BRUSSELS, BELGIUM.

★Ⓟ**Moore Stephens Limited** *(C N S Barton, C O L Dixon, B L Hazell, A T J Moll, J T B Pickles, L E Spurrier)* P O Box 743, Suite 5, Watergardens 4, Waterport, GIBRALTAR, GIBRALTAR.

★ⓉⒶ**Moore Stephens LLP** *(C R Alliston-Greiner, L M Bay, S J Baylis, S N Bill, A G Brook, M J C Butler, D M Chopping, P A Clark, D R Elliott, M Finch, A J Gallagher, S P Gallagher, A Galli, D Gregory, D M Hayes, M A Henderson, J C Herniman, S H Hillary Lesquerre, N D Hilton, J S Hurrell, M Kotsapas, C Lazarevic, G A Luck, S J Markley, R J S Mason, C R Moore, R H J D C Moore, R Noye-Allen, P Osborne, L A Paler, P H A Parr, A Potts, D A Rolph, P T Short, M E Simms, G W Smith, P D Stewart, P R Stockton, P R Sykes, T S Ward, V D Watson, T West, J A Wilkinson, G E H Williams, J M Willmont, K J Wolstenholme, G W Woodhouse, T J Woodward)* 150 Aldersgate Street, LONDON, EC1A 4AB. and at BIRMINGHAM, BRISTOL, CHATHAM, WATFORD

★Ⓣ**Moore Stephens Mauritius** *(D Busgeeth, A Rogbeer, R Rogbeer)* 6th Floor, Newton Tower, Sir William Newton Steet, PORT LOUIS, MAURITIUS.

★Ⓣ**Moore Stephens Stylianou & Co** *(C Ioannou, Y Ioannou, C Schizas)* Iris Tower, Office 602, 5B Archbishop Makarios Avenue, 1302 NICOSIA, CYPRUS.

ⒻⒶ**Moore Stephens, trading name of Moore Stephens (Guildford) LLP** *(C Goodwin, L A Paler)* Priory House, Pilgrims Court, Sydenham Road, GUILDFORD, SURREY, GU1 3RX.

Ⓟ**Moore Stephens, trading name of Moore Stephens (Limassol) limited** *(C Efstratiou)* Areil Corner, 1st Floor Office 101, 196 Arch Makarios Avenue, CY 3030 LIMASSOL, CYPRUS.

ⓉⒻⒶ**Moore Stephens, trading name of Moore Stephens (North West) LLP** *(A I McGain, B McGain, S T McGain, K J Miller, M P Platt)* 110-114 Duke Street, LIVERPOOL, L1 5AG. and at MANCHESTER, WIDNES

ⓉⒻⒶ**Moore Stephens, trading name of Moore Stephens (South) LLP** *(A Coldwell, K R Cooper, S E Datlen, G J Francis, A D Henshaw, S Lucas, R Newman, M Rule, M J Scott, A L Stevens, M I Wakeford, M F J Weil, A Williams, A S Wulff)* City Gates, 2-4 Southgate, CHICHESTER, WEST SUSSEX, PO19 8DJ. and at NEWPORT, SALISBURY, SOUTHAMPTON

★ⓉⒻⒶ**Moore Thompson** *(A P Heskin, M Hildred, M D Longley, K J Maggs, T I Martin, C W Wright)* Bank House, Broad Street, SPALDING, LINCOLNSHIRE, PE11 1TB. and at PETERBOROUGH, WISBECH

Moores Rowland *(K F Sim)* 701 Sunning Plaza, 10 Hysan Avenue, CAUSEWAY BAY, HONG KONG ISLAND, HONG KONG SAR.

★**Moores Rowland Levey & Jung** *(M Levey)* Biskupsky Dvur 2095/8, 110 00 PRAGUE, CZECH REPUBLIC.

Moorfields Corporate Finance, trading name of Moorfields Corporate Finance LLP *(S R Thomas)* Moorfields, 88 Wood Street, LONDON, EC2V 7RS.

Moorfields Corporate Recovery LLP *(R H Pick, S R Thomas)* 88 Wood Street, LONDON, EC2V 7QR. and at LEEDS

ⓅⒶ**Moorgate, trading name of Coolbell Limited** *(R S Gale, S L Moore)* Wigley Manor, Romsey Road, Ower, ROMSEY, HAMPSHIRE, SO51 6AF.

ⓅⒶ**Moorlands Book Keeping Services, Moorlands Business Advisory Services, Moorlands Payroll Services, trading names of Tavistock Business Consultancy Limited** *(F A S Harris)* 28 Glanville Road, TAVISTOCK, DEVON, PL19 0EB.

ⒻⒶ**Moors Andrew McClusky & Co** *(A McClusky)* Halton View Villas, 3-5 Wilson Patten Street, WARRINGTON, WA1 1PG.

ⒻⒶ**Moors Andrew Thomas & Co LLP** *(A G Thomas)* 94 Wilderspool Causeway, WARRINGTON, WA4 6PU.

Ⓟ**Moors Andrew Thomas, trading name of Moors Andrew Thomas (Private Clients) Limited** *(A G Thomas)* 94 Wilderspool Causeway, WARRINGTON, WA4 6PU.

Ⓟ**Moors Gibson, trading name of Moors Gibson Limited** *(G S Moors)* 31 Holland Road, Kensal Rise, LONDON, NW10 5AH.

Morag Reid *(M E Reid)* Blackhillock, Glenbuchat, STRATHDON, ABERDEENSHIRE, AB36 8TQ.

Morchard Bishop & Co *(C V Barker-Benfield)* 4 Dene Walk, Lower Bourne, FARNHAM, SURREY, GU10 3PL.

Moreton & Co *(J W E Moreton)* Armscote House, Upper Dowdeswell, Andoversford, CHELTENHAM, GLOUCESTERSHIRE, GL54 4LU.

Morgan & Co *(P M Morgan)* Cockshott Farmhouse, Highgate Hill, Hawkhurst, CRANBROOK, KENT, TN18 4LS.

Ⓟ**Morgan & Co, trading name of Hendraws Limited** *(Ian D Morgan, J W Spry)* 23 Blatchington Road, TUNBRIDGE WELLS, KENT, TN2 5EG.

Morgan & Morgan *(J E Morgan)* 9 Lakeside Gardens, MERTHYR TYDFIL, MID GLAMORGAN, CF48 1EN.

Ⓟ**Morgan AVN Limited** *(R D Morgan)* 59 Victoria Road, SURBITON, SURREY, KT6 4NQ.

ⓉⒻⓅⒶ**Morgan Cameron, trading name of Morgan Cameron Limited** *(A F Thornton, M R Thornton)* Wittas House, Two Rivers, Station Lane, WITNEY, OXFORDSHIRE, OX28 4BH.

Ⓐ**Morgan Griffiths LLP** *(M R Corfield, D T Jones, S Lewis, R J Osment)* Cross Chambers, 9 High Street, NEWTOWN, POWYS, SY16 2NY.

★**Morgan Revill Accountants** *(B A Morgan)* 73 Sheepwalk Lane, Ravenshead, NOTTINGHAM, NG15 9FD.

ⓅⒶ**Morgan Rose** *(S E Humphreys)* 37 Marlowes, HEMEL HEMPSTEAD, HERTFORDSHIRE, HP1 1LD.

Morgan-Jones & Co *(D Morgan-Jones)* Wychwood Cottage, 38 High Street, Riseley, BEDFORD, MK44 1DX.

Ⓟ**Morgans, trading name of G C Morgan Limited** *(G C Morgan, D G Owen)* Clive House, Severn Road, WELSHPOOL, POWYS, SY21 7AL.

Ⓟ**Morgans, trading name of Iterix Limited** *(R J C Morgan)* 86 High Street, CARSHALTON, SURREY, SM5 3AE.

Ⓟ**Morgwn Atkins Limited** *(M D Atkins)* Eight Bells House, 14 Church Street, TETBURY, GLOUCESTERSHIRE, GL8 8JG.

Morley & Co *(N Morley)* 83 Marathon House, 200 Marylebone Road, LONDON, NW1 5PL.

Ⓐ**Morley & Co, trading name of Morley & Co (UK) LLP** *(N Morley)* 2 Cricklade Court, Old Town, SWINDON, SN1 2JR.

Ⓐ**Morley Haswell** *(R S E Haswell, S R Morley)* 4 St James Court, Bridgnorth Road, Wollaston, STOURBRIDGE, DY8 3QG.

Ⓟ**Morley Haswell Consultants Limited** *(R S E Haswell, S R Morley)* 4 St. James Court, Bridgnorth Road, Wollaston, STOURBRIDGE, WEST MIDLANDS, DY8 3QG.

Morley Tippett *(J C M Tippett)* White Park Barn, Loseley Park, GUILDFORD, SURREY, GU3 1HS.

Ⓐ**Morleys** *(M C J Morley)* Nabobs, Kings Lane, Chipperfield, KINGS LANGLEY, WD4 9EP.

ⓉⒻⒶ**Morphakis Stelios & Co** *(S Morphakis)* 22 Parkway, Southgate, LONDON, N14 6QU.

Morris & Associates *(A H Morris)* 1st Floor, 4 Henrietta Street, LONDON, WC2E 8SF.

ⓉⒻⓅⒶ**Morris & Co, trading name of Morris & Co (2011) Limited** *(S Barker, W O R Benoy, J M Carr, E W Greeves, P J Harrison, D D Lea, N O Ledingham)* Chester House, Lloyd Drive, Chesire Oaks Business Park, ELLESMERE PORT, CHESHIRE, CH65 9HQ.

Ⓟ**Morris & Co, trading name of Morris Hartdene Limited** *(A H Morris, G A Morris)* 1 Hartdene House, Bridge Road, BAGSHOT, SURREY, GU19 5AT.

Morris & Thomas LLP *(J R Thomas)* 9 Court Road, BRIDGEND, MID GLAMORGAN, CF31 1BE.

★ⓉⒻⒶ**Morris Cook** *(A C S Clarke, M A Jones)* 6 Salop Road, OSWESTRY, SHROPSHIRE, SY11 2NU. and at ELLESMERE, LLANGOLLEN, TELFORD

ⓉⒻⒶ**Morris Crocker** *(V A Fenner, K M Gilbert, R M L Perry)* Station House, 50 North Street, HAVANT, PO9 1QU.

ⒻⓅ**Morris Crocker Limited** *(V A Fenner, K M Gilbert, R M L Perry)* Station House, 50 North Street, HAVANT, HAMPSHIRE, PO9 1QU.

Ⓟ**Morris Green Accountants Limited** *(V J S Green)* 1 Tregaron Court, Ash Bank, STOKE-ON-TRENT, ST2 9QL.

ⒻⒶ**Morris Gregory** *(A Brooks, J A Ormiston)* County End Business Centre, Jackson Street, Springhead, OLDHAM, OL4 4TZ.

Ⓟ**Morris Gregory Ltd** *(A Brooks, J A Ormiston)* County End Business Centre, Jackson Street, Springhead, OLDHAM, OL4 4TZ.

★ⓉⒻⒶ**Morris Lane** *(R P Morris)* 31/33 Commercial Road, POOLE, DORSET, BH14 0HU.

★ⓉⒶ**Morris Owen** *(Robert Beale, D W Bond, R J Harman, Michael Johnson)* 43-45 Devizes Road, SWINDON, SN1 4BG. and at CIRENCESTER

ⓉⓅⒶ**Morris Palmer Limited** *(M A C Carter)* Barttelot Court, Barttelot Road, HORSHAM, WEST SUSSEX, RH12 1DQ.

★**Morris Snelling & Co.** *(D R Cottingham)* P.O. Box HM 1806, Century House, Richmond Road, HAMILTON HM HX, BERMUDA.

ⓉⒻⓅⒶ**Morris Wheeler & Co, trading name of Morris Wheeler & Co Limited** *(M S Burrows, P C Morris)* 26 Church Street, BISHOP'S STORTFORD, HERTFORDSHIRE, CM23 2LY.

Ⓟ**Morris White Limited** *(F J Morris, J R Morris, G White)* 38 Triscombe Drive, CARDIFF, CF5 2PN.

Ⓟ**Morris White, trading name of JFM Growing Business Solutions Limited** *(F J Morris, J R Morris, G White)* 38 Triscombe Drive, CARDIFF, SOUTH GLAMORGAN, CF5 2PN.

★**Morris, Cottingham & Co** *(D R Cottingham)* Hibiscus Square, Pond Street, GRAND TURK, TURKS AND CAICOS ISLANDS.

Morrison & Co *(D P Morrison)* The Tile House, Bagshot Road, Worplesdon Hill, WOKING, SURREY, GU22 0QY. and at LONDON

Morrison Forensic *(D N Morrison)* 97 Camden Road, LONDON, NW1 9HA.

Morrison Govan *(P M Govan)* Bull Farm Barn, Hartley, CRANBROOK, TN17 3QE.

ⓉⒻ**Morrisons** *(K S Morrison)* 7 Grove Place, BEDFORD, MK40 3JJ.

★**Morrisons Business Advisers** *(K S Morrison)* 7 Grove Place, BEDFORD, MK40 3JJ.

Mortimer & Co *(I L Mortimer)* Ashfield Hse., 304 High St., Boston Spa, WETHERBY, LS23 6AJ.

ⓅⒶ**Morton Smithies, trading name of Morton Smithies Consultancy Limited** *(J M Smithies)* The Studio, Lower Lodge, Weetwood Lane, LEEDS, LS16 5PH.

Ⓐ**Mortons** *(C B Cotton)* 7A Brooklands Avenue, SHEFFIELD, S10 4GA.

Ⓐ**Morwood-Leyland & Co** *(A M Morwood-Leyland)* Suite 48, 88-90 Hatton Garden, LONDON, EC1N 8PN.

ⓉⒶ**Mosley & Co.** *(N H Chamberlain)* 14 Market Place, Ramsbottom, BURY, BL0 9HT.

ⓉⒻⒶ**Moss & Williamson** *(A E Booth, D Evans, M G Foote, P Lee, C H McLean)* Booth Street Chambers, Booth Street, ASHTON-UNDER-LYNE, OL6 7LQ. and at CHEADLE, STALYBRIDGE

Ⓟ**Moss & Williamson Ltd** *(A E Booth, D Evans, M G Foote, P Lee, C H McLean)* Booth Street Chambers, Booth Street, ASHTON-UNDER-LYNE, LANCASHIRE, OL6 7LQ.

Moss Goodman *(J H M Goodman)* 24 Lyndhurst Gardens, Finchley, LONDON, N3 1TB.

ⓅⒶ**Moss James, trading name of Moss James Limited** *(R J Moss)* Titsey Estate Office, Pilgrims Lane, OXTED, SURREY, RH8 0SE.

★ⒻⒶ**Mossgroves, trading name of Mossgroves LLP** *(J B Wells)* 3 The Deans, Bridge Road, BAGSHOT, SURREY, GU19 5AT.

★**Mostafa Shawki & Co** *(A M Shawki)* 153 Mohamed Farid St., Bank Misr Tower P.O.Box 2095, CAIRO, 11511, EGYPT. and at ALEXANDRIA

ⓉⒶ**Mostons** *(P J Moston)* 29 The Green, Winchmore Hill, LONDON, N21 1HS.

Motashaw's *(M M Motashaw)* 110 Ward Avenue, GRAYS, RM17 5RL.

Ⓟ**Mouat Accountancy Limited** *(C E Mouat)* Newton Red House, Mitford, MORPETH, NORTHUMBERLAND, NE61 3QW.

ⓉⒻⒶ**Mouktaris & Co** *(G A Mouktaris)* 156A Burnt Oak Broadway, EDGWARE, HA8 0AX.

Ⓟ**Moulds & Co Ltd** *(S J Reynolds)* Unit 10, York Road Estate, WETHERBY, WEST YORKSHIRE, LS22 7SU.

Moulsdale & Co *(N G Moulsdale)* Ivy Cottage, Castley, OTLEY, WEST YORKSHIRE, LS21 2PY.

ⓉⓅⒶ**Moulsham Audits Limited** *(B I Watkinson)* 683 Galleywood Road, CHELMSFORD, CM2 8BT. and at HALSTEAD

ⒻⒶ**Moulton Johnson** *(I K Johnson, P S Moulton)* Lutidine House, Newark Lane, Ripley, WOKING, SURREY, GU23 6BS.

★ⒻⓅⒶ**Moulton Johnson Limited** *(I K Johnson, P S Moulton)* 25a Crown Street, BRENTWOOD, ESSEX, CM14 4BA.

Mount Katten & Co. *(I Katzenberg)* 35 Temple Gardens, LONDON, NW11 0LP.

ⒻⓅⒶ**Mountsides Limited** *(H Alibhai, C J Andrews, J R Dutton, J W Rowe, K J Wright)* 2 Mountside, STANMORE, MIDDLESEX, HA7 2DT.

Ⓟ**Mouzouris & Polyviou Limited** *(N M Mouzouris, P Polyviou)* 1 Karatza Str and Makariou Ave, Thelma Court, 1st Floor, 3021 LIMASSOL, CYPRUS.

Movie Accounting LLP *(S C Power, C D Whitley-Jones)* Kingfisher House, Hurstwood Grange, Hurstwood Lane, HAYWARDS HEATH, WEST SUSSEX, RH17 7QX.

ⒻⒶ**Moynihan & Co** *(E J Moynihan)* Suite 7, Claremont House, 22-24 Claremont Road, SURBITON, SURREY, KT6 4QU.

Ⓟ**MP Associates (Warwick) Ltd** *(P Duckworth)* Holly Cottage, Moreton Paddox, Moreton Morrell, WARWICK, CV35 9BU.

Ⓐ**MPC, trading name of Miles & Partners Consulting LLP** *(D J Miles)* Harella House, 90-98 Goswell Road, LONDON, EC1V 7RD.

ⓅⒶ**MPS Associates, trading name of MPS Associates Ltd** *(N Morley)* 2 Cricklade Court, Old Town, SWINDON, SN1 2JR.

Ⓟ**MR Mellor & Co Ltd** *(M R Mellor)* Panton House, Panton Place, High Street, HOLYWELL, CH8 7LD.

MRM Accounting *(M R Martin)* 90 Albert Road, Grappenhall, WARRINGTON, WA4 2PG.

MRMA *(M J Rogers)* MRM Office Park, 10 Village Road, KLOOF, 3610, SOUTH AFRICA.

Mrs C M Cowgill ACA *(C M Cowgill)* 4 Penny Meadow, Capel St. Mary, IPSWICH, IP9 2UU.

Mrs C.M. Edge BSc FCA *(C M Edge)* 2 Kingswood Road, LONDON, SW19 3NE.

Mrs D Tams *(D Tams)* 4 Conway Court, Stirling Close, NEW MILTON, BH25 6AR.

Mrs G.E.Cashmore *(G E Cashmore)* The Old Post Office, Edwalton, NOTTINGHAM, NG12 4AB.

Mrs Julia Todd FCA *(J M Todd)* 22 Mayfair Avenue, WORCESTER PARK, KT4 7SL.

Mrs M Featherstone ACA *(M D Featherstone)* 13 Wentworth Road, Harborne, BIRMINGHAM, B17 9SH.

Mrs Mary Osborne *(M Osborne)* 6 Russet Gardens, CAMBERLEY, SURREY, GU15 2LG.

Mrs P.J.Taylor *(P J Taylor)* 3 Ninnings Road, Chalfont St Peter, GERRARDS CROSS, SL9 0EF.

Ⓕ**Mrs P.V.R. Richards** *(P V R Richards)* 34 Queensmill Road, LONDON, SW6 6JS.

Mrs R V Perera *(R V Perera)* 484 Bideford Green, LEIGHTON BUZZARD, BEDFORDSHIRE, LU7 2TZ.

Ⓐ**Mrs S.M. Rowley FCA** *(S M Rowley)* 223 Fullingdale Road, NORTHAMPTON, NN3 2QH.

Mrs Sarah Keeble BA(Hons) ACA CTA *(S L Keeble)* 51 Pembury Road, BEXLEYHEATH, KENT, DA7 5LN.

Mrs T. Storan, trading name of Tracy Storan *(T F Storan)* Highlands, 72 Stevenage Road, KNEBWORTH, HERTFORDSHIRE, SG3 6NN.

Ms Susan Kemp ACA *(S Kemp)* 100 Welsford Road, NORWICH, NR4 6QH.

MS&Co *(M J Sandle)* First Floor, Park Court, Park Street, St. Peter Port, GUERNSEY, GY1 1EE. and at LONDON

MSCO *(M Miah)* Suda House, 100a Mile End Road, LONDON, E1 4UN.

Muallah Weissbraun & Co *(M Weissbraun)* 220 The Vale, LONDON, NW11 8SR.

Ⓐ**Muallah Weissbraun, trading name of Michael, Pasha & Co** *(M Weissbraun)* 220 The Vale, LONDON, NW11 8SR.

MueDelta Accounting & Finance Consulting *(M Dev)* 37 Quickswood Drive, LIVERPOOL, L25 4TP.

Muggleston & Co *(J Muggleston)* 50 Southway, Eldwick, BINGLEY, BD16 3DT.

Mulberry Accountancy *(F C Hindley)* 40 Mill Road, Frettenham, NORWICH, NR12 2LQ.

Mulhall & Company *(J B Mulhall)* 2 Langdon Av, AYLESBURY, HP21 9UX.

★Ⓐ**Mullen Stoker** *(N Mullen)* Mullen Stoker House, Mandale Business Park, Belmont Industrial Estate, DURHAM, DH1 1TH.

★ⒻⒶ**Mulligan Williams** *(L T Mulligan, T F Mulligan)* 4 Long Street, Stoney Stanton, LEICESTER, LE9 4DQ.

Ⓟ**Multisolo Limited** *(P Stansfield)* Regency House, 45-51 Chorley New Road, BOLTON, BL1 4QR.

Ⓐ**Mumby Heppenstall** *(C Heppenstall, J A D Mumby)* Wellingore Hall, Wellingore, LINCOLN, LN5 0HX.

ⒻⒶ**Mumford & Co** *(B F Mumford)* The Old Rectory, Church Street, WEYBRIDGE, SURREY, KT13 8DE.

Ⓟ**Mumford & Co Ltd** *(S A N Milburn)* Sandall House, 230 High Street, HERNE BAY, KENT, CT6 5AX.

Munaver Rasul *(M H Rasul)* Entrance 2a, Part 1st Floor, Crossford Court, Dane Road, SALE, CHESHIRE M33 7BZ.

Ⓟ**Munday Long & Co Limited** *(R J I Long)* Alton House, 66 High Street, NORTHWOOD, HA6 1BL.

Ⓟ**Munday Long Accounting Services Ltd** *(R J I Long)* Alton House, 66 High Street, NORTHWOOD, MIDDLESEX, HA6 1BL.

Mundy & Co *(N H W Mundy)* 15 Williams Mead, Bartestree, HEREFORD, HR1 4BT.

Munir Tatar & Associates *(M H Tatar)* 32 Willoughby Road, Hornsey, LONDON, N8 0JG.

Ⓟ**Munro Harradine Ltd** *(D A Oakensen)* 31 Stallard Street, TROWBRIDGE, WILTSHIRE, BA14 9AA.

Munro Moore *(M Y Moore)* Glynsk, Liscarney, WESTPORT, COUNTY MAYO, IRELAND.

Ⓟ**Munro, trading name of Munro Accountants Limited** *(D A Oakensen)* 31 Stallard Street, TROWBRIDGE, WILTSHIRE, BA14 9AA.

ⓅⒶ**Munro, trading name of Munro Audit Limited** *(D A Oakensen)* 31 Stallard Street, TROWBRIDGE, WILTSHIRE, BA14 9AA.

★**Munro's** *(M E Ceeney, B M Collins)* 1341 High Road, Whetstone, LONDON, N20 9HR.

Ⓟ**Munro's (Accounting Services) Limited** *(M E Ceeney, B M Collins)* 1341 High Road, Whetstone, LONDON, N20 9HR.

★**Munslows** *(S C Parsons, N A Steinberg)* 2nd Floor, Manfield House, 1 Southampton Street, LONDON, WC2R 0LR.

Ⓟ**Muras Gill, trading name of Muras Gill Ltd** *(G C Bate)* Thomas House, Croxstalls Place, Bloxwich, WALSALL, WS3 2PP.

Ⓟ**Muras Management Services Ltd** *(T P Brueton, C A Morris)* Regent House, Bath Avenue, WOLVERHAMPTON, WV1 4EG.

Murgatroyd & Co *(G Murgatroyd)* 12 Popples Drive, HALIFAX, WEST YORKSHIRE, HX2 9SQ.

Ⓐ**Murphy & Co** *(P Murphy)* The Coach House, 24b Park Hill Street, BOLTON, LANCASHIRE, BL1 4AR.

ⒻⒶ**Murphy Salisbury** *(M Bullock, B K Gupta, S R Smith)* 15 Warwick Road, STRATFORD-UPON-AVON, CV37 6YW.

Murray *(I B Murray)* Murray House, 58 High Street, Biddulph, STOKE-ON-TRENT, ST8 6AR.

★ⒻⓅ**Murray & Lamb, Paul & Co, trading names of Murray & Lamb Accountants Ltd** *(S Lamb, G S Murray)* 25-27 Medomsley Road, CONSETT, COUNTY DURHAM, DH8 5HE. and at BARNARD CASTLE, STANLEY

Ⓟ**Murray Accounting Services Limited** *(I F C Murray)* Mead Court, 10 The Mead Business Centre, 176-178 Berkhamstead Road, CHESHAM, BUCKINGHAMSHIRE, HP5 3EE. and at HIGH WYCOMBE

Ⓟ**Murray CA Limited** *(I B Murray)* Murray House, 58 High Street, Biddulph, STOKE-ON-TRENT, ST8 6AR.

Ⓣ**Murray McIntosh O'Brien** *(G McIntosh, S P Murray, R B Pennington)* Wellesley House, 204 London Road, WATERLOOVILLE, PO7 7AN.

ⓉⒻⒶ**Murray Smith, trading name of Murray Smith LLP** *(M G Benson, P R Daniel, M J M Jones, D B Watkinson, S A Williams)* Darland House, 44 Winnington Hill, NORTHWICH, CHESHIRE, CW8 1AU. and at WINSFORD

Murray Walne, trading name of Murray Walne LLP *(M Walne)* The Willows, 10a Vicarage Road, OAKHAM, LE15 6EG.

ⒻⓅⒶ**Murrayoung, trading name of MurraYoung Limited** *(S Murray, A P Smart, J Young)* 15 Home Farm, Luton Hoo Estate, LUTON, LU1 3TD.

Murrays, trading name of Cranleigh-Swash & Co *(P A Cranleigh-Swash)* Greenford Business Centre, I C G House, Station Approach, Oldfield Lane North, GREENFORD, MIDDLESEX UB6 0AL. and at HEMEL HEMPSTEAD

Ⓟ**Murrell Consultancy Limited** *(D J Roberts)* 39 Manor Road, SUTTON COLDFIELD, B73 6EE.

Murrells *(J D Willis)* Cedar House, 41 Thorpe Road, NORWICH, NR1 1ES.

Ⓐ**Muscat & Co** *(J S Muscat)* Kingswood Lodge, Kingswood Lane, WARLINGHAM, CR6 9AB.

★**Mushtaq & Co** *(M A Vohra)* 407 Commerce Centre, Hasrat Mohani Road, KARACHI 74200, PAKISTAN. and at LAHORE

Ⓟ**Music Business Associates Limited** *(C J Bevis)* Apex House, 6 West Street, EPSOM, SURREY, KT18 7RG.

ⓉⓅⒶ**Musker & Garrett, trading name of Musker & Garrett Limited** *(J Garrett, R Musker)* Edward House, North Mersey Business Centre, Woodward Road, Knowsley Industrial Park, LIVERPOOL, L33 7UY. and at WIDNES

Ⓟ**Musket Lane Enterprises Limited** *(P J Lee)* Autumn Cottage, Musket Lane, Hollingbourne, MAIDSTONE, KENT, ME17 1UY.

Ⓟ**Mustafa A Datoo, trading name of Mustafa A Datoo Ltd** *(M A L Datoo)* 144 Dorset Road, Merton Park, LONDON, SW19 3EF.

★Ⓣ**MustaphaRaj** *(Dato Ratnaswamy)* E-33-05 Dataran 32, No 2 Jalan 19/1, 46300 PETALING JAYA, SELANGOR, MALAYSIA.

MW & Co LLP *(R J Chandler, M D Harknett)* 100 High Road, Byfleet, WEST BYFLEET, SURREY, KT14 7QT.

Ⓟ**MW Denton, trading name of MW Denton Limited** *(M W Denton)* 29 Devonshire Street, KEIGHLEY, WEST YORKSHIRE, BD21 2BH.

MW Martin J Wright *(M J Wright)* Grove House, Pond Hall Road, Hadleigh, IPSWICH, SUFFOLK, IP7 5PQ.

MW Roberts & Co *(M W Roberts)* 8 Kings Oak, COLWYN BAY, CLWYD, LL29 6AJ.

MWForensics *(M Woof)* Beech Cottage, Slad, STROUD, GLOUCESTERSHIRE, GL6 7QA.

Ⓟ**MWI Accountants Ltd** *(W Iqbal)* 9-11 St. Andrews Street, BLACKBURN, LANCASHIRE, BB1 8AE.

★Ⓕ**MWM** *(P Walker)* 24 Oxford Street, WELLINGBOROUGH, NN8 4JE.

ⓅⒶ**MWM, trading name of Mooney Williams May Limited** *(M T Mooney, C G Williams)* 11 Great George Street, BRISTOL, BS1 5RR.

ⓉⒻⒶ**MWS** *(J R Gorridge, N P Kleinfeld, D McCartney, D A Nice, F A Read, G R M Simons, C R Smith)* Kingsridge House, 601 London Road, WESTCLIFF-ON-SEA, ESSEX, SS0 9PE.

ⒻⓅ**MWS Business Management Limited** *(M W Sadofsky)* 6 Earls Court, Priory Park East, HULL, HU4 7DY.

Ⓟ**My Bean Counter Limited** *(M M Little)* 1 Rusthall Avenue, LONDON, W4 1BW.

Ⓟ**My Business Centre Ltd** *(F Rook)* Bridge House, 25 Fore Street, OKEHAMPTON, DEVON, EX20 1DL.

My FD Richmond.co.uk, trading name of S D Williams FCA BSc *(S D Williams)* 20 Manor Road, RICHMOND, SURREY, TW9 1YB.

Ⓟ**My Online Accountant, trading name of Online Accounting Solutions Limited** *(P J Bird)* 65A Liverpool Road, Penwortham, PRESTON, PR1 9XD.

ⓉⒻⓅⒶ**Myers Clark, trading name of Myers Clark Limited** *(J C Crook, R G Marsden, J P Shaw, P J Windmill)* Iveco House, Station Road, WATFORD, WD17 1DL.

Myers Hogg & Co *(G M Hogg)* 3 Lemna Road, Leytenstone, LONDON, E11 1JL.

Myles T. Stott *(M T Stott)* 12 Chemin du Hameau, 1255 VEYRIER, SWITZERLAND.

Ⓟ**Mynotts Ltd** *(T J Mynott)* Long Cottage, Homington Road, Coombe Bissett, SALISBURY, SP5 4LR.

ⓉⒻⒶ**Myrus Smith** *(K C Fisher, S A Jones)* Norman House, 8 Burnell Road, SUTTON, SURREY, SM1 4BW.

MZ Accountants *(N Cyroos)* 51 Creighton Road, Ealing, LONDON, W5 4SH.

Ⓟ**N & P Accounting Solutions Limited** *(K C Keller)* Lynwood House, 373-375 Station Road, HARROW, MIDDLESEX, HA1 2AW.

★**N A Yamakis, trading name of Yamakis & Co** *(N A Yamakis)* Regaena House, 4a Regaena Street, PO Box 21082, 1501 NICOSIA, CYPRUS.

N Anayiotos & Co *(N Anayiotos)* 20 Bishops Avenue, ELSTREE, WD6 3LZ.

N Anson *(N Anson)* 3 Swan Grove, Exning, NEWMARKET, SUFFOLK, CB8 7HX.

Ⓟ**N Armes & Co Ltd** *(N Armes)* 1 Pelmark House, 11 Amwell End, WARE, HERTFORDSHIRE, SG12 9HP.

Ⓟ**N Constantinou & Co Audit Ltd** *(N Constantinou)* Limassol Centre PO Box 54039, Block B. Office 508, Rega Fereou St., 3720 LIMASSOL, CYPRUS.

N D Myatt & Co *(N D Myatt)* 194 Coombe Lane, LONDON, SW20 0QT.

N Din *(N Din)* 60 Sydney Road, West Ealing, LONDON, W13 9EY.

N Dunhill & Co *(N V A Dunhill)* 23A Moreton Terrace, Pimlico, LONDON, SW1V 2NS.

Ⓐ**N Harris & Co, trading name of N H & Co LLP** *(N Harris, I E Mawji, F Meghani)* Jaybee House, 155-157a Clapham High Street, LONDON, SW4 7SY.

N J Charman *(N J Charman)* The Coppice, 184 Medstead Road, Beech, ALTON, HAMPSHIRE, GU34 4AJ.

Ⓟ**N J Duncumb, trading name of N 4 Tax Limited** *(N J Duncumb)* The Old Vicarage, Scamblesby, LOUTH, LN11 9XL.

N J Hadfield *(N J Hadfield)* Tobys Cottage, Blythburgh, HALESWORTH, SUFFOLK, IP19 9NG.

N K Consultancy *(N J Kassam)* 37 Clarence Gate Gardens, Glentworth Street, LONDON, NW1 6BA.

N L Tuchband *(N L Tuchband)* 925 Finchley Road, LONDON, NW11 7PE.

Ⓟ**N Mouzouris Ltd** *(N M Mouzouris)* 12 Navarinou Str, 3041 LIMASSOL, CYPRUS.

N P D Jackson FCA *(N P D Jackson)* 14 Gronant Road, PRESTATYN, CLWYD, LL19 9DS.

N P Sharpe *(N P Sharpe)* 84 Nettleham Road, LINCOLN, LN2 1RR.

Ⓟ**N P Smith & Co Limited** *(N P Smith)* 10 Tudman Close, SUTTON COLDFIELD, WEST MIDLANDS, B76 1GP.

Ⓟ**N R Bacon & Co, trading name of N R Bacon Ltd** *(N R Bacon)* 19 Queens Road, Sketty, SWANSEA, SA2 0SD.

Ⓟ**N R Betts & Co, trading name of Professional Tax & Accounting Services Ltd** *(N R Betts)* 44 Squires Lane, Finchley, LONDON, N3 2AT.

Ⓟ**N R Peplow & Co Ltd** *(N R Peplow)* 2nd Floor, 150 Upper New Walk, LEICESTER, LEICESTERSHIRE, LE1 7QA.

ⓅⒶ**N Saha & Co, trading name of N Saha & Co Limited** *(T Saha)* Flat 21 Parade Mansions, Hendon Central, LONDON, NW4 3JR.

N Seerungum & Co *(N Seerungum)* 25 Vicarage Lane, ILFORD, ESSEX, IG1 4AG.

Ⓐ**N T Chew** *(N Chew)* 2nd Floor Cathay Building, 86 Holloway Head, BIRMINGHAM, B1 1NB.

Ⓟ**N Tate & Co, trading name of N Tate & Co Limited** *(N L Tate)* 42 St. Andrews Road, RAMSGATE, KENT, CT11 7EQ.

Ⓟ**N Towers & Co Limited** *(N C Towers)* 63 Spring Meadow, Clayton-le-Woods, LEYLAND, PR25 5UR.

N White & Co *(N White)* 14 Abbey Walk, GREAT MISSENDEN, BUCKINGHAMSHIRE, HP16 0AY.

N. Bahl & Co *(N Bahl)* A 9/34 Vasant Vihar, NEW DELHI 110057, INDIA.

N. Elliott & Co. *(N Elliott)* 2 Gilsland Grove, Northburn Vale, CRAMLINGTON, NORTHUMBERLAND, NE23 3SY.

Ⓐ**N. Haggart & Co** *(N R Haggart)* 114 Copse Avenue, WEST WICKHAM, BR4 9NP.

N. Kumar & Co *(N Kumar)* J-14 Hauz Khas, Yusaf Sarai, Mehrauli Road, NEW DELHI 16, INDIA.

N. Nabi & Co *(T I M Nurun Nabi)* 75 Hillside Gardens, WALLINGTON, SURREY, SM6 9NX.

N. Tree *(N Tree)* Flat 17, Gun Wharf, 124 Wapping High Street, LONDON, E1W 2NJ.

N. Zaman & Co *(A K M Nuruzzaman)* 35a Westbury Avenue, LONDON, N22 6BS.

N.A. Allen *(N A Allen)* 2 Dewhurst Terrace, Sunniside, NEWCASTLE UPON TYNE, NE16 5LP.

N.A. Lane *(N A Lane)* 17394 N 77th Street, SCOTTSDALE, AZ 85255, UNITED STATES.

N.A. Norman & Co. *(N A Norman)* 31 High Street, Winslow, BUCKINGHAM, MK18 3HE.

Ⓐ**N.B. Lancaster & Co** *(I C Lancaster)* 6 Brunswick Street, CARLISLE, CA1 1PN.

N.C. Youngman *(N C Youngman)* The Pines, Thakeham Copse, Storrington, PULBOROUGH, WEST SUSSEX, RH20 3JW.

N.J. Brown *(N J Brown)* 36 Kingsleigh Place, MITCHAM, CR4 4NU.

N.J. Liddell & Co *(N J Liddell)* Moor Farm, Kings Lane, Sotherton, BECCLES, NR34 8AF.

Ⓐ**N.J. Patel & Co** *(N J Patel)* 345 Bearwood Road, SMETHWICK, WEST MIDLANDS, B66 4DB.

N.K. Phillips *(N K Phillips)* 30 Laneham Place, KENILWORTH, WARWICKSHIRE, CV8 2UN.

N.K. Sutaria & Co *(N K Sutaria)* Unison, Epping Road, Roydon, HARLOW, CM19 5HN.

ⒻⒶ**N.M. Shah & Co.** *(N M Shah)* Miller House, Rosslyn Crescent, HARROW, MIDDLESEX, HA1 2RZ.

N.N. Kothari & Co *(N N Kothari)* 19 Collins Avenue, STANMORE, HA7 1DL.

N.P. Shah & Co *(N P Shah)* 26 Willowcourt Avenue, Kenton, HARROW, MIDDLESEX, HA3 8ES.

Ⓐ**N.P. Shah & Company** *(N P Shah)* Unit A2 Livingstone Court, 55 Peel Road, Wealdstone, HARROW, HA3 7QT.

Ⓐ**N.P. Smith & Co** *(N P Smith)* 10 Tudman Close, Walmley, SUTTON COLDFIELD, WEST MIDLANDS, B76 1GP.

★ⓉⒻⒶ**N.R. Barton** *(G H Potter, C M Rogers, J Schofield, D J Shirley)* 19-21 Bridgeman Terrace, WIGAN, WN1 1TD.

N.R. Patel & Co *(N R Patel)* 19 Hill Crescent, HARROW, HA1 2PW.

N.R. Ward *(N R Ward)* 36 Brushwood Road, HORSHAM, RH12 4PE.

Ⓐ**N.S. Amin & Co** *(N S Amin)* 334-336 Goswell Rd, LONDON, EC1V 7RP.

N.S. Lucas & Co *(N S Lucas)* The Courtyard, 80 High Street, AMERSHAM, BUCKINGHAMSHIRE, HP7 0DS.

N.T.Butler *(N T Butler)* 26 Rose Lane, Melbourn, ROYSTON, SG8 6AD.

N.W. Rivett *(N W Rivett)* 41 Thompson Avenue, COLCHESTER, CO3 4HW.

NA Associates, trading name of NA Associates LLP *(S R Hunt)* 1st Floor, Woodgate Studios, 2-8 Games Road, Cockfosters, BARNET, HERTFORDSHIRE EN4 9HN.

ⒻⓅ**NA Judd Corporate Finance, trading name of NA Judd Limited** *(N A Judd)* Milton Keynes Business Centre, Foxhunter Drive, Linford Wood, MILTON KEYNES, MK14 6GD.

Ⓟ**Nabarro Poole, trading name of Nabarro Poole Ltd** *(A K Nabarro)* 31 Church Road, Northenden, MANCHESTER, M22 4NN.

Ⓐ**Nagaria & Co** *(R S Shah)* 21 Alverstone Road, NEW MALDEN, SURREY, KT3 4BA.

ⓅⒶ**Nagle James Associates Limited** *(K C Nathwani)* 51/53 Station Road, HARROW, HA1 2TY.

Ⓟ**Nagle James Financial Planning Ltd** *(K C Nathwani)* 51/53 Station Road, HARROW, HA1 2TY.

ⒻⓅ**Nagle Jay Ltd** *(J S Lakhani)* 100 College Road, HARROW, HA1 1BQ.

ⒻⒶ**Nagler Simmons** *(P J Simmons)* 5 Beaumont Gate, Shenley Hill, RADLETT, HERTFORDSHIRE, WD7 7AR.

Naik & Co *(H R Naik)* 66 Montpelier Rise, WEMBLEY, MIDDLESEX, HA9 8RQ.

ⓉⒶ**Naim Ahmed & Co** *(N Ahmed)* 79 College Road, HARROW, MIDDLESEX, HA1 1BD.

ⓉⒻⒶ**Nairne, Son & Green** *(J M Edge, C Roberts)* 477 Chester Road, MANCHESTER, M16 9HF.

Ⓐ**Najefy & Co** *(S Najefy)* 46 Victoria Road, WORTHING, WEST SUSSEX, BN11 1XE.

Najem D Toor *(N U D Toor)* 37-A PCSIR Housing Society, Canal Bank, LAHORE, PAKISTAN.

Nanavati & Co *(P G Nanavati)* 34 Burwell Avenue, GREENFORD, UB6 0NU.

Nankivells *(G D Nankivell)* 45 Green Drift, ROYSTON, SG8 5BX.

Naren Patel & Co *(N N Patel)* 126 Royal College Street, LONDON, NW1 0TA.

Naren Unadkat & Co *(N R Unadkat)* 50 Wychwood Avenue, EDGWARE, HA8 6TH.

Ⓐ**Nash & Co** *(J A Luker)* 77 Fore Street, BODMIN, CORNWALL, PL31 2JB.

Nash & Co *(D H Nash)* Highclose Farm, Bath Road, HUNGERFORD, BERKSHIRE, RG17 0SP.

Ⓐ**Nash Harvey LLP** *(J W B Alder, D A Smith)* The Granary, Hermitage Court, Hermitage Lane, MAIDSTONE, KENT, ME16 9NT.

Ⓟ**Nash Harvey Payroll Services Ltd** *(J W B Alder, D A Smith)* The Granary, Hermitage Court, Hermitage Lane, MAIDSTONE, KENT, ME16 9NT.

Ⓟ**Nash Harvey Taxation Services Ltd** *(J W B Alder, D A Smith)* The Granary, Hermitage Court, Hermitage Lane, MAIDSTONE, KENT, ME16 9NT.

Nasim Ahmad & Co *(N Ahmad)* 48 Woodend, Handsworth Wood, BIRMINGHAM, B20 1EN.

ⒻⒶ**Nasir Mahmud** *(N Mahmud)* Falcon House, 257 Burlington Road, NEW MALDEN, KT3 4NE.

Natalie Backes *(N Backes)* 93 Listria Park, LONDON, N16 5SP.

Ⓐ**Natalie Green & Co** *(N U Green)* 7G Mobbs Miller House, Christchurch Road, NORTHAMPTON, NN1 5LL.

Natalie Powell ACA *(N A Powell)* 7 Shorefield Road, Marchwood, SOUTHAMPTON, SO40 4SR.

Ⓐ**Nath Luthra & Co** *(V N Luthra)* Minavil House, 1st Floor, Ealing Road, WEMBLEY, HA0 4EL.

Ⓟ**Nathan Evans Limited** *(N C Evans, S J Evans)* 16 Cambrian Way, Marshfield, CARDIFF, CF3 2WB.

ⓉⒻⒶ**Nathan Maknight** *(M A Khan)* 326a Limpsfield Road, SOUTH CROYDON, SURREY, CR2 9DH. and at LONDON

Naughten & Co *(E A Naughten)* 2 Carlton Bank, Station Road, HARPENDEN, AL5 4SU.

★**Naunton Jones Le Masurier** *(D P Le Masurier)* 5 St. Andrews Crescent, CARDIFF, CF10 3DA. and at BARRY, PENARTH

Ⓟ**Navitas Advisors, trading name of Navitas Advisors Limited** *(J J Le Fort)* Albany House, 4th Floor Office 404, 324-326 Regent Street, LONDON, W1B 3HH.

★ⒻⓅⒶ**Naylor Wintersgill, trading name of Naylor Wintersgill Ltd** *(V Fryer, V M Houldsworth, G Lamb, P Naylor, P L Venter, A M Whalley, A Wintersgill)* Carlton House, Grammar School Street, BRADFORD, WEST YORKSHIRE, BD1 4NS.

ⓉⒻⒶ**Nazim & Co** *(M Nazim-Ud-Din)* Suite 1C, Cranbrook House, 61 Cranbrook Road, ILFORD, ESSEX, IG1 4PG.

Ⓣ**Nazman** *(M A Choudhury)* Rutland House, 114-116 Manningham Lane, BRADFORD, WEST YORKSHIRE, BD8 7JF.

ⓅⒶ**NB Consulting Limited** *(N D Beeson)* 2 Foxglove Close, BUCKINGHAM, MK18 1FU.

NCL & Co, trading name of Nicholas Charles Lewis & Co *(N C Lewis)* 5 Leycroft Close, CANTERBURY, KENT, CT2 7LD.

Ⓟ**NCR Accountants Ltd** *(C J Backhouse)* Miller House, Rosslyn Crescent, HARROW, MIDDLESEX, HA1 2RZ.

Ⓟ**NCTS Limited** *(C W K Hinton)* Ross House, The Square, Stow on the Wold, CHELTENHAM, GLOUCESTERSHIRE, GL54 1AF.

Ⓟ**ND Partners, trading name of New Door Partnerships Limited** *(K Orbeck)* 12 Crow Hill, BROADSTAIRS, KENT, CT10 1HT. and at RAMSGATE

Ⓟ**NE Accountancy Services Limited** *(S Gibson)* 9 Park Parade, Roker, SUNDERLAND, SR6 9LU.

ⓅⒶ**Neal Carter Limited** *(N Carter)* 2a Alton House Office Park, Gatehouse Way, Gatehouse Industrial Area, AYLESBURY, BUCKINGHAMSHIRE, HP19 8YF.

ⓉⒻⒶ**Neal Frain** *(P A Hazlehurst)* 53 York Street, HEYWOOD, LANCASHIRE, OL10 4NR.

Ⓟ**Needham Hall & Co, trading name of N H Accountants Limited** *(D W Hall)* 6 Bedford Road, Barton-le-Clay, BEDFORD, MK45 4JU.

Ⓐ**Needham, Chipchase, Manners & Co** *(R I Crisop, M E Needham)* 30b Market Place, RICHMOND, DL10 4QG.

Ⓟ**Needle's Eye, trading name of Needle's Eye Limited** *(C S Wright)* 14 Catherine Drive, SUTTON COLDFIELD, B73 6AX.

Neeld Wellings *(A N Wellings)* Rawlings Barn, Wambrook, CHARD, TA20 3DF.

Neil & Co *(R G Neil)* 30 Cedar Avenue, BARNET, HERTFORDSHIRE, EN4 8DX.

★Ⓕ**Neil Davies Associates** *(N Davies)* Bude Business Centre, Kings Hill Industrial Estate, BUDE, CORNWALL, EX23 8QN.

Ⓟ**Neil Ellis Consulting, trading name of Neil Ellis Consulting Limited** *(N G Ellis)* 1 Friary, Temple Quay, BRISTOL, BS1 6EU.

ⓅⒶ**Neil Graham Limited** *(N R Graham)* Berg Kaprow Lewis LLP, 35 Ballards Lane, LONDON, N3 1XW.

Neil H MacGregor *(N H MacGregor)* 177-4 Craigmillar Castle Ave, EDINBURGH, EH16 4DN.

ⓅⒶ**Neil Hodge & Co Limited** *(N A Hodge)* 106A Commercial Street, Risca, NEWPORT, NP11 6EE.

Ⓟ**Neil Hooton Accountancy Services Limited** *(N E Hooton)* Suite 36 The Studio, Nortex Business Centre, 105 Chorley Old Road, BOLTON, BL1 3AS.

Ⓐ**Neil Scott & Company** *(N S Scott)* 107 Kenton Road, Kenton, HARROW, HA3 0AN.

Neil Sharman *(N W Sharman)* 91 Manchester Road, Slaithwaite, HUDDERSFIELD, HD7 5HP.

Ⓐ**Neil Simpson & Co** *(N F Simpson)* 12 Church Road, Bengeo, HERTFORD, SG14 3DP. and at LONDON

Ⓐ**Neil Summer LLP** *(N Summer)* 25 Harley Street, LONDON, W1G 9BR.

Ⓟ**Neil Walton Ltd** *(N Walton)* Bank Foot Farm, Ingleby Greenhow, Great Ayton, MIDDLESBROUGH, CLEVELAND, TS9 6LP.

ⒻⒶ**Neil Westwood & Co** *(N A Westwood)* 101 Dixons Green Road, DUDLEY, DY2 7DJ.

ⓅⒶ**Neil Wilson & Co, trading name of Neil Wilson Accountancy and Bookkeeping Limited** *(N D F Wilson)* 42A Walnut Road, Chelston, TORQUAY, TQ2 6HS.

Ⓐ**Neil Wright & Co** *(N J Wright)* 166 Linacre Road, Litherland, LIVERPOOL, L21 8JU.

Neill & Co *(J A Kiernander)* 26 New Broadway, Ealing, LONDON, W5 2XA.

Ⓟ**Neils Limited** *(D N Gungah)* 3 Dukes Court, Wellington Street, LUTON, BEDFORDSHIRE, LU1 5AF. and at LONDON

Ⓟ**Neilson Renton & Co Ltd** *(G S Neilson)* 101 Main Street, Uddingston, GLASGOW, G71 7EW.

Ⓟ**Nelson & Co, trading name of Greg Nelson Limited** *(G C Nelson)* The Anchorage, Malpas Village, TRURO, TR1 1SN.

Ⓟ**Nene Business Services Limited** *(M A Oxby)* Unit 3, Bramley Road, ST. IVES, CAMBRIDGESHIRE, PE27 3WS.

Ⓟ**Neoserve Audit Limited** *(N Nicolaides)* P.O Box 70585, 3800 LIMASSOL, CYPRUS.

Ⓟ**Nero Accounting Limited** *(N J Duncan, R J Palk)* Crows Nest Business Park, Ashton Road, Billinge, WIGAN, LANCASHIRE, WN5 7XX.

Ⓐ**Nesbits** *(S Nesbit)* Robertsfield, Holland Road, Hurst Green, OXTED, SURREY, RH8 9BQ.

Ⓟ**Nettleton Management Services Limited** *(M V R Heaven)* Quadrant Court, 48 Calthorpe Road, Edgbaston, BIRMINGHAM, B15 1TH.

Ⓟ**Network 4M Limited** *(M G Ede, S J MacRae, T S Spencer)* Suite 1, Park Farm Barn, Brabourne, ASHFORD, KENT, TN25 6RG.

ⒻⒶ**Neuhoff & Co** *(M E Neuhoff)* Claydons Barns, 11 Towcester Road, Whittlebury, TOWCESTER, NN12 8XU.

ⓉⓅⒶ**Nevill Hovey & Co Limited** *(T J Smith, H M Williams)* Southgate Close, LAUNCESTON, CORNWALL, PL15 9DU.

Nevill, Stormont & Co *(R A C Nevill)* 1155 A London Road, LEIGH-ON-SEA, ESSEX, SS9 3JE.

Neville & Co *(R P Neville)* 10-11Lynher Buildings, Queen Anne Battery, PLYMOUTH, PL4 0LP.

Neville A. Joseph *(N A Joseph)* Marlowe House, Hale Road, Wendover, AYLESBURY, HP22 6NE.

Ⓟ**Neville Levy & Co Limited** *(N Levy)* 26 Gables Avenue, BOREHAMWOOD, WD6 4SP.

Neville R. Bull *(N R Bull)* 32 Well Lane, Stock, INGATESTONE, CM4 9LZ.

Neville T. Stanton *(N T Stanton)* 3 Buckingham Road West, Heaton Moor, STOCKPORT, SK4 4AZ.

★**Neville Weston & Company** *(J L French)* 3 High Street, St. Lawrence, RAMSGATE, KENT, CT11 0QL.

Ⓐ**Newbery Chapman LLP** *(I H Gokmen)* Adam House, 14 New Burlington Street, LONDON, W1S 3BQ.

Newbound & Co. *(C P Newbound)* 578 St Mary's Road, WINNIPEG R2M 3L5, MB, CANADA.

★ⓉⒻⒶ**Newby Castleman** *(C J Castleman, M D Castleman, S D Castleman, D M Hastings)* West Walk Building, 110 Regent Road, LEICESTER, LE1 7LT. and at LOUGHBOROUGH

ⓉⒶ**Newby Crouch** *(P J C Crouch)* Ember House, 35-37 Creek Road, EAST MOLESEY, KT8 9BE.

Newfield & Co *(R Shaw)* 2 Broadwaters Drive, Hagley, STOURBRIDGE, DY9 0JU.

ⒻⒶ**Newman & Co** *(F T Chin, C Newman)* Regent House, 1 Pratt Mews, LONDON, NW1 0AD.

ⒻⓅⒶ**Newman & Co, trading name of Waveney Accountants Limited** *(L R Newman)* 4b Church Street, DISS, NORFOLK, IP22 4DD. and at BECCLES, LOWESTOFT

Newman Brown *(D A Newman)* Kinetic Centre, Theobald Street, BOREHAMWOOD, WD6 4BA.

Ⓟ**Newman James, trading name of Newman James Limited** *(Y C Newman)* 43 St. Francis Avenue, SOLIHULL, WEST MIDLANDS, B91 1EB.

★ⓉⒻⓅⒶ**Newman Morris, trading name of Newman Morris Ltd** *(C G Morris)* Wellington House, 273-275 High Street, London Colney, ST. ALBANS, HERTFORDSHIRE, AL2 1HA.

ⓉⒻⒶ**Newman Peters** *(Y M A Bulmer, R H Newman, R J Peters)* 19 Fitzroy Square, LONDON, W1T 6EQ.

Ⓟ**Newman Raphael Limited** *(F R Newman)* 3 Elderberry Court, 39b Bycullah Road, ENFIELD, MIDDLESEX, EN2 8FF.

Ⓟ**Newman Stevens, trading name of Newman Stevens Limited** *(Y C Newman)* 43 St. Francis Avenue, SOLIHULL, WEST MIDLANDS, B91 1EB.

★**Newmans** *(M V Pandya)* Jubilee House, Merrion Avenue, STANMORE, MIDDLESEX, HA7 4RY.

ⒻⒶ**Newnham & Co** *(E R Newnham)* 65 Morden Hill, LONDON, SE13 7NP.

Ⓟ**Newsham & Co, trading name of Newsham & Co Ltd** *(H Newsham)* 11 Allanhall Way, Kirk Ella, HULL, HU10 7QU.

Newsham Tax *(K Newsham)* 1 New Mills, Forest Road, LYDNEY, GL15 4ET.

★**Newsham, Hanson & Company** *(D R Hanson)* 1-5 Bellevue Road, CLEVEDON, AVON, BS21 7NP.

Newstone & Co. *(R E Newstone)* 2 Pepper Court, Great Chesterford, SAFFRON WALDEN, ESSEX, CB10 1NZ.

Newsum-Smith & Co *(A M Newsum-Smith)* 17 Burleigh Road, West Bridgford, NOTTINGHAM, NG2 6FP.

ⒻⒶ**Newton & Co.** *(D H Jennings)* Ranmore House, 19 Ranmore Road, DORKING, SURREY, RH4 1HE.

★ⓉⓅⒶ**Newton & Garner Limited** *(S J Poley, D L Watts)* Building 2, 30 Friern Park, North Finchley, LONDON, N12 9DA.

Ⓟ**Newton Green & Co, trading name of R J Lewin & Co Ltd** *(R J Lewin)* 17 Wyelands View, Mathern, CHEPSTOW, GWENT, NP16 6HN.

Ⓟ**Newton Magnus Ltd** *(S I Magnus, S J Wood)* Arrowsmith Court, Station Approach, BROADSTONE, BH18 8AT.

★**Nexia Charles Mar Fan & Co** *(S Mar, Y T T Wong)* 11/F Fortis Tower, 77-79 Gloucester Road, WAN CHAI, HONG KONG ISLAND, HONG KONG SAR.

★Ⓣ**Nexia Poyiadjis** *(I P Poyiadjis, S Poyiadjis, P S Prodromides)* 2 Sophouli St, Chanteclair House 8th Flr, P O Box 21814, 1513 NICOSIA, CYPRUS. and at LIMASSOL, LONDON

ⒻⓅⒶ**Nexia Smith & Williamson, trading name of Nexia Smith & Williamson Audit Limited** *(J C Appleton, M D Bishop, A D Bond, I T Burns, I S Cooper, C Deane, S D Drew, A J Edmonds, R D Green, K Jackman, Y J Lang, N Lee, G A S G Murphy, J A Mutton, M J Neale, S J Peskett, A J Pryor, P A Quigley, J R Selden, N S Simmonds, K L Smith, J M Talbot, P W Treadgold)* Nexia Smith & Williamson Audit Limited, 25 Moorgate, LONDON, EC2R 6AY. and at BELFAST, BIRMINGHAM, BRISTOL, DUBLIN, GLASGOW, GUILDFORD, SALISBURY, SOUTHAMPTON, WORCESTER

Ⓟ**Next Level Financial Management Ltd** *(Les Hodgson)* Willow House, 17 East Grange, SUNDERLAND, SR5 1NX.

Ⓟ**NFCA Limited** *(N F Appleby)* Brookside Farm, Forest Road, Burley, RINGWOOD, HAMPSHIRE, BH24 4DQ.

Ⓟ**NFW Accounting Services Limited** *(N F West)* 1 Bailey Close, Frimley, CAMBERLEY, SURREY, GU16 7EN.

Ng & Co *(K Ng)* 7 Lyndhurst Avenue, LONDON, NW7 2AD.

NG Accountancy Services *(S H Ng)* 36 Sutherland Place, WICKFORD, ESSEX, SS12 9HD.

Ng Fuk Yan Samuel *(F S Ng)* 2003 Wayson Commercial House, 68 Lockhart Road, WAN CHAI, HONG KONG ISLAND, HONG KONG SAR.

Ng, Ho & Partners *(P Y Ng)* No 4, Jalan 14-52, PETALING JAYA, Selangor, MALAYSIA.

Ng, Lee & Partners *(P Y Ng)* Suite Nos. A 23-1 & 2 23rd Floor, Menara UOA Bangsar, No.5 Jalan Bangsar Utama 1, 59000 KUALA LUMPUR, FEDERAL TERRITORY, MALAYSIA.

Ⓟ**Niall Murphy, trading name of NMTC Limited** *(N K D Murphy)* Five Acres, Prinsted Lane, Prinsted, EMSWORTH, HAMPSHIRE, PO10 8HS.

Ⓟ**Nichol Goodwill Brown Ltd** *(I G Brown, D Nichol)* 112 Whitley Road, WHITLEY BAY, TYNE AND WEAR, NE26 2NE. and at BLYTH

Nichola Hall ACA *(N L Hall)* 65 Oakwood Close, MIDHURST, WEST SUSSEX, GU29 9QP.

★ⒻⓅ**Nicholas & Walters Ltd** *(M A T Wilson)* 54-56 Victoria Street, Shirebrook, MANSFIELD, NOTTINGHAMSHIRE, NG20 8AQ.

Ⓟ**Nicholas Andrew & Co Limited** *(N A S Andrew)* 49 Berkeley Square, LONDON, W1J 5AZ.

ⓉⒻⓅⒶ**Nicholas Barwell & Co Ltd** *(N M Barwell)* Stirling House, Carriers Fold, Church Road, Wombourne, WOLVERHAMPTON, WV5 9DJ.

Nicholas Brooks BA FCA *(N Brooks)* 10 School Road, Elmswell, BURY ST. EDMUNDS, SUFFOLK, IP30 9EQ.

Nicholas C.E. Hayward *(N C E Hayward)* 5 Higher Actis, GLASTONBURY, SOMERSET, BA6 8DR.

ⒻⓅⒶ**Nicholas Cliffe & Co Limited** *(A N Cliffe)* Mill House, Mill Court, Great Shelford, CAMBRIDGE, CB22 5LD.

Nicholas Coates *(N R J Coates)* Fawley House, 4A Station Approach, Somersham, HUNTINGDON, CAMBRIDGESHIRE, PE28 3JD.

Nicholas D Morgan *(N D Morgan)* 5 Walnut Paddock, Harby, MELTON MOWBRAY, LEICESTERSHIRE, LE14 4BD.

Nicholas Filose *(N J Filose)* Greenmead, Waters Grn, BROCKENHURST, SO42 7RG.

Nicholas Ford Martin *(N F Martin)* 61 Temple Road, Kew, RICHMOND, SURREY, TW9 2EB.

Nicholas Gee & Co *(N Gee)* 6 Devonshire Close, AMERSHAM, BUCKINGHAMSHIRE, HP6 5JG.

Ⓐ**Nicholas Hadjinicolaou** *(N Hadjinicolaou)* 151 Longsight, Harwood, BOLTON, BL2 3JE.

Nicholas J. Grimes *(N J Grimes)* Spindrift, 39 Dunthorne Road, COLCHESTER, CO4 0HZ.

Nicholas Jenner & Co *(N Jenner)* PO Box 4001, Pangbourne, READING, RG8 7FN.

ⓉⒻⓅⒶ**Nicholas Ng and Company, trading name of Nicholas Ng and Company Ltd** *(C K Ng)* 201 Lordship Lane, LONDON, SE22 8HA.

★ⓉⒻⒶ**Nicholas Peters & Co** *(P Petrou)* 18-22 Wigmore Street, LONDON, W1U 2RG. and at BARNET

Nicholas Ridge, CTA *(N B Ridge)* Oakleaf, Ludwells Lane, Waltham Chase, SOUTHAMPTON, SO32 2NP.

Nicholas Taylor *(N R Taylor)* 57 Willows Road, BOURNE END, BUCKINGHAMSHIRE, SL8 5HG.

Nicholas Wells *(N R Wells)* 7 Fenbrook Close, Hambrook, BRISTOL, BS16 1QJ.

ⓉⓅⒶ**Nichols & Co (Accountancy) Ltd** *(S Nichols)* Unit 7, Mulberry Place, Pinnell Road, LONDON, SE9 6AR.

Nichols & Co, trading name of Nichols Financial LLP *(L M Nichols, S Nichols)* 7 Mulberry Place, Pinnell Road, Eltham, LONDON, SE9 6AR.

Nicholson & Co *(N A Nicholson)* Suite 21, 3 Ludgate Square, LONDON, EC4M 7AS.

Nicholson & Co. *(F B M Lai Cheong, J R Nicholson)* Monument House, 215 Marsh Road, PINNER, HA5 5NE.

★Ⓟ**Nicholson Blythe, trading name of Nicholson Blythe Limited** *(A J Stebbings)* Claremont House, 223 Branston Road, BURTON-ON-TRENT, STAFFORDSHIRE, DE14 3BT.

▽ⓉⒶ**Nicholsons** *(R Grayson, R J Hallsworth, S M Kerby, E L Murray)* Newland House, The Point, Weaver Road, LINCOLN, LN6 3QN. and at MARKET RASEN

ⒻⒶ**Nicholsons** *(P McKay)* Watermead House, 2 Codicote Road, WELWYN, AL6 9NB.

ⓅⒶ**Nick Brajkovich Limited** *(N Brajkovich)* 29 Withers Avenue, Orford, WARRINGTON, WA2 8EU.

Nick Cottrill *(N M Cottrill)* 73 Burley Lane, Quarndon, DERBY, DE22 5JR.

Nick Dillow, trading name of N.J. Dillow *(N J Dillow)* Vine Cottage, Hampton Hill, Swanmore, SOUTHAMPTON, SO32 2QN.

Nick Froud *(N E Froud)* 16 Shorewood Close, Warsash, SOUTHAMPTON, SO31 9LB.

Nick Gerzimbke *(N S R Gerzimbke)* 25 Woodside, ASHBY-DE-LA-ZOUCH, LEICESTERSHIRE, LE65 2NJ.

Ⓕ**Nick Hulme Corporate Finance** *(N A Hulme)* Atria, Spa Road, BOLTON, BL1 4AG.

Nick James *(N C James)* Yew Tree Cottage, Scot Lane, Chew Stoke, BRISTOL, BS40 8UW.

Nick Pritchard *(J N D Pritchard)* 1 Church Street, STOURBRIDGE, WEST MIDLANDS, DY8 1LT.

★ⒻⓅⒶ**Nickalls & Co Ltd** *(D G S Nickalls)* 4 Bridge Street, Amble, MORPETH, NORTHUMBERLAND, NE65 0DR.

Ⓟ**Nicklin Accountancy Services Limited** *(C R Cook, H J Owen)* Church Court, Stourbridge Road, HALESOWEN, WEST MIDLANDS, B63 3TT.

ⓉⒻⒶ**Nicklin LLP** *(C R Cook, H J Owen)* Church Court, Stourbridge Road, HALESOWEN, WEST MIDLANDS, B63 3TT.

Ⓟ**Nicklin Management Services Limited** *(C R Cook, H J Owen)* Church Court, Stourbridge Road, HALESOWEN, WEST MIDLANDS, B63 3TT.

Nicola A Birch *(N A Hill)* 91 Greaves Lane, Stannington, SHEFFIELD, S6 6BD.

Nicola Anderson FCA FCIE *(N J Anderson)* 189 Baldwins Lane, Croxley Green, RICKMANSWORTH, HERTFORDSHIRE, WD3 3LL.

Ⓟ**Nicola Bowker & Co Limited** *(N J Bowker)* Alexander Buildings, 37 New Road, Laxey, ISLE OF MAN, IM4 7BQ.

Ⓟ**Nicola Brookes, trading name of Nicola Brookes Limited** *(N D Brookes)* Mole End, Shorts Green Lane, Motcombe, SHAFTESBURY, DORSET, SP7 9PA.

Ⓟ**Nicola Fisher Financial Planning Limited** *(N J Fisher)* 2 Inchford Close, NUNEATON, WARWICKSHIRE, CV11 6UF.

Nicola Hopkinson *(N G Hopkinson)* 23 Leyborne Park, Kew, RICHMOND, SURREY, TW9 3HB.

Nicola J Russell *(N J Russell)* 27 Valley Road, RICKMANSWORTH, WD3 4DT.

Nicola Jones *(N Jones)* 30 Tamar Close, Whitefield, MANCHESTER, M45 8SJ.

Nicola Rhind -Tutt ACA MAAT *(N A Rhind-Tutt)* 9 Castle Mount, Tisbury, SALISBURY, WILTSHIRE, SP3 6PP.

Nicola Woodburn *(N J Woodburn)* 100 Station Road, Bannockburn, STIRLING, FK7 8JP.

Nicolaou & Co *(A Nicolaou)* 25 Heath Drive, POTTERS BAR, EN6 1EN.

Ⓟ**Nicolaou Dearle & Co, trading name of Nicolaou Dearle & Co (2005) Ltd** *(R J H Dearle)* 13 Highpoint Business Village, Henwood, ASHFORD, KENT, TN24 8DH.

Ⓐ**Nicolaou Dearle (Audit) LLP** *(R J H Dearle)* Unit 13, Highpoint Business Village, Henwood, ASHFORD, KENT, TN24 8DH.

Nicolas Gerra FCA MBA *(N J Gerra)* 6 Lambpark Court, Churchinford, TAUNTON, SOMERSET, TA3 7PL.

Nicolas Gollings & Co *(N A Gollings)* Haddon Cottage, Victoria Road, WEYBRIDGE, SURREY, KT13 9QH.

Ⓟ**Nicos A. Vassiliades & Sons Limited** *(A N Vassiliades)* PO Box 60112, 8100 PAPHOS, CYPRUS.

Nicos Voskarides *(N C Voskarides)* P O Box 25081, 1306 NICOSIA, CYPRUS.

ⓉⒺⒶ**Nielsens** *(S P Dubb, M R Mandalia, D U Shah)* 453 Cranbrook Road, ILFORD, ESSEX, IG2 6EW.

ⒺⓅ**Nigel Allison Ltd** *(N D Allison)* Bridge Farmhouse, Crowfield Road, Coddenham, IPSWICH, IP6 9PX.

Nigel Arnold & Co *(N W Arnold)* 18 Norfolk House, Courtlands Sheen Road, RICHMOND, TW10 5AT.

Nigel Beck Taxation Consultant *(N R Beck)* Ashfield, Rookery Lane, Broughton, STOCKBRIDGE, HAMPSHIRE, SO20 8AZ.

Ⓟ**Nigel Coyle & Co, trading name of Nigel Coyle & Co Limited** *(N E Coyle)* 25 Hall Walk, COTTINGHAM, NORTH HUMBERSIDE, HU16 4RL.

Nigel D. Sara *(N D Sara)* 12 Paulton Drive, Bishopston, BRISTOL, BS7 8JJ.

Nigel Edwards *(N D Edwards)* Cross Gate, Shute Hill, Bishopsteignton, TEIGNMOUTH, DEVON, TQ14 9QL.

Nigel Gorski Consulting *(N H Gorski)* 23 Hollinwood View, BINGLEY, WEST YORKSHIRE, BD16 2EF.

Nigel H Hart & Co *(N H Hart)* 99 Old Church Lane, STANMORE, MIDDLESEX, HA7 2RT.

Ⓔ**Nigel H. Gilroy & Co** *(N H Gilroy)* 6 Broomfield Road, SURBITON, KT5 9AZ.

Ⓟ**Nigel House ACA - AIMS Accountants for Business, trading name of Nigel House Limited** *(N M D House)* 1 Westminster Close, SHAFTESBURY, DORSET, SP7 9JY.

Ⓟ**Nigel K Wayne FCA, trading name of Nigel K Wayne & Co Limited** *(N K Wayne)* 15a East Street, OKEHAMPTON, DEVON, EX20 1AS.

Nigel M Hunt FCA *(N M Hunt)* 4 Millburgh Hall, Selham Road, Graffham, PETWORTH, WEST SUSSEX, GU28 0QH.

Nigel M Reese FCA *(N M Reese)* 48 Dalkeith Grove, STANMORE, HA7 4SF.

Nigel Price *(D N Price)* Highfield, Green Lane, Appledore, BIDEFORD, DEVON, EX39 1QZ.

ⒺⓅⒶ**Nigel Ricks & Company Limited** *(F N Ricks)* Rose Villa, 42 Glebe Street, LOUGHBOROUGH, LEICESTERSHIRE, LE11 1JR.

Ⓟ**Nigel Singleton, trading name of B D & M Limited** *(N J Singleton)* Skies, 20 St. Martinsfield, Martinstown, DORCHESTER, DORSET, DT2 9JU.

Nigel Smith *(N R Smith)* The Old Church, Shelton New Road, STOKE-ON-TRENT, ST4 6DP.

Ⓐ**Nigel Spence & Co** *(N A Spence)* Tan House, 15 South End, Bassingbourn, ROYSTON, HERTFORDSHIRE, SG8 5NJ.

Ⓟ**Nigel Watts Consultancy Limited** *(N A Watts)* Watch House, The Ridge, Winchelsea Beach, WINCHELSEA, EAST SUSSEX, TN36 4LU. and at HORSHAM

Nigel West & Co *(N R S West)* 18 Rother View, Burwash, ETCHINGHAM, TN19 7BN.

Ⓐ**Nigel Whittle** *(N J Whittle)* Parkside House, 167 Chorley New Road, BOLTON, BL1 4RA.

★Ⓐ**Nigel Wilson & Co** *(N K Wilson)* Third Floor, 111 Charterhouse Street, LONDON, EC1M 6AW.

ⓉⓅⒶ**Nigel Wordingham Ltd** *(N J Wordingham)* 5 Recorder Road, NORWICH, NR1 1NR.

Ⓔ**Nigel Wright Corporate Finance** *(N C C Wright)* 11 Danemere Street, LONDON, SW15 1LT.

ⓉⓅ**Nihonbo Ltd** *(J P A Snelling)* PO Box 497, Godalming, SURREY, GU8 5WB.

Nijhawan *(S Nijhawan)* The Old Queen Victoria, High Street, Rattlesden, BURY ST. EDMUNDS, SUFFOLK, IP30 0RA.

Ⓐ**Niren Blake LLP** *(C J Niren)* Brook Point, 1412 High Road, LONDON, N20 9BH.

Ⓟ**Nirius Consulting Limited** *(L T Heycock)* D5 Culham Science Centre, ABINGDON, OXFORDSHIRE, OX14 3DB.

Nixon D M *(D M Nixon)* 25 Castlegate, NEWARK, NG24 1AZ.

ⒺⓅⒶ**Nixon Mee, trading name of Nixon Mee Ltd** *(R S Mee)* Unit 9, Whitwick Business Centre, Stenson Road, COALVILLE, LEICESTERSHIRE, LE67 4JP.

Nizar Kanji & Co *(N T Kanji)* 18 The Fairway, NORTHWOOD, HA6 3DY.

NJB *(N Brand)* 40 Lawrence Avenue, WARE, HERTFORDSHIRE, SG12 8JL.

ⒺⒶ**NJHCO** *(N J Heeramaneck)* 8th Floor, Tolworth Tower, Ewell Road, SURBITON, KT6 7EL.

Ⓟ**NJJT, trading name of NJJT Limited** *(J A C Wood)* 95a Connaught Avenue, FRINTON-ON-SEA, ESSEX, CO13 9PS.

NMC *(J Ng Man Chuen)* Suite 306, St James Court, St Denis Street, PORT LOUIS, MAURITIUS.

Ⓟ**No Nonsense Limited** *(P J Grafton, P Lingham)* 7-8 Raleigh Walk, Waterfront 2000, Brigantine Place, CARDIFF, CF10 4LN.

Noble & Co *(G C Noble)* Abacus House, Mona Street, Douglas, ISLE OF MAN, IM1 3AE.

Ⓟ**Noble Accountancy Ltd** *(E J Noble)* 41 Guildford Road, West End, WOKING, SURREY, GU24 9PW.

Noble Accountancy Services *(R A Draper)* Unit 4, Denby Dale Industrial Park, Wakefield Road, Denby Dale, HUDDERSFIELD, HD8 8QH.

Ⓟ**Noble Pondus (CPA) Limited** *(S S Wong)* Room B 7/F, Man Hing Commercial Building, 79-83 Queen's Road Central, CENTRAL, HONG KONG ISLAND, HONG KONG SAR.

ⓅⒶ**Noble, trading name of Noble Accountants Ltd** *(L Noble)* Tarn Villa, Culgaith, PENRITH, CUMBRIA, CA10 1QL.

Ⓟ**Nobot Limited** *(B J E Morton)* 30 Woolpack Lane, The Lace Market, NOTTINGHAM, NG1 1GA.

ⓉⒺⒶ**Nockels Hornsey** *(J R Hornsey, A G Nockels)* 24 Bath Street, ABINGDON, OX14 3QH.

ⒺⒶ**Noel & Co.** *(A H Noel, L M Noel)* 4 Parliament Close, Prestwood, GREAT MISSENDEN, HP16 9DT.

Noel M. Periton *(N M Periton)* 14 Claremont Avenue, ESHER, KT10 9JD.

Noel Popplewell & Co *(N Popplewell)* 18 Vaughan Way, Connah's Quay, DEESIDE, CH5 4NG.

ⓅⒶ**Noel Williams Business Services Ltd** *(N Williams)* Cedar House, Hazell Drive, NEWPORT, GWENT, NP10 8FY.

★ⓉⓅⒶ**Nolan James, trading name of Nolan James Limited** *(R H James)* Suite 1, Armcon Business Park, London Road South, Poynton, STOCKPORT, CHESHIRE SK12 1LQ.

ⓅⒶ**Nolan Williams Ltd** *(N L Brown, M J Nolan)* Kintyre House, 70 High Street, FAREHAM, HAMPSHIRE, PO16 7BB.

Nomizon Associates *(J E Toppin)* The Old Rectory, Sutton Road, Langley, MAIDSTONE, KENT, ME17 3LY.

ⓉⒺⓅ**Nordens, trading name of Mark Norden & Co Limited** *(M Norden)* 158 Hermon Hill, South Woodford, LONDON, E18 1QH.

Noreen Todd FCA *(N Todd)* Wheal Betty, Trevenen Bal, HELSTON, CORNWALL, tr13 0pr.

Ⓟ**Norman C Sands Limited** *(N C Sands)* 333 Hagley Road, Pedmore, STOURBRIDGE, WEST MIDLANDS, DY9 0RF.

★ⒺⒶ**Norman Cox and Ashby** *(N M Gower-Smith)* Grosvenor Lodge, 72 Grosvenor Road, TUNBRIDGE WELLS, TN1 2AZ.

Norman Ewen & Co *(N E Ewen)* The Barn, Monument Offices, Maldon Road, Woodham Mortimer, MALDON, ESSEX CM9 6SN.

Ⓔ**Norman J. Wigley & Partners** *(M J Wigley)* Edgar House, 12 Birmingham Road, WALSALL, WS1 2NA.

Norman Oakey ACA *(N T Oakey)* Cwm Islwyn, Cwm y Gaist, Llanbister Road, LLANDRINDOD WELLS, POWYS, LD1 5UW.

Ⓟ**Norman R Evans & Co Limited** *(N R Evans)* 25-27 Station Street, Cheslyn Hay, WALSALL, WS6 7ED.

ⒺⒶ**Norman Stanley** *(N Schuman, R J Schuman)* Suite 1R10, Elstree Business Centre, Elstree Way, BOREHAMWOOD, HERTFORDSHIRE, WD6 1RX.

Norman T. Rea *(N T Rea)* 41 Plantation Rd, AMERSHAM, HP6 6HL.

Norman You *(J You)* 72 Rodney Street, LIVERPOOL, L1 9AF.

ⓉⒺⓅⒶ**Norrie Gibson & Co, trading name of Norrie Gibson & Co Ltd** *(A B Rowland)* Grosvenor House, 102 Beverley Road, HULL, HU3 1YA.

Norris Gilbert *(N Gilbert)* 143 Ivor Court, 209 Gloucester Place, LONDON, NW1 6BT.

Ⓐ**Norris-Small** *(L E Norris-Small)* 2 Camino Road, Harborne, BIRMINGHAM, B32 3XE.

Ⓟ**North & Co (Accounts & Tax) Limited** *(B E North)* Suite 3, The Old Stables, Hillhurst Farm, Westenhanger, HYTHE, KENT CT21 4HU.

ⓉⓅ**North London Accountancy Services, trading name of W Accountancy Limited** *(C R K Wheatley, M S Wood)* 369 Hertford Road, ENFIELD, MIDDLESEX, EN3 5JW. and at WOKING

Ⓟ**North Staffs Accountancy Services Ltd** *(D W T Birkin)* 153-155 High Street, Wolstanton, NEWCASTLE, STAFFORDSHIRE, ST5 0EJ.

ⒺⓅ**North West Accounting Services Ltd** *(E J Shew)* 46 Crank Road, Billinge, WIGAN, LANCASHIRE, WN5 7EZ.

North West Office Services *(A M McCartney)* Grove House, 27 Hawkin Street, LONDONDERRY, BT48 6RE.

Ⓔ**Northams** *(C H Gillard)* 21/23 New Street, HONITON, EX14 1HA.

Ⓟ**Northcliffe Accountancy Services Limited** *(B J Roberts)* 7-8 Raleigh Walk, Brigantine Place, CARDIFF, CF10 4LN.

Northcote, trading name of Stuart Phillips *(S Phillips)* 154 West End Avenue, HARROGATE, NORTH YORKSHIRE, HG2 9BT.

ⓉⒺⒶ**Northcott Trumfield** *(G I Northcott, D E Trumfield)* Devonshire Villa, 52 Stuart Road, Stoke, PLYMOUTH, PL3 4EE.

Ⓟ**Northern Alliance, trading name of Northern Alliance Limited** *(M Kelly)* 47 White Rose Lane, WOKING, GU22 7CB. and at LONDON

Ⓔ**Northfield Accountancy Services** *(M Snaith)* Unit 2, St Catherines Court, Sunderland Enterprise Park, SUNDERLAND, TYNE AND WEAR, SR5 3XJ.

Ⓟ**Northline Business Consultants Ltd** *(N P Hooper, S Tatlock)* 2nd Floor, Clarendon Centre, 38 Clarendon Road, Monton, Eccles, MANCHESTER M30 9ES.

ⓉⒺⓅ**Northover Bennett & Co Ltd** *(M A Northover)* 130 Bournemouth Road, Chandler's Ford, EASTLEIGH, HAMPSHIRE, SO53 3AL.

Northpoint Accountants *(S C Rawlinson)* 61a High Street, ALTON, HAMPSHIRE, GU34 1AB. and at POOLE

Ⓟ**Northwest Trust Company Limited** *(J M Cryer, P E Dearden, D A R Drewett, P A Seaward)* PO Box 16, Analyst House, Douglas, ISLE OF MAN, IM99 1AP.

★**Northwood Management Services** *(L F Magee)* 40 Kewferry Road, NORTHWOOD, HA6 2PB.

Ⓟ**Northwood Payroll Services Ltd** *(B W Harley)* Iveco House, Station Road, WATFORD, WD17 1TA.

Ⓟ**Northwood Registrars Ltd** *(R I Jacob, N G Lachman)* 136 Pinner Road, NORTHWOOD, MIDDLESEX, HA6 1BP.

ⒺⒶ**Norton Lewis & Co** *(G N Norton)* 246/248 Great Portland St, LONDON, W1W 5JL.

Nortons Group LLP *(P Doyle, A H Norton, C J Owens)* Highlands House, Basingstoke Road, Spencers Wood, READING, RG7 1NT.

Ⓟ**Nortons Recovery Limited** *(P Doyle, A H Norton)* Highlands House, Basingstoke Road, Spencers Wood, READING, RG7 1NT.

Note for Note, trading name of C.R. Turner & Co. *(C R Turner)* 15 Marroway, Weston Turville, AYLESBURY, HP22 5TQ.

ⒺⒶ**Nott & Co** *(P C Nott)* 24 Chase Road, Southgate, LONDON, N14 4EU.

Ⓟ**Nott & Co(Accountants) Ltd** *(P C Nott)* 24 Chase Road, Southgate, LONDON, N14 4EU.

ⓉⒺⓅⒶ**Notts Ltd** *(C G Nott)* 38 Rothesay Road, LUTON, LU1 1QZ.

Ⓟ**Novatax Limited** *(L R Thomson)* 50 Regent Street, RUGBY, WARWICKSHIRE, CV21 2PU.

Noviga Consulting *(M D Barker)* 28 Woodbine Road, Gosforth, NEWCASTLE UPON TYNE, NE3 1DD.

★ⓉⒺⓅⒶ**Novis & Co., trading name of Novis Howarth Limited** *(C M Howarth)* 1 Victoria Court, Bank Square, Morley, LEEDS, LS27 9SE.

Novis Business Servicess LLP *(C M Howarth)* 1 Victoria Court, Bank Square, Morley, LEEDS, LS27 9SE.

ⓅⒶ**Novitt Bamford Limited** *(B Novitt)* Pennyfarthing House, 560 Brighton Road, SOUTH CROYDON, SURREY, CR2 6AW. and at BARNET

Ⓟ**Novitt Harris & Co Limited** *(M S Novitt)* Unit H Ver House, London Road, Markyate, ST. ALBANS, HERTFORDSHIRE, AL3 8JP.

Ⓟ**Noy & Partners, trading name of Noy & Partners Accountants Ltd** *(D Bell)* 144 Nottingham Road, Eastwood, NOTTINGHAM, NG16 3GE.

ⒺⒶ**NR Pulver & Co** *(N R Pulver)* Rear Office, 1st Floor, 43-45 High Road, BUSHEY, WD23 1EE.

NRW *(N R Welch)* 1480a London Road, LEIGH-ON-SEA, ESSEX, SS9 2UR.

NSO Associates LLP *(E A Oddie)* 75 Springfield Road, CHELMSFORD, CM2 6JB.

Nsobiari George & Co *(O N George)* 12 Ijora Causeway, P.O. Box 8342, LAGOS, NIGERIA.

Ⓟ**Number Solutions Limited** *(T F Chizana)* Rolling Woods, Walpole Drive, Ramsey, ISLE OF MAN, IM8 1LX.

Ⓣ**Numera, trading name of Numera Partners LLP** *(C E Attle, G Cohen)* 6th Floor, Charles House, 108-110 Finchley Road, LONDON, NW3 5JJ.

ⓉⒺⒶ**Numerion Associates LLP** *(I I Aziz, S Aziz)* 2 London Wall Buildings, London Wall, LONDON, EC2M 5UU.

ⓉⓅⒶ**Numis Limited** *(T I Skittles, K Wells)* 1st Floor, Brook House, Mount Pleasant, CROWBOROUGH, EAST SUSSEX, TN6 2NE.

★ⓉⒺⒶ**Nunn Hayward** *(S Dodd, M D Duke, P S Hayward, J M Hemmings, I M Nunn, D J Palmer)* Sterling House, 20 Station Road, GERRARDS CROSS, SL9 8EL. and at NEW MALDEN

Nursen Karafistan *(N Karafistan)* Flat 3, Christchurch Place, Christ Church Mount, EPSOM, SURREY, KT19 8RS.

Ⓟ**Nutshell Accountants, trading name of Nutshell Accountants Limited** *(M Lonsdale)* 153 Cavendish Road, Clapham, LONDON, SW12 0BW.

ⓅⒶ**NW Accounts Audit Limited** *(N Warburton)* 40 Buxton Road West, Disley, STOCKPORT, CHESHIRE, SK12 2LY.

Ⓟ**NW Accounts Limited** *(N Warburton)* 40 Buxton Road West, Disley, STOCKPORT, SK12 2LY.

ⓅⒶ**NW Consultants Limited** *(N D Watson)* 55 Crown Street, BRENTWOOD, ESSEX, CM14 4BD.

ⒺⓅ**NWHI Limited** *(D G Kipling)* 194a Ferry Road, EDINBURGH, EH6 4NW.

Ⓟ**NWN Blue Squared Ltd** *(S Harris, E B Niman)* 7 Bourne Court, Southend Road, WOODFORD GREEN, ESSEX, IG8 8HD. and at ST. ALBANS

★**nyc** *(N Y Chundrigar)* 36 Birkbeck Road, LONDON, N12 8DZ.

★ⓉⒺⒶ**Nyman Libson Paul** *(P J Decker, K P Dias, J I Fraser, A S Katten, R Lloyd, D Morrison, J Newman, R J Paul, R S Paul, A D Pins, L E Pittal, J M Pope, I H Segal, A R Shah, P G Taiano)* Regina House, 124 Finchley Road, LONDON, NW3 5JS.

ⒺⒶ**Nyman Linden** *(M J Linden, M Marks, R Patel, A J Plaskow)* 105 Baker Street, LONDON, W1U 6NY.

ⓉⓅⒶ**NYO, trading name of NYO Limited** *(N Y Oztoprak)* Rowlandson House, 289-293 Ballards Lane, LONDON, N12 8NP.

O M Morgan & Co *(O M Morgan)* 153 Verulam Road, ST. ALBANS, AL3 4DN.

O. Evans-Jones *(O Evans-Jones)* Bod Marian, Glan Conwy, COLWYN BAY, LL28 5SY.

O. Lewis, trading name of O. Lewis & Co *(O Lewis)* Cefni Chambers, 10A High Street, LLANGEFNI, LL77 7LT.

O.A.Adefeso & Co *(O O Johnson)* Sennia House, 41a Joel Ogunnaike Street, GRA-Ikeja PO Box 2067, LAGOS, NIGERIA.

O.L. Yeo & Co *(O L Yeo)* 110 A & B, Jalan Melaka Raya 25, Taman Melaka Raya, 75000 MALACCA CITY, MALACCA STATE, MALAYSIA.

O.M. Holmes *(O M Holmes)* Holly Cottage, Main Road, Knockholt, SEVENOAKS, TN14 7LT.

Oak *(J S Aujla)* 4 Hampton Close, SUTTON COLDFIELD, WEST MIDLANDS, B73 6RQ.

Oak Tree *(C G Anderson, K J Anderson)* 6 Oak Tree Road, MARLOW, BUCKINGHAMSHIRE, SL7 3EE.

Oaken Accountancy Services *(D L Sadler)* Fairfields, Oaken Lane, Oaken, WOLVERHAMPTON, WV8 2BD.

Oakes & Co *(R J Oakes)* Bramble Hill Lodge, Main Street, Dry Doddington, NEWARK, NOTTINGHAMSHIRE, NG23 5HU.

Ⓟ**Oaklea Accounting Limited** *(P Spurden)* Oaklea, Cowards Lane, Codicote, HITCHIN, HERTFORDSHIRE, SG4 8UN.

Ⓟ**Oaks Financial Ltd** *(C J Vale)* Race Course Farm, Mary Lane, Bescaby, MELTON MOWBRAY, LEICESTERSHIRE, LE14 4AU.

Ⓟ**Oakwoods, trading name of Oakwoods Accountancy Limited** *(M T Jones)* 8 Morston Court, Kingswood Lakeside, CANNOCK, STAFFORDSHIRE, WS11 8JB.

Ⓟ**OASYS, trading name of Open Administration Systems Limited** *(D V Buxton)* Ampney House, Falcon Close, Quedgeley, GLOUCESTER, GL2 4LS.

★**Obiora Monu & Co.** *(A Ononye)* 19 Martins Street, P.O. Box 4130, LAGOS, NIGERIA.

Ⓐ**O'Brien & Co** *(S.W. O'Brien)* 31A Finkle Street, SELBY, YO8 4DT.

ⓉⒺⓅⒶ**O'Brien & Partners, trading name of The AOB Group Limited** *(D L Griffiths, L Van Emden)* 7a Nevill Street, ABERGAVENNY, GWENT, NP7 5AA. and at PONTYPRIDD

O'Byrne & Kennedy LLP *(P M Kennedy)* East Wing, Goffs Oak House, Goffs Lane, Goffs Oak, WALTHAM CROSS, HERTFORDSHIRE EN7 5BW.

Ⓟ**Occleston & Co Limited** *(D Occleston)* The Old Post Office, East Rounton, NORTHALLERTON, NORTH YORKSHIRE, DL6 2LF.

ⒺⓅ**Ocean Consultancy Ltd** *(D J Park)* Parliament Square, Parliament Street, CREDITON, DEVON, EX17 2AW.

Ⓔ**O'Connell & Co** *(S.P. O'Connell)* The Barn, 12a High Street, Wheathampstead, ST. ALBANS, AL4 8AA.

O'Connor & Co *(N G O'Connor)* 22 Kendals Close, RADLETT, HERTFORDSHIRE, WD7 8NQ.

ⓉⓅ**Octokhan, trading name of Octokhan Investment Services Ltd** *(F A Khan)* 60 Torrens Drive, CARDIFF, CF23 6DS. and at DHAKA

Oddpenny *(K L Wimpenny)* 3 Howbeck Road, PRENTON, MERSEYSIDE, CH43 6TD.

Odoom & Co *(R S Odoom)* 59 Upper Tollington Park, LONDON, N4 4DD.

Odyssey Accounting and Tax Services *(D Robinson)* 167 Ramsden Road, LONDON, SW12 8RF.

ⒺⓅ**Odyssey Corporate Finance, trading name of Odyssey Advisers Limited** *(M Y Michael)* Baskerville House, Centenary Square, BIRMINGHAM, B1 2ND.

Ⓐ**O'Farrell** *(W O'Farrell)* 1 Chaucer Drive, LONDON, SE1 5TA.

Ⓟ**Off The Square Limited** *(C I Owen)* Wheelwright Cottage, Cherington, SHIPSTON-ON-STOUR, CV36 5HS.

ⒺⓅⒶ**Ogilvie & Company, trading name of Ogilvie & Company Limited** *(D C N Ogilvie)* 25 Rutland Square, EDINBURGH, EH1 2BW.

Ogstons *(A Ogston)* 6 Norfolk Road, ST. IVES, CAMBRIDGESHIRE, PE27 3DP.

ⓉⒺⓅⒶ**O'Hara Wood, trading name of O'Hara Wood Limited** *(A W Wood)* 29 Gay Street, BATH, BA1 2NT. and at MELKSHAM

OJC Accountancy Services *(R L Owen-Jones)* 17 King Henrys Road, KINGSTON UPON THAMES, SURREY, KT1 3QA.

★**Ojike, Okechukwu & Co** *(Chief Ojike)* 5th Floor, 18 Oba Akran Avenue, Ikeja, GPO Box 2495, Marina, LAGOS 101221 NIGERIA.

Ⓟ**OJK (Audit) Limited** *(R J Shafto)* 19 Portland Place, LONDON, W1B 1PX.

Ⓟ**Old Mill Associates (BA) Ltd** *(P R Newbold)* 53 Old Mill Road, Broughton Astley, LEICESTER, LE9 6PQ.

Ⓐ**Old Mill Audit LLP** *(M J Butler, I J Carlson, G D C Eggleton, S J Grimster, J H Jackson, D J Maslen, A D Moore, P Neate, D C Perks, I M Sharpe, J R G Stonehouse, P G Treby)* The Old Mill, Park Road, SHEPTON MALLET, SOMERSET, BA4 5BS. and at DORCHESTER, EXETER, YEOVIL

ⓉⒺ**Old Mill, trading name of Old Mill Accountancy LLP** *(M J Butler, I J Carlson, G D C Eggleton, S J Grimster, J H Jackson, A D Moore, P Neate, D C Perks, I M Sharpe, J R G Stonehouse, P G Treby)* The Old Mill, Park Road, SHEPTON MALLET, SOMERSET, BA4 5BS. and at DORCHESTER, EXETER, MELKSHAM, YEOVIL

Oldfield & Co *(A G Oldfield)* 2A Hutcliffe Wood Road, SHEFFIELD, S8 0EX.

ⒺⒶ**Oliver & Co** *(S J Oliver)* 259 Otley Road, West Park, LEEDS, LS16 5LQ.

Oliver Plummer & Co *(O J Plummer)* 9 Seagrave Road, LONDON, SW6 1RP.

★**Oliver Wong & Co.** *(S K O Wong)* 12/F Goodfit Commercial Building, 7 Fleming Road, WAN CHAI, HONG KONG SAR.

Ⓟ**Olivine, trading name of Olivine Capital Partners Ltd** *(S R Cumberland)* 1 Grosvenor Crescent, LONDON, SW1X 7EF.

ⒺⓅⒶ**Ollis & Co, trading name of The Ollis Partnership Limited** *(J A Davies, D L Page, W R Preston, I Randle, R M Smith)* 2 Hamilton Terrace, Holly Walk, LEAMINGTON SPA, WARWICKSHIRE, CV32 4LY.

Olukayode Akindele & Co *(Chief Akindele)* 208/212 Broad Street, P.O. Box 70828, LAGOS, NIGERIA.

★**Oluseye Johnson & Co** *(O O Johnson)* 16 Modupe Johnson Crecent, Surulere P.O. Box 6206, LAGOS, NIGERIA.

★**Olusola Aigbe & Co** *(F O Aigbe)* 21 Fagbile Street, Surulere, PO Box 432 Yaba, LAGOS, NIGERIA.

Ⓟ**OMB Accountants, trading name of OMB Accountants Ltd** *(C R Gray)* Holmwood Farm, Horsham Road, North Holmwood, DORKING, SURREY, RH5 4JR.

★**OmniLogic Systems Group, trading name of PricewaterhouseCoopers** *(R M Bosshard, P Challinor, P J Feetham)* 95 King Street South, Suite 201, WATERLOO N2J 5A2, ON, CANADA. and at CALGARY, CHARLOTTETOWN, EDMONTON, HALIFAX, HAMILTON, MISSISSAUGA, MONTREAL, NORTH YORK, OTTAWA, REGINA, RICHMOND, SAINT JOHN, SASKATOON, ST JOHN'S, TORONTO, TRURO, VANCOUVER, WINDSOR, WINNIPEG

Ⓟ**On the spot, trading name of Alison Morrison Limited** *(A T Morrison)* Austens, Chestnut Walk, Tangmere, CHICHESTER, WEST SUSSEX, PO20 2HH.

Ⓟ**On The Spot, trading name of On The Spot Tax Limited** *(P J Tomlinson)* 3 Springfield Close, Bolney, HAYWARDS HEATH, WEST SUSSEX, RH17 5PQ.

★Ⓟ**On Time Payroll, The Tax & Accountancy Practice, trading names of Underwood Barron Associates Limited** *(C S Baker, N R B Barron, C Lewis, A J McDougal)* Monks Brook House, 13-17 Hursley Road, Chandler's Ford, EASTLEIGH, HAMPSHIRE, SO53 2FW. and at LYMINGTON

Ⓟ**One 2 One Accountants Ltd** *(M J Richards)* The School House, 108 Bedminster Down Road, BRISTOL, BS13 7AF.

Ⓟ**One 4 Tax and Accounts Ltd** *(H Hupje)* 20 Woodmere Avenue, WATFORD, WD24 7LN.

Ⓟ**One Company Formation Ltd** *(H Hupje)* 20 Woodmere Avenue, WATFORD, WD24 7LN.

Ⓟ**One Stop Business Advisers Limited** *(D J Oates)* Suite 59, 42 St Johns Road, SCARBOROUGH, NORTH YORKSHIRE, YO12 5ET.

Ⓟ**One Zone Tax Solutions, trading name of One Zone Tax Solutions Ltd** *(J C Middleton)* 5 Chelsea Close, Biddulph, STOKE-ON-TRENT, ST8 6UA.

Ong Boon Bah & Co *(K B Lim)* B10-1 Megan Phileo Promenade, 189 Jalan Tun Razak, 50400 KUALA LUMPUR, FEDERAL TERRITORY, MALAYSIA.

Ⓟ**On-Line Accountants Ltd** *(J W Walsh)* Albion House, 163-167 King Street, DUKINFIELD, CHESHIRE, SK16 4LF.

Ⓟ**Online Financial & Accountancy Ltd** *(R G B Duthie)* 71 Bexley High Street, BEXLEY, DA5 1AA.

Ⓟ**Online Tax Returns Limited** *(A Doggett)* 5 Crossborough Gardens, BASINGSTOKE, HAMPSHIRE, RG21 4LB.

ⒺⓅⒶ**Oppenheim and Company Limited** *(B H Oppenheim)* 52 Great Eastern Street, LONDON, EC2A 3EP.

ⒺⓅ**Oppenheim Scroxton Limited** *(J M Scroxton)* 52 Great Eastern Street, LONDON, EC2A 3EP.

Ⓐ**Oppenheims** *(N S Oppenheim)* PO Box 3578, MAIDENHEAD, BERKSHIRE, SL6 3WH.

Ⓟ**Oppenheims Accountancy Limited** *(M J M Oppenheim)* PO Box 2385, MAIDENHEAD, BERKSHIRE, SL6 7WQ.

Ⓟ**Optima Corporate Finance LLP** *(P D Ellis, G M Kaye)* 32 Bedford Row, LONDON, WC1R 4HE.

ⓉⓅⒶ**Optima Financial Solutions, trading name of Optima Financial Solutions Limited** *(K H Bexley)* Elms Farm, Upper Minety, MALMESBURY, WILTSHIRE, SN16 9PR. and at SWINDON

ⒺⓅ**Opus Health Capital Limited** *(G M Kaye)* Ground Floor, 17 Red Lion Square, LONDON, WC1R 4QH.

Ⓟ**Opus, trading name of Opus Services Limited** *(J B Halstead)* The Laurels, 2 St Leonards Road, HARROGATE, NORTH YORKSHIRE, HG2 8NX.

Ⓔ**Orbis Partners LLP** *(G D Ecob, C Gregory, S Zaki)* Third Floor, 35 Newhall Street, BIRMINGHAM, B3 3PU.

Orco Services *(Thomas Peter Spencer-Smith)* The Old Rectory, Llanvetherine, ABERGAVENNY, GWENT, NP7 8RG.

ⓉⒺⒶ**O'Reilly** *(A Little, G Ritzema)* Ullswater House, Duke Street, PENRITH, CUMBRIA, CA11 7LY. and at HAWES, KIRKBY STEPHEN, LEYBURN

Ⓟ**Oriel Accounting, trading name of Oriel Accounting Ltd** *(B P Pursey)* Cheltenham House, Clarence Street, CHELTENHAM, GLOUCESTERSHIRE, GL50 3JR.

Ⓟ**Oriental Link CPA Limited** *(S T Ho)* Suites 1303 - 1306A, 13/F, Asian House, 1 Hennessy Road, WAN CHAI, HONG KONG SAR.

Ⓟ**Orion Accountancy Limited** *(A J Pickard, C M Pickard)* 30 Garners Road, Chalfont St. Peter, GERRARDS CROSS, BUCKINGHAMSHIRE, SL9 0EZ.

Orion Network Consultants LLP *(N D Pilbrow)* 12 Wootton Rivers, MARLBOROUGH, WILTSHIRE, SN8 4NH. and at LONDON

Ⓟ**Ormerod Rutter Solutions Ltd** *(C A McGrory)* The Oakley, Kidderminster Road, DROITWICH, WORCESTERSHIRE, WR9 9AY.

ⓉⒺⓅⒶ**Ormerod Rutter, trading name of Ormerod Rutter Limited** *(C A McGrory, N Ormerod, G T Rutter)* The Oakley, Kidderminster Road, DROITWICH, WORCESTERSHIRE, WR9 9AY.

ⓉⓅ**Orwin Oliver, trading name of Orwin Oliver Ltd** *(N W Bell, A Orwin)* 24 King Street, ULVERSTON, CUMBRIA, LA12 7DZ.

ⓅⒶ**Osbornes Accountants Limited** *(P J Osborne)* 20 Market Place, KINGSTON UPON THAMES, SURREY, KT1 1JP.

Oscar Ip & Co *(O K H Ip)* 42 General Drive, LIVERPOOL, L12 4ZB.

ⒺⒶ**O'Shea & Owen** *(M Owen)* 5 Willow Walk, COWBRIDGE, CF71 7EE.

Ⓟ**Osiris Management Services Limited** *(D J Hopkins, B M Le Claire)* PO Box 437, 13 Castle Street, St Helier, JERSEY, JE4 0ZE.

Ⓟ**Ottoline Ferdinand, trading name of Ottoline Ferdinand Ltd** *(E L Holmes)* 38A Thompson Road, East Dulwich, LONDON, SE22 9JR.

ⓉⒶ**Oury Clark** *(I Friend, E H Green, S E Harris, E Johnson, R M Lockwood, A C Oury, J E Oury, R A Oury, I Phipps, D A Smith, D G Taylor Rea, H J Williams)* PO Box 150, Herschel House, 58 Herschel Street, SLOUGH, SL1 1HD.

Ouston, Sidders & Co. *(M C G Ouston)* 9 Aplins Close, HARPENDEN, HERTFORDSHIRE, AL5 2PZ.

ⓅⒶ**Outre-Manche Expertise Limited** *(B P R Nedelec)* 17 Trinity House, Station Road, BOREHAMWOOD, HERTFORDSHIRE, WD6 1DA.

Ⓟ**Outsourced Accountancy Services Ltd** *(N P Yardley)* Flat 11, Randolph Court, 11 The Avenue, Hatch End, PINNER, MIDDLESEX HA5 4HQ.

Ⓟ**Outsourced Accounts Department Ltd** *(D Halpern)* 32 Winders Way, SALFORD, M6 6AR.

Ⓟ**Outsourced Bookeeping Solutions, trading name of Berley Accountants Limited** *(J H Berman, M Levy)* 76 New Cavendish Street, LONDON, W1G 9TB.

Ow Fook Sheng & Co *(F S Ow)* 76 Tanjong Pagar Road, SINGAPORE 088497, SINGAPORE.

★ⒺⒶ**Owain Bebb a'i Gwmni** *(A E Evans, R R Harris)* 32 Y Maes, CAERNARFON, GWYNEDD, LL55 2NN. and at PWLLHELI

Owen & Co *(A G Owen)* 41 Ashley Terrace, EDINBURGH, EH11 1RY.

Owen A. Parry & Co *(O A Parry)* 14 Tavistock Road, Sketty, SWANSEA, SA2 0SL.

Owen Accountancy *(M A Owen)* April Cottage, Poundfield Lane, Cookham, MAIDENHEAD, BERKSHIRE, SL6 9RY.

Ⓟ**Owen Business Solutions Limited** *(G Owen)* 1 Cobham Close, ENFIELD, MIDDLESEX, EN1 3SD.

ⓅⒶ**Owen John & Co Ltd** *(R I Bevan-Jones)* Mardy Chambers, 6 Wind Street, SWANSEA, SA1 1DH.

Ⓐ**Owers & Co** *(D J Owers)* Round Maples, Edwardstone, SUDBURY, SUFFOLK, CO10 5PR.

Ⓟ**Oxford Accountant Ltd** *(A J Walton)* March Cottage, The Green, Great Milton, OXFORD, OX44 7NS.

Ⓟ**Oxford Book-Keepers Limited** *(R D Potts)* 6 Jacobs Yard, Middle Barton, CHIPPING NORTON, OXFORDSHIRE, OX7 7BY.

ⒺⓅⒶ**Oxlade Limited** *(J A Oxlade, M J Plastow)* The Old Bakehouse, Holton, OXFORD, OX33 1PZ.

ⓅⒶ**Oxley & Co, trading name of Oxley Accountants & Business Advisors Limited** *(G W Oxley, S S Whyte)* 17 Manor Road, EAST MOLESEY, SURREY, KT8 9JU.

Ⓟ**Oxley Accountants Limited** *(L T Oxley)* Top Floor, The Greyhound Building, 17 Moor Street, CHEPSTOW, GWENT, NP16 5DB.

Ⓟ**P A Cook & Co (Oxford) Ltd** *(P A Cook)* Crown House, London Road, Loudwater, HIGH WYCOMBE, BUCKINGHAMSHIRE, HP10 9TJ.

ⓉⒺⒶ**P A Hull & Co** *(C M Hothersall, M T Hothersall, G A Hull, C H Jady)* 41 Bridgeman Terrace, WIGAN, LANCASHIRE, WN1 1TT. and at BOLTON, NEWTON-LE-WILLOWS

Ⓟ**P A Hutchinson & Co, trading name of P A Hutchinson & Co Ltd** *(P A Hutchinson)* Old Courts Road, BRIGG, LINCOLNSHIRE, DN20 8JD.

P A Ryan MA(Ed) FCA DChA *(P A Ryan)* 66 Fountain Road, LONDON, SW17 0HQ.

Ⓐ**P and Co, trading name of P and Co LLP** *(S Pitayanukul)* Unit 13, 2 Artichoke Hill, LONDON, E1W 2DE. and at LEEDS, MANCHESTER

Ⓟ**P B Support Services Limited** *(L Y Statham)* Cliveden Chambers, Cliveden Place, STOKE-ON-TRENT, ST3 4JB.

P Clarke FCA *(P Clarke)* 48 Dorothy Avenue, Glen Parva, LEICESTER, LE2 9JD.

P D Eaton & Co *(P D Eaton)* 32 Main Street, Lambley, NOTTINGHAM, NG4 4PN.

ⓅⒶ**P E Garside Limited** *(P E Garside)* Deeks Evans, 3 Boyne Park, TUNBRIDGE WELLS, KENT, TN4 8EN. and at HASTINGS

ⓅⒶ**P E M Cowdy Limited** *(P E M Cowdy)* Whittingham Riddell LLP, Belmont House, Shrewsbury Business Park, SHREWSBURY, SY2 6LG.

Ⓟ**P G & S A Watson Ltd** *(P G Watson)* Denstone, 6 Park Road, Chandlers Ford, EASTLEIGH, SO53 2EU.

P G Dyer *(P G Dyer)* 133 Bramcote Avenue, Chilwell, NOTTINGHAM, NG9 4EY.

P G. Patel & Co *(P G Patel)* 48 Clarendon Gardens, WEMBLEY, HA9 7QN.

Ⓟ**P H Crook FCA, trading name of Bradavon Financial Services Limited** *(P H Crook)* Bradavon, 45 The Dales, COTTINGHAM, HU16 5JS.

P H Tang & Co *(P Tang)* 3rd Floor, Rammon House, 101 Sai Yeung Choi Street South, MONG KOK, KOWLOON, HONG KONG SAR.

P Hadjimichael *(P M Hadjimichael)* Office 5, 44 Hakket, 6045 LARNACA, CYPRUS.

P Haywood *(P Haywood)* 61 Moxon Way, Manor Park, Ashton-in-Makerfield, WIGAN, WN4 8SW.

ⓅⒶ**P Hinchliffe Limited** *(P Hinchliffe)* 1 The Villas, Blackergreen Lane, Silkstone, BARNSLEY, SOUTH YORKSHIRE, S75 4NF.

Ⓟ**P J Beedham & Co, trading name of P J Beedham Limited** *(P J G Beedham)* Graffix House, Newtown Road, HENLEY-ON-THAMES, OXFORDSHIRE, RG9 1HG.

P J Finnegan *(P J Finnegan)* 10 Rutland Drive, Mickleover, DERBY, DE3 9FW.

Ⓟ**P J Greenacre & Co Limited** *(P J Greenacre)* The Old Bakery, Tiptoe Road, Wootton, NEW MILTON, BH25 5SJ.

Ⓟ**P J Hamson & Co Limited** *(P J Hamson, D Spooner)* 99 Wilsthorpe Road, Long Eaton, NOTTINGHAM, NG10 3LE.

Ⓟ**P Jackson Ltd** *(P Jackson)* Avtech House, Bird Hall Lane, Cheadle Heath, STOCKPORT, SK3 0XX.

Ⓟ**P K Hardy Ltd** *(P K Hardy)* 12 Shropshire Close, MIDDLEWICH, CW10 9ES.

Ⓟ**P Leiwy & Co Ltd** *(P Leiwy)* 74 Salisbury Road, HARROW, HA1 1NZ.

ⓅⒶ**P M Brown & Company, trading name of P M Brown & Company Limited** *(P M Brown)* 37 Haighton Drive, Fulwood, PRESTON, PR2 9LU.

P M Stafford *(P M Stafford)* 22 Foyle Street, SUNDERLAND, SR1 1LE.

Ⓟ**P P Evans Limited** *(P P Evans)* 125 Woodside Road, AMERSHAM, BUCKINGHAMSHIRE, HP6 6AW.

Ⓟ**P Polyviou & Partners Limited** *(P Polyviou)* Proteas House, 155 Arch. Makarios III Avenue, Office 202, 3026 LIMASSOL, CYPRUS.

Ⓟ**P R Bateman Financial Management Ltd** *(P R Bateman)* 9 Pembroke Close, CHESTER, CH4 7BS.

ⒺⓅⒶ**P R Hornsby & Company, trading name of P R Hornsby & Company Limited** *(T J Croft, Mandy Wilson)* 5 Yeomans Court, Ware Road, HERTFORD, SG13 7HJ.

Ⓐ**P R Patel & Co** *(P R Patel)* 2 Admiral House, Cardinal Way, HARROW, MIDDLESEX, HA3 5TE.

P R Wilby *(P R Wilby)* 13 Alan Drive, BARNET, EN5 2PP.

P Rethinasamy & Co *(P Rethinasamy)* Kompleks Skomk, Block A 2nd Floor, Jalan Mahkamah, PO Box 117, 36008 DR TELUK INTAN, PERAK MALAYSIA.

Ⓟ**P Ross & Co Ltd** *(P Ross)* 18 Woodcock Dell Avenue, Kenton, HARROW, MIDDLESEX, HA3 0NS.

P S Accounting *(P M Spragg)* 41 Sycamore Drive, Hollywood, BIRMINGHAM, B47 5QX.

ⒺⓅⒶ**P T Davies & Co Limited** *(P T Davies)* Hazeldene Lodge, Thame Road, Longwick, PRINCES RISBOROUGH, BUCKINGHAMSHIRE, HP27 9SW. and at GERRARDS CROSS

ⓉⓅ**P W Accountants Ltd** *(P E Whitmell)* 82b High Street, Sawston, CAMBRIDGE, CB22 3HJ.

P W Osborne & Co *(P W Osborne)* 29 Westbridge Road, Trewoon, ST AUSTELL, CORNWALL, PL25 5TF.

★**P&A Associates** *(P B Stapleton)* 30 Offham Slope, Woodside Park, LONDON, N12 7BZ.

P. Bradford *(P A Bradford)* Abbey Cottage, Kings Road, MALVERN, WR14 4HL.

P. C. Chiu & Co *(P Chiu)* Room 1303, Cameron Commercial Centre, 458-468 Hennessy Road, CAUSEWAY BAY, HONG KONG SAR.

Ⓐ**P. C. Daruwalla & Co** *(P C Daruwalla)* 4 Raisins Hill, PINNER, HA5 2BS.

Ⓟ**P. D. Hughes Consultancy Services Ltd** *(P D Hughes)* 11 Sails Drive, Heslington, YORK, YO10 3LR.

Ⓐ**P. David Levinson** *(P D Levinson)* 20 Moor End Avenue, SALFORD, M7 3NX.

P. Furmston & Co *(P Willis)* Longburgh Farmhouse, Burgh by Sands, CARLISLE, CA5 6AF.

P. Greensmith & Co *(P Greensmith)* 35 Pinecrest Drive, Thornhill, CARDIFF, CF14 9DS.

P. Haley & Co *(P Haley)* Poverty Hall, Lower Ellistones, Greetland, HALIFAX, HX4 8NG.

P. Patel *(P G Patel)* 71 Park Road, Great Sankey, WARRINGTON, WA5 3EA.

★Ⓐ**P. Willson & Co** *(T D Kirk)* Carlton House, High Street, Higham Ferrers, RUSHDEN, NN10 8BW.

P.A. Brown *(P A Brown)* 52 Northbrook Road, Shirley, SOLIHULL, B90 3NP.

Ⓕ**P.A. Cook And Co** *(P A Cook)* Crown House, London Road, Loudwater, HIGH WYCOMBE, HP10 9TJ.

P.A. Field & Co *(P M A Field)* Hare Knap, Lewes Road, Ditchling, HASSOCKS, WEST SUSSEX, BN6 8TY.

P.A. Goulden *(P A Goulden)* Beechings, Water Street, Hampstead Norreys, THATCHAM, RG18 0SB.

P.A. Kershaw *(P A Kershaw)* Meadowbank, Willington Road, Willington, TARPORLEY, CW6 0ND.

P.A. Thomas *(P A Thomas)* 6 Poole Road, WIMBORNE, DORSET, BH21 1QE.

P.A. Walford *(P A Walford)* Bannatyne Cottage, BANNATYNE, CHRIST CHURCH, BARBADOS.

Ⓟ**P.A.N. Grimley, trading name of P.A.N. Grimley Ltd** *(P A N Grimley)* Hillcrest, Lawrenny Road, Cresselly, KILGETTY, DYFED, SA68 0TB.

P.A.P. Leach *(P A P Leach)* 14 Manilla Rd, Clifton, BRISTOL, BS8 4ED.

P.B. Reast *(P B Reast)* 78 Cedar Road, Mickleton, CHIPPING CAMPDEN, GLOUCESTERSHIRE, GL55 6SZ.

ⓉⒻⒶ**P.B. Syddall & Co** *(N W Polding, J Ridings, P B Syddall)* Grafton House, 81 Chorley Old Road, BOLTON, BL1 3AJ.

P.C Marks & Co *(P C Marks)* 10 Carlton Close, West Heath Road, LONDON, NW3 7UA.

P.C. Roberts & Co *(P C Roberts)* P.O.Box 561, PMB 6803 International, Commercial Central, GIBRALTAR, GIBRALTAR.

P.D. Root *(P D Root)* 95 Jumpers Road, CHRISTCHURCH, BH23 2JS.

P.E. Shirley LLP *(P E Shirley)* 24 Lime Street, LONDON, EC3M 7HS.

P.F.Hope *(P F Hope)* 17 Agatha Gardens, Fernhill Heath, WORCESTER, WR3 8PB.

ⒻⒶ**P.G. Fry & Co** *(P G Fry)* Hatherley House, Bisley Green, Bisley, WOKING, GU24 9EW.

Ⓕ**P.G. Thompson & Co** *(P G Thompson)* 239B High Street, ALDERSHOT, HAMPSHIRE, GU11 1TJ.

P.G.Jeffery *(P G Jeffery)* 84 Townside, Haddenham, AYLESBURY, BUCKINGHAMSHIRE, HP17 8AW.

ⓅⒶ**P.H. Michell & Co Ltd** *(P H Michell)* Providence Cottage, Bracken Lane, Storrington, PULBOROUGH, WEST SUSSEX, RH20 3HS.

Ⓐ**P.H. Ross and Co** *(P Ross)* 18 Woodcock Dell Avenue, Kenton, HARROW, HA3 0NS.

P.H.J. Brunton & Co *(P H J Brunton)* 14 The Brackens, Locks Heath, SOUTHAMPTON, SO31 6TU.

P.H.Lam & Company *(P H Lam)* Room 1602, Tung Hip Commercial Building, 244-252 Des Voeux Road, CENTRAL, HONG KONG ISLAND, HONG KONG SAR.

P.J Fray *(P J Fray)* Keepers Cottage, Upton Bishop, ROSS-ON-WYE, HR9 7UE.

P.J. Davis *(P J Davis)* 2 Essenden Court, Stony Stratford, MILTON KEYNES, MK11 1NW.

P.J. Dickerson *(P J Dickerson)* 133 Marlborough Crescent, Riverhead, SEVENOAKS, TN13 2HN.

P.J. Doyle & Co. *(P J Doyle)* 45 Heather Drive, Rednal, BIRMINGHAM, B45 9RA.

P.J. Field *(P J Field)* Monkey Lodge, Skirmett Road, Hambleden, HENLEY-ON-THAMES, RG9 6SX.

P.J. Hewitt & Co *(P J Hewitt)* Crown House, High Road, LOUGHTON, ESSEX, IG10 4LG.

Ⓐ**P.J. Higgins & Co** *(P J Higgins)* 2 Cuchulainn Place, COBH, COUNTY CORK, IRELAND.

P.J. Kir-on *(P J Kir-On)* 3 Shatner Centre, 95461 JERUSALEM, ISRAEL.

P.J. Lindsay *(P J Lindsay)* 13 Beech Rd, REIGATE, RH2 9LS.

P.J. Narramore *(P J Narramore)* 3 Williams Way, Higham Ferrers, RUSHDEN, NN10 8AJ.

P.J. Reed *(P J Reed)* 20a Pantbach Road, Birchgrove, CARDIFF, CF14 1UA.

Ⓐ**P.J. Seal** *(P J Seal)* 5 Beechbank Drive, Thorpe End Gardens, Gt Plumstead, NORWICH, NR13 5BW.

P.J.I. Lowther *(P J I Lowther)* 15 Duncan Road, RICHMOND, TW9 2JD.

P.J.Spicer *(P J Spicer)* 43 Turners Hill, Cheshunt, WALTHAM CROSS, EN8 8NJ.

P.J.Williams & Co, trading name of P.J.Williams *(P J Williams)* 45 Baginton Road, Styvechale, COVENTRY, CV3 6JX.

Ⓕ**P.K. Mankelow & Co** *(P K Mankelow)* P.O.Box 45, CRAWLEY, RH10 3YP.

P.K. Wong & Co *(P K I Wong)* Unit 909 Tower 1, Silvercod, 30 Canton Road, TSIM SHA TSUI, KOWLOON, HONG KONG SAR.

P.L. Tan *(P L Tan)* 80 Druid Stoke Avenue, Stoke Bishop, BRISTOL, BS9 1DQ.

P.L. Wood *(P L Wood)* 20 Lonsdale Meadows, Boston Spa, WETHERBY, LS23 6DQ.

P.L.T. Maw & Co. *(P L T Maw)* 192 Harestone Valley Road, CATERHAM, CR3 6BT.

Ⓟ**P.Lavery & Company Limited** *(P J Lavery)* 64 Grosvenor Road, Muswell Hill, LONDON, N10 2DS.

ⓉⒶ**P.M. Humphreys & Co** *(P M Humphreys)* 82a Whitchurch Road, CARDIFF, CF14 3LX.

ⓉⒶ**P.M. Randall & Co** *(P M Randall)* PO Box 131, Harold Hill, ROMFORD, ESSEX, RM3 9LZ.

P.O'N. Carden *(P O Carden)* 1st Floor (Rear Suite), 56-58 High Street, Ewell, EPSOM, KT17 1RW.

ⓉⒻⒶ**P.P.S.** *(P A Papworth-Smith, I Willoughby)* 29 Devizes Road, SWINDON, SN1 4BG.

P.R Bateman *(P R Bateman)* 9 Pembroke Close, CHESTER, CH4 7BS.

P.R. Moss *(P R Moss)* 12 Hawkshaw Bank Road, BLACKBURN, BB1 8JS.

P.R. Stratton *(P R Stratton)* 2 Butlers Yard, 7 Main Road, EMSWORTH, PO10 8AP.

P.R. Whittaker *(P R Whittaker)* 49 Woodfield Road, Cheadle Hulme, CHEADLE, CHESHIRE, SK8 7JT.

Ⓐ**P.R. Willans & Co** *(P R Willans)* 21 The Fairway, BROMLEY, BR1 2JZ.

P.R.A Palfreyman *(P R A Palfreyman)* 83 Nottingham Road, Codnor, RIPLEY, DE5 9RH.

ⒻⒶ**P.R.Hartley** *(P R Hartley)* PO Box 27075, LONDON, N2 0FZ.

P.S. Loe & Co. *(P S Loe)* Edgecombe, Amberley, STROUD, GLOUCESTERSHIRE, GL5 5AB.

P.S. Moon and Company *(P S Moon)* 22 The Piece, Churchdown, GLOUCESTER, GL3 2EX.

ⓉⒶ**P.S. Nagarajah** *(P S Nagarajah)* 64 Oakington Avenue, WEMBLEY, MIDDLESEX, HA9 8HZ.

Ⓕ**P.S. Vora & Co** *(P S Vora)* 32 Doeshill Drive, WICKFORD, ESSEX, SS12 9RD.

P.S. Wallace & Co *(P S Wallace)* 284 Clifton Drive South, St Annes, LYTHAM ST. ANNES, FY8 1LH. and at NEWCASTLE UPON TYNE

ⓉⒻⒶ**P.S.J. Alexander & Co** *(M Shah, V N Shah)* 1 Doughty Street, LONDON, WC1N 2PH.

P.T. Bhimjiyani & Co *(P T Bhimjiyani)* 124 Chatsworth Road, LONDON, NW2 5QU.

P.T. Looker & Co *(P T Looker)* 3 Stonards Hill, EPPING, CM16 4QE.

P.T. Patel & Co. *(P T Patel)* Avad House, Belvue Road, NORTHOLT, UB5 5HY.

P.T. Vaughan *(P T Vaughan)* 31 Temples Court, Helpston, PETERBOROUGH, PE6 7EU.

P.T.Walsh *(P T Walsh)* 11 Griffiths Drive, SOUTHPORT, PR9 7DP.

Ⓟ**P3 Learning Limited** *(D J Starr, P Wignall)* 30 Brudenell Drive, Stoke Mandeville, AYLESBURY, BUCKINGHAMSHIRE, HP22 5UR.

Ⓟ**PA Bishop & Co Limited** *(P A Bishop)* Unit 316, Ettrick Riverside Business Centre, Dunsdale Road, SELKIRK, TD7 5EB.

ⓅⒶ**PAAM THIRTEEN LIMITED** *(K K J Shah)* 16 Beaufort Court, Admirals Way, Docklands, LONDON, E14 9XL.

Pabani & Co *(S Pabani)* 30 Wertheim Court, Suite 14B, RICHMOND HILL L4B 1B9, ON, CANADA.

Ⓟ**Pace Accountancy Ltd** *(L J C G Pace)* 3 The Retreat, Glebe Lane, Abberton, COLCHESTER, CO5 7NW.

Ⓟ**Pace Tax Ltd** *(L J C G Pace)* 3 The Retreat, Glebe Lane, Abberton, COLCHESTER, CO5 7NW.

Ⓟ**Pace, trading name of PC Accountancy Ltd** *(L J C G Pace)* 3 The Retreat, Glebe Lane, Abberton, COLCHESTER, CO5 7NW.

ⓅⒶ**Pacific Ltd** *(B J Cluer)* 1st Floor Woburn House, 84 St. Benedicts Street, NORWICH, NR2 4AB.

★ⒻⒶ**Packman, Leslie & Co.** *(J D Packman)* Gresham House, 144 High Street, EDGWARE, MIDDLESEX, HA8 7EZ.

Packwood Associates LLP *(R J Parsons)* Cedar Court, Packwood Lane, Lapworth, SOLIHULL, B94 6AU.

★ⓉⒻⒶ**Page Kirk, trading name of Page Kirk LLP** *(I D Barker, G S Cree, M P Mellor, P G Staniforth, L A Tooley, J S Wallis)* Sherwood House, 7 Gregory Boulevard, NOTTINGHAM, NG7 6LB.

Ⓟ**Page Maddox Limited** *(G Maddox)* 21 Honeysuckle Gardens, Everton, LYMINGTON, HAMPSHIRE, SO41 0EH.

Ⓟ**Page One Limited** *(A S Brookes)* 19 Claydon Road, KINGSWINFORD, WEST MIDLANDS, DY6 0HR.

Ⓟ**Painswick Accounting & Taxation Services Ltd** *(S J Dandy)* Green Ridges, Cotswold Mead, Painswick, STROUD, GLOUCESTERSHIRE, GL6 6XB.

Pak Yee & Co *(P Y Yee)* 6 The Cleave, HARPENDEN, AL5 5SJ.

Palmer *(I P Palmer)* 64 Northbourne Avenue, Northbourne, BOURNEMOUTH, BH10 6DQ.

Palmer Accounting Services *(L A Palmer)* Lincoln House, 21 Dunstable Street, Ampthill, BEDFORD, BEDFORDSHIRE, MK45 2NJ.

★**Palmer McCarthy** *(M H Brain)* Toronto House, 49a South End, CROYDON, CR9 1LT.

Ⓣ**Palmer, Riley & Co** *(J Metherell)* First Floor, Wallington Court, Fareham Heights, Standard Way, FAREHAM, HAMPSHIRE PO16 8XT.

ⒻⓅ**PalmerMoore, trading name of Palmer Moore Limited** *(P H J Beadsmoore)* C/O Harwoods, 1 Trinity Place, Midland Drive, SUTTON COLDFIELD, WEST MIDLANDS, B72 1TX.

Ⓐ**Palmers** *(C M J Palmer)* 28 Chipstead Station Parade, Chipstead, COULSDON, SURREY, CR5 3TF.

Pamela J Legg *(P J Legg)* Doric House, Wraylands Drive, REIGATE, SURREY, RH2 0LG.

Pamela Morrow *(P Morrow)* 30 Church Way, LONDON, N20 0LA.

Pamela Stoney *(P Stoney)* 61 Earith Road, Willingham, CAMBRIDGE, CB24 5LS.

Ⓟ**Panaco International Limited** *(M L T Pang)* First Floor, 27 Gloucester Place, LONDON, W1U 8HU.

★**Panayiotou Kittos Soteriou & Co** *(P Panayiotou)* 68 Spyrou Kyprianou Av, Nicolaides Shopping City, Joanna Ct 2nd FL, PO Box 42529, 6500 LARNACA, CYPRUS.

Ⓟ**Pan-China (Hong Kong) CPA Limited** *(M M Choi, P C Fung, W P Ng)* 20/F, HONG KONG SAR Trade Centre, 161-167 Des Voeux Road, CENTRAL, HONG KONG SAR.

ⓅⒶ**Pandey & Co, trading name of Pandey & Co Limited** *(D Pandey)* Cambridge House, 32 Padwell Road, SOUTHAMPTON, SO14 6QZ.

Pang Chan & Co. *(Y Chan)* Unit A 13th Floor, E.I.B. Centre, 40-44 Bonham Strand, SHEUNG WAN, HONG KONG ISLAND, HONG KONG SAR.

Panicos Y Komodromos & Co *(P Komodromos)* Karantokis Building, 16 Zenas De Tyras Office 6, P.O. Box 27162, NICOSIA, CYPRUS. and at LARNACA

Ⓟ**Papademetriou & Partners Ltd** *(C D Papademetriou, L D Papademetriou)* P.O.Box 21865, 1514 NICOSIA, CYPRUS.

ⓉⒻⓅⒶ**Paper Park, Price Pearson, Taxshield, Taxwise, trading names of Price Pearson Ltd** *(V Brassington, C Cooper, N C Davis, S Garrington, A J Homer, F J McKay, D E Price, P C Rayney, K A Turner, A Williams)* Finch House, 28-30 Wolverhampton Street, DUDLEY, DY1 1DB. and at KIDDERMINSTER

Paradigm Accountancy Services *(T P J Bailey)* The Chestnuts, Lanham Green, Cressing, BRAINTREE, ESSEX, CM77 8DT.

Paragon *(I Younus)* 155 Normanton Road, DERBY, DE23 6UR.

Ⓟ**Paragon Financial Management Limited** *(D J McGonigle, D J Parker)* 11 Ferrands Close, Harden, BINGLEY, WEST YORKSHIRE, BD16 1JA.

Param & Co *(K Parameswaran)* 18 Foxley Lane, PURLEY, CR8 3ED.

Ⓐ**Parcell & Associates** *(N R Parcell)* Aldreth, Pearcroft Road, STONEHOUSE, GL10 2JY.

Parekhs *(R R D Parekh)* 16 Sevington Street, Maida Hill, LONDON, W9 2QN.

ⓅⒶ**Paresh Shah, trading name of Paresh Shah Ltd** *(P L Shah)* 128 Malvern Gardens, HARROW, MIDDLESEX, HA3 9PG.

Pareto, trading name of Pareto Tax and Wealth LLP *(R Woolley)* 8 St. John Street, MANCHESTER, M3 4DU.

★**Parfitt & Co** *(J M Parfitt)* 22 High Street, Rowledge, FARNHAM, SURREY, GU10 4BS.

Pargetters *(R P Durber)* 19 Church Avenue, STOKE-ON-TRENT, ST2 7DA.

Ⓟ**Paris & Co, trading name of Paris & Co UK Limited** *(R P Aristotelous)* 9 Leys Gardens, Cockfosters, BARNET, EN4 9NA.

Ⓟ**Park Associates, trading name of Apaz Ltd** *(M F Zuzga)* Gretton House, Waterside Court, Third Avenue, Centrum 100, BURTON-ON-TRENT, STAFFORDSHIRE DE14 2WQ.

Ⓟ**Park Place Corporate Finance, trading name of Park Place Corporate Finance LLP** *(D R Hardless, J E Stones)* 19 Park Place, LEEDS, LS1 2SJ.

ⓅⒶ**Parker Business Development, trading name of Parker Business Development Ltd** *(A G Parker)* 1192 Warwick Road, Acocks Green, BIRMINGHAM, B27 6BT.

★ⓉⒶ**Parker Cavendish** *(J C C Carruth, R A Rubenstein, P B K Shah)* 28 Church Road, STANMORE, HA7 4XR.

★Ⓟ**Parker Cavendish Limited** *(J C C Carruth, R A Rubenstein, P B K Shah)* 28 Church Road, STANMORE, MIDDLESEX, HA7 4XR.

Parker Gradwell & Co *(S W Johnson)* 17 Chapel Street, HYDE, SK14 1LF.

ⓅⒶ**Parker Lloyd, trading name of Clenton Limited** *(D P Patel)* 11 Old Court House, Old Court Place, LONDON, W8 4PD.

★**Parker Randall** *(J H Parker)* Mehmet Akif Cad, Mine Apt D4, Koskliciflik, NICOSIA, CYPRUS. and at KYRENIA

Parker Randall, trading name of Parker Randall LLP *(J H Parker)* 9 Bickels Yard, 151-153 Bermondsey Street, London Bridge, LONDON, SE1 3HA.

Ⓟ**Parker Simm Consulting Limited** *(H E Parker)* 7 Audley Drive, WARLINGHAM, SURREY, CR6 9AH.

★**Parker Wood** *(R A Rubenstein, P B K Shah)* 28 Church Road, STANMORE, MIDDLESEX, HA7 4XR.

ⒻⓅⒶ**Parkers, trading name of Parkers Business Services Limited** *(C J Arbenz, D I Jemmett, S G Monk)* Cornelius House, 178-180 Church Road, HOVE, EAST SUSSEX, BN3 2DJ.

Parkes & Co *(L E Parkes)* 5 Crondal Place, Edgbaston, BIRMINGHAM, B15 2LB.

Ⓟ**Parkes & Swan Limited** *(L J Parkes, L J Swan)* White Rose Farm, Hextalls Lane, Bletchingley, REDHILL, RH1 4QT.

ⓉⒻⒶ**Parkhurst Hill** *(K S Clay, L Price, P D Stapleton, D B Tromans)* Torrington Chambers, 58 North Road East, PLYMOUTH, PL4 6AJ.

ⒻⓅⒶ**Parkhurst Hill, trading name of Parkhurst Hill Limited** *(K S Clay, L Price, P D Stapleton, D B Tromans)* Torrington Chambers, 58 North Road East, PLYMOUTH, DEVON, PL4 6AJ.

★**Parkin S. Booth & Co** *(P J Fleming)* Yorkshire House, 18 Chapel Street, LIVERPOOL, L3 9AG. and at CHESTER, LLANDUDNO, WARRINGTON

ⓉⒻⒶ**Parkinson Matthews LLP** *(R J Matthews, K Parkinson)* Cedar House, 35 Ashbourne Road, DERBY, DE22 3FS.

Parkside *(A P Aiken)* 12 Stuart Road, BARNET, HERTFORDSHIRE, EN4 8XG.

Parkson & Company *(L E Tse)* Unit 1301, 13/F Lemmi Centre, 50 Hoi Yuen Road, KWUN TONG, KOWLOON, HONG KONG SAR.

Ⓟ**Parkwell Business Solutions Limited** *(M M Vekaria)* 36 St. Andrews Drive, STANMORE, MIDDLESEX, HA7 2NB.

Ⓟ**Parkwood Financial Solutions Ltd** *(K Baker)* Madon & Co, 8th Floor Tolworth Tower, Ewell Road, SURBITON, SURREY, KT6 7EL.

ⓉⒶ**Parlane Purkis & Co** *(J Purkis, N D Smeeton)* 177 London Road, SOUTHEND-ON-SEA, SS1 1PW.

Ⓟ**Parlow Associates Limited** *(I G Parker)* 16 Brockwood Close, Gamlingay, SANDY, BEDFORDSHIRE, SG19 3EG.

Ⓐ**Parr & Company** *(C J Parr)* Parsimony Towers, Brighton Road, Shermanbury, HORSHAM, WEST SUSSEX, RH13 8HQ.

Parry & Co *(C L Crewe, P J Parry)* Unit 1, Temple House Estate, 6 West Road, HARLOW, ESSEX, CM20 2DU.

Parry & Co *(W Parry)* Ynys Hir, Sandy Lane, RHOSNEIGR, GWYNEDD, LL64 5XA.

Ⓟ**Parry Business Services Limited** *(S M Parry)* 28 Briarwood, Westbury on Trym, BRISTOL, BS9 3SS.

Parry Consulting *(M Parry)* 20 Holly Avenue, Jesmond, NEWCASTLE UPON TYNE, NE2 2PY.

ⓅⒶ**Parry Scholes & Co Ltd** *(P T Scholes)* A9 Trem Y Duffryn, Colomendy Industrial Estate, Rhyl Road, DENBIGH, CLWYD, LL16 5TA.

Parsons & Co *(I W Parsons)* St John's Business Centre, St. Johns North, WAKEFIELD, WEST YORKSHIRE, WF1 3QA.

Parsons & Co. *(P A Parsons)* Denendeh House, Mount Hermon Road, Palestine, ANDOVER, HAMPSHIRE, SP11 7EW.

Ⓟ**Parsons Royle & Co, trading name of Parsons Royle & Co Ltd** *(P C Carroll)* Capital House, 2 Market Street, Atherton, MANCHESTER, M46 0DN. and at BOLTON

Partha Mitra - PCLG
Members in Practice and Firms - Alphabetical

Partha Mitra *(P Mitra)* Plot No. Y-14 Block EP, Sector V, Lake Electronic Complex, Bidhan Nagar, KOLKATA 700091, WEST BENGAL INDIA.

Partridge & Co. *(M R Partridge)* The Old Malt House, The Green, Clipston, MARKET HARBOROUGH, LE16 9RS.

ⓉⒶ**Parvez & Co** *(P A Khan)* 20 Greyhound Road, LONDON, W6 8NX.

Pascall & Co. *(P Paschali)* 47 Park Way, Whetstone, LONDON, N20 0XN.

Ⓐ**Passer, Chevern & Co** *(S Chevern)* 5 Spring Villa Road, EDGWARE, MIDDLESEX, HA8 7EB.

Ⓟ**Passman Leonard, trading name of Passman Leonard Limited** *(P Watson, R M Watson)* Bentinck House, Bentinck Road, WEST DRAYTON, MIDDLESEX, UB7 7RQ.

ⒻⓅⒶ**Passmore Weeks & Richardson, trading name of PWR Accountants Limited** *(M I W Passmore, K A Richardson)* 2 Beacon End Courtyard, London Road, Stanway, COLCHESTER, CO3 0NU. and at EYE, SUDBURY

Ⓟ**Patara & Co Limited** *(T S Patara)* Financial House, 352 Bearwood Road, Bearwood, BIRMINGHAM, B66 4ET.

Ⓕ**Patel Dodhia & Co** *(R P Dodhia)* 4 Trinity Street, LONDON, SE1 1DB.

Ⓐ**Patel Khanderia & Co** *(V S N Khanderia, C V Patel)* 9 Hitherwood Drive, LONDON, SE19 1XA.

Patel, Shah & Joshi *(M Shah, V N Shah)* 1 Doughty Street, LONDON, WC1N 2PH.

Ⓟ**Patens & Co Limited** *(R Patel)* 20a Selsdon Road, SOUTH CROYDON, SURREY, CR2 6PA.

Ⓟ**Paterson Boyd & Co, trading name of Paterson Boyd & Co Limited** *(S Boardman)* 18 North Street, GLENROTHES, KY7 5NA. and at LEVEN

ⒻⒶ**Paterson Brodie** *(L Y Statham)* Cliveden Chambers, Cliveden Place, Longton, STOKE-ON-TRENT, ST3 4JB.

Ⓕ**Pathfinder Strategic Partners LLP** *(C S Burford)* The Royd, 40 Duchy Road, HARROGATE, NORTH YORKSHIRE, HG1 2ER.

Ⓐ**Patmans** *(R Patel)* 94 Brinkburn Gardens, EDGWARE, MIDDLESEX, HA8 5PP.

Ⓐ**Patmore & Co** *(A W Patmore)* Isabella Mews, The Avenue, Combe Down, BATH, BA2 5EH.

Patricia A Jones *(P A Jones)* 316 Bristol Road, Edgbaston, BIRMINGHAM, B5 7SN.

Patricia Bernard *(P J Bernard)* 1 Chapel Close, Leigh Sinton, MALVERN, WR13 5BP.

Patricia Cook *(P Cook)* 1 Rib Vale, Bengeo, HERTFORD, SG14 3LE.

Patricia Gera FCA *(P Gera)* 11 Dr Zammit Street, BALZAN BZN 1430, MALTA.

ⒻⓅ**Patricia J Arnold & Co Ltd** *(P J R Arnold)* Black House, Dipton Mill Road, HEXHAM, NORTHUMBERLAND, NE46 1RZ.

Patricia Moss FCA *(P J Moss)* Maytime, High Street, Little Chesterford, SAFFRON WALDEN, ESSEX, CB10 1TS.

Patricia Rizan *(P M Rizan)* 21 Chervil Way, Burghfield Common, READING, RG7 3YX.

Patrick Ford *(P Ford)* Leybourne Lodge, Combe Lane, Wormley, GODALMING, GU8 5TP.

Patrick Herelle *(P Herelle)* 88 Daneby Road, Catford, LONDON, SE6 2QG.

Patrick J Knight FCA *(P J Knight)* Marlow, Manorial Road, Parkgate, NESTON, CH64 6QW.

Patrick J. Manners *(P J Manners)* Oak House, Tetchill Moor, ELLESMERE, SHROPSHIRE, SY12 9AL.

Patrick Kan & Co *(P M G Kan)* 80 Marine Parade Road, #16-09, Parkway Parade, SINGAPORE 449269, SINGAPORE.

★**Patrick Kong & Associates** *(P F K Kong)* 2nd Floor Lot 19, Luyang Phase 8 Kota Kinabalu, Specialist Ctr POB 11835, 88830 KOTA KINABALU, SABAH, MALAYSIA.

★**Patrick Lai & Co.** *(W W P Lai)* Room 1106, Capitol Centre, 5-19 Jardine's Bazaar, CAUSEWAY BAY, HONG KONG SAR.

Patrick NG & Company *(W P Ng)* 20th Floor, HONG KONG SAR Trade Centre, 161-167 Des Voeux Road, CENTRAL, HONG KONG ISLAND, HONG KONG SAR.

Patrick O'Conor BSc FCA *(P F O'Conor)* 51 Downs Park West, Westbury Park, BRISTOL, BS6 7QL.

ⓅⒶ**Patro Limited** *(N C D Taylor)* Holly House, Burnsall, SKIPTON, NORTH YORKSHIRE, BD23 6BN.

Patsalides & Co *(T Patsalides)* 60 Larnacos Avenue, Flat 301, Aglantzia, 2101 NICOSIA, CYPRUS.

Ⓐ**Patson & Co** *(D Patel)* 9 Limes Road, BECKENHAM, BR3 6NS.

ⓅⒶ**Patsons Accountancy Limited** *(R Patel, R K Patel)* Suraj Chambers, 53 Islington Park Street, LONDON, N1 1QB.

Paul & Co *(P B E Quayle)* 5 Peel Market Place, ISLE OF MAN, IM5 1AB.

Ⓐ**Paul & Co** *(V K Paul)* 11-12 Freetrade House, Lowther Road, STANMORE, MIDDLESEX, HA7 1EP.

Paul & Maundrell *(C N Maundrell)* 13 Church Street, HELSTON, CORNWALL, TR13 8TD. and at FALMOUTH

ⒻⓅⒶ**Paul A Hill & Co, trading name of Paul A Hill & Co Limited** *(P A Hill, K T Upton)* 3 Bull Lane, ST. IVES, CAMBRIDGESHIRE, PE27 5AX. and at CHATTERIS

Paul Alton *(P Alton)* Admin House, 6 North Street, DROITWICH, WORCESTERSHIRE, WR9 8JB.

Ⓐ**Paul Austen Associates** *(P J Austen)* Charter House, 7-9 Wagg Street, CONGLETON, CHESHIRE, CW12 4BA.

Paul Beasley *(P J Beasley)* Dampier House, Dampier Street, LEEK, STAFFORDSHIRE, ST13 5PF.

Paul Boothroyd *(P Boothroyd)* 1 Potters Walk, Golcar, HUDDERSFIELD, HD7 4HH.

Paul Broadhurst & Co *(P Broadhurst)* 74-76 High Street, WINSFORD, CW7 2AP.

Paul C Singleton, trading name of Paul C. Singleton Ltd *(P C Singleton)* Riverdale, 89 Graham Road, SHEFFIELD, S10 3GP.

Paul Catherall *(P G Catherall)* Holm Oak, Mount Park Avenue, Harrow on the Hill, HARROW, HA1 3JN.

Ⓟ**Paul Chappell, trading name of Astracon Limited** *(P R Chappell)* 2 The Firs, Moorfield Road, Duxford, CAMBRIDGE, CB2 4PY.

ⓉⒶ**Paul Clegg & Company** *(Paul Clegg)* Riverside Offices, Second Floor, 26 St Georges Quay, LANCASTER, LA1 1RD.

Ⓐ**Paul Clixby** *(P A Clixby)* 27 Hornyold Road, MALVERN, WORCESTERSHIRE, WR14 1QQ.

Paul Conron FCA *(P A Conron)* 4 Robin Hood Lane, Wrightington, WIGAN, WN6 9QG.

Paul Craik *(J P P Craik)* 51 Mead Way, BROMLEY, BR2 9ER.

Paul Creasy *(P Creasy)* St. Davids, Meavy Bourne, YELVERTON, DEVON, PL20 6AR.

ⒻⓅⒶ**Paul Crowdy Partnership Limited** *(R Smith, T J White)* Redmayne House, 4 Whiteladies Road, Clifton, BRISTOL, BS8 1PD.

Paul Cumming *(P J Cumming)* Warwick House, Church Lane, Little Witley, WORCESTER, WR6 6LP.

Paul D. Camp *(P D Camp)* Jarrards, Church Hill, Radwinter, SAFFRON WALDEN, CB10 2SX.

Paul D. Faulconbridge *(P D Faulconbridge)* 16 Trinity Gardens, THORNTON-CLEVELEYS, FY5 2UA.

Paul Davis *(P A Davis)* 27 Hill Road, Oakley, BASINGSTOKE, RG23 7HS.

Paul Davis *(P C Davis)* 57 Chiltern Road, Quedgeley, GLOUCESTER, GL2 4TU.

Paul de Keyser *(P D De Keyser)* 2 Constable Close, LONDON, NW11 6TY.

Ⓐ**Paul Dixon & Associates** *(P F Dixon)* Byeways, Mill Road, Lower Shiplake, HENLEY-ON-THAMES, RG9 3LW.

Paul E Marshall ACA BSc *(P E Marshall)* 28 Ryder Crescent, SOUTHPORT, MERSEYSIDE, PR8 3AE.

Paul E. Wildermuth *(P E Wildermuth)* Pentre Farm, Pentre, Cilcain, MOLD, FLINTSHIRE, CH7 5PF.

Paul Eddins Chartered Accountantts, trading name of Paul Eddins *(P F R Eddins)* 214 Whitchurch Road, CARDIFF, CF14 3ND.

Paul Ford & Co *(P W Ford)* 26 Cherwell Road, Keynsham, BRISTOL, BS31 1QT.

Ⓕ**Paul Furrer & Co** *(P S Furrer)* 2nd Floor Tuition House, 27-37 St. Georges Road, Wimbledon, LONDON, SW19 4EU.

Paul G. Lewis *(P G Lewis)* 2 Le Clos de la Vallee, La Vallee de St. Pierre, St. Lawrence, JERSEY, JE3 1LF.

Paul Gaywood *(P Gaywood)* 2 Fairways, Fulwood, PRESTON, PR2 8FX.

Paul Goodman *(P J Goodman)* Mortons Cottage, The Green, Sarratt, RICKMANSWORTH, HERTFORDSHIRE, WD3 6BH.

Paul H. Dawson *(P H Dawson)* 104 Clarence Road, Four Oaks, SUTTON COLDFIELD, B74 4AS.

Paul Handley *(P J W Handley)* 6 Highbury Road, Streetly, SUTTON COLDFIELD, B74 4TF.

Paul Harris & Company *(P Harris)* PO Box 61 GT, GEORGE TOWN, GRAND CAYMAN, KY1 1102, CAYMAN ISLANDS.

Paul Higgins *(P R Higgins)* 10 Ritherdon Road, Tooting, LONDON, SW17 8QD.

Ⓟ**Paul Hindle Limited** *(P G Hindle)* The Old Gamedealers, Dereham Road, Garvestone, NORWICH, NR9 4QT.

Ⓟ**Paul Horton and Associates Limited** *(P A Horton)* 86 Stannington View Road, Crookes, SHEFFIELD, S10 1SR.

Ⓟ**Paul Howley & Co, trading name of Paul Howley & Co Limited** *(P H Bowden)* 42 Pitt Street, BARNSLEY, SOUTH YORKSHIRE, S70 1BB.

Paul J Cooper *(P J Cooper)* Crumps Cottage, Harlow Common, HARLOW, ESSEX, CM17 9NE.

Paul James Associates *(J P James)* Turnstile Cottage, Firle Road, SEAFORD, BN25 2JD.

Paul Jenkins *(T P Jenkins)* 39 High Street, PERSHORE, WR10 1EU.

Paul K Haynes *(P K Haynes)* 128 Malines Avenue, PEACEHAVEN, BN10 7RZ.

Ⓟ**Paul Kirby & Co, trading name of Paul Kirby & Company Ltd** *(P Kirby)* Davenport House, Bawtry Road, Everton, DONCASTER, SOUTH YORKSHIRE, DN10 5BP.

Paul Lederman *(P Lederman)* 18 Wheatley Close, LONDON, NW4 4LG.

Paul Lynton ACA *(P R Lynton)* 36 Mutrix Road, LONDON, NW6 4QG.

Ⓕ**Paul M Bowers** *(P M Bowers)* 3 Herewood Close, NEWBURY, BERKSHIRE, RG14 1PY.

Paul M Tate *(P M Tate)* 3 Hanwell Court, Hanwell, BANBURY, OX17 1HF.

Paul Marks & Co *(P M Stankiewicz)* Flat 1, 3 Lansdowne Road, Wimbledon, LONDON, SW20 8AP.

Paul Marshall & Co *(P F Marshall)* 138 George V Avenue, WORTHING, BN11 5RX.

Paul Monaghan *(P Monaghan)* 18 Hartshill Close, Hillingdon, UXBRIDGE, MIDDLESEX, UB10 9LH.

Paul Mulley *(P Mulley)* 13 Newmans Drive, Hutton, BRENTWOOD, ESSEX, CM13 2PZ.

Ⓟ**Paul Neasham Accountancy Limited** *(P Neasham)* 6 Oak Tree Road, BEDALE, NORTH YORKSHIRE, DL8 1UE.

Ⓐ**Paul Ng & Associates** *(P H S Ng)* 15 Halifax Way, WELWYN GARDEN CITY, AL7 2QH.

ⓅⒶ**Paul Phillis & Co Limited** *(P Phillis)* Unit 16, Leeway Estate, NEWPORT, GWENT, NP19 4SL.

Paul Purdham *(P Purdham)* 26 Millers Hill, HOUGHTON LE SPRING, DH4 7AJ.

Paul R Bowes *(P R Bowes)* 57 Centurion Road, BRIGHTON, BN1 3LN.

Paul Raby *(P Raby)* 45 The Roundway, Morley, LEEDS, LS27 0JR.

Paul S Axcell *(P S Axcell)* Kiln Cottage, Fourstones, HEXHAM, NE47 5DH.

Ⓟ**Paul S Hammond FCA, trading name of Hammond Taxation Services Limited** *(P S Hammond)* Glenbrook, Torwoodhill Road, Rhu, HELENSBURGH, DUNBARTONSHIRE, G84 8TG.

Ⓟ**Paul Sharman Limited** *(P Sharman)* 33 Watling Close, Bracebridge Heath, LINCOLN, LN4 2BD.

★Ⓐ**Paul Slater & Co** *(P Slater)* 1 Washington Street, NORTHAMPTON, NN2 6NL.

★Ⓟ**Paul Steele, trading name of Paul Steele Limited** *(P C Steele)* 18 Newport Street, TIVERTON, DEVON, EX16 6NL.

Paul Suckling & Co *(P W Suckling)* Mousetraps, Hall Green, Little Yeldham, HALSTEAD, CO9 4LF.

Paul T Wenham *(P T C Wenham)* GPO Box 2551, SYDNEY, NSW 2001, AUSTRALIA.

Paul Tay & Co *(P G H Tay)* 63 Stead Street, MELBOURNE, VIC 3205, AUSTRALIA.

Ⓟ**Paul Taylor, trading name of Taylor Long 2008 Limited** *(P E Taylor)* 22 Middleton Street, WYMONDHAM, NORFOLK, NR18 0AD.

Paul Tranter & Company *(P A Tranter)* 31 High Street, STOKESLEY, NORTH YORKSHIRE, TS9 5AD.

Ⓐ**Paul Trodden & Co** *(P J Trodden)* 30 St Mary's Row, Moseley, BIRMINGHAM, B13 8JG.

Ⓟ**Paul Turner - AIMS Accountants for Business, trading name of Charmes Limited** *(P A Turner)* 14a Farlands Road, Oldswinford, STOURBRIDGE, WEST MIDLANDS, DY8 2DD.

Ⓐ**Paul Varty** *(P A Varty)* 24 St Cuthberts Way, DARLINGTON, DL1 1GB.

ⒻⒶ**Paul Venn Accountants** *(P B Venn)* 40 Woodborough Road, WINSCOMBE, SOMERSET, BS25 1AG.

Paul W. Maher & Co. *(P W Maher)* Oakley House, 46 Old Pound Close, Lytchett Matravers, POOLE, DORSET, BH16 6BW.

Paul W.C. Ho & Company *(P W C Ho)* 20th Floor Golden Centre, No. 188 Des Voeux Road, CENTRAL, HONG KONG ISLAND, HONG KONG SAR.

Paul Wakefield *(Paul Wakefield)* Myrtle Cottage, Lower End, Great Milton, OXFORD, OX44 7NJ.

★**Paul Wan & Co** *(P T C Wan)* 10 Anson Road, No. 35-08 International Plaza, SINGAPORE 079903, SINGAPORE.

Paul Webster & Associates *(P Webster)* 27 Cavendish Road, SUTTON, SURREY, SM2 5EY.

ⒻⓅⒶ**Paul Winston Limited** *(P Winston)* 23 Alleyn Place, WESTCLIFF-ON-SEA, ESSEX, SS0 8AT.

Paul Wooddisse *(P A Wooddisse)* 2 Chantry Road, STOURBRIDGE, DY7 6SA.

Paula Comley ACA, trading name of Paula Comley *(P A Comley)* Ingles Manor, Castle Hill Avenue, FOLKESTONE, KENT, CT20 2RD.

Paula Thomas *(P Thomas)* 25 Westcote Road, Streatham, LONDON, SW16 6BN.

Paula Vanninen *(P H Vanninen)* Flat 3, 50 Eardley Crescent, LONDON, SW5 9JZ.

Pauline Hegarty *(P A Hegarty)* 18 Footherley Road, Shenstone, LICHFIELD, STAFFORDSHIRE, WS14 0NJ.

Ⓕ**Pauline Lonsdale** *(P A Lonsdale)* 26 Elmfield Road, BROMLEY, BR1 1WA.

ⓉⒻⒶ**Pawley & Malyon** *(D Malyon, P J Neville, W J Terry)* 15 Bedford Square, LONDON, WC1B 3JA. and at SAWBRIDGEWORTH

Ⓟ**Payacademy Ltd** *(M S Caister, N S Caister)* Prosperity House, 121 Green Lane, DERBY, DE1 1RZ.

★Ⓐ**Paylings** *(J C Brearton)* 7 The Office Campus, Paragon Business Village, Red Hall Court, WAKEFIELD, WEST YORKSHIRE, WF1 2UY. and at NORMANTON

PayMatters Accountancy Services LLP *(M D Grady)* Barons Court, Manchester Road, WILMSLOW, CHESHIRE, SK9 1BQ.

Payne & Co *(S A Allen)* 76 Grove Vale Avenue, Great Barr, BIRMINGHAM, B43 6BZ.

Ⓐ**Payne & Co** *(M A Payne)* 16 Ingham Road, West Hampstead, LONDON, NW6 1DE.

★ⓅⒶ**Payne & Co, trading name of Payne & Co Accountants Limited** *(A Payne)* Holly Cottage, Over Lane, Almondsbury, BRISTOL, BS32 4DF.

Ⓟ**Payne & Payne Ltd** *(L Payne)* 14 Kennedy Road, BICESTER, OXFORDSHIRE, OX26 2BG.

Payne Allen *(F C Dauppe)* 45 Whitelands Avenue, Chorleywood, RICKMANSWORTH, HERTFORDSHIRE, WD3 5RE.

ⓅⒶ**Payne Walker Limited** *(P Stephenson)* Suite 2, 10 High Street, MELTON MOWBRAY, LEICESTERSHIRE, LE13 0TR.

Ⓟ**Payplan, trading name of Payplan Bespoke Solutions Limited** *(N T Payne)* Kempton House, Dysart Road, GRANTHAM, LINCOLNSHIRE, NG31 7LE.

Ⓟ**Payplan, trading name of Payplan Partnership Limited** *(N T Payne)* Kempton House, Dysart Road, GRANTHAM, LINCOLNSHIRE, NG31 7LE.

Ⓟ**Payroll Services Limited** *(A Schick-Maier)* 21 Culverlands Close, STANMORE, MIDDLESEX, HA7 3AG.

Ⓟ**Payroll Specialists Limited** *(M E Bishop)* Merryhills, Dulcote, WELLS, SOMERSET, BA5 3NU.

Ⓟ**Paystream Accounting Services Ltd** *(P M Malley)* Mansion House, Manchester Road, ALTRINCHAM, CHESHIRE, WA14 4RW.

ⒻⒶ**PB Associates** *(R J Clement, G P Rees, A Sharif)* 2 Castle Business Village, Station Road, HAMPTON, MIDDLESEX, TW12 2BX.

Ⓟ**PB Financial Planning Ltd** *(P F Gillman, C W Olley)* Causeway House, 1 Dane Street, BISHOP'S STORTFORD, HERTFORDSHIRE, CM23 3BT. and at CAMBRIDGE

Ⓟ**PB Recovery, trading name of Marsh Hammond Limited** *(C R Hammond)* Peek House, 20 Eastcheap, LONDON, EC3M 1EB.

★ⒻⒶ**PBA Accountants** *(C S Bissell)* 130 High Street, HUNGERFORD, BERKSHIRE, RG17 0DL.

Ⓟ**PBA Accounting Limited** *(P A Baker)* Grover House, Grover Walk, Corringham, STANFORD-LE-HOPE, ESSEX, SS17 7LS.

★ⓉⒻⒶ**PBA Group, trading name of P Baker & Associates** *(P A Baker)* Grover House, Grover Walk, Corringham, STANFORD-LE-HOPE, ESSEX, SS17 7LS.

Ⓟ**PBV Services, trading name of Shaw Austin Limited** *(C A Goy, D H Shaw)* 45 City Road, CHESTER, CH1 3AE.

Ⓟ**PC & Chan Limited** *(P W K Chan)* 14 The Village Square, Netherne on the Hill, COULSDON, SURREY, CR5 1LZ.

Ⓟ**PC & Co, trading name of Light Fantastic (UK) Limited** *(P W Challenor)* 44 Lower Town Street, Bramley, LEEDS, LS13 2BW.

Ⓟ**PC Accounting Services Limited** *(P J Barber, C Horsley)* 2 Jardine House, Harrovian Business Village, Bessborough Road, HARROW, MIDDLESEX, HA1 3EX.

Ⓟ**PC Accounting Solutions Limited** *(M E M Hughes)* 61 Cowbridge Road East, CARDIFF, CF11 9AE.

★**PC Secretarial Services** *(H J Cohen)* Tall Trees, 15a Dean Park Road, BOURNEMOUTH, BH1 1HU.

Ⓟ**PCK & Co, trading name of PCK Accounting Ltd** *(P Karageorghis)* 11 Dove Lane, POTTERS BAR, EN6 2SG.

ⓉⒻⓅ**PCLG, trading name of PCLG Limited** *(Ian Peter Broadley, L R Elliot)* Equinox House, Clifton Park Avenue, Clifton Park, Shipton Road, YORK, YO30 5PA.

Members in Practice and Firms - Alphabetical PCP CPA Limited - Peter L Hood

Ⓟ**PCP CPA Limited** *(S I Chua)* 34/F The Lee Gardens, 33 Hysan Avenue, CAUSEWAY BAY, HONG KONG SAR.

PD Accountancy Services *(P Dodd)* 9 Coolidge Avenue, LANCASTER, LA1 5ER.

Ⓟ**PDH Accountants Limited** *(P D Hawes)* Timbers, Southview Road, CROWBOROUGH, TN6 1HW.

Ⓕ**Peach & Co** *(S L Hall)* 115 Byrkley Street, BURTON-ON-TRENT, DE14 2EG.

Ⓟ**Peach Wilkinson Limited** *(J S Williams)* 78 Cross Hill, Ecclesfield, SHEFFIELD, S35 9TU.

Ⓟ**Peachey & Co (Accountants) Ltd** *(D Peachey)* 4 Sunny Rise, Chaldon, CATERHAM, SURREY, CR3 5PR.

ⒻⒶ**Pearce & Co** *(R G Pearce)* First Floor, 39 Gay Street, BATH, BA1 2NT.

Pearce & Co *(M Pearce)* 44 Barker Hill, Lowdham, NOTTINGHAM, NG14 7BH.

Ⓐ**Pearce Aitchison** *(C F Pearce)* 1 Church Square, LEIGHTON BUZZARD, LU7 1AE.

Pearce Wills *(A H Pearce)* Meridian House, Heron Way, TRURO, CORNWALL, TR1 2XN.

★Ⓟ**Pearl Accountants Ltd** *(J Aslam)* 359 Willington Road South, HOUNSLOW, TW4 5HU.

Pearl Hargood BA ACA *(P Hargood)* Hafan, Heol y Mynydd, Penbre, Llanelli, BURRY PORT, DYFED SA16 0AJ.

★Ⓐ**Pearlman Rose** *(M W S Jilani)* 2 St. Georges Mews, 43 Westminster Bridge Road, LONDON, SE1 7JB.

Ⓟ**Pearsense Ltd** *(A D A Pearse)* White Cottage, Cold Ashby Road, Guilsborough, NORTHAMPTON, NN6 8QN.

Ⓟ**Pearson & Associates, trading name of P&A Accountants Ltd** *(A Howarth)* North Barn, Broughton Hall, SKIPTON, BD23 3AE.

Ⓐ**Pearson & Co** *(R A Pearson)* 113 Smug Oak Business Centre, Lye Lane, Bricket Wood, ST. ALBANS, AL2 3UG.

Pearson & Co *(A Pearson)* Endover House, Rodborough Common, STROUD, GL5 5BT.

★ⓉⒻⓅⒶ**Pearson Buchholz Limited** *(L F Buchholz, S J Daniels, R D Pearson, I M Woollard)* North House, 5 Farmoor Court, Farmoor, OXFORD, OX2 9LU.

ⓉⒻⒶ**Pearson May** *(J Bowden, N S A Oliver, D J Richards, J R Rose, K R S Surry, M D Taylor)* 37 Great Pulteney Street, BATH, BA2 4DA. and at CHIPPENHAM, TROWBRIDGE

Ⓟ**Pearson, trading name of PCA Limited** *(D L P Goodwin)* 12 Old Park Avenue, LONDON, SW12 8RH.

Pearsons *(A Pearson)* 20 Irongate, DERBY, DE1 3GP.

Ⓟ**Peasemore Business Services Ltd** *(G Anderson)* Holwell, Stainfield Road, Kirkby Underwood, BOURNE, LINCOLNSHIRE, PE10 0SG.

★**Peats** *(N J Peat)* Canford House, Discovery Court, 551-553 Wallisdown Road, POOLE, DORSET, BH12 5AG.

Ⓐ**Peaty & Co** *(Gerald Peaty)* 163 - 164 Moulsham Street, CHELMSFORD, CM2 0LD.

ⓉⒶ**Peel Walker** *(S Cousen, P A Nutton)* 11 Victoria Rd, ELLAND, HX5 0AE.

ⓉⓅ**Peers Roberts, trading name of Peer Roberts Limited** *(D D Shah)* The Pavilion, 56 Rosslyn Crescent, HARROW, MIDDLESEX, HA1 2SZ.

Pegasus & Co *(S C Au Yeung)* 7/F Chuang's Enterprises Building, 382 Lockhart Road, WAN CHAI, HONG KONG SAR.

ⒻⒶ**Pelham** *(C B Hunt, J N White)* Pelham Business Centre, 16 Dudley Street, GRIMSBY, DN31 2AB.

ⒻⓅ**Pelican Consultancy Ltd** *(V F N Blackburn)* 6 Cockhaise Cottages, Monteswood Lane, Lindfield, HAYWARDS HEATH, WEST SUSSEX, RH16 2QP.

★ⒻⒶ**Pells** *(M A Burnell, S W Merriman, F T C Pell, A R R Price)* 1 Derby Road, Eastwood, NOTTINGHAM, NG16 3PA.

PEM Corporate Finance LLP *(P Chapman, R D C Guthrie, J A Lettice, J H Parry, S M Peak, C Walklett, R Webster, P H F Wilsdon)* Salisbury House, Station Road, CAMBRIDGE, CB1 2LA.

★ⓉⒶ**PEM Technology, trading name of Peters Elworthy & Moore** *(P Chapman, R D C Guthrie, L A Jeanroy, J A Lettice, J H Parry, S M Peak, C Walklett, R Webster, K Whitehouse, P H F Wilsdon)* Salisbury House, Station Road, CAMBRIDGE, CB1 2LA.

PEM VAT Services LLP *(P Chapman, R D C Guthrie, J A Lettice, J H Parry, S M Peak, C Walklett, R Webster, P H F Wilsdon)* Salisbury House, Station Road, CAMBRIDGE, CB1 2LA.

Ⓣ**Pembertons, trading name of Sefton Solomon** *(S A Solomon)* Peterden House, 1a Leighton Road, West Ealing, LONDON, W13 9EL.

★**Pembroke Accountancy Services** *(I M W Latham)* 5 College Mews, Saint Ann's Hill, LONDON, SW18 2SJ.

Ⓐ**Pembroke Consulting** *(S R J Briggs)* Clive House, 12-18 Queens Road, WEYBRIDGE, SURREY, KT13 9XB.

Pendray & Co *(S E Pendray)* The Hylands, 244 Chipstead Way, Woodmansterne, BANSTEAD, SM7 3LQ.

Peninsula Accounting *(G Schoeb)* 66 Sandtoft Road, LONDON, SE7 7LR.

Ⓟ**Penlee Consulting Ltd** *(J A Thorpe)* 32 Chiltern Road, Wendover, AYLESBURY, BUCKINGHAMSHIRE, HP22 6DA.

Penn & Company LLP *(C A Penn, M S Penn)* Tordown, 5 Ashwell Lane, GLASTONBURY, BA6 8BG.

★**Penn Accountants & Tax Consultants** *(Z D Penn)* Swale Folly, The Street, Doddington, SITTINGBOURNE, KENT, ME9 0BG.

ⒻⓅⒶ**Pennington Hunter Limited** *(D I H Hunter, M R Pennington)* Stanhope House, Mark Rake, Bromborough, WIRRAL, MERSEYSIDE, CH62 2DN.

Ⓟ**Pennington Silver, trading name of Pennington Silver Limited** *(P E Silver)* 30 Union Street, SOUTHPORT, MERSEYSIDE, PR9 0QE.

Pennington Williams *(D I H Hunter, M R Pennington)* Stanhope House, Mark Rake, Bromborough, WIRRAL, MERSEYSIDE, CH62 2DN.

Ⓐ**Penningtons** *(M Kripalani)* Wellington House, 209-217 High Street, Hampton Hill, HAMPTON, MIDDLESEX, TW12 1NP.

Penny Howitt *(P A Howitt)* 4 Canvey Close, WIGSTON, LE18 3WS.

Penny Lane *(K Walji)* Third Floor, Borough House, 78-80 Borough High Street, LONDON, SE1 1LL.

Ⓟ**Pennywise Accounting, trading name of Pennywise Accounting Limited** *(C M Warrington)* Dickhurst House, Rodgate Lane, HASLEMERE, SURREY, GU27 2EW.

Ⓟ**Pension Accounts Limited** *(K Archer)* Cob Suite Old Swan House, 29 High Street, HEMEL HEMPSTEAD, HERTFORDSHIRE, HP1 3AA.

Ⓟ**Penson Associates, trading name of Penson & Penson Limited** *(A A Penson)* Fairfield House, Dodds Lane, CHALFONT ST. GILES, BUCKINGHAMSHIRE, HP8 4EL.

Ⓟ**Penta Associates, trading name of Penta Associates Limited** *(A Chiotis)* 244 Long Lane, LONDON, N3 2RN.

Ⓣ**Pentins** *(A Davidson, J N Hawkins)* Lullingstone House, 5 Castle Street, CANTERBURY, CT1 2FG.

ⓅⒶ**Pentins, trading name of Pentins Business Advisers Limited** *(A Davidson, J N Hawkins)* 5 Castle Street, CANTERBURY, KENT, CT1 2FG.

★ⓉⒻⒶ**Peplows** *(P Guest, L Lugger, G C Rooke, M D Young)* Moorgate House, King Street, NEWTON ABBOT, TQ12 2LG. and at CARLISLE, EXETER, TORQUAY

Ⓟ**Pepper Ideas Limited** *(K Blecher)* 18a Rothschild Road, LONDON, W4 5HS.

Ⓟ**Per Annum Accounting Limited** *(E R French)* Flat A, The Chestnuts, 5 Kenilworth Road, NOTTINGHAM, NG7 1DD.

ⒻⒶ**Percy Gore & Co** *(A R J Leal, H N Mockett, G C Simpson, N G F Wreford)* 39 Hawley Square, MARGATE, KENT, CT9 1NZ.

Percy Pemberton & Co *(R D Mason)* 11 Sandal Cliff, Sandal, WAKEFIELD, WF2 6AU.

ⓉⒻⒶ**Percy Westhead & Company** *(R J Adams, T A R Elston)* Greg's Buildings, 1 Booth Street, MANCHESTER, M2 4AD.

ⒻⓅⒶ**Peregrine, trading name of Peregrine Accountants & Business Advisers Ltd** *(G P Banwell, N C F Miles)* The Old Bank, The Triangle, Paulton, BRISTOL, BS39 7LE.

Perera Lynch *(R J C Lynch)* Hornhatch Hatch Farm, Rices Corner, New Road, Shalford, GUILDFORD, SURREY GU4 8HS.

Ⓟ**Perfitt Consultants Limited** *(A J Perfitt)* Cornet Street, St. Peter Port, GUERNSEY, GY1 1LF.

★**Perkins** *(M Bubb)* The Albany, South Esplanade, St. Peter Port, GUERNSEY, GY1 1AE.

Perkins & Co *(C H Perkins)* 20 Taylor Avenue, Kew, RICHMOND, TW9 4ED.

ⒻⒶ**Perkins Copeland** *(C P Freeman, S A Gausden)* 15 Gildredge Rd, EASTBOURNE, BN21 4RA.

ⒻⓅⒶ**Perlin Franco, trading name of Perlin Franco Ltd** *(F Franco, P L Perlin)* Trojan House, 34 Arcadia Avenue, LONDON, N3 2JU.

ⓉⒻⓅⒶ**Perrins Limited** *(C L Birch, W P Harvey, S Osment)* Custom House, The Strand, BARNSTAPLE, DEVON, EX31 1EU.

Perry Douglass & Co *(D J Perry)* 4 Market Hill, Clare, SUDBURY, CO10 8NN.

★ⒻⒶ**Perrys** *(S Hale, D E McCusker, S M Pope, S M Rustrick)* 32-34 St. Johns Road, TUNBRIDGE WELLS, KENT, TN4 9NT. and at LONDON, SEVENOAKS, SNODLAND, WEST MALLING

Ⓟ**Pershore Management Services Ltd** *(C T A Meredith)* Suite No 1, Royal Arcade, Broad Street, PERSHORE, WORCESTERSHIRE, WR10 1AG.

ⒻⓅ**Personal Debt Solutions (PDS), The MacDonald Partnership, TMP, trading names of The MacDonald Partnership plc** *(N D Chesterton, D C Macdonald)* Level 25, Tower 42, 25 Old Broad Street, LONDON, EC2N 1HQ.

Ⓟ**Personal Numbers Ltd** *(J P Parkinson)* 2 Fawns Keep, WILMSLOW, CHESHIRE, SK9 2BQ.

Ⓐ**Pestell & Co** *(J P Pestell)* 2A Nicola Close, SOUTH CROYDON, SURREY, CR2 6NB.

Ⓟ**Peter Angel & Co, trading name of Peter Angel & Co Ltd** *(P B Angel)* Finance House, 77 Queens Road, BUCKHURST HILL, IG9 5BW.

Peter Arrowsmith FCA *(P Arrowsmith)* Office 4 Knights Farm, Newton Road, RUSHDEN, NORTHAMPTONSHIRE, NN10 0SX.

ⓉⒻⒶ**Peter Auguste & Co** *(P Auguste)* 1 Dukes Passage, Off Duke Street, BRIGHTON, EAST SUSSEX, BN1 1BS.

Ⓟ**Peter Barclay Limited** *(P J Barclay)* 1st Floor, 11 Church Street, MELKSHAM, WILTSHIRE, SN12 6LS.

Ⓟ**Peter Barratt, trading name of Barramsgate Limited** *(P D Barratt)* 105 London Road, RAMSGATE, KENT, CT11 0DR.

Peter Barrett *(P C Barrett)* The Manor, Little Clanfield, BAMPTON, OX18 2RX.

Ⓟ**Peter Bennetts Ltd** *(P L Bennetts)* 51 Albert Street, LONDON, NW1 7LX.

Peter Bradley *(P Bradley)* 63 Kingswood Road, TADWORTH, KT20 5EF.

Peter Braithwaite FCA *(P G Braithwaite)* 40 Kingswood Avenue, Shortlands, BROMLEY, BR2 0NY.

Peter Brandl FCA *(P L J Brandl)* 30 St Cuthberts Lane, Locks Heath, SOUTHAMPTON, HAMPSHIRE, SO31 6TE.

Ⓐ**Peter Brook** *(P J Brook)* 15 Luxemburg Gardens, Brook Green, LONDON, W6 7EA.

Peter Bruff & Co *(P F J Bruff)* Cherry Court, 5 Cherry Orchard, Littlebourne, CANTERBURY, CT3 1QG.

Peter Burrows *(P H Burrows)* 11 Telford Close, Preston, WEYMOUTH, DT3 6PG.

Peter C. Yates *(P C Yates)* 100 Baker Street, POTTERS BAR, HERTFORDSHIRE, EN6 2EP.

Ⓟ**Peter Chan (CPA) Limited** *(P P Chan)* 2nd Floor, Caltex House, 258 Hennessy Road, WAN CHAI, HONG KONG SAR.

Peter Chant *(P J Chant)* 22 Cottage Offices, Latimer Park, Latimer Road, CHESHAM, BUCKINGHAMSHIRE, HP5 1TU.

Ⓣ**Peter Chong & Co** *(P T N Chong)* 51 Changkat Bukit Bintang, 50200 KUALA LUMPUR, FEDERAL TERRITORY, MALAYSIA. and at PENANG

Peter Clark *(P J Clark)* Milestones, 98 Woodside Road, AMERSHAM, BUCKINGHAMSHIRE, HP6 6AP.

Peter Copp *(P R Copp)* Mawenzi, Muir of Fowlis, ALFORD, ABERDEENSHIRE, AB33 8JX.

ⒻⓅⒶ**Peter Crane & Co, trading name of Peter Crane & Co Ltd** *(P A Crane)* 30/32 Trebarwith Crescent, NEWQUAY, TR7 1DX.

Peter Crowther & Co *(P L Crowther)* 17 Springwood Drive, Skircoat Green, HALIFAX, WEST YORKSHIRE, HX3 0TQ.

Peter D. Lace *(P D Lace)* First Floor, 18 Hope Street, Douglas, ISLE OF MAN, IM1 1AQ.

Peter da Costa & Co *(P M W Da Costa)* 56 Richmond Park Road, KINGSTON UPON THAMES, SURREY, KT2 6AJ.

★**Peter Deane & Co** *(P M Deane)* 21 Guildford Drive, Chandlers Ford, EASTLEIGH, SO53 3PR.

Peter Dew *(P A Dew)* 22 Lattimore Road, Wheathampstead, ST. ALBANS, HERTFORDSHIRE, AL4 8QE.

Peter Di Giuseppe *(P E Di Giuseppe)* Witsend, 10 Poplar Close, Aller Park, NEWTON ABBOT, TQ12 4PG.

Peter Dingley *(P C Dingley)* Buckland Place, Southampton Road, LYMINGTON, HAMPSHIRE, SO41 9GZ.

Peter Duffell *(P M Duffell)* 32 The Ridgeway, ENFIELD, EN2 8QH.

ⓅⒶ**Peter Durbin & Company Limited** *(M D Tomlinson)* Holiday House, Valley Road, ILKLEY, LS29 8PA.

Peter E Campbell & Co *(P E Campbell)* Burnside Cottage, Strachur, CAIRNDOW, ARGYLL, PA27 8DG.

Peter E. Byrne *(P E Byrne)* 68 Lavender Avenue, Kingsbury, LONDON, NW9 8HE.

Peter E. Doyle *(P E Doyle)* 18 Borrowbydale Avenue, KNARESBOROUGH, NORTH YORKSHIRE, HG5 0NF.

Peter Edney & Co *(P W Edney)* 95 Station Road, HAMPTON, MIDDLESEX, TW12 2BD.

Peter F Selley & Co *(P F Selley)* 84 Belleville Road, LONDON, SW11 6PP.

Peter F. Wollen *(P F Wollen)* 7 Cleeve Lake Court, Bishops Cleeve, CHELTENHAM, GLOUCESTERSHIRE, GL52 8SN.

Peter Fitt *(P W E Fitt)* 7 Coast Road, West Mersea, COLCHESTER, CO5 8QE.

Peter Geary & Co *(P M G Geary)* 31 Church Street, BISHOPS CASTLE, SHROPSHIRE, SY9 5AD.

★Ⓟ**Peter Geary & Co Limited** *(P M G Geary)* 31 Church Street, BISHOPS CASTLE, SHROPSHIRE, SY9 5AD.

Peter H. Hubbard *(P H Hubbard)* 5 Broadway Market, Fencepiece Road, Barkingside, ILFORD, ESSEX, IG6 2JT.

Peter Haigh *(P J Haigh)* The Old Estate Office, Westway Farm, Bishop Sutton, BRISTOL, BS39 5XP.

Peter Harris & Company *(P J Harris)* Audley House, Northbridge Road, BERKHAMSTED, HP4 1EH.

Ⓟ**Peter Harris & Company, trading name of All About Numbers Ltd** *(P J Harris)* Audley House, North Bridge Road, BERKHAMSTED, HERTFORDSHIRE, HP4 1EH.

Peter Harrison *(P Harrison)* Riggs House, Riggs Head, SCARBOROUGH, YO12 5TG.

Peter Heatherington *(P Heatherington)* Dene House, Hartburn, MORPETH, NORTHUMBERLAND, NE61 4JB.

Ⓟ**Peter Hill, trading name of Peter Hill (Accountant) Limited** *(P Hill)* 76 Holburn Park, STOCKTON-ON-TEES, CLEVELAND, TS19 8BJ.

Peter Hirst & Co *(P G Hirst)* The Coach House, Outwood Lane, Horsforth, LEEDS, LS18 4HR.

★**Peter Howard & Co** *(S C Foreman)* Wharfe Mews House, 1 Wharfe Mews, Cliffe Terrace, WETHERBY, LS22 6LX.

★Ⓣ**Peter Howard Foreman & Co** *(S C Foreman)* 1 Wharfe Mews Cliffe Terrace, WETHERBY, LS22 6LX.

ⒻⓅⒶ**Peter Howard Foreman Limited** *(S C Foreman)* 1 Wharfe Mews, Cliffe Terrace, WETHERBY, LS22 6LX.

ⒻⓅⒶ**Peter Howard-Jones Ltd** *(P N Howard-Jones)* Unit 8, Quy Court, Colliers Lane, Stow-cum-Quy, CAMBRIDGE, CB25 9AU.

Ⓐ**Peter Howes Associates** *(P K Howes)* 6 Abbey Hill Close, WINCHESTER, SO23 7AZ.

ⒻⓅⒶ**Peter Hunt & Co, trading name of Peter Hunt & Co Limited** *(J G Cook, P C P Hunt)* Argon House, Argon Mews, Fulham Broadway, LONDON, SW6 1BJ.

Ⓣ**Peter I M Chieng & Co** *(I M Chieng)* A-5-4A 5th Floor, Northpoint Office, Northpoint Mid Valley City, No 1 Medan Syed Putra Utara, 59200 KUALA LUMPUR, FEDERAL TERRITORY MALAYSIA.

Peter J Cooney *(P J Cooney)* 42 London Road, Oadby, LEICESTER, LE2 5DH.

ⒻⓅ**Peter J Delf FCA, trading name of Corporate Management Services Limited** *(Peter J Delf)* 16 Park View, Winchmore Hill, LONDON, N21 1QX.

Peter J Fish *(P J Fish)* Culvers Hill, Rowington, WARWICK, CV35 7AB.

Peter J Stevenson *(P J Stevenson)* 8 Harbord Road, OXFORD, OX2 8LJ.

Peter J Swift ACA FCCA Accounting Services *(P J Swift)* 23 Parkland View, BARNSLEY, S71 5LG.

Peter J. Ball *(P J Ball)* 25 Kersteman Road, BRISTOL, BS6 7BX.

Ⓕ**Peter J. Burgess** *(P J Burgess)* 113 High Street, Yelling, ST. NEOTS, PE19 6SB.

Peter J. Hearnshaw & Co *(P J Hearnshaw)* 2 Sankyns Green, Little Witley, WORCESTER, WR6 6LQ.

Ⓕ**Peter J. Monahan & Co** *(P J Monahan)* 16 Farmhill Park, Douglas, ISLE OF MAN, IM2 2EE.

Ⓕ**Peter J. Thompson** *(P J Thompson)* 3 Streatley Farm Cottages, Wallingford Road, Streatley, READING, RG8 9PX.

Peter James *(P R James)* 71 Washford Road, SHREWSBURY, SHROPSHIRE, SY3 9HW.

Ⓐ**Peter Jensen** *(P A Jensen)* 5 Bridge Street, BISHOP'S STORTFORD, HERTFORDSHIRE, CM23 2JU.

Peter John Norman FCA *(P J Norman)* Bosgarrack, Hellangove Farm, Gulval, PENZANCE, CORNWALL, TR20 8XD.

Peter Katz & Co, trading name of P.D. Katz *(P D Katz)* Apartment 8, Alexandra House, Richmond Drive, Repton Park, WOODFORD GREEN, ESSEX IG8 8RF.

Peter Kay *(P Kay)* 14 Hamond Close, SOUTH CROYDON, SURREY, CR2 6BZ.

ⓅⒶ**Peter Kemp Ltd** *(P J Kemp)* Critchleys LLP, Critchleys, Avalon House, Marcham Road, ABINGDON, OXFORDSHIRE OX14 1UD.

Peter L Hood *(Peter L Hood)* 20 Neville Crescent, Bromham, BEDFORD, MK43 8JE.

★**Peter Lam & Co.** *(K C P Lam)* Suite 1807 The Gateway, Tower II Harbour City, 25 Canton Road, TSIM SHA TSUI, KOWLOON, HONG KONG SAR.

Ⓟ**Peter Lickiss Chartered Tax Adviser Limited** *(P A J Lickiss)* 35 Honiton Way, Aldridge, WALSALL, WS9 0JS.

Ⓕ**Peter Lobbenberg & Co** *(P Lobbenberg)* 74 Chancery Lane, LONDON, WC2A 1AD.

Peter Louth and Company *(P Louth)* 18 Westdown Road, Catford, LONDON, SE6 4RL.

Peter Lucas & Co *(P R Lucas)* 54 Pilsdon Drive, Canford Heath, POOLE, BH17 9HS.

Peter Lynch & Co *(P D Lynch)* Regus House, Malthouse Avenue, Cardiff Gate Business Park, CARDIFF, CF23 8RU.

Peter M N Jennings FCA *(P M N Jennings)* Mariners, Longs Wharf, YARMOUTH, ISLE OF WIGHT, PO41 0PW.

Peter M. Holiday *(P M Holiday)* Western House, 44 Western Road, Urmston, MANCHESTER, M41 6LF.

Peter M. Raven *(P M Raven)* The White House, 318 Manchester Road, West Timperley, ALTRINCHAM, CHESHIRE, WA14 5NB.

Peter Marshall *(P I Marshall)* 38 Oakley Street, LONDON, SW3 5HA.

Peter Marshall *(P W Marshall)* 20 Highfield Road, Keyworth, NOTTINGHAM, NG12 5JE.

Ⓕ**Peter Mayston** *(A P Mayston)* Jacobs Farm, Wiggens Green, Helions Bumpstead, HAVERHILL, SUFFOLK, CB9 7AD.

Peter McKay *(P H McKay)* 73 High Street, Yardley Hastings, NORTHAMPTON, NN7 1ER.

Peter Mitchell & Co *(B A Makinson, P J D Mitchell)* 95 High Street, GREAT MISSENDEN, HP16 0AL.

Peter Moore *(P J Moore)* 5 Sillwood Hall, Montpelier Road, BRIGHTON, BN1 2LQ.

Ⓟ**Peter Mossman Consultants Ltd** *(P L Mossman)* Cushy Dingle, Watery Lane, Llanishen, CHEPSTOW, GWENT, NP16 6QT.

Peter Murgatroyd *(P Murgatroyd)* 347 Whitehall Road, LEEDS, LS12 6LB.

Peter N Olsen *(P N Olsen)* Norse Cottage, Elwick, HARTLEPOOL, CLEVELAND, TS27 3EF.

Peter O'Connell FCA *(P O'Connell)* Bickley, Westerdunes Park, NORTH BERWICK, EAST LOTHIAN, EH39 5HJ.

Peter P Blomeley FCA *(P P Blomeley)* 6 Christopher Acre, ROCHDALE, LANCASHIRE, OL11 5FE.

Peter Price & Co *(P G Price)* 9 Broad Street, LLANDOVERY, DYFED, SA20 0AR.

Ⓟ**Peter Price & Company (Pontypool) Limited** *(D Sherrington)* Park Royal House, Hanbury Road, PONTYPOOL, GWENT, NP4 6LL.

Peter R Little FCA, trading name of P R Little *(P R Little)* 16 Kenwyn Close, West End, SOUTHAMPTON, SO18 3PJ.

Peter R. Dennis *(P R Dennis)* 37 Saxonbury Road, Southbourne, BOURNEMOUTH, BH6 5NB.

Peter R. Moore *(P R Moore)* 20 Carisbrooke Drive, Napperley Park, NOTTINGHAM, NG3 5DS.

ⒻⓅ**Peter Rayney Tax Consulting Limited** *(P C Rayney)* 91 Eighth Avenue, LUTON, LU3 3DP.

Peter Reeves *(P T Reeves)* The Old Orchard, Sandy Lane, Southmoor, ABINGDON, OXFORDSHIRE, OX13 5HX.

Peter Riley *(P W Riley)* 21 New Road, BRIXHAM, TQ5 8NB.

Peter S Kirkland *(P S Kirkland)* 30 Sunningdale Drive, Woodborough, NOTTINGHAM, NG14 6EQ.

Ⓕ**Peter S. Whitfield** *(P S Whitfield)* 13 Briarwood, Westbury on Trym, BRISTOL, BS9 3SS.

Peter Sabine & Co *(P G Sabine)* 17 Keble Place, LONDON, SW13 8HJ.

Peter Sanders *(P H Sanders)* 68 Hayle Terrace, HAYLE, CORNWALL, TR27 4BT.

Peter Shaw *(P J Shaw)* 1 Radcliffe Gardens, Radcliffe Lane, PUDSEY, WEST YORKSHIRE, LS28 8BG.

Ⓟ**Peter Simon & Co Limited** *(J P Carrington, S Davies)* The Old Maids Head, 110 High Street, Stalham, NORWICH, NR12 9AU.

Peter Smith *(P J Smith)* Rose Cottage, Brill Road, Horton-Cum-Studley, OXFORD, OX33 1BN.

Peter Smith & Co *(P Smith)* 12 Bonneycroft Lane, Easingwold, YORK, YO61 3AR.

Peter Stables *(P Stables)* 77 Smith House Lane, BRIGHOUSE, WEST YORKSHIRE, HD6 2LF.

Peter Thorn *(P Thorn)* 38 Greenways, CHELMSFORD, CM1 4EF.

Ⓘ**Peter Torino BSc ACA - AIMS Accountants for Business** *(P A Torino)* 25 Leith Mansions, Grantully Road, LONDON, W9 1LQ.

Peter Travers & Co. *(P M Travers)* 28 Manor Road Extension, Oadby, LEICESTER, LE2 4FF.

ⓅⒶ**Peter Upton, trading name of Peter Upton Limited** *(P J H Upton)* The Counting House, 7 Bridge Street, MAIDENHEAD, BERKSHIRE, SL6 8PA.

Peter W Shephard *(P W Shephard)* 2 Brinsley Close, SOLIHULL, WEST MIDLANDS, B91 3FR.

Peter W. Lacey *(P W Lacey)* The Old Forge, West Buckland, WELLINGTON, TA21 9JS.

Peter W. Seaman *(P W Seaman)* 32 Offley Road, SANDBACH, CHESHIRE, CW11 1GY.

Peter Walker *(P Walker)* 6 Aspin Lane, KNARESBOROUGH, HG5 8ED.

Peter Walton *(P Walton)* 23 Castleknowe Gardens, Kirkton Park, CARLUKE, ML8 5UX.

Peter Warburton & Co *(P Warburton)* Gwalia, Llangynhafal, DENBIGH, CLWYD, LL16 4LN.

Ⓟ**Peter Waren Consultancy Limited** *(P J Warren)* Home Farm, Gatcombe, NEWPORT, ISLE OF WIGHT, PO30 3HL.

Peter Watts & Co *(P M Watts)* Berrylands, Hawthorne Lane, ROSS-ON-WYE, HEREFORDSHIRE, HR9 5BG. and at CAMBRIDGE

ⓅⒶ**Peter Weldon & Co, trading name of Peter Weldon & Co Ltd** *(P Weldon)* 87 Station Road, ASHINGTON, NORTHUMBERLAND, NE63 8RS.

Peter Wicksteed *(P Wicksteed)* El Calvario 12, San Lorenzo, 35018 LAS PALMAS, GRAN CANARIA, SPAIN.

ⒻⒶ**Peter Wilkins & Co** *(P J D Wilkins)* 16 Cathedral Road, CARDIFF, CF11 9LJ.

Peter Williams & Co *(P J Williams)* 68 Herbert Gardens, LONDON, NW10 3BU.

Peter Willson *(P E Willson)* Bowood, The Ropewalk, Penpol Point, TRURO, TR3 6NS.

Peter Wilson *(P Wilson)* Suite 6, Rockfield House, 512 Darwen Road, Bromley Cross, BOLTON, BL7 9DX.

Ⓐ**Peter Young** *(P C R Young)* Orchard Cottage, Stanford Lane, Hadlow, TONBRIDGE, TN11 0JP.

★**Peters & Co** *(M Holder)* 1 Park Road, CATERHAM, CR3 5TB.

ⒻⒶ**Peters & Co** *(C Peters)* 41A Mottram Old Road, STALYBRIDGE, SK15 2TF.

Peters & Wright *(Caroline Peters)* 387 Ongar Road, Pilgrim's Hatch, BRENTWOOD, ESSEX, CM15 9JA.

ⒾⓅ**Petersons, trading name of AVN Petersons Limited** *(P G Rollison)* Church House, 94 Felpham Road, BOGNOR REGIS, WEST SUSSEX, PO22 7PG.

ⒾⓅⒶ**Petersons, trading name of Petersons Accountants Limited** *(P J Hellawell, M J Sinfield)* 28 High Street, WITNEY, OXFORDSHIRE, OX28 6RA.

Petrou & Co *(S Petrou)* 4 Heddon Court, Cockfosters Road, BARNET, HERTFORDSHIRE, EN4 0DE.

Pett Franklin & Co LLP *(W Franklin)* Victoria House, 116 Colmore Row, BIRMINGHAM, B3 3BD.

ⒾⒻⒶ**Peyton Tyler Mears** *(M E Mears, T C Peyton, M Tyler)* Middleborough House, 16 Middleborough, COLCHESTER, CO1 1QT.

ⓅⒶ**PG&E Professional Services Limited** *(S Edrich)* 3 Novara Row, Calabria Road, LONDON, N5 1JL.

★Ⓟ**PGK Associates Limited** *(P R Gokani)* Talbot House Business Centre, 204-226 Imperial Drive, Raynes Lane, HARROW, MIDDLESEX, HA2 7HH.

ⒻⒶ**PGM** *(P G McAreavey)* 405 Lisburn Road, BELFAST, COUNTY ANTRIM, BT9 7EW. and at CRAIGAVON

Ⓟ**PGS Accountancy Ltd** *(P G Stark)* 54 Ridgestone Avenue, Bilton Kingston-Upon-Hull, HULL, HU11 4AJ.

Ⓕ**Pharos Associates** *(C J Powell)* PO Box 21, TEDDINGTON, MIDDLESEX, TW11 9SW.

Ⓟ**Pheonix Consultancy Limited** *(D M Allman)* 17 Collinbrook Avenue, CREWE, CHESHIRE, CW2 6PN.

ⒻⓅⒶ**Phil Dodgson & Partners Limited** *(P W Dodgson, E Podmore)* 49 Chapeltown, PUDSEY, WEST YORKSHIRE, LS28 7RZ. and at SKIPTON

Ⓟ**Phil McPhail & Co, trading name of PMC Limited** *(P A McPhail)* 124 Main Street, Burley in Wharfedale, ILKLEY, WEST YORKSHIRE, LS29 7JP.

Phil Thomas FCA *(P S G Thomas)* 18 Home Close, Middleton Cheney, BANBURY, OXFORDSHIRE, OX17 2LD.

Ⓟ**Philbys, trading name of Philbys Limited** *(M Philby)* Bank Chambers, 27a Market Place, Market Deeping, PETERBOROUGH, PE6 8EA.

Ⓟ**Philip A Dickinson Accountants Ltd** *(P A Dickinson)* 103 High Street, HERNE BAY, KENT, CT6 5LA.

★ⒻⓅⒶ**Philip Barnes & Co Ltd** *(P M Barnes, F Bates, P C J Bird, J Clark, C J Humphreys)* The Old Council Chambers, Halford Street, TAMWORTH, B79 7RB.

Ⓟ**Philip Beck Limited** *(P A Beck)* 41 Kingston Street, CAMBRIDGE, CB1 2NU.

Ⓟ**Philip Burley & Co, trading name of Philip Burley (Whitby) Limited** *(A Walker)* 28 Bagdale, WHITBY, YO21 1QL.

Ⓐ**Philip Collins** *(P Collins)* 37 Carmarthen Road, Up Hatherley, CHELTENHAM, GLOUCESTERSHIRE, GL51 3JZ.

Philip Davies *(P J Davies)* 3 Park Hall Crescent, Castle Bromwich, BIRMINGHAM, B36 9SN.

Ⓟ**Philip Dykes & Co, trading name of Formaco Ltd** *(P Dykes, R Dykes)* 1 Roebuck Lane, SALE, M33 7SY.

Philip E Kanas *(P E Kanas)* Downs Court, 29 The Downs, ALTRINCHAM, WA14 2QD.

Ⓟ**Philip Friede & Co, trading name of Philip Friede & Co Ltd** *(P M Friede)* Third Floor, Premier House, 12-13 Hatton Garden, LONDON, EC1N 8AN.

Ⓟ**Philip Gee & Company Limited** *(P W S Gee)* 15-16 Bond Street, WOLVERHAMPTON, WV2 4AS.

Philip Goodmaker *(P H Goodmaker)* 18 Fallowfield, Middlesex, STANMORE, HA7 3DF.

Philip Gorrod *(P J Gorrod)* High Hill House, 30 London Road, HALESWORTH, SUFFOLK, IP19 8LR.

Philip Green - AIMS Accountants For Business *(P A Green)* Copper Glade, Moss Lane, Yarnfield, STONE, STAFFORDSHIRE, ST15 0PW.

Philip Harris & Co *(P Harris)* 38 Woodruff Way, Thornhill, CARDIFF, CF14 9FP.

Ⓕ**Philip Haynes FCA** *(P E Haynes)* Briarsmead, Old Road, Buckland, BETCHWORTH, RH3 7DU.

ⓅⒶ**Philip Hector & Co Limited** *(J P Hector)* Unit 6, Grange Road Workshops, Grange Road, Geddington, KETTERING, NORTHAMPTONSHIRE NN14 1AL.

Philip Howard Accounting Services *(P V Howard)* 10 Manston Drive, Crossgates, LEEDS, LS15 8RA.

Philip Howes *(P C F Howes)* 37 Heather Lea Avenue, SHEFFIELD, S17 3DL.

ⒻⒶ**Philip Hudson & Co** *(P J Hudson)* 454-458 Chiswick High Road, LONDON, W4 5TT.

Ⓐ**Philip I. Macorison** *(P I Macorison)* 1 Abingdon Way, ORPINGTON, BR6 9WA.

Philip J. Hodges FCA *(P J Hodges)* 123 Birchfield Road, Headless Cross, REDDITCH, WORCESTERSHIRE, B97 4LE.

Ⓐ**Philip Kendell** *(P J Kendell)* 4 Wheelwrights Corner, Nailsworth, STROUD, GL6 0DB.

★**Philip Lee & Co.** *(C S Law, C P Lee)* Office B, 22nd floor, Guangdong Investment Tower, 148 Connaught Road, CENTRAL, HONG KONG ISLAND HONG KONG SAR.

Philip M Doe *(P M Doe)* 24 The Ridgeway, Codicote, HITCHIN, HERTFORDSHIRE, SG4 8YP.

Philip M Hollins MA FCA *(P M Hollins)* Lavant Gate, Lavant, CHICHESTER, WEST SUSSEX, PO18 0BB.

Philip M Tucker *(P M Tucker)* 58 Park Grange Croft, SHEFFIELD, S2 3QL.

Ⓟ**Philip Marshall Limited** *(P R Marshall)* Gatwick Farm House, Stantway Lane, WESTBURY-ON-SEVERN, GLOUCESTERSHIRE, GL14 1QG.

ⓅⒶ**Philip Martin Limited** *(P J Martin)* Crown House, 4 High Street, Tyldesley, MANCHESTER, M29 8AL.

Philip Moore *(P G Moore)* Torridon, Wood Road, HINDHEAD, SURREY, GU26 6PX.

Philip Morgan *(P Morgan)* 9 Lakeside Gardens, MERTHYR TYDFIL, CF48 1EN.

ⓅⒶ**Philip Munk Limited** *(P J Munk)* TWP Accounting LLP, The Old Rectory, Church Street, WEYBRIDGE, SURREY, KT13 8DE.

Ⓟ**Philip Nickson & Co Ltd** *(P Nickson)* 10 Lancaster Road, Kempsford, FAIRFORD, GLOUCESTERSHIRE, GL7 4DW.

Philip Oddy *(P D Oddy)* Albion House, 24 Roundhay Road, LEEDS, LS7 1BT.

Philip Ogilvie *(P J Ogilvie)* PO Box 29, 1st Floor, 6 Casemates Square, GIBRALTAR, GB1 1ZZ, GIBRALTAR.

Philip P L Choi & Co *(P P Choi)* 2702-6 Lucky Commercial Centre, 103-9 Des Voeux Road West, CENTRAL, HONG KONG SAR.

Philip P. Couldrey *(P P Couldrey)* 93 Avenue Besme, 1190 BRUSSELS, BELGIUM.

Ⓕ**Philip Patten & Co** *(B P Patten)* 54 Oakington Avenue, Little Chalfont, AMERSHAM, HP6 6ST.

Philip Potter *(P Potter)* 20 Egerton Road, Monton, Eccles, MANCHESTER, M30 9LR.

Philip Saunders BA ACA *(P K Saunders)* 6 Vyvyans Terrace, Praze, CAMBORNE, CORNWALL, TR14 0LD.

Ⓐ**Philip T. Chave & Co** *(P T Chave)* Belfry House, Bell Lane, HERTFORD, SG14 1BP.

Philip Thomas & Co *(D P G Thomas)* 72 Station Road, Llanishen, CARDIFF, CF14 5UT.

Philip Walker *(P O Walker)* Anthony's Well, Chew Stoke, BRISTOL, BS40 8XG.

Philip Wong & Co *(P Wong)* 142 Jalan Datuk Sulaiman 6, Taman Tun Dr Ismail, 60000 KUALA LUMPUR, FEDERAL TERRITORY, MALAYSIA.

Ⓟ**Philip Wood & Co Ltd** *(P E Wood)* 12 Main North Road, Woodend 7610, NORTH CANTERBURY, NEW ZEALAND.

Philippa Verzhbitskaya *(P H Verzhbitskaya)* 33A Hitchin Lane, Clifton, SHEFFORD, BEDFORDSHIRE, SG17 5RS.

Ⓐ**Philips** *(P K Soteri)* 1160 High Rd, LONDON, N20 0RA.

ⒾⒻⓅⒶ**Phillip Bates & Co, trading name of Phillip Bates & Co Limited** *(P N Bates)* 1-3 Chester Road, NESTON, CH64 9PA.

Phillip Cooper & Co *(P Cooper)* 9 Dock Street, HULL, HU1 3DL.

Ⓕ**Phillip Corbin & Associates** *(P A Corbin)* Trym Lodge, 1 Henbury Road, Westbury-on-Trym, BRISTOL, BS9 3HQ.

ⓅⒶ**Phillip Jenkins Limited** *(P Jenkins)* 16 Parkfields, Pen-Y-Fai, BRIDGEND, MID GLAMORGAN, CF31 4NQ.

Ⓟ**Phillip Lee Management Consultants Pte Ltd** *(S H Lee)* Blk 166 Woodlands St 13, Apartment 02-521, SINGAPORE 730166, SINGAPORE.

Phillip P. Evans *(P P Evans)* Crown House, London Road, Loudwater, HIGH WYCOMBE, HP10 9TJ.

Ⓐ**Phillips & Co.** *(M J Phillips)* 52 The Chase, Newhall, HARLOW, ESSEX, CM17 9JA.

Ⓟ**Phillips Dinnes Limited** *(M C Dinnes, Stephen Phillips)* Lyddons, Nailsbourne, TAUNTON, SOMERSET, TA2 8AF.

★ⒾⒻⒶ**Phillips Frith, trading name of Phillips Frith LLP** *(I W Chalmers)* 9 Tregarne Terrace, ST. AUSTELL, CORNWALL, PL25 4DD.

Phillips Parkinson & Co *(J P Parkinson)* 2 Fawns Keep, WILMSLOW, SK9 2BQ.

Phillips Spyrou LLP *(L A Phillips, S P Spyrou)* 2 Old Court Mews, 311a Chase Road, LONDON, N14 6JS.

ⒾⓅⒶ**Phillips, trading name of Phillips Ltd** *(N C Phillips)* Kingsland House, Stafford Court, Stafford Park 1, TELFORD, SHROPSHIRE, TF3 3BD.

ⒾⒻⓅⒶ**Phipp & Co, trading name of Phipp & Co (Accountants) Ltd** *(G R Hill, S C Payne)* 6 Nottingham Road, Long Eaton, NOTTINGHAM, NG10 1HP.

ⒻⒶ**Phipps Henson McAllister** *(J Austin, S M Chambers, C Henson, P J Phipps, R A Phipps, M S Smith, R Whitehouse)* 22/24 Harborough Road, Kingsthorpe, NORTHAMPTON, NN2 7AZ. and at BANBURY

Ⓕ**Pickering** *(D Pickering)* 10 Oxford Street, MALMESBURY, SN16 9AZ.

★**Pickerings** *(J C G Pickering)* 48 South Street, ALDERLEY EDGE, SK9 7ES.

Ⓟ**Pickup Investigative Accounting & Forensics Pty Ltd** *(H E Pickup)* 23 Emerald Tce, PERTH, WA 6005, AUSTRALIA.

ⒾⒻⓅⒶ**Pierce Corporate Finance, trading name of Pierce C A Ltd** *(G G Boyes, J D Green, M Maden-Wilkinson, T E Nutter, P Warren)* Mentor House, Ainsworth Street, BLACKBURN, BB1 6AY.

ⓅⒶ**Pierce Group, trading name of Pierce Group Limited** *(S J Baxendale, G G Boyes, J D Green, M Maden-Wilkinson, D K Sharpe, P Warren)* Mentor House, Ainsworth Street, BLACKBURN, BB1 6AY.

Ⓐ**Piercy & Co** *(M W Piercy)* Tudor Lodge, The Drive, Hook Heath, WOKING, GU22 0JS.

Ⓟ**Pilkingtons, trading name of Dunne & Pilkington Limited** *(C B Pilkington, S Pilkington)* 135 Towngate, LEYLAND, PR25 2LH.

Ⓟ**Pillow May Ltd** *(J Pillow)* Bremhill Grove Farmhouse, East Tytherton, CHIPPENHAM, WILTSHIRE, SN15 4LX.

ⓅⒶ**Pinard & Co Limited** *(J A Pinard)* Berkley House, 18 Station Road, EAST GRINSTEAD, WEST SUSSEX, RH19 1DJ.

Ⓟ**Pinard Wright & Co Ltd** *(J A Pinard, E K H Wright)* Berkeley House, 18 Station Road, EAST GRINSTEAD, WEST SUSSEX, RH19 1DJ.

ⒻⒶ**Pinder & Ratki** *(H Eales, M Ratki)* 7 Lansdowne Terrace, Gosforth, NEWCASTLE UPON TYNE, NE3 1HN.

ⒾⒻⓅⒶ**Pinfields, trading name of Pinfields Limited** *(A Hess, P Tivey, M Warman)* Meryll House, 57 Worcester Road, BROMSGROVE, WORCESTERSHIRE, B61 7DN.

Ⓟ**Pinfold Secretarial Services Limited** *(S W Bygott)* 1-3 Dudley Street, GRIMSBY, LINCOLNSHIRE, DN31 2AW.

ⒻⒶ**Pinkham Blair** *(D A Blair, D J Pinkham)* 87A High Street, The Old Town, HEMEL HEMPSTEAD, HERTFORDSHIRE, HP1 3AH.

Ⓟ**Pinnacle Bookkeeping Ltd** *(R G Barrs, P S Bird, J A Cowan)* 6th Floor, Victory House, Prospect Hill, Douglas, ISLE OF MAN, IM1 1EQ.

Ⓟ**Pinnacle Freelance Services Limited** *(L Ramm)* Fifth Floor, Kingmaker House, Station Road, New Barnet, BARNET, HERTFORDSHIRE EN5 1NZ.

Ⓟ**Pinnacle Ltd** *(R J Macaulay)* Tyn y Mynydd, Llanddona, BEAUMARIS, GWYNEDD, LL58 8TR.

ⓅⒶ**Pinnacle, trading name of DeMontfort Solutions Ltd** *(A Kataria)* 32 De Montfort Street, LEICESTER, LE1 7GD.

ⒻⒶ**Pinner Darlington** *(K Fullerton, K Minett, R Pinner)* Broughton House, 187 Wolverhampton Street, DUDLEY, DY1 3AD. and at BRIDGNORTH, KIDDERMINSTER

★**Pinnick Lewis** *(H J Daniel)* Handel House, 95 High Street, EDGWARE, HA8 7DB.

Pinstripe Busines Solutions *(L M Hannan)* 28 Foxglove Close, NEWTON AYCLIFFE, COUNTY DURHAM, DL5 4PF.

Ⓐ**Piper Thompson** *(T J Thompson)* Mulberry House, 53 Church Street, WEYBRIDGE, KT13 8DJ.

Pippa Warren *(P J Warren)* 7 Dane Close, Winsley, BRADFORD-ON-AVON, BA15 2NA.

ⓉⓅⒶ**Pitayanukul & Co Ltd** *(S Pitayanukul)* No. 13, 2 Artichoke Hill, LONDON, E1W 2DE.

Pitman Cohen Recoveries LLP *(S Cohen, J A Swan)* Great Central House, Great Central Avenue, RUISLIP, MIDDLESEX, HA4 6TS.

ⒻⒶ**Pitt, Godden & Taylor** *(M D Godden, P T Shiers, P J Taylor)* Brunel House, George Street, GLOUCESTER, GL1 1BZ.

ⓉⒻⒶ**PJE** *(P J Evans, M A Salter)* 3 Oakfield Court, Oakfield Road, Clifton, BRISTOL, BS8 2BD.

ⒻⓅⒶ**PJE, trading name of Cyfri Cyfrifwyr Cyfyngedig** *(S C Evans, S A Longworth, D R Patterson)* 23 College Street, LAMPETER, DYFED, SA48 7DY. and at ABERAERON, ABERYSTWYTH

PJH & Company *(P Hoszowskyj)* 39A Mottram Moor, Mottram, HYDE, SK14 6LA.

PJM Accountancy *(P J McAughey)* Trevean, Yeolmbridge, LAUNCESTON, CORNWALL, PL15 8NJ.

PJMA *(P J Macdonald)* PO Box 58218, LONDON, N1 4XN.

Ⓟ**PJP Tax Consultancy, trading name of PJP Tax Consultancy Ltd** *(P J Preston)* Longbridge Farm, WARWICK, CV34 6RB.

ⓅⒶ**PJW Accounting Limited** *(P J Woodcock)* Suite 15, Hawkesyard Hall, Armitage Park, Armitage, RUGELEY, STAFFORDSHIRE WS15 1PU.

Ⓐ**PK Audit London, trading name of PK Audit LLP** *(P W Kennedy, M J C Penny, K Shah, J M Waller)* 22 The Quadrant, RICHMOND, SURREY, TW9 1BP.

★ⓉⒶ**PK Group, trading name of PK Partners LLP** *(P W Kennedy, M J C Penny, K Shah, J M Waller)* 22 The Quadrant, RICHMOND, SURREY, TW9 1BP.

PK Kwong & Co *(P Kwong)* Unit 2011, 20/F Hopewell Centre, 183 Queens Road East, WAN CHAI, HONG KONG ISLAND, HONG KONG SAR.

PKB UK LLP *(A J Hindley)* Beechey House, 87 Church Street, CROWTHORNE, RG45 7AW.

PKB, trading name of Peter K Blackwell FCA *(P K Blackwell)* 11 Farndale, WIGSTON, LEICESTERSHIRE, LE18 3XP.

★**PKF** *(L K Hui)* 26/F Citicorp Centre, 18 Whitfield Road, CAUSEWAY BAY, HONG KONG ISLAND, HONG KONG SAR.

★**PKF** *(A J Skelchy)* 9th Floor, MCB Plaza, No 6 Changkat Raja, Chulan, 50200 KUALA LUMPUR, FEDERAL TERRITORY MALAYSIA.

ⓉⓅⒶ**PKF (Channel Islands) Ltd** *(J S Bradley, S M Phillips, S J Thornton)* PO Box 296, Sarnia House, Le Truchot, St Peter Port, GUERNSEY, GY1 4NA.

ⓉⓅⒶ**PKF (Isle of Man) LLC** *(M H Crowe, J M Cryer, P E Dearden, D A R Drewett, M J Kneale, P A Seaward)* PO Box 16, Analyst House, Douglas, ISLE OF MAN, IM99 1AP.

★ⓉⒶ**PKF (UK) LLP** *(D G Bancroft, S J Barnsdall, N Bathia, I A Bingham, R S Bint, T N Birch, M Bridge, S J Browning, N J Buxton, P M Cassell, J B Cassidy, P M Clarke, S C Collins, M R G Cook, L M Cooper, C Cox, D M Dearman, N E S Dimes, T A Drew, D P Eagles, P J Ellis, T J Entwistle, C W A Escott, M Fairhurst, R J Faulkner, K Ferguson, H Ghafoor, M D Gibson, M J Gill, M R Goodchild, B J Hamblin, J P Hamilton, J A Harris, S P Harrison, P J Harrup, R A Hawkins, J D Hiley, J W M Hills, S P Holgate, J R Homewood, D K Horner, A J Huddleston, R L F Hudson, C P Humphreys, S P Jessop, A M Kerry, S King, J A Kirkham, N Y Kissun, D G Liddell, J M Lister, M Martin, V A Martin-Long, H R Mathew-Jones, I F Mathieson, R F McNaughton, D H Mead, R L Merchant, K R Mistry, J D E Money, M J Muskett, J D Newell, P R Pallett, R H M Plews, D J Pomfret, G J Randall, B G Ricketts, I C Schofield, H F Sharpe, L J Shaw, E M Shepherd, G M Singleton, T D Smith, T R Stephenson, C W Stewart, A C Stringer, M Sykes, B D Tash, K J Thompson, H G Voisey, J D Welch, N M Whitaker, R R Whitlock, R D Wilson)* Farringdon Place, 20 Farringdon Road, LONDON, EC1M 3AP. and at ALTON, BIRMINGHAM, BRISTOL, CARDIFF, DERBY, EDINBURGH, GLASGOW, GREAT YARMOUTH, GUILDFORD, IPSWICH, LEEDS, LEICESTER, LINCOLN, LIVERPOOL, MANCHESTER, NORWICH, NOTTINGHAM, SHEFFIELD

PKF Cayman *(S B Leung)* Century Yard, Cricket Square, 171 Elgin Avenue, PO Box 1782, GEORGE TOWN, GRAND CAYMAN KY1-1109 CAYMAN ISLANDS.

★**PKF Kenya** *(H R Shah)* Jubilee Insurance Building, 3rd Floor, Moi Avenue, PO Box 90553, MOMBASA, 80100 KENYA.

★**PKF, PKF Pannell Kerr Forster, PKF Professional Services, Safecon SARL, trading names of PKF S.A.R.L** *(P N Adibe)* 304 Boulevard du 13 Janvier, LOME, TOGO. and at ABUJA, ACCRA, BAUCHI, DOUALA, FREETOWN, JOS, KADUNA, KANO, KUMASI, MINNA, TEMA, ZARIA

ⓉⓅ**PKF/ATCO, PKF/ATCO Limited, trading names of PKF Savvides & Co Ltd** *(C D Antoniou, G A Koukoumas, F Savvides, S Stavrou)* Meliza Court, 4th & 7th Floors, 229 Arch Makarios III Ave, 3105 LIMASSOL, CYPRUS. and at NICOSIA

PKIB Accounting LLP *(I M Beardall, K Patel)* 132 Leicester Road, LOUGHBOROUGH, LEICESTERSHIRE, LE11 2AQ.

Ⓟ**PKM Admin Services Limited** *(P K Mankelow)* PO Box 45, CRAWLEY, WEST SUSSEX, RH10 3YP.

ⓉⒶ**PKN Parkins** *(J R Parkin, J S Parkin)* 63 Bawtry Road, Bramley, ROTHERHAM, S66 2TN.

Ⓟ**PKS, trading name of PK Shah & Co Ltd** *(P K Shah)* 60 Fairlands Avenue, THORNTON HEATH, SURREY, CR7 6HA.

ⓅⒶ**PKW Accountancy Limited** *(P K West)* Second Floor, 1 Church Square, LEIGHTON BUZZARD, BEDFORDSHIRE, LU7 1AE.

ⓉⒻⒶ**PKW LLP** *(M Kershaw, M J Pickup, J Wild)* Cloth Hall, 150 Drake Street, ROCHDALE, LANCASHIRE, OL16 1PX.

★ⒻⒶ**Place Campbell** *(N J Avis, R G C Bridger, E A Monk, M D Watkins)* Wilmington House, High Street, EAST GRINSTEAD, RH19 3AU.

ⒻⒶ**Place Flight** *(G L Flight)* Montrose House, 22 Christopher Road, EAST GRINSTEAD, RH19 3BT.

Plan For Success *(C A Hotson)* 4 Murray Road, HUDDERSFIELD, HD2 2AD.

ⒻⓅ**PlanIT Services Limited** *(A D Learer)* Lansdowne House, City Forum, 250 City Road, LONDON, EC1V 2QZ.

Ⓐ**Plant & Co** *(P J Plant)* 17 Lichfield Street, STONE, STAFFORDSHIRE, ST15 8NA.

Platinum Capital Partners LLP *(S Thelwall-Jones)* The Hayloft, Mulsford Lane, Sarn, MALPAS, CHESHIRE, SY14 7LW.

ⓉⒻⒶ**Platt Rushton LLP** *(M J Hallybone, A P Mate, G M Powling, D A Sheekey)* Sutherland House, 1759 London Road, LEIGH-ON-SEA, ESSEX, SS9 2RZ.

ⒻⒶ**Platts** *(A M Platt)* 643 Watford Way, Apex Corner Mill Hill, LONDON, NW7 3JR.

Playter & Co *(S Playter)* 18 Stinchar Drive, Badgers Copse, Chandlers Ford, EASTLEIGH, SO53 4QH.

Ⓟ**PLG Consulting Ltd** *(P Guiduzzi)* 2nd Floor Victory House, 99-101 Regent Street, LONDON, W1B 4EZ.

ⓅⒶ**PLH Limited** *(P L Hunkin)* Woodfield House, Castle Walk, NEATH, WEST GLAMORGAN, SA11 3LN.

ⓉⒻⒶ**Plummer Parsons** *(N C Beckhurst, N J H Brown, C M Gorringe, S J Griffen, K L McCurdy, A W Saunders, P Thursfield)* 18 Hyde Gardens, EASTBOURNE, BN21 4PT. and at BRIGHTON, HAILSHAM

Ⓟ**Plummer Parsons, trading name of Plummer Parsons Accountants Limited** *(N C Beckhurst, N J H Brown, C M Gorringe, S J Griffen, K L McCurdy, A W Saunders, P Thursfield)* 4 Frederick Terrace, Frederick Place, BRIGHTON, BN1 1AX. and at EASTBOURNE, HAILSHAM

Ⓟ**Plus Minus, trading name of Plus Minus Ltd** *(S C Saha)* C/6, 417 Wick Lane, Fish Island, LONDON, E3 2JG.

Ⓟ**Plushcourt Estates Limited** *(J R Chenery)* 2 The Estate Yard, Ixworth, BURY ST. EDMUNDS, SUFFOLK, IP31 2HE.

ⒻⓅ**PM & M Corporate Finance, trading name of PM & M Corporate Finance Limited** *(R A Ainscough, J E Akrill, S M Anderson, D P Bradley, A R Brierley, D L Eatough, J Parry, A Tinker)* Greenbank Technology Park, Challenge Way, BLACKBURN, BB1 5QB.

ⓅⓂ**PM Cook & Co, trading name of PM Cook & Co Ltd** *(P M Cook)* 2 Hunters Buildings, Bowesfield Lane, STOCKTON-ON-TEES, CLEVELAND, TS18 3QZ.

PM Johnson *(P M Johnson)* Tarag', 48 Rectory Road, Gosforth, NEWCASTLE UPON TYNE, NE3 1XP.

ⓅⒶ**PM&G, trading name of PM&G Limited** *(P Gladwin, P Mitchell)* Mainwood Farm, Kneesall, NEWARK, NOTTINGHAMSHIRE, NG22 0AH.

ⓉⒻⒶ**PM+M Solutions for Business LLP** *(R A Ainscough, J E Akrill, S M Anderson, D P Bradley, A R Brierley, D L Eatough, J Parry, A Tinker)* Greenbank Technology Park, Challenge Way, BLACKBURN, BB1 5QB. and at BURNLEY

PMB *(P M Barrett)* Maseru Book Centre Building, P.O. Box 1252, Kingsway, MASERU, 100, LESOTHO.

Ⓟ**PMM Services Limited** *(M S Silver)* Flat 4, 7 Gordon Avenue, STANMORE, MIDDLESEX, HA7 3QE.

PN Philis & Co *(P N Philis)* 16 Macquarie Drive, CHERRYBROOK, NSW 2126, AUSTRALIA.

Pocknells LLP *(C M Pocknell)* 46 Hullbridge Road, South Woodham Ferrers, CHELMSFORD, ESSEX, CM3 5NG.

Pococks *(M Pocock)* 3 Thamesgate Close, Ham, RICHMOND, TW10 7YS.

★Ⓣ**Poh & Tan** *(B L B Poh)* 19-1 Jalan 3/146, Bandar Tasik Selatan, 57000 KUALA LUMPUR, FEDERAL TERRITORY, MALAYSIA.

★Ⓐ**Pointon Young** *(S A J Brown)* 33 Ludgate Hill, BIRMINGHAM, B3 1EH.

Ⓐ**Pollard Goodman** *(C V Pollard)* 49 High Street, Westbury on Trym, BRISTOL, BS9 3ED.

Ⓟ**Pollards Accountancy Services Limited** *(L E Coulter)* 54 Ebury Road, RICKMANSWORTH, HERTFORDSHIRE, WD3 1BN.

Pollorosso *(S D McCletchie)* Flat 2, Redcliffe House, 33 Cavendish Road East, NOTTINGHAM, NG7 1BB.

Ⓟ**Polydoros Xenophontos Ltd** *(P K Xenophontos)* Athienitis Building, 8 Kennedy Avenue Suite 305, 1087 NICOSIA, CYPRUS.

★**Pool & Patel** *(S Patel, B L Pool)* Maison La Rosiere, P.O. Box 117, VICTORIA, SEYCHELLES.

★**Poole Mordant, trading name of Poole Mordant LLP** *(M R Poole)* 35 City Business Centre, St Olav's Court, Rotherhithe, LONDON, SE16 2XB.

★**Poole Waterfield** *(R K Groseley)* Priory House, Priory Road, DUDLEY, WEST MIDLANDS, DY1 1HH. and at STOURBRIDGE

Ⓟ**Poole Waterfield Limited** *(D L Gibbens, H C Gibbens, R K Groseley)* Priory House, Priory Road, DUDLEY, WEST MIDLANDS, DY1 1HH.

ⓉⒻⒶ**Pooleys** *(D H Pooley)* 45 Lemon Street, TRURO, TR1 2NS.

★**Poon & Co.** *(W C Poon, Y S Poon Wong)* Dominion Centre, 6th Floor, 43-59 Queen's Road East, WAN CHAI, HONG KONG ISLAND, HONG KONG SAR.

Poonja & Company *(M Poonja)* P O Box 1510, LOS ALTOS, CA 94023-1510, UNITED STATES.

Pope & Co *(J B Pope)* 1 Drayton Close, Swindon Village, CHELTENHAM, GL51 9QB.

★**Poppleton and Appleby** *(M T Coyne)* 35 Ludgate Hill, BIRMINGHAM, B3 1EH. and at COVENTRY

ⓉⒻⒶ**Porritt Rainey** *(A R E Peal)* 9 Pembroke Road, SEVENOAKS, KENT, TN13 1XR.

ⓉⒻⓅⒶ**Porter Garland, trading name of Porter Garland Limited** *(P G Peel, T C A Pottinger, A Williams)* Portland House, Park Street, BAGSHOT, SURREY, GU19 5PG.

ⒻⒶ**Portlock & Company** *(D I Macleod)* Ash House, Ash Road, New Ash Green, LONGFIELD, KENT, DA3 8JD.

Portman & Co *(P S Patel)* 5 High Street, Hornsey, LONDON, N8 7PS.

Ⓟ**Positive Accountants, trading name of A Lock & Co Limited** *(A D Lock)* Elmwood House, York Road, Kirk Hammerton, YORK, YO26 8DH.

Posner Lyons *(J L Posner)* 38a Northiam, Woodside Park, LONDON, N12 7HA.

Potter & Co *(R J Potter, W S Potter)* 79 Friar Gate, DERBY, DE1 1FL.

ⓅⒶ**Potter & Pollard, trading name of Potter & Pollard Ltd** *(R E Bagshawe)* Richmond Court, 216 Capstone Road, BOURNEMOUTH, BH8 8RX.

Ⓟ**Potter Adams Limited** *(D M Young)* 89 Gillards Close, Rockwell Green, WELLINGTON, SOMERSET, TA21 9DX.

Ⓟ**Potter Associates Ltd** *(R J Potter, W S Potter)* 79 Friar Gate, DERBY, DE1 1FL.

ⓉⒶ**Potter Baker** *(A D Baker, M J Wevill)* 20 Western Road, LAUNCESTON, PL15 7BA. and at TAVISTOCK

ⒻⒶ**Potter McGregor & Co.** *(M J Holt, J A Potter)* 5 Willmott Close, SUTTON COLDFIELD, WEST MIDLANDS, B75 5NP. and at BURTON-ON-TRENT

★**Potts & Co** *(R D Potts)* 6 Jacobs Yard, Middle Barton, CHIPPING NORTON, OXFORDSHIRE, OX7 7BY.

Poulton & Co *(S N Poulton)* 15 Oakdene, BEACONSFIELD, BUCKINGHAMSHIRE, HP9 2BZ.

ⓉⒶ**Povey Little** *(A M Povey)* 12 Hatherley Road, SIDCUP, KENT, DA14 4DT.

Powdrill & Smith *(P R W Smith)* 120 Bull Head Street, Wigston Magna, WIGSTON, LE18 1PB.

Powell & Co *(R T W Powell)* 5 High Street, KINGTON, HEREFORDSHIRE, HR5 3AX.

Ⓐ**Powell & Co.** *(S A W Powell)* Manor Cottage, Shamley Green, GUILDFORD, GU5 0UD.

ⒻⓅⒶ**Powell & Powell, trading name of Powell & Powell Limited** *(C F Mellalieu, S M Tattersall)* 107 Wellington Road, STOCKPORT, CHESHIRE, SK1 3TL.

Ⓐ**Power & Co** *(S J Power)* 12 Queen Eleanors Drive, Knowle, SOLIHULL, WEST MIDLANDS, B93 9LY.

ⒻⓅⒶ**Power Accountax, trading name of Power Accountax Limited** *(R P Kohli)* 8c High Street, SOUTHAMPTON, SO14 2DH.

★ⓉⒻⒶ**Power Thompson** *(C J Thompson)* 199 Clarendon Park Road, LEICESTER, LE2 3AN.

Powrie Appleby LLP *(D Powrie, C P Walker)* Queen Anne House, 4 6 & 8 New Street, LEICESTER, LE1 5NR.

ⒻⓅ**PPG Accountants Limited** *(D T Guest)* Ferndale House, 3 Firs Street, DUDLEY, WEST MIDLANDS, DY2 7DN.

Ⓟ**PPK Accountants Limited** *(W D Coupland)* Evolution House, 2-6 Easthampstead Road, WOKINGHAM, BERKSHIRE, RG40 2EG.

ⓅⒶ**PPK Auditors, trading name of PPK Auditors Limited** *(W D Coupland)* Evolution House, 2-6 Easthampstead Road, WOKINGHAM, BERKSHIRE, RG40 2EG.

PPK Professional Services LLP *(W D Coupland)* Evolution House, 2- 6 Easthampstead Road, WOKINGHAM, BERKSHIRE, RG40 2EG.

Ⓟ**Pracserve Limited** *(U K Ray)* Falcon House, 257 Burlington Road, NEW MALDEN, KT3 4NE.

Practical Financial Management, trading name of David Bowman *(D Bowman)* 40 Hurdeswell, Long Hanborough, WITNEY, OX29 8DH.

Ⓟ**Practical Tax Consultants Limited** *(M E Bell)* 4 Greenfield Road, HOLMFIRTH, WEST YORKSHIRE, HD9 2JT.

Pradip D. Patel *(P D Patel)* 41 Warwick Road, New Southgate, LONDON, N11 2SD.

ⓉⒻⒶ**Prager and Fenton, trading name of Prager and Fenton LLP** *(M A Boomla, A K Jacobs)* 8th Floor, Imperial House, 15-19 Kingsway, LONDON, WC2B 6UN.

Prakash Raithatha & Co *(P C Raithatha)* 11 Grove Farm Park, NORTHWOOD, HA6 2BQ.

ⓉⒶ**PRB Accountants LLP** *(M J Cole, K M Lo, S C Power, C D Whitley-Jones)* Kingfisher House, Hurstwood Grange, Hurstwood Lane, HAYWARDS HEATH, WEST SUSSEX, RH17 7QX.

Ⓟ**Premier Accountants Limited** *(A Chrysostomou)* Suite 1A 3rd Floor, Hillside House, 2-6 Friern Park, LONDON, N12 9BT.

Ⓟ**Premier Financial Direction Ltd** *(C J Gahagan)* Kestrel Court, Harbour Road, Portishead, BRISTOL, BS20 7AN.

Ⓟ**Premier Payroll Centre Limited** *(A D Richards, N Wilson)* 68 Argyle Street, BIRKENHEAD, MERSEYSIDE, CH41 6AF.

Ⓟ**Premier Payroll Limited** *(D J Topping)* 1 Long Street, TETBURY, GLOUCESTERSHIRE, GL8 8AA.

Ⓟ**Premier Strategies Limited** *(R A Coombs, M D Edmond, C S Jackson, R S McBurnie, A P Raynor)* The Poynt, 45 Wollaton Street, NOTTINGHAM, NG1 5FW.

Ⓟ**Premier Tax Consultancy Ltd** *(K A Salter)* Calico House, Calico Lane, Furness Vale, HIGH PEAK, DERBYSHIRE, SK23 7SW.

★ⒻⒶ**Prentis & Co LLP** *(N A Prentis)* 115c Milton Road, CAMBRIDGE, CB4 1XE.

Preseli Management Accounting *(S T Warner)* Ranelagh, Precelly Crescent, GOODWICK, DYFED, SA64 0HF.

Ⓟ**Preston Accountants Limited** *(D W Aston)* 132 Walham Green Court, Moore Park Road, Fulham, LONDON, SW6 2PX.

ⓉⒻ**Prestons** *(S J Preston)* The Old Stables, Ilex Farm, Handley Lane, Handley, Clay Cross, CHESTERFIELD DERBYSHIRE S45 9AT.

ⒻⒶ**Prestons** *(A Mehta, A H Patel)* 364-368 Cranbrook Road, Gants Hill, ILFORD, ESSEX, IG2 6HY.

Ⓐ**Prestons & Jacksons Partnership LLP** *(A Mehta, A H Patel)* 364-368 Cranbrook Road, ILFORD, ESSEX, IG2 6HY.

Ⓟ**Pretium Consulting Limited** *(H Patel)* 16 Martock Gardens, LONDON, N11 3GH.

Price & Company *(M J E Price)* Meadsted House, 80 Jacklyns Lane, ALRESFORD, SO24 9LJ.

▽ⓉⒻⓅⒶ**Price & Company** *(M J Neilan, M N Preece, P A Severn, S Wood)* 30/32 Gildredge Road, EASTBOURNE, BN21 4SH.

★**Price Bailey LLP** *(S J Blake, M W H Clapson, P F Gillman, P G Martin, N Mayhew, G W Miller, C W Olley, C J Pickard, A J Sanderson, T J Smith, R L Vass, J S Warren)* Causeway House, 1 Dane Street, BISHOP'S STORTFORD, HERTFORDSHIRE, CM23 3BT. and at CAMBRIDGE, ELY, LONDON, NORWICH

★ⓉⒶ**Price Bailey LLP** *(S J Blake, M W H Clapson, P F Gillman, P G Martin, N Mayhew, G W Miller, C W Olley, C J Pickard, A J Sanderson, T J Smith, R L Vass, J S Warren)* Causeway House, 1 Dane Street, BISHOP'S STORTFORD, HERTFORDSHIRE, CM23 3BT. and at CAMBRIDGE, ELY, GUERNSEY, LONDON, NORWICH

Ⓟ**Price Bailey, trading name of Price Bailey Ltd** *(M W H Clapson, P F Gillman, C W Olley, C J Pickard)* PO Box 511, 2nd Floor Elizabeth House, Les Ruetles' Brayes, St. Peter Port, GUERNSEY, GY1 6DU.

Ⓟ**Price Davis, trading name of Price Davis Limited** *(H Davis)* The Old Baptist Chapel, New Street, Painswick, STROUD, GL6 6XH.

ⒻⒶ**Price Firman** *(M N Cox, M Firman, S J Richards, V Underhill)* Prince Consort House, Albert Embankment, LONDON, SE1 7TJ.

Price Jenkins & Co *(S P Jenkins)* 14 Plas y Ddol, Johnstown, CARMARTHEN, DYFED, SA31 3PL.

Price Mann & Co *(B T G Hindocha, V T Hindocha)* 447 Kenton Road, HARROW, HA3 0XY.

★**Price Pearson Wheatley** *(J S Wheatley)* Clarendon House, 14 St Andrews Street, DROITWICH, WR9 8DY.

ⓅⒶ**PriceDeacon Witham, trading name of Price Deacon Witham Ltd** *(D J Witham)* 9 Millar Court, Station Road, KENILWORTH, WARWICKSHIRE, CV8 1JD. and at SOLIHULL

★Ⓣ**PricewaterhouseCoopers** *(G J Davies, F J Konings, M L Poelman, S C B Wray)* P O Box 7067, 1007 JB AMSTERDAM, NETHERLANDS. and at ALKMAAR, AMERSFOORT, ARNHEM, BREDA, DORDRECHT, EINDHOVEN, GRONINGEN, HENGELO, LEEUWARDEN, MAASTRICHT, NIJMEGEN, ROTTERDAM, THE HAGUE, UTRECHT, ZWOLLE

★Ⓣ**PricewaterhouseCoopers** *(A Yiannopoulos)* 268-270 Kifissias Avenue, Halandri, 15232 ATHENS, GREECE. and at PIRAEUS, THESSALONIKI

★**PricewaterhouseCoopers** *(N Haines, E R Lucas, A S Wotton)* Level 21, PWC Tower, 188 Quay Street, Private Bag 92162, AUCKLAND 1142, NEW ZEALAND. and at CHRISTCHURCH, DUNEDIN, NAPIER, NEW PLYMOUTH, WELLINGTON, WHANGAREI

★**PricewaterhouseCoopers** *(C C Sifri)* SNA Building 5th Floor, PO Box 11-3155, Tabaris Square, BEIRUT, LEBANON.

★**PricewaterhouseCoopers** *(R M Bynoe, M A Hatch)* Financial Services Centre, Bishop's Court Hill, BRIDGETOWN, BARBADOS.

★**PricewaterhouseCoopers** *(P A Cunningham, M F Pottle)* namesti Svobody 20, 602 00 BRNO, CZECH REPUBLIC. and at OSTRAVA, PRAGUE

★**PricewaterhouseCoopers** *(C Chan, R A Clementson, S C Copley, J W Donker, S W Y S Doo, C A Farrell, M R Fenez, R A Gazzi, R J Knight, M Kohli, Y Lam, K T Lo, T L Lui, F Y Lyn, W T L Mak, C D Po, R S Punia, C S Shaftesley, K H Spooner, C W Tsang, P A Whalley, S S S Yang, K F F Yip, C Yu)* Prince's Building, 22/F, 10 Chater Road, CENTRAL, HONG KONG ISLAND, HONG KONG SAR. and at KWUN TONG, SHEUNG WAN

★Ⓣ**PricewaterhouseCoopers** *(S Drake, A Garrett, W E Hunt, V D Lodhia, I Schneider, M K Speller, P Suddaby, J S Todd)* Emirates Towers Offices, PO Box 11987, Level 40, Sheikh Zayed Road, PO Box 11987, DUBAI UNITED ARAB EMIRATES. and at ABU DHABI

PricewaterhouseCoopers *(C Kohli, A E O'Callaghan)* One Spencer Dock, North Wall Quay, DUBLIN 1, COUNTY DUBLIN, IRELAND. and at CORK, GALWAY, KILKENNY, LIMERICK, WATERFORD, WEXFORD

★Ⓣ**PricewaterhouseCoopers** *(R M A Bonieux, L M Levehang, M M O Noormohamed-Oosman)* 18 CyberCity, EBENE, MAURITIUS. and at PORT LOUIS

★**PricewaterhouseCoopers** *(P R Anderton, C J F Bolland, J I N Freeland, R C Jenkinson)* Strathvale House, PO Box 258, GEORGE TOWN, GRAND CAYMAN, KY1-1104, CAYMAN ISLANDS.

★Ⓣ**PricewaterhouseCoopers** *(E C A Lavarello, K C Menez)* Intnl Commercial Centre, Casemates Square, GIBRALTAR, GIBRALTAR.

★Ⓣ**PricewaterhouseCoopers** *(R C Patching)* Dorchester House, 7 Church Street West, PO Box HM1171, HAMILTON HM EX, BERMUDA.

★**PricewaterhouseCoopers** *(K S Wood)* Building No 4, Arundel Office Park, Norfolk Road Mount Pleasant, HARARE, ZIMBABWE. and at GABORONE

▽ⓉⒶ**PricewaterhouseCoopers** *(D B Churcher, I G Clague, M Simpson)* Sixty Circular Road, Douglas, ISLE OF MAN, IM1 1SA.

★**PricewaterhouseCoopers** *(S J D Humphries, C D Rees)* Gedung PricewaterhouseCoopers, 5/F Jl HR Rasuna Said Kav C-3, Kuningan JAKARTA, 12920, INDONESIA.

▽**PricewaterhouseCoopers** *(K U Igbokwe)* Plot 252E Muri Okunola Street, Victoria Island, P O Box 2419, LAGOS, NIGERIA. and at ABUJA

★**PricewaterhouseCoopers** *(K M Carpenter)* ADL House, 3rd Floor, P O Box 30379, Capital City, LILONGWE, 3 MALAWI. and at BLANTYRE

★**PricewaterhouseCoopers** *(A.J.S.D'silva, P Fitzgerald)* Paseo de la Castellana 53, 28046 MADRID, SPAIN. and at BARCELONA, VALENCIA, ZARAGOZA

★**PricewaterhouseCoopers** *(W D Bailey)* Multinational Bancorp., Centre 14th Floor, 6805 Ayala Avenue, MAKATI CITY 1226, PHILIPPINES. and at MANILA

★**PricewaterhouseCoopers** *(R D P Walker)* Rovuma Carlton Hotel, Centro de Escritorios Piso 3, Sala 1 Rua de Se MAPUTO, 114, MOZAMBIQUE.

★**PricewaterhouseCoopers** *(J P E Lewis)* PO Box 569, MBABANE, SWAZILAND.

★**PricewaterhouseCoopers** *(P K B Kinisu, R K Shah, M J Whitehead)* Rahimtulla Tower, Upper Hill Road, PO Box 43963, NAIROBI, 00100, KENYA. and at MOMBASA

★**PricewaterhouseCoopers** *(S C Beach)* Credit House, P O Box 484, Cuthbertson Street, PORT MORESBY, PAPUA NEW GUINEA. and at LAE

★**PricewaterhouseCoopers** *(A J F Dawes, L S Hemery)* Avenida Andres Bello 2711, Torre Costanera Piso 5, SANTIAGO, CHILE. and at ANTOFAGASTA, CONCEPCION, PUERTO MONTT

★**PricewaterhouseCoopers** *(M A Hopkin)* Avenida Francisco Matarazzo 1400, Torre Torino, Aqua Branca, SAO PAULO, 05001-903, BRAZIL. and at BELO HORIZONTE, BRASILIA, CAMPINAS, CURITIBA, PORTO ALEGRE, RECIFE, RIBEIRAO PRETO, RIO DE JANEIRO, SALVADOR, SOROCABA, VITORIA

★Ⓣ**PricewaterhouseCoopers** *(S W Gee, K Leong, D J Ryley)* 12th Floor Shui On Plaza, 333 Huai Hai Zhong Road, SHANGHAI 200021, CHINA. and at BEIJING, CHONGQING, DALIAN, GUANGZHOU, QINGDAO, SHENZHEN, SUZHOU, TIANJIN, XI'AN

★**PricewaterhouseCoopers** *(R J Wilkinson)* P O Box 1531, Old Parham Road, ST JOHNS, ANTIGUA AND BARBUDA.

★Ⓣ**PricewaterhouseCoopers** *(J Camilleri, F J Mifsud Bonnici, D A Valenzia, K J Valenzia)* 167 Merchants Street, VALLETTA VLT 1174, MALTA.

Ⓟ**PricewaterhouseCoopers (Vietnam) Ltd** *(P S Coleman, S Gaskill, R J Irwin, I S Lydall, R B Peters)* 4th Floor Saigon Tower, 29 Le Duan Boulevard, District 1, HO CHI MINH CITY, VIETNAM.

PricewaterhouseCoopers Aarata, trading name of PricewaterhouseCoopers *(M G Falconer, S D Hunt, M J Wyborn)* Kasumigaseki Building 15F, Kasumigaseki 3-2-5, Chiyoda-Ku, TOKYO, 100-6015 JAPAN. and at SEOUL

★**PricewaterhouseCoopers AG** *(S S L Di Paola, I D Mason, R A Van Alphen)* St Jakobs-Strasse 25, Postfach 4152, 4052 BASEL, SWITZERLAND. and at GENEVA

★**PricewaterhouseCoopers AS** *(S M Constant)* Bj°rvika, Postboks 748, Sentrum, NO-0106 OSLO, NORWAY. and at ALESUND, ARENDAL, DRAMMEN, FORDE, FREDRIKSTAD, HAMAR, KRISTIANSAND, MO I RANA, STAVANGER, TROMSO, TRONDHEIM

Ⓐ**PricewaterhouseCoopers AS LLP** *(R G Sexton)* 1 Embankment Place, LONDON, WC2N 6RH.

ⓉⒶ**PricewaterhouseCoopers CI LLP** *(W J Dorman, K J Hairon, M W James, S J Le Page)* Twenty Two Colomberie, St Helier, JERSEY, JE1 4XA. and at GUERNSEY

★Ⓣ**PricewaterhouseCoopers GmbH** *(R W Burton, E Hummitzsch, P Marshall, V J Price, S M Roberts)* Bockenheimer Anlage 15, Postfach 111842, 60053 FRANKFURT AM MAIN, GERMANY. and at ACHERN, BERLIN, BIELEFELD, DRESDEN, DUSSELDORF, ESSEN, FREIBURG, HALLE, HAMBURG, HANNOVER, KARLSRUHE, KASSEL, LEIPZIG, MAGDEBURG, MAINZ, MUNICH, NURNBERG, OLDENBURG, PIRMASENS, POTSDAM, RECKLINGHAUSEN, SAARBRUCKEN, SCHWERIN, SIEGEN, STUTTGART, WALLDORF

★**PricewaterhouseCoopers Inc** *(D M Fairbank, A D Seccombe)* 90 Rivonia Road, Sandown, JOHANNESBURG, GAUTENG, 2196, SOUTH AFRICA. and at BELLVILLE, BETHAL, BISHO, BLOEMFONTEIN, CAPE TOWN, CERES, DURBAN, EAST LONDON, ESHOWE, GEORGE, GREENACRES, GROENKLOOF, KIMBERLEY, KLERKSDORP, LICHTENBURG, MAFIKENG, MOORREESBURG, NELSPRUIT, PAARL, PIETERSBURG, PRETORIA, RICHARDS BAY, ROBERTSON, STELLENBOSCH, SUNNINGHILL, TZANEEN, UMTATA, WELKOM, WORCESTER

★**PricewaterhouseCoopers KFT** *(L M Birch, N R N Blower, G A Johnstone, J C Mozley, A M Simonds)* Wesselenyi u 16, BUDAPEST, H-1077, HUNGARY.

PriceWaterhouseCoopers LDA *(A A Baird, P C Q Mallett)* Palacio Sottomayor, Rue Sousa Martins, No 1 - 2 Esq, 1050-217 LISBON, PORTUGAL.

ⓉⓅ**PricewaterhouseCoopers Limited** *(M S Andreou, N Chimarides, A T Constantinides, C Constantinou, S C Constantinou, E Eftychiou, E Evgeniou, G K Foradaris, A Hadjiloucas, V P Hadjivassiliou, P Y Kaouris, Y A Kaponides, G Kazamias, G C Lambrou, A M Loizou, L A Markides, P Maroudias, C L Mavrocordatos, S C Michail, C M Nicolaides, T N Nolas, C N Papadopoulos, T C Parperis, C Pelekanos, P Petrakis, P K Pilides, A S Pittas, C K Santis, P Soseilos, S Stephanides, A Tavitian, C Themistocleous, E Theodorou, N A Theodoulou, C Tsolakis)* City House, 6 Karaiskakis Street, CY-3032 LIMASSOL, CYPRUS. and at LARNACA, NICOSIA, PAPHOS, POLIS CHRYSOHOUS, STROVOLOS

★**PricewaterhouseCoopers LLP** *(C Dempsey, I L Gardner, E Hodgeon, G E Johnson, E L Myall-Schofield, A J O'Reilly, D H Ricketts, P Sheward, R J Veysey, R J Withey)* 488 Almaden Boulevard, SAN JOSE, CA 95110, UNITED STATES. and at ATLANTA, BOSTON, CHICAGO, FLORHAM PARK, FORT WORTH, HOUSTON, LOS ANGELES, NEW YORK, ORLANDO, PHILADELPHIA, RALEIGH, SAN FRANCISCO, SOUTH JERSEY, TOLEDO, WASHINGTON, WOODLAND HILLS

Ⓣ**PricewaterhouseCoopers LLP** *(G Banerjee, P M Eastwood, Y K Kan, P Low Eng Huat, D A Nixon, C Ooi, G W S Tan)* 17-00 PWC Building, 8 Cross Street, SINGAPORE 048424, SINGAPORE.

Ⓟ**PricewaterhouseCoopers Ltd** *(K Dasgupta, P Ghosh, P M Kanakia, P Mitra, V Nijhawan, K H Vachha)* 252 Veer Savarkar Marg, Shivaji Park Dadr, MUMBAI 400028, MAHARASHTRA, INDIA. and at BANGALORE, BHUBANESWAR, CALCUTTA, GURGAON, HYDERABAD, MADRAS, NEW DELHI, PUNE

★**PricewaterhouseCoopers Ltd** *(D M T Bruton, J P Connolly)* Abacus House, P O Box 63, PROVIDENCIALES, TURKS AND CAICOS ISLANDS.

★Ⓣ**PricewaterhouseCoopers S.a.r.l.** *(D A Roach)* 400 route d'Esch, B P 1443, L-1014 LUXEMBOURG, LUXEMBOURG.

★**PricewaterhouseCoopers Sp. z o.o.** *(O B Grygier, P Peplinski, K Sinclair)* Al.Armii Ludowej 14, WARSAW, 00638, POLAND. and at KRAKOW

★**PricewaterhouseCoopers UAB** *(C C Butler)* Jasinskio 16B, VILNIUS LT-01112, LITHUANIA.

ⓅⒶ**PricewaterhouseCoopers, trading name of PricewaterhouseCoopers LLC** *(D B Churcher, I G Clague, K M Cowley, P C Craig, N M Halsall, M Simpson)* Sixty Circular Road, Circular Road, Douglas, ISLE OF MAN, IM1 1SA.

Pride *(C E Jones)* Polymer Court, Hope Street, DUDLEY, DY2 8RS.

Pridham Accountancy *(R L Pridham)* Pear Tree House, Pebworth Road, Ullington, EVESHAM, WORCESTERSHIRE, WR11 8QG.

Prime Virtue CPA & Co *(Y K H Tsui)* Unit 1603, 16/F, Omega Plaza, 32 Dundas Street, MONG KOK, KOWLOON HONG KONG SAR.

★ⓉⒻⓅⒶ**Prime, trading name of Prime Accountants & Business Advisers Limited** *(M N Davies, K H Johns, L P Moore)* 5 Argosy Court, Scimitar Way, Whitley Business Park, COVENTRY, CV3 4GA. and at SOLIHULL

★ⓅⒶ**Prime, trading name of Prime Accountants Group Limited** *(M N Davies, K H Johns, L P Moore)* 5 Argosy Court, Scimitar Way, Whitley Business Park, COVENTRY, CV3 4GA.

Ⓟ**Primul Consulting, trading name of Blitz The Bug Limited** *(R J Harvey)* Apartment 1202, Vallea Court, 1 Red Bank, MANCHESTER, M4 4FH.

Prince & Co *(D J Prince)* 23 Willes Road, LONDON, NW5 3DT.

ⓉⒻⒶ**Princecroft Willis, trading name of Princecroft Willis LLP** *(J Belinger, A N Bunston, A Gates, M A Johns, W J Law, N J Love, J I Robinson, D K Watton)* Towngate House, 2-8 Parkstone Road, POOLE, DORSET, BH15 2PW. and at NEW MILTON

Ⓣ**Princep Pardoe** *(K A Biggs)* 794 High Street, KINGSWINFORD, WEST MIDLANDS, DY6 8BQ.

Ⓟ**Priority Payroll Services Limited** *(C Gray)* 26 Lower Kings Road, BERKHAMSTED, HERTFORDSHIRE, HP4 2AE.

Ⓟ**Priory Checkpoint Limited** *(A J Croft)* 6 Bull Ring, MUCH WENLOCK, SHROPSHIRE, TF13 6HS.

Ⓟ**Prism Group Limited** *(S A Gardner)* The Old Sawmill, Copyhold Lane, Lindfield, HAYWARDS HEATH, WEST SUSSEX, RH16 1XT.

Ⓟ**Pristine Data Limited** *(M A Cooper)* 1a High Street, EPSOM, SURREY, KT19 8DA.

Ⓟ**Pritchard & Co, trading name of Pritchard A'I Gwmni Cyf** *(I R Williams)* 74 High Street, FISHGUARD, DYFED, SA65 9AU. and at CARDIGAN, HAVERFORDWEST

Ⓟ**Pritchard Evans & Co Ltd** *(E J Lewis)* 21 Carmarthen Street, LLANDEILO, CARMARTHENSHIRE, SA19 6AN.

Ⓟ**Pritchard Jones Accountancy Services Limited** *(H Jones)* 3 Quay Street, CARMARTHEN, DYFED, SA31 3JT.

Pritchard Roberts & Co *(D G Roberts)* 108A Lammas Street, CARMARTHEN, SA31 3AP.

ⓅⒶ**Pritchett & Co, trading name of Pritchett & Co Limited** *(R Kenwell, D H Pritchett)* 16 Wynnstay Road, COLWYN BAY, CLWYD, LL29 8NB.

Ⓟ**Pritchett & Co, trading name of Pritchett & Co Limited** *(R Kenwell, D H Pritchett)* 16 Wynnstay Road, COLWYN BAY, CONWY, LL29 8NB.

Pritchett Consulting, trading name of Pritchett Consulting BSc FCA *(P A Pritchett)* 2 Sweep Close, Market Weighton, YORK, YO43 3NH.

Ⓟ**Privilege Accounts, trading name of Privilege Accounts Limited** *(B P Roback, V R Stanton)* Catalyst House, 720 Centennial Avenue, Centennial Park, Elstree, BOREHAMWOOD, HERTFORDSHIRE WD6 3SY.

★**PRK Accountants** *(P A Baker)* Grover House, Grover Walk, Corringham, STANFORD-LE-HOPE, ESSEX, SS17 7LS.

Ⓟ**Proactive Accounting, trading name of Proactive Accounting (South East) Limited** *(W J Kyne)* 31 Oakwood Avenue, PURLEY, SURREY, CR8 1AR.

Ⓟ**Proactive Tax Ltd** *(L S Wagner)* 9 Hopetoun Drive, Bridge of Allan, STIRLING, FK9 4QQ.

ⒻⒶ**Probitts & Co** *(C M Probitts)* No 1 Carrera House, Merlin Court, Gatehouse Close, AYLESBURY, BUCKINGHAMSHIRE, HP19 8DP.

Ⓟ**ProBiz CPA Limited** *(H Poon)* 20/F, On Hong Commercial Building, 145 Hennessy Road, WAN CHAI, HONG KONG ISLAND, HONG KONG SAR.

Ⓟ**Procuro Payroll Services Ltd** *(A Brocklehurst, C Knaggs)* Princes House, Wright Street, HULL, HU2 8HX.

Prof. R.H. Macve FCA *(R H Macve)* Bronwydd, 3 Trefor Road, ABERYSTWYTH, SY23 2EH.

Ⓟ**Professional Financial Consultants Ltd** *(P S Baker, B J McKenzie)* 14-16 Station Road West, OXTED, RH8 9EP.

Ⓟ**Professional Link Limited** *(S Atkins, G C Whitehouse)* 39-40 Calthorpe Road, Edgbaston, BIRMINGHAM, B15 1TS.

Ⓟ**Profitplus, trading name of Profitplus Corporate Services Limited** *(D Griffiths)* Westville, Ober Road, BROCKENHURST, HAMPSHIRE, SO42 7ST.

Ⓟ**Profitsevolution.co.uk Ltd** *(C A Penn, M S Penn)* Tordown, 5 Ashwell Lane, GLASTONBURY, SOMERSET, BA6 8BG.

Ⓟ**Prolific Payroll Limited** *(J M Andrews, R S Andrews)* 9 Nimrod Close, Sandpit Lane, ST. ALBANS, HERTFORDSHIRE, AL4 9XY.

Ⓟ**Prontax Ltd** *(W A Swaddle)* 25 Briardene Drive, South Wardley, GATESHEAD, NE10 8AN.

Ⓟ**Property FD, trading name of AS Collaborative Consulting Ltd** *(A B A Samuels)* 12 Park Mount, HARPENDEN, HERTFORDSHIRE, AL5 3AR.

Prophet & Collinson *(G M Prophet)* Tregolds, 20 Moorlands Road, Fishponds, BRISTOL, BS16 3LF.

Prosper Accounting Services *(R J Abolins)* 6 Arundel Close, Tuffley, GLOUCESTER, GL4 0TW.

Prospero *(D M Butler)* 12 Hockerley New Road, Whaley Bridge, HIGH PEAK, DERBYSHIRE, SK23 7GA.

ⓅⒶ**Prospero Accounting Ltd** *(R G Evans)* 1 Portland Street, MANCHESTER, M1 3BE.

Ⓐ**Proto & Co** *(P R Proto)* 41 Kingsmead Avenue, WORCESTER PARK, SURREY, KT4 8XA.

Ⓐ**Proud Goulbourn** *(K A Rogers)* 608 Liverpool Road, Irlam, MANCHESTER, M44 5AA.

Ⓟ**Proud Goulbourn Accountants Ltd** *(K A Rogers)* 608 Liverpool Road, Irlam, MANCHESTER, M44 5AA.

Ⓐ**Proudler Hiser & Co** *(R H Johnson)* 46/48 Coatham Road, REDCAR, TS10 1RS.

ⒺⓅ**Prowting & Partners Limited** *(K D J Prowting, S C Prowting)* 6 West Park, Clifton, BRISTOL, BS8 2LT.

Prue Mitchell *(P G Mitchell)* 130 Canford Cliffs Road, POOLE, DORSET, BH13 7ER.

Prue Stopford FCA *(P J L Stopford)* Pilgrim Cottage, Polson Hill, Morchard Bishop, CREDITON, DEVON, EX17 6SD.

Ⓟ**PRW Financial Services Limited** *(P R F Weatherseed)* 10 The Minnels, HASSOCKS, WEST SUSSEX, BN6 8QW.

ⓅⒶ**PRWS (Bristol) Limited** *(S J Whitby-Smyth)* 53 High Street, Keynsham, BRISTOL, BS31 1DS.

ⓉⒺⒶ**Pryor, Begent, Fry & Co.** *(S M Coates, A J Fry, E T Pascoe)* 97 Meneage Street, HELSTON, TR13 8RE. and at HAYLE

Ⓟ**PS Accounting Services (UK) Ltd** *(N K D Desai)* 144-146 King's Cross Road, LONDON, WC1X 9DU.

PSH & Company *(P S Ho)* 12/F, Nathan Commercial Building, 430-436 Nathan Road, YAU MA TEI, KOWLOON, HONG KONG SAR.

★**PSJ & Associates** *(P M Gandhi)* Capitol Hill Towers, 3rd Floor, Cathedral Road, NAIROBI, KENYA. and at MOMBASA

PSM *(P S Marshall)* 32 Worsley Road, NEWPORT, ISLE OF WIGHT, PO30 5JD.

★**PT Davies & Co** *(P T Davies)* Hazeldene Lodge, Thame Road, Longwick, PRINCES RISBOROUGH, BUCKINGHAMSHIRE, HP27 9SW. and at GERRARDS CROSS

Ⓟ**PTL Accountancy Services Limited** *(P T Looker)* 3 Stonards Hill, EPPING, ESSEX, CM16 4QE.

Ⓟ**Pubtax Limited** *(C B F Lawson)* Hendomen Farmhouse, Hen-Domen, MONTGOMERY, POWYS, SY15 6HB.

Pugh Clarke & Co *(K E Clarke)* 175 Manor Road, CHIGWELL, IG7 5QB.

★ⓉⒺⒶ**Pugsley Revill** *(D Revill)* 18 High West Street, DORCHESTER, DT1 1UW. and at POOLE

ⒺⓅⒶ**Pullan Barnes, trading name of Pullan Barnes Limited** *(Y Bari, M Barnes, K Pullan)* Stephenson House, Richard Street, Hetton-le-Hole, HOUGHTON LE SPRING, TYNE AND WEAR, DH5 9HW. and at DURHAM

★Ⓟ**Pulse, trading name of Pulse Accountants Limited** *(R Masters)* 1a Carrera House, Gatehouse Close, AYLESBURY, BUCKINGHAMSHIRE, HP19 8DP.

ⓉⒶ**Purcells** *(E H Feingold, A H Finn)* 4 Quex Road, LONDON, NW6 4PJ.

Ⓟ**Purcells UK Limited** *(M J M Purcell)* 342 Bloomfield Road, BATH, BA2 2PB.

Ⓟ**Pure FD Limited** *(C A Graham, K W J Saunders)* Wellesley House, Duke of Wellington Avenue, Royal Arsenal, LONDON, SE18 6SS.

Ⓟ**Purely Financial, trading name of Its Purely Financial Limited** *(T J Mitchell, G M Tomlinson)* Laurel Cottage, The Batch, Butcombe, BRISTOL, BS40 7UY. and at HORSHAM

Ⓟ**Purple Cat Accountancy Limited** *(J L Watkin)* 87 Highgate Road, WALSALL, WS1 3JA.

ⓉⒺⓅⒶ**Pursglove & Brown, trading name of Military House Limited** *(S M Greensill, J A Hunt, F Patterson, C N H Pursglove)* Military House, 24 Castle Street, CHESTER, CH1 2DS.

Purshotam Dhir *(P Dhir)* A3 Chiragh Enclave, NEW DELHI 110048, INDIA.

Ⓟ**PW Business Solutions Ltd** *(J Belinger, A N Bunston, A Gates, M A Johns, W J Law, N J Love, J I Robinson, D K Watton)* The Coach House, George Business Centre, Christchurch Road, NEW MILTON, HAMPSHIRE, BH25 6QJ.

★Ⓣ**PWC Malaysia, trading name of PricewaterhouseCoopers** *(M F Azmi, K F Chin, C M Cho, M A B Haji Yahya, T K Lim, M L Ng, A L Ong, A J Raslan, S Sammanthan, T Sangarapillai, T Somasundaram, U K Vivekananda)* P.O.Box 10192, Level 10 1 Sentral, Jalan Travers, 50470 KUALA LUMPUR, FEDERAL TERRITORY, MALAYSIA. and at IPOH, JOHOR BAHRU, KOTA KINABALU, KUANTAN, KUCHING, LABUAN, MALACCA CITY, PULAU PINANG

PWP Accounting Services *(P M Ward)* Bournemouth Indoor Bowls Club, Kings Park Drive, Kings Park, BOURNEMOUTH, BH7 6JD.

Ⓟ**PWPlus CPA Limited** *(S K Yu)* Room 2003, CC Wu Building, 302-308 Hennersey Road, WAN CHAI, HONG KONG ISLAND, HONG KONG SAR. and at CAUSEWAY BAY

Pyliotis Associates *(R S Pyliotis)* 157 Great North Way, LONDON, NW4 1PP.

Ⓟ**Pyplacz Ltd** *(B Pyplacz)* 6 Bexley Square, SALFORD, M3 6BZ.

Ⓟ**Qaisar Johnson Associates Limited** *(M J Johnson)* 208 A Roundhay Road, LEEDS, WEST YORKSHIRE, LS8 5AA.

Ⓐ**Qayyum & Co** *(A Qayyum)* Portland House, 431 Chester Road, MANCHESTER, M16 9HA.

Ⓟ**Qazi M Husain, trading name of Q M Husain & Co Limited** *(Q M Husain)* 37 Grove Avenue, Muswell Hill, LONDON, N10 2AS.

Ⓒ**Quanast Services** *(R T McDonagh)* Rutland House, 44 Masons Hill, BROMLEY, BR2 9EQ.

Quantico *(N J Clayton, R F Matusiewicz)* Nottingham Castle Marina, Marina Road, Castle Marina Park, NOTTINGHAM, NG7 1TN.

Ⓟ**Quantis, trading name of Quantis Limited** *(P M Smith)* 13 Newgate Street, MORPETH, NORTHUMBERLAND, NE61 1AL.

Ⓟ**Quantum Accountancy Services Limited** *(G W Robson)* The Quadrus Centre, Woodstock Way, Boldon Business Park, BOLDON COLLIERY, TYNE AND WEAR, NE35 9PF.

Quantum Accounts & Taxation Services *(F M Shaida)* 208 Redbridge Lane East, ILFORD, ESSEX, IG4 5BH.

Ⓟ**Quantum ATS Limited** *(F M Shaida)* 208 Redbridge Lane East, ILFORD, ESSEX, IG4 5BH.

Ⓟ**Quantum Financial Solutions Limited** *(P J Gravett)* Ellerslie, Crawley End, Chrishall, ROYSTON, SG8 8QJ.

Ⓟ**Quantum, trading name of Anglopol Limited** *(R R Wisniowski)* Oxford House, 24 Oxford Road North, LONDON, W4 4DH.

Ⓟ**Quantum, trading name of Quantum Accountancy Ltd** *(S D Pearce, M R Studd)* 4 Forest Court, Oaklands Park, WOKINGHAM, BERKSHIRE, RG41 2FD.

★ⓅⒶ**Quay Business Advice Limited** *(L A Sessions)* 1 Town Quay Wharf, Abbey Road, BARKING, ESSEX, IG11 7BZ.

ⓉⒺⓅ**Qubic, trading name of Qubic Associates Limited** *(D M Graham)* 1 Staithes, The Watermark, GATESHEAD, TYNE AND WEAR, NE11 9SN. and at LONDON

Ⓟ**Queensgate Management (East Midlands) LLP** *(J Wetherall)* Unit 4, Henley Way, LINCOLN, LN6 3QR.

Quentin Caisley *(Q Caisley)* Unit 6, Bearl, STOCKSFIELD, NORTHUMBERLAND, NE43 7AJ.

Quentin Wong & Co Certified Public Accountants *(C Q Wong)* Room 907, 9/F, Wayson Commercial Building, 28 Connaught Road West, SHEUNG WAN, HONG KONG ISLAND HONG KONG SAR.

ⓅⒶ**Queripel and Kettlewell Limited** *(J S Kettlewell, P G Queripel)* The Barn, Hall Mews, Boston Spa, WETHERBY, WEST YORKSHIRE, LS23 6DT.

ⒺⓅⒶ**Quest Duthoit Limited** *(E V Curtis)* 19 Farncombe Road, WORTHING, BN11 2AY.

ⒺⒶ**Quiney & Co** *(P L Quiney)* Trinley Cottage, Main Road, Tirley, GLOUCESTER, GL19 4EU.

ⓅⒶ**Quinneys, trading name of Quinney and Company Ltd** *(W J Quinney)* Bank Chambers, Market Place, Reepham, NORWICH, NR10 4JJ.

Ⓟ**Quove Accounting Ltd** *(A N Mole)* Talpa Hall, Station Road, Old Newton, STOWMARKET, SUFFOLK, IP14 4HQ.

Ⓟ**QX Accounting Services Ltd** *(C E Robinson)* Castle Chambers, Off Mill Bridge, SKIPTON, NORTH YORKSHIRE, BD23 1NJ.

Ⓟ**R & L Giles Limited** *(L A Giles, R E Giles)* 21 St Ives Gardens, BOURNEMOUTH, BH2 6NS.

R & M *(S Redhead)* Repeat House, Bright Road, MANCHESTER, M30 0WG.

Ⓟ**R A Cave Limited** *(R A Cave)* Yew tree, 13 Leeds Road, MIRFIELD, WEST YORKSHIRE, WF14 0BY.

ⓅⒶ**R A French Ltd** *(R A French)* 12 Lychgate, Higher Walton, WARRINGTON, WA4 6TF.

ⒺⒶ**R A Jones & Co** *(R A Jones)* 38 Rumbridge Street, Totton, SOUTHAMPTON, SO40 9DS.

Ⓟ**R A Lister Limited** *(R A Lister)* 14 Rishworth Street, WAKEFIELD, WEST YORKSHIRE, WF1 3BY.

R A Lock & Co *(R A Lock)* 256 Old Church Road, Chingford, LONDON, E4 8BT.

ⓉⓅⒶ**R A McLeod & Co, trading name of R A McLeod (Financial Services) Limited** *(R A McLeod)* 10 Portland Business Centre, Manor House Lane, Datchet, SLOUGH, SL3 9EG. and at LONDON

Ⓟ**R A Swift Financial Consulting, trading name of R A Swift Financial Consulting Limited** *(R A Swift)* 221 Station Road, Knowle, SOLIHULL, WEST MIDLANDS, B93 0PU.

R Ahmed & Co. *(A Ahmed)* 37 New Road, LONDON, E1 1HE.

Ⓟ**R Ashdown & Company Limited** *(R V Ashdown)* 75 Brookville Road, LONDON, SW6 7BH.

Ⓟ**R Bath & Co Ltd** *(R N Bath)* 8 Northwood Park Road, Hanley, STOKE-ON-TRENT, ST1 2DT.

R C Penfold *(R C Penfold)* 238 Corbets Tey Road, UPMINSTER, ESSEX, RM14 2BL.

R D Martin & Co *(R D Martin)* 28 Church Road, STANMORE, MIDDLESEX, HA7 4XR.

Ⓟ**R D Owen & Co, trading name of R D Owen Services Limited** *(R N Browning, I D Gillard)* Queen Caroline House, 18a Queen Square, BATH, BA1 2HR. and at WARMINSTER

★ⓅⒶ**R D Owen, trading name of Pethericks & Gillard Ltd** *(R N Browning, I D Gillard, M J Petherick)* 124 High Street, Midsomer Norton, BATH, BA3 2DA. and at WELLS

R E Bishop *(R E Bishop)* Little Orchard, 97 Westbury Road, NORTHWOOD, HA6 3DA.

R E Needs *(R E Needs)* 42 Huddersfield Road, BARNSLEY, SOUTH YORKSHIRE, S75 1DW.

R F Cornish *(R F Cornish)* 22 Bayview Road, WHITSTABLE, KENT, CT5 4NP.

R F Lander *(R F Lander)* Spinney Corner, Green Lane, Aspley Guise, MILTON KEYNES, MK17 8EN.

R F Love and Company *(R F Love)* 23 Chudleigh Road, EXETER, EX2 8TS.

Ⓟ**R Foster & Co, trading name of R Foster & Co (Accountants) Ltd** *(R W Foster)* Orchid House, 243 Elliott Street, Tyldesley, MANCHESTER, M29 8DG.

Ⓐ**R Fulena And Co** *(R Fulena)* 41 Britten Close, LONDON, NW11 7HQ.

R G Clark FCA *(R G Clark)* Brunel House, Ediva Road, Meopham, GRAVESEND, KENT, DA13 0ND.

R G Consultancy *(R Glatter)* 12 York Gate, Regent's Park, LONDON, NW1 4QS.

Ⓟ**R G Holder & Co Limited** *(R G Holder)* Whetcombe Whey, Ropers Lane, Wrington, BRISTOL, BS40 5NH.

Ⓟ**R G Thakrar & Co, trading name of AT & RT Consultants Ltd** *(R G Thakrar)* 7 Michleham Down, LONDON, N12 7JJ.

Ⓟ**R H Accountancy Services Limited** *(R B Hearne)* 22 Beresford Road, HARROW, HA1 4QZ.

R H Froom BBS FCA *(R H Froom)* 93 Mill Green, CONGLETON, CHESHIRE, CW12 1GD.

R H Jackson and Co *(R H Jackson)* 1 Wroth Tyes Cottage, Upper Hartfield, HARTFIELD, EAST SUSSEX, TN7 4DY.

Ⓟ**R Holden & Co Accountants Ltd** *(R Holden)* Ashleigh House, 81 Birmingham Road, WEST BROMWICH, WEST MIDLANDS, B70 0PX.

R Hoyle *(R Hoyle)* 51 Oakwood Avenue, BECKENHAM, BR3 6PT.

Ⓟ**R J Anderton Limited** *(R J Anderton)* Suite 110, First Floor, Malthouse Business Centre, 48 Southport Road, ORMSKIRK, LANCASHIRE L39 1QR.

R J Barwick *(R J Barwick)* Maybury Copse, The Ridge, WOKING, SURREY, GU22 7EQ.

R J Bentley *(R J Bentley)* Milsons Cottage, Wellhouse, Hermitage, THATCHAM, BERKSHIRE, RG18 9UG.

★ⓅⒶ**R J Francis & Co, trading name of R J Francis & Co Limited** *(R J Francis)* Franklin House, 3 Commercial Road, HEREFORD, HR1 2AZ.

R J M Banbury *(R J M Banbury)* 44 Bounds Oak Way, TUNBRIDGE WELLS, TN4 0TN.

R J Rice *(R J Rice)* 144 Cromwell Way, KIDLINGTON, OX5 2LJ.

R J Springfield *(R J Springfield)* Kelani, 32 Teign View Road, Bishopsteignton, TEIGNMOUTH, TQ14 9SZ.

R J Stanton & Co *(R J Stanton)* Mill Hill, Chop Gate, Stokesley, MIDDLESBROUGH, TS9 7HY. and at HARROGATE

R J Symms Financial Services *(R J Symms)* 5 Coniston Road, Gatley, CHEADLE, CHESHIRE, SK8 4AP.

R J Taylor *(R J Taylor)* 26 Midholm, Hampstead Garden Suburb, LONDON, NW11 6LN.

ⓅⒶ**R J Young Limited** *(R J Young)* Deeks Evans, 3 Boyne Park, TUNBRIDGE WELLS, KENT, TN4 8EN. and at HASTINGS

R K Thomas *(R K Thomas)* Pools Close House, Pools Close, Chapel Street, Welford on Avon, STRATFORD-UPON-AVON, WARWICKSHIRE CV37 8QB.

ⓅⒶ**R L Charles Limited** *(P Charles)* Robson Laidler LLP, Fernwood House, Fernwood Road, Jesmond, NEWCASTLE UPON TYNE, NE2 1TJ.

Ⓟ**R L Ferris, trading name of R L Ferris Limited** *(J M Heppenstall)* 64 Derby Lane, LIVERPOOL, L13 3DN.

ⓅⒶ**R L Moran Limited** *(M T Moran)* Robson Laidler LLP, Fernwood House, Fernwood Road, Jesmond, NEWCASTLE UPON TYNE, NE2 1TJ.

Ⓐ**R Learmonth Dick** *(R L Dick)* 3a Headley Road, Woodley, READING, RG5 4JB.

R Lewes *(R Lewes)* 15 Guldrey Lane, SEDBERGH, CUMBRIA, LA10 5DS.

R M A *(R Miller)* 86 Park Lane, Whitefield, MANCHESTER, M45 7PL.

R M Batchelor ACA *(R M Batchelor)* 70 Chesterton Avenue, HARPENDEN, HERTFORDSHIRE, AL5 5SU.

R M Sargeant *(R M Sargeant)* 13 Fairgreen, Cockfosters, BARNET, EN4 0QS.

ⓉⒶ**R P Imray** *(R P Imray)* 6 The Old Maltings, Ditton Walk, CAMBRIDGE, CB5 8PY.

R P Rendle & Co *(R P Rendle)* No 9 Hockley Court, Hockley Heath, SOLIHULL, WEST MIDLANDS, B94 6NW.

ⒺⓅⒶ**R P Smith & Co, trading name of R P Smith & Co Limited** *(D P Abbott, K M Brophy, S J Worswick)* 71 Chorley Old Road, BOLTON, LANCASHIRE, BL1 3AJ.

Ⓟ**R Rose & Co, trading name of R Rose & Co Ltd** *(R Rose)* 213 Derbyshire Lane, Norton Lees, SHEFFIELD, S8 8SA.

R S Hall and Co *(R S Hall)* Dragon's Lair, 27 Belle Meade Close, Woodgate, CHICHESTER, WEST SUSSEX, PO20 3YD.

ⓅⒶ**R S Harding, trading name of R S Harding Ltd** *(R S Harding)* 15 High Street, Redbourn, ST. ALBANS, HERTFORDSHIRE, AL3 7LE.

R Sadlier *(R J Sadlier)* 22 Heather Close, Whittoncroft, ISLEWORTH, MIDDLESEX, TW7 7PR.

R Somers - Accountancy *(R Somers)* Grafton, Waterlane, Oakridge, STROUD, GLOUCESTERSHIRE, GL6 7PL.

ⓉⓅⒶ**R T Marke & Co Limited** *(N T Marke, E R Meardon, D B Sims)* 69 High Street, BIDEFORD, DEVON, EX39 2AT.

ⓅⒶ**R Thompson & Co Ltd** *(R G Thompson)* Sterling Offices, 30a Mill Street, BEDFORD, MK40 3HD.

R W Golder *(R W Golder)* 28 Beaufort Avenue, New Cubbington, LEAMINGTON SPA, CV32 7TA.

R. Bicknell & Co *(R Bicknell)* 71 Bedford Road, READING, RG1 7EY.

R. Black & Co *(R Black)* 11 Vernon Road, SALFORD, M7 4NW.

R. Clapshaw *(R E A Clapshaw)* Norney Grange, Shackleford, GODALMING, GU8 6AY.

R. David Anderson *(R D Anderson)* West Gables, Westgate, Thornton-le-Dale, PICKERING, YO18 7SG.

R. G. Burnand & Co *(R G Burnand)* Suite 4, Thamesbourne Lodge, Station Road, BOURNE END, BUCKINGHAMSHIRE, SL8 5QH.

R. Herbert & Co *(R L Herbert)* 53 Cedar Lawn Avenue, BARNET, HERTFORDSHIRE, EN5 2LP.

R. Jackson *(R Jackson)* 18 Plane Tree Croft, LEEDS, LS17 8UQ.

R. Jagpal & Co *(R K Jagpal)* 51 Harrowdene Road, WEMBLEY, HA0 2JQ.

R. Livesley BCom FCA *(R Livesley)* 25 Groveland Road, WALLASEY, MERSEYSIDE, CH45 8JY.

Ⓔ**R. Marchant & Co** *(R Marchant)* 42 Oakleigh Park South, LONDON, N20 9JN.

Ⓐ**R. Mullick** *(R Mullick)* 10 Chatteris Way, Lower Earley, READING, RG6 4JA.

R. Pickup *(R Pickup)* Keepers Cottage, Sowerby Road, Sowerby, PRESTON, PR3 0TT.

R. Pyatt *(R Pyatt)* 10 Friary Close, Hamstead Hall Road, Handsworth Wood, BIRMINGHAM, B20 1HP.

R. Robinson *(R Robinson)* Broadstones Farm, Mill Brow, Marple, STOCKPORT, SK6 5DG.

R. Sutton & Co *(W D Williams)* 25 Park Street, MACCLESFIELD, SK11 6SS.

R. Tennant & Co *(R Tennant)* Mellowbrook House, 1A Stratford Lane, Hilton, BRIDGNORTH, SHROPSHIRE, WV15 5PF.

R. Thirkettle *(R Thirkettle)* 1 Atwell Close, WALLINGFORD, OX10 0LH.

R. Thompson & Co *(R Thompson)* 6 Worthington Crescent, POOLE, DORSET, BH14 8BW.

Ⓟ**R. W. & CO Ltd** *(R A J Wood)* Bishops Farm, Coldharbour, WEYMOUTH, DORSET, DT3 4BG.

R. Weare & Co. *(R D M Weare)* Brook House, Llandevaud, NEWPORT, NP18 2AA.

R.A Bodoano *(R A Bodoano)* Rowanberries, Linton, ROSS-ON-WYE, HR9 7RY.

Ⓣ**R.A. & D.A. Thompson** *(D A Thompson)* 30 High Street, LEIGHTON BUZZARD, BEDFORDSHIRE, LU7 1EA.

R.A. Ellis & Co *(R A Ellis)* 9 The Elms, Church Road, Claygate, ESHER, KT10 0JT.

R.A. Hughes *(R A Hughes)* 76 Oxford Road, Old Marston, OXFORD, OX3 0RD.

R.A. Leslie & Co., trading name of R.A. Leslie & Co LLP *(H C Cutting, R A Leslie)* Gowran House, 56 Broad Street, Chipping Sodbury, BRISTOL, BS37 6AG.

R.A. Lister *(R A Lister)* Suite 2, 14 Rishworth Street, WAKEFIELD, WEST YORKSHIRE, WF1 3BY.

R.A. Moore *(R A Moore)* 421 Middleton Rd, Middleton, MANCHESTER, M24 4QZ.

ⓉⒻⒶ**R.A. Pick & Co** *(R A Pick)* Cobham House, 9 Warwick Court, Grays Inn, LONDON, WC1R 5DJ.

Ⓐ**R.A. Randall** *(R A Randall)* 166 Kempshott Lane, Kempshott, BASINGSTOKE, RG22 5LA.

Ⓐ**R.A. Spires & Co** *(R A Spires)* 97 Stonald Road, Whittlesey, PETERBOROUGH, PE7 1QP.

ⒻⒶ**R.A. Vowles & Co** *(R A Vowles)* 148 Commercial Road, Totton, SOUTHAMPTON, SO40 3AA.

R.A. Woollard *(R A Woollard)* 19 Annetyard Drive, SKELMORLIE, PA17 5BN.

R.A.B. Viner & Co *(R A B Viner)* Systems House, 42 Broad Street, KIDDERMINSTER, WORCESTERSHIRE, DY10 2LY.

Ⓐ**R.A.C. West & Co** *(R A C West)* 1 St. Peter Street, TIVERTON, DEVON, EX16 6NE.

R.B. Dubash & Co *(R B Dubash)* Firuz-Ara, 160 Maharishi Karve Road, Cooperage, MUMBAI 400021, MAHARASHTRA, INDIA.

Ⓕ**R.B. Platt & Co** *(R B Platt)* Alpine House, 28 Church Road, Rainford, ST. HELENS, MERSEYSIDE, WA11 8HE.

R.C Smith *(R C Smith)* 1 Tower Close, ORPINGTON, BR6 0SP.

R.C. Butler *(R C Butler)* 83 Strathcona Avenue, Bookham, LEATHERHEAD, KT23 4HS.

R.C. Dobson & Co *(R C Dobson)* Bredon View, Hollybush, LEDBURY, HR8 1ET.

R.C. Taylor *(R C Taylor)* Brailsford Green, Church Lane, Brailsford, ASHBOURNE, DE6 3BX.

R.C. Turner *(R C Turner)* Almond House, Grange Street, Clifton, SHEFFORD, BEDFORDSHIRE, SG17 5EW.

R.C.H. Stanley *(R C H Stanley)* Hoth Farm House, Danegate, Eridge Green, TUNBRIDGE WELLS, TN3 9HU.

R.D. Gale FCA *(R D Gale)* 94a Strines Road, Marple, STOCKPORT, CHESHIRE, SK6 7DU.

R.D. Hill Associates *(R D Hill)* 5 Whinslee Drive, Lostock, BOLTON, BL6 4NB.

R.D. Rangeley FCA *(R D A Rangeley)* Abbey House, 25 Clarendon Road, REDHILL, RH1 1QZ.

R.D. Sutton & Company *(R D Sutton)* 544 Leeds Road, Thackley, BRADFORD, BD10 8JH.

Ⓟ**R.D. Uttley, trading name of R D Uttley Limited** *(R D Uttley)* Shaw Cottage, Shaw Wood Road, Langfield, TODMORDEN, OL14 6HP.

R.D.I. Scott & Co *(R E Scott)* 4a China Street, LLANIDLOES, SY18 6AB.

R.E. Coates *(R E Coates)* 48 Countess Wear Road, EXETER, EX2 6LR.

R.E. Matthews *(R E Matthews)* Garn Hebogydd, Gwbert on Sea, CARDIGAN, SA43 1PR.

Ⓟ**R.E. Needs Ltd** *(R E Needs)* 42 Huddersfield Road, BARNSLEY, S75 1DW.

R.E. Smithson *(R E Smithson)* 14 Lister Avenue, HITCHIN, SG4 9ES.

R.E. Stratford & Co *(P T S Wyatt)* 100 Queen Street, NEWTON ABBOT, DEVON, TQ12 2EU.

Ⓐ**R.E.Jones & Co** *(L J Cox, S E W Jones)* 132 Burnt Ash Road, Lee, LONDON, SE12 8PU.

R.F. Bavington-Jones *(R.F. Bavington-Jones)* 1 Oak Cottages, Cox Hill, Shepherdswell, DOVER, KENT, CT15 7NB.

R.F. Carey *(R F Carey)* 5 Courtrai, Lansdown Castle Drive, CHELTENHAM, GL51 7AF.

R.F. Frazer & Co *(J B McGlashan)* 112a Wallasey Road, WALLASEY, MERSEYSIDE, CH44 2AE.

R.F. George & Co *(R F George)* 110 Ferring Street, Ferring, WORTHING, BN12 5JP.

Ⓕ**R.G. Hilton & Co.** *(B W Hobbs)* 10a Bank Street, CASTLEFORD, WF10 1HZ.

R.G. Holder & Co *(R G Holder)* Whetcombe Whey, Ropers Lane, Wrington, SOMERSET, BS40 5NH.

R.G. Jenyns *(R G Jenyns)* Bottisham Hall, Bottisham, CAMBRIDGE, CB5 9ED.

R.G. Justice & Co *(R G Justice)* 36 Heath Street, STOURBRIDGE, WEST MIDLANDS, DY8 1SB.

R.G. Major *(R G Major)* The Burrows, Windmill Hill, Ashill, ILMINSTER, TA19 9NT.

R.G. Mendelssohn *(R G Mendelssohn)* 31 Bromsgrove Road, STUDLEY, B80 7PH.

Ⓟ**R.G. Rupal Ltd** *(R G Rupal)* 30 Fernhall Drive, ILFORD, IG4 5BW.

R.G.D. Maunsell & Co *(R G D Maunsell)* Pear Tree Cottage, 27 Rasen Road, Tealby, MARKET RASEN, LINCOLNSHIRE, LN8 3XL.

R.H. Bird & Co *(R H Bird)* Spencer House, 114 High Street, Wordsley, STOURBRIDGE, DY8 5QR.

ⓉⒻⒶ**R.H. Jeffs & Rowe** *(H T W Jones, R E Thomas)* 27-28 Gelliwastad Road, PONTYPRIDD, CF37 2BW.

R.H. Phillips *(R H Phillips)* Wychwood, 86 Kimpton Road Blackmore End, Wheathampstead, ST. ALBANS, AL4 8LX.

R.H. Renwick *(R H Renwick)* 121-123 High Street, NORTHALLERTON, DL7 8PQ.

R.I. Cavell *(R I Cavell)* 155 Reepham Road, Hellesdon, NORWICH, NR6 5PW.

ⒻⒶ**R.J. Cladd** *(R J Cladd)* Suite 134, Milton Keynes Business Centre, Foxhunter Drive, Linford Wood, MILTON KEYNES, MK14 6GD.

R.J. Dennis *(R J Dennis)* Kerian, Corkscrew Lane, Woolston, YEOVIL, BA22 7BP.

R.J. Dunscombe *(R J Dunscombe)* 68 Hillmead, HORSHAM, RH12 2PX.

R.J. Holcombe & Co *(R J Holcombe)* Apple Tree Cottage, Church Street, Appleford, ABINGDON, OX14 4PA.

R.J. Kettlewell & Co *(R J Kettlewell)* 43 Ann Beaumont Way, Hadleigh, IPSWICH, IP7 6SB.

R.J. Littlechild *(R J Littlechild)* 5 Tintagel Court, St. Neots, ST. NEOTS, PE19 2RZ.

R.J. Scurrah *(R J Scurrah)* 8 Bonds Lane, Elswick, PRESTON, PR4 3ZE.

Ⓟ**R.J. Taylor & Co, trading name of R.J. Taylor Limited** *(R J Taylor)* Unit A2, Imex Business Park, Flaxley Road, Stechford, BIRMINGHAM, B33 9AL.

R.J. Webb & Co *(R J Webb)* 26 Ben Rhydding Road, ILKLEY, LS29 8RL.

R.J. Whittaker *(R J Whittaker)* Rivelin Cottage, Wynne Cresent, Lower Penn, WOLVERHAMPTON, WV4 4SW.

R.J.C. Davey *(R J C Davey)* 124 Old Park Ridings, Grange Park, LONDON, N21 2EP.

R.J.Dixon & Co *(G J Watts)* 6 Woodland Way, Marden Ash, ONGAR, CM5 9EP.

★ⓉⒻⒶ**R.J.G. Palmer Gardner** *(S J L Gardner)* Norgar House, 10 East Street, FAREHAM, PO16 0BN.

R.J.W. Associates *(R J Wyeth)* 44 Kirby Drive, Bramley Green, TADLEY, HAMPSHIRE, RG26 5FN.

R.K. Dobson *(R K Dobson)* 37 Walton Gardens, FOLKESTONE, CT19 5PR.

R.K. Gupta & Co *(R K Gupta)* 89 Hook Rise South, SURBITON, SURREY, KT6 7NA.

★**R.K. Khanna & Co** *(A K Khanna)* D-41, NDSE Dart II, NEW DELHI 110049, INDIA.

★Ⓣ**R.K. Lawrence & Co** *(R K Lawrence)* 94 Brook Street, ERITH, DA8 1JF.

Ⓐ**R.K. Raja & Co** *(R K Raja)* 21 Whitehouse Way, LONDON, N14 7LX.

R.K. Rattan *(R K Rattan)* 51 Paxford Road, WEMBLEY, HA0 3RQ.

R.K. Riddle *(R K Riddle)* 121 Imperial Way, ASHFORD, KENT, TN23 5HT.

R.K. Sethi & Co *(R K Sethi)* 140 Springwell Road, HOUNSLOW, TW5 9BP.

R.K. Sharma *(R K Sharma)* 22 Bisley Road, STROUD, GL5 1HE.

ⒻⒶ**R.K.Groseley** *(R K Groseley)* Lynwood House, Dudley Road, Lye, STOURBRIDGE, DY9 8DU.

R.Kerridge *(R Kerridge)* 32 Queens Road, READING, RG1 4AU.

R.L. Hine *(R L Hine)* 72 Yew Tree Road, Southborough, TUNBRIDGE WELLS, TN4 0BN.

R.L. Vaughan & Co *(A E Clifford, R L Vaughan)* Mortimer House, 40 Chatsworth Parade, Queensway, Petts Wood, ORPINGTON, KENT BR5 1DE.

R.L.B. Marshall *(R L B Marshall)* 51 Clare Crescent, LEATHERHEAD, SURREY, KT22 7RA.

R.M. Johnson *(R M Johnson)* 36 Wolds Rise, MATLOCK, DE4 3HJ.

R.M. Rahim & Co. *(R M Rahim)* 164 Lincoln Road, PETERBOROUGH, PE1 2NW.

R.M. Slack *(R M Slack)* 278 Skinburness Road, Skinburness, WIGTON, CA7 4QU.

R.M. Walmsley *(R M Walmsley)* 21 Clinton Terrace, BUDLEIGH SALTERTON, DEVON, EX9 6RY.

R.M. Willgoose *(R M Willgoose)* Chestnut End, Leddington, LEDBURY, HR8 2LG.

R.M.Saltmarsh *(R M Saltmarsh)* P.O. Box 21145, Orchard Park P.O., KELOWNA VIY 9N8, BC, CANADA.

Ⓐ**R.N. Store & Co** *(B Dalby)* 26 Hickman Street, GAINSBOROUGH, DN21 2DZ.

R.N. Thomas & Co *(R N Thomas)* 31 Silver Street, BRADFORD-ON-AVON, BA15 1JX.

R.N. Virk & Co *(R N Virk)* 25 Anley Road, West Kensington, LONDON, W14 0BZ.

R.P. Denyer *(R P Denyer)* 11 Stuarts Green, STOURBRIDGE, WEST MIDLANDS, DY9 0XR.

Ⓐ**R.P. Ellis** *(R P Ellis)* The Priory, 414 Newark Road, LINCOLN, LN6 8RX.

R.P. Harker *(R P Harker)* Maskani Yetu, 2 Garey Close, Foxdale, ISLE OF MAN, IM4 3EU.

ⒻⒶ**R.P. Smith & Co** *(D P Abbott, K M Brophy, S J Worswick)* 28 St Thomas's Rd, CHORLEY, PR7 1HX.

R.P.Mitchell & Co *(R P Mitchell)* 81 Rochestown Avenue, Dun Laoire, DUBLIN, COUNTY DUBLIN, IRELAND.

Ⓕ**R.R. Hallett** *(R R Hallett)* Orleton Grange, Orleton, Stanford Bridge, WORCESTER, WR6 6SU.

ⓉⒶ**R.R. Shah & Co** *(R R Shah)* 78 Wembley Park Drive, WEMBLEY, HA9 8HB.

R.R. Spiegel *(R R Spiegel)* 5 Ledway Drive, WEMBLEY, HA9 9TH.

R.Rendle *(R Rendle)* 38 Antonio Nani Street, TA'XBIEX XBX 1086, MALTA.

R.S. Benson *(R S Benson)* Bell Lane House, Bell Lane, Minchinhampton, STROUD, GL6 9BP.

R.S. Patel & Co *(R S Patel)* 43 Costons Avenue, GREENFORD, MIDDLESEX, UB6 8RJ.

ⓉⒻⒶ**R.S. Porter & Co** *(C J Keates-Porter)* 77/81 Alma Rd, Clifton, BRISTOL, BS8 2DP.

Ⓟ**R.T Brighton, trading name of R.T Brighton Ltd** *(R T Brighton)* 12 Wensleydale, DROITWICH, WR9 8PF.

R.V. Hoad & Co *(R V Hoad)* Suite 11, Keynes House, Chester Park, Alfreton Road, DERBY, DE21 4AS.

R.V. Kent *(R V Kent)* Philpot House, Station Road, RAYLEIGH, SS6 7HH.

R.W. Davidson *(R W Davidson)* 47 Squire Bakers Lane, MARKHAM L3P 3G8, ON, CANADA.

R.W. Honour *(R W Honour)* Bramhope, 72 Mill Lane, Whaplode, SPALDING, LINCOLNSHIRE, PE12 6TS.

ⒻⒶ**R.W. Pain and Co** *(R W Pain)* The Old Post Office, Main Street, Burton Overy, LEICESTER, LE8 9DL.

ⒻⒶ**R.W. Womwell** *(R W Womwell)* Suite 11, Woodside House, 18 Walsworth Road, HITCHIN, HERTFORDSHIRE, SG4 9SP.

R.W.Mercer & Co *(R W Mercer)* Welford House, Matlock Street, BAKEWELL, DE45 1EE.

R.W.Meredith *(R W Meredith)* 256 Higham Lane, NUNEATON, CV11 6AR.

★Ⓣ**RA Accountants LLP** *(A Hafeez)* Audit House, 260 Field End Road, RUISLIP, MIDDLESEX, HA4 9LT.

Ⓟ**RA Payroll Services Ltd** *(A Levy, R I Simons, P A Taylor)* 13-15 Station Road, LONDON, N3 2SB.

Rabet & Co *(A J D Rabet)* 2 Old Farm Close, La Route Du Mont Mado, St. John, JERSEY, JE3 4DS.

★**Rabinraj & Partners** *(Dato Ratnaswamy)* A6-05 Level 6 Carlton Court, Punchak Prima Condominium, Jalan Sri Hartamas 17, 50480 KUALA LUMPUR, FEDERAL TERRITORY, MALAYSIA.

★**Rabjohns LLP** *(I J C Smith)* 1-3 College Yard, WORCESTER, WR1 2LB.

Rachael Hart ACA *(R Hart)* 3 Evelench Barns, Evelench Lane, Tibberton, DROITWICH, WORCESTERSHIRE, WR9 7NY.

Rachael Prideaux ACA *(R E Prideaux)* 64 Queens Crescent, BODMIN, CORNWALL, PL31 1QW.

Rachel Dunhill *(R A Dunhill)* 31 Crown Street, Scissett, HUDDERSFIELD, HD8 9JN.

Rachel E. Scott & Co *(R E Scott)* The Old Vicarage, Wellington, HEREFORD, HR4 8AU.

Rachel Hollox *(R L Hollox)* Jesmond, Ridgeway, OTTERY ST. MARY, DEVON, EX11 1DT.

Ⓟ**Rachel Keenan & Co Ltd** *(R J Keenan)* 16 Thornfield Hey, Spital, WIRRAL, MERSEYSIDE, CH63 9JT.

Rachel Mason *(R A Mason)* 31 Harefield Road, COVENTRY, CV2 4BX.

Rachel Roberts *(R J S Roberts)* Brookfield, Thorpe Road, MELTON MOWBRAY, LEICESTERSHIRE, LE13 1SH.

Rachel Sykes *(R E Jay)* The Old Church, West Allerdean, BERWICK-UPON-TWEED, TD15 2TD.

ⓅⒶ**Radford & Sergeant, Swain & Co, trading names of Swain & Company (Accountants) Limited** *(K Swain)* 73 High Street, ALDERSHOT, HAMPSHIRE, GU11 1BY.

Raedan *(C A Bareham)* Maple House, High Street, POTTERS BAR, HERTFORDSHIRE, EN6 5BS.

Rafaqat Mansha Mohsin Dossani Masoom & Co *(A H Dossani)* Suite 113 3rd Floor, Hafeez Centre, KCHS Block 7&8, Shahra-e-Faisal, KARACHI 75350, PAKISTAN.

★Ⓣ**Raffingers Stuart** *(T Beeharry)* 19-20 Bourne Court, Southend Road, WOODFORD GREEN, IG8 8HD.

ⓉⓅ**Rahman & Co, trading name of Rahman & Co Ltd** *(K M A Rahman)* 7 Meadows Bridge, Parc Menter, Cross Hands, LLANELLI, DYFED, SA14 6RA.

Rahman & Co. *(M R Rahman)* 3 Narcissus Road, LONDON, NW6 1TJ.

Ⓣ**Rahman Rahman Huq** *(A Ashfaq, S A Hafiz, A H Khan, A N A H Siddiqui)* 9 Mohakhali Commercial Area, 11th & 12th Floors, DHAKA 1212, BANGLADESH.

Rahman Sarfaraz Rahim Iqbal Rafiq *(I R Malik)* 4-B, 90 Canal Park, Gulberg-II, LAHORE, PAKISTAN.

★**Raif Omer & Co** *(R Omer)* P.K. 533, Atacag Ishani, 9 Ali Ruhi Sokak, LEFKOSA MERSIN 10, TURKEY.

Rainsford & Co *(V M Rainsford)* Low Leas House, Lea, MATLOCK, DE4 5JR.

ⓅⒶ**Raise, trading name of Raise Associates Limited** *(S Rai)* 10th Floor, 3 Hardman Street, Spinning Fields, MANCHESTER, M3 3HF.

Ⓐ**Raj Nair** *(R Nair)* CRC Cabinet de Revision & Conseil SA, Pl. des Eaux-Vives 6, P O Box 3444, 1211 GENEVA, SWITZERLAND. and at LUGANO

Raj Shah & Co *(R S Shah)* 46 Heddon Court Avenue, BARNET, HERTFORDSHIRE, EN4 9NG.

ⓉⒻⒶ**Raja & Co** *(M K Raja)* Aknam, 56 Chorley New Road, BOLTON, BL1 4AP.

★Ⓟ**Rajani & Co, trading name of R Rajani & Co Ltd** *(R Rajani)* Midland House, 50-52 Midland Road, WELLINGBOROUGH, NN8 1LU.

Ⓟ**Ralph Bettany Associates Limited** *(R C Bettany)* 1st Floor, 13 Vardre Road, Clydach, SWANSEA, SA6 5LP.

ⓅⒶ**Ralph Crump Accountants Limited** *(R Crump)* 14 Bakers Drove, Rownhams, SOUTHAMPTON, SO16 8AD.

ⓅⒶ**Ramar Accounting Services Limited** *(R Waran)* 111 Aldwick Road, BOGNOR REGIS, WEST SUSSEX, PO21 2NY.

Ramesh A. Patel & Co *(R A Patel)* 10 Harrow Place, Off Middlesex Street, LONDON, E1 7DB.

Ⓐ**Ramm Louis & Co** *(L Ramm)* Fifth Floor, Kingmaker House, Station Road, New Barnet, BARNET, HERTFORDSHIRE EN5 1NZ.

ⓉⒻⒶ**Ramon Lee & Partners** *(B F Jones, D Terry)* Kemp House, 152-160 City Road, LONDON, EC1V 2DW.

Ramsay & Co *(S N Ramsay)* 28 Carpenters Wood Drive, Chorleywood, RICKMANSWORTH, WD3 5RJ.

ⓉⒻⒶ**Ramsay Brown and Partners** *(K L Perry, S Singer, L M Slavin, J A Stone)* Ramsay House, 18 Vera Avenue, Grange Park, LONDON, N21 1RA.

Ⓟ**Ramshaw & Co Ltd** *(D S Ramshaw)* 2nd Floor, Yarm House, Roseworth Crescent, Gosforth, NEWCASTLE UPON TYNE, NE3 1NR.

Ⓟ**Randall & Company, trading name of Framecall Ltd** *(R W Randall)* 21 Clarence Road, Kew Gardens, RICHMOND, TW9 3NL.

ⓉⒻⒶ**Randall & Payne, trading name of Randall & Payne LLP** *(W J Abbott, M A Anthony, I Selwood, T J Watkins)* Rodborough Court, Walkley Hill, STROUD, GLOUCESTERSHIRE, GL5 3LR. and at CHELTENHAM, GLOUCESTER

Randall Greene *(R A Edwards, C R Greene)* Parallel House, 32/34 London Road, GUILDFORD, SURREY, GU1 2AB.

Ⓟ**Rapid Relief Consultancy, trading name of Rapid Relief Consultancy Limited** *(A E J S Wilson)* Cedar Cottage, Burrough Green, NEWMARKET, SUFFOLK, CB8 9NE.

Ⓐ**Rashed Shaheedee & Co** *(R A Shaheedee)* Chytel House, 160-164 Mile End Road, LONDON, E1 4LJ.

Rashid Ebrahim *(A R A Ebrahim)* 71 Dr. Lesur Street, Unit 7, BEAU BASSIN, MAURITIUS.

Rashmi Shah & Co *(R R Shah)* 62 Bertram Road, Hendon, LONDON, NW4 3PP.

Ratcliffe & Co *(A G Ratcliffe)* 74 Chancery Lane, LONDON, WC2A 1AD.

Ⓟ**Ratigan & Co Ltd** *(P A Ratigan)* 43 South Avenue, BUXTON, DERBYSHIRE, SK17 6NQ.

Ⓟ**Ratio Business Services Limited** *(G Purvis)* 10 Mardley Hill, WELWYN, HERTFORDSHIRE, AL6 0TN.

Ravine & Co *(R G Patel)* 783 Harrow Road, WEMBLEY, HA0 2LP.

★ⓉⒻⒶ**Rawcliffe & Co** *(M G Ashton, D A Harben, I C Harrison)* West Park House, 7/9 Wilkinson Avenue, BLACKPOOL, LANCASHIRE, FY3 9XG. and at PRESTON

Ⓐ**Rawi & Co LLP** *(R A Rawi, B C Vyas)* 128 Ebury Street, LONDON, SW1W 9QQ.

★**Rawlinson & Hunter** *(R E Douglas)* Windward 1, Regatta Office Park, PO Box 897, GEORGE TOWN, GRAND CAYMAN, KY1 - 1103 CAYMAN ISLANDS.

★ⓉⒻⒶ**Rawlinson & Hunter** *(P A Baker, C J A Bliss, D C Davies, M Harris, F J Jennings, S P Jennings, R B Melling, K S Nagra, P M Prettejohn, D C Rawlings, A Shilling)* Eighth Floor, 6 New Street Square, New Fetter Lane, LONDON, EC4A 3AQ. and at EPSOM

★ⓉⓅ**Rawlinson & Hunter, trading name of Rawlinson & Hunter Limited** *(D G Goar, S A James, S P Jennings, A D M Morgan)* Trafalgar Court, 3rd Floor, West Wing, St Peter Port, GUERNSEY, GY1 2JA.

★**Rawlinson Pryde & Partners** *(G Pryde, D J Rawlinson)* Argent House, 5 Goldington Road, BEDFORD, MK40 3JY.

ⓅⒶ**Rawlinson Pryde Limited** *(G Pryde, D J Rawlinson)* Argent House, 5 Goldington Road, BEDFORD, MK40 3JY.

ⒻⒶ**Rawlinsons** *(R J Hayter)* Marian House, 3 Colton Mill, Bullerthorpe Lane, LEEDS, LS15 9JN.

★ⓉⒶ**Rawlinsons** *(C J Collier, A J Cox, C J Crowley, M A Jackson, G H Jones, K N Woodthorpe)* Ruthlyn House, 90 Lincoln Road, PETERBOROUGH, PE1 2SP.

Ⓟ**Rawlinsons Payroll and HR Limited** *(C J Crowley)* Ruthlyn House, 90 Lincoln Road, PETERBOROUGH, PE1 2SP.

ⒻⒶ**Rawse, Varley & Co** *(J M Rawse, K R Varley, P M Varley)* Lloyds Bank Chambers, Hustlergate, BRADFORD, BD1 1UQ.

Ⓐ**Ray Adams** *(R J Adams)* Wellington House, 273-275 High Street, London Colney, ST. ALBANS, HERTFORDSHIRE, AL2 1HA.

Ray Cockrem ACA *(R J Cockrem)* 38 Elmgate Drive, Littledown, BOURNEMOUTH, BH7 7EG.

Ⓟ**Ray Dyer, trading name of Ray Dyer Accountants Ltd** *(R C Dyer)* Inglenook, Main Road, Nutbourne, CHICHESTER, PO18 8RR.

Ray Graves & Co *(R J Graves)* 158 Cemetery Road, IPSWICH, IP4 2HL.

ⓉⓅⒶ**Raymond & Co, trading name of A R Raymond & Co Limited** *(E J Cruttenden, E H Jenman, C O Jones)* 67 London Road, ST. LEONARDS-ON-SEA, EAST SUSSEX, TN37 6AR.

Raymond Birns *(R Birns)* 20 Woodstock Avenue, LONDON, NW11 9SL.

Raymond Bissex *(R A Bissex)* The Vicarage, 4 St. Andrews Road, BOOTLE, MERSEYSIDE, L20 5EX.

Raymond Brett Associates, trading name of Raymond M A Brett *(R M A Brett)* Woodside, Westfields, Whiteleaf, PRINCES RISBOROUGH, HP27 0LH.

Raymond Carter & Co *(J A Carter)* 1b Haling Road, SOUTH CROYDON, Surrey, CR2 6HS.

Raymond F.L. Wong *(R F L Wong)* Room 1305 13F, Universal Trade Centre, 3-5A Arbuthnot Road, CENTRAL, HONG KONG ISLAND, HONG KONG SAR.

Raymond Harris *(R I Harris)* 3 Golfside Close, LONDON, N20 0RD.

Raymond Hecek *(R V Hecek)* 615 London Road, WESTCLIFF-ON-SEA, ESSEX, SS0 9PE.

Raymond M. Green *(R M Green)* 25 Croft Close, Spondon, DERBY, DE21 7EF.

Raymond O'Leary *(R O'Leary)* 62 Ski View, SUNDERLAND, SR3 1NP.

Raymond Sentance & Co *(R G A Sentance)* 4 Dunsmore, The Hoe, Carpenders Park, WATFORD, WD19 5AU.

ⓉⒻⒶ**Rayner Essex, Tax First, trading names of Rayner Essex LLP** *(C R Essex, S J Essex, A H C Federer, K A Goldfarb, C W Goodkind, N M Heyes, S C Jacobs, T F Sansom, C A Walters)* Faulkner House, Victoria Street, ST. ALBANS, HERTFORDSHIRE, AL1 3SE. and at LONDON

Ⓟ**RB Chartered Accountant, trading name of RB Chartered Accountant Ltd** *(R J Barnett)* Offices 1 & 2 Top Corner, Market Street, PENKRIDGE, STAFFORDSHIRE, ST19 5DH.

ⒻⓅⒶ**RBA Accountancy Limited** *(S J Smale)* 8 Victoria Road, BRIDLINGTON, NORTH HUMBERSIDE, YO15 2BW.

ⒻⒶ**RBC** *(R W Brown)* 1 Victoria Square, BIRMINGHAM, B1 1BD.

RBS Accountancy & Bookkeeping, trading name of Gerald F Hayter *(G F Hayter)* 324 London Road, WOKINGHAM, BERKSHIRE, RG40 1RD.

ⒻⓅⒶ**RBS Accountants Limited** *(K K J Shah)* Suite 16, Beaufort Court, Admirals Way, LONDON, E14 9XL.

Ⓟ**RCA Corporate Finance, trading name of Richard Coppock Associates Limited** *(R J Coppock)* 80 Beulah Road, CARDIFF, CF14 6LZ.

Ⓟ**RCC Processing Limited** *(D Clarke, S R Rhodes)* 42 Market Street, Eckington, SHEFFIELD, S21 4JH.

Ⓟ**RCi (Birmingham) Limited** *(M S I Choudhury)* 45 Villa Road, Handsworth, BIRMINGHAM, B19 1BH.

Ⓟ**RCi (Exeter) Limited** *(M S I Choudhury)* 49 Fore Street, Heavitree, EXETER, EX1 2QN.

ⓅⒶ**RCi Audit and Assurance Services Limited** *(M S I Choudhury)* 3rd Floor, 2-12 Victoria Street, LUTON, BEDFORDSHIRE, LU1 2UA.

ⓉⓅ**RCi, RCi Global, trading names of RCi (Luton) Limited** *(M S I Choudhury)* 3rd Floor, 2-12 Victoria Street, LUTON, BEDFORDSHIRE, LU1 2UA.

Ⓟ**RCi, RCiglobal, trading names of RCi (Peterborough) Limited** *(M S I Choudhury)* First Floor, 254-256 Lincoln Road, PETERBOROUGH, CAMBRIDGESHIRE, PE1 2ND.

Ⓟ**RD Accountancy Solutions Ltd** *(R L Davies)* 18 Poplar Road, NEWTOWN, POWYS, SY16 2AQ.

RD Batho & Co *(R D Batho)* 12A West Beach, LYTHAM ST. ANNES, FY8 5QH.

RDATS, trading name of Ronnie Davidson Accountancy & Taxation Services *(R E Davidson)* 17 Murray Crescent, PINNER, MIDDLESEX, HA5 3QF. and at LONDON

★ⒻⒶ**RDP Newmans, trading name of RDP Newmans LLP** *(D M Finn, A R Gangola, C J Humpage, R Nyman, L R Perez, P Radia, M Sachdev)* Lynwood House, 373/375 Station Road, HARROW, MIDDLESEX, HA1 2AW. and at SOUTHEND-ON-SEA

RE Elliott & Co *(R E Elliott)* 25 Westrow Gardens, Seven Kings, ILFORD, ESSEX, IG3 9NE.

Re:Accounts *(E M Prior)* 18 Highpoint, Lyonsdown Road, New Barnet, BARNET, HERTFORDSHIRE, EN5 1LS.

★**Re10 (UK) Plc** *(N Patel)* Albemarle House, 1 Albemarle Street, LONDON, W1S 4HA.

Ⓟ**Re10, trading name of Shasens & Re10 (South East) Ltd** *(B R Shah)* 165 High Street, RICKMANSWORTH, HERTFORDSHIRE, WD3 1AY. and at HARROW

ⒻⒶ**Read & Co** *(S R Read)* 3c Sopwith Crescent, Hurricane Way, WICKFORD, ESSEX, SS11 8YU.

★ⓉⓅ**Read & Co, trading name of Derek J Read Limited** *(D Hallett, J Tomsett)* 107 North Street, MARTOCK, SOMERSET, TA12 6EJ. and at SHERBORNE

Ⓟ**Read Business Consulting Ltd** *(L A Read)* Leys House, Alveston, STRATFORD-UPON-AVON, WARWICKSHIRE, CV37 7QT.

Ⓟ**Read Woodruff, trading name of Read Woodruff Limited** *(N R Woodruff)* 24 Cornwall Road, DORCHESTER, DORSET, DT1 1RX.

ⓉⒶ**Read, Milburn & Co** *(D Hodgson, N J Liley)* 71 Howard Street, NORTH SHIELDS, TYNE AND WEAR, NE30 1AF.

Ⓟ**Reads & Co, trading name of Reads & Co Limited** *(P J Crosby, C J Moulder)* PO Box 179, 40 Esplanade, St Helier, JERSEY, JE4 9RJ.

ⓉⓅⒶ**Reads & Co., trading name of Reads & Co. Group Limited** *(P J Crosby, C J Moulder)* PO Box 179, 40 Esplanade, St. Helier, JERSEY, JE4 9RJ.

ⓅⒶ**Reads & Co., trading name of Reads (Audit) Limited** *(P J Crosby, C J Moulder)* 3rd Floor, 40 Esplanade, St. Helier, JERSEY, JE4 9RJ.

Ⓟ**Real Time Accounting Limited** *(G M Thorneycroft)* 11-13 Lonsdale Gardens, TUNBRIDGE WELLS, KENT, TN1 1NU.

ⓅⒶ**Reardon & Co Limited** *(N J Diss)* Ash House, Breckenwood Road, Fulbourn, CAMBRIDGE, CB21 5DQ.

ⓅⒶ**Reardon Holdings Limited** *(N J Diss)* Ash House, Breckenwood Road, Fulbourn, CAMBRIDGE, CB21 5DQ.

ⒻⒶ**Reay & King** *(R J Evans)* 87 High Street, Wimbledon, LONDON, SW19 5EG.

Rebbeck & Company *(D J Rebbeck)* Bramley Cottage, 45 Haconby Lane, Morton, BOURNE, LINCOLNSHIRE, PE10 0NP.

Rebecca Benneyworth *(R A Benneyworth)* Woodhouse, Rodborough Lane, Rodborough, STROUD, GL5 2LN.

Rebecca Blake *(R L Blake)* The Studio, 2 Kings End Road, Powick, WORCESTER, WR2 4RA.

Rebecca Taylor *(R L Taylor)* 11 Sea View Road, SKEGNESS, LINCOLNSHIRE, PE25 1BW.

Rebecca Wilber *(R Wilber)* 63 Marleigh Road, Bidford-on-Avon, ALCESTER, WARWICKSHIRE, B50 4EE.

Rebecca Williams BSc ACA *(R J Williams)* 62 Derbyshire Road, SALE, CHESHIRE, M33 3EL.

Ⓐ**Rebello & Co** *(T P Rebello)* 200 Brighton Road, PURLEY, CR8 4HB.

★**Reconta Ernst & Young** *(R N A Franchini, P G Smith)* Via Della Chiusa 2, 20123 MILAN, ITALY. and at BARI, BOLOGNA, BRESCIA, FLORENCE, NAPLES, ROME, TURIN

Ⓟ**Red Emerald, trading name of Red Emerald Ltd** *(J Patel)* Hadley House, 17 Park Road, High Barnet, BARNET, HERTFORDSHIRE, EN5 5RY.

Reddaway & Co *(R G Pulsford)* 30 St. Peter Street, TIVERTON, EX16 6NR.

★ⓉⒶ**Reddy Siddiqui & Kabani** *(F A Muddassir, A M Siddiqui, O F Siddiqui, S H Siddiqui)* Park View, 183-189 The Vale, LONDON, W3 7RW.

ⓉⒻⓅⒶ**Redford & Co, trading name of Redford & Co Limited** *(M J Redford)* 1st Floor, 64 Baker Street, LONDON, W1U 7GB.

Ⓟ**Redland Business Consultancy Limited** *(F E Small)* 4 Branksome Road, Redland, BRISTOL, BS6 7LL.

Redman Nichols Butler *(J W Butler, A J Nichols)* Maclaren House, Skerne Road, DRIFFIELD, YO25 6PN. and at YORK

Ⓟ**Redshield Business Solutions Limited** *(J C Dinnage, J S A Morris)* Unit 2, Birchden Farm, Broadwater Forest Lane, Groombridge, TUNBRIDGE WELLS, KENT TN3 9NR.

★Ⓕ**Reece Hulme & Co** *(G Hulme)* 1 Wilson Patten Street, WARRINGTON, WA1 1PG.

ⓅⒶ**Reed & Co, trading name of Reed Accounts & Tax Limited** *(C M Reed)* Hallings Hatch, Parkgate Road, Newdigate, DORKING, SURREY, RH5 5DY.

Ⓐ**Reed Ransted** *(D A Ransted)* Finance House, 522 Uxbridge Road, PINNER, MIDDLESEX, HA5 3PU.

Reeds *(C R Reed)* Copperfields, Mount Pleasant, CROWBOROUGH, TN6 2NF.

Rees & Co *(D B Rees)* 10 Dryden Mansions, Queens Club Gardens, LONDON, W14 9RG.

Rees Beaufort & Co *(P A Rees)* 38 Beaufort Avenue, Langland, SWANSEA, SA3 4PB.

ⓉⒻⒶ**Rees Pollock** *(C Barnett, C Dimmick, C A Kimberlin, A J Macpherson, J M Moulsdale, J M Munday, S P Rees, P A Vipond)* 35 New Bridge Street, LONDON, EC4V 6BW.

Ⓟ**ReesRussell Taxation Services Limited** *(J M Russell)* 37 Market Square, WITNEY, OXFORDSHIRE, OX28 6RE.

★ⒻⒶ**ReesRussell, trading name of ReesRussell LLP** *(J M Russell)* 37 Market Square, WITNEY, OXFORDSHIRE, OX28 6RE.

Ⓐ**Reeves & Co** *(C Vaughan)* Argyle commercial Centre, Argyle Street, SWINDON, SN2 6AR.

ⓉⒻⒶ**Reeves, trading name of Reeves & Co LLP** *(N J Alder, D J Ashman, E Clapton, M M Connolly, M J Cook, M K R Dyer, A J Q Griggs, R W Heasman, P D Hudson, G H Jones, S J Ledger, T P W Levey, S T Linley, P A R Manser, A H Miller, T E Mills, J C O'Brien, M O'Brien, M S T Procter, C S Reeve-Tucker, C N Relf, S M Robinson, O S Skinner, C R Stevens, R A Stevens, R M Sutton, S J Tancock, S P Tanner, A C J Tinham, P N Wood)* 37 St. Margarets Street, CANTERBURY, KENT, CT1 2TU. and at CHATHAM, HORLEY, LONDON

Reeve-Young & Co *(H D R Young)* Silverbirch Cottage, Watford Road, Elstree, BOREHAMWOOD, WD6 3BE.

Ⓟ**Refresh Business Group, trading name of Refresh Recovery Limited** *(G Craig)* West Lancashire Investment Centre, Maple View, Whitemoss Business Park, SKELMERSDALE, LANCASHIRE, WN8 9TG.

Ⓟ**Regent Consultancy Limited** *(A Dave)* 18 Fitzhardinge Street, Manchester Square, LONDON, W1H 6EQ.

Ⓟ**Regent Services Ltd** *(H A Adamjee)* Bridge House, 11 Creek Road, EAST MOLESEY, SURREY, KT8 9BE.

Regina L.S. Chow *(L R Chow)* 5/F, Dahsing Life Building, 99 -105 Des Voeux Road, CENTRAL, HONG KONG SAR.

Ⓟ**Reginald J Coade & Co Limited** *(P A Rudge)* 90-92 High Street, Bidford-on-Avon, ALCESTER, WARWICKSHIRE, B50 4AF.

Ⓟ**Rehman Michael & Co, trading name of Rehman Michael(Accountants) Limited** *(M A Malik)* 277 Roundhay Road, LEEDS, WEST YORKSHIRE, LS8 4HS. and at BRADFORD

★Ⓣ**RehncyShaheen** *(J S Rehncy)* 1276-1278 Greenford Road, GREENFORD, MIDDLESEX, UB6 0HH. and at LONDON

ⒻⓅ**Reid & Co, trading name of Reid & Co Corporate Services Limited** *(J E Lewis)* Witan Court, 305 Upper Fourth Street, Central, MILTON KEYNES, MK9 1EH.

Ⓟ**Reid Moffat & Co Limited** *(W Moffat)* 15 Niffany Gardens, SKIPTON, NORTH YORKSHIRE, BD23 1SZ.

ⓉⒻⒶ**reidwilliams** *(C R H Williams)* Prince Regent House, 108 London Street, READING, RG1 4SJ.

Ⓕ**Reifer & Co** *(A Reifer)* 23 Craven Walk, LONDON, N16 6BS.

Reisman & Co *(M S Reisman)* 63 High Road, Bushey Heath, BUSHEY, WD23 1EE.

Renaud Desvaux De Marigny *(R J Desvaux De Marigny)* 29 Brown Sequard Street, CUREPIPE, MAURITIUS.

Rendell & Co *(J C Rendell)* 125 Portway, WELLS, BA5 2BR.

★**Rendell Thompson** *(J C Rendell)* 125 Portway, WELLS, BA5 2BR. and at CHRISTCHURCH, FLEET

Renton & Co *(S N Renton)* Chalkwell Park House, 700 London Road, WESTCLIFF-ON-SEA, SS0 9HQ.

Ⓟ**Resolve - Tax and Accounts Limited** *(R F Arnold)* 7 Braybrooke Road, Wargrave, READING, RG10 8DU.

Ⓟ**Resolve Business Solutions, trading name of Resolve Cambridge Ltd** *(P Reid)* Tyburn House, Station Road, Oakington, CAMBRIDGE, CB24 3AH.

Ⓕ**ReSolve, trading name of ReSolve Partners LLP** *(C F Gunn)* One America Square, LONDON, EC3N 2LB. and at BIRMINGHAM

Resource Revision S.A.R.L *(C F Medlyn)* 36 Rue Gabriel Lippmann, L-1943 LUXEMBOURG, LUXEMBOURG.

Ⓟ**Resources, trading name of Financial Resources Limited** *(J Heaton)* The Hermitage Tower, Elston Lane, Grimsargh, PRESTON, PR2 5LE.

Ⓐ**Retout Capel & Co** *(P G Retout)* Unit 4, Ffordd yr onnen, Lon Parcwr Business Park, RUTHIN, CLWYD, LL15 1NJ.

Ⓟ**Revelation, trading name of Revelation Business Solutions Limited** *(M C Wakerley)* Woodland House, Bowson Square, Bream, LYDNEY, GLOUCESTERSHIRE, GL15 6LB.

ⓉⒻⒶ**Revell Ward, trading name of Revell Ward LLP** *(K G Borowski, J A Davies, J D Wilson)* 7th Floor, 30 Market Street, HUDDERSFIELD, HD1 2HG.

Revill Pearce *(A J Prevett)* Stane House, Salmons Corner, Nr. Coggeshall, COLCHESTER, CO6 1RX. and at LONDON

Rex Harrold & Co *(R Harrold)* The Old Coach House, Theobalds Park Road, ENFIELD, EN2 9BD.

Ⓐ**Reynolds & Co** *(R J Reynolds)* Square Root Business Centre, 102-116 Windmill Road, CROYDON, CR0 2XQ.

Reynolds & Co *(J W Reynolds)* 4 Thorpe Hall Close, Thorpe Bay, SOUTHEND-ON-SEA, SS1 3SQ.

ⒻⒶ**Reynolds & Company** *(N P Reynolds)* Meridian House, 7 The Avenue, Highams Park, LONDON, E4 9LB.

Ⓟ**Reynolds 2000 (Taxation Services) Ltd** *(A L Bunn)* Whitstone Farm, Bovey Tracey, NEWTON ABBOT, TQ13 9NA.

Ⓐ**Reza Samii** *(G Rahmat-Samii)* 5 Calico Row, Plantation Wharf, Battersea, LONDON, SW11 3YH.

RFM Associates *(R F Messik)* 10 Carew Way, WATFORD, WD19 5BG.

RFS *(R C Farnell-Smith)* The Coach House, 1A Watt Place, Cheadle, STOKE-ON-TRENT, STAFFORDSHIRE, ST10 1NY.

ⒻⓅⒶ**RFW Rutherfords, trading name of RFW Rutherfords Ltd** *(D G Griffiths, J D Rose)* Ardenham Court, Oxford Road, AYLESBURY, BUCKINGHAMSHIRE, HP19 8HT.

Ⓟ**RGD, trading name of Deri Consultants Limited** *(R G Deri)* The Old Vicarage, Main Street, Boynton, BRIDLINGTON, NORTH HUMBERSIDE, YO16 4XJ.

Ⓣ**RGL Forensic Accountants (Singapore) Pte Ltd, RGL International (Australasia) Pty Ltd, trading names of RGL LLP** *(J Crick, K J Harding, A S Levitt, C M Rawlin, J H F Stanbury)* 8th Floor, Dashwood, 69 Old Broad Street, LONDON, EC2M 1QS. and at SINGAPORE, SYDNEY

Ⓟ**RH Jeffs & Rowe Ltd** *(H T W Jones, R E Thomas)* 27-28 Gelliwastad Road, PONTYPRIDD, MID GLAMORGAN, CF37 2BW.

RHCO *(A R Hakim)* 727-729 High Road, Finchley, LONDON, N12 0BP.

★ⓉⒻⒶ**RHK, trading name of RHK Business Advisers LLP** *(D C Hall, G Miller, D J Thompson)* Coburg House, 1 Coburg Street, GATESHEAD, TYNE AND WEAR, NE8 1NS.

Rhodes & Co *(J H Rhodes)* 7 Richmond Bridge House, 419 Richmond Road, TWICKENHAM, TW1 2EX.

ⓉⒻⒶ**Rhodes & Rhodes** *(J Katz, S A Levinson, G J West)* 42 Doughty Street, LONDON, WC1N 2LY.

Rhodes Clarke & Co *(D Clarke, S R Rhodes)* 42 Market Street, Eckington, SHEFFIELD, S21 4JH.

ⓉⒻⒶ**RHP Partnership** *(M G Hurst, K Mayfield, S M Pring, N A Rudd, N A Rudd)* Lancaster House, 87 Yarmouth Road, NORWICH, NORFOLK, NR7 0HF.

★**Riaz Ahmad & Co** *(I E Sheikh)* 10B St Marys Park, Main Boulevard, Gulberg III, LAHORE, PAKISTAN.

ⓉⒻⒶ**Ribchester Smith & Law, trading name of Ribchesters** *(D M Armstrong, D Holloway, J W T Law)* 67 Saddler Street, DURHAM, DH1 3NP. and at NEWCASTLE UPON TYNE

ⓉⒻⒶ**Rice & Co** *(S M Dale, M S Gibbs, K J Preece, C Stonier)* Harance House, Rumer Hill Business Estate, Rumer Hill Road, CANNOCK, STAFFORDSHIRE, WS11 0ET. and at UTTOXETER

ⓉⒻⒶ**Rice Associates, trading name of Rice Associates Ltd** *(A M Beet, D Rice, S E Wildey)* Market Chambers, 3-4 Market Place, WOKINGHAM, BERKSHIRE, RG40 1AL.

Richard & Sue Garner *(R W Garner, S Garner)* 7 Kingsland House, 135 Andover Road, NEWBURY, BERKSHIRE, RG14 6JL.

Richard A Fogg MA ACA *(R A Fogg)* 98 Erddig Road, WREXHAM, LL13 7DR.

Ⓐ**Richard A. Crocker** *(R A Crocker)* 181 Chester Road, Hazel Grove, STOCKPORT, CHESHIRE, SK7 6EN.

Richard A. Fell *(R A Fell)* Albion Lodge, Fordham Road, NEWMARKET, SUFFOLK, CB8 7AQ.

Richard A. Pepper *(R A Pepper)* 8 Apple Tree Close, PONTEFRACT, WEST YORKSHIRE, WF8 4RH.

Richard A. Sinclair *(R Sinclair)* 122 Lickhill Road, STOURPORT-ON-SEVERN, DY13 8SF.

Richard Abel & Co *(R J Abel)* 14 Shelwick Grove, Dorridge, SOLIHULL, WEST MIDLANDS, B93 8UH.

Ⓟ**Richard Airey Limited** *(R A Airey)* 2 Church Lane, Clayton West, HUDDERSFIELD, HD8 9LY.

Ⓟ**Richard Alsept Limited** *(R J Alsept)* 58 Kings Field, Seahouses, SEAHOUSES, NORTHUMBERLAND, NE68 7PA.

ⓉⒻⒶ**Richard Anthony & Company** *(M Barnett, A M Hassan, P Horesh, A Levy, A V Simons, R I Simons, B Singh, P A Taylor)* 13 Station Road, Finchley, LONDON, N3 2SB.

Richard Apps *(R V Apps)* 3 Strickland Avenue, Shadwell, LEEDS, LS17 8JX.

Richard B. Pennington *(R B Pennington)* Firnook, Linkside East, HINDHEAD, GU26 6NY.

Richard Brown & Co *(R S S Brown)* 1 High Street, Roydon, HARLOW, CM19 5HJ.

Ⓟ**Richard Bunker & Company, trading name of Richard Bunker & Co Limited** *(R W Bunker)* Colkin House, 16 Oakfield Road, Clifton, BRISTOL, BS8 2AP.

Richard C. Yates *(R C Yates)* 16 Arnold Grove, Shirley, SOLIHULL, WEST MIDLANDS, B90 3JR.

Ⓟ**Richard Caley Ltd** *(R M Caley)* Havenside, Trewent Hill, Freshwater East, PEMBROKE, SA71 5LJ.

Ⓐ**Richard Clerey & Co** *(R A Clerey)* 18 Brenkley Way, Blezard Business Park, Seaton Burn, NEWCASTLE UPON TYNE, NE13 6DS.

Richard Coleman *(R H Coleman)* 3 Pentland Drive, Warren Wood Arnold, NOTTINGHAM, NG5 9PZ.

Richard Crosby *(R W V Crosby)* Shrublands Farmhouse, Barston Lane, Barston, SOLIHULL, B92 0JU.

Ⓟ**Richard Crosby Limited** *(R W V Crosby)* The Shrublands Farmhouse, Barston Lane, Barston, SOLIHULL, WEST MIDLANDS, B92 0JU.

Richard D. Warman *(R D Warman)* Silver Birches, Heronsgate, RICKMANSWORTH, WD3 5DN.

Richard Davison Associates *(R L Davison)* Studio 320, Highgate Studios, 53-79 Highgate Road, LONDON, NW5 1TL.

Richard Deane FCA *(R J Deane)* 58 Oldfields Close, LEOMINSTER, HEREFORDSHIRE, HR6 8TL.

Richard Diamond *(R E Diamond)* 01 BP 7168, ABIDJAN, COTE d'IVOIRE.

Richard Dovey & Co *(R P Dovey)* 61 Malmains Way, BECKENHAM, BR3 6SB.

Ⓐ**Richard Dunford & Co** *(R J Dunford)* 26 High Trees Avenue, BOURNEMOUTH, BH8 9JX.

Ⓟ**Richard Dunford Limited** *(R J Dunford)* 26 High Trees Avenue, BOURNEMOUTH, BH8 9JX.

Ⓟ**Richard F Hawkins Ltd** *(R F Hawkins)* Linport, 59 Oaklands Avenue, Porthill, NEWCASTLE, STAFFORDSHIRE, ST5 0DR.

Ⓕ**Richard F. Hopper** *(R F Hopper)* Chinthurst, 30 St. Stephens Hill, LAUNCESTON, CORNWALL, PL15 8HN.

Richard Falkner & Co *(R I Falkner)* Lowfield House, 222 Wellington Road South, STOCKPORT, CHESHIRE, SK2 6RS.

ⒻⒶ**Richard Freedman** *(R A Freedman)* Suite 2, Fountain House, 1a Elm Park, STANMORE, MIDDLESEX, HA7 4AU.

Richard Green *(R P Green)* Smithwood Farmhouse, Smithwood Common, CRANLEIGH, GU6 8QY.

Richard H. Hartley *(R H Hartley)* 142 Broadhurst Gardens, LONDON, NW6 3BH.

Richard H. Hudson *(R H Hudson)* Lilyhurst House, Lilyhurst, SHIFNAL, TF11 8RL.

Ⓐ**Richard H. Snelling** *(R H Snelling)* 9 West Hill, Sanderstead, SOUTH CROYDON, Surrey, CR2 0SB.

Richard Hanmer *(W R Hanmer)* Rua Ambrizette 180-11, 05704-020 SAO PAULO, BRAZIL.

Richard Hewson & Co *(R C Hewson)* 21 Corner Green, LONDON, SE3 9JJ.

Ⓟ**Richard Hopes Limited** *(R J Hopes)* Bell House, Ashford Hill, THATCHAM, BERKSHIRE, RG19 8BB.

Ⓟ**Richard Horsley & Co Ltd** *(R G C Horsley)* Acorn House, 395d Midsummer Boulevard, MILTON KEYNES, MK9 3HP.

Ⓟ**Richard Hughes & Co Ltd** *(R J W Hughes)* 95 St. Peters Close, Moreton-on-Lugg, HEREFORD, HR4 8DN.

Richard Ian & Co *(R Basch)* Suite 7, 2nd Floor Elstree House, Elstree Way, BOREHAMWOOD, HERTFORDSHIRE, WD6 1SD.

Richard J Allen *(R J Allen)* Glengarry Lodge, INVERGARRY, INVERNESS-SHIRE, PH35 4HG.

Richard J Gower *(R J Gower)* Redferns, 35 The Lagger, CHALFONT ST. GILES, BUCKINGHAMSHIRE, HP8 4DH.

ⓅⒶ**Richard J Miller Limited** *(R J Miller)* Dafferns LLP, 1 Eastwood, Harry Weston Road, Binley Business Park, COVENTRY, CV3 2UB.

Richard J. Hilton *(R J Hilton)* 11 Crow Park Drive, Burton Joyce, NOTTINGHAM, NG14 5AS.

★**Richard J. Smith & Co** *(G R Frampton)* 53 Fore Street, IVYBRIDGE, PL21 9AE. and at TRURO

Richard J. Wilkins *(R J Wilkins)* 1 Wentworth Close, Barnham, BOGNOR REGIS, WEST SUSSEX, PO22 0HS.

ⒻⒶ**Richard Joseph & Co** *(R L Joseph)* 2nd Floor, 65 Station Road, EDGWARE, HA8 7HX.

Richard Juett *(R A Juett)* 2 St Mary's Road, Bishopstoke, EASTLEIGH, SO50 6BP.

ⓅⒶ**Richard Juneman Limited** *(R J Juneman)* 8 Great James Street, LONDON, WC1N 3DF.

Richard Kemp & Co *(R G Kemp)* 33a Crook Log, BEXLEYHEATH, DA6 8EB.

Ⓟ**Richard Kendall & Co, trading name of Richard Kendall & Co Ltd** *(R J Kendall)* 15 Victoria Road, TEDDINGTON, MIDDLESEX, TW11 0BB.

Richard Kiew & Co *(R J F Kiew)* 1st Floor No. 10 A, Lorong 4, Jalan Nanas, PO Box 2536, 93750 KUCHING, SARAWAK MALAYSIA.

Ⓐ**Richard Kleiner LLP** *(R H Kleiner)* 25 Harley Street, LONDON, W1G 9BR.

Richard L Hudson FCA *(R L Hudson)* The Elms, 29 North Bar Without, BEVERLEY, HU17 7AG.

ⓅⒶ**Richard Malone Associates Ltd** *(R J Malone)* 64 Clarendon Road, WATFORD, WD17 1DA.

Ⓟ**Richard Matthew Associates, trading name of RM Professional Practice Ltd** *(S R M Knights)* Forge House, Ansell Road, DORKING, RH4 1UN.

Ⓟ**Richard Matthew, trading name of Richard Matthew Ltd** *(P Adams)* 17 Broomfield Park, Westcott, DORKING, RH4 3QQ.

Richard Mawhood *(R Mawhood)* 9 Far Lane, Wadsley, SHEFFIELD, S6 4FA.

Richard Moore & Co *(R A Moore)* 6 Bridge End, Dorchester on Thames, WALLINGFORD, OX10 7JP.

ⒻⒶ**Richard Morgan and Company** *(R D Morgan)* 59 Victoria Road, SURBITON, SURREY, KT6 4NQ.

Richard Newton *(R J E Newton)* Church View, 162 Main Street, Alrewas, BURTON-ON-TRENT, STAFFORDSHIRE, DE13 7ED.

Richard Newton *(R Newton)* 15 Manningford Close, WINCHESTER, SO23 7EU.

Ⓕ**Richard Norton & Co** *(R J Norton)* 342 Regents Park Road, LONDON, N3 2LJ.

Richard P Braysher *(R P Braysher)* 2 High Road, Eastcote, PINNER, MIDDLESEX, HA5 2EW.

Richard P G Lewis *(R P G Lewis)* Brick Kiln Cottage, 20 Comfort Road, Mylor Bridge, FALMOUTH, CORNWALL, TR11 5SE.

ⓅⒶ**Richard Percy Limited** *(R C S J Percy)* Sandhills Farm, Braintree Road, Wethersfield, BRAINTREE, ESSEX, CM7 4AG.

Ⓟ**Richard Perkins & Company, trading name of Brookfield Realisation Ltd** *(R C Perkins, P A Rudge)* 50 Brookfield Close, Hunt End, REDDITCH, WORCESTERSHIRE, B97 5LL.

Richard Place & Co *(D H Andrews, C C James)* Here House, Second Avenue, Batchmere, CHICHESTER, WEST SUSSEX, PO20 7LF. and at BEVERLEY

★**Richard Place Dobson LLP** *(M N Frost, P R Hayden, M R Tyson)* Brackenhurst, Little London, Selsfield Road, Ardingly, HAYWARDS HEATH, WEST SUSSEX RH17 6TJ.

★ⓉⒻⓅⒶ**Richard Place Dobson, trading name of Richard Place Dobson Services Limited** *(M N Frost, P R Hayden, M R Tyson)* Ground Floor, 1-7 Station Road, CRAWLEY, WEST SUSSEX, RH10 1HT.

ⒻⒶ**Richard Place Palmer** *(J F Palmer)* 52a Carfax, HORSHAM, WEST SUSSEX, RH12 1EQ.

Ⓕ**Richard Ramalingum & Co** *(R Ramalingum)* 30 West Gardens, Ewell Village, EPSOM, SURREY, KT17 1NE.

Ⓟ**Richard S Burton, trading name of Richard S Burton Ltd** *(R S Burton)* 48c Main Street, Meadow Lane, Burton Joyce, NOTTINGHAM, NG14 5EX.

★Ⓟ**Richard S Harris & Co Ltd** *(R S Harris)* 45 Bell Common, EPPING, CM16 4DY.

Richard S K Chan & Co *(S K R Chan)* Room 1601, Yu Sung Boon Building, 107 Des Voeux Road C, CENTRAL, HONG KONG ISLAND, HONG KONG SAR.

Richard Samson *(R Samson)* 21 Coldharbour Lane, LONDON, SE5 9NR.

Richard Seddon *(R J Seddon)* 4 Hardy Drive, Bramhall, STOCKPORT, SK7 2BW.

Ⓐ**Richard Sexton** *(R G Sexton)* 1 Embankment Place, LONDON, WC2N 6RH.

ⓉⒶ**Richard Sexton & Co** *(S M Hamilton, K G Simpson)* St. Margaret's, 3 Manor Road, COLCHESTER, CO3 3LU.

ⒻⓅ**Richard Shaw, trading name of Richard G Shaw Limited** *(R G Shaw)* The Granary, Caldewell Farm Barns, Pershore Road, Stoulton, WORCESTER PARK, WR7 4RL.

Richard Shears *(R J Shears)* Parallel House, 32 London Road, GUILDFORD, SURREY, GU1 2AB.

Ⓣ**Richard Small & Co** *(R E Small)* 24 Central Precinct, Winchester Road, Chandlers Ford, EASTLEIGH, SO53 2GA.

ⓉⒻⓅⒶ**Richard Smedley, trading name of Richard Smedley Limited** *(R W Smedley)* Oakford House, 291 Low Lane, Horsforth, LEEDS, LS18 5NU.

Richard Sparkes *(R W Sparkes)* Garden Cottage, Barking, IPSWICH, IP6 8HJ.

Ⓟ**Richard Stapley, trading name of Richard Stapley Limited** *(R J Stapley)* PO Box 349, Maison de Haut, La Grande Rue, St Saviours, GUERNSEY, GY1 3UZ.

Richard Tarr & Co *(R L Tarr)* Wood Park, East Down, BARNSTAPLE, EX31 4LZ.

Richard Taylor & Co *(R C C Taylor)* Orchard Chambers, 4 Rocky Lane, Heswall, WIRRAL, CH60 0BY.

Richard Thompson & Company *(R W G Thompson)* 15 Swanswell Road, Olton, SOLIHULL, B92 7ET.

Richard Tozer LLP *(R Tozer)* Tricor Suite, 7th Floor, 52-54 Gracechurch Street, LONDON, EC3V 0EH.

Richard W. Wesley & Co *(R W Wesley)* 68 Waddon Court Road, CROYDON, SURREY, CR0 4AJ.

Richard W.J. Walker *(R W J Walker)* Bracken Hills, Surby Road, Port Erin, ISLE OF MAN, IM9 6TD.

Richard Walsh *(R W Walsh)* Jonquils, Marlow Common, MARLOW, SL7 2JQ.

Richard Webb FCA *(A R Webb)* 71 Osborne Parc, HELSTON, CORNWALL, TR13 8TZ.

Richard Willoughby *(R G W Willoughby)* 3 Ashlands Grove, Harpfields, STOKE-ON-TRENT, ST4 6QU.

Ⓟ**Richard Wood, trading name of Richard F Wood Ltd** *(R F Wood)* Oakwood House, 51a Lucknow Avenue, Mapperley Park, NOTTINGHAM, NG3 5AZ.

Ⓐ**Richard Woods & Co** *(R L Woods)* Southwold House, Boston Road, Swineshead, BOSTON, PE20 3HB.

Ⓐ**Richard Wyatt & Co.** *(R D Wyatt)* 109c High Street, CHESHAM, HP5 1DE.

Ⓐ**Richard Yong & Co** *(R C K Yong)* 100 Hale Lane, LONDON, NW7 3SE.

Richards & Co *(T R Richards)* The Dormer House, 159 Rough Common Road, CANTERBURY, CT2 9BS. and at FOLKESTONE

Richards & Co. *(B Richards)* Owners Business Centre, High Street, Newburn, NEWCASTLE UPON TYNE, NE15 8LN.

ⓉⓅⒶ**Richards Associates, trading name of Richards Associates Limited** *(A M Richards)* Suite 10 & 11, Hawkesyard Hall, Armitage Road, RUGELEY, STAFFORDSHIRE, WS15 1PU.

Ⓟ**Richards Sandy Partnership, trading name of The Richards Sandy Partnership Limited** *(R I Richards, N P Sandy)* 6 Edgar Street, WORCESTER, WR1 2LR.

Richardson & Co *(E K Richardson)* Summerville, 65 Daisy Bank Rd, Victoria Pk, MANCHESTER, M14 5QL.

Richardson Business Services *(J C Richardson)* 29 Bolton Road North, Edenfield, BURY, LANCASHIRE, BL0 0HB.

ⓉⒻⓅⒶ**Richardson Jones, trading name of Richardson Jones Limited** *(C D Jones, D C Porter, G A Thrush)* Mercury House, 19/21 Chapel Street, MARLOW, BUCKINGHAMSHIRE, SL7 3HN.

ⓅⒶ**Richardson Nutt Limited** *(D Sisson)* Unit 7, Stadium Business Court, Millennium Way, Pride Park, DERBY, DE24 8HP.

★ⒻⓅⒶ**Richardson Swift, trading name of Richardson Swift Ltd** *(M T Richardson)* 11 Laura Place, BATH, BA2 4BL.

★Ⓐ**Richardson, Watson & Co** *(P Charge, D T T Tan)* Mint House, 6 Stanley Park Road, WALLINGTON, SM6 0HA.

Ⓐ**Richardsons** *(E A Richardson)* 99 London Street, READING, RG1 4QA.

ⓉⓅⒶ**Richardsons, trading name of Richardsons Financial Group Limited** *(B A Hawkes, I S Husband, A R King, A Richardson)* 30 Upper High Street, THAME, OXFORDSHIRE, OX9 3EZ.

ⓉⒻⒶ**Riches & Company** *(R G Bolton, N J Caso)* 34 Anyards Road, COBHAM, SURREY, KT11 2LA. and at LONDON, SHARJAH

Riches Consulting *(K I Riches)* Little Coombe, Longfield Road, DORKING, SURREY, RH4 3DE.

Richman & Co *(M Richman)* 293 Kenton Lane, HARROW, HA3 8RR.

ⓉⒻⒶ**Rickard Keen LLP** *(K E Davies, W J Gould, N C Kelleway, A Worsdale)* 7 Nelson Street, SOUTHEND-ON-SEA, SS1 1EH. and at BASILDON

Ⓟ**Ricketts & Co, trading name of Ricketts & Co Limited** *(C M W Ricketts)* 43 Bugle Street, SOUTHAMPTON, SO14 2AG.

Ⓟ**Rickman, trading name of Leonard Rickman Accountancy Services Limited** *(L Rickman)* Devonshire House, Manor Way, BOREHAMWOOD, HERTFORDSHIRE, WD6 1QQ.

Ricky Leung & Co. *(R Y C Leung)* Unit 505 5th Floor, Tower 2, Cheung Sha Wan Plaza, 833 Cheung Sha Wan Road, LAI CHI KOK, KOWLOON HONG KONG SAR.

★ⒻⓅⒶ**Ridehalgh Limited** *(S Henry)* Guardian House, 42 Preston New Road, BLACKBURN, BB2 6AH.

Ⓟ**Ridge House Associates Limited** *(G E Jell)* Ridge House, Over Old Road, Hartpury, GLOUCESTER, GL19 3DH.

Ⓕ**Ridgetown LLP** *(P H Waxman)* 4 Fernacre, SALE, CHESHIRE, M33 2BA.

Ⓟ**Ridgeway Accountancy Practice, trading name of Belmont Services (Southwest) Limited** *(D A Rice)* 117 The Ridgeway, Plympton, PLYMOUTH, PL7 2AA.

ⓅⒶ**Ridley Marreco & Co, trading name of Ridley Marreco & Co Limited** *(S W Bunce)* Dove House, Mill Lane, Barford St. Michael, BANBURY, OXFORDSHIRE, OX15 0RH.

ⓉⒶ**Rigbey Harrison** *(D Collett, M J Holder, J Smith)* 4 Church Green East, REDDITCH, B98 8BT.

ⓉⒻⒶ**Rigby Lennon & Co** *(A F Harrison, A Lennon, J P Rigby)* 20 Winmarleigh Street, WARRINGTON, WA1 1JY.

Ⓟ**Rigel Wolf Limited** *(S R Smith)* Orion House, 28a Spital Terrace, GAINSBOROUGH, LINCOLNSHIRE, DN21 2HQ.

Ⓟ**Rightway Accounting Services Ltd** *(L S Dale)* 39 Finchley Avenue, CHELMSFORD, CM2 9BX.

ⓉⒻⒶ**Riley** *(B E Constantine, V P Doyle, J Stacey)* 51 North Hill, PLYMOUTH, PL4 8HZ.

ⓉⒻⓅⒶ**Riley & Co, trading name of Riley & Co Limited** *(V Atkinson, A K Riley, S J Walton)* 52 St. Johns Lane, HALIFAX, WEST YORKSHIRE, HX1 2BW.

Ⓐ**Riley Moss Audit LLP** *(F A Patel, W Yasin)* 183-185 North Road, PRESTON, PR1 1YQ. and at MANCHESTER

ⒻⓅ**Riley Moss, trading name of Riley Moss Limited** *(F A Patel, W Yasin)* Riley House, 183-185 North Road, PRESTON, PR1 1YQ. and at MANCHESTER

Ⓟ**Rilis Limited** *(M J Riley)* 4 High Street, STOURPORT-ON-SEVERN, WORCESTERSHIRE, DY13 8DH.

Ⓟ**Rily Accountancy and Business Solutions Ltd** *(R D Tunnicliffe)* Rily House, 55 Stryd Hywel Harris, HENGOED, MID GLAMORGAN, CF82 7DN.

Rimingtons *(C L Rimington)* 14 Hill Brow, Kirk Ella, HULL, HU10 7PP.

★ⓉⒶ**Rimmer & May** *(A M Evans, E Truman)* 19 Murray Street, LLANELLI, DYFED, SA15 1AQ.

★**Rimmer Case Partnership** *(B E Case, C F Rimmer)* Fir Tree House, Truemans Way, Hawarden, DEESIDE, CLWYD, CH5 3LS.

★**Ring** *(R R Ring)* 443 C Queen Street E, TORONTO M5A 1T6, ON, CANADA.

ⓅⒶ**Ringwood Accounting, trading name of Ringwood Accounting Limited** *(L E Weeks)* 1 Folly Farm Lane, Ashley, RINGWOOD, HAMPSHIRE, BH24 2NN.

Members in Practice and Firms - Alphabetical **Ripe - Robinson & Co**

★ⓉⒻⒶ**Ripe, trading name of Ripe LLP** *(R D Glazer)* 9a Burroughs Gardens, LONDON, NW4 4AU.
Ⓐ**Ritchie Burge & Co** *(N D R Burge)* 14 Earlish, Portree, ISLE OF SKYE, IV51 9XL.
Ⓐ**Ritchie Phillips, trading name of Ritchie Phillips LLP** *(S D Ritchie)* The Old Granary, Field Place Estate, Field Place, Broadbridge Heath, HORSHAM, WEST SUSSEX RH12 3PB.
▽**Ritsons** *(D Newton)* The Tower, 103 High Street, ELGIN, MORAYSHIRE, IV30 1EB. and at BUCKIE, FORRES, INVERNESS, KEITH
Riverside Accountancy *(P J McNicoll)* 52 Ray Park Avenue, MAIDENHEAD, BERKSHIRE, SL6 8DX.
Ⓟ**Riverside Financial Consultancy Ltd** *(S J M Dent)* 22A Bradmore Park Road, LONDON, W6 0DT.
Rizvi & Co *(S M M Rizvi)* Wonea House, 2 Richmond Road, ISLEWORTH, MIDDLESEX, TW7 7BL.
RJ & CA Perkins *(C A Perkins, R J Perkins)* Clemenstone Court, Clemenstone, COWBRIDGE, CF71 7PZ.
RJ Accountancy *(R M Bonehill)* Crows Cottage, Low Road, Friskney, BOSTON, LINCOLNSHIRE, PE22 8NW.
Ⓟ**RJ Cromar Ltd** *(R J Cromar)* 7 Kinnaird Avenue, Newton Mearns, GLASGOW, G77 5EL.
RJ Hall *(R J Hall)* Great Danegate, Danegate, Eridge Green, TUNBRIDGE WELLS, KENT, TN3 9HU.
Ⓕ**RJ Marsden** *(R J Marsden)* Park House, 9 Park Town, OXFORD, OX2 6SN.
Ⓟ**RJA Accountants Ltd** *(R J Adams)* Wellington House, 273-275 High Street, London Colney, ST. ALBANS, HERTFORDSHIRE, AL2 1HA.
RJB *(R J Billups)* Warlingham Court Farm, Tithepit Shaw Lane, WARLINGHAM, CR6 9AT.
RJF Hamon FCA *(R J F Hamon)* Le Mahier, La Rue Mahier, St Ouen, JERSEY, JE3 2DW.
RJG Accountants LLP *(S J L Gardner)* Norgar House, 10 East Street, FAREHAM, HAMPSHIRE, PO16 0BN.
Ⓟ**RJI Consulting Ltd** *(R J Illingworth)* 18 White Oak Drive, Bishops Wood, STAFFORD, ST19 9AH.
Ⓟ**RJN Associates Ltd** *(R J Andrews)* 28 Penny Croft, HARPENDEN, AL5 2PB.
RK Baldwin FCA CTA - Consultant *(R K Baldwin)* Tanglewood, Long Bottom Lane, Seer Green, BEACONSFIELD, BUCKINGHAMSHIRE, HP9 2UL.
RKT Business Solutions *(R Turnock)* 28 Fairfield Road, TADCASTER, NORTH YORKSHIRE, LS24 9SN.
ⓅⒶ**RL Wiseman Ltd** *(D Wiseman)* Robson Laidler LLP, Fernwood House, Fernwood Road, Jesmond, NEWCASTLE UPON TYNE, NE2 1TJ.
Ⓟ**RLJ, trading name of RLJ & Co Limited** *(R Lewis - James)* Chapel Cottage, Michaelston-y-Fedw, CARDIFF, CF3 6XT.
Ⓟ**RLP Accounting Limited** *(B F Jones, D Terry)* Kemp House, 152-160 City Road, LONDON, EC1V 2DW.
RLW Accountants *(R L Whiting)* 5 Elms Paddock, Little Stretton, CHURCH STRETTON, SHROPSHIRE, SY6 6RD.
RLW Associates Ltd, trading name of SDW Associates *(S D Wyatt)* 57 Brockhurst Road, GOSPORT, HAMPSHIRE, PO12 3AP.
RM Accountants *(R Mustafa)* 1 Slowmans Close, Park Street, ST. ALBANS, HERTFORDSHIRE, AL2 2DJ.
Ⓟ**RM Crowder Ltd** *(R M Crowder)* Rest Haven, North Kelsey Road, Caistor, MARKET RASEN, LINCOLNSHIRE, LN7 6SF.
RM Hall *(R M Hall)* Farm View, High Row, Kirby Misperton, MALTON, NORTH YORKSHIRE, YO17 6XN.
ⒻⓅ**RMCA Ltd** *(R Masters)* The Counting House, 9 High Street, TRING, HERTFORDSHIRE, HP23 5TE.
RMJ Accounting *(R Johnson)* Top Barn, Greensforge Lane, Stourton, STOURBRIDGE, WEST MIDLANDS, DY7 5BD.
Ⓟ**RMS, trading name of Randall Management Services Limited** *(M J Randall)* 12 Furniss Avenue, Dore, SHEFFIELD, S17 3QL.
ⓉⒻⒶ**RMT Accountants and Business Advisors** *(M H Gilbert, A A Josephs, J M Pott, S D Slater)* RMT Accountants and Business Advisors, Gosforth Park Avenue, NEWCASTLE UPON TYNE, NE12 8EG.
ⓅⒶ**RMT Accountants and Business Advisors Limited** *(A A Josephs, J M Pott, S D Slater)* Unit 2, Gosforth Park Avenue, NEWCASTLE UPON TYNE, NE12 8EG.
ⓉⒶ**RNS** *(R J Abbott, J Camm, A J Clayton, J P Heeney, A Ingleton, R F Marris, I M Pounder, R A Smith)* The Poplars, Bridge Street, BRIGG, NORTH LINCOLNSHIRE, DN20 8NQ. and at SCUNTHORPE
ⒻⓅⒶ**RNS, trading name of RNS Business Solutions Limited** *(R N Sangani)* 276 Preston Road, HARROW, MIDDLESEX, HA3 0QA.
Ⓟ**RNV Limited** *(P G Randall)* 21-23 West Street, Oundle, PETERBOROUGH, PE8 4EJ.
Rob Barrigan Consulting *(R Barrigan)* Stoer House, 1 Polam Road, DARLINGTON, COUNTY DURHAM, DL1 5NW.
ⓉⓅ**Rob Jones & Co, trading name of Robert Jones (Wales) Limited** *(R F G Jones)* The Forge, Glanusk Park, CRICKHOWELL, POWYS, NP8 1LP.
Ⓟ**Rob McCulloch Limited** *(R McCulloch)* 18 Barn Close, Cumnor Hill, OXFORD, OX2 9JP.
Rob Meek FCA CTA *(R C Meek)* Woodland Lodge, White House Drive, Barnt Green, BIRMINGHAM, B45 8HF.
Robb & Co *(L C Robb)* 26 Mayes Close, WARLINGHAM, CR6 9LB.
Ⓐ**Robbins Partnership** *(A Ioannou, D C Robbins)* 176 Monton Road, Monton, Eccles, MANCHESTER, M30 9GA.
Robert A. Lewis & Co *(R A Lewis)* Manor Farm, West End, Ashton, CHESTER, CH3 8DG.
Robert Affleck FCA *(R A Affleck)* 3 The Knoll, COBHAM, SURREY, KT11 2PN.
Ⓐ**Robert Anthony** *(R N Anthony)* 36 Merdon Avenue, Chandlers Ford, EASTLEIGH, SO53 1EP.
Robert Bailey *(R Bailey)* Slater House, Meadowcroft Business Park, Pope Lane, Whitestake, PRESTON, PR4 4BA.
Ⓟ**Robert Billingham Limited** *(R Billingham)* Spring Fields, Leasowes Lane, Lapal, HALESOWEN, WEST MIDLANDS, B62 8QE.
Robert Boot & Co *(G R Boot)* Cotleigh, 6A Windermere Way, REIGATE, RH2 0LW.
Robert Brown *(R Brown)* 30 Thornbridge Close, RUSHDEN, NORTHAMPTONSHIRE, NN10 9NJ.
Ⓐ**Robert Brown & Co** *(R W I Brown)* 21 Westley Street, DUDLEY, DY1 1TS.
ⒻⒶ**Robert Brown & Co.** *(R T Brown)* Monarch House, 1 Smyth Road, BRISTOL, BS3 2BX.
Robert C. Bennett *(R C Bennett)* Willow House, 69 Ridgeway Road, Long Ashton, BRISTOL, BS41 9EZ.
Robert C. Lea *(R C Lea)* 20 Hawthorn Road, SHREWSBURY, SY3 7NB.
★**Robert Chin Lee & Associates** *(R K C Chin)* 2nd Floor, Lot 15 Bl.B Lintus Sq, Jalan Lintus, 88300 KOTA KINABALU Sabah, MALAYSIA.
ⒻⓅⒶ**Robert Clow & Co, trading name of Robert Clow & Co Ltd** *(R C Clow, D Lakhani)* 40-44 High Street, NORTHWOOD, MIDDLESEX, HA6 1BN.
Robert Coombes Ltd *(R H Coombes)* 6 Smith Barry Circus, Upper Rissington, CHELTENHAM, GL54 2NQ.
Ⓟ**Robert Culver Limited** *(R Culver)* Field House, Brackley Avenue, Hartley Wintney, HOOK, HAMPSHIRE, RG27 8QU.
Ⓐ**Robert Davies & Co** *(R G Davies)* Marche Manor, Halfway House, SHREWSBURY, SY5 9DE.
Robert Dewar *(R D Dewar)* 31 Rivermill, 151 Grosvenor Road, LONDON, SW1V 3JN.
Robert E. Long *(R E Long)* 21 Gresham Road, EDGWARE, HA8 6NU.
Ⓐ**Robert Evans** *(R J Evans)* 23 Clifton Hill, St Johns Wood, LONDON, NW8 0QE.
Robert Farquhar *(R M Farquhar)* 55 High Street, Topsham, EXETER, EX3 0DY.
Robert Felix *(R D Felix)* 33 Broomhill Road, WOODFORD GREEN, ESSEX, IG8 9HD.
ⓅⒶ**Robert G Tudor Limited** *(R G Tudor)* 21 Heycroft, COVENTRY, CV4 7HE.
Ⓟ**Robert G W Doney Limited** *(R G W Doney)* Sunnyfield, Church Road, West Lavington, MIDHURST, WEST SUSSEX, GU29 0EH.
ⒻⒶ**Robert Gale & Co** *(R Gale)* 8 Adelaide Row, SEAHAM, SR7 7EF.
★**Robert Gale and Company** *(R Gale)* 8 Adelaide Row, SEAHAM, COUNTY DURHAM, SR7 7EF.
Ⓟ**Robert Gray Accountancy Services Limited** *(R E Gray)* 12 Exchange Street, RETFORD, NOTTINGHAMSHIRE, DN22 6BL.
Robert H. Nelson *(R H Nelson)* 15 South Drive, WOKINGHAM, RG40 2DH.
Robert Hayden & Co *(A J Duffy, R L Hayden)* 195 Bramhall Lane, Davenport, STOCKPORT, SK2 6JA.
Robert Hill *(R I Hill)* 10 Townsway, Lostock Hall, PRESTON, PR5 5YQ.
ⓅⒶ**Robert Hugh, trading name of Robert Hugh Limited** *(R Hugh)* 15 Dan-y-Bryn Avenue, Radyr, CARDIFF, CF15 8DD.
Robert I.K. Duroe *(R I K Duroe)* 4 Lansdowne Road, Frimley, CAMBERLEY, GU16 9UW.
Robert J Gill FCA *(R J Gill)* 4 Rutland Drive, Mickleover, DERBY, DE3 9FW.
ⒻⓅ**Robert J Gogarty, trading name of Robgog Limited** *(R J Gogarty)* Bank House, Southwick Square, Southwick, BRIGHTON, BN42 4FN.
Robert J Smith *(R J Smith)* 17 Meadow Close, Hinchley Wood, ESHER, SURREY, KT10 0AY.
ⓉⒻⒶ**Robert J. Bass & Co** *(R J Bass)* 339 High Street, WEST BROMWICH, B70 9QG.
Robert J. Crowe & Co *(J Crowe)* 93 Jesmond Park West, High Heaton, NEWCASTLE UPON TYNE, NE7 7BY.
Robert J. Twist *(R J Twist)* 42 Rue de Bassano, 75008 PARIS, FRANCE.
Ⓟ**Robert Jackson Management Limited** *(R I Jackson)* 41 Avondale Avenue, Woodside Pk, Finchley, LONDON, N12 8ER.
Ⓟ**Robert Jones Accountants Limited** *(R D P Jones)* Office 9, Neston Centre, High Street, NESTON, CH64 9TZ.
Robert K. Bendell *(R K Bendell)* 10 Holmesdale Road, BEXHILL-ON-SEA, TN39 3QE.
Robert Keats *(R D Keats)* 29 Lyndhurst, SKELMERSDALE, LANCASHIRE, WN8 6UH.
Robert Kerr *(R Kerr)* Doonane, Ingleby Road, Stanton-by-Bridge, DERBY, DE73 7HT.
ⓅⒶ**Robert Kirtland Ltd** *(R M Kirtland)* Critchleys LLP, Greyfriars Court, Paradise Square, OXFORD, OX1 1BE.
Robert Knight *(C F Knight, R I Knight)* 34A Statton Road, Cuffley, Potters Bar, POTTERS BAR, HERTFORDSHIRE, EN6 4HE.
Ⓐ**Robert Ko & Company** *(R S W Ko)* 33 Crofton Avenue, LONDON, W4 3EW.
ⒻⒶ**Robert L. Wiles** *(R L Wiles)* 33 Bush Hill, Winchmore Hill, LONDON, N21 2BT.
Ⓕ**Robert Lee** *(C R Lee)* 18 The Village, West Hallam, ILKESTON, DERBYSHIRE, DE7 6GR.
Robert Lynn FCA *(R Lynn)* 1 Pitt Court, Nymet Rowland, CREDITON, DEVON, EX17 6AN.
Robert Lyons & Co *(R E Lyons)* Flat 1, 42 Marryat Road, Wimbledon, LONDON, SW19 5BD.
Robert M Howes *(R M Howes)* Catochil Farm, Glenfarg, PERTH, PH2 9PX.
Ⓟ**Robert M Humphry Limited** *(R M Humphry)* 2 East Street, OKEHAMPTON, DEVON, EX20 1AS.
Robert M Spencer FCA *(R M Spencer)* Heritage House, 6 Wragby Road, Sudbrooke, LINCOLN, LN2 2QU.
Robert M W Wood *(R M W Wood)* 27 Silver Birch Drive, Hollywood, BIRMINGHAM, B47 5RB.
Robert M. Walters *(R M Walters)* 5 Glen Drive, Stoke Bishop, BRISTOL, BS9 1SA.
Robert McDonald *(R McDonald)* 15 Vicarage Gate, LONDON, W8 4AA.
Ⓟ**Robert Miller & Co, trading name of Robert Miller & Company (Cleadon) Limited** *(P N Brown, S P Fletcher)* 43a Front Street, Cleadon Village, SUNDERLAND, SR6 7PG.
Ⓟ**Robert Miller & Co, trading name of Robert Miller & Company (Houghton) Limited** *(P N Brown, S P Fletcher)* Kings Hall, Imperial Buildings, HOUGHTON LE SPRING, TYNE AND WEAR, DH4 4DJ.
Robert Moss *(R H Moss)* 94 Malthouse Lane, Earlswood, SOLIHULL, WEST MIDLANDS, B94 5SA.
Ⓟ**Robert Ogle** *(R C Ogle)* 6 The Elms, Doncaster Road, ROTHERHAM, S65 1DY.
Robert P.C. Goddard *(R P C Goddard)* 42 Theobalds Way, Frimley, CAMBERLEY, GU16 9RF.
Ⓟ**Robert Parry & Co Limited** *(R Parry)* Nat. Westminster Bank Chambers, 2 Dundas Street, Queensferry, DEESIDE, CH5 1SZ.
Ⓟ**Robert Perry Limited** *(R E Perry)* Parkside House, Old Stafford Road, Slade Heath. Near Coven, WOLVERHAMPTON, WV10 7PH.
Robert Pinnock *(R L Pinnock)* Tower House, High Street, Hurstpierpoint, HASSOCKS, WEST SUSSEX, BN6 9RQ.
Ⓐ**Robert Pola** *(R M F Pola)* The Dormers, Low Road, Congham, KING'S LYNN, PE32 1AE.
Ⓐ**Robert Powell** *(R W Powell)* A4 Spinnaker House, Spinnaker Road, Hempsted Lane, GLOUCESTER, GL2 5FD.
Robert Raynes *(R V M Raynes)* Bridleway Cottage, 85 Priors Hill, Wroughton, SWINDON, SN4 0RL.
Robert Richardson & Co *(R M Richardson)* The Citadel, Old Clare Street, LIMERICK, COUNTY LIMERICK, IRELAND.
Robert S Bowden *(R S Bowden)* Apple Tree, White Gritt, Minsterley, SHREWSBURY, SY5 0JN.
Ⓟ**Robert S Boys, trading name of Robert S Boys Limited** *(A R Boston, R S Boys, M L Byrne, R I Coulthard)* 28-30 Grange Road West, BIRKENHEAD, MERSEYSIDE, CH41 4DA.
ⓉⒶ**Robert S. Boys** *(A R Boston, R S Boys, M L Byrne, R I Coulthard)* 28-30 Grange Road West, BIRKENHEAD, CH41 4DA.
Robert S. Dearing *(R S Dearing)* Meadowbank, Parsonage Lane, Farnham Common, SLOUGH, SL2 3PA.
ⓉⒻⒶ**Robert Sadler & Company** *(R A Sadler)* Hargroves Cycles, 30b Southgate, CHICHESTER, WEST SUSSEX, PO19 1DP.
Robert Shaw FCA *(R W G Shaw)* 5 Thorley Hill, BISHOP'S STORTFORD, HERTFORDSHIRE, CM23 3ND.
Ⓟ**Robert Stone & Co, trading name of Robert Stone Accountancy Limited** *(R E Stone)* Old Magistrates Court, East Street, ILMINSTER, SOMERSET, TA19 9AJ.
Robert Stubbs *(R Stubbs)* Briarmead, St. Johns Park, Menston, ILKLEY, LS29 6ES.
Robert Tooley *(R G Tooley)* 38 Farm Way, NORTHWOOD, HA6 3EF.
ⒻⒶ**Robert Tydeman & Co** *(R K Tydeman)* 58 Gipsy Hill, Upper Norwood, LONDON, SE19 1PD.
ⒻⒶ**Robert V. Ashdown** *(R V Ashdown)* 75 Brookville Road, LONDON, SW6 7BH.
Ⓟ**Robert W Belcher Limited** *(R W Belcher)* 26 Station Approach, Hayes, BROMLEY, BR2 7EH. and at CROWBOROUGH
Robert W. Belcher *(R W Belcher)* 26 Station Approach, Hayes, BROMLEY, BR2 7EH. and at CROWBOROUGH
Robert W. Robinson *(R W Robinson)* 58 Coppice Farm Road, Penn, HIGH WYCOMBE, HP10 8AH.
Robert Warner *(R H Warner)* 14 Hanborough Business Park, Long Hanborough, WITNEY, OXFORDSHIRE, OX29 8LH.
Robert Watson *(R C Watson)* 71 Hayes Hill, Hayes, BROMLEY, KENT, BR2 7HN.
ⓉⒶ**Robert Whowell & Partners** *(I C F S Agar, J W Mills, B Peake, J R Whowell, R H Whowell)* 78 Loughborough Road, Quorn, LOUGHBOROUGH, LEICESTERSHIRE, LE12 8DX.
Ⓣ**Robert Yam & Co** *(R M L Yam)* Fortune Centre, Apt. 16-03, 190 Middle Road, SINGAPORE 188979, SINGAPORE.
Roberts & Co *(R A Roberts)* The Pheasants, Digging Lane, Fyfield, ABINGDON, OXFORDSHIRE, OX13 5LY.
ⒻⒶ**Roberts & Co** *(C M Clarke, D N Roberts, P H Roberts)* 136 Kensington Church Street, LONDON, W8 4BH.
ⒻⓅⒶ**Roberts & Co, trading name of Roberts & Co (Accountants) Ltd** *(D G Roberts, J A Roberts)* 2 Tower House, HODDESDON, EN11 8UR.
ⓅⒶ**Roberts & Co, trading name of Roberts & Co (Bristol) Limited** *(P J Roberts)* 24 High Street, Chipping Sodbury, BRISTOL, BS37 6AH.
ⓉⒻⒶ**Roberts & Partners** *(F Dizadji, M K Niemann)* 47 Queen Anne Street, LONDON, W1G 9JG.
Roberts Redman *(J B Roberts)* 27 St Johns Avenue, LEATHERHEAD, KT22 7HT.
ⒻⒶ**Roberts Toner, trading name of Roberts Toner LLP** *(D B Roberts)* Melbourne House, 44-46 Grosvenor Street, STALYBRIDGE, CHESHIRE, SK15 2JN.
ⓉⒻⒶ**Robertshaw Myers** *(P Bailey, M D Bottomley, R Day, T D Lodge, D A Richmond)* Number 3, Acorn Business Park, Keighley Road, SKIPTON, NORTH YORKSHIRE, BD23 2UE.
ⒻⒶ**Robertson & Co** *(J D Robertson)* 169 Spencefield Lane, LEICESTER, LE5 6GG.
★Ⓕ**Robertson Craig** *(J Fowlie, B Fox, I Gillies, S S Merry)* 3 Clairmont Gardens, GLASGOW, G3 7LW.
Ⓟ**Robertson Craig Ltd** *(S S Merry)* 3 Clairmont Gardens, GLASGOW, G3 7LW.
★**Robertson Milroy & Co** *(M P Robertson)* Coopers House, 65 Wingletye Lane, HORNCHURCH, RM11 3AT.
ⓉⓅⒶ**Robertson Milroy Limited** *(M P Robertson)* Coopers House, 65 Wingletye Road, HORNCHURCH, RM11 3AT.
Ⓟ**Robin Atkins Limited** *(R V Atkins)* 7 Lindley Gardens, ALRESFORD, SO24 9PU.
Robin Blackburn *(R B Blackburn)* Field House, 29 Adlington Road, WILMSLOW, SK9 2BJ.
Robin Darbyshire FCA *(R V Darbyshire)* 43 Ethelbert Road, Wimbledon, LONDON, SW20 8QE.
Robin Fielding MA ACA, trading name of RDF Financial Solutions *(R D Fielding)* Dove Cottage, Liphook Road, Headley, BORDON, HAMPSHIRE, GU35 8LL.
Robin G. Fautley *(R G Fautley)* 9 Lynton Road, Thorpe Bay, SOUTHEND-ON-SEA, SS1 3BE.
Robin Pang & Co *(H R Pang)* 2/F, Xiu Ping Comm. Bldg, 104 Jervois Street, SHEUNG WAN, HONG KONG SAR.
Robin Upton Insolvency *(R A Upton)* 284 Clifton Drive South, St Annes, LYTHAM ST. ANNES, FY8 1LH. and at NEWCASTLE UPON TYNE
Robin Youle *(E R G Youle)* 6 Malpas Drive, PINNER, MIDDLESEX, HA5 1DF.
Robins *(R N Cooke)* Leonard House, 12-14 Silver Street, TAMWORTH, STAFFORDSHIRE, B79 7NH.
Robinson *(C A Robinson)* 9 Costins Walk, BERKHAMSTED, HERTFORDSHIRE, HP4 2WG.
Robinson & Co *(W C F Robinson)* 5 Pinehurst, SEVENOAKS, TN14 5AQ.

ⓉⒶ**Robinson & Co** *(P E Ellwood, J.D.O'Hare, J D Plaskett, J Spires, R Troughton, M A Wood)* Oxford Chambers, New Oxford Street, WORKINGTON, CA14 2LR. and at WHITEHAVEN

Ⓟ**Robinson Consulting, trading name of Robconsult Limited** *(P J Robinson)* 3 Tunnel Hill Mews, Knock Lane, Blisworth, NORTHAMPTON, NN7 3DA.

Ⓟ**Robinson Financial Consultancy Ltd** *(T J Robinson)* 31 Elmswood Gardens, Sherwood, NOTTINGHAM, NG5 4AY.

Ⓐ**Robinson Miller** *(D H Miller)* 68 West Street, WARMINSTER, WILTSHIRE, BA12 8JW.

ⓉⒺⒶ**Robinson Reed Layton** *(G D Boulton, S L Gainey, T P Reed)* Peat House, Newham Road, TRURO, TR1 2DP.

ⓉⓅⒶ**Robinson Rice Associates Ltd** *(B E Rice, A P Williams)* 49 Station Road, Ainsdale, SOUTHPORT, MERSEYSIDE, PR8 3HH. and at WIRRAL

Ⓔ**Robinson Rushen** *(K D Rushen)* 47 Queen Anne Street, LONDON, W1G 9JG.

★ⒺⒶ**Robinson Sterling** *(D Vijh)* 551 Green Lane, ILFORD, ESSEX, IG3 9RJ.

ⒺⒶ**Robinson Stewart & Co.** *(J S Robinson)* 7 Granard Business Centre, Bunns Lane, Mill Hill, LONDON, NW7 2DQ.

ⓉⓅⒶ**Robinson Udale Limited** *(D M Brookes, A J Meeks, R Udale)* The Old Bank, 41 King Street, PENRITH, CUMBRIA, CA11 7AY.

Ⓐ**Roblins** *(A J Prankerd, L A Roblin)* 3 Deryn Court, Wharfedale Road, Pentwyn, CARDIFF, CF23 7HA.

Robson & Co *(S M Pneh)* 51 Wayside Avenue, Bushey Heath, BUSHEY, WD23 4SH.

ⓉⒺ**Robson Laidler LLP** *(D Wiseman)* Fernwood House, Fernwood Road, Jesmond, NEWCASTLE UPON TYNE, NE2 1TJ.

Ⓟ**Robson Welsh, trading name of Robson Welsh Limited** *(B F Welsh)* 4 The Goose Green, WIRRAL, MERSEYSIDE, CH47 6BQ.

ⓉⒶ**Robsons** *(K M Robson)* 1a Sykes Grove, HARROGATE, HG1 2DB.

ⒺⓅⒶ**Robsons, trading name of Robson & Co Limited** *(I P Robson, S J Smale, R G Worthington)* Kingfisher Court, Plaxton Bridge Road, Woodmansey, BEVERLEY, NORTH HUMBERSIDE, HU17 0RT.

Roccia LLP *(M Spano)* 19 Crown Passage, St James, LONDON, SW1Y 6PP.

Roche & Co *(C P Roche)* Barnswood, 64 Orton Lane, Wombourne, WOLVERHAMPTON, WV5 9AW.

ⒺⒶ**Roches** *(R A Roche)* 40 Locks Heath Centre, Centre Way, Locks Heath, SOUTHAMPTON, SO31 6DX.

Roche-Saunders & Co *(R D K Roche-Saunders)* 34 The Watton, BRECON, POWYS, LD3 7EF.

ⒺⓅⒶ**Rochesters, trading name of Rochesters Audit Services Limited** *(P Hewston, S G Rochester)* No 3 Caroline Court, 13 Caroline Street, St Pauls Square, BIRMINGHAM, B3 1TR.

Ⓣ**Rochesters, trading name of Rochesters LLP** *(P Hewston, S G Rochester)* 3 Caroline Court, 13 Caroline Street, St Pauls Square, BIRMINGHAM, B3 1TR.

Rochman Goodmans *(P H Rochman)* 29 Barrett Road, Fetcham, LEATHERHEAD, KT22 9HL. and at LONDON

★Ⓐ**Rockett & Co** *(N A Rockett)* 16 Rickmansworth Road, NORTHWOOD, HA6 1HA.

Ⓟ**Rockwells, trading name of Rockwells Ltd** *(P R Edwards)* 17 Church Road, TUNBRIDGE WELLS, KENT, TN1 1LG.

Rocky Shek & Co *(R Shek)* Room 901, Yip Fung Building, 9/F No 2, D'Aguilar Street, CENTRAL, HONG KONG ISLAND HONG KONG SAR.

Ⓟ**Rod George Limited** *(R E George)* The Red House, 18 High Street, Collingham, NEWARK, NOTTINGHAMSHIRE, NG23 7LA.

★ⓉⒺⒶ**Roddis Taylor Robinson** *(G P Robinson)* Unit 6, Acorn Business Park, Woodseats Close, SHEFFIELD, S8 0TB.

Roderick C Hole *(R C Hole)* 28 Rouse Gardens, Alleyn Park, LONDON, SE21 8AF.

Ⓟ**Rodl & Partner Limited** *(I M Lewis)* Concorde House, Trinity Park, Solihull, BIRMINGHAM, B37 7UQ.

Rodney H. de Mello *(R H De Mello)* The Orangery, 12a Lawn Road, Milford-on-Sea, LYMINGTON, HAMPSHIRE, SO41 0QZ.

Rodney M. Dossett *(R M Dossett)* 55 Grand Parade, LEIGH-ON-SEA, SS9 1DT.

Rodney Pangbourne *(R B Pangbourne)* 33 Pennal Grove, Ingleby Barwick, STOCKTON-ON-TEES, CLEVELAND, TS17 5HP.

ⒺⒶ**Rodney Pitts** *(J R G Pitts)* 4 Fairways, 1240 Warwick Road, Knowle, SOLIHULL, B93 9LL.

Rodney S. W. Richards *(R S W Richards)* 3 Shaftesbury Villas, Allen Street, LONDON, W8 6UZ.

Ⓟ**Rodney Taylor Ltd** *(R B Taylor)* 119 Norman Road, Barton-le-Clay, BEDFORD, MK45 4QG.

Roebuck & Co *(R C R Roebuck)* 165 Bournville Lane, Bournville, BIRMINGHAM, B30 1LY.

ⓉⒺⒶ**Roffe Swayne** *(C R Baxter, J R Fisher, J A K Gardner, M E F Katz, A Kelly, M S Leigh, S E Ward, L A Warner, E F Way)* Ashcombe Court, Woolsack Way, GODALMING, GU7 1LQ.

Roger Bell & Co *(R W Bell)* 25 Purfield Drive, Wargrave, READING, RG10 8AP.

Roger Bryant MSc BSc (Econ) FCA FCCA *(R G Bryant)* Linden House, Chapel Hill, Clayton West, HUDDERSFIELD, HD8 9NH.

Roger Burns *(R Burns)* 125 Tamworth Road, Long Eaton, NOTTINGHAM, NG10 1BH.

ⓉⒺⓅ**Roger C Bloomer, trading name of AccounTax Services (Swindon) Limited** *(R C Bloomer)* 2 Charnwood Court, Newport Street, SWINDON, SN1 3DX.

★ⓉⒶ**Roger C. Oaten** *(R C Oaten)* First Floor, 23 Westfield Park, Redland, BRISTOL, BS6 6LT.

Roger Celia *(R Celia)* 23 Lodge Close, HERTFORD, SG14 3DH.

Roger Chadwick FCA *(R A H Chadwick)* 11 Oakfield Court, 252 Pampisford Road, SOUTH CROYDON, SURREY, CR2 6DD.

Roger Claxton *(R J Claxton)* 7 Indigo Yard, NORWICH, NR3 3QZ.

Roger D Pearce *(R D Pearce)* 11 Upper Bourne Lane, FARNHAM, GU10 4RQ.

Roger D. Neville *(R D Neville)* 97 Rous Road, BUCKHURST HILL, IG9 6BU.

Ⓔ**Roger Denton** *(R Denton)* 8A Church Street, RUSHDEN, NN10 9YT.

Roger Edmonds *(R J Edmonds)* 18 Bradley Croft, Balsall Common, COVENTRY, CV7 7PZ.

Roger Guillebaud & Co *(J R Guillebaud)* Sweet Meadows, Clifford Bridge, Drewsteignton, EXETER, EX6 6QB.

Roger Harper *(R Harper)* PO Box 4, Castletown, ISLE OF MAN, IM99 9YU.

ⓉⒺⒶ**Roger Hopkins** *(R D Hopkins)* 18 Princes Street, NORWICH, NR3 1AE.

Roger Jenkins & Co *(R G Jenkins)* Skyburriowe Vean, Skyburriowe Lane, Garras, HELSTON, CORNWALL, TR12 6LR.

Roger K C Lee & Co *(R K Lee)* Room 1109, 11/F, 118 Connaught Road West, SAI YING POON, HONG KONG ISLAND, HONG KONG SAR.

Roger King S.R.L *(R G King)* Via Amilcare Ponchielli 3, 20129 MILAN, ITALY.

Roger Levey & Co *(R J Levey)* 26 Conifer Drive, Tilehurst, READING, RG31 6YU.

Ⓟ**Roger Lugg & Co Limited** *(H D Barrett, B W Chapman, R B Lugg)* 12-14 High Street, CATERHAM, SURREY, CR3 5UA.

ⒺⓅⒶ**Roger M Darby Limited** *(R M Darby)* 85 High Street, Kinver, STOURBRIDGE, WEST MIDLANDS, DY7 6HD.

Roger M. Porteous *(R M Porteous)* 10 Windermere Road, Babbacombe, TORQUAY, TQ1 3RF.

Roger M. Salisbury *(R M Salisbury)* Cedar Cottage, Denham Lane, Chalfont St Peter, GERRARDS CROSS, SL9 0QQ.

Roger Mathews *(R G Mathews)* 10 Durrington Park Road, Wimbledon, LONDON, SW20 8NX.

Roger Newnes-Smith *(R Newnes-Smith)* Woodend, Lower Moushill Lane, Milford, GODALMING, GU8 5JX.

Roger Price Aims Accounting Beaconsfield *(R C Price)* 36 Wattleton Road, BEACONSFIELD, HP9 1SE.

Roger Purcell LLP *(R B A Purcell)* 202 Old Brompton Road, LONDON, SW5 0BU.

ⓉⓅ**Roger Smallman & Co Limited** *(R C B Smallman)* 30A Bedford Place, SOUTHAMPTON, SO15 2DG.

ⒺⓅⒶ**Roger Sutton & Co., trading name of Roger Sutton & Co. Limited** *(R W Sutton)* 79 High Street, TEDDINGTON, MIDDLESEX, TW11 8HG.

Roger W. Tovey *(R W Tovey)* 30 Maidenhall, Highnam, GLOUCESTER, GL2 8DL.

Roger Yeates *(R Yeates)* 4 Petrel Croft, Kempshott, BASINGSTOKE, RG22 5JY.

Rogers *(F J Rogers)* 20 St. Georges Close, TODDINGTON, BEDFORDSHIRE, LU5 6AT.

Ⓟ**Rogers & Co, trading name of CJR Accountants Limited** *(C J Rogers)* Oxford House, 8 Church Street, Arnold, NOTTINGHAM, NG5 8FB.

Rogers & Company *(N D Rogers)* Suite E, 102A Longstone Road, EASTBOURNE, BN21 3SJ.

Rogers Evans *(T C Evans)* 20 Brunswick Place, SOUTHAMPTON, SO15 2AQ. and at BRISTOL

Ⓟ**Rogers Evans (Bristol) Limited** *(V H Ellaby, T C Evans)* Suite B1, The White House, Forest Road, Kingswood, BRISTOL, BS15 8DH. and at SOUTHAMPTON, TRURO

ⓅⒶ**Rogers Paulley, trading name of Rogers Paulley Limited** *(C S Rogers)* Arclight House, 3 Unity Street, BRISTOL, BS1 5HH.

ⓉⒺⓅⒶ**Rogers Spencer, trading name of Rogers Spencer Limited** *(S P Allcock)* Newstead House, Pelham Road, NOTTINGHAM, NG5 1AP.

Rogger & Co *(J R Rogger)* 5 Grass Park, Finchley, LONDON, N3 1UB.

ⒺⓅ**Rogove & Company, trading name of Eppy Limited** *(A I Rogove, I J Rogove)* 101 White Lion Street, LONDON, N1 9PF.

ⓅⒶ**Rohans, trading name of Rohans Auditors (UK) Ltd** *(K J Richards)* Rohans House, 92-96 Wellington Road South, STOCKPORT, CHESHIRE, SK1 3TJ.

Roland Hepworth *(R Hepworth)* 2 Hall Croft, NORMANTON, WEST YORKSHIRE, WF6 2DN.

Ⓔ**Roland J. Adamson** *(R J Adamson)* 1 North Parade Passage, BATH, BA1 1NX.

Roland J. Boggon *(R J Boggon)* Moorea, Pitchcombe, STROUD, GL6 6LJ.

ⓅⒶ**Roland Klepzig Limited** *(R P Klepzig)* 42 Copperfield Street, LONDON, SE1 0DY.

Roland Worthington-Eyre *(R Worthington-Eyre)* Quartz Lodge, Kildalton, Port Ellen, ISLE OF ISLAY, ARGYLL, PA42 7EF.

Ⓟ**Rollason Accountancy Limited** *(M A Rollason)* 26 Langdale Drive, ASCOT, BERKSHIRE, SL5 8TQ.

ⒺⒶ**Rolt Harrison & Hewitt** *(N A Hewitt, H E A Rolt)* 110/112 Lancaster Road, BARNET, EN4 8AL.

Ⓟ**Rolyat Limited** *(R J Taylor)* Unit A/2, Imex Business Park, Flaxley Road, BIRMINGHAM, B33 9AL.

Ⓟ**Romsey Capital Limited** *(M J Hodgson)* 156 New Street, CAMBRIDGE, CB1 2QX.

Ⓟ**Ron Coates & Co Limited** *(R A Coates)* 374 Cowbridge Rd East, CARDIFF, CF5 1JJ.

Ron Machell *(R Machell)* 204 Northfield Avenue, Ealing, LONDON, W13 9SJ.

Ⓟ**Ron Welsh & Co, trading name of Ron Welsh (North West) Limited** *(R C Welsh)* Mannamead, Church Lane, NESTON, CH64 9US.

Rona Maccallum *(R K MacCallum)* 127 Atherstone Avenue, PETERBOROUGH, PE3 9UJ.

Ronald B. Cronin *(R B Cronin)* 2 Holly Hill Drive, BANSTEAD, SM7 2BD.

Ⓐ**Ronald Elliott & Co** *(R Elliott)* 26 Catsey Woods, Bushey Heath, BUSHEY, WD23 4HS.

Ronald Fuss & Co *(R L Fuss)* Flat 7, Aspen Court, 86 Holders Hill Road, LONDON, NW4 1LW.

★**Ronald H. T. Lee & Co.** *(H R Lee)* Room 1002, 10/F, Malaysia Building, 50 Gloucester Road, WAN CHAI, HONG KONG ISLAND HONG KONG SAR.

Ronald Hendon & Co *(R Hendon)* 16 The Callenders, Heathbourne Road, BUSHEY HEATH, WD23 1PU.

ⒺⒶ**Ronald Picardo** *(R Picardo)* 15 Woodridge Way, NORTHWOOD, HA6 2BE.

ⒺⒶ**Ronald Shaw & Co** *(R J Pawlowski)* Ashford House, 95 Dixons Green, DUDLEY, DY2 7DJ.

Ronald W. F. Chan & Co. *(W R Chan)* Room 1901, 19/F Henan Building, 90-92 Jaffe Road, WAN CHAI, HONG KONG SAR.

★**Ronald W.F. Ko & Co** *(P Au, W R Ko)* 4th Floor Winbase Centre, 208 Queen's Road Central, CENTRAL, HONG KONG ISLAND, HONG KONG SAR.

ⒺⓅⒶ**Ronkowski & Hall, trading name of Ronkowski & Hall Ltd** *(A Hall, P K Ronkowski)* 12 Westgate, Baildon, SHIPLEY, WEST YORKSHIRE, BD17 5EJ.

Ⓟ**Rooke Holt, trading name of Rooke Holt Limited** *(J P C C Hasoon, P D Kaye)* Giffords Farm, Giffords Cross, Bampton, TIVERTON, DEVON, EX16 9DR.

Ⓟ**Rootcorz, trading name of Rootcorz Limited** *(M G Jesper)* 21 Washington Terrace, NORTH SHIELDS, TYNE AND WEAR, NE30 2HG.

Ⓟ**Ropas Limited** *(R Bebbington)* PO Box 63531, NAIROBI, 00619, KENYA.

Ros Garrett Tax Services *(R J Garrett-Bowes)* Maple Lodge, Sycamore Close, AMERSHAM, BUCKINGHAMSHIRE, HP6 6BW.

Ⓟ**Rose Green Consultancy Ltd** *(S E Payne)* 26 Blondell Drive, Aldwick, BOGNOR REGIS, WEST SUSSEX, PO21 4BQ.

Rosemary A Campbell *(R A Campbell)* Butterscotch House, 32 Besford Court Estate, Besford, WORCESTER, WR8 9LZ.

Rosemary J. Steinson *(R J Steinson)* Glenesk, Holbrook, IPSWICH, IP9 2PZ.

Rosemary Tomlinson *(R O Tomlinson)* 2 Bank Farm Cottages, Bran Mill Lane, Paxford, CHIPPING CAMPDEN, GL55 6XJ.

Rosemary Unthank *(R A Unthank)* 15 Thornley Road, FELIXSTOWE, IP11 7LA.

Ⓐ**Rosenberg & Co** *(H Rosenberg)* 28A Bury New Road, Prestwich, MANCHESTER, M25 0LD.

Ⓐ**Rosenfeld & Co** *(Z M Rosenfeld)* 6 Vivian Avenue, LONDON, NW4 3YA.

Ⓐ**Rosenthal & Co** *(M Rosenthal)* 106 High West Street, GATESHEAD, NE8 1NA.

Ⓔ**Rosenthal & Co** *(R C Rosenthal)* 39 Fairlawn Avenue, Chiswick, LONDON, W4 5EF.

Ⓟ**Rosh Finance Ltd, trading name of Rosh FD Ltd** *(M B Hyman)* 33 Richmond Hill Road, CHEADLE, CHESHIRE, SK8 1QF.

ⒺⒶ**Ross Bennet-Smith** *(A Bennet-Smith, S L Ross)* Charles House, 5-11 Regent Street, St James, LONDON, SW1Y 4LR.

★ⓉⒺⓅⒶ**Ross Brooke Limited** *(M R W Brooke, P S Brown)* 2 Old Bath Road, NEWBURY, BERKSHIRE, RG14 1QL. and at SWINDON

Ⓟ**Ross Financial Consultancy Limited** *(N Ross)* 33 Campbell Road, EDINBURGH, EH12 6DT.

Ⓟ**Ross Franklin Limited** *(J C Ross)* 18 Park Hall Road, East Finchley, LONDON, N2 9PU.

ⓅⒶ**Ross Kit & Co Limited** *(K Rossides)* Victoria House, 18 Dalston Gardens, STANMORE, MIDDLESEX, HA7 1BU.

Ⓟ**Ross Martin Tax Consultancy Limited** *(N Ross Martin)* The Roost, The Orchard, Uploders, BRIDPORT, DORSET, DT6 4PF.

Ⓐ**Ross, Edwards** *(S Sen)* 70 Claremont Road, SURBITON, KT6 4RH.

ⓅⒶ**Rosscot Assurance, trading name of Rosscot Assurance Limited** *(K G Bates, T M Brown, S P O'Flaherty, C H Taylor)* Thomas Edge House, Tunnell Street, St. Helier, JERSEY, JE2 4LU.

ⓉⓅ**Rosscot, trading name of Rosscot Limited** *(K G Bates, S P O'Flaherty, C H Taylor)* Thomas Edge House, Tunnell Street, St Helier, JERSEY, JE2 4LU.

Rossiter Smith & Co *(K E Innoles, D B Smith)* Bank House, 1 Burlington Road, BRISTOL, BS6 6TJ.

Ⓟ**Rosstax Ltd** *(H J Ross)* Britannia House, 958 High Road, Finchley, LONDON, N12 9RY.

ⒺⓅⒶ**Rostance Edwards Limited** *(D A Rostance)* 1 & 2 Heritage Park, Hayes Way, CANNOCK, STAFFORDSHIRE, WS11 7LT.

ⓉⒶ**Rostrons** *(S N Clarke, E J Claxton, M Raper)* St Peter's House, Cattle Market Street, NORWICH, NR1 3DY.

Ⓟ**Rosy Jeffery, trading name of Rosy Jeffery Ltd** *(R J Jeffery)* Highdown, Lime Kiln Lane, Uplyme, LYME REGIS, DT7 3XG.

★ⒺⓅⒶ**Rotherham Taylor, trading name of Rotherham Taylor Limited** *(M W Barton)* Unit 21-22, Navigation Business Village, Navigation Way, Ashton-on-Ribble, PRESTON, PR2 2YP. and at CHORLEY

ⓅⒶ**Rothman Accountancy Services Ltd** *(R L E Rothman)* The Old Butchery, High Street, Twyford, WINCHESTER, HAMPSHIRE, SO21 1NH.

ⓉⒶ**Rothmans, trading name of Rothman Pantall LLP** *(A W Bennett, C H Cable, G J B Corlett, C S Cox, P J Dawson, S T Elliott, D P P Laidlaw, B Lynch, A D Miller, M P Osborne, A J Perriam, J Poulter, J L Shaw, R D L Showan, T D Stocker, S A Sullivan)* Fryern House, 125 Winchester Road, CHANDLERS FORD, SOUTHAMPTON, HAMPSHIRE, SO53 2DR. and at EASTLEIGH, FAREHAM, HAVANT, PORTSMOUTH, RINGWOOD, SALISBURY, SUTTON, WINCHESTER

Ⓟ**Rothwell & Co, trading name of S & R Rothwell Ltd** *(R E Rothwell, S C Rothwell)* 4 Hall Close, Bramhope, LEEDS, LS16 9JQ.

Ⓣ**Rotsas & Co** *(C C Rotsas)* 44 Epias Street, 2411 ENGOMI, CYPRUS.

ⒺⒶ**Rouse, trading name of Rouse Audit LLP** *(L M Bower, G H Gaffney, B Palmer, N A Relph, D A Sharp)* 55 Station Road, BEACONSFIELD, BUCKINGHAMSHIRE, HP9 1QL.

ⓉⒺ**Rouse, trading name of Rouse Partners LLP** *(L M Bower, K P M Brewer, A E M Child, G H Gaffney, B Palmer, N A Relph, D A Sharp, P F Wagstaff)* 55 Station Road, BEACONSFIELD, BUCKINGHAMSHIRE, HP9 1QL.

★Ⓟ**Routeglow Limited** *(M A Haydon)* 83 Timberbank, Vigo, GRAVESEND, KENT, DA13 0SN.

Routledge Taylor, trading name of AbacusHouse.com LLP *(J W Holman, P Routledge)* Abacus House, Wickhurst Lane, Broadbridge Heath, HORSHAM, RH12 3LY.

Rowan & Co, trading name of Account Ability *(K C Rowan, S M Rowan)* 4 Gibbs Hill, Headcorn, ASHFORD, KENT, TN27 9UD. and at LONDON

Ⓣ**Rowan Blaxland** *(R F Blaxland)* Grove Lodge, Grove Road, Brockdish, DISS, IP21 4JP.

Ⓟ**Rowan Business Solutions Limited** *(C M Lamb)* 4 Craig Meadows, Ringmer, LEWES, EAST SUSSEX, BN8 5FB.

ⓅⒶ**Rowdens, trading name of Rowdens Ltd** *(J B Rowden, P A Rowden)* Unit 3E, Vinnetrow Business Park, Vinnetrow Road, Runcton, CHICHESTER, WEST SUSSEX PO20 1QH.

Rowena M Marsh FCA MAE *(R M Marsh)* 9 St. Ives Park, Ashley Heath, RINGWOOD, HAMPSHIRE, BH24 2JX.

★**Rowes Accountants** *(W E R Oatridge)* 57 Newgate Lane, Whitestake, PRESTON, PR4 4JU.

Rowett Bookkeeping Services *(S J Smith)* 5 Franklin Street, EXETER, EX2 4HF.

Rowland Cowen & Co *(J D Cowen)* 1 Holders Meadows, Holders Green, Lindsell, DUNMOW, ESSEX, CM6 3QQ.

★Ⓣ**Rowland Hall** *(Richard Snoxall, David Stewart)* 44-54 Orsett Road, GRAYS, RM17 5ED.

Rowland Hogg *(R A R Hogg)* 11 Wood Street, WALLINGFORD, OX10 0BD.

Rowland Stratford & Co *(R C Stratford)* 53 The Mews, Newton Croft, SUDBURY, CO10 2RW.

ⒻⓅ**Rowlands Limited** *(E Brannigan, D Nairn, D T Taylor)* Rowlands House, Portobello Road, Portobello Trading Estate, Birtley, CHESTER LE STREET, COUNTY DURHAM DH3 2RY. and at CROOK, HEXHAM, NEWCASTLE UPON TYNE

Rowles & Co, trading name of Griffiths & Co *(M J Rowles)* 97a High Street, LYMINGTON, HAMPSHIRE, SO41 9AP. and at SOUTHAMPTON

Rowley Ward *(M Ward)* Tower House, 4 Tower Street, YORK, YO1 9SB. and at SCARBOROUGH

★Ⓐ**Rowleys Group LLP** *(M O Hook, A H Jarvis, R J Radford, P T Swann-Jones)* 6 Dominus Way, Meridian Business Park, LEICESTER, LE19 1RP.

ⓉⒻⓅⒶ**Rowley's, trading name of The Rowleys Partnership Limited** *(M O Hook, A H Jarvis, R J Radford, P T Swann-Jones)* 6 Dominus Way, Meridian Business Park, LEICESTER, LE19 1RP.

Rowmic *(K L Jackson)* 3 Meadway, Harrold, BEDFORD, MK43 7DP.

Ⓟ**Roxburgh Consulting Limited** *(A C Roxburgh)* 9 Valley Court, Craig Road, STOCKPORT, SK4 2AW.

Roy Barraclough *(R Barraclough)* 36 Victoria Road, Fulwood, PRESTON, PR2 8NE.

Roy C. Martin *(R C Martin)* 7 Hawkridge, Shoeburyness, SOUTHEND-ON-SEA, SS3 8AU.

Ⓣ**Roy D. Brown** *(R D Brown)* 13 Mountain Road, Coppull, CHORLEY, PR7 5EL.

Roy F. Gentry *(R F Gentry)* 67 Broad Street, SEAFORD, BN25 1NR.

Roy Goldsbrough *(R Goldsbrough)* 10 Quantock Grove, Bingham, NOTTINGHAM, NG13 8SE.

Roy Gresham FCA *(R Gresham)* 40 Barcombe Road, Barnston, Heswall, WIRRAL, MERSEYSIDE, CH60 1UZ.

Roy J. Hutchings *(R J Hutchings)* Brenacre, Ford Street, WELLINGTON, TA21 9PE.

ⓅⒶ**Roy Joseph & Company, trading name of Roy Joseph & Company Limited** *(R J Medayil)* 19 Bradmore Green, Brookmans Park, HATFIELD, HERTFORDSHIRE, AL9 7QR.

Roy K. Phillips *(R K Phillips)* 21 Spencers Close, Stanford-in-the-Vale, FARINGDON, OXFORDSHIRE, SN7 8NG.

Roy Lote FCA, trading name of Roy Lote *(A R Lote)* Exchequer House, 117 Lea Street, KIDDERMINSTER, WORCESTERSHIRE, DY10 1SN.

Roy Macfarlane *(R. Macfarlane)* Saville Court, Saville Place, Clifton, BRISTOL, BS8 4EJ.

★Ⓐ**Roy Pinnock & Co, trading name of Roy Pinnock & Co LLP** *(N B S Grimson)* Wren House, 68 London Road, ST. ALBANS, HERTFORDSHIRE, AL1 1NG.

Roy Sandey *(P Margetts)* 31 High Cross Street, ST AUSTELL, CORNWALL, PL25 4AN.

Roy Trigger & Associates *(R Trigger)* 22 Brickfield Avenue, HEMEL HEMPSTEAD, HERTFORDSHIRE, HP3 8NP.

Ⓟ**Roy Truscott, trading name of Backtobusiness Limited** *(H R Truscott)* 5 Wheatfield, Leybourne, WEST MALLING, KENT, ME19 5QB.

Roy W. Novis *(R W Novis)* Stone Lodge, Ling Lane, Scarcroft, LEEDS, LS14 3HY.

ⓉⒻⓅⒶ**Royce Peeling Green, RPG, trading names of Royce Peeling Green Limited** *(J S Brownson, P J Buckley, A R Burnett, M A Chatten, D P Million, S Murrills, I Paramor, C Poston, P Randall, J J Redmond, C Slater)* The Copper Room, Deva Centre, Trinity Way, MANCHESTER, M3 7BG. and at LONDON

Ⓟ**Royles** *(J C Royle)* 18 Heaton Gardens, 25 Heaton Moor Road, STOCKPORT, CHESHIRE, SK4 4LT.

Ⓟ**Royles (Heaton Moor) Ltd** *(J C Royle)* 18 Heaton Gardens, 25 Heaton Moor Road, STOCKPORT, CHESHIRE, SK4 4LT.

Ⓟ**Royston Parkin Limited** *(L C Pridmore)* 5 Railway Court, Ten Pound Walk, DONCASTER, SOUTH YORKSHIRE, DN4 5FB. and at SHEFFIELD

ⓅⒶ**RP Accounting, trading name of RPFCA Limited** *(R S Perren)* The Counting House, 22 Bellrope Meadow, Thaxted, DUNMOW, ESSEX, CM6 2FE.

Ⓟ**RP Taxation Services Limited** *(L C Pridmore)* 95 Queen Street, SHEFFIELD, S1 1WG.

ⓅⒶ**RPG Holdings Limited** *(J S Brownson, P J Buckley, C Slater)* The Copper Room, Deva Centre, Trinity Way, SALFORD, M3 7BG. and at LONDON

Ⓟ**RPG Services Limited** *(J S Brownson, C Poston, C Slater)* The Copper Room, Deva Centre, Trinity Way, SALFORD, M3 7BG.

Ⓐ**RPM Associates** *(R P Mehta)* 22 Chestnut Avenue, RICKMANSWORTH, HERTFORDSHIRE, WD3 4HB.

Ⓟ**RS Liddell Consulting Ltd** *(R S Liddell)* Treyarnon, Lonning Foot, Rockcliffe, CARLISLE, CA6 4AB.

ⒻⒶ**RS Partnership, trading name of RS Partnership LLP** *(W Stannard)* Riverside House, 14 Prospect Place, WELWYN, HERTFORDSHIRE, AL6 9EN.

RSH Accounting *(R S Hunt)* Waters Edge, 4 Sydney Loader Place, Darby Green, CAMBERLEY, SURREY, GU17 0AF.

★**RSM Nelson Wheeler** *(W K Chu, P W Wong, T M S Wong, W C Wong, R T F Yam)* 29th Floor Caroline Centre, Lee Gardens Two, 28 Yun Ping Road, CAUSEWAY BAY, HONG KONG ISLAND, HONG KONG SAR. and at MELBOURNE

★Ⓣ**RSM Robert Teo, Kuan & Co** *(R K T Teo, K F Yong)* Penthouse Wisma RKT Block A No2, Jalan Raja Abdullah, Off Jalan Sultan Ismail, 50300 KUALA LUMPUR, FEDERAL TERRITORY, MALAYSIA.

ⓉⓅⒶ**RSM Tenon Audit, trading name of RSM Tenon Audit Limited** *(P D Coleman, A J Hunt, D J Parish, J M Pinder, P C Wright)* The Poynt, 45 Wollaton Street, NOTTINGHAM, NG1 5FW. and at BASINGSTOKE, BIRMINGHAM, BOLTON, BOURNEMOUTH, BRISTOL, CARDIFF, CHORLEY, EASTLEIGH, EDINBURGH, GLASGOW, GRANGEMOUTH, HARROGATE, LEEDS, LEICESTER, LONDON, MANCHESTER, MILTON KEYNES, PERTH, READING, ROCHDALE, STOKE-ON-TRENT, SUNDERLAND, SWINDON, TELFORD

ⓉⓅ**RSM Tenon, RSM Tenon (Isle of Man) Limited, RSM Tenon Forensic, RSM Tenon Recovery, trading names of RSM Tenon Limited** *(C S Jackson, B J Marsh, C Ratten, A P Raynor, M R Rossiter)* International House, 66 Chiltern Street, LONDON, W1U 4JT. and at ABERDEEN, BACUP, BASINGSTOKE, BIRMINGHAM, BOLTON, BOURNEMOUTH, BRIGHTON, BRISTOL, CARDIFF, CHELMSFORD, CHORLEY, CROYDON, DERBY, EASTLEIGH, EDINBURGH, GLASGOW, GRANGEMOUTH, GRIMSBY, HARROGATE, HULL, INVERNESS, ISLE OF MAN, LEEDS, LEICESTER, MANCHESTER, MARLOW, MILTON KEYNES, NOTTINGHAM, PERTH, PORTSMOUTH, READING, ROCHDALE, STOKE-ON-TRENT, SUNDERLAND, SWINDON, TELFORD, WAKEFIELD, WATFORD, WELLS, WORCESTER

RSW *(R C H Wong)* Unit 6-17, 17 Thorpe Street, BIRMINGHAM, B5 4AT.

Ⓟ**RTA Limited** *(P D Le Seelleur, R A S Taylor)* PO Box 851, 2nd Floor, 24-26 Broad Street, JERSEY, JE4 0XE.

Rubicon Projects LLP *(C S Brown, S P Jenkinson)* 72 Lairgate, BEVERLEY, NORTH HUMBERSIDE, HU17 8EU.

Ⓕ**Rucklidge & Co** *(J F Rucklidge)* Blakes Farm, Ashurst, STEYNING, BN44 3AN.

ⓅⒶ**Rudge & Co, trading name of Rudge & Co Ltd** *(P A Rudge)* Bordesley Hall, The Holloway, Alvechurch, BIRMINGHAM, B48 7QA.

ⒻⒶ**Rumford & Co** *(M A M Sharkey, E Vangelatos)* Conex House, 148 Field End Road, Eastcote, PINNER, MIDDLESEX, HA5 1RJ.

Rupert H Allibone FCA *(R H Allibone)* Hunters View, Stemborough Lane, Leire, LUTTERWORTH, LE17 5EX.

Ⓟ**Rupert King & Company, trading name of Rupert King & Company Limited** *(J R C King)* Stanton House, 31 Westgate, GRANTHAM, LINCOLNSHIRE, NG31 6LX.

Rupert Merson LLP *(J K Merson, R J Merson)* 24 Ribblesdale Road, LONDON, SW16 6SE.

ⓈⒶ**Rupp & Fraser** *(I S Fraser, C D Rupp)* 7 St. Paul's Road, NEWTON ABBOT, TQ12 2HP.

ⓉⓅ**RUS, trading name of RUS & Company (UK) Ltd** *(R U Samar)* 1190a - 1192 Stratford Road, Hall Green, BIRMINGHAM, B28 8AB.

ⒻⓅⒶ**Rushton Osborne & Co, trading name of Rushton Osborne & Co Limited** *(J J R Austin, D H Jones)* Ringley Park House, 59 Reigate Road, REIGATE, SURREY, RH2 0QJ.

ⒻⓅⒶ**Rushtons (NW) Limited** *(N M Calvert)* Shorrock House, 1 Faraday Court, Fulwood, PRESTON, PR2 9NB.

ⓅⒶ**Ruskells, trading name of Ruskells Limited** *(D J Ruskell)* The Tall House, 29a West Street, MARLOW, BUCKINGHAMSHIRE, SL7 2LS.

Russell & Co *(D R Perrett)* 50 Bridge Road, Litherland, LIVERPOOL, L21 6PH.

Ⓟ**Russell & Co, trading name of Profit Ability North East Limited** *(B V Russell)* Unit 1, Meadowfield Court, Meadowfield, Ponteland, NEWCASTLE UPON TYNE, NE20 9SD.

Ⓐ**Russell & Co, trading name of Russell & Co Partnership LLP** *(A R Russell)* Station House, Station Approach, East Horsley, LEATHERHEAD, SURREY, KT24 6QX.

Ⓟ**Russell Associates Ltd** *(D Russell)* 40 Birchdale Gardens, Chadwell Heath, ROMFORD, RM6 4DU.

Ⓢ**Russell Bedford Ltd** *(A L Sober)* Russell Bedford House, City Forum, 250 City Road, LONDON, EC1V 2QQ.

★Ⓟ**Russell Payne & Co, trading name of Russell Payne & Co Ltd** *(D W Nicholson, R I Payne)* Landmark House, 1 Riseholme Road, LINCOLN, LN1 3SN.

ⓅⒶ**Russell Phillips, trading name of Russell Phillips Ltd** *(H T Phillips, J M Russell)* 23 Station Road, GERRARDS CROSS, BUCKINGHAMSHIRE, SL9 8ES.

ⓉⓅ**Russell Smith, trading name of Russell Smith Tax & Accountancy Services Limited** *(K J Barker, R P H Smith)* G3 Round Foundry, Media Centre, Foundry Street, LEEDS, LS11 5QP.

Ruth Naftalin *(R M Naftalin)* 14 Park Crescent, LONDON, N3 2NJ.

Ⓟ**Rutherford Accountancy Limited** *(M K Edwards)* 34 Pettitts Lane, Dry Drayton, CAMBRIDGE, CB23 8BT.

ⓅⒶ**Rutton B Viccajee, trading name of Rutton B Viccajee Limited** *(R B Viccajee)* Red Lion House, London Road, Bentley, FARNHAM, SURREY, GU10 5HY.

ⒻⓅⒶ**RWB, trading name of RWB CA Limited** *(R W Bonnello, N Coupland)* Northgate House, North Gate, Basford, NOTTINGHAM, NG7 7BE.

RWF, trading name of RWF Rubinstein *(M J Rubinstein)* 171 Bury New Road, Whitefield, MANCHESTER, M45 6AB.

ⒻⓅ**Ryan & Co, trading name of Cliff Ryan** *(C A Ryan)* 4F Shirland Mews, LONDON, W9 3DY.

Ryan Consulting *(N J Ryan)* Halasto UTCA 21, 1039 BUDAPEST, HUNGARY.

★**Ryan IP & Co.** *(H C R Ip)* Room 1801, The Centre Mark, 287-299 Queen's Road Central, CENTRAL, HONG KONG ISLAND, HONG KONG SAR.

★ⒻⒶ**Ryans** *(K R Bell, C A Chisnall)* 67 Chorley Old Road, BOLTON, BL1 3AJ.

ⓉⒻⒶ**Ryecroft Glenton** *(D R Anderson, D Armstrong, G Cawthorn, C Charlton, P Charlton, A A E Glenton, D J Graham, T J Mallon, G Maughan, D Milligan, C N Pearson, C R Robson, I M Smith, G White, A E Woolhead, N R Wyrley-Birch)* 32 Portland Terrace, Jesmond, NEWCASTLE UPON TYNE, NE2 1QP. and at MORPETH, WHITLEY BAY

Ryedale Accountancy *(P E Derby)* Bridge Farm, Station Road, Gilling East, YORK, YO62 4JW.

Ⓟ**Ryland Consulting Limited** *(S A Ryland)* 5 Yeading Avenue, Rayners Lane, HARROW, MIDDLESEX, HA2 9RL.

Ⓟ**Rytax Consultants Ltd** *(R C Yates)* 16 Arnold Grove, Shirley, SOLIHULL, WEST MIDLANDS, B90 3JR.

★**S & J Accountants** *(J W Evans)* 27 Wildmoor Lane, Catshill, BROMSGROVE, B61 0NT.

Ⓟ**S 9, trading name of S 9 Limited** *(D P Miller)* 18 Merlin Way, Mickleover, DERBY, DE3 0SL.

S A V Buchanan *(S A V Buchanan)* Heathfield, 49 Raglan Road, REIGATE, RH2 0DY.

★ⒶⓈ **Burgess & Co** *(S Burgess)* 11 Slayleigh Avenue, Fulwood, SHEFFIELD, S10 3RA.

ⓅⒶ**S C Hosker & Co, trading name of S C Hosker & Co Limited** *(S C Hosker)* Endeavour House, 98 Waters Meeting Road, Navigation Business Park, The Valley, BOLTON, BL1 8SW.

ⓉⓅⒶ**S C Miller Ltd** *(S C Miller)* Clock Offices, High Street, Bishops Waltham, SOUTHAMPTON, SO32 1AA.

Ⓐ**S Charles Mesher & Co** *(S C Mesher)* 4 Newnham Park, HOOK, RG27 9QL.

Ⓟ**S Chowdhury & Co, trading name of S Chowdhury & Co Ltd** *(S Chowdhury)* 17 Midholm, Wembley Park, WEMBLEY, MIDDLESEX, HA9 9LJ.

ⓉⓅⒶ**S Cobbin & Co Limited** *(S Cobbin)* The Old Surgery, 15a Station Road, EPPING, ESSEX, CM16 4HG.

S Cook Bookkeeping Services *(S L Cook)* Kinta Cottage, Edwin Road, West Horsley, LEATHERHEAD, SURREY, KT24 6LN.

Ⓟ**S D K Educational Consultancy Limited** *(S D Knee)* 10 Bath Road, SWINDON, SN1 4BA.

S F Kwok & Co *(S Kwok)* Room 1609-11, 16/F Tai Yau Building, 181Johnston Road, WAN CHAI, HONG KONG SAR.

S G D Accountancy *(S G Dillon)* 27 Linden Lea, Down Ampney, CIRENCESTER, GLOUCESTERSHIRE, GL7 5PF.

ⓅⒶ**S G Todd Limited** *(S G Todd)* Little Mount, 9b Southfield Road, PAIGNTON, TQ3 2SW.

S Garrett ACA *(S G Garrett)* 21 Cottonwood, Biddick Woods, HOUGHTON LE SPRING, TYNE AND WEAR, DH4 7TA.

ⓉⒶ**S H Hellmuth & Co, trading name of Devine & Co** *(B W J Devine)* 242/242a Farnham Road, SLOUGH, SL1 4XE.

ⓉⒻⒶ**S H Landes LLP** *(S H Landes)* 3rd Floor, Fairgate House, 78 New Oxford Street, LONDON, WC1A 1HB.

ⒻⓅ**S Hall Associates, trading name of S Hall Associates Limited** *(S J Hall)* 9 Wimpole Street, LONDON, W1G 9SG.

S Harrison *(S C Harrison)* 6 Albany, 38-40 Alexandra Grove, North Finchley, LONDON, N12 8NN.

S J Anderson BA ACA *(S J Anderson)* Walton House, 10 Mapperley Road, Mapperley Park, NOTTINGHAM, NG3 5AA.

Ⓟ**S J Ball, trading name of Sphere Management Limited** *(S J Ball)* PO Box 587, St Peter Port, GUERNSEY, GY1 6LS.

S J Balmont *(S J Balmont)* 11 Lodge Road, Fetcham, LEATHERHEAD, KT22 9QY.

Ⓟ**S J Bastable, trading name of SJB Accountancy Limited** *(S J Bastable)* 41 Lochaber Street, Roath, CARDIFF, CF24 3LS.

S J Faulkner *(S J Faulkner)* Willow Farm, Wood Lane, Quadring Eaudyke, SPALDING, LINCOLNSHIRE, PE11 4SS.

S J Flory LLP *(S J Flory)* 66 Haven Way, NEWHAVEN, EAST SUSSEX, BN9 9TD.

S J Hook *(S J Hook)* 38A Ledbury Road, LONDON, W11 2AB.

Ⓟ**S J Pickup & Co, trading name of S.J. Pickup & Co Limited** *(L Hughes)* Long Acre, Milton Street, POLEGATE, EAST SUSSEX, BN26 5RW.

S Johnson & Co *(S C Johnson)* 100 Overstone Road, Sywell, NORTHAMPTON, NN6 0AW.

ⒻⓅⒶ**S Johnston & Co, trading name of S. Johnston & Co Limited** *(S M Johnston)* 24 Picton House, Hussar Court, WATERLOOVILLE, HAMPSHIRE, PO7 7SQ.

S K Chan & Co *(S Chan)* Flat D 8th Floor, Tak Lee Commercial Building, 113-117 Wanchai Road, WAN CHAI, HONG KONG SAR.

Ⓟ**S Kainth & Co, trading name of S Kainth & Co Limited** *(S Kainth)* 34 Belvedere Avenue, Clayhall, ILFORD, ESSEX, IG5 0UE.

Ⓟ**S L Lee & Lau CPA Limited** *(Y Lau, S Lee)* Room 1702, 17/F, Tung Hip Commercial Building, 248 Des Voeux Road, CENTRAL, HONG KONG SAR.

S L Wong & Co *(S L Wong)* 2nd Floor, Teng Fuh Commercial Building, 333 Queen's Road Central, SHEUNG WAN, HONG KONG SAR. and at SAN PO KONG

Ⓟ**S M Smith, trading name of S M Smith Ltd** *(S M Smith)* 7 Slingsby Close, Apperley Bridge, BRADFORD, WEST YORKSHIRE, BD10 0UJ.

Ⓟ**S McCombie & Co Ltd** *(G V Penasa)* First Floor, 99 Bancroft, HITCHIN, HERTFORDSHIRE, SG5 1NQ.

S N Pochkhanawala & Co *(S N Pochkhanawala)* 86 Braeside Square, UNIONVILLE L3R 0A5, ON, CANADA.

ⒻⓅ**S P 2 Consulting Limited** *(S E Parker)* Long Spinney, Burrows Lane, Gomshall, GUILDFORD, GU5 9QE.

ⓉⓅⒶ**S P Crowther & Co Limited** *(S P Crowther)* Woodland View House, 675 Leeds Road, HUDDERSFIELD, HD2 1YY.

S P Graves *(S P Graves)* 27 All Saints Street, HASTINGS, EAST SUSSEX, TN34 3BJ.

ⓅⒶ**S P K Shah & Co Ltd** *(P K Shah, S K Shah)* 216 Melton Road, LEICESTER, LE4 7PG.

Ⓐ**S P Spyrou & Co** *(S P Spyrou)* Unit 2, Old Court Mews, 311a Chase Road, Southgate, LONDON, N14 6JS.

Ⓟ**S R Renvoize Limited** *(S R Renvoize)* St Edmunds House, 1 Arwela Road, FELIXSTOWE, IP11 2DG.

S Shaikh *(S Shaikh)* 19 Faber Gardens, Hendon, LONDON, NW4 4NP.

S T Bennett & Co *(S T Bennett)* 36 Bracken Drive, CHIGWELL, ESSEX, IG7 5RF.

Ⓟ**S Theodorou Accountants Limited** *(S G Theodorou)* 14 Souliou, Aglantzia, 2102 NICOSIA, CYPRUS.

ⓉⒻⒶ**S V Bye** *(M A Beeforth, E F Gosney, E Hamilton, D C Robinson)* New Garth House, Upper Garth Gardens, GUISBOROUGH, TS14 6HA.

S Walker *(S D Walker)* 6 Woodside, Methley, LEEDS, LS26 9HB.

S Y Kwong, Foong & Co *(S Y Kwong)* 4/F 108 Jalan Tun H.S. Lee, 50000 KUALA LUMPUR, FEDERAL TERRITORY, MALAYSIA.

S. Akbar & Co *(S R Akbar)* 1st Floor Rear, Hamilton House, 84-86 High Street, Rainham, GILLINGHAM, KENT ME8 7JH.

S. Amin & Co. *(S P Amin)* 10 The Covert, NORTHWOOD, HA6 2UD.

Ⓐ**S. C. Telfer** *(S C Richardson)* 24 High Street, Holme-on-Spalding Moor, YORK, YO43 4HL.

Ⓐ**S. Collins-Dryer** *(S J Collins-Dryer)* 23 Millpond Court, ADDLESTONE, SURREY, KT15 2JY.

S. Crowther & Co *(S A Crowther)* 19 Fieldhouse Drive, Slaithwaite, HUDDERSFIELD, HD7 5BY.

Ⓐ**S. Davies & Co** *(S Davies)* 148 Bury New Road, Whitefield, MANCHESTER, M45 6AD.

S. Dunning FCA *(S Dunning)* 8 Dunlin Rise, Merrow, GUILDFORD, GU4 7DX.

S. Ebrahim *(S Ebrahim)* 5 Porlock Avenue, HARROW, MIDDLESEX, HA2 0AP.

★**S. F. Cheung & Co.** *(S F Cheung)* Room 704 Belgian Bank Building, 721-725 Nathan Road, TSIM SHA TSUI, KOWLOON, HONG KONG SAR.

Ⓟ**S. G. Ripley & Co Ltd** *(M J Hodgson-Barker)* 157 Lewisham Road, LONDON, SE13 7PZ.

S. Husain & Co *(S Husain)* 83 Corbins Lane, South Harrow, HARROW, HA2 8EN.

★**S. K. Luk & Co.** *(S K Luk)* Rooms 502-503 5th Floor, Wanchai Commercial Centre, 194-204 Johnston Road, WAN CHAI, HONG KONG ISLAND, HONG KONG SAR.

Ⓐ**S. Kapur & Co** *(S Kapur)* 6 Hartfield Close, Elstree, BOREHAMWOOD, WD6 3JD.

S. Keith Rhodes BSc FCA *(Keith Rhodes)* 14 Limetree Gardens, Lowdham, NOTTINGHAM, NG14 7DJ.

★**S. Lim & Co.** *(S Lim)* Lot 46-2 Block E, Damai Plaza Phase IV Luyang, 88300 KOTA KINABALU Sabah, MALAYSIA.

ⒻⒶ**S. McCombie & Co** *(G V Penasa)* First Floor, 99 Bancroft, HITCHIN, SG5 1NQ.

S. Poole & Co *(S A Poole)* 220 Barnet Road, POTTERS BAR, HERTFORDSHIRE, EN6 2SH.

ⒻⒶ**S. Ray & Co** *(S Rai)* 52 Royston Park Road, Hatch End, PINNER, HA5 4AF.

S. S. Lau & Co. *(S S Lau)* Unit A, 13/F, Empire Land Commercial Centre, 81-85 Lockhart Road, WAN CHAI, HONG KONG ISLAND HONG KONG SAR.

S. Samuels & Co *(S Samuels)* 205 Bury Old Road, Prestwich, MANCHESTER, M25 1JF.

ⒻⒶ**S. Shah & Co.** *(S Z Shah)* 17 Lovatt Close, EDGWARE, HA8 9XG.

S. Sharma & Co *(S Sharma)* 42 Kathleen Ave, WEMBLEY, HA0 4JH.

★Ⓐ**S. Syedain & Co** *(S Husain)* 2nd Floor Heron House, 109 Wembley Hill Road, WEMBLEY, HA9 8DA.

S.A. Buhariwalla & Associates, trading name of S.A. Buhariwalla & Co *(M S Buhariwalla)* 203 Konark Classic, 55 Hill Road, Bandai, MUMBAI, INDIA.

S.A. Mann *(S A Mann)* 4 Canons Close, EDGWARE, MIDDLESEX, HA8 7QR.

ⓉⒻⒶ**S.Asghar & Co** *(S Asghar)* 69 Headstone Road, HARROW, MIDDLESEX, HA1 1PQ.

S.B.Shah & Co. *(S B Shah)* 97 Brim Hill, LONDON, N2 0EZ.

Ⓟ**S.B.T.S Limited** *(J L Beattie)* 72a Thornbury Wood, Chandler's Ford, EASTLEIGH, HAMPSHIRE, SO53 5DQ.

ⒻⒶ**S.C. Devani & Co** *(S C Devani)* 37 High Street, Acton, LONDON, W3 6ND.

Ⓟ**S.C. M. Accountancy Services Ltd** *(S C Matejtschuk)* 28 Witter Avenue, Ickleford, HITCHIN, SG5 3UF.

S.D. Janmohamed *(S D H Janmohamed)* 235-2903 Rabbit Hill Road, EDMONTON T6R 3A3, AB, CANADA.

Ⓐ**S.D. Modi & Co** *(S D Modi)* Windsor Chambers, 367a Bearwood Road, SMETHWICK, WEST MIDLANDS, B66 4DL.

Ⓟ**S.D. Whiting & Co, trading name of S.D. Whiting & Co Limited** *(S D Whiting)* 76 Ouseley Road, Wraysbury, STAINES, TW19 5JH.

S.E. Bibby & Co *(S E Bibby)* 1 Wych Elm Close, HORNCHURCH, RM11 3AJ.

S.E. Brown *(S E Brown)* 2 Chancel Way, Charlton Kings, CHELTENHAM, GL53 7RR.

Ⓟ**S.E.S. Consultancy Limited** *(S E Drummond)* 6 Fallowfield, Beyton, BURY ST. EDMUNDS, SUFFOLK, IP30 9BN.

S.E.Wood *(S E Wood)* Fieldings, 6 Wheelers Way, Felbridge, EAST GRINSTEAD, RH19 2QJ.

Ⓐ**S.F. Brocklehurst & Co.** *(S F Brocklehurst)* Forest Lodge, Forest Road, Pyrford, WOKING, SURREY, GU22 8NA.

★**S.F.Ahmed & Co.** *(S F Ali)* House No 25D, Road No 13A, Block D, Banani, DHAKA 1213, BANGLADESH. and at CHITTAGONG

Ⓕ**S.G. Beale & Co.** *(S G J Beale)* 3 Redman Court, Bell Street, PRINCES RISBOROUGH, HP27 0AA.

S.G. Ripley & Co *(M J Hodgson-Barker)* 157 Lewisham Road, LONDON, SE13 7PZ.

S.G. Schanschieff, trading name of S.G. Schanschieff FCA *(S G Schanschieff)* Rushworth, Church Farm, Church Brampton, NORTHAMPTON, NN6 8BN.

Ⓐ**S.G. Talati** *(S G Talati)* 17 St Georges Road, SOUTHSEA, PO4 9PL.

Ⓐ**S.G.Banister & Co** *(T A Clunie)* 40 Great James Street, LONDON, WC1N 3HB.

S.H. Bettaney *(S H Bettaney)* 78 Harrowes Meade, EDGWARE, HA8 8RP.

Ⓕ**S.I. Gompels & Co** *(S I Gompels)* 7 Heathfield, Stoke D'Abernon, COBHAM, KT11 2QY.

S.J. Burns & Co *(S J Burns)* Jubilee House, Suite 9A Altcar Road, Formby, LIVERPOOL, L37 8DL.

S.J. Cooke & Company *(S J Cooke)* Stone Farm, Borough Lane, Great Finborough, STOWMARKET, IP14 3AS.

S.J. Earl *(S J Earl)* 22 The Fairway, LEIGH-ON-SEA, SS9 4QL.

S.J. Gaunt *(S J Gaunt)* 42 Wike Ridge Avenue, Alwoodley, LEEDS, LS17 9NL.

S.J. Haydon *(S J Haydon)* The Conifers, Stone Lane, Lydiard Millicent, SWINDON, SN5 3LD.

S.J. Hertzberg & Co *(S J Hertzberg)* 18 Glebelands Avenue, South Woodford, LONDON, E18 2AB.

S.J. Rose & Co *(S J Rose)* 2 Oak Lodge, 6 Oak Lodge Drive, WEST WICKHAM, KENT, BR4 0RQ.

S.J. Simpson *(S J Simpson)* Anchor & Hope Cottage, 1 Cove Hill, Perranarworthal, TRURO, CORNWALL, TR3 7QQ.

S.J. Wetherall *(S J Wetherall)* 264 Banbury Road, OXFORD, OX2 7DY.

ⒻⒶ**S.J.M. Dent** *(S J M Dent)* 22a Bradmore Park Road, LONDON, W6 0DT.

S.K. Bhatt *(S K Bhatt)* 178 Stroud Road, GLOUCESTER, GL1 5JX.

S.K. Duggal *(S K Duggal)* 13 Pelham Court, NEWCASTLE UPON TYNE, NE3 2YL.

S.K. Sharma & Co *(S K Sharma)* Gable House, Black Pond Lane, Farnham Common, SLOUGH, SL2 3EN.

S.L. Lam & Company *(S S L Lam)* Rooms 1804-5, The Centre Mark, 287-299 Queen's Road, CENTRAL, HONG KONG ISLAND, HONG KONG SAR.

S.L. Scott *(S L Scott)* 235 New London Road, CHELMSFORD, CM2 9AA.

Ⓐ**S.L. Smith & Co** *(S L Smith)* Barbican House, 26-34 Old Street, LONDON, EC1V 9QR.

S.M. Jaufuraully & Co *(S M Jaufuraully)* 122 Northover Road, Westbury On Trym, BRISTOL, BS9 3LG.

S.M.C Bruce *(S M C Bruce)* 28 Pheasants Way, RICKMANSWORTH, WD3 7ES.

S.M.G. Daya & Co *(S M Gulamhusein)* P.O.Box 90071, MOMBASA, KENYA.

Ⓣ**S.N. Bartarya** *(S N Bartarya)* Chartwell House 1st Floor, 292 Hale Lane, EDGWARE, HA8 8NP.

S.R. Anthony *(S R Anthony)* 26 Beachway, CANVEY ISLAND, SS8 0BD.

S.R. Connellan & Co *(S R Connellan)* Our Shell, Hempnall Road, Bedingham, BUNGAY, SUFFOLK, NR35 2NW.

Ⓣ**S.R. Dawson** *(S R Dawson)* 37 Adelaide Road, SHEFFIELD, S7 1SQ.

S.R. Jones *(S R Jones)* Middle Lane Ends Farm, Lane Ends Lane, Cowling, KEIGHLEY, BD22 0LD.

★**S.R. Lynn & Co** *(S R Lynn)* 11 Warren Yard, Wolverton Mill, MILTON KEYNES, MK12 5NW.

S.R. Warburton *(S R Warburton)* 34 Cherry Tree Avenue, Kirby Muxloe, LEICESTER, LE9 2HN.

S.S. McDermott *(S S McDermott)* 15 Childwall Crescent, Childwall, LIVERPOOL, L16 7PG.

S.U. Tamuri *(S U Tamuri)* 1 Forrest Gardens, LONDON, SW16 4LP.

S.W. Kan & Co. *(L H Tong)* Room 501 502 & 508, 5th Floor, Mirror Tower, 61 Mody Road, Tsunshatsui East, TSIM SHA TSUI KOWLOON HONG KONG SAR. and at MONG KOK

ⓉⒶ**S.W.Frankson & Co** *(M C Finch, C E Harte, B Ruddick)* Bridge House, 119-123 Station Road, HAYES, MIDDLESEX, UB3 4BX.

S.W.M. Reynolds *(S W M Reynolds)* Morar, 20 Delavor Road, Heswall, WIRRAL, MERSEYSIDE, CH60 4RW.

S.Y. Yu *(S Wu)* Unit 1007 10/F, Focal Industrial Building, 21 Man Lok Street, HUNG HOM, KOWLOON, HONG KONG SAR.

Ⓟ**S2 Solutions, trading name of S2 Solutions Limited** *(S H Michaels)* 34 Hillview Road, PINNER, MIDDLESEX, HA5 4PA.

Ⓐ**Sabera & Co** *(S Patel)* 126 Middlesex Street, LONDON, E1 7HY.

Ⓟ**Sable & Argent Limited** *(J White)* 2 Elvetham Crescent, FLEET, HAMPSHIRE, GU51 1BU.

Ⓟ**Sable Accounting, trading name of Sable Accounting Ltd** *(A M Deakin, R J Phillips)* Castlewood House, 77-91 New Oxford Street, LONDON, WC1A 1DG.

Ⓟ**Sabre Management Services Limited** *(B E Salmon)* Anglo International House, Lord Street, Douglas, ISLE OF MAN, IM1 4LN.

ⓉⒻⒶ**Sachdevs** *(R Sachdev)* 63 Cromwell Lane, Westwood Heath, COVENTRY, CV4 8AQ.

ⒻⓅ**Sackman & Co, trading name of Sackman & Co Limited** *(M Sackman)* Unit L32, MK Two Business Centre, Barton Road, Water Eaton, MILTON KEYNES, MK2 3HU. and at LONDON

Ⓟ**Saddique & Co, trading name of Ray (Accountants) Mcr Ltd** *(M Saddique)* 78 Dickenson Road, Rusholme, MANCHESTER, M14 5HF.

ⓉⒶ**Sadiq, Metcalfe & Co.** *(M Sadiq)* 94 Dickenson Road, MANCHESTER, M14 5HJ.

Ⓣ**Sadler Davies & Co LLP** *(G L Fogarty, G E J Sadler)* 25A Essex Road, DARTFORD, DA1 2AU.

ⓉⒻⒶ**Sadofskys** *(A Brocklehurst, C Knaggs)* Princes House, Wright Street, HULL, HU2 8HX.

★**Saeed Methani Mushtaq & Co** *(F H Arbab, S Hassan)* 10/7 Al-Karam, Faiz Road, Old Muslim Town, LAHORE, PAKISTAN. and at KARACHI, PESHAWAR

ⓉⒶ**Saffery Champness** *(R A Angliss, R J Collis, R T Elliott, S J Garrard, H F Green, M P Johnson, C A H Nicholson)* P O Box 141, La Tonnelle House, Les Banques, St. Sampson, GUERNSEY, GY1 3HS.

★ⓉⒻⒶ**Saffery Champness** *(C J H Adams, P R N Adams, T P L Adams, A G D Arnott, K T Bartlett, L Brennan, E Brierley, D L Caira, S R Collins, R J Collis, C E Cromwell, M Di Leto, R T Elliott, N F Fernyhough, M J Floydd, S J Garrard, A N Gaskell, T M T Gregory, M J Harrison, P J Horsman, D Hughes, M P Johnson, D T Kakkad, N J Kelsey, S R Kite, P F Langdon, D Lemon, C W D Macey, M D McGarry, L G Mosca, C A H Nicholson, A R Robinson, J R Shuffrey, C H M Simpson, L J Sowden, S W Swift, J J Sykes, C J Turtington, D C Wragg)* Lion House, Red Lion Street, LONDON, WC1R 4GB. and at EDINBURGH, HIGH WYCOMBE, INVERNESS

★ⒻⒶ**Saffery Champness** *(C J H Adams, P R N Adams, T P L Adams, A G D Arnott, K T Bartlett, L Brennan, E Brierley, D L Caira, S R Collins, R J Collis, C E Cromwell, M Di Leto, R T Elliott, N F Fernyhough, M J Floydd, S J Garrard, A N Gaskell, T M T Gregory, M J Harrison, P J Horsman, D Hughes, M P Johnson, D T Kakkad, N J Kelsey, S R Kite, P F Langdon, D Lemon, C W D Macey, M D McGarry, L G Mosca, C A H Nicholson, A R Robinson, J R Shuffrey, C H M Simpson, L J Sowden, S W Swift, J J Sykes, C J Turtington, D C Wragg)* Stuart House, City Road, PETERBOROUGH, PE1 1QF. and at BOURNEMOUTH, BRISTOL, HARROGATE, LONDON, MANCHESTER

Ⓟ**Saga, trading name of Saga Business Solutions Limited** *(M P Shah)* Unit 5, 20 High Street, LONDON, E15 2PP.

Sagar & Co *(P Sagar)* 2 Ambleside Close, STONE, STAFFORDSHIRE, ST15 8FU.

ⓉⒻⒶ**Sagars LLP** *(J Beevers, C W Jones, K Naylor, C D M Smetham)* Gresham House, 5-7 St. Pauls Street, LEEDS, LS1 2JG.

ⓉⒻⒶ**Sage & Co** *(S K Sangani)* 38A High Street, NORTHWOOD, HA6 1BN.

ⓉⒻⓅⒶ**Sage & Company, trading name of Sage & Company Business Advisors Limited** *(M F Gilmartin, C N Porter)* 102 Bowen Court, St Asaph Business Park, ST. ASAPH, CLWYD, LL17 0JE.

Ⓣ**Sager & Co.** *(A M Sager)* 7 Water End Close, BOREHAMWOOD, HERTFORDSHIRE, WD6 4PW.

ⓉⒻⓅ**Sagoo & Co, trading name of CSJ Financial Solutions Limited** *(S S Sagoo)* 122 High Street, LONDON, W3 6QX.

ⓅⒶ**Sahni & Co Limited** *(B S Sahni)* 55 Maresfield Gardens, LONDON, NW3 5TE.

Ⓐ**Saifuddin & Co** *(A Saifuddin)* 62 Widmore Road, BROMLEY, BR1 3BD.

★ⓉⒶ**Saint & Co.** *(P A J Boothroyd, P R Dhillon, L M Farrer, S Farrer, D A Gibson, A P Irving, D E Johnson, D A Liddle, J Little, W G P Moore, Marion Nolan, I Scott, E J Southward, I Thompson)* Sterling House, Wavell Drive, Rosehill, CARLISLE, CA1 2SA. and at AMBLESIDE, ANNAN, COCKERMOUTH, KESWICK, MILLOM, PENRITH, WHITEHAVEN, WIGTON

Ⓟ**Sajid & Sajid, trading name of Sajid & Sajid Limited** *(J P Oldoni, A A Sajid)* 26 Dover Street, Mayfair, LONDON, W1S 4LY.

Ⓣ**Sajjad Haider & Co** *(S Haider, S B S Haider)* P.O. Box 3251, DUBAI, UNITED ARAB EMIRATES.

Ⓟ**Salary and Accounting Services Limited** *(K M Halliwell, R Thirkettle)* Adam House, 71 Bell Street, HENLEY-ON-THAMES, OXFORDSHIRE, RG9 2BD.

Ⓟ**Salary Solutions Limited** *(G Dickinson, S P Mell, R I Watson)* 12 Victoria Road, BARNSLEY, SOUTH YORKSHIRE, S70 2BB.

Ⓟ**Sale Accounting Services Limited** *(K H Rourke)* 35 Hillington Road, SALE, CHESHIRE, M33 6GQ.

Ⓐ**Saleemi Associates** *(M A Saleemi)* 792 Wickham Road, CROYDON, SURREY, CR0 8EA.

Saleha and Co *(I Islam)* 40 Cranley Drive, ILFORD, ESSEX, IG2 6AH.

Ⓟ**Saleport Limited** *(A C Short)* Merewood, Pond Road, WOKING, SURREY, GU22 0JZ.

ⓉⒻⓅⒶ**Salisbury & Company, trading name of Salisbury & Company Business Solutions Limited** *(A O Roberts, J C Salisbury)* Irish Square, Upper Denbigh Road, ST. ASAPH, CLWYD, LL17 0RN. and at CONWY

Salisbury Accounting & Payroll Services *(N C Rimer)* Sunrize House, Downton, SALISBURY, SP5 3JJ.

Ⓟ**Sally Currin Ltd** *(S A Currin)* 33 Lower Blackfriars Crescent, St. Marys Water Lane, SHREWSBURY, SY1 2BA.

Sally Ferguson & Co *(S R Ferguson)* 66 Luton Road, HARPENDEN, AL5 2UR.

Ⓟ**Sally French Accountancy Services, trading name of Greenman French Limited** *(S K French)* Byways, The Batch, Bishop Sutton, BRISTOL, BS39 5US.

Ⓟ**Sally Grant Limited** *(S A Walker)* El Villa, 3 Ladybridge Road, WATERLOOVILLE, PO7 5RP.

Sally Haynes *(S E Haynes)* 8 Burcott Road, WELLS, SOMERSET, BA5 2EQ.

Sally Morris Accountancy *(S E Morris)* 15 Broadway Road, Bishopston, BRISTOL, BS7 8ES.

ⓉⒻⓅ**Sally Reed Ltd** *(S A Reed)* 27F Pennygillam Way, LAUNCESTON, CORNWALL, PL15 7ED.

Sally Shepard *(S J Shepard)* Hopesay, 8 Glebe Close, Moulsford, WALLINGFORD, OX10 9JA.

Salman Ross *(F J Islam)* 141 Woodlands Road, ILFORD, IG1 1JR.

Ⓕ**Salmon & Co** *(R C Salmon)* 4 Buckingham Place, Bellfield Road, HIGH WYCOMBE, HP13 5HQ.

Salmon & Co *(P Salmon)* PO Box 71, Farnham Royal, SLOUGH, SL2 3SH.

Salter & Co *(K J Salter)* 34 Byron Avenue, LONDON, E18 2HQ.

ⒻⓅⒶ**Saltrick & Saltrick Ltd** *(C J Saltrick, C R Saltrick)* 5 The Glasshouse Studios, Fryern Court Road, Burgate, FORDINGBRIDGE, HAMPSHIRE, SP6 1QX.

ⒻⓅ**Salway Wright, trading name of Salway and Wright (Spalding) Limited** *(A M Smith, A D Wood)* 32 The Crescent, SPALDING, LINCOLNSHIRE, PE11 1AF.

Sam Binks *(S G Binks)* Coombe Farm Cottage, Canford Lane, BRISTOL, BS9 3PE.

Sam Farren BSc ACA DChA *(S Farren)* 107 Noahs Ark, Kemsing, SEVENOAKS, KENT, TN15 6PD.

Sam Merchant *(S A Merchant)* 73 Gorsewood Road, St. John's, WOKING, GU21 8XG.

ⓉⓅⒶ**Sam Rogoff & Co, trading name of Sam Rogoff & Co Limited** *(J L Buse, S Rogoff)* 2nd Floor, 167-169 Great Portland Street, LONDON, W1W 5PF.

Samantha Adnrew BSc ACA *(S Andrew)* 1 Knighton Road, Wembury, PLYMOUTH, PL9 0EA.

Samantha Cutting ACA *(S J Cutting)* 7 Beechwood Close, Whitfield, DOVER, KENT, CT16 3JZ.

Ⓟ**Samantha Frize Ltd** *(S M V Frize)* Lhag Dhoo, Pinfold Hill, Laxey, ISLE OF MAN, IM4 7HJ.

Samantha Kelly ACA *(S Kelly)* 10 Ferniefields, HIGH WYCOMBE, BUCKINGHAMSHIRE, HP12 4SP.

Samantha Taylor ACA *(S L Taylor)* 72 Mid Street, South Nutfield, REDHILL, SURREY, RH1 4JX.

Samantha Thompson *(S J Thompson)* Westside, 1 Halliford Drive, Barnham, BOGNOR REGIS, WEST SUSSEX, PO22 0AB.

Ⓟ**Samera Ltd** *(A Mehra)* Samera House, 138 High Street, ESHER, SURREY, KT10 9QJ.

Samjis *(A M P Samji)* 4 Fulwood Court, Kenton Rd, HARROW, HA3 8AA.

Ⓟ**Sammar & Co Limited** *(S A Farooqi)* Baet-Ul-Zafar, 14 Albury Avenue, Cheam, SUTTON, SM2 7JT.

Sammy K. K. Ng *(K S Ng)* Unit 302, Kam On Building, 176a Queens Road, CENTRAL, HONG KONG ISLAND, HONG KONG SAR.

ⓉⒶ**Sampson West** *(N J Hickling, M A Sampson, L F West)* 34 Ely Place, LONDON, EC1N 6TD.

Ⓟ**Samuel George Limited** *(T Gill)* 14 Rogers Way, WARWICK, CV34 6PY.

Samuel S. Dicker *(S S Dicker)* 32 Chatterton, LETCHWORTH GARDEN CITY, HERTFORDSHIRE, SG6 2JY.
Samuel Slater & Sons *(R Butterworth)* 11 Queen Street, OLDHAM, OL1 1RG.
ⒻⓅ**Samuels Corporate Limited** *(P T Samuels)* The Old Forge, 36A West Street, REIGATE, SURREY, RH2 9BX.
ⓉⒶ**Samuels, trading name of Samuels LLP** *(S Narula)* 3 Locks Yard, High Street, SEVENOAKS, KENT, TN13 1LT.
Ⓣ**Sanderlings LLP** *(A Fender)* Sanderling House, 1071 Warwick Road, Acocks Green, BIRMINGHAM, B27 6QT. and at ASHBY-DE-LA-ZOUCH, SOLIHULL, WHITCHURCH
ⒻⒶ**Sanders** *(I C McManus, S B Sanders)* 1 Bickenhall Mansions, Bickenhall Street, LONDON, W1U 6BP.
Sanders & Co *(V Sanders)* The Old Rectory, Long Lane, South Hykeham, LINCOLN, LN6 9NX.
ⓉⒻⓅ**Sanders Geeson, trading name of Sanders Geeson Limited** *(J Szczepanski)* Raines Business Centre, Raines House, Denby Dale Road, WAKEFIELD, WEST YORKSHIRE, WF1 1HR.
ⓉⓅⒶ**Sanders Swinbank Limited** *(D Sanders, S M A Swinbank)* 7 Victoria Road, DARLINGTON, DL1 5SN.
Sandes *(H S A Raperport)* 45 Arden Road, LONDON, N3 3AD.
★**Sandison Easson & Co** *(M D Murray, A S Thomson, I R Tongue)* Rex Buildings, Alderley Road, WILMSLOW, CHESHIRE, SK9 1HY.
ⒻⒶ**Sandison Lang & Co** *(A C D Lang)* 2 St.Mary's Road, TONBRIDGE, TN9 2LB.
Ⓕ**Sandison Rouse & Co** *(P J Edwards, G F R Rouse)* Richmond House, 48 Bromyard Road, St Johns, WORCESTER, WR2 5BT.
Ⓟ**Sandisons, trading name of Sandisons Limited** *(N H Cooke)* Badger House, Salisbury Road, BLANDFORD FORUM, DORSET, DT11 7QD.
Sandra Aldworth *(S Aldworth)* The School House, Clayhidon, CULLOMPTON, DEVON, EX15 3PL.
Sandra Brown & Co *(S K Brown)* Sunnyside, Holyport Street, Holyport, MAIDENHEAD, BERKSHIRE, SL6 2JR.
★**Sandra McNamara & Co** *(S M McNamara)* 9 Vernon Grove, Rathgar, DUBLIN 6, COUNTY DUBLIN, IRELAND.
Ⓟ**Sansom & Co, trading name of Sansom & Company Accountants Limited** *(B T Sansom)* 1st Floor, 3 Charles Court, Budbrooke Road, WARWICK, CV34 5LZ.
ⓉⒶ**Sansons** *(S Sood)* 35 Beaufort Court, Admirals Way, South Quay Waterside, LONDON, E14 9XL.
Ⓟ**Sarah Abbott and Co, trading name of Sarah Abbott and Co Limited** *(S E Abbott)* 4 Lancaster Road, IPSWICH, IP4 2NY.
Sarah Adamson *(S L Adamson)* Digges Barn, Out Elmstead Lane, Barham, CANTERBURY, KENT, CT4 6PH.
Sarah Buttars & Company *(S L Buttars)* Brensham Cottage, Malting Lane, Aldbury, TRING, HERTFORDSHIRE, HP23 5RH.
Sarah Cleminson Consultancy *(S Cleminson)* Island Chase, Steep, PETERSFIELD, HAMPSHIRE, GU32 1AE.
Sarah E Lamb BSc ACA *(S E Lamb)* 23 Park Drive, Midgey, WHITEHAVEN, CUMBRIA, CA28 7RY.
Sarah Fox *(S F S Fox)* Edgeworth House, Edgeworth, STROUD, GL6 7JQ.
Ⓐ**Sarah Hardy Accountancy** *(K S Hardy)* 2 Quarry Bank, LIGHTWATER, SURREY, GU18 5PE.
Sarah Harvey & Company *(S A Harvey)* Swallows Barn, St Sampsons Close, Tywardreath, PAR, PL24 2QZ.
Sarah Henry *(S M Henry)* 24 Frewin Road, LONDON, SW18 3LP.
Sarah J Fitzgerald *(S J Fitzgerald)* Briar Cottage, Hurston Lane, Storrington, PULBOROUGH, WEST SUSSEX, RH20 4HH.
Sarah M. Goodwin *(S M Goodwin)* Amber Hill, Amberley, STROUD, GL5 5AN.
Ⓟ**Sarbacco, trading name of Sarbacco Limited** *(S S Chauhan)* 18 Coldershaw Road, LONDON, W13 9DX.
Sargent & Co *(A C Sargent)* 37 Albury Drive, PINNER, MIDDLESEX, HA5 3RL.
Ⓐ**Sargent & Co** *(A G Sargent)* 194b Addington Road, Selsdon, SOUTH CROYDON, SURREY, CR2 8LD.
Sargent Services LLP *(H N Painter, J Salt)* 26 Sansome Walk, WORCESTER, WR1 1LX.
Sarmad & Co *(S A Khan)* 115 London Road, MORDEN, SURREY, SM4 5HP.
Ⓟ**Sarmad Global Accountancy Services Ltd** *(S A Khan, A A Mahamadi)* 115 London Road, MORDEN, SURREY, SM4 5HP.
Saron Rusden *(S R Rusden)* 3 The Paddock, 73a Mudeford, CHRISTCHURCH, BH23 3NJ.
★**Sashi Kala Devi Associates** *(S K D Renganathan)* 31 Cantonment Road, SINGAPORE 089747, SINGAPORE.
Sassoon Saleh *(S Saleh)* 13 Woodward Avenue, LONDON, NW4 4NU.
SAT & Co *(S Singh)* 331 Torbay Road, HARROW, MIDDLESEX, HA2 9QD.
Satish R. Khimasia *(S R Khimasia)* P.O. Box 40214, NAIROBI, KENYA.
Satish Shah *(S Shah)* PO Box 82675, MOMBASA, KENYA.
Sattar & Co *(A Sattar)* 95 Oldham Road, ROCHDALE, LANCASHIRE, OL16 5QR.
ⒻⓅⒶ**Saul Fairholm, trading name of Saul Fairholm Limited** *(S L Tointon, R M Welsh, R M White)* 12 Tentercroft Street, LINCOLN, LINCOLNSHIRE, LN5 7DB. and at RETFORD
Ⓐ**Saunders & Co** *(P B Saunders)* 29 Harcourt Street, LONDON, W1H 4HS.
Saunders Accounting *(V A Saunders)* 34 Shaftesbury Mount, Blackwater, CAMBERLEY, SURREY, GU17 9JR.
ⓉⒶ**Saunders, Wood & Co.** *(J A Wood, N J Wood)* The White House, 140A Tachbrook Street, LONDON, SW1V 2NE.
Ⓟ**Savage & Company, trading name of P R Savage & Company Limited** *(P R Savage)* 3a Warwick Road, BEACONSFIELD, BUCKINGHAMSHIRE, HP9 2PE.
Ⓟ**Savvas E Savvides Ltd** *(S E Savvides)* Pelekanos Court 21, 12 Prometheus Str, Office 102, PO Box 28743, 2082 NICOSIA, CYPRUS.
Ⓟ**Savvides Audit Limited** *(G Savvides)* Loucaides Court, 3 Makarios Avenue, 4th Floor, Mesa Geitonia, 4000 LIMASSOL, CYPRUS.
★ⒻⒶ**Sawford Bullard** *(C P Fletcher)* 6 Hazelwood Road, NORTHAMPTON, NN1 1LW.
★ⒻⒶ**Sawin & Edwards** *(W K Sawin)* 15 Southampton Place, LONDON, WC1A 2AJ.
Ⓟ**Saxby & Sinden, trading name of Saxby & Sinden Limited** *(A J Sinden)* 18 High Street, BUDLEIGH SALTERTON, DEVON, EX9 6LQ.
ⒻⓅ**Saxbys, trading name of Saxbys Limited** *(N S Saxby)* Maple House, Rookery Road, Monewden, WOODBRIDGE, SUFFOLK, IP13 7DD.
Ⓐ**Saxon & Co** *(A A Saxon)* Kings Chambers, Queens Cross, DUDLEY, DY1 1QT.
Saxon & Co *(J C Saxon)* Crowley, 85 Hope Road, SALE, M33 3AW.
Ⓟ**Saxons Limited** *(A A Saxon)* Kings Chambers, Queens Cross, DUDLEY, WEST MIDLANDS, DY1 1QT.
ⓉⒶ**Sayer Vincent** *(P M Craig, H C E Elliott, J A Miller, C L Sayer)* 8 Angel Gate, City Road, LONDON, EC1V 2SJ.
ⓉⒻⒶ**Sayers Butterworth LLP** *(A K Burch, M C Dunne, P E Ffitch, A G Mahoney, M W Wright)* 3rd Floor, 12 Gough Square, LONDON, EC4A 3DW.
ⓅⒶ**Saymur Accountants, trading name of Saymur Accountants Limited** *(M M Gulamhusein)* 1st Floor, 27 Peterborough Road, HARROW, MIDDLESEX, HA1 2AU.
Sazan & Company *(A M A I Sazan)* 93 Crayford Road, Crayford, DARTFORD, DA1 4AS.
SB & Company *(S S Bawa)* 55 Syon Park Gardens, ISLEWORTH, MIDDLESEX, TW7 5NE.
Ⓟ**SB&P Corporate Finance Ltd** *(W J Shore, J R Sumner, R J R Young)* Oriel House, 2-8 Oriel Road, BOOTLE, MERSEYSIDE, L20 7EP.
ⓉⒻⒶ**SB&P LLP** *(A G Bruford, W J Shore, J R Sumner, R J R Young)* Oriel House, 2-8 Oriel Road, BOOTLE, MERSEYSIDE, L20 7EP.
ⓅⒶ**SBCA, trading name of Crystal Securities Practice Limited** *(C P Bond, S F Bond)* Park House, 17 Moor Park Avenue, PRESTON, PR1 6AS.
SBLR LLP *(H S Lerner)* 2345 Yonge Street, Suite 300, TORONTO M4P 2E5, ON, CANADA.
Ⓐ**SBM & Co** *(P McAlpine, S B McAlpine)* 117 Fentiman Road, LONDON, SW8 1JZ.
SBM Resources *(P J A Press)* 48 Wycombe Road, Prestwood, GREAT MISSENDEN, BUCKINGHAMSHIRE, HP16 0PQ.
★**Scannell & Associates** *(M Scannell)* 180 Piccadilly, LONDON, W1J 9HF.
Ⓟ**Scarsdale Trust Limited** *(A C Drennan)* 73 Ashgate Avenue, CHESTERFIELD, DERBYSHIRE, S40 1JD.
Scheermann & Partners *(S A Scheermann)* 31b Lyndhurst Road, LONDON, NW3 5PB.
★**Schmitz & de Grace** *(L C Ross)* 1116 Sixth Avenue, PRINCE GEORGE V2L 3M6, BC, CANADA.
Ⓟ**Schofield Smith & Co, trading name of Schofield Smith & Co Limited** *(J S R Smith)* 69 East Craigs Rigg, EDINBURGH, EH12 8JA.
ⓉⒶ**Schofields, trading name of Schofields Partnership LLP** *(D Leatham, P J Schofield)* Dean Park House, Dean Park Crescent, BOURNEMOUTH, BH1 1HP.
ⒻⒶ**Schonhut Carr & Co** *(J G Carr, T Carr)* Thames House, Mayo Road, WALTON-ON-THAMES, SURREY, KT12 2QA.
Ⓟ**SCI Kakofengitis & Co Ltd** *(A Kakofengitis)* PO Box 57489, 3316 LIMASSOL, CYPRUS.
★ⓉⒻⒶ**Scodie Deyong LLP** *(L S Deyong, M G Jacobs, M Scodie, S J Sefton, L C Warde)* 85 Frampton Street, LONDON, NW8 8NQ.
Ⓟ**Scorer Accounting Services, trading name of City Financial Trust Limited** *(M F Scorer)* 33 Waring Drive, Green Street Green, ORPINGTON, BR6 6DN.
★ⓉⒻⒶ**Scott & Wilkinson, trading name of Scott & Wilkinson LLP** *(S W Hinnigan, N J Martin, P Wilkinson)* Dalton House, 9 Dalton Square, LANCASTER, LA1 1WD.
Scott Baird & Co. *(John H.Scott-Baird)* Ardbeg, Drominane, KILLEAGH, COUNTY CORK, IRELAND.
ⒻⓅⒶ**Scott Vevers, trading name of Scott Vevers Ltd** *(M J Cridland)* 65 East Street, BRIDPORT, DORSET, DT6 3LB.
▽**Scott-Moncrieff** *(N B Bennett)* Exchange Place 3, Semple Street, EDINBURGH, EH3 8BL. and at GLASGOW
Scovells *(M G Scovell)* Mennadews, Windlesham Road, Chobham, WOKING, SURREY, GU24 8SY.
Ⓣ**Screaton & Co** *(B Screaton)* 49 Station Street, ATHERSTONE, CV9 1DB.
ⓉⒻⒶ**Scrutton Bland** *(N L Banks, S S Gravener, S V Gull, J B McElhinney, T E O'Connor, J C Pickering, A P Strickland)* Sanderson House, Museum Street, IPSWICH, IP1 1HE. and at COLCHESTER
Scruttons *(C M Scrutton, H G Scrutton)* 2A Bickerton Road, Headington, OXFORD, OX3 7LS.
Ⓟ**Scullard & Co Ltd** *(C D P Scullard)* 14 Vetchwood Gardens, West Timperley, ALTRINCHAM, CHESHIRE, WA14 5ZG.
★Ⓟ**SD Knee, trading name of SD Knee Ltd** *(S D Knee)* 10 Bath Road, Old Town, SWINDON, SN1 4BA.
Ⓟ**SDP Financials Ltd** *(S J Parsons)* 28 Fordwich Drive, Frindsbury, ROCHESTER, KENT, ME2 3FA.
Ⓟ**Seafields, trading name of Nittin Accountancy Services Limited** *(N B Shah)* 50 Bullescroft Road, EDGWARE, HA8 8RW.
Ⓣ**Seah & Associates** *(T P Lim, C W Seah)* Suite 15.05 Level 15, City Square Office Tower, 106-108 Jalan Wong Ah Fook, 80000 JOHOR BAHRU, MALAYSIA.
Ⓟ**Seahurst Limited** *(S C Griffiths)* 156 Bath Road, SOUTHSEA, HAMPSHIRE, PO4 0HU.
Ⓟ**Seal, trading name of Strategy Engineering Associates Limited** *(J A Loveless)* The Lilacs, 25 Church Road, LEATHERHEAD, SURREY, KT22 8AT.
ⓉⒻⓅ**Seals King & Co Limited** *(R Seals)* 17 Brunts Street, MANSFIELD, NOTTINGHAMSHIRE, NG18 1AX. and at CHESTERFIELD
Ⓟ**Seamark Forensic Services Limited** *(M J P Seamark)* Stella House, 82 Greenway Road, TAUNTON, SOMERSET, TA2 6LE.
Ⓟ**Sean Rowe Limited** *(S D Rowe)* 169 New London Road, CHELMSFORD, CM2 0AE.
Searby & Co *(D N Searby, G D Searby)* Princes House, Wright Street, HULL, HU2 8HX.
Searle & Co *(K H Searle)* Camelot, 32 Diddington Lane, Hampton in Arden, SOLIHULL, B92 0BZ.
Searle Inskip Freed & Co *(R Inskip)* Beke Lodge, Beke Hall Chase North, Rawreth, RAYLEIGH, ESSEX, SS6 9EZ.
Ⓟ**Secretarial Administration Ltd** *(D M Mason)* Lee House, 6a Highfield Road, Edgbaston, BIRMINGHAM, B15 3ED.
Ⓟ**Secretarial Law Ltd** *(M Howson-Green)* Ashton House, 12 The Precinct, Winchester Road, Chandler's Ford, EASTLEIGH, HAMPSHIRE SO53 2GB.
★ⓅⒶ**Seddon Smith, trading name of Seddon Smith Limited** *(D C Seddon)* Milton House, Gatehouse Road, AYLESBURY, BUCKINGHAMSHIRE, HP19 8EA.
ⓅⒶ**Sedulo Business Services Limited** *(D L Clegg)* 42-44 Chorley New Road, BOLTON, BL1 4AP.
ⒻⒶ**Segrave & Pocknell** *(C M Pocknell)* 46 Hullbridge Road, South Woodham Ferrers, CHELMSFORD, CM3 5NG.
★**Sekhar & Tan** *(A B M Don, G K Tan)* Suite 16-8 Level 16, Wisma UOA II, 21 Jalan Pinang, 50450 KUALA LUMPUR, FEDERAL TERRITORY, MALAYSIA.
Ⓟ**Seles Limited** *(R Seligmann)* 17 St. Marys Road, LONDON, NW11 9UE.
Self Assessment Taxation Services *(C C Z Ramsay)* The Barn, The Old Farm House, Pewit Lane, NANTWICH, CHESHIRE, CW5 7PP.
ⓅⒶ**Seligman Percy** *(B E Percy, P M Seligman)* Hilton House, Lord Street, STOCKPORT, SK1 3NA.
ⓉⒻⒶ**Sellens French** *(J French, D A Hargreaves, K Sellens)* 93/97 Bohemia Road, ST. LEONARDS-ON-SEA, EAST SUSSEX, TN37 6RJ.
Ⓟ**Sellers & Co Ltd** *(N D Sellers)* 2a Brookfield Avenue, Bredbury, STOCKPORT, CHESHIRE, SK6 1DF.
Selwyns *(J G Selwyn)* Hillside, Letton Close, BLANDFORD FORUM, DORSET, DT11 7SS.
Senn & Co *(T J Senn)* 36 Robert Moffat, High Legh, KNUTSFORD, CHESHIRE, WA16 6PS.
Ⓟ**Senn Payroll Limited** *(A J Carroll)* 335 Jockey Road, SUTTON COLDFIELD, WEST MIDLANDS, B73 5XE.
Sensible Finance *(E J Judd)* 15 Lower Evingar Road, WHITCHURCH, HAMPSHIRE, RG28 7BX.
Ⓟ**Sentinel Trustees Limited** *(M P Bassford)* 50 Palmerston Road, Wimbledon, LONDON, SW19 1PQ.
★**Sephton & Company LLP** *(P L Houlston)* Marston House, 5 Elmdon Lane, Marston Green, BIRMINGHAM, B37 7DL.
Serco *(S A Rahman)* 133 Nork Way, BANSTEAD, SURREY, SM7 1HR.
Serfaty & Co *(M W Serfaty)* Suite 4 1st Floor, 123 Main Street, GIBRALTAR, GIBRALTAR.
ⓉⒻⒶ**Sergents** *(A W Sergent)* 4 Leyland Street, PRESCOT, MERSEYSIDE, L34 5QP.
Ⓟ**Service Charge Assurance Ltd** *(C Harmer, P Seccombe, T W Slater)* Salatin House, 19 Cedar Road, SUTTON, SURREY, SM2 5DA.
Ⓟ**Service Industry Support Limited** *(B S Connolly)* Covertside, Kings Mill Lane, South Nutfield, REDHILL, RH1 5JX.
Sewell & Co *(S J Sewell)* Rafters, 31 Luton Avenue, BROADSTAIRS, CT10 2DH.
★**Sexty & Co.** *(A M Orves, C B Peck, D S Yapp)* 124 Thorpe Road, NORWICH, NR1 1RS. and at NORTH WALSHAM
Ⓐ**Seymour King** *(S H Kazmi)* 3 Accommodation Road, LONDON, NW11 8ED.
ⓉⒻⓅⒶ**Seymour Taylor, trading name of Seymour Taylor Audit Ltd** *(C J Baker, F W Johnston, S J Turner)* 57 London Road, HIGH WYCOMBE, BUCKINGHAMSHIRE, HP11 1BS.
Ⓟ**SFB Consultants Limited** *(P Carvell, J Sargent, P R White)* 126 Manor Court Road, NUNEATON, WARWICKSHIRE, CV11 5HL.
ⒻⓅ**SG Associates Limited** *(D R Gray)* 82z Portland Place, LONDON, W1B 1NS.
SGB Consulting *(S G Barrell)* Woodridings, Landscape Road, WARLINGHAM, SURREY, CR6 9JB.
SGW & Co *(S G Whitaker)* Fairfields, 39 Main Street, Bunny, NOTTINGHAM, NG11 6QU.
Ⓐ**Shabbir & Co** *(G Shabbir)* 248 Brockley Road, LONDON, SE4 2SF.
Shabir Velji *(S Velji)* 260 Hollingham Rd, UNIONVILLE LR3 8J6, ON, CANADA.
Ⓟ**Shacklefords Limited** *(T D Shackleford)* 3 Essex Road, Four Oaks, SUTTON COLDFIELD, WEST MIDLANDS, B75 6NR.
ⒻⒶ**Shackleton & Co** *(J D Shackleton, M F Shackleton)* 8 Huxley Drive, Bramhall, STOCKPORT, SK7 2PH.
ⓅⒶ**Shacter Cohen & Bor, trading name of SCB (Accountants) Limited** *(J A Bor, E V Cohen)* 31 Sackville Street, MANCHESTER, M1 3LZ.
Shacter Cohen & Bor, trading name of Shacter Cohen & Bor LLP *(J A Bor, E V Cohen)* 31 Sackville Street, MANCHESTER, M1 3LZ.
Ⓟ**Shaddick Consultancy Services Ltd** *(P B Shaddick)* Bank Chambers, 7 Market Street, LEIGH, LANCASHIRE, WN7 1ED.
ⒻⒶ**Shaddick Smith, trading name of Shaddick Smith LLP** *(B Lewis, P B Shaddick)* Bank Chambers, 7 Market Street, LEIGH, LANCASHIRE, WN7 1ED.
Shaffers *(A L Shaffer)* 90 Moorlands Drive, Shirley, SOLIHULL, B90 3RE.
Shafiq & Co *(S Shafiq)* 1 Lark Street, BOLTON, BL1 2UA.
Ⓐ**Shah And Shin** *(M N Shah, Y L Shin)* 42a The Broadway, Joel Street, NORTHWOOD, HA6 1PA.
ⓉⒶ**Shah Dodhia & Co** *(C Shah, S B Shah)* 173 Cleveland Street, LONDON, W1T 6QR.
Shah Patel & Company *(S K Shah)* Laxmi Plaza, Biashara Street, PO Box 41652, NAIROBI, 00100, KENYA.
ⓉⒻⓅⒶ**Shahabuddin & Co Limited** *(K Shahabuddin, K F Shahabuddin, K I Shahabuddin)* Lombard Chambers, Ormond Street, LIVERPOOL, L3 9NA.
ⓅⒶ**Shaik & Co Ltd** *(A A Shaik)* 1145 Oldham Road, Newton Heath, MANCHESTER, M40 2FU.
Shaikh & Co *(M Shaikh)* 174 Canterbury Road, CROYDON, SURREY, CR0 3HE.
Ⓟ**Shan Kennedy, trading name of Shan Kennedy Limited** *(S M Kennedy)* 71 Palewell Park, LONDON, SW14 8JJ.

Shane O'Neill Esq. BA ACA - Simon Storvik & Company Limited **Members in Practice and Firms - Alphabetical**

Shane O'Neill Esq. BA ACA *(S O F O'Neill)* 26 Montreal Street, Levenshulme, MANCHESTER, M19 3BY.

Shanker Iyer & Co *(S Iyer)* 3 Phillip Street, Unit 18-00, Commerce Point, SINGAPORE 048693, SINGAPORE.

ⒻⓅ**Shankley Enterprises Limited** *(D M Shankley)* 32 Market Place, KENDAL, CUMBRIA, LA9 4TN.

ⓉⓅⒶ**Shannon Callister & Co, trading name of Harding Lewis Limited** *(M R Callister, D L Cooper, M J Estella, A M Gerrard)* 34 Athol Street, Douglas, ISLE OF MAN, IM1 1JB.

Shapiro Dymant & Co *(A Shapiro)* 17 Cawkwell Close, CHELMSFORD, CM2 6SG.

Ⓟ**Shapiro Dymant & Co, trading name of October Marketing Limited** *(A Shapiro)* 17 Cawkwell Close, CHELMSFORD, CM2 6SG.

Sharad Badhwar BSc ACA CTA *(S Badhwar)* 17 Balmoral Road, HARROW, MIDDLESEX, HA2 8TF.

ⓅⒶ**Shareef & Co, trading name of Shareef & Co Ltd** *(N M Shareef)* 18-22 Stoney Lane, Yardley, BIRMINGHAM, B25 8YP.

Ⓟ**Shareway, trading name of Shareway Financial Services Limited** *(S Bumpsteed)* Penns Grange, 9 Netherdale Close, Wylde Green, SUTTON COLDFIELD, WEST MIDLANDS, B72 1YW.

Ⓐ**Sharma & Co.** *(S K Sharma)* 5 St. Denys Road, Portswood, SOUTHAMPTON, SO17 2GN.

★ⓉⒶ**Sharman Fielding** *(S F Hardy, A R Patel)* 9 University Road, LEICESTER, LE1 7RA.

Ⓐ**Sharnock & Co** *(P J Sharnock)* First Floor, 8B Lonsdale Gardens, TUNBRIDGE WELLS, KENT, TN1 1NU.

Sharon Faulkner *(S Faulkner)* 6795 Lake Rd, PONCA CITY, OK 74604-5179, UNITED STATES.

Sharon Huffen *(S Huffen)* Woodman House, 18 Main Street, Ryther, TADCASTER, LS24 9EE.

Ⓐ**Sharon Kilbane** *(S A Kilbane)* 87 How Wood, Park Street, ST. ALBANS, HERTFORDSHIRE, AL2 2RW.

Sharon R Ryan *(S R Ryan)* 1 The Limes, Priory Road, SHANKLIN, ISLE OF WIGHT, PO37 6SB.

Sharon Ramdenee *(S Ramdenee)* Deburg Edwards Street, FLOREAL, MAURITIUS.

Ⓟ**Sharp Consulting (UK) Limited** *(J C Sharp)* 182 White Hill, CHESHAM, BUCKINGHAMSHIRE, HP5 1AZ.

Sharpe, Perry & Co. *(G V J Sharpe)* 8 Spring Grove, Woburn Sands, MILTON KEYNES, MK17 8RY.

Ⓣ**Shaw Gibbs LLP** *(A G Caiger, S H Neal, D P O'Connell, L Watson, S J Wetherall)* 264 Banbury Road, OXFORD, OX2 7DY.

ⓅⒶ**Shaw Wallace Limited** *(H V Gadhia)* 43 Manchester Street, LONDON, W1U 7LP.

Ⓟ**Shaws ATS Limited** *(P H Shaw)* Mingulay, Farleton, LANCASTER, LA2 9LF.

★Ⓟ**Shea & Co Limited** *(J B Shea)* 105 Stansted Road, LONDON, SE23 1HH.

ⒻⓅⒶ**Sheards, trading name of Sheards Accountancy Ltd** *(C Atkinson, R J Lay, K Winterburn)* Vernon House, 40 New North Road, HUDDERSFIELD, HD1 5LS.

★**Shears & Dube'** *(S Husain)* Cardinal Point, Park Road, RICKMANSWORTH, HERTFORDSHIRE, WD3 1RE.

ⓅⒶ**Shears & Partners, trading name of Shears & Partners Limited** *(S H Sacks)* 88 Edgware Way, EDGWARE, MIDDLESEX, HA8 8JS.

Ⓟ**Sheen Consulting Services Ltd** *(P T Coulson)* 169 Sheen Lane, LONDON, SW14 8NA.

ⓉⒻⒶ**Sheen Stickland LLP** *(T E James, C A Matthissen, D A Sanders, P J Sharpe, P E H Wright)* 4 High Street, ALTON, HAMPSHIRE, GU34 1BU. and at CHICHESTER

Sheeten Amin *(S R Amin)* 8 Langley Grove, NEW MALDEN, KT3 3AL.

▽**Sheikh & Co** *(M S I Ibrahim)* Aboulela New Building, Gamhoria Street, P O Box 1608, KHARTOUM, 1111, SUDAN.

Shelagh Wilkinson ACA *(S M Wilkinson)* Runtlings Grange, Runtlings, OSSETT, WEST YORKSHIRE, WF5 8JJ.

ⓉⒻⒶ**Shelley & Partners** *(K D Buddhdev, L I Finn)* Brentmead House, Britannia Road, LONDON, N12 9RU.

ⓉⒻⒶ**Shelley Stock Hutter, trading name of Shelley Stock Hutter LLP** *(S P Adler, R W R Churchill, S F Hutter, B Lane, L R Stock)* 7-10 Chandos Street, LONDON, W1G 9DQ.

Shelly Kaufman, trading name of R Kaufman *(R E Kaufman)* 7 Mayfield Gardens, LONDON, NW4 2PY.

Shelvoke, Pickering, Janney & Co *(A G Hough, B Matthews)* 57-61 Market Place, CANNOCK, WS11 1BP.

ⒻⒶ**Shenkers, trading name of Shenkers LLP** *(M M Shenker, R S Shenker)* 5 Wellesley Court, Apsley Way, LONDON, NW2 7HF.

Shepheard Accounting *(M R Shepheard)* Westview, Hayes Lane, Slinfold, HORSHAM, WEST SUSSEX, RH13 0SJ.

Shepherd & Co *(W R Shepherd)* 1st Floor, 4 Fisher Street, CARLISLE, CA3 8RN.

Shepherd & Company *(A C Shepherd)* Old London House, High Street, Stoke Row, HENLEY-ON-THAMES, RG9 5QL.

Ⓟ**Shepherd Accountancy Ltd** *(A E Shepherd)* 27 Nursery Close, HOOK, RG27 9QX.

ⒻⒶ**Shepherd Smail** *(R J Shepherd, A T K Smail)* Northway House, The Forum, CIRENCESTER, GLOUCESTERSHIRE, GL7 2QY.

Ⓐ**Sheppard and Co** *(J M Sheppard)* International House, George Curl Way, SOUTHAMPTON, SO18 2RZ.

ⒻⓅ**Sheppard Rockey & Williams, trading name of Sheppard Rockey & Williams Ltd** *(E T Rockey, S L Williams)* Sannerville Chase, Exminster, EXETER, EX6 8AT.

★ⒻⓅⒶ**Sheppards, trading name of John Sheppard & Co Limited** *(C J Levine)* Oak House, Barrington Road, ALTRINCHAM, CHESHIRE, WA14 1HZ.

★ⒻⓅⒶ**Sheppards, trading name of Sheppards Accountants Limited** *(I F Sheppard)* 22 The Square, The Millfields, PLYMOUTH, PL1 3JX.

ⓅⒶ**Sheridan Brooks Limited** *(S S Jackson, A P Sheridan)* Sheridan Brooks Ltd, 176 Brighton Road, COULSDON, SURREY, CR5 2NF.

ⓉⓅⒶ**Sheridan Clarke Ltd** *(A T Clarke)* Bridge House, 25-27 The Bridge, Wealdstone, HARROW, MIDDLESEX, HA3 5AB.

Sheridan Swallow *(J B S Swallow)* Brickhill House, North Oakley, TADLEY, HAMPSHIRE, RG26 5TT.

Sherman Bass Trent & Co *(B Trent)* 1 Ormonde Court, 70 Parson Street, LONDON, NW4 1RE.

Sherman Chong & Co *(Y S Chong)* Suite 902, 9th Floor, Parkes Commercial Centre, No. 2-8 Parkes Street, TSIM SHA TSUI, KOWLOON HONG KONG SAR.

Ⓐ**Sherrington & Co** *(D Sherrington)* 16 Gold Tops, NEWPORT, GWENT, NP20 4PH.

ⓉⓅⒶ**Sherwood Hall Associates Limited** *(C W Flanagan)* 1st Floor, Langton House, Bird Street, LICHFIELD, STAFFORDSHIRE, WS13 6PY.

Ⓟ**Sherwood Harborne Ltd** *(G P Harborne)* Sherwood House, 548 Birmingham Road, Lydiate Ash, BROMSGROVE, B61 0HT.

★ⓉⒻⒶ**Sherwoods** *(A C Brown)* 30 Addiscombe Grove, CROYDON, CR9 5AY.

Sherwoods *(M H Faulknall)* 1 Ferndale Grove, HINCKLEY, LEICESTERSHIRE, LE10 0EH.

Ⓟ**Sheryl Cain Limited** *(S M Cain)* 237 Sheen Lane, LONDON, SW14 8LE.

Ⓐ**Sheth & Co** *(V P Sheth)* 270-272 Radford Road, COVENTRY, CV6 3BU.

Shewrings *(J A Shewring)* 17 Tynewydd Drive, Castleton, CARDIFF, CF3 2SB.

Ⓟ**Shiakallis & Co Audit Services Ltd** *(N Shiakallis)* 44-46 Acropolis Avenue, 1st Floor Office 101, CY2012 NICOSIA, CYPRUS.

Shillito Partners LLP *(J R Shillito)* 43-45 Portman Square, LONDON, W1H 6HN.

ⓉⒶ**Shimmin Wilson & Co** *(A J Clark-Wilson, A P Shimmin)* 13-15 Hope Street, Douglas, ISLE OF MAN, IM1 1AQ.

Ⓟ**Shine Garfen & Co** *(D L Garfen, G Garfen)* 210 Hendon Way, LONDON, NW4 3NE.

Ⓟ**ShineWing (HK) CPA Limited** *(Y B Ip, W Lo)* 43/F The Lee Gardens, 33 Hysan Avenue, CAUSEWAY BAY, HONG KONG SAR.

Ⓟ**Shinewood Professional Services, trading name of Shinewood Ltd** *(I G Andow)* 4 Orchard Place, Harvington, EVESHAM, WORCESTERSHIRE, WR11 8NF.

★ⓉⒻⒶ**Shipleys LLP** *(G N Fisher, J M A Henman, S J Jeffcott, S A E Jell, S L Joberns, J Kinton, A W Mein, K S Roberts, S W Robinson, S B Ryman, J Sanghrajka, D Vassiliou)* 10 Orange Street, Haymarket, LONDON, WC2H 7DQ. and at BIRMINGHAM, GODALMING, SAFFRON WALDEN

Ⓟ**Shirtcliffe & Co, trading name of Shirtcliffe & Co Limited** *(S J Shirtcliffe)* 668 Woodborough Road, Mapperley, NOTTINGHAM, NG3 5FS.

Shoaie, Zahedi & Co *(C Y H Zahedi, S M A Zahedi)* 10 Clive Avenue, Goring-by-Sea, WORTHING, WEST SUSSEX, BN12 4SG. and at WEMBLEY

ⒻⒶ**Shoesmiths** *(G W Cross, E R Shoesmith)* Suites 1 & 2, Ground Floor, 54 Hagley Road, Edgbaston, BIRMINGHAM, B16 8PE.

Ⓟ**Shoesmiths Business Solutions Ltd** *(E R Shoesmith)* 54 Hagley Road, BIRMINGHAM, B16 8PE.

Ⓟ**Shooter Greene & Co, trading name of Begbies Chettle Agar Ltd** *(R G Maples, J Payne, C P Wain)* Epworth House, 25 City Road, LONDON, EC1Y 1AR.

Shore Accountancy Services *(A C Shore)* Frew Toll Cottage, Thornhill, STIRLING, FK8 3QU.

Ⓟ**Shoreout Services Limited** *(D D Freeman)* Gateway Lodge, 76A Oakleigh Park North, LONDON, N20 9AS.

Shortlands Ltd *(A P G Thompson)* Shortlands, Frimley Road, Ash Vale, ALDERSHOT, HAMPSHIRE, GU12 5PP.

ⓉⒶ**Shorts** *(P D Beeson, J A Bown, J A Brier, H K Freeman, P E Freeman, M P Pope)* 6 Fairfield Road, CHESTERFIELD, DERBYSHIRE, S40 4TP. and at SHEFFIELD

Ⓟ**Shorts (Management Consultants) Ltd** *(M J Short)* 7 Waterloo Road, WHITSTABLE, KENT, CT5 1BP.

Shrinivas Honap *(S M Honap)* 178 Kineton Green Road, SOLIHULL, B92 7ES.

Shroff & Associates *(C P Shroff)* Flat 52 5t Floor, Goolestan Building, (Besides Mahalaxmi Temple), 34 Bhulabhai Desai Road, MUMBAI 400 026, INDIA.

ⓉⒶ**Shroff Accountancy Services** *(J Shroff)* Excel House, 1 Hornminster Glen, HORNCHURCH, RM11 3XL.

Ⓟ**Shu Lun Pan Horwath Hong Kong CPA Limited** *(P Li)* 20th Floor, Central Plaza, 18 Harbour Road, WAN CHAI, HONG KONG ISLAND, HONG KONG SAR.

Ⓟ**Shu Lun Pan Horwath Hong Kong CPA Limited** *(S H Ng)* 2001-2005 Central Plaza, 18 Harbour Road, WAN CHAI, HONG KONG ISLAND, HONG KONG SAR.

★ⒻⒶ**Shulman & Company** *(N Shulman)* 52 Redington Road, Hampstead, LONDON, NW3 7RS.

Sian Tindal *(S A Tindal)* The Brew House, School Lane, Cookham, MAIDENHEAD, BERKSHIRE, SL6 9QN.

Ⓐ**Siba & Co** *(M Siba)* 308 High Street, CROYDON, CR0 1NG.

Ⓟ**Sibbald Young, trading name of S Y Accountancy Services Ltd** *(P Sibbald, T K Young)* Unit 6D Planet Business Centre, Planet Place, West Moor, NEWCASTLE UPON TYNE, NE12 6DY.

ⓉⓅⒶ**Sibbalds, trading name of Sibbalds Ltd** *(T B Grant, H O Vasdev)* Oakhurst House, 57 Ashbourne Road, DERBY, DE22 3FS.

ⓉⓅⒶ**Sidaways Limited** *(J F J Sidaway, S A Sidaway)* Unit 5, Providence Court, Pynes Hill, EXETER, EX2 5JL.

Sidery & Co *(G J Sidery)* Ashfield, Wrexham Road, CHESTER, CH4 7QQ.

Sidikies *(A Siddiqi)* 1-3 Sun Street, LONDON, EC2A 2EP.

Sidney A. Beale & Co. *(S A Beale)* 338 Yardley Road, Yardley, BIRMINGHAM, B25 8LT.

Sidney Berman FCA *(S Berman)* 24 Riverside Gardens, LONDON, N3 3GR.

Ⓣ**Sigma Partnership, trading name of Sigma 2002 LLP** *(M J Crisp, A Dysch, J L P Seet)* 45-47 Cornhill, LONDON, EC3V 3PF.

ⓉⒻⒶ**Sigma Solutions, trading name of Smailes Goldie** *(J N Allison, P D Duffield, I R Lamb, M Overfield, J M Sharpley, N Shipley)* Regents Court, Princess Street, HULL, HU2 8BA. and at BARTON-UPON-HUMBER

ⓉⓅ**Sigma, trading name of Alhambra Accounting Limited** *(J Yakoob)* Crown House, 28 George Street, BIRMINGHAM, B12 9RG.

Sigma, trading name of Sigma (Accounting Tax & Business Advice) LLP *(P S James)* Vale House, Over Compton, SHERBORNE, DORSET, DT9 4QS.

ⓉⓅⒶ**Sigma, trading name of Sigmaca Ltd** *(N Malik)* J O Hunter House, 409 Bradford Road, HUDDERSFIELD, HD2 2RB.

Ⓟ**Signet Accounting Services Limited** *(D A Brazier)* 7 Gloucester Road, BARNET, HERTFORDSHIRE, EN5 1RS.

Ⓟ**Signia Associates, trading name of Signia Associates Ltd** *(A Chiotis)* 103 First Floor, 100 Pall Mall, St James London, LONDON, SW1Y 5NQ.

ⒻⓅ**Signia Corporate Finance, trading name of Signia Corporate Finance Limited** *(S Lees)* Springfield, Macclesfield Road, ALDERLEY EDGE, CHESHIRE, SK9 7BW.

ⓉⒻⓅⒶ**Silbury, trading name of Silbury Business Advisers Ltd** *(C E Baylis, A C Eustace)* Venture House, Calne Road, Lyneham, CHIPPENHAM, WILTSHIRE, SN15 4PP.

Ⓟ**Silbury, trading name of Silbury Woking Ltd** *(J R Aughterson, C E Baylis, A C Eustace)* Elizabeth House, Duke Street, WOKING, SURREY, GU21 5AS.

ⓅⒶ**Silfern Accountancy, trading name of Silfern Limited** *(B C Hogg)* 2 Market Lane, Selby, SELBY, NORTH YORKSHIRE, YO8 4QA.

ⓉⒻⒶ**Silk & Co** *(A P Silk)* 23 Havelock Road, HASTINGS, TN34 1BP.

ⓉⒻⒶ**Silver & Co** *(P J Silver)* The Hollies, 16 St. Johns Street, BRIDGNORTH, SHROPSHIRE, WV15 6AG. and at CANNOCK, STAFFORD, WOLVERHAMPTON

Silver Levene LLP *(M I Franks, P R A Grossmark, H E Mehta, U J Modi, R B Perez, C C Rosenthal)* 37 Warren Street, LONDON, W1T 6AD.

★Ⓕ**Silver, Sevket & Co** *(S Sevket)* 16 Bromley Road, BECKENHAM, KENT, BR3 5JE.

Ⓟ**Silverghost Consultancy Ltd** *(H W S Royse)* 11 Warrens Way, Tacolneston, NORWICH, NR16 1DH.

ⒻⓅ**Silvermans, trading name of Silvermans AP Limited** *(J A Silverman)* 2 Castleham Court, 180 High Street, EDGWARE, MIDDLESEX, HA8 7EX.

ⓅⒶ**Silverstone Group, trading name of Silverstone Audit Limited** *(N D Beeson, N G Jones)* Fairfield Farm Cottage, Upper Weald, MILTON KEYNES, MK19 6EL.

Ⓟ**Silvertribe Limited** *(H W Johnston)* 7 Manor Farm Way, Seer Green, BEACONSFIELD, HP9 2YD.

Silvester Parker & Co, trading name of Silvester Parker & Co LLP *(C M Silvester)* The Spinney, Beausale, WARWICK, CV35 7NU.

Ⓐ**Sim Kapila** *(R Kapila, G E Sim)* St. George's House, 14-17 Wells Street, LONDON, W1T 3PD.

Ⓟ**Simalls Limited** *(S D Hall)* PO Box 773, Charles Bisson House, 30-32 New Street, St Helier, JERSEY, JE4 0RZ.

★**Simia Wall, trading name of Fisher Berger & Associates** *(B J Fisher)* Devonshire House, 582 Honeypot Lane, STANMORE, MIDDLESEX, HA7 1JS. and at LONDON

Simm Associates *(M Simm)* Hillside Cottage, Agneash, Lonan, ISLE OF MAN, IM4 7NS.

Ⓕ**Simmonds & Co** *(G M Simmonds)* 23 Links Way, NORTHWOOD, HA6 2XA. and at LONDON

ⓉⒻⒶ**Simmons Gainsford LLP** *(P Austin, O A H W Dodd, J Goldman, S M Jennings, A Pisavadi, M S Pizer, D J Pumfrey, C G Stebbing, S M Strauss, H Sze, R C Thakerar)* 5th Floor, 7-10 Chandos Street, Cavendish Square, LONDON, W1G 9DQ. and at UCKFIELD

★**Simms Hanson** *(R H Simms)* 51 Windy Arbour, KENILWORTH, WARWICKSHIRE, CV8 2BB.

Simon Bevan *(S J P Bevan)* Cheviot View, Holy Island, BERWICK-UPON-TWEED, TD15 2SQ.

Simon Bown Associates *(S E Bown)* Highfield Court, Highfield Park, Creaton, NORTHAMPTON, NN6 8NT.

ⓅⒶ**Simon Coles & Co, trading name of Simon Coles Limited** *(S G Coles)* P O Box 600, LONDON, WC1H 0XB.

Simon Cowley *(S C Cowley)* 73 Arthur Road, LONDON, SW19 7DP.

Ⓐ**Simon Cross** *(S G Cross)* 34 Church Avenue, Swillington, LEEDS, LS26 8QH.

Simon D H Pullar *(S D H Pullar)* Monks Tower, Honeywood Lane, Okewood Hill, DORKING, RH5 5PZ.

Ⓟ**Simon Day & Co, trading name of Simon Day Limited** *(S Day)* Unit 2, Uffcott Farm, Uffcott, SWINDON, SN4 9NB.

Ⓟ**Simon Goldstrong ACA, trading name of Goldstrong Accountants Ltd** *(S K Goldstrong)* 55 Heaton Road, Grange Park, BILLINGHAM, CLEVELAND, TS23 3GP.

Simon Granger *(S J Granger)* Little Mede, Blundel Lane, Stoke D'Abernon, COBHAM, KT11 2SF.

Simon Groves & Co *(S N Groves)* 227 Cassiobury Drive, WATFORD, HERTFORDSHIRE, WD17 3AN.

Simon J Ackers *(S J Ackers)* 37 Brandreth Drive, Parbold, WIGAN, LANCASHIRE, WN8 7HB.

Ⓟ**Simon J Gibson, trading name of Simon J Gibson Limited** *(S J Gibson)* 7 Eskdale Close, Sleights, WHITBY, YO22 5EW.

Ⓟ**Simon John Christopher Ltd** *(S J Christopher)* First Floor Suite, Drapers House, Market Place, STURMINSTER NEWTON, DORSET, DT10 1AS. and at BRIDPORT

Simon Kingsley *(S P D S J Kingsley)* 58 Montague Road, Hackney, LONDON, E8 2HW.

Ⓟ**Simon Ling & Co, trading name of Simon Ling & Co Ltd** *(S J Ling)* Woodstock House, 29a Agates Lane, ASHTEAD, SURREY, KT21 2ND.

ⒻⒶ**Simon Murray & Co** *(S A Murray)* Woburn House, YELVERTON, PL20 6BS.

Simon N. Cowman *(S N Cowman)* Mayfield, 8 Brooksby Road, Hoby, MELTON MOWBRAY, LEICESTERSHIRE, LE14 3EA.

Ⓟ**Simon Owers, trading name of Simon Owers Corporate Limited** *(S J Owers)* Fairfield Cottage, Warrington Road, Great Budworth, NORTHWICH, CHESHIRE, CW9 6HB.

Simon S W Lui & Co *(S Lui)* Bank Centre 1013, Nathan Road 636, MONG KOK, KOWLOON, HONG KONG SAR.

★Ⓕ**Simon Silver-Myer** *(M J Simon)* 8 Durweston Street, LONDON, W1H 1EW.

ⓅⒶ**Simon Speller Limited** *(S J Speller)* 64 Clarendon Road, WATFORD, WD17 1DA.

Ⓟ**Simon Storvik & Company Limited** *(S Storvik)* 7 Rockleaze Avenue, BRISTOL, BS9 1NG.

Members in Practice and Firms - Alphabetical   Simon Tee Business Services Limited - Sopher + Co

ⓅⒶ**Simon Tee Business Services Limited** *(S R Tee)* Cedar House, Hazell Drive, NEWPORT, GWENT, NP10 8FY.

Simon Tesler And Associates *(S Tesler)* 149 Albion Road, LONDON, N16 9JU.

Ⓟ**Simon Whiteley Consulting Limited** *(S W A Whiteley, W Whiteley)* 74 Lyndhurst Grove, LONDON, SE15 5AH.

Ⓐ**Simon Winegarten and Co** *(S Winegarten)* 13 Hurstdene Gardens, LONDON, N15 6NA.

Ⓟ**Simone Harvey, trading name of SLH Accounting Ltd** *(S L Harvey)* 62a High Street, Hampton Hill, HAMPTON, MIDDLESEX, TW12 1PD.

★ⓉⒻⒶ**Simpkins Edwards, trading name of Simpkins Edwards LLP** *(D G Clapp, J L Coombs, A Hemmings, J C House, I A Huggett, C J Nightingale, L Sommerville-Woodward, J M Watson)* Michael House, Castle Street, EXETER, EX4 3LQ. and at BARNSTAPLE, HOLSWORTHY, OKEHAMPTON

Ⓟ**Simple Debt Solutions, trading name of Simple Debt Solutions Limited** *(S R Penn, A Poxon, J M Titley)* D T E House, Hollins Mount, BURY, LANCASHIRE, BL9 8AT.

Ⓟ**Simplified Accounting Limited** *(R A Savage)* 34 Brackley Road, TOWCESTER, NORTHAMPTONSHIRE, NN12 6DJ.

Simply Accounting *(R A Board)* 39 Barnfield, CREDITON, DEVON, EX17 3HS.

Ⓟ**Simply Churches, trading name of Simply Churches Limited** *(J M M Helm)* 17 Heathville Road, LONDON, N19 3AL.

ⒻⓅⒶ**Simpson & Co, trading name of Simpson & Co (Accountants) Limited** *(M D R Shave, L A Simpson)* 21 High Street, LUTTERWORTH, LEICESTERSHIRE, LE17 4AT.

Ⓟ**Simpson Accountants, trading name of Simpson Accountants Limited** *(P E Simpson)* 24 Oxfield Park Drive, Old Stratford, MILTON KEYNES, MK19 6DP.

Ⓟ**Simpson Associates, trading name of Simpson & Associates (Accountants) Limited** *(A Simpson)* 23 Browning Avenue, BOURNEMOUTH, DORSET, BH5 1NR.

ⓅⒶ**Simpson Burgess Nash, trading name of Simpson Burgess Nash Ltd** *(M L Burgess, R M Simpson)* Ground Floor, Maclaren House, Lancastrian Office Centre, Talbot Road, Old Trafford, MANCHESTER M32 0FP.

ⓉⒶ**Simpson Wood** *(P J Carson, G D T Cliffe, M Fielding, D J McAllister, C M Stratford)* Bank Chambers, Market Street, HUDDERSFIELD, HD1 2EW. and at SHEFFIELD

ⓉⒻⒶ**Simpson Wreford & Partners** *(C J Atkinson, T P Lindfield, A Weaks, D J Wilkes)* Suffolk House, George Street, CROYDON, CR0 0YN.

★ⓉⒻⒶ**Simpson, Wreford & Co** *(C A Graham, K W J Saunders)* Wellesley House, Duke of Wellington Avenue, Royal Arsenal, LONDON, SE18 6SS.

ⒻⓅⒶ**Simpsons, trading name of J L Simpson Ltd** *(D W Richards)* Hunters, Headley Road, Grayshott, HINDHEAD, SURREY, GU26 6DL.

Ⓕ**Simson Jones** *(B M Jones)* Calle Ostrero, Posthouse Suite 88, Chiclana, 11130 CADIZ, SPAIN.

Sinclair & Co *(D A P Sinclair)* 10 Colson Road, CROYDON, CR0 6UA.

ⓅⒶ**Sinclair & Co, trading name of Sinclair & Co (Accountants) Limited** *(F D Robinson)* 7 Portland Road, Edgbaston, BIRMINGHAM, B16 9HN.

ⒻⓅ**Sinclair Associates, trading name of Sinclair UK Associates Limited** *(D G Sinclair)* Roman House, 296 Golders Green Road, LONDON, NW11 9PT.

Sinclair Harris *(J H Sinclair)* 46 Vivian Avenue, Hendon Central, LONDON, NW4 3XP.

ⒻⓅⒶ**Sinclairs, trading name of Sinclairs Carston Ltd** *(K M Munn, R J O Rees)* 32 Queen Anne Street, LONDON, W1G 8HD.

Singhania Associates *(S Singhania)* 25 Lodge Close, HUNTINGDON, CAMBRIDGESHIRE, PE29 6GR.

Ⓟ**Singla & Co Ltd** *(S K Singla)* 12 Devereux Court, LONDON, WC2R 3JJ.

Sinnett & Co *(S J Sinnett)* 61-63 Church Street, Caversham, READING, RG4 8AX.

ⓅⒶ**Sinnett & Tansley Limited** *(H T W Goodman, D S Tansley)* 3 Richfield Place, Richfield Avenue, READING, RG1 8EQ.

Ⓟ**Sirius Business Solutions Limited** *(J Flynn)* 2 Wimpole Close, YORK, YO30 5GG.

SIS *(M M Pissourios, S E Socratous, E E Sykopetritis)* 38 Karaiskaki Street, KANIKA Alexander Center, Block 1, Office 113 C/D, PC 3032 LIMASSOL, CYPRUS.

Siva Palan & Co. *(K Sivapalan)* 69-75 Boston Manor Road, BRENTFORD, MIDDLESEX, TW8 9JJ.

Ⓣ**Siva Yogan & Co** *(N Ariaratnam)* Hounslow Business Park, Unit 6, HOUNSLOW, TW3 3UD.

Ⓟ**SJ Ferriter, trading name of S&J Accounting Services Ltd** *(S J Ferriter)* 65 Chestnut Grove, Wilmington, DARTFORD, DA2 7PQ. and at WILMINGTON

★Ⓣ**SJ Grant Thornton** *(N K Jasani)* No 11, Faber Imperial Court, Jalan Sultan Ismail, 50250 KUALA LUMPUR, FEDERAL TERRITORY, MALAYSIA.

SJ Griffiths Consultancy *(S J Griffiths)* 16 Glenfield Close, SUTTON COLDFIELD, WEST MIDLANDS, B76 1LD.

Ⓟ**SJ Males & Co, trading name of SJ Males & Co Limited** *(C J Males)* Basepoint Business & Innovation Centre, 110 Butterfield, Great Marlings, LUTON, BEDFORDSHIRE, LU2 8DL.

SJ Morrell *(S J Morrell)* The Triangle, Grafton Villas, Crossgates, LEEDS, LS15 8SH.

SJB *(S Brook)* Pleasant Place, The Street, Great Tey, COLCHESTER, CO6 1JS.

SJB & Co *(S J Bell)* 8 Barnfield, Feering, COLCHESTER, CO5 9HP.

Ⓟ**SJB Accounting Ltd** *(S J G Briginshaw)* 24 Elstow Avenue, Caversham, READING, RG4 6RX.

SJH Accountancy *(S Hakeem)* 295 Evesham Road, REDDITCH, WORCESTERSHIRE, B97 5HL.

SJR Associates *(S J Roberts)* 5 Rodens Close, Rossett, WREXHAM, CLWYD, LL12 0EZ.

Ⓟ**SJS Tax, trading name of SJS Tax Limited** *(S J Saady)* Symal House, Suite C2, 423 Edgware Road, LONDON, NW9 0HU.

Skeeles & Zanini *(J W Skeeles)* 1a Bearton Green, HITCHIN, SG5 1UN.

Ⓕ**Skingle Helps & Co** *(J V R Helps)* 28 Southway, Carshalton Beeches, CARSHALTON, SURREY, SM5 4HW.

Skinner & Co *(D J Skinner)* The Old Vicarage, 10 Church Street, RICKMANSWORTH, HERTFORDSHIRE, WD3 1BS.

ⒻⓅⒶ**SKM, trading name of SKM Accountants (North West) Ltd** *(S Mahomed)* Pegasus House, 5 Winckley Court, Mount Street, PRESTON, PR1 8BU.

★Ⓟ**SKN, trading name of SKN Services Ltd** *(S Uddin)* SKN Business Centre, 1 Guildford Street, BIRMINGHAM, B19 2HN.

ⒻⓅ**Skye Corporate Finance, trading name of Skye Corporate Finance Limited** *(J G Sykes)* 307 High Road, Chilwell, Beeston, NOTTINGHAM, NG9 5DL.

Ⓟ**SL Accountancy Ltd** *(S D Cohen)* Lear House, 259 Cranbrook Road, ILFORD, ESSEX, IG1 4TG.

Ⓟ**SL Accountants Ltd** *(S E Green, L A Hartley)* 294 Warwick Road, SOLIHULL, WEST MIDLANDS, B92 7AF.

Ⓟ**SLA Tax Ltd** *(S E Green, L A Hartley)* 17 Jacobean Lane, Knowle, SOLIHULL, WEST MIDLANDS, B93 8LD.

ⓅⒶ**Slade & Cooper, trading name of Slade & Cooper Limited** *(P M Cowham)* 6 Mount Street, MANCHESTER, M2 5NS.

Ⓐ**Slaney & Co** *(C G H Jubb, R K Ryder)* 26 St. John Street, MANSFIELD, NOTTINGHAMSHIRE, NG18 1QJ. and at WORKSOP

ⒻⒶ**Slater Johnstone** *(E R Slater, F C Slater)* 3 Thimble Lane, Knowle, SOLIHULL, WEST MIDLANDS, B93 0LY.

ⓉⒻⒶ**Slaters** *(S P Slater)* Lymore Villa, 162a London Road, Chesterton, NEWCASTLE, STAFFORDSHIRE, ST5 7JB.

SLD Accountants *(S L Conway)* 30 Wyatt Place, Strood, ROCHESTER, KENT, ME2 2DQ.

Ⓟ**Sleigh & Story, trading name of Sleigh & Story Limited** *(D J Story)* 46b Bradford Road, BRIGHOUSE, WEST YORKSHIRE, HD6 1RY.

SLL Accounts *(S L Lacey)* Burnside, Station Road, EDENBRIDGE, KENT, TN8 5NB.

ⒻⒶ**Sloan & Co** *(R B Alvis, S W Kayne)* Granite Buildings, 6 Stanley Street, LIVERPOOL, L1 6AF.

Ⓟ**Sloane Walker, trading name of Sloane Walker Ltd** *(N T Walker)* 33 Rosedale Close, Hardwicke, GLOUCESTER, GL2 4JL. and at OTTERY ST. MARY

ⓉⒻⓅⒶ**Sloane Winckless & Co, trading name of Sloane Winckless & Co Limited** *(Neil A R Winckless)* Britannia Chambers, 181-185 High Street, NEW MALDEN, SURREY, KT3 4BH.

SM & Co *(S E Marsh)* 1 Cranmer House, Maybush Lane, FELIXSTOWE, SUFFOLK, IP11 7NA.

Ⓟ**Small Business Centre, trading name of SB Centre Ltd** *(J Piper)* 14 Somer Fields, LYME REGIS, DT7 3EL.

Ⓟ**Smallfield, Cody & Co.** *(M A Kennedy)* 5 Harley Place, Harley Street, LONDON, W1G 8QD.

Smart & Co. *(D M Smart)* 17 Liverpool Road, WORTHING, BN11 1SU.

Ⓟ**SMB Total Accounting Limited** *(S Blitz)* 14 Edgecliffe Drive, ILFORD, ESSEX, IG6 1LL.

★Ⓟ**SME Accountancy Limited** *(S K Bhaduri, U K Ray)* 46-48 High Street, BARNET, HERTFORDSHIRE, EN5 5SJ.

Ⓟ**SME Accounting Services Ltd** *(L Coulson)* 24 Speen Lane, Speen, NEWBURY, BERKSHIRE, RG14 1RN.

Ⓟ**SME Corporate Finance Limited** *(J S Jeffrey)* Suite 6, 43 Bedford Street, LONDON, WC2E 9HA.

Ⓟ**SME Payroll Services Limited** *(S J T Askew, R J Calderwood)* Denning House, 1 London Road, MAIDSTONE, KENT, ME16 8HS. and at DEAL

Smethers & Co *(N Smethers)* 41 Albion Road, Pitstone, LEIGHTON BUZZARD, LU7 9AY.

ⓉⒻⓅⒶ**Smethurst & Buckton, trading name of Smethurst & Buckton Ltd** *(P T Gallant, J M Mulholland)* 12 Abbey Road, GRIMSBY, SOUTH HUMBERSIDE, DN32 0HL.

Ⓟ**Smith & Eades, trading name of Eades Limited** *(N P Smith)* 2b Haddo Street, Greenwich, LONDON, SE10 9RN.

ⓉⒻⓅ**Smith & Williamson Ltd** *(S J Adshead, F A M Akers-Douglas, D P Alexander, J C Appleton, C P Aylott, J Barnes, M D Bishop, D J Blenkarn, J T Boadle, A D Bond, I T Burns, N J Cartwright, I S Cooper, W P Cotton, M R Courtney, J H Dalrymple, C Deane, H V Demuth, S D Drew, A J Edmonds, P F Garwood, R D Green, D J Hall, R P H Harris, G J Healy, K Jackman, Y J Lang, M D Lea, N Lee, B K Livingston, T J Lyford, S J Mabey, J C B Major, R F Mannion, M K McMullen, P E Moody, D J Mouncey, G A S G Murphy, J A Mutton, M J Neale, N C Osler, J N Oswell, G A Palfrey, G D Pearce, J A Peters, A J Pryor, P A Quigley, N J Reeve, G A Rigby, D W Roper, P J Sayers, J R Selden, R Sharma, N S Simmonds, D A Smart, K L Smith, A C Spicer, K P Stopps, J M Talbot, S L Thompson, P W Treadgold, A Walton, A T R Wilkes, M J Wingate)* 25 Moorgate, LONDON, EC2R 6AY. and at BELFAST, BIRMINGHAM, BRISTOL, DUBLIN, GLASGOW, GUILDFORD, SALISBURY, SOUTHAMPTON, WORCESTER

★Ⓟ**Smith Austin, trading name of Smith Austin Limited** *(N J Smith)* 50 Hoyland Road, Hoyland Common, BARNSLEY, S74 0PB.

ⓉⒻⓅⒶ**Smith Cookson, trading name of Smith Cookson Accountants Limited** *(I Dutton)* 4 Yorke Street, Hucknall, NOTTINGHAM, NG15 7BT.

★ⓉⒶ**Smith Cooper** *(C L Beachell, J A Cope, A R Delve, P W Duffin, A M Durbin, J P Farnsworth, R G Hives, B J Montgomery, J Morgan, J C Taylor, S R Tysoe, G J Whiting)* 2 Lace Market Square, NOTTINGHAM, NG1 1PB. and at ALFRETON, ASHBOURNE, BIRMINGHAM, BURTON-ON-TRENT, BUXTON, DERBY, ILKESTON, LEICESTER

★ⓅⒶ**Smith Cooper Nottingham, trading name of F B 40 Limited** *(A R Delve, P W Duffin, J C Taylor, S R Tysoe, G J Whiting)* 2 Lace Market Square, NOTTINGHAM, NG1 1PB.

★ⓉⒻⒶ**Smith Craven** *(A R Cribb, K Fitton, H R Mee, W S Reay)* Kelham House, Kelham Street, DONCASTER, DN1 3RE. and at CHESTERFIELD, SHEFFIELD, WORKSOP

ⓅⒶ**Smith Emmerson Audit Limited** *(P Emmerson)* H5 Ash Tree Court, Mellors Way, Nottingham Business Park, NOTTINGHAM, NG8 6PY.

★**Smith Emmerson, trading name of Smith Emmerson Accountants LLP** *(P Emmerson)* H5 Ash Tree Court, Nottingham Business Park, NOTTINGHAM, NG8 6PY.

ⒻⓅ**Smith Kennedy Limited** *(A J Kennedy)* 14 Stanton Harcourt Road, WITNEY, OXFORDSHIRE, OX28 3LD.

ⓉⓅⒶ**Smith Malhotra Limited** *(R Malhotra)* 40-42 High Street, Newington, SITTINGBOURNE, KENT, ME9 7JL. and at WEST MALLING

Ⓟ**Smith McBride, trading name of Smith McBride Limited** *(J C Smith)* Copthall Bridge House, Station Bridge, HARROGATE, NORTH YORKSHIRE, HG1 1SP.

Smith Mercia Accountancy Services *(D Smith)* 4 Sudeley, Dosthill, TAMWORTH, B77 1JR.

Ⓟ**Smith Munir Accountancy, trading name of Smith Munir Accountancy Limited** *(J B Smith)* First Floor, 1 Edmund Street, BRADFORD, BD5 0BH.

Smith Partnership *(R A Smith)* 5 Sedgefield Drive, Thurnby, LEICESTER, LE7 9PT.

ⒻⓅⒶ**Smith Pearman, trading name of Smith Pearman Limited** *(K J Hardy, T E Hardy)* Hurst House, High Street, Ripley, WOKING, SURREY, GU23 6AY.

★ⓉⒻⒶ**Smith, Hodge & Baxter** *(A P Armer, I J Chown, J G Hatcher)* Thorpe House, 93 Headlands, KETTERING, NN15 6BL.

★**Smithaston** *(T Smith)* The Royal, 25 Bank Plain, NORWICH, NR2 4SF.

ⓉⒻⒶ**Smithfield Accountants LLP** *(E Poli)* 117 Charterhouse Street, LONDON, EC1M 6AA.

Smiths *(C M Smith)* P O Box 487, PORT MORESBY, PAPUA NEW GUINEA.

Smiths *(M R Smith)* Unit 114, Boston House, Grove Technology Park, WANTAGE, OX12 9FF.

Ⓟ**Smiths Accounting & Tax, trading name of SATS Ltd** *(A P Smith)* Milton House, Gatehouse Road, AYLESBURY, HP19 8EA.

ⓅⒶ**SMJH Limited** *(S Harries)* Woodfield House, Castle Walk, NEATH, WEST GLAMORGAN, SA11 3LN.

Ⓟ**SMP Accounting and Tax Limited** *(A J Dowling, P N Eckersley, J J Scott, S J Turner)* PO Box 227, Clinch's House, Lord Street, Douglas, ISLE OF MAN, IM99 1RZ.

Ⓟ**SMR Associates, trading name of SMR Business & Tax Associates Limited** *(S M Ruback)* 25 Woodhall Gate, PINNER, MIDDLESEX, HA5 4TN.

ⓉⒻⓅⒶ**SMS Abacus & Co Ltd** *(J C Mehta, K Shahabuddin, K F Shahabuddin)* Rowlandson House, 289-293 Ballards Lane, LONDON, N12 8NP.

Ⓟ**Smyth & Co, trading name of Smyth & Co Limited** *(G D Smyth)* 4 High Street, Langford, BIGGLESWADE, BEDFORDSHIRE, SG18 9RR.

SN Bartarya & Co, trading name of S.N. Bartarya *(S N Bartarya)* 75 Weston Street, LONDON, SE1 3RS. and at OBERARTH

ⓅⒶ**Snedkers Accountants Ltd** *(N D Snedker)* Angel House, Hardwick, WITNEY, OXFORDSHIRE, OX29 7QE.

ⓅⒶ**Sneekers & Co, trading name of S Nunn & Co Limited** *(S M Nunn)* Unit 2, Guards Avenue, The Village, CATERHAM, SURREY, CR3 5XL.

★**Snelson & Co** *(K Snelson)* 26 Denholme, Upholland, SKELMERSDALE, WN8 0AU.

Ⓟ**SNH Tax, trading name of SN Hayes Tax Partners Ltd** *(A M Hayes)* PO Box 318, 9 Hope Street, St Helier, JERSEY, JE4 9XQ.

SNK *(S Kazamia)* 13 Machera Street, 2650 NICOSIA, CYPRUS.

Ⓐ**Snowdon Robertson & Co** *(A W S Robertson)* The Old Pheasant, Parmoor, Hambleden, HENLEY-ON-THAMES, RG9 6NH.

Ⓟ**Soar Valley Accountancy Services Limited** *(S J McAra)* 49 High Street, Kegworth, DERBY, DE74 2DA.

Soares & Co. *(A L S Soares)* 1A Colin Parade, Edgware Road Colindale, LONDON, NW9 6SG.

ⒻⒶ**Sobell Rhodes LLP** *(S J Arnold)* 1st Floor Monument House, 215 Marsh Road, PINNER, MIDDLESEX, HA5 5NE. and at LONDON

★ⓉⒻⓅⒶ**Sochall Smith Limited** *(A S Charles, D J G Paylor)* 3 Park Square, LEEDS, LS1 2NE. and at MIDDLESBROUGH, SHEFFIELD

★Ⓐ**Sochalls** *(B D Sochall)* 9 Wimpole Street, LONDON, W1G 9SR.

Sohans *(M Singh)* 44a Bradford Street, WALSALL, WEST MIDLANDS, WS1 3QA.

ⓅⒶ**Solazzo & Co Ltd** *(S Solazzo)* Woodlands, 27 Ferney Road, Cheshunt, WALTHAM CROSS, EN7 6XQ.

Ⓟ**Solution 121 Limited** *(C P Bodimeade)* Brandon House, King Street, KNUTSFORD, CHESHIRE, WA16 6DX.

Ⓐ**Solutions 4 Business LLP** *(J F O'Mahony, J S T O'Mahony)* 5 Fairmile, HENLEY-ON-THAMES, OXFORDSHIRE, RG9 2JR.

ⓉⓅ**Solutions 4 Caterers, trading name of Your Finance Team Limited** *(P E Flaxman)* The Meads Business Centre, 19 Kingsmead, FARNBOROUGH, HAMPSHIRE, GU14 7SR.

Ⓟ**Solutions For Evolution, trading name of Solutions For Evolution Limited** *(D V Buxton)* Ampney House, Falcon Close, Quedgeley, GLOUCESTER, GL2 4LS.

ⒻⓅⒶ**Somerbys, trading name of Somerbys Limited** *(M P Jinks, A R West)* 30 Nelson Street, LEICESTER, LE1 7BA.

Ⓟ**Somerfield Consultants Limited** *(M A Collier, M J Hurdman, K Luxford, J A Williamson)* West Hill, 61 London Road, MAIDSTONE, KENT, ME16 8TX.

Somers Baker Prince Kurz LLP *(S L Kurz, F M Weinberg)* 45 Ealing Road, WEMBLEY, HA0 4BA.

Ⓟ**Somersby Consulting Limited** *(S R Adcock)* 100 Somersby Road, Woodthorpe, NOTTINGHAM, NG5 4LT.

Ⓐ**Somerton & Co** *(R N Bharkhada)* Challenge House, 616 Mitcham Road, CROYDON, CR0 3AA.

Sonam Frasi & Co *(S T Frasi)* The Bridge House, 256a Ladysmith Road, ENFIELD, MIDDLESEX, EN1 3AF.

Sonneborn & Co *(P M Sonneborn)* High Holborn House, 52-54 High Holborn, LONDON, WC1V 6RL.

Soon & Associates *(P S Soon)* 8 Jalan Edgecumbe, 10250 PENANG, MALAYSIA.

★ⓉⒻⒶ**Sopher + Co** *(I Sopher)* 5 Elstree Gate, Elstree Way, BOREHAMWOOD, HERTFORDSHIRE, WD6 1JD. and at LONDON

Ⓟ**Sopher + Traqs International Taxation Limited** *(D R M Sopher, I Sopher)* 38 Berkeley Square, LONDON, W1J 5AL.

Sophia Dickens BSc ACA *(S E Dickens)* 27 West Way, HARPENDEN, AL5 4RD.

Sophie Peters *(S E Peters)* 33 Park Road, BURY ST. EDMUNDS, SUFFOLK, IP33 3QW.

Sophie Trafford *(S C Trafford)* Church Lodge, Station Road, Wrington, BRISTOL, BS40 5LG.

Sophie Wheeler *(S E Wheeler)* Church Farm, Podington, WELLINGBOROUGH, NORTHAMPTONSHIRE, NN29 7HS.

Ⓟ**Sorrell, trading name of Sorrell Ltd** *(J S Sorrell)* Glaven Farm Barn, Thornage Road, Letheringsett, HOLT, NORFOLK, NR25 7JE.

ⒾⒻⒶ**Soteriou Banerji** *(P T Soteriou, R Soteriou)* 253 Grays Inn Road, LONDON, WC1X 8QT.

ⓅⒶ**Soteriou Christou, trading name of Soteriou Christou Ltd** *(P Soteriou)* 6a Dickenson's Place, LONDON, SE25 5HL.

Sotinwa Business Services *(K A Sotinwa)* 51 Elm Park, READING, RG30 2HT.

Soulla Clarkson *(C L Clarkson)* Rowgate, Thorpe Bassett, MALTON, NORTH YORKSHIRE, YO17 8LU.

Sound Accounting *(J M Turner, P A E Turner)* Wingfield House, 13 Thorn Park, Mannamead, PLYMOUTH, PL3 4TG.

Ⓟ**South Coast Accounting Services Limited** *(J L Shaw)* 24 Park Road South, HAVANT, HAMPSHIRE, PO9 1HB.

ⓅⒶ**South East Accountancy Services Ltd** *(K R Joiner)* 34 Wells Way, FAVERSHAM, KENT, ME13 7QP.

Southam & Co *(K H Southam)* 23 Penshurst Road, POTTERS BAR, HERTFORDSHIRE, EN6 5JR.

Ⓟ**Southbourne Business Solutions Ltd** *(P D Hill)* Archer House, Britland Estate, Northbourne Road, EASTBOURNE, EAST SUSSEX, BN22 8PW.

Ⓟ**Southeringtons Limited** *(N J Southerington)* 71 Church Street, Langham, OAKHAM, LEICESTERSHIRE, LE15 7JE.

Southerns & Carter *(G W Pearce)* October House, 17 Dudley Street, Sedgley, DUDLEY, WEST MIDLANDS, DY3 1SA.

Ⓟ**Southgate Accounting, trading name of Southgate Accounting and Computer Consultants Ltd** *(W B Flynn)* 81 Ulleswater Road, Southgate, LONDON, N14 7BN.

Ⓐ**Southon & Co** *(R J Preston)* 6 The Parade, EXMOUTH, EX8 1RL.

ⒾⒻⒶ**Southwell, Tyrrell & Co** *(S R Clark, P E F Marshall)* 9 Newbury Street, LONDON, EC1A 7HU. and at WARE

Ⓟ**Southwinds Consulting Limited** *(A N Bennett)* 2nd Floor, Nadine House, 13 North Quay, Douglas, ISLE OF MAN, IM1 4LE.

Ⓐ**Southworth & Co** *(I G Southworth)* Unit 3 Investment House, 28 Queens Road, WEYBRIDGE, SURREY, KT13 9UT.

Ⓟ**Southworth & Co Ltd** *(J P Southworth)* Woodlea, Four Elms, EDENBRIDGE, TN8 6NE.

Sovereign Accounting Solutions *(J R Donald)* Langarth House, Rejerrah, NEWQUAY, CORNWALL, TR8 5QB.

ⓅⒶ**Sovereign Business Services Ltd** *(W E Robinson)* 7 Portland Terrace, NEWCASTLE UPON TYNE, NE2 1QQ.

ⒾⒻⓅⒶ**Sovereign Business Services, trading name of OBC The Accountants Limited** *(A P Hill, M J D Ogilvie)* 2 Upperton Gardens, EASTBOURNE, EAST SUSSEX, BN21 2AH.

Sovereign Payroll Services *(G L Pickering)* First Floor Office, Wharf Road, Whaley Bridge, HIGH PEAK, DERBYSHIRE, SK23 7AD.

ⒾⓅ**Sowerbutts & Co Ltd** *(L G Sowerbutts)* Fiscal House, 367 London Road, CAMBERLEY, GU15 3HQ.

★ⒻⒶ**Sowerby FRS, trading name of Sowerby FRS LLP** *(A M Allen, J C Hackney)* Beckside Court, Annie Reed Road, BEVERLEY, NORTH HUMBERSIDE, HU17 0LF. and at HORNSEA

SP Accounting *(S D I Powe)* Hermida, 97 Ilsham Road, Wellswood, TORQUAY, TQ1 2JD.

SP Kell *(S P Kell)* Clwyd House, 3c Clwyd Street, RUTHIN, CLWYD, LL15 1HF.

Ⓟ**SP Redrupp, trading name of SP Redrupp Limited** *(S P Redrupp)* 10 Dover Road, Branksome Park, POOLE, DORSET, BH13 6DZ.

Spain Accountants *(P Greene)* Avenida Diagonal 468 6, 08006 BARCELONA, SPAIN.

ⒾⒻⒶ**Spain Brothers & Co** *(F P Cheney, A J Dixon, P A Flood, J R Glenister, M E J Minus)* 29 Manor Road, FOLKESTONE, KENT, CT20 2SE. and at CANTERBURY, DOVER

★**Spain, Fewer, Quinlan & Co** *(J J Quinlan)* The Mall, THURLES, COUNTY TIPPERARY, IRELAND.

Sparkes & Co *(R E Sparkes)* Tarquin, Brinsea Road, Congresbury, BRISTOL, BS49 5JF.

Speechleys *(P M T Rees)* Princes Chambers, 23 Wynnstay Road, COLWYN BAY, CLWYD, LL29 8NT.

★**Spence Clarke & Co** *(A M A Spence Clarke)* Edificio Los Pinos L-1, Calle Jacinto Benavente 32, 29600 MARBELLA, SPAIN.

ⒻⒶ**Spencer Fellows & Co** *(R J Harman, R Worboys)* 169 New London Road, CHELMSFORD, CM2 0AE.

Ⓐ**Spencer Gardner Dickins, trading name of Spencer Gardner Dickins Audit LLP** *(P V R Dickins, D S Thomas)* Unit 3, Coventry Innovation Village, Cheetah Road, COVENTRY, CV1 2TL.

ⒻⓅ**Spencer Gardner Dickins, trading name of Spencer Gardner Dickins Limited** *(D Burton, P V R Dickins, D S Thomas)* 3 Coventry Innovation Village, Cheetah Road, COVENTRY, CV1 2TL.

ⒻⓅⒶ**Spencer Hyde Limited** *(S J McGuinness)* 272 Regents Park Road, LONDON, N3 3HN.

Ⓟ**Spencer Wood & Associates, trading name of HCA Spencer Woods Limited** *(M J Johnson)* Roundhay Chambers, 199 Roundhay Road, LEEDS, LS8 5AN. and at HARROGATE, WAKEFIELD

Ⓟ**Spencer Woods & Associates, trading name of HCA Spencer Woods Overseas Limited** *(M J Johnson)* Roundhay Chambers, 199 Roundhay Road, LEEDS, LS8 5AN. and at HARROGATE, WAKEFIELD

Spencer-Smith & Co *(Thomas Peter Spencer-Smith)* The Old Rectory, Llanvetherine, ABERGAVENNY, GWENT, NP7 8RG.

ⒾⒻⒶ**Spenser, Wilson & Co** *(R Hemblys, P Seton, E A Short, J C Yewdall)* Equitable House, 55 Pellon Lane, HALIFAX, WEST YORKSHIRE, HX1 5SP.

ⒾⓅ**SPGM Limited** *(S Polyviou)* Galatariotis Building, 3rd Floor, 11 Limassol Avenue, 2112 NICOSIA, CYPRUS.

ⒾⒻⒶ**Spiers & Company** *(P T Falvey, H P Singh)* 72 Fielding Road, Chiswick, LONDON, W4 1DB.

Spiro Neil *(D N Gungah)* Unit 3, Dukes Court, Wellington Street, LUTON, LU1 5AF. and at LONDON

★Ⓐ**SPL Associates** *(C Watson)* 2nd Floor, De Burgh House, Market Road, WICKFORD, ESSEX, SS12 0BB. and at LONDON, ROCHDALE

★ⒾⒻⒶ**Spofforths, trading name of Spofforths LLP** *(R A Dunlop, S G Ediss, J P Fautley, J R Frean, D J Grainge, J Haulkham, P J W Hussey, A J F Jones, S P J Kirkham, A J Pearce, A J Spofforth, D M Spofforth, R C P P Spofforth, C J Took, S L Webber)* 9 Donnington Park, 85 Birdham Road, CHICHESTER, WEST SUSSEX, PO20 7AJ. and at BRIGHTON, HORSHAM, PULBOROUGH, WORTHING

Ⓟ**Spofforths, trading name of Spofforths Private Client Services LLP** *(S P J Kirkham, P R Lansberry)* Comewell House, North Street, HORSHAM, WEST SUSSEX, RH12 1RL. and at CHICHESTER

Ⓐ**Spooner & Co** *(R M Spooner)* Mulberry, Shrubbs Hill Lane, Sunningdale, ASCOT, SL5 0LD.

Ⓟ**Spooner & Co Ltd** *(R M Spooner)* Mulberry, Shrubbs Hill Lane, ASCOT, BERKSHIRE, SL5 0LD.

ⒻⓅ**Springboard Corporate Finance Limited** *(D R C Neate, J Sparks)* Baskerville House, Centenary Square, BIRMINGHAM, B1 2ND.

Ⓟ**Springfield Tax Services Ltd** *(Richard Lane, T G Somers)* Springfield House, 99-101 Crossbrook Street, Cheshunt, WALTHAM CROSS, HERTFORDSHIRE, EN8 8JR.

Springfords LLP *(J F Kerr)* Dundas House, Westfield Park, Eskbank, DALKEITH, MIDLOTHIAN, EH22 3FB.

Ⓟ**Springtide Accountancy Ltd** *(S J Reeves)* 21 Lentune Way, LYMINGTON, HAMPSHIRE, SO41 3PE.

ⒾⒻⒶ**Sproull & Co** *(P A R Cole, C J Robinson, D A Spriggs)* 31-33 College Road, HARROW, MIDDLESEX, HA1 1EJ.

Spry & Associates, trading name of J W Spry FCA *(J W Spry)* 21 Hildenfields, TONBRIDGE, KENT, TN10 3DQ.

Spurling & Co *(R D Spurling)* 18 Marlborough Drive, WEYBRIDGE, SURREY, KT13 8PA.

Ⓟ**Spurling Cannon, trading name of Spurling Cannon Limited** *(M D Studham)* 424 Margate Road, Westwood, RAMSGATE, KENT, CT12 6SR.

ⒻⒶ**SPW, SPW Poppleton Appleby, trading names of SPW (UK) LLP** *(D L Platt, S A Shah, H J Sorsky, P J Winter)* 51 New Cavendish Street, LONDON, W1G 9TG.

SQ Associates *(T P Lim, C W Seah)* Suite 15.05 Level 15, City Square Office Tower, 106-108 Jalan Wong Ah Fook, 80000 JOHOR BAHRU, MALAYSIA. and at KOTA, KOTA KINABALU

SQM *(T P Lim, C W Seah)* Suite 15.05 Level 15, City Square Office Tower, 106-108 Jalan Wong Ah Fook, 80000 JOHOR BAHRU, MALAYSIA.

SR Pooley & Co *(S R Pooley)* 56 Corner Farm Road, Staplehurst, TONBRIDGE, TN12 0PS. and at TORQUAY

SR&A, trading name of Steve Russell and Associates *(S P Russell)* Paddock Hill House, Sacombe Green, Sacombe, WARE, HERTFORDSHIRE, SG12 0JH.

ⒻⓅⒶ**SRC Taxation Consultancy, trading name of SRC Taxation Consultancy Ltd** *(J S Flavell)* Blenheim House, 56 Old Steine, BRIGHTON, BN1 1NH.

Ⓟ**SRE Associates Limited** *(S R Eldridge)* 15 Ryeish Green Cottages, Hyde End Lane, Spencers Wood, READING, RG7 1ET.

Ⓟ**SRE Consultancy Limited** *(S R Eldridge)* 15 Ryeish Green Cottages, Hyde End Lane, Spencers Wood, READING, RG7 1ET.

ⓅⒶ**Sri & Co Accountants Ltd** *(G Sri Ragavan, M Sri Ragavan)* 36 Brent House, 214 Kenton Road, HARROW, MIDDLESEX, HA3 8BT.

Ⓟ**SRK Accounting Limited** *(S R Kallu)* 27 Holmes Court, Paradise Road, LONDON, SW4 6QJ.

★ⒾⒶ**SRLV** *(L W Finger, S P Jeffery, S Marks, M H L Ossman, R B Rosenberg, A Verma, M Voulters)* 89 New Bond Street, LONDON, W1S 1DA.

ⒻⒶ**SRN Sonico** *(J S Thind)* 60 Wensleydale Road, HAMPTON, MIDDLESEX, TW12 2LX.

Ⓟ**SRP Accounts Limited** *(R I D B Pethick)* The Old Customs House, Torwood Gardens Rd, TORQUAY, TQ1 1EG.

Ⓟ**St James Accounting, trading name of St James Accounting Limited** *(T J Cheesman)* 53 Manor Way, Deeping St. James, PETERBOROUGH, PE6 8PS.

St James Consultancy *(P Benney)* 1 Emperor Way, Exeter Business Park, EXETER, DEVON, EX1 3QS.

St. Mellion Accounting Services *(P M Caiden)* 1 Edwy Parade, GLOUCESTER, GL1 2QH.

ⒾⓅⒶ**Stables Thompson & Briscoe, trading name of Stables Thompson & Briscoe Ltd** *(D Briscoe, H M Holmes)* Lowther House, Lowther Street, KENDAL, CUMBRIA, LA9 4DX.

Ⓟ**Stacey & Co Limited** *(I Stacey)* Prime House, 14 Porters Wood, ST. ALBANS, HERTFORDSHIRE, AL3 6PQ.

ⒻⒶ**Stacey & Partners** *(R D Alliban, M J Nicholls, E J Wager, M A Wallace)* 30 Bridge Street, THETFORD, NORFOLK, IP24 3AG. and at BURY ST. EDMUNDS, NEWMARKET, SUDBURY

Ⓟ**Stacey & Partners Limited** *(M J Nicholls, E J Wager, M A Wallace)* The Beeches, 30 Bridge Street, THETFORD, NORFOLK, IP24 3AG. and at BURY ST. EDMUNDS, NEWMARKET, SUDBURY

★**Stacey Business Services** *(E J Wager, M A Wallace)* 88 High Street, NEWMARKET, SUFFOLK, CB8 8JX.

Stacey D Charleston ACA *(S D Stevens)* 7 Tug Wilson Close, Northway, TEWKESBURY, GLOUCESTERSHIRE, GL20 8RJ.

ⒾⓅⒶ**Stafford & Co, trading name of SCCA Ltd** *(K J Stafford, R J Stafford)* 2nd Floor, Nelson Mill, Gaskell Street, BOLTON, BL1 2QE.

Ⓐ**Stafford Challis & Co** *(R A Bushell)* Stafford Challis & Co, PO Box 344, Mont Crevelt House, Bulwer Avenue, St Sampson, GUERNSEY GY1 3US.

Ⓐ**Stafford Thursz** *(R T Stafford)* Cavendish House, Clarke Street, POULTON-LE-FYLDE, LANCASHIRE, FY6 8JW.

ⒾⒻⒶ**Staffords, trading name of Staffords Cambridge LLP** *(S D Ellis, M C A Pettifer, J R Stafford)* CPC1, Capital Park, Fulbourn, CAMBRIDGE, CB21 5XE.

Ⓟ**Stanbridge Associates Limited** *(V Sanders)* The Old Rectory, Long Lane, South Hykeham, LINCOLN, LN6 9NX.

ⒾⒻⒶ**Stanes Rand & Co** *(A S Rand)* 10 Jesus Lane, CAMBRIDGE, CB5 8BA.

Stanes Rand LLP *(S J Kilshaw, A S Rand)* 10 Jesus Lane, CAMBRIDGE, CB5 8BA.

Staniszewski & Richter, trading name of Staniszewski & Richter Sp. z.o.o. *(M E Richter, A M Staniszewski)* ul.Lwowska 10/21, 00-658 WARSAW, POLAND.

Ⓟ**Stanley House Consulting, trading name of Stanley House Consulting Limited** *(L A S Jay)* Stanley House, Trevellance Lane, PERRANPORTH, CORNWALL, TR6 0AX.

ⒾⒻⓅⒶ**Stanley Joseph Limited** *(P S Helps)* Suite 1, Liberty House, South Liberty Lane, BRISTOL, BS3 2ST.

Ⓟ**Stanley Kenner & Co Limited** *(S T Kenner)* 3 Walbrook, Woodford Road, South Woodford, LONDON, E18 2EG.

ⒻⒶ**Stanley Wilkinson & Co** *(S Wilkinson)* 139 Red Bank Road, Bispham, BLACKPOOL, LANCASHIRE, FY2 9HZ.

ⒻⒶ**Stanley Yule** *(I T Bidmead)* 79 Church Hill, Northfield, BIRMINGHAM, B31 3UB. and at WALSALL

Ⓟ**Stanley Yule Ltd** *(I T Bidmead, B Saunders)* 79 Church Hill, Northfield, BIRMINGHAM, B31 3UB.

Ⓐ**Stansfield & Co** *(A Stansfield)* Suite 303, Queens Dock Business Centre, Norfolk Street, LIVERPOOL, L1 0BG.

Stansfield & Co *(S M Stansfield)* 2 Fountain Place, Barbourne, WORCESTER, WR1 3HW.

Stanton & Co *(J S Cooper)* 6 Princes Park Avenue, LONDON, NW11 0JP.

Ⓕ**Stanton Partners** *(S D Stanton)* Warren House, Carrington Close, Arkley, BARNET, HERTFORDSHIRE, EN5 3NA.

★Ⓕ**Stanton Partnership** *(M J Stanton)* 55 Lynwood Drive, WORCESTER PARK, KT4 7AE.

★**Stapletons** *(C P Bird)* 4 Market Street, CREDITON, EX17 2AJ.

Ⓟ**Stardata Business Services Limited** *(T F Berkley, T Curzon, J Landau, M L Marks, J H Simmons)* Harben House, Harben Parade, Finchley Road, LONDON, NW3 6JP.

Ⓟ**Starfield Management Ltd** *(S N Poulton)* 15 Oakdene, BEACONSFIELD, BUCKINGHAMSHIRE, HP9 2BZ.

Starfish Accounting *(G R Rollings)* Littledene, Ellington Road, MAIDENHEAD, BERKSHIRE, SL6 0AX.

Ⓕ**Starkey Saunders** *(D R Starkey)* 4 Clare Road, HALIFAX, HX1 2HX.

Ⓕ**Starr & Co** *(L Starr)* 76 Wellington Road South, STOCKPORT, SK1 3SU.

Ⓟ**Startax Accountancy Services Ltd** *(N Seerungum)* 122-126 Kilburn High Road, West Hampstead, LONDON, NW6 4HY.

Startup Consultancy *(H M Etty)* 67 Endowood Road, Millhouses, SHEFFIELD, S7 2LY.

Ⓟ**STAS Ltd** *(S P Turner)* 11 Marguerites Way, St Fagans, CARDIFF, CF5 4QW.

Statton & Co, trading name of R.L. Statton *(R L Statton)* 1st Floor, Regency Arcade, Molesworth Street, WADEBRIDGE, PL27 7DH.

Ⓐ**Statutory Auditors LLP** *(A Varma)* Suite 2.9, Central House, 1 Ballards Lane, LONDON, N3 1QL.

Staub & Co *(F I Staub)* 5 Mansfield Avenue, Denton, MANCHESTER, M34 3NS.

ⒾⓅ**Stead Flintoff & Company, trading name of Cummins Young Ltd** *(J Cummins, A D Young)* 39 Westgate, THIRSK, NORTH YORKSHIRE, YO7 1QR.

ⒻⓅⒶ**Stead Robinson, trading name of Stead Robinson Limited** *(P J Lofthouse)* Whitby Court, Abbey Road, Shepley, HUDDERSFIELD, HD8 8ER.

Stedman & Co *(J F Stedman)* Cassel, 33 Foley Road, Claygate, ESHER, SURREY, KT10 0LU.

Steeds & Co *(D W H Steeds)* 1 Littleworth Avenue, ESHER, KT10 9PB.

ⒾⒶ**Steele Robertson Goddard** *(A N Bloom, T R S J Meadows, D J Skeet, H C Wood)* 28 Ely Place, LONDON, EC1N 6AA. and at GLASGOW

Steeles Support Services *(R J Steele)* c/o Stoneleigh, 6 Carlton Gardens, Stanwix, CARLISLE, CA3 9NP.

Ⓐ**Steggles & Co** *(A Steggles)* 2a Peel Street, Farnworth, BOLTON, BL4 8AA.

ⒾⒻⓅⒶ**Stein Richards, trading name of Stein Richards Limited** *(R G Hyams, R I Nissen)* 10 London Mews, LONDON, W2 1HY.

ⒾⒶ**Steiner & Co.** *(T A Steiner)* 50 Cowick Street, EXETER, EX4 1AP.

Ⓟ**Steiner Management Ltd** *(T A Steiner)* 50 Cowick Street, EXETER, EX4 1AP.

Stella Jensen, trading name of Jensen & Co *(S Jensen)* 15 Water Wheel Close, Quedgeley, GLOUCESTER, GL2 4XH.

Ⓟ**Stema Services Ltd** *(S J Hackett)* 198 Station Road, LEIGH-ON-SEA, ESSEX, SS9 3BS.

Stephanie Brass *(S R Brass)* 12 Snowdrop Grove, Winnersh, WOKINGHAM, RG41 5UP.

Stephanie James *(S S James)* 44 Lincoln Hill, Ironbridge, TELFORD, SHROPSHIRE, TF8 7NY.

Stephen A Howell *(S A Howell)* Pant Y Fedwen, Gelli'r Haidd, Tonyrefail, PORTH, MID GLAMORGAN, CF39 8AP.

Stephen Baughan *(S W Baughan)* 3 Ormond Drive, HAMPTON, MIDDLESEX, TW12 2TP.

Stephen Booth *(S C E Booth)* 17 Ivyhouse Road, Ickenham, UXBRIDGE, UB10 8NF.

Stephen C Hudson *(S C Hudson)* 24 Westfield Close, Brampton, CHESTERFIELD, S40 3RS.

Stephen C Ranscombe & Co *(S C Ranscombe)* Tigh Ceilidh, NAIRN, IV12 5NX.

Ⓐ**Stephen C Stone & Co** *(S C Stone)* 32 Green Lane, LONDON, NW4 2NG.

Stephen CJ Garner *(S C J Garner)* Rookery Farm, Back Lane, Kingston Seymour, CLEVEDON, AVON, BS21 6XB.

Ⓐ**Stephen Coleman LLP** *(S P Coleman)* Gerald Edelman, 25 Harley Street, LONDON, W1G 9BR.

Stephen Cunningham & Co *(J S C Cunningham)* Silversprings, 140 The Burn Road, Templepatrick, BALLYCLARE, COUNTY ANTRIM, BT39 0DQ.

Stephen Daniel & Co. *(B S Freedman, M J Kraus)* 138 Pinner Road, HARROW, HA1 4JE.

ⒻⓅ**Stephen Daniels, trading name of Practical Accounting Limited** *(S Daniels)* 50 Ashby Road, TAMWORTH, STAFFORDSHIRE, B79 8AD.

Stephen Deutsch *(S S Deutsch)* 102 Green Lane, EDGWARE, HA8 8EJ.

Ⓟ**Stephen Dilley & Associates Limited** *(S W Dilley)* 12 Barton Close, St. Annes Park, BRISTOL, BS4 4BA.

Stephen Everall FCA *(S R Everall)* 12 Hillside, Sawston, CAMBRIDGE, CB22 5BL.

Ⓟ**Stephen Farra Associates, trading name of Stephen Farra Associates Ltd** *(A Ross)* Synergy House, 98 Hornchurch Road, HORNCHURCH, ESSEX, RM11 1JS.

Stephen Franklin FCA CTA *(S Franklin)* 45 Membris Way, Woodford Halse, DAVENTRY, NN11 3QZ.

Stephen G Donald MA (Hons) MBA ACA *(S G Donald)* 12 Kincarrathie Crescent, PERTH, PH2 7HH.

Ⓟ**Stephen Green, trading name of Greens Accountancy & Tax Services Limited** *(S M Green)* 106a Commercial Street, Risca, NEWPORT, NP11 6EE.

Ⓕ**Stephen Harris & Co** *(S M Harris)* Belgrave Place, 8 Manchester Road, BURY, LANCASHIRE, BL9 0ED.

ⓉⓅⒶ**Stephen Hill Mid Kent, trading name of Stephen Hill Mid Kent Ltd** *(T N B Lister, P Shillinglaw)* 44 High Street, NEW ROMNEY, TN28 8BZ. and at MAIDSTONE

★ⓅⒶ**Stephen Hill Partnership (Holdings) Limited** *(M T Sackett)* 139 Watling Street, GILLINGHAM, KENT, ME7 2YY.

★ⓉⓅ**Stephen Hill Partnership Limited** *(M T Sackett)* 139-141 Watling Street, GILLINGHAM, KENT, ME7 2YY.

Stephen Hobson *(S M Hobson)* 3 Sona Merg Close, Heamoor, PENZANCE, TR18 3QL.

ⒻⒶ**Stephen Hobson BA FCA** *(S Hobson)* 84 New Street, ALTRINCHAM, CHESHIRE, WA14 2QP.

ⒻⒶ**Stephen Iseman & Co.** *(S M Iseman)* 30 Oakridge Avenue, RADLETT, HERTFORDSHIRE, WD7 8ER.

Ⓟ**Stephen J Bright, trading name of Britac Limited** *(S J Bright)* 10 Highcroft, EXETER, EX4 4JQ.

Ⓐ**Stephen J. Bright** *(S J Bright)* 10 High Croft, Lower Argyll Road, EXETER, EX4 4JQ.

Stephen J. Kerry *(S J Kerry)* 90 Hilltop, TONBRIDGE, TN9 2UP.

Stephen Jasper *(S G Jasper)* 912 Wellbourne Commercial Centre, 8 Java Road, NORTH POINT, HONG KONG ISLAND, HONG KONG SAR.

Stephen Jay *(S J Jay)* 17 Geraldine Road, Wandsworth, LONDON, SW18 2NR.

Ⓟ**Stephen Joslin & Co, trading name of Joslin & Co Limited** *(S R Joslin)* 30 Milton Road, WESTCLIFF-ON-SEA, ESSEX, SS0 7JX.

Ⓟ**Stephen Kent & Company Ltd** *(S M Kent)* 456 Gower Road, Killay, SWANSEA, SA2 7AL.

Stephen Ketteringham *(S J Ketteringham)* 24 Cae Gwylan, BORTH, CEREDIGION, SY24 5LD.

Stephen Koh & Co *(L K Koh)* 90 Cecil Street #08-03, RHB Bank Building, SINGAPORE 069531, SINGAPORE.

Stephen Le Bras *(S J A J Le Bras)* 6 Queen Anne's Court, Peascod Street, WINDSOR, SL4 1DG.

Stephen Lightley *(S J Lightley)* 36 Graham Park Road, NEWCASTLE UPON TYNE, NE3 4BJ.

Stephen Lockwood *(S Lockwood)* Swallow Barn, Manor Road, Stutton, TADCASTER, NORTH YORKSHIRE, LS24 9BR.

Stephen M. Joseph *(S M B Joseph)* 29 Bentley Way, STANMORE, HA7 3RR.

Stephen Malme *(S E C Malme)* 51 Mornington Road, North Chingford, LONDON, E4 7DT.

Stephen Matthews *(S H Mathews)* 5 Detillens Lane, OXTED, SURREY, RH8 0DH.

Ⓟ**Stephen Mayled & Associates, Stephen Mayled & Associates Business Development Specialists, Stephen Mayled & Associates Dental Business Specialists, trading names of Stephen Mayled & Associates Ltd** *(S J Mayled)* Cottage Farm, Michaelston-le-Pit, DINAS POWYS, SOUTH GLAMORGAN, CF64 4HE.

Stephen Miller *(S D Miller)* 117 George Lane, South Woodford, LONDON, E18 1AN.

Stephen Mortimer, trading name of Mortimer S *(S Mortimer)* 1 Chilwell Close, SOLIHULL, B91 3YL.

Stephen Napier & Company *(S Napier)* First Floor, Hodges Chambers, Crane Street, PONTYPOOL, NP4 6LY.

Ⓐ**Stephen Pearl & Co** *(S Pearl)* 3 Bentalls Close, SOUTHEND-ON-SEA, SS2 5PS.

ⓉⒻⒶ**Stephen Pearn & Co** *(S C Pearn)* 20 Henver Road, NEWQUAY, TR7 3BJ.

★ⒻⒶ**Stephen Penny and Partners** *(R E Bagshawe)* 898/902 Wimborne Road, Moordown, BOURNEMOUTH, DORSET, BH9 2DW.

Stephen Pritchard & Co. *(S Pritchard)* 144 Folkestone Road, SOUTHPORT, MERSEYSIDE, PR8 5PP.

Stephen R Marsh *(S R Marsh)* 7 Worths Way, STRATFORD-UPON-AVON, WARWICKSHIRE, CV37 0RR.

Stephen R Thomas *(S R Thomas)* Hawthorn House, Tunnel Lane, North Warnborough, HOOK, HAMPSHIRE, RG29 1JT.

Stephen R Winton FCA *(S R Winton)* 17 Canterbury Close, SWINDON, SN3 1HU.

Stephen R. Allen & Co *(S R Allen)* Appletree Court, 2A Vicarage Lane, HESSLE, HU13 9LQ.

Stephen R. Bell *(S R Bell)* 30 Avon Way, South Woodford, LONDON, E18 2AR.

Stephen Rosser *(S J Rosser)* 43 Bridge Road, GRAYS, RM17 6BU.

Ⓐ**Stephen Samuel & Co** *(S Samuel)* 141 Stanmore Hill, STANMORE, MIDDLESEX, HA7 3ED.

Stephen Schick *(S E Schick)* 31 Abbey Gardens, LONDON, NW8 9AS.

Ⓟ**Stephen Shaw Accountancy Services Limited** *(S Shaw)* 9 Blue Haze Close, PLYMOUTH, PL6 7HR.

ⓅⒶ**Stephen Starr, trading name of Stephen Starr Limited** *(S G Starr)* 12 Aldenham Avenue, RADLETT, HERTFORDSHIRE, WD7 8HX.

Ⓟ**Stephen T. Clarke Limited** *(S T Clarke)* 23 Rolleston Crescent, Watnall, NOTTINGHAM, NG16 1JU.

Stephen Thomas *(S Thomas)* Greenlands, Parkside Drive South, Whittle-Le Woods, CHORLEY, PR6 7PH.

Ⓐ**Stephen W. Jones** *(S W Jones)* King Edward House, 82 Stourbridge Road, HALESOWEN, B63 3UP.

Stephen Waxman & Company *(S A Waxman)* Canada House, 29 Hampton Road, TWICKENHAM, TW2 5QE.

Stephen Willcox *(S R Willcox)* Frogwell House, Cotesbach, LUTTERWORTH, LE17 4HZ.

Stephen Woodcock *(S R Woodcock)* 69 Maudlin Drive, TEIGNMOUTH, DEVON, TQ14 8SB.

Stephens Paul *(B Bates, N T Paul)* 24 Cuddington Avenue, WORCESTER PARK, KT4 7DA.

Ⓐ**Stephenson & Co** *(C K Bailey, M R Smith)* Ground Floor Austin House, 43 Poole Road, Westbourne, BOURNEMOUTH, BH4 9DN.

ⓉⒻⒶ**Stephenson Coates** *(A W Coates, J H Oswald)* Asama Court, West 2, Newcastle Business Park, NEWCASTLE UPON TYNE, NE4 7YD.

ⓉⒶ**Stephenson Nuttall & Co** *(A P Haigh, T F Hudson, Sir Peter Parker)* Ossington Chambers, 6-8 Castle Gate, NEWARK, NG24 1AX.

Ⓟ**Stephenson Sheppard & Co Limited** *(G G Stone)* Albany House, 5 New Street, SALISBURY, SP1 2PH. and at SOUTHAMPTON

★ⓉⒻⒶ**Stephenson Smart** *(M J Andrews, P E Carter, A C Dodds, P Lofting, N R Ward)* 22-26 King Street, KING'S LYNN, NORFOLK, PE30 1HJ. and at FAKENHAM, WISBECH

★ⓉⒻⒶ**Stephenson Smart & Co** *(P H Evans, P J Lawson, I Walker, G M Wiles)* Stephenson House, 15 Church Walk, PETERBOROUGH, PE1 2TP.

Ⓟ**Stephenson Smart & Co, trading name of The SS Partnership Limited** *(K D Cross)* Barclays Bank Chambers, 9a Market Place, BRIGG, SOUTH HUMBERSIDE, DN20 8ES. and at BARTON-UPON-HUMBER, SCUNTHORPE

Ⓟ**Steps for Success, trading name of Steps for Success Ltd** *(S D Philpott)* 19 Quail Green, WOLVERHAMPTON, WV6 8DF.

★ⓉⒻⒶ**Sterling** *(D K Doshi, B A Vanza)* 505 Pinner Road, HARROW, MIDDLESEX, HA2 6EH.

ⒻⒶ**Sterling Associates** *(J J Ved)* 5 Theobald Court, Theobald Street, BOREHAMWOOD, HERTFORDSHIRE, WD6 4RN.

Ⓕ**Sterling Corporate Finance, trading name of Sterling Corporate Finance LLP** *(A N Exley, A S Rose, J G Smith)* 12 York Place, LEEDS, LS1 2DS.

ⓉⓅⒶ**Sterling Financial, trading name of Sterling Financial Accountancy Services Limited** *(K L M Noble)* 27 Lincoln Croft, Shenstone, LICHFIELD, STAFFORDSHIRE, WS14 0ND.

ⒻⒶ**Sterling Hay** *(J S Wasu)* PO Box 970, BROMLEY, BR1 9JF.

★Ⓟ**Sterling Informia Limited** *(M S Seyed Mokhtassi, A Youshani)* Grove House, 774-780 Wilmslow Road, Didsbury, MANCHESTER, M20 2DR.

ⓉⒻⒶ**Sterling Partners LLP** *(M S Seyed Mokhtassi, A Youshani)* Grove House, 774-780 Wilmslow Road, Didsbury, MANCHESTER, M20 2DR.

★Ⓟ**Sterling Pay Limited** *(M S Seyed Mokhtassi, A Youshani)* Grove House, 774-780 Wilmslow Road, Didsbury, MANCHESTER, M20 2DR.

Sterling Tax *(R W Mann)* 84 Smugglers Lane North, Highcliffe, CHRISTCHURCH, DORSET, BH23 4NL.

Ⓟ**Sterlings Accountancy Solutions Limited** *(D J Parker)* 18 Springfield Avenue, Hutton, BRENTWOOD, ESSEX, CM13 1RE.

ⓉⒻⓅⒶ**Sterlings Ltd** *(A A Cohen, G J Moss)* Lawford House, Albert Place, LONDON, N3 1QA.

Stern & Co *(G G Stern)* 12-15 Hanger Green, LONDON, W5 3AY.

ⓉⒻⓅⒶ**Stern & Company, trading name of Stern & Company Limited** *(G G Stern)* 12-15 Hanger Green, Ealing, LONDON, W5 3AY.

ⒻⒶ**Stern Associates** *(S D Stern)* 2 Helenslea Avenue, LONDON, NW11 8ND.

★Ⓟ**Steve Astbury & Partners Ltd** *(S J Astbury)* 9 Manchester Road, HEYWOOD, LANCASHIRE, OL10 2DZ.

Ⓟ**Steve Astbury Ltd** *(S J Astbury)* 379 Stitch-Mi-Lane, Harwood, BOLTON, BL2 3PR.

★**Steve Au Yeung & Co** *(S K S Au Yeung)* Room 1901 19/F, Ka Nin Wah Commercial Building, 423-425 Hennessy Road, CAUSEWAY BAY, HONG KONG ISLAND, HONG KONG SAR.

Ⓟ**Steve Ellum & Associates Limited** *(S F Ellum)* 18 Bryn Terrace, LLANELLI, SA15 2PD.

Ⓟ**Steve Jones (Bath) Limited** *(S L Jones)* 74 Newbridge Road, BATH, BA1 3LA.

ⓅⒶ**Steve Monico, trading name of Steve Monico Limited** *(S N Monico)* 19 Goldington Road, BEDFORD, MK40 3JY.

Ⓟ**Steve Morris Accountants, trading name of Steve Morris Accountants Limited** *(S Morris)* 84 Robertson Drive, St. Annes Park, BRISTOL, BS4 4RG.

Ⓐ**Steve Reynolds** *(S M Reynolds)* Suite 125, 6 The Broadway, Mill Hill, LONDON, NW7 3LL.

Steve Smith FCA *(S P Smith)* 38 Timbertree Road, CRADLEY HEATH, WEST MIDLANDS, B64 7LE.

Steve Watt & Associates, trading name of Steve Watt Bsc FCA CTA *(S M Watt)* 1 Connaught Road, FOLKESTONE, KENT, CT20 1DA.

ⓉⒻ**Steven Carey & Co** *(S H Carey)* Countrywide House, 166 Fore Street, SALTASH, CORNWALL, PL12 6JR.

Steven Ellwood *(S J Ellwood)* 94 Biddulph Road, CONGLETON, CW12 3LY.

ⒻⒶ**Steven Glicher & Co.** *(S V Glicher)* Eden Point, Three Acres Lane, Cheadle Hulme, CHEADLE, CHESHIRE, SK8 6RL.

Steven Gurmin *(S Gurmin)* 122 Hamilton Avenue, HALESOWEN, B62 8SJ.

ⓅⒶ**Steven Hocking-Robinson Limited** *(S Hocking-Robinson)* Berg Kaprow Lewis LLP, 35 Ballards Lane, LONDON, N3 1XW.

★**Steven Tan Russell Bedford PAC** *(S C C Tan)* 25 International Business Park, #04 - 22/26 German Centre, SINGAPORE 609916, SINGAPORE.

Steven Wainwright FCA *(S R Wainwright)* 11 Sandling Avenue, Horfield, BRISTOL, BS7 0HS.

★**Stevens & Willey** *(H L Mansford)* Grenville House, 9 Boutport Street, BARNSTAPLE, EX31 1TZ.

Ⓟ**Stevens & Willey Ltd** *(H L Mansford)* Grenville House, 9 Boutport Street, BARNSTAPLE, DEVON, EX31 1TZ.

Ⓐ**Stevensons** *(A L Stevenson)* 6 Sylvan Gardens, SURBITON, SURREY, KT6 6PP.

ⓉⒶ**Steward & Co** *(J A Steward)* 5 East Lane, LONDON, SE16 4UD.

ⓉⒻⒶ**Stewart & Co** *(P J Clennell, A N Cousins, D A Hartley, D A McCusker, G Robinson)* Knoll House, Knoll Road, CAMBERLEY, GU15 3SY. and at BAGSHOT

Ⓟ**Stewart & Co Accountancy Services Ltd** *(P J Clennell, S L Clennell, A N Cousins, D A Hartley, D A McCusker, G Robinson)* Knoll House, Knoll Road, CAMBERLEY, SURREY, GU15 3SY.

ⒻⒶ**Stewart & Co LLP** *(C J Stewart)* Ebenezer House, 5a Poole Road, BOURNEMOUTH, BH2 5QJ.

Ⓟ**Stewart & Co, trading name of Professional Accountancy & Business Services Limited** *(C E Stewart)* 5 Plainview Close, Aldridge, WALSALL, WS9 0YY.

ⒻⒶ**Stewart & Partners** *(S A Lever)* 6 Regent Gate, High Street, WALTHAM CROSS, HERTFORDSHIRE, EN8 7AF.

★Ⓟ**Stewart Associates Shrewsbury Ltd** *(I P Stewart)* Emstrey House North, Shrewsbury Business Park, SHREWSBURY, SY2 6LG.

Stewart Aylward FCA *(B S M Aylward)* Isbourne, Chandos Street, Winchcombe, CHELTENHAM, GLOUCESTERSHIRE, GL54 5HX.

Stewart Laitner & Co *(S A Laitner)* 17 Bancroft Avenue, East Finchley, LONDON, N2 0AR.

ⓉⒻⒶ**Stewart, Fletcher and Barrett** *(A J S Bexon, P Carvell, J Sargent, P R White)* Manor Court Chambers, 126 Manor Court Road, NUNEATON, CV11 5HL.

Stewarts Accountancy Services, trading name of Peter G Stewart *(P G Stewart)* 41 Warren Road, BANSTEAD, SM7 1LG.

ⒻⓅ**Stewarts Accountants Limited** *(C N Stewart)* 271 High Street, BERKHAMSTED, HERTFORDSHIRE, HP4 1AA.

Ⓟ**STFS, trading name of Silver Tree Financial Support (STFS) Ltd** *(D J Wilson)* 79 St. Leonards Road, AMERSHAM, BUCKINGHAMSHIRE, HP6 6DR.

ⓅⒶ**Stiddard, trading name of Stiddard Mathers Limited** *(A M Mathers)* Kent CCC, Worsley Bridge Road, BECKENHAM, KENT, BR3 1RL.

★ⒻⒶ**Stiles & Company** *(A Rees)* 2 Lake End Court, Taplow Road, Taplow, MAIDENHEAD, SL6 0JQ.

ⓉⒻⒶ**Stirk Lambert & Co** *(C Hill, R J Hudson)* Russell Chambers, 61A North Street, KEIGHLEY, BD21 3DS.

★**Stirling International** *(R C Williams)* 11th Floor, St James Centre, 111 Elizabeth Street, GPO Box 7019, SYDNEY, NSW 2001 AUSTRALIA.

Stokes Accountants *(G R Stokes)* 1 Bentley Way, Coton Green, TAMWORTH, STAFFORDSHIRE, B79 8LJ.

Stokoe Loughlin *(A M Stokoe)* 1 The Parade, CHESTER LE STREET, COUNTY DURHAM, DH3 3LR.

ⓉⒻⒶ**Stokoe Rodger** *(M M Bradley, S G Charlton, I R Christer, D E Stokoe)* St Matthews House, Haugh Lane, HEXHAM, NORTHUMBERLAND, NE46 3PU. and at GATESHEAD

ⓉⒻⓅ**Stone & Co, trading name of Innisfree 2000 Limited** *(R A Stone)* Charnwood House, Marsh Road, Ashton, BRISTOL, BS3 2NA.

Ⓐ**Stone & Partners** *(J Stone)* 571 Fishponds Road, Fishponds, BRISTOL, BS16 3AF.

ⒻⓅⒶ**Stone Osmond Limited** *(P G Stone)* 75 Bournemouth Road, Chandlers Ford, EASTLEIGH, SO53 3AP.

Stone R. Duncan & Co *(R D Stone)* Sunrise House, Newdigate Road, Beare Green, DORKING, RH5 4QD.

★Ⓟ**Stonebridge Partnership, trading name of The Stonebridge Partnership Ltd** *(N K Privett)* 1 Chalkpit Terrace, DORKING, SURREY, RH4 1HX.

ⒻⒶ**Stonebridge Stewart** *(S G Lawrence)* Daryl House, 76a Pensby Road, Heswall, WIRRAL, CH60 7RF. and at RUTHIN

Stonegate Trinity LLP *(W Godley)* 3rd Floor, 3 Brindley Place, BIRMINGHAM, B1 2JB.

ⒻⒶ**Stoner Cottingham** *(S R Cottingham, D J Stoner)* 42 London Rd, HORSHAM, RH12 1AY.

ⓉⒻⓅⒶ**Stones Accountancy Limited** *(P N O'Donnell)* Outset House, Turkey Mill, Ashford Road, MAIDSTONE, KENT, ME14 5PP.

Stonham.Co *(E J Stonham)* 1 Market Avenue, CHICHESTER, WEST SUSSEX, PO19 1JU. and at BRISTOL, EXETER, GUILDFORD, LONDON, REDRUTH, SOUTHAMPTON, WITNEY

Stonycroft Business Support, trading name of Brian Johnson B.Com FCA *(B Johnson)* 9 Shrublands Road, BERKHAMSTED, HERTFORDSHIRE, HP4 3HY.

ⒻⓅⒶ**Stopford Associates, trading name of Stopford Associates Limited** *(P M Nicholson, B J Stopford)* Synergy House, 7 Acorn Business Park, Commercial Gate, MANSFIELD, NOTTINGHAMSHIRE, NG18 1EX.

ⓉⒶ**ST-Partnership** *(V N Shah, N J Thakker)* Mandeville House, 45-47 Tudor Road, HARROW, HA3 5PQ.

Strachan & Co *(D A Strachan)* Summerhill Cottage, 9 Summerhill Road, DARTFORD, KENT, DA1 2LP.

Strategic Corporate Finance Partners LLP *(A M Coates)* 27 Gander Lane, Napier Court, Barlborough, CHESTERFIELD, DERBYSHIRE, S43 4PZ.

Ⓟ**Strategic Corporate Finance, trading name of Strategic Corporate Finance Transactions Ltd** *(A M Coates)* 27 Gander Lane, Napier Court, Barlborough, CHESTERFIELD, DERBYSHIRE, S43 4PZ.

Ⓟ**Strategic FD, trading name of Strategic Finance Director Limited** *(A L Clayden)* 18 Roughgrove Copse, Binfield, BRACKNELL, BERKSHIRE, RG42 4EZ.

Ⓟ**Strathbraid Limited** *(R J Sweetman)* 22 Braid Farm Road, EDINBURGH, EH10 6LF.

Ⓟ**Strathmore Audit Limited** *(D Johnson)* 3rd Floor, Ivy Mill, Crown Street, Failsworth, MANCHESTER, M35 9BG.

Ⓟ**Strathmore Business Services, trading name of Strathmore Accountants Limited** *(D Johnson)* 3rd Floor, Ivy Mill, Crown Street, Failsworth, MANCHESTER, M35 9BG.

ⓉⒻⓅⒶ**Straughans, trading name of Straughans Limited** *(M J H Tait)* Hadrian House, Front Street, CHESTER LE STREET, COUNTY DURHAM, DH3 3DB.

Ⓐ**Strauss Phillips & Co** *(B M Strauss)* PO Box 585, EDGWARE, MIDDLESEX, HA8 4DU.

Stredder & Co *(D Stredder)* Rose Cottage, Manley Road, Alvanley, FRODSHAM, WA6 9DE.

★Ⓟ**Street & Berg, trading name of Street & Berg Limited** *(J R Jones)* The Media Centre, Culverhouse Cross, CARDIFF, CF5 6XJ.

Ⓐ**Streets Audit, trading name of Streets Audit LLP** *(R Godley, A R Manderfield, S W Sargent, P F Tutin, R J Ward)* Tower House, Lucy Tower Street, LINCOLN, LN1 1XW. and at BEDFORD, CAMBRIDGE, GRANTHAM, HULL, NEWMARKET, PETERBOROUGH, SHEFFIELD, STEVENAGE

★Ⓟ**Streets ISA Limited** *(R Godley, S W Sargent, P F Tutin, R J Ward)* Tower House, Lucy Tower Street, LINCOLN, LN1 1XW.

★Ⓟ**Streets ISA, trading name of Streets ISA Ltd** *(R Godley, A R Manderfield, S W Sargent, P F Tutin, R J Ward)* 30 Great Portland Street, LONDON, W1W 8QU. and at HULL

★**Streets Tax, trading name of Streets Tax LLP** *(R Godley, S W Sargent, P F Tutin, R J Ward)* Tower House, Lucy Tower Street, LINCOLN, LN1 1XW.

★Ⓟ**Streets, Streets Corporate Finance, trading names of SMS Corporate Partner Unlimited** *(R Godley, S W Sargent, P F Tutin, R J Ward)* Tower House, Lucy Tower Street, LINCOLN, LN1 1XW. and at SHEFFIELD

★Ⓣ**Streets, trading name of Streets LLP** *(M P Bradshaw, J Day, R Godley, R C Lee, L J Lord, S W Sargent, P F Tutin, R J Ward)* Tower House, Lucy Tower Street, LINCOLN, LINCOLNSHIRE, LN1 1XW. and at GRANTHAM, SHEFFIELD

★**Streets, trading name of Streets Whitmarsh Sterland LLP** *(A R Blake, J Day, R Godley, B Halstead, D L Martin, S W Sargent, J K Sinfield, H J Tanner, S L Tharby, P F Tutin, R J Ward)* Tower House, Lucy Tower Street, LINCOLN, LN1 1XW. and at BEDFORD, CAMBRIDGE, NEWMARKET, PETERBOROUGH, STEVENAGE

Ⓟ**Stressfree Bookkeeping, trading name of Stressfree Bookkeeping Limited** *(G Robinson)* Sovereign House, 37 Middle Road, Park Gate, SOUTHAMPTON, SO31 7GH.

Stringer & Co *(D J Stringer)* 5 Bassett Wood Drive, SOUTHAMPTON, SO16 3PT.

Ⓟ**Stringer Mallard, trading name of CTA (Leeds) Ltd** *(P A Houlton)* 20b Main Street, Barwick in Elmet, LEEDS, LS15 4JQ.

Strother Alexander *(D S Alexander)* 5 Ballyshannon Road, KILLARNEY HEIGHTS, NSW 2087, AUSTRALIA.

Ⓐ**Strover, Leader & Co** *(J A R Ironmonger, D L Roberts)* Barry House, 20/22 Worple Road, Wimbledon, LONDON, SW19 4DH.

Stuart A. Griggs *(S A Griggs)* 99 High Street, Yatton, BRISTOL, BS49 4DR.

Ⓟ**Stuart Anderson, trading name of Stuart Anderson Accountants Limited** *(S Anderson)* Newland, Ely Valley Road, Talbot Green, PONTYCLUN, MID GLAMORGAN, CF72 8AP.

Ⓐ**Stuart Arrandale** *(S L Arrandale)* 23-25 Gwydir Street, CAMBRIDGE, CB1 2LG.

Ⓕ**Stuart B. Lodge & Co** *(S B Lodge)* 44 Bradford Road, Idle, BRADFORD, BD10 9PE.

Stuart Ballantine *(S D Ballantine)* 9 Oak Avenue, Ickenham, UXBRIDGE, MIDDLESEX, UB10 8LP.

Stuart Brampton *(S R Brampton)* 95 Hollywood Lane, Hollywood, BIRMINGHAM, B47 5PY.

Stuart Brandreth *(S Brandreth)* 41 Chestnut Drive, Berry Hill, MANSFIELD, NOTTINGHAMSHIRE, NG18 4PW.

Ⓐ**Stuart Burton & Co** *(B S Burton)* 18 Crosby Road North, Waterloo, LIVERPOOL, L22 4QF.

Ⓟ**Stuart Cardwell Ltd** *(S J P Cardwell)* 9a Alexandra Parade, WESTON-SUPER-MARE, AVON, BS23 1QT.

Stuart Cowen Prof Corp'n *(S Cowen)* 11148-81 Avenue, EDMONTON T6G 0S5, AB, CANADA.

ⓅⒶ**Stuart Dick & Co Limited** *(N W Wylde)* Suite 8 & 9, Courtyard House, Mill Lane, GODALMING, SURREY, GU7 1EY.

Ⓐ**Stuart Dunstan & Co** *(S A Dunstan)* 105 Oak Hill, WOODFORD GREEN, IG8 9PF.

Ⓐ**Stuart Edwards & Company** *(S Edwards)* Garden Studios, 11-15 Betterton Street, LONDON, WC2H 9BP.

Stuart Gordon *(S T Gordon)* Suite 3 Capital House, Speke Hall Road, Hunts Cross, LIVERPOOL, L24 9GB.

Ⓐ**Stuart Hoare** *(S E Hoare)* 87 London Road, Cowplain, WATERLOOVILLE, PO8 8XB.

Stuart K Jones FCA *(S K Jones)* 56-58 Warwick Road, KENILWORTH, WARWICKSHIRE, CV8 1HH.

Stuart Kay *(S J Kay)* Elmdene, Ridgley Road, Chiddingfold, GODALMING, GU8 4QN.

Stuart Moffatt *(S Moffatt)* 53 Crestway, LONDON, SW15 5DB.

Stuart Noad BA FCA *(S I Noad)* 34 Brighton Road, SOUTHPORT, MERSEYSIDE, PR8 4DD.

Ⓟ**Stuart Oake Limited** *(S N Oake)* 3 Portland Place, PENRITH, CUMBRIA, CA11 7QN.

Ⓐ**Stuart Rosenberg LLP** *(S H Rosenberg)* 25 Harley Street, LONDON, W1G 9BR.

Stuart S.E. Green *(S S E Green)* The Glen, 19 Lingfield Common Road, LINGFIELD, RH7 6BU.

Ⓟ**Stuart Vine & Co, trading name of Innerview Limited** *(S M Vine)* Station House, 2 Station Road, RADLETT, WD7 8JX.

Stuart Whiteley FCA CMI *(J S Whiteley)* 50 Alma Road, COLNE, LANCASHIRE, BB8 7JJ.

Stuart Wright *(S N H Wright)* 79 Churchill Road, THETFORD, IP24 2JZ.

Stubbs & Co *(N J Stubbs)* 21 Bridle Lane, Streetly, SUTTON COLDFIELD, B74 3QE.

★ⓉⒶ**Stubbs Parkin South** *(J M A Birtles, D J Kelsall, N D G Shanks)* 28 Cheshire Street, MARKET DRAYTON, SHROPSHIRE, TF9 1PF. and at SHREWSBURY, WHITCHURCH

ⓉⒻⓅⒶ**Stubbs Parkin Taylor & Co, trading name of Stubbs Parkin Taylor & Co Limited** *(D A Taylor, K E Thompson)* 18a London Street, SOUTHPORT, MERSEYSIDE, PR9 0UE.

Ⓐ**Stuckeys** *(J G H Stuckey)* 19 Highfield Road, Edgbaston, BIRMINGHAM, B15 3BH.

ⓉⓅⒶ**Studholme-Bell Limited** *(A W J Bell)* Vantage House, East Terrace Business Park, Euxton Lane, Euxton, CHORLEY, PR7 6TB.

Ⓟ**Stuff Ltd** *(G H Sedgwick)* PO Box 417, 2nd Floor Abbott Building, Waterfront Drive, ROAD TOWN, TORTOLA ISLAND, VIRGIN ISLANDS (BRITISH).

Ⓟ**Sturgess Hutchinson, trading name of Sturgess Hutchinson Limited** *(D G Goodwin)* 10 Station Road, Earl Shilton, LEICESTER, LE9 7GA.

Ⓐ**Sturmans** *(B A Sturman)* The Seedbed Centre, Langston Road, LOUGHTON, ESSEX, IG10 3TQ.

★Ⓟ**Style Accountants Limited** *(A C Style)* Bank House, Southwick Square, Southwick, BRIGHTON, BN42 4FN.

ⓅⒶ**Styles & Co, trading name of Styles & Co Accountants Limited** *(I Lloyd, L Styles)* Heather House, 473 Warrington Road, Culcheth, WARRINGTON, WA3 5QU.

Su Mace *(S J Mace)* 140 Old Norwich Road, Horsham St. Faith, NORWICH, NR10 3JF.

Success Story Builder LLP *(G P D'silva)* Pendragon House, 170 Merton High Street, LONDON, SW19 1AY.

Sudhir Sinha & Co *(S K Sinha)* 2 Silver Street, CARDIFF, CF24 0LG.

Sue Gale, trading name of S.A. Gale *(S A Gale)* The Tile House, Marston St Lawrence, BANBURY, OX17 2DA.

Sue Lewis Accountancy Services *(S J Lewis)* Dove Cottage, 18 Style Road, Wiveliscombe, TAUNTON, SOMERSET, TA4 2LN.

Sue Moore *(S E Moore)* Orchard House, Main Street, Countesthorpe, LEICESTER, LE8 5QX.

Sue Stone Bookkeeping Services *(S B Stone)* Longfield, Boraston Lane, TENBURY WELLS, WORCESTERSHIRE, WR15 8RB.

Ⓟ**Sue Wickham, trading name of Quartrange Limited** *(S C Wickham)* 30 Gwynne Close, TRING, HP23 5EN.

Sue Woodgate *(S M Woodgate)* 42 St. Nicholas Drive, SHEPPERTON, MIDDLESEX, TW17 9LD.

Sufraz & Co *(H Sufraz)* 13 Newton Road, Canford Cliffs, POOLE, BH13 7EX.

ⓉⒻⒶ**Sugarwhite Associates** *(D Davis, J Sugarwhite)* 5 Windus Road, LONDON, N16 6UT.

Ⓣ**Sugdens, trading name of Sugdens LLP** *(A B Sugden)* Unit 20, Zenith Park, Whaley Road, BARNSLEY, SOUTH YORKSHIRE, S75 1HT.

Sullivan & Co *(N J A Sullivan)* 7 Newry Park, CHESTER, CH2 2AR.

ⒻⓅ**Sullivans, trading name of Sullivans Associates Limited** *(N P Mahoney, K M Munn, R J O Rees, P M H Teng)* 14 Gelliwastad Road, PONTYPRIDD, MID GLAMORGAN, CF37 2BW.

Ⓟ**Sully & Co** *(J B Edwards)* Sully House, 7 Clovelly Road Industrial Estate, BIDEFORD, DEVON, EX39 3HN.

ⒻⒶ**Sully & Co** *(S J Cartledge, J S Hale)* 18-22 Angel Crescent, BRIDGWATER, SOMERSET, TA6 3AL.

ⓉⒻ**Sully & Co** *(J R Kelly, N S L Williams)* 75 South Street, SOUTH MOLTON, EX36 4AG.

ⒻⓅⒶ**Sully Partnership, trading name of Sully Partnership Limited** *(I C Bascombe, N J Chivers)* 8 Unity Street, BRISTOL, BS1 5HH.

Ⓟ**Sultan Business Management Ltd** *(A A Sultan)* Elm Point, East End Way, PINNER, MIDDLESEX, HA5 3BS.

Ⓟ**Sum It, trading name of Sum It Accounts Ltd** *(S J Devlin)* 29 Greenlands Road, NEWBURY, BERKSHIRE, RG14 7JS.

Sumer Rustem & Co *(Sumer Rustem)* Ecevit Sokak No 58, Gonyeli, PO Box 6, LEFKOSA MERSIN 10, TURKEY.

Ⓟ**Sumit (UK) Limited** *(S I Martin)* 17 Cosgrove Road, Old Stratford, MILTON KEYNES, MK19 6AG.

Summ.it, trading name of Summit Accounting Solutions LLP *(S J Dunbar)* 74 Gartside Street, Spinningfields, MANCHESTER, M3 3EL.

ⒻⒶ**Summerhayes** *(J F Rudge)* Compass House, 6 Billetfield, TAUNTON, SOMERSET, TA1 3NN.

ⒻⒶ**Summers & Co.** *(A G Summers, R Summers)* 6 Jacobs Well Mews, LONDON, W1U 3DY.

Summers Accountancy and Book Keeping Services *(R N Lewis)* 70 New Road, Skewen, NEATH, WEST GLAMORGAN, SA10 6HA.

ⒻⒶ**Summers Morgan** *(N Corden, D J Manning)* Sheraton House, Lower Road, Chorleywood, RICKMANSWORTH, WD3 5LH.

Ⓟ**Summit Office Services Ltd** *(T Allen, S J Coke, C B Heslop)* 1 High Street, THATCHAM, BERKSHIRE, RG19 3JG.

Ⓟ**Sumup Limited** *(M J Williams)* 28 Pangfield Park, Allesley Park, COVENTRY, CV5 9NL.

Ⓟ**Sunaxis Ltd** *(C B Chadwick)* Checkpoint House, Unit 8 Checkpoint Court, Sadler Road, LINCOLN, LINCOLNSHIRE, LN6 3PW.

Ⓟ**Sunderland & Co, trading name of Dagas Limited** *(D G Sunderland)* 1 Gate Lodge Way, Laindon, BASILDON, ESSEX, SS15 4AR.

Sunderland Driver *(R Greenwood)* Orchard House, Aire Valley Business Centre, KEIGHLEY, BD21 3DU.

Sundip Shah BSc (Econ) ACA *(S Shah)* 135 Northwood Way, NORTHWOOD, MIDDLESEX, HA6 1RF.

Susan Atkins *(S J Atkins)* Yew House, Barnet Wood Road, BROMLEY, BR2 8HJ.

Ⓐ**Susan Barnwell** *(S M Barnwell)* The Former Vicarage, Much Marcle, LEDBURY, HEREFORDSHIRE, HR8 2NL.

Susan Baron *(S Mensforth)* The Old School, Over Haddon, BAKEWELL, DERBYSHIRE, DE45 1JE.

Susan C. Stott *(S C Stott)* 34 Tom Lane, Crosland Moor, HUDDERSFIELD, HD4 5PS.

Susan Church Accountancy Services *(S J Church)* 8 Dandridge Drive, BOURNE END, SL8 5UW.

Susan Davies ACA *(S J Davies)* 26 Sion Court, Sion Road, TWICKENHAM, TW1 3DD.

Susan E. Ainley *(S E Ainley)* 39 Fourth Avenue, HOVE, BN3 2PN.

Susan Ellison *(S T Ellison)* 30 Whitchurch Close, Padgate, WARRINGTON, WA1 4JZ.

ⓉⒻⓅⒶ**Susan Field, trading name of Susan Field Limited** *(S Field)* Neptune House, 70 Royal Hill, LONDON, SE10 8RF.

Ⓟ**Susan Goldsmith Limited** *(S Goldsmith)* 3 Kings Drive, EDGWARE, HA8 8EB.

ⓅⒶ**Susan Hinchliffe & Co Ltd** *(S J Hinchliffe)* 4 Newton Close, Newton Ferrers, PLYMOUTH, PL8 1AL.

Susan J Royce *(S J Royce)* Flat 29, Speed House, Barbican, LONDON, EC2Y 8AT.

Susan King ACA *(Susan King)* Hazlemere, 115 London Road, Temple Ewell, DOVER, CT16 3BY.

Susan Knowles ACA *(S E Knowles)* 210 Rockingham Road, KETTERING, NORTHAMPTONSHIRE, NN16 9AH.

Susan Singleton *(S L Singleton)* 475 Whirlowdale Road, Whirlow, SHEFFIELD, S11 9NH.

ⒻⒶ**Susan Stelfox** *(S Stelfox)* 46 The Keep, Blackheath, LONDON, SE3 0AF.

Susan Watson Accountancy Services *(S C Watson)* 28 Oak Drive, HENLOW, SG16 6BX.

Susanna Russell-Smith FCA *(Susanna Russell-Smith)* 249 Upper Richmond Road, Putney, LONDON, SW15 6SW.

Ⓟ**Sussex Accountancy Services Ltd** *(K L Headicar)* 5 Bankside, HASSOCKS, BN6 8EL.

ⓅⒶ**Sussex Tax Shop, The Property Tax Shop, trading names of Cohen Davidson Limited** *(I M Cohen)* 7 Marlborough Place, BRIGHTON-LE-SANDS, BN1 1UB.

Ⓟ**Sussex Taxation & Business Serv. Ltd** *(A A Hobbs)* 27 Albany Road, ST. LEONARDS-ON-SEA, EAST SUSSEX, TN38 0LP.

Ⓟ**Sustainable Opportunity Solutions, trading name of Sustainable Opportunity Solutions Limited** *(P R Adderley)* 14 Ravensheugh Road, Levenhall, MUSSELBURGH, MIDLOTHIAN, EH21 7PU.

Sutcliffe & Co *(S G Sutcliffe)* 3 Branch Road, BATLEY, WEST YORKSHIRE, WF17 5RY.

Ⓟ**Sutcliffe & Co, trading name of Sutcliffe & Co Ltd** *(J K A Coward, N J Huzal, M Langhelt)* Old Bank House, STURMINSTER NEWTON, DT10 1AN.

★Ⓐ**Sutcliffe & Riley** *(J M Bairstow, E Beaumont)* 3 Central Street, HALIFAX, HX1 1HU.

Ⓟ**Sutherland Corporate Services Ltd** *(M J Hallybone, A P Mate, G M Powling, D A Sheekey)* Sutherland House, 1759 London Road, LEIGH-ON-SEA, ESSEX, SS9 2RZ.

Ⓟ**Sutton Dipple Limited** *(S T Dipple, I R Sutton)* 8 Wheelwright's Corner, Old Market, Nailsworth, STROUD, GL6 0DB.

★ⓉⓅⒶ**Sutton McGrath Ltd** *(D I Sutton)* 5 Westbrook Court, Sharrow Vale Road, SHEFFIELD, S11 8YZ. and at CHESTERFIELD

Suzanne Cater, trading name of S.L. Cater *(S L Cater)* 6 Terminal House, Station Approach, SHEPPERTON, TW17 8AS.

Ⓟ**Suzanne Hill & Co, trading name of Suzanne Hill & Co Limited** *(S M Hill)* Rose Cottage, Cross Lanes, Oscroft Tarvin, CHESTER, CH3 8NQ.

Suzanne Spicer *(S Spicer)* 7 Keswick Close, DUNSTABLE, LU6 3AW.

Suzanne Wong & Co *(S S Wong)* Unit 704 Gee Tuck Building, Gee Tuck Building, 18 Bonham Strand, CENTRAL, HONG KONG SAR.

ⓅⒶ**SW Accountants Ltd** *(D P Smith)* 51 Eaton Hill, Cookridge, LEEDS, LS16 6SE.

Ⓟ**SW Corporate Services Ltd** *(C A Graham, K W J Saunders)* Wellesley House, Duke of Wellington Avenue, LONDON, SE18 6SS.

Ⓟ**SW Executor & Trustee Company Ltd** *(K W J Saunders)* Wellesley House, Duke of Wellington Avenue, Royal Arsenal, LONDON, SE18 6SS.

ⓉⒻ**Swallow & Co** *(D A Swallow)* Commercial House, 10 Bridge Road, Stokesley, MIDDLESBROUGH, TS9 5AA.

Ⓟ**Swallow, trading name of Swallow Associates (Stokesley) Limited** *(P J Wright)* Commercial House, 10 Bridge Road, Stokesley, MIDDLESBROUGH, CLEVELAND, TS9 5AA.

Ⓟ**Swan Accountancy Solutions Limited** *(M Spicer)* 21 Leacroft Close, STAINES, MIDDLESEX, TW18 4NP.

ⓉⓅ**Swandec, trading name of Swandec Limited** *(A West)* 550 Valley Road, Basford, NOTTINGHAM, NG5 1JJ.

Ⓟ**Swat UK Limited** *(R G Brown, A H R Gibbons, M J Sturgess)* Tor View House, Darklake View, Estover, PLYMOUTH, PL6 7TL. and at HESSLE, LONDON, PONTYCLUN

SWC *(S W Crew)* Hollywood, Furze Vale Road, Headley Down, BORDON, HAMPSHIRE, GU35 8EP.

Sweeting & Co *(R C A Sweeting)* 22 Willowbrook Close, Broughton Astley, LEICESTER, LE9 6HF.

Ⓟ**Swift Resolutions Limited** *(G M Swift)* 84 Brimstage Road, Heswall, WIRRAL, MERSEYSIDE, CH60 1XQ.

★ⓉⒻⒶ**Swindells, trading name of Swindells LLP** *(J Fackler, P J Gale, I K Jenkins, P I Moorey, M J Richardson)* New Olives, High Street, UCKFIELD, EAST SUSSEX, TN22 1QE. and at SEAFORD

Swinford House LLP *(I R Baker, P G Simpson)* Swinford House, Albion Street, BRIERLEY HILL, WEST MIDLANDS, DY5 3EE.

Ⓟ**Switchcourt Limited** *(A B A Samuels)* 12 Park Mount, HARPENDEN, HERTFORDSHIRE, AL5 3AR.

Sycamore Accounting Services *(D E Betteridge)* 42 New Lane, Huntington, YORK, YO32 9NT.

Ⓟ**Sycamore, trading name of Sycamore Accountancy Services Limited** *(N W Ramage)* 29 Blenheim Road, Moseley, BIRMINGHAM, B13 9TY.

ⒻⒶ**Sydney Parker & Co** *(S S Parker)* Parke House, 77 Edgwarebury Lane, EDGWARE, MIDDLESEX, HA8 8NJ.

ⒻⒶ**Sykes, Dalby & Truelove** *(A H B Dalby, C R Truelove)* 63 High Street, Hurstpierpoint, HASSOCKS, WEST SUSSEX, BN6 9RE. and at CAMBERLEY

Sylva & Co *(S I C Okoye)* 105 Loampit Vale, Lewisham, LONDON, SE13 7TG.

Symonds & Co *(R L Symonds)* Sunny Nook, Barhatch Road, CRANLEIGH, SURREY, GU6 7DJ.

Ⓐ**Symons** *(K D Symons, P Symons)* Willow Corner, 7 Ackrells Mead, SANDHURST, BERKSHIRE, GU47 8JJ.

ⒻⓅ**Synergee, trading name of Synergee Limited** *(M Allen, D P Austin)* 2nd Floor, 8 Lonsdale Gardens, TUNBRIDGE WELLS, KENT, TN1 1NU.

Synergy *(M D Harrad)* 3-4 Moorside Court, Yelverton Business Park, YELVERTON, DEVON, PL20 7PE.
Ⓟ**Synergy Business Solutions UK Limited** *(D J Woods)* 1 Fordyce Close, HORNCHURCH, ESSEX, RM11 3LE.
Ⓟ**Synergy Services(SW) Ltd** *(M D Harrad)* 3-4 Moorside Court, Yelverton Business Park, YELVERTON, DEVON, PL20 7PE.
Syron & Company *(D V Syron)* 7 Bell Villas, Ponteland, NEWCASTLE UPON TYNE, NE20 9BD.
Systematic Tax & Accountancy *(M J Wilson)* Hudson House, 8 Albany Street, EDINBURGH, EH1 3QB.
Ⓟ**T & I (Wisbech) Ltd** *(A D Davies)* 107 Elm Low Road, WISBECH, CAMBRIDGESHIRE, PE14 0DF.
★ⒻⓅⒶ**T A Gittins & Company, trading name of Gittins Limited** *(V E Jones)* 28 Salop Road, OSWESTRY, SHROPSHIRE, SY11 2NZ. and at WREXHAM
Ⓟ**T Cheung & Co, trading name of Chadsworth Limited** *(T K Cheung)* Unit 3A Wing Yip Centre, 278 Thimble Mill Lane, Nechells, BIRMINGHAM, B7 5HD.
T D Brown & Co *(T D Brown)* 50 The Ridings, SURBITON, SURREY, KT5 8HQ.
ⒻⓅ**T D G Keyworth & Co Limited** *(T D G Keyworth)* 158 Hemper Lane, Greenhill, SHEFFIELD, S8 7FE.
T D M Crees *(T D M Crees)* 29 Summerdown Lane, East Dean, EASTBOURNE, BN20 0LE.
T Hussain & Co *(T Hussain)* 123-E/1, Unit B, Hali Road, Gulberg III, LAHORE, PAKISTAN. and at LONDON
ⓅⒶ**T I Garner Limited** *(T I Garner)* 74 Ben Bank Road, Silkstone Common, BARNSLEY, SOUTH YORKSHIRE, S75 4PE.
ⓅⒶ**T J Jones Limited** *(T J Jones)* Whittingham Riddell LLP, Belmont House, Shrewsbury Business Park, SHREWSBURY, SY2 6LG.
Ⓟ**T J Loughnane, trading name of T J Loughnane Limited** *(T J Loughnane)* The Studio, Broad Street Walk, WOKINGHAM, BERKSHIRE, RG40 1BW.
Ⓟ**T J Medano Ltd** *(T J Williams)* 12 Stonehill Close, Ranskill, RETFORD, DN22 8NG.
T J Pearce FCA *(T J Pearce)* 2 The Fieldings, SITTINGBOURNE, KENT, ME10 4HA.
T J Shaw *(T J Shaw)* 6 Cherrington Manor Court, Cherrington, NEWPORT, TF10 8PA.
T M Accountancy *(T A Machova)* 42 Edendale Road, BEXLEYHEATH, KENT, DA7 6RW.
T M Rounsefell FCA *(T M Rounsefell)* 8 Alexandra Close, CREDITON, DEVON, EX17 2DY.
T M Webster & Co *(T M Webster)* 6 Lanheverne Parc, St Keverne, HELSTON, TR12 6LX.
Ⓟ**T Nawaz & Co Ltd** *(T Nawaz)* Cambridge House, 66 Little Horton Lane, BRADFORD, WEST YORKSHIRE, BD5 0HU.
T O SYLVESTER *(T O Sylvester)* 87 Winsley Hill, Limpley Stoke, BATH, WILTSHIRE, BA2 7FA.
T P Au & Co *(T Au)* Units B-C, 15th Floor Sun House, 90 Connaught Road, CENTRAL, HONG KONG ISLAND, HONG KONG SAR.
ⓉⓅ**T Rawlinson & Co Limited** *(R K Cowling)* 127 Cleethorpe Road, GRIMSBY, SOUTH HUMBERSIDE, DN31 3EW.
ⓉⒻⓅⒶ**T S Patara and Co, trading name of T S Patara & Co Ltd** *(T S Patara)* Financial House, 352 Bearwood Road, Bearwood, BIRMINGHAM, B66 4ET.
Ⓟ**T W Tax Services Limited** *(B W MacNay)* 3 Clanricarde Gardens, TUNBRIDGE WELLS, TN1 1HQ.
T Wood & Co (Birmingham) Limited *(T Wood)* 129 Hazelhurst Road, Kings Heath, BIRMINGHAM, B14 6AG.
Ⓕ**T. Burton & Co** *(T Burton)* 178 Brownhill Rd, Catford, LONDON, SE6 2DJ.
Ⓟ**T. C. Ng & Co. CPA Ltd.** *(E K C Man)* Amber Commercial Building, 13th Floor, 70-74 Morrison Hill Road, WAN CHAI, HONG KONG ISLAND, HONG KONG SAR.
T. Casillas & Co *(T N A Casillas)* 27 St Lawrence Drive, Eastcote, PINNER, HA5 2RL.
Ⓟ**T. King & Co Ltd** *(T King)* 72 Mill Road, ERITH, DA8 1HN.
T. Rashid *(T Rashid)* 20 Sundew Court, Elmore Close, WEMBLEY, HA0 1YY.
Ⓐ**T. Staplehurst** *(T Staplehurst)* April Cottage, Sturt's Lane, TADWORTH, KT20 7RQ.
T.A. Jehan & Co *(T A Jehan)* Ingouville House, Ingouville Lane, St Helier, JERSEY, JE4 8SP.
T.A. Parkinson *(E A Parkinson, T A Parkinson)* Linton Close, Trip Lane, Linton, WETHERBY, WEST YORKSHIRE, LS22 4HX.
T.B. Bollen *(T B Bollen)* 89 Groundwell Road, SWINDON, SN1 2NA.
T.D Marcuson *(T D Marcuson)* 15 West Hill Road, Foxton, CAMBRIDGE, CB22 6SZ.
T.D. Brooks & Co *(T D Brooks)* Flat 8, The Ferns, 90 Golf Links Road, FERNDOWN, DORSET, BH22 8BZ.
Ⓐ**T.E. Carpenter** *(T E Carpenter)* 362 Pickhurst Rise, WEST WICKHAM, BR4 0AY.
T.E.T.Gower *(T E T Gower)* 12 Birdwood Road, MAIDENHEAD, SL6 5AP.
T.F. Brown & Co *(T F Brown)* West Farm, Eavestone, RIPON, HG4 3HD.
T.F. Raishbrook *(T F Raishbrook)* 28 Highsted Road, SITTINGBOURNE, KENT, ME10 4PS.
T.G. Deakin *(T G Deakin)* 36 Berkeley, LETCHWORTH GARDEN CITY, HERTFORDSHIRE, SG6 2HA.
T.H. Bates *(T H Bates)* 27 Clarendon Road, Boston Spa, WETHERBY, LS23 6NG.
T.H. Chua & Co. *(T H Chua)* No 5-2 1st Floor, Jalan Othman, 84000 MUAR, JOHOR, MALAYSIA.
T.H. Graves *(T H Graves)* 73 Fairfax Road, TEDDINGTON, TW11 9DA.
T.J. Abrey *(T J Abrey)* 2 Swallow Close, Clopton Hill, STRATFORD-UPON-AVON, CV37 6TT.
T.J. Hussey *(T J Hussey)* Andrew Hill Cottage, Andrew Hill Lane, Hedgerley, SLOUGH, SL2 3UL.
T.J. Moorby *(T J Moorby)* 8 Melton Grange Road, Melton, WOODBRIDGE, SUFFOLK, IP12 1SA.
T.J. Pinton & Company *(T J Pinton)* 15 Hazel Avenue, Cove, FARNBOROUGH, HAMPSHIRE, GU14 0HA.
T.J. Rider *(T J Rider)* 36 Oaken Lane, Claygate, ESHER, KT10 0RG.
Ⓐ**T.J. Saxon** *(T J Saxon)* 43 Hagley Road, STOURBRIDGE, DY8 1QR.
T.J. Walker *(T J Walker)* 173 Wellington Road, Bush Hill Park, ENFIELD, EN1 2RL.
T.K. Choi & Co *(T Y B Yu)* 15th Floor, Empire Land Commercial Centre, 81-85 Lockhart, WAN CHAI, HONG KONG ISLAND, HONG KONG SAR.
T.L. Burton *(T L Burton)* Accountants Place, Heath Road, Linton, MAIDSTONE, ME17 4NU.
T.M. McMullen FCA *(T M McMullen)* 5 Milnthorpe Lane, Bramham, WETHERBY, WEST YORKSHIRE, LS23 6SW.
T.M. Watts & Co *(T M Watts)* 42 Wentworth Gardens, Palmers Green, LONDON, N13 5SN.
T.M.J. Norton *(T M J Norton)* 25 Beauworth Avenue, Greasby, WIRRAL, CH49 3QY.
T.P. Winnell & Co *(P Winnell)* 7 Hill Street, Douglas, ISLE OF MAN, IM1 1EF.
T.R. Stebbings & Co. *(T R Stebbings)* Onega House, 112 Main Road, SIDCUP, KENT, DA14 6NE.
T.R.H. McOwat *(T R H McOwat)* 8 Armley Grange Drive, LEEDS, LS12 3QH.
T.S. Batt *(T S Batt)* Crown House, Home Gardens, DARTFORD, DA1 1DZ.
T.S. Hope & Co *(T S Hope)* 56a Bury Road, Edenfield, Ramsbottom, BURY, LANCASHIRE, BL0 0ET.
Ⓐ**T.W. Tasker** *(T W Tasker)* 52a Station Rd, ASHINGTON, NE63 9UJ.
Ⓟ**TAB Associates Ltd** *(T A Bomber)* 59 King Street, Darlaston, WEDNESBURY, WEST MIDLANDS, WS10 8DE.
Ⓟ**Tacconi Green & Co (2000) Ltd** *(H Tacconi)* 32a East Street, ST. IVES, CAMBRIDGESHIRE, PE27 5PD.
Ⓐ**Tacconi Green & Co, trading name of H Tacconi** *(H Tacconi)* 32a East Street, ST.IVES, PE27 5PD.
ⓉⓅ**Tacconi Green & Co. Ltd** *(H Tacconi)* 32a East Street, ST.IVES, PE27 5PD.
TAD Consultancy *(T A Dabbs)* 41 Valentines Lea, Northchapel, PETWORTH, WEST SUSSEX, GU28 9HY.
Taddesse Woldegabriel & Co *(T Woldegabriel)* P.O. Box 22848 - Code 1000, ADDIS ABABA, ETHIOPIA.
Tadmans *(M R Tadman)* Blandford House, Church Walk, Combe, WITNEY, OX29 8NQ.
★**TadvinCo - Ernst & Young Iran** *(J Fararooy)* 1303 Vali-e-Asr Avenue, TEHRAN, 15178, IRAN.
Tahir & Co *(T Hussain)* 96 Boundary Road, Plaistow, LONDON, E13 9QG.
Tailored Tax Solutions LLP *(H Rafique)* No 3 Scott House, Admirals Way, LONDON, E14 9UG.
Tait Walker Corporate Finance, Tait Walker Corporate Recovery, trading names of Tait Walker Advisory Services LLP *(D R Arthur, M R C Brunton, A Crawley, G S Goldie, A J Moorby, G Moore, S C Plaskitt, M A Smith)* Bulman House, Regent Centre, Gosforth, NEWCASTLE UPON TYNE, NE3 3LS.
ⓉⒶ**Tait Walker, trading name of Tait Walker LLP** *(D R Arthur, M R C Brunton, A Crawley, G S Goldie, A J Moorby, G Moore, S C Plaskitt, M A Smith)* Bulman House, Regent Centre, Gosforth, NEWCASTLE UPON TYNE, NE3 3LS. and at MORPETH, STOCKTON-ON-TEES
Tallon Tax *(P C Tallon)* 33 Cavendish Square, LONDON, W1G 0PW.
Ⓕ**Talukdar & Co** *(M N H Talukdar)* 158 Whitworth Road, ROCHDALE, OL12 0JG.
Talyarkhan & Co *(D R Talyarkhan)* Lyndewode House, Bomanji Petit Road, Cumballa Hill, MUMBAI 400036, MAHARASHTRA, INDIA.
Ⓟ**TAM & Sons Limited** *(T A Marshall)* 12 Market Street, HEBDEN BRIDGE, WEST YORKSHIRE, HX7 6AD.
Tam Au & Co *(F Tam)* Unit B, 22/F Tak Lee Commercial Building, 113 Wan Chai Road, WAN CHAI, HONG KONG ISLAND, HONG KONG SAR.
Tam Chi Ming *(C M Tam)* Room 1805 18th Floor, Wellborne Commercial Centre, 8 Java Road, NORTH POINT, HONG KONG ISLAND, HONG KONG SAR.
Tambayah & Co *(N P Tambayah)* 7 Norland Square, Holland Park, LONDON, W11 4PX.
ⓅⒶ**Tamblyn & Co Limited** *(S E Tamblyn)* Kinnersley House, Kinnersley, Nr Severn Stoke, WORCESTER, WR8 9JR.
★**Tang and Fok** *(H Y P Fok)* Rooms 1801-3 18/ Floor, Tung Ning Building, 249-253 Des Voeux Road Central, CENTRAL, HONG KONG ISLAND, HONG KONG SAR.
Tang Yuen Shun *(Y Tang)* Unit K 18/F, World Tech Centre, 95 How Ming Street, KWUN TONG, KOWLOON, HONG KONG SAR.
Ⓟ**Tania Wilkie & Co Ltd** *(T Wilkie)* 52 Portsmouth Road, LEE-ON-THE-SOLENT, HAMPSHIRE, PO13 9AG.
ⒻⒶ**Tanna & Co.** *(P Tanna)* 13 Sheaveshill Parade, Sheaveshill Avenue, LONDON, NW9 6RS.
Tanna & Co. *(D P Tanna)* 6 Ravenscroft Avenue, WEMBLEY, MIDDLESEX, HA9 9TL.
Tanner & Co, trading name of C.J. Tanner *(C J Tanner)* 6 Rose Hill, DORKING, SURREY, RH4 2EG.
Tanzeela Samad *(T Samad)* 2 Hawksnest Gardens East, Alwoodley, LEEDS, LS17 7JQ.
ⓉⒻⓅⒶ**Taparia & Co, trading name of Taparia Consultants Limited** *(S Taparia)* Taparia House, 1096 Uxbridge Road, HAYES, MIDDLESEX, UB4 8QH.
ⓉⓅ**Tarbun & Company, trading name of Tarbun & Company Limited** *(P J Tarbun)* 10 Bishopdale Close, MORECAMBE, LANCASHIRE, LA3 3SU.
ⓅⒶ**Target Consulting Group, trading name of Target Consulting Group Limited** *(A L Bennett, A P Sandiford, K Seeley)* Lawrence House, Lower Bristol Road, BATH, BA2 9ET.
ⓉⒻⓅⒶ**Target, Target Corporate Finance, Target HR Consultancy, Target Tax Consultancy, trading names of Target Consulting Limited** *(A L Bennett, A P Sandiford, K Seeley)* Lawrence House, Lower Bristol Road, BATH, BA2 9ET. and at BRISTOL, READING, RUGBY
ⒻⓅⒶ**Target, trading name of Target Accountants Limited** *(A L Bennett, A P Sandiford, K Seeley)* Lawrence House, Lower Bristol Road, BATH, BA2 9ET. and at LONDON
Ⓟ**Tarima, trading name of Tarima Consulting Limited** *(T Khan)* 1a Becket Gardens, WELWYN, HERTFORDSHIRE, AL6 9JE.
★**Tariq Ayub, Anwar & Co** *(T A Qureshi)* 84-B-1 Gulberg III, LAHORE, PAKISTAN.
Tarrant Green & Co *(R T B Green)* 27 Old Gloucester Street, LONDON, WC1N 3AX.
ⓅⒶ**Tasker Accounting Services Limited** *(C J Tasker)* 14 Sunnybank Crescent, Yeadon, LEEDS, LS19 7TE.
Tasos Papaloizou *(T Papaloizou)* 260 Sussex Way, LONDON, N19 4HY.
ⓅⒶ**TAT Accounting, trading name of TAT Accounting Limited** *(T A Tzouliou)* 26 Hillfield Park, LONDON, N21 3QH.
★**Tatar & Co** *(H T Muftizade, E R Tatar, R Z Tatar, Z E R Tatar)* 11 Hasene Ilgaz Str, P.O. Box 768, LEFKOSA MERSIN 10, TURKEY.
Tate & Co. *(H B K Tate)* 11 Bridge Wharf Road, ISLEWORTH, MIDDLESEX, TW7 6BS.
ⓅⒶ**Tattersalls, trading name of Tattersalls Accountancy Services Limited** *(J A Tattersall)* Concept House, 3 Dene Street, DORKING, SURREY, RH4 2DR.
ⓅⒶ**Tatum Guest Associates, trading name of Hicks Randles Limited** *(A L S Hicks, D G Hicks, I V Roberts)* 7 Grove Park Road, WREXHAM, CLWYD, LL12 7AA. and at MOLD, NEWTOWN
Tax - Easy *(A Knapper)* Mayfield Cottage, Eastham Street, CLITHEROE, LANCASHIRE, BB7 2HY.
Ⓟ**Tax & Accounts Solutions Ltd** *(C E Faint)* The Old School House, Lyndhurst Road, BROCKENHURST, HAMPSHIRE, SO42 7RH.
Ⓟ**Tax 24-7.Com Limited** *(M Broadhead)* PO Box 47-118, LONDON, W6 0NX.
Ⓟ**Tax Accountants Ltd** *(A D Patel)* 9 Griffith Close, STRATFORD-UPON-AVON, WARWICKSHIRE, CV37 0TP.
Tax Accounting Consultancy Service *(A C Spooner)* 31 Ullswater Road, LONDON, SW13 9PL.
Ⓟ**Tax Advice Shop Limited** *(R W Davies)* West Lodge, Rainbow Street, LEOMINSTER, HEREFORDSHIRE, HR6 8DQ.
Tax and Figures LLP *(R Insalaco)* The Coach House, 77a Marlowes, HEMEL HEMPSTEAD, HERTFORDSHIRE, HP1 1LF.
Tax Assist Accountants *(K Shah)* 121 Dugdale Hill Lane, POTTERS BAR, HERTFORDSHIRE, EN6 2DS.
Ⓟ**Tax Assist Accountants Grimsby, trading name of Hassle Free Tax Ltd** *(S Parker)* 57 Kingsway, CLEETHORPES, SOUTH HUMBERSIDE, DN35 0AD.
Tax Assist Accountants, trading name of P Cornish *(P R Cornish)* 4 Deacon Close, Bowdon, ALTRINCHAM, CHESHIRE, WA14 3ND.
Ⓟ**Tax Assist Accountants, trading name of Tax and Accounts Shop Limited** *(D R Roberts)* 12 Hibel Road, MACCLESFIELD, CHESHIRE, SK10 2AB.
Ⓟ**Tax Assured Limited** *(R J Wynniatt-Husey)* Threefields, Church Lane, Marchington, UTTOXETER, STAFFORDSHIRE, ST14 8LJ.
Ⓟ**Tax Beans & Law, trading name of Tax Beans & Law Ltd** *(K Samuels)* 111 Stratford Road, Wolverton, MILTON KEYNES, MK12 5LW.
ⓉⒻⓅⒶ**Tax Champion, trading name of Knowles Warwick Limited** *(S D Knowles)* 183 Fraser Road, SHEFFIELD, S8 0JP.
Tax Consulting Solutions *(M J Bell)* 53 The Business Centre, Metcalf Way, CRAWLEY, WEST SUSSEX, RH11 7XX.
Tax Credit Strategies LLP *(D T Scott)* 15 Colburn Avenue, NEWTON AYCLIFFE, COUNTY DURHAM, DL5 7HX.
Ⓟ**Tax Investigation Services, trading name of Astacx Limited** *(K A Anderson)* Longcroft Farmhouse, 31 Derby Road, Aston-on-Trent, DERBY, DE72 2AE.
Tax Investigation Services, trading name of Chris Madge & Co *(C B Madge)* The Stables, Clevedon Hall, CLEVEDON, BS21 7SJ. and at CARDIFF, LONDON
Ⓟ**Tax Key Limited** *(L Y C Fung)* 2nd Floor, Astoria House, 62 Shaftesbury Avenue, LONDON, W1D 6LT.
Ⓟ**Tax Partner Ltd** *(J M Baker, R C Baker, R P Batchelor, L P Girling)* 21 Dennyview Road, Abbots Leigh, BRISTOL, BS8 3RD.
Ⓟ**Tax Processing Limited** *(G R Randall, A Ward)* The Parade, LISKEARD, CORNWALL, PL14 6AF.
ⓉⓅⒶ**Tax Processing Limited, trading name of Ward Randall Limited** *(G R Randall, A Ward)* The Parade, LISKEARD, CORNWALL, PL14 6AF.
Ⓟ**Tax Returns Nationwide Ltd** *(D R Curtis, P Curtis)* 1 Tape Street, Cheadle, STOKE-ON-TRENT, ST10 1BB.
Tax Right *(G Wilkinson)* 35 Montgomery Close, Whiston Knowsley, PRESCOT, L35 3RD.
Ⓟ**Tax Solutions (North West) Limited** *(K Pope)* 35 Woodside Lane, Poynton, STOCKPORT, CHESHIRE, SK12 1BB.
Ⓟ**Tax Support Limited** *(K M Pitchford)* Building 67, Europa Business Park, Bird Hall Lane, Cheadle Heath, STOCKPORT, CHESHIRE SK3 0XA.
Tax Training Solutions *(H Stainton)* 19 Vale Coppice, Ramsbottom, BURY, LANCASHIRE, BL0 9FJ.
Tax Unravelled, trading name of Jane Jennings ACA *(J A Jennings)* 28 Barbaras Meadow, Tilehurst, READING, RG31 6YF.
ⓅⒶ**Tax, Audit and Accounts Solutions Limited** *(C S Homan)* Southgate Chambers, 37-39 Southgate Street, WINCHESTER, HAMPSHIRE, SO23 9EH.
Ⓟ**Tax4You.co.uk Limited** *(M Sheezan)* Castle Court, 41 London Road, REIGATE, SURREY, RH2 9RJ.
Taxadjusters LLP *(D A Dodds)* Boundary Farm, South Scarle Lane, Swinderby, LINCOLN, LN6 9JA.
TaxAssist Accountants *(R A Brookes)* 173 Mill Road, CAMBRIDGE, CB1 3AN.
TaxAssist Accountants *(B F Combe)* 41 High Street, EAST GRINSTEAD, WEST SUSSEX, RH19 3AF.
Taxassist Accountants *(B A Piercy)* Hutchinson House, 21 Sandown Lane, Wavertree, LIVERPOOL, L15 7LQ.
TaxAssist Accountants *(A G Coles)* 3 Boldmere Road, SUTTON COLDFIELD, WEST MIDLANDS, B73 5UY.
TaxAssist Accountants - Gary Richards *(G A Richards)* 714 London Road, Larkfield, AYLESFORD, KENT, ME20 6BL.
Ⓟ**Taxassist Accountants, trading name of Accounting Concepts (Cheshire) Ltd** *(S Rotherham)* 134 Liverpool Road, WIDNES, CHESHIRE, WA8 7JB.
Ⓟ**TaxAssist Accountants, trading name of BS Tax and Accountancy Limited** *(J E Sheard)* Phoenix House, 2 Huddersfield Road, STALYBRIDGE, CHESHIRE, SK15 2QA. and at MANCHESTER
Taxassist Accountants, trading name of Donovan Crutchfield *(D A Crutchfield)* 34 Lower Richmond Road, LONDON, SW15 1JP.

Ⓟ**TaxAssist Accountants, trading name of My Tax Accountant Limited** *(A E Smith)* 38 Bretonside, PLYMOUTH, PL4 0AU.

Taxassist Accountants, trading name of Peter Stoddart FCA *(P Stoddart)* 226 Chester Road, SUNDERLAND, SR4 7HR.

Taxassist Accountants, trading name of RJ Parkin *(R J Parkin)* 7 Solihull Lane, Hall Green, BIRMINGHAM, B28 9LS.

Ⓟ**TaxAssist Accountants, trading name of Tax Matters Accountants Ltd** *(D J Rodick)* 259 Edleston Road, CREWE, CHESHIRE, CW2 7EA. and at WARRINGTON

Ⓟ**Taxation Advice & Consultancy Ltd** *(N Pugh, K A Smith)* Elfed House, Oak Tree Court, Mulberry Drive, Cardiff Gate Business Park, Pontprennau, CARDIFF CF23 8RS.

Ⓟ**Taxbak, The Melia Partnership, trading names of Taxbak Limited** *(S Childs)* Park House, 91 Garstang Road, PRESTON, PR1 1LD.

Taxbase Accountancy Services *(J M Payne)* 32 West Burnside, DOLLAR, CLACKMANNANSHIRE, FK14 7DR.

Ⓟ**TaxCo Global, trading name of TaxCo Global Limited** *(B J Sacher)* 38 Wigmore Street, LONDON, W1U 2RU.

Taxdore *(V H Parnell)* Collingwood, 6 Oxshott Rise, COBHAM, KT11 2RN.

Taxing Nannies - Payroll Agents, trading name of Sara Graff & Co *(S J Graff)* 28 Minchenden Crescent, Southgate, LONDON, N14 7EL.

Ⓟ**TaxiTax, trading name of Your Exit Strategy Ltd** *(A J Solomons)* Suite 213, 2 Gayton Road, HARROW, MIDDLESEX, HA1 2XU.

Ⓟ**Taxline 3d, trading name of Chiltern Tax Support for Professionals Limited** *(P M Eagland)* 55 Baker Street, LONDON, W1U 7EU.

Ⓟ**Taxmaster Solutions Limited** *(D A Dodds)* Boundary Farm, South Scarle Lane, Swinderby, LINCOLN, LN6 9JA.

Ⓟ**Taxsavers Accountants, trading name of Taxsavers Direct Ltd** *(G C Booth)* 26 Orchard Way, OXTED, SURREY, RH8 9DJ.

Ⓟ**Taxsolve UK Limited** *(D S George)* 57A High Street, FELTHAM, MIDDLESEX, TW13 4EZ.

Ⓟ**Taxwrite.co.uk Limited** *(J S Speller)* 1436 London Road, LEIGH-ON-SEA, ESSEX, SS9 2UL.

ⓅⒶ**Tayabali Tomlin & White, trading name of TT&W Limited** *(I Z Tayabali, S R F White)* 5 High Green, Great Shelford, CAMBRIDGE, CB22 5EG.

ⒾⓅⒶ**Tayabali-Tomlin, trading name of Tayabali-Tomlin Limited** *(A N Damery, A F Noorani)* Kenton House, Oxford Street, MORETON-IN-MARSH, GLOUCESTERSHIRE, GL56 0LA. and at CHELTENHAM

Ⓐ**Taylor & Co** *(H C E Downing)* 20 Edenhurst Court, Parkhill Road, TORQUAY, TQ1 2DD.

ⓅⒶ**Taylor & Co Accountancy Services Ltd** *(D Taylor)* 64 Lewin Street, MIDDLEWICH, CHESHIRE, CW10 9AS.

Ⓟ**Taylor & Company, trading name of N C Taylor Limited** *(N C Taylor)* Temple Chambers, 4 Abbey Road, GRIMSBY, DN32 0HF.

Ⓟ**Taylor Brooker, TB-a, trading names of Taylor Brooker Accountancy Limited** *(R D Sutton)* Barham Court, Teston, MAIDSTONE, KENT, ME18 5BZ.

Taylor Cocks Medical LLP *(S Beaumont)* 3 Acorn Business Centre, Northarbour Road, Cosham, PORTSMOUTH, PO6 3TH.

★ⒾⒻⓅⒶ**Taylor Cocks, trading name of The Taylor Cocks Partnership Limited** *(S Beaumont, P N Taylor)* Taylor Cocks LLP, 3 Acorn Business Centre, Northarbour Road, Cosham, PORTSMOUTH, PO6 3TH. and at FARNHAM, HENLEY-ON-THAMES, OXFORD, READING, SOUTHAMPTON, WIMBORNE

★ⓅⒶ**Taylor Dawson Plumb, trading name of Taylor Dawson Plumb Limited** *(G M Plumb, J P Taylor)* 2 King Street, NOTTINGHAM, NG1 2AS.

ⒾⒻⓅ**Taylor Edward, trading name of Taylor Edward Limited** *(A A T Miah)* 3 Broadway Court, High Street, CHESHAM, BUCKINGHAMSHIRE, HP5 1EG.

Taylor Gillam & Co *(R W Lloyd)* 28 Hillcroft Avenue, PURLEY, SURREY, CR8 3DJ.

ⒻⒶ**Taylor Roberts** *(N Roberts, M O Taylor)* Unit 9B, Wingbury Business Village, Upper Wingbury Farm, AYLESBURY, HP22 4LW. and at WATERLOOVILLE

★ⒾⒻⒶ**Taylor Rowlands, trading name of Rowlands** *(E Brannigan, C Chater, E C Glover, P M Millar, D Nairn, D T Taylor, D G Waugh)* Rowlands House, Portobello Road, Birtley, CHESTER LE STREET, COUNTY DURHAM, DH3 2RY. and at CROOK, YARM

ⓅⒶ**Taylor Rushby, trading name of Taylor Rushby Limited** *(N E Taylor)* 32 Crouch Street, COLCHESTER, CO3 3HH.

Ⓐ**Taylor, Croft & Winder** *(D A Taylor)* 16 Bond Street, WAKEFIELD, WF1 2QP.

ⒾⒻⒶ**Taylor, Viney & Marlow** *(P A Brown, S McCallum, S L Pinion, A J Smith, D J Stevens, C J Taylor)* 46-54 High Street, INGATESTONE, CM4 9DW. and at LEIGH-ON-SEA

Taylored Accountancy Services *(K Taylor)* Northfield, Low Street, Carlton, GOOLE, NORTH HUMBERSIDE, DN14 9PN.

Ⓟ**Taylored Accounting Solutions, trading name of Taylored Business Solutions Ltd** *(M J Taylor)* 15 Junction Gardens, PLYMOUTH, PL4 9AR.

Ⓐ**Taylors** *(R Gulabivala)* Battle House, 1 East Barnet Road, BARNET, EN4 8RR.

ⒻⒶ**Taylors** *(C R N Taylor)* 203 London Road, Hadleigh, BENFLEET, SS7 2RD.

Taylors *(A J Taylor)* 51 High Street, Stokesley, MIDDLESBROUGH, CLEVELAND, TS9 5AD.

ⒾⒻⒶ**TBW** *(M M Chan, R L O Tang)* E3 The Premier Centre, Abbey Park, ROMSEY, SO51 9DG. and at LONDON

TC Greenwood *(T C Greenwood)* 22 Ullswater Road, Handforth, WILMSLOW, CHESHIRE, SK9 3NQ.

Ⓟ**TCG Accountancy Limited** *(C Gibson)* 19 Chesterholm, CARLISLE, CA2 7XH.

Ⓐ**TCP (GB) Audit LLP** *(R Wheldon)* 10 The Triangle, NOTTINGHAM, NG2 1AE.

ⓅⒶ**TCP Holdings Ltd** *(P N Taylor)* 3 Acorn Business Centre, Northarbour Road, PORTSMOUTH, PO6 3TH.

Teal Strategy, trading name of Snowden & Co *(J F H Snowden)* Dial House, High Street, Hook Norton, BANBURY, OXFORDSHIRE, OX15 5NQ.

Ⓟ**Team 4 Accounting Ltd** *(J A Mills)* Cressfield House, School Lane, Headbourne Worthy, WINCHESTER, SO23 7JX.

Ⓐ**Team Audit, trading name of Team Audit LLP** *(P Kingham, N Y S Liu)* Kingham House, 161 College Street, ST. HELENS, MERSEYSIDE, WA10 1TY.

Ⓟ**Teamwork Financial Services Limited** *(A M Mandalia)* 31 Cheyneys Avenue, EDGWARE, MIDDLESEX, HA8 6SA.

ⒾⒻⓅⒶ**Tearle & Carver, trading name of Tearle & Carver Limited** *(A Carver, K A Harrison)* Chandos House, School Lane, BUCKINGHAM, MK18 1HD.

Ⓟ**Teather & Co, trading name of Teather & Co Limited** *(K M Teather)* Tile Oak, Old Slade Lane, Richings Park, IVER, SL0 9DR.

Ⓟ**Ted Henderson Limited** *(J E Henderson)* Ben-y-Hone Cottage, 21 Dundas Street, Comrie, CRIEFF, PERTHSHIRE, PH6 2LN.

Ⓟ**Teddington Tax Services Ltd** *(R A Chalk)* 6 Marina Way, TEDDINGTON, MIDDLESEX, TW11 9PN.

teleologica, trading name of Brian J Coutanche *(B J Coutanche)* Egret House, Mount Bingham, St. Helier, JERSEY, JE2 4XY.

Telling R.C. *(R C Telling)* Warecott, Old Worcester Road, Hartlebury, KIDDERMINSTER, DY11 7XL.

Ⓟ**Tempest Forensice Accounting Ltd** *(G L Mesher)* Nant-Yr-Arian, Llandefalle, BRECON, POWYS, LD3 0NS.

ⒾⒻⓅ**Temple & Co, trading name of T and C Services Ltd** *(K B Last)* 76 Townsend Lane, HARPENDEN, AL5 2RQ.

★**Temple Gothard Johnson Abioy e & Co** *(O O Johnson)* 13 Norman Williams Street, off Awolowo Road SW Ikoyo, LAGOS, NIGERIA. and at KANO

ⓅⒶ**Temple West Limited** *(S M Davies)* PO Box 454, WEST BYFLEET, SURREY, KT14 9BD.

ⒻⓅⒶ**Templetons (UK) Ltd** *(S K Lakhani)* 309 Hoe Street, LONDON, E17 9BG.

ⓅⒶ**Temporal Lennon & Company Limited** *(J M G Richardson)* Suite 1A, Realtex House, Leeds Road, Rawdon, LEEDS, LS19 6AX.

ⒾⓅ**Tenbury Ltd** *(P M Bramall)* Brenchley Mews, School Road, Charing, ASHFORD, KENT, TN27 0JW.

Tendler & Co *(G P Tendler, M J Tendler)* 7 Frithwood Avenue, NORTHWOOD, HA6 3LY.

Ⓟ**Terence Houghton & Co Ltd** *(J Cousins Woodrow, J Healy, R M Johnson)* Saddlers Courtyard, 4-6 South Parade, Bawtry, DONCASTER, SOUTH YORKSHIRE, DN10 6JH.

Ⓐ**Terence J. Down & Co.** *(T J Down)* Brook House, Park Avenue, VENTNOR, ISLE OF WIGHT, PO38 1LE.

Terrance G. Chang *(T G Chang)* PO Box 3037, Tragarete Road Post Office, PORT OF SPAIN, TRINIDAD AND TOBAGO.

Terry Beak & Co *(T J Beak)* 5 Hamilton Close, Littlestone, NEW ROMNEY, TN28 8NU.

Terry Bickenson *(T E Bickenson)* 96 Broadmoor Lane, BATH, BA1 4LB.

Terry Burrells *(T Burrells)* 33 Rectory Avenue, Corfe Mullen, WIMBORNE, BH21 3EZ.

Ⓟ**Terry J Greaves, trading name of 4U Management Ltd** *(T J Greaves)* 8 Hodgson Fold, Addingham, ILKLEY, WEST YORKSHIRE, LS29 0HA.

Terry Marsh *(T G Marsh)* Barley Mow House, Woods Lane, Cliddesden, BASINGSTOKE, RG25 2JG.

Terry R. Wellstood & Co *(T R Wellstood)* Copse Lodge, Cogges Lane, Stanton Harcourt, WITNEY, OXFORDSHIRE, OX29 5AJ.

ⒻⓅⒶ**Tesciuba Limited** *(A J Tesciuba)* The Chambers, 13 Police Street, MANCHESTER, M2 7LQ.

Ⓟ**Tessa Davidson Limited** *(T L Davidson)* The Ashridge Business Centre, 121 High Street, BERKHAMSTED, HERTFORDSHIRE, HP4 2DJ.

Ⓟ**Tester Accountancy & Bookkeeping Ltd** *(D M Samothrakis)* 34 Fairoak Road, CARDIFF, CF24 4PY.

★**Tetlow & Smith** *(A G Phillips)* 1 Osborne Road, Jesmond, NEWCASTLE UPON TYNE, NE2 2AA.

TF Lam & Company *(T Lam)* Unit 2105, 21/F Exchange Tower, 33 Wang Chiu Road, KOWLOON BAY, HONG KONG SAR.

★ⒾⒻⒶ**TFD Dunhams** *(M F Dunham, P G O'Brien)* 11 Warwick Road, Old Trafford, MANCHESTER, M16 0QQ.

Ⓟ**TG Associates, trading name of TG Associates Limited** *(R Gudka, A K Thakrar)* Monument House, 215 Marsh Road, PINNER, HA5 5NE.

★ⒻⓅⒶ**TGFP, trading name of TGFP Limited** *(B R Reynolds)* Fulford House, Newbold Terrace, LEAMINGTON SPA, WARWICKSHIRE, CV32 4EA.

Thain Osborne & Co. *(C A Thain)* 1st Floor, 94A High Street, SEVENOAKS, KENT, TN13 1LP.

★ⒻⓅⒶ**Thain Wildbur, trading name of Anglian Accountancy Services Ltd** *(J Hodson)* 36-38 King Street, KING'S LYNN, NORFOLK, PE30 1ES.

ⒻⒶ**Thaker & Co.** *(B J Thaker)* 31 Southwood Gardens, Gants Hill, ILFORD, ESSEX, IG2 6YF.

Ⓐ**Thakrar & Co** *(V S Thakrar)* 48 Dean Road, LEICESTER, LE4 6GN.

★**Thakrar Coombs & Co** *(R A Coombs, L Shah)* The Dairy House, Moneyrow Green, Holyport, MAIDENHEAD, SL6 2ND.

Ⓟ**Thanki Associates Limited** *(N D Thanki)* 16 Wembley Park Drive, WEMBLEY, MIDDLESEX, HA9 8HA.

Ⓐ**Thapers** *(A K Mangal)* 14 Holyhead Road, Handsworth, BIRMINGHAM, B21 0LT.

Thatchers *(J E Bassil)* 13 Dunstable Road, Studham, DUNSTABLE, LU6 2QG.

Thauoos & Co *(O F Thauoos)* 201 High Street, Penge, LONDON, SE20 7PF.

Ⓟ**The A9 Partnership (Highland) Ltd** *(P A Capewell, E L Smart)* Elm House, Cradlehall Business Park, INVERNESS, IV2 5GH.

★Ⓟ**The Accountancy Fellowship, trading name of Accountancy Fellowship Limited** *(W G Belcher)* 9 Queens Road, BOURNEMOUTH, DORSET, BH2 6BA.

Ⓟ**The Accountancy Service, trading name of Accountancy Services (New Malden) Limited** *(R S Shah)* The Offices, 1 Park Road, NEW MALDEN, SURREY, KT3 5AF.

Ⓓ**The Accounting Centre** *(M I Somers)* 60 Croham Valley Road, SOUTH CROYDON, Surrey, CR2 7NB.

ⒾⓅ**The Accounts Bureau Limited** *(M M Weston)* 2nd Floor, 1 Warwick Row, LONDON, SW1E 5ER.

Ⓟ**The Accounts Company.Com, trading name of The Accounts Company.Com Ltd** *(P S Rushton)* Unit 1 City Point, 156 Chapel Street, MANCHESTER, M3 6BF. and at SALFORD

Ⓓ**The Accounts Department** *(A J Solomons)* Computer House, 390/394 Kenton Road, HARROW, HA3 9HB.

Ⓟ**The Accounts Dept. Limited** *(P T Soteriou, R Soteriou)* 3 Cromer Street, LONDON, WC1H 8LS.

Ⓟ**The Accounts Factory, trading name of The Accounts Factory Ltd** *(M D Lamburn, B E Turner)* 1 Place Farm, Wheathampstead, ST. ALBANS, HERTFORDSHIRE, AL4 8SB.

★**The Accounts People** *(K J Nicholson)* 25 Priory Mead, Doddinghurst, BRENTWOOD, ESSEX, CM15 0NB.

ⒻⓅⒶ**The Alnwick Accountants Ltd** *(F Robson, J H Spowart)* 16 Bondgate Without, ALNWICK, NORTHUMBERLAND, NE66 1PP.

Ⓐ**The Bailey Partnership** *(C F Bailey)* Sterling House, 27 Hatchlands Road, REDHILL, RH1 6RW.

★ⒾⒻⒶ**The Barker Partnership** *(C Gill, W G Pearson, P B Triffitt)* Bank Chambers, 17 Central Buildings, Market Place, THIRSK, YO7 1HD. and at LEYBURN, RIPON

ⒻⓅⒶ**The Barker Partnership, trading name of The Barker Partnership Limited** *(C Gill, W G Pearson, P B Triffitt)* 17 Market Place, THIRSK, NORTH YORKSHIRE, YO7 1HD. and at HARROGATE

The Burns Partnership *(P A Osborn)* 138 Peperharow Road, GODALMING, SURREY, GU7 2PW. and at BANFF

Ⓐ**The Business Services Office** *(S J Trobridge)* 57 Moorview Way, SKIPTON, NORTH YORKSHIRE, BD23 2JW.

Ⓟ**The Campbell Parker Partnership Limited** *(H Sheridan)* 2 City Limits, Danehill, Lower Earley, READING, RG6 4UP.

★ⒾⒻⒶ**The Carley Partnership** *(A J Gooch, B J Hensman, B Owen)* St. James's House, 8 Overcliffe, GRAVESEND, DA11 0HJ.

ⒾⒶ**The cba Partnership** *(C S Brown, S P Jenkinson, M K Todd)* 72 Lairgate, BEVERLEY, HU17 8EU.

The Chamber of Experts *(T J Vogel)* 48 The Street, Sporle, KING'S LYNN, PE32 2DR.

ⒾⒻⒶ**The Chartwell Practice** *(M J Chilver, F D Startin)* Chartwell House, 4 St. Pauls Square, BURTON-ON-TRENT, STAFFORDSHIRE, DE14 2EF.

Ⓟ**The Chiltern Partnership Ltd** *(K M Best)* Grafton House, Bulls Head Yard, ALCESTER, WARWICKSHIRE, B49 5BX. and at WATLINGTON

The Clifton Tax Practice LLP *(K L White)* The Pavilions, Eden Park, Ham Green, BRISTOL, BS20 0DD.

★Ⓟ**The Company Specialists (Accounting Services) Ltd** *(S M Matthews, P M Sutton)* 53 Rodney Street, LIVERPOOL, L1 9ER.

Ⓟ**The Cook Partnership Ltd** *(D J Cook)* Suites 11 &12, Akeman Business Park, Akeman Street, TRING, HERTFORDSHIRE, HP23 6AF.

The Counting House *(P M Mitchell)* Flat 64, Exeter House, Putney Heath, LONDON, SW15 3SX.

The Counting House Partnership LLP *(J P Bradney, M J Worrall)* 6 Hanover Road, TUNBRIDGE WELLS, KENT, TN1 1EY.

Ⓜ**The Crossgrove Partnership Ltd** *(D J Crossgrove)* 40 Belmont Road, Bramhall, STOCKPORT, SK7 1LE.

The Curtis Partnership *(D R Curtis, P Curtis)* 1 Tape Street, Cheadle, STOKE-ON-TRENT, ST10 1BB.

ⒻⒶ**The Davison Partnership** *(D B Leese, A Pope)* Reliance House, Moorland Road, Burslem, STOKE-ON-TRENT, ST6 1DP.

Ⓟ**The Debt People, trading name of MoneyPlus Group Limited** *(S M Quinn)* Lawson House, 22-26 Stockport Road, ALTRINCHAM, CHESHIRE, WA15 8EX.

Ⓟ**The Decimal Place, trading name of Razzle Limited** *(R J Everall)* 8 Blandfield Road, LONDON, SW12 8BG.

Ⓟ**The Dinsdale Young Practice Ltd** *(B Singh)* First Floor, 10 College Road, HARROW, MIDDLESEX, HA1 1BE.

The Doran Consultancy *(J Doran)* 1-2 Hill End House, Norwood Green, HALIFAX, HX3 8QE.

★ⓅⒶ**The DPC Group Limited** *(D Griffiths, C Kane, S J Webster, V A Wood)* Vernon Road, STOKE-ON-TRENT, ST4 2QY.

Ⓟ**The Dyer Partnership, trading name of The Dyer Partnership Limited** *(M E Dyer)* 17 Westminster Court, Hipley Street, WOKING, SURREY, GU22 9LG.

Ⓟ**The Financial Management Centre - Hammersmith, trading name of Zein Contractors Limited** *(M C Zein)* Unit 71, 61 Praed Street, LONDON, W2 1NS.

Ⓟ**The Financial Management Centre Newcastle upon Tyne, trading name of Key Accountancy Services Limited** *(W E R Tombs)* 92 Whitton View, Rothbury, MORPETH, NORTHUMBERLAND, NE65 7QN.

Ⓟ**The Financial Management Centre, trading name of My Accounts Centre Limited** *(H S Tack)* 89 Shaggy Calf Lane, SLOUGH, SL2 5HP. and at LONDON

Ⓟ**The Focus Practice, trading name of Graham Potter & Co Limited** *(G C Potter)* 3 Sandringham Road, Birkdale, SOUTHPORT, MERSEYSIDE, PR8 2JZ.

Ⓟ**The Fresh Accountancy Company, trading name of The Fresh Accountancy Company Limited** *(T Baker)* 1 Brownings End, Ogwell, NEWTON ABBOT, DEVON, TQ12 6YZ.

★ⓅⒶ**The Greene Partnership** *(G M Greene)* Durkan House, 5th Floor, 155 East Barnet Road, BARNET, HERTFORDSHIRE, EN4 8QZ.

ⒻⓅⒶ**The Gretton Partnership Limited** *(C W Gretton, R J Gretton)* 9 Brook Lane, Corfe Mullen, WIMBORNE, DORSET, BH21 3RD.

Ⓕ**The Hall Liddy Partnership** *(D J Hall, D P Liddy, A J Pow)* 12 St. John Street, MANCHESTER, M3 4DY.

The Hanson Partnership LLP *(C K Hanson)* Suite A, Unit 16, Cirencester Office Park, Tetbury Road, CIRENCESTER, GLOUCESTERSHIRE GL7 6JJ.

ⓉⓅ**The Hay Group, trading name of Hay Tax Limited** *(L D F Hill, S. Macwhirter)* Berkeley House, Dix's Field, EXETER, EX1 1PZ.

Ⓐ**The Highgrove Practice** *(R C Matthews)* 6 Highgrove Gardens, WORTHING, BN11 4SN.

ⒻⒶ**The Hopkins Partnership** *(N L Hopkins)* 1 South Newton Trading Estate, Warminster Road, South Newton, SALISBURY, SP2 0QW.

The Hughes Consultancy *(D S Hughes)* 4a Church Court, RICHMOND, TW9 1JL.

Ⓟ**The Hunters Wood Partnership Ltd** *(R D F Clarke)* Hunters Wood, Heath Ride, Finchampstead, WOKINGHAM, BERKSHIRE, RG40 3QJ.

ⓅⒶ**The Hutchinson Partnership, trading name of The Hutchinson Partnership Limited** *(S R Bennett, J Hutchinson, J M Hutchinson)* The Bull Pen, Amberley Court, Sutton St. Nicholas, HEREFORD, HR1 3BX.

★Ⓟ**The Integrity Partnership Ltd** *(T J Shaw, M W Wellsbury)* 36 High Street, Madeley, TELFORD, SHROPSHIRE, TF7 5AS.

Ⓟ**The Internet Retailer Limited** *(B Sunderland)* 12 Riverview Business Park, Station Road, FOREST ROW, EAST SUSSEX, RH18 5DW.

★Ⓐ**The Janes Partnership** *(J P Janes)* Suite 4C, 35 High Street, Sandridge, ST. ALBANS, HERTFORDSHIRE, AL4 9DD.

ⒻⒶ**The JMO Practice** *(J M O'Sullivan)* 631 Linen Hall, 162-168 Regent Street, LONDON, W1B 5TE.

▽**The JRW Group** *(S D Cove)* Riverside House, Ladhope Vale, GALASHIELS, SELKIRKSHIRE, TD1 1BT. and at HAWICK, LANGHOLM, PEEBLES

★ⓉⒻⒶ**The Kings Mill Partnership** *(P Haining, D J Mitchell, P A Taylor)* 75 Park Lane, CROYDON, CR9 1XS. and at HEATHFIELD

ⓉⒶ**The Lawford Company** *(R M Smith, M J Woolford)* Lawford House, Leacroft, STAINES, TW18 4NN.

Ⓐ**The Lawrence Woolfson Partnership** *(H N Lawrence, R M Woolfson)* 1 Bentinck Street, LONDON, W1U 2ED.

★ⒻⒶ**The Leaman Partnership LLP** *(D H Fieldman, J Swansborough)* 51 Queen Anne Street, LONDON, W1G 9HS.

The Mak Practice *(M A Kimbery)* Chiltlee Manor, Haslemere Road, LIPHOOK, HAMPSHIRE, GU30 7AZ.

The Martlet Partnership LLP *(D C Macdonald, M D Pedder)* Martlet House, E1 Yeoman Gate, Yeoman Way, WORTHING, WEST SUSSEX, BN13 3QZ. and at LONDON

Ⓐ**The McCay Partnership** *(J B McCay, J Mon)* Financial House, 14 Barclay Road, CROYDON, CR0 1JN.

ⒻⓅⒶ**The McWhirter Partnership, trading name of The McWhirter Partnership Limited** *(P R McWhirter)* 1 Foley Place, Common Road, Claygate, ESHER, SURREY, KT10 0HU.

The MGroup Corporate Finance LLP *(P M Casterton, G C Lane)* Cranbrook House, 287-291 Banbury Road, OXFORD, OX2 7JQ.

★Ⓐ**The MGroup Partnership** *(P M Casterton, G C Lane)* Cranbrook House, 287/291 Banbury Road, OXFORD, OX2 7JQ.

Ⓟ**The Mill Consultancy, trading name of The Mill Consultancy Limited** *(J R Davison)* The Mill, Village Road, Christow, EXETER, EX6 7LX.

The Moore Scarrott Partnership LLP *(S R Headon, C M S Longbottom, M W Shelton)* Calyx House, South Road, TAUNTON, SOMERSET, TA1 3DY.

★ⓉⒶ**The Mudd Partnership** *(P Alexandrou, C M Jones, G T McGhie, J A Stanley, C Walby)* Lakeview House, 4 Woodbrook Crescent, BILLERICAY, ESSEX, CM12 0EQ.

Ⓟ**The North West Business Support Centre Limited** *(A D Newbold)* 15 St. Peters Place, FLEETWOOD, LANCASHIRE, FY7 6EB.

The Norton Partnership *(D E Norton)* The Croft, Park Road, Cross Hills, KEIGHLEY, WEST YORKSHIRE, BD20 8BG.

ⓉⒶ**The Norton Practice, trading name of Nortons Group** *(A S Campbell, P Doyle, A H Norton)* Highlands House, Basingstoke Road, Spencers Wood, READING, RG7 1NT.

The Objectivity Partnership LLP *(S D Barber, M R S Beadle)* 12 York Gate, Regent's Park, LONDON, NW1 4QS.

Ⓟ**The Old Coach House Services Limited** *(M Green)* The Old Coach House, 40 Carey Street, READING, RG1 7JS.

Ⓟ**The Orange Partnership, trading name of The Orange Partnership Ltd** *(P C Joyce, D L Ward)* 17 Crane Mews, Gould Road, TWICKENHAM, TW2 6RS. and at KENILWORTH

★**The P&A Partnership** *(B A Guilfoyle, P A Revill, D E Simpson, C M White)* 93 Queen Street, SHEFFIELD, S1 1WF. and at GLASGOW, LEEDS, LONDON

ⓉⒻⒶ**The Paris Partnership LLP** *(L A R Paris)* Russell House, 140 High Street, EDGWARE, MIDDLESEX, HA8 7LW.

Ⓟ**The PayCompany Ltd** *(M J Chilver, F D Startin)* Chartwell House, 4 St. Pauls Square, BURTON-ON-TRENT, STAFFORDSHIRE, DE14 2EF.

Ⓟ**The Payroll Agency Limited** *(I Dutton)* 4 Yorke Street, Hucknall, NOTTINGHAM, NG15 7BT.

The Price Consultancy, trading name of Price *(P G Price)* 81 Park Square East, Jaywick, CLACTON-ON-SEA, ESSEX, CO15 2NP.

The Print Partner Practice *(F J Knight)* 4 Denning Close, MAIDSTONE, KENT, ME16 0WT.

ⓉⒻⓅⒶ**The Priory Partnership, trading name of Priory Practice Limited** *(A P Morse, M.R. O'Donnell, K Penny, S P Penny, M D Sergi)* 1 Abbots Quay, Monks Ferry, BIRKENHEAD, CH41 5LH. and at CHESTER

Ⓟ**The Professional Payroll Limited** *(L S Deyong, M G Jacobs, M Scodie, S J Sefton)* 85 Frampton Street, LONDON, NW8 8NQ.

ⓅⒶ**The Red Sky Partnership Ltd** *(G Sisman)* Red Sky House, Fairclough Hall, Halls Green, Weston, HITCHIN, HERTFORDSHIRE SG4 7DP.

★**The Redfern Partnership** *(D R Morris)* Redfern House, 29 Jury Street, WARWICK, CV34 4EH.

ⓉⒶ**The Roy Sokhal Group** *(J P R Sokhal)* Suite 235, 2nd Floor, Island Business Centre, 18-36 Wellington Street, Woolwich, LONDON SE18 6PF.

The Sharman Partnership *(P D Sharman)* 4 Coronation Road, Crosby, LIVERPOOL, L23 3BJ.

★ⓅⒶ**The Shepherd Partnership Limited** *(A J McManus, A W Webb)* Albion House, Rope Walk, Otley Street, SKIPTON, NORTH YORKSHIRE, BD23 1ED.

★**The Simlers Partnership** *(G J Simler)* 83 Baker Street, LONDON, W1U 6AG.

ⓉⒻⒶ**The Sinden Thackeray Partnership** *(V A Thackeray)* 23 Star Hill, ROCHESTER, KENT, ME1 1XF.

The Small Accounts Company *(S Manger)* 3 Nutmead Close, BEXLEY, KENT, DA5 2DT.

Ⓟ**The Solutions Centre Limited** *(M Davis)* 218 Malvern Road, BOURNEMOUTH, BH9 3BX.

ⒻⓅⒶ**The Southill Partnership, trading name of The Southill Partnership Limited** *(K E Gooding, M Leggett)* Southill Business Park, Cornbury Park, Charlbury, CHIPPING NORTON, OXFORDSHIRE, OX7 3EW.

Ⓟ**The Springfield Accountancy Network Ltd** *(M Foti)* 17 The Ridgeway, Fetcham, LEATHERHEAD, SURREY, KT22 9BA.

Ⓟ**The Studio Practice Limited** *(S Shell)* Holly House, 2 Hardy Close, Swarland, MORPETH, NORTHUMBERLAND, NE65 9PG.

Ⓟ**The Surrey Practice Limited** *(J P Chittock)* Tara, Tite Hill, Englefield Green, EGHAM, TW20 0NH.

ⓅⒶ**The Swillett Portfolio Limited** *(P R Willey)* Berry Cottage, Bullsland Lane, Chorleywood, RICKMANSWORTH, WD3 5BD.

★**The TACS Partnership** *(M D Blake, S A Willcox)* Graylaw House, Mersey Square, STOCKPORT, CHESHIRE, SK1 1AL.

Ⓟ**The Tax Advisor Ltd** *(S B Badcock)* 1 Adam Business Centre, Henson Way, Industrial Estate, KETTERING, NORTHAMPTONSHIRE, NN16 8PX.

★**The Tax Partnership** *(T C Heaton)* Spring Cottage, 90 Monkton Deverill, WARMINSTER, WILTSHIRE, BA12 7EX.

Ⓟ**The Tax People Limited** *(A J Rodway)* Apple Pie Cottage, Woodside Road, Chiddingfold, GODALMING, GU8 4RA.

The Tax Place Solutions LLP *(R W J Brown, M R Wrigglesworth)* Suite 26, Century Building, Tower Street, Brunswick Business Park, LIVERPOOL, L3 4BJ.

Ⓟ**The Tax Return Service(Sheffield) Ltd** *(A J Russell)* Sovereign House, 4 Machon Bank, SHEFFIELD, S7 1GP.

ⓉⒻⓅⒶ**The Tax Shop of Fareham, trading name of Alliott Wingham Limited** *(N L Brown, M J Nolan, M Wingham)* Kintyre House, 70 High Street, FAREHAM, HAMPSHIRE, PO16 7BB.

Ⓟ**The Tax Shop, trading name of The Tax Shop(Falmouth) Ltd** *(N G Matthews)* 52 Killigrew Street, FALMOUTH, CORNWALL, TR11 3PP.

Ⓟ**The Taxation Compliance Company Limited** *(A B Lovett)* 9 Manor Road, Wheathampstead, ST. ALBANS, AL4 8JG.

★**The Thomas Consulting Group** *(H Thomas)* 532 Pine Wood Court, LOS GATOS, CA 95032, UNITED STATES.

The Walker Brown Partnership LLP *(D J Wright)* 32 Trafalgar Road, Portslade, BRIGHTON, BN41 1LD.

The Workhouse *(B R Kehoe)* Allstone Cottage, Cold Bath Road, Caerleon, NEWPORT, GWENT, NP18 1NF.

ⒻⒶ**The Young Company** *(R A Young)* Ground Floor, 2B Vantage Park, Washingley Road, HUNTINGDON, CAMBRIDGESHIRE, PE29 6SR.

Ⓐ**The Zane Partnership** *(R S Banga)* 925 Finchley Road, LONDON, NW11 7PE.

Themis & Co. *(T Themistocli)* 80 Lyonsdown Road, BARNET, EN5 1JL.

Themistocleous Themis *(T Themistocleous)* 20a Mouson Street, Egkomi, 2412 NICOSIA, CYPRUS.

Theresa M. Bolton *(T Bolton)* 32 Granville Road, BARNET, EN5 4DS.

Thiang & Co *(K G Thiang)* 10 Lebuh Gopeng, 41400 KLANG, SELANGOR, MALAYSIA.

ⓉⒻⒶ**Thickbroom Coventry** *(M A Payne, D C Timbers)* 147a High Street, WALTHAM CROSS, EN8 7AP.

Think Business Figures, trading name of R G Waller *(R G Waller)* 106 Lakeview Way, Hampton Hargate, PETERBOROUGH, PE7 8DH.

Ⓟ**Think Map Corporation Limited** *(B H Oppenheim, J M Scroxton)* 52 Great Eastern Street, LONDON, EC2A 3EP.

ⓉⓅ**Thinkfine Limited** *(I De Silva)* 158 Buckingham Palace Road, LONDON, SW1W 9TR.

Ⓟ**Thinking Book-keeping Ltd** *(M Thompson)* Units 7-8, Cargo Workspace, 41-43 George Place, PLYMOUTH, PL1 3DX.

Ⓟ**Third Millennium Consultants Limited** *(G D Wilkins)* Kelly Park, St. Dominick, SALTASH, CORNWALL, PL12 6SQ.

ⒻⓅⒶ**Thoburn and Chapman Limited** *(F J Thoburn, R W Thoburn)* 14 Barrington Street, SOUTH SHIELDS, TYNE AND WEAR, NE33 1AJ.

Ⓕ**Thomas & Co** *(S R Thomas)* Coolibah House, Polhorman Lane, Mullion, HELSTON, CORNWALL, TR12 7JD.

Thomas & Co *(N J Thomas)* Oxwich Green Farmhouse, Oxwich, SWANSEA, SA3 1LX.

ⒻⒶ**Thomas & Company** *(C R Thomas)* 261 Hatherley Road, CHELTENHAM, GL51 6HF.

★**Thomas & Woolven** *(P A Thomas)* 6 Poole Road, WIMBORNE, DORSET, BH21 1QE. and at FAREHAM

ⒻⒶ**Thomas & Young, trading name of Thomas & Young LLP** *(M J Blamire-Brown, J Carty, R J Gaunt, R J Parry, C G Thomas, M E Vousden, V J Young)* 240-244 Stratford Road, Shirley, SOLIHULL, WEST MIDLANDS, B90 3AE.

ⓅⒶ**Thomas Alexander & Company Ltd** *(V Chrysostomou, A Odysseos)* 590 Green Lanes, LONDON, N13 5RY.

Ⓐ**Thomas and Company** *(P J G Thomas)* 2a Lord Street, Douglas, ISLE OF MAN, IM1 2BD.

Thomas and Company *(M D Thomas)* 11a Silver Street, TROWBRIDGE, BA14 8AA.

ⒻⒶ**Thomas Associates** *(M A Thomas)* 5 Union Court, LIVERPOOL, L2 4SJ.

ⓅⒶ**Thomas Bell-Richards Ltd** *(T A M Bell-Richards)* Bowman & Hillier Building, The Old Brewery, Priory Lane, BURFORD, OX18 4SG.

Thomas C.I. Leung & Co. *(T C I Leung)* Room 1301-1302, Kowloon Building, 555 Nathan Road, MONG KOK, KOWLOON, HONG KONG SAR.

Thomas Cheng & Co *(C T Cheng)* Units 803-4, 8/F, Nan Fung Tower, 173 Des Voeux Road, CENTRAL, HONG KONG SAR.

Thomas Chippendale *(T Chippendale)* 39 Market Place, CHIPPENHAM, SN15 3HT.

ⓉⒶ**Thomas Cooke** *(T J M Cooke)* 1 Kilmarsh Road, LONDON, W6 0PL.

ⓉⒻⒶ**Thomas Coombs, trading name of Thomas Coombs & Son** *(S M Adam, C Darwin, G W D Jenkinson, J C Murtland)* Century House, 29 Clarendon Road, LEEDS, LS2 9PG.

Thomas Cox & Co *(P R Cox)* 4 Home farm, Luton Hoo Estate, LUTON, BEDFORDSHIRE, LU1 3TD.

Ⓐ**Thomas David** *(D Brown, T J Mines)* 6-7 Castle Gate, Castle Street, HERTFORD, HERTFORDSHIRE, SG14 1HD.

★**Thomas Edward Dixon & Company** *(I D Francis, R J Wells)* 376 London Road, Hadleigh, BENFLEET, SS7 2DA.

Thomas Gare *(T Gare)* 44 Ramillies Avenue, Cheadle Hulme, CHEADLE, SK8 7AL.

★ⓉⓅⒶ**Thomas Harris, trading name of Thomas Harris Limited** *(C R Thomas)* The 1929 Building, 18 Watermill Way, LONDON, SW19 2RD.

Thomas Harvey *(T Harvey)* 157 Lower Blandford Road, BROADSTONE, DORSET, BH18 8NU.

Thomas Lane *(T A Lane)* Little Hill Cottage, Buckland St Mary, CHARD, TA20 3SS.

★ⓉⒻⒶ**Thomas May & Co** *(K Bathia, B S Carruthers, Mrs S D Major, S E Marshall, D M Radford)* Allen House, Newarke Street, LEICESTER, LE1 5SG.

Ⓐ**Thomas Neilson** *(S Naik)* 108 Catlins Lane, PINNER, MIDDLESEX, HA5 2BX.

ⒻⓅ**Thomas Nock Martin, trading name of Thomas Nock Martin Ltd** *(D L Martin)* 5 Hagley Court South, The Waterfront, Level Street, BRIERLEY HILL, WEST MIDLANDS, DY5 1XE.

Thomas R. Knowles & Williams *(C D Williams)* Stanley House, Market Square, HOLYHEAD, GWYNEDD, LL65 1UF.

Thomas R. Layzell & Co *(T R Layzell)* 185 Winchester Road, Chandlers Ford, EASTLEIGH, SO53 2DU.

Ⓟ**Thomas Tax Consultancy Limited** *(J L Thomas)* 17 Oldfield Mews, LONDON, N6 5XA.

★ⓉⒻⒶ**Thomas Westcott** *(S J Carrington, S A Cresswell, J Flood, R Gillard, M J Marsh, I McMurtry, M Ohlsen, V Parnell, P B Petrides, J Potter, J S Poyner, D H Simpson, G J Sindle, S R Smith, N Smy, R B Thomas)* 26-28 Southernhay East, EXETER, DEVON, EX1 1NS. and at AXMINSTER, BARNSTAPLE, BIDEFORD, CREDITON, HOLSWORTHY, HONITON, ILFRACOMBE, OKEHAMPTON, PLYMOUTH, SEATON, TIVERTON, TORQUAY

ⓅⒶ**Thomas, Wood & Co, trading name of Wadock Limited** *(A D Wood)* 2nd Floor, 33a High Street, Stony Stratford, MILTON KEYNES, MK11 1AA.

Thompson & Co *(R G Thompson)* Sterling Offices, 60 Midland Road, WELLINGBOROUGH, NN8 1LU. and at BEDFORD, NORTHAMPTON

Thompson & Co. *(J C Thompson)* 33 New Street, CARNFORTH, LA5 9BX.

ⒻⒶ**Thompson & Hunter** *(W S A Hunter)* 43/45 High Street, SEVENOAKS, TN13 1JF. and at LONDON

Ⓟ**Thompson Accountancy Limited** *(L F Thompson)* 2 Gloucester Way, Heath Hayes, CANNOCK, STAFFORDSHIRE, WS11 7YN.

ⓅⒶ**Thompson Balch Limited** *(D M Balch, S A Balch)* Sovereign House, 15 Towcester Road, Old Stratford, MILTON KEYNES, MK19 6AN.

Ⓟ**Thompson Elphick, trading name of Thompson Elphick Limited** *(M J Thompson)* The Corner House, 2 High Street, AYLESFORD, KENT, ME20 7BG.

★ⓉⒻⒶ**Thompson Jenner LLP** *(N R Curtis, M Hart, S J Lewis, J P Westley, R H B Wilson)* Thompson Jenner, 1 Colleton Crescent, EXETER, EX2 4DG. and at EXMOUTH

ⒻⓅ**Thompson Jones Business Solutions Limited** *(P Boddis, P D Carlin, J K Stone)* 2 Heap Bridge, BURY, LANCASHIRE, BL9 7HR.

ⓉⒶ**Thompson Jones LLP** *(P Boddis, P D Carlin, J K Stone)* 2 Heap Bridge, BURY, LANCASHIRE, BL9 7HR.

Ⓟ**Thompson Prior, trading name of Thompson Prior Accountancy Services Limited** *(K L M Noble)* The Old Bank Chambers, 27 Lincoln Croft, Shenstone, LICHFIELD, STAFFORDSHIRE, WS14 0ND. and at BRIDGNORTH

ⒻⒶ**Thompson Taraz, trading name of Thompson Taraz LLP** *(A D Grieve, M M Heffernan, D E Suter, A Taraz)* 35 Grosvenor Street, Mayfair, LONDON, W1K 4QX.

ⒻⓅⒶ**Thompson Wright Limited** *(K Evans, R L Thompson, D Wright)* Ebeneezer House, Ryecroft, NEWCASTLE, STAFFORDSHIRE, ST5 2BE. and at LEEK

ⒻⒶ**Thompsons** *(D D Thompson)* 19 East Parade, HARROGATE, NORTH YORKSHIRE, HG1 5LF. and at BRADFORD

Thompsons Accountancy, trading name of Thompsons Accountancy Limited *(C S Thompson)* 7 Kingsway, HAYLING ISLAND, HAMPSHIRE, PO11 0LZ.

Ⓟ**Thompsons Corporate Services Ltd** *(A K Trigg)* 1 Grove Place, BEDFORD, MK40 3JJ.

Ⓟ**Thompsons MK Limited** *(J A Thompson, P D Thompson)* 1 Hathaway Court, Crownhill, MILTON KEYNES, MK8 0LG.

★ⒻⓅⒶ**Thompsons, trading name of Thompsons Accountants and Advisors Limited** *(A K Trigg, T Wiseman)* 1 Grove Place, BEDFORD, MK40 3JJ.

Thomson & Co *(R B Thomson)* 2 Oakfield Lane, KESTON, BR2 6BY.

★**Thong & Lim** *(J H Lim)* 27 Cantonment Road, SINGAPORE 089745, SINGAPORE.

ⓅⒶ**Thornalley & Co, trading name of Thornalley & Co Limited** *(H R Lovett)* 143 Burton Road, LINCOLN, LN1 3LN.

ⒻⓅⒶ**Thorne & Co, trading name of Thorne & Co (Ross-on-Wye) Limited** *(C J Briggs, B E Clare)* 1 St. Marys Street, ROSS-ON-WYE, HEREFORDSHIRE, HR9 5HT. and at HEREFORD

ⓉⒻⒶ**Thorne Lancaster Parker** *(R Cameron-Clarke, C D Kay, S R Parker, P C Schonberger, Z C Sethna, N R Usher)* 8th Floor, Aldwych House, 81 Aldwych, LONDON, WC2B 4HN.

Thorne Widgery & Jones LLP *(P G Lewis, A M F Smallwood, V E Williams)* 33 Bridge Street, HEREFORD, HR4 9DQ.

ⒻⓅⒶ**Thorne Widgery, trading name of Thorne Widgery Accountancy Ltd** *(P G Lewis, A M F Smallwood, V E Williams)* 33 Bridge Street, HEREFORD, HR4 9DQ.

Thornhill Accountancy Services *(G D Brown)* 88 Thornhill Street, Calverley, PUDSEY, WEST YORKSHIRE, LS28 5PD.

ⓅⒶ**Thornhill Scott Ltd** *(R P Scott)* Albert Buildings, 49 Queen Victoria Street, LONDON, EC4N 4SA.

Ⓟ**ThorntonRones, trading name of ThorntonRones Ltd** *(R J Rones)* 311 High Road, LOUGHTON, ESSEX, IG10 1AH.

Thorntons *(J R Thornton)* 2 Tuffnells Way, HARPENDEN, AL5 3HH.

ⒻⒶ**Thorpe Thompson** *(C J Thompson)* 1st Floor Lincoln Lodge, 2 Tettenhall Road, WOLVERHAMPTON, WV1 4SA.

Ⓟ**Thorpes, trading name of Thorpes Limited** *(P Thorpe)* Moorgate Crofts Business Centre, South Grove, ROTHERHAM, SOUTH YORKSHIRE, S60 2DH.

Ⓟ**Thorsten Orr, trading name of Thorsten Orr Limited** *(T J Orr)* Flat 7, 5 Little Stanhope Street, BATH, BA1 2BH.

THP Company Secretarial LLP *(A C Hart, C D Johnson)* 34-40 High Street, Wanstead, LONDON, E11 2RJ.

THP Tax Solutions LLP *(A C Hart)* 34-40 High Street, Wanstead, LONDON, E11 2RJ.

★ⒹⒻⓅⒶ**THP Total Accounting, trading name of THP Limited** *(M Boulter, A C Hart, J B Hearne, C D Johnson)* 34-40 High Street, Wanstead, LONDON, E11 2RJ. and at CHELMSFORD, SAFFRON WALDEN, SUTTON

THP Wealth Structuring, trading name of THP Wealth Structuring LLP *(M Boulter, A C Hart)* 34-40 High Street, Wanstead, LONDON, E11 2RJ.

Ⓟ**Three Kings Accounting Ltd** *(V Cresswell)* Mede House, St. Judes Road, Englefield Green, EGHAM, SURREY, TW20 0DH.

Ⓟ**Three Lines Management Limited** *(D N Seaman)* Unit 17, Sandleheath Industrial Estate, FORDINGBRIDGE, HAMPSHIRE, SP6 1PA.

Three Sixty *(J Lun Leung, E Ng Yim On)* #02-A8 Cybertower 1, EBENE, MAURITIUS.

ⒹⓅ**Throgmorton UK Limited** *(T A Brown, R I Ganpatsingh)* 4th Floor, Reading Bridge House, Reading Bridge, George Street, READING, RG1 8LS.

Ⓕ**Thurston Watts & Co** *(S N Samji)* 39-41 North Road, LONDON, N7 9DP.

ⒻⓅⒶ**Thwaites Blackwell Bailey & Co Limited** *(S J Williams)* Delaport Coach House, Wheathampstead, ST. ALBANS, HERTFORDSHIRE, AL4 8RQ.

ⒻⒶ**Thwaites Blackwell Warwick & Co, trading name of Warwick Durham & Co.** *(A H Warwick)* Senator House, 2 Graham Road, Hendon Central, LONDON, NW4 3HJ.

Thwaites, trading name of N R Gillhespy *(N R Gillhespy)* 172 Birmingham Road, SUTTON COLDFIELD, WEST MIDLANDS, B72 1BX.

Ⓟ**Tick Accountancy Limited** *(A L Boronte)* 168 Fairview Road, STEVENAGE, HERTFORDSHIRE, SG1 2NE.

Tickett & Co *(J Tickett)* 97 Wilmot Way, BANSTEAD, SURREY, SM7 2QA.

Ⓕ**Tidmarsh & Co.** *(R J S Tidmarsh)* Wallace House, 45 Portland Road, HOVE, BN3 5DQ.

ⒹⒻⒶ**TiernayFedrick** *(S Roberts, J P B Tiernay, N F Tiernay)* 19 Trinity Square, LLANDUDNO, GWYNEDD, LL30 2RD.

Tierney Tax Consultancy *(R M Tierney)* Kilcorran House, Kilcorran, SMITHBORO, COUNTY MONAGHAN, IRELAND.

★**Tiffin Green** *(N O Tidbury)* 11 Queens Road, BRENTWOOD, ESSEX, CM14 4HE.

Ⓟ**Tiffin Green Accounting Limited** *(N O Tidbury)* 11 Queens Road, BRENTWOOD, ESSEX, CM14 4HE.

Ⓟ**Tilbrook & Co Ltd** *(P M Tilbrook)* The Lawn, 9 Cross Road, TADWORTH, KT20 5SP.

ⓅⒶ**Tilbury Young Limited** *(M C Young)* Almac House, Church Lane, Bisley, WOKING, GU24 9DR.

ⒻⓅⒶ**Tildesley & Tonks Limited** *(M J Evans)* Unit 8, Pendeford Place, Pendeford Business Park, Wobaston Road, WOLVERHAMPTON, WV9 5HD.

ⒹⒻⒶ**Tile & Co** *(J W Tile, J G Wyncoll)* Warden House, 37 Manor Road, COLCHESTER, CO3 3LX.

Ⓐ**Tiley & Co** *(A Tiley, M S Tiley)* Parkway Cottage, Andover Road, Highclere, NEWBURY, RG20 9QU.

Till & Cloake *(R S Cloake)* 70 South Street, LANCING, WEST SUSSEX, BN15 8AJ.

Tilman & Co *(J A Tilman)* 15 Searle Way, Eight Ash Green, COLCHESTER, CO6 3QS.

Ⓟ**Tim Allatson, trading name of Tim Allatson Limited** *(T Allatson)* 4 Brompton Way, West Bridgford, NOTTINGHAM, NG2 7SU.

Tim Chapple *(T J Chapple)* 10 St. Mellion Close, Monkton Park, CHIPPENHAM, WILTSHIRE, SN15 3XN.

Ⓕ**Tim Dowling** *(T H Dowling)* 16 Gordon Road, Claygate, ESHER, SURREY, KT10 0PQ.

ⒻⒶ**Tim Drake** *(T W Drake)* Garden Cottage Ockham Lane, Hatchford, COBHAM, KT11 1LP.

Tim Fox *(T G Fox)* Pawlies Farm, Loxwood, BILLINGSHURST, WEST SUSSEX, RH14 0QN.

Tim Gage *(T J Gage)* 45 Flitwick Road, Ampthill, BEDFORD, BEDFORDSHIRE, MK45 2NS.

Tim Gilson *(T R Gilson)* 6 Homestead Close, Bredon, TEWKESBURY, GLOUCESTERSHIRE, GL20 7NN.

Tim Harris *(T G Harris)* Mill Cottage, Windmill Hill, Brenchley, TONBRIDGE, KENT, TN12 7NR.

Tim Lawrence *(T G R Lawrence)* Whitethorn, Collinswood Road, Farnham Common, SLOUGH, SL2 3LH.

Tim Morgan *(T D Morgan)* 7 Fowberry Crescent, Fenham, NEWCASTLE UPON TYNE, NE4 9XH.

Tim O'Brien *(D T J O'Brien)* The Green, Datchet, SLOUGH, SL3 9AS.

Tim Patterson *(T J Patterson)* Ropewalk Cottage, Ropewalk, KINGSBRIDGE, DEVON, TQ7 1HH.

Tim Phillips *(T R H Phillips)* The Steading, Knockmuir, AVOCH, ROSS-SHIRE, IV9 8RD.

Ⓟ**Tim Pollard Ltd** *(C S Pollard, T N Pollard)* Creeds Farm, Elkington, NORTHAMPTON, NN6 6NJ.

Ⓐ**Tim R Anderson** *(T R Anderson)* 56 Glebelands Road, KNUTSFORD, CHESHIRE, WA16 9DZ.

Tim Smith *(T R Smith)* 14 Newton Park, Newton Solney, BURTON-ON-TRENT, DE15 0SX.

Tim Williamson *(T J G Williamson)* WG Hospitality (SA) cc, PO Box 53, ST LUCIA, KWAZULU NATAL, 3936, SOUTH AFRICA.

Tim Wood FCA *(T N Wood)* Moresdale Lodge, Lambrigg, KENDAL, CUMBRIA, LA8 0DH.

Ⓟ**Timberfield Ltd** *(P J L Floyd)* 87a Hadlow Road, TONBRIDGE, KENT, TN9 1QD.

Ⓟ**Timbrell & Co Ltd** *(J D Timbrell, S E Timbrell)* Chiltern House Business Centre, 45 Station Road, HENLEY-ON-THAMES, OXFORDSHIRE, RG9 1AT.

Time Business Services *(A A M Riazi, H C Thatcher)* 250 Harbour Way, SHOREHAM-BY-SEA, WEST SUSSEX, BN43 5HZ. and at EASTBOURNE

Ⓟ**Timecount Ltd** *(D Koshal)* Gautam House, 1-3 Shenley Avenue, RUISLIP, MIDDLESEX, HA4 6BP.

★**Timenides & Evangeli** *(E Evangelou)* PO Box 21560, 1510 NICOSIA, CYPRUS.

Ⓟ**Timewise Limited** *(D S George)* 246 High Road, HARROW, MIDDLESEX, HA3 7BB.

Timothy Coomer *(T Coomer)* 3 Greenfields, Dunhills Lane, Enham Alamein, ANDOVER, HAMPSHIRE, SP11 6RB.

Timothy Dubens *(T S D Dubens)* 10 Mermaid Quay, NOOSAVILLE, QLD 4566, AUSTRALIA.

Ⓟ**Timothy Johnson Limited** *(T A A Johnson)* 8 Rhodesia Road, LONDON, SW9 9EL.

Ⓐ**Timothy Jones & Co** *(T S Jones)* 1 Arbrook Lane, ESHER, SURREY, KT10 9EG.

Timothy M Rogerson *(T M Rogerson)* 18 Saxon Way, ROMSEY, HAMPSHIRE, SO51 5PT.

ⓅⒶ**Timothy N. Horne Ltd** *(T N Horne)* Bay Villa, 40 Church Road, Otley, IPSWICH, IP6 9NP.

Timothy P. Bolton *(T P Bolton)* Latchmere House, Watling Street, CANTERBURY, CT1 2UD.

Timothy S Cockcroft *(T S Cockcroft)* Vale Cottage, 16 Watsons Lane, Harby, MELTON MOWBRAY, LE14 4DD.

ⒹⒶ**Tindle's, trading name of Tindle's LLP** *(A Foster, R R Tindle)* Scotswood House, Teesdale South, STOCKTON-ON-TEES, CLEVELAND, TS17 6SB.

Ting Ho Kwan & Chan *(S K Chan, C T Chow, S C Ho, L H S Ting, S K C Ting)* 9th Floor Tung Ning Bldg, 249-253 Des Voeux Road C, CENTRAL, HONG KONG ISLAND, HONG KONG SAR.

ⒹⓅⒶ**Tingle Ashmore Ltd** *(B P Ashmore, K A Tingle)* Enterprise House, Broadfield Court, SHEFFIELD, S8 0XF.

Ⓟ**Tippings, trading name of Tippings Accountants Limited** *(A Tipping)* 115 Chapel Lane, Longton, PRESTON, PR4 5NA.

★**Tiptaft Smith & Co Secretarial Services** *(D H P Tiptaft)* Montagu Chambers, Montagu Square, MEXBOROUGH, SOUTH YORKSHIRE, S64 9AJ.

Ⓐ**Tiptaft, Smith & Co** *(D H P Tiptaft)* Montagu Chambers, Montagu Square, MEXBOROUGH, S64 9AJ.

★Ⓕ**Tish Leibovitch** *(M J Green, B Leibovitch)* 249 Cranbrook Road, ILFORD, IG1 4TG.

Tittensor & Co LLP *(C A Mead, H V Tittensor)* Fourwinds, Wengeo Lane, WARE, HERTFORDSHIRE, SG12 0EH.

ⒻⓅⒶ**Titus Thorp & Ainsworth Limited** *(M Muschamp, B H Taylor)* 212 North Road, PRESTON, PR1 1YP. and at BLACKPOOL

Tiwari & Co *(S S Tiwari)* 25 Knighton Close, New Duston, NORTHAMPTON, NN5 6NE.

TJ Lelliott FCA *(T J Lelliott)* 7 The Lilacs, Barkham, WOKINGHAM, RG41 4UT.

Ⓟ**TJM Dougherty, trading name of TJM Dougherty Ltd** *(T J Dougherty)* 7 The Coppice, Great Barton, BURY ST. EDMUNDS, SUFFOLK, IP31 2TT.

TJS Consultants *(T J Seckel)* Ridgeway, Westfield, Hoe Lane, Abinger Hammer, DORKING, SURREY RH5 6RS.

ⒻⓅⒶ**TKG Partnership, trading name of TKG Partnership Limited** *(C Kyprianou)* Unit 3, Gateway Mews, Ringway, Bounds Green, LONDON, N11 2UT.

Ⓟ**TLC CPA Limited** *(C M Tam)* Room 1203, 12/F Wing on Centre, 111 Connaught Road, CENTRAL, HONG KONG SAR.

★ⒹⒻⓅⒶ**TLL, TLL Company Services, Turpin Lucas Lees, trading names of TLL Accountants Limited** *(P Buck, D P Lucas)* 7-9 Station Road, Hesketh Bank, PRESTON, PR4 6SN. and at BLACKBURN

ⒹⒻ**TLP** *(P D Land, A V Wild)* 3 Greengate, Cardale Park, HARROGATE, NORTH YORKSHIRE, HG3 1GY.

ⓅⒶ**TLP Audit Limited** *(P D Land, A V Wild)* 3 Greengate, Cardale Park, HARROGATE, NORTH YORKSHIRE, HG3 1GY.

TLP Consulting LLP *(P D Land, A V Wild)* 3 Greengate, Cardale Park, HARROGATE, NORTH YORKSHIRE, HG3 1GY.

Ⓟ**TM Accounting Limited** *(T M Manning)* 120 Allington Close, TAUNTON, SOMERSET, TA1 2NF.

TMB & Co *(T Evans)* Tynycae, Briw, Llangedwyn, OSWESTRY, SY10 9LB.

Ⓟ**TMC Accountancy Limited** *(C Glass)* 14 Clifton Moor Business Village, James Nicolson Link, YORK, YO30 4XG.

Ⓟ**TMF Management (UK) Limited** *(R N Arthur)* 400 Capability Green, LUTON, BEDFORDSHIRE, LU1 3AE.

Ⓓ**TMG Corporate Finance LLP** *(J D Casstles, P J Travis)* 16 Oxford Court, MANCHESTER, M2 3WQ.

Ⓟ**TMH Simpson Limited** *(T Simpson)* 1 Heather Way, Countesthorpe, LEICESTER, LE8 5WU.

To Wai Kum *(W K To)* 1711 North Tower, Concordia Plaza, 1 Science Museum Road, TSIM SHA TSUI, KOWLOON, HONG KONG SAR.

Ⓟ**Tolverne Tax Services, trading name of Tolverne Tax Services Limited** *(I R Forbes)* Tolverne, White Cross, Cury, HELSTON, CORNWALL, TR12 7BH.

Tom Burgess *(T E Burgess)* 27 Ellesmere Road, Uphill, WESTON-SUPER-MARE, AVON, BS23 4UT.

ⓅⒶ**Tom Carroll Associates Ltd** *(T G Carroll, R W Theckston)* 166 Prescot Road, ST. HELENS, MERSEYSIDE, WA10 3TS. and at WALLASEY

Tom Day *(T H B Day)* Ashleigh, Barton Blount, Church Broughton, DERBY, DE65 5AP.

Tom Madge *(T A Madge)* 18 Chilcot Close, LONDON, E14 6AN.

Tom Main *(T A Main)* Mill Cottage, Upper Neatham Mill Lane, Holybourne, ALTON, HAMPSHIRE, GU34 4EP.

Tom Morton *(T M Morton)* Carcosa, 2 Forbes Park, Bramhall, STOCKPORT, SK7 2RE.

★ⒹⒻⒶ**Tomkinson Teal LLP** *(K J Teal, D W Tomkinson)* Hanover Court, 5 Queen Street, LICHFIELD, STAFFORDSHIRE, WS13 6QD.

Tommy C.P. Sze & Company *(C T Sze)* Flat 2003, 20/F, Wellborne Commercial Centre, 8 Java Road, NORTH POINT, HONG KONG SAR.

Tommy Ng & Co *(F L Ng)* Suite B, 11/F Foo Cheong Building, 82-86 Wing Lok Street, SHEUNG WAN, HONG KONG ISLAND, HONG KONG SAR.

Tony Cole & Co *(A M Cole)* 227 London Road, North End, PORTSMOUTH, PO2 9AJ.

Ⓟ**Tony Dicker & Co, trading name of Tony Dicker Ltd** *(A R Dicker)* 29 Courtenay Road, Keynsham, BRISTOL, BS31 1JU.

Tony Dover FCA *(A Dover)* 11 Defender Court, Hylton Riverside Enterprise Park, SUNDERLAND, SR5 3PE.

Tony Eginton & Co *(A C T Eginton)* 1 Upper Gladstone Road, CHESHAM, BUCKINGHAMSHIRE, HP5 3AF.

Tony Everitt *(T K Everitt)* 11B Soham Road, Fordham, ELY, CAMBRIDGESHIRE, CB7 5LB.

ⒻⓅⒶ**Tony Freeman & Company, trading name of TF & Partners Limited** *(A L Conway)* New Maxdov House, 130 Bury New Road, Prestwich, MANCHESTER, M25 0AA.

Tony Freeman FCA MIPA *(M A Freeman)* New Maxdov House, 130 Bury New Road, Prestwich, MANCHESTER, M25 0AA.

Ⓟ**Tony Hailwood Ltd** *(A G Hailwood)* 14 Davenport Road, Heswall, WIRRAL, MERSEYSIDE, CH60 9LF.

Ⓐ**Tony Hine & Co** *(A Hine)* Herne House, 68 Birchanger Lane, Birchanger, BISHOP'S STORTFORD, CM23 5QA.

Ⓟ**Tony J Smart** *(T J Smart)* 29 Lancaster Way, Glen Parva, LEICESTER, LE2 9UA.

Ⓟ**Tony Jopson & Co, trading name of Tony Jopson & Co Limited** *(Anthony Jopson)* 246 Peverell Park Road, Peverell, PLYMOUTH, PL3 4QG.

Ⓟ**Tony Robbins FCA, trading name of Tony Robbins FCA Limited** *(A T Robbins)* 8 Redwood Close, West End, SOUTHAMPTON, SO30 3SG.

Tony Rowell *(A J Rowell)* 1a Middle Way, LEWES, EAST SUSSEX, BN7 1NH.

Ⓟ**Tony Stitt** *(A V P Stitt)* 257 Goldhurst Terrace, LONDON, NW6 3EP.

Ⓟ**Too Much Tax Ltd** *(C G Brown)* 9 Alburys, Wrington, BRISTOL, BS40 5NZ.

TOP, trading name of The Onboard Partnership LLP *(G S A Montgomery)* Chilton House, Charnham Lane, HUNGERFORD, BERKSHIRE, RG17 0EY.

ⓅⒶ**Topaz Solutions Ltd** *(V J Graham)* 19 Osborne Road, NORTHAMPTON, NN2 6NU.

ⓅⒶ**Topping & Company, trading name of Topping Consultancy Limited** *(J Topping)* 209 Liverpool Road, SOUTHPORT, MERSEYSIDE, PR8 4PH.

ⒻⓅ**Topping & Van Gerwen, trading name of Topping & Van Gerwen Limited** *(D J Topping)* 1 Long Street, TETBURY, GLOUCESTERSHIRE, GL8 8AA.

ⒻⒶ**Topping Partnership** *(P J Bentham, M Topping)* 9th Floor, 8 Exchange Quay, SALFORD, M5 3EJ. and at LEIGH

Ⓟ**Topping Partnership Limited** *(M Topping)* 9th Floor, 8 Exchange Quay, SALFORD, M5 3EJ.

★**Torevell Dent Audit LLP** *(M B Fox)* 4th Floor, 153/155 Sunbridge Road, BRADFORD, BD1 2NU. and at HALIFAX, HUDDERSFIELD

Ⓟ**Torevell Dent Ltd** *(M B Fox)* 1-3 St. Annes Place, HALIFAX, WEST YORKSHIRE, HX1 5RB.

Ⓟ**Torr Waterfield, trading name of Torr Waterfield Ltd** *(T Simpson)* Park House, 37 Clarence Street, LEICESTER, LE1 3RW.

Torrance Accountancy Services *(G L Torrance)* 6 Hillcrest, RYE, EAST SUSSEX, TN31 7HP.

ⓅⒶ**Torringtons, trading name of Torringtons Limited** *(B L Jackson)* Hillside House, 2-6 Friern Park, North Finchley, LONDON, N12 9FB.

Tosh & Co *(P M Tosh)* 105B High Str, HONITON, EX14 1PE.

Ⓟ**Total Accounting Solutions Limited** *(A Whitehouse)* 68 Habgood Road, LOUGHTON, ESSEX, IG10 1HE.

Ⓟ**Totality Solutions Ltd** *(J D Shaw)* PO Box 138, FRODSHAM, WA6 6AY.

Ⓐ**Totally Taxation, trading name of Channon & Co** *(R O Channon)* The Mill, Balls Corner, Kingsteignton Road, NEWTON ABBOT, DEVON, TQ12 2QA.

Ⓟ**Totteridge Associates Limited** *(N R Hughes)* 9 Ash Grove, Weedon Lane, AMERSHAM, BUCKINGHAMSHIRE, HP6 5QU.

Ⓐ**Toumbas & Co** *(P G Toumbas)* 5 Long Road, CANVEY ISLAND, SS8 0JA.

★**Towers & Gornall** *(T Bennett)* Abacus House, The Ropewalk, Garstang, PRESTON, PR3 1NS. and at CLITHEROE, LANCASTER

Towne & Co *(S D Towne)* Norbreck House, Landmere Lane, Edwalton, NOTTINGHAM, NG12 4DG.

Townend English *(F D Townend)* 80 Market Street, Pocklington, YORK, YO42 2AB.

Ⓟ**Townend English Ltd** *(F D Townend)* 80 Market Street, Pocklington, YORK, YO42 2AB.

★ⒹⒻⒶ**Townends** *(B J Barker, A Carroll, A Cooper, T J Maeer, J P Shand, P Sharpe, F C Verney, J Williamson)* Carlisle Chambers, Carlisle Street, GOOLE, DN14 5DX. and at PONTEFRACT, SELBY, YORK

★ⒻⓅⒶ**Townends, trading name of Townends Accountants Limited** *(A Carroll, B B Davis, S M Green, J P Shand, P Sharpe, F C Verney, J Williamson)* Fulford Lodge, 1 Heslington Lane, YORK, YO10 4HW. and at GOOLE, PONTEFRACT, SELBY

Ⓟ**Townsend & Co Accountants Ltd** *(D J Townsend)* Office 3, The Kings Head Centre, 38 High Street, MALDON, ESSEX, CM9 5PN.

★ⒹⓅⒶ**Townsend Harrison Limited** *(S P Harrison)* 13 Yorkersgate, MALTON, NORTH YORKSHIRE, YO17 7AA.

ⓉⒻⓅⒶ**TP Lewis & Partners, trading name of T P Lewis & Partners (BOS) Limited** *(T P Lewis, R K Searle)* 3/5 College Street, BURNHAM-ON-SEA, SOMERSET, TA8 1AR. and at WEDMORE

TPA Accountancy Services *(J T Hogg)* 38 Stanhope Road, SOUTH SHIELDS, NE33 4BT.

Ⓟ**Tracy Newman & Co Ltd** *(T L Newman)* 14 High Street, Wilburton, ELY, CAMBRIDGESHIRE, CB6 3RB. and at CAMBRIDGE

Ⓟ**Trading Skills Limited** *(D M Styles)* 3 Rushmere Close, Adlington, MACCLESFIELD, CHESHIRE, SK10 5SR.

Trafalgar Accounting and Taxation Services LLP *(T J Richardson)* 8 Emsons Close, Linton, CAMBRIDGE, CB21 4NB.

ⓅⒶ**Trafalgars, trading name of Trafalgar Accountancy & Tax Limited** *(J L Bill, C R Pate)* Trafalgar House, 261 Alcester Road South, BIRMINGHAM, B14 6DT.

Ⓟ**Train Consulting Limited** *(G S C Train)* 42 Ryecroft Road, LONDON, SW16 3EQ.

Ⓟ**Transfer Pricing Consultants Ltd** *(J C Paul)* 8 Southall Drive, Hartlebury, KIDDERMINSTER, WORCESTERSHIRE, DY11 7LD.

Ⓟ**Transparent Accountancy, trading name of Transparent Accountancy Limited** *(H L Clarke, C P Downing)* 48 Dean Park Road, BOURNEMOUTH, BH1 1QA.

ⓉⒻⒶ**Tranter Lowe (D&W) LLP** *(I Davies, M J Lowe)* Bank House, 66 High Street, Dawley, TELFORD, SHROPSHIRE, TF4 2HD.

ⒻⓅⒶ**Tranter Lowe, trading name of Tranter Lowe (Oakengates) Ltd** *(A J Poole, J Tranter)* International House, 6 Market Street, Oakengates, TELFORD, SHROPSHIRE, TF2 6EF.

ⓉⒻⒶ**Traviss & Co** *(M J Traviss)* Newtown House, Newtown Road, LIPHOOK, HAMPSHIRE, GU30 7DX.

Ⓟ**TRC Accountancy Ltd** *(T R Cooney)* 26 Coopers Row, LYTHAM ST. ANNES, LANCASHIRE, FY8 4UD.

★Ⓟ**Treasury Accounting Limited** *(A K Sainsbury)* The Old Treasury, 7 Kings Road, SOUTHSEA, HAMPSHIRE, PO5 4DJ. and at LYNDHURST

ⓅⒶ**Treetops, trading name of TTCA Ltd** *(T W McManners)* 269 Farnborough Road, FARNBOROUGH, HAMPSHIRE, GU14 7LY.

Ⓟ**Trenchard Carnie Limited** *(N J Carnie)* 3 Rhododendron Close, CARDIFF, CF23 7HS.

ⒻⓅⒶ**Trenfield Williams Ltd** *(J R D Haigh, D E Richardson)* 1st Floor, The Old Railway Station, Sea Mills Lane, BRISTOL, BS9 1FF.

Trent, Raymond & Co *(J Gold)* 4 Chartley Avenue, STANMORE, MIDDLESEX, HA7 3QZ.

Tresise & Company *(W A Tresise)* Brockhurst, 28 Evesham Walk, Sandhurst, SANDHURST, GU47 0YU.

ⓅⒶ**Trevelyan & Company, trading name of Trevelyan & Company Ltd** *(M Gara)* Charles House, 20/22 Elland Road, Churwell Hill, LEEDS, LS27 7SS.

Trevor A. Bomber FCA *(T A Bomber)* 59 King Street, Darlaston, WEDNESBURY, WS10 8DE.

Ⓐ**Trevor Aldridge** *(T A Aldridge)* 64 Old Hadlow Road, TONBRIDGE, TN10 4EX.

Ⓟ**Trevor Aldridge Limited** *(T A Aldridge)* 64 Old Hadlow Road, TONBRIDGE, KENT, TN10 4EX.

Trevor B. Poole *(T B Poole)* 109 Barnett Wood Lane, ASHTEAD, SURREY, KT21 2LR.

Trevor C. Davies *(T C Davies)* Brent Cottage, Hilltop, Cley-next-the-Sea, HOLT, NR25 7SD.

Trevor Dowson *(T C A Dowson)* Sackville Place, 44-48 Magdalen Street, NORWICH, NR3 1JU.

Trevor J Mathew-Jones *(T J Mathew-Jones)* 30 Bertram Drive, Hoylake, WIRRAL, MERSEYSIDE, CH47 0LQ.

Trevor JF Day *(T J F Day)* 13 Heythrop Close, Oadby, LEICESTER, LE2 4SL.

▽ⓉⒻⒶ**Trevor Jones & Co.** *(Y Hadjimarcou, S M Lewis, A J P McKeown)* Old Bank Chambers, 582-586 Kingsbury Road, Erdington, BIRMINGHAM, B24 9ND.

Ⓐ**Trevor Jones, trading name of The Trevor Jones Partnership LLP** *(T J Hall, Richard Lane, T G Somers)* Springfield House, 99-101 Crossbrook Street, Cheshunt, WALTHAM CROSS, HERTFORDSHIRE, EN8 8JR.

Ⓐ**Trevor L. Newell & Co** *(T L Newell)* 155 Wellingborough Road, RUSHDEN, NN10 9TB.

Trevor Leach & Co *(T Leach)* Bradda House, Bradda Road, Port Erin, ISLE OF MAN, IM9 6PQ.

Trevor M Ball, trading name of Trevor M Ball & Co *(T M Ball)* 46 The Close, NORWICH, NR1 4EG.

Ⓐ**Trevor T. Harden FCA** *(T T Harden)* 35 Meadow Way, Farnborough Park, ORPINGTON, BR6 8LN.

Trevor Watts *(T Watts)* P O Box 2162, PULBOROUGH, RH20 2WZ.

Trevor Wright *(T Wright)* 2 Wayside Drive, Oadby, LEICESTER, LE2 4NU.

Trewen Consultancy *(J R Jenkins)* Trewen, Lon ty Llwyd, Llanfarian, ABERYSTWYTH, DYFED, SY23 4UH.

Ⓟ**Tricom Services Limited** *(D Sinnett)* 22 High Street, BUCKINGHAM, MK18 1NU.

Trigg & Co *(T J Trigg)* 1 Merton Mansions, Bushey Road, LONDON, SW20 8DQ.

Ⓟ**Trigg Management Limited** *(M A Trigg)* 117 Layhams Road, WEST WICKHAM, KENT, BR4 9HE.

Ⓟ**Trilogic Family Office Limited** *(R J Southgate)* May Cottage, Ashfield Road, Norton, BURY ST. EDMUNDS, SUFFOLK, IP31 3NF.

Ⓣ**Trinity Corporate Services Romania SRL** *(H R Watkins)* 24 Paleologu Street, 3rd District, 030552 BUCHAREST, ROMANIA.

ⒻⓅⒶ**Tripp & Co, trading name of Tripp Accountancy Ltd** *(M B Tripp)* The Old Brewery, Newtown, BRADFORD-ON-AVON, WILTSHIRE, BA15 1NF.

Ⓟ**Triquetra Limited** *(M P Kelly)* 3 Meadow Close, SEVENOAKS, TN13 3HZ.

Trood Pratt & Co *(P Lockyer)* GPO Box 3437, SYDNEY, NSW 1043, AUSTRALIA.

Trotman & Co *(G R Trotman)* Queensborough House, 2 Claremont Road, SURBITON, KT6 4QU.

Trouble Shooter *(R G Shooter)* 39 Castle Street, LEICESTER, LE1 5WN.

ⓉⒶ**Trudgeon Halling** *(J H Anderson-Riley, R G Hatch)* The Platt, WADEBRIDGE, PL27 7AE.

Ⓟ**Trudgeon Halling Limited** *(J H Anderson-Riley, R G Hatch)* The Platt, WADEBRIDGE, CORNWALL, PL27 7AE.

Ⓟ**True Capital, trading name of True Capital Two Limited** *(D R Gordon-Smith, D C W Reid)* Prince Albert House, 20 King Street, MAIDENHEAD, BERKSHIRE, SL6 1DT.

True Partners Consulting, trading name of True Partners Consulting (UK) LLP *(L Secular)* 68 Lombard Street, LONDON, EC3V 9LJ.

Ⓟ**Truefair Limited** *(N M Khan)* 69 Plumstead Common Road, Plumstead, LONDON, SE18 3AX.

Ⓟ**Truequest Limited** *(J S Cooper)* 6 Princes Park Avenue, LONDON, NW11 0JP.

Ⓟ**Trustax Services Ltd** *(L V Hindocha)* Unit V15, Lenton Business Centre, Lenton Boulevard, NOTTINGHAM, NG7 2BY.

Ⓟ**Trustee Training & Support Limited** *(C H Dicker)* Hill House, Ranworth, NORFOLK, NR13 6AB.

ⓉⒻⒶ**Try Lunn & Co** *(J J Buckley, C C Try)* Roland House, Princes Dock Street, HULL, HU1 2LD.

Tryhorn and Hall *(N A Tryhorn)* 153 Stafford Road, WALLINGTON, SM6 9BN.

Trystram Alley & Co *(C R T Alley)* P.O. Box 4377, 29 St Ann's Road, PORT OF SPAIN, TRINIDAD AND TOBAGO.

TS Birley *(T S Birley)* West Suite, Level 5, Mill Court, La Charroterie, St. Peter Port, GUERNSEY GY1 1EJ.

ⒻⒶ**Tsalikis & Co** *(A Tsalikis)* 30 Carrwood Avenue, Bramhall, STOCKPORT, CHESHIRE, SK7 2PY.

Tsang Cho Tai *(C T Tsang)* Unit 1411, 14/F Lippo Sun Plaza, 28 Canton Road, TSIM SHA TSUI, KOWLOON, HONG KONG SAR.

Tsang Tam & Company *(C Y Tam)* Room 704, 7/F Kai Wong Commercial Building, 222-226 Queens Road, CENTRAL, HONG KONG ISLAND, HONG KONG SAR.

Ⓟ**Tsavo Accounts Limited** *(D M Carter)* Amador, Tower Road, St. Helier, JERSEY, JE2 3HR.

★**Tse & Lam** *(Y L Lam, R C L Tse)* Unit A, 5F China Overseas Building, 139 Hennessy Road, WAN CHAI, HONG KONG ISLAND, HONG KONG SAR.

Ⓟ**Tserkezos Sawides Associates Limited** *(D V Tserkezos)* PO Box 23452, 1683 NICOSIA, CYPRUS.

TSW Accountancy and Taxation Services, trading name of Tina Wakeling FCA *(T S Wakeling)* 25 Southcote Close, South Cave, BROUGH, NORTH HUMBERSIDE, HU15 2BQ.

TSW International Taxation Consulting *(S R Weeden)* Lower Floor, 41 Forehill, ELY, CAMBRIDGESHIRE, CB7 4AA. and at FERRYSIDE

Ⓟ**TT Turner Limited** *(N K Turner)* 21 Greenbank Road, Marple Bridge, STOCKPORT, SK6 5ED.

★ⓉⒻⓅⒶ**TTR Barnes, trading name of TTR Barnes Limited** *(R B Huntley, A Russell, J T Thorne)* 3-5 Grange Terrace, Stockton Road, SUNDERLAND, SR2 7DG.

ⓅⒶ**TTRB Limited** *(A Russell)* 3-5 Grange Terrace, Stockton Road, SUNDERLAND, SR2 7DG.

★ⓉⒻⒶ**Tuchbands** *(N L Tuchband, P A Woolfson)* 925 Finchley Road, LONDON, NW11 7PE.

Ⓟ**Tuchbands Accounting Services Ltd** *(P A Woolfson)* 925 Finchley Road, LONDON, NW11 7PE.

ⓉⒻⒶ**Tudor John** *(P D Davies, H M Mulhall, D C S Nelson)* Nightingale House, 46/48 East Street, EPSOM, KT17 1HQ.

ⒻⓅⒶ**Tudor John Ltd** *(P D Davies, H M Mulhall, D C S Nelson)* Nightingale House, 46-48 East Street, EPSOM, SURREY, KT17 1HQ.

Ⓟ**Tudor Payne & Co, trading name of Tudor Payne & Co Ltd** *(A T Payne)* 52 Parkstone Road, POOLE, DORSET, BH15 2PU.

ⒻⓅⒶ**Tung Sing & Co, trading name of Tung Sing & Co Limited** *(C M Y Tung Sing)* 26 Oakleigh Park South, LONDON, N20 9JU.

ⓅⒶ**Turnbull & Co Accountants Limited** *(I J Taberner, M R Turnbull)* Pilgrim House, Oxford Place, PLYMOUTH, PL1 5AJ.

ⒻⓅⒶ**Turnbull Associates, trading name of Turnbull Associates Limited** *(J C Crook, R G Marsden, J P Shaw, P J Windmill)* Iveco House, Station Road, WATFORD, WD17 1TA.

Ⓐ**Turner & Co** *(M Turner)* 10A White Hart Parade, London Road, Blackwater, CAMBERLEY, SURREY, GU17 9AD.

Turner & Co *(C M Turner)* 4 Bridle Ways, East Bridgford, NOTTINGHAM, NG13 8PT.

★ⒻⒶ**Turner & Ellerby** *(R D Baker)* The Guildhall, Framlingham, WOODBRIDGE, IP13 9AZ.

Turner & Partners *(P W Rose)* 8 The Crescent, WISBECH, CAMBRIDGESHIRE, PE13 1EN.

★ⒻⒶ**Turner & Smith** *(R Neal)* Westgate House, Royland Road, LOUGHBOROUGH, LE11 2EH.

ⒻⓅⒶ**Turner & Turner, trading name of Turner & Turner (Preston) Ltd** *(M R Turner)* Bank House, 9 Victoria Road, Fulwood, PRESTON, PR2 8ND.

ⓉⒻⓅⒶ**Turner and Brown Limited** *(J L Thomas, N A Thomas)* 105 Garstang Road, PRESTON, PR1 1LD.

Ⓟ**Turner Barratt Corporate Finance Limited** *(D C Turner)* 15 Market Place, NEWBURY, BERKSHIRE, RG14 5AA.

★Ⓟ**Turner Beaumont & Co Limited** *(D P Turner)* Thorncliffe Mews, Thorncliffe Park Estate, Newton Chambers Road, Chapeltown, SHEFFIELD, S35 2PH.

★ⓉⒻⒶ**Turner Peachey** *(S Allum, J I Morris, J Ollier, D C Owen, C Perry, E E Turner, R Whitfield)* Column House, London Road, SHREWSBURY, SY2 6NN. and at OSWESTRY, SHIFNAL, WELSHPOOL

★ⒻⒶ**Turner Peachey Incorporating Ridgway Wall & Co** *(S Allum, N J Freeman)* 12 West Castle St, BRIDGNORTH, WV16 4AB.

ⓅⒶ**Turner Warran Accounting Ltd** *(S J Warran)* 101 Ferriby High Road, NORTH FERRIBY, NORTH HUMBERSIDE, HU14 3LA.

Ⓟ**Turners Accounting & Business Solutions Ltd** *(C J Turner)* Suite 170, Lomeshaye Business Village, Turner Road, NELSON, LANCASHIRE, BB9 7DR.

★**Turpin Barker Armstrong** *(D Payne)* Allen House, 1 Westmead Road, SUTTON, SURREY, SM1 4LA. and at SEVENOAKS

Ⓟ**Tuson & Partners Limited** *(J C A Chivers, D V Shah)* 5th Floor, Minories House, 2-5 Minories, LONDON, EC3N 1BJ.

ⓉⒻⓅ**Tussies Limited** *(R D Tussie)* 31 Wilmslow Road, Cheadle Hulme, CHEADLE, SK8 1DR.

Tuveys, trading name of S.J.E Tuvey *(S J E Tuvey)* The Old Farmhouse, Chapel Lane, Shotteswell, BANBURY, OX17 1JB.

TW Business Solutions LLP *(P G Lewis, A M F Smallwood, V E Williams)* 33 Bridge Street, HEREFORD, HR4 9DQ.

TW Chan & Co *(T Chan)* Unit 2203, 22/F Malaysia Building, 50 Gloucester Road, WAN CHAI, HONG KONG ISLAND, HONG KONG SAR.

Ⓐ**Twamley and Co** *(A Twamley)* Enterprise House, 7 Coventry Road, COLESHILL, WARWICKSHIRE, B46 3BB.

Ⓟ**TWD Tax Services Ltd** *(B M Oster)* Grosvenor House, St. Thomas's Place, STOCKPORT, CHESHIRE, SK1 3TZ.

Ⓟ**Twinemanda Limited** *(A C Brown)* 30 Addiscombe Grove, CROYDON, CR9 5AY.

Ⓟ**Twissell Neilson Budd & Co Limited** *(M J Twissell)* Belgravia House, High Street, Hartley Wintney, HOOK, RG27 8NS.

Ⓐ**TWJ, trading name of TWJ Partnership LLP** *(A R Whitehead)* The Moorings, Dane Road Industrial Estate, SALE, CHESHIRE, M33 7BP.

Ⓟ**Two Plus Two Accounting Limited** *(E J Noel)* Tous Ensamble, La Rue de Haut, St Lawrence, JERSEY, JE3 1JQ.

ⒻⒶ**TWP, trading name of TWP Accounting LLP** *(B K Morley)* The Old Rectory, Church Street, WEYBRIDGE, SURREY, KT13 8DE.

ⓉⒶ**Tyas & Company** *(S N Ayres, S R Tyas)* 5 East Park, CRAWLEY, RH10 6AN.

Ⓟ**Tye Limited** *(E V Lindsey)* The Red Barn, Thornend, Christian Malford, CHIPPENHAM, WILTSHIRE, SN15 4BX.

Tyler & Co *(J S Tyler)* 3 Home Farm Way, Easter Compton, BRISTOL, BS35 5SE.

ⒻⓅ**Tyler Redmore, trading name of Tyler Redmore Limited** *(P G Tyler)* 157 Redland Road, BRISTOL, BS6 6YE.

Ⓐ**Tyler Waddington** *(E A G Tyler-Waddington)* The Gables, 15 Old Watling Street, Flamstead, ST. ALBANS, HERTFORDSHIRE, AL3 8HL.

Ⓟ**Tyler-Waddington Ltd** *(C M Tyler-Waddington, E A G Tyler-Waddington)* 15 Old Watling Street, Flamstead, ST. ALBANS, HERTFORDSHIRE, AL3 8HL.

Ⓟ**Tyrrell's, trading name of Tyrrells Limited** *(A J Procter, D F Tyrrell)* 69 Princess Victoria Street, Clifton, BRISTOL, BS8 4DD.

Ⓟ**Udai Parmar & Co Ltd** *(U S Parmar)* 29 New Way Road, LONDON, NW9 6PL.

Uddin & Co *(M R Uddin)* 12 Fairlawns, SUNBURY-ON-THAMES, TW16 6QR.

ⓉⓅ**UHY Antonis Kassapis Ltd** *(A E Kassapis, G E Kassapis)* 89 Kennedy Avenue, Off 201, Floor 2, P O Box 26624, 1640 NICOSIA, CYPRUS.

ⓉⒻⒶ**UHY Calvert Smith** *(J M Judson Smith, N J Pearce, H L Priest, K W Ward)* 31 St Saviourgate, YORK, YO1 8NQ.

Ⓟ**UHY Corporate Finance Limited** *(M P W Egan, C J Lowry, L Sacker)* Quadrant House, 4 Thomas More Square, LONDON, E1W 1YW.

ⓉⒶ**UHY Hacker Young** *(J G Ierston, N S Jenkins)* St John's Chambers, Love Street, CHESTER, CH1 1QN.

ⓉⒹ**UHY Hacker Young** *(G Davies, D A Guest, R B Simmons, S Thantrey)* 168 Church Road, HOVE, BN3 2DL.

ⒻⒶ**UHY Hacker Young** *(T Harris, A H Thomas)* First Floor, Pembroke House, Ellice Way, Wrexham Technology Park, WREXHAM, CLWYD LL13 7YT.

ⓅⒶ**UHY Hacker Young, trading name of UHY Hacker Young (S E) Ltd** *(D A Guest, R B Simmons, S Thantrey)* 168 Church Road, HOVE, EAST SUSSEX, BN3 2DL.

ⓉⒻⒶ**UHY Hacker Young, trading name of UHY Kent LLP** *(R J Bursey, A D Cooper, A R Hickie, E M Jordan)* Thames House, Roman Square, SITTINGBOURNE, KENT, ME10 4BJ.

★ⓉⒻⒶ**UHY Hacker Young, UHY Hacker Young City Registrars, UHY Hacker Young Corporate Finance, UHY Hacker Young Turnaround and Recovery, UHY Jackson Bly, trading names of UHY Hacker Young LLP** *(A Andronikou, M A Carney, G C K Chong, I R Cohen, J E Easton, M P W Egan, M Giddens, C N Jones, D S Levy, C J Lowry, C R Maugham, P Oliver, L Sacker, E M Searby, J A Simmonds, H P Spencer, J P Warsop, M Waterman)* Quadrant House, 4 Thomas More Square, LONDON, E1W 1YW. and at MANCHESTER, NOTTINGHAM

ⒻⒶ**UHY Hacker Young, UHY Hacker Young Turnaround and Recovery, trading names of UHY Hacker Young Manchester LLP** *(N C Gawthorpe, S J Lawson, D Symonds, M D Wasinski)* St. James Buildings, 79 Oxford Street, MANCHESTER, M1 6HT.

ⓉⒻⓅⒶ**UHY Hacker Young, UHY Peacheys, trading names of Peacheys CA Limited** *(P Byett, J P Griffiths, S M Theaker)* Lanyon House, Mission Court, NEWPORT, GWENT, NP20 2DW. and at ABERGAVENNY, BRISTOL

★ⓉⒻⒶ**UHY Torgersens** *(B Howells, D M Johnson, P K McMahon, P N Newbold, S J Torgersen)* Somerford Buildings, Norfolk Street, SUNDERLAND, SR1 1EE.

ⒻⓅⒶ**UHY Torgersens incorporating Brian Green & Co, trading name of UHY Torgersens Limited** *(D M Johnson, P N Newbold, S J Torgersen)* 7 Grange Road West, JARROW, TYNE AND WEAR, NE32 3JA.

ⓉⒻⒶ**UHY Wingfield Slater** *(R J Givans, D N Hemmingfield, P F Newsam, J L Wingfield)* 6 Broadfield Court, Broadfield Way, SHEFFIELD, S8 0XF.

Ⓟ**UK Accounting Limited** *(M J Kinson)* 5 Saxon Close, Breedon-on-the-Hill, DERBY, DE73 8LS.

Ⓟ**UK Expat, trading name of UK Expat Pty Ltd** *(J G Connolly)* 5/491 Nicholson Street, Carlton North, MELBOURNE, VIC 3054, AUSTRALIA. and at VICTORIA

Ⓟ**UK Tax Returns Ltd** *(B S Sahni)* 55 Maresfield Gardens, LONDON, NW3 5TE.

ⓅⒶ**UK Taxation Services, trading name of UKTS Audit Limited** *(D A Waters)* 221 High Street, BLACKWOOD, GWENT, NP12 1AL.

ⓉⒻⓅ**Ullyott, trading name of Ullyott Limited** *(S J Ullyott)* 6 George Street, DRIFFIELD, NORTH HUMBERSIDE, YO25 6RA.

★**Ulysses Yuen & Co.** *(N L U Yuen)* 13/F Foo Hoo Centre, 3 Austin Avenue, TSIM SHA TSIU, KOWLOON, HONG KONG SAR.

Ⓐ**Umesh Patel & Co** *(U D Patel)* 1 Kings Court, Harwood Road, HORSHAM, RH13 5UR.

ⓉⓅⒶ**Unadkat & Co, trading name of Unadkat & Co Limited** *(N R Unadkat)* 12 The Wharf, Bridge Street, BIRMINGHAM, B1 2JS.

ⓉⒻⒶ**Underwood Barron, trading name of Underwood Barron LLP** *(C S Baker, N R B Barron, A J McDougal)* Monks Brook House, 13-17 Hursley Road, Chandler's Ford, EASTLEIGH, HAMPSHIRE, SO53 2FW.

Ⓐ**Underwood Kinson** *(M J Kinson)* 5 Saxon Close, Breedon-on-the-Hill, DERBY, DE73 8LS.

Ⓟ**Union Alpha CPA Limited** *(S Y Lau, M C F Wong)* 19/F No. 3 Lockhart Road, WAN CHAI, HONG KONG ISLAND, HONG KONG SAR.

Ⓟ**Union Partners, trading name of Union Partners Limited** *(P C Mavron, C Stoakes)* 38 South Molton Street, Mayfair, LONDON, W1K 5RL.

Ⓟ**Unique Debt Solutions Ltd** *(G N Ratcliffe)* Bridgeman Court, Salop Street, BOLTON, BL2 1DQ. and at CARLISLE

Unthank & Co *(J A S Unthank)* 4 Coniston Close, FELIXSTOWE, IP11 9SW.

★**Unuigbe, Akintola & Co.** *(S U Unuigbe)* Marble House (2nd Floor), 1 Kingsway Road, P.O. Ikoyi, LAGOS, NIGERIA. and at BENIN CITY

ⓉⒻⒶ**UNW LLP** *(N Bearpark, S Lant, M J Morris, A M Suggett, A J G Wilson)* Citygate, St. James Boulevard, NEWCASTLE UPON TYNE, NE1 4JE.

Ⓟ**Upminster Accountants, trading name of Upminster Limited** *(D D T Gricks)* 1 Engayne Gardens, UPMINSTER, ESSEX, RM14 1UY.

Ⓐ**Uppal & Warr** *(I H Uppal)* 452 Manchester Road, Heaton Chapel, STOCKPORT, SK4 5DL.

ⓅⒶ**Upper Street Accounts Ltd** *(S J Hodgson, J K Reynolds)* 3 Tolpuddle Street, Islington, LONDON, N1 0XT.

Upton Neenan Lees *(D V Upton)* 6a Croydon Road, CATERHAM, SURREY, CR3 6QB.

Urban Accountancy *(H C Urban)* 20 Alverton Avenue, POOLE, DORSET, BH15 2QG.

★ⓉⒻⓅⒶ**Usher Spiby & Co, trading name of Ushers Limited** *(D T Lever, A C Walton)* 76 Manchester Road, Denton, MANCHESTER, M34 3PS. and at STOCKPORT

Usman Accountancy *(A Usman)* Communications House, 26 York Street, LONDON, W1U 6PZ.

V & A Monkshead Preece LLP *(H C Fairpo)* The Chapel, Silver Street, Witcham, ELY, CAMBRIDGESHIRE, CB6 2LF.

V & A Vigar & Co LLP *(A A Vigar)* Stoneygate House, 2 Greenfield Road, HOLMFIRTH, HD9 2JT.

V A McGowan *(V A McGowan)* 5 Hartington Road, Bramhall, STOCKPORT, SK7 2DZ.

Ⓟ**V Clemas Ltd** *(V E Clemas)* Vicarage Farm, Daggons Road, Alderholt, FORDINGBRIDGE, HAMPSHIRE, SP6 3DN.

V F Mather & Co *(V F Mather)* 4 Houldsworth Square, Reddish, STOCKPORT, SK5 7AF.

ⓉⒻⓅⒶ**V K Mehta & Co, trading name of VKM Accountants Limited** *(V K Mehta)* 25 Balham High Road, LONDON, SW12 9AL.

ⒻⒶ**V Kapadia & Co** *(V V Kapadia)* 53 Sheen Lane, LONDON, SW14 8AB. and at RICHMOND

Ⓟ**V Kapadia & Co, trading name of V Kapadia & Co Limited** *(V V Kapadia)* 53 Sheen Lane, LONDON, SW14 8AB. and at RICHMOND

V O ODIASE & CO *(V O Odiase)* GPO Box 9209, Marina, LAGOS, NIGERIA.

Ⓟ**V V Patel & Co, trading name of Freshfield Associates Ltd** *(V V Patel)* 71a Knighton Way Lane, Denham, UXBRIDGE, UB9 4EH.

V&A Bell Brown LLP *(A A Vigar)* Stoneygate House, 2 Greenfield Road, HOLMFIRTH, HD9 2JT.

ⒻⓅ**V&A Corporate Finance, trading name of Steam Corporate Finance Limited** *(H C Fairpo, A A Vigar)* The Chapel, Silver Street, Witcham, ELY, CAMBRIDGESHIRE, CB6 2LF. and at HOLMFIRTH, PETERBOROUGH

ⓉⓅ**V&A Vigar Group Ltd** *(H C Fairpo, A A Vigar)* V&A Bell Brown LLP, Stoneygate House, 2 Greenfield Road, HOLMFIRTH, HD9 2JT.

Ⓟ**V. Komodromos & Co Accountants & Consultants Ltd** *(P Komodromos, V Komodromos)* PO Box 27162, 1642 NICOSIA, CYPRUS. and at PAPHOS

V. Mistry & Co *(V Mistry)* Premier House, 112 Station Road, EDGWARE, HA8 7BJ.

V.G. Cundy & Co *(V G Cundy)* 175 Ladybank Road, Mickleover, DERBY, DE3 0QF.

V.L. Rainsford *(V L Rainsford)* 31b Thirsk Road, Battersea, LONDON, SW11 5SU.

ⒻⒶ**V.M. Murphy & Co** *(V M Murphy)* Finsbury House, New Street, CHIPPING NORTON, OX7 5LL.

V.R. Andreae FCA *(V R Andreae)* 57a Chilkwell Street, GLASTONBURY, BA6 8DE.

V.R. Patel *(V R Patel)* 7 Greenway, HEMEL HEMPSTEAD, HERTFORDSHIRE, HP2 4QG.

Ⓕ**V.S. Shah & Co** *(V S Shah)* 3 Lakenheath, Oakwood, LONDON, N14 4RJ.

VA Corporate Finance, trading name of Zia Mursaleen *(Z Mursaleen)* 53 Leatherhead Road, ASHTEAD, KT21 2TP.

Vainker & Associates Sarl *(N M Vainker)* 17bd Royal, L-2449 LUXEMBOURG, LUXEMBOURG.

★ⓉⒻⒶ**Vale & West** *(K M Cutts, P R W Ringrow)* Victoria House, 26 Queen Victoria Street, READING, RG1 1TG.

★**Valentine Ellis & Co** *(R E Coward)* Preacher's Court, The Charterhouse, Charterhouse Square, LONDON, EC1M 6AS.

★Ⓟ**Valeur Accountancy Limited** *(A M Sinel)* Oaklands, La Rue de la Frontiere, St Mary, JERSEY, JE3 3EG.

Vallance Lodge & Co *(M Y Manjra)* Units 082 - 086, 555 White Hart Lane, LONDON, N17 7RN.

Vanessa Fletcher FCA *(V A Fletcher)* Wrentham House, Southwold Road, Wrentham, BECCLES, SUFFOLK, NR34 7JF.

Ⓕ**Vanguard Corporate Finance** *(B F McCann)* Liverpool Science Park, 131 Mount Pleasant, LIVERPOOL, L3 5TF.

Ⓟ**Vanilla Accounting, trading name of Vanilla Accounting Limited** *(P J Edwards)* 3 Oakmere Close, Edwalton, NOTTINGHAM, NG12 4FJ.

Vantage *(R P J Allen)* Lower Ground Floor, 20-24 Kirby Street, LONDON, EC1N 8TS.

Ⓟ**Varden Nuttall Limited** *(P A Nuttall)* Release House, Heap Bridge, BURY, LANCASHIRE, BL9 7JR.

Varney & Co *(K B Varney)* 46 Mile End Road, Highweek, NEWTON ABBOT, TQ12 1RW.

Ⓟ**Vasco de Gouveia, trading name of Vasco de Gouveia Limited** *(V G De Gouveia)* 10 Lindens Close, Effingham, LEATHERHEAD, SURREY, KT24 5NZ.

Vaswani & Co *(M Vaswani)* 29a Hendon Avenue, Finchley Central, LONDON, N3 1UJ.

Ⓟ**VAT Assist Limited** *(D W Breger, A R W Parfitt)* Acre House, 11-15 William Road, LONDON, NW1 3ER.

Ⓐ**Vaughan & Company** *(D B Vaughan)* Telford House, 1 Claremont Bank, SHREWSBURY, SY1 1RW.

VBP & Co *(V B Patel)* 19 Morden Court Parade, London Road, MORDEN, SURREY, SM4 5HJ.

Ⓐ**Ved Dhaun & Co** *(V P Dhaun)* 20 Lansdowne Terrace, Gosforth, NEWCASTLE UPON TYNE, NE3 1HP.

Ⓐ**Venitt and Greaves** *(M A Venitt)* 115 Craven Park Road, LONDON, N15 6BL.

ⓉⒻⓅⒶ**Venthams, trading name of Venthams Limited** *(S R Baldwin, M S Cragg, R J Green, S P Harrison, A Mathers, S A Rowson, M J Taylor, P G Warburton)* Millhouse, 32-38 East Street, ROCHFORD, SS4 1DB. and at LONDON, REDHILL

Ventour & Co *(L Ventour)* 18 Oldfield Lane South, GREENFORD, MIDDLESEX, UB6 9LD.

Ⓟ**Venture Alliance Corporate Finance Ltd** *(P G Catherall, S C Radford)* 18 Chinthurst Park, Shalford, GUILDFORD, GU4 8JH.

Verinder & Associates *(A L Verinder)* 1-3 Crosby Road South, LIVERPOOL, L22 1RG.

Vernon & Company *(R W P Vernon)* Fairfields, Pennypot Lane, Chobham, WOKING, GU24 8DJ.

Vernon J. George *(V J George)* 29 Taylors Avenue, HODDESDON, HERTFORDSHIRE, EN11 8QE.

Ⓐ**Versant, trading name of Versant Associates LLP** *(M Illingsworth)* The Old Mill, 9 Soar Lane, LEICESTER, LE3 5DE.

Verulam Business Services *(C Hunt)* Willow Cottage, 19 Pancake Lane, Leverstock Green, HEMEL HEMPSTEAD, HERTFORDSHIRE, HP2 4NB.

Ⓟ**Very Useful Solutions Limited** *(V R Du Preez)* BM 6885, LONDON, WC1N 3XX.

Ⓟ**Vetiver, trading name of Vetiver Ltd** *(B G Williams)* East Ballarobin, Kerrowkeil Road, Grenaby, ISLE OF MAN, IM9 3BB.

Ⓟ**VFDnet, trading name of VFD Ltd** *(J D A Shand)* Magdalen Centre, Robert Robinson Avenue, OXFORD, OX4 4GA.

★**VI Partnership** *(V E Ioannou)* 20-21 Wolsey Mews, Kentish Town Road, LONDON, NW5 2DX.

Ⓟ**Via Executive Limited** *(I M Burns)* PO Box 46, Envoy House, St Peter Port, GUERNSEY, GY1 4AY.

Vicki Johnson *(V C Johnson)* 86 Sywell Road, Overstone, NORTHAMPTON, NN6 0AQ.

Ⓕ**Vicky Platt** *(Vicky C Platt)* 8 Moreton Avenue, HARPENDEN, HERTFORDSHIRE, AL5 2ET.

★ⒻⒶ**Victor Boorman & Co** *(S R A Holmes, K B Jordan)* Europa House, Goldstone Villas, HOVE, BN3 3RQ.

Victor Davis & Co *(V E Davis)* Horning Reach, Royston Park Road, Hatch End, PINNER, HA5 4AD.

Ⓟ**Victor Green Services Ltd** *(V S Green)* 7 Inchlaggan Road, Fallings Park, WOLVERHAMPTON, WV10 9QX.

Ⓟ**Victor Kirby & Co Limited** *(V G Kirby)* Business & Technology Centre, Shire Hill, SAFFRON WALDEN, ESSEX, CB11 3AQ. and at WOODFORD GREEN

Victor S. Green & Co *(V S Green)* 7 Inchlaggan Road, Fallings Park, WOLVERHAMPTON, WV10 9QX.

Victor Stanton Associates *(V R Stanton)* Steden, Reenglass Road, STANMORE, MIDDLESEX, HA7 4NT.

Ⓟ**Victoria Accountancy Limited** *(P A Hardwick)* 3 St Augustines Mansions, Bloomburg Street, LONDON, SW1V 2RG.

Victoria Barnard Accountancy *(V C Barnard)* 13 Pitfold Avenue, HASLEMERE, SURREY, GU27 1PN.

Ⓟ**Viewman Investments Ltd** *(J C Barnard)* Brelston Court, Marstow, ROSS-ON-WYE, HEREFORDSHIRE, HR9 6HF.

Ⓟ**Viewpoint Business Services Ltd** *(D J Porter)* Suite 3, Unit 8, Kingsdale Business Centre, Regina Road, CHELMSFORD, CM1 1PE.

Vikram Patel *(V S Patel)* 168 Lavender Hill, Battersea, LONDON, SW11 5TG.

ⓉⒻⒶ**Villars Hayward LLP** *(J Hayward, N M Smith)* Boston House, 2a Boston Road, HENLEY-ON-THAMES, OXFORDSHIRE, RG9 1DY.

Ⓟ**Vincent Bifulco & Co, trading name of Vincent Bifulco & Co Ltd** *(V Bifulco)* 47 Cumberland Park, LONDON, W3 6SX.

Ⓐ**Vincent Blake** *(V C Blake)* The Old Farmhouse, Town Row Green, CROWBOROUGH, TN6 3QU.

ⓉⒻⒶ**Vincent Clemas** *(V E Clemas)* Cornerways House, School Lane, RINGWOOD, BH24 1LG.

Vincent Clemas LLP *(V E Clemas)* Cornerways House, School Lane, RINGWOOD, HAMPSHIRE, BH24 1LG.

★**Vincent Lee & Co.** *(T C V Lee)* 1/F Xiu Ping Commercial Building, 104 Jervois Street, SHEUNG WAN, HONG KONG ISLAND, HONG KONG SAR.

Vincent Loh *(V C Loh)* 30-16-3, Jamnah View Condominium, Jalan Buluh Perindu, Taman SA, 59000 KUALA LUMPUR, MALAYSIA.

Vincent Mak & Company *(L Shum)* Room 1617-18, Star House, 3 Salisbury Road, TSIM SHA TSUI, KOWLOON, HONG KONG SAR.

Ⓟ**Vincent Ventures Limited** *(M R Vincent)* 2 Karen Drive, Backwell, BRISTOL, BS48 3JT.

Vincere Partners LLP *(T Lumb)* 1The Corner House, Aimson Road West, Timperley, ALTRINCHAM, CHESHIRE, WA15 7XP.

Vine & Co *(G Vine)* Beyond The Pond, 1 Bicester Road, Marsh Gibbon, BICESTER, OXFORDSHIRE, OX27 0EU.

Vinod Shah *(V D P Shah)* 25 Montpelier Rise, WEMBLEY, MIDDLESEX, HA9 8RG.

ⓅⒶ**Vinshaw & Co, trading name of Vinshaw Limited** *(N D Shah)* 1 Promenade Chambers, 1-8 Edgwarebury Lane, EDGWARE, MIDDLESEX, HA8 7JZ.

ⓅⒶ**Vipin Raja & CO, trading name of V R Accountants Limited** *(V M Raja)* Vipin Raja & Co, 100 College Road, HARROW, MIDDLESEX, HA1 1BQ.

ⓅⒶ**Virash Bach & Co, trading name of Virash Bach & Co Limited** *(V Patel)* 72 Lyndhurst Road, THORNTON HEATH, SURREY, CR7 7PW.

Ⓟ**Virbix, trading name of Virbix Ltd** *(S C Bruce)* North Lodge, South Horrington Village, WELLS, SOMERSET, BA5 3DZ.

Ⓟ**Viridis Consulting Ltd** *(J E Green)* 9 Kenyons, West Horsley, LEATHERHEAD, SURREY, KT24 6HX.

Ⓟ**Virtual Back Office Limited** *(R K Dua)* 3 Century Court, Tolpits Lane, WATFORD, WD18 9RS.

Ⓟ**Virtual Business Source Limited** *(S F Guyton, T R Maris, C D Maylin, D H Smyth, N D Willimer, P M Woodhall)* PO Box 501, The Nexus Building, Broadway, LETCHWORTH GARDEN CITY, HERTFORDSHIRE, SG6 9BL.

Ⓟ**Virtual Finance Limited** *(D B Maniar)* Devonshire House, 582 Honeypot Lane, STANMORE, HA7 1JS.

Ⓐ**Visana** *(R J Visana)* 43 Parade House, 135 The Parade, High Street, WATFORD, WD17 1NS.

Ⓟ**Visana Limited** *(R J Visana)* 43 Parade House, 135 The Parade, High Street, WATFORD, WD17 1NS.

ⓉⒶ**Vision Consulting** *(G Alahi)* 555 Cranbrook Road, ILFORD, ESSEX, IG2 6HE.

Ⓐ**Vista Audit LLP** *(S Jones)* Chancery House, 3 Hatchlands Road, REDHILL, RH1 6AA.

ⓉⒻⓅ**Vista Partners Limited** *(S Jones)* Chancery House, 3 Hatchlands Road, REDHILL, RH1 6AA.

Ⓟ**Vitag Limited** *(T A Graves)* 9 Laurel Avenue, GRAVESEND, KENT, DA12 5QP.

Ⓟ**Vital Accounting Limited** *(R L Shah)* Empire House, Empire Way, WEMBLEY, MIDDLESEX, HA9 0EW.

Vittis & Co *(M Christou)* 21 Hillfield Park, Winchmore Hill, LONDON, N21 3QJ.

Ⓟ**VIVA Accounting Limited** *(A Valembois)* 115 Whitby Road, IPSWICH, IP4 4AG.

Vive & Co *(R Vive)* The Isles, 203 Reading Road, WOKINGHAM, BERKSHIRE, RG41 1LJ.

Vivien M. Hirst *(V M Rieden)* 4 White Rose Lane, Lower Bourne, FARNHAM, GU10 3NG.

VN Tax & Accounts *(Y Van Niekerk)* Mashbury Hall, Mashbury, CHELMSFORD, ESSEX, CM1 4TF.

Ⓟ**Vogue Management Services Limited** *(R G K Griffith)* Units 6-10, Strawberry Lane Industrial Estate, Strawberry Lane, WILLENHALL, WV13 3RS.

★**Vohora & Company** *(P K Vohora)* Suite 309A, 15252 - 32nd Avenue, SURREY V3S 0R7, BC, CANADA.

ⓉⓅⒶ**Voice & Co, trading name of Voice & Co Accountancy Services Limited** *(H A Voice)* 14 Jessops Riverside, 800 Brightside Lane, SHEFFIELD, S9 2RX.

ⓉⒻⒶ**Voisey & Co.** *(C J Thomson, P Urmston, L M Warburton)* 8 Winmarleigh Street, WARRINGTON, WA1 1JW.

ⓅⒶ**Volans Leach & Schofield, trading name of Volans Limited** *(C S K Smart)* 10 Blenheim Terrace, LEEDS, LS2 9HX.

Vora & Co *(N N Vora)* 30 Pasture Field Road, Peel Hall, MANCHESTER, M22 5JU.

ⒻⓅⒶ**Vora & Company, trading name of R Vora & Co Limited** *(R S Vora)* 6 Carlton Road, ROMFORD, ESSEX, RM2 5AA.

Ⓟ**VS Consultancy, trading name of VS Consultancy Limited** *(V E Steward)* Greenfield Farm, 23 West Street, Hibaldstow, BRIGG, SOUTH HUMBERSIDE, DN20 9NY.

ⓅⒶ**VSP, trading name of VSP Limited** *(J P Patel)* 23a Lyttleton Road, Hampstead Gardens Suburb, LONDON, N2 0DN.

ⓉⒻⒶ**W & H, trading name of Whitehead & Howarth** *(M W Cronshaw, J C Dugdale, C L Higgins, G R Maddock)* 327 Clifton Drive South, LYTHAM ST. ANNES, FY8 1HN.

Ⓟ**W A Willis Ltd** *(W A Willis)* Wyre Hill Cottage, Buildwas, TELFORD, SHROPSHIRE, TF8 7BX.

Ⓟ**W G Chadwick, trading name of W.G. Chadwick Ltd** *(W G Chadwick)* 20 Colne Road, BARNOLDSWICK, LANCASHIRE, BB18 5QU.

Ⓟ**W G Financial Outsourcing Solutions Ltd** *(D C Williams)* Elfed House, Oak Tree Court, Mulberry Drive, Cardiff Gate Business Park, Pontprennau, CARDIFF CF23 8RS.

ⓉⓅ**W Glynne Owen & Co Limited** *(W G Owen)* 2 Caradog Villas, Glanhwfa Road, LLANGEFNI, GWYNEDD, LL77 7EN.

W H. Levings *(W H Levings)* 46 College Road, RINGWOOD, HAMPSHIRE, BH24 1NX.

ⓉⒻⓅⒶ**W J James & Co, trading name of W J James & Co Limited** *(N J Morrell, K R Saunders-Jones, W Williams)* Bishop House, 10 Wheat Street, BRECON, LD3 7DG. and at HEREFORD

W J Shepherd *(W J Shepherd)* 33 West Road, Bowdon, ALTRINCHAM, CHESHIRE, WA14 2LA.

W K Corporate Finance LLP *(C B Baynes)* Bridge House, 4 Borough High Street, LONDON, SE1 9QR.

W M M Jed & Co *(W M M Jedrzejewski)* 6 Old Barn Close, Hempstead, GILLINGHAM, KENT, ME7 3PJ.

W M Wong & Co *(W Wong)* Room 1517, 15/F, Nan Fung Centre, 264-298 Castle Peak Road, TSUEN WAN, NEW TERRITORIES HONG KONG SAR.

W M Yu & Co *(W M Yu)* Flat B1, 11/F, Loyong Court Commercial Building, 212-220 Lockhart Road, WAN CHAI, HONG KONG SAR.

W R Fell & Co *(W R Fell)* 11 Lingdales, Formby, LIVERPOOL, L37 7HA.

ⓉⓅⒶ**W R Frost & Co, trading name of W R Frost & Co Limited** *(M J Marriott, P D Vooght)* Riversdale, Ashburton Road, TOTNES, DEVON, TQ9 5JU.

W R Lowe MA FCA *(W R Lowe)* 48 Copperfields, Kemsing, SEVENOAKS, TN15 6QG.

W S Mantz & Co *(W S Mantz)* 90 Brixton Hill, LONDON, SW2 1QN.

W S Wong & Co *(S T Leung, Y M S Leung)* 16th Floor, Jonsim Place, 228 Queen's Road East, WAN CHAI, HONG KONG ISLAND, HONG KONG SAR.

W T Wynter MA FCA *(M T Wynter)* Thornton Cottage, Puckpool Hill, RYDE, PO33 1PJ.

W. Brian Copley *(W B Copley)* Barn Cottage, 5 Crossland Gardens, Tickhill, DONCASTER, SOUTH YORKSHIRE, DN11 9QS.

W. Crawford *(W Crawford)* 38 Oak Avenue, BINGLEY, WEST YORKSHIRE, BD16 1ES.

W. English & Co *(W English)* 121 London Road, KNEBWORTH, HERTFORDSHIRE, SG3 6EX.

W. Howard *(W Howard)* 102 Bluehouse Lane, Limpsfield, OXTED, RH8 0AJ.

Ⓐ**W. John Baker** *(W J Baker)* 4 Corbar Road, STOCKPORT, SK2 6EP.

Ⓕ**W. Osborne & Co** *(M W Osborne, W Osborne)* Harwood House, Park Road, MELTON MOWBRAY, LE13 1TX.

Ⓐ**W. Rowland Waller & Co.** *(P M Taylor)* 6 Trinity Rd, SHEERNESS, ME12 2PJ.

W. Winward F.C.A *(W Winward)* The Old Vicarage, North End Road, Yapton, ARUNDEL, WEST SUSSEX, BN18 0DT.

W.A. Gilmour *(W A Gilmour)* 4 St Gilberts Close, Pointon, SLEAFORD, LINCOLNSHIRE, NG34 0NG.

W.A. Hodgetts *(W A Hodgetts)* Berachah, 1a Laustan Close, Merrow, GUILDFORD, GU1 2TS.

W.A. Sheret *(W A Sheret)* Meadowcroft, Yarm Road, Hilton, YARM, TS15 9LF.

W.B. Henderson *(W B Henderson)* Pachesham Gates, Oxshott Road, LEATHERHEAD, KT22 0ER.

W.G. Belcher & Co *(W G Belcher)* 9 Queens Road, Westbourne, BOURNEMOUTH, BH2 6BA.

Ⓕ**W.G.Rastall** *(W G Rastall)* Crest Acre House, Sedbury Lane, Tutshill, CHEPSTOW, NP16 7DU.

W.Glyn Evans & Co *(W A G Evans)* Wyecroft, Holme Lacy, HEREFORD, HR2 6LJ.

W.H. Roberts & Co *(W H Roberts)* The Old Rectory, Church Lane, Hoby, MELTON MOWBRAY, LE14 3DR.

W.H. Wong & Co *(W C Wong)* Room 6, 16/ Floor, Enterprise Square 3, 39 Wang Chiu Road, KOWLOON BAY, KOWLOON HONG KONG SAR.

W.J. Cowell *(W J Cowell)* 7 Spinney Close, Douglas, ISLE OF MAN, IM2 1NF.

ⒻⒶ**W.J. Matthews & Son** *(D A Chidley, B O Jones, J M Pritchard)* 11 - 15 Bridge Street, CAERNARFON, LL55 1AB.

W.J. Palmer & Co. *(W J Palmer)* 21 Jesmond Way, STANMORE, MIDDLESEX, HA7 4QR.

W.K. Sui *(W K Siu)* 8th Floor, Prince's Building, CENTRAL, Hong Kong Island, HONG KONG SAR.

W.L. Bland & Co *(W L Bland)* 141 High Street, AMERSHAM, BUCKINGHAMSHIRE, HP7 0DY.

W.M.A Carroll *(W M A Carroll)* 16 Ormonde Place, Old Avenue, WEYBRIDGE, KT13 0PE.

W.M.J. Pope *(W M J Pope)* 54 Kings Avenue, Parkstone, POOLE, BH14 9QJ.

W.N. Tolfree *(W N Tolfree)* 6 Ledsgrove, Ipplepen, NEWTON ABBOT, TQ12 5QY.

W.O. Lo & Co *(W Lo)* Room 1901-2, Park-In Commercial Centre, 56 Dundas Street, MONG KOK, KOWLOON, HONG KONG SAR.

W.R. Kewley & Co *(J Massingberd-Mundy)* The Old Post Office, The Street, West Raynham, FAKENHAM, NORFOLK, NR21 7AD.

W.Y.Thomson & Co *(R G Snook)* 7 Telgarth Road, Ferring, WORTHING, WEST SUSSEX, BN12 5PX.

Ⓟ**WAB Grove Ltd** *(D Koshal)* Gautam House, 1-3 Shenley Avenue, Ruislip Manor, RUISLIP, MIDDLESEX, HA4 6BP.

ⒻⓅ**WAC (Whale & Company) Limited** *(B J Whale)* Holly Berry House, Rough Park, RUGELEY, STAFFORDSHIRE, WS15 3SQ.

Waddells *(J E F Waddell)* P.O. Box 140, PORT OF SPAIN, TRINIDAD AND TOBAGO.

Ⓟ**Waddington Tax Consultancy Ltd** *(D Waddington)* Cragside, Delph Lane, Daresbury, WARRINGTON, WA4 4AN.

Wade Stevens *(G W Stevens)* 7a The Broadway, Cheam, SUTTON, SURREY, SM3 8BH.

Ⓟ**WadeX Limited** *(D L Wade)* 11 Richmond Road, SUTTON COLDFIELD, WEST MIDLANDS, B73 6BJ.

Ⓐ**Wadlan Ley** *(J Ley)* 119 Battersea Business Centre, Lavender Hill, LONDON, SW11 5QL.

ⒻⒶ**Wadud Patwari & Co.** *(M A W Patwari)* 10 Tooting Bec Road, LONDON, SW17 8BD.

Ⓟ**Wages Bureau (Manchester) Ltd** *(B Pyplacz)* 6 Bexley Square, SALFORD, M3 6BZ.

Ⓟ**Wagner Associates Limited** *(L S Wagner)* 34 West George Street, GLASGOW, G2 1DA. and at EDINBURGH

★**Wagstaff, Rowland & Huntley** *(M J Boxall)* 27 Lewisham High St, LONDON, SE13 5AF.

ⓉⒻⒶ**Wagstaffs, trading name of Wags LLP** *(A E Dagless, M R Hubbocks, N D Savjani)* Richmond House, Walkern Road, STEVENAGE, HERTFORDSHIRE, SG1 3QP.

Wai S Chui *(W Chui)* 100 Lafayette Circle, Suite 204, LAFAYETTE, CA 94549, UNITED STATES.

ⓉⓅⒶ**Waight & Co Limited** *(P C S Waight)* 8 Lonsdale Gardens, TUNBRIDGE WELLS, KENT, TN1 1NU.

Ⓟ**Waining Accountancy, trading name of Waining Accountancy Limited** *(J P Waining)* 6 Bramlyn Close, Clowne, CHESTERFIELD, DERBYSHIRE, S43 4QP.

Ⓐ**Waite & Hartley** *(D N Hartley)* 66 North Street, WETHERBY, WEST YORKSHIRE, LS22 6NR.

ⓉⒶ**Wakelin & Day** *(A Day, T A McClure)* 9 Pound Lane, GODALMING, GU7 1BX.

Ⓟ**Walbrook Bureau Services Limited** *(J I Graveney)* 34 High Street, Westbury-on-Trym, BRISTOL, BS9 3DZ.

Walji & Co, trading name of Walji & Co (UK) LLP *(R Hooda, S M H Walji)* Prospect House, 50 Leigh Road, EASTLEIGH, HAMPSHIRE, SO50 9DT.

ⓅⒶ**Walji & Co, trading name of Walji & Co Private Clients Ltd** *(R Hooda, S M H Walji)* Prospect House, 50 Leigh Road, EASTLEIGH, HAMPSHIRE, SO50 9DT.

Walkden I.J. *(I J Walkden)* Lower Hill Farm, Tockholes, DARWEN, BB3 0NF.

Ⓟ**Walker & Associates Ltd** *(D G Walker)* 47 Orrin Close, Woodthorpe, YORK, YO24 2RA.

★Ⓣ**Walker & Co.** *(A Walker)* Belgrave House, 15 Belgrave Crescent, SCARBOROUGH, NORTH YORKSHIRE, YO11 1UB.

ⓉⒻⒶ**Walker & Sutcliffe** *(N A Ledgard, D A Walker)* 12 Greenhead Road, HUDDERSFIELD, HD1 4EN.

Ⓟ**Walker & Sutcliffe (Bookkeeping Services) Limited** *(N A Ledgard, D A Walker)* 12 Greenhead Road, HUDDERSFIELD, HD1 4EN.

Ⓟ**Walker Accountancy Limited** *(C A Walker)* 2 Biscay Court, Oakwood, DERBY, DE21 2SG.

ⓉⒻⓅⒶ**Walker Begley Limited** *(K G Begley, K Walker)* 207 Knutsford Road, Grappenhall, WARRINGTON, WA4 2QL.

ⓅⒶ**Walker Broadbent Associates, trading name of Walker Broadbent Associates Limited** *(M V Walker)* Westgate House, 25 Westgate, OTLEY, WEST YORKSHIRE, LS21 3AT.

Walker Harris *(D H Harris)* 27 St. David Street, BRECHIN, ANGUS, DD9 6EG. and at MONTROSE

ⒻⒶ**Walker Hubble** *(D A Walker)* 5 Parsons Street, DUDLEY, DY1 1JJ.

ⓉⒶ**Walker Moyle** *(D G W Bishop, R M Crookes, C A Moyle, P J Thomas)* Alverton Pavilion, Trewithen Road, PENZANCE, CORNWALL, TR18 4LS. and at REDRUTH, ST. IVES

Walker Sharp & Co *(T C Walker-Sharp)* 15 Hillside Avenue, ASHBOURNE, DERBYSHIRE, DE6 1EG.

ⒻⒶ**Walker Sutcliffe & Cooper** *(B J Cooper, S G Sutcliffe, D A Walker)* 4 The Square, Aspley Guise, MILTON KEYNES, MK17 8DF.

▽**Walker, Dunnett & Co** *(R P Dunnett)* 29 Commercial Street, DUNDEE, DD1 3DG. and at CARNOUSTIE

ⒻⓅⒶ**Walkers, trading name of Walkers Accountants Limited** *(A Day, N L Hudson, M W Procter, A F Simpson, R F Walker)* 16-18 Devonshire Street, KEIGHLEY, WEST YORKSHIRE, BD21 2DG.

★ⒻⒶ**Wall and Partners** *(M Longden, S N Robinson)* 3 & 5 Commercial Gate, MANSFIELD, NG18 1EJ.

Wall Green *(G S Wall)* 119 High Street, Clay Cross, CHESTERFIELD, S45 9DZ.

ⒻⒶ**Walla Leete** *(R B Walla)* The Mews, Northlands, Grey Road, ALTRINCHAM, CHESHIRE, WA14 4BT.

★ⓉⒻⒶ**Wallace Crooke** *(A P Holles, M P H Jones)* Wallace House, 20 Birmingham Road, WALSALL, WS1 2LT. and at BRIDGNORTH

★**Wallace Ko & Co.** *(Y W W Ko)* 19th Floor, Kam Chung Commercial Building, 19-21 Hennessy Road, WAN CHAI, HONG KONG ISLAND, HONG KONG SAR.

Wallace Simson *(W Simson)* 4 Holland Close, STANMORE, MIDDLESEX, HA7 3AN.

Wallace Williams & Co *(R F King)* 4 Island Farm Close, BRIDGEND, CF31 3LY.

ⒻⓅ**Wallace Williams Austin Ltd** *(T J Robinson)* 57 Cowbridge Road East, CARDIFF, CF11 9AE.

ⓉⒻⒶ**Waller & Byford** *(D A Byford, M R Byford)* Clements House, 1279 London Road, LEIGH-ON-SEA, SS9 2AD.

Waller Wilson & Co *(J D Waller, S P Wilson)* The Forge Cottage, 2 High Street, Mildenhall, BURY ST. EDMUNDS, IP28 7EJ.

ⓉⒻⒶ**Wallwork, Nelson & Johnson** *(P Woodburn)* Chandler House, 7 Ferry Road Office Park, Riversway, PRESTON, PR2 2YH.

Ⓟ**Walmsley & Co Accountants Ltd** *(B T Walmsley)* 8 Eastway, SALE, CHESHIRE, M33 4DX.

★**Walsh & Co** *(G M Walsh)* 977 London Road, LEIGH-ON-SEA, ESSEX, SS9 3LB.

Walsh & Co *(I J Walsh)* First Floor Offices, 59 Appletree Gardens, WHITLEY BAY, TYNE AND WEAR, NE25 8XD.

Ⓟ**Walshe & Co Ltd** *(W G Howell)* 2 Seabrook Drive, WEST WICKHAM, KENT, BR4 9AJ.

Ⓟ**Walshtax, trading name of Walshtax Limited** *(G M Walsh)* 977 London Road, LEIGH-ON-SEA, ESSEX, SS9 3LB.

ⓉⒻⒶ**Walter Dawson & Son** *(G D Atkinson, J Hall, A Mitchell)* 7 Wellington Road East, DEWSBURY, WF13 1HF. and at BRADFORD, HUDDERSFIELD, LEEDS, LEYBURN

ⓉⒻⓅⒶ**Walter Hunter & Co, trading name of Walter Hunter & Co Limited** *(J Rhodes, D R Thomas)* 24 Bridge Street, NEWPORT, GWENT, NP20 4SF.

ⒻⓅ**Walter Ridgway & Son Limited** *(D Pick)* Walter Ridgway & Son Ltd, 69 Flixton Road, Urmston, MANCHESTER, M41 5AN.

Walter Scott *(W Scott)* 3 Clonard Avenue, Sandyford Road, DUBLIN 16, COUNTY DUBLIN, IRELAND.

Walter Sinclair & Co *(W I Sinclair)* 81 Wembley Park Drive, WEMBLEY, HA9 8HE.

★ⓉⒻⒶ**Walter Wright** *(K N Brown, P R Garrard, D Simcox)* 89 High Street, Hadleigh, IPSWICH, IP7 5EA.

Ⓟ**Walter Wright Consultancy Ltd** *(K N Brown, P R Garrard, D Simcox)* 89 High Street, Hadleigh, IPSWICH, IP7 5EA.

ⒻⓅⒶ**Walters and Tufnell, trading name of Walters and Tufnell Limited** *(R G Tufnell)* 122 New London Road, CHELMSFORD, CM2 0RG.

Ⓟ**Walters Associates, trading name of Walters Associates Limited** *(A N B Mehta)* Suite 21, Third Floor, Barkat House, 116-118 Finchley Road, LONDON, NW3 5HT.

ⓅⒶ**Walters Hawson Limited** *(K D Hawson, D I Walters)* 26 Percy Street, ROTHERHAM, S65 1ED.

Ⓐ**Walters Shah** *(A G S Shah)* Unit B, 15 Bell Yard Mews, LONDON, SE1 3TY.

Ⓐ**Walton & Co** *(D A Walton)* The Chimes Bannister Green, Felsted, DUNMOW, ESSEX, CM6 3NL.

Walton Accounting Services *(S J Walton)* 11 Pargate Close, RIPLEY, DERBYSHIRE, DE5 8JU.

Ⓟ**Walton Dodge Forensic, trading name of Walton Dodge Forensic Limited** *(J R Dodge, R Walton)* Dencora Court, 2 Meridian Way, NORWICH, NR7 0TA.

ⓉⒻⒶ**Waltons Clark Whitehill, trading name of Waltons Clark Whitehill LLP** *(S A M M Adams, D R Boyd, C J Davey, P Harrison, H A O'Driscoll)* Oakland House, 40 Victoria Road, HARTLEPOOL, CLEVELAND, TS26 8DD.

Wan Man Tsang *(W M Tsang)* Room 2303-04, Wing on Centre, 111 Connaught Road, CENTRAL, HONG KONG ISLAND, HONG KONG SAR.

Wandle House Associates *(H Carter Pegg, C H Leong)* Wandle House, 47 Wandle Road, CROYDON, SURREY, CR0 1DF.

Wanta Bookkeeper *(W D Miskin)* 2 Forest Close, LONDON, E11 1PY.

Ⓐ**Ward & Co** *(C W J Ward)* First Floor, 15 Young Street, LONDON, W8 5EH.

Ⓐ**Ward & Co.** *(A M Ward)* Wallington Cottage, Drift Road, FAREHAM, PO16 8SY. and at HAVANT

Ⓟ**Ward Accountancy Services Limited** *(R D Ward)* 7 Manns Way, Rayleigh, ESSEX, SS6 9QB.

Ward Davis *(A R Davis)* 10 Fusilier Way, Weedon, NORTHAMPTON, NN7 4TH.

ⓉⒻⓅⒶ**Ward Divecha Limited** *(A R Divecha)* 29 Welbeck Street, LONDON, W1G 8DA.

★ⓉⓅⒶ**Ward Goodman, trading name of Ward Goodman Limited** *(G G Ball, D E R Lapthorn, I M Rodd)* 4 Cedar Park, Cobham Road, Ferndown Industrial Estate, WIMBORNE, DORSET, BH21 7SF.

★**Ward Mackenzie** *(J F Green)* Sussex House, Farningham Road, CROWBOROUGH, EAST SUSSEX, TN6 2JP. and at CRAWLEY, TUNBRIDGE WELLS

Ward Sheldrake Consultancy *(B J Ward)* Lower Barrow Kiln, Acton Mill Lane, Suckley, WORCESTER, WR6 5EJ.

★Ⓟ**Ward Williams, trading name of Ward Williams Business Advisers Limited** *(R J Hayward)* Bay Lodge, 36 Harefield Road, UXBRIDGE, MIDDLESEX, UB8 1PH.

ⓅⒶ**Ward Williams, trading name of Ward Williams Group Limited** *(P J Grainger, R J Hayward, M.W.McKinnell)* Park House, 25-27 Monument Hill, WEYBRIDGE, SURREY, KT13 8RT.

★ⓉⒻⓅⒶ**Ward Williams, trading name of Ward Williams Limited** *(P J Grainger, R J Hayward, M.W.McKinnell)* Park House, 25 - 27 Monument Hill, WEYBRIDGE, SURREY, KT13 8RT.

Ward, Patel & Co *(J W Ward)* The Gables, Haggatt Hall, St Michael, BRIDGETOWN, BARBADOS.

Wardell Accounting Services *(J Wardell)* 10 Meadowgate Croft, Lofthouse, WAKEFIELD, WEST YORKSHIRE, WF3 3SS.

ⒻⒶ**Warings, trading name of Warings Business Advisers LLP** *(H Chambers, R Darby, P A Lydon, N M Roby)* Bedford House, 60 Chorley New Road, BOLTON, BL1 4DA.

▽**Warmingtons Inc** *(P Warmington)* Suite 6, 21B Cascades Crescent, Chase Valley, PIETERMARITZBURG, 3201, SOUTH AFRICA.

★**Warneford Gibbs** *(B R Warneford)* College House, 17 King Edwards Road, RUISLIP, HA4 7AE.

Ⓐ**Warner & Co** *(P S Warner)* Lowe House, 55 Townsend Street, CHELTENHAM, GL51 9HA.

ⒻⒶ**Warners** *(B D Warner)* 12-14 Greenhill Crescent, Watford Business Park, WATFORD, WD18 8JA.

Ⓐ**Warr & Co** *(S C Barnes, D F Bowers, S Dhokia, P J Edwards, T V Warr)* Mynshull House, 78 Churchgate, STOCKPORT, SK1 1YJ.

Ⓐ**Warren & Co (Partnership)** *(C R Warren, L J Warren)* Meadhaven, Church Lane, Flax Bourton, BRISTOL, BS48 3QF.

Ⓟ**Warren & Co Business Consultancy Ltd** *(C R Warren, L J Warren)* Meadhaven, Church Lane, Flax Bourton, BRISTOL, BS48 3QF.

Ⓐ**Warren Clare** *(R A Warren)* 5-6 George Street, ST. ALBANS, HERTFORDSHIRE, AL3 4ER.

Ⓐ**Warren D Miskin** *(W D Miskin)* 2 Forest Close, Snaresbrook, LONDON, E11 1PY.

ⒻⓅⒶ**Warrener Stewart, trading name of Warrener Stewart Limited** *(J A P Broers, G J Chapman, C P Edney, J E Last, N D Morgan, D M Talbot)* Harwood House, 43 Harwood Road, LONDON, SW6 4QP.

Warwick Pendarves & Co *(S Pendarves)* 38 Hound Road, Netley Abbey, SOUTHAMPTON, SO31 5FX.

Ⓟ**Waterman Brown-London, trading name of Accounting & Financial Solutions (London) Ltd** *(M T Brown)* 66 Norman Road, Wimbledon, LONDON, SW19 1BN.

Ⓐ**Waters & Atkinson** *(R Jump, D S J Sissons)* The Old Court House, Clark Street, MORECAMBE, LA4 5HR.

Waterton Park Accountancy *(R J Atkinson)* Holly Cottage, Brockswood Court, Walton, WAKEFIELD, WEST YORKSHIRE, WF2 6RU.

★**Watkins Odendaal** *(A G Watkins)* No. 300 Windsor Square, 1959 152nd Street, WHITE ROCK V4A 9E3, BC, CANADA.

ⓉⒶ**Watkinson Black** *(D J Watkinson)* 1st Floor, 264 Manchester Road, WARRINGTON, WA1 3RB.

Watling & Co *(S C G Watling)* Beach House, La Route de St. Aubin, St. Lawrence, JERSEY, JE3 1LP.

ⓅⒶ**Watson and Darbyshire Audit Ltd** *(A J Watson)* Nymrod House, 85 King Street, Whalley, CLITHEROE, LANCASHIRE, BB7 9SW.

★**Watson Associates (Audit Services) Ltd, trading name of Watson Associates** *(I D Hamblyn, R C Harris, J C Males, G D Slater, M G Wickens)* 30-34 North Street, HAILSHAM, EAST SUSSEX, BN27 1DW.

★ⓉⒻⒶ**Watson Buckle, trading name of Watson Buckle LLP** *(C R Padgett, S M Sedgwick, D K Warren, M C Wilcock)* York House, Cottingley Business Park, BRADFORD, BD16 1PE.

Ⓟ**Watson Jones Accounting Limited** *(R Watson Jones)* 18 Hillside, Lilleshall, NEWPORT, SHROPSHIRE, TF10 9HG.

Watson Lenney *(S L Lenney)* Pendell Court Farmhouse, Pendell Road, Bletchingley, REDHILL, RH1 4QH.

★ⓉⒻⒶ**Watts Gregory LLP** *(D P Challenger, C D Hatcher, N Pugh, K A Smith, D C Williams)* Elfed House, Oak Tree Court, Mulberry Drive, Cardiff Gate Business Park Pontprennau, CARDIFF, CF23 8RS.

Waugh & Co. *(E P G Waugh)* Springs, Millhayes, Stockland, HONITON, DEVON, EX14 9DB.

ⓅⒶ**Waugh Haines Rigby Limited** *(C Biggs, L W Buchanan, D J Phillips)* 18 Miller Court, Severn Drive, Tewkesbury Business Park, TEWKESBURY, GLOUCESTERSHIRE, GL20 8DN.

Waverley Tax Consultancy *(J J Inman)* 36 New Road, Milford, GODALMING, SURREY, GU8 5BE.

Ⓟ**Wayne Fleming Associates, trading name of Wayne Fleming Associates Limited** *(W P Fleming)* Greenfields, Swanton Road, DEREHAM, NORFOLK, NR20 4PS.

Wayne T. King & Co - Wilkins Kennedy **Members in Practice and Firms - Alphabetical**

ⓉⒶ**Wayne T. King & Co** *(W T King)* 2 High Street, MENAI BRIDGE, GWYNEDD, LL59 5EE.

Ⓟ**wcs, trading name of Wessex Commercial Solutions Ltd** *(G M Potts)* Suite 29, Yeovil Innovation Centre, Barracks Close, Copse Road, YEOVIL, SOMERSET BA22 8RN.

Ⓟ**WD & GR Allsopp Ltd** *(W D Allsopp)* 7 Daisy Close, Bagworth, COALVILLE, LEICESTERSHIRE, LE67 1HP.

Ⓟ**Weald Accountancy & Bookkeeping Services Limited** *(K J Clipston)* 1 Brook Farm Cottages, Bowzell Road, Weald, SEVENOAKS, KENT, TN14 6NE.

Wealthy Creations LLP *(F J Thoburn, R W Thoburn)* 14 Barrington Street, SOUTH SHIELDS, TYNE AND WEAR, NE33 1AJ.

Weatherer Bailey Bragg LLP *(D J Horsley, R J Miner)* Victoria Chambers, 100 Boldmere Road, SUTTON COLDFIELD, WEST MIDLANDS, B73 5UB.

Ⓟ**Weaver, trading name of Weaver Financial Limited** *(S E Parker)* 9 Newland Way, NANTWICH, CHESHIRE, CW5 7JH.

ⒻⓅⒶ**Weavers, trading name of Weaver Buckworth & Partners** *(E W Buckworth)* 18 Queens Road, COVENTRY, CV1 3EG.

ⒻⓅⒶ**Webb & Company Accountants and Business Advisers, trading name of Webb & Co Limited** *(B Davidson, M F Webb)* 1 New Street, WELLS, SOMERSET, BA5 2LA.

ⒻⓅⒶ**Webb Accountancy Services Ltd** *(J D Webb)* 19 Diamond Court, Opal Drive, Fox Milne, MILTON KEYNES, MK15 0DU.

ⓅⒶ**Webb House, trading name of Webb House Limited** *(J Jarman, M Webb)* 11 Duncan Close, Moulton Park Industrial Estate, NORTHAMPTON, NN3 6WL.

Ⓟ**Webster & Co, trading name of Webster & Co (York) limited** *(J A Webster)* The Paddocks, Wetherby Road, Rufforth, YORK, YO23 3QB.

Ⓟ**Webster Associates, trading name of Lawrence Webster Associates Limited** *(L A Webster)* Eastlands Court, St Peters Road, RUGBY, WARWICKSHIRE, CV21 3QP.

★**Webster Ng & Co.** *(K W W Ng)* Rooms 1306-7 13/F, Park-In Commerical Centre, 56 Dundas Street, MONG KOK, KOWLOON, HONG KONG SAR.

ⓉⒻⒶ**Websters** *(D J Goddard, A M Salmon, I D Stubbs)* Baker Street Chambers, 136 Baker Street, LONDON, W1U 6UD. and at BIRMINGHAM

Ⓟ**Weeden Ltd** *(D Weeden)* Orchard House, 15 Elizabeth Close, Scotter, GAINSBOROUGH, LINCOLNSHIRE, DN21 3TA.

Ⓟ**Weedens, trading name of Good Care Business Support Limited** *(N D Weeden)* 21 Orchard Avenue, Southgate, LONDON, N14 4NB.

Ⓕ**Weiler & Co** *(F H D Weiler)* 12 Marchmont Road, RICHMOND, SURREY, TW10 6HQ.

ⒻⓅⒶ**Welbeck Associates, trading name of Welbeck Associates Limited** *(J Bradley-Hoare, P M Clark, P McBride)* 31 Harley Street, LONDON, W1G 9QS.

Ⓟ**Wellborne Limited** *(S A Beale)* 338 Yardley Road, Yardley, BIRMINGHAM, B25 8LT.

ⓉⒻⒶ**Wellden Turnbull LLP** *(R W John, S A Spevack)* 78 Portsmouth Road, COBHAM, SURREY, KT11 1PP.

Ⓟ**Weller Mackrill, trading name of Weller Mackrill Ltd** *(L J Mackrill)* South Building, Upper Farm, Wootton St. Lawrence, BASINGSTOKE, HAMPSHIRE, RG23 8PE.

★Ⓣ**Wellers** *(N S Beck, S P Crook, A M Dore, B J Morris, R W O Paterson, P J Sharp, D J Stanbury, M P Wyatt)* 8 King Edward Street, OXFORD, OX1 4HL. and at BANBURY, LONDON, THAME

Ⓟ**Wellers Contractors Limited** *(N S Beck, A M Dore, P J Sharp)* 55 Catherine Place, LONDON, SW1E 6DY.

Ⓟ**Wellington Guscott Limited** *(R L Cunningham)* No.1 Booths Hall, Chelford Road, KNUTSFORD, CHESHIRE, WA16 8QZ. and at LONDON

Wellkept Financial Services *(R B Welch)* 10 Newent Road, Northfield, BIRMINGHAM, B31 2ED.

Ⓐ**Wells & Co.** *(T A Wells)* Telford House, Hamilton Close, BASINGSTOKE, RG21 6YT.

★ⓉⒻⒶ**Wells Associates, trading name of Wells Professional Partnership LLP** *(N J Fellows)* 10 Lonsdale Gardens, TUNBRIDGE WELLS, KENT, TN1 1NU.

★ⓉⒻⒶ**Wells Richardson** *(A I T Ostrowski, G Wade)* Cannon House, Rutland Road, SHEFFIELD, S3 8DP.

★ⓅⒶ**Wellway Accountants Limited** *(R Thompson)* Borough Hall, Wellway, MORPETH, NORTHUMBERLAND, NE61 1BN.

Ⓟ**Wellway Business Advisers Limited** *(R Thompson)* Borough Hall, Wellway, MORPETH, NORTHUMBERLAND, NE61 1BN.

Wellway LLP *(R Thompson)* Borough Hall, Wellway, MORPETH, NORTHUMBERLAND, NE61 1BN.

Ⓟ**Welsby Associates Limited** *(G R J Welsby)* Sintra, Bethesda Street, Upper Basildon, READING, RG8 8NU.

ⒻⒶ**Wem & Co** *(A I Wem)* Savoy House, Savoy Circus, LONDON, W3 7DA.

Wendy W F Yee *(W W F Yee)* Unit B, 8/F Tin Fung Industrial Mansion, 63 Wong Chuk Hang Road, ABERDEEN, HONG KONG ISLAND, HONG KONG SAR.

★ⓉⒻⒶ**Wenn Townsend** *(A K Bahl, S J Bates, G L Cole, J V Gould, A E Haines, J A Layzell, K Middleton, L J Palmer, D J Pluck, S M Shelley)* 30 St Giles', OXFORD, OX1 3LE. and at ABINGDON, CIRENCESTER

Ⓟ**Wenn Townsend Accountants Limited** *(A K Bahl, S J Bates, G L Cole, J V Gould, A E Haines, J A Layzell, K Middleton, L J Palmer, D J Pluck, S M Shelley)* 30 St. Giles, OXFORD, OX1 3LE.

Ⓐ**Wernham Wallace Skinner & Co** *(D J Skinner, F Wernham)* Summit House, 2A Highfield Road, DARTFORD, DA1 2JY.

Ⓟ**Wesley & Co, trading name of Chargedeep Limited** *(M W Pratt)* 42 Shevington Moor, Standish, WIGAN, LANCASHIRE, WN6 0SA.

Ⓐ**Wesley Pemberton LLP** *(M Anthonisz, I R Gunesh)* 89 Vicars Moor Lane, LONDON, N21 1BL.

ⓅⒶ**Wesley Wilson Audit Ltd** *(R W Wesley, A R Wilson)* Parker House, 44 Stafford Road, WALLINGTON, SURREY, SM6 9AA.

Wesley Wilson LLP *(R W Wesley, A R Wilson)* Park House, 44 Stafford Road, WALLINGTON, SURREY, SM6 9AA.

Ⓐ**West** *(S West)* Office 2 Greswolde House, 197b Station Road, Knowle, SOLIHULL, WEST MIDLANDS, B93 0PU.

Ⓐ**West & Co** *(J W Waters, S J West)* Old Hempstead House, 10 Queensway, HEMEL HEMPSTEAD, HERTFORDSHIRE, HP1 1LR.

ⒻⓅⒶ**West and Foster, trading name of West and Foster Limited** *(J M G Foster, P J P Miles)* 2 Broomgrove Road, SHEFFIELD, SOUTH YORKSHIRE, S10 2LR. and at BAKEWELL

Ⓟ**West Country Finance Ltd** *(J L White)* 46 Engine Lane, Nailsea, BRISTOL, BS48 4RL.

Ⓟ**West Hill Tax Services Limited** *(A K Lea)* Cedar Haven, Toadpit Lane, West Hill, OTTERY ST. MARY, DEVON, EX11 1TR.

Ⓟ**West House Accountants, trading name of West House Accountants Ltd** *(J B Guy)* 14 High Street, Tettenhall, WOLVERHAMPTON, WV6 8QT.

★Ⓐ**West Reynolds** *(N A W Reynolds)* 42 Windmill Street, GRAVESEND, KENT, DA12 1BA.

Ⓐ**West Wake Price LLP** *(R A Kapadia, M J Peters, M J Silcock)* 4 Chiswell Street, LONDON, EC1Y 4UP.

Ⓐ**West, Wake, Price & Co** *(P R Webb)* Abacus House, Cranbrook Road, HAWKHURST, KENT, TN18 4AR.

Ⓟ**Westbournes Limited** *(K P Tanner)* 16 Glastonbury Road, HOVE, EAST SUSSEX, BN3 4PL.

★ⓉⒻⒶ**Westbury Business Services, Westbury Computer Services, Westbury Payroll Services, Westbury Secretarial Services, trading names of Westbury** *(J R Dabek, A J Gittins, H Graham, K Graham, P D Klinger, N Padden, N C Pearson, N S Springer)* 145/157 St John Street, LONDON, EC1V 4PY.

Ⓟ**Westcas, trading name of West Country Accounting Services Ltd** *(L J Levan)* D2 White House Business Centre, Forest Road, Kingswood, BRISTOL, BS15 8DH. and at WOTTON-UNDER-EDGE

Ⓟ**Westcliff Finance Limited** *(M Britt, P E Britt)* Westcliff House, 106 Southlands Road, BROMLEY, BR2 9QY.

Ⓟ**Westcountry Payroll Ltd** *(N Bamber, R P Carne, I E Powell, S Truran)* 2 Barnfield Crescent, EXETER, EX1 1QT.

ⒻⒶ**Westlake Clark** *(P D Clegg, F J Legris, Z K Redmill)* Nat West Bank Chambers, 55 Station Road, NEW MILTON, HAMPSHIRE, BH25 6JA. and at LYMINGTON

Ⓟ**Westmere Services Limited** *(F Sham)* 15 Burleigh Gardens, LONDON, N14 5AH.

Weston & Co *(R C Weston)* 10 Chendre Close, Hayfield, HIGH PEAK, SK22 2PH.

Weston & Co *(D J Weston)* 1 Arundel Close, Lynchborough Road, Passfield, LIPHOOK, GU30 7RW.

ⓉⒻⒶ**Weston Kay** *(M C Kay, K D Patel, J L Springbett, J H L Weston)* 73/75 Mortimer Street, LONDON, W1W 7SQ.

Weston Underwood *(C Weston Underwood)* 63 Agar Road, Illogan Highway, REDRUTH, CORNWALL, TR15 3EJ.

Weston, Whalley & Jackson *(C R Worthy)* 12 Skipton House, Thanets Yard, SKIPTON, NORTH YORKSHIRE, BD23 1EE.

ⒻⓅⒶ**Westons, trading name of Westons Business Solutions Ltd** *(J S Hinsley)* Queens Buildings, 55 Queen Street, SHEFFIELD, S1 2DX.

WGD LLP *(C P Woodward, S A Woodward)* 900 Elveden House, 717-7 Seventh Avenue SW, CALGARY T2P 0Z3, AB, CANADA.

★**WH Parker** *(R J Sarjeant, N F Williams)* 174 High Street, Harborne, BIRMINGHAM, B17 9PP.

ⓉⓅ**Whale Rock Professional Services Group, trading name of Whale Rock Accounting Limited** *(S M Muir, J Ward)* 4th Floor, 15 Basinghall Street, LONDON, EC2V 5BR.

Ⓐ**Whalley & Co.** *(D I Whalley)* Whalley & Co, 29 Chester Road, Castle Bromwich, BIRMINGHAM, B36 9DA.

Wheat & Butler *(S D Butler, N R Wheat)* 19 Holbrook Lane, CHISLEHURST, BR7 6PE.

Wheatley *(D J Wheatley)* 5 Robin Close, Huntington, CANNOCK, STAFFORDSHIRE, WS12 4PQ.

ⓅⒶ**Wheatley Pearce Limited** *(G P Bemment, K L Butcher)* 11 Winchester Place, North Street, POOLE, DORSET, BH15 1NX.

ⓉⒻⒶ**Wheawill & Sudworth** *(C E Barratt, H V Beaumont, M S Bland, D M Butterworth, A Hayer, A J Lee, D Sinclair)* P.O. Box B30, 35 Westgate, HUDDERSFIELD, HD1 1PA.

Ⓐ**Wheeler & Co** *(K Wheeler)* The Shrubbery, 14 Church Street, WHITCHURCH, Hampshire, RG28 7AB.

ⓅⒶ**Wheeler & Co, trading name of Wheeler & Co CA Ltd** *(P J Wheeler)* 24 Dukes Wood Avenue, GERRARDS CROSS, BUCKINGHAMSHIRE, SL9 7JT.

Ⓟ**Wheeler Rennen Limited** *(J P Dignum)* Dorset House, Regent Park, 297 Kingston Road, LEATHERHEAD, SURREY, KT22 7PL.

Wheeler, Hegarty & Co *(B P Hegarty)* Forest Lodge, Kingston Hill, KINGSTON UPON THAMES, SURREY, KT2 7JZ.

★ⓉⒻⒶ**Wheelers** *(M R Baker, A J Cave, H Garrett)* 16 North Street, WISBECH, CAMBRIDGESHIRE, PE13 1NE.

ⓉⓅ**Wheelers, trading name of Wheelers (2020) Limited** *(D H J Danes)* 6 Providence Court, Pynes Hill, EXETER, EX2 5JL.

Wheelhouse Hulme *(R S Hulme)* Westfield House, Woodhouse Lane, Biddulph, STOKE-ON-TRENT, ST8 7DR.

Whins Associates LLP *(F E Kershaw)* 12 Draycott Place, LONDON, SW3 2SB.

ⓉⒶ**Whitakers** *(D P Bennett, S G Hawkey, N C Powell)* Bryndon House, 5-7 Berry Road, NEWQUAY, TR7 1AD. and at ST COLUMB

ⓉⒻⓅⒶ**White & Company, trading name of White & Company (UK) Limited** *(B P White, E S White)* 6th Floor, Blackfriars House, Parsonage, MANCHESTER, M3 2JA.

ⒻⒶ**White Adams & Co** *(C J White-Adams)* 1 Famona House, Bridgwater Road, WINSCOMBE, SOMERSET, BS25 1NA.

Ⓟ**White Corfield & Fry Limited** *(E C Fry)* 420 Brighton Road, SOUTH CROYDON, SURREY, CR2 6AN.

★Ⓐ**White Hart Associates LLP** *(M J Siddiqui)* East House, 109 South Worple Way, LONDON, SW14 8TN.

Ⓕ**White Kite** *(A Walker)* 8 Forest Farm Business Park, Fulford, YORK, YO19 4RH.

ⓉⒻⒶ**Whitehead & Aldrich** *(D Greenwood, J D Hughes-Deane, A J Makin, R J D Mullineaux)* 5 Ribblesdale Place, PRESTON, PR1 8BZ.

Whitehead & Co *(I M Whitehead)* Penfold, Cannington Lane, Uplyme, LYME REGIS, DT7 3SW.

ⓅⒶ**Whitehead & Co, trading name of Whitehead Accountants Limited** *(A G Whitehead)* 40 Lord Street, STOCKPORT, CHESHIRE, SK1 3NA.

ⒻⒶ**Whitehouse Ridsdale** *(T J Luckin, A Phillips)* 26 Birmingham Road, WALSALL, WS1 2LZ.

▽**Whitelaw Wells** *(S C Jarvie)* 9 Ainslie Place, EDINBURGH, EH3 6AT. and at GLASGOW

Whites *(P L Levey)* 99 Preston Grove, YEOVIL, SOMERSET, BA20 2DB.

ⓉⓅⒶ**Whitesides, trading name of Whiteside Limited** *(J L Whiteside)* 6 & 7 Feast Field, Horsforth, LEEDS, LS18 4TJ.

★ⓉⒻⒶ**Whiting & Partners** *(A Band, B J Carroll, J D Cater, J J Harrison, M N Haydon, C Kelly, R C Meadows, T J Nunn, I G C Piper, P N Tatum, A Winearls)* Garland House, Garland Street, BURY ST. EDMUNDS, SUFFOLK, IP33 1EZ. and at ELY, HUNTINGDON, KING'S LYNN, MARCH, MILDENHALL, WISBECH

★ⒻⓅ**Whiting & Partners Limited** *(J J Harrison, P M Peters)* Garland House, Garland Street, BURY ST. EDMUNDS, SUFFOLK, IP33 1EZ. and at HUNTINGDON

★ⓉⒻⒶ**Whitley Stimpson, trading name of Whitley Stimpson LLP** *(M J Anson, N P R Bullen, M K Higgs, J M Walton, M Wyatt)* Penrose House, 67 Hightown Road, BANBURY, OXFORDSHIRE, OX16 9BE.

Whitmill Prescott & Co *(S F L Bulling)* The Green Garages, Cambridge Road, Newport, SAFFRON WALDEN, ESSEX, CB11 3TN.

Whitmill Wilson & Co. *(A J Wilson)* 40 Union St, RYDE, PO33 2LF.

★Ⓐ**Whitnalls** *(J Beesley)* 1st Floor, Cotton House, Old Hall Street, LIVERPOOL, L3 9TX.

Ⓟ**Whittaker Financials, trading name of Whittaker & Company Limited** *(G B Whittaker)* 13 Doolittle Mill, Froghall Road, Ampthill, BEDFORD, MK45 2ND.

Ⓟ**Whitten Spencer Limited** *(T D Spencer)* 29 High Street, Bridge, CANTERBURY, KENT, CT4 5JZ.

ⓉⒻⒶ**Whittingham Riddell LLP** *(P I Lane, A M Malpass, R J Paris, P M Sheppard)* Belmont House, Shrewsbury Business Park, SHREWSBURY, SY2 6LG. and at LUDLOW, NEWTOWN

Ⓕ**Whittington & Co** *(C C Whittington)* 83 South Street, DORKING, RH4 2JU.

ⓅⒶ**Whittingtons, trading name of Whittingtons Business Services Ltd** *(M I Joseph, P D Raper)* 1 High Street, GUILDFORD, SURREY, GU2 4HP.

ⓉⒻⒶ**Whittle & Co, trading name of Whittle & Partners LLP** *(T M Moriarty, R M Skells, R Ward, P J Whittle)* Century House South, North Station Road, COLCHESTER, CO1 1RE.

ⓉⒶ**Whittles, trading name of Whittles LLP** *(R A Andrews, M C Whittle, P J Whittle)* 1 Richmond Road, LYTHAM ST. ANNES, LANCASHIRE, FY8 1PE.

Ⓟ**Whittocks End Accountancy Ltd** *(A A Smith)* Whittocks End, Kempley, DYMOCK, GLOUCESTERSHIRE, GL18 2BS.

ⓉⒻⓅⒶ**WHS Accountants Limited** *(C J Hill, G Sheard)* Elmville House, 305 Roundhay Road, LEEDS, LS8 4HT.

Ⓐ**Whyatt & Co** *(C R J Whyatt)* 3 Pinford Dell, Wigmore Park, LUTON, LU2 9SD.

ⓉⒻⒶ**Whyatt Pakeman Partners** *(R W Bunker, D K Golledge, R Pimblett)* Colkin House, 16 Oakfield Rd, Clifton, BRISTOL, BS8 2AP.

Whyton Roberts *(A J Whyton)* Clouds, Soldridge Road, Medstead, ALTON, GU34 5JF.

ⓉⒶ**Wiggin's** *(A C D Wiggin)* Soane Point, 6-8 Market Place, READING, RG1 2EG.

Wiggins & Co. *(L M Wiggins)* The Old Stables, East Lenham Farm, Ashford Road, Lenham, MAIDSTONE, KENT ME17 2DP.

Ⓡ**Wigmore Registrars Ltd** *(S Cowan, J Diner, P Goldstein)* 201 Great Portland Street, LONDON, W1W 5AB.

▽**Wikramanayake & Co** *(P S Wikramanayake)* 50 Hardy Street, DOVER HEIGHTS, NSW 2030, AUSTRALIA.

Ⓐ**Wilcox & Co** *(G B Wilcox)* Smithy Farm, Twyford, Barrow on Trent, DERBY, DE73 7HJ.

Ⓟ**Wild & Co, trading name of Wild Accountancy Limited** *(E C Wild)* 16 Green Way, HARROGATE, NORTH YORKSHIRE, HG2 9LR.

Wild & Co. *(C B Wild)* 34 Dringthorpe Road, Dringhouses, YORK, NORTH YORKSHIRE, YO24 1LG.

★**Wilde Timmons Michaud Inc** *(P F Wilde)* 32 Glendale Avenue, LOWER SACKVILLE B4C 3M1, NS, CANADA.

★ⒻⒶ**Wilder Coe** *(C J Rebbetts)* Gloucester House, Church Walk, BURGESS HILL, RH15 9AS.

Ⓣ**Wilder Coe** *(R S Berry, M Bordoley, B L Chew, R M Coe, N Cowan, S S Landy, J Pattani, M R Saunders)* 233-237 Old Marylebone Road, LONDON, NW1 5QT. and at STEVENAGE

ⓉⒻⒶ**Wilder Coe LLP** *(R S Berry, M Bordoley, B L Chew, R M Coe, N Cowan, F J B Hudson, S S Landy, J Pattani, M R Saunders)* 233-237 Old Marylebone Road, LONDON, NW1 5QT. and at STEVENAGE

Wilder Jayakar & Company *(A W Jayakar)* 15 Heathermount Gardens, CROWTHORNE, RG45 6HW.

ⓉⒶ**Wildin & Co** *(R L Lewis, G M Wildin, J A Wildin)* Kings Buildings, Hill Street, LYDNEY, GLOUCESTERSHIRE, GL15 5HE.

ⒻⒶ**Wilding, Hudson & Co** *(J R Wilding)* Saxon House, 17 Lewis Road, SUTTON, SM1 4BR.

Ⓐ**Wildman & Co** *(M R Wildman)* Goss Court, 36a High Street, Thrapston, KETTERING, NN14 4JH.

ⓉⒻⓅⒶ**Wilds, trading name of Wilds Limited** *(A J Buchsbaum, M J Rayner, M J Seddon, J A Wild)* Lancaster House, 70-76 Blackburn Street, Radcliffe, MANCHESTER, M26 2JW.

ⒻⓅⒶ**Wilkes Tranter & Co Limited** *(P J Arch, S E W Tranter)* Brook House, Moss Grove, KINGSWINFORD, WEST MIDLANDS, DY6 9HS.

Wilkins & Co *(R J Forsyth)* 36 Chalklands, BOURNE END, BUCKINGHAMSHIRE, SL8 5TJ.

★ⓉⒻⒶ**Wilkins Kennedy** *(P J Barton, C B Baynes, J W Beames, R S Butterfield, D Carey, T E A Collerton, A E Dodsworth, T B L Feller, D M Fenn, S R Golder, J E Golding, P A Goodman, S P Grant, D R Graves, S Hannaford, S J Harrison, R T Haslam, J Howard, R Howard, I A Jefferson, R N G*

Johnson, K J Lee, M.J. Macdonald, A L Magagnin, P R Manning, J R Natt, A L Nayler, D Nixon, M J Norton, N J Parrett, W J B Payne, L J Penny, R D Reynolds, R Shastri, R C P Smith, R J Southey, I M Talbot, M R Tizard, M A Wilkes, R W Williams, C G Wiseman, R K Young) Bridge House, London Bridge, LONDON, SE1 9QR. and at AMERSHAM, EGHAM, GUILDFORD, HERTFORD, ORPINGTON, READING, ROMSEY, SOUTHEND-ON-SEA, STANLEY, WINCHESTER

ⓉⒻⓅⒶ**Wilkins Kennedy FKC Limited** *(R S Butterfield, J M McIntyre, R D Reynolds, H J E Summerfield, M D Swan, M A Wilkes)* 35-41 Stourside Place, Station Road, ASHFORD, KENT, TN23 1PP.

Wilkinson & Co *(A H Wilkinson)* 68 Thorpe Lane, Almondbury, HUDDERSFIELD, HD5 8UF.

Ⓟ**Wilkinson & Partners Business Services Limited** *(D Wilkinson)* Victoria Mews, 19 Mill Field Road, Cottingley Business Park, Cottingley, BINGLEY, WEST YORKSHIRE BD16 1PY.

★ⓉⒶ**Wilkinson and Partners** *(P Raistrick, D Wilkinson)* Victoria Mews, 19 Mill Field Road, Cottingley Business Park, Cottingley, BINGLEY, WEST YORKSHIRE BD16 1PY.

★Ⓐ**Wilkinson Latham** *(I M W Latham)* 5 College Mews, Saint Ann's Hill, LONDON, SW18 2SJ.

Wilks & Associates *(H C Wilks)* 19 Church Lane, West Tytherley, SALISBURY, SP5 1JY.

Willan & Willan *(M J Willan)* The Old Post Office, High Street, Hartley Wintney, HOOK, HAMPSHIRE, RG27 8NZ.

Willcox & Co *(A K Willcox)* 10 Chilcott Court, SOUTHAMPTON, SO52 9PS.

★ⒻⒶ**Willey & Co** *(P J Willey)* Bainbridge House, 379 Stamfordham Road, Westerhope, NEWCASTLE UPON TYNE, NE5 2LH.

William A Sankey FCA *(W A Sankey)* 10 Portland Road, Bowdon, ALTRINCHAM, WA14 2PA.

William B. Preston *(W B Preston)* 1 Montrouge Crescent, EPSOM, KT17 3PB.

Ⓕ**William Dann & Co** *(W E Dann)* 30-32 Norwich Street, DEREHAM, NR19 1BX.

▽Ⓣ**William Duncan & CO** *(G W B Bryson, H A Murphy)* 30 Miller Road, AYR, AYRSHIRE, KA7 2AY. and at HAMILTON, TARBERT

William George *(W J George)* 3 Maple Spring, BISHOP'S STORTFORD, CM23 2PU.

William H. Chetham *(W H Chetham)* 10 Arnesby Avenue, SALE, CHESHIRE, M33 2WJ.

Ⓕ**William Harling & Co** *(J A Baggaley)* 23 Abingdon Street, BLACKPOOL, FY1 1DG.

★ⓉⒻⓅⒶ**William Hinton, trading name of William Hinton Limited** *(C W K Hinton, I R Quartermaine)* Ross House, The Square, Stow on the Wold, CHELTENHAM, GLOUCESTERSHIRE, GL54 1AF.

ⒻⒶ**William Howell & Co** *(W G Howell)* 2 Seabrook Drive, WEST WICKHAM, BR4 9AJ.

William J Mayes *(B W Mayes, W J Mayes)* Vansittart Estate, Arthur Road, WINDSOR, SL4 1SE.

William Jukes *(W D Jukes)* 30 Parkway, Meols, WIRRAL, MERSEYSIDE, CH47 7BT.

William L. Thompson & Co *(W L Thompson)* Arbeia Business Centre, 8 Stanhope Parade, SOUTH SHIELDS, TYNE AND WEAR, NE33 4BA.

Ⓟ**William M. L. Ho & Co. Limited** *(W M L Ho)* Unit Nos. 301-02 3/F, New East Ocean Centre, No. 9 Science Museum Road, TSIM SHA TSIU, KOWLOON, HONG KONG SAR.

William Oxley *(W Oxley)* 6 The Mount, Furzeham, BRIXHAM, TQ5 8QY.

ⓉⒶ**William Price & Co** *(J I Graveney, R J Holcombe)* Westbury Court, Church Road, Westbury-on-Trym, BRISTOL, BS9 3EF.

William Saddleton *(W Saddleton)* 94 Cowper Road, HARPENDEN, AL5 5NH.

ⓉⓅ**William Withers & Co, trading name of William Withers & Co Limited** *(W J Withers)* Town Farm, Templeton, TIVERTON, EX16 8BL.

ⒻⒶ**Williams** *(D A Dias)* Jade House, 67 Park Royal Road, LONDON, NW10 7JJ.

Williams & Co *(T R J Williams)* Bramley Cottage, Town Row Green, Rotherfield, CROWBOROUGH, TN6 3QU.

ⓉⒶ**Williams & Co** *(P Smith, M Williams)* 8-10 South Street, EPSOM, KT18 7PF.

★**Williams & Co** *(R M Jones, R A Williams)* 4 Cambridge Gardens, HASTINGS, TN34 1EH.

Williams & Co *(J O R Williams)* Longmead, 3 Heol Gwermont, Llansaint, KIDWELLY, DYFED, SA17 5JA.

Ⓕ**Williams & Co** *(R I Williams)* New Maxdov House, 130 Bury New Road, Prestwich, MANCHESTER, M25 0AA.

Williams & Co *(E M Williams)* Quietways, Old Walls, Llanrhidian, SWANSEA, SA3 1HA.

ⓅⒶ**Williams & Co. Ltd** *(J Williams)* Ebor House, 1 Knott Lane, Easingwold, YORK, YO61 3LX.

Ⓟ**Williams Denton Cyf** *(P R Denton, H A P Jones)* Glaslyn, Ffordd y Parc, Parc Menai, BANGOR, GWYNEDD, LL57 4FE. and at LLANDUDNO

★ⒻⓅⒶ**Williams Giles, trading name of Williams Giles Limited** *(R P Bristow, A C Crawford, M Williams)* 12 Conqueror Court, SITTINGBOURNE, KENT, ME10 5BH.

Ⓟ**Williams Grant Ltd** *(S J Chalmers)* 83 Liverpool Street, SOUTHAMPTON, SO14 6FU.

Ⓐ**Williams Knowles & Co** *(N M Knowles)* Lloyd Chambers, 139 Carlton Road, WORKSOP, S81 7AD.

ⒻⒶ**Williams Naylor** *(M S Williams)* 1st Floor, 454 Gower Road, Killay, SWANSEA, SA2 7AL.

Ⓟ**Williams Resource Management Ltd** *(A K Taylor)* The Oval, 14 West Walk, LEICESTER, LE1 7NA.

ⒻⓅⒶ**Williams Ross Ltd** *(J B Chown, K W Jones, G Moses)* 4 Ynys Bridge Court, Gwaelod Y Garth, CARDIFF, CF15 9SS.

ⒻⒶ**Williamson West** *(D Horton, A R Matthews, A P Spokes, J A West, S Williamson)* 10 Langdale Gate, WITNEY, OX28 6EX.

Williamsons *(M N Williamson)* Rosewood, Raemoir Road, BANCHORY, KINCARDINESHIRE, AB31 4ET.

ⓅⒶ**Willis Burnell Ltd** *(S W Burnell)* Spectrum House, Bromells Road, LONDON, SW4 0BN.

ⓉⓅⒶ**Willis Cooper, trading name of Willis Cooper Limited** *(R J Cooper)* Unit 6, Heritage Business Centre, Derby Road, BELPER, DERBYSHIRE, DE56 1SW.

ⓉⒻⒶ**Willis Jones** *(A D W Jones)* 64 Walter Road, SWANSEA, SA1 4PT.

▽**Willow Accountancy** *(M J Roberts)* Willow Cottage, Valley Road, WOTTON-UNDER-EDGE, GLOUCESTERSHIRE, GL12 7NP.

Willow Accountants *(S E Webb)* Rivers Lodge, West Common, HARPENDEN, HERTFORDSHIRE, AL5 2JD.

Ⓟ**Wills & Co, trading name of R Wills Accountants Limited** *(R Wills)* Chaparral, Windsor Lane, Little Kingshill, GREAT MISSENDEN, HP16 0DP.

Ⓟ**Wills Accountants, trading name of Wills Accountants Limited** *(S P Wills, W J Wills)* 10 The Crescent, PLYMOUTH, PL1 3AB.

★ⓉⓅⒶ**Wills Bingley, trading name of Wills Bingley Limited** *(G W Bingley, W E Wills)* St. Denys House, 22 East Hill, ST. AUSTELL, CORNWALL, PL25 4TR.

Ⓕ**Wilson & Co** *(D P Wilson)* Joseph's Well, Hanover Walk, Park Lane, LEEDS, LS3 1AB.

Ⓟ**Wilson Andrews Limited** *(B J Stewart)* 145 St. Vincent Street, GLASGOW, G2 5JF.

Wilson Durrant *(P A Durrant)* 2 The Quadrant, COVENTRY, CV1 2DX.

ⓉⒻⒶ**Wilson Henry, trading name of Wilson Henry LLP** *(P A Alcock, H S Henry, D J Kirby)* 145 Edge Lane, Edge Hill, LIVERPOOL, L7 2PF.

ⒻⓅⒶ**Wilson Sandford & Co, trading name of Wilson Sandford (Brighton) Limited** *(A C Sandford, R F S Wilson)* 97 Church Street, BRIGHTON, BN1 1UJ.

ⓉⒻⓅⒶ**Wilson Sandford Ltd** *(J H Mainwood, A C Sandford, R F S Wilson)* 85 Church Road, HOVE, EAST SUSSEX, BN3 2BB.

ⓉⒶ**Wilson Sharpe & Co** *(C Sharpe, Stewart Wilson)* 27 Osborne Street, GRIMSBY, NORTH LINCOLNSHIRE, DN31 1NU.

Ⓕ**Wilson Stevens LLP** *(G C Davis, N K Wilson)* 3rd Floor, 111 Charterhouse Street, LONDON, EC1M 6AW.

★ⓉⒻⒶ**Wilson Wright, trading name of Wilson Wright LLP** *(W Baker, B A Carmel, A P Cramer, J Grossman, M Lerner)* First Floor, Thavies Inn House, 3-4 Holborn Circus, LONDON, EC1N 2HA.

Wilsons Accounting Services *(S Wilson)* Cherry Lodge, West Haddon Road, Watford, NORTHAMPTON, NN6 7UN.

Wilton Audit *(L M Levehang)* 3 Leoville L' Homme St, PORT LOUIS, MAURITIUS.

ⒻⒶ**Wilton Mutlow & Co** *(Roy Mutlow)* 3 College Yard, Lower Dagnall Street, ST. ALBANS, HERTFORDSHIRE, AL3 4PA.

ⓉⒶ**Winburn Glass Norfolk** *(C Glass, R Stubley, M J Tindall, M Winburn)* Convention House, St. Mary's Street, LEEDS, LS9 7DP.

Winch & Co *(J R Winch)* Yew Tree Cottage, Great Bradley, NEWMARKET, Suffolk, CB8 9LH.

Windell & Co *(D M Windell)* 45 Downview Road, Barnham, BOGNOR REGIS, WEST SUSSEX, PO22 0EF.

Ⓟ**Windell & Co Accountants Limited** *(D M Windell)* 45 Downview Road, Barnham, BOGNOR REGIS, PO22 0EF.

ⓉⓅⒶ**Windle & Bowker, trading name of Windle & Bowker Limited** *(S T Briggs, E R Hargreaves, M C Heming, N P C Stead)* Croft House, Station Road, BARNOLDSWICK, LANCASHIRE, BB18 5NA. and at SKIPTON

Ⓟ**Windows Bookkeeping Ltd** *(M G Bettridge)* 2nd Floor, 27 High Street, HIGH WYCOMBE, BUCKINGHAMSHIRE, HP11 2AG.

ⓉⓅⒶ**Windsor Audit Limited** *(H A Fell)* 111 Eddington Crescent, WELWYN GARDEN CITY, HERTFORDSHIRE, AL7 4SX.

ⓅⒶ**Windy Ridge Consulting Limited** *(M S Harrison)* 1st Floor, Monument House, 215 Marsh Road, PINNER, MIDDLESEX, HA5 5NE.

ⓉⒶ**Wine & Co** *(S M Lewis, J I Wine)* 20-22 Bridge End, LEEDS, LS1 4DJ.

Ⓟ**Wingrave Yeats Limited** *(C C Jenkins, M L Jones, Miss K L Moran)* 101 Wigmore Street, LONDON, W1U 1QU.

ⓉⒻⒶ**Wingrave Yeats Partnership LLP** *(G L Bates, C C Jenkins, M L Jones, Miss K L Moran, P Owen)* 101 Wigmore Street, LONDON, W1U 1QU.

ⓉⒻⓅⒶ**Winn & Co, trading name of Winn & Co (Yorkshire) Limited** *(S K Clipperton, S R Lloyd)* 62/63 Westborough, SCARBOROUGH, YO11 1TS. and at BRIDLINGTON

Ⓐ**Winningtons** *(J B Grant, L J Grant)* 1 Winnington Road, LONDON, N2 0TP.

Ⓐ**Winston Fox & Co** *(A J Winston)* 34 Arlington Road, LONDON, NW1 7HU.

Ⓐ**Winston Fox Nur & Co** *(N M Tafsirullah)* Crown House, 2A Ashfield Parade, Southgate, LONDON, N14 5EJ.

ⒻⒶ**Winston Gross & Co** *(B Gross, A J Winston)* 34 Arlington Road, LONDON, NW1 7HU.

Ⓐ**Winter & Co** *(C P A Winter)* Melbury House, 34 Southborough Road, Bickley, BROMLEY, BR1 2EB.

Winters Consulting *(P J C Winter)* 59A North Street, Nailsea, BRISTOL, BS48 4BS.

Ⓟ**Wintersgill Associates, trading name of Wintersgill Associates Limited** *(P Wintersgill)* Suite 1, 10/12 The Grove, ILKLEY, WEST YORKSHIRE, LS29 9EG.

ⓅⒶ**Winterstoke Financial Management Limited** *(J M Handley Potts)* Unit 1, Rivermead, Pipers Way, THATCHAM, BERKSHIRE, RG19 4EP.

Ⓟ**Wintons Limited** *(R J Winton)* First Floor, 6 Ferranti Court, Staffordshire Technology Park, STAFFORD, ST18 0LQ.

ⓉⒻⒶ**Wise & Co** *(M J Dickinson, R A Lock, S G Morgan, S M South, T J Turner, R F Wise)* Wey Court West, Union Road, FARNHAM, SURREY, GU9 7PT.

ⒻⒶ**Wise & Co** *(C J Wise)* The Old Star, Church Street, PRINCES RISBOROUGH, HP27 9AA.

Wise & Co. *(P G Wise)* 24 Woodside Road, WOODFORD GREEN, ESSEX, IG8 0TR.

★Ⓟ**Wisteria, trading name of Wisteria Limited** *(A Millet)* Cavendish House, 369 Burnt Oak Broadway, EDGWARE, MIDDLESEX, HA8 5AW.

Ⓟ**Witchert Associates Limited** *(N G Pledger, K R Smith)* 133 Sheerstock, Haddenham, AYLESBURY, BUCKINGHAMSHIRE, HP17 8EY.

Ⓐ**Witcombs** *(S J Witcomb)* Turnfields Gate, THATCHAM, BERKSHIRE, RG19 4PT.

Ⓟ**Withall & Co, trading name of Withall & Co Ltd** *(S E Withall)* Squires House, 205A High Street, WEST WICKHAM, BR4 0PH.

Witham Accounting & Taxation Services *(S C Peck)* South Lodge, Ropsley, GRANTHAM, LINCOLNSHIRE, NG33 4AS.

Ⓟ**Witherington & Co Ltd** *(A F R Mendes)* 55A London Road, LEICESTER, LE2 0PE.

★ⓉⓅ**Wittich & Co Limited** *(P C Wittich)* Holly Grove, Hatching Green, HARPENDEN, HERTFORDSHIRE, AL5 2JS.

★**WJ & JA Frisby** *(W J Frisby)* 27a Park Road, BUXTON, DERBYSHIRE, SK17 6SG.

WK Accountants *(W Kilborn)* 5 Welland Court, Desborough, KETTERING, NN14 2PQ.

WK Ng & Co *(W Ng)* Room 2001, 20/F Grandtech Centre, 8 On Ping Road, SHA TIN, NEW TERRITORIES, HONG KONG SAR.

★ⓉⒻⒶ**WKH** *(T R Maris, C D Maylin, J I Price, J P Sheehan, D H Smyth, N D Willimer, P M Woodhall)* PO Box 501, The Nexus Building, Broadway, LETCHWORTH GARDEN CITY, HERTFORDSHIRE, SG6 9BL. and at CAMBRIDGE, ROYSTON

Ⓟ**WKL & Partners C.P.A Limited** *(M W Lui)* 20/F, Ka Wah Bank Centre, 232 Des Voeux Road Central, CENTRAL, HONG KONG SAR.

ⓉⒻⒶ**Wm Fortune & Son** *(T A Atkinson)* Collingwood House, Church Square, HARTLEPOOL, TS24 7EN.

Wm. E. Price & Co *(W E Price)* Nyth Glyd, Ffrwd Road, Abersychan, PONTYPOOL, NP4 8PF.

Ⓟ**WMM Consulting Limited** *(M R Macrow)* 70 Briggate, KNARESBOROUGH, NORTH YORKSHIRE, HG5 8BH.

ⓉⒻⒶ**WMT, trading name of Williamson Morton Thornton LLP** *(J R Banks, J I Childs, A Dunn, E E Irvine, R W Thornton, A L Williamson, G D Wintle)* 47 Holywell Hill, ST. ALBANS, HERTFORDSHIRE, AL1 1HD.

WMW Consultants *(W M Warfield)* Bedford Heights, Manton Lane, BEDFORD, MK41 7PH.

Ⓟ**Wolfson Associates Services Ltd** *(K Wolfson)* 1st Floor, 314 Regents Park Road, Finchley, LONDON, N3 2LT.

ⒻⓅⒶ**Wolfson Associates, trading name of Wolfson Associates Limited** *(I Wolfson, K Wolfson)* 1st Floor, 314 Regents Park Road, Finchley, LONDON, N3 2LT.

Ⓟ**Wolstenholme McIlwee Limited** *(F E McIlwee, T V Wolstenholme)* Marlet House, E1 Yeoman Gate, Yeoman Way, WORTHING, WEST SUSSEX, BN13 1QZ.

★**Wong & Associates** *(Sames Wong)* 5403 - 48 Street, YELLOWKNIFE X1A 1N7, NT, CANADA.

Ⓐ**Wong & Co** *(K K S Wong)* 2nd Floor Astoria House, 62 Shaftesbury Avenue, LONDON, W1D 6LT.

Wong & Company *(F S C Wong)* 70 Airthrie Road, Goodmayes, ILFORD, IG3 9QU.

Wong & Kwan *(C M Wong)* Room A, 7/F Queen Centre, 58-64 Queens Road East, WAN CHAI, HONG KONG ISLAND, HONG KONG SAR.

★**Wong Brothers & Co** *(C P G Cheng)* 19th Fl Mass Mutual Tower, 38 Gloucester Road, WAN CHAI, HONG KONG ISLAND, HONG KONG SAR.

Ⓟ**Wong Chan Lau C.P.A. Ltd** *(S J Chan)* Rooms 805 - 6, 8/F, Tai Yau Building, 181 Johnston Road, WAN CHAI, HONG KONG SAR.

Ⓟ**Wong Chan Lau CPA Co Ltd** *(S Lau)* Rooms 805-6, 8/F, Tai Yau Building, 181 Johnston Road, WAN CHAI, HONG KONG SAR.

Ⓟ**Wong Kok Yee Tax Services Pte Ltd** *(K Y Wong)* 78 Shenton Way, Apartment 30 - 01, Lippo Centre, SINGAPORE 079120, SINGAPORE.

Ⓟ**Wong Lam Leung & Kwok C.P.A Ltd** *(K K Leung, L T P Wong)* Room 1101, 11/F China Insurance Group Building, 141 Des Voeux Road Central, CENTRAL, HONG KONG ISLAND, HONG KONG SAR.

Wong Miu Ting, Ivy *(M I Wong)* Rm. 1311 13/F. Leighton Centre, 77 Leighton Road, CAUSEWAY BAY, HONG KONG SAR.

Ⓐ**Wood & Co** *(J G Wood)* 53b Calle Romo, Jimena de la Frontera, 11330 CADIZ, SPAIN.

Ⓟ**Wood & Disney Ltd** *(P Disney)* 1 Lodge Court, Lodge Lane, Langham, COLCHESTER, CO4 5NE.

Wood Berry & Co *(S Berry)* 5 Anderson Court, Sullart Street, COCKERMOUTH, CUMBRIA, CA13 0EB.

★ⓉⒻⓅⒶ**Wood Branson Dickinson, trading name of WBD Accountants Ltd** *(A D Branson, P W J Dickinson)* Norton House, Fircroft Way, EDENBRIDGE, KENT, TN8 6EJ.

ⓉⒶ**Wood, Hicks & Co** *(G K Hicks)* Units 1-2 Warrior Court, 9-11 Mumby Road, GOSPORT, HAMPSHIRE, PO12 1BS.

Woodbridge & Co, trading name of Matthew J Woodbridge ACA *(M J Woodbridge)* PO Box 6400, Pitstone, LEIGHTON BUZZARD, BEDFORDSHIRE, LU7 6DS.

Woodgates *(G W Khan)* Century House, 100 London Road, LEICESTER, LE2 0QS.

ⓅⒶ**Woodland & Woodland Limited** *(A M Woodland, D B Woodland)* Dragon House, Princes Way, Bridgend Industrial Estate, BRIDGEND, MID GLAMORGAN, CF31 3AQ.

Woods & Co *(D J Woods)* 1 Fordyce Close, HORNCHURCH, ESSEX, RM11 3LE.

★ⓉⒻ**Woodward Hale** *(V E Cowling, R K Hale, M J Hewlett)* 38 Dollar Street, CIRENCESTER, GL7 2AN.

ⓅⒶ**Woodward Hale Limited** *(V E Cowling, R K Hale, M J Hewlett)* 38 Dollar Street, CIRENCESTER, GLOUCESTERSHIRE, GL7 2AN.

ⒻⒶ**Woolford & Co, trading name of Woolford & Co LLP** *(L Binge, J C Dunne, J M F Wigram, P Wilman)* Hillbrow House, Hillbrow Road, ESHER, SURREY, KT10 9NW.

Ⓐ**Woolmer & Kennedy** *(J F M Kennedy, P T Woolmer)* 30 Star Hill, ROCHESTER, ME1 1XB.

Wootton & Co *(M W Jeffries)* 29 Tidmarsh Road, Leek Wootton, WARWICK, CV35 7QP.

Ⓟ**Working Finance, trading name of Working Finance Ltd** *(R J Dodds)* 127 Queen Alexandra Mansions, Tonbridge Street, LONDON, WC1H 9DW.

★**Worley Pritchard & Co** *(K M Pritchard)* 34 Hydes Road, WEDNESBURY, WS10 9SY.

★ⓉⒻⒶ**Wormald & Partners** *(N A Dando, D R Patel)* Redland House, 157 Redland Road, BRISTOL, BS6 6YE.

ⓉⒻⒶ**Wortham Jaques** *(D G Wortham)* 130a High Street, CREDITON, DEVON, EX17 3LQ.

★Ⓕ**Worton Rock, trading name of Worton LLP** *(D J Burrows, G B Holmes, P J Trinham)* Beauchamp House, 402/403 Stourport Road, KIDDERMINSTER, WORCESTERSHIRE, DY11 7BG.

ⓉⒻⓅⒶ**Worton Rock, trading name of Worton Rock Limited** *(D J Burrows, P J Trinham)* Churchfield House, 36 Vicar Street, DUDLEY, WEST MIDLANDS, DY2 8RG.

Ⓐ**Wortons** *(Derrick Worton)* 23 Bull Plain, HERTFORD, SG14 1DX.

ⓅⒶ**WP Audit Limited** *(P J H Upton)* 7 Bridge Street, MAIDENHEAD, BERKSHIRE, SL6 8PA.

ⓅⒶ**WPA Audit Limited** *(R J Wynniatt-Husey)* 26 Grosvenor Street, Mayfair, LONDON, W1K 4QW.

Wray & Company *(S Deakin Wray)* 36 Berkeley, LETCHWORTH GARDEN CITY, HERTFORDSHIRE, SG6 2HA.

Ⓟ**Wray Accountants Ltd** *(P F Wray)* PO Box 413, KEIGHLEY, BD22 9WX.

Wren Accountancy *(G Wren)* 26 Saxton Lane, Saxton, TADCASTER, NORTH YORKSHIRE, LS24 9QD.

Ⓟ**Wren Accounting Ltd** *(N B S Grimson)* 68 London Road, ST. ALBANS, HERTFORDSHIRE, AL1 1NG.

Ⓐ**Wright & Co** *(G M Edie, H G Nichols)* 57 High Street, South Norwood, LONDON, SE25 6EF.

Wright & Co *(A P Wright)* 2 Longrood Road, Bilton, RUGBY, CV22 7RG.

Wright & Co *(L W P Wright)* 51 Oxhey Avenue, WATFORD, WD19 4HB.

ⓉⒻⓅⒶ**Wright & Co Partnership Ltd** *(M Atkinson)* The Squires, 5 Walsall Street, WEDNESBURY, WS10 9BZ. and at STAFFORD

Ⓣ**Wright Associates** *(K J Wright)* First Floor, 56-57 High Street, STOURBRIDGE, WEST MIDLANDS, DY8 1DE.

ⓅⒶ**Wright Connections Limited** *(C M Brown, S M Goodson)* Bedford Business Centre, 61-63 St. Peters Street, BEDFORD, MK40 2PR.

ⓉⒻⓅⒶ**Wright Vigar Limited** *(P D Harrison, J E O'Hern, N M Roberts, J P Sewell, C J Shelbourne, B M Starling, R L J Vigar)* 15 Newland, LINCOLN, LN1 1XG. and at GAINSBOROUGH, LONDON, NEWARK, RETFORD, SLEAFORD

ⓉⒻⒶ**Wrigley Partington** *(N C Daniels, A P Dixon, R M Dixon, D N Ducie, D J Huxley, P G Quinn, G R Wilkinson)* Sterling House, 501 Middleton Road, Chadderton, OLDHAM, OL9 9LY.

Ⓟ**WriteTax Consultancy Services Limited** *(S D Bradford)* 6 Eider Close, BUCKINGHAM, MK18 1GL.

WS Lui & Co *(W S Lui)* Unit B, 12/F, Ka Nin Wah Commercial Building, 423 - 425 Hennessy Road, WAN CHAI, HONG KONG SAR.

Ⓟ**WS, trading name of WS Accountants Limited** *(W Smart)* 114 Park Avenue North, NORTHAMPTON, NN3 2JB.

ⓅⒶ**WSM Business Advisors, trading name of WSM Advisors Limited** *(S C C Marsh, W Patterson, G F M Stebbing, P J Windsor)* Pinnacle House, 17-25 Hartfield Road, LONDON, SW19 3SE.

ⓉⒻⒶ**WSM, WSM Property, trading names of WSM Partners LLP** *(S C C Marsh, W Patterson, G F M Stebbing, P J Windsor)* Pinnacle House, 17/25 Hartfield Road, Wimbledon, LONDON, SW19 3SE.

WSS Forensic Accounting *(W S Starr)* 25 Manchester Square, LONDON, W1U 3PY.

Ⓟ**WT Accountants Ltd** *(R W John, S A Spevack)* 78 Portsmouth Road, COBHAM, SURREY, KT11 1PP.

Wular Kaul Dhoul & Co, trading name of Wular Kaul & Co *(S N Kaul)* 61 Colin Crescent, LONDON, NW9 6EU.

www.Forensic.HK, trading name of B Kwok & Co *(B K B Kwok)* Units 2003 & 2004, 20/F Hua Qin, International Building, 340 Queens Road, CENTRAL, HONG KONG SAR. and at SHEUNG WAN

Ⓟ**Wyatt & Co, trading name of Nigel Wyatt & Company Limited** *(N P L Wyatt)* 125 Main Street, Garforth, LEEDS, LS25 1AF.

Ⓟ**Wyatt & Co, trading name of Wyatt & Co (Scarborough) Limited** *(M C Husler, I E A Wyatt)* 50-51 Albemarle Crescent, SCARBOROUGH, NORTH YORKSHIRE, YO11 1XX.

Ⓟ**Wyatt Husler Cook Limited** *(J J Cook, M C Husler, I E A Wyatt)* 10 Quay Road, BRIDLINGTON, NORTH HUMBERSIDE, YO15 2AP.

Ⓟ**Wyatt Husler Cook, trading name of Wyatt Husler Cook(Accountants) Limited** *(J J Cook, M C Husler, I E A Wyatt)* 50-51 Albemarle Crescent, SCARBOROUGH, NORTH YORKSHIRE, YO11 1XX.

ⓉⒶ**Wyatt, Morris, Golland & Co** *(D Bentley, S N Chadwick, N K Greenhalgh, J B Hoyle, C P J Morris, G Morris, P A Richards)* Park House, 200 Drake Street, ROCHDALE, OL16 1PJ.

ⒻⒶ**Wyatts** *(G C Wyatt, K M Wyatt)* York House, 1 Seagrave Road, LONDON, SW6 1RP.

Ⓜ**Wyck Consultancy** *(J P A Adams)* Wyck House, Woods Green, WADHURST, EAST SUSSEX, TN5 6QS.

ⓉⒻⓅⒶ**Wynniatt-Husey Ltd** *(I A McIntosh, R J Wynniatt-Husey)* The Old Coach House, Horse Fair, RUGELEY, STAFFORDSHIRE, WS15 2EL.

ⓉⓅ**Xhi Accounting Limited** *(C Neophytou)* United House, North Road, LONDON, N7 9DP.

★**XL Bookkeeping Services** *(J Shroff)* Excel House, 1 Hornminster Glen, HORNCHURCH, ESSEX, RM11 3XL.

Ⓐ**Y Drydedd Ddraig Cyf** *(R D Taylor)* RFOZ, Orbit Business Centre, Rhydycar Business Park, MERTHYR TYDFIL, MID GLAMORGAN, CF48 1DL.

Y L Ngan & Company *(Y L Ngan)* Suite 1019, 10/F China Chem Golden Plaza, 77 Mody Road, TSIM SHA TSUI, KOWLOON, HONG KONG SAR.

Ⓣ**Y P Lazarou** *(Y P Lazarou)* 79 Ellados Avenue, 8020 PAPHOS, CYPRUS.

Y.A. Peerbaye *(Y A Peerbaye)* Richard House, 6th Floor, Remy Ollier Street, PORT LOUIS, MAURITIUS.

Y.F.Pang & Co *(Y F Pang)* Unit 1801-2, 18/F Jubilee Centre, 46 Gloucester Road, WAN CHAI, HONG KONG SAR.

Y.H. Ong *(Y H Ong)* 8 Chee Hoon Avenue, SINGAPORE 1129, SINGAPORE.

Y.K. Leung & Co *(Y K Leung)* Room 804 8th Floor, Lap Fai Building, 6-8 Pottinger Street, CENTRAL, HONG KONG ISLAND, HONG KONG SAR.

★**Y.L. Law and Company** *(Y L Law)* Room 502 5/F, Prosperous Building, 48-52 Des Voeux Road, CENTRAL, HONG KONG ISLAND, HONG KONG SAR.

Y.P.Sennik *(Y P Sennik)* P.O. Box 45551, NAIROBI, KENYA.

Y.T. Yee & Co *(Y T Yee)* 8-12-11a Menara Bangsar, Jalan Liku, P.O. Box 12536, 50782 KUALA LUMPUR, FEDERAL TERRITORY, MALAYSIA.

Yadav & Co *(V R Yadav)* 87 Lansdowne Road, Seven Kings, ILFORD, IG3 8NG.

Ⓟ**Yannons, trading name of Yannons Limited** *(D O'Connor)* The Basement, 5 Orchard Gardens, TEIGNMOUTH, DEVON, TQ14 8DP.

Ⓟ**Yaqub & Co, trading name of Yaqub & Co Limited** *(M Yaqub)* 274 Stapleton Road, Easton, BRISTOL, BS5 0NW.

Yardley & Co *(M J Yardley)* 27 Hoxton Street, LONDON, N1 6NH.

Yates & Co *(C M Yates)* 27 Rosewood Gardens, Marchwood, SOUTHAMPTON, SO40 4YX.

Ⓟ**YBP Consultants, trading name of Your Business Partners Limited** *(L M Renak)* Bowmans House, Bessemer Drive, STEVENAGE, HERTFORDSHIRE, SG1 2DL.

Ⓟ**YD Associates, trading name of Thought Revolution Limited** *(Y Dharsi)* 38a Station Road, North Harrow, HARROW, MIDDLESEX, HA2 7SE.

ⓉⓅ**Year End Accounting, trading name of Year End Accounting Limited** *(I M Bavill)* 1st Floor, 9 East Parade, LEEDS, LS1 2AJ.

Ⓟ**Year End Solutions, trading name of Year End Solutions Limited** *(W A Smith)* 26 Stockham Close, Cricklade, SWINDON, SN6 6EF.

Ⓐ**Yeung & Co** *(K K W Yeung)* 14 Grange Drive, CHISLEHURST, BR7 5ES.

Ⓟ**Yeung, Chan & Associates CPA Limited** *(C H Yeung)* 1703-1705 Easey Commercial Building, 253-261 Hennessy Road, WAN CHAI, HONG KONG SAR.

Ⓟ**YG Eaton & Co Limited** *(R Barve, Y K Gupta)* Alpine House, Unit 2, 1st Floor, Honeypot Lane, LONDON, NW9 9RX.

ⓉⓅ**Yiakoumi & Partners Ltd** *(P N Yiacoumi, I N Yiakoumi)* 1 Ayias Lavras Street, Office 304 Engomi, 2414 NICOSIA, CYPRUS.

Ⓟ**Yianni Neil & Co, trading name of Yianni Neil & Co Limited** *(G Georgiou)* Everlast House, 1 Cranbrook Lane, New Southgate, LONDON, N11 1PF.

Yip Tai Him *(T Yip)* 7/F New York House, 60 Connaught Road, CENTRAL, HONG KONG ISLAND, HONG KONG SAR.

Yip, Ng & Company *(T F Ng)* Room A-B, 15/F, Ritz Plaza, 122 Austin Road, TSIM SHA TSUI, KOWLOON HONG KONG SAR.

Ⓟ**YN Services Limited** *(G Georgiou)* Everlast House, 1 Cranbrook Lane, New Southgate, LONDON, N11 1PF.

ⓅⒶ**York Sly, trading name of York Sly Ltd** *(Chris Sly)* Charterhouse, 5 Hill Rise View, BROMSGROVE, WORCESTERSHIRE, B60 1GA.

Ⓟ**Yorkshire Corporate Services Ltd** *(G M Aitken)* 18 High Street, NORTH FERRIBY, NORTH HUMBERSIDE, HU14 3JP.

Ⓟ**Yorkshire Financial Management Limited** *(C Salkeld)* The Old Hall, Bramham, WETHERBY, WEST YORKSHIRE, LS23 6QR.

Yorkshire Medical Accountants LLP *(J D Horrabin)* Unit 1, Milestone Court Business Park, Town Street, Stanningley, LEEDS, LS28 6HE.

Youden & Co *(J C Youden)* Old Stocks, Crowbrook Road, Monks Risborough, PRINCES RISBOROUGH, HP27 9LW.

ⓉⒻⒶ**Young & Co** *(G M John, L J Rogers)* Bewell House, Bewell Street, HEREFORD, HR4 0BA. and at MALVERN

Young & Company *(T Layland)* Church Farm House, Lodge Lane, Tendring, CLACTON-ON-SEA, ESSEX, CO16 0BS.

ⓉⓅⒶ**Young & Phillips, trading name of Young & Phillips Limited** *(D M Phillips, P A Young)* Inspiration House, Williams Place, Cardiff Road, PONTYPRIDD, MID GLAMORGAN, CF37 5BH. and at TREORCHY

Ⓟ**Youngman & Co** *(B J Youngman)* 11 Lynn Road, ELY, CB7 4EG. and at CAMBRIDGE

ⓅⒶ**Younis Bhatti & Co Ltd** *(M Y Bhatti)* 1st Floor, 93 Broad Street, BIRMINGHAM, B15 1AU.

Ⓟ**Your Profit Coach, trading name of Planning & Control Solutions Limited** *(C P Simister)* 17 Beachburn Way, Handsworth Wood, BIRMINGHAM, B20 2AU.

Ⓟ**YP Finance Limited** *(Y Patas)* Hawthorne House, 17A Hawthorne Drive, LEICESTER, LE5 6DL.

ⒻⒶ**YPO** *(W R Gilbert, K A Weston)* The Granary, Haggs Farm Business Park, Haggs Road, HARROGATE, NORTH YORKSHIRE, HG3 1EQ.

★**Yu How Yuen & Co.** *(H Y Yu)* Room 1104-1105 New Victory House, 93-103 Wing Lok Street, CENTRAL, HONG KONG ISLAND, HONG KONG SAR.

Yuen Tang & Co *(K K M Yuen)* 301 Bangunan Lee Yan Lian, Jalan Tun Perak, 50050 KUALA LUMPUR, FEDERAL TERRITORY, MALAYSIA.

ⓅⒶ**Yussouf & Co, trading name of Accountancy Services London Ltd** *(F Yussouf)* Suite 401/402, Cumberland House, 80 Scrubs Lane, LONDON, NW10 6RF.

★**YWC & Partners** *(T K S Choi, T Y B Yu)* 15th Floor, Empire Land Commercial Centre, 81-85 Lockhart Road, WAN CHAI, HONG KONG ISLAND, HONG KONG SAR.

Ⓟ**Z Dudhia & Company Limited** *(Z Dudhia)* 4 Hornton Place, LONDON, W8 4LZ.

ⒻⒶ**Zaidi & Co** *(M H Zaidi, M H Zaidi)* Amen Corner, 241 Mitcham Road, LONDON, SW17 9JQ.

Zakariya & Company *(A Zakariya)* Al Shaheed Tower, 4th Floor, Khaled Ben Al Waleed Street, PO Box 1773, SAFAT, 13018 KUWAIT.

Ⓐ**Zaman & Co.** *(T Zaman)* 27 Dollis Hill Lane, LONDON, NW2 6JH.

Ⓟ**Zane Accounting Services Limited** *(R S Banga)* 925 Finchley Road, LONDON, NW11 7PE.

Ⓣ**ZAO Deloitte & Touche CIS** *(J J W Robarts)* 5 Lesnaya Street, Building B, 125047 MOSCOW, RUSSIAN FEDERATION.

★Ⓣ**ZAO PricewaterhouseCoopers (Audit), trading name of PricewaterhouseCoopers** *(A T Antoniou, S J Ferrers-Dunn, D W Gray, G Latimir, C W M Skirrow, S J Snaith)* White Square Office Center, 10 Butyrsky Val, 125047 MOSCOW, RUSSIAN FEDERATION. and at ST PETERSBURG, TOGLIATTI

Ⓟ**ZDP Limited** *(G Conway)* 4 Station Terrace, CAERPHILLY, MID GLAMORGAN, CF83 1HD.

Ⓟ**Zebra Accounting (Thames Valley) Ltd** *(J A Foulds, R W Garner)* 7 Kingsland House, 135 Andover Road, NEWBURY, BERKSHIRE, RG14 6JL.

Zenith Corporate Finance LLP *(A Sharma)* 109-110 Viglen House, Alperton Lane, Alperton, WEMBLEY, MIDDLESEX, HA0 1HD. and at LEICESTER

Ⓟ**Zenon Secretarial Services Limited** *(R W Price)* 51 The Stream, Ditton, AYLESFORD, KENT, ME20 6AG.

Ⓟ**Zenon Tax Limited** *(R W Price)* 51 The Stream, Ditton, AYLESFORD, KENT, ME20 6AG.

Zenon Training Services LLP *(R W Price)* 51 The Stream, Ditton, AYLESFORD, KENT, ME20 6AG.

Ⓟ**Zenon Transaction Services Limited** *(R W Price)* 51 The Stream, Ditton, AYLESFORD, KENT, ME20 6AG.

Ⓟ**Zenon TTAS Limited** *(R W Price)* 51 The Stream, Ditton, AYLESFORD, KENT, ME20 6AG.

Ⓟ**Zeros Ltd** *(C Reid)* Brick House, 150a Station Road, Woburn Sands, MILTON KEYNES, MK17 8SG.

Ⓟ**Zerotwotwenty, trading name of Zero Two Twenty Limited** *(S R Jones)* 7 Beaumont Avenue, RICHMOND, SURREY, TW9 2HE.

ZHM Consultants *(Z H M Vahora)* 53 De Vere Gardens, ILFORD, ESSEX, IG1 3EB.

Zinaida Silins FCA *(Z B Silins)* Hybank, 12 Old Road, Walgrave, NORTHAMPTON, NN6 9QW.

Ⓟ**Zintin Ltd** *(M W Gerard)* 21 Manor Close, TUNBRIDGE WELLS, KENT, TN4 8YB.

Zoe Pettman *(K Z V Pettman)* Broomfield, Cherry Gardens Hill, Groombridge, TUNBRIDGE WELLS, KENT, TN3 9NY.

Ⓟ**Zolfo Cooper (BVI) Limited** *(W R Tacon)* 2nd Floor, Palm Grove House, Wickhams Cay, PO Box 4571, TORTOLA, VIRGIN ISLANDS (BRITISH).

Zolfo Cooper LLP *(S J Appell, A W Brierley, L A Causer, M J Flower, S V Freakley, P G E Hemming, D F Hughes, A Laing, S J Longfield, G J Smith, N J Tinker, J M Turner)* 10 Fleet Place, LONDON, EC4M 7RB. and at LEEDS, MANCHESTER

ⓉⓅ**Zolfo Cooper, trading name of Zolfo Cooper Ltd** *(M A Lewis)* The Zenith Building, 26 Spring Gardens, MANCHESTER, M2 1AB. and at BIRMINGHAM, GLASGOW, LEEDS, LONDON